MW00774355

The Message–NKJV Parallel Bible

THE MESSAGE–NKJV PARALLEL BIBLE

THOMAS NELSON
Since 1798

NASHVILLE DALLAS MEXICO CITY RIO DE JANEIRO BEIJING

The Message-NKJV Parallel Bible

1 2 3 4 5 6 7 8 9 10 — 14 13 12 11 10 09 08 07

Contents

Welcome to *The Message–NKJV Parallel Bible* vii
Preface to the New King James Version ix
Preface to *The Message* xv

Old Testament

Book	Page
Genesis	1
Exodus	76
Leviticus	137
Numbers	180
Deuteronomy	244
Joshua	299
Judges	336
Ruth	373
1 Samuel	379
2 Samuel	428
1 Kings	470
2 Kings	518
1 Chronicles	565
2 Chronicles	608
Ezra	661
Nehemiah	677
Esther	701
Job	712
Psalms	763
Proverbs	897
Ecclesiastes	946
Song of Solomon (Song of Songs)	961
Isaiah	970
Jeremiah	1073
Lamentations	1175
Ezekiel	1186
Daniel	1263
Hosea	1287
Joel	1303
Amos	1309
Obadiah	1322
Jonah	1324
Micah	1327
Nahum	1337
Habakkuk	1341
Zephaniah	1346
Haggai	1351
Zechariah	1354
Malachi	1370

New Testament

Book	Page
Matthew	1379
Mark	1432
Luke	1464
John	1520
Acts	1563
Romans	1617
1 Corinthians	1645
2 Corinthians	1670
Galatians	1686
Ephesians	1696
Philippians	1704
Colossians	1710
1 Thessalonians	1716
2 Thessalonians	1721
1 Timothy	1724
2 Timothy	1730
Titus	1734
Philemon	1737
Hebrews	1738
James	1755
1 Peter	1761
2 Peter	1767
1 John	1771
2 John	1777
3 John	1778
Jude	1779
Revelation	1781

Harmony of the Gospels 1809
Concordance (NKJV) 1815

BOOKS OF THE BIBLE IN ALPHABETICAL ORDER

Acts 1563
Amos 1309
1 Chronicles 565
2 Chronicles 608
Colossians 1710
1 Corinthians 1645
2 Corinthians 1670
Daniel 1263
Deuteronomy 244
Ecclesiastes 946
Ephesians 1696
Esther 701
Exodus 76
Ezekiel 1186
Ezra 661
Galatians 1686
Genesis 1
Habakkuk 1341
Haggai 1351
Hebrews 1738
Hosea 1287
Isaiah 970
James 1755
Jeremiah 1073
Job 712
Joel 1303
John 1520
1 John 1771
2 John 1777
3 John 1778
Jonah 1324
Joshua 299
Jude 1779
Judges 336
1 Kings 470
2 Kings 518
Lamentations 1175
Leviticus 137
Luke 1464
Malachi 1370
Mark 1432
Matthew 1379
Micah 1327
Nahum 1337
Nehemiah 677
Numbers 180
Obadiah 1322
1 Peter 1761
2 Peter 1767
Philemon 1737
Philippians 1704
Proverbs 897
Psalms 763
Revelation 1781
Romans 1617
Ruth 373
1 Samuel 379
2 Samuel 428
Song of Solomon (Song of Songs) 961
1 Thessalonians 1716
2 Thessalonians 1721
1 Timothy 1724
2 Timothy 1730
Titus 1734
Zechariah 1354
Zephaniah 1346

Welcome to *The Message–NKJV Parallel Bible*

This parallel Bible gives you the best contrast available in a parallel Bible. It features two very different translations that are outstanding examples in their respective categories.

The New King James Version is the most popular example of a formal or "word-for-word" Bible translation, where every *word* from the original languages is carefully transmitted in modern English as precisely as clarity, taste, and grammar will allow. This makes it an excellent translation for study. The NKJV is current and clear, yet it is accurate and reliable, and it is majestic enough for those who want "a Bible that sounds like a Bible." The NKJV New Testament is translated from the traditional text of the Greek New Testament, on which its predecessor the King James Version was also based. Here's how the NKJV renders a beloved passage, John 3:16–21:

> "For God so loved the world that He gave His only begotten Son, that whoever believes in Him should not perish but have everlasting life. For God did not send His Son into the world to condemn the world, but that the world through Him might be saved.
>
> "He who believes in Him is not condemned; but he who does not believe is condemned already, because he has not believed in the name of the only begotten Son of God. And this is the condemnation, that the light has come into the world, and men loved darkness rather than light, because their deeds were evil. For everyone practicing evil hates the light and does not come to the light, lest his deeds should be exposed. But he who does the truth comes to the light, that his deeds may be clearly seen, that they have been done in God."

The Message takes a very different approach. Its translator, the innovative Christian author Eugene Peterson, calls it "a translation into American," a supplement to other translations, whose tone "stabs us awake to a beauty and hope that connects us with our real lives." *The Message* is by far the most imaginative, lively, and compelling interpretation of the scriptures available, and Thomas Nelson appreciates the opportunity to partner with the primary publisher of *The Message,* NavPress, in presenting it here. *The Message* New Testament is translated from a recently edited critical text of the Greek New Testament. Here is *The Message* rendering of John 3:16–21:

> "This is how much God loved the world: He gave his Son, his one and only Son. And this is why: so that no one need be destroyed; by believing in him, anyone can have a whole and lasting life. God didn't go to all the trouble of sending his Son merely to point an accusing finger, telling the world how bad it was. He came to help, to put the world right again. Anyone who trusts in him is acquitted; anyone who refuses to trust him has long since been under the death sentence without knowing it. And why? Because of that person's failure to believe in the one-of-a-kind Son of God when introduced to him.

> "This is the crisis we're in: God-light streamed into the world, but men and women everywhere ran for darkness. They went for the darkness because they were not really interested in pleasing God. Everyone who makes a practice of doing evil, addicted to denial and illusion, hates God-light and won't come near it, fearing a painful exposure. But anyone working and living in truth and reality welcomes God-light so the work can be seen for the God-work it is."

That's quite a difference! This parallel edition of the Bible allows you to compare two radically distinct Bible translations. It provides amazing "depth perception" for your study of God's Word, as you consider the startling dissimilarities of these two approaches to Bible translation when you view them side by side.

We have also included a harmony of the gospels and a concordance (geared to the familiar wording of the NKJV). We pray that God will use this parallel Bible to instruct, encourage, and bless you in your study of His message to you.

The Publishers

Preface to the New King James Version®

Purpose

In the preface to the 1611 edition, the translators of the Authorized Version, known popularly as the King James Bible, state that it was not their purpose "to make a new translation . . . but to make a good one better." Indebted to the earlier work of William Tyndale and others, they saw their best contribution to consist in revising and enhancing the excellence of the English versions which had sprung from the Reformation of the sixteenth century. In harmony with the purpose of the King James scholars, the translators and editors of the present work have not pursued a goal of innovation. They have perceived the Holy Bible, New King James Version, as a continuation of the labors of the earlier translators, thus unlocking for today's readers the spiritual treasures found especially in the Authorized Version of the Holy Scriptures.

A Living Legacy

For nearly four hundred years, and throughout several revisions of its English form, the King James Bible has been deeply revered among the English-speaking peoples of the world. The precision of translation for which it is historically renowned, and its majesty of style, have enabled that monumental version of the word of God to become the mainspring of the religion, language, and legal foundations of our civilization.

Although the Elizabethan period and our own era share in zeal for technical advance, the former period was more aggressively devoted to classical learning. Along with this awakened concern for the classics came a flourishing companion interest in the Scriptures, an interest that was enlivened by the conviction that the manuscripts were providentially handed down and were a trustworthy record of the inspired Word of God. The King James translators were committed to producing an English Bible that would be a precise translation, and by no means a paraphrase or a broadly approximate rendering. On the one hand, the scholars were almost as familiar with the original languages of the Bible as with their native English. On the other hand, their reverence for the divine Author and His Word assured a translation of the Scriptures in which only a principle of utmost accuracy could be accepted.

In 1786 Catholic scholar Alexander Geddes said of the King James Bible, "If accuracy and strictest attention to the letter of the text be supposed to constitute an excellent version, this is of all versions the most excellent." George Bernard Shaw became a literary legend in our century because of his severe and often humorous criticisms of our most cherished values. Surprisingly, however, Shaw pays the following tribute to the scholars commissioned by King James: "The translation was extraordinarily well done because to the translators what they were translating was not merely a curious collection of ancient books written by different authors in different stages of culture, but the Word of God divinely revealed through His chosen and expressly inspired scribes. In this conviction they carried out their work with boundless reverence and care and achieved a beautifully artistic result." History agrees with these estimates. Therefore, while seeking to unveil the excellent *form* of the traditional English Bible, special care has also been taken in the present edition to preserve the work of *precision* which is the legacy of the 1611 translators.

COMPLETE EQUIVALENCE IN TRANSLATION

Where new translation has been necessary in the New King James Version, the most complete representation of the original has been rendered by considering the history of usage and etymology of words in their contexts. This principle of complete equivalence seeks to preserve *all* of the information in the text, while presenting it in good literary form. Dynamic equivalence, a recent procedure in Bible translation, commonly results in paraphrasing where a more literal rendering is needed to reflect a specific and vital sense. For example, complete equivalence truly renders the original text in expressions such as "lifted her voice and wept" (Gen. 21:16); "I gave you cleanness of teeth" (Amos 4:6); "Jesus met them, saying, 'Rejoice!'" (Matt. 28:9); and "Woman, what does your concern have to do with Me?" (John 2:4). Complete equivalence translates fully, in order to provide an English text that is both accurate and readable.

In keeping with the principle of complete equivalence, it is the policy to translate interjections which are commonly omitted in modern language renderings of the Bible. As an example, the interjection *behold,* in the older King James editions, continues to have a place in English usage, especially in dramatically calling attention to a spectacular scene, or an event of profound importance such as the Immanuel prophecy of Isaiah 7:14. Consequently, *behold* is retained for these occasions in the present edition. However, the Hebrew and Greek originals for this word can be translated variously, depending on the circumstances in the passage. Therefore, in addition to *behold,* words such as *indeed, look, see,* and *surely* are also rendered to convey the appropriate sense suggested by the context in each case.

In faithfulness to God and to our readers, it was deemed appropriate that all participating scholars sign a statement affirming their belief in the verbal and plenary inspiration of Scripture, and in the inerrancy of the original autographs.

DEVOTIONAL QUALITY

The King James scholars readily appreciated the intrinsic beauty of divine revelation. They accordingly disciplined their talents to render well-chosen English words of their time, as well as a graceful, often musical arrangement of language, which has stirred the hearts of Bible readers through the years. The translators, the committees, and the editors of the present edition, while sensitive to the late twentieth-century English idiom, and while adhering faithfully to the Hebrew, Aramaic, and Greek texts, have sought to maintain those lyrical and devotional qualities that are so highly regarded in the Authorized Version. This devotional quality is especially apparent in the poetic and prophetic books, although even the relatively plain style of the Gospels and Epistles cannot strictly be likened, as sometimes suggested, to modern newspaper style. The Koine Greek of the New Testament is influenced by the Hebrew background of the writers, for whom even the gospel narratives were not merely flat utterance, but often song in various degrees of rhythm.

THE STYLE

Students of the Bible applaud the timeless devotional character of our historic Bible. Yet it is also universally understood that our language, like all living languages, has undergone profound change since 1611. Subsequent revisions of the King James Bible have sought to keep abreast of changes in English speech. The present work is a further step toward this objective. Where obsolescence and other reading difficulties exist, present day vocabulary, punctuation, and grammar have been carefully integrated. Words representing ancient objects, such as *chariot* and *phylactery,* have no modern substitutes and are therefore retained.

A special feature of the New King James Version is its conformity to the thought flow of the

1611 Bible. The reader discovers that the sequence and selection of words, phrases, and clauses of the new edition, while much clearer, are so close to the traditional that there is remarkable ease in listening to the reading of either edition while following with the other.

In the discipline of translating biblical and other ancient languages, a standard method of transliteration, that is, the English spelling of untranslated words, such as names of persons and places, has never been commonly adopted. In keeping with the design of the present work, the King James spelling of untranslated words is retained, although made uniform throughout. For example, instead of the spellings *Isaiah* and *Elijah* in the Old Testament, and *Esaias* and *Elias* in the New Testament, *Isaiah* and *Elijah* now appear in both Testaments.

King James doctrinal and theological terms, for example, *propitiation, justification,* and *sanctification,* are generally familiar to English-speaking peoples. Such terms have been retained except where the original language indicates need for a more precise translation.

Readers of the Authorized Version will immediately be struck by the absence of several pronouns: *thee, thou,* and *ye* are replaced by the simple *you,* while *your* and *yours* are substituted for *thy* and *thine* as applicable. *Thee, thou, thy* and *thine* were once forms of address to express a special relationship to human as well as divine persons. These pronouns are no longer part of our language. However, reverence for God in the present work is preserved by capitalizing pronouns, including *You, Your,* and *Yours,* which refer to Him. Additionally, capitalization of these pronouns benefits the reader by clearly distinguishing divine and human persons referred to in a passage. Without such capitalization the distinction is often obscure, because the antecedent of a pronoun is not always clear in the English translation.

In addition to the pronoun usages of the seventeenth century, the *-eth* and *-est* verb endings, so familiar in the earlier King James editions, are now obsolete. Unless a speaker is schooled in these verb endings, there is common difficulty in selecting the correct form to be used with a given subject of the verb in vocal prayer. That is, should we use *love, loveth,* or *lovest? do, doeth, doest,* or *dost? have, hath,* or *hast?* Because these forms are obsolete, contemporary English usage has been substituted for the previous verb endings.

In older editions of the King James Version, the frequency of the connective *and* far exceeded the limits of present English usage. Also, biblical linguists agree that the Hebrew and Greek original words for this conjunction may commonly be translated otherwise, depending on the immediate context. Therefore, instead of *and,* alternatives such as *also, but, however, now, so, then,* and *thus* are accordingly rendered in the present edition, when the original language permits.

The real character of the Authorized Version does not reside in its archaic pronouns or verbs or other grammatical forms of the seventeenth century, but rather in the care taken by its scholars to impart the letter and spirit of the original text in a majestic and reverent style.

THE FORMAT

The format of the New King James Version is designed to enhance the vividness and devotional quality of the Holy Scriptures:

- Subject headings assist the reader to identify topics and transitions in the biblical content.
- Words or phrases in *italics* indicate expressions in the original language which require clarification by additional English words, as also done throughout the history of the King James Bible.
- Oblique type in the New Testament indicates a quotation from the Old Testament.
- Prose is divided into paragraphs to indicate the structure of thought.

- Poetry is structured as contemporary verse to reflect the poetic form and beauty of the passage in the original language.
- The covenant name of God was usually translated from the Hebrew as LORD or GOD (using capital letters as shown) in the King James Old Testament. This tradition is maintained. In the present edition the name is so capitalized whenever the covenant name is quoted in the New Testament from a passage in the Old Testament.

THE OLD TESTAMENT TEXT

The Hebrew Bible has come down to us through the scrupulous care of ancient scribes who copied the original text in successive generations. By the sixth century A.D. the scribes were succeeded by a group known as the Masoretes, who continued to preserve the sacred Scriptures for another five hundred years in a form known as the Masoretic Text. Babylonia, Palestine, and Tiberias were the main centers of Masoretic activity; but by the tenth century A.D. the Masoretes of Tiberias, led by the family of ben Asher, gained the ascendancy. Through subsequent editions, the ben Asher text became in the twelfth century the only recognized form of the Hebrew Scriptures.

Daniel Bomberg printed the first Rabbinic Bible in 1516–17; that work was followed in 1524–25 by a second edition prepared by Jacob ben Chayyim and also published by Bomberg. The text of ben Chayyim was adopted in most subsequent Hebrew Bibles, including those used by the King James translators. The ben Chayyim text was also used for the first two editions of Rudolph Kittel's *Biblia Hebraica* of 1906 and 1912. In 1937 Paul Kahle published a third edition of *Biblia Hebraica.* This edition was based on the oldest dated manuscript of the ben Asher text, the Leningrad Manuscript B19a (A.D. 1008), which Kahle regarded as superior to that used by ben Chayyim.

For the New King James Version the text used was the 1967/1977 Stuttgart edition of the *Biblia Hebraica,* with frequent comparisons being made with the Bomberg edition of 1524–25. The Septuagint (Greek) Version of the Old Testament and the Latin Vulgate also were consulted. In addition to referring to a variety of ancient versions of the Hebrew Scriptures, the New King James Version draws on the resources of relevant manuscripts from the Dead Sea caves. In the few places where the Hebrew was so obscure that the 1611 King James was compelled to follow one of the versions, but where information is now available to resolve the problems, the New King James Version follows the Hebrew text. Significant variations are recorded in the New King James translators' notes.

THE NEW TESTAMENT TEXT

There is more manuscript support for the New Testament than for any other body of ancient literature. Over five thousand Greek, eight thousand Latin, and many more manuscripts in other languages attest the integrity of the New Testament. There is only one basic New Testament used by Protestants, Roman Catholics, and Orthodox, by conservatives and liberals. Minor variations in hand copying have appeared through the centuries, before mechanical printing began about A.D. 1450.

Some variations exist in the spelling of Greek words, in word order, and in similar details. These ordinarily do not show up in translation and do not affect the sense of the text in any way.

Other manuscript differences such as omission or inclusion of a word or a clause, and two paragraphs in the Gospels, should not overshadow the overwhelming degree of *agreement* which exists among the ancient records. Bible readers may be assured that the most important differences in English New Testaments of today are due, not to manuscript divergence, but to the way in which translators view the task of translation: How literally should the text be rendered? How does the translator view the matter of biblical inspiration? Does the translator adopt a paraphrase when a literal rendering would be quite clear and more to the point? The New King James Version follows the historic precedent of the Authorized Version in maintaining a literal approach to translation, except where the idiom of the original language cannot be translated directly into our tongue.

The King James New Testament was based on the traditional text of the Greek-speaking churches, first published in 1516, and later called the Textus Receptus or Received Text. Although based on the relatively few available manuscripts, these were representative of many more which existed at the time but only became known later. In the late nineteenth century, B. Westcott and F. Hort taught that this text had been officially edited by the fourth century church, but a total lack of historical evidence for this event has forced a revision of the theory. It is now widely held that the Byzantine Text that largely supports the Textus Receptus has as much right as the Alexandrian or any other tradition to be weighed in determining the text of the New Testament.

Since the 1880s most contemporary translations of the New Testament have relied upon a relatively few manuscripts discovered chiefly in the late nineteenth and early twentieth centuries. Such translations depend primarily on two manuscripts, Codex Vaticanus and Codex Sinaiticus, because of their greater age. The Greek text obtained by using these sources and the related papyri (our most ancient manuscripts) is known as the Alexandrian Text. However, some scholars have grounds for doubting the faithfulness of Vaticanus and Sinaiticus, since they often disagree with one another, and Sinaiticus exhibits excessive omission.

A third viewpoint of New Testament scholarship holds that the best text is based on the consensus of the majority of existing Greek manuscripts. This text is called the Majority Text. Most of these manuscripts are in substantial agreement. Even though many are late, and none is earlier than the fifth century, usually their readings are verified by papyri, ancient versions, quotations from the early church fathers, or a combination of these. The Majority Text is similar to the Textus Receptus, but it corrects those readings which have little or no support in the Greek manuscript tradition.

Today, scholars agree that the science of New Testament textual criticism is in a state of flux. Very few scholars still favor the Textus Receptus as such, and then often for its historical prestige as the text of Luther, Calvin, Tyndale, and the King James Version. For about a century most have followed a Critical Text (so called because it is edited according to specific principles of textual criticism) which depends heavily upon the Alexandrian type of text. More recently many have abandoned this Critical Text (which is quite similar to the one edited by Westcott and Hort) for one that is more eclectic. Finally, a small but growing number of scholars prefer the Majority Text, which is close to the traditional text except in the Revelation.

In light of these facts, and also because the New King James Version is the fifth revision of a historic document translated from specific Greek texts, the editors decided to retain the traditional text in the body of the New Testament and to indicate major Critical and Majority Text variant readings in the translators' notes. Although these variations are duly indicated in the translators' notes of the present edition, it is most important to emphasize that fully eighty-five percent of the New Testament text is the same in the Textus Receptus, the Alexandrian Text, and the Majority Text.

NEW KING JAMES TRANSLATORS' NOTES

Significant textual explanations, alternate translations, and New Testament citations of Old Testament passages are supplied in the New King James translators' notes.

Important textual variants in the Old Testament are identified in a standard form.

The textual notes in the present edition of the New Testament make no evaluation of readings, but do clearly indicate the manuscript sources of readings. They objectively present the facts without such tendentious remarks as "the best manuscripts omit" or "the most reliable manuscripts read." Such notes are value judgments that differ according to varying viewpoints on the text. By giving a clearly defined set of variants the New King James Version benefits readers of all textual persuasions.

Where significant variations occur in the New Testament Greek manuscripts, textual notes are classified as follows:

NU-Text
These variations from the traditional text generally represent the Alexandrian or Egyptian type of text described previously in "The New Testament Text." They are found in the Critical Text published in the twenty-seventh edition of the Nestle-Aland Greek New Testament (N) and in the United Bible Societies' fourth edition (U), hence the acronym, "NU-Text."

M-Text
This symbol indicates points of variation in the Majority Text from the traditional text, as also previously discussed in "The New Testament Text." It should be noted that M stands for whatever reading is printed in the published *Greek New Testament According to the Majority Text,* whether supported by overwhelming, strong, or only a divided majority textual tradition.

The textual notes reflect the scholarship of the past two centuries and will assist the reader to observe the variations between the different manuscript traditions of the New Testament. Such information is generally not available in English translations of the New Testament.

Preface to *The Message*

To the Reader

If there is anything distinctive about *The Message*, perhaps it is because the text is shaped by the hand of a working pastor. For most of my adult life I have been given a primary responsibility for getting the message of the Bible into the lives of the men and women with whom I worked. I did it from pulpit and lectern, in home Bible studies and at mountain retreats, through conversations in hospitals and nursing homes, over coffee in kitchens and while strolling on an ocean beach. *The Message* grew from the soil of forty years of pastoral work.

As I worked at this task, this Word of God, which forms and transforms human lives, did form and transform human lives. Planted in the soil of my congregation and community the seed words of the Bible germinated and grew and matured. When it came time to do the work that is now *The Message*, I often felt that I was walking through an orchard at harvest time, plucking fully formed apples and peaches and plums from laden branches. There's hardly a page in the Bible I did not see lived in some way or other by the men and women, saints and sinners, to whom I was pastor—and then verified in my nation and culture.

I didn't start out as a pastor. I began my vocational life as a teacher and for several years taught the biblical languages of Hebrew and Greek in a theological seminary. I expected to live the rest of my life as a professor and scholar, teaching and writing and studying. But then my life took a sudden vocational turn to pastoring in a congregation.

I was now plunged into quite a different world. The first noticeable difference was that nobody seemed to care much about the Bible, which so recently people had been paying me to teach them. Many of the people I worked with now knew virtually nothing about it, had never read it, and weren't interested in learning. Many others had spent years reading it but for them it had gone flat through familiarity, reduced to clichés. Bored, they dropped it. And there weren't many people in between. Very few were interested in what I considered my primary work, getting the words of the Bible into their heads and hearts, getting the message lived. They found newspapers and magazines, videos and pulp fiction more to their taste.

Meanwhile I had taken on as my life work the responsibility of getting these very people to listen, really listen, to the message in this book. I knew I had my work cut out for me.

I lived in two language worlds, the world of the Bible and the world of Today. I had always assumed they were the same world. But these people didn't see it that way. So out of necessity I became a "translator" (although I wouldn't have called it that then), daily standing on the border between two worlds, getting the language of the Bible that God uses to create and save us, heal and bless us, judge and rule over us, into the language of Today that we use to gossip and tell stories, give directions and do business, sing songs, and talk to our children.

And all the time those old biblical languages, those powerful and vivid Hebrew and Greek originals, kept working their way underground in my speech, giving energy and sharpness to words and phrases, expanding the imagination of the people with whom I was working to hear the language of the Bible in the language of Today and the language of Today in the language of the Bible.

I did that for thirty years in one congregation. And then one day (it was April 30, 1990) I got a letter from an editor asking me to work on a new version of the Bible along the lines of what I had been doing as a pastor. I agreed. The next ten years was harvest time. *The Message* is the result.

The Message is a reading Bible. It is not intended to replace the excellent study Bibles that are available. My intent here (as it was earlier in my congregation and community) is simply to get people reading it who don't know that the Bible is read-able at all, at least by them, and to get people who long ago lost interest in the Bible to read it again. But I haven't tried to make it easy—there is much in the Bible that is hard to understand. So at some point along the way, soon or late, it will be important to get a standard study Bible to facilitate further study. Meanwhile, read in order to live, praying as you read, "God, let it be with me just as you say."

—EUGENE H. PETERSON

THE MESSAGE

Reading is the first thing, just reading the Bible. As we read we enter a new world of words and find ourselves in on a conversation in which God has the first and last words. We soon realize that we are included in the conversation. We didn't expect this. But this is precisely what generation after generation of Bible readers do find: The Bible is not only written about us but to us. In these pages we become insiders to a conversation in which God uses words to form and bless us, to teach and guide us, to forgive and save us.

We aren't used to this. We are used to reading books that explain things, or tell us what to do, or inspire or entertain us. But this is different. This is a world of revelation: God revealing to people just like us—men and women created in God's image—how God works and what is going on in this world in which we find ourselves. At the same time that God reveals all this, God draws us in by invitation and command to participate in God's working life. We gradually (or suddenly) realize that we are insiders in the most significant action of our time as God establishes his grand rule of love and justice on this earth (as it is in heaven). "Revelation" means that we are reading something we couldn't have guessed or figured out on our own. Revelation is what makes the Bible unique.

And so just reading this Bible, *The Message,* and listening to what we read, is the first thing. There will be time enough for study later on. But first, it is important simply to read, leisurely and thoughtfully. We need to get a feel for the way these stories and songs, these prayers and conversations, these sermons and visions, invite us into this large, large world in which the invisible God is behind and involved in everything visible and illuminates what it means to live here—really live, not just get across the street. As we read, and the longer we read, we begin to "get it"—we are in conversation with God. We find ourselves listening and answering in matters that most concern us: who we are, where we came from, where we are going, what makes us tick, the texture of the world and the communities we live in, and—most of all—the incredible love of God among us, doing for us what we cannot do for ourselves.

Through reading the Bible, we see that there is far more to the world, more to us, more to what we see and more to what we don't see—more to everything!—than we had ever dreamed, and that this "more" has to do with God.

This is new for many of us, a different sort of book—a book that reads us even as we read it. We are used to picking up and reading books for what we can get out of them: information we can use, inspiration to energize us, instructions on how to do something or other, entertainment to while away a rainy day, wisdom that will guide us into living better. These things can and do take place when reading the Bible, but the Bible is given to us in the first place simply to invite us to make ourselves at home in the world of God, God's word and world, and become familiar with the way God speaks and the ways in which we answer him with our lives.

Our reading turns up some surprises. The biggest surprise for many is how accessible this book is to those who simply open it up and read it. Virtually anyone can read this Bible with understanding. The reason that new translations are made every couple of generations or so is to keep the language of the Bible current with the common speech we use, the very language in which it was first written. We don't have to be smart or well-educated to understand it, for it is written in the words and sentences we hear in the marketplace, on school playgrounds, and around the dinner table. Because the Bible is so famous and revered, many assume that we need experts to explain and interpret it for us—and, of course, there are some things that need to be explained. But the first men and women who listened to these words now written in our Bibles were ordinary, everyday, working-class people. One of the greatest of the early translators of the Bible into English, William Tyndale, said that he was translating so that "the boy that driveth the plough" would be able to read the Scriptures.

One well-educated African man, who later became one of the most influential Bible teachers in our history (Augustine), was greatly offended when he first read the Bible. Instead of a book cultivated and polished in the literary style he admired so much, he found it full of homespun, earthy stories of plain, unimportant people. He read it in a Latin translation full of slang and jargon. He took one look at what he considered the "unspiritual" quality of so many of its characters and the everydayness of Jesus, and contemptuously abandoned it. It was years before he realized that God had not taken the form of a sophisticated intellectual to teach us about highbrow heavenly culture so we could appreciate the finer things of God. When he saw that God entered our lives as a Jewish servant in order to save us from our sins, he started reading the Book gratefully and believingly.

Some are also surprised that Bible reading does not introduce us to a "nicer" world. This biblical world is decidedly not an ideal world, the kind we see advertised in travel posters. Suffering and injustice and ugliness are not purged from the world in which God works and loves and saves. Nothing is glossed over. God works patiently and deeply, but often in hidden ways, in the mess of our humanity and history. Ours is not a neat and tidy world in which we are assured that we can get everything under our control. This takes considerable getting used to—there is mystery everywhere. The Bible does not give us a predictable cause-effect world in which we can plan our careers and secure our futures. It is not a dream world in which everything works out according to our adolescent expectations—there is pain and poverty and abuse at which we cry out in indignation, "You can't let this happen!" For most of us it takes years and years and years to exchange our dream world for this real world of grace and mercy, sacrifice and love, freedom and joy—the God-saved world.

Yet another surprise is that the Bible does not flatter us. It is not trying to sell us anything that promises to make life easier. It doesn't offer secrets to what we often think of as prosperity or pleasure or high adventure. The reality that comes into focus as we read the Bible has to do with what God is doing in a saving love that includes us and everything we do. This is quite different from what our sin-stunted and culture-cluttered minds imagined. But our Bible reading does not give us access to a mail-order catalog of idols from which we can pick and choose to satisfy our fantasies. The Bible begins with God speaking creation and us into being. It continues with God entering into personalized and complex relationships with us, helping and blessing us, teaching and training us, correcting and disciplining us, loving and saving us. This is not an escape from reality but a plunge into more reality—a sacrificial but altogether better life all the way.

God doesn't force any of this on us: God's word is personal address, inviting, commanding, challenging, rebuking, judging, comforting, directing—but not forcing. Not coercing. We are given space and freedom to answer, to enter the conversation. For more than anything else the Bible invites our participation in the work and language of God.

As we read, we find that there is a connection between the Word Read and the Word Lived. Everything in this book is live-able. Many of us find that the most important question we ask as we read is not "What does it mean?" but "How can I live it?" So we read personally, not impersonally. We read in order to live our true selves, not just get information that we can use to raise our standard of living. Bible reading is a means of listening to and obeying God, not gathering religious data by which we can be our own gods.

You are going to hear stories in this Book that will take you out of your preoccupation with yourself and into the spacious freedom in which God is working the world's salvation. You are going to come across words and sentences that stab you awake to a beauty and hope that will connect you with your real life.

Be sure to answer.

THE OLD TESTAMENT

GENESIS

New King James Version

The History of Creation

1 In the beginning God created the heavens
and the earth. 2The earth was without form,
and void; and darkness *was*[a] on the face of the
deep. And the Spirit of God was hovering over
the face of the waters.
3Then God said, "Let there be light"; and
there was light. 4And God saw the light, that *it
was* good; and God divided the light from the
darkness. 5God called the light Day, and the
darkness He called Night. So the evening and
the morning were the first day.
6Then God said, "Let there be a firmament in
the midst of the waters, and let it divide the wa-
ters from the waters." 7Thus God made the fir-
mament, and divided the waters which *were* un-
der the firmament from the waters which *were*
above the firmament; and it was so. 8And God
called the firmament Heaven. So the evening
and the morning were the second day.
9Then God said, "Let the waters under the
heavens be gathered together into one place,
and let the dry *land* appear"; and it was so.
10And God called the dry *land* Earth, and the
gathering together of the waters He called Seas.
And God saw that *it was* good.
11Then God said, "Let the earth bring forth
grass, the herb *that* yields seed, *and* the fruit
tree *that* yields fruit according to its kind,
whose seed *is* in itself, on the earth"; and it was
so. 12And the earth brought forth grass, the herb
that yields seed according to its kind, and the
tree *that* yields fruit, whose seed *is* in itself ac-
cording to its kind. And God saw that *it was*
good. 13So the evening and the morning were
the third day.
14Then God said, "Let there be lights in the
firmament of the heavens to divide the day from
the night; and let them be for signs and seasons,
and for days and years; 15and let them be for
lights in the firmament of the heavens to give
light on the earth"; and it was so. 16Then God
made two great lights: the greater light to rule
the day, and the lesser light to rule the night. *He
made* the stars also. 17God set them in the firma-
ment of the heavens to give light on the earth,

1:2 [a]Words in italic type have been added for clarity. They are not found in the original Hebrew or Aramaic.

The Message

Heaven and Earth

1-2 1 First this: God created the Heavens and Earth—all you see, all you don't see. Earth was a soup of nothingness, a bottomless emptiness, an inky blackness. God's Spirit brooded like a bird above the watery abyss.

3-5 God spoke: "Light!"
And light appeared.
God saw that light was good
and separated light from dark.
God named the light Day,
he named the dark Night.
It was evening, it was morning—
Day One.

6-8 God spoke: "Sky! In the middle of the waters;
separate water from water!"
God made sky.
He separated the water under sky
from the water above sky.
And there it was:
he named sky the Heavens;
It was evening, it was morning—
Day Two.

9-10 God spoke: "Separate!
Water-beneath-Heaven, gather into one place;
Land, appear!"
And there it was.
God named the land Earth.
He named the pooled water Ocean.
God saw that it was good.

11-13 God spoke: "Earth, green up! Grow all varieties
of seed-bearing plants,
Every sort of fruit-bearing tree."
And there it was.
Earth produced green seed-bearing plants,
all varieties,
And fruit-bearing trees of all sorts.
God saw that it was good.
It was evening, it was morning—
Day Three.

14-15 God spoke: "Lights! Come out!
Shine in Heaven's sky!
Separate Day from Night.
Mark seasons and days and years,
Lights in Heaven's sky to give light to Earth."
And there it was.

16-19 God made two big lights, the larger
to take charge of Day,
The smaller to be in charge of Night;
and he made the stars.
God placed them in the heavenly sky
to light up Earth

New King James Version

18and to rule over the day and over the night, and to divide the light from the darkness. And God saw that *it was* good. 19So the evening and the morning were the fourth day.

20Then God said, "Let the waters abound with an abundance of living creatures, and let birds fly above the earth across the face of the firmament of the heavens." 21So God created great sea creatures and every living thing that moves, with which the waters abounded, according to their kind, and every winged bird according to its kind. And God saw that *it was* good. 22And God blessed them, saying, "Be fruitful and multiply, and fill the waters in the seas, and let birds multiply on the earth." 23So the evening and the morning were the fifth day.

24Then God said, "Let the earth bring forth the living creature according to its kind: cattle and creeping thing and beast of the earth, *each* according to its kind"; and it was so. 25And God made the beast of the earth according to its kind, cattle according to its kind, and everything that creeps on the earth according to its kind. And God saw that *it was* good.

26Then God said, "Let Us make man in Our image, according to Our likeness; let them have dominion over the fish of the sea, over the birds of the air, and over the cattle, over all[a] the earth and over every creeping thing that creeps on the earth." 27So God created man in His *own* image; in the image of God He created him; male and female He created them. 28Then God blessed them, and God said to them, "Be fruitful and multiply; fill the earth and subdue it; have dominion over the fish of the sea, over the birds of the air, and over every living thing that moves on the earth."

29And God said, "See, I have given you every herb *that* yields seed which *is* on the face of all the earth, and every tree whose fruit yields seed; to you it shall be for food. 30Also, to every beast of the earth, to every bird of the air, and to everything that creeps on the earth, in which *there is* life, *I have given* every green herb for food"; and it was so. 31Then God saw everything that He had made, and indeed *it was* very good. So the evening and the morning were the sixth day.

1:26 [a]Syriac reads *all the wild animals of.*

The Message

And oversee Day and Night,
to separate light and dark.
God saw that it was good.
It was evening, it was morning—
Day Four.

20-23 God spoke: "Swarm, Ocean, with fish
and all sea life!
Birds, fly through the sky over Earth!"
God created the huge whales,
all the swarm of life in the waters,
And every kind and species of flying
birds.
God saw that it was good.
God blessed them: "Prosper! Reproduce!
Fill Ocean!
Birds, reproduce on Earth!"
It was evening, it was morning—
Day Five.

24-25 God spoke: "Earth, generate life! Every
sort and kind:
cattle and reptiles and wild
animals—all kinds."
And there it was:
wild animals of every kind,
Cattle of all kinds, every sort of reptile
and bug.
God saw that it was good.

26-28 God spoke: "Let us make human beings
in our image, make them
reflecting our nature
So they can be responsible for the fish
in the sea,
the birds in the air, the cattle,
And, yes, Earth itself,
and every animal that moves on the
face of Earth."
God created human beings;
he created them godlike,
Reflecting God's nature.
He created them male and female.
God blessed them:
"Prosper! Reproduce! Fill Earth! Take
charge!
Be responsible for fish in the sea and
birds in the air,
for every living thing that moves on
the face of Earth."

29-30 Then God said, "I've given you
every sort of seed-bearing plant on
Earth
And every kind of fruit-bearing tree,
given them to you for food.
To all animals and all birds,
everything that moves and breathes,
I give whatever grows out of the ground
for food."
And there it was.

31 God looked over everything he had
made;
it was so good, so very good!
It was evening, it was morning—
Day Six.

NEW KING JAMES VERSION

2 Thus the heavens and the earth, and all the host of them, were finished. 2And on the seventh day God ended His work which He had done, and He rested on the seventh day from all His work which He had done. 3Then God blessed the seventh day and sanctified it, because in it He rested from all His work which God had created and made.

4This *is* the history[a] of the heavens and the earth when they were created, in the day that the LORD God made the earth and the heavens, 5before any plant of the field was in the earth and before any herb of the field had grown. For the LORD God had not caused it to rain on the earth, and *there was* no man to till the ground; 6but a mist went up from the earth and watered the whole face of the ground.

7And the LORD God formed man *of* the dust of the ground, and breathed into his nostrils the breath of life; and man became a living being.

LIFE IN GOD'S GARDEN

8The LORD God planted a garden eastward in Eden, and there He put the man whom He had formed. 9And out of the ground the LORD God made every tree grow that is pleasant to the sight and good for food. The tree of life *was* also in the midst of the garden, and the tree of the knowledge of good and evil.

10Now a river went out of Eden to water the garden, and from there it parted and became four riverheads. 11The name of the first *is* Pishon; it *is* the one which skirts the whole land of Havilah, where *there is* gold. 12And the gold of that land *is* good. Bdellium and the onyx stone *are* there. 13The name of the second river *is* Gihon; it *is* the one which goes around the whole land of Cush. 14The name of the third river *is* Hiddekel;[a] it *is* the one which goes toward the east of Assyria. The fourth river *is* the Euphrates.

15Then the LORD God took the man and put him in the garden of Eden to tend and keep it. 16And the LORD God commanded the man, saying, "Of every tree of the garden you may freely eat; 17but of the tree of the knowledge of good and evil you shall not eat, for in the day that you eat of it you shall surely die."

18And the LORD God said, "*It is* not good that man should be alone; I will make him a helper comparable to him." 19Out of the ground the LORD God formed every beast of the field and every bird of the air, and brought *them* to Adam to see what he would call them. And whatever Adam called each living creature, that *was* its name. 20So Adam gave names to all cattle, to the birds of the air, and to every beast of the field. But for Adam there was not found a helper comparable to him.

21And the LORD God caused a deep sleep to fall on Adam, and he slept; and He took one of his ribs, and closed up the flesh in its place. 22Then the rib which the LORD God had taken from man He made into a woman, and He brought her to the man.

2:4 [a]Hebrew *toledoth,* literally *generations* **2:14** [a]Or *Tigris*

THE MESSAGE

1 2 Heaven and Earth were finished,
down to the last detail.

2-4 By the seventh day
God had finished his work.
On the seventh day
he rested from all his work.
God blessed the seventh day.
He made it a Holy Day
Because on that day he rested from his work,
all the creating God had done.

This is the story of how it all started,
of Heaven and Earth when they were created.

ADAM AND EVE

5-7 At the time GOD made Earth and Heaven, before any grasses or shrubs had sprouted from the ground—GOD hadn't yet sent rain on Earth, nor was there anyone around to work the ground (the whole Earth was watered by underground springs)—GOD formed Man out of dirt from the ground and blew into his nostrils the breath of life. The Man came alive—a living soul!

8-9 Then GOD planted a garden in Eden, in the east. He put the Man he had just made in it. GOD made all kinds of trees grow from the ground, trees beautiful to look at and good to eat. The Tree-of-Life was in the middle of the garden, also the Tree-of-Knowledge-of-Good-and-Evil.

10-14 A river flows out of Eden to water the garden and from there divides into four rivers. The first is named Pishon; it flows through Havilah where there is gold. The gold of this land is good. The land is also known for a sweet-scented resin and the onyx stone. The second river is named Gihon; it flows through the land of Cush. The third river is named Hiddekel and flows east of Assyria. The fourth river is the Euphrates.

15 GOD took the Man and set him down in the Garden of Eden to work the ground and keep it in order.

16-17 GOD commanded the Man, "You can eat from any tree in the garden, except from the Tree-of-Knowledge-of-Good-and-Evil. Don't eat from it. The moment you eat from that tree, you're dead."

18-20 GOD said, "It's not good for the Man to be alone; I'll make him a helper, a companion." So GOD formed from the dirt of the ground all the animals of the field and all the birds of the air. He brought them to the Man to see what he would name them. Whatever the Man called each living creature, that was its name. The Man named the cattle, named the birds of the air, named the wild animals; but he didn't find a suitable companion.

21-22 GOD put the Man into a deep sleep. As he slept he removed one of his ribs and replaced it with flesh. GOD then used the rib that he had taken from the Man to make Woman and presented her to the Man.

New King James Version

23And Adam said:

"This *is* now bone of my bones
And flesh of my flesh;
She shall be called Woman,
Because she was taken out of Man."

24Therefore a man shall leave his father and
mother and be joined to his wife, and they shall
become one flesh.
25And they were both naked, the man and his
wife, and were not ashamed.

The Temptation and Fall of Man

3 Now the serpent was more cunning than any
beast of the field which the LORD God had
made. And he said to the woman, "Has God in-
deed said, 'You shall not eat of every tree of the
garden'?"
2And the woman said to the serpent, "We
may eat the fruit of the trees of the garden; 3but
of the fruit of the tree which *is* in the midst of
the garden, God has said, 'You shall not eat it,
nor shall you touch it, lest you die.' "
4Then the serpent said to the woman, "You
will not surely die. 5For God knows that in the
day you eat of it your eyes will be opened, and
you will be like God, knowing good and evil."
6So when the woman saw that the tree *was*
good for food, that it *was* pleasant to the eyes,
and a tree desirable to make *one* wise, she took
of its fruit and ate. She also gave to her husband
with her, and he ate. 7Then the eyes of both of
them were opened, and they knew that they
were naked; and they sewed fig leaves together
and made themselves coverings.
8And they heard the sound of the LORD God
walking in the garden in the cool of the day, and
Adam and his wife hid themselves from the
presence of the LORD God among the trees of
the garden.
9Then the LORD God called to Adam and said
to him, "Where *are* you?"
10So he said, "I heard Your voice in the gar-
den, and I was afraid because I was naked; and
I hid myself."
11And He said, "Who told you that you *were*
naked? Have you eaten from the tree of which I
commanded you that you should not eat?"
12Then the man said, "The woman whom You
gave *to be* with me, she gave me of the tree, and
I ate."
13And the LORD God said to the woman,
"What *is* this you have done?"
The woman said, "The serpent deceived me,
and I ate."
14So the LORD God said to the serpent:

"Because you have done this,
You *are* cursed more than all cattle,
And more than every beast of the field;
On your belly you shall go,
And you shall eat dust
All the days of your life.
15And I will put enmity
Between you and the woman,
And between your seed and her Seed;
He shall bruise your head,
And you shall bruise His heel."

The Message

23-25 The Man said,
"Finally! Bone of my bone,
flesh of my flesh!
Name her Woman
for she was made from Man."
Therefore a man leaves his father and
mother and embraces his wife.
They become one flesh.
The two of them, the Man and his
Wife, were naked, but they felt no
shame.

1 3 The serpent was clever, more clever than
any wild animal GOD had made. He spoke
to the Woman: "Do I understand that God told
you not to eat from any tree in the garden?"
2-3 The Woman said to the serpent, "Not at
all. We can eat from the trees in the garden.
It's only about the tree in the middle of the
garden that God said, 'Don't eat from it;
don't even touch it or you'll die.' "
4-5 The serpent told the Woman, "You won't
die. God knows that the moment you eat
from that tree, you'll see what's really going
on. You'll be just like God, knowing every-
thing, ranging all the way from good to evil."
6 When the Woman saw that the tree
looked like good eating and realized what
she would get out of it—she'd know every-
thing!—she took and ate the fruit and then
gave some to her husband, and he ate.
7 Immediately the two of them did "see
what's really going on"—saw themselves
naked! They sewed fig leaves together as
makeshift clothes for themselves.
8 When they heard the sound of GOD
strolling in the garden in the evening
breeze, the Man and his Wife hid in the trees
of the garden, hid from GOD.
9 GOD called to the Man: "Where are you?"
10 He said, "I heard you in the garden and I
was afraid because I was naked. And I hid."
11 GOD said, "Who told you you were
naked? Did you eat from that tree I told you
not to eat from?"
12 The Man said, "The Woman you gave me
as a companion, she gave me fruit from the
tree, and, yes, I ate it."
GOD said to the Woman, "What is this that
you've done?"
13 "The serpent seduced me," she said, "and
I ate."

14-15 GOD told the serpent:
"Because you've done this, you're
cursed,
cursed beyond all cattle and wild
animals,
Cursed to slink on your belly
and eat dirt all your life.
I'm declaring war between you and the
Woman,
between your offspring and hers.
He'll wound your head,
you'll wound his heel."

NEW KING JAMES VERSION

16To the woman He said:

"I will greatly multiply your sorrow and your
conception;
In pain you shall bring forth children;
Your desire *shall be* for your husband,
And he shall rule over you."

17Then to Adam He said, "Because you have
heeded the voice of your wife, and have eaten
from the tree of which I commanded you, say-
ing, 'You shall not eat of it':

"Cursed *is* the ground for your sake;
In toil you shall eat *of* it
All the days of your life.
18Both thorns and thistles it shall bring forth
for you,
And you shall eat the herb of the field.
19In the sweat of your face you shall eat bread
Till you return to the ground,
For out of it you were taken;
For dust you *are*,
And to dust you shall return."

20And Adam called his wife's name Eve, be-
cause she was the mother of all living.
21Also for Adam and his wife the LORD God
made tunics of skin, and clothed them.
22Then the LORD God said, "Behold, the man
has become like one of Us, to know good and
evil. And now, lest he put out his hand and take
also of the tree of life, and eat, and live for-
ever"— 23therefore the LORD God sent him out of
the garden of Eden to till the ground from which
he was taken. 24So He drove out the man; and
He placed cherubim at the east of the garden of
Eden, and a flaming sword which turned every
way, to guard the way to the tree of life.

CAIN MURDERS ABEL

4 Now Adam knew Eve his wife, and she con-
ceived and bore Cain, and said, "I have ac-
quired a man from the LORD." 2Then she bore
again, this time his brother Abel. Now Abel was
a keeper of sheep, but Cain was a tiller of the
ground. 3And in the process of time it came to
pass that Cain brought an offering of the fruit of
the ground to the LORD. 4Abel also brought of the
firstborn of his flock and of their fat. And the
LORD respected Abel and his offering, 5but He
did not respect Cain and his offering. And Cain
was very angry, and his countenance fell.
6So the LORD said to Cain, "Why are you an-
gry? And why has your countenance fallen? 7If
you do well, will you not be accepted? And if
you do not do well, sin lies at the door. And its
desire *is* for you, but you should rule over it."

THE MESSAGE

16 He told the Woman:
"I'll multiply your pains in childbirth;
you'll give birth to your babies in pain.
You'll want to please your husband,
but he'll lord it over you."

17-19 He told the Man:
"Because you listened to your wife
and ate from the tree
That I commanded you not to eat from,
'Don't eat from this tree,'
The very ground is cursed because of
you;
getting food from the ground
Will be as painful as having babies is for
your wife;
you'll be working in pain all your life
long.
The ground will sprout thorns and
weeds,
you'll get your food the hard way,
Planting and tilling and harvesting,
sweating in the fields from dawn to
dusk,
Until you return to that ground yourself,
dead and buried;
you started out as dirt, you'll end up
dirt."

20 The Man, known as Adam, named his
wife Eve because she was the mother of all
the living.
21 GOD made leather clothing for Adam and
his wife and dressed them.
22 GOD said, "The Man has become like one
of us, capable of knowing everything, rang-
ing from good to evil. What if he now should
reach out and take fruit from the Tree-of-
Life and eat, and live forever? Never—this
cannot happen!"
23-24 So GOD expelled them from the Garden
of Eden and sent them to work the ground,
the same dirt out of which they'd been
made. He threw them out of the garden and
stationed angel-cherubim and a revolving
sword of fire east of it, guarding the path to
the Tree-of-Life.

1 4 Adam slept with Eve his wife. She con-
ceived and had Cain. She said, "I've gotten
a man, with GOD's help!"
2 Then she had another baby, Abel. Abel
was a herdsman and Cain a farmer.
3-5 Time passed. Cain brought an offering to
GOD from the produce of his farm. Abel also
brought an offering, but from the firstborn
animals of his herd, choice cuts of meat.
GOD liked Abel and his offering, but Cain
and his offering didn't get his approval.
Cain lost his temper and went into a sulk.
6-7 GOD spoke to Cain: "Why this tantrum?
Why the sulking? If you do well, won't you
be accepted? And if you don't do well, sin is
lying in wait for you, ready to pounce; it's
out to get you, you've got to master it."

New King James Version

8 Now Cain talked with Abel his brother;[a] and
it came to pass, when they were in the field, that
Cain rose up against Abel his brother and killed
him.
9 Then the LORD said to Cain, "Where *is* Abel
your brother?"
He said, "I do not know. *Am* I my brother's
keeper?"
10 And He said, "What have you done? The
voice of your brother's blood cries out to Me
from the ground. 11 So now you *are* cursed from
the earth, which has opened its mouth to receive
your brother's blood from your hand. 12 When
you till the ground, it shall no longer yield its
strength to you. A fugitive and a vagabond you
shall be on the earth."
13 And Cain said to the LORD, "My punish-
ment *is* greater than I can bear! 14 Surely You
have driven me out this day from the face of the
ground; I shall be hidden from Your face; I shall
be a fugitive and a vagabond on the earth, and
it will happen *that* anyone who finds me will
kill me."
15 And the LORD said to him, "Therefore,[a]
whoever kills Cain, vengeance shall be taken on
him sevenfold." And the LORD set a mark on
Cain, lest anyone finding him should kill him.

The Family of Cain

16 Then Cain went out from the presence of
the LORD and dwelt in the land of Nod on the
east of Eden. 17 And Cain knew his wife, and she
conceived and bore Enoch. And he built a city,
and called the name of the city after the name of
his son—Enoch. 18 To Enoch was born Irad; and
Irad begot Mehujael, and Mehujael begot
Methushael, and Methushael begot Lamech.
19 Then Lamech took for himself two wives:
the name of one *was* Adah, and the name of the
second *was* Zillah. 20 And Adah bore Jabal. He
was the father of those who dwell in tents and
have livestock. 21 His brother's name *was* Jubal.
He was the father of all those who play the harp
and flute. 22 And as for Zillah, she also bore
Tubal-Cain, an instructor of every craftsman in
bronze and iron. And the sister of Tubal-Cain
was Naamah.
23 Then Lamech said to his wives:

"Adah and Zillah, hear my voice;
Wives of Lamech, listen to my speech!
For I have killed a man for wounding me,
Even a young man for hurting me.
24 If Cain shall be avenged sevenfold,
Then Lamech seventy-sevenfold."

A New Son

25 And Adam knew his wife again, and she
bore a son and named him Seth, "For God has
appointed another seed for me instead of Abel,
whom Cain killed." 26 And as for Seth, to him
also a son was born; and he named him Enosh.[a]
Then *men* began to call on the name of the
LORD.

4:8 [a]Samaritan Pentateuch, Septuagint, Syriac, and Vulgate add *"Let us go out to the field."* 4:15 [a]Following Masoretic Text and Targum; Septuagint, Syriac, and Vulgate read *Not so.* 4:26 [a]Greek *Enos*

The Message

8 Cain had words with his brother. They were out in the field; Cain came at Abel his brother and killed him.

9 GOD said to Cain, "Where is Abel your brother?"

He said, "How should I know? Am I his babysitter?"

10-12 GOD said, "What have you done! The voice of your brother's blood is calling to me from the ground. From now on you'll get nothing but curses from this ground; you'll be driven from this ground that has opened its arms to receive the blood of your murdered brother. You'll farm this ground, but it will no longer give you its best. You'll be a homeless wanderer on Earth."

13-14 Cain said to GOD, "My punishment is too much. I can't take it! You've thrown me off the land and I can never again face you. I'm a homeless wanderer on Earth and whoever finds me will kill me."

15 GOD told him, "No. Anyone who kills Cain will pay for it seven times over." GOD put a mark on Cain to protect him so that no one who met him would kill him.

16 Cain left the presence of GOD and lived in No-Man's-Land, east of Eden.

17-18 Cain slept with his wife. She conceived and had Enoch. He then built a city and named it after his son, Enoch.
Enoch had Irad,
Irad had Mehujael,
Mehujael had Methushael,
Methushael had Lamech.

19-22 Lamech married two wives, Adah and Zillah. Adah gave birth to Jabal, the ancestor of all who live in tents and herd cattle. His brother's name was Jubal, the ancestor of all who play the lyre and flute. Zillah gave birth to Tubal-Cain, who worked at the forge making bronze and iron tools. Tubal-Cain's sister was Naamah.

23-24 Lamech said to his wives,
Adah and Zillah, listen to me;
you wives of Lamech, hear me out:
I killed a man for wounding me,
a young man who attacked me.
If Cain is avenged seven times,
for Lamech it's seventy-seven!

25-26 Adam slept with his wife again. She had a son whom she named Seth. She said, "God has given me another child in place of Abel whom Cain killed." And then Seth had a son whom he named Enosh.

That's when men and women began praying and worshiping in the name of GOD.

New King James Version

The Family of Adam

5 This is the book of the genealogy of Adam. In
the day that God created man, He made him
in the likeness of God. 2He created them male
and female, and blessed them and called them
Mankind in the day they were created. 3And
Adam lived one hundred and thirty years, and
begot *a son* in his own likeness, after his image,
and named him Seth. 4After he begot Seth, the
days of Adam were eight hundred years; and he
had sons and daughters. 5So all the days that
Adam lived were nine hundred and thirty years;
and he died.
6Seth lived one hundred and five years, and
begot Enosh. 7After he begot Enosh, Seth lived
eight hundred and seven years, and had sons
and daughters. 8So all the days of Seth were
nine hundred and twelve years; and he died.
9Enosh lived ninety years, and begot
Cainan.[a] 10After he begot Cainan, Enosh lived
eight hundred and fifteen years, and had sons
and daughters. 11So all the days of Enosh were
nine hundred and five years; and he died.
12Cainan lived seventy years, and begot Ma-
halalel. 13After he begot Mahalalel, Cainan lived
eight hundred and forty years, and had sons and
daughters. 14So all the days of Cainan were nine
hundred and ten years; and he died.
15Mahalalel lived sixty-five years, and begot
Jared. 16After he begot Jared, Mahalalel lived
eight hundred and thirty years, and had sons
and daughters. 17So all the days of Mahalalel
were eight hundred and ninety-five years; and
he died.
18Jared lived one hundred and sixty-two
years, and begot Enoch. 19After he begot Enoch,
Jared lived eight hundred years, and had sons
and daughters. 20So all the days of Jared were
nine hundred and sixty-two years; and he died.
21Enoch lived sixty-five years, and begot
Methuselah. 22After he begot Methuselah,
Enoch walked with God three hundred years,
and had sons and daughters. 23So all the days of
Enoch were three hundred and sixty-five years.
24And Enoch walked with God; and he *was* not,
for God took him.
25Methuselah lived one hundred and eighty-
seven years, and begot Lamech. 26After he begot
Lamech, Methuselah lived seven hundred and
eighty-two years, and had sons and daughters.
27So all the days of Methuselah were nine hun-
dred and sixty-nine years; and he died.
28Lamech lived one hundred and eighty-two
years, and had a son. 29And he called his name
Noah, saying, "This *one* will comfort us con-
cerning our work and the toil of our hands, be-
cause of the ground which the LORD has cursed."
30After he begot Noah, Lamech lived five hun-
dred and ninety-five years, and had sons and
daughters. 31So all the days of Lamech were
seven hundred and seventy-seven years; and he
died.
32And Noah was five hundred years old, and
Noah begot Shem, Ham, and Japheth.

5:9 [a]Hebrew *Qenan*

The Message

The Family Tree of the Human Race

1-2 5 This is the family tree of the human race:
When God created the human race, he
made it godlike, with a nature akin to God.
He created both male and female and
blessed them, the whole human race.
3-5 When Adam was 130 years old, he had a
son who was just like him, his very spirit
and image, and named him Seth. After the
birth of Seth, Adam lived another 800 years,
having more sons and daughters. Adam
lived a total of 930 years. And he died.
6-8 When Seth was 105 years old, he had
Enosh. After Seth had Enosh, he lived an-
other 807 years, having more sons and
daughters. Seth lived a total of 912 years.
And he died.
9-11 When Enosh was ninety years old, he had
Kenan. After he had Kenan, he lived another
815 years, having more sons and daughters.
Enosh lived a total of 905 years. And he
died.
12-14 When Kenan was seventy years old, he
had Mahalalel. After he had Mahalalel, he
lived another 840 years, having more sons
and daughters. Kenan lived a total of 910
years. And he died.
15-17 When Mahalalel was sixty-five years old,
he had Jared. After he had Jared, he lived
another 830 years, having more sons and
daughters. Mahalalel lived a total of 895
years. And he died.
18-20 When Jared was 162 years old, he had
Enoch. After he had Enoch, he lived another
800 years, having more sons and daughters.
Jared lived a total of 962 years. And he died.
21-23 When Enoch was sixty-five years old, he
had Methuselah. Enoch walked steadily
with God. After he had Methuselah, he lived
another 300 years, having more sons and
daughters. Enoch lived a total of 365 years.
24 Enoch walked steadily with God. And
then one day he was simply gone: God took
him.
25-27 When Methuselah was 187 years old, he
had Lamech. After he had Lamech, he lived
another 782 years. Methuselah lived a total
of 969 years. And he died.
28-31 When Lamech was 182 years old, he had
a son. He named him Noah, saying, "This
one will give us a break from the hard work
of farming the ground that GOD cursed." Af-
ter Lamech had Noah, he lived another 595
years, having more sons and daughters.
Lamech lived a total of 777 years. And he
died.
32 When Noah was 500 years old, he had
Shem, Ham, and Japheth.

New King James Version

The Wickedness and Judgment of Man

6 Now it came to pass, when men began to
multiply on the face of the earth, and daugh-
ters were born to them, [2]that the sons of God
saw the daughters of men, that they *were* beau-
tiful; and they took wives for themselves of all
whom they chose.
[3]And the LORD said, "My Spirit shall not
strive[a] with man forever, for he *is* indeed flesh;
yet his days shall be one hundred and twenty
years." [4]There were giants on the earth in those
days, and also afterward, when the sons of God
came in to the daughters of men and they bore
children to them. Those *were* the mighty men
who *were* of old, men of renown.
[5]Then the LORD[a] saw that the wickedness of
man *was* great in the earth, and *that* every in-
tent of the thoughts of his heart *was* only evil
continually. [6]And the LORD was sorry that He
had made man on the earth, and He was grieved
in His heart. [7]So the LORD said, "I will destroy
man whom I have created from the face of the
earth, both man and beast, creeping thing and
birds of the air, for I am sorry that I have made
them." [8]But Noah found grace in the eyes of the
LORD.

Noah Pleases God

[9]This is the genealogy of Noah. Noah was a
just man, perfect in his generations. Noah
walked with God. [10]And Noah begot three sons:
Shem, Ham, and Japheth.
[11]The earth also was corrupt before God, and
the earth was filled with violence. [12]So God
looked upon the earth, and indeed it was cor-
rupt; for all flesh had corrupted their way on the
earth.

The Ark Prepared

[13]And God said to Noah, "The end of all flesh
has come before Me, for the earth is filled with
violence through them; and behold, I will de-
stroy them with the earth. [14]Make yourself an
ark of gopherwood; make rooms in the ark, and
cover it inside and outside with pitch. [15]And this
is how you shall make it: The length of the ark
shall be three hundred cubits, its width fifty cu-
bits, and its height thirty cubits. [16]You shall
make a window for the ark, and you shall finish
it to a cubit from above; and set the door of the
ark in its side. You shall make it *with* lower, sec-
ond, and third *decks*. [17]And behold, I Myself am
bringing floodwaters on the earth, to destroy
from under heaven all flesh in which *is* the
breath of life; everything that *is* on the earth
shall die. [18]But I will establish My covenant with
you; and you shall go into the ark—you, your
sons, your wife, and your sons' wives with you.
[19]And of every living thing of all flesh you shall
bring two of every *sort* into the ark, to keep
them alive with you; they shall be male and fe-
male. [20]Of the birds after their kind, of animals
after their kind, and of every creeping thing of
the earth after its kind, two of every *kind* will

6:3 [a]Septuagint, Syriac, Targum, and Vulgate read *abide*.
6:5 [a]Following Masoretic Text and Targum; Vulgate reads *God;* Septuagint reads *LORD God*.

The Message

Giants in the Land

1-2 6 When the human race began to increase, with more and more daughters being born, the sons of God noticed that the daughters of men were beautiful. They looked them over and picked out wives for themselves.

3 Then GOD said, "I'm not going to breathe life into men and women endlessly. Eventually they're going to die; from now on they can expect a life span of 120 years."

4 This was back in the days (and also later) when there were giants in the land. The giants came from the union of the sons of God and the daughters of men. These were the mighty men of ancient lore, the famous ones.

Noah and His Sons

5-7 GOD saw that human evil was out of control. People thought evil, imagined evil—evil, evil, evil from morning to night. GOD was sorry that he had made the human race in the first place; it broke his heart. GOD said, "I'll get rid of my ruined creation, make a clean sweep: people, animals, snakes and bugs, birds—the works. I'm sorry I made them."

8 But Noah was different. GOD liked what he saw in Noah.

9-10 This is the story of Noah: Noah was a good man, a man of integrity in his community. Noah walked with God. Noah had three sons: Shem, Ham, and Japheth.

11-12 As far as God was concerned, the Earth had become a sewer; there was violence everywhere. God took one look and saw how bad it was, everyone corrupt and corrupting—life itself corrupt to the core.

13 God said to Noah, "It's all over. It's the end of the human race. The violence is everywhere; I'm making a clean sweep.

14-16 "Build yourself a ship from teakwood. Make rooms in it. Coat it with pitch inside and out. Make it 450 feet long, seventy-five feet wide, and forty-five feet high. Build a roof for it and put in a window eighteen inches from the top; put in a door on the side of the ship; and make three decks, lower, middle, and upper.

17 "I'm going to bring a flood on the Earth that will destroy everything alive under Heaven. Total destruction.

18-21 "But I'm going to establish a covenant with you: You'll board the ship, and your sons, your wife and your sons' wives will come on board with you. You are also to take two of each living creature, a male and a female, on board the ship, to preserve their lives with you: two of every species of bird, mammal, and reptile—two of everything so

NEW KING JAMES VERSION

come to you to keep *them* alive. 21And you shall
take for yourself of all food that is eaten, and
you shall gather *it* to yourself; and it shall be
food for you and for them."
22Thus Noah did; according to all that God
commanded him, so he did.

THE GREAT FLOOD

7Then the LORD said to Noah, "Come into the
ark, you and all your household, because I
have seen *that* you *are* righteous before Me in
this generation. 2You shall take with you seven
each of every clean animal, a male and his fe-
male; two each of animals that *are* unclean, a
male and his female; 3also seven each of birds of
the air, male and female, to keep the species
alive on the face of all the earth. 4For after seven
more days I will cause it to rain on the earth
forty days and forty nights, and I will destroy
from the face of the earth all living things that I
have made." 5And Noah did according to all that
the LORD commanded him. 6Noah *was* six hun-
dred years old when the floodwaters were on
the earth.
7So Noah, with his sons, his wife, and his
sons' wives, went into the ark because of the
waters of the flood. 8Of clean animals, of ani-
mals that *are* unclean, of birds, and of every-
thing that creeps on the earth, 9two by two they
went into the ark to Noah, male and female, as
God had commanded Noah. 10And it came to
pass after seven days that the waters of the
flood were on the earth. 11In the six hundredth
year of Noah's life, in the second month, the sev-
enteenth day of the month, on that day all the
fountains of the great deep were broken up, and
the windows of heaven were opened. 12And the
rain was on the earth forty days and forty
nights.
13On the very same day Noah and Noah's
sons, Shem, Ham, and Japheth, and Noah's wife
and the three wives of his sons with them, en-
tered the ark— 14they and every beast after its
kind, all cattle after their kind, every creeping
thing that creeps on the earth after its kind, and
every bird after its kind, every bird of every sort.
15And they went into the ark to Noah, two by
two, of all flesh in which *is* the breath of life.
16So those that entered, male and female of all
flesh, went in as God had commanded him; and
the LORD shut him in.
17Now the flood was on the earth forty days.
The waters increased and lifted up the ark, and
it rose high above the earth. 18The waters pre-
vailed and greatly increased on the earth, and
the ark moved about on the surface of the wa-
ters. 19And the waters prevailed exceedingly on
the earth, and all the high hills under the whole
heaven were covered. 20The waters prevailed fif-
teen cubits upward, and the mountains were
covered. 21And all flesh died that moved on the
earth: birds and cattle and beasts and every
creeping thing that creeps on the earth, and
every man. 22All in whose nostrils *was* the
breath of the spirit[a] of life, all that *was* on the
dry *land,* died. 23So He destroyed all living
things which were on the face of the ground:

7:22 [a]Septuagint and Vulgate omit *of the spirit.*

THE MESSAGE

as to preserve their lives along with yours.
Also get all the food you'll need and store it
up for you and them."
22 Noah did everything God commanded
him to do.

1 7Next GOD said to Noah, "Now board the
ship, you and all your family—out of every-
one in this generation, you're the righteous
one.
2-4 "Take on board with you seven pairs of
every clean animal, a male and a female;
one pair of every unclean animal, a male
and a female; and seven pairs of every kind
of bird, a male and a female, to insure their
survival on Earth. In just seven days I will
dump rain on Earth for forty days and forty
nights. I'll make a clean sweep of everything
that I've made."
5 Noah did everything GOD commanded
him.
6-10 Noah was 600 years old when the flood-
waters covered the Earth. Noah and his wife
and sons and their wives boarded the ship
to escape the flood. Clean and unclean ani-
mals, birds, and all the crawling creatures
came in pairs to Noah and to the ship, male
and female, just as God had commanded
Noah. In seven days the floodwaters came.
11-12 It was the six-hundredth year of Noah's
life, in the second month, on the seventeenth
day of the month that it happened: all the
underground springs erupted and all the
windows of Heaven were thrown open. Rain
poured for forty days and forty nights.
13-16 That's the day Noah and his sons Shem,
Ham, and Japheth, accompanied by his wife
and his sons' wives, boarded the ship. And
with them every kind of wild and domestic
animal, right down to all the kinds of crea-
tures that crawl and all kinds of birds and
anything that flies. They came to Noah and
to the ship in pairs—everything and any-
thing that had the breath of life in it, male
and female of every creature came just as
God had commanded Noah. Then GOD shut
the door behind him.
17-23 The flood continued forty days and the
waters rose and lifted the ship high over the
Earth. The waters kept rising, the flood
deepened on the Earth, the ship floated on
the surface. The flood got worse until all the
highest mountains were covered—the high-
water mark reached twenty feet above the
crest of the mountains. Everything died.
Anything that moved—dead. Birds, farm an-
imals, wild animals, the entire teeming exu-
berance of life—dead. And all people—dead.
Every living, breathing creature that lived
on dry land died; he wiped out the whole

NEW KING JAMES VERSION

both man and cattle, creeping thing and bird of the air. They were destroyed from the earth. Only Noah and those who *were* with him in the ark remained *alive.* 24And the waters prevailed on the earth one hundred and fifty days.

NOAH'S DELIVERANCE

8 Then God remembered Noah, and every living thing, and all the animals that *were* with him in the ark. And God made a wind to pass over the earth, and the waters subsided. 2The fountains of the deep and the windows of heaven were also stopped, and the rain from heaven was restrained. 3And the waters receded continually from the earth. At the end of the hundred and fifty days the waters decreased. 4Then the ark rested in the seventh month, the seventeenth day of the month, on the mountains of Ararat. 5And the waters decreased continually until the tenth month. In the tenth *month,* on the first *day* of the month, the tops of the mountains were seen.

6So it came to pass, at the end of forty days, that Noah opened the window of the ark which he had made. 7Then he sent out a raven, which kept going to and fro until the waters had dried up from the earth. 8He also sent out from himself a dove, to see if the waters had receded from the face of the ground. 9But the dove found no resting place for the sole of her foot, and she returned into the ark to him, for the waters *were* on the face of the whole earth. So he put out his hand and took her, and drew her into the ark to himself. 10And he waited yet another seven days, and again he sent the dove out from the ark. 11Then the dove came to him in the evening, and behold, a freshly plucked olive leaf *was* in her mouth; and Noah knew that the waters had receded from the earth. 12So he waited yet another seven days and sent out the dove, which did not return again to him anymore.

13And it came to pass in the six hundred and first year, in the first *month,* the first *day* of the month, that the waters were dried up from the earth; and Noah removed the covering of the ark and looked, and indeed the surface of the ground was dry. 14And in the second month, on the twenty-seventh day of the month, the earth was dried.

15Then God spoke to Noah, saying, 16"Go out of the ark, you and your wife, and your sons and your sons' wives with you. 17Bring out with you every living thing of all flesh that *is* with you: birds and cattle and every creeping thing that creeps on the earth, so that they may abound on the earth, and be fruitful and multiply on the earth." 18So Noah went out, and his sons and his wife and his sons' wives with him. 19Every animal, every creeping thing, every bird, *and* whatever creeps on the earth, according to their families, went out of the ark.

GOD'S COVENANT WITH CREATION

20Then Noah built an altar to the LORD, and took of every clean animal and of every clean bird, and offered burnt offerings on the altar. 21And the LORD smelled a soothing aroma. Then the LORD said in His heart, "I will never again

THE MESSAGE

works—people and animals, crawling creatures and flying birds, every last one of them, gone. Only Noah and his company on the ship lived.

24 The floodwaters took over for 150 days.

1-3 8 Then God turned his attention to Noah and all the wild animals and farm animals with him on the ship. God caused the wind to blow and the floodwaters began to go down. The underground springs were shut off, the windows of Heaven closed and the rain quit. Inch by inch the water lowered. After 150 days the worst was over.

4-6 On the seventeenth day of the seventh month, the ship landed on the Ararat mountain range. The water kept going down until the tenth month. On the first day of the tenth month the tops of the mountains came into view. After forty days Noah opened the window that he had built into the ship.

7-9 He sent out a raven; it flew back and forth waiting for the floodwaters to dry up. Then he sent a dove to check on the flood conditions, but it couldn't even find a place to perch—water still covered the Earth. Noah reached out and caught it, brought it back into the ship.

10-11 He waited seven more days and sent out the dove again. It came back in the evening with a freshly picked olive leaf in its beak. Noah knew that the flood was about finished.

12 He waited another seven days and sent the dove out a third time. This time it didn't come back.

13-14 In the six-hundred-first year of Noah's life, on the first day of the first month, the flood had dried up. Noah opened the hatch of the ship and saw dry ground. By the twenty-seventh day of the second month, the Earth was completely dry.

15-17 God spoke to Noah: "Leave the ship, you and your wife and your sons and your sons' wives. And take all the animals with you, the whole menagerie of birds and mammals and crawling creatures, all that brimming prodigality of life, so they can reproduce and flourish on the Earth."

18-19 Noah disembarked with his sons and wife and his sons' wives. Then all the animals, crawling creatures, birds—every creature on the face of the Earth—left the ship family by family.

20-21 Noah built an altar to GOD. He selected clean animals and birds from every species and offered them as burnt offerings on the altar. GOD smelled the sweet fragrance and thought to himself, "I'll never again curse

NEW KING JAMES VERSION

curse the ground for man's sake, although the imagination of man's heart *is* evil from his youth; nor will I again destroy every living thing as I have done.

22"While the earth remains,
Seedtime and harvest,
Cold and heat,
Winter and summer,
And day and night
Shall not cease."

9 So God blessed Noah and his sons, and said to them: "Be fruitful and multiply, and fill the earth.[a] 2And the fear of you and the dread of you shall be on every beast of the earth, on every bird of the air, on all that move *on* the earth, and on all the fish of the sea. They are given into your hand. 3Every moving thing that lives shall be food for you. I have given you all things, even as the green herbs. 4But you shall not eat flesh with its life, *that is,* its blood. 5Surely for your lifeblood I will demand *a reckoning;* from the hand of every beast I will require it, and from the hand of man. From the hand of every man's brother I will require the life of man.

6"Whoever sheds man's blood,
By man his blood shall be shed;
For in the image of God
He made man.
7And as for you, be fruitful and multiply;
Bring forth abundantly in the earth
And multiply in it."

8Then God spoke to Noah and to his sons with him, saying: 9"And as for Me, behold, I establish My covenant with you and with your descendants[a] after you, 10and with every living creature that *is* with you: the birds, the cattle, and every beast of the earth with you, of all that go out of the ark, every beast of the earth. 11Thus I establish My covenant with you: Never again shall all flesh be cut off by the waters of the flood; never again shall there be a flood to destroy the earth."

12And God said: "This *is* the sign of the covenant which I make between Me and you, and every living creature that *is* with you, for perpetual generations: 13I set My rainbow in the cloud, and it shall be for the sign of the covenant between Me and the earth. 14It shall be, when I bring a cloud over the earth, that the rainbow shall be seen in the cloud; 15and I will remember My covenant which *is* between Me and you and every living creature of all flesh; the waters shall never again become a flood to destroy all flesh. 16The rainbow shall be in the cloud, and I will look on it to remember the everlasting covenant between God and every living creature of all flesh that *is* on the earth." 17And God said to Noah, "This *is* the sign of the covenant which I have established between Me and all flesh that *is* on the earth."

9:1 [a]Compare Genesis 1:28 9:9 [a]Literally *seed*

THE MESSAGE

the ground because of people. I know they
have this bent toward evil from an early age,
but I'll never again kill off everything living
as I've just done.

22 For as long as Earth lasts,
planting and harvest, cold and heat,
Summer and winter, day and night
will never stop."

1-4 9 God blessed Noah and his sons: He said,
"Prosper! Reproduce! Fill the Earth! Every
living creature—birds, animals, fish—will
fall under your spell and be afraid of you.
You're responsible for them. All living crea-
tures are yours for food; just as I gave you
the plants, now I give you everything else.
Except for meat with its lifeblood still in it—
don't eat that.
5 "But your own lifeblood I will avenge; I
will avenge it against both animals and
other humans.

6-7 Whoever sheds human blood,
by humans let his blood be shed,
Because God made humans in his image
reflecting God's very nature.
You're here to bear fruit, reproduce,
lavish life on the Earth, live
bountifully!"

8-11 Then God spoke to Noah and his sons:
"I'm setting up my covenant with you in-
cluding your children who will come after
you, along with everything alive around
you—birds, farm animals, wild animals—
that came out of the ship with you. I'm set-
ting up my covenant with you that never
again will everything living be destroyed by
floodwaters; no, never again will a flood de-
stroy the Earth."
12-16 God continued, "This is the sign of the
covenant I am making between me and you
and everything living around you and every-
one living after you. I'm putting my rainbow
in the clouds, a sign of the covenant be-
tween me and the Earth. From now on,
when I form a cloud over the Earth and the
rainbow appears in the cloud, I'll remember
my covenant between me and you and
everything living, that never again will
floodwaters destroy all life. When the rain-
bow appears in the cloud, I'll see it and re-
member the eternal covenant between God
and everything living, every last living crea-
ture on Earth."
17 And God said, "This is the sign of the
covenant that I've set up between me and
everything living on the Earth."

New King James Version

Noah and His Sons

18Now the sons of Noah who went out of the
ark were Shem, Ham, and Japheth. And Ham
was the father of Canaan. 19These three *were*
the sons of Noah, and from these the whole
earth was populated.
20And Noah began *to be* a farmer, and he
planted a vineyard. 21Then he drank of the wine
and was drunk, and became uncovered in his
tent. 22And Ham, the father of Canaan, saw the
nakedness of his father, and told his two broth-
ers outside. 23But Shem and Japheth took a gar-
ment, laid *it* on both their shoulders, and went
backward and covered the nakedness of their
father. Their faces *were* turned away, and they
did not see their father's nakedness.
24So Noah awoke from his wine, and knew
what his younger son had done to him. 25Then
he said:

"Cursed *be* Canaan;
A servant of servants
He shall be to his brethren."

26And he said:

"Blessed *be* the LORD,
The God of Shem,
And may Canaan be his servant.
27May God enlarge Japheth,
And may he dwell in the tents of Shem;
And may Canaan be his servant."

28And Noah lived after the flood three hun-
dred and fifty years. 29So all the days of Noah
were nine hundred and fifty years; and he died.

Nations Descended from Noah

10 Now this *is* the genealogy of the sons of
Noah: Shem, Ham, and Japheth. And sons
were born to them after the flood.
2The sons of Japheth *were* Gomer, Magog,
Madai, Javan, Tubal, Meshech, and Tiras. 3The
sons of Gomer *were* Ashkenaz, Riphath,[a] and
Togarmah. 4The sons of Javan *were* Elishah,
Tarshish, Kittim, and Dodanim.[a] 5From these the
coastland *peoples* of the Gentiles were sepa-
rated into their lands, everyone according to his
language, according to their families, into their
nations.
6The sons of Ham *were* Cush, Mizraim, Put,[a]
and Canaan. 7The sons of Cush *were* Seba, Hav-
ilah, Sabtah, Raamah, and Sabtechah; and the
sons of Raamah *were* Sheba and Dedan.
8Cush begot Nimrod; he began to be a
mighty one on the earth. 9He was a mighty
hunter before the LORD; therefore it is said,
"Like Nimrod the mighty hunter before the
LORD." 10And the beginning of his kingdom was
Babel, Erech, Accad, and Calneh, in the land of
Shinar. 11From that land he went to Assyria and
built Nineveh, Rehoboth Ir, Calah, 12and Resen
between Nineveh and Calah (that *is* the princi-
pal city).

10:3 [a]Spelled *Diphath* in 1 Chronicles 1:6 **10:4** [a]Spelled *Rodanim* in Samaritan Pentateuch and 1 Chronicles 1:7 **10:6** [a]Or *Phut*

The Message

18-19 The sons of Noah who came out of the
ship were Shem, Ham, and Japheth. Ham
was the father of Canaan. These are the
three sons of Noah; from these three the
whole Earth was populated.

20-23 Noah, a farmer, was the first to plant a
vineyard. He drank from its wine, got drunk
and passed out, naked in his tent. Ham, the
father of Canaan, saw that his father was
naked and told his two brothers who were
outside the tent. Shem and Japheth took a
cloak, held it between them from their
shoulders, walked backward and covered
their father's nakedness, keeping their faces
turned away so they did not see their fa-
ther's exposed body.
24-27 When Noah woke up with his hangover,
he learned what his youngest son had done.
He said,

Cursed be Canaan! A slave of slaves,
a slave to his brothers!
Blessed be GOD, the God of Shem,
but Canaan shall be his slave.
God prosper Japheth,
living spaciously in the tents of Shem.
But Canaan shall be his slave.

28-29 Noah lived another 350 years following
the flood. He lived a total of 950 years. And
he died.

The Family Tree of Noah's Sons

1 10 This is the family tree of the sons of
Noah: Shem, Ham, and Japheth. After
the flood, they themselves had sons.
2 The sons of Japheth: Gomer, Magog,
Madai, Javan, Tubal, Meshech, Tiras.
3 The sons of Gomer: Ashkenaz, Riphath,
Togarmah.
4-5 The sons of Javan: Elishah, Tarshish, Kit-
tim, Rodanim. The seafaring peoples devel-
oped from these, each in its own place by
family, each with its own language.

6 The sons of Ham: Cush, Egypt, Put,
Canaan.
7 The sons of Cush: Seba, Havilah, Sabtah,
Raamah, Sabteca.
The sons of Raamah: Sheba, Dedan.
8-12 Cush also had Nimrod. He was the first
great warrior on Earth. He was a great
hunter before GOD. There was a saying,
"Like Nimrod, a great hunter before GOD."
His kingdom got its start with Babel; then
Erech, Akkad, and Calneh in the country of
Shinar. From there he went up to Asshur
and built Nineveh, Rehoboth Ir, Calah, and
Resen between Nineveh and the great city
Calah.

New King James Version

13Mizraim begot Ludim, Anamim, Lehabim, Naphtuhim, 14Pathrusim, and Casluhim (from whom came the Philistines and Caphtorim).

15Canaan begot Sidon his firstborn, and Heth; 16the Jebusite, the Amorite, and the Girgashite; 17the Hivite, the Arkite, and the Sinite; 18the Arvadite, the Zemarite, and the Hamathite. Afterward the families of the Canaanites were dispersed. 19And the border of the Canaanites was from Sidon as you go toward Gerar, as far as Gaza; then as you go toward Sodom, Gomorrah, Admah, and Zeboiim, as far as Lasha. 20These *were* the sons of Ham, according to their families, according to their languages, in their lands *and* in their nations.

21And *children* were born also to Shem, the father of all the children of Eber, the brother of Japheth the elder. 22The sons of Shem *were* Elam, Asshur, Arphaxad, Lud, and Aram. 23The sons of Aram *were* Uz, Hul, Gether, and Mash.[a] 24Arphaxad begot Salah,[a] and Salah begot Eber. 25To Eber were born two sons: the name of one *was* Peleg, for in his days the earth was divided; and his brother's name *was* Joktan. 26Joktan begot Almodad, Sheleph, Hazarmaveth, Jerah, 27Hadoram, Uzal, Diklah, 28Obal,[a] Abimael, Sheba, 29Ophir, Havilah, and Jobab. All these *were* the sons of Joktan. 30And their dwelling place was from Mesha as you go toward Sephar, the mountain of the east. 31These *were* the sons of Shem, according to their families, according to their languages, in their lands, according to their nations.

32These *were* the families of the sons of Noah, according to their generations, in their nations; and from these the nations were divided on the earth after the flood.

The Tower of Babel

11 Now the whole earth had one language and one speech. 2And it came to pass, as they journeyed from the east, that they found a plain in the land of Shinar, and they dwelt there. 3Then they said to one another, "Come, let us make bricks and bake *them* thoroughly." They had brick for stone, and they had asphalt for mortar. 4And they said, "Come, let us build ourselves a city, and a tower whose top *is* in the heavens; let us make a name for ourselves, lest we be scattered abroad over the face of the whole earth."

5But the LORD came down to see the city and the tower which the sons of men had built. 6And the LORD said, "Indeed the people *are* one and they all have one language, and this is what they begin to do; now nothing that they propose to do will be withheld from them. 7Come, let Us go down and there confuse their language, that they may not understand one another's speech." 8So the LORD scattered them abroad from there

10:23 [a]Called *Meshech* in Septuagint and 1 Chronicles 1:17 **10:24** [a]Following Masoretic Text, Vulgate, and Targum; Septuagint reads *Arphaxad begot Cainan, and Cainan begot Salah* (compare Luke 3:35, 36). **10:28** [a]Spelled *Ebal* in 1 Chronicles 1:22

The Message

13-14 Egypt was ancestor to the Ludim, the Anamim, the Lehabim, the Naphtuhim, the Pathrusim, the Casluhim (the origin of the Philistines), and the Kaphtorim.

15-19 Canaan had Sidon his firstborn, Heth, the Jebusites, the Amorites, the Girgashites, the Hivites, the Arkites, the Sinites, the Arvadites, the Zemarites, and the Hamathites. Later the Canaanites spread out, going from Sidon toward Gerar, as far south as Gaza, and then east all the way over to Sodom, Gomorrah, Admah, Zeboiim, and on to Lasha.

20 These are the descendants of Ham by family, language, country, and nation.

21 Shem, the older brother of Japheth, also had sons. Shem was ancestor to all the children of Eber.

22 The sons of Shem: Elam, Asshur, Arphaxad, Lud, and Aram.

23 The sons of Aram: Uz, Hul, Gether, Meshech.

24-25 Arphaxad had Shelah and Shelah had Eber. Eber had two sons, Peleg (so named because in his days the human race divided) and Joktan.

26-30 Joktan had Almodad, Sheleph, Hazarmaveth, Jerah, Hadoram, Uzal, Diklah, Obal, Abimael, Sheba, Ophir, Havilah, and Jobab—all sons of Joktan. Their land goes from Mesha toward Sephar as far as the mountain ranges in the east.

31 These are the descendants of Shem by family, language, country, and nation.

32 This is the family tree of the sons of Noah as they developed into nations. From them nations developed all across the Earth after the flood.

"God Turned Their Language into 'Babble' "

1-2 11 At one time, the whole Earth spoke the same language. It so happened that as they moved out of the east, they came upon a plain in the land of Shinar and settled down.

3 They said to one another, "Come, let's make bricks and fire them well." They used brick for stone and tar for mortar.

4 Then they said, "Come, let's build ourselves a city and a tower that reaches Heaven. Let's make ourselves famous so we won't be scattered here and there across the Earth."

5 GOD came down to look over the city and the tower those people had built.

6-9 GOD took one look and said, "One people, one language; why, this is only a first step. No telling what they'll come up with next—they'll stop at nothing! Come, we'll go down and garble their speech so they won't understand each other." Then GOD scattered them from there all over the world. And they

NEW KING JAMES VERSION

over the face of all the earth, and they ceased
building the city. 9Therefore its name is called
Babel, because there the LORD confused the lan-
guage of all the earth; and from there the LORD
scattered them abroad over the face of all the
earth.

SHEM'S DESCENDANTS

10This *is* the genealogy of Shem: Shem *was*
one hundred years old, and begot Arphaxad two
years after the flood. 11After he begot Arphaxad,
Shem lived five hundred years, and begot sons
and daughters.
12Arphaxad lived thirty-five years, and begot
Salah. 13After he begot Salah, Arphaxad lived
four hundred and three years, and begot sons
and daughters.
14Salah lived thirty years, and begot Eber.
15After he begot Eber, Salah lived four hundred
and three years, and begot sons and daughters.
16Eber lived thirty-four years, and begot Pe-
leg. 17After he begot Peleg, Eber lived four hun-
dred and thirty years, and begot sons and
daughters.
18Peleg lived thirty years, and begot Reu.
19After he begot Reu, Peleg lived two hundred
and nine years, and begot sons and daughters.
20Reu lived thirty-two years, and begot
Serug. 21After he begot Serug, Reu lived two
hundred and seven years, and begot sons and
daughters.
22Serug lived thirty years, and begot Nahor.
23After he begot Nahor, Serug lived two hundred
years, and begot sons and daughters.
24Nahor lived twenty-nine years, and begot
Terah. 25After he begot Terah, Nahor lived one
hundred and nineteen years, and begot sons
and daughters.
26Now Terah lived seventy years, and begot
Abram, Nahor, and Haran.

TERAH'S DESCENDANTS

27This *is* the genealogy of Terah: Terah begot
Abram, Nahor, and Haran. Haran begot Lot.
28And Haran died before his father Terah in his
native land, in Ur of the Chaldeans. 29Then
Abram and Nahor took wives: the name of
Abram's wife *was* Sarai, and the name of Na-
hor's wife, Milcah, the daughter of Haran the fa-
ther of Milcah and the father of Iscah. 30But
Sarai was barren; she had no child.
31And Terah took his son Abram and his
grandson Lot, the son of Haran, and his daugh-
ter-in-law Sarai, his son Abram's wife, and they
went out with them from Ur of the Chaldeans to
go to the land of Canaan; and they came to
Haran and dwelt there. 32So the days of Terah
were two hundred and five years, and Terah
died in Haran.

PROMISES TO ABRAM

12 Now the LORD had said to Abram:

"Get out of your country,
From your family
And from your father's house,
To a land that I will show you.

THE MESSAGE

had to quit building the city. That's how it came to be called Babel, because there GOD turned their language into "babble." From there GOD scattered them all over the world.

10-11 This is the story of Shem. When Shem was 100 years old, he had Arphaxad. It was two years after the flood. After he had Arphaxad, he lived 500 more years and had other sons and daughters.

12-13 When Arphaxad was thirty-five years old, he had Shelah. After Arphaxad had Shelah, he lived 403 more years and had other sons and daughters.

14-15 When Shelah was thirty years old, he had Eber. After Shelah had Eber, he lived 403 more years and had other sons and daughters.

16-17 When Eber was thirty-four years old, he had Peleg. After Eber had Peleg, he lived 430 more years and had other sons and daughters.

18-19 When Peleg was thirty years old, he had Reu. After he had Reu, he lived 209 more years and had other sons and daughters.

20-21 When Reu was thirty-two years old, he had Serug. After Reu had Serug, he lived 207 more years and had other sons and daughters.

22-23 When Serug was thirty years old, he had Nahor. After Serug had Nahor, he lived 200 more years and had other sons and daughters.

24-25 When Nahor was twenty-nine years old, he had Terah. After Nahor had Terah, he lived 119 more years and had other sons and daughters.

26 When Terah was seventy years old, he had Abram, Nahor, and Haran.

THE FAMILY TREE OF TERAH

27-28 This is the story of Terah. Terah had Abram, Nahor, and Haran.

Haran had Lot. Haran died before his father, Terah, in the country of his family, Ur of the Chaldees.

29 Abram and Nahor each got married. Abram's wife was Sarai; Nahor's wife was Milcah, the daughter of his brother Haran. Haran had two daughters, Milcah and Iscah.

30 Sarai was barren; she had no children.

31 Terah took his son Abram, his grandson Lot (Haran's son), and Sarai his daughter-in-law (his son Abram's wife) and set out with them from Ur of the Chaldees for the land of Canaan. But when they got as far as Haran, they settled down there.

32 Terah lived 205 years. He died in Haran.

ABRAM AND SARAI

1 12 GOD told Abram: "Leave your country, your family, and your father's home for a land that I will show you.

NEW KING JAMES VERSION

2I will make you a great nation;
I will bless you
And make your name great;
And you shall be a blessing.
3I will bless those who bless you,
And I will curse him who curses you;
And in you all the families of the earth shall
be blessed."

4So Abram departed as the LORD had spoken
to him, and Lot went with him. And Abram *was*
seventy-five years old when he departed from
Haran. 5Then Abram took Sarai his wife and Lot
his brother's son, and all their possessions that
they had gathered, and the people whom they
had acquired in Haran, and they departed to go
to the land of Canaan. So they came to the land
of Canaan. 6Abram passed through the land to
the place of Shechem, as far as the terebinth
tree of Moreh.[a] And the Canaanites *were* then in
the land.
7Then the LORD appeared to Abram and said,
"To your descendants I will give this land." And
there he built an altar to the LORD, who had ap-
peared to him. 8And he moved from there to the
mountain east of Bethel, and he pitched his tent
with Bethel on the west and Ai on the east; there
he built an altar to the LORD and called on the
name of the LORD. 9So Abram journeyed, going
on still toward the South.[a]

ABRAM IN EGYPT

10Now there was a famine in the land, and
Abram went down to Egypt to dwell there, for
the famine *was* severe in the land. 11And it came
to pass, when he was close to entering Egypt,
that he said to Sarai his wife, "Indeed I know
that you *are* a woman of beautiful countenance.
12Therefore it will happen, when the Egyptians
see you, that they will say, 'This *is* his wife'; and
they will kill me, but they will let you live.
13Please say you *are* my sister, that it may be
well with me for your sake, and that I[a] may live
because of you."
14So it was, when Abram came into Egypt,
that the Egyptians saw the woman, that she *was*
very beautiful. 15The princes of Pharaoh also
saw her and commended her to Pharaoh. And
the woman was taken to Pharaoh's house. 16He
treated Abram well for her sake. He had sheep,
oxen, male donkeys, male and female servants,
female donkeys, and camels.
17But the LORD plagued Pharaoh and his
house with great plagues because of Sarai,
Abram's wife. 18And Pharaoh called Abram and
said, "What *is* this you have done to me? Why
did you not tell me that she *was* your wife?
19Why did you say, 'She *is* my sister'? I might
have taken her as my wife. Now therefore, here
is your wife; take *her* and go your way." 20So
Pharaoh commanded *his* men concerning him;
and they sent him away, with his wife and all
that he had.

12:6 [a]Hebrew *Alon Moreh* **12:9** [a]Hebrew *Negev* **12:13** [a]Literally *my soul*

THE MESSAGE

2-3 I'll make you a great nation
and bless you.
I'll make you famous;
you'll be a blessing.
I'll bless those who bless you;
those who curse you I'll curse.
All the families of the Earth
will be blessed through you."

4-6 So Abram left just as GOD said, and Lot left with him. Abram was seventy-five years old when he left Haran. Abram took his wife Sarai and his nephew Lot with him, along with all the possessions and people they had gotten in Haran, and set out for the land of Canaan and arrived safe and sound.

Abram passed through the country as far as Shechem and the Oak of Moreh. At that time the Canaanites occupied the land.

7 GOD appeared to Abram and said, "I will give this land to your children." Abram built an altar at the place GOD had appeared to him.

8 He moved on from there to the hill country east of Bethel and pitched his tent between Bethel to the west and Ai to the east. He built an altar there and prayed to GOD.

9 Abram kept moving, steadily making his way south, to the Negev.

10-13 Then a famine came to the land. Abram went down to Egypt to live; it was a hard famine. As he drew near to Egypt, he said to his wife, Sarai, "Look. We both know that you're a beautiful woman. When the Egyptians see you they're going to say, 'Aha! That's his wife!' and kill me. But they'll let you live. Do me a favor: tell them you're my sister. Because of you, they'll welcome me and let me live."

14-15 When Abram arrived in Egypt, the Egyptians took one look and saw that his wife was stunningly beautiful. Pharaoh's princes raved over her to Pharaoh. She was taken to live with Pharaoh.

16-17 Because of her, Abram got along very well: he accumulated sheep and cattle, male and female donkeys, men and women servants, and camels. But GOD hit Pharaoh hard because of Abram's wife Sarai; everybody in the palace got seriously sick.

18-19 Pharaoh called for Abram, "What's this that you've done to me? Why didn't you tell me that she's your wife? Why did you say, 'She's my sister' so that I'd take her as my wife? Here's your wife back—take her and get out!"

20 Pharaoh ordered his men to get Abram out of the country. They sent him and his wife and everything he owned on their way.

New King James Version

Abram Inherits Canaan

13 Then Abram went up from Egypt, he and
his wife and all that he had, and Lot with
him, to the South.[a] 2Abram *was* very rich in live-
stock, in silver, and in gold. 3And he went on his
journey from the South as far as Bethel, to the
place where his tent had been at the beginning,
between Bethel and Ai, 4to the place of the altar
which he had made there at first. And there
Abram called on the name of the LORD.
5Lot also, who went with Abram, had flocks
and herds and tents. 6Now the land was not able
to support them, that they might dwell together,
for their possessions were so great that they
could not dwell together. 7And there was strife
between the herdsmen of Abram's livestock and
the herdsmen of Lot's livestock. The Canaanites
and the Perizzites then dwelt in the land.
8So Abram said to Lot, "Please let there be
no strife between you and me, and between my
herdsmen and your herdsmen; for we *are*
brethren. 9*Is* not the whole land before you?
Please separate from me. If *you take* the left,
then I will go to the right; or, if *you go* to the
right, then I will go to the left."
10And Lot lifted his eyes and saw all the plain
of Jordan, that it *was* well watered everywhere
(before the LORD destroyed Sodom and Gomor-
rah) like the garden of the LORD, like the land of
Egypt as you go toward Zoar. 11Then Lot chose
for himself all the plain of Jordan, and Lot jour-
neyed east. And they separated from each other.
12Abram dwelt in the land of Canaan, and Lot
dwelt in the cities of the plain and pitched *his*
tent even as far as Sodom. 13But the men of
Sodom *were* exceedingly wicked and sinful
against the LORD.
14And the LORD said to Abram, after Lot had
separated from him: "Lift your eyes now and
look from the place where you are—northward,
southward, eastward, and westward; 15for all the
land which you see I give to you and your de-
scendants[a] forever. 16And I will make your de-
scendants as the dust of the earth; so that if a
man could number the dust of the earth, *then*
your descendants also could be numbered.
17Arise, walk in the land through its length and
its width, for I give it to you."
18Then Abram moved *his* tent, and went and
dwelt by the terebinth trees of Mamre,[a] which
are in Hebron, and built an altar there to the
LORD.

Lot's Captivity and Rescue

14 And it came to pass in the days of Am-
raphel king of Shinar, Arioch king of El-
lasar, Chedorlaomer king of Elam, and Tidal
king of nations,[a] 2*that* they made war with Bera
king of Sodom, Birsha king of Gomorrah,
Shinab king of Admah, Shemeber king of Ze-
boiim, and the king of Bela (that is, Zoar). 3All
these joined together in the Valley of Siddim
(that is, the Salt Sea). 4Twelve years they served
Chedorlaomer, and in the thirteenth year they
rebelled.

13:1 [a]Hebrew *Negev* **13:15** [a]Literally *seed,* and so throughout the book **13:18** [a]Hebrew *Alon Mamre* **14:1** [a]Hebrew *goyim*

The Message

1-2 13 So Abram left Egypt and went back to
the Negev, he and his wife and every-
thing he owned, and Lot still with him. By
now Abram was very rich, loaded with cat-
tle and silver and gold.
3-4 He moved on from the Negev, camping
along the way, to Bethel, the place he had
first set up his tent between Bethel and Ai
and built his first altar. Abram prayed there
to GOD.
5-7 Lot, who was traveling with Abram, was
also rich in sheep and cattle and tents. But
the land couldn't support both of them; they
had too many possessions. They couldn't
both live there—quarrels broke out between
Abram's shepherds and Lot's shepherds.
The Canaanites and Perizzites were also liv-
ing on the land at the time.
8-9 Abram said to Lot, "Let's not have fight-
ing between us, between your shepherds
and my shepherds. After all, we're family.
Look around. Isn't there plenty of land out
there? Let's separate. If you go left, I'll go
right; if you go right, I'll go left."
10-11 Lot looked. He saw the whole plain of the
Jordan spread out, well watered (this was
before GOD destroyed Sodom and Gomor-
rah), like GOD's garden, like Egypt, and
stretching all the way to Zoar. Lot took the
whole plain of the Jordan. Lot set out to the
east.
11-12 That's how they came to part company,
uncle and nephew. Abram settled in
Canaan; Lot settled in the cities of the plain
and pitched his tent near Sodom.
13 The people of Sodom were evil—flagrant
sinners against GOD.
14-17 After Lot separated from him, GOD said
to Abram, "Open your eyes, look around.
Look north, south, east, and west. Every-
thing you see, the whole land spread out be-
fore you, I will give to you and your children
forever. I'll make your descendants like
dust—counting your descendants will be as
impossible as counting the dust of the
Earth. So—on your feet, get moving! Walk
through the country, its length and breadth;
I'm giving it all to you."
18 Abram moved his tent. He went and set-
tled by the Oaks of Mamre in Hebron. There
he built an altar to GOD.

1-2 14 Then this: Amraphel king of Shinar,
Arioch king of Ellasar, Kedorlaomer
king of Elam, and Tidal king of Goiim went
off to war to fight Bera king of Sodom, Bir-
sha king of Gomorrah, Shinab king of
Admah, Shemeber king of Zeboiim, and the
king of Bela, that is, Zoar.
3-4 This second group of kings, the attacked,
came together at the Valley of Siddim, that
is, the Salt Sea. They had been under the
thumb of Kedorlaomer for twelve years. In
the thirteenth year, they revolted.

New King James Version

5In the fourteenth year Chedorlaomer and
the kings that *were* with him came and attacked
the Rephaim in Ashteroth Karnaim, the Zuzim
in Ham, the Emim in Shaveh Kiriathaim, 6and
the Horites in their mountain of Seir, as far as El
Paran, which *is* by the wilderness. 7Then they
turned back and came to En Mishpat (that *is*,
Kadesh), and attacked all the country of the
Amalekites, and also the Amorites who dwelt in
Hazezon Tamar.

8And the king of Sodom, the king of Gomor-
rah, the king of Admah, the king of Zeboiim,
and the king of Bela (that *is*, Zoar) went out and
joined together in battle in the Valley of Siddim
9against Chedorlaomer king of Elam, Tidal king
of nations,[a] Amraphel king of Shinar, and Ari-
och king of Ellasar—four kings against five.
10Now the Valley of Siddim *was full of* asphalt
pits; and the kings of Sodom and Gomorrah
fled; *some* fell there, and the remainder fled to
the mountains. 11Then they took all the goods of
Sodom and Gomorrah, and all their provisions,
and went their way. 12They also took Lot,
Abram's brother's son who dwelt in Sodom, and
his goods, and departed.

13Then one who had escaped came and told
Abram the Hebrew, for he dwelt by the terebinth
trees of Mamre[a] the Amorite, brother of Eshcol
and brother of Aner; and they *were* allies with
Abram. 14Now when Abram heard that his
brother was taken captive, he armed his three
hundred and eighteen trained *servants* who
were born in his own house, and went in pursuit
as far as Dan. 15He divided his forces against
them by night, and he and his servants attacked
them and pursued them as far as Hobah, which
is north of Damascus. 16So he brought back all
the goods, and also brought back his brother
Lot and his goods, as well as the women and the
people.

17And the king of Sodom went out to meet
him at the Valley of Shaveh (that *is*, the King's
Valley), after his return from the defeat of Ched-
orlaomer and the kings who *were* with him.

Abram and Melchizedek

18Then Melchizedek king of Salem brought
out bread and wine; he *was* the priest of God
Most High. 19And he blessed him and said:

"Blessed be Abram of God Most High,
Possessor of heaven and earth;
20And blessed be God Most High,
Who has delivered your enemies into your
hand."

And he gave him a tithe of all.
21Now the king of Sodom said to Abram,
"Give me the persons, and take the goods for
yourself."

22But Abram said to the king of Sodom, "I
have raised my hand to the LORD, God Most
High, the Possessor of heaven and earth, 23that I
will take nothing, from a thread to a sandal
strap, and that I will not take anything that *is*
yours, lest you should say, 'I have made Abram

14:9 [a]Hebrew *goyim* **14:13** [a]Hebrew *Alon Mamre*

The Message

5-7 In the fourteenth year, Kedorlaomer and the kings allied with him set out and defeated the Rephaim in Ashteroth Karnaim, the Zuzim in Ham, the Emim in Shaveh Kiriathaim, and the Horites in their hill country of Seir as far as El Paran on the far edge of the desert. On their way back they stopped at En Mishpat, that is, Kadesh, and conquered the whole region of the Amalekites as well as that of the Amorites who lived in Hazazon Tamar.

8-9 That's when the king of Sodom marched out with the king of Gomorrah, the king of Admah, the king of Zeboiim, and the king of Bela, that is, Zoar. They drew up in battle formation against their enemies in the Valley of Siddim—against Kedorlaomer king of Elam, Tidal king of Goiim, Amraphel king of Shinar, and Arioch king of Ellasar, four kings against five.

10-12 The Valley of Siddim was full of tar pits. When the kings of Sodom and Gomorrah fled, they fell into the tar pits, but the rest escaped into the mountains. The four kings captured all the possessions of Sodom and Gomorrah, all their food and equipment, and went on their way. They captured Lot, Abram's nephew who was living in Sodom at the time, taking everything he owned with them.

13-16 A fugitive came and reported to Abram the Hebrew. Abram was living at the Oaks of Mamre the Amorite, brother of Eshcol and Aner. They were allies of Abram. When Abram heard that his nephew had been taken prisoner, he lined up his servants, all of them born in his household—there were 318 of them—and chased after the captors all the way to Dan. Abram and his men split into small groups and attacked by night. They chased them as far as Hobah, just north of Damascus. They recovered all the plunder along with nephew Lot and his possessions, including the women and the people.

17-20 After Abram returned from defeating Kedorlaomer and his allied kings, the king of Sodom came out to greet him in the Valley of Shaveh, the King's Valley. Melchizedek, king of Salem, brought out bread and wine—he was priest of The High God—and blessed him:

Blessed be Abram by The High God,
Creator of Heaven and Earth.
And blessed be The High God,
who handed your enemies over to
you.

Abram gave him a tenth of all the recovered plunder.

21 The king of Sodom said to Abram, "Give me back the people but keep all the plunder for yourself."

22-24 But Abram told the king of Sodom, "I swear to GOD, The High God, Creator of Heaven and Earth, this solemn oath, that I'll take nothing from you, not so much as a thread or a shoestring. I'm not going to have

NEW KING JAMES VERSION

rich'— 24except only what the young men have
eaten, and the portion of the men who went with
me: Aner, Eshcol, and Mamre; let them take
their portion."

GOD'S COVENANT WITH ABRAM

15 After these things the word of the LORD
came to Abram in a vision, saying, "Do not
be afraid, Abram. I *am* your shield, your exceed-
ingly great reward."
2But Abram said, "Lord GOD, what will You
give me, seeing I go childless, and the heir of my
house *is* Eliezer of Damascus?" 3Then Abram
said, "Look, You have given me no offspring; in-
deed one born in my house is my heir!"
4And behold, the word of the LORD *came* to
him, saying, "This one shall not be your heir, but
one who will come from your own body shall be
your heir." 5Then He brought him outside and
said, "Look now toward heaven, and count the
stars if you are able to number them." And He
said to him, "So shall your descendants be."
6And he believed in the LORD, and He ac-
counted it to him for righteousness.
7Then He said to him, "I *am* the LORD, who
brought you out of Ur of the Chaldeans, to give
you this land to inherit it."
8And he said, "Lord GOD, how shall I know
that I will inherit it?"
9So He said to him, "Bring Me a three-year-
old heifer, a three-year-old female goat, a three-
year-old ram, a turtledove, and a young pigeon."
10Then he brought all these to Him and cut them
in two, down the middle, and placed each piece
opposite the other; but he did not cut the birds
in two. 11And when the vultures came down on
the carcasses, Abram drove them away.
12Now when the sun was going down, a deep
sleep fell upon Abram; and behold, horror *and*
great darkness fell upon him. 13Then He said to
Abram: "Know certainly that your descendants
will be strangers in a land *that is* not theirs, and
will serve them, and they will afflict them four
hundred years. 14And also the nation whom they
serve I will judge; afterward they shall come out
with great possessions. 15Now as for you, you
shall go to your fathers in peace; you shall be
buried at a good old age. 16But in the fourth gen-
eration they shall return here, for the iniquity of
the Amorites *is* not yet complete."
17And it came to pass, when the sun went
down and it was dark, that behold, there ap-
peared a smoking oven and a burning torch that
passed between those pieces. 18On the same day
the LORD made a covenant with Abram, saying:
"To your descendants I have given this land,
from the river of Egypt to the great river, the
River Euphrates— 19the Kenites, the Kenezzites,
the Kadmonites, 20the Hittites, the Perizzites, the
Rephaim, 21the Amorites, the Canaanites, the
Girgashites, and the Jebusites."

HAGAR AND ISHMAEL

16 Now Sarai, Abram's wife, had borne him
no *children.* And she had an Egyptian
maidservant whose name was Hagar. 2So Sarai

THE MESSAGE

you go around saying, 'I made Abram rich.'
Nothing for me other than what the young
men ate and the share of the men who went
with me, Aner, Eshcol, and Mamre; they're
to get their share of the plunder."

1 15 After all these things, this word of GOD
came to Abram in a vision: "Don't be
afraid, Abram. I'm your shield. Your reward
will be grand!"
2-3 Abram said, "GOD, Master, what use are
your gifts as long as I'm childless and
Eliezer of Damascus is going to inherit
everything?" Abram continued, "See, you've
given me no children, and now a mere
house servant is going to get it all."
4 Then GOD's Message came: "Don't worry,
he won't be your heir; a son from your body
will be your heir."
5 Then he took him outside and said, "Look
at the sky. Count the stars. Can you do it?
Count your descendants! You're going to
have a big family, Abram!"
6 And he believed! Believed GOD! God de-
clared him "Set-Right-with-God."
7 GOD continued, "I'm the same GOD who
brought you from Ur of the Chaldees and
gave you this land to own."
8 Abram said, "Master GOD, how am I to
know this, that it will all be mine?"
9 GOD said, "Bring me a heifer, a goat, and
a ram, each three years old, and a dove and
a young pigeon."
10-12 He brought all these animals to him, split
them down the middle, and laid the halves
opposite each other. But he didn't split the
birds. Vultures swooped down on the car-
casses, but Abram scared them off. As the
sun went down a deep sleep overcame
Abram and then a sense of dread, dark and
heavy.
13-16 GOD said to Abram, "Know this: your de-
scendants will live as outsiders in a land not
theirs; they'll be enslaved and beaten down
for 400 years. Then I'll punish their slave
masters; your offspring will march out of
there loaded with plunder. But not you;
you'll have a long and full life and die a
good and peaceful death. Not until the
fourth generation will your descendants re-
turn here; sin is still a thriving business
among the Amorites."
17-21 When the sun was down and it was dark,
a smoking firepot and a flaming torch
moved between the split carcasses. That's
when GOD made a covenant with Abram:
"I'm giving this land to your children, from
the Nile River in Egypt to the River Eu-
phrates in Assyria—the country of the Ken-
ites, Kenizzites, Kadmonites, Hittites, Per-
izzites, Rephaim, Amorites, Canaanites,
Girgashites, and Jebusites."

1-2 16 Sarai, Abram's wife, hadn't yet pro-
duced a child.
She had an Egyptian maid named Hagar.

NEW KING JAMES VERSION

said to Abram, "See now, the LORD has re-
strained me from bearing *children.* Please, go in
to my maid; perhaps I shall obtain children by
her." And Abram heeded the voice of Sarai.
[3]Then Sarai, Abram's wife, took Hagar her
maid, the Egyptian, and gave her to her husband
Abram to be his wife, after Abram had dwelt ten
years in the land of Canaan. [4]So he went in to
Hagar, and she conceived. And when she saw
that she had conceived, her mistress became de-
spised in her eyes.
[5]Then Sarai said to Abram, "My wrong *be*
upon you! I gave my maid into your embrace;
and when she saw that she had conceived, I be-
came despised in her eyes. The LORD judge be-
tween you and me."
[6]So Abram said to Sarai, "Indeed your maid
is in your hand; do to her as you please." And
when Sarai dealt harshly with her, she fled from
her presence.
[7]Now the Angel of the LORD found her by a
spring of water in the wilderness, by the spring
on the way to Shur. [8]And He said, "Hagar,
Sarai's maid, where have you come from, and
where are you going?"
She said, "I am fleeing from the presence of
my mistress Sarai."
[9]The Angel of the LORD said to her, "Return
to your mistress, and submit yourself under her
hand." [10]Then the Angel of the LORD said to her,
"I will multiply your descendants exceedingly,
so that they shall not be counted for multitude."
[11]And the Angel of the LORD said to her:

"Behold, you *are* with child,
And you shall bear a son.
You shall call his name Ishmael,
Because the LORD has heard your affliction.
[12]He shall be a wild man;
His hand *shall be* against every man,
And every man's hand against him.
And he shall dwell in the presence of all his
brethren."

[13]Then she called the name of the LORD who
spoke to her, You-Are-the-God-Who-Sees; for
she said, "Have I also here seen Him who sees
me?" [14]Therefore the well was called Beer Lahai
Roi;[a] observe, *it is* between Kadesh and Bered.
[15]So Hagar bore Abram a son; and Abram
named his son, whom Hagar bore, Ishmael.
[16]Abram *was* eighty-six years old when Hagar
bore Ishmael to Abram.

THE SIGN OF THE COVENANT

17 When Abram was ninety-nine years old,
the LORD appeared to Abram and said to
him, "I *am* Almighty God; walk before Me and
be blameless. [2]And I will make My covenant be-
tween Me and you, and will multiply you ex-
ceedingly." [3]Then Abram fell on his face, and
God talked with him, saying: [4]"As for Me, be-
hold, My covenant is with you, and you shall be
a father of many nations. [5]No longer shall your
name be called Abram, but your name shall be
Abraham; for I have made you a father of many
nations. [6]I will make you exceedingly fruitful;

16:14 [a]Literally *Well of the One Who Lives and Sees Me*

THE MESSAGE

Sarai said to Abram, "GOD has not seen fit to
let me have a child. Sleep with my maid.
Maybe I can get a family from her." Abram
agreed to do what Sarai said.
3-4 So Sarai, Abram's wife, took her Egyp-
tian maid Hagar and gave her to her hus-
band Abram as a wife. Abram had been liv-
ing ten years in Canaan when this took
place. He slept with Hagar and she got preg-
nant. When Hagar learned she was preg-
nant, she looked down on her mistress.
5 Sarai told Abram, "It's all your fault that
I'm suffering this abuse. I put my maid in
bed with you and the minute she knows
she's pregnant, she treats me like I'm noth-
ing. May GOD decide which of us is right."
6 "You decide," said Abram. "Your maid is
your business."
Sarai was abusive to Hagar and Hagar
ran away.
7-8 An angel of GOD found her beside a
spring in the desert; it was the spring on the
road to Shur. He said, "Hagar, maid of Sarai,
what are you doing here?"
She said, "I'm running away from Sarai
my mistress."
9-12 The angel of GOD said, "Go back to your
mistress. Put up with her abuse." He contin-
ued, "I'm going to give you a big family, chil-
dren past counting.

From this pregnancy, you'll get a son:
Name him Ishmael;
for GOD heard you, GOD answered you.
He'll be a bucking bronco of a man,
a real fighter, fighting and being
fought,
Always stirring up trouble,
always at odds with his family."

13 She answered GOD by name, praying to
the God who spoke to her, "You're the God
who sees me!
"Yes! He saw me; and then I saw him!"
14 That's how that desert spring got named
"God-Alive-Sees-Me Spring." That spring is
still there, between Kadesh and Bered.
15-16 Hagar gave Abram a son. Abram named
him Ishmael. Abram was eighty-six years
old when Hagar gave him his son, Ishmael.

1-2 **17** When Abram was ninety-nine years
old, GOD showed up and said to him, "I
am The Strong God, live entirely before me,
live to the hilt! I'll make a covenant between
us and I'll give you a huge family."
3-8 Overwhelmed, Abram fell flat on his face.
Then God said to him, "This is my
covenant with you: You'll be the father of
many nations. Your name will no longer be
Abram, but Abraham, meaning that 'I'm
making you the father of many nations.' I'll
make you a father of fathers—I'll make na-

NEW KING JAMES VERSION

and I will make nations of you, and kings shall
come from you. 7And I will establish My
covenant between Me and you and your descen-
dants after you in their generations, for an ever-
lasting covenant, to be God to you and your de-
scendants after you. 8Also I give to you and your
descendants after you the land in which you are
a stranger, all the land of Canaan, as an ever-
lasting possession; and I will be their God."

9And God said to Abraham: "As for you, you
shall keep My covenant, you and your descen-
dants after you throughout their generations.
10This *is* My covenant which you shall keep, be-
tween Me and you and your descendants after
you: Every male child among you shall be cir-
cumcised; 11and you shall be circumcised in the
flesh of your foreskins, and it shall be a sign of
the covenant between Me and you. 12He who is
eight days old among you shall be circumcised,
every male child in your generations, he who is
born in your house or bought with money from
any foreigner who is not your descendant. 13He
who is born in your house and he who is bought
with your money must be circumcised, and My
covenant shall be in your flesh for an everlast-
ing covenant. 14And the uncircumcised male
child, who is not circumcised in the flesh of his
foreskin, that person shall be cut off from his
people; he has broken My covenant."

15Then God said to Abraham, "As for Sarai
your wife, you shall not call her name Sarai, but
Sarah *shall be* her name. 16And I will bless her
and also give you a son by her; then I will bless
her, and she shall be *a mother* of nations; kings
of peoples shall be from her."

17Then Abraham fell on his face and
laughed, and said in his heart, "Shall *a child* be
born to a man who is one hundred years old?
And shall Sarah, who is ninety years old, bear *a
child?*" 18And Abraham said to God, "Oh, that
Ishmael might live before You!"

19Then God said: "No, Sarah your wife shall
bear you a son, and you shall call his name
Isaac; I will establish My covenant with him for
an everlasting covenant, *and* with his descen-
dants after him. 20And as for Ishmael, I have
heard you. Behold, I have blessed him, and will
make him fruitful, and will multiply him exceed-
ingly. He shall beget twelve princes, and I will
make him a great nation. 21But My covenant I
will establish with Isaac, whom Sarah shall bear
to you at this set time next year." 22Then He fin-
ished talking with him, and God went up from
Abraham.

23So Abraham took Ishmael his son, all who
were born in his house and all who were bought
with his money, every male among the men of
Abraham's house, and circumcised the flesh of
their foreskins that very same day, as God had
said to him. 24Abraham *was* ninety-nine years old
when he was circumcised in the flesh of his fore-
skin. 25And Ishmael his son *was* thirteen years
old when he was circumcised in the flesh of his
foreskin. 26That very same day Abraham was cir-
cumcised, and his son Ishmael; 27and all the men
of his house, born in the house or bought with
money from a foreigner, were circumcised with
him.

THE MESSAGE

tions from you, kings will issue from you. I'm establishing my covenant between me and you, a covenant that includes your descendants, a covenant that goes on and on and on, a covenant that commits me to be your God and the God of your descendants. And I'm giving you and your descendants this land where you're now just camping, this whole country of Canaan, to own forever. And I'll be their God."

9-14 God continued to Abraham, "And you: You will honor my covenant, you and your descendants, generation after generation. This is the covenant that you are to honor, the covenant that pulls in all your descendants: Circumcise every male. Circumcise by cutting off the foreskin of the penis; it will be the sign of the covenant between us. Every male baby will be circumcised when he is eight days old, generation after generation—this includes house-born slaves and slaves bought from outsiders who are not blood kin. Make sure you circumcise both your own children and anyone brought in from the outside. That way my covenant will be cut into your body, a permanent mark of my permanent covenant. An uncircumcised male, one who has not had the foreskin of his penis cut off, will be cut off from his people—he has broken my covenant."

15-16 God continued speaking to Abraham, "And Sarai your wife: Don't call her Sarai any longer; call her Sarah. I'll bless her—yes! I'll give you a son by her! Oh, how I'll bless her! Nations will come from her; kings of nations will come from her."

17 Abraham fell flat on his face. And then he laughed, thinking, "Can a hundred-year-old man father a son? And can Sarah, at ninety years, have a baby?"

18 Recovering, Abraham said to God, "Oh, keep Ishmael alive and well before you!"

19 But God said, "That's not what I mean. Your wife, Sarah, will have a baby, a son. Name him Isaac (Laughter). I'll establish my covenant with him and his descendants, a covenant that lasts forever.

20-21 "And Ishmael? Yes, I heard your prayer for him. I'll also bless him; I'll make sure he has plenty of children—a huge family. He'll father twelve princes; I'll make him a great nation. But I'll establish my covenant with Isaac whom Sarah will give you about this time next year."

22 God finished speaking with Abraham and left.

23 Then Abraham took his son Ishmael and all his servants, whether houseborn or purchased—every male in his household—and circumcised them, cutting off their foreskins that very day, just as God had told him.

24-27 Abraham was ninety-nine years old when he was circumcised. His son Ishmael was thirteen years old when he was circumcised. Abraham and Ishmael were circumcised the same day together with all the servants of his household, those born there and those purchased from outsiders—all were circumcised with him.

NEW KING JAMES VERSION

THE SON OF PROMISE

18 Then the LORD appeared to him by the terebinth trees of Mamre,[a] as he was sitting in the tent door in the heat of the day. 2So he lifted his eyes and looked, and behold, three men were standing by him; and when he saw *them,* he ran from the tent door to meet them, and bowed himself to the ground, 3and said, "My Lord, if I have now found favor in Your sight, do not pass on by Your servant. 4Please let a little water be brought, and wash your feet, and rest yourselves under the tree. 5And I will bring a morsel of bread, that you may refresh your hearts. After that you may pass by, inasmuch as you have come to your servant."

They said, "Do as you have said."

6So Abraham hurried into the tent to Sarah and said, "Quickly, make ready three measures of fine meal; knead *it* and make cakes." 7And Abraham ran to the herd, took a tender and good calf, gave *it* to a young man, and he hastened to prepare it. 8So he took butter and milk and the calf which he had prepared, and set *it* before them; and he stood by them under the tree as they ate.

9Then they said to him, "Where *is* Sarah your wife?"

So he said, "Here, in the tent."

10And He said, "I will certainly return to you according to the time of life, and behold, Sarah your wife shall have a son."

(Sarah was listening in the tent door which *was* behind him.) 11Now Abraham and Sarah were old, well advanced in age; *and* Sarah had passed the age of childbearing.[a] 12Therefore Sarah laughed within herself, saying, "After I have grown old, shall I have pleasure, my lord being old also?"

13And the LORD said to Abraham, "Why did Sarah laugh, saying, 'Shall I surely bear *a child,* since I am old?' 14Is anything too hard for the LORD? At the appointed time I will return to you, according to the time of life, and Sarah shall have a son."

15But Sarah denied *it,* saying, "I did not laugh," for she was afraid.

And He said, "No, but you did laugh!"

ABRAHAM INTERCEDES FOR SODOM

16Then the men rose from there and looked toward Sodom, and Abraham went with them to send them on the way. 17And the LORD said, "Shall I hide from Abraham what I am doing, 18since Abraham shall surely become a great and mighty nation, and all the nations of the earth shall be blessed in him? 19For I have known him, in order that he may command his children and his household after him, that they keep the way of the LORD, to do righteousness and justice, that the LORD may bring to Abraham what He has spoken to him." 20And the LORD said, "Because the outcry against Sodom and Gomorrah is great, and because their sin is very grave, 21I will go down now and see whether they have done altogether according to the outcry against it that has come to Me; and if not, I will know."

18:1 [a]Hebrew *Alon Mamre* **18:11** [a]Literally *the manner of women had ceased to be with Sarah*

THE MESSAGE

1-2 18 GOD appeared to Abraham at the Oaks of Mamre while he was sitting at the entrance of his tent. It was the hottest part of the day. He looked up and saw three men standing. He ran from his tent to greet them and bowed before them.

3-5 He said, "Master, if it please you, stop for a while with your servant. I'll get some water so you can wash your feet. Rest under this tree. I'll get some food to refresh you on your way, since your travels have brought you across my path."

They said, "Certainly. Go ahead."

6 Abraham hurried into the tent to Sarah. He said, "Hurry. Get three cups of our best flour; knead it and make bread."

7-8 Then Abraham ran to the cattle pen and picked out a nice plump calf and gave it to the servant who lost no time getting it ready. Then he got curds and milk, brought them with the calf that had been roasted, set the meal before the men, and stood there under the tree while they ate.

9 The men said to him, "Where is Sarah your wife?"

He said, "In the tent."

10 One of them said, "I'm coming back about this time next year. When I arrive, your wife Sarah will have a son." Sarah was listening at the tent opening, just behind the man.

11-12 Abraham and Sarah were old by this time, very old. Sarah was far past the age for having babies. Sarah laughed within herself, "An old woman like me? Get pregnant? With this old man of a husband?"

13-14 GOD said to Abraham, "Why did Sarah laugh saying, 'Me? Have a baby? An old woman like me?' Is anything too hard for GOD? I'll be back about this time next year and Sarah will have a baby."

15 Sarah lied. She said, "I didn't laugh," because she was afraid.

But he said, "Yes you did; you laughed."

16 When the men got up to leave, they set off for Sodom. Abraham walked with them to say good-bye.

17-19 Then GOD said, "Shall I keep back from Abraham what I'm about to do? Abraham is going to become a large and strong nation; all the nations of the world are going to find themselves blessed through him. Yes, I've settled on him as the one to train his children and future family to observe GOD's way of life, live kindly and generously and fairly, so that GOD can complete in Abraham what he promised him."

20-21 GOD continued, "The cries of the victims in Sodom and Gomorrah are deafening; the sin of those cities is immense. I'm going down to see for myself, see if what they're doing is as bad as it sounds. Then I'll know."

NEW KING JAMES VERSION

[22]Then the men turned away from there and went toward Sodom, but Abraham still stood before the LORD. [23]And Abraham came near and said, "Would You also destroy the righteous with the wicked? [24]Suppose there were fifty righteous within the city; would You also destroy the place and not spare *it* for the fifty righteous that were in it? [25]Far be it from You to do such a thing as this, to slay the righteous with the wicked, so that the righteous should be as the wicked; far be it from You! Shall not the Judge of all the earth do right?"

[26]So the LORD said, "If I find in Sodom fifty righteous within the city, then I will spare all the place for their sakes."

[27]Then Abraham answered and said, "Indeed now, I who *am but* dust and ashes have taken it upon myself to speak to the Lord: [28]Suppose there were five less than the fifty righteous; would You destroy all of the city for *lack of* five?"

So He said, "If I find there forty-five, I will not destroy *it*."

[29]And he spoke to Him yet again and said, "Suppose there should be forty found there?"

So He said, "I will not do *it* for the sake of forty."

[30]Then he said, "Let not the Lord be angry, and I will speak: Suppose thirty should be found there?"

So He said, "I will not do *it* if I find thirty there."

[31]And he said, "Indeed now, I have taken it upon myself to speak to the Lord: Suppose twenty should be found there?"

So He said, "I will not destroy *it* for the sake of twenty."

[32]Then he said, "Let not the Lord be angry, and I will speak but once more: Suppose ten should be found there?"

And He said, "I will not destroy *it* for the sake of ten." [33]So the LORD went His way as soon as He had finished speaking with Abraham; and Abraham returned to his place.

SODOM'S DEPRAVITY

19 Now the two angels came to Sodom in the evening, and Lot was sitting in the gate of Sodom. When Lot saw *them*, he rose to meet them, and he bowed himself with his face toward the ground. [2]And he said, "Here now, my lords, please turn in to your servant's house and spend the night, and wash your feet; then you may rise early and go on your way."

And they said, "No, but we will spend the night in the open square."

[3]But he insisted strongly; so they turned in to him and entered his house. Then he made them a feast, and baked unleavened bread, and they ate.

[4]Now before they lay down, the men of the city, the men of Sodom, both old and young, all the people from every quarter, surrounded the house. [5]And they called to Lot and said to him, "Where are the men who came to you tonight? Bring them out to us that we may know them *carnally*."

[6]So Lot went out to them through the doorway, shut the door behind him, [7]and said,

THE MESSAGE

22 The men set out for Sodom, but Abraham stood in GOD's path, blocking his way.

23-25 Abraham confronted him, "Are you serious? Are you planning on getting rid of the good people right along with the bad? What if there are fifty decent people left in the city; will you lump the good with the bad and get rid of the lot? Wouldn't you spare the city for the sake of those fifty innocents? I can't believe you'd do that, kill off the good and the bad alike as if there were no difference between them. Doesn't the Judge of all the Earth judge with justice?"

26 GOD said, "If I find fifty decent people in the city of Sodom, I'll spare the place just for them."

27-28 Abraham came back, "Do I, a mere mortal made from a handful of dirt, dare open my mouth again to my Master? What if the fifty fall short by five—would you destroy the city because of those missing five?"

He said, "I won't destroy it if there are forty-five."

29 Abraham spoke up again, "What if you only find forty?"

"Neither will I destroy it if for forty."

30 He said, "Master, don't be irritated with me, but what if only thirty are found?"

"No, I won't do it if I find thirty."

31 He pushed on, "I know I'm trying your patience, Master, but how about for twenty?"

"I won't destroy it for twenty."

32 He wouldn't quit, "Don't get angry, Master—this is the last time. What if you only come up with ten?"

"For the sake of only ten, I won't destroy the city."

33 When GOD finished talking with Abraham, he left. And Abraham went home.

1-2 **19** The two angels arrived at Sodom in the evening. Lot was sitting at the city gate. He saw them and got up to welcome them, bowing before them and said, "Please, my friends, come to my house and stay the night. Wash up. You can rise early and be on your way refreshed."

They said, "No, we'll sleep in the street."

3 But he insisted, wouldn't take no for an answer; and they relented and went home with him. Lot fixed a hot meal for them and they ate.

4-5 Before they went to bed men from all over the city of Sodom, young and old, descended on the house from all sides and boxed them in. They yelled to Lot, "Where are the men who are staying with you for the night? Bring them out so we can have our sport with them!"

6-8 Lot went out, barring the door behind him, and said, "Brothers, please, don't be

NEW KING JAMES VERSION

"Please, my brethren, do not do so wickedly!
8See now, I have two daughters who have not
known a man; please, let me bring them out to
you, and you may do to them as you wish; only
do nothing to these men, since this is the reason
they have come under the shadow of my roof."
9And they said, "Stand back!" Then they
said, "This one came in to stay *here,* and he
keeps acting as a judge; now we will deal worse
with you than with them." So they pressed hard
against the man Lot, and came near to break
down the door. 10But the men reached out their
hands and pulled Lot into the house with them,
and shut the door. 11And they struck the men
who *were* at the doorway of the house with
blindness, both small and great, so that they be-
came weary *trying* to find the door.

SODOM AND GOMORRAH DESTROYED

12Then the men said to Lot, "Have you any-
one else here? Son-in-law, your sons, your
daughters, and whomever you have in the city—
take *them* out of this place! 13For we will destroy
this place, because the outcry against them has
grown great before the face of the LORD, and the
LORD has sent us to destroy it."
14So Lot went out and spoke to his sons-in-
law, who had married his daughters, and said,
"Get up, get out of this place; for the LORD will
destroy this city!" But to his sons-in-law he
seemed to be joking.
15When the morning dawned, the angels
urged Lot to hurry, saying, "Arise, take your wife
and your two daughters who are here, lest you be
consumed in the punishment of the city." 16And
while he lingered, the men took hold of his hand,
his wife's hand, and the hands of his two daugh-
ters, the LORD being merciful to him, and they
brought him out and set him outside the city. 17So
it came to pass, when they had brought them out-
side, that he[a] said, "Escape for your life! Do not
look behind you nor stay anywhere in the plain.
Escape to the mountains, lest you be destroyed."
18Then Lot said to them, "Please, no, my
lords! 19Indeed now, your servant has found fa-
vor in your sight, and you have increased your
mercy which you have shown me by saving my
life; but I cannot escape to the mountains, lest
some evil overtake me and I die. 20See now, this
city *is* near *enough* to flee to, and it *is* a little
one; please let me escape there (*is* it not a little
one?) and my soul shall live."
21And he said to him, "See, I have favored
you concerning this thing also, in that I will not
overthrow this city for which you have spoken.
22Hurry, escape there. For I cannot do anything
until you arrive there."
Therefore the name of the city was called
Zoar.
23The sun had risen upon the earth when Lot
entered Zoar. 24Then the LORD rained brimstone
and fire on Sodom and Gomorrah, from the
LORD out of the heavens. 25So He overthrew
those cities, all the plain, all the inhabitants of
the cities, and what grew on the ground.
26But his wife looked back behind him, and
she became a pillar of salt.

19:17 [a]Septuagint, Syriac, and Vulgate read *they.*

THE MESSAGE

vile! Look, I have two daughters, virgins; let me bring them out; you can take your pleasure with them, but don't touch these men—they're my guests."

9 They said, "Get lost! You drop in from nowhere and now you're going to tell us how to run our lives. We'll treat you worse than them!" And they charged past Lot to break down the door.

10-11 But the two men reached out and pulled Lot inside the house, locking the door. Then they struck blind the men who were trying to break down the door, both leaders and followers, leaving them groping in the dark.

12-13 The two men said to Lot, "Do you have any other family here? Sons, daughters—anybody in the city? Get them out of here, and now! We're going to destroy this place. The outcries of victims here to GOD are deafening; we've been sent to blast this place into oblivion."

14 Lot went out and warned the fiancés of his daughters, "Evacuate this place; GOD is about to destroy this city!" But his daughters' would-be husbands treated it as a joke.

15 At break of day, the angels pushed Lot to get going, "Hurry. Get your wife and two daughters out of here before it's too late and you're caught in the punishment of the city."

16-17 Lot was dragging his feet. The men grabbed Lot's arm, and the arms of his wife and daughters—GOD was so merciful to them!—and dragged them to safety outside the city. When they had them outside, Lot was told, "Now run for your life! Don't look back! Don't stop anywhere on the plain—run for the hills or you'll be swept away."

18-20 But Lot protested, "No, masters, you can't mean it! I know that you've taken a liking to me and have done me an immense favor in saving my life, but I can't run for the mountains—who knows what terrible thing might happen to me in the mountains and leave me for dead. Look over there—that town is close enough to get to. It's a small town, hardly anything to it. Let me escape there and save my life—it's a mere wide place in the road."

21-22 "All right, Lot. If you insist. I'll let you have your way. And I won't stamp out the town you've spotted. But hurry up. Run for it! I can't do anything until you get there." That's why the town was called Zoar, that is, Smalltown.

23 The sun was high in the sky when Lot arrived at Zoar.

24-25 Then GOD rained brimstone and fire down on Sodom and Gomorrah—a river of lava from GOD out of the sky!—and destroyed these cities and the entire plain and everyone who lived in the cities and everything that grew from the ground.

26 But Lot's wife looked back and turned into a pillar of salt.

New King James Version

27And Abraham went early in the morning to
the place where he had stood before the Lord.
28Then he looked toward Sodom and Gomorrah,
and toward all the land of the plain; and he saw,
and behold, the smoke of the land which went
up like the smoke of a furnace. 29And it came to
pass, when God destroyed the cities of the plain,
that God remembered Abraham, and sent Lot
out of the midst of the overthrow, when He over-
threw the cities in which Lot had dwelt.

The Descendants of Lot

30Then Lot went up out of Zoar and dwelt in
the mountains, and his two daughters were with
him; for he was afraid to dwell in Zoar. And he
and his two daughters dwelt in a cave. 31Now the
firstborn said to the younger, "Our father *is* old,
and *there is* no man on the earth to come in to
us as is the custom of all the earth. 32Come, let
us make our father drink wine, and we will lie
with him, that we may preserve the lineage of
our father." 33So they made their father drink
wine that night. And the firstborn went in and
lay with her father, and he did not know when
she lay down or when she arose.
34It happened on the next day that the first-
born said to the younger, "Indeed I lay with my
father last night; let us make him drink wine
tonight also, and you go in *and* lie with him, that
we may preserve the lineage of our father."
35Then they made their father drink wine that
night also. And the younger arose and lay with
him, and he did not know when she lay down or
when she arose.
36Thus both the daughters of Lot were with
child by their father. 37The firstborn bore a son
and called his name Moab; he *is* the father of the
Moabites to this day. 38And the younger, she also
bore a son and called his name Ben-Ammi; he *is*
the father of the people of Ammon to this day.

Abraham and Abimelech

20 And Abraham journeyed from there to the
South, and dwelt between Kadesh and
Shur, and stayed in Gerar. 2Now Abraham said
of Sarah his wife, "She *is* my sister." And Abim-
elech king of Gerar sent and took Sarah.
3But God came to Abimelech in a dream by
night, and said to him, "Indeed you *are* a dead
man because of the woman whom you have
taken, for she *is* a man's wife."
4But Abimelech had not come near her; and
he said, "Lord, will You slay a righteous nation
also? 5Did he not say to me, 'She *is* my sister'?
And she, even she herself said, 'He *is* my
brother.' In the integrity of my heart and inno-
cence of my hands I have done this."
6And God said to him in a dream, "Yes, I
know that you did this in the integrity of your
heart. For I also withheld you from sinning
against Me; therefore I did not let you touch her.
7Now therefore, restore the man's wife; for he *is*
a prophet, and he will pray for you and you shall
live. But if you do not restore *her*, know that you
shall surely die, you and all who *are* yours."

The Message

27-28 Abraham got up early the next morning and went to the place he had so recently stood with God. He looked out over Sodom and Gomorrah, surveying the whole plain. All he could see was smoke belching from the Earth, like smoke from a furnace.

29 And that's the story: When God destroyed the Cities of the Plain, he was mindful of Abraham and first got Lot out of there before he blasted those cities off the face of the Earth.

30 Lot left Zoar and went into the mountains to live with his two daughters; he was afraid to stay in Zoar. He lived in a cave with his daughters.

31-32 One day the older daughter said to the younger, "Our father is getting old and there's not a man left in the country by whom we can get pregnant. Let's get our father drunk with wine and lie with him. We'll get children through our father—it's our only chance to keep our family alive."

33-35 They got their father drunk with wine that very night. The older daughter went and lay with him. He was oblivious, knowing nothing of what she did. The next morning the older said to the younger, "Last night I slept with my father. Tonight, it's your turn. We'll get him drunk again and then you sleep with him. We'll both get a child through our father and keep our family alive." So that night they got their father drunk again and the younger went in and slept with him. Again he was oblivious, knowing nothing of what she did.

36-38 Both daughters became pregnant by their father, Lot. The older daughter had a son and named him Moab, the ancestor of the present-day Moabites. The younger daughter had a son and named him Ben-Ammi, the ancestor of the present-day Ammonites.

1-2 20 Abraham traveled from there south to the Negev and settled down between Kadesh and Shur. While he was camping in Gerar, Abraham said of his wife Sarah, "She's my sister."

2-3 So Abimelech, king of Gerar, sent for Sarah and took her. But God came to Abimelech in a dream that night and told him, "You're as good as dead—that woman you took, she's a married woman."

4-5 Now Abimelech had not yet slept with her, hadn't so much as touched her. He said, "Master, would you kill an innocent man? Didn't he tell me, 'She's my sister'? And didn't she herself say, 'He's my brother'? I had no idea I was doing anything wrong when I did this."

6-7 God said to him in the dream, "Yes, I know your intentions were pure, that's why I kept you from sinning against me; I was the one who kept you from going to bed with her. So now give the man's wife back to him. He's a prophet and will pray for you—pray for your life. If you don't give her back, know that it's certain death both for you and everyone in your family."

NEW KING JAMES VERSION

8So Abimelech rose early in the morning,
called all his servants, and told all these things
in their hearing; and the men were very much
afraid. 9And Abimelech called Abraham and
said to him, "What have you done to us? How
have I offended you, that you have brought on
me and on my kingdom a great sin? You have
done deeds to me that ought not to be done."
10Then Abimelech said to Abraham, "What did
you have in view, that you have done this
thing?"

11And Abraham said, "Because I thought,
surely the fear of God *is* not in this place; and
they will kill me on account of my wife. 12But in-
deed *she is* truly my sister. She *is* the daughter
of my father, but not the daughter of my mother;
and she became my wife. 13And it came to pass,
when God caused me to wander from my fa-
ther's house, that I said to her, 'This *is* your
kindness that you should do for me: in every
place, wherever we go, say of me, "He *is* my
brother." ' "

14Then Abimelech took sheep, oxen, and
male and female servants, and gave *them* to
Abraham; and he restored Sarah his wife to
him. 15And Abimelech said, "See, my land *is* be-
fore you; dwell where it pleases you." 16Then to
Sarah he said, "Behold, I have given your
brother a thousand *pieces* of silver; indeed this
vindicates you[a] before all who *are* with you and
before everybody." Thus she was rebuked.

17So Abraham prayed to God; and God
healed Abimelech, his wife, and his female ser-
vants. Then they bore *children;* 18for the LORD
had closed up all the wombs of the house of
Abimelech because of Sarah, Abraham's wife.

ISAAC IS BORN

21 And the LORD visited Sarah as He had
said, and the LORD did for Sarah as He had
spoken. 2For Sarah conceived and bore Abra-
ham a son in his old age, at the set time of which
God had spoken to him. 3And Abraham called
the name of his son who was born to him—
whom Sarah bore to him—Isaac. 4Then Abra-
ham circumcised his son Isaac when he was
eight days old, as God had commanded him.
5Now Abraham was one hundred years old
when his son Isaac was born to him. 6And Sarah
said, "God has made me laugh, *and* all who hear
will laugh with me." 7She also said, "Who would
have said to Abraham that Sarah would nurse
children? For I have borne *him* a son in his old
age."

HAGAR AND ISHMAEL DEPART

8So the child grew and was weaned. And
Abraham made a great feast on the same day
that Isaac was weaned.

9And Sarah saw the son of Hagar the Egyp-
tian, whom she had borne to Abraham, scoffing.

20:16 [a]Literally *it is a covering of the eyes for you*

THE MESSAGE

8-9 Abimelech was up first thing in the morn-
ing. He called all his house servants to-
gether and told them the whole story. They
were shocked. Then Abimelech called in
Abraham and said, "What have you done to
us? What have I ever done to you that you
would bring on me and my kingdom this
huge offense? What you've done to me
ought never to have been done."

10 Abimelech went on to Abraham, "What-
ever were you thinking of when you did this
thing?"

11-13 Abraham said, "I just assumed that there
was no fear of God in this place and that
they'd kill me to get my wife. Besides, the
truth is that she is my half sister; she's my
father's daughter but not my mother's.
When God sent me out as a wanderer from
my father's home, I told her, 'Do me a favor;
wherever we go, tell people that I'm your
brother.' "

14-15 Then Abimelech gave Sarah back to
Abraham, and along with her sent sheep
and cattle and servants, both male and fe-
male. He said, "My land is open to you; live
wherever you wish."

16 And to Sarah he said, "I've given your
brother a thousand pieces of silver—that
clears you of even a shadow of suspicion be-
fore the eyes of the world. You're vindi-
cated."

17-18 Then Abraham prayed to God and God
healed Abimelech, his wife and his maidser-
vants, and they started having babies again.
For GOD had shut down every womb in
Abimelech's household on account of
Sarah, Abraham's wife.

1-4 21 GOD visited Sarah exactly as he said
he would; GOD did to Sarah what he
promised: Sarah became pregnant and gave
Abraham a son in his old age, and at the
very time God had set. Abraham named him
Isaac. When his son was eight days old,
Abraham circumcised him just as God had
commanded.

5-6 Abraham was a hundred years old when
his son Isaac was born.

Sarah said,

God has blessed me with laughter
and all who get the news will laugh
with me!

7 She also said,

Whoever would have suggested to
Abraham
that Sarah would one day nurse a
baby!
Yet here I am! I've given the old man a
son!

8 The baby grew and was weaned. Abra-
ham threw a big party on the day Isaac was
weaned.

9-10 One day Sarah saw the son that Hagar
the Egyptian had borne to Abraham, poking

NEW KING JAMES VERSION

10Therefore she said to Abraham, "Cast out this
bondwoman and her son; for the son of this
bondwoman shall not be heir with my son,
namely with Isaac." 11And the matter was very
displeasing in Abraham's sight because of his
son.
12But God said to Abraham, "Do not let it be
displeasing in your sight because of the lad or
because of your bondwoman. Whatever Sarah
has said to you, listen to her voice; for in Isaac
your seed shall be called. 13Yet I will also make
a nation of the son of the bondwoman, because
he *is* your seed."
14So Abraham rose early in the morning, and
took bread and a skin of water; and putting *it* on
her shoulder, he gave *it* and the boy to Hagar,
and sent her away. Then she departed and wan-
dered in the Wilderness of Beersheba. 15And the
water in the skin was used up, and she placed
the boy under one of the shrubs. 16Then she
went and sat down across from *him* at a dis-
tance of about a bowshot; for she said to herself,
"Let me not see the death of the boy." So she sat
opposite *him,* and lifted her voice and wept.
17And God heard the voice of the lad. Then
the angel of God called to Hagar out of heaven,
and said to her, "What ails you, Hagar? Fear not,
for God has heard the voice of the lad where he
is. 18Arise, lift up the lad and hold him with your
hand, for I will make him a great nation."
19Then God opened her eyes, and she saw a
well of water. And she went and filled the skin
with water, and gave the lad a drink. 20So God
was with the lad; and he grew and dwelt in the
wilderness, and became an archer. 21He dwelt in
the Wilderness of Paran; and his mother took a
wife for him from the land of Egypt.

A COVENANT WITH ABIMELECH

22And it came to pass at that time that Abim-
elech and Phichol, the commander of his army,
spoke to Abraham, saying, "God *is* with you in
all that you do. 23Now therefore, swear to me by
God that you will not deal falsely with me, with
my offspring, or with my posterity; but that ac-
cording to the kindness that I have done to you,
you will do to me and to the land in which you
have dwelt."
24And Abraham said, "I will swear."
25Then Abraham rebuked Abimelech be-
cause of a well of water which Abimelech's ser-
vants had seized. 26And Abimelech said, "I do
not know who has done this thing; you did not
tell me, nor had I heard *of it* until today." 27So
Abraham took sheep and oxen and gave them to
Abimelech, and the two of them made a
covenant. 28And Abraham set seven ewe lambs
of the flock by themselves.
29Then Abimelech asked Abraham, "What *is
the meaning of* these seven ewe lambs which
you have set by themselves?"
30And he said, "You will take *these* seven
ewe lambs from my hand, that they may be my
witness that I have dug this well." 31Therefore he
called that place Beersheba,[a] because the two of
them swore an oath there.
32Thus they made a covenant at Beersheba.

21:31 [a]Literally *Well of the Oath* or *Well of the Seven*

THE MESSAGE

fun at her son Isaac. She told Abraham, "Get
rid of this slave woman and her son. No
child of this slave is going to share inheri-
tance with my son Isaac!"
11-13 The matter gave great pain to Abraham—
after all, Ishmael was his son. But God
spoke to Abraham, "Don't feel badly about
the boy and your maid. Do whatever Sarah
tells you. Your descendants will come
through Isaac. Regarding your maid's son,
be assured that I'll also develop a great na-
tion from him—he's your son, too."
14-16 Abraham got up early the next morning,
got some food together and a canteen of wa-
ter for Hagar, put them on her back and sent
her away with the child. She wandered off
into the desert of Beersheba. When the wa-
ter was gone, she left the child under a
shrub and went off, fifty yards or so. She
said, "I can't watch my son die." As she sat,
she broke into sobs.
17-18 Meanwhile, God heard the boy crying.
The angel of God called from Heaven to Ha-
gar, "What's wrong, Hagar? Don't be afraid.
God has heard the boy and knows the fix
he's in. Up now; go get the boy. Hold him
tight. I'm going to make of him a great na-
tion."
19 Just then God opened her eyes. She
looked. She saw a well of water. She went to
it and filled her canteen and gave the boy a
long, cool drink.
20-21 God was on the boy's side as he grew up.
He lived out in the desert and became a
skilled archer. He lived in the Paran wilder-
ness. And his mother got him a wife from
Egypt.

22-23 At about that same time, Abimelech and
the captain of his troops, Phicol, spoke to
Abraham: "No matter what you do, God is
on your side. So swear to me that you won't
do anything underhanded to me or any of
my family. For as long as you live here,
swear that you'll treat me and my land as
well as I've treated you."
24 Abraham said, "I swear it."
25-26 At the same time, Abraham confronted
Abimelech over the matter of a well of wa-
ter that Abimelech's servants had taken.
Abimelech said, "I have no idea who did
this; you never told me about it; this is the
first I've heard of it."
27-28 So the two of them made a covenant.
Abraham took sheep and cattle and gave
them to Abimelech. Abraham set aside
seven sheep from his flock.
29 Abimelech said, "What does this mean?
These seven sheep you've set aside."
30 Abraham said, "It means that when you
accept these seven sheep, you take it as
proof that I dug this well, that it's my well."
31-32 That's how the place got named Beer-
sheba (the Oath-Well), because the two of
them swore a covenant oath there. After
they had made the covenant at Beersheba,

NEW KING JAMES VERSION

So Abimelech rose with Phichol, the com-
mander of his army, and they returned to the
land of the Philistines. 33Then *Abraham* planted
a tamarisk tree in Beersheba, and there called
on the name of the LORD, the Everlasting God.
34And Abraham stayed in the land of the
Philistines many days.

ABRAHAM'S FAITH CONFIRMED

22 Now it came to pass after these things that
God tested Abraham, and said to him,
"Abraham!"
And he said, "Here I am."
2Then He said, "Take now your son, your
only *son* Isaac, whom you love, and go to the
land of Moriah, and offer him there as a burnt
offering on one of the mountains of which I
shall tell you."
3So Abraham rose early in the morning and
saddled his donkey, and took two of his young
men with him, and Isaac his son; and he split the
wood for the burnt offering, and arose and went
to the place of which God had told him. 4Then
on the third day Abraham lifted his eyes and
saw the place afar off. 5And Abraham said to his
young men, "Stay here with the donkey; the lad[a]
and I will go yonder and worship, and we will
come back to you."
6So Abraham took the wood of the burnt of-
fering and laid *it* on Isaac his son; and he took
the fire in his hand, and a knife, and the two of
them went together. 7But Isaac spoke to Abra-
ham his father and said, "My father!"
And he said, "Here I am, my son."
Then he said, "Look, the fire and the wood,
but where *is* the lamb for a burnt offering?"
8And Abraham said, "My son, God will pro-
vide for Himself the lamb for a burnt offering."
So the two of them went together.
9Then they came to the place of which God
had told him. And Abraham built an altar there
and placed the wood in order; and he bound
Isaac his son and laid him on the altar, upon the
wood. 10And Abraham stretched out his hand
and took the knife to slay his son.
11But the Angel of the LORD called to him
from heaven and said, "Abraham, Abraham!"
So he said, "Here I am."
12And He said, "Do not lay your hand on the
lad, or do anything to him; for now I know that
you fear God, since you have not withheld your
son, your only *son*, from Me."
13Then Abraham lifted his eyes and looked,
and there behind *him was* a ram caught in a
thicket by its horns. So Abraham went and took
the ram, and offered it up for a burnt offering in-
stead of his son. 14And Abraham called the
name of the place, The-LORD-Will-Provide;[a] as it
is said *to* this day, "In the Mount of the LORD it
shall be provided."
15Then the Angel of the LORD called to Abra-
ham a second time out of heaven, 16and said:
"By Myself I have sworn, says the LORD, because
you have done this thing, and have not withheld
your son, your only *son*— 17blessing I will bless
you, and multiplying I will multiply your de-
scendants as the stars of the heaven and as the

22:5 [a]Or *young man* **22:14** [a]Hebrew *YHWH Yireh*

THE MESSAGE

Abimelech and his commander, Phicol, left
and went back to Philistine territory.
33-34 Abraham planted a tamarisk tree in
Beersheba and worshiped GOD there, pray-
ing to the Eternal God. Abraham lived in
Philistine country for a long time.

1 22 After all this, God tested Abraham.
God said, "Abraham!"
"Yes?" answered Abraham. "I'm listen-
ing."
2 He said, "Take your dear son Isaac whom
you love and go to the land of Moriah. Sac-
rifice him there as a burnt offering on one of
the mountains that I'll point out to you."
3-5 Abraham got up early in the morning and
saddled his donkey. He took two of his
young servants and his son Isaac. He had
split wood for the burnt offering. He set out
for the place God had directed him. On the
third day he looked up and saw the place in
the distance. Abraham told his two young
servants, "Stay here with the donkey. The
boy and I are going over there to worship;
then we'll come back to you."
6 Abraham took the wood for the burnt of-
fering and gave it to Isaac his son to carry.
He carried the flint and the knife. The two of
them went off together.
7 Isaac said to Abraham his father, "Fa-
ther?"
"Yes, my son."
"We have flint and wood, but where's the
sheep for the burnt offering?"
8 Abraham said, "Son, God will see to it
that there's a sheep for the burnt offering."
And they kept on walking together.
9-10 They arrived at the place to which God
had directed him. Abraham built an altar.
He laid out the wood. Then he tied up Isaac
and laid him on the wood. Abraham reached
out and took the knife to kill his son.
11 Just then an angel of GOD called to him
out of Heaven, "Abraham! Abraham!"
"Yes, I'm listening."
12 "Don't lay a hand on that boy! Don't
touch him! Now I know how fearlessly you
fear God; you didn't hesitate to place your
son, your dear son, on the altar for me."
13 Abraham looked up. He saw a ram
caught by its horns in the thicket. Abraham
took the ram and sacrificed it as a burnt of-
fering instead of his son.
14 Abraham named that place GOD-Yireh
(GOD-Sees-to-It). That's where we get the
saying, "On the mountain of GOD, he sees to
it."
15-18 The angel of GOD spoke from Heaven a
second time to Abraham: "I swear—GOD's
sure word!—because you have gone through
with this, and have not refused to give me
your son, your dear, dear son, I'll bless
you—oh, how I'll bless you! And I'll make
sure that your children flourish—like stars
in the sky! like sand on the beaches! And

NEW KING JAMES VERSION

sand which *is* on the seashore; and your descen-
dants shall possess the gate of their enemies.
18 In your seed all the nations of the earth shall
be blessed, because you have obeyed My voice."
19 So Abraham returned to his young men, and
they rose and went together to Beersheba; and
Abraham dwelt at Beersheba.

THE FAMILY OF NAHOR

20 Now it came to pass after these things that
it was told Abraham, saying, "Indeed Milcah
also has borne children to your brother Nahor:
21 Huz his firstborn, Buz his brother, Kemuel the
father of Aram, 22 Chesed, Hazo, Pildash, Jid-
laph, and Bethuel." 23 And Bethuel begot Re-
bekah.[a] These eight Milcah bore to Nahor, Abra-
ham's brother. 24 His concubine, whose name
was Reumah, also bore Tebah, Gaham, Tha-
hash, and Maachah.

SARAH'S DEATH AND BURIAL

23 Sarah lived one hundred and twenty-seven
years; *these were* the years of the life of
Sarah. 2 So Sarah died in Kirjath Arba (that *is,*
Hebron) in the land of Canaan, and Abraham
came to mourn for Sarah and to weep for her.
3 Then Abraham stood up from before his
dead, and spoke to the sons of Heth, saying, 4 "I
am a foreigner and a visitor among you. Give
me property for a burial place among you, that I
may bury my dead out of my sight."
5 And the sons of Heth answered Abraham,
saying to him, 6 "Hear us, my lord: You *are* a
mighty prince among us; bury your dead in the
choicest of our burial places. None of us will
withhold from you his burial place, that you
may bury your dead."
7 Then Abraham stood up and bowed himself
to the people of the land, the sons of Heth. 8 And
he spoke with them, saying, "If it is your wish
that I bury my dead out of my sight, hear me,
and meet with Ephron the son of Zohar for me,
9 that he may give me the cave of Machpelah
which he has, which *is* at the end of his field. Let
him give it to me at the full price, as property for
a burial place among you."
10 Now Ephron dwelt among the sons of
Heth; and Ephron the Hittite answered Abra-
ham in the presence of the sons of Heth, all who
entered at the gate of his city, saying, 11 "No, my
lord, hear me: I give you the field and the cave
that *is* in it; I give it to you in the presence of the
sons of my people. I give it to you. Bury your
dead!"
12 Then Abraham bowed himself down before
the people of the land; 13 and he spoke to Ephron
in the hearing of the people of the land, saying,
"If you *will give it,* please hear me. I will give
you money for the field; take *it* from me and I
will bury my dead there."
14 And Ephron answered Abraham, saying to
him, 15 "My lord, listen to me; the land *is worth*
four hundred shekels of silver. What *is* that be-
tween you and me? So bury your dead." 16 And
Abraham listened to Ephron; and Abraham

22:23 [a]Spelled *Rebecca* in Romans 9:10

THE MESSAGE

your descendants will defeat their enemies. All nations on Earth will find themselves blessed through your descendants because you obeyed me."

19 Then Abraham went back to his young servants. They got things together and returned to Beersheba. Abraham settled down in Beersheba.

20-23 After all this, Abraham got the news: "Your brother Nahor is a father! Milcah has given him children: Uz, his firstborn, his brother Buz, Kemuel (he was the father of Aram), Kesed, Hazo, Pildash, Jidlaph, and Bethuel." (Bethuel was the father of Rebekah.) Milcah gave these eight sons to Nahor, Abraham's brother.

24 His concubine, Reumah, gave him four more children: Tebah, Gaham, Tahash, and Maacah.

1-2 23 Sarah lived 127 years. Sarah died in Kiriath Arba, present-day Hebron, in the land of Canaan. Abraham mourned for Sarah and wept.

3-4 Then Abraham got up from mourning his dead wife and spoke to the Hittites: "I know I'm only an outsider here among you, but sell me a burial plot so that I can bury my dead decently."

5-6 The Hittites responded, "Why, you're no mere outsider here with us, you're a prince of God! Bury your dead wife in the best of our burial sites. None of us will refuse you a place for burial."

7-9 Then Abraham got up, bowed respectfully to the people of the land, the Hittites, and said, "If you're serious about helping me give my wife a proper burial, intercede for me with Ephron son of Zohar. Ask him to sell me the cave of Machpelah that he owns, the one at the end of his land. Ask him to sell it to me at its full price for a burial plot, with you as witnesses."

10-11 Ephron was part of the local Hittite community. Then Ephron the Hittite spoke up, answering Abraham with all the Hittites who were part of the town council listening: "Oh no, my master! I couldn't do that. The field is yours—a gift. I'll give it and the cave to you. With my people as witnesses, I give it to you. Bury your deceased wife."

12-13 Abraham bowed respectfully before the assembled council and answered Ephron: "Please allow me—I want to pay the price of the land; take my money so that I can go ahead and bury my wife."

14-15 Then Ephron answered Abraham, "If you insist, master. What's four hundred silver shekels between us? Now go ahead and bury your wife."

16 Abraham accepted Ephron's offer and paid out the sum that Ephron had named

NEW KING JAMES VERSION

weighed out the silver for Ephron which he had named in the hearing of the sons of Heth, four hundred shekels of silver, currency of the merchants.

17So the field of Ephron which *was* in Machpelah, which *was* before Mamre, the field and the cave which *was* in it, and all the trees that *were* in the field, which *were* within all the surrounding borders, were deeded 18to Abraham as a possession in the presence of the sons of Heth, before all who went in at the gate of his city.

19And after this, Abraham buried Sarah his wife in the cave of the field of Machpelah, before Mamre (that *is,* Hebron) in the land of Canaan. 20So the field and the cave that *is* in it were deeded to Abraham by the sons of Heth as property for a burial place.

A BRIDE FOR ISAAC

24 Now Abraham was old, well advanced in age; and the LORD had blessed Abraham in all things. 2So Abraham said to the oldest servant of his house, who ruled over all that he had, "Please, put your hand under my thigh, 3and I will make you swear by the LORD, the God of heaven and the God of the earth, that you will not take a wife for my son from the daughters of the Canaanites, among whom I dwell; 4but you shall go to my country and to my family, and take a wife for my son Isaac."

5And the servant said to him, "Perhaps the woman will not be willing to follow me to this land. Must I take your son back to the land from which you came?"

6But Abraham said to him, "Beware that you do not take my son back there. 7The LORD God of heaven, who took me from my father's house and from the land of my family, and who spoke to me and swore to me, saying, 'To your descendants[a] I give this land,' He will send His angel before you, and you shall take a wife for my son from there. 8And if the woman is not willing to follow you, then you will be released from this oath; only do not take my son back there." 9So the servant put his hand under the thigh of Abraham his master, and swore to him concerning this matter.

10Then the servant took ten of his master's camels and departed, for all his master's goods *were in* his hand. And he arose and went to Mesopotamia, to the city of Nahor. 11And he made his camels kneel down outside the city by a well of water at evening time, the time when women go out to draw *water.* 12Then he said, "O LORD God of my master Abraham, please give me success this day, and show kindness to my master Abraham. 13Behold, *here* I stand by the well of water, and the daughters of the men of the city are coming out to draw water. 14Now let it be that the young woman to whom I say, 'Please let down your pitcher that I may drink,' and she says, 'Drink, and I will also give your camels a drink'—*let* her *be the one* You have appointed for Your servant Isaac. And by this I will know that You have shown kindness to my master."

15And it happened, before he had finished speaking, that behold, Rebekah, who was born

24:7 [a]Literally *seed*

THE MESSAGE

before the town council of Hittites—four hundred silver shekels at the current exchange rate.

17-20 That's how Ephron's field next to Mamre—the field, its cave, and all the trees within its borders—became Abraham's property. The town council of Hittites witnessed the transaction. Abraham then proceeded to bury his wife Sarah in the cave in the field of Machpelah that is next to Mamre, present-day Hebron, in the land of Canaan. The field and its cave went from the Hittites into Abraham's possession as a burial plot.

ISAAC AND REBEKAH

1 24 Abraham was now an old man. GOD had blessed Abraham in every way.

2-4 Abraham spoke to the senior servant in his household, the one in charge of everything he had, "Put your hand under my thigh and swear by GOD—God of Heaven, God of Earth—that you will not get a wife for my son from among the young women of the Canaanites here, but will go to the land of my birth and get a wife for my son Isaac."

5 The servant answered, "But what if the woman refuses to leave home and come with me? Do I then take your son back to your home country?"

6-8 Abraham said, "Oh no. Never. By no means are you to take my son back there. GOD, the God of Heaven, took me from the home of my father and from the country of my birth and spoke to me in solemn promise, 'I'm giving *this* land to your descendants.' This God will send his angel ahead of you to get a wife for my son. And if the woman won't come, you are free from this oath you've sworn to me. But under no circumstances are you to take my son back there."

9 So the servant put his hand under the thigh of his master Abraham and gave his solemn oath.

10-14 The servant took ten of his master's camels and, loaded with gifts from his master, traveled to Aram Naharaim and the city of Nahor. Outside the city, he made the camels kneel at a well. It was evening, the time when the women came to draw water. He prayed, "O GOD, God of my master Abraham, make things go smoothly this day; treat my master Abraham well! As I stand here by the spring while the young women of the town come out to get water, let the girl to whom I say, 'Lower your jug and give me a drink,' and who answers, 'Drink, and let me also water your camels'—let her be the woman you have picked out for your servant Isaac. Then I'll know that you're working graciously behind the scenes for my master."

15-17 It so happened that the words were barely out of his mouth when Rebekah, the

NEW KING JAMES VERSION

to Bethuel, son of Milcah, the wife of Nahor,
Abraham's brother, came out with her pitcher
on her shoulder. 16Now the young woman *was*
very beautiful to behold, a virgin; no man had
known her. And she went down to the well,
filled her pitcher, and came up. 17And the ser-
vant ran to meet her and said, "Please let me
drink a little water from your pitcher."
18So she said, "Drink, my lord." Then she
quickly let her pitcher down to her hand, and
gave him a drink. 19And when she had finished
giving him a drink, she said, "I will draw *water*
for your camels also, until they have finished
drinking." 20Then she quickly emptied her
pitcher into the trough, ran back to the well to
draw *water,* and drew for all his camels. 21And
the man, wondering at her, remained silent so as
to know whether the LORD had made his jour-
ney prosperous or not.
22So it was, when the camels had finished
drinking, that the man took a golden nose ring
weighing half a shekel, and two bracelets for
her wrists weighing ten *shekels* of gold, 23and
said, "Whose daughter *are* you? Tell me, please,
is there room *in* your father's house for us to
lodge?"
24So she said to him, "I *am* the daughter of
Bethuel, Milcah's son, whom she bore to Na-
hor." 25Moreover she said to him, "We have both
straw and feed enough, and room to lodge."
26Then the man bowed down his head and
worshiped the LORD. 27And he said, "Blessed *be*
the LORD God of my master Abraham, who has
not forsaken His mercy and His truth toward my
master. As for me, being on the way, the LORD
led me to the house of my master's brethren."
28So the young woman ran and told her
mother's household these things.
29Now Rebekah had a brother whose name
was Laban, and Laban ran out to the man by the
well. 30So it came to pass, when he saw the nose
ring, and the bracelets on his sister's wrists, and
when he heard the words of his sister Rebekah,
saying, "Thus the man spoke to me," that he
went to the man. And there he stood by the
camels at the well. 31And he said, "Come in, O
blessed of the LORD! Why do you stand outside?
For I have prepared the house, and a place for
the camels."
32Then the man came to the house. And he
unloaded the camels, and provided straw and
feed for the camels, and water to wash his feet
and the feet of the men who *were* with him.
33*Food* was set before him to eat, but he said, "I
will not eat until I have told about my errand."
And he said, "Speak on."
34So he said, "I *am* Abraham's servant. 35The
LORD has blessed my master greatly, and he has
become great; and He has given him flocks and
herds, silver and gold, male and female ser-
vants, and camels and donkeys. 36And Sarah my
master's wife bore a son to my master when she
was old; and to him he has given all that he has.
37Now my master made me swear, saying, 'You
shall not take a wife for my son from the daugh-
ters of the Canaanites, in whose land I dwell;
38but you shall go to my father's house and to

THE MESSAGE

daughter of Bethuel whose mother was
Milcah the wife of Nahor, Abraham's
brother, came out with a water jug on her
shoulder. The girl was stunningly beautiful,
a pure virgin. She went down to the spring,
filled her jug, and came back up. The ser-
vant ran to meet her and said, "Please, can I
have a sip of water from your jug?"
18-21 She said, "Certainly, drink!" And she held
the jug so that he could drink. When he had
satisfied his thirst she said, "I'll get water for
your camels, too, until they've drunk their
fill." She promptly emptied her jug into the
trough and ran back to the well to fill it, and
she kept at it until she had watered all the
camels.
The man watched, silent. Was this GOD's
answer? Had GOD made his trip a success or
not?
22-23 When the camels had finished drinking,
the man brought out gifts, a gold nose ring
weighing a little over a quarter of an ounce
and two arm bracelets weighing about four
ounces, and gave them to her. He asked her,
"Tell me about your family? Whose daugh-
ter are you? Is there room in your father's
house for us to stay the night?"
24-25 She said, "I'm the daughter of Bethuel the
son of Milcah and Nahor. And there's plenty
of room in our house for you to stay—and
lots of straw and feed besides."
26-27 At this the man bowed in worship before
GOD and prayed, "Blessed be GOD, God of
my master Abraham: How generous and
true you've been to my master; you've held
nothing back. You led me right to the door of
my master's brother!"
28 And the girl was off and running, telling
everyone in her mother's house what had
happened.
29-31 Rebekah had a brother named Laban.
Laban ran outside to the man at the spring.
He had seen the nose ring and the bracelets
on his sister and had heard her say, "The
man said this and this and this to me." So he
went to the man and there he was, still
standing with his camels at the spring. La-
ban welcomed him: "Come on in, blessed of
GOD! Why are you standing out here? I've
got the house ready for you; and there's also
a place for your camels."
32-33 So the man went into the house. The
camels were unloaded and given straw and
feed. Water was brought to bathe the feet of
the man and the men with him. Then Laban
brought out food. But the man said, "I won't
eat until I tell my story."
Laban said, "Go ahead; tell us."
34-41 The servant said, "I'm the servant of
Abraham. GOD has blessed my master—he's
a great man; GOD has given him sheep and
cattle, silver and gold, servants and maid-
servants, camels and donkeys. And then to
top it off, Sarah, my master's wife, gave him
a son in her old age and he has passed
everything on to his son. My master made
me promise, 'Don't get a wife for my son
from the daughters of the Canaanites in
whose land I live. No, go to my father's

NEW KING JAMES VERSION

my family, and take a wife for my son.’ 39And I
said to my master, ‘Perhaps the woman will not
follow me.’ 40But he said to me, ‘The LORD, be-
fore whom I walk, will send His angel with you
and prosper your way; and you shall take a wife
for my son from my family and from my father’s
house. 41You will be clear from this oath when
you arrive among my family; for if they will not
give *her* to you, then you will be released from
my oath.’
42“And this day I came to the well and said,
‘O LORD God of my master Abraham, if You will
now prosper the way in which I go, 43behold, I
stand by the well of water; and it shall come to
pass that when the virgin comes out to draw *wa-
ter,* and I say to her, “Please give me a little wa-
ter from your pitcher to drink,” 44and she says to
me, “Drink, and I will draw for your camels
also,”—*let* her *be* the woman whom the LORD
has appointed for my master’s son.’
45“But before I had finished speaking in my
heart, there was Rebekah, coming out with her
pitcher on her shoulder; and she went down to
the well and drew *water.* And I said to her,
‘Please let me drink.’ 46And she made haste and
let her pitcher down from her *shoulder,* and
said, ‘Drink, and I will give your camels a drink
also.’ So I drank, and she gave the camels a
drink also. 47Then I asked her, and said, ‘Whose
daughter *are* you?’ And she said, ‘The daughter
of Bethuel, Nahor’s son, whom Milcah bore to
him.’ So I put the nose ring on her nose and the
bracelets on her wrists. 48And I bowed my head
and worshiped the LORD, and blessed the LORD
God of my master Abraham, who had led me in
the way of truth to take the daughter of my mas-
ter’s brother for his son. 49Now if you will deal
kindly and truly with my master, tell me. And if
not, tell me, that I may turn to the right hand or
to the left.”
50Then Laban and Bethuel answered and
said, “The thing comes from the LORD; we can-
not speak to you either bad or good. 51Here *is*
Rebekah before you; take *her* and go, and let
her be your master’s son’s wife, as the LORD has
spoken.”
52And it came to pass, when Abraham’s ser-
vant heard their words, that he worshiped the
LORD, *bowing himself* to the earth. 53Then the
servant brought out jewelry of silver, jewelry of
gold, and clothing, and gave *them* to Rebekah.
He also gave precious things to her brother and
to her mother.
54And he and the men who *were* with him ate
and drank and stayed all night. Then they arose
in the morning, and he said, “Send me away to
my master.”
55But her brother and her mother said, “Let
the young woman stay with us *a few* days, at
least ten; after that she may go.”
56And he said to them, “Do not hinder me,
since the LORD has prospered my way; send me
away so that I may go to my master.”
57So they said, “We will call the young
woman and ask her personally.” 58Then they
called Rebekah and said to her, “Will you go
with this man?”
And she said, “I will go.”

THE MESSAGE

home, back to my family, and get a wife for
my son there.’ I said to my master, ‘But what
if the woman won’t come with me?’ He said,
‘GOD before whom I’ve walked faithfully
will send his angel with you and he’ll make
things work out so that you’ll bring back a
wife for my son from my family, from the
house of my father. Then you’ll be free from
the oath. If you go to my family and they
won’t give her to you, you will also be free
from the oath.’
42-44 “Well, when I came this very day to the
spring, I prayed, ‘GOD, God of my master
Abraham, make things turn out well in this
task I’ve been given. I’m standing at this
well. When a young woman comes here to
draw water and I say to her, Please, give me
a sip of water from your jug, and she says,
Not only will I give you a drink, I’ll also wa-
ter your camels—let that woman be the wife
GOD has picked out for my master’s son.’
45-48 “I had barely finished offering this
prayer, when Rebekah arrived, her jug on
her shoulder. She went to the spring and
drew water and I said, ‘Please, can I have a
drink?’ She didn’t hesitate. She held out her
jug and said, ‘Drink; and when you’re fin-
ished I’ll also water your camels.’ I drank,
and she watered the camels. I asked her,
‘Whose daughter are you?’ She said, ‘The
daughter of Bethuel whose parents were
Nahor and Milcah.’ I gave her a ring for her
nose, bracelets for her arms, and bowed in
worship to GOD. I praised GOD, the God of
my master Abraham who had led me
straight to the door of my master’s family to
get a wife for his son.
49 “Now, tell me what you are going to do. If
you plan to respond with a generous *yes*, tell
me. But if not, tell me plainly so I can figure
out what to do next.”
50-51 Laban and Bethuel answered, “This is to-
tally from GOD. We have no say in the mat-
ter, either yes or no. Rebekah is yours: Take
her and go; let her be the wife of your mas-
ter’s son, as GOD has made plain.”
52-54 When Abraham’s servant heard their de-
cision, he bowed in worship before GOD.
Then he brought out gifts of silver and gold
and clothing and gave them to Rebekah. He
also gave expensive gifts to her brother and
mother. He and his men had supper and
spent the night. But first thing in the morn-
ing they were up. He said, “Send me back to
my master.”
55 Her brother and mother said, “Let the girl
stay a while, say another ten days, and then
go.”
56 He said, “Oh, don’t make me wait! GOD
has worked everything out so well—send
me off to my master.”
57 They said, “We’ll call the girl; we’ll ask
her.”
They called Rebekah and asked her, “Do
you want to go with this man?”
58 She said, “I’m ready to go.”

New King James Version

59So they sent away Rebekah their sister and her nurse, and Abraham's servant and his men. 60And they blessed Rebekah and said to her:

"Our sister, *may* you *become*
The mother of thousands of ten thousands;
And may your descendants possess
The gates of those who hate them."

61Then Rebekah and her maids arose, and they rode on the camels and followed the man. So the servant took Rebekah and departed.

62Now Isaac came from the way of Beer Lahai Roi, for he dwelt in the South. 63And Isaac went out to meditate in the field in the evening; and he lifted his eyes and looked, and there, the camels *were* coming. 64Then Rebekah lifted her eyes, and when she saw Isaac she dismounted from her camel; 65for she had said to the servant, "Who *is* this man walking in the field to meet us?"

The servant said, "It *is* my master." So she took a veil and covered herself.

66And the servant told Isaac all the things that he had done. 67Then Isaac brought her into his mother Sarah's tent; and he took Rebekah and she became his wife, and he loved her. So Isaac was comforted after his mother's *death.*

Abraham and Keturah

25 Abraham again took a wife, and her name *was* Keturah. 2And she bore him Zimran, Jokshan, Medan, Midian, Ishbak, and Shuah. 3Jokshan begot Sheba and Dedan. And the sons of Dedan were Asshurim, Letushim, and Leummim. 4And the sons of Midian *were* Ephah, Epher, Hanoch, Abidah, and Eldaah. All these *were* the children of Keturah.

5And Abraham gave all that he had to Isaac. 6But Abraham gave gifts to the sons of the concubines which Abraham had; and while he was still living he sent them eastward, away from Isaac his son, to the country of the east.

Abraham's Death and Burial

7This *is* the sum of the years of Abraham's life which he lived: one hundred and seventy-five years. 8Then Abraham breathed his last and died in a good old age, an old man and full *of years,* and was gathered to his people. 9And his sons Isaac and Ishmael buried him in the cave of Machpelah, which *is* before Mamre, in the field of Ephron the son of Zohar the Hittite, 10the field which Abraham purchased from the sons of Heth. There Abraham was buried, and Sarah his wife. 11And it came to pass, after the death of Abraham, that God blessed his son Isaac. And Isaac dwelt at Beer Lahai Roi.

The Families of Ishmael and Isaac

12Now this *is* the genealogy of Ishmael, Abraham's son, whom Hagar the Egyptian, Sarah's maidservant, bore to Abraham. 13And these *were* the names of the sons of Ishmael, by their names, according to their generations: The firstborn of Ishmael, Nebajoth; then Kedar, Adbeel, Mibsam, 14Mishma, Dumah, Massa,

The Message

59-60 So they sent them off, their sister Rebekah with her nurse, and Abraham's servant with his men. And they blessed Rebekah saying,

You're our sister—live bountifully!
And your children, triumphantly!

61 Rebekah and her young maids mounted the camels and followed the man. The servant took Rebekah and set off for home.

62-65 Isaac was living in the Negev. He had just come back from a visit to Beer Lahai Roi. In the evening he went out into the field; while meditating he looked up and saw camels coming. When Rebekah looked up and saw Isaac, she got down from her camel and asked the servant, "Who is that man out in the field coming toward us?"

"That is my master."

She took her veil and covered herself.

66-67 After the servant told Isaac the whole story of the trip, Isaac took Rebekah into the tent of his mother Sarah. He married Rebekah and she became his wife and he loved her. So Isaac found comfort after his mother's death.

1-2 25 Abraham married a second time; his new wife was named Keturah. She gave birth to Zimran, Jokshan, Medan, Midian, Ishbak, and Shuah.

3 Jokshan had Sheba and Dedan.

Dedan's descendants were the Asshurim, the Letushim, and the Leummim.

4 Midian had Ephah, Epher, Hanoch, Abida, and Eldaah—all from the line of Keturah.

5-6 But Abraham gave everything he possessed to Isaac. While he was still living, he gave gifts to the sons he had by his concubines, but then sent them away to the country of the east, putting a good distance between them and his son Isaac.

7-11 Abraham lived 175 years. Then he took his final breath. He died happy at a ripe old age, full of years, and was buried with his family. His sons Isaac and Ishmael buried him in the cave of Machpelah in the field of Ephron son of Zohar the Hittite, next to Mamre. It was the field that Abraham had bought from the Hittites. Abraham was buried next to his wife Sarah. After Abraham's death, God blessed his son Isaac. Isaac lived at Beer Lahai Roi.

The Family Tree of Ishmael

12 This is the family tree of Ishmael son of Abraham, the son that Hagar the Egyptian, Sarah's maid, bore to Abraham.

13-16 These are the names of Ishmael's sons in the order of their births: Nebaioth, Ishmael's firstborn, Kedar, Adbeel, Mibsam, Mishma, Dumah, Massa, Hadad, Tema, Je-

New King James Version

15 Hadar,[a] Tema, Jetur, Naphish, and Kedemah.
16 These *were* the sons of Ishmael and these *were*
their names, by their towns and their settle-
ments, twelve princes according to their na-
tions. 17 These *were* the years of the life of Ish-
mael: one hundred and thirty-seven years; and
he breathed his last and died, and was gathered
to his people. 18 (They dwelt from Havilah as far
as Shur, which *is* east of Egypt as you go toward
Assyria.) He died in the presence of all his
brethren.

19 This *is* the genealogy of Isaac, Abraham's
son. Abraham begot Isaac. 20 Isaac was forty
years old when he took Rebekah as wife, the
daughter of Bethuel the Syrian of Padan Aram,
the sister of Laban the Syrian. 21 Now Isaac
pleaded with the LORD for his wife, because she
was barren; and the LORD granted his plea, and
Rebekah his wife conceived. 22 But the children
struggled together within her; and she said, "If
all is well, why *am I like* this?" So she went to in-
quire of the LORD.
23 And the LORD said to her:

"Two nations *are* in your womb,
Two peoples shall be separated from your
body;
One people shall be stronger than the other,
And the older shall serve the younger."

24 So when her days were fulfilled *for her* to
give birth, indeed *there were* twins in her
womb. 25 And the first came out red. *He was* like
a hairy garment all over; so they called his name
Esau.[a] 26 Afterward his brother came out, and his
hand took hold of Esau's heel; so his name was
called Jacob.[a] Isaac *was* sixty years old when
she bore them.
27 So the boys grew. And Esau was a skillful
hunter, a man of the field; but Jacob was a mild
man, dwelling in tents. 28 And Isaac loved Esau
because he ate *of his* game, but Rebekah loved
Jacob.

Esau Sells His Birthright

29 Now Jacob cooked a stew; and Esau came
in from the field, and he *was* weary. 30 And Esau
said to Jacob, "Please feed me with that same
red *stew,* for I *am* weary." Therefore his name
was called Edom.[a]
31 But Jacob said, "Sell me your birthright as
of this day."
32 And Esau said, "Look, I *am* about to die; so
what *is* this birthright to me?"
33 Then Jacob said, "Swear to me as of this
day."
So he swore to him, and sold his birthright to
Jacob. 34 And Jacob gave Esau bread and stew of
lentils; then he ate and drank, arose, and went
his way. Thus Esau despised *his* birthright.

25:15 [a]Masoretic Text reads *Hadad.* **25:25** [a]Literally *Hairy*
25:26 [a]Literally *Supplanter* **25:30** [a]Literally *Red*

The Message

tur, Naphish, and Kedemah—all the sons of Ishmael. Their settlements and encampments were named after them. Twelve princes with their twelve tribes.

17-18 Ishmael lived 137 years. When he breathed his last and died he was buried with his family. His children settled down all the way from Havilah near Egypt eastward to Shur in the direction of Assyria. The Ishmaelites didn't get along with any of their kin.

Jacob and Esau

19-20 This is the family tree of Isaac son of Abraham: Abraham had Isaac. Isaac was forty years old when he married Rebekah daughter of Bethuel the Aramean of Paddan Aram. She was the sister of Laban the Aramean.

21-23 Isaac prayed hard to GOD for his wife because she was barren. GOD answered his prayer and Rebekah became pregnant. But the children tumbled and kicked inside her so much that she said, "If this is the way it's going to be, why go on living?" She went to GOD to find out what was going on. GOD told her,

Two nations are in your womb,
two peoples butting heads while still
in your body.
One people will overpower the other,
and the older will serve the younger.

24-26 When her time to give birth came, sure enough, there were twins in her womb. The first came out reddish, as if snugly wrapped in a hairy blanket; they named him Esau (Hairy). His brother followed, his fist clutched tight to Esau's heel; they named him Jacob (Heel). Isaac was sixty years old when they were born.

27-28 The boys grew up. Esau became an expert hunter, an outdoorsman. Jacob was a quiet man preferring life indoors among the tents. Isaac loved Esau because he loved his game, but Rebekah loved Jacob.

29-30 One day Jacob was cooking a stew. Esau came in from the field, starved. Esau said to Jacob, "Give me some of that red stew—I'm starved!" That's how he came to be called Edom (Red).

31 Jacob said, "Make me a trade: my stew for your rights as the firstborn."

32 Esau said, "I'm starving! What good is a birthright if I'm dead?"

33-34 Jacob said, "First, swear to me." And he did it. On oath Esau traded away his rights as the firstborn. Jacob gave him bread and the stew of lentils. He ate and drank, got up and left. That's how Esau shrugged off his rights as the firstborn.

NEW KING JAMES VERSION

ISAAC AND ABIMELECH

26 There was a famine in the land, besides the first famine that was in the days of Abraham. And Isaac went to Abimelech king of the Philistines, in Gerar.

2Then the LORD appeared to him and said: "Do not go down to Egypt; live in the land of which I shall tell you. 3Dwell in this land, and I will be with you and bless you; for to you and your descendants I give all these lands, and I will perform the oath which I swore to Abraham your father. 4And I will make your descendants multiply as the stars of heaven; I will give to your descendants all these lands; and in your seed all the nations of the earth shall be blessed; 5because Abraham obeyed My voice and kept My charge, My commandments, My statutes, and My laws."

6So Isaac dwelt in Gerar. 7And the men of the place asked about his wife. And he said, "She *is* my sister"; for he was afraid to say, "*She is* my wife," *because he thought,* "lest the men of the place kill me for Rebekah, because she *is* beautiful to behold." 8Now it came to pass, when he had been there a long time, that Abimelech king of the Philistines looked through a window, and saw, and there was Isaac, showing endearment to Rebekah his wife. 9Then Abimelech called Isaac and said, "Quite obviously she *is* your wife; so how could you say, 'She *is* my sister'?"

Isaac said to him, "Because I said, 'Lest I die on account of her.' "

10And Abimelech said, "What *is* this you have done to us? One of the people might soon have lain with your wife, and you would have brought guilt on us." 11So Abimelech charged all *his* people, saying, "He who touches this man or his wife shall surely be put to death."

12Then Isaac sowed in that land, and reaped in the same year a hundredfold; and the LORD blessed him. 13The man began to prosper, and continued prospering until he became very prosperous; 14for he had possessions of flocks and possessions of herds and a great number of servants. So the Philistines envied him. 15Now the Philistines had stopped up all the wells which his father's servants had dug in the days of Abraham his father, and they had filled them with earth. 16And Abimelech said to Isaac, "Go away from us, for you are much mightier than we."

17Then Isaac departed from there and pitched his tent in the Valley of Gerar, and dwelt there. 18And Isaac dug again the wells of water which they had dug in the days of Abraham his father, for the Philistines had stopped them up after the death of Abraham. He called them by the names which his father had called them.

19Also Isaac's servants dug in the valley, and found a well of running water there. 20But the herdsmen of Gerar quarreled with Isaac's herdsmen, saying, "The water *is* ours." So he called the name of the well Esek,[a] because they quarreled with him. 21Then they dug another well, and they quarreled over that *one* also. So he called its name Sitnah.[a] 22And he moved

26:20 [a]Literally *Quarrel* **26:21** [a]Literally *Enmity*

THE MESSAGE

1 **26** There was a famine in the land, as bad as the famine during the time of Abraham. And Isaac went down to Abimelech, king of the Philistines, in Gerar.

2-5 GOD appeared to him and said, "Don't go down to Egypt; stay where I tell you. Stay here in this land and I'll be with you and bless you. I'm giving you and your children all these lands, fulfilling the oath that I swore to your father Abraham. I'll make your descendants as many as the stars in the sky and give them all these lands. All the nations of the Earth will get a blessing for themselves through your descendants. And why? Because Abraham obeyed my summons and kept my charge—my commands, my guidelines, my teachings."

6 So Isaac stayed put in Gerar.

7 The men of the place questioned him about his wife. He said, "She's my sister." He was afraid to say "She's my wife." He was thinking, "These men might kill me to get Rebekah, she's so beautiful."

8-9 One day, after they had been there quite a long time, Abimelech, king of the Philistines, looked out his window and saw Isaac fondling his wife Rebekah. Abimelech sent for Isaac and said, "So, she's your wife. Why did you tell us 'She's my sister'?"

Isaac said, "Because I thought I might get killed by someone who wanted her."

10 Abimelech said, "But think of what you might have done to *us*! Given a little more time, one of the men might have slept with your wife; you would have been responsible for bringing guilt down on us."

11 Then Abimelech gave orders to his people: "Anyone who so much as lays a hand on this man or his wife dies."

12-15 Isaac planted crops in that land and took in a huge harvest. GOD blessed him. The man got richer and richer by the day until he was very wealthy. He accumulated flocks and herds and many, many servants, so much so that the Philistines began to envy him. They got back at him by throwing dirt and debris into all the wells that his father's servants had dug back in the days of his father Abraham, clogging up all the wells.

16 Finally, Abimelech told Isaac: "Leave. You've become far too big for us."

17-18 So Isaac left. He camped in the valley of Gerar and settled down there. Isaac dug again the wells which were dug in the days of his father Abraham but had been clogged up by the Philistines after Abraham's death. And he renamed them, using the original names his father had given them.

19-24 One day, as Isaac's servants were digging in the valley, they came on a well of spring water. The shepherds of Gerar quarreled with Isaac's shepherds, claiming, "This water is ours." So Isaac named the well Esek (Quarrel) because they quarreled over it. They dug another well and there was a difference over that one also, so he named it Sitnah (Accusation). He went on from there

NEW KING JAMES VERSION

from there and dug another well, and they did
not quarrel over it. So he called its name Re-
hoboth,[a] because he said, "For now the LORD has
made room for us, and we shall be fruitful in the
land."
[23]Then he went up from there to Beersheba.
[24]And the LORD appeared to him the same night
and said, "I *am* the God of your father Abraham;
do not fear, for I *am* with you. I will bless you
and multiply your descendants for My servant
Abraham's sake." [25]So he built an altar there
and called on the name of the LORD, and he
pitched his tent there; and there Isaac's servants
dug a well.
[26]Then Abimelech came to him from Gerar
with Ahuzzath, one of his friends, and Phichol
the commander of his army. [27]And Isaac said to
them, "Why have you come to me, since you
hate me and have sent me away from you?"
[28]But they said, "We have certainly seen that
the LORD is with you. So we said, 'Let there now
be an oath between us, between you and us; and
let us make a covenant with you, [29]that you will
do us no harm, since we have not touched you,
and since we have done nothing to you but good
and have sent you away in peace. You *are* now
the blessed of the LORD.'"
[30]So he made them a feast, and they ate and
drank. [31]Then they arose early in the morning
and swore an oath with one another; and Isaac
sent them away, and they departed from him in
peace.
[32]It came to pass the same day that Isaac's
servants came and told him about the well
which they had dug, and said to him, "We have
found water." [33]So he called it Shebah.[a] There-
fore the name of the city *is* Beersheba[b] to this
day.
[34]When Esau was forty years old, he took as
wives Judith the daughter of Beeri the Hittite,
and Basemath the daughter of Elon the Hittite.
[35]And they were a grief of mind to Isaac and
Rebekah.

ISAAC BLESSES JACOB

27 Now it came to pass, when Isaac was old
and his eyes were so dim that he could not
see, that he called Esau his older son and said to
him, "My son."
And he answered him, "Here I am."
[2]Then he said, "Behold now, I am old. I do not
know the day of my death. [3]Now therefore,
please take your weapons, your quiver and your
bow, and go out to the field and hunt game for
me. [4]And make me savory food, such as I love,
and bring *it* to me that I may eat, that my soul
may bless you before I die."
[5]Now Rebekah was listening when Isaac
spoke to Esau his son. And Esau went to the
field to hunt game and to bring *it*. [6]So Rebekah
spoke to Jacob her son, saying, "Indeed I heard

26:22 [a]Literally *Spaciousness* **26:33** [a]Literally *Oath* or *Seven*
[b]Literally *Well of the Oath* or *Well of the Seven*

THE MESSAGE

and dug yet another well. But there was no fighting over this one so he named it Rehoboth (Wide-Open Spaces), saying, "Now GOD has given us plenty of space to spread out in the land." From there he went up to Beersheba. That very night GOD appeared to him and said,

I am the God of Abraham your father;
don't fear a thing because I'm with
you.
I'll bless you and make your children
flourish
because of Abraham my servant.

25 Isaac built an altar there and prayed, calling on GOD by name. He pitched his tent and his servants started digging another well.

26-27 Then Abimelech came to him from Gerar with Ahuzzath his advisor and Phicol the head of his troops. Isaac asked them, "Why did you come to me? You hate me; you threw me out of your country."

28-29 They said, "We've realized that GOD is on your side. We'd like to make a deal between us—a covenant that we maintain friendly relations. We haven't bothered you in the past; we treated you kindly and let you leave us in peace. So—GOD's blessing be with you!"

30-31 Isaac laid out a feast and they ate and drank together. Early in the morning they exchanged oaths. Then Isaac said good-bye and they parted as friends.

32-33 Later that same day, Isaac's servants came to him with news about the well they had been digging, "We've struck water!" Isaac named the well Sheba (Oath), and that's the name of the city, Beersheba (Oath-Well), to this day.

34-35 When Esau was forty years old he married Judith, daughter of Beeri the Hittite, and Basemath, daughter of Elon the Hittite. They turned out to be thorns in the sides of Isaac and Rebekah.

1 **27** When Isaac had become an old man and was nearly blind, he called his eldest son, Esau, and said, "My son."

"Yes, Father?"

2-4 "I'm an old man," he said; "I might die any day now. Do me a favor: Get your quiver of arrows and your bow and go out in the country and hunt me some game. Then fix me a hearty meal, the kind that you know I like, and bring it to me to eat so that I can give you my personal blessing before I die."

5-7 Rebekah was eavesdropping as Isaac spoke to his son Esau. As soon as Esau had gone off to the country to hunt game for his father, Rebekah spoke to her son Jacob. "I just overheard your father talking with your

New King James Version

your father speak to Esau your brother, saying,
7'Bring me game and make savory food for me,
that I may eat it and bless you in the presence of
the LORD before my death.' 8Now therefore, my
son, obey my voice according to what I com-
mand you. 9Go now to the flock and bring me
from there two choice kids of the goats, and I
will make savory food from them for your fa-
ther, such as he loves. 10Then you shall take *it* to
your father, that he may eat *it*, and that he may
bless you before his death."

11And Jacob said to Rebekah his mother,
"Look, Esau my brother *is* a hairy man, and I *am*
a smooth-*skinned* man. 12Perhaps my father will
feel me, and I shall seem to be a deceiver to him;
and I shall bring a curse on myself and not a
blessing."

13But his mother said to him, "*Let* your curse
be on me, my son; only obey my voice, and go,
get *them* for me." 14And he went and got *them*
and brought *them* to his mother, and his mother
made savory food, such as his father loved.
15Then Rebekah took the choice clothes of her
elder son Esau, which *were* with her in the
house, and put them on Jacob her younger son.
16And she put the skins of the kids of the goats
on his hands and on the smooth part of his neck.
17Then she gave the savory food and the bread,
which she had prepared, into the hand of her
son Jacob.

18So he went to his father and said, "My fa-
ther."

And he said, "Here I am. Who *are* you, my
son?"

19Jacob said to his father, "I *am* Esau your
firstborn; I have done just as you told me; please
arise, sit and eat of my game, that your soul may
bless me."

20But Isaac said to his son, "How *is it* that
you have found *it* so quickly, my son?"

And he said, "Because the LORD your God
brought *it* to me."

21Isaac said to Jacob, "Please come near, that
I may feel you, my son, whether you *are* really
my son Esau or not." 22So Jacob went near to
Isaac his father, and he felt him and said, "The
voice *is* Jacob's voice, but the hands *are* the
hands of Esau." 23And he did not recognize him,
because his hands were hairy like his brother
Esau's hands; so he blessed him.

24Then he said, "*Are* you really my son
Esau?"

He said, "I *am*."

25He said, "Bring *it* near to me, and I will eat
of my son's game, so that my soul may bless
you." So he brought *it* near to him, and he ate;
and he brought him wine, and he drank. 26Then
his father Isaac said to him, "Come near now
and kiss me, my son." 27And he came near and
kissed him; and he smelled the smell of his
clothing, and blessed him and said:

"Surely, the smell of my son
Is like the smell of a field
Which the LORD has blessed.
28Therefore may God give you
Of the dew of heaven,
Of the fatness of the earth,
And plenty of grain and wine.

The Message

brother, Esau. He said, 'Bring me some
game and fix me a hearty meal so that I can
eat and bless you with GOD's blessing before
I die.'

8-10 "Now, my son, listen to me. Do what I tell
you. Go to the flock and get me two young
goats. Pick the best; I'll prepare them into a
hearty meal, the kind that your father loves.
Then you'll take it to your father, he'll eat
and bless you before he dies."

11-12 "But Mother," Jacob said, "my brother
Esau is a hairy man and I have smooth skin.
What happens if my father touches me?
He'll think I'm playing games with him. I'll
bring down a curse on myself instead of a
blessing."

13 "If it comes to that," said his mother, "I'll
take the curse on myself. Now, just do what
I say. Go and get the goats."

14 So he went and got them and brought
them to his mother and she cooked a hearty
meal, the kind his father loved so much.

15-17 Rebekah took the dress-up clothes of her
older son Esau and put them on her younger
son Jacob. She took the goatskins and cov-
ered his hands and the smooth nape of his
neck. Then she placed the hearty meal she
had fixed and fresh bread she'd baked into
the hands of her son Jacob.

18 He went to his father and said, "My fa-
ther!"

"Yes?" he said. "Which son are you?"

19 Jacob answered his father, "I'm your
firstborn son Esau. I did what you told me.
Come now; sit up and eat of my game so you
can give me your personal blessing."

20 Isaac said, "So soon? How did you get it
so quickly?"

"Because your GOD cleared the way for
me."

21 Isaac said, "Come close, son; let me touch
you—are you really my son Esau?"

22-23 So Jacob moved close to his father Isaac.
Isaac felt him and said, "The voice is Jacob's
voice but the hands are the hands of Esau."
He didn't recognize him because his hands
were hairy, like his brother Esau's.

23-24 But as he was about to bless him he
pressed him, "You're sure? *You* are my son
Esau?"

"Yes. I am."

25 Isaac said, "Bring the food so I can eat of
my son's game and give you my personal
blessing." Jacob brought it to him and he
ate. He also brought him wine and he drank.

26 Then Isaac said, "Come close, son, and
kiss me."

27-29 He came close and kissed him and Isaac
smelled the smell of his clothes. Finally, he
blessed him,

Ahhh. The smell of my son
is like the smell of the open country
blessed by GOD.
May God give you
of Heaven's dew
and Earth's bounty of grain and wine.

NEW KING JAMES VERSION

29 Let peoples serve you,
And nations bow down to you.
Be master over your brethren,
And let your mother's sons bow down to
you.
Cursed *be* everyone who curses you,
And blessed *be* those who bless you!"

ESAU'S LOST HOPE

30 Now it happened, as soon as Isaac had fin-
ished blessing Jacob, and Jacob had scarcely
gone out from the presence of Isaac his father,
that Esau his brother came in from his hunting.
31 He also had made savory food, and brought it
to his father, and said to his father, "Let my fa-
ther arise and eat of his son's game, that your
soul may bless me."
32 And his father Isaac said to him, "Who *are*
you?"
So he said, "I *am* your son, your firstborn,
Esau."
33 Then Isaac trembled exceedingly, and said,
"Who? Where *is* the one who hunted game and
brought *it* to me? I ate all *of it* before you came,
and I have blessed him—*and* indeed he shall be
blessed."
34 When Esau heard the words of his father,
he cried with an exceedingly great and bitter
cry, and said to his father, "Bless me—me also, O
my father!"
35 But he said, "Your brother came with deceit
and has taken away your blessing."
36 And *Esau* said, "Is he not rightly named Ja-
cob? For he has supplanted me these two times.
He took away my birthright, and now look, he
has taken away my blessing!" And he said,
"Have you not reserved a blessing for me?"
37 Then Isaac answered and said to Esau, "In-
deed I have made him your master, and all his
brethren I have given to him as servants; with
grain and wine I have sustained him. What shall
I do now for you, my son?"
38 And Esau said to his father, "Have you only
one blessing, my father? Bless me—me also, O
my father!" And Esau lifted up his voice and
wept.
39 Then Isaac his father answered and said to
him:

"Behold, your dwelling shall be of the fatness
of the earth,
And of the dew of heaven from above.
40 By your sword you shall live,
And you shall serve your brother;
And it shall come to pass, when you become
restless,
That you shall break his yoke from your
neck."

JACOB ESCAPES FROM ESAU

41 So Esau hated Jacob because of the bless-
ing with which his father blessed him, and Esau
said in his heart, "The days of mourning for my
father are at hand; then I will kill my brother Ja-
cob."
42 And the words of Esau her older son were
told to Rebekah. So she sent and called Jacob
her younger son, and said to him, "Surely your
brother Esau comforts himself concerning you

THE MESSAGE

May peoples serve you
and nations honor you.
You will master your brothers,
and your mother's sons will honor
you.
Those who curse you will be cursed,
those who bless you will be blessed.

30-31 And then right after Isaac had blessed Ja-
cob and Jacob had left, Esau showed up
from the hunt. He also had prepared a
hearty meal. He came to his father and said,
"Let my father get up and eat of his son's
game, that he may give me his personal
blessing."
32 His father Isaac said, "And who are you?"
"I am your son, your firstborn, Esau."
33 Isaac started to tremble, shaking vio-
lently. He said, "Then who hunted game and
brought it to me? I finished the meal just
now, before you walked in. And I blessed
him—he's blessed for good!"
34 Esau, hearing his father's words, sobbed
violently and most bitterly, and cried to his
father, "My father! Can't you also bless me?"
35 "Your brother," he said, "came here
falsely and took your blessing."
36 Esau said, "Not for nothing was he
named Jacob, the Heel. Twice now he's
tricked me: first he took my birthright and
now he's taken my blessing."
He begged, "Haven't you kept back any
blessing for me?"
37 Isaac answered Esau, "I've made him
your master, and all his brothers his ser-
vants, and lavished grain and wine on him.
I've given it all away. What's left for you, my
son?"
38 "But don't you have just one blessing for
me, Father? Oh, bless me my father! Bless
me!" Esau sobbed inconsolably.
39-40 Isaac said to him,

You'll live far from Earth's bounty,
remote from Heaven's dew.
You'll live by your sword, hand-to-
mouth,
and you'll serve your brother.
But when you can't take it any more
you'll break loose and run free.

41 Esau seethed in anger against Jacob be-
cause of the blessing his father had given
him; he brooded, "The time for mourning
my father's death is close. And then I'll kill
my brother Jacob."
42-45 When these words of her older son Esau
were reported to Rebekah, she called her
younger son Jacob and said, "Your brother
Esau is plotting vengeance against you. He's

NEW KING JAMES VERSION

by intending to kill you. 43Now therefore, my
son, obey my voice: arise, flee to my brother La-
ban in Haran. 44And stay with him a few days,
until your brother's fury turns away, 45until your
brother's anger turns away from you, and he
forgets what you have done to him; then I will
send and bring you from there. Why should I be
bereaved also of you both in one day?"

46And Rebekah said to Isaac, "I am weary of
my life because of the daughters of Heth; if Ja-
cob takes a wife of the daughters of Heth, like
these *who are* the daughters of the land, what
good will my life be to me?"

28 Then Isaac called Jacob and blessed him,
and charged him, and said to him: "You
shall not take a wife from the daughters of
Canaan. 2Arise, go to Padan Aram, to the house
of Bethuel your mother's father; and take your-
self a wife from there of the daughters of Laban
your mother's brother.

3"May God Almighty bless you,
And make you fruitful and multiply you,
That you may be an assembly of peoples;
4And give you the blessing of Abraham,
To you and your descendants with you,
That you may inherit the land
In which you are a stranger,
Which God gave to Abraham."

5So Isaac sent Jacob away, and he went to Padan
Aram, to Laban the son of Bethuel the Syrian,
the brother of Rebekah, the mother of Jacob
and Esau.

ESAU MARRIES MAHALATH

6Esau saw that Isaac had blessed Jacob and
sent him away to Padan Aram to take himself a
wife from there, *and that* as he blessed him he
gave him a charge, saying, "You shall not take a
wife from the daughters of Canaan," 7and that
Jacob had obeyed his father and his mother and
had gone to Padan Aram. 8Also Esau saw that
the daughters of Canaan did not please his fa-
ther Isaac. 9So Esau went to Ishmael and took
Mahalath the daughter of Ishmael, Abraham's
son, the sister of Nebajoth, to be his wife in ad-
dition to the wives he had.

JACOB'S VOW AT BETHEL

10Now Jacob went out from Beersheba and
went toward Haran. 11So he came to a certain
place and stayed there all night, because the sun
had set. And he took one of the stones of that
place and put it at his head, and he lay down in
that place to sleep. 12Then he dreamed, and be-
hold, a ladder *was* set up on the earth, and its
top reached to heaven; and there the angels of
God were ascending and descending on it.

13And behold, the LORD stood above it and
said: "I *am* the LORD God of Abraham your fa-
ther and the God of Isaac; the land on which you
lie I will give to you and your descendants.
14Also your descendants shall be as the dust of
the earth; you shall spread abroad to the west
and the east, to the north and the south; and in
you and in your seed all the families of the earth

THE MESSAGE

going to kill you. Son, listen to me. Get out
of here. Run for your life to Haran, to my
brother Laban. Live with him for a while un-
til your brother cools down, until his anger
subsides and he forgets what you did to him.
I'll then send for you and bring you back.
Why should I lose both of you the same
day?"

46 Rebekah spoke to Isaac, "I'm sick to
death of these Hittite women. If Jacob also
marries a native Hittite woman, why live?"

1-2 28 So Isaac called in Jacob and blessed
him. Then he ordered him, "Don't take
a Caananite wife. Leave at once. Go to Pad-
dan Aram to the family of your mother's fa-
ther, Bethuel. Get a wife for yourself from
the daughters of your uncle Laban.

3-4 "And may The Strong God bless you and
give you many, many children, a congrega-
tion of peoples; and pass on the blessing of
Abraham to you and your descendants so
that you will get this land in which you live,
this land God gave Abraham."

5 So Isaac sent Jacob off. He went to Pad-
dan Aram, to Laban son of Bethuel the
Aramean, the brother of Rebekah who was
the mother of Jacob and Esau.

6-9 Esau learned that Isaac had blessed Ja-
cob and sent him to Paddan Aram to get a
wife there, and while blessing him com-
manded, "Don't marry a Canaanite woman,"
and that Jacob had obeyed his parents and
gone to Paddan Aram. When Esau realized
how deeply his father Isaac disliked the
Canaanite women, he went to Ishmael and
married Mahalath the sister of Nebaioth
and daughter of Ishmael, Abraham's son.
This was in addition to the wives he already
had.

10-12 Jacob left Beersheba and went to Haran. He
came to a certain place and camped for the
night since the sun had set. He took one of
the stones there, set it under his head and
lay down to sleep. And he dreamed: A stair-
way was set on the ground and it reached all
the way to the sky; angels of God were go-
ing up and going down on it.

13-15 Then GOD was right before him, saying, "I
am GOD, the God of Abraham your father
and the God of Isaac. I'm giving the ground
on which you are sleeping to you and to
your descendants. Your descendants will be
as the dust of the Earth; they'll stretch from
west to east and from north to south. All the
families of the Earth will bless themselves

NEW KING JAMES VERSION

shall be blessed. 15Behold, I *am* with you and
will keep you wherever you go, and will bring
you back to this land; for I will not leave you un-
til I have done what I have spoken to you."
16Then Jacob awoke from his sleep and said,
"Surely the LORD is in this place, and I did not
know *it*." 17And he was afraid and said, "How
awesome *is* this place! This *is* none other than
the house of God, and this *is* the gate of
heaven!"
18Then Jacob rose early in the morning, and
took the stone that he had put at his head, set it
up as a pillar, and poured oil on top of it. 19And
he called the name of that place Bethel;[a] but the
name of that city had been Luz previously.
20Then Jacob made a vow, saying, "If God will be
with me, and keep me in this way that I am go-
ing, and give me bread to eat and clothing to put
on, 21so that I come back to my father's house in
peace, then the LORD shall be my God. 22And
this stone which I have set as a pillar shall be
God's house, and of all that You give me I will
surely give a tenth to You."

JACOB MEETS RACHEL

29So Jacob went on his journey and came to
the land of the people of the East. 2And he
looked, and saw a well in the field; and behold,
there *were* three flocks of sheep lying by it; for
out of that well they watered the flocks. A large
stone *was* on the well's mouth. 3Now all the
flocks would be gathered there; and they would
roll the stone from the well's mouth, water the
sheep, and put the stone back in its place on the
well's mouth.
4And Jacob said to them, "My brethren,
where *are* you from?"
And they said, "We *are* from Haran."
5Then he said to them, "Do you know Laban
the son of Nahor?"
And they said, "We know him."
6So he said to them, "Is he well?"
And they said, "*He is* well. And look, his
daughter Rachel is coming with the sheep."
7Then he said, "Look, *it is* still high day; *it is*
not time for the cattle to be gathered together.
Water the sheep, and go and feed *them*."
8But they said, "We cannot until all the flocks
are gathered together, and they have rolled the
stone from the well's mouth; then we water the
sheep."
9Now while he was still speaking with them,
Rachel came with her father's sheep, for she
was a shepherdess. 10And it came to pass, when
Jacob saw Rachel the daughter of Laban his
mother's brother, and the sheep of Laban his
mother's brother, that Jacob went near and
rolled the stone from the well's mouth, and wa-
tered the flock of Laban his mother's brother.
11Then Jacob kissed Rachel, and lifted up his
voice and wept. 12And Jacob told Rachel that he
was her father's relative and that he *was* Re-
bekah's son. So she ran and told her father.
13Then it came to pass, when Laban heard

28:19 [a]Literally *House of God*

THE MESSAGE

in you and your descendants. Yes. I'll stay with you, I'll protect you wherever you go, and I'll bring you back to this very ground. I'll stick with you until I've done everything I promised you."

16-17 Jacob woke up from his sleep. He said, "GOD is in this place—truly. And I didn't even know it!" He was terrified. He whispered in awe, "Incredible. Wonderful. Holy. This is God's House. This is the Gate of Heaven."

18-19 Jacob was up first thing in the morning. He took the stone he had used for his pillow and stood it up as a memorial pillar and poured oil over it. He christened the place Bethel (God's House). The name of the town had been Luz until then.

20-22 Jacob vowed a vow: "If God stands by me and protects me on this journey on which I'm setting out, keeps me in food and clothing, and brings me back in one piece to my father's house, *this* GOD will be my God. This stone that I have set up as a memorial pillar will mark this as a place where God lives. And everything you give me, I'll return a tenth to you."

1-3 29 Jacob set out again on his way to the people of the east. He noticed a well out in an open field with three flocks of sheep bedded down around it. This was the common well from which the flocks were watered. The stone over the mouth of the well was huge. When all the flocks were gathered, the shepherds would roll the stone from the well and water the sheep; then they would return the stone, covering the well.

4 Jacob said, "Hello friends. Where are you from?"

They said, "We're from Haran."

5 Jacob asked, "Do you know Laban son of Nahor?"

"We do."

6 "Are things well with him?" Jacob continued.

"Very well," they said. "And here is his daughter Rachel coming with the flock."

7 Jacob said, "There's a lot of daylight still left; it isn't time to round up the sheep yet, is it? So why not water the flocks and go back to grazing?"

8 "We can't," they said. "Not until all the shepherds get here. It takes all of us to roll the stone from the well. Not until then can we water the flocks."

9-13 While Jacob was in conversation with them, Rachel came up with her father's sheep. She was the shepherd. The moment Jacob spotted Rachel, daughter of Laban his mother's brother, saw her arriving with his uncle Laban's sheep, he went and single-handedly rolled the stone from the mouth of the well and watered the sheep of his uncle Laban. Then he kissed Rachel and broke into tears. He told Rachel that he was related to her father, that he was Rebekah's son. She ran and told her father. When La-

NEW KING JAMES VERSION

the report about Jacob his sister's son, that he
ran to meet him, and embraced him and kissed
him, and brought him to his house. So he told
Laban all these things. [14]And Laban said to him,
"Surely you *are* my bone and my flesh." And he
stayed with him for a month.

JACOB MARRIES LEAH AND RACHEL

[15]Then Laban said to Jacob, "Because you
are my relative, should you therefore serve me
for nothing? Tell me, what *should* your wages
be?" [16]Now Laban had two daughters: the name
of the elder *was* Leah, and the name of the
younger *was* Rachel. [17]Leah's eyes *were* deli-
cate, but Rachel was beautiful of form and ap-
pearance.

[18]Now Jacob loved Rachel; so he said, "I will
serve you seven years for Rachel your younger
daughter."

[19]And Laban said, "*It is* better that I give her
to you than that I should give her to another
man. Stay with me." [20]So Jacob served seven
years for Rachel, and they seemed *only* a few
days to him because of the love he had for her.

[21]Then Jacob said to Laban, "Give *me* my
wife, for my days are fulfilled, that I may go in
to her." [22]And Laban gathered together all the
men of the place and made a feast. [23]Now it
came to pass in the evening, that he took Leah
his daughter and brought her to Jacob; and he
went in to her. [24]And Laban gave his maid Zil-
pah to his daughter Leah *as* a maid. [25]So it came
to pass in the morning, that behold, it *was* Leah.
And he said to Laban, "What is this you have
done to me? Was it not for Rachel that I served
you? Why then have you deceived me?"

[26]And Laban said, "It must not be done so in
our country, to give the younger before the first-
born. [27]Fulfill her week, and we will give you
this one also for the service which you will serve
with me still another seven years."

[28]Then Jacob did so and fulfilled her week.
So he gave him his daughter Rachel as wife
also. [29]And Laban gave his maid Bilhah to his
daughter Rachel as a maid. [30]Then *Jacob* also
went in to Rachel, and he also loved Rachel
more than Leah. And he served with Laban still
another seven years.

THE CHILDREN OF JACOB

[31]When the LORD saw that Leah *was*
unloved, He opened her womb; but Rachel *was*
barren. [32]So Leah conceived and bore a son, and
she called his name Reuben;[a] for she said, "The
LORD has surely looked on my affliction. Now
therefore, my husband will love me." [33]Then she
conceived again and bore a son, and said, "Be-
cause the LORD has heard that I *am* unloved, He
has therefore given me this *son* also." And she
called his name Simeon.[a] [34]She conceived again
and bore a son, and said, "Now this time my
husband will become attached to me, because I
have borne him three sons." Therefore his name
was called Levi.[a] [35]And she conceived again and
bore a son, and said, "Now I will praise the

29:32 [a]Literally *See, a Son* **29:33** [a]Literally *Heard* **29:34** [a]Lit-
erally *Attached*

THE MESSAGE

ban heard the news—Jacob, his sister's
son!—he ran out to meet him, embraced and
kissed him and brought him home. Jacob
told Laban the story of everything that had
happened.

14-15 Laban said, "You're family! My flesh and
blood!"

When Jacob had been with him for a
month, Laban said, "Just because you're my
nephew, you shouldn't work for me for
nothing. Tell me what you want to be paid.
What's a fair wage?"

16-18 Now Laban had two daughters; Leah was
the older and Rachel the younger. Leah had
nice eyes, but Rachel was stunningly beauti-
ful. And it was Rachel that Jacob loved.

So Jacob answered, "I will work for you
seven years for your younger daughter
Rachel."

19 "It is far better," said Laban, "that I give
her to you than marry her to some outsider.
Yes. Stay here with me."

20 So Jacob worked seven years for Rachel.
But it only seemed like a few days, he loved
her so much.

21-24 Then Jacob said to Laban, "Give me my
wife; I've completed what we agreed I'd do.
I'm ready to consummate my marriage." La-
ban invited everyone around and threw a
big feast. At evening, though, he got his
daughter Leah and brought her to the mar-
riage bed, and Jacob slept with her. (Laban
gave his maid Zilpah to his daughter Leah
as her maid.)

25 Morning came: There was Leah in the
marriage bed!

Jacob confronted Laban, "What have you
done to me? Didn't I work all this time for
the hand of Rachel? Why did you cheat me?"

26-27 "We don't do it that way in our country,"
said Laban. "We don't marry off the younger
daughter before the older. Enjoy your week
of honeymoon, and then we'll give you the
other one also. But it will cost you another
seven years of work."

28-30 Jacob agreed. When he'd completed the
honeymoon week, Laban gave him his
daughter Rachel to be his wife. (Laban gave
his maid Bilhah to his daughter Rachel as
her maid.) Jacob then slept with her. And he
loved Rachel more than Leah. He worked
for Laban another seven years.

31-32 When GOD realized that Leah was
unloved, he opened her womb. But Rachel
was barren. Leah became pregnant and had
a son. She named him Reuben (Look-It's-a-
Boy!). "This is a sign," she said, "that GOD
has seen my misery; and a sign that now my
husband will love me."

33-35 She became pregnant again and had an-
other son. "GOD heard," she said, "that I was
unloved and so he gave me this son also."
She named this one Simeon (GOD-Heard).
She became pregnant yet again—another
son. She said, "Now maybe my husband will
connect with me—I've given him three
sons!" That's why she named him Levi
(Connect). She became pregnant a final
time and had a fourth son. She said, "This

New King James Version

LORD." Therefore she called his name Judah.[a] Then she stopped bearing.

30 Now when Rachel saw that she bore Jacob no children, Rachel envied her sister, and said to Jacob, "Give me children, or else I die!"

2 And Jacob's anger was aroused against Rachel, and he said, "*Am* I in the place of God, who has withheld from you the fruit of the womb?"

3 So she said, "Here is my maid Bilhah; go in to her, and she will bear *a child* on my knees, that I also may have children by her." 4 Then she gave him Bilhah her maid as wife, and Jacob went in to her. 5 And Bilhah conceived and bore Jacob a son. 6 Then Rachel said, "God has judged my case; and He has also heard my voice and given me a son." Therefore she called his name Dan.[a] 7 And Rachel's maid Bilhah conceived again and bore Jacob a second son. 8 Then Rachel said, "With great wrestlings I have wrestled with my sister, *and* indeed I have prevailed." So she called his name Naphtali.[a]

9 When Leah saw that she had stopped bearing, she took Zilpah her maid and gave her to Jacob as wife. 10 And Leah's maid Zilpah bore Jacob a son. 11 Then Leah said, "A troop comes!"[a] So she called his name Gad.[b] 12 And Leah's maid Zilpah bore Jacob a second son. 13 Then Leah said, "I am happy, for the daughters will call me blessed." So she called his name Asher.[a]

14 Now Reuben went in the days of wheat harvest and found mandrakes in the field, and brought them to his mother Leah. Then Rachel said to Leah, "Please give me *some* of your son's mandrakes."

15 But she said to her, "*Is it* a small matter that you have taken away my husband? Would you take away my son's mandrakes also?"

And Rachel said, "Therefore he will lie with you tonight for your son's mandrakes."

16 When Jacob came out of the field in the evening, Leah went out to meet him and said, "You must come in to me, for I have surely hired you with my son's mandrakes." And he lay with her that night.

17 And God listened to Leah, and she conceived and bore Jacob a fifth son. 18 Leah said, "God has given me my wages, because I have given my maid to my husband." So she called his name Issachar.[a] 19 Then Leah conceived again and bore Jacob a sixth son. 20 And Leah said, "God has endowed me *with* a good endowment; now my husband will dwell with me, because I have borne him six sons." So she called his name Zebulun.[a] 21 Afterward she bore a daughter, and called her name Dinah.

22 Then God remembered Rachel, and God listened to her and opened her womb. 23 And she conceived and bore a son, and said, "God has taken away my reproach." 24 So she called his name Joseph,[a] and said, "The LORD shall add to me another son."

29:35 [a]Literally *Praise* **30:6** [a]Literally *Judge* **30:8** [a]Literally *My Wrestling* **30:11** [a]Following Qere, Syriac, and Targum; Kethib, Septuagint, and Vulgate read *in fortune.* [b]Literally *Troop* or *Fortune* **30:13** [a]Literally *Happy* **30:18** [a]Literally *Wages* **30:20** [a]Literally *Dwelling* **30:24** [a]Literally *He Will Add*

The Message

time I'll praise GOD." So she named him Judah (Praise-GOD). Then she stopped having children.

1 30 When Rachel realized that she wasn't having any children for Jacob, she became jealous of her sister. She told Jacob, "Give me sons or I'll die!"

2 Jacob got angry with Rachel and said, "Am I God? Am I the one who refused you babies?"

3-5 Rachel said, "Here's my maid Bilhah. Sleep with her. Let her substitute for me so I can have a child through her and build a family." So she gave him her maid Bilhah for a wife and Jacob slept with her. Bilhah became pregnant and gave Jacob a son.

6-8 Rachel said, "God took my side and vindicated me. He listened to me and gave me a son." She named him Dan (Vindication). Rachel's maid Bilhah became pregnant again and gave Jacob a second son. Rachel said, "I've been in an all-out fight with my sister—and I've won." So she named him Naphtali (Fight).

9-13 When Leah saw that she wasn't having any more children, she gave her maid Zilpah to Jacob for a wife. Zilpah had a son for Jacob. Leah said, "How fortunate!" and she named him Gad (Lucky). When Leah's maid Zilpah had a second son for Jacob, Leah said, "A happy day! The women will congratulate me in my happiness." So she named him Asher (Happy).

14 One day during the wheat harvest Reuben found some mandrakes in the field and brought them home to his mother Leah. Rachel asked Leah, "Could I please have some of your son's mandrakes?"

15 Leah said, "Wasn't it enough that you got my husband away from me? And now you also want my son's mandrakes?"

Rachel said, "All right. I'll let him sleep with you tonight in exchange for your son's love-apples."

16-21 When Jacob came home that evening from the fields, Leah was there to meet him: "Sleep with me tonight; I've bartered my son's mandrakes for a night with you." So he slept with her that night. God listened to Leah; she became pregnant and gave Jacob a fifth son. She said, "God rewarded me for giving my maid to my husband." She named him Issachar (Bartered). Leah became pregnant yet again and gave Jacob a sixth son, saying, "God has given me a great gift. This time my husband will honor me with gifts—I've given him six sons!" She named him Zebulun (Honor). Last of all she had a daughter and named her Dinah.

22-24 And then God remembered Rachel. God listened to her and opened her womb. She became pregnant and had a son. She said, "God has taken away my humiliation." She named him Joseph (Add), praying, "May GOD add yet another son to me."

NEW KING JAMES VERSION

JACOB'S AGREEMENT WITH LABAN

25And it came to pass, when Rachel had
borne Joseph, that Jacob said to Laban, "Send
me away, that I may go to my own place and to
my country. 26Give *me* my wives and my chil-
dren for whom I have served you, and let me go;
for you know my service which I have done for
you."

27And Laban said to him, "Please *stay,* if I
have found favor in your eyes, *for* I have learned
by experience that the LORD has blessed me for
your sake." 28Then he said, "Name me your
wages, and I will give *it.*"

29So *Jacob* said to him, "You know how I
have served you and how your livestock has
been with me. 30For what you had before I *came*
was little, and it has increased to a great
amount; the LORD has blessed you since my
coming. And now, when shall I also provide for
my own house?"

31So he said, "What shall I give you?"

And Jacob said, "You shall not give me any-
thing. If you will do this thing for me, I will
again feed and keep your flocks: 32Let me pass
through all your flock today, removing from
there all the speckled and spotted sheep, and all
the brown ones among the lambs, and the spot-
ted and speckled among the goats; and *these*
shall be my wages. 33So my righteousness will
answer for me in time to come, when the subject
of my wages comes before you: every one that *is*
not speckled and spotted among the goats, and
brown among the lambs, will be considered
stolen, if *it is* with me."

34And Laban said, "Oh, that it were accord-
ing to your word!" 35So he removed that day the
male goats that were speckled and spotted, all
the female goats that were speckled and spot-
ted, every one that had *some* white in it, and all
the brown ones among the lambs, and gave
them into the hand of his sons. 36Then he put
three days' journey between himself and Jacob,
and Jacob fed the rest of Laban's flocks.

37Now Jacob took for himself rods of green
poplar and of the almond and chestnut trees,
peeled white strips in them, and exposed the
white which *was* in the rods. 38And the rods
which he had peeled, he set before the flocks in
the gutters, in the watering troughs where the
flocks came to drink, so that they should con-
ceive when they came to drink. 39So the flocks
conceived before the rods, and the flocks
brought forth streaked, speckled, and spotted.
40Then Jacob separated the lambs, and made the
flocks face toward the streaked and all the
brown in the flock of Laban; but he put his own
flocks by themselves and did not put them with
Laban's flock.

41And it came to pass, whenever the stronger
livestock conceived, that Jacob placed the rods
before the eyes of the livestock in the gutters,
that they might conceive among the rods. 42But
when the flocks were feeble, he did not put
them in; so the feebler were Laban's and the
stronger Jacob's. 43Thus the man became ex-
ceedingly prosperous, and had large flocks, fe-
male and male servants, and camels and don-
keys.

THE MESSAGE

25-26 After Rachel had had Joseph, Jacob spoke to Laban, "Let me go back home. Give me my wives and children for whom I've served you. You know how hard I've worked for you."

27-28 Laban said, "If you please, I have learned through divine inquiry that GOD has blessed me because of you." He went on, "So name your wages. I'll pay you."

29-30 Jacob replied, "You know well what my work has meant to you and how your livestock has flourished under my care. The little you had when I arrived has increased greatly; everything I did resulted in blessings for you. Isn't it about time that I do something for my own family?"

31-33 "So, what should I pay you?"

Jacob said, "You don't have to pay me a thing. But how about this? I will go back to pasture and care for your flocks. Go through your entire flock today and take out every speckled or spotted sheep, every dark-colored lamb, every spotted or speckled goat. They will be my wages. That way you can check on my honesty when you assess my wages. If you find any goat that's not speckled or spotted or a sheep that's not black, you will know that I stole it."

34 "Fair enough," said Laban. "It's a deal."

35-36 But that very day Laban removed all the mottled and spotted billy goats and all the speckled and spotted nanny goats, every animal that had even a touch of white on it plus all the black sheep and placed them under the care of his sons. Then he put a three-day journey between himself and Jacob. Meanwhile Jacob went on tending what was left of Laban's flock.

37-42 But Jacob got fresh branches from poplar, almond, and plane trees and peeled the bark, leaving white stripes on them. He stuck the peeled branches in front of the watering troughs where the flocks came to drink. When the flocks were in heat, they came to drink and mated in front of the streaked branches. Then they gave birth to young that were streaked or spotted or speckled. Jacob placed the ewes before the dark-colored animals of Laban. That way he got distinctive flocks for himself which he didn't mix with Laban's flocks. And when the sturdier animals were mating, Jacob placed branches at the troughs in view of the animals so that they mated in front of the branches. But he wouldn't set up the branches before the feebler animals. That way the feeble animals went to Laban and the sturdy ones to Jacob.

43 The man got richer and richer, acquiring huge flocks, lots and lots of servants, not to mention camels and donkeys.

New King James Version

Jacob Flees from Laban

31 Now *Jacob* heard the words of Laban's sons, saying, "Jacob has taken away all that was our father's, and from what was our father's he has acquired all this wealth." 2And Jacob saw the countenance of Laban, and indeed it *was* not *favorable* toward him as before. 3Then the LORD said to Jacob, "Return to the land of your fathers and to your family, and I will be with you."

4So Jacob sent and called Rachel and Leah to the field, to his flock, 5and said to them, "I see your father's countenance, that it *is* not *favorable* toward me as before; but the God of my father has been with me. 6And you know that with all my might I have served your father. 7Yet your father has deceived me and changed my wages ten times, but God did not allow him to hurt me. 8If he said thus: 'The speckled shall be your wages,' then all the flocks bore speckled. And if he said thus: 'The streaked shall be your wages,' then all the flocks bore streaked. 9So God has taken away the livestock of your father and given *them* to me.

10"And it happened, at the time when the flocks conceived, that I lifted my eyes and saw in a dream, and behold, the rams which leaped upon the flocks *were* streaked, speckled, and gray-spotted. 11Then the Angel of God spoke to me in a dream, saying, 'Jacob.' And I said, 'Here I am.' 12And He said, 'Lift your eyes now and see, all the rams which leap on the flocks *are* streaked, speckled, and gray-spotted; for I have seen all that Laban is doing to you. 13I *am* the God of Bethel, where you anointed the pillar *and* where you made a vow to Me. Now arise, get out of this land, and return to the land of your family.' "

14Then Rachel and Leah answered and said to him, "Is there still any portion or inheritance for us in our father's house? 15Are we not considered strangers by him? For he has sold us, and also completely consumed our money. 16For all these riches which God has taken from our father are *really* ours and our children's; now then, whatever God has said to you, do it."

17Then Jacob rose and set his sons and his wives on camels. 18And he carried away all his livestock and all his possessions which he had gained, his acquired livestock which he had gained in Padan Aram, to go to his father Isaac in the land of Canaan. 19Now Laban had gone to shear his sheep, and Rachel had stolen the household idols that were her father's. 20And Jacob stole away, unknown to Laban the Syrian, in that he did not tell him that he intended to flee. 21So he fled with all that he had. He arose and crossed the river, and headed toward the mountains of Gilead.

Laban Pursues Jacob

22And Laban was told on the third day that Jacob had fled. 23Then he took his brethren with him and pursued him for seven days' journey, and he overtook him in the mountains of Gilead. 24But God had come to Laban the Syrian in a dream by night, and said to him, "Be careful that you speak to Jacob neither good nor bad."

The Message

1-2 31 Jacob learned that Laban's sons were talking behind his back: "Jacob has used our father's wealth to make himself rich at our father's expense." At the same time, Jacob noticed that Laban had changed toward him. He wasn't treating him the same.

3 That's when GOD said to Jacob, "Go back home where you were born. I'll go with you."

4-9 So Jacob sent word for Rachel and Leah to meet him out in the field where his flocks were. He said, "I notice that your father has changed toward me; he doesn't treat me the same as before. But the God of my father hasn't changed; he's still with me. You know how hard I've worked for your father. Still, your father has cheated me over and over, changing my wages time and again. But God never let him really hurt me. If he said, 'Your wages will consist of speckled animals' the whole flock would start having speckled lambs and kids. And if he said, 'From now on your wages will be streaked animals' the whole flock would have streaked ones. Over and over God used your father's livestock to reward me.

10-11 "Once, while the flocks were mating, I had a dream and saw the billy goats, all of them streaked, speckled, and mottled, mounting their mates. In the dream an angel of God called out to me, 'Jacob!'

"I said, 'Yes?'

12-13 "He said, 'Watch closely. Notice that all the goats in the flock that are mating are streaked, speckled, and mottled. I know what Laban's been doing to you. I'm the God of Bethel where you consecrated a pillar and made a vow to me. Now be on your way, get out of this place, go home to your birthplace.' "

14-16 Rachel and Leah said, "Has he treated us any better? Aren't we treated worse than outsiders? All he wanted was the money he got from selling us, and he's spent all that. Any wealth that God has seen fit to return to us from our father is justly ours and our children's. Go ahead. Do what God told you."

17-18 Jacob did it. He put his children and his wives on camels and gathered all his livestock and everything he had gotten, everything acquired in Paddan Aram, to go back home to his father Isaac in the land of Canaan.

19-21 Laban was off shearing sheep. Rachel stole her father's household gods. And Jacob had concealed his plans so well that Laban the Aramean had no idea what was going on—he was totally in the dark. Jacob got away with everything he had and was soon across the Euphrates headed for the hill country of Gilead.

22-24 Three days later, Laban got the news: "Jacob's run off." Laban rounded up his relatives and chased after him. Seven days later they caught up with him in the hill country of Gilead. That night God came to Laban the Aramean in a dream and said, "Be careful what you do to Jacob, whether good or bad."

NEW KING JAMES VERSION

25So Laban overtook Jacob. Now Jacob had pitched his tent in the mountains, and Laban with his brethren pitched in the mountains of Gilead.

26And Laban said to Jacob: "What have you done, that you have stolen away unknown to me, and carried away my daughters like captives *taken* with the sword? 27Why did you flee away secretly, and steal away from me, and not tell me; for I might have sent you away with joy and songs, with timbrel and harp? 28And you did not allow me to kiss my sons and my daughters. Now you have done foolishly in *so* doing. 29It is in my power to do you harm, but the God of your father spoke to me last night, saying, 'Be careful that you speak to Jacob neither good nor bad.' 30And now you have surely gone because you greatly long for your father's house, *but* why did you steal my gods?"

31Then Jacob answered and said to Laban, "Because I was afraid, for I said, 'Perhaps you would take your daughters from me by force.' 32With whomever you find your gods, do not let him live. In the presence of our brethren, identify what I have of yours and take *it* with you." For Jacob did not know that Rachel had stolen them.

33And Laban went into Jacob's tent, into Leah's tent, and into the two maids' tents, but he did not find *them.* Then he went out of Leah's tent and entered Rachel's tent. 34Now Rachel had taken the household idols, put them in the camel's saddle, and sat on them. And Laban searched all about the tent but did not find *them.* 35And she said to her father, "Let it not displease my lord that I cannot rise before you, for the manner of women *is* with me." And he searched but did not find the household idols.

36Then Jacob was angry and rebuked Laban, and Jacob answered and said to Laban: "What *is* my trespass? What *is* my sin, that you have so hotly pursued me? 37Although you have searched all my things, what part of your household things have you found? Set *it* here before my brethren and your brethren, that they may judge between us both! 38These twenty years I *have been* with you; your ewes and your female goats have not miscarried their young, and I have not eaten the rams of your flock. 39That which was torn *by beasts* I did not bring to you; I bore the loss of it. You required it from my hand, *whether* stolen by day or stolen by night. 40*There* I was! In the day the drought consumed me, and the frost by night, and my sleep departed from my eyes. 41Thus I have been in your house twenty years; I served you fourteen years for your two daughters, and six years for your flock, and you have changed my wages ten times. 42Unless the God of my father, the God of Abraham and the Fear of Isaac, had been with me, surely now you would have sent me away empty-handed. God has seen my affliction and the labor of my hands, and rebuked *you* last night."

LABAN'S COVENANT WITH JACOB

43And Laban answered and said to Jacob, "*These* daughters *are* my daughters, and *these*

THE MESSAGE

25 When Laban reached him, Jacob's tents were pitched in the Gilead mountains; Laban pitched his tents there, too.

26-30 "What do you mean," said Laban, "by keeping me in the dark and sneaking off, hauling my daughters off like prisoners of war? Why did you run off like a thief in the night? Why didn't you tell me? Why, I would have sent you off with a great celebration—music, timbrels, flutes! But you wouldn't permit me so much as a kiss for my daughters and grandchildren. It was a stupid thing for you to do. If I had a mind to, I could destroy you right now, but the God of your father spoke to me last night, 'Be careful what you do to Jacob, whether good or bad.' I understand. You left because you were homesick. But why did you steal my household gods?"

31-32 Jacob answered Laban, "I was afraid. I thought you would take your daughters away from me by brute force. But as far as your gods are concerned, if you find that anybody here has them, that person dies. With all of us watching, look around. If you find anything here that belongs to you, take it." Jacob didn't know that Rachel had stolen the gods.

33-35 Laban went through Jacob's tent, Leah's tent, and the tents of the two maids but didn't find them. He went from Leah's tent to Rachel's. But Rachel had taken the household gods, put them inside a camel cushion, and was sitting on them. When Laban had gone through the tent, searching high and low without finding a thing, Rachel said to her father, "Don't think I'm being disrespectful, my master, that I can't stand before you, but I'm having my period." So even though he turned the place upside down in his search, he didn't find the household gods.

36-37 Now it was Jacob's turn to get angry. He lit into Laban: "So what's my crime, what wrong have I done you that you badger me like this? You've ransacked the place. Have you turned up a single thing that's yours? Let's see it—display the evidence. Our two families can be the jury and decide between us.

38-42 "In the twenty years I've worked for you, ewes and she-goats never miscarried. I never feasted on the rams from your flock. I never brought you a torn carcass killed by wild animals but that I paid for it out of my own pocket—actually, you made me pay whether it was my fault or not. I was out in all kinds of weather, from torrid heat to freezing cold, putting in many a sleepless night. For twenty years I've done this: I slaved away fourteen years for your two daughters and another six years for your flock and you changed my wages ten times. If the God of my father, the God of Abraham and the Fear of Isaac, had not stuck with me, you would have sent me off penniless. But God saw the fix I was in and how hard I had worked and last night rendered his verdict."

43-44 Laban defended himself: "The daughters are my daughters, the children are my chil-

NEW KING JAMES VERSION

children *are* my children, and *this* flock *is* my flock; all that you see *is* mine. But what can I do this day to these my daughters or to their children whom they have borne? 44Now therefore, come, let us make a covenant, you and I, and let it be a witness between you and me."

45So Jacob took a stone and set it up *as* a pillar. 46Then Jacob said to his brethren, "Gather stones." And they took stones and made a heap, and they ate there on the heap. 47Laban called it Jegar Sahadutha,[a] but Jacob called it Galeed.[b] 48And Laban said, "This heap *is* a witness between you and me this day." Therefore its name was called Galeed, 49also Mizpah,[a] because he said, "May the LORD watch between you and me when we are absent one from another. 50If you afflict my daughters, or if you take *other* wives besides my daughters, *although* no man *is* with us—see, God *is* witness between you and me!"

51Then Laban said to Jacob, "Here is this heap and here is *this* pillar, which I have placed between you and me. 52This heap *is* a witness, and *this* pillar *is* a witness, that I will not pass beyond this heap to you, and you will not pass beyond this heap and this pillar to me, for harm. 53The God of Abraham, the God of Nahor, and the God of their father judge between us." And Jacob swore by the Fear of his father Isaac. 54Then Jacob offered a sacrifice on the mountain, and called his brethren to eat bread. And they ate bread and stayed all night on the mountain. 55And early in the morning Laban arose, and kissed his sons and daughters and blessed them. Then Laban departed and returned to his place.

ESAU COMES TO MEET JACOB

32 So Jacob went on his way, and the angels of God met him. 2When Jacob saw them, he said, "This *is* God's camp." And he called the name of that place Mahanaim.[a]

3Then Jacob sent messengers before him to Esau his brother in the land of Seir, the country of Edom. 4And he commanded them, saying, "Speak thus to my lord Esau, 'Thus your servant Jacob says: "I have dwelt with Laban and stayed there until now. 5I have oxen, donkeys, flocks, and male and female servants; and I have sent to tell my lord, that I may find favor in your sight." ' "

6Then the messengers returned to Jacob, saying, "We came to your brother Esau, and he also is coming to meet you, and four hundred men *are* with him." 7So Jacob was greatly afraid and distressed; and he divided the people that *were* with him, and the flocks and herds and camels, into two companies. 8And he said, "If Esau comes to the one company and attacks it, then the other company which is left will escape."

31:47 [a]Literally, in Aramaic, *Heap of Witness* [b]Literally, in Hebrew, *Heap of Witness* **31:49** [a]Literally *Watch* **32:2** [a]Literally *Double Camp*

THE MESSAGE

dren, the flock is my flock—everything you see is mine. But what can I do about my daughters or for the children they've had? So let's settle things between us, make a covenant—God will be the witness between us."

45 Jacob took a stone and set it upright as a pillar.

46-47 Jacob called his family around, "Get stones!" They gathered stones and heaped them up and then ate there beside the pile of stones. Laban named it in Aramaic, Yegar-sahadutha (Witness Monument); Jacob echoed the naming in Hebrew, Galeed (Witness Monument).

48-50 Laban said, "This monument of stones will be a witness, beginning now, between you and me." (That's why it is called Galeed—Witness Monument.) It is also called Mizpah (Watchtower) because Laban said, "GOD keep watch between you and me when we are out of each other's sight. If you mistreat my daughters or take other wives when there's no one around to see you, God will see you and stand witness between us."

51-53 Laban continued to Jacob, "This monument of stones and this stone pillar that I have set up is a witness, a witness that I won't cross this line to hurt you and you won't cross this line to hurt me. The God of Abraham and the God of Nahor (the God of their ancestor) will keep things straight between us."

53-55 Jacob promised, swearing by the Fear, the God of his father Isaac. Then Jacob offered a sacrifice on the mountain and worshiped, calling in all his family members to the meal. They ate and slept that night on the mountain. Laban got up early the next morning, kissed his grandchildren and his daughters, blessed them, and then set off for home.

1-2 32 And Jacob went his way. Angels of God met him. When Jacob saw them he said, "Oh! God's Camp!" And he named the place Mahanaim (Campground).

3-5 Then Jacob sent messengers on ahead to his brother Esau in the land of Seir in Edom. He instructed them: "Tell my master Esau this, 'A message from your servant Jacob: I've been staying with Laban and couldn't get away until now. I've acquired cattle and donkeys and sheep; also men and women servants. I'm telling you all this, my master, hoping for your approval.' "

6 The messengers came back to Jacob and said, "We talked to your brother Esau and he's on his way to meet you. But he has four hundred men with him."

7-8 Jacob was scared. Very scared. Panicked, he divided his people, sheep, cattle, and camels into two camps. He thought, "If Esau comes on the first camp and attacks it, the other camp has a chance to get away."

New King James Version

9 Then Jacob said, "O God of my father Abra-
ham and God of my father Isaac, the LORD who
said to me, 'Return to your country and to your
family, and I will deal well with you': 10 I am not
worthy of the least of all the mercies and of all
the truth which You have shown Your servant;
for I crossed over this Jordan with my staff, and
now I have become two companies. 11 Deliver
me, I pray, from the hand of my brother, from
the hand of Esau; for I fear him, lest he come
and attack me *and* the mother with the children.
12 For You said, 'I will surely treat you well, and
make your descendants as the sand of the sea,
which cannot be numbered for multitude.' "

13 So he lodged there that same night, and
took what came to his hand as a present for
Esau his brother: 14 two hundred female goats
and twenty male goats, two hundred ewes and
twenty rams, 15 thirty milk camels with their
colts, forty cows and ten bulls, twenty female
donkeys and ten foals. 16 Then he delivered *them*
to the hand of his servants, every drove by itself,
and said to his servants, "Pass over before me,
and put some distance between successive
droves." 17 And he commanded the first one, say-
ing, "When Esau my brother meets you and asks
you, saying, 'To whom do you belong, and where
are you going? Whose *are* these in front of you?'
18 then you shall say, 'They *are* your servant Ja-
cob's. It *is* a present sent to my lord Esau; and
behold, he also *is* behind us.' " 19 So he com-
manded the second, the third, and all who fol-
lowed the droves, saying, "In this manner you
shall speak to Esau when you find him; 20 and
also say, 'Behold, your servant Jacob *is* behind
us.' " For he said, "I will appease him with the
present that goes before me, and afterward I
will see his face; perhaps he will accept me."
21 So the present went on over before him, but he
himself lodged that night in the camp.

Wrestling with God

22 And he arose that night and took his two
wives, his two female servants, and his eleven
sons, and crossed over the ford of Jabbok. 23 He
took them, sent them over the brook, and sent
over what he had. 24 Then Jacob was left alone;
and a Man wrestled with him until the breaking
of day. 25 Now when He saw that He did not pre-
vail against him, He touched the socket of his
hip; and the socket of Jacob's hip was out of
joint as He wrestled with him. 26 And He said,
"Let Me go, for the day breaks."

But he said, "I will not let You go unless You
bless me!"

27 So He said to him, "What *is* your name?"

He said, "Jacob."

28 And He said, "Your name shall no longer
be called Jacob, but Israel;[a] for you have strug-
gled with God and with men, and have pre-
vailed."

29 Then Jacob asked, saying, "Tell *me* Your
name, I pray."

And He said, "Why *is* it *that* you ask about
My name?" And He blessed him there.

30 So Jacob called the name of the place Pe-
niel:[a] "For I have seen God face to face, and my

32:28 [a]Literally *Prince with God* **32:30** [a]Literally *Face of God*

The Message

9-12 And then Jacob prayed, "God of my father Abraham, God of my father Isaac, GOD who told me, 'Go back to your parents' homeland and I'll treat you well.' I don't deserve all the love and loyalty you've shown me. When I left here and crossed the Jordan I only had the clothes on my back, and now look at me—two camps! Save me, please, from the violence of my brother, my angry brother! I'm afraid he'll come and attack us all, me, the mothers and the children. You yourself said, 'I will treat you well; I'll make your descendants like the sands of the sea, far too many to count.' "

13-16 He slept the night there. Then he prepared a present for his brother Esau from his possessions: two hundred female goats, twenty male goats, two hundred ewes and twenty rams, thirty camels with their nursing young, forty cows and ten bulls, twenty female donkeys and ten male donkeys. He put a servant in charge of each herd and said, "Go ahead of me and keep a healthy space between each herd."

17-18 Then he instructed the first one out: "When my brother Esau comes close and asks, 'Who is your master? Where are you going? Who owns these?'—answer him like this, 'Your servant Jacob. They are a gift to my master Esau. He's on his way.' "

19-20 He gave the same instructions to the second servant and to the third—to each in turn as they set out with their herds: "Say 'Your servant Jacob is on his way behind us.' " He thought, "I will soften him up with the succession of gifts. Then when he sees me face-to-face, maybe he'll be glad to welcome me."

21 So his gifts went before him while he settled down for the night in the camp.

22-23 But during the night he got up and took his two wives, his two maidservants, and his eleven children and crossed the ford of the Jabbok. He got them safely across the brook along with all his possessions.

24-25 But Jacob stayed behind by himself, and a man wrestled with him until daybreak. When the man saw that he couldn't get the best of Jacob as they wrestled, he deliberately threw Jacob's hip out of joint.

26 The man said, "Let me go; it's daybreak."

Jacob said, "I'm not letting you go 'til you bless me."

27 The man said, "What's your name?"

He answered, "Jacob."

28 The man said, "But no longer. Your name is no longer Jacob. From now on it's Israel (God-Wrestler); you've wrestled with God and you've come through."

29 Jacob asked, "And what's your name?"

The man said, "Why do you want to know my name?" And then, right then and there, he blessed him.

30 Jacob named the place Peniel (God's Face) because, he said, "I saw God face-to-face and lived to tell the story!"

NEW KING JAMES VERSION

life is preserved." [31]Just as he crossed over
Penuel[a] the sun rose on him, and he limped on
his hip. [32]Therefore to this day the children of Is-
rael do not eat the muscle that shrank, which *is*
on the hip socket, because He touched the
socket of Jacob's hip in the muscle that shrank.

JACOB AND ESAU MEET

33 Now Jacob lifted his eyes and looked, and
there, Esau was coming, and with him
were four hundred men. So he divided the chil-
dren among Leah, Rachel, and the two maidser-
vants. [2]And he put the maidservants and their
children in front, Leah and her children behind,
and Rachel and Joseph last. [3]Then he crossed
over before them and bowed himself to the
ground seven times, until he came near to his
brother.
[4]But Esau ran to meet him, and embraced
him, and fell on his neck and kissed him, and
they wept. [5]And he lifted his eyes and saw the
women and children, and said, "Who *are* these
with you?"
So he said, "The children whom God has gra-
ciously given your servant." [6]Then the maidser-
vants came near, they and their children, and
bowed down. [7]And Leah also came near with
her children, and they bowed down. Afterward
Joseph and Rachel came near, and they bowed
down.
[8]Then Esau said, "What *do* you *mean by* all
this company which I met?"
And he said, "*These are* to find favor in the
sight of my lord."
[9]But Esau said, "I have enough, my brother;
keep what you have for yourself."
[10]And Jacob said, "No, please, if I have now
found favor in your sight, then receive my pres-
ent from my hand, inasmuch as I have seen your
face as though I had seen the face of God, and
you were pleased with me. [11]Please, take my
blessing that is brought to you, because God has
dealt graciously with me, and because I have
enough." So he urged him, and he took *it*.
[12]Then Esau said, "Let us take our journey;
let us go, and I will go before you."
[13]But Jacob said to him, "My lord knows that
the children *are* weak, and the flocks and herds
which are nursing *are* with me. And if the men
should drive them hard one day, all the flock
will die. [14]Please let my lord go on ahead before
his servant. I will lead on slowly at a pace which
the livestock that go before me, and the chil-
dren, are able to endure, until I come to my lord
in Seir."
[15]And Esau said, "Now let me leave with you
some of the people who *are* with me."
But he said, "What need is there? Let me find
favor in the sight of my lord." [16]So Esau returned
that day on his way to Seir. [17]And Jacob jour-
neyed to Succoth, built himself a house, and
made booths for his livestock. Therefore the
name of the place is called Succoth.[a]

JACOB COMES TO CANAAN

[18]Then Jacob came safely to the city of
Shechem, which *is* in the land of Canaan, when

32:31 [a]Same as *Peniel*, verse 30 **33:17** [a]Literally *Booths*

THE MESSAGE

31-32 The sun came up as he left Peniel, limp-
ing because of his hip. (This is why Israelites
to this day don't eat the hip muscle; because
Jacob's hip was thrown out of joint.)

1-4 33 Jacob looked up and saw Esau coming
with his four hundred men. He divided
the children between Leah and Rachel and
the two maidservants. He put the maidser-
vants out in front, Leah and her children
next, and Rachel and Joseph last. He led the
way and, as he approached his brother,
bowed seven times, honoring his brother.
But Esau ran up and embraced him, held
him tight and kissed him. And they both
wept.
5 Then Esau looked around and saw the
women and children: "And who are these
with you?"
Jacob said, "The children that God saw fit
to bless me with."
6-7 Then the maidservants came up with
their children and bowed; then Leah and
her children, also bowing; and finally,
Joseph and Rachel came up and bowed to
Esau.
8 Esau then asked, "And what was the
meaning of all those herds that I met?"
"I was hoping that they would pave the
way for my master to welcome me."
9 Esau said, "Oh, brother. I have plenty of
everything—keep what is yours for your-
self."
10-11 Jacob said, "Please. If you can find it in
your heart to welcome me, accept these
gifts. When I saw your face, it was as the
face of God smiling on me. Accept the gifts
I have brought for you. God has been good
to me and I have more than enough." Jacob
urged the gifts on him and Esau accepted.
12 Then Esau said, "Let's start out on our
way; I'll take the lead."
13-14 But Jacob said, "My master can see that
the children are frail. And the flocks and
herds are nursing, making for slow going. If
I push them too hard, even for a day, I'd lose
them all. So, master, you go on ahead of
your servant, while I take it easy at the pace
of my flocks and children. I'll catch up with
you in Seir."
15 Esau said, "Let me at least lend you some
of my men."
"There's no need," said Jacob. "Your gen-
erous welcome is all I need or want."
16 So Esau set out that day and made his
way back to Seir.
17 And Jacob left for Succoth. He built a
shelter for himself and sheds for his live-
stock. That's how the place came to be
called Succoth (Sheds).
18-20 And that's how it happened that Jacob
arrived all in one piece in Shechem in the
land of Canaan—all the way from Paddan

NEW KING JAMES VERSION

he came from Padan Aram; and he pitched his tent before the city. 19And he bought the parcel of land, where he had pitched his tent, from the children of Hamor, Shechem's father, for one hundred pieces of money. 20Then he erected an altar there and called it El Elohe Israel.[a]

THE DINAH INCIDENT

34 Now Dinah the daughter of Leah, whom she had borne to Jacob, went out to see the daughters of the land. 2And when Shechem the son of Hamor the Hivite, prince of the country, saw her, he took her and lay with her, and violated her. 3His soul was strongly attracted to Dinah the daughter of Jacob, and he loved the young woman and spoke kindly to the young woman. 4So Shechem spoke to his father Hamor, saying, "Get me this young woman as a wife."

5And Jacob heard that he had defiled Dinah his daughter. Now his sons were with his livestock in the field; so Jacob held his peace until they came. 6Then Hamor the father of Shechem went out to Jacob to speak with him. 7And the sons of Jacob came in from the field when they heard *it;* and the men were grieved and very angry, because he had done a disgraceful thing in Israel by lying with Jacob's daughter, a thing which ought not to be done. 8But Hamor spoke with them, saying, "The soul of my son Shechem longs for your daughter. Please give her to him as a wife. 9And make marriages with us; give your daughters to us, and take our daughters to yourselves. 10So you shall dwell with us, and the land shall be before you. Dwell and trade in it, and acquire possessions for yourselves in it."

11Then Shechem said to her father and her brothers, "Let me find favor in your eyes, and whatever you say to me I will give. 12Ask me ever so much dowry and gift, and I will give according to what you say to me; but give me the young woman as a wife."

13But the sons of Jacob answered Shechem and Hamor his father, and spoke deceitfully, because he had defiled Dinah their sister. 14And they said to them, "We cannot do this thing, to give our sister to one who is uncircumcised, for that *would be* a reproach to us. 15But on this *condition* we will consent to you: If you will become as we *are,* if every male of you is circumcised, 16then we will give our daughters to you, and we will take your daughters to us; and we will dwell with you, and we will become one people. 17But if you will not heed us and be circumcised, then we will take our daughter and be gone."

18And their words pleased Hamor and Shechem, Hamor's son. 19So the young man did not delay to do the thing, because he delighted in Jacob's daughter. He *was* more honorable than all the household of his father.

20And Hamor and Shechem his son came to the gate of their city, and spoke with the men of their city, saying: 21"These men *are* at peace with us. Therefore let them dwell in the land and trade in it. For indeed the land *is* large enough for them. Let us take their daughters to us as

33:20 [a]Literally *God, the God of Israel*

THE MESSAGE

Aram. He camped near the city. He bought the land where he pitched his tent from the sons of Hamor, the father of Shechem. He paid a hundred silver coins for it. Then he built an altar there and named it El-Elohe-Israel (Mighty Is the God of Israel).

1-4 34 One day Dinah, the daughter Leah had given Jacob, went to visit some of the women in that country. Shechem, the son of Hamor the Hivite who was chieftain there, saw her and raped her. Then he felt a strong attraction to Dinah, Jacob's daughter, fell in love with her, and wooed her. Shechem went to his father Hamor, "Get me this girl for my wife."

5-7 Jacob heard that Shechem had raped his daughter Dinah, but his sons were out in the fields with the livestock so he didn't say anything until they got home. Hamor, Shechem's father, went to Jacob to work out marriage arrangements. Meanwhile Jacob's sons on their way back from the fields heard what had happened. They were outraged, explosive with anger. Shechem's rape of Jacob's daughter was intolerable in Israel and not to be put up with.

8-10 Hamor spoke with Jacob and his sons, "My son Shechem is head over heels in love with your daughter—give her to him as his wife. Intermarry with us. Give your daughters to us and we'll give our daughters to you. Live together with us as one family. Settle down among us and make yourselves at home. Prosper among us."

11-12 Shechem then spoke for himself, addressing Dinah's father and brothers: "Please, say yes. I'll pay anything. Set the bridal price as high as you will—the sky's the limit! Only give me this girl for my wife."

13-17 Jacob's sons answered Shechem and his father with cunning. Their sister, after all, had been raped. They said, "This is impossible. We could never give our sister to a man who was uncircumcised. Why, we'd be disgraced. The only condition on which we can talk business is if all your men become circumcised like us. Then we will freely exchange daughters in marriage and make ourselves at home among you and become one big, happy family. But if this is not an acceptable condition, we will take our sister and leave."

18 That seemed fair enough to Hamor and his son Shechem.

19 The young man was so smitten with Jacob's daughter that he proceeded to do what had been asked. He was also the most admired son in his father's family.

20-23 So Hamor and his son Shechem went to the public square and spoke to the town council: "These men like us; they are our friends. Let them settle down here and make themselves at home; there's plenty of room in the country for them. And, just think, we can even exchange our daughters

New King James Version

wives, and let us give them our daughters. [22]Only on this *condition* will the men consent to dwell with us, to be one people: if every male among us is circumcised as they *are* circumcised. [23]*Will* not their livestock, their property, and every animal of theirs *be* ours? Only let us consent to them, and they will dwell with us." [24]And all who went out of the gate of his city heeded Hamor and Shechem his son; every male was circumcised, all who went out of the gate of his city.

[25]Now it came to pass on the third day, when they were in pain, that two of the sons of Jacob, Simeon and Levi, Dinah's brothers, each took his sword and came boldly upon the city and killed all the males. [26]And they killed Hamor and Shechem his son with the edge of the sword, and took Dinah from Shechem's house, and went out. [27]The sons of Jacob came upon the slain, and plundered the city, because their sister had been defiled. [28]They took their sheep, their oxen, and their donkeys, what *was* in the city and what *was* in the field, [29]and all their wealth. All their little ones and their wives they took captive; and they plundered even all that *was* in the houses.

[30]Then Jacob said to Simeon and Levi, "You have troubled me by making me obnoxious among the inhabitants of the land, among the Canaanites and the Perizzites; and since I *am* few in number, they will gather themselves together against me and kill me. I shall be destroyed, my household and I."

[31]But they said, "Should he treat our sister like a harlot?"

Jacob's Return to Bethel

35 Then God said to Jacob, "Arise, go up to Bethel and dwell there; and make an altar there to God, who appeared to you when you fled from the face of Esau your brother."

[2]And Jacob said to his household and to all who *were* with him, "Put away the foreign gods that *are* among you, purify yourselves, and change your garments. [3]Then let us arise and go up to Bethel; and I will make an altar there to God, who answered me in the day of my distress and has been with me in the way which I have gone." [4]So they gave Jacob all the foreign gods which *were* in their hands, and the earrings which *were* in their ears; and Jacob hid them under the terebinth tree which *was* by Shechem.

[5]And they journeyed, and the terror of God was upon the cities that *were* all around them, and they did not pursue the sons of Jacob. [6]So Jacob came to Luz (that *is,* Bethel), which *is* in the land of Canaan, he and all the people who *were* with him. [7]And he built an altar there and called the place El Bethel,[a] because there God appeared to him when he fled from the face of his brother.

[8]Now Deborah, Rebekah's nurse, died, and she was buried below Bethel under the terebinth tree. So the name of it was called Allon Bachuth.[a]

[9]Then God appeared to Jacob again, when he

35:7 [a]Literally *God of the House of God* **35:8** [a]Literally *Terebinth of Weeping*

The Message

in marriage. But these men will only accept our invitation to live with us and become one big family on one condition, that all our males become circumcised just as they themselves are. This is a very good deal for us—these people are very wealthy with great herds of livestock and we're going to get our hands on it. So let's do what they ask and have them settle down with us."

24 Everyone who was anyone in the city agreed with Hamor and his son, Shechem; every male was circumcised.

25-29 Three days after the circumcision, while all the men were still very sore, two of Jacob's sons, Simeon and Levi, Dinah's brothers, each with his sword in hand, walked into the city as if they owned the place and murdered every man there. They also killed Hamor and his son Shechem, rescued Dinah from Shechem's house, and left. When the rest of Jacob's sons came on the scene of slaughter, they looted the entire city in retaliation for Dinah's rape. Flocks, herds, donkeys, belongings—everything, whether in the city or the fields—they took. And then they took all the wives and children captive and ransacked their homes for anything valuable.

30 Jacob said to Simeon and Levi, "You've made my name stink to high heaven among the people here, these Canaanites and Perizzites. If they decided to gang up on us and attack, as few as we are we wouldn't stand a chance; they'd wipe me and my people right off the map."

31 They said, "Nobody is going to treat our sister like a whore and get by with it."

1 **35** God spoke to Jacob: "Go back to Bethel. Stay there and build an altar to the God who revealed himself to you when you were running for your life from your brother Esau."

2-3 Jacob told his family and all those who lived with him, "Throw out all the alien gods which you have, take a good bath and put on clean clothes, we're going to Bethel. I'm going to build an altar there to the God who answered me when I was in trouble and has stuck with me everywhere I've gone since."

4-5 They turned over to Jacob all the alien gods they'd been holding on to, along with their lucky-charm earrings. Jacob buried them under the oak tree in Shechem. Then they set out. A paralyzing fear descended on all the surrounding villages so that they were unable to pursue the sons of Jacob.

6-7 Jacob and his company arrived at Luz, that is, Bethel, in the land of Canaan. He built an altar there and named it El-Bethel (God-of-Bethel) because that's where God revealed himself to him when he was running from his brother.

8 And that's when Rebekah's nurse, Deborah, died. She was buried just below Bethel under the oak tree. It was named Allon-Bacuth (Weeping-Oak).

9-10 God revealed himself once again to Ja-

NEW KING JAMES VERSION

came from Padan Aram, and blessed him. 10 And
God said to him, "Your name *is* Jacob; your
name shall not be called Jacob anymore, but Is-
rael shall be your name." So He called his name
Israel. 11 Also God said to him: "I *am* God
Almighty. Be fruitful and multiply; a nation and
a company of nations shall proceed from you,
and kings shall come from your body. 12 The land
which I gave Abraham and Isaac I give to you;
and to your descendants after you I give this
land." 13 Then God went up from him in the place
where He talked with him. 14 So Jacob set up a
pillar in the place where He talked with him, a
pillar of stone; and he poured a drink offering
on it, and he poured oil on it. 15 And Jacob called
the name of the place where God spoke with
him, Bethel.

DEATH OF RACHEL

16 Then they journeyed from Bethel. And
when there was but a little distance to go to
Ephrath, Rachel labored *in childbirth,* and she
had hard labor. 17 Now it came to pass, when she
was in hard labor, that the midwife said to her,
"Do not fear; you will have this son also." 18 And
so it was, as her soul was departing (for she
died), that she called his name Ben-Oni;[a] but his
father called him Benjamin.[b] 19 So Rachel died
and was buried on the way to Ephrath (that *is,*
Bethlehem). 20 And Jacob set a pillar on her
grave, which *is* the pillar of Rachel's grave to
this day.

21 Then Israel journeyed and pitched his tent
beyond the tower of Eder. 22 And it happened,
when Israel dwelt in that land, that Reuben went
and lay with Bilhah his father's concubine; and
Israel heard *about it.*

JACOB'S TWELVE SONS

Now the sons of Jacob were twelve: 23 the
sons of Leah *were* Reuben, Jacob's firstborn,
and Simeon, Levi, Judah, Issachar, and Zebulun;
24 the sons of Rachel *were* Joseph and Benjamin;
25 the sons of Bilhah, Rachel's maidservant, *were*
Dan and Naphtali; 26 and the sons of Zilpah,
Leah's maidservant, *were* Gad and Asher. These
were the sons of Jacob who were born to him in
Padan Aram.

35:18 [a]Literally *Son of My Sorrow* [b]Literally *Son of the Right Hand*

THE MESSAGE

cob, after he had come back from Paddan Aram and blessed him: "Your name is Jacob (Heel); but that's your name no longer. From now on your name is Israel (God-Wrestler)."

11-12 God continued,

I am The Strong God.
Have children! Flourish!
A nation—a whole company of nations!—
will come from you.
Kings will come from your loins;
the land I gave Abraham and Isaac
I now give to you,
and pass it on to your descendants.

13 And then God was gone, ascended from the place where he had spoken with him.

14-15 Jacob set up a stone pillar on the spot where God had spoken with him. He poured a drink offering on it and anointed it with oil. Jacob dedicated the place where God had spoken with him, Bethel (God's-House).

16-17 They left Bethel. They were still quite a ways from Ephrath when Rachel went into labor—hard, hard labor. When her labor pains were at their worst, the midwife said to her, "Don't be afraid—you have another boy."

18 With her last breath, for she was now dying, she named him Ben-oni (Son-of-My-Pain), but his father named him Ben-jamin (Son-of-Good-Fortune).

19-20 Rachel died and was buried on the road to Ephrath, that is, Bethlehem. Jacob set up a pillar to mark her grave. It is still there today, "Rachel's Grave Stone."

21-22 Israel kept on his way and set up camp at Migdal Eder. While Israel was living in that region, Reuben went and slept with his father's concubine, Bilhah. And Israel heard of what he did.

22-26 There were twelve sons of Jacob.
The sons by Leah:
Reuben, Jacob's firstborn
Simeon
Levi
Judah
Issachar
Zebulun.
The sons by Rachel:
Joseph
Benjamin.
The sons by Bilhah, Rachel's maid:
Dan
Naphtali.
The sons by Zilpah, Leah's maid:
Gad
Asher.
These were Jacob's sons, born to him in Paddan Aram.

New King James Version

Death of Isaac

[27]Then Jacob came to his father Isaac at Mamre, or Kirjath Arba[a] (that *is,* Hebron), where Abraham and Isaac had dwelt. [28]Now the days of Isaac were one hundred and eighty years. [29]So Isaac breathed his last and died, and was gathered to his people, *being* old and full of days. And his sons Esau and Jacob buried him.

The Family of Esau

36 Now this *is* the genealogy of Esau, who is Edom. [2]Esau took his wives from the daughters of Canaan: Adah the daughter of Elon the Hittite; Aholibamah the daughter of Anah, the daughter of Zibeon the Hivite; [3]and Basemath, Ishmael's daughter, sister of Nebajoth. [4]Now Adah bore Eliphaz to Esau, and Basemath bore Reuel. [5]And Aholibamah bore Jeush, Jaalam, and Korah. These *were* the sons of Esau who were born to him in the land of Canaan.

[6]Then Esau took his wives, his sons, his daughters, and all the persons of his household, his cattle and all his animals, and all his goods which he had gained in the land of Canaan, and went to a country away from the presence of his brother Jacob. [7]For their possessions were too great for them to dwell together, and the land where they were strangers could not support them because of their livestock. [8]So Esau dwelt in Mount Seir. Esau *is* Edom.

[9]And this *is* the genealogy of Esau the father of the Edomites in Mount Seir. [10]These *were* the names of Esau's sons: Eliphaz the son of Adah the wife of Esau, and Reuel the son of Basemath the wife of Esau. [11]And the sons of Eliphaz were Teman, Omar, Zepho,[a] Gatam, and Kenaz.

[12]Now Timna was the concubine of Eliphaz, Esau's son, and she bore Amalek to Eliphaz. These *were* the sons of Adah, Esau's wife.

[13]These *were* the sons of Reuel: Nahath, Zerah, Shammah, and Mizzah. These were the sons of Basemath, Esau's wife.

[14]These were the sons of Aholibamah, Esau's wife, the daughter of Anah, the daughter of Zibeon. And she bore to Esau: Jeush, Jaalam, and Korah.

The Chiefs of Edom

[15]These *were* the chiefs of the sons of Esau. The sons of Eliphaz, the firstborn *son* of Esau, were Chief Teman, Chief Omar, Chief Zepho, Chief Kenaz, [16]Chief Korah,[a] Chief Gatam, *and* Chief Amalek. These *were* the chiefs of Eliphaz in the land of Edom. They *were* the sons of Adah.

[17]These *were* the sons of Reuel, Esau's son: Chief Nahath, Chief Zerah, Chief Shammah, and Chief Mizzah. These *were* the chiefs of Reuel in the land of Edom. These *were* the sons of Basemath, Esau's wife.

[18]And these *were* the sons of Aholibamah, Esau's wife: Chief Jeush, Chief Jaalam, and

35:27 [a]Literally *Town of Arba* **36:11** [a]Spelled *Zephi* in 1 Chronicles 1:36 **36:16** [a]Samaritan Pentateuch omits *Chief Korah.*

The Message

27-29 Finally, Jacob made it back home to his father Isaac at Mamre in Kiriath Arba, present-day Hebron, where Abraham and Isaac had lived. Isaac was now 180 years old. Isaac breathed his last and died—an old man full of years. He was buried with his family by his sons Esau and Jacob.

1 36 This is the family tree of Esau, who is also called Edom.

2-3 Esau married women of Canaan: Adah, daughter of Elon the Hittite; Oholibamah, daughter of Anah and the granddaughter of Zibeon the Hivite; and Basemath, daughter of Ishmael and sister of Nebaioth.

4 Adah gave Esau Eliphaz;
Basemath had Reuel;
5 Oholibamah had Jeush, Jalam, and Korah.
These are the sons of Esau who were born to him in the land of Canaan.

6-8 Esau gathered up his wives, sons and daughters, and everybody in his household, along with all his livestock—all the animals and possessions he had gotten in Canaan—and moved a considerable distance away from his brother Jacob. The brothers had too many possessions to live together in the same place; the land couldn't support their combined herds of livestock. So Esau ended up settling in the hill country of Seir (Esau and Edom are the same).

9-10 So this is the family tree of Esau, ancestor of the people of Edom, in the hill country of Seir. The names of Esau's sons:
Eliphaz, son of Esau's wife Adah;
Reuel, son of Esau's wife Basemath.

11-12 The sons of Eliphaz: Teman, Omar, Zepho, Gatam, and Kenaz. (Eliphaz also had a concubine Timna, who had Amalek.) These are the grandsons of Esau's wife Adah.

13 And these are the sons of Reuel: Nahath, Zerah, Shammah, and Mizzah—grandsons of Esau's wife Basemath.

14 These are the sons of Esau's wife Oholibamah, daughter of Anah the son of Zibeon. She gave Esau his sons Jeush, Jalam, and Korah.

15-16 These are the chieftains in Esau's family tree. From the sons of Eliphaz, Esau's firstborn, came the chieftains Teman, Omar, Zepho, Kenaz, Korah, Gatam, and Amalek—the chieftains of Eliphaz in the land of Edom; all of them sons of Adah.

17 From the sons of Esau's son Reuel came the chieftains Nahath, Zerah, Shammah, and Mizzah. These are the chieftains of Reuel in the land of Edom; all these were sons of Esau's wife Basemath.

18 These are the sons of Esau's wife Oholibamah: the chieftains Jeush, Jalam,

NEW KING JAMES VERSION

Chief Korah. These *were* the chiefs *who de-*
scended from Aholibamah, Esau's wife, the
daughter of Anah. 19These *were* the sons of
Esau, who is Edom, and these *were* their chiefs.

THE SONS OF SEIR

20These *were* the sons of Seir the Horite who
inhabited the land: Lotan, Shobal, Zibeon,
Anah, 21Dishon, Ezer, and Dishan. These *were*
the chiefs of the Horites, the sons of Seir, in the
land of Edom.
22And the sons of Lotan were Hori and
Hemam.[a] Lotan's sister *was* Timna.
23These *were* the sons of Shobal: Alvan,[a]
Manahath, Ebal, Shepho,[b] and Onam.
24These *were* the sons of Zibeon: both Ajah
and Anah. This *was the* Anah who found the
water[a] in the wilderness as he pastured the don-
keys of his father Zibeon. 25These *were* the chil-
dren of Anah: Dishon and Aholibamah the
daughter of Anah.
26These *were* the sons of Dishon:[a] Hemdan,[b]
Eshban, Ithran, and Cheran. 27These *were* the
sons of Ezer: Bilhan, Zaavan, and Akan.[a]
28These *were* the sons of Dishan: Uz and Aran.
29These *were* the chiefs of the Horites: Chief
Lotan, Chief Shobal, Chief Zibeon, Chief Anah,
30Chief Dishon, Chief Ezer, and Chief Dishan.
These *were* the chiefs of the Horites, according
to their chiefs in the land of Seir.

THE KINGS OF EDOM

31Now these *were* the kings who reigned in
the land of Edom before any king reigned over
the children of Israel: 32Bela the son of Beor
reigned in Edom, and the name of his city *was*
Dinhabah. 33And when Bela died, Jobab the son
of Zerah of Bozrah reigned in his place. 34When
Jobab died, Husham of the land of the Teman-
ites reigned in his place. 35And when Husham
died, Hadad the son of Bedad, who attacked
Midian in the field of Moab, reigned in his place.
And the name of his city *was* Avith. 36When
Hadad died, Samlah of Masrekah reigned in his
place. 37And when Samlah died, Saul of Re-
hoboth-*by*-the-River reigned in his place.
38When Saul died, Baal-Hanan the son of Ach-
bor reigned in his place. 39And when Baal-
Hanan the son of Achbor died, Hadar[a] reigned
in his place; and the name of his city *was* Pau.[b]
His wife's name *was* Mehetabel, the daughter of
Matred, the daughter of Mezahab.

THE CHIEFS OF ESAU

40And these *were* the names of the chiefs of
Esau, according to their families and their
places, by their names: Chief Timnah, Chief Al-
vah,[a] Chief Jetheth, 41Chief Aholibamah, Chief
Elah, Chief Pinon, 42Chief Kenaz, Chief Teman,

36:22 [a]Spelled *Homam* in 1 Chronicles 1:39 **36:23** [a]Spelled *Alian* in 1 Chronicles 1:40 [b]Spelled *Shephi* in 1 Chronicles 1:40 **36:24** [a]Following Masoretic Text and Vulgate (*hot springs*); Septuagint reads *Jamin;* Targum reads *mighty men;* Talmud interprets as *mules.* **36:26** [a]Hebrew *Dishan* [b]Spelled *Hamran* in 1 Chronicles 1:41 **36:27** [a]Spelled *Jaakan* in 1 Chronicles 1:42 **36:39** [a]Spelled *Hadad* in Samaritan Pentateuch, Syriac, and 1 Chronicles 1:50 [b]Spelled *Pai* in 1 Chronicles 1:50 **36:40** [a]Spelled *Aliah* in 1 Chronicles 1:51

THE MESSAGE

and Korah—chieftains born of Esau's wife
Oholibamah, daughter of Anah.
19 These are the sons of Esau, that is, Edom,
and these are their chieftains.

20-21 This is the family tree of Seir the Horite,
who were native to that land: Lotan, Shobal,
Zibeon, Anah, Dishon, Ezer, and Dishan.
These are the chieftains of the Horites, the
sons of Seir in the land of Edom.
22 The sons of Lotan were Hori and
Homam; Lotan's sister was Timna.
23 The sons of Shobal were Alvan, Mana-
hath, Ebal, Shepho, and Onam.
24 The sons of Zibeon were Aiah and
Anah—this is the same Anah who found the
hot springs in the wilderness while herding
his father Zibeon's donkeys.
25 The children of Anah were Dishon and
his daughter Oholibamah.
26 The sons of Dishon were Hemdan, Esh-
ban, Ithran, and Keran.
27 The sons of Ezer: Bilhan, Zaavan, and
Akan.
28 The sons of Dishan: Uz and Aran.
29-30 And these were the Horite chieftains:
Lotan, Shobal, Zibeon, Anah, Dishon, Ezer,
and Dishan—the Horite chieftains clan by
clan in the land of Seir.

31-39 And these are the kings who ruled in
Edom before there was a king in Israel: Bela
son of Beor was the king of Edom; the name
of his city was Dinhabah. When Bela died,
Jobab son of Zerah from Bozrah became the
next king. When Jobab died, he was fol-
lowed by Hushan from the land of the Te-
manites. When Hushan died, he was fol-
lowed by Hadad son of Bedad; he was the
king who defeated the Midianites in Moab;
the name of his city was Avith. When Hadad
died, Samlah of Masrekah became the next
king. When Samlah died, Shaul from Re-
hoboth-on-the-River became king. When
Shaul died, he was followed by Baal-Hanan
son of Acbor. When Baal-Hanan son of Ac-
bor died, Hadad became king; the name of
his city was Pau; his wife's name was
Mehetabel daughter of Matred, daughter of
Me-Zahab.

40-43 And these are the chieftains from the line
of Esau, clan by clan, region by region:
Timna, Alvah, Jetheth, Oholibamah, Elah,
Pinon, Kenaz, Teman, Mibzar, Magdiel, and

NEW KING JAMES VERSION

Chief Mibzar, 43Chief Magdiel, and Chief Iram.
These *were* the chiefs of Edom, according to
their dwelling places in the land of their posses-
sion. Esau *was* the father of the Edomites.

JOSEPH DREAMS OF GREATNESS

37 Now Jacob dwelt in the land where his fa-
ther was a stranger, in the land of Canaan.
2This *is* the history of Jacob.
Joseph, *being* seventeen years old, was feed-
ing the flock with his brothers. And the lad *was*
with the sons of Bilhah and the sons of Zilpah,
his father's wives; and Joseph brought a bad re-
port of them to his father.
3Now Israel loved Joseph more than all his
children, because he *was* the son of his old age.
Also he made him a tunic of *many* colors. 4But
when his brothers saw that their father loved
him more than all his brothers, they hated him
and could not speak peaceably to him.
5Now Joseph had a dream, and he told *it* to
his brothers; and they hated him even more. 6So
he said to them, "Please hear this dream which
I have dreamed: 7There we were, binding
sheaves in the field. Then behold, my sheaf
arose and also stood upright; and indeed your
sheaves stood all around and bowed down to my
sheaf."
8And his brothers said to him, "Shall you in-
deed reign over us? Or shall you indeed have do-
minion over us?" So they hated him even more
for his dreams and for his words.
9Then he dreamed still another dream and
told it to his brothers, and said, "Look, I have
dreamed another dream. And this time, the sun,
the moon, and the eleven stars bowed down to
me."
10So he told *it* to his father and his brothers;
and his father rebuked him and said to him,
"What *is* this dream that you have dreamed?
Shall your mother and I and your brothers in-
deed come to bow down to the earth before
you?" 11And his brothers envied him, but his fa-
ther kept the matter *in mind.*

JOSEPH SOLD BY HIS BROTHERS

12Then his brothers went to feed their fa-
ther's flock in Shechem. 13And Israel said to
Joseph, "Are not your brothers feeding *the flock*
in Shechem? Come, I will send you to them."
So he said to him, "Here I am."
14Then he said to him, "Please go and see if it
is well with your brothers and well with the
flocks, and bring back word to me." So he sent
him out of the Valley of Hebron, and he went to
Shechem.
15Now a certain man found him, and there he
was, wandering in the field. And the man asked
him, saying, "What are you seeking?"
16So he said, "I am seeking my brothers.
Please tell me where they are feeding *their
flocks.*"
17And the man said, "They have departed
from here, for I heard them say, 'Let us go to
Dothan.' " So Joseph went after his brothers and
found them in Dothan.
18Now when they saw him afar off, even be-
fore he came near them, they conspired against

THE MESSAGE

Iram—the chieftains of Edom as they occu-
pied their various regions.
This accounts for the family tree of Esau,
ancestor of all Edomites.

1 37 Meanwhile Jacob had settled down
where his father had lived, the land of
Canaan.

JOSEPH AND HIS BROTHERS

2 This is the story of Jacob. The story contin-
ues with Joseph, seventeen years old at the
time, helping out his brothers in herding the
flocks. These were his half brothers actu-
ally, the sons of his father's wives Bilhah
and Zilpah. And Joseph brought his father
bad reports on them.
3-4 Israel loved Joseph more than any of his
other sons because he was the child of his
old age. And he made him an elaborately
embroidered coat. When his brothers real-
ized that their father loved him more than
them, they grew to hate him—they wouldn't
even speak to him.
5-7 Joseph had a dream. When he told it to
his brothers, they hated him even more. He
said, "Listen to this dream I had. We were all
out in the field gathering bundles of wheat.
All of a sudden my bundle stood straight up
and your bundles circled around it and
bowed down to mine."
8 His brothers said, "So! You're going to
rule us? You're going to boss us around?"
And they hated him more than ever because
of his dreams and the way he talked.
9 He had another dream and told this one
also to his brothers: "I dreamed another
dream—the sun and moon and eleven stars
bowed down to me!"
10-11 When he told it to his father and broth-
ers, his father reprimanded him: "What's
with all this dreaming? Am I and your
mother and your brothers all supposed to
bow down to you?" Now his brothers were
really jealous; but his father brooded over
the whole business.
12-13 His brothers had gone off to Shechem
where they were pasturing their father's
flocks. Israel said to Joseph, "Your brothers
are with flocks in Shechem. Come, I want to
send you to them."
Joseph said, "I'm ready."
14 He said, "Go and see how your brothers
and the flocks are doing and bring me back
a report." He sent him off from the valley of
Hebron to Shechem.
15 A man met him as he was wandering
through the fields and asked him, "What are
you looking for?"
16 "I'm trying to find my brothers. Do you
have any idea where they are grazing their
flocks?"
17 The man said, "They've left here, but I
overheard them say, 'Let's go to Dothan.' "
So Joseph took off, tracked his brothers
down, and found them in Dothan.
18-20 They spotted him off in the distance. By
the time he got to them they had cooked up

New King James Version

him to kill him. 19 Then they said to one another, "Look, this dreamer is coming! 20 Come therefore, let us now kill him and cast him into some pit; and we shall say, 'Some wild beast has devoured him.' We shall see what will become of his dreams!"

21 But Reuben heard *it,* and he delivered him out of their hands, and said, "Let us not kill him." 22 And Reuben said to them, "Shed no blood, *but* cast him into this pit which *is* in the wilderness, and do not lay a hand on him"—that he might deliver him out of their hands, and bring him back to his father.

23 So it came to pass, when Joseph had come to his brothers, that they stripped Joseph *of* his tunic, the tunic of *many* colors that *was* on him. 24 Then they took him and cast him into a pit. And the pit *was* empty; *there was* no water in it.

25 And they sat down to eat a meal. Then they lifted their eyes and looked, and there was a company of Ishmaelites, coming from Gilead with their camels, bearing spices, balm, and myrrh, on their way to carry *them* down to Egypt. 26 So Judah said to his brothers, "What profit *is there* if we kill our brother and conceal his blood? 27 Come and let us sell him to the Ishmaelites, and let not our hand be upon him, for he *is* our brother *and* our flesh." And his brothers listened. 28 Then Midianite traders passed by; so *the brothers* pulled Joseph up and lifted him out of the pit, and sold him to the Ishmaelites for twenty *shekels* of silver. And they took Joseph to Egypt.

29 Then Reuben returned to the pit, and indeed Joseph *was* not in the pit; and he tore his clothes. 30 And he returned to his brothers and said, "The lad *is* no *more;* and I, where shall I go?"

31 So they took Joseph's tunic, killed a kid of the goats, and dipped the tunic in the blood. 32 Then they sent the tunic of *many* colors, and they brought *it* to their father and said, "We have found this. Do you know whether it *is* your son's tunic or not?"

33 And he recognized it and said, "*It is* my son's tunic. A wild beast has devoured him. Without doubt Joseph is torn to pieces." 34 Then Jacob tore his clothes, put sackcloth on his waist, and mourned for his son many days. 35 And all his sons and all his daughters arose to comfort him; but he refused to be comforted, and he said, "For I shall go down into the grave to my son in mourning." Thus his father wept for him.

36 Now the Midianites[a] had sold him in Egypt to Potiphar, an officer of Pharaoh *and* captain of the guard.

Judah and Tamar

38 It came to pass at that time that Judah departed from his brothers, and visited a certain Adullamite whose name *was* Hirah. 2 And Judah saw there a daughter of a certain Canaanite whose name *was* Shua, and he married her and went in to her. 3 So she conceived and bore a son, and he called his name Er. 4 She conceived again and bore a son, and she called

37:36 [a]Masoretic Text reads *Medanites.*

The Message

a plot to kill him. The brothers were saying, "Here comes that dreamer. Let's kill him and throw him into one of these old cisterns; we can say that a vicious animal ate him up. We'll see what his dreams amount to."

21-22 Reuben heard the brothers talking and intervened to save him, "We're not going to kill him. No murder. Go ahead and throw him in this cistern out here in the wild, but don't hurt him." Reuben planned to go back later and get him out and take him back to his father.

23-24 When Joseph reached his brothers, they ripped off the fancy coat he was wearing, grabbed him, and threw him into a cistern. The cistern was dry; there wasn't any water in it.

25-27 Then they sat down to eat their supper. Looking up, they saw a caravan of Ishmaelites on their way from Gilead, their camels loaded with spices, ointments, and perfumes to sell in Egypt. Judah said, "Brothers, what are we going to get out of killing our brother and concealing the evidence? Let's sell him to the Ishmaelites, but let's not kill him—he is, after all, our brother, our own flesh and blood." His brothers agreed.

28 By that time the Midianite traders were passing by. His brothers pulled Joseph out of the cistern and sold him for twenty pieces of silver to the Ishmaelites who took Joseph with them down to Egypt.

29-30 Later Reuben came back and went to the cistern—no Joseph! He ripped his clothes in despair. Beside himself, he went to his brothers. "The boy's gone! What am I going to do!"

31-32 They took Joseph's coat, butchered a goat, and dipped the coat in the blood. They took the fancy coat back to their father and said, "We found this. Look it over—do you think this is your son's coat?"

33 He recognized it at once. "My son's coat—a wild animal has eaten him. Joseph torn limb from limb!"

34-35 Jacob tore his clothes in grief, dressed in rough burlap, and mourned his son a long, long time. His sons and daughters tried to comfort him but he refused their comfort. "I'll go to the grave mourning my son." Oh, how his father wept for him.

36 In Egypt the Midianites sold Joseph to Potiphar, one of Pharaoh's officials, manager of his household affairs.

1-5 **38** About that time, Judah separated from his brothers and hooked up with a man in Adullam named Hirah. While there, Judah met the daughter of a Canaanite named Shua. He married her, they went to bed, she became pregnant and had a son named Er. She got pregnant again and had a son

NEW KING JAMES VERSION

his name Onan. 5And she conceived yet again and bore a son, and called his name Shelah. He was at Chezib when she bore him.

6Then Judah took a wife for Er his firstborn, and her name *was* Tamar. 7But Er, Judah's firstborn, was wicked in the sight of the LORD, and the LORD killed him. 8And Judah said to Onan, "Go in to your brother's wife and marry her, and raise up an heir to your brother." 9But Onan knew that the heir would not be his; and it came to pass, when he went in to his brother's wife, that he emitted on the ground, lest he should give an heir to his brother. 10And the thing which he did displeased the LORD; therefore He killed him also.

11Then Judah said to Tamar his daughter-in-law, "Remain a widow in your father's house till my son Shelah is grown." For he said, "Lest he also die like his brothers." And Tamar went and dwelt in her father's house.

12Now in the process of time the daughter of Shua, Judah's wife, died; and Judah was comforted, and went up to his sheepshearers at Timnah, he and his friend Hirah the Adullamite. 13And it was told Tamar, saying, "Look, your father-in-law is going up to Timnah to shear his sheep." 14So she took off her widow's garments, covered *herself* with a veil and wrapped herself, and sat in an open place which *was* on the way to Timnah; for she saw that Shelah was grown, and she was not given to him as a wife. 15When Judah saw her, he thought she *was* a harlot, because she had covered her face. 16Then he turned to her by the way, and said, "Please let me come in to you"; for he did not know that she *was* his daughter-in-law.

So she said, "What will you give me, that you may come in to me?"

17And he said, "I will send a young goat from the flock."

So she said, "Will you give *me* a pledge till you send *it*?"

18Then he said, "What pledge shall I give you?"

So she said, "Your signet and cord, and your staff that *is* in your hand." Then he gave *them* to her, and went in to her, and she conceived by him. 19So she arose and went away, and laid aside her veil and put on the garments of her widowhood.

20And Judah sent the young goat by the hand of his friend the Adullamite, to receive *his* pledge from the woman's hand, but he did not find her. 21Then he asked the men of that place, saying, "Where is the harlot who *was* openly by the roadside?"

And they said, "There was no harlot in this *place*."

22So he returned to Judah and said, "I cannot find her. Also, the men of the place said there was no harlot in this *place*."

23Then Judah said, "Let her take *them* for herself, lest we be shamed; for I sent this young goat and you have not found her."

THE MESSAGE

named Onan. She had still another son; she named this one Shelah. They were living at Kezib when she had him.

6-7 Judah got a wife for Er, his firstborn. Her name was Tamar. But Judah's firstborn, Er, grievously offended GOD and GOD took his life.

8-10 So Judah told Onan, "Go and sleep with your brother's widow; it's the duty of a brother-in-law to keep your brother's line alive." But Onan knew that the child wouldn't be his, so whenever he slept with his brother's widow he spilled his semen on the ground so he wouldn't produce a child for his brother. GOD was much offended by what he did and also took his life.

11 So Judah stepped in and told his daughter-in-law Tamar, "Live as a widow at home with your father until my son Shelah grows up." He was worried that Shelah would also end up dead, just like his brothers. So Tamar went to live with her father.

12 Time passed. Judah's wife, Shua's daughter, died. When the time of mourning was over, Judah with his friend Hirah of Adullam went to Timnah for the sheep shearing.

13-14 Tamar was told, "Your father-in-law has gone to Timnah to shear his sheep." She took off her widow's clothes, put on a veil to disguise herself, and sat at the entrance to Enaim which is on the road to Timnah. She realized by now that even though Shelah was grown up, she wasn't going to be married to him.

15 Judah saw her and assumed she was a prostitute since she had veiled her face. He left the road and went over to her. He said, "Let me sleep with you." He had no idea that she was his daughter-in-law.

16 She said, "What will you pay me?"

17 "I'll send you," he said, "a kid goat from the flock."

She said, "Not unless you give me a pledge until you send it."

18 "So what would you want in the way of a pledge?"

She said, "Your personal seal-and-cord and the staff you carry."

He handed them over to her and slept with her. And she got pregnant.

19 She then left and went home. She removed her veil and put her widow's clothes back on.

20-21 Judah sent the kid goat by his friend from Adullam to recover the pledge from the woman. But he couldn't find her. He asked the men of that place, "Where's the prostitute that used to sit by the road here near Enaim?"

They said, "There's never been a prostitute here."

22 He went back to Judah and said, "I couldn't find her. The men there said there never has been a prostitute there."

23 Judah said, "Let her have it then. If we keep looking, everyone will be poking fun at us. I kept my part of the bargain—I sent the kid goat but you couldn't find her."

New King James Version

24 And it came to pass, about three months after, that Judah was told, saying, "Tamar your daughter-in-law has played the harlot; furthermore she *is* with child by harlotry."

So Judah said, "Bring her out and let her be burned!"

25 When she *was* brought out, she sent to her father-in-law, saying, "By the man to whom these belong, I *am* with child." And she said, "Please determine whose these *are*—the signet and cord, and staff."

26 So Judah acknowledged *them* and said, "She has been more righteous than I, because I did not give her to Shelah my son." And he never knew her again.

27 Now it came to pass, at the time for giving birth, that behold, twins *were* in her womb.
28 And so it was, when she was giving birth, that *the one* put out *his* hand; and the midwife took a scarlet *thread* and bound it on his hand, saying, "This one came out first."
29 Then it happened, as he drew back his hand, that his brother came out unexpectedly; and she said, "How did you break through? *This* breach *be* upon you!" Therefore his name was called Perez.[a]
30 Afterward his brother came out who had the scarlet *thread* on his hand. And his name was called Zerah.

Joseph a Slave in Egypt

39 Now Joseph had been taken down to Egypt. And Potiphar, an officer of Pharaoh, captain of the guard, an Egyptian, bought him from the Ishmaelites who had taken him down there.
2 The LORD was with Joseph, and he was a successful man; and he was in the house of his master the Egyptian.
3 And his master saw that the LORD *was* with him and that the LORD made all he did to prosper in his hand.
4 So Joseph found favor in his sight, and served him. Then he made him overseer of his house, and all *that* he had he put under his authority.
5 So it was, from the time *that* he had made him overseer of his house and all that he had, that the LORD blessed the Egyptian's house for Joseph's sake; and the blessing of the LORD was on all that he had in the house and in the field.
6 Thus he left all that he had in Joseph's hand, and he did not know what he had except for the bread which he ate.

Now Joseph was handsome in form and appearance.

7 And it came to pass after these things that his master's wife cast longing eyes on Joseph, and she said, "Lie with me."

8 But he refused and said to his master's wife, "Look, my master does not know what *is* with me in the house, and he has committed all that he has to my hand.
9 *There is* no one greater in this house than I, nor has he kept back anything from me but you, because you *are* his wife. How then can I do this great wickedness, and sin against God?"

10 So it was, as she spoke to Joseph day by day, that he did not heed her, to lie with her *or* to be with her.

38:29 [a]Literally *Breach* or *Breakthrough*

The Message

24 Three months or so later, Judah was told, "Your daughter-in-law has been playing the whore—and now she's a pregnant whore."

Judah yelled, "Get her out here. Burn her up!"

25 As they brought her out, she sent a message to her father-in-law, "I'm pregnant by the man who owns these things. Identify them, please. Who's the owner of the seal-and-cord and the staff?"

26 Judah saw they were his. He said, "She's in the right; I'm in the wrong—I wouldn't let her marry my son Shelah." He never slept with her again.

27-30 When her time came to give birth, it turned out that there were twins in her womb. As she was giving birth, one put his hand out; the midwife tied a red thread on his hand, saying, "This one came first." But then he pulled it back and his brother came out. She said, "Oh! A breakout!" So she named him Perez (Breakout). Then his brother came out with the red thread on his hand. They named him Zerah (Bright).

1 39 After Joseph had been taken to Egypt by the Ishmaelites, Potiphar an Egyptian, one of Pharaoh's officials and the manager of his household, bought him from them.

2-6 As it turned out, GOD was with Joseph and things went very well with him. He ended up living in the home of his Egyptian master. His master recognized that GOD was with him, saw that GOD was working for good in everything he did. He became very fond of Joseph and made him his personal aide. He put him in charge of all his personal affairs, turning everything over to him. From that moment on, GOD blessed the home of the Egyptian—all because of Joseph. The blessing of GOD spread over everything he owned, at home and in the fields, and all Potiphar had to concern himself with was eating three meals a day.

6-7 Joseph was a strikingly handsome man. As time went on, his master's wife became infatuated with Joseph and one day said, "Sleep with me."

8-9 He wouldn't do it. He said to his master's wife, "Look, with me here, my master doesn't give a second thought to anything that goes on here—he's put me in charge of everything he owns. He treats me as an equal. The only thing he hasn't turned over to me is you. You're his wife, after all! How could I violate his trust and sin against God?"

10 She pestered him day after day after day, but he stood his ground. He refused to go to bed with her.

NEW KING JAMES VERSION

11 But it happened about this time, when Joseph went into the house to do his work, and none of the men of the house *was* inside, 12 that she caught him by his garment, saying, "Lie with me." But he left his garment in her hand, and fled and ran outside. 13 And so it was, when she saw that he had left his garment in her hand and fled outside, 14 that she called to the men of her house and spoke to them, saying, "See, he has brought in to us a Hebrew to mock us. He came in to me to lie with me, and I cried out with a loud voice. 15 And it happened, when he heard that I lifted my voice and cried out, that he left his garment with me, and fled and went outside."

16 So she kept his garment with her until his master came home. 17 Then she spoke to him with words like these, saying, "The Hebrew servant whom you brought to us came in to me to mock me; 18 so it happened, as I lifted my voice and cried out, that he left his garment with me and fled outside."

19 So it was, when his master heard the words which his wife spoke to him, saying, "Your servant did to me after this manner," that his anger was aroused. 20 Then Joseph's master took him and put him into the prison, a place where the king's prisoners *were* confined. And he was there in the prison. 21 But the LORD was with Joseph and showed him mercy, and He gave him favor in the sight of the keeper of the prison. 22 And the keeper of the prison committed to Joseph's hand all the prisoners who *were* in the prison; whatever they did there, it was his doing. 23 The keeper of the prison did not look into anything *that was* under *Joseph's* authority,[a] because the LORD was with him; and whatever he did, the LORD made *it* prosper.

THE PRISONERS' DREAMS

40 It came to pass after these things *that* the butler and the baker of the king of Egypt offended their lord, the king of Egypt. 2 And Pharaoh was angry with his two officers, the chief butler and the chief baker. 3 So he put them in custody in the house of the captain of the guard, in the prison, the place where Joseph *was* confined. 4 And the captain of the guard charged Joseph with them, and he served them; so they were in custody for a while.

5 Then the butler and the baker of the king of Egypt, who *were* confined in the prison, had a dream, both of them, each man's dream in one night *and* each man's dream with its *own* interpretation. 6 And Joseph came in to them in the morning and looked at them, and saw that they *were* sad. 7 So he asked Pharaoh's officers who *were* with him in the custody of his lord's house, saying, "Why do you look *so* sad today?"

8 And they said to him, "We each have had a dream, and *there is* no interpreter of it."

So Joseph said to them, "Do not interpretations belong to God? Tell *them* to me, please."

9 Then the chief butler told his dream to Joseph, and said to him, "Behold, in my dream a vine *was* before me, 10 and in the vine *were* three

39:23 [a]Literally *his hand*

THE MESSAGE

11-15 On one of these days he came to the house to do his work and none of the household servants happened to be there. She grabbed him by his cloak, saying, "Sleep with me!" He left his coat in her hand and ran out of the house. When she realized that he had left his coat in her hand and run outside, she called to her house servants: "Look—this Hebrew shows up and before you know it he's trying to seduce us. He tried to make love to me but I yelled as loud as I could. With all my yelling and screaming, he left his coat beside me here and ran outside."

16-18 She kept his coat right there until his master came home. She told him the same story. She said, "The Hebrew slave, the one you brought to us, came after me and tried to use me for his plaything. When I yelled and screamed, he left his coat with me and ran outside."

19-23 When his master heard his wife's story, telling him, "These are the things your slave did to me," he was furious. Joseph's master took him and threw him into the jail where the king's prisoners were locked up. But there in jail GOD was still with Joseph: He reached out in kindness to him; he put him on good terms with the head jailer. The head jailer put Joseph in charge of all the prisoners—he ended up managing the whole operation. The head jailer gave Joseph free rein, never even checked on him, because GOD was with him; whatever he did GOD made sure it worked out for the best.

1-4 40 As time went on, it happened that the cupbearer and the baker of the king of Egypt crossed their master, the king of Egypt. Pharaoh was furious with his two officials, the head cupbearer and the head baker, and put them in custody under the captain of the guard; it was the same jail where Joseph was held. The captain of the guard assigned Joseph to see to their needs.

4-7 After they had been in custody for a while, the king's cupbearer and baker, while being held in the jail, both had a dream on the same night, each dream having its own meaning. When Joseph arrived in the morning, he noticed that they were feeling low. So he asked them, the two officials of Pharaoh who had been thrown into jail with him, "What's wrong? Why the long faces?"

8 They said, "We dreamed dreams and there's no one to interpret them."

Joseph said, "Don't interpretations come from God? Tell me the dreams."

9-11 First the head cupbearer told his dream to Joseph: "In my dream there was a vine in front of me with three branches on it: It bud-

NEW KING JAMES VERSION

branches; it *was* as though it budded, its blos-
soms shot forth, and its clusters brought forth
ripe grapes. [11]Then Pharaoh's cup *was* in my
hand; and I took the grapes and pressed them
into Pharaoh's cup, and placed the cup in
Pharaoh's hand."
[12]And Joseph said to him, "This *is* the inter-
pretation of it: The three branches *are* three
days. [13]Now within three days Pharaoh will lift
up your head and restore you to your place, and
you will put Pharaoh's cup in his hand accord-
ing to the former manner, when you were his
butler. [14]But remember me when it is well with
you, and please show kindness to me; make
mention of me to Pharaoh, and get me out of
this house. [15]For indeed I was stolen away from
the land of the Hebrews; and also I have done
nothing here that they should put me into the
dungeon."
[16]When the chief baker saw that the interpre-
tation was good, he said to Joseph, "I also *was* in
my dream, and there *were* three white baskets
on my head. [17]In the uppermost basket *were* all
kinds of baked goods for Pharaoh, and the birds
ate them out of the basket on my head."
[18]So Joseph answered and said, "This *is* the
interpretation of it: The three baskets *are* three
days. [19]Within three days Pharaoh will lift off
your head from you and hang you on a tree; and
the birds will eat your flesh from you."
[20]Now it came to pass on the third day, *which*
was Pharaoh's birthday, that he made a feast for
all his servants; and he lifted up the head of the
chief butler and of the chief baker among his
servants. [21]Then he restored the chief butler to
his butlership again, and he placed the cup in
Pharaoh's hand. [22]But he hanged the chief
baker, as Joseph had interpreted to them. [23]Yet
the chief butler did not remember Joseph, but
forgot him.

PHARAOH'S DREAMS

41 Then it came to pass, at the end of two full
years, that Pharaoh had a dream; and be-
hold, he stood by the river. [2]Suddenly there
came up out of the river seven cows, fine look-
ing and fat; and they fed in the meadow. [3]Then
behold, seven other cows came up after them
out of the river, ugly and gaunt, and stood by the
other cows on the bank of the river. [4]And the
ugly and gaunt cows ate up the seven fine look-
ing and fat cows. So Pharaoh awoke. [5]He slept
and dreamed a second time; and suddenly seven
heads of grain came up on one stalk, plump and
good. [6]Then behold, seven thin heads, blighted
by the east wind, sprang up after them. [7]And the
seven thin heads devoured the seven plump and
full heads. So Pharaoh awoke, and indeed, *it*
was a dream. [8]Now it came to pass in the morn-
ing that his spirit was troubled, and he sent and
called for all the magicians of Egypt and all its
wise men. And Pharaoh told them his dreams,
but *there was* no one who could interpret them
for Pharaoh.
[9]Then the chief butler spoke to Pharaoh, say-
ing: "I remember my faults this day. [10]When
Pharaoh was angry with his servants, and put
me in custody in the house of the captain of the
guard, *both* me and the chief baker, [11]we each

THE MESSAGE

ded, blossomed, and the clusters ripened into
grapes. I was holding Pharaoh's cup; I took
the grapes, squeezed them into Pharaoh's
cup, and gave the cup to Pharaoh."

12-15 Joseph said, "Here's the meaning. The
three branches are three days. Within three
days, Pharaoh will get you out of here and
put you back to your old work—you'll be
giving Pharaoh his cup just as you used to
do when you were his cupbearer. Only re-
member me when things are going well with
you again—tell Pharaoh about me and get
me out of this place. I was kidnapped from
the land of the Hebrews. And since I've been
here, I've done nothing to deserve being put
in this hole."

16-17 When the head baker saw how well
Joseph's interpretation turned out, he spoke
up: "My dream went like this: I saw three
wicker baskets on my head; the top basket
had assorted pastries from the bakery and
birds were picking at them from the basket
on my head."

18-19 Joseph said, "This is the interpretation:
The three baskets are three days; within
three days Pharaoh will take off your head,
impale you on a post, and the birds will pick
your bones clean."

20-22 And sure enough, on the third day it was
Pharaoh's birthday and he threw a feast for
all his servants. He set the head cupbearer
and the head baker in places of honor in the
presence of all the guests. Then he restored
the head cupbearer to his cupbearing post;
he handed Pharaoh his cup just as before.
And then he impaled the head baker on a
post, following Joseph's interpretations ex-
actly.

23 But the head cupbearer never gave
Joseph another thought; he forgot all about
him.

1-4 41 Two years passed and Pharaoh had a
dream: He was standing by the Nile
River. Seven cows came up out of the Nile,
all shimmering with health, and grazed on
the marsh grass. Then seven other cows, all
skin and bones, came up out of the river af-
ter them and stood by them on the bank of
the Nile. The skinny cows ate the seven
healthy cows. Then Pharaoh woke up.

5-7 He went back to sleep and dreamed a
second time: Seven ears of grain, full-bodied
and lush, grew out of a single stalk. Then
seven more ears grew up, but these were
thin and dried out by the east wind. The thin
ears swallowed up the full, healthy ears.
Then Pharaoh woke up—another dream.

8 When morning came, he was upset. He
sent for all the magicians and sages of
Egypt. Pharaoh told them his dreams, but
they couldn't interpret them to him.

9-13 The head cupbearer then spoke up and
said to Pharaoh, "I just now remembered
something—I'm sorry, I should have told
you this long ago. Once when Pharaoh got
angry with his servants, he locked me and
the head baker in the house of the captain of

NEW KING JAMES VERSION

had a dream in one night, he and I. Each of us
dreamed according to the interpretation of his
own dream. [12]Now there *was* a young Hebrew
man with us there, a servant of the captain of
the guard. And we told him, and he interpreted
our dreams for us; to each man he interpreted
according to his *own* dream. [13]And it came to
pass, just as he interpreted for us, so it hap-
pened. He restored me to my office, and he
hanged him."
[14]Then Pharaoh sent and called Joseph, and
they brought him quickly out of the dungeon;
and he shaved, changed his clothing, and came
to Pharaoh. [15]And Pharaoh said to Joseph, "I
have had a dream, and *there is* no one who can
interpret it. But I have heard it said of you *that*
you can understand a dream, to interpret it."
[16]So Joseph answered Pharaoh, saying, "*It is*
not in me; God will give Pharaoh an answer of
peace."
[17]Then Pharaoh said to Joseph: "Behold, in
my dream I stood on the bank of the river.
[18]Suddenly seven cows came up out of the river,
fine looking and fat; and they fed in the
meadow. [19]Then behold, seven other cows came
up after them, poor and very ugly and gaunt,
such ugliness as I have never seen in all the land
of Egypt. [20]And the gaunt and ugly cows ate up
the first seven, the fat cows. [21]When they had
eaten them up, no one would have known that
they had eaten them, for they *were* just as ugly
as at the beginning. So I awoke. [22]Also I saw in
my dream, and suddenly seven heads came up
on one stalk, full and good. [23]Then behold, seven
heads, withered, thin, *and* blighted by the east
wind, sprang up after them. [24]And the thin
heads devoured the seven good heads. So I told
this to the magicians, but *there was* no one who
could explain *it* to me."
[25]Then Joseph said to Pharaoh, "The dreams
of Pharaoh *are* one; God has shown Pharaoh
what He *is* about to do: [26]The seven good cows
are seven years, and the seven good heads *are*
seven years; the dreams *are* one. [27]And the seven
thin and ugly cows which came up after them
are seven years, and the seven empty heads
blighted by the east wind are seven years of
famine. [28]This *is* the thing which I have spoken
to Pharaoh. God has shown Pharaoh what He *is*
about to do. [29]Indeed seven years of great plenty
will come throughout all the land of Egypt; [30]but
after them seven years of famine will arise, and
all the plenty will be forgotten in the land of
Egypt; and the famine will deplete the land. [31]So
the plenty will not be known in the land because
of the famine following, for it *will be* very severe.
[32]And the dream was repeated to Pharaoh twice
because the thing *is* established by God, and God
will shortly bring it to pass.
[33]"Now therefore, let Pharaoh select a dis-
cerning and wise man, and set him over the land
of Egypt. [34]Let Pharaoh do *this*, and let him ap-
point officers over the land, to collect one-fifth
of the produce of the land of Egypt in the seven
plentiful years. [35]And let them gather all the
food of those good years that are coming, and
store up grain under the authority of Pharaoh,
and let them keep food in the cities. [36]Then that

THE MESSAGE

the guard. We both had dreams on the same
night, each dream with its own meaning. It
so happened that there was a young Hebrew
slave there with us; he belonged to the cap-
tain of the guard. We told him our dreams
and he interpreted them for us, each dream
separately. Things turned out just as he in-
terpreted. I was returned to my position and
the head baker was impaled."

14 Pharaoh at once sent for Joseph. They
brought him on the run from the jail cell. He
cut his hair, put on clean clothes, and came
to Pharaoh.

15 "I dreamed a dream," Pharaoh told
Joseph. "Nobody can interpret it. But I've
heard that just by hearing a dream you can
interpret it."

16 Joseph answered, "Not I, but God. God
will set Pharaoh's mind at ease."

17-21 Then Pharaoh said to Joseph, "In my
dream I was standing on the bank of the
Nile. Seven cows, shimmering with health,
came up out of the river and grazed on the
marsh grass. On their heels seven more
cows, all skin and bones, came up. I've never
seen uglier cows anywhere in Egypt. Then
the seven skinny, ugly cows ate up the first
seven healthy cows. But you couldn't tell by
looking—after eating them up they were
just as skinny and ugly as before. Then I
woke up.

22-24 "In my second dream I saw seven ears of
grain, full-bodied and lush, growing out of a
single stalk, and right behind them, seven
other ears, shriveled, thin, and dried out by
the east wind. And the thin ears swallowed
up the full ears. I've told all this to the magi-
cians but they can't figure it out."

25-27 Joseph said to Pharaoh, "Pharaoh's two
dreams both mean the same thing. God is
telling Pharaoh what he is going to do. The
seven healthy cows are seven years and the
seven healthy ears of grain are seven
years—they're the same dream. The seven
sick and ugly cows that followed them up
are seven years and the seven scrawny ears
of grain dried out by the east wind are the
same—seven years of famine.

28-32 "The meaning is what I said earlier: God
is letting Pharaoh in on what he is going to
do. Seven years of plenty are on their way
throughout Egypt. But on their heels will
come seven years of famine, leaving no
trace of the Egyptian plenty. As the country
is emptied by famine, there won't be even a
scrap left of the previous plenty—the famine
will be total. The fact that Pharaoh dreamed
the same dream twice emphasizes God's de-
termination to do this and do it soon.

33-36 "So, Pharaoh needs to look for a wise and
experienced man and put him in charge of
the country. Then Pharaoh needs to appoint
managers throughout the country of Egypt
to organize it during the years of plenty.
Their job will be to collect all the food pro-
duced in the good years ahead and stockpile
the grain under Pharaoh's authority, storing
it in the towns for food. This grain will be

NEW KING JAMES VERSION

food shall be as a reserve for the land for the
seven years of famine which shall be in the land
of Egypt, that the land may not perish during
the famine."

JOSEPH'S RISE TO POWER

37 So the advice was good in the eyes of
Pharaoh and in the eyes of all his servants.
38 And Pharaoh said to his servants, "Can we
find *such a one* as this, a man in whom *is* the
Spirit of God?"
39 Then Pharaoh said to Joseph, "Inasmuch
as God has shown you all this, *there is* no one as
discerning and wise as you. 40 You shall be over
my house, and all my people shall be ruled ac-
cording to your word; only in regard to the
throne will I be greater than you." 41 And
Pharaoh said to Joseph, "See, I have set you
over all the land of Egypt."
42 Then Pharaoh took his signet ring off his
hand and put it on Joseph's hand; and he
clothed him in garments of fine linen and put a
gold chain around his neck. 43 And he had him
ride in the second chariot which he had; and
they cried out before him, "Bow the knee!" So
he set him over all the land of Egypt. 44 Pharaoh
also said to Joseph, "I *am* Pharaoh, and without
your consent no man may lift his hand or foot in
all the land of Egypt." 45 And Pharaoh called
Joseph's name Zaphnath-Paaneah. And he gave
him as a wife Asenath, the daughter of Poti-
Pherah priest of On. So Joseph went out over *all*
the land of Egypt.
46 Joseph was thirty years old when he stood
before Pharaoh king of Egypt. And Joseph went
out from the presence of Pharaoh, and went
throughout all the land of Egypt. 47 Now in the
seven plentiful years the ground brought forth
abundantly. 48 So he gathered up all the food of
the seven years which were in the land of Egypt,
and laid up the food in the cities; he laid up in
every city the food of the fields which sur-
rounded them. 49 Joseph gathered very much
grain, as the sand of the sea, until he stopped
counting, for *it was* immeasurable.
50 And to Joseph were born two sons before
the years of famine came, whom Asenath, the
daughter of Poti-Pherah priest of On, bore to
him. 51 Joseph called the name of the firstborn
Manasseh:[a] "For God has made me forget all my
toil and all my father's house." 52 And the name
of the second he called Ephraim:[a] "For God has
caused me to be fruitful in the land of my afflic-
tion."
53 Then the seven years of plenty which were
in the land of Egypt ended, 54 and the seven
years of famine began to come, as Joseph had
said. The famine was in all lands, but in all the
land of Egypt there was bread. 55 So when all the
land of Egypt was famished, the people cried to
Pharaoh for bread. Then Pharaoh said to all the
Egyptians, "Go to Joseph; whatever he says to
you, do."

41:51 [a]Literally *Making Forgetful* **41:52** [a]Literally *Fruitfulness*

THE MESSAGE

held back to be used later during the seven years of famine that are coming on Egypt. This way the country won't be devastated by the famine."

37 This seemed like a good idea to Pharaoh and his officials.

38 Then Pharaoh said to his officials, "Isn't this the man we need? Are we going to find anyone else who has God's spirit in him like this?"

39-40 So Pharaoh said to Joseph, "You're the man for us. God has given you the inside story—no one is as qualified as you in experience and wisdom. From now on, you're in charge of my affairs; all my people will report to you. Only as king will I be over you."

41-43 So Pharaoh commissioned Joseph: "I'm putting you in charge of the entire country of Egypt." Then Pharaoh removed his signet ring from his finger and slipped it on Joseph's hand. He outfitted him in robes of the best linen and put a gold chain around his neck. He put the second-in-command chariot at his disposal, and as he rode people shouted "Bravo!"

Joseph was in charge of the entire country of Egypt.

44 Pharaoh told Joseph, "I am Pharaoh, but no one in Egypt will make a single move without your stamp of approval."

45 Then Pharaoh gave Joseph an Egyptian name, Zaphenath-Paneah (God Speaks and He Lives). He also gave him an Egyptian wife, Asenath, the daughter of Potiphera, the priest of On (Heliopolis).

And Joseph took up his duties over the land of Egypt.

46 Joseph was thirty years old when he went to work for Pharaoh the king of Egypt. As soon as Joseph left Pharaoh's presence, he began his work in Egypt.

47-49 During the next seven years of plenty the land produced bumper crops. Joseph gathered up the food of the seven good years in Egypt and stored the food in cities. In each city he stockpiled surplus from the surrounding fields. Joseph collected so much grain—it was like the sand of the ocean!—that he finally quit keeping track.

50-52 Joseph had two sons born to him before the years of famine came. Asenath, daughter of Potiphera the priest of On, was their mother. Joseph named the firstborn Manasseh (Forget), saying, "God made me forget all my hardships and my parental home." He named his second son Ephraim (Double Prosperity), saying, "God has prospered me in the land of my sorrow."

53-54 Then Egypt's seven good years came to an end and the seven years of famine arrived, just as Joseph had said. All countries experienced famine; Egypt was the only country that had bread.

55 When the famine spread throughout Egypt, the people called out in distress to Pharaoh, calling for bread. He told the Egyptians, "Go to Joseph. Do what he tells you."

NEW KING JAMES VERSION

56 The famine was over all the face of the earth,
and Joseph opened all the storehouses[a] and sold
to the Egyptians. And the famine became severe
in the land of Egypt. 57 So all countries came to
Joseph in Egypt to buy *grain*, because the famine
was severe in all lands.

JOSEPH'S BROTHERS GO TO EGYPT

42 When Jacob saw that there was grain in
Egypt, Jacob said to his sons, "Why do you
look at one another?" 2 And he said, "Indeed I
have heard that there is grain in Egypt; go down
to that place and buy for us there, that we may
live and not die."
3 So Joseph's ten brothers went down to buy
grain in Egypt. 4 But Jacob did not send Joseph's
brother Benjamin with his brothers, for he said,
"Lest some calamity befall him." 5 And the sons
of Israel went to buy *grain* among those who
journeyed, for the famine was in the land of
Canaan.
6 Now Joseph *was* governor over the land;
and it was he who sold to all the people of the
land. And Joseph's brothers came and bowed
down before him with *their* faces to the earth.
7 Joseph saw his brothers and recognized them,
but he acted as a stranger to them and spoke
roughly to them. Then he said to them, "Where
do you come from?"
And they said, "From the land of Canaan to
buy food."
8 So Joseph recognized his brothers, but they
did not recognize him. 9 Then Joseph remem-
bered the dreams which he had dreamed about
them, and said to them, "You *are* spies! You have
come to see the nakedness of the land!"
10 And they said to him, "No, my lord, but
your servants have come to buy food. 11 We *are*
all one man's sons; we *are* honest *men;* your ser-
vants are not spies."
12 But he said to them, "No, but you have
come to see the nakedness of the land."
13 And they said, "Your servants *are* twelve
brothers, the sons of one man in the land of
Canaan; and in fact, the youngest *is* with our fa-
ther today, and one *is* no more."
14 But Joseph said to them, "It *is* as I spoke to
you, saying, 'You *are* spies!' 15 In this *manner* you
shall be tested: By the life of Pharaoh, you shall
not leave this place unless your youngest
brother comes here. 16 Send one of you, and let
him bring your brother; and you shall be kept in
prison, that your words may be tested to see
whether *there is* any truth in you; or else, by the
life of Pharaoh, surely you *are* spies!" 17 So he
put them all together in prison three days.
18 Then Joseph said to them the third day, "Do
this and live, *for* I fear God: 19 If you *are* honest
men, let one of your brothers be confined to
your prison house; but you, go and carry grain
for the famine of your houses. 20 And bring your
youngest brother to me; so your words will be
verified, and you shall not die."
And they did so. 21 Then they said to one an-
other, "We *are* truly guilty concerning our
brother, for we saw the anguish of his soul when

41:56 [a] Literally *all that was in them*

THE MESSAGE

56-57 As the famine got worse all over the
country, Joseph opened the storehouses and
sold emergency supplies to the Egyptians.
The famine was very bad. Soon the whole
world was coming to buy supplies from
Joseph. The famine was bad all over.

1-2 **42** When Jacob learned that there was
food in Egypt, he said to his sons,
"Why do you sit around here and look at
one another? I've heard that there is food in
Egypt. Go down there and buy some so that
we can survive and not starve to death."
3-5 Ten of Joseph's brothers went down to
Egypt to get food. Jacob didn't send
Joseph's brother Benjamin with them; he
was afraid that something bad might hap-
pen to him. So Israel's sons joined everyone
else that was going to Egypt to buy food, for
Canaan, too, was hit hard by the famine.
6-7 Joseph was running the country; he was
the one who gave out rations to all the peo-
ple. When Joseph's brothers arrived, they
treated him with honor, bowing to him.
Joseph recognized them immediately, but
treated them as strangers and spoke
roughly to them.
He said, "Where do you come from?"
"From Canaan," they said. "We've come
to buy food."
8 Joseph knew who they were, but they
didn't know who he was.
9 Joseph, remembering the dreams he had
dreamed of them, said, "You're spies. You've
come to look for our weak spots."
10-11 "No, master," they said. "We've only come
to buy food. We're all the sons of the same
man; we're honest men; we'd never think of
spying."
12 He said, "No. You're spies. You've come to
look for our weak spots."
13 They said, "There were twelve of us
brothers—sons of the same father in the
country of Canaan. The youngest is with our
father, and one is no more."
14-16 But Joseph said, "It's just as I said, you're
spies. This is how I'll test you. As Pharaoh
lives, you're not going to leave this place un-
til your younger brother comes here. Send
one of you to get your brother while the rest
of you stay here in jail. We'll see if you're
telling the truth or not. As Pharaoh lives, I
say you're spies."
17 Then he threw them into jail for three
days.
18-20 On the third day, Joseph spoke to them.
"Do this and you'll live. I'm a God-fearing
man. If you're as honest as you say you are,
one of your brothers will stay here in jail
while the rest of you take the food back to
your hungry families. But you have to bring
your youngest brother back to me, confirm-
ing the truth of your speech—and not one of
you will die." They agreed.
21 Then they started talking among them-
selves. "Now we're paying for what we did
to our brother—we saw how terrified he was

NEW KING JAMES VERSION

he pleaded with us, and we would not hear;
therefore this distress has come upon us."
22And Reuben answered them, saying, "Did I
not speak to you, saying, 'Do not sin against the
boy'; and you would not listen? Therefore be-
hold, his blood is now required of us." 23But they
did not know that Joseph understood *them,* for
he spoke to them through an interpreter. 24And
he turned himself away from them and wept.
Then he returned to them again, and talked with
them. And he took Simeon from them and
bound him before their eyes.

THE BROTHERS RETURN TO CANAAN

25Then Joseph gave a command to fill their
sacks with grain, to restore every man's money
to his sack, and to give them provisions for the
journey. Thus he did for them. 26So they loaded
their donkeys with the grain and departed from
there. 27But as one *of them* opened his sack to
give his donkey feed at the encampment, he saw
his money; and there it was, in the mouth of his
sack. 28So he said to his brothers, "My money
has been restored, and there it is, in my sack!"
Then their hearts failed *them* and they were
afraid, saying to one another, "What *is* this *that*
God has done to us?"
29Then they went to Jacob their father in the
land of Canaan and told him all that had hap-
pened to them, saying: 30"The man *who is* lord of
the land spoke roughly to us, and took us for
spies of the country. 31But we said to him, 'We
are honest *men;* we are not spies. 32We *are*
twelve brothers, sons of our father; one *is* no
more, and the youngest *is* with our father this
day in the land of Canaan.' 33Then the man, the
lord of the country, said to us, 'By this I will
know that you *are* honest *men:* Leave one of
your brothers *here* with me, take *food for* the
famine of your households, and be gone. 34And
bring your youngest brother to me; so I shall
know that you *are* not spies, but *that* you *are*
honest *men.* I will grant your brother to you, and
you may trade in the land.' "
35Then it happened as they emptied their
sacks, that surprisingly each man's bundle of
money *was* in his sack; and when they and their
father saw the bundles of money, they were
afraid. 36And Jacob their father said to them,
"You have bereaved me: Joseph is no *more,*
Simeon is no *more,* and you want to take Ben-
jamin. All these things are against me."
37Then Reuben spoke to his father, saying,
"Kill my two sons if I do not bring him *back* to
you; put him in my hands, and I will bring him
back to you."
38But he said, "My son shall not go down
with you, for his brother is dead, and he is left
alone. If any calamity should befall him along
the way in which you go, then you would bring
down my gray hair with sorrow to the grave."

JOSEPH'S BROTHERS RETURN WITH BENJAMIN

43 Now the famine *was* severe in the land.
2And it came to pass, when they had eaten
up the grain which they had brought from
Egypt, that their father said to them, "Go back,
buy us a little food."

THE MESSAGE

when he was begging us for mercy. We
wouldn't listen to him and now we're the
ones in trouble."
22 Reuben broke in. "Didn't I tell you, 'Don't
hurt the boy'? But no, you wouldn't listen.
And now we're paying for his murder."
23-24 Joseph had been using an interpreter, so
they didn't know that Joseph was under-
standing every word. Joseph turned away
from them and cried. When he was able to
speak again, he took Simeon and had him
tied up, making a prisoner of him while they
all watched.
25 Then Joseph ordered that their sacks be
filled with grain, that their money be put
back in each sack, and that they be given ra-
tions for the road. That was all done for
them.
26 They loaded their food supplies on their
donkeys and set off.
27-28 When they stopped for the night, one of
them opened his sack to get food for his
donkey; there at the mouth of his bag was
his money. He called out to his brothers,
"My money has been returned; it's right
here in my bag!" They were puzzled—and
frightened. "What's God doing to us?"
29-32 When they got back to their father Jacob,
back in the land of Canaan, they told him
everything that had happened, saying, "The
man who runs the country spoke to us
roughly and accused us of being spies. We
told him, 'We are honest men and in no way
spies. There were twelve of us brothers,
sons of one father; one is gone and the
youngest is with our father in Canaan.'
33-34 "But the master of the country said,
'Leave one of your brothers with me, take
food for your starving families, and go.
Bring your youngest brother back to me,
proving that you're honest men and not
spies. And then I'll give your brother back to
you and you'll be free to come and go in this
country.' "
35 As they were emptying their food sacks,
each man came on his purse of money. On
seeing their money, they and their father
were upset.
36 Their father said to them, "You're taking
everything I've got! Joseph's gone, Simeon's
gone, and now you want to take Benjamin.
If you have your way, I'll be left with noth-
ing."
37 Reuben spoke up: "I'll put my two sons in
your hands as hostages. If I don't bring Ben-
jamin back, you can kill them. Trust me with
Benjamin; I'll bring him back."
38 But Jacob refused. "My son will not go
down with you. His brother is dead and he is
all I have left. If something bad happens to
him on the road, you'll put my gray, sorrow-
ing head in the grave."

1-2 43 The famine got worse. When they had
eaten all the food they had brought
back from Egypt, their father said, "Go back
and get some more food."

NEW KING JAMES VERSION

3But Judah spoke to him, saying, "The man solemnly warned us, saying, 'You shall not see my face unless your brother *is* with you.' 4If you send our brother with us, we will go down and buy you food. 5But if you will not send *him*, we will not go down; for the man said to us, 'You shall not see my face unless your brother *is* with you.' "

6And Israel said, "Why did you deal *so* wrongfully with me *as* to tell the man whether you had still *another* brother?"

7But they said, "The man asked us pointedly about ourselves and our family, saying, '*Is* your father still alive? Have you *another* brother?' And we told him according to these words. Could we possibly have known that he would say, 'Bring your brother down'?"

8Then Judah said to Israel his father, "Send the lad with me, and we will arise and go, that we may live and not die, both we and you *and* also our little ones. 9I myself will be surety for him; from my hand you shall require him. If I do not bring him *back* to you and set him before you, then let me bear the blame forever. 10For if we had not lingered, surely by now we would have returned this second time."

11And their father Israel said to them, "If *it must be* so, then do this: Take some of the best fruits of the land in your vessels and carry down a present for the man—a little balm and a little honey, spices and myrrh, pistachio nuts and almonds. 12Take double money in your hand, and take back in your hand the money that was returned in the mouth of your sacks; perhaps it was an oversight. 13Take your brother also, and arise, go back to the man. 14And may God Almighty give you mercy before the man, that he may release your other brother and Benjamin. If I am bereaved, I am bereaved!"

15So the men took that present and Benjamin, and they took double money in their hand, and arose and went down to Egypt; and they stood before Joseph. 16When Joseph saw Benjamin with them, he said to the steward of his house, "Take *these* men to my home, and slaughter an animal and make ready; for *these* men will dine with me at noon." 17Then the man did as Joseph ordered, and the man brought the men into Joseph's house.

18Now the men were afraid because they were brought into Joseph's house; and they said, "*It is* because of the money, which was returned in our sacks the first time, that we are brought in, so that he may make a case against us and seize us, to take us as slaves with our donkeys."

19When they drew near to the steward of Joseph's house, they talked with him at the door of the house, 20and said, "O sir, we indeed came down the first time to buy food; 21but it happened, when we came to the encampment, that we opened our sacks, and there, *each* man's money *was* in the mouth of his sack, our money in full weight; so we have brought it back in our hand. 22And we have brought down other money in our hands to buy food. We do not know who put our money in our sacks."

THE MESSAGE

3-5 But Judah said, "The man warned us most emphatically, 'You won't so much as see my face if you don't have your brother with you.' If you're ready to release our brother to go with us, we'll go down and get you food. But if you're not ready, we aren't going. What would be the use? The man told us, 'You won't so much as see my face if you don't have your brother with you.' "

6 Israel said, "Why are you making my life so difficult! Why did you ever tell the man you had another brother?"

7 They said, "The man pressed us hard, asking pointed questions about our family: 'Is your father alive? Do you have another brother?' So we answered his questions. How did we know that he'd say, 'Bring your brother here'?"

8-10 Judah pushed his father Israel. "Let the boy go; I'll take charge of him. Let us go and be on our way—if we don't get going, we're all going to starve to death—we and you and our children, too! I'll take full responsibility for his safety; it's my life on the line for his. If I don't bring him back safe and sound, I'm the guilty one; I'll take all the blame. If we had gone ahead in the first place instead of procrastinating like this, we could have been there and back twice over."

11-14 Their father Israel gave in. "If it has to be, it has to be. But do this: stuff your packs with the finest products from the land you can find and take them to the man as gifts—some balm and honey, some spices and perfumes, some pistachios and almonds. And take plenty of money—pay back double what was returned to your sacks; that might have been a mistake. Take your brother and get going. Go back to the man. And may The Strong God give you grace in that man's eyes so that he'll send back your other brother along with Benjamin. For me, nothing's left; I've lost everything."

15-16 The men took the gifts, double the money, and Benjamin. They lost no time in getting to Egypt and meeting Joseph. When Joseph saw that they had Benjamin with them, he told his house steward, "Take these men into the house and make them at home. Butcher an animal and prepare a meal; these men are going to eat with me at noon."

17-18 The steward did what Joseph had said and took them inside. But they became anxious when they were brought into Joseph's home, thinking, "It's the money; he thinks we ran off with the money on our first trip down here. And now he's got us where he wants us—he's going to turn us into slaves and confiscate our donkeys."

19-22 So they went up to Joseph's house steward and talked to him in the doorway. They said, "Listen, master. We came down here one other time to buy food. On our way home, the first night out we opened our bags and found our money at the mouth of the bag—the exact amount we'd paid. We've brought it all back and have plenty more to buy more food with. We have no idea who put the money in our bags."

New King James Version

23 But he said, "Peace *be* with you, do not be
afraid. Your God and the God of your father has
given you treasure in your sacks; I had your
money." Then he brought Simeon out to them.
24 So the man brought the men into Joseph's
house and gave *them* water, and they washed
their feet; and he gave their donkeys feed.
25 Then they made the present ready for Joseph's
coming at noon, for they heard that they would
eat bread there.
26 And when Joseph came home, they
brought him the present which *was* in their
hand into the house, and bowed down before
him to the earth. 27 Then he asked them about
their well-being, and said, "*Is* your father well,
the old man of whom you spoke? *Is* he still
alive?"
28 And they answered, "Your servant our fa-
ther *is* in good health; he *is* still alive." And they
bowed their heads down and prostrated them-
selves.
29 Then he lifted his eyes and saw his brother
Benjamin, his mother's son, and said, "*Is* this
your younger brother of whom you spoke to
me?" And he said, "God be gracious to you, my
son." 30 Now his heart yearned for his brother; so
Joseph made haste and sought *somewhere* to
weep. And he went into *his* chamber and wept
there. 31 Then he washed his face and came out;
and he restrained himself, and said, "Serve the
bread."
32 So they set him a place by himself, and
them by themselves, and the Egyptians who ate
with him by themselves; because the Egyptians
could not eat food with the Hebrews, for that *is*
an abomination to the Egyptians. 33 And they sat
before him, the firstborn according to his
birthright and the youngest according to his
youth; and the men looked in astonishment at
one another. 34 Then he took servings to them
from before him, but Benjamin's serving was
five times as much as any of theirs. So they
drank and were merry with him.

Joseph's Cup

44 And he commanded the steward of his
house, saying, "Fill the men's sacks with
food, as much as they can carry, and put each
man's money in the mouth of his sack. 2 Also put
my cup, the silver cup, in the mouth of the sack
of the youngest, and his grain money." So he did
according to the word that Joseph had spoken.
3 As soon as the morning dawned, the men were
sent away, they and their donkeys. 4 When they
had gone out of the city, *and* were not *yet* far off,
Joseph said to his steward, "Get up, follow the
men; and when you overtake them, say to them,
'Why have you repaid evil for good? 5 *Is* not this
the one from which my lord drinks, and with
which he indeed practices divination? You have
done evil in so doing.' "
6 So he overtook them, and he spoke to them
these same words. 7 And they said to him, "Why
does my lord say these words? Far be it from us
that your servants should do such a thing.
8 Look, we brought back to you from the land of
Canaan the money which we found in the
mouth of our sacks. How then could we steal sil-
ver or gold from your lord's house? 9 With

The Message

23 The steward said, "Everything's in order. Don't worry. Your God and the God of your father must have given you a bonus. I was paid in full." And with that, he presented Simeon to them.

24-25 He then took them inside Joseph's house and made them comfortable—gave them water to wash their feet and saw to the feeding of their donkeys. The brothers spread out their gifts as they waited for Joseph to show up at noon—they had been told that they were to have dinner with him.

26 When Joseph got home, they presented him with the gifts they had brought and bowed respectfully before him.

27 Joseph welcomed them and said, "And your old father whom you mentioned to me, how is he? Is he still alive?"

28 They said, "Yes—your servant our father is quite well, very much alive." And they again bowed respectfully before him.

29 Then Joseph picked out his brother Benjamin, his own mother's son. He asked, "And is this your youngest brother that you told me about?" Then he said, "God be gracious to you, my son."

30-31 Deeply moved on seeing his brother and about to burst into tears, Joseph hurried out into another room and had a good cry. Then he washed his face, got a grip on himself, and said, "Let's eat."

32-34 Joseph was served at his private table, the brothers off by themselves and the Egyptians off by themselves (Egyptians won't eat at the same table with Hebrews; it's repulsive to them). The brothers were seated facing Joseph, arranged in order of their age, from the oldest to the youngest. They looked at one another wide-eyed, wondering what would happen next. When the brothers' plates were served from Joseph's table, Benjamin's plate came piled high, far more so than his brothers. And so the brothers feasted with Joseph, drinking freely.

1-2 44 Joseph ordered his house steward: "Fill the men's bags with food—all they can carry—and replace each one's money at the top of the bag. Then put my chalice, my silver chalice, in the top of the bag of the youngest, along with the money for his food." He did as Joseph ordered.

3-5 At break of day the men were sent off with their donkeys. They were barely out of the city when Joseph said to his house steward, "Run after them. When you catch up with them, say, 'Why did you pay me back evil for good? This is the chalice my master drinks from; he also uses it for divination. This is outrageous!' "

6 He caught up with them and repeated all this word for word.

7-9 They said, "What is my master talking about? We would never do anything like that! Why, the money we found in our bags earlier, we brought back all the way from Canaan—do you think we'd turn right around and steal it back from your master?

NEW KING JAMES VERSION

whomever of your servants it is found, let him
die, and we also will be my lord's slaves."
10And he said, "Now also *let* it *be* according
to your words; he with whom it is found shall be
my slave, and you shall be blameless." 11Then
each man speedily let down his sack to the
ground, and each opened his sack. 12So he
searched. He began with the oldest and left off
with the youngest; and the cup was found in
Benjamin's sack. 13Then they tore their clothes,
and each man loaded his donkey and returned
to the city.
14So Judah and his brothers came to
Joseph's house, and he *was* still there; and they
fell before him on the ground. 15And Joseph said
to them, "What deed *is* this you have done? Did
you not know that such a man as I can certainly
practice divination?"
16Then Judah said, "What shall we say to my
lord? What shall we speak? Or how shall we
clear ourselves? God has found out the iniquity
of your servants; here we are, my lord's slaves,
both we and *he* also with whom the cup was
found."
17But he said, "Far be it from me that I should
do so; the man in whose hand the cup was
found, he shall be my slave. And as for you, go
up in peace to your father."

JUDAH INTERCEDES FOR BENJAMIN

18Then Judah came near to him and said: "O
my lord, please let your servant speak a word in
my lord's hearing, and do not let your anger
burn against your servant; for you *are* even like
Pharaoh. 19My lord asked his servants, saying,
'Have you a father or a brother?' 20And we said
to my lord, 'We have a father, an old man, and a
child of *his* old age, *who is* young; his brother is
dead, and he alone is left of his mother's chil-
dren, and his father loves him.' 21Then you said
to your servants, 'Bring him down to me, that I
may set my eyes on him.' 22And we said to my
lord, 'The lad cannot leave his father, for *if* he
should leave his father, *his father* would die.'
23But you said to your servants, 'Unless your
youngest brother comes down with you, you
shall see my face no more.'
24"So it was, when we went up to your ser-
vant my father, that we told him the words of my
lord. 25And our father said, 'Go back *and* buy us
a little food.' 26But we said, 'We cannot go down;
if our youngest brother is with us, then we will
go down; for we may not see the man's face un-
less our youngest brother *is* with us.' 27Then
your servant my father said to us, 'You know
that my wife bore me two sons; 28and the one
went out from me, and I said, "Surely he is torn
to pieces"; and I have not seen him since. 29But
if you take this one also from me, and calamity
befalls him, you shall bring down my gray hair
with sorrow to the grave.'
30"Now therefore, when I come to your ser-
vant my father, and the lad *is* not with us, since

THE MESSAGE

If that chalice is found on any of us, he'll die;
and the rest of us will be your master's
slaves."
10 The steward said, "Very well then, but we
won't go that far. Whoever is found with the
chalice will be my slave; the rest of you can
go free."
11-12 They outdid each other in putting their
bags on the ground and opening them up for
inspection. The steward searched their
bags, going from oldest to youngest. The
chalice showed up in Benjamin's bag.
13 They ripped their clothes in despair,
loaded up their donkeys, and went back to
the city.
14 Joseph was still at home when Judah and
his brothers got back. They threw them-
selves down on the ground in front of him.
15 Joseph accused them: "How can you have
done this? You have to know that a man in
my position would have discovered this."
16 Judah as spokesman for the brothers
said, "What can we say, master? What *is*
there to say? How can we prove our inno-
cence? God is behind this, exposing how
bad we are. We stand guilty before you and
ready to be your slaves—we're all in this to-
gether, the rest of us as guilty as the one
with the chalice."
17 "I'd never do that to you," said Joseph.
"Only the one involved with the chalice will
be my slave. The rest of you are free to go
back to your father."
18-20 Judah came forward. He said, "Please,
master; can I say just one thing to you?
Don't get angry. Don't think I'm presumptu-
ous—you're the same as Pharaoh as far as
I'm concerned. You, master, asked us, 'Do
you have a father and a brother?' And we
answered honestly, 'We have a father who is
old and a younger brother who was born to
him in his old age. His brother is dead and
he is the only son left from that mother. And
his father loves him more than anything.'
21-22 "Then you told us, 'Bring him down here
so I can see him.' We told you, master, that it
was impossible: 'The boy can't leave his fa-
ther; if he leaves, his father will die.'
23 "And then you said, 'If your youngest
brother doesn't come with you, you won't be
allowed to see me.'
24-26 "When we returned to our father, we told
him everything you said to us. So when our
father said, 'Go back and buy some more
food,' we told him flatly, 'We can't. The only
way we can go back is if our youngest
brother is with us. We aren't allowed to even
see the man if our youngest brother doesn't
come with us.'
27-29 "Your servant, my father, told us, 'You
know very well that my wife gave me two
sons. One turned up missing. I concluded
that he'd been ripped to pieces. I've never
seen him since. If you now go and take this
one and something bad happens to him,
you'll put my old gray, grieving head in the
grave for sure.'
30-32 "And now, can't you see that if I show up
before your servant, my father, without the

NEW KING JAMES VERSION

his life is bound up in the lad's life, 31it will hap-
pen, when he sees that the lad *is* not *with us*,
that he will die. So your servants will bring
down the gray hair of your servant our father
with sorrow to the grave. 32For your servant be-
came surety for the lad to my father, saying, 'If I
do not bring him *back* to you, then I shall bear
the blame before my father forever.' 33Now
therefore, please let your servant remain in-
stead of the lad as a slave to my lord, and let the
lad go up with his brothers. 34For how shall I go
up to my father if the lad *is* not with me, lest per-
haps I see the evil that would come upon my fa-
ther?"

JOSEPH REVEALED TO HIS BROTHERS

45 Then Joseph could not restrain himself be-
fore all those who stood by him, and he
cried out, "Make everyone go out from me!" So
no one stood with him while Joseph made him-
self known to his brothers. 2And he wept aloud,
and the Egyptians and the house of Pharaoh
heard *it*.
3Then Joseph said to his brothers, "I *am*
Joseph; does my father still live?" But his broth-
ers could not answer him, for they were dis-
mayed in his presence. 4And Joseph said to his
brothers, "Please come near to me." So they
came near. Then he said: "I *am* Joseph your
brother, whom you sold into Egypt. 5But now, do
not therefore be grieved or angry with your-
selves because you sold me here; for God sent
me before you to preserve life. 6For these two
years the famine *has been* in the land, and *there
are* still five years in which *there will be* neither
plowing nor harvesting. 7And God sent me be-
fore you to preserve a posterity for you in the
earth, and to save your lives by a great deliver-
ance. 8So now *it was* not you *who* sent me here,
but God; and He has made me a father to
Pharaoh, and lord of all his house, and a ruler
throughout all the land of Egypt.
9"Hurry and go up to my father, and say to
him, 'Thus says your son Joseph: "God has made
me lord of all Egypt; come down to me, do not
tarry. 10You shall dwell in the land of Goshen,
and you shall be near to me, you and your chil-
dren, your children's children, your flocks and
your herds, and all that you have. 11There I will
provide for you, lest you and your household,
and all that you have, come to poverty; for *there
are* still five years of famine." '
12"And behold, your eyes and the eyes of my
brother Benjamin see that *it is* my mouth that
speaks to you. 13So you shall tell my father of all
my glory in Egypt, and of all that you have seen;
and you shall hurry and bring my father down
here."
14Then he fell on his brother Benjamin's
neck and wept, and Benjamin wept on his neck.
15Moreover he kissed all his brothers and wept
over them, and after that his brothers talked
with him.

THE MESSAGE

boy, this son with whom his life is so bound
up, the moment he realizes the boy is gone,
he'll die on the spot. He'll die of grief and
we, your servants who are standing here be-
fore you, will have killed him. And that's not
all. I got my father to release the boy to
show him to you by promising, 'If I don't
bring him back, I'll stand condemned before
you, Father, all my life.'
33-34 "So let me stay here as your slave, not
this boy. Let the boy go back with his broth-
ers. How can I go back to my father if the
boy is not with me? Oh, don't make me go
back and watch my father die in grief!"

1-2 45 Joseph couldn't hold himself in any
longer, keeping up a front before all
his attendants. He cried out, "Leave! Clear
out—everyone leave!" So there was no one
with Joseph when he identified himself to his
brothers. But his sobbing was so violent that
the Egyptians couldn't help but hear him. The
news was soon reported to Pharaoh's palace.
3 Joseph spoke to his brothers: "I am
Joseph. Is my father really still alive?" But
his brothers couldn't say a word. They were
speechless—they couldn't believe what they
were hearing and seeing.
4-8 "Come closer to me," Joseph said to his
brothers. They came closer. "I am Joseph
your brother whom you sold into Egypt. But
don't feel badly, don't blame yourselves for
selling me. God was behind it. God sent me
here ahead of you to save lives. There has
been a famine in the land now for two years;
the famine will continue for five more
years—neither plowing nor harvesting. God
sent me on ahead to pave the way and make
sure there was a remnant in the land, to save
your lives in an amazing act of deliverance.
So you see, it wasn't you who sent me here
but God. He set me in place as a father to
Pharaoh, put me in charge of his personal
affairs, and made me ruler of all Egypt.
9-11 "Hurry back to my father. Tell him, 'Your
son Joseph says: I'm master of all of Egypt.
Come as fast as you can and join me here.
I'll give you a place to live in Goshen where
you'll be close to me—you, your children,
your grandchildren, your flocks, your herds,
and anything else you can think of. I'll take
care of you there completely. There are still
five more years of famine ahead; I'll make
sure all your needs are taken care of, you
and everyone connected with you—you
won't want for a thing.'
12-13 "Look at me. You can see for yourselves,
and my brother Benjamin can see for him-
self, that it's me, my own mouth, telling you
all this. Tell my father all about the high po-
sition I hold in Egypt, tell him everything
you've seen here, but don't take all day—
hurry up and get my father down here."
14-15 Then Joseph threw himself on his brother
Benjamin's neck and wept, and Benjamin
wept on his neck. He then kissed all his
brothers and wept over them. Only then
were his brothers able to talk with him.

New King James Version

16Now the report of it was heard in Pharaoh's house, saying, "Joseph's brothers have come." So it pleased Pharaoh and his servants well. 17And Pharaoh said to Joseph, "Say to your brothers, 'Do this: Load your animals and depart; go to the land of Canaan. 18Bring your father and your households and come to me; I will give you the best of the land of Egypt, and you will eat the fat of the land. 19Now you are commanded—do this: Take carts out of the land of Egypt for your little ones and your wives; bring your father and come. 20Also do not be concerned about your goods, for the best of all the land of Egypt *is* yours.' "

21Then the sons of Israel did so; and Joseph gave them carts, according to the command of Pharaoh, and he gave them provisions for the journey. 22He gave to all of them, to each man, changes of garments; but to Benjamin he gave three hundred *pieces* of silver and five changes of garments. 23And he sent to his father these *things:* ten donkeys loaded with the good things of Egypt, and ten female donkeys loaded with grain, bread, and food for his father for the journey. 24So he sent his brothers away, and they departed; and he said to them, "See that you do not become troubled along the way."

25Then they went up out of Egypt, and came to the land of Canaan to Jacob their father. 26And they told him, saying, "Joseph *is* still alive, and he *is* governor over all the land of Egypt." And Jacob's heart stood still, because he did not believe them. 27But when they told him all the words which Joseph had said to them, and when he saw the carts which Joseph had sent to carry him, the spirit of Jacob their father revived. 28Then Israel said, "*It is* enough. Joseph my son *is* still alive. I will go and see him before I die."

Jacob's Journey to Egypt

46 So Israel took his journey with all that he had, and came to Beersheba, and offered sacrifices to the God of his father Isaac. 2Then God spoke to Israel in the visions of the night, and said, "Jacob, Jacob!"

And he said, "Here I am."

3So He said, "I *am* God, the God of your father; do not fear to go down to Egypt, for I will make of you a great nation there. 4I will go down with you to Egypt, and I will also surely bring you up *again;* and Joseph will put his hand on your eyes."

5Then Jacob arose from Beersheba; and the sons of Israel carried their father Jacob, their little ones, and their wives, in the carts which Pharaoh had sent to carry him. 6So they took their livestock and their goods, which they had acquired in the land of Canaan, and went to Egypt, Jacob and all his descendants with him. 7His sons and his sons' sons, his daughters and his sons' daughters, and all his descendants he brought with him to Egypt.

8Now these *were* the names of the children of Israel, Jacob and his sons, who went to Egypt: Reuben *was* Jacob's firstborn.

The Message

16 The story was reported in Pharaoh's
palace: "Joseph's brothers have come." It
was good news to Pharaoh and all who
worked with him.
17-18 Pharaoh said to Joseph, "Tell your brothers, 'This is the plan: Load up your pack animals; go to Canaan, get your father and your families and bring them back here. I'll settle you on the best land in Egypt—you'll live off the fat of the land.'
19-20 "Also tell them this: 'Here's what I want you to do: Take wagons from Egypt to carry your little ones and your wives and load up your father and come back. Don't worry about having to leave things behind; the best in all of Egypt will be yours.' "
21-23 And they did just that, the sons of Israel. Joseph gave them the wagons that Pharaoh had promised and food for the trip. He outfitted all the brothers in brand-new clothes, but he gave Benjamin three hundred pieces of silver and several suits of clothes. He sent his father these gifts: ten donkeys loaded with Egypt's best products and another ten donkeys loaded with grain and bread, provisions for his father's journey back.
24 Then he sent his brothers off. As they left he told them, "Take it easy on the journey; try to get along with each other."
25-28 They left Egypt and went back to their father Jacob in Canaan. When they told him, "Joseph is still alive—and he's the ruler over the whole land of Egypt!" he went numb; he couldn't believe his ears. But the more they talked, telling him everything that Joseph had told them and when he saw the wagons that Joseph had sent to carry him back, the blood started to flow again—their father Jacob's spirit revived. Israel said, "I've heard enough—my son Joseph is still alive. I've got to go and see him before I die."

1 46 So Israel set out on the journey with everything he owned. He arrived at Beersheba and worshiped, offering sacrifices to the God of his father Isaac.
2 God spoke to Israel in a vision that night: "Jacob! Jacob!"

"Yes?" he said. "I'm listening."
3-4 God said, "I am the God of your father. Don't be afraid of going down to Egypt. I'm going to make you a great nation there. I'll go with you down to Egypt; I'll also bring you back here. And when you die, Joseph will be with you; with his own hand he'll close your eyes."
5-7 Then Jacob left Beersheba. Israel's sons loaded their father and their little ones and their wives on the wagons Pharaoh had sent to carry him. They arrived in Egypt with the livestock and the wealth they had accumulated in Canaan. Jacob brought everyone in his family with him—sons and grandsons, daughters and granddaughters. Everyone.
8 These are the names of the Israelites, Jacob and his descendants, who went to Egypt:

Reuben, Jacob's firstborn.

NEW KING JAMES VERSION

9 The sons of Reuben *were* Hanoch, Pallu,
Hezron, and Carmi. 10 The sons of Simeon *were*
Jemuel,[a] Jamin, Ohad, Jachin,[b] Zohar,[c] and
Shaul, the son of a Canaanite woman. 11 The sons
of Levi *were* Gershon, Kohath, and Merari. 12 The
sons of Judah *were* Er, Onan, Shelah, Perez, and
Zerah (but Er and Onan died in the land of
Canaan). The sons of Perez were Hezron and
Hamul. 13 The sons of Issachar *were* Tola, Puvah,[a]
Job,[b] and Shimron. 14 The sons of Zebulun *were*
Sered, Elon, and Jahleel. 15 These *were* the sons
of Leah, whom she bore to Jacob in Padan Aram,
with his daughter Dinah. All the persons, his
sons and his daughters, *were* thirty-three.
16 The sons of Gad *were* Ziphion,[a] Haggi,
Shuni, Ezbon,[b] Eri, Arodi,[c] and Areli. 17 The sons
of Asher *were* Jimnah, Ishuah, Isui, Beriah, and
Serah, their sister. And the sons of Beriah *were*
Heber and Malchiel. 18 These *were* the sons of
Zilpah, whom Laban gave to Leah his daughter;
and these she bore to Jacob: sixteen persons.
19 The sons of Rachel, Jacob's wife, *were*
Joseph and Benjamin. 20 And to Joseph in the
land of Egypt were born Manasseh and
Ephraim, whom Asenath, the daughter of Poti-
Pherah priest of On, bore to him. 21 The sons of
Benjamin *were* Belah, Becher, Ashbel, Gera,
Naaman, Ehi, Rosh, Muppim, Huppim,[a] and
Ard. 22 These *were* the sons of Rachel, who were
born to Jacob: fourteen persons in all.
23 The son of Dan *was* Hushim.[a] 24 The sons of
Naphtali *were* Jahzeel,[a] Guni, Jezer, and
Shillem.[b] 25 These *were* the sons of Bilhah,
whom Laban gave to Rachel his daughter, and
she bore these to Jacob: seven persons in all.
26 All the persons who went with Jacob to
Egypt, who came from his body, besides Jacob's
sons' wives, *were* sixty-six persons in all. 27 And
the sons of Joseph who were born to him in
Egypt *were* two persons. All the persons of the
house of Jacob who went to Egypt were seventy.

JACOB SETTLES IN GOSHEN

28 Then he sent Judah before him to Joseph,
to point out before him *the way* to Goshen. And
they came to the land of Goshen. 29 So Joseph
made ready his chariot and went up to Goshen
to meet his father Israel; and he presented him-
self to him, and fell on his neck and wept on his
neck a good while.
30 And Israel said to Joseph, "Now let me die,
since I have seen your face, because you *are* still
alive."
31 Then Joseph said to his brothers and to his
father's household, "I will go up and tell
Pharaoh, and say to him, 'My brothers and
those of my father's house, who *were* in the land
of Canaan, have come to me. 32 And the men *are*
shepherds, for their occupation has been to feed

46:10 [a]Spelled *Nemuel* in 1 Chronicles 4:24 [b]Called *Jarib* in 1 Chronicles 4:24 [c]Called *Zerah* in 1 Chronicles 4:24 **46:13** [a]Spelled *Puah* in 1 Chronicles 7:1 [b]Same as *Jashub* in Numbers 26:24 and 1 Chronicles 7:1 **46:16** [a]Spelled *Zephon* in Samaritan Pentateuch, Septuagint, and Numbers 26:15 [b]Called *Ozni* in Numbers 26:16 [c]Spelled *Arod* in Numbers 26:17 **46:21** [a]Called *Hupham* in Numbers 26:39 **46:23** [a]Called *Shuham* in Numbers 26:42 **46:24** [a]Spelled *Jahziel* in 1 Chronicles 7:13 [b]Spelled *Shallum* in 1 Chronicles 7:13

THE MESSAGE

9 Reuben's sons: Hanoch, Pallu, Hezron, and Carmi.

10 Simeon's sons: Jemuel, Jamin, Ohad, Jakin, Zohar, and Shaul the son of a Canaanite woman.

11 Levi's sons: Gershon, Kohath, and Merari.

12 Judah's sons: Er, Onan, Shelah, Perez, and Zerah (Er and Onan had already died in the land of Canaan). The sons of Perez were Hezron and Hamul.

13 Issachar's sons: Tola, Puah, Jashub, and Shimron.

14 Zebulun's sons: Sered, Elon, and Jahleel.

15 These are the sons that Leah bore to Jacob in Paddan Aram. There was also his daughter Dinah. Altogether, sons and daughters, they numbered thirty-three.

16 Gad's sons: Zephon, Haggi, Shuni, Ezbon, Eri, Arodi, and Areli.

17 Asher's sons: Imnah, Ishvah, Ishvi, and Beriah. Also their sister Serah, and Beriah's sons, Heber and Malkiel.

18 These are the children that Zilpah, the maid that Laban gave to his daughter Leah, bore to Jacob—sixteen of them.

19-21 The sons of Jacob's wife Rachel were Joseph and Benjamin. Joseph was the father of two sons, Manasseh and Ephraim, from his marriage to Asenath daughter of Potiphera, priest of On. They were born to him in Egypt. Benjamin's sons were Bela, Beker, Ashbel, Gera, Naaman, Ehi, Rosh, Muppim, Huppim, and Ard.

22 These are the children born to Jacob through Rachel—fourteen.

23 Dan's son: Hushim.

24 Naphtali's sons: Jahziel, Guni, Jezer, and Shillem.

25 These are the children born to Jacob through Bilhah, the maid Laban had given to his daughter Rachel—seven.

26-27 Summing up, all those who went down to Egypt with Jacob—his own children, not counting his sons' wives—numbered sixty-six. Counting in the two sons born to Joseph in Egypt, the members of Jacob's family who ended up in Egypt numbered seventy.

28-29 Jacob sent Judah on ahead to get directions to Goshen from Joseph. When they got to Goshen, Joseph gave orders for his chariot and went to Goshen to meet his father Israel. The moment Joseph saw him, he threw himself on his neck and wept. He wept a long time.

30 Israel said to Joseph, "I'm ready to die. I've looked into your face—you are indeed alive."

31-34 Joseph then spoke to his brothers and his father's family. "I'll go and tell Pharaoh, 'My brothers and my father's family, all of whom lived in Canaan, have come to me. The men are shepherds; they've always made their

NEW KING JAMES VERSION

livestock; and they have brought their flocks, their herds, and all that they have.' 33So it shall be, when Pharaoh calls you and says, 'What is your occupation?' 34that you shall say, 'Your servants' occupation has been with livestock from our youth even till now, both we *and* also our fathers,' that you may dwell in the land of Goshen; for every shepherd *is* an abomination to the Egyptians."

47 Then Joseph went and told Pharaoh, and said, "My father and my brothers, their flocks and their herds and all that they possess, have come from the land of Canaan; and indeed they *are* in the land of Goshen." 2And he took five men from among his brothers and presented them to Pharaoh. 3Then Pharaoh said to his brothers, "What *is* your occupation?"

And they said to Pharaoh, "Your servants *are* shepherds, both we *and* also our fathers." 4And they said to Pharaoh, "We have come to dwell in the land, because your servants have no pasture for their flocks, for the famine *is* severe in the land of Canaan. Now therefore, please let your servants dwell in the land of Goshen."

5Then Pharaoh spoke to Joseph, saying, "Your father and your brothers have come to you. 6The land of Egypt *is* before you. Have your father and brothers dwell in the best of the land; let them dwell in the land of Goshen. And if you know *any* competent men among them, then make them chief herdsmen over my livestock."

7Then Joseph brought in his father Jacob and set him before Pharaoh; and Jacob blessed Pharaoh. 8Pharaoh said to Jacob, "How old *are* you?"

9And Jacob said to Pharaoh, "The days of the years of my pilgrimage *are* one hundred and thirty years; few and evil have been the days of the years of my life, and they have not attained to the days of the years of the life of my fathers in the days of their pilgrimage." 10So Jacob blessed Pharaoh, and went out from before Pharaoh.

11And Joseph situated his father and his brothers, and gave them a possession in the land of Egypt, in the best of the land, in the land of Rameses, as Pharaoh had commanded. 12Then Joseph provided his father, his brothers, and all his father's household with bread, according to the number in *their* families.

JOSEPH DEALS WITH THE FAMINE

13Now *there was* no bread in all the land; for the famine *was* very severe, so that the land of Egypt and the land of Canaan languished because of the famine. 14And Joseph gathered up all the money that was found in the land of Egypt and in the land of Canaan, for the grain which they bought; and Joseph brought the money into Pharaoh's house.

15So when the money failed in the land of Egypt and in the land of Canaan, all the Egyptians came to Joseph and said, "Give us bread, for why should we die in your presence? For the money has failed."

16Then Joseph said, "Give your livestock, and I will give you *bread* for your livestock, if the money is gone." 17So they brought their live-

THE MESSAGE

living by raising livestock. And they've
brought their flocks and herds with them,
along with everything else they own.' When
Pharaoh calls you in and asks what kind of
work you do, tell him, 'Your servants have
always kept livestock for as long as we can
remember—we and our parents also.' That
way he'll let you stay apart in the area of
Goshen—for Egyptians look down on anyone who is a shepherd."

1 47 Joseph went to Pharaoh and told him,
"My father and brothers with their
flocks and herds and everything they own
have come from Canaan. Right now they are
in Goshen."

2-3 He had taken five of his brothers with
him and introduced them to Pharaoh.
Pharaoh asked them, "What kind of work
do you do?"

3-4 "Your servants are shepherds, the same
as our fathers were. We have come to this
country to find a new place to live. There is
no pasture for our flocks in Canaan. The
famine has been very bad there. Please,
would you let your servants settle in the region of Goshen?"

5-6 Pharaoh looked at Joseph. "So, your father and brothers have arrived—a reunion!
Egypt welcomes them. Settle your father
and brothers on the choicest land—yes, give
them Goshen. And if you know any among
them that are especially good at their work,
put them in charge of my own livestock."

7-8 Next Joseph brought his father Jacob in
and introduced him to Pharaoh. Jacob
blessed Pharaoh. Pharaoh asked Jacob,
"How old are you?"

9-10 Jacob answered Pharaoh, "The years of
my sojourning are 130—a short and hard
life and not nearly as long as my ancestors
were given." Then Jacob blessed Pharaoh
and left.

11-12 Joseph settled his father and brothers in
Egypt, made them proud owners of choice
land—it was the region of Rameses (that is,
Goshen)—just as Pharaoh had ordered.
Joseph took good care of them—his father
and brothers and all his father's family,
right down to the smallest baby. He made
sure they had plenty of everything.

13-15 The time eventually came when there was
no food anywhere. The famine was very
bad. Egypt and Canaan alike were devastated by the famine. Joseph collected all the
money that was to be found in Egypt and
Canaan to pay for the distribution of food.
He banked the money in Pharaoh's palace.
When the money from Egypt and Canaan
had run out, the Egyptians came to Joseph.
"Food! Give us food! Are you going to watch
us die right in front of you? The money is all
gone."

16-17 Joseph said, "Bring your livestock. I'll
trade you food for livestock since your

NEW KING JAMES VERSION

stock to Joseph, and Joseph gave them bread *in*
exchange for the horses, the flocks, the cattle of
the herds, and for the donkeys. Thus he fed
them with bread *in exchange* for all their live-
stock that year.
18When that year had ended, they came to
him the next year and said to him, "We will not
hide from my lord that our money is gone; my
lord also has our herds of livestock. There is
nothing left in the sight of my lord but our bod-
ies and our lands. 19Why should we die before
your eyes, both we and our land? Buy us and our
land for bread, and we and our land will be ser-
vants of Pharaoh; give *us* seed, that we may live
and not die, that the land may not be desolate."
20Then Joseph bought all the land of Egypt
for Pharaoh; for every man of the Egyptians
sold his field, because the famine was severe
upon them. So the land became Pharaoh's.
21And as for the people, he moved them into the
cities,[a] from *one* end of the borders of Egypt to
the *other* end. 22Only the land of the priests he
did not buy; for the priests had rations *allotted*
to them by Pharaoh, and they ate their rations
which Pharaoh gave them; therefore they did
not sell their lands.
23Then Joseph said to the people, "Indeed I
have bought you and your land this day for
Pharaoh. Look, *here is* seed for you, and you
shall sow the land. 24And it shall come to pass in
the harvest that you shall give one-fifth to
Pharaoh. Four-fifths shall be your own, as seed
for the field and for your food, for those of your
households and as food for your little ones."
25So they said, "You have saved our lives; let
us find favor in the sight of my lord, and we will
be Pharaoh's servants." 26And Joseph made it a
law over the land of Egypt to this day, *that*
Pharaoh should have one-fifth, except for the
land of the priests only, *which* did not become
Pharaoh's.

JOSEPH'S VOW TO JACOB

27So Israel dwelt in the land of Egypt, in the
country of Goshen; and they had possessions
there and grew and multiplied exceedingly.
28And Jacob lived in the land of Egypt seventeen
years. So the length of Jacob's life was one hun-
dred and forty-seven years. 29When the time
drew near that Israel must die, he called his son
Joseph and said to him, "Now if I have found fa-
vor in your sight, please put your hand under
my thigh, and deal kindly and truly with me.
Please do not bury me in Egypt, 30but let me lie
with my fathers; you shall carry me out of Egypt
and bury me in their burial place."
And he said, "I will do as you have said."
31Then he said, "Swear to me." And he swore
to him. So Israel bowed himself on the head of
the bed.

47:21 [a]Following Masoretic Text and Targum; Samaritan Pentateuch, Septuagint, and Vulgate read *made the people virtual slaves.*

THE MESSAGE

money's run out." So they brought Joseph their livestock. He traded them food for their horses, sheep, cattle, and donkeys. He got them through that year in exchange for all their livestock.

18-19 When that year was over, the next year rolled around and they were back, saying, "Master, it's no secret to you that we're broke: our money's gone and we've traded you all our livestock. We've nothing left to barter with but our bodies and our farms. What use are our bodies and our land if we stand here and starve to death right in front of you? Trade us food for our bodies and our land. We'll be slaves to Pharaoh and give up our land—all we ask is seed for survival, just enough to live on and keep the farms alive."

20-21 So Joseph bought up all the farms in Egypt for Pharaoh. Every Egyptian sold his land—the famine was that bad. That's how Pharaoh ended up owning all the land and the people ended up slaves; Joseph reduced the people to slavery from one end of Egypt to the other.

22 Joseph made an exception for the priests. He didn't buy their land because they received a fixed salary from Pharaoh and were able to live off of that salary. So they didn't need to sell their land.

23-24 Joseph then announced to the people: "Here's how things stand: I've bought you and your land for Pharaoh. In exchange I'm giving you seed so you can plant the ground. When the crops are harvested, you must give a fifth to Pharaoh and keep four-fifths for yourselves, for seed for yourselves and your families—you're going to be able to feed your children!"

25 They said, "You've saved our lives! Master, we're grateful and glad to be slaves to Pharaoh."

26 Joseph decreed a land law in Egypt that is still in effect, *A Fifth Goes to Pharaoh.* Only the priests' lands were not owned by Pharaoh.

27-28 And so Israel settled down in Egypt in the region of Goshen. They acquired property and flourished. They became a large company of people. Jacob lived in Egypt for seventeen years. In all, he lived 147 years.

29-30 When the time came for Israel to die, he called his son Joseph and said, "Do me this favor. Put your hand under my thigh, a sign that you're loyal and true to me to the end. Don't bury me in Egypt. When I lie down with my fathers, carry me out of Egypt and bury me alongside them."

"I will," he said. "I'll do what you've asked."

31 Israel said, "Promise me." Joseph promised.

Israel bowed his head in submission and gratitude from his bed.

NEW KING JAMES VERSION

JACOB BLESSES JOSEPH'S SONS

48 Now it came to pass after these things that
Joseph was told, "Indeed your father *is*
sick"; and he took with him his two sons, Ma-
nasseh and Ephraim. 2And Jacob was told,
"Look, your son Joseph is coming to you"; and
Israel strengthened himself and sat up on the
bed. 3Then Jacob said to Joseph: "God Almighty
appeared to me at Luz in the land of Canaan
and blessed me, 4and said to me, 'Behold, I will
make you fruitful and multiply you, and I will
make of you a multitude of people, and give this
land to your descendants after you *as* an ever-
lasting possession.' 5And now your two sons,
Ephraim and Manasseh, who were born to you
in the land of Egypt before I came to you in
Egypt, *are* mine; as Reuben and Simeon, they
shall be mine. 6Your offspring whom you beget
after them shall be yours; they will be called by
the name of their brothers in their inheritance.
7But as for me, when I came from Padan, Rachel
died beside me in the land of Canaan on the
way, when *there was* but a little distance to go
to Ephrath; and I buried her there on the way to
Ephrath (that is, Bethlehem)."

8Then Israel saw Joseph's sons, and said,
"Who *are* these?"

9Joseph said to his father, "They *are* my sons,
whom God has given me in this *place*."

And he said, "Please bring them to me, and I
will bless them." 10Now the eyes of Israel were
dim with age, *so that* he could not see. Then
Joseph brought them near him, and he kissed
them and embraced them. 11And Israel said to
Joseph, "I had not thought to see your face; but
in fact, God has also shown me your offspring!"

12So Joseph brought them from beside his
knees, and he bowed down with his face to the
earth. 13And Joseph took them both, Ephraim
with his right hand toward Israel's left hand,
and Manasseh with his left hand toward Israel's
right hand, and brought *them* near him. 14Then
Israel stretched out his right hand and laid *it* on
Ephraim's head, who *was* the younger, and his
left hand on Manasseh's head, guiding his
hands knowingly, for Manasseh *was* the first-
born. 15And he blessed Joseph, and said:

"God, before whom my fathers Abraham and
Isaac walked,
The God who has fed me all my life long to
this day,
16The Angel who has redeemed me from all
evil,
Bless the lads;
Let my name be named upon them,
And the name of my fathers Abraham and
Isaac;
And let them grow into a multitude in the
midst of the earth."

17Now when Joseph saw that his father laid
his right hand on the head of Ephraim, it dis-
pleased him; so he took hold of his father's hand
to remove it from Ephraim's head to Ma-
nasseh's head. 18And Joseph said to his father,
"Not so, my father, for this *one is* the firstborn;
put your right hand on his head."

THE MESSAGE

1-2 48 Some time after this conversation,
Joseph was told, "Your father is ill." He
took his two sons, Manasseh and Ephraim,
and went to Jacob. When Jacob was told,
"Your son Joseph has come," he roused him-
self and sat up in bed.

3-7 Jacob said to Joseph, "The Strong God
appeared to me at Luz in the land of Canaan
and blessed me. He said, 'I'm going to make
you prosperous and numerous, turn you into
a congregation of tribes; and I'll turn this
land over to your children coming after you
as a permanent inheritance.' I'm adopting
your two sons who were born to you here in
Egypt before I joined you; they have equal
status with Reuben and Simeon. But any
children born after them are yours; they will
come after their brothers in matters of in-
heritance. I want it this way because, as I
was returning from Paddan, your mother
Rachel, to my deep sorrow, died as we were
on our way through Canaan when we were
only a short distance from Ephrath, now
called Bethlehem."

8 Just then Jacob noticed Joseph's sons
and said, "Who are these?"

9-11 Joseph told his father, "They are my sons
whom God gave to me in this place."

"Bring them to me," he said, "so I can
bless them." Israel's eyesight was poor from
old age; he was nearly blind. So Joseph
brought them up close. Old Israel kissed and
embraced them and then said to Joseph, "I
never expected to see your face again, and
now God has let me see your children as
well!"

12-16 Joseph took them from Israel's knees and
bowed respectfully, his face to the ground.
Then Joseph took the two boys, Ephraim with
his right hand setting him to Israel's left, and
Manasseh with his left hand setting him to Is-
rael's right, and stood them before him. But
Israel crossed his arms and put his right hand
on the head of Ephraim who was the younger
and his left hand on the head of Manasseh,
the firstborn. Then he blessed them:

The God before whom walked
my fathers Abraham and Isaac,
The God who has been my shepherd
all my life long to this very day,
The Angel who delivered me from every
evil,
Bless the boys.
May my name be echoed in their lives,
and the names of Abraham and Isaac,
my fathers,
And may they grow
covering the Earth with their children.

17-18 When Joseph saw that his father had
placed his right hand on Ephraim's head, he
thought he had made a mistake, so he took
hold of his father's hand to move it from
Ephraim's head to Manasseh's, saying,
"That's the wrong head, Father; the other
one is the firstborn; place your right hand
on his head."

New King James Version

19 But his father refused and said, "I know, my
son, I know. He also shall become a people, and
he also shall be great; but truly his younger
brother shall be greater than he, and his descen-
dants shall become a multitude of nations."
20 So he blessed them that day, saying, "By
you Israel will bless, saying, 'May God make
you as Ephraim and as Manasseh!' " And thus
he set Ephraim before Manasseh.
21 Then Israel said to Joseph, "Behold, I am
dying, but God will be with you and bring you
back to the land of your fathers. 22 Moreover I
have given to you one portion above your broth-
ers, which I took from the hand of the Amorite
with my sword and my bow."

Jacob's Last Words to His Sons

49 And Jacob called his sons and said,
"Gather together, that I may tell you what
shall befall you in the last days:

2 "Gather together and hear, you sons of
Jacob,
And listen to Israel your father.

3 "Reuben, you are my firstborn,
My might and the beginning of my strength,
The excellency of dignity and the excellency
of power.
4 Unstable as water, you shall not excel,
Because you went up to your father's bed;
Then you defiled *it*—
He went up to my couch.

5 "Simeon and Levi *are* brothers;
Instruments of cruelty *are in* their dwelling
place.
6 Let not my soul enter their council;
Let not my honor be united to their
assembly;
For in their anger they slew a man,
And in their self-will they hamstrung an ox.
7 Cursed *be* their anger, for *it is* fierce;
And their wrath, for it is cruel!
I will divide them in Jacob
And scatter them in Israel.

8 "Judah, you *are he* whom your brothers shall
praise;
Your hand *shall be* on the neck of your
enemies;
Your father's children shall bow down
before you.
9 Judah *is* a lion's whelp;
From the prey, my son, you have gone up.
He bows down, he lies down as a lion;
And as a lion, who shall rouse him?
10 The scepter shall not depart from Judah,
Nor a lawgiver from between his feet,
Until Shiloh comes;
And to Him *shall be* the obedience of the
people.

The Message

19-20 But his father wouldn't do it. He said, "I
know, my son; but I know what I'm doing.
He also will develop into a people, and he
also will be great. But his younger brother
will be even greater and his descendants
will enrich nations." Then he blessed them
both:

Israel will use your names to give
blessings:
May God make you like Ephraim and
Manasseh.

In that he made it explicit: he put
Ephraim ahead of Manasseh.
21-22 Israel then said to Joseph, "I'm about to
die. God be with you and give you safe pas-
sage back to the land of your fathers. As for
me, I'm presenting you, as the first among
your brothers, the ridge of land I took from
Amorites with my sword and bow."

1 **49** Jacob called his sons and said, "Gather
around. I want to tell you what you can
expect in the days to come."

2 Come together, listen sons of Jacob,
listen to Israel your father.

3-4 Reuben, you're my firstborn,
my strength, first proof of my
manhood,
at the top in honor and at the top in
power,
But like a bucket of water spilled,
you'll be at the top no more,
Because you climbed into your father's
marriage bed,
mounting that couch, and you defiled it.

5-6 Simeon and Levi are two of a kind,
ready to fight at the drop of a hat.
I don't want anything to do with their
vendettas,
want no part in their bitter feuds;
They kill men in fits of temper,
slash oxen on a whim.
7 A curse on their uncontrolled anger,
on their indiscriminate wrath.
I'll throw them out with the trash;
I'll shred and scatter them like confetti
throughout Israel.

8-12 You, Judah, your brothers will praise
you:
Your fingers on your enemies' throat,
while your brothers honor you.
You're a lion's cub, Judah,
home fresh from the kill, my son.
Look at him, crouched like a lion, king
of beasts;
who dares mess with him?
The scepter shall not leave Judah;
he'll keep a firm grip on the command
staff
Until the ultimate ruler comes
and the nations obey him.

NEW KING JAMES VERSION

11 Binding his donkey to the vine,
And his donkey's colt to the choice vine,
He washed his garments in wine,
And his clothes in the blood of grapes.
12 His eyes *are* darker than wine,
And his teeth whiter than milk.

13 "Zebulun shall dwell by the haven of the sea;
He *shall become* a haven for ships,
And his border shall adjoin Sidon.

14 "Issachar is a strong donkey,
Lying down between two burdens;
15 He saw that rest *was* good,
And that the land *was* pleasant;
He bowed his shoulder to bear *a burden*,
And became a band of slaves.

16 "Dan shall judge his people
As one of the tribes of Israel.
17 Dan shall be a serpent by the way,
A viper by the path,
That bites the horse's heels
So that its rider shall fall backward.
18 I have waited for your salvation, O LORD!

19 "Gad, a troop shall tramp upon him,
But he shall triumph at last.

20 "Bread from Asher *shall be* rich,
And he shall yield royal dainties.

21 "Naphtali *is* a deer let loose;
He uses beautiful words.

22 "Joseph *is* a fruitful bough,
A fruitful bough by a well;
His branches run over the wall.
23 The archers have bitterly grieved him,
Shot *at him* and hated him.
24 But his bow remained in strength,
And the arms of his hands were made strong
By the hands of the Mighty *God* of Jacob
(From there *is* the Shepherd, the Stone of Israel),
25 By the God of your father who will help you,
And by the Almighty who will bless you
With blessings of heaven above,
Blessings of the deep that lies beneath,
Blessings of the breasts and of the womb.
26 The blessings of your father
Have excelled the blessings of my ancestors,
Up to the utmost bound of the everlasting hills.
They shall be on the head of Joseph,
And on the crown of the head of him who was separate from his brothers.

THE MESSAGE

He'll tie up his donkey to the grapevine,
his purebred prize to a sturdy branch.
He will wash his shirt in wine
and his cloak in the blood of grapes,
His eyes will be darker than wine,
his teeth whiter than milk.

13 Zebulun settles down on the seashore;
he's a safe harbor for ships,
right alongside Sidon.

14-15 Issachar is one tough donkey
crouching between the corrals;
When he saw how good the place was,
how pleasant the country,
He gave up his freedom
and went to work as a slave.

16-17 Dan will handle matters of justice for his people;
he will hold his own just fine among the tribes of Israel.
Dan is only a small snake in the grass,
a lethal serpent in ambush by the road
When he strikes a horse in the heel,
and brings its huge rider crashing down.

18 I wait in hope
for your salvation, GOD.

19 Gad will be attacked by bandits,
but he will trip them up.

20 Asher will become famous for rich foods,
candies and sweets fit for kings.

21-26 Naphtali is a deer running free
that gives birth to lovely fawns.

Joseph is a wild donkey,
a wild donkey by a spring,
spirited donkeys on a hill.
The archers with malice attacked,
shooting their hate-tipped arrows;
But he held steady under fire,
his bow firm, his arms limber,
With the backing of the Champion of Jacob,
the Shepherd, the Rock of Israel.
The God of your father—may he help you!
And may The Strong God—may he give you his blessings,
Blessings tumbling out of the skies,
blessings bursting up from the Earth—
blessings of breasts and womb.
May the blessings of your father
exceed the blessings of the ancient mountains,
surpass the delights of the eternal hills;
May they rest on the head of Joseph,
on the brow of the one consecrated among his brothers.

New King James Version

27“Benjamin is a ravenous wolf;
In the morning he shall devour the prey,
And at night he shall divide the spoil.”

28All these *are* the twelve tribes of Israel, and this *is* what their father spoke to them. And he blessed them; he blessed each one according to his own blessing.

Jacob's Death and Burial

29Then he charged them and said to them: “I am to be gathered to my people; bury me with my fathers in the cave that *is* in the field of Ephron the Hittite, 30in the cave that *is* in the field of Machpelah, which *is* before Mamre in the land of Canaan, which Abraham bought with the field of Ephron the Hittite as a possession for a burial place. 31There they buried Abraham and Sarah his wife, there they buried Isaac and Rebekah his wife, and there I buried Leah. 32The field and the cave that *is* there *were* purchased from the sons of Heth.” 33And when Jacob had finished commanding his sons, he drew his feet up into the bed and breathed his last, and was gathered to his people.

50 Then Joseph fell on his father's face and wept over him, and kissed him. 2And Joseph commanded his servants the physicians to embalm his father. So the physicians embalmed Israel. 3Forty days were required for him, for such are the days required for those who are embalmed; and the Egyptians mourned for him seventy days.

4Now when the days of his mourning were past, Joseph spoke to the household of Pharaoh, saying, “If now I have found favor in your eyes, please speak in the hearing of Pharaoh, saying, 5‘My father made me swear, saying, “Behold, I am dying; in my grave which I dug for myself in the land of Canaan, there you shall bury me.” Now therefore, please let me go up and bury my father, and I will come back.’ ”

6And Pharaoh said, “Go up and bury your father, as he made you swear.”

7So Joseph went up to bury his father; and with him went up all the servants of Pharaoh, the elders of his house, and all the elders of the land of Egypt, 8as well as all the house of Joseph, his brothers, and his father's house. Only their little ones, their flocks, and their herds they left in the land of Goshen. 9And there went up with him both chariots and horsemen, and it was a very great gathering.

10Then they came to the threshing floor of Atad, which *is* beyond the Jordan, and they mourned there with a great and very solemn lamentation. He observed seven days of mourning for his father. 11And when the inhabitants of the land, the Canaanites, saw the mourning at the threshing floor of Atad, they said, “This *is* a deep mourning of the Egyptians.” Therefore its name was called Abel Mizraim,[a] which *is* beyond the Jordan.

50:11 [a]Literally *Mourning of Egypt*

The Message

27 Benjamin is a ravenous wolf;
all morning he gorges on his kill,
at evening divides up what's left over.

28 All these are the tribes of Israel, the twelve tribes. And this is what their father said to them as he blessed them, blessing each one with his own special farewell blessing.

29-32 Then he instructed them: “I am about to be gathered to my people. Bury me with my fathers in the cave which is in the field of Ephron the Hittite, the cave in the field of Machpelah facing Mamre in the land of Canaan, the field Abraham bought from Ephron the Hittite for a burial plot. Abraham and his wife Sarah were buried there; Isaac and his wife Rebekah were buried there; I also buried Leah there. The field and the cave were bought from the Hittites.”

33 Jacob finished instructing his sons, pulled his feet into bed, breathed his last, and was gathered to his people.

1 50 Joseph threw himself on his father, wept over him, and kissed him.

2-3 Joseph then instructed the physicians in his employ to embalm his father. The physicians embalmed Israel. The embalming took forty days, the period required for embalming. There was public mourning by the Egyptians for seventy days.

4-5 When the period of mourning was completed, Joseph petitioned Pharaoh's court: “If you have reason to think kindly of me, present Pharaoh with my request: My father made me swear, saying, ‘I am ready to die. Bury me in the grave plot that I prepared for myself in the land of Canaan.’ Please give me leave to go up and bury my father. Then I'll come back.”

6 Pharaoh said, “Certainly. Go and bury your father as he made you promise under oath.”

7-9 So Joseph left to bury his father. And all the high-ranking officials from Pharaoh's court went with him, all the dignitaries of Egypt, joining Joseph's family—his brothers and his father's family. Their children and flocks and herds were left in Goshen. Chariots and horsemen accompanied them. It was a huge funeral procession.

10 Arriving at the Atad Threshing Floor just across the Jordan River, they stopped for a period of mourning, letting their grief out in loud and lengthy lament. For seven days, Joseph engaged in these funeral rites for his father.

11 When the Canaanites who lived in that area saw the grief being poured out at the Atad Threshing Floor, they said, “Look how deeply the Egyptians are mourning.” That is how the site at the Jordan got the name Abel Mizraim (Egyptian Lament).

New King James Version

12So his sons did for him just as he had com-
manded them. 13For his sons carried him to the
land of Canaan, and buried him in the cave of
the field of Machpelah, before Mamre, which
Abraham bought with the field from Ephron the
Hittite as property for a burial place. 14And after
he had buried his father, Joseph returned to
Egypt, he and his brothers and all who went up
with him to bury his father.

Joseph Reassures His Brothers

15When Joseph's brothers saw that their fa-
ther was dead, they said, "Perhaps Joseph will
hate us, and may actually repay us for all the
evil which we did to him." 16So they sent *mes-
sengers* to Joseph, saying, "Before your father
died he commanded, saying, 17'Thus you shall
say to Joseph: "I beg you, please forgive the tres-
pass of your brothers and their sin; for they did
evil to you." ' Now, please, forgive the trespass
of the servants of the God of your father." And
Joseph wept when they spoke to him.
18Then his brothers also went and fell down
before his face, and they said, "Behold, we *are*
your servants."
19Joseph said to them, "Do not be afraid, for
am I in the place of God? 20But as for you, you
meant evil against me; *but* God meant it for
good, in order to bring it about as *it is* this day,
to save many people alive. 21Now therefore, do
not be afraid; I will provide for you and your lit-
tle ones." And he comforted them and spoke
kindly to them.

Death of Joseph

22So Joseph dwelt in Egypt, he and his fa-
ther's household. And Joseph lived one hundred
and ten years. 23Joseph saw Ephraim's children
to the third *generation*. The children of Machir,
the son of Manasseh, were also brought up on
Joseph's knees.
24And Joseph said to his brethren, "I am dy-
ing; but God will surely visit you, and bring you
out of this land to the land of which He swore to
Abraham, to Isaac, and to Jacob." 25Then Joseph
took an oath from the children of Israel, saying,
"God will surely visit you, and you shall carry
up my bones from here." 26So Joseph died, *being*
one hundred and ten years old; and they
embalmed him, and he was put in a coffin in
Egypt.

The Message

12-13 Jacob's sons continued to carry out his instructions to the letter. They took him on into Canaan and buried him in the cave in the field of Machpelah facing Mamre, the field that Abraham had bought as a burial plot from Ephron the Hittite.

14-15 After burying his father, Joseph went back to Egypt. All his brothers who had come with him to bury his father returned with him. After the funeral, Joseph's brothers talked among themselves: "What if Joseph is carrying a grudge and decides to pay us back for all the wrong we did him?"

16-17 So they sent Joseph a message, "Before his death, your father gave this command: Tell Joseph, 'Forgive your brothers' sin—all that wrongdoing. They did treat you very badly.' Will you do it? Will you forgive the sins of the servants of your father's God?"

When Joseph received their message, he wept.

18 Then the brothers went in person to him, threw themselves on the ground before him and said, "We'll be your slaves."

19-21 Joseph replied, "Don't be afraid. Do I act for God? Don't you see, you planned evil against me but God used those same plans for my good, as you see all around you right now—life for many people. Easy now, you have nothing to fear; I'll take care of you and your children." He reassured them, speaking with them heart-to-heart.

22-23 Joseph continued to live in Egypt with his father's family. Joseph lived 110 years. He lived to see Ephraim's sons into the third generation. The sons of Makir, Manasseh's son, were also recognized as Joseph's.

24 At the end, Joseph said to his brothers, "I am ready to die. God will most certainly pay you a visit and take you out of this land and back to the land he so solemnly promised to Abraham, Isaac, and Jacob."

25 Then Joseph made the sons of Israel promise under oath, "When God makes his visitation, make sure you take my bones with you as you leave here."

26 Joseph died at the age of 110 years. They embalmed him and placed him in a coffin in Egypt.

EXODUS

New King James Version

Israel's Suffering in Egypt

1 Now these *are* the names of the children of Israel who came to Egypt; each man and his household came with Jacob: 2Reuben, Simeon, Levi, and Judah; 3Issachar, Zebulun, and Benjamin; 4Dan, Naphtali, Gad, and Asher. 5All those who were descendants[a] of Jacob were seventy[b] persons (for Joseph was in Egypt *already*). 6And Joseph died, all his brothers, and all that generation. 7But the children of Israel were fruitful and increased abundantly, multiplied and grew exceedingly mighty; and the land was filled with them.

8Now there arose a new king over Egypt, who did not know Joseph. 9And he said to his people, "Look, the people of the children of Israel *are* more and mightier than we; 10come, let us deal shrewdly with them, lest they multiply, and it happen, in the event of war, that they also join our enemies and fight against us, and *so* go up out of the land." 11Therefore they set taskmasters over them to afflict them with their burdens. And they built for Pharaoh supply cities, Pithom and Raamses. 12But the more they afflicted them, the more they multiplied and grew. And they were in dread of the children of Israel. 13So the Egyptians made the children of Israel serve with rigor. 14And they made their lives bitter with hard bondage—in mortar, in brick, and in all manner of service in the field. All their service in which they made them serve *was* with rigor.

15Then the king of Egypt spoke to the Hebrew midwives, of whom the name of one *was* Shiphrah and the name of the other Puah; 16and he said, "When you do the duties of a midwife for the Hebrew women, and see *them* on the birthstools, if it *is* a son, then you shall kill him; but if it *is* a daughter, then she shall live." 17But the midwives feared God, and did not do as the king of Egypt commanded them, but saved the male children alive. 18So the king of Egypt called for the midwives and said to them, "Why have you done this thing, and saved the male children alive?"

19And the midwives said to Pharaoh, "Because the Hebrew women *are* not like the Egyptian women; for they *are* lively and give birth before the midwives come to them."

20Therefore God dealt well with the midwives, and the people multiplied and grew very mighty. 21And so it was, because the midwives feared God, that He provided households for them.

22So Pharaoh commanded all his people, saying, "Every son who is born[a] you shall cast into the river, and every daughter you shall save alive."

1:5 [a]Literally *who came from the loins of* [b]Dead Sea Scrolls and Septuagint read *seventy-five* (compare Acts 7:14). **1:22** [a]Samaritan Pentateuch, Septuagint, and Targum add *to the Hebrews.*

The Message

1-5 1 These are the names of the Israelites who went to Egypt with Jacob, each bringing his family members:

Reuben, Simeon, Levi, and Judah,
Issachar, Zebulun, and Benjamin,
Dan and Naphtali, Gad and Asher.

Seventy persons in all generated by Jacob's seed. Joseph was already in Egypt.

6-7 Then Joseph died, and all his brothers—that whole generation. But the children of Israel kept on reproducing. They were very prolific—a population explosion in their own right—and the land was filled with them.

"A New King . . . Who Didn't Know Joseph"

8-10 A new king came to power in Egypt who didn't know Joseph. He spoke to his people in alarm, "There are way too many of these Israelites for us to handle. We've got to do something: Let's devise a plan to contain them, lest if there's a war they should join our enemies, or just walk off and leave us."

11-14 So they organized them into work-gangs and put them to hard labor under gang-foremen. They built the storage cities Pithom and Rameses for Pharaoh. But the harder the Egyptians worked them the more children the Israelites had—children everywhere! The Egyptians got so they couldn't stand the Israelites and treated them worse than ever, crushing them with slave labor. They made them miserable with hard labor—making bricks and mortar and back-breaking work in the fields. They piled on the work, crushing them under the cruel workload.

15-16 The king of Egypt had a talk with the two Hebrew midwives; one was named Shiphrah and the other Puah. He said, "When you deliver the Hebrew women, look at the sex of the baby. If it's a boy, kill him; if it's a girl, let her live."

17-18 But the midwives had far too much respect for God and didn't do what the king of Egypt ordered; they let the boy babies live. The king of Egypt called in the midwives. "Why didn't you obey my orders? You've let those babies live!"

19 The midwives answered Pharaoh, "The Hebrew women aren't like the Egyptian women; they're vigorous. Before the midwife can get there, they've already had the baby."

20-21 God was pleased with the midwives. The people continued to increase in number—a very strong people. And because the midwives honored God, God gave them families of their own.

22 So Pharaoh issued a general order to all his people: "Every boy that is born, drown him in the Nile. But let the girls live."

NEW KING JAMES VERSION

MOSES IS BORN

2 And a man of the house of Levi went and
took *as wife* a daughter of Levi. [2]So the
woman conceived and bore a son. And when
she saw that he *was* a beautiful *child,* she hid
him three months. [3]But when she could no
longer hide him, she took an ark of bulrushes
for him, daubed it with asphalt and pitch, put
the child in it, and laid *it* in the reeds by the
river's bank. [4]And his sister stood afar off, to
know what would be done to him.

[5]Then the daughter of Pharaoh came down
to bathe at the river. And her maidens walked
along the riverside; and when she saw the ark
among the reeds, she sent her maid to get it.
[6]And when she opened *it,* she saw the child, and
behold, the baby wept. So she had compassion
on him, and said, "This is one of the Hebrews'
children."

[7]Then his sister said to Pharaoh's daughter,
"Shall I go and call a nurse for you from the He-
brew women, that she may nurse the child for
you?"

[8]And Pharaoh's daughter said to her, "Go."
So the maiden went and called the child's
mother. [9]Then Pharaoh's daughter said to her,
"Take this child away and nurse him for me, and
I will give *you* your wages." So the woman took
the child and nursed him. [10]And the child grew,
and she brought him to Pharaoh's daughter, and
he became her son. So she called his name
Moses,[a] saying, "Because I drew him out of the
water."

MOSES FLEES TO MIDIAN

[11]Now it came to pass in those days, when
Moses was grown, that he went out to his
brethren and looked at their burdens. And he
saw an Egyptian beating a Hebrew, one of his
brethren. [12]So he looked this way and that way,
and when he saw no one, he killed the Egyptian
and hid him in the sand. [13]And when he went
out the second day, behold, two Hebrew men
were fighting, and he said to the one who did
the wrong, "Why are you striking your compan-
ion?"

[14]Then he said, "Who made you a prince and
a judge over us? Do you intend to kill me as you
killed the Egyptian?"

So Moses feared and said, "Surely this thing
is known!" [15]When Pharaoh heard of this mat-
ter, he sought to kill Moses. But Moses fled from
the face of Pharaoh and dwelt in the land of
Midian; and he sat down by a well.

[16]Now the priest of Midian had seven daugh-
ters. And they came and drew water, and they
filled the troughs to water their father's flock.
[17]Then the shepherds came and drove them
away; but Moses stood up and helped them, and
watered their flock.

[18]When they came to Reuel their father, he
said, "How *is it that* you have come so soon to-
day?"

[19]And they said, "An Egyptian delivered us
from the hand of the shepherds, and he also
drew enough water for us and watered the
flock."

2:10 [a]Literally *Drawn Out*

THE MESSAGE

MOSES

1-3 2 A man from the family of Levi married a
Levite woman. The woman became preg-
nant and had a son. She saw there was
something special about him and hid him.
She hid him for three months. When she
couldn't hide him any longer she got a little
basket-boat made of papyrus, waterproofed
it with tar and pitch, and placed the child in
it. Then she set it afloat in the reeds at the
edge of the Nile.

4-6 The baby's older sister found herself a
vantage point a little way off and watched to
see what would happen to him. Pharaoh's
daughter came down to the Nile to bathe;
her maidens strolled on the bank. She saw
the basket-boat floating in the reeds and
sent her maid to get it. She opened it and
saw the child—a baby crying! Her heart
went out to him. She said, "This must be one
of the Hebrew babies."

7 Then his sister was before her: "Do you
want me to go and get a nursing mother
from the Hebrews so she can nurse the baby
for you?"

8 Pharaoh's daughter said, "Yes. Go." The
girl went and called the child's mother.

9 Pharaoh's daughter told her, "Take this
baby and nurse him for me. I'll pay you."
The woman took the child and nursed him.

10 After the child was weaned, she pre-
sented him to Pharaoh's daughter who
adopted him as her son. She named him
Moses (Pulled-Out), saying, "I pulled him
out of the water."

11-12 Time passed. Moses grew up. One day he
went and saw his brothers, saw all that hard
labor. Then he saw an Egyptian hit a He-
brew—one of his relatives! He looked this
way and then that; when he realized there
was no one in sight, he killed the Egyptian
and buried him in the sand.

13 The next day he went out there again.
Two Hebrew men were fighting. He spoke to
the man who started it: "Why are you hitting
your neighbor?"

14 The man shot back: "Who do you think
you are, telling us what to do? Are you going
to kill me the way you killed that Egyptian?"

Then Moses panicked: "Word's gotten
out—people know about this."

15 Pharaoh heard about it and tried to kill
Moses, but Moses got away to the land of
Midian. He sat down by a well.

16-17 The priest of Midian had seven daugh-
ters. They came and drew water, filling the
troughs and watering their father's sheep.
When some shepherds came and chased the
girls off, Moses came to their rescue and
helped them water their sheep.

18 When they got home to their father,
Reuel, he said, "That didn't take long. Why
are you back so soon?"

19 "An Egyptian," they said, "rescued us
from a bunch of shepherds. Why, he even
drew water for us and watered the sheep."

NEW KING JAMES VERSION

20 So he said to his daughters, "And where *is*
he? Why *is* it *that* you have left the man? Call
him, that he may eat bread."
21 Then Moses was content to live with the
man, and he gave Zipporah his daughter to
Moses. 22 And she bore *him* a son. He called his
name Gershom,[a] for he said, "I have been a
stranger in a foreign land."
23 Now it happened in the process of time that
the king of Egypt died. Then the children of Is-
rael groaned because of the bondage, and they
cried out; and their cry came up to God because
of the bondage. 24 So God heard their groaning,
and God remembered His covenant with Abra-
ham, with Isaac, and with Jacob. 25 And God
looked upon the children of Israel, and God ac-
knowledged *them.*

MOSES AT THE BURNING BUSH

3 Now Moses was tending the flock of Jethro
his father-in-law, the priest of Midian. And he
led the flock to the back of the desert, and came
to Horeb, the mountain of God. 2 And the Angel
of the LORD appeared to him in a flame of fire
from the midst of a bush. So he looked, and be-
hold, the bush was burning with fire, but the
bush *was* not consumed. 3 Then Moses said, "I
will now turn aside and see this great sight, why
the bush does not burn."
4 So when the LORD saw that he turned aside
to look, God called to him from the midst of the
bush and said, "Moses, Moses!"
And he said, "Here I am."
5 Then He said, "Do not draw near this place.
Take your sandals off your feet, for the place
where you stand *is* holy ground." 6 Moreover He
said, "I *am* the God of your father—the God of
Abraham, the God of Isaac, and the God of Ja-
cob." And Moses hid his face, for he was afraid
to look upon God.
7 And the LORD said: "I have surely seen the
oppression of My people who *are* in Egypt, and
have heard their cry because of their taskmas-
ters, for I know their sorrows. 8 So I have come
down to deliver them out of the hand of the
Egyptians, and to bring them up from that land
to a good and large land, to a land flowing with
milk and honey, to the place of the Canaanites
and the Hittites and the Amorites and the Per-
izzites and the Hivites and the Jebusites. 9 Now
therefore, behold, the cry of the children of Is-
rael has come to Me, and I have also seen the
oppression with which the Egyptians oppress
them. 10 Come now, therefore, and I will send you
to Pharaoh that you may bring My people, the
children of Israel, out of Egypt."
11 But Moses said to God, "Who *am* I that I
should go to Pharaoh, and that I should bring
the children of Israel out of Egypt?"
12 So He said, "I will certainly be with you.
And this *shall be* a sign to you that I have sent
you: When you have brought the people out of
Egypt, you shall serve God on this mountain."

2:22 [a]Literally *Stranger There*

THE MESSAGE

20 He said, "So where is he? Why did you
leave him behind? Invite him so he can have
something to eat with us."
21-22 Moses agreed to settle down there with
the man, who then gave his daughter Zippo-
rah (Bird) to him for his wife. She had a son,
and Moses named him Gershom (So-
journer), saying, "I'm a sojourner in a for-
eign country."

23 Many years later the king of Egypt died. The
Israelites groaned under their slavery and
cried out. Their cries for relief from their
hard labor ascended to God:
24 God listened to their groanings.
God remembered his covenant with
Abraham, with Isaac, and with Jacob.
25 God saw what was going on with Israel.
God understood.

1-2 3 Moses was shepherding the flock of Jethro,
his father-in-law, the priest of Midian. He
led the flock to the west end of the wilder-
ness and came to the mountain of God,
Horeb. The angel of GOD appeared to him in
flames of fire blazing out of the middle of a
bush. He looked. The bush was blazing
away but it didn't burn up.
3 Moses said, "What's going on here? I
can't believe this! Amazing! Why doesn't the
bush burn up?"
4 GOD saw that he had stopped to look. God
called to him from out of the bush, "Moses!
Moses!"
He said, "Yes? I'm right here!"
5 God said, "Don't come any closer. Re-
move your sandals from your feet. You're
standing on holy ground."
6 Then he said, "I am the God of your fa-
ther: The God of Abraham, the God of Isaac,
the God of Jacob."
Moses hid his face, afraid to look at God.
7-8 GOD said, "I've taken a good, long look at
the affliction of my people in Egypt. I've
heard their cries for deliverance from their
slave masters; I know all about their pain.
And now I have come down to help them,
pry them loose from the grip of Egypt, get
them out of that country and bring them to
a good land with wide-open spaces, a land
lush with milk and honey, the land of the
Canaanite, the Hittite, the Amorite, the Per-
izzite, the Hivite, and the Jebusite.
9-10 "The Israelite cry for help has come to
me, and I've seen for myself how cruelly
they're being treated by the Egyptians. It's
time for you to go back: I'm sending you to
Pharaoh to bring my people, the People of
Israel, out of Egypt."
11 Moses answered God, "But why me?
What makes you think that I could ever go
to Pharaoh and lead the children of Israel
out of Egypt?"
12 "I'll be with you," God said. "And this will
be the proof that I am the one who sent you:
When you have brought my people out of
Egypt, you will worship God right here at
this very mountain."

NEW KING JAMES VERSION

13Then Moses said to God, "Indeed, *when* I come to the children of Israel and say to them, 'The God of your fathers has sent me to you,' and they say to me, 'What *is* His name?' what shall I say to them?"

14And God said to Moses, "I AM WHO I AM." And He said, "Thus you shall say to the children of Israel, 'I AM has sent me to you.' " 15Moreover God said to Moses, "Thus you shall say to the children of Israel: 'The LORD God of your fathers, the God of Abraham, the God of Isaac, and the God of Jacob, has sent me to you. This *is* My name forever, and this *is* My memorial to all generations.' 16Go and gather the elders of Israel together, and say to them, 'The LORD God of your fathers, the God of Abraham, of Isaac, and of Jacob, appeared to me, saying, "I have surely visited you and *seen* what is done to you in Egypt; 17and I have said I will bring you up out of the affliction of Egypt to the land of the Canaanites and the Hittites and the Amorites and the Perizzites and the Hivites and the Jebusites, to a land flowing with milk and honey." ' 18Then they will heed your voice; and you shall come, you and the elders of Israel, to the king of Egypt; and you shall say to him, 'The LORD God of the Hebrews has met with us; and now, please, let us go three days' journey into the wilderness, that we may sacrifice to the LORD our God.' 19But I am sure that the king of Egypt will not let you go, no, not even by a mighty hand. 20So I will stretch out My hand and strike Egypt with all My wonders which I will do in its midst; and after that he will let you go. 21And I will give this people favor in the sight of the Egyptians; and it shall be, when you go, that you shall not go empty-handed. 22But every woman shall ask of her neighbor, namely, of her who dwells near her house, articles of silver, articles of gold, and clothing; and you shall put *them* on your sons and on your daughters. So you shall plunder the Egyptians."

MIRACULOUS SIGNS FOR PHARAOH

4 Then Moses answered and said, "But suppose they will not believe me or listen to my voice; suppose they say, 'The LORD has not appeared to you.' "

2So the LORD said to him, "What *is* that in your hand?"

He said, "A rod."

3And He said, "Cast it on the ground." So he cast it on the ground, and it became a serpent; and Moses fled from it. 4Then the LORD said to Moses, "Reach out your hand and take *it* by the tail" (and he reached out his hand and caught it, and it became a rod in his hand), 5"that they may believe that the LORD God of their fathers, the God of Abraham, the God of Isaac, and the God of Jacob, has appeared to you."

6Furthermore the LORD said to him, "Now put your hand in your bosom." And he put his hand in his bosom, and when he took it out, behold, his hand *was* leprous, like snow. 7And He said, "Put your hand in your bosom again." So he put his hand in his bosom again, and drew it out of his bosom, and behold, it was restored like his *other* flesh. 8"Then it will be, if they do not believe you, nor heed the message of the

THE MESSAGE

13 Then Moses said to God, "Suppose I go to the People of Israel and I tell them, 'The God of your fathers sent me to you'; and they ask me, 'What is his name?' What do I tell them?"

14 God said to Moses, "I-AM-WHO-I-AM. Tell the People of Israel, 'I-AM sent me to you.' "

15 God continued with Moses: "This is what you're to say to the Israelites: 'GOD, the God of your fathers, the God of Abraham, the God of Isaac, and the God of Jacob sent me to you.' This has always been my name, and this is how I always will be known.

16-17 "Now be on your way. Gather the leaders of Israel. Tell them, 'GOD, the God of your fathers, the God of Abraham, Isaac, and Jacob, appeared to me, saying, "I've looked into what's being done to you in Egypt, and I've determined to get you out of the affliction of Egypt and take you to the land of the Canaanite, the Hittite, the Amorite, the Perizzite, the Hivite, and the Jebusite, a land brimming over with milk and honey." '

18 "Believe me, they will listen to you. Then you and the leaders of Israel will go to the king of Egypt and say to him: 'GOD, the God of the Hebrews, has met with us. Let us take a three-day journey into the wilderness where we will worship GOD—*our* God.'

19-22 "I know that the king of Egypt won't let you go unless forced to, so I'll intervene and hit Egypt where it hurts—oh, my miracles will send them reeling!—after which they'll be glad to send you off. I'll see to it that this people get a hearty send-off by the Egyptians—when you leave, you won't leave empty-handed! Each woman will ask her neighbor and any guests in her house for objects of silver and gold, for jewelry and extra clothes; you'll put them on your sons and daughters. Oh, you'll clean the Egyptians out!"

1 4 Moses objected, "They won't trust me. They won't listen to a word I say. They're going to say, 'GOD? Appear to him? Hardly!' "

2 So GOD said, "What's that in your hand?"

"A staff."

3 "Throw it on the ground." He threw it. It became a snake; Moses jumped back—fast!

4-5 GOD said to Moses, "Reach out and grab it by the tail." He reached out and grabbed it—and he was holding his staff again. "That's so they will trust that GOD appeared to you, the God of their fathers, the God of Abraham, the God of Isaac, and the God of Jacob."

6 GOD then said, "Put your hand inside your shirt." He slipped his hand under his shirt, then took it out. His hand had turned leprous, like snow.

7 He said, "Put your hand back under your shirt." He did it, then took it back out—as healthy as before.

8-9 "So if they don't trust you and aren't convinced by the first sign, the second sign

NEW KING JAMES VERSION

first sign, that they may believe the message of
the latter sign. 9And it shall be, if they do not be-
lieve even these two signs, or listen to your
voice, that you shall take water from the river[a]
and pour *it* on the dry *land*. The water which
you take from the river will become blood on
the dry *land*."
10Then Moses said to the LORD, "O my Lord,
I *am* not eloquent, neither before nor since You
have spoken to Your servant; but I *am* slow of
speech and slow of tongue."
11So the LORD said to him, "Who has made
man's mouth? Or who makes the mute, the deaf,
the seeing, or the blind? *Have* not I, the LORD?
12Now therefore, go, and I will be with your
mouth and teach you what you shall say."
13But he said, "O my Lord, please send by the
hand of whomever *else* You may send."
14So the anger of the LORD was kindled
against Moses, and He said: "Is not Aaron the
Levite your brother? I know that he can speak
well. And look, he is also coming out to meet
you. When he sees you, he will be glad in his
heart. 15Now you shall speak to him and put the
words in his mouth. And I will be with your
mouth and with his mouth, and I will teach you
what you shall do. 16So he shall be your
spokesman to the people. And he himself shall
be as a mouth for you, and you shall be to him
as God. 17And you shall take this rod in your
hand, with which you shall do the signs."

MOSES GOES TO EGYPT

18So Moses went and returned to Jethro his
father-in-law, and said to him, "Please let me go
and return to my brethren who *are* in Egypt,
and see whether they are still alive."
And Jethro said to Moses, "Go in peace."
19Now the LORD said to Moses in Midian,
"Go, return to Egypt; for all the men who sought
your life are dead." 20Then Moses took his wife
and his sons and set them on a donkey, and he
returned to the land of Egypt. And Moses took
the rod of God in his hand.
21And the LORD said to Moses, "When you go
back to Egypt, see that you do all those wonders
before Pharaoh which I have put in your hand.
But I will harden his heart, so that he will not let
the people go. 22Then you shall say to Pharaoh,
'Thus says the LORD: "Israel *is* My son, My first-
born. 23So I say to you, let My son go that he
may serve Me. But if you refuse to let him go, in-
deed I will kill your son, your firstborn." ' "
24And it came to pass on the way, at the en-
campment, that the LORD met him and sought to
kill him. 25Then Zipporah took a sharp stone
and cut off the foreskin of her son and cast *it* at
Moses'[a] feet, and said, "Surely you *are* a hus-
band of blood to me!" 26So He let him go. Then
she said, "*You are* a husband of blood!"—be-
cause of the circumcision.

4:9 [a]That is, the Nile 4:25 [a]Literally *his*

THE MESSAGE

should do it. But if it doesn't, if even after these two signs they don't trust you and listen to your message, take some water out of the Nile and pour it out on the dry land; the Nile water that you pour out will turn to blood when it hits the ground."

10 Moses raised another objection to GOD: "Master, please, I don't talk well. I've never been good with words, neither before nor after you spoke to me. I stutter and stammer."

11-12 GOD said, "And who do you think made the human mouth? And who makes some mute, some deaf, some sighted, some blind? Isn't it I, GOD? So, get going. I'll be right there with you—with your mouth! I'll be right there to teach you what to say."

13 He said, "Oh, Master, please! Send somebody else!"

14-17 GOD got angry with Moses: "Don't you have a brother, Aaron the Levite? He's good with words, I know he is. He speaks very well. In fact, at this very moment he's on his way to meet you. When he sees you he's going to be glad. You'll speak to him and tell him what to say. I'll be right there with you as you speak and with him as he speaks, teaching you step by step. He will speak to the people for you. He'll act as your mouth, but you'll decide what comes out of it. Now take this staff in your hand; you'll use it to do the signs."

18 Moses went back to Jethro his father-in-law and said, "I need to return to my relatives who are in Egypt. I want to see if they're still alive."

Jethro said, "Go. And peace be with you."

19 GOD said to Moses in Midian: "Go. Return to Egypt. All the men who wanted to kill you are dead."

20 So Moses took his wife and sons and put them on a donkey for the return trip to Egypt. He had a firm grip on the staff of God.

21-23 GOD said to Moses, "When you get back to Egypt, be prepared: All the wonders that I will do through you, you'll do before Pharaoh. But I will make him stubborn so that he will refuse to let the people go. Then you are to tell Pharaoh, 'GOD's Message: Israel is my son, my firstborn! I told you, "Free my son so that he can serve me." But you refused to free him. So now I'm going to kill *your* son, *your* firstborn.' "

24-26 On the journey back, as they camped for the night, GOD met Moses and would have killed him but Zipporah took a flint knife and cut off her son's foreskin, and touched Moses' member with it. She said, "Oh! You're a bridegroom of blood to me!" Then GOD let him go. She used the phrase "bridegroom of blood" because of the circumcision.

NEW KING JAMES VERSION

[27]And the LORD said to Aaron, "Go into the
wilderness to meet Moses." So he went and met
him on the mountain of God, and kissed him.
[28]So Moses told Aaron all the words of the LORD
who had sent him, and all the signs which He
had commanded him. [29]Then Moses and Aaron
went and gathered together all the elders of the
children of Israel. [30]And Aaron spoke all the
words which the LORD had spoken to Moses.
Then he did the signs in the sight of the people.
[31]So the people believed; and when they heard
that the LORD had visited the children of Israel
and that He had looked on their affliction, then
they bowed their heads and worshiped.

FIRST ENCOUNTER WITH PHARAOH

5 Afterward Moses and Aaron went in and told
Pharaoh, "Thus says the LORD God of Israel:
'Let My people go, that they may hold a feast to
Me in the wilderness.' "
[2]And Pharaoh said, "Who *is* the LORD, that I
should obey His voice to let Israel go? I do not
know the LORD, nor will I let Israel go."
[3]So they said, "The God of the Hebrews has
met with us. Please, let us go three days' journey
into the desert and sacrifice to the LORD our
God, lest He fall upon us with pestilence or with
the sword."
[4]Then the king of Egypt said to them, "Moses
and Aaron, why do you take the people from
their work? Get *back* to your labor." [5]And
Pharaoh said, "Look, the people of the land *are*
many now, and you make them rest from their
labor!"
[6]So the same day Pharaoh commanded the
taskmasters of the people and their officers,
saying, [7]"You shall no longer give the people
straw to make brick as before. Let them go and
gather straw for themselves. [8]And you shall lay
on them the quota of bricks which they made
before. You shall not reduce it. For they are idle;
therefore they cry out, saying, 'Let us go *and*
sacrifice to our God.' [9]Let more work be laid on
the men, that they may labor in it, and let them
not regard false words."
[10]And the taskmasters of the people and
their officers went out and spoke to the people,
saying, "Thus says Pharaoh: 'I will not give you
straw. [11]Go, get yourselves straw where you can
find it; yet none of your work will be reduced.' "
[12]So the people were scattered abroad through-
out all the land of Egypt to gather stubble in-
stead of straw. [13]And the taskmasters forced
them to hurry, saying, "Fulfill your work, *your*
daily quota, as when there was straw." [14]Also the
officers of the children of Israel, whom
Pharaoh's taskmasters had set over them, were
beaten *and* were asked, "Why have you not ful-
filled your task in making brick both yesterday
and today, as before?"
[15]Then the officers of the children of Israel
came and cried out to Pharaoh, saying, "Why
are you dealing thus with your servants?
[16]There is no straw given to your servants, and
they say to us, 'Make brick!' And indeed your
servants *are* beaten, but the fault *is* in your *own*
people."

THE MESSAGE

27-28 GOD spoke to Aaron, "Go and meet Moses in
the wilderness." He went and met him at the
mountain of God and kissed him. Moses
told Aaron the message that GOD had sent
him to speak and the wonders he had com-
manded him to do.
29-31 So Moses and Aaron proceeded to round
up all the leaders of Israel. Aaron told them
everything that GOD had told Moses and
demonstrated the wonders before the peo-
ple. And the people trusted and listened be-
lievingly that GOD was concerned with what
was going on with the Israelites and knew
all about their affliction. They bowed low
and they worshiped.

MOSES AND AARON AND PHARAOH

1 5 After that Moses and Aaron approached
Pharaoh. They said, "GOD, the God of Is-
rael, says, 'Free my people so that they can
hold a festival for me in the wilderness.' "
2 Pharaoh said, "And who is GOD that I
should listen to him and send Israel off? I
know nothing of this so-called 'GOD' and I'm
certainly not going to send Israel off."
3 They said, "The God of the Hebrews has
met with us. Let us take a three-day journey
into the wilderness so we can worship our
GOD lest he strike us with either disease or
death."
4-5 But the king of Egypt said, "Why on
earth, Moses and Aaron, would you suggest
the people be given a holiday? Back to
work!" Pharaoh went on, "Look, I've got all
these people bumming around, and now you
want to reward them with time off?"
6-9 Pharaoh took immediate action. He sent
down orders to the slave-drivers and their
underlings: "Don't provide straw for the
people for making bricks as you have been
doing. Make them get their own straw. And
make them produce the same number of
bricks—no reduction in their daily quotas!
They're getting lazy. They're going around
saying, 'Give us time off so we can worship
our God.' Crack down on them. That'll cure
them of their whining, their god-fantasies."
10-12 The slave-drivers and their underlings
went out to the people with their new in-
structions. "Pharaoh's orders: No more
straw provided. Get your own straw wher-
ever you can find it. And not one brick less
in your daily work quota!" The people scat-
tered all over Egypt scrabbling for straw.
13 The slave-drivers were merciless, saying,
"Complete your daily quota of bricks—the
same number as when you were given
straw."
14 The Israelite foremen whom the slave-
drivers had appointed were beaten and
badgered. "Why didn't you finish your quota
of bricks yesterday or the day before—and
now again today?"
15-16 The Israelite foremen came to Pharaoh
and cried out for relief: "Why are you treat-
ing your servants like this? Nobody gives us
any straw and they tell us, 'Make bricks!'
Look at us—we're being beaten. And it's not
our fault."

NEW KING JAMES VERSION

17But he said, "You *are* idle! Idle! Therefore
you say, 'Let us go *and* sacrifice to the LORD.'
18Therefore go now *and* work; for no straw shall
be given you, yet you shall deliver the quota of
bricks." 19And the officers of the children of Is-
rael saw *that* they *were* in trouble after it was
said, "You shall not reduce *any* bricks from your
daily quota."
20Then, as they came out from Pharaoh, they
met Moses and Aaron who stood there to meet
them. 21And they said to them, "Let the LORD
look on you and judge, because you have made
us abhorrent in the sight of Pharaoh and in the
sight of his servants, to put a sword in their
hand to kill us."

ISRAEL'S DELIVERANCE ASSURED

22So Moses returned to the LORD and said,
"Lord, why have You brought trouble on this
people? Why *is* it You have sent me? 23For since
I came to Pharaoh to speak in Your name, he has
done evil to this people; neither have You deliv-
ered Your people at all."

6Then the LORD said to Moses, "Now you shall
see what I will do to Pharaoh. For with a
strong hand he will let them go, and with a
strong hand he will drive them out of his land."
2And God spoke to Moses and said to him: "I
am the LORD. 3I appeared to Abraham, to Isaac,
and to Jacob, as God Almighty, but *by* My name
LORD[a] I was not known to them. 4I have also es-
tablished My covenant with them, to give them
the land of Canaan, the land of their pilgrimage,
in which they were strangers. 5And I have also
heard the groaning of the children of Israel
whom the Egyptians keep in bondage, and I
have remembered My covenant. 6Therefore say
to the children of Israel: 'I *am* the LORD; I will
bring you out from under the burdens of the
Egyptians, I will rescue you from their bondage,
and I will redeem you with an outstretched arm
and with great judgments. 7I will take you as My
people, and I will be your God. Then you shall
know that I *am* the LORD your God who brings
you out from under the burdens of the Egyp-
tians. 8And I will bring you into the land which
I swore to give to Abraham, Isaac, and Jacob;
and I will give it to you *as* a heritage: I *am* the
LORD.' " 9So Moses spoke thus to the children of
Israel; but they did not heed Moses, because of
anguish of spirit and cruel bondage.
10And the LORD spoke to Moses, saying,
11"Go in, tell Pharaoh king of Egypt to let the
children of Israel go out of his land."
12And Moses spoke before the LORD, saying,
"The children of Israel have not heeded me.
How then shall Pharaoh heed me, for I *am* of
uncircumcised lips?"
13Then the LORD spoke to Moses and Aaron,
and gave them a command for the children of
Israel and for Pharaoh king of Egypt, to bring
the children of Israel out of the land of Egypt.

6:3 [a]Hebrew *YHWH*, traditionally *Jehovah*

THE MESSAGE

17-18 But Pharaoh said, "Lazy! That's what you
are! Lazy! That's why you whine, 'Let us go
so we can worship GOD.' Well then, go—go
back to work. Nobody's going to give you
straw, and at the end of the day you better
bring in your full quota of bricks."

19 The Israelite foremen saw that they were
in a bad way, having to go back and tell their
workers, "Not one brick short in your daily
quota."

20-21 As they left Pharaoh, they found Moses
and Aaron waiting to meet them. The fore-
men said to them, "May GOD see what
you've done and judge you—you've made us
stink before Pharaoh and his servants!
You've put a weapon in his hand that's go-
ing to kill us!"

22-23 Moses went back to GOD and said, "My
Master, why are you treating this people so
badly? And why did you ever send me?
From the moment I came to Pharaoh to
speak in your name, things have only gotten
worse for this people. And rescue? Does this
look like rescue to you?"

1 6GOD said to Moses, "Now you'll see what
I'll do to Pharaoh: With a strong hand
he'll send them out free; with a strong hand
he'll drive them out of his land."

2-6 God continued speaking to Moses, reas-
suring him, "I am GOD. I appeared to Abra-
ham, Isaac, and Jacob as The Strong God,
but by my name GOD (I-Am-Present) I was
not known to them. I also established my
covenant with them to give them the land of
Canaan, the country in which they lived as
sojourners. But now I've heard the groan-
ings of the Israelites whom the Egyptians
continue to enslave and I've remembered
my covenant. Therefore tell the Israelites:

6-8 "I am GOD. I will bring you out from un-
der the cruel hard labor of Egypt. I will res-
cue you from slavery. I will redeem you, in-
tervening with great acts of judgment. I'll
take you as my own people and I'll be God
to you. You'll know that I am GOD, *your* God
who brings you out from under the cruel
hard labor of Egypt. I'll bring you into the
land that I promised to give Abraham, Isaac,
and Jacob and give it to you as your own
country. *I AM GOD.*"

9 But when Moses delivered this message
to the Israelites, they didn't even hear him—
they were that beaten down in spirit by the
harsh slave conditions.

10-11 Then GOD said to Moses, "Go and speak
to Pharaoh king of Egypt so that he will re-
lease the Israelites from his land."

12 Moses answered GOD, "Look—the Is-
raelites won't even listen to me. How do you
expect Pharaoh to? And besides, I stutter."

13 But GOD again laid out the facts to Moses
and Aaron regarding the Israelites and
Pharaoh king of Egypt, and he again com-
manded them to lead the Israelites out of the
land of Egypt.

New King James Version

The Family of Moses and Aaron

14These *are* the heads of their fathers'
houses: The sons of Reuben, the firstborn of Is-
rael, *were* Hanoch, Pallu, Hezron, and Carmi.
These are the families of Reuben. 15And the sons
of Simeon *were* Jemuel,[a] Jamin, Ohad, Jachin,
Zohar, and Shaul the son of a Canaanite
woman. These *are* the families of Simeon.
16These *are* the names of the sons of Levi ac-
cording to their generations: Gershon, Kohath,
and Merari. And the years of the life of Levi
were one hundred and thirty-seven. 17The sons
of Gershon *were* Libni and Shimi according to
their families. 18And the sons of Kohath *were*
Amram, Izhar, Hebron, and Uzziel. And the
years of the life of Kohath *were* one hundred
and thirty-three. 19The sons of Merari *were*
Mahli and Mushi. These *are* the families of Levi
according to their generations.

20Now Amram took for himself Jochebed, his
father's sister, as wife; and she bore him Aaron
and Moses. And the years of the life of Amram
were one hundred and thirty-seven. 21The sons
of Izhar *were* Korah, Nepheg, and Zichri. 22And
the sons of Uzziel *were* Mishael, Elzaphan, and
Zithri. 23Aaron took to himself Elisheba, daugh-
ter of Amminadab, sister of Nahshon, as wife;
and she bore him Nadab, Abihu, Elemazar, and
Ithamar. 24And the sons of Korah *were* Assir,
Elkanah, and Abiasaph. These are the families
of the Korahites. 25Eleazar, Aaron's son, took for
himself one of the daughters of Putiel as wife;
and she bore him Phinehas. These *are* the heads
of the fathers' houses of the Levites according to
their families.

26These *are the same* Aaron and Moses to
whom the LORD said, "Bring out the children of
Israel from the land of Egypt according to their
armies." 27These *are* the ones who spoke to
Pharaoh king of Egypt, to bring out the children
of Israel from Egypt. These *are the same* Moses
and Aaron.

Aaron Is Moses' Spokesman

28And it came to pass, on the day the LORD
spoke to Moses in the land of Egypt, 29that the
LORD spoke to Moses, saying, "I *am* the LORD.
Speak to Pharaoh king of Egypt all that I say to
you."

30But Moses said before the LORD, "Behold, I
am of uncircumcised lips, and how shall
Pharaoh heed me?"

7 So the LORD said to Moses: "See, I have made
you *as* God to Pharaoh, and Aaron your
brother shall be your prophet. 2You shall speak all
that I command you. And Aaron your brother
shall tell Pharaoh to send the children of Israel
out of his land. 3And I will harden Pharaoh's
heart, and multiply My signs and My wonders in
the land of Egypt. 4But Pharaoh will not heed you,
so that I may lay My hand on Egypt and bring My
armies *and* My people, the children of Israel, out
of the land of Egypt by great judgments. 5And the
Egyptians shall know that I *am* the LORD, when I
stretch out My hand on Egypt and bring out the
children of Israel from among them."

6:15 [a]Spelled *Nemuel* in Numbers 26:12

The Message

The Family Tree of Moses and Aaron

14 These are the heads of the tribes:

The sons of Reuben, Israel's firstborn: Hanoch, Pallu, Hezron, and Carmi—these are the families of Reuben.

15 The sons of Simeon: Jemuel, Jamin, Ohad, Jakin, Zohar, and Saul, the son of a Canaanite woman—these are the families of Simeon.

16 These are the names of the sons of Levi in the order of their birth: Gershon, Kohath, and Merari. Levi lived 137 years.

17 The sons of Gershon by family: Libni and Shimei.

18 The sons of Kohath: Amram, Izhar, Hebron, and Uzziel. Kohath lived to be 133.

19 The sons of Merari: Mahli and Mushi.

These are the sons of Levi in the order of their birth.

20 Amram married his aunt Jochebed and she had Aaron and Moses. Amram lived to be 137.

21 The sons of Izhar: Korah, Nepheg, and Zicri.

22 The sons of Uzziel: Mishael, Elzaphan, and Sithri.

23 Aaron married Elisheba, the daughter of Amminadab and sister of Nahshon, and she had Nadab and Abihu, Eleazar and Ithamar.

24 The sons of Korah: Assir, Elkanah, and Abiasaph. These are the families of the Korahites.

25 Aaron's son Eleazar married one of the daughters of Putiel and she had Phinehas.

These are the heads of the Levite families, family by family.

26-27 This is the Aaron and Moses whom GOD ordered: "Bring the Israelites out of the land of Egypt clan by clan." These are the men, Moses and Aaron, who told Pharaoh king of Egypt to release the Israelites from Egypt.

"I'll Make You as a God to Pharaoh"

28 And that's how things stood when GOD next spoke to Moses in Egypt.

29 God addressed Moses, saying, "I am GOD. Tell Pharaoh king of Egypt everything I say to you."

30 And Moses answered, "Look at me. I stutter. Why would Pharaoh listen to me?"

1-5 7 GOD told Moses, "Look at me. I'll make you as a god to Pharaoh and your brother Aaron will be your prophet. You are to speak everything I command you, and your brother Aaron will tell it to Pharaoh. Then he will release the Israelites from his land. At the same time I am going to put Pharaoh's back up and follow it up by filling Egypt with signs and wonders. Pharaoh is not going to listen to you, but I will have my way against Egypt and bring out my soldiers, my people the Israelites, from Egypt by mighty acts of judgment. The Egyptians will realize that I am GOD when I step in and take the Israelites out of their country."

NEW KING JAMES VERSION

6Then Moses and Aaron did *so;* just as the LORD commanded them, so they did. 7And Moses *was* eighty years old and Aaron eighty-three years old when they spoke to Pharaoh.

AARON'S MIRACULOUS ROD

8Then the LORD spoke to Moses and Aaron, saying, 9"When Pharaoh speaks to you, saying, 'Show a miracle for yourselves,' then you shall say to Aaron, 'Take your rod and cast *it* before Pharaoh, *and* let it become a serpent.' " 10So Moses and Aaron went in to Pharaoh, and they did so, just as the LORD commanded. And Aaron cast down his rod before Pharaoh and before his servants, and it became a serpent.

11But Pharaoh also called the wise men and the sorcerers; so the magicians of Egypt, they also did in like manner with their enchantments. 12For every man threw down his rod, and they became serpents. But Aaron's rod swallowed up their rods. 13And Pharaoh's heart grew hard, and he did not heed them, as the LORD had said.

THE FIRST PLAGUE: WATERS BECOME BLOOD

14So the LORD said to Moses: "Pharaoh's heart *is* hard; he refuses to let the people go. 15Go to Pharaoh in the morning, when he goes out to the water, and you shall stand by the river's bank to meet him; and the rod which was turned to a serpent you shall take in your hand. 16And you shall say to him, 'The LORD God of the Hebrews has sent me to you, saying, "Let My people go, that they may serve Me in the wilderness"; but indeed, until now you would not hear! 17Thus says the LORD: "By this you shall know that I *am* the LORD. Behold, I will strike the waters which *are* in the river with the rod that *is* in my hand, and they shall be turned to blood. 18And the fish that *are* in the river shall die, the river shall stink, and the Egyptians will loathe to drink the water of the river." ' "

19Then the LORD spoke to Moses, "Say to Aaron, 'Take your rod and stretch out your hand over the waters of Egypt, over their streams, over their rivers, over their ponds, and over all their pools of water, that they may become blood. And there shall be blood throughout all the land of Egypt, both in *buckets of* wood and *pitchers of* stone.' " 20And Moses and Aaron did so, just as the LORD commanded. So he lifted up the rod and struck the waters that *were* in the river, in the sight of Pharaoh and in the sight of his servants. And all the waters that *were* in the river were turned to blood. 21The fish that *were* in the river died, the river stank, and the Egyptians could not drink the water of the river. So there was blood throughout all the land of Egypt.

22Then the magicians of Egypt did so with their enchantments; and Pharaoh's heart grew hard, and he did not heed them, as the LORD had said. 23And Pharaoh turned and went into his house. Neither was his heart moved by this. 24So all the Egyptians dug all around the river for water to drink, because they could not drink the water of the river. 25And seven days passed after the LORD had struck the river.

THE MESSAGE

6-7 Moses and Aaron did exactly what GOD
commanded. Moses was eighty and Aaron
eighty-three when they spoke to Pharaoh.

8-9 Then GOD spoke to Moses and Aaron. He
said, "When Pharaoh speaks to you and
says, 'Prove yourselves. Perform a miracle,'
then tell Aaron, 'Take your staff and throw it
down in front of Pharaoh: It will turn into a
snake.' "

10 Moses and Aaron went to Pharaoh and
did what GOD commanded. Aaron threw his
staff down in front of Pharaoh and his ser-
vants, and it turned into a snake.

11-12 Pharaoh called in his wise men and sor-
cerers. The magicians of Egypt did the same
thing by their incantations: each man threw
down his staff and they all turned into
snakes. But then Aaron's staff swallowed
their staffs.

13 Yet Pharaoh was as stubborn as ever—he
wouldn't listen to them, just as GOD had
said.

STRIKE ONE: BLOOD

14-18 GOD said to Moses: "Pharaoh is a stubborn
man. He refuses to release the people. First
thing in the morning, go and meet Pharaoh
as he goes down to the river. At the shore of
the Nile take the staff that turned into a
snake and say to him, 'GOD, the God of the
Hebrews, sent me to you with this message,
"Release my people so that they can wor-
ship me in the wilderness." So far you
haven't listened. This is how you'll know
that I am GOD. I am going to take this staff
that I'm holding and strike this Nile River
water: The water will turn to blood; the fish
in the Nile will die; the Nile will stink; and
the Egyptians won't be able to drink the
Nile water.' "

19 GOD said to Moses, "Tell Aaron, 'Take
your staff and wave it over the waters of
Egypt—over its rivers, its canals, its ponds,
all its bodies of water—so that they turn to
blood.' There'll be blood everywhere in
Egypt—even in the pots and pans."

20-21 Moses and Aaron did exactly as GOD
commanded them. Aaron raised his staff
and hit the water in the Nile with Pharaoh
and his servants watching. All the water in
the Nile turned into blood. The fish in the
Nile died; the Nile stank; and the Egyptians
couldn't drink the Nile water. The blood was
everywhere in Egypt.

22-25 But the magicians of Egypt did the same
thing with their incantations. Still Pharaoh
remained stubborn. He wouldn't listen to
them as GOD had said. He turned on his heel
and went home, never giving it a second
thought. But all the Egyptians had to dig in-
land from the river for water because they
couldn't drink the Nile water.

Seven days went by after GOD had struck
the Nile.

NEW KING JAMES VERSION

THE SECOND PLAGUE: FROGS

8 And the LORD spoke to Moses, "Go to
Pharaoh and say to him, 'Thus says the LORD:
"Let My people go, that they may serve Me. 2 But
if you refuse to let *them* go, behold, I will smite
all your territory with frogs. 3 So the river shall
bring forth frogs abundantly, which shall go up
and come into your house, into your bedroom,
on your bed, into the houses of your servants, on
your people, into your ovens, and into your
kneading bowls. 4 And the frogs shall come up
on you, on your people, and on all your ser-
vants." ' "
5 Then the LORD spoke to Moses, "Say to
Aaron, 'Stretch out your hand with your rod
over the streams, over the rivers, and over the
ponds, and cause frogs to come up on the land
of Egypt.' " 6 So Aaron stretched out his hand
over the waters of Egypt, and the frogs came up
and covered the land of Egypt. 7 And the magi-
cians did so with their enchantments, and
brought up frogs on the land of Egypt.
8 Then Pharaoh called for Moses and Aaron,
and said, "Entreat the LORD that He may take
away the frogs from me and from my people;
and I will let the people go, that they may sacri-
fice to the LORD."
9 And Moses said to Pharaoh, "Accept the
honor of saying when I shall intercede for you,
for your servants, and for your people, to de-
stroy the frogs from you and your houses, *that*
they may remain in the river only."
10 So he said, "Tomorrow." And he said, "*Let
it be* according to your word, that you may
know that *there is* no one like the LORD our God.
11 And the frogs shall depart from you, from your
houses, from your servants, and from your peo-
ple. They shall remain in the river only."
12 Then Moses and Aaron went out from
Pharaoh. And Moses cried out to the LORD con-
cerning the frogs which He had brought against
Pharaoh. 13 So the LORD did according to the word
of Moses. And the frogs died out of the houses,
out of the courtyards, and out of the fields. 14 They
gathered them together in heaps, and the land
stank. 15 But when Pharaoh saw that there was re-
lief, he hardened his heart and did not heed them,
as the LORD had said.

THE THIRD PLAGUE: LICE

16 So the LORD said to Moses, "Say to Aaron,
'Stretch out your rod, and strike the dust of the
land, so that it may become lice throughout all
the land of Egypt.' " 17 And they did so. For
Aaron stretched out his hand with his rod and
struck the dust of the earth, and it became lice
on man and beast. All the dust of the land be-
came lice throughout all the land of Egypt.
18 Now the magicians so worked with their
enchantments to bring forth lice, but they could
not. So there were lice on man and beast. 19 Then
the magicians said to Pharaoh, "This *is* the fin-
ger of God." But Pharaoh's heart grew hard, and
he did not heed them, just as the LORD had said.

THE MESSAGE

STRIKE TWO: FROGS

1-4 8 GOD said to Moses, "Go to Pharaoh and tell him, 'GOD'S Message: Release my people so they can worship me. If you refuse to release them, I'm warning you, I'll hit the whole country with frogs. The Nile will swarm with frogs—they'll come up into your houses, into your bedrooms and into your beds, into your servants' quarters, among the people, into your ovens and pots and pans. They'll be all over you, all over everyone—frogs everywhere, on and in everything!' "

5 GOD said to Moses, "Tell Aaron, 'Wave your staff over the rivers and canals and ponds. Bring up frogs on the land of Egypt.' "

6 Aaron stretched his staff over the waters of Egypt and a mob of frogs came up and covered the country.

7 But again the magicians did the same thing using their incantations—they also produced frogs in Egypt.

8 Pharaoh called in Moses and Aaron and said, "Pray to GOD to rid us of these frogs. I'll release the people so that they can make their sacrifices and worship GOD."

9 Moses said to Pharaoh, "Certainly. Set the time. When do you want the frogs out of here, away from your servants and people and out of your houses? You'll be rid of frogs except for those in the Nile."

10-11 "Make it tomorrow."

Moses said, "Tomorrow it is—so you'll realize that there is no God like our GOD. The frogs will be gone. You and your houses and your servants and your people, free of frogs. The only frogs left will be the ones in the Nile."

12-14 Moses and Aaron left Pharaoh, and Moses prayed to GOD about the frogs he had brought on Pharaoh. GOD responded to Moses' prayer: The frogs died off—houses, courtyards, fields, all free of frogs. They piled the frogs in heaps. The country reeked of dead frogs.

15 But when Pharaoh saw that he had some breathing room, he got stubborn again and wouldn't listen to Moses and Aaron. Just as GOD had said.

STRIKE THREE: GNATS

16 GOD said to Moses, "Tell Aaron, 'Take your staff and strike the dust. The dust will turn into gnats all over Egypt.' "

17 He did it. Aaron grabbed his staff and struck the dust of the Earth; it turned into gnats, gnats all over people and animals. All the dust of the Earth turned into gnats, gnats everywhere in Egypt.

18 The magicians tried to produce gnats with their incantations but this time they couldn't do it. There were gnats everywhere, all over people and animals.

19 The magicians said to Pharaoh, "This is God's doing." But Pharaoh was stubborn and wouldn't listen. Just as GOD had said.

NEW KING JAMES VERSION

THE FOURTH PLAGUE: FLIES

20And the LORD said to Moses, "Rise early in
the morning and stand before Pharaoh as he
comes out to the water. Then say to him, 'Thus
says the LORD: "Let My people go, that they may
serve Me. 21Or else, if you will not let My people
go, behold, I will send swarms *of flies* on you
and your servants, on your people and into your
houses. The houses of the Egyptians shall be full
of swarms *of flies*, and also the ground on which
they *stand*. 22And in that day I will set apart the
land of Goshen, in which My people dwell, that
no swarms *of flies* shall be there, in order that
you may know that I *am* the LORD in the midst
of the land. 23I will make a difference[a] between
My people and your people. Tomorrow this sign
shall be." ' " 24And the LORD did so. Thick
swarms *of flies* came into the house of Pharaoh,
into his servants' houses, and into all the land of
Egypt. The land was corrupted because of the
swarms *of flies*.

25Then Pharaoh called for Moses and Aaron,
and said, "Go, sacrifice to your God in the land."

26And Moses said, "It is not right to do so, for
we would be sacrificing the abomination of the
Egyptians to the LORD our God. If we sacrifice
the abomination of the Egyptians before their
eyes, then will they not stone us? 27We will go
three days' journey into the wilderness and sac-
rifice to the LORD our God as He will command
us."

28So Pharaoh said, "I will let you go, that you
may sacrifice to the LORD your God in the
wilderness; only you shall not go very far away.
Intercede for me."

29Then Moses said, "Indeed I am going out
from you, and I will entreat the LORD, that the
swarms *of flies* may depart tomorrow from
Pharaoh, from his servants, and from his peo-
ple. But let Pharaoh not deal deceitfully any-
more in not letting the people go to sacrifice to
the LORD."

30So Moses went out from Pharaoh and en-
treated the LORD. 31And the LORD did according
to the word of Moses; He removed the swarms
of flies from Pharaoh, from his servants, and
from his people. Not one remained. 32But
Pharaoh hardened his heart at this time also;
neither would he let the people go.

THE FIFTH PLAGUE: LIVESTOCK DISEASED

9 Then the LORD said to Moses, "Go in to
Pharaoh and tell him, 'Thus says the LORD God
of the Hebrews: "Let My people go, that they may
serve Me. 2For if you refuse to let *them* go, and
still hold them, 3behold, the hand of the LORD will
be on your cattle in the field, on the horses, on the
donkeys, on the camels, on the oxen, and on the
sheep—a very severe pestilence. 4And the LORD
will make a difference between the livestock of Is-
rael and the livestock of Egypt. So nothing shall
die of all *that* belongs to the children of Israel." ' "
5Then the LORD appointed a set time, saying, "To-
morrow the LORD will do this thing in the land."

8:23 [a]Literally *set a ransom* (compare Exodus 9:4 and 11:7)

THE MESSAGE

STRIKE FOUR: FLIES

20-23 GOD said to Moses, "Get up early in the
morning and confront Pharaoh as he goes
down to the water. Tell him, 'GOD's Message:
Release my people so they can worship me.
If you don't release my people, I'll release
swarms of flies on you, your servants, your
people, and your homes. The houses of the
Egyptians and even the ground under their
feet will be thick with flies. But when it hap-
pens, I'll set Goshen where my people live
aside as a sanctuary—no flies in Goshen.
That will show you that I am GOD in this
land. I'll make a sharp distinction between
your people and mine. This sign will occur
tomorrow.' "

24 And GOD did just that. Thick swarms of
flies in Pharaoh's palace and the houses of
his servants. All over Egypt, the country ru-
ined by flies.

25 Pharaoh called in Moses and Aaron and
said, "Go ahead. Sacrifice to your God—but
do it here in this country."

26-27 Moses said, "That would not be wise.
What we sacrifice to our GOD would give
great offense to Egyptians. If we openly sac-
rifice what is so deeply offensive to Egyp-
tians, they'll kill us. Let us go three days'
journey into the wilderness and sacrifice to
our GOD, just as he instructed us."

28 Pharaoh said, "All right. I'll release you to
go and sacrifice to your GOD in the wilder-
ness. Only don't go too far. Now pray for
me."

29 Moses said, "As soon as I leave here, I will
pray to GOD that tomorrow the flies will
leave Pharaoh, his servants, and his people.
But don't play games with us and change
your mind about releasing us to sacrifice to
GOD."

30-32 Moses left Pharaoh and prayed to GOD.
GOD did what Moses asked. He got rid of the
flies from Pharaoh and his servants and his
people. There wasn't a fly left. But Pharaoh
became stubborn once again and wouldn't
release the people.

STRIKE FIVE: ANIMALS

1-4 9 GOD said to Moses, "Go to Pharaoh and
tell him, 'GOD, the God of the Hebrews,
says: Release my people so they can wor-
ship me. If you refuse to release them and
continue to hold on to them, I'm giving you
fair warning: GOD will come down hard on
your livestock out in the fields—horses,
donkeys, camels, cattle, sheep—striking
them with a severe disease. GOD will draw a
sharp line between the livestock of Israel
and the livestock of Egypt. Not one animal
that belongs to the Israelites will die.' "

5 Then GOD set the time: "Tomorrow GOD
will do this thing."

NEW KING JAMES VERSION

6So the LORD did this thing on the next day,
and all the livestock of Egypt died; but of the
livestock of the children of Israel, not one died.
7Then Pharaoh sent, and indeed, not even one of
the livestock of the Israelites was dead. But the
heart of Pharaoh became hard, and he did not
let the people go.

THE SIXTH PLAGUE: BOILS

8So the LORD said to Moses and Aaron, "Take
for yourselves handfuls of ashes from a furnace,
and let Moses scatter it toward the heavens in
the sight of Pharaoh. 9And it will become fine
dust in all the land of Egypt, and it will cause
boils that break out in sores on man and beast
throughout all the land of Egypt." 10Then they
took ashes from the furnace and stood before
Pharaoh, and Moses scattered *them* toward
heaven. And *they* caused boils that break out in
sores on man and beast. 11And the magicians
could not stand before Moses because of the
boils, for the boils were on the magicians and on
all the Egyptians. 12But the LORD hardened the
heart of Pharaoh; and he did not heed them, just
as the LORD had spoken to Moses.

THE SEVENTH PLAGUE: HAIL

13Then the LORD said to Moses, "Rise early in
the morning and stand before Pharaoh, and say
to him, 'Thus says the LORD God of the Hebrews:
"Let My people go, that they may serve Me, 14for
at this time I will send all My plagues to your
very heart, and on your servants and on your
people, that you may know that *there is* none
like Me in all the earth. 15Now if I had stretched
out My hand and struck you and your people
with pestilence, then you would have been cut
off from the earth. 16But indeed for this *purpose*
I have raised you up, that I may show My power
in you, and that My name may be declared in all
the earth. 17As yet you exalt yourself against My
people in that you will not let them go. 18Behold,
tomorrow about this time I will cause very
heavy hail to rain down, such as has not been in
Egypt since its founding until now. 19Therefore
send now *and* gather your livestock and all that
you have in the field, for the hail shall come
down on every man and every animal which is
found in the field and is not brought home; and
they shall die." ' "

20He who feared the word of the LORD among
the servants of Pharaoh made his servants and
his livestock flee to the houses. 21But he who did
not regard the word of the LORD left his servants
and his livestock in the field.

22Then the LORD said to Moses, "Stretch out
your hand toward heaven, that there may be hail
in all the land of Egypt—on man, on beast, and
on every herb of the field, throughout the land
of Egypt." 23And Moses stretched out his rod to-
ward heaven; and the LORD sent thunder and
hail, and fire darted to the ground. And the LORD
rained hail on the land of Egypt. 24So there was
hail, and fire mingled with the hail, so very
heavy that there was none like it in all the land
of Egypt since it became a nation. 25And the hail
struck throughout the whole land of Egypt, all
that *was* in the field, both man and beast; and

THE MESSAGE

6-7 And the next day GOD did it. All the livestock of Egypt died, but not one animal of the Israelites died. Pharaoh sent men to find out what had happened and there it was: none of the livestock of the Israelites had died—not one death. But Pharaoh stayed stubborn. He wouldn't release the people.

STRIKE SIX: BOILS

8-11 GOD said to Moses and Aaron, "Take fistfuls of soot from a furnace and have Moses throw it into the air right before Pharaoh's eyes; it will become a film of fine dust all over Egypt and cause sores, an eruption of boils on people and animals throughout Egypt." So they took soot from a furnace, stood in front of Pharaoh, and threw it up into the air. It caused boils to erupt on people and animals. The magicians weren't able to compete with Moses this time because of the boils—they were covered with boils just like everyone else in Egypt.

12 GOD hardened Pharaoh in his stubbornness. He wouldn't listen, just as GOD had said to Moses.

STRIKE SEVEN: HAIL

13-19 GOD said to Moses, "Get up early in the morning and confront Pharaoh. Tell him, 'GOD, the God of the Hebrews, says: Release my people so they can worship me. This time I am going to strike you and your servants and your people with the full force of my power so you'll get it into your head that there's no one like me anywhere in all the Earth. You know that by now I could have struck you and your people with deadly disease and there would be nothing left of you, not a trace. But for one reason only I've kept you on your feet: To make you recognize my power so that my reputation spreads in all the Earth. You are still building yourself up at my people's expense. You are not letting them go. So here's what's going to happen: At this time tomorrow I'm sending a terrific hailstorm—there's never been a storm like this in Egypt from the day of its founding until now. So get your livestock under roof—everything exposed in the open fields, people and animals, will die when the hail comes down.' "

20-21 All of Pharaoh's servants who had respect for GOD's word got their workers and animals under cover as fast as they could, but those who didn't take GOD's word seriously left their workers and animals out in the field.

22 GOD said to Moses: "Stretch your hands to the skies. Signal the hail to fall all over Egypt on people and animals and crops exposed in the fields of Egypt."

23-26 Moses lifted his staff to the skies and GOD sent peals of thunder and hail shot through with lightning strikes. GOD rained hail down on the land of Egypt. The hail came, hail and lightning—a fierce hailstorm. There had been nothing like it in Egypt in its entire history. The hail hit hard all over Egypt. Everything exposed out in the fields, people and

New King James Version

the hail struck every herb of the field and broke every tree of the field. 26Only in the land of Goshen, where the children of Israel *were,* there was no hail.

27And Pharaoh sent and called for Moses and Aaron, and said to them, "I have sinned this time. The LORD *is* righteous, and my people and I *are* wicked. 28Entreat the LORD, that there may be no *more* mighty thundering and hail, for *it is* enough. I will let you go, and you shall stay no longer."

29So Moses said to him, "As soon as I have gone out of the city, I will spread out my hands to the LORD; the thunder will cease, and there will be no more hail, that you may know that the earth *is* the LORD's. 30But as for you and your servants, I know that you will not yet fear the LORD God."

31Now the flax and the barley were struck, for the barley *was* in the head and the flax *was* in bud. 32But the wheat and the spelt were not struck, for they *are* late crops.

33So Moses went out of the city from Pharaoh and spread out his hands to the LORD; then the thunder and the hail ceased, and the rain was not poured on the earth. 34And when Pharaoh saw that the rain, the hail, and the thunder had ceased, he sinned yet more; and he hardened his heart, he and his servants. 35So the heart of Pharaoh was hard; neither would he let the children of Israel go, as the LORD had spoken by Moses.

The Eighth Plague: Locusts

10 Now the LORD said to Moses, "Go in to Pharaoh; for I have hardened his heart and the hearts of his servants, that I may show these signs of Mine before him, 2and that you may tell in the hearing of your son and your son's son the mighty things I have done in Egypt, and My signs which I have done among them, that you may know that I *am* the LORD."

3So Moses and Aaron came in to Pharaoh and said to him, "Thus says the LORD God of the Hebrews: 'How long will you refuse to humble yourself before Me? Let My people go, that they may serve Me. 4Or else, if you refuse to let My people go, behold, tomorrow I will bring locusts into your territory. 5And they shall cover the face of the earth, so that no one will be able to see the earth; and they shall eat the residue of what is left, which remains to you from the hail, and they shall eat every tree which grows up for you out of the field. 6They shall fill your houses, the houses of all your servants, and the houses of all the Egyptians—which neither your fathers nor your fathers' fathers have seen, since the day that they were on the earth to this day.' " And he turned and went out from Pharaoh.

7Then Pharaoh's servants said to him, "How long shall this man be a snare to us? Let the men go, that they may serve the LORD their God. Do you not yet know that Egypt is destroyed?"

8So Moses and Aaron were brought again to Pharaoh, and he said to them, "Go, serve the LORD your God. Who *are* the ones that are going?"

The Message

animals and crops, was smashed. Even the trees in the fields were shattered. Except for Goshen where the Israelites lived; there was no hail in Goshen.

27-28 Pharaoh summoned Moses and Aaron. He said, "I've sinned for sure this time—GOD is in the right and I and my people are in the wrong. Pray to GOD. We've had enough of GOD's thunder and hail. I'll let you go. The sooner you're out of here the better."

29-30 Moses said, "As soon as I'm out of the city, I'll stretch out my arms to GOD. The thunder will stop and the hail end so you'll know that the land is GOD's land. Still, I know that you and your servants have no respect for GOD."

31-32 (The flax and the barley were ruined, for they were just ripening, but the wheat and spelt weren't hurt—they ripen later.)

33 Moses left Pharaoh and the city and stretched out his arms to GOD. The thunder and hail stopped; the storm cleared.

34-35 But when Pharaoh saw that the rain and hail and thunder had stopped, he kept right on sinning, stubborn as ever, both he and his servants. Pharaoh's heart turned rock-hard. He refused to release the Israelites, as GOD had ordered through Moses.

Strike Eight: Locusts

1-2 10 GOD said to Moses: "Go to Pharaoh. I've made him stubborn, him and his servants, so that I can force him to look at these signs and so you'll be able to tell your children and grandchildren how I toyed with the Egyptians, like a cat with a mouse; you'll tell them the stories of the signs that I brought down on them, so that you'll all know that I am GOD."

3-6 Moses and Aaron went to Pharaoh and said to him, "GOD, the God of the Hebrews, says, 'How long are you going to refuse to knuckle under? Release my people so that they can worship me. If you refuse to release my people, watch out; tomorrow I'm bringing locusts into your country. They'll cover every square inch of ground; no one will be able to see the ground. They'll devour everything left over from the hailstorm, even the saplings out in the fields—they'll clear-cut the trees. And they'll invade your houses, filling the houses of your servants, filling every house in Egypt. Nobody will have ever seen anything like this, from the time your ancestors first set foot on this soil until today.' "

Then he turned on his heel and left Pharaoh.

7 Pharaoh's servants said to him, "How long are you going to let this man harass us? Let these people go and worship their GOD. Can't you see that Egypt is on its last legs?"

8 So Moses and Aaron were brought back to Pharaoh. He said to them, "Go ahead then. Go worship your GOD. But just who exactly is going with you?"

New King James Version

9 And Moses said, "We will go with our young and our old; with our sons and our daughters, with our flocks and our herds we will go, for we must hold a feast to the LORD."

10 Then he said to them, "The LORD had better be with you when I let you and your little ones go! Beware, for evil is ahead of you. 11 Not so! Go now, you *who are* men, and serve the LORD, for that is what you desired." And they were driven out from Pharaoh's presence.

12 Then the LORD said to Moses, "Stretch out your hand over the land of Egypt for the locusts, that they may come upon the land of Egypt, and eat every herb of the land—all that the hail has left." 13 So Moses stretched out his rod over the land of Egypt, and the LORD brought an east wind on the land all that day and all *that* night. When it was morning, the east wind brought the locusts. 14 And the locusts went up over all the land of Egypt and rested on all the territory of Egypt. *They were* very severe; previously there had been no such locusts as they, nor shall there be such after them. 15 For they covered the face of the whole earth, so that the land was darkened; and they ate every herb of the land and all the fruit of the trees which the hail had left. So there remained nothing green on the trees or on the plants of the field throughout all the land of Egypt.

16 Then Pharaoh called for Moses and Aaron in haste, and said, "I have sinned against the LORD your God and against you. 17 Now therefore, please forgive my sin only this once, and entreat the LORD your God, that He may take away from me this death only." 18 So he went out from Pharaoh and entreated the LORD. 19 And the LORD turned a very strong west wind, which took the locusts away and blew them into the Red Sea. There remained not one locust in all the territory of Egypt. 20 But the LORD hardened Pharaoh's heart, and he did not let the children of Israel go.

The Ninth Plague: Darkness

21 Then the LORD said to Moses, "Stretch out your hand toward heaven, that there may be darkness over the land of Egypt, darkness *which* may even be felt." 22 So Moses stretched out his hand toward heaven, and there was thick darkness in all the land of Egypt three days. 23 They did not see one another; nor did anyone rise from his place for three days. But all the children of Israel had light in their dwellings.

24 Then Pharaoh called to Moses and said, "Go, serve the LORD; only let your flocks and your herds be kept back. Let your little ones also go with you."

25 But Moses said, "You must also give us sacrifices and burnt offerings, that we may sacrifice to the LORD our God. 26 Our livestock also shall go with us; not a hoof shall be left behind. For we must take some of them to serve the LORD our God, and even we do not know with what we must serve the LORD until we arrive there."

27 But the LORD hardened Pharaoh's heart, and he would not let them go. 28 Then Pharaoh said to him, "Get away from me! Take heed to

The Message

9 Moses said, "We're taking young and old, sons and daughters, flocks and herds—this is our worship-celebration of GOD."

10-11 He said, "I'd sooner send you off with GOD's blessings than let you go with your children. Look, you're up to no good—it's written all over your faces. Nothing doing. Just the men are going—go ahead and worship GOD. That's what you want so badly." And they were thrown out of Pharaoh's presence.

12 GOD said to Moses: "Stretch your hand over Egypt and signal the locusts to cover the land of Egypt, devouring every blade of grass in the country, everything that the hail didn't get."

13 Moses stretched out his staff over the land of Egypt. GOD let loose an east wind. It blew that day and night. By morning the east wind had brought in the locusts.

14-15 The locusts covered the country of Egypt, settling over every square inch of Egypt; the place was thick with locusts. There never was an invasion of locusts like it in the past, and never will be again. The ground was completely covered, black with locusts. They ate everything, every blade of grass, every piece of fruit, anything that the hail didn't get. Nothing left but bare trees and bare fields—not a sign of green in the whole land of Egypt.

16-17 Pharaoh had Moses and Aaron back in no time. He said, "I've sinned against your GOD and against you. Overlook my sin one more time. Pray to your GOD to get me out of this—get death out of here!"

18-19 Moses left Pharaoh and prayed to GOD. GOD reversed the wind—a powerful west wind took the locusts and dumped them into the Red Sea. There wasn't a single locust left in the whole country of Egypt.

20 But GOD made Pharaoh stubborn as ever. He still didn't release the Israelites.

Strike Nine: Darkness

21 GOD said to Moses: "Stretch your hand to the skies. Let darkness descend on the land of Egypt—a darkness so dark you can touch it."

22-23 Moses stretched out his hand to the skies. Thick darkness descended on the land of Egypt for three days. Nobody could see anybody. For three days no one could so much as move. Except for the Israelites: they had light where they were living.

24 Pharaoh called in Moses: "Go and worship GOD. Leave your flocks and herds behind. But go ahead and take your children."

25-26 But Moses said, "You have to let us take our sacrificial animals and offerings with us so we can sacrifice them in worship to our GOD. Our livestock has to go with us with not a hoof left behind; they are part of the worship of our GOD. And we don't know just what will be needed until we get there."

27 But GOD kept Pharaoh stubborn as ever. He wouldn't agree to release them.

28 Pharaoh said to Moses: "Get out of my sight! And watch your step. I don't want to

NEW KING JAMES VERSION

yourself and see my face no more! For in the day
you see my face you shall die!"
29So Moses said, "You have spoken well. I
will never see your face again."

DEATH OF THE FIRSTBORN ANNOUNCED

11 And the LORD said to Moses, "I will bring
one more plague on Pharaoh and on
Egypt. Afterward he will let you go from here.
When he lets *you* go, he will surely drive you out
of here altogether. 2Speak now in the hearing of
the people, and let every man ask from his
neighbor and every woman from her neighbor,
articles of silver and articles of gold." 3And the
LORD gave the people favor in the sight of the
Egyptians. Moreover the man Moses *was* very
great in the land of Egypt, in the sight of
Pharaoh's servants and in the sight of the peo-
ple.
4Then Moses said, "Thus says the LORD:
'About midnight I will go out into the midst of
Egypt; 5and all the firstborn in the land of Egypt
shall die, from the firstborn of Pharaoh who sits
on his throne, even to the firstborn of the female
servant who *is* behind the handmill, and all the
firstborn of the animals. 6Then there shall be a
great cry throughout all the land of Egypt, such
as was not like it *before,* nor shall be like it
again. 7But against none of the children of Israel
shall a dog move its tongue, against man or
beast, that you may know that the LORD does
make a difference between the Egyptians and
Israel.' 8And all these your servants shall come
down to me and bow down to me, saying, 'Get
out, and all the people who follow you!' After
that I will go out." Then he went out from
Pharaoh in great anger.
9But the LORD said to Moses, "Pharaoh will
not heed you, so that My wonders may be mul-
tiplied in the land of Egypt." 10So Moses and
Aaron did all these wonders before Pharaoh;
and the LORD hardened Pharaoh's heart, and he
did not let the children of Israel go out of his
land.

THE PASSOVER INSTITUTED

12 Now the LORD spoke to Moses and Aaron
in the land of Egypt, saying, 2"This month
shall be your beginning of months; it *shall be*
the first month of the year to you. 3Speak to all
the congregation of Israel, saying: 'On the tenth
of this month every man shall take for himself a
lamb, according to the house of *his* father, a
lamb for a household. 4And if the household is
too small for the lamb, let him and his neighbor
next to his house take *it* according to the num-
ber of the persons; according to each man's
need you shall make your count for the lamb.
5Your lamb shall be without blemish, a male of
the first year. You may take *it* from the sheep or
from the goats. 6Now you shall keep it until the
fourteenth day of the same month. Then the
whole assembly of the congregation of Israel
shall kill it at twilight. 7And they shall take *some*

THE MESSAGE

ever see you again. If I lay eyes on you
again, you're dead."
29 Moses said, "Have it your way. You won't
see my face again."

STRIKE TEN: DEATH

1 11 GOD said to Moses: "I'm going to hit
Pharaoh and Egypt one final time, and
then he'll let you go. When he releases you,
that will be the end of Egypt for you; he
won't be able to get rid of you fast enough.
2-3 "So here's what you do. Tell the people to
ask, each man from his neighbor and each
woman from her neighbor, for things made
of silver and gold." GOD saw to it that the
Egyptians liked the people. Also, Moses was
greatly admired by the Egyptians, a re-
spected public figure among both Pharaoh's
servants and the people at large.
4-7 Then Moses confronted Pharaoh: "GOD's
Message: 'At midnight I will go through
Egypt and every firstborn child in Egypt
will die, from the firstborn of Pharaoh, who
sits on his throne, to the firstborn of the
slave girl working at her hand mill. Also the
firstborn of animals. Widespread wailing
will erupt all over the country, lament such
as has never been and never will be again.
But against the Israelites—man, woman, or
animal—there won't be so much as a dog's
bark, so that you'll know that GOD makes a
clear distinction between Egypt and Israel.'
8 "Then all these servants of yours will go
to their knees, begging me to leave, 'Leave!
You and all the people who follow you!' And
I will most certainly leave."
Moses, seething with anger, left Pharaoh.
9 GOD said to Moses, "Pharaoh's not going
to listen to a thing you say so that the signs
of my presence and work are going to mul-
tiply in the land of Egypt."

10 Moses and Aaron had performed all
these signs in Pharaoh's presence, but GOD
turned Pharaoh more stubborn than ever—
yet again he refused to release the Israelites
from his land.

1-10 12 GOD said to Moses and Aaron while
still in Egypt, "This month is to be the
first month of the year for you. Address the
whole community of Israel; tell them that on
the tenth of this month each man is to take
a lamb for his family, one lamb to a house. If
the family is too small for a lamb, then share
it with a close neighbor, depending on the
number of persons involved. Be mindful of
how much each person will eat. Your lamb
must be a healthy male, one year old; you
can select it from either the sheep or the
goats. Keep it penned until the fourteenth
day of this month and then slaughter it—the
entire community of Israel will do this—at
dusk. Then take some of the blood and

New King James Version

of the blood and put *it* on the two doorposts and on the lintel of the houses where they eat it. 8Then they shall eat the flesh on that night; roasted in fire, with unleavened bread *and* with bitter *herbs* they shall eat it. 9Do not eat it raw, nor boiled at all with water, but roasted in fire—its head with its legs and its entrails. 10You shall let none of it remain until morning, and what remains of it until morning you shall burn with fire. 11And thus you shall eat it: *with* a belt on your waist, your sandals on your feet, and your staff in your hand. So you shall eat it in haste. It *is* the LORD's Passover.

12'For I will pass through the land of Egypt on that night, and will strike all the firstborn in the land of Egypt, both man and beast; and against all the gods of Egypt I will execute judgment: I *am* the LORD. 13Now the blood shall be a sign for you on the houses where you *are*. And when I see the blood, I will pass over you; and the plague shall not be on you to destroy *you* when I strike the land of Egypt.

14'So this day shall be to you a memorial; and you shall keep it as a feast to the LORD throughout your generations. You shall keep it as a feast by an everlasting ordinance. 15Seven days you shall eat unleavened bread. On the first day you shall remove leaven from your houses. For whoever eats leavened bread from the first day until the seventh day, that person shall be cut off from Israel. 16On the first day *there shall be* a holy convocation, and on the seventh day there shall be a holy convocation for you. No manner of work shall be done on them; but *that* which everyone must eat—that only may be prepared by you. 17So you shall observe *the Feast of* Unleavened Bread, for on this same day I will have brought your armies out of the land of Egypt. Therefore you shall observe this day throughout your generations as an everlasting ordinance. 18In the first *month*, on the fourteenth day of the month at evening, you shall eat unleavened bread, until the twenty-first day of the month at evening. 19For seven days no leaven shall be found in your houses, since whoever eats what is leavened, that same person shall be cut off from the congregation of Israel, whether *he is* a stranger or a native of the land. 20You shall eat nothing leavened; in all your dwellings you shall eat unleavened bread.' "

21Then Moses called for all the elders of Israel and said to them, "Pick out and take lambs for yourselves according to your families, and kill the Passover *lamb*. 22And you shall take a bunch of hyssop, dip *it* in the blood that *is* in the basin, and strike the lintel and the two doorposts with the blood that *is* in the basin. And none of you shall go out of the door of his house until morning. 23For the LORD will pass through to strike the Egyptians; and when He sees the blood on the lintel and on the two doorposts, the LORD will pass over the door and not allow the destroyer to come into your houses to strike *you*. 24And you shall observe this thing as an ordinance for you and your sons forever. 25It will come to pass when you come to the land which the LORD will give you, just as He promised, that you shall keep this service. 26And it shall be, when your children say to you, 'What do you mean by this service?' 27that

The Message

smear it on the two doorposts and the lintel of the houses in which you will eat it. You are to eat the meat, roasted in the fire, that night, along with bread, made without yeast, and bitter herbs. Don't eat any of it raw or boiled in water; make sure it's roasted—the whole animal, head, legs, and innards. Don't leave any of it until morning; if there are leftovers, burn them in the fire.

11 "And here is how you are to eat it: Be fully dressed with your sandals on and your stick in your hand. Eat in a hurry; it's the Passover to GOD.

12-13 "I will go through the land of Egypt on this night and strike down every firstborn in the land of Egypt, whether human or animal, and bring judgment on all the gods of Egypt. I am GOD. The blood will serve as a sign on the houses where you live. When I see the blood I will pass over you—no disaster will touch you when I strike the land of Egypt.

14-16 "This will be a memorial day for you; you will celebrate it as a festival to GOD down through the generations, a fixed festival celebration to be observed always. You will eat unraised bread (matzoth) for seven days: On the first day get rid of all yeast from your houses—anyone who eats anything with yeast from the first day to the seventh day will be cut off from Israel. The first and the seventh days are set aside as holy; do no work on those days. Only what you have to do for meals; each person can do that.

17-20 "Keep the Festival of Unraised Bread! This marks the exact day I brought you out in force from the land of Egypt. Honor the day down through your generations, a fixed festival to be observed always. In the first month, beginning on the fourteenth day at evening until the twenty-first day at evening, you are to eat unraised bread. For those seven days not a trace of yeast is to be found in your houses. Anyone, whether a visitor or a native of the land, who eats anything raised shall be cut off from the community of Israel. Don't eat anything raised. Only matzoth."

21-23 Moses assembled all the elders of Israel. He said, "Select a lamb for your families and slaughter the Passover lamb. Take a bunch of hyssop and dip it in the bowl of blood and smear it on the lintel and on the two doorposts. No one is to leave the house until morning. GOD will pass through to strike Egypt down. When he sees the blood on the lintel and the two doorposts, GOD will pass over the doorway; he won't let the destroyer enter your house to strike you down with ruin.

24-27 "Keep this word. It's the law for you and your children, forever. When you enter the land which GOD will give you as he promised, keep doing this. And when your children say to you, 'Why are we doing this?'

NEW KING JAMES VERSION

you shall say, 'It *is* the Passover sacrifice of the
LORD, who passed over the houses of the children
of Israel in Egypt when He struck the Egyptians
and delivered our households.' " So the people
bowed their heads and worshiped. 28Then the
children of Israel went away and did *so;* just as
the LORD had commanded Moses and Aaron, so
they did.

THE TENTH PLAGUE: DEATH OF THE FIRSTBORN

29And it came to pass at midnight that the
LORD struck all the firstborn in the land of
Egypt, from the firstborn of Pharaoh who sat on
his throne to the firstborn of the captive who
was in the dungeon, and all the firstborn of live-
stock. 30So Pharaoh rose in the night, he, all his
servants, and all the Egyptians; and there was a
great cry in Egypt, for *there was* not a house
where *there was* not one dead.

THE EXODUS

31Then he called for Moses and Aaron by
night, and said, "Rise, go out from among my
people, both you and the children of Israel. And
go, serve the LORD as you have said. 32Also take
your flocks and your herds, as you have said,
and be gone; and bless me also."

33And the Egyptians urged the people, that
they might send them out of the land in haste.
For they said, "We *shall* all *be* dead." 34So the
people took their dough before it was leavened,
having their kneading bowls bound up in their
clothes on their shoulders. 35Now the children of
Israel had done according to the word of Moses,
and they had asked from the Egyptians articles
of silver, articles of gold, and clothing. 36And the
LORD had given the people favor in the sight of
the Egyptians, so that they granted them *what
they requested.* Thus they plundered the Egyp-
tians.

37Then the children of Israel journeyed from
Rameses to Succoth, about six hundred thou-
sand men on foot, besides children. 38A mixed
multitude went up with them also, and flocks
and herds—a great deal of livestock. 39And they
baked unleavened cakes of the dough which
they had brought out of Egypt; for it was not
leavened, because they were driven out of Egypt
and could not wait, nor had they prepared pro-
visions for themselves.

40Now the sojourn of the children of Israel
who lived in Egypt[a] *was* four hundred and thirty
years. 41And it came to pass at the end of the
four hundred and thirty years—on that very
same day—it came to pass that all the armies of
the LORD went out from the land of Egypt. 42It *is*
a night of solemn observance to the LORD for
bringing them out of the land of Egypt. This *is*
that night of the LORD, a solemn observance for
all the children of Israel throughout their gener-
ations.

PASSOVER REGULATIONS

43And the LORD said to Moses and Aaron,
"This *is* the ordinance of the Passover: No for-

12:40 [a]Samaritan Pentateuch and Septuagint read *Egypt and Canaan.*

THE MESSAGE

tell them: 'It's the Passover-sacrifice to GOD
who passed over the homes of the Israelites
in Egypt when he hit Egypt with death but
rescued us.' "

The people bowed and worshiped.

28 The Israelites then went and did what
GOD had commanded Moses and Aaron.
They did it all.

29 At midnight GOD struck every firstborn in
the land of Egypt, from the firstborn of
Pharaoh, who sits on his throne, right down
to the firstborn of the prisoner locked up in
jail. Also the firstborn of the animals.

30 Pharaoh got up that night, he and all his
servants and everyone else in Egypt—what
wild wailing and lament in Egypt! There
wasn't a house in which someone wasn't
dead.

31-32 Pharaoh called in Moses and Aaron that
very night and said, "Get out of here and be
done with you—you and your Israelites! Go
worship GOD on your own terms. And yes,
take your sheep and cattle as you've in-
sisted, but go. And bless me."

33 The Egyptians couldn't wait to get rid of
them; they pushed them to hurry up, saying,
"We're all as good as dead."

34-36 The people grabbed their bread dough
before it had risen, bundled their bread
bowls in their cloaks and threw them over
their shoulders. The Israelites had already
done what Moses had told them; they had
asked the Egyptians for silver and gold
things and clothing. GOD saw to it that the
Egyptians liked the people and so readily
gave them what they asked for. Oh yes!
They picked those Egyptians clean.

37-39 The Israelites moved on from Rameses to
Succoth, about 600,000 on foot, besides their
dependents. There was also a crowd of
riffraff tagging along, not to mention the
large flocks and herds of livestock. They
baked unraised cakes with the bread dough
they had brought out of Egypt; it hadn't
raised—they'd been rushed out of Egypt and
hadn't time to fix food for the journey.

THE PASSOVER

40-42 The Israelites had lived in Egypt 430 years.
At the end of the 430 years, to the very day,
GOD'S entire army left Egypt. GOD kept
watch all night, watching over the Israelites
as he brought them out of Egypt. Because
GOD kept watch, all Israel for all generations
will honor GOD by keeping watch this
night—a watchnight.

43-47 GOD said to Moses and Aaron, "These are
the rules for the Passover:

No foreigners are to eat it.

NEW KING JAMES VERSION

eigner shall eat it. [44]But every man's servant who is bought for money, when you have circumcised him, then he may eat it. [45]A sojourner and a hired servant shall not eat it. [46]In one house it shall be eaten; you shall not carry any of the flesh outside the house, nor shall you break one of its bones. [47]All the congregation of Israel shall keep it. [48]And when a stranger dwells with you *and wants* to keep the Passover to the LORD, let all his males be circumcised, and then let him come near and keep it; and he shall be as a native of the land. For no uncircumcised person shall eat it. [49]One law shall be for the native-born and for the stranger who dwells among you."

[50]Thus all the children of Israel did; as the LORD commanded Moses and Aaron, so they did. [51]And it came to pass, on that very same day, that the LORD brought the children of Israel out of the land of Egypt according to their armies.

THE FIRSTBORN CONSECRATED

13 Then the LORD spoke to Moses, saying, [2]"Consecrate to Me all the firstborn, whatever opens the womb among the children of Israel, *both* of man and beast; it is Mine."

THE FEAST OF UNLEAVENED BREAD

[3]And Moses said to the people: "Remember this day in which you went out of Egypt, out of the house of bondage; for by strength of hand the LORD brought you out of this *place.* No leavened bread shall be eaten. [4]On this day you are going out, in the month Abib. [5]And it shall be, when the LORD brings you into the land of the Canaanites and the Hittites and the Amorites and the Hivites and the Jebusites, which He swore to your fathers to give you, a land flowing with milk and honey, that you shall keep this service in this month. [6]Seven days you shall eat unleavened bread, and on the seventh day *there shall be* a feast to the LORD. [7]Unleavened bread shall be eaten seven days. And no leavened bread shall be seen among you, nor shall leaven be seen among you in all your quarters. [8]And you shall tell your son in that day, saying, '*This is done* because of what the LORD did for me when I came up from Egypt.' [9]It shall be as a sign to you on your hand and as a memorial between your eyes, that the LORD's law may be in your mouth; for with a strong hand the LORD has brought you out of Egypt. [10]You shall therefore keep this ordinance in its season from year to year.

THE LAW OF THE FIRSTBORN

[11]"And it shall be, when the LORD brings you into the land of the Canaanites, as He swore to you and your fathers, and gives it to you, [12]that you shall set apart to the LORD all that open the womb, that is, every firstborn that comes from an animal which you have; the males *shall be* the LORD's. [13]But every firstborn of a donkey you shall redeem with a lamb; and if you will not redeem *it,* then you shall break its neck.

THE MESSAGE

Any slave, if he's paid for and circumcised, can eat it.

No casual visitor or hired hand can eat it.

Eat it in one house—don't take the meat outside the house.

Don't break any of the bones.

The whole community of Israel is to be included in the meal.

48 "If an immigrant is staying with you and wants to keep the Passover to GOD, every male in his family must be circumcised, then he can participate in the Meal—he will then be treated as a native son. But no uncircumcised person can eat it.

49 "The same law applies both to the native and the immigrant who is staying with you."

50-51 All the Israelites did exactly as GOD commanded Moses and Aaron. That very day GOD brought the Israelites out of the land of Egypt, tribe by tribe.

1-2 13 GOD spoke to Moses, saying, "Consecrate every firstborn to me—the first one to come from the womb among the Israelites, whether person or animal, is mine."

3 Moses said to the people, "Always remember this day. This is the day when you came out of Egypt from a house of slavery. GOD brought you out of here with a powerful hand. Don't eat any raised bread.

4-5 "You are leaving in the spring month of Abib. When GOD brings you into the land of the Canaanite, the Hittite, the Amorite, the Hivite, and the Jebusite, which he promised to your fathers to give you, a land lavish with milk and honey, you are to observe this service during this month:

6 "You are to eat unraised bread for seven days; on the seventh day there is a festival celebration to GOD.

7 "Only unraised bread is to be eaten for seven days. There is not to be a trace of anything fermented—no yeast anywhere.

8 "Tell your child on that day: 'This is because of what GOD did for me when I came out of Egypt.'

9-10 "The day of observance will be like a sign on your hand, a memorial between your eyes, and the teaching of GOD in your mouth. It was with a powerful hand that GOD brought you out of Egypt. Follow these instructions at the set time, year after year after year.

11-13 "When GOD brings you into the land of the Canaanites, as he promised you and your fathers, and turns it over to you, you are to set aside the first birth out of every womb to GOD. Every first birth from your livestock belongs to GOD. You can redeem every first birth of a donkey if you want to by substituting a lamb; if you decide not to redeem it, you must break its neck.

New King James Version

And all the firstborn of man among your sons you shall redeem. 14 So it shall be, when your son asks you in time to come, saying, 'What *is* this?' that you shall say to him, 'By strength of hand the LORD brought us out of Egypt, out of the house of bondage. 15 And it came to pass, when Pharaoh was stubborn about letting us go, that the LORD killed all the firstborn in the land of Egypt, both the firstborn of man and the firstborn of beast. Therefore I sacrifice to the LORD all males that open the womb, but all the firstborn of my sons I redeem.' 16 It shall be as a sign on your hand and as frontlets between your eyes, for by strength of hand the LORD brought us out of Egypt."

The Wilderness Way

17 Then it came to pass, when Pharaoh had let the people go, that God did not lead them *by* way of the land of the Philistines, although that *was* near; for God said, "Lest perhaps the people change their minds when they see war, and return to Egypt." 18 So God led the people around *by* way of the wilderness of the Red Sea. And the children of Israel went up in orderly ranks out of the land of Egypt.

19 And Moses took the bones of Joseph with him, for he had placed the children of Israel under solemn oath, saying, "God will surely visit you, and you shall carry up my bones from here with you."[a]

20 So they took their journey from Succoth and camped in Etham at the edge of the wilderness. 21 And the LORD went before them by day in a pillar of cloud to lead the way, and by night in a pillar of fire to give them light, so as to go by day and night. 22 He did not take away the pillar of cloud by day or the pillar of fire by night *from* before the people.

The Red Sea Crossing

14 Now the LORD spoke to Moses, saying: 2 "Speak to the children of Israel, that they turn and camp before Pi Hahiroth, between Migdol and the sea, opposite Baal Zephon; you shall camp before it by the sea. 3 For Pharaoh will say of the children of Israel, 'They *are* bewildered by the land; the wilderness has closed them in.' 4 Then I will harden Pharaoh's heart, so that he will pursue them; and I will gain honor over Pharaoh and over all his army, that the Egyptians may know that I *am* the LORD." And they did so.

5 Now it was told the king of Egypt that the people had fled, and the heart of Pharaoh and his servants was turned against the people; and they said, "Why have we done this, that we have let Israel go from serving us?" 6 So he made ready his chariot and took his people with him. 7 Also, he took six hundred choice chariots, and all the chariots of Egypt with captains over every one of them. 8 And the LORD hardened the heart of Pharaoh king of Egypt, and he pursued the children of Israel; and the children of Israel went out with boldness. 9 So the Egyptians pur-

13:19 [a]Genesis 50:25

The Message

13-16 "Redeem every firstborn child among
your sons. When the time comes and your
son asks you, 'What does this mean?' you
tell him, 'GOD brought us out of Egypt, out of
a house of slavery, with a powerful hand.
When Pharaoh stubbornly refused to let us
go, GOD killed every firstborn in Egypt, the
firstborn of both humans and animals.
That's why I make a sacrifice for every first
male birth from the womb to GOD and re-
deem every firstborn son.' The observance
functions like a sign on your hands or a
symbol on the middle of your forehead: GOD
brought us out of Egypt with a powerful
hand."

17 It so happened that after Pharaoh re-
leased the people, God didn't lead them by
the road through the land of the Philistines,
which was the shortest route, for God
thought, "If the people encounter war,
they'll change their minds and go back to
Egypt."

18 So God led the people on the wilderness
road, looping around to the Red Sea. The Is-
raelites left Egypt in military formation.

19 Moses took the bones of Joseph with him,
for Joseph had made the Israelites solemnly
swear to do it, saying, "God will surely hold
you accountable, so make sure you bring my
bones from here with you."

20-22 They moved on from Succoth and then
camped at Etham at the edge of the wilder-
ness. GOD went ahead of them in a Pillar of
Cloud during the day to guide them on the
way, and at night in a Pillar of Fire to give
them light; thus they could travel both day
and night. The Pillar of Cloud by day and
the Pillar of Fire by night never left the peo-
ple.

The Story and Song of Salvation

1-2 14 GOD spoke to Moses: "Tell the Is-
raelites to turn around and make camp
at Pi Hahiroth, between Migdol and the sea.
Camp on the shore of the sea opposite Baal
Zephon.

3-4 "Pharaoh will think, 'The Israelites are
lost; they're confused. The wilderness has
closed in on them.' Then I'll make Pharaoh's
heart stubborn again and he'll chase after
them. And I'll use Pharaoh and his army to
put my Glory on display. Then the Egyptians
will realize that I am GOD."

And that's what happened.

5-7 When the king of Egypt was told that the
people were gone, he and his servants
changed their minds. They said, "What have
we done, letting Israel, our slave labor, go
free?" So he had his chariots harnessed up
and got his army together. He took six hun-
dred of his best chariots, with the rest of the
Egyptian chariots and their drivers coming
along.

8-9 GOD made Pharaoh king of Egypt stub-
born, determined to chase the Israelites as
they walked out on him without even look-
ing back. The Egyptians gave chase and

NEW KING JAMES VERSION

sued them, all the horses *and* chariots of
Pharaoh, his horsemen and his army, and over-
took them camping by the sea beside Pi Hahi-
roth, before Baal Zephon.
10And when Pharaoh drew near, the children
of Israel lifted their eyes, and behold, the Egyp-
tians marched after them. So they were very
afraid, and the children of Israel cried out to the
LORD. 11Then they said to Moses, "Because *there*
were no graves in Egypt, have you taken us
away to die in the wilderness? Why have you so
dealt with us, to bring us up out of Egypt? 12*Is*
this not the word that we told you in Egypt, say-
ing, 'Let us alone that we may serve the Egyp-
tians'? For *it would have been* better for us to
serve the Egyptians than that we should die in
the wilderness."
13And Moses said to the people, "Do not be
afraid. Stand still, and see the salvation of the
LORD, which He will accomplish for you today.
For the Egyptians whom you see today, you
shall see again no more forever. 14The LORD will
fight for you, and you shall hold your peace."
15And the LORD said to Moses, "Why do you
cry to Me? Tell the children of Israel to go for-
ward. 16But lift up your rod, and stretch out your
hand over the sea and divide it. And the children
of Israel shall go on dry *ground* through the
midst of the sea. 17And I indeed will harden the
hearts of the Egyptians, and they shall follow
them. So I will gain honor over Pharaoh and
over all his army, his chariots, and his horse-
men. 18Then the Egyptians shall know that I *am*
the LORD, when I have gained honor for Myself
over Pharaoh, his chariots, and his horsemen."
19And the Angel of God, who went before the
camp of Israel, moved and went behind them;
and the pillar of cloud went from before them
and stood behind them. 20So it came between
the camp of the Egyptians and the camp of Is-
rael. Thus it was a cloud and darkness *to the*
one, and it gave light by night *to the other*, so
that the one did not come near the other all that
night.
21Then Moses stretched out his hand over the
sea; and the LORD caused the sea to go *back* by
a strong east wind all that night, and made the
sea into dry *land*, and the waters were divided.
22So the children of Israel went into the midst of
the sea on the dry *ground*, and the waters *were*
a wall to them on their right hand and on their
left. 23And the Egyptians pursued and went after
them into the midst of the sea, all Pharaoh's
horses, his chariots, and his horsemen.
24Now it came to pass, in the morning watch,
that the LORD looked down upon the army of the
Egyptians through the pillar of fire and cloud,
and He troubled the army of the Egyptians.
25And He took off[a] their chariot wheels, so that
they drove them with difficulty; and the Egyp-
tians said, "Let us flee from the face of Israel, for
the LORD fights for them against the Egyptians."
26Then the LORD said to Moses, "Stretch out
your hand over the sea, that the waters may

14:25 [a]Samaritan Pentateuch, Septuagint, and Syriac read *bound*.

THE MESSAGE

caught up with them where they had made
camp by the sea—all Pharaoh's horse-
drawn chariots and their riders, all his foot
soldiers there at Pi Hahiroth opposite Baal
Zephon.
10-12 As Pharaoh approached, the Israelites
looked up and saw them—Egyptians! Com-
ing at them!
They were totally afraid. They cried out
in terror to GOD. They told Moses, "Weren't
the cemeteries large enough in Egypt so
that you had to take us out here in the
wilderness to die? What have you done to
us, taking us out of Egypt? Back in Egypt
didn't we tell you this would happen? Didn't
we tell you, 'Leave us alone here in Egypt—
we're better off as slaves in Egypt than as
corpses in the wilderness.' "
13 Moses spoke to the people: "Don't be
afraid. Stand firm and watch GOD do his
work of salvation for you today. Take a good
look at the Egyptians today for you're never
going to see them again.

14 GOD will fight the battle for you.
And you? You keep your mouths shut!"

15-16 GOD said to Moses: "Why cry out to me?
Speak to the Israelites. Order them to get
moving. Hold your staff high and stretch
your hand out over the sea: Split the sea!
The Israelites will walk through the sea on
dry ground.
17-18 "Meanwhile I'll make sure the Egyptians
keep up their stubborn chase—I'll use
Pharaoh and his entire army, his chariots
and horsemen, to put my Glory on display
so that the Egyptians will realize that I am
GOD."
19-20 The angel of God that had been leading
the camp of Israel now shifted and got be-
hind them. And the Pillar of Cloud that had
been in front also shifted to the rear. The
Cloud was now between the camp of Egypt
and the camp of Israel. The Cloud en-
shrouded one camp in darkness and flooded
the other with light. The two camps didn't
come near each other all night.
21 Then Moses stretched out his hand over
the sea and GOD, with a terrific east wind all
night long, made the sea go back. He made
the sea dry ground. The seawaters split.
22-25 The Israelites walked through the sea on
dry ground with the waters a wall to the
right and to the left. The Egyptians came af-
ter them in full pursuit, every horse and
chariot and driver of Pharaoh racing into
the middle of the sea. It was now the morn-
ing watch. GOD looked down from the Pillar
of Fire and Cloud on the Egyptian army and
threw them into a panic. He clogged the
wheels of their chariots; they were stuck in
the mud.
The Egyptians said, "Run from Israel!
GOD is fighting on their side and against
Egypt!"
26 GOD said to Moses, "Stretch out your
hand over the sea and the waters will come

NEW KING JAMES VERSION

come back upon the Egyptians, on their chari-
ots, and on their horsemen." 27And Moses
stretched out his hand over the sea; and when
the morning appeared, the sea returned to its
full depth, while the Egyptians were fleeing into
it. So the LORD overthrew the Egyptians in the
midst of the sea. 28Then the waters returned and
covered the chariots, the horsemen, *and* all the
army of Pharaoh that came into the sea after
them. Not so much as one of them remained.
29But the children of Israel had walked on dry
land in the midst of the sea, and the waters *were*
a wall to them on their right hand and on their
left.

30So the LORD saved Israel that day out of the
hand of the Egyptians, and Israel saw the Egyp-
tians dead on the seashore. 31Thus Israel saw
the great work which the LORD had done in
Egypt; so the people feared the LORD, and be-
lieved the LORD and His servant Moses.

THE SONG OF MOSES

15 Then Moses and the children of Israel sang this song to the LORD, and spoke, saying:

"I will sing to the LORD,
For He has triumphed gloriously!
The horse and its rider
He has thrown into the sea!
2The LORD *is* my strength and song,
And He has become my salvation;
He *is* my God, and I will praise Him;
My father's God, and I will exalt Him.
3The LORD *is* a man of war;
The LORD *is* His name.
4Pharaoh's chariots and his army He has cast into the sea;
His chosen captains also are drowned in the Red Sea.
5The depths have covered them;
They sank to the bottom like a stone.

6"Your right hand, O LORD, has become glorious in power;
Your right hand, O LORD, has dashed the enemy in pieces.
7And in the greatness of Your excellence
You have overthrown those who rose against You;
You sent forth Your wrath;
It consumed them like stubble.
8And with the blast of Your nostrils
The waters were gathered together;
The floods stood upright like a heap;
The depths congealed in the heart of the sea.
9The enemy said, 'I will pursue,
I will overtake,
I will divide the spoil;
My desire shall be satisfied on them.
I will draw my sword,
My hand shall destroy them.'
10You blew with Your wind,
The sea covered them;
They sank like lead in the mighty waters.

THE MESSAGE

back over the Egyptians, over their chariots, over their horsemen."

27-28 Moses stretched his hand out over the sea: As the day broke and the Egyptians were running, the sea returned to its place as before. GOD dumped the Egyptians in the middle of the sea. The waters returned, drowning the chariots and riders of Pharaoh's army that had chased after Israel into the sea. Not one of them survived.

29-31 But the Israelites walked right through the middle of the sea on dry ground, the waters forming a wall to the right and to the left. GOD delivered Israel that day from the oppression of the Egyptians. And Israel looked at the Egyptian dead, washed up on the shore of the sea, and realized the tremendous power that GOD brought against the Egyptians. The people were in reverent awe before GOD and trusted in GOD and his servant Moses.

1-8 15 Then Moses and the Israelites sang this song to GOD, giving voice together,

I'm singing my heart out to GOD—what a victory!
He pitched horse and rider into the sea.
GOD is my strength, GOD is my song,
and, yes! GOD is my salvation.
This is the kind of God I have
and I'm telling the world!
This is the God of my father—
I'm spreading the news far and wide!
GOD is a fighter,
pure GOD, through and through.
Pharaoh's chariots and army
he dumped in the sea,
The elite of his officers
he drowned in the Red Sea.
Wild ocean waters poured over them;
they sank like a rock in the deep blue sea.
Your strong right hand, GOD, shimmers with power;
your strong right hand shatters the enemy.
In your mighty majesty
you smash your upstart enemies,
You let loose your hot anger
and burn them to a crisp.
At a blast from your nostrils
the waters piled up;
Tumbling streams dammed up,
wild oceans curdled into a swamp.

9 The enemy spoke,
"I'll pursue, I'll hunt them down,
I'll divide up the plunder,
I'll glut myself on them;
I'll pull out my sword,
my fist will send them reeling."

10-11 You blew with all your might
and the sea covered them.
They sank like a lead weight
in the majestic waters.

NEW KING JAMES VERSION

11 “Who *is* like You, O LORD, among the gods?
Who *is* like You, glorious in holiness,
Fearful in praises, doing wonders?
12 You stretched out Your right hand;
The earth swallowed them.
13 You in Your mercy have led forth
The people whom You have redeemed;
You have guided *them* in Your strength
To Your holy habitation.
14 “The people will hear *and* be afraid;
Sorrow will take hold of the inhabitants of
Philistia.
15 Then the chiefs of Edom will be dismayed;
The mighty men of Moab,
Trembling will take hold of them;
All the inhabitants of Canaan will melt
away.
16 Fear and dread will fall on them;
By the greatness of Your arm
They will be *as* still as a stone,
Till Your people pass over, O LORD,
Till the people pass over
Whom You have purchased.
17 You will bring them in and plant them
In the mountain of Your inheritance,
In the place, O LORD, *which* You have made
For Your own dwelling,
The sanctuary, O Lord, *which* Your hands
have established.

18 “The LORD shall reign forever and ever.”

19 For the horses of Pharaoh went with his
chariots and his horsemen into the sea, and the
LORD brought back the waters of the sea upon
them. But the children of Israel went on dry *land*
in the midst of the sea.

THE SONG OF MIRIAM

20 Then Miriam the prophetess, the sister of
Aaron, took the timbrel in her hand; and all the
women went out after her with timbrels and
with dances. 21 And Miriam answered them:

“Sing to the LORD,
For He has triumphed gloriously!
The horse and its rider
He has thrown into the sea!”

BITTER WATERS MADE SWEET

22 So Moses brought Israel from the Red Sea;
then they went out into the Wilderness of Shur.
And they went three days in the wilderness and
found no water. 23 Now when they came to
Marah, they could not drink the waters of
Marah, for they *were* bitter. Therefore the name
of it was called Marah.[a] 24 And the people com-
plained against Moses, saying, “What shall we
drink?” 25 So he cried out to the LORD, and the
LORD showed him a tree. When he cast *it* into
the waters, the waters were made sweet.

There He made a statute and an ordinance
for them, and there He tested them,

15:23 [a]Literally *Bitter*

THE MESSAGE

Who compares with you
among gods, O GOD?
Who compares with you in power,
in holy majesty,
In awesome praises,
wonder-working God?

12-13 You stretched out your right hand
and the Earth swallowed them up.
But the people you redeemed,
you led in merciful love;
You guided them under your protection
to your holy pasture.

14-18 When people heard, they were scared;
Philistines writhed and trembled;
Yes, even the head men in Edom were
shaken,
and the big bosses in Moab.
Everybody in Canaan
panicked and fell faint.
Dread and terror
sent them reeling.
Before your brandished right arm
they were struck dumb like a stone,
Until your people crossed over and
entered, O GOD,
until the people you made crossed
over and entered.
You brought them and planted them
on the mountain of your heritage,
The place where you live,
the place you made,
Your sanctuary, Master,
that you established with your own
hands.
Let GOD rule
forever, for eternity!

19 Yes, Pharaoh’s horses and chariots and
riders went into the sea and GOD turned the
waters back on them; but the Israelites
walked on dry land right through the middle
of the sea.

20-21 Miriam the prophetess, Aaron’s sister, took
a tambourine, and all the women followed
her with tambourines, dancing. Miriam led
them in singing,

Sing to GOD—
what a victory!
He pitched horse and rider
into the sea!

TRAVELING THROUGH THE WILDERNESS

22-24 Moses led Israel from the Red Sea on to the
Wilderness of Shur. They traveled for three
days through the wilderness without finding
any water. They got to Marah, but they
couldn’t drink the water at Marah; it was
bitter. That’s why they called the place
Marah (Bitter). And the people complained
to Moses, “So what are we supposed to
drink?”

25 So Moses cried out in prayer to GOD. GOD
pointed him to a stick of wood. Moses threw
it into the water and the water turned sweet.

NEW KING JAMES VERSION

26and said, "If you diligently heed the voice of
the LORD your God and do what is right in His
sight, give ear to His commandments and keep
all His statutes, I will put none of the diseases on
you which I have brought on the Egyptians. For
I *am* the LORD who heals you."
27Then they came to Elim, where there *were*
twelve wells of water and seventy palm trees; so
they camped there by the waters.

BREAD FROM HEAVEN

16And they journeyed from Elim, and all the
congregation of the children of Israel
came to the Wilderness of Sin, which is between
Elim and Sinai, on the fifteenth day of the sec-
ond month after they departed from the land of
Egypt. 2Then the whole congregation of the chil-
dren of Israel complained against Moses and
Aaron in the wilderness. 3And the children of Is-
rael said to them, "Oh, that we had died by the
hand of the LORD in the land of Egypt, when we
sat by the pots of meat *and* when we ate bread
to the full! For you have brought us out into this
wilderness to kill this whole assembly with
hunger."
4Then the LORD said to Moses, "Behold, I will
rain bread from heaven for you. And the people
shall go out and gather a certain quota every day,
that I may test them, whether they will walk in
My law or not. 5And it shall be on the sixth day
that they shall prepare what they bring in, and it
shall be twice as much as they gather daily."
6Then Moses and Aaron said to all the chil-
dren of Israel, "At evening you shall know that
the LORD has brought you out of the land of
Egypt. 7And in the morning you shall see the
glory of the LORD; for He hears your complaints
against the LORD. But what *are* we, that you
complain against us?" 8Also Moses said, "*This
shall be seen* when the LORD gives you meat to
eat in the evening, and in the morning bread to
the full; for the LORD hears your complaints
which you make against Him. And what *are* we?
Your complaints *are* not against us but against
the LORD."
9Then Moses spoke to Aaron, "Say to all the
congregation of the children of Israel, 'Come
near before the LORD, for He has heard your
complaints.' " 10Now it came to pass, as Aaron
spoke to the whole congregation of the children
of Israel, that they looked toward the wilder-
ness, and behold, the glory of the LORD ap-
peared in the cloud.
11And the LORD spoke to Moses, saying, 12"I
have heard the complaints of the children of Is-
rael. Speak to them, saying, 'At twilight you
shall eat meat, and in the morning you shall be
filled with bread. And you shall know that I *am*
the LORD your God.' "
13So it was that quails came up at evening and
covered the camp, and in the morning the dew
lay all around the camp. 14And when the layer of
dew lifted, there, on the surface of the wilderness,
was a small round substance, *as* fine as frost on
the ground. 15So when the children of Israel saw
it, they said to one another, "What is it?" For they
did not know what it *was*.

THE MESSAGE

26 That's the place where GOD set up rules
and procedures; that's where he started test-
ing them.
GOD said, "If you listen, listen obediently
to how GOD tells you to live in his presence,
obeying his commandments and keeping all
his laws, then I won't strike you with all the
diseases that I inflicted on the Egyptians; I
am GOD your healer."
27 They came to Elim where there were
twelve springs of water and seventy palm
trees. They set up camp there by the water.

1-3 16On the fifteenth day of the second
month after they had left Egypt, the
whole company of Israel moved on from
Elim to the Wilderness of Sin which is be-
tween Elim and Sinai. The whole company
of Israel complained against Moses and
Aaron there in the wilderness. The Israelites
said, "Why didn't GOD let us die in comfort
in Egypt where we had lamb stew and all
the bread we could eat? You've brought us
out into this wilderness to starve us to
death, the whole company of Israel!"
4-5 GOD said to Moses, "I'm going to rain
bread down from the skies for you. The peo-
ple will go out and gather each day's ration.
I'm going to test them to see if they'll live ac-
cording to my Teaching or not. On the sixth
day, when they prepare what they have
gathered, it will turn out to be twice as much
as their daily ration."
6-7 Moses and Aaron told the People of Is-
rael, "This evening you will know that it is
GOD who brought you out of Egypt; and in
the morning you will see the Glory of GOD.
Yes, he's listened to your complaints against
him. You haven't been complaining against
us, you know, but against GOD."
8 Moses said, "Since it will be GOD who
gives you meat for your meal in the evening
and your fill of bread in the morning, it's
GOD who will have listened to your com-
plaints against him. Who are we in all this?
You haven't been complaining to us—you've
been complaining to GOD!"
9 Moses instructed Aaron: "Tell the whole
company of Israel: 'Come near to GOD. He's
heard your complaints.' "
10 When Aaron gave out the instructions to
the whole company of Israel, they turned to
face the wilderness. And there it was: the
Glory of GOD visible in the Cloud.
11-12 GOD spoke to Moses, "I've listened to the
complaints of the Israelites. Now tell them:
'At dusk you will eat meat and at dawn
you'll eat your fill of bread; and you'll real-
ize that I am GOD, *your* God.' "
13-15 That evening quail flew in and covered
the camp and in the morning there was a
layer of dew all over the camp. When the
layer of dew had lifted, there on the wilder-
ness ground was a fine flaky something, fine
as frost on the ground. The Israelites took
one look and said to one another, *man-hu*
(What is it?). They had no idea what it was.
15-16 So Moses told them, "It's the bread GOD
has given you to eat. And these are GOD's in-

NEW KING JAMES VERSION

And Moses said to them, "This *is* the bread
which the LORD has given you to eat. 16This is
the thing which the LORD has commanded: 'Let
every man gather it according to each one's
need, one omer for each person, *according to
the* number of persons; let every man take for
those who *are* in his tent.' "
17Then the children of Israel did so and gath-
ered, some more, some less. 18So when they
measured *it* by omers, he who gathered much
had nothing left over, and he who gathered little
had no lack. Every man had gathered according
to each one's need. 19And Moses said, "Let no
one leave any of it till morning." 20Notwithstand-
ing they did not heed Moses. But some of them
left part of it until morning, and it bred worms
and stank. And Moses was angry with them.
21So they gathered it every morning, every man
according to his need. And when the sun be-
came hot, it melted.
22And so it was, on the sixth day, *that* they
gathered twice as much bread, two omers for
each one. And all the rulers of the congregation
came and told Moses. 23Then he said to them,
"This *is what* the LORD has said: 'Tomorrow *is* a
Sabbath rest, a holy Sabbath to the LORD. Bake
what you will bake *today,* and boil what you will
boil; and lay up for yourselves all that remains,
to be kept until morning.' " 24So they laid it up
till morning, as Moses commanded; and it did
not stink, nor were there any worms in it. 25Then
Moses said, "Eat that today, for today *is* a Sab-
bath to the LORD; today you will not find it in the
field. 26Six days you shall gather it, but on the
seventh day, the Sabbath, there will be none."
27Now it happened *that some* of the people
went out on the seventh day to gather, but they
found none. 28And the LORD said to Moses,
"How long do you refuse to keep My command-
ments and My laws? 29See! For the LORD has
given you the Sabbath; therefore He gives you
on the sixth day bread for two days. Let every
man remain in his place; let no man go out of his
place on the seventh day." 30So the people rested
on the seventh day.
31And the house of Israel called its name
Manna.[a] And it *was* like white coriander seed,
and the taste of it *was* like wafers *made* with
honey.
32Then Moses said, "This *is* the thing which
the LORD has commanded: 'Fill an omer with it,
to be kept for your generations, that they may
see the bread with which I fed you in the wilder-
ness, when I brought you out of the land of
Egypt.' " 33And Moses said to Aaron, "Take a pot
and put an omer of manna in it, and lay it up be-
fore the LORD, to be kept for your generations."
34As the LORD commanded Moses, so Aaron laid
it up before the Testimony, to be kept. 35And the
children of Israel ate manna forty years, until
they came to an inhabited land; they ate manna
until they came to the border of the land of
Canaan. 36Now an omer *is* one-tenth of an
ephah.

16:31 [a]Literally *What?* (compare Exodus 16:15)

THE MESSAGE

structions: 'Gather enough for each person, about two quarts per person; gather enough for everyone in your tent.' "

17-18 The People of Israel went to work and started gathering, some more, some less, but when they measured out what they had gathered, those who gathered more had no extra and those who gathered less weren't short—each person had gathered as much as was needed.

19 Moses said to them, "Don't leave any of it until morning."

20 But they didn't listen to Moses. A few of the men kept back some of it until morning. It got wormy and smelled bad. And Moses lost his temper with them.

21-22 They gathered it every morning, each person according to need. Then the sun heated up and it melted. On the sixth day they gathered twice as much bread, about four quarts per person.

Then the leaders of the company came to Moses and reported.

23-24 Moses said, "This is what GOD was talking about: Tomorrow is a day of rest, a holy Sabbath to GOD. Whatever you plan to bake, bake today; and whatever you plan to boil, boil today. Then set aside the leftovers until morning." They set aside what was left until morning, as Moses had commanded. It didn't smell bad and there were no worms in it.

25-26 Moses said, "Now eat it; this is the day, a Sabbath for GOD. You won't find any of it on the ground today. Gather it every day for six days, but the seventh day is Sabbath; there won't be any of it on the ground."

27 On the seventh day, some of the people went out to gather anyway but they didn't find anything.

28-29 GOD said to Moses, "How long are you going to disobey my commands and not follow my instructions? Don't you see that GOD has given you the Sabbath? So on the sixth day he gives you bread for *two* days. So, each of you, stay home. Don't leave home on the seventh day."

30 So the people quit working on the seventh day.

31 The Israelites named it manna (What is it?). It looked like coriander seed, whitish. And it tasted like a cracker with honey.

32 Moses said, "This is GOD's command: 'Keep a two-quart jar of it, an omer, for future generations so they can see the bread that I fed you in the wilderness after I brought you out of Egypt.' "

33 Moses told Aaron, "Take a jar and fill it with two quarts of manna. Place it before GOD, keeping it safe for future generations."

34 Aaron did what GOD commanded Moses. He set it aside before The Testimony to preserve it.

35 The Israelites ate the manna for forty years until they arrived at the land where they would settle down. They ate manna until they reached the border into Canaan.

36 According to ancient measurements, an omer is one-tenth of an ephah.

NEW KING JAMES VERSION

WATER FROM THE ROCK

17Then all the congregation of the children
of Israel set out on their journey from the
Wilderness of Sin, according to the command-
ment of the LORD, and camped in Rephidim; but
there was no water for the people to drink.
2Therefore the people contended with Moses,
and said, "Give us water, that we may drink."
So Moses said to them, "Why do you contend
with me? Why do you tempt the LORD?"
3And the people thirsted there for water, and
the people complained against Moses, and said,
"Why *is* it you have brought us up out of Egypt,
to kill us and our children and our livestock
with thirst?"
4So Moses cried out to the LORD, saying,
"What shall I do with this people? They are al-
most ready to stone me!"
5And the LORD said to Moses, "Go on before
the people, and take with you some of the elders
of Israel. Also take in your hand your rod with
which you struck the river, and go. 6Behold, I
will stand before you there on the rock in
Horeb; and you shall strike the rock, and water
will come out of it, that the people may drink."
And Moses did so in the sight of the elders of
Israel. 7So he called the name of the place Mas-
sah[a] and Meribah,[b] because of the contention of
the children of Israel, and because they tempted
the LORD, saying, "Is the LORD among us or not?"

VICTORY OVER THE AMALEKITES

8Now Amalek came and fought with Israel in
Rephidim. 9And Moses said to Joshua, "Choose
us some men and go out, fight with Amalek. To-
morrow I will stand on the top of the hill with
the rod of God in my hand." 10So Joshua did as
Moses said to him, and fought with Amalek.
And Moses, Aaron, and Hur went up to the top
of the hill. 11And so it was, when Moses held up
his hand, that Israel prevailed; and when he let
down his hand, Amalek prevailed. 12But Moses'
hands *became* heavy; so they took a stone and
put *it* under him, and he sat on it. And Aaron
and Hur supported his hands, one on one side,
and the other on the other side; and his hands
were steady until the going down of the sun.
13So Joshua defeated Amalek and his people
with the edge of the sword.
14Then the LORD said to Moses, "Write this
for a memorial in the book and recount *it* in the
hearing of Joshua, that I will utterly blot out the
remembrance of Amalek from under heaven."
15And Moses built an altar and called its name,
The-LORD-Is-My-Banner;[a] 16for he said, "Be-
cause the LORD has sworn: the LORD *will have*
war with Amalek from generation to genera-
tion."

JETHRO'S ADVICE

18And Jethro, the priest of Midian, Moses'
father-in-law, heard of all that God had
done for Moses and for Israel His people—that
the LORD had brought Israel out of Egypt. 2Then

17:7 [a]Literally *Tempted* [b]Literally *Contention* **17:15** [a]Hebrew *YHWH Nissi*

THE MESSAGE

1-2 17Directed by GOD, the whole company of Israel moved on by stages from the Wilderness of Sin. They set camp at Rephidim. And there wasn't a drop of water for the people to drink. The people took Moses to task: "Give us water to drink." But Moses said, "Why pester me? Why are you testing GOD?"

3 But the people were thirsty for water there. They complained to Moses, "Why did you take us from Egypt and drag us out here with our children and animals to die of thirst?"

4 Moses cried out in prayer to GOD, "What can I do with these people? Any minute now they'll kill me!"

5-6 GOD said to Moses, "Go on out ahead of the people, taking with you some of the elders of Israel. Take the staff you used to strike the Nile. And go. I'm going to be present before you there on the rock at Horeb. You are to strike the rock. Water will gush out of it and the people will drink."

6-7 Moses did what he said, with the elders of Israel right there watching. He named the place Massah (Testing-Place) and Meribah (Quarreling) because of the quarreling of the Israelites and because of their testing of GOD when they said, "Is GOD here with us, or not?"

8-9 Amalek came and fought Israel at Rephidim. Moses ordered Joshua: "Select some men for us and go out and fight Amalek. Tomorrow I will take my stand on top of the hill holding God's staff."

10-13 Joshua did what Moses ordered in order to fight Amalek. And Moses, Aaron, and Hur went to the top of the hill. It turned out that whenever Moses raised his hands, Israel was winning, but whenever he lowered his hands, Amalek was winning. But Moses' hands got tired. So they got a stone and set it under him. He sat on it and Aaron and Hur held up his hands, one on each side. So his hands remained steady until the sun went down. Joshua defeated Amalek and its army in battle.

14 GOD said to Moses, "Write this up as a reminder to Joshua, to keep it before him, because I will most certainly wipe the very memory of Amalek off the face of the Earth."

15-16 Moses built an altar and named it "GOD My Banner." He said,

Salute GOD's rule!
GOD at war with Amalek
Always and forever!

1-4 18Jethro, priest of Midian and father-in-law to Moses, heard the report of all that God had done for Moses and Israel his people, the news that GOD had delivered Israel from Egypt. Jethro, Moses' father-in-

NEW KING JAMES VERSION

Jethro, Moses' father-in-law, took Zipporah,
Moses' wife, after he had sent her back, 3with
her two sons, of whom the name of one *was*
Gershom (for he said, "I have been a stranger in
a foreign land")[a] 4and the name of the other *was*
Eliezer[a] (for *he said,* "The God of my father *was*
my help, and delivered me from the sword of
Pharaoh"); 5and Jethro, Moses' father-in-law,
came with his sons and his wife to Moses in the
wilderness, where he was encamped at the
mountain of God. 6Now he had said to Moses, "I,
your father-in-law Jethro, am coming to you
with your wife and her two sons with her."
7So Moses went out to meet his father-in-law,
bowed down, and kissed him. And they asked
each other about *their* well-being, and they
went into the tent. 8And Moses told his father-in-
law all that the LORD had done to Pharaoh and
to the Egyptians for Israel's sake, all the hard-
ship that had come upon them on the way, and
how the LORD had delivered them. 9Then Jethro
rejoiced for all the good which the LORD had
done for Israel, whom He had delivered out of
the hand of the Egyptians. 10And Jethro said,
"Blessed *be* the LORD, who has delivered you out
of the hand of the Egyptians and out of the hand
of Pharaoh, *and* who has delivered the people
from under the hand of the Egyptians. 11Now I
know that the LORD *is* greater than all the gods;
for in the very thing in which they behaved
proudly, *He was* above them." 12Then Jethro,
Moses' father-in-law, took[a] a burnt offering and
other sacrifices *to offer* to God. And Aaron
came with all the elders of Israel to eat bread
with Moses' father-in-law before God.
13And so it was, on the next day, that Moses
sat to judge the people; and the people stood be-
fore Moses from morning until evening. 14So
when Moses' father-in-law saw all that he did
for the people, he said, "What *is* this thing that
you are doing for the people? Why do you alone
sit, and all the people stand before you from
morning until evening?"
15And Moses said to his father-in-law, "Be-
cause the people come to me to inquire of God.
16When they have a difficulty, they come to me,
and I judge between one and another; and I
make known the statutes of God and His laws."
17So Moses' father-in-law said to him, "The
thing that you do *is* not good. 18Both you and
these people who *are* with you will surely wear
yourselves out. For this thing *is* too much for
you; you are not able to perform it by yourself.
19Listen now to my voice; I will give you coun-
sel, and God will be with you: Stand before God
for the people, so that you may bring the diffi-
culties to God. 20And you shall teach them the
statutes and the laws, and show them the way in
which they must walk and the work they must
do. 21Moreover you shall select from all the peo-
ple able men, such as fear God, men of truth,
hating covetousness; and place *such* over them
to be rulers of thousands, rulers of hundreds,
rulers of fifties, and rulers of tens. 22And let
them judge the people at all times. Then it will

18:3 [a]Compare Exodus 2:22 **18:4** [a]Literally *My God Is Help*
18:12 [a]Following Masoretic Text and Septuagint; Syriac, Targum, and Vulgate read *offered.*

THE MESSAGE

law, had taken in Zipporah, Moses' wife
who had been sent back home, and her two
sons. The name of the one was Gershom
(Sojourner) for he had said, "I'm a sojourner
in a foreign land"; the name of the other was
Eliezer (God's-Help) because "The God of
my father is my help and saved me from
death by Pharaoh."
5-6 Jethro, Moses' father-in-law, brought
Moses his sons and his wife there in the
wilderness where he was camped at the
mountain of God. He had sent a message
ahead to Moses: "I, your father-in-law, am
coming to you with your wife and two sons."
7-8 Moses went out to welcome his father-in-
law. He bowed to him and kissed him. Each
asked the other how things had been with
him. Then they went into the tent. Moses
told his father-in-law the story of all that
GOD had done to Pharaoh and Egypt in
helping Israel, all the trouble they had expe-
rienced on the journey, and how GOD had
delivered them.
9-11 Jethro was delighted in all the good that
GOD had done for Israel in delivering them
from Egyptian oppression. Jethro said,
"Blessed be GOD who has delivered you
from the power of Egypt and Pharaoh, who
has delivered his people from the oppres-
sion of Egypt. Now I know that GOD is
greater than all gods because he's done this
to all those who treated Israel arrogantly."
12 Jethro, Moses' father-in-law, brought a
Whole-Burnt-Offering and sacrifices to
God. And Aaron, along with all the elders of
Israel, came and ate the meal with Moses'
father-in-law in the presence of God.
13-14 The next day Moses took his place to
judge the people. People were standing be-
fore him all day long, from morning to
night. When Moses' father-in-law saw all
that he was doing for the people, he said,
"What's going on here? Why are you doing
all this, and all by yourself, letting every-
body line up before you from morning to
night?"
15-16 Moses said to his father-in-law, "Because
the people come to me with questions about
God. When something comes up, they come
to me. I judge between a man and his neigh-
bor and teach them God's laws and instruc-
tions."
17-23 Moses' father-in-law said, "This is no way
to go about it. You'll burn out, and the peo-
ple right along with you. This is way too
much for you—you can't do this alone. Now
listen to me. Let me tell you how to do this
so that God will be in this with you. Be there
for the people before God, but let the mat-
ters of concern be presented to God. Your
job is to teach them the rules and instruc-
tions, to show them how to live, what to do.
And then you need to keep a sharp eye out
for competent men—men who fear God,
men of integrity, men who are incorrupt-
ible—and appoint them as leaders over
groups organized by the thousand, by the
hundred, by fifty, and by ten. They'll be re-
sponsible for the everyday work of judging

NEW KING JAMES VERSION

be *that* every great matter they shall bring to
you, but every small matter they themselves
shall judge. So it will be easier for you, for they
will bear *the burden* with you. [23]If you do this
thing, and God *so* commands you, then you will
be able to endure, and all this people will also
go to their place in peace."

[24]So Moses heeded the voice of his father-in-
law and did all that he had said. [25]And Moses
chose able men out of all Israel, and made them
heads over the people: rulers of thousands,
rulers of hundreds, rulers of fifties, and rulers of
tens. [26]So they judged the people at all times; the
hard cases they brought to Moses, but they
judged every small case themselves.

[27]Then Moses let his father-in-law depart,
and he went his way to his own land.

ISRAEL AT MOUNT SINAI

19 In the third month after the children of Is-
rael had gone out of the land of Egypt, on
the same day, they came *to* the Wilderness of
Sinai. [2]For they had departed from Rephidim,
had come *to* the Wilderness of Sinai, and
camped in the wilderness. So Israel camped
there before the mountain.

[3]And Moses went up to God, and the LORD
called to him from the mountain, saying, "Thus
you shall say to the house of Jacob, and tell the
children of Israel: [4]'You have seen what I did to
the Egyptians, and *how* I bore you on eagles'
wings and brought you to Myself. [5]Now there-
fore, if you will indeed obey My voice and keep
My covenant, then you shall be a special trea-
sure to Me above all people; for all the earth *is*
Mine. [6]And you shall be to Me a kingdom of
priests and a holy nation.' These *are* the words
which you shall speak to the children of Israel."

[7]So Moses came and called for the elders of
the people, and laid before them all these words
which the LORD commanded him. [8]Then all the
people answered together and said, "All that the
LORD has spoken we will do." So Moses brought
back the words of the people to the LORD. [9]And
the LORD said to Moses, "Behold, I come to you
in the thick cloud, that the people may hear
when I speak with you, and believe you forever."

So Moses told the words of the people to the
LORD.

[10]Then the LORD said to Moses, "Go to the
people and consecrate them today and tomor-
row, and let them wash their clothes. [11]And let
them be ready for the third day. For on the third
day the LORD will come down upon Mount Sinai
in the sight of all the people. [12]You shall set
bounds for the people all around, saying, 'Take
heed to yourselves *that* you do *not* go up to the
mountain or touch its base. Whoever touches
the mountain shall surely be put to death. [13]Not
a hand shall touch him, but he shall surely be
stoned or shot *with an arrow;* whether man or
beast, he shall not live.' When the trumpet
sounds long, they shall come near the moun-
tain."

THE MESSAGE

among the people. They'll bring the hard cases to you, but in the routine cases they'll be the judges. They will share your load and that will make it easier for you. If you handle the work this way, you'll have the strength to carry out whatever God commands you, and the people in their settings will flourish also."

24-27 Moses listened to the counsel of his father-in-law and did everything he said. Moses picked competent men from all Israel and set them as leaders over the people who were organized by the thousand, by the hundred, by fifty, and by ten. They took over the everyday work of judging among the people. They brought the hard cases to Moses, but in the routine cases they were the judges. Then Moses said good-bye to his father-in-law who went home to his own country.

MOUNT SINAI

1-2 19 Three months after leaving Egypt the Israelites entered the Wilderness of Sinai. They followed the route from Rephidim, arrived at the Wilderness of Sinai, and set up camp. Israel camped there facing the mountain.

3-6 As Moses went up to meet God, GOD called down to him from the mountain: "Speak to the House of Jacob, tell the People of Israel: 'You have seen what I did to Egypt and how I carried you on eagles' wings and brought you to me. If you will listen obediently to what I say and keep my covenant, out of all peoples you'll be my special treasure. The whole Earth is mine to choose from, but you're special: a kingdom of priests, a holy nation.'

"This is what I want you to tell the People of Israel."

7 Moses came back and called the elders of Israel together and set before them all these words which GOD had commanded him.

8 The people were unanimous in their response: "Everything GOD says, we will do." Moses took the people's answer back to GOD.

9 GOD said to Moses, "Get ready. I'm about to come to you in a thick cloud so that the people can listen in and trust you completely when I speak with you." Again Moses reported the people's answer to GOD.

10-13 GOD said to Moses, "Go to the people. For the next two days get these people ready to meet the Holy GOD. Have them scrub their clothes so that on the third day they'll be fully prepared, because on the third day GOD will come down on Mount Sinai and make his presence known to all the people. Post boundaries for the people all around, telling them, 'Warning! Don't climb the mountain. Don't even touch its edge. Whoever touches the mountain dies—a certain death. And no one is to touch that person, he's to be stoned. That's right—stoned. Or shot with arrows, shot to death. Animal or man, whichever—put to death.'

"A long blast from the horn will signal that it's safe to climb the mountain."

NEW KING JAMES VERSION

14So Moses went down from the mountain to
the people and sanctified the people, and they
washed their clothes. 15And he said to the peo-
ple, "Be ready for the third day; do not come
near *your* wives."
16Then it came to pass on the third day, in the
morning, that there were thunderings and light-
nings, and a thick cloud on the mountain; and
the sound of the trumpet was very loud, so that
all the people who *were* in the camp trembled.
17And Moses brought the people out of the camp
to meet with God, and they stood at the foot of
the mountain. 18Now Mount Sinai *was* com-
pletely in smoke, because the LORD descended
upon it in fire. Its smoke ascended like the
smoke of a furnace, and the whole mountain[a]
quaked greatly. 19And when the blast of the
trumpet sounded long and became louder and
louder, Moses spoke, and God answered him by
voice. 20Then the LORD came down upon Mount
Sinai, on the top of the mountain. And the LORD
called Moses to the top of the mountain, and
Moses went up.
21And the LORD said to Moses, "Go down and
warn the people, lest they break through to gaze
at the LORD, and many of them perish. 22Also let
the priests who come near the LORD consecrate
themselves, lest the LORD break out against
them."
23But Moses said to the LORD, "The people
cannot come up to Mount Sinai; for You warned
us, saying, 'Set bounds around the mountain
and consecrate it.' "
24Then the LORD said to him, "Away! Get
down and then come up, you and Aaron with
you. But do not let the priests and the people
break through to come up to the LORD, lest He
break out against them." 25So Moses went down
to the people and spoke to them.

THE TEN COMMANDMENTS

20 And God spoke all these words, saying:
2"I *am* the LORD your God, who brought you
out of the land of Egypt, out of the house
of bondage.
3"You shall have no other gods before Me.
4"You shall not make for yourself a carved
image—any likeness *of anything* that *is*
in heaven above, or that *is* in the earth
beneath, or that *is* in the water under the
earth; 5you shall not bow down to them
nor serve them. For I, the LORD your God,
am a jealous God, visiting the iniquity of
the fathers upon the children to the third
and fourth *generations* of those who hate
Me, 6but showing mercy to thousands, to
those who love Me and keep My
commandments.
7"You shall not take the name of the LORD
your God in vain, for the LORD will not
hold *him* guiltless who takes His name in
vain.
8"Remember the Sabbath day, to keep it holy.
9Six days you shall labor and do all your
work, 10but the seventh day *is* the
Sabbath of the LORD your God. *In it* you

19:18 [a]Septuagint reads *all the people*.

THE MESSAGE

14-15 Moses went down the mountain to the
people and prepared them for the holy
meeting. They gave their clothes a good
scrubbing. Then he addressed the people:
"Be ready in three days. Don't sleep with a
woman."
16 On the third day at daybreak, there were
loud claps of thunder, flashes of lightning, a
thick cloud covering the mountain, and an
ear-piercing trumpet blast. Everyone in the
camp shuddered in fear.
17 Moses led the people out of the camp to
meet God. They stood at attention at the
base of the mountain.
18-20 Mount Sinai was all smoke because GOD
had come down on it as fire. Smoke poured
from it like smoke from a furnace. The
whole mountain shuddered in huge spasms.
The trumpet blasts grew louder and louder.
Moses spoke and God answered in thunder.
GOD descended to the peak of Mount Sinai.
GOD called Moses up to the peak and Moses
climbed up.
21-22 GOD said to Moses, "Go down. Warn the
people not to break through the barricades
to get a look at GOD lest many of them die.
And the priests also, warn them to prepare
themselves for the holy meeting, lest GOD
break out against them."
23 Moses said to GOD, "But the people can't
climb Mount Sinai. You've already warned
us well telling us: 'Post boundaries around
the mountain. Respect the holy mountain.'"
24 GOD told him, "Go down and then bring
Aaron back up with you. But make sure that
the priests and the people don't break
through and come up to GOD, lest he break
out against them."
25 So Moses went down to the people. He
said to them:

1-2 20 GOD spoke all these words:
I am GOD, your God,
who brought you out of the land of Egypt,
out of a life of slavery.
3 No other gods, only me.
4-6 No carved gods of any size, shape, or form
of anything whatever, whether of things
that fly or walk or swim. Don't bow down
to them and don't serve them because *I*
am GOD, your God, and I'm a most jeal-
ous God, punishing the children for any
sins their parents pass on to them to the
third, and yes, even to the fourth genera-
tion of those who hate me. But I'm
unswervingly loyal to the thousands who
love me and keep my commandments.
7 No using the name of GOD, your God, in
curses or silly banter; GOD won't put up
with the irreverent use of his name.
8-11 Observe the Sabbath day, to keep it holy.
Work six days and do everything you
need to do. But the seventh day is a Sab-
bath to GOD, your God. Don't do any

NEW KING JAMES VERSION

shall do no work: you, nor your son, nor
your daughter, nor your male servant,
nor your female servant, nor your cattle,
nor your stranger who *is* within your
gates. 11For *in* six days the LORD made
the heavens and the earth, the sea, and
all that *is* in them, and rested the seventh
day. Therefore the LORD blessed the
Sabbath day and hallowed it.
12"Honor your father and your mother, that
your days may be long upon the land
which the LORD your God is giving you.
13"You shall not murder.
14"You shall not commit adultery.
15"You shall not steal.
16"You shall not bear false witness against
your neighbor.
17"You shall not covet your neighbor's house;
you shall not covet your neighbor's wife,
nor his male servant, nor his female
servant, nor his ox, nor his donkey, nor
anything that *is* your neighbor's."

THE PEOPLE AFRAID OF GOD'S PRESENCE

18Now all the people witnessed the thunder-
ings, the lightning flashes, the sound of the
trumpet, and the mountain smoking; and when
the people saw *it,* they trembled and stood afar
off. 19Then they said to Moses, "You speak with
us, and we will hear; but let not God speak with
us, lest we die."
20And Moses said to the people, "Do not fear;
for God has come to test you, and that His fear
may be before you, so that you may not sin."
21So the people stood afar off, but Moses drew
near the thick darkness where God *was.*

THE LAW OF THE ALTAR

22Then the LORD said to Moses, "Thus you
shall say to the children of Israel: 'You have
seen that I have talked with you from heaven.
23You shall not make *anything to be* with Me—
gods of silver or gods of gold you shall not make
for yourselves. 24An altar of earth you shall
make for Me, and you shall sacrifice on it your
burnt offerings and your peace offerings, your
sheep and your oxen. In every place where I
record My name I will come to you, and I will
bless you. 25And if you make Me an altar of
stone, you shall not build it of hewn stone; for if
you use your tool on it, you have profaned it.
26Nor shall you go up by steps to My altar, that
your nakedness may not be exposed on it.'

THE LAW CONCERNING SERVANTS

21 "Now these *are* the judgments which you
shall set before them: 2If you buy a He-
brew servant, he shall serve six years; and in the
seventh he shall go out free and pay nothing. 3If
he comes in by himself, he shall go out by him-
self; if he *comes in* married, then his wife shall
go out with him. 4If his master has given him a
wife, and she has borne him sons or daughters,
the wife and her children shall be her master's,
and he shall go out by himself. 5But if the ser-
vant plainly says, 'I love my master, my wife,
and my children; I will not go out free,' 6then his
master shall bring him to the judges. He shall

THE MESSAGE

work—not you, nor your son, nor your
daughter, nor your servant, nor your
maid, nor your animals, not even the for-
eign guest visiting in your town. For in
six days GOD made Heaven, Earth, and
sea, and everything in them; he rested on
the seventh day. Therefore GOD blessed
the Sabbath day; he set it apart as a holy
day.
12 Honor your father and mother so that you'll
live a long time in the land that God, your
God, is giving you.
13 No murder.
14 No adultery.
15 No stealing.
16 No lies about your neighbor.
17 No lusting after your neighbor's house—or
wife or servant or maid or ox or donkey.
Don't set your heart on anything that is
your neighbor's.

18-19 All the people, experiencing the thunder
and lightning, the trumpet blast and the
smoking mountain, were afraid—they
pulled back and stood at a distance. They
said to Moses, "You speak to us and we'll lis-
ten, but don't have God speak to us or we'll
die."
20 Moses spoke to the people: "Don't be
afraid. God has come to test you and instill
a deep and reverent awe within you so that
you won't sin."
21 The people kept their distance while
Moses approached the thick cloud where
God was.

22-26 GOD said to Moses, "Give this Message to
the People of Israel: 'You've experienced
firsthand how I spoke with you from Heaven.
Don't make gods of silver and gods of gold
and then set them alongside me. Make me an
earthen Altar. Sacrifice your Whole-Burnt-
Offerings, your Peace-Offerings, your sheep,
and your cattle on it. Every place where I
cause my name to be honored in your wor-
ship, I'll be there myself and bless you. If you
use stones to make my Altar, don't use
dressed stones. If you use a chisel on the
stones you'll profane the Altar. Don't use
steps to climb to my Altar because that will
expose your nakedness.' "

1 21 "These are the laws that you are to
place before them:
2-6 "When you buy a Hebrew slave, he will
serve six years. The seventh year he goes
free, for nothing. If he came in single he
leaves single. If he came in married he
leaves with his wife. If the master gives him
a wife and she gave him sons and daugh-
ters, the wife and children stay with the
master and he leaves by himself. But sup-
pose the slave should say, 'I love my master
and my wife and children—I don't want my
freedom,' then his master is to bring him be-

NEW KING JAMES VERSION

also bring him to the door, or to the doorpost,
and his master shall pierce his ear with an awl;
and he shall serve him forever.
7“And if a man sells his daughter to be a fe-
male slave, she shall not go out as the male
slaves do. 8If she does not please her master,
who has betrothed her to himself, then he shall
let her be redeemed. He shall have no right to
sell her to a foreign people, since he has dealt
deceitfully with her. 9And if he has betrothed
her to his son, he shall deal with her according
to the custom of daughters. 10If he takes another
wife, he shall not diminish her food, her cloth-
ing, and her marriage rights. 11And if he does
not do these three for her, then she shall go out
free, without *paying* money.

THE LAW CONCERNING VIOLENCE

12“He who strikes a man so that he dies shall
surely be put to death. 13However, if he did not
lie in wait, but God delivered *him* into his hand,
then I will appoint for you a place where he may
flee.
14“But if a man acts with premeditation
against his neighbor, to kill him by treachery,
you shall take him from My altar, that he may
die.
15“And he who strikes his father or his
mother shall surely be put to death.
16“He who kidnaps a man and sells him, or if
he is found in his hand, shall surely be put to
death.
17“And he who curses his father or his
mother shall surely be put to death.
18“If men contend with each other, and one
strikes the other with a stone or with *his* fist,
and he does not die but is confined to *his* bed,
19if he rises again and walks about outside with
his staff, then he who struck *him* shall be acquit-
ted. He shall only pay *for* the loss of his time,
and shall provide *for him* to be thoroughly
healed.
20“And if a man beats his male or female ser-
vant with a rod, so that he dies under his hand,
he shall surely be punished. 21Notwithstanding,
if he remains alive a day or two, he shall not be
punished; for he *is* his property.
22“If men fight, and hurt a woman with child,
so that she gives birth prematurely, yet no harm
follows, he shall surely be punished accordingly
as the woman’s husband imposes on him; and
he shall pay as the judges *determine.* 23But if
any harm follows, then you shall give life for
life, 24eye for eye, tooth for tooth, hand for hand,
foot for foot, 25burn for burn, wound for wound,
stripe for stripe.
26“If a man strikes the eye of his male or fe-
male servant, and destroys it, he shall let him go
free for the sake of his eye. 27And if he knocks
out the tooth of his male or female servant, he
shall let him go free for the sake of his tooth.

ANIMAL CONTROL LAWS

28“If an ox gores a man or a woman to death,
then the ox shall surely be stoned, and its flesh
shall not be eaten; but the owner of the ox *shall
be* acquitted. 29But if the ox tended to thrust
with its horn in times past, and it has been made

THE MESSAGE

fore God and to a door or doorpost and pierce his ear with an awl, a sign that he is a slave for life.

7-11 “When a man sells his daughter to be a handmaid, she doesn’t go free after six years like the men. If she doesn’t please her master, her family must buy her back; her master doesn’t have the right to sell her to foreigners since he broke his word to her. If he turns her over to his son, he has to treat her like a daughter. If he marries another woman, she retains all her full rights to meals, clothing, and marital relations. If he won’t do any of these three things for her, she goes free, for nothing.

12-14 “If someone hits another and death results, the penalty is death. But if there was no intent to kill—if it was an accident, an ‘act of God’—I’ll set aside a place to which the killer can flee for refuge. But if the murder was premeditated, cunningly plotted, then drag the killer away, even if it’s from my Altar, to be put to death.

15 “If someone hits father or mother, the penalty is death.

16 “If someone kidnaps a person, the penalty is death, regardless of whether the person has been sold or is still held in possession.

17 “If someone curses father or mother, the penalty is death.

18-19 “If a quarrel breaks out and one hits the other with a rock or a fist and the injured one doesn’t die but is confined to bed and then later gets better and can get about on a crutch, the one who hit him is in the clear, except to pay for the loss of time and make sure of complete recovery.

20-21 “If a slave owner hits a slave, male or female, with a stick and the slave dies on the spot, the slave must be avenged. But if the slave survives a day or two, he’s not to be avenged—the slave is the owner’s property.

22-25 “When there’s a fight and in the fight a pregnant woman is hit so that she miscarries but is not otherwise hurt, the one responsible has to pay whatever the husband demands in compensation. But if there is further damage, then you must give life for life—eye for eye, tooth for tooth, hand for hand, foot for foot, burn for burn, wound for wound, bruise for bruise.

26-27 “If a slave owner hits the eye of a slave or handmaid and ruins it, the owner must let the slave go free because of the eye. If the owner knocks out the tooth of the male or female slave, the slave must be released and go free because of the tooth.

28-32 “If an ox gores a man or a woman to death, the ox must be stoned. The meat cannot be eaten but the owner of the ox is in the clear. But if the ox has a history of goring and the owner knew it and did nothing to

NEW KING JAMES VERSION

known to his owner, and he has not kept it con-
fined, so that it has killed a man or a woman, the
ox shall be stoned and its owner also shall be
put to death. 30If there is imposed on him a sum
of money, then he shall pay to redeem his life,
whatever is imposed on him. 31Whether it has
gored a son or gored a daughter, according to
this judgment it shall be done to him. 32If the ox
gores a male or female servant, he shall give to
their master thirty shekels of silver, and the ox
shall be stoned.

33"And if a man opens a pit, or if a man digs
a pit and does not cover it, and an ox or a don-
key falls in it, 34the owner of the pit shall make
it good; he shall give money to their owner, but
the dead *animal* shall be his.

35"If one man's ox hurts another's, so that it
dies, then they shall sell the live ox and divide
the money from it; and the dead *ox* they shall
also divide. 36Or if it was known that the ox
tended to thrust in time past, and its owner has
not kept it confined, he shall surely pay ox for
ox, and the dead animal shall be his own.

RESPONSIBILITY FOR PROPERTY

22 "If a man steals an ox or a sheep, and
slaughters it or sells it, he shall restore five
oxen for an ox and four sheep for a sheep. 2If the
thief is found breaking in, and he is struck so
that he dies, *there shall be* no guilt for his blood-
shed. 3If the sun has risen on him, *there shall be*
guilt for his bloodshed. He should make full
restitution; if he has nothing, then he shall be
sold for his theft. 4If the theft is certainly found
alive in his hand, whether it is an ox or donkey
or sheep, he shall restore double.

5"If a man causes a field or vineyard to be
grazed, and lets loose his animal, and it feeds in
another man's field, he shall make restitution
from the best of his own field and the best of his
own vineyard.

6"If fire breaks out and catches in thorns, so
that stacked grain, standing grain, or the field is
consumed, he who kindled the fire shall surely
make restitution.

7"If a man delivers to his neighbor money or
articles to keep, and it is stolen out of the man's
house, if the thief is found, he shall pay double.
8If the thief is not found, then the master of the
house shall be brought to the judges *to see*
whether he has put his hand into his neighbor's
goods.

9"For any kind of trespass, *whether it con-
cerns* an ox, a donkey, a sheep, or clothing, *or*
for any kind of lost thing which *another* claims
to be his, the cause of both parties shall come
before the judges; *and* whomever the judges
condemn shall pay double to his neighbor. 10If a
man delivers to his neighbor a donkey, an ox, a
sheep, or any animal to keep, and it dies, is hurt,
or driven away, no one seeing *it*, 11*then* an oath
of the LORD shall be between them both, that he
has not put his hand into his neighbor's goods;
and the owner of it shall accept *that*, and he
shall not make *it* good. 12But if, in fact, it is

THE MESSAGE

guard against it, then if the ox kills a man or
a woman, the ox is to be stoned and the
owner given the death penalty. If a ransom
is agreed upon instead of death, he must pay
it in full as a redemption for his life. If a son
or daughter is gored, the same judgment
holds. If it is a slave or a handmaid the ox
gores, thirty shekels of silver is to be paid to
the owner and the ox stoned.

33-34 "If someone uncovers a cistern or digs a
pit and leaves it open and an ox or donkey
falls into it, the owner of the pit must pay
whatever the animal is worth to its owner
but can keep the dead animal.

35-36 "If someone's ox injures a neighbor's ox
and the ox dies, they must sell the live ox
and split the price; they must also split the
dead animal. But if the ox had a history of
goring and the owner knew it and did noth-
ing to guard against it, the owner must pay
an ox for an ox but can keep the dead ani-
mal."

1-3 22 "If someone steals an ox or a lamb and
slaughters or sells it, the thief must
pay five cattle in place of the ox and four
sheep in place of the lamb. If the thief is
caught while breaking in and is hit hard and
dies, there is no bloodguilt. But if it happens
after daybreak, there is bloodguilt.

3-4 "A thief must make full restitution for
what is stolen. The thief who is unable to
pay is to be sold for his thieving. If caught
red-handed with the stolen goods, and the
ox or donkey or lamb is still alive, the thief
pays double.

5 "If someone grazes livestock in a field or
vineyard but lets them loose so they graze in
someone else's field, restitution must be
made from the best of the owner's field or
vineyard.

6 "If fire breaks out and spreads to the
brush so that the sheaves of grain or the
standing grain or even the whole field is
burned up, whoever started the fire must
pay for the damages.

7-8 "If someone gives a neighbor money or
things for safekeeping and they are stolen
from the neighbor's house, the thief, if
caught, must pay back double. If the thief is
not caught, the owner must be brought be-
fore God to determine whether the owner
was the one who took the neighbor's goods.

9 "In all cases of stolen goods, whether
oxen, donkeys, sheep, clothing, anything in
fact missing of which someone says, 'That's
mine,' both parties must come before the
judges. The one the judges pronounce guilty
must pay double to the other.

10-13 "If someone gives a donkey or ox or lamb
or any kind of animal to another for safe-
keeping and it dies or is injured or lost and
there is no witness, an oath before GOD must
be made between them to decide whether
one has laid hands on the property of the
other. The owner must accept this and no
damages are assessed. But if it turns out it

NEW KING JAMES VERSION

stolen from him, he shall make restitution to the owner of it. [13]If it is torn to pieces *by a beast, then* he shall bring it as evidence, *and* he shall not make good what was torn.

[14]"And if a man borrows *anything* from his neighbor, and it becomes injured or dies, the owner of it not *being* with it, he shall surely make *it* good. [15]If its owner *was* with it, he shall not make *it* good; if it *was* hired, it came for its hire.

MORAL AND CEREMONIAL PRINCIPLES

[16]"If a man entices a virgin who is not betrothed, and lies with her, he shall surely pay the bride-price for her *to be* his wife. [17]If her father utterly refuses to give her to him, he shall pay money according to the bride-price of virgins.

[18]"You shall not permit a sorceress to live.

[19]"Whoever lies with an animal shall surely be put to death.

[20]"He who sacrifices to *any* god, except to the LORD only, he shall be utterly destroyed.

[21]"You shall neither mistreat a stranger nor oppress him, for you were strangers in the land of Egypt.

[22]"You shall not afflict any widow or fatherless child. [23]If you afflict them in any way, *and* they cry at all to Me, I will surely hear their cry; [24]and My wrath will become hot, and I will kill you with the sword; your wives shall be widows, and your children fatherless.

[25]"If you lend money to *any of* My people *who are* poor among you, you shall not be like a moneylender to him; you shall not charge him interest. [26]If you ever take your neighbor's garment as a pledge, you shall return it to him before the sun goes down. [27]For that *is* his only covering, it *is* his garment for his skin. What will he sleep in? And it will be that when he cries to Me, I will hear, for I *am* gracious.

[28]"You shall not revile God, nor curse a ruler of your people.

[29]"You shall not delay *to offer* the first of your ripe produce and your juices. The firstborn of your sons you shall give to Me. [30]Likewise you shall do with your oxen *and* your sheep. It shall be with its mother seven days; on the eighth day you shall give it to Me.

[31]"And you shall be holy men to Me: you shall not eat meat torn *by beasts* in the field; you shall throw it to the dogs.

JUSTICE FOR ALL

23 "You shall not circulate a false report. Do not put your hand with the wicked to be an unrighteous witness. [2]You shall not follow a crowd to do evil; nor shall you testify in a dispute so as to turn aside after many to pervert *justice.* [3]You shall not show partiality to a poor man in his dispute.

[4]"If you meet your enemy's ox or his donkey going astray, you shall surely bring it back to him again. [5]If you see the donkey of one who hates you lying under its burden, and you would refrain from helping it, you shall surely help him with it.

[6]"You shall not pervert the judgment of your poor in his dispute.

THE MESSAGE

was stolen, the owner must be compensated. If it has been torn by wild beasts, the torn animal must be brought in as evidence; no damages have to be paid.

14-15 "If someone borrows an animal from a neighbor and it gets injured or dies while the owner is not present, he must pay for it. But if the owner was with it, he doesn't have to pay. If the animal was hired, the payment covers the loss.

16-17 "If a man seduces a virgin who is not engaged to be married and sleeps with her, he must pay the marriage price and marry her. If her father absolutely refuses to give her away, the man must still pay the marriage price for virgins.

18 "Don't let a sorceress live.

19 "Anyone who has sex with an animal gets the death penalty.

20 "Anyone who sacrifices to a god other than GOD alone must be put to death.

21 "Don't abuse or take advantage of strangers; you, remember, were once strangers in Egypt.

22-24 "Don't mistreat widows or orphans. If you do and they cry out to me, you can be sure I'll take them most seriously; I'll show my anger and come raging among you with the sword, and your wives will end up widows and your children orphans.

25 "If you lend money to my people, to any of the down-and-out among you, don't come down hard on them and gouge them with interest.

26-27 "If you take your neighbor's coat as security, give it back before nightfall; it may be your neighbor's only covering—what else does the person have to sleep in? And if I hear the neighbor crying out from the cold, I'll step in—I'm compassionate.

28 "Don't curse God; and don't damn your leaders.

29-30 "Don't be stingy as your wine vats fill up.

"Dedicate your firstborn sons to me. The same with your cattle and sheep—they are to stay for seven days with their mother, then give them to me.

31 "Be holy for my sake.

"Don't eat mutilated flesh you find in the fields; throw it to the dogs."

1-3 **23** "Don't pass on malicious gossip.

"Don't link up with a wicked person and give corrupt testimony. Don't go along with the crowd in doing evil and don't fudge your testimony in a case just to please the crowd. And just because someone is poor, don't show favoritism in a dispute.

4-5 "If you find your enemy's ox or donkey loose, take it back to him. If you see the donkey of someone who hates you lying helpless under its load, don't walk off and leave it. Help it up.

6 "When there is a dispute concerning your poor, don't tamper with the justice due them.

NEW KING JAMES VERSION

7Keep yourself far from a false matter; do not
kill the innocent and righteous. For I will not
justify the wicked. 8And you shall take no bribe,
for a bribe blinds the discerning and perverts
the words of the righteous.
9"Also you shall not oppress a stranger, for
you know the heart of a stranger, because you
were strangers in the land of Egypt.

THE LAW OF SABBATHS

10"Six years you shall sow your land and
gather in its produce, 11but the seventh *year* you
shall let it rest and lie fallow, that the poor of
your people may eat; and what they leave, the
beasts of the field may eat. In like manner you
shall do with your vineyard *and* your olive
grove. 12Six days you shall do your work, and on
the seventh day you shall rest, that your ox and
your donkey may rest, and the son of your female servant and the stranger may be refreshed.
13"And in all that I have said to you, be circumspect and make no mention of the name of
other gods, nor let it be heard from your mouth.

THREE ANNUAL FEASTS

14"Three times you shall keep a feast to Me in
the year: 15You shall keep the Feast of Unleavened Bread (you shall eat unleavened bread
seven days, as I commanded you, at the time appointed in the month of Abib, for in it you came
out of Egypt; none shall appear before Me
empty); 16and the Feast of Harvest, the firstfruits
of your labors which you have sown in the field;
and the Feast of Ingathering at the end of the
year, when you have gathered in *the fruit of*
your labors from the field.
17"Three times in the year all your males
shall appear before the Lord GOD.[a]
18"You shall not offer the blood of My sacrifice with leavened bread; nor shall the fat of My
sacrifice remain until morning. 19The first of the
firstfruits of your land you shall bring into the
house of the LORD your God. You shall not boil a
young goat in its mother's milk.

THE ANGEL AND THE PROMISES

20"Behold, I send an Angel before you to
keep you in the way and to bring you into the
place which I have prepared. 21Beware of Him
and obey His voice; do not provoke Him, for He
will not pardon your transgressions; for My
name *is* in Him. 22But if you indeed obey His
voice and do all that I speak, then I will be an
enemy to your enemies and an adversary to
your adversaries. 23For My Angel will go before
you and bring you in to the Amorites and the
Hittites and the Perizzites and the Canaanites
and the Hivites and the Jebusites; and I will cut
them off. 24You shall not bow down to their
gods, nor serve them, nor do according to their
works; but you shall utterly overthrow them and
completely break down their *sacred* pillars.

23:17 [a]Hebrew *YHWH*, usually translated LORD

THE MESSAGE

7 "Stay clear of false accusations. Don't contribute to the death of innocent and good people. I don't let the wicked off the hook.

8 "Don't take bribes. Bribes blind perfectly good eyes and twist the speech of good people.

9 "Don't take advantage of a stranger. You know what it's like to be a stranger; you were strangers in Egypt.

10-11 "Sow your land for six years and gather in its crops, but in the seventh year leave it alone and give it a rest so that your poor may eat from it. What they leave, let the wildlife have. Do the same with your vineyards and olive groves.

12 "Work for six days and rest the seventh so your ox and donkey may rest and your servant and migrant workers may have time to get their needed rest.

13 "Listen carefully to everything I tell you. Don't pay attention to other gods—don't so much as mention their names.

14 "Three times a year you are to hold a festival for me.

15 "Hold the spring Festival of Unraised Bread when you eat unraised bread for seven days at the time set for the month of Abib, as I commanded you. That was the month you came out of Egypt. No one should show up before me empty-handed.

16 "Hold the summer Festival of Harvest when you bring in the firstfruits of all your work in the fields.

"Hold the autumn Festival of Ingathering at the end of the season when you bring in the year's crops.

17 "Three times a year all your males are to appear before the Master, GOD.

18 "Don't offer the blood of a sacrifice to me with anything that has yeast in it.

"Don't leave the fat from my festival offering out overnight.

19 "Bring the choice first produce of the year to the house of your GOD.

"Don't boil a kid in its mother's milk.

20-24 "Now get yourselves ready. I'm sending my Angel ahead of you to guard you in your travels, to lead you to the place that I've prepared. Pay close attention to him. Obey him. Don't go against him. He won't put up with your rebellions because he's acting on my authority. But if you obey him and do everything I tell you, I'll be an enemy to your enemies, I'll fight those who fight you. When my Angel goes ahead of you and leads you to the land of the Amorites, the Hittites, the Perizzites, the Canaanites, the Hivites, and the Jebusites, I'll clear the country of them. So don't worship or serve their gods; don't do anything they do because I'm going to wipe them right off the face of the Earth and smash their sacred phallic pillars to bits.

New King James Version

25“So you shall serve the LORD your God, and He will bless your bread and your water. And I will take sickness away from the midst of you. 26No one shall suffer miscarriage or be barren in your land; I will fulfill the number of your days.

27“I will send My fear before you, I will cause confusion among all the people to whom you come, and will make all your enemies turn *their* backs to you. 28And I will send hornets before you, which shall drive out the Hivite, the Canaanite, and the Hittite from before you. 29I will not drive them out from before you in one year, lest the land become desolate and the beasts of the field become too numerous for you. 30Little by little I will drive them out from before you, until you have increased, and you inherit the land. 31And I will set your bounds from the Red Sea to the sea, Philistia, and from the desert to the River.[a] For I will deliver the inhabitants of the land into your hand, and you shall drive them out before you. 32You shall make no covenant with them, nor with their gods. 33They shall not dwell in your land, lest they make you sin against Me. For *if* you serve their gods, it will surely be a snare to you.”

Israel Affirms the Covenant

24 Now He said to Moses, “Come up to the LORD, you and Aaron, Nadab and Abihu, and seventy of the elders of Israel, and worship from afar. 2And Moses alone shall come near the LORD, but they shall not come near; nor shall the people go up with him.”

3So Moses came and told the people all the words of the LORD and all the judgments. And all the people answered with one voice and said, “All the words which the LORD has said we will do.” 4And Moses wrote all the words of the LORD. And he rose early in the morning, and built an altar at the foot of the mountain, and twelve pillars according to the twelve tribes of Israel. 5Then he sent young men of the children of Israel, who offered burnt offerings and sacrificed peace offerings of oxen to the LORD. 6And Moses took half the blood and put *it* in basins, and half the blood he sprinkled on the altar. 7Then he took the Book of the Covenant and read in the hearing of the people. And they said, “All that the LORD has said we will do, and be obedient.” 8And Moses took the blood, sprinkled *it* on the people, and said, “This is the blood of the covenant which the LORD has made with you according to all these words.”

On the Mountain with God

9Then Moses went up, also Aaron, Nadab, and Abihu, and seventy of the elders of Israel, 10and they saw the God of Israel. And *there was* under His feet as it were a paved work of sapphire stone, and it was like the very heavens in *its* clarity. 11But on the nobles of the children of Israel He did not lay His hand. So they saw God, and they ate and drank.

23:31 [a]Hebrew *Nahar*, the Euphrates

The Message

25-26 “But you—you serve your GOD and he'll bless your food and your water. I'll get rid of the sickness among you; there won't be any miscarriages nor barren women in your land. I'll make sure you live full and complete lives.

27 “I'll send my Terror on ahead of you and throw those peoples you're approaching into a panic. All you'll see of your enemies is the backs of their necks.

28-31 “And I'll send Despair on ahead of you. It will push the Hivites, the Canaanites, and the Hittites out of your way. I won't get rid of them all at once lest the land grow up in weeds and the wild animals take over. Little by little I'll get them out of there while you have a chance to get your crops going and make the land your own. I will make your borders stretch from the Red Sea to the Mediterranean Sea and from the Wilderness to the Euphrates River. I'm turning everyone living in that land over to you; go ahead and drive them out.

32-33 “Don't make any deals with them or their gods. They are not to stay in the same country with you lest they get you to sin by worshiping their gods. Beware. That's a huge danger.”

1-2 24 He said to Moses, “Climb the mountain to GOD, you and Aaron, Nadab, Abihu, and seventy of the elders of Israel. They will worship from a distance; only Moses will approach GOD. The rest are not to come close. And the people are not to climb the mountain at all.”

3 So Moses went to the people and told them everything GOD had said—all the rules and regulations. They all answered in unison: “Everything GOD said, we'll do.”

4-6 Then Moses wrote it all down, everything GOD had said. He got up early the next morning and built an Altar at the foot of the mountain using twelve pillar-stones for the twelve tribes of Israel. Then he directed young Israelite men to offer Whole-Burnt-Offerings and sacrifice Peace-Offerings of bulls. Moses took half the blood and put it in bowls; the other half he threw against the Altar.

7 Then he took the Book of the Covenant and read it as the people listened. They said, “Everything GOD said, we'll do. Yes, we'll obey.”

8 Moses took the rest of the blood and threw it out over the people, saying, “This is the blood of the covenant which GOD has made with you out of all these words I have spoken.”

9-11 Then they climbed the mountain—Moses and Aaron, Nadab and Abihu, and seventy of the elders of Israel—and saw the God of Israel. He was standing on a pavement of something like sapphires—pure, clear sky-blue. He didn't hurt these pillar-leaders of the Israelites: They saw God; and they ate and drank.

NEW KING JAMES VERSION

12Then the LORD said to Moses, "Come up to Me on the mountain and be there; and I will give you tablets of stone, and the law and commandments which I have written, that you may teach them."

13So Moses arose with his assistant Joshua, and Moses went up to the mountain of God. 14And he said to the elders, "Wait here for us until we come back to you. Indeed, Aaron and Hur *are* with you. If any man has a difficulty, let him go to them." 15Then Moses went up into the mountain, and a cloud covered the mountain.

16Now the glory of the LORD rested on Mount Sinai, and the cloud covered it six days. And on the seventh day He called to Moses out of the midst of the cloud. 17The sight of the glory of the LORD *was* like a consuming fire on the top of the mountain in the eyes of the children of Israel. 18So Moses went into the midst of the cloud and went up into the mountain. And Moses was on the mountain forty days and forty nights.

OFFERINGS FOR THE SANCTUARY

25 Then the LORD spoke to Moses, saying: 2"Speak to the children of Israel, that they bring Me an offering. From everyone who gives it willingly with his heart you shall take My offering. 3And this *is* the offering which you shall take from them: gold, silver, and bronze; 4blue, purple, and scarlet *thread,* fine linen, and goats' *hair;* 5ram skins dyed red, badger skins, and acacia wood; 6oil for the light, and spices for the anointing oil and for the sweet incense; 7onyx stones, and stones to be set in the ephod and in the breastplate. 8And let them make Me a sanctuary, that I may dwell among them. 9According to all that I show you, *that is,* the pattern of the tabernacle and the pattern of all its furnishings, just so you shall make *it.*

THE ARK OF THE TESTIMONY

10"And they shall make an ark of acacia wood; two and a half cubits *shall be* its length, a cubit and a half its width, and a cubit and a half its height. 11And you shall overlay it with pure gold, inside and out you shall overlay it, and shall make on it a molding of gold all around. 12You shall cast four rings of gold for it, and put *them* in its four corners; two rings *shall be* on one side, and two rings on the other side. 13And you shall make poles *of* acacia wood, and overlay them with gold. 14You shall put the poles into the rings on the sides of the ark, that the ark may be carried by them. 15The poles shall be in the rings of the ark; they shall not be taken from it. 16And you shall put into the ark the Testimony which I will give you.

17"You shall make a mercy seat of pure gold; two and a half cubits *shall be* its length and a cubit and a half its width. 18And you shall make two cherubim of gold; of hammered work you shall make them at the two ends of the mercy seat. 19Make one cherub at one end, and the other cherub at the other end; you shall make the cherubim at the two ends of it *of one piece* with the mercy seat. 20And the cherubim shall stretch out *their* wings above, covering the mercy seat with their wings, and they shall face

THE MESSAGE

12-13 GOD said to Moses, "Climb higher up the mountain and wait there for me; I'll give you tablets of stone, the teachings and commandments that I've written to instruct them." So Moses got up, accompanied by Joshua his aide. And Moses climbed up the mountain of God.

14 He told the elders of Israel, "Wait for us here until we return to you. You have Aaron and Hur with you; if there are any problems, go to them."

15-17 Then Moses climbed the mountain. The Cloud covered the mountain. The Glory of GOD settled over Mount Sinai. The Cloud covered it for six days. On the seventh day he called out of the Cloud to Moses. In the view of the Israelites below, the Glory of God looked like a raging fire at the top of the mountain.

18 Moses entered the middle of the Cloud and climbed the mountain. Moses was on the mountain forty days and forty nights.

INSTRUCTIONS ON THE MOUNTAIN: THE OFFERINGS

1-9 25 GOD spoke to Moses: "Tell the Israelites that they are to set aside offerings for me. Receive the offerings from everyone who is willing to give. These are the offerings I want you to receive from them: gold, silver, bronze; blue, purple, and scarlet material; fine linen; goats' hair; tanned rams' skins; dolphin skins; acacia wood; lamp oil; spices for anointing oils and for fragrant incense; onyx stones and other stones for setting in the Ephod and the Breastpiece. Let them construct a Sanctuary for me so that I can live among them. You are to construct it following the plans I've given you, the design for The Dwelling and the design for all its furnishings.

THE CHEST

10-15 "First let them make a Chest using acacia wood: make it three and three-quarters feet long and two and one-quarter feet wide and deep. Cover it with a veneer of pure gold inside and out and make a molding of gold all around it. Cast four gold rings and attach them to its four feet, two rings on one side and two rings on the other. Make poles from acacia wood and cover them with a veneer of gold and insert them into the rings on the sides of the Chest for carrying the Chest. The poles are to stay in the rings; they must not be removed.

16 "Place The Testimony that I give you in the Chest.

17 "Now make a lid of pure gold for the Chest, an Atonement-Cover, three and three-quarters feet long and two and one-quarter feet wide.

18-22 "Sculpt two winged angels out of hammered gold for either end of the Atonement-Cover, one angel at one end, one angel at the other. Make them of one piece with the Atonement-Cover. Make the angels with their wings spread, hovering over the Atonement-Cover, facing one another but

NEW KING JAMES VERSION

one another; the faces of the cherubim *shall be*
toward the mercy seat. 21You shall put the mercy
seat on top of the ark, and in the ark you shall
put the Testimony that I will give you. 22And
there I will meet with you, and I will speak with
you from above the mercy seat, from between
the two cherubim which *are* on the ark of the
Testimony, about everything which I will give
you in commandment to the children of Israel.

THE TABLE FOR THE SHOWBREAD

23"You shall also make a table of acacia
wood; two cubits *shall be* its length, a cubit its
width, and a cubit and a half its height. 24And
you shall overlay it with pure gold, and make a
molding of gold all around. 25You shall make for
it a frame of a handbreadth all around, and you
shall make a gold molding for the frame all
around. 26And you shall make for it four rings of
gold, and put the rings on the four corners that
are at its four legs. 27The rings shall be close to
the frame, as holders for the poles to bear the
table. 28And you shall make the poles of acacia
wood, and overlay them with gold, that the table
may be carried with them. 29You shall make its
dishes, its pans, its pitchers, and its bowls for
pouring. You shall make them of pure gold.
30And you shall set the showbread on the table
before Me always.

THE GOLD LAMPSTAND

31"You shall also make a lampstand of pure
gold; the lampstand shall be of hammered work.
Its shaft, its branches, its bowls, its *ornamental*
knobs, and flowers shall be *of one piece.* 32And
six branches shall come out of its sides: three
branches of the lampstand out of one side, and
three branches of the lampstand out of the other
side. 33Three bowls *shall be* made like almond
blossoms on one branch, *with* an *ornamental*
knob and a flower, and three bowls made like
almond *blossoms* on the other branch, *with* an
ornamental knob and a flower—and so for the
six branches that come out of the lampstand.
34On the lampstand itself four bowls *shall be*
made like almond *blossoms, each with* its *orna-
mental* knob and flower. 35And *there shall be* a
knob under the *first* two branches of the same,
a knob under the *second* two branches of the
same, and a knob under the *third* two branches
of the same, according to the six branches that
extend from the lampstand. 36Their knobs and
their branches *shall be of one piece;* all of it
shall be one hammered piece of pure gold. 37You
shall make seven lamps for it, and they shall
arrange its lamps so that they give light in front
of it. 38And its wick-trimmers and their trays
shall be of pure gold. 39It shall be made of a tal-
ent of pure gold, with all these utensils. 40And
see to it that you make *them* according to the
pattern which was shown you on the mountain.

THE TABERNACLE

26 "Moreover you shall make the tabernacle
with ten curtains *of* fine woven linen and
blue, purple, and scarlet *thread;* with artistic de-
signs of cherubim you shall weave them. 2The

THE MESSAGE

looking down on it. Set the Atonement-
Cover as a lid over the Chest and place in
the Chest The Testimony that I will give you.
I will meet you there at set times and speak
with you from above the Atonement-Cover
and from between the angel-figures that are
on it, speaking the commands that I have for
the Israelites.

THE TABLE

23-28 "Next make a Table from acacia wood.
Make it three feet long, one and one-half
feet wide and two and one-quarter feet high.
Cover it with a veneer of pure gold. Make a
molding all around it of gold. Make the bor-
der a handbreadth wide all around it and a
rim of gold for the border. Make four rings
of gold and attach the rings to the four legs
parallel to the tabletop. They will serve as
holders for the poles used to carry the Table.
Make the poles of acacia wood and cover
them with a veneer of gold. They will be
used to carry the Table.

29 "Make plates, bowls, jars, and jugs for
pouring out offerings. Make them of pure
gold.

30 "Always keep fresh Bread of the Presence
on the Table before me.

THE LAMPSTAND

31-36 "Make a Lampstand of pure hammered
gold. Make its stem and branches, cups, ca-
lyxes, and petals all of one piece. Give it six
branches, three from one side and three
from the other; put three cups shaped like
almond blossoms, each with calyx and
petals, on one branch, three on the next, and
so on—the same for all six branches. On the
main stem of the Lampstand, make four
cups shaped like almonds, with calyx and
petals, a calyx extending from under each
pair of the six branches, the entire Lamp-
stand fashioned from one piece of ham-
mered pure gold.

37-38 "Make seven of these lamps for the Table.
Arrange the lamps so they throw their light
out in front. Make the candle snuffers and
trays out of pure gold.

39-40 "Use a seventy-five-pound brick of pure
gold to make the Lampstand and its acces-
sories. Study the design you were given on
the mountain and make everything accord-
ingly."

THE DWELLING

1-6 26 "Make The Dwelling itself from ten
panels of tapestry woven from fine
twisted linen, blue and purple and scarlet
material, with an angel-cherubim design. A
skilled craftsman should do it. The panels of

New King James Version

length of each curtain *shall be* twenty-eight cubits, and the width of each curtain four cubits. And every one of the curtains shall have the same measurements. 3Five curtains shall be coupled to one another, and *the other* five curtains *shall be* coupled to one another. 4And you shall make loops of blue *yarn* on the edge of the curtain on the selvedge of *one* set, and likewise you shall do on the outer edge of *the other* curtain of the second set. 5Fifty loops you shall make in the one curtain, and fifty loops you shall make on the edge of the curtain that *is* on the end of the second set, that the loops may be clasped to one another. 6And you shall make fifty clasps of gold, and couple the curtains together with the clasps, so that it may be one tabernacle.

7"You shall also make curtains of goats' *hair,* to be a tent over the tabernacle. You shall make eleven curtains. 8The length of each curtain *shall be* thirty cubits, and the width of each curtain four cubits; and the eleven curtains shall all have the same measurements. 9And you shall couple five curtains by themselves and six curtains by themselves, and you shall double over the sixth curtain at the forefront of the tent. 10You shall make fifty loops on the edge of the curtain that is outermost in *one* set, and fifty loops on the edge of the curtain of the second set. 11And you shall make fifty bronze clasps, put the clasps into the loops, and couple the tent together, that it may be one. 12The remnant that remains of the curtains of the tent, the half curtain that remains, shall hang over the back of the tabernacle. 13And a cubit on one side and a cubit on the other side, of what remains of the length of the curtains of the tent, shall hang over the sides of the tabernacle, on this side and on that side, to cover it.

14"You shall also make a covering of ram skins dyed red for the tent, and a covering of badger skins above that.

15"And for the tabernacle you shall make the boards of acacia wood, standing upright. 16Ten cubits *shall be* the length of a board, and a cubit and a half *shall be* the width of each board. 17Two tenons *shall be* in each board for binding one to another. Thus you shall make for all the boards of the tabernacle. 18And you shall make the boards for the tabernacle, twenty boards for the south side. 19You shall make forty sockets of silver under the twenty boards: two sockets under each of the boards for its two tenons. 20And for the second side of the tabernacle, the north side, *there shall be* twenty boards 21and their forty sockets of silver: two sockets under each of the boards. 22For the far side of the tabernacle, westward, you shall make six boards. 23And you shall also make two boards for the two back corners of the tabernacle. 24They shall be coupled together at the bottom and they shall be coupled together at the top by one ring. Thus it shall be for both of them. They shall be for the two corners. 25So there shall be eight boards with their sockets of silver—sixteen sockets—two sockets under each of the boards.

26"And you shall make bars of acacia wood: five for the boards on one side of the tabernacle, 27five bars for the boards on the other side of the tabernacle, and five bars for the boards of the side of the tabernacle, for the far side westward.

The Message

tapestry are each to be forty-six feet long and six feet wide. Join five of the panels together, and then the other five together. Make loops of blue along the edge of the outside panel of the first set and the same on the outside panel of the second set. Make fifty loops on each panel. Then make fifty gold clasps and join the tapestries together so that The Dwelling is one whole.

7-11 "Next make tapestries of goat hair for a tent that will cover The Dwelling. Make eleven panels of these tapestries. The length of each panel will be forty-five feet long and six feet wide. Join five of the panels together, and then the other six. Fold the sixth panel double at the front of the tent. Now make fifty loops along the edge of the end panel and fifty loops along the edge of the joining panel. Make fifty clasps of bronze and connect the clasps with the loops, bringing the tent together.

12-14 "Hang half of the overlap of the tapestry panels over the rear of The Dwelling. The eighteen inches of overlap on either side will cover the sides of the tent. Finally, make a covering for the tapestries of tanned rams' skins dyed red and over that a covering of dolphin skins.

15-25 "Frame The Dwelling with planks of acacia wood, each section of frame fifteen feet long and two and one-quarter feet wide, with two pegs for securing them. Make all the frames identical: twenty frames for the south side with forty silver sockets to receive the two pegs from each of the twenty frames; the same construction on the north side of The Dwelling; for the rear of The Dwelling, which faces west, make six frames with two additional frames for the rear corners. Both of the two corner frames need to be double in thickness from top to bottom and fit into a single ring—eight frames altogether with sixteen sockets of silver, two under each frame.

26-30 "Now make crossbars of acacia wood, five for the frames on one side of The Dwelling, five for the other side, and five for the back side facing west. The center cross-

NEW KING JAMES VERSION

[28]The middle bar shall pass through the midst of the boards from end to end. [29]You shall overlay the boards with gold, make their rings of gold *as* holders for the bars, and overlay the bars with gold. [30]And you shall raise up the tabernacle according to its pattern which you were shown on the mountain.

[31]“You shall make a veil woven of blue, purple, and scarlet *thread,* and fine woven linen. It shall be woven with an artistic design of cherubim. [32]You shall hang it upon the four pillars of acacia *wood* overlaid with gold. Their hooks *shall be* gold, upon four sockets of silver. [33]And you shall hang the veil from the clasps. Then you shall bring the ark of the Testimony in there, behind the veil. The veil shall be a divider for you between the holy *place* and the Most Holy. [34]You shall put the mercy seat upon the ark of the Testimony in the Most Holy. [35]You shall set the table outside the veil, and the lampstand across from the table on the side of the tabernacle toward the south; and you shall put the table on the north side.

[36]“You shall make a screen for the door of the tabernacle, *woven of* blue, purple, and scarlet *thread,* and fine woven linen, made by a weaver. [37]And you shall make for the screen five pillars of acacia *wood,* and overlay them with gold; their hooks *shall be* gold, and you shall cast five sockets of bronze for them.

THE ALTAR OF BURNT OFFERING

27 “You shall make an altar of acacia wood, five cubits long and five cubits wide—the altar shall be square—and its height *shall be* three cubits. [2]You shall make its horns on its four corners; its horns shall be of one piece with it. And you shall overlay it with bronze. [3]Also you shall make its pans to receive its ashes, and its shovels and its basins and its forks and its firepans; you shall make all its utensils of bronze. [4]You shall make a grate for it, a network of bronze; and on the network you shall make four bronze rings at its four corners. [5]You shall put it under the rim of the altar beneath, that the network may be midway up the altar. [6]And you shall make poles for the altar, poles of acacia wood, and overlay them with bronze. [7]The poles shall be put in the rings, and the poles shall be on the two sides of the altar to bear it. [8]You shall make it hollow with boards; as it was shown you on the mountain, so shall they make *it.*

THE COURT OF THE TABERNACLE

[9]“You shall also make the court of the tabernacle. For the south side *there shall be* hangings for the court *made of* fine woven linen, one hundred cubits long for one side. [10]And its twenty pillars and their twenty sockets *shall be* bronze. The hooks of the pillars and their bands *shall be* silver. [11]Likewise along the length of the north side *there shall be* hangings one hundred *cubits* long, with its twenty pillars and their twenty sockets of bronze, and the hooks of the pillars and their bands of silver.

[12]“And along the width of the court on the west side *shall be* hangings of fifty cubits, with their ten pillars and their ten sockets. [13]The

THE MESSAGE

bar runs from end to end halfway up the frames. Cover the frames with a veneer of gold and make gold rings to hold the crossbars. And cover the crossbars with a veneer of gold. Then put The Dwelling together, following the design you were shown on the mountain.

31-35 “Make a curtain of blue, purple, and scarlet material and fine twisted linen. Have a design of angel-cherubim woven into it by a skilled craftsman. Fasten it with gold hooks to four posts of acacia wood covered with a veneer of gold, set on four silver bases. After hanging the curtain from the clasps, bring the Chest of The Testimony in behind the curtain. The curtain will separate the Holy Place from the Holy-of-Holies. Now place the Atonement-Cover lid on the Chest of The Testimony in the Holy-of-Holies. Place the Table and the Lampstand outside the curtain, the Lampstand on the south side of The Dwelling and the Table opposite it on the north side.

36-37 “Make a screen for the door of the tent. Weave it from blue, purple, and scarlet material and fine twisted linen. Frame the weaving with five poles of acacia wood covered with a veneer of gold and make gold hooks to hang the weaving. Cast five bronze bases for the poles.”

THE ALTAR

1-8 27 “Make an Altar of acacia wood. Make it seven and a half feet square and four and a half feet high. Make horns at each of the four corners. The horns are to be of one piece with the Altar and covered with a veneer of bronze. Make buckets for removing the ashes, along with shovels, basins, forks, and fire pans. Make all these utensils from bronze. Make a grate of bronze mesh and attach bronze rings at each of the four corners. Put the grate under the ledge of the Altar at the halfway point of the Altar. Make acacia wood poles for the Altar and cover them with a veneer of bronze. Insert the poles through the rings on the two sides of the Altar for carrying. Use boards to make the Altar, keeping the interior hollow.

THE COURTYARD

9-11 “Make a Courtyard for The Dwelling. The south side is to be 150 feet long. The hangings for the Courtyard are to be woven from fine twisted linen, with their twenty posts, twenty bronze bases, and fastening hooks and bands of silver. The north side is to be exactly the same.

12-19 “For the west end of the Courtyard you will need seventy-five feet of hangings with their ten posts and bases. Across the

NEW KING JAMES VERSION

width of the court on the east side *shall be* fifty cubits. 14The hangings on *one* side *of the gate shall be* fifteen cubits, *with* their three pillars and their three sockets. 15And on the other side *shall be* hangings of fifteen *cubits, with* their three pillars and their three sockets.

16"For the gate of the court *there shall be* a screen twenty cubits long, *woven of* blue, purple, and scarlet *thread,* and fine woven linen, made by a weaver. It *shall have* four pillars and four sockets. 17All the pillars around the court shall have bands of silver; their hooks *shall be* of silver and their sockets of bronze. 18The length of the court *shall be* one hundred cubits, the width fifty throughout, and the height five cubits, *made of* fine woven linen, and its sockets of bronze. 19All the utensils of the tabernacle for all its service, all its pegs, and all the pegs of the court, *shall be* of bronze.

THE CARE OF THE LAMPSTAND

20"And you shall command the children of Israel that they bring you pure oil of pressed olives for the light, to cause the lamp to burn continually. 21In the tabernacle of meeting, outside the veil which *is* before the Testimony, Aaron and his sons shall tend it from evening until morning before the LORD. *It shall be* a statute forever to their generations on behalf of the children of Israel.

GARMENTS FOR THE PRIESTHOOD

28 "Now take Aaron your brother, and his sons with him, from among the children of Israel, that he may minister to Me as priest, Aaron *and* Aaron's sons: Nadab, Abihu, Eleazar, and Ithamar. 2And you shall make holy garments for Aaron your brother, for glory and for beauty. 3So you shall speak to all *who are* gifted artisans, whom I have filled with the spirit of wisdom, that they may make Aaron's garments, to consecrate him, that he may minister to Me as priest. 4And these *are* the garments which they shall make: a breastplate, an ephod,[a] a robe, a skillfully woven tunic, a turban, and a sash. So they shall make holy garments for Aaron your brother and his sons, that he may minister to Me as priest.

THE EPHOD

5"They shall take the gold, blue, purple, and scarlet *thread,* and the fine linen, 6and they shall make the ephod of gold, blue, purple, *and* scarlet *thread,* and fine woven linen, artistically worked. 7It shall have two shoulder straps joined at its two edges, and *so* it shall be joined together. 8And the intricately woven band of the ephod, which *is* on it, shall be of the same workmanship, *made of* gold, blue, purple, and scarlet *thread,* and fine woven linen.

9"Then you shall take two onyx stones and engrave on them the names of the sons of Israel: 10six of their names on one stone and six names on the other stone, in order of their birth. 11With the work of an engraver in stone, *like* the engravings of a signet, you shall engrave the two

28:4 [a]That is, an ornamented vest

THE MESSAGE

seventy-five feet at the front, or east end, you will need twenty-two and a half feet of hangings, with their three posts and bases on one side and the same for the other side. At the door of the Courtyard make a screen thirty feet long woven from blue, purple, and scarlet stuff, with fine twisted linen, embroidered by a craftsman, and hung on its four posts and bases. All the posts around the Courtyard are to be banded with silver, with hooks of silver and bases of bronze. The Courtyard is to be 150 feet long and seventy-five feet wide. The hangings of fine twisted linen set on their bronze bases are to be seven and a half feet high. All the tools used for setting up The Holy Dwelling, including all the pegs in it and the Courtyard, are to be made of bronze.

20-21 "Now, order the Israelites to bring you pure, clear olive oil for light so that the lamps can be kept burning. In the Tent of Meeting, the area outside the curtain that veils The Testimony, Aaron and his sons will keep this light burning from evening until morning before GOD. This is to be a permanent practice down through the generations for Israelites."

THE VESTMENTS

1-5 28 "Get your brother Aaron and his sons from among the Israelites to serve me as priests: Aaron and his sons Nadab, Abihu, Eleazar, Ithamar. Make sacred vestments for your brother Aaron to symbolize glory and beauty. Consult with the skilled craftsmen, those whom I have gifted in this work, and arrange for them to make Aaron's vestments, to set him apart as holy, to act as priest for me. These are the articles of clothing they are to make: Breastpiece, Ephod, robe, woven tunic, turban, sash. They are making holy vestments for your brother Aaron and his sons as they work as priests for me. They will need gold; blue, purple, and scarlet material; and fine linen.

THE EPHOD

6-14 "Have the Ephod made from gold; blue, purple, and scarlet material; and fine twisted linen by a skilled craftsman. Give it two shoulder pieces at two of the corners so it can be fastened. The decorated band on it is to be just like it and of one piece with it: made of gold; blue, purple, and scarlet material; and of fine twisted linen. Next take two onyx stones and engrave the names of the sons of Israel on them in the order of their birth, six names on one stone and the remaining six on the other. Engrave the names of the sons of Israel on the two stones the way a jeweler engraves a seal.

NEW KING JAMES VERSION

stones with the names of the sons of Israel. You
shall set them in settings of gold. [12]And you
shall put the two stones on the shoulders of the
ephod *as* memorial stones for the sons of Israel.
So Aaron shall bear their names before the
LORD on his two shoulders as a memorial. [13]You
shall also make settings of gold, [14]and you shall
make two chains of pure gold like braided
cords, and fasten the braided chains to the set-
tings.

THE BREASTPLATE

[15]"You shall make the breastplate of judg-
ment. Artistically woven according to the work-
manship of the ephod you shall make it: of gold,
blue, purple, and scarlet *thread,* and fine woven
linen, you shall make it. [16]It shall be doubled
into a square: a span *shall be* its length, and a
span *shall be* its width. [17]And you shall put set-
tings of stones in it, four rows of stones: *The
first* row *shall be* a sardius, a topaz, and an
emerald; *this shall be* the first row; [18]the second
row *shall be* a turquoise, a sapphire, and a dia-
mond; [19]the third row, a jacinth, an agate, and an
amethyst; [20]and the fourth row, a beryl, an onyx,
and a jasper. They shall be set in gold settings.
[21]And the stones shall have the names of the
sons of Israel, twelve according to their names,
like the engravings of a signet, each one with its
own name; they shall be according to the twelve
tribes.

[22]"You shall make chains for the breastplate
at the end, like braided cords of pure gold. [23]And
you shall make two rings of gold for the breast-
plate, and put the two rings on the two ends of
the breastplate. [24]Then you shall put the two
braided *chains* of gold in the two rings which
are on the ends of the breastplate; [25]and the
other two ends of the two braided *chains* you
shall fasten to the two settings, and put them on
the shoulder straps of the ephod in the front.

[26]"You shall make two rings of gold, and put
them on the two ends of the breastplate, on the
edge of it, which is on the inner side of the
ephod. [27]And two *other* rings of gold you shall
make, and put them on the two shoulder straps,
underneath the ephod toward its front, right at
the seam above the intricately woven band of
the ephod. [28]They shall bind the breastplate by
means of its rings to the rings of the ephod, us-
ing a blue cord, so that it is above the intricately
woven band of the ephod, and so that the breast-
plate does not come loose from the ephod.

[29]"So Aaron shall bear the names of the sons
of Israel on the breastplate of judgment over his
heart, when he goes into the holy *place,* as a me-
morial before the LORD continually. [30]And you
shall put in the breastplate of judgment the
Urim and the Thummim,[a] and they shall be over
Aaron's heart when he goes in before the LORD.
So Aaron shall bear the judgment of the chil-
dren of Israel over his heart before the LORD
continually.

28:30 [a]Literally *the Lights and the Perfections* (compare Leviticus 8:8)

THE MESSAGE

Then mount the stones in settings of fili-
greed gold. Fasten the two stones on the
shoulder pieces of the Ephod—they are me-
morial stones for the Israelites. Aaron will
wear these names on his shoulders as a me-
morial before GOD. Make the settings of
gold filigree. Make two chains of pure gold
and braid them like cords, then attach the
corded chains to the settings.

THE BREASTPIECE

15-20 "Now make a Breastpiece of Judgment, us-
ing skilled craftsmen, the same as with the
Ephod. Use gold; blue, purple, and scarlet
material; and fine twisted linen. Make it
nine inches square and folded double.
Mount four rows of precious gemstones on
it.

First row: carnelian, topaz, emerald.
Second row: ruby, sapphire, crystal.
Third row: jacinth, agate, amethyst.
Fourth row: beryl, onyx, jasper.

20-21 "Set them in gold filigree. The twelve
stones correspond to the names of the Is-
raelites, with twelve names engraved, one
on each, as on a seal for the twelve tribes.

22-28 "Then make braided chains of pure gold
for the Breastpiece, like cords. Make two
rings of gold for the Breastpiece and fasten
them to the two ends. Fasten the two golden
cords to the rings at the ends of the Breast-
piece. Then fasten the other ends of the two
cords to the two settings of filigree, attach-
ing them to the shoulder pieces of the
Ephod in front. Then make two rings of gold
and fasten them to the two ends of the
Breastpiece on its inside edge facing the
Ephod. Then make two more rings of gold
and fasten them in the front of the Ephod to
the lower part of the two shoulder pieces,
near the seam above the decorated band.
Fasten the Breastpiece in place by running a
cord of blue through its rings to the rings of
the Ephod so that it rests secure on the dec-
orated band of the Ephod and won't come
loose.

29-30 "Aaron will regularly carry the names of
the sons of Israel on the Breastpiece of
Judgment over his heart as he enters the
Sanctuary into the presence of GOD for re-
membrance. Place the Urim and Thummim
in the Breastpiece of Judgment. They will be
over Aaron's heart when he enters the pres-
ence of GOD. In this way Aaron will regu-
larly carry the Breastpiece of Judgment into
the presence of GOD.

NEW KING JAMES VERSION

OTHER PRIESTLY GARMENTS

31“You shall make the robe of the ephod all of
blue. 32There shall be an opening for his head in
the middle of it; it shall have a woven binding all
around its opening, like the opening in a coat of
mail, so that it does not tear. 33And upon its hem
you shall make pomegranates of blue, purple,
and scarlet, all around its hem, and bells of gold
between them all around: 34a golden bell and a
pomegranate, a golden bell and a pomegranate,
upon the hem of the robe all around. 35And it
shall be upon Aaron when he ministers, and its
sound will be heard when he goes into the holy
place before the LORD and when he comes out,
that he may not die.

36“You shall also make a plate of pure gold
and engrave on it, *like* the engraving of a signet:

HOLINESS TO THE LORD.

37And you shall put it on a blue cord, that it may
be on the turban; it shall be on the front of the
turban. 38So it shall be on Aaron’s forehead, that
Aaron may bear the iniquity of the holy things
which the children of Israel hallow in all their
holy gifts; and it shall always be on his fore-
head, that they may be accepted before the
LORD.

39“You shall skillfully weave the tunic of fine
linen *thread,* you shall make the turban of fine
linen, and you shall make the sash of woven
work.

40“For Aaron’s sons you shall make tunics,
and you shall make sashes for them. And you
shall make hats for them, for glory and beauty.
41So you shall put them on Aaron your brother
and on his sons with him. You shall anoint them,
consecrate them, and sanctify them, that they
may minister to Me as priests. 42And you shall
make for them linen trousers to cover their
nakedness; they shall reach from the waist to
the thighs. 43They shall be on Aaron and on his
sons when they come into the tabernacle of
meeting, or when they come near the altar to
minister in the holy *place,* that they do not incur
iniquity and die. *It shall be* a statute forever to
him and his descendants after him.

AARON AND HIS SONS CONSECRATED

29 “And this is what you shall do to them to
hallow them for ministering to Me as
priests: Take one young bull and two rams with-
out blemish, 2and unleavened bread, unleavened
cakes mixed with oil, and unleavened wafers
anointed with oil (you shall make them of wheat
flour). 3You shall put them in one basket and
bring them in the basket, with the bull and the
two rams.

4“And Aaron and his sons you shall bring to
the door of the tabernacle of meeting, and you
shall wash them with water. 5Then you shall
take the garments, put the tunic on Aaron, and
the robe of the ephod, the ephod, and the breast-
plate, and gird him with the intricately woven
band of the ephod. 6You shall put the turban on
his head, and put the holy crown on the turban.
7And you shall take the anointing oil, pour *it* on
his head, and anoint him. 8Then you shall bring
his sons and put tunics on them. 9And you shall

THE MESSAGE

THE ROBE

31-35 “Make the robe for the Ephod entirely of blue, with an opening for the head at the center and a hem on the edge so that it won’t tear. For the edge of the skirts make pomegranates of blue, purple, and scarlet material all around and alternate them with bells of gold—gold bell and pomegranate, gold bell and pomegranate—all around the hem of the robe. Aaron has to wear it when he does his priestly work. The bells will be heard when he enters the Holy Place and comes into the presence of GOD, and again when he comes out so that he won’t die.

THE TURBAN, TUNIC, UNDERWEAR

36-38 “Make a plate of pure gold. Engrave on it as on a seal: ‘Holy to GOD.’ Tie it with a blue cord to the front of the turban. It is to rest there on Aaron’s forehead. He’ll take on any guilt involved in the sacred offerings that the Israelites consecrate, no matter what they bring. It will always be on Aaron’s forehead so that the offerings will be acceptable before GOD.

39-41 “Weave the tunic of fine linen. Make the turban of fine linen. The sash will be the work of an embroiderer. Make tunics, sashes, and hats for Aaron’s sons to express glory and beauty. Dress your brother Aaron and his sons in them. Anoint, ordain, and consecrate them to serve me as priests.

42-43 “Make linen underwear to cover their nakedness from waist to thigh. Aaron and his sons must wear it whenever they enter the Tent of Meeting or approach the Altar to minister in the Holy Place so that they won’t incur guilt and die. This is a permanent rule for Aaron and all his priest-descendants.”

CONSECRATION OF PRIESTS

1-4 29 “This is the ceremony for consecrating them as priests. Take a young bull and two rams, healthy and without defects. Using fine wheat flour but no yeast make bread and cakes mixed with oil and wafers spread with oil. Place them in a basket and carry them along with the bull and the two rams. Bring Aaron and his sons to the entrance of the Tent of Meeting and wash them with water.

5-9 “Then take the vestments and dress Aaron in the tunic, the robe of the Ephod, the Ephod, and the Breastpiece, belting the Ephod on him with the embroidered waistband. Set the turban on his head and place the sacred crown on the turban. Then take the anointing oil and pour it on his head, anointing him. Then bring his sons, put tunics on them and gird them with sashes, both Aaron and his sons, and set hats on them. Their priesthood is upheld by law and is permanent.

NEW KING JAMES VERSION

gird them with sashes, Aaron and his sons, and
put the hats on them. The priesthood shall be
theirs for a perpetual statute. So you shall con-
secrate Aaron and his sons.
10“You shall also have the bull brought be-
fore the tabernacle of meeting, and Aaron and
his sons shall put their hands on the head of the
bull. 11Then you shall kill the bull before the
LORD, *by* the door of the tabernacle of meeting.
12You shall take *some* of the blood of the bull
and put *it* on the horns of the altar with your fin-
ger, and pour all the blood beside the base of the
altar. 13And you shall take all the fat that covers
the entrails, the fatty lobe *attached* to the liver,
and the two kidneys and the fat that *is* on them,
and burn *them* on the altar. 14But the flesh of the
bull, with its skin and its offal, you shall burn
with fire outside the camp. It *is* a sin offering.
15“You shall also take one ram, and Aaron
and his sons shall put their hands on the head of
the ram; 16and you shall kill the ram, and you
shall take its blood and sprinkle *it* all around on
the altar. 17Then you shall cut the ram in pieces,
wash its entrails and its legs, and put *them* with
its pieces and with its head. 18And you shall
burn the whole ram on the altar. It *is* a burnt of-
fering to the LORD; it *is* a sweet aroma, an offer-
ing made by fire to the LORD.
19“You shall also take the other ram, and
Aaron and his sons shall put their hands on the
head of the ram. 20Then you shall kill the ram,
and take some of its blood and put *it* on the tip
of the right ear of Aaron and on the tip of the
right ear of his sons, on the thumb of their right
hand and on the big toe of their right foot, and
sprinkle the blood all around on the altar. 21And
you shall take some of the blood that is on the
altar, and some of the anointing oil, and sprinkle
it on Aaron and on his garments, on his sons
and on the garments of his sons with him; and
he and his garments shall be hallowed, and his
sons and his sons' garments with him.
22“Also you shall take the fat of the ram, the
fat tail, the fat that covers the entrails, the fatty
lobe *attached to* the liver, the two kidneys and
the fat on them, the right thigh (for it *is* a ram of
consecration), 23one loaf of bread, one cake
made with oil, and one wafer from the basket of
the unleavened bread that *is* before the LORD;
24and you shall put all these in the hands of
Aaron and in the hands of his sons, and you
shall wave them *as* a wave offering before the
LORD. 25You shall receive them back from their
hands and burn *them* on the altar as a burnt of-
fering, as a sweet aroma before the LORD. It *is* an
offering made by fire to the LORD.
26“Then you shall take the breast of the ram
of Aaron's consecration and wave it *as* a wave
offering before the LORD; and it shall be your
portion. 27And from the ram of the consecration
you shall consecrate the breast of the wave offer-
ing which is waved, and the thigh of the heave
offering which is raised, of *that* which *is* for
Aaron and of *that* which is for his sons. 28It shall
be from the children of Israel *for* Aaron and his
sons by a statute forever. For it is a heave offer-
ing; it shall be a heave offering from the children
of Israel from the sacrifices of their peace offer-
ings, *that is,* their heave offering to the LORD.

THE MESSAGE

9-14 “This is how you will ordain Aaron and his sons: Bring the bull to the Tent of Meeting. Aaron and his sons will place their hands on the head of the bull. Then you will slaughter the bull in the presence of GOD at the entrance to the Tent of Meeting. Take some of the bull's blood and smear it on the horns of the Altar with your finger; pour the rest of the blood on the base of the Altar. Next take all the fat that covers the innards, fat from around the liver and the two kidneys, and burn it on the Altar. But the flesh of the bull, including its hide and dung, you will burn up outside the camp. It is an Absolution-Offering.

15-18 “Then take one of the rams. Have Aaron and his sons place their hands on the head of the ram. Slaughter the ram and take its blood and throw it against the Altar, all around. Cut the ram into pieces; wash its innards and legs, then gather the pieces and its head and burn the whole ram on the Altar. It is a Whole-Burnt-Offering to GOD, a pleasant fragrance, an offering by fire to GOD.

19-21 “Then take the second ram. Have Aaron and his sons place their hands on the ram's head. Slaughter the ram. Take some of its blood and rub it on Aaron's right earlobe and on the right earlobes of his sons, on the thumbs of their right hands and on the big toes of their right feet. Sprinkle the rest of the blood against all sides of the Altar. Then take some of the blood that is on the Altar, mix it with some of the anointing oil, and splash it on Aaron and his clothes and on his sons and their clothes so that Aaron and his clothes and his sons and his sons' clothes will be made holy.

22-23 “Take the fat from the ram, the fat tail, the fat that covers the innards, the long lobe of the liver, the two kidneys and the fat on them, and the right thigh: this is the ordination ram. Also take one loaf of bread, an oil cake, and a wafer from the breadbasket that is in the presence of GOD.

24-25 “Place all of these in the open hands of Aaron and his sons who will wave them before GOD, a Wave-Offering. Then take them from their hands and burn them on the Altar with the Whole-Burnt-Offering—a pleasing fragrance before GOD, a gift to GOD.

26 “Now take the breast from Aaron's ordination ram and wave it before GOD, a Wave-Offering. That will be your portion.

27-28 “Consecrate the Wave-Offering breast and the thigh that was held up. These are the parts of the ordination ram that are for Aaron and his sons. Aaron and his sons are always to get this offering from the Israelites; the Israelites are to make this offering regularly from their Peace-Offerings.

New King James Version

29“And the holy garments of Aaron shall be his sons’ after him, to be anointed in them and to be consecrated in them. 30That son who becomes priest in his place shall put them on for seven days, when he enters the tabernacle of meeting to minister in the holy *place*.

31“And you shall take the ram of the consecration and boil its flesh in the holy place. 32Then Aaron and his sons shall eat the flesh of the ram, and the bread that *is* in the basket, *by* the door of the tabernacle of meeting. 33They shall eat those things with which the atonement was made, to consecrate *and* to sanctify them; but an outsider shall not eat *them*, because they *are* holy. 34And if any of the flesh of the consecration offerings, or of the bread, remains until the morning, then you shall burn the remainder with fire. It shall not be eaten, because it *is* holy.

35“Thus you shall do to Aaron and his sons, according to all that I have commanded you. Seven days you shall consecrate them. 36And you shall offer a bull every day *as* a sin offering for atonement. You shall cleanse the altar when you make atonement for it, and you shall anoint it to sanctify it. 37Seven days you shall make atonement for the altar and sanctify it. And the altar shall be most holy. Whatever touches the altar must be holy.[a]

The Daily Offerings

38“Now this *is* what you shall offer on the altar: two lambs of the first year, day by day continually. 39One lamb you shall offer in the morning, and the other lamb you shall offer at twilight. 40With the one lamb shall be one-tenth *of an ephah* of flour mixed with one-fourth of a hin of pressed oil, and one-fourth of a hin of wine *as* a drink offering. 41And the other lamb you shall offer at twilight; and you shall offer with it the grain offering and the drink offering, as in the morning, for a sweet aroma, an offering made by fire to the LORD. 42*This shall be* a continual burnt offering throughout your generations *at* the door of the tabernacle of meeting before the LORD, where I will meet you to speak with you. 43And there I will meet with the children of Israel, and *the tabernacle* shall be sanctified by My glory. 44So I will consecrate the tabernacle of meeting and the altar. I will also consecrate both Aaron and his sons to minister to Me as priests. 45I will dwell among the children of Israel and will be their God. 46And they shall know that I *am* the LORD their God, who brought them up out of the land of Egypt, that I may dwell among them. I *am* the LORD their God.

The Altar of Incense

30 “You shall make an altar to burn incense on; you shall make it of acacia wood. 2A cubit *shall be* its length and a cubit its width—it shall be square—and two cubits *shall be* its height. Its horns *shall be* of one piece with it. 3And you shall overlay its top, its sides all around, and its horns with pure gold; and you shall make for it a molding of gold all around.

29:37 [a]Compare Numbers 4:15 and Haggai 2:11–13

The Message

29-30 “Aaron’s sacred garments are to be handed down to his descendants so they can be anointed and ordained in them. The son who succeeds him as priest is to wear them for seven days and enter the Tent of Meeting to minister in the Holy Place.

31-34 “Take the ordination ram and boil the meat in the Holy Place. At the entrance to the Tent of Meeting, Aaron and his sons will eat the boiled ram and the bread that is in the basket. Atoned by these offerings, ordained and consecrated by them, they are the only ones who are to eat them. No outsiders are to eat them; they’re holy. Anything from the ordination ram or from the bread that is left over until morning you are to burn up. Don’t eat it; it’s holy.

35-37 “Do everything for the ordination of Aaron and his sons exactly as I’ve commanded you throughout the seven days. Offer a bull as an Absolution-Offering for atonement each day. Offer it on the Altar when you make atonement for it: Anoint and consecrate it. Make atonement for the Altar and consecrate it for seven days; the Altar will become soaked in holiness—anyone who so much as touches the Altar will become holy.

38-41 “This is what you are to offer on the Altar: two year-old lambs each and every day, one lamb in the morning and the second lamb at evening. With the sacrifice of the first lamb offer two quarts of fine flour with a quart of virgin olive oil, plus a quart of wine for a Drink-Offering. The sacrifice of the second lamb, the one at evening, is also to be accompanied by the same Grain-Offering and Drink-Offering of the morning sacrifice to give a pleasing fragrance, a gift to GOD.

42-46 “This is to be your regular, daily Whole-Burnt-Offering before GOD, generation after generation, sacrificed at the entrance of the Tent of Meeting. That’s where I’ll meet you; that’s where I’ll speak with you; that’s where I’ll meet the Israelites, at the place made holy by my Glory. I’ll make the Tent of Meeting and the Altar holy. I’ll make Aaron and his sons holy in order to serve me as priests. I’ll move in and live with the Israelites. I’ll be their God. They’ll realize that I am their GOD who brought them out of the land of Egypt so that I could live with them. I am GOD, *your* God.”

The Altar of Incense

1-5 30 “Make an Altar for burning incense. Construct it from acacia wood, one and one-half feet square and three feet high with its horns of one piece with it. Cover it with a veneer of pure gold, its top, sides, and horns, and make a gold molding around it

NEW KING JAMES VERSION

4 Two gold rings you shall make for it, under the molding on both its sides. You shall place *them* on its two sides, and they will be holders for the poles with which to bear it. 5 You shall make the poles of acacia wood, and overlay them with gold. 6 And you shall put it before the veil that *is* before the ark of the Testimony, before the mercy seat that *is* over the Testimony, where I will meet with you.

7 "Aaron shall burn on it sweet incense every morning; when he tends the lamps, he shall burn incense on it. 8 And when Aaron lights the lamps at twilight, he shall burn incense on it, a perpetual incense before the LORD throughout your generations. 9 You shall not offer strange incense on it, or a burnt offering, or a grain offering; nor shall you pour a drink offering on it. 10 And Aaron shall make atonement upon its horns once a year with the blood of the sin offering of atonement; once a year he shall make atonement upon it throughout your generations. It *is* most holy to the LORD."

THE RANSOM MONEY

11 Then the LORD spoke to Moses, saying: 12 "When you take the census of the children of Israel for their number, then every man shall give a ransom for himself to the LORD, when you number them, that there may be no plague among them when *you* number them. 13 This is what everyone among those who are numbered shall give: half a shekel according to the shekel of the sanctuary (a shekel *is* twenty gerahs). The half-shekel *shall be* an offering to the LORD. 14 Everyone included among those who are numbered, from twenty years old and above, shall give an offering to the LORD. 15 The rich shall not give more and the poor shall not give less than half a shekel, when *you* give an offering to the LORD, to make atonement for yourselves. 16 And you shall take the atonement money of the children of Israel, and shall appoint it for the service of the tabernacle of meeting, that it may be a memorial for the children of Israel before the LORD, to make atonement for yourselves."

THE BRONZE LAVER

17 Then the LORD spoke to Moses, saying: 18 "You shall also make a laver of bronze, with its base also of bronze, for washing. You shall put it between the tabernacle of meeting and the altar. And you shall put water in it, 19 for Aaron and his sons shall wash their hands and their feet in water from it. 20 When they go into the tabernacle of meeting, or when they come near the altar to minister, to burn an offering made by fire to the LORD, they shall wash with water, lest they die. 21 So they shall wash their hands and their feet, lest they die. And it shall be a statute forever to them—to him and his descendants throughout their generations."

THE HOLY ANOINTING OIL

22 Moreover the LORD spoke to Moses, saying: 23 "Also take for yourself quality spices—five hundred *shekels* of liquid myrrh, half as much sweet-smelling cinnamon (two hundred and fifty *shekels*), two hundred and fifty *shekels* of

THE MESSAGE

with two rings of gold beneath the molding. Place the rings on the two opposing sides to serve as holders for poles by which it will be carried. Make the poles of acacia wood and cover them with a veneer of gold.

6-10 "Place the Altar in front of the curtain that hides the Chest of The Testimony, in front of the Atonement-Cover that is over The Testimony where I will meet you. Aaron will burn fragrant incense on it every morning when he polishes the lamps, and again in the evening as he prepares the lamps for lighting, so that there will always be incense burning before GOD, generation after generation. But don't burn on this Altar any unholy incense or Whole-Burnt-Offering or Grain-Offering. And don't pour out Drink-Offerings on it. Once a year Aaron is to purify the Altar horns. Using the blood of the Absolution-Offering of atonement, he is to make this atonement every year down through the generations. It is most holy to GOD."

THE ATONEMENT-TAX

11-16 GOD spoke to Moses: "When you take a head count of the Israelites to keep track of them, all must pay an atonement-tax to GOD for their life at the time of being registered so that nothing bad will happen because of the registration. Everyone who gets counted is to give a half-shekel (using the standard Sanctuary shekel of a fifth of an ounce to the shekel)—a half-shekel offering to GOD. Everyone counted, age twenty and up, is to make the offering to GOD. The rich are not to pay more nor the poor less than the half-shekel offering to GOD, the atonement-tax for your lives. Take the atonement-tax money from the Israelites and put it to the maintenance of the Tent of Meeting. It will be a memorial fund for the Israelites in honor of GOD, making atonement for your lives."

THE WASHBASIN

17-21 GOD spoke to Moses: "Make a bronze Washbasin; make it with a bronze base. Place it between the Tent of Meeting and the Altar. Put water in it. Aaron and his sons will wash their hands and feet in it. When they enter the Tent of Meeting or approach the Altar to serve there or offer gift offerings to GOD, they are to wash so they will not die. They are to wash their hands and their feet so they will not die. This is the rule forever, for Aaron and his sons down through the generations."

HOLY ANOINTING OIL

22-25 GOD spoke to Moses: "Take the best spices: twelve and a half pounds of liquid myrrh; half that much, six and a quarter pounds, of fragrant cinnamon; six and a quarter

NEW KING JAMES VERSION

sweet-smelling cane, [24]five hundred *shekels* of cassia, according to the shekel of the sanctuary, and a hin of olive oil. [25]And you shall make from these a holy anointing oil, an ointment compounded according to the art of the perfumer. It shall be a holy anointing oil. [26]With it you shall anoint the tabernacle of meeting and the ark of the Testimony; [27]the table and all its utensils, the lampstand and its utensils, and the altar of incense; [28]the altar of burnt offering with all its utensils, and the laver and its base. [29]You shall consecrate them, that they may be most holy; whatever touches them must be holy.[a] [30]And you shall anoint Aaron and his sons, and consecrate them, that *they* may minister to Me as priests.

[31]"And you shall speak to the children of Israel, saying: 'This shall be a holy anointing oil to Me throughout your generations. [32]It shall not be poured on man's flesh; nor shall you make *any other* like it, according to its composition. It *is* holy, *and* it shall be holy to you. [33]Whoever compounds *any* like it, or whoever puts *any* of it on an outsider, shall be cut off from his people.' "

THE INCENSE

[34]And the LORD said to Moses: "Take sweet spices, stacte and onycha and galbanum, and pure frankincense with *these* sweet spices; there shall be equal amounts of each. [35]You shall make of these an incense, a compound according to the art of the perfumer, salted, pure, *and* holy. [36]And you shall beat *some* of it very fine, and put some of it before the Testimony in the tabernacle of meeting where I will meet with you. It shall be most holy to you. [37]But *as for* the incense which you shall make, you shall not make any for yourselves, according to its composition. It shall be to you holy for the LORD. [38]Whoever makes *any* like it, to smell it, he shall be cut off from his people."

ARTISANS FOR BUILDING THE TABERNACLE

31 Then the LORD spoke to Moses, saying: [2]"See, I have called by name Bezalel the son of Uri, the son of Hur, of the tribe of Judah. [3]And I have filled him with the Spirit of God, in wisdom, in understanding, in knowledge, and in all *manner of* workmanship, [4]to design artistic works, to work in gold, in silver, in bronze, [5]in cutting jewels for setting, in carving wood, and to work in all *manner of* workmanship.

[6]"And I, indeed I, have appointed with him Aholiab the son of Ahisamach, of the tribe of Dan; and I have put wisdom in the hearts of all the gifted artisans, that they may make all that I have commanded you: [7]the tabernacle of meeting, the ark of the Testimony and the mercy seat that *is* on it, and all the furniture of the tabernacle—[8]the table and its utensils, the pure *gold* lampstand with all its utensils, the altar of incense, [9]the altar of burnt offering with all its utensils, and the laver and its base—[10]the garments of ministry,[a] the holy garments for Aaron the priest and the garments of his sons, to minister as priests, [11]and the anointing oil and sweet

30:29 [a]Compare Numbers 4:15 and Haggai 2:11–13 **31:10** [a]Or *woven garments*

THE MESSAGE

pounds of fragrant cane; twelve and a half pounds of cassia—using the standard Sanctuary weight for all of them—and a gallon of olive oil. Make these into a holy anointing oil, a perfumer's skillful blend.

26-29 "Use it to anoint the Tent of Meeting, the Chest of The Testimony, the Table and all its utensils, the Lampstand and its utensils, the Altar of Incense, the Altar of Whole-Burnt-Offerings and all its utensils, and the Washbasin and its base. Consecrate them so they'll be soaked in holiness, so that anyone who so much as touches them will become holy.

30-33 "Then anoint Aaron and his sons. Consecrate them as priests to me. Tell the Israelites, 'This will be my holy anointing oil throughout your generations.' Don't pour it on ordinary men. Don't copy this mixture to use for yourselves. It's holy; keep it holy. Whoever mixes up anything like it, or puts it on an ordinary person, will be expelled."

HOLY INCENSE

34-38 GOD spoke to Moses: "Take fragrant spices—gum resin, onycha, galbanum—and add pure frankincense. Mix the spices in equal proportions to make an aromatic incense, the art of a perfumer, salted and pure—holy. Now crush some of it into powder and place some of it before The Testimony in the Tent of Meeting where I will meet with you; it will be for you the holiest of holy places. When you make this incense, you are not to copy the mixture for your own use. It's holy to GOD; keep it that way. Whoever copies it for personal use will be excommunicated."

BEZALEL AND OHOLIAB

1-5 31 GOD spoke to Moses: "See what I've done; I've personally chosen Bezalel son of Uri, son of Hur of the tribe of Judah. I've filled him with the Spirit of God, giving him skill and know-how and expertise in every kind of craft to create designs and work in gold, silver, and bronze; to cut and set gemstones; to carve wood—he's an all-around craftsman.

6-11 "Not only that, but I've given him Oholiab, son of Ahisamach of the tribe of Dan, to work with him. And to all who have an aptitude for crafts I've given the skills to make all the things I've commanded you: the Tent of Meeting, the Chest of The Testimony and its Atonement-Cover, all the implements for the Tent, the Table and its implements, the pure Lampstand and all its implements, the Altar of Incense, the Altar of Whole-Burnt-Offering and all its implements, the Washbasin and its base, the official vestments, the holy vestments for Aaron the priest and his sons in their priestly duties, the anointing oil, and the aromatic in-

NEW KING JAMES VERSION

incense for the holy *place*. According to all that
I have commanded you they shall do."

THE SABBATH LAW

12And the LORD spoke to Moses, saying,
13"Speak also to the children of Israel, saying:
'Surely My Sabbaths you shall keep, for it *is* a
sign between Me and you throughout your gen-
erations, that *you* may know that I *am* the LORD
who sanctifies you. 14You shall keep the Sab-
bath, therefore, for *it is* holy to you. Everyone
who profanes it shall surely be put to death; for
whoever does *any* work on it, that person shall
be cut off from among his people. 15Work shall
be done for six days, but the seventh *is* the Sab-
bath of rest, holy to the LORD. Whoever does *any*
work on the Sabbath day, he shall surely be put
to death. 16Therefore the children of Israel shall
keep the Sabbath, to observe the Sabbath
throughout their generations *as* a perpetual
covenant. 17It *is* a sign between Me and the chil-
dren of Israel forever; for *in* six days the LORD
made the heavens and the earth, and on the sev-
enth day He rested and was refreshed.' "
18And when He had made an end of speak-
ing with him on Mount Sinai, He gave Moses
two tablets of the Testimony, tablets of stone,
written with the finger of God.

THE GOLD CALF

32 Now when the people saw that Moses de-
layed coming down from the mountain,
the people gathered together to Aaron, and said
to him, "Come, make us gods that shall go be-
fore us; for *as for* this Moses, the man who
brought us up out of the land of Egypt, we do
not know what has become of him."
2And Aaron said to them, "Break off the
golden earrings which *are* in the ears of your
wives, your sons, and your daughters, and bring
them to me." 3So all the people broke off the
golden earrings which *were* in their ears, and
brought *them* to Aaron. 4And he received *the
gold* from their hand, and he fashioned it with
an engraving tool, and made a molded calf.
Then they said, "This *is* your god, O Israel,
that brought you out of the land of Egypt!"
5So when Aaron saw *it*, he built an altar be-
fore it. And Aaron made a proclamation and
said, "Tomorrow *is* a feast to the LORD." 6Then
they rose early on the next day, offered burnt of-
ferings, and brought peace offerings; and the
people sat down to eat and drink, and rose up to
play.
7And the LORD said to Moses, "Go, get down!
For your people whom you brought out of the
land of Egypt have corrupted *themselves*. 8They
have turned aside quickly out of the way which
I commanded them. They have made them-
selves a molded calf, and worshiped it and sac-
rificed to it, and said, 'This *is* your god, O Israel,
that brought you out of the land of Egypt!' "
9And the LORD said to Moses, "I have seen this
people, and indeed it *is* a stiff-necked people!

THE MESSAGE

cense for the Holy Place—they'll make
everything just the way I've commanded
you."

SABBATH

12-17 GOD spoke to Moses: "Tell the Israelites,
'Above all, keep my Sabbaths, the sign be-
tween me and you, generation after genera-
tion, to keep the knowledge alive that I am
the GOD who makes you holy. Keep the Sab-
bath; it's holy to you. Whoever profanes it
will most certainly be put to death. Whoever
works on it will be excommunicated from
the people. There are six days for work but
the seventh day is Sabbath, pure rest, holy
to GOD. Anyone who works on the Sabbath
will most certainly be put to death. The Is-
raelites will keep the Sabbath, observe Sab-
bath-keeping down through the genera-
tions, as a standing covenant. It's a fixed
sign between me and the Israelites. Yes, be-
cause in six days GOD made the Heavens
and the Earth and on the seventh day he
stopped and took a long, deep breath.' "
18 When he finished speaking with him on
Mount Sinai, he gave Moses two tablets of
Testimony, slabs of stone, written with the
finger of God.

"MAKE GODS FOR US"

1 32 When the people realized that Moses
was taking forever in coming down off
the mountain, they rallied around Aaron
and said, "Do something. Make gods for us
who will lead us. That Moses, the man who
got us out of Egypt—who knows what's
happened to him?"
2-4 So Aaron told them, "Take off the gold
rings from the ears of your wives and sons
and daughters and bring them to me." They
all did it; they removed the gold rings from
their ears and brought them to Aaron. He
took the gold from their hands and cast it in
the form of a calf, shaping it with an engrav-
ing tool.
The people responded with enthusiasm:
"These are your gods, O Israel, who brought
you up from Egypt!"
5 Aaron, taking in the situation, built an al-
tar before the calf.
Aaron then announced, "Tomorrow is a
feast day to GOD!"
6 Early the next morning, the people got up
and offered Whole-Burnt-Offerings and
brought Peace-Offerings. The people sat
down to eat and drink and then began to
party. It turned into a wild party!
7-8 GOD spoke to Moses, "Go! Get down
there! Your people whom you brought up
from the land of Egypt have fallen to pieces.
In no time at all they've turned away from
the way I commanded them: They made a
molten calf and worshiped it. They've sacri-
ficed to it and said, 'These are the gods, O Is-
rael, that brought you up from the land of
Egypt!' "
9-10 GOD said to Moses, "I look at this peo-
ple—oh! what a stubborn, hard-headed peo-

NEW KING JAMES VERSION

10Now therefore, let Me alone, that My wrath
may burn hot against them and I may consume
them. And I will make of you a great nation."
11Then Moses pleaded with the LORD his
God, and said: "LORD, why does Your wrath burn
hot against Your people whom You have brought
out of the land of Egypt with great power and
with a mighty hand? 12Why should the Egyp-
tians speak, and say, 'He brought them out to
harm them, to kill them in the mountains, and to
consume them from the face of the earth'? Turn
from Your fierce wrath, and relent from this
harm to Your people. 13Remember Abraham,
Isaac, and Israel, Your servants, to whom You
swore by Your own self, and said to them, 'I will
multiply your descendants as the stars of
heaven; and all this land that I have spoken of I
give to your descendants, and they shall inherit
it forever.' "[a] 14So the LORD relented from the
harm which He said He would do to His people.
15And Moses turned and went down from the
mountain, and the two tablets of the Testimony
were in his hand. The tablets *were* written on
both sides; on the one *side* and on the other they
were written. 16Now the tablets *were* the work of
God, and the writing *was* the writing of God en-
graved on the tablets.
17And when Joshua heard the noise of the
people as they shouted, he said to Moses, "*There
is* a noise of war in the camp."
18But he said:

"*It is* not the noise of the shout of victory,
Nor the noise of the cry of defeat,
But the sound of singing I hear."

19So it was, as soon as he came near the
camp, that he saw the calf *and* the dancing. So
Moses' anger became hot, and he cast the
tablets out of his hands and broke them at the
foot of the mountain. 20Then he took the calf
which they had made, burned *it* in the fire, and
ground *it* to powder; and he scattered *it* on the
water and made the children of Israel drink *it*.
21And Moses said to Aaron, "What did this peo-
ple do to you that you have brought *so* great a
sin upon them?"
22So Aaron said, "Do not let the anger of my
lord become hot. You know the people, that they
are set on evil. 23For they said to me, 'Make us
gods that shall go before us; *as for* this Moses,
the man who brought us out of the land of
Egypt, we do not know what has become of
him.' 24And I said to them, 'Whoever has any
gold, let them break *it* off.' So they gave *it* to me,
and I cast it into the fire, and this calf came out."
25Now when Moses saw that the people *were*
unrestrained (for Aaron had not restrained
them, to *their* shame among their enemies),
26then Moses stood in the entrance of the camp,
and said, "Whoever *is* on the LORD's side—*come*
to me!" And all the sons of Levi gathered them-
selves together to him. 27And he said to them,
"Thus says the LORD God of Israel: 'Let every
man put his sword on his side, and go in and out

32:13 [a]Genesis 13:15 and 22:17

THE MESSAGE

ple! Let me alone now, give my anger free
reign to burst into flames and incinerate
them. But I'll make a great nation out of
you."

11-13 Moses tried to calm his GOD down. He
said, "Why, GOD, would you lose your tem-
per with your people? Why, you brought
them out of Egypt in a tremendous demon-
stration of power and strength. Why let the
Egyptians say, 'He had it in for them—he
brought them out so he could kill them in
the mountains, wipe them right off the face
of the Earth.' Stop your anger. Think twice
about bringing evil against your people!
Think of Abraham, Isaac, and Israel, your
servants to whom you gave your word,
telling them 'I will give you many children,
as many as the stars in the sky, and I'll give
this land to your children as their land for-
ever.' "

14 And GOD did think twice. He decided not
to do the evil he had threatened against his
people.

15-16 Moses turned around and came down
from the mountain, carrying the two tablets
of The Testimony. The tablets were written
on both sides, front and back. God made the
tablets and God wrote the tablets—en-
graved them.

17 When Joshua heard the sound of the peo-
ple shouting noisily, he said to Moses,
"That's the sound of war in the camp!"

18 But Moses said,

Those aren't songs of victory,
And those aren't songs of defeat,
I hear songs of people throwing a
party.

19-20 And that's what it was. When Moses
came near to the camp and saw the calf and
the people dancing, his anger flared. He
threw down the tablets and smashed them
to pieces at the foot of the mountain. He
took the calf that they had made, melted it
down with fire, pulverized it to powder, then
scattered it on the water and made the Is-
raelites drink it.

21 Moses said to Aaron, "What on Earth did
these people ever do to you that you in-
volved them in this huge sin?"

22-23 Aaron said, "Master, don't be angry. You
know this people and how set on evil they
are. They said to me, 'Make us gods who
will lead us. This Moses, the man who
brought us out of Egypt, we don't know
what's happened to him.'

24 "So I said, 'Who has gold?' And they took
off their jewelry and gave it to me. I threw it
in the fire and out came this calf."

25-26 Moses saw that the people were simply
running wild—Aaron had let them run wild,
disgracing themselves before their enemies.
He took up a position at the entrance to the
camp and said, "Whoever is on GOD's side,
join me!" All the Levites stepped up.

27 He then told them, "GOD's orders, the God
of Israel: 'Strap on your swords and go to

NEW KING JAMES VERSION

from entrance to entrance throughout the camp,
and let every man kill his brother, every man his
companion, and every man his neighbor.' " 28 So
the sons of Levi did according to the word of
Moses. And about three thousand men of the
people fell that day. 29 Then Moses said, "Conse-
crate yourselves today to the LORD, that He may
bestow on you a blessing this day, for every man
has opposed his son and his brother."
30 Now it came to pass on the next day that
Moses said to the people, "You have committed
a great sin. So now I will go up to the LORD; per-
haps I can make atonement for your sin." 31 Then
Moses returned to the LORD and said, "Oh, these
people have committed a great sin, and have
made for themselves a god of gold! 32 Yet now, if
You will forgive their sin—but if not, I pray, blot
me out of Your book which You have written."
33 And the LORD said to Moses, "Whoever has
sinned against Me, I will blot him out of My
book. 34 Now therefore, go, lead the people to *the*
place of which I have spoken to you. Behold, My
Angel shall go before you. Nevertheless, in the
day when I visit for punishment, I will visit pun-
ishment upon them for their sin."
35 So the LORD plagued the people because of
what they did with the calf which Aaron made.

THE COMMAND TO LEAVE SINAI

33 Then the LORD said to Moses, "Depart *and*
go up from here, you and the people whom
you have brought out of the land of Egypt, to the
land of which I swore to Abraham, Isaac, and
Jacob, saying, 'To your descendants I will give
it.' 2 And I will send *My* Angel before you, and I
will drive out the Canaanite and the Amorite
and the Hittite and the Perizzite and the Hivite
and the Jebusite. 3 *Go up* to a land flowing with
milk and honey; for I will not go up in your
midst, lest I consume you on the way, for you *are*
a stiff-necked people."
4 And when the people heard this bad news,
they mourned, and no one put on his ornaments.
5 For the LORD had said to Moses, "Say to the chil-
dren of Israel, 'You *are* a stiff-necked people. I
could come up into your midst in one moment
and consume you. Now therefore, take off your
ornaments, that I may know what to do to you.' "
6 So the children of Israel stripped themselves of
their ornaments by Mount Horeb.

MOSES MEETS WITH THE LORD

7 Moses took his tent and pitched it outside
the camp, far from the camp, and called it the
tabernacle of meeting. And it came to pass *that*
everyone who sought the LORD went out to the
tabernacle of meeting which *was* outside the
camp. 8 So it was, whenever Moses went out to
the tabernacle, *that* all the people rose, and
each man stood *at* his tent door and watched
Moses until he had gone into the tabernacle.
9 And it came to pass, when Moses entered the
tabernacle, that the pillar of cloud descended
and stood *at* the door of the tabernacle, and *the*
LORD talked with Moses. 10 All the people saw
the pillar of cloud standing *at* the tabernacle
door, and all the people rose and worshiped,
each man *in* his tent door.

THE MESSAGE

work. Crisscross the camp from one end to the other: Kill brother, friend, neighbor.' "

28 The Levites carried out Moses' orders. Three thousand of the people were killed that day.

29 Moses said, "You confirmed your ordination today—and at great cost, even killing your sons and brothers! And GOD has blessed you."

30 The next day Moses addressed the people: "You have sinned an enormous sin! But I am going to go up to GOD; maybe I'll be able to clear you of your sin."

31-32 Moses went back to GOD and said, "This is terrible. This people has sinned—it's an enormous sin! They made gods of gold for themselves. And now, if you will only forgive their sin. . . . But if not, erase me out of the book you've written."

33-34 GOD said to Moses, "I'll only erase from my book those who sin against me. For right now, you go and lead the people to where I told you. Look, my Angel is going ahead of you. On the day, though, when I settle accounts, their sins will certainly be part of the settlement."

35 GOD sent a plague on the people because of the calf they and Aaron had made.

1-3 33 GOD said to Moses: "Now go. Get on your way from here, you and the people you brought up from the land of Egypt. Head for the land which I promised to Abraham, Isaac, and Jacob, saying 'I will give it to your descendants.' I will send an angel ahead of you and I'll drive out the Canaanites, Amorites, Hittites, Perizzites, Hivites, and Jebusites. It's a land flowing with milk and honey. But I won't be with you in person—you're such a stubborn, hard-headed people!—lest I destroy you on the journey."

4 When the people heard this harsh verdict, they were plunged into gloom and wore long faces. No one put on jewelry.

5-6 GOD said to Moses, "Tell the Israelites, 'You're one hard-headed people. I couldn't stand being with you for even a moment—I'd destroy you. So take off all your jewelry until I figure out what to do with you.' " So the Israelites stripped themselves of their jewelry from Mount Horeb on.

7-10 Moses used to take the Tent and set it up outside the camp, some distance away. He called it the Tent of Meeting. Anyone who sought GOD would go to the Tent of Meeting outside the camp. It went like this: When Moses would go to the Tent, all the people would stand at attention; each man would take his position at the entrance to his tent with his eyes on Moses until he entered the Tent; whenever Moses entered the Tent, the Pillar of Cloud descended to the entrance to the Tent and GOD spoke with Moses. All the people would see the Pillar of Cloud at the entrance to the Tent, stand at attention, and then bow down in worship, each man at the entrance to his tent.

New King James Version

11So the LORD spoke to Moses face to face, as a man speaks to his friend. And he would return to the camp, but his servant Joshua the son of Nun, a young man, did not depart from the tabernacle.

The Promise of God's Presence

12Then Moses said to the LORD, "See, You say to me, 'Bring up this people.' But You have not let me know whom You will send with me. Yet You have said, 'I know you by name, and you have also found grace in My sight.' 13Now therefore, I pray, if I have found grace in Your sight, show me now Your way, that I may know You and that I may find grace in Your sight. And consider that this nation *is* Your people."

14And He said, "My Presence will go *with you,* and I will give you rest."

15Then he said to Him, "If Your Presence does not go *with us,* do not bring us up from here. 16For how then will it be known that Your people and I have found grace in Your sight, except You go with us? So we shall be separate, Your people and I, from all the people who *are* upon the face of the earth."

17So the LORD said to Moses, "I will also do this thing that you have spoken; for you have found grace in My sight, and I know you by name."

18And he said, "Please, show me Your glory."

19Then He said, "I will make all My goodness pass before you, and I will proclaim the name of the LORD before you. I will be gracious to whom I will be gracious, and I will have compassion on whom I will have compassion." 20But He said, "You cannot see My face; for no man shall see Me, and live." 21And the LORD said, "Here is a place by Me, and you shall stand on the rock. 22So it shall be, while My glory passes by, that I will put you in the cleft of the rock, and will cover you with My hand while I pass by. 23Then I will take away My hand, and you shall see My back; but My face shall not be seen."

Moses Makes New Tablets

34 And the LORD said to Moses, "Cut two tablets of stone like the first *ones,* and I will write on *these* tablets the words that were on the first tablets which you broke. 2So be ready in the morning, and come up in the morning to Mount Sinai, and present yourself to Me there on the top of the mountain. 3And no man shall come up with you, and let no man be seen throughout all the mountain; let neither flocks nor herds feed before that mountain."

4So he cut two tablets of stone like the first *ones.* Then Moses rose early in the morning and went up Mount Sinai, as the LORD had commanded him; and he took in his hand the two tablets of stone.

5Now the LORD descended in the cloud and stood with him there, and proclaimed the name of the LORD. 6And the LORD passed before him and proclaimed, "The LORD, the LORD God, merciful and gracious, longsuffering, and abounding in goodness and truth, 7keeping mercy for thousands, forgiving iniquity and transgression

The Message

11 And GOD spoke with Moses face-to-face,
as neighbors speak to one another. When he
would return to the camp, his attendant, the
young man Joshua, stayed—he didn't leave
the Tent.

12-13 Moses said to GOD, "Look, you tell me, 'Lead
this people,' but you don't let me know
whom you're going to send with me. You tell
me, 'I know you well and you are special to
me.' If I am so special to you, let me in on
your plans. That way, I will continue being
special to you. Don't forget, this is *your* people, your responsibility."

14 GOD said, "My presence will go with you.
I'll see the journey to the end."

15-16 Moses said, "If your presence doesn't take
the lead here, call this trip off right now. How
else will it be known that you're with me in
this, with me and your people? Are you traveling with us or not? How else will we know
that we're special, I and your people, among
all other people on this planet Earth?"

17 GOD said to Moses: "All right. Just as you
say; this also I will do, for I know you well
and you are special to me. I know you by
name."

18 Moses said, "Please. Let me see your
Glory."

19 GOD said, "I will make my Goodness pass
right in front of you; I'll call out the name,
GOD, right before you. I'll treat well
whomever I want to treat well and I'll be
kind to whomever I want to be kind."

20 GOD continued, "But you may not see my
face. No one can see me and live."

21-23 GOD said, "Look, here is a place right beside me. Put yourself on this rock. When my
Glory passes by, I'll put you in the cleft of
the rock and cover you with my hand until
I've passed by. Then I'll take my hand away
and you'll see my back. But you won't see
my face."

1-3 34 GOD spoke to Moses: "Cut out two
tablets of stone just like the originals
and engrave on them the words that were on
the original tablets you smashed. Be ready
in the morning to climb Mount Sinai and get
set to meet me on top of the mountain. Not
a soul is to go with you; the whole mountain
must be clear of people, even animals—not
even sheep or oxen can be grazing in front
of the mountain."

4-7 So Moses cut two tablets of stone just like
the originals. He got up early in the morning
and climbed Mount Sinai as GOD had commanded him, carrying the two tablets of
stone. GOD descended in the cloud and took
up his position there beside him and called
out the name, GOD. GOD passed in front of
him and called out, "GOD, GOD, a God of
mercy and grace, endlessly patient—so
much love, so deeply true—loyal in love for
a thousand generations, forgiving iniquity,

NEW KING JAMES VERSION

and sin, by no means clearing *the guilty,* visiting
the iniquity of the fathers upon the children and
the children's children to the third and the
fourth generation."
[8]So Moses made haste and bowed his head
toward the earth, and worshiped. [9]Then he said,
"If now I have found grace in Your sight, O Lord,
let my Lord, I pray, go among us, even though
we *are* a stiff-necked people; and pardon our in-
iquity and our sin, and take us as Your inheri-
tance."

THE COVENANT RENEWED

[10]And He said: "Behold, I make a covenant.
Before all your people I will do marvels such as
have not been done in all the earth, nor in any
nation; and all the people among whom you *are*
shall see the work of the LORD. For it *is* an awe-
some thing that I will do with you. [11]Observe
what I command you this day. Behold, I am driv-
ing out from before you the Amorite and the
Canaanite and the Hittite and the Perizzite and
the Hivite and the Jebusite. [12]Take heed to your-
self, lest you make a covenant with the inhabi-
tants of the land where you are going, lest it be
a snare in your midst. [13]But you shall destroy
their altars, break their *sacred* pillars, and cut
down their wooden images [14](for you shall wor-
ship no other god, for the LORD, whose name *is*
Jealous, *is* a jealous God), [15]lest you make a
covenant with the inhabitants of the land, and
they play the harlot with their gods and make
sacrifice to their gods, and *one of them* invites
you and you eat of his sacrifice, [16]and you take
of his daughters for your sons, and his daugh-
ters play the harlot with their gods and make
your sons play the harlot with their gods.
[17]"You shall make no molded gods for your-
selves.
[18]"The Feast of Unleavened Bread you shall
keep. Seven days you shall eat unleavened
bread, as I commanded you, in the appointed
time of the month of Abib; for in the month of
Abib you came out from Egypt.
[19]"All that open the womb *are* Mine, and
every male firstborn among your livestock,
whether ox or sheep. [20]But the firstborn of a
donkey you shall redeem with a lamb. And if
you will not redeem *him,* then you shall break
his neck. All the firstborn of your sons you shall
redeem.
"And none shall appear before Me empty-
handed.
[21]"Six days you shall work, but on the sev-
enth day you shall rest; in plowing time and in
harvest you shall rest.
[22]"And you shall observe the Feast of Weeks,
of the firstfruits of wheat harvest, and the Feast
of Ingathering at the year's end.
[23]"Three times in the year all your men shall
appear before the Lord, the LORD God of Israel.
[24]For I will cast out the nations before you and
enlarge your borders; neither will any man
covet your land when you go up to appear be-
fore the LORD your God three times in the year.
[25]"You shall not offer the blood of My sacri-
fice with leaven, nor shall the sacrifice of the
Feast of the Passover be left until morning.

THE MESSAGE

rebellion, and sin. Still, he doesn't ignore
sin. He holds sons and grandsons responsi-
ble for a father's sins to the third and even
fourth generation."

8-9 At once, Moses fell to the ground and
worshiped, saying, "Please, O Master, if you
see anything good in me, please Master,
travel with us, hard-headed as these people
are. Forgive our iniquity and sin. Own us,
possess us."

10-12 And GOD said, "As of right now, I'm mak-
ing a covenant with you: In full sight of your
people I will work wonders that have never
been created in all the Earth, in any nation.
Then all the people with whom you're living
will see how tremendous GOD's work is, the
work I'll do for you. Take careful note of all
I command you today. I'm clearing your way
by driving out Amorites, Canaanites, Hit-
tites, Perizzites, Hivites, and Jebusites. Stay
vigilant. Don't let down your guard lest you
make covenant with the people who live in
the land that you are entering and they trip
you up.

13-16 "Tear down their altars, smash their phal-
lic pillars, chop down their fertility poles.
Don't worship any other god. GOD—his
name is The-Jealous-One—is a jealous God.
Be careful that you don't make a covenant
with the people who live in the land and
take up with their sex-and-religion life, join
them in meals at their altars, marry your
sons to their women, women who take up
with any convenient god or goddess and
will get your sons to do the same thing.

17 "Don't make molten gods for yourselves.

18 "Keep the Feast of Unraised Bread. Eat
only unraised bread for seven days in the
month of Abib—it was in the month of Abib
that you came out of Egypt.

19 "Every firstborn from the womb is mine,
all the males of your herds, your firstborn
oxen and sheep.

20 "Redeem your firstborn donkey with a
lamb. If you don't redeem it you must break
its neck.

"Redeem each of your firstborn sons.

"No one is to show up in my presence
empty-handed.

21 "Work six days and rest the seventh. Stop
working even during plowing and harvest-
ing.

22 "Keep the Feast of Weeks with the first
cutting of the wheat harvest, and the Feast
of Ingathering at the turn of the year.

23-24 "All your men are to appear before the
Master, the GOD of Israel, three times a year.
You won't have to worry about your land
when you appear before your GOD three
times each year, for I will drive out the na-
tions before you and give you plenty of land.
Nobody's going to be hanging around plot-
ting ways to get it from you.

25 "Don't mix the blood of my sacrifices
with anything fermented.

"Don't leave leftovers from the Passover
Feast until morning.

NEW KING JAMES VERSION

26“The first of the firstfruits of your land you
shall bring to the house of the LORD your God.
You shall not boil a young goat in its mother’s
milk.”
27Then the LORD said to Moses, “Write these
words, for according to the tenor of these words
I have made a covenant with you and with Is-
rael.” 28So he was there with the LORD forty days
and forty nights; he neither ate bread nor drank
water. And He wrote on the tablets the words of
the covenant, the Ten Commandments.[a]

THE SHINING FACE OF MOSES

29Now it was so, when Moses came down
from Mount Sinai (and the two tablets of the
Testimony *were* in Moses’ hand when he came
down from the mountain), that Moses did not
know that the skin of his face shone while he
talked with Him. 30So when Aaron and all the
children of Israel saw Moses, behold, the skin of
his face shone, and they were afraid to come
near him. 31Then Moses called to them, and
Aaron and all the rulers of the congregation re-
turned to him; and Moses talked with them.
32Afterward all the children of Israel came near,
and he gave them as commandments all that the
LORD had spoken with him on Mount Sinai.
33And when Moses had finished speaking with
them, he put a veil on his face. 34But whenever
Moses went in before the LORD to speak with
Him, he would take the veil off until he came
out; and he would come out and speak to the
children of Israel whatever he had been com-
manded. 35And whenever the children of Israel
saw the face of Moses, that the skin of Moses’
face shone, then Moses would put the veil on his
face again, until he went in to speak with Him.

SABBATH REGULATIONS

35 Then Moses gathered all the congregation
of the children of Israel together, and said
to them, “These *are* the words which the LORD
has commanded *you* to do: 2Work shall be done
for six days, but the seventh day shall be a holy
day for you, a Sabbath of rest to the LORD. Who-
ever does any work on it shall be put to death.
3You shall kindle no fire throughout your
dwellings on the Sabbath day.”

OFFERINGS FOR THE TABERNACLE

4And Moses spoke to all the congregation of
the children of Israel, saying, “This *is* the thing
which the LORD commanded, saying: 5‘Take
from among you an offering to the LORD. Who-
ever *is* of a willing heart, let him bring it as an
offering to the LORD: gold, silver, and bronze;
6blue, purple, and scarlet *thread,* fine linen, and
goats’ *hair;* 7ram skins dyed red, badger skins,
and acacia wood; 8oil for the light, and spices for
the anointing oil and for the sweet incense;
9onyx stones, and stones to be set in the ephod
and in the breastplate.

ARTICLES OF THE TABERNACLE

10‘All *who are* gifted artisans among you
shall come and make all that the LORD has com-

34:28 [a]Literally *Ten Words*

THE MESSAGE

26 “Bring the finest of the firstfruits of your
produce to the house of your GOD.
“Don’t boil a kid in its mother’s milk.”

27 GOD said to Moses: “Now write down
these words, for by these words I’ve made a
covenant with you and Israel.”
28 Moses was there with GOD forty days and
forty nights. He didn’t eat any food; he didn’t
drink any water. And he wrote on the tablets
the words of the covenant, the Ten Words.
29-30 When Moses came down from Mount
Sinai carrying the two Tablets of The Testi-
mony, he didn’t know that the skin of his
face glowed because he had been speaking
with GOD. Aaron and all the Israelites saw
Moses, saw his radiant face, and held back,
afraid to get close to him.
31-32 Moses called out to them. Aaron and the
leaders in the community came back and
Moses talked with them. Later all the Is-
raelites came up to him and he passed on
the commands, everything that GOD had
told him on Mount Sinai.
33-35 When Moses finished speaking with
them, he put a veil over his face, but when
he went into the presence of GOD to speak
with him, he removed the veil until he came
out. When he came out and told the Is-
raelites what he had been commanded, they
would see Moses’ face, its skin glowing, and
then he would again put the veil on his face
until he went back in to speak with GOD.

BUILDING THE PLACE OF WORSHIP

1 35 Moses spoke to the entire congrega-
tion of Israel, saying, “These are the
things that GOD has commanded you to do:
2-3 “Work six days, but the seventh day will
be a holy rest day, GOD’s holy rest day. Any-
one who works on this day must be put to
death. Don’t light any fires in your homes
on the Sabbath day.”

THE OFFERINGS

4 Moses spoke to the entire congregation of
Israel, saying, “This is what GOD has com-
manded:
5-9 “Gather from among you an offering for
GOD. Receive on GOD’s behalf what every-
one is willing to give as an offering: gold,
silver, bronze; blue, purple, and scarlet ma-
terial; fine linen; goats’ hair; tanned rams’
skins; dolphin skins; acacia wood; lamp oil;
spices for anointing oils and for fragrant in-
cense; onyx stones and other stones for set-
ting in the Ephod and the Breastpiece.
10-19 “Come—all of you who have skills—come
and make everything that GOD has com-

NEW KING JAMES VERSION

manded: 11the tabernacle, its tent, its covering, its clasps, its boards, its bars, its pillars, and its sockets; 12the ark and its poles, *with* the mercy seat, and the veil of the covering; 13the table and its poles, all its utensils, and the showbread; 14also the lampstand for the light, its utensils, its lamps, and the oil for the light; 15the incense altar, its poles, the anointing oil, the sweet incense, and the screen for the door at the entrance of the tabernacle; 16the altar of burnt offering with its bronze grating, its poles, all its utensils, *and* the laver and its base; 17the hangings of the court, its pillars, their sockets, and the screen for the gate of the court; 18the pegs of the tabernacle, the pegs of the court, and their cords; 19the garments of ministry,[a] for ministering in the holy *place*—the holy garments for Aaron the priest and the garments of his sons, to minister as priests.' "

THE TABERNACLE OFFERINGS PRESENTED

20And all the congregation of the children of Israel departed from the presence of Moses. 21Then everyone came whose heart was stirred, and everyone whose spirit was willing, *and* they brought the LORD's offering for the work of the tabernacle of meeting, for all its service, and for the holy garments. 22They came, both men and women, as many as had a willing heart, *and* brought earrings and nose rings, rings and necklaces, all jewelry of gold, that is, every man who *made* an offering of gold to the LORD. 23And every man, with whom was found blue, purple, and scarlet *thread,* fine linen, goats' *hair,* red skins of rams, and badger skins, brought *them.* 24Everyone who offered an offering of silver or bronze brought the LORD's offering. And everyone with whom was found acacia wood for any work of the service, brought *it.* 25All the women *who were* gifted artisans spun yarn with their hands, and brought what they had spun, of blue, purple, *and* scarlet, and fine linen. 26And all the women whose hearts stirred with wisdom spun yarn of goats' *hair.* 27The rulers brought onyx stones, and the stones to be set in the ephod and in the breastplate, 28and spices and oil for the light, for the anointing oil, and for the sweet incense. 29The children of Israel brought a freewill offering to the LORD, all the men and women whose hearts were willing to bring *material* for all kinds of work which the LORD, by the hand of Moses, had commanded to be done.

THE ARTISANS CALLED BY GOD

30And Moses said to the children of Israel, "See, the LORD has called by name Bezalel the son of Uri, the son of Hur, of the tribe of Judah; 31and He has filled him with the Spirit of God, in wisdom and understanding, in knowledge and all manner of workmanship, 32to design artistic works, to work in gold and silver and bronze, 33in cutting jewels for setting, in carving wood, and to work in all manner of artistic workmanship.

34"And He has put in his heart the ability to teach, *in* him and Aholiab the son of Ahisamach,

35:19 [a]Or *woven garments*

THE MESSAGE

manded: The Dwelling with its tent and cover, its hooks, frames, crossbars, posts, and bases; the Chest with its poles, the Atonement-Cover and veiling curtain; the Table with its poles and implements and the Bread of the Presence; the Lampstand for giving light with its furnishings and lamps and the oil for lighting; the Altar of Incense with its poles, the anointing oil, the fragrant incense; the screen for the door at the entrance to The Dwelling; the Altar of Whole-Burnt-Offering with its bronze grate and poles and all its implements; the Washbasin with its base; the tapestry hangings for the Courtyard with the posts and bases, the screen for the Courtyard gate; the pegs for The Dwelling, the pegs for the Courtyard with their cords; the official vestments for ministering in the Holy Place, the sacred vestments for Aaron the priest and for his sons serving as priests."

20-26 So everyone in the community of Israel left the presence of Moses. Then they came back, every one whose heart was roused, whose spirit was freely responsive, bringing offerings to GOD for building the Tent of Meeting, furnishing it for worship and making the holy vestments. They came, both men and women, all the willing spirits among them, offering brooches, earrings, rings, necklaces—anything made of gold—offering up their gold jewelry to GOD. And anyone who had blue, purple, and scarlet fabrics; fine linen; goats' hair; tanned leather; and dolphin skins brought them. Everyone who wanted to offer up silver or bronze as a gift to GOD brought it. Everyone who had acacia wood that could be used in the work, brought it. All the women skilled at weaving brought their weavings of blue and purple and scarlet fabrics and their fine linens. And all the women who were gifted in spinning, spun the goats' hair.

27-29 The leaders brought onyx and other precious stones for setting in the Ephod and the Breastpiece. They also brought spices and olive oil for lamp oil, anointing oil, and incense. Every man and woman in Israel whose heart moved them freely to bring something for the work that GOD through Moses had commanded them to make, brought it, a voluntary offering for GOD.

BEZALEL AND OHOLIAB

30-35 Moses told the Israelites, "See, GOD has selected Bezalel son of Uri, son of Hur, of the tribe of Judah. He's filled him with the Spirit of God, with skill, ability, and know-how for making all sorts of things, to design and work in gold, silver, and bronze; to carve stones and set them; to carve wood, working in every kind of skilled craft. And he's also made him a teacher, he and Oholiab son of Ahisamach, of the tribe of Dan. He's gifted

NEW KING JAMES VERSION

of the tribe of Dan. 35He has filled them with skill to do all manner of work of the engraver and the designer and the tapestry maker, in blue, purple, and scarlet *thread,* and fine linen, and of the weaver—those who do every work and those who design artistic works.

36 "And Bezalel and Aholiab, and every gifted artisan in whom the LORD has put wisdom and understanding, to know how to do all manner of work for the service of the sanctuary, shall do according to all that the LORD has commanded."

THE PEOPLE GIVE MORE THAN ENOUGH

2Then Moses called Bezalel and Aholiab, and every gifted artisan in whose heart the LORD had put wisdom, everyone whose heart was stirred, to come and do the work. 3And they received from Moses all the offering which the children of Israel had brought for the work of the service of making the sanctuary. So they continued bringing to him freewill offerings every morning. 4Then all the craftsmen who were doing all the work of the sanctuary came, each from the work he was doing, 5and they spoke to Moses, saying, "The people bring much more than enough for the service of the work which the LORD commanded *us* to do."

6So Moses gave a commandment, and they caused it to be proclaimed throughout the camp, saying, "Let neither man nor woman do any more work for the offering of the sanctuary." And the people were restrained from bringing, 7for the material they had was sufficient for all the work to be done—indeed too much.

BUILDING THE TABERNACLE

8Then all the gifted artisans among them who worked on the tabernacle made ten curtains woven of fine linen, and of blue, purple, and scarlet *thread; with* artistic designs of cherubim they made them. 9The length of each curtain *was* twenty-eight cubits, and the width of each curtain four cubits; the curtains *were* all the same size. 10And he coupled five curtains to one another, and *the other* five curtains he coupled to one another. 11He made loops of blue *yarn* on the edge of the curtain on the selvedge of one set; likewise he did on the outer edge of *the other* curtain of the second set. 12Fifty loops he made on one curtain, and fifty loops he made on the edge of the curtain on the end of the second set; the loops held one *curtain* to another. 13And he made fifty clasps of gold, and coupled the curtains to one another with the clasps, that it might be one tabernacle.

14He made curtains of goats' *hair* for the tent over the tabernacle; he made eleven curtains. 15The length of each curtain *was* thirty cubits, and the width of each curtain four cubits; the eleven curtains *were* the same size. 16He coupled five curtains by themselves and six curtains by themselves. 17And he made fifty loops on the edge of the curtain that is outermost in one set, and fifty loops he made on the edge of the curtain of the second set. 18He also made fifty bronze clasps to couple the tent together,

THE MESSAGE

them with the know-how needed for carving, designing, weaving, and embroidering in blue, purple, and scarlet fabrics, and in fine linen. They can make anything and design anything."

1 36 "Bezalel and Oholiab, along with
everyone whom GOD has given the
skill and know-how for making everything
involved in the worship of the Sanctuary as
commanded by GOD, are to start to work."

2-3 Moses summoned Bezalel and Oholiab
along with all whom GOD had gifted with
the ability to work skillfully with their
hands. The men were eager to get started
and engage in the work. They took from
Moses all the offerings that the Israelites
had brought for the work of constructing
the Sanctuary. The people kept on bringing
in their freewill offerings, morning after
morning.

4-5 All the artisans who were at work mak-
ing everything involved in constructing the
Sanctuary came, one after another, to
Moses, saying, "The people are bringing
more than enough for doing this work that
GOD has commanded us to do!"

6-7 So Moses sent out orders through the
camp: "Men! Women! No more offerings for
the building of the Sanctuary!"

The people were ordered to stop bringing offerings! There was plenty of material for all the work to be done. Enough and more than enough.

THE TAPESTRIES

8-13 Then all the skilled artisans on The
Dwelling made ten tapestries of fine twisted
linen and blue, purple, and scarlet fabric
with an angel-cherubim design worked into
the material. Each panel of tapestry was
forty-six feet long and six feet wide. Five of
the panels were joined together, and then
the other five. Loops of blue were made
along the edge of the outside panel of the
first set, and the same on the outside panel
of the second set. They made fifty loops on
each panel, with the loops opposite each
other. Then they made fifty gold clasps and
joined the tapestries together so that The
Dwelling was one whole.

14-19 Next they made tapestries of woven goat
hair for a tent that would cover The
Dwelling. They made eleven panels of these
tapestries. The length of each panel was
forty-five feet long and six feet wide. They
joined five of the panels together, and then
the other six, by making fifty loops along
the edge of the end panel and fifty loops
along the edge of the joining panel, then
making fifty clasps of bronze, connecting
the clasps to the loops, bringing the tent to-

NEW KING JAMES VERSION

that it might be one. [19]Then he made a covering
for the tent of ram skins dyed red, and a cover-
ing of badger skins above *that.*
[20]For the tabernacle he made boards of aca-
cia wood, standing upright. [21]The length of each
board *was* ten cubits, and the width of each
board a cubit and a half. [22]Each board had two
tenons for binding one to another. Thus he
made for all the boards of the tabernacle. [23]And
he made boards for the tabernacle, twenty
boards for the south side. [24]Forty sockets of sil-
ver he made to go under the twenty boards: two
sockets under each of the boards for its two
tenons. [25]And for the other side of the taberna-
cle, the north side, he made twenty boards [26]and
their forty sockets of silver: two sockets under
each of the boards. [27]For the west side of the tab-
ernacle he made six boards. [28]He also made two
boards for the two back corners of the taberna-
cle. [29]And they were coupled at the bottom and
coupled together at the top by one ring. Thus he
made both of them for the two corners. [30]So
there were eight boards and their sockets—six-
teen sockets of silver—two sockets under each
of the boards.
[31]And he made bars of acacia wood: five for
the boards on one side of the tabernacle, [32]five
bars for the boards on the other side of the tab-
ernacle, and five bars for the boards of the tab-
ernacle on the far side westward. [33]And he made
the middle bar to pass through the boards from
one end to the other. [34]He overlaid the boards
with gold, made their rings of gold *to be* holders
for the bars, and overlaid the bars with gold.
[35]And he made a veil of blue, purple, and
scarlet *thread,* and fine woven linen; it was
worked *with* an artistic design of cherubim.
[36]He made for it four pillars of acacia *wood,* and
overlaid them with gold, with their hooks of
gold; and he cast four sockets of silver for them.
[37]He also made a screen for the tabernacle
door, of blue, purple, and scarlet *thread,* and
fine woven linen, made by a weaver, [38]and its
five pillars with their hooks. And he overlaid
their capitals and their rings with gold, but their
five sockets *were* bronze.

MAKING THE ARK OF THE TESTIMONY

37 Then Bezalel made the ark of acacia wood;
two and a half cubits *was* its length, a cu-
bit and a half its width, and a cubit and a half its
height. [2]He overlaid it with pure gold inside and
outside, and made a molding of gold all around
it. [3]And he cast for it four rings of gold *to be set*
in its four corners: two rings on one side, and
two rings on the other side of it. [4]He made poles
of acacia wood, and overlaid them with gold.
[5]And he put the poles into the rings at the sides
of the ark, to bear the ark. [6]He also made the
mercy seat of pure gold; two and a half cubits
was its length and a cubit and a half its width.
[7]He made two cherubim of beaten gold; he made
them of one piece at the two ends of the mercy
seat: [8]one cherub at one end on this side, and the
other cherub at the *other* end on that side. He
made the cherubim at the two ends *of one piece*
with the mercy seat. [9]The cherubim spread out

THE MESSAGE

gether. They finished it off by covering the
tapestries with tanned rams' skins dyed red,
and covered that with dolphin skins.

THE FRAMING

20-30 They framed The Dwelling with vertical
planks of acacia wood, each section of
frame fifteen feet long and two and a quar-
ter feet wide, with two pegs for securing
them. They made all the frames identical:
twenty frames for the south side, with forty
silver sockets to receive the two tenons from
each of the twenty frames; they repeated
that construction on the north side of The
Dwelling. For the rear of The Dwelling fac-
ing west, they made six frames, with two ad-
ditional frames for the rear corners. Both of
the two corner frames were double in thick-
ness from top to bottom and fit into a single
ring—eight frames altogether with sixteen
sockets of silver, two under each frame.
31-34 They made crossbars of acacia wood, five
for the frames on one side of The Dwelling,
five for the other side, and five for the back
side facing west. The center crossbar ran
from end to end halfway up the frames.
They covered the frames with a veneer of
gold, made gold rings to hold the crossbars,
and covered the crossbars with a veneer of
gold.
35-36 They made the curtain of blue, purple,
and scarlet material and fine twisted linen.
They wove a design of angel-cherubim into
it. They made four posts of acacia wood,
covered them with a veneer of gold, and cast
four silver bases for them.
37-38 They made a screen for the door of the
tent, woven from blue, purple, and scarlet
material and fine twisted linen with embroi-
dery. They framed the weaving with five
poles of acacia wood covered with a veneer
of gold, and made gold hooks to hang the
weaving and five bronze bases for the poles.

THE CHEST

1-5 37 Bezalel made the Chest using acacia
wood: He made it three and three-
quarters feet long and two and a quarter
feet wide and deep. He covered it inside and
out with a veneer of pure gold and made a
molding of gold all around it. He cast four
gold rings and attached them to its four feet,
two rings on one side and two rings on the
other. He made poles from acacia wood,
covered them with a veneer of gold, and in-
serted the poles for carrying the Chest into
the rings on the sides.
6 Next he made a lid of pure gold for the
Chest, an Atonement-Cover, three and
three-quarters feet long and two and a quar-
ter feet wide.
7-9 He sculpted two winged angel-cherubim
out of hammered gold for the ends of the
Atonement-Cover, one angel at one end, one
angel at the other. He made them of one
piece with the Atonement-Cover. The angels

NEW KING JAMES VERSION

their wings above, *and* covered the mercy seat
with their wings. They faced one another; the
faces of the cherubim were toward the mercy
seat.

MAKING THE TABLE FOR THE SHOWBREAD

10He made the table of acacia wood; two cu-
bits *was* its length, a cubit its width, and a cu-
bit and a half its height. 11And he overlaid it
with pure gold, and made a molding of gold all
around it. 12Also he made a frame of a hand-
breadth all around it, and made a molding of
gold for the frame all around it. 13And he cast
for it four rings of gold, and put the rings on
the four corners that *were* at its four legs. 14The
rings were close to the frame, as holders for
the poles to bear the table. 15And he made the
poles of acacia wood to bear the table, and
overlaid them with gold. 16He made of pure
gold the utensils which were on the table: its
dishes, its cups, its bowls, and its pitchers for
pouring.

MAKING THE GOLD LAMPSTAND

17He also made the lampstand of pure gold;
of hammered work he made the lampstand. Its
shaft, its branches, its bowls, its *ornamental*
knobs, and its flowers were of the same piece.
18And six branches came out of its sides: three
branches of the lampstand out of one side, and
three branches of the lampstand out of the other
side. 19There were three bowls made like al-
mond *blossoms* on one branch, with an *orna-
mental* knob and a flower, and three bowls
made like almond *blossoms* on the other
branch, with an *ornamental* knob and a
flower—and so for the six branches coming out
of the lampstand. 20And on the lampstand itself
were four bowls made like almond *blossoms*,
each with its *ornamental* knob and flower.
21*There was* a knob under the *first* two branches
of the same, a knob under the *second* two
branches of the same, and a knob under the
third two branches of the same, according to the
six branches extending from it. 22Their knobs
and their branches were of one piece; all of it
was one hammered piece of pure gold. 23And he
made its seven lamps, its wick-trimmers, and its
trays of pure gold. 24Of a talent of pure gold he
made it, with all its utensils.

MAKING THE ALTAR OF INCENSE

25He made the incense altar of acacia wood.
Its length *was* a cubit and its width a cubit—*it
was* square—and two cubits *was* its height. Its
horns were *of one piece* with it. 26And he over-
laid it with pure gold: its top, its sides all around,
and its horns. He also made for it a molding of
gold all around it. 27He made two rings of gold
for it under its molding, by its two corners on
both sides, as holders for the poles with which
to bear it. 28And he made the poles of acacia
wood, and overlaid them with gold.

MAKING THE ANOINTING OIL AND THE INCENSE

29He also made the holy anointing oil and the
pure incense of sweet spices, according to the
work of the perfumer.

THE MESSAGE

had outstretched wings and appeared to
hover over the Atonement-Cover, facing one
another but looking down on the Atone-
ment-Cover.

THE TABLE

10-15 He made the Table from acacia wood. He
made it three feet long, one and a half feet
wide and two and a quarter feet high. He
covered it with a veneer of pure gold and
made a molding of gold all around it. He
made a border a handbreadth wide all
around it and a rim of gold for the border. He
cast four rings of gold for it and attached the
rings to the four legs parallel to the tabletop.
They will serve as holders for the poles used
to carry the Table. He made the poles of aca-
cia wood and covered them with a veneer of
gold. They will be used to carry the Table.

16 Out of pure gold he made the utensils for
the Table: its plates, bowls, jars, and jugs
used for pouring.

THE LAMPSTAND

17-23 He made a Lampstand of pure hammered
gold, making its stem and branches, cups,
calyxes, and petals all of one piece. It had
six branches, three from one side and three
from the other; three cups shaped like al-
mond blossoms with calyxes and petals on
one branch, three on the next, and so on—
the same for all six branches. On the main
stem of the Lampstand, there were four
cups shaped like almonds, with calyxes and
petals, a calyx extending from under each
pair of the six branches. The entire Lamp-
stand with its calyxes and stems was fash-
ioned from one piece of hammered pure
gold. He made seven of these lamps with
their candle snuffers, all out of pure gold.

24 He used a seventy-five-pound brick of
pure gold to make the Lampstand and its
accessories.

THE ALTAR OF INCENSE

25-28 He made an Altar for burning incense from
acacia wood. He made it a foot and a half
square and three feet high, with its horns of
one piece with it. He covered it with a ve-
neer of pure gold, its top, sides, and horns,
and made a gold molding around it with two
rings of gold beneath the molding. He
placed the rings on the two opposing sides
to serve as holders for poles by which it will
be carried. He made the poles of acacia
wood and covered them with a veneer of
gold.

29 He also prepared with the art of a per-
fumer the holy anointing oil and the pure
aromatic incense.

NEW KING JAMES VERSION

MAKING THE ALTAR OF BURNT OFFERING

38 He made the altar of burnt offering of acacia wood; five cubits *was* its length and five cubits its width—*it was* square—and its height *was* three cubits. 2He made its horns on its four corners; the horns were *of one piece* with it. And he overlaid it with bronze. 3He made all the utensils for the altar: the pans, the shovels, the basins, the forks, and the firepans; all its utensils he made of bronze. 4And he made a grate of bronze network for the altar, under its rim, midway from the bottom. 5He cast four rings for the four corners of the bronze grating, *as* holders for the poles. 6And he made the poles of acacia wood, and overlaid them with bronze. 7Then he put the poles into the rings on the sides of the altar, with which to bear it. He made the altar hollow with boards.

MAKING THE BRONZE LAVER

8He made the laver of bronze and its base of bronze, from the bronze mirrors of the serving women who assembled at the door of the tabernacle of meeting.

MAKING THE COURT OF THE TABERNACLE

9Then he made the court on the south side; the hangings of the court *were of* fine woven linen, one hundred cubits long. 10There *were* twenty pillars for them, with twenty bronze sockets. The hooks of the pillars and their bands *were* silver. 11On the north side *the hangings were* one hundred cubits *long,* with twenty pillars and their twenty bronze sockets. The hooks of the pillars and their bands *were* silver. 12And on the west side *there were* hangings of fifty cubits, with ten pillars and their ten sockets. The hooks of the pillars and their bands *were* silver. 13For the east side *the hangings were* fifty cubits. 14The hangings of one side *of the gate were* fifteen cubits *long, with* their three pillars and their three sockets, 15and the same for the other side of the court gate; on this side and that *were* hangings of fifteen cubits, *with* their three pillars and their three sockets. 16All the hangings of the court all around *were of* fine woven linen. 17The sockets for the pillars *were* bronze, the hooks of the pillars and their bands *were* silver, and the overlay of their capitals *was* silver; and all the pillars of the court had bands of silver. 18The screen for the gate of the court *was* woven of blue, purple, and scarlet *thread,* and of fine woven linen. The length *was* twenty cubits, and the height along its width *was* five cubits, corresponding to the hangings of the court. 19And *there were* four pillars *with* their four sockets of bronze; their hooks *were* silver, and the overlay of their capitals and their bands *was* silver. 20All the pegs of the tabernacle, and of the court all around, *were* bronze.

MATERIALS OF THE TABERNACLE

21This is the inventory of the tabernacle, the tabernacle of the Testimony, which was counted according to the commandment of Moses, for the service of the Levites, by the hand of Ithamar, son of Aaron the priest.

22Bezalel the son of Uri, the son of Hur, of the

THE MESSAGE

THE ALTAR OF WHOLE-BURNT-OFFERING

1-7 **38** He made the Altar of Whole-Burnt-
Offering from acacia wood. He made it
seven and a half feet square and four and a
half feet high. He made horns at each of the
four corners. The horns were made of one
piece with the Altar and covered with a ve-
neer of bronze. He made from bronze all the
utensils for the Altar: the buckets for remov-
ing the ashes, shovels, basins, forks, and fire
pans. He made a grate of bronze mesh un-
der the ledge halfway up the Altar. He cast
four rings at each of the four corners of the
bronze grating to hold the poles. He made
the poles of acacia wood and covered them
with a veneer of bronze. He inserted the
poles through the rings on the two sides of
the Altar for carrying it. The Altar was made
out of boards; it was hollow.

THE WASHBASIN

8 He made the Bronze Washbasin and its
bronze stand from the mirrors of the
women's work group who were assigned to
serve at the entrance to the Tent of Meeting.

THE COURTYARD

9-11 And he made the Courtyard. On the south
side the hangings for the Courtyard, woven
from fine twisted linen, were 150 feet long,
with their twenty posts and twenty bronze
bases, and fastening hooks and bands of sil-
ver. The north side was exactly the same.
12-20 The west end of the Courtyard had sev-
enty-five feet of hangings with ten posts and
bases, and fastening hooks and bands of sil-
ver. Across the seventy-five feet at the front,
or east end, were twenty-two and a half feet
of hangings, with their three posts and
bases on one side and the same for the other
side. All the hangings around the Courtyard
were of fine twisted linen. The bases for the
posts were bronze and the fastening hooks
and bands on the posts were of silver. The
posts of the Courtyard were both capped
and banded with silver. The screen at the
door of the Courtyard was embroidered in
blue, purple, and scarlet fabric with fine
twisted linen. It was thirty feet long and
seven and a half feet high, matching the
hangings of the Courtyard. There were four
posts with bases of bronze and fastening
hooks of silver; they were capped and
banded in silver. All the pegs for The
Dwelling and the Courtyard were made of
bronze.

21-23 This is an inventory of The Dwelling that
housed The Testimony drawn up by order of
Moses for the work of the Levites under
Ithamar, son of Aaron the priest. Bezalel, the
son of Uri, son of Hur, of the tribe of Judah,

NEW KING JAMES VERSION

tribe of Judah, made all that the LORD had com-
manded Moses. 23And with him *was* Aholiab the
son of Ahisamach, of the tribe of Dan, an en-
graver and designer, a weaver of blue, purple,
and scarlet *thread,* and of fine linen.
24All the gold that was used in all the work of
the holy *place,* that is, the gold of the offering,
was twenty-nine talents and seven hundred and
thirty shekels, according to the shekel of the
sanctuary. 25And the silver from those who were
numbered of the congregation *was* one hundred
talents and one thousand seven hundred and
seventy-five shekels, according to the shekel of
the sanctuary: 26a bekah for each man (*that is,*
half a shekel, according to the shekel of the
sanctuary), for everyone included in the num-
bering from twenty years old and above, for six
hundred and three thousand, five hundred and
fifty *men.* 27And from the hundred talents of sil-
ver were cast the sockets of the sanctuary and
the bases of the veil: one hundred sockets from
the hundred talents, one talent for each socket.
28Then from the one thousand seven hundred
and seventy-five *shekels* he made hooks for the
pillars, overlaid their capitals, and made bands
for them.
29The offering of bronze *was* seventy talents
and two thousand four hundred shekels. 30And
with it he made the sockets for the door of the tab-
ernacle of meeting, the bronze altar, the bronze
grating for it, and all the utensils for the altar,
31the sockets for the court all around, the bases
for the court gate, all the pegs for the tabernacle,
and all the pegs for the court all around.

MAKING THE GARMENTS OF THE PRIESTHOOD

39 Of the blue, purple, and scarlet *thread* they
made garments of ministry,[a] for minister-
ing in the holy *place,* and made the holy gar-
ments for Aaron, as the LORD had commanded
Moses.

MAKING THE EPHOD

2He made the ephod of gold, blue, purple,
and scarlet *thread,* and of fine woven linen.
3And they beat the gold into thin sheets and cut
it into threads, to work *it* in *with* the blue, pur-
ple, and scarlet *thread,* and the fine linen, *into*
artistic designs. 4They made shoulder straps for
it to couple *it* together; it was coupled together
at its two edges. 5And the intricately woven
band of his ephod that *was* on it *was* of the same
workmanship, *woven of* gold, blue, purple, and
scarlet *thread,* and of fine woven linen, as the
LORD had commanded Moses.
6And they set onyx stones, enclosed in set-
tings of gold; they were engraved, as signets are
engraved, with the names of the sons of Israel.
7He put them on the shoulders of the ephod *as*
memorial stones for the sons of Israel, as the
LORD had commanded Moses.

MAKING THE BREASTPLATE

8And he made the breastplate, artistically
woven like the workmanship of the ephod, of

39:1 [a]Or *woven garments*

THE MESSAGE

made everything that GOD had commanded Moses. Working with Bezalel was Oholiab, the son of Ahisamach, of the tribe of Dan, an artisan, designer, and embroiderer in blue, purple, and scarlet fabrics and fine linen.

24 Gold. The total amount of gold used in construction of the Sanctuary, all of it contributed freely, weighed out at 1,900 pounds according to the Sanctuary standard.

25-28 Silver. The silver from those in the community who were registered in the census came to 6,437 pounds according to the Sanctuary standard—that amounted to a *beka,* or half-shekel, for every registered person aged twenty and over, a total of 603,550 men. They used the three and one-quarter tons of silver to cast the bases for the Sanctuary and for the hangings, one hundred bases at sixty-four pounds each. They used the remaining thirty-seven pounds to make the connecting hooks on the posts, and the caps and bands for the posts.

29-31 Bronze. The bronze that was brought in weighed 4,522 pounds. It was used to make the door of the Tent of Meeting, the Bronze Altar with its bronze grating, all the utensils of the Altar, the bases around the Courtyard, the bases for the gate of the Courtyard, and all the pegs for The Dwelling and the Courtyard.

1 39 Vestments. Using the blue, purple, and scarlet fabrics, they made the woven vestments for ministering in the Sanctuary. Also they made the sacred vestments for Aaron, as GOD had commanded Moses.

2-5 Ephod. They made the Ephod using gold and blue, purple, and scarlet fabrics and finely twisted linen. They hammered out gold leaf and sliced it into threads that were then worked into designs in the blue, purple, and scarlet fabric and fine linen. They made shoulder pieces fastened at the two ends. The decorated band was made of the same material—gold, blue, purple, and scarlet material, and of fine twisted linen—and of one piece with it, just as GOD had commanded Moses.

6-7 They mounted the onyx stones in a setting of filigreed gold and engraved the names of the sons of Israel on them, then fastened them on the shoulder pieces of the Ephod as memorial stones for the Israelites, just as GOD had commanded Moses.

8-10 Breastpiece. They made a Breastpiece designed like the Ephod from gold, blue, pur-

NEW KING JAMES VERSION

gold, blue, purple, and scarlet *thread,* and of
fine woven linen. 9They made the breastplate
square by doubling it; a span *was* its length and
a span its width when doubled. 10And they set in
it four rows of stones: a row with a sardius, a
topaz, and an emerald was the first row; 11the
second row, a turquoise, a sapphire, and a dia-
mond; 12the third row, a jacinth, an agate, and an
amethyst; 13the fourth row, a beryl, an onyx, and
a jasper. *They were* enclosed in settings of gold
in their mountings. 14*There were* twelve stones
according to the names of the sons of Israel: ac-
cording to their names, *engraved like* a signet,
each one with its own name according to the
twelve tribes. 15And they made chains for the
breastplate at the ends, like braided cords of
pure gold. 16They also made two settings of gold
and two gold rings, and put the two rings on the
two ends of the breastplate. 17And they put the
two braided *chains* of gold in the two rings on
the ends of the breastplate. 18The two ends of
the two braided *chains* they fastened in the two
settings, and put them on the shoulder straps of
the ephod in the front. 19And they made two
rings of gold and put *them* on the two ends of
the breastplate, on the edge of it, which *was* on
the inward side of the ephod. 20They made two
other gold rings and put them on the two shoul-
der straps, underneath the ephod toward its
front, right at the seam above the intricately wo-
ven band of the ephod. 21And they bound the
breastplate by means of its rings to the rings of
the ephod with a blue cord, so that it would be
above the intricately woven band of the ephod,
and that the breastplate would not come loose
from the ephod, as the LORD had commanded
Moses.

MAKING THE OTHER PRIESTLY GARMENTS

22He made the robe of the ephod of woven
work, all of blue. 23And *there was* an opening in
the middle of the robe, like the opening in a coat
of mail, *with* a woven binding all around the
opening, so that it would not tear. 24They made
on the hem of the robe pomegranates of blue,
purple, and scarlet, and of fine woven *linen.*
25And they made bells of pure gold, and put the
bells between the pomegranates on the hem of
the robe all around between the pomegranates:
26a bell and a pomegranate, a bell and a pome-
granate, all around the hem of the robe to min-
ister in, as the LORD had commanded Moses.
27They made tunics, artistically woven of fine
linen, for Aaron and his sons, 28a turban of fine
linen, exquisite hats of fine linen, short trousers
of fine woven linen, 29and a sash of fine woven
linen with blue, purple, and scarlet *thread,*
made by a weaver, as the LORD had commanded
Moses.
30Then they made the plate of the holy crown
of pure gold, and wrote on it an inscription *like*
the engraving of a signet:

HOLINESS TO THE LORD.

31And they tied to it a blue cord, to fasten *it*
above on the turban, as the LORD had com-
manded Moses.

THE MESSAGE

ple, and scarlet material, and fine twisted linen. Doubled, the Breastpiece was nine inches square. They mounted four rows of precious gemstones on it.

First row: carnelian, topaz, emerald.

11 Second row: ruby, sapphire, crystal.

12 Third row: jacinth, agate, amethyst.

13-14 Fourth row: beryl, onyx, jasper.

The stones were mounted in a gold filigree. The twelve stones corresponded to the names of the sons of Israel, twelve names engraved as on a seal, one for each of the twelve tribes.

15-21 They made braided chains of pure gold for the Breastpiece, like cords. They made two settings of gold filigree and two rings of gold, put the two rings at the two ends of the Breastpiece, and fastened the two ends of the cords to the two rings at the end of the Breastpiece. Then they fastened the cords to the settings of filigree, attaching them to the shoulder pieces of the Ephod in front. Then they made two rings of gold and fastened them to the two ends of the Breastpiece on its inside edge facing the Ephod. They made two more rings of gold and fastened them in the front of the Ephod to the lower part of the two shoulder pieces, near the seam above the decorated band of the Ephod. The Breastpiece was fastened by running a cord of blue through its rings to the rings of the Ephod so that it rested secure on the decorated band of the Ephod and wouldn't come loose, just as GOD had commanded Moses.

22-26 Robe. They made the robe for the Ephod entirely of blue. The opening of the robe at the center was like a collar, the edge hemmed so that it wouldn't tear. On the hem of the robe they made pomegranates of blue, purple, and scarlet material and fine twisted linen. They also made bells of pure gold and alternated the bells and pomegranates—a bell and a pomegranate, a bell and a pomegranate—all around the hem of the robe that was worn for ministering, just as GOD had commanded Moses.

27-29 They also made the tunics of fine linen, the work of a weaver, for Aaron and his sons, the turban of fine linen, the linen hats, the linen underwear made of fine twisted linen, and sashes of fine twisted linen, blue, purple, and scarlet material and embroidered, just as GOD had commanded Moses.

30-31 They made the plate, the sacred crown, of pure gold and engraved on it as on a seal: "Holy to GOD." They attached a blue cord to it and fastened it to the turban, just as GOD had commanded Moses.

New King James Version

The Work Completed
[32]Thus all the work of the tabernacle of the
tent of meeting was finished. And the children
of Israel did according to all that the LORD had
commanded Moses; so they did. [33]And they
brought the tabernacle to Moses, the tent and all
its furnishings: its clasps, its boards, its bars, its
pillars, and its sockets; [34]the covering of ram
skins dyed red, the covering of badger skins,
and the veil of the covering; [35]the ark of the Tes-
timony with its poles, and the mercy seat; [36]the
table, all its utensils, and the showbread; [37]the
pure *gold* lampstand with its lamps (the lamps
set in order), all its utensils, and the oil for light;
[38]the gold altar, the anointing oil, and the sweet
incense; the screen for the tabernacle door; [39]the
bronze altar, its grate of bronze, its poles, and all
its utensils; the laver with its base; [40]the hang-
ings of the court, its pillars and its sockets, the
screen for the court gate, its cords, and its pegs;
all the utensils for the service of the tabernacle,
for the tent of meeting; [41]and the garments of
ministry,[a] to minister in the holy *place:* the holy
garments for Aaron the priest, and his sons' gar-
ments, to minister as priests.
[42]According to all that the LORD had com-
manded Moses, so the children of Israel did all
the work. [43]Then Moses looked over all the
work, and indeed they had done it; as the LORD
had commanded, just so they had done it. And
Moses blessed them.

The Tabernacle Erected and Arranged
40 Then the LORD spoke to Moses, saying:
[2]"On the first day of the first month you
shall set up the tabernacle of the tent of meet-
ing. [3]You shall put in it the ark of the Testimony,
and partition off the ark with the veil. [4]You shall
bring in the table and arrange the things that
are to be set in order on it; and you shall bring
in the lampstand and light its lamps. [5]You shall
also set the altar of gold for the incense before
the ark of the Testimony, and put up the screen
for the door of the tabernacle. [6]Then you shall
set the altar of the burnt offering before the
door of the tabernacle of the tent of meeting.
[7]And you shall set the laver between the taber-
nacle of meeting and the altar, and put water in it.

39:41 [a]Or *woven garments*

The Message

32 That completed the work of The Dwelling, the Tent of Meeting. The People of Israel did what GOD had commanded Moses. They did it all.

33-41 They presented The Dwelling to Moses, the Tent and all its furnishings:

fastening hooks
frames
crossbars
posts
bases
tenting of tanned ram skins
tenting of dolphin skins
veil of the screen
Chest of The Testimony
  with its poles
  and Atonement-Cover
Table
  with its utensils
  and the Bread of the Presence
Lampstand of pure gold
  and its lamps all fitted out
  and all its utensils
  and the oil for the light
Gold Altar
anointing oil
fragrant incense
screen for the entrance to the Tent
Bronze Altar
  with its bronze grate
  its poles and all its utensils
Washbasin
  and its base
hangings for the Courtyard
  its posts and bases
screen for the gate of the Courtyard
  its cords and its pegs
utensils for ministry in The Dwelling,
  the Tent of Meeting
woven vestments for ministering in
  the Sanctuary
sacred vestments for Aaron the priest,
  and his sons when serving as priests

42-43 The Israelites completed all the work, just as GOD had commanded. Moses saw that they had done all the work and done it exactly as GOD had commanded. Moses blessed them.

"Moses Finished the Work"

1-3 **40** GOD spoke to Moses: "On the first day of the first month, set up The Dwelling, the Tent of Meeting. Place the Chest of The Testimony in it and screen the Chest with the curtain.

4 "Bring in the Table and set it, arranging its Lampstand and lamps.

5 "Place the Gold Altar of Incense before the Chest of The Testimony and hang the curtain at the door of The Dwelling.

6 "Place the Altar of Whole-Burnt-Offering at the door of The Dwelling, the Tent of Meeting.

7 "Place the Washbasin between the Tent of Meeting and the Altar and fill it with water.

New King James Version

8You shall set up the court all around, and hang up the screen at the court gate.

9"And you shall take the anointing oil, and anoint the tabernacle and all that *is* in it; and you shall hallow it and all its utensils, and it shall be holy. 10You shall anoint the altar of the burnt offering and all its utensils, and consecrate the altar. The altar shall be most holy. 11And you shall anoint the laver and its base, and consecrate it.

12"Then you shall bring Aaron and his sons to the door of the tabernacle of meeting and wash them with water. 13You shall put the holy garments on Aaron, and anoint him and consecrate him, that he may minister to Me as priest. 14And you shall bring his sons and clothe them with tunics. 15You shall anoint them, as you anointed their father, that they may minister to Me as priests; for their anointing shall surely be an everlasting priesthood throughout their generations."

16Thus Moses did; according to all that the LORD had commanded him, so he did.

17And it came to pass in the first month of the second year, on the first *day* of the month, *that* the tabernacle was raised up. 18So Moses raised up the tabernacle, fastened its sockets, set up its boards, put in its bars, and raised up its pillars. 19And he spread out the tent over the tabernacle and put the covering of the tent on top of it, as the LORD had commanded Moses. 20He took the Testimony and put *it* into the ark, inserted the poles through the rings of the ark, and put the mercy seat on top of the ark. 21And he brought the ark into the tabernacle, hung up the veil of the covering, and partitioned off the ark of the Testimony, as the LORD had commanded Moses.

22He put the table in the tabernacle of meeting, on the north side of the tabernacle, outside the veil; 23and he set the bread in order upon it before the LORD, as the LORD had commanded Moses. 24He put the lampstand in the tabernacle of meeting, across from the table, on the south side of the tabernacle; 25and he lit the lamps before the LORD, as the LORD had commanded Moses. 26He put the gold altar in the tabernacle of meeting in front of the veil; 27and he burned sweet incense on it, as the LORD had commanded Moses. 28He hung up the screen *at* the door of the tabernacle. 29And he put the altar of burnt offering *before* the door of the tabernacle of the tent of meeting, and offered upon it the burnt offering and the grain offering, as the LORD had commanded Moses. 30He set the laver between the tabernacle of meeting and the altar, and put water there for washing; 31and Moses, Aaron, and his sons would wash their hands and their feet *with water* from it. 32Whenever they went into the tabernacle of meeting, and when they came near the altar, they washed, as the LORD had commanded Moses. 33And he raised up the court all around the tabernacle and the altar, and hung up the screen of the court gate. So Moses finished the work.

The Message

8 "Set up the Courtyard on all sides and hang the curtain at the entrance to the Courtyard.

9-11 "Then take the anointing oil and anoint The Dwelling and everything in it; consecrate it and all its furnishings so that it becomes holy. Anoint the Altar of Whole-Burnt-Offering and all its utensils, consecrating the Altar so that it is completely holy. Anoint the Washbasin and its base: consecrate it.

12-15 "Finally, bring Aaron and his sons to the entrance of the Tent of Meeting and wash them with water. Dress Aaron in the sacred vestments. Anoint him. Consecrate him to serve me as priest. Bring his sons and put tunics on them. Anoint them, just as you anointed their father, to serve me as priests. Their anointing will bring them into a perpetual priesthood, down through the generations."

16 Moses did everything GOD commanded. He did it all.

17-19 On the first day of the first month of the second year, The Dwelling was set up. Moses set it up: He laid its bases, erected the frames, placed the crossbars, set the posts, spread the tent over The Dwelling, and put the covering over the tent, just as GOD had commanded Moses.

20-21 He placed The Testimony in the Chest, inserted the poles for carrying the Chest, and placed the lid, the Atonement-Cover, on it. He brought the Chest into The Dwelling and set up the curtain, screening off the Chest of The Testimony, just as GOD had commanded Moses.

22-23 He placed the Table in the Tent of Meeting on the north side of The Dwelling, outside the curtain, and arranged the Bread there before GOD, just as GOD had commanded him.

24-25 He placed the Lampstand in the Tent of Meeting opposite the Table on the south side of The Dwelling and set up the lamps before GOD, just as GOD had commanded him.

26-27 Moses placed the Gold Altar in the Tent of Meeting in front of the curtain and burned fragrant incense on it, just as GOD had commanded him.

28 He placed the screen at the entrance to The Dwelling.

29 He set the Altar of Whole-Burnt-Offering at the door of The Dwelling, the Tent of Meeting, and offered up the Whole-Burnt-Offerings and the Grain-Offerings, just as GOD had commanded Moses.

30-32 He placed the Washbasin between the Tent of Meeting and the Altar, and filled it with water for washing. Moses and Aaron and his sons washed their hands and feet there. When they entered the Tent of Meeting and when they served at the Altar, they washed, just as GOD had commanded Moses.

33 Finally, he erected the Courtyard all around The Dwelling and the Altar, and put up the screen for the Courtyard entrance.

Moses finished the work.

NEW KING JAMES VERSION

THE CLOUD AND THE GLORY

[34]Then the cloud covered the tabernacle of
meeting, and the glory of the LORD filled the tab-
ernacle. [35]And Moses was not able to enter the
tabernacle of meeting, because the cloud rested
above it, and the glory of the LORD filled the tab-
ernacle. [36]Whenever the cloud was taken up
from above the tabernacle, the children of Israel
would go onward in all their journeys. [37]But if
the cloud was not taken up, then they did not
journey till the day that it was taken up. [38]For
the cloud of the LORD *was* above the tabernacle
by day, and fire was over it by night, in the sight
of all the house of Israel, throughout all their
journeys.

THE MESSAGE

34-35 The Cloud covered the Tent of Meeting,
and the Glory of GOD filled The Dwelling.
Moses couldn't enter the Tent of Meeting be-
cause the Cloud was upon it, and the Glory
of GOD filled The Dwelling.
36-38 Whenever the Cloud lifted from The
Dwelling, the People of Israel set out on
their travels, but if the Cloud did not lift,
they wouldn't set out until it did lift. The
Cloud of GOD was over The Dwelling during
the day and the fire was in it at night, visible
to all the Israelites in all their travels.

LEVITICUS

New King James Version

The Burnt Offering

1 Now the LORD called to Moses, and spoke to
him from the tabernacle of meeting, saying,
2“Speak to the children of Israel, and say to
them: ‘When any one of you brings an offering
to the LORD, you shall bring your offering of the
livestock—of the herd and of the flock.
3‘If his offering *is* a burnt sacrifice of the
herd, let him offer a male without blemish; he
shall offer it of his own free will at the door of
the tabernacle of meeting before the LORD.
4Then he shall put his hand on the head of the
burnt offering, and it will be accepted on his be-
half to make atonement for him. 5He shall kill
the bull before the LORD; and the priests,
Aaron’s sons, shall bring the blood and sprinkle
the blood all around on the altar that *is by* the
door of the tabernacle of meeting. 6And he shall
skin the burnt offering and cut it into its pieces.
7The sons of Aaron the priest shall put fire on
the altar, and lay the wood in order on the fire.
8Then the priests, Aaron’s sons, shall lay the
parts, the head, and the fat in order on the wood
that *is* on the fire upon the altar; 9but he shall
wash its entrails and its legs with water. And the
priest shall burn all on the altar as a burnt sac-
rifice, an offering made by fire, a sweet aroma to
the LORD.
10‘If his offering *is* of the flocks—of the sheep
or of the goats—as a burnt sacrifice, he shall
bring a male without blemish. 11He shall kill it
on the north side of the altar before the LORD;
and the priests, Aaron’s sons, shall sprinkle its
blood all around on the altar. 12And he shall cut
it into its pieces, with its head and its fat; and
the priest shall lay them in order on the wood
that *is* on the fire upon the altar; 13but he shall
wash the entrails and the legs with water. Then
the priest shall bring *it* all and burn *it* on the al-
tar; it *is* a burnt sacrifice, an offering made by
fire, a sweet aroma to the LORD.
14‘And if the burnt sacrifice of his offering to
the LORD *is* of birds, then he shall bring his of-
fering of turtledoves or young pigeons. 15The
priest shall bring it to the altar, wring off its
head, and burn *it* on the altar; its blood shall be
drained out at the side of the altar. 16And he
shall remove its crop with its feathers and cast
it beside the altar on the east side, into the place
for ashes. 17Then he shall split it at its wings, *but*
shall not divide *it* completely; and the priest
shall burn it on the altar, on the wood that *is* on
the fire. It *is* a burnt sacrifice, an offering made
by fire, a sweet aroma to the LORD.

The Grain Offering

2 ‘When anyone offers a grain offering to the
LORD, his offering shall be *of* fine flour. And
he shall pour oil on it, and put frankincense on
it. 2He shall bring it to Aaron’s sons, the priests,
one of whom shall take from it his handful of
fine flour and oil with all the frankincense. And
the priest shall burn *it as* a memorial on the al-
tar, an offering made by fire, a sweet aroma to

The Message

Whole-Burnt-Offering

1-2 1 God called Moses and spoke to him from
the Tent of Meeting: “Speak to the People
of Israel. Tell them, When anyone presents
an offering to GOD, present an animal from
either the herd or the flock.
3-9 “If the offering is a Whole-Burnt-Offering
from the herd, present a male without a de-
fect at the entrance to the Tent of Meeting
that it may be accepted by GOD. Lay your
hand on the head of the Whole-Burnt-Offer-
ing so that it may be accepted on your be-
half to make atonement for you. Slaughter
the bull in GOD’s presence. Aaron’s sons, the
priests, will make an offering of the blood
by splashing it against all sides of the Altar
that stands at the entrance to the Tent of
Meeting. Next, skin the Whole-Burnt-Offer-
ing and cut it up. Aaron’s sons, the priests,
will prepare a fire on the Altar, carefully lay-
ing out the wood, and then arrange the body
parts, including the head and the suet, on
the wood prepared for the fire on the Altar.
Scrub the entrails and legs clean. The priest
will burn it all on the Altar: a Whole-Burnt-
Offering, a Fire-Gift, a pleasing fragrance to
GOD.
10-13 “If the Whole-Burnt-Offering comes from
the flock, whether sheep or goat, present a
male without defect. Slaughter it on the
north side of the Altar in GOD’s presence.
The sons of Aaron, the priests, will throw
the blood against all sides of the Altar. Cut it
up and the priest will arrange the pieces, in-
cluding the head and the suet, on the wood
prepared for burning on the Altar. Scrub the
entrails and legs clean. The priest will offer
it all, burning it on the Altar: a Whole-Burnt-
Offering, a Fire-Gift, a pleasing fragrance to
GOD.
14-17 “If a bird is presented to GOD for the
Whole-Burnt-Offering it can be either a
dove or a pigeon. The priest will bring it to
the Altar, wring off its head, and burn it on
the Altar. But he will first drain the blood on
the side of the Altar, remove the gizzard and
its contents, and throw them on the east side
of the Altar where the ashes are piled. Then
rip it open by its wings but leave it in one
piece and burn it on the Altar on the wood
prepared for the fire: a Whole-Burnt-Offer-
ing, a Fire-Gift, a pleasing fragrance to
GOD.”

Grain-Offering

1-3 2 “When you present a Grain-Offering to
GOD, use fine flour. Pour oil on it, put in-
cense on it, and bring it to Aaron’s sons, the
priests. One of them will take a handful of
the fine flour and oil, with all the incense,
and burn it on the Altar for a memorial: a
Fire-Gift, a pleasing fragrance to GOD. The

NEW KING JAMES VERSION

the LORD. [3]The rest of the grain offering *shall be*
Aaron's and his sons'. *It is* most holy of the of-
ferings to the LORD made by fire.
[4]'And if you bring as an offering a grain of-
fering baked in the oven, *it shall be* unleavened
cakes of fine flour mixed with oil, or unleavened
wafers anointed with oil. [5]But if your offering *is*
a grain offering *baked* in a pan, *it shall be of* fine
flour, unleavened, mixed with oil. [6]You shall
break it in pieces and pour oil on it; it *is* a grain
offering.
[7]'If your offering *is* a grain offering *baked* in
a covered pan, it shall be made *of* fine flour with
oil. [8]You shall bring the grain offering that is
made of these things to the LORD. And when it is
presented to the priest, he shall bring it to the al-
tar. [9]Then the priest shall take from the grain of-
fering a memorial portion, and burn *it* on the al-
tar. *It is* an offering made by fire, a sweet aroma
to the LORD. [10]And what is left of the grain offer-
ing *shall be* Aaron's and his sons'. *It is* most
holy of the offerings to the LORD made by fire.
[11]'No grain offering which you bring to the
LORD shall be made with leaven, for you shall
burn no leaven nor any honey in any offering to
the LORD made by fire. [12]As for the offering of
the firstfruits, you shall offer them to the LORD,
but they shall not be burned on the altar for a
sweet aroma. [13]And every offering of your grain
offering you shall season with salt; you shall not
allow the salt of the covenant of your God to be
lacking from your grain offering. With all your
offerings you shall offer salt.
[14]'If you offer a grain offering of your first-
fruits to the LORD, you shall offer for the grain of-
fering of your firstfruits green heads of grain
roasted on the fire, grain beaten from full heads.
[15]And you shall put oil on it, and lay frankincense
on it. It *is* a grain offering. [16]Then the priest shall
burn the memorial portion: *part* of its beaten
grain and *part* of its oil, with all the frankincense,
as an offering made by fire to the LORD.

THE PEACE OFFERING

3 'When his offering *is* a sacrifice of a peace of-
fering, if he offers *it* of the herd, whether
male or female, he shall offer it without blemish
before the LORD. [2]And he shall lay his hand on
the head of his offering, and kill it *at* the door of
the tabernacle of meeting; and Aaron's sons, the
priests, shall sprinkle the blood all around on
the altar. [3]Then he shall offer from the sacrifice
of the peace offering an offering made by fire to
the LORD. The fat that covers the entrails and all
the fat that *is* on the entrails, [4]the two kidneys
and the fat that *is* on them by the flanks, and the
fatty lobe *attached* to the liver above the kid-
neys, he shall remove; [5]and Aaron's sons shall
burn it on the altar upon the burnt sacrifice,
which *is* on the wood that *is* on the fire, *as* an of-
fering made by fire, a sweet aroma to the LORD.
[6]'If his offering as a sacrifice of a peace of-
fering to the LORD *is* of the flock, *whether* male
or female, he shall offer it without blemish. [7]If
he offers a lamb as his offering, then he shall of-
fer it before the LORD. [8]And he shall lay his hand
on the head of his offering, and kill it before the
tabernacle of meeting; and Aaron's sons shall
sprinkle its blood all around on the altar.

THE MESSAGE

rest of the Grain-Offering is for Aaron and
his sons—a most holy part of the Fire-Gifts
to GOD.
4 "When you present a Grain-Offering of
oven-baked loaves, use fine flour, mixed
with oil but no yeast. Or present wafers
made without yeast and spread with oil.
5-6 "If you bring a Grain-Offering cooked on
a griddle, use fine flour mixed with oil but
without yeast. Crumble it and pour oil on
it—it's a Grain-Offering.
7 "If you bring a Grain-Offering deep-fried
in a pan, make it of fine flour with oil.
8-10 "Bring the Grain-Offering you make from
these ingredients and present it to the
priest. He will bring it to the Altar, break off
a memorial piece from the Grain-Offering,
and burn it on the Altar: a Fire-Gift, a pleas-
ing fragrance to GOD. The rest of the Grain-
Offering is for Aaron and his sons—a most
holy part of the gifts to GOD.
11-13 "All the Grain-Offerings that you present
to GOD must be made without yeast; you
must never burn any yeast or honey as a
Fire-Gift to GOD. You may offer them to GOD
as an offering of firstfruits but not on the Al-
tar as a pleasing fragrance. Season every
presentation of your Grain-Offering with
salt. Don't leave the salt of the covenant
with your God out of your Grain-Offerings.
Present all your offerings with salt.
14-16 "If you present a Grain-Offering of first-
fruits to GOD, bring crushed heads of the
new grain roasted. Put oil and incense on
it—it's a Grain-Offering. The priest will
burn some of the mixed grain and oil with
all the incense as a memorial—a Fire-Gift to
GOD."

THE PEACE-OFFERING

1-5 3 "If your offering is a Peace-Offering and
you present an animal from the herd,
either male or female, it must be an animal
without any defect. Lay your hand on the
head of your offering and slaughter it at the
entrance of the Tent of Meeting. Aaron's
sons, the priests, will throw the blood on all
sides of the Altar. As a Fire-Gift to GOD from
the Peace-Offering, present all the fat that
covers or is connected to the entrails, the
two kidneys and the fat around them at the
loins, and the lobe of the liver that is re-
moved along with the kidneys. Aaron and
his sons will burn it on the Altar along with
the Whole-Burnt-Offering that is on the
wood prepared for the fire: a Fire-Gift, a
pleasing fragrance to GOD.
6-11 "If your Peace-Offering to GOD comes
from the flock, bring a male or female with-
out defect. If you offer a lamb, offer it to
GOD. Lay your hand on the head of your of-
fering and slaughter it at the Tent of Meet-
ing. The sons of Aaron will throw its blood
on all sides of the Altar. As a Fire-Gift to

NEW KING JAMES VERSION

[9]'Then he shall offer from the sacrifice of the peace offering, as an offering made by fire to the LORD, its fat *and* the whole fat tail which he shall remove close to the backbone. And the fat that covers the entrails and all the fat that *is* on the entrails, [10]the two kidneys and the fat that *is* on them by the flanks, and the fatty lobe *attached* to the liver above the kidneys, he shall remove; [11]and the priest shall burn *them* on the altar *as* food, an offering made by fire to the LORD.

[12]'And if his offering *is* a goat, then he shall offer it before the LORD. [13]He shall lay his hand on its head and kill it before the tabernacle of meeting; and the sons of Aaron shall sprinkle its blood all around on the altar. [14]Then he shall offer from it his offering, as an offering made by fire to the LORD. The fat that covers the entrails and all the fat that *is* on the entrails, [15]the two kidneys and the fat that *is* on them by the flanks, and the fatty lobe *attached* to the liver above the kidneys, he shall remove; [16]and the priest shall burn them on the altar *as* food, an offering made by fire for a sweet aroma; all the fat *is* the LORD's.

[17]'*This shall be* a perpetual statute throughout your generations in all your dwellings: you shall eat neither fat nor blood.' "

THE SIN OFFERING

4 Now the LORD spoke to Moses, saying, [2]"Speak to the children of Israel, saying: 'If a person sins unintentionally against any of the commandments of the LORD *in anything* which ought not to be done, and does any of them, [3]if the anointed priest sins, bringing guilt on the people, then let him offer to the LORD for his sin which he has sinned a young bull without blemish as a sin offering. [4]He shall bring the bull to the door of the tabernacle of meeting before the LORD, lay his hand on the bull's head, and kill the bull before the LORD. [5]Then the anointed priest shall take some of the bull's blood and bring it to the tabernacle of meeting. [6]The priest shall dip his finger in the blood and sprinkle some of the blood seven times before the LORD, in front of the veil of the sanctuary. [7]And the priest shall put some of the blood on the horns of the altar of sweet incense before the LORD, which is in the tabernacle of meeting; and he shall pour the remaining blood of the bull at the base of the altar of the burnt offering, which is at the door of the tabernacle of meeting. [8]He shall take from it all the fat of the bull as the sin offering. The fat that covers the entrails and all the fat which *is* on the entrails, [9]the two kidneys and the fat that *is* on them by the flanks, and the fatty lobe *attached* to the liver above the kidneys, he shall remove, [10]as it was taken from the bull of the sacrifice of the peace offering; and the priest shall burn them on the altar of the burnt offering. [11]But the bull's hide and all its flesh, with its head and legs, its entrails and offal— [12]the whole bull he shall carry outside the camp to a clean place, where the ashes are poured out, and burn it on wood with fire; where the ashes are poured out it shall be burned.

[13]'Now if the whole congregation of Israel sins unintentionally, and the thing is hidden

THE MESSAGE

GOD from the Peace-Offering, present its fat, the entire fat tail cut off close to the backbone, all the fat on and connected to the entrails, the two kidneys and the fat around them on the loins, and the lobe of the liver which is removed along with the kidneys. The priest will burn it on the Altar: a meal, a Fire-Gift to GOD.

12-16 "If the offering is a goat, bring it into the
presence of GOD, lay your hand on its head,
and slaughter it in front of the Tent of Meet-
ing. Aaron's sons will throw the blood on all
sides of the Altar. As a Fire-Gift to GOD pre-
sent the fat that covers and is connected to
the entrails, the two kidneys and the fat
which is around them on the loins, and the
lobe of the liver which is removed along
with the kidneys. The priest will burn them
on the Altar: a meal, a Fire-Gift, a pleasing
fragrance.
16-17 "All the fat belongs to GOD. This is the
fixed rule down through the generations,
wherever you happen to live: Don't eat the
fat; don't eat the blood. None of it."

THE ABSOLUTION-OFFERING

1-12 4 GOD spoke to Moses: "Tell the Israelites,
When a person sins unintentionally by
straying from any of GOD's commands,
breaking what must not be broken, if it's the
anointed priest who sins and so brings guilt
on the people, he is to bring a bull without
defect to GOD as an Absolution-Offering for
the sin he has committed. Have him bring
the bull to the entrance of the Tent of Meet-
ing in the presence of GOD, lay his hand on
the bull's head, and slaughter the bull be-
fore GOD. He is then to take some of the
bull's blood, bring it into the Tent of Meet-
ing, dip his finger in the blood, and sprinkle
some of it seven times before GOD, before
the curtain of the Sanctuary. He is to smear
some of the blood on the horns of the Altar
of Fragrant Incense before GOD which is in
the Tent of Meeting. He is to pour the rest of
the bull's blood out at the base of the Altar
of Whole-Burnt-Offering at the entrance of
the Tent of Meeting. He is to remove all the
fat from the bull of the Absolution-Offering,
the fat which covers and is connected to the
entrails, the two kidneys and the fat that is
around them at the loins, and the lobe of the
liver which he takes out along with the kid-
neys—the same procedure as when the fat is
removed from the bull of the Peace-Offering.
Finally, he is to burn all this on the Altar of
Burnt Offering. Everything else—the bull's
hide, meat, head, legs, organs, and guts—he
is to take outside the camp to a clean place
where the ashes are dumped and is to burn
it on a wood fire.
13-21 "If the whole congregation sins uninten-
tionally by straying from one of the com-

New King James Version

from the eyes of the assembly, and they have
done *something against* any of the command-
ments of the LORD *in anything* which should not
be done, and are guilty; 14when the sin which
they have committed becomes known, then the
assembly shall offer a young bull for the sin,
and bring it before the tabernacle of meeting.
15And the elders of the congregation shall lay
their hands on the head of the bull before the
LORD. Then the bull shall be killed before the
LORD. 16The anointed priest shall bring some of
the bull's blood to the tabernacle of meeting.
17Then the priest shall dip his finger in the blood
and sprinkle *it* seven times before the LORD, in
front of the veil. 18And he shall put *some* of the
blood on the horns of the altar which *is* before
the LORD, which *is* in the tabernacle of meeting;
and he shall pour the remaining blood at the
base of the altar of burnt offering, which is at
the door of the tabernacle of meeting. 19He shall
take all the fat from it and burn *it* on the altar.
20And he shall do with the bull as he did with the
bull as a sin offering; thus he shall do with it. So
the priest shall make atonement for them, and it
shall be forgiven them. 21Then he shall carry the
bull outside the camp, and burn it as he burned
the first bull. It *is* a sin offering for the assembly.

22'When a ruler has sinned, and done *some-
thing* unintentionally *against* any of the com-
mandments of the LORD his God *in anything*
which should not be done, and is guilty, 23or if
his sin which he has committed comes to his
knowledge, he shall bring as his offering a kid
of the goats, a male without blemish. 24And he
shall lay his hand on the head of the goat, and
kill it at the place where they kill the burnt of-
fering before the LORD. It *is* a sin offering. 25The
priest shall take some of the blood of the sin of-
fering with his finger, put *it* on the horns of the
altar of burnt offering, and pour its blood at the
base of the altar of burnt offering. 26And he shall
burn all its fat on the altar, like the fat of the sac-
rifice of the peace offering. So the priest shall
make atonement for him concerning his sin, and
it shall be forgiven him.

27'If anyone of the common people sins unin-
tentionally by doing *something against* any of
the commandments of the LORD *in anything*
which ought not to be done, and is guilty, 28or if
his sin which he has committed comes to his
knowledge, then he shall bring as his offering a
kid of the goats, a female without blemish, for
his sin which he has committed. 29And he shall
lay his hand on the head of the sin offering, and
kill the sin offering at the place of the burnt of-
fering. 30Then the priest shall take *some* of its
blood with his finger, put *it* on the horns of the
altar of burnt offering, and pour all *the remain-
ing* blood at the base of the altar. 31He shall re-
move all its fat, as fat is removed from the sacri-
fice of the peace offering; and the priest shall
burn it on the altar for a sweet aroma to the
LORD. So the priest shall make atonement for
him, and it shall be forgiven him.

32'If he brings a lamb as his sin offering, he
shall bring a female without blemish. 33Then he
shall lay his hand on the head of the sin offer-
ing, and kill it as a sin offering at the place
where they kill the burnt offering. 34The priest

The Message

mandments of GOD that must not be bro-
ken, they become guilty even though no one
is aware of it. When they do become aware
of the sin they've committed, the congrega-
tion must bring a bull as an Absolution-Of-
fering and present it at the Tent of Meeting.
The elders of the congregation will lay their
hands on the bull's head in the presence of
GOD and one of them will slaughter it be-
fore GOD. The anointed priest will then
bring some of the blood into the Tent of
Meeting, dip his finger in the blood, and
sprinkle some of it seven times before GOD
in front of the curtain. He will smear some
of the blood on the horns of the Altar which
is before GOD in the Tent of Meeting and
pour the rest of it at the base of the Altar of
Whole-Burnt-Offering at the entrance of
the Tent of Meeting. He will remove all the
fat and burn it on the Altar. He will follow
the same procedure with this bull as with
the bull for the Absolution-Offering. The
priest makes atonement for them and they
are forgiven. They then will take the bull
outside the camp and burn it just as they
burned the first bull. It's the Absolution-
Offering for the congregation.

22-26 "When a ruler sins unintentionally by
straying from one of the commands of his
GOD which must not be broken, he is guilty.
When he becomes aware of the sin he has
committed, he must bring a goat for his of-
fering, a male without any defect, lay his
hand on the head of the goat, and slaughter
it in the place where they slaughter the
Whole-Burnt-Offering in the presence of
GOD—it's an Absolution-Offering. The priest
will then take some of the blood of the
Absolution-Offering with his finger, smear
it on the horns of the Altar of Whole-Burnt-
Offering, and pour the rest at the base of the
Altar. He will burn all its fat on the Altar, the
same as with the fat of the Peace-Offering.

"The priest makes atonement for him on
account of his sin and he's forgiven.

27-31 "When an ordinary member of the con-
gregation sins unintentionally, straying
from one of the commandments of GOD
which must not be broken, he is guilty.
When he is made aware of his sin, he shall
bring a goat, a female without any defect,
and offer it for his sin, lay his hand on the
head of the Absolution-Offering, and
slaughter it at the place of the Whole-Burnt-
Offering. The priest will take some of its
blood with his finger, smear it on the horns
of the Altar of Whole-Burnt-Offering, and
pour the rest at the base of the Altar. Finally,
he'll take out all the fat, the same as with the
Peace-Offerings, and burn it on the Altar for
a pleasing fragrance to GOD.

"In this way, the priest makes atonement
for him and he's forgiven.

32-35 "If he brings a lamb for an Absolution-
Offering, he shall present a female without
any defect, lay his hand on the head of the
Absolution-Offering, and slaughter it at the
same place they slaughter the Whole-Burnt-
Offering. The priest will take some of the

NEW KING JAMES VERSION

shall take *some* of the blood of the sin offering with his finger, put *it* on the horns of the altar of burnt offering, and pour all *the remaining* blood at the base of the altar. 35He shall remove all its fat, as the fat of the lamb is removed from the sacrifice of the peace offering. Then the priest shall burn it on the altar, according to the offerings made by fire to the LORD. So the priest shall make atonement for his sin that he has committed, and it shall be forgiven him.

THE TRESPASS OFFERING

5 'If a person sins in hearing the utterance of an oath, and *is* a witness, whether he has seen or known *of the matter*—if he does not tell *it*, he bears guilt.

2'Or if a person touches any unclean thing, whether *it is* the carcass of an unclean beast, or the carcass of unclean livestock, or the carcass of unclean creeping things, and he is unaware of it, he also shall be unclean and guilty. 3Or if he touches human uncleanness—whatever uncleanness with which a man may be defiled, and he is unaware of it—when he realizes *it*, then he shall be guilty.

4'Or if a person swears, speaking thoughtlessly with *his* lips to do evil or to do good, whatever *it is* that a man may pronounce by an oath, and he is unaware of it—when he realizes *it*, then he shall be guilty in any of these *matters*.

5'And it shall be, when he is guilty in any of these *matters*, that he shall confess that he has sinned in that *thing*; 6and he shall bring his trespass offering to the LORD for his sin which he has committed, a female from the flock, a lamb or a kid of the goats as a sin offering. So the priest shall make atonement for him concerning his sin.

7'If he is not able to bring a lamb, then he shall bring to the LORD, for his trespass which he has committed, two turtledoves or two young pigeons: one as a sin offering and the other as a burnt offering. 8And he shall bring them to the priest, who shall offer *that* which *is* for the sin offering first, and wring off its head from its neck, but shall not divide *it* completely. 9Then he shall sprinkle *some* of the blood of the sin offering on the side of the altar, and the rest of the blood shall be drained out at the base of the altar. It *is* a sin offering. 10And he shall offer the second *as* a burnt offering according to the prescribed manner. So the priest shall make atonement on his behalf for his sin which he has committed, and it shall be forgiven him.

11'But if he is not able to bring two turtledoves or two young pigeons, then he who sinned shall bring for his offering one-tenth of an ephah of fine flour as a sin offering. He shall put no oil on it, nor shall he put frankincense on it, for it *is* a sin offering. 12Then he shall bring it to the priest, and the priest shall take his handful of it as a memorial portion, and burn *it* on the altar according to the offerings made by fire to the LORD. It *is* a sin offering. 13The priest shall make atonement for him, for his sin that he has committed in any of these matters; and it shall be forgiven him. *The rest* shall be the priest's as a grain offering.' "

THE MESSAGE

blood of the Absolution-Offering with his finger, smear it on the horns of the Altar of Burnt-Offering, and pour the rest at the base of the Altar. He shall remove all the fat, the same as for the lamb of the Peace-Offering. Finally, the priest will burn it on the Altar on top of the gifts to GOD.

"In this way, the priest makes atonement for him on account of his sin and he's forgiven."

1 5 "If you sin by not stepping up and offering
yourself as a witness to something you've
heard or seen in cases of wrongdoing, you'll
be held responsible.
2 "Or if you touch anything ritually un-
clean, like the carcass of an unclean animal,
wild or domestic, or a dead reptile, and you
weren't aware of it at the time, but you're
contaminated and you're guilty;
3 "Or if you touch human uncleanness, any
sort of ritually contaminating uncleanness,
and you're not aware of it at the time, but
later you realize it and you're guilty;
4 "Or if you impulsively swear to do some-
thing, whether good or bad—some rash oath
that just pops out—and you aren't aware of
what you've done at the time, but later you
come to realize it and you're guilty in any of
these cases;
5-6 "When you are guilty, immediately con-
fess the sin that you've committed and bring
as your penalty to GOD for the sin you have
committed a female lamb or goat from the
flock for an Absolution-Offering.
"In this way, the priest will make atone-
ment for your sin.
7-10 "If you can't afford a lamb, bring as your
penalty to GOD for the sin you have committed
two doves or two pigeons, one for the Absolu-
tion-Offering and the other for the Whole-
Burnt-Offering. Bring them to the priest who
will first offer the one for the Absolution-
Offering: He'll wring its neck but not sever it,
splash some of the blood of the Absolution-
Offering against the Altar, and squeeze the
rest of it out at the base. It's an Absolution-
Offering. He'll then take the second bird and
offer it as a Whole-Burnt-Offering, following
the procedures step-by-step.
"In this way, the priest will make atone-
ment for your sin and you're forgiven.
11-12 "If you cannot afford the two doves or pi-
geons, bring two quarts of fine flour for
your Absolution-Offering. Don't put oil or
incense on it—it's an Absolution-Offering.
Bring it to the priest; he'll take a handful
from it as a memorial and burn it on the Al-
tar with the gifts for GOD. It's an Absolution-
Offering.
13 "The priest will make atonement for you
and any of these sins you've committed and
you're forgiven. The rest of the offering be-
longs to the priest, the same as with the
Grain-Offering."

New King James Version

Offerings with Restitution

[14]Then the LORD spoke to Moses, saying: [15]"If
a person commits a trespass, and sins uninten-
tionally in regard to the holy things of the LORD,
then he shall bring to the LORD as his trespass
offering a ram without blemish from the flocks,
with your valuation in shekels of silver accord-
ing to the shekel of the sanctuary, as a trespass
offering. [16]And he shall make restitution for the
harm that he has done in regard to the holy
thing, and shall add one-fifth to it and give it to
the priest. So the priest shall make atonement
for him with the ram of the trespass offering,
and it shall be forgiven him.

[17]"If a person sins, and commits any of these
things which are forbidden to be done by the
commandments of the LORD, though he does not
know *it*, yet he is guilty and shall bear his iniq-
uity. [18]And he shall bring to the priest a ram
without blemish from the flock, with your valu-
ation, as a trespass offering. So the priest shall
make atonement for him regarding his igno-
rance in which he erred and did not know *it*,
and it shall be forgiven him. [19]It is a trespass of-
fering; he has certainly trespassed against the
LORD."

6 And the LORD spoke to Moses, saying: [2]"If a
person sins and commits a trespass against
the LORD by lying to his neighbor about what
was delivered to him for safekeeping, or about a
pledge, or about a robbery, or if he has extorted
from his neighbor, [3]or if he has found what was
lost and lies concerning it, and swears falsely—
in any one of these things that a man may do in
which he sins: [4]then it shall be, because he has
sinned and is guilty, that he shall restore what
he has stolen, or the thing which he has ex-
torted, or what was delivered to him for safe-
keeping, or the lost thing which he found, [5]or all
that about which he has sworn falsely. He shall
restore its full value, add one-fifth more to it,
and give it to whomever it belongs, on the day of
his trespass offering. [6]And he shall bring his
trespass offering to the LORD, a ram without
blemish from the flock, with your valuation, as a
trespass offering, to the priest. [7]So the priest
shall make atonement for him before the LORD,
and he shall be forgiven for any one of these
things that he may have done in which he tres-
passes."

The Law of the Burnt Offering

[8]Then the LORD spoke to Moses, saying,
[9]"Command Aaron and his sons, saying, 'This *is*
the law of the burnt offering: The burnt offering
shall be on the hearth upon the altar all night
until morning, and the fire of the altar shall be
kept burning on it. [10]And the priest shall put on
his linen garment, and his linen trousers he
shall put on his body, and take up the ashes of
the burnt offering which the fire has consumed
on the altar, and he shall put them beside the al-
tar. [11]Then he shall take off his garments, put on
other garments, and carry the ashes outside the
camp to a clean place. [12]And the fire on the altar
shall be kept burning on it; it shall not be put
out. And the priest shall burn wood on it every

The Message

Compensation-Offering

14-16 GOD spoke to Moses: "When a person be-
trays his trust and unknowingly sins by
straying against any of the holy things of
GOD, he is to bring as his penalty to GOD a
ram without any defect from the flock, the
value of the ram assessed in shekels, ac-
cording to the Sanctuary shekel for a Com-
pensation-Offering. He is to make addi-
tional compensation for the sin he has
committed against any holy thing by adding
twenty percent to the ram and giving it to
the priest.

"Thus the priest will make atonement for
him with the ram of the Compensation-
Offering and he's forgiven.

17-18 "If anyone sins by breaking any of the
commandments of GOD which must not be
broken, but without being aware of it at the
time, the moment he does realize his guilt
he is held responsible. He is to bring to the
priest a ram without any defect, assessed at
the value of the Compensation-Offering.

18-19 "Thus the priest will make atonement for
him for his error that he was unaware of
and he's forgiven. It is a Compensation-
Offering; he was surely guilty before God."

1-6 6 GOD spoke to Moses: "When anyone sins
by betraying trust with GOD by deceiving
his neighbor regarding something entrusted
to him, or by robbing or cheating or threat-
ening him; or if he has found something lost
and lies about it and swears falsely regard-
ing any of these sins that people commonly
commit—when he sins and is found guilty,
he must return what he stole or extorted, re-
store what was entrusted to him, return the
lost thing he found, or anything else about
which he swore falsely. He must make full
compensation, add twenty percent to it, and
hand it over to the owner on the same day
he brings his Compensation-Offering. He
must present to GOD as his Compensation-
Offering a ram without any defect from the
flock, assessed at the value of a Compensa-
tion-Offering.

7 "Thus the priest will make atonement for
him before GOD and he's forgiven of any of
the things that one does that bring guilt."

Further Instructions

8-13 GOD spoke to Moses: "Command Aaron and
his sons. Tell them, These are the instruc-
tions for the Whole-Burnt-Offering. Leave
the Whole-Burnt-Offering on the Altar
hearth through the night until morning,
with the fire kept burning on the Altar. Then
dress in your linen clothes with linen under-
wear next to your body. Remove the ashes
remaining from the Whole-Burnt-Offering
and place them beside the Altar. Then
change clothes and carry the ashes outside
the camp to a clean place. Meanwhile keep
the fire on the Altar burning; it must not go
out. Replenish the wood for the fire every

NEW KING JAMES VERSION

morning, and lay the burnt offering in order on
it; and he shall burn on it the fat of the peace of-
ferings. 13 A fire shall always be burning on the
altar; it shall never go out.

THE LAW OF THE GRAIN OFFERING

14 'This *is* the law of the grain offering: The
sons of Aaron shall offer it on the altar before
the LORD. 15 He shall take from it his handful of
the fine flour of the grain offering, with its oil,
and all the frankincense which *is* on the grain of-
fering, and shall burn *it* on the altar *for* a sweet
aroma, as a memorial to the LORD. 16 And the re-
mainder of it Aaron and his sons shall eat; with
unleavened bread it shall be eaten in a holy
place; in the court of the tabernacle of meeting
they shall eat it. 17 It shall not be baked with
leaven. I have given it *as* their portion of My of-
ferings made by fire; it *is* most holy, like the sin
offering and the trespass offering. 18 All the males
among the children of Aaron may eat it. *It shall
be* a statute forever in your generations concern-
ing the offerings made by fire to the LORD. Every-
one who touches them must be holy.' "[a]
19 And the LORD spoke to Moses, saying,
20 "This *is* the offering of Aaron and his sons,
which they shall offer to the LORD, *beginning* on
the day when he is anointed: one-tenth of an
ephah of fine flour as a daily grain offering, half
of it in the morning and half of it at night. 21 It
shall be made in a pan with oil. *When it is*
mixed, you shall bring it in. The baked pieces of
the grain offering you shall offer *for* a sweet
aroma to the LORD. 22 The priest from among his
sons, who is anointed in his place, shall offer it.
It is a statute forever to the LORD. It shall be
wholly burned. 23 For every grain offering for the
priest shall be wholly burned. It shall not be
eaten."

THE LAW OF THE SIN OFFERING

24 Also the LORD spoke to Moses, saying,
25 "Speak to Aaron and to his sons, saying, 'This
is the law of the sin offering: In the place where
the burnt offering is killed, the sin offering shall
be killed before the LORD. It *is* most holy. 26 The
priest who offers it for sin shall eat it. In a holy
place it shall be eaten, in the court of the taber-
nacle of meeting. 27 Everyone who touches its
flesh must be holy.[a] And when its blood is sprin-
kled on any garment, you shall wash that on
which it was sprinkled, in a holy place. 28 But the
earthen vessel in which it is boiled shall be bro-
ken. And if it is boiled in a bronze pot, it shall be
both scoured and rinsed in water. 29 All the
males among the priests may eat it. It *is* most
holy. 30 But no sin offering from which *any* of the
blood is brought into the tabernacle of meeting,
to make atonement in the holy *place*,[a] shall be
eaten. It shall be burned in the fire.

THE LAW OF THE TRESPASS OFFERING

7 'Likewise this *is* the law of the trespass offer-
ing (it *is* most holy): 2 In the place where they

6:18 [a]Compare Numbers 4:15 and Haggai 2:11–13 **6:27** [a]Compare Numbers 4:15 and Haggai 2:11–13 **6:30** [a]The Most Holy Place when capitalized

THE MESSAGE

morning, arrange the Whole-Burnt-Offering on it, and burn the fat of the Peace-Offering on top of it all. Keep the fire burning on the Altar continuously. It must not go out.

14-18 "These are the instructions for the Grain-Offering. Aaron's sons are to present it to GOD in front of the Altar. The priest takes a handful of the fine flour of the Grain-Offering with its oil and all its incense and burns this as a memorial on the Altar, a pleasing fragrance to GOD. Aaron and his sons eat the rest of it. It is unraised bread and so eaten in a holy place—in the Courtyard of the Tent of Meeting. They must not bake it with yeast. I have designated it as their share of the gifts presented to me. It is very holy, like the Absolution-Offering and the Compensation-Offering. Any male descendant among Aaron's sons may eat it. This is a fixed rule regarding GOD's gifts, stretching down the generations. Anyone who touches these offerings must be holy."

19-23 GOD spoke to Moses: "This is the offering which Aaron and his sons each are to present to GOD on the day he is anointed: two quarts of fine flour as a regular Grain-Offering, half in the morning and half in the evening. Prepare it with oil on a griddle. Bring it well-mixed and then present it crumbled in pieces as a pleasing fragrance to GOD. Aaron's son who is anointed to succeed him offers it to GOD—this is a fixed rule. The whole thing is burned. Every Grain-Offering of a priest is burned completely; it must not be eaten."

24-30 GOD spoke to Moses: "Tell Aaron and his sons, These are the instructions for the Absolution-Offering. Slaughter the Absolution-Offering in the place where the Whole-Burnt-Offering is slaughtered before GOD—the offering is most holy. The priest in charge eats it in a holy place, the Courtyard of the Tent of Meeting. Anyone who touches any of the meat must be holy. A garment that gets blood spattered on it must be washed in a holy place. Break the clay pot in which the meat was cooked. If it was cooked in a bronze pot, scour it and rinse it with water. Any male among the priestly families may eat it; it is most holy. But any Absolution-Offering whose blood is brought into the Tent of Meeting to make atonement in the Sanctuary must not be eaten, it has to be burned."

1-6 7 "These are the instructions for the Compensation-Offering. It is most holy. Slaughter the Compensation-Offering in the same

NEW KING JAMES VERSION

kill the burnt offering they shall kill the trespass offering. And its blood he shall sprinkle all around on the altar. [3]And he shall offer from it all its fat. The fat tail and the fat that covers the entrails, [4]the two kidneys and the fat that *is* on them by the flanks, and the fatty lobe *attached* to the liver above the kidneys, he shall remove; [5]and the priest shall burn them on the altar *as* an offering made by fire to the LORD. It *is* a trespass offering. [6]Every male among the priests may eat it. It shall be eaten in a holy place. It *is* most holy. [7]The trespass offering *is* like the sin offering; *there is* one law for them both: the priest who makes atonement with it shall have *it*. [8]And the priest who offers anyone's burnt offering, that priest shall have for himself the skin of the burnt offering which he has offered. [9]Also every grain offering that is baked in the oven and all that is prepared in the covered pan, or in a pan, shall be the priest's who offers it. [10]Every grain offering, *whether* mixed with oil or dry, shall belong to all the sons of Aaron, to one *as much* as the other.

THE LAW OF PEACE OFFERINGS

[11]'This *is* the law of the sacrifice of peace offerings which he shall offer to the LORD: [12]If he offers it for a thanksgiving, then he shall offer, with the sacrifice of thanksgiving, unleavened cakes mixed with oil, unleavened wafers anointed with oil, or cakes of blended flour mixed with oil. [13]Besides the cakes, *as* his offering he shall offer leavened bread with the sacrifice of thanksgiving of his peace offering. [14]And from it he shall offer one cake from each offering *as* a heave offering to the LORD. It shall belong to the priest who sprinkles the blood of the peace offering.

[15]'The flesh of the sacrifice of his peace offering for thanksgiving shall be eaten the same day it is offered. He shall not leave any of it until morning. [16]But if the sacrifice of his offering *is* a vow or a voluntary offering, it shall be eaten the same day that he offers his sacrifice; but on the next day the remainder of it also may be eaten; [17]the remainder of the flesh of the sacrifice on the third day must be burned with fire. [18]And if *any* of the flesh of the sacrifice of his peace offering is eaten at all on the third day, it shall not be accepted, nor shall it be imputed to him; it shall be an abomination *to* him who offers it, and the person who eats of it shall bear guilt.

[19]'The flesh that touches any unclean thing shall not be eaten. It shall be burned with fire. And as for the *clean* flesh, all who are clean may eat of it. [20]But the person who eats the flesh of the sacrifice of the peace offering that *belongs* to the LORD, while he is unclean, that person shall be cut off from his people. [21]Moreover the person who touches any unclean thing, *such as* human uncleanness, *an* unclean animal, or any abominable unclean thing,[a] and who eats the flesh of the sacrifice of the peace offering that *belongs* to the LORD, that person shall be cut off from his people.' "

7:21 [a]Following Masoretic Text, Septuagint, and Vulgate; Samaritan Pentateuch, Syriac, and Targum read *swarming thing* (compare 5:2).

THE MESSAGE

place that the Whole-Burnt-Offering is slaughtered. Splash its blood against all sides of the Altar. Offer up all the fat: the fat tail, the fat covering the entrails, the two kidneys and the fat encasing them at the loins, and the lobe of the liver that is removed with the kidneys. The priest burns them on the Altar as a gift to GOD. It is a Compensation-Offering. Any male from among the priests' families may eat it. But it must be eaten in a holy place; it is most holy.

7-10 "The Compensation-Offering is the same as the Absolution-Offering—the same rules apply to both. The offering belongs to the priest who makes atonement with it. The priest who presents a Whole-Burnt-Offering for someone gets the hide for himself. Every Grain-Offering baked in an oven or prepared in a pan or on a griddle belongs to the priest who presents it. It's his. Every Grain-Offering, whether dry or mixed with oil, belongs equally to all the sons of Aaron.

11-15 "These are the instructions for the Peace-Offering which is presented to GOD. If you bring it to offer thanksgiving, then along with the Thanksgiving-Offering present unraised loaves of bread mixed with oil, unraised wafers spread with oil, and cakes of fine flour, well-kneaded and mixed with oil. Along with the Peace-Offering of thanksgiving, present loaves of yeast bread as an offering. Bring one of each kind as an offering, a Contribution-Offering to GOD; it goes to the priest who throws the blood of the Peace-Offering. Eat the meat from the Peace-Offering of thanksgiving the same day it is offered. Don't leave any of it overnight.

16-21 "If the offering is a Votive-Offering or a Freewill-Offering, it may be eaten the same day it is sacrificed and whatever is left over on the next day may also be eaten. But any meat from the sacrifice that is left to the third day must be burned up. If any of the meat from the Peace-Offering is eaten on the third day, the person who has brought it will not be accepted. It won't benefit him a bit—it has become defiled meat. And whoever eats it must take responsibility for his iniquity. Don't eat meat that has touched anything ritually unclean; burn it up. Any other meat can be eaten by those who are ritually clean. But if you're not ritually clean and eat meat from the Peace-Offering for GOD, you will be excluded from the congregation. And if you touch anything ritually unclean, whether human or animal uncleanness or an obscene object, and go ahead and eat from a Peace-Offering for GOD, you'll be excluded from the congregation."

NEW KING JAMES VERSION

FAT AND BLOOD MAY NOT BE EATEN
22 And the LORD spoke to Moses, saying,
23 "Speak to the children of Israel, saying: 'You
shall not eat any fat, of ox or sheep or goat.
24 And the fat of an animal that dies *naturally*,
and the fat of what is torn by wild beasts, may
be used in any other way; but you shall by no
means eat it. 25 For whoever eats the fat of the
animal of which men offer an offering made by
fire to the LORD, the person who eats *it* shall be
cut off from his people. 26 Moreover you shall not
eat any blood in any of your dwellings, *whether*
of bird or beast. 27 Whoever eats any blood, that
person shall be cut off from his people.' "

THE PORTION OF AARON AND HIS SONS
28 Then the LORD spoke to Moses, saying,
29 "Speak to the children of Israel, saying: 'He
who offers the sacrifice of his peace offering to
the LORD shall bring his offering to the LORD
from the sacrifice of his peace offering. 30 His
own hands shall bring the offerings made by
fire to the LORD. The fat with the breast he shall
bring, that the breast may be waved *as* a wave
offering before the LORD. 31 And the priest shall
burn the fat on the altar, but the breast shall be
Aaron's and his sons'. 32 Also the right thigh you
shall give to the priest *as* a heave offering from
the sacrifices of your peace offerings. 33 He
among the sons of Aaron, who offers the blood
of the peace offering and the fat, shall have the
right thigh for *his* part. 34 For the breast of the
wave offering and the thigh of the heave offer-
ing I have taken from the children of Israel,
from the sacrifices of their peace offerings, and
I have given them to Aaron the priest and to his
sons from the children of Israel by a statute for-
ever.' "

35 This *is* the consecrated portion for Aaron
and his sons, from the offerings made by fire to
the LORD, on the day when *Moses* presented
them to minister to the LORD as priests. 36 The
LORD commanded this to be given to them by
the children of Israel, on the day that He
anointed them, *by* a statute forever throughout
their generations.

37 This *is* the law of the burnt offering, the
grain offering, the sin offering, the trespass of-
fering, the consecrations, and the sacrifice of
the peace offering, 38 which the LORD com-
manded Moses on Mount Sinai, on the day
when He commanded the children of Israel to
offer their offerings to the LORD in the Wilder-
ness of Sinai.

AARON AND HIS SONS CONSECRATED
8 And the LORD spoke to Moses, saying: 2 "Take
Aaron and his sons with him, and the gar-
ments, the anointing oil, a bull as the sin offer-
ing, two rams, and a basket of unleavened
bread; 3 and gather all the congregation together
at the door of the tabernacle of meeting."

4 So Moses did as the LORD commanded him.
And the congregation was gathered together at
the door of the tabernacle of meeting. 5 And
Moses said to the congregation, "This *is* what
the LORD commanded to be done."

6 Then Moses brought Aaron and his sons

THE MESSAGE

22-27 GOD spoke to Moses: "Speak to the People
of Israel. Tell them, Don't eat any fat of cat-
tle or sheep or goats. The fat of an animal
found dead or torn by wild animals can be
put to some other purpose, but you may not
eat it. If you eat fat from an animal from
which a gift has been presented to GOD,
you'll be excluded from the congregation.
And don't eat blood, whether of birds or an-
imals, no matter where you end up living. If
you eat blood you'll be excluded from the
congregation."

28-34 GOD spoke to Moses: "Speak to the People of
Israel. Tell them, When you present a Peace-
Offering to GOD, bring some of your Peace-
Offering as a special sacrifice to GOD, a gift
to GOD in your own hands. Bring the fat with
the breast and then wave the breast before
GOD as a Wave-Offering. The priest will burn
the fat on the Altar; Aaron and his sons get
the breast. Give the right thigh from your
Peace-Offerings as a Contribution-Offering
to the priest. Give a portion of the right thigh
to the son of Aaron who offers the blood and
fat of the Peace-Offering as his portion. From
the Peace-Offerings of Israel, I'm giving the
breast of the Wave-Offering and the thigh of
the Contribution-Offering to Aaron the
priest and his sons. This is their fixed com-
pensation from the People of Israel."

35-36 From the day they are presented to serve
as priests to GOD, Aaron and his sons can
expect to receive these allotments from the
gifts of GOD. This is what GOD commanded
the People of Israel to give the priests from
the day of their anointing. This is the fixed
rule down through the generations.

37-38 These are the instructions for the Whole-
Burnt-Offering, the Grain-Offering, the Abso-
lution-Offering, the Compensation-Offering,
the Ordination-Offering, and the Peace-Offer-
ing which GOD gave Moses at Mount Sinai on
the day he commanded the People of Israel to
present their offerings to GOD in the wilder-
ness of Sinai.

THE ORDINATION OF PRIESTS
1-4 8 GOD spoke to Moses: He said, "Take Aaron
and with him his sons, the garments, the
anointing oil, the bull for the Absolution-
Offering, the two rams, and the basket of
unraised bread. Gather the entire congrega-
tion at the entrance of the Tent of Meeting."
Moses did just as GOD commanded him and
the congregation gathered at the entrance
of the Tent of Meeting.

5 Moses addressed the congregation: "This
is what GOD has commanded to be done."

6-9 Moses brought Aaron and his sons for-

NEW KING JAMES VERSION

and washed them with water. 7And he put the
tunic on him, girded him with the sash, clothed
him with the robe, and put the ephod on him;
and he girded him with the intricately woven
band of the ephod, and with it tied *the ephod* on
him. 8Then he put the breastplate on him, and he
put the Urim and the Thummim[a] in the breast-
plate. 9And he put the turban on his head. Also
on the turban, on its front, he put the golden
plate, the holy crown, as the LORD had com-
manded Moses.

10Also Moses took the anointing oil, and
anointed the tabernacle and all that *was* in it,
and consecrated them. 11He sprinkled some of it
on the altar seven times, anointed the altar and
all its utensils, and the laver and its base, to con-
secrate them. 12And he poured some of the
anointing oil on Aaron's head and anointed
him, to consecrate him.

13Then Moses brought Aaron's sons and put
tunics on them, girded them with sashes, and
put hats on them, as the LORD had commanded
Moses.

14And he brought the bull for the sin offer-
ing. Then Aaron and his sons laid their hands on
the head of the bull for the sin offering, 15and
Moses killed *it*. Then he took the blood, and put
some on the horns of the altar all around with
his finger, and purified the altar. And he poured
the blood at the base of the altar, and conse-
crated it, to make atonement for it. 16Then he
took all the fat that *was* on the entrails, the fatty
lobe *attached to* the liver, and the two kidneys
with their fat, and Moses burned *them* on the al-
tar. 17But the bull, its hide, its flesh, and its offal,
he burned with fire outside the camp, as the
LORD had commanded Moses.

18Then he brought the ram as the burnt offer-
ing. And Aaron and his sons laid their hands on
the head of the ram, 19and Moses killed *it*. Then
he sprinkled the blood all around on the altar.
20And he cut the ram into pieces; and Moses
burned the head, the pieces, and the fat. 21Then
he washed the entrails and the legs in water.
And Moses burned the whole ram on the altar.
It *was* a burnt sacrifice for a sweet aroma, an of-
fering made by fire to the LORD, as the LORD had
commanded Moses.

22And he brought the second ram, the ram of
consecration. Then Aaron and his sons laid their
hands on the head of the ram, 23and Moses
killed *it*. Also he took *some* of its blood and put
it on the tip of Aaron's right ear, on the thumb of
his right hand, and on the big toe of his right
foot. 24Then he brought Aaron's sons. And
Moses put *some* of the blood on the tips of their
right ears, on the thumbs of their right hands,
and on the big toes of their right feet. And
Moses sprinkled the blood all around on the al-
tar. 25Then he took the fat and the fat tail, all the
fat that *was* on the entrails, the fatty lobe *at-
tached to* the liver, the two kidneys and their fat,
and the right thigh; 26and from the basket of un-
leavened bread that was before the LORD he
took one unleavened cake, a cake of bread
anointed with oil, and one wafer, and put *them*

8:8 [a]Literally *the Lights and the Perfections* (compare Exodus 28:30)

THE MESSAGE

ward and washed them with water. He put
the tunic on Aaron and tied it around him
with a sash. Then he put the robe on him
and placed the Ephod on him. He fastened
the Ephod with a woven belt, making it
snug. He put the Breastpiece on him and put
the Urim and Thummim in the pouch of the
Breastpiece. He placed the turban on his
head with the gold plate fixed to the front of
it, the holy crown, just as GOD had com-
manded Moses.

10-12 Then Moses took the anointing oil and
anointed The Dwelling and everything that
was in it, consecrating them. He sprinkled
some of the oil on the Altar seven times,
anointing the Altar and all its utensils, the
Washbasin and its stand, consecrating
them. He poured some of the anointing oil
on Aaron's head, anointing him and thus
consecrating him.

13 Moses brought Aaron's sons forward and
put tunics on them, belted them with sashes,
and put caps on them, just as GOD had com-
manded Moses.

14-17 Moses brought out the bull for the Abso-
lution-Offering. Aaron and his sons placed
their hands on its head. Moses slaughtered
the bull and purified the Altar by smearing
the blood on each of the horns of the Altar
with his finger. He poured out the rest of the
blood at the base of the Altar. He conse-
crated it so atonement could be made on it.
Moses took all the fat on the entrails and the
lobe of liver and the two kidneys with their
fat and burned it all on the Altar. The bull
with its hide and meat and guts he burned
outside the camp, just as GOD had com-
manded Moses.

18-21 Moses presented the ram for the Whole-
Burnt-Offering. Aaron and his sons laid
their hands on the head of the ram. Moses
slaughtered it and splashed the blood
against all sides of the Altar. He cut the ram
up into pieces and then burned the head, the
pieces, and the fat. He washed the entrails
and the legs with water and then burned the
whole ram on the Altar. It was a Whole-
Burnt-Offering, a pleasing fragrance—a gift
to GOD, just as GOD had commanded Moses.

22-29 Moses then presented the second ram, the
ram for the Ordination-Offering. Aaron and
his sons laid their hands on the ram's head.
Moses slaughtered it and smeared some of
its blood on the lobe of Aaron's right ear, on
the thumb of his right hand, and on the big
toe of his right foot. Then Aaron's sons were
brought forward and Moses smeared some
of the blood on the lobes of their right ears,
on the thumbs of their right hands, and on
the big toes of their right feet. Moses threw
the remaining blood against each side of the
Altar. He took the fat, the fat tail, all the fat
that was on the entrails, the lobe of the liver,
the two kidneys with their fat, and the right
thigh. From the basket of unraised bread
that was in the presence of GOD he took one
loaf of the unraised bread made with oil and
one wafer. He placed these on the fat por-

NEW KING JAMES VERSION

on the fat and on the right thigh; 27and he put all *these* in Aaron's hands and in his sons' hands, and waved them *as* a wave offering before the LORD. 28Then Moses took them from their hands and burned *them* on the altar, on the burnt offering. They *were* consecration offerings for a sweet aroma. That *was* an offering made by fire to the LORD. 29And Moses took the breast and waved it *as* a wave offering before the LORD. It was Moses' part of the ram of consecration, as the LORD had commanded Moses.

30Then Moses took some of the anointing oil and some of the blood which *was* on the altar, and sprinkled *it* on Aaron, on his garments, on his sons, and on the garments of his sons with him; and he consecrated Aaron, his garments, his sons, and the garments of his sons with him.

31And Moses said to Aaron and his sons, "Boil the flesh *at* the door of the tabernacle of meeting, and eat it there with the bread that *is* in the basket of consecration offerings, as I commanded, saying, 'Aaron and his sons shall eat it.' 32What remains of the flesh and of the bread you shall burn with fire. 33And you shall not go outside the door of the tabernacle of meeting *for* seven days, until the days of your consecration are ended. For seven days he shall consecrate you. 34As he has done this day, *so* the LORD has commanded to do, to make atonement for you. 35Therefore you shall stay *at* the door of the tabernacle of meeting day and night for seven days, and keep the charge of the LORD, so that you may not die; for so I have been commanded." 36So Aaron and his sons did all the things that the LORD had commanded by the hand of Moses.

THE PRIESTLY MINISTRY BEGINS

9 It came to pass on the eighth day that Moses called Aaron and his sons and the elders of Israel. 2And he said to Aaron, "Take for yourself a young bull as a sin offering and a ram as a burnt offering, without blemish, and offer *them* before the LORD. 3And to the children of Israel you shall speak, saying, 'Take a kid of the goats as a sin offering, and a calf and a lamb, *both* of the first year, without blemish, as a burnt offering, 4also a bull and a ram as peace offerings, to sacrifice before the LORD, and a grain offering mixed with oil; for today the LORD will appear to you.' "

5So they brought what Moses commanded before the tabernacle of meeting. And all the congregation drew near and stood before the LORD. 6Then Moses said, "This *is* the thing which the LORD commanded you to do, and the glory of the LORD will appear to you." 7And Moses said to Aaron, "Go to the altar, offer your sin offering and your burnt offering, and make atonement for yourself and for the people. Offer the offering of the people, and make atonement for them, as the LORD commanded."

8Aaron therefore went to the altar and killed the calf of the sin offering, which *was* for himself. 9Then the sons of Aaron brought the blood

THE MESSAGE

tions and the right thigh. He put all this in the hands of Aaron and his sons who waved them before GOD as a Wave-Offering. Then Moses took it all back from their hands and burned them on the Altar on top of the Whole-Burnt-Offering. These were the Ordination-Offerings, a pleasing fragrance to GOD, a gift to GOD. Then Moses took the breast and raised it up as a Wave-Offering before GOD; it was Moses' portion from the Ordination-Offering ram, just as GOD had commanded Moses.

30 Moses took some of the anointing oil and some of the blood from the Altar and sprinkled Aaron and his garments, and his sons and their garments, consecrating Aaron and his garments and his sons and their garments.

31-35 Moses spoke to Aaron and his sons: "Boil the meat at the entrance of the Tent of Meeting and eat it there with the bread from the basket of ordination, just as I commanded, saying, 'Aaron and his sons are to eat it.' Burn up the leftovers from the meat and bread. Don't leave through the entrance of the Tent of Meeting for the seven days that will complete your ordination. Your ordination will last seven days. GOD commanded what has been done this day in order to make atonement for you. Stay at the entrance of the Tent of Meeting day and night for seven days. Be sure to do what GOD requires, lest you die. This is what I have been commanded."

36 Aaron and his sons did everything that GOD had commanded by Moses.

THE PRIESTS GO TO WORK

1-2 9 On the eighth day, Moses called in Aaron and his sons and the leaders of Israel. He spoke to Aaron: "Take a bull-calf for your Absolution-Offering and a ram for your Whole-Burnt Offering, both without defect, and offer them to GOD.

3-4 "Then tell the People of Israel, Take a male goat for an Absolution-Offering and a calf and a lamb, both yearlings without defect, for a Whole-Burnt-Offering and a bull and a ram for a Peace-Offering, to be sacrificed before GOD with a Grain-Offering mixed with oil, because GOD will appear to you today."

5-6 They brought the things that Moses had ordered to the Tent of Meeting. The whole congregation came near and stood before GOD. Moses said, "This is what GOD commanded you to do so that the Shining Glory of GOD will appear to you."

7 Moses instructed Aaron, "Approach the Altar and sacrifice your Absolution-Offering and your Whole-Burnt-Offering. Make atonement for yourself and for the people. Sacrifice the offering that is for the people and make atonement for them, just as GOD commanded."

8-11 Aaron approached the Altar and slaughtered the calf as an Absolution-Offering for himself. Aaron's sons brought the blood to

NEW KING JAMES VERSION

to him. And he dipped his finger in the blood, put *it* on the horns of the altar, and poured the blood at the base of the altar. 10But the fat, the kidneys, and the fatty lobe from the liver of the sin offering he burned on the altar, as the LORD had commanded Moses. 11The flesh and the hide he burned with fire outside the camp.

12And he killed the burnt offering; and Aaron's sons presented to him the blood, which he sprinkled all around on the altar. 13Then they presented the burnt offering to him, with its pieces and head, and he burned *them* on the altar. 14And he washed the entrails and the legs, and burned *them* with the burnt offering on the altar.

15Then he brought the people's offering, and took the goat, which *was* the sin offering for the people, and killed it and offered it for sin, like the first one. 16And he brought the burnt offering and offered it according to the prescribed manner. 17Then he brought the grain offering, took a handful of it, and burned *it* on the altar, besides the burnt sacrifice of the morning.

18He also killed the bull and the ram *as* sacrifices of peace offerings, which *were* for the people. And Aaron's sons presented to him the blood, which he sprinkled all around on the altar, 19and the fat from the bull and the ram—the fatty tail, what covers *the entrails* and the kidneys, and the fatty lobe *attached to* the liver; 20and they put the fat on the breasts. Then he burned the fat on the altar; 21but the breasts and the right thigh Aaron waved *as* a wave offering before the LORD, as Moses had commanded.

22Then Aaron lifted his hand toward the people, blessed them, and came down from offering the sin offering, the burnt offering, and peace offerings. 23And Moses and Aaron went into the tabernacle of meeting, and came out and blessed the people. Then the glory of the LORD appeared to all the people, 24and fire came out from before the LORD and consumed the burnt offering and the fat on the altar. When all the people saw *it,* they shouted and fell on their faces.

THE PROFANE FIRE OF NADAB AND ABIHU

10 Then Nadab and Abihu, the sons of Aaron, each took his censer and put fire in it, put incense on it, and offered profane fire before the LORD, which He had not commanded them. 2So fire went out from the LORD and devoured them, and they died before the LORD. 3And Moses said to Aaron, "This is what the LORD spoke, saying:

'By those who come near Me
I must be regarded as holy;
And before all the people
I must be glorified.' "

So Aaron held his peace.

THE MESSAGE

him. He dipped his finger in the blood and smeared some of it on the horns of the Altar. He poured out the rest of the blood at the base of the Altar. He burned the fat, the kidneys, and the lobe of the liver from the Absolution-Offering on the Altar, just as GOD had commanded Moses. He burned the meat and the skin outside the camp.

12-14 Then he slaughtered the Whole-Burnt-Offering. Aaron's sons handed him the blood and he threw it against each side of the Altar. They handed him the pieces and the head and he burned these on the Altar. He washed the entrails and the legs and burned them on top of the Whole-Burnt-Offering on the Altar.

15-21 Next Aaron presented the offerings of the people. He took the male goat, the Absolution-Offering for the people, slaughtered it, and offered it as an Absolution-Offering just as he did with the first offering. He presented the Whole-Burnt-Offering following the same procedures. He presented the Grain-Offering by taking a handful of it and burning it on the Altar along with the morning Whole-Burnt-Offering. He slaughtered the bull and the ram, the people's Peace-Offerings. Aaron's sons handed him the blood and he threw it against each side of the Altar. The fat pieces from the bull and the ram—the fat tail and the fat that covers the kidney and the lobe of the liver—they laid on the breasts and Aaron burned it on the Altar. Aaron waved the breasts and the right thigh before GOD as a Wave-Offering, just as GOD commanded.

22-24 Aaron lifted his hands over the people and blessed them. Having completed the rituals of the Absolution-Offering, the Whole-Burnt-Offering, and the Peace-Offering, he came down from the Altar. Moses and Aaron entered the Tent of Meeting. When they came out they blessed the people and the Glory of GOD appeared to all the people. Fire blazed out from GOD and consumed the Whole-Burnt-Offering and the fat pieces on the Altar. When all the people saw it happen they cheered loudly and then fell down, bowing in reverence.

NADAB AND ABIHU

1-2 **10** That same day Nadab and Abihu, Aaron's sons, took their censers, put hot coals and incense in them, and offered "strange" fire to GOD—something GOD had not commanded. Fire blazed out from GOD and consumed them—they died in GOD's presence.

3 Moses said to Aaron, "This is what GOD meant when he said,

To the one who comes near me,
I will show myself holy;
Before all the people,
I will show my glory."

Aaron was silent.

NEW KING JAMES VERSION

4Then Moses called Mishael and Elzaphan, the sons of Uzziel the uncle of Aaron, and said to them, "Come near, carry your brethren from before the sanctuary out of the camp." 5So they went near and carried them by their tunics out of the camp, as Moses had said.

6And Moses said to Aaron, and to Eleazar and Ithamar, his sons, "Do not uncover your heads nor tear your clothes, lest you die, and wrath come upon all the people. But let your brethren, the whole house of Israel, bewail the burning which the LORD has kindled. 7You shall not go out from the door of the tabernacle of meeting, lest you die, for the anointing oil of the LORD *is* upon you." And they did according to the word of Moses.

CONDUCT PRESCRIBED FOR PRIESTS

8Then the LORD spoke to Aaron, saying: 9"Do not drink wine or intoxicating drink, you, nor your sons with you, when you go into the tabernacle of meeting, lest you die. *It shall be* a statute forever throughout your generations, 10that you may distinguish between holy and unholy, and between unclean and clean, 11and that you may teach the children of Israel all the statutes which the LORD has spoken to them by the hand of Moses."

12And Moses spoke to Aaron, and to Eleazar and Ithamar, his sons who were left: "Take the grain offering that remains of the offerings made by fire to the LORD, and eat it without leaven beside the altar; for it *is* most holy. 13You shall eat it in a holy place, because it *is* your due and your sons' due, of the sacrifices made by fire to the LORD; for so I have been commanded. 14The breast of the wave offering and the thigh of the heave offering you shall eat in a clean place, you, your sons, and your daughters with you; for *they are* your due and your sons' due, *which* are given from the sacrifices of peace offerings of the children of Israel. 15The thigh of the heave offering and the breast of the wave offering they shall bring with the offerings of fat made by fire, to offer *as* a wave offering before the LORD. And it shall be yours and your sons' with you, by a statute forever, as the LORD has commanded."

16Then Moses made careful inquiry about the goat of the sin offering, and there it was—burned up. And he was angry with Eleazar and Ithamar, the sons of Aaron *who were* left, saying, 17"Why have you not eaten the sin offering in a holy place, since it *is* most holy, and *God* has given it to you to bear the guilt of the congregation, to make atonement for them before the LORD? 18See! Its blood was not brought inside the holy *place;*[a] indeed you should have eaten it in a holy *place*, as I commanded."

19And Aaron said to Moses, "Look, this day they have offered their sin offering and their burnt offering before the LORD, and such things have befallen me! *If* I had eaten the sin offering today, would it have been accepted in the sight of the LORD?" 20So when Moses heard *that*, he was content.

10:18 [a]The Most Holy Place when capitalized

THE MESSAGE

4-5 Moses called for Mishael and Elzaphan, sons of Uzziel, Aaron's uncle. He said, "Come. Carry your dead cousins outside the camp, away from the Sanctuary." They came and carried them off, outside the camp, just as Moses had directed.

6-7 Moses then said to Aaron and his remaining sons, Eleazar and Ithamar, "No mourning rituals for you—unkempt hair, torn clothes—or you'll also die and GOD will be angry with the whole congregation. Your relatives—all the People of Israel, in fact—will do the mourning over those GOD has destroyed by fire. And don't leave the entrance to the Tent of Meeting lest you die, because GOD's anointing oil is on you."

They did just as Moses said.

8-11 GOD instructed Aaron: "When you enter the Tent of Meeting, don't drink wine or strong drink, neither you nor your sons, lest you die. This is a fixed rule down through the generations. Distinguish between the holy and the common, between the ritually clean and unclean. Teach the People of Israel all the decrees that GOD has spoken to them through Moses."

12-15 Moses spoke to Aaron and his surviving sons, Eleazar and Ithamar, "Take the leftovers of the Grain-Offering from the Fire-Gifts for GOD and eat beside the Altar that which has been prepared without yeast, for it is most holy. Eat it in the Holy Place because it is your portion and the portion of your sons from the Fire-Gifts for GOD. This is what GOD commanded me. Also, you and your sons and daughters are to eat the breast of the Wave-Offering and the thigh of the Contribution-Offering in a clean place. They are provided as your portion and the portion of your children from the Peace-Offerings presented by the People of Israel. Bring the thigh of the Contribution-Offering and the breast of the Wave-Offering and the fat pieces of the Fire-Gifts and lift them up as a Wave-Offering. This will be the regular share for you and your children as ordered by GOD."

16-18 When Moses looked into the matter of the goat of the Absolution-Offering, he found that it had been burned up. He became angry with Eleazar and Ithamar, Aaron's remaining sons, and asked, "Why didn't you eat the Absolution-Offering in the Holy Place since it is most holy? The offering was given to you for taking away the guilt of the community by making atonement for them before GOD. Since its blood was not taken into the Holy Place, you should have eaten the goat in the Sanctuary as I commanded."

19 Aaron replied to Moses, "Look. They sacrificed their Absolution-Offering and Whole-Burnt-Offering before GOD today, and you see what has happened to me—I've lost two sons. Do you think GOD would have been pleased if I had gone ahead and eaten the Absolution-Offering today?"

20 When Moses heard this response, he accepted it.

New King James Version

Foods Permitted and Forbidden

11 Now the LORD spoke to Moses and Aaron,
saying to them, 2“Speak to the children of
Israel, saying, ‘These *are* the animals which you
may eat among all the animals that *are* on the
earth: 3Among the animals, whatever divides
the hoof, having cloven hooves *and* chewing the
cud—that you may eat. 4Nevertheless these you
shall not eat among those that chew the cud or
those that have cloven hooves: the camel, be-
cause it chews the cud but does not have cloven
hooves, is unclean to you; 5the rock hyrax, be-
cause it chews the cud but does not have cloven
hooves, *is* unclean to you; 6the hare, because it
chews the cud but does not have cloven hooves,
is unclean to you; 7and the swine, though it di-
vides the hoof, having cloven hooves, yet does
not chew the cud, *is* unclean to you. 8Their flesh
you shall not eat, and their carcasses you shall
not touch. They *are* unclean to you.

9‘These you may eat of all that *are* in the wa-
ter: whatever in the water has fins and scales,
whether in the seas or in the rivers—that you
may eat. 10But all in the seas or in the rivers that
do not have fins and scales, all that move in the
water or any living thing which *is* in the water,
they *are* an abomination to you. 11They shall be
an abomination to you; you shall not eat their
flesh, but you shall regard their carcasses as an
abomination. 12Whatever in the water does not
have fins or scales—that *shall be* an abomina-
tion to you.

13‘And these you shall regard as an abomina-
tion among the birds; they shall not be eaten,
they *are* an abomination: the eagle, the vulture,
the buzzard, 14the kite, and the falcon after its
kind; 15every raven after its kind, 16the ostrich,
the short-eared owl, the sea gull, and the hawk
after its kind; 17the little owl, the fisher owl, and
the screech owl; 18the white owl, the jackdaw,
and the carrion vulture; 19the stork, the heron
after its kind, the hoopoe, and the bat.

20‘All flying insects that creep on *all* fours
shall be an abomination to you. 21Yet these you
may eat of every flying insect that creeps on *all*
fours: those which have jointed legs above their
feet with which to leap on the earth. 22These you
may eat: the locust after its kind, the destroying
locust after its kind, the cricket after its kind,
and the grasshopper after its kind. 23But all
other flying insects which have four feet *shall
be* an abomination to you.

Unclean Animals

24‘By these you shall become unclean; who-
ever touches the carcass of any of them shall be
unclean until evening; 25whoever carries part of
the carcass of any of them shall wash his clothes
and be unclean until evening: 26*The carcass* of
any animal which divides the foot, but is not
cloven-hoofed or does not chew the cud, *is* un-
clean to you. Everyone who touches it shall be
unclean. 27And whatever goes on its paws,
among all kinds of animals that go on *all* fours,
those *are* unclean to you. Whoever touches any
such carcass shall be unclean until evening.
28Whoever carries *any such* carcass shall wash
his clothes and be unclean until evening. It *is*
unclean to you.

The Message

Foods

1-2 11 GOD spoke to Moses and Aaron: “Speak to the People of Israel. Tell them, Of all the animals on Earth, these are the animals that you may eat:

3-8 “You may eat any animal that has a split hoof, divided in two, and that chews the cud, but not an animal that only chews the cud or only has a split hoof. For instance, the camel chews the cud but doesn’t have a split hoof, so it’s unclean. The rock badger chews the cud but doesn’t have a split hoof and so it’s unclean. The rabbit chews the cud but doesn’t have a split hoof so is unclean. The pig has a split hoof, divided in two, but doesn’t chew the cud and so is unclean. You may not eat their meat nor touch their carcasses; they are unclean to you.

9-12 “Among the creatures that live in the water of the seas and streams, you may eat any that have fins and scales. But anything that doesn’t have fins and scales, whether in seas or streams, whether small creatures in the shallows or huge creatures in the deeps, you are to detest. Yes, detest them. Don’t eat their meat; detest their carcasses. Anything living in the water that doesn’t have fins and scales is detestable to you.

13-19 “These are the birds you are to detest. Don’t eat them. They are detestable: eagle, vulture, osprey, kite, all falcons, all ravens, ostrich, nighthawk, sea gull, all hawks, owl, cormorant, ibis, water hen, pelican, Egyptian vulture, stork, all herons, hoopoe, bat.

20-23 “All flying insects that walk on all fours are detestable to you. But you can eat some of these, namely, those that have jointed legs for hopping on the ground: all locusts, katydids, crickets, and grasshoppers. But all the other flying insects that have four legs you are to detest.

24-25 “You will make yourselves ritually unclean until evening if you touch their carcasses. If you pick up one of their carcasses you must wash your clothes and you’ll be unclean until evening.

26 “Every animal that has a split hoof that’s not completely divided, or that doesn’t chew the cud is unclean for you; if you touch the carcass of any of them you become unclean.

27-28 “Every four-footed animal that goes on its paws is unclean for you; if you touch its carcass you are unclean until evening. If you pick up its carcass you must wash your clothes and are unclean until evening. They are unclean for you.

NEW KING JAMES VERSION

29'These also *shall be* unclean to you among
the creeping things that creep on the earth: the
mole, the mouse, and the large lizard after its
kind; 30the gecko, the monitor lizard, the sand
reptile, the sand lizard, and the chameleon.
31These *are* unclean to you among all that creep.
Whoever touches them when they are dead
shall be unclean until evening. 32Anything on
which *any* of them falls, when they are dead
shall be unclean, whether *it is* any item of wood
or clothing or skin or sack, whatever item *it is*,
in which *any* work is done, it must be put in wa-
ter. And it shall be unclean until evening; then it
shall be clean. 33Any earthen vessel into which
any of them falls you shall break; and whatever
is in it shall be unclean: 34in such a vessel, any
edible food upon which water falls becomes un-
clean, and any drink that may be drunk from it
becomes unclean. 35And everything on which *a
part* of *any such* carcass falls shall be unclean;
whether it is an oven or cooking stove, it shall
be broken down; *for* they *are* unclean, and shall
be unclean to you. 36Nevertheless a spring or a
cistern, *in which there is* plenty of water, shall
be clean, but whatever touches any such carcass
becomes unclean. 37And if a part of *any such*
carcass falls on any planting seed which is to be
sown, it *remains* clean. 38But if water is put on
the seed, and if *a part* of *any such* carcass falls
on it, it *becomes* unclean to you.

39'And if any animal which you may eat dies,
he who touches its carcass shall be unclean un-
til evening. 40He who eats of its carcass shall
wash his clothes and be unclean until evening.
He also who carries its carcass shall wash his
clothes and be unclean until evening.

41'And every creeping thing that creeps on
the earth *shall be* an abomination. It shall not be
eaten. 42Whatever crawls on its belly, whatever
goes on *all* fours, or whatever has many feet
among all creeping things that creep on the
earth—these you shall not eat, for they *are* an
abomination. 43You shall not make yourselves
abominable with any creeping thing that creeps;
nor shall you make yourselves unclean with
them, lest you be defiled by them. 44For I *am* the
LORD your God. You shall therefore consecrate
yourselves, and you shall be holy; for I *am* holy.
Neither shall you defile yourselves with any
creeping thing that creeps on the earth. 45For I
am the LORD who brings you up out of the land
of Egypt, to be your God. You shall therefore be
holy, for I *am* holy.

46'This *is* the law of the animals and the birds
and every living creature that moves in the wa-
ters, and of every creature that creeps on the
earth, 47to distinguish between the unclean and
the clean, and between the animal that may be
eaten and the animal that may not be eaten.' "

THE RITUAL AFTER CHILDBIRTH

12 Then the LORD spoke to Moses, saying,
2"Speak to the children of Israel, saying: 'If
a woman has conceived, and borne a male child,
then she shall be unclean seven days; as in the
days of her customary impurity she shall be un-
clean. 3And on the eighth day the flesh of his
foreskin shall be circumcised. 4She shall then
continue in the blood of *her* purification thirty-

THE MESSAGE

29-38 "Among the creatures that crawl on the
ground, the following are unclean for you:
weasel, rat, all lizards, gecko, monitor
lizard, wall lizard, skink, chameleon.
Among the crawling creatures, these are un-
clean for you. If you touch them when they
are dead, you are ritually unclean until
evening. When one of them dies and falls on
something, that becomes unclean no matter
what it's used for, whether it's made of
wood, cloth, hide, or sackcloth. Put it in the
water—it's unclean until evening, and then
it's clean. If one of these dead creatures falls
into a clay pot, everything in the pot is un-
clean and you must break the pot. Any food
that could be eaten but has water on it from
such a pot is unclean, and any liquid that
could be drunk from it is unclean. Anything
that one of these carcasses falls on is un-
clean—an oven or cooking pot must be bro-
ken up; they're unclean and must be treated
as unclean. A spring, though, or a cistern for
collecting water remains clean, but if you
touch one of these carcasses you're ritually
unclean. If a carcass falls on any seeds that
are to be planted, they remain clean. But if
water has been put on the seed and a car-
cass falls on it, you must treat it as unclean.

39-40 "If an animal that you are permitted to
eat dies, anyone who touches the carcass is
ritually unclean until evening. If you eat
some of the carcass you must wash your
clothes and you are unclean until evening. If
you pick up the carcass you must wash your
clothes and are unclean until evening.

41-43 "Creatures that crawl on the ground are
detestable and not to be eaten. Don't eat
creatures that crawl on the ground, whether
on their belly or on all fours or on many
feet—they are detestable. Don't make your-
selves unclean or be defiled by them, be-
cause I am your GOD.

44-45 "Make yourselves holy for I am holy.
Don't make yourselves ritually unclean by
any creature that crawls on the ground. I am
GOD who brought you up out of the land of
Egypt. Be holy because I am holy.

46-47 "These are the instructions on animals,
birds, fish, and creatures that crawl on the
ground. You have to distinguish between the
ritually unclean and the clean, between liv-
ing creatures that can be eaten and those
that cannot be eaten."

CHILDBIRTH

1-5 **12** GOD spoke to Moses: "Tell the People
of Israel, A woman who conceives and
gives birth to a boy is ritually unclean for
seven days, the same as during her menstru-
ation. On the eighth day circumcise the boy.
The mother must stay home another thirty-

NEW KING JAMES VERSION

three days. She shall not touch any hallowed
thing, nor come into the sanctuary until the days
of her purification are fulfilled.
5‘But if she bears a female child, then she
shall be unclean two weeks, as in her customary
impurity, and she shall continue in the blood of
her purification sixty-six days.
6‘When the days of her purification are ful-
filled, whether for a son or a daughter, she shall
bring to the priest a lamb of the first year as a
burnt offering, and a young pigeon or a turtle-
dove as a sin offering, to the door of the taber-
nacle of meeting. 7Then he shall offer it before
the LORD, and make atonement for her. And she
shall be clean from the flow of her blood. This *is*
the law for her who has borne a male or a fe-
male.
8‘And if she is not able to bring a lamb, then
she may bring two turtledoves or two young pi-
geons—one as a burnt offering and the other as
a sin offering. So the priest shall make atone-
ment for her, and she will be clean.’ ”

THE LAW CONCERNING LEPROSY

13 And the LORD spoke to Moses and Aaron,
saying: 2“When a man has on the skin of
his body a swelling, a scab, or a bright spot, and
it becomes on the skin of his body *like* a leprous[a]
sore, then he shall be brought to Aaron the priest
or to one of his sons the priests. 3The priest shall
examine the sore on the skin of the body; and if
the hair on the sore has turned white, and the
sore appears *to be* deeper than the skin of his
body, it *is* a leprous sore. Then the priest shall ex-
amine him, and pronounce him unclean. 4But if
the bright spot *is* white on the skin of his body,
and does not appear *to be* deeper than the skin,
and its hair has not turned white, then the priest
shall isolate *the one who has* the sore seven
days. 5And the priest shall examine him on the
seventh day; and indeed *if* the sore appears to be
as it was, *and* the sore has not spread on the
skin, then the priest shall isolate him another
seven days. 6Then the priest shall examine him
again on the seventh day; and indeed *if* the sore
has faded, *and* the sore has not spread on the
skin, then the priest shall pronounce him clean;
it *is only* a scab, and he shall wash his clothes
and be clean. 7But if the scab should at all spread
over the skin, after he has been seen by the
priest for his cleansing, he shall be seen by the
priest again. 8And *if* the priest sees that the scab
has indeed spread on the skin, then the priest
shall pronounce him unclean. It *is* leprosy.
9“When the leprous sore is on a person, then
he shall be brought to the priest. 10And the
priest shall examine *him;* and indeed *if* the
swelling on the skin *is* white, and it has turned
the hair white, and *there is* a spot of raw flesh in
the swelling, 11it *is* an old leprosy on the skin of
his body. The priest shall pronounce him un-
clean, and shall not isolate him, for he *is* un-
clean.

13:2 [a]Hebrew *saraath,* disfiguring skin diseases, including leprosy, and so in verses 2–46 and 14:1–32

THE MESSAGE

three days for purification from her bleed-
ing. She may not touch anything conse-
crated or enter the Sanctuary until the days
of her purification are complete. If she gives
birth to a girl, she is unclean for fourteen
days, the same as during her menstruation.
She must stay home for sixty-six days for
purification from her bleeding.
6-7 “When the days for her purification for
either a boy or a girl are complete, she will
bring a yearling lamb for a Whole-Burnt-
Offering and a pigeon or dove for an Abso-
lution-Offering to the priest at the entrance
of the Tent of Meeting. He will offer it to
GOD and make atonement for her. She is
then clean from her flow of blood.
“These are the instructions for a woman
who gives birth to either a boy or a girl.
8 “If she can’t afford a lamb, she can bring
two doves or two pigeons, one for the Whole-
Burnt-Offering and one for the Absolution-
Offering. The priest will make atonement for
her and she will be clean.”

INFECTIONS

1-3 13 GOD spoke to Moses and Aaron:
“When someone has a swelling or a
blister or a shiny spot on the skin that might
signal a serious skin disease on the body,
bring him to Aaron the priest or to one of his
priest sons. The priest will examine the sore
on the skin. If the hair in the sore has turned
white and the sore appears more than skin
deep, it is a serious skin disease and infec-
tious. After the priest has examined it, he
will pronounce the person unclean.
4-8 “If the shiny spot on the skin is white but
appears to be only on the surface and the
hair has not turned white, the priest will
quarantine the person for seven days. On
the seventh day the priest will examine it
again; if, in his judgment, the sore is the
same and has not spread, the priest will
keep him in quarantine for another seven
days. On the seventh day the priest will ex-
amine him a second time; if the sore has
faded and hasn’t spread, the priest will de-
clare him clean—it is a harmless rash. The
person can go home and wash his clothes;
he is clean. But if the sore spreads after he
has shown himself to the priest and been de-
clared clean, he must come back again to
the priest who will conduct another exami-
nation. If the sore has spread, the priest will
pronounce him unclean—it is a serious skin
disease and infectious.
9-17 “Whenever someone has a serious and
infectious skin disease, you must bring him
to the priest. The priest will examine him; if
there is a white swelling in the skin, the hair
is turning white, and there is an open sore in
the swelling, it is a chronic skin disease. The
priest will pronounce him unclean. But he

NEW KING JAMES VERSION

12“And if leprosy breaks out all over the skin,
and the leprosy covers all the skin of *the one*
who has the sore, from his head to his foot,
wherever the priest looks, 13then the priest shall
consider; and indeed *if* the leprosy has covered
all his body, he shall pronounce *him* clean *who*
has the sore. It has all turned white. He *is* clean.
14But when raw flesh appears on him, he shall
be unclean. 15And the priest shall examine the
raw flesh and pronounce him to be unclean; *for*
the raw flesh *is* unclean. It *is* leprosy. 16Or if the
raw flesh changes and turns white again, he
shall come to the priest. 17And the priest shall
examine him; and indeed *if* the sore has turned
white, then the priest shall pronounce *him* clean
who has the sore. He *is* clean.
18“If the body develops a boil in the skin, and
it is healed, 19and in the place of the boil there
comes a white swelling or a bright spot, reddish-
white, then it shall be shown to the priest; 20and
if, when the priest sees it, it indeed appears
deeper than the skin, and its hair has turned
white, the priest shall pronounce him unclean. It
is a leprous sore which has broken out of the
boil. 21But if the priest examines it, and indeed
there are no white hairs in it, and it *is* not deeper
than the skin, but has faded, then the priest
shall isolate him seven days; 22and if it should at
all spread over the skin, then the priest shall
pronounce him unclean. It *is* a leprous sore.
23But if the bright spot stays in one place, *and*
has not spread, it *is* the scar of the boil; and the
priest shall pronounce him clean.
24“Or if the body receives a burn on its skin
by fire, and the raw *flesh* of the burn becomes a
bright spot, reddish-white or white, 25then the
priest shall examine it; and indeed *if* the hair of
the bright spot has turned white, and it appears
deeper than the skin, it *is* leprosy broken out in
the burn. Therefore the priest shall pronounce
him unclean. It *is* a leprous sore. 26But if the
priest examines it, and indeed *there are* no
white hairs in the bright spot, and it *is* not
deeper than the skin, but has faded, then the
priest shall isolate him seven days. 27And the
priest shall examine him on the seventh day. If it
has at all spread over the skin, then the priest
shall pronounce him unclean. It *is* a leprous
sore. 28But if the bright spot stays in one place,
and has not spread on the skin, but has faded, it
is a swelling from the burn. The priest shall pro-
nounce him clean, for it *is* the scar from the
burn.
29“If a man or woman has a sore on the head or
the beard, 30then the priest shall examine the sore;
and indeed if it appears deeper than the skin, *and*
there is in it thin yellow hair, then the priest shall
pronounce him unclean. It *is* a scaly leprosy of
the head or beard. 31But if the priest examines
the scaly sore, and indeed it does not appear
deeper than the skin, and *there is* no black hair
in it, then the priest shall isolate *the one who*
has the scale seven days. 32And on the seventh
day the priest shall examine the sore; and in-
deed *if* the scale has not spread, and there is no
yellow hair in it, and the scale does not appear

THE MESSAGE

doesn't need to quarantine him because he's
already given his diagnosis of unclean. If a
serious disease breaks out that covers all
the skin from head to foot, wherever the
priest looks, the priest will make a thorough
examination; if the disease covers his entire
body, he will pronounce the person with the
sore clean—since it has turned all white, he
is clean. But if they are open, running sores,
he is unclean. The priest will examine the
open sores and pronounce him unclean. The
open sores are unclean; they are evidence of
a serious skin disease. But if the open sores
dry up and turn white, he is to come back to
the priest who will reexamine him; if the
sores have turned white, the priest will pro-
nounce the person with the sores clean. He
is clean.
18-23 “When a person has a boil and it heals
and in place of the boil there is white
swelling or a reddish-white shiny spot, the
person must present himself to the priest for
an examination. If it looks like it has pene-
trated the skin and the hair in it has turned
white, the priest will pronounce him un-
clean. It is a serious skin disease that has
broken out in the boil. But if the examina-
tion shows that there is no white hair in it
and it is only skin deep and has faded, the
priest will put him in quarantine for seven
days. If it then spreads over the skin, the
priest will diagnose him as unclean. It is in-
fectious. But if the shiny spot has not
changed and hasn't spread, it's only a scar
from the boil. The priest will pronounce him
clean.
24-28 “When a person has a burn on his skin
and the raw flesh turns into a reddish-white
or white shiny spot, the priest is to examine
it. If the hair has turned white in the shiny
spot and it looks like it's more than skin
deep, a serious skin disease has erupted in
the area of the burn. The priest will pro-
nounce him unclean; it is a serious skin dis-
ease and infectious. But if on examination
there is no white hair in the shiny spot and
it doesn't look to be more than skin deep but
has faded, the priest will put him in quaran-
tine for seven days. On the seventh day the
priest will reexamine him. If by then it has
spread over the skin, the priest will diag-
nose him as unclean; it is a serious skin dis-
ease and infectious. If by that time the shiny
spot has stayed the same and has not spread
but has faded, it is only a swelling from the
burn. The priest will pronounce him clean;
it's only a scar from the burn.
29-37 “If a man or woman develops a sore on
the head or chin, the priest will offer a diag-
nosis. If it looks as if it is under the skin and
the hair in it is yellow and thin, he will pro-
nounce the person ritually unclean. It is an
itch, an infectious skin disease. But if when
he examines the itch, he finds it is only skin
deep and there is no black hair in it, he will
put the person in quarantine for seven days.
On the seventh day he will reexamine the
sore; if the itch has not spread, there is no
yellow hair in it, and it looks as if the itch is

NEW KING JAMES VERSION

deeper than the skin, [33]he shall shave himself, but the scale he shall not shave. And the priest shall isolate *the one who has* the scale another seven days. [34]On the seventh day the priest shall examine the scale; and indeed *if* the scale has not spread over the skin, and does not appear deeper than the skin, then the priest shall pronounce him clean. He shall wash his clothes and be clean. [35]But if the scale should at all spread over the skin after his cleansing, [36]then the priest shall examine him; and indeed *if* the scale has spread over the skin, the priest need not seek for yellow hair. He *is* unclean. [37]But if the scale appears to be at a standstill, and there is black hair grown up in it, the scale has healed. He *is* clean, and the priest shall pronounce him clean.

[38]"If a man or a woman has bright spots on the skin of the body, *specifically* white bright spots, [39]then the priest shall look; and indeed *if* the bright spots on the skin of the body *are* dull white, it *is* a white spot *that* grows on the skin. He *is* clean.

[40]"As for the man whose hair has fallen from his head, he *is* bald, *but* he *is* clean. [41]He whose hair has fallen from his forehead, he *is* bald on the forehead, *but* he *is* clean. [42]And if there is on the bald head or bald forehead a reddish-white sore, it *is* leprosy breaking out on his bald head or his bald forehead. [43]Then the priest shall examine it; and indeed *if* the swelling of the sore *is* reddish-white on his bald head or on his bald forehead, as the appearance of leprosy on the skin of the body, [44]he is a leprous man. He *is* unclean. The priest shall surely pronounce him unclean; his sore *is* on his head.

[45]"Now the leper on whom the sore *is*, his clothes shall be torn and his head bare; and he shall cover his mustache, and cry, 'Unclean! Unclean!' [46]He shall be unclean. All the days he has the sore he shall be unclean. He *is* unclean, and he shall dwell alone; his dwelling *shall be* outside the camp.

THE LAW CONCERNING LEPROUS GARMENTS

[47]"Also, if a garment has a leprous plague[a] in it, *whether it is* a woolen garment or a linen garment, [48]whether *it is* in the warp or woof of linen or wool, whether in leather or in anything made of leather, [49]and if the plague is greenish or reddish in the garment or in the leather, whether in the warp or in the woof, or in anything made of leather, it *is* a leprous plague and shall be shown to the priest. [50]The priest shall examine the plague and isolate *that which has* the plague seven days. [51]And he shall examine the plague on the seventh day. If the plague has spread in the garment, either in the warp or in the woof, in the leather *or* in anything made of leather, the plague *is* an active leprosy. It *is* unclean. [52]He shall therefore burn that garment in which is the plague, whether warp or woof, in wool or in linen, or anything of leather, for it *is* an active leprosy; *the garment* shall be burned in the fire.

[53]"But if the priest examines *it*, and indeed the plague has not spread in the garment, either

13:47 [a]A mold, fungus, or similar infestation, and so in verses 47–59

THE MESSAGE

only skin deep, the person must shave, except for the itch; the priest will send him back to quarantine for another seven days. If the itch has not spread, and looks to be only skin deep, the priest will pronounce him clean. The person can go home and wash his clothes; he is clean. But if the itch spreads after being pronounced clean, the priest must reexamine it; if the itch has spread in the skin, he doesn't have to look any farther, for yellow hair, for instance; he is unclean. But if he sees that the itch is unchanged and black hair has begun to grow in it, the itch is healed. The person is clean and the priest will pronounce him clean.

38-39 "When a man or woman gets shiny or white shiny spots on the skin, the priest is to make an examination; if the shiny spots are dull white, it is only a rash that has broken out: The person is clean.

40-44 "When a man loses his hair and goes bald, he is clean. If he loses his hair from his forehead, he is bald and he is clean. But if he has a reddish-white sore on scalp or forehead, it means a serious skin disease is breaking out. The priest is to examine it; if the swollen sore on his scalp or forehead is reddish-white like the appearance of the sore of a serious skin disease, he has a serious skin disease and is unclean. The priest has to pronounce him unclean because of the sore on his head.

45-46 "Any person with a serious skin disease must wear torn clothes, leave his hair loose and unbrushed, cover his upper lip, and cry out, 'Unclean! Unclean!' As long as anyone has the sores, that one continues to be ritually unclean. That person must live alone; he or she must live outside the camp.

47-58 "If clothing—woolen or linen clothing, woven or knitted cloth of linen or wool, leather or leatherwork—is infected with a patch of serious fungus and if the spot in the clothing or the leather or the woven or the knitted material or anything made of leather is greenish or rusty, that is a sign of serious fungus. Show it to the priest. The priest will examine the spot and then confiscate the material for seven days. On the seventh day he will reexamine the spot. If it has spread in the garment—the woven or knitted or leather material—it is the spot of a persistent serious fungus and the material is unclean. He must burn the garment. Because of the persistent and contaminating fungus, the material must be burned. But if when the priest examines it the spot has not spread in the garment, the priest will com-

New King James Version

in the warp or in the woof, or in anything made
of leather, [54]then the priest shall command that
they wash *the thing* in which *is* the plague; and
he shall isolate it another seven days. [55]Then the
priest shall examine the plague after it has been
washed; and indeed *if* the plague has not
changed its color, though the plague has not
spread, it *is* unclean, and you shall burn it in the
fire; it continues eating away, *whether* the dam-
age *is* outside or inside. [56]If the priest examines
it, and indeed the plague has faded after wash-
ing it, then he shall tear it out of the garment,
whether out of the warp or out of the woof, or
out of the leather. [57]But if it appears again in the
garment, either in the warp or in the woof, or in
anything made of leather, it *is* a spreading
plague; you shall burn with fire that in which is
the plague. [58]And if you wash the garment, ei-
ther warp or woof, or whatever is made of
leather, if the plague has disappeared from it,
then it shall be washed a second time, and shall
be clean.

[59]"This *is* the law of the leprous plague in a
garment of wool or linen, either in the warp or
woof, or in anything made of leather, to pro-
nounce it clean or to pronounce it unclean."

The Ritual for Cleansing Healed Lepers

14 Then the LORD spoke to Moses, saying,
[2]"This shall be the law of the leper for the
day of his cleansing: He shall be brought to the
priest. [3]And the priest shall go out of the camp,
and the priest shall examine *him;* and indeed, *if*
the leprosy is healed in the leper, [4]then the
priest shall command to take for him who is to
be cleansed two living *and* clean birds, cedar
wood, scarlet, and hyssop. [5]And the priest shall
command that one of the birds be killed in an
earthen vessel over running water. [6]As for the
living bird, he shall take it, the cedar wood and
the scarlet and the hyssop, and dip them and the
living bird in the blood of the bird *that was*
killed over the running water. [7]And he shall
sprinkle it seven times on him who is to be
cleansed from the leprosy, and shall pronounce
him clean, and shall let the living bird loose in
the open field. [8]He who is to be cleansed shall
wash his clothes, shave off all his hair, and wash
himself in water, that he may be clean. After that
he shall come into the camp, and shall stay out-
side his tent seven days. [9]But on the seventh day
he shall shave all the hair off his head and his
beard and his eyebrows—all his hair he shall
shave off. He shall wash his clothes and wash
his body in water, and he shall be clean.

[10]"And on the eighth day he shall take two
male lambs without blemish, one ewe lamb of
the first year without blemish, three-tenths *of an*
ephah of fine flour mixed with oil as a grain of-
fering, and one log of oil. [11]Then the priest who
makes *him* clean shall present the man who is to
be made clean, and those things, before the
LORD, *at* the door of the tabernacle of meeting.
[12]And the priest shall take one male lamb and
offer it as a trespass offering, and the log of oil,
and wave them *as* a wave offering before the
LORD. [13]Then he shall kill the lamb in the place
where he kills the sin offering and the burnt of-
fering, in a holy place; for as the sin offering *is*

The Message

mand the owner to wash the material that
has the spot, and he will confiscate it for an-
other seven days. He'll then make another
examination after it has been washed; if the
spot hasn't changed in appearance, even
though it hasn't spread, it is still unclean.
Burn it up, whether the fungus has affected
the back or the front. If, when the priest
makes his examination, the spot has faded
after it has been washed, he is to tear the
spot from the garment. But if it reappears, it
is a fresh outbreak—throw whatever has the
spot in the fire. If the garment is washed and
the spot has gone away, then wash it a sec-
ond time; it is clean.

59 "These are the instructions regarding a
spot of serious fungus in clothing of wool or
linen, woven or knitted material, or any ar-
ticle of leather, for pronouncing them clean
or unclean."

1-9 14 GOD spoke to Moses: "These are the in-
structions for the infected person at
the time of his cleansing. First, bring him to
the priest. The priest will take him outside the
camp and make an examination; if the in-
fected person has been healed of the serious
skin disease, the priest will order two live,
clean birds, some cedar wood, scarlet
thread, and hyssop to be brought for the one
to be cleansed. The priest will order him to
kill one of the birds over fresh water in a
clay pot. The priest will then take the live
bird with the cedar wood, the scarlet thread,
and the hyssop and dip them in the blood of
the dead bird over fresh water and then
sprinkle the person being cleansed from the
serious skin disease seven times and pro-
nounce him clean. Finally, he will release
the live bird in the open field. The cleansed
person, after washing his clothes, shaving
off all his hair, and bathing with water, is
clean. Afterwards he may again enter the
camp, but he has to live outside his tent for
seven days. On the seventh day, he must
shave off all his hair—from his head, beard,
eyebrows, all of it. He then must wash his
clothes and bathe all over with water. He
will be clean.

10-18 "The next day, the eighth day, he will
bring two lambs without defect and a year-
ling ewe without defect, along with roughly
six quarts of fine flour mixed with oil. The
priest who pronounces him clean will place
him and the materials for his offerings in
the presence of GOD at the entrance to the
Tent of Meeting. The priest will take one of
the lambs and present it and the pint of oil
as a Compensation-Offering and lift them
up as a Wave-Offering before GOD. He will
slaughter the lamb in the place where the
Absolution-Offering and the Whole-Burnt-

NEW KING JAMES VERSION

the priest's, so *is* the trespass offering. It *is* most holy. 14The priest shall take *some* of the blood of the trespass offering, and the priest shall put *it* on the tip of the right ear of him who is to be cleansed, on the thumb of his right hand, and on the big toe of his right foot. 15And the priest shall take *some* of the log of oil, and pour *it* into the palm of his own left hand. 16Then the priest shall dip his right finger in the oil that *is* in his left hand, and shall sprinkle some of the oil with his finger seven times before the LORD. 17And of the rest of the oil in his hand, the priest shall put *some* on the tip of the right ear of him who is to be cleansed, on the thumb of his right hand, and on the big toe of his right foot, on the blood of the trespass offering. 18The rest of the oil that *is* in the priest's hand he shall put on the head of him who is to be cleansed. So the priest shall make atonement for him before the LORD.

19"Then the priest shall offer the sin offering, and make atonement for him who is to be cleansed from his uncleanness. Afterward he shall kill the burnt offering. 20And the priest shall offer the burnt offering and the grain offering on the altar. So the priest shall make atonement for him, and he shall be clean.

21"But if he *is* poor and cannot afford it, then he shall take one male lamb *as* a trespass offering to be waved, to make atonement for him, one-tenth *of an ephah* of fine flour mixed with oil as a grain offering, a log of oil, 22and two turtledoves or two young pigeons, such as he is able to afford: one shall be a sin offering and the other a burnt offering. 23He shall bring them to the priest on the eighth day for his cleansing, to the door of the tabernacle of meeting, before the LORD. 24And the priest shall take the lamb of the trespass offering and the log of oil, and the priest shall wave them *as* a wave offering before the LORD. 25Then he shall kill the lamb of the trespass offering, and the priest shall take *some* of the blood of the trespass offering and put *it* on the tip of the right ear of him who is to be cleansed, on the thumb of his right hand, and on the big toe of his right foot. 26And the priest shall pour some of the oil into the palm of his own left hand. 27Then the priest shall sprinkle with his right finger *some* of the oil that *is* in his left hand seven times before the LORD. 28And the priest shall put *some* of the oil that *is* in his hand on the tip of the right ear of him who is to be cleansed, on the thumb of the right hand, and on the big toe of his right foot, on the place of the blood of the trespass offering. 29The rest of the oil that *is* in the priest's hand he shall put on the head of him who is to be cleansed, to make atonement for him before the LORD. 30And he shall offer one of the turtledoves or young pigeons, such as he can afford— 31such as he is able to afford, the one *as* a sin offering and the other *as* a burnt offering, with the grain offering. So the priest shall make atonement for him who is to be cleansed before the LORD. 32This *is* the law *for one* who had a leprous sore, who cannot afford the usual cleansing."

THE MESSAGE

Offering are slaughtered, in the Holy Place, because like the Absolution-Offering, the Compensation-Offering belongs to the priest; it is most holy. The priest will now take some of the blood of the Compensation-Offering and put it on the right earlobe of the man being cleansed, on the thumb of his right hand, and on the big toe of his right foot. Following that he will take some oil and pour it into the palm of his left hand and then with the finger of his right hand sprinkle oil seven times before GOD. The priest will put some of the remaining oil on the right earlobe of the one being cleansed, on the thumb of his right hand, and on the big toe of his right foot, placing it on top of the blood of the Compensation-Offering. He will put the rest of the oil on the head of the man being cleansed and make atonement for him before GOD.

19-20 "Finally the priest will sacrifice the Absolution-Offering and make atonement for the one to be cleansed from his uncleanness, slaughter the Whole-Burnt-Offering and offer it with the Grain-Offering on the Altar. He has made atonement for him. He is clean.

21-22 "If he is poor and cannot afford these offerings, he will bring one male lamb as a Compensation-Offering to be offered as a Wave-Offering to make atonement for him, and with it a couple of quarts of fine flour mixed with oil for a Grain-Offering, a pint of oil, and two doves or pigeons which he can afford, one for an Absolution-Offering and the other for a Whole-Burnt-Offering.

23-29 "On the eighth day he will bring them to the priest at the entrance to the Tent of Meeting before the presence of GOD. The priest will take the lamb for the Compensation-Offering together with the pint of oil and wave them before GOD as a Wave-Offering. He will slaughter the lamb for the Compensation-Offering, take some of its blood and put it on the lobe of the right ear of the one to be cleansed, on the thumb of his right hand, and on the big toe of his right foot. The priest will pour some of the oil into the palm of his left hand, and with his right finger sprinkle some of the oil from his palm seven times before GOD. He will put some of the oil that is in his palm on the same places he put the blood of the Compensation-Offering, on the lobe of the right ear of the one to be cleansed, on the thumb of his right hand, and on the big toe of his right foot. The priest will take what is left of the oil in his palm and put it on the head of the one to be cleansed, making atonement for him before GOD.

30-31 "At the last, he will sacrifice the doves or pigeons which are within his means, one as an Absolution-Offering and the other as a Whole-Burnt-Offering along with the Grain-Offering. Following this procedure the priest will make atonement for the one to be cleansed before GOD."

32 These are the instructions to be followed for anyone who has a serious skin disease and cannot afford the regular offerings for his cleansing.

New King James Version

The Law Concerning Leprous Houses

[33]And the LORD spoke to Moses and Aaron, saying: [34]"When you have come into the land of Canaan, which I give you as a possession, and I put the leprous plague[a] in a house in the land of your possession, [35]and he who owns the house comes and tells the priest, saying, 'It seems to me that *there is* some plague in the house,' [36]then the priest shall command that they empty the house, before the priest goes *into it* to examine the plague, that all that *is* in the house may not be made unclean; and afterward the priest shall go in to examine the house. [37]And he shall examine the plague; and indeed *if* the plague *is* on the walls of the house with ingrained streaks, greenish or reddish, which appear to be deep in the wall, [38]then the priest shall go out of the house, to the door of the house, and shut up the house seven days. [39]And the priest shall come again on the seventh day and look; and indeed *if* the plague has spread on the walls of the house, [40]then the priest shall command that they take away the stones in which *is* the plague, and they shall cast them into an unclean place outside the city. [41]And he shall cause the house to be scraped inside, all around, and the dust that they scrape off they shall pour out in an unclean place outside the city. [42]Then they shall take other stones and put *them* in the place of *those* stones, and he shall take other mortar and plaster the house.

[43]"Now if the plague comes back and breaks out in the house, after he has taken away the stones, after he has scraped the house, and after it is plastered, [44]then the priest shall come and look; and indeed *if* the plague has spread in the house, it *is* an active leprosy in the house. It *is* unclean. [45]And he shall break down the house, its stones, its timber, and all the plaster of the house, and he shall carry *them* outside the city to an unclean place. [46]Moreover he who goes into the house at all while it is shut up shall be unclean until evening. [47]And he who lies down in the house shall wash his clothes, and he who eats in the house shall wash his clothes.

[48]"But if the priest comes in and examines *it*, and indeed the plague has not spread in the house after the house was plastered, then the priest shall pronounce the house clean, because the plague is healed. [49]And he shall take, to cleanse the house, two birds, cedar wood, scarlet, and hyssop. [50]Then he shall kill one of the birds in an earthen vessel over running water; [51]and he shall take the cedar wood, the hyssop, the scarlet, and the living bird, and dip them in the blood of the slain bird and in the running water, and sprinkle the house seven times. [52]And he shall cleanse the house with the blood of the bird and the running water and the living bird, with the cedar wood, the hyssop, and the scarlet. [53]Then he shall let the living bird loose outside the city in the open field, and make atonement for the house, and it shall be clean.

[54]"This *is* the law for any leprous sore and scale, [55]for the leprosy of a garment and of a house, [56]for a swelling and a scab and a bright spot, [57]to teach when *it is* unclean and when *it is* clean. This *is* the law of leprosy."

14:34 [a]Decomposition by mildew, mold, dry rot, etc., and so in verses 34–53

The Message

33-42 GOD spoke to Moses and Aaron: "When you
enter the land of Canaan, which I'm giving
to you as a possession, and I put a serious
fungus in a house in the land of your posses-
sion, the householder is to go and tell the
priest, 'I have some kind of fungus in my
house.' The priest is to order the house va-
cated until he can come to examine the fun-
gus, so that nothing in the house is declared
unclean. When the priest comes and exam-
ines the house, if the fungus on the walls of
the house has greenish or rusty swelling
that appears to go deeper than the surface
of the wall, the priest is to walk out the door
and shut the house up for seven days. On
the seventh day he is to come back and con-
duct another examination; if the fungus has
spread in the walls of the house, he is to or-
der that the stones affected by the fungus be
torn out and thrown in a garbage dump out-
side the city. He is to make sure the entire
inside of the house is scraped and the plas-
ter that is removed be taken away to the
garbage dump outside the city. Then he is to
replace the stones and replaster the house.
43-47 "If the fungus breaks out again in the
house after the stones have been torn out
and the house has been scraped and plas-
tered, the priest is to come and conduct an
examination; if the fungus has spread, it is a
malignant fungus. The house is unclean.
The house has to be demolished—its stones,
wood, and plaster are to be removed to the
garbage dump outside the city. Anyone who
enters the house while it is closed up is un-
clean until evening. Anyone who sleeps or
eats in the house must wash his clothes.
48-53 "But if when the priest comes and con-
ducts his examination, he finds that the fun-
gus has not spread after the house has been
replastered, the priest is to declare that the
house is clean; the fungus is cured. He then
is to purify the house by taking two birds,
some cedar wood, scarlet thread, and hys-
sop. He will slaughter one bird over fresh
water in a clay pot. Then he will take the
cedar wood, the hyssop, the scarlet thread,
and the living bird, dip them in the blood of
the killed bird and the fresh water and
sprinkle the house seven times, cleansing
the house with the blood of the bird, the
fresh water, the living bird, the cedar wood,
the hyssop, and the scarlet thread. Last of
all, he will let the living bird loose outside
the city in the open field. He has made
atonement for the house; the house is clean.
54-57 "These are the procedures to be followed
for every kind of serious skin disease or
itch, for mildew or fungus on clothing or in
a house, and for a swelling or blister or
shiny spot in order to determine when it is
unclean and when it is clean. These are the
procedures regarding infectious skin dis-
eases and mildew and fungus."

NEW KING JAMES VERSION

THE LAW CONCERNING BODILY DISCHARGES

15 And the LORD spoke to Moses and Aaron, saying, 2"Speak to the children of Israel, and say to them: 'When any man has a discharge from his body, his discharge *is* unclean. 3And this shall be his uncleanness in regard to his discharge—whether his body runs with his discharge, or his body is stopped up by his discharge, it *is* his uncleanness. 4Every bed is unclean on which he who has the discharge lies, and everything on which he sits shall be unclean. 5And whoever touches his bed shall wash his clothes and bathe in water, and be unclean until evening. 6He who sits on anything on which he who has the discharge sat shall wash his clothes and bathe in water, and be unclean until evening. 7And he who touches the body of him who has the discharge shall wash his clothes and bathe in water, and be unclean until evening. 8If he who has the discharge spits on him who is clean, then he shall wash his clothes and bathe in water, and be unclean until evening. 9Any saddle on which he who has the discharge rides shall be unclean. 10Whoever touches anything that was under him shall be unclean until evening. He who carries *any of* those things shall wash his clothes and bathe in water, and be unclean until evening. 11And whomever the one who has the discharge touches, and has not rinsed his hands in water, he shall wash his clothes and bathe in water, and be unclean until evening. 12The vessel of earth that he who has the discharge touches shall be broken, and every vessel of wood shall be rinsed in water.

13'And when he who has a discharge is cleansed of his discharge, then he shall count for himself seven days for his cleansing, wash his clothes, and bathe his body in running water; then he shall be clean. 14On the eighth day he shall take for himself two turtledoves or two young pigeons, and come before the LORD, to the door of the tabernacle of meeting, and give them to the priest. 15Then the priest shall offer them, the one *as* a sin offering and the other *as* a burnt offering. So the priest shall make atonement for him before the LORD because of his discharge.

16'If any man has an emission of semen, then he shall wash all his body in water, and be unclean until evening. 17And any garment and any leather on which there is semen, it shall be washed with water, and be unclean until evening. 18Also, when a woman lies with a man, and *there is* an emission of semen, they shall bathe in water, and be unclean until evening.

19'If a woman has a discharge, *and* the discharge from her body is blood, she shall be set apart seven days; and whoever touches her shall be unclean until evening. 20Everything that she lies on during her impurity shall be unclean; also everything that she sits on shall be unclean. 21Whoever touches her bed shall wash his clothes and bathe in water, and be unclean until evening. 22And whoever touches anything that she sat on shall wash his clothes and bathe in water, and be unclean until evening. 23If *anything* is on *her* bed or on anything on which she sits, when he touches it, he shall be unclean until evening.

THE MESSAGE

BODILY DISCHARGES

1-3 15 GOD spoke to Moses and Aaron: "Speak to the People of Israel. Tell them, When a man has a discharge from his genitals, the discharge is unclean. Whether it comes from a seepage or an obstruction he is unclean. He is unclean all the days his body has a seepage or an obstruction.

4-7 "Every bed on which he lies is ritually unclean, everything on which he sits is unclean. If someone touches his bed or sits on anything he's sat on, or touches the man with the discharge, he has to wash his clothes and bathe in water; he remains unclean until evening.

8-11 "If the man with the discharge spits on someone who is clean, that person has to wash his clothes and bathe in water; he remains unclean until evening. Every saddle on which the man with the discharge rides is unclean. Whoever touches anything that has been under him becomes unclean until evening. Anyone who carries such an object must wash his clothes and bathe with water; he remains unclean until evening. If the one with the discharge touches someone without first rinsing his hands with water, the one touched must wash his clothes and bathe with water; he remains unclean until evening.

12 "If a pottery container is touched by someone with a discharge, you must break it; a wooden article is to be rinsed in water.

13-15 "When a person with a discharge is cleansed from it, he is to count off seven days for his cleansing, wash his clothes, and bathe in running water. Then he is clean. On the eighth day he is to take two doves or two pigeons and come before GOD at the entrance of the Tent of Meeting and give them to the priest. The priest then offers one as an Absolution-Offering and one as a Whole-Burnt-Offering and makes atonement for him in the presence of GOD because of his discharge.

16-18 "When a man has an emission of semen, he must bathe his entire body in water; he remains unclean until evening. Every piece of clothing and everything made of leather which gets semen on it must be washed with water; it remains unclean until evening. When a man sleeps with a woman and has an emission of semen, both are to wash in water; they remain unclean until evening.

19-23 "When a woman has a discharge of blood, the impurity of her menstrual period lasts seven days. Anyone who touches her is unclean until evening. Everything on which she lies or sits during her period is unclean. Anyone who touches her bed or anything on which she sits must wash his clothes and bathe in water; he remains unclean until evening.

NEW KING JAMES VERSION

24 And if any man lies with her at all, so that her
impurity is on him, he shall be unclean seven
days; and every bed on which he lies shall be
unclean.

25 'If a woman has a discharge of blood for
many days, other than at the time of her *cus-
tomary* impurity, or if it runs beyond her *usual
time of* impurity, all the days of her unclean dis-
charge shall be as the days of her *customary* im-
purity. She *shall be* unclean. 26 Every bed on
which she lies all the days of her discharge shall
be to her as the bed of her impurity; and what-
ever she sits on shall be unclean, as the unclean-
ness of her impurity. 27 Whoever touches those
things shall be unclean; he shall wash his
clothes and bathe in water, and be unclean until
evening.

28 'But if she is cleansed of her discharge,
then she shall count for herself seven days, and
after that she shall be clean. 29 And on the eighth
day she shall take for herself two turtledoves or
two young pigeons, and bring them to the priest,
to the door of the tabernacle of meeting. 30 Then
the priest shall offer the one *as* a sin offering
and the other *as* a burnt offering, and the priest
shall make atonement for her before the LORD
for the discharge of her uncleanness.

31 'Thus you shall separate the children of Is-
rael from their uncleanness, lest they die in their
uncleanness when they defile My tabernacle
that *is* among them. 32 This *is* the law for one
who has a discharge, and *for him* who emits se-
men and is unclean thereby, 33 and for her who is
indisposed because of her *customary* impurity,
and for one who has a discharge, either man or
woman, and for him who lies with her who is
unclean.' "

THE DAY OF ATONEMENT

16 Now the LORD spoke to Moses after the
death of the two sons of Aaron, when they
offered *profane fire* before the LORD, and died;
2 and the LORD said to Moses: "Tell Aaron your
brother not to come at *just* any time into the
Holy *Place* inside the veil, before the mercy seat
which *is* on the ark, lest he die; for I will appear
in the cloud above the mercy seat.

3 "Thus Aaron shall come into the Holy *Place*:
with *the blood of* a young bull as a sin offering,
and *of* a ram as a burnt offering. 4 He shall put
the holy linen tunic and the linen trousers on his
body; he shall be girded with a linen sash, and
with the linen turban he shall be attired. These
are holy garments. Therefore he shall wash his
body in water, and put them on. 5 And he shall
take from the congregation of the children of Is-
rael two kids of the goats as a sin offering, and
one ram as a burnt offering.

6 "Aaron shall offer the bull as a sin offering,
which *is* for himself, and make atonement for
himself and for his house. 7 He shall take the two
goats and present them before the LORD *at* the
door of the tabernacle of meeting. 8 Then Aaron
shall cast lots for the two goats: one lot for the
LORD and the other lot for the scapegoat. 9 And
Aaron shall bring the goat on which the LORD's
lot fell, and offer it *as* a sin offering. 10 But the

THE MESSAGE

24 "If a man sleeps with her and her menstrual blood gets on him, he is unclean for seven days and every bed on which he lies becomes unclean.

25-27 "If a woman has a discharge of blood for many days, but not at the time of her monthly period, or has a discharge that continues beyond the time of her period, she is unclean the same as during the time of her period. Every bed on which she lies during the time of the discharge and everything on which she sits becomes unclean the same as in her monthly period. Anyone who touches these things becomes unclean and must wash his clothes and bathe in water; he remains unclean until evening.

28-30 "When she is cleansed from her discharge, she is to count off seven days; then she is clean. On the eighth day she is to take two doves or two pigeons and bring them to the priest at the entrance to the Tent of Meeting. The priest will offer one for an Absolution-Offering and the other for a Whole-Burnt-Offering. The priest will make atonement for her in the presence of GOD because of the discharge that made her unclean.

31 "You are responsible for keeping the People of Israel separate from that which makes them ritually unclean, lest they die in their unclean condition by defiling my Dwelling which is among them.

32-33 "These are the procedures to follow for a man with a discharge or an emission of semen that makes him unclean, and for a woman in her menstrual period—any man or woman with a discharge and also for a man who sleeps with a woman who is unclean."

THE DAY OF ATONEMENT

1-2 16 After the death of Aaron's two sons—they died when they came before GOD with strange fire—GOD spoke to Moses: "Tell your brother Aaron not to enter into the Holy of Holies, barging inside the curtain that's before the Atonement-Cover on the Chest whenever he feels like it, lest he die, because I am present in the Cloud over the Atonement-Cover.

3-5 "This is the procedure for Aaron when he enters the Holy Place: He will bring a young bull for an Absolution-Offering and a ram for a Whole-Burnt-Offering; he will put on the holy linen tunic and the linen underwear, tie the linen sash around him, and put on the linen turban. These are the sacred vestments so he must bathe himself with water before he puts them on. Then from the Israelite community he will bring two male goats for an Absolution-Offering and a Whole-Burnt-Offering.

6-10 "Aaron will offer the bull for his own Absolution-Offering in order to make atonement for himself and his household. Then he will set the two goats before GOD at the entrance to the Tent of Meeting and cast lots over the two goats, one lot for GOD and the other lot for Azazel. He will offer the goat on which the lot to GOD falls as an Absolu-

NEW KING JAMES VERSION

goat on which the lot fell to be the scapegoat
shall be presented alive before the LORD, to
make atonement upon it, *and* to let it go as the
scapegoat into the wilderness.
11"And Aaron shall bring the bull of the sin
offering, which is for himself, and make atone-
ment for himself and for his house, and shall kill
the bull as the sin offering which *is* for himself.
12Then he shall take a censer full of burning
coals of fire from the altar before the LORD, with
his hands full of sweet incense beaten fine, and
bring *it* inside the veil. 13And he shall put the in-
cense on the fire before the LORD, that the cloud
of incense may cover the mercy seat that *is* on
the Testimony, lest he die. 14He shall take some
of the blood of the bull and sprinkle *it* with his
finger on the mercy seat on the east *side;* and
before the mercy seat he shall sprinkle some of
the blood with his finger seven times.
15"Then he shall kill the goat of the sin offer-
ing, which *is* for the people, bring its blood in-
side the veil, do with that blood as he did with
the blood of the bull, and sprinkle it on the
mercy seat and before the mercy seat. 16So he
shall make atonement for the Holy *Place,* be-
cause of the uncleanness of the children of Is-
rael, and because of their transgressions, for all
their sins; and so he shall do for the tabernacle
of meeting which remains among them in the
midst of their uncleanness. 17There shall be no
man in the tabernacle of meeting when he goes
in to make atonement in the Holy *Place,* until he
comes out, that he may make atonement for
himself, for his household, and for all the as-
sembly of Israel. 18And he shall go out to the al-
tar that *is* before the LORD, and make atonement
for it, and shall take some of the blood of the
bull and some of the blood of the goat, and put
it on the horns of the altar all around. 19Then he
shall sprinkle some of the blood on it with his
finger seven times, cleanse it, and consecrate it
from the uncleanness of the children of Israel.
20"And when he has made an end of atoning
for the Holy *Place,* the tabernacle of meeting,
and the altar, he shall bring the live goat.
21Aaron shall lay both his hands on the head of
the live goat, confess over it all the iniquities of
the children of Israel, and all their transgres-
sions, concerning all their sins, putting them on
the head of the goat, and shall send *it* away into
the wilderness by the hand of a suitable man.
22The goat shall bear on itself all their iniquities
to an uninhabited land; and he shall release the
goat in the wilderness.
23"Then Aaron shall come into the tabernacle
of meeting, shall take off the linen garments
which he put on when he went into the Holy
Place, and shall leave them there. 24And he shall
wash his body with water in a holy place, put on
his garments, come out and offer his burnt of-
fering and the burnt offering of the people, and
make atonement for himself and for the people.
25The fat of the sin offering he shall burn on the
altar. 26And he who released the goat as the
scapegoat shall wash his clothes and bathe his
body in water, and afterward he may come into

THE MESSAGE

tion-Offering. The goat on which the lot for Azazel falls will be sent out into the wilderness to Azazel to make atonement.

11-14 "Aaron will present his bull for an Absolution-Offering to make atonement for himself and his household. He will slaughter his bull for the Absolution-Offering. He will take a censer full of burning coals from the Altar before GOD and two handfuls of finely ground aromatic incense and bring them inside the curtain and put the incense on the fire before GOD; the smoke of the incense will cover the Atonement-Cover which is over The Testimony so that he doesn't die. He will take some of the bull's blood and sprinkle it with his finger on the front of the Atonement-Cover, then sprinkle the blood before the Atonement-Cover seven times.

15-17 "Next he will slaughter the goat designated as the Absolution-Offering for the people and bring the blood inside the curtain. He will repeat what he does with the bull's blood, sprinkling it on and before the Atonement-Cover. In this way he will make atonement for the Holy of Holies because of the uncleannesses of the Israelites, their acts of rebellion, and all their other sins. He will do the same thing for the Tent of Meeting which dwells among the people in the midst of their uncleanness. There is to be no one in the Tent of Meeting from the time Aaron goes in to make atonement in the Holy of Holies until he comes out, having made atonement for himself, his household, and the whole community of Israel.

18-19 "Then he will come out to the Altar that is before GOD and make atonement for it. He will take some of the bull's blood and some of the goat's blood and smear it all around the four horns of the Altar. With his finger he will sprinkle some of the blood on it seven times to purify and consecrate it from the uncleannesses of the Israelites.

20-22 "When Aaron finishes making atonement for the Holy of Holies, the Tent of Meeting, and the Altar, he will bring up the live goat, lay both hands on the live goat's head, and confess all the iniquities of the People of Israel, all their acts of rebellion, all their sins. He will put all the sins on the goat's head and send it off into the wilderness, led out by a man standing by and ready. The goat will carry all their iniquities to an empty wasteland; the man will let him loose out there in the wilderness.

23-25 "Finally, Aaron will come into the Tent of Meeting and take off the linen clothes in which he dressed to enter the Holy of Holies and leave them there. He will bathe in water in a Holy Place, put on his priestly vestments, offer the Whole-Burnt-Offering for himself and the Whole-Burnt-Offering for the people, making atonement for himself and the people, and burn the fat of the Absolution-Offering on the Altar.

26-28 "The man who takes the goat out to Azazel in the wilderness then will wash his clothes and bathe himself with water. After that he will be permitted to come back into

NEW KING JAMES VERSION

the camp. 27 The bull *for* the sin offering and the goat *for* the sin offering, whose blood was brought in to make atonement in the Holy *Place,* shall be carried outside the camp. And they shall burn in the fire their skins, their flesh, and their offal. 28 Then he who burns them shall wash his clothes and bathe his body in water, and afterward he may come into the camp.

29 "*This* shall be a statute forever for you: In the seventh month, on the tenth *day* of the month, you shall afflict your souls, and do no work at all, *whether* a native of your own country or a stranger who dwells among you. 30 For on that day *the priest* shall make atonement for you, to cleanse you, *that* you may be clean from all your sins before the LORD. 31 It *is* a sabbath of solemn rest for you, and you shall afflict your souls. *It is* a statute forever. 32 And the priest, who is anointed and consecrated to minister as priest in his father's place, shall make atonement, and put on the linen clothes, the holy garments; 33 then he shall make atonement for the Holy Sanctuary,[a] and he shall make atonement for the tabernacle of meeting and for the altar, and he shall make atonement for the priests and for all the people of the assembly. 34 This shall be an everlasting statute for you, to make atonement for the children of Israel, for all their sins, once a year." And he did as the LORD commanded Moses.

THE SANCTITY OF BLOOD

17 And the LORD spoke to Moses, saying, 2 "Speak to Aaron, to his sons, and to all the children of Israel, and say to them, 'This *is* the thing which the LORD has commanded, saying: 3 "Whatever man of the house of Israel who kills an ox or lamb or goat in the camp, or who kills *it* outside the camp, 4 and does not bring it to the door of the tabernacle of meeting to offer an offering to the LORD before the tabernacle of the LORD, the guilt of bloodshed shall be imputed to that man. He has shed blood; and that man shall be cut off from among his people, 5 to the end that the children of Israel may bring their sacrifices which they offer in the open field, that they may bring them to the LORD at the door of the tabernacle of meeting, to the priest, and offer them *as* peace offerings to the LORD. 6 And the priest shall sprinkle the blood on the altar of the LORD *at* the door of the tabernacle of meeting, and burn the fat for a sweet aroma to the LORD. 7 They shall no more offer their sacrifices to demons, after whom they have played the harlot. This shall be a statute forever for them throughout their generations." '

8 "Also you shall say to them: 'Whatever man of the house of Israel, or of the strangers who dwell among you, who offers a burnt offering or sacrifice, 9 and does not bring it to the door of the tabernacle of meeting, to offer it to the LORD, that man shall be cut off from among his people.

16:33 [a]That is, the Most Holy Place

THE MESSAGE

the camp. The bull for the Absolution-Offering and the goat for the Absolution-Offering, whose blood has been taken into the Holy of Holies to make atonement, are to be taken outside the camp and burned—their hides, their meat, and their entrails. The man assigned to burn them up will then wash his clothes and bathe himself in water. Then he is free to come back into the camp.

29-31 "This is standard practice for you, a per-
petual ordinance. On the tenth day of the
seventh month, both the citizen and the for-
eigner living with you are to enter into a
solemn fast and refrain from all work, be-
cause on this day atonement will be made
for you, to cleanse you. In the presence of
GOD you will be made clean of all your sins.
It is a Sabbath of all Sabbaths. You must
fast. It is a perpetual ordinance.
32 "The priest who is anointed and ordained
to succeed his father is to make the atone-
ment:
He puts on the sacred linen garments;
33 He purges the Holy of Holies by making
atonement;
He purges the Tent of Meeting and the Al-
tar by making atonement;
He makes atonement for the priests and
all the congregation.
34 "This is a perpetual ordinance for you:
Once a year atonement is to be made for all
the sins of the People of Israel."
And Aaron did it, just as GOD com-
manded Moses.

HOLY LIVING: SACRIFICES AND BLOOD

1-7 17 GOD spoke to Moses: "Speak to Aaron
and his sons and all the Israelites. Tell
them, This is what GOD commands: Any and
every man who slaughters an ox or lamb or
goat inside or outside the camp instead of
bringing it to the entrance of the Tent of
Meeting to offer it to GOD in front of The
Dwelling of GOD—that man is considered
guilty of bloodshed; he has shed blood and
must be cut off from his people. This is so
the Israelites will bring to GOD the sacrifices
that they're in the habit of sacrificing out in
the open fields. They must bring them to
GOD and the priest at the entrance to the
Tent of Meeting and sacrifice them as Peace-
Offerings to GOD. The priest will splash the
blood on the Altar of GOD at the entrance to
the Tent of Meeting and burn the fat as a
pleasing fragrance to GOD. They must no
longer offer their sacrifices to goat-
demons—a kind of religious orgy. This is a
perpetual decree down through the genera-
tions.
8-9 "Tell them, Any Israelite or foreigner liv-
ing among them who offers a Whole-Burnt-
Offering or Peace-Offering but doesn't bring
it to the entrance of the Tent of Meeting to
sacrifice it to GOD, that person must be cut
off from his people.

NEW KING JAMES VERSION

10 ‘And whatever man of the house of Israel,
or of the strangers who dwell among you, who
eats any blood, I will set My face against that
person who eats blood, and will cut him off from
among his people. 11 For the life of the flesh *is* in
the blood, and I have given it to you upon the al-
tar to make atonement for your souls; for it *is*
the blood *that* makes atonement for the soul.’
12 Therefore I said to the children of Israel, ‘No
one among you shall eat blood, nor shall any
stranger who dwells among you eat blood.’

13 “Whatever man of the children of Israel, or
of the strangers who dwell among you, who
hunts and catches any animal or bird that may
be eaten, he shall pour out its blood and cover it
with dust; 14 for *it is* the life of all flesh. Its blood
sustains its life. Therefore I said to the children
of Israel, ‘You shall not eat the blood of any
flesh, for the life of all flesh is its blood. Who-
ever eats it shall be cut off.’

15 “And every person who eats what died *nat-
urally* or what was torn *by beasts, whether he is*
a native of your own country or a stranger, he
shall both wash his clothes and bathe in water,
and be unclean until evening. Then he shall be
clean. 16 But if he does not wash *them* or bathe
his body, then he shall bear his guilt.”

LAWS OF SEXUAL MORALITY

18 Then the LORD spoke to Moses, saying,
2 “Speak to the children of Israel, and say
to them: ‘I am the LORD your God. 3 According to
the doings of the land of Egypt, where you
dwelt, you shall not do; and according to the do-
ings of the land of Canaan, where I am bringing
you, you shall not do; nor shall you walk in their
ordinances. 4 You shall observe My judgments
and keep My ordinances, to walk in them: I *am*
the LORD your God. 5 You shall therefore keep
My statutes and My judgments, which if a man
does, he shall live by them: I *am* the LORD.

6 ‘None of you shall approach anyone who is
near of kin to him, to uncover his nakedness: I
am the LORD. 7 The nakedness of your father or
the nakedness of your mother you shall not un-
cover. She *is* your mother; you shall not uncover
her nakedness. 8 The nakedness of your father’s
wife you shall not uncover; it *is* your father’s
nakedness. 9 The nakedness of your sister, the
daughter of your father, or the daughter of your
mother, *whether* born at home or elsewhere,
their nakedness you shall not uncover. 10 The
nakedness of your son’s daughter or your
daughter’s daughter, their nakedness you shall
not uncover; for theirs *is* your own nakedness.
11 The nakedness of your father’s wife’s daugh-
ter, begotten by your father—she *is* your sister—
you shall not uncover her nakedness. 12 You shall
not uncover the nakedness of your father’s sis-
ter; she *is* near of kin to your father. 13 You shall
not uncover the nakedness of your mother’s sis-
ter, for she *is* near of kin to your mother. 14 You
shall not uncover the nakedness of your father’s
brother. You shall not approach his wife; she *is*
your aunt. 15 You shall not uncover the naked-
ness of your daughter-in-law—she *is* your son’s
wife—you shall not uncover her nakedness.
16 You shall not uncover the nakedness of your
brother’s wife; it *is* your brother’s nakedness.

THE MESSAGE

10-12 “If any Israelite or foreigner living among
them eats blood, I will disown that person
and cut him off from his people, for the life
of an animal is in the blood. I have provided
the blood for you to make atonement for
your lives on the Altar; it is the blood, the
life, that makes atonement. That’s why I tell
the People of Israel, ‘Don’t eat blood.’ The
same goes for the foreigner who lives
among you, ‘Don’t eat blood.’

13-14 “Any and every Israelite—this also goes
for the foreigners—who hunts down an ani-
mal or bird that is edible, must bleed it and
cover the blood with dirt, because the life of
every animal is its blood—the blood is its
life. That’s why I tell the Israelites, ‘Don’t eat
the blood of any animal because the life of
every animal is its blood. Anyone who eats
the blood must be cut off.’

15-16 “Anyone, whether native or foreigner,
who eats from an animal that is found dead
or mauled must wash his clothes and bathe
in water; he remains unclean until evening
and is then clean. If he doesn’t wash or
bathe his body, he’ll be held responsible for
his actions.”

SEX

1-5 18 GOD spoke to Moses: “Speak to the
People of Israel. Tell them, I am GOD,
your God. Don’t live like the people of Egypt
where you used to live, and don’t live like
the people of Canaan where I’m bringing
you. Don’t do what they do. Obey my laws
and live by my decrees. I am your GOD. Keep
my decrees and laws: The person who obeys
them lives by them. I am GOD.

6 “Don’t have sex with a close relative. I am
GOD.

7 “Don’t violate your father by having sex
with your mother. She is your mother. Don’t
have sex with her.

8 “Don’t have sex with your father’s wife.
That violates your father.

9 “Don’t have sex with your sister, whether
she’s your father’s daughter or your
mother’s, whether she was born in the same
house or elsewhere.

10 “Don’t have sex with your son’s daughter
or your daughter’s daughter. That would vi-
olate your own body.

11 “Don’t have sex with the daughter of
your father’s wife born to your father. She is
your sister.

12 “Don’t have sex with your father’s sister;
she is your aunt, closely related to your fa-
ther.

13 “Don’t have sex with your mother’s sis-
ter; she is your aunt, closely related to your
mother.

14 “Don’t violate your father’s brother, your
uncle, by having sex with his wife. She is
your aunt.

15 “Don’t have sex with your daughter-in-
law. She is your son’s wife; don’t have sex
with her.

16 “Don’t have sex with your brother’s wife;
that would violate your brother.

NEW KING JAMES VERSION

17You shall not uncover the nakedness of a
woman and her daughter, nor shall you take her
son's daughter or her daughter's daughter, to
uncover her nakedness. They *are* near of kin to
her. It *is* wickedness. 18Nor shall you take a
woman as a rival to her sister, to uncover her
nakedness while the other is alive.
19'Also you shall not approach a woman to
uncover her nakedness as long as she is in her
customary impurity. 20Moreover you shall not
lie carnally with your neighbor's wife, to defile
yourself with her. 21And you shall not let any of
your descendants pass through *the fire* to Mo-
lech, nor shall you profane the name of your
God: I *am* the LORD. 22You shall not lie with a
male as with a woman. It *is* an abomination.
23Nor shall you mate with any animal, to defile
yourself with it. Nor shall any woman stand be-
fore an animal to mate with it. It *is* perversion.
24'Do not defile yourselves with any of these
things; for by all these the nations are defiled,
which I am casting out before you. 25For the land
is defiled; therefore I visit the punishment of its
iniquity upon it, and the land vomits out its in-
habitants. 26You shall therefore keep My
statutes and My judgments, and shall not com-
mit *any* of these abominations, *either* any of
your own nation or any stranger who dwells
among you 27(for all these abominations the
men of the land have done, who *were* before
you, and thus the land is defiled), 28lest the land
vomit you out also when you defile it, as it vom-
ited out the nations that *were* before you. 29For
whoever commits any of these abominations,
the persons who commit *them* shall be cut off
from among their people.
30'Therefore you shall keep My ordinance, so
that *you* do not commit *any* of these abominable
customs which were committed before you, and
that you do not defile yourselves by them: I *am*
the LORD your God.' "

MORAL AND CEREMONIAL LAWS

19 And the LORD spoke to Moses, saying,
2"Speak to all the congregation of the chil-
dren of Israel, and say to them: 'You shall be
holy, for I the LORD your God *am* holy.
3'Every one of you shall revere his mother
and his father, and keep My Sabbaths: I *am* the
LORD your God.
4'Do not turn to idols, nor make for your-
selves molded gods: I *am* the LORD your God.
5'And if you offer a sacrifice of a peace offer-
ing to the LORD, you shall offer it of your own
free will. 6It shall be eaten the same day you of-
fer *it*, and on the next day. And if any remains
until the third day, it shall be burned in the fire.
7And if it is eaten at all on the third day, it *is* an
abomination. It shall not be accepted. 8There-
fore *everyone* who eats it shall bear his iniquity,
because he has profaned the hallowed *offering*
of the LORD; and that person shall be cut off
from his people.
9'When you reap the harvest of your land,
you shall not wholly reap the corners of your
field, nor shall you gather the gleanings of your
harvest. 10And you shall not glean your vine-
yard, nor shall you gather *every* grape of your

THE MESSAGE

17 "Don't have sex with both a woman and
her daughter. And don't have sex with her
granddaughters either. They are her close
relatives. That is wicked.
18 "Don't marry your wife's sister as a rival
wife and have sex with her while your wife
is living.
19 "Don't have sex with a woman during the
time of her menstrual period when she is
unclean.
20 "Don't have sex with your neighbor's
wife and violate yourself by her.
21 "Don't give any of your children to be
burned in sacrifice to the god Molech—an
act of sheer blasphemy of your God. I am
GOD.
22 "Don't have sex with a man as one does
with a woman. That is abhorrent.
23 "Don't have sex with an animal and vio-
late yourself by it.
"A woman must not have sex with an an-
imal. That is perverse.
24-28 "Don't pollute yourself in any of these
ways. This is how the nations became pol-
luted, the ones that I am going to drive out
of the land before you. Even the land itself
became polluted and I punished it for its in-
iquities—the land vomited up its inhabi-
tants. You must keep my decrees and laws—
natives and foreigners both. You must not do
any of these abhorrent things. The people
who lived in this land before you arrived did
all these things and polluted the land. And if
you pollute it, the land will vomit you up just
as it vomited up the nations that preceded
you.
29-30 "Those who do any of these abhorrent
things will be cut off from their people. Keep
to what I tell you; don't engage in any of the
abhorrent acts that were practiced before
you came. Don't pollute yourselves with
them. I am GOD, *your* God."

"I AM GOD, YOUR GOD"

1-2 19 GOD spoke to Moses: "Speak to the
congregation of Israel. Tell them, Be
holy because I, GOD, your God, am holy.
3 "Every one of you must respect his
mother and father.
"Keep my Sabbaths. I am GOD, your God.
4 "Don't take up with no-god idols. Don't
make gods of cast metal. I am GOD, your
God.
5-8 "When you sacrifice a Peace-Offering to
GOD, do it as you've been taught so it is ac-
ceptable. Eat it on the day you sacrifice it
and the day following. Whatever is left until
the third day is to be burned up. If it is eaten
on the third day it is polluted meat and not
acceptable. Whoever eats it will be held re-
sponsible because he has violated what is
holy to GOD. That person will be cut off from
his people.
9-10 "When you harvest your land, don't har-
vest right up to the edges of your field or
gather the gleanings from the harvest. Don't
strip your vineyard bare or go back and pick

New King James Version

vineyard; you shall leave them for the poor and
the stranger: I *am* the LORD your God.
11 'You shall not steal, nor deal falsely, nor lie
to one another. 12 And you shall not swear by My
name falsely, nor shall you profane the name of
your God: I *am* the LORD.
13 'You shall not cheat your neighbor, nor rob
him. The wages of him who is hired shall not re-
main with you all night until morning. 14 You
shall not curse the deaf, nor put a stumbling
block before the blind, but shall fear your God:
I *am* the LORD.
15 'You shall do no injustice in judgment. You
shall not be partial to the poor, nor honor the
person of the mighty. In righteousness you shall
judge your neighbor. 16 You shall not go about *as*
a talebearer among your people; nor shall you
take a stand against the life of your neighbor: I
am the LORD.
17 'You shall not hate your brother in your
heart. You shall surely rebuke your neighbor,
and not bear sin because of him. 18 You shall not
take vengeance, nor bear any grudge against
the children of your people, but you shall love
your neighbor as yourself: I *am* the LORD.
19 'You shall keep My statutes. You shall not
let your livestock breed with another kind. You
shall not sow your field with mixed seed. Nor
shall a garment of mixed linen and wool come
upon you.
20 'Whoever lies carnally with a woman who
is betrothed to a man as a concubine, and who
has not at all been redeemed nor given her free-
dom, for this there shall be scourging; *but* they
shall not be put to death, because she was not
free. 21 And he shall bring his trespass offering
to the LORD, to the door of the tabernacle of
meeting, a ram as a trespass offering. 22 The
priest shall make atonement for him with the
ram of the trespass offering before the LORD for
his sin which he has committed. And the sin
which he has committed shall be forgiven him.
23 'When you come into the land, and have
planted all kinds of trees for food, then you shall
count their fruit as uncircumcised. Three years
it shall be as uncircumcised to you. *It* shall not
be eaten. 24 But in the fourth year all its fruit
shall be holy, a praise to the LORD. 25 And in the
fifth year you may eat its fruit, that it may yield
to you its increase: I *am* the LORD your God.
26 'You shall not eat *anything* with the blood,
nor shall you practice divination or soothsay-
ing. 27 You shall not shave around the sides of
your head, nor shall you disfigure the edges of
your beard. 28 You shall not make any cuttings
in your flesh for the dead, nor tattoo any marks
on you: I *am* the LORD.
29 'Do not prostitute your daughter, to cause
her to be a harlot, lest the land fall into harlotry,
and the land become full of wickedness.
30 'You shall keep My Sabbaths and rever-
ence My sanctuary: I *am* the LORD.
31 'Give no regard to mediums and familiar
spirits; do not seek after them, to be defiled by
them: I *am* the LORD your God.

The Message

up the fallen grapes. Leave them for the poor and the foreigner. I am GOD, your God.

11 "Don't steal.

"Don't lie.

"Don't deceive anyone.

12 "Don't swear falsely using my name, violating the name of your God. I am GOD.

13 "Don't exploit your friend or rob him.

"Don't hold back the wages of a hired hand overnight.

14 "Don't curse the deaf; don't put a stumbling block in front of the blind; fear your God. I am GOD.

15 "Don't pervert justice. Don't show favoritism to either the poor or the great. Judge on the basis of what is right.

16 "Don't spread gossip and rumors.

"Don't just stand by when your neighbor's life is in danger. I am GOD.

17 "Don't secretly hate your neighbor. If you have something against him, get it out into the open; otherwise you are an accomplice in his guilt.

18 "Don't seek revenge or carry a grudge against any of your people.

"Love your neighbor as yourself. I am GOD.

19 "Keep my decrees.

"Don't mate two different kinds of animals.

"Don't plant your fields with two kinds of seed.

"Don't wear clothes woven of two kinds of material.

20-22 "If a man has sex with a slave girl who is engaged to another man but has not yet been ransomed or given her freedom, there must be an investigation. But they aren't to be put to death because she wasn't free. The man must bring a Compensation-Offering to GOD at the entrance to the Tent of Meeting, a ram of compensation. The priest will perform the ritual of atonement for him before GOD with the ram of compensation for the sin he has committed. Then he will stand forgiven of the sin he committed.

23-25 "When you enter the land and plant any kind of fruit tree, don't eat the fruit for three years; consider it inedible. By the fourth year its fruit is holy, an offering of praise to GOD. Beginning in the fifth year you can eat its fruit; you'll have richer harvests this way. I am GOD, your God.

26 "Don't eat meat with blood in it.

"Don't practice divination or sorcery.

27 "Don't cut the hair on the sides of your head or trim your beard.

28 "Don't gash your bodies on behalf of the dead.

"Don't tattoo yourselves. I am GOD.

29 "Don't violate your daughter by making her a whore—the whole country would soon become a brothel, filled with sordid sex.

30 "Keep my Sabbaths and revere my Sanctuary: I am GOD.

31 "Don't dabble in the occult or traffic with mediums; you'll pollute your souls. I am GOD, your God.

New King James Version

32‘You shall rise before the gray headed and honor the presence of an old man, and fear your God: I *am* the LORD.

33‘And if a stranger dwells with you in your land, you shall not mistreat him. 34The stranger who dwells among you shall be to you as one born among you, and you shall love him as yourself; for you were strangers in the land of Egypt: I *am* the LORD your God.

35‘You shall do no injustice in judgment, in measurement of length, weight, or volume. 36You shall have honest scales, honest weights, an honest ephah, and an honest hin: I *am* the LORD your God, who brought you out of the land of Egypt.

37‘Therefore you shall observe all My statutes and all My judgments, and perform them: I *am* the LORD.’ ”

PENALTIES FOR BREAKING THE LAW

20 Then the LORD spoke to Moses, saying, 2“Again, you shall say to the children of Israel: ‘Whoever of the children of Israel, or of the strangers who dwell in Israel, who gives *any* of his descendants to Molech, he shall surely be put to death. The people of the land shall stone him with stones. 3I will set My face against that man, and will cut him off from his people, because he has given *some* of his descendants to Molech, to defile My sanctuary and profane My holy name. 4And if the people of the land should in any way hide their eyes from the man, when he gives *some* of his descendants to Molech, and they do not kill him, 5then I will set My face against that man and against his family; and I will cut him off from his people, and all who prostitute themselves with him to commit harlotry with Molech.

6‘And the person who turns to mediums and familiar spirits, to prostitute himself with them, I will set My face against that person and cut him off from his people. 7Consecrate yourselves therefore, and be holy, for I *am* the LORD your God. 8And you shall keep My statutes, and perform them: I *am* the LORD who sanctifies you.

9‘For everyone who curses his father or his mother shall surely be put to death. He has cursed his father or his mother. His blood *shall be* upon him.

10‘The man who commits adultery with *another* man’s wife, *he* who commits adultery with his neighbor’s wife, the adulterer and the adulteress, shall surely be put to death. 11The man who lies with his father’s wife has uncovered his father’s nakedness; both of them shall surely be put to death. Their blood *shall be* upon them. 12If a man lies with his daughter-in-law, both of them shall surely be put to death. They have committed perversion. Their blood *shall be* upon them. 13If a man lies with a male as he lies with a woman, both of them have committed an abomination. They shall surely be put to death. Their blood *shall be* upon them. 14If a man marries a woman and her mother, it *is* wickedness. They shall be burned with fire, both he and they, that there may be no wickedness among you.

The Message

32 “Show respect to the aged; honor the presence of an elder; fear your God. I am GOD.

33-34 “When a foreigner lives with you in your land, don’t take advantage of him. Treat the foreigner the same as a native. Love him like one of your own. Remember that you were once foreigners in Egypt. I am GOD, your God.

35-36 “Don’t cheat when measuring length, weight, or quantity. Use honest scales and weights and measures. I am GOD, your God. I brought you out of Egypt.

37 “Keep all my decrees and all my laws. Yes, *do* them. I am GOD.”

1-5 20 GOD spoke to Moses: “Tell the Israelites, Each and every Israelite and foreigner in Israel who gives his child to the god Molech must be put to death. The community must kill him by stoning. I will resolutely reject that man and cut him off from his people. By giving his child to the god Molech he has polluted my Sanctuary and desecrated my holy name. If the people of the land look the other way as if nothing had happened when that man gives his child to the god Molech and fail to kill him, I will resolutely reject that man and his family, and him and all who join him in prostituting themselves in the rituals of the god Molech I will cut off from their people.

6 “I will resolutely reject persons who dabble in the occult or traffic with mediums, prostituting themselves in their practices. I will cut them off from their people.

7-8 “Set yourselves apart for a holy life. *Live* a holy life, because I am GOD, your God. Do what I tell you; *live* the way I tell you. I am the GOD who makes you holy.

9 “Any and every person who curses his father or mother must be put to death. By cursing his father or mother he is responsible for his own death.

10 “If a man commits adultery with another man’s wife—the wife, say, of his neighbor—both the man and the woman, the adulterer and adulteress, must be put to death.

11 “If a man has sex with his father’s wife, he has violated his father. Both the man and woman must be put to death; they are responsible for their own deaths.

12 “If a man has sex with his daughter-in-law, both of them must be put to death. What they have done is perverse. And they are responsible for their own deaths.

13 “If a man has sex with a man as one does with a woman, both of them have done what is abhorrent. They must be put to death; they are responsible for their own deaths.

14 “If a man marries both a woman and her mother, that’s wicked. All three of them must be burned at the stake, purging the wickedness from the community.

NEW KING JAMES VERSION

15 If a man mates with an animal, he shall surely
be put to death, and you shall kill the animal. 16 If
a woman approaches any animal and mates
with it, you shall kill the woman and the animal.
They shall surely be put to death. Their blood *is*
upon them.
17 'If a man takes his sister, his father's
daughter or his mother's daughter, and sees her
nakedness and she sees his nakedness, it *is* a
wicked thing. And they shall be cut off in the
sight of their people. He has uncovered his sis-
ter's nakedness. He shall bear his guilt. 18 If a
man lies with a woman during her sickness and
uncovers her nakedness, he has exposed her
flow, and she has uncovered the flow of her
blood. Both of them shall be cut off from their
people.
19 'You shall not uncover the nakedness of
your mother's sister nor of your father's sister,
for that would uncover his near of kin. They
shall bear their guilt. 20 If a man lies with his un-
cle's wife, he has uncovered his uncle's naked-
ness. They shall bear their sin; they shall die
childless. 21 If a man takes his brother's wife, it *is*
an unclean thing. He has uncovered his
brother's nakedness. They shall be childless.
22 'You shall therefore keep all My statutes
and all My judgments, and perform them, that
the land where I am bringing you to dwell may
not vomit you out. 23 And you shall not walk in
the statutes of the nation which I am casting out
before you; for they commit all these things, and
therefore I abhor them. 24 But I have said to you,
"You shall inherit their land, and I will give it to
you to possess, a land flowing with milk and
honey." I *am* the LORD your God, who has sepa-
rated you from the peoples. 25 You shall therefore
distinguish between clean animals and unclean,
between unclean birds and clean, and you shall
not make yourselves abominable by beast or by
bird, or by any kind of living thing that creeps
on the ground, which I have separated from you
as unclean. 26 And you shall be holy to Me, for I
the LORD *am* holy, and have separated you from
the peoples, that you should be Mine.
27 'A man or a woman who is a medium, or
who has familiar spirits, shall surely be put to
death; they shall stone them with stones. Their
blood *shall be* upon them.' "

REGULATIONS FOR CONDUCT OF PRIESTS

21 And the LORD said to Moses, "Speak to the
priests, the sons of Aaron, and say to them:
'None shall defile himself for the dead among
his people, 2 except for his relatives who are
nearest to him: his mother, his father, his son,
his daughter, and his brother; 3 also his virgin
sister who is near to him, who has had no hus-
band, for her he may defile himself. 4 *Otherwise*
he shall not defile himself, *being* a chief man
among his people, to profane himself.
5 'They shall not make any bald *place* on their
heads, nor shall they shave the edges of their
beards nor make any cuttings in their flesh.
6 They shall be holy to their God and not profane
the name of their God, for they offer the offer-
ings of the LORD made by fire, *and* the bread of
their God; therefore they shall be holy.

THE MESSAGE

15 "If a man has sex with an animal, he must
be put to death and you must kill the animal.
16 "If a woman has sex with an animal, you
must kill both the woman and the animal.
They must be put to death. And they are re-
sponsible for their deaths.
17 "If a man marries his sister, the daughter
of either his father or mother, and they have
sex, that's a disgrace. They must be publicly
cut off from their people. He has violated his
sister and will be held responsible.
18 "If a man sleeps with a woman during her
period and has sex with her, he has uncov-
ered her 'fountain' and she has revealed her
'fountain'—both of them must be cut off
from their people.
19 "Don't have sex with your aunt on either
your mother's or father's side. That violates
a close relative. Both of you are held respon-
sible.
20 "If a man has sex with his aunt, he has
dishonored his uncle. They will be held re-
sponsible and die childless.
21 "If a man marries his brother's wife, it's a
defilement. He has shamed his brother.
They will be childless.
22-23 "Do what I tell you, all my decrees and
laws; live by them so that the land where I'm
bringing you won't vomit you out. You sim-
ply must not live like the nations I'm driving
out before you. They did all these things and
I hated every minute of it.
24-26 "I've told you, remember, that you will
possess their land that I'm giving to you as
an inheritance, a land flowing with milk and
honey. I am GOD, your God, who has distin-
guished you from the nations. So live like it:
Distinguish between ritually clean and un-
clean animals and birds. Don't pollute your-
selves with any animal or bird or crawling
thing which I have marked out as unclean
for you. Live holy lives before me because I,
GOD, am holy. I have distinguished you from
the nations to be my very own.
27 "A man or woman who is a medium or
sorcerer among you must be put to death.
You must kill them by stoning. They're re-
sponsible for their own deaths."

HOLY PRIESTS

1-4 **21** GOD spoke to Moses: "Speak to the
priests, the sons of Aaron. Tell them, A
priest must not ritually contaminate himself
by touching the dead, except for close rela-
tives: mother, father, son, daughter, brother,
or an unmarried sister who is dependent on
him since she has no husband; for these he
may make himself ritually unclean, but he
must not contaminate himself with the dead
who are only related to him by marriage
and thus profane himself.
5-6 "Priests must not shave their heads or
trim their beards or gash their bodies. They
must be holy to their God and must not pro-
fane the name of their God. Because their
job is to present the gifts of GOD, the food of
their God, they are to be holy.

New King James Version

7They shall not take a wife *who is* a harlot or a defiled woman, nor shall they take a woman divorced from her husband; for *the priest*[a] is holy to his God. 8Therefore you shall consecrate him, for he offers the bread of your God. He shall be holy to you, for I the LORD, who sanctify you, *am* holy. 9The daughter of any priest, if she profanes herself by playing the harlot, she profanes her father. She shall be burned with fire.

10'*He who is* the high priest among his brethren, on whose head the anointing oil was poured and who is consecrated to wear the garments, shall not uncover his head nor tear his clothes; 11nor shall he go near any dead body, nor defile himself for his father or his mother; 12nor shall he go out of the sanctuary, nor profane the sanctuary of his God; for the consecration of the anointing oil of his God *is* upon him: I *am* the LORD. 13And he shall take a wife in her virginity. 14A widow or a divorced woman or a defiled woman *or* a harlot—these he shall not marry; but he shall take a virgin of his own people as wife. 15Nor shall he profane his posterity among his people, for I the LORD sanctify him.' "

16And the LORD spoke to Moses, saying, 17"Speak to Aaron, saying: 'No man of your descendants in *succeeding* generations, who has *any* defect, may approach to offer the bread of his God. 18For any man who has a defect shall not approach: a man blind or lame, who has a marred *face* or any *limb* too long, 19a man who has a broken foot or broken hand, 20or is a hunchback or a dwarf, or *a man* who has a defect in his eye, or eczema or scab, or is a eunuch. 21No man of the descendants of Aaron the priest, who has a defect, shall come near to offer the offerings made by fire to the LORD. He has a defect; he shall not come near to offer the bread of his God. 22He may eat the bread of his God, *both* the most holy and the holy; 23only he shall not go near the veil or approach the altar, because he has a defect, lest he profane My sanctuaries; for I the LORD sanctify them.' "

24And Moses told *it* to Aaron and his sons, and to all the children of Israel.

22 Then the LORD spoke to Moses, saying, 2"Speak to Aaron and his sons, that they separate themselves from the holy things of the children of Israel, and that they do not profane My holy name *by* what they dedicate to Me: I *am* the LORD. 3Say to them: 'Whoever of all your descendants throughout your generations, who goes near the holy things which the children of Israel dedicate to the LORD, while he has uncleanness upon him, that person shall be cut off from My presence: I *am* the LORD.

4'Whatever man of the descendants of Aaron, who *is* a leper or has a discharge, shall not eat the holy offerings until he is clean. And whoever touches anything made unclean *by* a corpse, or a man who has had an emission of semen, 5or whoever touches any creeping thing by

21:7 [a]Literally *he*

The Message

7-8 "Because a priest is holy to his God he must not marry a woman who has been a harlot or a cult prostitute or a divorced woman. Make sure he is holy because he serves the food of your God. Treat him as holy because I, GOD, who make you holy, am holy.

9 "If a priest's daughter defiles herself in prostitution, she disgraces her father. She must be burned at the stake.

10-12 "The high priest, the one among his brothers who has received the anointing oil poured on his head and been ordained to wear the priestly vestments, must not let his hair go wild and tangled nor wear ragged and torn clothes. He must not enter a room where there is a dead body. He must not ritually contaminate himself, even for his father or mother; and he must neither abandon nor desecrate the Sanctuary of his God because of the dedication of the anointing oil which is upon him. I am GOD.

13-15 "He is to marry a young virgin, not a widow, not a divorcee, not a cult prostitute—he is only to marry a virgin from his own people. He must not defile his descendants among his people because I am GOD who makes him holy."

16-23 GOD spoke to Moses: "Tell Aaron, None of your descendants, in any generation to come, who has a defect of any kind may present as an offering the food of his God. That means anyone who is blind or lame, disfigured or deformed, crippled in foot or hand, hunchbacked or dwarfed, who has anything wrong with his eyes, who has running sores or damaged testicles. No descendant of Aaron the priest who has any defect is to offer gifts to GOD; he has a defect and so must not offer the food of his God. He may eat the food of his God, both the most holy and the holy, but because of his defect he must not go near the curtain or approach the Altar. It would desecrate my Sanctuary. I am GOD who makes them holy."

24 Moses delivered this message to Aaron, his sons, and to all the People of Israel.

1-2 22 GOD spoke to Moses: "Tell Aaron and his sons to treat the holy offerings that the Israelites consecrate to me with reverence so they won't desecrate my holy name. I am GOD.

3 "Tell them, From now on, if any of your descendants approaches in a state of ritual uncleanness the holy offerings that the Israelites consecrate to GOD, he will be cut off from my presence. I am GOD.

4-8 "Each and every one of Aaron's descendants who has an infectious skin disease or a discharge may not eat any of the holy offerings until he is clean. Also, if he touches anything defiled by a corpse, or has an emission of semen, or is contaminated by touching a crawling creature, or touches a

NEW KING JAMES VERSION

which he would be made unclean, or any person
by whom he would become unclean, whatever
his uncleanness may be— 6the person who has
touched any such thing shall be unclean until
evening, and shall not eat the holy *offerings* un-
less he washes his body with water. 7And when
the sun goes down he shall be clean; and after-
ward he may eat the holy *offerings*, because it *is*
his food. 8Whatever dies *naturally* or is torn *by
beasts* he shall not eat, to defile himself with it:
I *am* the LORD.

9'They shall therefore keep My ordinance,
lest they bear sin for it and die thereby, if they
profane it: I the LORD sanctify them.

10'No outsider shall eat the holy *offering;* one
who dwells with the priest, or a hired servant,
shall not eat the holy thing. 11But if the priest
buys a person with his money, he may eat it; and
one who is born in his house may eat his food.
12If the priest's daughter is married to an out-
sider, she may not eat of the holy offerings. 13But
if the priest's daughter is a widow or divorced,
and has no child, and has returned to her fa-
ther's house as in her youth, she may eat her fa-
ther's food; but no outsider shall eat it.

14'And if a man eats the holy *offering* unin-
tentionally, then he shall restore a holy *offering*
to the priest, and add one-fifth to it. 15They shall
not profane the holy *offerings* of the children of
Israel, which they offer to the LORD, 16or allow
them to bear the guilt of trespass when they eat
their holy *offerings;* for I the LORD sanctify
them.' "

OFFERINGS ACCEPTED AND NOT ACCEPTED

17And the LORD spoke to Moses, saying,
18"Speak to Aaron and his sons, and to all the
children of Israel, and say to them: 'Whatever
man of the house of Israel, or of the strangers in
Israel, who offers his sacrifice for any of his
vows or for any of his freewill offerings, which
they offer to the LORD as a burnt offering—
19*you shall offer* of your own free will a male
without blemish from the cattle, from the sheep,
or from the goats. 20Whatever has a defect, you
shall not offer, for it shall not be acceptable on
your behalf. 21And whoever offers a sacrifice of
a peace offering to the LORD, to fulfill *his* vow, or
a freewill offering from the cattle or the sheep,
it must be perfect to be accepted; there shall be
no defect in it. 22Those *that are* blind or broken
or maimed, or have an ulcer or eczema or scabs,
you shall not offer to the LORD, nor make an of-
fering by fire of them on the altar to the LORD.
23Either a bull or a lamb that has any limb too
long or too short you may offer *as* a freewill of-
fering, but for a vow it shall not be accepted.

24'You shall not offer to the LORD what is
bruised or crushed, or torn or cut; nor shall you
make *any offering of them* in your land. 25Nor
from a foreigner's hand shall you offer any of
these as the bread of your God, because their
corruption *is* in them, *and* defects *are* in them.
They shall not be accepted on your behalf.' "

26And the LORD spoke to Moses, saying:
27"When a bull or a sheep or a goat is born, it
shall be seven days with its mother; and from
the eighth day and thereafter it shall be ac-
cepted as an offering made by fire to the LORD.

THE MESSAGE

person who is contaminated for whatever reason—a person who touches any such thing will be ritually unclean until evening and may not eat any of the holy offerings unless he has washed well with water. After the sun goes down he is clean and may go ahead and eat the holy offerings; they are his food. But he must not contaminate himself by eating anything found dead or torn by wild animals. I am GOD.

9 "The priests must observe my instructions lest they become guilty and die by treating the offerings with irreverence. I am GOD who makes them holy.

10-13 "No layperson may eat anything set apart as holy. Nor may a priest's guest or his hired hand eat anything holy. But if a priest buys a slave, the slave may eat of it; also the slaves born in his house may eat his food. If a priest's daughter marries a layperson, she may no longer eat from the holy contributions. But if the priest's daughter is widowed or divorced and without children and returns to her father's household as before, she may eat of her father's food. But no layperson may eat of it.

14 "If anyone eats from a holy offering accidentally, he must give back the holy offering to the priest and add twenty percent to it.

15-16 "The priests must not treat with irreverence the holy offerings of the Israelites that they contribute to GOD lest they desecrate themselves and make themselves guilty when they eat the holy offerings. I am GOD who makes them holy."

17-25 GOD spoke to Moses: "Tell Aaron and his sons and all the People of Israel, Each and every one of you, whether native born or foreigner, who presents a Whole-Burnt-Offering to GOD to fulfill a vow or as a Freewill-Offering, must make sure that it is a male without defect from cattle, sheep, or goats for it to be acceptable. Don't try slipping in some creature that has a defect—it won't be accepted. Whenever anyone brings an offering from cattle or sheep as a Peace-Offering to GOD to fulfill a vow or as a Freewill-Offering, it has to be perfect, without defect, to be acceptable. Don't try giving GOD an animal that is blind, crippled, mutilated, an animal with running sores, a rash, or mange. Don't place any of these on the Altar as a gift to GOD. You may, though, offer an ox or sheep that is deformed or stunted as a Freewill-Offering, but it is not acceptable in fulfilling a vow. Don't offer to GOD an animal with bruised, crushed, torn, or cut-off testicles. Don't do this in your own land but don't accept them from foreigners and present them as food for your GOD either. Because of deformities and defects they will not be acceptable."

26-30 GOD spoke to Moses: "When a calf or lamb or goat is born, it is to stay with its mother for seven days. After the eighth day, it is acceptable as an offering, a gift to GOD.

NEW KING JAMES VERSION

[28]*Whether it is* a cow or ewe, do not kill both her and her young on the same day. [29]And when you offer a sacrifice of thanksgiving to the LORD, offer *it* of your own free will. [30]On the same day it shall be eaten; you shall leave none of it until morning: I *am* the LORD.

[31]"Therefore you shall keep My commandments, and perform them: I *am* the LORD. [32]You shall not profane My holy name, but I will be hallowed among the children of Israel. I *am* the LORD who sanctifies you, [33]who brought you out of the land of Egypt, to be your God: I *am* the LORD."

FEASTS OF THE LORD

23 And the LORD spoke to Moses, saying, [2]"Speak to the children of Israel, and say to them: 'The feasts of the LORD, which you shall proclaim *to be* holy convocations, these *are* My feasts.

THE SABBATH

[3]'Six days shall work be done, but the seventh day *is* a Sabbath of solemn rest, a holy convocation. You shall do no work *on it;* it *is* the Sabbath of the LORD in all your dwellings.

THE PASSOVER AND UNLEAVENED BREAD

[4]'These *are* the feasts of the LORD, holy convocations which you shall proclaim at their appointed times. [5]On the fourteenth *day* of the first month at twilight *is* the LORD's Passover. [6]And on the fifteenth day of the same month *is* the Feast of Unleavened Bread to the LORD; seven days you must eat unleavened bread. [7]On the first day you shall have a holy convocation; you shall do no customary work on it. [8]But you shall offer an offering made by fire to the LORD for seven days. The seventh day *shall be* a holy convocation; you shall do no customary work *on it.*' "

THE FEAST OF FIRSTFRUITS

[9]And the LORD spoke to Moses, saying, [10]"Speak to the children of Israel, and say to them: 'When you come into the land which I give to you, and reap its harvest, then you shall bring a sheaf of the firstfruits of your harvest to the priest. [11]He shall wave the sheaf before the LORD, to be accepted on your behalf; on the day after the Sabbath the priest shall wave it. [12]And you shall offer on that day, when you wave the sheaf, a male lamb of the first year, without blemish, as a burnt offering to the LORD. [13]Its grain offering *shall be* two-tenths *of an ephah* of fine flour mixed with oil, an offering made by fire to the LORD, for a sweet aroma; and its drink offering *shall be* of wine, one-fourth of a hin. [14]You shall eat neither bread nor parched grain nor fresh grain until the same day that you have brought an offering to your God; *it shall be* a statute forever throughout your generations in all your dwellings.

THE FEAST OF WEEKS

[15]'And you shall count for yourselves from the day after the Sabbath, from the day that you brought the sheaf of the wave offering: seven

THE MESSAGE

Don't slaughter both a cow or ewe and its young on the same day. When you sacrifice a Thanksgiving-Offering to GOD, do it right so it will be acceptable. Eat it on the same day; don't leave any leftovers until morning. I am GOD.

31 "Do what I tell you; *live* what I tell you. I am GOD.

32-33 "Don't desecrate my holy name. I insist on being treated with holy reverence among the People of Israel. I am GOD who makes you holy and brought you out of Egypt to be your God. I am GOD."

THE FEASTS

1-2 **23** GOD spoke to Moses: "Tell the People of Israel, These are my appointed feasts, the appointed feasts of GOD which you are to decree as sacred assemblies.

3 "Work six days. The seventh day is a Sabbath, a day of total and complete rest, a sacred assembly. Don't do any work. Wherever you live, it is a Sabbath to GOD.

4 "These are the appointed feasts of GOD, the sacred assemblies which you are to announce at the times set for them:

5 "GOD's Passover, beginning at sundown on the fourteenth day of the first month.

6-8 "GOD's Feast of Unraised Bread, on the fifteenth day of this same month. You are to eat unraised bread for seven days. Hold a sacred assembly on the first day; don't do any regular work. Offer Fire-Gifts to GOD for seven days. On the seventh day hold a sacred assembly; don't do any regular work."

9-14 GOD spoke to Moses: "Tell the People of Israel, When you arrive at the land that I am giving you and reap its harvest, bring to the priest a sheaf of the first grain that you harvest. He will wave the sheaf before GOD for acceptance on your behalf; on the morning after Sabbath, the priest will wave it. On the same day that you wave the sheaf, offer a year-old male lamb without defect for a Whole-Burnt-Offering to GOD and with it the Grain-Offering of four quarts of fine flour mixed with oil—a Fire-Gift to GOD, a pleasing fragrance—and also a Drink-Offering of a quart of wine. Don't eat any bread or roasted or fresh grain until you have presented this offering to your God. This is a perpetual decree for all your generations to come, wherever you live.

15-21 "Count seven full weeks from the morning after the Sabbath when you brought the sheaf as a Wave-Offering, fifty days until the

NEW KING JAMES VERSION

Sabbaths shall be completed. [16]Count fifty days
to the day after the seventh Sabbath; then you
shall offer a new grain offering to the LORD.
[17]You shall bring from your dwellings two wave
loaves of two-tenths *of an ephah.* They shall be
of fine flour; they shall be baked with leaven.
They are the firstfruits to the LORD. [18]And you
shall offer with the bread seven lambs of the
first year, without blemish, one young bull, and
two rams. They shall be *as* a burnt offering to
the LORD, with their grain offering and their
drink offerings, an offering made by fire for a
sweet aroma to the LORD. [19]Then you shall sac-
rifice one kid of the goats as a sin offering, and
two male lambs of the first year as a sacrifice of
a peace offering. [20]The priest shall wave them
with the bread of the firstfruits *as* a wave offer-
ing before the LORD, with the two lambs. They
shall be holy to the LORD for the priest. [21]And
you shall proclaim on the same day *that* it is a
holy convocation to you. You shall do no custom-
ary work *on it. It shall be* a statute forever in all
your dwellings throughout your generations.
[22]'When you reap the harvest of your land,
you shall not wholly reap the corners of your
field when you reap, nor shall you gather any
gleaning from your harvest. You shall leave
them for the poor and for the stranger: I *am* the
LORD your God.' "

THE FEAST OF TRUMPETS

[23]Then the LORD spoke to Moses, saying,
[24]"Speak to the children of Israel, saying: 'In the
seventh month, on the first *day* of the month,
you shall have a sabbath-*rest,* a memorial of
blowing of trumpets, a holy convocation. [25]You
shall do no customary work *on it;* and you shall
offer an offering made by fire to the LORD.' "

THE DAY OF ATONEMENT

[26]And the LORD spoke to Moses, saying:
[27]"Also the tenth *day* of this seventh month *shall
be* the Day of Atonement. It shall be a holy con-
vocation for you; you shall afflict your souls,
and offer an offering made by fire to the LORD.
[28]And you shall do no work on that same day,
for it *is* the Day of Atonement, to make atone-
ment for you before the LORD your God. [29]For
any person who is not afflicted *in soul* on that
same day shall be cut off from his people. [30]And
any person who does any work on that same
day, that person I will destroy from among his
people. [31]You shall do no manner of work; *it
shall be* a statute forever throughout your gen-
erations in all your dwellings. [32]It *shall be* to you
a sabbath of *solemn* rest, and you shall afflict
your souls; on the ninth *day* of the month at
evening, from evening to evening, you shall cel-
ebrate your sabbath."

THE FEAST OF TABERNACLES

[33]Then the LORD spoke to Moses, saying,
[34]"Speak to the children of Israel, saying: 'The
fifteenth day of this seventh month *shall be* the
Feast of Tabernacles *for* seven days to the LORD.
[35]On the first day *there shall be* a holy convoca-
tion. You shall do no customary work *on it.* [36]*For*
seven days you shall offer an offering made by

THE MESSAGE

morning of the seventh Sabbath. Then pre-
sent a new Grain-Offering to GOD. Bring
from wherever you are living two loaves of
bread made from four quarts of fine flour
and baked with yeast as a Wave-Offering of
the first ripe grain to GOD. In addition to the
bread, offer seven yearling male lambs
without defect, plus one bull and two rams.
They will be a Whole-Burnt-Offering to GOD
together with their Grain-Offerings and
Drink-Offerings—offered as Fire-Gifts, a
pleasing fragrance to GOD. Offer one male
goat for an Absolution-Offering and two
yearling lambs for a Peace-Offering. The
priest will wave the two lambs before GOD
as a Wave-Offering, together with the bread
of the first ripe grain. They are sacred offer-
ings to GOD for the priest. Proclaim the day
as a sacred assembly. Don't do any ordinary
work. It is a perpetual decree wherever you
live down through your generations.
22 "When you reap the harvest of your land,
don't reap the corners of your field or
gather the gleanings. Leave them for the
poor and the foreigners. I am GOD, *your*
God."

23-25 GOD said to Moses: "Tell the People of Is-
rael, On the first day of the seventh month,
set aside a day of rest, a sacred assembly—
mark it with loud blasts on the ram's horn.
Don't do any ordinary work. Offer a Fire-
Gift to GOD."

26-32 GOD said to Moses: "The tenth day of the
seventh month is the Day of Atonement.
Hold a sacred assembly, fast, and offer a
Fire-Gift to GOD. Don't work on that day be-
cause it is a day of atonement to make
atonement for you before your GOD. Anyone
who doesn't fast on that day must be cut off
from his people. I will destroy from among
his people anyone who works on that day.
Don't do any work that day—none. This is a
perpetual decree for all the generations to
come, wherever you happen to be living. It
is a Sabbath of complete and total rest, a
fast day. Observe your Sabbath from the
evening of the ninth day of the month until
the following evening."

33-36 GOD said to Moses: "Tell the People of Is-
rael, GOD's Feast of Booths begins on the fif-
teenth day of the seventh month. It lasts
seven days. The first day is a sacred assem-
bly; don't do any ordinary work. Offer Fire-

New King James Version

fire to the LORD. On the eighth day you shall have a holy convocation, and you shall offer an offering made by fire to the LORD. It *is* a sacred assembly, *and* you shall do no customary work *on it*.

37‘These *are* the feasts of the LORD which you shall proclaim *to be* holy convocations, to offer an offering made by fire to the LORD, a burnt offering and a grain offering, a sacrifice and drink offerings, everything on its day— 38besides the Sabbaths of the LORD, besides your gifts, besides all your vows, and besides all your freewill offerings which you give to the LORD.

39‘Also on the fifteenth day of the seventh month, when you have gathered in the fruit of the land, you shall keep the feast of the LORD *for* seven days; on the first day *there shall be* a sabbath-*rest*, and on the eighth day a sabbath-*rest*. 40And you shall take for yourselves on the first day the fruit of beautiful trees, branches of palm trees, the boughs of leafy trees, and willows of the brook; and you shall rejoice before the LORD your God for seven days. 41You shall keep it as a feast to the LORD for seven days in the year. *It shall be* a statute forever in your generations. You shall celebrate it in the seventh month. 42You shall dwell in booths for seven days. All who are native Israelites shall dwell in booths, 43that your generations may know that I made the children of Israel dwell in booths when I brought them out of the land of Egypt: I *am* the LORD your God.’ ”

44So Moses declared to the children of Israel the feasts of the LORD.

Care of the Tabernacle Lamps

24 Then the LORD spoke to Moses, saying: 2“Command the children of Israel that they bring to you pure oil of pressed olives for the light, to make the lamps burn continually. 3Outside the veil of the Testimony, in the tabernacle of meeting, Aaron shall be in charge of it from evening until morning before the LORD continually; *it shall be* a statute forever in your generations. 4He shall be in charge of the lamps on the pure *gold* lampstand before the LORD continually.

The Bread of the Tabernacle

5“And you shall take fine flour and bake twelve cakes with it. Two-tenths *of an ephah* shall be in each cake. 6You shall set them in two rows, six in a row, on the pure *gold* table before the LORD. 7And you shall put pure frankincense on *each* row, that it may be on the bread for a memorial, an offering made by fire to the LORD. 8Every Sabbath he shall set it in order before the LORD continually, *being taken* from the children of Israel by an everlasting covenant. 9And it shall be for Aaron and his sons, and they shall eat it in a holy place; for it *is* most holy to him from the offerings of the LORD made by fire, by a perpetual statute.”

The Message

Gifts to GOD for seven days. On the eighth day hold a sacred assembly and offer a gift to GOD. It is a solemn convocation. Don't do any ordinary work.

37-38 “These are the appointed feasts of GOD which you will decree as sacred assemblies for presenting Fire-Gifts to GOD: the Whole-Burnt-Offerings, Grain-Offerings, sacrifices, and Drink-Offerings assigned to each day. These are in addition to offerings for GOD's Sabbaths and also in addition to other gifts connected with whatever you have vowed and all the Freewill-Offerings you give to GOD.

39-43 “So, summing up: On the fifteenth day of the seventh month, after you have brought your crops in from your fields, celebrate the Feast of GOD for seven days. The first day is a complete rest and the eighth day is a complete rest. On the first day, pick the best fruit from the best trees; take fronds of palm trees and branches of leafy trees and from willows by the brook and celebrate in the presence of your GOD for seven days—yes, for seven full days celebrate it as a festival to GOD. Every year from now on, celebrate it in the seventh month. Live in booths for seven days—every son and daughter of Israel is to move into booths so that your descendants will know that I made the People of Israel live in booths when I brought them out of the land of Egypt. I am GOD, *your* God.”

44 Moses posted the calendar for the annual appointed feasts of GOD which Israel was to celebrate.

Light and Bread

1-4 24 GOD spoke to Moses: “Order the People of Israel to bring you virgin olive oil for light so that the lamps may be kept burning continually. Aaron is in charge of keeping these lamps burning in front of the curtain that screens The Testimony in the Tent of Meeting from evening to morning continually before GOD. This is a perpetual decree down through the generations. Aaron is responsible for keeping the lamps burning continually on the Lampstand of pure gold before GOD.

5-9 “Take fine flour and bake twelve loaves of bread, using about four quarts of flour to a loaf. Arrange them in two rows of six each on the Table of pure gold before GOD. Along each row spread pure incense, marking the bread as a memorial; it is a gift to GOD. Regularly, every Sabbath, this bread is to be set before GOD, a perpetual covenantal response from Israel. The bread then goes to Aaron and his sons, who are to eat it in a Holy Place. It is their most holy share from the gifts to GOD. This is a perpetual decree.”

New King James Version

The Penalty for Blasphemy

10Now the son of an Israelite woman, whose father *was* an Egyptian, went out among the children of Israel; and this Israelite *woman's* son and a man of Israel fought each other in the camp. 11And the Israelite woman's son blasphemed the name *of the* LORD and cursed; and so they brought him to Moses. (His mother's name *was* Shelomith the daughter of Dibri, of the tribe of Dan.) 12Then they put him in custody, that the mind of the LORD might be shown to them.

13And the LORD spoke to Moses, saying, 14"Take outside the camp him who has cursed; then let all who heard *him* lay their hands on his head, and let all the congregation stone him.

15"Then you shall speak to the children of Israel, saying: 'Whoever curses his God shall bear his sin. 16And whoever blasphemes the name of the LORD shall surely be put to death. All the congregation shall certainly stone him, the stranger as well as him who is born in the land. When he blasphemes the name *of the* LORD, he shall be put to death.

17'Whoever kills any man shall surely be put to death. 18Whoever kills an animal shall make it good, animal for animal.

19'If a man causes disfigurement of his neighbor, as he has done, so shall it be done to him— 20fracture for fracture, eye for eye, tooth for tooth; as he has caused disfigurement of a man, so shall it be done to him. 21And whoever kills an animal shall restore it; but whoever kills a man shall be put to death. 22You shall have the same law for the stranger and for one from your own country; for I *am* the LORD your God.' "

23Then Moses spoke to the children of Israel; and they took outside the camp him who had cursed, and stoned him with stones. So the children of Israel did as the LORD commanded Moses.

The Sabbath of the Seventh Year

25 And the LORD spoke to Moses on Mount Sinai, saying, 2"Speak to the children of Israel, and say to them: 'When you come into the land which I give you, then the land shall keep a sabbath to the LORD. 3Six years you shall sow your field, and six years you shall prune your vineyard, and gather its fruit; 4but in the seventh year there shall be a sabbath of solemn rest for the land, a sabbath to the LORD. You shall neither sow your field nor prune your vineyard. 5What grows of its own accord of your harvest you shall not reap, nor gather the grapes of your untended vine, *for* it is a year of rest for the land. 6And the sabbath *produce* of the land shall be food for you: for you, your male and female servants, your hired man, and the stranger who dwells with you, 7for your livestock and the beasts that *are* in your land—all its produce shall be for food.

The Year of Jubilee

8'And you shall count seven sabbaths of years for yourself, seven times seven years; and the time of the seven sabbaths of years shall be to you forty-nine years. 9Then you shall cause

The Message

10-12 One day the son of an Israelite mother and an Egyptian father went out among the Israelites. A fight broke out in the camp between him and an Israelite. The son of the Israelite woman blasphemed the Name of GOD and cursed. They brought him to Moses. His mother's name was Shelomith, daughter of Dibri of the tribe of Dan. They put him in custody waiting for GOD's will to be revealed to them.

13-16 Then GOD spoke to Moses: "Take the blasphemer outside the camp. Have all those who heard him place their hands on his head; then have the entire congregation stone him. Then tell the Israelites, Anyone who curses God will be held accountable; anyone who blasphemes the Name of GOD must be put to death. The entire congregation must stone him. It makes no difference whether he is a foreigner or a native, if he blasphemes the Name, he will be put to death.

17-22 "Anyone who hits and kills a fellow human must be put to death. Anyone who kills someone's animal must make it good—a life for a life. Anyone who injures his neighbor will get back the same as he gave: fracture for fracture, eye for eye, tooth for tooth. What he did to hurt that person will be done to him. Anyone who hits and kills an animal must make it good, but whoever hits and kills a fellow human will be put to death. And no double standards: the same rule goes for foreigners and natives. I am GOD, *your* God."

23 Moses then spoke to the People of Israel. They brought the blasphemer outside the camp and stoned him. The People of Israel followed the orders GOD had given Moses.

"The Land Will Observe a Sabbath to God"

1-7 25 GOD spoke to Moses at Mount Sinai: "Speak to the People of Israel. Tell them, When you enter the land which I am going to give you, the land will observe a Sabbath to GOD. Sow your fields, prune your vineyards, and take in your harvests for six years. But the seventh year the land will take a Sabbath of complete and total rest, a Sabbath to GOD; you will not sow your fields or prune your vineyards. Don't reap what grows of itself; don't harvest the grapes of your untended vines. The land gets a year of complete and total rest. But you can eat from what the land volunteers during the Sabbath year—you and your men and women servants, your hired hands, and the foreigners who live in the country, and, of course, also your livestock and the wild animals in the land can eat from it. Whatever the land volunteers of itself can be eaten.

"The Fiftieth Year Shall Be a Jubilee for You"

8-12 "Count off seven Sabbaths of years—seven times seven years: Seven Sabbaths of years adds up to forty-nine years. Then sound

NEW KING JAMES VERSION

the trumpet of the Jubilee to sound on the tenth *day* of the seventh month; on the Day of Atonement you shall make the trumpet to sound throughout all your land. 10And you shall consecrate the fiftieth year, and proclaim liberty throughout *all* the land to all its inhabitants. It shall be a Jubilee for you; and each of you shall return to his possession, and each of you shall return to his family. 11That fiftieth year shall be a Jubilee to you; in it you shall neither sow nor reap what grows of its own accord, nor gather *the grapes* of your untended vine. 12For it *is* the Jubilee; it shall be holy to you; you shall eat its produce from the field.

13'In this Year of Jubilee, each of you shall return to his possession. 14And if you sell anything to your neighbor or buy from your neighbor's hand, you shall not oppress one another. 15According to the number of years after the Jubilee you shall buy from your neighbor, and according to the number of years of crops he shall sell to you. 16According to the multitude of years you shall increase its price, and according to the fewer number of years you shall diminish its price; for he sells to you *according* to the number *of the years* of the crops. 17Therefore you shall not oppress one another, but you shall fear your God; for I *am* the LORD your God.

PROVISIONS FOR THE SEVENTH YEAR

18'So you shall observe My statutes and keep My judgments, and perform them; and you will dwell in the land in safety. 19Then the land will yield its fruit, and you will eat your fill, and dwell there in safety.

20'And if you say, "What shall we eat in the seventh year, since we shall not sow nor gather in our produce?" 21Then I will command My blessing on you in the sixth year, and it will bring forth produce enough for three years. 22And you shall sow in the eighth year, and eat old produce until the ninth year; until its produce comes in, you shall eat of the old *harvest*.

REDEMPTION OF PROPERTY

23'The land shall not be sold permanently, for the land *is* Mine; for you *are* strangers and sojourners with Me. 24And in all the land of your possession you shall grant redemption of the land.

25'If one of your brethren becomes poor, and has sold *some* of his possession, and if his redeeming relative comes to redeem it, then he may redeem what his brother sold. 26Or if the man has no one to redeem it, but he himself becomes able to redeem it, 27then let him count the years since its sale, and restore the remainder to the man to whom he sold it, that he may return to his possession. 28But if he is not able to have *it* restored to himself, then what was sold shall remain in the hand of him who bought it until the Year of Jubilee; and in the Jubilee it shall be released, and he shall return to his possession.

29'If a man sells a house in a walled city, then he may redeem it within a whole year after it is sold; *within* a full year he may redeem it. 30But if it is not redeemed within the space of a full year, then the house in the walled city shall belong permanently to him who bought it,

THE MESSAGE

loud blasts on the ram's horn on the tenth day of the seventh month, the Day of Atonement. Sound the ram's horn all over the land. Sanctify the fiftieth year; make it a holy year. Proclaim freedom all over the land to everyone who lives in it—a Jubilee for you: Each person will go back to his family's property and reunite with his extended family. The fiftieth year is your Jubilee year: Don't sow; don't reap what volunteers itself in the fields; don't harvest the untended vines because it's the Jubilee and a holy year for you. You're permitted to eat from whatever volunteers itself in the fields.

13 "In this year of Jubilee everyone returns home to his family property.

14-17 "If you sell or buy property from one of your countrymen, don't cheat him. Calculate the purchase price on the basis of the number of years since the Jubilee. He is obliged to set the sale price on the basis of the number of harvests remaining until the next Jubilee. The more years left, the more money; you can raise the price. But the fewer years left, the less money; decrease the price. What you are buying and selling in fact is the number of crops you're going to harvest. Don't cheat each other. Fear your God. I am GOD, your God.

18-22 "Keep my decrees and observe my laws and you will live secure in the land. The land will yield its fruit; you will have all you can eat and will live safe and secure. Do I hear you ask, 'What are we going to eat in the seventh year if we don't plant or harvest?' I assure you, I will send such a blessing in the sixth year that the land will yield enough for three years. While you plant in the eighth year, you will eat from the old crop and continue until the harvest of the ninth year comes in.

23-24 "The land cannot be sold permanently because the land is mine and you are foreigners—you're my tenants. You must provide for the right of redemption for any of the land that you own.

25-28 "If one of your brothers becomes poor and has to sell any of his land, his nearest relative is to come and buy back what his brother sold. If a man has no one to redeem it but he later prospers and earns enough for its redemption, he is to calculate the value since he sold it and refund the balance to the man to whom he sold it; he can then go back to his own land. If he doesn't get together enough money to repay him, what he sold remains in the possession of the buyer until the year of Jubilee. In the Jubilee it will be returned and he can go back and live on his land.

29-31 "If a man sells a house in a walled city, he retains the right to buy it back for a full year after the sale. At any time during that year he can redeem it. But if it is not redeemed before the full year has passed, it becomes the permanent possession of the buyer and

NEW KING JAMES VERSION

throughout his generations. It shall not be re-
leased in the Jubilee. 31However the houses of
villages which have no wall around them shall
be counted as the fields of the country. They
may be redeemed, and they shall be released in
the Jubilee. 32Nevertheless the cities of the
Levites, *and* the houses in the cities of their pos-
session, the Levites may redeem at any time.
33And if a man purchases a house from the
Levites, then the house that was sold in the city
of his possession shall be released in the Ju-
bilee; for the houses in the cities of the Levites
are their possession among the children of Is-
rael. 34But the field of the common-land of their
cities may not be sold, for it *is* their perpetual
possession.

LENDING TO THE POOR

35'If one of your brethren becomes poor, and
falls into poverty among you, then you shall
help him, like a stranger or a sojourner, that he
may live with you. 36Take no usury or interest
from him; but fear your God, that your brother
may live with you. 37You shall not lend him your
money for usury, nor lend him your food at a
profit. 38I *am* the LORD your God, who brought
you out of the land of Egypt, to give you the land
of Canaan *and* to be your God.

THE LAW CONCERNING SLAVERY

39'And if *one of* your brethren *who dwells* by
you becomes poor, and sells himself to you, you
shall not compel him to serve as a slave. 40As a
hired servant *and* a sojourner he shall be with
you, *and* shall serve you until the Year of Jubilee.
41And *then* he shall depart from you—he and his
children with him—and shall return to his own
family. He shall return to the possession of his
fathers. 42For they *are* My servants, whom I
brought out of the land of Egypt; they shall not
be sold as slaves. 43You shall not rule over him
with rigor, but you shall fear your God. 44And as
for your male and female slaves whom you may
have—from the nations that are around you,
from them you may buy male and female slaves.
45Moreover you may buy the children of the
strangers who dwell among you, and their fam-
ilies who are with you, which they beget in your
land; and they shall become your property.
46And you may take them as an inheritance for
your children after you, to inherit *them as* a pos-
session; they shall be your permanent slaves.
But regarding your brethren, the children of Is-
rael, you shall not rule over one another with
rigor.

47'Now if a sojourner or stranger close to you
becomes rich, and *one of* your brethren *who
dwells* by him becomes poor, and sells himself
to the stranger *or* sojourner close to you, or to a
member of the stranger's family, 48after he is
sold he may be redeemed again. One of his
brothers may redeem him; 49or his uncle or his
uncle's son may redeem him; or *anyone* who is
near of kin to him in his family may redeem
him; or if he is able he may redeem himself.
50Thus he shall reckon with him who bought
him: The price of his release shall be according
to the number of years, from the year that he
was sold to him until the Year of Jubilee; *it shall*

THE MESSAGE

his descendants. It is not returned in the Ju-
bilee. However, houses in unwalled villages
are treated the same as fields. They can be
redeemed and have to be returned at the Ju-
bilee.

32-34 "As to the Levitical cities, houses in the
cities owned by the Levites are always sub-
ject to redemption. Levitical property is al-
ways redeemable if it is sold in a town that
they hold and reverts to them in the Jubilee,
because the houses in the towns of the
Levites are their property among the People
of Israel. The pastures belonging to their
cities may not be sold; they are their perma-
nent possession.

35-38 "If one of your brothers becomes indigent
and cannot support himself, help him, the
same as you would a foreigner or a guest so
that he can continue to live in your neigh-
borhood. Don't gouge him with interest
charges; out of reverence for your God help
your brother to continue to live with you in
the neighborhood. Don't take advantage of
his plight by running up big interest charges
on his loans, and don't give him food for
profit. I am your GOD who brought you out
of Egypt to give you the land of Canaan and
to be your God.

39-43 "If one of your brothers becomes indigent
and has to sell himself to you, don't make
him work as a slave. Treat him as a hired
hand or a guest among you. He will work for
you until the Jubilee, after which he and his
children are set free to go back to his clan
and his ancestral land. Because the People
of Israel are my servants whom I brought
out of Egypt, they must never be sold as
slaves. Don't tyrannize them; fear your God.

44-46 "The male and female slaves which you
have are to come from the surrounding na-
tions; you are permitted to buy slaves from
them. You may also buy the children of for-
eign workers who are living among you
temporarily and from their clans which are
living among you and have been born in
your land. They become your property. You
may will them to your children as property
and make them slaves for life. But you must
not tyrannize your brother Israelites.

47-53 "If a foreigner or temporary resident
among you becomes rich and one of your
brothers becomes poor and sells himself to
the foreigner who lives among you or to a
member of the foreigner's clan, he still has
the right of redemption after he has sold
himself. One of his relatives may buy him
back. An uncle or cousin or any close rela-
tive of his extended family may redeem him.
Or, if he gets the money together, he can re-
deem himself. What happens then is that he
and his owner count out the time from the
year he sold himself to the year of Jubilee;

NEW KING JAMES VERSION

be according to the time of a hired servant for
him. 51If *there are* still many years *remaining*,
according to them he shall repay the price of his
redemption from the money with which he was
bought. 52And if there remain but a few years
until the Year of Jubilee, then he shall reckon
with him, *and* according to his years he shall re-
pay him the price of his redemption. 53He shall
be with him as a yearly hired servant, and he
shall not rule with rigor over him in your sight.
54And if he is not redeemed in these *years*, then
he shall be released in the Year of Jubilee—he
and his children with him. 55For the children of
Israel *are* servants to Me; they *are* My servants
whom I brought out of the land of Egypt: I *am*
the LORD your God.

PROMISE OF BLESSING AND RETRIBUTION

26 'You shall not make idols for yourselves;
neither a carved image nor a *sacred* pillar
shall you rear
up for yourselves;
nor shall you set up an engraved stone in
your land, to bow down to it;
for I *am* the LORD your God.
2You shall keep My Sabbaths and reverence
My sanctuary:
I *am* the LORD.

3'If you walk in My statutes and keep My
commandments, and perform them,
4then I will give you rain in its season, the
land shall yield its produce, and the trees
of the field shall yield their fruit.
5Your threshing shall last till the time of
vintage, and the vintage shall last till the
time of sowing;
you shall eat your bread to the full, and
dwell in your land safely.
6I will give peace in the land, and you shall
lie down, and none will make *you* afraid;
I will rid the land of evil beasts,
and the sword will not go through your
land.
7You will chase your enemies, and they shall
fall by the sword before you.
8Five of you shall chase a hundred, and a
hundred of you shall put ten thousand to
flight;
your enemies shall fall by the sword before
you.
9'For I will look on you favorably and make
you fruitful, multiply you and confirm
My covenant with you.
10You shall eat the old harvest, and clear out
the old because of the new.
11I will set My tabernacle among you, and My
soul shall not abhor you.
12I will walk among you and be your God, and
you shall be My people.
13I *am* the LORD your God, who brought you
out of the land of Egypt, that *you* should
not be their slaves;
I have broken the bands of your yoke and
made you walk upright.

14'But if you do not obey Me, and do not
observe all these commandments,

THE MESSAGE

the buy-back price is set according to the wages of a hired hand for that number of years. If many years remain before the Jubilee, he must pay back a larger share of his purchase price, but if only a few years remain until the Jubilee, he is to calculate his redemption price accordingly. He is to be treated as a man hired from year to year. You must make sure that his owner does not tyrannize him.

54-55 "If he is not redeemed in any of these ways, he goes free in the year of Jubilee, he and his children, because the People of Israel are my servants, my servants whom I brought out of Egypt. I am GOD, *your* God.

1 26 "Don't make idols for yourselves; don't set up an image or a sacred pillar for yourselves, and don't place a carved stone in your land that you can bow down to in worship. I am GOD, *your* God.

2 "Keep my Sabbaths; treat my Sanctuary with reverence. I am GOD.

"IF YOU LIVE BY MY DECREES . . ."

3-5 "If you live by my decrees and obediently keep my commandments, I will send the rains in their seasons, the ground will yield its crops and the trees of the field their fruit. You will thresh until the grape harvest and the grape harvest will continue until planting time; you'll have more than enough to eat and will live safe and secure in your land.

6-10 "I'll make the country a place of peace—you'll be able to go to sleep at night without fear; I'll get rid of the wild beasts; I'll eliminate war. You'll chase out your enemies and defeat them: Five of you will chase a hundred, and a hundred of you will chase ten thousand and do away with them. I'll give you my full attention: I'll make sure you prosper, make sure you grow in numbers, and keep my covenant with you in good working order. You'll still be eating from last year's harvest when you have to clean out the barns to make room for the new crops.

11-13 "I'll set up my residence in your neighborhood; I won't avoid or shun you; I'll stroll through your streets. I'll be your God; you'll be my people. I am GOD, your personal God who rescued you from Egypt so that you would no longer be slaves to the Egyptians. I ripped off the harness of your slavery so that you can move about freely.

"BUT IF YOU REFUSE TO OBEY ME . . ."

14-17 "But if you refuse to obey me and won't observe my commandments, despising my de-

New King James Version

15and if you despise My statutes, or if your
soul abhors My judgments, so that you
do not perform all My commandments,
but break My covenant,
16I also will do this to you:
I will even appoint terror over you, wasting
disease and fever which shall consume
the eyes and cause sorrow of heart.
And you shall sow your seed in vain, for
your enemies shall eat it.
17I will set My face against you, and you shall
be defeated by your enemies.
Those who hate you shall reign over you,
and you shall flee when no one pursues
you.

18'And after all this, if you do not obey Me,
then I will punish you seven times more
for your sins.
19I will break the pride of your power;
I will make your heavens like iron and your
earth like bronze.
20And your strength shall be spent in vain;
for your land shall not yield its produce, nor
shall the trees of the land yield their
fruit.
21'Then, if you walk contrary to Me, and are
not willing to obey Me, I will bring on
you seven times more plagues, according
to your sins.
22I will also send wild beasts among you,
which shall rob you of your children,
destroy your livestock, and make you
few in number;
and your highways shall be desolate.

23'And if by these things you are not reformed
by Me, but walk contrary to Me,
24then I also will walk contrary to you, and I
will punish you yet seven times for your
sins.
25And I will bring a sword against you that
will execute the vengeance of the
covenant;
when you are gathered together within your
cities I will send pestilence among you;
and you shall be delivered into the hand of
the enemy.
26When I have cut off your supply of bread,
ten women shall bake your bread in one
oven, and they shall bring back your
bread by weight, and you shall eat and
not be satisfied.

27'And after all this, if you do not obey Me, but
walk contrary to Me,
28then I also will walk contrary to you in fury;
and I, even I, will chastise you seven times
for your sins.
29You shall eat the flesh of your sons, and you
shall eat the flesh of your daughters.
30I will destroy your high places, cut down
your incense altars, and cast your
carcasses on the lifeless forms of your
idols;
and My soul shall abhor you.
31I will lay your cities waste and bring your
sanctuaries to desolation, and I will not
smell the fragrance of your sweet
aromas.

The Message

crees and holding my laws in contempt by
your disobedience, making a shambles of
my covenant, I'll step in and pour on the
trouble: debilitating disease, high fevers,
blindness, your life leaking out bit by bit.
You'll plant seed but your enemies will eat
the crops. I'll turn my back on you and stand
by while your enemies defeat you. People
who hate you will govern you. You'll run
scared even when there's no one chasing
you.

18-20 "And if none of this works in getting your
attention, I'll discipline you seven times over
for your sins. I'll break your strong pride: I'll
make the skies above you like a sheet of tin
and the ground under you like cast iron. No
matter how hard you work, nothing will
come of it: No crops out of the ground, no
fruit off the trees.

21-22 "If you defy me and refuse to listen, your
punishment will be seven times more than
your sins: I'll set wild animals on you; they'll
rob you of your children, kill your cattle,
and decimate your numbers until you'll
think you are living in a ghost town.

23-26 "And if even this doesn't work and you
refuse my discipline and continue your defi-
ance, then it will be my turn to defy you. I,
yes I, will punish you for your sins seven
times over: I'll let war loose on you, aveng-
ing your breaking of the covenant; when
you huddle in your cities for protection, I'll
send a deadly epidemic on you and you'll be
helpless before your enemies; when I cut off
your bread supply, ten women will bake
bread in one oven and ration it out. You'll
eat, but barely—no one will get enough.

27-35 "And if this—*even this!*—doesn't work
and you still won't listen, still defy me, I'll
have had enough and in hot anger will defy
you, punishing you for your sins seven times
over: famine will be so severe that you'll end
up cooking and eating your sons in stews
and your daughters in barbecues; I'll smash
your sex-and-religion shrines and all the
paraphernalia that goes with them, and then
stack your corpses and the idol-corpses in
the same piles—I'll abhor you; I'll turn your
cities into rubble; I'll clean out your sanctu-
aries; I'll hold my nose at the "pleasing
aroma" of your sacrifices. I'll turn your land

NEW KING JAMES VERSION

32I will bring the land to desolation, and your
enemies who dwell in it shall be
astonished at it.
33I will scatter you among the nations and
draw out a sword after you;
your land shall be desolate and your cities
waste.
34Then the land shall enjoy its sabbaths as
long as it lies desolate and you *are* in
your enemies' land;
then the land shall rest and enjoy its
sabbaths.
35As long as *it* lies desolate it shall rest—
for the time it did not rest on your sabbaths
when you dwelt in it.

36'And as for those of you who are left, I will
send faintness into their hearts in the
lands of their enemies;
the sound of a shaken leaf shall cause them
to flee;
they shall flee as though fleeing from a
sword, and they shall fall when no one
pursues.
37They shall stumble over one another, as it
were before a sword, when no one
pursues;
and you shall have no *power* to stand before
your enemies.
38You shall perish among the nations, and the
land of your enemies shall eat you up.
39And those of you who are left shall waste
away in their iniquity in your enemies'
lands;
also in their fathers' iniquities, which are
with them, they shall waste away.

40'*But* if they confess their iniquity and the
iniquity of their fathers, with their
unfaithfulness in which they were
unfaithful to Me, and that they also have
walked contrary to Me,
41and *that* I also have walked contrary to
them and have brought them into the
land of their enemies;
if their uncircumcised hearts are humbled,
and they accept their guilt—
42then I will remember My covenant with
Jacob, and My covenant with Isaac and
My covenant with Abraham I will
remember;
I will remember the land.
43The land also shall be left empty by them,
and will enjoy its sabbaths while it lies
desolate without them;
they will accept their guilt, because they
despised My judgments and because
their soul abhorred My statutes.
44Yet for all that, when they are in the land of
their enemies, I will not cast them away,
nor shall I abhor them, to utterly destroy
them and break My covenant with them;
for I *am* the LORD their God.
45But for their sake I will remember the
covenant of their ancestors, whom I
brought out of the land of Egypt in the
sight of the nations, that I might be their
God:
I *am* the LORD.' "

THE MESSAGE

into a lifeless moonscape—your enemies who come in to take over will be shocked at what they see. I'll scatter you all over the world and keep after you with the point of my sword in your backs. There'll be nothing left in your land, nothing going on in your cities. With you gone and dispersed in the countries of your enemies, the land, empty of you, will finally get a break and enjoy its Sabbath years. All the time it's left there empty, the land will get rest, the Sabbaths it never got when you lived there.

36-39 "As for those among you still alive, I'll give them over to fearful timidity—even the rustle of a leaf will throw them into a panic. They'll run here and there, back and forth, as if running for their lives even though no one is after them, tripping and falling over one another in total confusion. You won't stand a chance against an enemy. You'll perish among the nations; the land of your enemies will eat you up. Any who are left will slowly rot away in the enemy lands. Rot. And all because of their sins, their sins compounded by their ancestors' sins.

"ON THE OTHER HAND, IF THEY CONFESS . . . "

40-42 "On the other hand, if they confess their sins and the sins of their ancestors, their treacherous betrayal, the defiance that set off my defiance that sent them off into enemy lands; if by some chance they soften their hard hearts and make amends for their sin, I'll remember my covenant with Jacob, I'll remember my covenant with Isaac, and, yes, I'll remember my covenant with Abraham. And I'll remember the land.

43-45 "The land will be empty of them and enjoy its Sabbaths while they're gone. They'll pay for their sins because they refused my laws and treated my decrees with contempt. But in spite of their behavior, while they are among their enemies I won't reject or abhor or destroy them completely. I won't break my covenant with them: I am GOD, their God. For their sake I will remember the covenant with their ancestors whom I, with all the nations watching, brought out of Egypt in order to be their God. I am GOD."

New King James Version

46These *are* the statutes and judgments and laws which the LORD made between Himself and the children of Israel on Mount Sinai by the hand of Moses.

Redeeming Persons and Property Dedicated to God

27 Now the LORD spoke to Moses, saying, 2"Speak to the children of Israel, and say to them: 'When a man consecrates by a vow certain persons to the LORD, according to your valuation, 3if your valuation is of a male from twenty years old up to sixty years old, then your valuation shall be fifty shekels of silver, according to the shekel of the sanctuary. 4If it *is* a female, then your valuation shall be thirty shekels; 5and if from five years old up to twenty years old, then your valuation for a male shall be twenty shekels, and for a female ten shekels; 6and if from a month old up to five years old, then your valuation for a male shall be five shekels of silver, and for a female your valuation shall be three shekels of silver; 7and if from sixty years old and above, if *it is* a male, then your valuation shall be fifteen shekels, and for a female ten shekels.

8'But if he is too poor to pay your valuation, then he shall present himself before the priest, and the priest shall set a value for him; according to the ability of him who vowed, the priest shall value him.

9'If *it is* an animal that men may bring as an offering to the LORD, all that *anyone* gives to the LORD shall be holy. 10He shall not substitute it or exchange it, good for bad or bad for good; and if he at all exchanges animal for animal, then both it and the one exchanged for it shall be holy. 11If *it is* an unclean animal which they do not offer as a sacrifice to the LORD, then he shall present the animal before the priest; 12and the priest shall set a value for it, whether it is good or bad; as you, the priest, value it, so it shall be. 13But if he *wants* at all *to* redeem it, then he must add one-fifth to your valuation.

14'And when a man dedicates his house *to be* holy to the LORD, then the priest shall set a value for it, whether it is good or bad; as the priest values it, so it shall stand. 15If he who dedicated it *wants to* redeem his house, then he must add one-fifth of the money of your valuation to it, and it shall be his.

16'If a man dedicates to the LORD *part* of a field of his possession, then your valuation shall be according to the seed for it. A homer of barley seed *shall be valued* at fifty shekels of silver. 17If he dedicates his field from the Year of Jubilee, according to your valuation it shall stand. 18But if he dedicates his field after the Jubilee, then the priest shall reckon to him the money due according to the years that remain till the Year of Jubilee, and it shall be deducted from your valuation. 19And if he who dedicates the field ever wishes to redeem it, then he must add one-fifth of the money of your valuation to it, and it shall belong to him. 20But if he does not want to redeem the field, or if he has sold the field to another man, it shall not be redeemed anymore; 21but the field, when it is released in the Jubilee, shall be holy to the LORD, as a devoted field; it shall be the possession of the priest.

The Message

46 These are the decrees, laws, and instructions that GOD established between himself and the People of Israel through Moses at Mount Sinai.

Vows, Dedications, and Redemptions

1-8 27 GOD spoke to Moses: He said, "Speak to the People of Israel. Tell them, If anyone wants to vow the value of a person to the service of GOD, set the value of a man between the ages of twenty and sixty at fifty shekels of silver, according to the Sanctuary shekel. For a woman the valuation is thirty shekels. If the person is between the ages of five and twenty, set the value at twenty shekels for a male and ten shekels for a female. If the person is between one month and five years, set the value at five shekels of silver for a boy and three shekels of silver for a girl. If the person is over sixty, set the value at fifteen shekels for a man and ten shekels for a woman. If anyone is too poor to pay the stated amount, he is to present the person to the priest, who will then set the value for him according to what the person making the vow can afford.

9-13 "If he vowed an animal that is acceptable as an offering to GOD, the animal is given to GOD and becomes the property of the Sanctuary. He must not exchange or substitute a good one for a bad one, or a bad one for a good one; if he should dishonestly substitute one animal for another, both the original and the substitute become property of the Sanctuary. If what he vowed is a ritually unclean animal, one that is not acceptable as an offering to GOD, the animal must be shown to the priest, who will set its value, either high or low. Whatever the priest sets will be its value. If the owner changes his mind and wants to redeem it, he must add twenty percent to its value.

14-15 "If a man dedicates his house to GOD, into the possession of the Sanctuary, the priest assesses its value, setting it either high or low. Whatever value the priest sets, that's what it is. If the man wants to buy it back, he must add twenty percent to its price and then it's his again.

16-21 "If a man dedicates to GOD part of his family land, its value is to be set according to the amount of seed that is needed for it at the rate of fifty shekels of silver to six bushels of barley seed. If he dedicates his field during the year of Jubilee, the set value stays. But if he dedicates it after the Jubilee, the priest will compute the value according to the years left until the next Jubilee, reducing the value proportionately. If the one dedicating it wants to buy it back, he must add twenty percent to its valuation, and then it's his again. But if he doesn't redeem it or sells the field to someone else, it can never be bought back. When the field is released in the Jubilee, it becomes holy to GOD, the possession of the Sanctuary, GOD's field. It goes into the hands of the priests.

New King James Version

[22]'And if a man dedicates to the LORD a field
which he has bought, which is not the field of
his possession, [23]then the priest shall reckon to
him the worth of your valuation, up to the Year
of Jubilee, and he shall give your valuation on
that day *as* a holy *offering* to the LORD. [24]In the
Year of Jubilee the field shall return to him from
whom it was bought, to the one who *owned* the
land as a possession. [25]And all your valuations
shall be according to the shekel of the sanctu-
ary: twenty gerahs to the shekel.

[26]'But the firstborn of the animals, which
should be the LORD's firstborn, no man shall
dedicate; whether *it is* an ox or sheep, it *is* the
LORD's. [27]And if *it is* an unclean animal, then he
shall redeem *it* according to your valuation, and
shall add one-fifth to it; or if it is not redeemed,
then it shall be sold according to your valuation.

[28]'Nevertheless no devoted *offering* that a
man may devote to the LORD of all that he has,
both man and beast, or the field of his posses-
sion, shall be sold or redeemed; every devoted
offering is most holy to the LORD. [29]No person
under the ban, who may become doomed to de-
struction among men, shall be redeemed, *but*
shall surely be put to death. [30]And all the tithe of
the land, *whether* of the seed of the land *or* of
the fruit of the tree, *is* the LORD's. It *is* holy to the
LORD. [31]If a man wants at all to redeem *any* of
his tithes, he shall add one-fifth to it. [32]And con-
cerning the tithe of the herd or the flock, of
whatever passes under the rod, the tenth one
shall be holy to the LORD. [33]He shall not inquire
whether it is good or bad, nor shall he exchange
it; and if he exchanges it at all, then both it and
the one exchanged for it shall be holy; it shall
not be redeemed.' "

[34]These *are* the commandments which the
LORD commanded Moses for the children of Is-
rael on Mount Sinai.

The Message

22-25 "If a man dedicates to GOD a field he has bought, a field which is not part of the family land, the priest will compute its proportionate value in relation to the next year of Jubilee. The man must pay its value on the spot as something that is now holy to GOD, belonging to the Sanctuary. In the year of Jubilee it goes back to its original owner, the man from whom he bought it. The valuations will be reckoned by the Sanctuary shekel, at twenty gerahs to the shekel.

26-27 "No one is allowed to dedicate the firstborn of an animal; the firstborn, as firstborn, already belongs to GOD. No matter if it's cattle or sheep, it already belongs to GOD. If it's one of the ritually unclean animals, he can buy it back at its assessed value by adding twenty percent to it. If he doesn't redeem it, it is to be sold at its assessed value.

28 "But nothing that a man irrevocably devotes to GOD from what belongs to him, whether human or animal or family land, may be either sold or bought back. Everything devoted is holy to the highest degree; it's GOD's inalienable property.

29 "No human who has been devoted to destruction can be redeemed. He must be put to death.

30-33 "A tenth of the land's produce, whether grain from the ground or fruit from the trees, is GOD's. It is holy to GOD. If a man buys back any of the tenth he has given, he must add twenty percent to it. A tenth of the entire herd and flock, every tenth animal that passes under the shepherd's rod, is holy to GOD. He is not permitted to pick out the good from the bad or make a substitution. If he dishonestly makes a substitution, both animals, the original and the substitute, become the possession of the Sanctuary and cannot be redeemed."

34 These are the commandments that GOD gave to Moses on Mount Sinai for the People of Israel.

NUMBERS

New King James Version

The First Census of Israel

1 Now the LORD spoke to Moses in the Wilderness of Sinai, in the tabernacle of meeting, on the first *day* of the second month, in the second year after they had come out of the land of Egypt, saying: 2“Take a census of all the congregation of the children of Israel, by their families, by their fathers’ houses, according to the number of names, every male individually, 3from twenty years old and above—all who *are able to* go to war in Israel. You and Aaron shall number them by their armies. 4And with you there shall be a man from every tribe, each one the head of his father’s house.

5“These are the names of the men who shall stand with you: from Reuben, Elizur the son of Shedeur; 6from Simeon, Shelumiel the son of Zurishaddai; 7from Judah, Nahshon the son of Amminadab; 8from Issachar, Nethanel the son of Zuar; 9from Zebulun, Eliab the son of Helon; 10from the sons of Joseph: from Ephraim, Elishama the son of Ammihud; from Manasseh, Gamaliel the son of Pedahzur; 11from Benjamin, Abidan the son of Gideoni; 12from Dan, Ahiezer the son of Ammishaddai; 13from Asher, Pagiel the son of Ocran; 14from Gad, Eliasaph the son of Deuel;[a] 15from Naphtali, Ahira the son of Enan.” 16These *were* chosen from the congregation, leaders of their fathers’ tribes, heads of the divisions in Israel.

17Then Moses and Aaron took these men who had been mentioned by name, 18and they assembled all the congregation together on the first *day* of the second month; and they recited their ancestry by families, by their fathers’ houses, according to the number of names, from twenty years old and above, each one individually. 19As the LORD commanded Moses, so he numbered them in the Wilderness of Sinai.

20Now the children of Reuben, Israel’s oldest son, their genealogies by their families, by their fathers’ house, according to the number of names, every male individually, from twenty years old and above, all who *were able to* go to war: 21those who were numbered of the tribe of Reuben *were* forty-six thousand five hundred.

22From the children of Simeon, their genealogies by their families, by their fathers’ house, of those who were numbered, according to the number of names, every male individually, from twenty years old and above, all who *were able to* go to war: 23those who were numbered of the tribe of Simeon *were* fifty-nine thousand three hundred.

24From the children of Gad, their genealogies by their families, by their fathers’ house, according to the number of names, from twenty years old and above, all who *were able to* go to war: 25those who were numbered of the tribe of Gad *were* forty-five thousand six hundred and fifty.

26From the children of Judah, their genealogies by their families, by their fathers’ house, according to the number of names, from twenty

1:14 [a]Spelled *Reuel* in 2:14

The Message

Census in the Wilderness of Sinai

1-5 1 God spoke to Moses in the Wilderness of Sinai at the Tent of Meeting on the first day of the second month in the second year after they had left Egypt. He said, “Number the congregation of the People of Israel by clans and families, writing down the names of every male. You and Aaron are to register, company by company, every man who is twenty years and older who is able to fight in the army. Pick one man from each tribe who is head of his family to help you. These are the names of the men who will help you:

from Reuben: Elizur son of Shedeur
6 from Simeon: Shelumiel son of Zurishaddai
7 from Judah: Nahshon son of Amminadab
8 from Issachar: Nethanel son of Zuar
9 from Zebulun: Eliab son of Helon
10 from the sons of Joseph,
from Ephraim: Elishama son of Ammihud
from Manasseh: Gamaliel son of Pedahzur
11 from Benjamin: Abidan son of Gideoni
12 from Dan: Ahiezer son of Ammishaddai
13 from Asher: Pagiel son of Ocran
14 from Gad: Eliasaph son of Deuel
15 from Naphtali: Ahira son of Enan.”

16 These were the men chosen from the congregation, leaders of their ancestral tribes, heads of Israel’s military divisions.

17-19 Moses and Aaron took these men who had been named to help and gathered the whole congregation together on the first day of the second month. The people registered themselves in their tribes according to their ancestral families, putting down the names of those who were twenty years old and older, just as GOD commanded Moses. He numbered them in the Wilderness of Sinai.

20-21 The line of Reuben, Israel’s firstborn: The men were counted off head by head, every male twenty years and older who was able to fight in the army, registered by tribes according to their ancestral families. The tribe of Reuben numbered 46,500.

22-23 The line of Simeon: The men were counted off head by head, every male twenty years and older who was able to fight in the army, registered by clans and families. The tribe of Simeon numbered 59,300.

24-25 The line of Gad: The men were counted off head by head, every male twenty years and older who was able to fight in the army, registered by clans and families. The tribe of Gad numbered 45,650.

26-27 The line of Judah: The men were counted off head by head, every male twenty years

New King James Version

years old and above, all who *were able to* go to war: [27]those who were numbered of the tribe of Judah *were* seventy-four thousand six hundred.

[28]From the children of Issachar, their genealogies by their families, by their fathers' house, according to the number of names, from twenty years old and above, all who *were able to* go to war: [29]those who were numbered of the tribe of Issachar *were* fifty-four thousand four hundred.

[30]From the children of Zebulun, their genealogies by their families, by their fathers' house, according to the number of names, from twenty years old and above, all who *were able to* go to war: [31]those who were numbered of the tribe of Zebulun *were* fifty-seven thousand four hundred.

[32]From the sons of Joseph, the children of Ephraim, their genealogies by their families, by their fathers' house, according to the number of names, from twenty years old and above, all who *were able to* go to war: [33]those who were numbered of the tribe of Ephraim *were* forty thousand five hundred.

[34]From the children of Manasseh, their genealogies by their families, by their fathers' house, according to the number of names, from twenty years old and above, all who *were able to* go to war: [35]those who were numbered of the tribe of Manasseh *were* thirty-two thousand two hundred.

[36]From the children of Benjamin, their genealogies by their families, by their fathers' house, according to the number of names, from twenty years old and above, all who *were able to* go to war: [37]those who were numbered of the tribe of Benjamin *were* thirty-five thousand four hundred.

[38]From the children of Dan, their genealogies by their families, by their fathers' house, according to the number of names, from twenty years old and above, all who *were able to* go to war: [39]those who were numbered of the tribe of Dan *were* sixty-two thousand seven hundred.

[40]From the children of Asher, their genealogies by their families, by their fathers' house, according to the number of names, from twenty years old and above, all who *were able to* go to war: [41]those who were numbered of the tribe of Asher *were* forty-one thousand five hundred.

[42]From the children of Naphtali, their genealogies by their families, by their fathers' house, according to the number of names, from twenty years old and above, all who *were able to* go to war: [43]those who were numbered of the tribe of Naphtali *were* fifty-three thousand four hundred.

[44]These are the ones who were numbered, whom Moses and Aaron numbered, with the leaders of Israel, twelve men, each one representing his father's house. [45]So all who were numbered of the children of Israel, by their fathers' houses, from twenty years old and above, all who *were able to* go to war in Israel— [46]all who were numbered were six hundred and three thousand five hundred and fifty.

[47]But the Levites were not numbered among them by their fathers' tribe; [48]for the LORD had spoken to Moses, saying: [49]"Only the tribe of

The Message

and older who was able to fight in the army, registered by clans and families. The tribe of Judah numbered 74,600.

28-29 The line of Issachar: The men were counted off head by head, every male twenty years and older who was able to fight in the army, registered by clans and families. The tribe of Issachar numbered 54,400.

30-31 The line of Zebulun: The men were counted off head by head, every male twenty years and older who was able to fight in the army, registered by clans and families. The tribe of Zebulun numbered 57,400.

32-33 The line of Joseph: From son Ephraim the men were counted off head by head, every male twenty years and older who was able to fight in the army, registered by clans and families. The tribe of Ephraim numbered 40,500.

34-35 And from son Manasseh the men were counted off head by head, every male twenty years and older who was able to fight in the army, registered by clans and families. The tribe of Manasseh numbered 32,200.

36-37 The line of Benjamin: The men were counted off head by head, every male twenty years and older who was able to fight in the army, registered by clans and families. The tribe of Benjamin numbered 35,400.

38-39 The line of Dan: The men were counted off head by head, every male twenty years and older who was able to fight in the army, registered by clans and families. The tribe of Dan numbered 62,700.

40-41 The line of Asher: The men were counted off head by head, every male twenty years and older who was able to fight in the army, registered by clans and families. The tribe of Asher numbered 41,500.

42-43 The line of Naphtali: The men were counted off head by head, every male twenty years and older who was able to fight in the army, registered by clans and families. The tribe of Naphtali numbered 53,400.

44-46 These are the numbers of those registered by Moses and Aaron, registered with the help of the leaders of Israel, twelve men, each representing his ancestral family. The sum total of the People of Israel twenty years old and over who were able to fight in the army, counted by ancestral family, was 603,550.

47-51 The Levites, however, were not counted by their ancestral family along with the others. GOD had told Moses, "The tribe of Levi

NEW KING JAMES VERSION

Levi you shall not number, nor take a census of
them among the children of Israel; 50but you
shall appoint the Levites over the tabernacle of
the Testimony, over all its furnishings, and over
all things that belong to it; they shall carry the
tabernacle and all its furnishings; they shall at-
tend to it and camp around the tabernacle. 51And
when the tabernacle is to go forward, the Levites
shall take it down; and when the tabernacle is to
be set up, the Levites shall set it up. The outsider
who comes near shall be put to death. 52The chil-
dren of Israel shall pitch their tents, everyone by
his own camp, everyone by his own standard, ac-
cording to their armies; 53but the Levites shall
camp around the tabernacle of the Testimony,
that there may be no wrath on the congregation
of the children of Israel; and the Levites shall
keep charge of the tabernacle of the Testimony."
54Thus the children of Israel did; according
to all that the LORD commanded Moses, so they
did.

THE TRIBES AND LEADERS BY ARMIES

2 And the LORD spoke to Moses and Aaron,
saying: 2"Everyone of the children of Israel
shall camp by his own standard, beside the em-
blems of his father's house; they shall camp
some distance from the tabernacle of meeting.
3On the east side, toward the rising of the sun,
those of the standard of the forces with Judah
shall camp according to their armies; and
Nahshon the son of Amminadab *shall be* the
leader of the children of Judah." 4And his army
was numbered at seventy-four thousand six
hundred.
5"Those who camp next to him *shall be* the
tribe of Issachar, and Nethanel the son of Zuar
shall be the leader of the children of Issachar."
6And his army was numbered at fifty-four thou-
sand four hundred.
7"Then *comes* the tribe of Zebulun, and Eliab
the son of Helon *shall be* the leader of the chil-
dren of Zebulun." 8And his army was numbered
at fifty-seven thousand four hundred. 9"All who
were numbered according to their armies of the
forces with Judah, one hundred and eighty-six
thousand four hundred—these shall break camp
first.
10"On the south side *shall be* the standard of
the forces with Reuben according to their armies,
and the leader of the children of Reuben *shall be*
Elizur the son of Shedeur." 11And his army was
numbered at forty-six thousand five hundred.
12"Those who camp next to him *shall be* the
tribe of Simeon, and the leader of the children
of Simeon *shall be* Shelumiel the son of Zuri-
shaddai." 13And his army was numbered at fifty-
nine thousand three hundred.
14"Then *comes* the tribe of Gad, and the
leader of the children of Gad *shall be* Eliasaph
the son of Reuel."[a] 15And his army was num-
bered at forty-five thousand six hundred and
fifty. 16"All who were numbered according to
their armies of the forces with Reuben, one hun-
dred and fifty-one thousand four hundred and
fifty—they shall be the second to break camp.

2:14 [a]Spelled *Deuel* in 1:14 and 7:42

THE MESSAGE

is an exception: Don't register them. Don't count the tribe of Levi; don't include them in the general census of the People of Israel. Instead, appoint the Levites to be in charge of The Dwelling of The Testimony—over all its furnishings and everything connected with it. Their job is to carry The Dwelling and all its furnishings, maintain it, and camp around it. When it's time to move The Dwelling, the Levites will take it down, and when it's time to set it up, the Levites will do it. Anyone else who even goes near it will be put to death.

52-53 "The rest of the People of Israel will set up their tents in companies, every man in his own camp under its own flag. But the Levites will set up camp around The Dwelling of The Testimony so that wrath will not fall on the community of Israel. The Levites are responsible for the security of The Dwelling of The Testimony."

54 The People of Israel did everything that GOD commanded Moses. They did it all.

MARCHING ORDERS

1-2 2 GOD spoke to Moses and Aaron. He said, "The People of Israel are to set up camp circling the Tent of Meeting and facing it. Each company is to camp under its distinctive tribal flag."

3-4 To the east toward the sunrise are the companies of the camp of Judah under its flag, led by Nahshon son of Amminadab. His troops number 74,600.

5-6 The tribe of Issachar will camp next to them, led by Nethanel son of Zuar. His troops number 54,400.

7-8 And the tribe of Zebulun is next to them, led by Eliab son of Helon. His troops number 57,400.

9 The total number of men assigned to Judah, troop by troop, is 186,400. They will lead the march.

10-11 To the south are the companies of the camp of Reuben under its flag, led by Elizur son of Shedeur. His troops number 46,500.

12-13 The tribe of Simeon will camp next to them, led by Shelumiel son of Zurishaddai. His troops number 59,300.

14-15 And the tribe of Gad is next to them, led by Eliasaph son of Deuel. His troops number 45,650.

16 The total number of men assigned to Reuben, troop by troop, is 151,450. They are second in the order of the march.

New King James Version

17“And the tabernacle of meeting shall move
out with the camp of the Levites in the middle of
the camps; as they camp, so they shall move out,
everyone in his place, by their standards.
18“On the west side *shall be* the standard of
the forces with Ephraim according to their
armies, and the leader of the children of
Ephraim *shall be* Elishama the son of Ammi-
hud.” 19And his army was numbered at forty
thousand five hundred.
20“Next to him *comes* the tribe of Manasseh,
and the leader of the children of Manasseh *shall*
be Gamaliel the son of Pedahzur.” 21And his
army was numbered at thirty-two thousand two
hundred.
22“Then *comes* the tribe of Benjamin, and the
leader of the children of Benjamin *shall be*
Abidan the son of Gideoni.” 23And his army was
numbered at thirty-five thousand four hundred.
24“All who were numbered according to their
armies of the forces with Ephraim, one hundred
and eight thousand one hundred—they shall be
the third to break camp.
25“The standard of the forces with Dan *shall*
be on the north side according to their armies,
and the leader of the children of Dan *shall be*
Ahiezer the son of Ammishaddai.” 26And his
army was numbered at sixty-two thousand
seven hundred.
27“Those who camp next to him *shall be* the
tribe of Asher, and the leader of the children of
Asher *shall be* Pagiel the son of Ocran.” 28And
his army was numbered at forty-one thousand
five hundred.
29“Then *comes* the tribe of Naphtali, and the
leader of the children of Naphtali *shall be* Ahira
the son of Enan.” 30And his army was numbered
at fifty-three thousand four hundred. 31“All who
were numbered of the forces with Dan, one hun-
dred and fifty-seven thousand six hundred—
they shall break camp last, with their stan-
dards.”
32These *are* the ones who were numbered of
the children of Israel by their fathers’ houses.
All who were numbered according to their
armies of the forces *were* six hundred and three
thousand five hundred and fifty. 33But the
Levites were not numbered among the children
of Israel, just as the LORD commanded Moses.
34Thus the children of Israel did according to
all that the LORD commanded Moses; so they
camped by their standards and so they broke
camp, each one by his family, according to their
fathers’ houses.

The Sons of Aaron

3 Now these *are* the records of Aaron and
Moses when the LORD spoke with Moses on
Mount Sinai. 2And these *are* the names of the
sons of Aaron: Nadab, the firstborn, and Abihu,
Eleazar, and Ithamar. 3These *are* the names of
the sons of Aaron, the anointed priests, whom
he consecrated to minister as priests. 4Nadab
and Abihu had died before the LORD when they
offered profane fire before the LORD in the
Wilderness of Sinai; and they had no children.
So Eleazar and Ithamar ministered as priests in
the presence of Aaron their father.

The Message

17 The Tent of Meeting with the camp of the Levites takes its place in the middle of the march. Each tribe will march in the same order in which they camped, each under its own flag.

18-19 To the west are the companies of the camp of Ephraim under its flag, led by Elishama son of Ammihud. His troops number 40,500.

20-21 The tribe of Manasseh will set up camp next to them, led by Gamaliel son of Pedahzur. His troops number 32,200.

22-23 And next to him is the camp of Benjamin, led by Abidan son of Gideoni. His troops number 35,400.

24 The total number of men assigned to the camp of Ephraim, troop by troop, is 108,100. They are third in the order of the march.

25-26 To the north are the companies of the camp of Dan under its flag, led by Ahiezer son of Ammishaddai. His troops number 62,700.

27-28 The tribe of Asher will camp next to them, led by Pagiel son of Ocran. His troops number 41,500.

29-30 And next to them is the tribe of Naphtali, led by Ahira son of Enan. His troops number 53,400.

31 The total number of men assigned to the camp of Dan number 157,600. They will set out, under their flags, last in the line of the march.

32-33 These are the People of Israel, counted according to their ancestral families. The total number in the camps, counted troop by troop, comes to 603,550. Following GOD’s command to Moses, the Levites were not counted in with the rest of Israel.

34 The People of Israel did everything the way GOD commanded Moses: They camped under their respective flags; they marched by tribe with their ancestral families.

The Levites

1 3 This is the family tree of Aaron and Moses at the time GOD spoke with Moses on Mount Sinai.

2 The names of the sons of Aaron: Nadab the firstborn, Abihu, Eleazar, and Ithamar—anointed priests ordained to serve as priests. But Nadab and Abihu fell dead in the presence of GOD when they offered unauthorized sacrifice to him in the Wilderness of Sinai. They left no sons, and so only Eleazar and Ithamar served as priests during the lifetime of their father, Aaron.

New King James Version

The Levites Serve in the Tabernacle

[5]And the LORD spoke to Moses, saying: [6]"Bring the tribe of Levi near, and present them before Aaron the priest, that they may serve him. [7]And they shall attend to his needs and the needs of the whole congregation before the tabernacle of meeting, to do the work of the tabernacle. [8]Also they shall attend to all the furnishings of the tabernacle of meeting, and to the needs of the children of Israel, to do the work of the tabernacle. [9]And you shall give the Levites to Aaron and his sons; they *are* given entirely to him[a] from among the children of Israel. [10]So you shall appoint Aaron and his sons, and they shall attend to their priesthood; but the outsider who comes near shall be put to death."

[11]Then the LORD spoke to Moses, saying: [12]"Now behold, I Myself have taken the Levites from among the children of Israel instead of every firstborn who opens the womb among the children of Israel. Therefore the Levites shall be Mine, [13]because all the firstborn *are* Mine. On the day that I struck all the firstborn in the land of Egypt, I sanctified to Myself all the firstborn in Israel, both man and beast. They shall be Mine: I *am* the LORD."

Census of the Levites Commanded

[14]Then the LORD spoke to Moses in the Wilderness of Sinai, saying: [15]"Number the children of Levi by their fathers' houses, by their families; you shall number every male from a month old and above."

[16]So Moses numbered them according to the word of the LORD, as he was commanded. [17]These were the sons of Levi by their names: Gershon, Kohath, and Merari. [18]And these *are* the names of the sons of Gershon by their families: Libni and Shimei. [19]And the sons of Kohath by their families: Amram, Izehar, Hebron, and Uzziel. [20]And the sons of Merari by their families: Mahli and Mushi. These *are* the families of the Levites by their fathers' houses.

[21]From Gershon *came* the family of the Libnites and the family of the Shimites; these *were* the families of the Gershonites. [22]Those who were numbered, according to the number of all the males from a month old and above—of those who were numbered *there were* seven thousand five hundred. [23]The families of the Gershonites were to camp behind the tabernacle westward. [24]And the leader of the father's house of the Gershonites *was* Eliasaph the son of Lael. [25]The duties of the children of Gershon in the tabernacle of meeting *included* the tabernacle, the tent with its covering, the screen for the door of the tabernacle of meeting, [26]the screen for the door of the court, the hangings of the court which *are* around the tabernacle and the altar, and their cords, according to all the work relating to them.

[27]From Kohath *came* the family of the Amramites, the family of the Izharites, the family of the Hebronites, and the family of the Uzzielites; these *were* the families of the Kohathites. [28]According to the number of all the males, from a month old and above, *there were* eight thousand

3:9 [a]Samaritan Pentateuch and Septuagint read *Me*.

The Message

5-10 GOD spoke to Moses. He said, "Bring forward the tribe of Levi and present them to Aaron so they can help him. They shall work for him and the whole congregation at the Tent of Meeting by doing the work of The Dwelling. Their job is to be responsible for all the furnishings of The Dwelling, ministering to the affairs of The Dwelling as the People of Israel come to perform their duties. Turn the Levites over to Aaron and his sons; they are the ones assigned to work full time for him. Appoint Aaron and his sons to minister as priests; anyone else who tries to elbow his way in will be put to death."

11-13 GOD spoke to Moses: "I have taken the Levites from among the People of Israel as a stand-in for every Israelite mother's firstborn son. The Levites belong to me. All the firstborn are mine—when I killed all the firstborn in Egypt, I consecrated for my own use every firstborn in Israel, whether human or animal. They belong to me. I am GOD."

14-16 GOD spoke to Moses in the Wilderness of Sinai: "Count the Levites by their ancestral families and clans. Count every male a month old and older." Moses counted them just as he was instructed by the mouth of GOD.

17 These are the names of the sons of Levi: Gershon, Kohath, and Merari.

18 These are the names of the Gershonite clans: Libni and Shimei.

19 The sons of Kohath by clan: Amram, Izhar, Hebron, and Uzziel.

20 The sons of Merari by clan: Mahli and Mushi.

These are the clans of Levi, family by family.

21-26 Gershon was ancestor to the clans of the Libnites and Shimeites, known as the Gershonite clans. All the males who were one month and older numbered 7,500. The Gershonite clans camped on the west, behind The Dwelling, led by Eliasaph son of Lael. At the Tent of Meeting the Gershonites were in charge of maintaining The Dwelling and its tent, its coverings, the screen at the entrance to the Tent of Meeting, the hangings of the Courtyard, the screen at the entrance to the Courtyard that surrounded The Dwelling and Altar, and the cords—in short, everything having to do with these things.

27-32 Kohath was ancestor to the clans of the Amramites, Izharites, Hebronites, and Uzzielites. These were known as the Kohathite clans. All the males who were one month and older numbered 8,600. The Ko-

NEW KING JAMES VERSION

six[a] hundred keeping charge of the sanctuary.
29 The families of the children of Kohath were to
camp on the south side of the tabernacle. 30 And
the leader of the fathers' house of the families of
the Kohathites *was* Elizaphan the son of Uzziel.
31 Their duty *included* the ark, the table, the
lampstand, the altars, the utensils of the sanctu-
ary with which they ministered, the screen, and
all the work relating to them.
32 And Eleazar the son of Aaron the priest
was to be chief over the leaders of the Levites,
with oversight of those who kept charge of the
sanctuary.
33 From Merari *came* the family of the
Mahlites and the family of the Mushites; these
were the families of Merari. 34 And those who
were numbered, according to the number of all
the males from a month old and above, *were* six
thousand two hundred. 35 The leader of the fa-
thers' house of the families of Merari *was* Zuriel
the son of Abihail. These *were* to camp on the
north side of the tabernacle. 36 And the ap-
pointed duty of the children of Merari *included*
the boards of the tabernacle, its bars, its pillars,
its sockets, its utensils, all the work relating to
them, 37 and the pillars of the court all around,
with their sockets, their pegs, and their cords.
38 Moreover those who were to camp before
the tabernacle on the east, before the tabernacle
of meeting, *were* Moses, Aaron, and his sons,
keeping charge of the sanctuary, to meet the
needs of the children of Israel; but the outsider
who came near was to be put to death. 39 All who
were numbered of the Levites, whom Moses and
Aaron numbered at the commandment of the
LORD, by their families, all the males from a
month old and above, *were* twenty-two thousand.

LEVITES DEDICATED INSTEAD OF THE FIRSTBORN

40 Then the LORD said to Moses: "Number all
the firstborn males of the children of Israel from
a month old and above, and take the number of
their names. 41 And you shall take the Levites for
Me—I *am* the LORD—instead of all the firstborn
among the children of Israel, and the livestock of
the Levites instead of all the firstborn among the
livestock of the children of Israel." 42 So Moses
numbered all the firstborn among the children
of Israel, as the LORD commanded him. 43 And all
the firstborn males, according to the number of
names from a month old and above, of those
who were numbered of them, were twenty-two
thousand two hundred and seventy-three.
44 Then the LORD spoke to Moses, saying:
45 "Take the Levites instead of all the firstborn
among the children of Israel, and the livestock
of the Levites instead of their livestock. The
Levites shall be Mine: I *am* the LORD. 46 And for
the redemption of the two hundred and seventy-
three of the firstborn of the children of Israel,
who are more than the number of the Levites,
47 you shall take five shekels for each one indi-
vidually; you shall take *them* in the currency of
the shekel of the sanctuary, the shekel of twenty
gerahs. 48 And you shall give the money, with
which the excess number of them is redeemed,
to Aaron and his sons."

3:28 [a]Some manuscripts of the Septuagint read *three.*

THE MESSAGE

hathites were in charge of the Sanctuary.
The Kohathite clans camped on the south
side of The Dwelling, led by Elizaphan son
of Uzziel. They were in charge of caring for
the Chest, the Table, the Lampstand, the Al-
tars, the articles of the Sanctuary used in
worship, and the screen—everything having
to do with these things. Eleazar, the son of
Aaron the priest, supervised the leaders of
the Levites and those in charge of the Sanc-
tuary.

33-37 Merari was ancestor to the clans of the
Mahlites and the Mushites, known as the
Merarite clans. The males who were one
month and older numbered 6,200. They
were led by Zuriel son of Abihail and
camped on the north side of The Dwelling.
The Merarites were in charge of the frames
of The Dwelling, its crossbars, posts, bases,
and all its equipment—everything having to
do with these things, as well as the posts of
the surrounding Courtyard with their bases,
tent pegs, and cords.

38 Moses and Aaron and his sons camped to
the east of The Dwelling, toward the rising
sun, in front of the Tent of Meeting. They
were in charge of maintaining the Sanctu-
ary for the People of Israel and the rituals of
worship. Anyone else who tried to perform
these duties was to be put to death.

39 The sum total of Levites counted at GOD's
command by Moses and Aaron, clan by
clan, all the males one month and older,
numbered 22,000.

40-41 GOD spoke to Moses: "Count all the first-
born males of the People of Israel who are
one month and older. List their names. Then
set apart for me the Levites—remember, I
am GOD—in place of all the firstborn among
the People of Israel, also the livestock of the
Levites in place of their livestock. I am
GOD."

42-43 So, just as GOD commanded him, Moses
counted all the firstborn of the People of Is-
rael. The total of firstborn males one month
and older, listed by name, numbered 22,273.

44-48 Again GOD spoke to Moses. He said,
"Take the Levites in place of all the firstborn
of Israel and the livestock of the Levites in
place of their livestock. The Levites are
mine, I am GOD. Redeem the 273 firstborn
Israelites who exceed the number of Levites
by collecting five shekels for each one, us-
ing the Sanctuary shekel (the shekel weigh-
ing twenty gerahs). Give that money to
Aaron and his sons for the redemption of
the excess number of Israelites."

NEW KING JAMES VERSION

49So Moses took the redemption money from those who were over and above those who were redeemed by the Levites. 50From the firstborn of the children of Israel he took the money, one thousand three hundred and sixty-five *shekels*, according to the shekel of the sanctuary. 51And Moses gave their redemption money to Aaron and his sons, according to the word of the LORD, as the LORD commanded Moses.

DUTIES OF THE SONS OF KOHATH

4 Then the LORD spoke to Moses and Aaron, saying: 2"Take a census of the sons of Kohath from among the children of Levi, by their families, by their fathers' house, 3from thirty years old and above, even to fifty years old, all who enter the service to do the work in the tabernacle of meeting.

4"This *is* the service of the sons of Kohath in the tabernacle of meeting, *relating to* the most holy things: 5When the camp prepares to journey, Aaron and his sons shall come, and they shall take down the covering veil and cover the ark of the Testimony with it. 6Then they shall put on it a covering of badger skins, and spread over *that* a cloth entirely of blue; and they shall insert its poles.

7"On the table of showbread they shall spread a blue cloth, and put on it the dishes, the pans, the bowls, and the pitchers for pouring; and the showbread[a] shall be on it. 8They shall spread over them a scarlet cloth, and cover the same with a covering of badger skins; and they shall insert its poles. 9And they shall take a blue cloth and cover the lampstand of the light, with its lamps, its wick-trimmers, its trays, and all its oil vessels, with which they service it. 10Then they shall put it with all its utensils in a covering of badger skins, and put *it* on a carrying beam.

11"Over the golden altar they shall spread a blue cloth, and cover it with a covering of badger skins; and they shall insert its poles. 12Then they shall take all the utensils of service with which they minister in the sanctuary, put *them* in a blue cloth, cover them with a covering of badger skins, and put *them* on a carrying beam. 13Also they shall take away the ashes from the altar, and spread a purple cloth over it. 14They shall put on it all its implements with which they minister there—the firepans, the forks, the shovels, the basins, and all the utensils of the altar—and they shall spread on it a covering of badger skins, and insert its poles. 15And when Aaron and his sons have finished covering the sanctuary and all the furnishings of the sanctuary, when the camp is set to go, then the sons of Kohath shall come to carry *them;* but they shall not touch any holy thing, lest they die.

"These *are* the things in the tabernacle of meeting which the sons of Kohath are to carry.

16"The appointed duty of Eleazar the son of Aaron the priest *is* the oil for the light, the sweet incense, the daily grain offering, the anointing oil, the oversight of all the tabernacle, of all that *is* in it, with the sanctuary and its furnishings."

4:7 [a]Literally *the continual bread*

THE MESSAGE

49-51 So Moses collected the redemption money from those who exceeded the number redeemed by the Levites. From the 273 firstborn Israelites he collected silver weighing 1,365 shekels according to the Sanctuary shekel. Moses turned over the redemption money to Aaron and his sons, as he was commanded by the word of GOD.

DUTIES OF THE KOHATHITES

1-3 4 GOD spoke to Moses and Aaron. He said, "Number the Kohathite line of Levites by clan and family. Count all the men from thirty to fifty years of age, all who enter the ministry to work in the Tent of Meeting.

4 "This is the assigned work of the Kohathites in the Tent of Meeting: care of the most holy things.

5-6 "When the camp is ready to set out, Aaron and his sons are to go in and take down the covering curtain and cover the Chest of The Testimony with it. Then they are to cover this with a dolphin skin, spread a solid blue cloth on top, and insert the poles.

7-8 "Then they are to spread a blue cloth on the Table of the Presence and set the Table with plates, incense dishes, bowls, and jugs for drink offerings. The bread that is always there stays on the Table. They are to cover these with a scarlet cloth, and on top of that spread the dolphin skin, and insert the poles.

9-10 "They are to use a blue cloth to cover the light-giving Lampstand and the lamps, snuffers, trays, and the oil jars that go with it. Then they are to wrap it all in a covering of dolphin skin and place it on a carrying frame.

11 "They are to spread a blue cloth over the Gold Altar and cover it with dolphin skins and place it on a carrying frame.

12 "They are to take all the articles used in ministering in the Sanctuary, wrap them in a blue cloth, cover them with dolphin skins, and place them on a carrying frame.

13-14 "They are to remove the ashes from the Altar and spread a purple cloth over it. They are to place on it all the articles used in ministering at the Altar—firepans, forks, shovels, bowls; everything used at the Altar—place them on the Altar, cover it with the dolphin skins, and insert the poles.

15 "When Aaron and his sons have finished covering the holy furnishings and all the holy articles, and the camp is ready to set out, the Kohathites are to come and do the carrying. But they must not touch the holy things or they will die. The Kohathites are in charge of carrying all the things that are in the Tent of Meeting.

16 "Eleazar son of Aaron the priest, is to be in charge of the oil for the light, the fragrant incense, the regular Grain-Offering, and the anointing oil. He is to be in charge of the entire Dwelling and everything in it, including its holy furnishings and articles."

NEW KING JAMES VERSION

17 Then the LORD spoke to Moses and Aaron,
saying: 18 "Do not cut off the tribe of the families
of the Kohathites from among the Levites; 19 but
do this in regard to them, that they may live and
not die when they approach the most holy
things: Aaron and his sons shall go in and ap-
point each of them to his service and his task.
20 But they shall not go in to watch while the holy
things are being covered, lest they die."

DUTIES OF THE SONS OF GERSHON

21 Then the LORD spoke to Moses, saying:
22 "Also take a census of the sons of Gershon, by
their fathers' house, by their families. 23 From
thirty years old and above, even to fifty years
old, you shall number them, all who enter to
perform the service, to do the work in the taber-
nacle of meeting. 24 This *is* the service of the fam-
ilies of the Gershonites, in serving and carrying:
25 They shall carry the curtains of the tabernacle
and the tabernacle of meeting *with* its covering,
the covering of badger skins that *is* on it, the
screen for the door of the tabernacle of meeting,
26 the screen for the door of the gate of the court,
the hangings of the court which *are* around the
tabernacle and altar, and their cords, all the fur-
nishings for their service and all that is made
for these things: so shall they serve.
27 "Aaron and his sons shall assign all the
service of the sons of the Gershonites, all their
tasks and all their service. And you shall ap-
point to them all their tasks as their duty. 28 This
is the service of the families of the sons of Ger-
shon in the tabernacle of meeting. And their du-
ties *shall be* under the authority[a] of Ithamar the
son of Aaron the priest.

DUTIES OF THE SONS OF MERARI

29 "*As for* the sons of Merari, you shall num-
ber them by their families and by their fathers'
house. 30 From thirty years old and above, even to
fifty years old, you shall number them, everyone
who enters the service to do the work of the tab-
ernacle of meeting. 31 And this *is* what they must
carry as all their service for the tabernacle of
meeting: the boards of the tabernacle, its bars,
its pillars, its sockets, 32 and the pillars around
the court with their sockets, pegs, and cords,
with all their furnishings and all their service;
and you shall assign *to each man* by name the
items he must carry. 33 This *is* the service of the
families of the sons of Merari, as all their service
for the tabernacle of meeting, under the author-
ity[a] of Ithamar the son of Aaron the priest."

CENSUS OF THE LEVITES

34 And Moses, Aaron, and the leaders of the
congregation numbered the sons of the Ko-
hathites by their families and by their fathers'
house, 35 from thirty years old and above, even to
fifty years old, everyone who entered the service
for work in the tabernacle of meeting; 36 and
those who were numbered by their families
were two thousand seven hundred and fifty.
37 These *were* the ones who were numbered of
the families of the Kohathites, all who might

4:28 [a]Literally *hand* 4:33 [a]Literally *hand*

THE MESSAGE

17-20 GOD spoke to Moses and Aaron, "Don't
let the tribal families of the Kohathites be
destroyed from among the Levites. Protect
them so they will live and not die when they
come near the most holy things. To protect
them, Aaron and his sons are to precede
them into the Sanctuary and assign each
man his task and what he is to carry. But the
Kohathites themselves must not go in to
look at the holy things, not even a glance at
them, or they will die."

DUTIES OF THE GERSHONITES

21-23 GOD spoke to Moses: "Number the Gershon-
ites by tribes according to their ancestral
families. Count all the men from thirty to
fifty years of age who enter the ministry of
work in the Tent of Meeting.
24-28 "The Gershonites by family and clan will
serve by carrying heavy loads: the curtains
of the Sanctuary and the Tent of Meeting;
the covering of the Tent and the outer cover-
ing of dolphin skins; the screens for the en-
trance to the Tent; the cords; and all the
equipment used in its ministries. The Ger-
shonites have the job of doing the work con-
nected with these things. All their work of
lifting and carrying and moving is to be
done under the supervision of Aaron and
his sons. Assign them specifically what they
are to carry. This is the work of the Ger-
shonite clans at the Tent of Meeting.
Ithamar son of Aaron the priest is to super-
vise their work.

DUTIES OF THE MERARITES

29-30 "Number the Merarites by their ancestral
families. Count all the men from thirty to
fifty years of age who enter the ministry of
work at the Tent of Meeting.
31-33 "This is their assigned duty as they go to
work at the Tent of Meeting: to carry the
frames of The Dwelling, its crossbars, posts,
and bases, as well as the posts of the sur-
rounding Courtyard with their bases, tent
pegs, cords, and all the equipment related to
their use. Assign to each man exactly what
he is to carry. This is the ministry of the
Merarite clans as they work at the Tent of
Meeting under the supervision of Ithamar
son of Aaron the priest."

34-37 Moses, Aaron, and the leaders of the congre-
gation counted the Kohathites by clan and
family. All the men from thirty to fifty years
of age who came to serve in the work in the
Tent of Meeting, counted by clans, were
2,750. This was the total from the Kohathite
clans who served in the Tent of Meeting.

NEW KING JAMES VERSION

serve in the tabernacle of meeting, whom Moses and Aaron numbered according to the commandment of the LORD by the hand of Moses.

38And those who were numbered of the sons of Gershon, by their families and by their fathers' house, 39from thirty years old and above, even to fifty years old, everyone who entered the service for work in the tabernacle of meeting— 40those who were numbered by their families, by their fathers' house, were two thousand six hundred and thirty. 41These *are* the ones who were numbered of the families of the sons of Gershon, of all who might serve in the tabernacle of meeting, whom Moses and Aaron numbered according to the commandment of the LORD.

42Those of the families of the sons of Merari who were numbered, by their families, by their fathers' house, 43from thirty years old and above, even to fifty years old, everyone who entered the service for work in the tabernacle of meeting— 44those who were numbered by their families were three thousand two hundred. 45These *are* the ones who were numbered of the families of the sons of Merari, whom Moses and Aaron numbered according to the word of the LORD by the hand of Moses.

46All who were numbered of the Levites, whom Moses, Aaron, and the leaders of Israel numbered, by their families and by their fathers' houses, 47from thirty years old and above, even to fifty years old, everyone who came to do the work of service and the work of bearing burdens in the tabernacle of meeting— 48those who were numbered were eight thousand five hundred and eighty.

49According to the commandment of the LORD they were numbered by the hand of Moses, each according to his service and according to his task; thus were they numbered by him, as the LORD commanded Moses.

CEREMONIALLY UNCLEAN PERSONS ISOLATED

5 And the LORD spoke to Moses, saying: 2"Command the children of Israel that they put out of the camp every leper, everyone who has a discharge, and whoever becomes defiled by a corpse. 3You shall put out both male and female; you shall put them outside the camp, that they may not defile their camps in the midst of which I dwell." 4And the children of Israel did so, and put them outside the camp; as the LORD spoke to Moses, so the children of Israel did.

CONFESSION AND RESTITUTION

5Then the LORD spoke to Moses, saying, 6"Speak to the children of Israel: 'When a man or woman commits any sin that men commit in unfaithfulness against the LORD, and that person is guilty, 7then he shall confess the sin which he has committed. He shall make restitution for his trespass in full, plus one-fifth of it, and give *it* to the one he has wronged. 8But if the man has no relative to whom restitution may be made for the wrong, the restitution for the wrong *must go* to the LORD for the priest, in addition to the ram of the atonement with which atonement is made for him. 9Every offering of all the holy things of the children of Israel, which they bring to the

THE MESSAGE

Moses and Aaron counted them just as GOD had commanded through Moses.

38-41 The Gershonites were counted by clan and family. All the men from thirty to fifty years of age who came to serve in the work in the Tent of Meeting, counted by clan and family, were 2,630. This was the total from the Gershonite clans who served in the Tent of Meeting. Moses and Aaron counted them just as GOD had commanded.

42-45 The Merarites were counted by clan and family. All the men from thirty to fifty years of age who came to serve in the work in the Tent of Meeting, counted by clan, were 3,200. This was the total from the Merarite clans. Moses and Aaron counted them just as GOD had commanded through Moses.

46-49 So Moses and Aaron and the leaders of Israel counted all the Levites by clan and family. All the men from thirty to fifty years of age who came to do the work of serving and carrying the Tent of Meeting numbered 8,580. At GOD's command through Moses, each man was assigned his work and told what to carry.

And that's the story of their numbering, as GOD commanded Moses.

SOME CAMP RULES

1-3 5 GOD spoke to Moses: "Command the People of Israel to ban from the camp anyone who has an infectious skin disease, anyone who has a discharge, and anyone who is ritually unclean from contact with a dead body. Ban male and female alike; send them outside the camp so that they won't defile their camp, the place I live among them."

4 The People of Israel did this, banning them from the camp. They did exactly what GOD had commanded through Moses.

5-10 GOD spoke to Moses: "Tell the People of Israel, When a man or woman commits any sin, the person has broken trust with GOD, is guilty, and must confess the sin. Full compensation plus twenty percent must be made to whoever was wronged. If the wronged person has no close relative who can receive the compensation, the compensation belongs to GOD and must be given to the priest, along with the ram by which atonement is made. All the sacred offerings that the People of Israel bring to a priest be-

NEW KING JAMES VERSION

priest, shall be his. 10And every man's holy things shall be his; whatever any man gives the priest shall be his.' "

CONCERNING UNFAITHFUL WIVES

11And the LORD spoke to Moses, saying, 12"Speak to the children of Israel, and say to them: 'If any man's wife goes astray and behaves unfaithfully toward him, 13and a man lies with her carnally, and it is hidden from the eyes of her husband, and it is concealed that she has defiled herself, and *there was* no witness against her, nor was she caught— 14if the spirit of jealousy comes upon him and he becomes jealous of his wife, who has defiled herself; or if the spirit of jealousy comes upon him and he becomes jealous of his wife, although she has not defiled herself— 15then the man shall bring his wife to the priest. He shall bring the offering required for her, one-tenth of an ephah of barley meal; he shall pour no oil on it and put no frankincense on it, because it *is* a grain offering of jealousy, an offering for remembering, for bringing iniquity to remembrance.

16'And the priest shall bring her near, and set her before the LORD. 17The priest shall take holy water in an earthen vessel, and take some of the dust that is on the floor of the tabernacle and put *it* into the water. 18Then the priest shall stand the woman before the LORD, uncover the woman's head, and put the offering for remembering in her hands, which *is* the grain offering of jealousy. And the priest shall have in his hand the bitter water that brings a curse. 19And the priest shall put her under oath, and say to the woman, "If no man has lain with you, and if you have not gone astray to uncleanness *while* under your husband's *authority,* be free from this bitter water that brings a curse. 20But if you have gone astray *while* under your husband's *authority,* and if you have defiled yourself and some man other than your husband has lain with you"— 21then the priest shall put the woman under the oath of the curse, and he shall say to the woman—"the LORD make you a curse and an oath among your people, when the LORD makes your thigh rot and your belly swell; 22and may this water that causes the curse go into your stomach, and make *your* belly swell and *your* thigh rot."

'Then the woman shall say, "Amen, so be it."

23'Then the priest shall write these curses in a book, and he shall scrape *them* off into the bitter water. 24And he shall make the woman drink the bitter water that brings a curse, and the water that brings the curse shall enter her *to become* bitter. 25Then the priest shall take the grain offering of jealousy from the woman's hand, shall wave the offering before the LORD, and bring it to the altar; 26and the priest shall take a handful of the offering, as its memorial portion, burn *it* on the altar, and afterward make the woman drink the water. 27When he has made her drink the water, then it shall be, if she has defiled herself and behaved unfaithfully toward her husband, that the water that brings a curse will enter her *and become* bitter, and her belly will swell, her thigh will rot, and the woman will become a curse among her people.

THE MESSAGE

long to the priest. Each person's sacred offerings are his own, but what one gives to the priest stays with the priest."

11-15 GOD spoke to Moses: "Tell the People of Israel, Say a man's wife goes off and has an affair, is unfaithful to him by sleeping with another man, but her husband knows nothing about it even though she has defiled herself. And then, even though there was no witness and she wasn't caught in the act, feelings of jealousy come over the husband and he suspects that his wife is impure. Even if she is innocent and his jealousy and suspicions are groundless, he is to take his wife to the priest. He must also take an offering of two quarts of barley flour for her. He is to pour no oil on it or mix incense with it because it is a Grain-Offering for jealousy, a Grain-Offering for bringing the guilt out into the open.

16-22 "The priest then is to take her and have her stand in the presence of GOD. He is to take some holy water in a pottery jar and put some dust from the floor of The Dwelling in the water. After the priest has her stand in the presence of GOD he is to uncover her hair and place the exposure-offering in her hands, the Grain-Offering for jealousy, while he holds the bitter water that delivers a curse. Then the priest will put the woman under oath and say, 'If no man has slept with you and you have not had an adulterous affair and become impure while married to your husband, may this bitter water that delivers a curse not harm you. But if you have had an affair while married to your husband and have defiled yourself by sleeping with a man other than your husband'—here the priest puts the woman under this curse—'may GOD cause your people to curse and revile you when he makes your womb shrivel and your belly swell. Let this water that delivers a curse enter your body so that your belly swells and your womb shrivels.'

"Then the woman shall say, 'Amen. Amen.'

23-28 "The priest is to write these curses on a scroll and then wash the words off into the bitter water. He then is to give the woman the bitter water that delivers a curse. This water will enter her body and cause acute pain. The priest then is to take from her hands a handful of the Grain-Offering for jealousy, wave it before GOD, and bring it to the Altar. The priest then is to take a handful of the Grain-Offering, using it as an exposure-offering, and burn it on the Altar; after this he is to make her drink the water. If she has defiled herself in being unfaithful to her husband, when she drinks the water that delivers a curse, it will enter her body and cause acute pain; her belly will swell and her womb shrivel. She will be cursed among her people. But if she has not defiled

New King James Version

28But if the woman has not defiled herself, and is clean, then she shall be free and may conceive children.

29'This *is* the law of jealousy, when a wife, *while* under her husband's *authority,* goes astray and defiles herself, 30or when the spirit of jealousy comes upon a man, and he becomes jealous of his wife; then he shall stand the woman before the LORD, and the priest shall execute all this law upon her. 31Then the man shall be free from iniquity, but that woman shall bear her guilt.' "

The Law of the Nazirite

6 Then the LORD spoke to Moses, saying, 2"Speak to the children of Israel, and say to them: 'When either a man or woman consecrates an offering to take the vow of a Nazirite, to separate himself to the LORD, 3he shall separate himself from wine and *similar* drink; he shall drink neither vinegar made from wine nor vinegar made from *similar* drink; neither shall he drink any grape juice, nor eat fresh grapes or raisins. 4All the days of his separation he shall eat nothing that is produced by the grapevine, from seed to skin.

5'All the days of the vow of his separation no razor shall come upon his head; until the days are fulfilled for which he separated himself to the LORD, he shall be holy. *Then* he shall let the locks of the hair of his head grow. 6All the days that he separates himself to the LORD he shall not go near a dead body. 7He shall not make himself unclean even for his father or his mother, for his brother or his sister, when they die, because his separation to God *is* on his head. 8All the days of his separation he shall be holy to the LORD.

9'And if anyone dies very suddenly beside him, and he defiles his consecrated head, then he shall shave his head on the day of his cleansing; on the seventh day he shall shave it. 10Then on the eighth day he shall bring two turtledoves or two young pigeons to the priest, to the door of the tabernacle of meeting; 11and the priest shall offer one as a sin offering and *the* other as a burnt offering, and make atonement for him, because he sinned in regard to the corpse; and he shall sanctify his head that same day. 12He shall consecrate to the LORD the days of his separation, and bring a male lamb in its first year as a trespass offering; but the former days shall be lost, because his separation was defiled.

13'Now this *is* the law of the Nazirite: When the days of his separation are fulfilled, he shall be brought to the door of the tabernacle of meeting. 14And he shall present his offering to the LORD: one male lamb in its first year without blemish as a burnt offering, one ewe lamb in its first year without blemish as a sin offering, one ram without blemish as a peace offering, 15a basket of unleavened bread, cakes of fine flour mixed with oil, unleavened wafers anointed with oil, and their grain offering with their drink offerings.

16'Then the priest shall bring *them* before the LORD and offer his sin offering and his burnt offering; 17and he shall offer the ram as a sacrifice

The Message

herself and is innocent of impurity, her
name will be cleared and she will be able to
have children.

29-31 "This is the law of jealousy in a case
where a woman goes off and has an affair
and defiles herself while married to her hus-
band, or a husband is tormented with feel-
ings of jealousy because he suspects his
wife. The priest is to have her stand in the
presence of GOD and go through this entire
procedure with her. The husband will be
cleared of wrong, but the woman will pay
for her wrong."

Nazirite Vows

1-4 6 GOD spoke to Moses: "Speak to the Peo-
ple of Israel; tell them, If any of you, man
or woman, wants to make a special Nazirite
vow, consecrating yourself totally to GOD,
you must not drink any wine or beer, no in-
toxicating drink of any kind, not even the
juice of grapes—in fact, you must not even
eat grapes or raisins. For the duration of the
consecration, nothing from the grapevine—
not even the seeds, not even the skin—may
be eaten.

5 "Also, for the duration of the consecration
you must not have your hair cut. Your long
hair will be a continuing sign of holy sepa-
ration to GOD.

6-7 "Also, for the duration of the consecration
to GOD, you must not go near a corpse. Even
if it's the body of your father or mother,
brother or sister, you must not ritually defile
yourself because the sign of consecration to
God is on your head.

8 "For the entire duration of your consecra-
tion you are holy to GOD.

9-12 "If someone should die suddenly in your
presence, so that your consecrated head is
ritually defiled, you must shave your head
on the day of your purifying, that is, the sev-
enth day. Then on the eighth day bring two
doves or two pigeons to the priest at the en-
trance to the Tent of Meeting. The priest will
offer one for the Absolution-Offering and
one for the Whole-Burnt-Offering, purifying
you from the ritual contamination of the
corpse. You resanctify your hair on that day
and reconsecrate your Nazirite consecra-
tion to GOD by bringing a yearling lamb for
a Compensation-Offering. You start over;
the previous days don't count because your
consecration was ritually defiled.

13-17 "These are the instructions for the time set
when your special consecration to GOD is up.
First, you are to be brought to the entrance to
the Tent of Meeting. Then you will present
your offerings to GOD: a healthy yearling
lamb for the Whole-Burnt-Offering, a healthy
yearling ewe for an Absolution-Offering, a
healthy ram for a Peace-Offering, a basket of
unraised bread made of fine flour, loaves
mixed with oil, and crackers spread with oil,
along with your Grain-Offerings and Drink-
Offerings. The priest will approach GOD and
offer up your Absolution-Offering and
Whole-Burnt-Offering. He will sacrifice the
ram as a Peace-Offering to GOD with the bas-

NEW KING JAMES VERSION

of a peace offering to the LORD, with the basket of unleavened bread; the priest shall also offer its grain offering and its drink offering. 18Then the Nazirite shall shave his consecrated head *at* the door of the tabernacle of meeting, and shall take the hair from his consecrated head and put *it* on the fire which is under the sacrifice of the peace offering.

19'And the priest shall take the boiled shoulder of the ram, one unleavened cake from the basket, and one unleavened wafer, and put *them* upon the hands of the Nazirite after he has shaved his consecrated *hair,* 20and the priest shall wave them as a wave offering before the LORD; they *are* holy for the priest, together with the breast of the wave offering and the thigh of the heave offering. After that the Nazirite may drink wine.'

21"This is the law of the Nazirite who vows to the LORD the offering for his separation, and besides that, whatever else his hand is able to provide; according to the vow which he takes, so he must do according to the law of his separation."

THE PRIESTLY BLESSING

22And the LORD spoke to Moses, saying: 23"Speak to Aaron and his sons, saying, 'This is the way you shall bless the children of Israel. Say to them:

24"The LORD bless you and keep you;
25The LORD make His face shine upon you,
And be gracious to you;
26The LORD lift up His countenance upon you,
And give you peace." '

27"So they shall put My name on the children of Israel, and I will bless them."

OFFERINGS OF THE LEADERS

7 Now it came to pass, when Moses had finished setting up the tabernacle, that he anointed it and consecrated it and all its furnishings, and the altar and all its utensils; so he anointed them and consecrated them. 2Then the leaders of Israel, the heads of their fathers' houses, who *were* the leaders of the tribes and over those who were numbered, made an offering. 3And they brought their offering before the LORD, six covered carts and twelve oxen, a cart for *every* two of the leaders, and for each one an ox; and they presented them before the tabernacle.

4Then the LORD spoke to Moses, saying, 5"Accept *these* from them, that they may be used in doing the work of the tabernacle of meeting; and you shall give them to the Levites, *to* every man according to his service." 6So Moses took the carts and the oxen, and gave them to the Levites. 7Two carts and four oxen he gave to the sons of Gershon, according to their service; 8and four carts and eight oxen he gave to the sons of Merari, according to their service, under the authority[a] of Ithamar the son of Aaron the priest. 9But to the sons of Kohath he gave none, because theirs *was* the service of the holy things, *which* they carried on their shoulders.

7:8 [a]Literally *hand*

THE MESSAGE

ket of unraised bread, and, last of all, the Grain-Offering and Drink-Offering.

18 "At the entrance to the Tent of Meeting, shave off the hair you consecrated and put it in the fire that is burning under the Peace-Offering.

19-20 "After you have shaved the hair of your consecration, the priest will take a shoulder from the ram, boiled, and a piece of unraised bread and a cracker from the basket and place them in your hands. The priest will then wave them before GOD, a Wave-Offering. They are holy and belong to the priest, along with the breast that was waved and the thigh that was offered.

"Now you are free to drink wine.

21 "These are the instructions for Nazirites as they bring offerings to GOD in their vow of consecration, beyond their other offerings. They must carry out the vow they have vowed following the instructions for the Nazirite."

THE AARONIC BLESSING

22-23 GOD spoke to Moses: "Tell Aaron and his sons, This is how you are to bless the People of Israel. Say to them,

24 GOD bless you and keep you,
25 GOD smile on you and gift you,
26 GOD look you full in the face
and make you prosper.

27 In so doing, they will place my name on the
People of Israel—
I will confirm it by blessing them."

OFFERINGS FOR THE DEDICATION

1 7 When Moses finished setting up The Dwelling, he anointed it and consecrated it along with all that went with it. At the same time he anointed and consecrated the Altar and its accessories.

2-3 The leaders of Israel, the heads of the ancestral tribes who had carried out the census, brought offerings. They presented before GOD six covered wagons and twelve oxen, a wagon from each pair of leaders and an ox from each leader.

4-5 GOD spoke to Moses: "Receive these so that they can be used to transport the Tent of Meeting. Give them to the Levites according to what they need for their work."

6-9 Moses took the wagons and oxen and gave them to the Levites. He gave two wagons and four oxen to the Gershonites for their work and four wagons and eight oxen to the Merarites for their work. They were all under the direction of Ithamar son of Aaron the priest. Moses didn't give any to the Kohathites because they had to carry the holy things for which they were responsible on their shoulders.

NEW KING JAMES VERSION

[10]Now the leaders offered the dedication *of-*
fering for the altar when it was anointed; so the
leaders offered their offering before the altar.
[11]For the LORD said to Moses, "They shall offer
their offering, one leader each day, for the dedi-
cation of the altar."
[12]And the one who offered his offering on
the first day *was* Nahshon the son of Ammi-
nadab, from the tribe of Judah. [13]His offering
was one silver platter, the weight of which *was*
one hundred and thirty *shekels,* and one silver
bowl of seventy shekels, according to the shekel
of the sanctuary, both of them full of fine flour
mixed with oil as a grain offering; [14]one gold
pan of ten *shekels,* full of incense; [15]one young
bull, one ram, and one male lamb in its first
year, as a burnt offering; [6]one kid of the goats as
a sin offering; [17]and for the sacrifice of peace of-
ferings: two oxen, five rams, five male goats,
and five male lambs in their first year. This *was*
the offering of Nahshon the son of Amminadab.
[18]On the second day Nethanel the son of
Zuar, leader of Issachar, presented *an offering.*
[19]*For* his offering he offered one silver platter,
the weight of which *was* one hundred and thirty
shekels, and one silver bowl of seventy shekels,
according to the shekel of the sanctuary, both of
them full of fine flour mixed with oil as a grain
offering; [20]one gold pan of ten *shekels,* full of in-
cense; [21]one young bull, one ram, and one male
lamb in its first year, as a burnt offering; [22]one
kid of the goats as a sin offering; [23]and as the
sacrifice of peace offerings: two oxen, five rams,
five male goats, and five male lambs in their
first year. This *was* the offering of Nethanel the
son of Zuar.
[24]On the third day Eliab the son of Helon,
leader of the children of Zebulun, *presented an*
offering. [25]His offering *was* one silver platter,
the weight of which *was* one hundred and thirty
shekels, and one silver bowl of seventy shekels,
according to the shekel of the sanctuary, both of
them full of fine flour mixed with oil as a grain
offering; [26]one gold pan of ten *shekels,* full of in-
cense; [27]one young bull, one ram, and one male
lamb in its first year, as a burnt offering; [28]one
kid of the goats as a sin offering; [29]and for the
sacrifice of peace offerings: two oxen, five rams,
five male goats, and five male lambs in their
first year. This *was* the offering of Eliab the son
of Helon.
[30]On the fourth day Elizur the son of
Shedeur, leader of the children of Reuben, *pre-*
sented an offering. [31]His offering *was* one silver
platter, the weight of which *was* one hundred

THE MESSAGE

10-11 When the Altar was anointed, the leaders
brought their offerings for its dedication
and presented them before the Altar be-
cause GOD had instructed Moses, "Each day
one leader is to present his offering for the
dedication of the Altar."

12-13 On the first day, Nahshon son of Ammi-
nadab, of the tribe of Judah, brought his of-
fering. His offering was:

a silver plate weighing three and a quar-
ter pounds and a silver bowl weighing one
and three-quarter pounds (according to the
standard Sanctuary weights), each filled
with fine flour mixed with oil as a Grain-
Offering;

14 a gold vessel weighing four ounces, filled
with incense;

15 a young bull, a ram, and a yearling lamb
for a Whole-Burnt-Offering;

16 a he-goat for an Absolution-Offering;
two oxen, five rams, five he-goats, and
five yearling lambs to be sacrificed as a
Peace-Offering.

17 This was the offering of Nahshon son of
Amminadab.

18-23 On the second day, Nethanel son of Zuar,
the leader of Issachar, brought his offering.
His offering was:

a silver plate weighing three and a quar-
ter pounds and a silver bowl weighing one
and three-quarter pounds (according to the
standard Sanctuary weights), each filled
with fine flour mixed with oil as a Grain-
Offering;

a gold vessel weighing four ounces, filled
with incense;

a young bull, a ram, and a yearling lamb
for a Whole-Burnt-Offering;

a he-goat for an Absolution-Offering;
two oxen, five rams, five he-goats, and
five yearling lambs to be sacrificed as a
Peace-Offering.

This was the offering of Nethanel son of
Zuar.

24-29 On the third day, Eliab son of Helon, the
leader of the people of Zebulun, brought his
offering. His offering was:

a silver plate weighing three and a quar-
ter pounds and a silver bowl weighing one
and three-quarter pounds (according to the
standard Sanctuary weights), each filled
with fine flour mixed with oil as a Grain-
Offering;

a gold vessel weighing four ounces, filled
with incense;

a young bull, a ram, and a yearling lamb
for a Whole-Burnt-Offering;

a he-goat for an Absolution-Offering;
two oxen, five rams, five he-goats, and
five yearling lambs to be sacrificed as a
Peace-Offering.

This was the offering of Eliab son of
Helon.

30-35 On the fourth day, Elizur son of Shedeur,
the leader of the people of Reuben, brought
his offering. His offering was:

NEW KING JAMES VERSION

and thirty *shekels,* and one silver bowl of sev-
enty shekels, according to the shekel of the
sanctuary, both of them full of fine flour mixed
with oil as a grain offering; [32]one gold pan of ten
shekels, full of incense; [33]one young bull, one
ram, and one male lamb in its first year, as a
burnt offering; [34]one kid of the goats as a sin of-
fering; [35]and as the sacrifice of peace offerings:
two oxen, five rams, five male goats, and five
male lambs in their first year. This *was* the of-
fering of Elizur the son of Shedeur.
[36]On the fifth day Shelumiel the son of Zur-
ishaddai, leader of the children of Simeon, *pre-
sented an offering.* [37]His offering *was* one silver
platter, the weight of which *was* one hundred
and thirty *shekels,* and one silver bowl of sev-
enty shekels, according to the shekel of the
sanctuary, both of them full of fine flour mixed
with oil as a grain offering; [38]one gold pan of ten
shekels, full of incense; [39]one young bull, one
ram, and one male lamb in its first year, as a
burnt offering; [40]one kid of the goats as a sin of-
fering; [41]and as the sacrifice of peace offerings:
two oxen, five rams, five male goats, and five
male lambs in their first year. This *was* the of-
fering of Shelumiel the son of Zurishaddai.
[42]On the sixth day Eliasaph the son of
Deuel,[a] leader of the children of Gad, *presented
an offering.* [43]His offering *was* one silver platter,
the weight of which *was* one hundred and thirty
shekels, and one silver bowl of seventy shekels,
according to the shekel of the sanctuary, both of
them full of fine flour mixed with oil as a grain
offering; [44]one gold pan of ten *shekels,* full of in-
cense; [45]one young bull, one ram, and one male
lamb in its first year, as a burnt offering; [46]one
kid of the goats as a sin offering; [47]and as the
sacrifice of peace offerings: two oxen, five rams,
five male goats, and five male lambs in their
first year. This *was* the offering of Eliasaph the
son of Deuel.
[48]On the seventh day Elishama the son of
Ammihud, leader of the children of Ephraim,
presented an offering. [49]His offering *was* one sil-
ver platter, the weight of which *was* one hun-
dred and thirty *shekels,* and one silver bowl of
seventy shekels, according to the shekel of the
sanctuary, both of them full of fine flour mixed
with oil as a grain offering; [50]one gold pan of ten
shekels, full of incense; [51]one young bull, one

7:42 [a]Spelled *Reuel* in 2:14

THE MESSAGE

a silver plate weighing three and a quarter pounds and a silver bowl weighing one and three-quarter pounds (according to the standard Sanctuary weights), each filled with fine flour mixed with oil as a Grain-Offering;

a gold vessel weighing four ounces, filled with incense;

a young bull, a ram, and a yearling lamb for a Whole-Burnt-Offering;

a he-goat for an Absolution-Offering;

two oxen, five rams, five he-goats, and five yearling lambs to be sacrificed as a Peace-Offering.

This was the offering of Elizur son of Shedeur.

36-41 On the fifth day, Shelumiel son of Zurishaddai, the leader of the people of Simeon, brought his offering. His offering was:

a silver plate weighing three and a quarter pounds and a silver bowl weighing one and three-quarter pounds (according to the standard Sanctuary weights), each filled with fine flour mixed with oil as a Grain-Offering;

a gold vessel weighing four ounces, filled with incense;

a young bull, a ram, and a yearling lamb for a Whole-Burnt-Offering;

a he-goat for an Absolution-Offering;

two oxen, five rams, five he-goats, and five yearling lambs to be sacrificed as a Peace-Offering.

This was the offering of Shelumiel son of Zurishaddai.

42-47 On the sixth day, Eliasaph son of Deuel, the leader of the people of Gad, brought his offering. His offering was:

a silver plate weighing three and a quarter pounds and a silver bowl weighing one and three-quarter pounds (according to the standard Sanctuary weights), each filled with fine flour mixed with oil as a Grain-Offering;

a gold vessel weighing four ounces, filled with incense;

a young bull, a ram, and a yearling lamb for a Whole-Burnt-Offering;

a he-goat for an Absolution-Offering;

two oxen, five rams, five he-goats, and five yearling lambs to be sacrificed as a Peace-Offering.

This was the offering of Eliasaph son of Deuel.

48-53 On the seventh day, Elishama son of Ammihud, the leader of the people of Ephraim, brought his offering. His offering was:

a silver plate weighing three and a quarter pounds and a silver bowl weighing one and three-quarter pounds (according to the standard Sanctuary weights), each filled with fine flour mixed with oil as a Grain-Offering;

a gold vessel weighing four ounces, filled with incense;

New King James Version

ram, and one male lamb in its first year, as a
burnt offering; 52one kid of the goats as a sin of-
fering; 53and as the sacrifice of peace offerings:
two oxen, five rams, five male goats, and five
male lambs in their first year. This *was* the of-
fering of Elishama the son of Ammihud.
54On the eighth day Gamaliel the son of
Pedahzur, leader of the children of Manasseh,
presented an offering. 55His offering *was* one sil-
ver platter, the weight of which *was* one hun-
dred and thirty *shekels,* and one silver bowl of
seventy shekels, according to the shekel of the
sanctuary, both of them full of fine flour mixed
with oil as a grain offering; 56one gold pan of ten
shekels, full of incense; 57one young bull, one
ram, and one male lamb in its first year, as a
burnt offering; 58one kid of the goats as a sin of-
fering; 59and as the sacrifice of peace offerings:
two oxen, five rams, five male goats, and five
male lambs in their first year. This *was* the of-
fering of Gamaliel the son of Pedahzur.
60On the ninth day Abidan the son of
Gideoni, leader of the children of Benjamin, *pre-
sented an offering.* 61His offering *was* one silver
platter, the weight of which *was* one hundred
and thirty *shekels,* and one silver bowl of sev-
enty shekels, according to the shekel of the
sanctuary, both of them full of fine flour mixed
with oil as a grain offering; 62one gold pan of ten
shekels, full of incense; 63one young bull, one
ram, and one male lamb in its first year, as a
burnt offering; 64one kid of the goats as a sin of-
fering; 65and as the sacrifice of peace offerings:
two oxen, five rams, five male goats, and five
male lambs in their first year. This *was* the of-
fering of Abidan the son of Gideoni.
66On the tenth day Ahiezer the son of Am-
mishaddai, leader of the children of Dan, *pre-
sented an offering.* 67His offering *was* one silver
platter, the weight of which *was* one hundred
and thirty *shekels,* and one silver bowl of sev-
enty shekels, according to the shekel of the
sanctuary, both of them full of fine flour mixed
with oil as a grain offering; 68one gold pan of ten
shekels, full of incense; 69one young bull, one
ram, and one male lamb in its first year, as a
burnt offering; 70one kid of the goats as a sin of-
fering; 71and as the sacrifice of peace offerings:
two oxen, five rams, five male goats, and five
male lambs in their first year. This *was* the of-
fering of Ahiezer the son of Ammishaddai.

The Message

a young bull, a ram, and a yearling lamb for a Whole-Burnt-Offering;

a he-goat for an Absolution-Offering;

two oxen, five rams, five he-goats, and five yearling lambs to be sacrificed as a Peace-Offering.

This was the offering of Elishama son of Ammihud.

54-59 On the eighth day, Gamaliel son of Pedahzur, the leader of the people of Manasseh, brought his offering. His offering was:

a silver plate weighing three and a quarter pounds and a silver bowl weighing one and three-quarter pounds (according to the standard Sanctuary weights), each filled with fine flour mixed with oil as a Grain-Offering;

a gold vessel weighing four ounces, filled with incense;

a young bull, a ram, and a yearling lamb for a Whole-Burnt-Offering;

a he-goat for an Absolution-Offering;

two oxen, five rams, five he-goats, and five yearling lambs to be sacrificed as a Peace-Offering.

This was the offering of Gamaliel son of Pedahzur.

60-65 On the ninth day, Abidan son of Gideoni, the leader of the people of Benjamin, brought his offering. His offering was:

a silver plate weighing three and a quarter pounds and a silver bowl weighing one and three-quarter pounds (according to the standard Sanctuary weights), each filled with fine flour mixed with oil as a Grain-Offering;

a gold vessel weighing four ounces, filled with incense;

a young bull, a ram, and a yearling lamb for a Whole-Burnt-Offering;

a he-goat for an Absolution-Offering;

two oxen, five rams, five he-goats, and five yearling lambs to be sacrificed as a Peace-Offering.

This was the offering of Abidan son of Gideoni.

66-71 On the tenth day, Ahiezer son of Ammishaddai, the leader of the people of Dan, brought his offering. His offering was:

a silver plate weighing three and a quarter pounds and a silver bowl weighing one and three-quarter pounds (according to the standard Sanctuary weights), each filled with fine flour mixed with oil as a Grain-Offering;

a gold vessel weighing four ounces, filled with incense;

a young bull, a ram, and a yearling lamb for a Whole-Burnt-Offering;

a he-goat for an Absolution-Offering;

two oxen, five rams, five he-goats, and five yearling lambs to be sacrificed as a Peace-Offering.

This was the offering of Ahiezer son of Ammishaddai.

NEW KING JAMES VERSION

72On the eleventh day Pagiel the son of
Ocran, leader of the children of Asher, *pre-
sented an offering.* 73His offering *was* one silver
platter, the weight of which *was* one hundred
and thirty *shekels,* and one silver bowl of sev-
enty shekels, according to the shekel of the
sanctuary, both of them full of fine flour mixed
with oil as a grain offering; 74one gold pan of ten
shekels, full of incense; 75one young bull, one
ram, and one male lamb in its first year, as a
burnt offering; 76one kid of the goats as a sin of-
fering; 77and as the sacrifice of peace offerings:
two oxen, five rams, five male goats, and five
male lambs in their first year. This *was* the of-
fering of Pagiel the son of Ocran.
78On the twelfth day Ahira the son of Enan,
leader of the children of Naphtali, *presented an
offering.* 79His offering *was* one silver platter,
the weight of which *was* one hundred and thirty
shekels, and one silver bowl of seventy shekels,
according to the shekel of the sanctuary, both of
them full of fine flour mixed with oil as a grain
offering; 80one gold pan of ten *shekels,* full of in-
cense; 81one young bull, one ram, and one male
lamb in its first year, as a burnt offering; 82one
kid of the goats as a sin offering; 83and as the
sacrifice of peace offerings: two oxen, five rams,
five male goats, and five male lambs in their
first year. This *was* the offering of Ahira the son
of Enan.
84This *was* the dedication *offering* for the al-
tar from the leaders of Israel, when it was
anointed: twelve silver platters, twelve silver
bowls, and twelve gold pans. 85Each silver plat-
ter *weighed* one hundred and thirty *shekels* and
each bowl seventy *shekels.* All the silver of the
vessels *weighed* two thousand four hundred
shekels, according to the shekel of the sanctu-
ary. 86The twelve gold pans full of incense
weighed ten *shekels* apiece, according to the
shekel of the sanctuary; all the gold of the pans
weighed one hundred and twenty *shekels.* 87All
the oxen for the burnt offering *were* twelve
young bulls, the rams twelve, the male lambs in
their first year twelve, with their grain offering,

THE MESSAGE

72-77 On the eleventh day, Pagiel son of Ocran, the leader of the people of Asher, brought his offering. His offering was:

a silver plate weighing three and a quarter pounds and a silver bowl weighing one and three-quarter pounds (according to the standard Sanctuary weights), each filled with fine flour mixed with oil as a Grain-Offering;

a gold vessel weighing four ounces, filled with incense;

a young bull, a ram, and a yearling lamb for a Whole-Burnt-Offering;

a he-goat for an Absolution-Offering;

two oxen, five rams, five he-goats, and five yearling lambs to be sacrificed as a Peace-Offering.

This was the offering of Pagiel son of Ocran.

78-83 On the twelfth day, Ahira son of Enan, the leader of the people of Naphtali, brought his offering. His offering was:

a silver plate weighing three and a quarter pounds and a silver bowl weighing one and three-quarter pounds (according to the standard Sanctuary weights), each filled with fine flour mixed with oil as a Grain-Offering;

a gold vessel weighing four ounces, filled with incense;

a young bull, a ram, and a yearling lamb for a Whole-Burnt-Offering;

a he-goat for an Absolution-Offering;

two oxen, five rams, five he-goats, and five yearling lambs to be sacrificed as a Peace-Offering.

This was the offering of Ahira son of Enan.

84 These were the dedication offerings of the leaders of Israel for the anointing of the Altar:

twelve silver plates,
twelve silver bowls,
twelve gold vessels.

85-86 Each plate weighed three and a quarter pounds and each bowl one and three-quarter pounds. All the plates and bowls together weighed about sixty pounds (using the official Sanctuary weight). The twelve gold vessels filled with incense weighed four ounces each (using the official Sanctuary weight). Altogether the gold vessels weighed about three pounds.

87 The sum total of animals used for the Whole-Burnt-Offering together with the Grain-Offering:

twelve bulls,
twelve rams,
twelve yearling lambs.

NEW KING JAMES VERSION

and the kids of the goats as a sin offering twelve. 88And all the oxen for the sacrifice of peace offerings were twenty-four bulls, the rams sixty, the male goats sixty, and the lambs in their first year sixty. This *was* the dedication *offering* for the altar after it was anointed.

89Now when Moses went into the tabernacle of meeting to speak with Him, he heard the voice of One speaking to him from above the mercy seat that *was* on the ark of the Testimony, from between the two cherubim; thus He spoke to him.

ARRANGEMENT OF THE LAMPS

8 And the LORD spoke to Moses, saying: 2"Speak to Aaron, and say to him, 'When you arrange the lamps, the seven lamps shall give light in front of the lampstand.' " 3And Aaron did so; he arranged the lamps to face toward the front of the lampstand, as the LORD commanded Moses. 4Now this workmanship of the lampstand *was* hammered gold; from its shaft to its flowers it *was* hammered work. According to the pattern which the LORD had shown Moses, so he made the lampstand.

CLEANSING AND DEDICATION OF THE LEVITES

5Then the LORD spoke to Moses, saying: 6"Take the Levites from among the children of Israel and cleanse them *ceremonially.* 7Thus you shall do to them to cleanse them: Sprinkle water of purification on them, and let them shave all their body, and let them wash their clothes, and *so* make themselves clean. 8Then let them take a young bull with its grain offering of fine flour mixed with oil, and you shall take another young bull as a sin offering. 9And you shall bring the Levites before the tabernacle of meeting, and you shall gather together the whole congregation of the children of Israel. 10So you shall bring the Levites before the LORD, and the children of Israel shall lay their hands on the Levites; 11and Aaron shall offer the Levites before the LORD *like* a wave offering from the children of Israel, that they may perform the work of the LORD. 12Then the Levites shall lay their hands on the heads of the young bulls, and you shall offer one as a sin offering and the other as a burnt offering to the LORD, to make atonement for the Levites.

13"And you shall stand the Levites before Aaron and his sons, and then offer them *like* a wave offering to the LORD. 14Thus you shall separate the Levites from among the children of Israel, and the Levites shall be Mine. 15After that the Levites shall go in to service the tabernacle of meeting. So you shall cleanse them and offer them *like* a wave offering. 16For they *are* wholly given to Me from among the children of Israel; I have taken them for Myself instead of all who

THE MESSAGE

For the Absolution-Offering:

twelve he-goats.

88 The sum total of animals used for the sacrifice of the Peace-Offering:

twenty-four bulls,
sixty rams,
sixty he-goats,
sixty yearling lambs.

These were the offerings for the dedication of the Altar after it was anointed.

89 When Moses entered the Tent of Meeting to speak with GOD, he heard the Voice speaking to him from between the two angel-cherubim above the Atonement-Cover on the Chest of The Testimony. He spoke with him.

THE LIGHTS

1-2 8 GOD spoke to Moses: "Tell Aaron, Install the seven lamps so they will throw light in front of the Lampstand."

3 Aaron did just that. He installed the lamps so they threw light in front of the Lampstand, as GOD had instructed Moses. The Lampstand was made of hammered gold from its stem to its petals. It was made precisely to the design GOD had shown Moses.

PURIFYING THE LEVITES

5-7 GOD spoke to Moses: "Take the Levites from the midst of the People of Israel and purify them for doing GOD's work. This is the way you will do it: Sprinkle water of absolution on them; have them shave their entire bodies; have them scrub their clothes. Then they will have purified themselves.

8-11 "Have them take a young bull with its accompanying Grain-Offering of fine flour mixed with oil, plus a second young bull for an Absolution-Offering. Bring the Levites to the front of the Tent of Meeting and gather the entire community of Israel. Present the Levites before GOD as the People of Israel lay their hands on them. Aaron will present the Levites before GOD as a Wave-Offering from the People of Israel so that they will be ready to do GOD's work.

12-14 "Have the Levites place their hands on the heads of the bulls, selecting one for the Absolution-Offering and another for the Whole-Burnt-Offering to GOD to make atonement for the Levites. Then have the Levites stand in front of Aaron and his sons and present them as a Wave-Offering to GOD. This is the procedure for setting apart the Levites from the rest of the People of Israel; the Levites are exclusively for my use.

15-19 "After you have purified the Levites and presented them as a Wave-Offering to GOD, they can go to work in the Tent of Meeting. The Levites have been selected out of the People of Israel for my exclusive use; they function in place of every firstborn male born to an Israelite woman. Every firstborn

NEW KING JAMES VERSION

open the womb, the firstborn of all the children of Israel. 17For all the firstborn among the children of Israel *are* Mine, *both* man and beast; on the day that I struck all the firstborn in the land of Egypt I sanctified them to Myself. 18I have taken the Levites instead of all the firstborn of the children of Israel. 19And I have given the Levites as a gift to Aaron and his sons from among the children of Israel, to do the work for the children of Israel in the tabernacle of meeting, and to make atonement for the children of Israel, that there be no plague among the children of Israel when the children of Israel come near the sanctuary."

20Thus Moses and Aaron and all the congregation of the children of Israel did to the Levites; according to all that the LORD commanded Moses concerning the Levites, so the children of Israel did to them. 21And the Levites purified themselves and washed their clothes; then Aaron presented them *like* a wave offering before the LORD, and Aaron made atonement for them to cleanse them. 22After that the Levites went in to do their work in the tabernacle of meeting before Aaron and his sons; as the LORD commanded Moses concerning the Levites, so they did to them.

23Then the LORD spoke to Moses, saying, 24"This *is* what *pertains* to the Levites: From twenty-five years old and above one may enter to perform service in the work of the tabernacle of meeting; 25and at the age of fifty years they must cease performing this work, and shall work no more. 26They may minister with their brethren in the tabernacle of meeting, to attend to needs, but they *themselves* shall do no work. Thus you shall do to the Levites regarding their duties."

THE SECOND PASSOVER

9 Now the LORD spoke to Moses in the Wilderness of Sinai, in the first month of the second year after they had come out of the land of Egypt, saying: 2"Let the children of Israel keep the Passover at its appointed time. 3On the fourteenth day of this month, at twilight, you shall keep it at its appointed time. According to all its rites and ceremonies you shall keep it." 4So Moses told the children of Israel that they should keep the Passover. 5And they kept the Passover on the fourteenth day of the first month, at twilight, in the Wilderness of Sinai; according to all that the LORD commanded Moses, so the children of Israel did.

6Now there were *certain* men who were defiled by a human corpse, so that they could not keep the Passover on that day; and they came before Moses and Aaron that day. 7And those men said to him, "We *became* defiled by a human corpse. Why are we kept from presenting the offering of the LORD at its appointed time among the children of Israel?"

8And Moses said to them, "Stand still, that I may hear what the LORD will command concerning you."

9Then the LORD spoke to Moses, saying, 10"Speak to the children of Israel, saying: 'If anyone of you or your posterity is unclean because of a corpse, or *is* far away on a journey, he may

THE MESSAGE

male in Israel, animal or human, is set apart for my use. When I struck down all the firstborn of Egypt, I consecrated them for my holy uses. But now I take the Levites as stand-ins in place of every firstborn son in Israel, selected out of the People of Israel, and I have given the Levites to Aaron and his sons to do all the work involved in the Tent of Meeting on behalf of all the People of Israel and to make atonement for them so that nothing bad will happen to them when they approach the Sanctuary."

20-22 Moses, Aaron, and the entire community of the People of Israel carried out these procedures with the Levites, just as GOD had commanded Moses. The Levites purified themselves and scrubbed their clothes. Then Aaron presented them as a Wave-Offering before GOD and made atonement for them to purify them. Only then did the Levites go to work at the Tent of Meeting. Aaron and his sons supervised them following the directions GOD had given.

23-26 GOD spoke to Moses: "These are your instructions regarding the Levites: At the age of twenty-five they will join the workforce in the Tent of Meeting; at the age of fifty they must retire from the work. They can assist their brothers in the tasks in the Tent of Meeting, but they are not permitted to do the actual work themselves. These are the ground rules for the work of the Levites."

PASSOVER

1-3 9 GOD spoke to Moses in the Wilderness of Sinai in the first month of the second year after leaving Egypt: "Have the People of Israel celebrate Passover at the set time. Celebrate it on schedule, on the evening of the fourteenth day of this month, following all the rules and procedures."

4-5 Moses told the People of Israel to celebrate the Passover and they did—in the Wilderness of Sinai at evening of the fourteenth day of the first month. The People of Israel did it all just as GOD had commanded Moses.

6-7 But some of them couldn't celebrate the Passover on the assigned day because they were ritually unclean on account of a corpse. So they presented themselves before Moses and Aaron on Passover and told Moses, "We have become ritually unclean because of a corpse, but why should we be barred from bringing GOD's offering along with other Israelites on the day set for Passover?"

8 Moses said, "Give me some time; I'll find out what GOD says in your circumstances."

9-12 GOD spoke to Moses: "Tell the People of Israel, If one or another of you is ritually unclean because of a corpse, or you happen to

NEW KING JAMES VERSION

still keep the LORD's Passover. [11]On the four-
teenth day of the second month, at twilight, they
may keep it. They shall eat it with unleavened
bread and bitter herbs. [12]They shall leave none
of it until morning, nor break one of its bones.
According to all the ordinances of the Passover
they shall keep it. [13]But the man who *is* clean
and is not on a journey, and ceases to keep the
Passover, that same person shall be cut off from
among his people, because he did not bring the
offering of the LORD at its appointed time; that
man shall bear his sin.
[14]'And if a stranger dwells among you, and
would keep the LORD's Passover, he must do so
according to the rite of the Passover and accord-
ing to its ceremony; you shall have one ordi-
nance, both for the stranger and the native of
the land.' "

THE CLOUD AND THE FIRE

[15]Now on the day that the tabernacle was
raised up, the cloud covered the tabernacle, the
tent of the Testimony; from evening until morn-
ing it was above the tabernacle like the appear-
ance of fire. [16]So it was always: the cloud cov-
ered it *by day,* and the appearance of fire by
night. [17]Whenever the cloud was taken up from
above the tabernacle, after that the children of
Israel would journey; and in the place where the
cloud settled, there the children of Israel would
pitch their tents. [18]At the command of the LORD
the children of Israel would journey, and at the
command of the LORD they would camp; as long
as the cloud stayed above the tabernacle they
remained encamped. [19]Even when the cloud
continued long, many days above the taberna-
cle, the children of Israel kept the charge of the
LORD and did not journey. [20]So it was, when the
cloud was above the tabernacle a few days: ac-
cording to the command of the LORD they would
remain encamped, and according to the com-
mand of the LORD they would journey. [21]So it
was, when the cloud remained only from
evening until morning: when the cloud was
taken up in the morning, then they would jour-
ney; whether by day or by night, whenever the
cloud was taken up, they would journey.
[22]*Whether it was* two days, a month, or a year
that the cloud remained above the tabernacle,
the children of Israel would remain encamped
and not journey; but when it was taken up, they
would journey. [23]At the command of the LORD
they remained encamped, and at the command
of the LORD they journeyed; they kept the
charge of the LORD, at the command of the LORD
by the hand of Moses.

TWO SILVER TRUMPETS

10 And the LORD spoke to Moses, saying:
[2]"Make two silver trumpets for yourself;
you shall make them of hammered work; you
shall use them for calling the congregation and
for directing the movement of the camps. [3]When
they blow both of them, all the congregation
shall gather before you at the door of the taber-
nacle of meeting. [4]But if they blow *only* one,
then the leaders, the heads of the divisions of Is-
rael, shall gather to you. [5]When you sound the

THE MESSAGE

be off on a long trip, you may still celebrate
GOD's Passover. But celebrate it on the four-
teenth day of the second month at evening.
Eat the lamb together with unraised bread
and bitter herbs. Don't leave any of it until
morning. Don't break any of its bones. Fol-
low all the procedures.
13 "But a man who is ritually clean and is
not off on a trip and still fails to celebrate
the Passover must be cut off from his people
because he did not present GOD's offering at
the set time. That man will pay for his sin.
14 "Any foreigner living among you who
wants to celebrate GOD's Passover is wel-
come to do it, but he must follow all the
rules and procedures. The same procedures
go for both foreigner and native-born."

THE CLOUD

15-16 The day The Dwelling was set up, the Cloud
covered The Dwelling of the Tent of Testi-
mony. From sunset until daybreak it was
over The Dwelling. It looked like fire. It was
like that all the time, the Cloud over The
Dwelling and at night looking like fire.
17-23 When the Cloud lifted above the Tent,
the People of Israel marched out; and when
the Cloud descended the people camped.
The People of Israel marched at GOD's com-
mand and they camped at his command. As
long as the Cloud was over The Dwelling,
they camped. Even when the Cloud hovered
over The Dwelling for many days, they hon-
ored GOD's command and wouldn't march.
They stayed in camp, obedient to GOD's
command, as long as the Cloud was over
The Dwelling, but the moment GOD issued
orders they marched. If the Cloud stayed
only from sunset to daybreak and then
lifted at daybreak, they marched. Night or
day, it made no difference—when the Cloud
lifted, they marched. It made no difference
whether the Cloud hovered over The
Dwelling for two days or a month or a year,
as long as the Cloud was there, they were
there. And when the Cloud went up, they
got up and marched. They camped at GOD's
command and they marched at GOD's com-
mand. They lived obediently by GOD's or-
ders as delivered by Moses.

THE TWO BUGLES

1-3 10 GOD spoke to Moses: "Make two bu-
gles of hammered silver. Use them to
call the congregation together and give
marching orders to the camps. When you
blow them, the whole community will meet
you at the entrance of the Tent of Meeting.
4-7 "When a bugle gives a single, short blast,
that's the signal for the leaders, the heads of
the clans, to assemble. When it gives a long
blast, that's the signal to march. At the first

NEW KING JAMES VERSION

advance, the camps that lie on the east side shall
then begin their journey. 6When you sound the
advance the second time, then the camps that lie
on the south side shall begin their journey; they
shall sound the call for them to begin their jour-
neys. 7And when the assembly is to be gathered
together, you shall blow, but not sound the ad-
vance. 8The sons of Aaron, the priests, shall
blow the trumpets; and these shall be to you as
an ordinance forever throughout your genera-
tions.
9"When you go to war in your land against
the enemy who oppresses you, then you shall
sound an alarm with the trumpets, and you will
be remembered before the LORD your God, and
you will be saved from your enemies. 10Also in
the day of your gladness, in your appointed
feasts, and at the beginning of your months, you
shall blow the trumpets over your burnt offer-
ings and over the sacrifices of your peace offer-
ings; and they shall be a memorial for you be-
fore your God: I *am* the LORD your God."

DEPARTURE FROM SINAI

11Now it came to pass on the twentieth *day* of
the second month, in the second year, that the
cloud was taken up from above the tabernacle
of the Testimony. 12And the children of Israel set
out from the Wilderness of Sinai on their jour-
neys; then the cloud settled down in the Wilder-
ness of Paran. 13So they started out for the first
time according to the command of the LORD by
the hand of Moses.
14The standard of the camp of the children of
Judah set out first according to their armies;
over their army was Nahshon the son of Ammi-
nadab. 15Over the army of the tribe of the chil-
dren of Issachar *was* Nethanel the son of Zuar.
16And over the army of the tribe of the children
of Zebulun *was* Eliab the son of Helon.
17Then the tabernacle was taken down; and
the sons of Gershon and the sons of Merari set
out, carrying the tabernacle.
18And the standard of the camp of Reuben
set out according to their armies; over their
army *was* Elizur the son of Shedeur. 19Over the
army of the tribe of the children of Simeon *was*
Shelumiel the son of Zurishaddai. 20And over
the army of the tribe of the children of Gad *was*
Eliasaph the son of Deuel.
21Then the Kohathites set out, carrying the
holy things. (The tabernacle would be prepared
for their arrival.)
22And the standard of the camp of the chil-
dren of Ephraim set out according to their
armies; over their army *was* Elishama the son of
Ammihud. 23Over the army of the tribe of the
children of Manasseh *was* Gamaliel the son of
Pedahzur. 24And over the army of the tribe of the
children of Benjamin *was* Abidan the son of
Gideoni.
25Then the standard of the camp of the chil-
dren of Dan (the rear guard of all the camps) set
out according to their armies; over their army
was Ahiezer the son of Ammishaddai. 26Over
the army of the tribe of the children of Asher
was Pagiel the son of Ocran. 27And over the
army of the tribe of the children of Naphtali *was*
Ahira the son of Enan.

THE MESSAGE

blast the tribes who were camped on the
east set out. At the second blast the camps
on the south set out. The long blasts are the
signals to march. The bugle call that gathers
the assembly is different from the signal to
march.
8-10 "The sons of Aaron, the priests, are in
charge of blowing the bugles; it's their as-
signed duty down through the generations.
When you go to war against an aggressor,
blow a long blast on the bugle so that GOD
will notice you and deliver you from your
enemies. Also at times of celebration, at the
appointed feasts and New Moon festivals,
blow the bugles over your Whole-Burnt-
Offerings and Peace-Offerings: they will
keep your attention on God. I am GOD, *your*
God."

THE MARCH FROM SINAI TO PARAN

11-13 In the second year, on the twentieth day of
the second month, the Cloud went up from
over The Dwelling of The Testimony. At that
the People of Israel set out on their travels
from the Wilderness of Sinai until the Cloud
finally settled in the Wilderness of Paran.
They began their march at the command of
GOD through Moses.
14-17 The flag of the camp of Judah led the
way, rank after rank under the command of
Nahshon son of Amminadab. Nethanel son
of Zuar commanded the forces of the tribe
of Issachar, and Eliab son of Helon com-
manded the forces of the tribe of Zebulun.
As soon as The Dwelling was taken down,
the Gershonites and the Merarites set out,
carrying The Dwelling.
18-21 The flag of the camp of Reuben was next
with Elizur son of Shedeur in command.
Shelumiel son of Zurishaddai commanded
the forces of the tribe of Simeon; Eliasaph
son of Deuel commanded the forces of the
tribe of Gad. Then the Kohathites left, carry-
ing the holy things. By the time they arrived
The Dwelling would be set up.
22-24 The flag of the tribe of Ephraim moved
out next, commanded by Elishama son of
Ammihud. Gamaliel son of Pedahzur com-
manded the forces of the tribe of Manasseh;
Abidan son of Gideoni commanded the
forces of the tribe of Benjamin.
25-27 Finally, under the flag of the tribe of Dan,
the rear guard of all the camps marched out
with Ahiezer son of Ammishaddai in com-
mand. Pagiel son of Ocran commanded the
forces of the tribe of Asher; Ahira son of
Enan commanded the forces of the tribe of
Naphtali.

NEW KING JAMES VERSION

28Thus *was* the order of march of the chil-
dren of Israel, according to their armies, when
they began their journey.
29Now Moses said to Hobab the son of Reuel[a]
the Midianite, Moses' father-in-law, "We are set-
ting out for the place of which the LORD said, 'I
will give it to you.' Come with us, and we will
treat you well; for the LORD has promised good
things to Israel."
30And he said to him, "I will not go, but I will
depart to my *own* land and to my relatives."
31So *Moses* said, "Please do not leave, inas-
much as you know how we are to camp in the
wilderness, and you can be our eyes. 32And it
shall be, if you go with us—indeed it shall be—
that whatever good the LORD will do to us, the
same we will do to you."
33So they departed from the mountain of the
LORD on a journey of three days; and the ark of
the covenant of the LORD went before them for
the three days' journey, to search out a resting
place for them. 34And the cloud of the LORD *was*
above them by day when they went out from the
camp.
35So it was, whenever the ark set out, that
Moses said:

"Rise up, O LORD!
Let Your enemies be scattered,
And let those who hate You flee before You."

36And when it rested, he said:

"Return, O LORD,
To the many thousands of Israel."

THE PEOPLE COMPLAIN

11 Now *when* the people complained, it dis-
pleased the LORD; for the LORD heard *it*,
and His anger was aroused. So the fire of the
LORD burned among them, and consumed *some*
in the outskirts of the camp. 2Then the people
cried out to Moses, and when Moses prayed to
the LORD, the fire was quenched. 3So he called
the name of the place Taberah,[a] because the fire
of the LORD had burned among them.
4Now the mixed multitude who were among
them yielded to intense craving; so the children
of Israel also wept again and said: "Who will
give us meat to eat? 5We remember the fish
which we ate freely in Egypt, the cucumbers, the
melons, the leeks, the onions, and the garlic;
6but now our whole being *is* dried up; *there is*
nothing at all except this manna *before* our
eyes!"
7Now the manna *was* like coriander seed,
and its color like the color of bdellium. 8The
people went about and gathered *it*, ground *it* on
millstones or beat *it* in the mortar, cooked *it* in
pans, and made cakes of it; and its taste was like
the taste of pastry prepared with oil. 9And when
the dew fell on the camp in the night, the manna
fell on it.
10Then Moses heard the people weeping

10:29 [a]Septuagint reads *Raguel* (compare Exodus 2:18).
11:3 [a]Literally *Burning*

THE MESSAGE

28 These were the marching units of the People of Israel. They were on their way.

29 Moses said to his brother-in-law Hobab son of Reuel the Midianite, Moses' father-in-law, "We're marching to the place about which GOD promised, 'I'll give it to you.' Come with us; we'll treat you well. GOD has promised good things for Israel."

30 But Hobab said, "I'm not coming; I'm going back home to my own country, to my own family."

31-32 Moses countered, "Don't leave us. You know all the best places to camp in the wilderness. We need your eyes. If you come with us, we'll make sure that you share in all the good things GOD will do for us."

33-36 And so off they marched. From the Mountain of GOD they marched three days with the Chest of the Covenant of GOD in the lead to scout out a campsite. The Cloud of GOD was above them by day when they marched from the camp. With the Chest leading the way, Moses would say,

Get up, GOD!
Put down your enemies!
Chase those who hate you to the hills!

And when the Chest was set down, he would say,

Rest with us, GOD,
Stay with the many,
Many thousands of Israel.

CAMP TABERAH

1-3 11 The people fell to grumbling over their hard life. GOD heard. When he heard his anger flared; then fire blazed up and burned the outer boundaries of the camp. The people cried out for help to Moses; Moses prayed to GOD and the fire died down. They named the place Taberah (Blaze) because fire from GOD had blazed up against them.

CAMP KIBROTH HATTAAVAH

4-6 The riffraff among the people had a craving and soon they had the People of Israel whining, "Why can't we have meat? We ate fish in Egypt—and got it free!—to say nothing of the cucumbers and melons, the leeks and onions and garlic. But nothing tastes good out here; all we get is manna, manna, manna."

7-9 Manna was a seedlike substance with a shiny appearance like resin. The people went around collecting it and ground it between stones or pounded it fine in a mortar. Then they boiled it in a pot and shaped it into cakes. It tasted like a delicacy cooked in olive oil. When the dew fell on the camp at night, the manna was right there with it.

10 Moses heard the whining, all those fami-

NEW KING JAMES VERSION

throughout their families, everyone at the door of his tent; and the anger of the LORD was greatly aroused; Moses also was displeased. 11So Moses said to the LORD, "Why have You afflicted Your servant? And why have I not found favor in Your sight, that You have laid the burden of all these people on me? 12Did I conceive all these people? Did I beget them, that You should say to me, 'Carry them in your bosom, as a guardian carries a nursing child,' to the land which You swore to their fathers? 13Where am I to get meat to give to all these people? For they weep all over me, saying, 'Give us meat, that we may eat.' 14I am not able to bear all these people alone, because the burden *is* too heavy for me. 15If You treat me like this, please kill me here and now—if I have found favor in Your sight—and do not let me see my wretchedness!"

THE SEVENTY ELDERS

16So the LORD said to Moses: "Gather to Me seventy men of the elders of Israel, whom you know to be the elders of the people and officers over them; bring them to the tabernacle of meeting, that they may stand there with you. 17Then I will come down and talk with you there. I will take of the Spirit that *is* upon you and will put *the same* upon them; and they shall bear the burden of the people with you, that you may not bear *it* yourself alone. 18Then you shall say to the people, 'Consecrate yourselves for tomorrow, and you shall eat meat; for you have wept in the hearing of the LORD, saying, "Who will give us meat to eat? For *it was* well with us in Egypt." Therefore the LORD will give you meat, and you shall eat. 19You shall eat, not one day, nor two days, nor five days, nor ten days, nor twenty days, 20but *for* a whole month, until it comes out of your nostrils and becomes loathsome to you, because you have despised the LORD who is among you, and have wept before Him, saying, "Why did we ever come up out of Egypt?" ' "

21And Moses said, "The people whom I *am* among *are* six hundred thousand men on foot; yet You have said, 'I will give them meat, that they may eat *for* a whole month.' 22Shall flocks and herds be slaughtered for them, to provide enough for them? Or shall all the fish of the sea be gathered together for them, to provide enough for them?"

23And the LORD said to Moses, "Has the LORD's arm been shortened? Now you shall see whether what I say will happen to you or not."

24So Moses went out and told the people the words of the LORD, and he gathered the seventy men of the elders of the people and placed them around the tabernacle. 25Then the LORD came down in the cloud, and spoke to him, and took of the Spirit that *was* upon him, and placed *the same* upon the seventy elders; and it happened, when the Spirit rested upon them, that they prophesied, although they never did *so* again.[a]

26But two men had remained in the camp: the name of one *was* Eldad, and the name of the other Medad. And the Spirit rested upon them. Now they *were* among those listed, but who had not gone out to the tabernacle; yet they prophesied in the camp.

11:25 [a]Targum and Vulgate read *did not cease.*

THE MESSAGE

lies whining in front of their tents. GOD's anger blazed up. Moses saw that things were in a bad way.

11-15 Moses said to GOD, "Why are you treating
me this way? What did I ever do to you to de-
serve this? Did I conceive them? Was I their
mother? So why dump the responsibility of
this people on me? Why tell me to carry
them around like a nursing mother, carry
them all the way to the land you promised to
their ancestors? Where am I supposed to get
meat for all these people who are whining to
me, 'Give us meat; we want meat.' I can't do
this by myself—it's too much, all these peo-
ple. If this is how you intend to treat me, do
me a favor and kill me. I've seen enough;
I've had enough. Let me out of here."

16-17 GOD said to Moses, "Gather together sev-
enty men from among the leaders of Israel,
men whom you know to be respected and
responsible. Take them to the Tent of Meet-
ing. I'll meet you there. I'll come down and
speak with you. I'll take some of the Spirit
that is on you and place it on them; they'll
then be able to take some of the load of this
people—you won't have to carry the whole
thing alone.

18-20 "Tell the people, Consecrate yourselves.
Get ready for tomorrow when you're going
to eat meat. You've been whining to GOD,
'We want meat; give us meat. We had a bet-
ter life in Egypt.' GOD has heard your whin-
ing and he's going to give you meat. You're
going to eat meat. And it's not just for a day
that you'll eat meat, and not two days, or
five or ten or twenty, but for a whole month.
You're going to eat meat until it's coming
out your nostrils. You're going to be so sick
of meat that you'll throw up at the mere
mention of it. And here's why: Because you
have rejected GOD who is right here among
you, whining to his face, 'Oh, why did we
ever have to leave Egypt?' "

21-22 Moses said, "I'm standing here sur-
rounded by 600,000 men on foot and you
say, 'I'll give them meat, meat every day for
a month.' So where's it coming from? Even
if all the flocks and herds were butchered,
would that be enough? Even if all the fish in
the sea were caught, would that be enough?"

23 GOD answered Moses, "So, do you think I
can't take care of you? You'll see soon
enough whether what I say happens for you
or not."

24-25 So Moses went out and told the people
what GOD had said. He called together sev-
enty of the leaders and had them stand
around the Tent. GOD came down in a cloud
and spoke to Moses and took some of the
Spirit that was on him and put it on the sev-
enty leaders. When the Spirit rested on them
they prophesied. But they didn't continue; it
was a onetime event.

26 Meanwhile two men, Eldad and Medad, had
stayed in the camp. They were listed as lead-
ers but they didn't leave camp to go to the
Tent. Still, the Spirit also rested on them and
they prophesied in the camp.

NEW KING JAMES VERSION

27 And a young man ran and told Moses, and
said, "Eldad and Medad are prophesying in the
camp."
28 So Joshua the son of Nun, Moses' assistant,
one of his choice men, answered and said,
"Moses my lord, forbid them!"
29 Then Moses said to him, "Are you zealous
for my sake? Oh, that all the LORD's people were
prophets *and* that the LORD would put His Spirit
upon them!" 30 And Moses returned to the camp,
he and the elders of Israel.

THE LORD SENDS QUAIL

31 Now a wind went out from the LORD, and it
brought quail from the sea and left *them* flutter-
ing near the camp, about a day's journey on this
side and about a day's journey on the other side,
all around the camp, and about two cubits above
the surface of the ground. 32 And the people
stayed up all that day, all night, and all the next
day, and gathered the quail (he who gathered
least gathered ten homers); and they spread
them out for themselves all around the camp.
33 But while the meat *was* still between their
teeth, before it was chewed, the wrath of the
LORD was aroused against the people, and the
LORD struck the people with a very great plague.
34 So he called the name of that place Kibroth
Hattaavah,[a] because there they buried the peo-
ple who had yielded to craving.
35 From Kibroth Hattaavah the people moved
to Hazeroth, and camped at Hazeroth.

DISSENSION OF AARON AND MIRIAM

12 Then Miriam and Aaron spoke against
Moses because of the Ethiopian woman
whom he had married; for he had married an
Ethiopian woman. 2 So they said, "Has the LORD
indeed spoken only through Moses? Has He not
spoken through us also?" And the LORD heard *it*.
3 (Now the man Moses *was* very humble, more
than all men who *were* on the face of the earth.)
4 Suddenly the LORD said to Moses, Aaron,
and Miriam, "Come out, you three, to the taber-
nacle of meeting!" So the three came out. 5 Then
the LORD came down in the pillar of cloud and
stood *in* the door of the tabernacle, and called
Aaron and Miriam. And they both went for-
ward. 6 Then He said,

"Hear now My words:
If there is a prophet among you,
I, the LORD, make Myself known to him in a
vision;
I speak to him in a dream.
7 Not so with My servant Moses;
He *is* faithful in all My house.
8 I speak with him face to face,
Even plainly, and not in dark sayings;
And he sees the form of the LORD.
Why then were you not afraid
To speak against My servant Moses?"

9 So the anger of the LORD was aroused
against them, and He departed.

11:34 [a]Literally *Graves of Craving*

THE MESSAGE

27 A young man ran and told Moses, "Eldad and Medad are prophesying in the camp!"

28 Joshua son of Nun, who had been Moses' right-hand man since his youth, said, "Moses, master! Stop them!"

29 But Moses said, "Are you jealous for me? Would that all GOD's people were prophets. Would that GOD would put his Spirit on all of them."

30-34 Then Moses and the leaders of Israel went back to the camp. A wind set in motion by GOD swept quails in from the sea. They piled up to a depth of about three feet in the camp and as far out as a day's walk in every direction. All that day and night and into the next day the people were out gathering the quail—huge amounts of quail; even the slowest person among them gathered at least sixty bushels. They spread them out all over the camp for drying. But while they were still chewing the quail and had hardly swallowed the first bites, GOD's anger blazed out against the people. He hit them with a terrible plague. They ended up calling the place Kibroth Hattaavah (Graves-of-the-Craving). There they buried the people who craved meat.

35 From Kibroth Hattaavah they marched on to Hazeroth. They remained at Hazeroth.

CAMP HAZEROTH

1-2 12 Miriam and Aaron talked against Moses behind his back of because his Cushite wife (he had married a Cushite woman). They said, "Is it only through Moses that GOD speaks? Doesn't he also speak through us?"

GOD overheard their talk.

3-8 Now the man Moses was a quietly humble man, more so than anyone living on Earth. GOD broke in suddenly on Moses and Aaron and Miriam saying, "Come out, you three, to the Tent of Meeting." The three went out. GOD descended in a Pillar of Cloud and stood at the entrance to the Tent. He called Aaron and Miriam to him. When they stepped out, he said,

Listen carefully to what I'm telling you.
If there is a prophet of GOD among
you,
I make myself known to him in visions,
I speak to him in dreams.
But I don't do it that way with my
servant Moses;
he has the run of my entire house;
I speak to him intimately, in person,
in plain talk without riddles:
He ponders the very form of GOD.
So why did you show no reverence or
respect
in speaking against my servant,
against Moses?

9 The anger of GOD blazed out against them. And then he left.

NEW KING JAMES VERSION

10 And when the cloud departed from above the
tabernacle, suddenly Miriam *became* leprous, as
white as snow. Then Aaron turned toward
Miriam, and there she was, a leper. 11 So Aaron
said to Moses, "Oh, my lord! Please do not lay
this sin on us, in which we have done foolishly
and in which we have sinned. 12 Please do not let
her be as one dead, whose flesh is half consumed
when he comes out of his mother's womb!"
13 So Moses cried out to the LORD, saying,
"Please heal her, O God, I pray!"
14 Then the LORD said to Moses, "If her father
had but spit in her face, would she not be
shamed seven days? Let her be shut out of the
camp seven days, and afterward she may be re-
ceived *again*." 15 So Miriam was shut out of the
camp seven days, and the people did not jour-
ney till Miriam was brought in *again*. 16 And af-
terward the people moved from Hazeroth and
camped in the Wilderness of Paran.

SPIES SENT INTO CANAAN

13 And the LORD spoke to Moses, saying,
2 "Send men to spy out the land of Canaan,
which I am giving to the children of Israel; from
each tribe of their fathers you shall send a man,
every one a leader among them."
3 So Moses sent them from the Wilderness of
Paran according to the command of the LORD,
all of them men who *were* heads of the children
of Israel. 4 Now these *were* their names: from the
tribe of Reuben, Shammua the son of Zaccur;
5 from the tribe of Simeon, Shaphat the son of
Hori; 6 from the tribe of Judah, Caleb the son of
Jephunneh; 7 from the tribe of Issachar, Igal the
son of Joseph; 8 from the tribe of Ephraim,
Hoshea[a] the son of Nun; 9 from the tribe of Ben-
jamin, Palti the son of Raphu; 10 from the tribe of
Zebulun, Gaddiel the son of Sodi; 11 from the
tribe of Joseph, *that is,* from the tribe of Ma-
nasseh, Gaddi the son of Susi; 12 from the tribe of
Dan, Ammiel the son of Gemalli; 13 from the
tribe of Asher, Sethur the son of Michael; 14 from
the tribe of Naphtali, Nahbi the son of Vophsi;
15 from the tribe of Gad, Geuel the son of Machi.
16 These *are* the names of the men whom
Moses sent to spy out the land. And Moses
called Hoshea[a] the son of Nun, Joshua.
17 Then Moses sent them to spy out the land
of Canaan, and said to them, "Go up this *way*
into the South, and go up to the mountains,
18 and see what the land is like: whether the peo-
ple who dwell in it *are* strong or weak, few or
many; 19 whether the land they dwell in *is* good
or bad; whether the cities they inhabit *are* like
camps or strongholds; 20 whether the land *is* rich
or poor; and whether there are forests there or
not. Be of good courage. And bring some of the
fruit of the land." Now the time *was* the season
of the first ripe grapes.

13:8 [a]Septuagint and Vulgate read *Oshea*. **13:16** [a]Septuagint and Vulgate read *Oshea*.

THE MESSAGE

10 When the Cloud moved off from the Tent, oh! Miriam had turned leprous, her skin like snow. Aaron took one look at Miriam—a leper!

11-12 He said to Moses, "Please, my master, please don't come down so hard on us for this foolish and thoughtless sin. Please don't make her like a stillborn baby coming out of its mother's womb with half its body decomposed."

13 And Moses prayed to GOD:

Please, God, heal her,
please heal her.

14-16 GOD answered Moses, "If her father had spat in her face, wouldn't she be ostracized for seven days? Quarantine her outside the camp for seven days. Then she can be readmitted to the camp." So Miriam was in quarantine outside the camp for seven days. The people didn't march on until she was readmitted. Only then did the people march from Hazeroth and set up camp in the Wilderness of Paran.

SCOUTING OUT CANAAN

1-2 13 GOD spoke to Moses: "Send men to scout out the country of Canaan that I am giving to the People of Israel. Send one man from each ancestral tribe, each one a tried-and-true leader in the tribe."

3-15 So Moses sent them off from the Wilderness of Paran at the command of GOD. All of them were leaders in Israel, one from each tribe. These were their names:

from Reuben: Shammua son of Zaccur
from Simeon: Shaphat son of Hori
from Judah: Caleb son of Jephunneh
from Issachar: Igal son of Joseph
from Ephraim: Hoshea son of Nun
from Benjamin: Palti son of Raphu
from Zebulun: Gaddiel son of Sodi
from Manasseh (a Joseph tribe): Gaddi son of Susi
from Dan: Ammiel son of Gemalli
from Asher: Sethur son of Michael
from Naphtali: Nahbi son of Vophsi
from Gad: Geuel son of Maki.

16 These are the names of the men Moses sent to scout out the land. Moses gave Hoshea (Salvation) son of Nun a new name—Joshua (GOD-Saves).

17-20 When Moses sent them off to scout out Canaan, he said, "Go up through the Negev and then into the hill country. Look the land over, see what it is like. Assess the people: Are they strong or weak? Are there few or many? Observe the land: Is it pleasant or harsh? Describe the towns where they live: Are they open camps or fortified with walls? And the soil: Is it fertile or barren? Are there forests? And try to bring back a sample of the produce that grows there—this is the season for the first ripe grapes."

New King James Version

21So they went up and spied out the land from the Wilderness of Zin as far as Rehob, near the entrance of Hamath. 22And they went up through the South and came to Hebron; Ahiman, Sheshai, and Talmai, the descendants of Anak, *were* there. (Now Hebron was built seven years before Zoan in Egypt.) 23Then they came to the Valley of Eshcol, and there cut down a branch with one cluster of grapes; they carried it between two of them on a pole. *They* also *brought* some of the pomegranates and figs. 24The place was called the Valley of Eshcol,[a] because of the cluster which the men of Israel cut down there. 25And they returned from spying out the land after forty days.

26Now they departed and came back to Moses and Aaron and all the congregation of the children of Israel in the Wilderness of Paran, at Kadesh; they brought back word to them and to all the congregation, and showed them the fruit of the land. 27Then they told him, and said: "We went to the land where you sent us. It truly flows with milk and honey, and this *is* its fruit. 28Nevertheless the people who dwell in the land *are* strong; the cities *are* fortified *and* very large; moreover we saw the descendants of Anak there. 29The Amalekites dwell in the land of the South; the Hittites, the Jebusites, and the Amorites dwell in the mountains; and the Canaanites dwell by the sea and along the banks of the Jordan."

30Then Caleb quieted the people before Moses, and said, "Let us go up at once and take possession, for we are well able to overcome it." 31But the men who had gone up with him said, "We are not able to go up against the people, for they *are* stronger than we." 32And they gave the children of Israel a bad report of the land which they had spied out, saying, "The land through which we have gone as spies *is* a land that devours its inhabitants, and all the people whom we saw in it *are* men of *great* stature. 33There we saw the giants[a] (the descendants of Anak came from the giants); and we were like grasshoppers in our own sight, and so we were in their sight."

Israel Refuses to Enter Canaan

14 So all the congregation lifted up their voices and cried, and the people wept that night. 2And all the children of Israel complained against Moses and Aaron, and the whole congregation said to them, "If only we had died in the land of Egypt! Or if only we had died in this wilderness! 3Why has the LORD brought us to this land to fall by the sword, that our wives and children should become victims? Would it not be better for us to return to Egypt?" 4So they said to one another, "Let us select a leader and return to Egypt."

5Then Moses and Aaron fell on their faces before all the assembly of the congregation of the children of Israel.

6But Joshua the son of Nun and Caleb the

13:24 [a]Literally *Cluster* 13:33 [a]Hebrew *nephilim*

The Message

21-25 With that they were on their way. They scouted out the land from the Wilderness of Zin as far as Rehob toward Lebo Hamath. Their route went through the Negev Desert to the town of Hebron. Ahiman, Sheshai, and Talmai, descendants of the giant Anak, lived there. Hebron had been built seven years before Zoan in Egypt. When they arrived at the Eshcol Valley they cut off a branch with a single cluster of grapes—it took two men to carry it—slung on a pole. They also picked some pomegranates and figs. They named the place Eshcol Valley (Grape-Cluster-Valley) because of the huge cluster of grapes they had cut down there. After forty days of scouting out the land, they returned home.

26-27 They presented themselves before Moses and Aaron and the whole congregation of the People of Israel in the Wilderness of Paran at Kadesh. They reported to the whole congregation and showed them the fruit of the land. Then they told the story of their trip:

27-29 "We went to the land to which you sent us and, oh! It *does* flow with milk and honey! Just look at this fruit! The only thing is that the people who live there are fierce, their cities are huge and well fortified. Worse yet, we saw descendants of the giant Anak. Amalekites are spread out in the Negev; Hittites, Jebusites, and Amorites hold the hill country; and the Canaanites are established on the Mediterranean Sea and along the Jordan."

30 Caleb interrupted, called for silence before Moses and said, "Let's go up and take the land—now. We can do it."

31-33 But the others said, "We can't attack those people; they're way stronger than we are." They spread scary rumors among the People of Israel. They said, "We scouted out the land from one end to the other—it's a land that swallows people whole. Everybody we saw was huge. Why, we even saw the Nephilim giants (the Anak giants come from the Nephilim). Alongside them we felt like grasshoppers. And they looked down on us as if we were grasshoppers."

1-3 14 The whole community was in an uproar, wailing all night long. All the People of Israel grumbled against Moses and Aaron. The entire community was in on it: "Why didn't we die in Egypt? Or in this wilderness? Why has GOD brought us to this country to kill us? Our wives and children are about to become plunder. Why don't we just head back to Egypt? And right now!"

4 Soon they were all saying it to one another: "Let's pick a new leader; let's head back to Egypt."

5 Moses and Aaron fell on their faces in front of the entire community, gathered in emergency session.

6-9 Joshua son of Nun and Caleb son of Je-

NEW KING JAMES VERSION

son of Jephunneh, *who were* among those who
had spied out the land, tore their clothes; 7and
they spoke to all the congregation of the chil-
dren of Israel, saying: "The land we passed
through to spy out *is* an exceedingly good land.
8If the LORD delights in us, then He will bring us
into this land and give it to us, 'a land which
flows with milk and honey.'[a] 9Only do not rebel
against the LORD, nor fear the people of the
land, for they *are* our bread; their protection has
departed from them, and the LORD *is* with us. Do
not fear them."
10And all the congregation said to stone
them with stones. Now the glory of the LORD ap-
peared in the tabernacle of meeting before all
the children of Israel.

MOSES INTERCEDES FOR THE PEOPLE

11Then the LORD said to Moses: "How long
will these people reject Me? And how long will
they not believe Me, with all the signs which I
have performed among them? 12I will strike
them with the pestilence and disinherit them,
and I will make of you a nation greater and
mightier than they."
13And Moses said to the LORD: "Then the
Egyptians will hear *it*, for by Your might You
brought these people up from among them,
14and they will tell *it* to the inhabitants of this
land. They have heard that You, LORD, *are*
among these people; that You, LORD, are seen
face to face and Your cloud stands above them,
and You go before them in a pillar of cloud by
day and in a pillar of fire by night. 15Now *if* You
kill these people as one man, then the nations
which have heard of Your fame will speak, say-
ing, 16'Because the LORD was not able to bring
this people to the land which He swore to give
them, therefore He killed them in the wilder-
ness.' 17And now, I pray, let the power of my
Lord be great, just as You have spoken, saying,
18'The LORD is longsuffering and abundant in
mercy, forgiving iniquity and transgression; but
He by no means clears *the guilty*, visiting the in-
iquity of the fathers on the children to the third
and fourth *generation*.'[a] 19Pardon the iniquity of
this people, I pray, according to the greatness of
Your mercy, just as You have forgiven this peo-
ple, from Egypt even until now."
20Then the LORD said: "I have pardoned, ac-
cording to your word; 21but truly, as I live, all the
earth shall be filled with the glory of the LORD—
22because all these men who have seen My glory
and the signs which I did in Egypt and in the
wilderness, and have put Me to the test now
these ten times, and have not heeded My voice,
23they certainly shall not see the land of which I
swore to their fathers, nor shall any of those
who rejected Me see it.

14:8 [a]Exodus 3:8 **14:18** [a]Exodus 34:6, 7

THE MESSAGE

phunneh, members of the scouting party,
ripped their clothes and addressed the as-
sembled People of Israel: "The land we
walked through and scouted out is a very
good land—very good indeed. If GOD is
pleased with us, he will lead us into that
land, a land that flows, as they say, with
milk and honey. And he'll give it to us. Just
don't rebel against GOD! And don't be afraid
of those people. Why, we'll have them for
lunch! They have no protection and GOD is
on our side. Don't be afraid of them!"

10-12 But, up in arms now, the entire commu-
nity was talking of hurling stones at them.

Just then the bright Glory of GOD ap-
peared at the Tent of Meeting. Every Israelite
saw it. GOD said to Moses, "How long will
these people treat me like dirt? How long re-
fuse to trust me? And with all these signs I've
done among them! I've had enough—I'm go-
ing to hit them with a plague and kill them.
But I'll make you into a nation bigger and
stronger than they ever were."

13-16 But Moses said to GOD, "The Egyptians
are going to hear about this! You delivered
this people from Egypt with a great show of
strength, and now this? The Egyptians will
tell everyone. They've already heard that you
are GOD, that you are on the side of this peo-
ple, that you are present among them, that
they see you with their own eyes in your
Cloud that hovers over them, in the Pillar of
Cloud that leads them by day and the Pillar
of Fire at night. If you kill this entire people
in one stroke, all the nations that have heard
what has been going on will say, 'Since GOD
couldn't get these people into the land which
he had promised to give them, he slaugh-
tered them out in the wilderness.'

17 "Now, please, let the power of the Master
expand, enlarge itself greatly, along the
lines you have laid out earlier when you
said,

18 GOD, slow to get angry and huge in loyal
love,
forgiving iniquity and rebellion and
sin;
Still, never just whitewashing sin.
But extending the fallout of parents'
sins
to children into the third,
even the fourth generation.

19 "Please forgive the wrongdoing of this
people out of the extravagance of your loyal
love just as all along, from the time they left
Egypt, you have been forgiving this people."

20-23 GOD said, "I forgive them, honoring your
words. But as I live and as the Glory of GOD
fills the whole Earth—not a single person of
those who saw my Glory, saw the miracle
signs I did in Egypt and the wilderness, and
who have tested me over and over and over
again, turning a deaf ear to me—not one of
them will set eyes on the land I so solemnly
promised to their ancestors. No one who
has treated me with such repeated contempt
will see it.

New King James Version

24But My servant Caleb, because he has a different spirit in him and has followed Me fully, I will bring into the land where he went, and his descendants shall inherit it. 25Now the Amalekites and the Canaanites dwell in the valley; tomorrow turn and move out into the wilderness by the Way of the Red Sea."

Death Sentence on the Rebels

26And the LORD spoke to Moses and Aaron, saying, 27"How long *shall I bear with* this evil congregation who complain against Me? I have heard the complaints which the children of Israel make against Me. 28Say to them, 'As I live,' says the LORD, 'just as you have spoken in My hearing, so I will do to you: 29The carcasses of you who have complained against Me shall fall in this wilderness, all of you who were numbered, according to your entire number, from twenty years old and above. 30Except for Caleb the son of Jephunneh and Joshua the son of Nun, you shall by no means enter the land which I swore I would make you dwell in. 31But your little ones, whom you said would be victims, I will bring in, and they shall know the land which you have despised. 32But *as for* you, your carcasses shall fall in this wilderness. 33And your sons shall be shepherds in the wilderness forty years, and bear the brunt of your infidelity, until your carcasses are consumed in the wilderness. 34According to the number of the days in which you spied out the land, forty days, for each day you shall bear your guilt one year, *namely* forty years, and you shall know My rejection. 35I the LORD have spoken this. I will surely do so to all this evil congregation who are gathered together against Me. In this wilderness they shall be consumed, and there they shall die.' "

36Now the men whom Moses sent to spy out the land, who returned and made all the congregation complain against him by bringing a bad report of the land, 37those very men who brought the evil report about the land, died by the plague before the LORD. 38But Joshua the son of Nun and Caleb the son of Jephunneh remained alive, of the men who went to spy out the land.

A Futile Invasion Attempt

39Then Moses told these words to all the children of Israel, and the people mourned greatly. 40And they rose early in the morning and went up to the top of the mountain, saying, "Here we are, and we will go up to the place which the LORD has promised, for we have sinned!"

41And Moses said, "Now why do you transgress the command of the LORD? For this will not succeed. 42Do not go up, lest you be defeated by your enemies, for the LORD *is* not among you. 43For the Amalekites and the Canaanites *are* there before you, and you shall fall by the sword; because you have turned away from the LORD, the LORD will not be with you."

The Message

24 "But my servant Caleb—this is a different story. He has a different spirit; he follows me passionately. I'll bring him into the land that he scouted and his children will inherit it.

25 "Since the Amalekites and Canaanites are so well established in the valleys, for right now change course and head back into the wilderness following the route to the Red Sea."

26-30 GOD spoke to Moses and Aaron: "How long is this going to go on, all this grumbling against me by this evil-infested community? I've had my fill of complaints from these grumbling Israelites. Tell them, As I live—GOD's decree—here's what I'm going to do: Your corpses are going to litter the wilderness—every one of you twenty years and older who was counted in the census, this whole generation of grumblers and grousers. Not one of you will enter the land and make your home there, the firmly and solemnly promised land, except for Caleb son of Jephunneh and Joshua son of Nun.

31-34 "Your children, the very ones that you said would be taken for plunder, I'll bring in to enjoy the land you rejected while your corpses will be rotting in the wilderness. These children of yours will live as shepherds in the wilderness for forty years, living with the fallout of your whoring unfaithfulness until the last of your generation lies a corpse in the wilderness. You scouted out the land for forty days; your punishment will be a year for each day, a forty-year sentence to serve for your sins—a long schooling in my displeasure.

35 "I, GOD, have spoken. I will most certainly carry out these things against this entire evil-infested community which has banded together against me. In this wilderness they will come to their end. There they will die."

36-38 So it happened that the men Moses sent to scout out the land returned to circulate false rumors about the land causing the entire community to grumble against Moses—all these men died. Having spread false rumors of the land, they died in a plague, confronted by GOD. Only Joshua son of Nun and Caleb son of Jephunneh were left alive of the men who went to scout out the land.

39-40 When Moses told all of this to the People of Israel, they mourned long and hard. But early the next morning they started out for the high hill country, saying, "We're here; we're ready—let's go up and attack the land that GOD promised us. We sinned, but now we're ready."

41-43 But Moses said, "Why are you crossing GOD's command yet again? This won't work. Don't attack. GOD isn't with you in this—you'll be beaten badly by your enemies. The Amalekites and Canaanites are ready for you and they'll kill you. Because you have left off obediently following GOD, GOD is not going to be with you in this."

NEW KING JAMES VERSION

44But they presumed to go up to the moun-
taintop. Nevertheless, neither the ark of the
covenant of the LORD nor Moses departed from
the camp. 45Then the Amalekites and the
Canaanites who dwelt in that mountain came
down and attacked them, and drove them back
as far as Hormah.

LAWS OF GRAIN AND DRINK OFFERINGS

15 And the LORD spoke to Moses, saying,
2"Speak to the children of Israel, and say
to them: 'When you have come into the land you
are to inhabit, which I am giving to you, 3and
you make an offering by fire to the LORD, a
burnt offering or a sacrifice, to fulfill a vow or as
a freewill offering or in your appointed feasts, to
make a sweet aroma to the LORD, from the herd
or the flock, 4then he who presents his offering
to the LORD shall bring a grain offering of one-
tenth *of an ephah* of fine flour mixed with one-
fourth of a hin of oil; 5and one-fourth of a hin of
wine as a drink offering you shall prepare with
the burnt offering or the sacrifice, for each
lamb. 6Or for a ram you shall prepare as a grain
offering two-tenths *of an ephah* of fine flour
mixed with one-third of a hin of oil; 7and as a
drink offering you shall offer one-third of a hin
of wine as a sweet aroma to the LORD. 8And
when you prepare a young bull as a burnt offer-
ing, or as a sacrifice to fulfill a vow, or as a
peace offering to the LORD, 9then shall be of-
fered with the young bull a grain offering of
three-tenths *of an ephah* of fine flour mixed
with half a hin of oil; 10and you shall bring as
the drink offering half a hin of wine as an offer-
ing made by fire, a sweet aroma to the LORD.
11'Thus it shall be done for each young bull,
for each ram, or for each lamb or young goat.
12According to the number that you prepare, so
you shall do with everyone according to their
number. 13All who are native-born shall do these
things in this manner, in presenting an offering
made by fire, a sweet aroma to the LORD. 14And
if a stranger dwells with you, or whoever *is*
among you throughout your generations, and
would present an offering made by fire, a sweet
aroma to the LORD, just as you do, so shall he do.
15One ordinance *shall be* for you of the assembly
and for the stranger who dwells *with you*, an or-
dinance forever throughout your generations;
as you are, so shall the stranger be before the
LORD. 16One law and one custom shall be for you
and for the stranger who dwells with you.' "[a]
17Again the LORD spoke to Moses, saying,
18"Speak to the children of Israel, and say to
them: 'When you come into the land to which I
bring you, 19then it will be, when you eat of the
bread of the land, that you shall offer up a heave
offering to the LORD. 20You shall offer up a cake
of the first of your ground meal *as* a heave offer-
ing; as a heave offering of the threshing floor, so
shall you offer it up. 21Of the first of your ground
meal you shall give to the LORD a heave offering
throughout your generations.

15:16 [a]Compare Exodus 12:49

THE MESSAGE

44-45 But they went anyway; recklessly and ar-
rogantly they climbed to the high hill coun-
try. But the Chest of the Covenant and
Moses didn't budge from the camp. The
Amalekites and the Canaanites who lived in
the hill country came out of the hills and at-
tacked and beat them, a rout all the way
down to Hormah.

MATTERS OF WORSHIP

1-5 15 GOD spoke to Moses: "Speak to the
People of Israel. Tell them, When you
enter your homeland that I am giving to you
and sacrifice a Fire-Gift to GOD, a Whole-
Burnt-Offering or any sacrifice from the
herd or flock for a Vow-Offering or Freewill-
Offering at one of the appointed feasts, as a
pleasing fragrance for GOD, the one bring-
ing the offering shall present to GOD a
Grain-Offering of two quarts of fine flour
mixed with a quart of oil. With each lamb
for the Whole-Burnt-Offering or other sacri-
fice, prepare a quart of oil and a quart of
wine as a Drink-Offering.
6-7 "For a ram prepare a Grain-Offering of
four quarts of fine flour mixed with one and
a quarter quarts of oil and one and a quar-
ter quarts of wine as a Drink-Offering. Pre-
sent it as a pleasing fragrance to GOD.
8-10 "When you prepare a young bull as a
Whole-Burnt-Offering or sacrifice for a spe-
cial vow or a Peace-Offering to GOD, bring
with the bull a Grain-Offering of six quarts
of fine flour and two quarts of oil. Also bring
two quarts of wine as a Drink-Offering. It
will be a Fire-Gift, a pleasing fragrance to
GOD.
11-12 "Each bull or ram, each lamb or young
goat, is to be prepared in this same way.
Carry out this procedure for each one, no
matter how many you have to prepare.
13-16 "Every native-born Israelite is to follow
this procedure when he brings a Fire-Gift as
a pleasing fragrance to GOD. In future gen-
erations, when a foreigner or visitor living
at length among you presents a Fire-Gift as
a pleasing fragrance to GOD, the same pro-
cedures must be followed. The community
has the same rules for you and the foreigner
living among you. This is the regular rule
for future generations. You and the foreigner
are the same before GOD. The same laws
and regulations apply to both you and the
foreigner who lives with you."

17-21 GOD spoke to Moses: "Speak to the Peo-
ple of Israel. Tell them, When you enter the
land into which I'm bringing you, and you
eat the food of that country, set some aside
as an offering for GOD. From the first batch
of bread dough make a round loaf for an of-
fering—an offering from the threshing floor.
Down through the future generations make
this offering to GOD from each first batch of
dough.

New King James Version

Laws Concerning Unintentional Sin

[22]'If you sin unintentionally, and do not ob-
serve all these commandments which the LORD
has spoken to Moses— [23]all that the LORD has
commanded you by the hand of Moses, from the
day the LORD gave commandment and onward
throughout your generations— [24]then it will be,
if it is unintentionally committed, without the
knowledge of the congregation, that the whole
congregation shall offer one young bull as a
burnt offering, as a sweet aroma to the LORD,
with its grain offering and its drink offering, ac-
cording to the ordinance, and one kid of the
goats as a sin offering. [25]So the priest shall
make atonement for the whole congregation of
the children of Israel, and it shall be forgiven
them, for it was unintentional; they shall bring
their offering, an offering made by fire to the
LORD, and their sin offering before the LORD, for
their unintended sin. [26]It shall be forgiven the
whole congregation of the children of Israel and
the stranger who dwells among them, because
all the people *did it* unintentionally.

[27]'And if a person sins unintentionally, then
he shall bring a female goat in its first year as a
sin offering. [28]So the priest shall make atone-
ment for the person who sins unintentionally,
when he sins unintentionally before the LORD, to
make atonement for him; and it shall be for-
given him. [29]You shall have one law for him who
sins unintentionally, *for* him who is native-born
among the children of Israel and for the
stranger who dwells among them.

Law Concerning Presumptuous Sin

[30]'But the person who does *anything* pre-
sumptuously, *whether he is* native-born or a
stranger, that one brings reproach on the LORD,
and he shall be cut off from among his people.
[31]Because he has despised the word of the LORD,
and has broken His commandment, that person
shall be completely cut off; his guilt *shall be*
upon him.' "

Penalty for Violating the Sabbath

[32]Now while the children of Israel were in
the wilderness, they found a man gathering
sticks on the Sabbath day. [33]And those who
found him gathering sticks brought him to
Moses and Aaron, and to all the congregation.
[34]They put him under guard, because it had not
been explained what should be done to him.

[35]Then the LORD said to Moses, "The man
must surely be put to death; all the congregation
shall stone him with stones outside the camp."
[36]So, as the LORD commanded Moses, all the
congregation brought him outside the camp and
stoned him with stones, and he died.

Tassels on Garments

[37]Again the LORD spoke to Moses, saying,
[38]"Speak to the children of Israel: Tell them to
make tassels on the corners of their garments
throughout their generations, and to put a blue
thread in the tassels of the corners. [39]And you
shall have the tassel, that you may look upon it
and remember all the commandments of the
LORD and do them, and that you *may* not follow

The Message

22-26 "But if you should get off the beaten track and not keep the commands which GOD spoke to Moses, any of the things that GOD commanded you under the authority of Moses from the time that GOD first commanded you right up to this present time, and if it happened more or less by mistake, with the congregation unaware of it, then the whole congregation is to sacrifice one young bull as a Whole-Burnt-Offering, a pleasing fragrance to GOD, accompanied by its Grain-Offering and Drink-Offering as stipulated in the rules, and a he-goat as an Absolution-Offering. The priest is to atone for the entire community of the People of Israel and they will stand forgiven. The sin was not deliberate, and they offered to GOD the Fire-Gift and Absolution-Offering for their inadvertence. The whole community of Israel including the foreigners living there will be absolved, because everyone was involved in the error.

27-28 "But if it's just one person who sins by mistake, not realizing what he's doing, he is to bring a yearling she-goat as an Absolution-Offering. The priest then is to atone for the person who accidentally sinned, to make atonement before GOD so that it won't be held against him.

29 "The same standard holds for everyone who sins by mistake; the native-born Israelites and the foreigners go by the same rules.

30-31 "But the person, native or foreigner, who sins defiantly, deliberately blaspheming GOD, must be cut off from his people: He has despised GOD's word, he has violated GOD's command; that person must be kicked out of the community, ostracized, left alone in his wrongdoing."

32-35 Once, during those wilderness years of the People of Israel, a man was caught gathering wood on the Sabbath. The ones who caught him hauled him before Moses and Aaron and the entire congregation. They put him in custody until it became clear what to do with him. Then GOD spoke to Moses: "Give the man the death penalty. Yes, kill him, the whole community hurling stones at him outside the camp."

36 So the whole community took him outside the camp and threw stones at him, an execution commanded by GOD and given through Moses.

37-41 GOD spoke to Moses: "Speak to the People of Israel. Tell them that from now on they are to make tassels on the corners of their garments and to mark each corner tassel with a blue thread. When you look at these tassels you'll remember and keep all the commandments of GOD, and not get dis-

NEW KING JAMES VERSION

the harlotry to which your own heart and your
own eyes are inclined, [40]and that you may re-
member and do all My commandments, and be
holy for your God. [41]I *am* the LORD your God,
who brought you out of the land of Egypt, to be
your God: I *am* the LORD your God."

REBELLION AGAINST MOSES AND AARON

16 Now Korah the son of Izhar, the son of Ko-
hath, the son of Levi, with Dathan and Abi-
ram the sons of Eliab, and On the son of Peleth,
sons of Reuben, took *men;* [2]and they rose up be-
fore Moses with some of the children of Israel,
two hundred and fifty leaders of the congrega-
tion, representatives of the congregation, men
of renown. [3]They gathered together against
Moses and Aaron, and said to them, "*You take*
too much upon yourselves, for all the congrega-
tion *is* holy, every one of them, and the LORD *is*
among them. Why then do you exalt yourselves
above the assembly of the LORD?"
[4]So when Moses heard *it,* he fell on his face;
[5]and he spoke to Korah and all his company,
saying, "Tomorrow morning the LORD will show
who *is* His and *who is* holy, and will cause *him*
to come near to Him. That one whom He
chooses He will cause to come near to Him. [6]Do
this: Take censers, Korah and all your company;
[7]put fire in them and put incense in them before
the LORD tomorrow, and it shall be *that* the man
whom the LORD chooses *is* the holy one. *You*
take too much upon yourselves, you sons of
Levi!"
[8]Then Moses said to Korah, "Hear now, you
sons of Levi: [9]*Is it* a small thing to you that the
God of Israel has separated you from the con-
gregation of Israel, to bring you near to Himself,
to do the work of the tabernacle of the LORD,
and to stand before the congregation to serve
them; [10]and that He has brought you near *to*
Himself, you and all your brethren, the sons of
Levi, with you? And are you seeking the priest-
hood also? [11]Therefore you and all your com-
pany *are* gathered together against the LORD.
And what *is* Aaron that you complain against
him?"
[12]And Moses sent to call Dathan and Abiram
the sons of Eliab, but they said, "We will not
come up! [13]*Is it* a small thing that you have
brought us up out of a land flowing with milk
and honey, to kill us in the wilderness, that you
should keep acting like a prince over us?
[14]Moreover you have not brought us into a land
flowing with milk and honey, nor given us in-
heritance of fields and vineyards. Will you put
out the eyes of these men? We will not come up!"
[15]Then Moses was very angry, and said to the
LORD, "Do not respect their offering. I have not
taken one donkey from them, nor have I hurt
one of them."
[16]And Moses said to Korah, "Tomorrow, you
and all your company be present before the
LORD—you and they, as well as Aaron. [17]Let
each take his censer and put incense in it, and

THE MESSAGE

tracted by everything you feel or see that se-
duces you into infidelities. The tassels will
signal remembrance and observance of all
my commandments, to live a holy life to
GOD. I am your GOD who rescued you from
the land of Egypt to be your personal God.
Yes, I am GOD, *your* God."

THE REBELS

1-3 16 Getting on his high horse one day, Ko-
rah son of Izhar, the son of Kohath, the
son of Levi, along with a few Reubenites—
Dathan and Abiram sons of Eliab, and On
son of Peleth—rebelled against Moses. He
had with him 250 leaders of the congrega-
tion of Israel, prominent men with positions
in the Council. They came as a group and
confronted Moses and Aaron, saying,
"You've overstepped yourself. This entire
community is holy and GOD is in their midst.
So why do you act like you're running the
whole show?"
4 On hearing this, Moses threw himself
facedown on the ground.
5 Then he addressed Korah and his gang:
"In the morning GOD will make clear who is
on his side, who is holy. GOD will take his
stand with the one he chooses.
6-7 "Now, Korah, here's what I want you, you
and your gang, to do: Tomorrow, take
censers. In the presence of GOD, put fire in
them and then incense. Then we'll see who
is holy, see whom GOD chooses. Sons of
Levi, you've overstepped *yourselves!*"
8-11 Moses continued with Korah, "Listen well
now, sons of Levi. Isn't it enough for you
that the God of Israel has selected you out of
the congregation of Israel to bring you near
him to serve in the ministries of The
Dwelling of GOD, and to stand before the
congregation to minister to them? He has
brought you and all your brother Levites
into his inner circle, and now you're grasp-
ing for the priesthood, too. It's GOD you've
ganged up against, not us. What do you have
against Aaron that you're bad-mouthing
him?"
12-14 Moses then ordered Dathan and Abiram,
sons of Eliab, to appear, but they said, "We're
not coming. Isn't it enough that you yanked
us out of a land flowing with milk and honey
to kill us in the wilderness? And now you
keep trying to boss us around! Face it, you
haven't produced: You haven't brought us
into a land flowing with milk and honey, you
haven't given us the promised inheritance of
fields and vineyards. You'd have to poke our
eyes out to keep us from seeing what's going
on. Forget it, we're not coming."
15 Moses' temper blazed white-hot. He said
to GOD, "Don't accept their Grain-Offering. I
haven't taken so much as a single donkey
from them; I haven't hurt a single hair of
their heads."
16-17 Moses said to Korah, "Bring your people
before GOD tomorrow. Appear there with
them and Aaron. Have each man bring his
censer filled with incense and present it to

NEW KING JAMES VERSION

each of you bring his censer before the LORD, two hundred and fifty censers; both you and Aaron, each *with* his censer." 18 So every man took his censer, put fire in it, laid incense on it, and stood at the door of the tabernacle of meeting with Moses and Aaron. 19 And Korah gathered all the congregation against them at the door of the tabernacle of meeting. Then the glory of the LORD appeared to all the congregation.

20 And the LORD spoke to Moses and Aaron, saying, 21 "Separate yourselves from among this congregation, that I may consume them in a moment."

22 Then they fell on their faces, and said, "O God, the God of the spirits of all flesh, shall one man sin, and You be angry with all the congregation?"

23 So the LORD spoke to Moses, saying, 24 "Speak to the congregation, saying, 'Get away from the tents of Korah, Dathan, and Abiram.' "

25 Then Moses rose and went to Dathan and Abiram, and the elders of Israel followed him. 26 And he spoke to the congregation, saying, "Depart now from the tents of these wicked men! Touch nothing of theirs, lest you be consumed in all their sins." 27 So they got away from around the tents of Korah, Dathan, and Abiram; and Dathan and Abiram came out and stood at the door of their tents, with their wives, their sons, and their little children.

28 And Moses said: "By this you shall know that the LORD has sent me to do all these works, for *I have* not *done them* of my own will. 29 If these men die naturally like all men, or if they are visited by the common fate of all men, *then* the LORD has not sent me. 30 But if the LORD creates a new thing, and the earth opens its mouth and swallows them up with all that belongs to them, and they go down alive into the pit, then you will understand that these men have rejected the LORD."

31 Now it came to pass, as he finished speaking all these words, that the ground split apart under them, 32 and the earth opened its mouth and swallowed them up, with their households and all the men with Korah, with all *their* goods. 33 So they and all those with them went down alive into the pit; the earth closed over them, and they perished from among the assembly. 34 Then all Israel who *were* around them fled at their cry, for they said, "Lest the earth swallow us up *also!*"

35 And a fire came out from the LORD and consumed the two hundred and fifty men who were offering incense.

36 Then the LORD spoke to Moses, saying: 37 "Tell Eleazar, the son of Aaron the priest, to pick up the censers out of the blaze, for they are holy, and scatter the fire some distance away. 38 The censers of these men who sinned against their own souls, let them be made into hammered plates as a covering for the altar. Because they presented them before the LORD, therefore they are holy; and they shall be a sign to the children of Israel."

THE MESSAGE

GOD—all 250 censers. And you and Aaron do the same, bring your censers."

18 So they all did it. They brought their censers filled with fire and incense and stood at the entrance of the Tent of Meeting. Moses and Aaron did the same.

19 It was Korah and his gang against Moses and Aaron at the entrance of the Tent of Meeting. The entire community could see the Glory of GOD.

20-21 GOD said to Moses and Aaron, "Separate yourselves from this congregation so that I can finish them off and be done with them."

22 They threw themselves on their faces and said, "O God, God of everything living, when one man sins are you going to take it out on the whole community?"

23-24 GOD spoke to Moses: "Speak to the community. Tell them, Back off from the tents of Korah, Dathan, and Abiram."

25-26 Moses got up and went to Dathan and Abiram. The leaders of Israel followed him. He then spoke to the community: "Back off from the tents of these bad men; don't touch a thing that belongs to them lest you be carried off on the flood of their sins."

27 So they all backed away from the tents of Korah, Dathan, and Abiram. Dathan and Abiram by now had come out and were standing at the entrance to their tents with their wives, children, and babies.

28-30 Moses continued to address the community: "This is how you'll know that it was GOD who sent me to do all these things and that it wasn't anything I cooked up on my own. If these men die a natural death like all the rest of us, you'll know that it wasn't GOD who sent me. But if GOD does something unprecedented—if the ground opens up and swallows the lot of them and they are pitched alive into Sheol—then you'll know that these men have been insolent with GOD."

31-33 The words were hardly out of his mouth when the Earth split open. Earth opened its mouth and in one gulp swallowed them down, the men and their families, all the human beings connected with Korah, along with everything they owned. And that was the end of them, pitched alive into Sheol. The Earth closed up over them and that was the last the community heard of them.

34 At the sound of their cries everyone around ran for dear life, shouting, "We're about to be swallowed up alive!"

35 Then GOD sent lightning. The fire cremated the 250 men who were offering the incense.

36-38 GOD spoke to Moses: "Tell Eleazar son of Aaron the priest, Gather up the censers from the smoldering cinders and scatter the coals a distance away for these censers have become holy. Take the censers of the men who have sinned and are now dead and hammer them into thin sheets for covering the Altar. They have been offered to GOD and are holy to GOD. Let them serve as a sign to Israel, evidence of what happened this day."

NEW KING JAMES VERSION

39 So Eleazar the priest took the bronze censers,
which those who were burned up had presented,
and they were hammered out as a covering on
the altar, 40 *to be* a memorial to the children of
Israel that no outsider, who *is* not a descendant
of Aaron, should come near to offer incense
before the LORD, that he might not become like
Korah and his companions, just as the LORD had
said to him through Moses.

COMPLAINTS OF THE PEOPLE

41 On the next day all the congregation of the
children of Israel complained against Moses
and Aaron, saying, "You have killed the people
of the LORD." 42 Now it happened, when the con-
gregation had gathered against Moses and
Aaron, that they turned toward the tabernacle
of meeting; and suddenly the cloud covered it,
and the glory of the LORD appeared. 43 Then
Moses and Aaron came before the tabernacle of
meeting.
44 And the LORD spoke to Moses, saying,
45 "Get away from among this congregation, that
I may consume them in a moment."
And they fell on their faces.
46 So Moses said to Aaron, "Take a censer and
put fire in it from the altar, put incense *on it,* and
take it quickly to the congregation and make
atonement for them; for wrath has gone out
from the LORD. The plague has begun." 47 Then
Aaron took *it* as Moses commanded, and ran
into the midst of the assembly; and already the
plague had begun among the people. So he put
in the incense and made atonement for the peo-
ple. 48 And he stood between the dead and the
living; so the plague was stopped. 49 Now those
who died in the plague were fourteen thousand
seven hundred, besides those who died in the
Korah incident. 50 So Aaron returned to Moses at
the door of the tabernacle of meeting, for the
plague had stopped.

THE BUDDING OF AARON'S ROD

17 And the LORD spoke to Moses, saying:
2 "Speak to the children of Israel, and get
from them a rod from each father's house, all
their leaders according to their fathers' houses—
twelve rods. Write each man's name on his rod.
3 And you shall write Aaron's name on the rod of
Levi. For there shall be one rod for the head of
each father's house. 4 Then you shall place them
in the tabernacle of meeting before the Testi-
mony, where I meet with you. 5 And it shall be
that the rod of the man whom I choose will blos-
som; thus I will rid Myself of the complaints of
the children of Israel, which they make against
you."
6 So Moses spoke to the children of Israel,
and each of their leaders gave him a rod apiece,
for each leader according to their fathers'
houses, twelve rods; and the rod of Aaron *was*
among their rods. 7 And Moses placed the rods
before the LORD in the tabernacle of witness.
8 Now it came to pass on the next day that
Moses went into the tabernacle of witness, and
behold, the rod of Aaron, of the house of Levi,
had sprouted and put forth buds, had produced

THE MESSAGE

39-40 So Eleazar gathered all the bronze censers that belonged to those who had been burned up and had them hammered flat and used to overlay the Altar, just as GOD had instructed him by Moses. This was to serve as a sign to Israel that only descendants of Aaron were allowed to burn incense before GOD; anyone else trying it would end up like Korah and his gang.

41 Grumbling broke out the next day in the community of Israel, grumbling against Moses and Aaron: "You have killed GOD's people!"

42 But it so happened that when the community got together against Moses and Aaron, they looked over at the Tent of Meeting and there was the Cloud—the Glory of GOD for all to see.

43-45 Moses and Aaron stood at the front of the Tent of Meeting. GOD spoke to Moses: "Back away from this congregation so that I can do away with them this very minute."

They threw themselves facedown on the ground.

46 Moses said to Aaron, "Take your censer and fill it with incense, along with fire from the Altar. Get to the congregation as fast as you can: make atonement for them. Anger is pouring out from GOD—the plague has started!"

47-48 Aaron grabbed the censer, as directed by Moses, and ran into the midst of the congregation. The plague had already begun. He put burning incense into the censer and atoned for the people. He stood there between the living and the dead and stopped the plague.

49-50 Fourteen thousand seven hundred people died from the plague, not counting those who died in the affair of Korah. Aaron then went back to join Moses at the entrance to the Tent of Meeting. The plague was stopped.

AARON'S STAFF

1-5 17 GOD spoke to Moses: "Speak to the People of Israel. Get staffs from them—twelve staffs in all, one from the leader of each of their ancestral tribes. Write each man's name on his staff. Start with Aaron; write Aaron's name on the staff of Levi and then proceed with the rest, a staff for the leader of each ancestral tribe. Now lay them out in the Tent of Meeting in front of The Testimony where I keep appointments with you. What will happen next is this: The staff of the man I choose will sprout. I'm going to put a stop to this endless grumbling by the People of Israel against you."

6-7 Moses spoke to the People of Israel. Their leaders handed over twelve staffs, one for the leader of each tribe. And Aaron's staff was one of them. Moses laid out the staffs before GOD in the Tent of Testimony.

8-9 Moses walked into the Tent of Testimony the next day and saw that Aaron's staff, the staff of the tribe of Levi, had in fact sprouted—buds, blossoms, and even ripe al-

New King James Version

blossoms and yielded ripe almonds. 9 Then
Moses brought out all the rods from before the
LORD to all the children of Israel; and they
looked, and each man took his rod.
10 And the LORD said to Moses, "Bring
Aaron's rod back before the Testimony, to be
kept as a sign against the rebels, that you may
put their complaints away from Me, lest they
die." 11 Thus did Moses; just as the LORD had
commanded him, so he did.
12 So the children of Israel spoke to Moses,
saying, "Surely we die, we perish, we all perish!
13 Whoever even comes near the tabernacle of
the LORD must die. Shall we all utterly die?"

Duties of Priests and Levites

18 Then the LORD said to Aaron: "You and
your sons and your father's house with
you shall bear the iniquity *related to* the sanctu-
ary, and you and your sons with you shall bear
the iniquity *associated with* your priesthood.
2 Also bring with you your brethren of the tribe
of Levi, the tribe of your father, that they may be
joined with you and serve you while you and
your sons *are* with you before the tabernacle of
witness. 3 They shall attend to your needs and all
the needs of the tabernacle; but they shall not
come near the articles of the sanctuary and the
altar, lest they die—they and you also. 4 They
shall be joined with you and attend to the needs
of the tabernacle of meeting, for all the work of
the tabernacle; but an outsider shall not come
near you. 5 And you shall attend to the duties of
the sanctuary and the duties of the altar, that
there *may* be no more wrath on the children
of Israel. 6 Behold, I Myself have taken your
brethren the Levites from among the children of
Israel; *they are* a gift to you, given by the LORD,
to do the work of the tabernacle of meeting.
7 Therefore you and your sons with you shall at-
tend to your priesthood for everything at the al-
tar and behind the veil; and you shall serve. I
give your priesthood *to you* as a gift for service,
but the outsider who comes near shall be put to
death."

Offerings for Support of the Priests

8 And the LORD spoke to Aaron: "Here, I My-
self have also given you charge of My heave of-
ferings, all the holy gifts of the children of Is-
rael; I have given them as a portion to you and
your sons, as an ordinance forever. 9 This shall
be yours of the most holy things *reserved* from
the fire: every offering of theirs, every grain of-
fering and every sin offering and every trespass
offering which they render to Me, *shall be* most
holy for you and your sons. 10 In a most holy
place you shall eat it; every male shall eat it. It
shall be holy to you.
11 "This also *is* yours: the heave offering of
their gift, with all the wave offerings of the chil-
dren of Israel; I have given them to you, and
your sons and daughters with you, as an ordi-
nance forever. Everyone who is clean in your
house may eat it.

The Message

monds! Moses brought out all the staffs
from GOD's presence and presented them to
the People of Israel. They took a good look.
Each leader took the staff with his name on
it.
10 GOD said to Moses, "Return Aaron's staff
to the front of The Testimony. Keep it there
as a sign to rebels. This will put a stop to the
grumbling against me and save their lives."
11 Moses did just as GOD commanded him.

12-13 The People of Israel said to Moses, "We're
as good as dead. This is our death sentence.
Anyone who even gets close to The
Dwelling of GOD is as good as dead. Are we
all doomed?"

Duties in the Tent of Testimony

1-4 18 GOD said to Aaron, "You and your
sons, along with your father's family,
are responsible for taking care of sins hav-
ing to do with the Sanctuary; you and your
sons are also responsible for sins involving
the priesthood. So enlist your brothers of
the tribe of Levi to join you and assist you
and your sons in your duties in the Tent of
Testimony. They will report to you as they
go about their duties related to the Tent, but
they must not have anything to do with the
holy things of the Altar under penalty of
death—both they and you will die! They are
to work with you in taking care of the Tent
of Meeting, whatever work is involved in the
Tent. Outsiders are not allowed to help you.
5-7 "Your job is to take care of the Sanctuary
and the Altar so that there will be no more
outbreaks of anger on the People of Israel. I
personally have picked your brothers, the
Levites, from Israel as a whole. I'm giving
them to you as a gift, a gift of GOD, to help
with the work of the Tent of Meeting. But
only you and your sons may serve as
priests, working around the Altar and inside
the curtain. The work of the priesthood is
my exclusive gift to you; it cannot be dele-
gated—anyone else who invades the Sanc-
tuary will be executed."

8-10 GOD spoke to Aaron, "I am personally put-
ting you in charge of my contributions, all
the holy gifts I get from the People of Israel.
I am turning them over to you and your chil-
dren for your personal use. This is the stand-
ing rule. You and your sons get what's left
from the offerings, whatever hasn't been to-
tally burned up on the Altar—the leftovers
from Grain-Offerings, Absolution-Offerings,
and Compensation-Offerings. Eat it rever-
ently; it is most holy; every male may eat it.
Treat it as holy.
11-13 "You also get the Wave-Offerings from
the People of Israel. I present them to you
and your sons and daughters as a gift. This
is the standing rule. Anyone in your house-
hold who is ritually clean may eat it. I also

New King James Version

12 “All the best of the oil, all the best of the new wine and the grain, their firstfruits which they offer to the LORD, I have given them to you. 13 Whatever first ripe fruit is in their land, which they bring to the LORD, shall be yours. Everyone who is clean in your house may eat it.

14 “Every devoted thing in Israel shall be yours.

15 “Everything that first opens the womb of all flesh, which they bring to the LORD, whether man or beast, shall be yours; nevertheless the firstborn of man you shall surely redeem, and the firstborn of unclean animals you shall redeem. 16 And those redeemed of the devoted things you shall redeem when one month old, according to your valuation, for five shekels of silver, according to the shekel of the sanctuary, which *is* twenty gerahs. 17 But the firstborn of a cow, the firstborn of a sheep, or the firstborn of a goat you shall not redeem; they *are* holy. You shall sprinkle their blood on the altar, and burn their fat *as* an offering made by fire for a sweet aroma to the LORD. 18 And their flesh shall be yours, just as the wave breast and the right thigh are yours.

19 “All the heave offerings of the holy things, which the children of Israel offer to the LORD, I have given to you and your sons and daughters with you as an ordinance forever; it *is* a covenant of salt forever before the LORD with you and your descendants with you.”

20 Then the LORD said to Aaron: “You shall have no inheritance in their land, nor shall you have any portion among them; I *am* your portion and your inheritance among the children of Israel.

TITHES FOR SUPPORT OF THE LEVITES

21 “Behold, I have given the children of Levi all the tithes in Israel as an inheritance in return for the work which they perform, the work of the tabernacle of meeting. 22 Hereafter the children of Israel shall not come near the tabernacle of meeting, lest they bear sin and die. 23 But the Levites shall perform the work of the tabernacle of meeting, and they shall bear their iniquity; *it shall be* a statute forever, throughout your generations, that among the children of Israel they shall have no inheritance. 24 For the tithes of the children of Israel, which they offer up *as* a heave offering to the LORD, I have given to the Levites as an inheritance; therefore I have said to them, ‘Among the children of Israel they shall have no inheritance.’ ”

THE TITHE OF THE LEVITES

25 Then the LORD spoke to Moses, saying, 26 “Speak thus to the Levites, and say to them: ‘When you take from the children of Israel the tithes which I have given you from them as your inheritance, then you shall offer up a heave offering of it to the LORD, a tenth of the tithe. 27 And your heave offering shall be reckoned to you as though *it were* the grain of the threshing floor and as the fullness of the winepress. 28 Thus you shall also offer a heave offering to the LORD from all your tithes which you receive from the children of Israel, and you shall give

The Message

give you all the best olive oil, the best new wine, and the grain that is offered to GOD as the firstfruits of their harvest—all the firstfruits they offer to GOD are yours. Anyone in your household who is ritually clean may eat it.

14-16 “You get every Totally-Devoted gift. Every firstborn that is offered to GOD, whether animal or person, is yours. Except you don’t get the firstborn itself, but its redemption price; firstborn humans and ritually clean animals are bought back and you get the redemption price. When the firstborn is a month old it must be redeemed at the redemption price of five shekels of silver, using the standard of the Sanctuary shekel, which weighs twenty gerahs.

17-19 “On the other hand, you don’t redeem a firstborn ox, sheep, or goat—they are holy. Instead splash their blood on the Altar and burn their fat as a Fire-Gift, a pleasing fragrance to GOD. But you get the meat, just as you get the breast from the Wave-Offering and the right thigh. All the holy offerings that the People of Israel set aside for GOD, I’m turning over to you and your children. That’s the standard rule and includes both you and your children—a Covenant-of-Salt, eternal and unchangeable before GOD.”

20 GOD said to Aaron, “You won’t get any inheritance in land, not so much as a small plot of ground: I am your plot of ground, I am your inheritance among the People of Israel.

21-24 “I’m giving the Levites all the tithes of Israel as their pay for the work they do in the Tent of Meeting. Starting now, the rest of the People of Israel cannot wander in and out of the Tent of Meeting; they’ll be penalized for their sin and the penalty is death. It’s the Levites and only the Levites who are to work in the Tent of Meeting and they are responsible for anything that goes wrong. This is the regular rule for all time. They get no inheritance among the People of Israel; instead I turn over to them the tithes that the People of Israel present as an offering to GOD. That’s why I give the ruling: They are to receive no land-inheritance among the People of Israel.”

25-29 GOD spoke to Moses: “Speak to the Levites. Tell them, When you get the tithe from the People of Israel, the inheritance that I have assigned to you, you must tithe that tithe and present it as an offering to GOD. Your offerings will be treated the same as other people’s gifts of grain from the threshing floor or wine from the wine vat. This is your procedure for making offerings to GOD from all the tithes you get from the People of Israel: give GOD’s portion from these tithes to

NEW KING JAMES VERSION

the LORD's heave offering from it to Aaron the priest. 29Of all your gifts you shall offer up every heave offering due to the LORD, from all the best of them, the consecrated part of them.' 30Therefore you shall say to them: 'When you have lifted up the best of it, then *the rest* shall be accounted to the Levites as the produce of the threshing floor and as the produce of the winepress. 31You may eat it in any place, you and your households, for it *is* your reward for your work in the tabernacle of meeting. 32And you shall bear no sin because of it, when you have lifted up the best of it. But you shall not profane the holy gifts of the children of Israel, lest you die.' "

LAWS OF PURIFICATION

19 Now the LORD spoke to Moses and Aaron, saying, 2"This *is* the ordinance of the law which the LORD has commanded, saying: 'Speak to the children of Israel, that they bring you a red heifer without blemish, in which there *is* no defect *and* on which a yoke has never come. 3You shall give it to Eleazar the priest, that he may take it outside the camp, and it shall be slaughtered before him; 4and Eleazar the priest shall take some of its blood with his finger, and sprinkle some of its blood seven times directly in front of the tabernacle of meeting. 5Then the heifer shall be burned in his sight: its hide, its flesh, its blood, and its offal shall be burned. 6And the priest shall take cedar wood and hyssop and scarlet, and cast *them* into the midst of the fire burning the heifer. 7Then the priest shall wash his clothes, he shall bathe in water, and afterward he shall come into the camp; the priest shall be unclean until evening. 8And the one who burns it shall wash his clothes in water, bathe in water, and shall be unclean until evening. 9Then a man *who is* clean shall gather up the ashes of the heifer, and store *them* outside the camp in a clean place; and they shall be kept for the congregation of the children of Israel for the water of purification;[a] it *is* for purifying from sin. 10And the one who gathers the ashes of the heifer shall wash his clothes, and be unclean until evening. It shall be a statute forever to the children of Israel and to the stranger who dwells among them.

11'He who touches the dead body of anyone shall be unclean seven days. 12He shall purify himself with the water on the third day and on the seventh day; *then* he will be clean. But if he does not purify himself on the third day and on the seventh day, he will not be clean. 13Whoever touches the body of anyone who has died, and does not purify himself, defiles the tabernacle of the LORD. That person shall be cut off from Israel. He shall be unclean, because the water of purification was not sprinkled on him; his uncleanness *is* still on him.

14'This *is* the law when a man dies in a tent: All who come into the tent and all who *are* in the tent shall be unclean seven days; 15and every open vessel, which has no cover fastened on it, *is* unclean. 16Whoever in the open field touches one who is slain by a sword or who has died, or

19:9 [a]Literally *impurity*

THE MESSAGE

Aaron the priest. Make sure that GOD's portion is the best and holiest of everything you get.

30-32 "Tell the Levites, When you offer the best part, the rest will be treated the same as grain from the threshing floor or wine from the wine vat that others give. You and your households are free to eat the rest of it anytime and anyplace—it's your wages for your work at the Tent of Meeting. By offering the best part, you'll avoid guilt, you won't desecrate the holy offerings of the People of Israel, and you won't die."

THE RED COW

1-4 **19** GOD spoke to Moses and Aaron: "This is the rule from the Revelation that GOD commands: Tell the People of Israel to get a red cow, a healthy specimen, ritually clean, that has never been in harness. Present it to Eleazar the priest, then take it outside the camp and butcher it while he looks on. Eleazar will take some of the blood on his finger and splash it seven times in the direction of the Tent of Meeting.

5-8 "Then under Eleazar's supervision burn the cow, the whole thing—hide, meat, blood, even its dung. The priest then will take a stick of cedar, some sprigs of hyssop, and a piece of scarlet material and throw them on the burning cow. Afterwards the priest must wash his clothes and bathe well with water. He can then come into the camp but he remains ritually unclean until evening. The man who burns the cow must also wash his clothes and bathe with water. He also is unclean until evening.

9 "Then a man who is ritually clean will gather the ashes of the cow and place them in a ritually clean place outside the camp. The congregation of Israel will keep them to use in the Water-of-Cleansing, an Absolution-Offering.

10 "The man who gathered up the ashes must scrub his clothes; he is ritually unclean until evening. This is to be a standing rule for both native-born Israelites and foreigners living among them.

11-13 "Anyone who touches a dead body is ritually unclean for seven days. He must purify himself with the Water-of-Cleansing on the third day; on the seventh day he will be clean. But if he doesn't follow the procedures for the third and seventh days, he won't be clean. Anyone who touches the dead body of anyone and doesn't get cleansed desecrates GOD's Dwelling and is to be excommunicated. For as long as the Water-of-Cleansing has not been sprinkled on him, he remains ritually unclean.

14-15 "This is the rule for someone who dies in his tent: Anyone who enters the tent or is already in the tent is ritually unclean for seven days, and every open container without a lid is unclean.

16-21 "Anyone out in the open field who touches a corpse, whether dead from violent

NEW KING JAMES VERSION

a bone of a man, or a grave, shall be unclean seven days.

17‘And for an unclean *person* they shall take some of the ashes of the heifer burnt for purification from sin, and running water shall be put on them in a vessel. 18A clean person shall take hyssop and dip *it* in the water, sprinkle *it* on the tent, on all the vessels, on the persons who were there, or on the one who touched a bone, the slain, the dead, or a grave. 19The clean *person* shall sprinkle the unclean on the third day and on the seventh day; and on the seventh day he shall purify himself, wash his clothes, and bathe in water; and at evening he shall be clean.

20‘But the man who is unclean and does not purify himself, that person shall be cut off from among the assembly, because he has defiled the sanctuary of the LORD. The water of purification has not been sprinkled on him; he *is* unclean. 21It shall be a perpetual statute for them. He who sprinkles the water of purification shall wash his clothes; and he who touches the water of purification shall be unclean until evening. 22Whatever the unclean *person* touches shall be unclean; and the person who touches *it* shall be unclean until evening.’ ”

MOSES’ ERROR AT KADESH

20 Then the children of Israel, the whole congregation, came into the Wilderness of Zin in the first month, and the people stayed in Kadesh; and Miriam died there and was buried there.

2Now there was no water for the congregation; so they gathered together against Moses and Aaron. 3And the people contended with Moses and spoke, saying: “If only we had died when our brethren died before the LORD! 4Why have you brought up the assembly of the LORD into this wilderness, that we and our animals should die here? 5And why have you made us come up out of Egypt, to bring us to this evil place? It *is* not a place of grain or figs or vines or pomegranates; nor *is* there any water to drink.” 6So Moses and Aaron went from the presence of the assembly to the door of the tabernacle of meeting, and they fell on their faces. And the glory of the LORD appeared to them.

7Then the LORD spoke to Moses, saying, 8“Take the rod; you and your brother Aaron gather the congregation together. Speak to the rock before their eyes, and it will yield its water; thus you shall bring water for them out of the rock, and give drink to the congregation and their animals.” 9So Moses took the rod from before the LORD as He commanded him.

10And Moses and Aaron gathered the assembly together before the rock; and he said to them, “Hear now, you rebels! Must we bring water for you out of this rock?” 11Then Moses lifted his hand and struck the rock twice with his rod; and water came out abundantly, and the congregation and their animals drank.

THE MESSAGE

or natural causes, or a human bone or a grave is unclean for seven days. For this unclean person, take some ashes from the burned Absolution-Offering and add some fresh water to it in a bowl. Find a ritually clean man to dip a sprig of hyssop into the water and sprinkle the tent and all its furnishings, the persons who were in the tent, the one who touched the bones of the person who was killed or died a natural death, and whoever may have touched a grave. Then he is to sprinkle the unclean person on the third and seventh days. On the seventh day he is considered cleansed. The cleansed person must then scrub his clothes and take a bath; by evening he is clean. But if an unclean person does not go through these cleansing procedures, he must be excommunicated from the community; he has desecrated the Sanctuary of GOD. The Water-of-Cleansing has not been sprinkled on him and he is ritually unclean. This is the standing rule for these cases.

“The man who sprinkles the Water-of-Cleansing has to scrub his clothes; anyone else who touched the Water-of-Cleansing is also ritually unclean until evening.

22 “Anything the ritually unclean man touches becomes unclean, and the person who touches what he touched is unclean until evening.”

CAMP KADESH

1 20 In the first month, the entire company of the People of Israel arrived in the Wilderness of Zin. The people stayed in Kadesh.

Miriam died there, and she was buried.

2-5 There was no water there for the community, so they ganged up on Moses and Aaron. They attacked Moses: “We wish we’d died when the rest of our brothers died before GOD. Why did you haul this congregation of GOD out here into this wilderness to die, people and cattle alike? And why did you take us out of Egypt in the first place, dragging us into this miserable country? No grain, no figs, no grapevines, no pomegranates—and now not even any water!”

6 Moses and Aaron walked from the assembled congregation to the Tent of Meeting and threw themselves facedown on the ground. And they saw the Glory of GOD.

7-8 GOD spoke to Moses: “Take the staff. Assemble the community, you and your brother Aaron. Speak to that rock that’s right in front of them and it will give water. You will bring water out of the rock for them; congregation and cattle will both drink.”

9-10 Moses took the staff away from GOD’s presence, as commanded. He and Aaron rounded up the whole congregation in front of the rock. Moses spoke: “Listen, rebels! Do we have to bring water out of this rock for you?”

11 With that Moses raised his arm and slammed his staff against the rock—once, twice. Water poured out. Congregation and cattle drank.

NEW KING JAMES VERSION

[12]Then the LORD spoke to Moses and Aaron,
"Because you did not believe Me, to hallow Me
in the eyes of the children of Israel, therefore
you shall not bring this assembly into the land
which I have given them."
[13]This *was* the water of Meribah,[a] because
the children of Israel contended with the LORD,
and He was hallowed among them.

PASSAGE THROUGH EDOM REFUSED

[14]Now Moses sent messengers from Kadesh
to the king of Edom. "Thus says your brother Is-
rael: 'You know all the hardship that has be-
fallen us, [15]how our fathers went down to Egypt,
and we dwelt in Egypt a long time, and the
Egyptians afflicted us and our fathers. [16]When
we cried out to the LORD, He heard our voice and
sent the Angel and brought us up out of Egypt;
now here we are in Kadesh, a city on the edge of
your border. [17]Please let us pass through your
country. We will not pass through fields or vine-
yards, nor will we drink water from wells; we
will go along the King's Highway; we will not
turn aside to the right hand or to the left until
we have passed through your territory.' "
[18]Then Edom said to him, "You shall not pass
through my *land,* lest I come out against you
with the sword."
[19]So the children of Israel said to him, "We
will go by the Highway, and if I or my livestock
drink any of your water, then I will pay for it; let
me only pass through on foot, nothing *more.*"
[20]Then he said, "You shall not pass through."
So Edom came out against them with many men
and with a strong hand. [21]Thus Edom refused to
give Israel passage through his territory; so Is-
rael turned away from him.

DEATH OF AARON

[22]Now the children of Israel, the whole con-
gregation, journeyed from Kadesh and came to
Mount Hor. [23]And the LORD spoke to Moses and
Aaron in Mount Hor by the border of the land of
Edom, saying: [24]"Aaron shall be gathered to his
people, for he shall not enter the land which I
have given to the children of Israel, because you
rebelled against My word at the water of
Meribah. [25]Take Aaron and Eleazar his son, and
bring them up to Mount Hor; [26]and strip Aaron
of his garments and put them on Eleazar his
son; for Aaron shall be gathered *to his people*
and die there." [27]So Moses did just as the LORD
commanded, and they went up to Mount Hor
in the sight of all the congregation. [28]Moses
stripped Aaron of his garments and put them on
Eleazar his son; and Aaron died there on the top
of the mountain. Then Moses and Eleazar came
down from the mountain. [29]Now when all the
congregation saw that Aaron was dead, all the
house of Israel mourned for Aaron thirty days.

20:13 [a]Literally *Contention*

THE MESSAGE

12 GOD said to Moses and Aaron, "Because you didn't trust me, didn't treat me with holy reverence in front of the People of Israel, you two aren't going to lead this company into the land that I am giving them."

13 These were the Waters of Meribah (Bickering) where the People of Israel bickered with GOD, and he revealed himself as holy.

14-16 Moses sent emissaries from Kadesh to the king of Edom with this message: "A message from your brother Israel: You are familiar with all the trouble we've run into. Our ancestors went down to Egypt and lived there a long time. The Egyptians viciously abused both us and our ancestors. But when we cried out for help to GOD, he heard our cry. He sent an angel and got us out of Egypt. And now here we are at Kadesh, a town at the border of your land.

17 "Will you give us permission to cut across your land? We won't trespass through your fields or orchards and we won't drink out of your wells; we'll keep to the main road, the King's Road, straying neither right nor left until we've crossed your border."

18 The king of Edom answered, "Not on your life. If you so much as set a foot on my land, I'll kill you."

19 The People of Israel said, "Look, we'll stay on the main road. If we or our animals drink any water, we'll pay you for it. We're harmless—just a company of footsore travelers."

20-21 He answered again: "No. You may *not* come through." And Edom came out and blocked the way with a crowd of people brandishing weapons. Edom refused to let them cross through his land. So Israel had to detour around him.

CAMP HOR

22 The People of Israel, the entire company, set out from Kadesh and traveled to Mount Hor.

23-26 GOD said to Moses and Aaron at Mount Hor at the border of Edom, "It's time for Aaron to be gathered into the company of his ancestors. He will not enter the land I am giving to the People of Israel because you both rebelled against my orders at the Waters of Meribah. So take Aaron and his son Eleazar and lead them up Mount Hor. Remove Aaron's clothes from him and put them on his son Eleazar. Aaron will be gathered there; Aaron will die."

27-29 Moses obeyed GOD's command. They climbed Mount Hor as the whole congregation watched. Moses took off Aaron's clothes and put them on his son Eleazar. Aaron died on top of the mountain. Then Moses and Eleazar came down from the mountain. The whole congregation, getting the news that Aaron had died, went into thirty days of mourning for him.

NEW KING JAMES VERSION

CANAANITES DEFEATED AT HORMAH

21 The king of Arad, the Canaanite, who
dwelt in the South, heard that Israel was
coming on the road to Atharim. Then he fought
against Israel and took *some* of them prisoners.
2So Israel made a vow to the LORD, and said, "If
You will indeed deliver this people into my
hand, then I will utterly destroy their cities."
3And the LORD listened to the voice of Israel and
delivered up the Canaanites, and they utterly
destroyed them and their cities. So the name of
that place was called Hormah.[a]

THE BRONZE SERPENT

4Then they journeyed from Mount Hor by the
Way of the Red Sea, to go around the land of
Edom; and the soul of the people became very
discouraged on the way. 5And the people spoke
against God and against Moses: "Why have you
brought us up out of Egypt to die in the wilder-
ness? For *there is* no food and no water, and our
soul loathes this worthless bread." 6So the LORD
sent fiery serpents among the people, and they
bit the people; and many of the people of Israel
died.
7Therefore the people came to Moses, and
said, "We have sinned, for we have spoken
against the LORD and against you; pray to the
LORD that He take away the serpents from us."
So Moses prayed for the people.
8Then the LORD said to Moses, "Make a fiery
serpent, and set it on a pole; and it shall be that
everyone who is bitten, when he looks at it, shall
live." 9So Moses made a bronze serpent, and put
it on a pole; and so it was, if a serpent had bitten
anyone, when he looked at the bronze serpent,
he lived.

FROM MOUNT HOR TO MOAB

10Now the children of Israel moved on and
camped in Oboth. 11And they journeyed from
Oboth and camped at Ije Abarim, in the wilder-
ness which *is* east of Moab, toward the sunrise.
12From there they moved and camped in the Val-
ley of Zered. 13From there they moved and
camped on the other side of the Arnon, which *is*
in the wilderness that extends from the border
of the Amorites; for the Arnon *is* the border of
Moab, between Moab and the Amorites.
14Therefore it is said in the Book of the Wars of
the LORD:

"Waheb in Suphah,[a]
The brooks of the Arnon,
15And the slope of the brooks
That reaches to the dwelling of Ar,
And lies on the border of Moab."

16From there *they went* to Beer, which *is* the
well where the LORD said to Moses, "Gather the
people together, and I will give them water."
17Then Israel sang this song:

"Spring up, O well!
All of you sing to it—

21:3 [a]Literally *Utter Destruction* **21:14** [a]Ancient unknown places; Vulgate reads *What He did in the Red Sea.*

THE MESSAGE

HORMAH

1 21 The Canaanite king of Arad, ruling in
the Negev, heard that Israel was ad-
vancing up the road to Atharim. He attacked
Israel and took prisoners of war.
2 Israel vowed a vow to GOD: "If you will
give this people into our power, we'll de-
stroy their towns and present the ruins to
you as a holy destruction."
3 GOD listened to Israel's prayer and gave
them the Canaanites. They destroyed both
them and their towns, a holy destruction.
They named the place Hormah (Holy De-
struction).

THE SNAKE OF FIERY COPPER

4-5 They set out from Mount Hor along the Red
Sea Road, a detour around the land of
Edom. The people became irritable and
cross as they traveled. They spoke out
against God and Moses: "Why did you drag
us out of Egypt to die in this godforsaken
country? No decent food; no water—we
can't stomach this stuff any longer."
6-7 So GOD sent poisonous snakes among the
people; they bit them and many in Israel
died. The people came to Moses and said,
"We sinned when we spoke out against GOD
and you. Pray to GOD; ask him to take these
snakes from us."
Moses prayed for the people.
8 GOD said to Moses, "Make a snake and
put it on a flagpole: Whoever is bitten and
looks at it will live."
9 So Moses made a snake of fiery copper
and put it on top of a flagpole. Anyone bit-
ten by a snake who then looked at the cop-
per snake lived.

CAMPING ON THE WAY TO MOAB

10-15 The People of Israel set out and camped at
Oboth. They left Oboth and camped at Iye
Abarim in the wilderness that faces Moab
on the east. They went from there and
pitched camp in the Zered Valley. Their next
camp was alongside the Arnon River, which
marks the border between Amorite country
and Moab. The Book of the Wars of GOD
refers to this place:

Waheb in Suphah,
the canyons of Arnon;
Along the canyon ravines
that lead to the village Ar
And lean hard against
the border of Moab.

16-18 They went on to Beer (The Well), where
GOD said to Moses, "Gather the people; I'll
give them water." That's where Israel sang
this song:

Erupt, Well!
Sing the Song of the Well,

NEW KING JAMES VERSION

18The well the leaders sank,
Dug by the nation's nobles,
By the lawgiver, with their staves."

And from the wilderness *they went* to Mat-
tanah, 19from Mattanah to Nahaliel, from Na-
haliel to Bamoth, 20and from Bamoth, *in* the val-
ley that *is* in the country of Moab, to the top of
Pisgah which looks down on the wasteland.[a]

KING SIHON DEFEATED

21Then Israel sent messengers to Sihon king
of the Amorites, saying, 22"Let me pass through
your land. We will not turn aside into fields or
vineyards; we will not drink water from wells.
We will go by the King's Highway until we have
passed through your territory." 23But Sihon
would not allow Israel to pass through his terri-
tory. So Sihon gathered all his people together
and went out against Israel in the wilderness,
and he came to Jahaz and fought against Israel.
24Then Israel defeated him with the edge of the
sword, and took possession of his land from the
Arnon to the Jabbok, as far as the people of Am-
mon; for the border of the people of Ammon
was fortified. 25So Israel took all these cities,
and Israel dwelt in all the cities of the Amorites,
in Heshbon and in all its villages. 26For Heshbon
was the city of Sihon king of the Amorites, who
had fought against the former king of Moab,
and had taken all his land from his hand as far
as the Arnon. 27Therefore those who speak in
proverbs say:

"Come to Heshbon, let it be built;
Let the city of Sihon be repaired.
28"For fire went out from Heshbon,
A flame from the city of Sihon;
It consumed Ar of Moab,
The lords of the heights of the Arnon.
29Woe to you, Moab!
You have perished, O people of Chemosh!
He has given his sons as fugitives,
And his daughters into captivity,
To Sihon king of the Amorites.

30"But we have shot at them;
Heshbon has perished as far as Dibon.
Then we laid waste as far as Nophah,
Which *reaches* to Medeba."

31Thus Israel dwelt in the land of the Amo-
rites. 32Then Moses sent to spy out Jazer; and
they took its villages and drove out the Amorites
who *were* there.

KING OG DEFEATED

33And they turned and went up by the way to
Bashan. So Og king of Bashan went out against
them, he and all his people, to battle at Edrei.
34Then the LORD said to Moses, "Do not fear
him, for I have delivered him into your hand,
with all his people and his land; and you shall
do to him as you did to Sihon king of the Amo-
rites, who dwelt at Heshbon."

21:20 [a]Hebrew *Jeshimon*

THE MESSAGE

the well sunk by princes,
Dug out by the peoples' leaders
digging with their scepters and staffs.

19-20 From the wilderness their route went from Mattanah to Nahaliel to Bamoth (The Heights) to the valley that opens into the fields of Moab from where Pisgah (The Summit) rises and overlooks Jeshimon (Wasteland).

21-22 Israel sent emissaries to Sihon, king of the Amorites, saying, "Let us cross your land. We won't trespass into your fields or drink water in your vineyards. We'll keep to the main road, the King's Road, until we're through your land."

23-27 But Sihon wouldn't let Israel go through. Instead he got his army together and marched into the wilderness to fight Israel. At Jahaz he attacked Israel. But Israel fought hard, beat him soundly, and took possession of his land from the Arnon all the way to the Jabbok right up to the Ammonite border. They stopped there because the Ammonite border was fortified. Israel took and occupied all the Amorite cities, including Heshbon and all its surrounding villages. Heshbon was the capital city of Sihon king of the Amorites. He had attacked the former king of Moab and captured all his land as far north as the river Arnon. That is why the folk singers sing,

Come to Heshbon to rebuild the city,
restore Sihon's town.

28-29 Fire once poured out of Heshbon,
flames from the city of Sihon;
Burning up Ar of Moab,
the natives of Arnon's heights.
Doom, Moab!
The people of Chemosh, done for!
Sons turned out as fugitives, daughters
abandoned as captives
to the king of the Amorites, to Sihon.

30 Oh, but we finished them off:
Nothing left of Heshbon as far as
Dibon;
Devastation as far off as Nophah,
scorched earth all the way to Medeba.

31-32 Israel moved in and lived in Amorite country. Moses sent men to scout out Jazer. They captured its villages and drove away the Amorites who lived there.

33 Then they turned north on the road to Bashan. Og king of Bashan marched out with his entire army to meet Moses in battle at Edrei.

34 GOD said to Moses, "Don't be afraid of him. I'm making a present of him to you, him and all his people and his land. Treat him the same as Sihon king of the Amorites who ruled in Heshbon."

NEW KING JAMES VERSION

35 So they defeated him, his sons, and all his peo-
ple, until there was no survivor left him; and
they took possession of his land.

BALAK SENDS FOR BALAAM

22 Then the children of Israel moved, and
camped in the plains of Moab on the side
of the Jordan *across from* Jericho.
2 Now Balak the son of Zippor saw all that Is-
rael had done to the Amorites. 3 And Moab was
exceedingly afraid of the people because they
were many, and Moab was sick with dread be-
cause of the children of Israel. 4 So Moab said to
the elders of Midian, "Now this company will
lick up everything around us, as an ox licks up
the grass of the field." And Balak the son of Zip-
por *was* king of the Moabites at that time. 5 Then
he sent messengers to Balaam the son of Beor at
Pethor, which *is* near the River[a] in the land of
the sons of his people,[b] to call him, saying:
"Look, a people has come from Egypt. See, they
cover the face of the earth, and are settling next
to me! 6 Therefore please come at once, curse
this people for me, for they *are* too mighty for
me. Perhaps I shall be able to defeat them and
drive them out of the land, for I know that he
whom you bless *is* blessed, and he whom you
curse is cursed."
7 So the elders of Moab and the elders of Mid-
ian departed with the diviner's fee in their hand,
and they came to Balaam and spoke to him the
words of Balak. 8 And he said to them, "Lodge
here tonight, and I will bring back word to you,
as the LORD speaks to me." So the princes of
Moab stayed with Balaam.
9 Then God came to Balaam and said, "Who
are these men with you?"
10 So Balaam said to God, "Balak the son of
Zippor, king of Moab, has sent to me, *saying*,
11 'Look, a people has come out of Egypt, and
they cover the face of the earth. Come now,
curse them for me; perhaps I shall be able to
overpower them and drive them out.' "
12 And God said to Balaam, "You shall not go
with them; you shall not curse the people, for
they *are* blessed."
13 So Balaam rose in the morning and said to
the princes of Balak, "Go back to your land, for
the LORD has refused to give me permission to
go with you."
14 And the princes of Moab rose and went to
Balak, and said, "Balaam refuses to come with
us."
15 Then Balak again sent princes, more nu-
merous and more honorable than they. 16 And
they came to Balaam and said to him, "Thus
says Balak the son of Zippor: 'Please let nothing
hinder you from coming to me; 17 for I will cer-
tainly honor you greatly, and I will do whatever
you say to me. Therefore please come, curse this
people for me.' "
18 Then Balaam answered and said to the ser-
vants of Balak, "Though Balak were to give me
his house full of silver and gold, I could not go
beyond the word of the LORD my God, to do less
or more. 19 Now therefore, please, you also stay

22:5 [a]That is, the Euphrates [b]Or *the people of Amau*

THE MESSAGE

35 So they attacked him, his sons, and all the
people—there was not a single survivor. Is-
rael took the land.

BALAAM

1 22 The People of Israel marched on and
camped on the Plains of Moab at Jor-
dan-Jericho.
2-3 Balak son of Zippor learned of all that Is-
rael had done to the Amorites. The people of
Moab were in a total panic because of Is-
rael. There were so many of them! They
were terrorized.
4-5 Moab spoke to the leaders of Midian:
"Look, this mob is going to clean us out—a
bunch of crows picking a carcass clean."
Balak son of Zippor, who was king of
Moab at that time, sent emissaries to get
Balaam son of Beor, who lived at Pethor on
the banks of the Euphrates River, his home-
land.
5-6 Balak's emissaries said, "Look. A people
has come up out of Egypt, and they're all
over the place! And they're pressing hard on
me. Come and curse them for me—they're
too much for me. Maybe then I can beat
them; we'll attack and drive them out of the
country. You have a reputation: Those you
bless stay blessed; those you curse stay
cursed."
7-8 The leaders of Moab and Midian were
soon on their way, with the fee for the curs-
ing tucked safely in their wallets. When they
got to Balaam, they gave him Balak's mes-
sage.
"Stay here for the night," Balaam said. "In
the morning I'll deliver the answer that GOD
gives me."
The Moabite nobles stayed with him.
9 Then God came to Balaam. He asked, "So
who are these men here with you?"
10-11 Balaam answered, "Balak son of Zippor,
king of Moab, sent them with a message:
'Look, the people that came up out of Egypt
are all over the place! Come and curse them
for me. Maybe then I'll be able to attack and
drive them out of the country.' "
12 God said to Balaam, "Don't go with them.
And don't curse the others—they are a
blessed people."
13 The next morning Balaam got up and
told Balak's nobles, "Go back home; GOD re-
fuses to give me permission to go with you."
14 So the Moabite nobles left, came back to
Balak, and said, "Balaam wouldn't come
with us."
15-17 Balak sent another group of nobles,
higher ranking and more distinguished.
They came to Balaam and said, "Balak son
of Zippor says, 'Please, don't refuse to come
to me. I will honor and reward you lav-
ishly—anything you tell me to do, I'll do; I'll
pay anything—only come and curse this
people.' "
18-19 Balaam answered Balak's servants:
"Even if Balak gave me his house stuffed
with silver and gold, I wouldn't be able to
defy the orders of my GOD to do anything,
whether big or little. But come along and

NEW KING JAMES VERSION

here tonight, that I may know what more the
LORD will say to me."
20And God came to Balaam at night and said
to him, "If the men come to call you, rise *and* go
with them; but only the word which I speak to
you—that you shall do." 21So Balaam rose in the
morning, saddled his donkey, and went with the
princes of Moab.

BALAAM, THE DONKEY, AND THE ANGEL

22Then God's anger was aroused because he
went, and the Angel of the LORD took His stand
in the way as an adversary against him. And he
was riding on his donkey, and his two servants
were with him. 23Now the donkey saw the Angel
of the LORD standing in the way with His drawn
sword in His hand, and the donkey turned aside
out of the way and went into the field. So Ba-
laam struck the donkey to turn her back onto
the road. 24Then the Angel of the LORD stood in
a narrow path between the vineyards, *with* a
wall on this side and a wall on that side. 25And
when the donkey saw the Angel of the LORD, she
pushed herself against the wall and crushed
Balaam's foot against the wall; so he struck her
again. 26Then the Angel of the LORD went fur-
ther, and stood in a narrow place where there
was no way to turn either to the right hand or to
the left. 27And when the donkey saw the Angel
of the LORD, she lay down under Balaam; so Ba-
laam's anger was aroused, and he struck the
donkey with his staff.
28Then the LORD opened the mouth of the
donkey, and she said to Balaam, "What have I
done to you, that you have struck me these three
times?"
29And Balaam said to the donkey, "Because
you have abused me. I wish there were a sword
in my hand, for now I would kill you!"
30So the donkey said to Balaam, "*Am* I not
your donkey on which you have ridden, ever
since *I became* yours, to this day? Was I ever dis-
posed to do this to you?"
And he said, "No."
31Then the LORD opened Balaam's eyes, and
he saw the Angel of the LORD standing in the
way with His drawn sword in His hand; and he
bowed his head and fell flat on his face. 32And
the Angel of the LORD said to him, "Why have
you struck your donkey these three times? Be-
hold, I have come out to stand against you, be-
cause *your* way is perverse before Me. 33The
donkey saw Me and turned aside from Me these
three times. If she had not turned aside from
Me, surely I would also have killed you by now,
and let her live."
34And Balaam said to the Angel of the LORD,
"I have sinned, for I did not know You stood in
the way against me. Now therefore, if it dis-
pleases You, I will turn back."
35Then the Angel of the LORD said to Balaam,
"Go with the men, but only the word that I speak
to you, that you shall speak." So Balaam went
with the princes of Balak.
36Now when Balak heard that Balaam was
coming, he went out to meet him at the city of
Moab, which *is* on the border at the Arnon, the
boundary of the territory.

THE MESSAGE

stay with me tonight as the others did; I'll see what GOD will say to me this time."

20 God came to Balaam that night and said, "Since these men have come all this way to see you, go ahead and go with them. But make sure you do absolutely nothing other than what I tell you."

21-23 Balaam got up in the morning, saddled his donkey, and went off with the noblemen from Moab. As he was going, though, God's anger flared. The angel of GOD stood in the road to block his way. Balaam was riding his donkey, accompanied by his two servants. When the donkey saw the angel blocking the road and brandishing a sword, she veered off the road into the ditch. Balaam beat the donkey and got her back on the road.

24-25 But as they were going through a vineyard, with a fence on either side, the donkey again saw GOD's angel blocking the way and veered into the fence, crushing Balaam's foot against the fence. Balaam hit her again.

26-27 GOD's angel blocked the way yet again—a very narrow passage this time; there was no getting through on the right or left. Seeing the angel, Balaam's donkey sat down under him. Balaam lost his temper; he beat the donkey with his stick.

28 Then GOD gave speech to the donkey. She said to Balaam: "What have I ever done to you that you have beat me these three times?"

29 Balaam said, "Because you've been playing games with me! If I had a sword I would have killed you by now."

30 The donkey said to Balaam, "Am I not your trusty donkey on whom you've ridden for years right up until now? Have I ever done anything like this to you before? Have I?"

He said, "No."

31 Then GOD helped Balaam see what was going on: He saw GOD's angel blocking the way, brandishing a sword. Balaam fell to the ground, his face in the dirt.

32-33 GOD's angel said to him: "Why have you beaten your poor donkey these three times? I have come here to block your way because you're getting way ahead of yourself. The donkey saw me and turned away from me these three times. If she hadn't, I would have killed you by this time, but not the donkey. I would have let her off."

34 Balaam said to GOD's angel, "I have sinned. I had no idea you were standing in the road blocking my way. If you don't like what I'm doing, I'll head back."

35 But GOD's angel said to Balaam, "Go ahead and go with them. But only say what I tell you to say—absolutely no other word."

And so Balaam continued to go with Balak's nobles.

36 When Balak heard that Balaam was coming, he went out to meet him in the Moabite town that was on the banks of the Arnon, right on the boundary of his land.

NEW KING JAMES VERSION

37Then Balak said to Balaam, "Did I not
earnestly send to you, calling for you? Why did
you not come to me? Am I not able to honor
you?"
38And Balaam said to Balak, "Look, I have
come to you! Now, have I any power at all to say
anything? The word that God puts in my mouth,
that I must speak." 39So Balaam went with
Balak, and they came to Kirjath Huzoth. 40Then
Balak offered oxen and sheep, and he sent *some*
to Balaam and to the princes who *were* with
him.

BALAAM'S FIRST PROPHECY

41So it was, the next day, that Balak took Ba-
laam and brought him up to the high places of
Baal, that from there he might observe the ex-
tent of the people.

23 Then Balaam said to Balak, "Build seven
altars for me here, and prepare for me
here seven bulls and seven rams."
2And Balak did just as Balaam had spoken,
and Balak and Balaam offered a bull and a ram
on *each* altar. 3Then Balaam said to Balak,
"Stand by your burnt offering, and I will go; per-
haps the LORD will come to meet me, and what-
ever He shows me I will tell you." So he went to
a desolate height. 4And God met Balaam, and he
said to Him, "I have prepared the seven altars,
and I have offered on *each* altar a bull and a
ram."
5Then the LORD put a word in Balaam's
mouth, and said, "Return to Balak, and thus you
shall speak." 6So he returned to him, and there
he was, standing by his burnt offering, he and
all the princes of Moab.
7And he took up his oracle and said:

"Balak the king of Moab has brought me
from Aram,
From the mountains of the east.
'Come, curse Jacob for me,
And come, denounce Israel!'

8"How shall I curse whom God has not
cursed?
And how shall I denounce *whom* the LORD
has not denounced?
9For from the top of the rocks I see him,
And from the hills I behold him;
There! A people dwelling alone,
Not reckoning itself among the nations.
10"Who can count the dust[a] of Jacob,
Or number one-fourth of Israel?
Let me die the death of the righteous,
And let my end be like his!"

11Then Balak said to Balaam, "What have
you done to me? I took you to curse my enemies,
and look, you have blessed *them* bountifully!"

23:10 [a]Or *dust cloud*

THE MESSAGE

37 Balak said to Balaam, "Didn't I send an urgent message for help? Why didn't you come when I called? Do you think I can't pay you enough?"

38 Balaam said to Balak, "Well, I'm here now. But I can't tell you just anything. I can speak only words that God gives me—no others."

39-40 Balaam then accompanied Balak to Kiriath Huzoth (Street-Town). Balak slaughtered cattle and sheep for sacrifices and presented them to Balaam and the nobles who were with him.

41 At daybreak Balak took Balaam up to Bamoth Baal (The Heights of Baal) so that he could get a good view of some of the people.

1 23 Balaam said, "Build me seven altars here, and then prepare seven bulls and seven rams."

Balak did it. Then Balaam and Balak sacrificed a bull and a ram on each of the altars.

3 Balaam instructed Balak: "Stand watch here beside your Whole-Burnt-Offering while I go off by myself. Maybe GOD will come and meet with me. Whatever he shows or tells me, I'll report to you." Then he went off by himself.

4 God did meet with Balaam. Balaam said, "I've set up seven altars and offered a bull and a ram on each altar."

5 Then GOD gave Balaam a message: "Return to Balak and give him this message."

6-10 He went back and found him stationed beside his Whole-Burnt-Offering and with him all the nobles of Moab. Then Balaam spoke his message-oracle:

Balak led me here from Aram,
the king of Moab all the way from the
eastern mountains.
"Go, curse Jacob for me;
go, damn Israel."
How can I curse whom God has not
cursed?
How can I damn whom GOD has not
damned?
From rock pinnacles I see them,
from hilltops I survey them:
Look! a people camping off by
themselves,
thinking themselves outsiders among
nations.
But who could ever count the dust of
Jacob
or take a census of cloud-of-dust
Israel?
I want to die like these right-living
people!
I want an end just like theirs!

11 Balak said to Balaam, "What's this? I brought you here to curse my enemies, and all you've done is bless them."

NEW KING JAMES VERSION

12 So he answered and said, "Must I not take
heed to speak what the LORD has put in my
mouth?"

BALAAM'S SECOND PROPHECY

13 Then Balak said to him, "Please come with
me to another place from which you may see
them; you shall see only the outer part of them,
and shall not see them all; curse them for me
from there." 14 So he brought him to the field of
Zophim, to the top of Pisgah, and built seven al-
tars, and offered a bull and a ram on *each* altar.
15 And he said to Balak, "Stand here by your
burnt offering while I meet[a] *the LORD* over
there."
16 Then the LORD met Balaam, and put a
word in his mouth, and said, "Go back to Balak,
and thus you shall speak." 17 So he came to him,
and there he was, standing by his burnt offer-
ing, and the princes of Moab were with him.
And Balak said to him, "What has the LORD
spoken?"
18 Then he took up his oracle and said:

"Rise up, Balak, and hear!
Listen to me, son of Zippor!
19 "God *is* not a man, that He should lie,
Nor a son of man, that He should repent.
Has He said, and will He not do?
Or has He spoken, and will He not make it
good?
20 Behold, I have received *a command* to bless;
He has blessed, and I cannot reverse it.

21 "He has not observed iniquity in Jacob,
Nor has He seen wickedness in Israel.
The LORD his God *is* with him,
And the shout of a King *is* among them.
22 God brings them out of Egypt;
He has strength like a wild ox.

23 "For *there is* no sorcery against Jacob,
Nor any divination against Israel.
It now must be said of Jacob
And of Israel, 'Oh, what God has done!'
24 Look, a people rises like a lioness,
And lifts itself up like a lion;
It shall not lie down until it devours the
prey,
And drinks the blood of the slain."

25 Then Balak said to Balaam, "Neither curse
them at all, nor bless them at all!"
26 So Balaam answered and said to Balak,
"Did I not tell you, saying, 'All that the LORD
speaks, that I must do'?"

BALAAM'S THIRD PROPHECY

27 Then Balak said to Balaam, "Please come, I
will take you to another place; perhaps it will
please God that you may curse them for me
from there." 28 So Balak took Balaam to the top
of Peor, that overlooks the wasteland.[a]

23:15 [a]Following Masoretic Text, Targum, and Vulgate; Syriac reads *call;* Septuagint reads *go and ask God.* **23:28** [a]Hebrew *Jeshimon*

THE MESSAGE

12 Balaam answered, "Don't I have to be careful to say what GOD gives me to say?"

13 Balak said to him, "Go with me to another place from which you can only see the outskirts of their camp—you won't be able to see the whole camp. From there, curse them for my sake."

14 So he took him to Watchmen's Meadow at the top of Pisgah. He built seven altars there and offered a bull and a ram on each altar.

15 Balaam said to Balak, "Take up your station here beside your Whole-Burnt-Offering while I meet with him over there."

16 GOD met with Balaam and gave him a message. He said, "Return to Balak and give him the message."

17-24 Balaam returned and found him stationed beside his Whole-Burnt-Offering and the nobles of Moab with him. Balak said to him, "What did GOD say?" Then Balaam spoke his message-oracle:

On your feet, Balak. Listen,
listen carefully son of Zippor:
God is not man, one given to lies,
and not a son of man changing his
mind.
Does he speak and not do what he says?
Does he promise and not come
through?
I was brought here to bless;
and now he's blessed—how can I
change that?
He has no bone to pick with Jacob,
he sees nothing wrong with Israel.
GOD is with them,
and they're with him, shouting praises
to their King.
God brought them out of Egypt,
rampaging like a wild ox.
No magic spells can bind Jacob,
no incantations can hold back Israel.
People will look at Jacob and Israel and
say,
"What a great thing has God done!"
Look, a people rising to its feet,
stretching like a lion,
a king-of-the-beasts, aroused,
Unsleeping, unresting until its hunt is
over
and it's eaten and drunk its fill.

25 Balak said to Balaam, "Well, if you can't curse them, at least don't bless them."

26 Balaam replied to Balak, "Didn't I tell you earlier: 'All God speaks, and only what he speaks, I speak'?"

27-28 Balak said to Balaam, "Please, let me take you to another place; maybe we can find the right place in God's eyes where you'll be able to curse them for me." So Balak took Balaam to the top of Peor, with a vista over the Jeshimon (Wasteland).

NEW KING JAMES VERSION

29Then Balaam said to Balak, "Build for me here
seven altars, and prepare for me here seven
bulls and seven rams." 30And Balak did as Bal-
aam had said, and offered a bull and a ram on
every altar.

24 Now when Balaam saw that it pleased the
LORD to bless Israel, he did not go as at
other times, to seek to use sorcery, but he set his
face toward the wilderness. 2And Balaam raised
his eyes, and saw Israel encamped according to
their tribes; and the Spirit of God came upon
him.
3Then he took up his oracle and said:

"The utterance of Balaam the son of Beor,
The utterance of the man whose eyes are
opened,
4The utterance of him who hears the words
of God,
Who sees the vision of the Almighty,
Who falls down, with eyes wide open:

5"How lovely are your tents, O Jacob!
Your dwellings, O Israel!
6Like valleys that stretch out,
Like gardens by the riverside,
Like aloes planted by the LORD,
Like cedars beside the waters.
7He shall pour water from his buckets,
And his seed *shall be* in many waters.

"His king shall be higher than Agag,
And his kingdom shall be exalted.

8"God brings him out of Egypt;
He has strength like a wild ox;
He shall consume the nations, his enemies;
He shall break their bones
And pierce *them* with his arrows.
9'He bows down, he lies down as a lion;
And as a lion, who shall rouse him?'[a]

"Blessed *is* he who blesses you,
And cursed *is* he who curses you."

10Then Balak's anger was aroused against
Balaam, and he struck his hands together; and
Balak said to Balaam, "I called you to curse my
enemies, and look, you have bountifully blessed
them these three times! 11Now therefore, flee to
your place. I said I would greatly honor you, but
in fact, the LORD has kept you back from honor."
12So Balaam said to Balak, "Did I not also
speak to your messengers whom you sent to me,
saying, 13'If Balak were to give me his house full
of silver and gold, I could not go beyond the
word of the LORD, to do good or bad of my own
will. What the LORD says, that I must speak'?
14And now, indeed, I am going to my people.
Come, I will advise you what this people will do
to your people in the latter days."

24:9 [a]Genesis 49:9

THE MESSAGE

29 Balaam said to Balak, "Build seven altars for me here and prepare seven bulls and seven rams for sacrifice."

30 Balak did it and presented an offering of a bull and a ram on each of the altars.

1-3 24 By now Balaam realized that GOD wanted to bless Israel. So he didn't work in any sorcery as he had done earlier. He turned and looked out over the wilderness. As Balaam looked, he saw Israel camped tribe by tribe. The Spirit of God came on him, and he spoke his oracle-message:

3-9 Decree of Balaam son of Beor,
yes, decree of a man with 20/20 vision;
Decree of a man who hears God speak,
who sees what The Strong God shows
him,
Who falls on his face in worship,
who sees what's really going on.

What beautiful tents, Jacob,
oh, your homes, Israel!
Like valleys stretching out in the
distance,
like gardens planted by rivers,
Like sweet herbs planted by the
gardener GOD,
like red cedars by pools and springs,
Their buckets will brim with water,
their seed will spread life everywhere.
Their king will tower over Agag and his
ilk,
their kingdom surpassingly majestic.
God brought them out of Egypt,
rampaging like a wild ox,
Gulping enemies like morsels of meat,
crushing their bones, snapping their
arrows.
Israel crouches like a lion and naps,
king-of-the-beasts—who dares
disturb him?
Whoever blesses you is blessed,
whoever curses you is cursed.

10-11 Balak lost his temper with Balaam. He shook his fist. He said to Balaam: "I got you in here to curse my enemies and what have you done? Blessed them! Blessed them three times! Get out of here! Go home! I told you I would pay you well, but you're getting nothing. You can blame GOD."

12-15 Balaam said to Balak, "Didn't I tell you up front when you sent your emissaries, 'Even if Balak gave me his palace stuffed with silver and gold, I couldn't do anything on my own, whether good or bad, that went against GOD's command'? I'm leaving for home and my people, but I warn you of what this people will do to your people in the days to come." Then he spoke his oracle-message:

NEW KING JAMES VERSION

BALAAM'S FOURTH PROPHECY

15So he took up his oracle and said:

"The utterance of Balaam the son of Beor,
And the utterance of the man whose eyes
are opened;
16The utterance of him who hears the words
of God,
And has the knowledge of the Most High,
Who sees the vision of the Almighty,
Who falls down, with eyes wide open:

17"I see Him, but not now;
I behold Him, but not near;
A Star shall come out of Jacob;
A Scepter shall rise out of Israel,
And batter the brow of Moab,
And destroy all the sons of tumult.[a]

18"And Edom shall be a possession;
Seir also, his enemies, shall be a possession,
While Israel does valiantly.
19Out of Jacob One shall have dominion,
And destroy the remains of the city."

20Then he looked on Amalek, and he took up
his oracle and said:

"Amalek *was* first among the nations,
But *shall be* last until he perishes."

21Then he looked on the Kenites, and he took
up his oracle and said:

"Firm is your dwelling place,
And your nest is set in the rock;
22Nevertheless Kain shall be burned.
How long until Asshur carries you away
captive?"

23Then he took up his oracle and said:

"Alas! Who shall live when God does this?
24But ships *shall come* from the coasts of
Cyprus,[a]
And they shall afflict Asshur and afflict
Eber,
And so shall *Amalek*,[b] until he perishes."

25So Balaam rose and departed and returned
to his place; Balak also went his way.

ISRAEL'S HARLOTRY IN MOAB

25 Now Israel remained in Acacia Grove,[a]
and the people began to commit harlotry
with the women of Moab. 2They invited the peo-
ple to the sacrifices of their gods, and the people
ate and bowed down to their gods. 3So Israel
was joined to Baal of Peor, and the anger of the
LORD was aroused against Israel.
4Then the LORD said to Moses, "Take all the
leaders of the people and hang the offenders be-
fore the LORD, out in the sun, that the fierce
anger of the LORD may turn away from Israel."

24:17 [a]Hebrew *Sheth* (compare Jeremiah 48:45) **24:24** [a]Hebrew *Kittim* [b]Literally *he* or *that one* **25:1** [a]Hebrew *Shittim*

THE MESSAGE

15-19 Decree of Balaam son of Beor,
decree of the man with 20/20 vision,
Decree of the man who hears godly
speech,
who knows what's going on with the
High God,
Who sees what The Strong God reveals,
who bows in worship and sees what's
real.
I see him, but not right now,
I perceive him, but not right here;
A star rises from Jacob
a scepter from Israel,
Crushing the heads of Moab,
the skulls of all the noisy windbags;
I see Edom sold off at auction,
enemy Seir marked down at the flea
market,
while Israel walks off with the
trophies.
A ruler is coming from Jacob
who'll destroy what's left in the city.

20 Then Balaam spotted Amalek and delivered
an oracle-message. He said,

Amalek, you're in first place among
nations right now,
but you're going to come in last,
ruined.

21-22 He saw the Kenites and delivered his oracle-
message to them:

Your home is in a nice secure place,
like a nest high on the face of a cliff.
Still, you Kenites will look stupid
when Asshur takes you prisoner.

23-24 Balaam spoke his final oracle-message:

Doom! Who stands a chance
when God starts in?
Sea-Peoples, raiders from across the sea,
will harass Asshur and Eber,
But they'll also come to nothing,
just like all the rest.

25 Balaam got up and went home. Balak
also went on his way.

THE ORGY AT SHITTIM

1-3 25 While Israel was camped at Shittim
(Acacia Grove), the men began to have
sex with the Moabite women. It started
when the women invited the men to their
sex-and-religion worship. They ate together
and then worshiped their gods. Israel ended
up joining in the worship of the Baal of Peor.
GOD was furious, his anger blazing out
against Israel.
4 GOD said to Moses, "Take all the leaders
of Israel and kill them by hanging, leaving
them publicly exposed in order to turn
GOD's anger away from Israel."

NEW KING JAMES VERSION

[5]So Moses said to the judges of Israel, "Every
one of you kill his men who were joined to Baal
of Peor."
[6]And indeed, one of the children of Israel
came and presented to his brethren a Midianite
woman in the sight of Moses and in the sight of
all the congregation of the children of Israel,
who *were* weeping at the door of the tabernacle
of meeting. [7]Now when Phinehas the son of
Eleazar, the son of Aaron the priest, saw *it*, he
rose from among the congregation and took a
javelin in his hand; [8]and he went after the man
of Israel into the tent and thrust both of them
through, the man of Israel, and the woman
through her body. So the plague was stopped
among the children of Israel. [9]And those who
died in the plague were twenty-four thousand.
[10]Then the LORD spoke to Moses, saying:
[11]"Phinehas the son of Eleazar, the son of Aaron
the priest, has turned back My wrath from the
children of Israel, because he was zealous with
My zeal among them, so that I did not consume
the children of Israel in My zeal. [12]Therefore
say, 'Behold, I give to him My covenant of peace;
[13]and it shall be to him and his descendants af-
ter him a covenant of an everlasting priesthood,
because he was zealous for his God, and made
atonement for the children of Israel.' "
[14]Now the name of the Israelite who was
killed, who was killed with the Midianite
woman, *was* Zimri the son of Salu, a leader of a
father's house among the Simeonites. [15]And the
name of the Midianite woman who was killed
was Cozbi the daughter of Zur; he *was* head of
the people of a father's house in Midian.
[16]Then the LORD spoke to Moses, saying:
[17]"Harass the Midianites, and attack them; [18]for
they harassed you with their schemes by which
they seduced you in the matter of Peor and in
the matter of Cozbi, the daughter of a leader of
Midian, their sister, who was killed in the day of
the plague because of Peor."

THE SECOND CENSUS OF ISRAEL

26 And it came to pass, after the plague, that
the LORD spoke to Moses and Eleazar the
son of Aaron the priest, saying: [2]"Take a census
of all the congregation of the children of Israel
from twenty years old and above, by their fa-
thers' houses, all who are able to go to war in Is-
rael." [3]So Moses and Eleazar the priest spoke
with them in the plains of Moab by the Jordan,
across from Jericho, saying: [4]"*Take a census of
the people* from twenty years old and above,
just as the LORD commanded Moses and the
children of Israel who came out of the land of
Egypt."
[5]Reuben *was* the firstborn of Israel. The chil-
dren of Reuben *were: of* Hanoch, the family of
the Hanochites; *of* Pallu, the family of the Pal-
luites; [6]*of* Hezron, the family of the Hezronites;
of Carmi, the family of the Carmites. [7]These *are*
the families of the Reubenites: those who were
numbered of them were forty-three thousand
seven hundred and thirty. [8]And the son of Pallu
was Eliab.

THE MESSAGE

5 Moses issued orders to the judges of Israel: "Each of you must execute the men under your jurisdiction who joined in the worship of Baal Peor."

6-9 Just then, while everyone was weeping in penitence at the entrance of the Tent of Meeting, an Israelite man, flaunting his behavior in front of Moses and the whole assembly, paraded a Midianite woman into his family tent. Phinehas son of Eleazar, the son of Aaron the priest, saw what he was doing, grabbed his spear, and followed them into the tent. With one thrust he drove the spear through the two of them, the man of Israel and the woman, right through their private parts. That stopped the plague from continuing among the People of Israel. But 24,000 had already died.

10-13 GOD spoke to Moses: "Phinehas son of Eleazar, son of Aaron the priest, has stopped my anger against the People of Israel. Because he was as zealous for my honor as I myself am, I didn't kill all the People of Israel in my zeal. So tell him that I am making a Covenant-of-Peace with him. He and his descendants are joined in a covenant of eternal priesthood, because he was zealous for his God and made atonement for the People of Israel."

14-15 The name of the man of Israel who was killed with the Midianite woman was Zimri son of Salu, the head of the Simeonite family. And the name of the Midianite woman who was killed was Cozbi daughter of Zur, a tribal chief of a Midianite family.

16-18 GOD spoke to Moses: "From here on make the Midianites your enemies. Fight them tooth and nail. They turned out to be your enemies when they seduced you in the business of Peor and that woman Cozbi, daughter of a Midianite leader, the woman who was killed at the time of the plague in the matter of Peor."

CENSUS ON THE PLAINS OF MOAB

1-2 26 After the plague GOD said to Moses and Eleazar son of Aaron the priest, "Number the entire community of Israel by families—count every person who is twenty years and older who is able to serve in the army of Israel."

3-4 Obeying GOD's command, Moses and Eleazar the priest addressed them on the Plains of Moab at Jordan-Jericho: "Count off from age twenty and older."

4-7 The People of Israel who came out of the land of Egypt:

Reuben, Israel's firstborn. The sons of Reuben were:

Hanoch and the Hanochite clan,
Pallu and the Palluite clan,
Hezron and the Hezronite clan,
Carmi and the Carmite clan.

These made up the Reubenite clans. They numbered 43,730.

8 The son of Pallu: Eliab.

NEW KING JAMES VERSION

9The sons of Eliab *were* Nemuel, Dathan, and
Abiram. These *are* the Dathan and Abiram, rep-
resentatives of the congregation, who con-
tended against Moses and Aaron in the com-
pany of Korah, when they contended against
the LORD; 10and the earth opened its mouth and
swallowed them up together with Korah when
that company died, when the fire devoured two
hundred and fifty men; and they became a sign.
11Nevertheless the children of Korah did not
die.

12The sons of Simeon according to their fam-
ilies *were: of* Nemuel,[a] the family of the Nem-
uelites; *of* Jamin, the family of the Jaminites; *of*
Jachin,[b] the family of the Jachinites; 13*of*
Zerah,[a] the family of the Zarhites; *of* Shaul, the
family of the Shaulites. 14These *are* the families
of the Simeonites: twenty-two thousand two
hundred.

15The sons of Gad according to their families
were: of Zephon,[a] the family of the Zephonites;
of Haggi, the family of the Haggites; *of* Shuni,
the family of the Shunites; 16*of* Ozni,[a] the family
of the Oznites; *of* Eri, the family of the Erites;
17*of* Arod,[a] the family of the Arodites; *of* Areli,
the family of the Arelites. 18These *are* the fami-
lies of the sons of Gad according to those who
were numbered of them: forty thousand five
hundred.

19The sons of Judah *were* Er and Onan; and
Er and Onan died in the land of Canaan. 20And
the sons of Judah according to their families
were: *of* Shelah, the family of the Shelanites; *of*
Perez, the family of the Parzites; *of* Zerah, the
family of the Zarhites. 21And the sons of Perez
were: *of* Hezron, the family of the Hezronites; *of*
Hamul, the family of the Hamulites. 22These *are*
the families of Judah according to those who
were numbered of them: seventy-six thousand
five hundred.

23The sons of Issachar according to their
families *were: of* Tola, the family of the Tolaites;
of Puah,[a] the family of the Punites;[b] 24of Jashub,
the family of the Jashubites; of Shimron, the
family of the Shimronites. 25These *are* the fami-
lies of Issachar according to those who were
numbered of them: sixty-four thousand three
hundred.

26The sons of Zebulun according to their
families *were:* of Sered, the family of the
Sardites; of Elon, the family of the Elonites; of
Jahleel, the family of the Jahleelites. 27These *are*
the families of the Zebulunites according to
those who were numbered of them: sixty thou-
sand five hundred.

28The sons of Joseph according to their fam-
ilies, by Manasseh and Ephraim, *were:* 29The
sons of Manasseh: of Machir, the family of the
Machirites; and Machir begot Gilead; of Gilead,
the family of the Gileadites. 30These *are* the sons

THE MESSAGE

9-11 The sons of Eliab: Nemuel, Dathan, and Abiram. (These were the same Dathan and Abiram, community leaders from Korah's gang, who rebelled against Moses and Aaron in the Korah Rebellion against GOD. The Earth opened its jaws and swallowed them along with Korah's gang who died when the fire ate them up, all 250 of them. After all these years, they're still a warning sign. But the line of Korah did not die out.)

12-14 The sons of Simeon by clans:
Nemuel and the Nemuelite clan,
Jamin and the Jaminite clan,
Jakin and the Jakinite clan,
Zerah and the Zerahite clan,
Shaul and the Shaulite clan.
These were the clans of Simeon. They numbered 22,200 men.

15-18 The sons of Gad by clans:
Zephon and the Zephonite clan,
Haggi and the Haggite clan,
Shuni and the Shunite clan,
Ozni and the Oznite clan,
Eri and the Erite clan,
Arodi and the Arodite clan,
Areli and the Arelite clan.
These were the clans of Gad. They numbered 40,500 men.

19-22 Er and Onan were sons of Judah who died early on in Canaan. The sons of Judah by clans:
Shelah and the Shelanite clan,
Perez and the Perezite clan,
Zerah and the Zerahite clan.
The sons of Perez:
Hezron and the Hezronite clan,
Hamul and the Hamulite clan.
These were the clans of Judah. They numbered 76,500.

23-25 The sons of Issachar by clans:
Tola and the Tolaite clan,
Puah and the Puite clan,
Jashub and the Jashubite clan,
Shimron and the Shimronite clan.
These were the clans of Issachar. They numbered 64,300.

26-27 The sons of Zebulun by clans:
Sered and the Seredite clan,
Elon and the Elonite clan,
Jahleel and the Jahleelite clan.
These were the clans of Zebulun. They numbered 60,500.

28-34 The sons of Joseph by clans through Manasseh and Ephraim. Through Manasseh:
Makir and the Makirite clan
(now Makir was the father of Gilead),
Gilead and the Gileadite clan.

26:12 [a]Spelled *Jemuel* in Genesis 46:10 and Exodus 6:15 [b]Called *Jarib* in 1 Chronicles 4:24 **26:13** [a]Called *Zohar* in Genesis 46:10 **26:15** [a]Called *Ziphion* in Genesis 46:16 **26:16** [a]Called *Ezbon* in Genesis 46:16 **26:17** [a]Spelled *Arodi* in Samaritan Pentateuch, Syriac, and Genesis 46:16 **26:23** [a]Hebrew *Puvah* (compare Genesis 46:13 and 1 Chronicles 7:1); Samaritan Pentateuch, Septuagint, Syriac, and Vulgate read *Puah.* [b]Samaritan Pentateuch, Septuagint, Syriac, and Vulgate read *Puaites.*

NEW KING JAMES VERSION

of Gilead: *of* Jeezer,[a] the family of the Jeezerites;
of Helek, the family of the Helekites; 31*of* Asriel,
the family of the Asrielites; *of* Shechem, the
family of the Shechemites; 32*of* Shemida, the
family of the Shemidaites; *of* Hepher, the family
of the Hepherites. 33Now Zelophehad the son of
Hepher had no sons, but daughters; and the
names of the daughters of Zelophehad *were*
Mahlah, Noah, Hoglah, Milcah, and Tirzah.
34These *are* the families of Manasseh; and those
who were numbered of them *were* fifty-two
thousand seven hundred.

35These *are* the sons of Ephraim according to
their families: of Shuthelah, the family of the
Shuthalhites; of Becher,[a] the family of the
Bachrites; of Tahan, the family of the Tahanites.
36And these *are* the sons of Shuthelah: of Eran,
the family of the Eranites. 37These *are* the fami-
lies of the sons of Ephraim according to those
who were numbered of them: thirty-two thou-
sand five hundred.

These *are* the sons of Joseph according to
their families.

38The sons of Benjamin according to their
families were: of Bela, the family of the Belaites;
of Ashbel, the family of the Ashbelites; of Ahi-
ram, the family of the Ahiramites; 39of
Shupham,[a] the family of the Shuphamites; of
Hupham,[b] the family of the Huphamites. 40And
the sons of Bela were Ard[a] and Naaman: *of Ard,*
the family of the Ardites; of Naaman, the family
of the Naamites. 41These *are* the sons of Ben-
jamin according to their families; and those who
were numbered of them *were* forty-five thou-
sand six hundred.

42These *are* the sons of Dan according to
their families: of Shuham,[a] the family of the
Shuhamites. These *are* the families of Dan ac-
cording to their families. 43All the families of the
Shuhamites, according to those who were num-
bered of them, *were* sixty-four thousand four
hundred.

44The sons of Asher according to their fami-
lies *were:* of Jimna, the family of the Jimnites; of
Jesui, the family of the Jesuites; of Beriah, the
family of the Beriites. 45Of the sons of Beriah: of
Heber, the family of the Heberites; of Malchiel,
the family of the Malchielites. 46And the name of
the daughter of Asher *was* Serah. 47These *are* the
families of the sons of Asher according to those
who were numbered of them: fifty-three thou-
sand four hundred.

48The sons of Naphtali according to their
families *were:* of Jahzeel,[a] the family of the
Jahzeelites; of Guni, the family of the Gunites;
49of Jezer, the family of the Jezerites; of Shillem,
the family of the Shillemites. 50These *are* the
families of Naphtali according to their families;
and those who were numbered of them *were*
forty-five thousand four hundred.

51These *are* those who were numbered of the
children of Israel: six hundred and one thou-
sand seven hundred and thirty.

26:30 [a]Called *Abiezer* in Joshua 17:2 **26:35** [a]Called *Bered* in 1 Chronicles 7:20 **26:39** [a]Masoretic Text reads *Shephupham,* spelled *Shephuphan* in 1 Chronicles 8:5. [b]Called *Huppim* in Genesis 46:21 **26:40** [a]Called *Addar* in 1 Chronicles 8:3 **26:42** [a]Called *Hushim* in Genesis 46:23 **26:48** [a]Spelled *Jahziel* in 1 Chronicles 7:13

THE MESSAGE

The sons of Gilead:
Iezer and the Iezerite clan,
Helek and the Helekite clan,
Asriel and the Asrielite clan,
Shechem and the Shechemite clan,
Shemida and the Shemidaite clan,
Hepher and the Hepherite clan.
Zelophehad son of Hepher had no sons, only daughters.
Their names were Mahlah, Noah, Hoglah, Milcah, and Tirzah.

These were the clans of Manasseh. They numbered 52,700.

35-37 The sons of Ephraim by clans:
Shuthelah and the Shuthelahite clan,
Beker and the Bekerite clan,
Tahan and the Tahanite clan.
The sons of Shuthelah:
Eran and the Eranite clan.
These were the clans of Ephraim. They numbered 32,500.

These are all the sons of Joseph by their clans.

38-41 The sons of Benjamin by clans:
Bela and the Belaite clan,
Ashbel and the Ashbelite clan,
Ahiram and the Ahiramite clan,
Shupham and the Shuphamite clan,
Hupham and the Huphamite clan.
The sons of Bela through Ard and Naaman:
Ard and the Ardite clan,
Naaman and the Naamite clan.
These were the clans of Benjamin. They numbered 45,600.

42-43 The sons of Dan by clan:
Shuham and the Shuhamite clan.
These are the clans of Dan, all Shuhamite clans. They numbered 64,400.

44-47 The sons of Asher by clan:
Imnah and the Imnite clan,
Ishvi and the Ishvite clan,
Beriah and the Beriite clan.
The sons of Beriah:
Heber and the Heberite clan,
Malkiel and the Malkielite clan.
Asher also had a daughter, Serah.
These were the clans of Asher. They numbered 53,400.

48-50 The sons of Naphtali by clans:
Jahzeel and the Jahzeelite clan,
Guni and the Gunite clan,
Jezer and the Jezerite clan,
Shillem and the Shillemite clan.
These were the clans of Naphtali. They numbered 45,400.

51 The total number of the People of Israel: 601,730.

NEW KING JAMES VERSION

52Then the LORD spoke to Moses, saying:
53"To these the land shall be divided as an inher-
itance, according to the number of names. 54To a
large *tribe* you shall give a larger inheritance,
and to a small *tribe* you shall give a smaller in-
heritance. Each shall be given its inheritance ac-
cording to those who were numbered of them.
55But the land shall be divided by lot; they shall
inherit according to the names of the tribes of
their fathers. 56According to the lot their inheri-
tance shall be divided between the larger and
the smaller."

57And these *are* those who were numbered of
the Levites according to their families: of Ger-
shon, the family of the Gershonites; of Kohath,
the family of the Kohathites; of Merari, the fam-
ily of the Merarites. 58These *are* the families of
the Levites: the family of the Libnites, the fam-
ily of the Hebronites, the family of the Mahlites,
the family of the Mushites, and the family of the
Korathites. And Kohath begot Amram. 59The
name of Amram's wife *was* Jochebed the
daughter of Levi, who was born to Levi in
Egypt; and to Amram she bore Aaron and
Moses and their sister Miriam. 60To Aaron were
born Nadab and Abihu, Eleazar and Ithamar.
61And Nadab and Abihu died when they offered
profane fire before the LORD.

62Now those who were numbered of them
were twenty-three thousand, every male from a
month old and above; for they were not num-
bered among the other children of Israel, be-
cause there was no inheritance given to them
among the children of Israel.

63These *are* those who were numbered by
Moses and Eleazar the priest, who numbered the
children of Israel in the plains of Moab by the
Jordan, *across from* Jericho. 64But among these
there was not a man of those who were num-
bered by Moses and Aaron the priest when they
numbered the children of Israel in the Wilderness
of Sinai. 65For the LORD had said of them, "They
shall surely die in the wilderness." So there was
not left a man of them, except Caleb the son of
Jephunneh and Joshua the son of Nun.

INHERITANCE LAWS

27 Then came the daughters of Zelophehad
the son of Hepher, the son of Gilead, the
son of Machir, the son of Manasseh, from the
families of Manasseh the son of Joseph; and
these *were* the names of his daughters: Mahlah,
Noah, Hoglah, Milcah, and Tirzah. 2And they
stood before Moses, before Eleazar the priest,
and before the leaders and all the congregation,
by the doorway of the tabernacle of meeting,
saying: 3"Our father died in the wilderness; but
he was not in the company of those who gath-
ered together against the LORD, in company
with Korah, but he died in his own sin; and he
had no sons. 4Why should the name of our fa-
ther be removed from among his family because
he had no son? Give us a possession among our
father's brothers."

THE MESSAGE

52-54 GOD spoke to Moses: "Divide up the inheritance of the land based on population. A larger group gets a larger inheritance; a smaller group gets a smaller inheritance—each gets its inheritance based on the population count.

55-56 "Make sure that the land is assigned by lot.

"Each group's inheritance is based on population, the number of names listed in its ancestral tribe, divided among the many and the few by lot."

57-58 These are the numberings of the Levites by clan:

Gershon and the Gershonite clan,
Kohath and the Kohathite clan,
Merari and the Merarite clan.

The Levite clans also included:

the Libnite clan,
the Hebronite clan,
the Mahlite clan,
the Mushite clan,
the Korahite clan.

58-61 Kohath was the father of Amram. Amram's wife was Jochebed, a descendant of Levi, born into the Levite family during the Egyptian years. Jochebed bore Aaron, Moses, and their sister Miriam to Amram. Aaron was the father of Nadab and Abihu, Eleazar and Ithamar; however, Nadab and Abihu died when they offered unauthorized sacrifice in the presence of GOD.

62 The numbering of Levite males one month and older came to 23,000. They hadn't been counted in with the rest of the People of Israel because they didn't inherit any land.

63-65 These are the ones numbered by Moses and Eleazar the priest, the People of Israel counted in the Plains of Moab at Jordan-Jericho. Not one of them had been among those counted by Moses and Aaron the priest in the census of the People of Israel taken in the Wilderness of Sinai. For GOD had said of them, "They'll die, die in the wilderness—not one of them will be left except for Caleb son of Jephunneh, and Joshua son of Nun."

THE DAUGHTERS OF ZELOPHEHAD

1 27 The daughters of Zelophehad showed up. Their father was the son of Hepher son of Gilead son of Makir son of Manasseh, belonging to the clans of Manasseh son of Joseph. The daughters were Mahlah, Noah, Hoglah, Milcah, and Tirzah.

2-4 They came to the entrance of the Tent of Meeting. They stood before Moses and Eleazar the priest and before the leaders and the congregation and said, "Our father died in the wilderness. He wasn't part of Korah's rebel anti-GOD gang. He died for his own sins. And he left no sons. But why should our father's name die out from his clan just because he had no sons? So give us an inheritance among our father's relatives."

New King James Version

5So Moses brought their case before the
Lord.
6And the Lord spoke to Moses, saying: 7"The
daughters of Zelophehad speak *what is* right;
you shall surely give them a possession of in-
heritance among their father's brothers, and
cause the inheritance of their father to pass to
them. 8And you shall speak to the children of Is-
rael, saying: 'If a man dies and has no son, then
you shall cause his inheritance to pass to his
daughter. 9If he has no daughter, then you shall
give his inheritance to his brothers. 10If he has
no brothers, then you shall give his inheritance
to his father's brothers. 11And if his father has
no brothers, then you shall give his inheritance
to the relative closest to him in his family, and
he shall possess it.' " And it shall be to the chil-
dren of Israel a statute of judgment, just as the
Lord commanded Moses.

Joshua the Next Leader of Israel

12Now the Lord said to Moses: "Go up into
this Mount Abarim, and see the land which I
have given to the children of Israel. 13And when
you have seen it, you also shall be gathered to
your people, as Aaron your brother was gath-
ered. 14For in the Wilderness of Zin, during the
strife of the congregation, you rebelled against
My command to hallow Me at the waters before
their eyes." (These *are* the waters of Meribah, at
Kadesh in the Wilderness of Zin.)
15Then Moses spoke to the Lord, saying:
16"Let the Lord, the God of the spirits of all
flesh, set a man over the congregation, 17who
may go out before them and go in before them,
who may lead them out and bring them in, that
the congregation of the Lord may not be like
sheep which have no shepherd."
18And the Lord said to Moses: "Take Joshua
the son of Nun with you, a man in whom *is* the
Spirit, and lay your hand on him; 19set him be-
fore Eleazar the priest and before all the con-
gregation, and inaugurate him in their sight.
20And you shall give *some* of your authority to
him, that all the congregation of the children of
Israel may be obedient. 21He shall stand before
Eleazar the priest, who shall inquire before the
Lord for him by the judgment of the Urim. At
his word they shall go out, and at his word they
shall come in, he and all the children of Israel
with him—all the congregation."
22So Moses did as the Lord commanded him.
He took Joshua and set him before Eleazar the
priest and before all the congregation. 23And he
laid his hands on him and inaugurated him, just
as the Lord commanded by the hand of Moses.

Daily Offerings

28 Now the Lord spoke to Moses, saying,
2"Command the children of Israel, and say
to them, 'My offering, My food for My offerings
made by fire as a sweet aroma to Me, you shall
be careful to offer to Me at their appointed time.'
3"And you shall say to them, 'This *is* the of-
fering made by fire which you shall offer to the
Lord: two male lambs in their first year without
blemish, day by day, as a regular burnt offering.
4The one lamb you shall offer in the morning,
the other lamb you shall offer in the evening,

The Message

5 Moses brought their case to God.
6-7 God ruled: "Zelophehad's daughters are right. Give them land as an inheritance among their father's relatives. Give them their father's inheritance.
8-11 "Then tell the People of Israel, If a man dies and leaves no son, give his inheritance to his daughter. If he has no daughter, give it to his brothers. If he has no brothers, give it to his father's brothers. If his father had no brothers, give it to the nearest relative so that the inheritance stays in the family. This is the standard procedure for the People of Israel, as commanded by God through Moses."

Joshua

12-14 God said to Moses, "Climb up into the Abarim Mountains and look over at the land that I am giving to the People of Israel. When you've had a good look you'll be joined to your ancestors in the grave—yes, you also along with Aaron your brother. This goes back to the day when the congregation quarreled in the Wilderness of Zin and you didn't honor me in holy reverence before them in the matter of the waters, the Waters of Meribah (Quarreling) at Kadesh in the Wilderness of Zin."
15-17 Moses responded to God: "Let God, the God of the spirits of everyone living, set a man over this community to lead them, to show the way ahead and bring them back home so God's community will not be like sheep without a shepherd."
18-21 God said to Moses, "Take Joshua the son of Nun—the Spirit is in him!—and place your hand on him. Stand him before Eleazar the priest in front of the entire congregation and commission him with everyone watching. Pass your magisterial authority over to him so that the whole congregation of the People of Israel will listen obediently to him. He is to consult with Eleazar the priest who, using the oracle-Urim, will prayerfully advise him in the presence of God. He will command the People of Israel, the entire community, in all their comings and goings."
22-23 Moses followed God's orders. He took Joshua and stood him before Eleazar the priest in front of the entire community. He laid his hands on him and commissioned him, following the procedures God had given Moses.

Offerings

1-8 28 God spoke to Moses: "Command the People of Israel. Tell them, You're in charge of presenting my food, my Fire-Gifts of pleasing fragrance, at the set times. Tell them, This is the Fire-Gift that you are to present to God: two healthy yearling lambs each day as a regular Whole-Burnt-Offering. Sacrifice one lamb in the morning, the other

NEW KING JAMES VERSION

5and one-tenth of an ephah of fine flour as a
grain offering mixed with one-fourth of a hin of
pressed oil. 6*It is* a regular burnt offering which
was ordained at Mount Sinai for a sweet aroma,
an offering made by fire to the LORD. 7And its
drink offering *shall be* one-fourth of a hin for
each lamb; in a holy *place* you shall pour out the
drink to the LORD as an offering. 8The other
lamb you shall offer in the evening; as the morn-
ing grain offering and its drink offering, you
shall offer *it* as an offering made by fire, a sweet
aroma to the LORD.

SABBATH OFFERINGS

9'And on the Sabbath day two lambs in their
first year, without blemish, and two-tenths *of an*
ephah of fine flour as a grain offering, mixed
with oil, with its drink offering— 10*this is* the
burnt offering for every Sabbath, besides the
regular burnt offering with its drink offering.

MONTHLY OFFERINGS

11'At the beginnings of your months you shall
present a burnt offering to the LORD: two young
bulls, one ram, and seven lambs in their first
year, without blemish; 12three-tenths *of an*
ephah of fine flour as a grain offering, mixed
with oil, for each bull; two-tenths *of an ephah* of
fine flour as a grain offering, mixed with oil, for
the one ram; 13and one-tenth *of an ephah* of fine
flour, mixed with oil, as a grain offering for each
lamb, as a burnt offering of sweet aroma, an of-
fering made by fire to the LORD. 14Their drink of-
fering shall be half a hin of wine for a bull, one-
third of a hin for a ram, and one-fourth of a hin
for a lamb; this *is* the burnt offering for each
month throughout the months of the year. 15Also
one kid of the goats as a sin offering to the LORD
shall be offered, besides the regular burnt offer-
ing and its drink offering.

OFFERINGS AT PASSOVER

16'On the fourteenth day of the first month *is*
the Passover of the LORD. 17And on the fifteenth
day of this month *is* the feast; unleavened bread
shall be eaten for seven days. 18On the first day
you shall have a holy convocation. You shall do
no customary work. 19And you shall present an
offering made by fire as a burnt offering to the
LORD: two young bulls, one ram, and seven
lambs in their first year. Be sure they are with-
out blemish. 20Their grain offering shall be of
fine flour mixed with oil: three-tenths *of an*
ephah you shall offer for a bull, and two-tenths
for a ram; 21you shall offer one-tenth *of an*
ephah for each of the seven lambs; 22also one
goat *as* a sin offering, to make atonement for
you. 23You shall offer these besides the burnt of-
fering of the morning, which *is* for a regular
burnt offering. 24In this manner you shall offer
the food of the offering made by fire daily for
seven days, as a sweet aroma to the LORD; it
shall be offered besides the regular burnt offer-
ing and its drink offering. 25And on the seventh
day you shall have a holy convocation. You shall
do no customary work.

THE MESSAGE

in the evening, together with two quarts of fine flour mixed with a quart of olive oil for a Grain-Offering. This is the standard Whole-Burnt-Offering instituted at Mount Sinai as a pleasing fragrance, a Fire-Gift to GOD. The Drink-Offering that goes with it is a quart of strong beer with each lamb. Pour out the Drink-Offering before GOD in the Sanctuary. Sacrifice the second lamb in the evening with the Grain-Offering and Drink-Offering the same as in the morning—a Fire-Gift of pleasing fragrance for GOD.

9-10 "On the Sabbath, sacrifice two healthy yearling lambs, together with the Drink-Offering and the Grain-Offering of four quarts of fine flour mixed with oil. This is the regular Sabbath Whole-Burnt-Offering, in addition to the regular Whole-Burnt-Offering and its Drink-Offering.

11 "On the first of the month offer a Whole-Burnt-Offering to GOD: two young bulls, one ram, and seven male yearling lambs—all healthy.

12-14 "A Grain-Offering of six quarts of fine flour mixed with oil goes with each bull, four quarts of fine flour mixed with oil with the ram, and two quarts of fine flour mixed with oil with each lamb. This is for a Whole-Burnt-Offering, a pleasing fragrance, a Fire-Gift to GOD. Also, Drink-Offerings of two quarts of wine for each bull, one and a quarter quarts of wine for the ram, and a quart of wine for each lamb are to be poured out.

14-15 "This is the first of the month Whole-Burnt-Offering to be made throughout the year. In addition to the regular Whole-Burnt-Offering with its accompanying Drink-Offering, a he-goat is to be offered to GOD as an Absolution-Offering.

16-17 "GOD's Passover is to be held on the fourteenth day of the first month. On the fifteenth day of this month hold a festival.

17-22 "For seven days, eat only unraised bread: Begin the first day in holy worship; don't do any regular work that day. Bring a Fire-Gift to GOD, a Whole-Burnt-Offering: two young bulls, one ram, and seven male yearling lambs—all healthy. Prepare a Grain-Offering of six quarts of fine flour mixed with oil for each bull, four quarts for the ram, and two quarts for each lamb, plus a goat as an Absolution-Offering to atone for you.

23-24 "Sacrifice these in addition to the regular morning Whole-Burnt-Offering. Prepare the food this way for the Fire-Gift, a pleasing fragrance to GOD, every day for seven days. Prepare it in addition to the regular Whole-Burnt-Offering and Drink-Offering.

25 "Conclude the seventh day in holy worship; don't do any regular work on that day.

New King James Version

Offerings at the Feast of Weeks

26'Also on the day of the firstfruits, when you bring a new grain offering to the LORD at your *Feast of* Weeks, you shall have a holy convocation. You shall do no customary work. 27You shall present a burnt offering as a sweet aroma to the LORD: two young bulls, one ram, and seven lambs in their first year, 28with their grain offering of fine flour mixed with oil: three-tenths *of an ephah* for each bull, two-tenths for the one ram, 29and one-tenth for each of the seven lambs; 30*also* one kid of the goats, to make atonement for you. 31Be sure they are without blemish. You shall present *them* with their drink offerings, besides the regular burnt offering with its grain offering.

Offerings at the Feast of Trumpets

29 'And in the seventh month, on the first *day* of the month, you shall have a holy convocation. You shall do no customary work. For you it is a day of blowing the trumpets. 2You shall offer a burnt offering as a sweet aroma to the LORD: one young bull, one ram, *and* seven lambs in their first year, without blemish. 3Their grain offering *shall be* fine flour mixed with oil: three-tenths *of an ephah* for the bull, two-tenths for the ram, 4and one-tenth for each of the seven lambs; 5also one kid of the goats *as* a sin offering, to make atonement for you; 6besides the burnt offering with its grain offering for the New Moon, the regular burnt offering with its grain offering, and their drink offerings, according to their ordinance, as a sweet aroma, an offering made by fire to the LORD.

Offerings on the Day of Atonement

7'On the tenth *day* of this seventh month you shall have a holy convocation. You shall afflict your souls; you shall not do any work. 8You shall present a burnt offering to the LORD *as* a sweet aroma: one young bull, one ram, *and* seven lambs in their first year. Be sure they are without blemish. 9Their grain offering *shall be of* fine flour mixed with oil: three-tenths *of an ephah* for the bull, two-tenths for the one ram, 10and one-tenth for each of the seven lambs; 11also one kid of the goats *as* a sin offering, besides the sin offering for atonement, the regular burnt offering with its grain offering, and their drink offerings.

Offerings at the Feast of Tabernacles

12'On the fifteenth day of the seventh month you shall have a holy convocation. You shall do no customary work, and you shall keep a feast to the LORD seven days. 13You shall present a burnt offering, an offering made by fire as a sweet aroma to the LORD: thirteen young bulls, two rams, *and* fourteen lambs in their first year. They shall be without blemish. 14Their grain offering *shall be of* fine flour mixed with oil: three-tenths *of an ephah* for each of the thirteen bulls, two-tenths for each of the two rams, 15and one-tenth for each of the fourteen lambs; 16also one kid of the goats *as* a sin offering, besides the regular burnt offering, its grain offering, and its drink offering.

The Message

26-30 "On the Day of Firstfruits when you bring an offering of new grain to GOD on your Feast-of-Weeks, gather in holy worship and don't do any regular work. Bring a Whole-Burnt-Offering of two young bulls, one ram, and seven male yearling lambs as a pleasing fragrance to GOD. Prepare a Grain-Offering of six quarts of fine flour mixed with oil for each bull, four quarts for the ram, and two quarts for each lamb, plus a he-goat as an Absolution-Offering to atone for you.

31 "These are all over and above the daily Whole-Burnt-Offering and its Grain-Offering and the Drink-Offering. Remember, the animals must be healthy.

1-5 29 "On the first day of the seventh month, gather in holy worship and do no regular work. This is your Day-of-Trumpet-Blasts. Sacrifice a Whole-Burnt-Offering: one young bull, one ram, and seven male yearling lambs—all healthy—as a pleasing fragrance to GOD. Prepare a Grain-Offering of six quarts of fine flour mixed with oil for the bull, four quarts for the ram, and two quarts for each lamb, plus a he-goat as an Absolution-Offering to atone for you.

6 "These are all over and above the monthly and daily Whole-Burnt-Offerings with their Grain-Offerings and Drink-Offerings as prescribed, a pleasing fragrance, a Fire-Gift to GOD.

7 "On the tenth day of this seventh month, gather in holy worship, humble yourselves, and do no work.

8-11 "Bring a Whole-Burnt-Offering to GOD as a pleasing fragrance: one young bull, one ram, and seven yearling male lambs—all healthy. Prepare a Grain-Offering of six quarts of fine flour mixed with oil for the bull, four quarts for the ram, and two quarts for each of the seven lambs. Also bring a he-goat as an Absolution-Offering to atone for you in addition to the regular Whole-Burnt-Offering with its Grain-Offering and Drink-Offering.

12-16 "Gather in holy worship on the fifteenth day of the seventh month; do no regular work. Celebrate a Festival to GOD for seven days. Bring a Whole-Burnt-Offering, a Fire-Gift of pleasing fragrance to GOD: thirteen young bulls, two rams, and fourteen yearling male lambs—all healthy. Prepare a Grain-Offering of six quarts of fine flour mixed with oil for each of the bulls, four quarts for each ram, and two quarts for each of the fourteen lambs. Also bring a he-goat as an Absolution-Offering in addition to the regular Whole-Burnt-Offering with its Grain-Offering and Drink-Offering.

NEW KING JAMES VERSION

17‘On the second day *present* twelve young
bulls, two rams, fourteen lambs in their first
year without blemish, 18and their grain offering
and their drink offerings for the bulls, for the
rams, and for the lambs, by their number, ac-
cording to the ordinance; 19also one kid of the
goats *as* a sin offering, besides the regular burnt
offering with its grain offering, and their drink
offerings.
20‘On the third day *present* eleven bulls, two
rams, fourteen lambs in their first year without
blemish, 21and their grain offering and their
drink offerings for the bulls, for the rams, and
for the lambs, by their number, according to the
ordinance; 22also one goat *as* a sin offering, be-
sides the regular burnt offering, its grain offer-
ing, and its drink offering.
23‘On the fourth day *present* ten bulls, two
rams, *and* fourteen lambs in their first year,
without blemish, 24and their grain offering and
their drink offerings for the bulls, for the rams,
and for the lambs, by their number, according to
the ordinance; 25also one kid of the goats *as* a
sin offering, besides the regular burnt offering,
its grain offering, and its drink offering.
26‘On the fifth day *present* nine bulls, two
rams, *and* fourteen lambs in their first year
without blemish, 27and their grain offering and
their drink offerings for the bulls, for the rams,
and for the lambs, by their number, according to
the ordinance; 28also one goat *as* a sin offering,
besides the regular burnt offering, its grain of-
fering, and its drink offering.
29‘On the sixth day *present* eight bulls, two
rams, *and* fourteen lambs in their first year
without blemish, 30and their grain offering and
their drink offerings for the bulls, for the rams,
and for the lambs, by their number, according to
the ordinance; 31also one goat *as* a sin offering,
besides the regular burnt offering, its grain of-
fering, and its drink offering.
32‘On the seventh day *present* seven bulls,
two rams, *and* fourteen lambs in their first year
without blemish, 33and their grain offering and
their drink offerings for the bulls, for the rams,
and for the lambs, by their number, according to
the ordinance; 34also one goat *as* a sin offering,
besides the regular burnt offering, its grain of-
fering, and its drink offering.
35‘On the eighth day you shall have a sacred
assembly. You shall do no customary work.
36You shall present a burnt offering, an offering
made by fire as a sweet aroma to the LORD: one
bull, one ram, seven lambs in their first year
without blemish, 37and their grain offering and
their drink offerings for the bull, for the ram,
and for the lambs, by their number, according to
the ordinance; 38also one goat *as* a sin offering,
besides the regular burnt offering, its grain of-
fering, and its drink offering.
39‘These you shall present to the LORD at
your appointed feasts (besides your vowed of-
ferings and your freewill offerings) as your
burnt offerings and your grain offerings, as
your drink offerings and your peace offerings.’ ”

THE MESSAGE

17-19 “On the second day: twelve young bulls,
two rams, and fourteen yearling male
lambs—all healthy. Prepare Grain-Offerings
and Drink-Offerings to go with the bulls,
rams, and lambs following the prescribed
recipes. And bring a he-goat as an Absolu-
tion-Offering in addition to the regular
Whole-Burnt-Offering with its Grain-Offer-
ing and Drink-Offering.
20-22 “On the third day: eleven bulls, two rams,
and fourteen male yearling lambs—all
healthy. Prepare Grain-Offerings and
Drink-Offerings to go with the bulls, rams,
and lambs following the prescribed recipes.
And bring a he-goat as an Absolution-
Offering in addition to the regular Whole-
Burnt-Offering with its Grain-Offering and
Drink-Offering.
23-25 “On the fourth day: ten bulls, two rams,
and fourteen male yearling lambs—all
healthy. Prepare Grain-Offerings and
Drink-Offerings to go with the bulls, rams,
and lambs following the prescribed recipes.
And bring a he-goat as an Absolution-
Offering in addition to the regular Whole-
Burnt-Offering with its Grain-Offering and
Drink-Offering.
26-28 “On the fifth day: nine bulls, two rams,
and fourteen male yearling lambs—all
healthy. Prepare Grain-Offerings and
Drink-Offerings to go with the bulls, rams,
and lambs following the prescribed recipes.
And bring a he-goat as an Absolution-
Offering in addition to the regular Whole-
Burnt-Offering with its Grain-Offering and
Drink-Offering.
29-31 “On the sixth day: eight bulls, two rams,
and fourteen male yearling lambs—all
healthy. Prepare Grain-Offerings and
Drink-Offerings to go with the bulls, rams,
and lambs following the prescribed recipes.
And bring a he-goat as an Absolution-
Offering in addition to the regular Whole-
Burnt-Offering with its Grain-Offering and
Drink-Offering.
32-34 “On the seventh day: seven bulls, two
rams, and fourteen male yearling lambs—all
healthy. Prepare Grain-Offerings and Drink-
Offerings to go with the bulls, rams, and
lambs following the prescribed recipes. And
bring a he-goat as an Absolution-Offering in
addition to the regular Whole-Burnt-Offering
with its Grain-Offering and Drink-Offering.
35-38 “On the eighth day: Gather in holy wor-
ship; do no regular work. Bring a Fire-Gift
of pleasing fragrance to GOD, a Whole-
Burnt-Offering: one bull, one ram, and
seven male yearling lambs—all healthy. Pre-
pare Grain-Offerings and Drink-Offerings
to go with the bulls, rams, and lambs follow-
ing the prescribed recipes. And bring a he-
goat as an Absolution-Offering in addition
to the regular Whole-Burnt-Offering with its
Grain-Offering and Drink-Offering.
39 “Sacrifice these to GOD as a congregation
at your set feasts: your Whole-Burnt-Offer-
ings, Grain-Offerings, Drink-Offerings, and
Peace-Offerings. These are all over and above
your personal Vow-Offerings and Freewill-
Offerings.”

NEW KING JAMES VERSION

40So Moses told the children of Israel every-
thing, just as the LORD commanded Moses.

THE LAW CONCERNING VOWS

30 Then Moses spoke to the heads of the
tribes concerning the children of Israel,
saying, "This *is* the thing which the LORD has
commanded: 2If a man makes a vow to the LORD,
or swears an oath to bind himself by some agree-
ment, he shall not break his word; he shall do ac-
cording to all that proceeds out of his mouth.
3"Or if a woman makes a vow to the LORD,
and binds *herself* by some agreement while in
her father's house in her youth, 4and her father
hears her vow and the agreement by which she
has bound herself, and her father holds his
peace, then all her vows shall stand, and every
agreement with which she has bound herself
shall stand. 5But if her father overrules her on
the day that he hears, then none of her vows nor
her agreements by which she has bound herself
shall stand; and the LORD will release her, be-
cause her father overruled her.
6"If indeed she takes a husband, while bound
by her vows or by a rash utterance from her lips
by which she bound herself, 7and her husband
hears *it*, and makes no response to her on the
day that he hears, then her vows shall stand,
and her agreements by which she bound herself
shall stand. 8But if her husband overrules her on
the day that he hears *it*, he shall make void her
vow which she took and what she uttered with
her lips, by which she bound herself, and the
LORD will release her.
9"Also any vow of a widow or a divorced
woman, by which she has bound herself, shall
stand against her.
10"If she vowed in her husband's house, or
bound herself by an agreement with an oath,
11and her husband heard *it*, and made no re-
sponse to her *and* did not overrule her, then all
her vows shall stand, and every agreement by
which she bound herself shall stand. 12But if her
husband truly made them void on the day he
heard *them*, then whatever proceeded from her
lips concerning her vows or concerning the
agreement binding her, it shall not stand; her
husband has made them void, and the LORD will
release her. 13Every vow and every binding oath
to afflict her soul, her husband may confirm it,
or her husband may make it void. 14Now if her
husband makes no response whatever to her
from day to day, then he confirms all her vows
or all the agreements that bind her; he confirms
them, because he made no response to her on
the day that he heard *them*. 15But if he does
make them void after he has heard *them*, then
he shall bear her guilt."
16These *are* the statutes which the LORD com-
manded Moses, between a man and his wife,
and between a father and his daughter in her
youth in her father's house.

VENGEANCE ON THE MIDIANITES

31 And the LORD spoke to Moses, saying:
2"Take vengeance on the Midianites for the
children of Israel. Afterward you shall be gath-
ered to your people."

THE MESSAGE

40 Moses instructed the People of Israel in
all that GOD commanded him.

VOWS

1-2 30 Moses spoke to the heads of the tribes
of the People of Israel: "This is what
GOD commands: When a man makes a vow
to GOD or binds himself by an oath to do
something, he must not break his word; he
must do exactly what he has said.
3-5 "When a woman makes a vow to GOD and
binds herself by a pledge as a young girl still
living in her father's house, and her father
hears of her vow or pledge but says nothing
to her, then she has to make good on all her
vows and pledges. But if her father holds
her back when he hears of what she has
done, none of her vows and pledges are
valid. GOD will release her since her father
held her back.
6-8 "If she marries after she makes a vow or
has made some rash promise or pledge, and
her husband hears of it but says nothing to
her, then she has to make good on whatever
she vowed or pledged. But if her husband
intervenes when he hears of it, he cancels
the vow or rash promise that binds her. And
GOD will release her.
9 "Any vow or pledge taken by a widow or
divorced woman is binding on her.
10-15 "When a woman who is living with her
husband makes a vow or takes a pledge un-
der oath and her husband hears about it but
says nothing and doesn't say she can't do it,
then all her vows and pledges are valid. But
if her husband cancels them when he hears
about them, then none of the vows and
pledges that she made are binding. Her hus-
band has canceled them and GOD will re-
lease her. Any vow and pledge that she
makes that may be to her detriment can be
either affirmed or annulled by her husband.
But if her husband is silent and doesn't
speak up day after day, he confirms her
vows and pledges—she has to make good
on them. By saying nothing to her when he
hears of them, he binds her to them. If, how-
ever, he cancels them sometime after he
hears of them, he takes her guilt on himself."
16 These are the rules that GOD gave Moses
regarding conduct between a man and his
wife and between a father and his young
daughter who is still living at home.

THE MIDIANITE WAR

1-2 31 GOD spoke to Moses: "Avenge the Peo-
ple of Israel on the Midianites. After-
ward you will go to be with your dead an-
cestors."

New King James Version

3So Moses spoke to the people, saying, "Arm
some of yourselves for war, and let them go
against the Midianites to take vengeance for the
LORD on Midian. 4A thousand from each tribe of
all the tribes of Israel you shall send to the war."
5So there were recruited from the divisions
of Israel one thousand from *each* tribe, twelve
thousand armed for war. 6Then Moses sent them
to the war, one thousand from *each* tribe; he
sent them to the war with Phinehas the son of
Eleazar the priest, with the holy articles and the
signal trumpets in his hand. 7And they warred
against the Midianites, just as the LORD com-
manded Moses, and they killed all the males.
8They killed the kings of Midian with *the rest of*
those who were killed—Evi, Rekem, Zur, Hur,
and Reba, the five kings of Midian. Balaam the
son of Beor they also killed with the sword.
9And the children of Israel took the women
of Midian captive, with their little ones, and
took as spoil all their cattle, all their flocks, and
all their goods. 10They also burned with fire all
the cities where they dwelt, and all their forts.
11And they took all the spoil and all the booty—
of man and beast.

Return from the War

12Then they brought the captives, the booty,
and the spoil to Moses, to Eleazar the priest, and
to the congregation of the children of Israel, to
the camp in the plains of Moab by the Jordan,
across from Jericho. 13And Moses, Eleazar the
priest, and all the leaders of the congregation,
went to meet them outside the camp. 14But
Moses was angry with the officers of the army,
with the captains over thousands and captains
over hundreds, who had come from the battle.
15And Moses said to them: "Have you kept all
the women alive? 16Look, these *women* caused
the children of Israel, through the counsel of
Balaam, to trespass against the LORD in the inci-
dent of Peor, and there was a plague among the
congregation of the LORD. 17Now therefore, kill
every male among the little ones, and kill every
woman who has known a man intimately. 18But
keep alive for yourselves all the young girls who
have not known a man intimately. 19And as for
you, remain outside the camp seven days; who-
ever has killed any person, and whoever has
touched any slain, purify yourselves and your
captives on the third day and on the seventh
day. 20Purify every garment, everything made of
leather, everything woven of goats' *hair,* and
everything made of wood."
21Then Eleazar the priest said to the men of
war who had gone to the battle, "This *is* the or-
dinance of the law which the LORD commanded
Moses: 22"Only the gold, the silver, the bronze,
the iron, the tin, and the lead, 23everything that
can endure fire, you shall put through the fire,
and it shall be clean; and it shall be purified
with the water of purification. But all that can-
not endure fire you shall put through water.
24And you shall wash your clothes on the sev-
enth day and be clean, and afterward you may
come into the camp."

The Message

3-4 Moses addressed the people: "Recruit men for a campaign against Midian, to exact GOD's vengeance on Midian, a thousand from each tribe of Israel to go to war."

5-6 A fighting force of a thousand from each tribe of Israel—twelve thousand in all—was recruited. Moses sent them off to war, a thousand from each tribe, and also Phinehas son of Eleazar, who went as priest to the army, in charge of holy vessels and the signaling bugles.

7-12 They attacked Midian, just as GOD had commanded Moses, and killed every last man. Among the fallen were Evi, Rekem, Zur, Hur, and Reba—the five kings of Midian. They also killed Balaam son of Beor with the sword. The People of Israel took the Midianite women and children captive and took all their animals and herds and goods as plunder. They burned to the ground all the towns in which Midianites lived and also their tent camps. They looted and plundered everything and everyone—stuff and people and animals. They took it all—captives and booty and plunder—back to Moses and Eleazar the priest and the company of Israel where they were camped on the Plains of Moab, at Jordan-Jericho.

13-18 Moses, Eleazar, and all the leaders of the congregation went to meet the returning army outside the camp. Moses was furious with the army officers—the commanders of thousands and commanders of hundreds—as they came back from the battlefield: "What's this! You've let these women live! They're the ones who, under Balaam's direction, seduced the People of Israel away from GOD in that mess at Peor, causing the plague that hit GOD's people. Finish your job: kill all the boys. Kill every woman who has slept with a man. The younger women who are virgins you can keep alive for yourselves.

19-20 "Now here's what you are to do: Pitch tents outside the camp. All who have killed anyone or touched a corpse must stay outside the camp for seven days. Purify yourselves and your captives on the third and seventh days. Purify every piece of clothing and every utensil—everything made of leather, goat hair, or wood."

21-24 Eleazar the priest then spoke to the soldiers who had fought in the battle: "This is the ruling from the Revelation that GOD gave Moses: Gold, silver, bronze, iron, tin, and lead—and anything else that can survive fire—must be passed through the fire; then it will be ritually purified. It must also be ritually washed in the Water-of-Cleansing. Further, whatever cannot survive fire must be put through that water. On the seventh day scrub your clothes; you will be ritually clean. Then you can return to camp."

New King James Version

Division of the Plunder
25Now the LORD spoke to Moses, saying:
26"Count up the plunder that was taken—of man
and beast—you and Eleazar the priest and the
chief fathers of the congregation; 27and divide
the plunder into two parts, between those who
took part in the war, who went out to battle, and
all the congregation. 28And levy a tribute for the
LORD on the men of war who went out to battle:
one of every five hundred of the persons, the
cattle, the donkeys, and the sheep; 29take *it* from
their half, and give *it* to Eleazar the priest as a
heave offering to the LORD. 30And from the chil-
dren of Israel's half you shall take one of every
fifty, drawn from the persons, the cattle, the
donkeys, and the sheep, from all the livestock,
and give them to the Levites who keep charge of
the tabernacle of the LORD." 31So Moses and
Eleazar the priest did as the LORD commanded
Moses.
32The booty remaining from the plunder,
which the men of war had taken, was six hun-
dred and seventy-five thousand sheep, 33sev-
enty-two thousand cattle, 34sixty-one thousand
donkeys, 35and thirty-two thousand persons in
all, of women who had not known a man inti-
mately. 36And the half, the portion for those who
had gone out to war, was in number three hun-
dred and thirty-seven thousand five hundred
sheep; 37and the LORD's tribute of the sheep was
six hundred and seventy-five. 38The cattle *were*
thirty-six thousand, of which the LORD's tribute
was seventy-two. 39The donkeys *were* thirty
thousand five hundred, of which the LORD's trib-
ute *was* sixty-one. 40The persons *were* sixteen
thousand, of which the LORD's tribute *was*
thirty-two persons. 41So Moses gave the tribute
which was the LORD's heave offering to Eleazar
the priest, as the LORD commanded Moses.
42And from the children of Israel's half,
which Moses separated from the men who
fought— 43now the half belonging to the congre-
gation was three hundred and thirty-seven thou-
sand five hundred sheep, 44thirty-six thousand
cattle, 45thirty thousand five hundred donkeys,
46and sixteen thousand persons— 47and from
the children of Israel's half Moses took one of
every fifty, drawn from man and beast, and gave
them to the Levites, who kept charge of the tab-
ernacle of the LORD, as the LORD commanded
Moses.
48Then the officers who *were* over thou-
sands of the army, the captains of thousands
and captains of hundreds, came near to Moses;
49and they said to Moses, "Your servants have
taken a count of the men of war who *are* under
our command, and not a man of us is missing.
50Therefore we have brought an offering for the
LORD, what every man found of ornaments of
gold: armlets and bracelets and signet rings
and earrings and necklaces, to make atonement
for ourselves before the LORD." 51So Moses and
Eleazar the priest received the gold from them,
all the fashioned ornaments. 52And all the gold
of the offering that they offered to the LORD,
from the captains of thousands and captains of
hundreds, was sixteen thousand seven hundred
and fifty shekels. 53(The men of war had taken
spoil, every man for himself.) 54And Moses and

The Message

25-27 GOD said to Moses, "I want you and Eleazar the priest and the family leaders in the community to count the captives, people and animals. Split the plunder between the soldiers who fought the battle and the rest of the congregation.

28-30 "Then tax the booty that goes to the soldiers at the rate of one life out of five hundred, whether humans, cattle, donkeys, or sheep. It's a GOD-tax taken from their half-share to be turned over to Eleazar the priest on behalf of GOD. Tax the congregation's half-share at the rate of one life out of fifty, whether persons, cattle, donkeys, sheep, goats, or other animals. Give this to the Levites who are in charge of the care of GOD's Dwelling."

31 Moses and Eleazar followed through with what GOD had commanded Moses.

32-35 The rest of the plunder taken by the army:

675,000 sheep
72,000 cattle
61,000 donkeys
32,000 women who were virgins

36-40 The half-share for those who had fought in the war:

337,500 sheep, with a tax of 675 for GOD
36,000 cattle, with a tax of 72 for GOD
30,500 donkeys, with a tax of 61 for GOD
16,000 people, with a tax of 32 for GOD

41 Moses turned the tax over to Eleazar the priest as GOD's part, following GOD's instructions to Moses.

42-46 The other half-share for the Israelite community that Moses set apart from what was given to the men who fought the war was:

337,500 sheep
36,000 cattle
30,500 donkeys
16,000 people

47 From the half-share going to the People of Israel, Moses, just as GOD had instructed him, picked one out of every fifty persons and animals and gave them to the Levites, who were in charge of maintaining GOD's Dwelling.

48-50 The military officers—commanders of thousands and commanders of hundreds—came to Moses and said, "We have counted the soldiers under our command and not a man is missing. We've brought offerings to GOD from the gold jewelry we got—armlets, bracelets, rings, earrings, ornaments—to make atonement for our lives before GOD."

51-54 Moses and Eleazar the priest received the gold from them, all that fine-crafted jewelry. In total, the gold from the commanders of thousands and hundreds that Moses and Eleazar offered as a gift to GOD weighed about six hundred pounds, all donated by the soldiers who had taken the booty. Moses

NEW KING JAMES VERSION

Eleazar the priest received the gold from the captains of thousands and of hundreds, and brought it into the tabernacle of meeting as a memorial for the children of Israel before the LORD.

THE TRIBES SETTLING EAST OF THE JORDAN

32 Now the children of Reuben and the children of Gad had a very great multitude of livestock; and when they saw the land of Jazer and the land of Gilead, that indeed the region *was* a place for livestock, 2the children of Gad and the children of Reuben came and spoke to Moses, to Eleazar the priest, and to the leaders of the congregation, saying, 3"Ataroth, Dibon, Jazer, Nimrah, Heshbon, Elealeh, Shebam, Nebo, and Beon, 4the country which the LORD defeated before the congregation of Israel, *is* a land for livestock, and your servants have livestock." 5Therefore they said, "If we have found favor in your sight, let this land be given to your servants as a possession. Do not take us over the Jordan."

6And Moses said to the children of Gad and to the children of Reuben: "Shall your brethren go to war while you sit here? 7Now why will you discourage the heart of the children of Israel from going over into the land which the LORD has given them? 8Thus your fathers did when I sent them away from Kadesh Barnea to see the land. 9For when they went up to the Valley of Eshcol and saw the land, they discouraged the heart of the children of Israel, so that they did not go into the land which the LORD had given them. 10So the LORD's anger was aroused on that day, and He swore an oath, saying, 11'Surely none of the men who came up from Egypt, from twenty years old and above, shall see the land of which I swore to Abraham, Isaac, and Jacob, because they have not wholly followed Me, 12except Caleb the son of Jephunneh, the Kenizzite, and Joshua the son of Nun, for they have wholly followed the LORD.' 13So the LORD's anger was aroused against Israel, and He made them wander in the wilderness forty years, until all the generation that had done evil in the sight of the LORD was gone. 14And look! You have risen in your fathers' place, a brood of sinful men, to increase still more the fierce anger of the LORD against Israel. 15For if you turn away from following Him, He will once again leave them in the wilderness, and you will destroy all these people."

16Then they came near to him and said: "We will build sheepfolds here for our livestock, and cities for our little ones, 17but we ourselves will be armed, ready *to go* before the children of Israel until we have brought them to their place; and our little ones will dwell in the fortified cities because of the inhabitants of the land. 18We will not return to our homes until every one of the children of Israel has received his inheritance. 19For we will not inherit with them on the other side of the Jordan and beyond, because our inheritance has fallen to us on this eastern side of the Jordan."

THE MESSAGE

and Eleazar took the gold from the commanders of thousands and hundreds and brought it to the Tent of Meeting, to serve as a reminder for the People of Israel before GOD.

TRIBES EAST OF THE JORDAN

1-4 32 The families of Reuben and Gad had huge herds of livestock. They saw that the country of Jazer and Gilead was just the place for grazing livestock. And so they came, the families of Gad and of Reuben, and spoke to Moses and Eleazar the priest and the leaders of the congregation, saying, "Ataroth, Dibon, Jazer, Nimrah, Heshbon, Elealeh, Sebam, Nebo, and Beon—the country that GOD laid low before the community of Israel—is a country just right for livestock, and we have livestock."

5 They continued, "If you think we've done a good job so far, give us this country for our inheritance. Don't make us go across the Jordan."

6-12 Moses answered the families of Gad and Reuben: "Do you mean that you are going to leave the fighting that's ahead to your brothers while you settle down here? Why would you even think of letting the People of Israel down, demoralizing them just as they're about to move into the land GOD gave them? That's exactly what your ancestors did when I sent them from Kadesh Barnea to survey the country. They went as far as the Valley of Eshcol, took one look and quit. They completely demoralized the People of Israel from entering the land GOD had given them. And GOD got angry—oh, did he get angry! He swore: 'They'll never get to see it; none of those who came up out of Egypt who are twenty years and older will ever get to see the land that I promised to Abraham, Isaac, and Jacob. They weren't interested in following me—their hearts weren't in it. None, except for Caleb son of Jephunneh the Kenizzite, and Joshua son of Nun; they followed me—their hearts were in it.'

13 "GOD's anger smoked against Israel. He made them wander in the wilderness for forty years, until that entire generation that acted out evil in his sight had died out.

14-15 "And now here you are, just one more mob of sinners stepping up to replace your ancestors, throwing fuel on the already blazing anger of GOD against Israel. If you won't follow him, he'll do it again. He'll dump them in the desert and the disaster will be all your fault."

16-19 They came close to him and said, "All we want to do is build corrals for our livestock and towns for our families. Then we'll take up arms and take the front lines, leading the People of Israel to their place. We'll be able to leave our families behind, secure in fortified towns, safe from those who live in the land. But we won't go back home until every Israelite is in full possession of his inheritance. We won't expect any inheritance west of the Jordan; we are claiming all our inheritance east of the Jordan."

New King James Version

20Then Moses said to them: "If you do this thing, if you arm yourselves before the LORD for the war, 21and all your armed men cross over the Jordan before the LORD until He has driven out His enemies from before Him, 22and the land is subdued before the LORD, then afterward you may return and be blameless before the LORD and before Israel; and this land shall be your possession before the LORD. 23But if you do not do so, then take note, you have sinned against the LORD; and be sure your sin will find you out. 24Build cities for your little ones and folds for your sheep, and do what has proceeded out of your mouth."

25And the children of Gad and the children of Reuben spoke to Moses, saying: "Your servants will do as my lord commands. 26Our little ones, our wives, our flocks, and all our livestock will be there in the cities of Gilead; 27but your servants will cross over, every man armed for war, before the LORD to battle, just as my lord says."

28So Moses gave command concerning them to Eleazar the priest, to Joshua the son of Nun, and to the chief fathers of the tribes of the children of Israel. 29And Moses said to them: "If the children of Gad and the children of Reuben cross over the Jordan with you, every man armed for battle before the LORD, and the land is subdued before you, then you shall give them the land of Gilead as a possession. 30But if they do not cross over armed with you, they shall have possessions among you in the land of Canaan."

31Then the children of Gad and the children of Reuben answered, saying: "As the LORD has said to your servants, so we will do. 32We will cross over armed before the LORD into the land of Canaan, but the possession of our inheritance *shall remain* with us on this side of the Jordan."

33So Moses gave to the children of Gad, to the children of Reuben, and to half the tribe of Manasseh the son of Joseph, the kingdom of Sihon king of the Amorites and the kingdom of Og king of Bashan, the land with its cities within the borders, the cities of the surrounding country. 34And the children of Gad built Dibon and Ataroth and Aroer, 35Atroth and Shophan and Jazer and Jogbehah, 36Beth Nimrah and Beth Haran, fortified cities, and folds for sheep. 37And the children of Reuben built Heshbon and Elealeh and Kirjathaim, 38Nebo and Baal Meon (*their* names being changed) and Shibmah; and they gave *other* names to the cities which they built.

39And the children of Machir the son of Manasseh went to Gilead and took it, and dispossessed the Amorites who *were* in it. 40So Moses gave Gilead to Machir the son of Manasseh, and he dwelt in it. 41Also Jair the son of Manasseh went and took its small towns, and called them Havoth Jair.[a] 42Then Nobah went and took Kenath and its villages, and he called it Nobah, after his own name.

32:41 [a]Literally *Towns of Jair*

The Message

20-22 Moses said, "If you do what you say, take up arms before GOD for battle and together go across the Jordan ready, before GOD, to fight until GOD has cleaned his enemies out of the land, then when the land is secure you will have fulfilled your duty to GOD and Israel. Then this land will be yours to keep before GOD.

23-24 "But if you don't do what you say, you will be sinning against GOD; you can be sure that your sin will track you down. So, go ahead. Build towns for your families and corrals for your livestock. Do what you said you'd do."

25-27 The families of Gad and Reuben told Moses: "We will do as our master commands. Our children and wives, our flocks and herds will stay behind here in the towns of Gilead. But we, every one of us fully armed, will cross the river to fight for GOD, just as our master has said."

28-30 So Moses issued orders for them to Eleazar the priest, Joshua the son of Nun, and the heads of the ancestral tribes of the People of Israel. Moses said, "If the families of Gad and Reuben cross the Jordan River with you and before GOD, all armed and ready to fight, then after the land is secure, you may give them the land of Gilead as their inheritance. But if they don't cross over with you, they'll have to settle up with you in Canaan."

31-32 The families of Gad and Reuben responded: "We will do what GOD has said. We will cross the Jordan before GOD, ready and willing to fight. But the land we inherit will be here, to the east of the Jordan."

33 Moses gave the families of Gad, Reuben, and the half-tribe of Manasseh son of Joseph the kingdom of Sihon, king of the Amorites, and the kingdom of Og, king of Bashan—the land, its towns, and all the territories connected with them—the works.

34-36 The Gadites rebuilt Dibon, Ataroth, Aroer, Atroth Shophan, Jazer, Jogbehah, Beth Nimrah, and Beth Haran as fortified cities; they also built corrals for their animals.

37-38 The Reubenites rebuilt Heshbon, Elealeh, and Kiriathaim, also Nebo and Baal Meon and Sibmah. They renamed the cities that they rebuilt.

39-40 The family of Makir son of Manasseh went to Gilead, captured it, and drove out the Amorites who lived there. Moses then gave Gilead to the Makirites, the descendants of Manasseh. They moved in and settled there.

41 Jair, another son of Manasseh, captured some villages and named them Havvoth Jair (Jair's Tent-Camps).

42 Nobah captured Kenath and its surrounding camps. He renamed it after himself, Nobah.

NEW KING JAMES VERSION

ISRAEL'S JOURNEY FROM EGYPT REVIEWED

33 These *are* the journeys of the children of
Israel, who went out of the land of Egypt
by their armies under the hand of Moses and
Aaron. 2Now Moses wrote down the starting
points of their journeys at the command of the
LORD. And these *are* their journeys according to
their starting points:
3They departed from Rameses in the first
month, on the fifteenth day of the first month;
on the day after the Passover the children of Is-
rael went out with boldness in the sight of all
the Egyptians. 4For the Egyptians were burying
all *their* firstborn, whom the LORD had killed
among them. Also on their gods the LORD had
executed judgments.
5Then the children of Israel moved from
Rameses and camped at Succoth. 6They de-
parted from Succoth and camped at Etham,
which *is* on the edge of the wilderness. 7They
moved from Etham and turned back to Pi Hahi-
roth, which *is* east of Baal Zephon; and they
camped near Migdol. 8They departed from be-
fore Hahiroth[a] and passed through the midst of
the sea into the wilderness, went three days'
journey in the Wilderness of Etham, and
camped at Marah. 9They moved from Marah
and came to Elim. At Elim *were* twelve springs
of water and seventy palm trees; so they
camped there.
10They moved from Elim and camped by the
Red Sea. 11They moved from the Red Sea and
camped in the Wilderness of Sin. 12They jour-
neyed from the Wilderness of Sin and camped at
Dophkah. 13They departed from Dophkah and
camped at Alush. 14They moved from Alush and
camped at Rephidim, where there was no water
for the people to drink.
15They departed from Rephidim and camped
in the Wilderness of Sinai. 16They moved from
the Wilderness of Sinai and camped at Kibroth
Hattaavah. 17They departed from Kibroth Hat-
taavah and camped at Hazeroth. 18They de-
parted from Hazeroth and camped at Rithmah.
19They departed from Rithmah and camped at
Rimmon Perez. 20They departed from Rimmon
Perez and camped at Libnah. 21They moved
from Libnah and camped at Rissah. 22They jour-
neyed from Rissah and camped at Kehelathah.
23They went from Kehelathah and camped at
Mount Shepher. 24They moved from Mount
Shepher and camped at Haradah. 25They moved
from Haradah and camped at Makheloth.
26They moved from Makheloth and camped at
Tahath. 27They departed from Tahath and
camped at Terah. 28They moved from Terah and
camped at Mithkah. 29They went from Mithkah
and camped at Hashmonah. 30They departed
from Hashmonah and camped at Moseroth.
31They departed from Moseroth and camped at
Bene Jaakan. 32They moved from Bene Jaakan
and camped at Hor Hagidgad. 33They went from
Hor Hagidgad and camped at Jotbathah. 34They
moved from Jotbathah and camped at Abronah.
35They departed from Abronah and camped at
Ezion Geber. 36They moved from Ezion Geber

33:8 [a]Many Hebrew manuscripts, Samaritan Pentateuch, Syriac, Targum, and Vulgate read *from Pi Hahiroth* (compare verse 7).

THE MESSAGE

CAMPSITES FROM RAMESES TO JORDAN-JERICHO

1-2 33 These are the camping sites in the journey of the People of Israel after they left Egypt, deployed militarily under the command of Moses and Aaron. Under GOD's instruction Moses kept a log of every time they moved, camp by camp:

3-4 They marched out of Rameses the day after the Passover. It was the fifteenth day of the first month. They marched out heads high and confident. The Egyptians, busy burying their firstborn whom GOD had killed, watched them go. GOD had exposed the nonsense of their gods.

5-36 The People of Israel:

left Rameses and camped at Succoth;

left Succoth and camped at Etham at the edge of the wilderness;

left Etham, circled back to Pi Hahiroth east of Baal Zephon, and camped near Migdol;

left Pi Hahiroth and crossed through the Sea into the wilderness; three days into the Wilderness of Etham they camped at Marah;

left Marah and came to Elim where there were twelve springs and seventy palm trees; they camped there;

left Elim and camped by the Red Sea;

left the Red Sea and camped in the Wilderness of Sin;

left the Wilderness of Sin and camped at Dophkah;

left Dophkah and camped at Alush;

left Alush and camped at Rephidim where there was no water for the people to drink;

left Rephidim and camped in the Wilderness of Sinai;

left the Wilderness of Sinai and camped at Kibroth Hattaavah;

left Kibroth Hattaavah and camped at Hazeroth;

left Hazeroth and camped at Rithmah;

left Rithmah and camped at Rimmon Perez;

left Rimmon Perez and camped at Libnah;

left Libnah and camped at Rissah;

left Rissah and camped at Kehelathah;

left Kehelathah and camped at Mount Shepher;

left Mount Shepher and camped at Haradah;

left Haradah and camped at Makheloth;

left Makheloth and camped at Tahath;

left Tahath and camped at Terah;

left Terah and camped at Mithcah;

left Mithcah and camped at Hashmonah;

left Hashmonah and camped at Moseroth;

left Moseroth and camped at Bene Jaakan;

left Bene Jaakan and camped at Hor Haggidgad;

left Hor Haggidgad and camped at Jotbathah;

left Jotbathah and camped at Abronah;

NEW KING JAMES VERSION

and camped in the Wilderness of Zin, which *is* Kadesh. 37They moved from Kadesh and camped at Mount Hor, on the boundary of the land of Edom.

38Then Aaron the priest went up to Mount Hor at the command of the LORD, and died there in the fortieth year after the children of Israel had come out of the land of Egypt, on the first *day* of the fifth month. 39Aaron *was* one hundred and twenty-three years old when he died on Mount Hor.

40Now the king of Arad, the Canaanite, who dwelt in the South in the land of Canaan, heard of the coming of the children of Israel.

41So they departed from Mount Hor and camped at Zalmonah. 42They departed from Zalmonah and camped at Punon. 43They departed from Punon and camped at Oboth. 44They departed from Oboth and camped at Ije Abarim, at the border of Moab. 45They departed from Ijim[a] and camped at Dibon Gad. 46They moved from Dibon Gad and camped at Almon Diblathaim. 47They moved from Almon Diblathaim and camped in the mountains of Abarim, before Nebo. 48They departed from the mountains of Abarim and camped in the plains of Moab by the Jordan, *across from* Jericho. 49They camped by the Jordan, from Beth Jesimoth as far as the Abel Acacia Grove[a] in the plains of Moab.

INSTRUCTIONS FOR THE CONQUEST OF CANAAN

50Now the LORD spoke to Moses in the plains of Moab by the Jordan, *across from* Jericho, saying, 51"Speak to the children of Israel, and say to them: 'When you have crossed the Jordan into the land of Canaan, 52then you shall drive out all the inhabitants of the land from before you, destroy all their engraved stones, destroy all their molded images, and demolish all their high places; 53you shall dispossess *the inhabitants of* the land and dwell in it, for I have given you the land to possess. 54And you shall divide the land by lot as an inheritance among your families; to the larger you shall give a larger inheritance, and to the smaller you shall give a smaller inheritance; there everyone's *inheritance* shall be whatever falls to him by lot. You shall inherit according to the tribes of your fathers. 55But if you do not drive out the inhabitants of the land from before you, then it shall be that those whom you let remain *shall be* irritants in your eyes and thorns in your sides, and they shall harass you in the land where you dwell. 56Moreover it shall be *that* I will do to you as I thought to do to them.' "

THE APPOINTED BOUNDARIES OF CANAAN

34 Then the LORD spoke to Moses, saying, 2"Command the children of Israel, and say to them: 'When you come into the land of Canaan, this *is* the land that shall fall to you as an inheritance—the land of Canaan to its boundaries. 3Your southern border shall be from the Wilderness of Zin along the border of Edom;

33:45 [a]Same as *Ije Abarim*, verse 44 **33:49** [a]Hebrew *Abel Shittim*

THE MESSAGE

left Abronah and camped at Ezion Geber;
left Ezion Geber and camped at Kadesh
in the Wilderness of Zin.

37-39 After they left Kadesh and camped at
Mount Hor at the border of Edom, Aaron the
priest climbed Mount Hor at GOD's com-
mand and died there. It was the first day of
the fifth month in the fortieth year after the
People of Israel had left Egypt. Aaron was
123 years old when he died on Mount Hor.

40 The Canaanite king of Arad—he ruled in the
Negev of Canaan—heard that the People of
Israel had arrived.

41-47 They left Mount Hor and camped at Zal-
monah;
left Zalmonah and camped at Punon;
left Punon and camped at Oboth;
left Oboth and camped at Iye Abarim on
the border of Moab;
left Iyim and camped at Dibon Gad;
left Dibon Gad and camped at Almon Di-
blathaim;
left Almon Diblathaim and camped in the
mountains of Abarim (Across-the-River),
within sight of Nebo.

48-49 After they left the mountains of Abarim
they camped on the Plains of Moab at Jor-
dan-Jericho. On the Plains of Moab their
camp stretched along the banks of the Jor-
dan from Beth Jeshimoth to Abel Shittim
(Acacia Meadow).

50-53 GOD spoke to Moses on the Plains of
Moab at Jordan-Jericho: "Tell the People of
Israel, When you cross the Jordan into the
country of Canaan, drive out the native pop-
ulation before you, destroy their carved
idols, destroy their cast images, level their
worship-mounds so that you take over the
land and make yourself at home in it; I've
given it to you. It's yours.

54 "Divide up the land by lot according to
the size of your clans: Large clans will get
large tracts of land, small clans will get
smaller tracts of land. However the lot falls,
that's it. Divide it up according to your an-
cestral tribes.

55-56 "But if you don't drive out the native pop-
ulation, everyone you let stay there will be-
come a cinder in your eye and a splinter in
your foot. They'll give you endless trouble
right in your own backyards. And I'll start
treating you the way I planned to treat
them."

LAND INHERITANCE

1-2 **34** GOD spoke to Moses: "Command the
People of Israel. Tell them, When you
enter Canaan, these are the borders of the
land you are getting as an inheritance:

3-5 "Your southern border will take in some
of the Wilderness of Zin where it touches

NEW KING JAMES VERSION

then your southern border shall extend east-
ward to the end of the Salt Sea; 4your border
shall turn from the southern side of the Ascent
of Akrabbim, continue to Zin, and be on the
south of Kadesh Barnea; then it shall go on to
Hazar Addar, and continue to Azmon; 5the bor-
der shall turn from Azmon to the Brook of
Egypt, and it shall end at the Sea.
6'As for the western border, you shall have
the Great Sea for a border; this shall be your
western border.
7'And this shall be your northern border:
From the Great Sea you shall mark out your
border line to Mount Hor; 8from Mount Hor you
shall mark out *your border* to the entrance of
Hamath; then the direction of the border shall
be toward Zedad; 9the border shall proceed to
Ziphron, and it shall end at Hazar Enan. This
shall be your northern border.
10'You shall mark out your eastern border
from Hazar Enan to Shepham; 11the border
shall go down from Shepham to Riblah on the
east side of Ain; the border shall go down and
reach to the eastern side of the Sea of Chin-
nereth; 12the border shall go down along the
Jordan, and it shall end at the Salt Sea. This
shall be your land with its surrounding bound-
aries.' "
13Then Moses commanded the children of Is-
rael, saying: "This *is* the land which you shall in-
herit by lot, which the LORD has commanded to
give to the nine tribes and to the half-tribe. 14For
the tribe of the children of Reuben according to
the house of their fathers, and the tribe of the
children of Gad according to the house of their
fathers, have received *their inheritance;* and the
half-tribe of Manasseh has received its inheri-
tance. 15The two tribes and the half-tribe have
received their inheritance on this side of the Jor-
dan, *across from* Jericho eastward, toward the
sunrise."

THE LEADERS APPOINTED TO DIVIDE THE LAND

16And the LORD spoke to Moses, saying,
17"These *are* the names of the men who shall di-
vide the land among you as an inheritance:
Eleazar the priest and Joshua the son of Nun.
18And you shall take one leader of every tribe to
divide the land for the inheritance. 19These *are*
the names of the men: from the tribe of Judah,
Caleb the son of Jephunneh; 20from the tribe of
the children of Simeon, Shemuel the son of Am-
mihud; 21from the tribe of Benjamin, Elidad the
son of Chislon; 22a leader from the tribe of the
children of Dan, Bukki the son of Jogli; 23from
the sons of Joseph: a leader from the tribe of the
children of Manasseh, Hanniel the son of
Ephod, 24and a leader from the tribe of the chil-
dren of Ephraim, Kemuel the son of Shiphtan;
25a leader from the tribe of the children of Zebu-
lun, Elizaphan the son of Parnach; 26a leader
from the tribe of the children of Issachar, Paltiel
the son of Azzan; 27a leader from the tribe of the
children of Asher, Ahihud the son of Shelomi;
28and a leader from the tribe of the children of
Naphtali, Pedahel the son of Ammihud."
29These *are* the ones the LORD commanded to
divide the inheritance among the children of Is-
rael in the land of Canaan.

THE MESSAGE

Edom. It starts in the east at the Dead Sea,
curves south of Scorpion Pass and on to Zin,
continues south of Kadesh Barnea, then to
Hazar Addar and on to Azmon, where it
takes a turn to the northwest to the Brook of
Egypt and on to the Mediterranean Sea.
6 "Your western border will be the Mediter-
ranean Sea.
7-9 "Your northern border runs on a line
from the Mediterranean Sea to Mount Hor,
and from Mount Hor to Lebo Hamath, con-
nects to Zedad, continues to Ziphron, and
ends at Hazar Enan. This is your northern
border.
10-12 "Your eastern border runs on a line from
Hazar Enan to Shepham. The border goes
south from Shepham to Riblah to the east of
Ain, and continues along the slopes east of
the Sea of Galilee. The border then follows
the Jordan River and ends at the Dead Sea.
"This is your land with its four borders."
13-15 Moses then commanded the People of Is-
rael: "This is the land: Divide up the inheri-
tance by lot. GOD has ordered it to be given
to the nine and a half tribes. The tribe of
Reuben, the tribe of Gad, and the half-tribe
of Manasseh have already received their in-
heritance; the two tribes and the half-tribe
got their inheritance east of Jordan-Jericho,
facing the sunrise."

16-19 GOD spoke to Moses: "These are the men
who will be in charge of distributing the in-
heritance of the land: Eleazar the priest and
Joshua son of Nun. Assign one leader from
each tribe to help them in distributing the
land. Assign these:
19-28 Caleb son of Jephunneh from the tribe of
Judah;
Shemuel son of Ammihud from the tribe
of Simeon;
Elidad son of Kislon from the tribe of
Benjamin;
Bukki son of Jogli, leader from the tribe
of Dan;
Hanniel son of Ephod, leader from the
tribe of Manasseh son of Joseph;
Kemuel son of Shiphtan, leader from the
tribe of Ephraim son of Joseph;
Elizaphan son of Parnach, leader from
the tribe of Zebulun;
Paltiel son of Azzan, leader from the tribe
of Issachar;
Ahihud son of Shelomi, leader from the
tribe of Asher;
Pedahel son of Ammihud, leader from the
tribe of Naphtali."
29 These are the men GOD commanded to
hand out the assignments of land-inheritance
to the People of Israel in the country of
Canaan.

New King James Version

Cities for the Levites

35 And the LORD spoke to Moses in the plains of Moab by the Jordan *across from* Jericho, saying: 2“Command the children of Israel that they give the Levites cities to dwell in from the inheritance of their possession, and you shall *also* give the Levites common-land around the cities. 3They shall have the cities to dwell in; and their common-land shall be for their cattle, for their herds, and for all their animals. 4The common-land of the cities which you will give the Levites *shall extend* from the wall of the city outward a thousand cubits all around. 5And you shall measure outside the city on the east side two thousand cubits, on the south side two thousand cubits, on the west side two thousand cubits, and on the north side two thousand cubits. The city *shall be* in the middle. This shall belong to them as common-land for the cities.

6“Now among the cities which you will give to the Levites *you shall appoint* six cities of refuge, to which a manslayer may flee. And to these you shall add forty-two cities. 7So all the cities you will give to the Levites *shall be* forty-eight; these *you shall give* with their common-land. 8And the cities which you will give *shall be* from the possession of the children of Israel; from the larger *tribe* you shall give many, from the smaller you shall give few. Each shall give some of its cities to the Levites, in proportion to the inheritance that each receives.”

Cities of Refuge

9Then the LORD spoke to Moses, saying, 10“Speak to the children of Israel, and say to them: ‘When you cross the Jordan into the land of Canaan, 11then you shall appoint cities to be cities of refuge for you, that the manslayer who kills any person accidentally may flee there. 12They shall be cities of refuge for you from the avenger, that the manslayer may not die until he stands before the congregation in judgment. 13And of the cities which you give, you shall have six cities of refuge. 14You shall appoint three cities on this side of the Jordan, and three cities you shall appoint in the land of Canaan, *which* will be cities of refuge. 15These six cities shall be for refuge for the children of Israel, for the stranger, and for the sojourner among them, that anyone who kills a person accidentally may flee there.

16‘But if he strikes him with an iron implement, so that he dies, he *is* a murderer; the murderer shall surely be put to death. 17And if he strikes him with a stone in the hand, by which one could die, and he does die, he *is* a murderer; the murderer shall surely be put to death. 18Or *if* he strikes him with a wooden hand weapon, by which one could die, and he does die, he *is* a murderer; the murderer shall surely be put to death. 19The avenger of blood himself shall put the murderer to death; when he meets him, he shall put him to death. 20If he pushes him out of hatred or, while lying in wait, hurls something at him so that he dies, 21or in enmity he strikes him with his hand so that he dies, the one who struck *him* shall surely be put to death. He *is* a murderer. The avenger of blood shall put the murderer to death when he meets him.

The Message

Cities for Levites and Asylum-Cities

1-3 35 Then GOD spoke to Moses on the Plains of Moab at Jordan-Jericho: “Command the People of Israel to give the Levites as their part of the total inheritance towns to live in. Make sure there is plenty of pasture around the towns. Then they will be well taken care of with towns to live in and pastures for their cattle, flocks, and other livestock.

4-5 “The pasture surrounding the Levites’ towns is to extend 1,500 feet in each direction from the city wall. The outside borders of the pasture are to measure three thousand feet on each of the four sides—east, south, west, and north—with the town at the center. Each city will be supplied with pasture.

6-8 “Six of these towns that you give the Levites will be asylum-cities to which anyone who accidentally kills another person may flee for asylum. In addition, you will give them forty-two other towns—forty-eight towns in all, together with their pastures. The towns that you give the Levites from the common inheritance of the People of Israel are to be taken in proportion to the size of each tribe—many towns from a tribe that has many, few from a tribe that has few.”

9-15 GOD spoke to Moses: “Speak to the People of Israel. Tell them, When you cross the River Jordan into the country of Canaan, designate your asylum-cities, towns to which a person who accidentally kills someone can flee for asylum. They will be places of refuge from the avenger so that the alleged murderer won’t be killed until he can appear before the community in court. Provide six asylum-cities. Designate three of the towns to the east side of the Jordan, the other three in Canaan proper—asylum-cities for the People of Israel, for the foreigner, and for any occasional visitors or guests—six asylum-cities to run to for anyone who accidentally kills another.

16 “But if the killer has used an iron object, that’s just plain murder; he’s obviously a murderer and must be put to death.

17 “Or if he has a rock in his hand big enough to kill and the man dies, that’s murder; he’s a murderer and must be put to death.

18 “Or if he’s carrying a wooden club heavy enough to kill and the man dies, that’s murder; he’s a murderer and must be put to death.

19 “In such cases the avenger has a right to kill the murderer when he meets him—he can kill him on the spot.

20-21 “And if out of sheer hatred a man pushes another or from ambush throws something at him and he dies, or angrily hits him with his fist and kills him, that’s murder—he must be put to death. The avenger has a right to kill him when he gets him.

NEW KING JAMES VERSION

22‘However, if he pushes him suddenly with-
out enmity, or throws anything at him without
lying in wait, 23or uses a stone, by which a man
could die, throwing *it* at him without seeing *him*,
so that he dies, while he was not his enemy or
seeking his harm, 24then the congregation shall
judge between the manslayer and the avenger of
blood according to these judgments. 25So the
congregation shall deliver the manslayer from
the hand of the avenger of blood, and the con-
gregation shall return him to the city of refuge
where he had fled, and he shall remain there un-
til the death of the high priest who was anointed
with the holy oil. 26But if the manslayer at any
time goes outside the limits of the city of refuge
where he fled, 27and the avenger of blood finds
him outside the limits of his city of refuge, and
the avenger of blood kills the manslayer, he shall
not be guilty of blood, 28because he should have
remained in his city of refuge until the death of
the high priest. But after the death of the high
priest the manslayer may return to the land of
his possession.
29‘And these *things* shall be a statute of judg-
ment to you throughout your generations in all
your dwellings. 30Whoever kills a person, the
murderer shall be put to death on the testimony
of witnesses; but one witness is not *sufficient*
testimony against a person for the death
penalty. 31Moreover you shall take no ransom
for the life of a murderer who *is* guilty of death,
but he shall surely be put to death. 32And you
shall take no ransom for him who has fled to his
city of refuge, that he may return to dwell in the
land before the death of the priest. 33So you
shall not pollute the land where you *are;* for
blood defiles the land, and no atonement can be
made for the land, for the blood that is shed on
it, except by the blood of him who shed it.
34Therefore do not defile the land which you in-
habit, in the midst of which I dwell; for I the
LORD dwell among the children of Israel.’ ”

MARRIAGE OF FEMALE HEIRS

36 Now the chief fathers of the families of the
children of Gilead the son of Machir, the
son of Manasseh, of the families of the sons of
Joseph, came near and spoke before Moses and
before the leaders, the chief fathers of the chil-
dren of Israel. 2And they said: “The LORD com-
manded my lord *Moses* to give the land as an in-
heritance by lot to the children of Israel, and my
lord was commanded by the LORD to give the in-
heritance of our brother Zelophehad to his
daughters. 3Now if they are married to any of
the sons of the *other* tribes of the children of Is-
rael, then their inheritance will be taken from
the inheritance of our fathers, and it will be
added to the inheritance of the tribe into which
they marry; so it will be taken from the lot of our
inheritance. 4And when the Jubilee of the chil-
dren of Israel comes, then their inheritance will
be added to the inheritance of the tribe into
which they marry; so their inheritance will be

THE MESSAGE

22-27 “If, however, he impulsively pushes some-
one and there is no history of hard feelings,
or he impetuously picks up something and
throws it, or he accidentally drops a stone
tool—a maul or hammer, say—and it hits
and kills someone he didn’t even know was
there, and there’s no suspicion that there
was bad blood between them, the commu-
nity is to judge between the killer and the
avenger following these guidelines. It’s the
task of the community to save the killer
from the hand of the avenger—the commu-
nity is to return him to his asylum-city to
which he fled. He must stay there until the
death of the High Priest who was anointed
with the holy oil. But if the murderer leaves
the asylum-city to which he has fled, and
the avenger finds him outside the borders of
his asylum-city, the avenger has a right to
kill the murderer. And he’s not considered
guilty of murder.
28 “So it’s important that he stay in his asy-
lum-city until the death of the High Priest.
After the death of the High Priest he is free
to return to his own place.

29 “These are the procedures for making judg-
ments from now on, wherever you live.
30 “Anyone who kills another may be exe-
cuted only on the testimony of eyewit-
nesses. But no one can be executed on the
testimony of only one witness.
31 “Don’t accept bribe money in exchange
for the life of a murderer. He’s guilty and de-
serves the death penalty. Put him to death.
32 “And don’t accept bribe money for any-
one who has fled to an asylum-city so as to
permit him to go back and live in his own
place before the death of the High Priest.
33 “Don’t pollute the land in which you live.
Murder pollutes the land. The land can’t be
cleaned up of the blood of murder except
through the blood of the murderer.
34 “Don’t desecrate the land in which you
live. I live here, too—I, GOD, live in the same
neighborhood with the People of Israel.”

THE DAUGHTERS OF ZELOPHEHAD

1 **36** The heads of the ancestral clan of
Gilead son of Makir, the son of Ma-
nasseh—they were from the clans of the de-
scendants of Joseph—approached Moses
and the leaders who were heads of the fam-
ilies in the People of Israel.
2-4 They said, “When GOD commanded my
master to hand over the inheritance-lands
by lot to the People of Israel, my master
was also commanded by GOD to hand over
the inheritance-land of Zelophehad our
brother to his daughters. But what happens
if they marry into another tribe in the Peo-
ple of Israel? Their inheritance-land will be
taken out of our ancestral tribe and get
added into the tribe into which they mar-
ried. And then when the year of Jubilee
comes for the People of Israel their inheri-
tance will be lumped in with the inheri-
tance of the tribe into which they mar-

NEW KING JAMES VERSION

taken away from the inheritance of the tribe of
our fathers."
5 Then Moses commanded the children of Is-
rael according to the word of the LORD, saying:
"What the tribe of the sons of Joseph speaks is
right. 6 This *is* what the LORD commands con-
cerning the daughters of Zelophehad, saying,
'Let them marry whom they think best, but they
may marry only within the family of their fa-
ther's tribe.' 7 So the inheritance of the children
of Israel shall not change hands from tribe to
tribe, for every one of the children of Israel shall
keep the inheritance of the tribe of his fathers.
8 And every daughter who possesses an inheri-
tance in any tribe of the children of Israel shall
be the wife of one of the family of her father's
tribe, so that the children of Israel each may
possess the inheritance of his fathers. 9 Thus no
inheritance shall change hands from *one* tribe
to another, but every tribe of the children of Is-
rael shall keep its own inheritance."
10 Just as the LORD commanded Moses, so did
the daughters of Zelophehad; 11 for Mahlah,
Tirzah, Hoglah, Milcah, and Noah, the daugh-
ters of Zelophehad, were married to the sons of
their father's brothers. 12 They were married into
the families of the children of Manasseh the son
of Joseph, and their inheritance remained in the
tribe of their father's family.
13 These *are* the commandments and the
judgments which the LORD commanded the chil-
dren of Israel by the hand of Moses in the plains
of Moab by the Jordan, *across from* Jericho.

THE MESSAGE

ried—their land will be removed from our
ancestors' inheritance!"

5-9 Moses, at GOD's command, issued this or-
der to the People of Israel: "What the tribe of
the sons of Joseph says is right. This is
GOD's command to Zelophehad's daughters:
They are free to marry anyone they choose
as long as they marry within their ancestral
clan. The inheritance-land of the People of
Israel must not get passed around from tribe
to tribe. No, keep the tribal inheritance-land
in the family. Every daughter who inherits
land, regardless of the tribe she is in, must
marry a man from within her father's tribal
clan. Every Israelite is responsible for mak-
ing sure the inheritance stays within the an-
cestral tribe. No inheritance-land may be
passed from tribe to tribe; each tribe of the
People of Israel must hold tight to its own
land."

10-12 Zelophehad's daughters did just as GOD
commanded Moses. Mahlah, Tirzah, Hoglah,
Milcah, and Noah, Zelophehad's daughters,
all married their cousins on their father's
side. They married within the families of
Manasseh son of Joseph and their inheri-
tance-lands stayed in their father's family.

13 These are the commands and regulations
that GOD commanded through the authority
of Moses to the People of Israel on the
Plains of Moab at Jordan-Jericho.

DEUTERONOMY

New King James Version

The Previous Command to Enter Canaan

1 These *are* the words which Moses spoke to all Israel on this side of the Jordan in the wilderness, in the plain[a] opposite Suph,[b] between Paran, Tophel, Laban, Hazeroth, and Dizahab. 2*It is* eleven days' *journey* from Horeb by way of Mount Seir to Kadesh Barnea. 3Now it came to pass in the fortieth year, in the eleventh month, on the first *day* of the month, *that* Moses spoke to the children of Israel according to all that the LORD had given him as commandments to them, 4after he had killed Sihon king of the Amorites, who dwelt in Heshbon, and Og king of Bashan, who dwelt at Ashtaroth in[a] Edrei.

5On this side of the Jordan in the land of Moab, Moses began to explain this law, saying, 6"The LORD our God spoke to us in Horeb, saying: 'You have dwelt long enough at this mountain. 7Turn and take your journey, and go to the mountains of the Amorites, to all the neighboring *places* in the plain,[a] in the mountains and in the lowland, in the South and on the seacoast, to the land of the Canaanites and to Lebanon, as far as the great river, the River Euphrates. 8See, I have set the land before you; go in and possess the land which the LORD swore to your fathers—to Abraham, Isaac, and Jacob—to give to them and their descendants after them.'

Tribal Leaders Appointed

9"And I spoke to you at that time, saying: 'I alone am not able to bear you. 10The LORD your God has multiplied you, and here you *are* today, as the stars of heaven in multitude. 11May the LORD God of your fathers make you a thousand times more numerous than you are, and bless you as He has promised you! 12How can I alone bear your problems and your burdens and your complaints? 13Choose wise, understanding, and knowledgeable men from among your tribes, and I will make them heads over you.' 14And you answered me and said, 'The thing which you have told *us* to do *is* good.' 15So I took the heads of your tribes, wise and knowledgeable men, and made them heads over you, leaders of thousands, leaders of hundreds, leaders of fifties, leaders of tens, and officers for your tribes.

16"Then I commanded your judges at that time, saying, 'Hear *the cases* between your brethren, and judge righteously between a man and his brother or the stranger who is with him. 17You shall not show partiality in judgment; you shall hear the small as well as the great; you shall not be afraid in any man's presence, for the judgment *is* God's. The case that is too hard for you, bring to me, and I will hear it.' 18And I commanded you at that time all the things which you should do.

1:1 [a]Hebrew *arabah* [b]One manuscript of the Septuagint, also Targum and Vulgate, read *Red Sea.* **1:4** [a]Septuagint, Syriac, and Vulgate read *and* (compare Joshua 12:4). **1:7** [a]Hebrew *arabah*

The Message

1-2 1 These are the sermons Moses preached to all Israel when they were east of the Jordan River in the Arabah Wilderness, opposite Suph, in the vicinity of Paran, Tophel, Laban, Hazeroth, and Dizahab. It takes eleven days to travel from Horeb to Kadesh Barnea following the Mount Seir route.

3-4 It was on the first day of the eleventh month of the fortieth year when Moses addressed the People of Israel, telling them everything GOD had commanded him concerning them. This came after he had defeated Sihon king of the Amorites, who ruled from Heshbon, and Og king of Bashan, who ruled from Ashtaroth in Edrei. It was east of the Jordan in the land of Moab that Moses set out to explain this Revelation.

Moses Preaches to Israel on the Plains of Moab

5 He said:

6-8 Back at Horeb, GOD, our God, spoke to us: "You've stayed long enough at this mountain. On your way now. Get moving. Head for the Amorite hills, wherever people are living in the Arabah, the mountains, the foothills, the Negev, the seashore—the Canaanite country and the Lebanon all the way to the big river, the Euphrates. Look, I've given you this land. Now go in and take it. It's the land GOD promised to give your ancestors Abraham, Isaac, and Jacob and their children after them."

9-13 At the time I told you, "I can't do this, can't carry you all by myself. GOD, your God, has multiplied your numbers. Why, look at you—you rival the stars in the sky! And may GOD, the God-of-Your-Fathers, keep it up and multiply you another thousand times, bless you just as he promised. But how can I carry, all by myself, your troubles and burdens and quarrels? So select some wise, understanding, and seasoned men from your tribes, and I will commission them as your leaders."

14 You answered me, "Good! A good solution."

15 So I went ahead and took the top men of your tribes, wise and seasoned, and made them your leaders—leaders of thousands, of hundreds, of fifties, and of tens, officials adequate for each of your tribes.

16-17 At the same time I gave orders to your judges: "Listen carefully to complaints and accusations between your fellow Israelites. Judge fairly between each person and his fellow or foreigner. Don't play favorites; treat the little and the big alike; listen carefully to each. Don't be impressed by big names. This is *God's* judgment you're dealing with. Hard cases you can bring to me; I'll deal with them."

18 I issued orders to you at that time regarding everything you would have to deal with.

New King James Version

Israel's Refusal to Enter the Land

19“So we departed from Horeb, and went
through all that great and terrible wilderness
which you saw on the way to the mountains of
the Amorites, as the LORD our God had com-
manded us. Then we came to Kadesh Barnea.
20And I said to you, ‘You have come to the moun-
tains of the Amorites, which the LORD our God
is giving us. 21Look, the LORD your God has set
the land before you; go up *and* possess *it*, as the
LORD God of your fathers has spoken to you; do
not fear or be discouraged.’

22“And every one of you came near to me and
said, ‘Let us send men before us, and let them
search out the land for us, and bring back word
to us of the way by which we should go up, and
of the cities into which we shall come.’

23“The plan pleased me well; so I took twelve
of your men, one man from *each* tribe. 24And
they departed and went up into the mountains,
and came to the Valley of Eshcol, and spied it
out. 25They also took *some* of the fruit of the
land in their hands and brought *it* down to us;
and they brought back word to us, saying, ‘*It is*
a good land which the LORD our God is giving
us.’

26“Nevertheless you would not go up, but re-
belled against the command of the LORD your
God; 27and you complained in your tents, and
said, ‘Because the LORD hates us, He has
brought us out of the land of Egypt to deliver us
into the hand of the Amorites, to destroy us.
28Where can we go up? Our brethren have dis-
couraged our hearts, saying, “The people *are*
greater and taller than we; the cities *are* great
and fortified up to heaven; moreover we have
seen the sons of the Anakim there.” ’

29“Then I said to you, ‘Do not be terrified, or
afraid of them. 30The LORD your God, who goes
before you, He will fight for you, according to all
He did for you in Egypt before your eyes, 31and
in the wilderness where you saw how the LORD
your God carried you, as a man carries his son,
in all the way that you went until you came to
this place.’ 32Yet, for all that, you did not believe
the LORD your God, 33who went in the way be-
fore you to search out a place for you to pitch
your tents, to show you the way you should go,
in the fire by night and in the cloud by day.

The Penalty for Israel's Rebellion

34“And the LORD heard the sound of your
words, and was angry, and took an oath, saying,
35‘Surely not one of these men of this evil gener-
ation shall see that good land of which I swore
to give to your fathers, 36except Caleb the son of
Jephunneh; he shall see it, and to him and his
children I am giving the land on which he
walked, because he wholly followed the LORD.’
37The LORD was also angry with me for your
sakes, saying, ‘Even you shall not go in there.
38Joshua the son of Nun, who stands before you,
he shall go in there. Encourage him, for he shall
cause Israel to inherit it.

39‘Moreover your little ones and your chil-
dren, who you say will be victims, who today
have no knowledge of good and evil, they shall
go in there; to them I will give it, and they shall
possess it. 40But *as for* you, turn and take your

The Message

19-21 Then we set out from Horeb and headed for the Amorite hill country, going through that huge and frightening wilderness that you've had more than an eyeful of by now—all under the command of GOD, our God—and finally arrived at Kadesh Barnea. There I told you, “You've made it to the Amorite hill country that GOD, our God, is giving us. Look, GOD, your God, has placed this land as a gift before you. Go ahead and take it now. GOD, the God-of-Your-Fathers, promised it to you. Don't be afraid. Don't lose heart.”

22 But then you all came to me and said, “Let's send some men on ahead to scout out the land for us and bring back a report on the best route to take and the kinds of towns we can expect to find.”

23-25 That seemed like a good idea to me, so I picked twelve men, one from each tribe. They set out, climbing through the hills. They came to the Eshcol Valley and looked it over. They took samples of the produce of the land and brought them back to us, saying, “It's a good land that GOD, our God, is giving us!”

26-28 But then you weren't willing to go up. You rebelled against GOD, your God's plain word. You complained in your tents: “GOD hates us. He hauled us out of Egypt in order to dump us among the Amorites—a death sentence for sure! How can we go up? We're trapped in a dead end. Our brothers took all the wind out of our sails, telling us, ‘The people are bigger and stronger than we are; their cities are huge, their defenses massive—we even saw Anakite giants there!’ ”

29-33 I tried to relieve your fears: “Don't be terrified of them. GOD, your God, is leading the way; he's fighting for you. You saw with your own eyes what he did for you in Egypt; you saw what he did in the wilderness, how GOD, your God, carried you as a father carries his child, carried you the whole way until you arrived here. But now that you're here, you won't trust GOD, your God—this same GOD who goes ahead of you in your travels to scout out a place to pitch camp, a fire by night and a cloud by day to show you the way to go.”

34-36 When GOD heard what you said, he exploded in anger. He swore, “Not a single person of this evil generation is going to get so much as a look at the good land that I promised to give to your parents. Not one—except for Caleb son of Jephunneh. He'll see it. I'll give him and his descendants the land he walked on because he was all for following GOD, heart and soul.”

37-40 But I also got it. Because of you GOD's anger spilled over onto me. He said, “You aren't getting in either. Your assistant, Joshua son of Nun, will go in. Build up his courage. He's the one who will claim the inheritance for Israel. And your babies of whom you said, ‘They'll be grabbed for plunder,’ and all these little kids who right now don't even know right from wrong—they'll get in. I'll give it to them. Yes, they'll be the new owners. But not you. Turn

New King James Version

journey into the wilderness by the Way of the
Red Sea.’
41“Then you answered and said to me, ‘We
have sinned against the LORD; we will go up and
fight, just as the LORD our God commanded us.’
And when everyone of you had girded on his
weapons of war, you were ready to go up into
the mountain.
42“And the LORD said to me, ‘Tell them, “Do
not go up nor fight, for I *am* not among you; lest
you be defeated before your enemies.” ’ 43So I
spoke to you; yet you would not listen, but re-
belled against the command of the LORD, and
presumptuously went up into the mountain.
44And the Amorites who dwelt in that mountain
came out against you and chased you as bees
do, and drove you back from Seir to Hormah.
45Then you returned and wept before the LORD,
but the LORD would not listen to your voice nor
give ear to you.
46“So you remained in Kadesh many days,
according to the days that you spent *there*.

The Desert Years

2 “Then we turned and journeyed into the
wilderness of the Way of the Red Sea, as the
LORD spoke to me, and we skirted Mount Seir
for many days.
2“And the LORD spoke to me, saying: 3‘You
have skirted this mountain long enough; turn
northward. 4And command the people, saying,
“You *are about to* pass through the territory of
your brethren, the descendants of Esau, who
live in Seir; and they will be afraid of you.
Therefore watch yourselves carefully. 5Do not
meddle with them, for I will not give you *any* of
their land, no, not so much as one footstep, be-
cause I have given Mount Seir to Esau *as* a pos-
session. 6You shall buy food from them with
money, that you may eat; and you shall also buy
water from them with money, that you may
drink.
7“For the LORD your God has blessed you in
all the work of your hand. He knows your trudg-
ing through this great wilderness. These forty
years the LORD your God *has been* with you; you
have lacked nothing.” ’
8“And when we passed beyond our brethren,
the descendants of Esau who dwell in Seir, away
from the road of the plain, away from Elath and
Ezion Geber, we turned and passed by way of
the Wilderness of Moab. 9Then the LORD said to
me, ‘Do not harass Moab, nor contend with
them in battle, for I will not give you *any* of their
land *as* a possession, because I have given Ar to
the descendants of Lot *as* a possession.’ ”
10(The Emim had dwelt there in times past, a
people as great and numerous and tall as the
Anakim. 11They were also regarded as giants,[a]
like the Anakim, but the Moabites call them
Emim. 12The Horites formerly dwelt in Seir, but
the descendants of Esau dispossessed them and
destroyed them from before them, and dwelt in
their place, just as Israel did to the land of their
possession which the LORD gave them.)

2:11 [a]Hebrew *rephaim*

The Message

around and head back into the wilderness
following the route to the Red Sea.”
41 You spoke up, “We’ve sinned against
GOD. We’ll go up and fight, following all the
orders that GOD, our God, has commanded.”
You took your weapons and dressed for bat-
tle—you thought it would be so easy going
into those hills!
42 But GOD told me, “Tell them, ‘Don’t do it;
don’t go up to fight—I’m not with you in
this. Your enemies will waste you.’ ”
43-46 I told you but you wouldn’t listen. You re-
belled at the plain word of GOD. You threw
out your chests and strutted into the hills.
And those Amorites, who had lived in those
hills all their lives, swarmed all over you like
a hive of bees, chasing you from Seir all the
way to Hormah, a stinging defeat. You came
back and wept in the presence of GOD, but
he didn’t pay a bit of attention to you; GOD
didn’t give you the time of day. You stayed
there in Kadesh a long time, about as long
as you had stayed there earlier.

1 2 Then we turned around and went back
into the wilderness following the route to
the Red Sea, as GOD had instructed me. We
worked our way in and around the hills of
Seir for a long, long time.

2-6 Then GOD said, “You’ve been going around
in circles in these hills long enough; go
north. Command the people, You’re about to
cut through the land belonging to your rela-
tives, the People of Esau who settled in Seir.
They are terrified of you, but restrain your-
selves. Don’t try and start a fight. I am not
giving you so much as a square inch of their
land. I’ve already given all the hill country
of Seir to Esau—he owns it all. Pay them up
front for any food or water you get from
them.”
7 GOD, your God, has blessed you in every-
thing you have done. He has guarded you in
your travels through this immense wilder-
ness. For forty years now, GOD, your God,
has been right here with you. You haven’t
lacked one thing.
8 So we detoured around our brothers, the
People of Esau who live in Seir, avoiding the
Arabah Road that comes up from Elath and
Ezion Geber; instead we used the road
through the Wilderness of Moab.

9 GOD told me, “And don’t try to pick a fight
with the Moabites. I am not giving you any
of their land. I’ve given ownership of Ar to
the People of Lot.”
10-12 The Emites (Monsters) used to live there—
mobs of hulking giants, like Anakites. Along
with the Anakites they were lumped in with
the Rephaites (Ghosts) but in Moab they
were called Emites. Horites also used to live
in Seir, but the descendants of Esau took over
and destroyed them, the same as Israel did in
the land GOD gave them to possess.

New King James Version

13“ ‘Now rise and cross over the Valley of the
Zered.’ So we crossed over the Valley of the
Zered. 14And the time we took to come from
Kadesh Barnea until we crossed over the Valley
of the Zered *was* thirty-eight years, until all the
generation of the men of war was consumed
from the midst of the camp, just as the LORD had
sworn to them. 15For indeed the hand of the
LORD was against them, to destroy them from
the midst of the camp until they were con-
sumed.
16“So it was, when all the men of war had fi-
nally perished from among the people, 17that the
LORD spoke to me, saying: 18‘This day you are to
cross over at Ar, the boundary of Moab. 19And
when you come near the people of Ammon, do
not harass them or meddle with them, for I will
not give you *any* of the land of the people of Am-
mon *as* a possession, because I have given it to
the descendants of Lot *as* a possession.’ ”
20(That was also regarded as a land of gi-
ants;[a] giants formerly dwelt there. But the Am-
monites call them Zamzummim, 21a people as
great and numerous and tall as the Anakim. But
the LORD destroyed them before them, and they
dispossessed them and dwelt in their place,
22just as He had done for the descendants of
Esau, who dwelt in Seir, when He destroyed the
Horites from before them. They dispossessed
them and dwelt in their place, even to this day.
23And the Avim, who dwelt in villages as far as
Gaza—the Caphtorim, who came from Caphtor,
destroyed them and dwelt in their place.)
24“ ‘Rise, take your journey, and cross over
the River Arnon. Look, I have given into your
hand Sihon the Amorite, king of Heshbon, and
his land. Begin to possess *it,* and engage him in
battle. 25This day I will begin to put the dread
and fear of you upon the nations under the
whole heaven, who shall hear the report of you,
and shall tremble and be in anguish because of
you.’

King Sihon Defeated

26“And I sent messengers from the Wilder-
ness of Kedemoth to Sihon king of Heshbon,
with words of peace, saying, 27‘Let me pass
through your land; I will keep strictly to the
road, and I will turn neither to the right nor to
the left. 28You shall sell me food for money, that
I may eat, and give me water for money, that I
may drink; only let me pass through on foot,
29just as the descendants of Esau who dwell in
Seir and the Moabites who dwell in Ar did for
me, until I cross the Jordan to the land which
the LORD our God is giving us.’
30“But Sihon king of Heshbon would not let
us pass through, for the LORD your God hard-
ened his spirit and made his heart obstinate,
that He might deliver him into your hand, as *it
is* this day.
31“And the LORD said to me, ‘See, I have be-
gun to give Sihon and his land over to you. Be-
gin to possess *it,* that you may inherit his land.’
32Then Sihon and all his people came out
against us to fight at Jahaz. 33And the LORD our
God delivered him over to us; so we defeated

2:20 [a]Hebrew *rephaim*

The Message

13 GOD said, “It’s time now to cross the
Brook Zered.” So we crossed the Brook
Zered.
14-15 It took us thirty-eight years to get from
Kadesh Barnea to the Brook Zered. That’s
how long it took for the entire generation of
soldiers from the camp to die off, as GOD
had sworn they would. GOD was relentless
against them until the last one was gone
from the camp.
16-23 When the last of these soldiers had died,
GOD said to me, “This is the day you cut
across the territory of Moab, at Ar. When
you approach the People of Ammon, don’t
try and pick a fight with them because I’m
not giving you any of the land of the People
of Ammon for yourselves—I’ve already
given it to the People of Lot.” It is also con-
sidered to have once been the land of the
Rephaites. Rephaites lived there long ago—
the Ammonites called them Zamzummites
(Barbarians)—huge mobs of them, giants
like the Anakites. GOD destroyed them and
the Ammonites moved in and took over. It
was the same with the People of Esau who
live in Seir—GOD got rid of the Horites who
lived there earlier and they moved in and
took over, as you can see. Regarding the
Avvites who lived in villages as far as Gaza,
the Caphtorites who came from Caphtor
(Crete) wiped them out and moved in.

24-25 “On your feet now. Get started. Cross the
Brook Arnon. Look: Here’s Sihon the Amo-
rite king of Heshbon and his land. I’m hand-
ing it over to you—it’s all yours. Go ahead,
take it. Go to war with him. Before the day
is out, I’ll make sure that all the people
around here are thoroughly terrified. Ru-
mors of you are going to spread like wild-
fire; they’ll totally panic.”
26-28 From the Wilderness of Kedemoth, I sent
messengers to Sihon, king of Heshbon.
They carried a friendly message: “Let me
cross through your land on the highway. I’ll
stay right on the highway; I won’t trespass
right or left. I’ll pay you for any food or wa-
ter we might need. Let me walk through.
29 “The People of Esau who live in Seir and
the Moabites who live in Ar did this, helping
me on my way until I can cross the Jordan
and enter the land that GOD, our God, is giv-
ing us.”
30 But Sihon king of Heshbon wouldn’t let
us cross his land. GOD, your God, turned his
spirit mean and his heart hard so he could
hand him over to you, as you can see that he
has done.
31 Then GOD said to me, “Look, I’ve got the
ball rolling—Sihon and his land are soon
yours. Go ahead. Take it. It’s practically
yours!”
32-36 So Sihon and his entire army confronted
us in battle at Jahaz. GOD handed him, his
sons, and his entire army over to us and we
utterly crushed them. While we were at it we

NEW KING JAMES VERSION

him, his sons, and all his people. 34We took all his cities at that time, and we utterly destroyed the men, women, and little ones of every city; we left none remaining. 35We took only the livestock as plunder for ourselves, with the spoil of the cities which we took. 36From Aroer, which *is* on the bank of the River Arnon, and *from* the city that *is* in the ravine, as far as Gilead, there was not one city too strong for us; the LORD our God delivered all to us. 37Only you did not go near the land of the people of Ammon—anywhere along the River Jabbok, or to the cities of the mountains, or wherever the LORD our God had forbidden us.

KING OG DEFEATED

3 "Then we turned and went up the road to Bashan; and Og king of Bashan came out against us, he and all his people, to battle at Edrei. 2And the LORD said to me, 'Do not fear him, for I have delivered him and all his people and his land into your hand; you shall do to him as you did to Sihon king of the Amorites, who dwelt at Heshbon.'

3"So the LORD our God also delivered into our hands Og king of Bashan, with all his people, and we attacked him until he had no survivors remaining. 4And we took all his cities at that time; there was not a city which we did not take from them: sixty cities, all the region of Argob, the kingdom of Og in Bashan. 5All these cities *were* fortified with high walls, gates, and bars, besides a great many rural towns. 6And we utterly destroyed them, as we did to Sihon king of Heshbon, utterly destroying the men, women, and children of every city. 7But all the livestock and the spoil of the cities we took as booty for ourselves.

8"And at that time we took the land from the hand of the two kings of the Amorites who *were* on this side of the Jordan, from the River Arnon to Mount Hermon 9(the Sidonians call Hermon Sirion, and the Amorites call it Senir), 10all the cities of the plain, all Gilead, and all Bashan, as far as Salcah and Edrei, cities of the kingdom of Og in Bashan.

11"For only Og king of Bashan remained of the remnant of the giants.[a] Indeed his bedstead *was* an iron bedstead. (*Is* it not in Rabbah of the people of Ammon?) Nine cubits *is* its length and four cubits its width, according to the standard cubit.

THE LAND EAST OF THE JORDAN DIVIDED

12"And this land, *which* we possessed at that time, from Aroer, which *is* by the River Arnon, and half the mountains of Gilead and its cities, I gave to the Reubenites and the Gadites. 13The rest of Gilead, and all Bashan, the kingdom of Og, I gave to half the tribe of Manasseh. (All the region of Argob, with all Bashan, was called the land of the giants.[a]

3:11 [a]Hebrew *rephaim* **3:13** [a]Hebrew *rephaim*

THE MESSAGE

captured all his towns and totally destroyed them, a holy destruction—men, women, and children. No survivors. We took the livestock and the plunder from the towns we had captured and carried them off for ourselves. From Aroer on the edge of the Brook Arnon and the town in the gorge, as far as Gilead, not a single town proved too much for us; GOD, our God, gave every last one of them to us.

37 The only land you didn't take, obeying GOD's command, was the land of the People of Ammon, the land along the Jabbok and around the cities in the hills.

1 3 Then we turned north and took the road to Bashan. Og king of Bashan, he and all his people, came out to meet us in battle at Edrei.

2 GOD said to me, "Don't be afraid of him; I'm turning him over to you, along with his whole army and his land. Treat him the way you treated Sihon king of the Amorites who ruled from Heshbon."

3-7 So GOD, our God, also handed Og king of Bashan over to us—Og and all his people—and we utterly crushed them. Again, no survivors. At the same time we took all his cities. There wasn't one of the sixty cities that we didn't take—the whole region of Argob, Og's kingdom in Bashan. All these cities were fortress cities with high walls and barred gates. There were also numerous unwalled villages. We totally destroyed them—a holy destruction. It was the same treatment we gave to Sihon king of Heshbon, a holy destruction of every city, man, woman, and child. But all the livestock and plunder from the cities we took for ourselves.

8-10 Throughout that time we took the land from under the control of the two kings of the Amorites who ruled the country east of the Jordan, all the way from the Brook Arnon to Mount Hermon. (Sirion is the name given Hermon by the Sidonians; the Amorites call it Senir.) We took all the towns of the plateau, everything in Gilead, everything in Bashan, as far as Salecah and Edrei, the border towns of Bashan, Og's kingdom.

11 Og king of Bashan was the last remaining Rephaite. His bed, made of iron, was over thirteen feet long and six wide. You can still see it on display in Rabbah of the People of Ammon.

12 Of the land that we possessed at that time, I gave the Reubenites and the Gadites the territory north of Aroer along the Brook Arnon and half the hill country of Gilead with its towns.

13 I gave the half-tribe of Manasseh the rest of Gilead and all of Bashan, Og's kingdom—all the region of Argob, which takes in all of Bashan. This used to be known as the Land of the Rephaites.

New King James Version

14 Jair the son of Manasseh took all the region of
Argob, as far as the border of the Geshurites
and the Maachathites, and called Bashan after
his own name, Havoth Jair,[a] to this day.)
15 "Also I gave Gilead to Machir. 16 And to the
Reubenites and the Gadites I gave from Gilead
as far as the River Arnon, the middle of the river
as *the* border, as far as the River Jabbok, the
border of the people of Ammon; 17 the plain also,
with the Jordan as *the* border, from Chinnereth
as far as the east side of the Sea of the Arabah
(the Salt Sea), below the slopes of Pisgah.
18 "Then I commanded you at that time, say-
ing: 'The LORD your God has given you this land
to possess. All you men of valor shall cross over
armed before your brethren, the children of Is-
rael. 19 But your wives, your little ones, and your
livestock (I know that you have much livestock)
shall stay in your cities which I have given you,
20 until the LORD has given rest to your brethren
as to you, and they also possess the land which
the LORD your God is giving them beyond the
Jordan. Then each of you may return to his pos-
session which I have given you.'
21 "And I commanded Joshua at that time,
saying, 'Your eyes have seen all that the LORD
your God has done to these two kings; so will
the LORD do to all the kingdoms through which
you pass. 22 You must not fear them, for the LORD
your God Himself fights for you.'

Moses Forbidden to Enter the Land

23 "Then I pleaded with the LORD at that time,
saying: 24 'O Lord GOD, You have begun to show
Your servant Your greatness and Your mighty
hand, for what god *is there* in heaven or on
earth who can do *anything* like Your works and
Your mighty *deeds*? 25 I pray, let me cross over
and see the good land beyond the Jordan, those
pleasant mountains, and Lebanon.'
26 "But the LORD was angry with me on your
account, and would not listen to me. So the
LORD said to me: 'Enough of that! Speak no
more to Me of this matter. 27 Go up to the top of
Pisgah, and lift your eyes toward the west, the
north, the south, and the east; behold *it* with
your eyes, for you shall not cross over this Jor-
dan. 28 But command Joshua, and encourage him
and strengthen him; for he shall go over before
this people, and he shall cause them to inherit
the land which you will see.'
29 "So we stayed in the valley opposite Beth
Peor.

3:14 [a]Literally *Towns of Jair*

The Message

14 Jair, a son of Manasseh, got the region of Argob to the borders of the Geshurites and Maacathites. He named the Bashan villages after himself, Havvoth Jair (Jair's Tent-Villages). They're still called that.

15 I gave Gilead to Makir.

16-17 I gave the Reubenites and Gadites the land from Gilead down to the Brook Arnon, whose middle was the boundary, and as far as the Jabbok River, the boundary line of the People of Ammon. The western boundary was the Jordan River in the Arabah all the way from the Kinnereth (the Sea of Galilee) to the Sea of the Arabah (the Salt Sea or Dead Sea) at the base of the slopes of Mount Pisgah on the east.

18-20 I commanded you at that time, "GOD, your God, has given you this land to possess. Your men, fit and armed for the fight, are to cross the river in advance of their brothers, the People of Israel. Only your wives, children, and livestock (I know you have much livestock) may go ahead and settle down in the towns I have already given you until GOD secures living space for your brothers as he has for you and they have taken possession of the country west of the Jordan that GOD, your God, is giving them. After that, each man may return to the land I've given you here."

21-22 I commanded Joshua at that time, "You've seen with your own two eyes everything GOD, your God, has done to these two kings. GOD is going to do the same thing to all the kingdoms over there across the river where you're headed. Don't be afraid of them. GOD, your God—he's fighting for you."

23-25 At that same time, I begged GOD: "GOD, my Master, you let me in on the beginnings, you let me see your greatness, you let me see your might—what god in Heaven or Earth can do anything like what you've done! Please, let me in also on the endings, let me cross the river and see the good land over the Jordan, the lush hills, the Lebanon mountains."

26-27 But GOD was still angry with me because of you. He wouldn't listen. He said, "Enough of that. Not another word from you on this. Climb to the top of Mount Pisgah and look around: look west, north, south, east. Take in the land with your own eyes. Take a good look because you're not going to cross this Jordan.

28 "Then command Joshua: Give him courage. Give him strength. Single-handed he will lead this people across the river. Single-handed he'll cause them to inherit the land at which you can only look."

29 That's why we have stayed in this valley near Beth Peor.

New King James Version

Moses Commands Obedience

4 "Now, O Israel, listen to the statutes and the judgments which I teach you to observe, that you may live, and go in and possess the land which the LORD God of your fathers is giving you. 2You shall not add to the word which I command you, nor take from it, that you may keep the commandments of the LORD your God which I command you. 3Your eyes have seen what the LORD did at Baal Peor; for the LORD your God has destroyed from among you all the men who followed Baal of Peor. 4But you who held fast to the LORD your God *are* alive today, every one of you.

5"Surely I have taught you statutes and judgments, just as the LORD my God commanded me, that you should act according *to them* in the land which you go to possess. 6Therefore be careful to observe *them;* for this *is* your wisdom and your understanding in the sight of the peoples who will hear all these statutes, and say, 'Surely this great nation *is* a wise and understanding people.'

7"For what great nation *is there* that has God *so* near to it, as the LORD our God *is* to us, for whatever *reason* we may call upon Him? 8And what great nation *is there* that has *such* statutes and righteous judgments as are in all this law which I set before you this day? 9Only take heed to yourself, and diligently keep yourself, lest you forget the things your eyes have seen, and lest they depart from your heart all the days of your life. And teach them to your children and your grandchildren, 10*especially concerning* the day you stood before the LORD your God in Horeb, when the LORD said to me, 'Gather the people to Me, and I will let them hear My words, that they may learn to fear Me all the days they live on the earth, and *that* they may teach their children.'

11"Then you came near and stood at the foot of the mountain, and the mountain burned with fire to the midst of heaven, with darkness, cloud, and thick darkness. 12And the LORD spoke to you out of the midst of the fire. You heard the sound of the words, but saw no form; *you* only *heard* a voice. 13So He declared to you His covenant which He commanded you to perform, the Ten Commandments; and He wrote them on two tablets of stone. 14And the LORD commanded me at that time to teach you statutes and judgments, that you might observe them in the land which you cross over to possess.

Beware of Idolatry

15"Take careful heed to yourselves, for you saw no form when the LORD spoke to you at Horeb out of the midst of the fire, 16lest you act corruptly and make for yourselves a carved image in the form of any figure: the likeness of male or female, 17the likeness of any animal that *is* on the earth or the likeness of any winged bird that flies in the air, 18the likeness of anything that creeps on the ground or the likeness of any fish that *is* in the water beneath the earth. 19And *take heed,* lest you lift your eyes to heaven, and *when* you see the sun, the moon, and the stars, all the host of heaven, you feel

The Message

1-2 4 Now listen, Israel, listen carefully to the rules and regulations that I am teaching you to follow so that you may live and enter and take possession of the land that GOD, the God-of-Your-Fathers, is giving to you. Don't add a word to what I command you, and don't remove a word from it. Keep the commands of GOD, your God, that I am commanding you.

3-4 You saw with your own eyes what GOD did at Baal Peor, how GOD destroyed from among you every man who joined in the Baal Peor orgies. But you, the ones who held tight to GOD, your God, are alive and well, every one of you, today.

5-6 Pay attention: I'm teaching you the rules and regulations that GOD commanded me, so that you may live by them in the land you are entering to take up ownership. Keep them. Practice them. You'll become wise and understanding. When people hear and see what's going on, they'll say, "What a great nation! So wise, so understanding! We've never seen anything like it."

7-8 Yes. What other great nation has gods that are intimate with them the way GOD, our God, is with us, always ready to listen to us? And what other great nation has rules and regulations as good and fair as this Revelation that I'm setting before you today?

9 Just make sure you stay alert. Keep close watch over yourselves. Don't forget anything of what you've seen. Don't let your heart wander off. Stay vigilant as long as you live. Teach what you've seen and heard to your children and grandchildren.

10 That day when you stood before GOD, your God, at Horeb, GOD said to me, "Assemble the people in my presence to listen to my words so that they will learn to fear me in holy fear for as long as they live on the land, and then they will teach these same words to their children."

11-13 You gathered. You stood in the shadow of the mountain. The mountain was ablaze with fire, blazing high into the very heart of Heaven. You stood in deep darkness and thick clouds. GOD spoke to you out of the fire. You heard the sound of words but you saw nothing—no form, only a voice. He announced his covenant, the Ten Words, by which he commanded you to live. Then he wrote them down on two slabs of stone.

14 And GOD commanded me at that time to teach you the rules and regulations that you are to live by in the land which you are crossing over the Jordan to possess.

15-20 You saw no form on the day GOD spoke to you at Horeb from out of the fire. Remember that. Carefully guard yourselves so that you don't turn corrupt and make a form, carving a figure that looks male or female, or looks like a prowling animal or a flying bird or a slithering snake or a fish in a stream. And also carefully guard yourselves so that you don't look up into the skies and see the sun and moon and stars, all the constellations of

NEW KING JAMES VERSION

driven to worship them and serve them, which
the LORD your God has given to all the peoples
under the whole heaven as a heritage. [20]But the
LORD has taken you and brought you out of the
iron furnace, out of Egypt, to be His people, an
inheritance, as you are this day. [21]Furthermore
the LORD was angry with me for your sakes, and
swore that I would not cross over the Jordan,
and that I would not enter the good land which
the LORD your God is giving you as an inheri-
tance. [22]But I must die in this land, I must not
cross over the Jordan; but you shall cross over
and possess that good land. [23]Take heed to your-
selves, lest you forget the covenant of the LORD
your God which He made with you, and make
for yourselves a carved image in the form of
anything which the LORD your God has forbid-
den you. [24]For the LORD your God *is* a consum-
ing fire, a jealous God.

[25]"When you beget children and grandchil-
dren and have grown old in the land, and act
corruptly and make a carved image in the form
of anything, and do evil in the sight of the LORD
your God to provoke Him to anger, [26]I call
heaven and earth to witness against you this
day, that you will soon utterly perish from the
land which you cross over the Jordan to pos-
sess; you will not prolong *your* days in it, but
will be utterly destroyed. [27]And the LORD will
scatter you among the peoples, and you will be
left few in number among the nations where the
LORD will drive you. [28]And there you will serve
gods, the work of men's hands, wood and stone,
which neither see nor hear nor eat nor smell.
[29]But from there you will seek the LORD your
God, and you will find *Him* if you seek Him with
all your heart and with all your soul. [30]When
you are in distress, and all these things come
upon you in the latter days, when you turn to the
LORD your God and obey His voice [31](for the
LORD your God *is* a merciful God), He will not
forsake you nor destroy you, nor forget the
covenant of your fathers which He swore to
them.

[32]"For ask now concerning the days that are
past, which were before you, since the day that
God created man on the earth, and *ask* from one
end of heaven to the other, whether *any* great
thing like this has happened, or *anything* like it
has been heard. [33]Did *any* people *ever* hear the
voice of God speaking out of the midst of the
fire, as you have heard, and live? [34]Or did God
ever try to go *and* take for Himself a nation from
the midst of *another* nation, by trials, by signs,
by wonders, by war, by a mighty hand and an
outstretched arm, and by great terrors, accord-
ing to all that the LORD your God did for you in
Egypt before your eyes?

THE MESSAGE

the skies, and be seduced into worshiping and serving them. GOD set them out for everybody's benefit, everywhere. But you—GOD took you right out of the iron furnace, out of Egypt, to become the people of his inheritance—and that's what you are this very day.

21-22 But GOD was angry with me because of you and the things you said. He swore that I'd never cross the Jordan, never get to enter the good land that GOD, your God, is giving you as an inheritance. This means that I am going to die here. I'm not crossing the Jordan. But you will cross; you'll possess the good land.

23-24 So stay alert. Don't for a minute forget the covenant which GOD, your God, made with you. And don't take up with any carved images, no forms of any kind—GOD, your God, issued clear commands on that. GOD, your God, is not to be trifled with—he's a consuming fire, a jealous God.

25-28 When the time comes that you have children and grandchildren, put on years, and start taking things for granted, if you then become corrupt and make any carved images, no matter what their form, by doing what is sheer evil in GOD's eyes and provoking his anger—I can tell you right now, with Heaven and Earth as witnesses, that it will be all over for you. You'll be kicked off the land that you're about to cross over the Jordan to possess. Believe me, you'll have a very short stay there. You'll be ruined, completely ruined. GOD will scatter you far and wide; a few of you will survive here and there in the nations where GOD will drive you. There you can worship your homemade gods to your hearts' content, your wonderful gods of wood and stone that can't see or hear or eat or smell.

29-31 But even there, if you seek GOD, your God, you'll be able to find him if you're serious, looking for him with your whole heart and soul. When troubles come and all these awful things happen to you, in future days you will come back to GOD, your God, and listen obediently to what he says. GOD, your God, is above all a compassionate God. In the end he will not abandon you, he won't bring you to ruin, he won't forget the covenant with your ancestors which he swore to them.

32-33 Ask questions. Find out what has been going on all these years before you were born. From the day God created man and woman on this Earth, and from the horizon in the east to the horizon in the west—as far back as you can imagine and as far away as you can imagine—has as great a thing as this ever happened? Has anyone ever heard of such a thing? Has a people ever heard, as you did, a god speaking out of the middle of the fire and lived to tell the story?

34 Or has a god ever tried to select for himself a nation from within a nation using trials, miracles, and war, putting his strong hand in, reaching his long arm out, a spectacle awesome and staggering, the way GOD, your God, did it for you in Egypt while you stood right there and watched?

NEW KING JAMES VERSION

35 To you it was shown, that you might know that
the LORD Himself *is* God; *there is* none other be-
sides Him. 36 Out of heaven He let you hear His
voice, that He might instruct you; on earth He
showed you His great fire, and you heard His
words out of the midst of the fire. 37 And because
He loved your fathers, therefore He chose their
descendants after them; and He brought you out
of Egypt with His Presence, with His mighty
power, 38 driving out from before you nations
greater and mightier than you, to bring you in,
to give you their land *as* an inheritance, as *it is*
this day. 39 Therefore know this day, and con-
sider *it* in your heart, that the LORD Himself *is*
God in heaven above and on the earth beneath;
there is no other. 40 You shall therefore keep His
statutes and His commandments which I com-
mand you today, that it may go well with you
and with your children after you, and that you
may prolong *your* days in the land which the
LORD your God is giving you for all time."

CITIES OF REFUGE EAST OF THE JORDAN

41 Then Moses set apart three cities on this
side of the Jordan, toward the rising of the sun,
42 that the manslayer might flee there, who kills
his neighbor unintentionally, without having
hated him in time past, and that by fleeing to
one of these cities he might live: 43 Bezer in the
wilderness on the plateau for the Reubenites,
Ramoth in Gilead for the Gadites, and Golan in
Bashan for the Manassites.

INTRODUCTION TO GOD'S LAW

44 Now this *is* the law which Moses set before
the children of Israel. 45 These *are* the testi-
monies, the statutes, and the judgments which
Moses spoke to the children of Israel after they
came out of Egypt, 46 on this side of the Jordan,
in the valley opposite Beth Peor, in the land of
Sihon king of the Amorites, who dwelt at Hesh-
bon, whom Moses and the children of Israel de-
feated after they came out of Egypt. 47 And they
took possession of his land and the land of Og
king of Bashan, two kings of the Amorites, who
were on this side of the Jordan, toward the ris-
ing of the sun, 48 from Aroer, which *is* on the
bank of the River Arnon, even to Mount Sion[a]
(that is, Hermon), 49 and all the plain on the east
side of the Jordan as far as the Sea of the
Arabah, below the slopes of Pisgah.

THE TEN COMMANDMENTS REVIEWED

5 And Moses called all Israel, and said to them:
"Hear, O Israel, the statutes and judgments
which I speak in your hearing today, that you
may learn them and be careful to observe them.
2 The LORD our God made a covenant with us in
Horeb. 3 The LORD did not make this covenant
with our fathers, but with us, those who *are* here
today, all of us who *are* alive. 4 The LORD talked
with you face to face on the mountain from the
midst of the fire. 5 I stood between the LORD and

4:48 [a]Syriac reads *Sirion* (compare 3:9).

THE MESSAGE

35-38 You were shown all this so that you would know that GOD is, well, God. He's the only God there is. He's it. He made it possible for you to hear his voice out of Heaven to discipline you. Down on Earth, he showed you the big fire and again you heard his words, this time out of the fire. He loved your ancestors and chose to work with their children. He personally and powerfully brought you out of Egypt in order to displace bigger and stronger and older nations with you, bringing you out and turning their land over to you as an inheritance. And now it's happening. This very day.

39-40 Know this well, then. Take it to heart right now: GOD is in Heaven above; GOD is on Earth below. He's the only God there is. Obediently live by his rules and commands which I'm giving you today so that you'll live well and your children after you—oh, you'll live a long time in the land that GOD, your God, is giving you.

41-42 Then Moses set aside three towns in the country on the east side of the Jordan to which someone who had unintentionally killed a person could flee and find refuge. If the murder was unintentional and there was no history of bad blood, the murderer could flee to one of these cities and save his life:

43 Bezer in the wilderness on the tableland for the Reubenites, Ramoth in Gilead for the Gadites, and Golan in Bashan for the Manassites.

44-49 This is the Revelation that Moses presented to the People of Israel. These are the testimonies, the rules and regulations Moses spoke to the People of Israel after their exodus from Egypt and arrival on the east side of the Jordan in the valley near Beth Peor. It was the country of Sihon king of the Amorites who ruled from Heshbon. Moses and the People of Israel fought and beat him after they left Egypt and took his land. They also took the land of Og king of Bashan. The two Amorite kings held the country on the east of the Jordan from Aroer on the bank of the Brook Arnon as far north as Mount Siyon, that is, Mount Hermon, all the Arabah plain east of the Jordan, and as far south as the Sea of the Arabah (the Dead Sea) beneath the slopes of Mount Pisgah.

MOSES TEACHES ISRAEL ON THE PLAINS OF MOAB

1 5 Moses called all Israel together. He said to them,

Attention, Israel. Listen obediently to the rules and regulations I am delivering to your listening ears today. Learn them. Live them.

2-5 GOD, our God, made a covenant with us at Horeb. GOD didn't just make this covenant with our parents; he made it also with us, with all of us who are alive right now. GOD spoke to you personally out of the fire on the mountain. At the time I stood between

NEW KING JAMES VERSION

you at that time, to declare to you the word of the
LORD; for you were afraid because of the fire,
and you did not go up the mountain. *He* said:

6 ‘I *am* the LORD your God who brought you
out of the land of Egypt, out of the house
of bondage.
7 ‘You shall have no other gods before Me.
8 ‘You shall not make for yourself a carved
image—any likeness *of anything* that *is*
in heaven above, or that *is* in the earth
beneath, or that *is* in the water under the
earth; 9 you shall not bow down to them
nor serve them. For I, the LORD your God,
am a jealous God, visiting the iniquity of
the fathers upon the children to the third
and fourth *generations* of those who hate
Me, 10 but showing mercy to thousands,
to those who love Me and keep My
commandments.
11 ‘You shall not take the name of the LORD
your God in vain, for the LORD will not
hold *him* guiltless who takes His name in
vain.
12 ‘Observe the Sabbath day, to keep it holy, as
the LORD your God commanded you.
13 Six days you shall labor and do all your
work, 14 but the seventh day *is* the
Sabbath of the LORD your God. *In it* you
shall do no work: you, nor your son, nor
your daughter, nor your male servant,
nor your female servant, nor your ox,
nor your donkey, nor any of your cattle,
nor your stranger who *is* within your
gates, that your male servant and your
female servant may rest as well as you.
15 And remember that you were a slave in
the land of Egypt, and the LORD your
God brought you out from there by a
mighty hand and by an outstretched
arm; therefore the LORD your God
commanded you to keep the Sabbath
day.
16 ‘Honor your father and your mother, as the
LORD your God has commanded you,
that your days may be long, and that it
may be well with you in the land which
the LORD your God is giving you.
17 ‘You shall not murder.
18 ‘You shall not commit adultery.
19 ‘You shall not steal.
20 ‘You shall not bear false witness against
your neighbor.
21 ‘You shall not covet your neighbor’s wife;
and you shall not desire your neighbor’s
house, his field, his male servant, his
female servant, his ox, his donkey, or
anything that *is* your neighbor’s.’
22 “These words the LORD spoke to all your
assembly, in the mountain from the
midst of the fire, the cloud, and the thick
darkness, with a loud voice; and He
added no more. And He wrote them on
two tablets of stone and gave them to
me.

THE PEOPLE AFRAID OF GOD’S PRESENCE

23 “So it was, when you heard the voice from
the midst of the darkness, while the mountain

THE MESSAGE

GOD and you, to tell you what GOD said. You
were afraid, remember, of the fire and
wouldn’t climb the mountain. He said:

6 I am GOD, your God,
who brought you out of the land of
Egypt,
out of a house of slaves.

7 No other gods, only me.
8-10 No carved gods of any size, shape, or form
of anything whatever, whether of things
that fly or walk or swim. Don’t bow down
to them and don’t serve them because *I*
am God, your God, and I’m a most jealous
God. I hold parents responsible for any
sins they pass on to their children to the
third, and yes, even to the fourth generation.
But I’m lovingly loyal to the thousands
who love me and keep my commandments.
11 No using the name of GOD, your God, in
curses or silly banter; GOD won’t put up
with the irreverent use of his name.
12-15 No working on the Sabbath; keep it holy
just as GOD, your God, commanded you.
Work six days, doing everything you have
to do, but the seventh day is a Sabbath, a
Rest Day—no work: not you, your son,
your daughter, your servant, your maid,
your ox, your donkey (or any of your animals),
and not even the foreigner visiting
your town. That way your servants and
maids will get the same rest as you. Don’t
ever forget that you were slaves in Egypt
and GOD, your God, got you out of there
in a powerful show of strength. That’s
why GOD, your God, commands you to
observe the day of Sabbath rest.
16 Respect your father and mother—GOD, your
God, commands it! You’ll have a long life;
the land that God is giving you will treat
you well.
17 No murder.
18 No adultery.
19 No stealing.
20 No lies about your neighbor.
21 No coveting your neighbor’s wife. And no
lusting for his house, field, servant, maid,
ox, or donkey either—nothing that belongs
to your neighbor!

22 These are the words that GOD spoke to
the whole congregation at the mountain. He
spoke in a tremendous voice from the fire
and cloud and dark mist. And that was it. No
more words. Then he wrote them on two
slabs of stone and gave them to me.
23-24 As it turned out, when you heard the
Voice out of that dark cloud and saw the

New King James Version

was burning with fire, that you came near to me, all the heads of your tribes and your elders. 24And you said: 'Surely the LORD our God has shown us His glory and His greatness, and we have heard His voice from the midst of the fire. We have seen this day that God speaks with man; yet he *still* lives. 25Now therefore, why should we die? For this great fire will consume us; if we hear the voice of the LORD our God anymore, then we shall die. 26For who *is there* of all flesh who has heard the voice of the living God speaking from the midst of the fire, as we *have,* and lived? 27You go near and hear all that the LORD our God may say, and tell us all that the LORD our God says to you, and we will hear and do *it.*'

28"Then the LORD heard the voice of your words when you spoke to me, and the LORD said to me: 'I have heard the voice of the words of this people which they have spoken to you. They are right *in* all that they have spoken. 29Oh, that they had such a heart in them that they would fear Me and always keep all My commandments, that it might be well with them and with their children forever! 30Go and say to them, "Return to your tents." 31But as for you, stand here by Me, and I will speak to you all the commandments, the statutes, and the judgments which you shall teach them, that they may observe *them* in the land which I am giving them to possess.'

32"Therefore you shall be careful to do as the LORD your God has commanded you; you shall not turn aside to the right hand or to the left. 33You shall walk in all the ways which the LORD your God has commanded you, that you may live and *that it may be* well with you, and *that* you may prolong *your* days in the land which you shall possess.

THE GREATEST COMMANDMENT

6 "Now this *is* the commandment, *and these are* the statutes and judgments which the LORD your God has commanded to teach you, that you may observe *them* in the land which you are crossing over to possess, 2that you may fear the LORD your God, to keep all His statutes and His commandments which I command you, you and your son and your grandson, all the days of your life, and that your days may be prolonged. 3Therefore hear, O Israel, and be careful to observe *it,* that it may be well with you, and that you may multiply greatly as the LORD God of your fathers has promised you—'a land flowing with milk and honey.'[a]

4"Hear, O Israel: The LORD our God, the LORD *is* one![a] 5You shall love the LORD your God with all your heart, with all your soul, and with all your strength.

6"And these words which I command you today shall be in your heart. 7You shall teach them diligently to your children, and shall talk of them when you sit in your house, when you walk by the way, when you lie down, and when you rise up. 8You shall bind them as a sign on your hand, and they shall be as frontlets be-

6:3 [a]Exodus 3:8 **6:4** [a]Or *The LORD is our God, the LORD alone* (that is, the only one)

The Message

mountain on fire, you approached me, all the heads of your tribes and your leaders, and said,

24-26 "Our GOD has revealed to us his glory and greatness. We've heard him speak from the fire today! We've seen that God can speak to humans and they can still live. But why risk it further? This huge fire will devour us if we stay around any longer. If we hear GOD's voice anymore, we'll die for sure. Has anyone ever known of anyone who has heard the Voice of GOD the way we have and lived to tell the story?

27 "From now on, *you* go and listen to what GOD, our God, says and then tell us what GOD tells you. We'll listen and we'll do it."

28-29 GOD heard what you said to me and told me, "I've heard what the people said to you. They're right—good and true words. What I wouldn't give if they'd always feel this way, continuing to revere me and always keep all my commands; they'd have a good life forever, they and their children!

30-31 "Go ahead and tell them to go home to their tents. But you, you stay here with me so I can tell you every commandment and all the rules and regulations that you must teach them so they'll know how to live in the land that I'm giving them as their own."

32-33 So be very careful to act exactly as GOD commands you. Don't veer off to the right or the left. Walk straight down the road GOD commands so that you'll have a good life and live a long time in the land that you're about to possess.

1-2 6 This is the commandment, the rules and regulations, that GOD, your God, commanded me to teach you to live out in the land you're about to cross into to possess. This is so that you'll live in deep reverence before GOD lifelong, observing all his rules and regulations that I'm commanding you, you and your children and your grandchildren, living good long lives.

3 Listen obediently, Israel. Do what you're told so that you'll have a good life, a life of abundance and bounty, just as GOD promised, in a land abounding in milk and honey.

4 Attention, Israel!
GOD, our God! GOD the one and only!

5 Love GOD, your God, with your whole heart: love him with all that's in you, love him with all you've got!

6-9 Write these commandments that I've given you today on your hearts. Get them inside of you and then get them inside your children. Talk about them wherever you are, sitting at home or walking in the street; talk about them from the time you get up in the morning to when you fall into bed at night. Tie them on your hands and foreheads as a

NEW KING JAMES VERSION

tween your eyes. 9You shall write them on the doorposts of your house and on your gates.

CAUTION AGAINST DISOBEDIENCE

10"So it shall be, when the LORD your God brings you into the land of which He swore to your fathers, to Abraham, Isaac, and Jacob, to give you large and beautiful cities which you did not build, 11houses full of all good things, which you did not fill, hewn-out wells which you did not dig, vineyards and olive trees which you did not plant—when you have eaten and are full—12*then* beware, lest you forget the LORD who brought you out of the land of Egypt, from the house of bondage. 13You shall fear the LORD your God and serve Him, and shall take oaths in His name. 14You shall not go after other gods, the gods of the peoples who *are* all around you 15(for the LORD your God *is* a jealous God among you), lest the anger of the LORD your God be aroused against you and destroy you from the face of the earth.

16"You shall not tempt the LORD your God as you tempted *Him* in Massah. 17You shall diligently keep the commandments of the LORD your God, His testimonies, and His statutes which He has commanded you. 18And you shall do *what is* right and good in the sight of the LORD, that it may be well with you, and that you may go in and possess the good land of which the LORD swore to your fathers, 19to cast out all your enemies from before you, as the LORD has spoken.

20"When your son asks you in time to come, saying, 'What *is the meaning of* the testimonies, the statutes, and the judgments which the LORD our God has commanded you?' 21then you shall say to your son: 'We were slaves of Pharaoh in Egypt, and the LORD brought us out of Egypt with a mighty hand; 22and the LORD showed signs and wonders before our eyes, great and severe, against Egypt, Pharaoh, and all his household. 23Then He brought us out from there, that He might bring us in, to give us the land of which He swore to our fathers. 24And the LORD commanded us to observe all these statutes, to fear the LORD our God, for our good always, that He might preserve us alive, as *it is* this day. 25Then it will be righteousness for us, if we are careful to observe all these commandments before the LORD our God, as He has commanded us.'

A CHOSEN PEOPLE

7 "When the LORD your God brings you into the land which you go to possess, and has cast out many nations before you, the Hittites and the Girgashites and the Amorites and the Canaanites and the Perizzites and the Hivites and the Jebusites, seven nations greater and mightier than you, 2and when the LORD your God delivers them over to you, you shall conquer them *and* utterly destroy them. You shall make no covenant with them nor show mercy to them.

THE MESSAGE

reminder; inscribe them on the doorposts of your homes and on your city gates.

10-12 When GOD, your God, ushers you into the land he promised through your ancestors Abraham, Isaac, and Jacob to give you, you're going to walk into large, bustling cities you didn't build, well-furnished houses you didn't buy, come upon wells you didn't dig, vineyards and olive orchards you didn't plant. When you take it all in and settle down, pleased and content, make sure you don't forget how you got there—GOD brought you out of slavery in Egypt.

13-19 Deeply respect GOD, your God. Serve and worship him exclusively. Back up your promises with his name only. Don't fool around with other gods, the gods of your neighbors, because GOD, your God, who is alive among you is a jealous God. Don't provoke him, igniting his hot anger that would burn you right off the face of the Earth. Don't push GOD, your God, to the wall as you did that day at Massah, the Testing-Place. Carefully keep the commands of GOD, your God, all the requirements and regulations he gave you. Do what is right; do what is good in GOD's sight so you'll live a good life and be able to march in and take this pleasant land that GOD so solemnly promised through your ancestors, throwing out your enemies left and right—exactly as GOD said.

20-24 The next time your child asks you, "What do these requirements and regulations and rules that GOD, our God, has commanded mean?" tell your child, "We were slaves to Pharaoh in Egypt and GOD powerfully intervened and got us out of that country. We stood there and watched as GOD delivered miracle-signs, great wonders, and evil-visitations on Egypt, on Pharaoh and his household. He pulled us out of there so he could bring us here and give us the land he so solemnly promised to our ancestors. That's why GOD commanded us to follow all these rules, so that we would live reverently before GOD, our God, as he gives us this good life, keeping us alive for a long time to come.

25 "It will be a set-right and put-together life for us if we make sure that we do this entire commandment in the Presence of GOD, our God, just as he commanded us to do."

1-2 7 When GOD, your God, brings you into the country that you are about to enter and take over, he will clear out the superpowers that were there before you: the Hittite, the Girgashite, the Amorite, the Canaanite, the Perizzite, the Hivite, and the Jebusite. Those seven nations are all bigger and stronger than you are. GOD, your God, will turn them over to you and you will conquer them. You must completely destroy them, offering them up as a holy destruction to GOD.

Don't make a treaty with them.
Don't let them off in any way.

NEW KING JAMES VERSION

3Nor shall you make marriages with them. You
shall not give your daughter to their son, nor
take their daughter for your son. 4For they will
turn your sons away from following Me, to serve
other gods; so the anger of the LORD will be
aroused against you and destroy you suddenly.
5But thus you shall deal with them: you shall de-
stroy their altars, and break down their *sacred*
pillars, and cut down their wooden images,[a] and
burn their carved images with fire.
6"For you *are* a holy people to the LORD your
God; the LORD your God has chosen you to be a
people for Himself, a special treasure above all
the peoples on the face of the earth. 7The LORD
did not set His love on you nor choose you be-
cause you were more in number than any other
people, for you were the least of all peoples; 8but
because the LORD loves you, and because He
would keep the oath which He swore to your fa-
thers, the LORD has brought you out with a
mighty hand, and redeemed you from the house
of bondage, from the hand of Pharaoh king of
Egypt.
9"Therefore know that the LORD your God,
He *is* God, the faithful God who keeps covenant
and mercy for a thousand generations with
those who love Him and keep His command-
ments; 10and He repays those who hate Him to
their face, to destroy them. He will not be slack
with him who hates Him; He will repay him to
his face. 11Therefore you shall keep the com-
mandment, the statutes, and the judgments
which I command you today, to observe them.

BLESSINGS OF OBEDIENCE

12"Then it shall come to pass, because you
listen to these judgments, and keep and do
them, that the LORD your God will keep with you
the covenant and the mercy which He swore to
your fathers. 13And He will love you and bless
you and multiply you; He will also bless the fruit
of your womb and the fruit of your land, your
grain and your new wine and your oil, the in-
crease of your cattle and the offspring of your
flock, in the land of which He swore to your fa-
thers to give you. 14You shall be blessed above
all peoples; there shall not be a male or female
barren among you or among your livestock.
15And the LORD will take away from you all sick-
ness, and will afflict you with none of the terri-
ble diseases of Egypt which you have known,
but will lay *them* on all those who hate you.
16Also you shall destroy all the peoples whom
the LORD your God delivers over to you; your
eye shall have no pity on them; nor shall you
serve their gods, for that *will be* a snare to you.
17"If you should say in your heart, 'These na-
tions are greater than I; how can I dispossess
them?'— 18you shall not be afraid of them, *but*
you shall remember well what the LORD your

7:5 [a]Hebrew *Asherim,* Canaanite deities

THE MESSAGE

3-4 Don't marry them: Don't give your
daughters to their sons and don't take their
daughters for your sons—before you know
it they'd involve you in worshiping their
gods, and GOD would explode in anger, put-
ting a quick end to you.
5 Here's what you are to do:

Tear apart their altars stone by stone,
smash their phallic pillars,
chop down their sex-and-religion
Asherah groves,
set fire to their carved god-images.

6 Do this because you are a people set
apart as holy to GOD, your God. GOD, your
God, chose you out of all the people on
Earth for himself as a cherished, personal
treasure.
7-10 GOD wasn't attracted to you and didn't
choose you because you were big and im-
portant—the fact is, there was almost noth-
ing to you. He did it out of sheer love, keep-
ing the promise he made to your ancestors.
GOD stepped in and mightily bought you
back out of that world of slavery, freed you
from the iron grip of Pharaoh king of Egypt.
Know this: GOD, your God, is God indeed, a
God you can depend upon. He keeps his
covenant of loyal love with those who love
him and observe his commandments for a
thousand generations. But he also pays
back those who hate him, pays them the
wages of death; he isn't slow to pay them
off—those who hate him, he pays right on
time.
11 So keep the command and the rules and
regulations that I command you today. Do
them.
12-13 And this is what will happen: When you,
on your part, will obey these directives,
keeping and following them, GOD, on his
part, will keep the covenant of loyal love
that he made with your ancestors:

He will love you,
he will bless you,
he will increase you.

13-15 He will bless the babies from your womb
and the harvest of grain, new wine, and oil
from your fields; he'll bless the calves from
your herds and lambs from your flocks in
the country he promised your ancestors that
he'd give you. You'll be blessed beyond all
other peoples: no sterility or barrenness in
you or your animals. GOD will get rid of all
sickness. And all the evil afflictions you ex-
perienced in Egypt he'll put not on you but
on those who hate you.
16 You'll make mincemeat of all the peoples
that GOD, your God, hands over to you.
Don't feel sorry for them. And don't worship
their gods—they'll trap you for sure.
17-19 You're going to think to yourselves, "Oh!
We're outnumbered ten to one by these na-
tions! We'll never even make a dent in
them!" But I'm telling you, Don't be afraid.
Remember, yes, remember in detail what

NEW KING JAMES VERSION

God did to Pharaoh and to all Egypt: [19]the great
trials which your eyes saw, the signs and the
wonders, the mighty hand and the outstretched
arm, by which the LORD your God brought you
out. So shall the LORD your God do to all the
peoples of whom you are afraid. [20]Moreover the
LORD your God will send the hornet among
them until those who are left, who hide them-
selves from you, are destroyed. [21]You shall not
be terrified of them; for the LORD your God, the
great and awesome God, *is* among you. [22]And
the LORD your God will drive out those nations
before you little by little; you will be unable to
destroy them at once, lest the beasts of the field
become *too* numerous for you. [23]But the LORD
your God will deliver them over to you, and will
inflict defeat upon them until they are de-
stroyed. [24]And He will deliver their kings into
your hand, and you will destroy their name from
under heaven; no one shall be able to stand
against you until you have destroyed them.
[25]You shall burn the carved images of their gods
with fire; you shall not covet the silver or gold
that is on them, nor take *it* for yourselves, lest
you be snared by it; for it *is* an abomination to
the LORD your God. [26]Nor shall you bring an
abomination into your house, lest you be
doomed to destruction like it. You shall utterly
detest it and utterly abhor it, for it *is* an accursed
thing.

REMEMBER THE LORD YOUR GOD

8 "Every commandment which I command you
today you must be careful to observe, that
you may live and multiply, and go in and pos-
sess the land of which the LORD swore to your
fathers. [2]And you shall remember that the LORD
your God led you all the way these forty years in
the wilderness, to humble you *and* test you, to
know what *was* in your heart, whether you
would keep His commandments or not. [3]So He
humbled you, allowed you to hunger, and fed
you with manna which you did not know nor
did your fathers know, that He might make you
know that man shall not live by bread alone; but
man lives by every *word* that proceeds from the
mouth of the LORD. [4]Your garments did not wear
out on you, nor did your foot swell these forty
years. [5]You should know in your heart that as a
man chastens his son, *so* the LORD your God
chastens you.

[6]"Therefore you shall keep the command-
ments of the LORD your God, to walk in His ways
and to fear Him. [7]For the LORD your God is bring-
ing you into a good land, a land of brooks of wa-
ter, of fountains and springs, that flow out of val-
leys and hills; [8]a land of wheat and barley, of
vines and fig trees and pomegranates, a land of
olive oil and honey; [9]a land in which you will eat
bread without scarcity, in which you will lack
nothing; a land whose stones *are* iron and out of
whose hills you can dig copper.

THE MESSAGE

GOD, your God, did to Pharaoh and all
Egypt. Remember the great contests to
which you were eyewitnesses: the miracle-
signs, the wonders, GOD's mighty hand as he
stretched out his arm and took you out of
there. GOD, your God, is going to do the
same thing to these people you're now so
afraid of.

20 And to top it off, the Hornet. GOD will un-
leash the Hornet on them until every survivor-
in-hiding is dead.

21-24 So don't be intimidated by them. GOD,
your God, is among you—GOD majestic, GOD
awesome. GOD, your God, will get rid of
these nations, bit by bit. You won't be per-
mitted to wipe them out all at once lest the
wild animals take over and overwhelm you.
But GOD, your God, will move them out of
your way—he'll throw them into a huge
panic until there's nothing left of them. He'll
turn their kings over to you and you'll re-
move all trace of them under Heaven. Not
one person will be able to stand up to you;
you'll put an end to them all.

25-26 Make sure you set fire to their carved
gods. Don't get greedy for the veneer of sil-
ver and gold on them and take it for your-
selves—you'll get trapped by it for sure. GOD
hates it; it's an abomination to GOD, your
God. And don't dare bring one of these
abominations home or you'll end up just
like it, burned up as a holy destruction. No:
It is forbidden! Hate it. Abominate it. De-
stroy it and preserve GOD's holiness.

1-5 8 Keep and live out the entire command-
ment that I'm commanding you today so
that you'll live and prosper and enter and
own the land that GOD promised to your an-
cestors. Remember every road that GOD led
you on for those forty years in the wilder-
ness, pushing you to your limits, testing you
so that he would know what you were made
of, whether you would keep his command-
ments or not. He put you through hard times.
He made you go hungry. Then he fed you
with manna, something neither you nor your
parents knew anything about, so you would
learn that men and women don't live by
bread only; we live by every word that comes
from GOD's mouth. Your clothes didn't wear
out and your feet didn't blister those forty
years. You learned deep in your heart that
GOD disciplines you in the same ways a fa-
ther disciplines his child.

6-9 So it's paramount that you keep the com-
mandments of GOD, your God, walk down
the roads he shows you and reverently re-
spect him. GOD is about to bring you into a
good land, a land with brooks and rivers,
springs and lakes, streams out of the hills
and through the valleys. It's a land of wheat
and barley, of vines and figs and pomegran-
ates, of olives, oil, and honey. It's land where
you'll never go hungry—always food on the
table and a roof over your head. It's a land
where you'll get iron out of rocks and mine
copper from the hills.

New King James Version

10When you have eaten and are full, then you shall bless the LORD your God for the good land which He has given you.

11"Beware that you do not forget the LORD your God by not keeping His commandments, His judgments, and His statutes which I command you today, 12lest—*when* you have eaten and are full, and have built beautiful houses and dwell *in them;* 13and *when* your herds and your flocks multiply, and your silver and your gold are multiplied, and all that you have is multiplied; 14when your heart is lifted up, and you forget the LORD your God who brought you out of the land of Egypt, from the house of bondage; 15who led you through that great and terrible wilderness, *in which were* fiery serpents and scorpions and thirsty land where there was no water; who brought water for you out of the flinty rock; 16who fed you in the wilderness with manna, which your fathers did not know, that He might humble you and that He might test you, to do you good in the end— 17then you say in your heart, 'My power and the might of my hand have gained me this wealth.'

18"And you shall remember the LORD your God, for *it is* He who gives you power to get wealth, that He may establish His covenant which He swore to your fathers, as *it is* this day. 19Then it shall be, if you by any means forget the LORD your God, and follow other gods, and serve them and worship them, I testify against you this day that you shall surely perish. 20As the nations which the LORD destroys before you, so you shall perish, because you would not be obedient to the voice of the LORD your God.

Israel's Rebellions Reviewed

9 "Hear, O Israel: You *are* to cross over the Jordan today, and go in to dispossess nations greater and mightier than yourself, cities great and fortified up to heaven, 2a people great and tall, the descendants of the Anakim, whom you know, and *of whom* you heard *it said,* 'Who can stand before the descendants of Anak?' 3Therefore understand today that the LORD your God *is* He who goes over before you *as* a consuming fire. He will destroy them and bring them down before you; so you shall drive them out and destroy them quickly, as the LORD has said to you.

4"Do not think in your heart, after the LORD your God has cast them out before you, saying, 'Because of my righteousness the LORD has brought me in to possess this land'; but *it is* because of the wickedness of these nations *that* the LORD is driving them out from before you. 5*It*

The Message

10 After a meal, satisfied, bless GOD, your God, for the good land he has given you.

11-16 Make sure you don't forget GOD, your God, by not keeping his commandments, his rules and regulations that I command you today. Make sure that when you eat and are satisfied, build pleasant houses and settle in, see your herds and flocks flourish and more and more money come in, watch your standard of living going up and up—make sure you don't become so full of yourself and your things that you forget GOD, your God,

the God who delivered you from
Egyptian slavery;
the God who led you through that huge
and fearsome wilderness, those
desolate, arid badlands crawling
with fiery snakes and scorpions;
the God who gave you water gushing
from hard rock;
the God who gave you manna to eat in
the wilderness, something your
ancestors had never heard of, in
order to give you a taste of the
hard life, to test you so that you
would be prepared to live well in
the days ahead of you.

17-18 If you start thinking to yourselves, "I did all this. And all by myself. I'm rich. It's all mine!"—well, think again. Remember that GOD, your God, gave you the strength to produce all this wealth so as to confirm the covenant that he promised to your ancestors—as it is today.

19-20 If you forget, forget GOD, your God, and start taking up with other gods, serving and worshiping them, I'm on record right now as giving you firm warning: that will be the end of you; I mean it—destruction. You'll go to your doom—the same as the nations GOD is destroying before you; doom because you wouldn't obey the Voice of GOD, your God.

1-2 9 Attention, Israel!

This very day you are crossing the Jordan to enter the land and dispossess nations that are much bigger and stronger than you are. You're going to find huge cities with sky-high fortress-walls and gigantic people, descendants of the Anakites—you've heard all about them; you've heard the saying, "No one can stand up to an Anakite."

3 Today know this: GOD, your God, is crossing the river ahead of you—he's a consuming fire. He will destroy the nations, he will put them under your power. You will dispossess them and very quickly wipe them out, just as GOD promised you would.

4-5 But when GOD pushes them out ahead of you, don't start thinking to yourselves, "It's because of all the good I've done that GOD has brought me in here to dispossess these nations." Actually it's because of all the evil these nations have done. No, it's nothing good that you've done, no record for de-

NEW KING JAMES VERSION

is not because of your righteousness or the up-
rightness of your heart *that* you go in to possess
their land, but because of the wickedness of
these nations *that* the LORD your God drives
them out from before you, and that He may ful-
fill the word which the LORD swore to your fa-
thers, to Abraham, Isaac, and Jacob. [6]Therefore
understand that the LORD your God is not giving
you this good land to possess because of your
righteousness, for you *are* a stiff-necked people.
[7]"Remember! Do not forget how you pro-
voked the LORD your God to wrath in the wilder-
ness. From the day that you departed from the
land of Egypt until you came to this place, you
have been rebellious against the LORD. [8]Also in
Horeb you provoked the LORD to wrath, so that
the LORD was angry *enough* with you to have de-
stroyed you. [9]When I went up into the mountain
to receive the tablets of stone, the tablets of the
covenant which the LORD made with you, then I
stayed on the mountain forty days and forty
nights. I neither ate bread nor drank water.
[10]Then the LORD delivered to me two tablets of
stone written with the finger of God, and on
them *were* all the words which the LORD had
spoken to you on the mountain from the midst
of the fire in the day of the assembly. [11]And it
came to pass, at the end of forty days and forty
nights, *that* the LORD gave me the two tablets of
stone, the tablets of the covenant.
[12]"Then the LORD said to me, 'Arise, go down
quickly from here, for your people whom you
brought out of Egypt have acted corruptly; they
have quickly turned aside from the way which I
commanded them; they have made themselves a
molded image.'
[13]"Furthermore the LORD spoke to me, say-
ing, 'I have seen this people, and indeed they are
a stiff-necked people. [14]Let Me alone, that I may
destroy them and blot out their name from un-
der heaven; and I will make of you a nation
mightier and greater than they.'
[15]"So I turned and came down from the
mountain, and the mountain burned with fire;
and the two tablets of the covenant *were* in my
two hands. [16]And I looked, and behold, you had
sinned against the LORD your God—had made
for yourselves a molded calf! You had turned
aside quickly from the way which the LORD had
commanded you. [17]Then I took the two tablets
and threw them out of my two hands and broke
them before your eyes. [18]And I fell down before
the LORD, as at the first, forty days and forty
nights; I neither ate bread nor drank water, be-
cause of all your sin which you committed in do-
ing wickedly in the sight of the LORD, to provoke
Him to anger. [19]For I was afraid of the anger and
hot displeasure with which the LORD was angry
with you, to destroy you. But the LORD listened
to me at that time also. [20]And the LORD was very
angry with Aaron *and* would have destroyed
him; so I prayed for Aaron also at the same time.
[21]Then I took your sin, the calf which you had
made, and burned it with fire and crushed it *and*
ground *it* very small, until it was as fine as dust;
and I threw its dust into the brook that de-
scended from the mountain.

THE MESSAGE

cency that you've built up, that got you here;
it's because of the vile wickedness of these
nations that GOD, your God, is dispossessing
them before you so that he can keep his
promised word to your ancestors, to Abra-
ham, Isaac, and Jacob.
6-10 Know this and don't ever forget it: It's not
because of any good that you've done that
GOD is giving you this good land to own.
Anything but! You're stubborn as mules.
Keep in mind and don't ever forget how an-
gry you made GOD, your God, in the wilder-
ness. You've kicked and screamed against
GOD from the day you left Egypt until you
got to this place, rebels all the way. You made
GOD angry at Horeb, made him so angry that
he wanted to destroy you. When I climbed
the mountain to receive the slabs of stone,
the tablets of the covenant that GOD made
with you, I stayed there on the mountain
forty days and nights: I ate no food; I drank
no water. Then GOD gave me the two slabs of
stone, engraved with the finger of God. They
contained word for word everything that
GOD spoke to you on the mountain out of the
fire, on the day of the assembly.
11-12 It was at the end of the forty days and
nights that GOD gave me the two slabs of
stone, the tablets of the covenant. GOD said
to me, "Get going, and quickly. Get down
there, because your people whom you led
out of Egypt have ruined everything. In al-
most no time at all they have left the road
that I laid out for them and gone off and
made for themselves a cast god."
13-14 GOD said, "I look at this people and all I see
are hardheaded, hardhearted rebels. Get out
of my way now so I can destroy them. I'm go-
ing to wipe them off the face of the map. Then
I'll start over with you to make a nation far
better and bigger than they could ever be."
15-17 I turned around and started down the
mountain—by now the mountain was blaz-
ing with fire—carrying the two tablets of the
covenant in my two arms. That's when I saw
it: There you were, sinning against GOD,
your God—you had made yourselves a cast
god in the shape of a calf! So soon you had
left the road that GOD had commanded you
to walk on. I held the two stone slabs high
and threw them down, smashing them to
bits as you watched.
18-20 Then I prostrated myself before GOD, just
as I had at the beginning of the forty days
and nights. I ate no food; I drank no water. I
did this because of you, all your sins, sin-
ning against GOD, doing what is evil in
GOD's eyes and making him angry. I was ter-
rified of GOD's furious anger, his blazing
anger. I was sure he would destroy you. But
once again GOD listened to me. And Aaron!
How furious he was with Aaron—ready to
destroy him. But I prayed also for Aaron at
that same time.
21 But that sin-thing that you made, that
calf-god, I took and burned in the fire,
pounded and ground it until it was crushed
into a fine powder, then threw it into the
stream that comes down the mountain.

NEW KING JAMES VERSION

22“Also at Taberah and Massah and Kibroth Hattaavah you provoked the LORD to wrath. 23Likewise, when the LORD sent you from Kadesh Barnea, saying, ‘Go up and possess the land which I have given you,’ then you rebelled against the commandment of the LORD your God, and you did not believe Him nor obey His voice. 24You have been rebellious against the LORD from the day that I knew you.

25“Thus I prostrated myself before the LORD; forty days and forty nights I kept prostrating myself, because the LORD had said He would destroy you. 26Therefore I prayed to the LORD, and said: ‘O Lord GOD, do not destroy Your people and Your inheritance whom You have redeemed through Your greatness, whom You have brought out of Egypt with a mighty hand. 27Remember Your servants, Abraham, Isaac, and Jacob; do not look on the stubbornness of this people, or on their wickedness or their sin, 28lest the land from which You brought us should say, “Because the LORD was not able to bring them to the land which He promised them, and because He hated them, He has brought them out to kill them in the wilderness.” 29Yet they *are* Your people and Your inheritance, whom You brought out by Your mighty power and by Your outstretched arm.’

THE SECOND PAIR OF TABLETS

10 “At that time the LORD said to me, ‘Hew for yourself two tablets of stone like the first, and come up to Me on the mountain and make yourself an ark of wood. 2And I will write on the tablets the words that were on the first tablets, which you broke; and you shall put them in the ark.’

3“So I made an ark of acacia wood, hewed two tablets of stone like the first, and went up the mountain, having the two tablets in my hand. 4And He wrote on the tablets according to the first writing, the Ten Commandments, which the LORD had spoken to you in the mountain from the midst of the fire in the day of the assembly; and the LORD gave them to me. 5Then I turned and came down from the mountain, and put the tablets in the ark which I had made; and there they are, just as the LORD commanded me.”

6(Now the children of Israel journeyed from the wells of Bene Jaakan to Moserah, where Aaron died, and where he was buried; and Eleazar his son ministered as priest in his stead. 7From there they journeyed to Gudgodah, and from Gudgodah to Jotbathah, a land of rivers of water. 8At that time the LORD separated the tribe of Levi to bear the ark of the covenant of the LORD, to stand before the LORD to minister to Him and to bless in His name, to this day. 9Therefore Levi has no portion nor inheritance with his brethren; the LORD *is* his inheritance, just as the LORD your God promised him.)

THE MESSAGE

22 And then there was Camp Taberah (Blaze), Massah (Testing-Place), and Camp Kibroth Hattaavah (Graves-of-the-Craving)—more occasions when you made GOD furious with you.

23-24 The most recent was when GOD sent you out from Kadesh Barnea, ordering you: “Go. Possess the land that I'm giving you.” And what did you do? You rebelled. Rebelled against the clear orders of GOD, your God. Refused to trust him. Wouldn't obey him. You've been rebels against GOD from the first day I knew you.

25-26 When I was on my face, prostrate before GOD those forty days and nights after GOD said he would destroy you, I prayed to GOD for you, “My Master, GOD, don't destroy your people, your inheritance whom, in your immense generosity, you redeemed, using your enormous strength to get them out of Egypt.

27-28 “Remember your servants Abraham, Isaac, and Jacob; don't make too much of the stubbornness of this people, their evil and their sin, lest the Egyptians from whom you rescued them say, ‘GOD couldn't do it; he got tired and wasn't able to take them to the land he promised them. He ended up hating them and dumped them in the wilderness to die.’

29 “They are your people still, your inheritance whom you powerfully and sovereignly rescued.”

1-2 10 GOD responded. He said, “Shape two slabs of stone similar to the first ones. Climb the mountain and meet me. Also make yourself a wooden chest. I will engrave the stone slabs with the words that were on the first ones, the ones you smashed. Then you will put them in the Chest.”

3-5 So I made a chest out of acacia wood, shaped two slabs of stone, just like the first ones, and climbed the mountain with the two slabs in my arms. He engraved the stone slabs the same as he had the first ones, the Ten Words that he addressed to you on the mountain out of the fire on the day of the assembly. Then GOD gave them to me. I turned around and came down the mountain. I put the stone slabs in the Chest that I made and they've been there ever since, just as GOD commanded me.

6-7 The People of Israel went from the wells of the Jaakanites to Moserah. Aaron died there and was buried. His son Eleazar succeeded him as priest. From there they went to Gudgodah, and then to Jotbathah, a land of streams of water.

8-9 That's when GOD set apart the tribe of Levi to carry GOD's Covenant Chest, to be on duty in the Presence of GOD, to serve him, and to bless in his name, as they continue to do today. And that's why Levites don't have a piece of inherited land as their kinsmen do. GOD is their inheritance, as GOD, your God, promised them.

NEW KING JAMES VERSION

10"As at the first time, I stayed in the mountain forty days and forty nights; the LORD also heard me at that time, *and* the LORD chose not to destroy you. 11Then the LORD said to me, 'Arise, begin *your* journey before the people, that they may go in and possess the land which I swore to their fathers to give them.'

THE ESSENCE OF THE LAW

12"And now, Israel, what does the LORD your God require of you, but to fear the LORD your God, to walk in all His ways and to love Him, to serve the LORD your God with all your heart and with all your soul, 13*and* to keep the commandments of the LORD and His statutes which I command you today for your good? 14Indeed heaven and the highest heavens belong to the LORD your God, *also* the earth with all that *is* in it. 15The LORD delighted only in your fathers, to love them; and He chose their descendants after them, you above all peoples, as *it is* this day. 16Therefore circumcise the foreskin of your heart, and be stiff-necked no longer. 17For the LORD your God *is* God of gods and Lord of lords, the great God, mighty and awesome, who shows no partiality nor takes a bribe. 18He administers justice for the fatherless and the widow, and loves the stranger, giving him food and clothing. 19Therefore love the stranger, for you were strangers in the land of Egypt. 20You shall fear the LORD your God; you shall serve Him, and to Him you shall hold fast, and take oaths in His name. 21He *is* your praise, and He *is* your God, who has done for you these great and awesome things which your eyes have seen. 22Your fathers went down to Egypt with seventy persons, and now the LORD your God has made you as the stars of heaven in multitude.

LOVE AND OBEDIENCE REWARDED

11 "Therefore you shall love the LORD your God, and keep His charge, His statutes, His judgments, and His commandments always. 2Know today that *I do* not *speak* with your children, who have not known and who have not seen the chastening of the LORD your God, His greatness and His mighty hand and His outstretched arm— 3His signs and His acts which He did in the midst of Egypt, to Pharaoh king of Egypt, and to all his land; 4what He did to the army of Egypt, to their horses and their chariots: how He made the waters of the Red Sea

THE MESSAGE

10 I stayed there on the mountain forty days and nights, just as I did the first time. And GOD listened to me, just as he did the first time: GOD decided not to destroy you.

11 GOD told me, "Now get going. Lead your people as they resume the journey to take possession of the land that I promised their ancestors that I'd give to them."

12-13 So now Israel, what do you think GOD expects from you? Just this: Live in his presence in holy reverence, follow the road he sets out for you, love him, serve GOD, your God, with everything you have in you, obey the commandments and regulations of GOD that I'm commanding you today—live a good life.

14-18 Look around you: Everything you see is GOD's—the heavens above and beyond, the Earth, and everything on it. But it was your ancestors who GOD fell in love with; he picked their children—that's *you!*—out of all the other peoples. That's where we are right now. So cut away the thick calluses from your heart and stop being so willfully hardheaded. GOD, your God, is the God of all gods, he's the Master of all masters, a God immense and powerful and awesome. He doesn't play favorites, takes no bribes, makes sure orphans and widows are treated fairly, takes loving care of foreigners by seeing that they get food and clothing.

19-21 You must treat foreigners with the same
loving care—
remember, you were once foreigners
in Egypt.
Reverently respect GOD, your God, serve
him, hold tight to him,
back up your promises with the
authority of his name.
He's your praise! He's your God!
He did all these tremendous, these
staggering things
that you saw with your own eyes.

22 When your ancestors entered Egypt, they numbered a mere seventy souls. And now look at you—you look more like the stars in the night skies in number. And your GOD did it.

1 **11** So love GOD, your God;
guard well his rules and regulations;
obey his commandments for the
rest of time.

2-7 Today it's very clear that it isn't your children who are front and center here: They weren't in on what GOD did, didn't see the acts, didn't experience the discipline, didn't marvel at his greatness, the way he displayed his power in the miracle-signs and deeds that he let loose in Egypt on Pharaoh king of Egypt and all his land, the way he took care of the Egyptian army, its horses and chariots, burying them in the waters of

NEW KING JAMES VERSION

overflow them as they pursued you, and *how* the
LORD has destroyed them to this day; 5what He
did for you in the wilderness until you came to
this place; 6and what He did to Dathan and Abi-
ram the sons of Eliab, the son of Reuben: how
the earth opened its mouth and swallowed them
up, their households, their tents, and all the sub-
stance that *was* in their possession, in the midst
of all Israel— 7but your eyes have seen every
great act of the LORD which He did.
8"Therefore you shall keep every command-
ment which I command you today, that you may
be strong, and go in and possess the land which
you cross over to possess, 9and that you may
prolong *your* days in the land which the LORD
swore to give your fathers, to them and their de-
scendants, 'a land flowing with milk and
honey.'[a] 10For the land which you go to possess
is not like the land of Egypt from which you
have come, where you sowed your seed and wa-
tered *it* by foot, as a vegetable garden; 11but the
land which you cross over to possess *is* a land of
hills and valleys, which drinks water from the
rain of heaven, 12a land for which the LORD your
God cares; the eyes of the LORD your God *are* al-
ways on it, from the beginning of the year to the
very end of the year.
13'And it shall be that if you earnestly obey
My commandments which I command you to-
day, to love the LORD your God and serve Him
with all your heart and with all your soul, 14then
I[a] will give *you* the rain for your land in its sea-
son, the early rain and the latter rain, that you
may gather in your grain, your new wine, and
your oil. 15And I will send grass in your fields for
your livestock, that you may eat and be filled.'
16Take heed to yourselves, lest your heart be de-
ceived, and you turn aside and serve other gods
and worship them, 17lest the LORD's anger be
aroused against you, and He shut up the heav-
ens so that there be no rain, and the land yield
no produce, and you perish quickly from the
good land which the LORD is giving you.
18"Therefore you shall lay up these words of
mine in your heart and in your soul, and bind
them as a sign on your hand, and they shall be
as frontlets between your eyes. 19You shall teach
them to your children, speaking of them when
you sit in your house, when you walk by the
way, when you lie down, and when you rise up.
20And you shall write them on the doorposts of
your house and on your gates, 21that your days
and the days of your children may be multiplied
in the land of which the LORD swore to your fa-
thers to give them, like the days of the heavens
above the earth.
22"For if you carefully keep all these com-
mandments which I command you to do—to
love the LORD your God, to walk in all His ways,
and to hold fast to Him— 23then the LORD will
drive out all these nations from before you, and
you will dispossess greater and mightier nations
than yourselves. 24Every place on which the sole
of your foot treads shall be yours: from the

11:9 [a]Exodus 3:8 **11:14** [a]Following Masoretic Text and Targum; Samaritan Pentateuch, Septuagint, and Vulgate read *He.*

THE MESSAGE

the Red Sea as they pursued you. GOD drowned them. And you're standing here today alive. Nor was it your children who saw how GOD took care of you in the wilderness up until the time you arrived here, what he did to Dathan and Abiram, the sons of Eliab son of Reuben, how the Earth opened its jaws and swallowed them with their families—their tents, and everything around them—right out of the middle of Israel. Yes, it was you—your eyes—that saw every great thing that GOD did.

8-9 So it's you who are in charge of keeping the entire commandment that I command you today so that you'll have the strength to invade and possess the land that you are crossing the river to make your own. Your obedience will give you a long life on the soil that GOD promised to give your ancestors and their children, a land flowing with milk and honey.

10-12 The land you are entering to take up ownership isn't like Egypt, the land you left, where you had to plant your own seed and water it yourselves as in a vegetable garden. But the land you are about to cross the river and take for your own is a land of mountains and valleys; it drinks water that rains from the sky. It's a land that GOD, your God, personally tends—he's the gardener—he alone keeps his eye on it all year long.

13-15 From now on if you listen obediently to the commandments that I am commanding you today, love GOD, your God, and serve him with everything you have within you, he'll take charge of sending the rain at the right time, both autumn and spring rains, so that you'll be able to harvest your grain, your grapes, your olives. He'll make sure there's plenty of grass for your animals. You'll have plenty to eat.

16-17 But be vigilant, lest you be seduced away and end up serving and worshiping other gods and GOD erupts in anger and shuts down Heaven so there's no rain and nothing grows in the fields, and in no time at all you're starved out—not a trace of you left on the good land that GOD is giving you.

18-21 Place these words on your hearts. Get them deep inside you. Tie them on your hands and foreheads as a reminder. Teach them to your children. Talk about them wherever you are, sitting at home or walking in the street; talk about them from the time you get up in the morning until you fall into bed at night. Inscribe them on the doorposts and gates of your cities so that you'll live a long time, and your children with you, on the soil that GOD promised to give your ancestors for as long as there is a sky over the Earth.

22-25 That's right. If you diligently keep all this commandment that I command you to obey—love GOD, your God, do what he tells you, stick close to him—GOD on his part will drive out all these nations that stand in your way. Yes, he'll drive out nations much bigger and stronger than you. Every square inch on which you place your foot will be yours.

New King James Version

wilderness and Lebanon, from the river, the River Euphrates, even to the Western Sea,[a] shall be your territory. 25No man shall be able to stand against you; the LORD your God will put the dread of you and the fear of you upon all the land where you tread, just as He has said to you.

26"Behold, I set before you today a blessing and a curse: 27the blessing, if you obey the commandments of the LORD your God which I command you today; 28and the curse, if you do not obey the commandments of the LORD your God, but turn aside from the way which I command you today, to go after other gods which you have not known. 29Now it shall be, when the LORD your God has brought you into the land which you go to possess, that you shall put the blessing on Mount Gerizim and the curse on Mount Ebal. 30*Are* they not on the other side of the Jordan, toward the setting sun, in the land of the Canaanites who dwell in the plain opposite Gilgal, beside the terebinth trees of Moreh? 31For you will cross over the Jordan and go in to possess the land which the LORD your God is giving you, and you will possess it and dwell in it. 32And you shall be careful to observe all the statutes and judgments which I set before you today.

A Prescribed Place of Worship

12 "These *are* the statutes and judgments which you shall be careful to observe in the land which the LORD God of your fathers is giving you to possess, all the days that you live on the earth. 2You shall utterly destroy all the places where the nations which you shall dispossess served their gods, on the high mountains and on the hills and under every green tree. 3And you shall destroy their altars, break their *sacred* pillars, and burn their wooden images with fire; you shall cut down the carved images of their gods and destroy their names from that place. 4You shall not worship the LORD your God *with* such *things*.

5"But you shall seek the place where the LORD your God chooses, out of all your tribes, to put His name for His dwelling place; and there you shall go. 6There you shall take your burnt offerings, your sacrifices, your tithes, the heave offerings of your hand, your vowed offerings, your freewill offerings, and the firstborn of your herds and flocks. 7And there you shall eat before the LORD your God, and you shall rejoice in all to which you have put your hand, you and your households, in which the LORD your God has blessed you.

8"You shall not at all do as we are doing here today—every man doing whatever *is* right in his own eyes— 9for as yet you have not come to the rest and the inheritance which the LORD your God is giving you. 10But *when* you cross over the Jordan and dwell in the land which the LORD your God is giving you to inherit, and He gives you rest from all your enemies round about, so

11:24 [a]That is, the Mediterranean

The Message

Your borders will stretch from the wilderness to the mountains of Lebanon, from the Euphrates River to the Mediterranean Sea. No one will be able to stand in your way. Everywhere you go, GOD-sent fear and trembling will precede you, just as he promised.

26 I've brought you today to the crossroads of Blessing and Curse.

27 The Blessing: if you listen obediently to the commandments of GOD, your God, which I command you today.

28 The Curse: if you don't pay attention to the commandments of GOD, your God, but leave the road that I command you today, following other gods of which you know nothing.

29-30 Here's what comes next: When GOD, your God, brings you into the land you are going into to make your own, you are to give out the Blessing from Mount Gerizim and the Curse from Mount Ebal. After you cross the Jordan River, follow the road to the west through Canaanite settlements in the valley near Gilgal and the Oaks of Moreh.

31-32 You are crossing the Jordan River to invade and take the land that GOD, your God, is giving you. Be vigilant. Observe all the regulations and rules I am setting before you today.

1 12 These are the rules and regulations that you must diligently observe for as long as you live in this country that GOD, the God-of-Your-Fathers, has given you to possess.

2-3 Ruthlessly demolish all the sacred shrines where the nations that you're driving out worship their gods—wherever you find them, on hills and mountains or in groves of green trees. Tear apart their altars. Smash their phallic pillars. Burn their sex-and-religion Asherah shrines. Break up their carved gods. Obliterate the names of those god sites.

4 Stay clear of those places—don't let what went on there contaminate the worship of GOD, your God.

5-7 Instead find the site that GOD, your God, will choose and mark it with his name as a common center for all the tribes of Israel. Assemble there. Bring to that place your Absolution-Offerings and sacrifices, your tithes and Tribute-Offerings, your Vow-Offerings, your Freewill-Offerings, and the firstborn of your herds and flocks. Feast there in the Presence of GOD, your God. Celebrate everything that you and your families have accomplished under the blessing of GOD, your God.

8-10 Don't continue doing things the way we're doing them at present, each of us doing as we wish. Until now you haven't arrived at the goal, the resting place, the inheritance that GOD, your God, is giving you. But the minute you cross the Jordan River and settle into the land GOD, your God, is enabling you to inherit, he'll give you rest from

New King James Version

that you dwell in safety, [11]then there will be the
place where the LORD your God chooses to
make His name abide. There you shall bring all
that I command you: your burnt offerings, your
sacrifices, your tithes, the heave offerings of
your hand, and all your choice offerings which
you vow to the LORD. [12]And you shall rejoice be-
fore the LORD your God, you and your sons and
your daughters, your male and female servants,
and the Levite who *is* within your gates, since he
has no portion nor inheritance with you. [13]Take
heed to yourself that you do not offer your burnt
offerings in every place that you see; [14]but in the
place which the LORD chooses, in one of your
tribes, there you shall offer your burnt offerings,
and there you shall do all that I command you.
[15]"However, you may slaughter and eat meat
within all your gates, whatever your heart de-
sires, according to the blessing of the LORD your
God which He has given you; the unclean and
the clean may eat of it, of the gazelle and the
deer alike. [16]Only you shall not eat the blood;
you shall pour it on the earth like water. [17]You
may not eat within your gates the tithe of your
grain or your new wine or your oil, of the first-
born of your herd or your flock, of any of your
offerings which you vow, of your freewill offer-
ings, or of the heave offering of your hand. [18]But
you must eat them before the LORD your God in
the place which the LORD your God chooses, you
and your son and your daughter, your male ser-
vant and your female servant, and the Levite
who *is* within your gates; and you shall rejoice
before the LORD your God in all to which you
put your hands. [19]Take heed to yourself that you
do not forsake the Levite as long as you live in
your land.
[20]"When the LORD your God enlarges your
border as He has promised you, and you say,
'Let me eat meat,' because you long to eat meat,
you may eat as much meat as your heart desires.
[21]If the place where the LORD your God chooses
to put His name is too far from you, then you
may slaughter from your herd and from your
flock which the LORD has given you, just as I
have commanded you, and you may eat within
your gates as much as your heart desires. [22]Just
as the gazelle and the deer are eaten, so you
may eat them; the unclean and the clean alike
may eat them. [23]Only be sure that you do not eat
the blood, for the blood *is* the life; you may not
eat the life with the meat. [24]You shall not eat it;
you shall pour it on the earth like water. [25]You
shall not eat it, that it may go well with you and
your children after you, when you do *what is*
right in the sight of the LORD. [26]Only the holy
things which you have, and your vowed offer-
ings, you shall take and go to the place which
the LORD chooses. [27]And you shall offer your
burnt offerings, the meat and the blood, on the
altar of the LORD your God; and the blood of

The Message

all your surrounding enemies. You'll be able
to settle down and live in safety.

11-12 From then on, at the place that GOD, your
God, chooses to mark with his name as the
place where you can meet him, bring every-
thing that I command you: your Absolution-
Offerings and sacrifices, tithes and Tribute-
Offerings, and the best of your Vow-Offerings
that you vow to GOD. Celebrate there in the
Presence of GOD, your God, you and your
sons and daughters, your servants and
maids, including the Levite living in your
neighborhood because he has no place of his
own in your inheritance.

13-14 Be extra careful: Don't offer your Absolu-
tion-Offerings just any place that strikes
your fancy. Offer your Absolution-Offerings
only in the place that GOD chooses in one of
your tribal regions. There and only there are
you to bring all that I command you.

15 It's permissible to slaughter your nonsac-
rificial animals like gazelle and deer in your
towns and eat all you want from them with
the blessing of GOD, your God. Both the rit-
ually clean and unclean may eat.

16-18 But you may not eat the blood. Pour the
blood out on the ground like water. Nor
may you eat there the tithe of your grain,
new wine, or olive oil; nor the firstborn of
your herds and flocks; nor any of the Vow-
Offerings that you vow; nor your Freewill-
Offerings and Tribute-Offerings. All these
you must eat in the Presence of GOD, your
God, in the place GOD, your God, chooses—
you, your son and daughter, your servant
and maid, and the Levite who lives in your
neighborhood. You are to celebrate in the
Presence of GOD, your God, all the things
you've been able to accomplish.

19 And make sure that for as long as you
live on your land you never, never neglect
the Levite.

20-22 When GOD, your God, expands your terri-
tory as he promised he would do, and you
say, "I'm hungry for meat," because you hap-
pen to be craving meat at the time, go ahead
and eat as much meat as you want. If you're
too far away from the place that GOD, your
God, has marked with his name, it's all right
to slaughter animals from your herds and
flocks that GOD has given you, as I've com-
manded you. In your own towns you may
eat as much of them as you want. Just as the
nonsacrificial animals like the gazelle and
deer are eaten, you may eat them; the ritu-
ally unclean and clean may eat them at the
same table.

23-25 Only this: Absolutely no blood. Don't eat
the blood. Blood is life; don't eat the life
with the meat. Don't eat it; pour it out on the
ground like water. Don't eat it; then you'll
have a good life, you and your children after
you. By all means, do the right thing in
GOD's eyes.

26-27 And this: Lift high your Holy-Offerings
and your Vow-Offerings and bring them to
the place GOD designates. Sacrifice your
Absolution-Offerings, the meat and blood,
on the Altar of GOD, your God; pour out the

NEW KING JAMES VERSION

your sacrifices shall be poured out on the altar of the LORD your God, and you shall eat the meat. [28]Observe and obey all these words which I command you, that it may go well with you and your children after you forever, when you do *what is* good and right in the sight of the LORD your God.

BEWARE OF FALSE GODS

[29]"When the LORD your God cuts off from before you the nations which you go to dispossess, and you displace them and dwell in their land, [30]take heed to yourself that you are not ensnared to follow them, after they are destroyed from before you, and that you do not inquire after their gods, saying, 'How did these nations serve their gods? I also will do likewise.' [31]You shall not worship the LORD your God in that way; for every abomination to the LORD which He hates they have done to their gods; for they burn even their sons and daughters in the fire to their gods.

[32]"Whatever I command you, be careful to observe it; you shall not add to it nor take away from it.

PUNISHMENT OF APOSTATES

13 "If there arises among you a prophet or a dreamer of dreams, and he gives you a sign or a wonder, [2]and the sign or the wonder comes to pass, of which he spoke to you, saying, 'Let us go after other gods'—which you have not known—'and let us serve them,' [3]you shall not listen to the words of that prophet or that dreamer of dreams, for the LORD your God is testing you to know whether you love the LORD your God with all your heart and with all your soul. [4]You shall walk after the LORD your God and fear Him, and keep His commandments and obey His voice; you shall serve Him and hold fast to Him. [5]But that prophet or that dreamer of dreams shall be put to death, because he has spoken in order to turn *you* away from the LORD your God, who brought you out of the land of Egypt and redeemed you from the house of bondage, to entice you from the way in which the LORD your God commanded you to walk. So you shall put away the evil from your midst.

[6]"If your brother, the son of your mother, your son or your daughter, the wife of your bosom, or your friend who is as your own soul, secretly entices you, saying, 'Let us go and serve other gods,' which you have not known, neither you nor your fathers, [7]of the gods of the people which *are* all around you, near to you or far off from you, from *one* end of the earth to the *other* end of the earth, [8]you shall not consent to him or listen to him, nor shall your eye pity him, nor shall you spare him or conceal him; [9]but you shall surely kill him; your hand shall be first against him to put him to death, and afterward the hand of all the people. [10]And you shall stone him with stones until he dies, because he sought to entice you away from the LORD your God, who brought you out of the land of Egypt, from the house of bondage. [11]So all Israel shall hear and fear, and not again do such wickedness as this among you.

THE MESSAGE

blood of the Absolution-Offering on the Al-
tar of GOD, your God; then you can go ahead
and eat the meat.
28 Be vigilant, listen obediently to these
words that I command you so that you'll
have a good life, you and your children, for
a long, long time, doing what is good and
right in the eyes of GOD, your God.

29-31 When GOD, your God, cuts off the nations
whose land you are invading, shoves them
out of your way so that you displace them
and settle in their land, be careful that you
don't get curious about them after they've
been destroyed before you. Don't get fasci-
nated with their gods, thinking, "I wonder
what it was like for them, worshiping their
gods. I'd like to try that myself." Don't do
this to GOD, your God. They commit every
imaginable abomination with their gods.
GOD hates it all with a passion. Why, they
even set their children on fire as offerings to
their gods!
32 Diligently do everything I command you,
the way I command you: don't add to it;
don't subtract from it.

1-4 13 When a prophet or visionary gets up in
your community and gives out a mirale-
sign or wonder, and the miracle-sign or
wonder that he gave out happens and he
says, "Let's follow other gods" (these are
gods you know nothing about), "let's wor-
ship them," don't pay any attention to what
that prophet or visionary says. GOD, your
God, is testing you to find out if you totally
love him with everything you have in you.
You are to follow only GOD, your God, hold
him in deep reverence, keep his command-
ments, listen obediently to what he says,
serve him—hold on to him for dear life!
5 And that prophet or visionary must be
put to death. He has urged mutiny against
GOD, your God, who rescued you from
Egypt, who redeemed you from a world of
slavery and put you on the road on which
GOD, your God, has commanded you to
walk. Purge the evil from your company.
6-10 And when your brother or son or daugh-
ter, or even your dear wife or lifelong friend,
comes to you in secret and whispers, "Let's
go and worship some other gods" (gods that
you know nothing about, neither you nor
your ancestors, the gods of the peoples
around you near and far, from one end of
the Earth to the other), don't go along with
him; shut your ears. Don't feel sorry for him
and don't make excuses for him. Kill him.
That's right, kill him. You throw the first
stone. Take action at once and swiftly with
everybody in the community getting in on it
at the end. Stone him with stones so that he
dies. He tried to turn you traitor against
GOD, your God, the one who got you out of
Egypt and the world of slavery.
11 Every man, woman, and child in Israel will
hear what's been done and be in awe. No one
will dare to do an evil thing like this again.

NEW KING JAMES VERSION

[12]"If you hear someone in one of your cities,
which the LORD your God gives you to dwell in,
saying, [13]'Corrupt men have gone out from
among you and enticed the inhabitants of their
city, saying, "Let us go and serve other gods" '—
which you have not known— [14]then you shall in-
quire, search out, and ask diligently. And *if it is*
indeed true *and* certain *that* such an abomina-
tion was committed among you, [15]you shall
surely strike the inhabitants of that city with the
edge of the sword, utterly destroying it, all that
is in it and its livestock—with the edge of the
sword. [16]And you shall gather all its plunder into
the middle of the street, and completely burn
with fire the city and all its plunder, for the LORD
your God. It shall be a heap forever; it shall not
be built again. [17]So none of the accursed things
shall remain in your hand, that the LORD may
turn from the fierceness of His anger and show
you mercy, have compassion on you and multi-
ply you, just as He swore to your fathers, [18]be-
cause you have listened to the voice of the LORD
your God, to keep all His commandments which
I command you today, to do *what is* right in the
eyes of the LORD your God.

IMPROPER MOURNING

14 "You *are* the children of the LORD your
God; you shall not cut yourselves nor
shave the front of your head for the dead. [2]For
you *are* a holy people to the LORD your God, and
the LORD has chosen you to be a people for Him-
self, a special treasure above all the peoples who
are on the face of the earth.

CLEAN AND UNCLEAN MEAT

[3]"You shall not eat any detestable thing.
[4]These *are* the animals which you may eat: the ox,
the sheep, the goat, [5]the deer, the gazelle, the roe
deer, the wild goat, the mountain goat,[a] the ante-
lope, and the mountain sheep. [6]And you may eat
every animal with cloven hooves, having the hoof
split into two parts, *and that* chews the cud,
among the animals. [7]Nevertheless, of those that
chew the cud or have cloven hooves, you shall not
eat, *such as* these: the camel, the hare, and the
rock hyrax; for they chew the cud but do not have
cloven hooves; they *are* unclean for you. [8]Also the
swine is unclean for you, because it has cloven
hooves, yet *does* not *chew* the cud; you shall not
eat their flesh or touch their dead carcasses.
[9]"These you may eat of all that *are* in the wa-
ters: you may eat all that have fins and scales.
[10]And whatever does not have fins and scales
you shall not eat; it *is* unclean for you.
[11]"All clean birds you may eat. [12]But these you
shall not eat: the eagle, the vulture, the buzzard,
[13]the red kite, the falcon, and the kite after their
kinds; [14]every raven after its kind; [15]the ostrich,
the short-eared owl, the sea gull, and the hawk
after their kinds; [16]the little owl, the screech owl,
the white owl, [17]the jackdaw, the carrion vulture,

14:5 [a]Or *addax*

THE MESSAGE

12-17 When word comes in from one of your
cities that GOD, your God, is giving you to
live in, reporting that evil men have gotten
together with some of the citizens of the city
and have broken away, saying, "Let's go and
worship other gods" (gods you know noth-
ing about), then you must conduct a careful
examination. Ask questions, investigate. If it
turns out that the report is true and this
abomination did in fact take place in your
community, you must execute the citizens of
that town. Kill them, setting that city apart
for holy destruction: the city and everything
in it including its animals. Gather the plun-
der in the middle of the town square and
burn it all—town and plunder together up in
smoke, a holy sacrifice to GOD, your God.
Leave it there, ashes and ruins. Don't build
on that site again. And don't let any of the
plunder devoted to holy destruction stick to
your fingers. Get rid of it so that GOD may
turn from anger to compassion, generously
making you prosper, just as he promised
your ancestors.
18 Yes. Obediently listen to GOD, your God.
Keep all his commands that I am giving you
today. Do the right thing in the eyes of GOD,
your God.

1-2 14 You are children of GOD, your God, so
don't mutilate your bodies or shave
your heads in funeral rites for the dead. You
only are a people holy to GOD, your God;
GOD chose you out of all the people on Earth
as his cherished personal treasure.
3-8 Don't eat anything abominable. These
are the animals you may eat: ox, sheep,
goat, deer, gazelle, roebuck, wild goat, ibex,
antelope, mountain sheep—any animal that
has a cloven hoof and chews the cud. But
you may not eat camels, rabbits, and rock
badgers because they chew the cud but they
don't have a cloven hoof—that makes them
ritually unclean. And pigs: Don't eat pigs—
they have a cloven hoof but don't chew the
cud, which makes them ritually unclean.
Don't even touch a pig's carcass.
9-10 This is what you may eat from the water:
anything that has fins and scales. But if it
doesn't have fins or scales, you may not eat
it. It's ritually unclean.
11-18 You may eat any ritually clean bird.
These are the exceptions, so don't eat these:
eagle, vulture, black vulture, kite, falcon, the
buzzard family, the raven family, ostrich,
nighthawk, the hawk family, little owl, great

NEW KING JAMES VERSION

the fisher owl, [18]the stork, the heron after its kind, and the hoopoe and the bat.

[19]"Also every creeping thing that flies is unclean for you; they shall not be eaten.

[20]"You may eat all clean birds.

[21]"You shall not eat anything that dies *of itself;* you may give it to the alien who *is* within your gates, that he may eat it, or you may sell it to a foreigner; for you *are* a holy people to the LORD your God.

"You shall not boil a young goat in its mother's milk.

TITHING PRINCIPLES

[22]"You shall truly tithe all the increase of your grain that the field produces year by year. [23]And you shall eat before the LORD your God, in the place where He chooses to make His name abide, the tithe of your grain and your new wine and your oil, of the firstborn of your herds and your flocks, that you may learn to fear the LORD your God always. [24]But if the journey is too long for you, so that you are not able to carry *the tithe, or* if the place where the LORD your God chooses to put His name is too far from you, when the LORD your God has blessed you, [25]then you shall exchange *it* for money, take the money in your hand, and go to the place which the LORD your God chooses. [26]And you shall spend that money for whatever your heart desires: for oxen or sheep, for wine or similar drink, for whatever your heart desires; you shall eat there before the LORD your God, and you shall rejoice, you and your household. [27]You shall not forsake the Levite who *is* within your gates, for he has no part nor inheritance with you.

[28]"At the end of *every* third year you shall bring out the tithe of your produce of that year and store *it* up within your gates. [29]And the Levite, because he has no portion nor inheritance with you, and the stranger and the fatherless and the widow who *are* within your gates, may come and eat and be satisfied, that the LORD your God may bless you in all the work of your hand which you do.

DEBTS CANCELED EVERY SEVEN YEARS

15 "At the end of *every* seven years you shall grant a release *of debts.* [2]And this *is* the form of the release: Every creditor who has lent *anything* to his neighbor shall release *it;* he shall not require *it* of his neighbor or his brother, because it is called the LORD's release. [3]Of a foreigner you may require *it;* but you shall give up your claim to what is owed by your brother, [4]except when there may be no poor among you; for the LORD will greatly bless you in the land which the LORD your God is giving you to possess *as* an inheritance— [5]only if you carefully obey the voice of the LORD your God, to observe with care all these commandments which I command you today. [6]For the LORD your God will bless you just as He promised you; you shall lend to many nations, but you shall not borrow; you shall reign over many nations, but they shall not reign over you.

THE MESSAGE

owl, white owl, pelican, osprey, cormorant, stork, the heron family, hoopoe, bat.

19-20 Winged insects are ritually unclean; don't eat them. But ritually clean winged creatures are permitted.

21 Because you are a people holy to GOD, your God, don't eat anything that you find dead. You can, though, give it to a foreigner in your neighborhood for a meal or sell it to a foreigner.

Don't boil a kid in its mother's milk.

22-26 Make an offering of ten percent, a tithe, of all the produce which grows in your fields year after year. Bring this into the Presence of GOD, your God, at the place he designates for worship and there eat the tithe from your grain, wine, and oil and the firstborn from your herds and flocks. In this way you will learn to live in deep reverence before GOD, your God, as long as you live. But if the place GOD, your God, designates for worship is too far away and you can't carry your tithe that far, GOD, your God, will still bless you: exchange your tithe for money and take the money to the place GOD, your God, has chosen to be worshiped. Use the money to buy anything you want: cattle, sheep, wine, or beer—anything that looks good to you. You and your family can then feast in the Presence of GOD, your God, and have a good time.

27 Meanwhile, don't forget to take good care of the Levites who live in your towns; they won't get any property or inheritance of their own as you will.

28-29 At the end of every third year, gather the tithe from all your produce of that year and put it aside in storage. Keep it in reserve for the Levite who won't get any property or inheritance as you will, and for the foreigner, the orphan, and the widow who live in your neighborhood. That way they'll have plenty to eat and GOD, your God, will bless you in all your work.

1-3 15 At the end of every seventh year, cancel all debts. This is the procedure: Everyone who has lent money to a neighbor writes it off. You must not press your neighbor or his brother for payment: All-Debts-Are-Canceled—GOD says so. You may collect payment from foreigners, but whatever you have lent to your fellow Israelite you must write off.

4-6 There must be no poor people among you because GOD is going to bless you lavishly in this land that GOD, your God, is giving you as an inheritance, your very own land. But only if you listen obediently to the Voice of GOD, your God, diligently observing every commandment that I command you today. Oh yes—GOD, your God, will bless you just as he promised. You will lend to many nations but won't borrow from any; you'll rule over many nations but none will rule over you.

New King James Version

Generosity to the Poor

7“If there is among you a poor man of your brethren, within any of the gates in your land which the LORD your God is giving you, you shall not harden your heart nor shut your hand from your poor brother, 8but you shall open your hand wide to him and willingly lend him sufficient for his need, whatever he needs. 9Beware lest there be a wicked thought in your heart, saying, ‘The seventh year, the year of release, is at hand,’ and your eye be evil against your poor brother and you give him nothing, and he cry out to the LORD against you, and it become sin among you. 10You shall surely give to him, and your heart should not be grieved when you give to him, because for this thing the LORD your God will bless you in all your works and in all to which you put your hand. 11For the poor will never cease from the land; therefore I command you, saying, ‘You shall open your hand wide to your brother, to your poor and your needy, in your land.’

The Law Concerning Bondservants

12“If your brother, a Hebrew man, or a Hebrew woman, is sold to you and serves you six years, then in the seventh year you shall let him go free from you. 13And when you send him away free from you, you shall not let him go away empty-handed; 14you shall supply him liberally from your flock, from your threshing floor, and from your winepress. *From what* the LORD your God has blessed you with, you shall give to him. 15You shall remember that you were a slave in the land of Egypt, and the LORD your God redeemed you; therefore I command you this thing today. 16And if it happens that he says to you, ‘I will not go away from you,’ because he loves you and your house, since he prospers with you, 17then you shall take an awl and thrust *it* through his ear to the door, and he shall be your servant forever. Also to your female servant you shall do likewise. 18It shall not seem hard to you when you send him away free from you; for he has been worth a double hired servant in serving you six years. Then the LORD your God will bless you in all that you do.

The Law Concerning Firstborn Animals

19“All the firstborn males that come from your herd and your flock you shall sanctify to the LORD your God; you shall do no work with the firstborn of your herd, nor shear the firstborn of your flock. 20You and your household shall eat *it* before the LORD your God year by year in the place which the LORD chooses. 21But if there is a defect in it, *if it is* lame or blind *or has* any serious defect, you shall not sacrifice it to the LORD your God. 22You may eat it within your gates; the unclean and the clean *person* alike *may eat it,* as *if it were* a gazelle or a deer. 23Only you shall not eat its blood; you shall pour it on the ground like water.

The Message

7-9 When you happen on someone who's in trouble or needs help among your people with whom you live in this land that GOD, your God, is giving you, don't look the other way pretending you don't see him. Don't keep a tight grip on your purse. No. Look at him, open your purse, lend whatever and as much as he needs. Don't count the cost. Don't listen to that selfish voice saying, “It's almost the seventh year, the year of All-Debts-Are-Canceled,” and turn aside and leave your needy neighbor in the lurch, refusing to help him. He'll call GOD's attention to you and your blatant sin.

10-11 Give freely and spontaneously. Don't have a stingy heart. The way you handle matters like this triggers GOD, your God's, blessing in everything you do, all your work and ventures. There are always going to be poor and needy people among you. So I command you: Always be generous, open purse and hands, give to your neighbors in trouble, your poor and hurting neighbors.

12-15 If a Hebrew man or Hebrew woman was sold to you and has served you for six years, in the seventh year you must set him or her free, released into a free life. And when you set them free don't send them off empty-handed. Provide them with some animals, plenty of bread and wine and oil. Load them with provisions from all the blessings with which GOD, your God, has blessed you. Don't for a minute forget that you were once slaves in Egypt and GOD, your God, redeemed you from that slave world.

For that reason, this day I command you to do this.

16-17 But if your slave, because he loves you and your family and has a good life with you, says, “I don't want to leave you,” then take an awl and pierce through his earlobe into the doorpost, marking him as your slave forever. Do the same with your women slaves who want to stay with you.

18 Don't consider this an unreasonable hardship, this setting your slave free. After all, he's worked six years for you at half the cost of a hired hand.

Believe me, GOD, your God, will bless you in everything you do.

19-23 Consecrate to GOD, your God, all the firstborn males in your herds and flocks. Don't use the firstborn from your herds as work animals; don't shear the firstborn from your flocks. These are for you to eat every year, you and your family, in the Presence of GOD, your God, at the place that GOD designates for worship. If the animal is defective, lame, say, or blind—anything wrong with it—don't slaughter it as a sacrifice to GOD, your God. Stay at home and eat it there. Both the ritually clean and unclean may eat it, the same as with a gazelle or a deer. Only you must not eat its blood. Pour the blood out on the ground like water.

NEW KING JAMES VERSION

THE PASSOVER REVIEWED

16 "Observe the month of Abib, and keep the Passover to the LORD your God, for in the month of Abib the LORD your God brought you out of Egypt by night. [2]Therefore you shall sacrifice the Passover to the LORD your God, from the flock and the herd, in the place where the LORD chooses to put His name. [3]You shall eat no leavened bread with it; seven days you shall eat unleavened bread with it, *that is*, the bread of affliction (for you came out of the land of Egypt in haste), that you may remember the day in which you came out of the land of Egypt all the days of your life. [4]And no leaven shall be seen among you in all your territory for seven days, nor shall *any* of the meat which you sacrifice the first day at twilight remain overnight until morning.

[5]"You may not sacrifice the Passover within any of your gates which the LORD your God gives you; [6]but at the place where the LORD your God chooses to make His name abide, there you shall sacrifice the Passover at twilight, at the going down of the sun, at the time you came out of Egypt. [7]And you shall roast and eat *it* in the place which the LORD your God chooses, and in the morning you shall turn and go to your tents. [8]Six days you shall eat unleavened bread, and on the seventh day there *shall be* a sacred assembly to the LORD your God. You shall do no work *on it*.

THE FEAST OF WEEKS REVIEWED

[9]"You shall count seven weeks for yourself; begin to count the seven weeks from *the time* you begin *to put* the sickle to the grain. [10]Then you shall keep the Feast of Weeks to the LORD your God with the tribute of a freewill offering from your hand, which you shall give as the LORD your God blesses you. [11]You shall rejoice before the LORD your God, you and your son and your daughter, your male servant and your female servant, the Levite who *is* within your gates, the stranger and the fatherless and the widow who *are* among you, at the place where the LORD your God chooses to make His name abide. [12]And you shall remember that you were a slave in Egypt, and you shall be careful to observe these statutes.

THE FEAST OF TABERNACLES REVIEWED

[13]"You shall observe the Feast of Tabernacles seven days, when you have gathered from your threshing floor and from your winepress. [14]And you shall rejoice in your feast, you and your son and your daughter, your male servant and your female servant and the Levite, the stranger and the fatherless and the widow, who *are* within your gates. [15]Seven days you shall keep a sacred feast to the LORD your God in the place which the LORD chooses, because the LORD your God will bless you in all your produce and in all the work of your hands, so that you surely rejoice.

[16]"Three times a year all your males shall appear before the LORD your God in the place which He chooses: at the Feast of Unleavened Bread, at the Feast of Weeks, and at the Feast of Tabernacles; and they shall not appear before the LORD empty-handed. [17]Every man *shall give* as he is able, according to the blessing of the LORD your God which He has given you.

THE MESSAGE

1-4 **16** Observe the month of Abib by celebrating the Passover to GOD, your God. It was in the month of Abib that GOD, your God, delivered you by night from Egypt. Offer the Passover-Sacrifice to GOD, your God, at the place GOD chooses to be worshiped by establishing his name there. Don't eat yeast bread with it; for seven days eat it with unraised bread, hard-times bread, because you left Egypt in a hurry—that bread will keep the memory fresh of how you left Egypt for as long as you live. There is to be no sign of yeast anywhere for seven days. And don't let any of the meat that you sacrifice in the evening be left over until morning.

5-7 Don't sacrifice the Passover in any of the towns that GOD, your God, gives you other than the one GOD, your God, designates for worship; there and there only you will offer the Passover-Sacrifice at evening as the sun goes down, marking the time that you left Egypt. Boil and eat it at the place designated by GOD, your God. Then, at daybreak, turn around and go home.

8 Eat unraised bread for six days. Set aside the seventh day as a holiday; don't do any work.

9-11 Starting from the day you put the sickle to the ripe grain, count out seven weeks. Celebrate the Feast-of-Weeks to GOD, your God, by bringing your Freewill-Offering—give as generously as GOD, your God, has blessed you. Rejoice in the Presence of GOD, your God: you, your son, your daughter, your servant, your maid, the Levite who lives in your neighborhood, the foreigner, the orphan and widow among you; rejoice at the place GOD, your God, will set aside to be worshiped.

12 Don't forget that you were once a slave in Egypt. So be diligent in observing these regulations.

13-15 Observe the Feast-of-Booths for seven days when you gather the harvest from your threshing-floor and your wine-vat. Rejoice at your festival: you, your son, your daughter, your servant, your maid, the Levite, the foreigner, and the orphans and widows who live in your neighborhood. Celebrate the Feast to GOD, your God, for seven days at the place GOD designates. GOD, your God, has been blessing you in your harvest and in all your work, so make a day of it—really celebrate!

16-17 All your men must appear before GOD, your God, three times each year at the place he designates: at the Feast-of-Unraised-Bread (Passover), at the Feast-of-Weeks, and at the Feast-of-Booths. No one is to show up in the Presence of GOD empty-handed; each man must bring as much as he can manage, giving generously in response to the blessings of GOD, your God.

NEW KING JAMES VERSION

JUSTICE MUST BE ADMINISTERED

18"You shall appoint judges and officers in all
your gates, which the LORD your God gives you,
according to your tribes, and they shall judge
the people with just judgment. 19You shall not
pervert justice; you shall not show partiality, nor
take a bribe, for a bribe blinds the eyes of the
wise and twists the words of the righteous. 20You
shall follow what is altogether just, that you
may live and inherit the land which the LORD
your God is giving you.

21"You shall not plant for yourself any tree,
as a wooden image, near the altar which you
build for yourself to the LORD your God. 22You
shall not set up a sacred pillar, which the LORD
your God hates.

17 "You shall not sacrifice to the LORD your
God a bull or sheep which has any blemish
or defect, for that *is* an abomination to the LORD
your God.

2"If there is found among you, within any of
your gates which the LORD your God gives you,
a man or a woman who has been wicked in the
sight of the LORD your God, in transgressing His
covenant, 3who has gone and served other gods
and worshiped them, either the sun or moon or
any of the host of heaven, which I have not com-
manded, 4and it is told you, and you hear *of it*,
then you shall inquire diligently. And if *it is* in-
deed true *and* certain that such an abomination
has been committed in Israel, 5then you shall
bring out to your gates that man or woman who
has committed that wicked thing, and shall
stone to death that man or woman with stones.
6Whoever is deserving of death shall be put to
death on the testimony of two or three wit-
nesses; he shall not be put to death on the testi-
mony of one witness. 7The hands of the wit-
nesses shall be the first against him to put him
to death, and afterward the hands of all the peo-
ple. So you shall put away the evil from among
you.

8"If a matter arises which is too hard for you
to judge, between degrees of guilt for blood-
shed, between one judgment or another, or be-
tween one punishment or another, matters of
controversy within your gates, then you shall
arise and go up to the place which the LORD
your God chooses. 9And you shall come to the
priests, the Levites, and to the judge *there* in
those days, and inquire *of them*; they shall pro-
nounce upon you the sentence of judgment.
10You shall do according to the sentence which
they pronounce upon you in that place which
the LORD chooses. And you shall be careful to do
according to all that they order you. 11According
to the sentence of the law in which they instruct
you, according to the judgment which they tell
you, you shall do; you shall not turn aside *to* the
right hand or *to* the left from the sentence
which they pronounce upon you. 12Now the man
who acts presumptuously and will not heed the
priest who stands to minister there before the
LORD your God, or the judge, that man shall die.
So you shall put away the evil from Israel. 13And
all the people shall hear and fear, and no longer
act presumptuously.

THE MESSAGE

18-19 Appoint judges and officers, organized by
tribes, in all the towns that GOD, your God,
is giving you. They are to judge the people
fairly and honestly. Don't twist the law.
Don't play favorites. Don't take a bribe—a
bribe blinds even a wise person; it under-
mines the intentions of the best of people.

20 The right! The right! Pursue only what's
right! It's the only way you can really live
and possess the land that GOD, your God, is
giving you.

21-22 Don't plant fertility Asherah trees alongside
the Altar of GOD, your God, that you build.
Don't set up phallic sex pillars—GOD, your
God, hates them.

1 17 And don't sacrifice to GOD, your God,
an ox or sheep that is defective or has
anything at all wrong with it. That's an
abomination, an insult to GOD, your God.

2-5 If you find anyone within the towns that
GOD, your God, is giving you doing what is
wrong in GOD's eyes, breaking his covenant
by going off to worship other gods, bowing
down to them—the sun, say, or the moon, or
any rebel sky-gods—look at the evidence
and investigate carefully. If you find that it is
true, that, in fact, an abomination has been
committed in Israel, then you are to take the
man or woman who did this evil thing out-
side your city gates and stone the man or
the woman. Hurl stones at the person until
dead.

6-7 But only on the testimony of two or three
witnesses may a person be put to death. No
one may be put to death on the testimony of
one witness. The witnesses must throw the
first stones in the execution, then the rest of
the community joins in. You have to purge
the evil from your community.

8-9 When matters of justice come up that are
too much for you—hard cases regarding
homicides, legal disputes, fights—take them
up to the central place of worship that GOD,
your God, has designated. Bring them to the
Levitical priests and the judge who is in of-
fice at the time. Consult them and they will
hand down the decision for you.

10-13 Then carry out their verdict at the place
designated by GOD, your God. Do what they
tell you, in exactly the way they tell you. Fol-
low their instructions precisely: Don't leave
out anything; don't add anything. Anyone
who presumes to override or twist the deci-
sion handed down by the priest or judge
who was acting in the Presence of GOD, your
God, is as good as dead—root him out, rid
Israel of the evil. Everyone will take notice
and be impressed. That will put an end to
presumptuous behavior.

New King James Version

Principles Governing Kings

[14]"When you come to the land which the LORD your God is giving you, and possess it and dwell in it, and say, 'I will set a king over me like all the nations that *are* around me,' [15]you shall surely set a king over you whom the LORD your God chooses; *one* from among your brethren you shall set as king over you; you may not set a foreigner over you, who *is* not your brother. [16]But he shall not multiply horses for himself, nor cause the people to return to Egypt to multiply horses, for the LORD has said to you, 'You shall not return that way again.' [17]Neither shall he multiply wives for himself, lest his heart turn away; nor shall he greatly multiply silver and gold for himself.

[18]"Also it shall be, when he sits on the throne of his kingdom, that he shall write for himself a copy of this law in a book, from *the one* before the priests, the Levites. [19]And it shall be with him, and he shall read it all the days of his life, that he may learn to fear the LORD his God and be careful to observe all the words of this law and these statutes, [20]that his heart may not be lifted above his brethren, that he may not turn aside from the commandment *to* the right hand or *to* the left, and that he may prolong *his* days in his kingdom, he and his children in the midst of Israel.

The Portion of the Priests and Levites

18 "The priests, the Levites—all the tribe of Levi—shall have no part nor inheritance with Israel; they shall eat the offerings of the LORD made by fire, and His portion. [2]Therefore they shall have no inheritance among their brethren; the LORD is their inheritance, as He said to them.

[3]"And this shall be the priest's due from the people, from those who offer a sacrifice, whether *it is* bull or sheep: they shall give to the priest the shoulder, the cheeks, and the stomach. [4]The firstfruits of your grain and your new wine and your oil, and the first of the fleece of your sheep, you shall give him. [5]For the LORD your God has chosen him out of all your tribes to stand to minister in the name of the LORD, him and his sons forever.

[6]"So if a Levite comes from any of your gates, from where he dwells among all Israel, and comes with all the desire of his mind to the place which the LORD chooses, [7]then he may serve in the name of the LORD his God as all his brethren the Levites *do,* who stand there before the LORD. [8]They shall have equal portions to eat, besides what comes from the sale of his inheritance.

Avoid Wicked Customs

[9]"When you come into the land which the LORD your God is giving you, you shall not learn to follow the abominations of those nations. [10]There shall not be found among you *anyone* who makes his son or his daughter pass through the fire, *or one* who practices witchcraft, *or* a soothsayer, or one who interprets omens, or a

The Message

14-17 When you enter the land that GOD, your God, is giving you and take it over and settle down, and then say, "I'm going to get me a king, a king like all the nations around me," make sure you get yourself a king whom GOD, your God, chooses. Choose your king from among your kinsmen; don't take a foreigner—only a kinsman. And make sure he doesn't build up a war machine, amassing military horses and chariots. He must not send people to Egypt to get more horses, because GOD told you, "You'll never go back there again!" And make sure he doesn't build up a harem, collecting wives who will divert him from the straight and narrow. And make sure he doesn't pile up a lot of silver and gold.

18-20 This is what must be done: When he sits down on the throne of his kingdom, the first thing he must do is make himself a copy of this Revelation on a scroll, copied under the supervision of the Levitical priests. That scroll is to remain at his side at all times; he is to study it every day so that he may learn what it means to fear his GOD, living in reverent obedience before these rules and regulations by following them. He must not become proud and arrogant, changing the commands at whim to suit himself or making up his own versions. If he reads and learns, he will have a long reign as king in Israel, he and his sons.

1-2 18 The Levitical priests—that's the entire tribe of Levi—don't get any land-inheritance with the rest of Israel. They get the Fire-Gift-Offerings of GOD—they will live on that inheritance. But they don't get land-inheritance like the rest of their kinsmen. GOD is their inheritance.

3-5 This is what the priests get from the people from any offering of an ox or a sheep: the shoulder, the two cheeks, and the stomach. You must also give them the firstfruits of your grain, wine, and oil and the first fleece of your sheep, because GOD, your God, has chosen only them and their children out of all your tribes to be present and serve always in the name of GOD, your God.

6-8 If a Levite moves from any town in Israel—and he is quite free to move wherever he desires—and comes to the place GOD designates for worship, he may serve there in the name of GOD along with all his brother Levites who are present and serving in the Presence of GOD. And he will get an equal share to eat, even though he has money from the sale of his parents' possessions.

9-12 When you enter the land that GOD, your God, is giving you, don't take on the abominable ways of life of the nations there. Don't you dare sacrifice your son or daughter in the fire. Don't practice divination, sorcery, fortunetelling, witchery, casting spells,

NEW KING JAMES VERSION

sorcerer, [11]or one who conjures spells, or a medium, or a spiritist, or one who calls up the dead. [12]For all who do these things *are* an abomination to the LORD, and because of these abominations the LORD your God drives them out from before you. [13]You shall be blameless before the LORD your God. [14]For these nations which you will dispossess listened to soothsayers and diviners; but as for you, the LORD your God has not appointed such for you.

A NEW PROPHET LIKE MOSES

[15]“The LORD your God will raise up for you a Prophet like me from your midst, from your brethren. Him you shall hear, [16]according to all you desired of the LORD your God in Horeb in the day of the assembly, saying, ‘Let me not hear again the voice of the LORD my God, nor let me see this great fire anymore, lest I die.’

[17]“And the LORD said to me: ‘What they have spoken is good. [18]I will raise up for them a Prophet like you from among their brethren, and will put My words in His mouth, and He shall speak to them all that I command Him. [19]And it shall be *that* whoever will not hear My words, which He speaks in My name, I will require *it* of him. [20]But the prophet who presumes to speak a word in My name, which I have not commanded him to speak, or who speaks in the name of other gods, that prophet shall die.’ [21]And if you say in your heart, ‘How shall we know the word which the LORD has not spoken?’— [22]when a prophet speaks in the name of the LORD, if the thing does not happen or come to pass, that *is* the thing which the LORD has not spoken; the prophet has spoken it presumptuously; you shall not be afraid of him.

THREE CITIES OF REFUGE

19 “When the LORD your God has cut off the nations whose land the LORD your God is giving you, and you dispossess them and dwell in their cities and in their houses, [2]you shall separate three cities for yourself in the midst of your land which the LORD your God is giving you to possess. [3]You shall prepare roads for yourself, and divide into three parts the territory of your land which the LORD your God is giving you to inherit, that any manslayer may flee there.

[4]“And this *is* the case of the manslayer who flees there, that he may live: Whoever kills his neighbor unintentionally, not having hated him in time past— [5]as when *a man* goes to the woods with his neighbor to cut timber, and his hand swings a stroke with the ax to cut down the tree, and the head slips from the handle and strikes his neighbor so that he dies—he shall flee to one of these cities and live; [6]lest the avenger of blood, while his anger is hot, pursue the manslayer and overtake him, because the way is long, and kill him, though he *was* not deserving of death, since he had not hated the victim in time past. [7]Therefore I command you, saying, ‘You shall separate three cities for yourself.’

THE MESSAGE

holding séances, or channeling with the dead. People who do these things are an abomination to GOD. It's because of just such abominable practices that GOD, your God, is driving these nations out before you.
13-14 Be completely loyal to GOD, your God.
These nations that you're about to run out of the country consort with sorcerers and witches. But not you. GOD, your God, forbids it.
15-16 GOD, your God, is going to raise up a
prophet for you. GOD will raise him up from among your kinsmen, a prophet like me. Listen obediently to him. This is what you asked GOD, your God, for at Horeb on the day you were all gathered at the mountain and said, “We can't hear any more from GOD, our God; we can't stand seeing any more fire. We'll die!”
17-19 And GOD said to me, “They're right;
they've spoken the truth. I'll raise up for them a prophet like you from their kinsmen. I'll tell him what to say and he will pass on to them everything I command him. And anyone who won't listen to my words spoken by him, I will personally hold responsible.
20 “But any prophet who fakes it, who
claims to speak in my name something I haven't commanded him to say, or speaks in the name of other gods, that prophet must die.”
21-22 You may be wondering among yourselves,
“How can we tell the difference, whether it was GOD who spoke or not?” Here's how: If what the prophet spoke in GOD's name doesn't happen, then obviously GOD wasn't behind it; the prophet made it up. Forget about him.

1-3 19 When GOD, your God, throws the nations
out of the country that GOD, your God, is giving you and you settle down in their cities and houses, you are to set aside three easily accessible cities in the land that GOD, your God, is giving you as your very own. Divide your land into thirds, this land that GOD, your God, is giving you to possess, and build roads to the towns so that anyone who accidentally kills another can flee there.
4-7 This is the guideline for the murderer
who flees there to take refuge: He has to have killed his neighbor without premeditation and with no history of bad blood between them. For instance, a man goes with his neighbor into the woods to cut a tree; he swings the ax, the head slips off the handle and hits his neighbor, killing him. He may then flee to one of these cities and save his life. If the city is too far away, the avenger of blood racing in hot-blooded pursuit might catch him since it's such a long distance, and kill him even though he didn't deserve it. It wasn't his fault. There was no history of hatred between them. Therefore I command you: Set aside the three cities for yourselves.

NEW KING JAMES VERSION

[8]"Now if the LORD your God enlarges your
territory, as He swore to your fathers, and gives
you the land which He promised to give to your
fathers, [9]and if you keep all these command-
ments and do them, which I command you to-
day, to love the LORD your God and to walk al-
ways in His ways, then you shall add three more
cities for yourself besides these three, [10]lest in-
nocent blood be shed in the midst of your land
which the LORD your God is giving you *as* an in-
heritance, and *thus* guilt of bloodshed be upon
you.

[11]"But if anyone hates his neighbor, lies in
wait for him, rises against him and strikes him
mortally, so that he dies, and he flees to one of
these cities, [12]then the elders of his city shall
send and bring him from there, and deliver him
over to the hand of the avenger of blood, that he
may die. [13]Your eye shall not pity him, but you
shall put away *the guilt of* innocent blood from
Israel, that it may go well with you.

PROPERTY BOUNDARIES

[14]"You shall not remove your neighbor's
landmark, which the men of old have set, in
your inheritance which you will inherit in the
land that the LORD your God is giving you to
possess.

THE LAW CONCERNING WITNESSES

[15]"One witness shall not rise against a man
concerning any iniquity or any sin that he com-
mits; by the mouth of two or three witnesses the
matter shall be established. [16]If a false witness
rises against any man to testify against him of
wrongdoing, [17]then both men in the controversy
shall stand before the LORD, before the priests
and the judges who serve in those days. [18]And
the judges shall make careful inquiry, and in-
deed, *if* the witness *is* a false witness, who has
testified falsely against his brother, [19]then you
shall do to him as he thought to have done to his
brother; so you shall put away the evil from
among you. [20]And those who remain shall hear
and fear, and hereafter they shall not again
commit such evil among you. [21]Your eye shall
not pity: life *shall be* for life, eye for eye, tooth
for tooth, hand for hand, foot for foot.

PRINCIPLES GOVERNING WARFARE

20 "When you go out to battle against your
enemies, and see horses and chariots *and*
people more numerous than you, do not be
afraid of them; for the LORD your God *is* with
you, who brought you up from the land of
Egypt. [2]So it shall be, when you are on the verge
of battle, that the priest shall approach and
speak to the people. [3]And he shall say to them,
'Hear, O Israel: Today you are on the verge of
battle with your enemies. Do not let your heart
faint, do not be afraid, and do not tremble or be
terrified because of them; [4]for the LORD your
God *is* He who goes with you, to fight for you
against your enemies, to save you.'

THE MESSAGE

8-10 When GOD, your God, enlarges your land, extending its borders as he solemnly promised your ancestors, by giving you the whole land he promised them because you are diligently living the way I'm commanding you today, namely, to love GOD, your God, and do what he tells you all your life; and when that happens, then add three more to these three cities so that there is no chance of innocent blood being spilled in your land. GOD, your God, is giving you this land as an inheritance—you don't want to pollute it with innocent blood and bring bloodguilt upon yourselves.

11-13 On the other hand, if a man with a history of hatred toward his neighbor waits in ambush, then jumps him, mauls and kills him, and then runs to one of these cities, that's a different story. The elders of his own city are to send for him and have him brought back. They are to hand him over to the avenger of blood for execution. Don't feel sorry for him. Clean out the pollution of wrongful murder from Israel so that you'll be able to live well and breathe clean air.

14 Don't move your neighbor's boundary markers, the longstanding landmarks set up by your pioneer ancestors defining their property.

15 You cannot convict anyone of a crime or sin on the word of one witness. You need two or three witnesses to make a case.

16-21 If a hostile witness stands to accuse someone of a wrong, then both parties involved in the quarrel must stand in the Presence of GOD before the priests and judges who are in office at that time. The judges must conduct a careful investigation; if the witness turns out to be a false witness and has lied against his fellow Israelite, give him the same medicine he intended for the other party. Clean the polluting evil from your company. People will hear of what you've done and be impressed; that will put a stop to this kind of evil among you. Don't feel sorry for the person: It's life for life, eye for eye, tooth for tooth, hand for hand, foot for foot.

1-4 20 When you go to war against your enemy and see horses and chariots and soldiers far outnumbering you, do not recoil in fear of them; GOD, your God, who brought you up out of Egypt is with you. When the battle is about to begin, let the priest come forward and speak to the troops. He'll say, "Attention, Israel. In a few minutes you're going to do battle with your enemies. Don't waver in resolve. Don't fear. Don't hesitate. Don't panic. GOD, your God, is right there with you, fighting with you against your enemies, fighting to win."

New King James Version

5“Then the officers shall speak to the people,
saying: ‘What man *is there* who has built a new
house and has not dedicated it? Let him go and
return to his house, lest he die in the battle and
another man dedicate it. 6Also what man *is*
there who has planted a vineyard and has not
eaten of it? Let him go and return to his house,
lest he die in the battle and another man eat of
it. 7And what man *is there* who is betrothed to a
woman and has not married her? Let him go
and return to his house, lest he die in the battle
and another man marry her.’
8“The officers shall speak further to the peo-
ple, and say, ‘What man *is there who is* fearful
and fainthearted? Let him go and return to his
house, lest the heart of his brethren faint[a] like
his heart.’ 9And so it shall be, when the officers
have finished speaking to the people, that they
shall make captains of the armies to lead the
people.
10“When you go near a city to fight against it,
then proclaim an offer of peace to it. 11And it
shall be that if they accept your offer of peace,
and open to you, then all the people *who are*
found in it shall be placed under tribute to you,
and serve you. 12Now if *the city* will not make
peace with you, but war against you, then you
shall besiege it. 13And when the LORD your God
delivers it into your hands, you shall strike
every male in it with the edge of the sword. 14But
the women, the little ones, the livestock, and all
that is in the city, all its spoil, you shall plunder
for yourself; and you shall eat the enemies’
plunder which the LORD your God gives you.
15Thus you shall do to all the cities *which are*
very far from you, which *are* not of the cities of
these nations.
16“But of the cities of these peoples which the
LORD your God gives you *as* an inheritance, you
shall let nothing that breathes remain alive,
17but you shall utterly destroy them: the Hittite
and the Amorite and the Canaanite and the Per-
izzite and the Hivite and the Jebusite, just as the
LORD your God has commanded you, 18lest they
teach you to do according to all their abomina-
tions which they have done for their gods, and
you sin against the LORD your God.
19“When you besiege a city for a long time,
while making war against it to take it, you shall
not destroy its trees by wielding an ax against
them; if you can eat of them, do not cut them
down to use in the siege, for the tree of the field
is man’s *food*. 20Only the trees which you know
are not trees for food you may destroy and cut
down, to build siegeworks against the city that
makes war with you, until it is subdued.

The Law Concerning Unsolved Murder

21 “If *anyone* is found slain, lying in the field
in the land which the LORD your God is
giving you to possess, *and* it is not known who

20:8 [a]Following Masoretic Text and Targum; Samaritan Penta-
teuch, Septuagint, Syriac, and Vulgate read *lest he make his
brother’s heart faint.*

The Message

5-7 Then let the officers step up and speak to the troops: “Is there a man here who has built a new house but hasn’t yet dedicated it? Let him go home right now lest he die in battle and another man dedicate it. And is there a man here who has planted a vineyard but hasn’t yet enjoyed the grapes? Let him go home right now lest he die in battle and another man enjoy the grapes. Is there a man here engaged to marry who hasn’t yet taken his wife? Let him go home right now lest he die in battle and another man take her.”

8 The officers will then continue, “And is there a man here who is wavering in resolve and afraid? Let him go home right now so that he doesn’t infect his fellows with his timidity and cowardly spirit.”

9 When the officers have finished speaking to the troops, let them appoint commanders of the troops who shall muster them by units.

10-15 When you come up against a city to attack it, call out, “Peace?” If they answer, “Yes, peace!” and open the city to you, then everyone found there will be conscripted as forced laborers and work for you. But if they don’t settle for peace and insist on war, then go ahead and attack. GOD, your God, will give them to you. Kill all the men with your swords. But don’t kill the women and children and animals. Everything inside the town you can take as plunder for you to use and eat—GOD, your God, gives it to you. This is the way you deal with the distant towns, the towns that don’t belong to the nations at hand.

16-18 But with the towns of the people that GOD, your God, is giving you as an inheritance, it’s different: don’t leave anyone alive. Consign them to holy destruction: the Hittites, Amorites, Canaanites, Perizzites, Hivites, and Jebusites, obeying the command of GOD, your God. This is so there won’t be any of them left to teach you to practice the abominations that they engage in with their gods and you end up sinning against GOD, your God.

19-20 When you mount an attack on a town and the siege goes on a long time, don’t start cutting down the trees, swinging your axes against them. Those trees are your future food; don’t cut them down. Are trees soldiers who come against you with weapons? The exception can be those trees which don’t produce food; you can chop them down and use the timbers to build siege engines against the town that is resisting you until it falls.

1-8 21 If a dead body is found on the ground, this ground that GOD, your God, has given you, lying out in the open, and no one

NEW KING JAMES VERSION

killed him, 2then your elders and your judges shall go out and measure *the distance* from the slain man to the surrounding cities. 3And it shall be *that* the elders of the city nearest to the slain man will take a heifer which has not been worked *and* which has not pulled with a yoke. 4The elders of that city shall bring the heifer down to a valley with flowing water, which is neither plowed nor sown, and they shall break the heifer's neck there in the valley. 5Then the priests, the sons of Levi, shall come near, for the LORD your God has chosen them to minister to Him and to bless in the name of the LORD; by their word every controversy and every assault shall be *settled.* 6And all the elders of that city nearest to the slain *man* shall wash their hands over the heifer whose neck was broken in the valley. 7Then they shall answer and say, 'Our hands have not shed this blood, nor have our eyes seen *it.* 8Provide atonement, O LORD, for Your people Israel, whom You have redeemed, and do not lay innocent blood to the charge of Your people Israel.' And atonement shall be provided on their behalf for the blood. 9So you shall put away the *guilt of* innocent blood from among you when you do *what is* right in the sight of the LORD.

FEMALE CAPTIVES

10"When you go out to war against your enemies, and the LORD your God delivers them into your hand, and you take them captive, 11and you see among the captives a beautiful woman, and desire her and would take her for your wife, 12then you shall bring her home to your house, and she shall shave her head and trim her nails. 13She shall put off the clothes of her captivity, remain in your house, and mourn her father and her mother a full month; after that you may go in to her and be her husband, and she shall be your wife. 14And it shall be, if you have no delight in her, then you shall set her free, but you certainly shall not sell her for money; you shall not treat her brutally, because you have humbled her.

FIRSTBORN INHERITANCE RIGHTS

15"If a man has two wives, one loved and the other unloved, and they have borne him children, *both* the loved and the unloved, and *if* the firstborn son is of her who is unloved, 16then it shall be, on the day he bequeaths his possessions to his sons, *that* he must not bestow firstborn status on the son of the loved wife in preference to the son of the unloved, the *true* firstborn. 17But he shall acknowledge the son of the unloved wife *as* the firstborn by giving him a double portion of all that he has, for he *is* the beginning of his strength; the right of the firstborn *is* his.

THE REBELLIOUS SON

18"If a man has a stubborn and rebellious son who will not obey the voice of his father or the voice of his mother, and *who,* when they have chastened him, will not heed them, 19then his father and his mother shall take hold of him and bring him out to the elders of his city, to the gate

THE MESSAGE

knows who killed him, your leaders and judges are to go out and measure the distance from the body to the nearest cities. The leaders and judges of the city that is nearest the corpse will then take a heifer that has never been used for work, never had a yoke on it. The leaders will take the heifer to a valley with a stream, a valley that has never been plowed or planted, and there break the neck of the heifer. The Levitical priests will then step up. GOD has chosen them to serve him in these matters by settling legal disputes and violent crimes and by pronouncing blessings in GOD's name. Finally, all the leaders of that town that is nearest the body will wash their hands over the heifer that had its neck broken at the stream and say, "We didn't kill this man and we didn't see who did it. Purify your people Israel whom you redeemed, O GOD. Clear your people Israel from any guilt in this murder."

8-9 That will clear them from any responsibility in the murder. By following these procedures you will have absolved yourselves of any part in the murder because you will have done what is right in GOD's sight.

10-14 When you go to war against your enemies and GOD, your God, gives you victory and you take prisoners, and then you notice among the prisoners of war a good-looking woman whom you find attractive and would like to marry, this is what you do: Take her home; have her trim her hair, cut her nails, and discard the clothes she was wearing when captured. She is then to stay in your home for a full month, mourning her father and mother. Then you may go to bed with her as husband and wife. If it turns out you don't like her, you must let her go and live wherever she wishes. But you can't sell her or use her as a slave since you've humiliated her.

15-17 When a man has two wives, one loved and the other hated, and they both give him sons, but the firstborn is from the hated wife, at the time he divides the inheritance with his sons he must not treat the son of the loved wife as the firstborn, cutting out the son of the hated wife, who is the actual firstborn. No, he must acknowledge the inheritance rights of the real firstborn, the son of the hated wife, by giving him a double share of the inheritance: that son is the first proof of his virility; the rights of the firstborn belong to him.

18-20 When a man has a stubborn son, a real rebel who won't do a thing his mother and father tell him, and even though they discipline him he still won't obey, his father and mother shall forcibly bring him before the leaders at the city gate and say to the city fa-

NEW KING JAMES VERSION

of his city. 20And they shall say to the elders of
his city, 'This son of ours is stubborn and rebel-
lious; he will not obey our voice; he is a glutton
and a drunkard.' 21Then all the men of his city
shall stone him to death with stones; so you
shall put away the evil from among you, and all
Israel shall hear and fear.

MISCELLANEOUS LAWS

22"If a man has committed a sin deserving of
death, and he is put to death, and you hang him
on a tree, 23his body shall not remain overnight
on the tree, but you shall surely bury him that
day, so that you do not defile the land which the
LORD your God is giving you *as* an inheritance;
for he who is hanged *is* accursed of God.

22 "You shall not see your brother's ox or his
sheep going astray, and hide yourself from
them; you shall certainly bring them back to
your brother. 2And if your brother *is* not near
you, or if you do not know him, then you shall
bring it to your own house, and it shall remain
with you until your brother seeks it; then you
shall restore it to him. 3You shall do the same
with his donkey, and so shall you do with his
garment; with any lost thing of your brother's,
which he has lost and you have found, you shall
do likewise; you must not hide yourself.
4"You shall not see your brother's donkey or
his ox fall down along the road, and hide your-
self from them; you shall surely help him lift
them up again.
5"A woman shall not wear anything that per-
tains to a man, nor shall a man put on a
woman's garment, for all who do so *are* an
abomination to the LORD your God.
6"If a bird's nest happens to be before you
along the way, in any tree or on the ground, with
young ones or eggs, with the mother sitting on
the young or on the eggs, you shall not take the
mother with the young; 7you shall surely let the
mother go, and take the young for yourself, that
it may be well with you and *that* you may pro-
long *your* days.
8"When you build a new house, then you
shall make a parapet for your roof, that you may
not bring guilt of bloodshed on your household
if anyone falls from it.
9"You shall not sow your vineyard with dif-
ferent kinds of seed, lest the yield of the seed
which you have sown and the fruit of your vine-
yard be defiled.
10"You shall not plow with an ox and a don-
key together.
11"You shall not wear a garment of different
sorts, *such as* wool and linen mixed together.
12"You shall make tassels on the four corners
of the clothing with which you cover *yourself*.

LAWS OF SEXUAL MORALITY

13"If any man takes a wife, and goes in to her,
and detests her, 14and charges her with shame-

THE MESSAGE

thers, "This son of ours is a stubborn rebel; he won't listen to a thing we say. He's a glutton and a drunk."

21 Then all the men of the town are to throw rocks at him until he's dead. You will have purged the evil pollution from among you. All Israel will hear what's happened and be in awe.

22-23 When a man has committed a capital crime, been given the death sentence, executed and hung from a tree, don't leave his dead body hanging overnight from the tree. Give him a decent burial that same day so that you don't desecrate your GOD-given land—a hanged man is an insult to God.

1-3 22 If you see your kinsman's ox or sheep wandering off loose, don't look the other way as if you didn't see it. Return promptly. If your fellow Israelite is not close by or you don't know whose it is, take the animal home with you and take care of it until your fellow asks about it. Then return it to him. Do the same if it's his donkey or a piece of clothing or anything else your fellow Israelite loses. Don't look the other way as if you didn't see it.

4 If you see your fellow's donkey or ox injured along the road, don't look the other way. Help him get it up and on its way.

5 A woman must not wear a man's clothing, nor a man wear women's clothing. This kind of thing is an abomination to GOD, your God.

6-7 When you come across a bird's nest alongside the road, whether in a tree or on the ground, and the mother is sitting on the young or on the eggs, don't take the mother with the young. You may take the babies, but let the mother go so that you will live a good and long life.

8 When you build a new house, make a parapet around your roof to make it safe so that someone doesn't fall off and die and your family become responsible for the death.

9 Don't plant two kinds of seed in your vineyard. If you do, you will forfeit what you've sown, the total production of the vineyard.

10 Don't plow with an ox and a donkey yoked together.

11 Don't wear clothes of mixed fabrics, wool and linen together.

12 Make tassels on the four corners of the cloak you use to cover yourself.

13-19 If a man marries a woman, sleeps with her, and then turns on her, calling her a slut,

NEW KING JAMES VERSION

ful conduct, and brings a bad name on her, and
says, 'I took this woman, and when I came to her
I found she *was* not a virgin,' 15then the father
and mother of the young woman shall take and
bring out *the evidence of* the young woman's
virginity to the elders of the city at the gate.
16And the young woman's father shall say to the
elders, 'I gave my daughter to this man as wife,
and he detests her. 17Now he has charged her
with shameful conduct, saying, "I found your
daughter *was* not a virgin," and yet these *are the*
evidences of my daughter's virginity.' And they
shall spread the cloth before the elders of the
city. 18Then the elders of that city shall take that
man and punish him; 19and they shall fine him
one hundred *shekels* of silver and give *them* to
the father of the young woman, because he has
brought a bad name on a virgin of Israel. And
she shall be his wife; he cannot divorce her all
his days.

20"But if the thing is true, *and evidences of*
virginity are not found for the young woman,
21then they shall bring out the young woman to
the door of her father's house, and the men of
her city shall stone her to death with stones, be-
cause she has done a disgraceful thing in Israel,
to play the harlot in her father's house. So you
shall put away the evil from among you.

22"If a man is found lying with a woman mar-
ried to a husband, then both of them shall die—
the man that lay with the woman, and the
woman; so you shall put away the evil from Is-
rael.

23"If a young woman *who is* a virgin is be-
trothed to a husband, and a man finds her in the
city and lies with her, 24then you shall bring
them both out to the gate of that city, and you
shall stone them to death with stones, the young
woman because she did not cry out in the city,
and the man because he humbled his neighbor's
wife; so you shall put away the evil from among
you.

25"But if a man finds a betrothed young
woman in the countryside, and the man forces
her and lies with her, then only the man who lay
with her shall die. 26But you shall do nothing to
the young woman; *there is* in the young woman
no sin *deserving* of death, for just as when a
man rises against his neighbor and kills him,
even so *is* this matter. 27For he found her in the
countryside, *and* the betrothed young woman
cried out, but *there was* no one to save her.

28"If a man finds a young woman *who is* a
virgin, who is not betrothed, and he seizes her
and lies with her, and they are found out, 29then
the man who lay with her shall give to the
young woman's father fifty *shekels* of silver, and
she shall be his wife because he has humbled
her; he shall not be permitted to divorce her all
his days.

30"A man shall not take his father's wife, nor
uncover his father's bed.

THE MESSAGE

giving her a bad name, saying, "I married
this woman, but when I slept with her I dis-
covered she wasn't a virgin," then the father
and mother of the girl are to take her with
the proof of her virginity to the town leaders
at the gate. The father is to tell the leaders,
"I gave my daughter to this man as wife and
he turned on her, rejecting her. And now he
has slanderously accused her, claiming that
she wasn't a virgin. But look at this, here is
the proof of my daughter's virginity." And
then he is to spread out her bloodstained
wedding garment before the leaders for
their examination. The town leaders then
are to take the husband, whip him, fine him
a hundred pieces of silver, and give it to the
father of the girl. The man gave a virgin girl
of Israel a bad name. He has to keep her as
his wife and can never divorce her.

20-21 But if it turns out that the accusation is
true and there is no evidence of the girl's
virginity, the men of the town are to take her
to the door of her father's house and stone
her to death. She acted disgracefully in Is-
rael. She lived like a whore while still in her
parents' home. Purge the evil from among
you.

22 If a man is found sleeping with another
man's wife, both must die. Purge that evil
from Israel.

23-24 If a man comes upon a virgin in town, a
girl who is engaged to another man, and
sleeps with her, take both of them to the
town gate and stone them until they die—
the girl because she didn't yell out for help
in the town and the man because he raped
her, violating the fiancée of his neighbor.
You must purge the evil from among you.

25-27 But if it was out in the country that the
man found the engaged girl and grabbed
and raped her, only the man is to die, the
man who raped her. Don't do anything to
the girl; she did nothing wrong. This is sim-
ilar to the case of a man who comes across
his neighbor out in the country and murders
him; when the engaged girl yelled out for
help, there was no one around to hear or
help her.

28-29 When a man comes upon a virgin who
has never been engaged and grabs and
rapes her and they are found out, the man
who raped her has to give her father fifty
pieces of silver. He has to marry her because
he took advantage of her. And he can never
divorce her.

30 A man may not marry his father's ex-
wife—that would violate his father's rights.

New King James Version

Those Excluded from the Congregation

23 “He who is emasculated by crushing or mutilation shall not enter the assembly of the LORD.

2“One of illegitimate birth shall not enter the assembly of the LORD; even to the tenth generation none of his *descendants* shall enter the assembly of the LORD.

3“An Ammonite or Moabite shall not enter the assembly of the LORD; even to the tenth generation none of his *descendants* shall enter the assembly of the LORD forever, 4because they did not meet you with bread and water on the road when you came out of Egypt, and because they hired against you Balaam the son of Beor from Pethor of Mesopotamia,[a] to curse you. 5Nevertheless the LORD your God would not listen to Balaam, but the LORD your God turned the curse into a blessing for you, because the LORD your God loves you. 6You shall not seek their peace nor their prosperity all your days forever.

7“You shall not abhor an Edomite, for he *is* your brother. You shall not abhor an Egyptian, because you were an alien in his land. 8The children of the third generation born to them may enter the assembly of the LORD.

Cleanliness of the Campsite

9“When the army goes out against your enemies, then keep yourself from every wicked thing. 10If there is any man among you who becomes unclean by some occurrence in the night, then he shall go outside the camp; he shall not come inside the camp. 11But it shall be, when evening comes, that he shall wash with water; and when the sun sets, he may come into the camp.

12“Also you shall have a place outside the camp, where you may go out; 13and you shall have an implement among your equipment, and when you sit down outside, you shall dig with it and turn and cover your refuse. 14For the LORD your God walks in the midst of your camp, to deliver you and give your enemies over to you; therefore your camp shall be holy, that He may see no unclean thing among you, and turn away from you.

Miscellaneous Laws

15“You shall not give back to his master the slave who has escaped from his master to you. 16He may dwell with you in your midst, in the place which he chooses within one of your gates, where it seems best to him; you shall not oppress him.

17“There shall be no *ritual* harlot[a] of the daughters of Israel, or a perverted[b] one of the sons of Israel. 18You shall not bring the wages of a harlot or the price of a dog to the house of the LORD your God for any vowed offering, for both of these *are* an abomination to the LORD your God.

19“You shall not charge interest to your brother—interest on money *or* food *or* anything that is lent out at interest. 20To a foreigner you

23:4 [a]Hebrew *Aram Naharaim* 23:17 [a]Hebrew *qedeshah*, feminine of *qadesh* (see note *b*) [b]Hebrew *qadesh*, that is, one practicing sodomy and prostitution in religious rituals

The Message

1 23 No eunuch is to enter the congregation
of GOD.
2 No bastard is to enter the congregation
of GOD, even to the tenth generation, nor
any of his children.
3-6 No Ammonite or Moabite is to enter the
congregation of GOD, even to the tenth generation, nor any of his children, ever. Those nations didn't treat you with hospitality on your travels out of Egypt, and on top of that they also hired Balaam son of Beor from Pethor in Mesopotamia to curse you. GOD, your God, refused to listen to Balaam but turned the curse into a blessing—how GOD, your God, loves you! Don't even try to get along with them or do anything for them, ever.
7 But don't spurn an Edomite; he's your
kin.

And don't spurn an Egyptian; you were a foreigner in his land.
8 Children born to Edomites and Egyptians
may enter the congregation of GOD in the third generation.

9-11 When you are camped out, at war with your
enemies, be careful to keep yourself from anything ritually defiling. If one of your men has become ritually unclean because of a nocturnal emission, he must go outside the camp and stay there until evening when he can wash himself, returning to the camp at sunset.
12-14 Mark out an area outside the camp where
you can go to relieve yourselves. Along with your weapons have a stick with you. After you relieve yourself, dig a hole with the stick and cover your excrement. GOD, your God, strolls through your camp; he's present to deliver you and give you victory over your enemies. Keep your camp holy; don't permit anything indecent or offensive in GOD's eyes.

15-16 Don't return a runaway slave to his master;
he's come to you for refuge. Let him live wherever he wishes within the protective gates of your city. Don't take advantage of him.

17-18 No daughter of Israel is to become a sa-
cred prostitute; and no son of Israel is to become a sacred prostitute. And don't bring the fee of a sacred whore or the earnings of a priest-pimp to the house of GOD, your God, to pay for any vow—they are both an abomination to GOD, your God.

19-20 Don't charge interest to your kinsmen on
any loan: not for money or food or clothing or anything else that could earn interest. You

New King James Version

may charge interest, but to your brother you
shall not charge interest, that the LORD your
God may bless you in all to which you set your
hand in the land which you are entering to pos-
sess.
21“When you make a vow to the LORD your
God, you shall not delay to pay it; for the LORD
your God will surely require it of you, and it
would be sin to you. 22But if you abstain from
vowing, it shall not be sin to you. 23That which
has gone from your lips you shall keep and per-
form, for you voluntarily vowed to the LORD
your God what you have promised with your
mouth.
24“When you come into your neighbor’s vine-
yard, you may eat your fill of grapes at your
pleasure, but you shall not put *any* in your con-
tainer. 25When you come into your neighbor’s
standing grain, you may pluck the heads with
your hand, but you shall not use a sickle on your
neighbor’s standing grain.

Law Concerning Divorce

24 “When a man takes a wife and marries
her, and it happens that she finds no favor
in his eyes because he has found some unclean-
ness in her, and he writes her a certificate of di-
vorce, puts *it* in her hand, and sends her out of
his house, 2when she has departed from his
house, and goes and becomes another man’s
wife, 3*if* the latter husband detests her and
writes her a certificate of divorce, puts *it* in her
hand, and sends her out of his house, or if the
latter husband dies who took her as his wife,
4*then* her former husband who divorced her
must not take her back to be his wife after she
has been defiled; for that *is* an abomination be-
fore the LORD, and you shall not bring sin on the
land which the LORD your God is giving you *as*
an inheritance.

Miscellaneous Laws

5“When a man has taken a new wife, he shall
not go out to war or be charged with any busi-
ness; he shall be free at home one year, and
bring happiness to his wife whom he has taken.
6“No man shall take the lower or the upper
millstone in pledge, for he takes *one’s* living in
pledge.
7“If a man is found kidnapping any of his
brethren of the children of Israel, and mistreats
him or sells him, then that kidnapper shall die;
and you shall put away the evil from among you.
8“Take heed in an outbreak of leprosy, that
you carefully observe and do according to all
that the priests, the Levites, shall teach you; just
as I commanded them, *so* you shall be careful to
do. 9Remember what the LORD your God did to
Miriam on the way when you came out of
Egypt!
10“When you lend your brother anything, you
shall not go into his house to get his pledge.
11You shall stand outside, and the man to whom
you lend shall bring the pledge out to you. 12And
if the man *is* poor, you shall not keep his pledge
overnight. 13You shall in any case return the
pledge to him again when the sun goes down,
that he may sleep in his own garment and bless

The Message

may charge foreigners interest, but you may not charge your brothers interest; that way GOD, your God, will bless all the work that you take up and the land that you are entering to possess.

21-23 When you make a vow to GOD, your God, don’t put off keeping it; GOD, your God, expects you to keep it and if you don’t you’re guilty. But if you don’t make a vow in the first place, there’s no sin. If you say you’re going to do something, do it. Keep the vow you willingly vowed to GOD, your God. You promised it, so do it.

24-25 When you enter your neighbor’s vineyard, you may eat all the grapes you want until you’re full, but you may not put any in your bucket or bag. And when you walk through the ripe grain of your neighbor, you may pick the heads of grain, but you may not swing your sickle there.

1-4 24 If a man marries a woman and then it happens that he no longer likes her because he has found something wrong with her, he may give her divorce papers, put them in her hand, and send her off. After she leaves, if she becomes another man’s wife and he also comes to hate her and this second husband also gives her divorce papers, puts them in her hand, and sends her off, or if he should die, then the first husband who divorced her can’t marry her again. She has made herself ritually unclean, and her remarriage would be an abomination in the Presence of GOD and defile the land with sin, this land that GOD, your God, is giving you as an inheritance.

5 When a man takes a new wife, he is not to go out with the army or be given any business or work duties. He gets one year off simply to be at home making his wife happy.

6 Don’t seize a handmill or an upper millstone as collateral for a loan. You’d be seizing someone’s very life.

7 If a man is caught kidnapping one of his kinsmen, someone of the People of Israel, to enslave or sell him, the kidnapper must die. Purge that evil from among you.

8-9 Warning! If a serious skin disease breaks out, follow exactly the rules set down by the Levitical priests. Follow them precisely as I commanded them. Don’t forget what GOD, your God, did to Miriam on your way out of Egypt.

10-13 When you make a loan of any kind to your neighbor, don’t enter his house to claim his pledge. Wait outside. Let the man to whom you made the pledge bring the pledge to you outside. And if he is destitute, don’t use his cloak as a bedroll; return it to him at nightfall so that he can sleep in his cloak and bless you. In the sight of GOD,

NEW KING JAMES VERSION

you; and it shall be righteousness to you before
the LORD your God.
14“You shall not oppress a hired servant *who*
is poor and needy, *whether* one of your brethren
or one of the aliens who *is* in your land within
your gates. 15Each day you shall give *him* his
wages, and not let the sun go down on it, for he
is poor and has set his heart on it; lest he cry out
against you to the LORD, and it be sin to you.
16“Fathers shall not be put to death for *their*
children, nor shall children be put to death for
their fathers; a person shall be put to death for
his own sin.
17“You shall not pervert justice due the
stranger or the fatherless, nor take a widow’s
garment as a pledge. 18But you shall remember
that you were a slave in Egypt, and the LORD
your God redeemed you from there; therefore I
command you to do this thing.
19“When you reap your harvest in your field,
and forget a sheaf in the field, you shall not go
back to get it; it shall be for the stranger, the fa-
therless, and the widow, that the LORD your God
may bless you in all the work of your hands.
20When you beat your olive trees, you shall not
go over the boughs again; it shall be for the
stranger, the fatherless, and the widow. 21When
you gather the grapes of your vineyard, you
shall not glean *it* afterward; it shall be for the
stranger, the fatherless, and the widow. 22And
you shall remember that you were a slave in the
land of Egypt; therefore I command you to do
this thing.

25 “If there is a dispute between men, and
they come to court, that *the judges* may
judge them, and they justify the righteous and
condemn the wicked, 2then it shall be, if the
wicked man deserves to be beaten, that the
judge will cause him to lie down and be beaten
in his presence, according to his guilt, with a
certain number of blows. 3Forty blows he may
give him *and* no more, lest he should exceed this
and beat him with many blows above these, and
your brother be humiliated in your sight.
4“You shall not muzzle an ox while it treads
out *the grain.*

MARRIAGE DUTY OF THE SURVIVING BROTHER

5“If brothers dwell together, and one of them
dies and has no son, the widow of the dead man
shall not be *married* to a stranger outside *the*
family; her husband’s brother shall go in to her,
take her as his wife, and perform the duty of a
husband’s brother to her. 6And it shall be *that*
the firstborn son which she bears will succeed
to the name of his dead brother, that his name
may not be blotted out of Israel. 7But if the man
does not want to take his brother’s wife, then let
his brother’s wife go up to the gate to the elders,
and say, ‘My husband’s brother refuses to raise
up a name to his brother in Israel; he will not
perform the duty of my husband’s brother.’
8Then the elders of his city shall call him and
speak to him. But *if* he stands firm and says, ‘I

THE MESSAGE

your God, that will be viewed as a righteous
act.

14-15 Don’t abuse a laborer who is destitute
and needy, whether he is a fellow Israelite
living in your land and in your city. Pay him
at the end of each workday; he’s living from
hand to mouth and needs it now. If you hold
back his pay, he’ll protest to GOD and you’ll
have sin on your books.

16 Parents shall not be put to death for their
children, nor children for their parents.
Each person shall be put to death for his
own sin.

17-18 Make sure foreigners and orphans get
their just rights. Don’t take the cloak of a
widow as security for a loan. Don’t ever for-
get that you were once slaves in Egypt and
GOD, your God, got you out of there. I com-
mand you: Do what I’m telling you.

19-22 When you harvest your grain and forget
a sheaf back in the field, don’t go back and
get it; leave it for the foreigner, the orphan,
and the widow so that GOD, your God, will
bless you in all your work. When you shake
the olives off your trees, don’t go back over
the branches and strip them bare—what’s
left is for the foreigner, the orphan, and the
widow. And when you cut the grapes in your
vineyard, don’t take every last grape—leave
a few for the foreigner, the orphan, and the
widow. Don’t ever forget that you were a
slave in Egypt. I command you: Do what I’m
telling you.

1-3 25 When men have a legal dispute, let
them go to court; the judges will decide
between them, declaring one innocent and
the other guilty. If the guilty one deserves
punishment, the judge will have him pros-
trate himself before him and lashed as many
times as his crime deserves, but not more
than forty. If you hit him more than forty
times, you will degrade him to something
less than human.

4 Don’t muzzle an ox while it is threshing.

5-6 When brothers are living together and
one of them dies without having had a son,
the widow of the dead brother shall not
marry a stranger from outside the family;
her husband’s brother is to come to her and
marry her and do the brother-in-law’s duty
by her. The first son that she bears shall be
named after her dead husband so his name
won’t die out in Israel.

7-10 But if the brother doesn’t want to marry
his sister-in-law, she is to go to the leaders at
the city gate and say, “My brother-in-law re-
fuses to keep his brother’s name alive in Is-
rael; he won’t agree to do the brother-in-
law’s duty by me.” Then the leaders will call
for the brother and confront him. If he
stands there defiant and says, “I don’t want

New King James Version

do not want to take her,' 9then his brother's wife shall come to him in the presence of the elders, remove his sandal from his foot, spit in his face, and answer and say, 'So shall it be done to the man who will not build up his brother's house.' 10And his name shall be called in Israel, 'The house of him who had his sandal removed.'

Miscellaneous Laws

11"If *two* men fight together, and the wife of one draws near to rescue her husband from the hand of the one attacking him, and puts out her hand and seizes him by the genitals, 12then you shall cut off her hand; your eye shall not pity *her.*

13"You shall not have in your bag differing weights, a heavy and a light. 14You shall not have in your house differing measures, a large and a small. 15You shall have a perfect and just weight, a perfect and just measure, that your days may be lengthened in the land which the LORD your God is giving you. 16For all who do such things, all who behave unrighteously, *are* an abomination to the LORD your God.

Destroy the Amalekites

17"Remember what Amalek did to you on the way as you were coming out of Egypt, 18how he met you on the way and attacked your rear ranks, all the stragglers at your rear, when you *were* tired and weary; and he did not fear God. 19Therefore it shall be, when the LORD your God has given you rest from your enemies all around, in the land which the LORD your God is giving you to possess *as* an inheritance, *that* you will blot out the remembrance of Amalek from under heaven. You shall not forget.

Offerings of Firstfruits and Tithes

26 "And it shall be, when you come into the land which the LORD your God is giving you *as* an inheritance, and you possess it and dwell in it, 2that you shall take some of the first of all the produce of the ground, which you shall bring from your land that the LORD your God is giving you, and put *it* in a basket and go to the place where the LORD your God chooses to make His name abide. 3And you shall go to the one who is priest in those days, and say to him, 'I declare today to the LORD your[a] God that I have come to the country which the LORD swore to our fathers to give us.'

4"Then the priest shall take the basket out of your hand and set it down before the altar of the LORD your God. 5And you shall answer and say before the LORD your God: 'My father *was* a Syrian,[a] about to perish, and he went down to Egypt and dwelt there, few in number; and there he became a nation, great, mighty, and populous. 6But the Egyptians mistreated us, afflicted us, and laid hard bondage on us. 7Then we cried out to the LORD God of our fathers, and the LORD

26:3 [a]Septuagint reads *my.* 26:5 [a]Or *Aramean*

The Message

her," his sister-in-law is to pull his sandal off his foot, spit in his face, and say, "This is what happens to the man who refuses to build up the family of his brother—his name in Israel will be Family-No-Sandal."

11-12 When two men are in a fight and the wife
of the one man, trying to rescue her husband, grabs the genitals of the man hitting him, you are to cut off her hand. Show no pity.

13-16 Don't carry around with you two weights,
one heavy and the other light, and don't keep two measures at hand, one large and the other small. Use only one weight, a true and honest weight, and one measure, a true and honest measure, so that you will live a long time on the land that GOD, your God, is giving you. Dishonest weights and measures are an abomination to GOD, your God—all this corruption in business deals!

17-19 Don't forget what Amalek did to you on
the road after you left Egypt, how he attacked you when you were tired, barely able to put one foot in front of another, mercilessly cut off your stragglers, and had no regard for God. When GOD, your God, gives you rest from all the enemies that surround you in the inheritance-land GOD, your God, is giving you to possess, you are to wipe the name of Amalek from off the Earth. Don't forget!

1-5 26 Once you enter the land that GOD, your
God, is giving you as an inheritance and take it over and settle down, you are to take some of all the firstfruits of what you grow in the land that GOD, your God, is giving you, put them in a basket and go to the place GOD, your God, sets apart for you to worship him. At that time, go to the priest who is there and say, "I announce to GOD, your God, today that I have entered the land that GOD promised our ancestors that he'd give to us." The priest will take the basket from you and place it on the Altar of GOD, your God. And there in the Presence of GOD, your God, you will recite:

5-10 A wandering Aramean was my father,
he went down to Egypt and sojourned
there,
he and just a handful of his brothers at
first, but soon
they became a great nation, mighty
and many.
The Egyptians abused and battered us,
in a cruel and savage slavery.
We cried out to GOD, the God-of-Our-
Fathers:

New King James Version

heard our voice and looked on our affliction and our labor and our oppression. [8]So the LORD brought us out of Egypt with a mighty hand and with an outstretched arm, with great terror and with signs and wonders. [9]He has brought us to this place and has given us this land, "a land flowing with milk and honey";[a] [10]and now, behold, I have brought the firstfruits of the land which you, O LORD, have given me.'

"Then you shall set it before the LORD your God, and worship before the LORD your God. [11]So you shall rejoice in every good *thing* which the LORD your God has given to you and your house, you and the Levite and the stranger who *is* among you.

[12]"When you have finished laying aside all the tithe of your increase in the third year—the year of tithing—and have given *it* to the Levite, the stranger, the fatherless, and the widow, so that they may eat within your gates and be filled, [13]then you shall say before the LORD your God: 'I have removed the holy *tithe* from *my* house, and also have given them to the Levite, the stranger, the fatherless, and the widow, according to all Your commandments which You have commanded me; I have not transgressed Your commandments, nor have I forgotten *them.* [14]I have not eaten any of it when in mourning, nor have I removed *any* of it for an unclean *use,* nor given *any* of it for the dead. I have obeyed the voice of the LORD my God, and have done according to all that You have commanded me. [15]Look down from Your holy habitation, from heaven, and bless Your people Israel and the land which You have given us, just as You swore to our fathers, "a land flowing with milk and honey." '[a]

A Special People of God

[16]"This day the LORD your God commands you to observe these statutes and judgments; therefore you shall be careful to observe them with all your heart and with all your soul. [17]Today you have proclaimed the LORD to be your God, and that you will walk in His ways and keep His statutes, His commandments, and His judgments, and that you will obey His voice. [18]Also today the LORD has proclaimed you to be His special people, just as He promised you, that *you* should keep all His commandments, [19]and that He will set you high above all nations which He has made, in praise, in name, and in honor, and that you may be a holy people to the LORD your God, just as He has spoken."

26:9 [a]Exodus 3:8 **26:15** [a]Exodus 3:8

The Message

He listened to our voice, he saw
our destitution, our trouble, our cruel
plight.
And GOD took us out of Egypt
with his strong hand and long arm,
terrible and great,
with signs and miracle-wonders.
And he brought us to this place,
gave us this land flowing with milk
and honey.
So here I am. I've brought the firstfruits
of what I've grown on this ground you
gave me, O GOD.

10-11 Then place it in the Presence of GOD, your God. Prostrate yourselves in the Presence of GOD, your God. And rejoice! Celebrate all the good things that GOD, your God, has given you and your family; you and the Levite and the foreigner who lives with you.

12-14 Every third year, the year of the tithe, give a tenth of your produce to the Levite, the foreigner, the orphan, and the widow so that they may eat their fill in your cities. And then, in the Presence of GOD, your God, say this:

I have brought the sacred share,
I've given it to the Levite, foreigner,
orphan, and widow.
What you commanded, I've done.
I haven't detoured around your
commands,
I haven't forgotten a single one.
I haven't eaten from the sacred share
while mourning,
I haven't removed any of it while
ritually unclean,
I haven't used it in funeral feasts.
I have listened obediently to the Voice
of GOD, my God,
I have lived the way you commanded
me.

15 Look down from your holy house in
Heaven!
Bless your people Israel and the
ground you gave us,
just as you promised our ancestors
you would,
this land flowing with milk and honey.

16-17 This very day GOD, your God, commands you to follow these rules and regulations, to live them out with everything you have in you. You've renewed your vows today that GOD is your God, that you'll live the way he shows you; do what he tells you in the rules, regulations, and commandments; and listen obediently to him.

18-19 And today GOD has reaffirmed that you are dearly held treasure just as he promised, a people entrusted with keeping his commandments, a people set high above all other nations that he's made, high in praise, fame, and honor: you're a people holy to GOD, your God. That's what he has promised.

New King James Version

The Law Inscribed on Stones

27 Now Moses, with the elders of Israel, com-
manded the people, saying: "Keep all the
commandments which I command you today.
2And it shall be, on the day when you cross over
the Jordan to the land which the LORD your God
is giving you, that you shall set up for your-
selves large stones, and whitewash them with
lime. 3You shall write on them all the words of
this law, when you have crossed over, that you
may enter the land which the LORD your God is
giving you, 'a land flowing with milk and
honey,'[a] just as the LORD God of your fathers
promised you. 4Therefore it shall be, when you
have crossed over the Jordan, *that* on Mount
Ebal you shall set up these stones, which I com-
mand you today, and you shall whitewash them
with lime. 5And there you shall build an altar to
the LORD your God, an altar of stones; you shall
not use an iron *tool* on them. 6You shall build
with whole stones the altar of the LORD your
God, and offer burnt offerings on it to the LORD
your God. 7You shall offer peace offerings, and
shall eat there, and rejoice before the LORD your
God. 8And you shall write very plainly on the
stones all the words of this law."
9Then Moses and the priests, the Levites,
spoke to all Israel, saying, "Take heed and listen,
O Israel: This day you have become the people
of the LORD your God. 10Therefore you shall
obey the voice of the LORD your God, and ob-
serve His commandments and His statutes
which I command you today."

Curses Pronounced from Mount Ebal

11And Moses commanded the people on the
same day, saying, 12"These shall stand on Mount
Gerizim to bless the people, when you have
crossed over the Jordan: Simeon, Levi, Judah,
Issachar, Joseph, and Benjamin; 13and these
shall stand on Mount Ebal to curse: Reuben,
Gad, Asher, Zebulun, Dan, and Naphtali.
14"And the Levites shall speak with a loud
voice and say to all the men of Israel: 15'Cursed
is the one who makes a carved or molded image,
an abomination to the LORD, the work of the
hands of the craftsman, and sets *it* up in secret.'
"And all the people shall answer and say,
'Amen!'
16'Cursed *is* the one who treats his father or
his mother with contempt.'
"And all the people shall say, 'Amen!'
17'Cursed *is* the one who moves his neigh-
bor's landmark.'
"And all the people shall say, 'Amen!'
18'Cursed *is* the one who makes the blind to
wander off the road.'
"And all the people shall say, 'Amen!'
19'Cursed *is* the one who perverts the justice
due the stranger, the fatherless, and widow.'
"And all the people shall say, 'Amen!'
20'Cursed *is* the one who lies with his father's
wife, because he has uncovered his father's bed.'
"And all the people shall say, 'Amen!'
21'Cursed *is* the one who lies with any kind of
animal.'

27:3 [a]Exodus 3:8

The Message

1-3 27 Moses commanded the leaders of Israel and charged the people: Keep every commandment that I command you today. On the day you cross the Jordan into the land that GOD, your God, is giving you, erect large stones and coat them with plaster. As soon as you cross over the river, write on the stones all the words of this Revelation so that you'll enter the land that GOD, your God, is giving you, that land flowing with milk and honey that GOD, the God-of-Your-Fathers, promised you.

4-7 So when you've crossed the Jordan, erect these stones on Mount Ebal. Then coat them with plaster. Build an Altar of stones for GOD, your God, there on the mountain. Don't use an iron tool on the stones; build the Altar to GOD, your God, with uncut stones and offer your Whole-Burnt-Offerings on it to GOD, your God. When you sacrifice your Peace-Offerings you will also eat them there, rejoicing in the Presence of GOD, your God.

8 Write all the words of this Revelation on the stones. Incise them sharply.

9-10 Moses and the Levitical priests addressed all Israel: Quiet. Listen obediently, Israel. This very day you have become the people of GOD, your God. Listen to the Voice of GOD, your God. Keep his commandments and regulations that I'm commanding you today.

11-13 That day Moses commanded: After you've crossed the Jordan, these tribes will stand on Mount Gerizim to bless the people: Simeon, Levi, Judah, Issachar, Joseph, and Benjamin. And these will stand on Mount Ebal for the curse: Reuben, Gad, Asher, Zebulun, Dan, and Naphtali.

14-26 The Levites, acting as spokesmen and speaking loudly, will address Israel:

GOD's curse on anyone who carves or
casts a god-image—an abomination to
GOD made by a craftsman—and sets it up
in secret.
All respond: *Yes. Absolutely.*
GOD's curse on anyone who demeans a
parent.
All respond: *Yes. Absolutely.*
GOD's curse on anyone who moves his
neighbor's boundary marker.
All respond: *Yes. Absolutely.*
GOD's curse on anyone who misdirects a
blind man on the road.
All respond: *Yes. Absolutely.*
GOD's curse on anyone who interferes
with justice due the foreigner, orphan, or
widow.
All respond: *Yes. Absolutely.*
GOD's curse on anyone who has sex with
his father's wife; he has violated the
woman who belongs to his father.
All respond: *Yes. Absolutely.*
GOD's curse on anyone who has sex with
an animal.

NEW KING JAMES VERSION

"And all the people shall say, 'Amen!'
22'Cursed *is* the one who lies with his sister,
the daughter of his father or the daughter of his
mother.'
"And all the people shall say, 'Amen!'
23'Cursed *is* the one who lies with his mother-
in-law.'
"And all the people shall say, 'Amen!'
24'Cursed *is* the one who attacks his neigh-
bor secretly.'
"And all the people shall say, 'Amen!'
25'Cursed *is* the one who takes a bribe to slay
an innocent person.'
"And all the people shall say, 'Amen!'
26'Cursed *is* the one who does not confirm *all*
the words of this law by observing them.'
"And all the people shall say, 'Amen!' "

BLESSINGS ON OBEDIENCE

28 "Now it shall come to pass, if you dili-
gently obey the voice of the LORD your
God, to observe carefully all His command-
ments which I command you today, that the
LORD your God will set you high above all na-
tions of the earth. 2And all these blessings shall
come upon you and overtake you, because you
obey the voice of the LORD your God:
3"Blessed *shall* you *be* in the city, and blessed
shall you *be* in the country.
4"Blessed *shall be* the fruit of your body, the
produce of your ground and the increase of your
herds, the increase of your cattle and the off-
spring of your flocks.
5"Blessed *shall be* your basket and your
kneading bowl.
6"Blessed *shall* you *be* when you come in,
and blessed *shall* you *be* when you go out.
7"The LORD will cause your enemies who rise
against you to be defeated before your face;
they shall come out against you one way and
flee before you seven ways.
8"The LORD will command the blessing on
you in your storehouses and in all to which you
set your hand, and He will bless you in the land
which the LORD your God is giving you.
9"The LORD will establish you as a holy peo-
ple to Himself, just as He has sworn to you, if
you keep the commandments of the LORD your
God and walk in His ways. 10Then all peoples of
the earth shall see that you are called by the
name of the LORD, and they shall be afraid of
you. 11And the LORD will grant you plenty of
goods, in the fruit of your body, in the increase
of your livestock, and in the produce of your
ground, in the land of which the LORD swore to
your fathers to give you. 12The LORD will open to
you His good treasure, the heavens, to give the
rain to your land in its season, and to bless all
the work of your hand. You shall lend to many
nations, but you shall not borrow. 13And the
LORD will make you the head and not the tail;
you shall be above only, and not be beneath, if
you heed the commandments of the LORD your
God, which I command you today, and are care-

THE MESSAGE

All respond: *Yes. Absolutely.*
GOD's curse on anyone who has sex with his sister, the daughter of his father or mother.
All respond: *Yes. Absolutely.*
GOD's curse on anyone who has sex with his mother-in-law.
All respond: *Yes. Absolutely.*
GOD's curse on anyone who kills his neighbor in secret.
All respond: *Yes. Absolutely.*
GOD's curse on anyone who takes a bribe to kill an innocent person.
All respond: *Yes. Absolutely.*
GOD's curse on whoever does not give substance to the words of this Revelation by living them.
All respond: *Yes. Absolutely.*

1-6 28 If you listen obediently to the Voice of GOD, your God, and heartily obey all his commandments that I command you today, GOD, your God, will place you on high, high above all the nations of the world. All these blessings will come down on you and spread out beyond you because you have responded to the Voice of GOD, your God:

GOD's blessing inside the city,
GOD's blessing in the country;
GOD's blessing on your children,
the crops of your land,
the young of your livestock,
the calves of your herds,
the lambs of your flocks.
GOD's blessing on your basket and bread bowl;
GOD's blessing in your coming in,
GOD's blessing in your going out.

7 GOD will defeat your enemies who attack you. They'll come at you on one road and run away on seven roads.
8 GOD will order a blessing on your barns and workplaces; he'll bless you in the land that GOD, your God, is giving you.
9 GOD will form you as a people holy to him, just as he promised you, if you keep the commandments of GOD, your God, and live the way he has shown you.

10 All the peoples on Earth will see you living under the Name of GOD and hold you in respectful awe.
11-14 GOD will lavish you with good things: children from your womb, offspring from your animals, and crops from your land, the land that GOD promised your ancestors that he would give you. GOD will throw open the doors of his sky vaults and pour rain on your land on schedule and bless the work you take in hand. You will lend to many nations but you yourself won't have to take out a loan. GOD will make you the head, not the tail; you'll always be the top dog, never the bottom dog, as you obediently listen to and diligently keep the commands of GOD, your God, that I am commanding you today.

New King James Version

ful to observe *them.* 14So you shall not turn
aside from any of the words which I command
you this day, *to* the right or the left, to go after
other gods to serve them.

Curses on Disobedience

15"But it shall come to pass, if you do not
obey the voice of the LORD your God, to observe
carefully all His commandments and His
statutes which I command you today, that all
these curses will come upon you and overtake
you:
16"Cursed *shall* you *be* in the city, and cursed
shall you *be* in the country.
17"Cursed *shall be* your basket and your
kneading bowl.
18"Cursed *shall be* the fruit of your body and
the produce of your land, the increase of your
cattle and the offspring of your flocks.
19"Cursed *shall* you *be* when you come in,
and cursed *shall* you *be* when you go out.
20"The LORD will send on you cursing, confu-
sion, and rebuke in all that you set your hand to
do, until you are destroyed and until you perish
quickly, because of the wickedness of your do-
ings in which you have forsaken Me. 21The LORD
will make the plague cling to you until He has
consumed you from the land which you are go-
ing to possess. 22The LORD will strike you with
consumption, with fever, with inflammation,
with severe burning fever, with the sword, with
scorching, and with mildew; they shall pursue
you until you perish. 23And your heavens which
are over your head shall be bronze, and the
earth which is under you *shall be* iron. 24The
LORD will change the rain of your land to pow-
der and dust; from the heaven it shall come
down on you until you are destroyed.
25"The LORD will cause you to be defeated be-
fore your enemies; you shall go out one way
against them and flee seven ways before them;
and you shall become troublesome to all the
kingdoms of the earth. 26Your carcasses shall be
food for all the birds of the air and the beasts of
the earth, and no one shall frighten *them* away.
27The LORD will strike you with the boils of
Egypt, with tumors, with the scab, and with the
itch, from which you cannot be healed. 28The
LORD will strike you with madness and blind-
ness and confusion of heart. 29And you shall
grope at noonday, as a blind man gropes in
darkness; you shall not prosper in your ways;
you shall be only oppressed and plundered con-
tinually, and no one shall save *you.*
30"You shall betroth a wife, but another man
shall lie with her; you shall build a house, but
you shall not dwell in it; you shall plant a vine-
yard, but shall not gather its grapes. 31Your ox
shall be slaughtered before your eyes, but you
shall not eat of it; your donkey *shall be* violently
taken away from before you, and shall not be re-
stored to you; your sheep *shall be* given to your
enemies, and you shall have no one to rescue
them.

The Message

Don't swerve an inch to the right or left from the words that I command you today by going off following and worshiping other gods.

15-19 Here's what will happen if you don't obediently listen to the Voice of GOD, your God, and diligently keep all the commandments and guidelines that I'm commanding you today. All these curses will come down hard on you:

GOD's curse in the city,
GOD's curse in the country;
GOD's curse on your basket and bread
  bowl;
GOD's curse on your children,
  the crops of your land,
  the young of your livestock,
  the calves of your herds,
  the lambs of your flocks.
GOD's curse in your coming in,
GOD's curse in your going out.

20 GOD will send The Curse, The Confusion, The Contrariness down on everything you try to do until you've been destroyed and there's nothing left of you—all because of your evil pursuits that led you to abandon me.

21 GOD will infect you with The Disease, wiping you right off the land that you're going in to possess.

22 GOD will set consumption and fever and rash and seizures and dehydration and blight and jaundice on you. They'll hunt you down until they kill you.

23-24 The sky over your head will become an iron roof, the ground under your feet, a slab of concrete. From out of the skies GOD will rain ash and dust down on you until you suffocate.

25-26 GOD will defeat you by enemy attack. You'll come at your enemies on one road and run away on seven roads. All the kingdoms of Earth will see you as a horror. Carrion birds and animals will boldly feast on your dead body with no one to chase them away.

27-29 GOD will hit you hard with the boils of Egypt, hemorrhoids, scabs, and an incurable itch. He'll make you go crazy and blind and senile. You'll grope around in the middle of the day like a blind person feeling his way through a lifetime of darkness; you'll never get to where you're going. Not a day will go by that you're not abused and robbed. And no one is going to help you.

30-31 You'll get engaged to a woman and another man will take her for his mistress; you'll build a house and never live in it; you'll plant a garden and never eat so much as a carrot; you'll watch your ox get butchered and not get a single steak from it; your donkey will be stolen from in front of you and you'll never see it again; your sheep will be sent off to your enemies and no one will lift a hand to help you.

New King James Version

32 Your sons and your daughters *shall be* given to
another people, and your eyes shall look and
fail *with longing* for them all day long; and
there shall be no strength in your hand. 33 A na-
tion whom you have not known shall eat the
fruit of your land and the produce of your labor,
and you shall be only oppressed and crushed
continually. 34 So you shall be driven mad be-
cause of the sight which your eyes see. 35 The
LORD will strike you in the knees and on the legs
with severe boils which cannot be healed, and
from the sole of your foot to the top of your
head.

36 "The LORD will bring you and the king
whom you set over you to a nation which nei-
ther you nor your fathers have known, and there
you shall serve other gods—wood and stone.
37 And you shall become an astonishment, a
proverb, and a byword among all nations where
the LORD will drive you.

38 "You shall carry much seed out to the field
but gather little in, for the locust shall consume
it. 39 You shall plant vineyards and tend *them*,
but you shall neither drink *of* the wine nor
gather the *grapes;* for the worms shall eat them.
40 You shall have olive trees throughout all your
territory, but you shall not anoint *yourself* with
the oil; for your olives shall drop off. 41 You shall
beget sons and daughters, but they shall not be
yours; for they shall go into captivity. 42 Locusts
shall consume all your trees and the produce of
your land.

43 "The alien who *is* among you shall rise
higher and higher above you, and you shall
come down lower and lower. 44 He shall lend to
you, but you shall not lend to him; he shall be
the head, and you shall be the tail.

45 "Moreover all these curses shall come upon
you and pursue and overtake you, until you are
destroyed, because you did not obey the voice of
the LORD your God, to keep His commandments
and His statutes which He commanded you.
46 And they shall be upon you for a sign and a
wonder, and on your descendants forever.

47 "Because you did not serve the LORD your
God with joy and gladness of heart, for the
abundance of everything, 48 therefore you shall
serve your enemies, whom the LORD will send
against you, in hunger, in thirst, in nakedness,
and in need of everything; and He will put a
yoke of iron on your neck until He has de-
stroyed you. 49 The LORD will bring a nation
against you from afar, from the end of the earth,
as swift as the eagle flies, a nation whose lan-
guage you will not understand, 50 a nation of
fierce countenance, which does not respect the
elderly nor show favor to the young. 51 And they
shall eat the increase of your livestock and the
produce of your land, until you are destroyed;
they shall not leave you grain or new wine or
oil, *or* the increase of your cattle or the offspring
of your flocks, until they have destroyed you.

52 "They shall besiege you at all your gates
until your high and fortified walls, in which you
trust, come down throughout all your land; and
they shall besiege you at all your gates through-
out all your land which the LORD your God has
given you.

The Message

32-34 Your sons and daughters will be shipped off to foreigners; you'll wear your eyes out looking vainly for them, helpless to do a thing. Your crops and everything you work for will be eaten and used by foreigners; you'll spend the rest of your lives abused and knocked around. What you see will drive you crazy.

35 GOD will hit you with painful boils on your knees and legs and no healing or relief from head to foot.

36-37 GOD will lead you and the king you set over you to a country neither you nor your ancestors have heard of; there you'll worship other gods, no-gods of wood and stone. Among all the peoples where GOD will take you, you'll be treated as a lesson or a proverb—a horror!

38-42 You'll plant sacks and sacks of seed in the field but get almost nothing—the grasshoppers will devour it. You'll plant and hoe and prune vineyards but won't drink or put up any wine—the worms will devour them. You'll have groves of olive trees everywhere, but you'll have no oil to rub on your face or hands—the olives will have fallen off. You'll have sons and daughters but they won't be yours for long—they'll go off to captivity. Locusts will take over all your trees and crops.

43-44 The foreigner who lives among you will climb the ladder, higher and higher, while you go deeper and deeper into the hole. He'll lend to you; you won't lend to him. He'll be the head; you'll be the tail.

45-46 All these curses are going to come on you. They're going to hunt you down and get you until there's nothing left of you because you didn't obediently listen to the Voice of GOD, your God, and diligently keep his commandments and guidelines that I commanded you. The curses will serve as signposts, warnings to your children ever after.

47-48 Because you didn't serve GOD, your God, out of the joy and goodness of your heart in the great abundance, you'll have to serve your enemies whom GOD will send against you. Life will be famine and drought, rags and wretchedness; then he'll put an iron yoke on your neck until he's destroyed you.

48-52 Yes, GOD will raise up a faraway nation against you, swooping down on you like an eagle, a nation whose language you can't understand, a mean-faced people, cruel to grandmothers and babies alike. They'll ravage the young of your animals and the crops from your fields until you're destroyed. They'll leave nothing behind: no grain, no wine, no oil, no calves, no lambs—and finally, no *you*. They'll lay siege to you while you're huddled behind your town gates. They'll knock those high, proud walls flat, those walls behind which you felt so safe. They'll lay siege to your fortified cities all over the country, this country that GOD, your God, has given you.

NEW KING JAMES VERSION

53You shall eat the fruit of your own body, the flesh of your sons and your daughters whom the LORD your God has given you, in the siege and desperate straits in which your enemy shall distress you. 54The sensitive and very refined man among you will be hostile toward his brother, toward the wife of his bosom, and toward the rest of his children whom he leaves behind, 55so that he will not give any of them the flesh of his children whom he will eat, because he has nothing left in the siege and desperate straits in which your enemy shall distress you at all your gates. 56The tender and delicate woman among you, who would not venture to set the sole of her foot on the ground because of her delicateness and sensitivity, will refuse[a] to the husband of her bosom, and to her son and her daughter, 57her placenta which comes out from between her feet and her children whom she bears; for she will eat them secretly for lack of everything in the siege and desperate straits in which your enemy shall distress you at all your gates.

58"If you do not carefully observe all the words of this law that are written in this book, that you may fear this glorious and awesome name, THE LORD YOUR GOD, 59then the LORD will bring upon you and your descendants extraordinary plagues—great and prolonged plagues—and serious and prolonged sicknesses. 60Moreover He will bring back on you all the diseases of Egypt, of which you were afraid, and they shall cling to you. 61Also every sickness and every plague, which *is* not written in this Book of the Law, will the LORD bring upon you until you are destroyed. 62You shall be left few in number, whereas you were as the stars of heaven in multitude, because you would not obey the voice of the LORD your God. 63And it shall be, *that* just as the LORD rejoiced over you to do you good and multiply you, so the LORD will rejoice over you to destroy you and bring you to nothing; and you shall be plucked from off the land which you go to possess.

64"Then the LORD will scatter you among all peoples, from one end of the earth to the other, and there you shall serve other gods, which neither you nor your fathers have known—wood and stone. 65And among those nations you shall find no rest, nor shall the sole of your foot have a resting place; but there the LORD will give you a trembling heart, failing eyes, and anguish of soul. 66Your life shall hang in doubt before you; you shall fear day and night, and have no assurance of life. 67In the morning you shall say, 'Oh, that it were evening!' And at evening you shall say, 'Oh, that it were morning!' because of the fear which terrifies your heart, and because of the sight which your eyes see.

68"And the LORD will take you back to Egypt in ships, by the way of which I said to you, 'You shall never see it again.' And there you shall be offered for sale to your enemies as male and female slaves, but no one will buy *you*."

28:56 [a]Literally *her eye shall be evil toward*

THE MESSAGE

53-55 And you'll end up cannibalizing your own sons and daughters that GOD, your God, has given you. When the suffering from the siege gets extreme, you're going to eat your own babies. The most gentle and caring man among you will turn hard, his eye evil, against his own brother, his cherished wife, and even the rest of his children who are still alive, refusing to share with them a scrap of meat from the cannibal child-stew he is eating. He's lost everything, even his humanity, in the suffering of the siege that your enemy mounts against your fortified towns.

56-57 And the most gentle and caring woman among you, a woman who wouldn't step on a wildflower, will turn hard, her eye evil, against her cherished husband, against her son, against her daughter, against even the afterbirth of her newborn infants; she plans to eat them in secret—she does eat them!—because she has lost everything, even her humanity, in the suffering of the siege that your enemy mounts against your fortified towns.

58-61 If you don't diligently keep all the words of this Revelation written in this book, living in holy awe before This Name glorious and terrible, GOD, your God, then GOD will pound you with catastrophes, you and your children, huge interminable catastrophes, hideous interminable illnesses. He'll bring back and stick you with every old Egyptian malady that once terrorized you. And yes, every disease and catastrophe imaginable—things not even written in the Book of this Revelation—GOD will bring on you until you're destroyed.

62 Because you didn't listen obediently to the Voice of GOD, your God, you'll be left with a few pitiful stragglers in place of the dazzling stars-in-the-heavens multitude you had become.

63-66 And this is how things will end up: Just as GOD once enjoyed you, took pleasure in making life good for you, giving you many children, so GOD will enjoy getting rid of you, clearing you off the Earth. He'll weed you out of the very soil that you are entering in to possess. He'll scatter you to the four winds, from one end of the Earth to the other. You'll worship all kinds of other gods, gods neither you nor your parents ever heard of, wood and stone no-gods. But you won't find a home there, you'll not be able to settle down. GOD will give you a restless heart, longing eyes, a homesick soul. You will live in constant jeopardy, terrified of every shadow, never knowing what you'll meet around the next corner.

67 In the morning you'll say, "I wish it were evening." In the evening you'll say, "I wish it were morning." Afraid, terrorized at what's coming next, afraid of the unknown, because of the sights you've witnessed.

68 GOD will ship you back to Egypt by a road I promised you'd never see again. There you'll offer yourselves for sale, both men and women, as slaves to your enemies. And not a buyer to be found.

New King James Version

The Covenant Renewed in Moab

29 These *are* the words of the covenant which the LORD commanded Moses to make with the children of Israel in the land of Moab, besides the covenant which He made with them in Horeb.

2Now Moses called all Israel and said to them: "You have seen all that the LORD did before your eyes in the land of Egypt, to Pharaoh and to all his servants and to all his land— 3the great trials which your eyes have seen, the signs, and those great wonders. 4Yet the LORD has not given you a heart to perceive and eyes to see and ears to hear, to this *very* day. 5And I have led you forty years in the wilderness. Your clothes have not worn out on you, and your sandals have not worn out on your feet. 6You have not eaten bread, nor have you drunk wine or *similar* drink, that you may know that I *am* the LORD your God. 7And when you came to this place, Sihon king of Heshbon and Og king of Bashan came out against us to battle, and we conquered them. 8We took their land and gave it as an inheritance to the Reubenites, to the Gadites, and to half the tribe of Manasseh. 9Therefore keep the words of this covenant, and do them, that you may prosper in all that you do.

10"All of you stand today before the LORD your God: your leaders and your tribes and your elders and your officers, all the men of Israel, 11your little ones and your wives—also the stranger who *is* in your camp, from the one who cuts your wood to the one who draws your water— 12that you may enter into covenant with the LORD your God, and into His oath, which the LORD your God makes with you today, 13that He may establish you today as a people for Himself, and *that* He may be God to you, just as He has spoken to you, and just as He has sworn to your fathers, to Abraham, Isaac, and Jacob.

14"I make this covenant and this oath, not with you alone, 15but with *him* who stands here with us today before the LORD our God, as well as with *him* who *is* not here with us today 16(for you know that we dwelt in the land of Egypt and that we came through the nations which you passed by, 17and you saw their abominations and their idols which *were* among them—wood and stone and silver and gold); 18so that there may not be among you man or woman or family or tribe, whose heart turns away today from the LORD our God, to go *and* serve the gods of these nations, and that there may not be among you a root bearing bitterness or wormwood; 19and so it may not happen, when he hears the words of this curse, that he blesses himself in his heart, saying, 'I shall have peace, even though I follow the dictates[a] of my heart'—as though the drunkard could be included with the sober.

20"The LORD would not spare him; for then the anger of the LORD and His jealousy would burn against that man, and every curse that is written in this book would settle on him, and the LORD would blot out his name from under heaven. 21And the LORD would separate him

29:19 [a]Or *stubbornness*

The Message

1 29 These are the terms of the Covenant that GOD commanded Moses to make with the People of Israel in the land of Moab, renewing the Covenant he made with them at Horeb.

Moses Blesses Israel on the Plains of Moab

2-4 Moses called all Israel together and said, You've seen with your own eyes everything that GOD did in Egypt to Pharaoh and his servants, and to the land itself—the massive trials to which you were eyewitnesses, the great signs and miracle-wonders. But GOD didn't give you an understanding heart or perceptive eyes or attentive ears until right now, this very day.

5-6 I took you through the wilderness for forty years and through all that time the clothes on your backs didn't wear out, the sandals on your feet didn't wear out, and you lived well without bread and wine and beer, proving to you that I am in fact GOD, your God.

7-8 When you arrived here in this place, Sihon king of Heshbon and Og king of Bashan met us primed for war but we beat them. We took their land and gave it as an inheritance to the Reubenites, the Gadites, and the half-tribe of Manasseh.

9 Diligently keep the words of this Covenant. Do what they say so that you will live well and wisely in every detail.

10-13 You are all standing here today in the Presence of GOD, your God—the heads of your tribes, your leaders, your officials, all Israel: your babies, your wives, the resident foreigners in your camps who fetch your firewood and water—ready to cross over into the solemnly sworn Covenant that GOD, your God, is making with you today, the Covenant that this day confirms that you are his people and he is GOD, your God, just as he promised you and your ancestors Abraham, Isaac, and Jacob.

14-21 I'm not making this Covenant and its oath with you alone. I *am* making it with you who are standing here today in the Presence of GOD, our God, yes, but also with those who are not here today. You know the conditions in which we lived in Egypt and how we crisscrossed through nations in our travels. You got an eyeful of their obscenities, their wood and stone, silver and gold junk-gods. Don't let down your guard lest even now, today, someone—man or woman, clan or tribe—gets sidetracked from GOD, our God, and gets involved with the no-gods of the nations; lest some poisonous weed sprout and spread among you, a person who hears the words of the Covenant-oath but exempts himself, thinking, "I'll live just the way I please, thank you," and ends up ruining life for everybody. GOD won't let him off the hook. GOD's anger and jealousy will erupt like a volcano against that person. The curses written in this book will bury him. GOD will delete his name from the records.

NEW KING JAMES VERSION

from all the tribes of Israel for adversity, accord-
ing to all the curses of the covenant that are
written in this Book of the Law, 22so that
the coming generation of your children who rise
up after you, and the foreigner who comes from
a far land, would say, when they see the plagues
of that land and the sicknesses which the LORD
has laid on it:
23'The whole land *is* brimstone, salt, and
burning; it is not sown, nor does it bear, nor
does any grass grow there, like the overthrow of
Sodom and Gomorrah, Admah, and Zeboiim,
which the LORD overthrew in His anger and His
wrath.' 24All nations would say, 'Why has the
LORD done so to this land? What does the heat of
this great anger mean?' 25Then *people* would
say: 'Because they have forsaken the covenant
of the LORD God of their fathers, which He made
with them when He brought them out of the
land of Egypt; 26for they went and served other
gods and worshiped them, gods that they did
not know and that He had not given to them.
27Then the anger of the LORD was aroused
against this land, to bring on it every curse that
is written in this book. 28And the LORD uprooted
them from their land in anger, in wrath, and in
great indignation, and cast them into another
land, as *it is* this day.'
29"The secret *things belong* to the LORD our
God, but those *things which are* revealed *belong*
to us and to our children forever, that *we* may do
all the words of this law.

THE BLESSING OF RETURNING TO GOD

30 "Now it shall come to pass, when all these
things come upon you, the blessing and
the curse which I have set before you, and you
call *them* to mind among all the nations where
the LORD your God drives you, 2and you return
to the LORD your God and obey His voice, ac-
cording to all that I command you today, you
and your children, with all your heart and with
all your soul, 3that the LORD your God will bring
you back from captivity, and have compassion
on you, and gather you again from all the na-
tions where the LORD your God has scattered
you. 4If *any* of you are driven out to the farthest
parts under heaven, from there the LORD your
God will gather you, and from there He will
bring you. 5Then the LORD your God will bring
you to the land which your fathers possessed,
and you shall possess it. He will prosper you
and multiply you more than your fathers. 6And
the LORD your God will circumcise your heart
and the heart of your descendants, to love the
LORD your God with all your heart and with all
your soul, that you may live.
7"Also the LORD your God will put all these
curses on your enemies and on those who hate
you, who persecuted you. 8And you will again
obey the voice of the LORD and do all His com-
mandments which I command you today. 9The
LORD your God will make you abound in all the
work of your hand, in the fruit of your body, in
the increase of your livestock, and in the pro-
duce of your land for good. For the LORD will
again rejoice over you for good as He rejoiced

THE MESSAGE

GOD will separate him out from all the tribes
of Israel for special punishment, according
to all the curses of the Covenant written in
this Book of Revelation.
22-23 The next generation, your children who
come after you and the foreigner who
comes from a far country, will be appalled
when they see the widespread devastation,
how GOD made the whole land sick. They'll
see a fire-blackened wasteland of brimstone
and salt flats, nothing planted, nothing
growing, not so much as a blade of grass
anywhere—like the overthrow of Sodom
and Gomorrah, Admah and Zeboiim, which
GOD overthrew in fiery rage.
24 All the nations will ask, "Why did GOD do
this to this country? What on earth could
have made him this angry?"
25-28 Your children will answer, "Because they
abandoned the Covenant of the GOD of their
ancestors that he made with them after he
got them out of Egypt; they went off and
worshiped other gods, submitted to gods
they'd never heard of before, gods they had
no business dealing with. So GOD's anger
erupted against that land and all the curses
written in this book came down on it. GOD,
furiously angry, pulled them, roots and all,
out of their land and dumped them in an-
other country, as you can see."
29 GOD, our God, will take care of the hidden
things but the revealed things are our busi-
ness. It's up to us and our children to attend
to all the terms in this Revelation.

1-5 30 Here's what will happen. While you're
out among the nations where GOD has
dispersed you and the blessings and curses
come in just the way I have set them before
you, and you and your children take them
seriously and come back to GOD, your God,
and obey him with your whole heart and
soul according to everything that I com-
mand you today, GOD, your God, will restore
everything you lost; he'll have compassion
on you; he'll come back and pick up the
pieces from all the places where you were
scattered. No matter how far away you end
up, GOD, your God, will get you out of there
and bring you back to the land your ances-
tors once possessed. It will be yours again.
He will give you a good life and make you
more numerous than your ancestors.
6-7 GOD, your God, will cut away the thick
calluses on your heart and your children's
hearts, freeing you to love GOD, your God,
with your whole heart and soul and live, re-
ally live. GOD, your God, will put all these
curses on your enemies who hated you and
were out to get you.
8-9 And you will make a new start, listening
obediently to GOD, keeping all his com-
mandments that I'm commanding you to-
day. GOD, your God, will outdo himself in
making things go well for you: you'll have
babies, get calves, grow crops, and enjoy an
all-around good life. Yes, GOD will start en-
joying you again, making things go well for

New King James Version

over your fathers, 10 if you obey the voice of the LORD your God, to keep His commandments and His statutes which are written in this Book of the Law, *and* if you turn to the LORD your God with all your heart and with all your soul.

The Choice of Life or Death

11 "For this commandment which I command you today *is* not *too* mysterious for you, nor *is* it far off. 12 It *is* not in heaven, that you should say, 'Who will ascend into heaven for us and bring it to us, that we may hear it and do it?' 13 Nor *is* it beyond the sea, that you should say, 'Who will go over the sea for us and bring it to us, that we may hear it and do it?' 14 But the word *is* very near you, in your mouth and in your heart, that you may do it.

15 "See, I have set before you today life and good, death and evil, 16 in that I command you today to love the LORD your God, to walk in His ways, and to keep His commandments, His statutes, and His judgments, that you may live and multiply; and the LORD your God will bless you in the land which you go to possess. 17 But if your heart turns away so that you do not hear, and are drawn away, and worship other gods and serve them, 18 I announce to you today that you shall surely perish; you shall not prolong *your* days in the land which you cross over the Jordan to go in and possess. 19 I call heaven and earth as witnesses today against you, *that* I have set before you life and death, blessing and cursing; therefore choose life, that both you and your descendants may live; 20 that you may love the LORD your God, that you may obey His voice, and that you may cling to Him, for He *is* your life and the length of your days; and that you may dwell in the land which the LORD swore to your fathers, to Abraham, Isaac, and Jacob, to give them."

Joshua the New Leader of Israel

31 Then Moses went and spoke these words to all Israel. 2 And he said to them: "I *am* one hundred and twenty years old today. I can no longer go out and come in. Also the LORD has said to me, 'You shall not cross over this Jordan.' 3 The LORD your God Himself crosses over before you; He will destroy these nations from before you, and you shall dispossess them. Joshua himself crosses over before you, just as the LORD has said. 4 And the LORD will do to them as He did to Sihon and Og, the kings of the Amorites and their land, when He destroyed them. 5 The LORD will give them over to you, that you may do to them according to every commandment which I have commanded you. 6 Be strong and of good courage, do not fear nor be afraid of them; for the LORD your God, He *is* the One who goes with you. He will not leave you nor forsake you."

The Message

you just as he enjoyed doing it for your ancestors.

10 But only if you listen obediently to GOD,
your God, and keep the commandments and
regulations written in this Book of Revelation.
Nothing halfhearted here; you must return
to GOD, your God, totally, heart and
soul, holding nothing back.

11-14 This commandment that I'm commanding
you today isn't too much for you, it's not
out of your reach. It's not on a high mountain—you
don't have to get mountaineers to
climb the peak and bring it down to your
level and explain it before you can live it.
And it's not across the ocean—you don't
have to send sailors out to get it, bring it
back, and then explain it before you can live
it. No. The word is right here and now—as
near as the tongue in your mouth, as near as
the heart in your chest. Just do it!

15 Look at what I've done for you today:
I've placed in front of you
Life and Good
Death and Evil.

16 And I command you today: Love GOD,
your God. Walk in his ways. Keep his commandments,
regulations, and rules so that
you will live, really live, live exuberantly,
blessed by GOD, your God, in the land you
are about to enter and possess.

17-18 But I warn you: If you have a change of
heart, refuse to listen obediently, and willfully
go off to serve and worship other gods,
you will most certainly die. You won't last
long in the land that you are crossing the
Jordan to enter and possess.

19-20 I call Heaven and Earth to witness
against you today: I place before you Life
and Death, Blessing and Curse. Choose life
so that you and your children will live. And
love GOD, your God, listening obediently to
him, firmly embracing him. Oh yes, he is life
itself, a long life settled on the soil that GOD,
your God, promised to give your ancestors,
Abraham, Isaac, and Jacob.

The Charge

1-2 **31** Moses went on and addressed these
words to all Israel. He said, "I'm 120
years old today. I can't get about as I used to.
And GOD told me, 'You're not going to cross
this Jordan River.'

3-5 "GOD, your God, will cross the river
ahead of you and destroy the nations in
your path so that you may dispossess them.
(And Joshua will cross the river before you,
as GOD said he would.) GOD will give the nations
the same treatment he gave the kings
of the Amorites, Sihon and Og, and their
land; he'll destroy them. GOD will hand the
nations over to you, and you'll treat them
exactly as I have commanded you.

6 "Be strong. Take courage. Don't be intimidated.
Don't give them a second thought
because GOD, your God, is striding ahead of
you. He's right there with you. He won't let
you down; he won't leave you."

New King James Version

7 Then Moses called Joshua and said to him in the sight of all Israel, "Be strong and of good courage, for you must go with this people to the land which the LORD has sworn to their fathers to give them, and you shall cause them to inherit it. 8 And the LORD, He *is* the One who goes before you. He will be with you, He will not leave you nor forsake you; do not fear nor be dismayed."

The Law to Be Read Every Seven Years

9 So Moses wrote this law and delivered it to the priests, the sons of Levi, who bore the ark of the covenant of the LORD, and to all the elders of Israel. 10 And Moses commanded them, saying: "At the end of *every* seven years, at the appointed time in the year of release, at the Feast of Tabernacles, 11 when all Israel comes to appear before the LORD your God in the place which He chooses, you shall read this law before all Israel in their hearing. 12 Gather the people together, men and women and little ones, and the stranger who *is* within your gates, that they may hear and that they may learn to fear the LORD your God and carefully observe all the words of this law, 13 and *that* their children, who have not known it, may hear and learn to fear the LORD your God as long as you live in the land which you cross the Jordan to possess."

Prediction of Israel's Rebellion

14 Then the LORD said to Moses, "Behold, the days approach when you must die; call Joshua, and present yourselves in the tabernacle of meeting, that I may inaugurate him."

So Moses and Joshua went and presented themselves in the tabernacle of meeting. 15 Now the LORD appeared at the tabernacle in a pillar of cloud, and the pillar of cloud stood above the door of the tabernacle.

16 And the LORD said to Moses: "Behold, you will rest with your fathers; and this people will rise and play the harlot with the gods of the foreigners of the land, where they go *to be* among them, and they will forsake Me and break My covenant which I have made with them. 17 Then My anger shall be aroused against them in that day, and I will forsake them, and I will hide My face from them, and they shall be devoured. And many evils and troubles shall befall them, so that they will say in that day, 'Have not these evils come upon us because our God *is* not among us?' 18 And I will surely hide My face in that day because of all the evil which they have done, in that they have turned to other gods.

19 "Now therefore, write down this song for yourselves, and teach it to the children of Israel; put it in their mouths, that this song may be a witness for Me against the children of Israel. 20 When I have brought them to the land flowing with milk and honey, of which I swore to their fathers, and they have eaten and filled themselves and grown fat, then they will turn to other gods and serve them; and they will provoke Me and break My covenant. 21 Then it shall be, when many evils and troubles have come upon them, that this song will testify against them as a wit-

The Message

7-8 Then Moses summoned Joshua. He said to him with all Israel watching, "Be strong. Take courage. You will enter the land with this people, this land that GOD promised their ancestors that he'd give them. You will make them the proud possessors of it. GOD is striding ahead of you. He's right there with you. He won't let you down; he won't leave you. Don't be intimidated. Don't worry."

9-13 Moses wrote out this Revelation and gave it to the priests, the sons of Levi, who carried the Chest of the Covenant of GOD, and to all the leaders of Israel. And he gave these orders: "At the end of every seven years, the Year-All-Debts-Are-Canceled, during the pilgrim Festival of Booths when everyone in Israel comes to appear in the Presence of GOD, your God, at the place he designates, read out this Revelation to all Israel, with everyone listening. Gather the people together—men, women, children, and the foreigners living among you—so they can listen well, so they may learn to live in holy awe before GOD, your God, and diligently keep everything in this Revelation. And do this so that their children, who don't yet know all this, will also listen and learn to live in holy awe before GOD, your God, for as long as you live on the land that you are crossing over the Jordan to possess."

14-15 GOD spoke to Moses: "You are about to die. So call Joshua. Meet me in the Tent of Meeting so that I can commission him."

So Moses and Joshua went and stationed themselves in the Tent of Meeting. GOD appeared in the Tent in a Pillar of Cloud. The Cloud was near the entrance of the Tent of Meeting.

16-18 GOD spoke to Moses: "You're about to die and be buried with your ancestors. You'll no sooner be in the grave than this people will be up and whoring after the foreign gods of this country that they are entering. They will abandon me and violate my Covenant that I've made with them. I'll get angry, oh so angry! I'll walk off and leave them on their own, won't so much as look back at them. Then many calamities and disasters will devastate them because they are defenseless. They'll say, 'Isn't it because our God wasn't here that all this evil has come upon us?' But I'll stay out of their lives, keep looking the other way because of all their evil: they took up with other gods!

19-21 "But for right now, copy down this song and teach the People of Israel to sing it by heart. They'll have it then as my witness against them. When I bring them into the land that I promised to their ancestors, a land flowing with milk and honey, and they eat and become full and get fat and then begin fooling around with other gods and worshiping them, and then things start falling apart, many terrible things happening, this song will be there with them as a witness to

NEW KING JAMES VERSION

ness; for it will not be forgotten in the mouths of
their descendants, for I know the inclination of
their behavior today, even before I have brought
them to the land of which I swore *to give them.*"
22 Therefore Moses wrote this song the same
day, and taught it to the children of Israel.
23 Then He inaugurated Joshua the son of Nun,
and said, "Be strong and of good courage; for
you shall bring the children of Israel into the
land of which I swore to them, and I will be with
you."
24 So it was, when Moses had completed writ-
ing the words of this law in a book, when they
were finished, 25 that Moses commanded the
Levites, who bore the ark of the covenant of the
LORD, saying: 26 "Take this Book of the Law, and
put it beside the ark of the covenant of the LORD
your God, that it may be there as a witness
against you; 27 for I know your rebellion and
your stiff neck. *If* today, while I am yet alive with
you, you have been rebellious against the LORD,
then how much more after my death? 28 Gather
to me all the elders of your tribes, and your offi-
cers, that I may speak these words in their hear-
ing and call heaven and earth to witness against
them. 29 For I know that after my death you will
become utterly corrupt, and turn aside from the
way which I have commanded you. And evil will
befall you in the latter days, because you will do
evil in the sight of the LORD, to provoke Him to
anger through the work of your hands."

THE SONG OF MOSES

30 Then Moses spoke in the hearing of all the
assembly of Israel the words of this song until
they were ended:

32 "Give ear, O heavens, and I will speak;
And hear, O earth, the words of my
mouth.
2 Let my teaching drop as the rain,
My speech distill as the dew,
As raindrops on the tender herb,
And as showers on the grass.
3 For I proclaim the name of the LORD:
Ascribe greatness to our God.
4 *He is* the Rock, His work *is* perfect;
For all His ways *are* justice,
A God of truth and without injustice;
Righteous and upright *is* He.

5 "They have corrupted themselves;
They are not His children,
Because of their blemish:
A perverse and crooked generation.
6 Do you thus deal with the LORD,
O foolish and unwise people?
Is He not your Father, *who* bought you?
Has He not made you and established you?

THE MESSAGE

who they are and what went wrong. Their
children won't forget this song; they'll be
singing it. Don't think I don't know what
they are already scheming to do, and they're
not even in the land yet, this land I promised
them."

22 So Moses wrote down this song that very
day and taught it to the People of Israel.

23 Then GOD commanded Joshua son of
Nun saying, "Be strong. Take courage. You
will lead the People of Israel into the land I
promised to give them. And I'll be right
there with you."

24-26 After Moses had finished writing down
the words of this Revelation in a book, right
down to the last word, he ordered the
Levites who were responsible for carrying
the Chest of the Covenant of GOD, saying,
"Take this Book of Revelation and place it
alongside the Chest of the Covenant of GOD,
your God. Keep it there as a witness.

27-29 "I know what rebels you are, how stub-
born and willful you can be. Even today,
while I'm still alive and present with you,
you're rebellious against GOD. How much
worse when I've died! So gather the leaders
of the tribes and the officials here. I have
something I need to say directly to them
with Heaven and Earth as witnesses. I know
that after I die you're going to make a mess
of things, abandoning the way I com-
manded, inviting all kinds of evil conse-
quences in the days ahead. You're deter-
mined to do evil in defiance of GOD—I know
you are—deliberately provoking his anger
by what you do."

30 So with everyone in Israel gathered and
listening, Moses taught them the words of
this song, from start to finish.

THE SONG

1-5 **32** Listen, Heavens, I have something to
tell you.
Attention, Earth, I've got a mouth full of
words.
My teaching, let it fall like a gentle rain,
my words arrive like morning dew,
Like a sprinkling rain on new grass,
like spring showers on the garden.
For it's GOD's Name I'm preaching—
respond to the greatness of our God!
The Rock: His works are perfect,
and the way he works is fair and just;
A God you can depend upon, no
exceptions,
a straight-arrow God.
His messed-up, mixed-up children, his
non-children,
throw mud at him but none of it sticks.

6-7 Don't you realize it is GOD you are
treating like this?
This is crazy; don't you have any sense
of reverence?
Isn't this your father who created you,
who made you and gave you a place
on Earth?

NEW KING JAMES VERSION

7"Remember the days of old,
Consider the years of many generations.
Ask your father, and he will show you;
Your elders, and they will tell you:
8When the Most High divided their
inheritance to the nations,
When He separated the sons of Adam,
He set the boundaries of the peoples
According to the number of the children of
Israel.
9For the LORD's portion *is* His people;
Jacob *is* the place of His inheritance.

10"He found him in a desert land
And in the wasteland, a howling wilderness;
He encircled him, He instructed him,
He kept him as the apple of His eye.
11As an eagle stirs up its nest,
Hovers over its young,
Spreading out its wings, taking them up,
Carrying them on its wings,
12*So* the LORD alone led him,
And *there was* no foreign god with him.

13"He made him ride in the heights of the
earth,
That he might eat the produce of the fields;
He made him draw honey from the rock,
And oil from the flinty rock;
14Curds from the cattle, and milk of the flock,
With fat of lambs;
And rams of the breed of Bashan, and goats,
With the choicest wheat;
And you drank wine, the blood of the
grapes.

15"But Jeshurun grew fat and kicked;
You grew fat, you grew thick,
You are obese!
Then he forsook God *who* made him,
And scornfully esteemed the Rock of his
salvation.
16They provoked Him to jealousy with foreign
gods;
With abominations they provoked Him to
anger.
17They sacrificed to demons, not to God,
To gods they did not know,
To new *gods,* new arrivals
That your fathers did not fear.
18Of the Rock *who* begot you, you are
unmindful,
And have forgotten the God who fathered
you.

19"And when the LORD saw *it,* He spurned
them,
Because of the provocation of His sons and
His daughters.
20And He said: 'I will hide My face from them,

THE MESSAGE

Read up on what happened before you
were born;
dig into the past, understand your
roots.
Ask your parents what it was like before
you were born;
ask the old-ones, they'll tell you a
thing or two.

8-9 When the High God gave the nations
their stake,
gave them their place on Earth,
He put each of the peoples within
boundaries
under the care of divine guardians.
But GOD himself took charge of his
people,
took Jacob on as his personal concern.

10-14 He found him out in the wilderness,
in an empty, windswept wasteland.
He threw his arms around him, lavished
attention on him,
guarding him as the apple of his eye.
He was like an eagle hovering over its
nest,
overshadowing its young,
Then spreading its wings, lifting them
into the air,
teaching them to fly.
GOD alone led him;
there was not a foreign god in sight.
GOD lifted him onto the hilltops,
so he could feast on the crops in the
fields.
He fed him honey from the rock,
oil from granite crags,
Curds of cattle and the milk of sheep,
the choice cuts of lambs and goats,
Fine Bashan rams, high-quality wheat,
and the blood of grapes: you drank
good wine!

15-18 Jeshurun put on weight and bucked;
you got fat, became obese, a tub of
lard.
He abandoned the God who made him,
he mocked the Rock of his salvation.
They made him jealous with their
foreign newfangled gods,
and with obscenities they vexed him
no end.
They sacrificed to no-god demons,
gods they knew nothing about,
The latest in gods, fresh from the
market,
gods your ancestors would never call
"gods."
You walked out on the Rock who gave
you your life,
forgot the birth-God who brought you
into the world.

19-25 GOD saw it and turned on his heel,
angered and hurt by his sons and
daughters.
He said, "From now on I'm looking the
other way.

NEW KING JAMES VERSION

I will see what their end *will be*,
For they *are* a perverse generation,
Children in whom *is* no faith.
21 They have provoked Me to jealousy by *what* is not God;
They have moved Me to anger by their foolish idols.
But I will provoke them to jealousy by *those who are* not a nation;
I will move them to anger by a foolish nation.
22 For a fire is kindled in My anger,
And shall burn to the lowest hell;
It shall consume the earth with her increase,
And set on fire the foundations of the mountains.

23 'I will heap disasters on them;
I will spend My arrows on them.
24 *They shall be* wasted with hunger,
Devoured by pestilence and bitter destruction;
I will also send against them the teeth of beasts,
With the poison of serpents of the dust.
25 The sword shall destroy outside;
There shall be terror within
For the young man and virgin,
The nursing child with the man of gray hairs.
26 I would have said, "I will dash them in pieces,
I will make the memory of them to cease from among men,"
27 Had I not feared the wrath of the enemy,
Lest their adversaries should misunderstand,
Lest they should say, "Our hand *is* high;
And it is not the LORD who has done all this." '

28 "For they *are* a nation void of counsel,
Nor *is there any* understanding in them.
29 Oh, that they were wise, *that* they understood this,
That they would consider their latter end!
30 How could one chase a thousand,
And two put ten thousand to flight,
Unless their Rock had sold them,
And the LORD had surrendered them?
31 For their rock *is* not like our Rock,
Even our enemies themselves *being* judges.
32 For their vine *is* of the vine of Sodom
And of the fields of Gomorrah;
Their grapes *are* grapes of gall,
Their clusters *are* bitter.
33 Their wine *is* the poison of serpents,
And the cruel venom of cobras.

34 '*Is* this not laid up in store with Me,
Sealed up among My treasures?
35 Vengeance is Mine, and recompense;
Their foot shall slip in *due* time;

THE MESSAGE

Wait and see what happens to them.
Oh, they're a turned-around, upside-down generation!
Who knows what they'll do from one moment to the next?
They've goaded me with their no-gods,
infuriated me with their hot-air gods;
I'm going to goad them with a no-people,
with a hollow nation incense them.
My anger started a fire,
a wildfire burning deep down in Sheol,
Then shooting up and devouring the Earth and its crops,
setting all the mountains, from bottom to top, on fire.
I'll pile catastrophes on them,
I'll shoot my arrows at them:
Starvation, blistering heat, killing disease;
I'll send snarling wild animals to attack from the forest
and venomous creatures to strike from the dust.
Killing in the streets,
terror in the houses,
Young men and virgins alike struck down,
and yes, breast-feeding babies and gray-haired old men."

26-27 I could have said, "I'll hack them to pieces,
wipe out all trace of them from the Earth,"
Except that I feared the enemy would grab the chance
to take credit for all of it,
Crowing, "Look what we did!
GOD had nothing to do with this."

28-33 They are a nation of ninnies,
they don't know enough to come in out of the rain.
If they had any sense at all, they'd know this;
they would see what's coming down the road.
How could one soldier chase a thousand enemies off,
or two men run off two thousand,
Unless their Rock had sold them,
unless GOD had given them away?
For their rock is nothing compared to our Rock;
even our enemies say that.
They're a vine that comes right out of Sodom,
who they are is rooted in Gomorrah;
Their grapes are poison grapes,
their grape-clusters bitter.
Their wine is rattlesnake venom,
mixed with lethal cobra poison.

34-35 Don't you realize that I have my shelves well stocked, locked behind iron doors?
I'm in charge of vengeance and payback,
just waiting for them to slip up;

NEW KING JAMES VERSION

For the day of their calamity *is* at hand,
And the things to come hasten upon them.’

36“For the LORD will judge His people
And have compassion on His servants,
When He sees that *their* power is gone,
And *there is* no one *remaining*, bond or free.
37He will say: ‘Where *are* their gods,
The rock in which they sought refuge?
38Who ate the fat of their sacrifices,
And drank the wine of their drink offering?
Let them rise and help you,
And be your refuge.

39‘Now see that I, *even* I, *am* He,
And *there is* no God besides Me;
I kill and I make alive;
I wound and I heal;
Nor *is there any* who can deliver from My hand.
40For I raise My hand to heaven,
And say, “*As* I live forever,
41If I whet My glittering sword,
And My hand takes hold on judgment,
I will render vengeance to My enemies,
And repay those who hate Me.
42I will make My arrows drunk with blood,
And My sword shall devour flesh,
With the blood of the slain and the captives,
From the heads of the leaders of the enemy.” ’

43“Rejoice, O Gentiles, *with* His people;[a]
For He will avenge the blood of His servants,
And render vengeance to His adversaries;
He will provide atonement for His land *and* His people.”

44So Moses came with Joshua[a] the son of
Nun and spoke all the words of this song in the
hearing of the people. 45Moses finished speak-
ing all these words to all Israel, 46and he said to
them: “Set your hearts on all the words which I
testify among you today, which you shall com-
mand your children to be careful to observe—all
the words of this law. 47For it *is* not a futile thing
for you, because it *is* your life, and by this word
you shall prolong *your* days in the land which
you cross over the Jordan to possess.”

MOSES TO DIE ON MOUNT NEBO

48Then the LORD spoke to Moses that very
same day, saying: 49“Go up this mountain of the
Abarim, Mount Nebo, which *is* in the land of
Moab, across from Jericho; view the land of
Canaan, which I give to the children of Israel as
a possession; 50and die on the mountain which
you ascend, and be gathered to your people, just
as Aaron your brother died on Mount Hor and
was gathered to his people; 51because you tres-
passed against Me among the children of Israel

32:43 [a]A Dead Sea Scroll fragment adds *And let all the gods (angels) worship Him* (compare Septuagint and Hebrews 1:6).
32:44 [a]Hebrew *Hoshea* (compare Numbers 13:8, 16)

THE MESSAGE

And the day of their doom is just around the corner,
sudden and swift and sure.

36-38 Yes, GOD will judge his people,
but oh how compassionately he’ll do it.
When he sees their weakened plight
and there is no one left, slave or free,
He’ll say, “So where are their gods,
the rock in which they sought refuge,
The gods who feasted on the fat of their sacrifices
and drank the wine of their drink-offerings?
Let them show their stuff and help you,
let them give you a hand!

39-42 “Do you see it now? Do you see that I’m the one?
Do you see that there’s no other god beside me?
I bring death and I give life, I wound and I heal—
there is no getting away from or around me!
I raise my hand in solemn oath;
I say, ‘I’m always around. By that very life I promise:
When I sharpen my lightning sword
and execute judgment,
I take vengeance on my enemies
and pay back those who hate me.
I’ll make my arrows drunk with blood,
my sword will gorge itself on flesh,
Feasting on slain and captive alike,
the proud and vain enemy corpses.’ ”

43 Celebrate, nations, join the praise of his people.
He avenges the deaths of his servants,
Pays back his enemies with vengeance,
and cleanses his land for his people.

44-47 Moses came and recited all the words of this song in the hearing of the people, he and Joshua son of Nun. When Moses had finished saying all these words to all Israel, he said, “Take to heart all these words to which I give witness today and urgently command your children to put them into practice, every single word of this Revelation. Yes. This is no small matter for you; it’s your life. In keeping this word you’ll have a good and long life in this land that you’re crossing the Jordan to possess.”

48-50 That same day GOD spoke to Moses: “Climb the Abarim Mountains to Mount Nebo in the land of Moab, overlooking Jericho, and view the land of Canaan that I’m giving the People of Israel to have and hold. Die on the mountain that you climb and join your people in the ground, just as your brother Aaron died on Mount Hor and joined his people.

51-52 “This is because you broke faith with me in the company of the People of Israel at the

NEW KING JAMES VERSION

at the waters of Meribah Kadesh, in the Wilder-
ness of Zin, because you did not hallow Me in
the midst of the children of Israel. 52 Yet you
shall see the land before *you,* though you shall
not go there, into the land which I am giving to
the children of Israel."

MOSES' FINAL BLESSING ON ISRAEL

33 Now this *is* the blessing with which Moses
the man of God blessed the children of Is-
rael before his death. 2 And he said:

"The LORD came from Sinai,
And dawned on them from Seir;
He shone forth from Mount Paran,
And He came with ten thousands of saints;
From His right hand
Came a fiery law for them.
3 Yes, He loves the people;
All His saints *are* in Your hand;
They sit down at Your feet;
Everyone receives Your words.
4 Moses commanded a law for us,
A heritage of the congregation of Jacob.
5 And He was King in Jeshurun,
When the leaders of the people were
gathered,
All the tribes of Israel together.

6 "Let Reuben live, and not die,
Nor let his men be few."

7 And this he said of Judah:

"Hear, LORD, the voice of Judah,
And bring him to his people;
Let his hands be sufficient for him,
And may You be a help against his enemies."

8 And of Levi he said:

"*Let* Your Thummim and Your Urim *be* with
Your holy one,
Whom You tested at Massah,
And with whom You contended at the waters
of Meribah,
9 Who says of his father and mother,
'I have not seen them';
Nor did he acknowledge his brothers,
Or know his own children;
For they have observed Your word
And kept Your covenant.
10 They shall teach Jacob Your judgments,
And Israel Your law.
They shall put incense before You,
And a whole burnt sacrifice on Your altar.
11 Bless his substance, LORD,
And accept the work of his hands;
Strike the loins of those who rise against
him,
And of those who hate him, that they rise
not again."

12 Of Benjamin he said:

"The beloved of the LORD shall dwell in
safety by Him,
Who shelters him all the day long;
And he shall dwell between His shoulders."

THE MESSAGE

Waters of Meribah Kadesh in the Wilder-
ness of Zin—you didn't honor my Holy
Presence in the company of the People of Is-
rael. You'll look at the land spread out before
you but you won't enter it, this land that I
am giving to the People of Israel."

THE BLESSING

1-5 33 Moses, man of God, blessed the People
of Israel with this blessing before his
death. He said,

GOD came down from Sinai,
he dawned from Seir upon them;
He radiated light from Mount Paran,
coming with ten thousand holy angels
And tongues of fire
streaming from his right hand.
Oh, how you love the people,
all his holy ones are palmed in your
left hand.
They sit at your feet,
honoring your teaching,
The Revelation commanded by Moses,
as the assembly of Jacob's inheritance.
Thus GOD became king in Jeshurun
as the leaders and tribes of Israel
gathered.

6 Reuben:
"Let Reuben live and not die,
but just barely, in diminishing
numbers."

7 Judah:
"Listen, GOD, to the Voice of Judah,
bring him to his people;
Strengthen his grip,
be his helper against his foes."

8-11 Levi:
"Let your Thummim and Urim
belong to your loyal saint;
The one you tested at Massah,
whom you fought with at the Waters of
Meribah,
Who said of his father and mother,
'I no longer recognize them.'
He turned his back on his brothers
and neglected his children,
Because he was guarding your sayings
and watching over your Covenant.
Let him teach your rules to Jacob
and your Revelation to Israel,
Let him keep the incense rising to your
nostrils
and the Whole-Burnt-Offerings on
your Altar.
GOD bless his commitment,
stamp your seal of approval on what
he does;
Disable the loins of those who defy him,
make sure we've heard the last from
those who hate him."

12 Benjamin:
"GOD's beloved;
GOD's permanent residence.
Encircled by GOD all day long,
within whom GOD is at home."

New King James Version

13And of Joseph he said:

"Blessed of the LORD *is* his land,
With the precious things of heaven, with the dew,
And the deep lying beneath,
14With the precious fruits of the sun,
With the precious produce of the months,
15With the best things of the ancient mountains,
With the precious things of the everlasting hills,
16With the precious things of the earth and its fullness,
And the favor of Him who dwelt in the bush.
Let *the blessing* come 'on the head of Joseph,
And on the crown of the head of him *who was* separate from his brothers.'[a]
17His glory *is like* a firstborn bull,
And his horns *like* the horns of the wild ox;
Together with them
He shall push the peoples
To the ends of the earth;
They *are* the ten thousands of Ephraim,
And they *are* the thousands of Manasseh."

18And of Zebulun he said:

"Rejoice, Zebulun, in your going out,
And Issachar in your tents!
19They shall call the peoples *to* the mountain;
There they shall offer sacrifices of righteousness;
For they shall partake *of* the abundance of the seas
And *of* treasures hidden in the sand."

20And of Gad he said:

"Blessed *is* he who enlarges Gad;
He dwells as a lion,
And tears the arm and the crown of his head.
21He provided the first *part* for himself,
Because a lawgiver's portion was reserved there.
He came *with* the heads of the people;
He administered the justice of the LORD,
And His judgments with Israel."

22And of Dan he said:

"Dan *is* a lion's whelp;
He shall leap from Bashan."

23And of Naphtali he said:

"O Naphtali, satisfied with favor,
And full of the blessing of the LORD,
Possess the west and the south."

24And of Asher he said:

"Asher *is* most blessed of sons;
Let him be favored by his brothers,
And let him dip his foot in oil.

33:16 [a]Genesis 49:26

The Message

13-17 Joseph:
"Blessed by GOD be his land:
The best fresh dew from high heaven,
and fountains springing from the depths;
The best radiance streaming from the sun
and the best the moon has to offer;
Beauty pouring off the tops of the mountains
and the best from the everlasting hills;
The best of Earth's exuberant gifts,
the smile of the Burning-Bush Dweller.
All this on the head of Joseph,
on the brow of the consecrated one among his brothers.
In splendor he's like a firstborn bull,
his horns the horns of a wild ox;
He'll gore the nations with those horns,
push them all to the ends of the Earth.
Ephraim by the ten thousands will do this,
Manasseh by the thousands will do this."

18-19 Zebulun and Issachar:
"Celebrate, Zebulun, as you go out,
and Issachar, as you stay home.
They'll invite people to the Mountain
and offer sacrifices of right worship,
For they will have hauled riches in from the sea
and gleaned treasures from the beaches."

20-21 Gad:
"Blessed is he who makes Gad large.
Gad roams like a lion,
tears off an arm, rips open a skull.
He took one look and grabbed the best place for himself,
the portion just made for someone in charge.
He took his place at the head,
carried out GOD's right ways
and his rules for life in Israel."

22 Dan:
"Dan is a lion's cub
leaping out of Bashan."

23 Naphtali:
"Naphtali brims with blessings,
spills over with GOD's blessings
As he takes possession
of the sea and southland."

24-25 Asher:
"Asher, best blessed of the sons!
May he be the favorite of his brothers,
his feet massaged in oil.

NEW KING JAMES VERSION

25 Your sandals *shall be* iron and bronze;
As your days, *so shall* your strength *be*.

26 "*There is* no one like the God of Jeshurun,
Who rides the heavens to help you,
And in His excellency on the clouds.
27 The eternal God *is your* refuge,
And underneath *are* the everlasting arms;
He will thrust out the enemy from before
you,
And will say, 'Destroy!'
28 Then Israel shall dwell in safety,
The fountain of Jacob alone,
In a land of grain and new wine;
His heavens shall also drop dew.
29 Happy *are* you, O Israel!
Who *is* like you, a people saved by the LORD,
The shield of your help
And the sword of your majesty!
Your enemies shall submit to you,
And you shall tread down their high places."

MOSES DIES ON MOUNT NEBO

34 Then Moses went up from the plains of
Moab to Mount Nebo, to the top of Pisgah,
which is across from Jericho. And the LORD
showed him all the land of Gilead as far as Dan,
2 all Naphtali and the land of Ephraim and Ma-
nasseh, all the land of Judah as far as the West-
ern Sea,[a] 3 the South, and the plain of the Valley
of Jericho, the city of palm trees, as far as Zoar.
4 Then the LORD said to him, "This *is* the land of
which I swore to give Abraham, Isaac, and Ja-
cob, saying, 'I will give it to your descendants.' I
have caused you to see *it* with your eyes, but you
shall not cross over there."

5 So Moses the servant of the LORD died there
in the land of Moab, according to the word of
the LORD. 6 And He buried him in a valley in the
land of Moab, opposite Beth Peor; but no one
knows his grave to this day. 7 Moses *was* one
hundred and twenty years old when he died. His
eyes were not dim nor his natural vigor dimin-
ished. 8 And the children of Israel wept for
Moses in the plains of Moab thirty days. So the
days of weeping *and* mourning for Moses
ended.

9 Now Joshua the son of Nun was full of the
spirit of wisdom, for Moses had laid his hands
on him; so the children of Israel heeded him,
and did as the LORD had commanded Moses.

10 But since then there has not arisen in Israel
a prophet like Moses, whom the LORD knew face
to face, 11 in all the signs and wonders which the
LORD sent him to do in the land of Egypt, before
Pharaoh, before all his servants, and in all his
land, 12 and by all that mighty power and all the
great terror which Moses performed in the sight
of all Israel.

34:2 [a]That is, the Mediterranean

THE MESSAGE

Safe behind iron-clad doors and gates,
your strength like iron as long as you
live."

26-28 There is none like God, Jeshurun,
riding to your rescue through the
skies,
his dignity haloed by clouds.
The ancient God is home
on a foundation of everlasting arms.
He drove out the enemy before you
and commanded, "Destroy!"
Israel lived securely,
the fountain of Jacob undisturbed
In grain and wine country
and, oh yes, his heavens drip dew.

29 Lucky Israel! Who has it as good as you?
A people *saved* by GOD!
The Shield who defends you,
the Sword who brings triumph.
Your enemies will come crawling on
their bellies
and you'll march on their backs.

THE DEATH OF MOSES

1-3 34 Moses climbed from the Plains of
Moab to Mount Nebo, the peak of Pis-
gah facing Jericho. GOD showed him all the
land from Gilead to Dan, all Naphtali,
Ephraim, and Manasseh; all Judah reaching
to the Mediterranean Sea; the Negev and
the plains which encircle Jericho, City of
Palms, as far south as Zoar.
4 Then and there GOD said to him, "This is
the land I promised to your ancestors, to
Abraham, Isaac, and Jacob with the words 'I
will give it to your descendants.' I've let you
see it with your own eyes. There it is. But
you're not going to go in."
5-6 Moses died there in the land of Moab,
Moses the servant of GOD, just as GOD said.
God buried him in the valley in the land of
Moab opposite Beth Peor. No one knows his
burial site to this very day.
7-8 Moses was 120 years old when he died.
His eyesight was sharp; he still walked with
a spring in his step. The People of Israel
wept for Moses in the Plains of Moab thirty
days. Then the days of weeping and mourn-
ing for Moses came to an end.
9 Joshua son of Nun was filled with the
spirit of wisdom because Moses had laid his
hands on him. The People of Israel listened
obediently to him and did the same as when
GOD had commanded Moses.
10-12 No prophet has risen since in Israel like
Moses, whom GOD knew face-to-face. Never
since has there been anything like the signs
and miracle-wonders that GOD sent him to
do in Egypt, to Pharaoh, to all his servants,
and to all his land—nothing to compare
with that all-powerful hand of his and all
the great and terrible things Moses did as
every eye in Israel watched.

JOSHUA

NEW KING JAMES VERSION

GOD'S COMMISSION TO JOSHUA

1 After the death of Moses the servant of the LORD, it came to pass that the LORD spoke to Joshua the son of Nun, Moses' assistant, saying: [2]"Moses My servant is dead. Now therefore, arise, go over this Jordan, you and all this people, to the land which I am giving to them—the children of Israel. [3]Every place that the sole of your foot will tread upon I have given you, as I said to Moses. [4]From the wilderness and this Lebanon as far as the great river, the River Euphrates, all the land of the Hittites, and to the Great Sea toward the going down of the sun, shall be your territory. [5]No man shall *be able to* stand before you all the days of your life; as I was with Moses, *so* I will be with you. I will not leave you nor forsake you. [6]Be strong and of good courage, for to this people you shall divide as an inheritance the land which I swore to their fathers to give them. [7]Only be strong and very courageous, that you may observe to do according to all the law which Moses My servant commanded you; do not turn from it to the right hand or to the left, that you may prosper wherever you go. [8]This Book of the Law shall not depart from your mouth, but you shall meditate in it day and night, that you may observe to do according to all that is written in it. For then you will make your way prosperous, and then you will have good success. [9]Have I not commanded you? Be strong and of good courage; do not be afraid, nor be dismayed, for the LORD your God *is* with you wherever you go."

THE ORDER TO CROSS THE JORDAN

[10]Then Joshua commanded the officers of the people, saying, [11]"Pass through the camp and command the people, saying, 'Prepare provisions for yourselves, for within three days you will cross over this Jordan, to go in to possess the land which the LORD your God is giving you to possess.' "

[12]And to the Reubenites, the Gadites, and half the tribe of Manasseh Joshua spoke, saying, [13]"Remember the word which Moses the servant of the LORD commanded you, saying, 'The LORD your God is giving you rest and is giving you this land.' [14]Your wives, your little ones, and your livestock shall remain in the land which Moses gave you on this side of the Jordan. But you shall pass before your brethren armed, all your mighty men of valor, and help them, [15]until the LORD has given your brethren rest, as He *gave* you, and they also have taken possession of the land which the LORD your God is giving them. Then you shall return to the land of your possession and enjoy it, which Moses the LORD's servant gave you on this side of the Jordan toward the sunrise."

[16]So they answered Joshua, saying, "All that you command us we will do, and wherever you send us we will go. [17]Just as we heeded Moses in all things, so we will heed you. Only the LORD your God be with you, as He was with Moses.

THE MESSAGE

1-9 1 After the death of Moses the servant of GOD, GOD spoke to Joshua, Moses' assistant:

"Moses my servant is dead. Get going. Cross this Jordan River, you and all the people. Cross to the country I'm giving to the People of Israel. I'm giving you every square inch of the land you set your foot on—just as I promised Moses. From the wilderness and this Lebanon east to the Great River, the Euphrates River—all the Hittite country—and then west to the Great Sea. It's all yours. All your life, no one will be able to hold out against you. In the same way I was with Moses, I'll be with you. I won't give up on you; I won't leave you. Strength! Courage! You are going to lead this people to inherit the land that I promised to give their ancestors. Give it everything you have, heart and soul. Make sure you carry out The Revelation that Moses commanded you, every bit of it. Don't get off track, either left or right, so as to make sure you get to where you're going. And don't for a minute let this Book of The Revelation be out of mind. Ponder and meditate on it day and night, making sure you practice everything written in it. Then you'll get where you're going; then you'll succeed. Haven't I commanded you? Strength! Courage! Don't be timid; don't get discouraged. GOD, your God, is with you every step you take."

THE TAKING OF THE LAND

10-11 Then Joshua gave orders to the people's leaders: "Go through the camp and give this order to the people: 'Pack your bags. In three days you will cross this Jordan River to enter and take the land GOD, your God, is giving you to possess.' "

12-15 Then Joshua addressed the Reubenites, the Gadites, and the half-tribe of Manasseh. He said, "Remember what Moses the servant of GOD commanded you: GOD, your God, gives you rest and he gives you this land. Your wives, your children, and your livestock can stay here east of the Jordan, the country Moses gave you; but you, tough soldiers all, must cross the River in battle formation, leading your brothers, helping them until GOD, your God, gives your brothers a place of rest just as he has done for you. They also will take possession of the land that GOD, your God, is giving them. Then you will be free to return to your possession, given to you by Moses the servant of GOD, across the Jordan to the east."

16-18 They answered Joshua: "Everything you commanded us, we'll do. Wherever you send us, we'll go. We obeyed Moses to the letter; we'll also obey you—we just pray that GOD, your God, will be with you as he was with

NEW KING JAMES VERSION

[18]Whoever rebels against your command and does not heed your words, in all that you command him, shall be put to death. Only be strong and of good courage."

RAHAB HIDES THE SPIES

2 Now Joshua the son of Nun sent out two men from Acacia Grove[a] to spy secretly, saying, "Go, view the land, especially Jericho."

So they went, and came to the house of a harlot named Rahab, and lodged there. [2]And it was told the king of Jericho, saying, "Behold, men have come here tonight from the children of Israel to search out the country."

[3]So the king of Jericho sent to Rahab, saying, "Bring out the men who have come to you, who have entered your house, for they have come to search out all the country."

[4]Then the woman took the two men and hid them. So she said, "Yes, the men came to me, but I did not know where they *were* from. [5]And it happened as the gate was being shut, when it was dark, that the men went out. Where the men went I do not know; pursue them quickly, for you may overtake them." [6](But she had brought them up to the roof and hidden them with the stalks of flax, which she had laid in order on the roof.) [7]Then the men pursued them by the road to the Jordan, to the fords. And as soon as those who pursued them had gone out, they shut the gate.

[8]Now before they lay down, she came up to them on the roof, [9]and said to the men: "I know that the LORD has given you the land, that the terror of you has fallen on us, and that all the inhabitants of the land are fainthearted because of you. [10]For we have heard how the LORD dried up the water of the Red Sea for you when you came out of Egypt, and what you did to the two kings of the Amorites who *were* on the other side of the Jordan, Sihon and Og, whom you utterly destroyed. [11]And as soon as we heard *these things*, our hearts melted; neither did there remain any more courage in anyone because of you, for the LORD your God, He *is* God in heaven above and on earth beneath. [12]Now therefore, I beg you, swear to me by the LORD, since I have shown you kindness, that you also will show kindness to my father's house, and give me a true token, [13]and spare my father, my mother, my brothers, my sisters, and all that they have, and deliver our lives from death."

[14]So the men answered her, "Our lives for yours, if none of you tell this business of ours. And it shall be, when the LORD has given us the land, that we will deal kindly and truly with you."

[15]Then she let them down by a rope through the window, for her house *was* on the city wall; she dwelt on the wall. [16]And she said to them, "Get to the mountain, lest the pursuers meet you. Hide there three days, until the pursuers have returned. Afterward you may go your way."

[17]So the men said to her: "We *will be* blameless of this oath of yours which you have made us swear, [18]unless, *when* we come into the land, you bind this line of scarlet cord in the window

2:1 [a]Hebrew *Shittim*

THE MESSAGE

Moses. Anyone who questions what you say
and refuses to obey whatever you command
him will be put to death. Strength! Courage!"

RAHAB

1 2 Joshua son of Nun secretly sent out from
Shittim two men as spies: "Go. Look over
the land. Check out Jericho." They left and
arrived at the house of a harlot named Ra-
hab and stayed there.
2 The king of Jericho was told, "We've just
learned that men arrived tonight to spy out
the land. They're from the People of Israel."
3 The king of Jericho sent word to Rahab:
"Bring out the men who came to you to stay
the night in your house. They're spies;
they've come to spy out the whole country."
4-7 The woman had taken the two men and
hidden them. She said, "Yes, two men did
come to me, but I didn't know where they'd
come from. At dark, when the gate was
about to be shut, the men left. But I have no
idea where they went. Hurry up! Chase
them—you can still catch them!" (She had
actually taken them up on the roof and hid-
den them under the stalks of flax that were
spread out for her on the roof.) So the men
set chase down the Jordan road toward the
fords. As soon as they were gone, the gate
was shut.
8-11 Before the spies were down for the night,
the woman came up to them on the roof and
said, "I know that GOD has given you the
land. We're all afraid. Everyone in the coun-
try feels hopeless. We heard how GOD dried
up the waters of the Red Sea before you
when you left Egypt, and what he did to the
two Amorite kings east of the Jordan, Sihon
and Og, whom you put under a holy curse
and destroyed. We heard it and our hearts
sank. We all had the wind knocked out of us.
And all because of you, you and GOD, your
God, God of the heavens above and God of
the earth below.
12-13 "Now promise me by GOD. I showed you
mercy; now show my family mercy. And
give me some tangible proof, a guarantee of
life for my father and mother, my brothers
and sisters—everyone connected with my
family. Save our souls from death!"
14 "Our lives for yours!" said the men. "But
don't tell anyone our business. When GOD
turns this land over to us, we'll do right by
you in loyal mercy."
15-16 She lowered them down out a window
with a rope because her house was on the
city wall to the outside. She told them, "Run
for the hills so your pursuers won't find you.
Hide out for three days and give your pur-
suers time to return. Then get on your way."
17-20 The men told her, "In order to keep this
oath you made us swear, here is what you
must do: Hang this red rope out the window

NEW KING JAMES VERSION

through which you let us down, and unless you bring your father, your mother, your brothers, and all your father's household to your own home. 19So it shall be *that* whoever goes outside the doors of your house into the street, his blood *shall be* on his own head, and we *will be* guiltless. And whoever is with you in the house, his blood *shall be* on our head if a hand is laid on him. 20And if you tell this business of ours, then we will be free from your oath which you made us swear."

21Then she said, "According to your words, so *be* it." And she sent them away, and they departed. And she bound the scarlet cord in the window.

22They departed and went to the mountain, and stayed there three days until the pursuers returned. The pursuers sought *them* all along the way, but did not find *them*. 23So the two men returned, descended from the mountain, and crossed over; and they came to Joshua the son of Nun, and told him all that had befallen them. 24And they said to Joshua, "Truly the LORD has delivered all the land into our hands, for indeed all the inhabitants of the country are fainthearted because of us."

ISRAEL CROSSES THE JORDAN

3 Then Joshua rose early in the morning; and they set out from Acacia Grove[a] and came to the Jordan, he and all the children of Israel, and lodged there before they crossed over. 2So it was, after three days, that the officers went through the camp; 3and they commanded the people, saying, "When you see the ark of the covenant of the LORD your God, and the priests, the Levites, bearing it, then you shall set out from your place and go after it. 4Yet there shall be a space between you and it, about two thousand cubits by measure. Do not come near it, that you may know the way by which you must go, for you have not passed *this* way before."

5And Joshua said to the people, "Sanctify yourselves, for tomorrow the LORD will do wonders among you." 6Then Joshua spoke to the priests, saying, "Take up the ark of the covenant and cross over before the people."

So they took up the ark of the covenant and went before the people.

7And the LORD said to Joshua, "This day I will begin to exalt you in the sight of all Israel, that they may know that, as I was with Moses, *so* I will be with you. 8You shall command the priests who bear the ark of the covenant, saying, 'When you have come to the edge of the water of the Jordan, you shall stand in the Jordan.' "

9So Joshua said to the children of Israel, "Come here, and hear the words of the LORD your God." 10And Joshua said, "By this you shall know that the living God *is* among you, and *that* He will without fail drive out from before you the Canaanites and the Hittites and the Hivites and the Perizzites and the Girgashites and the Amorites and the Jebusites: 11Behold, the ark of the covenant of the Lord of all the earth is crossing over before you into the Jordan. 12Now

3:1 [a]Hebrew *Shittim*

THE MESSAGE

through which you let us down and gather your entire family with you in your house—father, mother, brothers, and sisters. Anyone who goes out the doors of your house into the street and is killed, it's his own fault—we aren't responsible. But for everyone within the house we take full responsibility. If anyone lays a hand on one of them, it's our fault. But if you tell anyone of our business here, the oath you made us swear is canceled—we're no longer responsible."

21 She said, "If that's what you say, that's the way it is," and sent them off. They left and she hung the red rope out the window.

22 They headed for the hills and stayed there for three days until the pursuers had returned. The pursuers had looked high and low but found nothing.

23-24 The men headed back. They came down out of the hills, crossed the river, and returned to Joshua son of Nun and reported all their experiences. They told Joshua, "Yes! GOD has given the whole country to us. Everybody there is in a state of panic because of us."

THE JORDAN

1-4 3 Joshua was up early and on his way from Shittim with all the People of Israel with him. He arrived at the Jordan and camped before crossing over. After three days, leaders went through the camp and gave out orders to the people: "When you see the Covenant-Chest of GOD, your God, carried by the Levitical priests, start moving. Follow it. Make sure you keep a proper distance between you and it, about half a mile—be sure now to keep your distance!—and you'll see clearly the route to take. You've never been on this road before."

5 Then Joshua addressed the people: "Sanctify yourselves. Tomorrow GOD will work miracle-wonders among you."

6 Joshua instructed the priests, "Take up the Chest of the Covenant and step out before the people." So they took it up and processed before the people.

7-8 GOD said to Joshua, "This very day I will begin to make you great in the eyes of all Israel. They'll see for themselves that I'm with you in the same way that I was with Moses. You will command the priests who are carrying the Chest of the Covenant: 'When you come to the edge of the Jordan's waters, stand there on the river bank.' "

9-13 Then Joshua addressed the People of Israel: "Attention! Listen to what GOD, your God, has to say. This is how you'll know that God is alive among you—he will completely dispossess before you the Canaanites, Hittites, Hivites, Perizzites, Girgashites, Amorites, and Jebusites. Look at what's before you: the Chest of the Covenant. Think of it—

New King James Version

therefore, take for yourselves twelve men from
the tribes of Israel, one man from every tribe.
13And it shall come to pass, as soon as the soles
of the feet of the priests who bear the ark of the
LORD, the Lord of all the earth, shall rest in the
waters of the Jordan, *that* the waters of the Jor-
dan shall be cut off, the waters that come down
from upstream, and they shall stand as a heap."
14So it was, when the people set out from
their camp to cross over the Jordan, with the
priests bearing the ark of the covenant before
the people, 15and as those who bore the ark
came to the Jordan, and the feet of the priests
who bore the ark dipped in the edge of the wa-
ter (for the Jordan overflows all its banks during
the whole time of harvest), 16that the waters
which came down from upstream stood *still,*
and rose in a heap very far away at Adam, the
city that *is* beside Zaretan. So the waters that
went down into the Sea of the Arabah, the Salt
Sea, failed, *and* were cut off; and the people
crossed over opposite Jericho. 17Then the priests
who bore the ark of the covenant of the LORD
stood firm on dry ground in the midst of the Jor-
dan; and all Israel crossed over on dry ground,
until all the people had crossed completely over
the Jordan.

The Memorial Stones

4 And it came to pass, when all the people had
completely crossed over the Jordan, that the
LORD spoke to Joshua, saying: 2"Take for your-
selves twelve men from the people, one man
from every tribe, 3and command them, saying,
'Take for yourselves twelve stones from here,
out of the midst of the Jordan, from the place
where the priests' feet stood firm. You shall
carry them over with you and leave them in the
lodging place where you lodge tonight.' "
4Then Joshua called the twelve men whom
he had appointed from the children of Israel,
one man from every tribe; 5and Joshua said to
them: "Cross over before the ark of the LORD
your God into the midst of the Jordan, and each
one of you take up a stone on his shoulder, ac-
cording to the number of the tribes of the chil-
dren of Israel, 6that this may be a sign among
you when your children ask in time to come,
saying, 'What do these stones *mean* to you?'
7Then you shall answer them that the waters of
the Jordan were cut off before the ark of the
covenant of the LORD; when it crossed over the
Jordan, the waters of the Jordan were cut off.
And these stones shall be for a memorial to the
children of Israel forever."
8And the children of Israel did so, just as
Joshua commanded, and took up twelve stones
from the midst of the Jordan, as the LORD had
spoken to Joshua, according to the number of
the tribes of the children of Israel, and carried
them over with them to the place where they
lodged, and laid them down there. 9Then Joshua
set up twelve stones in the midst of the Jordan,
in the place where the feet of the priests who
bore the ark of the covenant stood; and they are
there to this day.
10So the priests who bore the ark stood in the
midst of the Jordan until everything was fin-
ished that the LORD had commanded Joshua to

The Message

the Master of the entire earth is crossing the
Jordan as you watch. Now take twelve men
from the tribes of Israel, one man from each
tribe. When the soles of the feet of the
priests carrying the Chest of GOD, Master of
all the earth, touch the Jordan's water, the
flow of water will be stopped—the water
coming from upstream will pile up in a
heap."
14-16 And that's what happened. The people
left their tents to cross the Jordan, led by the
priests carrying the Chest of the Covenant.
When the priests got to the Jordan and their
feet touched the water at the edge (the Jor-
dan overflows its banks throughout the har-
vest), the flow of water stopped. It piled up
in a heap—a long way off—at Adam, which
is near Zarethan. The river went dry all the
way down to the Arabah Sea (the Salt Sea).
And the people crossed, facing Jericho.
17 And there they stood; those priests carry-
ing the Chest of the Covenant stood firmly
planted on dry ground in the middle of the
Jordan while all Israel crossed on dry
ground. Finally the whole nation was across
the Jordan, and not one wet foot.

1-3 4 When the whole nation was finally across,
GOD spoke to Joshua: "Select twelve
men from the people, a man from each tribe,
and tell them, 'From right here, the middle
of the Jordan where the feet of the priests
are standing firm, take twelve stones. Carry
them across with you and set them down in
the place where you camp tonight.' "
4-7 Joshua called out the twelve men whom
he selected from the People of Israel, one
man from each tribe. Joshua directed them,
"Cross to the middle of the Jordan and take
your place in front of the Chest of GOD, your
God. Each of you heft a stone to your shoul-
der, a stone for each of the tribes of the Peo-
ple of Israel, so you'll have something later
to mark the occasion. When your children
ask you, 'What are these stones to you?'
you'll say, 'The flow of the Jordan was
stopped in front of the Chest of the
Covenant of GOD as it crossed the Jordan—
stopped in its tracks. These stones are a per-
manent memorial for the People of Israel.' "
8-9 The People of Israel did exactly as Joshua
commanded: They took twelve stones from
the middle of the Jordan—a stone for each
of the twelve tribes, just as GOD had in-
structed Joshua—carried them across with
them to the camp, and set them down there.
Joshua set up the twelve stones taken from
the middle of the Jordan that had marked
the place where the priests who carried the
Chest of the Covenant had stood. They are
still there today.
10-11 The priests carrying the Chest continued
standing in the middle of the Jordan until
everything God had instructed Joshua to tell

NEW KING JAMES VERSION

speak to the people, according to all that Moses
had commanded Joshua; and the people hurried
and crossed over. [11]Then it came to pass, when
all the people had completely crossed over, that
the ark of the LORD and the priests crossed over
in the presence of the people. [12]And the men of
Reuben, the men of Gad, and half the tribe of
Manasseh crossed over armed before the chil-
dren of Israel, as Moses had spoken to them.
[13]About forty thousand prepared for war
crossed over before the LORD for battle, to the
plains of Jericho. [14]On that day the LORD exalted
Joshua in the sight of all Israel; and they feared
him, as they had feared Moses, all the days of
his life.

[15]Then the LORD spoke to Joshua, saying,
[16]"Command the priests who bear the ark of
the Testimony to come up from the Jordan."
[17]Joshua therefore commanded the priests, say-
ing, "Come up from the Jordan." [18]And it came
to pass, when the priests who bore the ark of the
covenant of the LORD had come from the midst
of the Jordan, *and* the soles of the priests' feet
touched the dry land, that the waters of the Jor-
dan returned to their place and overflowed all
its banks as before.

[19]Now the people came up from the Jordan
on the tenth *day* of the first month, and they
camped in Gilgal on the east border of Jericho.
[20]And those twelve stones which they took out
of the Jordan, Joshua set up in Gilgal. [21]Then he
spoke to the children of Israel, saying: "When
your children ask their fathers in time to come,
saying, 'What *are* these stones?' [22]then you shall
let your children know, saying, 'Israel crossed
over this Jordan on dry land'; [23]for the LORD
your God dried up the waters of the Jordan be-
fore you until you had crossed over, as the LORD
your God did to the Red Sea, which He dried
up before us until we had crossed over, [24]that all
the peoples of the earth may know the hand of
the LORD, that it *is* mighty, that you may fear the
LORD your God forever."

THE SECOND GENERATION CIRCUMCISED

5 So it was, when all the kings of the Amorites
who *were* on the west side of the Jordan, and
all the kings of the Canaanites who *were* by the
sea, heard that the LORD had dried up the waters
of the Jordan from before the children of Israel
until we[a] had crossed over, that their heart
melted; and there was no spirit in them any
longer because of the children of Israel.

[2]At that time the LORD said to Joshua, "Make
flint knives for yourself, and circumcise the sons
of Israel again the second time." [3]So Joshua
made flint knives for himself, and circumcised
the sons of Israel at the hill of the foreskins.[a]

5:1 [a]Following Kethib; Qere, some Hebrew manuscripts and editions, Septuagint, Syriac, Targum, and Vulgate read *they*.
5:3 [a]Hebrew *Gibeath Haaraloth*

THE MESSAGE

the people to do was done (confirming what Moses had instructed Joshua). The people crossed; no one dawdled. When the crossing of all the people was complete, they watched as the Chest of the Covenant and the priests crossed over.

12-13 The Reubenites, Gadites, and the half-tribe of Manasseh had crossed over in battle formation in front of the People of Israel, obedient to Moses' instructions. All told, about forty thousand armed soldiers crossed over before GOD to the plains of Jericho, ready for battle.

14 GOD made Joshua great that day in the sight of all Israel. They were in awe of him just as they had been in awe of Moses all his life.

15-16 GOD told Joshua, "Command the priests carrying the Chest of The Testimony to come up from the Jordan."

17 Joshua commanded the priests, "Come up out of the Jordan."

18 They did it. The priests carrying GOD's Chest of the Covenant came up from the middle of the Jordan. As soon as the soles of the priests' feet touched dry land, the Jordan's waters resumed their flow within the banks, just as before.

19-22 The people came up out of the Jordan on the tenth day of the first month. They set up camp at The Gilgal (The Circle) to the east of Jericho. Joshua erected a monument at The Gilgal, using the twelve stones that they had taken from the Jordan. And then he told the People of Israel, "In the days to come, when your children ask their fathers, 'What are these stones doing here?' tell your children this: 'Israel crossed over this Jordan on dry ground.'

23-24 "Yes, GOD, your God, dried up the Jordan's waters for you until you had crossed, just as GOD, your God, did at the Red Sea, which had dried up before us until we had crossed. This was so that everybody on earth would recognize how strong GOD's rescuing hand is and so that you would hold GOD in solemn reverence always."

1 5 When all the Amorite kings west of the Jordan and the Canaanite kings along the seacoast heard how GOD had stopped the Jordan River before the People of Israel until they had crossed over, their hearts sank; the courage drained out of them just thinking about the People of Israel.

2-3 At that time GOD said to Joshua, "Make stone knives and circumcise the People of Israel a second time." So Joshua made stone knives and circumcised the People of Israel at Foreskins Hill.

NEW KING JAMES VERSION

4And this *is* the reason why Joshua circumcised
them: All the people who came out of Egypt *who*
were males, all the men of war, had died in the
wilderness on the way, after they had come out
of Egypt. 5For all the people who came out had
been circumcised, but all the people born in the
wilderness, on the way as they came out of
Egypt, had not been circumcised. 6For the chil-
dren of Israel walked forty years in the wilder-
ness, till all the people *who were* men of war,
who came out of Egypt, were consumed, be-
cause they did not obey the voice of the LORD—
to whom the LORD swore that He would not
show them the land which the LORD had sworn
to their fathers that He would give us, "a land
flowing with milk and honey."[a] 7Then Joshua
circumcised their sons *whom* He raised up in
their place; for they were uncircumcised, be-
cause they had not been circumcised on the
way.

8So it was, when they had finished circum-
cising all the people, that they stayed in their
places in the camp till they were healed. 9Then
the LORD said to Joshua, "This day I have rolled
away the reproach of Egypt from you." There-
fore the name of the place is called Gilgal[a] to
this day.

10Now the children of Israel camped in Gil-
gal, and kept the Passover on the fourteenth day
of the month at twilight on the plains of Jericho.
11And they ate of the produce of the land on the
day after the Passover, unleavened bread and
parched grain, on the very same day. 12Then the
manna ceased on the day after they had eaten
the produce of the land; and the children of Is-
rael no longer had manna, but they ate the food
of the land of Canaan that year.

THE COMMANDER OF THE ARMY OF THE LORD

13And it came to pass, when Joshua was by
Jericho, that he lifted his eyes and looked, and
behold, a Man stood opposite him with His
sword drawn in His hand. And Joshua went to
Him and said to Him, "*Are* You for us or for our
adversaries?"

14So He said, "No, but *as* Commander of the
army of the LORD I have now come."

And Joshua fell on his face to the earth and
worshiped, and said to Him, "What does my
Lord say to His servant?"

15Then the Commander of the LORD's army
said to Joshua, "Take your sandal off your foot,
for the place where you stand *is* holy." And
Joshua did so.

THE DESTRUCTION OF JERICHO

6 Now Jericho was securely shut up because of
the children of Israel; none went out, and
none came in. 2And the LORD said to Joshua:
"See! I have given Jericho into your hand, its
king, *and* the mighty men of valor. 3You shall
march around the city, all *you* men of war; you
shall go all around the city once. This you shall

5:6 [a]Exodus 3:8 5:9 [a]Literally *Rolling*

THE MESSAGE

4-7 This is why Joshua conducted the circumcision. All the males who had left Egypt, the soldiers, had died in the wilderness on the journey out of Egypt. All the people who had come out of Egypt, of course, had been circumcised, but all those born in the wilderness along the way since leaving Egypt had not been. The fact is that the People of Israel had walked through that wilderness for forty years until the entire nation died out, all the men of military age who had come out of Egypt but had disobeyed the call of GOD. GOD vowed that these would never lay eyes on the land GOD had solemnly promised their ancestors to give us, a land flowing with milk and honey. But their children had replaced them. These are the ones Joshua circumcised. They had never been circumcised; no one had circumcised them along the way.

8 When they had completed the circumcising of the whole nation, they stayed where they were in camp until they were healed.

9 GOD said to Joshua, "Today I have rolled away the reproach of Egypt." That's why the place is called The Gilgal. It's still called that.

10 The People of Israel continued to camp at The Gilgal. They celebrated the Passover on the evening of the fourteenth day of the month on the plains of Jericho.

11-12 Right away, the day after the Passover, they started eating the produce of that country, unraised bread and roasted grain. And then no more manna; the manna stopped. As soon as they started eating food grown in the land, there was no more manna for the People of Israel. That year they ate from the crops of Canaan.

13 And then this, while Joshua was there near Jericho: He looked up and saw right in front of him a man standing, holding his drawn sword. Joshua stepped up to him and said, "Whose side are you on—ours or our enemies'?"

14 He said, "Neither. I'm commander of GOD's army. I've just arrived." Joshua fell, face to the ground, and worshiped. He asked, "What orders does my Master have for his servant?"

15 GOD's army commander ordered Joshua, "Take your sandals off your feet. The place you are standing is holy."

Joshua did it.

JERICHO

1 6 Jericho was shut up tight as a drum because of the People of Israel: no one going in, no one coming out.

2-5 GOD spoke to Joshua, "Look sharp now. I've already given Jericho to you, along with its king and its crack troops. Here's what you are to do: March around the city, all your soldiers. Circle the city once. Repeat

New King James Version

do six days. [4]And seven priests shall bear seven trumpets of rams' horns before the ark. But the seventh day you shall march around the city seven times, and the priests shall blow the trumpets. [5]It shall come to pass, when they make a long *blast* with the ram's horn, *and* when you hear the sound of the trumpet, that all the people shall shout with a great shout; then the wall of the city will fall down flat. And the people shall go up every man straight before him."

[6]Then Joshua the son of Nun called the priests and said to them, "Take up the ark of the covenant, and let seven priests bear seven trumpets of rams' horns before the ark of the LORD." [7]And he said to the people, "Proceed, and march around the city, and let him who is armed advance before the ark of the LORD."

[8]So it was, when Joshua had spoken to the people, that the seven priests bearing the seven trumpets of rams' horns before the LORD advanced and blew the trumpets, and the ark of the covenant of the LORD followed them. [9]The armed men went before the priests who blew the trumpets, and the rear guard came after the ark, while *the priests* continued blowing the trumpets. [10]Now Joshua had commanded the people, saying, "You shall not shout or make any noise with your voice, nor shall a word proceed out of your mouth, until the day I say to you, 'Shout!' Then you shall shout." [11]So he had the ark of the LORD circle the city, going around *it* once. Then they came into the camp and lodged in the camp.

[12]And Joshua rose early in the morning, and the priests took up the ark of the LORD. [13]Then seven priests bearing seven trumpets of rams' horns before the ark of the LORD went on continually and blew with the trumpets. And the armed men went before them. But the rear guard came after the ark of the LORD, while *the priests* continued blowing the trumpets. [14]And the second day they marched around the city once and returned to the camp. So they did six days.

[15]But it came to pass on the seventh day that they rose early, about the dawning of the day, and marched around the city seven times in the same manner. On that day only they marched around the city seven times. [16]And the seventh time it happened, when the priests blew the trumpets, that Joshua said to the people: "Shout, for the LORD has given you the city! [17]Now the city shall be doomed by the LORD to destruction, it and all who *are* in it. Only Rahab the harlot shall live, she and all who *are* with her in the house, because she hid the messengers that we sent. [18]And you, by all means abstain from the accursed things, lest you become accursed when you take of the accursed things, and make the camp of Israel a curse, and trouble it. [19]But all the silver and gold, and vessels of bronze and iron, *are* consecrated to the LORD; they shall come into the treasury of the LORD."

[20]So the people shouted when *the priests* blew the trumpets. And it happened when the people heard the sound of the trumpet, and the people shouted with a great shout, that the wall fell down flat. Then the people went up into the city, every man straight before him, and they took the city.

The Message

this for six days. Have seven priests carry seven ram's horn trumpets in front of the Chest. On the seventh day march around the city seven times, the priests blowing away on the trumpets. And then, a long blast on the ram's horn—when you hear that, all the people are to shout at the top of their lungs. The city wall will collapse at once. All the people are to enter, every man straight on in."

6 So Joshua son of Nun called the priests and told them, "Take up the Chest of the Covenant. Seven priests are to carry seven ram's horn trumpets leading GOD's Chest."

7 Then he told the people, "Set out! March around the city. Have the armed guard march before the Chest of GOD."

8-9 And it happened. Joshua spoke, the people moved: Seven priests with their seven ram's horn trumpets set out before GOD. They blew the trumpets, leading GOD's Chest of the Covenant. The armed guard marched ahead of the trumpet-blowing priests; the rear guard was marching after the Chest, marching and blowing their trumpets.

10 Joshua had given orders to the people, "Don't shout. In fact, don't even speak—not so much as a whisper until you hear me say, 'Shout!'—then shout away!"

11-13 He sent the Chest of GOD on its way around the city. It circled once, came back to camp, and stayed for the night. Joshua was up early the next morning and the priests took up the Chest of GOD. The seven priests carrying the seven ram's horn trumpets marched before the Chest of GOD, marching and blowing the trumpets, with the armed guard marching before and the rear guard marching after. Marching and blowing of trumpets!

14 On the second day they again circled the city once and returned to camp. They did this six days.

15-17 When the seventh day came, they got up early and marched around the city this same way but seven times—yes, this day they circled the city seven times. On the seventh time around the priests blew the trumpets and Joshua signaled the people, "Shout!—GOD has given you the city! The city and everything in it is under a holy curse and offered up to GOD.

"Except for Rahab the harlot—she is to live, she and everyone in her house with her, because she hid the agents we sent.

18-19 "As for you, watch yourselves in the city under holy curse. Be careful that you don't covet anything in it and take something that's cursed, endangering the camp of Israel with the curse and making trouble for everyone. All silver and gold, all vessels of bronze and iron are holy to GOD. Put them in GOD's treasury."

20 The priests blew the trumpets.

When the people heard the blast of the trumpets, they gave a thunderclap shout. The wall fell at once. The people rushed straight into the city and took it.

NEW KING JAMES VERSION

21 And they utterly destroyed all that *was* in the
city, both man and woman, young and old, ox
and sheep and donkey, with the edge of the
sword.
22 But Joshua had said to the two men who
had spied out the country, "Go into the harlot's
house, and from there bring out the woman and
all that she has, as you swore to her." 23 And the
young men who had been spies went in and
brought out Rahab, her father, her mother, her
brothers, and all that she had. So they brought
out all her relatives and left them outside the
camp of Israel. 24 But they burned the city and all
that *was* in it with fire. Only the silver and gold,
and the vessels of bronze and iron, they put into
the treasury of the house of the LORD. 25 And
Joshua spared Rahab the harlot, her father's
household, and all that she had. So she dwells in
Israel to this day, because she hid the messen-
gers whom Joshua sent to spy out Jericho.
26 Then Joshua charged *them* at that time,
saying, "Cursed *be* the man before the LORD
who rises up and builds this city Jericho;
he shall lay its foundation with his firstborn,
and with his youngest he shall set up its gates."
27 So the LORD was with Joshua, and his fame
spread throughout all the country.

DEFEAT AT AI

7 But the children of Israel committed a tres-
pass regarding the accursed things, for
Achan the son of Carmi, the son of Zabdi,[a] the
son of Zerah, of the tribe of Judah, took of the
accursed things; so the anger of the LORD
burned against the children of Israel.
2 Now Joshua sent men from Jericho to Ai,
which *is* beside Beth Aven, on the east side of
Bethel, and spoke to them, saying, "Go up and spy
out the country." So the men went up and spied
out Ai. 3 And they returned to Joshua and said to
him, "Do not let all the people go up, but let about
two or three thousand men go up and attack Ai.
Do not weary all the people there, for *the people
of Ai are* few." 4 So about three thousand men went
up there from the people, but they fled before the
men of Ai. 5 And the men of Ai struck down about
thirty-six men, for they chased them *from* before
the gate as far as Shebarim, and struck them
down on the descent; therefore the hearts of the
people melted and became like water.
6 Then Joshua tore his clothes, and fell to the
earth on his face before the ark of the LORD un-
til evening, he and the elders of Israel; and they
put dust on their heads. 7 And Joshua said, "Alas,
Lord GOD, why have You brought this people
over the Jordan at all—to deliver us into the
hand of the Amorites, to destroy us? Oh, that we
had been content, and dwelt on the other side of

7:1 [a]Called *Zimri* in 1 Chronicles 2:6

THE MESSAGE

21 They put everything in the city under the
holy curse, killing man and woman, young
and old, ox and sheep and donkey.
22-24 Joshua ordered the two men who had
spied out the land, "Enter the house of the
harlot and rescue the woman and everyone
connected with her, just as you promised
her." So the young spies went in and
brought out Rahab, her father, mother, and
brothers—everyone connected with her.
They got the whole family out and gave
them a place outside the camp of Israel. But
they burned down the city and everything in
it, except for the gold and silver and the
bronze and iron vessels—all that they put in
the treasury of GOD's house.
25 But Joshua let Rahab the harlot live—Ra-
hab and her father's household and every-
one connected to her. She is still alive and
well in Israel because she hid the agents
whom Joshua sent to spy out Jericho.

26 Joshua swore a solemn oath at that time:

Cursed before GOD is the man
who sets out to rebuild this city
Jericho.
He'll pay for the foundation with his
firstborn son,
he'll pay for the gates with his
youngest son.

27 GOD was with Joshua. He became famous
all over the land.

ACHAN

1 7 Then the People of Israel violated the
holy curse. Achan son of Carmi, the son
of Zabdi, the son of Zerah of the tribe of Ju-
dah, took some of the cursed things. GOD be-
came angry with the People of Israel.
2 Joshua sent men from Jericho to Ai (The
Ruin), which is near Beth Aven just east of
Bethel. He instructed them, "Go up and spy
out the land." The men went up and spied
out Ai.
3 They returned to Joshua and reported,
"Don't bother sending a lot of people—two
or three thousand men are enough to defeat
Ai. Don't wear out the whole army; there
aren't that many people there."
4-5 So three thousand men went up—and
then fled in defeat before the men of Ai! The
men of Ai killed thirty-six—chased them
from the city gate as far as The Quarries,
killing them at the descent. The heart of the
people sank, all spirit knocked out of them.
6 Joshua ripped his clothes and fell on his
face to the ground before the Chest of GOD,
he and the leaders throwing dirt on their
heads, prostrate until evening.
7-9 Joshua said, "Oh, oh, oh . . . Master, GOD.
Why did you insist on bringing this people
across the Jordan? To make us victims of the
Amorites? To wipe us out? Why didn't we
just settle down on the east side of the Jor-

NEW KING JAMES VERSION

the Jordan! 8O Lord, what shall I say when Is-
rael turns its back before its enemies? 9For the
Canaanites and all the inhabitants of the land
will hear *it,* and surround us, and cut off our
name from the earth. Then what will You do for
Your great name?"

THE SIN OF ACHAN

10So the LORD said to Joshua: "Get up! Why
do you lie thus on your face? 11Israel has sinned,
and they have also transgressed My covenant
which I commanded them. For they have even
taken some of the accursed things, and have
both stolen and deceived; and they have also put
it among their own stuff. 12Therefore the chil-
dren of Israel could not stand before their ene-
mies, *but* turned *their* backs before their ene-
mies, because they have become doomed to
destruction. Neither will I be with you anymore,
unless you destroy the accursed from among
you. 13Get up, sanctify the people, and say,
'Sanctify yourselves for tomorrow, because thus
says the LORD God of Israel: "*There is* an ac-
cursed thing in your midst, O Israel; you cannot
stand before your enemies until you take away
the accursed thing from among you." 14In the
morning therefore you shall be brought accord-
ing to your tribes. And it shall be *that* the tribe
which the LORD takes shall come according to
families; and the family which the LORD takes
shall come by households; and the household
which the LORD takes shall come man by man.
15Then it shall be *that* he who is taken with the
accursed thing shall be burned with fire, he and
all that he has, because he has transgressed the
covenant of the LORD, and because he has done
a disgraceful thing in Israel.' "
16So Joshua rose early in the morning and
brought Israel by their tribes, and the tribe of
Judah was taken. 17He brought the clan of Ju-
dah, and he took the family of the Zarhites; and
he brought the family of the Zarhites man by
man, and Zabdi was taken. 18Then he brought
his household man by man, and Achan the son
of Carmi, the son of Zabdi, the son of Zerah, of
the tribe of Judah, was taken.
19Now Joshua said to Achan, "My son, I beg
you, give glory to the LORD God of Israel, and
make confession to Him, and tell me now what
you have done; do not hide *it* from me."
20And Achan answered Joshua and said, "In-
deed I have sinned against the LORD God of Is-
rael, and this is what I have done: 21When I saw
among the spoils a beautiful Babylonian gar-
ment, two hundred shekels of silver, and a
wedge of gold weighing fifty shekels, I coveted
them and took them. And there they are, hidden
in the earth in the midst of my tent, with the sil-
ver under it."
22So Joshua sent messengers, and they ran to
the tent; and there it was, hidden in his tent,
with the silver under it. 23And they took them
from the midst of the tent, brought them to
Joshua and to all the children of Israel, and laid
them out before the LORD. 24Then Joshua, and
all Israel with him, took Achan the son of Zerah,
the silver, the garment, the wedge of gold, his
sons, his daughters, his oxen, his donkeys, his
sheep, his tent, and all that he had, and they

THE MESSAGE

dan? Oh, Master, what can I say after this, after Israel has been run off by its enemies? When the Canaanites and all the others living here get wind of this, they'll gang up on us and make short work of us—and then how will you keep up *your* reputation?"

10-12 GOD said to Joshua, "Get up. Why are you groveling? Israel has sinned: They've broken the covenant I commanded them; they've taken forbidden plunder—stolen and then covered up the theft, squirreling it away with their own stuff. The People of Israel can no longer look their enemies in the eye—they themselves are plunder. I can't continue with you if you don't rid yourselves of the cursed things.

13 "So get started. Purify the people. Tell them: Get ready for tomorrow by purifying yourselves. For this is what GOD, the God of Israel, says: There are cursed things in the camp. You won't be able to face your enemies until you have gotten rid of these cursed things.

14-15 "First thing in the morning you will be called up by tribes. The tribe GOD names will come up clan by clan; the clan GOD names will come up family by family; and the family GOD names will come up man by man. The person found with the cursed things will be burned, he and everything he has, because he broke GOD's covenant and did this despicable thing in Israel."

16-18 Joshua was up at the crack of dawn and called Israel up tribe by tribe. The tribe of Judah was singled out. Then he called up the clans and singled out the Zerahites. He called up the Zerahite families and singled out the Zabdi family. He called up the family members one by one and singled out Achan son of Carmi, the son of Zabdi, the son of Zerah of the tribe of Judah.

19 Joshua spoke to Achan, "My son, give glory to GOD, the God of Israel. Make your confession to him. Tell me what you did. Don't keep back anything from me."

20-21 Achan answered Joshua, "It's true. I sinned against GOD, the God of Israel. This is how I did it. In the plunder I spotted a beautiful Shinar robe, two hundred shekels of silver, and a fifty-shekel bar of gold, and I coveted and took them. They are buried in my tent with the silver at the bottom."

22-23 Joshua sent off messengers. They ran to the tent. And there it was, buried in the tent with the silver at the bottom. They took the stuff from the tent and brought it to Joshua and to all the People of Israel and spread it out before GOD.

24 Joshua took Achan son of Zerah, took the silver, the robe, the gold bar, his sons and daughters, his ox, donkey, sheep, and tent—everything connected with him. All Israel

New King James Version

brought them to the Valley of Achor. 25And
Joshua said, "Why have you troubled us? The
LORD will trouble you this day." So all Israel
stoned him with stones; and they burned them
with fire after they had stoned them with stones.
26Then they raised over him a great heap of
stones, still there to this day. So the LORD turned
from the fierceness of His anger. Therefore the
name of that place has been called the Valley of
Achor[a] to this day.

The Fall of Ai

8Now the LORD said to Joshua: "Do not be
afraid, nor be dismayed; take all the people of
war with you, and arise, go up to Ai. See, I have
given into your hand the king of Ai, his people,
his city, and his land. 2And you shall do to Ai
and its king as you did to Jericho and its king.
Only its spoil and its cattle you shall take as
booty for yourselves. Lay an ambush for the city
behind it."
3So Joshua arose, and all the people of war, to
go up against Ai; and Joshua chose thirty thou-
sand mighty men of valor and sent them away
by night. 4And he commanded them, saying: "Be-
hold, you shall lie in ambush against the city, be-
hind the city. Do not go very far from the city, but
all of you be ready. 5Then I and all the people
who *are* with me will approach the city; and it
will come about, when they come out against us
as at the first, that we shall flee before them. 6For
they will come out after us till we have drawn
them from the city, for they will say, '*They are*
fleeing before us as at the first.' Therefore we
will flee before them. 7Then you shall rise from
the ambush and seize the city, for the LORD your
God will deliver it into your hand. 8And it will be,
when you have taken the city, *that* you shall set
the city on fire. According to the commandment
of the LORD you shall do. See, I have commanded
you."
9Joshua therefore sent them out; and they
went to lie in ambush, and stayed between
Bethel and Ai, on the west side of Ai; but Joshua
lodged that night among the people. 10Then
Joshua rose up early in the morning and mus-
tered the people, and went up, he and the elders
of Israel, before the people to Ai. 11And all the
people of war who *were* with him went up and
drew near; and they came before the city and
camped on the north side of Ai. Now a valley *lay*
between them and Ai. 12So he took about five
thousand men and set them in ambush between
Bethel and Ai, on the west side of the city. 13And
when they had set the people, all the army that
was on the north of the city, and its rear guard
on the west of the city, Joshua went that night
into the midst of the valley.
14Now it happened, when the king of Ai saw
it, that the men of the city hurried and rose
early and went out against Israel to battle, he
and all his people, at an appointed place before
the plain. But he did not know that *there was* an
ambush against him behind the city. 15And
Joshua and all Israel made as if they were
beaten before them, and fled by the way of the
wilderness. 16So all the people who *were* in Ai

7:26 [a]Literally *Trouble*

The Message

was there. They led them off to the Valley of Achor (Trouble Valley).

25-26 Joshua said, "Why have you troubled us? GOD will now trouble you. Today!" And all Israel stoned him—burned him with fire and stoned him with stones. They piled a huge pile of stones over him. It's still there. Only then did GOD turn from his hot anger. That's how the place came to be called Trouble Valley right up to the present time.

Ai

1 8GOD said to Joshua, "Don't be timid and don't so much as hesitate. Take all your soldiers with you and go back to Ai. I have turned the king of Ai over to you—his people, his city, and his land.

2 "Do to Ai and its king what you did to Jericho and its king. Only this time you may plunder its stuff and cattle to your heart's content. Set an ambush behind the city."

3-8 Joshua and all his soldiers got ready to march on Ai. Joshua chose thirty thousand men, tough, seasoned fighters, and sent them off at night with these orders: "Look sharp now. Lie in ambush behind the city. Get as close as you can. Stay alert. I and the troops with me will approach the city head-on. When they come out to meet us just as before, we'll turn and run. They'll come after us, leaving the city. As we are off and running, they'll say, 'They're running away just like the first time.' That's your signal to spring from your ambush and take the city. GOD, your God, will hand it to you on a platter. Once you have the city, burn it down. GOD says it, you do it. Go to it. I've given you your orders."

9 Joshua sent them off. They set their ambush and waited between Bethel and Ai, just west of Ai. Joshua spent the night with the people.

10-13 Joshua was up early in the morning and mustered his army. He and the leaders of Israel led the troops to Ai. The whole army, fighting men all, marched right up within sight of the city and set camp on the north side of Ai. There was a valley between them and Ai. He had taken about five thousand men and put them in ambush between Bethel and Ai, west of the city. They were all deployed, the main army to the north of the city and the ambush to the west. Joshua spent the night in the valley.

14 So it happened that when the king of Ai saw all this, the men of the city lost no time; they were out of there at the crack of dawn to join Israel in battle, the king and his troops, at a field en route to the Arabah. The king didn't know of the ambush set against him behind the city.

15-17 Joshua and all Israel let themselves be chased; they ran toward the wilderness. Everybody in the city was called to the chase. They pursued Joshua and were led

NEW KING JAMES VERSION

were called together to pursue them. And they
pursued Joshua and were drawn away from the
city. 17There was not a man left in Ai or Bethel
who did not go out after Israel. So they left the
city open and pursued Israel.
18Then the LORD said to Joshua, "Stretch out
the spear that *is* in your hand toward Ai, for I
will give it into your hand." And Joshua
stretched out the spear that *was* in his hand to-
ward the city. 19So *those in* ambush arose
quickly out of their place; they ran as soon as he
had stretched out his hand, and they entered the
city and took it, and hurried to set the city on
fire. 20And when the men of Ai looked behind
them, they saw, and behold, the smoke of the
city ascended to heaven. So they had no power
to flee this way or that way, and the people who
had fled to the wilderness turned back on the
pursuers.
21Now when Joshua and all Israel saw that
the ambush had taken the city and that the
smoke of the city ascended, they turned back
and struck down the men of Ai. 22Then the oth-
ers came out of the city against them; so they
were *caught* in the midst of Israel, some on this
side and some on that side. And they struck
them down, so that they let none of them remain
or escape. 23But the king of Ai they took alive,
and brought him to Joshua.
24And it came to pass when Israel had made
an end of slaying all the inhabitants of Ai in the
field, in the wilderness where they pursued
them, and when they all had fallen by the edge
of the sword until they were consumed, that all
the Israelites returned to Ai and struck it with
the edge of the sword. 25So it was *that* all who
fell that day, both men and women, *were* twelve
thousand—all the people of Ai. 26For Joshua did
not draw back his hand, with which he
stretched out the spear, until he had utterly de-
stroyed all the inhabitants of Ai. 27Only the live-
stock and the spoil of that city Israel took as
booty for themselves, according to the word of
the LORD which He had commanded Joshua.
28So Joshua burned Ai and made it a heap for-
ever, a desolation to this day. 29And the king of
Ai he hanged on a tree until evening. And as
soon as the sun was down, Joshua commanded
that they should take his corpse down from the
tree, cast it at the entrance of the gate of the city,
and raise over it a great heap of stones *that re-*
mains to this day.

JOSHUA RENEWS THE COVENANT

30Now Joshua built an altar to the LORD God
of Israel in Mount Ebal, 31as Moses the servant
of the LORD had commanded the children of Is-
rael, as it is written in the Book of the Law of
Moses: "an altar of whole stones over which no
man has wielded an iron *tool.*"[a] And they of-
fered on it burnt offerings to the LORD, and sac-
rificed peace offerings. 32And there, in the pres-
ence of the children of Israel, he wrote on the
stones a copy of the law of Moses, which he had
written. 33Then all Israel, with their elders and
officers and judges, stood on either side of the
ark before the priests, the Levites, who bore the

8:31 [a]Deuteronomy 27:5, 6

THE MESSAGE

away from the city. There wasn't a soul left
in Ai or Bethel who wasn't out there chasing
after Israel. The city was left empty and un-
defended as they were chasing Israel down.
18-19 Then GOD spoke to Joshua: "Stretch out
the javelin in your hand toward Ai—I'm giv-
ing it to you." Joshua stretched out the
javelin in his hand toward Ai. At the signal
the men in ambush sprang to their feet, ran
to the city, took it, and quickly had it up in
flames.
20-21 The men of Ai looked back and, oh! saw
the city going up in smoke. They found
themselves trapped with nowhere to run.
The army on the run toward the wilderness
did an about-face—Joshua and all Israel,
seeing that the ambush had taken the city,
saw it going up in smoke, turned and at-
tacked the men of Ai.
22-23 Then the men in the ambush poured out
of the city. The men of Ai were caught in the
middle with Israelites on both sides—a real
massacre. And not a single survivor. Except
for the king of Ai; they took him alive and
brought him to Joshua.
24-25 When it was all over, Israel had killed
everyone in Ai, whether in the fields or in
the wilderness where they had chased them.
When the killing was complete, the Is-
raelites returned to Ai and completed the
devastation. The death toll that day came to
twelve thousand men and women—every-
one in Ai.
26-27 Joshua didn't lower his outstretched
javelin until the sacred destruction of Ai and
all its people was completed. Israel did get
to take the livestock and loot left in the city;
GOD's instructions to Joshua allowed for
that.
28-29 Joshua burned Ai to the ground. A "heap"
of nothing forever, a "no-place"—go see for
yourself. He hanged the king of Ai from a
tree. At evening, with the sun going down,
Joshua ordered the corpse cut down. They
dumped it at the entrance to the city and
piled it high with stones—you can go see
that also.

30-32 Then Joshua built an altar to the GOD of Is-
rael on Mount Ebal. He built it following the
instructions of Moses the servant of GOD to
the People of Israel and written in the Book
of The Revelation of Moses, an altar of
whole stones that hadn't been chiseled or
shaped by an iron tool. On it they offered to
GOD Whole-Burnt-Offerings and sacrificed
Peace-Offerings. He also wrote out a copy of
The Revelation of Moses on the stones. He
wrote it with the People of Israel looking on.
33 All Israel was there, foreigners and citi-
zens alike, with their elders, officers, and
judges, standing on opposite sides of the
Chest, facing the Levitical priests who carry

NEW KING JAMES VERSION

ark of the covenant of the LORD, the stranger as well as he who was born among them. Half of them *were* in front of Mount Gerizim and half of them in front of Mount Ebal, as Moses the servant of the LORD had commanded before, that they should bless the people of Israel. 34And afterward he read all the words of the law, the blessings and the cursings, according to all that is written in the Book of the Law. 35There was not a word of all that Moses had commanded which Joshua did not read before all the assembly of Israel, with the women, the little ones, and the strangers who were living among them.

THE TREATY WITH THE GIBEONITES

9 And it came to pass when all the kings who *were* on this side of the Jordan, in the hills and in the lowland and in all the coasts of the Great Sea toward Lebanon—the Hittite, the Amorite, the Canaanite, the Perizzite, the Hivite, and the Jebusite—heard *about it,* 2that they gathered together to fight with Joshua and Israel with one accord.

3But when the inhabitants of Gibeon heard what Joshua had done to Jericho and Ai, 4they worked craftily, and went and pretended to be ambassadors. And they took old sacks on their donkeys, old wineskins torn and mended, 5old and patched sandals on their feet, and old garments on themselves; and all the bread of their provision was dry *and* moldy. 6And they went to Joshua, to the camp at Gilgal, and said to him and to the men of Israel, "We have come from a far country; now therefore, make a covenant with us."

7Then the men of Israel said to the Hivites, "Perhaps you dwell among us; so how can we make a covenant with you?"

8But they said to Joshua, "We *are* your servants."

And Joshua said to them, "Who *are* you, and where do you come from?"

9So they said to him: "From a very far country your servants have come, because of the name of the LORD your God; for we have heard of His fame, and all that He did in Egypt, 10and all that He did to the two kings of the Amorites who *were* beyond the Jordan—to Sihon king of Heshbon, and Og king of Bashan, who was at Ashtaroth. 11Therefore our elders and all the inhabitants of our country spoke to us, saying, 'Take provisions with you for the journey, and go to meet them, and say to them, "We *are* your servants; now therefore, make a covenant with us." ' 12This bread of ours we took hot *for* our provision from our houses on the day we departed to come to you. But now look, it is dry and moldy. 13And these wineskins which we filled *were* new, and see, they are torn; and these our garments and our sandals have become old because of the very long journey."

14Then the men of Israel took some of their provisions; but they did not ask counsel of the LORD. 15So Joshua made peace with them, and made a covenant with them to let them live; and the rulers of the congregation swore to them.

16And it happened at the end of three days, after they had made a covenant with them, that they heard that they *were* their neighbors who

THE MESSAGE

GOD's Covenant Chest. Half of the people
stood with their backs to Mount Gerizim
and half with their backs to Mount Ebal to
bless the People of Israel, just as Moses the
servant of GOD had instructed earlier.
34-35 After that, he read out everything written
in The Revelation, the Blessing and the
Curse, everything in the Book of The Revelation.
There wasn't a word of all that Moses
commanded that Joshua didn't read to the
entire congregation—men, women, children,
and foreigners who had been with
them on the journey.

GIBEON

1-2 9 All the kings west of the Jordan in the
hills and foothills and along the Mediterranean
seacoast north toward Lebanon—
the Hittites, Amorites, Canaanites, Perizzites,
Hivites, Girgashites, and Jebusites—
got the news. They came together in a
coalition to fight against Joshua and Israel
under a single command.
3-6 The people of Gibeon heard what Joshua
had done to Jericho and Ai and cooked up a
ruse. They posed as travelers: their donkeys
loaded with patched sacks and mended
wineskins, threadbare sandals on their feet,
tattered clothes on their bodies, nothing but
dry crusts and crumbs for food. They came
to Joshua at Gilgal and spoke to the men of
Israel, "We've come from a far-off country;
make a covenant with us."
7 The men of Israel said to these Hivites,
"How do we know you aren't local people?
How could we then make a covenant with
you?"
8 They said to Joshua, "We'll be your servants."
Joshua said, "Who are you now? Where
did you come from?"
9-11 They said, "From a far-off country, very
far away. Your servants came because we'd
heard such great things about GOD, your
God—all those things he did in Egypt! And
the two Amorite kings across the Jordan,
King Sihon of Heshbon and King Og of
Bashan, who ruled in Ashtaroth! Our leaders
and everybody else in our country told
us, 'Pack up some food for the road and go
meet them. Tell them, We're your servants;
make a covenant with us.'
12-13 "This bread was warm from the oven
when we packed it and left to come and see
you. Now look at it—crusts and crumbs.
And our cracked and mended wineskins,
good as new when we filled them. And our
clothes and sandals, in tatters from the long,
hard traveling."
14 The men of Israel looked them over and
accepted the evidence. But they didn't ask
GOD about it.
15 So Joshua made peace with them and
formalized it with a covenant to guarantee
their lives. The leaders of the congregation
swore to it.
16-18 And then, three days after making this
covenant, they learned that they were next-door
neighbors who had been living there

NEW KING JAMES VERSION

dwelt near them. [17]Then the children of Israel journeyed and came to their cities on the third day. Now their cities *were* Gibeon, Chephirah, Beeroth, and Kirjath Jearim. [18]But the children of Israel did not attack them, because the rulers of the congregation had sworn to them by the LORD God of Israel. And all the congregation complained against the rulers.

[19]Then all the rulers said to all the congregation, "We have sworn to them by the LORD God of Israel; now therefore, we may not touch them. [20]This we will do to them: We will let them live, lest wrath be upon us because of the oath which we swore to them." [21]And the rulers said to them, "Let them live, but let them be woodcutters and water carriers for all the congregation, as the rulers had promised them."

[22]Then Joshua called for them, and he spoke to them, saying, "Why have you deceived us, saying, 'We *are* very far from you,' when you dwell near us? [23]Now therefore, you *are* cursed, and none of you shall be freed from being slaves—woodcutters and water carriers for the house of my God."

[24]So they answered Joshua and said, "Because your servants were clearly told that the LORD your God commanded His servant Moses to give you all the land, and to destroy all the inhabitants of the land from before you; therefore we were very much afraid for our lives because of you, and have done this thing. [25]And now, here we are, in your hands; do with us as it seems good and right to do to us." [26]So he did to them, and delivered them out of the hand of the children of Israel, so that they did not kill them. [27]And that day Joshua made them woodcutters and water carriers for the congregation and for the altar of the LORD, in the place which He would choose, even to this day.

THE SUN STANDS STILL

10 Now it came to pass when Adoni-Zedek king of Jerusalem heard how Joshua had taken Ai and had utterly destroyed it—as he had done to Jericho and its king, so he had done to Ai and its king—and how the inhabitants of Gibeon had made peace with Israel and were among them, [2]that they feared greatly, because Gibeon *was* a great city, like one of the royal cities, and because it *was* greater than Ai, and all its men *were* mighty. [3]Therefore Adoni-Zedek king of Jerusalem sent to Hoham king of Hebron, Piram king of Jarmuth, Japhia king of Lachish, and Debir king of Eglon, saying, [4]"Come up to me and help me, that we may attack Gibeon, for it has made peace with Joshua and with the children of Israel." [5]Therefore the five kings of the Amorites, the king of Jerusalem, the king of Hebron, the king of Jarmuth, the king of Lachish, *and* the king of Eglon, gathered together and went up, they and all their armies, and camped before Gibeon and made war against it.

[6]And the men of Gibeon sent to Joshua at the camp at Gilgal, saying, "Do not forsake your servants; come up to us quickly, save us and help us, for all the kings of the Amorites who dwell in the mountains have gathered together against us."

THE MESSAGE

all along! The People of Israel broke camp and set out; three days later they reached their towns—Gibeon, Kephirah, Beeroth, and Kiriath Jearim. But the People of Israel didn't attack them; the leaders of the congregation had given their word before the GOD of Israel. But the congregation was up in arms over their leaders.

19-21 The leaders were united in their response to the congregation: "We promised them in the presence of the GOD of Israel. We can't lay a hand on them now. But we can do this: We will let them live so we don't get blamed for breaking our promise." Then the leaders continued, "We'll let them live, but they will be woodcutters and water carriers for the entire congregation."

And that's what happened; the leaders' promise was kept.

22-23 But Joshua called the Gibeonites together and said, "Why did you lie to us, telling us, 'We live far, far away from you,' when you're our next-door neighbors? For that you are cursed. From now on it's menial labor for you—woodcutters and water carriers for the house of my God."

24-25 They answered Joshua, "We got the message loud and clear that GOD, your God, commanded through his servant Moses: to give you the whole country and destroy everyone living in it. We were terrified because of you; that's why we did this. That's it. We're at your mercy. Whatever you decide is right for us, do it."

26-27 And that's what they did. Joshua delivered them from the power of the People of Israel so they didn't kill them. But he made them woodcutters and water carriers for the congregation and for the Altar of GOD at the place GOD chooses. They still are.

THE FIVE KINGS

1-2 10 It wasn't long before My-Master-Zedek king of Jerusalem heard that Joshua had taken Ai and destroyed it and its king under a holy curse, just as he had done to Jericho and its king. He also learned that the people of Gibeon had come to terms with Israel and were living as neighbors. He and his people were alarmed: Gibeon was a big city—as big as any with a king and bigger than Ai—and all its men were seasoned fighters.

3-4 Adoni-Zedek king of Jerusalem sent word to Hoham king of Hebron, Piram king of Jarmuth, Japhia king of Lachish, and Debir king of Eglon: "Come and help me. Let's attack Gibeon; they've joined up with Joshua and the People of Israel."

5 So the five Amorite (Western) kings—the king of Jerusalem, the king of Hebron, the king of Jarmuth, the king of Lachish, and the king of Eglon—combined their armies and set out to attack Gibeon.

6 The men of Gibeon sent word to Joshua camped at Gilgal, "Don't let us down now! Come up here quickly! Save us! Help us! All the Amorite kings who live up in the hills have ganged up on us."

NEW KING JAMES VERSION

7So Joshua ascended from Gilgal, he and all
the people of war with him, and all the mighty
men of valor. 8And the LORD said to Joshua, "Do
not fear them, for I have delivered them into
your hand; not a man of them shall stand before
you." 9Joshua therefore came upon them sud-
denly, having marched all night from Gilgal.
10So the LORD routed them before Israel, killed
them with a great slaughter at Gibeon, chased
them along the road that goes to Beth Horon,
and struck them down as far as Azekah and
Makkedah. 11And it happened, as they fled be-
fore Israel *and* were on the descent of Beth
Horon, that the LORD cast down large hailstones
from heaven on them as far as Azekah, and they
died. *There were* more who died from the hail-
stones than the children of Israel killed with the
sword.

12Then Joshua spoke to the LORD in the day
when the LORD delivered up the Amorites before
the children of Israel, and he said in the sight of
Israel:

"Sun, stand still over Gibeon;
And Moon, in the Valley of Aijalon."
13So the sun stood still,
And the moon stopped,
Till the people had revenge
Upon their enemies.

Is this not written in the Book of Jasher? So the
sun stood still in the midst of heaven, and did
not hasten to go *down* for about a whole day.
14And there has been no day like that, before it
or after it, that the LORD heeded the voice of a
man; for the LORD fought for Israel.

15Then Joshua returned, and all Israel with
him, to the camp at Gilgal.

THE AMORITE KINGS EXECUTED

16But these five kings had fled and hidden
themselves in a cave at Makkedah. 17And it was
told Joshua, saying, "The five kings have been
found hidden in the cave at Makkedah."
18So Joshua said, "Roll large stones against
the mouth of the cave, and set men by it to guard
them. 19And do not stay *there* yourselves, *but*
pursue your enemies, and attack their rear
guard. Do not allow them to enter their cities,
for the LORD your God has delivered them into
your hand." 20Then it happened, while Joshua
and the children of Israel made an end of slay-
ing them with a very great slaughter, till they
had finished, that those who escaped entered
fortified cities. 21And all the people returned to
the camp, to Joshua at Makkedah, in peace.

No one moved his tongue against any of the
children of Israel.

22Then Joshua said, "Open the mouth of the
cave, and bring out those five kings to me from
the cave." 23And they did so, and brought out
those five kings to him from the cave: the king
of Jerusalem, the king of Hebron, the king of
Jarmuth, the king of Lachish, *and* the king of
Eglon.
24So it was, when they brought out those
kings to Joshua, that Joshua called for all the
men of Israel, and said to the captains of the
men of war who went with him, "Come near, put

THE MESSAGE

7-8 So Joshua set out from Gilgal, his whole army with him—all those tough soldiers! GOD told him, "Don't give them a second thought. I've put them under your thumb—not one of them will stand up to you."

9-11 Joshua marched all night from Gilgal and took them by total surprise. GOD threw them into total confusion before Israel, a major victory at Gibeon. Israel chased them along the ridge to Beth Horon and fought them all the way down to Azekah and Makkedah. As they ran from the People of Israel, down from the Beth Horon ridge and all the way to Azekah, GOD pitched huge stones on them out of the sky and many died. More died from the hailstones than the People of Israel killed with the sword.

12-13 The day GOD gave the Amorites up to Israel, Joshua spoke to GOD, with all Israel listening:

"Stop, Sun, over Gibeon;
Halt, Moon, over Aijalon Valley."
And Sun stopped,
Moon stood stock still
Until he defeated his enemies.

13-14 (You can find this written in the Book of Jashar.) The sun stopped in its tracks in mid sky; just sat there all day. There's never been a day like that before or since—GOD took orders from a human voice! Truly, GOD fought for Israel.

15 Then Joshua returned, all Israel with him, to the camp at Gilgal.

16-17 Meanwhile the five kings had hidden in the cave at Makkedah. Joshua was told, "The five kings have been found, hidden in the cave at Makkedah."

18-19 Joshua said, "Roll big stones against the mouth of the cave and post guards to keep watch. But don't you hang around—go after your enemies. Cut off their retreat. Don't let them back into their cities. GOD has given them to you."

20-21 Joshua and the People of Israel then finished them off, total devastation. Only a few got away to the fortified towns. The whole army then returned intact to the camp and to Joshua at Makkedah. There was no criticism that day from the People of Israel!

22 Then Joshua said, "Open the mouth of the cave and bring me those five kings."

23 They did it. They brought him the five kings from the cave: the king of Jerusalem, the king of Hebron, the king of Jarmuth, the king of Lachish, and the king of Eglon.

24 When they had them all there in front of Joshua, he called up the army and told the field commanders who had been with him, "Come here. Put your feet on the necks of these kings."

NEW KING JAMES VERSION

your feet on the necks of these kings." And they
drew near and put their feet on their necks.
25Then Joshua said to them, "Do not be afraid,
nor be dismayed; be strong and of good
courage, for thus the LORD will do to all your en-
emies against whom you fight." 26And afterward
Joshua struck them and killed them, and
hanged them on five trees; and they were hang-
ing on the trees until evening. 27So it was at the
time of the going down of the sun *that* Joshua
commanded, and they took them down from the
trees, cast them into the cave where they had
been hidden, and laid large stones against the
cave's mouth, *which remain* until this very day.

CONQUEST OF THE SOUTHLAND

28On that day Joshua took Makkedah, and
struck it and its king with the edge of the sword.
He utterly destroyed them[a]—all the people who
were in it. He let none remain. He also did to the
king of Makkedah as he had done to the king of
Jericho.

29Then Joshua passed from Makkedah, and
all Israel with him, to Libnah; and they fought
against Libnah. 30And the LORD also delivered it
and its king into the hand of Israel; he struck it
and all the people who *were* in it with the edge
of the sword. He let none remain in it, but did to
its king as he had done to the king of Jericho.

31Then Joshua passed from Libnah, and all
Israel with him, to Lachish; and they encamped
against it and fought against it. 32And the LORD
delivered Lachish into the hand of Israel, who
took it on the second day, and struck it and all
the people who *were* in it with the edge of the
sword, according to all that he had done to Lib-
nah. 33Then Horam king of Gezer came up to
help Lachish; and Joshua struck him and his
people, until he left him none remaining.

34From Lachish Joshua passed to Eglon, and
all Israel with him; and they encamped against
it and fought against it. 35They took it on that
day and struck it with the edge of the sword; all
the people who *were* in it he utterly destroyed
that day, according to all that he had done to
Lachish.

36So Joshua went up from Eglon, and all Is-
rael with him, to Hebron; and they fought
against it. 37And they took it and struck it with
the edge of the sword—its king, all its cities, and
all the people who *were* in it; he left none re-
maining, according to all that he had done to
Eglon, but utterly destroyed it and all the people
who *were* in it.

38Then Joshua returned, and all Israel with
him, to Debir; and they fought against it. 39And
he took it and its king and all its cities; they
struck them with the edge of the sword and ut-
terly destroyed all the people who *were* in it. He
left none remaining; as he had done to Hebron,
so he did to Debir and its king, as he had done
also to Libnah and its king.

40So Joshua conquered all the land: the
mountain country and the South[a] and the low-
land and the wilderness slopes, and all their

10:28 [a]Following Masoretic Text and most authorities; many Hebrew manuscripts, some manuscripts of the Septuagint, and some manuscripts of the Targum read *it*. **10:40** [a]Hebrew *Negev*, and so throughout this book

THE MESSAGE

They stepped up and put their feet on
their necks.

25 Joshua told them, "Don't hold back.
Don't be timid. Be strong! Be confident! This
is what GOD will do to all your enemies
when you fight them."

26-27 Then Joshua struck and killed the kings.
He hung them on five trees where they re-
mained until evening. At sunset Joshua gave
the command. They took them down from
the trees and threw them into the cave
where they had hidden. They put large
stones at the mouth of the cave. The kings
are still in there.

NO SURVIVORS

28 That same day Joshua captured Makkedah,
a massacre that included the king. He car-
ried out the holy curse. No survivors.
Makkedah's king got the same treatment as
Jericho's king.

29-30 Joshua, all Israel with him, moved on
from Makkedah to Libnah and fought
against Libnah. GOD gave Libnah to Israel.
They captured city and king and massacred
the lot. No survivors. Libnah's king got the
same treatment as Jericho's king.

31-32 Joshua, all Israel with him, moved on
from Libnah to Lachish. He set up camp
nearby and attacked. GOD gave Lachish to
Israel. Israel took it in two days and killed
everyone. He carried out the holy curse, the
same as with Libnah.

33 Horam, king of Gezer, arrived to help
Lachish. Joshua attacked him and his army
until there was nothing left of them. No sur-
vivors.

34-35 Joshua, all Israel with him, moved on
from Lachish to Eglon. They set up camp
and attacked. They captured it and killed
everyone, carrying out the holy curse, the
same as they had done with Lachish.

36-37 Joshua, all Israel with him, went up from
Eglon to Hebron. He attacked and captured
it. They killed everyone, including its king,
its villages, and their people. No survivors,
the same as with Eglon. They carried out the
holy curse on city and people.

38-39 Then Joshua, all Israel with him, turned
toward Debir and attacked it. He captured
it, its king, and its villages. They killed
everyone. They put everyone and everything
under the holy curse. No survivors. Debir
and its king got the same treatment as He-
bron and its king, and Libnah and its king.

40-42 Joshua took the whole country: hills, desert,
foothills, and mountain slopes, including all

NEW KING JAMES VERSION

kings; he left none remaining, but utterly de-
stroyed all that breathed, as the LORD God of Is-
rael had commanded. 41And Joshua conquered
them from Kadesh Barnea as far as Gaza, and
all the country of Goshen, even as far as Gibeon.
42All these kings and their land Joshua took at
one time, because the LORD God of Israel fought
for Israel. 43Then Joshua returned, and all Israel
with him, to the camp at Gilgal.

THE NORTHERN CONQUEST

11 And it came to pass, when Jabin king of
Hazor heard *these things*, that he sent to
Jobab king of Madon, to the king of Shimron, to
the king of Achshaph, 2and to the kings who
were from the north, in the mountains, in the
plain south of Chinneroth, in the lowland, and
in the heights of Dor on the west, 3to the
Canaanites in the east and in the west, the
Amorite, the Hittite, the Perizzite, the Jebusite in
the mountains, and the Hivite below Hermon in
the land of Mizpah. 4So they went out, they and
all their armies with them, *as* many people *as*
the sand that *is* on the seashore in multitude,
with very many horses and chariots. 5And when
all these kings had met together, they came and
camped together at the waters of Merom to fight
against Israel.
6But the LORD said to Joshua, "Do not be afraid
because of them, for tomorrow about this time I
will deliver all of them slain before Israel. You
shall hamstring their horses and burn their char-
iots with fire." 7So Joshua and all the people of
war with him came against them suddenly by the
waters of Merom, and they attacked them. 8And
the LORD delivered them into the hand of Israel,
who defeated them and chased them to Greater
Sidon, to the Brook Misrephoth,[a] and to the Valley
of Mizpah eastward; they attacked them until
they left none of them remaining. 9So Joshua did
to them as the LORD had told him: he hamstrung
their horses and burned their chariots with fire.
10Joshua turned back at that time and took
Hazor, and struck its king with the sword; for
Hazor was formerly the head of all those king-
doms. 11And they struck all the people who *were*
in it with the edge of the sword, utterly destroy-
ing *them*. There was none left breathing. Then
he burned Hazor with fire.
12So all the cities of those kings, and all their
kings, Joshua took and struck with the edge of
the sword. He utterly destroyed them, as Moses
the servant of the LORD had commanded. 13But
as for the cities that stood on their mounds,[a] Is-
rael burned none of them, except Hazor only,
which Joshua burned. 14And all the spoil of these
cities and the livestock, the children of Israel
took as booty for themselves; but they struck
every man with the edge of the sword until they
had destroyed them, and they left none breath-
ing. 15As the LORD had commanded Moses his
servant, so Moses commanded Joshua, and so
Joshua did. He left nothing undone of all that the
LORD had commanded Moses.

11:8 [a]Hebrew *Misrephoth Maim* 11:13 [a]Hebrew *tel*, a heap of successive city ruins

THE MESSAGE

kings. He left no survivors. He carried out the holy curse on everything that breathed, just as GOD, the God of Israel, had commanded. Joshua's conquest stretched from Kadesh Barnea to Gaza and from the entire region of Goshen to Gibeon. Joshua took all these kings and their lands in a single campaign because GOD, the God of Israel, fought for Israel.

43 Then Joshua, all Israel with him, went back to the camp at Gilgal.

1-3 11 When Jabin king of Hazor heard of all this, he sent word to Jobab king of Madon; to the king of Shimron; to the king of Acshaph; to all the kings in the northern mountains; to the kings in the valley south of Kinnereth; to the kings in the western foothills and Naphoth Dor; to the Canaanites both east and west; to the Amorites, Hittites, Perizzites, and Jebusites in the hill country; and to the Hivites below Hermon in the region of Mizpah.

4-5 They came out in full force, all their troops massed together—a huge army, in number like sand on an ocean beach—to say nothing of all the horses and chariots. All these kings met and set up camp together at the Waters of Merom, ready to fight against Israel.

6 GOD said to Joshua: "Don't worry about them. This time tomorrow I'll hand them over to Israel, all dead. You'll hamstring their horses. You'll set fire to their chariots."

7-9 Joshua, his entire army with him, took them by surprise, falling on them at the Waters of Merom. GOD gave them to Israel, who struck and chased them all the way to Greater Sidon, to Misrephoth Maim, and then to the Valley of Mizpah on the east. No survivors. Joshua treated them following GOD's instructions: he hamstrung their horses; he burned up their chariots.

10-11 Then Joshua came back and took Hazor, killing its king. Early on Hazor had been head of all these kingdoms. They killed every person there, carrying out the holy curse—not a breath of life left anywhere. Then he burned down Hazor.

12-14 Joshua captured and massacred all the royal towns with their kings, the holy curse commanded by Moses the servant of GOD. But Israel didn't burn the cities that were built on mounds, except for Hazor—Joshua did burn down Hazor. The People of Israel plundered all the loot, including the cattle, from these towns for themselves. But they killed the people—total destruction. They left nothing human that breathed.

15 Just as GOD commanded his servant Moses, so Moses commanded Joshua, and Joshua did it. He didn't leave incomplete one thing that GOD had commanded Moses.

NEW KING JAMES VERSION

SUMMARY OF JOSHUA'S CONQUESTS

16 Thus Joshua took all this land: the moun-
tain country, all the South, all the land of
Goshen, the lowland, and the Jordan plain[a]—the
mountains of Israel and its lowlands, 17 from
Mount Halak and the ascent to Seir, even as far
as Baal Gad in the Valley of Lebanon below
Mount Hermon. He captured all their kings, and
struck them down and killed them. 18 Joshua
made war a long time with all those kings.
19 There was not a city that made peace with the
children of Israel, except the Hivites, the inhab-
itants of Gibeon. All *the others* they took in bat-
tle. 20 For it was of the LORD to harden their
hearts, that they should come against Israel in
battle, that He might utterly destroy them, *and*
that they might receive no mercy, but that He
might destroy them, as the LORD had com-
manded Moses.

21 And at that time Joshua came and cut off
the Anakim from the mountains: from Hebron,
from Debir, from Anab, from all the mountains
of Judah, and from all the mountains of Israel;
Joshua utterly destroyed them with their cities.
22 None of the Anakim were left in the land of the
children of Israel; they remained only in Gaza,
in Gath, and in Ashdod.

23 So Joshua took the whole land, according
to all that the LORD had said to Moses; and
Joshua gave it as an inheritance to Israel ac-
cording to their divisions by their tribes. Then
the land rested from war.

THE KINGS CONQUERED BY MOSES

12 These *are* the kings of the land whom the
children of Israel defeated, and whose
land they possessed on the other side of the Jor-
dan toward the rising of the sun, from the River
Arnon to Mount Hermon, and all the eastern
Jordan plain: 2 *One king was* Sihon king of the
Amorites, who dwelt in Heshbon *and* ruled half
of Gilead, from Aroer, which is on the bank of
the River Arnon, from the middle of that river,
even as far as the River Jabbok, *which is* the
border of the Ammonites, 3 and the eastern Jor-
dan plain from the Sea of Chinneroth as far as
the Sea of the Arabah (the Salt Sea), the road to
Beth Jeshimoth, and southward below the
slopes of Pisgah. 4 *The other king was* Og king of
Bashan and his territory, *who was* of the rem-
nant of the giants, who dwelt at Ashtaroth and
at Edrei, 5 and reigned over Mount Hermon, over
Salcah, over all Bashan, as far as the border of
the Geshurites and the Maachathites, and over
half of Gilead *to* the border of Sihon king of
Heshbon.

6 These Moses the servant of the LORD and
the children of Israel had conquered; and Moses
the servant of the LORD had given it *as* a posses-
sion to the Reubenites, the Gadites, and half the
tribe of Manasseh.

11:16 [a]Hebrew *arabah*

THE MESSAGE

16-20 Joshua took the whole country: the moun-
tains, the southern desert, all of Goshen, the
foothills, the valley (the Arabah), and the Is-
rael mountains with their foothills, from
Mount Halak, which towers over the region
of Seir, all the way to Baal Gad in the Valley
of Lebanon in the shadows of Mount Her-
mon. He captured their kings and then
killed them. Joshua fought against these
kings for a long time. Not one town made
peace with the People of Israel, with the one
exception of the Hivites who lived in
Gibeon. Israel fought and took all the rest. It
was GOD's idea that they all would stub-
bornly fight the Israelites so he could put
them under the holy curse without mercy.
That way he could destroy them just as GOD
had commanded Moses.

21-22 Joshua came out at that time also to root out
the Anakim from the hills, from Hebron,
from Debir, from Anab, from the mountains
of Judah, from the mountains of Israel.
Joshua carried out the holy curse on them
and their cities. No Anakim were left in the
land of the People of Israel, except in Gaza,
Gath, and Ashdod—there were a few left
there.

23 Joshua took the whole region. He did
everything that GOD had told Moses. Then
he parceled it out as an inheritance to Israel
according to their tribes.

And Israel had rest from war.

THE DEFEATED KINGS

1 12 These are the kings that the People of
Israel defeated and whose land they
took on the east of the Jordan, from the
Arnon Gorge to Mount Hermon, with the
whole eastern side of the Arabah Valley.

2-3 Sihon king of the Amorites, who reigned
from Heshbon: His rule extended from
Aroer, which sits at the edge of the Arnon
Gorge, from the middle of the gorge and
over half of Gilead to the Gorge of the Jab-
bok River, which is the border of the Am-
monites. His rule included the eastern
Arabah Valley from the Sea of Kinnereth to
the Arabah Sea (the Salt Sea), eastward to-
ward Beth Jeshimoth and southward to the
slopes of Pisgah.

4-5 And Og king of Bashan, one of the last of
the Rephaim who reigned from Ashtaroth
and Edrei: His rule extended from Mount
Hermon and Salecah over the whole of
Bashan to the border of the Geshurites and
the Maacathites (the other half of Gilead) to
the border of Sihon king of Heshbon.

6 Moses the servant of GOD and the People
of Israel defeated them. And Moses the ser-
vant of GOD gave this land as an inheritance
to the Reubenites, the Gadites, and half of
the tribe of Manasseh.

NEW KING JAMES VERSION

THE KINGS CONQUERED BY JOSHUA

7And these *are* the kings of the country
which Joshua and the children of Israel con-
quered on this side of the Jordan, on the west,
from Baal Gad in the Valley of Lebanon as far as
Mount Halak and the ascent to Seir, which
Joshua gave to the tribes of Israel *as* a posses-
sion according to their divisions, 8in the moun-
tain country, in the lowlands, in the *Jordan*
plain, in the slopes, in the wilderness, and in the
South—the Hittites, the Amorites, the Canaan-
ites, the Perizzites, the Hivites, and the Jeb-
usites: 9the king of Jericho, one; the king of Ai,
which *is* beside Bethel, one; 10the king of
Jerusalem, one; the king of Hebron, one; 11the
king of Jarmuth, one; the king of Lachish, one;
12the king of Eglon, one; the king of Gezer,
one; 13the king of Debir, one; the king of Geder,
one; 14the king of Hormah, one; the king of
Arad, one; 15the king of Libnah, one; the king of
Adullam, one; 16the king of Makkedah, one; the
king of Bethel, one; 17the king of Tappuah, one;
the king of Hepher, one; 18the king of Aphek,
one; the king of Lasharon, one; 19the king of
Madon, one; the king of Hazor, one; 20the king of
Shimron Meron, one; the king of Achshaph,
one; 21the king of Taanach, one; the king of
Megiddo, one; 22the king of Kedesh, one; the
king of Jokneam in Carmel, one; 23the king of
Dor in the heights of Dor, one; the king of the
people of Gilgal, one; 24the king of Tirzah, one—
all the kings, thirty-one.

REMAINING LAND TO BE CONQUERED

13 Now Joshua was old, advanced in years.
And the LORD said to him: "You are old, ad-
vanced in years, and there remains very much
land yet to be possessed. 2This is the land that
yet remains: all the territory of the Philistines
and all *that of* the Geshurites, 3from Sihor,
which *is* east of Egypt, as far as the border of
Ekron northward (*which* is counted as Canaan-
ite); the five lords of the Philistines—the
Gazites, the Ashdodites, the Ashkelonites, the
Gittites, and the Ekronites; also the Avites;
4from the south, all the land of the Canaanites,
and Mearah that belongs to the Sidonians as far
as Aphek, to the border of the Amorites; 5the
land of the Gebalites,[a] and all Lebanon, toward
the sunrise, from Baal Gad below Mount Her-
mon as far as the entrance to Hamath; 6all the

13:5 [a]Or *Giblites*

THE MESSAGE

7-24 And these are the kings of the land that Joshua and the People of Israel defeated in the country west of the Jordan, from Baal Gad in the Valley of Lebanon south to Mount Halak, which towers over Seir. Joshua gave this land to the tribes of Israel as a possession, according to their divisions: lands in the mountains, the western foothills, and the Arabah Valley, on the slopes, and in the wilderness and the Negev desert (lands on which Hittites, Amorites and Canaanites, Perizzites, Hivites, and Jebusites had lived). The kings were:

The king of Jericho	one
The king of Ai (near Bethel)	one
The king of Jerusalem	one
The king of Hebron	one
The king of Jarmuth	one
The king of Lachish	one
The king of Eglon	one
The king of Gezer	one
The king of Debir	one
The king of Geder	one
The king of Hormah	one
The king of Arad	one
The king of Libnah	one
The king of Adullam	one
The king of Makkedah	one
The king of Bethel	one
The king of Tappuah	one
The king of Hepher	one
The king of Aphek	one
The king of Lasharon	one
The king of Madon	one
The king of Hazor	one
The king of Shimron Meron	one
The king of Acshaph	one
The king of Taanach	one
The king of Megiddo	one
The king of Kedesh	one
The king of Jokneam in Carmel	one
The king of Dor (Naphoth Dor)	one
The king of Goyim in Gilgal	one
The king of Tirzah	one

A total of thirty-one kings.

THE RECEIVING OF THE LAND

1-6 13 When Joshua had reached a venerable age, GOD said to him, "You've had a good, long life, but there is a lot of land still to be taken. This is the land that remains:

all the districts of the Philistines and Geshurites;

the land from the Shihor River east of Egypt to the border of Ekron up north, Canaanite country (there were five Philistine tyrants—in Gaza, in Ashdod, in Ashkelon, in Gath, in Ekron); also the Avvim from the south;

all the Canaanite land from Arah (belonging to the Sidonians) to Aphek at the Amorite border;

the country of the Gebalites;

all Lebanon eastward from Baal Gad in the shadow of Mount Hermon to the Entrance of Hamath;

NEW KING JAMES VERSION

inhabitants of the mountains from Lebanon as
far as the Brook Misrephoth,[a] *and* all the Sidonians—them I will drive out from before the
children of Israel; only divide it by lot to Israel
as an inheritance, as I have commanded you.
7Now therefore, divide this land as an inheritance to the nine tribes and half the tribe of Manasseh."

THE LAND DIVIDED EAST OF THE JORDAN

8With the other half-tribe the Reubenites and
the Gadites received their inheritance, which
Moses had given them, beyond the Jordan eastward, as Moses the servant of the LORD had
given them: 9from Aroer which *is* on the bank of
the River Arnon, and the town that *is* in the
midst of the ravine, and all the plain of Medeba
as far as Dibon; 10all the cities of Sihon king of
the Amorites, who reigned in Heshbon, as far as
the border of the children of Ammon; 11Gilead,
and the border of the Geshurites and Maachathites, all Mount Hermon, and all Bashan as far
as Salcah; 12all the kingdom of Og in Bashan,
who reigned in Ashtaroth and Edrei, who remained of the remnant of the giants; for Moses
had defeated and cast out these.

13Nevertheless the children of Israel did not
drive out the Geshurites or the Maachathites,
but the Geshurites and the Maachathites dwell
among the Israelites until this day.

14Only to the tribe of Levi he had given no inheritance; the sacrifices of the LORD God of Israel made by fire *are* their inheritance, as He
said to them.

THE LAND OF REUBEN

15And Moses had given to the tribe of the
children of Reuben *an inheritance* according to
their families. 16Their territory was from Aroer,
which *is* on the bank of the River Arnon, and the
city that *is* in the midst of the ravine, and all the
plain by Medeba; 17Heshbon and all its cities that
are in the plain: Dibon, Bamoth Baal, Beth Baal
Meon, 18Jahaza, Kedemoth, Mephaath, 19Kirjathaim, Sibmah, Zereth Shahar on the mountain of the valley, 20Beth Peor, the slopes of Pisgah, and Beth Jeshimoth— 21all the cities of the
plain and all the kingdom of Sihon king of the
Amorites, who reigned in Heshbon, whom
Moses had struck with the princes of Midian:
Evi, Rekem, Zur, Hur, and Reba, who *were*
princes of Sihon dwelling in the country. 22The
children of Israel also killed with the sword Balaam the son of Beor, the soothsayer, among
those who were killed by them. 23And the border
of the children of Reuben was the bank of the
Jordan. This *was* the inheritance of the children
of Reuben according to their families, the cities
and their villages.

13:6 [a]Hebrew *Misrephoth Maim*

THE MESSAGE

all who live in the mountains, from
Lebanon to Misrephoth Maim;
all the Sidonians.

6-7 "I myself will drive them out before the People of Israel. All you have to do is allot this land to Israel as an inheritance, as I have instructed you. Do it now: Allot this land as an inheritance to the nine tribes and the half-tribe of Manasseh."

LAND EAST OF THE JORDAN

8 The other half-tribe of Manasseh, with the Reubenites and Gadites, had been given their inheritance by Moses on the other side of the Jordan eastward. Moses the servant of GOD gave it to them.

9-13 This land extended from Aroer at the edge of the Arnon Gorge and the city in the middle of the valley, taking in the entire tableland of Medeba as far as Dibon, and all the towns of Sihon king of the Amorites, who ruled from Heshbon, and out to the border of the Ammonites. It also included Gilead, the country of the people of Geshur and Maacah, all of Mount Hermon, and all Bashan as far as Salecah—the whole kingdom of Og in Bashan, who reigned in Ashtaroth and Edrei. He was one of the last survivors of the Rephaim. Moses had defeated them and taken their land. The People of Israel never did drive out the Geshurites and the Maacathites—they're still there, living in Israel.

14 Levi was the only tribe that did not receive an inheritance. The Fire-Gift-Offerings to GOD, the God of Israel, are their inheritance, just as he told them.

REUBEN

15-22 To the tribe of Reuben, clan by clan, Moses gave:

the land from Aroer at the edge of the Arnon Gorge and the town in the middle of the valley, including the tableland around Medeba;

Heshbon on the tableland with all its towns (Dibon, Bamoth Baal, Beth Baal Meon, Jahaz, Kedemoth, Mephaath, Kiriathaim, Sibmah, Zereth Shahar on Valley Mountain, Beth Peor, the slopes of Pisgah, Beth Jeshimoth);

and all the cities of the tableland, the whole kingdom of Sihon king of the Amorites, who ruled at Heshbon, whom Moses put to death along with the princes of Midian: Evi, Rekem, Zur, Hur, and Reba, who lived in that country, all puppets of Sihon. (In addition to those killed in battle, Balaam son of Beor, the soothsayer, was put to death by the People of Israel.)

23 The boundary for the Reubenites was the bank of the Jordan River. This was the inheritance of the Reubenites, their villages and cities, according to their clans.

NEW KING JAMES VERSION

THE LAND OF GAD

24 Moses also had given *an inheritance* to the tribe of Gad, to the children of Gad according to their families. 25 Their territory was Jazer, and all the cities of Gilead, and half the land of the Ammonites as far as Aroer, which *is* before Rabbah, 26 and from Heshbon to Ramath Mizpah and Betonim, and from Mahanaim to the border of Debir, 27 and in the valley Beth Haram, Beth Nimrah, Succoth, and Zaphon, the rest of the kingdom of Sihon king of Heshbon, with the Jordan as *its* border, as far as the edge of the Sea of Chinnereth, on the other side of the Jordan eastward. 28 This *is* the inheritance of the children of Gad according to their families, the cities and their villages.

HALF THE TRIBE OF MANASSEH (EAST)

29 Moses also had given *an inheritance* to half the tribe of Manasseh; it was for half the tribe of the children of Manasseh according to their families: 30 Their territory was from Mahanaim, all Bashan, all the kingdom of Og king of Bashan, and all the towns of Jair which are in Bashan, sixty cities; 31 half of Gilead, and Ashtaroth and Edrei, cities of the kingdom of Og in Bashan, *were* for the children of Machir the son of Manasseh, for half of the children of Machir according to their families.

32 These *are the areas* which Moses had distributed as an inheritance in the plains of Moab on the other side of the Jordan, by Jericho eastward. 33 But to the tribe of Levi Moses had given no inheritance; the LORD God of Israel *was* their inheritance, as He had said to them.

THE LAND DIVIDED WEST OF THE JORDAN

14 These *are the areas* which the children of Israel inherited in the land of Canaan, which Eleazar the priest, Joshua the son of Nun, and the heads of the fathers of the tribes of the children of Israel distributed as an inheritance to them. 2 Their inheritance *was* by lot, as the LORD had commanded by the hand of Moses, for the nine tribes and the half-tribe. 3 For Moses had given the inheritance of the two tribes and the half-tribe on the other side of the Jordan; but to the Levites he had given no inheritance among them. 4 For the children of Joseph were two tribes: Manasseh and Ephraim. And they gave no part to the Levites in the land, except cities to dwell *in*, with their common-lands for their livestock and their property. 5 As the LORD had commanded Moses, so the children of Israel did; and they divided the land.

CALEB INHERITS HEBRON

6 Then the children of Judah came to Joshua in Gilgal. And Caleb the son of Jephunneh the Kenizzite said to him: "You know the word which the LORD said to Moses the man of God concerning you and me in Kadesh Barnea. 7 I *was* forty years old when Moses the servant of the LORD sent me from Kadesh Barnea to spy

THE MESSAGE

GAD

24-27 To the tribe of Gad, clan by clan, Moses gave:
the territory of Jazer and all the towns of Gilead and half the Ammonite country as far as Aroer near Rabbah;
the land from Heshbon to Ramath Mizpah and Betonim, and from Mahanaim to the region of Debir;
in the valley: Beth Haram, Beth Nimrah, Succoth, and Zaphon, with the rest of the kingdom of Sihon king of Heshbon (the east side of the Jordan, north to the end of the Sea of Kinnereth).

28 This was the inheritance of the Gadites, their cities and villages, clan by clan.

HALF-TRIBE OF MANASSEH

29-31 To the half-tribe of Manasseh, clan by clan, Moses gave:
the land stretching out from Mahanaim;
all of Bashan, which is the entire kingdom of Og king of Bashan, and all the settlements of Jair in Bashan—sixty towns in all.
Half of Gilead with Ashtaroth and Edrei, the royal cities of Og in Bashan, belong to the descendants of Makir, a son of Manasseh (in other words, the half-tribe of the children of Makir) for their clans.

32-33 This is the inheritance that Moses gave out when he was on the plains of Moab across the Jordan east of Jericho. But Moses gave no inheritance to the tribe of Levi. GOD, the God of Israel, is their inheritance, just as he told them.

LAND WEST OF THE JORDAN

1-2 14 Here are the inheritance allotments that the People of Israel received in the land of Canaan. Eleazar the priest, Joshua son of Nun, and the heads of the family clans made the allotments. Each inheritance was assigned by lot to the nine and a half tribes, just as GOD had commanded Moses.

3-4 Moses had given the two and a half tribes their inheritance east of the Jordan, but hadn't given an inheritance to the Levites, as he had to the others. Because the sons of Joseph had become two tribes, Manasseh and Ephraim, they gave no allotment to the Levites; but they did give them cities to live in with pasture rights for their flocks and herds.

5 The People of Israel followed through exactly as GOD had commanded Moses. They apportioned the land.

CALEB

6-12 The people of Judah came to Joshua at Gilgal. Caleb son of Jephunneh the Kenizzite spoke: "You'll remember what GOD said to Moses the man of God concerning you and me back at Kadesh Barnea. I was forty years old when Moses the servant of GOD

NEW KING JAMES VERSION

out the land, and I brought back word to him as *it was* in my heart. 8Nevertheless my brethren who went up with me made the heart of the people melt, but I wholly followed the LORD my God. 9So Moses swore on that day, saying, 'Surely the land where your foot has trodden shall be your inheritance and your children's forever, because you have wholly followed the LORD my God.' 10And now, behold, the LORD has kept me alive, as He said, these forty-five years, ever since the LORD spoke this word to Moses while Israel wandered in the wilderness; and now, here I am this day, eighty-five years old. 11As yet I *am as* strong this day as on the day that Moses sent me; just as my strength *was* then, so now *is* my strength for war, both for going out and for coming in. 12Now therefore, give me this mountain of which the LORD spoke in that day; for you heard in that day how the Anakim *were* there, and *that* the cities *were* great *and* fortified. It may be that the LORD *will be* with me, and I shall be able to drive them out as the LORD said."

13And Joshua blessed him, and gave Hebron to Caleb the son of Jephunneh as an inheritance. 14Hebron therefore became the inheritance of Caleb the son of Jephunneh the Kenizzite to this day, because he wholly followed the LORD God of Israel. 15And the name of Hebron formerly was Kirjath Arba (*Arba was* the greatest man among the Anakim).

Then the land had rest from war.

THE LAND OF JUDAH

15 So *this* was the lot of the tribe of the children of Judah according to their families:

The border of Edom at the Wilderness of Zin southward *was* the extreme southern boundary. 2And their southern border began at the shore of the Salt Sea, from the bay that faces southward. 3Then it went out to the southern side of the Ascent of Akrabbim, passed along to Zin, ascended on the south side of Kadesh Barnea, passed along to Hezron, went up to Adar, and went around to Karkaa. 4*From there* it passed toward Azmon and went out to the Brook of Egypt; and the border ended at the sea. This shall be your southern border.

5The east border *was* the Salt Sea as far as the mouth of the Jordan.

And the border on the northern quarter *began* at the bay of the sea at the mouth of the Jordan. 6The border went up to Beth Hoglah and passed north of Beth Arabah; and the border went up to the stone of Bohan the son of Reuben. 7Then the border went up toward Debir from the Valley of Achor, and it turned northward toward Gilgal, which *is* before the Ascent of Adummim, which *is* on the south side of the valley. The border continued toward the waters of En Shemesh and ended at En Rogel. 8And the border went up by the Valley of the Son of Hinnom to the southern slope of the Jebusite *city* (which *is* Jerusalem). The border went up to the top of the mountain that *lies* before the Valley of Hinnom westward, which *is* at the end of the Valley of Rephaim[a] northward. 9Then the border

15:8 [a]Literally *Giants*

THE MESSAGE

sent me from Kadesh Barnea to spy out the land. And I brought back an honest and accurate report. My companions who went with me discouraged the people, but I stuck to my guns, totally with GOD, my God. That was the day that Moses solemnly promised, 'The land on which your feet have walked will be your inheritance, you and your children's, forever. Yes, you have lived totally for GOD.' Now look at me: GOD has kept me alive, as he promised. It is now forty-five years since GOD spoke this word to Moses, years in which Israel wandered in the wilderness. And here I am today, eighty-five years old! I'm as strong as I was the day Moses sent me out. I'm as strong as ever in battle, whether coming or going. So give me this hill country that GOD promised me. You yourself heard the report, that the Anakim were there with their great fortress cities. If GOD goes with me, I will drive them out, just as GOD said."

13-14 Joshua blessed him. He gave Hebron to Caleb son of Jephunneh as an inheritance. Hebron belongs to Caleb son of Jephunneh the Kenizzite still today, because he gave himself totally to GOD, the God of Israel.

15 The name of Hebron used to be Kiriath Arba, named after Arba, the greatest man among the Anakim.

And the land had rest from war.

JUDAH

1 15 The lot for the people of Judah, their clans, extended south to the border of Edom, to the wilderness of Zin in the extreme south.

2-4 The southern border ran from the tip of the Salt Sea south of The Tongue; it ran southward from Scorpions Pass, went around Zin and just south of Kadesh Barnea; then it ran past Hezron, ascended to Addar, and curved around to Karka; from there it passed along to Azmon, came out at the Brook of Egypt, ending at the Sea. This is the southern boundary.

5-11 The eastern boundary: the Salt Sea up to the mouth of the Jordan.

The northern boundary started at the shallows of the Sea at the mouth of the Jordan, went up to Beth Hoglah and around to the north of Beth Arabah and to the Stone of Bohan son of Reuben. The border then ascended to Debir from Trouble Valley and turned north toward Gilgal, which lies opposite Red Pass, just south of the gorge. The border then followed the Waters of En Shemesh and ended at En Rogel. The border followed the Valley of Ben Hinnom along the southern slope of the Jebusite ridge (that is, Jerusalem). It ascended to the top of the mountain opposite Hinnom Valley on the west, at the northern end of Rephaim Valley;

NEW KING JAMES VERSION

went around from the top of the hill to the foun-
tain of the water of Nephtoah, and extended to
the cities of Mount Ephron. And the border went
around to Baalah (which *is* Kirjath Jearim).
10Then the border turned westward from Baalah
to Mount Seir, passed along to the side of Mount
Jearim on the north (which *is* Chesalon), went
down to Beth Shemesh, and passed on to Tim-
nah. 11And the border went out to the side of
Ekron northward. Then the border went around
to Shicron, passed along to Mount Baalah, and
extended to Jabneel; and the border ended at
the sea.
12The west border *was* the coastline of the
Great Sea. This *is* the boundary of the children
of Judah all around according to their families.

CALEB OCCUPIES HEBRON AND DEBIR

13Now to Caleb the son of Jephunneh he
gave a share among the children of Judah, ac-
cording to the commandment of the LORD to
Joshua, *namely,* Kirjath Arba, which *is* Hebron
(*Arba was* the father of Anak). 14Caleb drove out
the three sons of Anak from there: Sheshai, Ahi-
man, and Talmai, the children of Anak. 15Then
he went up from there to the inhabitants of De-
bir (formerly the name of Debir *was* Kirjath
Sepher).
16And Caleb said, "He who attacks Kirjath
Sepher and takes it, to him I will give Achsah
my daughter as wife." 17So Othniel the son of
Kenaz, the brother of Caleb, took it; and he gave
him Achsah his daughter as wife. 18Now it was
so, when she came *to him,* that she persuaded
him to ask her father for a field. So she dis-
mounted from *her* donkey, and Caleb said to
her, "What do you wish?" 19She answered, "Give
me a blessing; since you have given me land in
the South, give me also springs of water." So he
gave her the upper springs and the lower
springs.

THE CITIES OF JUDAH

20This *was* the inheritance of the tribe of the
children of Judah according to their families:
21The cities at the limits of the tribe of the
children of Judah, toward the border of Edom in
the South, were Kabzeel, Eder, Jagur, 22Kinah,
Dimonah, Adadah, 23Kedesh, Hazor, Ithnan,
24Ziph, Telem, Bealoth, 25Hazor, Hadattah, Ker-
ioth, Hezron (which *is* Hazor), 26Amam, Shema,
Moladah, 27Hazar Gaddah, Heshmon, Beth
Pelet, 28Hazar Shual, Beersheba, Bizjothjah,
29Baalah, Ijim, Ezem, 30Eltolad, Chesil, Hormah,
31Ziklag, Madmannah, Sansannah, 32Lebaoth,
Shilhim, Ain, and Rimmon: all the cities *are*
twenty-nine, with their villages.

THE MESSAGE

the border then took a turn at the top of the mountain to the spring, the Waters of Nephtoah, and followed the valley out to Mount Ephron, turned toward Baalah (that is, Kiriath Jearim), took another turn west of Baalah to Mount Seir, curved around to the northern shoulder of Mount Jearim (that is, Kesalon), descended to Beth Shemesh, and crossed to Timnah. The border then went north to the ridge of Ekron, turned toward Shikkeron, passed along to Mount Baalah, and came out at Jabneel. The border ended at the Sea.

12 The western border: the coastline of the Great Sea.

This is the boundary around the people of Judah for their clans.

13 Joshua gave Caleb son of Jephunneh a section among the people of Judah, according to GOD's command. He gave him Kiriath Arba, that is, Hebron. Arba was the ancestor of Anak.

14-15 Caleb drove out three Anakim from Hebron: Sheshai, Ahiman, and Talmai, all descendants of Anak. He marched up from there against the people of Debir. Debir used to be called Kiriath Sepher.

16-17 Caleb said, "Whoever attacks Kiriath Sepher and takes it, I'll give my daughter Acsah to him as his wife." Othniel son of Kenaz, Caleb's brother, took it; so Caleb gave him his daughter Acsah as his wife.

18-19 When she arrived she got him
to ask for farmland from her father.
As she dismounted from her donkey
Caleb asked her, "What would you like?"
She said, "Give me a marriage gift.
You've given me desert land;
Now give me pools of water!"
And he gave her the upper and the lower pools.

20-32 This is the inheritance of the tribe of the people of Judah, clan by clan.

The southern towns of the tribe of Judah in the Negev were near the boundary of Edom:

Kabzeel, Eder, Jagur,
Kinah, Dimonah, Adadah,
Kedesh, Hazor, Ithnan,
Ziph, Telem, Bealoth,
Hazor Hadattah, Kerioth Hezron (that is, Hazor),
Amam, Shema, Moladah,
Hazar Gaddah, Heshmon, Beth Pelet,
Hazar Shual, Beersheba, Biziothiah,
Baalah, Iim, Ezem,
Eltolad, Kesil, Hormah,
Ziklag, Madmannah, Sansannah,
Lebaoth, Shilhim, Ain, and Rimmon—
a total of twenty-nine towns and their villages.

NEW KING JAMES VERSION

33In the lowland: Eshtaol, Zorah, Ashnah,
34Zanoah, En Gannim, Tappuah, Enam, 35Jar-
muth, Adullam, Socoh, Azekah, 36Sharaim,
Adithaim, Gederah, and Gederothaim: fourteen
cities with their villages; 37Zenan, Hadashah,
Migdal Gad, 38Dilean, Mizpah, Joktheel,
39Lachish, Bozkath, Eglon, 40Cabbon, Lahmas,[a]
Kithlish, 41Gederoth, Beth Dagon, Naamah, and
Makkedah: sixteen cities with their villages;
42Libnah, Ether, Ashan, 43Jiphtah, Ashnah,
Nezib, 44Keilah, Achzib, and Mareshah: nine
cities with their villages; 45Ekron, with its towns
and villages; 46from Ekron to the sea, all that *lay*
near Ashdod, with their villages; 47Ashdod with
its towns and villages, Gaza with its towns and
villages—as far as the Brook of Egypt and the
Great Sea with *its* coastline.

48And in the mountain country: Shamir, Jat-
tir, Sochoh, 49Dannah, Kirjath Sannah (which *is*
Debir), 50Anab, Eshtemoh, Anim, 51Goshen,
Holon, and Giloh: eleven cities with their vil-
lages; 52Arab, Dumah, Eshean, 53Janum, Beth
Tappuah, Aphekah, 54Humtah, Kirjath Arba
(which *is* Hebron), and Zior: nine cities with
their villages; 55Maon, Carmel, Ziph, Juttah,
56Jezreel, Jokdeam, Zanoah, 57Kain, Gibeah, and
Timnah: ten cities with their villages; 58Halhul,
Beth Zur, Gedor, 59Maarath, Beth Anoth, and
Eltekon: six cities with their villages; 60Kirjath
Baal (which *is* Kirjath Jearim) and Rabbah: two
cities with their villages.

61In the wilderness: Beth Arabah, Middin,
Secacah, 62Nibshan, the City of Salt, and En
Gedi: six cities with their villages.

63As for the Jebusites, the inhabitants of
Jerusalem, the children of Judah could not drive
them out; but the Jebusites dwell with the chil-
dren of Judah at Jerusalem to this day.

EPHRAIM AND WEST MANASSEH

16 The lot fell to the children of Joseph from
the Jordan, by Jericho, to the waters of
Jericho on the east, to the wilderness that goes
up from Jericho through the mountains to
Bethel, 2then went out from Bethel to Luz,[a]
passed along to the border of the Archites at

15:40 [a]Or *Lahmam* 16:2 [a]Septuagint reads *Bethel* (that is, Luz).

THE MESSAGE

33-47 In the Shephelah (the western foothills) there were:
Eshtaol, Zorah, Ashnah,
Zanoah, En Gannim, Tappuah, Enam,
Jarmuth, Adullam, Socoh, Azekah,
Shaaraim, Adithaim, and Gederah (or Gederothaim)—
fourteen towns and their villages.
Zenan, Hadashah, Migdal Gad,
Dilean, Mizpah, Joktheel,
Lachish, Bozkath, Eglon,
Cabbon, Lahmas, Kitlish,
Gederoth, Beth Dagon, Naamah, and Makkedah—
sixteen towns and their villages.
Libnah, Ether, Ashan,
Iphtah, Ashnah, Nezib,
Keilah, Aczib, and Mareshah—
nine towns and their villages.
Ekron with its towns and villages;
From Ekron, west to the sea, all that bordered Ashdod with its villages;
Ashdod with its towns and villages;
Gaza with its towns and villages all the way to the Brook of Egypt.
The Great Sea is the western border.

48-60 In the hill country:
Shamir, Jattir, Socoh,
Dannah, Kiriath Sannah (that is, Debir),
Anab, Eshtemoh, Anim,
Goshen, Holon, and Giloh—
eleven towns and their villages.
Arab, Dumah, Eshan,
Janim, Beth Tappuah, Aphekah,
Humtah, Kiriath Arba (that is, Hebron), and Zior—
nine towns and their villages.
Maon, Carmel, Ziph, Juttah,
Jezreel, Jokdeam, Zanoah,
Kain, Gibeah, and Timnah—
ten towns and their villages.
Halhul, Beth Zur, Gedor,
Maarath, Beth Anoth, and Eltekon—
six towns and their villages.
Kiriath Baal (that is, Kiriath Jearim) and Rabbah—
two towns and their villages.

61-62 In the wilderness:
Beth Arabah, Middin, Secacah,
Nibshan, the City of Salt, and En Gedi—
six towns and their villages.

63 The people of Judah couldn't get rid of the Jebusites who lived in Jerusalem. The Jebusites stayed put, living alongside the people of Judah. They are still living there in Jerusalem.

JOSEPH

1-3 **16** The lot for the people of Joseph went
from the Jordan near Jericho, east of
the spring of Jericho, north through the
desert mountains to Bethel. It went on from
Bethel (that is, Luz) to the territory of the
Arkites in Ataroth. It then descended west-

NEW KING JAMES VERSION

Ataroth, 3 and went down westward to the boundary of the Japhletites, as far as the boundary of Lower Beth Horon to Gezer; and it ended at the sea.

4 So the children of Joseph, Manasseh and Ephraim, took their inheritance.

THE LAND OF EPHRAIM

5 The border of the children of Ephraim, according to their families, was *thus:* The border of their inheritance on the east side was Ataroth Addar as far as Upper Beth Horon.

6 And the border went out toward the sea on the north side of Michmethath; then the border went around eastward to Taanath Shiloh, and passed by it on the east of Janohah. 7 Then it went down from Janohah to Ataroth and Naarah,[a] reached to Jericho, and came out at the Jordan.

8 The border went out from Tappuah westward to the Brook Kanah, and it ended at the sea. This *was* the inheritance of the tribe of the children of Ephraim according to their families. 9 The separate cities for the children of Ephraim *were* among the inheritance of the children of Manasseh, all the cities with their villages.

10 And they did not drive out the Canaanites who dwelt in Gezer; but the Canaanites dwell among the Ephraimites to this day and have become forced laborers.

THE OTHER HALF-TRIBE OF MANASSEH (WEST)

17 There was also a lot for the tribe of Manasseh, for he *was* the firstborn of Joseph: *namely* for Machir the firstborn of Manasseh, the father of Gilead, because he was a man of war; therefore he was given Gilead and Bashan. 2 And there was *a lot* for the rest of the children of Manasseh according to their families: for the children of Abiezer,[a] the children of Helek, the children of Asriel, the children of Shechem, the children of Hepher, and the children of Shemida; these *were* the male children of Manasseh the son of Joseph according to their families.

3 But Zelophehad the son of Hepher, the son of Gilead, the son of Machir, the son of Manasseh, had no sons, but only daughters. And these *are* the names of his daughters: Mahlah, Noah, Hoglah, Milcah, and Tirzah. 4 And they came near before Eleazar the priest, before Joshua the son of Nun, and before the rulers, saying, "The LORD commanded Moses to give us an inheritance among our brothers." Therefore, according to the commandment of the LORD, he gave them an inheritance among their father's brothers. 5 Ten shares fell to Manasseh, besides the land of Gilead and Bashan, which *were* on the other side of the Jordan, 6 because the daughters of Manasseh received an inheritance among his sons; and the rest of Manasseh's sons had the land of Gilead.

7 And the territory of Manasseh was from Asher to Michmethath, that *lies* east of Shechem; and the border went along south to the inhabitants of En Tappuah. 8 Manasseh had

16:7 [a]Or *Naaran* (compare 1 Chronicles 7:28) **17:2** [a]Called *Jeezer* in Numbers 26:30

THE MESSAGE

ward to the territory of the Japhletites to the region of Lower Beth Horon and on to Gezer, ending at the Sea.

4 This is the region from which the people of Joseph—Manasseh and Ephraim—got their inheritance.

5-9 Ephraim's territory by clans:

The boundary of their inheritance went from Ataroth Addar in the east to Upper Beth Horon and then west to the Sea. From Micmethath on the north it turned eastward to Taanath Shiloh and passed along, still eastward, to Janoah. The border then descended from Janoah to Ataroth and Naarah; it touched Jericho and came out at the Jordan. From Tappuah the border went westward to the Brook Kanah and ended at the Sea. This was the inheritance of the tribe of Ephraim by clans, including the cities set aside for Ephraim within the inheritance of Manasseh—all those towns and their villages.

10 But they didn't get rid of the Canaanites who were living in Gezer. Canaanites are still living among the people of Ephraim, but they are made to do forced labor.

1-2 17 This is the lot that fell to the people of Manasseh, Joseph's firstborn. (Gilead and Bashan had already been given to Makir, Manasseh's firstborn and father of Gilead, because he was an outstanding fighter.) So the lot that follows went to the rest of the people of Manasseh and their clans, the clans of Abiezer, Helek, Asriel, Shechem, Hepher, and Shemida. These are the male descendants of Manasseh son of Joseph by their clans.

3-4 Zelophehad son of Hepher, the son of Gilead, the son of Makir, the son of Manasseh, had no sons, only daughters. Their names were Mahlah, Noah, Hoglah, Milcah, and Tirzah. They went to Eleazar the priest, Joshua son of Nun, and the leaders and said, "GOD commanded Moses to give us an inheritance among our kinsmen." And Joshua did it; he gave them, as GOD commanded, an inheritance amid their father's brothers.

5-6 Manasseh's lot came to ten portions, in addition to the land of Gilead and Bashan on the other side of the Jordan, because Manasseh's daughters got an inheritance along with his sons. The land of Gilead belonged to the rest of the people of Manasseh.

7-10 The boundary of Manasseh went from Asher all the way to Micmethath, just opposite Shechem, then ran southward to the people living at En Tappuah. (The land of Tappuah belonged to Manasseh, but Tap-

NEW KING JAMES VERSION

the land of Tappuah, but Tappuah on the border of Manasseh *belonged* to the children of Ephraim. 9And the border descended to the Brook Kanah, southward to the brook. These cities of Ephraim *are* among the cities of Manasseh. The border of Manasseh *was* on the north side of the brook; and it ended at the sea.

10Southward *it was* Ephraim's, northward *it was* Manasseh's, and the sea was its border. Manasseh's territory was adjoining Asher on the north and Issachar on the east. 11And in Issachar and in Asher, Manasseh had Beth Shean and its towns, Ibleam and its towns, the inhabitants of Dor and its towns, the inhabitants of En Dor and its towns, the inhabitants of Taanach and its towns, and the inhabitants of Megiddo and its towns—three hilly regions. 12Yet the children of Manasseh could not drive out *the inhabitants of* those cities, but the Canaanites were determined to dwell in that land. 13And it happened, when the children of Israel grew strong, that they put the Canaanites to forced labor, but did not utterly drive them out.

MORE LAND FOR EPHRAIM AND MANASSEH

14Then the children of Joseph spoke to Joshua, saying, "Why have you given us *only* one lot and one share to inherit, since we *are* a great people, inasmuch as the LORD has blessed us until now?"

15So Joshua answered them, "If you *are* a great people, *then* go up to the forest *country* and clear a place for yourself there in the land of the Perizzites and the giants, since the mountains of Ephraim are too confined for you."

16But the children of Joseph said, "The mountain country is not enough for us; and all the Canaanites who dwell in the land of the valley have chariots of iron, *both those* who *are* of Beth Shean and its towns and *those* who *are* of the Valley of Jezreel."

17And Joshua spoke to the house of Joseph—to Ephraim and Manasseh—saying, "You *are* a great people and have great power; you shall not have *only* one lot, 18but the mountain country shall be yours. Although it *is* wooded, you shall cut it down, and its farthest extent shall be yours; for you shall drive out the Canaanites, though they have iron chariots *and* are strong."

THE REMAINDER OF THE LAND DIVIDED

18 Now the whole congregation of the children of Israel assembled together at Shiloh, and set up the tabernacle of meeting there. And the land was subdued before them. 2But there remained among the children of Israel seven tribes which had not yet received their inheritance.

3Then Joshua said to the children of Israel: "How long will you neglect to go and possess the land which the LORD God of your fathers has given you? 4Pick out from among you three men for *each* tribe, and I will send them; they shall rise and go through the land, survey it according to their inheritance, and come *back* to me. 5And they shall divide it into seven parts. Judah shall remain in their territory on the south, and the

THE MESSAGE

puah itself on the border of Manasseh belonged to the Ephraimites.) The boundary continued south to the Brook Kanah. (The cities there belonged to Ephraim although they lay among the cities of Manasseh.) The boundary of Manasseh ran north of the brook and ended at the Sea. The land to the south belonged to Ephraim; the land to the north to Manasseh, with the Sea as their western border; they meet Asher on the north and Issachar on the east.

11 Within Issachar and Asher, Manasseh
also held Beth Shan, Ibleam, and the people
of Dor, Endor, Taanach, and Megiddo, together with their villages, and the third in
the list is Naphoth.

12-13 The people of Manasseh never were able
to take over these towns—the Canaanites
wouldn't budge. But later, when the Israelites got stronger, they put the Canaanites to forced labor. But they never did get
rid of them.

14 The people of Joseph spoke to Joshua: "Why
did you give us just one allotment, one solitary share? There are a lot of us, and growing—GOD has extravagantly blessed us."

15 Joshua responded, "Since there are so
many of you, and you find the hill country of
Ephraim too confining, climb into the forest
and clear ground there for yourselves in the
land of the Perizzites and the Rephaim."

16 But the people of Joseph said, "There's
not enough hill country for us; and the
Canaanites who live down in the plain, both
those in Beth Shan and its villages and in
the Valley of Jezreel, have iron chariots."

17-18 Joshua said to the family of Joseph (to
Ephraim and Manasseh): "Yes, there are a
lot of you, and you are very strong. One lot
is not enough for you. You also get the hill
country. It's nothing but trees now, but you
will clear the land and make it your own
from one end to the other. The powerful
Canaanites, even with their iron chariots,
won't stand a chance against you."

THE SHILOH SURVEY

1-2 18 Then the entire congregation of the
People of Israel got together at Shiloh.
They put up the Tent of Meeting.

The land was under their control but
there were still seven Israelite tribes who
had yet to receive their inheritance.

3-5 Joshua addressed the People of Israel:
"How long are you going to sit around on
your hands, putting off taking possession of
the land that GOD, the God of your ancestors, has given you? Pick three men from
each tribe so I can commission them. They
will survey and map the land, showing the
inheritance due each tribe, and report back
to me. They will divide it into seven parts.
Judah will stay in its territory in the south

NEW KING JAMES VERSION

house of Joseph shall remain in their territory
on the north. 6You shall therefore survey the
land in seven parts and bring *the survey* here to
me, that I may cast lots for you here before the
LORD our God. 7But the Levites have no part
among you, for the priesthood of the LORD *is*
their inheritance. And Gad, Reuben, and half
the tribe of Manasseh have received their inher-
itance beyond the Jordan on the east, which
Moses the servant of the LORD gave them."
8Then the men arose to go away; and Joshua
charged those who went to survey the land, say-
ing, "Go, walk through the land, survey it, and
come back to me, that I may cast lots for you
here before the LORD in Shiloh." 9So the men
went, passed through the land, and wrote the
survey in a book in seven parts by cities; and
they came to Joshua at the camp in Shiloh.
10Then Joshua cast lots for them in Shiloh be-
fore the LORD, and there Joshua divided the land
to the children of Israel according to their divi-
sions.

THE LAND OF BENJAMIN

11Now the lot of the tribe of the children of
Benjamin came up according to their families,
and the territory of their lot came out between
the children of Judah and the children of
Joseph. 12Their border on the north side began
at the Jordan, and the border went up to the side
of Jericho on the north, and went up through the
mountains westward; it ended at the Wilderness
of Beth Aven. 13The border went over from there
toward Luz, to the side of Luz (which *is* Bethel)
southward; and the border descended to
Ataroth Addar, near the hill that *lies* on the
south side of Lower Beth Horon.
14Then the border extended around the west
side to the south, from the hill that *lies* before
Beth Horon southward; and it ended at Kirjath
Baal (which *is* Kirjath Jearim), a city of the chil-
dren of Judah. This *was* the west side.
15The south side *began* at the end of Kirjath
Jearim, and the border extended on the west
and went out to the spring of the waters of
Nephtoah. 16Then the border came down to the
end of the mountain that *lies* before the Valley of
the Son of Hinnom, which *is* in the Valley of the
Rephaim[a] on the north, descended to the Valley
of Hinnom, to the side of the Jebusite *city* on the
south, and descended to En Rogel. 17And it went
around from the north, went out to En Shemesh,
and extended toward Geliloth, which is before
the Ascent of Adummim, and descended to the
stone of Bohan the son of Reuben. 18Then it
passed along toward the north side of Arabah,[a]
and went down to Arabah. 19And the border
passed along to the north side of Beth Hoglah;
then the border ended at the north bay at the
Salt Sea, at the south end of the Jordan. This
was the southern boundary.
20The Jordan was its border on the east side.
This *was* the inheritance of the children of Ben-
jamin, according to its boundaries all around,
according to their families.

18:16 [a]Literally *Giants* **18:18** [a]Or *Beth Arabah* (compare 15:6 and 18:22)

THE MESSAGE

and the people of Joseph will keep to their place in the north.

6 "You are responsible for preparing a survey map showing seven portions. Then bring it to me so that I can cast lots for you here in the presence of our GOD.

7 "Only the Levites get no portion among you because the priesthood of GOD is their inheritance. And Gad, Reuben, and the half-tribe of Manasseh already have their inheritance on the east side of the Jordan, given to them by Moses the servant of GOD."

8 So the men set out. As they went out to survey the land, Joshua charged them: "Go. Survey the land and map it. Then come back to me and I will cast lots for you here at Shiloh in the presence of GOD."

9 So off the men went. They covered the ground and mapped the country by towns in a scroll. Then they reported back to Joshua at the camp at Shiloh.

10 Joshua cast the lots for them at Shiloh in the presence of GOD. That's where Joshua divided up the land to the People of Israel, according to their tribal divisions.

BENJAMIN

11 The first lot turned up for the tribe of Benjamin with its clans. The border of the allotment went between the peoples of Judah and Joseph.

12-13 The northern border began at the Jordan, then went up to the ridge north of Jericho, ascending west into the hill country into the wilderness of Beth Aven. From there the border went around to Luz, to its southern ridge (that is, Bethel), and then down from Ataroth Addar to the mountain to the south of Lower Beth Horon.

14 There the border took a turn on the west side and swung south from the mountain to the south of Beth Horon and ended at Kiriath Baal (that is, Kiriath Jearim), a town of the people of Judah. This was the west side.

15-19 The southern border began at the edge of Kiriath Jearim on the west, then ran west until it reached the spring, the Waters of Nephtoah. It then descended to the foot of the mountain opposite the Valley of Ben Hinnom (which flanks the Valley of Rephaim to the north), descended to the Hinnom Valley, just south of the Jebusite ridge, and went on to En Rogel. From there it curved north to En Shemesh and Geliloth, opposite the Red Pass (Adummim), down to the Stone of Bohan the son of Reuben, continued toward the north flank of Beth Arabah, then plunged to the Arabah. It then followed the slope of Beth Hoglah north and came out at the northern bay of the Salt Sea—the south end of the Jordan. This was the southern border.

20 The east border was formed by the Jordan.

This was the inheritance of the people of Benjamin for their clans, marked by these borders on all sides.

NEW KING JAMES VERSION

21 Now the cities of the tribe of the children of Benjamin, according to their families, were Jericho, Beth Hoglah, Emek Keziz, 22 Beth Arabah, Zemaraim, Bethel, 23 Avim, Parah, Ophrah, 24 Chephar Haammoni, Ophni, and Gaba: twelve cities with their villages; 25 Gibeon, Ramah, Beeroth, 26 Mizpah, Chephirah, Mozah, 27 Rekem, Irpeel, Taralah, 28 Zelah, Eleph, Jebus (which *is* Jerusalem), Gibeath, *and* Kirjath: fourteen cities with their villages. This was the inheritance of the children of Benjamin according to their families.

SIMEON'S INHERITANCE WITH JUDAH

19 The second lot came out for Simeon, for the tribe of the children of Simeon according to their families. And their inheritance was within the inheritance of the children of Judah. 2 They had in their inheritance Beersheba (Sheba), Moladah, 3 Hazar Shual, Balah, Ezem, 4 Eltolad, Bethul, Hormah, 5 Ziklag, Beth Marcaboth, Hazar Susah, 6 Beth Lebaoth, and Sharuhen: thirteen cities and their villages; 7 Ain, Rimmon, Ether, and Ashan: four cities and their villages; 8 and all the villages that *were* all around these cities as far as Baalath Beer, Ramah of the South. This *was* the inheritance of the tribe of the children of Simeon according to their families.

9 The inheritance of the children of Simeon *was included* in the share of the children of Judah, for the share of the children of Judah was too much for them. Therefore the children of Simeon had *their* inheritance within the inheritance of that people.

THE LAND OF ZEBULUN

10 The third lot came out for the children of Zebulun according to their families, and the border of their inheritance was as far as Sarid. 11 Their border went toward the west and to Maralah, went to Dabbasheth, and extended along the brook that is east of Jokneam. 12 Then from Sarid it went eastward toward the sunrise along the border of Chisloth Tabor, and went out toward Daberath, bypassing Japhia. 13 And from there it passed along on the east of Gath Hepher, toward Eth Kazin, and extended to Rimmon, which borders on Neah. 14 Then the border went around it on the north side of Hannathon, and it ended in the Valley of Jiphthah El. 15 Included were Kattath, Nahallal, Shimron, Idalah, and Bethlehem: twelve cities with their villages. 16 This *was* the inheritance of the children of Zebulun according to their families, these cities with their villages.

THE LAND OF ISSACHAR

17 The fourth lot came out to Issachar, for the children of Issachar according to their families. 18 And their territory went to Jezreel, and *included* Chesulloth, Shunem, 19 Haphraim, Shion,

THE MESSAGE

21-28 The cities of the tribe of Benjamin, clan by clan, were:

Jericho, Beth Hoglah, Emek Keziz,
Beth Arabah, Zemaraim, Bethel,
Avvim, Parah, Ophrah,
Kephar Ammoni, Ophni, and Geba—
twelve towns with their villages.
Gibeon, Ramah, Beeroth,
Mizpah, Kephirah, Mozah,
Rekem, Irpeel, Taralah,
Zelah, Haeleph, the Jebusite city (that is, Jerusalem), Gibeah, and Kiriath Jearim—
fourteen cities with their villages.

This was the inheritance for Benjamin, according to its clans.

SIMEON

1-8 19 The second lot went to Simeon for its clans. Their inheritance was within the territory of Judah. In their inheritance they had:

Beersheba (or Sheba), Moladah,
Hazar Shual, Balah, Ezem,
Eltolad, Bethul, Hormah,
Ziklag, Beth Marcaboth, Hazar Susah,
Beth Lebaoth, and Sharuhen—
thirteen towns and their villages.
Ain, Rimmon, Ether, and Ashan—
four towns and their villages—plus all the villages around these towns as far as Baalath Beer, the Ramah of the Negev.

8-9 This is the inheritance of the tribe of Simeon according to its clans. The inheritance of Simeon came out of the share of Judah, because Judah's portion turned out to be more than they needed. That's how the people of Simeon came to get their lot from within Judah's portion.

ZEBULUN

10-15 The third lot went to Zebulun, clan by clan:

The border of their inheritance went all the way to Sarid. It ran west to Maralah, met Dabbesheth, and then went to the brook opposite Jokneam. In the other direction from Sarid, the border ran east; it followed the sunrise to the border of Kisloth Tabor, on to Daberath and up to Japhia. It continued east to Gath Hepher and Eth Kazin, came out at Rimmon, and turned toward Neah. There the border went around on the north to Hannathon and ran out into the Valley of Iphtah El. It included Kattath, Nahalal, Shimron, Idalah, and Bethlehem—twelve cities with their villages.

16 This is the inheritance of the people of Zebulun for their clans—these towns and their villages.

ISSACHAR

17-21 The fourth lot went to Issachar, clan by clan. Their territory included:

NEW KING JAMES VERSION

Anaharath, 20Rabbith, Kishion, Abez, 21Remeth,
En Gannim, En Haddah, and Beth Pazzez. 22And
the border reached to Tabor, Shahazimah, and
Beth Shemesh; their border ended at the Jordan:
sixteen cities with their villages. 23This *was* the
inheritance of the tribe of the children of Is-
sachar according to their families, the cities and
their villages.

THE LAND OF ASHER

24The fifth lot came out for the tribe of the
children of Asher according to their families.
25And their territory included Helkath, Hali,
Beten, Achshaph, 26Alammelech, Amad, and
Mishal; it reached to Mount Carmel westward,
along *the Brook* Shihor Libnath. 27It turned to-
ward the sunrise to Beth Dagon; and it reached
to Zebulun and to the Valley of Jiphthah El, then
northward beyond Beth Emek and Neiel, by-
passing Cabul *which was* on the left, 28including
Ebron,[a] Rehob, Hammon, and Kanah, as far as
Greater Sidon. 29And the border turned to
Ramah and to the fortified city of Tyre; then the
border turned to Hosah, and ended at the sea by
the region of Achzib. 30Also Ummah, Aphek,
and Rehob *were included:* twenty-two cities
with their villages. 31This *was* the inheritance of
the tribe of the children of Asher according to
their families, these cities with their villages.

THE LAND OF NAPHTALI

32The sixth lot came out to the children of
Naphtali, for the children of Naphtali according
to their families. 33And their border began at
Heleph, enclosing the territory from the tere-
binth tree in Zaanannim, Adami Nekeb, and
Jabneel, as far as Lakkum; it ended at the Jor-
dan. 34From Heleph the border extended west-
ward to Aznoth Tabor, and went out from there
toward Hukkok; it adjoined Zebulun on the
south side and Asher on the west side, and
ended at Judah by the Jordan toward the sun-
rise. 35And the fortified cities *are* Ziddim, Zer,
Hammath, Rakkath, Chinnereth, 36Adamah,
Ramah, Hazor, 37Kedesh, Edrei, En Hazor,
38Iron, Migdal El, Horem, Beth Anath, and Beth
Shemesh: nineteen cities with their villages.
39This *was* the inheritance of the tribe of the
children of Naphtali according to their families,
the cities and their villages.

THE LAND OF DAN

40The seventh lot came out for the tribe of the
children of Dan according to their families.
41And the territory of their inheritance was Zo-
rah, Eshtaol, Ir Shemesh, 42Shaalabbin, Aijalon,
Jethlah, 43Elon, Timnah, Ekron, 44Eltekeh, Gib-
bethon, Baalath, 45Jehud, Bene Berak, Gath
Rimmon, 46Me Jarkon, and Rakkon, with the re-
gion near Joppa.

19:28 [a]Following Masoretic Text, Targum, and Vulgate; a few Hebrew manuscripts read *Abdon* (compare 21:30 and 1 Chronicles 6:74).

THE MESSAGE

Jezreel, Kesulloth, Shunem,
Hapharaim, Shion, Anaharath,
Rabbith, Kishion, Ebez,
Remeth, En Gannim, En Haddah, and
Beth Pazzez.

22 The boundary touched Tabor, Shahazu-
mah, and Beth Shemesh and ended at the
Jordan—sixteen towns and their villages.
23 These towns with their villages were the
inheritance of the tribe of Issachar, clan by
clan.

ASHER

24 The fifth lot went to the tribe of Asher, clan
by clan:
25-30 Their territory included Helkath, Hali,
Beten, Acshaph, Allammelech, Amad, and
Mishal. The western border touched Carmel
and Shihor Libnath, then turned east to-
ward Beth Dagon, touched Zebulun and the
Valley of Iphtah El, and went north to Beth
Emek and Neiel, skirting Cabul on the left.
It went on to Abdon, Rehob, Hammon, and
Kanah, all the way to Greater Sidon. The
border circled back toward Ramah, ex-
tended to the fort city of Tyre, turned toward
Hosah, and came out at the Sea in the re-
gion of Aczib, Ummah, Aphek, and Rehob—
twenty-two towns and their villages.

31 These towns and villages were the inher-
itance of the tribe of Asher, clan by clan.

NAPHTALI

32 The sixth lot came to Naphtali and its clans.
33 Their border ran from Heleph, from the
oak at Zaanannim, passing Adami Nekeb
and Jabneel to Lakkum and ending at the
Jordan.
34 The border returned on the west at
Aznoth Tabor and came out at Hukkok,
meeting Zebulun on the south, Asher on the
west, and the Jordan on the east.
The fort cities were:
35-38 Ziddim, Zer, Hammath, Rakkath,
Kinnereth,
Adamah, Ramah, Hazor,
Kedesh, Edrei, En Hazor,
Iron, Migdal El, Horem, Beth Anath, and
Beth Shemesh—
nineteen towns and their villages.

39 This is the inheritance of the tribe of
Naphtali, the cities and their villages, clan
by clan.

DAN

40-46 The seventh lot fell to Dan. The territory of
their inheritance included:

Zorah, Eshtaol, Ir Shemesh,
Shaalabbin, Aijalon, Ithlah,
Elon, Timnah, Ekron,
Eltekeh, Gibbethon, Baalath,
Jehud, Bene Berak, Gath Rimmon,
Me Jarkon, and Rakkon, with the region
facing Joppa.

NEW KING JAMES VERSION

47And the border of the children of Dan went be-
yond these, because the children of Dan went up
to fight against Leshem and took it; and they
struck it with the edge of the sword, took pos-
session of it, and dwelt in it. They called
Leshem, Dan, after the name of Dan their father.
48This *is* the inheritance of the tribe of the chil-
dren of Dan according to their families, these
cities with their villages.

JOSHUA'S INHERITANCE

49When they had made an end of dividing
the land as an inheritance according to their
borders, the children of Israel gave an inheri-
tance among them to Joshua the son of Nun.
50According to the word of the LORD they gave
him the city which he asked for, Timnath Serah
in the mountains of Ephraim; and he built the
city and dwelt in it.
51These *were* the inheritances which Eleazar
the priest, Joshua the son of Nun, and the heads
of the fathers of the tribes of the children of Israel
divided as an inheritance by lot in Shiloh before
the LORD, at the door of the tabernacle of meet-
ing. So they made an end of dividing the country.

THE CITIES OF REFUGE

20 The LORD also spoke to Joshua, saying,
2"Speak to the children of Israel, saying:
'Appoint for yourselves cities of refuge, of which
I spoke to you through Moses, 3that the slayer
who kills a person accidentally *or* unintention-
ally may flee there; and they shall be your
refuge from the avenger of blood. 4And when he
flees to one of those cities, and stands at the en-
trance of the gate of the city, and declares his
case in the hearing of the elders of that city, they
shall take him into the city as one of them, and
give him a place, that he may dwell among
them. 5Then if the avenger of blood pursues
him, they shall not deliver the slayer into his
hand, because he struck his neighbor uninten-
tionally, but did not hate him beforehand. 6And
he shall dwell in that city until he stands before
the congregation for judgment, *and* until the
death of the one who is high priest in those
days. Then the slayer may return and come to
his own city and his own house, to the city from
which he fled.' "
7So they appointed Kedesh in Galilee, in the
mountains of Naphtali, Shechem in the moun-
tains of Ephraim, and Kirjath Arba (which *is*
Hebron) in the mountains of Judah. 8And on the
other side of the Jordan, by Jericho eastward,
they assigned Bezer in the wilderness on the
plain, from the tribe of Reuben, Ramoth in
Gilead, from the tribe of Gad, and Golan in
Bashan, from the tribe of Manasseh. 9These
were the cities appointed for all the children of
Israel and for the stranger who dwelt among
them, that whoever killed a person accidentally
might flee there, and not die by the hand of the
avenger of blood until he stood before the con-
gregation.

THE MESSAGE

47 But the people of Dan failed to get rid of the Westerners (Amorites), who pushed them back into the hills. The Westerners kept them out of the plain and they didn't have enough room. So the people of Dan marched up and attacked Leshem. They took it, killed the inhabitants, and settled in. They renamed it Leshem Dan after the name of Dan their ancestor.

48 This is the inheritance of the tribe of Dan, according to its clans, these towns with their villages.

49-50 They completed the dividing of the land as inheritance and the setting of its boundaries. The People of Israel then gave an inheritance among them to Joshua son of Nun. In obedience to GOD's word, they gave him the city which he had requested, Timnath Serah in the hill country of Ephraim. He rebuilt the city and settled there.

51 These are the inheritances which Eleazar the priest and Joshua son of Nun and the ancestral leaders assigned by lot to the tribes of Israel at Shiloh in the presence of GOD at the entrance of the Tent of Meeting. They completed the dividing of the land.

ASYLUM-CITIES

1-3 20 Then GOD spoke to Joshua: "Tell the People of Israel: Designate the asylum-cities, as I instructed you through Moses, so that anyone who kills a person accidentally—that is, unintentionally—may flee there as a safe place of asylum from the avenger of blood.

4 "A person shall escape for refuge to one of these cities, stand at the entrance to the city gate, and lay out his case before the city's leaders. The leaders must then take him into the city among them and give him a place to live with them.

5-6 "If the avenger of blood chases after him, they must not give him up—he didn't intend to kill the person; there was no history of ill-feeling. He may stay in that city until he has stood trial before the congregation and until the death of the current high priest. Then he may go back to his own home in his hometown from which he fled."

7 They set apart Kedesh in Galilee in the hills of Naphtali, Shechem in the hills of Ephraim, and Kiriath Arba (that is, Hebron) in the hills of Judah.

8-9 On the other side of the Jordan, east of Jericho, they designated Bezer on the desert plateau from the tribe of Reuben, Ramoth in Gilead from the tribe of Gad, and Golan in Bashan from the tribe of Manasseh. These were the designated cities for the People of Israel and any resident foreigner living among them, so that anyone who killed someone unintentionally could flee there and not die by the hand of the avenger of blood without a fair trial before the congregation.

New King James Version

Cities of the Levites

21 Then the heads of the fathers' *houses* of the Levites came near to Eleazar the priest, to Joshua the son of Nun, and to the heads of the fathers' *houses* of the tribes of the children of Israel. 2And they spoke to them at Shiloh in the land of Canaan, saying, "The LORD commanded through Moses to give us cities to dwell in, with their common-lands for our livestock." 3So the children of Israel gave to the Levites from their inheritance, at the commandment of the LORD, these cities and their common-lands:

4Now the lot came out for the families of the Kohathites. And the children of Aaron the priest, *who were* of the Levites, had thirteen cities by lot from the tribe of Judah, from the tribe of Simeon, and from the tribe of Benjamin. 5The rest of the children of Kohath had ten cities by lot from the families of the tribe of Ephraim, from the tribe of Dan, and from the half-tribe of Manasseh.

6And the children of Gershon had thirteen cities by lot from the families of the tribe of Issachar, from the tribe of Asher, from the tribe of Naphtali, and from the half-tribe of Manasseh in Bashan.

7The children of Merari according to their families had twelve cities from the tribe of Reuben, from the tribe of Gad, and from the tribe of Zebulun.

8And the children of Israel gave these cities with their common-lands by lot to the Levites, as the LORD had commanded by the hand of Moses.

9So they gave from the tribe of the children of Judah and from the tribe of the children of Simeon these cities which are designated by name, 10which were for the children of Aaron, one of the families of the Kohathites, *who were* of the children of Levi; for the lot was theirs first. 11And they gave them Kirjath Arba (*Arba was* the father of Anak), which *is* Hebron, in the mountains of Judah, with the common-land surrounding it. 12But the fields of the city and its villages they gave to Caleb the son of Jephunneh as his possession.

13Thus to the children of Aaron the priest they gave Hebron with its common-land (a city of refuge for the slayer), Libnah with its common-land, 14Jattir with its common-land, Eshtemoa with its common-land, 15Holon with its common-land, Debir with its common-land, 16Ain with its common-land, Juttah with its common-land, and Beth Shemesh with its common-land: nine cities from those two tribes; 17and from the tribe of Benjamin, Gibeon with its common-land, Geba with its common-land, 18Anathoth with its common-land, and Almon with its common-land: four cities. 19All the cities of the children of Aaron, the priests, *were* thirteen cities with their common-lands.

20And the families of the children of Kohath, the Levites, the rest of the children of Kohath, even they had the cities of their lot from the tribe of Ephraim. 21For they gave them Shechem with its common-land in the mountains of Ephraim (a city of refuge for the slayer), Gezer with its common-land, 22Kibzaim with its com-

The Message

Cities for the Levites

1-2 21 The ancestral heads of the Levites came to Eleazar the priest and Joshua son of Nun and to the heads of the other tribes of the People of Israel. This took place at Shiloh in the land of Canaan. They said, "GOD commanded through Moses that you give us cities to live in with access to pastures for our cattle."

3 So the People of Israel, out of their own inheritance, gave the Levites, just as GOD commanded, the following cities and pastures:

4-5 The lot came out for the families of the Kohathites this way: Levites descended from Aaron the priest received by lot thirteen cities out of the tribes of Judah, Simeon, and Benjamin. The rest of the Kohathites received by lot ten cities from the families of the tribes of Ephraim, Dan, and the half-tribe of Manasseh.

6 The Gershonites received by lot thirteen cities from the families of the tribes of Issachar, Asher, Naphtali, and the half-tribe of Manasseh in Bashan.

7 The families of the Merarites received twelve towns from the tribes of Reuben, Gad, and Zebulun.

8 So the People of Israel gave these cities with their pastures to the Levites just as GOD had ordered through Moses, that is, by lot.

Cities for the Descendants of Aaron

9-10 They assigned from the tribes of Judah, Simeon, and Benjamin the following towns, here named individually (these were for the descendants of Aaron who were from the families of the Kohathite branch of Levi because the first lot fell to them):

11-12 Kiriath Arba (Arba was the ancestor of Anak), that is, Hebron, in the hills of Judah, with access to the pastures around it. The fields of the city and its open lands they had already given to Caleb son of Jephunneh as his possession.

13-16 To the descendants of Aaron the priest they gave Hebron (the asylum-city for the unconvicted killers), Libnah, Jattir, Eshtemoa, Holon, Debir, Ain, Juttah, and Beth Shemesh, all with their accompanying pastures—nine towns from these two tribes.

17-18 And from the tribe of Benjamin: Gibeon, Geba, Anathoth, and Almon, together with their pastures—four towns.

19 The total for the cities and pastures for the priests descended from Aaron came to thirteen.

20-22 The rest of the Kohathite families from the tribe of Levi were assigned their cities by lot from the tribe of Ephraim: Shechem (the asylum-city for the unconvicted killer) in the hills of Ephraim, Gezer, Kibzaim, and

NEW KING JAMES VERSION

mon-land, and Beth Horon with its common-land: four cities; 23and from the tribe of Dan, Eltekeh with its common-land, Gibbethon with its common-land, 24Aijalon with its common-land, *and* Gath Rimmon with its common-land: four cities; 25and from the half-tribe of Manasseh, Tanach with its common-land and Gath Rimmon with its common-land: two cities. 26All the ten cities with their common-lands were for the rest of the families of the children of Kohath.

27Also to the children of Gershon, of the families of the Levites, from the *other* half-tribe of Manasseh, *they gave* Golan in Bashan with its common-land (a city of refuge for the slayer), and Be Eshterah with its common-land: two cities; 28and from the tribe of Issachar, Kishion with its common-land, Daberath with its common-land, 29Jarmuth with its common-land, *and* En Gannim with its common-land: four cities; 30and from the tribe of Asher, Mishal with its common-land, Abdon with its common-land, 31Helkath with its common-land, and Rehob with its common-land: four cities; 32and from the tribe of Naphtali, Kedesh in Galilee with its common-land (a city of refuge for the slayer), Hammoth Dor with its common-land, and Kartan with its common-land: three cities. 33All the cities of the Gershonites according to their families *were* thirteen cities with their common-lands.

34And to the families of the children of Merari, the rest of the Levites, from the tribe of Zebulun, Jokneam with its common-land, Kartah with its common-land, 35Dimnah with its common-land, *and* Nahalal with its common-land: four cities; 36and from the tribe of Reuben, Bezer with its common-land, Jahaz with its common-land, 37Kedemoth with its common-land, and Mephaath with its common-land: four cities;[a] 38and from the tribe of Gad, Ramoth in Gilead with its common-land (a city of refuge for the slayer), Mahanaim with its common-land, 39Heshbon with its common-land, *and* Jazer with its common-land: four cities in all. 40So all the cities for the children of Merari according to their families, the rest of the families of the Levites, were *by* their lot twelve cities.

41All the cities of the Levites within the possession of the children of Israel *were* forty-eight cities with their common-lands. 42Every one of these cities had its common-land surrounding it; thus *were* all these cities.

THE PROMISE FULFILLED

43So the LORD gave to Israel all the land of which He had sworn to give to their fathers, and they took possession of it and dwelt in it. 44The LORD gave them rest all around, according to all that He had sworn to their fathers. And not a man of all their enemies stood against them; the LORD delivered all their enemies into their hand. 45Not a word failed of any good thing which the LORD had spoken to the house of Israel. All came to pass.

21:37 [a]Following Septuagint and Vulgate (compare 1 Chronicles 6:78, 79); Masoretic Text, Bomberg, and Targum omit verses 36 and 37.

THE MESSAGE

Beth Horon, with their pastures—four towns.

23-24 From the tribe of Dan they received Eltekeh, Gibbethon, Aijalon, and Gath Rimmon, all with their pastures—four towns.

25 And from the half-tribe of Manasseh they received Taanach and Gath Rimmon with their pastures—two towns.

26 All told, ten cities with their pastures went to the remaining Kohathite families.

27 The Gershonite families of the tribe of Levi were given from the half-tribe of Manasseh: Golan in Bashan (an asylum-city for the unconvicted killer), and Be Eshtarah, with their pastures—two cities.

28-29 And from the tribe of Issachar: Kishion, Daberath, Jarmuth, and En Gannim, with their pastures—four towns.

30-31 From the tribe of Asher: Mishal, Abdon, Helkath, and Rehob, with their pastures—four towns.

32 From the tribe of Naphtali: Kedesh in Galilee (an asylum-city for the unconvicted killer), Hammoth Dor, and Kartan, with their pastures—three towns.

33 For the Gershonites and their families: thirteen towns with their pastures.

34-35 The Merari families, the remaining Levites, were given from the tribe of Zebulun: Jokneam, Kartah, Dimnah, and Nahalal, with their pastures—four cities.

36-37 From the tribe of Reuben: Bezer, Jahaz, Kedemoth, and Mephaath, with their pastures—four towns.

38-39 From the tribe of Gad: Ramoth in Gilead (an asylum-city for the unconvicted killer), Mahanaim, Heshbon, and Jazer, with their pastures—a total of four towns.

40 All these towns were assigned by lot to the Merarites, the remaining Levites—twelve towns.

41-42 The Levites held forty-eight towns with their accompanying pastures within the territory of the People of Israel. Each of these towns had pastures surrounding it—this was the case for all these towns.

43-44 And so GOD gave Israel the entire land that he had solemnly vowed to give to their ancestors. They took possession of it and made themselves at home in it. And GOD gave them rest on all sides, as he had also solemnly vowed to their ancestors. Not a single one of their enemies was able to stand up to them—GOD handed over all their enemies to them.

45 Not one word failed from all the good words GOD spoke to the house of Israel. Everything came out right.

New King James Version

Eastern Tribes Return to Their Lands

22 Then Joshua called the Reubenites, the Gadites, and half the tribe of Manasseh, 2and said to them: "You have kept all that Moses the servant of the LORD commanded you, and have obeyed my voice in all that I commanded you. 3You have not left your brethren these many days, up to this day, but have kept the charge of the commandment of the LORD your God. 4And now the LORD your God has given rest to your brethren, as He promised them; now therefore, return and go to your tents *and* to the land of your possession, which Moses the servant of the LORD gave you on the other side of the Jordan. 5But take careful heed to do the commandment and the law which Moses the servant of the LORD commanded you, to love the LORD your God, to walk in all His ways, to keep His commandments, to hold fast to Him, and to serve Him with all your heart and with all your soul." 6So Joshua blessed them and sent them away, and they went to their tents.

7Now to half the tribe of Manasseh Moses had given a possession in Bashan, but to the *other* half of it Joshua gave *a possession* among their brethren on this side of the Jordan, westward. And indeed, when Joshua sent them away to their tents, he blessed them, 8and spoke to them, saying, "Return with much riches to your tents, with very much livestock, with silver, with gold, with bronze, with iron, and with very much clothing. Divide the spoil of your enemies with your brethren."

9So the children of Reuben, the children of Gad, and half the tribe of Manasseh returned, and departed from the children of Israel at Shiloh, which *is* in the land of Canaan, to go to the country of Gilead, to the land of their possession, which they had obtained according to the word of the LORD by the hand of Moses.

An Altar by the Jordan

10And when they came to the region of the Jordan which *is* in the land of Canaan, the children of Reuben, the children of Gad, and half the tribe of Manasseh built an altar there by the Jordan—a great, impressive altar. 11Now the children of Israel heard *someone* say, "Behold, the children of Reuben, the children of Gad, and half the tribe of Manasseh have built an altar on the frontier of the land of Canaan, in the region of the Jordan—on the children of Israel's side." 12And when the children of Israel heard *of it,* the whole congregation of the children of Israel gathered together at Shiloh to go to war against them.

13Then the children of Israel sent Phinehas the son of Eleazar the priest to the children of Reuben, to the children of Gad, and to half the tribe of Manasseh, into the land of Gilead, 14and with him ten rulers, one ruler each from the chief house of every tribe of Israel; and each one *was* the head of the house of his father among the divisions[a] of Israel. 15Then they came to the children of Reuben, to the children of Gad, and to half the tribe of Manasseh, to the land of Gilead, and they spoke with them, saying,

22:14 [a]Literally *thousands*

The Message

1-5 22 Then Joshua called together the Reubenites, Gadites, and the half-tribe of Manasseh. He said: "You have carried out everything Moses the servant of GOD commanded you, and you have obediently done everything I have commanded you. All this time and right down to this very day you have not abandoned your brothers; you've shouldered the task laid on you by GOD, your God. And now GOD, your God, has given rest to your brothers just as he promised them. You're now free to go back to your homes, the country of your inheritance that Moses the servant of GOD gave you on the other side of the Jordan. Only this: Be vigilant in keeping the Commandment and The Revelation that Moses the servant of GOD laid on you: Love GOD, your God, walk in all his ways, do what he's commanded, embrace him, serve him with everything you are and have."

6-7 Then Joshua blessed them and sent them on their way. They went home. (To the half-tribe of Manasseh, Moses had assigned a share in Bashan. To the other half, Joshua assigned land with their brothers west of the Jordan.)

7-8 When Joshua sent them off to their homes, he blessed them. He said: "Go home. You're going home rich—great herds of cattle, silver and gold, bronze and iron, huge piles of clothing. Share the wealth with your friends and families—all this plunder from your enemies!"

9 The Reubenites, Gadites, and the half-tribe of Manasseh left the People of Israel at Shiloh in the land of Canaan to return to Gilead, the land of their possession, which they had taken under the command of Moses as ordered by GOD.

10 They arrived at Geliloth on the Jordan (touching on Canaanite land). There the Reubenites, Gadites, and the half-tribe of Manasseh built an altar on the banks of the Jordan—a huge altar!

11 The People of Israel heard of it: "What's this? The Reubenites, Gadites, and the half-tribe of Manasseh have built an altar facing the land of Canaan at Geliloth on the Jordan, across from the People of Israel!"

12-14 When the People of Israel heard this, the entire congregation mustered at Shiloh to go to war against them. They sent Phinehas son of Eleazar the priest to the Reubenites, Gadites, and the half-tribe of Manasseh (that is, to the land of Gilead). Accompanying him were ten chiefs, one chief for each of the ten tribes, each the head of his ancestral family. They represented the military divisions of Israel.

15-18 They went to the Reubenites, Gadites, and the half-tribe of Manasseh and spoke to them: "The entire congregation of GOD

NEW KING JAMES VERSION

16“Thus says the whole congregation of the
LORD: ‘What treachery *is* this that you have com-
mitted against the God of Israel, to turn away
this day from following the LORD, in that you
have built for yourselves an altar, that you might
rebel this day against the LORD? 17*Is* the iniquity
of Peor not enough for us, from which we are
not cleansed till this day, although there was a
plague in the congregation of the LORD, 18but
that you must turn away this day from following
the LORD? And it shall be, if you rebel today
against the LORD, that tomorrow He will be an-
gry with the whole congregation of Israel.
19Nevertheless, if the land of your possession *is*
unclean, *then* cross over to the land of the pos-
session of the LORD, where the LORD’s taberna-
cle stands, and take possession among us; but
do not rebel against the LORD, nor rebel against
us, by building yourselves an altar besides the
altar of the LORD our God. 20Did not Achan the
son of Zerah commit a trespass in the accursed
thing, and wrath fell on all the congregation of
Israel? And that man did not perish alone in his
iniquity.’ ”

21Then the children of Reuben, the children
of Gad, and half the tribe of Manasseh an-
swered and said to the heads of the divisions[a] of
Israel: 22“The LORD God of gods, the LORD God
of gods, He knows, and let Israel itself know—if
it is in rebellion, or if in treachery against the
LORD, do not save us this day. 23If we have built
ourselves an altar to turn from following the
LORD, or if to offer on it burnt offerings or grain
offerings, or if to offer peace offerings on it, let
the LORD Himself require *an account*. 24But in
fact we have done it for fear, for a reason, say-
ing, ‘In time to come your descendants may
speak to our descendants, saying, “What have
you to do with the LORD God of Israel? 25For the
LORD has made the Jordan a border between
you and us, *you* children of Reuben and children
of Gad. You have no part in the LORD.” So your
descendants would make our descendants cease
fearing the LORD.’ 26Therefore we said, ‘Let us
now prepare to build ourselves an altar, not for
burnt offering nor for sacrifice, 27but *that* it *may*
be a witness between you and us and our gener-
ations after us, that we may perform the service
of the LORD before Him with our burnt offer-
ings, with our sacrifices, and with our peace of-
ferings; that your descendants may not say to
our descendants in time to come, “You have no
part in the LORD.” ’ 28Therefore we said that it
will be, when they say *this* to us or to our gener-
ations in time to come, that we may say, ‘Here is
the replica of the altar of the LORD which our fa-
thers made, though not for burnt offerings nor
for sacrifices; but it *is* a witness between you
and us.’ 29Far be it from us that we should rebel
against the LORD, and turn from following the
LORD this day, to build an altar for burnt offer-
ings, for grain offerings, or for sacrifices, be-
sides the altar of the LORD our God which *is* be-
fore His tabernacle.”

22:21 [a]Literally *thousands*

THE MESSAGE

wants to know: What is this violation against
the God of Israel that you have committed,
turning your back on GOD and building your
own altar—a blatant act of rebellion against
GOD? Wasn’t the crime of Peor enough for
us? Why, to this day we aren’t rid of it, still
living with the fallout of the plague on the
congregation of GOD! Look at you—turning
your back on GOD! If you rebel against GOD
today, tomorrow he’ll vent his anger on all of
us, the entire congregation of Israel.

19-20 “If you think the land of your possession
isn’t holy enough but somehow contami-
nated, come back over to GOD’s possession,
where GOD’s Dwelling is set up, and take
your land there, but don’t rebel against GOD.
And don’t rebel against us by building your
own altar apart from the Altar of our GOD.
When Achan son of Zerah violated the holy
curse, didn’t anger fall on the whole congre-
gation of Israel? He wasn’t the only one to
die for his sin.”

21-22 The Reubenites, Gadites, and the half-
tribe of Manasseh replied to the heads of the
tribes of Israel:

The God of Gods is GOD,
The God of Gods is GOD!

22-23 “He knows and he’ll let Israel know if this
is a rebellious betrayal of GOD. And if it is,
don’t bother saving us. If we built ourselves
an altar in rebellion against GOD, if we did it
to present on it Whole-Burnt-Offerings or
Grain-Offerings or to enact there sacrificial
Peace-Offerings, let GOD decide.

24-25 “But that’s not it. We did it because we
cared. We were anxious lest someday your
children should say to our children, ‘You’re
not connected with GOD, the God of Israel!
GOD made the Jordan a boundary between
us and you. You Reubenites and Gadites
have no part in GOD.’ And then your chil-
dren might cause our children to quit wor-
shiping GOD.

26 “So we said to ourselves, ‘Let’s do some-
thing. Let’s build an altar—but not for
Whole-Burnt-Offerings, not for sacrifices.’

27 “We built this altar as a witness between
us and you and our children coming after
us, a witness to the Altar where we worship
GOD in his Sacred Dwelling with our Whole-
Burnt-Offerings and our sacrifices and our
Peace-Offerings.

“This way, your children won’t be able to
say to our children in the future, ‘You have
no part in GOD.’

28 “We said to ourselves, ‘If anyone speaks
disparagingly to us or to our children in the
future, we’ll say: Look at this model of
GOD’s Altar which our ancestors made. It’s
not for Whole-Burnt-Offerings, not for sacri-
fices. It’s a witness connecting us with you.’

29 “Rebelling against or turning our backs
on GOD is the last thing on our minds right
now. We never dreamed of building an altar
for Whole-Burnt-Offerings or Grain-Offer-
ings to rival the Altar of our GOD in front of
his Sacred Dwelling.”

NEW KING JAMES VERSION

30Now when Phinehas the priest and the rulers of the congregation, the heads of the divisions[a] of Israel who *were* with him, heard the words that the children of Reuben, the children of Gad, and the children of Manasseh spoke, it pleased them. 31Then Phinehas the son of Eleazar the priest said to the children of Reuben, the children of Gad, and the children of Manasseh, "This day we perceive that the LORD *is* among us, because you have not committed this treachery against the LORD. Now you have delivered the children of Israel out of the hand of the LORD."

32And Phinehas the son of Eleazar the priest, and the rulers, returned from the children of Reuben and the children of Gad, from the land of Gilead to the land of Canaan, to the children of Israel, and brought back word to them. 33So the thing pleased the children of Israel, and the children of Israel blessed God; they spoke no more of going against them in battle, to destroy the land where the children of Reuben and Gad dwelt.

34The children of Reuben and the children of Gad[a] called the altar, *Witness*, "For *it is* a witness between us that the LORD *is* God."

JOSHUA'S FAREWELL ADDRESS

23 Now it came to pass, a long time after the LORD had given rest to Israel from all their enemies round about, that Joshua was old, advanced in age. 2And Joshua called for all Israel, for their elders, for their heads, for their judges, and for their officers, and said to them:

"I am old, advanced in age. 3You have seen all that the LORD your God has done to all these nations because of you, for the LORD your God *is* He who has fought for you. 4See, I have divided to you by lot these nations that remain, to be an inheritance for your tribes, from the Jordan, with all the nations that I have cut off, as far as the Great Sea westward. 5And the LORD your God will expel them from before you and drive them out of your sight. So you shall possess their land, as the LORD your God promised you. 6Therefore be very courageous to keep and to do all that is written in the Book of the Law of Moses, lest you turn aside from it to the right hand or to the left, 7*and* lest you go among these nations, these who remain among you. You shall not make mention of the name of their gods, nor cause *anyone* to swear *by them;* you shall not serve them nor bow down to them, 8but you shall hold fast to the LORD your God, as you have done to this day. 9For the LORD has driven out from before you great and strong nations; but *as for* you, no one has been able to stand against you to this day. 10One man of you shall chase a thousand, for the LORD your God *is* He who fights for you, as He promised you. 11Therefore take careful heed to yourselves, that you love the LORD your God. 12Or else, if indeed you do go back, and cling to the remnant of these nations—these that remain among you—and make marriages with them, and go in to them

22:30 [a]Literally *thousands* **22:34** [a]Septuagint adds *and half the tribe of Manasseh.*

THE MESSAGE

30 Phinehas the priest, all the heads of the congregation, and the heads of the military divisions of Israel who were also with him heard what the Reubenites, Gadites, and the half-tribe of Manasseh had to say. They were satisfied.

31 Priest Phinehas son of Eleazar said to Reuben, Gad, and Manasseh, "Now we're convinced that GOD is present with us since you haven't been disloyal to GOD in this matter. You saved the People of Israel from GOD's discipline."

32-33 Then Priest Phinehas son of Eleazar left the Reubenites, Gadites, and the half-tribe of Manasseh (from Gilead) and, with the chiefs, returned to the land of Canaan to the People of Israel and gave a full report. They were pleased with the report. The People of Israel blessed God—there was no more talk of attacking and destroying the land in which the Reubenites and Gadites were living.

34 Reuben and Gad named the altar:

A Witness Between Us.
GOD Alone Is God.

JOSHUA'S CHARGE

1-2 23 A long time later, after GOD had given Israel rest from all their surrounding enemies, and Joshua was a venerable old man, Joshua called all Israel together—elders, chiefs, judges, and officers. Then he spoke to them:

2-3 "I'm an old man. I've lived a long time. You have seen everything that GOD has done to these nations because of you. He did it because he's GOD, your God. He fought for you.

4-5 "Stay alert: I have assigned to you by lot these nations that remain as an inheritance to your tribes—these in addition to the nations I have already cut down—from the Jordan to the Great Sea in the west. GOD, your God, will drive them out of your path until there's nothing left of them and you'll take over their land just as GOD, your God, promised you.

6-8 "Now, stay strong and steady. Obediently do everything written in the *Book of The Revelation of Moses*—don't miss a detail. Don't get mixed up with the nations that are still around. Don't so much as speak the names of their gods or swear by them. And by all means don't worship or pray to them. Hold tight to GOD, your God, just as you've done up to now.

9-10 "GOD has driven out superpower nations before you. And up to now, no one has been able to stand up to you. Think of it—one of you, single-handedly, putting a thousand on the run! Because GOD is GOD, your God. Because he fights for you, just as he promised you.

11-13 "Now, vigilantly guard your souls: Love GOD, your God. Because if you wander off and start taking up with these remaining nations still among you (intermarry, say, and have other dealings with them), know

NEW KING JAMES VERSION

and they to you, 13know for certain that the LORD your God will no longer drive out these nations from before you. But they shall be snares and traps to you, and scourges on your sides and thorns in your eyes, until you perish from this good land which the LORD your God has given you.

14"Behold, this day I *am* going the way of all the earth. And you know in all your hearts and in all your souls that not one thing has failed of all the good things which the LORD your God spoke concerning you. All have come to pass for you; not one word of them has failed. 15Therefore it shall come to pass, that as all the good things have come upon you which the LORD your God promised you, so the LORD will bring upon you all harmful things, until He has destroyed you from this good land which the LORD your God has given you. 16When you have transgressed the covenant of the LORD your God, which He commanded you, and have gone and served other gods, and bowed down to them, then the anger of the LORD will burn against you, and you shall perish quickly from the good land which He has given you."

THE COVENANT AT SHECHEM

24 Then Joshua gathered all the tribes of Israel to Shechem and called for the elders of Israel, for their heads, for their judges, and for their officers; and they presented themselves before God. 2And Joshua said to all the people, "Thus says the LORD God of Israel: 'Your fathers, *including* Terah, the father of Abraham and the father of Nahor, dwelt on the other side of the River[a] in old times; and they served other gods. 3Then I took your father Abraham from the other side of the River, led him throughout all the land of Canaan, and multiplied his descendants and gave him Isaac. 4To Isaac I gave Jacob and Esau. To Esau I gave the mountains of Seir to possess, but Jacob and his children went down to Egypt. 5Also I sent Moses and Aaron, and I plagued Egypt, according to what I did among them. Afterward I brought you out.

6'Then I brought your fathers out of Egypt, and you came to the sea; and the Egyptians pursued your fathers with chariots and horsemen to the Red Sea. 7So they cried out to the LORD; and He put darkness between you and the Egyptians, brought the sea upon them, and covered them. And your eyes saw what I did in Egypt. Then you dwelt in the wilderness a long time. 8And I brought you into the land of the Amorites, who dwelt on the other side of the Jordan, and they fought with you. But I gave them into your hand, that you might possess their land, and I destroyed them from before you. 9Then Balak the son of Zippor, king of Moab, arose to make war against Israel, and sent and called Balaam the son of Beor to curse you. 10But I would not listen to Balaam; therefore he continued to bless you. So I delivered you out of his hand. 11Then you went over the Jordan and came to Jericho. And the men of Jericho fought against you—*also* the Amorites, the Perizzites,

24:2 [a]Hebrew *Nahar,* the Euphrates, and so in verses 3, 14, and 15

THE MESSAGE

for certain that GOD, your God, will not get rid of these nations for you. They'll be nothing but trouble to you—horsewhips on your backs and sand in your eyes—until you're the ones who will be driven out of this good land that GOD, your God, has given you.
14 "As you can see, I'm about to go the way
we all end up going. Know this with all your heart, with everything in you, that not one detail has failed of all the good things GOD, your God, promised you. It has all happened. Nothing's left undone—not so much as a word.
15-16 "But just as sure as everything good that
GOD, your God, has promised has come true, so also GOD will bring to pass every bad thing until there's nothing left of you in this good land that GOD has given you. If you leave the path of the Covenant of GOD, your God, that he commanded you, go off and serve and worship other gods, GOD's anger will blaze out against you. In no time at all there'll be nothing left of you, no sign that you've ever been in this good land he gave you."

THE COVENANT AT SHECHEM

1-2 24 Joshua called together all the tribes of
Israel at Shechem. He called in the elders, chiefs, judges, and officers. They presented themselves before God. Then Joshua addressed all the people:
2-6 "This is what GOD, the God of Israel, says:
A long time ago your ancestors, Terah and his sons Abraham and Nahor, lived to the east of the River Euphrates. They worshiped other gods. I took your ancestor Abraham from the far side of The River. I led him all over the land of Canaan and multiplied his descendants. I gave him Isaac. Then I gave Isaac Jacob and Esau. I let Esau have the mountains of Seir as home, but Jacob and his sons ended up in Egypt. I sent Moses and Aaron. I hit Egypt hard with plagues and then led you out of there. I brought your ancestors out of Egypt. You came to the sea, the Egyptians in hot pursuit with chariots and cavalry, to the very edge of the Red Sea!
7-10 "Then they cried out for help to GOD. He
put a cloud between you and the Egyptians and then let the sea loose on them. It drowned them.

"You watched the whole thing with your own eyes, what I did to Egypt. And then you lived in the wilderness for a long time. I brought you to the country of the Amorites, who lived east of the Jordan, and they fought you. But I fought for you and you took their land. I destroyed them for you. Then Balak son of Zippor made his appearance. He was the king of Moab. He got ready to fight Israel by sending for Balaam son of Beor to come and curse you. But I wouldn't listen to Balaam—he ended up blessing you over and over! I saved you from him.
11 "You then crossed the Jordan and came
to Jericho. The Jericho leaders ganged up on you as well as the Amorites, Perizzites,

NEW KING JAMES VERSION

the Canaanites, the Hittites, the Girgashites, the
Hivites, and the Jebusites. But I delivered them
into your hand. 12I sent the hornet before you
which drove them out from before you, *also* the
two kings of the Amorites, *but* not with your
sword or with your bow. 13I have given you a
land for which you did not labor, and cities
which you did not build, and you dwell in them;
you eat of the vineyards and olive groves which
you did not plant.'
14"Now therefore, fear the LORD, serve Him
in sincerity and in truth, and put away the gods
which your fathers served on the other side of
the River and in Egypt. Serve the LORD! 15And if
it seems evil to you to serve the LORD, choose for
yourselves this day whom you will serve,
whether the gods which your fathers served that
were on the other side of the River, or the gods
of the Amorites, in whose land you dwell. But as
for me and my house, we will serve the LORD."
16So the people answered and said: "Far be it
from us that we should forsake the LORD to
serve other gods; 17for the LORD our God *is* He
who brought us and our fathers up out of the
land of Egypt, from the house of bondage, who
did those great signs in our sight, and preserved
us in all the way that we went and among all the
people through whom we passed. 18And the
LORD drove out from before us all the people, in-
cluding the Amorites who dwelt in the land. We
also will serve the LORD, for He *is* our God."
19But Joshua said to the people, "You cannot
serve the LORD, for He *is* a holy God. He *is* a jeal-
ous God; He will not forgive your transgressions
nor your sins. 20If you forsake the LORD and
serve foreign gods, then He will turn and do you
harm and consume you, after He has done you
good."
21And the people said to Joshua, "No, but we
will serve the LORD!"
22So Joshua said to the people, "You *are* wit-
nesses against yourselves that you have chosen
the LORD for yourselves, to serve Him."
And they said, "*We are* witnesses!"
23"Now therefore," *he said*, "put away the for-
eign gods which *are* among you, and incline
your heart to the LORD God of Israel."
24And the people said to Joshua, "The LORD
our God we will serve, and His voice we will
obey!"
25So Joshua made a covenant with the peo-
ple that day, and made for them a statute and an
ordinance in Shechem.
26Then Joshua wrote these words in the
Book of the Law of God. And he took a large
stone, and set it up there under the oak that *was*
by the sanctuary of the LORD.

THE MESSAGE

Canaanites, Hittites, Girgashites, Hivites,
and Jebusites, but I turned them over to you.
12 "I sent the Hornet ahead of you. It drove
out the two Amorite kings—did your work
for you. You didn't have to do a thing, not so
much as raise a finger.
13 "I handed you a land for which you did
not work, towns you did not build. And here
you are now living in them and eating from
vineyards and olive groves you did not
plant.
14 "So now: Fear GOD. Worship him in total
commitment. Get rid of the gods your ances-
tors worshiped on the far side of The River
(the Euphrates) and in Egypt. You, worship
GOD.
15 "If you decide that it's a bad thing to wor-
ship GOD, then choose a god you'd rather
serve—and do it today. Choose one of the
gods your ancestors worshiped from the
country beyond The River, or one of the gods
of the Amorites, on whose land you're now
living. As for me and my family, we'll wor-
ship GOD."
16 The people answered, "We'd never for-
sake GOD! Never! We'd never leave GOD to
worship other gods.
17-18 "GOD is our God! He brought up our an-
cestors from Egypt and from slave condi-
tions. He did all those great signs while we
watched. He has kept his eye on us all along
the roads we've traveled and among the na-
tions we've passed through. Just for us he
drove out all the nations, Amorites and all,
who lived in the land.
"Count us in: We too are going to worship
GOD. He's our God."

19-20 Then Joshua told the people: "You can't
do it; you're not able to worship GOD. He is
a holy God. He is a jealous God. He won't
put up with your fooling around and sin-
ning. When you leave GOD and take up the
worship of foreign gods, he'll turn right
around and come down on you hard. He'll
put an end to you—and after all the good he
has done for you!"
21 But the people told Joshua: "No! No! We
worship GOD!"
22 And so Joshua addressed the people:
"You are witnesses against yourselves that
you have chosen GOD for yourselves—to
worship him."
And they said, "We are witnesses."
23 Joshua said, "Now get rid of all the for-
eign gods you have with you. Say an unqual-
ified Yes to GOD, the God of Israel."
24 The people answered Joshua, "We will
worship GOD. What he says, we'll do."

25-26 Joshua completed a Covenant for the
people that day there at Shechem. He made
it official, spelling it out in detail. Joshua
wrote out all the directions and regulations
into the Book of The Revelation of God.
Then he took a large stone and set it up un-
der the oak that was in the holy place of
GOD.

NEW KING JAMES VERSION

27And Joshua said to all the people, "Behold, this
stone shall be a witness to us, for it has heard all
the words of the LORD which He spoke to us. It
shall therefore be a witness to you, lest you deny
your God." 28So Joshua let the people depart,
each to his own inheritance.

DEATH OF JOSHUA AND ELEAZAR

29Now it came to pass after these things that
Joshua the son of Nun, the servant of the LORD,
died, *being* one hundred and ten years old.
30And they buried him within the border of his
inheritance at Timnath Serah, which *is* in the
mountains of Ephraim, on the north side of
Mount Gaash.

31Israel served the LORD all the days of
Joshua, and all the days of the elders who out-
lived Joshua, who had known all the works of
the LORD which He had done for Israel.

32The bones of Joseph, which the children of
Israel had brought up out of Egypt, they buried
at Shechem, in the plot of ground which Jacob
had bought from the sons of Hamor the father
of Shechem for one hundred pieces of silver,
and which had become an inheritance of the
children of Joseph.

33And Eleazar the son of Aaron died. They
buried him in a hill *belonging to* Phinehas his
son, which was given to him in the mountains of
Ephraim.

THE MESSAGE

27 Joshua spoke to all the people: "This stone is a witness against us. It has heard every word that GOD has said to us. It is a standing witness against you lest you cheat on your God."

28 Then Joshua dismissed the people, each to his own place of inheritance.

29-30 After all this, Joshua son of Nun, the servant of GOD, died. He was 110 years old. They buried him in the land of his inheritance at Timnath Serah in the mountains of Ephraim, north of Mount Gaash.

31 Israel served GOD through the lifetime of Joshua and of the elders who outlived him, who had themselves experienced all that GOD had done for Israel.

32 Joseph's bones, which the People of Israel had brought from Egypt, they buried in Shechem in the plot of ground that Jacob had purchased from the sons of Hamor (who was the father of Shechem). He paid a hundred silver coins for it. It belongs to the inheritance of the family of Joseph.

33 Eleazar son of Aaron died. They buried him at Gibeah, which had been allotted to his son Phinehas in the mountains of Ephraim.

JUDGES

New King James Version

The Continuing Conquest of Canaan

1 Now after the death of Joshua it came to pass
that the children of Israel asked the LORD,
saying, "Who shall be first to go up for us
against the Canaanites to fight against them?"
2And the LORD said, "Judah shall go up. In-
deed I have delivered the land into his hand."
3So Judah said to Simeon his brother, "Come
up with me to my allotted territory, that we may
fight against the Canaanites; and I will likewise
go with you to your allotted territory." And
Simeon went with him. 4Then Judah went up,
and the LORD delivered the Canaanites and the
Perizzites into their hand; and they killed ten
thousand men at Bezek. 5And they found Adoni-
Bezek in Bezek, and fought against him; and
they defeated the Canaanites and the Perizzites.
6Then Adoni-Bezek fled, and they pursued him
and caught him and cut off his thumbs and big
toes. 7And Adoni-Bezek said, "Seventy kings
with their thumbs and big toes cut off used to
gather *scraps* under my table; as I have done, so
God has repaid me." Then they brought him to
Jerusalem, and there he died.
8Now the children of Judah fought against
Jerusalem and took it; they struck it with the
edge of the sword and set the city on fire. 9And
afterward the children of Judah went down to
fight against the Canaanites who dwelt in the
mountains, in the South,[a] and in the lowland.
10Then Judah went against the Canaanites who
dwelt in Hebron. (Now the name of Hebron *was*
formerly Kirjath Arba.) And they killed Sheshai,
Ahiman, and Talmai.
11From there they went against the inhabi-
tants of Debir. (The name of Debir *was* formerly
Kirjath Sepher.)
12Then Caleb said, "Whoever attacks Kirjath
Sepher and takes it, to him I will give my daugh-
ter Achsah as wife." 13And Othniel the son of
Kenaz, Caleb's younger brother, took it; so he
gave him his daughter Achsah as wife. 14Now it
happened, when she came *to him*, that she
urged him[a] to ask her father for a field. And she
dismounted from *her* donkey, and Caleb said to
her, "What do you wish?" 15So she said to him,
"Give me a blessing; since you have given me
land in the South, give me also springs of wa-
ter."
And Caleb gave her the upper springs and
the lower springs.
16Now the children of the Kenite, Moses' fa-
ther-in-law, went up from the City of Palms with
the children of Judah into the Wilderness of Ju-
dah, which *lies* in the South *near* Arad; and they
went and dwelt among the people. 17And Judah
went with his brother Simeon, and they at-
tacked the Canaanites who inhabited Zephath,

1:9 [a]Hebrew *Negev*, and so throughout this book **1:14** [a]Septuagint and Vulgate read *he urged her*.

The Message

1 1 A time came after the death of Joshua when the People of Israel asked GOD, "Who will take the lead in going up against the Canaanites to fight them?"

2 And GOD said, "Judah will go. I've given the land to him."

3 The men of Judah said to those of their brother Simeon, "Go up with us to our territory and we'll fight the Canaanites. Then we'll go with you to your territory." And Simeon went with them.

4 So Judah went up. GOD gave them the Canaanites and the Perizzites. They defeated them at Bezek—ten military units!

5-7 They caught up with My-Master-Bezek there and fought him. They smashed the Canaanites and the Perizzites. My-Master-Bezek ran, but they gave chase and caught him. They cut off his thumbs and big toes. My-Master-Bezek said, "Seventy kings with their thumbs and big toes cut off used to crawl under my table, scavenging. Now God has done to me what I did to them."

They brought him to Jerusalem and he died there.

8-10 The people of Judah attacked and captured Jerusalem, subduing the city by sword and then sending it up in flames. After that they had gone down to fight the Canaanites who were living in the hill country, the Negev, and the foothills. Judah had gone on to the Canaanites who lived in Hebron (Hebron used to be called Kiriath Arba) and brought Sheshai, Ahiman, and Talmai to their knees.

11-12 From there they had marched against the population of Debir (Debir used to be called Kiriath Sepher). Caleb had said, "Whoever attacks Kiriath Sepher and takes it, I'll give my daughter Acsah to him as his wife."

13 Othniel son of Kenaz, Caleb's brother, took it, so Caleb gave him his daughter Acsah as his wife.

14-15 When she arrived she got him
to ask for farmland from her father.
As she dismounted from her donkey
Caleb asked her, "What would you like?"
She said, "Give me a marriage gift.
You've given me desert land;
Now give me pools of water!"
And he gave her the upper and the lower pools.

16 The people of Hobab the Kenite, Moses' relative, went up with the people of Judah from the City of Palms to the wilderness of Judah at the descent of Arad. They settled down there with the Amalekites.

17 The people of Judah went with their kin the Simeonites and struck the Canaanites

NEW KING JAMES VERSION

and utterly destroyed it. So the name of the city was called Hormah. 18 Also Judah took Gaza with its territory, Ashkelon with its territory, and Ekron with its territory. 19 So the LORD was with Judah. And they drove out the mountaineers, but they could not drive out the inhabitants of the lowland, because they had chariots of iron. 20 And they gave Hebron to Caleb, as Moses had said. Then he expelled from there the three sons of Anak. 21 But the children of Benjamin did not drive out the Jebusites who inhabited Jerusalem; so the Jebusites dwell with the children of Benjamin in Jerusalem to this day.

22 And the house of Joseph also went up against Bethel, and the LORD *was* with them. 23 So the house of Joseph sent men to spy out Bethel. (The name of the city *was* formerly Luz.) 24 And when the spies saw a man coming out of the city, they said to him, "Please show us the entrance to the city, and we will show you mercy." 25 So he showed them the entrance to the city, and they struck the city with the edge of the sword; but they let the man and all his family go. 26 And the man went to the land of the Hittites, built a city, and called its name Luz, which *is* its name to this day.

INCOMPLETE CONQUEST OF THE LAND

27 However, Manasseh did not drive out *the inhabitants of* Beth Shean and its villages, or Taanach and its villages, or the inhabitants of Dor and its villages, or the inhabitants of Ibleam and its villages, or the inhabitants of Megiddo and its villages; for the Canaanites were determined to dwell in that land. 28 And it came to pass, when Israel was strong, that they put the Canaanites under tribute, but did not completely drive them out.

29 Nor did Ephraim drive out the Canaanites who dwelt in Gezer; so the Canaanites dwelt in Gezer among them.

30 Nor did Zebulun drive out the inhabitants of Kitron or the inhabitants of Nahalol; so the Canaanites dwelt among them, and were put under tribute.

31 Nor did Asher drive out the inhabitants of Acco or the inhabitants of Sidon, or of Ahlab, Achzib, Helbah, Aphik, or Rehob. 32 So the Asherites dwelt among the Canaanites, the inhabitants of the land; for they did not drive them out.

33 Nor did Naphtali drive out the inhabitants of Beth Shemesh or the inhabitants of Beth Anath; but they dwelt among the Canaanites, the inhabitants of the land. Nevertheless the inhabitants of Beth Shemesh and Beth Anath were put under tribute to them.

34 And the Amorites forced the children of Dan into the mountains, for they would not allow them to come down to the valley; 35 and the Amorites were determined to dwell in Mount Heres, in Aijalon, and in Shaalbim;[a] yet when the strength of the house of Joseph became greater, they were put under tribute.

36 Now the boundary of the Amorites *was* from the Ascent of Akrabbim, from Sela, and upward.

1:35 [a]Spelled *Shaalabbin* in Joshua 19:42

THE MESSAGE

who lived in Zephath. They carried out the holy curse and named the city Curse-town.

18-19 But Judah didn't manage to capture Gaza, Ashkelon, and Ekron with their territories. GOD was certainly with Judah in that they took over the hill country. But they couldn't oust the people on the plain because they had iron chariots.

20 They gave Hebron to Caleb, as Moses had directed. Caleb drove out the three sons of Anak.

21 But the people of Benjamin couldn't get rid of the Jebusites living in Jerusalem. Benjaminites and Jebusites live side by side in Jerusalem to this day.

22-26 The house of Joseph went up to attack Bethel. GOD was with them. Joseph sent out spies to look the place over. Bethel used to be known as Luz. The spies saw a man leaving the city and said to him, "Show us a way into the city and we'll treat you well." The man showed them a way in. They killed everyone in the city but the man and his family. The man went to Hittite country and built a city. He named it Luz; that's its name to this day.

27-28 But Manasseh never managed to drive out Beth Shan, Taanach, Dor, Ibleam, and Megiddo with their territories. The Canaanites dug in their heels and wouldn't budge. When Israel became stronger they put the Canaanites to forced labor, but they never got rid of them.

29 Neither did Ephraim drive out the Canaanites who lived in Gezer. The Canaanites stuck it out and lived there with them.

30 Nor did Zebulun drive out the Canaanites in Kitron or Nahalol. They kept living there, but they were put to forced labor.

31-32 Nor did Asher drive out the people of Acco, Sidon, Ahlab, Aczib, Helbah, Aphek, and Rehob. Asher went ahead and settled down with the Canaanites since they could not get rid of them.

33 Naphtali fared no better. They couldn't drive out the people of Beth Shemesh or Beth Anath so they just moved in and lived with them. They did, though, put them to forced labor.

34-35 The Amorites pushed the people of Dan up into the hills and wouldn't let them down on the plains. The Amorites stubbornly continued to live in Mount Heres, Aijalon, and Shaalbim. But when the house of Joseph got the upper hand, they were put to forced labor.

36 The Amorite border extended from Scorpions' Pass and Sela upward.

New King James Version

Israel's Disobedience

2 Then the Angel of the Lord came up from
Gilgal to Bochim, and said: "I led you up from
Egypt and brought you to the land of which I
swore to your fathers; and I said, 'I will never
break My covenant with you. 2And you shall
make no covenant with the inhabitants of this
land; you shall tear down their altars.' But you
have not obeyed My voice. Why have you done
this? 3Therefore I also said, 'I will not drive them
out before you; but they shall be *thorns* in your
side,[a] and their gods shall be a snare to you.' "
4So it was, when the Angel of the Lord spoke
these words to all the children of Israel, that the
people lifted up their voices and wept.
5Then they called the name of that place
Bochim;[a] and they sacrificed there to the Lord.
6And when Joshua had dismissed the people,
the children of Israel went each to his own in-
heritance to possess the land.

Death of Joshua

7So the people served the Lord all the days
of Joshua, and all the days of the elders who
outlived Joshua, who had seen all the great
works of the Lord which He had done for Israel.
8Now Joshua the son of Nun, the servant of the
Lord, died *when he was* one hundred and ten
years old. 9And they buried him within the bor-
der of his inheritance at Timnath Heres, in the
mountains of Ephraim, on the north side of
Mount Gaash. 10When all that generation had
been gathered to their fathers, another genera-
tion arose after them who did not know the
Lord nor the work which He had done for Is-
rael.

Israel's Unfaithfulness

11Then the children of Israel did evil in the
sight of the Lord, and served the Baals; 12and
they forsook the Lord God of their fathers, who
had brought them out of the land of Egypt; and
they followed other gods from *among* the gods
of the people who *were* all around them, and
they bowed down to them; and they provoked
the Lord to anger. 13They forsook the Lord and
served Baal and the Ashtoreths.[a] 14And the
anger of the Lord was hot against Israel. So He
delivered them into the hands of plunderers
who despoiled them; and He sold them into the
hands of their enemies all around, so that they
could no longer stand before their enemies.
15Wherever they went out, the hand of the Lord
was against them for calamity, as the Lord had
said, and as the Lord had sworn to them. And
they were greatly distressed.
16Nevertheless, the Lord raised up judges
who delivered them out of the hand of those
who plundered them. 17Yet they would not listen
to their judges, but they played the harlot with
other gods, and bowed down to them. They
turned quickly from the way in which their fa-
thers walked, in obeying the commandments of
the Lord; they did not do so. 18And when the
Lord raised up judges for them, the Lord was
with the judge and delivered them out of the

2:3 [a]Septuagint, Targum, and Vulgate read *enemies to you.*
2:5 [a]Literally *Weeping* **2:13** [a]Canaanite goddesses

The Message

1-2 2 God's angel went up from Gilgal to Bokim
and said, "I brought you out of Egypt; I led
you to the land that I promised to your fa-
thers; and I said, I'll never break my
covenant with you—never! And you're
never to make a covenant with the people
who live in this land. Tear down their altars!
But you haven't obeyed me! What's this that
you're doing?
3 "So now I'm telling you that I won't drive
them out before you. They'll trip you up and
their gods will become a trap."
4-5 When God's angel had spoken these
words to all the People of Israel, they cried
out—oh! how they wept! They named the
place Bokim (Weepers). And there they sac-
rificed to God.

6-9 After Joshua had dismissed them, the Peo-
ple of Israel went off to claim their allotted
territories and take possession of the land.
The people worshiped God throughout the
lifetime of Joshua and the time of the lead-
ers who survived him, leaders who had been
in on all of God's great work that he had
done for Israel. Then Joshua son of Nun, the
servant of God, died. He was 110 years old.
They buried him in his allotted inheritance
at Timnath Heres in the hills of Ephraim
north of Mount Gaash.
10 Eventually that entire generation died
and was buried. Then another generation
grew up that didn't know anything of God
or the work he had done for Israel.

11-15 The People of Israel did evil in God's sight:
they served Baal-gods; they deserted God,
the God of their parents who had led them
out of Egypt; they took up with other gods,
gods of the peoples around them. They actu-
ally worshiped them! And oh, how they an-
gered God as they worshiped god Baal and
goddess Astarte! God's anger was hot
against Israel: He handed them off to plun-
derers who stripped them; he sold them
cheap to enemies on all sides. They were
helpless before their enemies. Every time
they walked out the door God was with
them—but for evil, just as God had said, just
as he had sworn he would do. They were in
a bad way.
16-17 But then God raised up judges who saved
them from their plunderers. But they wouldn't
listen to their judges; they prostituted them-
selves to other gods—worshiped them! They
lost no time leaving the road walked by their
parents, the road of obedience to God's
commands. They refused to have anything
to do with it.
18-19 When God was setting up judges for
them, he would be right there with the
judge: He would save them from their ene-

NEW KING JAMES VERSION

hand of their enemies all the days of the judge;
for the LORD was moved to pity by their groan-
ing because of those who oppressed them and
harassed them. 19And it came to pass, when the
judge was dead, that they reverted and behaved
more corruptly than their fathers, by following
other gods, to serve them and bow down to
them. They did not cease from their own doings
nor from their stubborn way.
20Then the anger of the LORD was hot against
Israel; and He said, "Because this nation has
transgressed My covenant which I commanded
their fathers, and has not heeded My voice, 21I
also will no longer drive out before them any of
the nations which Joshua left when he died, 22so
that through them I may test Israel, whether
they will keep the ways of the LORD, to walk in
them as their fathers kept *them*, or not."
23Therefore the LORD left those nations, without
driving them out immediately; nor did He de-
liver them into the hand of Joshua.

THE NATIONS REMAINING IN THE LAND

3 Now these *are* the nations which the LORD
left, that He might test Israel by them, *that is*,
all who had not known any of the wars in
Canaan 2(*this was* only so that the generations
of the children of Israel might be taught to know
war, at least those who had not formerly known
it), 3*namely*, five lords of the Philistines, all the
Canaanites, the Sidonians, and the Hivites who
dwelt in Mount Lebanon, from Mount Baal Her-
mon to the entrance of Hamath. 4And they were
left, that He might test Israel by them, to know
whether they would obey the commandments of
the LORD, which He had commanded their fa-
thers by the hand of Moses.
5Thus the children of Israel dwelt among the
Canaanites, the Hittites, the Amorites, the Per-
izzites, the Hivites, and the Jebusites. 6And they
took their daughters to be their wives, and gave
their daughters to their sons; and they served
their gods.

OTHNIEL

7So the children of Israel did evil in the sight
of the LORD. They forgot the LORD their God,
and served the Baals and Asherahs.[a] 8Therefore
the anger of the LORD was hot against Israel,
and He sold them into the hand of Cushan-
Rishathaim king of Mesopotamia; and the chil-
dren of Israel served Cushan-Rishathaim eight
years. 9When the children of Israel cried out to
the LORD, the LORD raised up a deliverer for the
children of Israel, who delivered them: Othniel
the son of Kenaz, Caleb's younger brother. 10The
Spirit of the LORD came upon him, and he
judged Israel. He went out to war, and the LORD
delivered Cushan-Rishathaim king of Mesopo-
tamia into his hand; and his hand prevailed over
Cushan-Rishathaim. 11So the land had rest for
forty years. Then Othniel the son of Kenaz died.

3:7 [a]Name or symbol for Canaanite goddesses

THE MESSAGE

mies' oppression as long as the judge was alive, for GOD was moved to compassion when he heard their groaning because of those who afflicted and beat them. But when the judge died, the people went right back to their old ways—but even worse than their parents!—running after other gods, serving and worshiping them. Stubborn as mules, they didn't drop a single evil practice.

20-22 And GOD's anger blazed against Israel. He said, "Because these people have thrown out my covenant that I commanded their parents and haven't listened to me, I'm not driving out one more person from the nations that Joshua left behind when he died. I'll use them to test Israel and see whether they stay on GOD's road and walk down it as their parents did."

23 That's why GOD let those nations remain. He didn't drive them out or let Joshua get rid of them.

1-4 3 These are the nations that GOD left there, using them to test the Israelites who had no experience in the Canaanite wars. He did it to train the descendants of Israel, the ones who had no battle experience, in the art of war. He left the five Philistine tyrants, all the Canaanites, the Sidonians, and the Hivites living on Mount Lebanon from Mount Baal Hermon to Hamath's Pass. They were there to test Israel and see whether they would obey GOD's commands that were given to their parents through Moses.

5-6 But the People of Israel made themselves at home among the Canaanites, Hittites, Amorites, Perizzites, Hivites, and Jebusites. They married their daughters and gave their own daughters to their sons in marriage. And they worshiped their gods.

OTHNIEL

7-8 The People of Israel did evil in GOD's sight. They forgot their GOD and worshiped the Baal gods and Asherah goddesses. GOD's hot anger blazed against Israel. He sold them off to Cushan-Rishathaim king of Aram Naharaim. The People of Israel were in servitude to Cushan-Rishathaim for eight years.

9-10 The People of Israel cried out to GOD and GOD raised up a savior who rescued them: Caleb's nephew Othniel, son of his younger brother Kenaz. The Spirit of GOD came on him and he rallied Israel. He went out to war and GOD gave him Cushan-Rishathaim king of Aram Naharaim. Othniel made short work of him.

11 The land was quiet for forty years. Then Othniel son of Kenaz died.

NEW KING JAMES VERSION

EHUD

12 And the children of Israel again did evil in the sight of the LORD. So the LORD strengthened Eglon king of Moab against Israel, because they had done evil in the sight of the LORD. 13 Then he gathered to himself the people of Ammon and Amalek, went and defeated Israel, and took possession of the City of Palms. 14 So the children of Israel served Eglon king of Moab eighteen years.

15 But when the children of Israel cried out to the LORD, the LORD raised up a deliverer for them: Ehud the son of Gera, the Benjamite, a left-handed man. By him the children of Israel sent tribute to Eglon king of Moab. 16 Now Ehud made himself a dagger (it was double-edged and a cubit in length) and fastened it under his clothes on his right thigh. 17 So he brought the tribute to Eglon king of Moab. (Now Eglon *was* a very fat man.) 18 And when he had finished presenting the tribute, he sent away the people who had carried the tribute. 19 But he himself turned back from the stone images that *were* at Gilgal, and said, "I have a secret message for you, O king."

He said, "Keep silence!" And all who attended him went out from him.

20 So Ehud came to him (now he was sitting upstairs in his cool private chamber). Then Ehud said, "I have a message from God for you." So he arose from *his* seat. 21 Then Ehud reached with his left hand, took the dagger from his right thigh, and thrust it into his belly. 22 Even the hilt went in after the blade, and the fat closed over the blade, for he did not draw the dagger out of his belly; and his entrails came out. 23 Then Ehud went out through the porch and shut the doors of the upper room behind him and locked them.

24 When he had gone out, *Eglon's*[a] servants came to look, and *to their* surprise, the doors of the upper room were locked. So they said, "He is probably attending to his needs in the cool chamber." 25 So they waited till they were embarrassed, and still he had not opened the doors of the upper room. Therefore they took the key and opened *them*. And there was their master, fallen dead on the floor.

26 But Ehud had escaped while they delayed, and passed beyond the stone images and escaped to Seirah. 27 And it happened, when he arrived, that he blew the trumpet in the mountains of Ephraim, and the children of Israel went down with him from the mountains; and he led them. 28 Then he said to them, "Follow *me*, for the LORD has delivered your enemies the Moabites into your hand." So they went down after him, seized the fords of the Jordan leading to Moab, and did not allow anyone to cross over. 29 And at that time they killed about ten thousand men of Moab, all stout men of valor; not a man escaped. 30 So Moab was subdued that day under the hand of Israel. And the land had rest for eighty years.

3:24 [a]Literally *his*

THE MESSAGE

EHUD

12-14 But the People of Israel went back to doing evil in GOD's sight. So GOD made Eglon king of Moab a power against Israel because they did evil in GOD's sight. He recruited the Ammonites and Amalekites and went out and struck Israel. They took the City of Palms. The People of Israel were in servitude to Eglon fourteen years.

15-19 The People of Israel cried out to GOD and GOD raised up for them a savior, Ehud son of Gera, a Benjaminite. He was left-handed. The People of Israel sent tribute by him to Eglon king of Moab. Ehud made himself a short two-edged sword and strapped it on his right thigh under his clothes. He presented the tribute to Eglon king of Moab. Eglon was grossly fat. After Ehud finished presenting the tribute, he went a little way with the men who had carried it. But when he got as far as the stone images near Gilgal, he went back and said, "I have a private message for you, O King."

The king told his servants, "Leave." They all left.

20-24 Ehud approached him—the king was now quite alone in his cool rooftop room—and said, "I have a word of God for you." Eglon stood up from his throne. Ehud reached with his left hand and took his sword from his right thigh and plunged it into the king's big belly. Not only the blade but the hilt went in. The fat closed in over it so he couldn't pull it out. Ehud slipped out by way of the porch and shut and locked the doors of the rooftop room behind him. Then he was gone.

When the servants came, they saw with surprise that the doors to the rooftop room were locked. They said, "He's probably relieving himself in the restroom."

25 They waited. And then they worried—no one was coming out of those locked doors. Finally, they got a key and unlocked them. There was their master, fallen on the floor, dead!

26-27 While they were standing around wondering what to do, Ehud was long gone. He got past the stone images and escaped to Seirah. When he got there, he sounded the trumpet on Mount Ephraim. The People of Israel came down from the hills and joined him. He took his place at their head.

28 He said, "Follow me, for GOD has given your enemies—yes, Moab!—to you." They went down after him and secured the fords of the Jordan against the Moabites. They let no one cross over.

29-30 At that time, they struck down about ten companies of Moabites, all of them well-fed and robust. Not one escaped. That day Moab was subdued under the hand of Israel.

The land was quiet for eighty years.

New King James Version

Shamgar

31After him was Shamgar the son of Anath,
who killed six hundred men of the Philistines
with an ox goad; and he also delivered Israel.

Deborah

4 When Ehud was dead, the children of Israel
again did evil in the sight of the LORD. 2So the
LORD sold them into the hand of Jabin king of
Canaan, who reigned in Hazor. The commander
of his army *was* Sisera, who dwelt in Harosheth
Hagoyim. 3And the children of Israel cried out
to the LORD; for Jabin had nine hundred chari-
ots of iron, and for twenty years he had harshly
oppressed the children of Israel.

4Now Deborah, a prophetess, the wife of
Lapidoth, was judging Israel at that time. 5And
she would sit under the palm tree of Deborah
between Ramah and Bethel in the mountains of
Ephraim. And the children of Israel came up to
her for judgment. 6Then she sent and called for
Barak the son of Abinoam from Kedesh in
Naphtali, and said to him, "Has not the LORD
God of Israel commanded, 'Go and deploy
troops at Mount Tabor; take with you ten thou-
sand men of the sons of Naphtali and of the
sons of Zebulun; 7and against you I will deploy
Sisera, the commander of Jabin's army, with his
chariots and his multitude at the River Kishon;
and I will deliver him into your hand'?"

8And Barak said to her, "If you will go with
me, then I will go; but if you will not go with me,
I will not go!"

9So she said, "I will surely go with you; nev-
ertheless there will be no glory for you in the
journey you are taking, for the LORD will sell
Sisera into the hand of a woman." Then Debo-
rah arose and went with Barak to Kedesh. 10And
Barak called Zebulun and Naphtali to Kedesh;
he went up with ten thousand men under his
command,[a] and Deborah went up with him.

11Now Heber the Kenite, of the children of
Hobab the father-in-law of Moses, had sepa-
rated himself from the Kenites and pitched his
tent near the terebinth tree at Zaanaim, which *is*
beside Kedesh.

12And they reported to Sisera that Barak the
son of Abinoam had gone up to Mount Tabor.
13So Sisera gathered together all his chariots,
nine hundred chariots of iron, and all the people
who *were* with him, from Harosheth Hagoyim
to the River Kishon.

14Then Deborah said to Barak, "Up! For this
is the day in which the LORD has delivered Sis-
era into your hand. Has not the LORD gone out
before you?" So Barak went down from Mount
Tabor with ten thousand men following him.
15And the LORD routed Sisera and all *his* chari-
ots and all *his* army with the edge of the sword
before Barak; and Sisera alighted from *his* char-
iot and fled away on foot. 16But Barak pursued
the chariots and the army as far as Harosheth
Hagoyim, and all the army of Sisera fell by the
edge of the sword; not a man was left.

17However, Sisera had fled away on foot to
the tent of Jael, the wife of Heber the Kenite; for

4:10 [a]Literally *at his feet*

The Message

Shamgar

31 Shamgar son of Anath came after Ehud. Us-
ing a cattle prod, he killed six hundred
Philistines single-handed. He too saved Is-
rael.

Deborah

1-3 4 The People of Israel kept right on doing
evil in GOD's sight. With Ehud dead, GOD
sold them off to Jabin king of Canaan who
ruled from Hazor. Sisera, who lived in
Harosheth Haggoyim, was the commander
of his army. The People of Israel cried out to
GOD because he had cruelly oppressed them
with his nine hundred iron chariots for
twenty years.

4-5 Deborah was a prophet, the wife of Lap-
pidoth. She was judge over Israel at that
time. She held court under Deborah's Palm
between Ramah and Bethel in the hills of
Ephraim. The People of Israel went to her in
matters of justice.

6-7 She sent for Barak son of Abinoam from
Kedesh in Naphtali and said to him, "It has
become clear that GOD, the God of Israel,
commands you: Go to Mount Tabor and pre-
pare for battle. Take ten companies of sol-
diers from Naphtali and Zebulun. I'll take
care of getting Sisera, the leader of Jabin's
army, to the Kishon River with all his chari-
ots and troops. And I'll make sure you win
the battle."

8 Barak said, "If you go with me, I'll go. But
if you don't go with me, I won't go."

9-10 She said, "Of course I'll go with you. But
understand that with an attitude like that,
there'll be no glory in it for you. GOD will
use a woman's hand to take care of Sisera."

Deborah got ready and went with Barak
to Kedesh. Barak called Zebulun and Naph-
tali together at Kedesh. Ten companies of
men followed him. And Deborah was with
him.

11-13 It happened that Heber the Kenite had
parted company with the other Kenites, the
descendants of Hobab, Moses' in-law. He
was now living at Zaanannim Oak near
Kedesh. They told Sisera that Barak son of
Abinoam had gone up to Mount Tabor. Sis-
era immediately called up all his chariots to
the Kishon River—nine hundred iron chari-
ots!—along with all his troops who were
with him at Harosheth Haggoyim.

14 Deborah said to Barak, "Charge! This
very day GOD has given you victory over
Sisera. Isn't GOD marching before you?"

Barak charged down the slopes of Mount
Tabor, his ten companies following him.

15-16 GOD routed Sisera—all those chariots, all
those troops!—before Barak. Sisera jumped
out of his chariot and ran. Barak chased the
chariots and troops all the way to Harosheth
Haggoyim. Sisera's entire fighting force was
killed—not one man left.

17-18 Meanwhile Sisera, running for his life,
headed for the tent of Jael, wife of Heber the
Kenite. Jabin king of Hazor and Heber the

NEW KING JAMES VERSION

there was peace between Jabin king of Hazor
and the house of Heber the Kenite. 18And Jael
went out to meet Sisera, and said to him, "Turn
aside, my lord, turn aside to me; do not fear."
And when he had turned aside with her into the
tent, she covered him with a blanket.
19Then he said to her, "Please give me a little
water to drink, for I am thirsty." So she opened
a jug of milk, gave him a drink, and covered
him. 20And he said to her, "Stand at the door of
the tent, and if any man comes and inquires of
you, and says, 'Is there any man here?' you shall
say, 'No.' "
21Then Jael, Heber's wife, took a tent peg and
took a hammer in her hand, and went softly to
him and drove the peg into his temple, and it
went down into the ground; for he was fast
asleep and weary. So he died. 22And then, as
Barak pursued Sisera, Jael came out to meet
him, and said to him, "Come, I will show you the
man whom you seek." And when he went into
her *tent,* there lay Sisera, dead with the peg in
his temple.
23So on that day God subdued Jabin king of
Canaan in the presence of the children of Israel.
24And the hand of the children of Israel grew
stronger and stronger against Jabin king of
Canaan, until they had destroyed Jabin king of
Canaan.

THE SONG OF DEBORAH

5 Then Deborah and Barak the son of Abinoam
sang on that day, saying:

2"When leaders lead in Israel,
When the people willingly offer themselves,
Bless the LORD!

3"Hear, O kings! Give ear, O princes!
I, *even* I, will sing to the LORD;
I will sing praise to the LORD God of Israel.

4"LORD, when You went out from Seir,
When You marched from the field of Edom,
The earth trembled and the heavens poured,
The clouds also poured water;
5The mountains gushed before the LORD,
This Sinai, before the LORD God of Israel.

6"In the days of Shamgar, son of Anath,
In the days of Jael,
The highways were deserted,
And the travelers walked along the byways.
7Village life ceased, it ceased in Israel,
Until I, Deborah, arose,
Arose a mother in Israel.
8They chose new gods;
Then *there was* war in the gates;
Not a shield or spear was seen among forty
thousand in Israel.
9My heart *is* with the rulers of Israel
Who offered themselves willingly with the
people.
Bless the LORD!

THE MESSAGE

Kenite were on good terms with one another.
Jael stepped out to meet Sisera and said,
"Come in, sir. Stay here with me. Don't be
afraid."
So he went with her into her tent. She
covered him with a blanket.
19 He said to her, "Please, a little water. I'm
thirsty."
She opened a bottle of milk, gave him a
drink, and then covered him up again.
20 He then said, "Stand at the tent flap. If
anyone comes by and asks you, 'Is there
anyone here?' tell him, 'No, not a soul.' "
21 Then while he was fast asleep from exhaustion, Jael wife of Heber took a tent peg
and hammer, tiptoed toward him, and drove
the tent peg through his temple and all the
way into the ground. He convulsed and died.
22 Barak arrived in pursuit of Sisera. Jael
went out to greet him. She said, "Come, I'll
show you the man you're looking for." He
went with her and there he was—Sisera,
stretched out, dead, with a tent peg through
his temple.
23-24 On that day God subdued Jabin king of
Canaan before the People of Israel. The People of Israel pressed harder and harder on
Jabin king of Canaan until there was nothing left of him.

1 5 That day Deborah and Barak son of Abinoam sang this song:

2 When they let down their hair in Israel,
they let it blow wild in the wind.
The people volunteered with abandon,
bless GOD!

3 Hear O kings! Listen O princes!
To GOD, yes to GOD, I'll sing,
Make music to GOD,
to the God of Israel.

4-5 GOD, when you left Seir,
marched across the fields of Edom,
Earth quaked, yes, the skies poured rain,
oh, the clouds made rivers.
Mountains leapt before GOD, the Sinai God,
before GOD, the God of Israel.

6-8 In the time of Shamgar son of Anath,
and in the time of Jael,
Public roads were abandoned,
travelers went by backroads.
Warriors became fat and sloppy,
no fight left in them.
Then you, Deborah, rose up;
you got up, a mother in Israel.
God chose new leaders,
who then fought at the gates.
And not a shield or spear to be seen
among the forty companies of Israel.

9 Lift your hearts high, O Israel,
with abandon, volunteering
yourselves with the people—bless
GOD!

NEW KING JAMES VERSION

10"Speak, you who ride on white donkeys,
Who sit in judges' attire,
And who walk along the road.
11Far from the noise of the archers, among the watering places,
There they shall recount the righteous acts of the LORD,
The righteous acts *for* His villagers in Israel;
Then the people of the LORD shall go down to the gates.

12"Awake, awake, Deborah!
Awake, awake, sing a song!
Arise, Barak, and lead your captives away,
O son of Abinoam!

13"Then the survivors came down, the people against the nobles;
The LORD came down for me against the mighty.
14From Ephraim *were* those whose roots were in Amalek.
After you, Benjamin, with your peoples,
From Machir rulers came down,
And from Zebulun those who bear the recruiter's staff.
15And the princes of Issachar[a] *were* with Deborah;
As Issachar, so *was* Barak
Sent into the valley under his command;[b]
Among the divisions of Reuben
There were great resolves of heart.
16Why did you sit among the sheepfolds,
To hear the pipings for the flocks?
The divisions of Reuben have great searchings of heart.
17Gilead stayed beyond the Jordan,
And why did Dan remain on ships?[a]
Asher continued at the seashore,
And stayed by his inlets.
18Zebulun *is* a people *who* jeopardized their lives to the point of death,
Naphtali also, on the heights of the battlefield.

19"The kings came *and* fought,
Then the kings of Canaan fought
In Taanach, by the waters of Megiddo;
They took no spoils of silver.
20They fought from the heavens;
The stars from their courses fought against Sisera.
21The torrent of Kishon swept them away,
That ancient torrent, the torrent of Kishon.
O my soul, march on in strength!
22Then the horses' hooves pounded,
The galloping, galloping of his steeds.
23'Curse Meroz,' said the angel[a] of the LORD,
'Curse its inhabitants bitterly,
Because they did not come to the help of the LORD,
To the help of the LORD against the mighty.'

5:15 [a]Following Septuagint, Syriac, Targum, and Vulgate; Masoretic Text reads *And my princes in Issachar.* [b]Literally *at his feet* **5:17** [a]Or *at ease* **5:23** [a]Or *Angel*

THE MESSAGE

10-11 You who ride on prize donkeys
comfortably mounted on blankets
And you who walk down the roads,
ponder, attend!
Gather at the town well
and listen to them sing,
Chanting the tale of GOD's victories,
his victories accomplished in Israel.

Then the people of GOD
went down to the city gates.

12 Wake up, wake up, Deborah!
Wake up, wake up, sing a song!
On your feet, Barak!
Take your prisoners, son of Abinoam!

13-18 Then the remnant went down to greet the brave ones.
The people of GOD joined the mighty ones.
The captains from Ephraim came to the valley,
behind you, Benjamin, with your troops.
Captains marched down from Makir,
from Zebulun high-ranking leaders came down.
Issachar's princes rallied to Deborah,
Issachar stood fast with Barak,
backing him up on the field of battle.
But in Reuben's divisions there was much second-guessing.
Why all those campfire discussions?
Diverted and distracted,
Reuben's divisions couldn't make up their minds.
Gilead played it safe across the Jordan,
and Dan, why did he go off sailing?
Asher kept his distance on the seacoast,
safe and secure in his harbors.
But Zebulun risked life and limb, defied death,
as did Naphtali on the battle heights.

19-23 The kings came, they fought,
the kings of Canaan fought.
At Taanach they fought, at Megiddo's brook,
but they took no silver, no plunder.
The stars in the sky joined the fight,
from their courses they fought against Sisera.
The torrent Kishon swept them away,
the torrent attacked them, the torrent Kishon.
Oh, you'll stomp on the necks of the strong!
Then the hoofs of the horses pounded,
charging, stampeding stallions.
"Curse Meroz," says GOD's angel.
"Curse, double curse, its people,
Because they didn't come when GOD needed them,
didn't rally to GOD's side with valiant fighters."

NEW KING JAMES VERSION

24 “Most blessed among women is Jael,
The wife of Heber the Kenite;
Blessed is she among women in tents.
25 He asked for water, she gave milk;
She brought out cream in a lordly bowl.
26 She stretched her hand to the tent peg,
Her right hand to the workmen’s hammer;
She pounded Sisera, she pierced his head,
She split and struck through his temple.
27 At her feet he sank, he fell, he lay still;
At her feet he sank, he fell;
Where he sank, there he fell dead.

28 “The mother of Sisera looked through the window,
And cried out through the lattice,
‘Why is his chariot *so* long in coming?
Why tarries the clatter of his chariots?’
29 Her wisest ladies answered her,
Yes, she answered herself,
30 ‘Are they not finding and dividing the spoil:
To every man a girl *or* two;
For Sisera, plunder of dyed garments,
Plunder of garments embroidered and dyed,
Two pieces of dyed embroidery for the neck of the looter?’

31 “Thus let all Your enemies perish, O LORD!
But *let* those who love Him *be* like the sun
When it comes out in full strength.”

So the land had rest for forty years.

MIDIANITES OPPRESS ISRAEL

6 Then the children of Israel did evil in the
sight of the LORD. So the LORD delivered them
into the hand of Midian for seven years, 2 and the
hand of Midian prevailed against Israel. Be-
cause of the Midianites, the children of Israel
made for themselves the dens, the caves, and
the strongholds which *are* in the mountains. 3 So
it was, whenever Israel had sown, Midianites
would come up; also Amalekites and the people
of the East would come up against them. 4 Then
they would encamp against them and destroy
the produce of the earth as far as Gaza, and
leave no sustenance for Israel, neither sheep nor
ox nor donkey. 5 For they would come up with
their livestock and their tents, coming in as nu-
merous as locusts; both they and their camels
were without number; and they would enter the
land to destroy it. 6 So Israel was greatly impov-
erished because of the Midianites, and the chil-
dren of Israel cried out to the LORD.
7 And it came to pass, when the children of Is-
rael cried out to the LORD because of the Midi-
anites, 8 that the LORD sent a prophet to the chil-
dren of Israel, who said to them, “Thus says the
LORD God of Israel: ‘I brought you up from

THE MESSAGE

24-27 Most blessed of all women is Jael,
wife of Heber the Kenite,
most blessed of homemaking women.
He asked for water,
she brought milk;
In a handsome bowl,
she offered cream.
She grabbed a tent peg in her left hand,
with her right hand she seized a hammer.
She hammered Sisera, she smashed his head,
she drove a hole through his temple.
He slumped at her feet. He fell. He sprawled.
He slumped at her feet. He fell.
Slumped. Fallen. Dead.

28-30 Sisera’s mother waited at the window,
a weary, anxious watch.
“What’s keeping his chariot?
What delays his chariot’s rumble?”
The wisest of her ladies-in-waiting answers
with calm, reassuring words,
“Don’t you think they’re busy at plunder,
dividing up the loot?
A girl, maybe two girls,
for each man,
And for Sisera a bright silk shirt,
a prize, fancy silk shirt!
And a colorful scarf—make it two scarves—
to grace the neck of the plunderer.”

31 Thus may all GOD’s enemies perish,
while his lovers be like the unclouded sun.

The land was quiet for forty years.

GIDEON

1-6 6 Yet again the People of Israel went back
to doing evil in GOD’s sight. GOD put them
under the domination of Midian for seven
years. Midian overpowered Israel. Because
of Midian, the People of Israel made for
themselves hideouts in the mountains—
caves and forts. When Israel planted its
crops, Midian and Amalek, the easterners,
would invade them, camp in their fields, and
destroy their crops all the way down to
Gaza. They left nothing for them to live on,
neither sheep nor ox nor donkey. Bringing
their cattle and tents, they came in and took
over, like an invasion of locusts. And their
camels—past counting! They marched in
and devastated the country. The People of
Israel, reduced to grinding poverty by Mid-
ian, cried out to GOD for help.
7-10 One time when the People of Israel had
cried out to GOD because of Midian, GOD
sent them a prophet with this message:
“GOD, the God of Israel, says,

I delivered you from Egypt,

NEW KING JAMES VERSION

Egypt and brought you out of the house of
bondage; 9and I delivered you out of the hand of
the Egyptians and out of the hand of all who op-
pressed you, and drove them out before you and
gave you their land. 10Also I said to you, "I *am*
the LORD your God; do not fear the gods of the
Amorites, in whose land you dwell." But you
have not obeyed My voice.' "

GIDEON

11Now the Angel of the LORD came and sat
under the terebinth tree which *was* in Ophrah,
which *belonged* to Joash the Abiezrite, while his
son Gideon threshed wheat in the winepress, in
order to hide *it* from the Midianites. 12And the
Angel of the LORD appeared to him, and said to
him, "The LORD *is* with you, you mighty man of
valor!"

13Gideon said to Him, "O my lord,[a] if the
LORD is with us, why then has all this happened
to us? And where *are* all His miracles which our
fathers told us about, saying, 'Did not the LORD
bring us up from Egypt?' But now the LORD has
forsaken us and delivered us into the hands of
the Midianites."

14Then the LORD turned to him and said, "Go
in this might of yours, and you shall save Israel
from the hand of the Midianites. Have I not sent
you?"

15So he said to Him, "O my Lord,[a] how can I
save Israel? Indeed my clan *is* the weakest in
Manasseh, and I *am* the least in my father's
house."

16And the LORD said to him, "Surely I will be
with you, and you shall defeat the Midianites as
one man."

17Then he said to Him, "If now I have found
favor in Your sight, then show me a sign that it
is You who talk with me. 18Do not depart from
here, I pray, until I come to You and bring out my
offering and set *it* before You."

And He said, "I will wait until you come
back."

19So Gideon went in and prepared a young
goat, and unleavened bread from an ephah of
flour. The meat he put in a basket, and he put
the broth in a pot; and he brought *them* out to
Him under the terebinth tree and presented
them. 20The Angel of God said to him, "Take the
meat and the unleavened bread and lay *them* on
this rock, and pour out the broth." And he did so.
21Then the Angel of the LORD put out the end
of the staff that *was* in His hand, and touched
the meat and the unleavened bread; and fire
rose out of the rock and consumed the meat and
the unleavened bread. And the Angel of the
LORD departed out of his sight.

22Now Gideon perceived that He *was* the An-
gel of the LORD. So Gideon said, "Alas, O Lord
GOD! For I have seen the Angel of the LORD face
to face."

23Then the LORD said to him, "Peace *be* with
you; do not fear, you shall not die." 24So Gideon
built an altar there to the LORD, and called it
The-LORD-*Is*-Peace.[a] To this day it *is* still in
Ophrah of the Abiezrites.

6:13 [a]Hebrew *adoni*, used of man **6:15** [a]Hebrew *Adonai*, used
of God **6:24** [a]Hebrew *YHWH Shalom*

THE MESSAGE

I freed you from a life of slavery;
I rescued you from Egypt's brutality
and then from every oppressor;
I pushed them out of your way
and gave you their land.

"And I said to you, 'I am GOD, your God.
Don't for a minute be afraid of the gods of
the Amorites in whose land you are living.'
But you didn't listen to me."

11-12 One day the angel of GOD came and sat
down under the oak in Ophrah that be-
longed to Joash the Abiezrite, whose son
Gideon was threshing wheat in the wine-
press, out of sight of the Midianites. The an-
gel of GOD appeared to him and said, "GOD
is with you, O mighty warrior!"

13 Gideon replied, "With *me*, my master? If
GOD is with us, why has all this happened to
us? Where are all the miracle-wonders our
parents and grandparents told us about,
telling us, 'Didn't GOD deliver us from
Egypt?' The fact is, GOD has nothing to do
with us—he has turned us over to Midian."

14 But GOD faced him directly: "Go in this
strength that is yours. Save Israel from Mid-
ian. Haven't I just sent you?"

15 Gideon said to him, "*Me*, my master?
How and with what could I ever save Israel?
Look at me. My clan's the weakest in Ma-
nasseh and I'm the runt of the litter."

16 GOD said to him, "I'll be with you. Believe
me, you'll defeat Midian as one man."

17-18 Gideon said, "If you're serious about this,
do me a favor: Give me a sign to back up
what you're telling me. Don't leave until I
come back and bring you my gift."

He said, "I'll wait till you get back."

19 Gideon went and prepared a young goat
and a huge amount of unraised bread (he
used over half a bushel of flour!). He put the
meat in a basket and the broth in a pot and
took them back under the shade of the oak
tree for a sacred meal.

20 The angel of God said to him, "Take the
meat and unraised bread, place them on
that rock, and pour the broth on them."
Gideon did it.

21-22 The angel of GOD stretched out the tip of
the stick he was holding and touched the
meat and the bread. Fire broke out of the
rock and burned up the meat and bread
while the angel of God slipped away out of
sight. And Gideon knew it was the angel of
God!

Gideon said, "Oh no! Master, GOD! I have
seen the angel of God face-to-face!"

23 But GOD reassured him, "Easy now. Don't
panic. You won't die."

24 Then Gideon built an altar there to GOD
and named it "GOD's Peace." It's still called
that at Ophrah of Abiezer.

New King James Version

25 Now it came to pass the same night that the
LORD said to him, "Take your father's young
bull, the second bull of seven years old, and tear
down the altar of Baal that your father has, and
cut down the wooden image[a] that *is* beside it;
26 and build an altar to the LORD your God on top
of this rock in the proper arrangement, and take
the second bull and offer a burnt sacrifice with
the wood of the image which you shall cut
down." 27 So Gideon took ten men from among
his servants and did as the LORD had said to
him. But because he feared his father's house-
hold and the men of the city too much to do *it* by
day, he did *it* by night.

Gideon Destroys the Altar of Baal

28 And when the men of the city arose early in
the morning, there was the altar of Baal, torn
down; and the wooden image that *was* beside it
was cut down, and the second bull was being of-
fered on the altar *which had been* built. 29 So
they said to one another, "Who has done this
thing?" And when they had inquired and asked,
they said, "Gideon the son of Joash has done
this thing." 30 Then the men of the city said to
Joash, "Bring out your son, that he may die, be-
cause he has torn down the altar of Baal, and
because he has cut down the wooden image that
was beside it."
31 But Joash said to all who stood against
him, "Would you plead for Baal? Would you save
him? Let the one who would plead for him be
put to death by morning! If he *is* a god, let him
plead for himself, because his altar has been
torn down!" 32 Therefore on that day he called
him Jerubbaal,[a] saying, "Let Baal plead against
him, because he has torn down his altar."
33 Then all the Midianites and Amalekites,
the people of the East, gathered together; and
they crossed over and encamped in the Valley of
Jezreel. 34 But the Spirit of the LORD came upon
Gideon; then he blew the trumpet, and the
Abiezrites gathered behind him. 35 And he sent
messengers throughout all Manasseh, who also
gathered behind him. He also sent messengers
to Asher, Zebulun, and Naphtali; and they came
up to meet them.

The Sign of the Fleece

36 So Gideon said to God, "If You will save Is-
rael by my hand as You have said— 37 look, I
shall put a fleece of wool on the threshing floor;
if there is dew on the fleece only, and *it is* dry on
all the ground, then I shall know that You will
save Israel by my hand, as You have said." 38 And
it was so. When he rose early the next morning
and squeezed the fleece together, he wrung the
dew out of the fleece, a bowlful of water. 39 Then
Gideon said to God, "Do not be angry with me,
but let me speak just once more: Let me test, I
pray, just once more with the fleece; let it now
be dry only on the fleece, but on all the ground
let there be dew." 40 And God did so that night. It
was dry on the fleece only, but there was dew on
all the ground.

6:25 [a]Hebrew *Asherah,* a Canaanite goddess **6:32** [a]Literally *Let Baal Plead*

The Message

25-26 That night this happened. GOD said to
him, "Take your father's best seven-year-old
bull, the prime one. Tear down your father's
Baal altar and chop down the Asherah fer-
tility pole beside it. Then build an altar to
GOD, your God, on the top of this hill. Take
the prime bull and present it as a Whole-
Burnt-Offering, using firewood from the
Asherah pole that you cut down."
27 Gideon selected ten men from his ser-
vants and did exactly what GOD had told
him. But because of his family and the peo-
ple in the neighborhood, he was afraid to do
it openly, so he did it that night.
28 Early in the morning, the people in town
were shocked to find Baal's altar torn down,
the Asherah pole beside it chopped down,
and the prime bull burning away on the al-
tar that had been built.
29 They kept asking, "Who did this?"
Questions and more questions, and then
the answer: "Gideon son of Joash did it."
30 The men of the town demanded of Joash:
"Bring out your son! He must die! Why, he
tore down the Baal altar and chopped down
the Asherah tree!"
31 But Joash stood up to the crowd pressing
in on him, "Are you going to fight Baal's bat-
tles for him? Are you going to save him?
Anyone who takes Baal's side will be dead
by morning. If Baal is a god in fact, let him
fight his own battles and defend his own al-
tar."
32 They nicknamed Gideon that day Jerub-
Baal because after he had torn down the
Baal altar, he had said, "Let Baal fight his
own battles."

33-35 All the Midianites and Amalekites (the east-
erners) got together, crossed the river, and
made camp in the Valley of Jezreel. GOD's
Spirit came over Gideon. He blew his ram's
horn trumpet and the Abiezrites came out,
ready to follow him. He dispatched messen-
gers all through Manasseh, calling them to
the battle; also to Asher, Zebulun, and
Naphtali. They all came.
36-37 Gideon said to God, "If this is right, if you
are using me to save Israel as you've said,
then look: I'm placing a fleece of wool on
the threshing floor. If dew is on the fleece
only, but the floor is dry, then I know that
you will use me to save Israel, as you said."
38 That's what happened. When he got up
early the next morning, he wrung out the
fleece—enough dew to fill a bowl with wa-
ter!
39 Then Gideon said to God, "Don't be impa-
tient with me, but let me say one more thing.
I want to try another time with the fleece.
But this time let the fleece stay dry, while the
dew drenches the ground."
40 God made it happen that very night. Only
the fleece was dry while the ground was wet
with dew.

NEW KING JAMES VERSION

GIDEON'S VALIANT THREE HUNDRED

7 Then Jerubbaal (that *is*, Gideon) and all the people who *were* with him rose early and encamped beside the well of Harod, so that the camp of the Midianites was on the north side of them by the hill of Moreh in the valley.

2And the LORD said to Gideon, "The people who *are* with you *are* too many for Me to give the Midianites into their hands, lest Israel claim glory for itself against Me, saying, 'My own hand has saved me.' 3Now therefore, proclaim in the hearing of the people, saying, 'Whoever *is* fearful and afraid, let him turn and depart at once from Mount Gilead.' " And twenty-two thousand of the people returned, and ten thousand remained.

4But the LORD said to Gideon, "The people *are* still *too* many; bring them down to the water, and I will test them for you there. Then it will be, *that* of whom I say to you, 'This one shall go with you,' the same shall go with you; and of whomever I say to you, 'This one shall not go with you,' the same shall not go." 5So he brought the people down to the water. And the LORD said to Gideon, "Everyone who laps from the water with his tongue, as a dog laps, you shall set apart by himself; likewise everyone who gets down on his knees to drink." 6And the number of those who lapped, *putting* their hand to their mouth, was three hundred men; but all the rest of the people got down on their knees to drink water. 7Then the LORD said to Gideon, "By the three hundred men who lapped I will save you, and deliver the Midianites into your hand. Let all the *other* people go, every man to his place." 8So the people took provisions and their trumpets in their hands. And he sent away all *the rest of* Israel, every man to his tent, and retained those three hundred men. Now the camp of Midian was below him in the valley.

9It happened on the same night that the LORD said to him, "Arise, go down against the camp, for I have delivered it into your hand. 10But if you are afraid to go down, go down to the camp with Purah your servant, 11and you shall hear what they say; and afterward your hands shall be strengthened to go down against the camp." Then he went down with Purah his servant to the outpost of the armed men who *were* in the camp. 12Now the Midianites and Amalekites, all the people of the East, were lying in the valley as numerous as locusts; and their camels *were* without number, as the sand by the seashore in multitude.

13And when Gideon had come, there was a man telling a dream to his companion. He said, "I have had a dream: *To my* surprise, a loaf of barley bread tumbled into the camp of Midian; it came to a tent and struck it so that it fell and overturned, and the tent collapsed."

14Then his companion answered and said, "This *is* nothing else but the sword of Gideon the son of Joash, a man of Israel! Into his hand God has delivered Midian and the whole camp."

15And so it was, when Gideon heard the telling of the dream and its interpretation, that he worshiped. He returned to the camp of Israel, and said, "Arise, for the LORD has delivered the camp of Midian into your hand."

THE MESSAGE

1 7 Jerub-Baal (Gideon) got up early the next
morning, all his troops right there with
him. They set up camp at Harod's Spring.
The camp of Midian was in the plain, north
of them near the Hill of Moreh.
2-3 GOD said to Gideon, "You have too large
an army with you. I can't turn Midian over to
them like this—they'll take all the credit, say-
ing, 'I did it all myself,' and forget about me.
Make a public announcement: 'Anyone
afraid, anyone who has any qualms at all,
may leave Mount Gilead now and go home.' "
Twenty-two companies headed for home. Ten
companies were left.
4-5 GOD said to Gideon: "There are still too
many. Take them down to the stream and I'll
make a final cut. When I say, 'This one goes
with you,' he'll go. When I say, 'This one
doesn't go,' he won't go." So Gideon took the
troops down to the stream.
5-6 GOD said to Gideon: "Everyone who laps
with his tongue, the way a dog laps, set on
one side. And everyone who kneels to drink,
drinking with his face to the water, set to the
other side." Three hundred lapped with their
tongues from their cupped hands. All the
rest knelt to drink.
7 GOD said to Gideon: "I'll use the three
hundred men who lapped at the stream to
save you and give Midian into your hands.
All the rest may go home."
8 After Gideon took all their provisions
and trumpets, he sent all the Israelites
home. He took up his position with the three
hundred. The camp of Midian stretched out
below him in the valley.
9-12 That night, GOD told Gideon: "Get up and
go down to the camp. I've given it to you. If
you have any doubts about going down, go
down with Purah your armor bearer; when
you hear what they're saying, you'll be bold
and confident." He and his armor bearer Pu-
rah went down near the place where sen-
tries were posted. Midian and Amalek, all
the easterners, were spread out on the plain
like a swarm of locusts. And their camels!
Past counting, like grains of sand on the
seashore!
13 Gideon arrived just in time to hear a man
tell his friend a dream. He said, "I had this
dream: A loaf of barley bread tumbled into
the Midianite camp. It came to the tent and
hit it so hard it collapsed. The tent fell!"
14 His friend said, "This has to be the sword
of Gideon son of Joash, the Israelite! God
has turned Midian—the whole camp!—over
to him."
15 When Gideon heard the telling of the
dream and its interpretation, he went to his
knees before God in prayer. Then he went
back to the Israelite camp and said, "Get up
and get going! GOD has just given us the
Midianite army!"

NEW KING JAMES VERSION

16 Then he divided the three hundred men *into*
three companies, and he put a trumpet into
every man's hand, with empty pitchers, and
torches inside the pitchers. 17 And he said to
them, "Look at me and do likewise; watch, and
when I come to the edge of the camp you shall
do as I do: 18 When I blow the trumpet, I and all
who *are* with me, then you also blow the trum-
pets on every side of the whole camp, and say,
'*The sword of* the LORD and of Gideon!' "

19 So Gideon and the hundred men who *were*
with him came to the outpost of the camp at the
beginning of the middle watch, just as they had
posted the watch; and they blew the trumpets
and broke the pitchers that *were* in their hands.
20 Then the three companies blew the trumpets
and broke the pitchers—they held the torches in
their left hands and the trumpets in their right
hands for blowing—and they cried, "The sword
of the LORD and of Gideon!" 21 And every man
stood in his place all around the camp; and the
whole army ran and cried out and fled. 22 When
the three hundred blew the trumpets, the LORD
set every man's sword against his companion
throughout the whole camp; and the army fled
to Beth Acacia,[a] toward Zererah, as far as the
border of Abel Meholah, by Tabbath.

23 And the men of Israel gathered together
from Naphtali, Asher, and all Manasseh, and
pursued the Midianites.

24 Then Gideon sent messengers throughout
all the mountains of Ephraim, saying, "Come
down against the Midianites, and seize from
them the watering places as far as Beth Barah
and the Jordan." Then all the men of Ephraim
gathered together and seized the watering
places as far as Beth Barah and the Jordan.
25 And they captured two princes of the Midian-
ites, Oreb and Zeeb. They killed Oreb at the
rock of Oreb, and Zeeb they killed at the wine-
press of Zeeb. They pursued Midian and
brought the heads of Oreb and Zeeb to Gideon
on the other side of the Jordan.

GIDEON SUBDUES THE MIDIANITES

8 Now the men of Ephraim said to him, "Why
have you done this to us by not calling us
when you went to fight with the Midianites?"
And they reprimanded him sharply.

2 So he said to them, "What have I done now
in comparison with you? *Is* not the gleaning *of*
the grapes of Ephraim better than the vintage of
Abiezer? 3 God has delivered into your hands the
princes of Midian, Oreb and Zeeb. And what
was I able to do in comparison with you?" Then
their anger toward him subsided when he said
that.

4 When Gideon came to the Jordan, he and
the three hundred men who *were* with him
crossed over, exhausted but still in pursuit.
5 Then he said to the men of Succoth, "Please
give loaves of bread to the people who follow
me, for they are exhausted, and I am pursuing
Zebah and Zalmunna, kings of Midian."

6 And the leaders of Succoth said, "*Are* the
hands of Zebah and Zalmunna now in your
hand, that we should give bread to your army?"

7:22 [a]Hebrew *Beth Shittah*

THE MESSAGE

16-18 He divided the three hundred men into
three companies. He gave each man a trum-
pet and an empty jar, with a torch in the jar.
He said, "Watch me and do what I do. When
I get to the edge of the camp, do exactly
what I do. When I and those with me blow
the trumpets, you also, all around the camp,
blow your trumpets and shout, 'For GOD and
for Gideon!' "

19-22 Gideon and his hundred men got to the
edge of the camp at the beginning of the
middle watch, just after the sentries had
been posted. They blew the trumpets, at the
same time smashing the jars they carried.
All three companies blew the trumpets and
broke the jars. They held the torches in their
left hands and the trumpets in their right
hands, ready to blow, and shouted, "A sword
for GOD and for Gideon!" They were sta-
tioned all around the camp, each man at his
post. The whole Midianite camp jumped to
its feet. They yelled and fled. When the three
hundred blew the trumpets, GOD aimed each
Midianite's sword against his companion,
all over the camp. They ran for their lives—
to Beth Shittah, toward Zererah, to the bor-
der of Abel Meholah near Tabbath.

23 Israelites rallied from Naphtali, from
Asher, and from all over Manasseh. They
had Midian on the run.

24 Gideon then sent messengers through all
the hill country of Ephraim, urging them,
"Come down against Midian! Capture the
fords of the Jordan at Beth Barah."

25 So all the men of Ephraim rallied and
captured the fords of the Jordan at Beth
Barah. They also captured the two Midianite
commanders Oreb (Raven) and Zeeb (Wolf).
They killed Oreb at Raven Rock; Zeeb they
killed at Wolf Winepress. And they pressed
the pursuit of Midian. They brought the
heads of Oreb and Zeeb to Gideon across
the Jordan.

1 8 Then the Ephraimites said to Gideon,
"Why did you leave us out of this, not call-
ing us when you went to fight Midian?"
They were indignant and let him know it.

2-3 But Gideon replied, "What have I done
compared to you? Why, even the gleanings
of Ephraim are superior to the vintage of
Abiezer. God gave you Midian's command-
ers, Oreb and Zeeb. What have I done com-
pared with you?"

When they heard this, they calmed down
and cooled off.

4-5 Gideon and his three hundred arrived at the
Jordan and crossed over. They were bone-
tired but still pressing the pursuit. He asked
the men of Succoth, "Please, give me some
loaves of bread for my troops I have with me.
They're worn out, and I'm hot on the trail of
Zebah and Zalmunna, the Midianite kings."

6 But the leaders in Succoth said, "You're
on a wild goose chase; why should we help
you on a fool's errand?"

NEW KING JAMES VERSION

7So Gideon said, "For this cause, when the
LORD has delivered Zebah and Zalmunna into
my hand, then I will tear your flesh with the
thorns of the wilderness and with briers!" 8Then
he went up from there to Penuel and spoke to
them in the same way. And the men of Penuel
answered him as the men of Succoth had an-
swered. 9So he also spoke to the men of Penuel,
saying, "When I come back in peace, I will tear
down this tower!"
10Now Zebah and Zalmunna *were* at Karkor,
and their armies with them, about fifteen thou-
sand, all who were left of all the army of the
people of the East; for one hundred and twenty
thousand men who drew the sword had fallen.
11Then Gideon went up by the road of those who
dwell in tents on the east of Nobah and Jogbe-
hah; and he attacked the army while the camp
felt secure. 12When Zebah and Zalmunna fled,
he pursued them; and he took the two kings of
Midian, Zebah and Zalmunna, and routed the
whole army.
13Then Gideon the son of Joash returned
from battle, from the Ascent of Heres. 14And he
caught a young man of the men of Succoth and
interrogated him; and he wrote down for him
the leaders of Succoth and its elders, seventy-
seven men. 15Then he came to the men of Suc-
coth and said, "Here are Zebah and Zalmunna,
about whom you ridiculed me, saying, '*Are* the
hands of Zebah and Zalmunna now in your
hand, that we should give bread to your weary
men?' " 16And he took the elders of the city, and
thorns of the wilderness and briers, and with
them he taught the men of Succoth. 17Then he
tore down the tower of Penuel and killed the
men of the city.
18And he said to Zebah and Zalmunna,
"What kind of men *were they* whom you killed
at Tabor?"
So they answered, "As you *are*, so *were* they;
each one resembled the son of a king."
19Then he said, "They *were* my brothers, the
sons of my mother. *As* the LORD lives, if you had
let them live, I would not kill you." 20And he said
to Jether his firstborn, "Rise, kill them!" But the
youth would not draw his sword; for he was
afraid, because he *was* still a youth.
21So Zebah and Zalmunna said, "Rise your-
self, and kill us; for as a man *is*, *so is* his
strength." So Gideon arose and killed Zebah
and Zalmunna, and took the crescent orna-
ments that *were* on their camels' necks.

GIDEON'S EPHOD

22Then the men of Israel said to Gideon,
"Rule over us, both you and your son, and your
grandson also; for you have delivered us from
the hand of Midian."
23But Gideon said to them, "I will not rule
over you, nor shall my son rule over you; the
LORD shall rule over you." 24Then Gideon said to
them, "I would like to make a request of you,
that each of you would give me the earrings
from his plunder." For they had golden earrings,
because they *were* Ishmaelites.
25So they answered, "We will gladly give
them." And they spread out a garment, and each

THE MESSAGE

7 Gideon said, "If you say so. But when GOD
gives me Zebah and Zalmunna, I'll give you
a thrashing, whip your bare flesh with
desert thorns and thistles!"
8-9 He went from there to Peniel and made
the same request. The men of Peniel, like the
men of Succoth, also refused. Gideon told
them, "When I return safe and sound, I'll de-
molish this tower."
10 Zebah and Zalmunna were in Karkor
with an army of about fifteen companies, all
that was left of the fighting force of the east-
erners—they had lost 120 companies of sol-
diers.
11-12 Gideon went up the caravan trail east of
Nobah and Jogbehah, found and attacked
the undefended camp. Zebah and Zalmunna
fled, but he chased and captured the two
kings of Midian. The whole camp had pan-
icked.

13-15 Gideon son of Joash returned from the
battle by way of the Heres Pass. He captured
a young man from Succoth and asked some
questions. The young man wrote down the
names of the officials and leaders of Suc-
coth, seventy-seven men. Then Gideon went
to the men of Succoth and said, "Here are
the wild geese, Zebah and Zalmunna, you
said I'd never catch. You wouldn't give so
much as a scrap of bread to my worn-
out men; you taunted us, saying that we
were on a fool's errand."
16-17 Then he took the seventy-seven leaders
of Succoth and thrashed them with desert
thorns and thistles. And he demolished the
tower of Peniel and killed the men of the
city.
18 He then addressed Zebah and Zalmunna:
"Tell me about the men you killed at Tabor."
"They were men much like you," they
said, "each one like a king's son."
19 Gideon said, "They were my brothers, my
mother's sons. As GOD lives, if you had let
them live, I would let you live."
20 Then he spoke to Jether, his firstborn:
"Get up and kill them." But he couldn't do it,
couldn't draw his sword. He was afraid—he
was still just a boy.
21 Zebah and Zalmunna said, "Do it your-
self—if you're man enough!" And Gideon
did it. He stepped up and killed Zebah and
Zalmunna. Then he took the crescents that
hung on the necks of their camels.

22 The Israelites said, "Rule over us, you and
your son and your grandson. You have saved
us from Midian's tyranny."
23 Gideon said, "I most certainly will not
rule over you, nor will my son. GOD will
reign over you."
24 Then Gideon said, "But I do have one re-
quest. Give me, each of you, an earring that
you took as plunder." Ishmaelites wore gold
earrings, and the men all had their pockets
full of them.
25-26 They said, "Of course. They're yours!"
They spread out a blanket and each man

NEW KING JAMES VERSION

man threw into it the earrings from his plunder. 26 Now the weight of the gold earrings that he requested was one thousand seven hundred *shekels* of gold, besides the crescent ornaments, pendants, and purple robes which *were* on the kings of Midian, and besides the chains that *were* around their camels' necks. 27 Then Gideon made it into an ephod and set it up in his city, Ophrah. And all Israel played the harlot with it there. It became a snare to Gideon and to his house.

28 Thus Midian was subdued before the children of Israel, so that they lifted their heads no more. And the country was quiet for forty years in the days of Gideon.

DEATH OF GIDEON

29 Then Jerubbaal the son of Joash went and dwelt in his own house. 30 Gideon had seventy sons who were his own offspring, for he had many wives. 31 And his concubine who *was* in Shechem also bore him a son, whose name he called Abimelech. 32 Now Gideon the son of Joash died at a good old age, and was buried in the tomb of Joash his father, in Ophrah of the Abiezrites.

33 So it was, as soon as Gideon was dead, that the children of Israel again played the harlot with the Baals, and made Baal-Berith their god. 34 Thus the children of Israel did not remember the LORD their God, who had delivered them from the hands of all their enemies on every side; 35 nor did they show kindness to the house of Jerubbaal (Gideon) in accordance with the good he had done for Israel.

ABIMELECH'S CONSPIRACY

9 Then Abimelech the son of Jerubbaal went to Shechem, to his mother's brothers, and spoke with them and with all the family of the house of his mother's father, saying, 2 "Please speak in the hearing of all the men of Shechem: 'Which is better for you, that all seventy of the sons of Jerubbaal reign over you, or that one reign over you?' Remember that I *am* your own flesh and bone."

3 And his mother's brothers spoke all these words concerning him in the hearing of all the men of Shechem; and their heart was inclined to follow Abimelech, for they said, "He is our brother." 4 So they gave him seventy *shekels* of silver from the temple of Baal-Berith, with which Abimelech hired worthless and reckless men; and they followed him. 5 Then he went to his father's house at Ophrah and killed his brothers, the seventy sons of Jerubbaal, on one stone. But Jotham the youngest son of Jerubbaal was left, because he hid himself. 6 And all the men of Shechem gathered together, all of Beth Millo, and they went and made Abimelech king beside the terebinth tree at the pillar that *was* in Shechem.

THE PARABLE OF THE TREES

7 Now when they told Jotham, he went and stood on top of Mount Gerizim, and lifted his voice and cried out. And he said to them:

THE MESSAGE

threw his plundered earrings on it. The gold earrings that Gideon had asked for weighed about forty-three pounds—and that didn't include the crescents and pendants, the purple robes worn by the Midianite kings, and the ornaments hung around the necks of their camels.

27 Gideon made the gold into a sacred ephod and put it on display in his hometown, Ophrah. All Israel prostituted itself there. Gideon and his family, too, were seduced by it.

28 Midian's tyranny was broken by the Israelites; nothing more was heard from them. The land was quiet for forty years in Gideon's time.

29-31 Jerub-Baal son of Joash went home and lived in his house. Gideon had seventy sons. He fathered them all—he had a lot of wives! His concubine, the one at Shechem, also bore him a son. He named him Abimelech.

32 Gideon son of Joash died at a good old age. He was buried in the tomb of his father Joash at Ophrah of the Abiezrites.

ABIMELECH

33-35 Gideon was hardly cool in the tomb when the People of Israel had gotten off track and were prostituting themselves to Baal—they made Baal-of-the-Covenant their god. The People of Israel forgot all about GOD, their God, who had saved them from all their enemies who had hemmed them in. And they didn't keep faith with the family of Jerub-Baal (Gideon), honoring all the good he had done for Israel.

1-2 9 Abimelech son of Jerub-Baal went to Shechem to his uncles and all his mother's relatives and said to them, "Ask all the leading men of Shechem, 'What do you think is best, that seventy men rule you—all those sons of Jerub-Baal—or that one man rule? You'll remember that I am your own flesh and blood.' "

3 His mother's relatives reported the proposal to the leaders of Shechem. They were inclined to take Abimelech. "Because," they said, "he is, after all, one of us."

4-5 They gave him seventy silver pieces from the shrine of Baal-of-the-Covenant. With the money he hired some reckless riffraff soldiers and they followed along after him. He went to his father's house in Ophrah and killed his half brothers, the sons of Jerub-Baal—seventy men! And on one stone! The youngest, Jotham son of Jerub-Baal, managed to hide, the only survivor.

6 Then all the leaders of Shechem and Beth Millo gathered at the Oak by the Standing Stone at Shechem and crowned Abimelech king.

7-9 When this was all told to Jotham, he climbed to the top of Mount Gerizim, raised his voice, and shouted:

NEW KING JAMES VERSION

“Listen to me, you men of Shechem,
That God may listen to you!

8“The trees once went forth to anoint a king
over them.
And they said to the olive tree,
‘Reign over us!’
9But the olive tree said to them,
‘Should I cease giving my oil,
With which they honor God and men,
And go to sway over trees?’

10“Then the trees said to the fig tree,
‘You come *and* reign over us!’
11But the fig tree said to them,
‘Should I cease my sweetness and my good
fruit,
And go to sway over trees?’

12“Then the trees said to the vine,
‘You come *and* reign over us!’
13But the vine said to them,
‘Should I cease my new wine,
Which cheers *both* God and men,
And go to sway over trees?’

14“Then all the trees said to the bramble,
‘You come *and* reign over us!’
15And the bramble said to the trees,
‘If in truth you anoint me as king over you,
Then come *and* take shelter in my shade;
But if not, let fire come out of the bramble
And devour the cedars of Lebanon!’

16“Now therefore, if you have acted in truth
and sincerity in making Abimelech king, and if
you have dealt well with Jerubbaal and his
house, and have done to him as he deserves—
17for my father fought for you, risked his life,
and delivered you out of the hand of Midian;
18but you have risen up against my father’s
house this day, and killed his seventy sons on
one stone, and made Abimelech, the son of his
female servant, king over the men of Shechem,
because he is your brother— 19if then you have
acted in truth and sincerity with Jerubbaal and
with his house this day, *then* rejoice in Abim-
elech, and let him also rejoice in you. 20But if
not, let fire come from Abimelech and devour
the men of Shechem and Beth Millo; and let fire
come from the men of Shechem and from Beth
Millo and devour Abimelech!” 21And Jotham ran
away and fled; and he went to Beer and dwelt
there, for fear of Abimelech his brother.

DOWNFALL OF ABIMELECH

22After Abimelech had reigned over Israel
three years, 23God sent a spirit of ill will be-
tween Abimelech and the men of Shechem; and

THE MESSAGE

Listen to me, leaders of Shechem.
And let God listen to you!
The trees set out one day
to anoint a king for themselves.
They said to Olive Tree,
“Rule over us.”
But Olive Tree told them,
“Am I no longer good for making oil
That gives glory to gods and men,
and to be demoted to waving over
trees?”

10-11 The trees then said to Fig Tree,
“You come and rule over us.”
But Fig Tree said to them,
“Am I no longer good for making
sweets,
My mouthwatering sweet fruits,
and to be demoted to waving over
trees?”

12-13 The trees then said to Vine,
“You come and rule over us.”
But Vine said to them,
“Am I no longer good for making
wine,
Wine that cheers gods and men,
and to be demoted to waving over
trees?”

14-15 All the trees then said to Tumbleweed,
“You come and reign over us.”
But Tumbleweed said to the trees:
“If you’re serious about making me
your king,
Come and find shelter in my shade.
But if not, let fire shoot from
Tumbleweed
and burn down the cedars of
Lebanon!”

16-20 “Now listen: Do you think you did a right and honorable thing when you made Abimelech king? Do you think you treated Jerub-Baal and his family well, did for him what he deserved? My father fought for you, risked his own life, and rescued you from Midian’s tyranny, and you have, just now, betrayed him. You massacred his sons—seventy men on a single stone! You made Abimelech, the son by his maidservant, king over Shechem’s leaders because he’s your relative. If you think that this is an honest day’s work, this way you have treated Jerub-Baal today, then enjoy Abimelech and let him enjoy you. But if not, let fire break from Abimelech and burn up the leaders of Shechem and Beth Millo. And let fire break from the leaders of Shechem and Beth Millo and burn up Abimelech.”

21 And Jotham fled. He ran for his life. He went to Beer and settled down there, because he was afraid of his brother Abimelech.

22-24 Abimelech ruled over Israel for three years. Then God brought bad blood between Abimelech and Shechem’s leaders, who

NEW KING JAMES VERSION

the men of Shechem dealt treacherously with
Abimelech, 24that the crime *done* to the seventy
sons of Jerubbaal might be settled and their
blood be laid on Abimelech their brother, who
killed them, and on the men of Shechem, who
aided him in the killing of his brothers. 25And
the men of Shechem set men in ambush against
him on the tops of the mountains, and they
robbed all who passed by them along that way;
and it was told Abimelech.

26Now Gaal the son of Ebed came with his
brothers and went over to Shechem; and the
men of Shechem put their confidence in him.
27So they went out into the fields, and gathered
grapes from their vineyards and trod *them*, and
made merry. And they went into the house of
their god, and ate and drank, and cursed Abim-
elech. 28Then Gaal the son of Ebed said, "Who *is*
Abimelech, and who *is* Shechem, that we should
serve him? *Is he* not the son of Jerubbaal, and *is*
not Zebul his officer? Serve the men of Hamor
the father of Shechem; but why should we serve
him? 29If only this people were under my au-
thority![a] Then I would remove Abimelech." So
he[b] said to Abimelech, "Increase your army and
come out!"

30When Zebul, the ruler of the city, heard the
words of Gaal the son of Ebed, his anger was
aroused. 31And he sent messengers to Abimelech
secretly, saying, "Take note! Gaal the son of Ebed
and his brothers have come to Shechem; and
here they are, fortifying the city against you.
32Now therefore, get up by night, you and the
people who *are* with you, and lie in wait in the
field. 33And it shall be, as soon as the sun is up in
the morning, *that* you shall rise early and rush
upon the city; and *when* he and the people who
are with him come out against you, you may
then do to them as you find opportunity."

34So Abimelech and all the people who *were*
with him rose by night, and lay in wait against
Shechem in four companies. 35When Gaal the
son of Ebed went out and stood in the entrance
to the city gate, Abimelech and the people who
were with him rose from lying in wait. 36And
when Gaal saw the people, he said to Zebul,
"Look, people are coming down from the tops of
the mountains!"

But Zebul said to him, "You see the shadows
of the mountains as *if they were* men."

37So Gaal spoke again and said, "See, people
are coming down from the center of the land,
and another company is coming from the Divin-
ers'[a] Terebinth Tree."

38Then Zebul said to him, "Where indeed *is*
your mouth now, with which you said, 'Who is
Abimelech, that we should serve him?' *Are* not
these the people whom you despised? Go out, if
you will, and fight with them now."

39So Gaal went out, leading the men of
Shechem, and fought with Abimelech. 40And
Abimelech chased him, and he fled from him;
and many fell wounded, to the *very* entrance of
the gate. 41Then Abimelech dwelt at Arumah,
and Zebul drove out Gaal and his brothers, so
that they would not dwell in Shechem.

9:29 [a]Literally *hand* [b]Following Masoretic Text and Targum; Dead Sea Scrolls read *they;* Septuagint reads *I.* **9:37** [a]Hebrew *Meonenim*

THE MESSAGE

now worked treacherously behind his back. Violence boomeranged: The murderous violence that killed the seventy brothers, the sons of Jerub-Baal, was now loose among Abimelech and Shechem's leaders, who had supported the violence.

25 To undermine Abimelech, Shechem's leaders put men in ambush on the mountain passes who robbed travelers on those roads. And Abimelech was told.

26-27 At that time Gaal son of Ebed arrived with his relatives and moved into Shechem. The leaders of Shechem trusted him. One day they went out into the fields, gathered grapes in the vineyards, and trod them in the winepress. Then they held a celebration in their god's temple, a feast, eating and drinking. And then they started putting down Abimelech.

28-29 Gaal son of Ebed said, "Who is this Abimelech? And who are we Shechemites to take orders from him? Isn't he the son of Jerub-Baal, and isn't this his henchman Zebul? We belong to the race of Hamor and bear the noble name of Shechem. Why should we be toadies of Abimelech? If I were in charge of this people, the first thing I'd do is get rid of Abimelech! I'd say, 'Show me your stuff, Abimelech—let's see who's boss here!' "

30-33 Zebul, governor of the city, heard what Gaal son of Ebed was saying and got angry. Secretly he sent messengers to Abimelech with the message, "Gaal son of Ebed and his relatives have come to Shechem and are stirring up trouble against you. Here's what you do: Tonight bring your troops and wait in ambush in the field. In the morning, as soon as the sun breaks, get moving and charge the city. Gaal and his troops will come out to you, and you'll know what to do next."

34-36 Abimelech and his troops, four companies of them, went up that night and waited in ambush approaching Shechem. Gaal son of Ebed had gotten up and was standing in the city gate. Abimelech and his troops left their cover. When Gaal saw them he said to Zebul, "Look at that, people coming down from the tops of the mountains!"

Zebul said, "That's nothing but mountain shadows; they just look like men." Gaal kept chattering away.

37 Then he said again, "Look at the troops coming down off Tabbur-erez (the Navel of the World)—and one company coming straight from the Oracle Oak."

38 Zebul said, "Where is that big mouth of yours now? You who said, 'And who is Abimelech that we should take orders from him?' Well, there he is with the troops you ridiculed. Here's your chance. Fight away!"

39-40 Gaal went out, backed by the leaders of Shechem, and did battle with Abimelech. Abimelech chased him, and Gaal turned tail and ran. Many fell wounded, right up to the city gate.

41 Abimelech set up his field headquarters at Arumah while Zebul kept Gaal and his relatives out of Shechem.

NEW KING JAMES VERSION

42And it came about on the next day that the
people went out into the field, and they told
Abimelech. 43So he took his people, divided
them into three companies, and lay in wait in
the field. And he looked, and there were the peo-
ple, coming out of the city; and he rose against
them and attacked them. 44Then Abimelech and
the company that *was* with him rushed forward
and stood at the entrance of the gate of the city;
and the *other* two companies rushed upon all
who *were* in the fields and killed them. 45So
Abimelech fought against the city all that day;
he took the city and killed the people who *were*
in it; and he demolished the city and sowed it
with salt.

46Now when all the men of the tower of
Shechem had heard *that*, they entered the
stronghold of the temple of the god Berith. 47And
it was told Abimelech that all the men of the
tower of Shechem were gathered together.
48Then Abimelech went up to Mount Zalmon, he
and all the people who *were* with him. And Abim-
elech took an ax in his hand and cut down a
bough from the trees, and took it and laid *it* on
his shoulder; then he said to the people who were
with him, "What you have seen me do, make
haste *and* do as I *have done*." 49So each of the
people likewise cut down his own bough and fol-
lowed Abimelech, put *them* against the strong-
hold, and set the stronghold on fire above them,
so that all the people of the tower of Shechem
died, about a thousand men and women.

50Then Abimelech went to Thebez, and he
encamped against Thebez and took it. 51But
there was a strong tower in the city, and all the
men and women—all the people of the city—
fled there and shut themselves in; then they
went up to the top of the tower. 52So Abimelech
came as far as the tower and fought against it;
and he drew near the door of the tower to burn
it with fire. 53But a certain woman dropped an
upper millstone on Abimelech's head and
crushed his skull. 54Then he called quickly to the
young man, his armorbearer, and said to him,
"Draw your sword and kill me, lest men say of
me, 'A woman killed him.' " So his young man
thrust him through, and he died. 55And when the
men of Israel saw that Abimelech was dead,
they departed, every man to his place.

56Thus God repaid the wickedness of Abim-
elech, which he had done to his father by killing
his seventy brothers. 57And all the evil of the
men of Shechem God returned on their own
heads, and on them came the curse of Jotham
the son of Jerubbaal.

TOLA

10 After Abimelech there arose to save Israel
Tola the son of Puah, the son of Dodo, a
man of Issachar; and he dwelt in Shamir in the
mountains of Ephraim. 2He judged Israel
twenty-three years; and he died and was buried
in Shamir.

JAIR

3After him arose Jair, a Gileadite; and he
judged Israel twenty-two years. 4Now he had

THE MESSAGE

42-45 The next day the people went out to the
fields. This was reported to Abimelech. He
took his troops, divided them into three
companies, and placed them in ambush in
the fields. When he saw that the people were
well out in the open, he sprang up and at-
tacked them. Abimelech and the company
with him charged ahead and took control of
the entrance to the city gate; the other two
companies chased down those who were in
the open fields and killed them. Abimelech
fought at the city all that day. He captured
the city and massacred everyone in it. He
leveled the city to the ground, then sowed it
with salt.

46-49 When the leaders connected with She-
chem's Tower heard this, they went into the
fortified God-of-the-Covenant temple. This
was reported to Abimelech that the
Shechem's Tower bunch were gathered to-
gether. He and his troops climbed Mount
Zalmon (Dark Mountain). Abimelech took
his ax and chopped a bundle of firewood,
picked it up, and put it on his shoulder. He
said to his troops, "Do what you've seen me
do, and quickly." So each of his men cut his
own bundle. They followed Abimelech, piled
their bundles against the Tower fortifica-
tions, and set the whole structure on fire.
Everyone in Shechem's Tower died, about a
thousand men and women.

50-54 Abimelech went on to Thebez. He camped
at Thebez and captured it. The Tower-of-
Strength stood in the middle of the city; all
the men and women of the city along with
the city's leaders had fled there and locked
themselves in. They were up on the tower
roof. Abimelech got as far as the tower and
assaulted it. He came up to the tower door to
set it on fire. Just then some woman dropped
an upper millstone on his head and crushed
his skull. He called urgently to his young ar-
mor bearer and said, "Draw your sword and
kill me so they can't say of me, 'A woman
killed him.' " His armor bearer drove in his
sword, and Abimelech died.

55 When the Israelites saw that Abimelech
was dead, they went home.

56-57 God avenged the evil Abimelech had done
to his father, murdering his seventy broth-
ers. And God brought down on the heads of
the men of Shechem all the evil that they
had done, the curse of Jotham son of Jerub-
Baal.

TOLA

1-2 **10** Tola son of Puah, the son of Dodo, was
next after Abimelech. He rose to the
occasion to save Israel. He was a man of Is-
sachar. He lived in Shamir in the hill coun-
try of Ephraim. He judged Israel for twenty-
three years and then died and was buried at
Shamir.

JAIR

3-5 After him, Jair the Gileadite stepped into
leadership. He judged Israel for twenty-two

NEW KING JAMES VERSION

thirty sons who rode on thirty donkeys; they also had thirty towns, which are called "Havoth Jair"[a] to this day, which *are* in the land of Gilead. 5And Jair died and was buried in Camon.

ISRAEL OPPRESSED AGAIN

6Then the children of Israel again did evil in the sight of the LORD, and served the Baals and the Ashtoreths, the gods of Syria, the gods of Sidon, the gods of Moab, the gods of the people of Ammon, and the gods of the Philistines; and they forsook the LORD and did not serve Him. 7So the anger of the LORD was hot against Israel; and He sold them into the hands of the Philistines and into the hands of the people of Ammon. 8From that year they harassed and oppressed the children of Israel for eighteen years—all the children of Israel who *were* on the other side of the Jordan in the land of the Amorites, in Gilead. 9Moreover the people of Ammon crossed over the Jordan to fight against Judah also, against Benjamin, and against the house of Ephraim, so that Israel was severely distressed.

10And the children of Israel cried out to the LORD, saying, "We have sinned against You, because we have both forsaken our God and served the Baals!"

11So the LORD said to the children of Israel, "*Did I* not *deliver you* from the Egyptians and from the Amorites and from the people of Ammon and from the Philistines? 12Also the Sidonians and Amalekites and Maonites[a] oppressed you; and you cried out to Me, and I delivered you from their hand. 13Yet you have forsaken Me and served other gods. Therefore I will deliver you no more. 14Go and cry out to the gods which you have chosen; let them deliver you in your time of distress."

15And the children of Israel said to the LORD, "We have sinned! Do to us whatever seems best to You; only deliver us this day, we pray." 16So they put away the foreign gods from among them and served the LORD. And His soul could no longer endure the misery of Israel.

17Then the people of Ammon gathered together and encamped in Gilead. And the children of Israel assembled together and encamped in Mizpah. 18And the people, the leaders of Gilead, said to one another, "Who *is* the man who will begin the fight against the people of Ammon? He shall be head over all the inhabitants of Gilead."

JEPHTHAH

11 Now Jephthah the Gileadite was a mighty man of valor, but he *was* the son of a harlot; and Gilead begot Jephthah. 2Gilead's wife bore sons; and when his wife's sons grew up, they drove Jephthah out, and said to him, "You shall have no inheritance in our father's house, for you *are* the son of another woman." 3Then Jephthah fled from his brothers and dwelt in the land of Tob; and worthless men banded together with Jephthah and went out *raiding* with him.

10:4 [a]Literally *Towns of Jair* (compare Numbers 32:41 and Deuteronomy 3:14) **10:12** [a]Some Septuagint manuscripts read *Midianites.*

THE MESSAGE

years. He had thirty sons who rode on thirty donkeys and had thirty towns in Gilead. The towns are still called Jair's Villages. Jair died and was buried in Kamon.

6-8 And then the People of Israel went back to doing evil in GOD's sight. They worshiped the Baal gods and Ashtoreth goddesses: gods of Aram, Sidon, and Moab; gods of the Ammonites and the Philistines. They just walked off and left GOD, quit worshiping him. And GOD exploded in hot anger at Israel and sold them off to the Philistines and Ammonites, who, beginning that year, bullied and battered the People of Israel mercilessly. For eighteen years they had them under their thumb, all the People of Israel who lived east of the Jordan in the Amorite country of Gilead.

9 Then the Ammonites crossed the Jordan to go to war also against Judah, Benjamin, and Ephraim. Israel was in a bad way!

10 The People of Israel cried out to GOD for help: "We've sinned against you! We left our God and worshiped the Baal gods!"

11-14 GOD answered the People of Israel: "When the Egyptians, Amorites, Ammonites, Philistines, Sidonians—even Amalek and Midian!—oppressed you and you cried out to me for help, I saved you from them. And now you've gone off and betrayed me, worshiping other gods. I'm not saving you anymore. Go ahead! Cry out for help to the gods you've chosen—let them get you out of the mess you're in!"

15 The People of Israel said to GOD: "We've sinned. Do to us whatever you think best, but please, get us out of this!"

16 Then they cleaned house of the foreign gods and worshiped only GOD. And GOD took Israel's troubles to heart.

JEPHTHAH

17-18 The Ammonites prepared for war, setting camp in Gilead. The People of Israel set their rival camp in Mizpah. The leaders in Gilead said, "Who will stand up for us against the Ammonites? We'll make him head over everyone in Gilead!"

1-3 11 Jephthah the Gileadite was one tough warrior. He was the son of a whore, but Gilead was his father. Meanwhile Gilead's legal wife had given him other sons, and when they grew up, his wife's sons threw Jephthah out. They told him: "You're not getting any of our family inheritance—you're the son of another woman." So Jephthah fled from his brothers and went to live in the land of Tob. Some riffraff joined him and went around with him.

NEW KING JAMES VERSION

[4]It came to pass after a time that the people of Ammon made war against Israel. [5]And so it was, when the people of Ammon made war against Israel, that the elders of Gilead went to get Jephthah from the land of Tob. [6]Then they said to Jephthah, "Come and be our commander, that we may fight against the people of Ammon."

[7]So Jephthah said to the elders of Gilead, "Did you not hate me, and expel me from my father's house? Why have you come to me now when you are in distress?"

[8]And the elders of Gilead said to Jephthah, "That is why we have turned again to you now, that you may go with us and fight against the people of Ammon, and be our head over all the inhabitants of Gilead."

[9]So Jephthah said to the elders of Gilead, "If you take me back home to fight against the people of Ammon, and the LORD delivers them to me, shall I be your head?"

[10]And the elders of Gilead said to Jephthah, "The LORD will be a witness between us, if we do not do according to your words." [11]Then Jephthah went with the elders of Gilead, and the people made him head and commander over them; and Jephthah spoke all his words before the LORD in Mizpah.

[12]Now Jephthah sent messengers to the king of the people of Ammon, saying, "What do you have against me, that you have come to fight against me in my land?"

[13]And the king of the people of Ammon answered the messengers of Jephthah, "Because Israel took away my land when they came up out of Egypt, from the Arnon as far as the Jabbok, and to the Jordan. Now therefore, restore those *lands* peaceably."

[14]So Jephthah again sent messengers to the king of the people of Ammon, [15]and said to him, "Thus says Jephthah: 'Israel did not take away the land of Moab, nor the land of the people of Ammon; [16]for when Israel came up from Egypt, they walked through the wilderness as far as the Red Sea and came to Kadesh. [17]Then Israel sent messengers to the king of Edom, saying, "Please let me pass through your land." But the king of Edom would not heed. And in like manner they sent to the king of Moab, but he would not *consent*. So Israel remained in Kadesh. [18]And they went along through the wilderness and bypassed the land of Edom and the land of Moab, came to the east side of the land of Moab, and encamped on the other side of the Arnon. But they did not enter the border of Moab, for the Arnon *was* the border of Moab. [19]Then Israel sent messengers to Sihon king of the Amorites, king of Heshbon; and Israel said to him, "Please let us pass through your land into our place." [20]But Sihon did not trust Israel to pass through his territory. So Sihon gathered all his people together, encamped in Jahaz, and fought against Israel. [21]And the LORD God of Israel delivered Sihon and all his people into the hand of Israel, and they defeated them. Thus Israel gained possession of all the land of the Amorites, who inhabited that country. [22]They took possession of all the territory of the Amorites, from the Arnon to the Jabbok and from the wilderness to the Jordan.

THE MESSAGE

4-6 Some time passed. And then the Ammonites started fighting Israel. With the Ammonites at war with them, the elders of Gilead went to get Jephthah from the land of Tob. They said to Jephthah: "Come. Be our general and we'll fight the Ammonites."

7 But Jephthah said to the elders of Gilead: "But you hate me. You kicked me out of my family home. So why are you coming to me now? Because you are in trouble. Right?"

8 The elders of Gilead replied, "That's it exactly. We've come to you to get you to go with us and fight the Ammonites. You'll be the head of all of us, all the Gileadites."

9 Jephthah addressed the elders of Gilead, "So if you bring me back home to fight the Ammonites and GOD gives them to me, I'll be your head—is that right?"

10-11 They said, "GOD is witness between us; whatever you say, we'll do." Jephthah went along with the elders of Gilead. The people made him their top man and general. And Jephthah repeated what he had said before GOD at Mizpah.

12 Then Jephthah sent messengers to the king of the Ammonites with a message: "What's going on here that you have come into my country picking a fight?"

13 The king of the Ammonites told Jephthah's messengers: "Because Israel took my land when they came up out of Egypt—from the Arnon all the way to the Jabbok and to the Jordan. Give it back peaceably and I'll go."

14-27 Jephthah again sent messengers to the king of the Ammonites with the message: "Jephthah's word: Israel took no Moabite land and no Ammonite land. When they came up from Egypt, Israel went through the desert as far as the Red Sea, arriving at Kadesh. There Israel sent messengers to the king of Edom saying, 'Let us pass through your land, please.' But the king of Edom wouldn't let them. Israel also requested permission from the king of Moab, but he wouldn't let them cross either. They were stopped in their tracks at Kadesh. So they traveled across the desert and circled around the lands of Edom and Moab. They came out east of the land of Moab and set camp on the other side of the Arnon—they didn't set foot in Moabite territory, for Arnon was the Moabite border. Israel then sent messengers to Sihon king of the Amorites at Heshbon the capital. Israel asked, 'Let us pass, please, through your land on the way to our country.' But Sihon didn't trust Israel to cut across his land; he got his entire army together, set up camp at Jahaz, and fought Israel. But GOD, the God of Israel, gave Sihon and all his troops to Israel. Israel defeated them. Israel took all the Amorite land, all Amorite land from Arnon to the Jabbok and from the desert to the Jordan. It was GOD, the God of Israel, who

NEW KING JAMES VERSION

23'And now the LORD God of Israel has dis-
possessed the Amorites from before His people
Israel; should you then possess it? 24Will you not
possess whatever Chemosh your god gives you
to possess? So whatever the LORD our God takes
possession of before us, we will possess. 25And
now, *are* you any better than Balak the son of
Zippor, king of Moab? Did he ever strive against
Israel? Did he ever fight against them? 26While
Israel dwelt in Heshbon and its villages, in
Aroer and its villages, and in all the cities along
the banks of the Arnon, for three hundred years,
why did you not recover *them* within that time?
27Therefore I have not sinned against you, but
you wronged me by fighting against me. May
the LORD, the Judge, render judgment this day
between the children of Israel and the people of
Ammon.' " 28However, the king of the people of
Ammon did not heed the words which Jephthah
sent him.

JEPHTHAH'S VOW AND VICTORY

29Then the Spirit of the LORD came upon
Jephthah, and he passed through Gilead and
Manasseh, and passed through Mizpah of
Gilead; and from Mizpah of Gilead he advanced
toward the people of Ammon. 30And Jephthah
made a vow to the LORD, and said, "If You will in-
deed deliver the people of Ammon into my
hands, 31then it will be that whatever comes out
of the doors of my house to meet me, when I re-
turn in peace from the people of Ammon, shall
surely be the LORD's, and I will offer it up as a
burnt offering."
32So Jephthah advanced toward the people
of Ammon to fight against them, and the LORD
delivered them into his hands. 33And he de-
feated them from Aroer as far as Minnith—
twenty cities—and to Abel Keramim,[a] with a
very great slaughter. Thus the people of Ammon
were subdued before the children of Israel.

JEPHTHAH'S DAUGHTER

34When Jephthah came to his house at Miz-
pah, there was his daughter, coming out to meet
him with timbrels and dancing; and she *was his*
only child. Besides her he had neither son nor
daughter. 35And it came to pass, when he saw
her, that he tore his clothes, and said, "Alas, my
daughter! You have brought me very low! You are
among those who trouble me! For I have given
my word to the LORD, and I cannot go back on it."
36So she said to him, "My father, *if* you have
given your word to the LORD, do to me according
to what has gone out of your mouth, because the
LORD has avenged you of your enemies, the peo-
ple of Ammon." 37Then she said to her father, "Let
this thing be done for me: let me alone for two
months, that I may go and wander on the moun-
tains and bewail my virginity, my friends and I."
38So he said, "Go." And he sent her away *for*
two months; and she went with her friends, and
bewailed her virginity on the mountains. 39And it
was so at the end of two months that she re-
turned to her father, and he carried out his vow
with her which he had vowed. She knew no man.

11:33 [a]Literally *Plain of Vineyards*

THE MESSAGE

pushed out the Amorites in favor of Israel; so who do you think you are to try to take it over? Why don't you just be satisfied with what your god Chemosh gives you and we'll settle for what GOD, our God, gives us? Do you think you're going to come off better than Balak son of Zippor, the king of Moab? Did he get anywhere in opposing Israel? Did he risk war? All this time—it's been three hundred years now!—that Israel has lived in Heshbon and its villages, in Aroer and its villages, and in all the towns along the Arnon, why didn't you try to snatch them away then? No, I haven't wronged you. But this is an evil thing that you are doing to me by starting a fight. Today GOD the Judge will decide between the People of Israel and the people of Ammon."

28 But the king of the Ammonites refused to listen to a word that Jephthah had sent him.

29-31 GOD's Spirit came upon Jephthah. He went across Gilead and Manasseh, went through Mizpah of Gilead, and from there approached the Ammonites. Jephthah made a vow before GOD: "If you give me a clear victory over the Ammonites, then I'll give to GOD whatever comes out of the door of my house to meet me when I return in one piece from among the Ammonites—I'll offer it up in a sacrificial burnt offering."

32-33 Then Jephthah was off to fight the Ammonites. And GOD gave them to him. He beat them soundly, all the way from Aroer to the area around Minnith as far as Abel Keramim—twenty cities! A massacre! Ammonites brought to their knees by the People of Israel.

34-35 Jephthah came home to Mizpah. His daughter ran from the house to welcome him home—dancing to tambourines! She was his only child. He had no son or daughter except her. When he realized who it was, he ripped his clothes, saying, "Ah, dearest daughter—I'm dirt. I'm despicable. My heart is torn to shreds. I made a vow to GOD and I can't take it back!"

36 She said, "Dear father, if you made a vow to GOD, do to me what you vowed; GOD did his part and saved you from your Ammonite enemies."

37 And then she said to her father, "But let this one thing be done for me. Give me two months to wander through the hills and lament my virginity since I will never marry, I and my dear friends."

38-39 "Oh yes, go," he said. He sent her off for two months. She and her dear girlfriends went among the hills, lamenting that she would never marry. At the end of the two months, she came back to her father. He fulfilled the vow with her that he had made. She had never slept with a man.

NEW KING JAMES VERSION

And it became a custom in Israel 40*that* the
daughters of Israel went four days each year to
lament the daughter of Jephthah the Gileadite.

JEPHTHAH'S CONFLICT WITH EPHRAIM

12 Then the men of Ephraim gathered to-
gether, crossed over toward Zaphon, and
said to Jephthah, "Why did you cross over to
fight against the people of Ammon, and did not
call us to go with you? We will burn your house
down on you with fire!"
2And Jephthah said to them, "My people and
I were in a great struggle with the people of Am-
mon; and when I called you, you did not deliver
me out of their hands. 3So when I saw that you
would not deliver *me,* I took my life in my hands
and crossed over against the people of Ammon;
and the LORD delivered them into my hand. Why
then have you come up to me this day to fight
against me?" 4Now Jephthah gathered together
all the men of Gilead and fought against
Ephraim. And the men of Gilead defeated
Ephraim, because they said, "You Gileadites *are*
fugitives of Ephraim among the Ephraimites
and among the Manassites." 5The Gileadites
seized the fords of the Jordan before the
Ephraimites *arrived.* And when *any* Ephraimite
who escaped said, "Let me cross over," the men
of Gilead would say to him, "*Are* you an
Ephraimite?" If he said, "No," 6then they would
say to him, "Then say, 'Shibboleth'!" And he
would say, "Sibboleth," for he could not pro-
nounce *it* right. Then they would take him and
kill him at the fords of the Jordan. There fell at
that time forty-two thousand Ephraimites.
7And Jephthah judged Israel six years. Then
Jephthah the Gileadite died and was buried
among the cities of Gilead.

IBZAN, ELON, AND ABDON

8After him, Ibzan of Bethlehem judged Is-
rael. 9He had thirty sons. And he gave away
thirty daughters in marriage, and brought in
thirty daughters from elsewhere for his sons. He
judged Israel seven years. 10Then Ibzan died and
was buried at Bethlehem.
11After him, Elon the Zebulunite judged Is-
rael. He judged Israel ten years. 12And Elon the
Zebulunite died and was buried at Aijalon in the
country of Zebulun.
13After him, Abdon the son of Hillel the Pir-
athonite judged Israel. 14He had forty sons and
thirty grandsons, who rode on seventy young
donkeys. He judged Israel eight years. 15Then
Abdon the son of Hillel the Pirathonite died and
was buried in Pirathon in the land of Ephraim,
in the mountains of the Amalekites.

THE BIRTH OF SAMSON

13 Again the children of Israel did evil in the
sight of the LORD, and the LORD delivered
them into the hand of the Philistines for forty
years.

THE MESSAGE

39-40 It became a custom in Israel that for four
days every year the young women of Israel
went out to mourn for the daughter of Jeph-
thah the Gileadite.

1 12 The men of Ephraim mustered their
troops, crossed to Zaphon, and said to
Jephthah, "Why did you go out to fight the
Ammonites without letting us go with you?
We're going to burn your house down on
you!"

2-3 Jephthah said, "I and my people had our
hands full negotiating with the Ammonites.
And I did call to you for help but you ignored
me. When I saw that you weren't coming, I
took my life in my hands and confronted the
Ammonites myself. And GOD gave them to
me! So why did you show up here today? Are
you spoiling for a fight with me?"

4 So Jephthah got his Gilead troops to-
gether and fought Ephraim. And the men of
Gilead hit them hard because they were say-
ing, "Gileadites are nothing but half breeds
and rejects from Ephraim and Manasseh."

5-6 Gilead captured the fords of the Jordan at
the crossing to Ephraim. If an Ephraimite
fugitive said, "Let me cross," the men of
Gilead would ask, "Are you an Ephraimite?"
and he would say, "No." And they would say,
"Say, 'Shibboleth.' " But he would always say,
"Sibboleth"—he couldn't say it right. Then
they would grab him and kill him there at the
fords of the Jordan. Forty-two Ephraimite di-
visions were killed on that occasion.

7 Jephthah judged Israel six years. Jeph-
thah the Gileadite died and was buried in
his city, Mizpah of Gilead.

IBZAN

8-9 After him, Ibzan of Bethlehem judged Is-
rael. He had thirty sons and thirty daugh-
ters. He gave his daughters in marriage
outside his clan and brought in thirty
daughters-in-law from the outside for his
sons.

10 He judged Israel seven years. Ibzan died
and was buried in Bethlehem.

ELON

11-12 After him, Elon the Zebulunite judged Israel.
He judged Israel ten years. Elon the Zeb-
ulunite died and was buried at Aijalon in the
land of Zebulun.

ABDON

13-15 After him, Abdon son of Hillel the Pir-
athonite judged Israel. He had forty sons
and thirty grandsons who rode on seventy
donkeys. He judged Israel eight years. Ab-
don son of Hillel the Pirathonite died and
was buried at Pirathon in the land of
Ephraim in the Amalekite hill country.

SAMSON

1 13 And then the People of Israel were
back at it again, doing what was evil in
GOD's sight. GOD put them under the domi-
nation of the Philistines for forty years.

NEW KING JAMES VERSION

2Now there was a certain man from Zorah, of
the family of the Danites, whose name *was*
Manoah; and his wife *was* barren and had no
children. 3And the Angel of the LORD appeared
to the woman and said to her, "Indeed now, you
are barren and have borne no children, but you
shall conceive and bear a son. 4Now therefore,
please be careful not to drink wine or *similar*
drink, and not to eat anything unclean. 5For be-
hold, you shall conceive and bear a son. And no
razor shall come upon his head, for the child
shall be a Nazirite to God from the womb; and
he shall begin to deliver Israel out of the hand of
the Philistines."
6So the woman came and told her husband,
saying, "A Man of God came to me, and His
countenance *was* like the countenance of the
Angel of God, very awesome; but I did not ask
Him where He *was* from, and He did not tell me
His name. 7And He said to me, 'Behold, you
shall conceive and bear a son. Now drink no
wine or *similar* drink, nor eat anything unclean,
for the child shall be a Nazirite to God from the
womb to the day of his death.' "
8Then Manoah prayed to the LORD, and said,
"O my Lord, please let the Man of God whom
You sent come to us again and teach us what we
shall do for the child who will be born."
9And God listened to the voice of Manoah,
and the Angel of God came to the woman again
as she was sitting in the field; but Manoah her
husband *was* not with her. 10Then the woman
ran in haste and told her husband, and said to
him, "Look, the Man who came to me the *other*
day has just now appeared to me!"
11So Manoah arose and followed his wife.
When he came to the Man, he said to Him, "Are
You the Man who spoke to this woman?"
And He said, "I *am.*"
12Manoah said, "Now let Your words come *to
pass!* What will be the boy's rule of life, and his
work?"
13So the Angel of the LORD said to Manoah,
"Of all that I said to the woman let her be care-
ful. 14She may not eat anything that comes from
the vine, nor may she drink wine or *similar*
drink, nor eat anything unclean. All that I com-
manded her let her observe."
15Then Manoah said to the Angel of the
LORD, "Please let us detain You, and we will pre-
pare a young goat for You."
16And the Angel of the LORD said to Manoah,
"Though you detain Me, I will not eat your food.
But if you offer a burnt offering, you must offer
it to the LORD." (For Manoah did not know He
was the Angel of the LORD.)
17Then Manoah said to the Angel of the
LORD, "What *is* Your name, that when Your words
come *to pass* we may honor You?"
18And the Angel of the LORD said to him, "Why
do you ask My name, seeing it *is* wonderful?"
19So Manoah took the young goat with the
grain offering, and offered it upon the rock to
the LORD. And He did a wondrous thing while
Manoah and his wife looked on— 20it happened
as the flame went up toward heaven from the al-
tar—the Angel of the LORD ascended in the
flame of the altar! When Manoah and his wife
saw *this,* they fell on their faces to the ground.

THE MESSAGE

2-5 At that time there was a man named
Manoah from Zorah from the tribe of Dan.
His wife was barren and childless. The an-
gel of God appeared to her and told her, "I
know that you are barren and childless, but
you're going to become pregnant and bear a
son. But take much care: Drink no wine or
beer; eat nothing ritually unclean. You are,
in fact, pregnant right now, carrying a son.
No razor will touch his head—the boy will
be God's Nazirite from the moment of his
birth. He will launch the deliverance from
Philistine oppression."
6-7 The woman went to her husband and
said, "A man of God came to me. He looked
like the angel of God—terror laced with
glory! I didn't ask him where he was from
and he didn't tell me his name, but he told
me, 'You're pregnant. You're going to give
birth to a son. Don't drink any wine or beer
and eat nothing ritually unclean. The boy
will be God's Nazirite from the moment of
birth to the day of his death.' "
8 Manoah prayed to GOD: "Master, let the
man of God you sent come to us again and
teach us how to raise this boy who is to be
born."
9-10 God listened to Manoah. God's angel
came again to the woman. She was sitting in
the field; her husband Manoah wasn't there
with her. She jumped to her feet and ran and
told her husband: "He's back! The man who
came to me that day!"
11 Manoah got up and, following his wife,
came to the man. He said to him, "Are you
the man who spoke to my wife?"
He said, "I am."
12 Manoah said, "So. When what you say
comes true, what do you have to tell us
about this boy and his work?"
13-14 The angel of God said to Manoah, "Keep
in mind everything I told the woman. Eat
nothing that comes from the vine: Drink no
wine or beer; eat no ritually unclean foods.
She's to observe everything I commanded
her."
15 Manoah said to the angel of God, "Please,
stay with us a little longer; we'll prepare a
meal for you—a young goat."
16 GOD's angel said to Manoah, "Even if I
stay, I won't eat your food. But if you want to
prepare a Whole-Burnt-Offering for GOD, go
ahead—offer it!" Manoah had no idea that
he was talking to the angel of God.
17 Then Manoah asked the angel of God,
"What's your name? When your words come
true, we'd like to honor you."
18 The angel of GOD said, "What's this? You
ask for my name? You wouldn't under-
stand—it's sheer wonder."
19-21 So Manoah took the kid and the Grain-
Offering and sacrificed them on a rock altar
to GOD who works wonders. As the flames
leapt up from the altar to heaven, GOD's an-
gel also ascended in the altar flames. When
Manoah and his wife saw this, they fell face-
down to the ground. Manoah and his wife
never saw the angel of GOD again.

NEW KING JAMES VERSION

21When the Angel of the LORD appeared no
more to Manoah and his wife, then Manoah
knew that He *was* the Angel of the LORD.
22And Manoah said to his wife, "We shall
surely die, because we have seen God!"
23But his wife said to him, "If the LORD had
desired to kill us, He would not have accepted a
burnt offering and a grain offering from our
hands, nor would He have shown us all these
things, nor would He have told us *such things* as
these at this time."
24So the woman bore a son and called his
name Samson; and the child grew, and the LORD
blessed him. 25And the Spirit of the LORD began
to move upon him at Mahaneh Dan[a] between
Zorah and Eshtaol.

SAMSON'S PHILISTINE WIFE

14 Now Samson went down to Timnah, and
saw a woman in Timnah of the daughters
of the Philistines. 2So he went up and told his fa-
ther and mother, saying, "I have seen a woman
in Timnah of the daughters of the Philistines;
now therefore, get her for me as a wife."
3Then his father and mother said to him, "*Is
there* no woman among the daughters of your
brethren, or among all my people, that you must
go and get a wife from the uncircumcised
Philistines?"
And Samson said to his father, "Get her for
me, for she pleases me well."
4But his father and mother did not know that
it was of the LORD—that He was seeking an oc-
casion to move against the Philistines. For at
that time the Philistines had dominion over Is-
rael.
5So Samson went down to Timnah with his
father and mother, and came to the vineyards of
Timnah.
Now *to his* surprise, a young lion *came* roar-
ing against him. 6And the Spirit of the LORD
came mightily upon him, and he tore the lion
apart as one would have torn apart a young
goat, though *he had* nothing in his hand. But he
did not tell his father or his mother what he had
done.
7Then he went down and talked with the
woman; and she pleased Samson well. 8After
some time, when he returned to get her, he
turned aside to see the carcass of the lion. And
behold, a swarm of bees and honey *were* in the
carcass of the lion. 9He took some of it in his
hands and went along, eating. When he came to
his father and mother, he gave *some* to them,
and they also ate. But he did not tell them that
he had taken the honey out of the carcass of the
lion.
10So his father went down to the woman.
And Samson gave a feast there, for young men
used to do so. 11And it happened, when they saw
him, that they brought thirty companions to be
with him.
12Then Samson said to them, "Let me pose a
riddle to you. If you can correctly solve and ex-
plain it to me within the seven days of the feast,
then I will give you thirty linen garments and
thirty changes of clothing. 13But if you cannot

13:25 [a]Literally *Camp of Dan* (compare 18:12)

THE MESSAGE

21-22 Only then did Manoah realize that this
was GOD's angel. He said to his wife, "We're
as good as dead! We've looked on God!"
23 But his wife said, "If GOD were planning
to kill us, he wouldn't have accepted our
Whole-Burnt-Offering and Grain-Offering,
or revealed all these things to us—given us
this birth announcement."
24-25 The woman gave birth to a son. They
named him Samson. The boy grew and GOD
blessed him. The Spirit of GOD began work-
ing in him while he was staying at a Danite
camp between Zorah and Eshtaol.

1-2 14 Samson went down to Timnah. There
in Timnah a woman caught his eye, a
Philistine girl. He came back and told his fa-
ther and mother, "I saw a woman in Timnah,
a Philistine girl; get her for me as my wife."
3 His parents said to him, "Isn't there a
woman among the girls in the neighbor-
hood of our people? Do you have to go get a
wife from the uncircumcised Philistines?"
But Samson said to his father, "Get her
for me. She's the one I want—she's the right
one."
4 (His father and mother had no idea that
GOD was behind this, that he was arranging
an opportunity against the Philistines. At
the time the Philistines lorded it over Israel.)
5-6 Samson went down to Timnah with his
father and mother. When he got to the vine-
yards of Timnah, a young lion came at him,
roaring. The Spirit of GOD came on him
powerfully and he ripped it open bare-
handed, like tearing a young goat. But he
didn't tell his parents what he had done.
7 Then he went on down and spoke to the
woman. In Samson's eyes, she was the one.
8-9 Some days later when he came back to
get her, he made a little detour to look at
what was left of the lion. And there a won-
der: a swarm of bees in the lion's carcass—
and honey! He scooped it up in his hands
and kept going, eating as he went. He re-
joined his father and mother and gave some
to them and they ate. But he didn't tell them
that he had scooped out the honey from the
lion's carcass.
10-11 His father went on down to make
arrangements with the woman, while Sam-
son prepared a feast there. That's what the
young men did in those days. Because the
people were wary of him, they arranged for
thirty friends to mingle with him.
12-13 Samson said to them: "Let me put a rid-
dle to you. If you can figure it out during the
seven days of the feast, I'll give you thirty
linen garments and thirty changes of fine
clothing. But if you can't figure it out then

NEW KING JAMES VERSION

explain *it* to me, then you shall give me thirty linen garments and thirty changes of clothing."

And they said to him, "Pose your riddle, that we may hear it."

14So he said to them:

"Out of the eater came something to eat,
And out of the strong came something
sweet."

Now for three days they could not explain the riddle.

15But it came to pass on the seventh[a] day that they said to Samson's wife, "Entice your husband, that he may explain the riddle to us, or else we will burn you and your father's house with fire. Have you invited us in order to take what is ours? *Is that* not *so*?"

16Then Samson's wife wept on him, and said, "You only hate me! You do not love me! You have posed a riddle to the sons of my people, but you have not explained *it* to me."

And he said to her, "Look, I have not explained *it* to my father or my mother; so should I explain *it* to you?" 17Now she had wept on him the seven days while their feast lasted. And it happened on the seventh day that he told her, because she pressed him so much. Then she explained the riddle to the sons of her people. 18So the men of the city said to him on the seventh day before the sun went down:

"What *is* sweeter than honey?
And what *is* stronger than a lion?"

And he said to them:

"If you had not plowed with my heifer,
You would not have solved my riddle!"

19Then the Spirit of the LORD came upon him mightily, and he went down to Ashkelon and killed thirty of their men, took their apparel, and gave the changes *of clothing* to those who had explained the riddle. So his anger was aroused, and he went back up to his father's house. 20And Samson's wife was *given* to his companion, who had been his best man.

SAMSON DEFEATS THE PHILISTINES

15 After a while, in the time of wheat harvest, it happened that Samson visited his wife with a young goat. And he said, "Let me go in to my wife, into *her* room." But her father would not permit him to go in.

2Her father said, "I really thought that you thoroughly hated her; therefore I gave her to your companion. *Is* not her younger sister better than she? Please, take her instead."

3And Samson said to them, "This time I shall be blameless regarding the Philistines if I harm them!" 4Then Samson went and caught three hundred foxes; and he took torches, turned *the foxes* tail to tail, and put a torch between each pair of tails. 5When he had set the torches on fire, he let *the foxes* go into the standing grain

THE MESSAGE

you'll give me thirty linen garments and thirty changes of fine clothing."

13-14 They said, "Put your riddle. Let's hear it."
So he said,

From the eater came something to eat,
From the strong came something sweet.

14-15 They couldn't figure it out. After three days they were still stumped. On the fourth day they said to Samson's bride, "Worm the answer out of your husband or we'll burn you and your father's household. Have you invited us here to bankrupt us?"

16 So Samson's bride turned on the tears, saying to him, "You hate me. You don't love me. You've told a riddle to my people but you won't even tell me the answer."

He said, "I haven't told my own parents—why would I tell you?"

17 But she turned on the tears all the seven days of the feast. On the seventh day, worn out by her nagging, he told her. Then she went and told it to her people.

18 The men of the town came to him on the seventh day, just before sunset and said,

What is sweeter than honey?
What is stronger than a lion?

And Samson said,

If you hadn't plowed with my heifer,
You wouldn't have found out my riddle.

19-20 Then the Spirit of GOD came powerfully on him. He went down to Ashkelon and killed thirty of their men, stripped them, and gave their clothing to those who had solved the riddle. Stalking out, smoking with anger, he went home to his father's house. Samson's bride became the wife of the best man at his wedding.

1-2 15 Later on—it was during the wheat harvest—Samson visited his bride, bringing a young goat. He said, "Let me see my wife—show me her bedroom."

But her father wouldn't let him in. He said, "I concluded that by now you hated her with a passion, so I gave her to your best man. But her little sister is even more beautiful. Why not take her instead?"

3 Samson said, "That does it. This time when I wreak havoc on the Philistines, I'm blameless."

4-5 Samson then went out and caught three hundred jackals. He lashed the jackals' tails together in pairs and tied a torch between each pair of tails. He then set fire to the torches and let them loose in the Philistine

14:15 [a]Following Masoretic Text, Targum, and Vulgate; Septuagint and Syriac read *fourth*.

NEW KING JAMES VERSION

of the Philistines, and burned up both the shocks and the standing grain, as well as the vineyards *and* olive groves.

6Then the Philistines said, "Who has done this?"

And they answered, "Samson, the son-in-law of the Timnite, because he has taken his wife and given her to his companion." So the Philistines came up and burned her and her father with fire.

7Samson said to them, "Since you would do a thing like this, I will surely take revenge on you, and after that I will cease." 8So he attacked them hip and thigh with a great slaughter; then he went down and dwelt in the cleft of the rock of Etam.

9Now the Philistines went up, encamped in Judah, and deployed themselves against Lehi. 10And the men of Judah said, "Why have you come up against us?"

So they answered, "We have come up to arrest Samson, to do to him as he has done to us."

11Then three thousand men of Judah went down to the cleft of the rock of Etam, and said to Samson, "Do you not know that the Philistines rule over us? What *is* this you have done to us?"

And he said to them, "As they did to me, so I have done to them."

12But they said to him, "We have come down to arrest you, that we may deliver you into the hand of the Philistines."

Then Samson said to them, "Swear to me that you will not kill me yourselves."

13So they spoke to him, saying, "No, but we will tie you securely and deliver you into their hand; but we will surely not kill you." And they bound him with two new ropes and brought him up from the rock.

14When he came to Lehi, the Philistines came shouting against him. Then the Spirit of the LORD came mightily upon him; and the ropes that *were* on his arms became like flax that is burned with fire, and his bonds broke loose from his hands. 15He found a fresh jawbone of a donkey, reached out his hand and took it, and killed a thousand men with it. 16Then Samson said:

"With the jawbone of a donkey,
Heaps upon heaps,
With the jawbone of a donkey
I have slain a thousand men!"

17And so it was, when he had finished speaking, that he threw the jawbone from his hand, and called that place Ramath Lehi.[a]

18Then he became very thirsty; so he cried out to the LORD and said, "You have given this great deliverance by the hand of Your servant; and now shall I die of thirst and fall into the hand of the uncircumcised?" 19So God split the hollow place that *is* in Lehi,[a] and water came out, and he drank; and his spirit returned, and he revived. Therefore he called its name En Hakkore,[b] which is in Lehi to this day.

15:17 [a]Literally *Jawbone Height* **15:19** [a]Literally *Jawbone* (compare verse 14) [b]Literally *Spring of the Caller*

THE MESSAGE

fields of ripe grain. Everything burned, both stacked and standing grain, vineyards and olive orchards—everything.

6 The Philistines said, "Who did this?"

They were told, "Samson, son-in-law of the Timnite who took his bride and gave her to his best man."

The Philistines went up and burned both her and her father to death.

7 Samson then said, "If this is the way you're going to act, I swear I'll get even with you. And I'm not quitting till the job's done!"

8 With that he tore into them, ripping them limb from limb—a huge slaughter. Then he went down and stayed in a cave at Etam Rock.

9-10 The Philistines set out and made camp in Judah, preparing to attack Lehi (Jawbone). When the men of Judah asked, "Why have you come up against us?" they said, "We're out to get Samson. We're going after Samson to do to him what he did to us."

11 Three companies of men from Judah went down to the cave at Etam Rock and said to Samson, "Don't you realize that the Philistines already bully and lord it over us? So what's going on with you, making things even worse?"

He said, "It was tit for tat. I only did to them what they did to me."

12 They said, "Well, we've come down here to tie you up and turn you over to the Philistines."

Samson said, "Just promise not to hurt me."

13 "We promise," they said. "We will tie you up and surrender you to them but, believe us, we won't kill you." They proceeded to tie him with new ropes and led him up from the Rock.

14-16 As he approached Lehi, the Philistines came to meet him, shouting in triumph. And then the Spirit of GOD came on him with great power. The ropes on his arms fell apart like flax on fire; the thongs slipped off his hands. He spotted a fresh donkey jawbone, reached down and grabbed it, and with it killed the whole company. And Samson said,

With a donkey's jawbone
I made heaps of donkeys of them.
With a donkey's jawbone
I killed an entire company.

17 When he finished speaking, he threw away the jawbone. He named that place Ramath Lehi (Jawbone Hill).

18-19 Now he was suddenly very thirsty. He called out to GOD, "You have given your servant this great victory. Are you going to abandon me to die of thirst and fall into the hands of the uncircumcised?" So God split open the rock basin in Lehi; water gushed out and Samson drank. His spirit revived—he was alive again! That's why it's called En Hakkore (Caller's Spring). It's still there at Lehi today.

NEW KING JAMES VERSION

[20]And he judged Israel twenty years in the days of the Philistines.

SAMSON AND DELILAH

16 Now Samson went to Gaza and saw a harlot there, and went in to her. [2]*When* the Gazites *were told,* "Samson has come here!" they surrounded *the place* and lay in wait for him all night at the gate of the city. They were quiet all night, saying, "In the morning, when it is daylight, we will kill him." [3]And Samson lay *low* till midnight; then he arose at midnight, took hold of the doors of the gate of the city and the two gateposts, pulled them up, bar and all, put *them* on his shoulders, and carried them to the top of the hill that faces Hebron.

[4]Afterward it happened that he loved a woman in the Valley of Sorek, whose name *was* Delilah. [5]And the lords of the Philistines came up to her and said to her, "Entice him, and find out where his great strength *lies,* and by what *means* we may overpower him, that we may bind him to afflict him; and every one of us will give you eleven hundred *pieces* of silver."

[6]So Delilah said to Samson, "Please tell me where your great strength *lies,* and with what you may be bound to afflict you."

[7]And Samson said to her, "If they bind me with seven fresh bowstrings, not yet dried, then I shall become weak, and be like any *other* man."

[8]So the lords of the Philistines brought up to her seven fresh bowstrings, not yet dried, and she bound him with them. [9]Now *men were* lying in wait, staying with her in the room. And she said to him, "The Philistines *are* upon you, Samson!" But he broke the bowstrings as a strand of yarn breaks when it touches fire. So the secret of his strength was not known.

[10]Then Delilah said to Samson, "Look, you have mocked me and told me lies. Now, please tell me what you may be bound with."

[11]So he said to her, "If they bind me securely with new ropes that have never been used, then I shall become weak, and be like any *other* man."

[12]Therefore Delilah took new ropes and bound him with them, and said to him, "The Philistines *are* upon you, Samson!" And *men were* lying in wait, staying in the room. But he broke them off his arms like a thread.

[13]Delilah said to Samson, "Until now you have mocked me and told me lies. Tell me what you may be bound with."

And he said to her, "If you weave the seven locks of my head into the web of the loom"—

[14]So she wove *it* tightly with the batten of the loom, and said to him, "The Philistines *are* upon you, Samson!" But he awoke from his sleep, and pulled out the batten and the web from the loom.

[15]Then she said to him, "How can you say, 'I love you,' when your heart *is* not with me? You

THE MESSAGE

20 Samson judged Israel for twenty years in the days of the Philistines.

1-2 **16** Samson went to Gaza and saw a prostitute. He went to her. The news got around: "Samson's here." They gathered around in hiding, waiting all night for him at the city gate, quiet as mice, thinking, "At sunrise we'll kill him."

3 Samson was in bed with the woman until midnight. Then he got up, seized the doors of the city gate and the two gateposts, bolts and all, hefted them on his shoulder, and carried them to the top of the hill that faces Hebron.

4-5 Some time later he fell in love with a woman in the Valley of Sorek (Grapes). Her name was Delilah. The Philistine tyrants approached her and said, "Seduce him. Discover what's behind his great strength and how we can tie him up and humble him. Each man's company will give you a hundred shekels of silver."

6 So Delilah said to Samson, "Tell me, dear, the secret of your great strength, and how you can be tied up and humbled."

7 Samson told her, "If they were to tie me up with seven bowstrings—the kind made from fresh animal tendons, not dried out—then I would become weak, just like anyone else."

8-9 The Philistine tyrants brought her seven bowstrings, not dried out, and she tied him up with them. The men were waiting in ambush in her room. Then she said, "The Philistines are on you, Samson!" He snapped the cords as though they were mere threads. The secret of his strength was still a secret.

10 Delilah said, "Come now, Samson—you're playing with me, making up stories. Be serious; tell me how you can be tied up."

11 He told her, "If you were to tie me up tight with new ropes, ropes never used for work, then I would be helpless, just like anybody else."

12 So Delilah got some new ropes and tied him up. She said, "The Philistines are on you, Samson!" The men were hidden in the next room. He snapped the ropes from his arms like threads.

13-14 Delilah said to Samson, "You're still playing games with me, teasing me with lies. Tell me how you can be tied up."

He said to her, "If you wove the seven braids of my hair into the fabric on the loom and drew it tight, then I would be as helpless as any other mortal."

When she had him fast asleep, Delilah took the seven braids of his hair and wove them into the fabric on the loom and drew it tight. Then she said, "The Philistines are on you, Samson!" He woke from his sleep and ripped loose from both the loom and fabric!

15 She said, "How can you say 'I love you' when you won't even trust me? Three times

NEW KING JAMES VERSION

have mocked me these three times, and have not
told me where your great strength *lies*." [16]And it
came to pass, when she pestered him daily with
her words and pressed him, *so* that his soul was
vexed to death, [17]that he told her all his heart,
and said to her, "No razor has ever come upon
my head, for I *have been* a Nazirite to God from
my mother's womb. If I am shaven, then my
strength will leave me, and I shall become weak,
and be like any *other* man."

[18]When Delilah saw that he had told her all his
heart, she sent and called for the lords of the
Philistines, saying, "Come up once more, for he
has told me all his heart." So the lords of the
Philistines came up to her and brought the money
in their hand. [19]Then she lulled him to sleep on
her knees, and called for a man and had him
shave off the seven locks of his head. Then she be-
gan to torment him,[a] and his strength left him.
[20]And she said, "The Philistines *are* upon you,
Samson!" So he awoke from his sleep, and said, "I
will go out as before, at other times, and shake
myself free!" But he did not know that the LORD
had departed from him.

[21]Then the Philistines took him and put out
his eyes, and brought him down to Gaza. They
bound him with bronze fetters, and he became a
grinder in the prison. [22]However, the hair of his
head began to grow again after it had been
shaven.

SAMSON DIES WITH THE PHILISTINES

[23]Now the lords of the Philistines gathered
together to offer a great sacrifice to Dagon their
god, and to rejoice. And they said:

"Our god has delivered into our hands
Samson our enemy!"

[24]When the people saw him, they praised their
god; for they said:

"Our god has delivered into our hands our
enemy,
The destroyer of our land,
And the one who multiplied our dead."

[25]So it happened, when their hearts were merry,
that they said, "Call for Samson, that he may
perform for us." So they called for Samson from
the prison, and he performed for them. And they
stationed him between the pillars. [26]Then Sam-
son said to the lad who held him by the hand,
"Let me feel the pillars which support the tem-
ple, so that I can lean on them." [27]Now the tem-
ple was full of men and women. All the lords of
the Philistines *were* there—about three thou-
sand men and women on the roof watching
while Samson performed.

[28]Then Samson called to the LORD, saying, "O
Lord GOD, remember me, I pray! Strengthen me,
I pray, just this once, O God, that I may with one
blow take vengeance on the Philistines for my
two eyes!"

16:19 [a]Following Masoretic Text, Targum, and Vulgate; Septuagint reads *he began to be weak*.

THE MESSAGE

now you've toyed with me, like a cat with a
mouse, refusing to tell me the secret of your
great strength."

16-17 She kept at it day after day, nagging and
tormenting him. Finally, he was fed up—he
couldn't take another minute of it. He
spilled it.

He told her, "A razor has never touched
my head. I've been God's Nazirite from con-
ception. If I were shaved, my strength would
leave me; I would be as helpless as any
other mortal."

18 When Delilah realized that he had told
her his secret, she sent for the Philistine
tyrants, telling them, "Come quickly—this
time he's told me the truth." They came,
bringing the bribe money.

19 When she got him to sleep, his head on her
lap, she motioned to a man to cut off the seven
braids of his hair. Immediately he began to
grow weak. His strength drained from him.

20 Then she said, "The Philistines are on
you, Samson!" He woke up, thinking, "I'll go
out, like always, and shake free." He didn't
realize that GOD had abandoned him.

21-22 The Philistines grabbed him, gouged out
his eyes, and took him down to Gaza. They
shackled him in irons and put him to the
work of grinding in the prison. But his hair,
though cut off, began to grow again.

23-24 The Philistine tyrants got together to of-
fer a great sacrifice to their god Dagon.
They celebrated, saying,

Our god has given us
Samson our enemy!

And when the people saw him, they joined
in, cheering their god,

Our god has given
Our enemy to us,
The one who ravaged our country,
Piling high the corpses among us.

25-27 Then this: Everyone was feeling high and
someone said, "Get Samson! Let him show
us his stuff!" They got Samson from the
prison and he put on a show for them.

They had him standing between the pil-
lars. Samson said to the young man who
was acting as his guide, "Put me where I can
touch the pillars that hold up the temple so
I can rest against them." The building was
packed with men and women, including all
the Philistine tyrants. And there were at
least three thousand in the stands watching
Samson's performance.

28 And Samson cried out to GOD:

Master, GOD!
Oh, please, look on me again,
Oh, please, give strength yet once
more.

God!
With one avenging blow let me be
avenged
On the Philistines for my two eyes!

NEW KING JAMES VERSION

29 And Samson took hold of the two middle pillars
which supported the temple, and he braced him-
self against them, one on his right and the other
on his left. 30 Then Samson said, "Let me die with
the Philistines!" And he pushed with *all his* might,
and the temple fell on the lords and all the people
who *were* in it. So the dead that he killed at his
death were more than he had killed in his life.
31 And his brothers and all his father's house-
hold came down and took him, and brought *him*
up and buried him between Zorah and Eshtaol
in the tomb of his father Manoah. He had judged
Israel twenty years.

MICAH'S IDOLATRY

17 Now there was a man from the mountains
of Ephraim, whose name *was* Micah. 2 And
he said to his mother, "The eleven hundred
shekels of silver that were taken from you, and
on which you put a curse, even saying it in my
ears—here *is* the silver with me; I took it."
And his mother said, "*May you be* blessed by
the LORD, my son!" 3 So when he had returned
the eleven hundred *shekels* of silver to his
mother, his mother said, "I had wholly dedicated
the silver from my hand to the LORD for my son,
to make a carved image and a molded image;
now therefore, I will return it to you." 4 Thus he
returned the silver to his mother. Then his
mother took two hundred *shekels* of silver and
gave them to the silversmith, and he made it into
a carved image and a molded image; and they
were in the house of Micah.
5 The man Micah had a shrine, and made an
ephod and household idols;[a] and he consecrated
one of his sons, who became his priest. 6 In those
days *there was* no king in Israel; everyone did
what was right in his own eyes.
7 Now there was a young man from Bethle-
hem in Judah, of the family of Judah; he *was* a
Levite, and was staying there. 8 The man de-
parted from the city of Bethlehem in Judah to
stay wherever he could find *a place*. Then he
came to the mountains of Ephraim, to the house
of Micah, as he journeyed. 9 And Micah said to
him, "Where do you come from?"
So he said to him, "I *am* a Levite from Beth-
lehem in Judah, and I am on my way to find *a*
place to stay."
10 Micah said to him, "Dwell with me, and be
a father and a priest to me, and I will give you
ten *shekels* of silver per year, a suit of clothes,
and your sustenance." So the Levite went in.
11 Then the Levite was content to dwell with the
man; and the young man became like one of his
sons to him. 12 So Micah consecrated the Levite,
and the young man became his priest, and lived
in the house of Micah. 13 Then Micah said, "Now
I know that the LORD will be good to me, since I
have a Levite as priest!"

17:5 [a]Hebrew *teraphim*

THE MESSAGE

29-30 Then Samson reached out to the two cen-
tral pillars that held up the building and
pushed against them, one with his right
arm, the other with his left. Saying, "Let me
die with the Philistines," Samson pushed
hard with all his might. The building
crashed on the tyrants and all the people in
it. He killed more people in his death than
he had killed in his life.

31 His brothers and all his relatives went down
to get his body. They carried him back and
buried him in the tomb of Manoah his fa-
ther, between Zorah and Eshtaol.
He judged Israel for twenty years.

MICAH

1-2 17 There was a man from the hill country
of Ephraim named Micah. He said to
his mother, "Remember that 1,100 pieces of
silver that were taken from you? I overheard
you when you pronounced your curse. Well,
I have the money; I stole it. But now I've
brought it back to you."
His mother said, "GOD bless you, my
son!"
3-4 As he returned the 1,100 silver pieces to
his mother, she said, "I had totally conse-
crated this money to GOD for my son to
make a statue, a cast god." Then she took
200 pieces of the silver and gave it to a
sculptor and he cast them into the form of a
god.
5 This man, Micah, had a private chapel.
He had made an ephod and some teraphim-
idols and had ordained one of his sons to be
his priest.
6 In those days there was no king in Israel.
People did whatever they felt like doing.

7-8 Meanwhile there was a young man from
Bethlehem in Judah and from a family of Ju-
dah. He was a Levite but was a stranger
there. He left that town, Bethlehem in Ju-
dah, seeking his fortune. He got as far as the
hill country of Ephraim and showed up at
Micah's house.
9 Micah asked him, "So where are you
from?"
He said, "I'm a Levite from Bethlehem in
Judah. I'm on the road, looking for a place
to settle down."
10 Micah said, "Stay here with me. Be my fa-
ther and priest. I'll pay you ten pieces of sil-
ver a year, whatever clothes you need, and
your meals."
11-12 The Levite agreed and moved in with
Micah. The young man fit right in and be-
came one of the family. Micah appointed the
young Levite as his priest. This all took
place in Micah's home.
13 Micah said, "Now I know that GOD will
make things go well for me—why, I've got a
Levite for a priest!"

NEW KING JAMES VERSION

THE DANITES ADOPT MICAH'S IDOLATRY

18 In those days *there was* no king in Israel. And in those days the tribe of the Danites was seeking an inheritance for itself to dwell in; for until that day *their* inheritance among the tribes of Israel had not fallen to them. 2 So the children of Dan sent five men of their family from their territory, men of valor from Zorah and Eshtaol, to spy out the land and search it. They said to them, "Go, search the land." So they went to the mountains of Ephraim, to the house of Micah, and lodged there. 3 While they *were* at the house of Micah, they recognized the voice of the young Levite. They turned aside and said to him, "Who brought you here? What are you doing in this *place*? What do you have here?"

4 He said to them, "Thus and so Micah did for me. He has hired me, and I have become his priest."

5 So they said to him, "Please inquire of God, that we may know whether the journey on which we go will be prosperous."

6 And the priest said to them, "Go in peace. The presence of the LORD *be* with you on your way."

7 So the five men departed and went to Laish. They saw the people who *were* there, how they dwelt safely, in the manner of the Sidonians, quiet and secure. *There were* no rulers in the land who might put *them* to shame for anything. They *were* far from the Sidonians, and they had no ties with anyone.[a]

8 Then *the spies* came back to their brethren at Zorah and Eshtaol, and their brethren said to them, "What *is* your *report?*"

9 So they said, "Arise, let us go up against them. For we have seen the land, and indeed it *is* very good. *Would* you *do* nothing? Do not hesitate to go, *and* enter to possess the land. 10 When you go, you will come to a secure people and a large land. For God has given it into your hands, a place where *there is* no lack of anything that *is* on the earth."

11 And six hundred men of the family of the Danites went from there, from Zorah and Eshtaol, armed with weapons of war. 12 Then they went up and encamped in Kirjath Jearim in Judah. (Therefore they call that place Mahaneh Dan[a] to this day. There *it is,* west of Kirjath Jearim.) 13 And they passed from there to the mountains of Ephraim, and came to the house of Micah.

14 Then the five men who had gone to spy out the country of Laish answered and said to their brethren, "Do you know that there are in these houses an ephod, household idols, a carved image, and a molded image? Now therefore, consider what you should do." 15 So they turned aside there, and came to the house of the young Levite man—to the house of Micah—and greeted him. 16 The six hundred men armed with their weapons of war, who *were* of the children of Dan, stood by the entrance of the gate. 17 Then the five men who had gone to spy out the land went up. Entering there, they took the carved image, the ephod, the household idols, and the molded image. The priest stood at the entrance

18:7 [a]Following Masoretic Text, Targum, and Vulgate; Septuagint reads *with Syria.* **18:12** [a]Literally *Camp of Dan*

THE MESSAGE

1 18 In those days there was no king in Israel. But also in those days, the tribe of Dan was looking for a place to settle down. They hadn't yet occupied their plot among the tribes of Israel.

2-3 The Danites sent out five robust warriors from Zorah and Eshtaol to look over the land and see what was out there suitable for their families. They said, "Go and explore the land."

They went into the hill country of Ephraim and got as far as the house of Micah. They camped there for the night. As they neared Micah's house, they recognized the voice of the young Levite. They went over and said to him, "How on earth did you get here? What's going on? What are you doing here?"

4 He said, "One thing led to another: Micah hired me and I'm now his priest."

5 They said, "Oh, good—inquire of God for us. Find out whether our mission will be a success."

6 The priest said, "Go assured. GOD's looking out for you all the way."

7 The five men left and headed north to Laish. They saw that the people there were living in safety under the umbrella of the Sidonians, quiet and unsuspecting. They had everything going for them. But the people lived a long way from the Sidonians to the west and had no treaty with the Arameans to the east.

8 When they got back to Zorah and Eshtaol, their brothers asked, "So, how did you find things?"

9-10 They said, "Let's go for it! Let's attack. We've seen the land and it is excellent. Are you going to just sit on your hands? Don't dawdle! Invade and conquer! When you get there, you'll find they're sitting ducks, totally unsuspecting. Wide open land—God is handing it over to you, everything you could ever ask for."

11-13 So six hundred Danite men set out from Zorah and Eshtaol, armed to the teeth. Along the way they made camp at Kiriath Jearim in Judah. That is why the place is still today called Dan's Camp—it's just west of Kiriath Jearim. From there they proceeded into the hill country of Ephraim and came to Micah's house.

14 The five men who earlier had explored the country of Laish told their companions, "Did you know there's an ephod, teraphim-idols, and a cast god-sculpture in these buildings? What do you think? Do you want to do something about it?"

15-18 So they turned off the road there, went to the house of the young Levite at Micah's place and asked how things had been with him. The six hundred Danites, all well-armed, stood guard at the entrance to the gate while the five scouts who had gone to explore the land went in and took the carved idol, the ephod, the teraphim-idols, and the god-sculpture. The priest was stand-

New King James Version

of the gate with the six hundred men *who were*
armed with weapons of war.
18When these went into Micah's house and
took the carved image, the ephod, the household
idols, and the molded image, the priest said to
them, "What are you doing?"
19And they said to him, "Be quiet, put your
hand over your mouth, and come with us; be a
father and a priest to us. *Is it* better for you to be
a priest to the household of one man, or that you
be a priest to a tribe and a family in Israel?" 20So
the priest's heart was glad; and he took the
ephod, the household idols, and the carved im-
age, and took his place among the people.
21Then they turned and departed, and put the
little ones, the livestock, and the goods in front
of them. 22When they were a good way from the
house of Micah, the men who *were* in the houses
near Micah's house gathered together and over-
took the children of Dan. 23And they called out
to the children of Dan. So they turned around
and said to Micah, "What ails you, that you have
gathered such a company?"
24So he said, "You have taken away my gods
which I made, and the priest, and you have gone
away. Now what more do I have? How can you
say to me, 'What ails you?' "
25And the children of Dan said to him, "Do
not let your voice be heard among us, lest angry
men fall upon you, and you lose your life, with
the lives of your household!" 26Then the children
of Dan went their way. And when Micah saw
that they *were* too strong for him, he turned and
went back to his house.

Danites Settle in Laish

27So they took *the things* Micah had made,
and the priest who had belonged to him, and
went to Laish, to a people quiet and secure; and
they struck them with the edge of the sword and
burned the city with fire. 28*There was* no deliv-
erer, because it *was* far from Sidon, and they
had no ties with anyone. It was in the valley that
belongs to Beth Rehob. So they rebuilt the city
and dwelt there. 29And they called the name of
the city Dan, after the name of Dan their father,
who was born to Israel. However, the name of
the city formerly *was* Laish.
30Then the children of Dan set up for them-
selves the carved image; and Jonathan the son
of Gershom, the son of Manasseh,[a] and his sons
were priests to the tribe of Dan until the day of
the captivity of the land. 31So they set up for
themselves Micah's carved image which he
made, all the time that the house of God was in
Shiloh.

The Levite's Concubine

19 And it came to pass in those days, when
there was no king in Israel, that there was
a certain Levite staying in the remote moun-
tains of Ephraim. He took for himself a concu-
bine from Bethlehem in Judah. 2But his concu-
bine played the harlot against him, and went
away from him to her father's house at Bethle-
hem in Judah, and was there four whole

18:30 [a]Septuagint and Vulgate read *Moses.*

The Message

ing at the gate entrance with the six hun-
dred armed men. When the five went into
Micah's house and took the carved idol, the
ephod, the teraphim-idols, and the sculpted
god, the priest said to them, "What do you
think you're doing?"
19 They said to him, "Hush! Don't make a
sound. Come with us. Be our father and
priest. Which is more important, that you be
a priest to one man or that you become
priest to a whole tribe and clan in Israel?"
20 The priest jumped at the chance. He took
the ephod, the teraphim-idols, and the idol
and fell in with the troops.
21-23 They turned away and set out, putting the
children, the cattle, and the gear in the lead.
They were well on their way from Micah's
house before Micah and his neighbors got
organized. But they soon overtook the Dan-
ites. They shouted at them. The Danites
turned around and said, "So what's all the
noise about?"
24 Micah said, "You took my god, the one I
made, and you took my priest. And you
marched off! What do I have left? How can
you now say, 'What's the matter?' "
25 But the Danites answered, "Don't yell at
us; you just might provoke some fierce, hot-
tempered men to attack you, and you'll end
up an army of dead men."
26 The Danites went on their way. Micah
saw that he didn't stand a chance against
their arms. He turned back and went home.

27 So they took the things that Micah had
made, along with his priest, and they ar-
rived at Laish, that city of quiet and unsus-
pecting people. They massacred the people
and burned down the city.
28-29 There was no one around to help. They
were a long way from Sidon and had no
treaty with the Arameans. Laish was in the
valley of Beth Rehob. When they rebuilt the
city they renamed it Dan after their ances-
tor who was a son of Israel, but its original
name was Laish.
30-31 The Danites set up the god-figure for
themselves. Jonathan son of Gershom, the
son of Moses, and his descendants were
priests to the tribe of Dan down to the time
of the land's captivity. All during the time
that there was a sanctuary of God in Shiloh,
they kept for their private use the god-figure
that Micah had made.

The Levite

1-4 19 It was an era when there was no king
in Israel. A Levite, living as a stranger
in the backwoods hill country of Ephraim,
got himself a concubine, a woman from
Bethlehem in Judah. But she quarreled with
him and left, returning to her father's house
in Bethlehem in Judah. She was there four

New King James Version

months. 3Then her husband arose and went af-
ter her, to speak kindly to her *and* bring her
back, having his servant and a couple of don-
keys with him. So she brought him into her fa-
ther's house; and when the father of the young
woman saw him, he was glad to meet him. 4Now
his father-in-law, the young woman's father, de-
tained him; and he stayed with him three days.
So they ate and drank and lodged there.
5Then it came to pass on the fourth day that
they arose early in the morning, and he stood to
depart; but the young woman's father said to his
son-in-law, "Refresh your heart with a morsel of
bread, and afterward go your way."
6So they sat down, and the two of them ate
and drank together. Then the young woman's
father said to the man, "Please be content to
stay all night, and let your heart be merry." 7And
when the man stood to depart, his father-in-law
urged him; so he lodged there again. 8Then he
arose early in the morning on the fifth day to de-
part, but the young woman's father said, "Please
refresh your heart." So they delayed until after-
noon; and both of them ate.
9And when the man stood to depart—he and
his concubine and his servant—his father-in-
law, the young woman's father, said to him,
"Look, the day is now drawing toward evening;
please spend the night. See, the day is coming to
an end; lodge here, that your heart may be
merry. Tomorrow go your way early, so that you
may get home."
10However, the man was not willing to spend
that night; so he rose and departed, and came
opposite Jebus (that *is,* Jerusalem). With him
were the two saddled donkeys; his concubine
was also with him. 11They *were* near Jebus, and
the day was far spent; and the servant said to
his master, "Come, please, and let us turn aside
into this city of the Jebusites and lodge in it."
12But his master said to him, "We will not
turn aside here into a city of foreigners, who *are*
not of the children of Israel; we will go on to
Gibeah." 13So he said to his servant, "Come, let
us draw near to one of these places, and spend
the night in Gibeah or in Ramah." 14And they
passed by and went their way; and the sun went
down on them near Gibeah, which belongs to
Benjamin. 15They turned aside there to go in to
lodge in Gibeah. And when he went in, he sat
down in the open square of the city, for no one
would take them into *his* house to spend the
night.
16Just then an old man came in from his
work in the field at evening, who also *was* from
the mountains of Ephraim; he was staying in
Gibeah, whereas the men of the place *were* Ben-
jamites. 17And when he raised his eyes, he saw
the traveler in the open square of the city; and
the old man said, "Where are you going, and
where do you come from?"
18So he said to him, "We *are* passing from
Bethlehem in Judah toward the remote moun-
tains of Ephraim; I *am* from there. I went to
Bethlehem in Judah; *now* I am going to the
house of the LORD. But there *is* no one who will
take me into his house, 19although we have both
straw and fodder for our donkeys, and bread

The Message

months. Then her husband decided to go after her and try to win her back. He had a servant and a pair of donkeys with him. When he arrived at her father's house, the girl's father saw him, welcomed him, and made him feel at home. His father-in-law, the girl's father, pressed him to stay. He stayed with him three days; they feasted and drank and slept.

5-6 On the fourth day, they got up at the crack of dawn and got ready to go. But the girl's father said to his son-in-law, "Strengthen yourself with a hearty breakfast and then you can go." So they sat down and ate breakfast together.

6-7 The girl's father said to the man, "Come now, be my guest. Stay the night—make it a holiday." The man got up to go, but his father-in-law kept after him, so he ended up spending another night.

8-9 On the fifth day, he was again up early, ready to go. The girl's father said, "You need some breakfast." They went back and forth, and the day slipped on as they ate and drank together. But the man and his concubine were finally ready to go. Then his father-in-law, the girl's father, said, "Look, the day's almost gone—why not stay the night? There's very little daylight left; stay another night and enjoy yourself. Tomorrow you can get an early start and set off for your own place."

10-11 But this time the man wasn't willing to spend another night. He got things ready, left, and went as far as Jebus (Jerusalem) with his pair of saddled donkeys, his concubine, and his servant. At Jebus, though, the day was nearly gone. The servant said to his master, "It's late; let's go into this Jebusite city and spend the night."

12-13 But his master said, "We're not going into any city of foreigners. We'll go on to Gibeah." He directed his servant, "Keep going. Let's go on ahead. We'll spend the night either at Gibeah or Ramah."

14-15 So they kept going. As they pressed on, the sun finally left them in the vicinity of Gibeah, which belongs to Benjamin. They left the road there to spend the night at Gibeah.

15-17 The Levite went and sat down in the town square, but no one invited them in to spend the night. Then, late in the evening, an old man came in from his day's work in the fields. He was from the hill country of Ephraim and lived temporarily in Gibeah where all the local citizens were Benjaminites. When the old man looked up and saw the traveler in the town square, he said, "Where are you going? And where are you from?"

18-19 The Levite said, "We're just passing through. We're coming from Bethlehem on our way to a remote spot in the hills of Ephraim. I come from there. I've just made a trip to Bethlehem in Judah and I'm on my way back home, but no one has invited us in for the night. We wouldn't be any trouble: We have food and straw for the donkeys,

NEW KING JAMES VERSION

and wine for myself, for your female servant, and for the young man *who is* with your servant; *there is* no lack of anything."

20And the old man said, "Peace *be* with you! However, *let* all your needs *be* my responsibility; only do not spend the night in the open square." 21So he brought him into his house, and gave fodder to the donkeys. And they washed their feet, and ate and drank.

GIBEAH'S CRIME

22As they were enjoying themselves, suddenly certain men of the city, perverted men,[a] surrounded the house *and* beat on the door. They spoke to the master of the house, the old man, saying, "Bring out the man who came to your house, that we may know him *carnally!*"

23But the man, the master of the house, went out to them and said to them, "No, my brethren! I beg you, do not act *so* wickedly! Seeing this man has come into my house, do not commit this outrage. 24Look, *here is* my virgin daughter and *the man's*[a] concubine; let me bring them out now. Humble them, and do with them as you please; but to this man do not do such a vile thing!" 25But the men would not heed him. So the man took his concubine and brought *her* out to them. And they knew her and abused her all night until morning; and when the day began to break, they let her go.

26Then the woman came as the day was dawning, and fell down at the door of the man's house where her master *was,* till it was light.

27When her master arose in the morning, and opened the doors of the house and went out to go his way, there was his concubine, fallen *at* the door of the house with her hands on the threshold. 28And he said to her, "Get up and let us be going." But there was no answer. So the man lifted her onto the donkey; and the man got up and went to his place.

29When he entered his house he took a knife, laid hold of his concubine, and divided her into twelve pieces, limb by limb,[a] and sent her throughout all the territory of Israel. 30And so it was that all who saw it said, "No such deed has been done or seen from the day that the children of Israel came up from the land of Egypt until this day. Consider it, confer, and speak up!"

ISRAEL'S WAR WITH THE BENJAMITES

20 So all the children of Israel came out, from Dan to Beersheba, as well as from the land of Gilead, and the congregation gathered together as one man before the LORD at Mizpah. 2And the leaders of all the people, all the tribes of Israel, presented themselves in the assembly of the people of God, four hundred thousand foot soldiers who drew the sword. 3(Now the children of Benjamin heard that the children of Israel had gone up to Mizpah.)

Then the children of Israel said, "Tell *us,* how did this wicked deed happen?"

4So the Levite, the husband of the woman who was murdered, answered and said, "My

19:22 [a]Literally *sons of Belial* **19:24** [a]Literally *his* **19:29** [a]Literally *with her bones*

THE MESSAGE

and bread and wine for the woman, the
young man, and me—we don't need any-
thing."
20-21 The old man said, "It's going to be all
right; I'll take care of you. You aren't going
to spend the night in the town square." He
took them home and fed the donkeys. They
washed up and sat down to a good meal.
22 They were relaxed and enjoying them-
selves when the men of the city, a gang of lo-
cal hell-raisers all, surrounded the house
and started pounding on the door. They
yelled for the owner of the house, the old
man, "Bring out the man who came to your
house. We want to have sex with him."
23-24 He went out and told them, "No, brothers!
Don't be obscene—this man is my guest.
Don't commit this outrage. Look, my virgin
daughter and his concubine are here. I'll
bring them out for you. Abuse them if you
must, but don't do anything so senselessly
vile to this man."
25-26 But the men wouldn't listen to him. Fi-
nally, the Levite pushed his concubine out
the door to them. They raped her repeatedly
all night long. Just before dawn they let her
go. The woman came back and fell at the
door of the house where her master was
sleeping. When the sun rose, there she was.
27 It was morning. Her master got up and
opened the door to continue his journey.
There she was, his concubine, crumpled in a
heap at the door, her hands on the thresh-
old.
28 "Get up," he said. "Let's get going." There
was no answer.
29-30 He lifted her onto his donkey and set out
for home. When he got home he took a knife
and dismembered his concubine—cut her
into twelve pieces. He sent her, piece by
piece, throughout the country of Israel. And
he ordered the men he sent out, "Say to
every man in Israel: 'Has such a thing as this
ever happened from the time the Israelites
came up from the land of Egypt until now?
Think about it! Talk it over. Do something!' "

1-2 20 Then all the People of Israel came out.
The congregation met in the presence
of GOD at Mizpah. They were all there, from
Dan to Beersheba, as one person! The lead-
ers of all the people, representing all the
tribes of Israel, took their places in the gath-
ering of God's people. There were four hun-
dred divisions of sword-wielding infantry.
3 Meanwhile the Benjaminites got wind
that the Israelites were meeting at Mizpah.
The People of Israel said, "Now tell us.
How did this outrageous evil happen?"
4-7 The Levite, the husband of the murdered
woman, spoke: "My concubine and I came

New King James Version

concubine and I went into Gibeah, which belongs to Benjamin, to spend the night. 5And the men of Gibeah rose against me, and surrounded the house at night because of me. They intended to kill me, but instead they ravished my concubine so that she died. 6So I took hold of my concubine, cut her in pieces, and sent her throughout all the territory of the inheritance of Israel, because they committed lewdness and outrage in Israel. 7Look! All of you *are* children of Israel; give your advice and counsel here and now!"

8So all the people arose as one man, saying, "None *of us* will go to his tent, nor will any turn back to his house; 9but now this *is* the thing which we will do to Gibeah: *We will go up* against it by lot. 10We will take ten men out of *every* hundred throughout all the tribes of Israel, a hundred out of *every* thousand, and a thousand out of *every* ten thousand, to make provisions for the people, that when they come to Gibeah in Benjamin, they may repay all the vileness that they have done in Israel." 11So all the men of Israel were gathered against the city, united together as one man.

12Then the tribes of Israel sent men through all the tribe of Benjamin, saying, "What *is* this wickedness that has occurred among you? 13Now therefore, deliver up the men, the perverted men[a] who *are* in Gibeah, that we may put them to death and remove the evil from Israel!" But the children of Benjamin would not listen to the voice of their brethren, the children of Israel. 14Instead, the children of Benjamin gathered together from their cities to Gibeah, to go to battle against the children of Israel. 15And from their cities at that time the children of Benjamin numbered twenty-six thousand men who drew the sword, besides the inhabitants of Gibeah, who numbered seven hundred select men. 16Among all this people *were* seven hundred select men *who were* left-handed; every one could sling a stone at a hair's *breadth* and not miss. 17Now besides Benjamin, the men of Israel numbered four hundred thousand men who drew the sword; all of these *were* men of war.

18Then the children of Israel arose and went up to the house of God[a] to inquire of God. They said, "Which of us shall go up first to battle against the children of Benjamin?"

The LORD said, "Judah first!"

19So the children of Israel rose in the morning and encamped against Gibeah. 20And the men of Israel went out to battle against Benjamin, and the men of Israel put themselves in battle array to fight against them at Gibeah. 21Then the children of Benjamin came out of Gibeah, and on that day cut down to the ground twenty-two thousand men of the Israelites. 22And the people, that is, the men of Israel, encouraged themselves and again formed the battle line at the place where they had put themselves in array on the first day. 23Then the children of Israel went up and wept before the LORD until evening, and asked counsel of the LORD, saying, "Shall I again draw near for battle against the children of my brother Benjamin?"

And the LORD said, "Go up against him."

20:13 [a]Literally *sons of Belial* **20:18** [a]Or *Bethel*

The Message

to spend the night at Gibeah, a Benjaminite town. That night the men of Gibeah came after me. They surrounded the house, intending to kill me. They gang-raped my concubine and she died. So I took my concubine, cut up her body, and sent her piece by piece—twelve pieces!—to every part of Israel's inheritance. This vile and outrageous crime was committed *in Israel!* So, Israelites, make up your minds. Decide on some action!"

8-11 All the people were at once and as one person on their feet. "None of us will go home; not a single one of us will go to his own house. Here's our plan for dealing with Gibeah: We'll march against it by drawing lots. We'll take ten of every hundred men from all the tribes of Israel (a hundred of every thousand, and a thousand of every ten thousand) to carry food for the army. When the troops arrive at Gibeah they will settle accounts for this outrageous and vile evil that was done in Israel." So all the men in Israel were gathered against the city, totally united.

12-13 The Israelite tribes sent messengers throughout the tribe of Benjamin saying, "What's the meaning of this outrage that took place among you? Surrender the men right here and now, these hell-raisers of Gibeah. We'll put them to death and burn the evil out of Israel."

13-16 But they wouldn't do it. The Benjaminites refused to listen to their brothers, the People of Israel. Instead they raised an army from all their cities and rallied at Gibeah to go to war against the People of Israel. In no time at all they had recruited from their cities twenty-six divisions of sword-wielding infantry. From Gibeah they got seven hundred hand-picked fighters, the best. There were another seven hundred supermarksmen who were ambidextrous—they could sling a stone at a hair and not miss.

17 The men of Israel, excluding Benjamin, mobilized four hundred divisions of sword-wielding fighting men.

18 They set out and went to Bethel to inquire of God. The People of Israel said, "Who of us shall be first to go into battle with the Benjaminites?"

GOD said, "Judah goes first."

19-21 The People of Israel got up the next morning and camped before Gibeah. The army of Israel marched out against Benjamin and took up their positions, ready to attack Gibeah. But the Benjaminites poured out of Gibeah and devastated twenty-two Israelite divisions on the ground.

22-23 The Israelites went back to the sanctuary and wept before GOD until evening. They again inquired of GOD, "Shall we again go into battle against the Benjaminites, our brothers?"

GOD said, "Yes. Attack."

NEW KING JAMES VERSION

24So the children of Israel approached the children of Benjamin on the second day. 25And Benjamin went out against them from Gibeah on the second day, and cut down to the ground eighteen thousand more of the children of Israel; all these drew the sword.

26Then all the children of Israel, that is, all the people, went up and came to the house of God[a] and wept. They sat there before the LORD and fasted that day until evening; and they offered burnt offerings and peace offerings before the LORD. 27So the children of Israel inquired of the LORD (the ark of the covenant of God *was* there in those days, 28and Phinehas the son of Eleazar, the son of Aaron, stood before it in those days), saying, "Shall I yet again go out to battle against the children of my brother Benjamin, or shall I cease?"

And the LORD said, "Go up, for tomorrow I will deliver them into your hand."

29Then Israel set men in ambush all around Gibeah. 30And the children of Israel went up against the children of Benjamin on the third day, and put themselves in battle array against Gibeah as at the other times. 31So the children of Benjamin went out against the people, *and* were drawn away from the city. They began to strike down *and* kill some of the people, as at the other times, in the highways (one of which goes up to Bethel and the other to Gibeah) and in the field, about thirty men of Israel. 32And the children of Benjamin said, "They *are* defeated before us, as at first."

But the children of Israel said, "Let us flee and draw them away from the city to the highways." 33So all the men of Israel rose from their place and put themselves in battle array at Baal Tamar. Then Israel's men in ambush burst forth from their position in the plain of Geba. 34And ten thousand select men from all Israel came against Gibeah, and the battle was fierce. But *the Benjamites*[a] did not know that disaster *was* upon them. 35The LORD defeated Benjamin before Israel. And the children of Israel destroyed that day twenty-five thousand one hundred Benjamites; all these drew the sword.

36So the children of Benjamin saw that they were defeated. The men of Israel had given ground to the Benjamites, because they relied on the men in ambush whom they had set against Gibeah. 37And the men in ambush quickly rushed upon Gibeah; the men in ambush spread out and struck the whole city with the edge of the sword. 38Now the appointed signal between the men of Israel and the men in ambush was that they would make a great cloud of smoke rise up from the city, 39whereupon the men of Israel would turn in battle. Now Benjamin had begun to strike *and* kill about thirty of the men of Israel. For they said, "Surely they are defeated before us, as *in* the first battle." 40But when the cloud began to rise from the city in a column of smoke, the Benjamites looked behind them, and there was the whole city going up *in smoke* to heaven. 41And when the men of Israel turned back, the men of Benjamin pan-

20:26 [a]Or *Bethel* **20:34** [a]Literally *they*

THE MESSAGE

24-25 The army took heart. The men of Israel took up the positions they had deployed on the first day.

On the second day, the Israelites again advanced against Benjamin. This time as the Benjaminites came out of the city, on this second day, they devastated another eighteen Israelite divisions, all swordsmen.

26 All the People of Israel, the whole army, were back at Bethel, weeping, sitting there in the presence of GOD. That day they fasted until evening. They sacrificed Whole-Burnt-Offerings and Peace-Offerings before GOD.

27-28 And they again inquired of GOD. The Chest of God's Covenant was there at that time with Phinehas son of Eleazar, the son of Aaron, as the ministering priest. They asked, "Shall we again march into battle against the Benjaminites, our brothers? Or should we call it quits?"

And GOD said, "Attack. Tomorrow I'll give you victory."

29-31 This time Israel placed men in ambush all around Gibeah. On the third day when Israel set out, they took up the same positions before the Benjaminites as before. When the Benjaminites came out to meet the army, they moved out from the city. Benjaminites began to cut down some of the troops just as they had before. About thirty men fell in the field and on the roads to Bethel and Gibeah.

32 The Benjaminites started bragging, "We're dropping them like flies, just as before!"

33 But the Israelites strategized: "Now let's retreat and pull them out of the city onto the main roads." So every Israelite moved farther out to Baal Tamar; at the same time the Israelite ambush rushed from its place west of Gibeah.

34-36 Ten crack divisions from all over Israel now arrived at Gibeah—intense, bloody fighting! The Benjaminites had no idea that they were about to go down in defeat—GOD routed them before Israel. The Israelites decimated twenty-five divisions of Benjamin that day—25,100 killed. They were all swordsmen. The Benjaminites saw that they were beaten.

The men of Israel acted like they were retreating before Benjamin, knowing that they could depend on the ambush they had prepared for Gibeah.

37-40 The ambush erupted and made quick work of Gibeah. The ambush spread out and massacred the city. The strategy for the main body of the ambush was that they send up a smoke signal from the city. Then the men of Israel would turn in battle. When that happened, Benjamin had killed about thirty Israelites and thought they were on their way to victory, yelling out, "They're on the run, just as in the first battle!" But then the signal went up from the city—a huge column of smoke. When the Benjaminites looked back, there it was, the whole city going up in smoke.

41-43 By the time the men of Israel had turned back on them, the men of Benjamin fell

NEW KING JAMES VERSION

icked, for they saw that disaster had come upon them. 42Therefore they turned *their backs* before the men of Israel in the direction of the wilderness; but the battle overtook them, and whoever *came* out of the cities they destroyed in their midst. 43They surrounded the Benjamites, chased them, *and* easily trampled them down as far as the front of Gibeah toward the east. 44And eighteen thousand men of Benjamin fell; all these *were* men of valor. 45Then they[a] turned and fled toward the wilderness to the rock of Rimmon; and they cut down five thousand of them on the highways. Then they pursued them relentlessly up to Gidom, and killed two thousand of them. 46So all who fell of Benjamin that day were twenty-five thousand men who drew the sword; all these *were* men of valor.

47But six hundred men turned and fled toward the wilderness to the rock of Rimmon, and they stayed at the rock of Rimmon for four months. 48And the men of Israel turned back against the children of Benjamin, and struck them down with the edge of the sword—from *every* city, men and beasts, all who were found. They also set fire to all the cities they came to.

WIVES PROVIDED FOR THE BENJAMITES

21 Now the men of Israel had sworn an oath at Mizpah, saying, "None of us shall give his daughter to Benjamin as a wife." 2Then the people came to the house of God,[a] and remained there before God till evening. They lifted up their voices and wept bitterly, 3and said, "O LORD God of Israel, why has this come to pass in Israel, that today there should be one tribe *missing* in Israel?"

4So it was, on the next morning, that the people rose early and built an altar there, and offered burnt offerings and peace offerings. 5The children of Israel said, "Who *is there* among all the tribes of Israel who did not come up with the assembly to the LORD?" For they had made a great oath concerning anyone who had not come up to the LORD at Mizpah, saying, "He shall surely be put to death." 6And the children of Israel grieved for Benjamin their brother, and said, "One tribe is cut off from Israel today. 7What shall we do for wives for those who remain, seeing we have sworn by the LORD that we will not give them our daughters as wives?"

8And they said, "What one *is there* from the tribes of Israel who did not come up to Mizpah to the LORD?" And, in fact, no one had come to the camp from Jabesh Gilead to the assembly. 9For when the people were counted, indeed, not one of the inhabitants of Jabesh Gilead *was* there. 10So the congregation sent out there twelve thousand of their most valiant men, and commanded them, saying, "Go and strike the inhabitants of Jabesh Gilead with the edge of the sword, including the women and children. 11And this *is* the thing that you shall do: You shall utterly destroy every male, and every woman who

20:45 [a]Septuagint reads *the rest.* **21:2** [a]Or *Bethel*

THE MESSAGE

apart—they could see that they were trapped. Confronted by the Israelites, they tried to get away down the wilderness road, but by now the battle was everywhere. The men of Israel poured out of the towns, killing them right and left, hot on their trail, picking them off east of Gibeah.

44 Eighteen divisions of Benjaminites were wiped out, all their best fighters.

45 Five divisions turned to escape to the wilderness, to Rimmon Rock, but the Israelites caught and slaughtered them on roads.

Keeping the pressure on, the Israelites brought down two more divisions.

46 The total of the Benjaminites killed that day came to twenty-five divisions of infantry, their best swordsmen.

47 Six hundred men got away. They made it to Rimmon Rock in the wilderness and held out there for four months.

48 The men of Israel came back and killed all the Benjaminites who were left, all the men and animals they found in every town, and then torched the towns, sending them up in flames.

WIVES

1 21 Back at Mizpah the men of Israel had taken an oath: "No man among us will give his daughter to a Benjaminite in marriage."

2-3 Now, back in Bethel, the people sat in the presence of God until evening. They cried loudly; there was widespread lamentation. They said, "Why, O GOD, God of Israel, has this happened? Why do we find ourselves today missing one whole tribe from Israel?"

4 Early the next morning, the people got busy and built an altar. They sacrificed Whole-Burnt-Offerings and Peace-Offerings.

5 Then the Israelites said, "Who from all the tribes of Israel didn't show up as we gathered in the presence of GOD?" For they had all taken a sacred oath that anyone who had not gathered in the presence of GOD at Mizpah had to be put to death.

6-7 But the People of Israel were feeling sorry for Benjamin, their brothers. They said, "Today, one tribe is cut off from Israel. How can we get wives for those who are left? We have sworn by GOD not to give any of our daughters to them in marriage."

8-9 They said, "Which one of the tribes of Israel didn't gather before GOD at Mizpah?"

It turned out that no one had come to the gathering from Jabesh Gilead. When they took a roll call of the people, not a single person from Jabesh Gilead was there.

10-11 So the congregation sent twelve divisions of their top men there with the command, "Kill everyone of Jabesh Gilead, including women and children. These are your instructions: Every man and woman who has

New King James Version

has known a man intimately." 12So they found among the inhabitants of Jabesh Gilead four hundred young virgins who had not known a man intimately; and they brought them to the camp at Shiloh, which is in the land of Canaan.

13Then the whole congregation sent *word* to the children of Benjamin who *were* at the rock of Rimmon, and announced peace to them. 14So Benjamin came back at that time, and they gave them the women whom they had saved alive of the women of Jabesh Gilead; and yet they had not found enough for them.

15And the people grieved for Benjamin, because the LORD had made a void in the tribes of Israel.

16Then the elders of the congregation said, "What shall we do for wives for those who remain, since the women of Benjamin have been destroyed?" 17And they said, "*There must be* an inheritance for the survivors of Benjamin, that a tribe may not be destroyed from Israel. 18However, we cannot give them wives from our daughters, for the children of Israel have sworn an oath, saying, 'Cursed *be* the one who gives a wife to Benjamin.' " 19Then they said, "In fact, *there is* a yearly feast of the LORD in Shiloh, which *is* north of Bethel, on the east side of the highway that goes up from Bethel to Shechem, and south of Lebonah."

20Therefore they instructed the children of Benjamin, saying, "Go, lie in wait in the vineyards, 21and watch; and just when the daughters of Shiloh come out to perform their dances, then come out from the vineyards, and every man catch a wife for himself from the daughters of Shiloh; then go to the land of Benjamin. 22Then it shall be, when their fathers or their brothers come to us to complain, that we will say to them, 'Be kind to them for our sakes, because we did not take a wife for any of them in the war; for *it is* not *as though* you have given the *women* to them at this time, making yourselves guilty of your oath.' "

23And the children of Benjamin did so; they took enough wives for their number from those who danced, whom they caught. Then they went and returned to their inheritance, and they rebuilt the cities and dwelt in them. 24So the children of Israel departed from there at that time, every man to his tribe and family; they went out from there, every man to his inheritance.

25In those days *there was* no king in Israel; everyone did *what was* right in his own eyes.

The Message

had sexual intercourse you must kill. But keep the virgins alive." And that's what they did.

12 And they found four hundred virgins among those who lived in Jabesh Gilead; they had never had sexual intercourse with a man. And they brought them to the camp at Shiloh, which is in the land of Canaan.

13-14 Then the congregation sent word to the Benjaminites who were at the Rimmon Rock and offered them peace. And Benjamin came. They gave them the women they had let live at Jabesh Gilead. But even then, there weren't enough for all the men.

15 The people felt bad for Benjamin; GOD had left out Benjamin—the missing piece from the Israelite tribes.

16-18 The elders of the congregation said, "How can we get wives for the rest of the men, since all the Benjaminite women have been killed? How can we keep the inheritance alive for the Benjaminite survivors? How can we prevent an entire tribe from extinction? We certainly can't give our own daughters to them as wives." (Remember, the Israelites had taken the oath: "Cursed is anyone who provides a wife to Benjamin.")

19 Then they said, "There is that festival of GOD held every year in Shiloh. It's north of Bethel, just east of the main road that goes up from Bethel to Shechem and a little south of Lebonah."

20-22 So they told the Benjaminites, "Go and hide in the vineyards. Stay alert—when you see the Shiloh girls come out to dance the dances, run out of the vineyards, grab one of the Shiloh girls for your wife, and then hightail it back to the country of Benjamin. When their fathers or brothers come to lay charges against us, we'll tell them, 'We did them a favor. After all we didn't go to war and kill to get wives for men. And it wasn't as if you were in on it by giving consent. But if you keep this up, you will incur blame.' "

23 And that's what the Benjaminites did: They carried off girls from the dance, wives enough for their number, got away, and went home to their inheritance. They rebuilt their towns and settled down.

24 From there the People of Israel dispersed, each man heading back to his own tribe and clan, each to his own plot of land.

25 At that time there was no king in Israel. People did whatever they felt like doing.

RUTH

New King James Version

Elimelech's Family Goes to Moab

1 Now it came to pass, in the days when the judges ruled, that there was a famine in the land. And a certain man of Bethlehem, Judah, went to dwell in the country of Moab, he and his wife and his two sons. [2]The name of the man *was* Elimelech, the name of his wife *was* Naomi, and the names of his two sons *were* Mahlon and Chilion—Ephrathites of Bethlehem, Judah. And they went to the country of Moab and remained there. [3]Then Elimelech, Naomi's husband, died; and she was left, and her two sons. [4]Now they took wives of the women of Moab: the name of the one *was* Orpah, and the name of the other Ruth. And they dwelt there about ten years. [5]Then both Mahlon and Chilion also died; so the woman survived her two sons and her husband.

Naomi Returns with Ruth

[6]Then she arose with her daughters-in-law that she might return from the country of Moab, for she had heard in the country of Moab that the LORD had visited His people by giving them bread. [7]Therefore she went out from the place where she was, and her two daughters-in-law with her; and they went on the way to return to the land of Judah. [8]And Naomi said to her two daughters-in-law, "Go, return each to her mother's house. The LORD deal kindly with you, as you have dealt with the dead and with me. [9]The LORD grant that you may find rest, each in the house of her husband."

So she kissed them, and they lifted up their voices and wept. [10]And they said to her, "Surely we will return with you to your people."

[11]But Naomi said, "Turn back, my daughters; why will you go with me? *Are* there still sons in my womb, that they may be your husbands? [12]Turn back, my daughters, go—for I am too old to have a husband. If I should say I have hope, *if* I should have a husband tonight and should also bear sons, [13]would you wait for them till they were grown? Would you restrain yourselves from having husbands? No, my daughters; for it grieves me very much for your sakes that the hand of the LORD has gone out against me!"

[14]Then they lifted up their voices and wept again; and Orpah kissed her mother-in-law, but Ruth clung to her.

[15]And she said, "Look, your sister-in-law has gone back to her people and to her gods; return after your sister-in-law."

[16]But Ruth said:

"Entreat me not to leave you,
Or to turn back from following after you;
For wherever you go, I will go;
And wherever you lodge, I will lodge;
Your people *shall be* my people,
And your God, my God.
[17]Where you die, I will die,
And there will I be buried.
The LORD do so to me, and more also,
If *anything but* death parts you and me."

The Message

1-2 **1** Once upon a time—it was back in the days when judges led Israel—there was a famine in the land. A man from Bethlehem in Judah left home to live in the country of Moab, he and his wife and his two sons. The man's name was Elimelech; his wife's name was Naomi; his sons were named Mahlon and Kilion—all Ephrathites from Bethlehem in Judah. They all went to the country of Moab and settled there.

3-5 Elimelech died and Naomi was left, she and her two sons. The sons took Moabite wives; the name of the first was Orpah, the second Ruth. They lived there in Moab for the next ten years. But then the two brothers, Mahlon and Kilion, died. Now the woman was left without either her young men or her husband.

6-7 One day she got herself together, she and her two daughters-in-law, to leave the country of Moab and set out for home; she had heard that GOD had been pleased to visit his people and give them food. And so she started out from the place she had been living, she and her two daughters-in-law with her, on the road back to the land of Judah.

8-9 After a short while on the road, Naomi told her two daughters-in-law, "Go back. Go home and live with your mothers. And may GOD treat you as graciously as you treated your deceased husbands and me. May GOD give each of you a new home and a new husband!" She kissed them and they cried openly.

10 They said, "No, we're going on with you to your people."

11-13 But Naomi was firm: "Go back, my dear daughters. Why would you come with me? Do you suppose I still have sons in my womb who can become your future husbands? Go back, dear daughters—on your way, please! I'm too old to get a husband. Why, even if I said, 'There's still hope!' and this very night got a man and had sons, can you imagine being satisfied to wait until they were grown? Would you wait that long to get married again? No, dear daughters; this is a bitter pill for me to swallow—more bitter for me than for you. GOD has dealt me a hard blow."

14 Again they cried openly. Orpah kissed her mother-in-law good-bye; but Ruth embraced her and held on.

15 Naomi said, "Look, your sister-in-law is going back home to live with her own people and gods; go with her."

16-17 But Ruth said, "Don't force me to leave you; don't make me go home. Where you go, I go; and where you live, I'll live. Your people are my people, your God is my god; where you die, I'll die, and that's where I'll be buried, so help me GOD—not even death itself is going to come between us!"

New King James Version

18When she saw that she was determined to
go with her, she stopped speaking to her.
19Now the two of them went until they came
to Bethlehem. And it happened, when they had
come to Bethlehem, that all the city was excited
because of them; and the women said, "*Is* this
Naomi?"
20But she said to them, "Do not call me
Naomi;[a] call me Mara,[b] for the Almighty has
dealt very bitterly with me. 21I went out full, and
the LORD has brought me home again empty.
Why do you call me Naomi, since the LORD has
testified against me, and the Almighty has af-
flicted me?"
22So Naomi returned, and Ruth the
Moabitess her daughter-in-law with her, who re-
turned from the country of Moab. Now they
came to Bethlehem at the beginning of barley
harvest.

Ruth Meets Boaz

2 There was a relative of Naomi's husband, a
man of great wealth, of the family of Elim-
elech. His name *was* Boaz. 2So Ruth the
Moabitess said to Naomi, "Please let me go to
the field, and glean heads of grain after *him* in
whose sight I may find favor."
And she said to her, "Go, my daughter."
3Then she left, and went and gleaned in the
field after the reapers. And she happened to
come to the part of the field *belonging* to Boaz,
who *was* of the family of Elimelech.
4Now behold, Boaz came from Bethlehem,
and said to the reapers, "The LORD *be* with you!"
And they answered him, "The LORD bless
you!"
5Then Boaz said to his servant who was in
charge of the reapers, "Whose young woman *is*
this?"
6So the servant who was in charge of the
reapers answered and said, "It *is* the young
Moabite woman who came back with Naomi
from the country of Moab. 7And she said,
'Please let me glean and gather after the reapers
among the sheaves.' So she came and has con-
tinued from morning until now, though she
rested a little in the house."
8Then Boaz said to Ruth, "You will listen, my
daughter, will you not? Do not go to glean in an-
other field, nor go from here, but stay close by
my young women. 9*Let* your eyes *be* on the field
which they reap, and go after them. Have I not
commanded the young men not to touch you?
And when you are thirsty, go to the vessels and
drink from what the young men have drawn."
10So she fell on her face, bowed down to the
ground, and said to him, "Why have I found fa-
vor in your eyes, that you should take notice of
me, since I *am* a foreigner?"
11And Boaz answered and said to her, "It has
been fully reported to me, all that you have done
for your mother-in-law since the death of your
husband, and *how* you have left your father and
your mother and the land of your birth, and
have come to a people whom you did not know

1:20 [a]Literally *Pleasant* [b]Literally *Bitter*

The Message

18-19 When Naomi saw that Ruth had her heart
set on going with her, she gave in. And so
the two of them traveled on together to
Bethlehem.
When they arrived in Bethlehem the
whole town was soon buzzing: "Is this re-
ally our Naomi? And after all this time!"
20-21 But she said, "Don't call me Naomi; call
me Bitter. The Strong One has dealt me a
bitter blow. I left here full of life, and GOD
has brought me back with nothing but the
clothes on my back. Why would you call me
Naomi? God certainly doesn't. The Strong
One ruined me."
22 And so Naomi was back, and Ruth the
foreigner with her, back from the country of
Moab. They arrived in Bethlehem at the be-
ginning of the barley harvest.

1 2 It so happened that Naomi had a relative
by marriage, a man prominent and rich,
connected with Elimelech's family. His
name was Boaz.
2 One day Ruth, the Moabite foreigner, said
to Naomi, "I'm going to work; I'm going out
to glean among the sheaves, following after
some harvester who will treat me kindly."
Naomi said, "Go ahead, dear daughter."
3-4 And so she set out. She went and started
gleaning in a field, following in the wake of
the harvesters. Eventually she ended up in
the part of the field owned by Boaz, her fa-
ther-in-law Elimelech's relative. A little later
Boaz came out from Bethlehem, greeting his
harvesters, "GOD be with you!" They replied,
"And GOD bless you!"
5 Boaz asked his young servant who was
foreman over the farm hands, "Who is this
young woman? Where did she come from?"
6-7 The foreman said, "Why, that's the
Moabite girl, the one who came with Naomi
from the country of Moab. She asked per-
mission. 'Let me glean,' she said, 'and
gather among the sheaves following after
your harvesters.' She's been at it steady ever
since, from early morning until now, with-
out so much as a break."
8-9 Then Boaz spoke to Ruth: "Listen, my
daughter. From now on don't go to any other
field to glean—stay right here in this one.
And stay close to my young women. Watch
where they are harvesting and follow them.
And don't worry about a thing; I've given or-
ders to my servants not to harass you. When
you get thirsty, feel free to go and drink
from the water buckets that the servants
have filled."
10 She dropped to her knees, then bowed
her face to the ground. "How does this hap-
pen that you should pick me out and treat
me so kindly—*me*, a foreigner?"
11-12 Boaz answered her, "I've heard all about
you—heard about the way you treated your
mother-in-law after the death of her hus-
band, and how you left your father and
mother and the land of your birth and have
come to live among a bunch of total

NEW KING JAMES VERSION

before. [12]The LORD repay your work, and a full reward be given you by the LORD God of Israel, under whose wings you have come for refuge."

[13]Then she said, "Let me find favor in your sight, my lord; for you have comforted me, and have spoken kindly to your maidservant, though I am not like one of your maidservants."

[14]Now Boaz said to her at mealtime, "Come here, and eat of the bread, and dip your piece of bread in the vinegar." So she sat beside the reapers, and he passed parched *grain* to her; and she ate and was satisfied, and kept some back. [15]And when she rose up to glean, Boaz commanded his young men, saying, "Let her glean even among the sheaves, and do not reproach her. [16]Also let *grain* from the bundles fall purposely for her; leave *it* that she may glean, and do not rebuke her."

[17]So she gleaned in the field until evening, and beat out what she had gleaned, and it was about an ephah of barley. [18]Then she took *it* up and went into the city, and her mother-in-law saw what she had gleaned. So she brought out and gave to her what she had kept back after she had been satisfied.

[19]And her mother-in-law said to her, "Where have you gleaned today? And where did you work? Blessed be the one who took notice of you."

So she told her mother-in-law with whom she had worked, and said, "The man's name with whom I worked today *is* Boaz."

[20]Then Naomi said to her daughter-in-law, "Blessed *be* he of the LORD, who has not forsaken His kindness to the living and the dead!" And Naomi said to her, "This man *is* a relation of ours, one of our close relatives."

[21]Ruth the Moabitess said, "He also said to me, 'You shall stay close by my young men until they have finished all my harvest.' "

[22]And Naomi said to Ruth her daughter-in-law, "*It is* good, my daughter, that you go out with his young women, and that people do not meet you in any other field." [23]So she stayed close by the young women of Boaz, to glean until the end of barley harvest and wheat harvest; and she dwelt with her mother-in-law.

RUTH'S REDEMPTION ASSURED

3 Then Naomi her mother-in-law said to her, "My daughter, shall I not seek security for you, that it may be well with you? [2]Now Boaz, whose young women you were with, *is he* not our relative? In fact, he is winnowing barley tonight at the threshing floor. [3]Therefore wash yourself and anoint yourself, put on your *best* garment and go down to the threshing floor; *but* do not make yourself known to the man until he

THE MESSAGE

strangers. GOD reward you well for what you've done—and with a generous bonus besides from GOD, to whom you've come seeking protection under his wings."

13 She said, "Oh sir, such grace, such kindness—I don't deserve it. You've touched my heart, treated me like one of your own. And I don't even belong here!"

14 At the lunch break, Boaz said to her, "Come over here; eat some bread. Dip it in the wine."

So she joined the harvesters. Boaz passed the roasted grain to her. She ate her fill and even had some left over.

15-16 When she got up to go back to work, Boaz ordered his servants: "Let her glean where there's still plenty of grain on the ground—make it easy for her. Better yet, pull some of the good stuff out and leave it for her to glean. Give her special treatment."

17-18 Ruth gleaned in the field until evening. When she threshed out what she had gathered, she ended up with nearly a full sack of barley! She gathered up her gleanings, went back to town, and showed her mother-in-law the results of her day's work; she also gave her the leftovers from her lunch.

19 Naomi asked her, "So where did you glean today? Whose field? GOD bless whoever it was who took such good care of you!"

Ruth told her mother-in-law, "The man with whom I worked today? His name is Boaz."

20 Naomi said to her daughter-in-law, "Why, GOD bless that man! GOD hasn't quite walked out on us after all! He still loves us, in bad times as well as good!"

Naomi went on, "That man, Ruth, is one of our circle of covenant redeemers, a close relative of ours!"

21 Ruth the Moabitess said, "Well, listen to this: He also told me, 'Stick with my workers until my harvesting is finished.' "

22 Naomi said to Ruth, "That's wonderful, dear daughter! Do that! You'll be safe in the company of his young women; no danger now of being raped in some stranger's field."

23 So Ruth did it—she stuck close to Boaz's young women, gleaning in the fields daily until both the barley and wheat harvesting were finished. And she continued living with her mother-in-law.

1-2 3 One day her mother-in-law Naomi said to Ruth, "My dear daughter, isn't it about time I arranged a good home for you so you can have a happy life? And isn't Boaz our close relative, the one with whose young women you've been working? Maybe it's time to make our move. Tonight is the night of Boaz's barley harvest at the threshing floor.

3-4 "Take a bath. Put on some perfume. Get all dressed up and go to the threshing floor. But don't let him know you're there until the party is well under way and he's had plenty

NEW KING JAMES VERSION

has finished eating and drinking. [4]Then it shall be, when he lies down, that you shall notice the place where he lies; and you shall go in, uncover his feet, and lie down; and he will tell you what you should do."

[5]And she said to her, "All that you say to me I will do."

[6]So she went down to the threshing floor and did according to all that her mother-in-law instructed her. [7]And after Boaz had eaten and drunk, and his heart was cheerful, he went to lie down at the end of the heap of grain; and she came softly, uncovered his feet, and lay down.

[8]Now it happened at midnight that the man was startled, and turned himself; and there, a woman was lying at his feet. [9]And he said, "Who *are* you?"

So she answered, "I *am* Ruth, your maidservant. Take your maidservant under your wing,[a] for you are a close relative."

[10]Then he said, "Blessed *are* you of the LORD, my daughter! For you have shown more kindness at the end than at the beginning, in that you did not go after young men, whether poor or rich. [11]And now, my daughter, do not fear. I will do for you all that you request, for all the people of my town know that you *are* a virtuous woman. [12]Now it is true that I *am* a close relative; however, there is a relative closer than I. [13]Stay this night, and in the morning it shall be *that* if he will perform the duty of a close relative for you—good; let him do it. But if he does not want to perform the duty for you, then I will perform the duty for you, *as* the LORD lives! Lie down until morning."

[14]So she lay at his feet until morning, and she arose before one could recognize another. Then he said, "Do not let it be known that the woman came to the threshing floor." [15]Also he said, "Bring the shawl that *is* on you and hold it." And when she held it, he measured six *ephahs* of barley, and laid *it* on her. Then she[a] went into the city.

[16]When she came to her mother-in-law, she said, "*Is* that you, my daughter?"

Then she told her all that the man had done for her. [17]And she said, "These six *ephahs* of barley he gave me; for he said to me, 'Do not go empty-handed to your mother-in-law.' "

[18]Then she said, "Sit still, my daughter, until you know how the matter will turn out; for the man will not rest until he has concluded the matter this day."

3:9 [a]Or *Spread the corner of your garment over your maidservant* **3:15** [a]Many Hebrew manuscripts, Syriac, and Vulgate read *she;* Masoretic Text, Septuagint, and Targum read *he.*

THE MESSAGE

of food and drink. When you see him slipping off to sleep, watch where he lies down and then go there. Lie at his feet to let him know that you are available to him for marriage. Then wait and see what he says. He'll tell you what to do."

5 Ruth said, "If you say so, I'll do it, just as you've told me."

6 She went down to the threshing floor and put her mother-in-law's plan into action.

7 Boaz had a good time, eating and drinking his fill—he felt great. Then he went off to get some sleep, lying down at the end of a stack of barley. Ruth quietly followed; she lay down to signal her availability for marriage.

8 In the middle of the night the man was suddenly startled and sat up. Surprise! This woman asleep at his feet!

9 He said, "And who are you?"

She said, "I am Ruth, your maiden; take me under your protecting wing. You're my close relative, you know, in the circle of covenant redeemers—you do have the right to marry me."

10-13 He said, "GOD bless you, my dear daughter! What a splendid expression of love! And when you could have had your pick of any of the young men around. And now, my dear daughter, don't you worry about a thing; I'll do all you could want or ask. Everybody in town knows what a courageous woman you are—a real prize! You're right, I am a close relative to you, but there is one even closer than I am. So stay the rest of the night. In the morning, if he wants to exercise his customary rights and responsibilities as the closest covenant redeemer, he'll have his chance; but if he isn't interested, as GOD lives, I'll do it. Now go back to sleep until morning."

14 Ruth slept at his feet until dawn, but she got up while it was still dark and wouldn't be recognized. Then Boaz said to himself, "No one must know that Ruth came to the threshing floor."

15 So Boaz said, "Bring the shawl you're wearing and spread it out."

She spread it out and he poured it full of barley, six measures, and put it on her shoulders. Then she went back to town.

16-17 When she came to her mother-in-law, Naomi asked, "And how did things go, my dear daughter?"

Ruth told her everything that the man had done for her, adding, "And he gave me all this barley besides—six quarts! He told me, 'You can't go back empty-handed to your mother-in-law!' "

18 Naomi said, "Sit back and relax, my dear daughter, until we find out how things turn out; that man isn't going to fool around. Mark my words, he's going to get everything wrapped up today."

New King James Version

Boaz Redeems Ruth

4 Now Boaz went up to the gate and sat down there; and behold, the close relative of whom Boaz had spoken came by. So Boaz said, "Come aside, friend,[a] sit down here." So he came aside and sat down. [2]And he took ten men of the elders of the city, and said, "Sit down here." So they sat down. [3]Then he said to the close relative, "Naomi, who has come back from the country of Moab, sold the piece of land which *belonged* to our brother Elimelech. [4]And I thought to inform you, saying, 'Buy *it* back in the presence of the inhabitants and the elders of my people. If you will redeem *it,* redeem *it;* but if you[a] will not redeem *it, then* tell me, that I may know; for *there is* no one but you to redeem *it,* and I *am* next after you.'"

And he said, "I will redeem *it.*"

[5]Then Boaz said, "On the day you buy the field from the hand of Naomi, you must also buy *it* from Ruth the Moabitess, the wife of the dead, to perpetuate[a] the name of the dead through his inheritance."

[6]And the close relative said, "I cannot redeem *it* for myself, lest I ruin my own inheritance. You redeem my right of redemption for yourself, for I cannot redeem *it.*"

[7]Now this *was the custom* in former times in Israel concerning redeeming and exchanging, to confirm anything: one man took off his sandal and gave *it* to the other, and this *was* a confirmation in Israel.

[8]Therefore the close relative said to Boaz, "Buy *it* for yourself." So he took off his sandal. [9]And Boaz said to the elders and all the people, "You *are* witnesses this day that I have bought all that was Elimelech's, and all that *was* Chilion's and Mahlon's, from the hand of Naomi. [10]Moreover, Ruth the Moabitess, the widow of Mahlon, I have acquired as my wife, to perpetuate the name of the dead through his inheritance, that the name of the dead may not be cut off from among his brethren and from his position at the gate.[a] You *are* witnesses this day."

[11]And all the people who *were* at the gate, and the elders, said, "*We are* witnesses. The LORD make the woman who is coming to your house like Rachel and Leah, the two who built the house of Israel; and may you prosper in Ephrathah and be famous in Bethlehem. [12]May your house be like the house of Perez, whom Tamar bore to Judah, because of the offspring which the LORD will give you from this young woman."

4:1 [a]Hebrew *peloni almoni;* literally *so and so* **4:4** [a]Following many Hebrew manuscripts, Septuagint, Syriac, Targum, and Vulgate; Masoretic Text reads *he.* **4:5** [a]Literally *raise up* **4:10** [a]Probably his civic office

The Message

1 4 Boaz went straight to the public square and took his place there. Before long the "closer relative," the one mentioned earlier by Boaz, strolled by.

"Step aside, old friend," said Boaz. "Take a seat." The man sat down.

2 Boaz then gathered ten of the town elders together and said, "Sit down here with us; we've got some business to take care of." And they sat down.

3-4 Boaz then said to his relative, "The piece of property that belonged to our relative Elimelech is being sold by his widow Naomi, who has just returned from the country of Moab. I thought you ought to know about it. Buy it back if you want it—you can make it official in the presence of those sitting here and before the town elders. You have first redeemer rights. If you don't want it, tell me so I'll know where I stand. You're first in line to do this and I'm next after you."

He said, "I'll buy it."

5 Then Boaz added, "You realize, don't you, that when you buy the field from Naomi, you also get Ruth the Moabite, the widow of our dead relative, along with the redeemer responsibility to have children with her to carry on the family inheritance."

6 Then the relative said, "Oh, I can't do that—I'd jeopardize my own family's inheritance. You go ahead and buy it—you can have my rights—I can't do it."

7 In the olden times in Israel, this is how they handled official business regarding matters of property and inheritance: a man would take off his shoe and give it to the other person. This was the same as an official seal or personal signature in Israel.

8 So when Boaz's "redeemer" relative said, "Go ahead and buy it," he signed the deal by pulling off his shoe.

9-10 Boaz then addressed the elders and all the people in the town square that day: "You are witnesses today that I have bought from Naomi everything that belonged to Elimelech and Kilion and Mahlon, including responsibility for Ruth the foreigner, the widow of Mahlon—I'll take her as my wife and keep the name of the deceased alive along with his inheritance. The memory and reputation of the deceased is not going to disappear out of this family or from his hometown. To all this you are witnesses this very day."

11-12 All the people in the town square that day, backing up the elders, said, "Yes, we are witnesses. May GOD make this woman who is coming into your household like Rachel and Leah, the two women who built the family of Israel. May GOD make you a pillar in Ephrathah and famous in Bethlehem! With the children GOD gives you from this young woman, may your family rival the family of Perez, the son Tamar bore to Judah."

New King James Version

Descendants of Boaz and Ruth

[13]So Boaz took Ruth and she became his
wife; and when he went in to her, the Lord gave
her conception, and she bore a son. [14]Then the
women said to Naomi, "Blessed *be* the Lord,
who has not left you this day without a close rel-
ative; and may his name be famous in Israel!
[15]And may he be to you a restorer of life and a
nourisher of your old age; for your daughter-in-
law, who loves you, who is better to you than
seven sons, has borne him." [16]Then Naomi took
the child and laid him on her bosom, and be-
came a nurse to him. [17]Also the neighbor
women gave him a name, saying, "There is a son
born to Naomi." And they called his name Obed.
He *is* the father of Jesse, the father of David.

[18]Now this *is* the genealogy of Perez: Perez
begot Hezron; [19]Hezron begot Ram, and Ram
begot Amminadab; [20]Amminadab begot
Nahshon, and Nahshon begot Salmon;[a]
[21]Salmon begot Boaz, and Boaz begot Obed;
[22]Obed begot Jesse, and Jesse begot David.

4:20 [a]Hebrew *Salmah*

The Message

13 Boaz married Ruth. She became his wife. Boaz slept with her. By God's gracious gift she conceived and had a son.

14-15 The town women said to Naomi, "Blessed be God! He didn't leave you without family to carry on your life. May this baby grow up to be famous in Israel! He'll make you young again! He'll take care of you in old age. And this daughter-in-law who has brought him into the world and loves you so much, why, she's worth more to you than seven sons!"

16 Naomi took the baby and held him in her arms, cuddling him, cooing over him, waiting on him hand and foot.

17 The neighborhood women started calling him "Naomi's baby boy!" But his real name was Obed. Obed was the father of Jesse, and Jesse the father of David.

18-22 This is the family tree of Perez:

Perez had Hezron,
Hezron had Ram,
Ram had Amminadab,
Amminadab had Nahshon,
Nahshon had Salmon,
Salmon had Boaz,
Boaz had Obed,
Obed had Jesse,
and Jesse had David.

1 SAMUEL

New King James Version

The Family of Elkanah

1 Now there was a certain man of Ramathaim Zophim, of the mountains of Ephraim, and his name *was* Elkanah the son of Jeroham, the son of Elihu,[a] the son of Tohu,[b] the son of Zuph, an Ephraimite. 2And he had two wives: the name of one *was* Hannah, and the name of the other Peninnah. Peninnah had children, but Hannah had no children. 3This man went up from his city yearly to worship and sacrifice to the LORD of hosts in Shiloh. Also the two sons of Eli, Hophni and Phinehas, the priests of the LORD, *were* there. 4And whenever the time came for Elkanah to make an offering, he would give portions to Peninnah his wife and to all her sons and daughters. 5But to Hannah he would give a double portion, for he loved Hannah, although the LORD had closed her womb. 6And her rival also provoked her severely, to make her miserable, because the LORD had closed her womb. 7So it was, year by year, when she went up to the house of the LORD, that she provoked her; therefore she wept and did not eat.

Hannah's Vow

8Then Elkanah her husband said to her, "Hannah, why do you weep? Why do you not eat? And why is your heart grieved? *Am* I not better to you than ten sons?"

9So Hannah arose after they had finished eating and drinking in Shiloh. Now Eli the priest was sitting on the seat by the doorpost of the tabernacle[a] of the LORD. 10And she *was* in bitterness of soul, and prayed to the LORD and wept in anguish. 11Then she made a vow and said, "O LORD of hosts, if You will indeed look on the affliction of Your maidservant and remember me, and not forget Your maidservant, but will give Your maidservant a male child, then I will give him to the LORD all the days of his life, and no razor shall come upon his head."

12And it happened, as she continued praying before the LORD, that Eli watched her mouth. 13Now Hannah spoke in her heart; only her lips moved, but her voice was not heard. Therefore Eli thought she was drunk. 14So Eli said to her, "How long will you be drunk? Put your wine away from you!"

15But Hannah answered and said, "No, my lord, I *am* a woman of sorrowful spirit. I have drunk neither wine nor intoxicating drink, but have poured out my soul before the LORD. 16Do

1:1 [a]Spelled *Eliel* in 1 Chronicles 6:34 [b]Spelled *Toah* in 1 Chronicles 6:34 **1:9** [a]Hebrew *heykal*, palace or temple

The Message

Hannah Pours Out Her Heart to God

1-2 1 There once was a man who lived in Ra-
mathaim. He was descended from the old
Zuph family in the Ephraim hills. His name
was Elkanah. (He was connected with the
Zuphs from Ephraim through his father
Jeroham, his grandfather Elihu, and his
great-grandfather Tohu.) He had two wives.
The first was Hannah; the second was
Peninnah. Peninnah had children; Hannah
did not.
3-7 Every year this man went from his home-
town up to Shiloh to worship and offer a
sacrifice to GOD-of-the-Angel-Armies. Eli
and his two sons, Hophni and Phinehas,
served as the priests of GOD there. When
Elkanah sacrificed, he passed helpings from
the sacrificial meal around to his wife
Peninnah and all her children, but he always
gave an especially generous helping to Han-
nah because he loved her so much, and be-
cause GOD had not given her children. But
her rival wife taunted her cruelly, rubbing it
in and never letting her forget that GOD had
not given her children. This went on year af-
ter year. Every time she went to the sanctu-
ary of GOD she could expect to be taunted.
Hannah was reduced to tears and had no
appetite.
8 Her husband Elkanah said, "Oh, Hannah,
why are you crying? Why aren't you eating?
And why are you so upset? Am I not of more
worth to you than ten sons?"
9-11 So Hannah ate. Then she pulled herself
together, slipped away quietly, and entered
the sanctuary. The priest Eli was on duty at
the entrance to GOD's Temple in the custom-
ary seat. Crushed in soul, Hannah prayed to
GOD and cried and cried—inconsolably.
Then she made a vow:

Oh, GOD-of-the-Angel-Armies,
If you'll take a good, hard look at my
pain,
If you'll quit neglecting me and go into
action for me
By giving me a son,
I'll give him completely, unreservedly to
you.
I'll set him apart for a life of holy
discipline.

12-14 It so happened that as she continued in
prayer before GOD, Eli was watching her
closely. Hannah was praying in her heart,
silently. Her lips moved, but no sound was
heard. Eli jumped to the conclusion that she
was drunk. He approached her and said,
"You're drunk! How long do you plan to
keep this up? Sober up, woman!"
15-16 Hannah said, "Oh no, sir—please! I'm a
woman hard used. I haven't been drinking.
Not a drop of wine or beer. The only thing
I've been pouring out is my heart, pouring it

New King James Version

not consider your maidservant a wicked
woman,[a] for out of the abundance of my com-
plaint and grief I have spoken until now."
17Then Eli answered and said, "Go in peace,
and the God of Israel grant your petition which
you have asked of Him."
18And she said, "Let your maidservant find
favor in your sight." So the woman went her
way and ate, and her face was no longer *sad.*

Samuel Is Born and Dedicated

19Then they rose early in the morning and
worshiped before the Lord, and returned and
came to their house at Ramah. And Elkanah
knew Hannah his wife, and the Lord remem-
bered her. 20So it came to pass in the process of
time that Hannah conceived and bore a son, and
called his name Samuel,[a] *saying,* "Because I
have asked for him from the Lord."
21Now the man Elkanah and all his house
went up to offer to the Lord the yearly sacrifice
and his vow. 22But Hannah did not go up, for she
said to her husband, "*Not* until the child is
weaned; then I will take him, that he may ap-
pear before the Lord and remain there forever."
23So Elkanah her husband said to her, "Do
what seems best to you; wait until you have
weaned him. Only let the Lord establish His[a]
word." Then the woman stayed and nursed her
son until she had weaned him.
24Now when she had weaned him, she took
him up with her, with three bulls,[a] one ephah of
flour, and a skin of wine, and brought him to the
house of the Lord in Shiloh. And the child *was*
young. 25Then they slaughtered a bull, and
brought the child to Eli. 26And she said, "O my
lord! As your soul lives, my lord, I *am* the
woman who stood by you here, praying to the
Lord. 27For this child I prayed, and the Lord has
granted me my petition which I asked of Him.
28Therefore I also have lent him to the Lord; as
long as he lives he shall be lent to the Lord." So
they worshiped the Lord there.

Hannah's Prayer

2 And Hannah prayed and said:

"My heart rejoices in the Lord;
My horn[a] is exalted in the Lord.
I smile at my enemies,
Because I rejoice in Your salvation.

2"No one is holy like the Lord,
For *there is* none besides You,
Nor *is there* any rock like our God.

3"Talk no more so very proudly;
Let no arrogance come from your mouth,
For the Lord *is* the God of knowledge;
And by Him actions are weighed.

1:16 [a]Literally *daughter of Belial* **1:20** [a]Literally *Heard by God* **1:23** [a]Following Masoretic Text, Targum, and Vulgate; Dead Sea Scrolls, Septuagint, and Syriac read *your.* **1:24** [a]Dead Sea Scrolls, Septuagint, and Syriac read *a three-year-old bull.* **2:1** [a]That is, strength

The Message

out to God. Don't for a minute think I'm a bad woman. It's because I'm so desperately unhappy and in such pain that I've stayed here so long."

17 Eli answered her, "Go in peace. And may the God of Israel give you what you have asked of him."

18 "Think well of me—and pray for me!" she said, and went her way. Then she ate heartily, her face radiant.

19 Up before dawn, they worshiped God and returned home to Ramah. Elkanah slept with Hannah his wife, and God began making the necessary arrangements in response to what she had asked.

Dedicating the Child to God

20 Before the year was out, Hannah had conceived and given birth to a son. She named him Samuel, explaining, "I asked God for him."

21-22 When Elkanah next took his family on their annual trip to Shiloh to worship God, offering sacrifices and keeping his vow, Hannah didn't go. She told her husband, "After the child is weaned, I'll bring him myself and present him before God—and that's where he'll stay, for good."

23-24 Elkanah said to his wife, "Do what you think is best. Stay home until you have weaned him. Yes! Let God complete what he has begun!"

So she did. She stayed home and nursed her son until she had weaned him. Then she took him up to Shiloh, bringing also the makings of a generous sacrificial meal—a prize bull, flour, and wine. The child was so young to be sent off!

25-26 They first butchered the bull, then brought the child to Eli. Hannah said, "Excuse me, sir. Would you believe that I'm the very woman who was standing before you at this very spot, praying to God? I prayed for this child, and God gave me what I asked for. And now I have dedicated him to God. He's dedicated to God for life."

Then and there, they worshiped God.

1 2 Hannah prayed:

I'm bursting with God-news!
I'm walking on air.
I'm laughing at my rivals.
I'm dancing my salvation.

2-5 Nothing and no one is holy like God,
no rock mountain like our God.
Don't dare talk pretentiously—
not a word of boasting, ever!
For God knows what's going on.
He takes the measure of everything
that happens.

NEW KING JAMES VERSION

[4]"The bows of the mighty men *are* broken,
And those who stumbled are girded with strength.
[5]*Those who were* full have hired themselves out for bread,
And the hungry have ceased *to hunger.*
Even the barren has borne seven,
And she who has many children has become feeble.
[6]"The LORD kills and makes alive;
He brings down to the grave and brings up.
[7]The LORD makes poor and makes rich;
He brings low and lifts up.
[8]He raises the poor from the dust
And lifts the beggar from the ash heap,
To set *them* among princes
And make them inherit the throne of glory.

"For the pillars of the earth *are* the LORD's,
And He has set the world upon them.
[9]He will guard the feet of His saints,
But the wicked shall be silent in darkness.

"For by strength no man shall prevail.
[10]The adversaries of the LORD shall be broken in pieces;
From heaven He will thunder against them.
The LORD will judge the ends of the earth.

"He will give strength to His king,
And exalt the horn of His anointed."

[11]Then Elkanah went to his house at Ramah.
But the child ministered to the LORD before Eli
the priest.

THE WICKED SONS OF ELI

[12]Now the sons of Eli *were* corrupt;[a] they did
not know the LORD. [13]And the priests' custom
with the people *was that* when any man offered
a sacrifice, the priest's servant would come with
a three-pronged fleshhook in his hand while the
meat was boiling. [14]Then he would thrust *it* into
the pan, or kettle, or caldron, or pot; and the
priest would take for himself all that the flesh-
hook brought up. So they did in Shiloh to all the
Israelites who came there. [15]Also, before they
burned the fat, the priest's servant would come
and say to the man who sacrificed, "Give meat
for roasting to the priest, for he will not take
boiled meat from you, but raw."
[16]And *if* the man said to him, "They should
really burn the fat first; *then* you may take *as
much* as your heart desires," he would then an-

2:12 [a]Literally *sons of Belial*

THE MESSAGE

The weapons of the strong are smashed to pieces,
while the weak are infused with fresh strength.
The well-fed are out begging in the streets for crusts,
while the hungry are getting second helpings.
The barren woman has a houseful of children,
while the mother of many is bereft.

6-10 GOD brings death and GOD brings life,
brings down to the grave and raises up.
GOD brings poverty and GOD brings wealth;
he lowers, he also lifts up.
He puts poor people on their feet again;
he rekindles burned-out lives with fresh hope,
Restoring dignity and respect to their lives—
a place in the sun!
For the very structures of earth are GOD's;
he has laid out his operations on a firm foundation.
He protectively cares for his faithful friends, step by step,
but leaves the wicked to stumble in the dark.
No one makes it in this life by sheer muscle!
GOD's enemies will be blasted out of the sky,
crashed in a heap and burned.
GOD will set things right all over the earth,
he'll give strength to his king,
he'll set his anointed on top of the world!

11 Elkanah went home to Ramah. The boy stayed and served GOD in the company of Eli the priest.

SAMUEL SERVES GOD

12-17 Eli's own sons were a bad lot. They didn't know GOD and could not have cared less about the customs of priests among the people. Ordinarily, when someone offered a sacrifice, the priest's servant was supposed to come up and, while the meat was boiling, stab a three-pronged fork into the cooking pot. The priest then got whatever came up on the fork. But this is how Eli's sons treated all the Israelites who came to Shiloh to offer sacrifices to GOD. Before they had even burned the fat to GOD, the priest's servant would interrupt whoever was sacrificing and say, "Hand over some of that meat for the priest to roast. He doesn't like boiled meat; he likes his rare." If the man objected, "First let the fat be burned—God's portion!—then take all you want," the servant

NEW KING JAMES VERSION

swer him, "*No,* but you must give *it* now; and if
not, I will take *it* by force."
17Therefore the sin of the young men was
very great before the LORD, for men abhorred
the offering of the LORD.

SAMUEL'S CHILDHOOD MINISTRY

18But Samuel ministered before the LORD,
even as a child, wearing a linen ephod. 19More-
over his mother used to make him a little robe,
and bring *it* to him year by year when she came
up with her husband to offer the yearly sacri-
fice. 20And Eli would bless Elkanah and his wife,
and say, "The LORD give you descendants from
this woman for the loan that was given to the
LORD." Then they would go to their own home.
21And the LORD visited Hannah, so that she
conceived and bore three sons and two daugh-
ters. Meanwhile the child Samuel grew before
the LORD.

PROPHECY AGAINST ELI'S HOUSEHOLD

22Now Eli was very old; and he heard every-
thing his sons did to all Israel,[a] and how they lay
with the women who assembled at the door of
the tabernacle of meeting. 23So he said to them,
"Why do you do such things? For I hear of your
evil dealings from all the people. 24No, my sons!
For *it is* not a good report that I hear. You make
the LORD's people transgress. 25If one man sins
against another, God will judge him. But if a
man sins against the LORD, who will intercede
for him?" Nevertheless they did not heed the
voice of their father, because the LORD desired
to kill them.
26And the child Samuel grew in stature, and
in favor both with the LORD and men.
27Then a man of God came to Eli and said to
him, "Thus says the LORD: 'Did I not clearly re-
veal Myself to the house of your father when
they were in Egypt in Pharaoh's house? 28Did I
not choose him out of all the tribes of Israel *to*
be My priest, to offer upon My altar, to burn in-
cense, and to wear an ephod before Me? And
did I not give to the house of your father all the
offerings of the children of Israel made by fire?
29Why do you kick at My sacrifice and My offer-
ing which I have commanded *in My* dwelling
place, and honor your sons more than Me, to
make yourselves fat with the best of all the of-
ferings of Israel My people?' 30Therefore the
LORD God of Israel says: 'I said indeed *that* your
house and the house of your father would walk
before Me forever.' But now the LORD says: 'Far
be it from Me; for those who honor Me I will
honor, and those who despise Me shall be
lightly esteemed. 31Behold, the days are coming
that I will cut off your arm and the arm of your
father's house, so that there will not be an old
man in your house. 32And you will see an enemy
in My dwelling place, *despite* all the good which
God does for Israel. And there shall not be an

2:22 [a]Following Masoretic Text, Targum, and Vulgate; Dead Sea Scrolls and Septuagint omit the rest of this verse.

THE MESSAGE

would demand, "No, I want it now. If you
won't give it, I'll take it." It was a horrible sin
these young servants were committing—
and right in the presence of GOD!—desecrat-
ing the holy offerings to GOD.
18-20 In the midst of all this, Samuel, a boy
dressed in a priestly linen tunic, served GOD.
Additionally, every year his mother would
make him a little robe cut to his size and
bring it to him when she and her husband
came for the annual sacrifice. Eli would
bless Elkanah and his wife, saying, "GOD
give you children to replace this child you
have dedicated to GOD." Then they would go
home.
21 GOD was most especially kind to Hannah.
She had three more sons and two daugh-
ters! The boy Samuel stayed at the sanctu-
ary and grew up with GOD.

A HARD LIFE WITH MANY TEARS

22-25 By this time Eli was very old. He kept get-
ting reports on how his sons were ripping
off the people and sleeping with the women
who helped out at the sanctuary. Eli took
them to task: "What's going on here? Why
are you doing these things? I hear story af-
ter story of your corrupt and evil carrying
on. Oh, my sons, this is not right! These are
terrible reports I'm getting, stories spread-
ing right and left among GOD's people! If
you sin against another person, there's
help—God's help. But if you sin against
GOD, who is around to help?"
25-26 But they were far gone in disobedience
and refused to listen to a thing their father
said. So GOD, who was fed up with them, de-
creed their death. But the boy Samuel was
very much alive, growing up, blessed by
GOD and popular with the people.
27-30 A holy man came to Eli and said: "This is
GOD's message: I revealed myself openly to
your ancestors when they were Pharaoh's
slaves in Egypt. Out of all the tribes of Is-
rael, I chose your family to be my priests: to
preside at the Altar, to burn incense, to wear
the priestly robes in my presence. I put your
ancestral family in charge of all the sacrifi-
cial offerings of Israel. So why do you now
treat as mere loot these very sacrificial of-
ferings that I commanded for my worship?
Why do you treat your sons better than me,
turning them loose to get fat on these offer-
ings, and ignoring me? Therefore—this is
GOD's word, the God of Israel speaking—I
once said that you and your ancestral fam-
ily would be my priests indefinitely, but
now—GOD's word, remember!—there is no
way this can continue.

I honor those who honor me;
those who scorn me I demean.

31-36 "Be well warned: It won't be long before I
wipe out both your family and your future
family. No one in your family will make it to
old age! You'll see good things that I'm do-
ing in Israel, but you'll see it and weep, for

NEW KING JAMES VERSION

old man in your house forever. 33But any of your men *whom* I do not cut off from My altar shall consume your eyes and grieve your heart. And all the descendants of your house shall die in the flower of their age. 34Now this *shall be* a sign to you that will come upon your two sons, on Hophni and Phinehas: in one day they shall die, both of them. 35Then I will raise up for Myself a faithful priest *who* shall do according to what *is* in My heart and in My mind. I will build him a sure house, and he shall walk before My anointed forever. 36And it shall come to pass that everyone who is left in your house will come *and* bow down to him for a piece of silver and a morsel of bread, and say, "Please, put me in one of the priestly positions, that I may eat a piece of bread." ' "

SAMUEL'S FIRST PROPHECY

3 Now the boy Samuel ministered to the LORD before Eli. And the word of the LORD was rare in those days; *there was* no widespread revelation. 2And it came to pass at that time, while Eli *was* lying down in his place, and when his eyes had begun to grow so dim that he could not see, 3and before the lamp of God went out in the tabernacle[a] of the LORD where the ark of God *was*, and while Samuel was lying down, 4that the LORD called Samuel. And he answered, "Here I am!" 5So he ran to Eli and said, "Here I am, for you called me."

And he said, "I did not call; lie down again." And he went and lay down.

6Then the LORD called yet again, "Samuel!"

So Samuel arose and went to Eli, and said, "Here I am, for you called me." He answered, "I did not call, my son; lie down again." 7(Now Samuel did not yet know the LORD, nor was the word of the LORD yet revealed to him.)

8And the LORD called Samuel again the third time. So he arose and went to Eli, and said, "Here I am, for you did call me."

Then Eli perceived that the LORD had called the boy. 9Therefore Eli said to Samuel, "Go, lie down; and it shall be, if He calls you, that you must say, 'Speak, LORD, for Your servant hears.' " So Samuel went and lay down in his place.

10Now the LORD came and stood and called as at other times, "Samuel! Samuel!"

And Samuel answered, "Speak, for Your servant hears."

11Then the LORD said to Samuel: "Behold, I will do something in Israel at which both ears of everyone who hears it will tingle. 12In that day I will perform against Eli all that I have spoken concerning his house, from beginning to end. 13For I have told him that I will judge his house forever for the iniquity which he knows, because his sons made themselves vile, and he did not restrain them. 14And therefore I have sworn to the house of Eli that the iniquity of Eli's house shall not be atoned for by sacrifice or offering forever."

3:3 [a]Hebrew *heykal*, palace or temple

THE MESSAGE

no one in your family will live to enjoy it. I will leave one person to serve at my Altar, but it will be a hard life, with many tears. Everyone else in your family will die before their time. What happens to your two sons, Hophni and Phinehas, will be the proof: Both will die the same day. Then I'll establish for myself a true priest. He'll do what I want him to do, be what I want him to be. I'll make his position secure and he'll do his work freely in the service of my anointed one. Survivors from your family will come to him begging for handouts, saying, 'Please, give me some priest work, just enough to put some food on the table.' "

"SPEAK, GOD. I'M READY TO LISTEN"

1-3 3 The boy Samuel was serving GOD under Eli's direction. This was at a time when the revelation of GOD was rarely heard or seen. One night Eli was sound asleep (his eyesight was very bad—he could hardly see). It was well before dawn; the sanctuary lamp was still burning. Samuel was still in bed in the Temple of GOD, where the Chest of God rested.

4-5 Then GOD called out, "Samuel, Samuel!"

Samuel answered, "Yes? I'm here." Then he ran to Eli saying, "I heard you call. Here I am."

Eli said, "I didn't call you. Go back to bed." And so he did.

6-7 GOD called again, "Samuel, Samuel!"

Samuel got up and went to Eli, "I heard you call. Here I am."

Again Eli said, "Son, I didn't call you. Go back to bed." (This all happened before Samuel knew GOD for himself. It was before the revelation of GOD had been given to him personally.)

8-9 GOD called again, "Samuel!"—the third time! Yet again Samuel got up and went to Eli, "Yes? I heard you call me. Here I am."

That's when it dawned on Eli that GOD was calling the boy. So Eli directed Samuel, "Go back and lie down. If the voice calls again, say, 'Speak, GOD. I'm your servant, ready to listen.' " Samuel returned to his bed.

10 Then GOD came and stood before him exactly as before, calling out, "Samuel! Samuel!"

Samuel answered, "Speak. I'm your servant, ready to listen."

11-14 GOD said to Samuel, "Listen carefully. I'm getting ready to do something in Israel that is going to shake everyone up and get their attention. The time has come for me to bring down on Eli's family everything I warned him of, every last word of it. I'm letting him know that the time's up. I'm bringing judgment on his family for good. He knew what was going on, that his sons were desecrating God's name and God's place, and he did nothing to stop them. This is my sentence on the family of Eli: The evil of Eli's family can never be wiped out by sacrifice or offering."

New King James Version

15So Samuel lay down until morning,[a] and opened the doors of the house of the LORD. And Samuel was afraid to tell Eli the vision. 16Then Eli called Samuel and said, "Samuel, my son!"

He answered, "Here I am."

17And he said, "What *is* the word that *the* LORD spoke to you? Please do not hide *it* from me. God do so to you, and more also, if you hide anything from me of all the things that He said to you." 18Then Samuel told him everything, and hid nothing from him. And he said, "It *is* the LORD. Let Him do what seems good to Him."

19So Samuel grew, and the LORD was with him and let none of his words fall to the ground. 20And all Israel from Dan to Beersheba knew that Samuel *had been* established as a prophet of the LORD. 21Then the LORD appeared again in Shiloh. For the LORD revealed Himself to Samuel in Shiloh by the word of the LORD.

4 And the word of Samuel came to all Israel.[a]

The Ark of God Captured

Now Israel went out to battle against the Philistines, and encamped beside Ebenezer; and the Philistines encamped in Aphek. 2Then the Philistines put themselves in battle array against Israel. And when they joined battle, Israel was defeated by the Philistines, who killed about four thousand men of the army in the field. 3And when the people had come into the camp, the elders of Israel said, "Why has the LORD defeated us today before the Philistines? Let us bring the ark of the covenant of the LORD from Shiloh to us, that when it comes among us it may save us from the hand of our enemies." 4So the people sent to Shiloh, that they might bring from there the ark of the covenant of the LORD of hosts, who dwells *between* the cherubim. And the two sons of Eli, Hophni and Phinehas, *were* there with the ark of the covenant of God.

5And when the ark of the covenant of the LORD came into the camp, all Israel shouted so loudly that the earth shook. 6Now when the Philistines heard the noise of the shout, they said, "What *does* the sound of this great shout in the camp of the Hebrews *mean*?" Then they understood that the ark of the LORD had come into the camp. 7So the Philistines were afraid, for they said, "God has come into the camp!" And they said, "Woe to us! For such a thing has never happened before. 8Woe to us! Who will deliver us from the hand of these mighty gods? These *are* the gods who struck the Egyptians with all

3:15 [a]Following Masoretic Text, Targum, and Vulgate; Septuagint adds *and he arose in the morning.* **4:1** [a]Following Masoretic Text and Targum; Septuagint and Vulgate add *And it came to pass in those days that the Philistines gathered themselves together to fight;* Septuagint adds further *against Israel.*

The Message

15 Samuel stayed in bed until morning, then rose early and went about his duties, opening the doors of the sanctuary, but he dreaded having to tell the vision to Eli.

16 But then Eli summoned Samuel: "Samuel, my son!"

Samuel came running: "Yes? What can I do for you?"

17 "What did he say? Tell it to me, all of it. Don't suppress or soften one word, as God is your judge! I want it all, word for word as he said it to you."

18 So Samuel told him, word for word. He held back nothing.

Eli said, "He is GOD. Let him do whatever he thinks best."

19-21 Samuel grew up. GOD was with him, and Samuel's prophetic record was flawless. Everyone in Israel, from Dan in the north to Beersheba in the south, recognized that Samuel was the real thing—a true prophet of GOD. GOD continued to show up at Shiloh, revealed through his word to Samuel at Shiloh.

The Chest of God Is Taken

1-3 4 Whatever Samuel said was broadcast all through Israel. Israel went to war against the Philistines. Israel set up camp at Ebenezer, the Philistines at Aphek. The Philistines marched out to meet Israel, the fighting spread, and Israel was badly beaten—about four thousand soldiers left dead on the field. When the troops returned to camp, Israel's elders said, "Why has GOD given us such a beating today by the Philistines? Let's go to Shiloh and get the Chest of GOD's Covenant. It will accompany us and save us from the grip of our enemies."

4 So the army sent orders to Shiloh. They brought the Chest of the Covenant of GOD, the GOD-of-the-Angel-Armies, the Cherubim-Enthroned-GOD. Eli's two sons, Hophni and Phinehas, accompanied the Chest of the Covenant of God.

5-6 When the Chest of the Covenant of GOD was brought into camp, everyone gave a huge cheer. The shouts were like thunderclaps shaking the very ground. The Philistines heard the shouting and wondered what on earth was going on: "What's all this shouting among the Hebrews?"

6-9 Then they learned that the Chest of GOD had entered the Hebrew camp. The Philistines panicked: "Their gods have come to their camp! Nothing like this has ever happened before. We're done for! Who can save us from the clutches of these super-gods? These are the same gods who hit the Egyptians with all kinds of plagues out in

NEW KING JAMES VERSION

the plagues in the wilderness. [9]Be strong and conduct yourselves like men, you Philistines, that you do not become servants of the Hebrews, as they have been to you. Conduct yourselves like men, and fight!"

[10]So the Philistines fought, and Israel was defeated, and every man fled to his tent. There was a very great slaughter, and there fell of Israel thirty thousand foot soldiers. [11]Also the ark of God was captured; and the two sons of Eli, Hophni and Phinehas, died.

DEATH OF ELI

[12]Then a man of Benjamin ran from the battle line the same day, and came to Shiloh with his clothes torn and dirt on his head. [13]Now when he came, there was Eli, sitting on a seat by the wayside watching,[a] for his heart trembled for the ark of God. And when the man came into the city and told *it,* all the city cried out. [14]When Eli heard the noise of the outcry, he said, "What *does* the sound of this tumult *mean?*" And the man came quickly and told Eli. [15]Eli was ninety-eight years old, and his eyes were so dim that he could not see.

[16]Then the man said to Eli, "I *am* he who came from the battle. And I fled today from the battle line."

And he said, "What happened, my son?"

[17]So the messenger answered and said, "Israel has fled before the Philistines, and there has been a great slaughter among the people. Also your two sons, Hophni and Phinehas, are dead; and the ark of God has been captured."

[18]Then it happened, when he made mention of the ark of God, that Eli fell off the seat backward by the side of the gate; and his neck was broken and he died, for the man was old and heavy. And he had judged Israel forty years.

ICHABOD

[19]Now his daughter-in-law, Phinehas' wife, was with child, *due* to be delivered; and when she heard the news that the ark of God was captured, and that her father-in-law and her husband were dead, she bowed herself and gave birth, for her labor pains came upon her. [20]And about the time of her death the women who stood by her said to her, "Do not fear, for you have borne a son." But she did not answer, nor did she regard *it.* [21]Then she named the child Ichabod,[a] saying, "The glory has departed from Israel!" because the ark of God had been captured and because of her father-in-law and her husband. [22]And she said, "The glory has departed from Israel, for the ark of God has been captured."

THE PHILISTINES AND THE ARK

5 Then the Philistines took the ark of God and brought it from Ebenezer to Ashdod. [2]When the Philistines took the ark of God, they brought it into the house of Dagon[a] and set it by Dagon. [3]And when the people of Ashdod arose early in

4:13 [a]Following Masoretic Text and Vulgate; Septuagint reads *beside the gate watching the road.* **4:21** [a]Literally *Inglorious*
5:2 [a]A Philistine idol

THE MESSAGE

the wilderness. On your feet, Philistines!
Courage! We're about to become slaves to
the Hebrews, just as they have been slaves
to us. Show what you're made of! Fight for
your lives!"
10-11 And did they ever fight! It turned into a
rout. They thrashed Israel so mercilessly
that the Israelite soldiers ran for their lives,
leaving behind an incredible thirty thou-
sand dead. As if that wasn't bad enough, the
Chest of God was taken and the two sons of
Eli—Hophni and Phinehas—were killed.

GLORY IS EXILED FROM ISRAEL

12-16 Immediately, a Benjaminite raced from the
front lines back to Shiloh. Shirt torn and
face smeared with dirt, he entered the town.
Eli was sitting on his stool beside the road
keeping vigil, for he was extremely worried
about the Chest of God. When the man ran
straight into town to tell the bad news,
everyone wept. They were appalled. Eli
heard the loud wailing and asked, "Why this
uproar?" The messenger hurried over and
reported. Eli was ninety-eight years old
then, and blind. The man said to Eli, "I've
just come from the front, barely escaping
with my life."
"And so, my son," said Eli, "what hap-
pened?"
17 The messenger answered, "Israel scat-
tered before the Philistines. The defeat was
catastrophic, with enormous losses. Your
sons Hophni and Phinehas died, and the
Chest of God was taken."
18 At the words, "Chest of God," Eli fell
backward off his stool where he sat next to
the gate. Eli was an old man, and very fat.
When he fell, he broke his neck and died. He
had led Israel forty years.
19-20 His daughter-in-law, the wife of Phine-
has, was pregnant and ready to deliver.
When she heard that the Chest of God had
been taken and that both her father-in-law
and her husband were dead, she went to her
knees to give birth, going into hard labor. As
she was about to die, her midwife said,
"Don't be afraid. You've given birth to a
son!" But she gave no sign that she had
heard.
21-22 The Chest of God gone, father-in-law
dead, husband dead, she named the boy Ich-
abod (Glory's-Gone), saying, "Glory is ex-
iled from Israel since the Chest of God was
taken."

THREATENED WITH MASS DEATH

1-2 5 Once the Philistines had seized the Chest
of God, they took it from Ebenezer to Ash-
dod, brought it into the shrine of Dagon, and
placed it alongside the idol of Dagon.
3-5 Next morning when the citizens of Ash-
dod got up, they were shocked to find

NEW KING JAMES VERSION

the morning, there was Dagon, fallen on its face
to the earth before the ark of the LORD. So they
took Dagon and set it in its place again. 4And
when they arose early the next morning, there
was Dagon, fallen on its face to the ground be-
fore the ark of the LORD. The head of Dagon and
both the palms of its hands *were* broken off on
the threshold; only Dagon's *torso*[a] was left of it.
5Therefore neither the priests of Dagon nor any
who come into Dagon's house tread on the
threshold of Dagon in Ashdod to this day.

6But the hand of the LORD was heavy on the
people of Ashdod, and He ravaged them and
struck them with tumors,[a] *both* Ashdod and its
territory. 7And when the men of Ashdod saw
how *it was*, they said, "The ark of the God of Is-
rael must not remain with us, for His hand is
harsh toward us and Dagon our god." 8There-
fore they sent and gathered to themselves all the
lords of the Philistines, and said, "What shall we
do with the ark of the God of Israel?"

And they answered, "Let the ark of the God
of Israel be carried away to Gath." So they car-
ried the ark of the God of Israel away. 9So it was,
after they had carried it away, that the hand of
the LORD was against the city with a very great
destruction; and He struck the men of the city,
both small and great, and tumors broke out on
them.

10Therefore they sent the ark of God to
Ekron. So it was, as the ark of God came to
Ekron, that the Ekronites cried out, saying,
"They have brought the ark of the God of Israel
to us, to kill us and our people!" 11So they sent
and gathered together all the lords of the
Philistines, and said, "Send away the ark of the
God of Israel, and let it go back to its own place,
so that it does not kill us and our people." For
there was a deadly destruction throughout all
the city; the hand of God was very heavy there.
12And the men who did not die were stricken
with the tumors, and the cry of the city went up
to heaven.

THE ARK RETURNED TO ISRAEL

6 Now the ark of the LORD was in the country
of the Philistines seven months. 2And the
Philistines called for the priests and the divin-
ers, saying, "What shall we do with the ark of
the LORD? Tell us how we should send it to its
place."

3So they said, "If you send away the ark of
the God of Israel, do not send it empty; but by all
means return *it* to Him *with* a trespass offering.
Then you will be healed, and it will be known to
you why His hand is not removed from you."

4Then they said, "What *is* the trespass offer-
ing which we shall return to Him?"

They answered, "Five golden tumors and five
golden rats, *according to* the number of the
lords of the Philistines. For the same plague *was*

5:4 [a]Following Septuagint, Syriac, Targum, and Vulgate; Masoretic Text reads *Dagon*. **5:6** [a]Probably bubonic plague. Septuagint and Vulgate add here *And in the midst of their land rats sprang up, and there was a great death panic in the city.*

THE MESSAGE

Dagon toppled from his place, flat on his
face before the Chest of GOD. They picked
him up and put him back where he be-
longed. First thing the next morning they
found him again, toppled and flat on his
face before the Chest of GOD. Dagon's head
and arms were broken off, strewn across the
entrance. Only his torso was in one piece.
(That's why even today, the priests of Dagon
and visitors to the Dagon shrine in Ashdod
avoid stepping on the threshold.)

6 GOD was hard on the citizens of Ashdod.
He devastated them by hitting them with tu-
mors. This happened in both the town and
the surrounding neighborhoods. He let
loose rats among them. Jumping from ships
there, rats swarmed all over the city! And
everyone was deathly afraid.

7-8 When the leaders of Ashdod saw what
was going on, they decided, "The chest of
the god of Israel has got to go. We can't han-
dle this, and neither can our god Dagon."
They called together all the Philistine lead-
ers and put it to them: "How can we get rid
of the chest of the god of Israel?"

The leaders agreed: "Move it to Gath." So
they moved the Chest of the God of Israel to
Gath.

9 But as soon as they moved it there, GOD
came down hard on that city, too. It was
mass hysteria! He hit them with tumors. Tu-
mors broke out on everyone in town, young
and old.

10-12 So they sent the Chest of God on to
Ekron, but as the Chest was being brought
into town, the people shouted in protest,
"You'll kill us all by bringing in this Chest of
the God of Israel!" They called the Philistine
leaders together and demanded, "Get it out
of here, this Chest of the God of Israel. Send
it back where it came from. We're threat-
ened with mass death!" For everyone was
scared to death when the Chest of God
showed up. God was already coming down
very hard on the place. Those who didn't die
were hit with tumors. All over the city cries
of pain and lament filled the air.

GOLD TUMORS AND RATS

1-2 6 After the Chest of GOD had been among
the Philistine people for seven months,
the Philistine leaders called together their
religious professionals, the priests, and ex-
perts on the supernatural for consultation:
"How can we get rid of this Chest of GOD,
get it off our hands without making things
worse? Tell us!"

3 They said, "If you're going to send the
Chest of the God of Israel back, don't just
dump it on them. Pay compensation. Then
you will be healed. After you're in the clear
again, God will let up on you. Why wouldn't
he?"

4-6 "And what exactly would make for ade-
quate compensation?"

"Five gold tumors and five gold rats,"
they said, "to match the number of Philistine
leaders. Since all of you—leaders and peo-
ple—suffered the same plague, make repli-

NEW KING JAMES VERSION

on all of you and on your lords. 5Therefore you shall make images of your tumors and images of your rats that ravage the land, and you shall give glory to the God of Israel; perhaps He will lighten His hand from you, from your gods, and from your land. 6Why then do you harden your hearts as the Egyptians and Pharaoh hardened their hearts? When He did mighty things among them, did they not let the people go, that they might depart? 7Now therefore, make a new cart, take two milk cows which have never been yoked, and hitch the cows to the cart; and take their calves home, away from them. 8Then take the ark of the LORD and set it on the cart; and put the articles of gold which you are returning to Him *as* a trespass offering in a chest by its side. Then send it away, and let it go. 9And watch: if it goes up the road to its own territory, to Beth Shemesh, *then* He has done us this great evil. But if not, then we shall know that *it is* not His hand *that* struck us—it happened to us by chance."

10Then the men did so; they took two milk cows and hitched them to the cart, and shut up their calves at home. 11And they set the ark of the LORD on the cart, and the chest with the gold rats and the images of their tumors. 12Then the cows headed straight for the road to Beth Shemesh, *and* went along the highway, lowing as they went, and did not turn aside to the right hand or the left. And the lords of the Philistines went after them to the border of Beth Shemesh.

13Now *the people of* Beth Shemesh *were* reaping their wheat harvest in the valley; and they lifted their eyes and saw the ark, and rejoiced to see *it*. 14Then the cart came into the field of Joshua of Beth Shemesh, and stood there; a large stone *was* there. So they split the wood of the cart and offered the cows as a burnt offering to the LORD. 15The Levites took down the ark of the LORD and the chest that *was* with it, in which *were* the articles of gold, and put *them* on the large stone. Then the men of Beth Shemesh offered burnt offerings and made sacrifices the same day to the LORD. 16So when the five lords of the Philistines had seen *it*, they returned to Ekron the same day.

17These *are* the golden tumors which the Philistines returned *as* a trespass offering to the LORD: one for Ashdod, one for Gaza, one for Ashkelon, one for Gath, one for Ekron; 18and the golden rats, *according to* the number of all the cities of the Philistines *belonging* to the five lords, *both* fortified cities and country villages, even as far as the large *stone of* Abel on which they set the ark of the LORD, *which stone remains* to this day in the field of Joshua of Beth Shemesh.

19Then He struck the men of Beth Shemesh, because they had looked into the ark of the LORD. He struck fifty thousand and seventy men[a] of the people, and the people lamented because the LORD had struck the people with a great slaughter.

6:19 [a]Or *He struck seventy men of the people and fifty oxen of a man*

THE MESSAGE

cas of the tumors and rats that are devastating the country and present them as an offering to the glory of the God of Israel. Then maybe he'll ease up and not be so hard on you and your gods, and on your country. Why be stubborn like the Egyptians and Pharaoh? God didn't quit pounding on them until they let the people go. Only then did he let up.

7-9 "So here's what you do: Take a brand-new oxcart and two cows that have never been in harness. Hitch the cows to the oxcart and send their calves back to the barn. Put the Chest of GOD on the cart. Secure the gold replicas of the tumors and rats that you are offering as compensation in a sack and set them next to the Chest. Then send it off. But keep your eyes on it. If it heads straight back home to where it came from, toward Beth Shemesh, it is clear that this catastrophe is a divine judgment, but if not, we'll know that God had nothing to do with it—it was just an accident."

10-12 So that's what they did: They hitched two cows to the cart, put their calves in the barn, and placed the Chest of GOD and the sack of gold rats and tumors on the cart. The cows headed straight for home, down the road to Beth Shemesh, straying neither right nor left, mooing all the way. The Philistine leaders followed them to the outskirts of Beth Shemesh.

13-15 The people of Beth Shemesh were harvesting wheat in the valley. They looked up and saw the Chest. Jubilant, they ran to meet it. The cart came into the field of Joshua, a Beth Shemeshite, and stopped there beside a huge boulder. The harvesters tore the cart to pieces, then chopped up the wood and sacrificed the cows as a burnt offering to GOD. The Levites took charge of the Chest of GOD and the sack containing the gold offerings, placing them on the boulder. Offering the sacrifices, everyone in Beth Shemesh worshiped GOD most heartily that day.

16 When the five Philistine leaders saw what they came to see, they returned the same day to Ekron.

17-18 The five gold replicas of the tumors were offered by the Philistines in compensation for the cities of Ashdod, Gaza, Ashkelon, Gath, and Ekron. The five gold rats matched the number of Philistine towns, both large and small, ruled by the five leaders. The big boulder on which they placed the Chest of GOD is still there in the field of Joshua of Beth Shemesh, a landmark.

IF YOU ARE SERIOUS ABOUT COMING BACK TO GOD

19-20 God struck some of the men of Beth Shemesh who, out of curiosity, irreverently peeked into the Chest of GOD. Seventy died. The whole town was in mourning, reeling

New King James Version

The Ark at Kirjath Jearim

20And the men of Beth Shemesh said, "Who
is able to stand before this holy LORD God? And
to whom shall it go up from us?" 21So they sent
messengers to the inhabitants of Kirjath Jearim,
saying, "The Philistines have brought back the
ark of the LORD; come down *and* take it up with
you."

7Then the men of Kirjath Jearim came and
took the ark of the LORD, and brought it into
the house of Abinadab on the hill, and conse-
crated Eleazar his son to keep the ark of the
LORD.

Samuel Judges Israel

2So it was that the ark remained in Kirjath
Jearim a long time; it was there twenty years.
And all the house of Israel lamented after the
LORD.
3Then Samuel spoke to all the house of Is-
rael, saying, "If you return to the LORD with all
your hearts, *then* put away the foreign gods and
the Ashtoreths[a] from among you, and prepare
your hearts for the LORD, and serve Him only;
and He will deliver you from the hand of the
Philistines." 4So the children of Israel put away
the Baals and the Ashtoreths,[a] and served the
LORD only.
5And Samuel said, "Gather all Israel to Miz-
pah, and I will pray to the LORD for you." 6So
they gathered together at Mizpah, drew water,
and poured *it* out before the LORD. And they
fasted that day, and said there, "We have sinned
against the LORD." And Samuel judged the chil-
dren of Israel at Mizpah.
7Now when the Philistines heard that the
children of Israel had gathered together at Miz-
pah, the lords of the Philistines went up against
Israel. And when the children of Israel heard *of
it,* they were afraid of the Philistines. 8So the
children of Israel said to Samuel, "Do not cease
to cry out to the LORD our God for us, that He
may save us from the hand of the Philistines."
9And Samuel took a suckling lamb and of-
fered *it as* a whole burnt offering to the LORD.
Then Samuel cried out to the LORD for Israel,
and the LORD answered him. 10Now as Samuel
was offering up the burnt offering, the
Philistines drew near to battle against Israel.
But the LORD thundered with a loud thunder
upon the Philistines that day, and so confused
them that they were overcome before Israel.
11And the men of Israel went out of Mizpah and
pursued the Philistines, and drove them back as
far as below Beth Car. 12Then Samuel took a
stone and set *it* up between Mizpah and Shen,
and called its name Ebenezer,[a] saying, "Thus far
the LORD has helped us."

7:3 [a]Canaanite goddesses **7:4** [a]Canaanite goddesses **7:12** [a]Literally *Stone of Help*

The Message

under the hard blow from GOD, and ques-
tioning, "Who can stand before GOD, this
holy God? And who can we get to take this
Chest off our hands?"

21 They sent emissaries to Kiriath Jearim,
saying, "The Philistines have returned the
Chest of GOD. Come down and get it."

1 7And they did. The men of Kiriath Jearim
came and got the Chest of GOD and deliv-
red it to the house of Abinadab on the hill.
They ordained his son, Eleazar, to take re-
sponsibility for the Chest of GOD.

2 From the time that the Chest came to rest
in Kiriath Jearim, a long time passed—
twenty years it was—and throughout Israel
there was a widespread, fearful movement
toward GOD.

3 Then Samuel addressed the house of Is-
rael: "If you are truly serious about coming
back to GOD, clean house. Get rid of the for-
eign gods and fertility goddesses, ground
yourselves firmly in GOD, worship him and
him alone, and he'll save you from Philistine
oppression."

4 They did it. They got rid of the gods and
goddesses, the images of Baal and Ash-
toreth, and gave their exclusive attention
and service to GOD.

5 Next Samuel said, "Get everybody to-
gether at Mizpah and I'll pray for you."

6 So everyone assembled at Mizpah. They
drew water from the wells and poured it out
before GOD in a ritual of cleansing. They
fasted all day and prayed, "We have sinned
against GOD."

So Samuel prepared the Israelites for
holy war there at Mizpah.

The Place Where God Helped Us

7 When the Philistines heard that Israel was
meeting at Mizpah, the Philistine leaders
went on the offensive. Israel got the report
and became frightened—Philistines on the
move again!

8 They pleaded with Samuel, "Pray with all
your might! And don't let up! Pray to GOD,
our God, that he'll save us from the boot of
the Philistines."

9 Samuel took a young lamb not yet
weaned and offered it whole as a Whole-
Burnt-Offering to GOD. He prayed fervently
to GOD, interceding for Israel. And GOD an-
swered.

10-12 While Samuel was offering the sacrifice,
the Philistines came within range to fight Is-
rael. Just then GOD thundered, a huge thun-
derclap exploding among the Philistines.
They panicked—mass confusion!—and ran
helter-skelter from Israel. Israel poured out
of Mizpah and gave chase, killing
Philistines right and left, to a point just be-
yond Beth Car. Samuel took a single rock
and set it upright between Mizpah and
Shen. He named it "Ebenezer" (Rock of
Help), saying, "This marks the place where
GOD helped us."

NEW KING JAMES VERSION

13So the Philistines were subdued, and they did not come anymore into the territory of Israel. And the hand of the LORD was against the Philistines all the days of Samuel. 14Then the cities which the Philistines had taken from Israel were restored to Israel, from Ekron to Gath; and Israel recovered its territory from the hands of the Philistines. Also there was peace between Israel and the Amorites.

15And Samuel judged Israel all the days of his life. 16He went from year to year on a circuit to Bethel, Gilgal, and Mizpah, and judged Israel in all those places. 17But he always returned to Ramah, for his home *was* there. There he judged Israel, and there he built an altar to the LORD.

ISRAEL DEMANDS A KING

8 Now it came to pass when Samuel was old that he made his sons judges over Israel. 2The name of his firstborn was Joel, and the name of his second, Abijah; *they were* judges in Beersheba. 3But his sons did not walk in his ways; they turned aside after dishonest gain, took bribes, and perverted justice.

4Then all the elders of Israel gathered together and came to Samuel at Ramah, 5and said to him, "Look, you are old, and your sons do not walk in your ways. Now make us a king to judge us like all the nations."

6But the thing displeased Samuel when they said, "Give us a king to judge us." So Samuel prayed to the LORD. 7And the LORD said to Samuel, "Heed the voice of the people in all that they say to you; for they have not rejected you, but they have rejected Me, that I should not reign over them. 8According to all the works which they have done since the day that I brought them up out of Egypt, even to this day—with which they have forsaken Me and served other gods—so they are doing to you also. 9Now therefore, heed their voice. However, you shall solemnly forewarn them, and show them the behavior of the king who will reign over them."

10So Samuel told all the words of the LORD to the people who asked him for a king. 11And he said, "This will be the behavior of the king who will reign over you: He will take your sons and appoint *them* for his own chariots and *to be* his horsemen, and *some* will run before his chariots. 12He will appoint captains over his thousands and captains over his fifties, *will set some* to plow his ground and reap his harvest, and *some* to make his weapons of war and equipment for his chariots. 13He will take your daughters *to be* perfumers, cooks, and bakers. 14And he will take the best of your fields, your vineyards, and your olive groves, and give *them* to his servants. 15He will take a tenth of your grain and your vintage, and give it to his officers and servants. 16And he will take your male servants, your female servants, your finest young men,[a] and your donkeys, and put *them* to his work. 17He will take a tenth of your sheep. And you will be his servants. 18And you will cry out in that day because of your king whom you have

8:16 [a]Septuagint reads *cattle*.

THE MESSAGE

13-14 The Philistines learned their lesson and stayed home—no more border crossings. GOD was hard on the Philistines all through Samuel's lifetime. All the cities from Ekron to Gath that the Philistines had taken from Israel were restored. Israel also freed the surrounding countryside from Philistine control. And there was peace between Israel and the Amorites.

15-17 Samuel gave solid leadership to Israel his entire life. Every year he went on a circuit from Bethel to Gilgal to Mizpah. He gave leadership to Israel in each of these places. But always he would return to Ramah, where he lived, and preside from there. That is where he built an altar to GOD.

REJECTING GOD AS THE KING

1-3 8 When Samuel got to be an old man, he set his sons up as judges in Israel. His firstborn son was named Joel, the name of his second, Abijah. They were assigned duty in Beersheba. But his sons didn't take after him; they were out for what they could get for themselves, taking bribes, corrupting justice.

4-5 Fed up, all the elders of Israel got together and confronted Samuel at Ramah. They presented their case: "Look, you're an old man, and your sons aren't following in your footsteps. Here's what we want you to do: Appoint a king to rule us, just like everybody else."

6 When Samuel heard their demand—"Give us a king to rule us!"—he was crushed. How awful! Samuel prayed to GOD.

7-9 GOD answered Samuel, "Go ahead and do what they're asking. They are not rejecting you. They've rejected me as their King. From the day I brought them out of Egypt until this very day they've been behaving like this, leaving me for other gods. And now they're doing it to you. So let them have their own way. But warn them of what they're in for. Tell them the way kings operate, just what they're likely to get from a king."

10-18 So Samuel told them, delivered GOD's warning to the people who were asking him to give them a king. He said, "This is the way the kind of king you're talking about operates. He'll take your sons and make soldiers of them—chariotry, cavalry, infantry, regimented in battalions and squadrons. He'll put some to forced labor on his farms, plowing and harvesting, and others to making either weapons of war or chariots in which he can ride in luxury. He'll put your daughters to work as beauticians and waitresses and cooks. He'll conscript your best fields, vineyards, and orchards and hand them over to his special friends. He'll tax your harvests and vintage to support his extensive bureaucracy. Your prize workers and best animals he'll take for his own use. He'll lay a tax on your flocks and you'll end up no better than slaves. The day will come when you will cry in desperation because of this king

New King James Version

chosen for yourselves, and the LORD will not
hear you in that day."
19 Nevertheless the people refused to obey
the voice of Samuel; and they said, "No, but we
will have a king over us, 20 that we also may be
like all the nations, and that our king may judge
us and go out before us and fight our battles."
21 And Samuel heard all the words of the peo-
ple, and he repeated them in the hearing of the
LORD. 22 So the LORD said to Samuel, "Heed their
voice, and make them a king."
And Samuel said to the men of Israel, "Every
man go to his city."

Saul Chosen to Be King

9 There was a man of Benjamin whose name
was Kish the son of Abiel, the son of Zeror,
the son of Bechorath, the son of Aphiah, a Ben-
jamite, a mighty man of power. 2 And he had a
choice and handsome son whose name *was*
Saul. *There was* not a more handsome person
than he among the children of Israel. From his
shoulders upward *he was* taller than any of the
people.
3 Now the donkeys of Kish, Saul's father,
were lost. And Kish said to his son Saul, "Please
take one of the servants with you, and arise, go
and look for the donkeys." 4 So he passed
through the mountains of Ephraim and through
the land of Shalisha, but they did not find *them*.
Then they passed through the land of Shaalim,
and *they were* not *there*. Then he passed
through the land of the Benjamites, but they did
not find *them*.
5 When they had come to the land of Zuph,
Saul said to his servant who *was* with him,
"Come, let us return, lest my father cease *caring*
about the donkeys and become worried about
us."
6 And he said to him, "Look now, *there is* in
this city a man of God, and *he is* an honorable
man; all that he says surely comes to pass. So let
us go there; perhaps he can show us the way
that we should go."
7 Then Saul said to his servant, "But look, *if*
we go, what shall we bring the man? For the
bread in our vessels is all gone, and *there is* no
present to bring to the man of God. What do we
have?"
8 And the servant answered Saul again and
said, "Look, I have here at hand one-fourth of a
shekel of silver. I will give *that* to the man of
God, to tell us our way." 9 (Formerly in Israel,
when a man went to inquire of God, he spoke
thus: "Come, let us go to the seer"; for *he who is*
now *called* a prophet was formerly called a
seer.)
10 Then Saul said to his servant, "Well said;
come, let us go." So they went to the city where
the man of God *was*.
11 As they went up the hill to the city, they met
some young women going out to draw water,
and said to them, "Is the seer here?"
12 And they answered them and said, "Yes,
there he is, just ahead of you. Hurry now; for to-
day he came to this city, because there is a sac-
rifice of the people today on the high place. 13 As
soon as you come into the city, you will surely
find him before he goes up to the high place to

The Message

you so much want for yourselves. But don't
expect GOD to answer."
19-20 But the people wouldn't listen to Samuel.
"No!" they said. "We will have a king to rule
us! Then we'll be just like all the other na-
tions. Our king will rule us and lead us and
fight our battles."
21-22 Samuel took in what they said and re-
hearsed it with GOD. GOD told Samuel, "Do
what they say. Make them a king."
Then Samuel dismissed the men of Israel:
"Go home, each of you to your own city."

Saul—Head and Shoulders Above the Crowd

1-2 9 There was a man from the tribe of Ben-
jamin named Kish. He was the son of
Abiel, grandson of Zeror, great-grandson of
Becorath, great-great-grandson of Aphiah—
a Benjaminite of stalwart character. He had
a son, Saul, a most handsome young man.
There was none finer—he literally stood
head and shoulders above the crowd!
3-4 Some of Kish's donkeys got lost. Kish
said to his son, "Saul, take one of the ser-
vants with you and go look for the donkeys."
Saul took one of the servants and went to
find the donkeys. They went into the hill
country of Ephraim around Shalisha, but
didn't find them. Then they went over to
Shaalim—no luck. Then to Jabin, and still
nothing.
5 When they got to Zuph, Saul said to the
young man with him, "Enough of this. Let's
go back. Soon my father is going to forget
about the donkeys and start worrying about
us."
6 He replied, "Not so fast. There's a holy
man in this town. He carries a lot of weight
around here. What he says is always right
on the mark. Maybe he can tell us where to
go."
7 Saul said, "If we go, what do we have to
give him? There's no more bread in our
sacks. We've nothing to bring as a gift to the
holy man. Do we have anything else?"
8-9 The servant spoke up, "Look, I just hap-
pen to have this silver coin! I'll give it to the
holy man and he'll tell us how to proceed!"
(In former times in Israel, a person who
wanted to seek God's word on a matter
would say, "Let's visit the Seer," because the
one we now call "the Prophet" used to be
called "the Seer.")
10 "Good," said Saul, "let's go." And they set
off for the town where the holy man lived.
11 As they were climbing up the hill into the
town, they met some girls who were coming
out to draw water. They said to them, "Is this
where the Seer lives?"
12-13 They answered, "It sure is—just ahead.
Hurry up. He's come today because the peo-
ple have prepared a sacrifice at the shrine.
As soon as you enter the town, you can
catch him before he goes up to the shrine to

NEW KING JAMES VERSION

eat. For the people will not eat until he comes,
because he must bless the sacrifice; afterward
those who are invited will eat. Now therefore, go
up, for about this time you will find him." 14So
they went up to the city. As they were coming
into the city, there was Samuel, coming out to-
ward them on his way up to the high place.
15Now the LORD had told Samuel in his ear
the day before Saul came, saying, 16"Tomorrow
about this time I will send you a man from the
land of Benjamin, and you shall anoint him
commander over My people Israel, that he may
save My people from the hand of the Philistines;
for I have looked upon My people, because their
cry has come to Me."
17So when Samuel saw Saul, the LORD said to
him, "There he is, the man of whom I spoke to
you. This one shall reign over My people."
18Then Saul drew near to Samuel in the gate,
and said, "Please tell me, where *is* the seer's
house?"
19Samuel answered Saul and said, "I *am* the
seer. Go up before me to the high place, for you
shall eat with me today; and tomorrow I will let
you go and will tell you all that *is* in your heart.
20But as for your donkeys that were lost three
days ago, do not be anxious about them, for they
have been found. And on whom *is* all the desire
of Israel? *Is it* not on you and on all your father's
house?"
21And Saul answered and said, "*Am* I not a
Benjamite, of the smallest of the tribes of Israel,
and my family the least of all the families of the
tribe[a] of Benjamin? Why then do you speak like
this to me?"
22Now Samuel took Saul and his servant and
brought them into the hall, and had them sit in
the place of honor among those who were in-
vited; there *were* about thirty persons. 23And
Samuel said to the cook, "Bring the portion
which I gave you, of which I said to you, 'Set it
apart.' " 24So the cook took up the thigh with its
upper part and set *it* before Saul. And *Samuel*
said, "Here it is, what was kept back. *It* was set
apart for you. Eat; for until this time it has been
kept for you, since I said I invited the people."
So Saul ate with Samuel that day.
25When they had come down from the high
place into the city, *Samuel* spoke with Saul on
the top of the house.[a] 26They arose early; and it
was about the dawning of the day that Samuel
called to Saul on the top of the house, saying,
"Get up, that I may send you on your way." And
Saul arose, and both of them went outside, he
and Samuel.

SAUL ANOINTED KING

27As they were going down to the outskirts of
the city, Samuel said to Saul, "Tell the servant to
go on ahead of us." And he went on. "But you
stand here awhile, that I may announce to you
the word of God."

10 Then Samuel took a flask of oil and
poured *it* on his head, and kissed him and

9:21 [a]Literally *tribes* 9:25 [a]Following Masoretic Text and Targum; Septuagint omits *He spoke with Saul on the top of the house;* Septuagint and Vulgate add *And he prepared a bed for Saul on the top of the house, and he slept.*

THE MESSAGE

eat. The people won't eat until he arrives, for
he has to bless the sacrifice. Only then can
everyone eat. So get going. You're sure to
find him!"
14 They continued their climb and entered
the city. And then there he was—Samuel!—
coming straight toward them on his way to
the shrine!
15-16 The very day before, GOD had confided in
Samuel, "This time tomorrow, I'm sending a
man from the land of Benjamin to meet you.
You're to anoint him as prince over my peo-
ple Israel. He will free my people from
Philistine oppression. Yes, I know all about
their hard circumstances. I've heard their
cries for help."
17 The moment Samuel laid eyes on Saul,
GOD said, "He's the one, the man I told you
about. This is the one who will keep my peo-
ple in check."
18 Saul came up to Samuel in the street and
said, "Pardon me, but can you tell me where
the Seer lives?"
19-20 "I'm the Seer," said Samuel. "Accompany
me to the shrine and eat with me. In the
morning I'll tell you all about what's on your
mind, and send you on your way. And by the
way, your lost donkeys—the ones you've
been hunting for the last three days—have
been found, so don't worry about them. At
this moment, Israel's future is in your
hands."
21 Saul answered, "But I'm only a Benjami-
nite, from the smallest of Israel's tribes, and
from the most insignificant clan in the tribe
at that. Why are you talking to me like this?"
22-23 Samuel took Saul and his servant and led
them into the dining hall at the shrine and
seated them at the head of the table. There
were about thirty guests. Then Samuel di-
rected the chef, "Bring the choice cut I
pointed out to you, the one I told you to re-
serve."
24 The chef brought it and placed it before
Saul with a flourish, saying, "This meal was
kept aside just for you. Eat! It was especially
prepared for this time and occasion with
these guests."
Saul ate with Samuel—a memorable day!
25 Afterward they went down from the
shrine into the city. A bed was prepared for
Saul on the breeze-cooled roof of Samuel's
house.
26 They woke at the break of day. Samuel
called to Saul on the roof, "Get up and I'll
send you off." Saul got up and the two of
them went out in the street.
27 As they approached the outskirts of
town, Samuel said to Saul, "Tell your ser-
vant to go on ahead of us. You stay with me
for a bit. I have a word of God to give you."

"YOU'LL BE A NEW PERSON"

1-2 10 Then Samuel took a flask of oil,
poured it on Saul's head, and kissed

NEW KING JAMES VERSION

said: "*Is it* not because the LORD has anointed
you commander over His inheritance?[a] 2When
you have departed from me today, you will find
two men by Rachel's tomb in the territory of
Benjamin at Zelzah; and they will say to you,
'The donkeys which you went to look for have
been found. And now your father has ceased
caring about the donkeys and is worrying about
you, saying, "What shall I do about my son?" '
3Then you shall go on forward from there and
come to the terebinth tree of Tabor. There three
men going up to God at Bethel will meet you,
one carrying three young goats, another carry-
ing three loaves of bread, and another carrying
a skin of wine. 4And they will greet you and give
you two *loaves* of bread, which you shall receive
from their hands. 5After that you shall come to
the hill of God where the Philistine garrison *is*.
And it will happen, when you have come there
to the city, that you will meet a group of
prophets coming down from the high place with
a stringed instrument, a tambourine, a flute, and
a harp before them; and they will be prophesy-
ing. 6Then the Spirit of the LORD will come upon
you, and you will prophesy with them and be
turned into another man. 7And let it be, when
these signs come to you, *that* you do as the oc-
casion demands; for God *is* with you. 8You shall
go down before me to Gilgal; and surely I will
come down to you to offer burnt offerings *and*
make sacrifices of peace offerings. Seven days
you shall wait, till I come to you and show you
what you should do."

9So it was, when he had turned his back to
go from Samuel, that God gave him another
heart; and all those signs came to pass that day.
10When they came there to the hill, there was a
group of prophets to meet him; then the Spirit of
God came upon him, and he prophesied among
them. 11And it happened, when all who knew
him formerly saw that he indeed prophesied
among the prophets, that the people said to one
another, "What *is* this *that* has come upon the
son of Kish? *Is* Saul also among the prophets?"
12Then a man from there answered and said,
"But who *is* their father?" Therefore it became a
proverb: "*Is* Saul also among the prophets?"
13And when he had finished prophesying, he
went to the high place.

14Then Saul's uncle said to him and his ser-
vant, "Where did you go?"

So he said, "To look for the donkeys. When
we saw that *they were* nowhere *to be found*, we
went to Samuel."

15And Saul's uncle said, "Tell me, please,
what Samuel said to you."

10:1 [a]Following Masoretic Text, Targum, and Vulgate; Septuagint reads *His people Israel; and you shall rule the people of the Lord;* Septuagint and Vulgate add *And you shall deliver His people from the hands of their enemies all around them. And this shall be a sign to you, that God has anointed you to be a prince.*

THE MESSAGE

him. He said, "Do you see what this means? GOD has anointed you prince over his people.

"This sign will confirm GOD's anointing of you as prince over his inheritance: After you leave me today, as you get closer to your home country of Benjamin, you'll meet two men near Rachel's Tomb. They'll say, 'The donkeys you went to look for are found. Your father has forgotten about the donkeys and is worried about you, wringing his hands—quite beside himself!'

3-4 "Leaving there, you'll arrive at the Oak of Tabor. There you'll meet three men going up to worship God at Bethel. One will be carrying three young goats, another carrying three sacks of bread, and the third a jug of wine. They'll say, 'Hello, how are you?' and offer you two loaves of bread, which you will accept.

5-6 "Next, you'll come to Gibeah of God, where there's a Philistine garrison. As you approach the town, you'll run into a bunch of prophets coming down from the shrine, playing harps and tambourines, flutes and drums. And they'll be prophesying. Before you know it, the Spirit of GOD will come on you and you'll be prophesying right along with them. And you'll be transformed. You'll be a new person!

7 "When these confirming signs are accomplished, you'll know that you're ready: Whatever job you're given to do, do it. God is with you!

8 "Now, go down to Gilgal and I will follow. I'll come down and join you in worship by sacrificing burnt offerings and peace offerings. Wait seven days. Then I'll come and tell you what to do next."

9 Saul turned and left Samuel. At that very moment God transformed him—made him a new person! And all the confirming signs took place the same day.

SAUL AMONG THE PROPHETS

10-12 When Saul and his party got to Gibeah, there were the prophets, right in front of them! Before he knew it, the Spirit of God came on Saul and he was prophesying right along with them. When those who had previously known Saul saw him prophesying with the prophets, they were totally surprised. "What's going on here? What's come over the son of Kish? How on earth did Saul get to be a prophet?" One man spoke up and said, "Who started this? Where did these people ever come from?"

That's how the saying got started, "Saul among the prophets! Who would have guessed?!"

13-14 When Saul was done prophesying, he returned home. His uncle asked him and his servant, "So where have you two been all this time?"

"Out looking for the donkeys. We looked and looked and couldn't find them. And then we found Samuel!"

15 "So," said Saul's uncle, "what did Samuel tell you?"

NEW KING JAMES VERSION

16 So Saul said to his uncle, "He told us plainly that the donkeys had been found." But about the matter of the kingdom, he did not tell him what Samuel had said.

SAUL PROCLAIMED KING

17 Then Samuel called the people together to the LORD at Mizpah, 18 and said to the children of Israel, "Thus says the LORD God of Israel: 'I brought up Israel out of Egypt, and delivered you from the hand of the Egyptians *and* from the hand of all kingdoms and from those who oppressed you.' 19 But you have today rejected your God, who Himself saved you from all your adversities and your tribulations; and you have said to Him, 'No, set a king over us!' Now therefore, present yourselves before the LORD by your tribes and by your clans."[a]

20 And when Samuel had caused all the tribes of Israel to come near, the tribe of Benjamin was chosen. 21 When he had caused the tribe of Benjamin to come near by their families, the family of Matri was chosen. And Saul the son of Kish was chosen. But when they sought him, he could not be found. 22 Therefore they inquired of the LORD further, "Has the man come here yet?"

And the LORD answered, "There he is, hidden among the equipment."

23 So they ran and brought him from there; and when he stood among the people, he was taller than any of the people from his shoulders upward. 24 And Samuel said to all the people, "Do you see him whom the LORD has chosen, that *there is* no one like him among all the people?"

So all the people shouted and said, "Long live the king!"

25 Then Samuel explained to the people the behavior of royalty, and wrote *it* in a book and laid *it* up before the LORD. And Samuel sent all the people away, every man to his house. 26 And Saul also went home to Gibeah; and valiant *men* went with him, whose hearts God had touched. 27 But some rebels said, "How can this man save us?" So they despised him, and brought him no presents. But he held his peace.

10:19 [a]Literally *thousands*

THE MESSAGE

16 Saul said, "He told us not to worry—the donkeys had been found." But Saul didn't breathe a word to his uncle of what Samuel said about the king business.

"WE WANT A KING!"

17-18 Samuel called the people to assemble before GOD at Mizpah. He addressed the children of Israel, "This is GOD's personal message to you:

18-19 "I brought Israel up out of Egypt. I delivered you from Egyptian oppression—yes, from all the bullying governments that made your life miserable. And now you want nothing to do with your God, the very God who has a history of getting you out of troubles of all sorts.

"And now you say, 'No! We want a king; give us a king!'

"Well, if that's what you want, that's what you'll get! Present yourselves formally before GOD, ranked in tribes and families."

20-21 After Samuel got all the tribes of Israel lined up, the Benjamin tribe was picked. Then he lined up the Benjamin tribe in family groups, and the family of Matri was picked. The family of Matri took its place in the lineup, and the name Saul, son of Kish, was picked. But when they went looking for him, he was nowhere to be found.

22 Samuel went back to GOD: "Is he anywhere around?"

GOD said, "Yes, he's right over there—hidden in that pile of baggage."

23 They ran and got him. He took his place before everyone, standing tall—head and shoulders above them.

24 Samuel then addressed the people, "Take a good look at whom GOD has chosen: the best! No one like him in the whole country!"

Then a great shout went up from the people: "Long live the king!"

25 Samuel went on to instruct the people in the rules and regulations involved in a kingdom, wrote it all down in a book, and placed it before GOD. Then Samuel sent everyone home.

26-27 Saul also went home to Gibeah, and with him some true and brave men whom GOD moved to join him. But the riffraff went off muttering, "Deliverer? Don't make me laugh!" They held him in contempt and refused to congratulate him. But Saul paid them no mind.

SAUL IS CROWNED KING

Nahash, king of the Ammonites, was brutalizing the tribes of Gad and Reuben, gouging out their right eyes and intimidating anyone who would come to Israel's help. There were very few Israelites living on the east side of the Jordan River who had not had their right eyes gouged out by Nahash. But seven thousand men had escaped from the Ammonites and were now living safely in Jabesh.

NEW KING JAMES VERSION

SAUL SAVES JABESH GILEAD

11 Then Nahash the Ammonite came up and encamped against Jabesh Gilead; and all the men of Jabesh said to Nahash, "Make a covenant with us, and we will serve you."

2And Nahash the Ammonite answered them, "On this *condition* I will make *a covenant* with you, that I may put out all your right eyes, and bring reproach on all Israel."

3Then the elders of Jabesh said to him, "Hold off for seven days, that we may send messengers to all the territory of Israel. And then, if *there is* no one to save us, we will come out to you."

4So the messengers came to Gibeah of Saul and told the news in the hearing of the people. And all the people lifted up their voices and wept. 5Now there was Saul, coming behind the herd from the field; and Saul said, "What *troubles* the people, that they weep?" And they told him the words of the men of Jabesh. 6Then the Spirit of God came upon Saul when he heard this news, and his anger was greatly aroused. 7So he took a yoke of oxen and cut them in pieces, and sent *them* throughout all the territory of Israel by the hands of messengers, saying, "Whoever does not go out with Saul and Samuel to battle, so it shall be done to his oxen."

And the fear of the LORD fell on the people, and they came out with one consent. 8When he numbered them in Bezek, the children of Israel were three hundred thousand, and the men of Judah thirty thousand. 9And they said to the messengers who came, "Thus you shall say to the men of Jabesh Gilead: 'Tomorrow, by *the time* the sun is hot, you shall have help.' " Then the messengers came and reported *it* to the men of Jabesh, and they were glad. 10Therefore the men of Jabesh said, "Tomorrow we will come out to you, and you may do with us whatever seems good to you."

11So it was, on the next day, that Saul put the people in three companies; and they came into the midst of the camp in the morning watch, and killed Ammonites until the heat of the day. And it happened that those who survived were scattered, so that no two of them were left together.

12Then the people said to Samuel, "Who *is* he who said, 'Shall Saul reign over us?' Bring the men, that we may put them to death."

13But Saul said, "Not a man shall be put to death this day, for today the LORD has accomplished salvation in Israel."

14Then Samuel said to the people, "Come, let us go to Gilgal and renew the kingdom there." 15So all the people went to Gilgal, and there they made Saul king before the LORD in Gilgal. There they made sacrifices of peace offerings before the LORD, and there Saul and all the men of Israel rejoiced greatly.

SAMUEL'S ADDRESS AT SAUL'S CORONATION

12 Now Samuel said to all Israel: "Indeed I have heeded your voice in all that you said to me, and have made a king over you. 2And now here is the king, walking before you; and I am old and grayheaded, and look, my sons *are*

THE MESSAGE

1 11 So Nahash went after them and prepared to go to war against Jabesh Gilead. The men of Jabesh petitioned Nahash: "Make a treaty with us and we'll serve you."

2 Nahash said, "I'll make a treaty with you on one condition: that every right eye among you be gouged out! I'll humiliate every last man and woman in Israel before I'm done!"

3 The town leaders of Jabesh said, "Give us time to send messengers around Israel—seven days should do it. If no one shows up to help us, we'll accept your terms."

4-5 The messengers came to Saul's place at Gibeah and told the people what was going on. As the people broke out in loud wails, Saul showed up. He was coming back from the field with his oxen.

Saul asked, "What happened? Why is everyone crying?"

And they repeated the message that had come from Jabesh.

6-7 The Spirit of God came on Saul when he heard the report and he flew into a rage. He grabbed the yoke of oxen and butchered them on the spot. He sent the messengers throughout Israel distributing the bloody pieces with this message: "Anyone who refuses to join up with Saul and Samuel, let this be the fate of his oxen!"

7-8 The terror of GOD seized the people, and they came out, one and all, not a laggard among them. Saul took command of the people at Bezek. There were 300,000 men from Israel, another 30,000 from Judah.

9-11 Saul instructed the messengers, "Tell this to the folk in Jabesh Gilead: 'Help is on the way. Expect it by noon tomorrow.' "

The messengers set straight off and delivered their message. Elated, the people of Jabesh Gilead sent word to Nahash: "Tomorrow we'll give ourselves up. You can deal with us on your terms." Long before dawn the next day, Saul had strategically placed his army in three groups. At first light they broke into the enemy camp and slaughtered Ammonites until noon. Those who were left ran for their lives, scattering every which way.

12 The people came to Samuel then and said, "Where are those men who said, 'Saul is not fit to rule over us'? Hand them over. We'll kill them!"

13-14 But Saul said, "Nobody is going to be executed this day. This is the day GOD saved Israel! Come, let's go to Gilgal and there reconsecrate the kingship."

15 They all trooped out to Gilgal. Before GOD, they crowned Saul king at Gilgal. And there they worshiped, sacrificing peace offerings. Saul and all Israel celebrated magnificently.

"DON'T CHASE AFTER GHOST-GODS"

1-3 12 Samuel addressed all Israel: "I've listened to everything you've said to me, listened carefully to every word, and I've given you a king. See for yourself: Your king among you, leading you! But now look at

NEW KING JAMES VERSION

with you. I have walked before you from my
childhood to this day. 3Here I am. Witness
against me before the LORD and before His
anointed: Whose ox have I taken, or whose don-
key have I taken, or whom have I cheated?
Whom have I oppressed, or from whose hand
have I received *any* bribe with which to blind
my eyes? I will restore *it* to you."
4And they said, "You have not cheated us or
oppressed us, nor have you taken anything from
any man's hand."
5Then he said to them, "The LORD *is* witness
against you, and His anointed *is* witness this
day, that you have not found anything in my
hand."
And they answered, "*He is* witness."
6Then Samuel said to the people, "*It is* the
LORD who raised up Moses and Aaron, and who
brought your fathers up from the land of Egypt.
7Now therefore, stand still, that I may reason
with you before the LORD concerning all the
righteous acts of the LORD which He did to you
and your fathers: 8When Jacob had gone into
Egypt,[a] and your fathers cried out to the LORD,
then the LORD sent Moses and Aaron, who
brought your fathers out of Egypt and made
them dwell in this place. 9And when they forgot
the LORD their God, He sold them into the hand
of Sisera, commander of the army of Hazor, into
the hand of the Philistines, and into the hand of
the king of Moab; and they fought against them.
10Then they cried out to the LORD, and said, 'We
have sinned, because we have forsaken the
LORD and served the Baals and Ashtoreths;[a] but
now deliver us from the hand of our enemies,
and we will serve You.' 11And the LORD sent
Jerubbaal,[a] Bedan,[b] Jephthah, and Samuel,[c] and
delivered you out of the hand of your enemies
on every side; and you dwelt in safety. 12And
when you saw that Nahash king of the Am-
monites came against you, you said to me, 'No,
but a king shall reign over us,' when the LORD
your God *was* your king.
13"Now therefore, here is the king whom you
have chosen *and* whom you have desired. And
take note, the LORD has set a king over you. 14If
you fear the LORD and serve Him and obey His
voice, and do not rebel against the commandment
of the LORD, then both you and the king who
reigns over you will continue following the LORD
your God. 15However, if you do not obey the voice
of the LORD, but rebel against the commandment
of the LORD, then the hand of the LORD will be
against you, as *it was* against your fathers.
16"Now therefore, stand and see this great
thing which the LORD will do before your eyes:
17*Is* today not the wheat harvest? I will call to
the LORD, and He will send thunder and rain,
that you may perceive and see that your wicked-
ness *is* great, which you have done in the sight
of the LORD, in asking a king for yourselves."
18So Samuel called to the LORD, and the LORD
sent thunder and rain that day; and all the peo-
ple greatly feared the LORD and Samuel.

12:8 [a]Following Masoretic Text, Targum, and Vulgate; Septuagint adds *and the Egyptians afflicted them.* **12:10** [a]Canaanite goddesses **12:11** [a]Syriac reads *Deborah;* Targum reads *Gideon.* [b]Septuagint and Syriac read *Barak;* Targum reads *Simson.* [c]Syriac reads *Simson.*

THE MESSAGE

me: I'm old and gray, and my sons are still
here. I've led you faithfully from my youth
until this very day. Look at me! Do you have
any complaints to bring before GOD and his
anointed? Have I ever stolen so much as an
ox or a donkey? Have I ever taken advan-
tage of you or exploited you? Have I ever
taken a bribe or played fast and loose with
the law? Bring your complaint and I'll make
it right."
4 "Oh no," they said, "never. You've never
done any of that—never abused us, never
lined your own pockets."
5 "That settles it then," said Samuel. "GOD
is witness, and his anointed is witness that
you find nothing against me—no faults, no
complaints."
6-8 And the people said, "He is witness."
Samuel continued, "This is the GOD who
made Moses and Aaron your leaders and
brought your ancestors out of Egypt. Take
your stand before him now as I review your
case before GOD in the light of all the righ-
teous ways in which GOD has worked with
you and your ancestors. When Jacob's sons
entered Egypt, the Egyptians made life hard
for them and they cried for help to GOD. GOD
sent Moses and Aaron, who led your ances-
tors out of Egypt and settled them here in
this place.
9 "They soon forgot their GOD, so he sold
them off to Sisera, commander of Hazor's
army, later to a hard life under the
Philistines, and still later to the king of
Moab. They had to fight for their lives.
10 "Then they cried for help to GOD. They
confessed, 'We've sinned! We've gone off
and left GOD and worshiped the fertility
gods and goddesses of Canaan. Oh, deliver
us from the brutalities of our enemies and
we'll worship you alone.'
11 "So GOD sent Jerub-Baal (Gideon), Bedan
(Barak), Jephthah, and Samuel. He saved
you from that hard life surrounded by ene-
mies, and you lived in peace.
12 "But when you saw Nahash, king of the
Ammonites, preparing to attack you, you
said to me, 'No more of this. We want a king
to lead us.' And GOD was already your king!
13-15 "So here's the king you wanted, the king
you asked for. GOD has let you have your own
way, given you a king. If you fear GOD, wor-
ship and obey him, and don't rebel against
what he tells you. If both you and your king
follow GOD, no problem. GOD will be sure to
save you. But if you don't obey him and rebel
against what he tells you, king or no king,
you will fare no better than your fathers.
16-17 "Pay attention! Watch this wonder that
GOD is going to perform before you now! It's
summer, as you well know, and the rainy
season is over. But I'm going to pray to GOD.
He'll send thunder and rain, a sign to con-
vince you of the great wrong you have done
to GOD by asking for a king."
18 Samuel prayed to GOD, and GOD sent
thunder and rain that same day. The people
were greatly afraid and in awe of GOD and
of Samuel.

NEW KING JAMES VERSION

19And all the people said to Samuel, "Pray for your servants to the LORD your God, that we may not die; for we have added to all our sins the evil of asking a king for ourselves."

20Then Samuel said to the people, "Do not fear. You have done all this wickedness; yet do not turn aside from following the LORD, but serve the LORD with all your heart. 21And do not turn aside; for *then you would go* after empty things which cannot profit or deliver, for they *are* nothing. 22For the LORD will not forsake His people, for His great name's sake, because it has pleased the LORD to make you His people. 23Moreover, as for me, far be it from me that I should sin against the LORD in ceasing to pray for you; but I will teach you the good and the right way. 24Only fear the LORD, and serve Him in truth with all your heart; for consider what great things He has done for you. 25But if you still do wickedly, you shall be swept away, both you and your king."

SAUL'S UNLAWFUL SACRIFICE

13 Saul reigned one year; and when he had reigned two years over Israel,[a] 2Saul chose for himself three thousand *men* of Israel. Two thousand were with Saul in Michmash and in the mountains of Bethel, and a thousand were with Jonathan in Gibeah of Benjamin. The rest of the people he sent away, every man to his tent.

3And Jonathan attacked the garrison of the Philistines that *was* in Geba, and the Philistines heard *of it*. Then Saul blew the trumpet throughout all the land, saying, "Let the Hebrews hear!" 4Now all Israel heard it said *that* Saul had attacked a garrison of the Philistines, and *that* Israel had also become an abomination to the Philistines. And the people were called together to Saul at Gilgal.

5Then the Philistines gathered together to fight with Israel, thirty[a] thousand chariots and six thousand horsemen, and people as the sand which *is* on the seashore in multitude. And they came up and encamped in Michmash, to the east of Beth Aven. 6When the men of Israel saw that they were in danger (for the people were distressed), then the people hid in caves, in thickets, in rocks, in holes, and in pits. 7And *some of* the Hebrews crossed over the Jordan to the land of Gad and Gilead.

As for Saul, he *was* still in Gilgal, and all the people followed him trembling. 8Then he waited seven days, according to the time set by Samuel. But Samuel did not come to Gilgal; and the people were scattered from him. 9So Saul said, "Bring a burnt offering and peace offerings here to me." And he offered the burnt offering. 10Now it happened, as soon as he had finished presenting the burnt offering, that Samuel came; and

13:1 [a]The Hebrew is difficult (compare 2 Samuel 5:4; 2 Kings 14:2; see also 2 Samuel 2:10; Acts 13:21). **13:5** [a]Following Masoretic Text, Septuagint, Targum, and Vulgate; Syriac and some manuscripts of the Septuagint read *three*.

THE MESSAGE

19 Then all the people begged Samuel, "Pray to your GOD for us, your servants. Pray that we won't die! On top of all our other sins, we've piled on one more—asking for a king!"

20-22 Samuel said to them, "Don't be fearful. It's true that you have done something very wrong. All the same, don't turn your back on GOD. Worship and serve him heart and soul! Don't chase after ghost-gods. There's nothing to them. They can't help you. They're nothing but ghost-gods! GOD, simply because of who he is, is not going to walk off and leave his people. GOD took delight in making you into his very own people.

23-25 "And neither will I walk off and leave you. That would be a sin against GOD! I'm staying right here at my post praying for you and teaching you the good and right way to live. But I beg of you, fear GOD and worship him honestly and heartily. You've seen how greatly he has worked among you! Be warned: If you live badly, both you and your king will be thrown out."

"GOD IS OUT LOOKING FOR YOUR REPLACEMENT"

1 13 Saul was a young man when he began as king. He was king over Israel for many years.

2 Saul conscripted enough men for three companies of soldiers. He kept two companies under his command at Micmash and in the Bethel hills. The other company was under Jonathan at Gibeah in Benjamin. He sent the rest of the men home.

3-4 Jonathan attacked and killed the Philistine governor stationed at Geba (Gibeah). When the Philistines heard the news, they raised the alarm: "The Hebrews are in revolt!" Saul ordered the reveille trumpets blown throughout the land. The word went out all over Israel, "Saul has killed the Philistine governor—drawn first blood! The Philistines are stirred up and mad as hornets!" Summoned, the army came to Saul at Gilgal.

5 The Philistines rallied their forces to fight Israel: three companies of chariots, six companies of cavalry, and so many infantry they looked like sand on the seashore. They went up into the hills and set up camp at Micmash, east of Beth Aven.

6-7 When the Israelites saw that they were way outnumbered and in deep trouble, they ran for cover, hiding in caves and pits, ravines and brambles and cisterns—wherever. They retreated across the Jordan River, refugees fleeing to the country of Gad and Gilead. But Saul held his ground in Gilgal, his soldiers still with him but scared to death.

8 He waited seven days, the time set by Samuel. Samuel failed to show up at Gilgal, and the soldiers were slipping away, right and left.

9-10 So Saul took charge: "Bring me the burnt offering and the peace offerings!" He went ahead and sacrificed the burnt offering. No

NEW KING JAMES VERSION

Saul went out to meet him, that he might greet
him.
[11]And Samuel said, "What have you done?"
Saul said, "When I saw that the people were
scattered from me, and *that* you did not come
within the days appointed, and *that* the
Philistines gathered together at Michmash,
[12]then I said, 'The Philistines will now come
down on me at Gilgal, and I have not made sup-
plication to the LORD.' Therefore I felt com-
pelled, and offered a burnt offering."
[13]And Samuel said to Saul, "You have done
foolishly. You have not kept the commandment
of the LORD your God, which He commanded
you. For now the LORD would have established
your kingdom over Israel forever. [14]But now
your kingdom shall not continue. The LORD has
sought for Himself a man after His own heart,
and the LORD has commanded him *to be* com-
mander over His people, because you have not
kept what the LORD commanded you."
[15]Then Samuel arose and went up from Gil-
gal to Gibeah of Benjamin.[a] And Saul numbered
the people present with him, about six hundred
men.

NO WEAPONS FOR THE ARMY

[16]Saul, Jonathan his son, and the people
present with them remained in Gibeah of Ben-
jamin. But the Philistines encamped in Mich-
mash. [17]Then raiders came out of the camp of
the Philistines in three companies. One com-
pany turned onto the road to Ophrah, to the
land of Shual, [18]another company turned to the
road *to* Beth Horon, and another company
turned *to* the road of the border that overlooks
the Valley of Zeboim toward the wilderness.
[19]Now there was no blacksmith to be found
throughout all the land of Israel, for the
Philistines said, "Lest the Hebrews make swords
or spears." [20]But all the Israelites would go
down to the Philistines to sharpen each man's
plowshare, his mattock, his ax, and his sickle;
[21]and the charge for a sharpening was a pim[a] for
the plowshares, the mattocks, the forks, and the
axes, and to set the points of the goads. [22]So it
came about, on the day of battle, that there was
neither sword nor spear found in the hand of
any of the people who *were* with Saul and
Jonathan. But they were found with Saul and
Jonathan his son.
[23]And the garrison of the Philistines went out
to the pass of Michmash.

JONATHAN DEFEATS THE PHILISTINES

14 Now it happened one day that Jonathan
the son of Saul said to the young man who
bore his armor, "Come, let us go over to the
Philistines' garrison that *is* on the other side."

13:15 [a]Following Masoretic Text and Targum; Septuagint and Vulgate add *And the rest of the people went up after Saul to meet the people who fought against them, going from Gilgal to Gibeah in the hill of Benjamin.* **13:21** [a]About two-thirds shekel weight

THE MESSAGE

sooner had he done it than Samuel showed
up! Saul greeted him.
11-12 Samuel said, "What on earth are you do-
ing?"
Saul answered, "When I saw I was losing
my army from under me, and that you hadn't
come when you said you would, and that the
Philistines were poised at Micmash, I said,
'The Philistines are about to come down on
me in Gilgal, and I haven't yet come before
GOD asking for his help.' So I took things into
my own hands, and sacrificed the burnt of-
fering."
13-14 "That was a fool thing to do," Samuel said
to Saul. "If you had kept the appointment
that your GOD commanded, by now GOD
would have set a firm and lasting founda-
tion under your kingly rule over Israel. As it
is, your kingly rule is already falling to
pieces. GOD is out looking for your replace-
ment right now. This time he'll do the choos-
ing. When he finds him, he'll appoint him
leader of his people. And all because you
didn't keep your appointment with GOD!"
15 At that, Samuel got up and left Gilgal.
What army there was left followed Saul into
battle. They went into the hills from Gilgal
toward Gibeah in Benjamin. Saul looked
over and assessed the soldiers still with
him—a mere six hundred!

JONATHAN AND HIS ARMOR BEARER

16-18 Saul, his son Jonathan, and the soldiers who
had remained made camp at Geba (Gibeah)
of Benjamin. The Philistines were camped
at Micmash. Three squads of raiding parties
were regularly sent out from the Philistine
camp. One squadron was assigned to the
Ophrah road going toward Shual country;
another was assigned to the Beth Horon
road; the third took the border road that
rimmed the Valley of Hyenas.
19-22 There wasn't a blacksmith to be found
anywhere in Israel. The Philistines made
sure of that—"Lest those Hebrews start
making swords and spears." That meant
that the Israelites had to go down among the
Philistines to keep their farm tools—plow-
shares and mattocks, axes and sickles—
sharp and in good repair. They charged a
silver coin for the plowshares and mattocks,
and half that for the rest. So when the battle
of Micmash was joined, there wasn't a
sword or spear to be found anywhere in Is-
rael—except for Saul and his son Jonathan;
they were both well-armed.
23 A patrol of Philistines took up a position
at Micmash Pass.

1-3 14 Later that day, Jonathan, Saul's son,
said to his armor bearer, "Come on, let's
go over to the Philistine garrison patrol on
the other side of the pass." But he didn't tell

NEW KING JAMES VERSION

But he did not tell his father. [2]And Saul was sit-
ting in the outskirts of Gibeah under a pome-
granate tree which *is* in Migron. The people who
were with him *were* about six hundred men.
[3]Ahijah the son of Ahitub, Ichabod's brother, the
son of Phinehas, the son of Eli, the LORD's priest
in Shiloh, was wearing an ephod. But the people
did not know that Jonathan had gone.
[4]Between the passes, by which Jonathan
sought to go over to the Philistines' garrison,
there was a sharp rock on one side and a sharp
rock on the other side. And the name of one *was*
Bozez, and the name of the other Seneh. [5]The
front of one faced northward opposite Mich-
mash, and the other southward opposite
Gibeah.
[6]Then Jonathan said to the young man who
bore his armor, "Come, let us go over to the gar-
rison of these uncircumcised; it may be that the
LORD will work for us. For nothing restrains the
LORD from saving by many or by few."
[7]So his armorbearer said to him, "Do all that
is in your heart. Go then; here I am with you, ac-
cording to your heart."
[8]Then Jonathan said, "Very well, let us cross
over to *these* men, and we will show ourselves
to them. [9]If they say thus to us, 'Wait until we
come to you,' then we will stand still in our place
and not go up to them. [10]But if they say thus,
'Come up to us,' then we will go up. For the LORD
has delivered them into our hand, and this *will
be* a sign to us."
[11]So both of them showed themselves to the
garrison of the Philistines. And the Philistines
said, "Look, the Hebrews are coming out of the
holes where they have hidden." [12]Then the men
of the garrison called to Jonathan and his ar-
morbearer, and said, "Come up to us, and we
will show you something."
Jonathan said to his armorbearer, "Come up
after me, for the LORD has delivered them into
the hand of Israel." [13]And Jonathan climbed up
on his hands and knees with his armorbearer
after him; and they fell before Jonathan. And as
he came after him, his armorbearer killed them.
[14]That first slaughter which Jonathan and his
armorbearer made was about twenty men
within about half an acre of land.[a]
[15]And there was trembling in the camp, in
the field, and among all the people. The garrison
and the raiders also trembled; and the earth
quaked, so that it was a very great trembling.
[16]Now the watchmen of Saul in Gibeah of Ben-
jamin looked, and *there* was the multitude,
melting away; and they went here and there.
[17]Then Saul said to the people who *were* with
him, "Now call the roll and see who has gone
from us." And when they had called the roll, sur-
prisingly, Jonathan and his armorbearer *were*
not *there.* [18]And Saul said to Ahijah, "Bring the
ark[a] of God here" (for at that time the ark[b] of
God was with the children of Israel). [19]Now it

14:14 [a]Literally *half the area plowed by a yoke* (of oxen in a day) **14:18** [a]Following Masoretic Text, Targum, and Vulgate; Septuagint reads *ephod.* [b]Following Masoretic Text, Targum, and Vulgate; Septuagint reads *ephod.*

THE MESSAGE

his father. Meanwhile, Saul was taking it easy under the pomegranate tree at the threshing floor on the edge of town at Geba (Gibeah). There were about six hundred men with him. Ahijah, wearing the priestly Ephod, was also there. (Ahijah was the son of Ahitub, brother of Ichabod, son of Phinehas, who was the son of Eli the priest of GOD at Shiloh.) No one there knew that Jonathan had gone off.

4-5 The pass that Jonathan was planning to cross over to the Philistine garrison was flanked on either side by sharp rock outcroppings, cliffs named Bozez and Seneh. The cliff to the north faced Micmash; the cliff to the south faced Geba (Gibeah).

6 Jonathan said to his armor bearer, "Come on now, let's go across to these uncircumcised pagans. Maybe GOD will work for us. There's no rule that says GOD can only deliver by using a big army. No one can stop GOD from saving when he sets his mind to it."

7 His armor bearer said, "Go ahead. Do what you think best. I'm with you all the way."

8-10 Jonathan said, "Here's what we'll do. We'll cross over the pass and let the men see we're there. If they say, 'Halt! Don't move until we check you out,' we'll stay put and not go up. But if they say, 'Come on up,' we'll go right up—and we'll know GOD has given them to us. That will be our sign."

11 So they did it, the two of them. They stepped into the open where they could be seen by the Philistine garrison. The Philistines shouted out, "Look at that! The Hebrews are crawling out of their holes!"

12 Then they yelled down to Jonathan and his armor bearer, "Come on up here! We've got a thing or two to show you!"

13 Jonathan shouted to his armor bearer, "Up! Follow me! GOD has turned them over to Israel!" Jonathan scrambled up on all fours, his armor bearer right on his heels. When the Philistines came running up to them, he knocked them flat, his armor bearer right behind finishing them off, bashing their heads in with stones.

14-15 In this first bloody encounter, Jonathan and his armor bearer killed about twenty men. That set off a terrific upheaval in both camp and field, the soldiers in the garrison and the raiding squad badly shaken up, the ground itself shuddering—panic like you've never seen before!

STRAIGHT TO THE BATTLE

16-18 Saul's sentries posted back at Geba (Gibeah) in Benjamin saw the confusion and turmoil raging in the camp. Saul commanded, "Line up and take the roll. See who's here and who's missing." When they called the roll, Jonathan and his armor bearer turned up missing.

18-19 Saul ordered Ahijah, "Bring the priestly Ephod. Let's see what GOD has to say here." (Ahijah was responsible for the Ephod in those days.) While Saul was in conversation

NEW KING JAMES VERSION

happened, while Saul talked to the priest, that
the noise which *was* in the camp of the
Philistines continued to increase; so Saul said to
the priest, "Withdraw your hand." 20Then Saul
and all the people who *were* with him assem-
bled, and they went to the battle; and indeed
every man's sword was against his neighbor,
and there was very great confusion. 21Moreover
the Hebrews *who* were with the Philistines be-
fore that time, who went up with them into the
camp *from the* surrounding *country,* they also
joined the Israelites who *were* with Saul and
Jonathan. 22Likewise all the men of Israel who
had hidden in the mountains of Ephraim, *when*
they heard that the Philistines fled, they also fol-
lowed hard after them in the battle. 23So the
LORD saved Israel that day, and the battle shifted
to Beth Aven.

SAUL'S RASH OATH

24And the men of Israel were distressed that
day, for Saul had placed the people under oath,
saying, "Cursed *is* the man who eats *any* food
until evening, before I have taken vengeance on
my enemies." So none of the people tasted food.
25Now all *the people* of the land came to a for-
est; and there was honey on the ground. 26And
when the people had come into the woods, there
was the honey, dripping; but no one put his hand
to his mouth, for the people feared the oath.
27But Jonathan had not heard his father charge
the people with the oath; therefore he stretched
out the end of the rod that *was* in his hand and
dipped it in a honeycomb, and put his hand to
his mouth; and his countenance brightened.
28Then one of the people said, "Your father
strictly charged the people with an oath, saying,
'Cursed *is* the man who eats food this day.' "
And the people were faint.

29But Jonathan said, "My father has troubled
the land. Look now, how my countenance has
brightened because I tasted a little of this honey.
30How much better if the people had eaten freely
today of the spoil of their enemies which they
found! For now would there not have been a
much greater slaughter among the Philistines?"

31Now they had driven back the Philistines
that day from Michmash to Aijalon. So the peo-
ple were very faint. 32And the people rushed on
the spoil, and took sheep, oxen, and calves, and
slaughtered *them* on the ground; and the people
ate *them* with the blood. 33Then they told Saul,
saying, "Look, the people are sinning against
the LORD by eating with the blood!"

So he said, "You have dealt treacherously;
roll a large stone to me this day." 34Then Saul
said, "Disperse yourselves among the people,
and say to them, 'Bring me here every man's ox
and every man's sheep, slaughter *them* here, and
eat; and do not sin against the LORD by eating
with the blood.' " So every one of the people
brought his ox with him that night, and slaugh-
tered *it* there.

THE MESSAGE

with the priest, the upheaval in the Philis-
tine camp became greater and louder. Then
Saul interrupted Ahijah: "Put the Ephod
away."

20-23 Saul immediately called his army to-
gether and they went straight to the battle.
When they got there they found total confu-
sion—Philistines swinging their swords
wildly, killing each other. Hebrews who had
earlier defected to the Philistine camp came
back. They now wanted to be with Israel un-
der Saul and Jonathan. Not only that, but
when all the Israelites who had been hiding
out in the backwoods of Ephraim heard that
the Philistines were running for their lives,
they came out and joined the chase. GOD
saved Israel! What a day!

The fighting moved on to Beth Aven. The
whole army was behind Saul now—ten
thousand strong!—with the fighting scatter-
ing into all the towns throughout the hills of
Ephraim.

24 Saul did something really foolish that
day. He addressed the army: "A curse on the
man who eats anything before evening, be-
fore I've wreaked vengeance on my ene-
mies!" None of them ate a thing all day.

25-27 There were honeycombs here and there
in the fields. But no one so much as put his
finger in the honey to taste it, for the sol-
diers to a man feared the curse. But
Jonathan hadn't heard his father put the
army under oath. He stuck the tip of his staff
into some honey and ate it. Refreshed, his
eyes lit up with renewed vigor.

28 A soldier spoke up, "Your father has put
the army under solemn oath, saying, 'A
curse on the man who eats anything before
evening!' No wonder the soldiers are droop-
ing!"

29-30 Jonathan said, "My father has imperiled
the country. Just look how quickly my en-
ergy has returned since I ate a little of this
honey! It would have been a lot better, be-
lieve me, if the soldiers had eaten their fill of
whatever they took from the enemy. Who
knows how much worse we could have
whipped them!"

31-32 They killed Philistines that day all the
way from Micmash to Aijalon, but the sol-
diers ended up totally exhausted. Then they
started plundering. They grabbed anything
in sight—sheep, cattle, calves—and butch-
ered it where they found it. Then they glut-
ted themselves—meat, blood, the works.

33-34 Saul was told, "Do something! The sol-
diers are sinning against GOD. They're eat-
ing meat with the blood still in it!"

Saul said, "You're biting the hand that
feeds you! Roll a big rock over here—now!"
He continued, "Disperse among the troops
and tell them, 'Bring your oxen and sheep to
me and butcher them properly here. Then
you can feast to your heart's content. Please
don't sin against GOD by eating meat with
the blood still in it.' "

And so they did. That night each soldier,
one after another, led his animal there to be
butchered.

New King James Version

35 Then Saul built an altar to the LORD. This was the first altar that he built to the LORD.

36 Now Saul said, "Let us go down after the Philistines by night, and plunder them until the morning light; and let us not leave a man of them."

And they said, "Do whatever seems good to you."

Then the priest said, "Let us draw near to God here."

37 So Saul asked counsel of God, "Shall I go down after the Philistines? Will You deliver them into the hand of Israel?" But He did not answer him that day. 38 And Saul said, "Come over here, all you chiefs of the people, and know and see what this sin was today. 39 For *as* the LORD lives, who saves Israel, though it be in Jonathan my son, he shall surely die." But not a man among all the people answered him. 40 Then he said to all Israel, "You be on one side, and my son Jonathan and I will be on the other side."

And the people said to Saul, "Do what seems good to you."

41 Therefore Saul said to the LORD God of Israel, "Give a perfect *lot.*"[a] So Saul and Jonathan were taken, but the people escaped. 42 And Saul said, "Cast *lots* between my son Jonathan and me." So Jonathan was taken. 43 Then Saul said to Jonathan, "Tell me what you have done."

And Jonathan told him, and said, "I only tasted a little honey with the end of the rod that *was* in my hand. So now I must die!"

44 Saul answered, "God do so and more also; for you shall surely die, Jonathan."

45 But the people said to Saul, "Shall Jonathan die, who has accomplished this great deliverance in Israel? Certainly not! *As* the LORD lives, not one hair of his head shall fall to the ground, for he has worked with God this day." So the people rescued Jonathan, and he did not die.

46 Then Saul returned from pursuing the Philistines, and the Philistines went to their own place.

Saul's Continuing Wars

47 So Saul established his sovereignty over Israel, and fought against all his enemies on every side, against Moab, against the people of Ammon, against Edom, against the kings of Zobah, and against the Philistines. Wherever he turned, he harassed *them.*[a] 48 And he gathered an army and attacked the Amalekites, and delivered Israel from the hands of those who plundered them.

14:41 [a]Following Masoretic Text and Targum; Septuagint and Vulgate read *Why do You not answer Your servant today? If the injustice is with me or Jonathan my son, O LORD God of Israel, give proof; and if You say it is with Your people Israel, give holiness.* **14:47** [a]Septuagint and Vulgate read *prospered.*

The Message

35 That's the story behind Saul's building an altar to GOD. It's the first altar to GOD that he built.

Find Out What God Thinks

36 Saul said, "Let's go after the Philistines tonight! We can spend the night looting and plundering. We won't leave a single live Philistine!"

"Sounds good to us," said the troops. "Let's do it!"

But the priest slowed them down: "Let's find out what God thinks about this."

37 So Saul prayed to God, "Shall I go after the Philistines? Will you put them in Israel's hand?" God didn't answer him on that occasion.

38-39 Saul then said, "All army officers, step forward. Some sin has been committed this day. We're going to find out what it is and who did it! As GOD lives, Israel's Savior God, whoever sinned will die, even if it should turn out to be Jonathan, my son!"

Nobody said a word.

40 Saul said to the Israelites, "You line up over on that side, and I and Jonathan my son will stand on this side."

The army agreed, "Fine. Whatever you say."

41 Then Saul prayed to GOD, "O God of Israel, why haven't you answered me today? Show me the truth. If the sin is in me or Jonathan, then, O GOD, give the sign Urim. But if the sin is in the army of Israel, give the sign Thummim."

The Urim sign turned up and pointed to Saul and Jonathan. That cleared the army.

42 Next Saul said, "Cast the lots between me and Jonathan—and death to the one GOD points to!"

The soldiers protested, "No—this is not right. Stop this!" But Saul pushed on anyway. They cast the lots, Urim and Thummim, and the lot fell to Jonathan.

43 Saul confronted Jonathan. "What did you do? Tell me!"

Jonathan said, "I licked a bit of honey off the tip of the staff I was carrying. That's it—and for that I'm to die?"

44 Saul said, "Yes. Jonathan most certainly will die. It's out of my hands—I can't go against God, can I?"

45 The soldiers rose up: "Jonathan—die? Never! He's just carried out this stunning salvation victory for Israel. As surely as GOD lives, not a hair on his head is going to be harmed. Why, he's been working hand-in-hand with God all day!" The soldiers rescued Jonathan and he didn't die.

46 Saul pulled back from chasing the Philistines, and the Philistines went home.

47-48 Saul extended his rule, capturing neighboring kingdoms. He fought enemies on every front—Moab, Ammon, Edom, the king of Zobah, the Philistines. Wherever he turned, he came up with a victory. He became invincible! He smashed Amalek, freeing Israel from the savagery and looting.

NEW KING JAMES VERSION

49The sons of Saul were Jonathan, Jishui,[a]
and Malchishua. And the names of his two
daughters *were these:* the name of the firstborn
Merab, and the name of the younger Michal.
50The name of Saul's wife *was* Ahinoam the
daughter of Ahimaaz. And the name of the com-
mander of his army *was* Abner the son of Ner,
Saul's uncle. 51Kish *was* the father of Saul, and
Ner the father of Abner *was* the son of Abiel.
52Now there was fierce war with the Philis-
tines all the days of Saul. And when Saul saw
any strong man or any valiant man, he took him
for himself.

SAUL SPARES KING AGAG

15 Samuel also said to Saul, "The LORD sent
me to anoint you king over His people,
over Israel. Now therefore, heed the voice of the
words of the LORD. 2Thus says the LORD of hosts:
'I will punish Amalek *for* what he did to Israel,
how he ambushed him on the way when he
came up from Egypt. 3Now go and attack
Amalek, and utterly destroy all that they have,
and do not spare them. But kill both man and
woman, infant and nursing child, ox and sheep,
camel and donkey.' "
4So Saul gathered the people together and
numbered them in Telaim, two hundred thou-
sand foot soldiers and ten thousand men of Ju-
dah. 5And Saul came to a city of Amalek, and
lay in wait in the valley.
6Then Saul said to the Kenites, "Go, depart,
get down from among the Amalekites, lest I de-
stroy you with them. For you showed kindness
to all the children of Israel when they came up
out of Egypt." So the Kenites departed from
among the Amalekites. 7And Saul attacked the
Amalekites, from Havilah all the way to Shur,
which is east of Egypt. 8He also took Agag king
of the Amalekites alive, and utterly destroyed all
the people with the edge of the sword. 9But Saul
and the people spared Agag and the best of the
sheep, the oxen, the fatlings, the lambs, and all
that was good, and were unwilling to utterly de-
stroy them. But everything despised and worth-
less, that they utterly destroyed.

SAUL REJECTED AS KING

10Now the word of the LORD came to Samuel,
saying, 11"I greatly regret that I have set up Saul
as king, for he has turned back from following
Me, and has not performed My command-
ments." And it grieved Samuel, and he cried out
to the LORD all night. 12So when Samuel rose
early in the morning to meet Saul, it was told
Samuel, saying, "Saul went to Carmel, and in-
deed, he set up a monument for himself; and he
has gone on around, passed by, and gone down
to Gilgal." 13Then Samuel went to Saul, and Saul
said to him, "Blessed *are* you of the LORD! I have
performed the commandment of the LORD."

14:49 [a]Called *Abinadab* in 1 Chronicles 8:33 and 9:39

THE MESSAGE

49-51 Saul's sons were Jonathan, Ishvi, and
Malki-Shua. His daughters were Merab, the
firstborn, and Michal, the younger. Saul's
wife was Ahinoam, daughter of Ahimaaz.
Abner son of Ner was commander of Saul's
army (Ner was Saul's uncle). Kish, Saul's fa-
ther, and Ner, Abner's father, were the sons
of Abiel.

52 All through Saul's life there was war, bit-
ter and relentless, with the Philistines. Saul
conscripted every strong and brave man he
laid eyes on.

1-2 15 Samuel said to Saul, "GOD sent me to
anoint you king over his people, Israel.
Now, listen again to what GOD says. This is
the GOD-of-the-Angel-Armies speaking:
2-3 "'I'm about to get even with Amalek for
ambushing Israel when Israel came up out
of Egypt. Here's what you are to do: Go to
war against Amalek. Put everything con-
nected with Amalek under a holy ban. And
no exceptions! This is to be total destruc-
tion—men and women, children and in-
fants, cattle and sheep, camels and don-
keys—the works.' "
4-5 Saul called the army together at Telaim
and prepared them to go to war—two hun-
dred companies of infantry from Israel and
another ten companies from Judah. Saul
marched to Amalek City and hid in the
canyon.
6 Then Saul got word to the Kenites: "Get
out of here while you can. Evacuate the city
right now or you'll get lumped in with the
Amalekites. I'm warning you because you
showed real kindness to the Israelites when
they came up out of Egypt."
And they did. The Kenites evacuated the
place.
7-9 Then Saul went after Amalek, from the
canyon all the way to Shur near the Egyptian
border. He captured Agag, king of Amalek,
alive. Everyone else was killed under the
terms of the holy ban. Saul and the army
made an exception for Agag, and for the
choice sheep and cattle. They didn't include
them under the terms of the holy ban. But all
the rest, which nobody wanted anyway, they
destroyed as decreed by the holy ban.
10-11 Then GOD spoke to Samuel: "I'm sorry I
ever made Saul king. He's turned his back
on me. He refuses to do what I tell him."
11-12 Samuel was angry when he heard this.
He prayed his anger and disappointment all
through the night. He got up early in the
morning to confront Saul but was told,
"Saul's gone. He went to Carmel to set up a
victory monument in his own honor, and
then was headed for Gilgal."
By the time Samuel caught up with him,
Saul had just finished an act of worship,
having used Amalekite plunder for the
burnt offerings sacrificed to GOD.
13 As Samuel came close, Saul called out,
"GOD's blessings on you! I accomplished
GOD's plan to the letter!"

NEW KING JAMES VERSION

14But Samuel said, "What then *is* this bleat-
ing of the sheep in my ears, and the lowing of
the oxen which I hear?"
15And Saul said, "They have brought them
from the Amalekites; for the people spared the
best of the sheep and the oxen, to sacrifice to
the LORD your God; and the rest we have utterly
destroyed."
16Then Samuel said to Saul, "Be quiet! And I
will tell you what the LORD said to me last
night."
And he said to him, "Speak on."
17So Samuel said, "When you *were* little in
your own eyes, *were* you not head of the tribes
of Israel? And did not the LORD anoint you king
over Israel? 18Now the LORD sent you on a mis-
sion, and said, 'Go, and utterly destroy the sin-
ners, the Amalekites, and fight against them un-
til they are consumed.' 19Why then did you not
obey the voice of the LORD? Why did you swoop
down on the spoil, and do evil in the sight of the
LORD?"
20And Saul said to Samuel, "But I have
obeyed the voice of the LORD, and gone on the
mission on which the LORD sent me, and
brought back Agag king of Amalek; I have ut-
terly destroyed the Amalekites. 21But the people
took of the plunder, sheep and oxen, the best of
the things which should have been utterly de-
stroyed, to sacrifice to the LORD your God in Gil-
gal."
22So Samuel said:

"Has the LORD *as great* delight in burnt
offerings and sacrifices,
As in obeying the voice of the LORD?
Behold, to obey is better than sacrifice,
And to heed than the fat of rams.
23For rebellion *is as* the sin of witchcraft,
And stubbornness *is as* iniquity and
idolatry.
Because you have rejected the word of the
LORD,
He also has rejected you from *being* king."

24Then Saul said to Samuel, "I have sinned,
for I have transgressed the commandment of
the LORD and your words, because I feared the
people and obeyed their voice. 25Now therefore,
please pardon my sin, and return with me, that I
may worship the LORD."
26But Samuel said to Saul, "I will not return
with you, for you have rejected the word of the
LORD, and the LORD has rejected you from being
king over Israel."
27And as Samuel turned around to go away,
Saul seized the edge of his robe, and it tore. 28So
Samuel said to him, "The LORD has torn the
kingdom of Israel from you today, and has given
it to a neighbor of yours, *who is* better than you.
29And also the Strength of Israel will not lie nor
relent. For He *is* not a man, that He should re-
lent."

THE MESSAGE

14 Samuel said, "So what's this I'm hear-
ing—this bleating of sheep, this mooing of
cattle?"
15 "Only some Amalekite loot," said Saul.
"The soldiers saved back a few of the choice
cattle and sheep to offer up in sacrifice to
GOD. But everything else we destroyed un-
der the holy ban."
16 "Enough!" interrupted Samuel. "Let me
tell you what GOD told me last night."
Saul said, "Go ahead. Tell me."
17-19 And Samuel told him. "When you started
out in this, you were nothing—and you
knew it. Then GOD put you at the head of Is-
rael—made you king over Israel. Then GOD
sent you off to do a job for him, ordering
you, 'Go and put those sinners, the
Amalekites, under a holy ban. Go to war
against them until you have totally wiped
them out.' So why did you not obey GOD?
Why did you grab all this loot? Why, with
GOD's eyes on you all the time, did you
brazenly carry out this evil?"
20-21 Saul defended himself. "What are you
talking about? I did obey GOD. I did the job
GOD set for me. I brought in King Agag and
destroyed the Amalekites under the terms of
the holy ban. So the soldiers saved back a
few choice sheep and cattle from the holy
ban for sacrifice to GOD at Gilgal—what's
wrong with that?"
22-23 Then Samuel said,

Do you think all GOD wants are
sacrifices—
empty rituals just for show?
He wants you to listen to him!
Plain listening is the thing,
not staging a lavish religious
production.
Not doing what GOD tells you
is far worse than fooling around in the
occult.
Getting self-important around GOD
is far worse than making deals with
your dead ancestors.
Because you said No to GOD's command,
he says No to your kingship.

24-25 Saul gave in and confessed, "I've sinned.
I've trampled roughshod over GOD's Word
and your instructions. I cared more about
pleasing the people. I let them tell me what
to do. Oh, absolve me of my sin! Take my
hand and lead me to the altar so I can wor-
ship GOD!"
26 But Samuel refused: "No, I can't come
alongside you in this. You rejected GOD's
command. Now GOD has rejected you as
king over Israel."
27-29 As Samuel turned to leave, Saul grabbed
at his priestly robe and a piece tore off.
Samuel said, "GOD has just now torn the
kingdom from you, and handed it over to
your neighbor, a better man than you are. Is-
rael's God-of-Glory doesn't deceive and he
doesn't dither. He says what he means and
means what he says."

New King James Version

30 Then he said, "I have sinned; *yet* honor me
now, please, before the elders of my people and
before Israel, and return with me, that I may
worship the LORD your God." 31 So Samuel
turned back after Saul, and Saul worshiped the
LORD.
32 Then Samuel said, "Bring Agag king of the
Amalekites here to me." So Agag came to him
cautiously.
And Agag said, "Surely the bitterness of
death is past."
33 But Samuel said, "As your sword has made
women childless, so shall your mother be child-
less among women." And Samuel hacked Agag
in pieces before the LORD in Gilgal.
34 Then Samuel went to Ramah, and Saul
went up to his house at Gibeah of Saul. 35 And
Samuel went no more to see Saul until the day
of his death. Nevertheless Samuel mourned for
Saul, and the LORD regretted that He had made
Saul king over Israel.

David Anointed King

16 Now the LORD said to Samuel, "How long
will you mourn for Saul, seeing I have re-
jected him from reigning over Israel? Fill your
horn with oil, and go; I am sending you to Jesse
the Bethlehemite. For I have provided Myself a
king among his sons."
2 And Samuel said, "How can I go? If Saul
hears *it*, he will kill me."
But the LORD said, "Take a heifer with you,
and say, 'I have come to sacrifice to the LORD.'
3 Then invite Jesse to the sacrifice, and I will
show you what you shall do; you shall anoint for
Me the one I name to you."
4 So Samuel did what the LORD said, and
went to Bethlehem. And the elders of the town
trembled at his coming, and said, "Do you come
peaceably?"
5 And he said, "Peaceably; I have come to sac-
rifice to the LORD. Sanctify yourselves, and
come with me to the sacrifice." Then he conse-
crated Jesse and his sons, and invited them to
the sacrifice.
6 So it was, when they came, that he looked at
Eliab and said, "Surely the LORD's anointed *is*
before Him!"
7 But the LORD said to Samuel, "Do not look
at his appearance or at his physical stature, be-
cause I have refused him. For *the LORD does* not
see as man sees;[a] for man looks at the outward
appearance, but the LORD looks at the heart."
8 So Jesse called Abinadab, and made him
pass before Samuel. And he said, "Neither has
the LORD chosen this one." 9 Then Jesse made
Shammah pass by. And he said, "Neither has the
LORD chosen this one." 10 Thus Jesse made seven
of his sons pass before Samuel. And Samuel
said to Jesse, "The LORD has not chosen these."
11 And Samuel said to Jesse, "Are all the young
men here?" Then he said, "There remains yet

16:7 [a]Septuagint reads *For God does not see as man sees;* Targum reads *It is not by the appearance of a man;* Vulgate reads *Nor do I judge according to the looks of a man.*

The Message

30 Saul tried again, "I have sinned. But don't
abandon me! Support me with your pres-
ence before the leaders and the people.
Come alongside me as I go back to worship
GOD."
31 Samuel did. He went back with him. And
Saul went to his knees before GOD and wor-
shiped.
32 Then Samuel said, "Present King Agag of
Amalek to me." Agag came, dragging his
feet, muttering that he'd be better off dead.
33 Samuel said, "Just as your sword made
many a woman childless, so your mother
will be childless among those women!" And
Samuel cut Agag down in the presence of
GOD right there in Gilgal.
34-35 Samuel left immediately for Ramah and
Saul went home to Gibeah. Samuel had
nothing to do with Saul from then on,
though he grieved long and deeply over
him. But GOD was sorry he had ever made
Saul king in the first place.

God Looks into the Heart

1 16 GOD addressed Samuel: "So, how long
are you going to mope over Saul? You
know I've rejected him as king over Israel.
Fill your flask with anointing oil and get go-
ing. I'm sending you to Jesse of Bethlehem.
I've spotted the very king I want among his
sons."
2-3 "I can't do that," said Samuel. "Saul will
hear about it and kill me."
GOD said, "Take a heifer with you and an-
nounce, 'I've come to lead you in worship of
GOD, with this heifer as a sacrifice.' Make
sure Jesse gets invited. I'll let you know
what to do next. I'll point out the one you
are to anoint."
4 Samuel did what GOD told him. When he
arrived at Bethlehem, the town fathers
greeted him, but apprehensively. "Is there
something wrong?"
5 "Nothing's wrong. I've come to sacrifice
this heifer and lead you in the worship of
GOD. Prepare yourselves, be consecrated,
and join me in worship." He made sure Jesse
and his sons were also consecrated and
called to worship.
6 When they arrived, Samuel took one look
at Eliab and thought, "Here he is! GOD's
anointed!"
7 But GOD told Samuel, "Looks aren't
everything. Don't be impressed with his
looks and stature. I've already eliminated
him. GOD judges persons differently than
humans do. Men and women look at the
face; GOD looks into the heart."
8 Jesse then called up Abinadab and pre-
sented him to Samuel. Samuel said, "This
man isn't GOD's choice either."
9 Next Jesse presented Shammah. Samuel
said, "No, this man isn't either."
10 Jesse presented his seven sons to
Samuel. Samuel was blunt with Jesse, "GOD
hasn't chosen any of these."
11 Then he asked Jesse, "Is this it? Are there
no more sons?"

NEW KING JAMES VERSION

the youngest, and there he is, keeping the
sheep."
And Samuel said to Jesse, "Send and bring
him. For we will not sit down[a] till he comes
here." 12So he sent and brought him in. Now he
was ruddy, with bright eyes, and good-looking.
And the LORD said, "Arise, anoint him; for this *is*
the one!" 13Then Samuel took the horn of oil and
anointed him in the midst of his brothers; and
the Spirit of the LORD came upon David from
that day forward. So Samuel arose and went to
Ramah.

A Distressing Spirit Troubles Saul

14But the Spirit of the LORD departed from
Saul, and a distressing spirit from the LORD
troubled him. 15And Saul's servants said to him,
"Surely, a distressing spirit from God is trou-
bling you. 16Let our master now command your
servants, *who are* before you, to seek out a man
who is a skillful player on the harp. And it shall
be that he will play it with his hand when the
distressing spirit from God is upon you, and you
shall be well."
17So Saul said to his servants, "Provide me
now a man who can play well, and bring *him* to
me."
18Then one of the servants answered and
said, "Look, I have seen a son of Jesse the Beth-
lehemite, *who is* skillful in playing, a mighty
man of valor, a man of war, prudent in speech,
and a handsome person; and the LORD *is* with
him."
19Therefore Saul sent messengers to Jesse,
and said, "Send me your son David, who *is* with
the sheep." 20And Jesse took a donkey *loaded
with* bread, a skin of wine, and a young goat,
and sent *them* by his son David to Saul. 21So
David came to Saul and stood before him. And
he loved him greatly, and he became his armor-
bearer. 22Then Saul sent to Jesse, saying, "Please
let David stand before me, for he has found fa-
vor in my sight." 23And so it was, whenever the
spirit from God was upon Saul, that David
would take a harp and play *it* with his hand.
Then Saul would become refreshed and well,
and the distressing spirit would depart from
him.

David and Goliath

17 Now the Philistines gathered their armies
together to battle, and were gathered at
Sochoh, which *belongs* to Judah; they en-
camped between Sochoh and Azekah, in Ephes
Dammim. 2And Saul and the men of Israel were
gathered together, and they encamped in the
Valley of Elah, and drew up in battle array
against the Philistines. 3The Philistines stood on
a mountain on one side, and Israel stood on a
mountain on the other side, with a valley be-
tween them.
4And a champion went out from the camp of
the Philistines, named Goliath, from Gath,

16:11 [a]Following Septuagint and Vulgate; Masoretic Text reads *turn around;* Targum and Syriac read *turn away.*

THE MESSAGE

"Well, yes, there's the runt. But he's out
tending the sheep."
Samuel ordered Jesse, "Go get him. We're
not moving from this spot until he's here."
12 Jesse sent for him. He was brought in, the
very picture of health—bright-eyed, good-
looking.
GOD said, "Up on your feet! Anoint him!
This is the one."
13 Samuel took his flask of oil and anointed
him, with his brothers standing around
watching. The Spirit of GOD entered David
like a rush of wind, God vitally empowering
him for the rest of his life.
Samuel left and went home to Ramah.

David—An Excellent Musician

14 At that very moment the Spirit of GOD left
Saul and in its place a black mood sent by
GOD settled on him. He was terrified.
15-16 Saul's advisors said, "This awful torment-
ing depression from God is making your life
miserable. O Master, let us help. Let us look
for someone who can play the harp. When
the black mood from God moves in, he'll
play his music and you'll feel better."
17 Saul told his servants, "Go ahead. Find
me someone who can play well and bring
him to me."
18 One of the young men spoke up, "I know
someone. I've seen him myself: the son of
Jesse of Bethlehem, an excellent musician.
He's also courageous, of age, well-spoken,
and good-looking. And GOD is with him."
19 So Saul sent messengers to Jesse re-
questing, "Send your son David to me, the
one who tends the sheep."
20-21 Jesse took a donkey, loaded it with a cou-
ple of loaves of bread, a flask of wine, and a
young goat, and sent his son David with it to
Saul. David came to Saul and stood before
him. Saul liked him immediately and made
him his right-hand man.
22 Saul sent word back to Jesse: "Thank
you. David will stay here. He's just the one I
was looking for. I'm very impressed by him."
23 After that, whenever the bad depression
from God tormented Saul, David got out his
harp and played. That would calm Saul
down, and he would feel better as the mood-
iness lifted.

Goliath

1-3 17 The Philistines drew up their troops
for battle. They deployed them at So-
coh in Judah, and set up camp between So-
coh and Azekah at Ephes Dammim. Saul
and the Israelites came together, camped at
Oak Valley, and spread out their troops in
battle readiness for the Philistines. The
Philistines were on one hill, the Israelites on
the opposing hill, with the valley between
them.
4-7 A giant nearly ten feet tall stepped out
from the Philistine line into the open, Go-

NEW KING JAMES VERSION

whose height *was* six cubits and a span. 5*He had* a bronze helmet on his head, and he *was* armed with a coat of mail, and the weight of the coat *was* five thousand shekels of bronze. 6And *he had* bronze armor on his legs and a bronze javelin between his shoulders. 7Now the staff of his spear *was* like a weaver's beam, and his iron spearhead *weighed* six hundred shekels; and a shield-bearer went before him. 8Then he stood and cried out to the armies of Israel, and said to them, "Why have you come out to line up for battle? *Am* I not a Philistine, and you the servants of Saul? Choose a man for yourselves, and let him come down to me. 9If he is able to fight with me and kill me, then we will be your servants. But if I prevail against him and kill him, then you shall be our servants and serve us." 10And the Philistine said, "I defy the armies of Israel this day; give me a man, that we may fight together." 11When Saul and all Israel heard these words of the Philistine, they were dismayed and greatly afraid.

12Now David *was* the son of that Ephrathite of Bethlehem Judah, whose name *was* Jesse, and who had eight sons. And the man was old, advanced *in years,* in the days of Saul. 13The three oldest sons of Jesse had gone to follow Saul to the battle. The names of his three sons who went to the battle *were* Eliab the firstborn, next to him Abinadab, and the third Shammah. 14David *was* the youngest. And the three oldest followed Saul. 15But David occasionally went and returned from Saul to feed his father's sheep at Bethlehem.

16And the Philistine drew near and presented himself forty days, morning and evening.

17Then Jesse said to his son David, "Take now for your brothers an ephah of this dried *grain* and these ten loaves, and run to your brothers at the camp. 18And carry these ten cheeses to the captain of *their* thousand, and see how your brothers fare, and bring back news of them." 19Now Saul and they and all the men of Israel *were* in the Valley of Elah, fighting with the Philistines.

20So David rose early in the morning, left the sheep with a keeper, and took *the things* and went as Jesse had commanded him. And he came to the camp as the army was going out to the fight and shouting for the battle. 21For Israel and the Philistines had drawn up in battle array, army against army. 22And David left his supplies in the hand of the supply keeper, ran to the army, and came and greeted his brothers. 23Then as he talked with them, there was the champion, the Philistine of Gath, Goliath by name, coming up from the armies of the Philistines; and he spoke according to the same words. So David heard *them.* 24And all the men of Israel, when they saw the man, fled from him and were dreadfully afraid. 25So the men of Israel said, "Have you seen this man who has come up? Surely he has come up to defy Israel; and it shall be *that* the man who kills him the king will enrich with great riches, will give him his daughter, and give his father's house exemption *from taxes* in Israel."

THE MESSAGE

liath from Gath. He had a bronze helmet on his head and was dressed in armor—126 pounds of it! He wore bronze shin guards and carried a bronze sword. His spear was like a fence rail—the spear tip alone weighed over fifteen pounds. His shield bearer walked ahead of him.

8-10 Goliath stood there and called out to the Israelite troops, "Why bother using your whole army? Am I not Philistine enough for you? And you're all committed to Saul, aren't you? So pick your best fighter and pit him against me. If he gets the upper hand and kills me, the Philistines will all become your slaves. But if I get the upper hand and kill him, you'll all become our slaves and serve us. I challenge the troops of Israel this day. Give me a man. Let us fight it out together!"

11 When Saul and his troops heard the Philistine's challenge, they were terrified and lost all hope.

12-15 Enter David. He was the son of Jesse the Ephrathite from Bethlehem in Judah. Jesse, the father of eight sons, was himself too old to join Saul's army. Jesse's three oldest sons had followed Saul to war. The names of the three sons who had joined up with Saul were Eliab, the firstborn; next, Abinadab; and third, Shammah. David was the youngest son. While his three oldest brothers went to war with Saul, David went back and forth from attending to Saul to tending his father's sheep in Bethlehem.

16 Each morning and evening for forty days, Goliath took his stand and made his speech.

17-19 One day, Jesse told David his son, "Take this sack of cracked wheat and these ten loaves of bread and run them down to your brothers in the camp. And take these ten wedges of cheese to the captain of their division. Check in on your brothers to see whether they are getting along all right, and let me know how they're doing—Saul and your brothers, and all the Israelites in their war with the Philistines in the Oak Valley."

20-23 David was up at the crack of dawn and, having arranged for someone to tend his flock, took the food and was on his way just as Jesse had directed him. He arrived at the camp just as the army was moving into battle formation, shouting the war cry. Israel and the Philistines moved into position, facing each other, battle-ready. David left his bundles of food in the care of a sentry, ran to the troops who were deployed, and greeted his brothers. While they were talking together, the Philistine champion, Goliath of Gath, stepped out from the front lines of the Philistines, and gave his usual challenge. David heard him.

24-25 The Israelites, to a man, fell back the moment they saw the giant—totally frightened. The talk among the troops was, "Have you ever seen anything like this, this man openly and defiantly challenging Israel? The man who kills the giant will have it made. The king will give him a huge reward, offer his daughter as a bride, and give his entire family a free ride."

NEW KING JAMES VERSION

26 Then David spoke to the men who stood by
him, saying, "What shall be done for the man
who kills this Philistine and takes away the re-
proach from Israel? For who *is* this uncircum-
cised Philistine, that he should defy the armies
of the living God?"
27 And the people answered him in this man-
ner, saying, "So shall it be done for the man who
kills him."
28 Now Eliab his oldest brother heard when
he spoke to the men; and Eliab's anger was
aroused against David, and he said, "Why did
you come down here? And with whom have you
left those few sheep in the wilderness? I know
your pride and the insolence of your heart, for
you have come down to see the battle."
29 And David said, "What have I done now? *Is*
there not a cause?" 30 Then he turned from him
toward another and said the same thing; and
these people answered him as the first ones *did*.
31 Now when the words which David spoke
were heard, they reported *them* to Saul; and he
sent for him. 32 Then David said to Saul, "Let no
man's heart fail because of him; your servant
will go and fight with this Philistine."
33 And Saul said to David, "You are not able
to go against this Philistine to fight with him; for
you *are* a youth, and he a man of war from his
youth."
34 But David said to Saul, "Your servant used
to keep his father's sheep, and when a lion or a
bear came and took a lamb out of the flock, 35 I
went out after it and struck it, and delivered *the*
lamb from its mouth; and when it arose against
me, I caught *it* by its beard, and struck and
killed it. 36 Your servant has killed both lion and
bear; and this uncircumcised Philistine will be
like one of them, seeing he has defied the armies
of the living God." 37 Moreover David said, "The
LORD, who delivered me from the paw of the lion
and from the paw of the bear, He will deliver me
from the hand of this Philistine."
And Saul said to David, "Go, and the LORD be
with you!"
38 So Saul clothed David with his armor, and
he put a bronze helmet on his head; he also
clothed him with a coat of mail. 39 David fas-
tened his sword to his armor and tried to walk,
for he had not tested *them*. And David said to
Saul, "I cannot walk with these, for I have not
tested *them*." So David took them off.
40 Then he took his staff in his hand; and he
chose for himself five smooth stones from the
brook, and put them in a shepherd's bag, in a
pouch which he had, and his sling was in his
hand. And he drew near to the Philistine. 41 So
the Philistine came, and began drawing near to
David, and the man who bore the shield *went*
before him. 42 And when the Philistine looked
about and saw David, he disdained him; for he
was *only* a youth, ruddy and good-looking. 43 So
the Philistine said to David, "*Am* I a dog, that
you come to me with sticks?" And the Philistine
cursed David by his gods. 44 And the Philistine
said to David, "Come to me, and I will give your
flesh to the birds of the air and the beasts of the
field!"

THE MESSAGE

FIVE SMOOTH STONES

26 David, who was talking to the men standing around him, asked, "What's in it for the man who kills that Philistine and gets rid of this ugly blot on Israel's honor? Who does he think he is, anyway, this uncircumcised Philistine, taunting the armies of God-Alive?"

27 They told him what everyone was saying about what the king would do for the man who killed the Philistine.

28 Eliab, his older brother, heard David fraternizing with the men and lost his temper: "What are you doing here! Why aren't you minding your own business, tending that scrawny flock of sheep? I know what you're up to. You've come down here to see the sights, hoping for a ringside seat at a bloody battle!"

29-30 "What is it with you?" replied David. "All I did was ask a question." Ignoring his brother, he turned to someone else, asked the same question, and got the same answer as before.

31 The things David was saying were picked up and reported to Saul. Saul sent for him.

32 "Master," said David, "don't give up hope. I'm ready to go and fight this Philistine."

33 Saul answered David, "You can't go and fight this Philistine. You're too young and inexperienced—and he's been at this fighting business since before you were born."

34-37 David said, "I've been a shepherd, tending sheep for my father. Whenever a lion or bear came and took a lamb from the flock, I'd go after it, knock it down, and rescue the lamb. If it turned on me, I'd grab it by the throat, wring its neck, and kill it. Lion or bear, it made no difference—I killed it. And I'll do the same to this Philistine pig who is taunting the troops of God-Alive. GOD, who delivered me from the teeth of the lion and the claws of the bear, will deliver me from this Philistine."

Saul said, "Go. And GOD help you!"

38-39 Then Saul outfitted David as a soldier in armor. He put his bronze helmet on his head and belted his sword on him over the armor. David tried to walk but he could hardly budge.

David told Saul, "I can't even move with all this stuff on me. I'm not used to this." And he took it all off.

40 Then David took his shepherd's staff, selected five smooth stones from the brook, and put them in the pocket of his shepherd's pack, and with his sling in his hand approached Goliath.

41-42 As the Philistine paced back and forth, his shield bearer in front of him, he noticed David. He took one look down on him and sneered—a mere youngster, apple-cheeked and peach-fuzzed.

43 The Philistine ridiculed David. "Am I a dog that you come after me with a stick?" And he cursed him by his gods.

44 "Come on," said the Philistine. "I'll make roadkill of you for the buzzards. I'll turn you into a tasty morsel for the field mice."

NEW KING JAMES VERSION

45Then David said to the Philistine, "You come to me with a sword, with a spear, and with a javelin. But I come to you in the name of the LORD of hosts, the God of the armies of Israel, whom you have defied. 46This day the LORD will deliver you into my hand, and I will strike you and take your head from you. And this day I will give the carcasses of the camp of the Philistines to the birds of the air and the wild beasts of the earth, that all the earth may know that there is a God in Israel. 47Then all this assembly shall know that the LORD does not save with sword and spear; for the battle *is* the LORD's, and He will give you into our hands."

48So it was, when the Philistine arose and came and drew near to meet David, that David hurried and ran toward the army to meet the Philistine. 49Then David put his hand in his bag and took out a stone; and he slung *it* and struck the Philistine in his forehead, so that the stone sank into his forehead, and he fell on his face to the earth. 50So David prevailed over the Philistine with a sling and a stone, and struck the Philistine and killed him. But *there was* no sword in the hand of David. 51Therefore David ran and stood over the Philistine, took his sword and drew it out of its sheath and killed him, and cut off his head with it.

And when the Philistines saw that their champion was dead, they fled. 52Now the men of Israel and Judah arose and shouted, and pursued the Philistines as far as the entrance of the valley[a] and to the gates of Ekron. And the wounded of the Philistines fell along the road to Shaaraim, even as far as Gath and Ekron. 53Then the children of Israel returned from chasing the Philistines, and they plundered their tents. 54And David took the head of the Philistine and brought it to Jerusalem, but he put his armor in his tent.

55When Saul saw David going out against the Philistine, he said to Abner, the commander of the army, "Abner, whose son *is* this youth?"

And Abner said, "As your soul lives, O king, I do not know."

56So the king said, "Inquire whose son this young man *is*."

57Then, as David returned from the slaughter of the Philistine, Abner took him and brought him before Saul with the head of the Philistine in his hand. 58And Saul said to him, "Whose son *are* you, young man?"

So David answered, "*I am* the son of your servant Jesse the Bethlehemite."

SAUL RESENTS DAVID

18 Now when he had finished speaking to Saul, the soul of Jonathan was knit to the soul of David, and Jonathan loved him as his own soul. 2Saul took him that day, and would

17:52 [a]Following Masoretic Text, Syriac, Targum, and Vulgate; Septuagint reads *Gath*.

THE MESSAGE

45-47 David answered, "You come at me with sword and spear and battle-ax. I come at you in the name of GOD-of-the-Angel-Armies, the God of Israel's troops, whom you curse and mock. This very day GOD is handing you over to me. I'm about to kill you, cut off your head, and serve up your body and the bodies of your Philistine buddies to the crows and coyotes. The whole earth will know that there's an extraordinary God in Israel. And everyone gathered here will learn that GOD doesn't save by means of sword or spear. The battle belongs to GOD—he's handing you to us on a platter!"

48-49 That roused the Philistine, and he started toward David. David took off from the front line, running toward the Philistine. David reached into his pocket for a stone, slung it, and hit the Philistine hard in the forehead, embedding the stone deeply. The Philistine crashed, facedown in the dirt.

50 That's how David beat the Philistine—with a sling and a stone. He hit him and killed him. No sword for David!

51 Then David ran up to the Philistine and stood over him, pulled the giant's sword from its sheath, and finished the job by cutting off his head. When the Philistines saw that their great champion was dead, they scattered, running for their lives.

52-54 The men of Israel and Judah were up on their feet, shouting! They chased the Philistines all the way to the outskirts of Gath and the gates of Ekron. Wounded Philistines were strewn along the Shaaraim road all the way to Gath and Ekron. After chasing the Philistines, the Israelites came back and looted their camp. David took the Philistine's head and brought it to Jerusalem. But the giant's weapons he placed in his own tent.

55 When Saul saw David go out to meet the Philistine, he said to Abner, commander of the army, "Tell me about this young man's family."

Abner said, "For the life of me, O King, I don't know."

56 The king said, "Well, find out the lineage of this raw youth."

57 As soon as David came back from killing the Philistine, Abner brought him, the Philistine's head still in his hand, straight to Saul.

58 Saul asked him, "Young man, whose son are you?"

"I'm the son of your servant Jesse," said David, "the one who lives in Bethlehem."

JONATHAN AND DAVID—SOUL FRIENDS

1 18 By the time David had finished reporting to Saul, Jonathan was deeply impressed with David—an immediate bond was forged between them. He became totally committed to David. From that point on he would be David's number-one advocate and friend.

2 Saul received David into his own house-

NEW KING JAMES VERSION

not let him go home to his father's house any-
more. [3]Then Jonathan and David made a
covenant, because he loved him as his own soul.
[4]And Jonathan took off the robe that *was* on
him and gave it to David, with his armor, even to
his sword and his bow and his belt.
[5]So David went out wherever Saul sent him,
and behaved wisely. And Saul set him over the
men of war, and he was accepted in the sight of
all the people and also in the sight of Saul's ser-
vants. [6]Now it had happened as they were com-
ing *home*, when David was returning from the
slaughter of the Philistine, that the women had
come out of all the cities of Israel, singing and
dancing, to meet King Saul, with tambourines,
with joy, and with musical instruments. [7]So the
women sang as they danced, and said:

"Saul has slain his thousands,
And David his ten thousands."

[8]Then Saul was very angry, and the saying dis-
pleased him; and he said, "They have ascribed
to David ten thousands, and to me they have as-
cribed only thousands. Now what more can he
have but the kingdom?" [9]So Saul eyed David
from that day forward.
[10]And it happened on the next day that the
distressing spirit from God came upon Saul, and
he prophesied inside the house. So David played
music with his hand, as at other times; but *there
was* a spear in Saul's hand. [11]And Saul cast the
spear, for he said, "I will pin David to the wall!"
But David escaped his presence twice.
[12]Now Saul was afraid of David, because the
LORD was with him, but had departed from Saul.
[13]Therefore Saul removed him from his pres-
ence, and made him his captain over a thou-
sand; and he went out and came in before the
people. [14]And David behaved wisely in all his
ways, and the LORD *was* with him. [15]Therefore,
when Saul saw that he behaved very wisely, he
was afraid of him. [16]But all Israel and Judah
loved David, because he went out and came in
before them.

DAVID MARRIES MICHAL

[17]Then Saul said to David, "Here is my older
daughter Merab; I will give her to you as a wife.
Only be valiant for me, and fight the LORD's bat-
tles." For Saul thought, "Let my hand not be
against him, but let the hand of the Philistines
be against him."
[18]So David said to Saul, "Who *am* I, and what
is my life *or* my father's family in Israel, that I
should be son-in-law to the king?" [19]But it hap-
pened at the time when Merab, Saul's daughter,
should have been given to David, that she was
given to Adriel the Meholathite as a wife.
[20]Now Michal, Saul's daughter, loved David.
And they told Saul, and the thing pleased him.
[21]So Saul said, "I will give her to him, that she
may be a snare to him, and that the hand of the

THE MESSAGE

hold that day, no more to return to the home
of his father.
3-4 Jonathan, out of his deep love for David,
made a covenant with him. He formalized it
with solemn gifts: his own royal robe and
weapons—armor, sword, bow, and belt.
5 Whatever Saul gave David to do, he did
it—and did it well. So well that Saul put him
in charge of his military operations. Every-
body, both the people in general and Saul's
servants, approved of and admired David's
leadership.

DAVID—THE NAME ON EVERYONE'S LIPS

6-9 As they returned home, after David had
killed the Philistine, the women poured out
of all the villages of Israel singing and danc-
ing, welcoming King Saul with tambou-
rines, festive songs, and lutes. In playful
frolic the women sang,

Saul kills by the thousand,
David by the ten thousand!

This made Saul angry—very angry. He took
it as a personal insult. He said, "They credit
David with 'ten thousands' and me with
only 'thousands.' Before you know it they'll
be giving him the kingdom!" From that mo-
ment on, Saul kept his eye on David.
10-11 The next day an ugly mood was sent by
God to afflict Saul, who became quite beside
himself, raving. David played his harp, as he
usually did at such times. Saul had a spear
in his hand. Suddenly Saul threw the spear,
thinking, "I'll nail David to the wall." David
ducked, and the spear missed. This hap-
pened twice.
12-16 Now Saul feared David. It was clear that
GOD was with David and had left Saul. So,
Saul got David out of his sight by making
him an officer in the army. David was in
combat frequently. Everything David did
turned out well. Yes, GOD was with him. As
Saul saw David becoming more successful,
he himself grew more fearful. He could see
the handwriting on the wall. But everyone
else in Israel and Judah loved David. They
loved watching him in action.

17 One day Saul said to David, "Here is
Merab, my eldest daughter. I want to give
her to you as your wife. Be brave and bold
for my sake. Fight GOD's battles!" But all the
time Saul was thinking, "The Philistines will
kill him for me. I won't have to lift a hand
against him."
18 David, embarrassed, answered, "Do you
really mean that? I'm from a family of no-
bodies! I can't be son-in-law to the king."
19 The wedding day was set, but as the time
neared for Merab and David to be married,
Saul reneged and married his daughter off
to Adriel the Meholathite.
20-21 Meanwhile, Saul's daughter Michal was
in love with David. When Saul was told of
this, he rubbed his hands in anticipation.
"Ah, a second chance. I'll use Michal as bait

NEW KING JAMES VERSION

Philistines may be against him." Therefore Saul
said to David a second time, "You shall be my
son-in-law today."
22And Saul commanded his servants, "Com-
municate with David secretly, and say, 'Look,
the king has delight in you, and all his servants
love you. Now therefore, become the king's son-
in-law.' "
23So Saul's servants spoke those words in the
hearing of David. And David said, "Does it seem
to you *a* light *thing* to be a king's son-in-law,
seeing I *am* a poor and lightly esteemed man?"
24And the servants of Saul told him, saying, "In
this manner David spoke."
25Then Saul said, "Thus you shall say to
David: 'The king does not desire any dowry but
one hundred foreskins of the Philistines, to take
vengeance on the king's enemies.' " But Saul
thought to make David fall by the hand of the
Philistines. 26So when his servants told David
these words, it pleased David well to become the
king's son-in-law. Now the days had not ex-
pired; 27therefore David arose and went, he and
his men, and killed two hundred men of the
Philistines. And David brought their foreskins,
and they gave them in full count to the king, that
he might become the king's son-in-law. Then
Saul gave him Michal his daughter as a wife.
28Thus Saul saw and knew that the LORD *was*
with David, and *that* Michal, Saul's daughter,
loved him; 29and Saul was still more afraid of
David. So Saul became David's enemy continu-
ally. 30Then the princes of the Philistines went
out *to war*. And so it was, whenever they went
out, *that* David behaved more wisely than all
the servants of Saul, so that his name became
highly esteemed.

SAUL PERSECUTES DAVID

19 Now Saul spoke to Jonathan his son and to
all his servants, that they should kill
David; but Jonathan, Saul's son, delighted
greatly in David. 2So Jonathan told David, say-
ing, "My father Saul seeks to kill you. Therefore
please be on your guard until morning, and stay
in a secret *place* and hide. 3And I will go out and
stand beside my father in the field where you
are, and I will speak with my father about you.
Then what I observe, I will tell you."
4Thus Jonathan spoke well of David to Saul
his father, and said to him, "Let not the king sin
against his servant, against David, because he
has not sinned against you, and because his
works *have been* very good toward you. 5For he
took his life in his hands and killed the Philis-
tine, and the LORD brought about a great deliv-
erance for all Israel. You saw *it* and rejoiced.
Why then will you sin against innocent blood, to
kill David without a cause?"
6So Saul heeded the voice of Jonathan, and
Saul swore, "*As* the LORD lives, he shall not be
killed." 7Then Jonathan called David, and
Jonathan told him all these things. So Jonathan
brought David to Saul, and he was in his pres-
ence as in times past.

THE MESSAGE

to get David out where the Philistines will
make short work of him." So again he said
to David, "You're going to be my son-in-
law."
22 Saul ordered his servants, "Get David off by
himself and tell him, 'The king is very taken
with you, and everyone at court loves you. Go
ahead, become the king's son-in-law!' "
23 The king's servants told all this to David,
but David held back. "What are you think-
ing of? I can't do that. I'm a nobody; I have
nothing to offer."
24-25 When the servants reported David's re-
sponse to Saul, he told them to tell David
this: "The king isn't expecting any money
from you; only this: Go kill a hundred
Philistines and bring evidence of your
vengeance on the king's behalf. Avenge the
king on his enemies." (Saul expected David
to be killed in action.)
26-27 On receiving this message, David was
pleased. There was something he could do
for the king that would qualify him to be his
son-in-law! He lost no time but went right
out, he and his men, killed the hundred
Philistines, brought their evidence back in a
sack, and counted it out before the king—
mission completed! Saul gave Michal his
daughter to David in marriage.
28-29 As Saul more and more realized that GOD
was with David, and how much his own
daughter, Michal, loved him, his fear of
David increased and settled into hate. Saul
hated David.
30 Whenever the Philistine warlords came
out to battle, David was there to meet
them—and beat them, upstaging Saul's
men. David's name was on everyone's lips.

THE BLACK MOOD OF SAUL

1-3 19 Saul called his son Jonathan together
with his servants and ordered them to
kill David. But because Jonathan treasured
David, he went and warned him: "My father
is looking for a way to kill you. Here's what
you are to do. Tomorrow morning, hide and
stay hidden. I'll go out with my father into
the field where you are hiding. I'll talk about
you with my father and we'll see what he
says. Then I'll report back to you."
4-5 Jonathan brought up David with his fa-
ther, speaking well of him. "Please," he said
to his father, "don't attack David. He hasn't
wronged you, has he? And just look at all
the good he has done! He put his life on the
line when he killed the Philistine. What a
great victory GOD gave Israel that day! You
were there. You saw it and were on your feet
applauding with everyone else. So why
would you even think of sinning against an
innocent person, killing David for no reason
whatever?"
6 Saul listened to Jonathan and said,
"You're right. As GOD lives, David lives. He
will not be killed."
7 Jonathan sent for David and reported to
him everything that was said. Then he
brought David back to Saul and everything
was as it was before.

NEW KING JAMES VERSION

8And there was war again; and David went
out and fought with the Philistines, and struck
them with a mighty blow, and they fled from
him.
9Now the distressing spirit from the LORD
came upon Saul as he sat in his house with his
spear in his hand. And David was playing *music*
with *his* hand. 10Then Saul sought to pin David
to the wall with the spear, but he slipped away
from Saul's presence; and he drove the spear
into the wall. So David fled and escaped that
night.
11Saul also sent messengers to David's house
to watch him and to kill him in the morning.
And Michal, David's wife, told him, saying, "If
you do not save your life tonight, tomorrow you
will be killed." 12So Michal let David down
through a window. And he went and fled and es-
caped. 13And Michal took an image and laid *it* in
the bed, put a cover of goats' *hair* for his head,
and covered *it* with clothes. 14So when Saul sent
messengers to take David, she said, "He *is* sick."
15Then Saul sent the messengers *back* to see
David, saying, "Bring him up to me in the bed,
that I may kill him." 16And when the messengers
had come in, there was the image in the bed,
with a cover of goats' *hair* for his head. 17Then
Saul said to Michal, "Why have you deceived me
like this, and sent my enemy away, so that he
has escaped?"

And Michal answered Saul, "He said to me,
'Let me go! Why should I kill you?' "
18So David fled and escaped, and went to
Samuel at Ramah, and told him all that Saul had
done to him. And he and Samuel went and
stayed in Naioth. 19Now it was told Saul, saying,
"Take note, David *is* at Naioth in Ramah!"
20Then Saul sent messengers to take David. And
when they saw the group of prophets prophesy-
ing, and Samuel standing *as* leader over them,
the Spirit of God came upon the messengers of
Saul, and they also prophesied. 21And when
Saul was told, he sent other messengers, and
they prophesied likewise. Then Saul sent mes-
sengers again the third time, and they prophe-
sied also. 22Then he also went to Ramah, and
came to the great well that *is* at Sechu. So he
asked, and said, "Where *are* Samuel and
David?"

And *someone* said, "Indeed *they are* at
Naioth in Ramah." 23So he went there to Naioth
in Ramah. Then the Spirit of God was upon him
also, and he went on and prophesied until he
came to Naioth in Ramah. 24And he also
stripped off his clothes and prophesied before
Samuel in like manner, and lay down naked all
that day and all that night. Therefore they say,
"*Is* Saul also among the prophets?"[a]

JONATHAN'S LOYALTY TO DAVID

20 Then David fled from Naioth in Ramah,
and went and said to Jonathan, "What
have I done? What *is* my iniquity, and what *is* my
sin before your father, that he seeks my life?"

19:24 [a]Compare 1 Samuel 10:12

THE MESSAGE

8 War broke out again and David went out
to fight Philistines. He beat them badly, and
they ran for their lives.
9-10 But then a black mood from God settled
over Saul and took control of him. He was
sitting at home, his spear in his hand, while
David was playing music. Suddenly, Saul
tried to skewer David with his spear, but
David ducked. The spear stuck in the wall
and David got away. It was night.
11-14 Saul sent men to David's house to stake it
out and then, first thing in the morning, to kill
him. But Michal, David's wife, told him what
was going on. "Quickly now—make your es-
cape tonight. If not, you'll be dead by morn-
ing!" She let him out of a window, and he
made his escape. Then Michal took a dummy
god and put it in the bed, placed a wig of
goat's hair on its head, and threw a quilt over
it. When Saul's men arrived to get David, she
said, "He's sick in bed."
15-16 Saul sent his men back, ordering them,
"Bring him, bed and all, so I can kill him."
When the men entered the room, all they
found in the bed was the dummy god with
its goat-hair wig!
17 Saul stormed at Michal: "How could you
play tricks on me like this? You sided with
my enemy, and now he's gotten away!"
18 Michal said, "He threatened me. He said,
'Help me out of here or I'll kill you.' "

David made good his escape and went to
Samuel at Ramah and told him everything
Saul had done to him. Then he and Samuel
withdrew to the privacy of Naioth.
19-20 Saul was told, "David's at Naioth in
Ramah." He immediately sent his men to
capture him. They saw a band of prophets
prophesying with Samuel presiding over
them. Before they knew it, the Spirit of God
was on them, too, and they were ranting and
raving right along with the prophets!
21 That was reported back to Saul, and he
dispatched more men. They, too, were soon
prophesying. So Saul tried a third time—a
third set of men—and they ended up mind-
lessly raving as well!
22 Fed up, Saul went to Ramah himself. He
came to the big cistern at Secu and inquired,
"Where are Samuel and David?"

A bystander said, "Over at Naioth in
Ramah."
23-24 As he headed out for Naioth in Ramah,
the Spirit of God was on him, too. All the
way to Naioth he was caught up in a bab-
bling trance! He ripped off his clothes and
lay there rambling gibberish before Samuel
for a day and a night, stretched out naked.
People are still talking about it: "Saul
among the prophets! Who would have
guessed?"

A COVENANT FRIENDSHIP IN GOD'S NAME

1 20 David got out of Naioth in Ramah alive
and went to Jonathan. "What do I do
now? What wrong have I inflicted on your
father that makes him so determined to kill
me?"

New King James Version

2 So Jonathan said to him, "By no means! You
shall not die! Indeed, my father will do nothing
either great or small without first telling me.
And why should my father hide this thing from
me? It *is* not *so!*"
3 Then David took an oath again, and said,
"Your father certainly knows that I have found
favor in your eyes, and he has said, 'Do not let
Jonathan know this, lest he be grieved.' But
truly, *as* the LORD lives and *as* your soul lives,
there is but a step between me and death."
4 So Jonathan said to David, "Whatever you
yourself desire, I will do *it* for you."
5 And David said to Jonathan, "Indeed tomor-
row *is* the New Moon, and I should not fail to sit
with the king to eat. But let me go, that I may
hide in the field until the third *day* at evening.
6 If
your father misses me at all, then say, 'David
earnestly asked *permission* of me that he might
run over to Bethlehem, his city, for *there is* a
yearly sacrifice there for all the family.'
7 If he
says thus: '*It is* well,' your servant will be safe.
But if he is very angry, be sure that evil is deter-
mined by him.
8 Therefore you shall deal kindly
with your servant, for you have brought your
servant into a covenant of the LORD with you.
Nevertheless, if there is iniquity in me, kill me
yourself, for why should you bring me to your
father?"
9 But Jonathan said, "Far be it from you! For
if I knew certainly that evil was determined by
my father to come upon you, then would I not
tell you?"
10 Then David said to Jonathan, "Who will tell
me, or what *if* your father answers you
roughly?"
11 And Jonathan said to David, "Come, let us
go out into the field." So both of them went out
into the field.
12 Then Jonathan said to David:
"The LORD God of Israel *is witness!* When I have
sounded out my father sometime tomorrow, *or*
the third *day,* and indeed *there is* good toward
David, and I do not send to you and tell you,
13 may the LORD do so and much more to
Jonathan. But if it pleases my father *to do* you
evil, then I will report it to you and send you
away, that you may go in safety. And the LORD
be with you as He has been with my father.
14 And you shall not only show me the kindness
of the LORD while I still live, that I may not die;
15 but you shall not cut off your kindness from
my house forever, no, not when the LORD has cut
off every one of the enemies of David from the
face of the earth."
16 So Jonathan made *a
covenant* with the house of David, *saying,* "Let
the LORD require *it* at the hand of David's ene-
mies."
17 Now Jonathan again caused David to vow,
because he loved him; for he loved him as he
loved his own soul.
18 Then Jonathan said to
David, "Tomorrow *is* the New Moon; and you
will be missed, because your seat will be empty.
19 And *when* you have stayed three days, go
down quickly and come to the place where you
hid on the day of the deed; and remain by the
stone Ezel.
20 Then I will shoot three arrows to
the side, as though I shot at a target;
21 and there
I will send a lad, *saying,* 'Go, find the arrows.' If
I expressly say to the lad, 'Look, the arrows *are*

The Message

2 "Nothing," said Jonathan. "You've done nothing wrong. And you're not going to die. Really, you're not! My father tells me everything. He does nothing, whether big or little, without confiding in me. So why would he do this behind my back? It can't be."

3 But David said, "Your father knows that we are the best of friends. So he says to himself, 'Jonathan must know nothing of this. If he does, he'll side with David.' But it's true—as sure as GOD lives, and as sure as you're alive before me right now—he's determined to kill me."

4 Jonathan said, "Tell me what you have in mind. I'll do anything for you."

5-8 David said, "Tomorrow marks the New Moon. I'm scheduled to eat dinner with the king. Instead, I'll go hide in the field until the evening of the third. If your father misses me, say, 'David asked if he could run down to Bethlehem, his hometown, for an anniversary reunion, and worship with his family.' If he says, 'Good!' then I'm safe. But if he gets angry, you'll know for sure that he's made up his mind to kill me. Oh, stick with me in this. You've entered into a covenant of GOD with me, remember! If I'm in the wrong, go ahead and kill me yourself. Why bother giving me up to your father?"

9 "Never!" exclaimed Jonathan. "I'd never do that! If I get the slightest hint that my father is fixated on killing you, I'll tell you."

10 David asked, "And whom will you get to tell me if your father comes back with a harsh answer?"

11-17 "Come outside," said Jonathan. "Let's go to the field." When the two of them were out in the field, Jonathan said, "As GOD, the God of Israel, is my witness, by this time tomorrow I'll get it out of my father how he feels about you. Then I'll let you know what I learn. May GOD do his worst to me if I let you down! If my father still intends to kill you, I'll tell you and get you out of here in one piece. And GOD be with you as he's been with my father! If I make it through this alive, continue to be my covenant friend. And if I die, keep the covenant friendship with my family—forever. And when GOD finally rids the earth of David's enemies, stay loyal to Jonathan!" Jonathan repeated his pledge of love and friendship for David. He loved David more than his own soul!

18-23 Jonathan then laid out his plan: "Tomorrow is the New Moon, and you'll be missed when you don't show up for dinner. On the third day, when they've quit expecting you, come to the place where you hid before, and wait beside that big boulder. I'll shoot three arrows in the direction of the boulder. Then I'll send off my servant, 'Go find the arrows.' If I yell after the servant, 'The arrows are on this side! Retrieve them!' that's the signal that you can return safely—as GOD lives, not a thing to fear! But if I yell, 'The arrows are

New King James Version

on this side of you; get them and come'—then, as the LORD lives, *there is* safety for you and no harm. 22But if I say thus to the young man, 'Look, the arrows *are* beyond you'—go your way, for the LORD has sent you away. 23And as for the matter which you and I have spoken of, indeed the LORD *be* between you and me forever."

24Then David hid in the field. And when the New Moon had come, the king sat down to eat the feast. 25Now the king sat on his seat, as at other times, on a seat by the wall. And Jonathan arose,[a] and Abner sat by Saul's side, but David's place was empty. 26Nevertheless Saul did not say anything that day, for he thought, "Something has happened to him; he *is* unclean, surely he *is* unclean." 27And it happened the next day, the second *day* of the month, that David's place was empty. And Saul said to Jonathan his son, "Why has the son of Jesse not come to eat, either yesterday or today?"

28So Jonathan answered Saul, "David earnestly asked *permission* of me *to go* to Bethlehem. 29And he said, 'Please let me go, for our family has a sacrifice in the city, and my brother has commanded me *to be there*. And now, if I have found favor in your eyes, please let me get away and see my brothers.' Therefore he has not come to the king's table."

30Then Saul's anger was aroused against Jonathan, and he said to him, "You son of a perverse, rebellious *woman!* Do I not know that you have chosen the son of Jesse to your own shame and to the shame of your mother's nakedness? 31For as long as the son of Jesse lives on the earth, you shall not be established, nor your kingdom. Now therefore, send and bring him to me, for he shall surely die."

32And Jonathan answered Saul his father, and said to him, "Why should he be killed? What has he done?" 33Then Saul cast a spear at him to kill him, by which Jonathan knew that it was determined by his father to kill David.

34So Jonathan arose from the table in fierce anger, and ate no food the second day of the month, for he was grieved for David, because his father had treated him shamefully.

35And so it was, in the morning, that Jonathan went out into the field at the time appointed with David, and a little lad *was* with him. 36Then he said to his lad, "Now run, find the arrows which I shoot." As the lad ran, he shot an arrow beyond him. 37When the lad had come to the place where the arrow was which Jonathan had shot, Jonathan cried out after the lad and said, "*Is* not the arrow beyond you?" 38And Jonathan cried out after the lad, "Make haste, hurry, do not delay!" So Jonathan's lad gathered up the arrows and came back to his master. 39But the lad did not know anything. Only Jonathan and David knew of the matter. 40Then Jonathan gave his weapons to his lad, and said to him, "Go, carry *them* to the city."

41As soon as the lad had gone, David arose from *a place* toward the south, fell on his face to the ground, and bowed down three times. And they kissed one another; and they wept together, but David more so.

20:25 [a]Following Masoretic Text, Syriac, Targum, and Vulgate; Septuagint reads *he sat across from Jonathan.*

The Message

farther out!' then run for it—GOD wants you out of here! Regarding all the things we've discussed, remember that GOD's in on this with us to the very end!"

24-26 David hid in the field. On the holiday of the New Moon, the king came to the table to eat. He sat where he always sat, the place against the wall, with Jonathan across the table and Abner at Saul's side. But David's seat was empty. Saul didn't mention it at the time, thinking, "Something's happened that's made him unclean. That's it—he's probably unclean for the holy meal."

27 But the day after the New Moon, day two of the holiday, David's seat was still empty. Saul asked Jonathan his son, "So where's that son of Jesse? He hasn't eaten with us either yesterday or today."

28-29 Jonathan said, "David asked my special permission to go to Bethlehem. He said, 'Give me leave to attend a family reunion back home. My brothers have ordered me to be there. If it seems all right to you, let me go and see my brothers.' That's why he's not here at the king's table."

30-31 Saul exploded in anger at Jonathan: "You son of a slut! Don't you think I know that you're in cahoots with the son of Jesse, disgracing both you and your mother? For as long as the son of Jesse is walking around free on this earth, your future in this kingdom is at risk. Now go get him. Bring him here. From this moment, he's as good as dead!"

32 Jonathan stood up to his father. "Why dead? What's he done?"

33 Saul threw his spear at him to kill him. That convinced Jonathan that his father was fixated on killing David.

34 Jonathan stormed from the table, furiously angry, and ate nothing the rest of the day, upset for David and smarting under the humiliation from his father.

35-39 In the morning, Jonathan went to the field for the appointment with David. He had his young servant with him. He told the servant, "Run and get the arrows I'm about to shoot." The boy started running and Jonathan shot an arrow way beyond him. As the boy came to the area where the arrow had been shot, Jonathan yelled out, "Isn't the arrow farther out?" He yelled again, "Hurry! Quickly! Don't just stand there!" Jonathan's servant then picked up the arrow and brought it to his master. The boy, of course, knew nothing of what was going on. Only Jonathan and David knew.

40-41 Jonathan gave his quiver and bow to the boy and sent him back to town. After the servant was gone, David got up from his hiding place beside the boulder, then fell on his face to the ground—three times prostrating himself! And then they kissed one another and wept, friend over friend, David weeping especially hard.

NEW KING JAMES VERSION

42Then Jonathan said to David, "Go in peace,
since we have both sworn in the name of the
LORD, saying, 'May the LORD be between you
and me, and between your descendants and my
descendants, forever.' " So he arose and de-
parted, and Jonathan went into the city.

DAVID AND THE HOLY BREAD

21 Now David came to Nob, to Ahimelech the
priest. And Ahimelech was afraid when he
met David, and said to him, "Why *are* you alone,
and no one is with you?"
2So David said to Ahimelech the priest, "The
king has ordered me on some business, and said
to me, 'Do not let anyone know anything about
the business on which I send you, or what I have
commanded you.' And I have directed *my* young
men to such and such a place. 3Now therefore,
what have you on hand? Give *me* five *loaves of*
bread in my hand, or whatever can be found."
4And the priest answered David and said,
"*There is* no common bread on hand; but there
is holy bread, if the young men have at least
kept themselves from women."
5Then David answered the priest, and said to
him, "Truly, women *have been* kept from us
about three days since I came out. And the ves-
sels of the young men are holy, and *the bread is*
in effect common, even though it was conse-
crated in the vessel this day."
6So the priest gave him holy *bread;* for there
was no bread there but the showbread which
had been taken from before the LORD, in order
to put hot bread *in its place* on the day when it
was taken away.
7Now a certain man of the servants of Saul
was there that day, detained before the LORD.
And his name *was* Doeg, an Edomite, the chief
of the herdsmen who *belonged* to Saul.
8And David said to Ahimelech, "Is there not
here on hand a spear or a sword? For I have
brought neither my sword nor my weapons with
me, because the king's business required haste."
9So the priest said, "The sword of Goliath the
Philistine, whom you killed in the Valley of Elah,
there it is, wrapped in a cloth behind the ephod.
If you will take that, take *it.* For *there is* no other
except that one here."
And David said, "*There is* none like it; give it
to me."

DAVID FLEES TO GATH

10Then David arose and fled that day from
before Saul, and went to Achish the king of
Gath. 11And the servants of Achish said to him,
"*Is* this not David the king of the land? Did they
not sing of him to one another in dances, saying:

'Saul has slain his thousands,
And David his ten thousands'?"[a]

12Now David took these words to heart, and
was very much afraid of Achish the king of
Gath. 13So he changed his behavior before them,
pretended madness in their hands, scratched on

THE MESSAGE

42 Jonathan said, "Go in peace! The two of us have vowed friendship in GOD's name, saying, 'GOD will be the bond between me and you, and between my children and your children forever!' "

DAVID PRETENDS TO GO CRAZY

1 21 David went on his way and Jonathan returned to town.

David went to Nob, to Ahimelech the Priest. Ahimelech was alarmed as he went out to greet David: "What are you doing here all by yourself—and not a soul with you?"

2-3 David answered Ahimelech the Priest, "The king sent me on a mission and gave strict orders: 'This is top secret—not a word of this to a soul.' I've arranged to meet up with my men in a certain place. Now, what's there here to eat? Do you have five loaves of bread? Give me whatever you can scrounge up!"

4 "I don't have any regular bread on hand," said the priest. "I only have holy bread. If your men have not slept with women recently, it's yours."

5 David said, "None of us has touched a woman. I always do it this way when I'm on a mission: My men abstain from sex. Even when it is an ordinary mission we do that—how much more on this holy mission."

6 So the priest gave them the holy bread. It was the only bread he had, Bread of the Presence that had been removed from GOD's presence and replaced by fresh bread at the same time.

7 One of Saul's officials was present that day keeping a religious vow. His name was Doeg the Edomite. He was chief of Saul's shepherds.

8 David asked Ahimelech, "Do you have a spear or sword of any kind around here? I didn't have a chance to grab my weapons. The king's mission was urgent and I left in a hurry."

9 The priest said, "The sword of Goliath, the Philistine you killed at Oak Valley—that's here! It's behind the Ephod wrapped in a cloth. If you want it, take it. There's nothing else here."

10-11 "Oh," said David, "there's no sword like that! Give it to me!"

And at that, David shot out of there, running for his life from Saul. He went to Achish, king of Gath. When the servants of Achish saw him, they said, "Can this be David, the famous David? Is this the one they sing of at their dances?

Saul kills by the thousand,
David by the ten thousand!"

12-15 When David realized that he had been recognized, he panicked, fearing the worst from Achish, king of Gath. So right there, while they were looking at him, he pre-

21:11 [a]Compare 1 Samuel 18:7

NEW KING JAMES VERSION

the doors of the gate, and let his saliva fall down on his beard. 14Then Achish said to his servants, "Look, you see the man is insane. Why have you brought him to me? 15Have I need of madmen, that you have brought this *fellow* to play the madman in my presence? Shall this *fellow* come into my house?"

DAVID'S FOUR HUNDRED MEN

22 David therefore departed from there and escaped to the cave of Adullam. So when his brothers and all his father's house heard *it*, they went down there to him. 2And everyone *who was* in distress, everyone who *was* in debt, and everyone *who was* discontented gathered to him. So he became captain over them. And there were about four hundred men with him.

3Then David went from there to Mizpah of Moab; and he said to the king of Moab, "Please let my father and mother come here with you, till I know what God will do for me." 4So he brought them before the king of Moab, and they dwelt with him all the time that David was in the stronghold.

5Now the prophet Gad said to David, "Do not stay in the stronghold; depart, and go to the land of Judah." So David departed and went into the forest of Hereth.

SAUL MURDERS THE PRIESTS

6When Saul heard that David and the men who *were* with him had been discovered—now Saul was staying in Gibeah under a tamarisk tree in Ramah, with his spear in his hand, and all his servants standing about him— 7then Saul said to his servants who stood about him, "Hear now, you Benjamites! Will the son of Jesse give every one of you fields and vineyards, *and* make you all captains of thousands and captains of hundreds? 8All of you have conspired against me, and *there is* no one who reveals to me that my son has made a covenant with the son of Jesse; and *there is* not one of you who is sorry for me or reveals to me that my son has stirred up my servant against me, to lie in wait, as *it is* this day."

9Then answered Doeg the Edomite, who was set over the servants of Saul, and said, "I saw the son of Jesse going to Nob, to Ahimelech the son of Ahitub. 10And he inquired of the LORD for him, gave him provisions, and gave him the sword of Goliath the Philistine."

11So the king sent to call Ahimelech the priest, the son of Ahitub, and all his father's house, the priests who *were* in Nob. And they all came to the king. 12And Saul said, "Hear now, son of Ahitub!"

He answered, "Here I am, my lord."

13Then Saul said to him, "Why have you conspired against me, you and the son of Jesse, in that you have given him bread and a sword, and have inquired of God for him, that he should rise against me, to lie in wait, as it is this day?"

THE MESSAGE

tended to go crazy, pounding his head on the city gate and foaming at the mouth, spit dripping from his beard. Achish took one look at him and said to his servants, "Can't you see he's crazy? Why did you let him in here? Don't you think I have enough crazy people to put up with as it is without adding another? Get him out of here!"

SAUL MURDERS THE PRIESTS OF GOD

1-2 22 So David got away and escaped to the
Cave of Adullam. When his brothers
and others associated with his family heard
where he was, they came down and joined
him. Not only that, but all who were down on
their luck came around—losers and vagrants
and misfits of all sorts. David became their
leader. There were about four hundred in all.

3-4 Then David went to Mizpah in Moab. He
petitioned the king of Moab, "Grant asylum
to my father and mother until I find out
what God has planned for me." David left
his parents in the care of the king of Moab.
They stayed there all through the time
David was hiding out.

5 The prophet Gad told David, "Don't go
back to the cave. Go to Judah." David did
what he told him. He went to the forest of
Hereth.

6-8 Saul got word of the whereabouts of
David and his men. He was sitting under the
big oak on the hill at Gibeah at the time,
spear in hand, holding court surrounded by
his officials. He said, "Listen here, you Ben-
jaminites! Don't think for a minute that you
have any future with the son of Jesse! Do
you think he's going to hand over choice
land, give you all influential jobs? Think
again. Here you are, conspiring against me,
whispering behind my back—not one of you
is man enough to tell me that my own son is
making deals with the son of Jesse, not one
of you who cares enough to tell me that my
son has taken the side of this, this . . . out-
law!"

9-10 Then Doeg the Edomite, who was stand-
ing with Saul's officials, spoke up: "I saw the
son of Jesse meet with Ahimelech son of
Ahitub, in Nob. I saw Ahimelech pray with
him for GOD's guidance, give him food, and
arm him with the sword of Goliath the
Philistine."

11 Saul sent for the priest Ahimelech son of
Ahitub, along with the whole family of
priests at Nob. They all came to the king.

12 Saul said, "You listen to me, son of Ahi-
tub!"

"Certainly, master," he said.

13 "Why have you ganged up against me
with the son of Jesse, giving him bread and
a sword, even praying with him for GOD's
guidance, setting him up as an outlaw, out to
get me?"

New King James Version

14So Ahimelech answered the king and said, "And who among all your servants *is as* faithful as David, who is the king's son-in-law, who goes at your bidding, and is honorable in your house? 15Did I then begin to inquire of God for him? Far be it from me! Let not the king impute anything to his servant, *or* to any in the house of my father. For your servant knew nothing of all this, little or much."

16And the king said, "You shall surely die, Ahimelech, you and all your father's house!" 17Then the king said to the guards who stood about him, "Turn and kill the priests of the LORD, because their hand also *is* with David, and because they knew when he fled and did not tell it to me." But the servants of the king would not lift their hands to strike the priests of the LORD. 18And the king said to Doeg, "You turn and kill the priests!" So Doeg the Edomite turned and struck the priests, and killed on that day eighty-five men who wore a linen ephod. 19Also Nob, the city of the priests, he struck with the edge of the sword, both men and women, children and nursing infants, oxen and donkeys and sheep—with the edge of the sword.

20Now one of the sons of Ahimelech the son of Ahitub, named Abiathar, escaped and fled after David. 21And Abiathar told David that Saul had killed the LORD's priests. 22So David said to Abiathar, "I knew that day, when Doeg the Edomite *was* there, that he would surely tell Saul. I have caused *the death* of all the persons of your father's house. 23Stay with me; do not fear. For he who seeks my life seeks your life, but with me you *shall be* safe."

David Saves the City of Keilah

23 Then they told David, saying, "Look, the Philistines are fighting against Keilah, and they are robbing the threshing floors."

2Therefore David inquired of the LORD, saying, "Shall I go and attack these Philistines?"

And the LORD said to David, "Go and attack the Philistines, and save Keilah."

3But David's men said to him, "Look, we are afraid here in Judah. How much more then if we go to Keilah against the armies of the Philistines?" 4Then David inquired of the LORD once again.

And the LORD answered him and said, "Arise, go down to Keilah. For I will deliver the Philistines into your hand." 5And David and his men went to Keilah and fought with the Philistines, struck them with a mighty blow, and took away their livestock. So David saved the inhabitants of Keilah.

6Now it happened, when Abiathar the son of Ahimelech fled to David at Keilah, *that* he went down *with* an ephod in his hand.

7And Saul was told that David had gone to Keilah. So Saul said, "God has delivered him into my hand, for he has shut himself in by entering a town that has gates and bars." 8Then Saul called all the people together for war, to go down to Keilah to besiege David and his men.

The Message

14-15 Ahimelech answered the king, "There's not an official in your administration as true to you as David, your own son-in-law and captain of your bodyguard. None more honorable either. Do you think that was the first time I prayed with him for God's guidance? Hardly! But don't accuse me of any wrongdoing, me or my family. I have no idea what you're trying to get at with this 'outlaw' talk."

16 The king said, "Death, Ahimelech! You're going to die—you and everyone in your family!"

17 The king ordered his henchmen, "Surround and kill the priests of GOD! They're hand in glove with David. They knew he was running away from me and didn't tell me." But the king's men wouldn't do it. They refused to lay a hand on the priests of GOD.

18-19 Then the king told Doeg, "You do it—massacre the priests!" Doeg the Edomite led the attack and slaughtered the priests, the eighty-five men who wore the sacred robes. He then carried the massacre into Nob, the city of priests, killing man and woman, child and baby, ox, donkey, and sheep—the works.

20-21 Only one son of Ahimelech son of Ahitub escaped: Abiathar. He got away and joined up with David. Abiathar reported to David that Saul had murdered the priests of GOD.

22-23 David said to Abiathar, "I knew it—that day I saw Doeg the Edomite there, I knew he'd tell Saul. I'm to blame for the death of everyone in your father's family. Stay here with me. Don't be afraid. The one out to kill you is out to kill me, too. Stick with me. I'll protect you."

Living in Desert Hideouts

1-2 23 It was reported to David that the Philistines were raiding Keilah and looting the grain. David went in prayer to GOD: "Should I go after these Philistines and teach them a lesson?"

GOD said, "Go. Attack the Philistines and save Keilah."

3 But David's men said, "We live in fear of our lives right here in Judah. How can you think of going to Keilah in the thick of the Philistines?"

4 So David went back to GOD in prayer. GOD said, "Get going. Head for Keilah. I'm placing the Philistines in your hands."

5-6 David and his men went to Keilah and fought the Philistines. He scattered their cattle, beat them decisively, and saved the people of Keilah. After Abiathar took refuge with David, he joined David in the raid on Keilah, bringing the Ephod with him.

7-8 Saul learned that David had gone to Keilah and thought immediately, "Good! God has handed him to me on a platter! He's in a walled city with locked gates, trapped!" Saul mustered his troops for battle and set out for Keilah to lay siege to David and his men.

New King James Version

9When David knew that Saul plotted evil
against him, he said to Abiathar the priest,
"Bring the ephod here." 10Then David said, "O
LORD God of Israel, Your servant has certainly
heard that Saul seeks to come to Keilah to de-
stroy the city for my sake. 11Will the men of
Keilah deliver me into his hand? Will Saul come
down, as Your servant has heard? O LORD God of
Israel, I pray, tell Your servant."
And the LORD said, "He will come down."
12Then David said, "Will the men of Keilah
deliver me and my men into the hand of Saul?"
And the LORD said, "They will deliver *you*."
13So David and his men, about six hundred,
arose and departed from Keilah and went wher-
ever they could go. Then it was told Saul that
David had escaped from Keilah; so he halted the
expedition.

David in Wilderness Strongholds

14And David stayed in strongholds in the
wilderness, and remained in the mountains in
the Wilderness of Ziph. Saul sought him every
day, but God did not deliver him into his hand.
15So David saw that Saul had come out to seek
his life. And David *was* in the Wilderness of
Ziph in a forest.[a] 16Then Jonathan, Saul's son,
arose and went to David in the woods and
strengthened his hand in God. 17And he said to
him, "Do not fear, for the hand of Saul my father
shall not find you. You shall be king over Israel,
and I shall be next to you. Even my father Saul
knows that." 18So the two of them made a
covenant before the LORD. And David stayed in
the woods, and Jonathan went to his own house.
19Then the Ziphites came up to Saul at
Gibeah, saying, "Is David not hiding with us in
strongholds in the woods, in the hill of Hachi-
lah, which *is* on the south of Jeshimon? 20Now
therefore, O king, come down according to all
the desire of your soul to come down; and our
part *shall be* to deliver him into the king's
hand."
21And Saul said, "Blessed *are* you of the
LORD, for you have compassion on me. 22Please
go and find out for sure, and see the place where
his hideout is, *and* who has seen him there. For
I am told he is very crafty. 23See therefore, and
take knowledge of all the lurking places where
he hides; and come back to me with certainty,
and I will go with you. And it shall be, if he is in
the land, that I will search for him throughout
all the clans[a] of Judah."
24So they arose and went to Ziph before
Saul. But David and his men *were* in the Wilder-
ness of Maon, in the plain on the south of Jeshi-
mon. 25When Saul and his men went to seek
him, they told David. Therefore he went down to
the rock, and stayed in the Wilderness of Maon.
And when Saul heard *that*, he pursued David in
the Wilderness of Maon. 26Then Saul went on
one side of the mountain, and David and his
men on the other side of the mountain. So David
made haste to get away from Saul, for Saul and
his men were encircling David and his men to
take them.

23:15 [a]Or *in Horesh* **23:23** [a]Literally *thousands*

The Message

9-11 But David got wind of Saul's strategy to
destroy him and said to Abiathar the priest,
"Get the Ephod." Then David prayed to GOD:
"God of Israel, I've just heard that Saul
plans to come to Keilah and destroy the city
because of me. Will the city fathers of Keilah
turn me over to him? Will Saul come down
and do what I've heard? O GOD, God of Is-
rael, tell me!"
GOD replied, "He's coming down."
12 "And will the head men of Keilah turn me
and my men over to Saul?"
And GOD said, "They'll turn you over."
13 So David and his men got out of there.
There were about six hundred of them. They
left Keilah and kept moving, going here,
there, wherever—always on the move.
When Saul was told that David had es-
caped from Keilah, he called off the raid.
14-15 David continued to live in desert hideouts
and the backcountry wilderness hills of
Ziph. Saul was out looking for him day after
day, but God never turned David over to
him. David kept out of the way in the wilder-
ness of Ziph, secluded at Horesh, since it
was plain that Saul was determined to hunt
him down.

16-18 Jonathan, Saul's son, visited David at
Horesh and encouraged him in God. He
said, "Don't despair. My father, Saul, can't
lay a hand on you. You will be Israel's king
and I'll be right at your side to help. And my
father knows it." Then the two of them made
a covenant before GOD. David stayed at
Horesh and Jonathan went home.

19-20 Some Ziphites went to Saul at Gibeah
and said, "Did you know that David is hid-
ing out near us in the caves and canyons of
Horesh? Right now he's at Hakilah Hill just
south of Jeshimon. So whenever you're
ready to come down, we'd count it an honor
to hand him over to the king."
21-23 Saul said, "GOD bless you for thinking
about me! Now go back and check every-
thing out. Learn his routines. Observe his
movements—where he goes, who he's with.
He's very shrewd, you know. Scout out all
his hiding places. Then meet me at Nacon
and I'll go with you. If he is anywhere to be
found in all the thousands of Judah, I'll
track him down!"
24-27 So the Ziphites set out on their recon-
naissance for Saul.
Meanwhile, David and his men were in
the wilderness of Maon, in the desert south
of Jeshimon. Saul and his men arrived and
began their search. When David heard of it,
he went south to Rock Mountain, camping
out in the wilderness of Maon. Saul heard
where he was and set off for the wilderness
of Maon in pursuit. Saul was on one side of
the mountain, David and his men on the
other. David was in full retreat, running,
with Saul and his men closing in, about to

New King James Version

27But a messenger came to Saul, saying, "Hurry and come, for the Philistines have invaded the land!" 28Therefore Saul returned from pursuing David, and went against the Philistines; so they called that place the Rock of Escape.[a] 29Then David went up from there and dwelt in strongholds at En Gedi.

David Spares Saul

24 Now it happened, when Saul had returned from following the Philistines, that it was told him, saying, "Take note! David *is* in the Wilderness of En Gedi." 2Then Saul took three thousand chosen men from all Israel, and went to seek David and his men on the Rocks of the Wild Goats. 3So he came to the sheepfolds by the road, where there *was* a cave; and Saul went in to attend to his needs. (David and his men were staying in the recesses of the cave.) 4Then the men of David said to him, "This is the day of which the LORD said to you, 'Behold, I will deliver your enemy into your hand, that you may do to him as it seems good to you.' " And David arose and secretly cut off a corner of Saul's robe. 5Now it happened afterward that David's heart troubled him because he had cut Saul's *robe.* 6And he said to his men, "The LORD forbid that I should do this thing to my master, the LORD's anointed, to stretch out my hand against him, seeing he *is* the anointed of the LORD." 7So David restrained his servants with *these* words, and did not allow them to rise against Saul. And Saul got up from the cave and went on *his* way.

8David also arose afterward, went out of the cave, and called out to Saul, saying, "My lord the king!" And when Saul looked behind him, David stooped with his face to the earth, and bowed down. 9And David said to Saul: "Why do you listen to the words of men who say, 'Indeed David seeks your harm'? 10Look, this day your eyes have seen that the LORD delivered you today into my hand in the cave, and *someone* urged *me* to kill you. But *my eye* spared you, and I said, 'I will not stretch out my hand against my lord, for he *is* the LORD's anointed.' 11Moreover, my father, see! Yes, see the corner of your robe in my hand! For in that I cut off the corner of your robe, and did not kill you, know and see that *there is* neither evil nor rebellion in my hand, and I have not sinned against you. Yet you hunt my life to take it. 12Let the LORD judge between you and me, and let the LORD avenge me on you. But my hand shall not be against you. 13As the proverb of the ancients says, 'Wickedness proceeds from the wicked.' But my hand shall not be against you. 14After whom has the king of Israel come out? Whom do you pursue? A dead dog? A flea? 15Therefore let the LORD be judge, and judge between you and me, and see and plead my case, and deliver me out of your hand."

16So it was, when David had finished speaking these words to Saul, that Saul said, "*Is* this your voice, my son David?" And Saul lifted up his voice and wept. 17Then he said to David: "You *are* more righteous than I; for you have rewarded me with good, whereas I have rewarded you with evil. 18And you have shown this day

23:28 [a]Hebrew *Sela Hammahlekoth*

The Message

get him. Just then a messenger came to Saul and said, "Hurry! Come back! The Philistines have just attacked the country!"

28-29 So Saul called off his pursuit of David and went back to deal with the Philistines. That's how that place got the name Narrow Escape. David left there and camped out in the caves and canyons of En Gedi.

"I'm No Rebel"

1-4 **24** When Saul came back after dealing with the Philistines, he was told, "David is now in the wilderness of En Gedi." Saul took three companies—the best he could find in all Israel—and set out in search of David and his men in the region of Wild Goat Rocks. He came to some sheep pens along the road. There was a cave there and Saul went in to relieve himself. David and his men were huddled far back in the same cave. David's men whispered to him, "Can you believe it? This is the day GOD was talking about when he said, 'I'll put your enemy in your hands. You can do whatever you want with him.' " Quiet as a cat, David crept up and cut off a piece of Saul's royal robe.

5-7 Immediately, he felt guilty. He said to his men, "GOD forbid that I should have done this to my master, GOD's anointed, that I should so much as raise a finger against him. He's GOD's anointed!" David held his men in check with these words and wouldn't let them pounce on Saul. Saul got up, left the cave, and went on down the road.

8-13 Then David stood at the mouth of the cave and called to Saul, "My master! My king!" Saul looked back. David fell to his knees and bowed in reverence. He called out, "Why do you listen to those who say 'David is out to get you'? This very day with your very own eyes you have seen that just now in the cave GOD put you in my hands. My men wanted me to kill you, but I wouldn't do it. I told them that I won't lift a finger against my master—he's GOD's anointed. Oh, my father, look at this, look at this piece that I cut from your robe. I could have cut you—killed you!—but I didn't. Look at the evidence! I'm not against you. I'm no rebel. I haven't sinned against you, and yet you're hunting me down to kill me. Let's decide which of us is in the right. GOD may avenge me, but it is in his hands, not mine. An old proverb says, 'Evil deeds come from evil people.' So be assured that my hand won't touch you.

14-15 "What does the king of Israel think he's doing? Who do you think you're chasing? A dead dog? A flea? GOD is our judge. He'll decide who is right. Oh, that he would look down right now, decide right now—and set me free of you!"

16-21 When David had finished saying all this, Saul said, "Can this be the voice of my son David?" and he wept in loud sobs. "You're the one in the right, not me," he continued. "You've heaped good on me; I've dumped evil on you. And now you've done it again—

NEW KING JAMES VERSION

how you have dealt well with me; for when the LORD delivered me into your hand, you did not kill me. [19]For if a man finds his enemy, will he let him get away safely? Therefore may the LORD reward you with good for what you have done to me this day. [20]And now I know indeed that you shall surely be king, and that the kingdom of Israel shall be established in your hand. [21]Therefore swear now to me by the LORD that you will not cut off my descendants after me, and that you will not destroy my name from my father's house."

[22]So David swore to Saul. And Saul went home, but David and his men went up to the stronghold.

DEATH OF SAMUEL

25 Then Samuel died; and the Israelites gathered together and lamented for him, and buried him at his home in Ramah. And David arose and went down to the Wilderness of Paran.[a]

DAVID AND THE WIFE OF NABAL

[2]Now *there was* a man in Maon whose business *was* in Carmel, and the man *was* very rich. He had three thousand sheep and a thousand goats. And he was shearing his sheep in Carmel. [3]The name of the man *was* Nabal, and the name of his wife Abigail. And *she was* a woman of good understanding and beautiful appearance; but the man *was* harsh and evil in *his* doings. He *was of the house of* Caleb.

[4]When David heard in the wilderness that Nabal was shearing his sheep, [5]David sent ten young men; and David said to the young men, "Go up to Carmel, go to Nabal, and greet him in my name. [6]And thus you shall say to him who lives *in prosperity:* 'Peace *be* to you, peace to your house, and peace to all that you have! [7]Now I have heard that you have shearers. Your shepherds were with us, and we did not hurt them, nor was there anything missing from them all the while they were in Carmel. [8]Ask your young men, and they will tell you. Therefore let *my* young men find favor in your eyes, for we come on a feast day. Please give whatever comes to your hand to your servants and to your son David.' "

[9]So when David's young men came, they spoke to Nabal according to all these words in the name of David, and waited.

[10]Then Nabal answered David's servants, and said, "Who *is* David, and who *is* the son of Jesse? There are many servants nowadays who break away each one from his master. [11]Shall I then take my bread and my water and my meat that I have killed for my shearers, and give *it* to men when I do not know where they *are* from?"

[12]So David's young men turned on their heels and went back; and they came and told him all these words. [13]Then David said to his men, "Every man gird on his sword." So every man girded on his sword, and David also girded

25:1 [a]Following Masoretic Text, Syriac, Targum, and Vulgate; Septuagint reads *Maon.*

THE MESSAGE

treated me generously. GOD put me in your hands and you didn't kill me. Why? When a man meets his enemy, does he send him down the road with a blessing? May GOD give you a bonus of blessings for what you've done for me today! I know now beyond doubt that you will rule as king. The kingdom of Israel is already in your grasp! Now promise me under GOD that you will not kill off my family or wipe my name off the books."

22 David promised Saul. Then Saul went home and David and his men went up to their wilderness refuge.

TO FIGHT GOD'S BATTLES

1 25 Samuel died. The whole country came to his funeral. Everyone grieved over his death, and he was buried in his hometown of Ramah. Meanwhile, David moved again, this time to the wilderness of Maon.

2-3 There was a certain man in Maon who carried on his business in the region of Carmel. He was very prosperous—three thousand sheep and a thousand goats, and it was sheep-shearing time in Carmel. The man's name was Nabal (Fool), a Calebite, and his wife's name was Abigail. The woman was intelligent and good-looking, the man brutish and mean.

4-8 David, out in the backcountry, heard that Nabal was shearing his sheep and sent ten of his young men off with these instructions: "Go to Carmel and approach Nabal. Greet him in my name, 'Peace! Life and peace to you. Peace to your household, peace to everyone here! I heard that it's sheep-shearing time. Here's the point: When your shepherds were camped near us we didn't take advantage of them. They didn't lose a thing all the time they were with us in Carmel. Ask your young men—they'll tell you. What I'm asking is that you be generous with my men—share the feast! Give whatever your heart tells you to your servants and to me, David your son.' "

9-11 David's young men went and delivered his message word for word to Nabal. Nabal tore into them, "Who is this David? Who is this son of Jesse? The country is full of runaway servants these days. Do you think I'm going to take good bread and wine and meat freshly butchered for my sheepshearers and give it to men I've never laid eyes on? Who knows where they've come from?"

12-13 David's men got out of there and went back and told David what he had said. David said, "Strap on your swords!" They all strapped on their swords, David and his

NEW KING JAMES VERSION

on his sword. And about four hundred men went with David, and two hundred stayed with the supplies.

14Now one of the young men told Abigail, Nabal's wife, saying, "Look, David sent messengers from the wilderness to greet our master; and he reviled them. 15But the men *were* very good to us, and we were not hurt, nor did we miss anything as long as we accompanied them, when we were in the fields. 16They were a wall to us both by night and day, all the time we were with them keeping the sheep. 17Now therefore, know and consider what you will do, for harm is determined against our master and against all his household. For he *is such* a scoundrel[a] that *one* cannot speak to him."

18Then Abigail made haste and took two hundred *loaves* of bread, two skins of wine, five sheep already dressed, five seahs of roasted *grain,* one hundred clusters of raisins, and two hundred cakes of figs, and loaded *them* on donkeys. 19And she said to her servants, "Go on before me; see, I am coming after you." But she did not tell her husband Nabal.

20So it was, *as* she rode on the donkey, that she went down under cover of the hill; and there were David and his men, coming down toward her, and she met them. 21Now David had said, "Surely in vain I have protected all that this *fellow* has in the wilderness, so that nothing was missed of all that *belongs* to him. And he has repaid me evil for good. 22May God do so, and more also, to the enemies of David, if I leave one male of all who *belong* to him by morning light."

23Now when Abigail saw David, she dismounted quickly from the donkey, fell on her face before David, and bowed down to the ground. 24So she fell at his feet and said: "On me, my lord, *on* me *let* this iniquity *be!* And please let your maidservant speak in your ears, and hear the words of your maidservant. 25Please, let not my lord regard this scoundrel Nabal. For as his name *is,* so *is* he: Nabal[a] *is* his name, and folly *is* with him! But I, your maidservant, did not see the young men of my lord whom you sent. 26Now therefore, my lord, *as* the LORD lives and *as* your soul lives, since the LORD has held you back from coming to bloodshed and from avenging yourself with your own hand, now then, let your enemies and those who seek harm for my lord be as Nabal. 27And now this present which your maidservant has brought to my lord, let it be given to the young men who follow my lord. 28Please forgive the trespass of your maidservant. For the LORD will certainly make for my lord an enduring house, because my lord fights the battles of the LORD, and evil is not found in you throughout your days. 29Yet a man has risen to pursue you and seek your life, but the life of my lord shall be bound in the bundle of the living with the LORD your God; and the lives of your enemies He shall sling out, *as from* the pocket of a sling.

25:17 [a]Literally *son of Belial* **25:25** [a]Literally *Fool*

THE MESSAGE

men, and set out, four hundred of them. Two hundred stayed behind to guard the camp.

14-17 Meanwhile, one of the young shepherds told Abigail, Nabal's wife, what had happened: "David sent messengers from the backcountry to salute our master, but he tore into them with insults. Yet these men treated us very well. They took nothing from us and didn't take advantage of us all the time we were in the fields. They formed a wall around us, protecting us day and night all the time we were out tending the sheep. Do something quickly because big trouble is ahead for our master and all of us. Nobody can talk to him. He's impossible—a real brute!"

18-19 Abigail flew into action. She took two hundred loaves of bread, two skins of wine, five sheep dressed out and ready for cooking, a bushel of roasted grain, a hundred raisin cakes, and two hundred fig cakes, and she had it all loaded on some donkeys. Then she said to her young servants, "Go ahead and pave the way for me. I'm right behind you." But she said nothing to her husband Nabal.

20-22 As she was riding her donkey, descending into a ravine, David and his men were descending from the other end, so they met there on the road. David had just said, "That sure was a waste, guarding everything this man had out in the wild so that nothing he had was lost—and now he rewards me with insults. A real slap in the face! May God do his worst to me if Nabal and every cur in his misbegotten brood aren't dead meat by morning!"

23-25 As soon as Abigail saw David, she got off her donkey and fell on her knees at his feet, her face to the ground in homage, saying, "My master, let me take the blame! Let me speak to you. Listen to what I have to say. Don't dwell on what that brute Nabal did. He acts out the meaning of his name: Nabal, Fool. Foolishness oozes from him.

25-27 "I wasn't there when the young men my master sent arrived. I didn't see them. And now, my master, as GOD lives and as you live, GOD has kept you from this avenging murder—and may your enemies, all who seek my master's harm, end up like Nabal! Now take this gift that I, your servant girl, have brought to my master, and give it to the young men who follow in the steps of my master.

28-29 "Forgive my presumption! But GOD is at work in my master, developing a rule solid and dependable. My master fights GOD's battles! As long as you live no evil will stick to you.

If anyone stands in your way,
if anyone tries to get you out of the way,
Know this: Your God-honored life is tightly bound
in the bundle of God-protected life;
But the lives of your enemies will be hurled aside
as a stone is thrown from a sling.

NEW KING JAMES VERSION

30And it shall come to pass, when the LORD has done for my lord according to all the good that He has spoken concerning you, and has appointed you ruler over Israel, 31that this will be no grief to you, nor offense of heart to my lord, either that you have shed blood without cause, or that my lord has avenged himself. But when the LORD has dealt well with my lord, then remember your maidservant."

32Then David said to Abigail: "Blessed *is* the LORD God of Israel, who sent you this day to meet me! 33And blessed *is* your advice and blessed *are* you, because you have kept me this day from coming to bloodshed and from avenging myself with my own hand. 34For indeed, *as* the LORD God of Israel lives, who has kept me back from hurting you, unless you had hurried and come to meet me, surely by morning light no males would have been left to Nabal!" 35So David received from her hand what she had brought him, and said to her, "Go up in peace to your house. See, I have heeded your voice and respected your person."

36Now Abigail went to Nabal, and there he was, holding a feast in his house, like the feast of a king. And Nabal's heart *was* merry within him, for he *was* very drunk; therefore she told him nothing, little or much, until morning light. 37So it was, in the morning, when the wine had gone from Nabal, and his wife had told him these things, that his heart died within him, and he became *like* a stone. 38Then it happened, *after* about ten days, that the LORD struck Nabal, and he died.

39So when David heard that Nabal was dead, he said, "Blessed *be* the LORD, who has pleaded the cause of my reproach from the hand of Nabal, and has kept His servant from evil! For the LORD has returned the wickedness of Nabal on his own head."

And David sent and proposed to Abigail, to take her as his wife. 40When the servants of David had come to Abigail at Carmel, they spoke to her saying, "David sent us to you, to ask you to become his wife."

41Then she arose, bowed her face to the earth, and said, "Here is your maidservant, a servant to wash the feet of the servants of my lord." 42So Abigail rose in haste and rode on a donkey, attended by five of her maidens; and she followed the messengers of David, and became his wife. 43David also took Ahinoam of Jezreel, and so both of them were his wives.

44But Saul had given Michal his daughter, David's wife, to Palti[a] the son of Laish, who *was* from Gallim.

DAVID SPARES SAUL A SECOND TIME

26 Now the Ziphites came to Saul at Gibeah, saying, "Is David not hiding in the hill of Hachilah, opposite Jeshimon?" 2Then Saul arose and went down to the Wilderness of Ziph, having three thousand chosen men of Israel with him, to seek David in the Wilderness of Ziph. 3And Saul encamped in the hill of Hachilah, which *is* opposite Jeshimon, by the road.

25:44 [a]Spelled *Paltiel* in 2 Samuel 3:15

THE MESSAGE

30-31 "When GOD completes all the goodness he has promised my master and sets you up as prince over Israel, my master will not have this dead weight in his heart, the guilt of an avenging murder. And when GOD has worked things for good for my master, remember me."

32-34 And David said, "Blessed be GOD, the God of Israel. He sent you to meet me! And blessed be your good sense! Bless you for keeping me from murder and taking charge of looking out for me. A close call! As GOD lives, the God of Israel who kept me from hurting you, if you had not come as quickly as you did, stopping me in my tracks, by morning there would have been nothing left of Nabal but dead meat."

35 Then David accepted the gift she brought him and said, "Return home in peace. I've heard what you've said and I'll do what you've asked."

36-38 When Abigail got home she found Nabal presiding over a huge banquet. He was in high spirits—and very, very drunk. So she didn't tell him anything of what she'd done until morning. But in the morning, after Nabal had sobered up, she told him the whole story. Right then and there he had a heart attack and fell into a coma. About ten days later GOD finished him off and he died.

39-40 When David heard that Nabal was dead he said, "Blessed be GOD who has stood up for me against Nabal's insults, kept me from an evil act, and let Nabal's evil boomerang back on him."

Then David sent for Abigail to tell her that he wanted her for his wife. David's servants went to Abigail at Carmel with the message, "David sent us to bring you to marry him."

41 She got up, and then bowed down, face to the ground, saying, "I'm your servant, ready to do anything you want. I'll even wash the feet of my master's servants!"

42 Abigail didn't linger. She got on her donkey and, with her five maids in attendance, went with the messengers to David and became his wife.

43-44 David also married Ahinoam of Jezreel. Both women were his wives. Saul had married off David's wife Michal to Palti (Paltiel) son of Laish, who was from Gallim.

OBSESSED WITH A SINGLE FLEA

1-3 26 Some Ziphites came to Saul at Gibeah and said, "Did you know that David is hiding out on the Hakilah Hill just opposite Jeshimon?" Saul was on his feet in a minute and on his way to the wilderness of Ziph, taking three thousand of his best men, the pick of the crop, to hunt for David in that wild desert. He camped just off the road at the Hakilah Hill, opposite Jeshimon.

3-5 David, still out in the backcountry, knew Saul had come after him. He sent scouts to

NEW KING JAMES VERSION

But David stayed in the wilderness, and he saw that Saul came after him into the wilderness. 4David therefore sent out spies, and understood that Saul had indeed come.

5So David arose and came to the place where Saul had encamped. And David saw the place where Saul lay, and Abner the son of Ner, the commander of his army. Now Saul lay within the camp, with the people encamped all around him. 6Then David answered, and said to Ahimelech the Hittite and to Abishai the son of Zeruiah, brother of Joab, saying, "Who will go down with me to Saul in the camp?"

And Abishai said, "I will go down with you."

7So David and Abishai came to the people by night; and there Saul lay sleeping within the camp, with his spear stuck in the ground by his head. And Abner and the people lay all around him. 8Then Abishai said to David, "God has delivered your enemy into your hand this day. Now therefore, please, let me strike him at once with the spear, right to the earth; and I will not *have to strike* him a second time!"

9But David said to Abishai, "Do not destroy him; for who can stretch out his hand against the LORD's anointed, and be guiltless?" 10David said furthermore, "*As* the LORD lives, the LORD shall strike him, or his day shall come to die, or he shall go out to battle and perish. 11The LORD forbid that I should stretch out my hand against the LORD's anointed. But please, take now the spear and the jug of water that *are* by his head, and let us go." 12So David took the spear and the jug of water *by* Saul's head, and they got away; and no man saw or knew *it* or awoke. For they *were* all asleep, because a deep sleep from the LORD had fallen on them.

13Now David went over to the other side, and stood on the top of a hill afar off, a great distance *being* between them. 14And David called out to the people and to Abner the son of Ner, saying, "Do you not answer, Abner?"

Then Abner answered and said, "Who *are* you, calling out to the king?"

15So David said to Abner, "*Are* you not a man? And who *is* like you in Israel? Why then have you not guarded your lord the king? For one of the people came in to destroy your lord the king. 16This thing that you have done *is* not good. *As* the LORD lives, you deserve to die, because you have not guarded your master, the LORD's anointed. And now see where the king's spear *is*, and the jug of water that *was* by his head."

17Then Saul knew David's voice, and said, "*Is* that your voice, my son David?"

David said, "*It is* my voice, my lord, O king." 18And he said, "Why does my lord thus pursue his servant? For what have I done, or what evil *is* in my hand? 19Now therefore, please, let my lord the king hear the words of his servant: If the LORD has stirred you up against me, let Him accept an offering. But if *it is* the children of men, *may* they *be* cursed before the LORD, for they have driven me out this day from sharing in the inheritance of the LORD, saying, 'Go, serve other gods.' 20So now, do not let my blood fall to

THE MESSAGE

determine his precise location. Then David set out and came to the place where Saul had set up camp and saw for himself where Saul and Abner, son of Ner, his general, were staying. Saul was safely inside the camp, encircled by the army.

6 Taking charge, David spoke to Ahimelech the Hittite and to Abishai son of Zeruiah, Joab's brother: "Who will go down with me and enter Saul's camp?"

Abishai whispered, "I'll go with you."

7 So David and Abishai entered the encampment by night, and there he was—Saul, stretched out asleep at the center of the camp, his spear stuck in the ground near his head, with Abner and the troops sound asleep on all sides.

8 Abishai said, "This is the moment! God has put your enemy in your grasp. Let me nail him to the ground with his spear. One hit will do it, believe me; I won't need a second!"

9 But David said to Abishai, "Don't you dare hurt him! Who could lay a hand on GOD's anointed and even think of getting away with it?"

10-11 He went on, "As GOD lives, either GOD will strike him, or his time will come and he'll die in bed, or he'll fall in battle, but GOD forbid that I should lay a finger on GOD's anointed. Now, grab the spear at his head and the water jug and let's get out of here."

12 David took the spear and water jug that were right beside Saul's head, and they slipped away. Not a soul saw. Not a soul knew. No one woke up! They all slept through the whole thing. A blanket of deep sleep from GOD had fallen on them.

13-14 Then David went across to the opposite hill and stood far away on the top of the mountain. With this safe distance between them, he shouted across to the army and Abner son of Ner, "Hey, Abner! How long do I have to wait for you to wake up and answer me?"

Abner said, "Who's calling?"

15-16 "Aren't you in charge there?" said David. "Why aren't you minding the store? Why weren't you standing guard over your master the king, when a soldier came to kill the king your master? Bad form! As GOD lives, your life should be forfeit, you and the entire bodyguard. Look what I have—the king's spear and water jug that were right beside his head!"

17-20 By now, Saul had recognized David's voice and said, "Is that you, my son David?"

David said, "Yes, it's me, O King, my master. Why are you after me, hunting me down? What have I done? What crime have I committed? Oh, my master, my king, listen to this from your servant: If GOD has stirred you up against me, then I gladly offer my life as a sacrifice. But if it's men who have done it, let them be banished from GOD's presence! They've expelled me from my rightful place in GOD's heritage, sneering, 'Out of here! Go get a job with some other god!' But you're not getting rid of me that

NEW KING JAMES VERSION

the earth before the face of the LORD. For the king of Israel has come out to seek a flea, as when one hunts a partridge in the mountains."

21Then Saul said, "I have sinned. Return, my son David. For I will harm you no more, because my life was precious in your eyes this day. Indeed I have played the fool and erred exceedingly."

22And David answered and said, "Here is the king's spear. Let one of the young men come over and get it. 23May the LORD repay every man *for* his righteousness and his faithfulness; for the LORD delivered you into *my* hand today, but I would not stretch out my hand against the LORD's anointed. 24And indeed, as your life was valued much this day in my eyes, so let my life be valued much in the eyes of the LORD, and let Him deliver me out of all tribulation."

25Then Saul said to David, "*May* you *be* blessed, my son David! You shall both do great things and also still prevail."

So David went on his way, and Saul returned to his place.

DAVID ALLIED WITH THE PHILISTINES

27 And David said in his heart, "Now I shall perish someday by the hand of Saul. *There is* nothing better for me than that I should speedily escape to the land of the Philistines; and Saul will despair of me, to seek me anymore in any part of Israel. So I shall escape out of his hand." 2Then David arose and went over with the six hundred men who *were* with him to Achish the son of Maoch, king of Gath. 3So David dwelt with Achish at Gath, he and his men, each man with his household, *and* David with his two wives, Ahinoam the Jezreelitess, and Abigail the Carmelitess, Nabal's widow. 4And it was told Saul that David had fled to Gath; so he sought him no more.

5Then David said to Achish, "If I have now found favor in your eyes, let them give me a place in some town in the country, that I may dwell there. For why should your servant dwell in the royal city with you?" 6So Achish gave him Ziklag that day. Therefore Ziklag has belonged to the kings of Judah to this day. 7Now the time that David dwelt in the country of the Philistines was one full year and four months.

8And David and his men went up and raided the Geshurites, the Girzites,[a] and the Amalekites. For those *nations* were the inhabitants of the land from of old, as you go to Shur, even as far as the land of Egypt. 9Whenever David attacked the land, he left neither man nor woman alive, but took away the sheep, the oxen, the donkeys, the camels, and the apparel, and returned and came to Achish. 10Then Achish would say, "Where have you made a raid today?" And David would say, "Against the southern *area* of Judah, or against the southern *area* of the Jerahmeelites, or against the southern *area* of the Kenites." 11David would save neither man nor woman alive, to bring *news* to Gath, saying, "Lest they should inform on us, saying, 'Thus David did.' " And thus *was* his behavior all the time he dwelt in the country of the Philistines.

27:8 [a]Or *Gezrites*

THE MESSAGE

easily; you'll not separate me from GOD in
life or death. The absurdity! The king of Is-
rael obsessed with a single flea! Hunting me
down—a mere partridge—out in the hills!"
21 Saul confessed, "I've sinned! Oh, come
back, my dear son David! I won't hurt you
anymore. You've honored me this day, treat-
ing my life as most precious. And I've acted
the fool—a moral dunce, a real clown."
22-24 David answered, "See what I have here?
The king's spear. Let one of your servants
come and get it. It's GOD's business to de-
cide what to do with each of us in regard to
what's right and who's loyal. GOD put your
life in my hands today, but I wasn't willing
to lift a finger against GOD's anointed. Just
as I honored your life today, may GOD honor
my life and rescue me from all trouble."
25 Saul said to David, "Bless you, dear son
David! Yes, do what you have to do! And,
yes, succeed in all you attempt!"
Then David went on his way, and Saul
went home.

1 27 David thought to himself, "Sooner or
later, Saul's going to get me. The best
thing I can do is escape to Philistine coun-
try. Saul will count me a lost cause and quit
hunting me down in every nook and cranny
of Israel. I'll be out of his reach for good."
2-4 So David left; he and his six hundred men
went to Achish son of Maoch, king of Gath.
They moved in and settled down in Gath,
with Achish. Each man brought his house-
hold; David brought his two wives, Ahin-
oam of Jezreel and Abigail, widow of Nabal
of Carmel. When Saul was told that David
had escaped to Gath, he called off the hunt.
5 Then David said to Achish, "If it's agree-
able to you, assign me a place in one of the
rural villages. It doesn't seem right that I,
your mere servant, should be taking up
space in the royal city."
6-7 So Achish assigned him Ziklag. (This is
how Ziklag got to be what it is now, a city of
the kings of Judah.) David lived in Philistine
country a year and four months.
8-9 From time to time David and his men
raided the Geshurites, the Girzites, and the
Amalekites—these people were longtime in-
habitants of the land stretching toward Shur
and on to Egypt. When David raided an area
he left no one alive, neither man nor
woman, but took everything else: sheep, cat-
tle, donkeys, camels, clothing—the works.
Then he'd return to Achish.
10-11 Achish would ask, "And whom did you
raid today?"
David would tell him, "Oh, the Negev of
Judah," or "The Negev of Jerahmeel," or
"The Negev of the Kenites." He never left a
single person alive lest one show up in Gath
and report what David had really been do-
ing. This is the way David operated all the
time he lived in Philistine country.

New King James Version

12 So Achish believed David, saying, "He has
made his people Israel utterly abhor him; there-
fore he will be my servant forever."

28 Now it happened in those days that the
Philistines gathered their armies together
for war, to fight with Israel. And Achish said to
David, "You assuredly know that you will go out
with me to battle, you and your men."
2 So David said to Achish, "Surely you know
what your servant can do."
And Achish said to David, "Therefore I will
make you one of my chief guardians forever."

Saul Consults a Medium

3 Now Samuel had died, and all Israel had
lamented for him and buried him in Ramah, in
his own city. And Saul had put the mediums and
the spiritists out of the land.
4 Then the Philistines gathered together, and
came and encamped at Shunem. So Saul gath-
ered all Israel together, and they encamped at
Gilboa. 5 When Saul saw the army of the
Philistines, he was afraid, and his heart trem-
bled greatly. 6 And when Saul inquired of the
LORD, the LORD did not answer him, either by
dreams or by Urim or by the prophets.
7 Then Saul said to his servants, "Find me a
woman who is a medium, that I may go to her
and inquire of her."
And his servants said to him, "In fact, *there
is* a woman who is a medium at En Dor."
8 So Saul disguised himself and put on other
clothes, and he went, and two men with him;
and they came to the woman by night. And he
said, "Please conduct a séance for me, and bring
up for me the one I shall name to you."
9 Then the woman said to him, "Look, you
know what Saul has done, how he has cut off
the mediums and the spiritists from the land.
Why then do you lay a snare for my life, to cause
me to die?"
10 And Saul swore to her by the LORD, saying,
"*As* the LORD lives, no punishment shall come
upon you for this thing."
11 Then the woman said, "Whom shall I bring
up for you?"
And he said, "Bring up Samuel for me."
12 When the woman saw Samuel, she cried
out with a loud voice. And the woman spoke to
Saul, saying, "Why have you deceived me? For
you *are* Saul!"
13 And the king said to her, "Do not be afraid.
What did you see?"
And the woman said to Saul, "I saw a spirit[a]
ascending out of the earth."
14 So he said to her, "What *is* his form?"
And she said, "An old man is coming up, and
he *is* covered with a mantle." And Saul per-
ceived that it *was* Samuel, and he stooped with
his face to the ground and bowed down.
15 Now Samuel said to Saul, "Why have you
disturbed me by bringing me up?"
And Saul answered, "I am deeply distressed;
for the Philistines make war against me, and

28:13 [a]Hebrew *elohim*

The Message

12 Achish came to trust David completely.
He thought, "He's made himself so repug-
nant to his people that he'll be in my camp
forever."

1 28 During this time the Philistines mus-
tered their troops to make war on Is-
rael. Achish said to David, "You can count
on this: You're marching with my troops,
you and your men."

2 And David said, "Good! Now you'll see
for yourself what I can do!"
"Great!" said Achish. "I'm making you
my personal bodyguard—for life!"

Saul Prayed, but God Didn't Answer

3 Samuel was now dead. All Israel had
mourned his death and buried him in
Ramah, his hometown. Saul had long since
cleaned out all those who held séances with
the dead.
4-5 The Philistines had mustered their troops
and camped at Shunem. Saul had assem-
bled all Israel and camped at Gilboa. But
when Saul saw the Philistine troops, he
shook in his boots, scared to death.
6 Saul prayed to GOD, but GOD didn't an-
swer—neither by dream nor by sign nor by
prophet.
7 So Saul ordered his officials, "Find me
someone who can call up spirits so I may go
and seek counsel from those spirits."
His servants said, "There's a witch at En-
dor."
8 Saul disguised himself by putting on dif-
ferent clothes. Then, taking two men with
him, he went under the cover of night to the
woman and said, "I want you to consult a
ghost for me. Call up the person I name."
9 The woman said, "Just hold on now! You
know what Saul did, how he swept the coun-
try clean of mediums. Why are you trying to
trap me and get me killed?"
10 Saul swore solemnly, "As GOD lives, you
won't get in any trouble for this."
11 The woman said, "So whom do you want
me to bring up?"
"Samuel. Bring me Samuel."
12 When the woman saw Samuel, she cried
out loudly to Saul, "Why did you lie to me?
You're Saul!"
13 The king told her, "You have nothing to
fear . . . but what do you see?"
"I see a spirit ascending from the under-
ground."
14 "And what does he look like?" Saul
asked.
"An old man ascending, robed like a
priest."
Saul knew it was Samuel. He fell down,
face to the ground, and worshiped.
15 Samuel said to Saul, "Why have you dis-
turbed me by calling me up?"
"Because I'm in deep trouble," said Saul.
"The Philistines are making war against me

NEW KING JAMES VERSION

God has departed from me and does not answer me anymore, neither by prophets nor by dreams. Therefore I have called you, that you may reveal to me what I should do."

16Then Samuel said: "So why do you ask me, seeing the LORD has departed from you and has become your enemy? 17And the LORD has done for Himself[a] as He spoke by me. For the LORD has torn the kingdom out of your hand and given it to your neighbor, David. 18Because you did not obey the voice of the LORD nor execute His fierce wrath upon Amalek, therefore the LORD has done this thing to you this day. 19Moreover the LORD will also deliver Israel with you into the hand of the Philistines. And tomorrow you and your sons *will be* with me. The LORD will also deliver the army of Israel into the hand of the Philistines."

20Immediately Saul fell full length on the ground, and was dreadfully afraid because of the words of Samuel. And there was no strength in him, for he had eaten no food all day or all night.

21And the woman came to Saul and saw that he was severely troubled, and said to him, "Look, your maidservant has obeyed your voice, and I have put my life in my hands and heeded the words which you spoke to me. 22Now therefore, please, heed also the voice of your maidservant, and let me set a piece of bread before you; and eat, that you may have strength when you go on *your* way."

23But he refused and said, "I will not eat."

So his servants, together with the woman, urged him; and he heeded their voice. Then he arose from the ground and sat on the bed. 24Now the woman had a fatted calf in the house, and she hastened to kill it. And she took flour and kneaded *it,* and baked unleavened bread from it. 25So she brought *it* before Saul and his servants, and they ate. Then they rose and went away that night.

THE PHILISTINES REJECT DAVID

29 Then the Philistines gathered together all their armies at Aphek, and the Israelites encamped by a fountain which *is* in Jezreel. 2And the lords of the Philistines passed in review by hundreds and by thousands, but David and his men passed in review at the rear with Achish. 3Then the princes of the Philistines said, "What *are* these Hebrews *doing here?*"

And Achish said to the princes of the Philistines, "*Is* this not David, the servant of Saul king of Israel, who has been with me these days, or these years? And to this day I have found no fault in him since he defected *to me.*"

4But the princes of the Philistines were angry with him; so the princes of the Philistines said to him, "Make this fellow return, that he may go back to the place which you have appointed for him, and do not let him go down with us to battle, lest in the battle he become our adversary. For with what could he reconcile himself to his master, if not with the heads of these men? 5*Is*

28:17 [a]Or *him,* that is, David

THE MESSAGE

and God has deserted me—he doesn't answer me any more, either by prophet or by dream. And so I'm calling on you to tell me what to do."

16-19 "Why ask me?" said Samuel. "GOD has turned away from you and is now on the side of your neighbor. GOD has done exactly what he told you through me—ripped the kingdom right out of your hands and given it to your neighbor. It's because you did not obey GOD, refused to carry out his seething judgment on Amalek, that GOD does to you what he is doing today. Worse yet, GOD is turning Israel, along with you, over to the Philistines. Tomorrow you and your sons will be with me. And, yes, indeed, GOD is giving Israel's army up to the Philistines."

20-22 Saul dropped to the ground, felled like a tree, terrified by Samuel's words. There wasn't an ounce of strength left in him—he'd eaten nothing all day and all night. The woman, realizing that he was in deep shock, said to him, "Listen to me. I did what you asked me to do, put my life in your hands in doing it, carried out your instructions to the letter. It's your turn to do what I tell you: Let me give you some food. Eat it. It will give you strength so you can get on your way."

23-25 He refused. "I'm not eating anything."

But when his servants joined the woman in urging him, he gave in to their pleas, picked himself up off the ground, and sat on the bed. The woman moved swiftly. She butchered a grain-fed calf she had, and took some flour, kneaded it, and baked some flat bread. Then she served it all up for Saul and his servants. After dining handsomely, they got up from the table and were on their way that same night.

1-2 **29** The Philistines mustered all their troops at Aphek. Meanwhile Israel had made camp at the spring at Jezreel. As the Philistine warlords marched forward by regiments and divisions, David and his men were bringing up the rear with Achish.

3 The Philistine officers said, "What business do these Hebrews have being here?"

Achish answered the officers, "Don't you recognize David, ex-servant of King Saul of Israel? He's been with me a long time. I've found nothing to be suspicious of, nothing to complain about, from the day he defected from Saul until now."

4-5 Angry with Achish, the Philistine officers said, "Send this man back to where he came from. Let him stick to his normal duties. He's not going into battle with us. He'd switch sides in the middle of the fight! What better chance to get back in favor with his master than by stabbing us in the back! Isn't this the

NEW KING JAMES VERSION

this not David, of whom they sang to one another in dances, saying:

'Saul has slain his thousands,
And David his ten thousands'?"[a]

6Then Achish called David and said to him, "Surely, *as* the LORD lives, you have been upright, and your going out and your coming in with me in the army *is* good in my sight. For to this day I have not found evil in you since the day of your coming to me. Nevertheless the lords do not favor you. 7Therefore return now, and go in peace, that you may not displease the lords of the Philistines."

8So David said to Achish, "But what have I done? And to this day what have you found in your servant as long as I have been with you, that I may not go and fight against the enemies of my lord the king?"

9Then Achish answered and said to David, "I know that you *are* as good in my sight as an angel of God; nevertheless the princes of the Philistines have said, 'He shall not go up with us to the battle.' 10Now therefore, rise early in the morning with your master's servants who have come with you.[a] And as soon as you are up early in the morning and have light, depart."

11So David and his men rose early to depart in the morning, to return to the land of the Philistines. And the Philistines went up to Jezreel.

DAVID'S CONFLICT WITH THE AMALEKITES

30 Now it happened, when David and his men came to Ziklag, on the third day, that the Amalekites had invaded the South and Ziklag, attacked Ziklag and burned it with fire, 2and had taken captive the women and those who *were* there, from small to great; they did not kill anyone, but carried *them* away and went their way. 3So David and his men came to the city, and there it was, burned with fire; and their wives, their sons, and their daughters had been taken captive. 4Then David and the people who *were* with him lifted up their voices and wept, until they had no more power to weep. 5And David's two wives, Ahinoam the Jezreelitess, and Abigail the widow of Nabal the Carmelite, had been taken captive. 6Now David was greatly distressed, for the people spoke of stoning him, because the soul of all the people was grieved, every man for his sons and his daughters. But David strengthened himself in the LORD his God.

7Then David said to Abiathar the priest, Ahimelech's son, "Please bring the ephod here to me." And Abiathar brought the ephod to David. 8So David inquired of the LORD, saying, "Shall I pursue this troop? Shall I overtake them?"

And He answered him, "Pursue, for you shall surely overtake *them* and without fail recover *all*."

29:5 [a]Compare 1 Samuel 18:7 **29:10** [a]Following Masoretic Text, Targum, and Vulgate; Septuagint adds *and go to the place which I have selected for you there; and set no bothersome word in your heart, for you are good before me. And rise on your way.*

THE MESSAGE

same David they celebrate at their parties,
singing,

Saul kills by the thousand,
David by the ten thousand!"

6-7 So Achish had to send for David and tell
him, "As GOD lives, you've been a trusty
ally—excellent in all the ways you have
worked with me, beyond reproach in the
ways you have conducted yourself. But the
warlords don't see it that way. So it's best
that you leave peacefully, now. It's not worth
it, displeasing the Philistine warlords."
8 "But what have I done?" said David.
"Have you had a single cause for complaint
from the day I joined up with you until now?
Why can't I fight against the enemies of my
master the king?"
9-10 "I agree," said Achish. "You're a good
man—as far as I'm concerned, God's angel!
But the Philistine officers were emphatic:
'He's not to go with us into battle.' So get an
early start, you and the men who came with
you. As soon as you have light enough to
travel, go."
11 David rose early, he and his men, and by
daybreak they were on their way back to
Philistine country. The Philistines went on
to Jezreel.

DAVID'S STRENGTH WAS IN HIS GOD

1-3 30 Three days later, David and his men ar-
rived back in Ziklag. Amalekites had
raided the Negev and Ziklag. They tore Zik-
lag to pieces and then burned it down. They
captured all the women, young and old.
They didn't kill anyone, but drove them like
a herd of cattle. By the time David and his
men entered the village, it had been burned
to the ground, and their wives, sons, and
daughters all taken prisoner.
4-6 David and his men burst out in loud
wails—wept and wept until they were ex-
hausted with weeping. David's two wives,
Ahinoam of Jezreel and Abigail widow of
Nabal of Carmel, had been taken prisoner
along with the rest. And suddenly David
was in even worse trouble. There was talk
among the men, bitter over the loss of their
families, of stoning him.
6-7 David strengthened himself with trust in
his GOD. He ordered Abiathar the priest, son
of Ahimelech, "Bring me the Ephod so I can
consult God." Abiathar brought it to David.
8 Then David prayed to GOD, "Shall I go af-
ter these raiders? Can I catch them?"
The answer came, "Go after them! Yes,
you'll catch them! Yes, you'll make the res-
cue!"

New King James Version

9 So David went, he and the six hundred men who *were* with him, and came to the Brook Besor, where those stayed who were left behind. 10 But David pursued, he and four hundred men; for two hundred stayed *behind,* who were so weary that they could not cross the Brook Besor.

11 Then they found an Egyptian in the field, and brought him to David; and they gave him bread and he ate, and they let him drink water. 12 And they gave him a piece of a cake of figs and two clusters of raisins. So when he had eaten, his strength came back to him; for he had eaten no bread nor drunk water for three days and three nights. 13 Then David said to him, "To whom do you *belong,* and where *are* you from?"

And he said, "I *am* a young man from Egypt, servant of an Amalekite; and my master left me behind, because three days ago I fell sick. 14 We made an invasion of the southern *area* of the Cherethites, in the *territory* which *belongs* to Judah, and of the southern *area* of Caleb; and we burned Ziklag with fire."

15 And David said to him, "Can you take me down to this troop?"

So he said, "Swear to me by God that you will neither kill me nor deliver me into the hands of my master, and I will take you down to this troop."

16 And when he had brought him down, there they were, spread out over all the land, eating and drinking and dancing, because of all the great spoil which they had taken from the land of the Philistines and from the land of Judah. 17 Then David attacked them from twilight until the evening of the next day. Not a man of them escaped, except four hundred young men who rode on camels and fled. 18 So David recovered all that the Amalekites had carried away, and David rescued his two wives. 19 And nothing of theirs was lacking, either small or great, sons or daughters, spoil or anything which they had taken from them; David recovered all. 20 Then David took all the flocks and herds they had driven before those *other* livestock, and said, "This *is* David's spoil."

21 Now David came to the two hundred men who had been so weary that they could not follow David, whom they also had made to stay at the Brook Besor. So they went out to meet David and to meet the people who *were* with him. And when David came near the people, he greeted them. 22 Then all the wicked and worthless men[a] of those who went with David answered and said, "Because they did not go with us, we will not give them *any* of the spoil that we have recovered, except for every man's wife and children, that they may lead *them* away and depart."

23 But David said, "My brethren, you shall not do so with what the LORD has given us, who has preserved us and delivered into our hand the troop that came against us. 24 For who will heed you in this matter? But as his part *is* who goes down to the battle, so *shall* his part *be* who stays by the supplies; they shall share alike." 25 So it was, from that day forward; he made it a statute and an ordinance for Israel to this day.

30:22 [a]Literally *men of Belial*

The Message

9-10 David went, he and the six hundred men with him. They arrived at the Brook Besor, where some of them dropped out. David and four hundred men kept up the pursuit, but two hundred of them were too fatigued to cross the Brook Besor, and stayed there.

11-12 Some who went on came across an Egyptian in a field and took him to David. They gave him bread and he ate. And he drank some water. They gave him a piece of fig cake and a couple of raisin muffins. Life began to revive in him. He hadn't eaten or drunk a thing for three days and nights!

13-14 David said to him, "Who do you belong to? Where are you from?"

"I'm an Egyptian slave of an Amalekite," he said. "My master walked off and left me when I got sick—that was three days ago. We had raided the Negev of the Kerethites, of Judah, and of Caleb. Ziklag we burned."

15 David asked him, "Can you take us to the raiders?"

"Promise me by God," he said, "that you won't kill me or turn me over to my old master, and I'll take you straight to the raiders."

16 He led David to them. They were scattered all over the place, eating and drinking, gorging themselves on all the loot they had plundered from Philistia and Judah.

17-20 David pounced. He fought them from before sunrise until evening of the next day. None got away except for four hundred of the younger men who escaped by riding off on camels. David rescued everything the Amalekites had taken. And he rescued his two wives! Nothing and no one was missing—young or old, son or daughter, plunder or whatever. David recovered the whole lot. He herded the sheep and cattle before them, and they all shouted, "David's plunder!"

21 Then David came to the two hundred who had been too tired to continue with him and had dropped out at the Brook Besor. They came out to welcome David and his band. As he came near he called out, "Success!"

22 But all the mean-spirited men who had marched with David, the rabble element, objected: "They didn't help in the rescue, they don't get any of the plunder we recovered. Each man can have his wife and children, but that's it. Take them and go!"

23-25 "Families don't do this sort of thing! Oh no, my brothers!" said David as he broke up the argument. "You can't act this way with what GOD gave us! God kept us safe. He handed over the raiders who attacked us. Who would ever listen to this kind of talk? The share of the one who stays with the gear is the share of the one who fights—equal shares. Share and share alike!" From that day on, David made that the rule in Israel—and it still is.

NEW KING JAMES VERSION

26Now when David came to Ziklag, he sent
some of the spoil to the elders of Judah, to his
friends, saying, "Here is a present for you from
the spoil of the enemies of the LORD"— 27to
those who *were* in Bethel, *those* who *were* in
Ramoth of the South, *those* who *were* in Jattir,
28*those* who *were* in Aroer, *those* who *were* in
Siphmoth, *those* who *were* in Eshtemoa, 29*those*
who *were* in Rachal, *those* who *were* in the
cities of the Jerahmeelites, *those* who *were* in
the cities of the Kenites, 30*those* who *were* in
Hormah, *those* who *were* in Chorashan,[a] *those*
who *were* in Athach, 31*those* who *were* in He-
bron, and to all the places where David himself
and his men were accustomed to rove.

THE TRAGIC END OF SAUL AND HIS SONS

31 Now the Philistines fought against Israel;
and the men of Israel fled from before the
Philistines, and fell slain on Mount Gilboa.
2Then the Philistines followed hard after Saul
and his sons. And the Philistines killed Jona-
than, Abinadab, and Malchishua, Saul's sons.
3The battle became fierce against Saul. The
archers hit him, and he was severely wounded
by the archers.
4Then Saul said to his armorbearer, "Draw
your sword, and thrust me through with it, lest
these uncircumcised men come and thrust me
through and abuse me."
But his armorbearer would not, for he was
greatly afraid. Therefore Saul took a sword and
fell on it. 5And when his armorbearer saw that
Saul was dead, he also fell on his sword, and
died with him. 6So Saul, his three sons, his ar-
morbearer, and all his men died together that
same day.
7And when the men of Israel who *were* on
the other side of the valley, and *those* who *were*
on the other side of the Jordan, saw that the men
of Israel had fled and that Saul and his sons
were dead, they forsook the cities and fled; and
the Philistines came and dwelt in them. 8So it
happened the next day, when the Philistines
came to strip the slain, that they found Saul and
his three sons fallen on Mount Gilboa. 9And
they cut off his head and stripped off his armor,
and sent *word* throughout the land of the
Philistines, to proclaim *it in* the temple of their
idols and among the people. 10Then they put his
armor in the temple of the Ashtoreths, and they
fastened his body to the wall of Beth Shan.[a]
11Now when the inhabitants of Jabesh
Gilead heard what the Philistines had done to
Saul, 12all the valiant men arose and traveled all
night, and took the body of Saul and the bodies
of his sons from the wall of Beth Shan; and they
came to Jabesh and burned them there. 13Then
they took their bones and buried *them* under
the tamarisk tree at Jabesh, and fasted seven
days.

30:30 [a]Or *Borashan* **31:10** [a]Spelled *Beth Shean* in Joshua 17:11 and elsewhere

THE MESSAGE

26-31 On returning to Ziklag, David sent portions of the plunder to the elders of Judah, his neighbors, with a note saying, "A gift from the plunder of GOD's enemies!" He sent them to the elders in Bethel, Ramoth Negev, Jattir, Aroer, Siphmoth, Eshtemoa, Racal, Jerahmeelite cities, Kenite cities, Hormah, Bor Ashan, Athach, and Hebron, along with a number of other places David and his men went to from time to time.

SAUL AND JONATHAN, DEAD ON THE MOUNTAIN

1-2 31 The Philistines made war on Israel. The men of Israel were in full retreat from the Philistines, falling left and right, wounded on Mount Gilboa. The Philistines caught up with Saul and his sons. They killed Jonathan, Abinadab, and Malki-Shua, Saul's sons.

3-4 The battle was hot and heavy around Saul. The archers got his range and wounded him badly. Saul said to his weapon bearer, "Draw your sword and put me out of my misery, lest these pagan pigs come and make a game out of killing me."

4-6 But his weapon bearer wouldn't do it. He was terrified. So Saul took the sword himself and fell on it. When the weapon bearer saw that Saul was dead, he too fell on his sword and died with him. So Saul, his three sons, and his weapon bearer—the men closest to him—died together that day.

7 When the Israelites in the valley opposite and those on the other side of the Jordan saw that their army was in full retreat and that Saul and his sons were dead, they left their cities and ran for their lives. The Philistines moved in and occupied the sites.

8-10 The next day, when the Philistines came to rob the dead, they found Saul and his three sons dead on Mount Gilboa. They cut off Saul's head and stripped off his armor. Then they spread the good news all through Philistine country in the shrines of their idols and among the people. They displayed his armor in the shrine of the Ashtoreth. They nailed his corpse to the wall at Beth Shan.

11-13 The people of Jabesh Gilead heard what the Philistines had done to Saul. Their valiant men sprang into action. They traveled all night, took the corpses of Saul and his three sons from the wall at Beth Shan, and carried them back to Jabesh and burned off the flesh. They then buried the bones under the tamarisk tree in Jabesh and fasted in mourning for seven days.

2 SAMUEL

New King James Version

The Report of Saul's Death

1 Now it came to pass after the death of Saul, when David had returned from the slaughter of the Amalekites, and David had stayed two days in Ziklag, [2]on the third day, behold, it happened that a man came from Saul's camp with his clothes torn and dust on his head. So it was, when he came to David, that he fell to the ground and prostrated himself.

[3]And David said to him, "Where have you come from?"

So he said to him, "I have escaped from the camp of Israel."

[4]Then David said to him, "How did the matter go? Please tell me."

And he answered, "The people have fled from the battle, many of the people are fallen and dead, and Saul and Jonathan his son are dead also."

[5]So David said to the young man who told him, "How do you know that Saul and Jonathan his son are dead?"

[6]Then the young man who told him said, "As I happened by chance *to be* on Mount Gilboa, there was Saul, leaning on his spear; and indeed the chariots and horsemen followed hard after him. [7]Now when he looked behind him, he saw me and called to me. And I answered, 'Here I am.' [8]And he said to me, 'Who *are* you?' So I answered him, 'I *am* an Amalekite.' [9]He said to me again, 'Please stand over me and kill me, for anguish has come upon me, but my life still *remains* in me.' [10]So I stood over him and killed him, because I was sure that he could not live after he had fallen. And I took the crown that *was* on his head and the bracelet that *was* on his arm, and have brought them here to my lord."

[11]Therefore David took hold of his own clothes and tore them, and *so did* all the men who *were* with him. [12]And they mourned and wept and fasted until evening for Saul and for Jonathan his son, for the people of the LORD and for the house of Israel, because they had fallen by the sword.

[13]Then David said to the young man who told him, "Where *are* you from?"

And he answered, "I *am* the son of an alien, an Amalekite."

[14]So David said to him, "How was it you were not afraid to put forth your hand to destroy the LORD's anointed?" [15]Then David called one of the young men and said, "Go near, *and* execute him!" And he struck him so that he died. [16]So David said to him, "Your blood *is* on your own head, for your own mouth has testified against you, saying, 'I have killed the LORD's anointed.' "

The Song of the Bow

[17]Then David lamented with this lamentation over Saul and over Jonathan his son, [18]and he told *them* to teach the children of Judah *the Song of* the Bow; indeed *it is* written in the Book of Jasher:

The Message

1-2 **1** Shortly after Saul died, David returned to Ziklag from his rout of the Amalekites. Three days later a man showed up unannounced from Saul's army camp.

2-3 Disheveled and obviously in mourning, he fell to his knees in respect before David. David asked, "What brings you here?"

He answered, "I've just escaped from the camp of Israel."

4 "So what happened?" said David. "What's the news?"

He said, "The Israelites have fled the battlefield, leaving a lot of their dead comrades behind. And Saul and his son Jonathan are dead."

5 David pressed the young soldier for details: "How do you know for sure that Saul and Jonathan are dead?"

6-8 "I just happened by Mount Gilboa and came on Saul, badly wounded and leaning on his spear, with enemy chariots and horsemen bearing down hard on him. He looked behind him, saw me, and called me to him. 'Yes sir,' I said, 'at your service.' He asked me who I was, and I told him, 'I'm an Amalekite.' "

9 "Come here," he said, "and put me out of my misery. I'm nearly dead already, but my life hangs on."

10 "So I did what he asked—I killed him. I knew he wouldn't last much longer anyway. I removed his royal headband and bracelet, and have brought them to my master. Here they are."

11-12 In lament, David ripped his clothes to ribbons. All the men with him did the same. They wept and fasted the rest of the day, grieving the death of Saul and his son Jonathan, and also the army of GOD and the nation Israel, victims in a failed battle.

13 Then David spoke to the young soldier who had brought the report: "Who are you, anyway?"

"I'm from an immigrant family—an Amalekite."

14-15 "Do you mean to say," said David, "that you weren't afraid to up and kill GOD's anointed king?" Right then he ordered one of his soldiers, "Strike him dead!" The soldier struck him, and he died.

16 "You asked for it," David told him. "You sealed your death sentence when you said you killed GOD's anointed king."

17-18 Then David sang this lament over Saul and his son Jonathan, and gave orders that everyone in Judah learn it by heart. Yes, it's even inscribed in The Book of Jashar.

NEW KING JAMES VERSION

[19]"The beauty of Israel is slain on your high places!
How the mighty have fallen!
[20]Tell *it* not in Gath,
Proclaim *it* not in the streets of Ashkelon—
Lest the daughters of the Philistines rejoice,
Lest the daughters of the uncircumcised triumph.

[21]"O mountains of Gilboa,
Let there be no dew nor rain upon you,
Nor fields of offerings.
For the shield of the mighty is cast away there!
The shield of Saul, not anointed with oil.
[22]From the blood of the slain,
From the fat of the mighty,
The bow of Jonathan did not turn back,
And the sword of Saul did not return empty.

[23]"Saul and Jonathan *were* beloved and pleasant in their lives,
And in their death they were not divided;
They were swifter than eagles,
They were stronger than lions.

[24]"O daughters of Israel, weep over Saul,
Who clothed you in scarlet, with luxury;
Who put ornaments of gold on your apparel.

[25]"How the mighty have fallen in the midst of the battle!
Jonathan *was* slain in your high places.
[26]I am distressed for you, my brother Jonathan;
You have been very pleasant to me;
Your love to me was wonderful,
Surpassing the love of women.

[27]"How the mighty have fallen,
And the weapons of war perished!"

DAVID ANOINTED KING OF JUDAH

2 It happened after this that David inquired of
the LORD, saying, "Shall I go up to any of the
cities of Judah?"
And the LORD said to him, "Go up."
David said, "Where shall I go up?"
And He said, "To Hebron."
[2]So David went up there, and his two wives
also, Ahinoam the Jezreelitess, and Abigail the
widow of Nabal the Carmelite. [3]And David
brought up the men who *were* with him, every
man with his household. So they dwelt in the
cities of Hebron.
[4]Then the men of Judah came, and there they
anointed David king over the house of Judah.
And they told David, saying, "The men of
Jabesh Gilead *were the ones* who buried Saul."
[5]So David sent messengers to the men of Jabesh
Gilead, and said to them, "You *are* blessed of the
LORD, for you have shown this kindness to your
lord, to Saul, and have buried him. [6]And now

THE MESSAGE

19-21 Oh, oh, Gazelles of Israel, struck down on your hills,
the mighty warriors—fallen, fallen!
Don't announce it in the city of Gath,
don't post the news in the streets of Ashkelon.
Don't give those coarse Philistine girls
one more excuse for a drunken party!
No more dew or rain for you, hills of Gilboa,
and not a drop from springs and wells,
For there the warriors' shields were dragged through the mud,
Saul's shield left there to rot.

22 Jonathan's bow was bold—
the bigger they were the harder they fell.
Saul's sword was fearless—
once out of the scabbard, nothing could stop it.

23 Saul and Jonathan—beloved, beautiful!
Together in life, together in death.
Swifter than plummeting eagles,
stronger than proud lions.

24-25 Women of Israel, weep for Saul.
He dressed you in finest cottons and silks,
spared no expense in making you elegant.
The mighty warriors—fallen, fallen
in the middle of the fight!
Jonathan—struck down on your hills!

26 O my dear brother Jonathan,
I'm crushed by your death.
Your friendship was a miracle-wonder,
love far exceeding anything I've known—
or ever hope to know.

27 The mighty warriors—fallen, fallen.
And the arms of war broken to bits.

1 2 After all this, David prayed. He asked
GOD, "Shall I move to one of the cities of
Judah?"
GOD said, "Yes, move."
"And to which city?"
"To Hebron."
2-3 So David moved to Hebron, along with
his two wives, Ahinoam of Jezreel and Abi-
gail the widow of Nabal of Carmel. David's
men, along with their families, also went
with him and made their home in and
around Hebron.
4-7 The citizens of Judah came to Hebron,
and then and there made David king over
the clans of Judah.

A report was brought to David that the
men of Jabesh Gilead had given Saul a de-
cent burial. David sent messengers to the
men of Jabesh Gilead: "GOD bless you for
this—for honoring your master, Saul, with a

NEW KING JAMES VERSION

may the LORD show kindness and truth to you. I
also will repay you this kindness, because you
have done this thing. 7Now therefore, let your
hands be strengthened, and be valiant; for your
master Saul is dead, and also the house of Judah
has anointed me king over them."

ISHBOSHETH MADE KING OF ISRAEL

8But Abner the son of Ner, commander of
Saul's army, took Ishbosheth[a] the son of Saul
and brought him over to Mahanaim; 9and he
made him king over Gilead, over the Ashurites,
over Jezreel, over Ephraim, over Benjamin, and
over all Israel. 10Ishbosheth, Saul's son, *was*
forty years old when he began to reign over Is-
rael, and he reigned two years. Only the house
of Judah followed David. 11And the time that
David was king in Hebron over the house of Ju-
dah was seven years and six months.

ISRAEL AND JUDAH AT WAR

12Now Abner the son of Ner, and the servants
of Ishbosheth the son of Saul, went out from
Mahanaim to Gibeon. 13And Joab the son of
Zeruiah, and the servants of David, went out
and met them by the pool of Gibeon. So they sat
down, one on one side of the pool and the other
on the other side of the pool. 14Then Abner said
to Joab, "Let the young men now arise and com-
pete before us."

And Joab said, "Let them arise."

15So they arose and went over by number,
twelve from Benjamin, *followers* of Ishbosheth
the son of Saul, and twelve from the servants of
David. 16And each one grasped his opponent by
the head and *thrust* his sword in his opponent's
side; so they fell down together. Therefore that
place was called the Field of Sharp Swords,[a]
which *is* in Gibeon. 17So there was a very fierce
battle that day, and Abner and the men of Israel
were beaten before the servants of David.

18Now the three sons of Zeruiah were there:
Joab and Abishai and Asahel. And Asahel *was*
as fleet of foot as a wild gazelle. 19So Asahel
pursued Abner, and in going he did not turn to
the right hand or to the left from following Ab-
ner.

20Then Abner looked behind him and said,
"*Are* you Asahel?"

He answered, "I *am*."

21And Abner said to him, "Turn aside to your
right hand or to your left, and lay hold on one of
the young men and take his armor for yourself."
But Asahel would not turn aside from following
him. 22So Abner said again to Asahel, "Turn
aside from following me. Why should I strike
you to the ground? How then could I face your
brother Joab?" 23However, he refused to turn
aside. Therefore Abner struck him in the stom-
ach with the blunt end of the spear, so that the
spear came out of his back; and he fell down
there and died on the spot. So it was *that* as
many as came to the place where Asahel fell
down and died, stood still.

24Joab and Abishai also pursued Abner. And
the sun was going down when they came to the

2:8 [a]Called *Esh-Baal* in 1 Chronicles 8:33 and 9:39 **2:16** [a]Hebrew *Helkath Hazzurim*

THE MESSAGE

funeral. GOD honor you and be true to you—
and I'll do the same, matching your gener-
ous act of goodness. Strengthen your re-
solve and do what must be done. Your
master, Saul, is dead. The citizens of Judah
have made me their king."

8-11 In the meantime, Abner son of Ner, com-
mander of Saul's army, had taken Saul's son
Ish-Bosheth to Mahanaim and made him
king over Gilead, over Asher, over Jezreel,
over Ephraim, over Benjamin—king, as it
turns out, over all Israel. Ish-Bosheth Saul's
son, was forty years old when he was made
king over Israel. He lasted only two years.
But the people of Judah stuck with David.
David ruled the people of Judah from He-
bron for seven and a half years.

12-13 One day Abner son of Ner set out from
Mahanaim with the soldiers of Ish-Bosheth
son of Saul, headed for Gibeon. Joab son of
Zeruiah, with David's soldiers, also set out.
They met at the Pool of Gibeon, Abner's
group on one side, Joab's on the other.

14 Abner challenged Joab, "Put up your best
fighters. Let's see them do their stuff."

Joab said, "Good! Let them go at it!"

15-16 So they lined up for the fight, twelve Ben-
jaminites from the side of Ish-Bosheth son
of Saul, and twelve soldiers from David's
side. The men from each side grabbed their
opponents' heads and stabbed them with
their daggers. They all fell dead—the whole
bunch together. So, they called the place
Slaughter Park. It's right there at Gibeon.

17-19 The fighting went from bad to worse
throughout the day. Abner and the men of
Israel were beaten to a pulp by David's men.
The three sons of Zeruiah were present:
Joab, Abishai, and Asahel. Asahel, as fast as
a wild antelope on the open plain, chased
Abner, staying hard on his heels.

20 Abner turned and said, "Is that you, Asa-
hel?"

"It surely is," he said.

21 Abner said, "Let up on me. Pick on some-
one you have a chance of beating and be
content with those spoils!" But Asahel
wouldn't let up.

22 Abner tried again, "Turn back. Don't
force me to kill you. How would I face your
brother Joab?"

23-25 When he refused to quit, Abner struck
him in the belly with the blunt end of his
spear so hard that it came out his back. Asa-
hel fell to the ground and died at once.
Everyone who arrived at the spot where
Asahel fell and died stood and gaped—Asa-
hel dead! But Joab and Abishai kept up the
chase after Abner. As the sun began to set,
they came to the hill of Ammah that faced

NEW KING JAMES VERSION

hill of Ammah, which *is* before Giah by the road
to the Wilderness of Gibeon. [25]Now the children
of Benjamin gathered together behind Abner
and became a unit, and took their stand on top
of a hill. [26]Then Abner called to Joab and said,
"Shall the sword devour forever? Do you not
know that it will be bitter in the latter end? How
long will it be then until you tell the people to re-
turn from pursuing their brethren?"
[27]And Joab said, "*As* God lives, unless you
had spoken, surely then by morning all the peo-
ple would have given up pursuing their
brethren." [28]So Joab blew a trumpet; and all the
people stood still and did not pursue Israel any-
more, nor did they fight anymore. [29]Then Abner
and his men went on all that night through the
plain, crossed over the Jordan, and went through
all Bithron; and they came to Mahanaim.
[30]So Joab returned from pursuing Abner.
And when he had gathered all the people to-
gether, there were missing of David's servants
nineteen men and Asahel. [31]But the servants of
David had struck down, of Benjamin and Ab-
ner's men, three hundred and sixty men who
died. [32]Then they took up Asahel and buried him
in his father's tomb, which *was in* Bethlehem.
And Joab and his men went all night, and they
came to Hebron at daybreak.

3 Now there was a long war between the house
of Saul and the house of David. But David
grew stronger and stronger, and the house of
Saul grew weaker and weaker.

SONS OF DAVID

[2]Sons were born to David in Hebron: His
firstborn was Amnon by Ahinoam the Jezreel-
itess; [3]his second, Chileab, by Abigail the widow
of Nabal the Carmelite; the third, Absalom the
son of Maacah, the daughter of Talmai, king of
Geshur; [4]the fourth, Adonijah the son of Hag-
gith; the fifth, Shephatiah the son of Abital; [5]and
the sixth, Ithream, by David's wife Eglah. These
were born to David in Hebron.

ABNER JOINS FORCES WITH DAVID

[6]Now it was so, while there was war between
the house of Saul and the house of David, that
Abner was strengthening *his hold* on the house
of Saul.
[7]And Saul had a concubine, whose name
was Rizpah, the daughter of Aiah. So *Ish-
bosheth* said to Abner, "Why have you gone in
to my father's concubine?"
[8]Then Abner became very angry at the
words of Ishbosheth, and said, "*Am* I a dog's
head that belongs to Judah? Today I show loy-
alty to the house of Saul your father, to his
brothers, and to his friends, and have not deliv-
ered you into the hand of David; and you charge
me today with a fault concerning this woman?
[9]May God do so to Abner, and more also, if I do
not do for David as the LORD has sworn to him—
[10]to transfer the kingdom from the house of
Saul, and set up the throne of David over Israel
and over Judah, from Dan to Beersheba." [11]And
he could not answer Abner another word, be-
cause he feared him.

THE MESSAGE

Giah on the road to the backcountry of Gibeon. The Benjaminites had taken their stand with Abner there, deployed strategically on a hill.

26 Abner called out to Joab, "Are we going to keep killing each other till doomsday? Don't you know that nothing but bitterness will come from this? How long before you call off your men from chasing their brothers?"

27-28 "As God lives," said Joab, "if you hadn't spoken up, we'd have kept up the chase until morning!" Then he blew the ram's horn trumpet and the whole army of Judah stopped in its tracks. They quit chasing Israel and called off the fighting.

29 Abner and his soldiers marched all that night up the Arabah Valley. They crossed the Jordan and, after a long morning's march, arrived at Mahanaim.

30-32 After Joab returned from chasing Abner, he took a head count of the army. Nineteen of David's men (besides Asahel) were missing. David's men had cut down 360 of Abner's men, all Benjaminites—all dead. They brought Asahel and buried him in the family tomb in Bethlehem. Joab and his men then marched all night, arriving in Hebron as the dawn broke.

1 3 The war between the house of Saul and the house of David dragged on and on. The longer it went on the stronger David became, with the house of Saul getting weaker.

2-5 During the Hebron years, sons were born to David:

Amnon, born of Ahinoam of Jezreel—the firstborn;
Kileab, born of Abigail of Carmel, Nabal's widow—his second;
Absalom, born of Maacah, daughter of Talmai, king of Geshur—the third;
Adonijah, born of Haggith—the fourth;
Shephatiah, born of Abital—the fifth;
Ithream, born of Eglah—the sixth.

These six sons of David were born in Hebron.

6-7 Abner took advantage of the continuing war between the house of Saul and the house of David to gain power for himself. Saul had had a concubine, Rizpah, the daughter of Aiah. One day Ish-Bosheth confronted Abner: "What business do you have sleeping with my father's concubine?"

8-10 Abner lost his temper with Ish-Bosheth, "Treat me like a dog, will you! Is this the thanks I get for sticking by the house of your father, Saul, and all his family and friends? I personally saved you from certain capture by David, and you make an issue out of my going to bed with a woman! What GOD promised David, I'll help accomplish—transfer the kingdom from the house of Saul and make David ruler over the whole country, both Israel and Judah, from Dan to Beersheba. If not, may God do his worst to me."

11 Ish-Bosheth, cowed by Abner's outburst, couldn't say another word.

NEW KING JAMES VERSION

12Then Abner sent messengers on his behalf
to David, saying, "Whose *is* the land?" saying
also, "Make your covenant with me, and indeed
my hand *shall be* with you to bring all Israel to
you."
13And *David* said, "Good, I will make a
covenant with you. But one thing I require of
you: you shall not see my face unless you first
bring Michal, Saul's daughter, when you come
to see my face." 14So David sent messengers to
Ishbosheth, Saul's son, saying, "Give *me* my
wife Michal, whom I betrothed to myself for a
hundred foreskins of the Philistines." 15And Ish-
bosheth sent and took her from *her* husband,
from Paltiel[a] the son of Laish. 16Then her hus-
band went along with her to Bahurim, weeping
behind her. So Abner said to him, "Go, return!"
And he returned.
17Now Abner had communicated with the
elders of Israel, saying, "In time past you were
seeking for David *to be* king over you. 18Now
then, do *it!* For the LORD has spoken of David,
saying, 'By the hand of My servant David, I[a] will
save My people Israel from the hand of the
Philistines and the hand of all their enemies.' "
19And Abner also spoke in the hearing of Ben-
jamin. Then Abner also went to speak in the
hearing of David in Hebron all that seemed
good to Israel and the whole house of Benjamin.
20So Abner and twenty men with him came
to David at Hebron. And David made a feast for
Abner and the men who *were* with him. 21Then
Abner said to David, "I will arise and go, and
gather all Israel to my lord the king, that they
may make a covenant with you, and that you
may reign over all that your heart desires." So
David sent Abner away, and he went in peace.

JOAB MURDERS ABNER

22At that moment the servants of David and
Joab came from a raid and brought much spoil
with them. But Abner *was* not with David in He-
bron, for he had sent him away, and he had gone
in peace. 23When Joab and all the troops that
were with him had come, they told Joab, saying,
"Abner the son of Ner came to the king, and he
sent him away, and he has gone in peace."
24Then Joab came to the king and said, "What
have you done? Look, Abner came to you; why
is it *that* you sent him away, and he has already
gone? 25Surely you realize that Abner the son of
Ner came to deceive you, to know your going
out and your coming in, and to know all that you
are doing."
26And when Joab had gone from David's
presence, he sent messengers after Abner, who
brought him back from the well of Sirah. But
David did not know *it*. 27Now when Abner had
returned to Hebron, Joab took him aside in the
gate to speak with him privately, and there
stabbed him in the stomach, so that he died for
the blood of Asahel his brother.
28Afterward, when David heard *it*, he said,
"My kingdom and I *are* guiltless before the
LORD forever of the blood of Abner the son of

3:15 [a]Spelled *Palti* in 1 Samuel 25:44 **3:18** [a]Following many Hebrew manuscripts, Septuagint, Syriac, and Targum; Masoretic Text reads *he*.

THE MESSAGE

12 Abner went ahead and sent personal
messengers to David: "Make a deal with me
and I'll help bring the whole country of Is-
rael over to you."
13 "Great," said David. "It's a deal. But only
on one condition: You're not welcome here
unless you bring Michal, Saul's daughter,
with you when you come to meet me."
14 David then sent messengers to Ish-
Bosheth son of Saul: "Give me back Michal,
whom I won as my wife at the cost of a hun-
dred Philistine foreskins."
15-16 Ish-Bosheth ordered that she be taken
from her husband Paltiel son of Laish. But
Paltiel followed her, weeping all the way, to
Bahurim. There Abner told him, "Go home."
And he went home.
17-18 Abner got the elders of Israel together
and said, "Only yesterday, it seems, you
were looking for a way to make David your
king. So do it—now! For GOD has given the
go-ahead on David: 'By my servant David's
hand, I'll save my people Israel from the op-
pression of the Philistines and all their other
enemies.' "
19 Abner took the Benjaminites aside and
spoke to them. Then he went to Hebron for
a private talk with David, telling him every-
thing that Israel in general and Benjamin in
particular were planning to do.
20 When Abner and the twenty men who
were with him met with David in Hebron,
David laid out a feast for them.
21 Abner then said, "I'm ready. Let me go
now to rally everyone in Israel for my mas-
ter, the king. They'll make a treaty with you,
authorizing you to rule them however you
see fit." Abner was sent off with David's
blessing.
22-23 Soon after that, David's men, led by Joab,
came back from a field assignment. Abner
was no longer in Hebron with David, having
just been dismissed with David's blessing.
As Joab and his raiding party arrived, they
were told that Abner the son of Ner had
been there with David and had been sent off
with David's blessing.
24-25 Joab went straight to the king: "What's
this you've done? Abner shows up, and you
let him walk away scot-free? You know Ab-
ner son of Ner better than that. This was no
friendly visit. He was here to spy on you, fig-
ure out your comings and goings, find out
what you're up to."
26-27 Joab left David and went into action. He
sent messengers after Abner; they caught
up with him at the well at Sirah and brought
him back. David knew nothing of all this.
When Abner got back to Hebron, Joab
steered him aside at the gate for a personal
word with him. There he stabbed him in the
belly, killed him in cold blood for the mur-
der of his brother Asahel.
28-30 Later on, when David heard what hap-
pened, he said, "Before GOD I and my king-
dom are totally innocent of this murder of
Abner son of Ner. Joab and his entire family

NEW KING JAMES VERSION

Ner. 29Let it rest on the head of Joab and on all his father's house; and let there never fail to be in the house of Joab one who has a discharge or is a leper, who leans on a staff or falls by the sword, or who lacks bread." 30So Joab and Abishai his brother killed Abner, because he had killed their brother Asahel at Gibeon in the battle.

DAVID'S MOURNING FOR ABNER

31Then David said to Joab and to all the people who were with him, "Tear your clothes, gird yourselves with sackcloth, and mourn for Abner." And King David followed the coffin. 32So they buried Abner in Hebron; and the king lifted up his voice and wept at the grave of Abner, and all the people wept. 33And the king sang *a lament* over Abner and said:

"Should Abner die as a fool dies?
34Your hands were not bound
Nor your feet put into fetters;
As a man falls before wicked men, *so* you fell."

Then all the people wept over him again.

35And when all the people came to persuade David to eat food while it was still day, David took an oath, saying, "God do so to me, and more also, if I taste bread or anything else till the sun goes down!" 36Now all the people took note *of it*, and it pleased them, since whatever the king did pleased all the people. 37For all the people and all Israel understood that day that it had not been the king's *intent* to kill Abner the son of Ner. 38Then the king said to his servants, "Do you not know that a prince and a great man has fallen this day in Israel? 39And I *am* weak today, though anointed king; and these men, the sons of Zeruiah, *are* too harsh for me. The LORD shall repay the evildoer according to his wickedness."

ISHBOSHETH IS MURDERED

4 When Saul's son[a] heard that Abner had died in Hebron, he lost heart, and all Israel was troubled. 2Now Saul's son *had* two men *who were* captains of troops. The name of one *was* Baanah and the name of the other Rechab, the sons of Rimmon the Beerothite, of the children of Benjamin. (For Beeroth also was *part* of Benjamin, 3because the Beerothites fled to Gittaim and have been sojourners there until this day.)

4Jonathan, Saul's son, had a son *who was* lame in *his* feet. He was five years old when the news about Saul and Jonathan came from Jezreel; and his nurse took him up and fled. And it happened, as she made haste to flee, that he fell and became lame. His name *was* Mephibosheth.[a]

5Then the sons of Rimmon the Beerothite, Rechab and Baanah, set out and came at about the heat of the day to the house of Ishbosheth, who was lying on his bed at noon. 6And they came there, all the way into the house, *as though* to get wheat, and they stabbed him in

4:1 [a]That is, Ishbosheth **4:4** [a]Called *Merib-Baal* in 1 Chronicles 8:34 and 9:40

THE MESSAGE

will always be under the curse of this blood-guilt. May they forever be victims of crippling diseases, violence, and famine." (Joab and his brother, Abishai, murdered Abner because he had killed their brother Asahel at the battle of Gibeon.)

31-32 David ordered Joab and all the men un-
der him, "Rip your cloaks into rags! Wear
mourning clothes! Lead Abner's funeral
procession with loud lament!" King David
followed the coffin. They buried Abner in
Hebron. The king's voice was loud in lament
as he wept at the side of Abner's grave. All
the people wept, too.
33-34 Then the king sang this tribute to Abner:

Can this be? Abner dead like a nameless bum?
You were a free man, free to go and do as you wished—
Yet you fell as a victim in a street brawl.

And all the people wept—a crescendo of crying!
35-37 They all came then to David, trying to get
him to eat something before dark. But David
solemnly swore, "I'll not so much as taste a
piece of bread, or anything else for that mat-
ter, before sunset, so help me God!" Every-
one at the funeral took notice—and liked
what they saw. In fact everything the king
did was applauded by the people. It was
clear to everyone that day, including all Is-
rael, that the king had nothing to do with
the death of Abner son of Ner.
38-39 The king spoke to his servants: "You real-
ize, don't you, that today a prince and hero
fell victim of foul play in Israel? And I,
though anointed king, was helpless to do
anything about it. These sons of Zeruiah are
too much for me. GOD, requite the criminal
for his crime!"

THE MURDER OF ISH-BOSHETH

1 4 Saul's son, Ish-Bosheth, heard that Abner
had died in Hebron. His heart sank. The
whole country was shaken.
2 Ish-Bosheth had two men who were cap-
tains of raiding bands—one was named
Baanah, the other Recab. They were sons of
Rimmon the Beerothite, a Benjaminite. (The
people of Beeroth had been assigned to Ben-
jamin ever since they escaped to Gittaim.
They still live there as resident aliens.)
4 It so happened that Saul's son, Jonathan,
had a son who was maimed in both feet.
When he was five years old, the report on
Saul and Jonathan came from Jezreel. His
nurse picked him up and ran, but in her
hurry to get away she fell, and the boy was
maimed. His name was Mephibosheth.
5-7 One day Baanah and Recab, the two sons
of Rimmon, headed out for the house of Ish-
Bosheth. They arrived at the hottest time of
the day, just as he was taking his afternoon
nap. They entered the house on a ruse, pre-
tending official business. The maid guard-
ing the bedroom had fallen asleep, so Recab

NEW KING JAMES VERSION

the stomach. Then Rechab and Baanah his brother escaped. 7For when they came into the house, he was lying on his bed in his bedroom; then they struck him and killed him, beheaded him and took his head, and were all night escaping through the plain. 8And they brought the head of Ishbosheth to David at Hebron, and said to the king, "Here is the head of Ishbosheth, the son of Saul your enemy, who sought your life; and the LORD has avenged my lord the king this day of Saul and his descendants."

9But David answered Rechab and Baanah his brother, the sons of Rimmon the Beerothite, and said to them, "*As* the LORD lives, who has redeemed my life from all adversity, 10when someone told me, saying, 'Look, Saul is dead,' thinking to have brought good news, I arrested him and had him executed in Ziklag—the one who *thought* I would give him a reward for *his* news. 11How much more, when wicked men have killed a righteous person in his own house on his bed? Therefore, shall I not now require his blood at your hand and remove you from the earth?" 12So David commanded his young men, and they executed them, cut off their hands and feet, and hanged *them* by the pool in Hebron. But they took the head of Ishbosheth and buried *it* in the tomb of Abner in Hebron.

DAVID REIGNS OVER ALL ISRAEL

5 Then all the tribes of Israel came to David at Hebron and spoke, saying, "Indeed we *are* your bone and your flesh. 2Also, in time past, when Saul was king over us, you were the one who led Israel out and brought them in; and the LORD said to you, 'You shall shepherd My people Israel, and be ruler over Israel.' " 3Therefore all the elders of Israel came to the king at Hebron, and King David made a covenant with them at Hebron before the LORD. And they anointed David king over Israel. 4David *was* thirty years old when he began to reign, *and* he reigned forty years. 5In Hebron he reigned over Judah seven years and six months, and in Jerusalem he reigned thirty-three years over all Israel and Judah.

THE CONQUEST OF JERUSALEM

6And the king and his men went to Jerusalem against the Jebusites, the inhabitants of the land, who spoke to David, saying, "You shall not come in here; but the blind and the lame will repel you," thinking, "David cannot come in here." 7Nevertheless David took the stronghold of Zion (that *is*, the City of David).

8Now David said on that day, "Whoever climbs up by way of the water shaft and defeats the Jebusites (the lame and the blind, *who are* hated by David's soul), *he shall be chief and captain.*"[a] Therefore they say, "The blind and the lame shall not come into the house."

5:8 [a]Compare 1 Chronicles 11:6

THE MESSAGE

and Baanah slipped by her and entered the
room where Ish-Bosheth was asleep on his
bed. They killed him and then cut off his
head, carrying it off as a trophy. They trav-
eled all night long, taking the route through
the Arabah Valley.
8 They presented the head of Ish-Bosheth
to David at Hebron, telling the king, "Here's
the head of Ish-Bosheth, Saul's son, your en-
emy. He was out to kill you, but GOD has
given vengeance to my master, the king—
vengeance this very day on Saul and his
children!"
9-11 David answered the brothers Recab and
Baanah, sons of Rimmon the Beerothite, "As
surely as GOD lives—the One who got me
out of every trouble I've ever been in—when
the messenger told me, 'Good news! Saul is
dead!' supposing I'd be delighted, I arrested
him and killed him on the spot in Ziklag.
That's what he got for his so-called good
news! And now you show up—evil men who
killed an innocent man in cold blood, a man
asleep in his own house! Don't think I won't
find you guilty of murder and rid the coun-
try of you!"
12 David then issued orders to his soldiers.
They killed the two—chopped off their
hands and feet, and hung the corpses at the
pool in Hebron. But Ish-Bosheth's head they
took and buried in Abner's tomb in Hebron.

1-2 5 Before long all the tribes of Israel ap-
proached David in Hebron and said,
"Look at us—your own flesh and blood! In
time past when Saul was our king, you were
the one who really ran the country. Even
then GOD said to you, 'You will shepherd my
people Israel and you'll be the prince.' "
3 All the leaders of Israel met with King
David at Hebron, and the king made a treaty
with them in the presence of GOD. And so
they anointed David king over Israel.

4-5 David was thirty years old when he became
king, and ruled for forty years. In Hebron he
ruled Judah for seven and a half years. In
Jerusalem he ruled all Israel and Judah for
thirty-three years.
6 David and his men immediately set out
for Jerusalem to take on the Jebusites, who
lived in that country. But they said, "You
might as well go home! Even the blind and
the lame could keep you out. You can't get in
here!" They had convinced themselves that
David couldn't break through.
7-8 But David went right ahead and captured
the fortress of Zion, known ever since as the
City of David. That day David said, "To get
the best of these Jebusites, one must target
the water system, not to mention this so-
called lame and blind bunch that David
hates." (In fact, he was so sick and tired of it,
people coined the expression, "No lame and
blind allowed in the palace.")

NEW KING JAMES VERSION

9Then David dwelt in the stronghold, and called it the City of David. And David built all around from the Millo[a] and inward. 10So David went on and became great, and the LORD God of hosts *was* with him.

11Then Hiram king of Tyre sent messengers to David, and cedar trees, and carpenters and masons. And they built David a house. 12So David knew that the LORD had established him as king over Israel, and that He had exalted His kingdom for the sake of His people Israel.

13And David took more concubines and wives from Jerusalem, after he had come from Hebron. Also more sons and daughters were born to David. 14Now these *are* the names of those who were born to him in Jerusalem: Shammua,[a] Shobab, Nathan, Solomon, 15Ibhar, Elishua,[a] Nepheg, Japhia, 16Elishama, Eliada, and Eliphelet.

THE PHILISTINES DEFEATED

17Now when the Philistines heard that they had anointed David king over Israel, all the Philistines went up to search for David. And David heard *of it* and went down to the stronghold. 18The Philistines also went and deployed themselves in the Valley of Rephaim. 19So David inquired of the LORD, saying, "Shall I go up against the Philistines? Will You deliver them into my hand?"

And the LORD said to David, "Go up, for I will doubtless deliver the Philistines into your hand."

20So David went to Baal Perazim, and David defeated them there; and he said, "The LORD has broken through my enemies before me, like a breakthrough of water." Therefore he called the name of that place Baal Perazim.[a] 21And they left their images there, and David and his men carried them away.

22Then the Philistines went up once again and deployed themselves in the Valley of Rephaim. 23Therefore David inquired of the LORD, and He said, "You shall not go up; circle around behind them, and come upon them in front of the mulberry trees. 24And it shall be, when you hear the sound of marching in the tops of the mulberry trees, then you shall advance quickly. For then the LORD will go out before you to strike the camp of the Philistines." 25And David did so, as the LORD commanded him; and he drove back the Philistines from Geba[a] as far as Gezer.

5:9 [a]Literally *The Landfill* **5:14** [a]Spelled *Shimea* in 1 Chronicles 3:5 **5:15** [a]Spelled *Elishama* in 1 Chronicles 3:6 **5:20** [a]Literally *Master of Breakthroughs* **5:25** [a]Following Masoretic Text, Targum, and Vulgate; Septuagint reads *Gibeon*.

THE MESSAGE

9-10 David made the fortress city his home and named it "City of David." He developed the city from the outside terraces inward. David proceeded with a longer stride, a larger embrace since the GOD-of-the-Angel-Armies was with him.

11-12 It was at this time that Hiram, king of Tyre, sent messengers to David, along with timbers of cedar. He also sent carpenters and masons to build a house for David. David took this as a sign that GOD had confirmed him as king of Israel, giving his kingship world prominence for the sake of Israel, his people.

13-16 David took on more concubines and wives from Jerusalem after he left Hebron. And more sons and daughters were born to him. These are the names of those born to him in Jerusalem:

Shammua,
Shobab,
Nathan,
Solomon,
Ibhar,
Elishua,
Nepheg,
Japhia,
Elishama,
Eliada,
Eliphelet.

17-18 When the Philistines got word that David had been made king over all Israel, they came on the hunt for him. David heard of it and went down to the stronghold. When the Philistines arrived, they deployed their forces in Raphaim Valley.

19 Then David prayed to GOD: "Shall I go up and fight the Philistines? Will you help me beat them?"

20-21 "Go up," GOD replied. "Count on me. I'll help you beat them."

David then went straight to Baal Perazim, and smashed them to pieces. Afterward David said, "GOD exploded on my enemies like a gush of water." That's why David named the place Baal Perazim (The-Master-Who-Explodes). The retreating Philistines dumped their idols, and David and his soldiers took them away.

22-23 Later there was a repeat performance. The Philistines came up again and deployed their troops in the Rephaim Valley. David again prayed to GOD.

23-24 This time GOD said, "Don't attack them head-on. Instead, circle around behind them and ambush them from the grove of sacred trees. When you hear the sound of shuffling in the trees, get ready to move out. It's a signal that GOD is going ahead of you to smash the Philistine camp."

25 David did exactly what GOD told him. He routed the Philistines all the way from Gibeon to Gezer.

NEW KING JAMES VERSION

THE ARK BROUGHT TO JERUSALEM

6 Again David gathered all *the* choice *men* of Israel, thirty thousand. 2And David arose and went with all the people who *were* with him from Baale Judah to bring up from there the ark of God, whose name is called by the Name,[a] the LORD of Hosts, who dwells *between* the cherubim. 3So they set the ark of God on a new cart, and brought it out of the house of Abinadab, which *was* on the hill; and Uzzah and Ahio, the sons of Abinadab, drove the new cart.[a] 4And they brought it out of the house of Abinadab, which *was* on the hill, accompanying the ark of God; and Ahio went before the ark. 5Then David and all the house of Israel played *music* before the LORD on all kinds of *instruments of* fir wood, on harps, on stringed instruments, on tambourines, on sistrums, and on cymbals.

6And when they came to Nachon's threshing floor, Uzzah put out *his hand* to the ark of God and took hold of it, for the oxen stumbled. 7Then the anger of the LORD was aroused against Uzzah, and God struck him there for *his* error; and he died there by the ark of God. 8And David became angry because of the LORD's outbreak against Uzzah; and he called the name of the place Perez Uzzah[a] to this day.

9David was afraid of the LORD that day; and he said, "How can the ark of the LORD come to me?" 10So David would not move the ark of the LORD with him into the City of David; but David took it aside into the house of Obed-Edom the Gittite. 11The ark of the LORD remained in the house of Obed-Edom the Gittite three months. And the LORD blessed Obed-Edom and all his household.

12Now it was told King David, saying, "The LORD has blessed the house of Obed-Edom and all that *belongs* to him, because of the ark of God." So David went and brought up the ark of God from the house of Obed-Edom to the City of David with gladness. 13And so it was, when those bearing the ark of the LORD had gone six paces, that he sacrificed oxen and fatted sheep. 14Then David danced before the LORD with all *his* might; and David *was* wearing a linen ephod. 15So David and all the house of Israel brought up the ark of the LORD with shouting and with the sound of the trumpet.

16Now as the ark of the LORD came into the City of David, Michal, Saul's daughter, looked through a window and saw King David leaping and whirling before the LORD; and she despised him in her heart. 17So they brought the ark of the LORD, and set it in its place in the midst of the tabernacle that David had erected for it. Then David offered burnt offerings and peace offerings before the LORD. 18And when David had finished offering burnt offerings and peace offerings, he blessed the people in the name of the LORD of hosts. 19Then he distributed among all the people, among the whole multitude of Israel, both the women and the men, to everyone a loaf of bread, a piece *of meat,* and a cake of raisins. So all the people departed, everyone to his house.

6:2 [a]Septuagint, Targum, and Vulgate omit *by the Name;* many Hebrew manuscripts and Syriac read *there.* **6:3** [a]Septuagint adds *with the ark.* **6:8** [a]Literally *Outburst Against Uzzah*

THE MESSAGE

1-2 6 David mustered the pick of the troops of Israel—thirty divisions of them. Together with his soldiers, David headed for Baalah to recover the Chest of God, which was called by the Name GOD-of-the-Angel-Armies, who was enthroned over the pair of angels on the Chest.

3-7 They placed the Chest of God on a brand-new oxcart and removed it from Abinadab's house on the hill. Uzzah and Ahio, Abinadab's sons, were driving the new cart loaded with the Chest of God, Ahio in the lead and Uzzah alongside the Chest. David and the whole company of Israel were in the parade, singing at the top of their lungs and playing mandolins, harps, tambourines, castanets, and cymbals. When they came to the threshing floor of Nacon, the oxen stumbled, so Uzzah reached out and grabbed the Chest of God. GOD blazed in anger against Uzzah and struck him hard because he had profaned the Chest. Uzzah died on the spot, right alongside the Chest.

8-11 Then David got angry because of GOD's deadly outburst against Uzzah. That place is still called Perez Uzzah (The-Explosion-Against-Uzzah). David became fearful of GOD that day and said, "This Chest is too hot to handle. How can I ever get it back to the City of David?" He refused to take the Chest of GOD a step farther. Instead, David removed it off the road and to the house of Obed-Edom the Gittite. The Chest of GOD stayed at the house of Obed-Edom the Gittite for three months. And GOD prospered Obed-Edom and his entire household.

12-16 It was reported to King David that GOD had prospered Obed-Edom and his entire household because of the Chest of God. So David thought, "I'll get that blessing for myself," and went and brought up the Chest of God from the house of Obed-Edom to the City of David, celebrating extravagantly all the way, with frequent sacrifices of choice bulls. David, ceremonially dressed in priest's linen, danced with great abandon before GOD. The whole country was with him as he accompanied the Chest of GOD with shouts and trumpet blasts. But as the Chest of GOD came into the City of David, Michal, Saul's daughter, happened to be looking out a window. When she saw King David leaping and dancing before GOD, her heart filled with scorn.

17-19 They brought the Chest of GOD and set it in the middle of the tent pavilion that David had pitched for it. Then and there David worshiped, offering burnt offerings and peace offerings. When David had completed the sacrifices of burnt and peace offerings, he blessed the people in the name of GOD-of-the-Angel-Armies and handed out to each person in the crowd, men and women alike, a loaf of bread, a date cake, and a raisin cake. Then everyone went home.

New King James Version

20Then David returned to bless his house-
hold. And Michal the daughter of Saul came out
to meet David, and said, "How glorious was the
king of Israel today, uncovering himself today in
the eyes of the maids of his servants, as one of
the base fellows shamelessly uncovers himself!"
21So David said to Michal, "*It was* before the
LORD, who chose me instead of your father and
all his house, to appoint me ruler over the peo-
ple of the LORD, over Israel. Therefore I will play
music before the LORD. 22And I will be even
more undignified than this, and will be humble
in my own sight. But as for the maidservants of
whom you have spoken, by them I will be held
in honor."
23Therefore Michal the daughter of Saul had
no children to the day of her death.

God's Covenant with David

7 Now it came to pass when the king was
dwelling in his house, and the LORD had
given him rest from all his enemies all around,
2that the king said to Nathan the prophet, "See
now, I dwell in a house of cedar, but the ark of
God dwells inside tent curtains."
3Then Nathan said to the king, "Go, do all
that *is* in your heart, for the LORD *is* with you."
4But it happened that night that the word of
the LORD came to Nathan, saying, 5"Go and tell
My servant David, 'Thus says the LORD: "Would
you build a house for Me to dwell in? 6For I have
not dwelt in a house since the time that I
brought the children of Israel up from Egypt,
even to this day, but have moved about in a tent
and in a tabernacle. 7Wherever I have moved
about with all the children of Israel, have I ever
spoken a word to anyone from the tribes of Is-
rael, whom I commanded to shepherd My peo-
ple Israel, saying, 'Why have you not built Me a
house of cedar?' " ' 8Now therefore, thus shall
you say to My servant David, 'Thus says the
LORD of hosts: "I took you from the sheepfold,
from following the sheep, to be ruler over My
people, over Israel. 9And I have been with you
wherever you have gone, and have cut off all
your enemies from before you, and have made
you a great name, like the name of the great
men who *are* on the earth. 10Moreover I will ap-
point a place for My people Israel, and will plant
them, that they may dwell in a place of their
own and move no more; nor shall the sons of
wickedness oppress them anymore, as previ-
ously, 11since the time that I commanded judges
to be over My people Israel, and have caused
you to rest from all your enemies. Also the LORD
tells you that He will make you a house.[a]
12"When your days are fulfilled and you rest
with your fathers, I will set up your seed after
you, who will come from your body, and I will
establish his kingdom. 13He shall build a house
for My name, and I will establish the throne of
his kingdom forever. 14I will be his Father, and
he shall be My son. If he commits iniquity, I will

7:11 [a]That is, a royal dynasty

The Message

20-22 David returned home to bless his family.
Michal, Saul's daughter, came out to greet
him: "How wonderfully the king has distin-
guished himself today—exposing himself to
the eyes of the servants' maids like some
burlesque street dancer!" David replied to
Michal, "In GOD's presence I'll dance all I
want! He chose me over your father and the
rest of our family and made me prince over
GOD's people, over Israel. Oh yes, I'll dance
to GOD's glory—more recklessly even than
this. And as far as I'm concerned . . . . I'll
gladly look like a fool . . . but among these
maids you're so worried about, I'll be hon-
ored no end."
23 Michal, Saul's daughter, was barren the
rest of her life.

God's Covenant with David

1-2 7 Before long, the king made himself at
home and GOD gave him peace from all
his enemies. Then one day King David said
to Nathan the prophet, "Look at this: Here I
am, comfortable in a luxurious house of
cedar, and the Chest of God sits in a plain
tent."
3 Nathan told the king, "Whatever is on
your heart, go and do it. GOD is with you."
4-7 But that night, the word of GOD came to
Nathan saying, "Go and tell my servant
David: This is GOD's word on the matter:
You're going to build a 'house' for me to live
in? Why, I haven't lived in a 'house' from the
time I brought the children of Israel up from
Egypt till now. All that time I've moved
about with nothing but a tent. And in all my
travels with Israel, did I ever say to any of
the leaders I commanded to shepherd Israel,
'Why haven't you built me a house of
cedar?'
8-11 "So here is what you are to tell my ser-
vant David: The GOD-of-the-Angel-Armies
has this word for you: I took you from the
pasture, tagging along after sheep, and
made you prince over my people Israel. I
was with you everywhere you went and
mowed your enemies down before you. Now
I'm making you famous, to be ranked with
the great names on earth. And I'm going to
set aside a place for my people Israel and
plant them there so they'll have their own
home and not be knocked around any more.
Nor will evil men afflict you as they always
have, even during the days I set judges over
my people Israel. Finally, I'm going to give
you peace from all your enemies.
11-16 "Furthermore, GOD has this message for
you: GOD himself will build you a house!
When your life is complete and you're
buried with your ancestors, then I'll raise up
your child, your own flesh and blood, to suc-
ceed you, and I'll firmly establish his rule.
He will build a house to honor me, and I will
guarantee his kingdom's rule permanently.
I'll be a father to him, and he'll be a son to
me. When he does wrong, I'll discipline him

NEW KING JAMES VERSION

chasten him with the rod of men and with the
blows of the sons of men. 15But My mercy shall
not depart from him, as I took *it* from Saul,
whom I removed from before you. 16And your
house and your kingdom shall be established
forever before you.[a] Your throne shall be estab-
lished forever." ' "
17According to all these words and according
to all this vision, so Nathan spoke to David.

DAVID'S THANKSGIVING TO GOD

18Then King David went in and sat before the
LORD; and he said: "Who *am* I, O Lord GOD? And
what is my house, that You have brought me this
far? 19And yet this was a small thing in Your
sight, O Lord GOD; and You have also spoken of
Your servant's house for a great while to come.
Is this the manner of man, O Lord GOD? 20Now
what more can David say to You? For You, Lord
GOD, know Your servant. 21For Your word's sake,
and according to Your own heart, You have done
all these great things, to make Your servant
know *them.* 22Therefore You are great, O Lord
GOD.[a] For *there is* none like You, nor *is there any*
God besides You, according to all that we have
heard with our ears. 23And who *is* like Your peo-
ple, like Israel, the one nation on the earth
whom God went to redeem for Himself as a peo-
ple, to make for Himself a name—and to do for
Yourself great and awesome deeds for Your
land—before Your people whom You redeemed
for Yourself from Egypt, the nations, and their
gods? 24For You have made Your people Israel
Your very own people forever; and You, LORD,
have become their God.
25"Now, O LORD God, the word which You
have spoken concerning Your servant and con-
cerning his house, establish *it* forever and do as
You have said. 26So let Your name be magnified
forever, saying, 'The LORD of hosts *is* the God
over Israel.' And let the house of Your servant
David be established before You. 27For You, O
LORD of hosts, God of Israel, have revealed *this*
to Your servant, saying, 'I will build you a house.'
Therefore Your servant has found it in his heart
to pray this prayer to You.
28"And now, O Lord GOD, You are God, and
Your words are true, and You have promised this
goodness to Your servant. 29Now therefore, let it
please You to bless the house of Your servant,
that it may continue before You forever; for You,
O Lord GOD, have spoken *it,* and with Your
blessing let the house of Your servant be blessed
forever."

DAVID'S FURTHER CONQUESTS

8 After this it came to pass that David attacked
the Philistines and subdued them. And David
took Metheg Ammah from the hand of the
Philistines.
2Then he defeated Moab. Forcing them down
to the ground, he measured them off with a line.
With two lines he measured off those to be put

7:16 [a]Septuagint reads *Me.* **7:22** [a]Targum and Syriac read *O LORD God.*

THE MESSAGE

in the usual ways, the pitfalls and obstacles of this mortal life. But I'll never remove my gracious love from him, as I removed it from Saul, who preceded you and whom I most certainly did remove. Your family and your kingdom are permanently secured. I'm keeping my eye on them! And your royal throne will always be there, rock solid."

17 Nathan gave David a complete and accurate account of everything he heard and saw in the vision.

18-21 King David went in, took his place before GOD, and prayed: "Who am I, my Master GOD, and what is my family, that you have brought me to this place in life? But that's nothing compared to what's coming, for you've also spoken of my family far into the future, given me a glimpse into tomorrow, my Master GOD! What can I possibly say in the face of all this? You know me, Master GOD, just as I am. You've done all this not because of who I am but because of who you are—out of your very heart!—but you've let me in on it.

22-24 "This is what makes you so great, Master GOD! There is none like you, no God but you, nothing to compare with what we've heard with our own ears. And who is like your people, like Israel, a nation unique in the earth, whom God set out to redeem for himself (and became most famous for it), performing great and fearsome acts, throwing out nations and their gods left and right as you saved your people from Egypt? You established for yourself a people—your very own Israel!—your people permanently. And you, GOD, became their God.

25-27 "So now, great GOD, this word that you have spoken to me and my family, guarantee it permanently! Do exactly what you've promised! Then your reputation will flourish always as people exclaim, 'The GOD-of-the-Angel-Armies is God over Israel!' And the house of your servant David will remain sure and solid in your watchful presence. For you, GOD-of-the-Angel-Armies, Israel's God, told me plainly, 'I will build you a house.' That's how I was able to find the courage to pray this prayer to you.

28-29 "And now, Master GOD, being the God you are, speaking sure words as you do, and having just said this wonderful thing to me, please, just one more thing: Bless my family; keep your eye on them always. You've already as much as said that you would, Master GOD! Oh, may your blessing be on my family permanently!"

1 8 In the days that followed, David struck hard at the Philistines—brought them to their knees and took control of the countryside.

2 He also fought and defeated Moab. He chose two-thirds of them randomly and executed them. The other third he spared. So

New King James Version

to death, and with one full line those to be kept alive. So the Moabites became David's servants, *and* brought tribute.

3David also defeated Hadadezer the son of Rehob, king of Zobah, as he went to recover his territory at the River Euphrates. 4David took from him one thousand *chariots,* seven hundred[a] horsemen, and twenty thousand foot soldiers. Also David hamstrung all the chariot horses, except that he spared *enough* of them for one hundred chariots.

5When the Syrians of Damascus came to help Hadadezer king of Zobah, David killed twenty-two thousand of the Syrians. 6Then David put garrisons in Syria of Damascus; and the Syrians became David's servants, *and* brought tribute. So the LORD preserved David wherever he went. 7And David took the shields of gold that had belonged to the servants of Hadadezer, and brought them to Jerusalem. 8Also from Betah[a] and from Berothai, cities of Hadadezer, King David took a large amount of bronze.

9When Toi[a] king of Hamath heard that David had defeated all the army of Hadadezer, 10then Toi sent Joram[a] his son to King David, to greet him and bless him, because he had fought against Hadadezer and defeated him (for Hadadezer had been at war with Toi); and *Joram* brought with him articles of silver, articles of gold, and articles of bronze. 11King David also dedicated these to the LORD, along with the silver and gold that he had dedicated from all the nations which he had subdued— 12from Syria,[a] from Moab, from the people of Ammon, from the Philistines, from Amalek, and from the spoil of Hadadezer the son of Rehob, king of Zobah.

13And David made *himself* a name when he returned from killing eighteen thousand Syrians[a] in the Valley of Salt. 14He also put garrisons in Edom; throughout all Edom he put garrisons, and all the Edomites became David's servants. And the LORD preserved David wherever he went.

David's Administration

15So David reigned over all Israel; and David administered judgment and justice to all his people. 16Joab the son of Zeruiah *was* over the army; Jehoshaphat the son of Ahilud *was* recorder; 17Zadok the son of Ahitub and Ahimelech the son of Abiathar *were* the priests; Seraiah[a] *was* the scribe; 18Benaiah the son of Jehoiada *was over* both the Cherethites and the Pelethites; and David's sons were chief ministers.

David's Kindness to Mephibosheth

9 Now David said, "Is there still anyone who is left of the house of Saul, that I may show him kindness for Jonathan's sake?"

8:4 [a]Or *seven thousand* (compare 1 Chronicles 18:4) 8:8 [a]Spelled *Tibhath* in 1 Chronicles 18:8 8:9 [a]Spelled *Tou* in 1 Chronicles 18:9 8:10 [a]Spelled *Hadoram* in 1 Chronicles 18:10 8:12 [a]Septuagint, Syriac, and some Hebrew manuscripts read *Edom.* 8:13 [a]Septuagint, Syriac, and some Hebrew manuscripts read *Edomites* (compare 1 Chronicles 18:12). 8:17 [a]Spelled *Shavsha* in 1 Chronicles 18:16

The Message

the Moabites fell under David's rule and were forced to bring tribute.

3-4 On his way to restore his sovereignty at the River Euphrates, David next defeated Hadadezer son of Rehob the king of Zobah. He captured from him a thousand chariots, seven thousand cavalry, and twenty thousand infantry. He hamstrung all the chariot horses, but saved back a hundred.

5-6 When the Arameans from Damascus came to the aid of Hadadezer king of Zobah, David killed twenty-two thousand of them. David set up a puppet government in Aram-Damascus. The Arameans became subjects of David and were forced to bring tribute. GOD gave victory to David wherever he marched.

7-8 David plundered the gold shields that belonged to the servants of Hadadezer and brought them to Jerusalem. He also looted a great quantity of bronze from Tebah and Berothai, cities of Hadadezer.

9-12 Toi, king of Hamath, heard that David had struck down the entire army of Hadadezer. So he sent his son Joram to King David to greet and congratulate him for fighting and defeating them, for Toi and Hadadezer were old enemies. He brought with him gifts of silver, gold, and bronze. King David consecrated these along with the silver and gold from all the nations he had conquered—from Aram, Moab, the Ammonites, the Philistines, and from Amalek, along with the plunder from Hadadezer son of Rehob king of Zobah.

13-14 David built a victory monument on his return from defeating the Arameans.

Abishai son of Zeruiah fought and defeated the Edomites in the Salt Valley. Eighteen thousand of them were killed. David set up a puppet government in Edom, and the Edomites became subjects under David.

GOD gave David victory wherever he marched.

15 Thus David ruled over all of Israel. He ruled well—fair and evenhanded in all his duties and relationships.

16 Joab son of Zeruiah was head of the army;

Jehoshaphat son of Ahilud was clerk;

17 Zadok son of Ahitub and Ahimelech son of Abiathar were priests;

Seraiah was secretary;

18 Benaiah son of Jehoiada was over the Kerethites and Pelethites;

And David's sons were priests.

An Open Table for Mephibosheth

1 9 One day David asked, "Is there anyone left of Saul's family? If so, I'd like to show him some kindness in honor of Jonathan."

NEW KING JAMES VERSION

2 And *there was* a servant of the house of
Saul whose name *was* Ziba. So when they had
called him to David, the king said to him, "*Are*
you Ziba?"
He said, "At your service!"
3 Then the king said, "*Is* there not still some-
one of the house of Saul, to whom I may show
the kindness of God?"
And Ziba said to the king, "There is still a
son of Jonathan *who is* lame in *his* feet."
4 So the king said to him, "Where *is* he?"
And Ziba said to the king, "Indeed he *is* in
the house of Machir the son of Ammiel, in Lo
Debar."
5 Then King David sent and brought him out
of the house of Machir the son of Ammiel, from
Lo Debar.
6 Now when Mephibosheth the son of
Jonathan, the son of Saul, had come to David, he
fell on his face and prostrated himself. Then
David said, "Mephibosheth?"
And he answered, "Here is your servant!"
7 So David said to him, "Do not fear, for I will
surely show you kindness for Jonathan your fa-
ther's sake, and will restore to you all the land
of Saul your grandfather; and you shall eat
bread at my table continually."
8 Then he bowed himself, and said, "What *is*
your servant, that you should look upon such a
dead dog as I?"
9 And the king called to Ziba, Saul's servant,
and said to him, "I have given to your master's
son all that belonged to Saul and to all his house.
10 You therefore, and your sons and your ser-
vants, shall work the land for him, and you shall
bring in *the harvest*, that your master's son may
have food to eat. But Mephibosheth your mas-
ter's son shall eat bread at my table always."
Now Ziba had fifteen sons and twenty servants.
11 Then Ziba said to the king, "According to
all that my lord the king has commanded his
servant, so will your servant do."
"As for Mephibosheth," *said the king*, "he
shall eat at my table[a] like one of the king's
sons." 12 Mephibosheth had a young son whose
name *was* Micha. And all who dwelt in the
house of Ziba *were* servants of Mephibosheth.
13 So Mephibosheth dwelt in Jerusalem, for he
ate continually at the king's table. And he was
lame in both his feet.

THE AMMONITES AND SYRIANS DEFEATED

10 It happened after this that the king of the
people of Ammon died, and Hanun his son
reigned in his place. 2 Then David said, "I will
show kindness to Hanun the son of Nahash, as
his father showed kindness to me."
So David sent by the hand of his servants to
comfort him concerning his father. And David's
servants came into the land of the people of Am-
mon. 3 And the princes of the people of Ammon
said to Hanun their lord, "Do you think that
David really honors your father because he has
sent comforters to you? Has David not *rather*
sent his servants to you to search the city, to spy
it out, and to overthrow it?"

9:11 [a]Septuagint reads *David's table.*

THE MESSAGE

2 It happened that a servant from Saul's
household named Ziba was there. They
called him into David's presence. The king
asked him, "Are you Ziba?"
"Yes sir," he replied.
3 The king asked, "Is there anyone left
from the family of Saul to whom I can show
some godly kindness?"
Ziba told the king, "Yes, there is
Jonathan's son, lame in both feet."
4 "Where is he?"
"He's living at the home of Makir son of
Ammiel in Lo Debar."
5 King David didn't lose a minute. He sent
and got him from the home of Makir son of
Ammiel in Lo Debar.
6 When Mephibosheth son of Jonathan
(who was the son of Saul), came before
David, he bowed deeply, abasing himself,
honoring David.
David spoke his name: "Mephibosheth."
"Yes sir?"
7 "Don't be frightened," said David. "I'd like
to do something special for you in memory
of your father Jonathan. To begin with, I'm
returning to you all the properties of your
grandfather Saul. Furthermore, from now
on you'll take all your meals at my table."
8 Shuffling and stammering, not looking him
in the eye, Mephibosheth said, "Who am I that
you pay attention to a stray dog like me?"
9-10 David then called in Ziba, Saul's right-
hand man, and told him, "Everything that
belonged to Saul and his family, I've handed
over to your master's grandson. You and
your sons and your servants will work his
land and bring in the produce, provisions
for your master's grandson. Mephibosheth
himself, your master's grandson, from now
on will take all his meals at my table." Ziba
had fifteen sons and twenty servants.
11-12 "All that my master the king has ordered
his servant," answered Ziba, "your servant
will surely do."
And Mephibosheth ate at David's table,
just like one of the royal family. Mephib-
osheth also had a small son named Mica. All
who were part of Ziba's household were
now the servants of Mephibosheth.
13 Mephibosheth lived in Jerusalem, taking
all his meals at the king's table. He was
lame in both feet.

1-2 10 Sometime after this, the king of the
Ammonites died and Hanun, his son,
succeeded him as king. David said, "I'd like
to show some kindness to Hanun, the son of
Nahash—treat him as well and as kindly as
his father treated me." So David sent Hanun
condolences regarding his father.
2-3 But when David's servants got to the land
of the Ammonites, the Ammonite leaders
warned Hanun, their head delegate, "Do you
for a minute suppose that David is honoring
your father by sending you comforters?
Don't you think it's because he wants to
snoop around the city and size it up that
David has sent his emissaries to you?"

NEW KING JAMES VERSION

4 Therefore Hanun took David's servants,
shaved off half of their beards, cut off their gar-
ments in the middle, at their buttocks, and sent
them away. 5 When they told David, he sent to
meet them, because the men were greatly
ashamed. And the king said, "Wait at Jericho
until your beards have grown, and *then* return."
6 When the people of Ammon saw that they
had made themselves repulsive to David, the peo-
ple of Ammon sent and hired the Syrians of Beth
Rehob and the Syrians of Zoba, twenty thousand
foot soldiers; and from the king of Maacah one
thousand men, and from Ish-Tob twelve thou-
sand men. 7 Now when David heard *of it,* he sent
Joab and all the army of the mighty men. 8 Then
the people of Ammon came out and put them-
selves in battle array at the entrance of the gate.
And the Syrians of Zoba, Beth Rehob, Ish-Tob,
and Maacah *were* by themselves in the field.
9 When Joab saw that the battle line was
against him before and behind, he chose some
of Israel's best and put *them* in battle array
against the Syrians. 10 And the rest of the people
he put under the command of Abishai his
brother, that he might set *them* in battle array
against the people of Ammon. 11 Then he said, "If
the Syrians are too strong for me, then you shall
help me; but if the people of Ammon are too
strong for you, then I will come and help you.
12 Be of good courage, and let us be strong for
our people and for the cities of our God. And
may the LORD do *what is* good in His sight."
13 So Joab and the people who *were* with him
drew near for the battle against the Syrians, and
they fled before him. 14 When the people of Am-
mon saw that the Syrians were fleeing, they also
fled before Abishai, and entered the city. So
Joab returned from the people of Ammon and
went to Jerusalem.
15 When the Syrians saw that they had been
defeated by Israel, they gathered together.
16 Then Hadadezer[a] sent and brought out the
Syrians who *were* beyond the River,[b] and they
came to Helam. And Shobach the commander
of Hadadezer's army *went* before them. 17 When
it was told David, he gathered all Israel, crossed
over the Jordan, and came to Helam. And the
Syrians set themselves in battle array against
David and fought with him. 18 Then the Syrians
fled before Israel; and David killed seven hun-
dred charioteers and forty thousand horsemen
of the Syrians, and struck Shobach the com-
mander of their army, who died there. 19 And
when all the kings *who were* servants to
Hadadezer[a] saw that they were defeated by Is-
rael, they made peace with Israel and served
them. So the Syrians were afraid to help the
people of Ammon anymore.

DAVID, BATHSHEBA, AND URIAH

11 It happened in the spring of the year, at the
time when kings go out *to battle,* that
David sent Joab and his servants with him, and

10:16 [a]Hebrew *Hadarezer* [b]That is, the Euphrates **10:19** [a]Hebrew *Hadarezer*

THE MESSAGE

4 So Hanun seized David's men, shaved off
half their beards, cut off their robes halfway
up their buttocks, and sent them packing.
5 When all this was reported to David, he
sent someone to meet them, for they were
seriously humiliated. The king told them,
"Stay in Jericho until your beards grow out.
Only then come back."
6 When it dawned on the Ammonites that
as far as David was concerned they stunk to
high heaven, they hired Aramean soldiers
from Beth-Rehob and Zobah—twenty thou-
sand infantry—and a thousand men from
the king of Maacah, and twelve thousand
men from Tob.
7 When David heard of this, he dispatched
Joab with his strongest fighters in full force.
8-12 The Ammonites marched out and arranged
themselves in battle formation at the city gate.
The Arameans of Zobah and Rehob and the
men of Tob and Maacah took up a position out
in the open fields. When Joab saw that he had
two fronts to fight, before and behind, he took
his pick of the best of Israel and deployed
them to confront the Arameans. The rest of
the army he put under the command of
Abishai, his brother, and deployed them to
confront the Ammonites. Then he said, "If
the Arameans are too much for me, you help
me. And if the Ammonites prove too much
for you, I'll come and help you. Courage!
We'll fight with might and main for our peo-
ple and for the cities of our God. And GOD
will do whatever he sees needs doing!"
13-14 But when Joab and his soldiers moved in
to fight the Arameans, they ran off in full re-
treat. Then the Ammonites, seeing the
Arameans run for dear life, took to their
heels from Abishai and went into the city.
So Joab left off fighting the Ammonites
and returned to Jerusalem.
15-17 When the Arameans saw how badly
they'd been beaten by Israel, they picked up
the pieces and regrouped. Hadadezer sent
for the Arameans who were across the
River. They came to Helam. Shobach, com-
mander of Hadadezer's army, led them. All
this was reported to David.
17-19 So David mustered Israel, crossed the Jor-
dan, and came to Helam. The Arameans
went into battle formation, ready for David,
and the fight was on. But the Arameans
again scattered before Israel. David killed
seven hundred chariot drivers and forty
thousand cavalry. And he mortally wounded
Shobach, the army commander, who died on
the battlefield. When all the kings who were
vassals of Hadadezer saw that they had been
routed by Israel, they made peace and be-
came Israel's vassals. The Arameans were
afraid to help the Ammonites ever again.

DAVID'S SIN AND SORROW

1 **11** When that time of year came around
again, the anniversary of the Ammonite
aggression, David dispatched Joab and his

NEW KING JAMES VERSION

all Israel; and they destroyed the people of Ammon and besieged Rabbah. But David remained at Jerusalem.

2Then it happened one evening that David arose from his bed and walked on the roof of the king's house. And from the roof he saw a woman bathing, and the woman *was* very beautiful to behold. 3So David sent and inquired about the woman. And *someone* said, "*Is* this not Bathsheba, the daughter of Eliam, the wife of Uriah the Hittite?" 4Then David sent messengers, and took her; and she came to him, and he lay with her, for she was cleansed from her impurity; and she returned to her house. 5And the woman conceived; so she sent and told David, and said, "I *am* with child."

6Then David sent to Joab, *saying*, "Send me Uriah the Hittite." And Joab sent Uriah to David. 7When Uriah had come to him, David asked how Joab was doing, and how the people were doing, and how the war prospered. 8And David said to Uriah, "Go down to your house and wash your feet." So Uriah departed from the king's house, and a gift *of food* from the king followed him. 9But Uriah slept at the door of the king's house with all the servants of his lord, and did not go down to his house. 10So when they told David, saying, "Uriah did not go down to his house," David said to Uriah, "Did you not come from a journey? Why did you not go down to your house?"

11And Uriah said to David, "The ark and Israel and Judah are dwelling in tents, and my lord Joab and the servants of my lord are encamped in the open fields. Shall I then go to my house to eat and drink, and to lie with my wife? *As* you live, and *as* your soul lives, I will not do this thing."

12Then David said to Uriah, "Wait here today also, and tomorrow I will let you depart." So Uriah remained in Jerusalem that day and the next. 13Now when David called him, he ate and drank before him; and he made him drunk. And at evening he went out to lie on his bed with the servants of his lord, but he did not go down to his house.

14In the morning it happened that David wrote a letter to Joab and sent *it* by the hand of Uriah. 15And he wrote in the letter, saying, "Set Uriah in the forefront of the hottest battle, and retreat from him, that he may be struck down and die." 16So it was, while Joab besieged the city, that he assigned Uriah to a place where he knew there *were* valiant men. 17Then the men of the city came out and fought with Joab. And *some* of the people of the servants of David fell; and Uriah the Hittite died also.

18Then Joab sent and told David all the things concerning the war, 19and charged the messenger, saying, "When you have finished telling the matters of the war to the king, 20if it happens that the king's wrath rises, and he says to you: 'Why did you approach so near to the city when you fought? Did you not know that they would shoot from the wall? 21Who struck Abimelech the son of Jerubbesheth?[a] Was it not a woman who cast a piece of a millstone on him from the wall, so that he died in Thebez? Why did you go near the wall?'—then you shall say, 'Your servant Uriah the Hittite is dead also.' "

11:21 [a]Same as *Jerubbaal* (Gideon), Judges 6:32ff

THE MESSAGE

fighting men of Israel in full force to destroy the Ammonites for good. They laid siege to Rabbah, but David stayed in Jerusalem.

2-5 One late afternoon, David got up from taking his nap and was strolling on the roof of the palace. From his vantage point on the roof he saw a woman bathing. The woman was stunningly beautiful. David sent to ask about her, and was told, "Isn't this Bathsheba, daughter of Eliam and wife of Uriah the Hittite?" David sent his agents to get her. After she arrived, he went to bed with her. (This occurred during the time of "purification" following her period.) Then she returned home. Before long she realized she was pregnant.

Later she sent word to David: "I'm pregnant."

6 David then got in touch with Joab: "Send Uriah the Hittite to me." Joab sent him.

7-8 When he arrived, David asked him for news from the front—how things were going with Joab and the troops and with the fighting. Then he said to Uriah, "Go home. Have a refreshing bath and a good night's rest."

8-9 After Uriah left the palace, an informant of the king was sent after him. But Uriah didn't go home. He slept that night at the palace entrance, along with the king's servants.

10 David was told that Uriah had not gone home. He asked Uriah, "Didn't you just come off a hard trip? So why didn't you go home?"

11 Uriah replied to David, "The Chest is out there with the fighting men of Israel and Judah—in tents. My master Joab and his servants are roughing it out in the fields. So, how can I go home and eat and drink and enjoy my wife? On your life, I'll not do it!"

12-13 "All right," said David, "have it your way. Stay for the day and I'll send you back tomorrow." So Uriah stayed in Jerusalem the rest of the day.

The next day David invited him to eat and drink with him, and David got him drunk. But in the evening Uriah again went out and slept with his master's servants. He didn't go home.

14-15 In the morning David wrote a letter to Joab and sent it with Uriah. In the letter he wrote, "Put Uriah in the front lines where the fighting is the fiercest. Then pull back and leave him exposed so that he's sure to be killed."

16-17 So Joab, holding the city under siege, put Uriah in a place where he knew there were fierce enemy fighters. When the city's defenders came out to fight Joab, some of David's soldiers were killed, including Uriah the Hittite.

18-21 Joab sent David a full report on the battle. He instructed the messenger, "After you have given to the king a detailed report on the battle, if he flares in anger, say, 'And by the way, your servant Uriah the Hittite is dead.' "

New King James Version

[22]So the messenger went, and came and told David all that Joab had sent by him. [23]And the messenger said to David, "Surely the men prevailed against us and came out to us in the field; then we drove them back as far as the entrance of the gate. [24]The archers shot from the wall at your servants; and *some* of the king's servants are dead, and your servant Uriah the Hittite is dead also."

[25]Then David said to the messenger, "Thus you shall say to Joab: 'Do not let this thing displease you, for the sword devours one as well as another. Strengthen your attack against the city, and overthrow it.' So encourage him."

[26]When the wife of Uriah heard that Uriah her husband was dead, she mourned for her husband. [27]And when her mourning was over, David sent and brought her to his house, and she became his wife and bore him a son. But the thing that David had done displeased the LORD.

Nathan's Parable and David's Confession

12 Then the LORD sent Nathan to David. And he came to him, and said to him: "There were two men in one city, one rich and the other poor. [2]The rich *man* had exceedingly many flocks and herds. [3]But the poor *man* had nothing, except one little ewe lamb which he had bought and nourished; and it grew up together with him and with his children. It ate of his own food and drank from his own cup and lay in his bosom; and it was like a daughter to him. [4]And a traveler came to the rich man, who refused to take from his own flock and from his own herd to prepare one for the wayfaring man who had come to him; but he took the poor man's lamb and prepared it for the man who had come to him."

[5]So David's anger was greatly aroused against the man, and he said to Nathan, "*As* the LORD lives, the man who has done this shall surely die! [6]And he shall restore fourfold for the lamb, because he did this thing and because he had no pity."

[7]Then Nathan said to David, "You *are* the man! Thus says the LORD God of Israel: 'I anointed you king over Israel, and I delivered you from the hand of Saul. [8]I gave you your master's house and your master's wives into your keeping, and gave you the house of Israel and Judah. And if *that had been* too little, I also would have given you much more! [9]Why have you despised the commandment of the LORD, to do evil in His sight? You have killed Uriah the Hittite with the sword; you have taken his wife *to be* your wife, and have killed him with the sword of the people of Ammon. [10]Now therefore,

The Message

22-24 Joab's messenger arrived in Jerusalem and gave the king a full report. He said, "The enemy was too much for us. They advanced on us in the open field, and we pushed them back to the city gate. But then arrows came hot and heavy on us from the city wall, and eighteen of the king's soldiers died."

25 When the messenger completed his report of the battle, David got angry at Joab. He vented it on the messenger: "Why did you get so close to the city? Didn't you know you'd be attacked from the wall? Didn't you remember how Abimelech son of Jerub-Besheth got killed? Wasn't it a woman who dropped a millstone on him from the wall and crushed him at Thebez? Why did you go close to the wall!"

"By the way," said Joab's messenger, "your servant Uriah the Hittite is dead."

Then David told the messenger, "Oh. I see. Tell Joab, 'Don't trouble yourself over this. War kills—sometimes one, sometimes another—you never know who's next. Redouble your assault on the city and destroy it.' Encourage Joab."

26-27 When Uriah's wife heard that her husband was dead, she grieved for her husband. When the time of mourning was over, David sent someone to bring her to his house. She became his wife and bore him a son.

27-3 **12** But GOD was not at all pleased with what David had done, and sent Nathan to David. Nathan said to him, "There were two men in the same city—one rich, the other poor. The rich man had huge flocks of sheep, herds of cattle. The poor man had nothing but one little female lamb, which he had bought and raised. It grew up with him and his children as a member of the family. It ate off his plate and drank from his cup and slept on his bed. It was like a daughter to him.

4 "One day a traveler dropped in on the rich man. He was too stingy to take an animal from his own herds or flocks to make a meal for his visitor, so he took the poor man's lamb and prepared a meal to set before his guest."

5-6 David exploded in anger. "As surely as GOD lives," he said to Nathan, "the man who did this ought to be lynched! He must repay for the lamb four times over for his crime and his stinginess!"

7-12 "You're the man!" said Nathan. "And here's what GOD, the God of Israel, has to say to you: I made you king over Israel. I freed you from the fist of Saul. I gave you your master's daughter and other wives to have and to hold. I gave you both Israel and Judah. And if that hadn't been enough, I'd have gladly thrown in much more. So why have you treated the word of GOD with brazen contempt, doing this great evil? You murdered Uriah the Hittite, then took his wife as your wife. Worse, you killed him with an Ammonite sword!

New King James Version

the sword shall never depart from your house,
because you have despised Me, and have taken
the wife of Uriah the Hittite to be your wife.'
11Thus says the LORD: 'Behold, I will raise up ad-
versity against you from your own house; and I
will take your wives before your eyes and give
them to your neighbor, and he shall lie with
your wives in the sight of this sun. 12For you did
it secretly, but I will do this thing before all Is-
rael, before the sun.' "
13So David said to Nathan, "I have sinned
against the LORD."
And Nathan said to David, "The LORD also
has put away your sin; you shall not die. 14How-
ever, because by this deed you have given great
occasion to the enemies of the LORD to blas-
pheme, the child also *who is* born to you shall
surely die." 15Then Nathan departed to his
house.

The Death of David's Son

And the LORD struck the child that Uriah's
wife bore to David, and it became ill. 16David
therefore pleaded with God for the child, and
David fasted and went in and lay all night on the
ground. 17So the elders of his house arose *and
went* to him, to raise him up from the ground.
But he would not, nor did he eat food with them.
18Then on the seventh day it came to pass that
the child died. And the servants of David were
afraid to tell him that the child was dead. For
they said, "Indeed, while the child was alive, we
spoke to him, and he would not heed our voice.
How can we tell him that the child is dead? He
may do some harm!"
19When David saw that his servants were
whispering, David perceived that the child was
dead. Therefore David said to his servants, "Is
the child dead?"
And they said, "He is dead."
20So David arose from the ground, washed
and anointed himself, and changed his clothes;
and he went into the house of the LORD and wor-
shiped. Then he went to his own house; and
when he requested, they set food before him,
and he ate. 21Then his servants said to him,
"What *is* this that you have done? You fasted and
wept for the child *while he was* alive, but when
the child died, you arose and ate food."
22And he said, "While the child was alive, I
fasted and wept; for I said, 'Who can tell
whether the LORD[a] will be gracious to me, that
the child may live?' 23But now he is dead; why
should I fast? Can I bring him back again? I
shall go to him, but he shall not return to me."

Solomon Is Born

24Then David comforted Bathsheba his wife,
and went in to her and lay with her. So she bore
a son, and he[a] called his name Solomon. Now
the LORD loved him, 25and He sent *word* by the
hand of Nathan the prophet: So he[a] called his
name Jedidiah,[b] because of the LORD.

12:22 [a]A few Hebrew manuscripts and Syriac read *God.*
12:24 [a]Following Kethib, Septuagint, and Vulgate; Qere, a few Hebrew manuscripts, Syriac, and Targum read *she.* **12:25** [a]Qere, some Hebrew manuscripts, Syriac, and Targum read *she.* [b]Literally *Beloved of the LORD*

The Message

And now, because you treated GOD with
such contempt and took Uriah the Hittite's
wife as your wife, killing and murder will
continually plague your family. This is GOD
speaking, remember! I'll make trouble for
you out of your own family. I'll take your
wives from right out in front of you. I'll give
them to some neighbor, and he'll go to bed
with them openly. You did your deed in se-
cret; I'm doing mine with the whole country
watching!"
13-14 Then David confessed to Nathan, "I've
sinned against GOD."
Nathan pronounced, "Yes, but that's not
the last word. GOD forgives your sin. You
won't die for it. But because of your blas-
phemous behavior, the son born to you will
die."
15-18 After Nathan went home, GOD afflicted
the child that Uriah's wife bore to David,
and he came down sick. David prayed des-
perately to God for the little boy. He fasted,
wouldn't go out, and slept on the floor. The
elders in his family came in and tried to get
him off the floor, but he wouldn't budge. Nor
could they get him to eat anything. On the
seventh day the child died. David's servants
were afraid to tell him. They said, "What do
we do now? While the child was living he
wouldn't listen to a word we said. Now, with
the child dead, if we speak to him there's no
telling what he'll do."
19 David noticed that the servants were
whispering behind his back, and realized
that the boy must have died.
He asked the servants, "Is the boy dead?"
"Yes," they answered. "He's dead."
20 David got up from the floor, washed his
face and combed his hair, put on a fresh
change of clothes, then went into the sanc-
tuary and worshiped. Then he came home
and asked for something to eat. They set it
before him and he ate.
21 His servants asked him, "What's going on
with you? While the child was alive you
fasted and wept and stayed up all night.
Now that he's dead, you get up and eat."
22-23 "While the child was alive," he said, "I
fasted and wept, thinking GOD might have
mercy on me and the child would live. But
now that he's dead, why fast? Can I bring
him back now? I can go to him, but he can't
come to me."
24-25 David went and comforted his wife
Bathsheba. And when he slept with her, they
conceived a son. When he was born they
named him Solomon. GOD had a special love
for him and sent word by Nathan the
prophet that GOD wanted him named Jed-
idiah (God's Beloved).

NEW KING JAMES VERSION

RABBAH IS CAPTURED

[26]Now Joab fought against Rabbah of the people of Ammon, and took the royal city. [27]And Joab sent messengers to David, and said, "I have fought against Rabbah, and I have taken the city's water *supply.* [28]Now therefore, gather the rest of the people together and encamp against the city and take it, lest I take the city and it be called after my name." [29]So David gathered all the people together and went to Rabbah, fought against it, and took it. [30]Then he took their king's crown from his head. Its weight *was* a talent of gold, with precious stones. And it was *set* on David's head. Also he brought out the spoil of the city in great abundance. [31]And he brought out the people who *were* in it, and put *them to work* with saws and iron picks and iron axes, and made them cross over to the brick works. So he did to all the cities of the people of Ammon. Then David and all the people returned to Jerusalem.

AMNON AND TAMAR

13 After this Absalom the son of David had a lovely sister, whose name *was* Tamar; and Amnon the son of David loved her. [2]Amnon was so distressed over his sister Tamar that he became sick; for she *was* a virgin. And it was improper for Amnon to do anything to her. [3]But Amnon had a friend whose name *was* Jonadab the son of Shimeah, David's brother. Now Jonadab *was* a very crafty man. [4]And he said to him, "Why *are* you, the king's son, becoming thinner day after day? Will you not tell me?"

Amnon said to him, "I love Tamar, my brother Absalom's sister."

[5]So Jonadab said to him, "Lie down on your bed and pretend to be ill. And when your father comes to see you, say to him, 'Please let my sister Tamar come and give me food, and prepare the food in my sight, that I may see *it* and eat it from her hand.' " [6]Then Amnon lay down and pretended to be ill; and when the king came to see him, Amnon said to the king, "Please let Tamar my sister come and make a couple of cakes for me in my sight, that I may eat from her hand."

[7]And David sent home to Tamar, saying, "Now go to your brother Amnon's house, and prepare food for him." [8]So Tamar went to her brother Amnon's house; and he was lying down. Then she took flour and kneaded *it,* made cakes in his sight, and baked the cakes. [9]And she took the pan and placed *them* out before him, but he refused to eat. Then Amnon said, "Have everyone go out from me." And they all went out from him. [10]Then Amnon said to Tamar, "Bring the food into the bedroom, that I may eat from your hand." And Tamar took the cakes which she had made, and brought *them* to Amnon her brother in the bedroom. [11]Now when she had brought *them* to him to eat, he took hold of her and said to her, "Come, lie with me, my sister."

THE MESSAGE

26-30 Joab, at war in Rabbah against the Am-
monites, captured the royal city. He sent
messengers to David saying, "I'm fighting at
Rabbah, and I've just captured the city's wa-
ter supply. Hurry and get the rest of the
troops together and set up camp here at the
city and complete the capture yourself. Oth-
erwise, I'll capture it and get all the credit
instead of you." So David marshaled all the
troops, went to Rabbah, and fought and cap-
tured it. He took the crown from their king's
head—very heavy with gold, and with a pre-
cious stone in it. It ended up on David's
head. And they plundered the city, carrying
off a great quantity of loot.

31 David emptied the city of its people and
put them to slave labor using saws, picks,
and axes, and making bricks. He did this to
all the Ammonite cities. Then David and the
whole army returned to Jerusalem.

1-4 13 Some time later, this happened: Absa-
lom, David's son, had a sister who was
very attractive. Her name was Tamar. Am-
non, also David's son, was in love with her.
Amnon was obsessed with his sister Tamar
to the point of making himself sick over her.
She was a virgin, so he couldn't see how he
could get his hands on her. Amnon had a
good friend, Jonadab, the son of David's
brother Shimeah. Jonadab was exception-
ally streetwise. He said to Amnon, "Why are
you moping around like this, day after day—
you, the son of the king! Tell me what's eat-
ing at you."

"In a word, Tamar," said Amnon. "My
brother Absalom's sister. I'm in love with
her."

5 "Here's what you do," said Jonadab. "Go
to bed and pretend you're sick. When your
father comes to visit you, say, 'Have my sis-
ter Tamar come and prepare some supper
for me here where I can watch her and she
can feed me.' "

6 So Amnon took to his bed and acted sick.
When the king came to visit, Amnon said,
"Would you do me a favor? Have my sister
Tamar come and make some nourishing
dumplings here where I can watch her and
be fed by her."

7 David sent word to Tamar who was home
at the time: "Go to the house of your brother
Amnon and prepare a meal for him."

8-9 So Tamar went to her brother Amnon's
house. She took dough, kneaded it, formed it
into dumplings, and cooked them while he
watched from his bed. But when she took the
cooking pot and served him, he wouldn't eat.

9-11 Amnon said, "Clear everyone out of the
house," and they all cleared out. Then he
said to Tamar, "Bring the food into my bed-
room, where we can eat in privacy." She
took the nourishing dumplings she had pre-
pared and brought them to her brother Am-
non in his bedroom. But when she got ready
to feed him, he grabbed her and said, "Come
to bed with me, sister!"

New King James Version

12But she answered him, "No, my brother, do not force me, for no such thing should be done in Israel. Do not do this disgraceful thing! 13And I, where could I take my shame? And as for you, you would be like one of the fools in Israel. Now therefore, please speak to the king; for he will not withhold me from you." 14However, he would not heed her voice; and being stronger than she, he forced her and lay with her.

15Then Amnon hated her exceedingly, so that the hatred with which he hated her *was* greater than the love with which he had loved her. And Amnon said to her, "Arise, be gone!"

16So she said to him, "No, indeed! This evil of sending me away *is* worse than the other that you did to me."

But he would not listen to her. 17Then he called his servant who attended him, and said, "Here! Put this *woman* out, away from me, and bolt the door behind her." 18Now she had on a robe of many colors, for the king's virgin daughters wore such apparel. And his servant put her out and bolted the door behind her.

19Then Tamar put ashes on her head, and tore her robe of many colors that *was* on her, and laid her hand on her head and went away crying bitterly. 20And Absalom her brother said to her, "Has Amnon your brother been with you? But now hold your peace, my sister. He *is* your brother; do not take this thing to heart." So Tamar remained desolate in her brother Absalom's house.

21But when King David heard of all these things, he was very angry. 22And Absalom spoke to his brother Amnon neither good nor bad. For Absalom hated Amnon, because he had forced his sister Tamar.

Absalom Murders Amnon

23And it came to pass, after two full years, that Absalom had sheepshearers in Baal Hazor, which *is* near Ephraim; so Absalom invited all the king's sons. 24Then Absalom came to the king and said, "Kindly note, your servant has sheepshearers; please, let the king and his servants go with your servant."

25But the king said to Absalom, "No, my son, let us not all go now, lest we be a burden to you." Then he urged him, but he would not go; and he blessed him.

26Then Absalom said, "If not, please let my brother Amnon go with us."

And the king said to him, "Why should he go with you?" 27But Absalom urged him; so he let Amnon and all the king's sons go with him.

28Now Absalom had commanded his servants, saying, "Watch now, when Amnon's heart is merry with wine, and when I say to you, 'Strike Amnon!' then kill him. Do not be afraid. Have I not commanded you? Be courageous and valiant." 29So the servants of Absalom did to Amnon as Absalom had commanded. Then all the king's sons arose, and each one got on his mule and fled.

The Message

12-13 "No, brother!" she said, "Don't hurt me! This kind of thing isn't done in Israel! Don't do this terrible thing! Where could I ever show my face? And you—you'll be out on the street in disgrace. Oh, please! Speak to the king—he'll let you marry me."

14 But he wouldn't listen. Being much stronger than she, he raped her.

15 No sooner had Amnon raped her than he hated her—an immense hatred. The hatred that he felt for her was greater than the love he'd had for her. "Get up," he said, "and get out!"

16-18 "Oh no, brother," she said. "Please! This is an even worse evil than what you just did to me!"

But he wouldn't listen to her. He called for his valet. "Get rid of this woman. Get her out of my sight! And lock the door after her." The valet threw her out and locked the door behind her.

18-19 She was wearing a long-sleeved gown. (That's how virgin princesses used to dress from early adolescence on.) Tamar poured ashes on her head, then she ripped the long-sleeved gown, held her head in her hands, and walked away, sobbing as she went.

20 Her brother Absalom said to her, "Has your brother Amnon had his way with you? Now, my dear sister, let's keep it quiet—a family matter. He is, after all, your brother. Don't take this so hard." Tamar lived in her brother Absalom's home, bitter and desolate.

21-22 King David heard the whole story and was enraged, but he didn't discipline Amnon. David doted on him because he was his firstborn. Absalom quit speaking to Amnon—not a word, whether good or bad—because he hated him for violating his sister Tamar.

23-24 Two years went by. One day Absalom threw a sheep-shearing party in Baal Hazor in the vicinity of Ephraim and invited all the king's sons. He also went to the king and invited him. "Look, I'm throwing a sheep-shearing party. Come, and bring your servants."

25 But the king said, "No, son—not this time, and not the whole household. We'd just be a burden to you." Absalom pushed, but David wouldn't budge. But he did give him his blessing.

26-27 Then Absalom said, "Well, if you won't come, at least let my brother Amnon come."

"And why," said the king, "should he go with you?" But Absalom was so insistent that he gave in and let Amnon and all the rest of the king's sons go.

28 Absalom prepared a banquet fit for a king. Then he instructed his servants, "Look sharp, now. When Amnon is well into the sauce and feeling no pain, and I give the order 'Strike Amnon,' kill him. And don't be afraid—I'm the one giving the command. Courage! You can do it!"

29-31 Absalom's servants did to Amnon exactly what their master ordered. All the king's sons got out as fast as they could, jumped on their mules, and rode off. While they were

NEW KING JAMES VERSION

30 And it came to pass, while they were on the way, that news came to David, saying, "Absalom has killed all the king's sons, and not one of them is left!" 31 So the king arose and tore his garments and lay on the ground, and all his servants stood by with their clothes torn. 32 Then Jonadab the son of Shimeah, David's brother, answered and said, "Let not my lord suppose they have killed all the young men, the king's sons, for only Amnon is dead. For by the command of Absalom this has been determined from the day that he forced his sister Tamar. 33 Now therefore, let not my lord the king take the thing to his heart, to think that all the king's sons are dead. For only Amnon is dead."

ABSALOM FLEES TO GESHUR

34 Then Absalom fled. And the young man who was keeping watch lifted his eyes and looked, and there, many people were coming from the road on the hillside behind him.[a] 35 And Jonadab said to the king, "Look, the king's sons are coming; as your servant said, so it is." 36 So it was, as soon as he had finished speaking, that the king's sons indeed came, and they lifted up their voice and wept. Also the king and all his servants wept very bitterly.

37 But Absalom fled and went to Talmai the son of Ammihud, king of Geshur. And *David* mourned for his son every day. 38 So Absalom fled and went to Geshur, and was there three years. 39 And King David[a] longed to go to[b] Absalom. For he had been comforted concerning Amnon, because he was dead.

ABSALOM RETURNS TO JERUSALEM

14 So Joab the son of Zeruiah perceived that the king's heart *was* concerned about Absalom. 2 And Joab sent to Tekoa and brought from there a wise woman, and said to her, "Please pretend to be a mourner, and put on mourning apparel; do not anoint yourself with oil, but act like a woman who has been mourning a long time for the dead. 3 Go to the king and speak to him in this manner." So Joab put the words in her mouth.

4 And when the woman of Tekoa spoke[a] to the king, she fell on her face to the ground and prostrated herself, and said, "Help, O king!"

5 Then the king said to her, "What troubles you?"

And she answered, "Indeed I *am* a widow, my husband is dead. 6 Now your maidservant had two sons; and the two fought with each other in the field, and *there was* no one to part them, but the one struck the other and killed him. 7 And now the whole family has risen up against your maidservant, and they said, 'Deliver him who struck his brother, that we may

13:34 [a]Septuagint adds *And the watchman went and told the king, and said, "I see men from the way of Horonaim, from the regions of the mountains."* **13:39** [a]Following Masoretic Text, Syriac, and Vulgate; Septuagint reads *the spirit of the king;* Targum reads *the soul of King David.* [b]Following Masoretic Text and Targum; Septuagint and Vulgate read *ceased to pursue after.* **14:4** [a]Many Hebrew manuscripts, Septuagint, Syriac, and Vulgate read *came.*

THE MESSAGE

still on the road, a rumor came to the king:
"Absalom just killed all the king's sons—not
one is left!" The king stood up, ripped his
clothes to shreds, and threw himself on the
floor. All his servants who were standing
around at the time did the same.
32-33 Just then, Jonadab, his brother Shim-
eah's son, stepped up. "My master must not
think that all the young men, the king's
sons, are dead. Only Amnon is dead. This
happened because of Absalom's outrage
since the day that Amnon violated his sister
Tamar. So my master, the king, mustn't
make things worse than they are, thinking
that all your sons are dead. Only Amnon is
dead."
34 Absalom fled.
Just then the sentry on duty looked up
and saw a cloud of dust on the road from
Horonaim alongside the mountain. He came
and told the king, "I've just seen a bunch of
men on the Horonaim road, coming around
the mountain."
35-37 Then Jonadab exclaimed to the king,
"See! It's the king's sons coming, just as I
said!" He had no sooner said the words than
the king's sons burst in—loud laments and
weeping! The king joined in, along with all
the servants—loud weeping, many tears.
David mourned the death of his son a long
time.
37-39 When Absalom fled, he went to Talmai
son of Ammihud, king of Geshur. He was
there three years. The king finally gave up
trying to get back at Absalom. He had come
to terms with Amnon's death.

1-3 14 Joab son of Zeruiah knew that the
king, deep down, still cared for Absa-
lom. So he sent to Tekoa for a wise woman
who lived there and instructed her, "Pretend
you are in mourning. Dress in black and
don't comb your hair, so you'll look like
you've been grieving over a dead loved one
for a long time. Then go to the king and tell
him this . . ." Joab then told her exactly
what to say.
4 The woman of Tekoa went to the king,
bowed deeply before him in homage, and
said, "O King, help!"
5-7 He said, "How can I help?"
"I'm a widow," she said. "My husband is
dead. I had two sons. The two of them got
into a fight out in the field and there was no
one around to step between them. The one
struck the other and killed him. Then the
whole family ganged up against me and de-
manded, 'Hand over this murderer so we
can kill him for the life of the brother he

New King James Version

execute him for the life of his brother whom he
killed; and we will destroy the heir also.' So they
would extinguish my ember that is left, and
leave to my husband *neither* name nor remnant
on the earth."
8 Then the king said to the woman, "Go to your
house, and I will give orders concerning you."
9 And the woman of Tekoa said to the king,
"My lord, O king, *let* the iniquity *be* on me and
on my father's house, and the king and his
throne *be* guiltless."
10 So the king said, "Whoever says *anything*
to you, bring him to me, and he shall not touch
you anymore."
11 Then she said, "Please let the king remem-
ber the LORD your God, and do not permit the
avenger of blood to destroy anymore, lest they
destroy my son."
And he said, "*As* the LORD lives, not one hair
of your son shall fall to the ground."
12 Therefore the woman said, "Please, let your
maidservant speak *another* word to my lord the
king."
And he said, "Say on."
13 So the woman said: "Why then have you
schemed such a thing against the people of God?
For the king speaks this thing as one who is guilty,
in that the king does not bring his banished one
home again. 14 For we will surely die and *become*
like water spilled on the ground, which cannot be
gathered up again. Yet God does not take away a
life; but He devises means, so that His banished
ones are not expelled from Him. 15 Now therefore,
I have come to speak of this thing to my lord the
king because the people have made me afraid.
And your maidservant said, 'I will now speak to
the king; it may be that the king will perform the
request of his maidservant. 16 For the king will
hear and deliver his maidservant from the hand
of the man *who would* destroy me and my son to-
gether from the inheritance of God.' 17 Your maid-
servant said, 'The word of my lord the king will
now be comforting; for as the angel of God, so *is*
my lord the king in discerning good and evil. And
may the LORD your God be with you.' "
18 Then the king answered and said to the
woman, "Please do not hide from me anything
that I ask you."
And the woman said, "Please, let my lord the
king speak."
19 So the king said, "*Is* the hand of Joab with
you in all this?" And the woman answered and
said, "*As* you live, my lord the king, no one can
turn to the right hand or to the left from any-
thing that my lord the king has spoken. For your
servant Joab commanded me, and he put all
these words in the mouth of your maidservant.
20 To bring about this change of affairs your ser-
vant Joab has done this thing; but my lord *is*
wise, according to the wisdom of the angel of
God, to know everything that *is* in the earth."
21 And the king said to Joab, "All right, I have
granted this thing. Go therefore, bring back the
young man Absalom."
22 Then Joab fell to the ground on his face and
bowed himself, and thanked the king. And Joab
said, "Today your servant knows that I have
found favor in your sight, my lord, O king, in that
the king has fulfilled the request of his servant."

The Message

murdered!' They want to wipe out the heir
and snuff out the one spark of life left to me.
And then there would be nothing left of my
husband—not so much as a name—on the
face of the earth.
15-17 "So now I've dared come to the king, my
master, about all this. They're making my
life miserable, and I'm afraid. I said to my-
self, 'I'll go to the king. Maybe he'll do some-
thing! When the king hears what's going on,
he'll step in and rescue me from the abuse of
the man who would get rid of me and my
son and God's inheritance—the works!' As
your handmaid, I decided ahead of time,
'The word of my master, the king, will be the
last word in this, for my master is like an an-
gel of God in discerning good and evil.' GOD
be with you!"
8 The king said, "Go home, and I'll take
care of this for you."
9 "I'll take all responsibility for what hap-
pens," the woman of Tekoa said. "I don't
want to compromise the king and his repu-
tation."
10 "Bring the man who has been harassing
you," the king continued. "I'll see to it that
he doesn't bother you anymore."
11 "Let the king invoke the name of GOD,"
said the woman, "so this self-styled vigilante
won't ruin everything, to say nothing of
killing my son."
"As surely as GOD lives," he said, "not so
much as a hair of your son's head will be
lost."
12 Then she asked, "May I say one more
thing to my master, the king?"
He said, "Go ahead."
13-14 "Why, then," the woman said, "have you
done this very thing against God's people?
In his verdict, the king convicts himself by
not bringing home his exiled son. We all die
sometime. Water spilled on the ground can't
be gathered up again. But God does not take
away life. He works out ways to get the ex-
ile back."
18 The king then said, "I'm going to ask you
something. Answer me truthfully."
"Certainly," she said. "Let my master, the
king, speak."
19-20 The king said, "Is the hand of Joab mixed
up in this?"
"On your life, my master king, a body
can't veer an inch right or left and get by
with it in the royal presence! Yes, it was your
servant Joab who put me up to this, and put
these very words in my mouth. It was be-
cause he wanted to turn things around that
your servant Joab did this. But my master is
as wise as God's angels in knowing how to
handle things on this earth."
21 The king spoke to Joab. "All right, I'll do
it. Go and bring the young man Absalom
back."
22 Joab bowed deeply in reverence and
blessed the king. "I'm reassured to know
that I'm still in your good graces and have
your confidence, since the king is taking the
counsel of his servant."

New King James Version

23So Joab arose and went to Geshur, and
brought Absalom to Jerusalem. 24And the king
said, "Let him return to his own house, but do
not let him see my face." So Absalom returned
to his own house, but did not see the king's
face.

David Forgives Absalom

25Now in all Israel there was no one who was
praised as much as Absalom for his good looks.
From the sole of his foot to the crown of his
head there was no blemish in him. 26And when
he cut the hair of his head—at the end of every
year he cut *it* because it was heavy on him—
when he cut it, he weighed the hair of his head
at two hundred shekels according to the king's
standard. 27To Absalom were born three sons,
and one daughter whose name *was* Tamar. She
was a woman of beautiful appearance.

28And Absalom dwelt two full years in
Jerusalem, but did not see the king's face.
29Therefore Absalom sent for Joab, to send him
to the king, but he would not come to him. And
when he sent again the second time, he would
not come. 30So he said to his servants, "See,
Joab's field is near mine, and he has barley
there; go and set it on fire." And Absalom's ser-
vants set the field on fire.

31Then Joab arose and came to Absalom's
house, and said to him, "Why have your ser-
vants set my field on fire?"

32And Absalom answered Joab, "Look, I sent
to you, saying, 'Come here, so that I may send
you to the king, to say, "Why have I come from
Geshur? *It would be* better for me *to be* there
still." ' Now therefore, let me see the king's face;
but if there is iniquity in me, let him execute
me."

33So Joab went to the king and told him. And
when he had called for Absalom, he came to the
king and bowed himself on his face to the
ground before the king. Then the king kissed
Absalom.

Absalom's Treason

15 After this it happened that Absalom pro-
vided himself with chariots and horses, and
fifty men to run before him. 2Now Absalom
would rise early and stand beside the way to the
gate. *So* it was, whenever anyone who had a law-
suit came to the king for a decision, that Absalom
would call to him and say, "What city *are* you
from?" And he would say, "Your servant *is* from
such and such a tribe of Israel." 3Then Absalom
would say to him, "Look, your case *is* good and
right; but *there is* no deputy of the king to hear
you." 4Moreover Absalom would say, "Oh, that I
were made judge in the land, and everyone who
has any suit or cause would come to me; then I
would give him justice." 5And *so* it was, whenever
anyone came near to bow down to him, that he
would put out his hand and take him and kiss
him. 6In this manner Absalom acted toward all Is-
rael who came to the king for judgment. So Ab-
salom stole the hearts of the men of Israel.

7Now it came to pass after forty[a] years that
Absalom said to the king, "Please, let me go to

15:7 [a]Septuagint manuscripts, Syriac, and Josephus read *four*.

The Message

23-24 Joab got up, went to Geshur, and brought Absalom to Jerusalem. The king said, "He may return to his house, but he is not to see me face-to-face." So Absalom returned home, but was not permitted to see the king.

25-27 This Absalom! There wasn't a man in all Israel talked about so much for his handsome good looks—and not a blemish on him from head to toe! When he cut his hair—he always cut it short in the spring because it had grown so heavy—the weight of the hair from his head was over two pounds! Three sons were born to Absalom, and one daughter. Her name was Tamar—and she was a beauty.

28-31 Absalom lived in Jerusalem for two years, and not once did he see the king face-to-face. He sent for Joab to get him in to see the king, but Joab still wouldn't budge. He tried a second time and Joab still wouldn't. So he told his servants, "Listen. Joab's field adjoins mine, and he has a crop of barley in it. Go set fire to it." So Absalom's servants set fire to the field. That got him moving—Joab came to Absalom at home and said, "Why did your servants set my field on fire?"

32 Absalom answered him, "Listen, I sent for you saying, 'Come, and soon. I want to send you to the king to ask, "What's the point of my coming back from Geshur? I'd be better off still there!" Let me see the king face-to-face. If he finds me guilty, then he can put me to death.' "

33 Joab went to the king and told him what was going on. Absalom was then summoned—he came and bowed deeply in reverence before him. And the king kissed Absalom.

1-2 15 As time went on, Absalom took to riding in a horse-drawn chariot, with fifty men running in front of him. Early each morning he would take up his post beside the road at the city gate. When anyone showed up with a case to bring to the king for a decision, Absalom would call him over and say, "Where do you hail from?"

And the answer would come, "Your servant is from one of the tribes of Israel."

3-6 Then Absalom would say, "Look, you've got a strong case; but the king isn't going to listen to you." Then he'd say, "Why doesn't someone make me a judge for this country? Anybody with a case could bring it to me and I'd settle things fair and square." Whenever someone would treat him with special honor, he'd shrug it off and treat him like an equal, making him feel important. Absalom did this to everyone who came to do business with the king and stole the hearts of everyone in Israel.

7-8 After four years of this, Absalom spoke to the king, "Let me go to Hebron to pay a vow

New King James Version

Hebron and pay the vow which I made to the LORD. 8For your servant took a vow while I dwelt at Geshur in Syria, saying, 'If the LORD indeed brings me back to Jerusalem, then I will serve the LORD.' "

9And the king said to him, "Go in peace." So he arose and went to Hebron.

10Then Absalom sent spies throughout all the tribes of Israel, saying, "As soon as you hear the sound of the trumpet, then you shall say, 'Absalom reigns in Hebron!' " 11And with Absalom went two hundred men invited from Jerusalem, and they went along innocently and did not know anything. 12Then Absalom sent for Ahithophel the Gilonite, David's counselor, from his city—from Giloh—while he offered sacrifices. And the conspiracy grew strong, for the people with Absalom continually increased in number.

David Escapes from Jerusalem

13Now a messenger came to David, saying, "The hearts of the men of Israel are with Absalom."

14So David said to all his servants who *were* with him at Jerusalem, "Arise, and let us flee, or we shall not escape from Absalom. Make haste to depart, lest he overtake us suddenly and bring disaster upon us, and strike the city with the edge of the sword."

15And the king's servants said to the king, "We *are* your servants, *ready to do* whatever my lord the king commands." 16Then the king went out with all his household after him. But the king left ten women, concubines, to keep the house. 17And the king went out with all the people after him, and stopped at the outskirts. 18Then all his servants passed before him; and all the Cherethites, all the Pelethites, and all the Gittites, six hundred men who had followed him from Gath, passed before the king.

19Then the king said to Ittai the Gittite, "Why are you also going with us? Return and remain with the king. For you *are* a foreigner and also an exile from your own place. 20In fact, you came *only* yesterday. Should I make you wander up and down with us today, since I go I know not where? Return, and take your brethren back. Mercy and truth *be* with you."

21But Ittai answered the king and said, "*As* the LORD lives, and *as* my lord the king lives, surely in whatever place my lord the king shall be, whether in death or life, even there also your servant will be."

22So David said to Ittai, "Go, and cross over." Then Ittai the Gittite and all his men and all the little ones who *were* with him crossed over. 23And all the country wept with a loud voice, and all the people crossed over. The king himself also crossed over the Brook Kidron, and all the people crossed over toward the way of the wilderness.

24There was Zadok also, and all the Levites with him, bearing the ark of the covenant of God. And they set down the ark of God, and Abiathar went up until all the people had finished crossing over from the city. 25Then the king said to Zadok, "Carry the ark of God back into the city. If I find favor in the eyes of the LORD, He

The Message

that I made to GOD. Your servant made a vow when I was living in Geshur in Aram saying, 'If GOD will bring me back to Jerusalem, I'll serve him with my life.' "

9 The king said, "Go with my blessing." And he got up and set off for Hebron.

10-12 Then Absalom sent undercover agents to all the tribes of Israel with the message, "When you hear the blast of the ram's horn trumpet, that's your signal: Shout, 'Absalom is king in Hebron!' " Two hundred men went with Absalom from Jerusalem. But they had been called together knowing nothing of the plot and made the trip innocently. While Absalom was offering sacrifices, he managed also to involve Ahithophel the Gilonite, David's advisor, calling him away from his hometown of Giloh. The conspiracy grew powerful and Absalom's supporters multiplied.

13 Someone came to David with the report, "The whole country has taken up with Absalom!"

14 "Up and out of here!" called David to all his servants who were with him in Jerusalem. "We've got to run for our lives or none of us will escape Absalom! Hurry, he's about to pull the city down around our ears and slaughter us all!"

15 The king's servants said, "Whatever our master, the king, says, we'll do; we're with you all the way!"

16-18 So the king and his entire household escaped on foot. The king left ten concubines behind to tend to the palace. And so they left, step by step by step, and then paused at the last house as the whole army passed by him—all the Kerethites, all the Pelethites, and the six hundred Gittites who had marched with him from Gath, went past.

19-20 The king called out to Ittai the Gittite, "What are you doing here? Go back with King Absalom. You're a stranger here and freshly uprooted from your own country. You arrived only yesterday, and am I going to let you take your chances with us as I live on the road like a gypsy? Go back, and take your family with you. And God's grace and truth go with you!"

21 But Ittai answered, "As GOD lives and my master the king lives, where my master is, that's where I'll be—whether it means life or death."

22 "All right," said David, "go ahead." And they went on, Ittai the Gittite with all his men and all the children he had with him.

23-24 The whole country was weeping in loud lament as all the people passed by. As the king crossed the Brook Kidron, the army headed for the road to the wilderness. Zadok was also there, the Levites with him, carrying GOD's Chest of the Covenant. They set the Chest of God down, Abiathar standing by, until all the people had evacuated the city.

25-26 Then the king ordered Zadok, "Take the Chest back to the city. If I get back in GOD's good graces, he'll bring me back and show

NEW KING JAMES VERSION

will bring me back and show me *both* it and His dwelling place. [26]But if He says thus: 'I have no delight in you,' here I am, let Him do to me as seems good to Him." [27]The king also said to Zadok the priest, "*Are* you *not* a seer? Return to the city in peace, and your two sons with you, Ahimaaz your son, and Jonathan the son of Abiathar. [28]See, I will wait in the plains of the wilderness until word comes from you to inform me." [29]Therefore Zadok and Abiathar carried the ark of God back to Jerusalem. And they remained there.

[30]So David went up by the Ascent of the *Mount of* Olives, and wept as he went up; and he had his head covered and went barefoot. And all the people who *were* with him covered their heads and went up, weeping as they went up. [31]Then *someone* told David, saying, "Ahithophel *is* among the conspirators with Absalom." And David said, "O LORD, I pray, turn the counsel of Ahithophel into foolishness!"

[32]Now it happened when David had come to the top *of the mountain,* where he worshiped God—there was Hushai the Archite coming to meet him with his robe torn and dust on his head. [33]David said to him, "If you go on with me, then you will become a burden to me. [34]But if you return to the city, and say to Absalom, 'I will be your servant, O king; *as* I *was* your father's servant previously, so I *will* now also *be* your servant,' then you may defeat the counsel of Ahithophel for me. [35]And *do* you not *have* Zadok and Abiathar the priests with you there? Therefore it will be *that* whatever you hear from the king's house, you shall tell to Zadok and Abiathar the priests. [36]Indeed *they have* there with them their two sons, Ahimaaz, Zadok's *son,* and Jonathan, Abiathar's *son;* and by them you shall send me everything you hear."

[37]So Hushai, David's friend, went into the city. And Absalom came into Jerusalem.

MEPHIBOSHETH'S SERVANT

16 When David was a little past the top *of the mountain,* there was Ziba the servant of Mephibosheth, who met him with a couple of saddled donkeys, and on them two hundred *loaves* of bread, one hundred clusters of raisins, one hundred summer fruits, and a skin of wine. [2]And the king said to Ziba, "What do you mean to do with these?"

So Ziba said, "The donkeys *are* for the king's household to ride on, the bread and summer fruit for the young men to eat, and the wine for those who are faint in the wilderness to drink."

[3]Then the king said, "And where *is* your master's son?"

And Ziba said to the king, "Indeed he is staying in Jerusalem, for he said, 'Today the house of Israel will restore the kingdom of my father to me.' "

[4]So the king said to Ziba, "Here, all that *belongs* to Mephibosheth *is* yours."

And Ziba said, "I humbly bow before you, *that* I may find favor in your sight, my lord, O king!"

THE MESSAGE

me where the Chest has been set down. But if he says, 'I'm not pleased with you'—well, he can then do with me whatever he pleases."

27-30 The king directed Zadok the priest, "Here's the plan: Return to the city peacefully, with Ahimaaz your son and Jonathan, Abiathar's son, with you. I'll wait at a spot in the wilderness across the river, until I get word from you telling us what's up." So Zadok and Abiathar took the Chest of God back to Jerusalem and placed it there, while David went up the Mount of Olives weeping, head covered but barefooted, and the whole army was with him, heads covered and weeping as they ascended.

31 David was told, "Ahithophel has joined the conspirators with Absalom." He prayed, "Oh, GOD—turn Ahithophel's counsel to foolishness."

32-36 As David approached the top of the hill where God was worshiped, Hushai the Arkite, clothes ripped to shreds and dirt on his head, was there waiting for him. David said, "If you come with me, you'll be just one more piece of luggage. Go back to the city and say to Absalom, 'I'm ready to be your servant, O King; I used to be your father's servant, now I'm your servant.' Do that and you'll be able to confuse Ahithophel's counsel for me. The priests Zadok and Abiathar are already there; whatever information you pick up in the palace, tell them. Their two sons—Zadok's son Ahimaaz and Abiathar's son Jonathan—are there with them—anything you pick up can be sent to me by them."

37 Hushai, David's friend, arrived at the same time Absalom was entering Jerusalem.

1 16 Shortly after David passed the crest of the hill, Mephibosheth's steward Ziba met him with a string of pack animals, saddled and loaded with a hundred loaves of bread, a hundred raisin cakes, a hundred baskets of fresh fruit, and a skin of wine.

2 The king said to Ziba, "What's all this?"

"The donkeys," said Ziba, "are for the king's household to ride, the bread and fruit are for the servants to eat, and the wine is for drinking, especially for those overcome by fatigue in the wilderness."

3 The king said, "And where is your master's grandson?"

"He stayed in Jerusalem," said Ziba. "He said, 'This is the day Israel is going to restore my grandfather's kingdom to me.' "

4 "Everything that belonged to Mephibosheth," said the king, "is now yours."

Ziba said, "How can I ever thank you? I'll be forever in your debt, my master and king; may you always look on me with such kindness!"

NEW KING JAMES VERSION

SHIMEI CURSES DAVID

5 Now when King David came to Bahurim, there was a man from the family of the house of Saul, whose name *was* Shimei the son of Gera, coming from there. He came out, cursing continuously as he came. 6 And he threw stones at David and at all the servants of King David. And all the people and all the mighty men *were* on his right hand and on his left. 7 Also Shimei said thus when he cursed: "Come out! Come out! You bloodthirsty man, you rogue! 8 The LORD has brought upon you all the blood of the house of Saul, in whose place you have reigned; and the LORD has delivered the kingdom into the hand of Absalom your son. So now you *are caught* in your own evil, because you are a bloodthirsty man!"

9 Then Abishai the son of Zeruiah said to the king, "Why should this dead dog curse my lord the king? Please, let me go over and take off his head!"

10 But the king said, "What have I to do with you, you sons of Zeruiah? So let him curse, because the LORD has said to him, 'Curse David.' Who then shall say, 'Why have you done so?' "

11 And David said to Abishai and all his servants, "See how my son who came from my own body seeks my life. How much more now *may this* Benjamite? Let him alone, and let him curse; for so the LORD has ordered him. 12 It may be that the LORD will look on my affliction,[a] and that the LORD will repay me with good for his cursing this day." 13 And as David and his men went along the road, Shimei went along the hillside opposite him and cursed as he went, threw stones at him and kicked up dust. 14 Now the king and all the people who *were* with him became weary; so they refreshed themselves there.

THE ADVICE OF AHITHOPHEL

15 Meanwhile Absalom and all the people, the men of Israel, came to Jerusalem; and Ahithophel *was* with him. 16 And so it was, when Hushai the Archite, David's friend, came to Absalom, that Hushai said to Absalom, "*Long* live the king! *Long* live the king!"

17 So Absalom said to Hushai, "*Is* this your loyalty to your friend? Why did you not go with your friend?"

18 And Hushai said to Absalom, "No, but whom the LORD and this people and all the men of Israel choose, his I will be, and with him I will remain. 19 "Furthermore, whom should I serve? *Should I* not *serve* in the presence of his son? As I have served in your father's presence, so will I be in your presence."

20 Then Absalom said to Ahithophel, "Give advice as to what we should do."

21 And Ahithophel said to Absalom, "Go in to your father's concubines, whom he has left to keep the house; and all Israel will hear that you are abhorred by your father. Then the hands of all who are with you will be strong." 22 So they pitched a tent for Absalom on the top of the house, and Absalom went in to his father's concubines in the sight of all Israel.

16:12 [a]Following Kethib, Septuagint, Syriac, and Vulgate; Qere reads *my eyes;* Targum reads *tears of my eyes.*

THE MESSAGE

5-8 When the king got to Bahurim, a man appeared who had connections with Saul's family. His name was Shimei son of Gera. As he followed along he shouted insults and threw rocks right and left at David and his company, servants and soldiers alike. To the accompaniment of curses he shouted, "Get lost, get lost, you butcher, you hellhound! GOD has paid you back for all your dirty work in the family of Saul and for stealing his kingdom. GOD has given the kingdom to your son Absalom. Look at you now—ruined! And good riddance, you pathetic old man!"

9 Abishai son of Zeruiah said, "This mangy dog can't insult my master the king this way—let me go over and cut off his head!"

10 But the king said, "Why are you sons of Zeruiah always interfering and getting in the way? If he's cursing, it's because GOD told him, 'Curse David.' So who dares raise questions?"

11-12 "Besides," continued David to Abishai and the rest of his servants, "my own son, my flesh and bone, is right now trying to kill me; compared to that this Benjaminite is small potatoes. Don't bother with him; let him curse; he's preaching GOD's word to me. And who knows, maybe GOD will see the trouble I'm in today and exchange the curses for something good."

13 David and his men went on down the road, while Shimei followed along on the ridge of the hill alongside, cursing, throwing stones down on them, and kicking up dirt.

14 By the time they reached the Jordan River, David and all the men of the company were exhausted. There they rested and were revived.

15 By this time Absalom and all his men were in Jerusalem.

And Ahithophel was with them.

16 Soon after, Hushai the Arkite, David's friend, came and greeted Absalom, "Long live the king! Long live the king!"

17 Absalom said to Hushai, "Is this the way you show devotion to your good friend? Why didn't you go with your friend David?"

18-19 "Because," said Hushai, "I want to be with the person that GOD and this people and all Israel have chosen. And I want to stay with him. Besides, who is there to serve other than the son? Just as I served your father, I'm now ready to serve you."

20 Then Absalom spoke to Ahithophel, "Are you ready to give counsel? What do we do next?"

21-22 Ahithophel told Absalom, "Go and sleep with your father's concubines, the ones he left to tend to the palace. Everyone will hear that you have openly disgraced your father, and the morale of everyone on your side will be strengthened." So Absalom pitched a tent up on the roof in public view, and went in and slept with his father's concubines.

New King James Version

23 Now the advice of Ahithophel, which he
gave in those days, *was* as if one had inquired at
the oracle of God. So *was* all the advice of
Ahithophel both with David and with Absalom.

17 Moreover Ahithophel said to Absalom,
"Now let me choose twelve thousand men,
and I will arise and pursue David tonight. 2 I will
come upon him while he *is* weary and weak, and
make him afraid. And all the people who *are*
with him will flee, and I will strike only the king.
3 Then I will bring back all the people to you.
When all return except the man whom you seek,
all the people will be at peace." 4 And the saying
pleased Absalom and all the elders of Israel.

The Advice of Hushai

5 Then Absalom said, "Now call Hushai the
Archite also, and let us hear what he says too."
6 And when Hushai came to Absalom, Absalom
spoke to him, saying, "Ahithophel has spoken in
this manner. Shall we do as he says? If not,
speak up."
7 So Hushai said to Absalom: "The advice
that Ahithophel has given *is* not good at this
time. 8 For," said Hushai, "you know your father
and his men, that they *are* mighty men, and they
are enraged in their minds, like a bear robbed of
her cubs in the field; and your father *is* a man of
war, and will not camp with the people. 9 Surely
by now he is hidden in some pit, or in some
other place. And it will be, when some of them
are overthrown at the first, that whoever hears
it will say, 'There is a slaughter among the peo-
ple who follow Absalom.' 10 And even he *who is*
valiant, whose heart *is* like the heart of a lion,
will melt completely. For all Israel knows that
your father *is* a mighty man, and *those* who *are*
with him *are* valiant men. 11 Therefore I advise
that all Israel be fully gathered to you, from Dan
to Beersheba, like the sand that *is* by the sea for
multitude, and that you go to battle in person.
12 So we will come upon him in some place
where he may be found, and we will fall on him
as the dew falls on the ground. And of him and
all the men who *are* with him there shall not be
left so much as one. 13 Moreover, if he has with-
drawn into a city, then all Israel shall bring
ropes to that city; and we will pull it into the
river, until there is not one small stone found
there."
14 So Absalom and all the men of Israel said,
"The advice of Hushai the Archite *is* better than
the advice of Ahithophel." For the LORD had pur-
posed to defeat the good advice of Ahithophel,
to the intent that the LORD might bring disaster
on Absalom.

Hushai Warns David to Escape

15 Then Hushai said to Zadok and Abiathar
the priests, "Thus and so Ahithophel advised
Absalom and the elders of Israel, and thus and
so I have advised. 16 Now therefore, send quickly
and tell David, saying, 'Do not spend this night
in the plains of the wilderness, but speedily
cross over, lest the king and all the people who
are with him be swallowed up.' "

The Message

23 The counsel that Ahithophel gave in those days was treated as if God himself had spoken. That was the reputation of Ahithophel's counsel to David; it was the same with Absalom.

1-3 17 Next Ahithophel advised Absalom, "Let me handpick twelve thousand men and go after David tonight. I'll come on him when he's bone tired and take him by complete surprise. The whole army will run off and I'll kill only David. Then I'll bring the army back to you—a bride brought back to her husband! You're only after one man, after all. Then everyone will be together in peace!"

4 Absalom thought it was an excellent strategy, and all the elders of Israel agreed.

5 But then Absalom said, "Call in Hushai the Arkite—let's hear what he has to say."

6 So Hushai came and Absalom put it to him, "This is what Ahithophel advised. Should we do it? What do you say?"

7-10 Hushai said, "The counsel that Ahithophel has given in this instance is not good. You know your father and his men, brave and bitterly angry—like a bear robbed of her cubs. And your father is an experienced fighter; you can be sure he won't be caught napping at a time like this. Even while we're talking, he's probably holed up in some cave or other. If he jumps your men from ambush, word will soon get back, 'A slaughter of Absalom's army!' Even if your men are valiant with hearts of lions, they'll fall apart at such news, for everyone in Israel knows the kind of fighting stuff your father's made of, and also the men with him.

11-13 "Here's what I'd advise: Muster the whole country, from Dan to Beersheba, an army like the sand of the sea, and you personally lead them. We'll smoke him out wherever he is, fall on him like dew falls on the earth, and, believe me, there won't be a single survivor. If he hides out in a city, then the whole army will bring ropes to that city and pull it down and into a gully—not so much as a pebble left of it!"

14 Absalom and all his company agreed that the counsel of Hushai the Arkite was better than the counsel of Ahithophel. (GOD had determined to discredit the counsel of Ahithophel so as to bring ruin on Absalom.)

15-16 Then Hushai told the priests Zadok and Abiathar, "Ahithophel advised Absalom and the elders of Israel thus and thus, and I advised them thus and thus. Now send this message as quickly as possible to David: 'Don't spend the night on this side of the river; cross immediately or the king and everyone with him will be swallowed up alive.' "

NEW KING JAMES VERSION

17Now Jonathan and Ahimaaz stayed at En Rogel, for they dared not be seen coming into the city; so a female servant would come and tell them, and they would go and tell King David. 18Nevertheless a lad saw them, and told Absalom. But both of them went away quickly and came to a man's house in Bahurim, who had a well in his court; and they went down into it. 19Then the woman took and spread a covering over the well's mouth, and spread ground grain on it; and the thing was not known. 20And when Absalom's servants came to the woman at the house, they said, "Where *are* Ahimaaz and Jonathan?"

So the woman said to them, "They have gone over the water brook."

And when they had searched and could not find *them*, they returned to Jerusalem. 21Now it came to pass, after they had departed, that they came up out of the well and went and told King David, and said to David, "Arise and cross over the water quickly. For thus has Ahithophel advised against you." 22So David and all the people who *were* with him arose and crossed over the Jordan. By morning light not one of them was left who had not gone over the Jordan.

23Now when Ahithophel saw that his advice was not followed, he saddled a donkey, and arose and went home to his house, to his city. Then he put his household in order, and hanged himself, and died; and he was buried in his father's tomb.

24Then David went to Mahanaim. And Absalom crossed over the Jordan, he and all the men of Israel with him. 25And Absalom made Amasa captain of the army instead of Joab. This Amasa *was* the son of a man whose name *was* Jithra,[a] an Israelite,[b] who had gone in to Abigail the daughter of Nahash, sister of Zeruiah, Joab's mother. 26So Israel and Absalom encamped in the land of Gilead.

27Now it happened, when David had come to Mahanaim, that Shobi the son of Nahash from Rabbah of the people of Ammon, Machir the son of Ammiel from Lo Debar, and Barzillai the Gileadite from Rogelim, 28brought beds and basins, earthen vessels and wheat, barley and flour, parched *grain* and beans, lentils and parched *seeds*, 29honey and curds, sheep and cheese of the herd, for David and the people who *were* with him to eat. For they said, "The people are hungry and weary and thirsty in the wilderness."

ABSALOM'S DEFEAT AND DEATH

18 And David numbered the people who *were* with him, and set captains of thousands and captains of hundreds over them. 2Then David sent out one third of the people under the hand of Joab, one third under the hand of Abishai the son of Zeruiah, Joab's brother, and one third under the hand of Ittai the Gittite. And the king said to the people, "I also will surely go out with you myself."

17:25 [a]Spelled *Jether* in 1 Chronicles 2:17 and elsewhere [b]Following Masoretic Text, some manuscripts of the Septuagint, and Targum; some manuscripts of the Septuagint read *Ishmaelite* (compare 1 Chronicles 2:17); Vulgate reads *of Jezrael.*

THE MESSAGE

17-20 Jonathan and Ahimaaz were waiting around at En Rogel. A servant girl would come and give them messages and then they would go and tell King David, for it wasn't safe to be seen coming into the city. But a soldier spotted them and told Absalom, so the two of them got out of there fast and went to a man's house in Bahurim. He had a well in his yard and they climbed into it. The wife took a rug and covered the well, then spread grain on it so no one would notice anything out of the ordinary. Shortly, Absalom's servants came to the woman's house and asked her, "Have you seen Ahimaaz and Jonathan?"

The woman said, "They were headed toward the river."

They looked but didn't find them, and then went back to Jerusalem.

21 When the coast was clear, Ahimaaz and Jonathan climbed out of the well and went on to make their report to King David, "Get up and cross the river quickly; Ahithophel has given counsel against you!"

22 David and his whole army were soon up and moving and crossed the Jordan. As morning broke there was not a single person who had not made it across the Jordan.

23 When Ahithophel realized that his counsel was not followed, he saddled his donkey and left for his hometown. After making out his will and putting his house in order, he hanged himself and died. He was buried in the family tomb.

24-26 About the time David arrived at Mahanaim, Absalom crossed the Jordan, and the whole army of Israel with him. Absalom had made Amasa head of the army, replacing Joab. (Amasa was the son of a man named Ithra, an Ishmaelite who had married Abigail, daughter of Nahash and sister of Zeruiah, the mother of Joab.) Israel and Absalom set camp in Gilead.

27-29 When David arrived at Mahanaim, Shobi son of Nahash from Ammonite Rabbah, and Makir son of Ammiel from Lo Debar, and Barzillai the Gileadite from Rogelim brought beds and blankets, bowls and jugs filled with wheat, barley, flour, roasted grain, beans and lentils, honey, and curds and cheese from the flocks and herds. They presented all this to David and his army to eat, "because," they said, "the army must be starved and exhausted and thirsty out in this wilderness."

1-2 18 David organized his forces. He appointed captains of thousands and captains of hundreds. Then David deployed his troops, a third under Joab, a third under Abishai son of Zeruiah, Joab's brother, and a third under Ittai the Gittite.

The king then announced, "I'm marching with you."

New King James Version

[3]But the people answered, "You shall not go out! For if we flee away, they will not care about us; nor if half of us die, will they care about us. But *you are* worth ten thousand of us now. For you are now more help to us in the city."

[4]Then the king said to them, "Whatever seems best to you I will do." So the king stood beside the gate, and all the people went out by hundreds and by thousands. [5]Now the king had commanded Joab, Abishai, and Ittai, saying, "*Deal* gently for my sake with the young man Absalom." And all the people heard when the king gave all the captains orders concerning Absalom.

[6]So the people went out into the field of battle against Israel. And the battle was in the woods of Ephraim. [7]The people of Israel were overthrown there before the servants of David, and a great slaughter of twenty thousand took place there that day. [8]For the battle there was scattered over the face of the whole countryside, and the woods devoured more people that day than the sword devoured.

[9]Then Absalom met the servants of David. Absalom rode on a mule. The mule went under the thick boughs of a great terebinth tree, and his head caught in the terebinth; so he was left hanging between heaven and earth. And the mule which *was* under him went on. [10]Now a certain man saw *it* and told Joab, and said, "I just saw Absalom hanging in a terebinth tree!"

[11]So Joab said to the man who told him, "You just saw *him!* And why did you not strike him there to the ground? I would have given you ten *shekels* of silver and a belt."

[12]But the man said to Joab, "Though I were to receive a thousand *shekels* of silver in my hand, I would not raise my hand against the king's son. For in our hearing the king commanded you and Abishai and Ittai, saying, 'Beware lest anyone *touch* the young man Absalom!'[a] [13]Otherwise I would have dealt falsely against my own life. For there is nothing hidden from the king, and you yourself would have set yourself against *me*."

[14]Then Joab said, "I cannot linger with you." And he took three spears in his hand and thrust them through Absalom's heart, while he was *still* alive in the midst of the terebinth tree. [15]And ten young men who bore Joab's armor surrounded Absalom, and struck and killed him.

[16]So Joab blew the trumpet, and the people returned from pursuing Israel. For Joab held back the people. [17]And they took Absalom and cast him into a large pit in the woods, and laid a very large heap of stones over him. Then all Israel fled, everyone to his tent.

[18]Now Absalom in his lifetime had taken and set up a pillar for himself, which *is* in the King's Valley. For he said, "I have no son to keep my name in remembrance." He called the pillar after his own name. And to this day it is called Absalom's Monument.

18:12 [a]The ancient versions read *'Protect the young man Absalom for me!'*

The Message

3 They said, "No, you mustn't march with us. If we're forced to retreat, the enemy won't give it a second thought. And if half of us die, they won't do so either. But you are worth ten thousand of us. It will be better for us if you stay in the city and help from there."

4 "If you say so," said the king. "I'll do what you think is best." And so he stood beside the city gate as the whole army marched out by hundreds and by thousands.

5 Then the king ordered Joab and Abishai and Ittai, "Deal gently for my sake with the young man Absalom." The whole army heard what the king commanded the three captains regarding Absalom.

6-8 The army took the field to meet Israel. It turned out that the battle was joined in the Forest of Ephraim. The army of Israel was beaten badly there that day by David's men, a terrific slaughter—twenty thousand men! There was fighting helter-skelter all over the place—the forest claimed more lives that day than the sword!

9-10 Absalom ran into David's men, but was out in front of them riding his mule, when the mule ran under the branches of a huge oak tree. Absalom's head was caught in the oak and he was left dangling between heaven and earth, the mule running right out from under him. A solitary soldier saw him and reported it to Joab, "I just saw Absalom hanging from an oak tree!"

11 Joab said to the man who told him, "If you saw him, why didn't you kill him then and there? I'd have rewarded you with ten pieces of silver and a fancy belt."

12-13 The man told Joab, "Even if I'd had a chance at a thousand pieces of silver, I wouldn't have laid a hand on the king's son. We all heard the king command you and Abishai and Ittai, 'For my sake, protect the young man Absalom.' Why, I'd be risking my life, for nothing is hidden from the king. And you would have just stood there!"

14-15 Joab said, "I can't waste my time with you." He then grabbed three knives and stabbed Absalom in the heart while he was still alive in the tree; by then Absalom was surrounded by ten of Joab's armor bearers; they hacked away at him and killed him.

16-17 Joab then blew the ram's horn trumpet, calling off the army in its pursuit of Israel. They took Absalom, dumped him into a huge pit in the forest, and piled an immense mound of rocks over him.

Meanwhile the whole army of Israel was in flight, each man making his own way home.

18 While alive, Absalom had erected for himself a pillar in the Valley of the King, "because," he said, "I have no son to carry on my name." He inscribed the pillar with his own name. To this day it is called "The Absalom Memorial."

New King James Version

David Hears of Absalom's Death

19 Then Ahimaaz the son of Zadok said, "Let
me run now and take the news to the king, how
the LORD has avenged him of his enemies."
20 And Joab said to him, "You shall not take
the news this day, for you shall take the news
another day. But today you shall take no news,
because the king's son is dead." 21 Then Joab
said to the Cushite, "Go, tell the king what you
have seen." So the Cushite bowed himself to
Joab and ran.
22 And Ahimaaz the son of Zadok said again
to Joab, "But whatever happens, please let me
also run after the Cushite."
So Joab said, "Why will you run, my son,
since you have no news ready?"
23 "But whatever happens," *he said,* "let me
run."
So he said to him, "Run." Then Ahimaaz ran
by way of the plain, and outran the Cushite.
24 Now David was sitting between the two
gates. And the watchman went up to the roof
over the gate, to the wall, lifted his eyes and
looked, and there was a man, running alone.
25 Then the watchman cried out and told the
king. And the king said, "If he *is* alone, *there is*
news in his mouth." And he came rapidly and
drew near.
26 Then the watchman saw *another* man run-
ning, and the watchman called to the gate-
keeper and said, "There is *another* man, run-
ning alone!"
And the king said, "He also brings news."
27 So the watchman said, "I think the running
of the first is like the running of Ahimaaz the
son of Zadok."
And the king said, "He *is* a good man, and
comes with good news."
28 So Ahimaaz called out and said to the king,
"All is well!" Then he bowed down with his face
to the earth before the king, and said, "Blessed
be the LORD your God, who has delivered up the
men who raised their hand against my lord the
king!"
29 The king said, "Is the young man Absalom
safe?"
Ahimaaz answered, "When Joab sent the
king's servant and *me* your servant, I saw a
great tumult, but I did not know what *it was
about.*"
30 And the king said, "Turn aside *and* stand
here." So he turned aside and stood still.
31 Just then the Cushite came, and the
Cushite said, "There is good news, my lord the
king! For the LORD has avenged you this day of
all those who rose against you."
32 And the king said to the Cushite, "Is the
young man Absalom safe?"
So the Cushite answered, "May the enemies
of my lord the king, and all who rise against you
to do harm, be like *that* young man!"

David's Mourning for Absalom

33 Then the king was deeply moved, and went
up to the chamber over the gate, and wept. And
as he went, he said thus: "O my son Absalom—
my son, my son Absalom—if only I had died in
your place! O Absalom my son, my son!"

The Message

19-20 Ahimaaz, Zadok's son, said, "Let me run
to the king and bring him the good news
that GOD has delivered him from his ene-
mies." But Joab said, "You're not the one to
deliver the good news today; some other
day, maybe, but it's not 'good news' today."
(This was because the king's son was dead.)
21 Then Joab ordered a Cushite, "You go.
Tell the king what you've seen."
"Yes sir," said the Cushite, and ran off.
22 Ahimaaz son of Zadok kept at it, begging
Joab, "What does it matter? Let me run, too,
following the Cushite."
Joab said, "Why all this 'Run, run'? You'll
get no thanks for it, I can tell you."
23 "I don't care; let me run."
"Okay," said Joab, "run." So Ahimaaz ran,
taking the lower valley road, and passed the
Cushite.
24-25 David was sitting between the two gates.
The sentry had gone up to the top of the gate
on the wall and looked around. He saw a
solitary runner. The sentry called down and
told the king. The king said, "If he's alone, it
must be good news!"
25-26 As the runner came closer, the sentry saw
another runner and called down to the gate,
"Another runner all by himself."
And the king said, "This also must be
good news."
27 Then the sentry said, "I can see the first
man now; he runs like Ahimaaz son of
Zadok."
"He's a good man," said the king. "He's
bringing good news for sure."
28 Then Ahimaaz called out and said to the
king, "Peace!" Then he bowed deeply before
the king, his face to the ground. "Blessed be
your GOD; he has handed over the men who
rebelled against my master the king."
29 The king asked, "But is the young man
Absalom all right?"
Ahimaaz said, "I saw a huge ruckus just
as Joab was sending me off, but I don't
know what it was about."
30 The king said, "Step aside and stand over
there." So he stepped aside.
31 Then the Cushite arrived and said, "Good
news, my master and king! GOD has given
victory today over all those who rebelled
against you!"
32 "But," said the king, "is the young man
Absalom all right?"
And the Cushite replied, "Would that all
of the enemies of my master the king and all
who maliciously rose against you end up
like that young man."

33 The king was stunned. Heartbroken, he
went up to the room over the gate and wept.
As he wept he cried out,

O my son Absalom, my dear, dear son
Absalom!
Why not me rather than you, my death
and not yours,
O Absalom, my dear, dear son!

NEW KING JAMES VERSION

19 And Joab was told, "Behold, the king is weeping and mourning for Absalom." [2]So the victory that day was *turned* into mourning for all the people. For the people heard it said that day, "The king is grieved for his son." [3]And the people stole back into the city that day, as people who are ashamed steal away when they flee in battle. [4]But the king covered his face, and the king cried out with a loud voice, "O my son Absalom! O Absalom, my son, my son!"

[5]Then Joab came into the house to the king, and said, "Today you have disgraced all your servants who today have saved your life, the lives of your sons and daughters, the lives of your wives and the lives of your concubines, [6]in that you love your enemies and hate your friends. For you have declared today that you regard neither princes nor servants; for today I perceive that if Absalom had lived and all of us had died today, then it would have pleased you well. [7]Now therefore, arise, go out and speak comfort to your servants. For I swear by the LORD, if you do not go out, not one will stay with you this night. And that will be worse for you than all the evil that has befallen you from your youth until now." [8]Then the king arose and sat in the gate. And they told all the people, saying, "There is the king, sitting in the gate." So all the people came before the king.

For everyone of Israel had fled to his tent.

DAVID RETURNS TO JERUSALEM

[9]Now all the people were in a dispute throughout all the tribes of Israel, saying, "The king saved us from the hand of our enemies, he delivered us from the hand of the Philistines, and now he has fled from the land because of Absalom. [10]But Absalom, whom we anointed over us, has died in battle. Now therefore, why do you say nothing about bringing back the king?"

[11]So King David sent to Zadok and Abiathar the priests, saying, "Speak to the elders of Judah, saying, 'Why are you the last to bring the king back to his house, since the words of all Israel have come to the king, to his *very* house? [12]You *are* my brethren, you *are* my bone and my flesh. Why then are you the last to bring back the king?' [13]And say to Amasa, '*Are* you not my bone and my flesh? God do so to me, and more also, if you are not commander of the army before me continually in place of Joab.' " [14]So he swayed the hearts of all the men of Judah, just as *the heart of* one man, so that they sent *this word* to the king: "Return, you and all your servants!"

[15]Then the king returned and came to the Jordan. And Judah came to Gilgal, to go to meet the king, to escort the king across the Jordan. [16]And Shimei the son of Gera, a Benjamite, who *was* from Bahurim, hurried and came down with the men of Judah to meet King David. [17]*There were* a thousand men of Benjamin with him, and Ziba the servant of the house of Saul, and his fifteen sons and his twenty servants

THE MESSAGE

DAVID'S GRIEF FOR ABSALOM

1-4 **19** Joab was told that David was weeping and lamenting over Absalom. The day's victory turned into a day of mourning as word passed through the army, "David is grieving over his son." The army straggled back to the city that day demoralized, dragging their tails. And the king held his face in his hands and lamented loudly,

O my son Absalom,
Absalom my dear, dear son!

5-7 But in private Joab rebuked the king: "Now you've done it—knocked the wind out of your loyal servants who have just saved your life, to say nothing of the lives of your sons and daughters, wives and concubines. What is this—loving those who hate you and hating those who love you? Your actions give a clear message: officers and soldiers mean nothing to you. You know that if Absalom were alive right now, we'd all be dead—would that make you happy? Get hold of yourself; get out there and put some heart into your servants! I swear to GOD that if you don't go to them they'll desert; not a soldier will be left here by nightfall. And that will be the worst thing that has happened yet."

8 So the king came out and took his place at the city gate. Soon everyone knew: "Oh, look! The king has come out to receive us." And his whole army came and presented itself to the king. But the Israelites had fled the field of battle and gone home.

9-10 Meanwhile, the whole populace was now complaining to its leaders, "Wasn't it the king who saved us time and again from our enemies, and rescued us from the Philistines? And now he has had to flee the country on account of Absalom. And now this Absalom whom we made king is dead in battle. So what are you waiting for? Why don't you bring the king back?"

11-13 When David heard what was being said, he sent word to Zadok and Abiathar, the priests, "Ask the elders of Judah, 'Why are you so laggard in bringing the king back home? You're my brothers! You're my own flesh and blood! So why are you the last ones to bring the king back home?' And tell Amasa, 'You, too, are my flesh and blood. As God is my witness, I'm making you the permanent commander of the army in place of Joab.' "

14 He captured the hearts of everyone in Judah. They were unanimous in sending for the king: "Come back, you and all your servants."

15-18 So the king returned. He arrived at the Jordan just as Judah reached Gilgal on their way to welcome the king and escort him across the Jordan. Even Shimei son of Gera, the Benjaminite from Bahurim, hurried down to join the men of Judah so he could welcome the king, a thousand Benjaminites with him. And Ziba, Saul's steward, with his fifteen sons and twenty servants, waded

New King James Version

with him; and they went over the Jordan before
the king. [18]Then a ferryboat went across to carry
over the king's household, and to do what he
thought good.

David's Mercy to Shimei

Now Shimei the son of Gera fell down before
the king when he had crossed the Jordan.
[19]Then he said to the king, "Do not let my lord
impute iniquity to me, or remember what wrong
your servant did on the day that my lord the
king left Jerusalem, that the king should take *it*
to heart. [20]For I, your servant, know that I have
sinned. Therefore here I am, the first to come to-
day of all the house of Joseph to go down to
meet my lord the king."
[21]But Abishai the son of Zeruiah answered
and said, "Shall not Shimei be put to death for
this, because he cursed the LORD's anointed?"
[22]And David said, "What have I to do with
you, you sons of Zeruiah, that you should be ad-
versaries to me today? Shall any man be put to
death today in Israel? For do I not know that to-
day I *am* king over Israel?" [23]Therefore the king
said to Shimei, "You shall not die." And the king
swore to him.

David and Mephibosheth Meet

[24]Now Mephibosheth the son of Saul came
down to meet the king. And he had not cared for
his feet, nor trimmed his mustache, nor washed
his clothes, from the day the king departed until
the day he returned in peace. [25]So it was, when
he had come to Jerusalem to meet the king, that
the king said to him, "Why did you not go with
me, Mephibosheth?"
[26]And he answered, "My lord, O king, my ser-
vant deceived me. For your servant said, 'I will
saddle a donkey for myself, that I may ride on it
and go to the king,' because your servant *is*
lame. [27]And he has slandered your servant to
my lord the king, but my lord the king *is* like the
angel of God. Therefore do *what is* good in your
eyes. [28]For all my father's house were but dead
men before my lord the king. Yet you set your
servant among those who eat at your own table.
Therefore what right have I still to cry out any-
more to the king?"
[29]So the king said to him, "Why do you speak
anymore of your matters? I have said, 'You and
Ziba divide the land.' "
[30]Then Mephibosheth said to the king,
"Rather, let him take it all, inasmuch as my lord
the king has come back in peace to his own
house."

David's Kindness to Barzillai

[31]And Barzillai the Gileadite came down
from Rogelim and went across the Jordan with
the king, to escort him across the Jordan. [32]Now
Barzillai was a very aged man, eighty years old.
And he had provided the king with supplies
while he stayed at Mahanaim, for he *was* a very
rich man. [33]And the king said to Barzillai,
"Come across with me, and I will provide for
you while you are with me in Jerusalem."

The Message

across the Jordan to meet the king and
brought his entourage across, doing what-
ever they could to make the king comfort-
able.

18-20 Shimei son of Gera bowed deeply in
homage to the king as soon as he was across
the Jordan and said, "Don't think badly of
me, my master! Overlook my irresponsible
outburst on the day my master the king left
Jerusalem—don't hold it against me! I know
I sinned, but look at me now—the first of all
the tribe of Joseph to come down and wel-
come back my master the king!"

21 Abishai son of Zeruiah interrupted,
"Enough of this! Shouldn't we kill him out-
right? Why, he cursed GOD's anointed!"

22 But David said, "What is it with you sons
of Zeruiah? Why do you insist on being so
contentious? Nobody is going to be killed
today. I am again king over Israel!"

23 Then the king turned to Shimei, "You're
not going to die." And the king gave him his
word.

24-25 Next Mephibosheth grandson of Saul ar-
rived from Jerusalem to welcome the king.
He hadn't combed his hair or trimmed his
beard or washed his clothes from the day
the king left until the day he returned safe
and sound. The king said, "And why didn't
you come with me, Mephibosheth?"

26-28 "My master the king," he said, "my ser-
vant betrayed me. I told him to saddle my
donkey so I could ride it and go with the
king, for, as you know, I am lame. And then
he lied to you about me. But my master the
king has been like one of God's angels: he
knew what was right and did it. Wasn't
everyone in my father's house doomed? But
you took me in and gave me a place at your
table. What more could I ever expect or
ask?"

29 "That's enough," said the king. "Say no
more. Here's my decision: You and Ziba di-
vide the property between you."

30 Mephibosheth said, "Oh, let him have it
all! All I care about is that my master the
king is home safe and sound!"

31-32 Barzillai the Gileadite had come down
from Rogelim. He crossed the Jordan with
the king to give him a good send-off. Barzil-
lai was a very old man—eighty years old! He
had supplied the king's needs all the while
he was in Mahanaim since he was very
wealthy.

33 "Join me in Jerusalem," the king said to
Barzillai. "Let me take care of you."

New King James Version

34But Barzillai said to the king, "How long
have I to live, that I should go up with the king
to Jerusalem? 35I *am* today eighty years old. Can
I discern between the good and bad? Can your
servant taste what I eat or what I drink? Can I
hear any longer the voice of singing men and
singing women? Why then should your servant
be a further burden to my lord the king? 36Your
servant will go a little way across the Jordan
with the king. And why should the king repay
me *with* such a reward? 37Please let your ser-
vant turn back again, that I may die in my own
city, near the grave of my father and mother. But
here is your servant Chimham; let him cross
over with my lord the king, and do for him what
seems good to you."
38And the king answered, "Chimham shall
cross over with me, and I will do for him what
seems good to you. Now whatever you request
of me, I will do for you." 39Then all the people
went over the Jordan. And when the king had
crossed over, the king kissed Barzillai and
blessed him, and he returned to his own place.

The Quarrel About the King

40Now the king went on to Gilgal, and
Chimham[a] went on with him. And all the people
of Judah escorted the king, and also half the
people of Israel. 41Just then all the men of Israel
came to the king, and said to the king, "Why
have our brethren, the men of Judah, stolen you
away and brought the king, his household, and
all David's men with him across the Jordan?"
42So all the men of Judah answered the men
of Israel, "Because the king *is* a close relative of
ours. Why then are you angry over this matter?
Have we ever eaten at the king's *expense*? Or
has he given us any gift?"
43And the men of Israel answered the men of
Judah, and said, "We have ten shares in the
king; therefore we also have more *right* to
David than you. Why then do you despise us—
were we not the first to advise bringing back our
king?"

Yet the words of the men of Judah were fiercer than the words of the men of Israel.

The Rebellion of Sheba

20 And there happened to be there a rebel,[a]
whose name *was* Sheba the son of Bichri,
a Benjamite. And he blew a trumpet, and said:

"We have no share in David,
Nor do we have inheritance in the son of
Jesse;
Every man to his tents, O Israel!"

2So every man of Israel deserted David, *and* fol-
lowed Sheba the son of Bichri. But the men of
Judah, from the Jordan as far as Jerusalem, re-
mained loyal to their king.
3Now David came to his house at Jerusalem.
And the king took the ten women, his concu-
bines whom he had left to keep the house, and
put them in seclusion and supported them, but

19:40 [a]Masoretic Text reads *Chimhan.* 20:1 [a]Literally *man of Belial*

The Message

34-37 But Barzillai declined the offer, "How long do you think I'd live if I went with the king to Jerusalem? I'm eighty years old and not much good anymore to anyone. Can't taste food; can't hear music. So why add to the burdens of my master the king? I'll just go a little way across the Jordan with the king. But why would the king need to make a great thing of that? Let me go back and die in my hometown and be buried with my father and mother. But my servant Kimham here; let him go with you in my place. But treat him well!"

38 The king said, "That's settled; Kimham goes with me. And I will treat him well! If you think of anything else, I'll do that for you, too."

39-40 The army crossed the Jordan but the king stayed. The king kissed and blessed Barzillai, who then returned home. Then the king, Kimham with him, crossed over at Gilgal.

40-41 The whole army of Judah and half the army of Israel processed with the king. The men of Israel came to the king and said, "Why have our brothers, the men of Judah, taken over as if they owned the king, escorting the king and his family and close associates across the Jordan?"

42 The men of Judah retorted, "Because the king is related to us, that's why! But why make a scene? You don't see us getting treated special because of it, do you?"

43 The men of Israel shot back, "We have ten shares in the king to your one. Besides we're the firstborn—so why are we having to play second fiddle? It was our idea to bring him back."

But the men of Judah took a harder line than the men of Israel.

1 20 Just then a good-for-nothing named Sheba son of Bicri the Benjaminite blew a blast on the ram's horn trumpet, calling out,

We've got nothing to do with David,
there's no future for us with the son
of Jesse!
Let's get out of here, Israel—head for
your tents!

2-3 So all the men of Israel deserted David and followed Sheba son of Bicri. But the men of Judah stayed committed, sticking with their king all the way from the Jordan to Jerusalem. When David arrived home in Jerusalem, the king took the ten concubines he had left to watch the palace and placed them in seclusion, under guard. He provided

NEW KING JAMES VERSION

did not go in to them. So they were shut up to
the day of their death, living in widowhood.
[4]And the king said to Amasa, "Assemble the
men of Judah for me within three days, and be
present here yourself." [5]So Amasa went to as-
semble *the men of* Judah. But he delayed longer
than the set time which David had appointed
him. [6]And David said to Abishai, "Now Sheba
the son of Bichri will do us more harm than Ab-
salom. Take your lord's servants and pursue
him, lest he find for himself fortified cities, and
escape us." [7]So Joab's men, with the Chere-
thites, the Pelethites, and all the mighty men,
went out after him. And they went out of
Jerusalem to pursue Sheba the son of Bichri.
[8]When they *were* at the large stone which *is* in
Gibeon, Amasa came before them. Now Joab
was dressed in battle armor; on it was a belt
with a sword fastened in its sheath at his hips;
and as he was going forward, it fell out. [9]Then
Joab said to Amasa, "*Are* you in health, my
brother?" And Joab took Amasa by the beard
with his right hand to kiss him. [10]But Amasa did
not notice the sword that *was* in Joab's hand.
And he struck him with it in the stomach, and
his entrails poured out on the ground; and he
did not *strike* him again. Thus he died.

Then Joab and Abishai his brother pursued
Sheba the son of Bichri. [11]Meanwhile one of
Joab's men stood near Amasa, and said, "Who-
ever favors Joab and whoever *is* for David—
follow Joab!" [12]But Amasa wallowed in *his*
blood in the middle of the highway. And when
the man saw that all the people stood still, he
moved Amasa from the highway to the field and
threw a garment over him, when he saw that
everyone who came upon him halted. [13]When he
was removed from the highway, all the people
went on after Joab to pursue Sheba the son of
Bichri.

[14]And he went through all the tribes of Israel
to Abel and Beth Maachah and all the Berites.
So they were gathered together and also went
after *Sheba*.[a] [15]Then they came and besieged
him in Abel of Beth Maachah; and they cast up
a siege mound against the city, and it stood by
the rampart. And all the people who *were* with
Joab battered the wall to throw it down.

[16]Then a wise woman cried out from the city,
"Hear, hear! Please say to Joab, 'Come nearby,
that I may speak with you.' " [17]When he had come
near to her, the woman said, "*Are* you Joab?"

He answered, "I *am*."

Then she said to him, "Hear the words of
your maidservant."

And he answered, "I am listening."

[18]So she spoke, saying, "They used to talk in
former times, saying, 'They shall surely seek
guidance at Abel,' and so they would end *dis-*
putes. [19]I *am among the* peaceable *and* faithful
in Israel. You seek to destroy a city and a mother
in Israel. Why would you swallow up the inheri-
tance of the LORD?"

[20]And Joab answered and said, "Far be it, far
be it from me, that I should swallow up or de-
stroy! [21]That *is* not so. But a man from the
mountains of Ephraim, Sheba the son of Bichri

20:14 [a]Literally *him*

THE MESSAGE

for their needs but didn't visit them. They
were virtual prisoners until they died, wid-
ows as long as they lived.

4-10 The king ordered Amasa, "Muster the
men of Judah for me in three days; then re-
port in." Amasa went to carry out his orders,
but he was late reporting back. So David told
Abishai, "Sheba son of Bicri is going to hurt
us even worse than Absalom did. Take your
master's servants and hunt him down before
he gets holed up in some fortress city where
we can't get to him." So under Abishai's
command, all the best men—Joab's men and
the Kerethites and Pelethites—left Jerusalem
to hunt down Sheba son of Bicri. They were
near the boulder at Gibeon when Amasa
came their way. Joab was wearing a tunic
with a sheathed sword strapped on his waist,
but the sword slipped out and fell to the
ground. Joab greeted Amasa, "How are you,
brother?" and took Amasa's beard in his
right hand as if to kiss him. Amasa didn't
notice the sword in Joab's other hand. Joab
stuck him in the belly and his guts spilled to
the ground. A second blow wasn't needed;
he was dead. Then Joab and his brother
Abishai continued to chase Sheba son of Bi-
cri.

11-14 One of Joab's soldiers took up his post
over the body and called out, "Everyone
who sides with Joab and supports David,
follow Joab!" Amasa was lying in a pool of
blood in the middle of the road; the man re-
alized that the whole army was going to
stop and take a look, so he pulled Amasa's
corpse off the road into the field and threw
a blanket over him so it wouldn't collect
spectators. As soon as he'd gotten him off
the road, the traffic flowed normally, follow-
ing Joab in the chase after Sheba son of Bi-
cri. Sheba passed through all the tribes of
Israel as far as Abel Beth Maacah; all the Bi-
crites clustered and followed him into the
city.

15 Joab's army arrived and laid siege to
Sheba in Abel Beth Maacah. They built a
siege-ramp up against the city's fortifica-
tion. The plan was to knock down the wall.

16-17 But a shrewd woman called out from the
city, "Listen, everybody! Please tell Joab to
come close so I can talk to him." When he
had come, the woman said, "Are you Joab?"

He said, "I am."

"Then," she said, "listen to what I have to
say."

He said, "I'm listening."

18-19 "There's an old saying in these parts: 'If
it's answers you want, come to Abel and get
it straight.' We're a peaceful people here,
and reliable. And here you are, trying to tear
down one of Israel's mother cities. Why
would you want to mess with GOD's legacy
like that?"

20-21 Joab protested, "Believe me, you've got
me all wrong. I'm not here to hurt anyone or
destroy anything—not on your life! But a
man from the hill country of Ephraim,
Sheba son of Bicri by name, revolted against

NEW KING JAMES VERSION

by name, has raised his hand against the king, against David. Deliver him only, and I will depart from the city."

So the woman said to Joab, "Watch, his head will be thrown to you over the wall." [22]Then the woman in her wisdom went to all the people. And they cut off the head of Sheba the son of Bichri, and threw *it* out to Joab. Then he blew a trumpet, and they withdrew from the city, every man to his tent. So Joab returned to the king at Jerusalem.

DAVID'S GOVERNMENT OFFICERS

[23]And Joab *was* over all the army of Israel; Benaiah the son of Jehoiada *was* over the Cherethites and the Pelethites; [24]Adoram *was* in charge of revenue; Jehoshaphat the son of Ahilud *was* recorder; [25]Sheva *was* scribe; Zadok and Abiathar *were* the priests; [26]and Ira the Jairite was a chief minister under David.

DAVID AVENGES THE GIBEONITES

21 Now there was a famine in the days of David for three years, year after year; and David inquired of the LORD. And the LORD answered, "*It is* because of Saul and *his* bloodthirsty house, because he killed the Gibeonites." [2]So the king called the Gibeonites and spoke to them. Now the Gibeonites *were* not of the children of Israel, but of the remnant of the Amorites; the children of Israel had sworn protection to them, but Saul had sought to kill them in his zeal for the children of Israel and Judah.

[3]Therefore David said to the Gibeonites, "What shall I do for you? And with what shall I make atonement, that you may bless the inheritance of the LORD?"

[4]And the Gibeonites said to him, "We will have no silver or gold from Saul or from his house, nor shall you kill any man in Israel for us."

So he said, "Whatever you say, I will do for you."

[5]Then they answered the king, "As for the man who consumed us and plotted against us, *that* we should be destroyed from remaining in any of the territories of Israel, [6]let seven men of his descendants be delivered to us, and we will hang them before the LORD in Gibeah of Saul, *whom* the LORD chose."

And the king said, "I will give *them.*"

[7]But the king spared Mephibosheth the son of Jonathan, the son of Saul, because of the LORD's oath that *was* between them, between David and Jonathan the son of Saul. [8]So the king took Armoni and Mephibosheth, the two sons of Rizpah the daughter of Aiah, whom she bore to Saul, and the five sons of Michal[a] the daughter of Saul, whom she brought up for Adriel the son of Barzillai the Meholathite; [9]and he delivered them into the hands of the Gibeonites, and they hanged them on the hill before the LORD. So they fell, *all* seven together, and were put to death in the days of harvest, in the first *days*, in the beginning of barley harvest.

21:8 [a]Or *Merab* (compare 1 Samuel 18:19 and 25:44; 2 Samuel 3:14 and 6:23)

THE MESSAGE

King David; hand him over, him only, and we'll get out of here."

The woman told Joab, "Sounds good. His head will be tossed to you from the wall."

22 The woman presented her strategy to the
whole city and they did it: They cut off the
head of Sheba son of Bicri and tossed it
down to Joab. He then blew a blast on the
ram's horn trumpet and the soldiers all went
home. Joab returned to the king in Jerusa-
lem.

FAMINE AND WAR

23-26 Joab was again commander of the whole
army of Israel. Benaiah son of Jehoiada
was over the Kerethites and Pelethites;
Adoniram over the work crews; Jehosha-
phat son of Ahilud was clerk; Sheva was
historian; Zadok and Abiathar were priests;
Ira the Jairite was David's chaplain.

1 21 There was a famine in David's time. It
went on year after year after year—
three years. David went to GOD seeking the
reason.

GOD said, "This is because there is blood
on Saul and his house, from the time he
massacred the Gibeonites."

2 So the king called the Gibeonites to-
gether for consultation. (The Gibeonites
were not part of Israel; they were what was
left of the Amorites, and protected by a
treaty with Israel. But Saul, a fanatic for the
honor of Israel and Judah, tried to kill them
off.)

3 David addressed the Gibeonites: "What
can I do for you? How can I compensate you
so that you will bless GOD's legacy of land
and people?"

4 The Gibeonites replied, "We don't want
any money from Saul and his family. And
it's not up to us to put anyone in Israel to
death."

But David persisted: "What are you say-
ing I should do for you?"

5-6 Then they told the king, "The man who
tried to get rid of us, who schemed to wipe
us off the map of Israel—well, let seven of
his sons be handed over to us to be exe-
cuted—hanged before GOD at Gibeah of
Saul, the holy mountain."

And David agreed, "I'll hand them over to
you."

7-9 The king spared Mephibosheth son of
Jonathan, the son of Saul, because of the
promise David and Jonathan had spoken
before GOD. But the king selected Armoni
and Mephibosheth, the two sons that Riz-
pah daughter of Aiah had borne to Saul,
plus the five sons that Saul's daughter
Merab had borne to Adriel son of Barzillai
the Meholathite. He turned them over to the
Gibeonites who hanged them on the moun-
tain before GOD—all seven died together.
Harvest was just getting underway, the be-
ginning of the barley harvest, when they
were executed.

NEW KING JAMES VERSION

10 Now Rizpah the daughter of Aiah took sackcloth and spread it for herself on the rock, from the beginning of harvest until the late rains poured on them from heaven. And she did not allow the birds of the air to rest on them by day nor the beasts of the field by night.

11 And David was told what Rizpah the daughter of Aiah, the concubine of Saul, had done. 12 Then David went and took the bones of Saul, and the bones of Jonathan his son, from the men of Jabesh Gilead who had stolen them from the street of Beth Shan,[a] where the Philistines had hung them up, after the Philistines had struck down Saul in Gilboa. 13 So he brought up the bones of Saul and the bones of Jonathan his son from there; and they gathered the bones of those who had been hanged. 14 They buried the bones of Saul and Jonathan his son in the country of Benjamin in Zelah, in the tomb of Kish his father. So they performed all that the king commanded. And after that God heeded the prayer for the land.

PHILISTINE GIANTS DESTROYED

15 When the Philistines were at war again with Israel, David and his servants with him went down and fought against the Philistines; and David grew faint. 16 Then Ishbi-Benob, who *was* one of the sons of the giant, the weight of whose bronze spear *was* three hundred *shekels*, who was bearing a new *sword*, thought he could kill David. 17 But Abishai the son of Zeruiah came to his aid, and struck the Philistine and killed him. Then the men of David swore to him, saying, "You shall go out no more with us to battle, lest you quench the lamp of Israel."

18 Now it happened afterward that there was again a battle with the Philistines at Gob. Then Sibbechai the Hushathite killed Saph,[a] who *was* one of the sons of the giant. 19 Again there was war at Gob with the Philistines, where Elhanan the son of Jaare-Oregim[a] the Bethlehemite killed *the brother of* Goliath the Gittite, the shaft of whose spear *was* like a weaver's beam.

20 Yet again there was war at Gath, where there was a man of *great* stature, who had six fingers on each hand and six toes on each foot, twenty-four in number; and he also was born to the giant. 21 So when he defied Israel, Jonathan the son of Shimea,[a] David's brother, killed him.

22 These four were born to the giant in Gath, and fell by the hand of David and by the hand of his servants.

PRAISE FOR GOD'S DELIVERANCE

22 Then David spoke to the LORD the words of this song, on the day when the LORD had delivered him from the hand of all his enemies, and from the hand of Saul. 2 And he said:[a]

"The LORD *is* my rock and my fortress and
 my deliverer;
3 The God of my strength, in whom I will
 trust;

21:12 [a]Spelled *Beth Shean* in Joshua 17:11 and elsewhere **21:18** [a]Spelled *Sippai* in 1 Chronicles 20:4 **21:19** [a]Spelled *Jair* in 1 Chronicles 20:5 **21:21** [a]Spelled *Shammah* in 1 Samuel 16:9 and elsewhere **22:2** [a]Compare Psalm 18

THE MESSAGE

10 Rizpah daughter of Aiah took rough burlap and spread it out for herself on a rock from the beginning of the harvest until the heavy rains started. She kept the birds away from the bodies by day and the wild animals by night.

11-14 David was told what she had done, this Rizpah daughter of Aiah and concubine of Saul. He then went and got the remains of Saul and Jonathan his son from the leaders at Jabesh Gilead (who had rescued them from the town square at Beth Shan where the Philistines had hung them after striking them down at Gilboa). He gathered up their remains and brought them together with the dead bodies of the seven who had just been hanged. The bodies were taken back to the land of Benjamin and given a decent burial in the tomb of Kish, Saul's father.

They did everything the king ordered to be done. That cleared things up: from then on God responded to Israel's prayers for the land.

15-17 War broke out again between the Philistines and Israel. David and his men went down to fight. David became exhausted. Ishbi-Benob, a warrior descended from Rapha, with a spear weighing nearly eight pounds and outfitted in brand-new armor, announced that he'd kill David. But Abishai son of Zeruiah came to the rescue, struck the Philistine, and killed him.

Then David's men swore to him, "No more fighting on the front-lines for you! Don't snuff out the lamp of Israel!"

18 Later there was another skirmish with the Philistines at Gob. That time Sibbecai the Hushathite killed Saph, another of the warriors descended from Rapha.

19 At yet another battle with the Philistines at Gob, Elhanan son of Jaar, the weaver of Bethlehem, killed Goliath the Gittite whose spear was as big as a flagpole.

20-21 Still another fight broke out in Gath. There was a giant there with six fingers on his hands and six toes on his feet—twenty-four fingers and toes! He was another of those descended from Rapha. He insulted Israel, and Jonathan son of Shimeah, David's brother, killed him.

22 These four were descended from Rapha in Gath. And they all were killed by David and his soldiers.

1 22 David prayed to GOD the words of this song after GOD saved him from all his enemies and from Saul.

2-3 GOD is bedrock under my feet,
 the castle in which I live,
 my rescuing knight.

NEW KING JAMES VERSION

My shield and the horn of my salvation,
My stronghold and my refuge;
My Savior, You save me from violence.
4I will call upon the LORD, *who is worthy* to be praised;
So shall I be saved from my enemies.

5"When the waves of death surrounded me,
The floods of ungodliness made me afraid.
6The sorrows of Sheol surrounded me;
The snares of death confronted me.
7In my distress I called upon the LORD,
And cried out to my God;
He heard my voice from His temple,
And my cry *entered* His ears.

8"Then the earth shook and trembled;
The foundations of heaven[a] quaked and were shaken,
Because He was angry.
9Smoke went up from His nostrils,
And devouring fire from His mouth;
Coals were kindled by it.
10He bowed the heavens also, and came down
With darkness under His feet.
11He rode upon a cherub, and flew;
And He was seen[a] upon the wings of the wind.
12He made darkness canopies around Him,
Dark waters *and* thick clouds of the skies.
13From the brightness before Him
Coals of fire were kindled.

14"The LORD thundered from heaven,
And the Most High uttered His voice.
15He sent out arrows and scattered them;
Lightning bolts, and He vanquished them.
16Then the channels of the sea were seen,
The foundations of the world were uncovered,
At the rebuke of the LORD,
At the blast of the breath of His nostrils.

17"He sent from above, He took me,
He drew me out of many waters.
18He delivered me from my strong enemy,
From those who hated me;
For they were too strong for me.
19They confronted me in the day of my calamity,
But the LORD was my support.
20He also brought me out into a broad place;
He delivered me because He delighted in me.

21"The LORD rewarded me according to my righteousness;
According to the cleanness of my hands
He has recompensed me.
22For I have kept the ways of the LORD,
And have not wickedly departed from my God.

22:8 [a]Following Masoretic Text, Septuagint, and Targum; Syriac and Vulgate read *hills* (compare Psalm 18:7). **22:11** [a]Following Masoretic Text and Septuagint; many Hebrew manuscripts, Syriac, and Vulgate read *He flew* (compare Psalm 18:10); Targum reads *He spoke with power.*

THE MESSAGE

My God—the high crag
where I run for dear life,
hiding behind the boulders,
safe in the granite hideout;
My mountaintop refuge,
he saves me from ruthless men.

4 I sing to GOD the Praise-Lofty,
and find myself safe and saved.

5-6 The waves of death crashed over me,
devil waters rushed over me.
Hell's ropes cinched me tight;
death traps barred every exit.

7 A hostile world! I called to GOD,
to my God I cried out.
From his palace he heard me call;
my cry brought me right into his presence—
a private audience!

8-16 Earth wobbled and lurched;
the very heavens shook like leaves,
Quaked like aspen leaves
because of his rage.
His nostrils flared, billowing smoke;
his mouth spit fire.
Tongues of fire darted in and out;
he lowered the sky.
He stepped down;
under his feet an abyss opened up.
He rode a winged creature,
swift on wind-wings.
He wrapped himself
in a trenchcoat of black rain-cloud darkness.
But his cloud-brightness burst through,
a grand comet of fireworks.
Then GOD thundered out of heaven;
the High God gave a great shout.
God shot his arrows—pandemonium!
He hurled his lightnings—a rout!
The secret sources of ocean were exposed,
the hidden depths of earth lay uncovered
The moment GOD roared in protest,
let loose his hurricane anger.

17-20 But me he caught—reached all the way
from sky to sea; he pulled me out
Of that ocean of hate, that enemy chaos,
the void in which I was drowning.
They hit me when I was down,
but GOD stuck by me.
He stood me up on a wide-open field;
I stood there saved—surprised to be loved!

21-25 GOD made my life complete
when I placed all the pieces before him.
When I cleaned up my act,
he gave me a fresh start.
Indeed, I've kept alert to GOD's ways;
I haven't taken God for granted.

NEW KING JAMES VERSION

23For all His judgments *were* before me;
And *as for* His statutes, I did not depart from them.
24I was also blameless before Him,
And I kept myself from my iniquity.
25Therefore the LORD has recompensed me according to my righteousness,
According to my cleanness in His eyes.[a]

26"With the merciful You will show Yourself merciful;
With a blameless man You will show Yourself blameless;
27With the pure You will show Yourself pure;
And with the devious You will show Yourself shrewd.
28You will save the humble people;
But Your eyes *are* on the haughty, *that* You may bring *them* down.

29"For You *are* my lamp, O LORD;
The LORD shall enlighten my darkness.
30For by You I can run against a troop;
By my God I can leap over a wall.
31*As for* God, His way *is* perfect;
The word of the LORD *is* proven;
He *is* a shield to all who trust in Him.

32"For who *is* God, except the LORD?
And who *is* a rock, except our God?
33God *is* my strength *and* power,[a]
And He makes my[b] way perfect.
34He makes my[a] feet like the *feet* of deer,
And sets me on my high places.
35He teaches my hands to make war,
So that my arms can bend a bow of bronze.

36"You have also given me the shield of Your salvation;
Your gentleness has made me great.
37You enlarged my path under me;
So my feet did not slip.

38"I have pursued my enemies and destroyed them;
Neither did I turn back again till they were destroyed.
39And I have destroyed them and wounded them,
So that they could not rise;
They have fallen under my feet.
40For You have armed me with strength for the battle;
You have subdued under me those who rose against me.
41You have also given me the necks of my enemies,
So that I destroyed those who hated me.
42They looked, but *there was* none to save;
Even to the LORD, but He did not answer them.

22:25 [a]Septuagint, Syriac, and Vulgate read *the cleanness of my hands in His sight* (compare Psalm 18:24); Targum reads *my cleanness before His word.* **22:33** [a]Dead Sea Scrolls, Septuagint, Syriac, and Vulgate read *It is God who arms me with strength* (compare Psalm 18:32); Targum reads *It is God who sustains me with strength.* [b]Following Qere, Septuagint, Syriac, Targum, and Vulgate (compare Psalm 18:32); Kethib reads *His.* **22:34** [a]Following Qere, Septuagint, Syriac, Targum, and Vulgate (compare Psalm 18:33); Kethib reads *His.*

THE MESSAGE

Every day I review the ways he works,
I try not to miss a trick.
I feel put back together,
and I'm watching my step.
GOD rewrote the text of my life
when I opened the book of my heart
to his eyes.

26-28 You stick by people who stick with you,
you're straight with people who're
straight with you,
You're good to good people,
you shrewdly work around the bad
ones.
You take the side of the down-and-out,
but the stuck-up you take down a
peg.

29-31 Suddenly, GOD, your light floods my
path,
GOD drives out the darkness.
I smash the bands of marauders,
I vault the high fences.
What a God! His road
stretches straight and smooth.
Every GOD-direction is road-tested.
Everyone who runs toward him
Makes it.

32-46 Is there any god like GOD?
Are we not at bedrock?
Is not this the God who armed me well,
then aimed me in the right direction?
Now I run like a deer;
I'm king of the mountain.
He shows me how to fight;
I can bend a bronze bow!
You protect me with salvation-armor;
you touch me and I feel ten feet tall.
You cleared the ground under me
so my footing was firm.
When I chased my enemies I caught
them;
I didn't let go till they were dead men.
I nailed them; they were down for good;
then I walked all over them.
You armed me well for this fight;
you smashed the upstarts.
You made my enemies turn tail,
and I wiped out the haters.
They cried "uncle"
but Uncle didn't come;
They yelled for GOD
and got no for an answer.

NEW KING JAMES VERSION

43Then I beat them as fine as the dust of the
earth;
I trod them like dirt in the streets,
And I spread them out.

44"You have also delivered me from the
strivings of my people;
You have kept me as the head of the nations.
A people I have not known shall serve me.
45The foreigners submit to me;
As soon as they hear, they obey me.
46The foreigners fade away,
And come frightened[a] from their hideouts.

47"The LORD lives!
Blessed *be* my Rock!
Let God be exalted,
The Rock of my salvation!
48*It is* God who avenges me,
And subdues the peoples under me;
49He delivers me from my enemies.
You also lift me up above those who rise
against me;
You have delivered me from the violent
man.
50Therefore I will give thanks to You, O LORD,
among the Gentiles,
And sing praises to Your name.

51*He is* the tower of salvation to His king,
And shows mercy to His anointed,
To David and his descendants forevermore."

DAVID'S LAST WORDS

23 Now these *are* the last words of David.

Thus says David the son of Jesse;
Thus says the man raised up on high,
The anointed of the God of Jacob,
And the sweet psalmist of Israel:

2"The Spirit of the LORD spoke by me,
And His word *was* on my tongue.
3The God of Israel said,
The Rock of Israel spoke to me:
'He who rules over men *must be* just,
Ruling in the fear of God.
4And *he shall be* like the light of the morning
when the sun rises,
A morning without clouds,
Like the tender grass *springing* out of the
earth,
By clear shining after rain.'

5"Although my house *is* not so with God,
Yet He has made with me an everlasting
covenant,
Ordered in all *things* and secure.
For *this is* all my salvation and all *my*
desire;
Will He not make *it* increase?
6But *the sons* of rebellion *shall* all *be* as
thorns thrust away,
Because they cannot be taken with hands.

22:46 [a]Following Septuagint, Targum, and Vulgate (compare Psalm 18:45); Masoretic Text reads *gird themselves.*

THE MESSAGE

I ground them to dust; they gusted in the
wind.
I threw them out, like garbage in the
gutter.
You rescued me from a squabbling
people;
you made me a leader of nations.
People I'd never heard of served me;
the moment they got wind of me they
submitted.
They gave up; they came trembling from
their hideouts.

47-51 Live, GOD! Blessing to my Rock,
my towering Salvation-God!
This God set things right for me
and shut up the people who talked
back.
He rescued me from enemy anger.
You pulled me from the grip of
upstarts,
You saved me from the bullies.
That's why I'm thanking you, GOD,
all over the world.
That's why I'm singing songs
that rhyme your name.
God's king takes the trophy;
God's chosen is beloved.
I mean David and all his children—
always.

1 23 These are David's last words:

The voice of the son of Jesse,
the voice of the man God took to the
top,
Whom the God of Jacob made king,
and Israel's most popular singer!

2-7 GOD's Spirit spoke through me,
his words took shape on my tongue.
The God of Israel spoke to me,
Israel's Rock-Mountain said,
"Whoever governs fairly and well,
who rules in the Fear-of-God,
Is like first light at daybreak
without a cloud in the sky,
Like green grass carpeting earth,
glistening under fresh rain."
And this is just how my regime has been,
for God guaranteed his covenant with
me,
Spelled it out plainly
and kept every promised word—
My entire salvation,
my every desire.
But the devil's henchmen are like thorns
culled and piled as trash;

NEW KING JAMES VERSION

7But the man *who* touches them
Must be armed with iron and the shaft of a spear,
And they shall be utterly burned with fire in *their* place."

DAVID'S MIGHTY MEN

8These *are* the names of the mighty men whom David had: Josheb-Basshebeth[a] the Tachmonite, chief among the captains.[b] He was called Adino the Eznite, because he had killed eight hundred men at one time. 9And after him *was* Eleazar the son of Dodo,[a] the Ahohite, *one* of the three mighty men with David when they defied the Philistines *who* were gathered there for battle, and the men of Israel had retreated. 10He arose and attacked the Philistines until his hand was weary, and his hand stuck to the sword. The LORD brought about a great victory that day; and the people returned after him only to plunder. 11And after him *was* Shammah the son of Agee the Hararite. The Philistines had gathered together into a troop where there was a piece of ground full of lentils. So the people fled from the Philistines. 12But he stationed himself in the middle of the field, defended it, and killed the Philistines. So the LORD brought about a great victory.

13Then three of the thirty chief men went down at harvest time and came to David at the cave of Adullam. And the troop of Philistines encamped in the Valley of Rephaim. 14David *was* then in the stronghold, and the garrison of the Philistines *was* then *in* Bethlehem. 15And David said with longing, "Oh, that someone would give me a drink of the water from the well of Bethlehem, which *is* by the gate!" 16So the three mighty men broke through the camp of the Philistines, drew water from the well of Bethlehem that *was* by the gate, and took it and brought *it* to David. Nevertheless he would not drink it, but poured it out to the LORD. 17And he said, "Far be it from me, O LORD, that I should do this! Is *this not* the blood of the men who went in *jeopardy of* their lives?" Therefore he would not drink it.

These things were done by the three mighty men.

18Now Abishai the brother of Joab, the son of Zeruiah, was chief of *another* three.[a] He lifted his spear against three hundred *men,* killed *them,* and won a name among *these* three. 19Was he not the most honored of three? Therefore he became their captain. However, he did not attain to the *first* three.

20Benaiah *was* the son of Jehoiada, the son of a valiant man from Kabzeel, who had done many deeds. He had killed two lion-like heroes of Moab. He also had gone down and killed a lion in the midst of a pit on a snowy day. 21And he killed an Egyptian, a spectacular man. The Egyptian *had* a spear in his hand; so he went down to him with a staff, wrested the spear out of the Egyptian's hand, and killed him with his own spear.

23:8 [a]Literally *One Who Sits in the Seat* (compare 1 Chronicles 11:11) [b]Following Masoretic Text and Targum; Septuagint and Vulgate read *the three.* **23:9** [a]Spelled *Dodai* in 1 Chronicles 27:4 **23:18** [a]Following Masoretic Text, Septuagint, and Vulgate; some Hebrew manuscripts and Syriac read *thirty;* Targum reads *the mighty men.*

THE MESSAGE

Better not try to touch them;
keep your distance with a rake or hoe.
They'll make a glorious bonfire!

8 This is the listing of David's top men.

Josheb-Basshebeth, the Tahkemonite. He was chief of the Three. He once put his spear to work against eight hundred—killed them all in a day.

9-10 Eleazar son of Dodai the Ahohite was the next of the elite Three. He was with David when the Philistines poked fun at them at Pas Dammim. When the Philistines drew up for battle, Israel retreated. But Eleazar stood his ground and killed Philistines right and left until he was exhausted—but he never let go of his sword! A big win for GOD that day. The army then rejoined Eleazar, but all there was left to do was the cleanup.

11-12 Shammah son of Agee the Hararite was the third of the Three. The Philistines had mustered for battle at Lehi, where there was a field full of lentils. Israel fled before the Philistines, but Shammah took his stand at the center of the field, successfully defended it, and routed the Philistines. Another great victory for GOD!

13-17 One day during harvest, the Three parted from the Thirty and joined David at the Cave of Adullam. A squad of Philistines had set up camp in the Valley of Rephaim. While David was holed up in the Cave, the Philistines had their base camp in Bethlehem. David had a sudden craving and said, "Would I ever like a drink of water from the well at the gate of Bethlehem!" So the Three penetrated the Philistine lines, drew water from the well at the gate of Bethlehem, and brought it back to David. But David wouldn't drink it; he poured it out as an offering to GOD, saying, "There is no way, GOD, that I'll drink this! This isn't mere water, it's their life-blood—they risked their very lives to bring it!" So David refused to drink it.

This is the sort of thing that the Three did.

18-19 Abishai brother of Joab and son of Zeruiah was the head of the Thirty. He once got credit for killing three hundred with his spear, but he was never named in the same breath as the Three. He was the most respected of the Thirty and was their captain, but never got included among the Three.

20-21 Benaiah son of Jehoiada from Kabzeel was a vigorous man who accomplished a great deal. He once killed two lion cubs in Moab. Another time, on a snowy day, he climbed down into a pit and killed a lion. Another time he killed a formidable Egyptian. The Egyptian was armed with a spear and Benaiah went against him with nothing but a walking stick; he seized the spear from his grip and killed him with his own spear.

NEW KING JAMES VERSION

[22]These *things* Benaiah the son of Jehoiada did,
and won a name among three mighty men. [23]He
was more honored than the thirty, but he did not
attain to the *first* three. And David appointed
him over his guard.
[24]Asahel the brother of Joab *was* one of the
thirty; Elhanan the son of Dodo of Bethlehem,
[25]Shammah the Harodite, Elika the Harodite,
[26]Helez the Paltite, Ira the son of Ikkesh the
Tekoite, [27]Abiezer the Anathothite, Mebunnai
the Hushathite, [28]Zalmon the Ahohite, Maharai
the Netophathite, [29]Heleb the son of Baanah (the
Netophathite), Ittai the son of Ribai from
Gibeah of the children of Benjamin, [30]Benaiah a
Pirathonite, Hiddai from the brooks of Gaash,
[31]Abi-Albon the Arbathite, Azmaveth the Barhu-
mite, [32]Eliahba the Shaalbonite (of the sons of
Jashen), Jonathan, [33]Shammah the Hararite,
Ahiam the son of Sharar the Hararite,
[34]Eliphelet the son of Ahasbai, the son of the
Maachathite, Eliam the son of Ahithophel the
Gilonite, [35]Hezrai[a] the Carmelite, Paarai the Ar-
bite, [36]Igal the son of Nathan of Zobah, Bani the
Gadite, [37]Zelek the Ammonite, Naharai the
Beerothite (armorbearer of Joab the son of
Zeruiah), [38]Ira the Ithrite, Gareb the Ithrite,
[39]*and* Uriah the Hittite: thirty-seven in all.

DAVID'S CENSUS OF ISRAEL AND JUDAH

24 Again the anger of the LORD was aroused
against Israel, and He moved David
against them to say, "Go, number Israel and Ju-
dah."
[2]So the king said to Joab the commander of
the army who *was* with him, "Now go through-
out all the tribes of Israel, from Dan to Beer-
sheba, and count the people, that I may know
the number of the people."
[3]And Joab said to the king, "Now may the
LORD your God add to the people a hundred
times more than there are, and may the eyes of
my lord the king see *it*. But why does my lord
the king desire this thing?" [4]Nevertheless the
king's word prevailed against Joab and against
the captains of the army. Therefore Joab and the
captains of the army went out from the presence
of the king to count the people of Israel.
[5]And they crossed over the Jordan and
camped in Aroer, on the right side of the town
which *is* in the midst of the ravine of Gad, and
toward Jazer. [6]Then they came to Gilead and to
the land of Tahtim Hodshi; they came to Dan

23:35 [a]Spelled *Hezro* in 1 Chronicles 11:37

THE MESSAGE

22-23 These are the things that Benaiah son of
Jehoiada is famous for. But neither did he
ever get ranked with the Three. He was held
in greatest respect among the Thirty, but he
never got included with the Three. David
put him in charge of his bodyguard.

THE THIRTY

24-39 "The Thirty" consisted of:
Asahel brother of Joab;
Elhanan son of Dodo of Bethlehem;
Shammah the Harodite;
Elika the Harodite;
Helez the Paltite;
Ira son of Ikkesh the Tekoite;
Abiezer the Anathothite;
Sibbecai the Hushathite;
Zalmon the Ahohite;
Maharai the Netophathite;
Heled son of Baanah the Netophathite;
Ithai son of Ribai from Gibeah of the
Benjaminites;
Benaiah the Pirathonite;
Hiddai from the badlands of Gaash;
Abi-Albon the Arbathite;
Azmaveth the Barhumite;
Eliahba the Shaalbonite;
Jashen the Gizonite;
Jonathan son of Shammah the Hararite;
Ahiam son of Sharar the Urite;
Eliphelet son of Ahasbai the Maacathite;
Eliam son of Ahithophel the Gilonite;
Hezro the Carmelite;
Paarai the Arbite;
Igal son of Nathan, commander of the
army of Hagrites;
Zelek the Ammonite;
Naharai the Beerothite, weapon bearer of
Joab son of Zeruiah;
Ira the Ithrite;
Gareb the Ithrite;
Uriah the Hittite.
Thirty-seven, all told.

1-2 **24** Once again GOD's anger blazed out
against Israel. He tested David by
telling him, "Go and take a census of Israel
and Judah." So David gave orders to Joab
and the army officers under him, "Canvass
all the tribes of Israel, from Dan to Beer-
sheba, and get a count of the population. I
want to know the number."
3 But Joab resisted the king: "May your
GOD multiply people by the hundreds right
before the eyes of my master the king, but
why on earth would you do a thing like
this?"
4-9 Nevertheless, the king insisted, and so
Joab and the army officers left the king to
take a census of Israel. They crossed the
Jordan and began with Aroer and the town
in the canyon of the Gadites near Jazer, pro-
ceeded through Gilead, passed Hermon,
then on to Dan, but detoured Sidon. They

NEW KING JAMES VERSION

Jaan and around to Sidon; 7and they came to the
stronghold of Tyre and to all the cities of the
Hivites and the Canaanites. Then they went out
to South Judah *as far as* Beersheba. 8So when
they had gone through all the land, they came to
Jerusalem at the end of nine months and twenty
days. 9Then Joab gave the sum of the number of
the people to the king. And there were in Israel
eight hundred thousand valiant men who drew
the sword, and the men of Judah were five hun-
dred thousand men.

THE JUDGMENT ON DAVID'S SIN

10And David's heart condemned him after he
had numbered the people. So David said to the
LORD, "I have sinned greatly in what I have done;
but now, I pray, O LORD, take away the iniquity of
Your servant, for I have done very foolishly."
11Now when David arose in the morning, the
word of the LORD came to the prophet Gad,
David's seer, saying, 12"Go and tell David, 'Thus
says the LORD: "I offer you three *things;* choose
one of them for yourself, that I may do *it* to
you." ' " 13So Gad came to David and told him;
and he said to him, "Shall seven[a] years of famine
come to you in your land? Or shall you flee three
months before your enemies, while they pursue
you? Or shall there be three days' plague in your
land? Now consider and see what answer I
should take back to Him who sent me."
14And David said to Gad, "I am in great dis-
tress. Please let us fall into the hand of the LORD,
for His mercies *are* great; but do not let me fall
into the hand of man."
15So the LORD sent a plague upon Israel from
the morning till the appointed time. From Dan
to Beersheba seventy thousand men of the peo-
ple died. 16And when the angel[a] stretched out
His hand over Jerusalem to destroy it, the LORD
relented from the destruction, and said to the
angel who was destroying the people, "It is
enough; now restrain your hand." And the angel
of the LORD was by the threshing floor of Arau-
nah[b] the Jebusite.
17Then David spoke to the LORD when he saw
the angel who was striking the people, and said,
"Surely I have sinned, and I have done wickedly;
but these sheep, what have they done? Let Your
hand, I pray, be against me and against my fa-
ther's house."

THE ALTAR ON THE THRESHING FLOOR

18And Gad came that day to David and said
to him, "Go up, erect an altar to the LORD on the
threshing floor of Araunah the Jebusite." 19So
David, according to the word of Gad, went up as
the LORD commanded. 20Now Araunah looked,
and saw the king and his servants coming to-
ward him. So Araunah went out and bowed be-
fore the king with his face to the ground.
21Then Araunah said, "Why has my lord the
king come to his servant?"
And David said, "To buy the threshing floor
from you, to build an altar to the LORD, that the
plague may be withdrawn from the people."

24:13 [a]Following Masoretic Text, Syriac, Targum, and Vulgate; Septuagint reads *three* (compare 1 Chronicles 21:12). **24:16** [a]Or *Angel* [b]Spelled *Ornan* in 1 Chronicles 21:15

THE MESSAGE

covered Fort Tyre and all the Hivite and
Canaanite cities, and finally reached the
Negev of Judah at Beersheba. They can-
vassed the whole country and after nine
months and twenty days arrived back in
Jerusalem. Joab gave the results of the cen-
sus to the king: 800,000 able-bodied fighting
men in Israel; in Judah 500,000.

10 But when it was all done, David was over-
whelmed with guilt because he had counted
the people, replacing trust with statistics.
And David prayed to GOD, "I have sinned
badly in what I have just done. But now GOD
forgive my guilt—I've been really stupid."

11-12 When David got up the next morning, the
word of GOD had already come to Gad the
prophet, David's spiritual advisor, "Go and
give David this message: 'GOD has spoken
thus: There are three things I can do to you;
choose one out of the three and I'll see that
it's done.' "

13 Gad came to deliver the message: "Do
you want three years of famine in the land,
or three months of running from your ene-
mies while they chase you down, or three
days of an epidemic on the country? Think
it over and make up your mind. What shall I
tell the one who sent me?"

14 David told Gad, "They're all terrible! But
I'd rather be punished by GOD, whose mercy
is great, than fall into human hands."

15-16 So GOD let loose an epidemic from morn-
ing until suppertime. From Dan to Beer-
sheba seventy thousand people died. But
when the angel reached out over Jerusalem
to destroy it, GOD felt the pain of the terror
and told the angel who was spreading death
among the people, "Enough's enough! Pull
back!"

The angel of GOD had just reached the
threshing floor of Araunah the Jebusite.
David looked up and saw the angel hovering
between earth and sky, sword drawn and
about to strike Jerusalem. David and the
elders bowed in prayer and covered them-
selves with rough burlap.

17 When David saw the angel about to de-
stroy the people, he prayed, "Please! I'm the
one who sinned; I, the shepherd, did the
wrong. But these sheep, what did they do
wrong? Punish me and my family, not
them."

18-19 That same day Gad came to David and
said, "Go and build an altar on the threshing
floor of Araunah the Jebusite." David did
what Gad told him, what GOD commanded.

20-21 Araunah looked up and saw David and
his men coming his way; he met them, bow-
ing deeply, honoring the king and saying,
"Why has my master the king come to see
me?"

"To buy your threshing floor," said David,
"so I can build an altar to GOD here and put
an end to this disaster."

NEW KING JAMES VERSION

22Now Araunah said to David, "Let my lord
the king take and offer up whatever *seems* good
to him. Look, *here are* oxen for burnt sacrifice,
and threshing implements and the yokes of the
oxen for wood. 23All these, O king, Araunah has
given to the king."

And Araunah said to the king, "May the
LORD your God accept you."

24Then the king said to Araunah, "No, but I
will surely buy *it* from you for a price; nor will I
offer burnt offerings to the LORD my God with
that which costs me nothing." So David bought
the threshing floor and the oxen for fifty shekels
of silver. 25And David built there an altar to the
LORD, and offered burnt offerings and peace of-
ferings. So the LORD heeded the prayers for the
land, and the plague was withdrawn from Israel.

THE MESSAGE

22-23 "Oh," said Araunah, "let my master the king take and sacrifice whatever he wants. Look, here's an ox for the burnt offering and threshing paddles and ox-yokes for fuel—Araunah gives it all to the king! And may GOD, your God, act in your favor."

24-25 But the king said to Araunah, "No. I've got to buy it from you for a good price; I'm not going to offer GOD, my God, sacrifices that are no sacrifice."

So David bought the threshing floor and the ox, paying out fifty shekels of silver. He built an altar to GOD there and sacrificed burnt offerings and peace offerings. GOD was moved by the prayers and that was the end of the disaster.

1 KINGS

New King James Version

Adonijah Presumes to Be King

1 Now King David was old, advanced in years; and they put covers on him, but he could not get warm. 2Therefore his servants said to him, "Let a young woman, a virgin, be sought for our lord the king, and let her stand before the king, and let her care for him; and let her lie in your bosom, that our lord the king may be warm." 3So they sought for a lovely young woman throughout all the territory of Israel, and found Abishag the Shunammite, and brought her to the king. 4The young woman *was* very lovely; and she cared for the king, and served him; but the king did not know her.

5Then Adonijah the son of Haggith exalted himself, saying, "I will be king"; and he prepared for himself chariots and horsemen, and fifty men to run before him. 6(And his father had not rebuked him at any time by saying, "Why have you done so?" He *was* also very good-looking. *His mother* had borne him after Absalom.) 7Then he conferred with Joab the son of Zeruiah and with Abiathar the priest, and they followed and helped Adonijah. 8But Zadok the priest, Benaiah the son of Jehoiada, Nathan the prophet, Shimei, Rei, and the mighty men who *belonged* to David were not with Adonijah.

9And Adonijah sacrificed sheep and oxen and fattened cattle by the stone of Zoheleth, which *is* by En Rogel; he also invited all his brothers, the king's sons, and all the men of Judah, the king's servants. 10But he did not invite Nathan the prophet, Benaiah, the mighty men, or Solomon his brother.

11So Nathan spoke to Bathsheba the mother of Solomon, saying, "Have you not heard that Adonijah the son of Haggith has become king, and David our lord does not know *it?* 12Come, please, let me now give you advice, that you may save your own life and the life of your son Solomon. 13Go immediately to King David and say to him, 'Did you not, my lord, O king, swear to your maidservant, saying, "Assuredly your son Solomon shall reign after me, and he shall sit on my throne"? Why then has Adonijah become king?' 14Then, while you are still talking there with the king, I also will come in after you and confirm your words."

15So Bathsheba went into the chamber to the king. (Now the king was very old, and Abishag the Shunammite was serving the king.) 16And Bathsheba bowed and did homage to the king. Then the king said, "What is your wish?"

17Then she said to him, "My lord, you swore by the LORD your God to your maidservant, *saying,* 'Assuredly Solomon your son shall reign after me, and he shall sit on my throne.' 18So now, look! Adonijah has become king; and now, my lord the king, you do not know about *it.* 19He has sacrificed oxen and fattened cattle and sheep in abundance, and has invited all the sons of the king, Abiathar the priest, and Joab the commander of the army; but Solomon your servant

The Message

David

1-4 1 King David grew old. The years had
caught up with him. Even though they
piled blankets on him, he couldn't keep
warm. So his servants said to him, "We're go-
ing to get a young virgin for our master the
king to be at his side and look after him;
she'll get in bed with you and arouse our
master the king." So they searched the coun-
try of Israel for the most ravishing girl they
could find; they found Abishag the Shunam-
mite and brought her to the king. The girl
was stunningly beautiful; she stayed at his
side and looked after the king, but the king
did not have sex with her.
5-6 At this time Adonijah, whose mother was
Haggith, puffed himself up saying, "I'm the
next king!" He made quite a splash, with
chariots and riders and fifty men to run
ahead of him. His father had spoiled him
rotten as a child, never once reprimanding
him. Besides that, he was very good-looking
and the next in line after Absalom.
7-8 Adonijah talked with Joab son of Zeruiah
and with Abiathar the priest, and they threw
their weight on his side. But neither the
priest Zadok, nor Benaiah son of Jehoiada,
nor Nathan the prophet, nor Shimei and
Rei, nor David's personal bodyguards sup-
ported Adonijah.
9-10 Next Adonijah held a coronation feast,
sacrificing sheep, cattle, and grain-fed
heifers at the Stone of Zoheleth near the Ro-
gel Spring. He invited all his brothers, the
king's sons, and everyone in Judah who had
position and influence—but he did not invite
the prophet Nathan, Benaiah, the body-
guards, or his brother Solomon.
11-14 Nathan went to Bathsheba, Solomon's
mother, "Did you know that Adonijah, Hag-
gith's son, has taken over as king, and our
master David doesn't know a thing about it?
Quickly now, let me tell you how you can
save both your own life and Solomon's. Go
immediately to King David. Speak up: 'Didn't
you, my master the king, promise me, "Your
son Solomon will be king after me and sit on
my throne"? So why is Adonijah now king?'
While you're there talking with the king, I'll
come in and corroborate your story."
15-16 Bathsheba went at once to the king in his
palace bedroom. He was so old! Abishag
was at his side making him comfortable. As
Bathsheba bowed low, honoring the king, he
said, "What do you want?"
17-21 "My master," she said, "you promised me
in GOD's name, 'Your son Solomon will be
king after me and sit on my throne.' And
now look what's happened—Adonijah has
taken over as king, and my master the king
doesn't even know it! He has thrown a huge
coronation feast—cattle and grain-fed
heifers and sheep—inviting all the king's
sons, the priest Abiathar, and Joab head of
the army. But your servant Solomon was *not*

NEW KING JAMES VERSION

he has not invited. 20And as for you, my lord, O king, the eyes of all Israel *are* on you, that you should tell them who will sit on the throne of my lord the king after him. 21Otherwise it will happen, when my lord the king rests with his fathers, that I and my son Solomon will be counted as offenders."

22And just then, while she was still talking with the king, Nathan the prophet also came in. 23So they told the king, saying, "Here is Nathan the prophet." And when he came in before the king, he bowed down before the king with his face to the ground. 24And Nathan said, "My lord, O king, have you said, 'Adonijah shall reign after me, and he shall sit on my throne'? 25For he has gone down today, and has sacrificed oxen and fattened cattle and sheep in abundance, and has invited all the king's sons, and the commanders of the army, and Abiathar the priest; and look! They are eating and drinking before him; and they say, '*Long* live King Adonijah!' 26But he has not invited me—me your servant—nor Zadok the priest, nor Benaiah the son of Jehoiada, nor your servant Solomon. 27Has this thing been done by my lord the king, and you have not told your servant who should sit on the throne of my lord the king after him?"

DAVID PROCLAIMS SOLOMON KING

28Then King David answered and said, "Call Bathsheba to me." So she came into the king's presence and stood before the king. 29And the king took an oath and said, "*As* the LORD lives, who has redeemed my life from every distress, 30just as I swore to you by the LORD God of Israel, saying, 'Assuredly Solomon your son shall be king after me, and he shall sit on my throne in my place,' so I certainly will do this day."

31Then Bathsheba bowed with *her* face to the earth, and paid homage to the king, and said, "Let my lord King David live forever!"

32And King David said, "Call to me Zadok the priest, Nathan the prophet, and Benaiah the son of Jehoiada." So they came before the king. 33The king also said to them, "Take with you the servants of your lord, and have Solomon my son ride on my own mule, and take him down to Gihon. 34There let Zadok the priest and Nathan the prophet anoint him king over Israel; and blow the horn, and say, '*Long* live King Solomon!' 35Then you shall come up after him, and he shall come and sit on my throne, and he shall be king in my place. For I have appointed him to be ruler over Israel and Judah."

36Benaiah the son of Jehoiada answered the king and said, "Amen! May the LORD God of my lord the king say so *too*. 37As the LORD has been with my lord the king, even so may He be with Solomon, and make his throne greater than the throne of my lord King David."

38So Zadok the priest, Nathan the prophet, Benaiah the son of Jehoiada, the Cherethites, and the Pelethites went down and had Solomon ride on King David's mule, and took him to Gihon. 39Then Zadok the priest took a horn of oil from the tabernacle and anointed Solomon. And

THE MESSAGE

invited. My master the king, every eye in Israel is watching you to see what you'll do—to see who will sit on the throne of my master the king after him. If you fail to act, the moment you're buried my son Solomon and I are as good as dead."

22-23 Abruptly, while she was telling the king all this, Nathan the prophet came in and was announced: "Nathan the prophet is here." He came before the king, honoring him by bowing deeply, his face touching the ground.

24-27 "My master the king," Nathan began, "did you say, 'Adonijah shall be king after me and sit on my throne'? Because that's what's happening. He's thrown a huge coronation feast—cattle, grain-fed heifers, sheep—inviting all the king's sons, the army officers, and Abiathar the priest. They're having a grand time, eating and drinking and shouting, 'Long live King Adonijah!' But I wasn't invited, nor was the priest Zadok, nor Benaiah son of Jehoiada, nor your servant Solomon. Is this something that my master the king has done behind our backs, not telling your servants who you intended to be king after you?"

28 King David took action: "Get Bathsheba back in here." She entered and stood before the king.

29-30 The king solemnly promised, "As GOD lives, the God who delivered me from every kind of trouble, I'll do exactly what I promised in GOD's name, the God of Israel: Your son Solomon will be king after me and take my place on the throne. And I'll make sure it happens this very day."

31 Bathsheba bowed low, her face to the ground. Kneeling in reverence before the king she said, "Oh, may my master, King David, live forever!"

32 King David said, "Call Zadok the priest, Nathan the prophet, and Benaiah son of Jehoiada." They came to the king.

33-35 Then he ordered, "Gather my servants, then mount my son Solomon on my royal mule and lead him in procession down to Gihon. When you get there, Zadok the priest and Nathan the prophet will anoint him king over Israel. Then blow the ram's horn trumpet and shout, 'Long live King Solomon!' You will then accompany him as he enters and takes his place on my throne, succeeding me as king. I have named him ruler over Israel and Judah."

36-37 Benaiah son of Jehoiada backed the king: "Yes! And may GOD, the God of my master the king, confirm it! Just as GOD has been with my master the king, may he also be with Solomon and make his rule even greater than that of my master King David!"

38-40 Then Zadok the priest, Nathan the prophet, Benaiah son of Jehoiada, and the king's personal bodyguard (the Kerethites and Pelethites) went down, mounted Solomon on King David's mule, and paraded with him to Gihon. Zadok the priest brought a flask of oil from the sanctuary and anointed Solomon. They blew the ram's

NEW KING JAMES VERSION

they blew the horn, and all the people said,
"*Long* live King Solomon!" 40And all the people
went up after him; and the people played the
flutes and rejoiced with great joy, so that the
earth *seemed to* split with their sound.
41Now Adonijah and all the guests who *were*
with him heard *it* as they finished eating. And
when Joab heard the sound of the horn, he said,
"Why *is* the city in such a noisy uproar?"
42While he was still speaking, there came
Jonathan, the son of Abiathar the priest. And
Adonijah said to him, "Come in, for you *are* a
prominent man, and bring good news."
43Then Jonathan answered and said to
Adonijah, "No! Our lord King David has made
Solomon king. 44The king has sent with him
Zadok the priest, Nathan the prophet, Benaiah
the son of Jehoiada, the Cherethites, and the
Pelethites; and they have made him ride on the
king's mule. 45So Zadok the priest and Nathan
the prophet have anointed him king at Gihon;
and they have gone up from there rejoicing, so
that the city is in an uproar. This *is* the noise that
you have heard. 46Also Solomon sits on the
throne of the kingdom. 47And moreover the
king's servants have gone to bless our lord King
David, saying, 'May God make the name of
Solomon better than your name, and may He
make his throne greater than your throne.' Then
the king bowed himself on the bed. 48Also the
king said thus, 'Blessed *be* the LORD God of Is-
rael, who has given *one* to sit on my throne this
day, while my eyes see *it!*' "
49So all the guests who were with Adonijah
were afraid, and arose, and each one went his
way.
50Now Adonijah was afraid of Solomon; so
he arose, and went and took hold of the horns of
the altar. 51And it was told Solomon, saying, "In-
deed Adonijah is afraid of King Solomon; for
look, he has taken hold of the horns of the altar,
saying, 'Let King Solomon swear to me today
that he will not put his servant to death with the
sword.' "
52Then Solomon said, "If he proves himself a
worthy man, not one hair of him shall fall to the
earth; but if wickedness is found in him, he shall
die." 53So King Solomon sent them to bring him
down from the altar. And he came and fell down
before King Solomon; and Solomon said to him,
"Go to your house."

DAVID'S INSTRUCTIONS TO SOLOMON

2 Now the days of David drew near that he
should die, and he charged Solomon his son,
saying: 2"I go the way of all the earth; be strong,
therefore, and prove yourself a man. 3And keep
the charge of the LORD your God: to walk in His
ways, to keep His statutes, His commandments,
His judgments, and His testimonies, as it is writ-
ten in the Law of Moses, that you may prosper
in all that you do and wherever you turn; 4that
the LORD may fulfill His word which He spoke
concerning me, saying, 'If your sons take heed
to their way, to walk before Me in truth with all
their heart and with all their soul,' He said, 'you
shall not lack a man on the throne of Israel.'

THE MESSAGE

horn trumpet and everyone shouted, "Long live King Solomon!" Everyone joined the fanfare, the band playing and the people singing, the very earth reverberating to the sound.

41 Adonijah and his retinue of guests were just finishing their "coronation" feast when they heard it. When Joab heard the blast of the ram's horn trumpet he said, "What's going on here? What's all this uproar?"

42 Suddenly, in the midst of the questioning, Jonathan son of Abiathar the priest, showed up. Adonijah said, "Welcome! A brave and good man like you must have good news."

43-48 But Jonathan answered, "Hardly! Our master King David has just made Solomon king! And the king has surrounded him with Zadok the priest, Nathan the prophet, Benaiah son of Jehoiada, with the Kerethites and Pelethites; and they've mounted Solomon on the royal mule. Zadok the priest and Nathan the prophet have anointed him king at Gihon and the parade is headed up this way singing—a great fanfare! The city is rocking! That's what you're hearing. Here's the crowning touch—Solomon is seated on the throne of the kingdom! And that's not all: The king's servants have come to give their blessing to our master King David saying, 'God make Solomon's name even more honored than yours, and make his rule greater than yours!' On his deathbed the king worshiped God and prayed, 'Blessed be GOD, Israel's God, who has provided a successor to my throne, and I've lived to see it!' "

49-50 Panicked, Adonijah's guests got out of there, scattering every which way. But Adonijah himself, afraid for his life because of Solomon, fled to the sanctuary and grabbed the horns of the Altar.

51 Solomon was told, "Adonijah, fearful of King Solomon, has taken sanctuary and seized the horns of the Altar and is saying, 'I'm not leaving until King Solomon promises that he won't kill me.' "

52-53 Solomon then said, "If he proves to be a man of honor, not a hair of his head will be hurt; but if there is evil in him, he'll die." Solomon summoned him and they brought him from the Altar. Adonijah came and bowed down, honoring the king. Solomon dismissed him, "Go home."

1-4 2 When David's time to die approached, he charged his son Solomon, saying, "I'm about to go the way of all the earth, but you—be strong; show what you're made of! Do what GOD tells you. Walk in the paths he shows you: Follow the life-map absolutely, keep an eye out for the signposts, his course for life set out in the revelation to Moses; then you'll get on well in whatever you do and wherever you go. Then GOD will confirm what he promised me when he said, 'If your sons watch their step, staying true to me heart and soul, you'll always have a successor on Israel's throne.'

New King James Version

5 “Moreover you know also what Joab the son
of Zeruiah did to me, *and* what he did to the two
commanders of the armies of Israel, to Abner
the son of Ner and Amasa the son of Jether,
whom he killed. And he shed the blood of war in
peacetime, and put the blood of war on his belt
that *was* around his waist, and on his sandals
that *were* on his feet. 6 Therefore do according to
your wisdom, and do not let his gray hair go
down to the grave in peace.

7 “But show kindness to the sons of Barzillai
the Gileadite, and let them be among those who
eat at your table, for so they came to me when I
fled from Absalom your brother.

8 “And see, *you have* with you Shimei the son
of Gera, a Benjamite from Bahurim, who cursed
me with a malicious curse in the day when I
went to Mahanaim. But he came down to meet
me at the Jordan, and I swore to him by the
LORD, saying, ‘I will not put you to death with
the sword.’ 9 Now therefore, do not hold him
guiltless, for you *are* a wise man and know what
you ought to do to him; but bring his gray hair
down to the grave with blood.”

Death of David

10 So David rested with his fathers, and was
buried in the City of David. 11 The period that
David reigned over Israel *was* forty years; seven
years he reigned in Hebron, and in Jerusalem he
reigned thirty-three years. 12 Then Solomon sat
on the throne of his father David; and his king-
dom was firmly established.

Solomon Executes Adonijah

13 Now Adonijah the son of Haggith came to
Bathsheba the mother of Solomon. So she said,
“Do you come peaceably?”

And he said, “Peaceably.” 14 Moreover he
said, “I have something *to say* to you.”

And she said, “Say it.”

15 Then he said, “You know that the kingdom
was mine, and all Israel had set their expecta-
tions on me, that I should reign. However, the
kingdom has been turned over, and has become
my brother’s; for it was his from the LORD.
16 Now I ask one petition of you; do not deny
me.”

And she said to him, “Say it.”

17 Then he said, “Please speak to King
Solomon, for he will not refuse you, that he may
give me Abishag the Shunammite as wife.”

18 So Bathsheba said, “Very well, I will speak
for you to the king.”

19 Bathsheba therefore went to King
Solomon, to speak to him for Adonijah. And the
king rose up to meet her and bowed down to
her, and sat down on his throne and had a
throne set for the king’s mother; so she sat at his
right hand. 20 Then she said, “I desire one small
petition of you; do not refuse me.”

And the king said to her, “Ask it, my mother,
for I will not refuse you.”

21 So she said, “Let Abishag the Shunammite
be given to Adonijah your brother as wife.”

22 And King Solomon answered and said to
his mother, “Now why do you ask Abishag the
Shunammite for Adonijah? Ask for him the

The Message

5-6 “And don’t forget what Joab son of Zeruiah did to the two commanders of Israel’s army, to Abner son of Ner and to Amasa son of Jether. He murdered them in cold blood, acting in peacetime as if he were at war, and has been stained with that blood ever since. Do what you think best with him, but by no means let him get off scot-free—make him pay.

7 “But be generous to the sons of Barzillai the Gileadite—extend every hospitality to them; that’s the way they treated me when I was running for my life from Absalom your brother.

8-9 “You also will have to deal with Shimei son of Gera the Benjaminite from Bahurim, the one who cursed me so viciously when I was on my way to Mahanaim. Later, when he welcomed me back at the Jordan, I promised him under GOD, ‘I won’t put you to death.’ But neither should you treat him as if nothing ever happened. You’re wise, you know how to handle these things. You’ll know what to do to make him pay before he dies.”

10-12 Then David joined his ancestors. He was buried in the City of David. David ruled Israel for forty years—seven years in Hebron and another thirty-three in Jerusalem. Solomon took over on the throne of his father David; he had a firm grip on the kingdom.

Solomon

13-14 Adonijah son of Haggith came to Bathsheba, Solomon’s mother. She said, “Do you come in peace?”

He said, “In peace.” And then, “May I say something to you?”

“Go ahead,” she said, “speak.”

15-16 “You know that I had the kingdom right in my hands and everyone expected me to be king, and then the whole thing backfired and the kingdom landed in my brother’s lap—GOD’s doing. So now I have one request to ask of you; please don’t refuse me.”

“Go ahead, ask,” she said.

17 “Ask King Solomon—he won’t turn *you* down—to give me Abishag the Shunammite as my wife.”

18 “Certainly,” said Bathsheba. “I’ll speak to the king for you.”

19 Bathsheba went to King Solomon to present Adonijah’s request. The king got up and welcomed her, bowing respectfully, and returned to his throne. Then he had a throne put in place for his mother, and she sat at his right hand.

20 She said, “I have a small favor to ask of you. Don’t refuse me.”

The king replied, “Go ahead, Mother; of course I won’t refuse you.”

21 She said, “Give Abishag the Shunammite to your brother Adonijah as his wife.”

22 King Solomon answered his mother, “What kind of favor is this, asking that Abishag the Shunammite be given to Adoni-

NEW KING JAMES VERSION

kingdom also—for he *is* my older brother—for
him, and for Abiathar the priest, and for Joab
the son of Zeruiah." [23]Then King Solomon swore
by the LORD, saying, "May God do so to me, and
more also, if Adonijah has not spoken this word
against his own life! [24]Now therefore, *as* the
LORD lives, who has confirmed me and set me
on the throne of David my father, and who has
established a house[a] for me, as He promised,
Adonijah shall be put to death today!"
[25]So King Solomon sent by the hand of Bena-
iah the son of Jehoiada; and he struck him
down, and he died.

ABIATHAR EXILED, JOAB EXECUTED

[26]And to Abiathar the priest the king said,
"Go to Anathoth, to your own fields, for you *are*
deserving of death; but I will not put you to
death at this time, because you carried the ark
of the Lord GOD before my father David, and be-
cause you were afflicted every time my father
was afflicted." [27]So Solomon removed Abiathar
from being priest to the LORD, that he might ful-
fill the word of the LORD which He spoke con-
cerning the house of Eli at Shiloh.
[28]Then news came to Joab, for Joab had de-
fected to Adonijah, though he had not defected
to Absalom. So Joab fled to the tabernacle of the
LORD, and took hold of the horns of the altar.
[29]And King Solomon was told, "Joab has fled to
the tabernacle of the LORD; there *he is*, by the al-
tar." Then Solomon sent Benaiah the son of Je-
hoiada, saying, "Go, strike him down." [30]So Be-
naiah went to the tabernacle of the LORD, and
said to him, "Thus says the king, 'Come out!' "
And he said, "No, but I will die here." And
Benaiah brought back word to the king, saying,
"Thus said Joab, and thus he answered me."
[31]Then the king said to him, "Do as he has
said, and strike him down and bury him, that
you may take away from me and from the house
of my father the innocent blood which Joab
shed. [32]So the LORD will return his blood on his
head, because he struck down two men more
righteous and better than he, and killed them
with the sword—Abner the son of Ner, the com-
mander of the army of Israel, and Amasa the
son of Jether, the commander of the army of Ju-
dah—though my father David did not know *it*.
[33]Their blood shall therefore return upon the
head of Joab and upon the head of his descen-
dants forever. But upon David and his descen-
dants, upon his house and his throne, there shall
be peace forever from the LORD."
[34]So Benaiah the son of Jehoiada went up
and struck and killed him; and he was buried in
his own house in the wilderness. [35]The king put
Benaiah the son of Jehoiada in his place over
the army, and the king put Zadok the priest in
the place of Abiathar.

SHIMEI EXECUTED

[36]Then the king sent and called for Shimei,
and said to him, "Build yourself a house in
Jerusalem and dwell there, and do not go out
from there anywhere. [37]For it shall be, on the
day you go out and cross the Brook Kidron,

2:24 [a]That is, a royal dynasty

THE MESSAGE

jah? Why don't you just ask me to hand over the whole kingdom to him on a platter since he is my older brother and has Abiathar the priest and Joab son of Zeruiah on his side!"

23-24 Then King Solomon swore under GOD, "May God do his worst to me if Adonijah doesn't pay for this with his life! As surely as GOD lives, the God who has set me firmly on the throne of my father David and has put me in charge of the kingdom just as he promised, Adonijah will die for this—today!"

25 King Solomon dispatched Benaiah son of Jehoiada; he struck Adonijah and he died.

26 The king then told Abiathar the priest, "You're exiled to your place in Anathoth. You deserve death but I'm not going to kill you—for now anyway—because you were in charge of the Chest of our ruling GOD in the company of David my father, and because you shared all the hard times with my father."

27 Solomon stripped Abiathar of his priesthood, fulfilling GOD's word at Shiloh regarding the family of Eli.

28-29 When this news reached Joab, this Joab who had conspired with Adonijah (although he had remained loyal in the Absalom affair), he took refuge in the sanctuary of GOD, seizing the horns of the Altar and holding on for dear life. King Solomon was told that Joab had escaped to the sanctuary of GOD and was clinging to the Altar; he immediately sent Benaiah son of Jehoiada with orders, "Kill him."

30 Benaiah went to the sanctuary of GOD and said, "King's orders: Come out."

He said, "No—I'll die right here."

Benaiah went back to the king and reported, "This was Joab's answer."

31-33 The king said, "Go ahead then, do what he says: Kill him and bury him. Absolve me and my father's family of the guilt from Joab's senseless murders. GOD is avenging those bloody murders on Joab's head. Two men he murdered, men better by far than he ever was: Behind my father's back he brutally murdered Abner son of Ner, commander of Israel's army, and Amasa son of Jether, commander of Judah's army. Responsibility for their murders is forever fixed on Joab and his descendants; but for David and his descendants, his family and kingdom, the final verdict is GOD's peace."

34-35 So Benaiah son of Jehoiada went back, struck Joab, and killed him. He was buried in his family plot out in the desert. The king appointed Benaiah son of Jehoiada over the army in place of Joab, and replaced Abiathar with Zadok the priest.

36-37 The king next called in Shimei and told him, "Build yourself a house in Jerusalem and live there, but you are not to leave the area. If you so much as cross the Brook

New King James Version

know for certain you shall surely die; your
blood shall be on your own head."
38And Shimei said to the king, "The saying *is*
good. As my lord the king has said, so your ser-
vant will do." So Shimei dwelt in Jerusalem
many days.
39Now it happened at the end of three years,
that two slaves of Shimei ran away to Achish the
son of Maachah, king of Gath. And they told
Shimei, saying, "Look, your slaves *are* in Gath!"
40So Shimei arose, saddled his donkey, and went
to Achish at Gath to seek his slaves. And Shimei
went and brought his slaves from Gath. 41And
Solomon was told that Shimei had gone from
Jerusalem to Gath and had come back. 42Then
the king sent and called for Shimei, and said to
him, "Did I not make you swear by the LORD,
and warn you, saying, 'Know for certain that on
the day you go out and travel anywhere, you
shall surely die'? And you said to me, 'The word
I have heard *is* good.' 43Why then have you not
kept the oath of the LORD and the command-
ment that I gave you?" 44The king said moreover
to Shimei, "You know, as your heart acknowl-
edges, all the wickedness that you did to my fa-
ther David; therefore the LORD will return your
wickedness on your own head. 45But King
Solomon *shall be* blessed, and the throne of
David shall be established before the LORD for-
ever."
46So the king commanded Benaiah the son of
Jehoiada; and he went out and struck him
down, and he died. Thus the kingdom was es-
tablished in the hand of Solomon.

Solomon Requests Wisdom

3 Now Solomon made a treaty with Pharaoh
king of Egypt, and married Pharaoh's daugh-
ter; then he brought her to the City of David un-
til he had finished building his own house, and
the house of the LORD, and the wall all around
Jerusalem. 2Meanwhile the people sacrificed at
the high places, because there was no house
built for the name of the LORD until those days.
3And Solomon loved the LORD, walking in the
statutes of his father David, except that he sac-
rificed and burned incense at the high places.
4Now the king went to Gibeon to sacrifice
there, for that *was* the great high place:
Solomon offered a thousand burnt offerings on
that altar. 5At Gibeon the LORD appeared to
Solomon in a dream by night; and God said,
"Ask! What shall I give you?"
6And Solomon said: "You have shown great
mercy to Your servant David my father, because
he walked before You in truth, in righteousness,
and in uprightness of heart with You; You have
continued this great kindness for him, and You
have given him a son to sit on his throne, as *it is*
this day. 7Now, O LORD my God, You have made
Your servant king instead of my father David,
but I *am* a little child; I do not know *how* to go
out or come in. 8And Your servant *is* in the midst

The Message

Kidron, you're as good as dead—you will
have decreed your own death sentence."
38 Shimei answered the king, "Oh, thank
you! Your servant will do exactly as my mas-
ter the king says." Shimei lived in Jerusalem
a long time.
39-40 But it so happened that three years later,
two of Shimei's slaves ran away to Achish
son of Maacah, king of Gath. Shimei was
told, "Your slaves are in Gath." Shimei
sprang into action, saddled his donkey, and
went to Achish in Gath looking for his
slaves. And then he came back, bringing his
slaves.
41 Solomon was told, "Shimei left Jerusalem
for Gath, and now he's back."
42-43 Solomon then called for Shimei and said,
"Didn't I make you promise me under GOD,
and give you a good warning besides, that
you would not leave this area? That if you left
you would have decreed your own death sen-
tence? And didn't you say, 'Oh, thank you—
I'll do exactly as you say'? So why didn't you
keep your sacred promise and do what I or-
dered?"
44-45 Then the king told Shimei, "Deep in your
heart you know all the evil that you did to
my father David; GOD will now avenge that
evil on you. But King Solomon will be
blessed and the rule of David will be a sure
thing under GOD forever."
46 The king then gave orders to Benaiah son
of Jehoiada; he went out and struck Shimei
dead.
The kingdom was now securely in
Solomon's grasp.

1-3 3 Solomon arranged a marriage contract
with Pharaoh, king of Egypt. He married
Pharaoh's daughter and brought her to the
City of David until he had completed build-
ing his royal palace and GOD's Temple and
the wall around Jerusalem. Meanwhile, the
people were worshiping at local shrines be-
cause at that time no temple had yet been
built to the Name of GOD. Solomon loved
GOD and continued to live in the God-honor-
ing ways of David his father, except that he
also worshiped at the local shrines, offering
sacrifices and burning incense.
4-5 The king went to Gibeon, the most pres-
tigious of the local shrines, to worship.
He sacrificed a thousand Whole-Burnt-
Offerings on that altar. That night, there in
Gibeon, GOD appeared to Solomon in a
dream: God said, "What can I give you?
Ask."
6 Solomon said, "You were extravagantly
generous in love with David my father, and
he lived faithfully in your presence, his rela-
tionships were just and his heart right. And
you have persisted in this great and gener-
ous love by giving him—and this very
day!—a son to sit on his throne.
7-8 "And now here I am: GOD, my God, you
have made me, your servant, ruler of the
kingdom in place of David my father. I'm
too young for this, a mere child! I don't
know the ropes, hardly know the 'ins' and

NEW KING JAMES VERSION

of Your people whom You have chosen, a great
people, too numerous to be numbered or
counted. [9]Therefore give to Your servant an un-
derstanding heart to judge Your people, that I
may discern between good and evil. For who is
able to judge this great people of Yours?”
[10]The speech pleased the LORD, that Solomon
had asked this thing. [11]Then God said to him:
“Because you have asked this thing, and have
not asked long life for yourself, nor have asked
riches for yourself, nor have asked the life of
your enemies, but have asked for yourself un-
derstanding to discern justice, [12]behold, I have
done according to your words; see, I have given
you a wise and understanding heart, so that
there has not been anyone like you before you,
nor shall any like you arise after you. [13]And I
have also given you what you have not asked:
both riches and honor, so that there shall not be
anyone like you among the kings all your days.
[14]So if you walk in My ways, to keep My statutes
and My commandments, as your father David
walked, then I will lengthen your days.”
[15]Then Solomon awoke; and indeed it had
been a dream. And he came to Jerusalem and
stood before the ark of the covenant of the
LORD, offered up burnt offerings, offered peace
offerings, and made a feast for all his servants.

SOLOMON'S WISE JUDGMENT

[16]Now two women *who were* harlots came to
the king, and stood before him. [17]And one
woman said, “O my lord, this woman and I dwell
in the same house; and I gave birth while she
was in the house. [18]Then it happened, the third
day after I had given birth, that this woman also
gave birth. And we *were* together; no one *was*
with us in the house, except the two of us in the
house. [19]And this woman's son died in the night,
because she lay on him. [20]So she arose in the
middle of the night and took my son from my
side, while your maidservant slept, and laid him
in her bosom, and laid her dead child in my
bosom. [21]And when I rose in the morning to
nurse my son, there he was, dead. But when I
had examined him in the morning, indeed, he
was not my son whom I had borne.”
[22]Then the other woman said, “No! But the
living one *is* my son, and the dead one *is* your
son.”

And the first woman said, “No! But the dead
one *is* your son, and the living one *is* my son.”

Thus they spoke before the king.
[23]And the king said, “The one says, ‘This *is*
my son, who lives, and your son *is* the dead one’;
and the other says, ‘No! But your son *is* the dead
one, and my son *is* the living one.’ ” [24]Then the
king said, “Bring me a sword.” So they brought
a sword before the king. [25]And the king said,
“Divide the living child in two, and give half to
one, and half to the other.”
[26]Then the woman whose son *was* living
spoke to the king, for she yearned with compas-
sion for her son; and she said, “O my lord, give
her the living child, and by no means kill him!”

But the other said, “Let him be neither mine
nor yours, *but* divide *him*.”

THE MESSAGE

‘outs’ of this job. And here I am, set down in the middle of the people you've chosen, a great people—far too many to ever count.

9 “Here's what I want: Give me a God-listening heart so I can lead your people well, discerning the difference between good and evil. For who on their own is capable of leading your glorious people?”

10-14 God, the Master, was delighted with Solomon's response. And God said to him, “Because you have asked for this and haven't grasped after a long life, or riches, or the doom of your enemies, but you have asked for the ability to lead and govern well, I'll give you what you've asked for—I'm giving you a wise and mature heart. There's never been one like you before; and there'll be no one after. As a bonus, I'm giving you both the wealth and glory you didn't ask for—there's not a king anywhere who will come up to your mark. And if you stay on course, keeping your eye on the life-map and the God-signs as your father David did, I'll also give you a long life.”

15 Solomon woke up—what a dream! He returned to Jerusalem, took his place before the Chest of the Covenant of God, and worshiped by sacrificing Whole-Burnt-Offerings and Peace-Offerings. Then he laid out a banquet for everyone in his service.

16-21 The very next thing, two prostitutes showed up before the king. The one woman said, “My master, this woman and I live in the same house. While we were living together, I had a baby. Three days after I gave birth, this woman also had a baby. We were alone—there wasn't anyone else in the house except for the two of us. The infant son of this woman died one night when she rolled over on him in her sleep. She got up in the middle of the night and took my son—I was sound asleep, mind you!—and put him at her breast and put her dead son at my breast. When I got up in the morning to nurse my son, here was this dead baby! But when I looked at him in the morning light, I saw immediately that he wasn't my baby.”

22 “Not so!” said the other woman. “The living one's mine; the dead one's yours.”

The first woman countered, “No! Your son's the dead one; mine's the living one.”

They went back and forth this way in front of the king.

23 The king said, “What are we to do? This woman says, ‘The living son is mine and the dead one is yours,’ and this woman says, ‘No, the dead one's yours and the living one's mine.’ ”

24 After a moment the king said, “Bring me a sword.” They brought the sword to the king.

25 Then he said, “Cut the living baby in two—give half to one and half to the other.”

26 The real mother of the living baby was overcome with emotion for her son and said, “Oh no, master! Give her the whole baby alive; don't kill him!”

But the other one said, “If I can't have him, you can't have him—cut away!”

New King James Version

27So the king answered and said, "Give the
first woman the living child, and by no means
kill him; she *is* his mother."
28And all Israel heard of the judgment which
the king had rendered; and they feared the king,
for they saw that the wisdom of God *was* in him
to administer justice.

Solomon's Administration

4 So King Solomon was king over all Israel.
2And these *were* his officials: Azariah the son
of Zadok, the priest; 3Elihoreph and Ahijah, the
sons of Shisha, scribes; Jehoshaphat the son of
Ahilud, the recorder; 4Benaiah the son of Je-
hoiada, over the army; Zadok and Abiathar, the
priests; 5Azariah the son of Nathan, over the of-
ficers; Zabud the son of Nathan, a priest *and* the
king's friend; 6Ahishar, over the household; and
Adoniram the son of Abda, over the labor force.
7And Solomon had twelve governors over all
Israel, who provided food for the king and his
household; each one made provision for one
month of the year. 8These *are* their names: Ben-
Hur,[a] in the mountains of Ephraim; 9Ben-
Deker,[a] in Makaz, Shaalbim, Beth Shemesh, and
Elon Beth Hanan; 10Ben-Hesed,[a] in Arubboth; to
him *belonged* Sochoh and all the land of He-
pher; 11Ben-Abinadab,[a] *in* all the regions of Dor;
he had Taphath the daughter of Solomon as
wife; 12Baana the son of Ahilud, *in* Taanach,
Megiddo, and all Beth Shean, which *is* beside
Zaretan below Jezreel, from Beth Shean to Abel
Meholah, as far as the other side of Jokneam;
13Ben-Geber,[a] in Ramoth Gilead; to him *be-
longed* the towns of Jair the son of Manasseh, in
Gilead; to him *also belonged* the region of Ar-
gob in Bashan—sixty large cities with walls and
bronze gate-bars; 14Ahinadab the son of Iddo, *in*
Mahanaim; 15Ahimaaz, in Naphtali; he also took
Basemath the daughter of Solomon as wife;
16Baanah the son of Hushai, in Asher and Aloth;
17Jehoshaphat the son of Paruah, in Issachar;
18Shimei the son of Elah, in Benjamin; 19Geber
the son of Uri, in the land of Gilead, *in* the coun-
try of Sihon king of the Amorites, and of Og
king of Bashan. *He was* the only governor who
was in the land.

Prosperity and Wisdom of Solomon's Reign

20Judah and Israel *were* as numerous as the
sand by the sea in multitude, eating and drink-

4:8 [a]Literally *Son of Hur* **4:9** [a]Literally *Son of Deker* **4:10** [a]Literally *Son of Hesed* **4:11** [a]Literally *Son of Abinadab* **4:13** [a]Literally *Son of Geber*

The Message

27 The king gave his decision: "Give the living baby to the first woman. Nobody is going to kill this baby. She is the real mother."

28 The word got around—everyone in Israel heard of the king's judgment. They were all in awe of the king, realizing that it was God's wisdom that enabled him to judge truly.

1-2 4 King Solomon was off to a good start ruling Israel.

These were the leaders in his government:

2-6 Azariah son of Zadok—the priest;
Elihoreph and Ahijah, sons of Shisha—secretaries;
Jehoshaphat son of Ahilud—historian;
Benaiah son of Jehoiada—commander of the army;
Zadok and Abiathar—priests;
Azariah son of Nathan—in charge of the regional managers;
Zabud son of Nathan—priest and friend to the king;
Ahishar—manager of the palace;
Adoniram son of Abda—manager of the slave labor.

7-19 Solomon had twelve regional managers distributed through-out Israel. They were responsible for supplying provisions for the king and his administration. Each was in charge of bringing supplies for one month of the year. These are the names:
Ben-Hur in the Ephraim hills;
Ben-Deker in Makaz, Shaalbim, Beth Shemesh, and Elon Bethhanan;
Ben-Hesed in Arubboth—this included Socoh and all of Hepher;
Ben-Abinadab in Naphoth Dor (he was married to Solomon's daughter Taphath);
Baana son of Ahilud in Taanach and Megiddo, all of Beth Shan next to Zarethan below Jezreel, and from Beth Shan to Abel Meholah over to Jokmeam;
Ben-Geber in Ramoth Gilead—this included the villages of Jair son of Manasseh in Gilead and the region of Argob in Bashan with its sixty large walled cities with bronze-studded gates;
Ahinadab son of Iddo in Mahanaim;
Ahimaaz in Naphtali (he was married to Solomon's daughter Basemath);
Baana son of Hushai in Asher and Aloth;
Jehoshaphat son of Paruah in Issachar;
Shimei son of Ela in Benjamin;
Geber son of Uri in Gilead—this was the country of Sihon king of the Amorites and also of Og king of Bashan; he managed the whole district by himself.

Solomon's Prosperity

20-21 Judah and Israel were densely populated—like sand on an ocean beach! All their needs

NEW KING JAMES VERSION

ing and rejoicing. 21So Solomon reigned over all
kingdoms from the River[a] *to* the land of the
Philistines, as far as the border of Egypt. *They*
brought tribute and served Solomon all the days
of his life.
22Now Solomon's provision for one day was
thirty kors of fine flour, sixty kors of meal, 23ten
fatted oxen, twenty oxen from the pastures, and
one hundred sheep, besides deer, gazelles, roe-
bucks, and fatted fowl.
24For he had dominion over all *the region* on
this side of the River[a] from Tiphsah even to
Gaza, namely over all the kings on this side of
the River; and he had peace on every side all
around him. 25And Judah and Israel dwelt
safely, each man under his vine and his fig tree,
from Dan as far as Beersheba, all the days of
Solomon.
26Solomon had forty[a] thousand stalls of
horses for his chariots, and twelve thousand
horsemen. 27And these governors, each man in
his month, provided food for King Solomon and
for all who came to King Solomon's table. There
was no lack in their supply. 28They also brought
barley and straw to the proper place, for the
horses and steeds, each man according to his
charge.
29And God gave Solomon wisdom and ex-
ceedingly great understanding, and largeness of
heart like the sand on the seashore. 30Thus
Solomon's wisdom excelled the wisdom of all
the men of the East and all the wisdom of Egypt.
31For he was wiser than all men—than Ethan the
Ezrahite, and Heman, Chalcol, and Darda, the
sons of Mahol; and his fame was in all the sur-
rounding nations. 32He spoke three thousand
proverbs, and his songs were one thousand and
five. 33Also he spoke of trees, from the cedar tree
of Lebanon even to the hyssop that springs out
of the wall; he spoke also of animals, of birds, of
creeping things, and of fish. 34And men of all na-
tions, from all the kings of the earth who had
heard of his wisdom, came to hear the wisdom
of Solomon.

SOLOMON PREPARES TO BUILD THE TEMPLE

5 Now Hiram king of Tyre sent his servants to
Solomon, because he heard that they had
anointed him king in place of his father, for Hi-
ram had always loved David. 2Then Solomon
sent to Hiram, saying:

> 3You know how my father David could not
> build a house for the name of the LORD his
> God because of the wars which were fought
> against him on every side, until the LORD
> put *his foes*[a] under the soles of his feet.

4:21 [a]That is, the Euphrates **4:24** [a]That is, the Euphrates **4:26** [a]Following Masoretic Text and most other authorities; some manuscripts of the Septuagint read *four* (compare 2 Chronicles 9:25). **5:3** [a]Literally *them*

THE MESSAGE

were met; they ate and drank and were happy. Solomon was sovereign over all the kingdoms from the River Euphrates in the east to the country of the Philistines in the west, all the way to the border of Egypt. They brought tribute and were vassals of Solomon all his life.

22-23 One day's food supply for Solomon's household was:

185 bushels of fine flour
375 bushels of meal
10 grain-fed cattle
20 range cattle
100 sheep
and miscellaneous deer, gazelles, roebucks, and choice fowl.

24-25 Solomon was sovereign over everything, countries and kings, west of the River Euphrates from Tiphsah to Gaza. Peace reigned everywhere. Throughout Solomon's life, everyone in Israel and Judah lived safe and sound, all of them from Dan in the north to Beersheba in the south—content with what they had.

26-28 Solomon had forty thousand stalls for chariot horses and twelve thousand horsemen. The district managers, each according to his assigned month, delivered food supplies for King Solomon and all who sat at the king's table; there was always plenty. They also brought to the designated place their assigned quota of barley and straw for the horses.

29-34 God gave Solomon wisdom—the deepest of understanding and the largest of hearts. There was nothing beyond him, nothing he couldn't handle. Solomon's wisdom outclassed the vaunted wisdom of wise men of the East, outshone the famous wisdom of Egypt. He was wiser than anyone—wiser than Ethan the Ezrahite, wiser than Heman, wiser than Calcol and Darda the sons of Mahol. He became famous among all the surrounding nations. He created 3,000 proverbs; his songs added up to 1,005. He knew all about plants, from the huge cedar that grows in Lebanon to the tiny hyssop that grows in the cracks of a wall. He understood everything about animals and birds, reptiles and fish. Sent by kings from all over the earth who had heard of his reputation, people came from far and near to listen to the wisdom of Solomon.

INTERNATIONAL FAME

1-4 5 Hiram king of Tyre sent ambassadors to Solomon when he heard that he had been crowned king in David's place. Hiram had loved David his whole life. Solomon responded, saying, "You know that David my father was not able to build a temple in honor of GOD because of the wars he had to fight on all sides, until GOD finally put them down. But now GOD has provided peace all

NEW KING JAMES VERSION

4But now the LORD my God has given me
rest on every side; *there is* neither adversary
nor evil occurrence.
5And behold, I propose to build a house for
the name of the LORD my God, as the LORD
spoke to my father David, saying, "Your son,
whom I will set on your throne in your place,
he shall build the house for My name."
6Now therefore, command that they cut
down cedars for me from Lebanon; and my
servants will be with your servants, and I
will pay you wages for your servants
according to whatever you say. For you
know *there is* none among us who has skill
to cut timber like the Sidonians.

7So it was, when Hiram heard the words of
Solomon, that he rejoiced greatly and said,

Blessed *be* the LORD this day, for He has given
David a wise son over this great people!

8Then Hiram sent to Solomon, saying:

I have considered *the message* which you
sent me, *and* I will do all you desire
concerning the cedar and cypress logs.
9My servants shall bring *them* down from
Lebanon to the sea; I will float them in rafts
by sea to the place you indicate to me, and
will have them broken apart there; then you
can take *them* away. And you shall fulfill my
desire by giving food for my household.

10Then Hiram gave Solomon cedar and cy-
press logs *according to* all his desire. 11And
Solomon gave Hiram twenty thousand kors of
wheat *as* food for his household, and twenty[a]
kors of pressed oil. Thus Solomon gave to Hi-
ram year by year.
12So the LORD gave Solomon wisdom, as He
had promised him; and there was peace be-
tween Hiram and Solomon, and the two of them
made a treaty together.
13Then King Solomon raised up a labor force
out of all Israel; and the labor force was thirty
thousand men. 14And he sent them to Lebanon,
ten thousand a month in shifts: they were one
month in Lebanon *and* two months at home;
Adoniram *was* in charge of the labor force.
15Solomon had seventy thousand who carried
burdens, and eighty thousand who quarried
stone in the mountains, 16besides three thousand
three hundred[a] from the chiefs of Solomon's
deputies, who supervised the people who la-
bored in the work. 17And the king commanded
them to quarry large stones, costly stones, *and*
hewn stones, to lay the foundation of the tem-
ple.[a] 18So Solomon's builders, Hiram's builders,
and the Gebalites quarried *them;* and they pre-
pared timber and stones to build the temple.

SOLOMON BUILDS THE TEMPLE

6And it came to pass in the four hundred and
eightieth[a] year after the children of Israel had

5:11 [a]Following Masoretic Text, Targum, and Vulgate; Septuagint and Syriac read *twenty thousand.* 5:16 [a]Following Masoretic Text, Targum, and Vulgate; Septuagint reads *three thousand six hundred.* 5:17 [a]Literally *house,* and so frequently throughout this book 6:1 [a]Following Masoretic Text, Targum, and Vulgate; Septuagint reads *fortieth.*

THE MESSAGE

around—no one against us, nothing at odds
with us.
5-6 "Now here is what I want to do: Build a
temple in honor of GOD, *my* God, following
the promise that GOD gave to David my fa-
ther, namely, 'Your son whom I will provide
to succeed you as king, he will build a house
in my honor.' And here is how you can help:
Give orders for cedars to be cut from the
Lebanon forest; my loggers will work along-
side yours and I'll pay your men whatever
wage you set. We both know that there is no
one like you Sidonians for cutting timber."
7 When Hiram got Solomon's message, he
was delighted, exclaiming, "Blessed be GOD
for giving David such a wise son to rule this
flourishing people!"
8-9 Then he sent this message to Solomon: "I
received your request for the cedars and cy-
presses. It's as good as done—your wish is
my command. My lumberjacks will haul the
timbers from the Lebanon forest to the sea,
assemble them into log rafts, float them to
the place you set, then have them disassem-
bled for you to haul away. All I want from
you is that you feed my crew."
10-12 In this way Hiram supplied all the cedar
and cypress timber that Solomon wanted. In
his turn, Solomon gave Hiram 125,000
bushels of wheat and 115,000 gallons of vir-
gin olive oil. He did this every year. And
GOD, for his part, gave Solomon wisdom,
just as he had promised. The healthy peace
between Hiram and Solomon was formal-
ized by a treaty.

THE TEMPLE WORK BEGINS

13-18 King Solomon raised a workforce of thirty
thousand men from all over Israel. He sent
them in shifts of ten thousand each month
to the Lebanon forest; they would work a
month in Lebanon and then be at home two
months. Adoniram was in charge of the
work crew. Solomon also had seventy thou-
sand unskilled workers and another eighty
thousand stonecutters up in the hills—plus
thirty-three hundred foremen managing the
project and supervising the work crews. Fol-
lowing the king's orders, they quarried huge
blocks of the best stone—dressed stone for
the foundation of The Temple. Solomon and
Hiram's construction workers, assisted by
the men of Gebal, cut and prepared the tim-
ber and stone for building The Temple.

1-6 6Four hundred and eighty years after the
Israelites came out of Egypt, in the fourth

NEW KING JAMES VERSION

come out of the land of Egypt, in the fourth year
of Solomon's reign over Israel, in the month of
Ziv, which *is* the second month, that he began to
build the house of the LORD. 2Now the house
which King Solomon built for the LORD, its
length *was* sixty cubits, its width twenty, and its
height thirty cubits. 3The vestibule in front of
the sanctuary[a] of the house *was* twenty cubits
long across the width of the house, *and* the
width of *the vestibule*[b] *extended* ten cubits from
the front of the house. 4And he made for the
house windows with beveled frames.

5Against the wall of the temple he built
chambers all around, *against* the walls of the
temple, all around the sanctuary and the inner
sanctuary.[a] Thus he made side chambers all
around it. 6The lowest chamber *was* five cubits
wide, the middle *was* six cubits wide, and the
third *was* seven cubits wide; for he made nar-
row ledges around the outside of the temple, so
that *the support beams* would not be fastened
into the walls of the temple. 7And the temple,
when it was being built, was built with stone fin-
ished at the quarry, so that no hammer or chisel
or any iron tool was heard in the temple while it
was being built. 8The doorway for the middle
story[a] *was* on the right side of the temple. They
went up by stairs to the middle *story,* and from
the middle to the third.

9So he built the temple and finished it, and
he paneled the temple with beams and boards of
cedar. 10And he built side chambers against the
entire temple, each five cubits high; they were
attached to the temple with cedar beams.

11Then the word of the LORD came to
Solomon, saying: 12"*Concerning* this temple
which you are building, if you walk in My
statutes, execute My judgments, keep all My
commandments, and walk in them, then I will
perform My word with you, which I spoke to
your father David. 13And I will dwell among the
children of Israel, and will not forsake My peo-
ple Israel."

14So Solomon built the temple and finished
it. 15And he built the inside walls of the temple
with cedar boards; from the floor of the temple
to the ceiling he paneled the inside with wood;
and he covered the floor of the temple with
planks of cypress. 16Then he built the twenty-
cubit room at the rear of the temple, from floor
to ceiling, with cedar boards; he built *it* inside as
the inner sanctuary, as the Most Holy *Place.*
17And in front of it the temple sanctuary was
forty cubits *long.* 18The inside of the temple was
cedar, carved with ornamental buds and open
flowers. All *was* cedar; there was no stone *to be*
seen.

19And he prepared the inner sanctuary inside
the temple, to set the ark of the covenant of the
LORD there. 20The inner sanctuary *was* twenty
cubits long, twenty cubits wide, and twenty cu-
bits high. He overlaid it with pure gold, and over-

6:3 [a]Hebrew *heykal;* here the main room of the temple, elsewhere called the holy place (compare Exodus 26:33 and Ezekiel 41:1) [b]Literally *it* **6:5** [a]Hebrew *debir;* here the inner room of the temple, elsewhere called the Most Holy Place (compare verse 16) **6:8** [a]Following Masoretic Text and Vulgate; Septuagint reads *upper story;* Targum reads *ground story.*

THE MESSAGE

year of Solomon's rule over Israel, in the month of Ziv, the second month, Solomon started building The Temple of GOD. The Temple that King Solomon built to GOD was ninety feet long, thirty feet wide, and forty-five feet high. There was a porch across the thirty-foot width of The Temple that extended out fifteen feet. Within The Temple he made narrow, deep-silled windows. Against the outside walls he built a supporting structure in which there were smaller rooms: The lower floor was seven and a half feet wide, the middle floor nine feet, and the third floor ten and a half feet. He had projecting ledges built into the outside Temple walls to support the buttressing beams.

7 The stone blocks for the building of The Temple were all dressed at the quarry so that the building site itself was reverently quiet—no noise from hammers and chisels and other iron tools.

8-10 The entrance to the ground floor was at the south end of The Temple; stairs led to the second floor and then to the third. Solomon built and completed The Temple, finishing it off with roof beams and planks of cedar. The supporting structure along the outside walls was attached to The Temple with cedar beams and the rooms in it were seven and a half feet tall.

11-13 The word of GOD came to Solomon saying, "About this Temple you are building—what's important is that you *live* the way I've set out for you and *do* what I tell you, following my instructions carefully and obediently. Then I'll complete in you the promise I made to David your father. I'll personally take up my residence among the Israelites—I won't desert my people Israel."

14-18 Solomon built and completed The Temple. He paneled the interior walls from floor to ceiling with cedar planks; for flooring he used cypress. The thirty feet at the rear of The Temple he made into an Inner Sanctuary, cedar planks from floor to ceiling—the Holy of Holies. The Main Sanctuary area in front was sixty feet long. The entire interior of The Temple was cedar, with carvings of fruits and flowers. All cedar—none of the stone was exposed.

19-22 The Inner Sanctuary within The Temple was for housing the Chest of the Covenant of God. This Inner Sanctuary was a cube, thirty feet each way, all plated with gold.

New King James Version

laid the altar of cedar. [21]So Solomon overlaid the inside of the temple with pure gold. He stretched gold chains across the front of the inner sanctuary, and overlaid it with gold. [22]The whole temple he overlaid with gold, until he had finished all the temple; also he overlaid with gold the entire altar that *was* by the inner sanctuary.

[23]Inside the inner sanctuary he made two cherubim *of* olive wood, *each* ten cubits high. [24]One wing of the cherub *was* five cubits, and the other wing of the cherub five cubits: ten cubits from the tip of one wing to the tip of the other. [25]And the other cherub *was* ten cubits; both cherubim *were* of the same size and shape. [26]The height of one cherub *was* ten cubits, and so *was* the other cherub. [27]Then he set the cherubim inside the inner room;[a] and they stretched out the wings of the cherubim so that the wing of the one touched *one* wall, and the wing of the other cherub touched the other wall. And their wings touched each other in the middle of the room. [28]Also he overlaid the cherubim with gold.

[29]Then he carved all the walls of the temple all around, both the inner and outer *sanctuaries,* with carved figures of cherubim, palm trees, and open flowers. [30]And the floor of the temple he overlaid with gold, both the inner and outer *sanctuaries.*

[31]For the entrance of the inner sanctuary he made doors *of* olive wood; the lintel *and* doorposts *were* one-fifth *of the wall.* [32]The two doors *were of* olive wood; and he carved on them figures of cherubim, palm trees, and open flowers, and overlaid *them* with gold; and he spread gold on the cherubim and on the palm trees. [33]So for the door of the sanctuary he also made doorposts *of* olive wood, one-fourth *of the wall.* [34]And the two doors *were of* cypress wood; two panels *comprised* one folding door, and two panels *comprised* the other folding door. [35]Then he carved cherubim, palm trees, and open flowers *on them,* and overlaid *them* with gold applied evenly on the carved work.

[36]And he built the inner court with three rows of hewn stone and a row of cedar beams.

[37]In the fourth year the foundation of the house of the LORD was laid, in the month of Ziv. [38]And in the eleventh year, in the month of Bul, which is the eighth month, the house was finished in all its details and according to all its plans. So he was seven years in building it.

Solomon's Other Buildings

7 But Solomon took thirteen years to build his own house; so he finished all his house.

[2]He also built the House of the Forest of Lebanon; its length *was* one hundred cubits, its width fifty cubits, and its height thirty cubits, with four rows of cedar pillars, and cedar beams on the pillars. [3]And *it was* paneled with cedar above the beams that *were* on forty-five pillars, fifteen *to* a row. [4]*There were* windows *with beveled frames in* three rows, and window *was* opposite window *in* three tiers. [5]And all the doorways and doorposts *had* rectangular frames; and window *was* opposite window *in* three tiers.

6:27 [a]Literally *house*

The Message

The Altar of cedar was also gold-plated. Everywhere you looked there was pure gold: gold chains strung in front of the gold-plated Inner Sanctuary—gold everywhere—walls, ceiling, floor, and Altar. Dazzling!

23-28 Then he made two cherubim, gigantic angel-like figures, from olivewood. Each was fifteen feet tall. The outstretched wings of the cherubim (they were identical in size and shape) measured another fifteen feet. He placed the two cherubim, their wings spread, in the Inner Sanctuary. The combined wingspread stretched the width of the room, the wing of one cherub touched one wall, the wing of the other the other wall, and the wings touched in the middle. The cherubim were gold-plated.

29-30 He then carved engravings of cherubim, palm trees, and flower blossoms on all the walls of both the Inner and the Main Sanctuary. And all the floors of both inner and outer rooms were gold-plated.

31-32 He constructed doors of olivewood for the entrance to the Inner Sanctuary; the lintel and doorposts were five-sided. The doors were also carved with cherubim, palm trees, and flowers, and then covered with gold leaf.

33-35 Similarly, he built the entrance to the Main Sanctuary using olivewood for the doorposts but these doorposts were four-sided. The doors were of cypress, split into two panels, each panel swinging separately. These also were carved with cherubim, palm trees, and flowers, and plated with finely hammered gold leaf.

36 He built the inner court with three courses of dressed stones topped with a course of planed cedar timbers.

37-38 The foundation for GOD's Temple was laid in the fourth year in the month of Ziv. It was completed in the eleventh year in the month of Bul (the eighth month) down to the last detail, just as planned. It took Solomon seven years to build it.

1-5 **7** It took Solomon another thirteen years to finish building his own palace complex. He built the Palace of the Forest of Lebanon a hundred and fifty feet long, seventy-five feet wide, and forty-five feet high. There were four rows of cedar columns supporting forty-five cedar beams, fifteen in each row, and then roofed with cedar. Windows in groupings of three were set high in the walls on either side. All the doors were rectangular and arranged symmetrically.

NEW KING JAMES VERSION

6He also made the Hall of Pillars: its length
was fifty cubits, and its width thirty cubits; and
in front of them *was* a portico with pillars, and
a canopy *was* in front of them.
7Then he made a hall for the throne, the Hall
of Judgment, where he might judge; and *it was*
paneled with cedar from floor to ceiling.[a]
8And the house where he dwelt *had* another
court inside the hall, of like workmanship.
Solomon also made a house like this hall for
Pharaoh's daughter, whom he had taken *as*
wife.
9All these *were of* costly stones cut to size,
trimmed with saws, inside and out, from the
foundation to the eaves, and also on the outside
to the great court. 10The foundation *was of*
costly stones, large stones, some ten cubits and
some eight cubits. 11And above *were* costly
stones, hewn to size, and cedar wood. 12The
great court *was* enclosed with three rows of
hewn stones and a row of cedar beams. So were
the inner court of the house of the LORD and the
vestibule of the temple.

HIRAM THE CRAFTSMAN

13Now King Solomon sent and brought Hu-
ram[a] from Tyre. 14He *was* the son of a widow
from the tribe of Naphtali, and his father *was* a
man of Tyre, a bronze worker; he was filled with
wisdom and understanding and skill in working
with all kinds of bronze work. So he came to
King Solomon and did all his work.

THE BRONZE PILLARS FOR THE TEMPLE

15And he cast two pillars of bronze, each one
eighteen cubits high, and a line of twelve cubits
measured the circumference of each. 16Then he
made two capitals *of* cast bronze, to set on the
tops of the pillars. The height of one capital *was*
five cubits, and the height of the other capital
was five cubits. 17*He made* a lattice network,
with wreaths of chainwork, for the capitals
which *were* on top of the pillars: seven chains
for one capital and seven for the other capital.
18So he made the pillars, and two rows of pome-
granates above the network all around to cover
the capitals that *were* on top; and thus he did for
the other capital.
19The capitals which *were* on top of the pil-
lars in the hall *were* in the shape of lilies, four
cubits. 20The capitals on the two pillars also *had*
pomegranates above, by the convex surface
which *was* next to the network; and there *were*
two hundred such pomegranates in rows on
each of the capitals all around.
21Then he set up the pillars by the vestibule
of the temple; he set up the pillar on the right
and called its name Jachin, and he set up the pil-
lar on the left and called its name Boaz. 22The
tops of the pillars were in the shape of lilies. So
the work of the pillars was finished.

THE SEA AND THE OXEN

23And he made the Sea of cast bronze, ten
cubits from one brim to the other; *it was* com-

7:7 [a]Literally *floor,* that is, of the upper level **7:13** [a]Hebrew *Hiram* (compare 2 Chronicles 2:13, 14)

THE MESSAGE

6 He built a colonnaded courtyard seventy-five feet long and forty-five wide. It had a roofed porch at the front with ample eaves.

7 He built a court room, the Hall of Justice, where he would decide judicial matters, and paneled it with cedar.

8 He built his personal residence behind the Hall on a similar plan. Solomon also built another one just like it for Pharaoh's daughter, whom he had married.

9-12 No expense was spared—everything here, inside and out, from foundation to roof was constructed using high-quality stone, accurately cut and shaped and polished. The foundation stones were huge, ranging in size from twelve to fifteen feet, and of the very best quality. The finest stone was used above the foundation, shaped to size and trimmed with cedar. The courtyard was enclosed with a wall made of three layers of stone and topped with cedar timbers, just like the one in the porch of The Temple of GOD.

13-14 King Solomon sent to Tyre and asked Hiram (not the king; another Hiram) to come. Hiram's mother was a widow from the tribe of Naphtali. His father was a Tyrian and a master worker in bronze. Hiram was a real artist—he could do anything with bronze. He came to King Solomon and did all the bronze work.

15-22 First he cast two pillars in bronze, each twenty-seven feet tall and eighteen feet in circumference. He then cast two capitals in bronze to set on the pillars; each capital was seven and a half feet high and flared at the top in the shape of a lily. Each capital was dressed with an elaborate filigree of seven braided chains and a double row of two hundred pomegranates, setting the pillars off magnificently. He set the pillars up in the entrance porch to The Temple; the pillar to the south he named Security (Jachin) and the pillar to the north Stability (Boaz). The capitals were in the shape of lilies.

22-24 When the pillars were finished, Hiram's next project was to make the Sea—an immense round basin of cast metal fifteen feet

NEW KING JAMES VERSION

pletely round. Its height *was* five cubits, and a
line of thirty cubits measured its circumference.
24Below its brim *were* ornamental buds en-
circling it all around, ten to a cubit, all the way
around the Sea. The ornamental buds *were* cast
in two rows when it was cast. 25It stood on
twelve oxen: three looking toward the north,
three looking toward the west, three looking to-
ward the south, and three looking toward the
east; the Sea *was set* upon them, and all their
back parts *pointed* inward. 26It *was* a hand-
breadth thick; and its brim was shaped like the
brim of a cup, *like* a lily blossom. It contained
two thousand[a] baths.

THE CARTS AND THE LAVERS

27He also made ten carts of bronze; four cu-
bits *was* the length of each cart, four cubits its
width, and three cubits its height. 28And this *was*
the design of the carts: They had panels, and the
panels *were* between frames; 29on the panels
that *were* between the frames *were* lions, oxen,
and cherubim. And on the frames *was* a
pedestal on top. Below the lions and oxen *were*
wreaths of plaited work. 30Every cart had four
bronze wheels and axles of bronze, and its four
feet had supports. Under the laver *were* sup-
ports of cast *bronze* beside each wreath. 31Its
opening inside the crown at the top *was* one cu-
bit in diameter; and the opening *was* round,
shaped *like* a pedestal, one and a half cubits in
outside diameter; and also on the opening *were*
engravings, but the panels were square, not
round. 32Under the panels *were* the four wheels,
and the axles of the wheels *were joined* to the
cart. The height of a wheel *was* one and a half
cubits. 33The workmanship of the wheels *was*
like the workmanship of a chariot wheel; their
axle pins, their rims, their spokes, and their
hubs *were* all of cast *bronze*. 34And *there were*
four supports at the four corners of each cart; its
supports *were* part of the cart itself. 35On the top
of the cart, at the height of half a cubit, *it was*
perfectly round. And on the top of the cart, its
flanges and its panels *were* of the same casting.
36On the plates of its flanges and on its panels he
engraved cherubim, lions, and palm trees, wher-
ever there was a clear space on each, with
wreaths all around. 37Thus he made the ten
carts. All of them were of the same mold, one
measure, *and* one shape.
38Then he made ten lavers of bronze; each
laver contained forty baths, *and* each laver *was*
four cubits. On each of the ten carts *was* a laver.
39And he put five carts on the right side of the
house, and five on the left side of the house. He
set the Sea on the right side of the house, toward
the southeast.

FURNISHINGS OF THE TEMPLE

40Huram[a] made the lavers and the shovels
and the bowls. So Huram finished doing all the
work that he was to do for King Solomon *for* the
house of the LORD: 41the two pillars, the *two*
bowl-shaped capitals that *were* on top of the

7:26 [a]Or *three thousand* (compare 2 Chronicles 4:5) **7:40** [a]Hebrew *Hiram* (compare 2 Chronicles 2:13, 14)

THE MESSAGE

in diameter, seven and a half feet tall, and
forty-five feet in circumference. Just under
the rim there were two bands of decorative
gourds, ten gourds to each foot and a half.
The gourds were cast in one piece with the
Sea.

25-26 The Sea was set on twelve bulls, three
facing north, three facing west, three facing
south, and three facing east; the bulls faced
outward supporting the Sea on their
hindquarters. The Sea was three inches
thick and flared at the rim like a cup, or like
a lily. It held about 11,500 gallons.

27-33 Hiram also made ten washstands of
bronze. Each was six feet square and four
and a half feet tall. They were made like
this: Panels were fastened to the uprights.
Lions, bulls, and cherubim were repre-
sented on the panels and uprights. Beveled
wreath-work bordered the lions and bulls
above and below. Each stand was mounted
on four bronze wheels with bronze axles.
The uprights were cast with decorative re-
lief work. Each stand held a basin on a cir-
cular engraved support a foot and a half
deep set on a pedestal two and a quarter feet
square. The washstand itself was square.
The axles were attached under the stand
and the wheels fixed to them. The wheels
were twenty-seven inches in diameter; they
were designed like chariot wheels. Every-
thing—axles, rims, spokes, and hubs—was
of cast metal.

34-37 There was a handle at the four corners of
each washstand, the handles cast in one
piece with the stand. At the top of the wash-
stand there was a ring about nine inches
deep. The uprights and handles were cast
with the stand. Everything and every avail-
able surface was engraved with cherubim,
lions, and palm trees, bordered by ara-
besques. The washstands were identical, all
cast in the same mold.

38-40 He also made ten bronze washbasins,
each six feet in diameter with a capacity of
230 gallons, one basin for each of the ten
washstands. He arranged five stands on the
south side of The Temple and five on the
north. The Sea was placed at the southeast
corner of The Temple. Hiram then fashioned
the various utensils: buckets and shovels
and bowls.

40-45 Hiram completed all the work he set out
to do for King Solomon on The Temple of
GOD:

two pillars;
two capitals on top of the pillars;

NEW KING JAMES VERSION

two pillars; the two networks covering the two bowl-shaped capitals which *were* on top of the pillars; [42]four hundred pomegranates for the two networks (two rows of pomegranates for each network, to cover the two bowl-shaped capitals that *were* on top of the pillars); [43]the ten carts, and ten lavers on the carts; [44]one Sea, and twelve oxen under the Sea; [45]the pots, the shovels, and the bowls.

All these articles which Huram[a] made for King Solomon *for* the house of the LORD *were of* burnished bronze. [46]In the plain of Jordan the king had them cast in clay molds, between Succoth and Zaretan. [47]And Solomon did not weigh all the articles, because *there were* so many; the weight of the bronze was not determined.

[48]Thus Solomon had all the furnishings made for the house of the LORD: the altar of gold, and the table of gold on which *was* the showbread; [49]the lampstands of pure gold, five on the right *side* and five on the left in front of the inner sanctuary, with the flowers and the lamps and the wick-trimmers of gold; [50]the basins, the trimmers, the bowls, the ladles, and the censers of pure gold; and the hinges of gold, *both* for the doors of the inner room (the Most Holy *Place*) *and* for the doors of the main hall of the temple.

[51]So all the work that King Solomon had done for the house of the LORD was finished; and Solomon brought in the things which his father David had dedicated: the silver and the gold and the furnishings. He put them in the treasuries of the house of the LORD.

THE ARK BROUGHT INTO THE TEMPLE

8 Now Solomon assembled the elders of Israel and all the heads of the tribes, the chief fathers of the children of Israel, to King Solomon in Jerusalem, that they might bring up the ark of the covenant of the LORD from the City of David, which *is* Zion. [2]Therefore all the men of Israel assembled with King Solomon at the feast in the month of Ethanim, which *is* the seventh month. [3]So all the elders of Israel came, and the priests took up the ark. [4]Then they brought up the ark of the LORD, the tabernacle of meeting, and all the holy furnishings that *were* in the tabernacle. The priests and the Levites brought them up. [5]Also King Solomon, and all the congregation of Israel who were assembled with him, *were* with him before the ark, sacrificing sheep and oxen that could not be counted or numbered for multitude.

7:45 [a]Hebrew *Hiram* (compare 2 Chronicles 2:13, 14)

THE MESSAGE

two decorative filigrees for the capitals;
four hundred pomegranates for the two filigrees
(a double row of pomegranates for each filigree);
ten washstands each with its washbasin;
one Sea;
twelve bulls under the Sea;
miscellaneous buckets, shovels, and bowls.

45-47 All these artifacts that Hiram made for King Solomon for The Temple of GOD were of burnished bronze. He cast them in clay in a foundry on the Jordan plain between Succoth and Zarethan. These artifacts were never weighed—there were far too many! Nobody has any idea how much bronze was used.

48-50 Solomon was also responsible for all the furniture and accessories in The Temple of GOD:

the gold Altar;
the gold Table that held the Bread of the Presence;
the pure gold candelabras, five to the right and five to the left in front of the Inner Sanctuary;
the gold flowers, lamps, and tongs;
the pure gold dishes, wick trimmers, sprinkling bowls, ladles, and censers;
the gold sockets for the doors of the Inner Sanctuary, the Holy of Holies, used also for the doors of the Main Sanctuary.

51 That completed all the work King Solomon did on The Temple of GOD. He then brought in the items consecrated by his father David, the silver and the gold and the artifacts. He placed them all in the treasury of GOD's Temple.

1-2 8 Bringing all this to a climax, King Solomon called in the leaders of Israel, all the heads of the tribes and the family patriarchs, to bring up the Chest of the Covenant of GOD from Zion, the City of David. And they came, all Israel before King Solomon in the month of Ethanim, the seventh month, for the great autumn festival.

3-5 With all Israel's leaders present, the priests took up the Chest of GOD and carried up the Chest and the Tent of Meeting and all the holy vessels that went with the Tent. King Solomon and the entire congregation of Israel were there at the Chest worshiping and sacrificing huge numbers of sheep and cattle—so many that no one could keep track.

New King James Version

6Then the priests brought in the ark of the
covenant of the LORD to its place, into the inner
sanctuary of the temple, to the Most Holy *Place*,
under the wings of the cherubim. 7For the cheru-
bim spread *their* two wings over the place of the
ark, and the cherubim overshadowed the ark
and its poles. 8The poles extended so that the
ends of the poles could be seen from the holy
place, in front of the inner sanctuary; but they
could not be seen from outside. And they are
there to this day. 9Nothing *was* in the ark except
the two tablets of stone which Moses put there
at Horeb, when the LORD made *a covenant* with
the children of Israel, when they came out of the
land of Egypt.

10And it came to pass, when the priests came
out of the holy *place*, that the cloud filled the
house of the LORD, 11so that the priests could not
continue ministering because of the cloud; for
the glory of the LORD filled the house of the
LORD.

12Then Solomon spoke:

"The LORD said He would dwell in the dark
cloud.
13I have surely built You an exalted house,
And a place for You to dwell in forever."

Solomon's Speech at Completion of the Work

14Then the king turned around and blessed
the whole assembly of Israel, while all the as-
sembly of Israel was standing. 15And he said:
"Blessed *be* the LORD God of Israel, who spoke
with His mouth to my father David, and with
His hand has fulfilled *it*, saying, 16'Since the day
that I brought My people Israel out of Egypt, I
have chosen no city from any tribe of Israel *in
which* to build a house, that My name might be
there; but I chose David to be over My people Is-
rael.' 17Now it was in the heart of my father
David to build a temple[a] for the name of the
LORD God of Israel. 18But the LORD said to my fa-
ther David, 'Whereas it was in your heart to
build a temple for My name, you did well that it
was in your heart. 19Nevertheless you shall not
build the temple, but your son who will come
from your body, he shall build the temple for My
name.' 20So the LORD has fulfilled His word
which He spoke; and I have filled the position of
my father David, and sit on the throne of Israel,
as the LORD promised; and I have built a temple
for the name of the LORD God of Israel. 21And
there I have made a place for the ark, in which
is the covenant of the LORD which He made with
our fathers, when He brought them out of the
land of Egypt."

Solomon's Prayer of Dedication

22Then Solomon stood before the altar of the
LORD in the presence of all the assembly of Is-
rael, and spread out his hands toward heaven;
23and he said: "LORD God of Israel, *there is* no
God in heaven above or on earth below like You,
who keep *Your* covenant and mercy with Your
servants who walk before You with all their
hearts. 24You have kept what You promised Your

8:17 [a]Literally *house*, and so in verses 18–20

The Message

6-9 Then the priests brought the Chest of the Covenant of GOD to its place in the Inner Sanctuary, the Holy of Holies, under the wings of the cherubim. The outspread wings of the cherubim stretched over the Chest and its poles. The poles were so long that their ends could be seen from the entrance to the Inner Sanctuary, but were not noticeable farther out. They're still there today. There was nothing in the Chest but the two stone tablets that Moses had placed in it at Horeb where GOD made a covenant with Israel after bringing them up from Egypt.

The Temple Finished, Dedicated, Filled

10-11 When the priests left the Holy Place, a cloud filled The Temple of GOD. The priests couldn't carry out their priestly duties because of the cloud—the glory of GOD filled The Temple of GOD!

12-13 Then Solomon spoke:

GOD has told us that he lives in the dark
where no one can see him;
I've built this splendid Temple, O God,
to mark your invisible presence
forever.

14 The king then turned to face the congregation and blessed them:

15-16 "Blessed be GOD, the God of Israel, who spoke personally to my father David. Now he has kept the promise he made when he said, 'From the day I brought my people Israel from Egypt, I haven't set apart one city among the tribes of Israel to build a Temple to fix my Name there. But I did choose David to rule my people Israel.'

17-19 "My father David had it in his heart to build a Temple honoring the Name of GOD, the God of Israel. But GOD told him 'It was good that you wanted to build a Temple in my honor—most commendable! But you are not the one to do it—your son will build it to honor my Name.'

20-21 "GOD has done what he said he would do: I have succeeded David my father and ruled over Israel just as GOD promised; and now I've built a Temple to honor GOD, the God of Israel, and I've secured a place for the Chest that holds the covenant of GOD, the covenant that he made with our ancestors when he brought them up from the land of Egypt."

22-25 Before the entire congregation of Israel, Solomon took a position before the Altar, spread his hands out before heaven, and prayed,

O GOD, God of Israel, there is no God
like you in the skies above or on the
earth below who unswervingly keeps
covenant with his servants and relent-
lessly loves them as they sincerely
live in obedience to your way. You kept
your word to David my father, your

NEW KING JAMES VERSION

servant David my father; You have both spoken
with Your mouth and fulfilled *it* with Your hand,
as *it is* this day. 25 Therefore, LORD God of Israel,
now keep what You promised Your servant
David my father, saying, 'You shall not fail to
have a man sit before Me on the throne of Israel,
only if your sons take heed to their way, that
they walk before Me as you have walked before
Me.' 26 And now I pray, O God of Israel, let Your
word come true, which You have spoken to Your
servant David my father.

27 "But will God indeed dwell on the earth?
Behold, heaven and the heaven of heavens can-
not contain You. How much less this temple
which I have built! 28 Yet regard the prayer of
Your servant and his supplication, O LORD my
God, and listen to the cry and the prayer which
Your servant is praying before You today: 29 that
Your eyes may be open toward this temple night
and day, toward the place of which You said, 'My
name shall be there,' that You may hear the
prayer which Your servant makes toward this
place. 30 And may You hear the supplication of
Your servant and of Your people Israel, when
they pray toward this place. Hear in heaven Your
dwelling place; and when You hear, forgive.

31 "When anyone sins against his neighbor,
and is forced to take an oath, and comes *and*
takes an oath before Your altar in this temple,
32 then hear in heaven, and act, and judge Your
servants, condemning the wicked, bringing his
way on his head, and justifying the righteous by
giving him according to his righteousness.

33 "When Your people Israel are defeated be-
fore an enemy because they have sinned against
You, and when they turn back to You and con-
fess Your name, and pray and make supplication
to You in this temple, 34 then hear in heaven, and
forgive the sin of Your people Israel, and bring
them back to the land which You gave to their
fathers.

35 "When the heavens are shut up and there is
no rain because they have sinned against You,
when they pray toward this place and confess
Your name, and turn from their sin because You
afflict them, 36 then hear in heaven, and forgive
the sin of Your servants, Your people Israel, that
You may teach them the good way in which they
should walk; and send rain on Your land which
You have given to Your people as an inheritance.

THE MESSAGE

personal word. You did exactly what you promised—every detail. The proof is before us today!

Keep it up, GOD, O God of Israel! Continue to keep the promises you made to David my father when you said, "You'll always have a descendant to represent my rule on Israel's throne, on the condition that your sons are as careful to live obediently in my presence as you have."

26 O God of Israel, let this all happen;
confirm and establish it!

27-32 Can it be that God will actually move into our neighborhood? Why, the cosmos itself isn't large enough to give you breathing room, let alone this Temple I've built. Even so, I'm bold to ask: Pay attention to these my prayers, both intercessory and personal, O GOD, my God. Listen to my prayers, energetic and devout, that I'm setting before you right now. Keep your eyes open to this Temple night and day, this place of which you said, "My Name will be honored there," and listen to the prayers that I pray at this place.

Listen from your home in heaven
and when you hear, forgive.

When someone hurts a neighbor and promises to make things right, and then comes and repeats the promise before your Altar in this Temple, listen from heaven and act accordingly: Judge your servants, making the offender pay for his offense and setting the offended free of any charges.

33-34 When your people Israel are beaten by an enemy because they've sinned against you, but then turn to you and acknowledge your rule in prayers desperate and devout in this Temple,

Listen from your home in heaven,
forgive the sin of your people
Israel,
return them to the land you gave
their ancestors.

35-36 When the skies shrivel up and there is no rain because your people have sinned against you, but then they pray at this place, acknowledging your rule and quitting their sins because you have scourged them,

Listen from your home in heaven,
forgive the sins of your servants,
your people Israel.

Then start over with them: Train them to live right and well; send rain on the land you gave your people as an inheritance.

New King James Version

37“When there is famine in the land, pesti-
lence *or* blight *or* mildew, locusts *or* grasshop-
pers; when their enemy besieges them in the
land of their cities; whatever plague or whatever
sickness *there is;* 38whatever prayer, whatever
supplication is made by anyone, *or* by all Your
people Israel, when each one knows the plague
of his own heart, and spreads out his hands to-
ward this temple: 39then hear in heaven Your
dwelling place, and forgive, and act, and give to
everyone according to all his ways, whose heart
You know (for You alone know the hearts of all
the sons of men), 40that they may fear You all the
days that they live in the land which You gave to
our fathers.
41“Moreover, concerning a foreigner, who *is*
not of Your people Israel, but has come from a
far country for Your name’s sake 42(for they will
hear of Your great name and Your strong hand
and Your outstretched arm), when he comes and
prays toward this temple, 43hear in heaven Your
dwelling place, and do according to all for
which the foreigner calls to You, that all peoples
of the earth may know Your name and fear You,
as *do* Your people Israel, and that they may
know that this temple which I have built is
called by Your name.
44“When Your people go out to battle against
their enemy, wherever You send them, and when
they pray to the LORD toward the city which You
have chosen and the temple which I have built
for Your name, 45then hear in heaven their
prayer and their supplication, and maintain
their cause.
46“When they sin against You (for *there is* no
one who does not sin), and You become angry
with them and deliver them to the enemy, and
they take them captive to the land of the enemy,
far or near; 47*yet* when they come to themselves
in the land where they were carried captive, and
repent, and make supplication to You in the land
of those who took them captive, saying, ‘We
have sinned and done wrong, we have commit-
ted wickedness’; 48and *when* they return to You
with all their heart and with all their soul in the
land of their enemies who led them away cap-
tive, and pray to You toward their land which
You gave to their fathers, the city which You
have chosen and the temple which I have built
for Your name: 49then hear in heaven Your

The Message

37-40 When disasters strike, famine or catastrophe, crop failure or disease, locust or beetle, or when an enemy attacks their defenses—calamity of any sort—any prayer that’s prayed from anyone at all among your people Israel, hearts penetrated by the disaster, hands and arms thrown out to this Temple for help,

Listen from your home in heaven.

Forgive and go to work on us. Give what each deserves, for you know each life from the inside (you’re the only one with such “inside knowledge”!) so that they’ll live before you in lifelong reverent and believing obedience on this land you gave our ancestors.

41-43 And don’t forget the foreigner who is not a member of your people Israel but has come from a far country because of your reputation. People *are* going to be attracted here by your great reputation, your wonder-working power, who come to pray at this Temple.

Listen from your home in heaven.

Honor the prayers of the foreigner so that people all over the world will know who you are and what you’re like and will live in reverent obedience before you, just as your own people Israel do; so they’ll know that you personally make this Temple that I’ve built what it is.

44-51 When your people go to war against their enemies at the time and place you send them and they pray to GOD toward the city you chose and this Temple I’ve built to honor your Name,

Listen from heaven to what they
pray and ask for,
and do what’s right for them.

When they sin against you—and they certainly will; there’s no one without sin!—and in anger you turn them over to the enemy and they are taken captive to the enemy’s land, whether far or near, but repent in the country of their captivity and pray with changed hearts in their exile, “We’ve sinned; we’ve done wrong; we’ve been most wicked,” and turn back to you heart and soul in the land of the enemy who conquered them, and pray to you toward their homeland, the land you gave their ancestors, toward the city you chose, and this Temple I have built to the honor of your Name,

NEW KING JAMES VERSION

dwelling place their prayer and their supplication, and maintain their cause, 50and forgive Your people who have sinned against You, and all their transgressions which they have transgressed against You; and grant them compassion before those who took them captive, that they may have compassion on them 51(for they *are* Your people and Your inheritance, whom You brought out of Egypt, out of the iron furnace), 52that Your eyes may be open to the supplication of Your servant and the supplication of Your people Israel, to listen to them whenever they call to You. 53For You separated them from among all the peoples of the earth *to be* Your inheritance, as You spoke by Your servant Moses, when You brought our fathers out of Egypt, O Lord GOD."

SOLOMON BLESSES THE ASSEMBLY

54And so it was, when Solomon had finished praying all this prayer and supplication to the LORD, that he arose from before the altar of the LORD, from kneeling on his knees with his hands spread up to heaven. 55Then he stood and blessed all the assembly of Israel with a loud voice, saying: 56"Blessed *be* the LORD, who has given rest to His people Israel, according to all that He promised. There has not failed one word of all His good promise, which He promised through His servant Moses. 57May the LORD our God be with us, as He was with our fathers. May He not leave us nor forsake us, 58that He may incline our hearts to Himself, to walk in all His ways, and to keep His commandments and His statutes and His judgments, which He commanded our fathers. 59And may these words of mine, with which I have made supplication before the LORD, be near the LORD our God day and night, that He may maintain the cause of His servant and the cause of His people Israel, as each day may require, 60that all the peoples of the earth may know that the LORD *is* God; *there is* no other. 61Let your heart therefore be loyal to the LORD our God, to walk in His statutes and keep His commandments, as at this day."

SOLOMON DEDICATES THE TEMPLE

62Then the king and all Israel with him offered sacrifices before the LORD. 63And Solomon offered a sacrifice of peace offerings, which he offered to the LORD, twenty-two thousand bulls and one hundred and twenty thousand sheep. So the king and all the children of Israel dedicated the house of the LORD. 64On the same day the king consecrated the middle of the court that *was* in front of the house of the LORD; for there he offered burnt offerings, grain offerings, and the fat of the peace offerings, because the bronze altar that *was* before the LORD *was* too small to receive the burnt offerings, the grain offerings, and the fat of the peace offerings.

THE MESSAGE

Listen from your home in heaven
to their prayers desperate and devout
and do what is best for them.

Forgive your people who have sinned
against you; forgive their gross rebellions and move their captors to treat them with compassion. They are, after all, your people and your precious inheritance whom you rescued from the heart of that iron-smelting furnace, Egypt!

52-53 O be alert and attentive to the
needy prayers of me, your servant, and your dear people Israel; listen every time they cry out to you! You handpicked them from all the peoples on earth to be your very own people, as you announced through your servant Moses when you, O GOD, in your masterful rule, delivered our ancestors from Egypt.

54-55 Having finished praying to GOD—all these bold and passionate prayers—Solomon stood up before GOD's Altar where he had been kneeling all this time, his arms stretched upward to heaven. Standing, he blessed the whole congregation of Israel, blessing them at the top of his lungs:
56-58 "Blessed be GOD, who has given peace to
his people Israel just as he said he'd do. Not one of all those good and wonderful words that he spoke through Moses has misfired. May GOD, our very own God, continue to be with us just as he was with our ancestors—may he never give up and walk out on us. May he keep us centered and devoted to him, following the life path he has cleared, watching the signposts, walking at the pace and rhythms he laid down for our ancestors.
59-61 "And let these words that I've prayed in
the presence of GOD be always right there before him, day and night, so that he'll do what is right for me, to guarantee justice for his people Israel day after day after day. Then all the people on earth will know GOD is the true God; there is no other God. And *you*, your lives must be totally obedient to GOD, our personal God, following the life path he has cleared, alert and attentive to everything he has made plain this day."

62-63 The king and all Israel with him then worshiped, offering sacrifices to GOD. Solomon offered Peace-Offerings, sacrificing to GOD 22,000 cattle, a hundred and 120,000 sheep. This is how the king and all Israel dedicated The Temple of GOD.

64 That same day, the king set apart the central area of the Courtyard in front of GOD's Temple for sacred use and there sacrificed the Whole-Burnt-Offerings, Grain-Offerings, and fat from the Peace-Offerings—the bronze Altar was too small to handle all these offerings.

New King James Version

65 At that time Solomon held a feast, and all Israel with him, a great assembly from the entrance of Hamath to the Brook of Egypt, before the LORD our God, seven days and seven *more* days—fourteen days. 66 On the eighth day he sent the people away; and they blessed the king, and went to their tents joyful and glad of heart for all the good that the LORD had done for His servant David, and for Israel His people.

God's Second Appearance to Solomon

9 And it came to pass, when Solomon had finished building the house of the LORD and the king's house, and all Solomon's desire which he wanted to do, 2 that the LORD appeared to Solomon the second time, as He had appeared to him at Gibeon. 3 And the LORD said to him: "I have heard your prayer and your supplication that you have made before Me; I have consecrated this house which you have built to put My name there forever, and My eyes and My heart will be there perpetually. 4 Now if you walk before Me as your father David walked, in integrity of heart and in uprightness, to do according to all that I have commanded you, *and* if you keep My statutes and My judgments, 5 then I will establish the throne of your kingdom over Israel forever, as I promised David your father, saying, 'You shall not fail to have a man on the throne of Israel.' 6 *But* if you or your sons at all turn from following Me, and do not keep My commandments *and* My statutes which I have set before you, but go and serve other gods and worship them, 7 then I will cut off Israel from the land which I have given them; and this house which I have consecrated for My name I will cast out of My sight. Israel will be a proverb and a byword among all peoples. 8 And *as for* this house, *which* is exalted, everyone who passes by it will be astonished and will hiss, and say, 'Why has the LORD done thus to this land and to this house?' 9 Then they will answer, 'Because they forsook the LORD their God, who brought their fathers out of the land of Egypt, and have embraced other gods, and worshiped them and served them; therefore the LORD has brought all this calamity on them.' "

Solomon and Hiram Exchange Gifts

10 Now it happened at the end of twenty years, when Solomon had built the two houses, the house of the LORD and the king's house 11 (Hiram the king of Tyre had supplied Solomon with cedar and cypress and gold, as much as he desired), *that* King Solomon then gave Hiram twenty cities in the land of Galilee. 12 Then Hiram went from Tyre to see the cities which Solomon had given him, but they did not please him. 13 So he said, "What *kind of* cities *are* these which you have given me, my brother?" And he called them the land of Cabul,[a] as they are to this day. 14 Then Hiram sent the king one hundred and twenty talents of gold.

9:13 [a]Literally *Good for Nothing*

The Message

65-66 This is how Solomon kept the great autumn feast, and all Israel with him, people there all the way from the far northeast (the Entrance to Hamath) to the far southwest (the Brook of Egypt)—a huge congregation. They started out celebrating for seven days—and then did it another seven days! Two solid weeks of celebration! Then he dismissed them. They blessed the king and went home, exuberant with heartfelt gratitude for all the good GOD had done for his servant David and for his people Israel.

1-2 9 After Solomon had completed building The Temple of GOD and his own palace, all the projects he had set his heart on doing, GOD appeared to Solomon again, just as he had appeared to him at Gibeon.

3-5 And GOD said to him, "I've listened to and received all your prayers, your ever-so-passionate prayers. I've sanctified this Temple that you have built: My Name is stamped on it forever; my eyes are on it and my heart in it always. As for you, if you live in my presence as your father David lived, pure in heart and action, living the life I've set out for you, attentively obedient to my guidance and judgments, then I'll back your kingly rule over Israel, make it a sure thing on a solid foundation. The same guarantee I gave David your father I'm giving you: 'You can count on always having a descendant on Israel's throne.'

6-9 "But if you or your sons betray me, ignoring my guidance and judgments, taking up with alien gods by serving and worshiping them, then the guarantee is off: I'll wipe Israel right off the map and repudiate this Temple I've just sanctified to honor my Name. And Israel will become nothing but a bad joke among the peoples of the world. And this Temple, splendid as it now is, will become an object of contempt; visitors will shake their heads, saying, 'Whatever happened here? What's the story behind these ruins?' Then they'll be told, 'The people who used to live here betrayed their GOD, the very God who rescued their ancestors from Egypt; they took up with alien gods, worshiping and serving them. That's what's behind this GOD-visited devastation.' "

10-12 At the end of twenty years, having built the two buildings, The Temple of GOD and his personal palace, Solomon rewarded Hiram king of Tyre with a gift of twenty villages in the district of Galilee. Hiram had provided him with all the cedar and cypress and gold that he had wanted. But when Hiram left Tyre to look over the villages that Solomon had given him, he didn't like what he saw.

13-14 He said, "What kind of reward is this, my friend? Twenty backwoods hick towns!" People still refer to them that way. This is all Hiram got from Solomon in exchange for four and a half tons of gold!

NEW KING JAMES VERSION

SOLOMON'S ADDITIONAL ACHIEVEMENTS

15And this *is* the reason for the labor force
which King Solomon raised: to build the house
of the LORD, his own house, the Millo,[a] the wall
of Jerusalem, Hazor, Megiddo, and Gezer.
16(Pharaoh king of Egypt had gone up and taken
Gezer and burned it with fire, had killed the
Canaanites who dwelt in the city, and had given
it *as* a dowry to his daughter, Solomon's wife.)
17And Solomon built Gezer, Lower Beth Horon,
18Baalath, and Tadmor in the wilderness, in the
land *of Judah,* 19all the storage cities that
Solomon had, cities for his chariots and cities
for his cavalry, and whatever Solomon desired
to build in Jerusalem, in Lebanon, and in all the
land of his dominion.

20All the people *who were* left of the Amo-
rites, Hittites, Perizzites, Hivites, and Jebusites,
who *were* not of the children of Israel— 21that is,
their descendants who were left in the land af-
ter them, whom the children of Israel had not
been able to destroy completely—from these
Solomon raised forced labor, as it is to this day.
22But of the children of Israel Solomon made no
forced laborers, because they *were* men of war
and his servants: his officers, his captains, com-
manders of his chariots, and his cavalry.

23Others *were* chiefs of the officials who
were over Solomon's work: five hundred and
fifty, who ruled over the people who did the
work.

24But Pharaoh's daughter came up from the
City of David to her house which *Solomon*[a] had
built for her. Then he built the Millo.

25Now three times a year Solomon offered
burnt offerings and peace offerings on the altar
which he had built for the LORD, and he burned
incense with them *on the altar* that *was* before
the LORD. So he finished the temple.

26King Solomon also built a fleet of ships at
Ezion Geber, which *is* near Elath[a] on the shore
of the Red Sea, in the land of Edom. 27Then Hi-
ram sent his servants with the fleet, seamen
who knew the sea, to work with the servants of
Solomon. 28And they went to Ophir, and ac-
quired four hundred and twenty talents of gold
from there, and brought *it* to King Solomon.

THE QUEEN OF SHEBA'S PRAISE OF SOLOMON

10 Now when the queen of Sheba heard of
the fame of Solomon concerning the name
of the LORD, she came to test him with hard
questions. 2She came to Jerusalem with a very
great retinue, with camels that bore spices, very
much gold, and precious stones; and when she
came to Solomon, she spoke with him about all
that was in her heart. 3So Solomon answered all
her questions; there was nothing so difficult for
the king that he could not explain *it* to her. 4And
when the queen of Sheba had seen all the wis-
dom of Solomon, the house that he had built,
5the food on his table, the seating of his ser-
vants, the service of his waiters and their ap-
parel, his cupbearers, and his entryway by

9:15 [a]Literally *The Landfill* **9:24** [a]Literally *he* (compare 2 Chronicles 8:11) **9:26** [a]Hebrew *Eloth* (compare 2 Kings 14:22)

THE MESSAGE

15 This is the work record of the labor force that King Solomon raised to build The Temple of GOD, his palace, the defense complex (the Millo), the Jerusalem wall, and the fortified cities of Hazor, Megiddo, and Gezer.

16-17 Pharaoh king of Egypt had come up and captured Gezer, torched it, and killed all the Canaanites who lived there. He gave it as a wedding present to his daughter, Solomon's wife. So Solomon rebuilt Gezer.

17-19 He also built Lower Beth Horon, Baalath, and Tamar in the desert, backcountry storehouse villages, and villages for chariots and horses. Solomon built widely and extravagantly in Jerusalem, in Lebanon, and wherever he fancied.

20-23 The remnants from the original inhabitants of the land (Amorites, Hittites, Perizzites, Hivites, and Jebusites—all non-Israelites), survivors of the holy wars, were rounded up by Solomon for his gangs of slave labor, a policy still in effect. But true Israelites were not treated this way; they were used in his army and administration—government leaders and commanders of his chariots and charioteers. They were also the project managers responsible for Solomon's building operations—550 of them in charge of the workforce.

24 It was after Pharaoh's daughter ceremonially ascended from the City of David and took up residence in the house built especially for her that Solomon built the defense complex (the Millo).

25 Three times a year Solomon worshiped at the Altar of GOD, sacrificing Whole-Burnt-Offerings and Peace-Offerings, and burning incense in the presence of GOD. Everything that had to do with The Temple he did generously and well; he didn't skimp.

26-28 And ships! King Solomon also built ships at Ezion Geber, located near Elath in Edom on the Red Sea. Hiram sent seaworthy sailors to assist Solomon's men with the fleet. They embarked for Ophir, brought back sixteen tons of gold, and presented it to King Solomon.

THE QUEEN OF SHEBA VISITS

1-5 10 The queen of Sheba heard about Solomon and his connection with the Name of GOD. She came to put his reputation to the test by asking tough questions. She made a grand and showy entrance into Jerusalem—camels loaded with spices, a huge amount of gold, and precious gems. She came to Solomon and talked about all the things that she cared about, emptying her heart to him. Solomon answered everything she put to him—nothing stumped him. When the queen of Sheba experienced for herself Solomon's wisdom and saw with her own eyes the palace he had built, the meals that were served, the impressive array of court officials and sharply dressed waiters, the lavish crystal, and the elaborate worship extravagant with Whole-Burnt-Offerings at

NEW KING JAMES VERSION

which he went up to the house of the LORD,
there was no more spirit in her. 6Then she said
to the king: "It was a true report which I heard
in my own land about your words and your wis-
dom. 7However I did not believe the words until
I came and saw with my own eyes; and indeed
the half was not told me. Your wisdom and pros-
perity exceed the fame of which I heard. 8Happy
are your men and happy *are* these your ser-
vants, who stand continually before you *and*
hear your wisdom! 9Blessed be the LORD your
God, who delighted in you, setting you on the
throne of Israel! Because the LORD has loved Is-
rael forever, therefore He made you king, to do
justice and righteousness."

10Then she gave the king one hundred and
twenty talents of gold, spices in great quantity,
and precious stones. There never again came
such abundance of spices as the queen of Sheba
gave to King Solomon. 11Also, the ships of Hi-
ram, which brought gold from Ophir, brought
great quantities of almug[a] wood and precious
stones from Ophir. 12And the king made steps of
the almug wood for the house of the LORD and
for the king's house, also harps and stringed in-
struments for singers. There never again came
such almug wood, nor has the like been seen to
this day.

13Now King Solomon gave the queen of
Sheba all she desired, whatever she asked, be-
sides what Solomon had given her according to
the royal generosity. So she turned and went to
her own country, she and her servants.

SOLOMON'S GREAT WEALTH

14The weight of gold that came to Solomon
yearly was six hundred and sixty-six talents of
gold, 15besides *that* from the traveling mer-
chants, from the income of traders, from all the
kings of Arabia, and from the governors of the
country.

16And King Solomon made two hundred
large shields *of* hammered gold; six hundred
shekels of gold went into each shield. 17He also
made three hundred shields *of* hammered gold;
three minas of gold went into each shield. The
king put them in the House of the Forest of
Lebanon.

18Moreover the king made a great throne of
ivory, and overlaid it with pure gold. 19The
throne had six steps, and the top of the throne
was round at the back; *there were* armrests on
either side of the place of the seat, and two lions
stood beside the armrests. 20Twelve lions stood
there, one on each side of the six steps; nothing
like *this* had been made for any *other* kingdom.

21All King Solomon's drinking vessels *were*
gold, and all the vessels of the House of the For-
est of Lebanon *were* pure gold. Not *one was* sil-
ver, for this was accounted as nothing in the
days of Solomon. 22For the king had merchant
ships[a] at sea with the fleet of Hiram. Once every
three years the merchant ships came bringing
gold, silver, ivory, apes, and monkeys.[b] 23So
King Solomon surpassed all the kings of the
earth in riches and wisdom.

10:11 [a]Or *algum* (compare 2 Chronicles 9:10, 11) **10:22** [a]Literally *ships of Tarshish*, deep-sea vessels [b]Or *peacocks*

THE MESSAGE

the steps leading up to The Temple of GOD, it took her breath away.

6-9 She said to the king, "It's all true! Your reputation for accomplishment and wisdom that reached all the way to my country is confirmed. I wouldn't have believed it if I hadn't seen it for myself; they didn't exaggerate! Such wisdom and elegance—far more than I could ever have imagined. Lucky the men and women who work for you, getting to be around you every day and hear your wise words firsthand! And blessed be GOD, your God, who took such a liking to you and made you king. Clearly, GOD's love for Israel is behind this, making you king to keep a just order and nurture a God-pleasing people."

10 She then gave the king four and a half tons of gold, and also sack after sack of spices and expensive gems. There hasn't been a cargo of spices like that since that shipload the queen of Sheba brought to King Solomon.

11-12 The ships of Hiram also imported gold from Ophir along with tremendous loads of fragrant sandalwood and expensive gems. The king used the sandalwood for fine cabinetry in The Temple of GOD and the palace complex, and for making harps and dulcimers for the musicians. Nothing like that shipment of sandalwood has been seen since.

13 King Solomon for his part gave the queen of Sheba all her heart's desire—everything she asked for, on top of what he had already so generously given her. Satisfied, she returned home with her train of servants.

14-15 Solomon received twenty-five tons of gold in tribute annually. This was above and beyond the taxes and profit on trade with merchants and assorted kings and governors.

16-17 King Solomon crafted two hundred body-length shields of hammered gold—seven and a half pounds of gold to each shield—and three hundred smaller shields about half that size. He stored the shields in the House of the Forest of Lebanon.

18-20 The king built a massive throne of ivory accented with a veneer of gold. The throne had six steps leading up to it, its back shaped like an arch. The armrests on each side were flanked by lions. Lions, twelve of them, were placed at either end of the six steps. There was no throne like it in any of the surrounding kingdoms.

21 King Solomon's chalices and tankards were made of gold and all the dinnerware and serving utensils in the House of the Forest of Lebanon were pure gold—nothing was made of silver; silver was considered common and cheap.

22 The king had a fleet of ocean-going ships at sea with Hiram's ships. Every three years the fleet would bring in a cargo of gold, silver, and ivory, and apes and peacocks.

23-25 King Solomon was wiser and richer than all the kings of the earth—he surpassed them all. People came from all over the

NEW KING JAMES VERSION

24Now all the earth sought the presence of Solomon to hear his wisdom, which God had put in his heart. 25Each man brought his present: articles of silver and gold, garments, armor, spices, horses, and mules, at a set rate year by year.

26And Solomon gathered chariots and horsemen; he had one thousand four hundred chariots and twelve thousand horsemen, whom he stationed[a] in the chariot cities and with the king at Jerusalem. 27The king made silver *as common* in Jerusalem as stones, and he made cedar trees as abundant as the sycamores which *are* in the lowland.

28Also Solomon had horses imported from Egypt and Keveh; the king's merchants bought them in Keveh at the *current* price. 29Now a chariot that was imported from Egypt cost six hundred *shekels* of silver, and a horse one hundred and fifty; and thus, through their agents,[a] they exported *them* to all the kings of the Hittites and the kings of Syria.

SOLOMON'S HEART TURNS FROM THE LORD

11 But King Solomon loved many foreign women, as well as the daughter of Pharaoh: women of the Moabites, Ammonites, Edomites, Sidonians, *and* Hittites— 2from the nations of whom the LORD had said to the children of Israel, "You shall not intermarry with them, nor they with you. Surely they will turn away your hearts after their gods." Solomon clung to these in love. 3And he had seven hundred wives, princesses, and three hundred concubines; and his wives turned away his heart. 4For it was so, when Solomon was old, that his wives turned his heart after other gods; and his heart was not loyal to the LORD his God, as *was* the heart of his father David. 5For Solomon went after Ashtoreth the goddess of the Sidonians, and after Milcom the abomination of the Ammonites. 6Solomon did evil in the sight of the LORD, and did not fully follow the LORD, as *did* his father David. 7Then Solomon built a high place for Chemosh the abomination of Moab, on the hill that *is* east of Jerusalem, and for Molech the abomination of the people of Ammon. 8And he did likewise for all his foreign wives, who burned incense and sacrificed to their gods.

9So the LORD became angry with Solomon, because his heart had turned from the LORD God of Israel, who had appeared to him twice, 10and had commanded him concerning this thing, that he should not go after other gods; but he did not keep what the LORD had commanded. 11Therefore the LORD said to Solomon, "Because you have done this, and have not kept My covenant and My statutes, which I have commanded you, I will surely tear the kingdom away from you and give it to your servant. 12Nevertheless I will not do it in your days, for the sake of your father David; I will tear it out of the hand of your son. 13However I will not tear away the whole kingdom; I will give one tribe to your son for the sake of My servant David, and for the sake of Jerusalem which I have chosen."

10:26 [a]Following Septuagint, Syriac, Targum, and Vulgate (compare 2 Chronicles 9:25); Masoretic Text reads *led*. **10:29** [a]Literally *by their hands*

THE MESSAGE

world to be with Solomon and drink in the
wisdom God had given him. And everyone
who came brought gifts—artifacts of gold and
silver, fashionable robes and gowns, the latest
in weapons, exotic spices, and horses and
mules—parades of visitors, year after year.
26-29 Solomon collected chariots and horses:
fourteen hundred chariots and twelve thou-
sand horses! He stabled them in the special
chariot cities as well as in Jerusalem. The
king made silver as common as rocks and
cedar as common as the fig trees in the low-
land hills. His horses were brought in from
Egypt and Cilicia, specially acquired by the
king's agents. Chariots from Egypt went for
fifteen pounds of silver and a horse for
about three and three-quarter pounds of sil-
ver. Solomon carried on a brisk horse-trad-
ing business with the Hittite and Aramean
royal houses.

1-5 11 King Solomon was obsessed with
women. Pharaoh's daughter was only
the first of the many foreign women he
loved—Moabite, Ammonite, Edomite,
Sidonian, and Hittite. He took them from the
surrounding pagan nations of which GOD
had clearly warned Israel, "You must not
marry them; they'll seduce you into infatua-
tions with their gods." Solomon fell in love
with them anyway, refusing to give them up.
He had seven hundred royal wives and three
hundred concubines—a thousand women in
all! And they did seduce him away from
God. As Solomon grew older, his wives be-
guiled him with their alien gods and he be-
came unfaithful—he didn't stay true to his
GOD as his father David had done. Solomon
took up with Ashtoreth, the whore goddess
of the Sidonians, and Molech, the horrible
god of the Ammonites.
6-8 Solomon openly defied GOD; he did not
follow in his father David's footsteps. He
went on to build a sacred shrine to
Chemosh, the horrible god of Moab, and to
Molech, the horrible god of the Ammonites,
on a hill just east of Jerusalem. He built sim-
ilar shrines for all his foreign wives, who
then polluted the countryside with the
smoke and stench of their sacrifices.
9-10 GOD was furious with Solomon for aban-
doning the GOD of Israel, the God who had
twice appeared to him and had so clearly
commanded him not to fool around with
other gods. Solomon faithlessly disobeyed
GOD's orders.
11-13 GOD said to Solomon, "Since this is the
way it is with you, that you have no intention
of keeping faith with me and doing what I
have commanded, I'm going to rip the king-
dom from you and hand it over to someone
else. But out of respect for your father David
I won't do it in your lifetime. It's your son
who will pay—I'll rip it right out of his grasp.
Even then I won't take it all; I'll leave him
one tribe in honor of my servant David and
out of respect for my chosen city Jerusalem."

New King James Version

Adversaries of Solomon

14Now the Lord raised up an adversary
against Solomon, Hadad the Edomite; he *was* a
descendant of the king in Edom. 15For it hap-
pened, when David was in Edom, and Joab the
commander of the army had gone up to bury the
slain, after he had killed every male in Edom
16(because for six months Joab remained there
with all Israel, until he had cut down every male
in Edom), 17that Hadad fled to go to Egypt, he
and certain Edomites of his father's servants
with him. Hadad *was* still a little child. 18Then
they arose from Midian and came to Paran; and
they took men with them from Paran and came
to Egypt, to Pharaoh king of Egypt, who gave
him a house, apportioned food for him, and gave
him land. 19And Hadad found great favor in the
sight of Pharaoh, so that he gave him as wife the
sister of his own wife, that is, the sister of Queen
Tahpenes. 20Then the sister of Tahpenes bore
him Genubath his son, whom Tahpenes weaned
in Pharaoh's house. And Genubath was in
Pharaoh's household among the sons of
Pharaoh.
21So when Hadad heard in Egypt that David
rested with his fathers, and that Joab the com-
mander of the army was dead, Hadad said to
Pharaoh, "Let me depart, that I may go to my
own country."
22Then Pharaoh said to him, "But what have
you lacked with me, that suddenly you seek to
go to your own country?"
So he answered, "Nothing, but do let me go
anyway."
23And God raised up *another* adversary
against him, Rezon the son of Eliadah, who had
fled from his lord, Hadadezer king of Zobah.
24So he gathered men to him and became cap-
tain over a band *of raiders,* when David killed
those *of Zobah.* And they went to Damascus and
dwelt there, and reigned in Damascus. 25He was
an adversary of Israel all the days of Solomon
(besides the trouble that Hadad *caused*); and he
abhorred Israel, and reigned over Syria.

Jeroboam's Rebellion

26Then Solomon's servant, Jeroboam the son
of Nebat, an Ephraimite from Zereda, whose
mother's name *was* Zeruah, a widow, also re-
belled against the king.
27And this *is* what caused him to rebel
against the king: Solomon had built the Millo
and repaired the damages to the City of David
his father. 28The man Jeroboam *was* a mighty
man of valor; and Solomon, seeing that the
young man was industrious, made him the offi-
cer over all the labor force of the house of
Joseph.
29Now it happened at that time, when Jer-
oboam went out of Jerusalem, that the prophet
Ahijah the Shilonite met him on the way; and he
had clothed himself with a new garment, and
the two *were* alone in the field. 30Then Ahijah
took hold of the new garment that *was* on him,
and tore it *into* twelve pieces.

The Message

14-20 God incited Hadad, a descendant of the
king of Edom, into hostile actions against
Solomon. Years earlier, when David devas-
tated Edom, Joab, commander of the army,
on his way to bury the dead, massacred all
the men of Edom. Joab and his army stayed
there for six months, making sure they had
killed every man in Edom. Hadad, just a boy
at the time, had escaped with some of the
Edomites who had worked for his father.
Their escape route took them through Mid-
ian to Paran. They picked up some men in
Paran and went on to Egypt and to Pharaoh
king of Egypt, who gave Hadad a house,
food, and even land. Pharaoh liked him so
well that he gave him the sister of his wife,
Queen Tahpenes, in marriage. She bore
Hadad a son named Genubath who was
raised like one of the royal family. Genubath
grew up in the palace with Pharaoh's chil-
dren.
21 While living in Egypt, Hadad heard that
both David and Joab, commander of the
army, were dead. He approached Pharaoh
and said, "Send me off with your blessing—
I want to return to my country."
22 "But why?" said Pharaoh. "Why would
you want to leave here? Hasn't everything
been to your liking?"
"Everything has been just fine," said
Hadad, "but I want to go home—give me a
good send-off!"

23-25 Then God incited another adversary against
Solomon, Rezon son of Eliada, who had de-
serted from his master, Hadadezer king of
Zobah. After David's slaughter of the
Arameans, Rezon collected a band of out-
laws and became their leader. They later
settled in Damascus, where Rezon eventu-
ally took over as king. Like Hadad, Rezon
was a thorn in Israel's side all of Solomon's
life. He was king over Aram, and he hated
Israel.

Adversaries Arise

26 And then, the last straw: Jeroboam son of
Nebat rebelled against the king. He was an
Ephraimite from Zeredah, his mother a
widow named Zeruah. He served in
Solomon's administration.
27-28 This is why he rebelled. Solomon had
built the outer defense system (the Millo)
and had restored the fortifications that were
in disrepair from the time of his father
David. Jeroboam stood out during the con-
struction as strong and able. When Solomon
observed what a good worker he was, he put
the young man in charge of the entire work-
force of the tribe of Joseph.
29-30 One day Jeroboam was walking down the
road out of Jerusalem. Ahijah the prophet of
Shiloh, wearing a brand-new cloak, met
him. The two of them were alone on that re-
mote stretch of road. Ahijah took off the
new cloak that he was wearing and ripped it
into twelve pieces.

NEW KING JAMES VERSION

31And he said to Jeroboam, "Take for yourself
ten pieces, for thus says the LORD, the God of Is-
rael: 'Behold, I will tear the kingdom out of the
hand of Solomon and will give ten tribes to you
32(but he shall have one tribe for the sake of My
servant David, and for the sake of Jerusalem,
the city which I have chosen out of all the tribes
of Israel), 33because they have[a] forsaken Me,
and worshiped Ashtoreth the goddess of the
Sidonians, Chemosh the god of the Moabites,
and Milcom the god of the people of Ammon,
and have not walked in My ways to do *what is*
right in My eyes and *keep* My statutes and My
judgments, as *did* his father David. 34However I
will not take the whole kingdom out of his hand,
because I have made him ruler all the days of
his life for the sake of My servant David, whom
I chose because he kept My commandments and
My statutes. 35But I will take the kingdom out of
his son's hand and give it to you—ten tribes.
36And to his son I will give one tribe, that My
servant David may always have a lamp before
Me in Jerusalem, the city which I have chosen
for Myself, to put My name there. 37So I will take
you, and you shall reign over all your heart de-
sires, and you shall be king over Israel. 38Then it
shall be, if you heed all that I command you,
walk in My ways, and do *what is* right in My
sight, to keep My statutes and My command-
ments, as My servant David did, then I will be
with you and build for you an enduring house,
as I built for David, and will give Israel to you.
39And I will afflict the descendants of David be-
cause of this, but not forever.' "

40Solomon therefore sought to kill Jer-
oboam. But Jeroboam arose and fled to Egypt,
to Shishak king of Egypt, and was in Egypt un-
til the death of Solomon.

DEATH OF SOLOMON

41Now the rest of the acts of Solomon, all
that he did, and his wisdom, *are* they not written
in the book of the acts of Solomon? 42And the
period that Solomon reigned in Jerusalem over
all Israel *was* forty years. 43Then Solomon
rested with his fathers, and was buried in the
City of David his father. And Rehoboam his son
reigned in his place.

THE REVOLT AGAINST REHOBOAM

12 And Rehoboam went to Shechem, for all
Israel had gone to Shechem to make him
king. 2So it happened, when Jeroboam the son
of Nebat heard *it* (he was still in Egypt, for he
had fled from the presence of King Solomon
and had been dwelling in Egypt), 3that they sent
and called him. Then Jeroboam and the whole
assembly of Israel came and spoke to Re-
hoboam, saying, 4"Your father made our yoke
heavy; now therefore, lighten the burdensome
service of your father, and his heavy yoke which
he put on us, and we will serve you."

5So he said to them, "Depart *for* three days,
then come back to me." And the people de-
parted.

11:33 [a]Following Masoretic Text and Targum; Septuagint, Syriac, and Vulgate read *he has*.

THE MESSAGE

31-33 Then he said to Jeroboam, "Take ten of these pieces for yourself; this is by order of the GOD of Israel: See what I'm doing—I'm ripping the kingdom out of Solomon's hands and giving you ten of the tribes. In honor of my servant David and out of respect for Jerusalem, the city I especially chose, he will get one tribe. And here's the reason: He faithlessly abandoned me and went off worshiping Ashtoreth goddess of the Sidonians, Chemosh god of the Moabites, and Molech god of the Ammonites. He hasn't lived the way I have shown him, hasn't done what I have wanted, and hasn't followed directions or obeyed orders as his father David did.

34-36 "Still, I won't take the whole kingdom away from him. I'll stick with him through his lifetime because of my servant David whom I chose and who did follow my directions and obey my orders. But after that I'll remove the kingdom from his son's control and give you ten tribes. I'll leave one tribe to his son, to maintain a witness to my servant David in Jerusalem, the city I chose as a memorial to my Name.

37-39 "But I have taken you in hand. Rule to your heart's content! You are to be the king of Israel. If you listen to what I tell you and live the way I show you and do what pleases me, following directions and obeying orders as my servant David did, I'll stick with you no matter what. I'll build you a kingdom as solid as the one I built for David. Israel will be yours! I am bringing pain and trouble on David's descendants, but the trials won't last forever."

40 Solomon ordered the assassination of Jeroboam, but he got away to Egypt and found asylum there with King Shishak. He remained in exile there until Solomon died.

41-43 The rest of Solomon's life and rule, his work and his wisdom, you can read for yourself in *The Chronicles of Solomon*. Solomon ruled in Jerusalem over all Israel for forty years. He died and was buried in the City of David his father. His son Rehoboam was the next king.

REHOBOAM

1-2 12 Rehoboam traveled to Shechem where all Israel had gathered to inaugurate him as king. Jeroboam had been in Egypt, where he had taken asylum from King Solomon; when he got the report of Solomon's death he had come back.

3-4 Rehoboam assembled Jeroboam and all the people. They said to Rehoboam, "Your father made life hard for us—worked our fingers to the bone. Give us a break; lighten up on us and we'll willingly serve you."

5 "Give me three days to think it over, then come back," Rehoboam said.

New King James Version

6 Then King Rehoboam consulted the elders
who stood before his father Solomon while he
still lived, and he said, "How do you advise *me*
to answer these people?"
7 And they spoke to him, saying, "If you will
be a servant to these people today, and serve
them, and answer them, and speak good words
to them, then they will be your servants forever."
8 But he rejected the advice which the elders
had given him, and consulted the young men
who had grown up with him, who stood before
him. 9 And he said to them, "What advice do you
give? How should we answer this people who
have spoken to me, saying, 'Lighten the yoke
which your father put on us'?"
10 Then the young men who had grown up
with him spoke to him, saying, "Thus you should
speak to this people who have spoken to you,
saying, 'Your father made our yoke heavy, but
you make *it* lighter on us'—thus you shall say to
them: 'My little *finger* shall be thicker than my
father's waist! 11 And now, whereas my father
put a heavy yoke on you, I will add to your yoke;
my father chastised you with whips, but I will
chastise you with scourges!' "[a]
12 So Jeroboam and all the people came to
Rehoboam the third day, as the king had di-
rected, saying, "Come back to me the third day."
13 Then the king answered the people roughly,
and rejected the advice which the elders had
given him; 14 and he spoke to them according to
the advice of the young men, saying, "My father
made your yoke heavy, but I will add to your
yoke; my father chastised you with whips, but I
will chastise you with scourges!"[a] 15 So the king
did not listen to the people; for the turn *of
events* was from the LORD, that He might fulfill
His word, which the LORD had spoken by Ahijah
the Shilonite to Jeroboam the son of Nebat.
16 Now when all Israel saw that the king did
not listen to them, the people answered the king,
saying:

"What share have we in David?
We have no inheritance in the son of Jesse.
To your tents, O Israel!
Now, see to your own house, O David!"

So Israel departed to their tents. 17 But Re-
hoboam reigned over the children of Israel who
dwelt in the cities of Judah.
18 Then King Rehoboam sent Adoram, who
was in charge of the revenue; but all Israel
stoned him with stones, and he died. Therefore
King Rehoboam mounted his chariot in haste to
flee to Jerusalem. 19 So Israel has been in rebel-
lion against the house of David to this day.
20 Now it came to pass when all Israel heard
that Jeroboam had come back, they sent for him
and called him to the congregation, and made
him king over all Israel. There was none who
followed the house of David, but the tribe of Ju-
dah only.
21 And when Rehoboam came to Jerusalem,
he assembled all the house of Judah with the

12:11 [a]Literally *scorpions* **12:14** [a]Literally *scorpions*

The Message

6 King Rehoboam talked it over with the
elders who had advised his father when he
was alive: "What's your counsel? How do
you suggest that I answer the people?"
7 They said, "If you will be a servant to this
people, be considerate of their needs and re-
spond with compassion, work things out with
them, they'll end up doing anything for you."
8-9 But he rejected the counsel of the elders
and asked the young men he'd grown up
with who were now currying his favor,
"What do you think? What should I say to
these people who are saying, 'Give us a
break from your father's harsh ways—
lighten up on us'?"
10-11 The young turks he'd grown up with said,
"These people who complain, 'Your father
was too hard on us; lighten up'—well, tell
them this: 'My little finger is thicker than
my father's waist. If you think life under my
father was hard, you haven't seen the half of
it. My father thrashed you with whips; I'll
beat you bloody with chains!' "
12-14 Three days later Jeroboam and the peo-
ple showed up, just as Rehoboam had di-
rected when he said, "Give me three days to
think it over, then come back." The king's
answer was harsh and rude. He spurned the
counsel of the elders and went with the ad-
vice of the younger set, "If you think life un-
der my father was hard, you haven't seen
the half of it. My father thrashed you with
whips; I'll beat you bloody with chains!"
15 Rehoboam turned a deaf ear to the peo-
ple. GOD was behind all this, confirming the
message that he had given to Jeroboam son
of Nebat through Ahijah of Shiloh.
16-17 When all Israel realized that the king
hadn't listened to a word they'd said, they
stood up to him and said,

Get lost, David!
We've had it with you, son of Jesse!
Let's get out of here, Israel, and fast!
From now on, David, mind your own
business.

And with that, they left. But Rehoboam
continued to rule those who lived in the
towns of Judah.

18-19 When King Rehoboam next sent out
Adoniram, head of the workforce, the Is-
raelites ganged up on him, pelted him with
stones, and killed him. King Rehoboam
jumped in his chariot and fled to Jerusalem
as fast as he could. Israel has been in rebel-
lion against the Davidic regime ever since.

Jeroboam of Israel

20 When the word was out that Jeroboam was
back and available, the assembled people
invited him and inaugurated him king over
all Israel. The only tribe left to the Davidic
dynasty was Judah.
21 When Rehoboam got back to Jerusalem,
he called up the men of Judah and the tribe

NEW KING JAMES VERSION

tribe of Benjamin, one hundred and eighty thou-
sand chosen *men* who were warriors, to fight
against the house of Israel, that he might restore
the kingdom to Rehoboam the son of Solomon.
22But the word of God came to Shemaiah the
man of God, saying, 23"Speak to Rehoboam the
son of Solomon, king of Judah, to all the house
of Judah and Benjamin, and to the rest of the
people, saying, 24'Thus says the LORD: "You shall
not go up nor fight against your brethren the
children of Israel. Let every man return to his
house, for this thing is from Me." ' " Therefore
they obeyed the word of the LORD, and turned
back, according to the word of the LORD.

JEROBOAM'S GOLD CALVES

25Then Jeroboam built Shechem in the
mountains of Ephraim, and dwelt there. Also he
went out from there and built Penuel. 26And Jer-
oboam said in his heart, "Now the kingdom may
return to the house of David: 27If these people go
up to offer sacrifices in the house of the LORD at
Jerusalem, then the heart of this people will turn
back to their lord, Rehoboam king of Judah, and
they will kill me and go back to Rehoboam king
of Judah."

28Therefore the king asked advice, made two
calves of gold, and said to the people, "It is too
much for you to go up to Jerusalem. Here are
your gods, O Israel, which brought you up from
the land of Egypt!" 29And he set up one in
Bethel, and the other he put in Dan. 30Now this
thing became a sin, for the people went *to wor-
ship* before the one as far as Dan. 31He made
shrines[a] on the high places, and made priests
from every class of people, who were not of the
sons of Levi.

32Jeroboam ordained a feast on the fifteenth
day of the eighth month, like the feast that *was*
in Judah, and offered sacrifices on the altar. So
he did at Bethel, sacrificing to the calves that he
had made. And at Bethel he installed the priests
of the high places which he had made. 33So he
made offerings on the altar which he had made
at Bethel on the fifteenth day of the eighth
month, in the month which he had devised in his
own heart. And he ordained a feast for the chil-
dren of Israel, and offered sacrifices on the altar
and burned incense.

THE MESSAGE OF THE MAN OF GOD

13 And behold, a man of God went from Ju-
dah to Bethel by the word of the LORD, and
Jeroboam stood by the altar to burn incense.
2Then he cried out against the altar by the word
of the LORD, and said, "O altar, altar! Thus says
the LORD: 'Behold, a child, Josiah by name, shall
be born to the house of David; and on you he
shall sacrifice the priests of the high places who
burn incense on you, and men's bones shall be
burned on you.' " 3And he gave a sign the same
day, saying, "This *is* the sign which the LORD has
spoken: Surely the altar shall split apart, and
the ashes on it shall be poured out."

4So it came to pass when King Jeroboam
heard the saying of the man of God, who cried

12:31 [a]Literally *a house*

THE MESSAGE

of Benjamin, a 180,000 of their best soldiers,
to go to war against Israel and recover the
kingdom for Rehoboam son of Solomon.

22-24 At this time the word of God came to She-
maiah, a man of God: "Tell this to Re-
hoboam son of Solomon king of Judah,
along with everyone in Judah and Benjamin
and anyone else who is around: This is
GOD's word: Don't march out; don't fight
against your brothers the Israelites; go back
home, every last one of you; *I'm* in charge
here." And they did it; they did what GOD
said and went home.

25 Jeroboam made a fort at Shechem in the
hills of Ephraim, and made that his head-
quarters. He also built a fort at Penuel.

26-27 But then Jeroboam thought, "It won't be
long before the kingdom is reunited under
David. As soon as these people resume wor-
ship at The Temple of GOD in Jerusalem,
they'll start thinking of Rehoboam king of
Judah as their ruler. They'll then kill me and
go back to King Rehoboam."

28-30 So the king came up with a plan: He
made two golden calves. Then he an-
nounced, "It's too much trouble for you to
go to Jerusalem to worship. Look at these—
the gods who brought you out of Egypt!" He
put one calf in Bethel; the other he placed in
Dan. This was blatant sin. Think of it—peo-
ple traveling all the way to Dan to worship a
calf!

31-33 And that wasn't the end of it. Jeroboam
built forbidden shrines all over the place
and recruited priests from wherever he
could find them, regardless of whether they
were fit for the job or not. To top it off, he
created a holy New Year festival to be held
on the fifteenth day of the eighth month to
replace the one in Judah, complete with
worship offered on the Altar at Bethel and
sacrificing before the calves he had set up
there. He staffed Bethel with priests from
the local shrines he had made. This was
strictly his own idea to compete with the
feast in Judah; and he carried it off with
flair, a festival exclusively for Israel, Jer-
oboam himself leading the worship at the
Altar.

1-3 13 And then this happened: Just as Jer-
oboam was at the Altar, about to make
an offering, a holy man came from Judah
by GOD's command and preached (these
were GOD's orders) to the Altar: "Altar, Al-
tar! GOD's message! 'A son will be born into
David's family named Josiah. The priests
from the shrines who are making offerings
on you, he will sacrifice—on you! Human
bones burned on you!' " At the same time he
announced a sign: "This is the proof GOD
gives—the Altar will split into pieces and
the holy offerings spill into the dirt."

4-5 When the king heard the message the
holy man preached against the Altar at

NEW KING JAMES VERSION

out against the altar in Bethel, that he stretched out his hand from the altar, saying, "Arrest him!" Then his hand, which he stretched out toward him, withered, so that he could not pull it back to himself. 5The altar also was split apart, and the ashes poured out from the altar, according to the sign which the man of God had given by the word of the LORD. 6Then the king answered and said to the man of God, "Please entreat the favor of the LORD your God, and pray for me, that my hand may be restored to me."

So the man of God entreated the LORD, and the king's hand was restored to him, and became as before. 7Then the king said to the man of God, "Come home with me and refresh yourself, and I will give you a reward."

8But the man of God said to the king, "If you were to give me half your house, I would not go in with you; nor would I eat bread nor drink water in this place. 9For so it was commanded me by the word of the LORD, saying, 'You shall not eat bread, nor drink water, nor return by the same way you came.' " 10So he went another way and did not return by the way he came to Bethel.

DEATH OF THE MAN OF GOD

11Now an old prophet dwelt in Bethel, and his sons came and told him all the works that the man of God had done that day in Bethel; they also told their father the words which he had spoken to the king. 12And their father said to them, "Which way did he go?" For his sons had seen[a] which way the man of God went who came from Judah. 13Then he said to his sons, "Saddle the donkey for me." So they saddled the donkey for him; and he rode on it, 14and went after the man of God, and found him sitting under an oak. Then he said to him, "*Are* you the man of God who came from Judah?"

And he said, "I *am.*"

15Then he said to him, "Come home with me and eat bread."

16And he said, "I cannot return with you nor go in with you; neither can I eat bread nor drink water with you in this place. 17For I have been told by the word of the LORD, 'You shall not eat bread nor drink water there, nor return by going the way you came.' "

18He said to him, "I too *am* a prophet as you *are*, and an angel spoke to me by the word of the LORD, saying, 'Bring him back with you to your house, that he may eat bread and drink water.' " (He was lying to him.)

19So he went back with him, and ate bread in his house, and drank water.

20Now it happened, as they sat at the table, that the word of the LORD came to the prophet who had brought him back; 21and he cried out to the man of God who came from Judah, saying, "Thus says the LORD: 'Because you have disobeyed the word of the LORD, and have not kept the commandment which the LORD your God commanded you, 22but you came back, ate bread, and drank water in the place of which *the LORD* said to you, "Eat no bread and drink

13:12 [a]Septuagint, Syriac, Targum, and Vulgate read *showed him.*

THE MESSAGE

Bethel, he reached out to grab him, yelling, "Arrest him!" But his arm was paralyzed and hung useless. At the same time the Altar broke apart and the holy offerings all spilled into the dirt—the very sign the holy man had announced by GOD's command.

6 The king pleaded with the holy man, "Help me! Pray to your GOD for the healing of my arm." The holy man prayed for him and the king's arm was healed—as good as new!

7 Then the king invited the holy man, "Join me for a meal; I have a gift for you."

8-10 The holy man told the king, "Not on your life! You couldn't pay me enough to get me to sit down with you at a meal in this place. I'm here under GOD's orders, and he commanded, 'Don't eat a crumb, don't drink a drop, and don't go back the way you came.' " Then he left by a different road than the one on which he had walked to Bethel.

11 There was an old prophet who lived in Bethel. His sons came and told him the story of what the holy man had done that day in Bethel, told him everything that had happened and what the holy man had said to the king.

12 Their father said, "Which way did he go?" His sons pointed out the road that the holy man from Judah had taken.

13-14 He told his sons, "Saddle my donkey." When they had saddled it, he got on and rode after the holy man. He found him sitting under an oak tree.

He asked him, "Are you the holy man who came from Judah?"

"Yes, I am," he said.

15 "Well, come home with me and have a meal."

16-17 "Sorry, I can't do that," the holy man said. "I can neither go back with you nor eat with you in this country. I'm under strict orders from GOD: 'Don't eat a crumb; don't drink a drop; and don't come back the way you came.' "

18-19 But he said, "I am also a prophet, just like you. And an angel came to me with a message from GOD: 'Bring him home with you, and give him a good meal!' " But the man was lying. So the holy man went home with him and they had a meal together.

20-22 There they were, sitting at the table together, when the word of GOD came to the prophet who had brought him back. He confronted the holy man who had come from Judah: "GOD's word to you: You disobeyed GOD's command; you didn't keep the strict orders your GOD gave you; you came back and sat down to a good meal in the very place GOD told you, 'Don't eat a crumb; don't drink a drop.' For that you're going to

NEW KING JAMES VERSION

no water," your corpse shall not come to the tomb of your fathers.' "

23So it was, after he had eaten bread and after he had drunk, that he saddled the donkey for him, the prophet whom he had brought back. 24When he was gone, a lion met him on the road and killed him. And his corpse was thrown on the road, and the donkey stood by it. The lion also stood by the corpse. 25And there, men passed by and saw the corpse thrown on the road, and the lion standing by the corpse. Then they went and told *it* in the city where the old prophet dwelt.

26Now when the prophet who had brought him back from the way heard *it*, he said, "It *is* the man of God who was disobedient to the word of the LORD. Therefore the LORD has delivered him to the lion, which has torn him and killed him, according to the word of the LORD which He spoke to him." 27And he spoke to his sons, saying, "Saddle the donkey for me." So they saddled *it*. 28Then he went and found his corpse thrown on the road, and the donkey and the lion standing by the corpse. The lion had not eaten the corpse nor torn the donkey. 29And the prophet took up the corpse of the man of God, laid it on the donkey, and brought it back. So the old prophet came to the city to mourn, and to bury him. 30Then he laid the corpse in his own tomb; and they mourned over him, *saying*, "Alas, my brother!" 31So it was, after he had buried him, that he spoke to his sons, saying, "When I am dead, then bury me in the tomb where the man of God *is* buried; lay my bones beside his bones. 32For the saying which he cried out by the word of the LORD against the altar in Bethel, and against all the shrines[a] on the high places which *are* in the cities of Samaria, will surely come to pass."

33After this event Jeroboam did not turn from his evil way, but again he made priests from every class of people for the high places; whoever wished, he consecrated him, and he became *one* of the priests of the high places. 34And this thing was the sin of the house of Jeroboam, so as to exterminate and destroy *it* from the face of the earth.

JUDGMENT ON THE HOUSE OF JEROBOAM

14 At that time Abijah the son of Jeroboam became sick. 2And Jeroboam said to his wife, "Please arise, and disguise yourself, that they may not recognize you as the wife of Jeroboam, and go to Shiloh. Indeed, Ahijah the prophet *is* there, who told me that *I would be* king over this people. 3Also take with you ten loaves, *some* cakes, and a jar of honey, and go to him; he will tell you what will become of the child." 4And Jeroboam's wife did so; she arose and went to Shiloh, and came to the house of Ahijah. But Ahijah could not see, for his eyes were glazed by reason of his age.

5Now the LORD had said to Ahijah, "Here is the wife of Jeroboam, coming to ask you some-

13:32 [a]Literally *houses*

THE MESSAGE

die far from home and not be buried in your ancestral tomb."

23-25 When the meal was over, the prophet who had brought him back saddled his donkey for him. Down the road a way, a lion met him and killed him. His corpse lay crumpled on the road, the lion on one side and the donkey on the other. Some passersby saw the corpse in a heap on the road, with the lion standing guard beside it. They went to the village where the old prophet lived and told what they had seen.

26 When the prophet who had gotten him off track heard it, he said, "It's the holy man who disobeyed GOD's strict orders. GOD turned him over to the lion who knocked him around and killed him, just as GOD had told him."

27-30 The prophet told his sons, "Saddle my donkey." They did it. He rode out and found the corpse in a heap in the road, with the lion and the donkey standing there. The lion hadn't bothered either the corpse or the donkey. The old prophet loaded the corpse of the holy man on his donkey and returned it to his own town to give it a decent burial. He placed the body in his own tomb. The people mourned, saying, "A sad day, brother!"

31-32 After the funeral, the prophet said to his sons, "When I die, bury me in the same tomb where the holy man is buried, my bones alongside his bones. The message that he preached by GOD's command against the Altar at Bethel and against all the sex-and-religion shrines in the towns of Samaria will come true."

33-34 After this happened, Jeroboam kept right on doing evil, recruiting priests for the forbidden shrines indiscriminately—anyone who wanted to could be a priest at one of the local shrines. This was the root sin of Jeroboam's government. And it was this that ruined him.

1-3 14 At about this time Jeroboam's son Abijah came down sick. Jeroboam said to his wife, "Do something. Disguise yourself so no one will know you are the queen and go to Shiloh. Ahijah the prophet lives there, the same Ahijah who told me I'd be king over this people. Take along ten loaves of bread, some sweet rolls, and a jug of honey. Make a visit to him and he'll tell you what's going on with our boy."

4-5 Jeroboam's wife did as she was told; she went straight to Shiloh and to Ahijah's house. Ahijah was an old man at this time, and blind, but GOD had warned Ahijah, "Jeroboam's wife is on her way to consult with you regarding her sick son; tell her this and this and this."

5-9 When she came in she was disguised. Ahijah heard her come through the door and said, "Welcome, wife of Jeroboam! But

NEW KING JAMES VERSION

thing about her son, for he *is* sick. Thus and thus
you shall say to her; for it will be, when she
comes in, that she will pretend *to be* another
woman."
[6]And so it was, when Ahijah heard the sound
of her footsteps as she came through the door,
he said, "Come in, wife of Jeroboam. Why do
you pretend *to be* another *person*? For I *have
been* sent to you *with* bad *news*. [7]Go, tell Jer-
oboam, 'Thus says the LORD God of Israel: "Be-
cause I exalted you from among the people, and
made you ruler over My people Israel, [8]and tore
the kingdom away from the house of David, and
gave it to you; and *yet* you have not been as My
servant David, who kept My commandments
and who followed Me with all his heart, to do
only *what was* right in My eyes; [9]but you have
done more evil than all who were before you, for
you have gone and made for yourself other gods
and molded images to provoke Me to anger, and
have cast Me behind your back— [10]therefore be-
hold! I will bring disaster on the house of Jer-
oboam, and will cut off from Jeroboam every
male in Israel, bond and free; I will take away
the remnant of the house of Jeroboam, as one
takes away refuse until it is all gone. [11]The dogs
shall eat whoever belongs to Jeroboam and dies
in the city, and the birds of the air shall eat who-
ever dies in the field; for the LORD has spoken!"
' [12]Arise therefore, go to your own house. When
your feet enter the city, the child shall die. [13]And
all Israel shall mourn for him and bury him, for
he is the only one of Jeroboam who shall come
to the grave, because in him there is found
something good toward the LORD God of Israel
in the house of Jeroboam.
[14]"Moreover the LORD will raise up for Him-
self a king over Israel who shall cut off the
house of Jeroboam; this is the day. What? Even
now! [15]For the LORD will strike Israel, as a reed
is shaken in the water. He will uproot Israel
from this good land which He gave to their fa-
thers, and will scatter them beyond the River,[a]
because they have made their wooden images,[b]
provoking the LORD to anger. [16]And He will give
Israel up because of the sins of Jeroboam, who
sinned and who made Israel sin."
[17]Then Jeroboam's wife arose and departed,
and came to Tirzah. When she came to the
threshold of the house, the child died. [18]And
they buried him; and all Israel mourned for him,
according to the word of the LORD which He
spoke through His servant Ahijah the prophet.

DEATH OF JEROBOAM

[19]Now the rest of the acts of Jeroboam, how
he made war and how he reigned, indeed they
are written in the book of the chronicles of the
kings of Israel. [20]The period that Jeroboam
reigned *was* twenty-two years. So he rested
with his fathers. Then Nadab his son reigned in
his place.

14:15 [a]That is, the Euphrates [b]Hebrew *Asherim*, Canaanite deities

THE MESSAGE

why the deception? I've got bad news for
you. Go and deliver this message I received
firsthand from GOD, the God of Israel, to Jer-
oboam: I raised you up from obscurity and
made you the leader of my people Israel. I
ripped the kingdom from the hands of
David's family and gave it to you, but you
weren't at all like my servant David who did
what I told him and lived from his undivided
heart, pleasing me. Instead you've set a new
record in works of evil by making alien
gods—tin gods! Pushing me aside and turn-
ing your back—you've made me mighty an-
gry.
10-11 "And I'll not put up with it: I'm bringing
doom on the household of Jeroboam, killing
the lot of them right down to the last male
wretch in Israel, whether slave or free.
They've become nothing but garbage and
I'm getting rid of them. The ones who die in
the city will be eaten by stray dogs; the ones
who die out in the country will be eaten by
carrion crows. GOD's decree!
12-13 "And that's it. Go on home—the minute
you step foot in town, the boy will die.
Everyone will come to his burial, mourning
his death. He is the only one in Jeroboam's
family who will get a decent burial; he's the
only one for whom GOD, the God of Israel,
has a good word to say.
14-16 "Then GOD will appoint a king over Israel
who will wipe out Jeroboam's family, wipe
them right off the map—doomsday for Jer-
oboam! He will hit Israel hard, as a storm
slaps reeds about; he'll pull them up by the
roots from this good land of their inheri-
tance, weeding them out, and then scatter
them to the four winds. And why? Because
they made GOD so angry with Asherah sex-
and-religion shrines. He'll wash his hands
of Israel because of Jeroboam's sins, which
have led Israel into a life of sin."
17-18 Jeroboam's wife left and went home to
Tirzah. The moment she stepped through
the door, the boy died. They buried him and
everyone mourned his death, just as GOD
had said through his servant the prophet
Ahijah.
19-20 The rest of Jeroboam's life, the wars he
fought and the way he ruled, is written in
The Chronicles of the Kings of Israel. He
ruled for twenty-two years. He died and was
buried with his ancestors. Nadab his son
was king after him.

New King James Version

Rehoboam Reigns in Judah

21And Rehoboam the son of Solomon reigned in Judah. Rehoboam *was* forty-one years old when he became king. He reigned seventeen years in Jerusalem, the city which the LORD had chosen out of all the tribes of Israel, to put His name there. His mother's name *was* Naamah, an Ammonitess. 22Now Judah did evil in the sight of the LORD, and they provoked Him to jealousy with their sins which they committed, more than all that their fathers had done. 23For they also built for themselves high places, *sacred* pillars, and wooden images on every high hill and under every green tree. 24And there were also perverted persons[a] in the land. They did according to all the abominations of the nations which the LORD had cast out before the children of Israel.

25It happened in the fifth year of King Rehoboam *that* Shishak king of Egypt came up against Jerusalem. 26And he took away the treasures of the house of the LORD and the treasures of the king's house; he took away everything. He also took away all the gold shields which Solomon had made. 27Then King Rehoboam made bronze shields in their place, and committed *them* to the hands of the captains of the guard, who guarded the doorway of the king's house. 28And whenever the king entered the house of the LORD, the guards carried them, then brought them back into the guardroom.

29Now the rest of the acts of Rehoboam, and all that he did, *are* they not written in the book of the chronicles of the kings of Judah? 30And there was war between Rehoboam and Jeroboam all *their* days. 31So Rehoboam rested with his fathers, and was buried with his fathers in the City of David. His mother's name *was* Naamah, an Ammonitess. Then Abijam[a] his son reigned in his place.

Abijam Reigns in Judah

15 In the eighteenth year of King Jeroboam the son of Nebat, Abijam became king over Judah. 2He reigned three years in Jerusalem. His mother's name *was* Maachah the granddaughter of Abishalom. 3And he walked in all the sins of his father, which he had done before him; his heart was not loyal to the LORD his God, as was the heart of his father David. 4Nevertheless for David's sake the LORD his God gave him a lamp in Jerusalem, by setting up his son after him and by establishing Jerusalem; 5because David did *what was* right in the eyes of the LORD, and had not turned aside from anything that He commanded him all the days of his life, except in the matter of Uriah the Hittite. 6And there was war between Rehoboam[a] and Jeroboam all the days of his life. 7Now the rest of the acts of Abijam, and all that he did, *are* they not written in the book of the chronicles of the kings of Judah? And there was war between Abijam and Jeroboam.

8So Abijam rested with his fathers, and they buried him in the City of David. Then Asa his son reigned in his place.

14:24 [a]Hebrew *qadesh*, that is, one practicing sodomy and prostitution in religious rituals **14:31** [a]Spelled *Abijah* in 2 Chronicles 12:16ff **15:6** [a]Following Masoretic Text, Septuagint, Targum, and Vulgate; some Hebrew manuscripts and Syriac read *Abijam*.

The Message

21-24 Rehoboam son of Solomon was king in Judah. He was forty-one years old when he took the throne and was king for seventeen years in Jerusalem, the city GOD selected from all the tribes of Israel for the worship of his Name. Rehoboam's mother was Naamah, an Ammonite. Judah was openly wicked before GOD, making him very angry. They set new records in sin, surpassing anything their ancestors had done. They built Asherah sex-and-religion shrines and set up sacred stones all over the place—on hills, under trees, wherever you looked. Worse, they had male sacred prostitutes, polluting the country outrageously—all the stuff that GOD had gotten rid of when he brought Israel into the land.

25-28 In the fifth year of King Rehoboam's rule, Shishak king of Egypt made war against Jerusalem. He plundered The Temple of GOD and the royal palace of their treasures, cleaned them out—even the gold shields that Solomon had made. King Rehoboam replaced them with bronze shields and outfitted the royal palace guards with them. Whenever the king went to GOD's Temple, the guards carried the shields but always returned them to the guardroom.

29-31 The rest of Rehoboam's life, what he said and did, is all written in *The Chronicles of the Kings of Judah*. There was war between Rehoboam and Jeroboam the whole time. Rehoboam died and was buried with his ancestors in the City of David. His mother was Naamah, an Ammonite. His son Abijah ruled after him.

Abijah of Judah

1-6 15 In the eighteenth year of the rule of Jeroboam son of Nebat, Abijah took over the throne of Judah. He ruled in Jerusalem three years. His mother was Maacah daughter of Absalom. He continued to sin just like his father before him. He was not truehearted to GOD as his great-grandfather David had been. But despite that, out of respect for David, his GOD graciously gave him a lamp, a son to follow him and keep Jerusalem secure. For David had lived an exemplary life before GOD all his days, not going off on his own in willful defiance of GOD's clear directions (except for that time with Uriah the Hittite). But war continued between Abijah and Jeroboam the whole time.

7-8 The rest of Abijah's life, everything he did, is written in *The Chronicles of the Kings of Judah*. But the war with Jeroboam was the dominant theme. Abijah died and was buried with his ancestors in the City of David. His son Asa was king after him.

NEW KING JAMES VERSION

ASA REIGNS IN JUDAH

9 In the twentieth year of Jeroboam king of
Israel, Asa became king over Judah. 10 And he
reigned forty-one years in Jerusalem. His
grandmother's name *was* Maachah the grand-
daughter of Abishalom. 11 Asa did *what was*
right in the eyes of the LORD, as *did* his father
David. 12 And he banished the perverted per-
sons[a] from the land, and removed all the idols
that his fathers had made. 13 Also he removed
Maachah his grandmother from *being* queen
mother, because she had made an obscene im-
age of Asherah.[a] And Asa cut down her obscene
image and burned *it* by the Brook Kidron. 14 But
the high places were not removed. Nevertheless
Asa's heart was loyal to the LORD all his days.
15 He also brought into the house of the LORD the
things which his father had dedicated, and the
things which he himself had dedicated: silver
and gold and utensils.

16 Now there was war between Asa and
Baasha king of Israel all their days. 17 And
Baasha king of Israel came up against Judah,
and built Ramah, that he might let none go out
or come in to Asa king of Judah. 18 Then Asa
took all the silver and gold *that was* left in the
treasuries of the house of the LORD and the
treasuries of the king's house, and delivered
them into the hand of his servants. And King
Asa sent them to Ben-Hadad the son of Tabrim-
mon, the son of Hezion, king of Syria, who dwelt
in Damascus, saying, 19 "*Let there be* a treaty be-
tween you and me, as there was between my fa-
ther and your father. See, I have sent you a pres-
ent of silver and gold. Come and break your
treaty with Baasha king of Israel, so that he will
withdraw from me."

20 So Ben-Hadad heeded King Asa, and sent
the captains of his armies against the cities of
Israel. He attacked Ijon, Dan, Abel Beth
Maachah, and all Chinneroth, with all the land
of Naphtali. 21 Now it happened, when Baasha
heard *it*, that he stopped building Ramah, and
remained in Tirzah.

22 Then King Asa made a proclamation
throughout all Judah; none *was* exempted. And
they took away the stones and timber of Ramah,
which Baasha had used for building; and with
them King Asa built Geba of Benjamin, and
Mizpah.

23 The rest of all the acts of Asa, all his might,
all that he did, and the cities which he built, *are*
they not written in the book of the chronicles of
the kings of Judah? But in the time of his old age
he was diseased in his feet. 24 So Asa rested with
his fathers, and was buried with his fathers in
the City of David his father. Then Jehoshaphat
his son reigned in his place.

NADAB REIGNS IN ISRAEL

25 Now Nadab the son of Jeroboam became
king over Israel in the second year of Asa king
of Judah, and he reigned over Israel two years.
26 And he did evil in the sight of the LORD, and
walked in the way of his father, and in his sin by
which he had made Israel sin.

15:12 [a]Hebrew *qedeshim*, that is, those practicing sodomy and prostitution in religious rituals **15:13** [a]A Canaanite goddess

THE MESSAGE

ASA OF JUDAH

9-10 In the twentieth year of Jeroboam king of Is-
rael, Asa began his rule over Judah. He
ruled for forty-one years in Jerusalem. His
grandmother's name was Maacah.

11-15 Asa conducted himself well before GOD,
reviving the ways of his ancestor David. He
cleaned house: He got rid of the sacred pros-
titutes and threw out all the idols his prede-
cessors had made. Asa spared nothing and
no one; he went so far as to remove Queen
Maacah from her position because she had
built a shockingly obscene memorial to the
whore goddess Asherah. Asa tore it down
and burned it up in the Kidron Valley. Unfor-
tunately, he didn't get rid of the local sex-
and-religion shrines. But he was well-inten-
tioned—his heart was in the right place, in
tune with GOD. All the gold and silver ves-
sels and artifacts that he and his father had
consecrated for holy use he installed in The
Temple.

16-17 But through much of his reign there was
war between Asa and Baasha king of Israel.
Baasha king of Israel started it by building a
fort at Ramah and closing the border be-
tween Israel and Judah so no one could en-
ter or leave Judah.

18-19 Asa took all the silver and gold that was
left in the treasuries of The Temple of GOD
and the royal palace, gave it to his servants,
and sent them to Ben-Hadad son of Tabrim-
mon, the son of Hezion king of Aram, who
was ruling in Damascus, with this message:
"Let's make a treaty like the one between
our fathers. I'm showing my good faith with
this gift of silver and gold. Break your deal
with Baasha king of Israel so he'll quit fight-
ing against me."

20-21 Ben-Hadad went along with King Asa
and sent out his troops against the towns of
Israel. He attacked Ijon, Dan, Abel Beth
Maacah, and the entire region of Kinnereth,
including Naphtali. When Baasha got the re-
port he quit fortifying Ramah and pulled
back to Tirzah.

22 Then King Asa issued orders to everyone
in Judah—no exemptions—to haul away the
logs and stones Baasha had used in the for-
tification of Ramah and use them to fortify
Geba in Benjamin and Mizpah.

23-24 A full account of Asa's life, all the great
things he did and the fortifications he con-
structed, is written in *The Chronicles of the*
Kings of Judah. In his old age he developed
severe gout. Then Asa died and was buried
with his ancestors in the City of David. His
son Jehoshaphat became king after him.

NADAB OF ISRAEL

25-26 Nadab son of Jeroboam became king over
Israel in the second year of Asa's rule in Ju-
dah. He was king of Israel two years. He was
openly evil before GOD—he followed in the
footsteps of his father who both sinned and
made Israel sin.

New King James Version

27Then Baasha the son of Ahijah, of the
house of Issachar, conspired against him. And
Baasha killed him at Gibbethon, which *be-
longed* to the Philistines, while Nadab and all Is-
rael laid siege to Gibbethon. 28Baasha killed him
in the third year of Asa king of Judah, and
reigned in his place. 29And it was so, when he
became king, *that* he killed all the house of Jer-
oboam. He did not leave to Jeroboam anyone
that breathed, until he had destroyed him, ac-
cording to the word of the LORD which He had
spoken by His servant Ahijah the Shilonite,
30because of the sins of Jeroboam, which he had
sinned and by which he had made Israel sin, be-
cause of his provocation with which he had pro-
voked the LORD God of Israel to anger.
31Now the rest of the acts of Nadab, and all
that he did, *are* they not written in the book of
the chronicles of the kings of Israel? 32And there
was war between Asa and Baasha king of Israel
all their days.

Baasha Reigns in Israel

33In the third year of Asa king of Judah,
Baasha the son of Ahijah became king over all
Israel in Tirzah, and *reigned* twenty-four years.
34He did evil in the sight of the LORD, and
walked in the way of Jeroboam, and in his sin by
which he had made Israel sin.

16 Then the word of the LORD came to Jehu
the son of Hanani, against Baasha, saying:
2"Inasmuch as I lifted you out of the dust and
made you ruler over My people Israel, and you
have walked in the way of Jeroboam, and have
made My people Israel sin, to provoke Me to
anger with their sins, 3surely I will take away
the posterity of Baasha and the posterity of his
house, and I will make your house like the
house of Jeroboam the son of Nebat. 4The dogs
shall eat whoever belongs to Baasha and dies in
the city, and the birds of the air shall eat who-
ever dies in the fields."
5Now the rest of the acts of Baasha, what he
did, and his might, *are* they not written in the
book of the chronicles of the kings of Israel? 6So
Baasha rested with his fathers and was buried
in Tirzah. Then Elah his son reigned in his
place.
7And also the word of the LORD came by the
prophet Jehu the son of Hanani against Baasha
and his house, because of all the evil that he did
in the sight of the LORD in provoking Him to
anger with the work of his hands, in being like
the house of Jeroboam, and because he killed
them.

Elah Reigns in Israel

8In the twenty-sixth year of Asa king of Ju-
dah, Elah the son of Baasha became king over
Israel, *and reigned* two years in Tirzah. 9Now his
servant Zimri, commander of half *his* chariots,
conspired against him as he was in Tirzah
drinking himself drunk in the house of Arza,
steward of *his* house in Tirzah. 10And Zimri
went in and struck him and killed him in the
twenty-seventh year of Asa king of Judah, and
reigned in his place.

The Message

27-28 Baasha son of Ahijah of the tribe of Issachar ganged up on him and attacked him at the Philistine town of Gibbethon while Nadab and the Israelites were doing battle there. Baasha killed Nadab in the third year of Asa king of Judah and became Israel's next king.

29-30 As soon as he was king he killed everyone in Jeroboam's family. There wasn't a living soul left to the name of Jeroboam; Baasha wiped them out totally, just as GOD's servant Ahijah of Shiloh had prophesied—punishment for Jeroboam's sins and for making Israel sin, for making the GOD of Israel thoroughly angry.

31-32 The rest of Nadab's life, everything else he did, is written in *The Chronicles of the Kings of Israel*. There was continuous war between Asa and Baasha king of Israel.

Baasha of Israel

33-34 In the third year of Asa king of Judah, Baasha son of Ahijah became king in Tirzah over all Israel. He ruled twenty-four years. He was openly evil before GOD, walking in the footsteps of Jeroboam, who both sinned and made Israel sin.

1-4 16 The word of GOD came to Jehu son of Hanani with this message for Baasha: "I took you from nothing—a complete nobody—and set you up as the leader of my people Israel, but you plodded along in the rut of Jeroboam, making my people Israel sin and making me seethe over their sin. And now the consequences—I will burn Baasha and his regime to cinders, the identical fate of Jeroboam son of Nebat. Baasha's people who die in the city will be eaten by scavenger dogs; carrion crows will eat the ones who die in the country."

5-6 The rest of Baasha's life, the record of his regime, is written in *The Chronicles of the Kings of Israel*. Baasha died and was buried with his ancestors in Tirzah. His son Elah was king after him.

7 That's the way it was with Baasha: Through the prophet Jehu son of Hanani, GOD's word came to him and his regime because of his life of open evil before GOD and his making GOD so angry—a chip off the block of Jeroboam, even though GOD had destroyed him.

Elah of Israel

8-10 In the twenty-sixth year of Asa king of Judah, Elah son of Baasha began his rule. He was king in Tirzah only two years. One day when he was at the house of Arza the palace manager, drinking himself drunk, Zimri, captain of half his chariot-force, conspired against him. Zimri slipped in, knocked Elah to the ground, and killed him. This happened in the twenty-seventh year of Asa king of Judah. Zimri then became the king.

NEW KING JAMES VERSION

11Then it came to pass, when he began to
reign, as soon as he was seated on his throne,
that he killed all the household of Baasha; he
did not leave him one male, neither of his rela-
tives nor of his friends. 12Thus Zimri destroyed
all the household of Baasha, according to the
word of the LORD, which He spoke against
Baasha by Jehu the prophet, 13for all the sins of
Baasha and the sins of Elah his son, by which
they had sinned and by which they had made Is-
rael sin, in provoking the LORD God of Israel to
anger with their idols.
14Now the rest of the acts of Elah, and all that
he did, *are* they not written in the book of the
chronicles of the kings of Israel?

ZIMRI REIGNS IN ISRAEL

15In the twenty-seventh year of Asa king of
Judah, Zimri had reigned in Tirzah seven days.
And the people *were* encamped against Gib-
bethon, which *belonged* to the Philistines.
16Now the people *who were* encamped heard it
said, "Zimri has conspired and also has killed
the king." So all Israel made Omri, the com-
mander of the army, king over Israel that day in
the camp. 17Then Omri and all Israel with him
went up from Gibbethon, and they besieged
Tirzah. 18And it happened, when Zimri saw that
the city was taken, that he went into the citadel
of the king's house and burned the king's house
down upon himself with fire, and died, 19be-
cause of the sins which he had committed in do-
ing evil in the sight of the LORD, in walking in
the way of Jeroboam, and in his sin which he
had committed to make Israel sin.
20Now the rest of the acts of Zimri, and the
treason he committed, *are* they not written in
the book of the chronicles of the kings of Israel?

OMRI REIGNS IN ISRAEL

21Then the people of Israel were divided into
two parts: half of the people followed Tibni the
son of Ginath, to make him king, and half fol-
lowed Omri. 22But the people who followed
Omri prevailed over the people who followed
Tibni the son of Ginath. So Tibni died and Omri
reigned. 23In the thirty-first year of Asa king of
Judah, Omri became king over Israel, *and
reigned* twelve years. Six years he reigned in
Tirzah. 24And he bought the hill of Samaria from
Shemer for two talents of silver; then he built on
the hill, and called the name of the city which he
built, Samaria, after the name of Shemer, owner
of the hill. 25Omri did evil in the eyes of the
LORD, and did worse than all who *were* before
him. 26For he walked in all the ways of Jer-
oboam the son of Nebat, and in his sin by which
he had made Israel sin, provoking the LORD God
of Israel to anger with their idols.
27Now the rest of the acts of Omri which he
did, and the might that he showed, *are* they not
written in the book of the chronicles of the
kings of Israel?
28So Omri rested with his fathers and was
buried in Samaria. Then Ahab his son reigned
in his place.

THE MESSAGE

11-13 Zimri had no sooner become king than he killed everyone connected with Baasha, got rid of them all like so many stray dogs—relatives and friends alike. Zimri totally wiped out the family of Baasha, just as GOD's word delivered by the prophet Jehu had said—wages for the sins of Baasha and his son Elah; not only for their sins but for dragging Israel into their sins and making the GOD of Israel angry with their stupid idols.

14 The rest of Elah's life, what he said and did, is written in *The Chronicles of the Kings of Israel.*

ZIMRI OF ISRAEL

15-19 Zimri was king in Tirzah for all of seven days during the twenty-seventh year of the reign of Asa king of Judah. The Israelite army was on maneuvers near the Philistine town of Gibbethon at the time. When they got the report, "Zimri has conspired against the king and killed him," right there in the camp they made Omri, commander of the army, king. Omri and the army immediately left Gibbethon and attacked Tirzah. When Zimri saw that he was surrounded and as good as dead, he entered the palace citadel, set the place on fire, and died. It was a fit end for his sins, for living a flagrantly evil life before GOD, walking in the footsteps of Jeroboam, sinning and then dragging Israel into his sins.

20 As for the rest of Zimri's life, along with his infamous conspiracy, it's all written in *The Chronicles of the Kings of Israel.*

OMRI OF ISRAEL

21-22 After that the people of Israel were split right down the middle: Half favored Tibni son of Ginath as king, and half wanted Omri. Eventually the Omri side proved stronger than the Tibni side. Tibni ended up dead and Omri king.

23-24 Omri took over as king of Israel in the thirty-first year of the reign of Asa king of Judah. He ruled for twelve years, the first six in Tirzah. He then bought the hill Samaria from Shemer for 150 pounds of silver. He developed the hill and named the city that he built Samaria, after its original owner Shemer.

25-26 But as far as GOD was concerned, Omri lived an evil life—set new records in evil. He walked in the footsteps of Jeroboam son of Nebat, who not only sinned but dragged Israel into his sins, making GOD angry—such an empty-headed, empty-hearted life!

27-28 The rest of Omri's life, the mark he made on his times, is written in *The Chronicles of the Kings of Israel.* Omri died and was buried in Samaria. His son Ahab was the next king after him.

NEW KING JAMES VERSION

AHAB REIGNS IN ISRAEL

29In the thirty-eighth year of Asa king of Judah, Ahab the son of Omri became king over Israel; and Ahab the son of Omri reigned over Israel in Samaria twenty-two years. 30Now Ahab the son of Omri did evil in the sight of the LORD, more than all who *were* before him. 31And it came to pass, as though it had been a trivial thing for him to walk in the sins of Jeroboam the son of Nebat, that he took as wife Jezebel the daughter of Ethbaal, king of the Sidonians; and he went and served Baal and worshiped him. 32Then he set up an altar for Baal in the temple of Baal, which he had built in Samaria. 33And Ahab made a wooden image.[a] Ahab did more to provoke the LORD God of Israel to anger than all the kings of Israel who were before him. 34In his days Hiel of Bethel built Jericho. He laid its foundation with Abiram his firstborn, and with his youngest *son* Segub he set up its gates, according to the word of the LORD, which He had spoken through Joshua the son of Nun.[a]

ELIJAH PROCLAIMS A DROUGHT

17 And Elijah the Tishbite, of the inhabitants of Gilead, said to Ahab, "*As* the LORD God of Israel lives, before whom I stand, there shall not be dew nor rain these years, except at my word."

2Then the word of the LORD came to him, saying, 3"Get away from here and turn eastward, and hide by the Brook Cherith, which flows into the Jordan. 4And it will be *that* you shall drink from the brook, and I have commanded the ravens to feed you there."

5So he went and did according to the word of the LORD, for he went and stayed by the Brook Cherith, which flows into the Jordan. 6The ravens brought him bread and meat in the morning, and bread and meat in the evening; and he drank from the brook. 7And it happened after a while that the brook dried up, because there had been no rain in the land.

ELIJAH AND THE WIDOW

8Then the word of the LORD came to him, saying, 9"Arise, go to Zarephath, which *belongs* to Sidon, and dwell there. See, I have commanded a widow there to provide for you." 10So he arose and went to Zarephath. And when he came to the gate of the city, indeed a widow *was* there gathering sticks. And he called to her and said, "Please bring me a little water in a cup, that I may drink." 11And as she was going to get *it*, he called to her and said, "Please bring me a morsel of bread in your hand."

12So she said, "As the LORD your God lives, I do not have bread, only a handful of flour in a bin, and a little oil in a jar; and see, I *am* gathering a couple of sticks that I may go in and prepare it for myself and my son, that we may eat it, and die."

13And Elijah said to her, "Do not fear; go *and* do as you have said, but make me a small cake

16:33 [a]Hebrew *Asherah*, a Canaanite goddess **16:34** [a]Compare Joshua 6:26

THE MESSAGE

AHAB OF ISRAEL

29-33 Ahab son of Omri became king of Israel in the thirty-eighth year of Asa king of Judah. Ahab son of Omri was king over Israel for twenty-two years. He ruled from Samaria. Ahab son of Omri did even more open evil before GOD than anyone yet—a new champion in evil! It wasn't enough for him to copy the sins of Jeroboam son of Nebat; no, he went all out, first by marrying Jezebel daughter of Ethbaal king of the Sidonians, and then by serving and worshiping the god Baal. He built a temple for Baal in Samaria, and then furnished it with an altar for Baal. Worse, he went on and built a shrine to the sacred whore Asherah. He made the GOD of Israel angrier than all the previous kings of Israel put together.

34 It was under Ahab's rule that Hiel of Bethel refortified Jericho, but at a terrible cost: He ritually sacrificed his firstborn son Abiram at the laying of the foundation, and his youngest son Segub at the setting up of the gates. This is exactly what Joshua son of Nun said would happen.

1 17 And then this happened: Elijah the Tishbite, from among the settlers of Gilead, confronted Ahab: "As surely as GOD lives, the God of Israel before whom I stand in obedient service, the next years are going to see a total drought—not a drop of dew or rain unless I say otherwise."

2-4 GOD then told Elijah, "Get out of here, and fast. Head east and hide out at the Kerith Ravine on the other side of the Jordan River. You can drink fresh water from the brook; I've ordered the ravens to feed you."

5-6 Elijah obeyed GOD's orders. He went and camped in the Kerith canyon on the other side of the Jordan. And sure enough, ravens brought him his meals, both breakfast and supper, and he drank from the brook.

7-9 Eventually the brook dried up because of the drought. Then GOD spoke to him: "Get up and go to Zarephath in Sidon and live there. I've instructed a woman who lives there, a widow, to feed you."

10-11 So he got up and went to Zarephath. As he came to the entrance of the village he met a woman, a widow, gathering firewood. He asked her, "Please, would you bring me a little water in a jug? I need a drink." As she went to get it, he called out, "And while you're at it, would you bring me something to eat?"

12 She said, "I swear, as surely as your GOD lives, I don't have so much as a biscuit. I have a handful of flour in a jar and a little oil in a bottle; you found me scratching together just enough firewood to make a last meal for my son and me. After we eat it, we'll die."

13-14 Elijah said to her, "Don't worry about a thing. Go ahead and do what you've said. But first make a small biscuit for me and

NEW KING JAMES VERSION

from it first, and bring *it* to me; and afterward make *some* for yourself and your son. 14For thus says the LORD God of Israel: 'The bin of flour shall not be used up, nor shall the jar of oil run dry, until the day the LORD sends rain on the earth.' "

15So she went away and did according to the word of Elijah; and she and he and her household ate for *many* days. 16The bin of flour was not used up, nor did the jar of oil run dry, according to the word of the LORD which He spoke by Elijah.

ELIJAH REVIVES THE WIDOW'S SON

17Now it happened after these things *that* the son of the woman who owned the house became sick. And his sickness was so serious that there was no breath left in him. 18So she said to Elijah, "What have I to do with you, O man of God? Have you come to me to bring my sin to remembrance, and to kill my son?"

19And he said to her, "Give me your son." So he took him out of her arms and carried him to the upper room where he was staying, and laid him on his own bed. 20Then he cried out to the LORD and said, "O LORD my God, have You also brought tragedy on the widow with whom I lodge, by killing her son?" 21And he stretched himself out on the child three times, and cried out to the LORD and said, "O LORD my God, I pray, let this child's soul come back to him." 22Then the LORD heard the voice of Elijah; and the soul of the child came back to him, and he revived.

23And Elijah took the child and brought him down from the upper room into the house, and gave him to his mother. And Elijah said, "See, your son lives!"

24Then the woman said to Elijah, "Now by this I know that you *are* a man of God, *and* that the word of the LORD in your mouth *is* the truth."

ELIJAH'S MESSAGE TO AHAB

18 And it came to pass *after* many days that the word of the LORD came to Elijah, in the third year, saying, "Go, present yourself to Ahab, and I will send rain on the earth."

2So Elijah went to present himself to Ahab; and *there was* a severe famine in Samaria. 3And Ahab had called Obadiah, who *was* in charge of *his* house. (Now Obadiah feared the LORD greatly. 4For so it was, while Jezebel massacred the prophets of the LORD, that Obadiah had taken one hundred prophets and hidden them, fifty to a cave, and had fed them with bread and water.) 5And Ahab had said to Obadiah, "Go into the land to all the springs of water and to all the brooks; perhaps we may find grass to keep the horses and mules alive, so that we will not have to kill any livestock." 6So they divided the land between them to explore it; Ahab went one way by himself, and Obadiah went another way by himself.

7Now as Obadiah was on his way, suddenly Elijah met him; and he recognized him, and fell on his face, and said, "*Is* that you, my lord Elijah?"

THE MESSAGE

bring it back here. Then go ahead and make
a meal from what's left for you and your
son. This is the word of the GOD of Israel:
'The jar of flour will not run out and the bot-
tle of oil will not become empty before GOD
sends rain on the land and ends this
drought.' "
15-16 And she went right off and did it, did just
as Elijah asked. And it turned out as he
said—daily food for her and her family. The
jar of meal didn't run out and the bottle of
oil didn't become empty: GOD's promise ful-
filled to the letter, exactly as Elijah had de-
livered it!
17 Later on the woman's son became sick.
The sickness took a turn for the worse—and
then he stopped breathing.
18 The woman said to Elijah, "Why did you
ever show up here in the first place—a holy
man barging in, exposing my sins, and
killing my son?"
19-20 Elijah said, "Hand me your son."
He then took him from her bosom, car-
ried him up to the loft where he was staying,
and laid him on his bed. Then he prayed, "O
GOD, my God, why have you brought this
terrible thing on this widow who has
opened her home to me? Why have you
killed her son?"
21-23 Three times he stretched himself out full-
length on the boy, praying with all his
might, "GOD, my God, put breath back into
this boy's body!" GOD listened to Elijah's
prayer and put breath back into his body—
he was alive! Elijah picked the boy up, car-
ried him downstairs from the loft, and gave
him to his mother. "Here's your son," said
Elijah, "alive!"
24 The woman said to Elijah, "I see it all
now—you *are* a holy man. When you speak,
GOD speaks—a true word!"

1-2 18 A long time passed. Then GOD's word
came to Elijah. The drought was now
in its third year. The message: "Go and pre-
sent yourself to Ahab; I'm about to make
it rain on the country." Elijah set out to pre-
sent himself to Ahab. The drought in
Samaria at the time was most severe.
3-4 Ahab called for Obadiah, who was in
charge of the palace. Obadiah feared GOD—
he was very devout. Earlier, when Jezebel
had tried to kill off all the prophets of GOD,
Obadiah had hidden away a hundred of
them in two caves, fifty in a cave, and then
supplied them with food and water.
5-6 Ahab ordered Obadiah, "Go through the
country; locate every spring and every
stream. Let's see if we can find enough
grass to keep our horses and mules from dy-
ing." So they divided the country between
them for the search—Ahab went one way,
Obadiah the other.
7 Obadiah went his way and suddenly
there he was—Elijah! Obadiah fell on his
knees, bowing in reverence, and exclaimed,
"Is it really you—my master Elijah?"

NEW KING JAMES VERSION

8And he answered him, "*It is* I. Go, tell your
master, 'Elijah *is here.*' "
9So he said, "How have I sinned, that you are
delivering your servant into the hand of Ahab,
to kill me? 10*As* the LORD your God lives, there is
no nation or kingdom where my master has not
sent someone to hunt for you; and when they
said, '*He is* not *here,*' he took an oath from the
kingdom or nation that they could not find you.
11And now you say, 'Go, tell your master, "Elijah
is here" '! 12And it shall come to pass, *as soon as*
I am gone from you, that the Spirit of the LORD
will carry you to a place I do not know; so when
I go and tell Ahab, and he cannot find you, he
will kill me. But I your servant have feared the
LORD from my youth. 13Was it not reported to my
lord what I did when Jezebel killed the prophets
of the LORD, how I hid one hundred men of the
LORD's prophets, fifty to a cave, and fed them
with bread and water? 14And now you say, 'Go,
tell your master, "Elijah *is here.*" ' He will kill
me!"
15Then Elijah said, "*As* the LORD of hosts
lives, before whom I stand, I will surely present
myself to him today."
16So Obadiah went to meet Ahab, and told
him; and Ahab went to meet Elijah.
17Then it happened, when Ahab saw Elijah,
that Ahab said to him, "*Is that* you, O troubler of
Israel?"
18And he answered, "I have not troubled Is-
rael, but you and your father's house *have,* in
that you have forsaken the commandments of
the LORD and have followed the Baals. 19Now
therefore, send *and* gather all Israel to me on
Mount Carmel, the four hundred and fifty
prophets of Baal, and the four hundred prophets
of Asherah,[a] who eat at Jezebel's table."

ELIJAH'S MOUNT CARMEL VICTORY

20So Ahab sent for all the children of Israel,
and gathered the prophets together on Mount
Carmel. 21And Elijah came to all the people, and
said, "How long will you falter between two
opinions? If the LORD *is* God, follow Him; but if
Baal, follow him." But the people answered him
not a word. 22Then Elijah said to the people, "I
alone am left a prophet of the LORD; but Baal's
prophets *are* four hundred and fifty men.
23Therefore let them give us two bulls; and let
them choose one bull for themselves, cut it in
pieces, and lay *it* on the wood, but put no fire
under it; and I will prepare the other bull, and
lay *it* on the wood, but put no fire *under it.*
24Then you call on the name of your gods, and I
will call on the name of the LORD; and the God
who answers by fire, He is God."
So all the people answered and said, "It is
well spoken."
25Now Elijah said to the prophets of Baal,
"Choose one bull for yourselves and prepare *it*
first, for you *are* many; and call on the name of
your god, but put no fire *under it.*"

18:19 [a]A Canaanite goddess

THE MESSAGE

8 "Yes," said Elijah, "the real me. Now go and tell your boss, 'I've seen Elijah.' "

9-14 Obadiah said, "But what have I done to deserve this? Ahab will kill me. As surely as your GOD lives, there isn't a country or kingdom where my master hasn't sent out search parties looking for you. And if they said, 'We can't find him; we've looked high and low,' he would make that country or kingdom swear that you were not to be found. And now you're telling me, 'Go and tell your master Elijah's found!' The minute I leave you the Spirit of GOD will whisk you away to who knows where. Then when I report to Ahab, you'll have disappeared and Ahab will kill me. And I've served GOD devoutly since I was a boy! Hasn't anyone told you what I did when Jezebel was out to kill the prophets of GOD, how I risked my life by hiding a hundred of them, fifty to a cave, and made sure they got food and water? And now you're telling me to draw attention to myself by announcing to my master, 'Elijah's been found.' Why, he'll kill me for sure."

15 Elijah said, "As surely as GOD-of-the-Angel-Armies lives, and before whom I take my stand, I'll meet with your master face-to-face this very day."

16 So Obadiah went straight to Ahab and told him. And Ahab went out to meet Elijah.

17-19 The moment Ahab saw Elijah he said, "So it's you, old troublemaker!"

"It's not I who has caused trouble in Israel," said Elijah, "but you and your government—you've dumped GOD's ways and commands and run off after the local gods, the Baals. Here's what I want you to do: Assemble everyone in Israel at Mount Carmel. And make sure that the special pets of Jezebel, the four hundred and fifty prophets of the local gods, the Baals, and the four hundred prophets of the whore goddess Asherah, are there."

20 So Ahab summoned everyone in Israel, particularly the prophets, to Mount Carmel.

21 Elijah challenged the people: "How long are you going to sit on the fence? If GOD is the real God, follow him; if it's Baal, follow him. Make up your minds!"

Nobody said a word; nobody made a move.

22-24 Then Elijah said, "I'm the only prophet of GOD left in Israel; and there are 450 prophets of Baal. Let the Baal prophets bring up two oxen; let them pick one, butcher it, and lay it out on an altar on firewood—but don't ignite it. I'll take the other ox, cut it up, and lay it on the wood. But neither will I light the fire. Then you pray to your gods and I'll pray to GOD. The god who answers with fire will prove to be, in fact, God."

All the people agreed: "A good plan—do it!"

25 Elijah told the Baal prophets, "Choose your ox and prepare it. You go first, you're the majority. Then pray to your god, but don't light the fire."

New King James Version

26 So they took the bull which was given them, and they prepared *it*, and called on the name of Baal from morning even till noon, saying, "O Baal, hear us!" But *there was* no voice; no one answered. Then they leaped about the altar which they had made.

27 And so it was, at noon, that Elijah mocked them and said, "Cry aloud, for he *is* a god; either he is meditating, or he is busy, or he is on a journey, *or* perhaps he is sleeping and must be awakened." 28 So they cried aloud, and cut themselves, as was their custom, with knives and lances, until the blood gushed out on them. 29 And when midday was past, they prophesied until the *time* of the offering of the *evening* sacrifice. But *there was* no voice; no one answered, no one paid attention.

30 Then Elijah said to all the people, "Come near to me." So all the people came near to him. And he repaired the altar of the LORD *that was* broken down. 31 And Elijah took twelve stones, according to the number of the tribes of the sons of Jacob, to whom the word of the LORD had come, saying, "Israel shall be your name."[a] 32 Then with the stones he built an altar in the name of the LORD; and he made a trench around the altar large enough to hold two seahs of seed. 33 And he put the wood in order, cut the bull in pieces, and laid *it* on the wood, and said, "Fill four waterpots with water, and pour *it* on the burnt sacrifice and on the wood." 34 Then he said, "Do *it* a second time," and they did *it* a second time; and he said, "Do *it* a third time," and they did *it* a third time. 35 So the water ran all around the altar; and he also filled the trench with water.

36 And it came to pass, at *the time of* the offering of the *evening* sacrifice, that Elijah the prophet came near and said, "LORD God of Abraham, Isaac, and Israel, let it be known this day that You *are* God in Israel and I *am* Your servant, and *that* I have done all these things at Your word. 37 Hear me, O LORD, hear me, that this people may know that You *are* the LORD God, and *that* You have turned their hearts back *to You* again."

38 Then the fire of the LORD fell and consumed the burnt sacrifice, and the wood and the stones and the dust, and it licked up the water that *was* in the trench. 39 Now when all the people saw *it*, they fell on their faces; and they said, "The LORD, He *is* God! The LORD, He *is* God!"

40 And Elijah said to them, "Seize the prophets of Baal! Do not let one of them escape!" So they seized them; and Elijah brought them down to the Brook Kishon and executed them there.

The Drought Ends

41 Then Elijah said to Ahab, "Go up, eat and drink; for *there is* the sound of abundance of rain." 42 So Ahab went up to eat and drink. And Elijah went up to the top of Carmel; then he bowed down on the ground, and put his face between his knees, 43 and said to his servant, "Go up now, look toward the sea."

18:31 [a]Genesis 32:28

The Message

26 So they took the ox he had given them, prepared it for the altar, then prayed to Baal. They prayed all morning long, "O Baal, answer us!" But nothing happened—not so much as a whisper of breeze. Desperate, they jumped and stomped on the altar they had made.

27-28 By noon, Elijah had started making fun of them, taunting, "Call a little louder—he is a god, after all. Maybe he's off meditating somewhere or other, or maybe he's gotten involved in a project, or maybe he's on vacation. You don't suppose he's overslept, do you, and needs to be waked up?" They prayed louder and louder, cutting themselves with swords and knives—a ritual common to them—until they were covered with blood.

29 This went on until well past noon. They used every religious trick and strategy they knew to make something happen on the altar, but nothing happened—not so much as a whisper, not a flicker of response.

30-35 Then Elijah told the people, "Enough of that—it's my turn. Gather around." And they gathered. He then put the altar back together for by now it was in ruins. Elijah took twelve stones, one for each of the tribes of Jacob, the same Jacob to whom GOD had said, "From now on your name is Israel." He built the stones into the altar in honor of GOD. Then Elijah dug a fairly wide trench around the altar. He laid firewood on the altar, cut up the ox, put it on the wood, and said, "Fill four buckets with water and drench both the ox and the firewood." Then he said, "Do it again," and they did it. Then he said, "Do it a third time," and they did it a third time. The altar was drenched and the trench was filled with water.

36-37 When it was time for the sacrifice to be offered, Elijah the prophet came up and prayed, "O GOD, God of Abraham, Isaac, and Israel, make it known right now that you are God in Israel, that I am your servant, and that I'm doing what I'm doing under your orders. Answer me, GOD; O answer me and reveal to this people that you are GOD, the true God, and that you are giving these people another chance at repentance."

38 Immediately the fire of GOD fell and burned up the offering, the wood, the stones, the dirt, and even the water in the trench.

39 All the people saw it happen and fell on their faces in awed worship, exclaiming, "GOD is the true God! GOD is the true God!"

40 Elijah told them, "Grab the Baal prophets! Don't let one get away!"

They grabbed them. Elijah had them taken down to the Brook Kishon and they massacred the lot.

41 Elijah said to Ahab, "Up on your feet! Eat and drink—celebrate! Rain is on the way; I hear it coming."

42-43 Ahab did it: got up and ate and drank. Meanwhile, Elijah climbed to the top of Carmel, bowed deeply in prayer, his face between his knees. Then he said to his young servant, "On your feet now! Look toward the sea."

New King James Version

So he went up and looked, and said, "*There is* nothing." And seven times he said, "Go again."
44Then it came to pass the seventh *time*, that he said, "There is a cloud, as small as a man's hand, rising out of the sea!" So he said, "Go up, say to Ahab, 'Prepare *your chariot*, and go down before the rain stops you.' "

45Now it happened in the meantime that the sky became black with clouds and wind, and there was a heavy rain. So Ahab rode away and went to Jezreel. 46Then the hand of the LORD came upon Elijah; and he girded up his loins and ran ahead of Ahab to the entrance of Jezreel.

Elijah Escapes from Jezebel

19 And Ahab told Jezebel all that Elijah had done, also how he had executed all the prophets with the sword. 2Then Jezebel sent a messenger to Elijah, saying, "So let the gods do *to me*, and more also, if I do not make your life as the life of one of them by tomorrow about this time." 3And when he saw *that*, he arose and ran for his life, and went to Beersheba, which *belongs* to Judah, and left his servant there.

4But he himself went a day's journey into the wilderness, and came and sat down under a broom tree. And he prayed that he might die, and said, "It is enough! Now, LORD, take my life, for I *am* no better than my fathers!"

5Then as he lay and slept under a broom tree, suddenly an angel[a] touched him, and said to him, "Arise *and* eat." 6Then he looked, and there by his head *was* a cake baked on coals, and a jar of water. So he ate and drank, and lay down again. 7And the angel[a] of the LORD came back the second time, and touched him, and said, "Arise *and* eat, because the journey *is* too great for you." 8So he arose, and ate and drank; and he went in the strength of that food forty days and forty nights as far as Horeb, the mountain of God.

9And there he went into a cave, and spent the night in that place; and behold, the word of the LORD *came* to him, and He said to him, "What are you doing here, Elijah?"

10So he said, "I have been very zealous for the LORD God of hosts; for the children of Israel have forsaken Your covenant, torn down Your altars, and killed Your prophets with the sword. I alone am left; and they seek to take my life."

God's Revelation to Elijah

11Then He said, "Go out, and stand on the mountain before the LORD." And behold, the LORD passed by, and a great and strong wind tore into the mountains and broke the rocks in pieces

19:5 [a]Or *Angel* 19:7 [a]Or *Angel*

The Message

He went, looked, and reported back, "I don't see a thing."

"Keep looking," said Elijah, "seven times if necessary."

44 And sure enough, the seventh time he said, "Oh yes, a cloud! But very small, no bigger than someone's hand, rising out of the sea."

"Quickly then, on your way. Tell Ahab, 'Saddle up and get down from the mountain before the rain stops you.' "

45-46 Things happened fast. The sky grew black with wind-driven clouds, and then a huge cloudburst of rain, with Ahab hightailing it in his chariot for Jezreel. And GOD strengthened Elijah mightily. Pulling up his robe and tying it around his waist, Elijah ran in front of Ahab's chariot until they reached Jezreel.

Revenge from Jezebel

1-2 19 Ahab reported to Jezebel everything that Elijah had done, including the massacre of the prophets. Jezebel immediately sent a messenger to Elijah with her threat: "The gods will get you for this and I'll get even with you! By this time tomorrow you'll be as dead as any one of those prophets."

3-5 When Elijah saw how things were, he ran for dear life to Beersheba, far in the south of Judah. He left his young servant there and then went on into the desert another day's journey. He came to a lone broom bush and collapsed in its shade, wanting in the worst way to be done with it all—to just die: "Enough of this, GOD! Take my life—I'm ready to join my ancestors in the grave!" Exhausted, he fell asleep under the lone broom bush.

Suddenly an angel shook him awake and said, "Get up and eat!"

6 He looked around and, to his surprise, right by his head were a loaf of bread baked on some coals and a jug of water. He ate the meal and went back to sleep.

7 The angel of GOD came back, shook him awake again, and said, "Get up and eat some more—you've got a long journey ahead of you."

8-9 He got up, ate and drank his fill, and set out. Nourished by that meal, he walked forty days and nights, all the way to the mountain of God, to Horeb. When he got there, he crawled into a cave and went to sleep.

Then the word of GOD came to him: "So Elijah, what are you doing here?"

10 "I've been working my heart out for the GOD-of-the-Angel-Armies," said Elijah. "The people of Israel have abandoned your covenant, destroyed the places of worship, and murdered your prophets. I'm the only one left, and now they're trying to kill me."

11-12 Then he was told, "Go, stand on the mountain at attention before GOD. GOD will pass by."

A hurricane wind ripped through the mountains and shattered the rocks before

NEW KING JAMES VERSION

before the LORD, *but* the LORD *was* not in the wind; and after the wind an earthquake, *but* the LORD *was* not in the earthquake; 12and after the earthquake a fire, *but* the LORD *was* not in the fire; and after the fire a still small voice.

13So it was, when Elijah heard *it*, that he wrapped his face in his mantle and went out and stood in the entrance of the cave. Suddenly a voice *came* to him, and said, "What are you doing here, Elijah?"

14And he said, "I have been very zealous for the LORD God of hosts; because the children of Israel have forsaken Your covenant, torn down Your altars, and killed Your prophets with the sword. I alone am left; and they seek to take my life."

15Then the LORD said to him: "Go, return on your way to the Wilderness of Damascus; and when you arrive, anoint Hazael *as* king over Syria. 16Also you shall anoint Jehu the son of Nimshi *as* king over Israel. And Elisha the son of Shaphat of Abel Meholah you shall anoint *as* prophet in your place. 17It shall be *that* whoever escapes the sword of Hazael, Jehu will kill; and whoever escapes the sword of Jehu, Elisha will kill. 18Yet I have reserved seven thousand in Israel, all whose knees have not bowed to Baal, and every mouth that has not kissed him."

ELISHA FOLLOWS ELIJAH

19So he departed from there, and found Elisha the son of Shaphat, who *was* plowing *with* twelve yoke *of oxen* before him, and he was with the twelfth. Then Elijah passed by him and threw his mantle on him. 20And he left the oxen and ran after Elijah, and said, "Please let me kiss my father and my mother, and *then* I will follow you."

And he said to him, "Go back again, for what have I done to you?"

21So *Elisha* turned back from him, and took a yoke of oxen and slaughtered them and boiled their flesh, using the oxen's equipment, and gave it to the people, and they ate. Then he arose and followed Elijah, and became his servant.

AHAB DEFEATS THE SYRIANS

20 Now Ben-Hadad the king of Syria gathered all his forces together; thirty-two kings *were* with him, with horses and chariots. And he went up and besieged Samaria, and made war against it. 2Then he sent messengers into the city to Ahab king of Israel, and said to him, "Thus says Ben-Hadad: 3'Your silver and your gold *are* mine; your loveliest wives and children are mine.' "

4And the king of Israel answered and said, "My lord, O king, just as you say, I and all that I have *are* yours."

5Then the messengers came back and said, "Thus speaks Ben-Hadad, saying, 'Indeed I have sent to you, saying, "You shall deliver to me your silver and your gold, your wives and your children"; 6but I will send my servants to you tomorrow about this time, and they shall search your house and the houses of your servants. And it shall be, *that* whatever is pleasant in your eyes, they will put *it* in their hands and take *it*.' "

THE MESSAGE

GOD, but GOD wasn't to be found in the wind; after the wind an earthquake, but GOD wasn't in the earthquake; and after the earthquake fire, but GOD wasn't in the fire; and after the fire a gentle and quiet whisper.

13-14 When Elijah heard the quiet voice, he muffled his face with his great cloak, went to the mouth of the cave, and stood there. A quiet voice asked, "So Elijah, now tell me, what are you doing here?" Elijah said it again, "I've been working my heart out for GOD, the GOD-of-the-Angel-Armies, because the people of Israel have abandoned your covenant, destroyed your places of worship, and murdered your prophets. I'm the only one left, and now they're trying to kill me."

15-18 GOD said, "Go back the way you came through the desert to Damascus. When you get there anoint Hazael; make him king over Aram. Then anoint Jehu son of Nimshi; make him king over Israel. Finally, anoint Elisha son of Shaphat from Abel Meholah to succeed you as prophet. Anyone who escapes death by Hazael will be killed by Jehu; and anyone who escapes death by Jehu will be killed by Elisha. Meanwhile, I'm preserving for myself seven thousand souls: the knees that haven't bowed to the god Baal, the mouths that haven't kissed his image."

19 Elijah went straight out and found Elisha son of Shaphat in a field where there were twelve pairs of yoked oxen at work plowing; Elisha was in charge of the twelfth pair. Elijah went up to him and threw his cloak over him.

20 Elisha deserted the oxen, ran after Elijah, and said, "Please! Let me kiss my father and mother good-bye—then I'll follow you."

"Go ahead," said Elijah, "but, mind you, don't forget what I've just done to you."

21 So Elisha left; he took his yoke of oxen and butchered them. He made a fire with the plow and tackle and then boiled the meat—a true farewell meal for the family. Then he left and followed Elijah, becoming his right-hand man.

1-3 20 At about this same time Ben-Hadad king of Aram mustered his troops. He recruited in addition thirty-two local sheiks, all outfitted with horses and chariots. He set out in force and surrounded Samaria, ready to make war. He sent an envoy into the city to set his terms before Ahab king of Israel: "Ben-Hadad lays claim to your silver and gold, and to the pick of your wives and sons."

4 The king of Israel accepted the terms: "As you say, distinguished lord; I and everything I have is yours."

5-6 But then the envoy returned a second time, saying, "On second thought, I want it all—your silver and gold and *all* your wives and sons. Hand them over—the whole works. I'll give you twenty-four hours; then my servants will arrive to search your palace and the houses of your officials and loot them; anything that strikes their fancy, they'll take."

New King James Version

7 So the king of Israel called all the elders of the land, and said, "Notice, please, and see how this *man* seeks trouble, for he sent to me for my wives, my children, my silver, and my gold; and I did not deny him."

8 And all the elders and all the people said to him, "Do not listen or consent."

9 Therefore he said to the messengers of Ben-Hadad, "Tell my lord the king, 'All that you sent for to your servant the first time I will do, but this thing I cannot do.' "

And the messengers departed and brought back word to him.

10 Then Ben-Hadad sent to him and said, "The gods do so to me, and more also, if enough dust is left of Samaria for a handful for each of the people who follow me."

11 So the king of Israel answered and said, "Tell *him*, 'Let not the one who puts on *his armor* boast like the one who takes *it off*.' "

12 And it happened when *Ben-Hadad* heard this message, as he and the kings *were* drinking at the command post, that he said to his servants, "Get ready." And they got ready to attack the city.

13 Suddenly a prophet approached Ahab king of Israel, saying, "Thus says the LORD: 'Have you seen all this great multitude? Behold, I will deliver it into your hand today, and you shall know that I *am* the LORD.' "

14 So Ahab said, "By whom?"

And he said, "Thus says the LORD: 'By the young leaders of the provinces.' "

Then he said, "Who will set the battle in order?"

And he answered, "You."

15 Then he mustered the young leaders of the provinces, and there were two hundred and thirty-two; and after them he mustered all the people, all the children of Israel—seven thousand.

16 So they went out at noon. Meanwhile Ben-Hadad and the thirty-two kings helping him were getting drunk at the command post. 17 The young leaders of the provinces went out first. And Ben-Hadad sent out *a patrol*, and they told him, saying, "Men are coming out of Samaria!" 18 So he said, "If they have come out for peace, take them alive; and if they have come out for war, take them alive."

19 Then these young leaders of the provinces went out of the city with the army which followed them. 20 And each one killed his man; so the Syrians fled, and Israel pursued them; and Ben-Hadad the king of Syria escaped on a horse with the cavalry. 21 Then the king of Israel went out and attacked the horses and chariots, and killed the Syrians with a great slaughter.

22 And the prophet came to the king of Israel and said to him, "Go, strengthen yourself; take note, and see what you should do, for in the spring of the year the king of Syria will come up against you."

The Message

7 The king of Israel called a meeting of all his tribal elders. He said, "Look at this—outrageous! He's just looking for trouble. He means to clean me out, demanding all my women and children. And after I already agreed to pay him off handsomely!"

8 The elders, backed by the people, said, "Don't cave in to him. Don't give an inch."

9 So he sent an envoy to Ben-Hadad, "Tell my distinguished lord, 'I agreed to the terms you delivered the first time, but this I can't do—this I *won't* do!' "

The envoy went back and delivered the answer.

10 Ben-Hadad shot back his response: "May the gods do their worst to me, and then worse again, if there'll be anything left of Samaria but rubble."

11 The king of Israel countered, "Think about it—it's easier to start a fight than end one."

12 It happened that when Ben-Hadad heard this retort he was into some heavy drinking, boozing it up with the sheiks in their field shelters. Drunkenly, he ordered his henchmen, "Go after them!" And they attacked the city.

13 Just then a lone prophet approached Ahab king of Israel and said, "GOD's word: Have you taken a good look at this mob? Well, look again—I'm turning it over to you this very day. And you'll know, beyond the shadow of a doubt, that I am GOD."

14 Ahab said, "Really? And who is going to make this happen?"

GOD said, "The young commandos of the regional chiefs."

"And who," said Ahab, "will strike the first blow?"

GOD said, "You."

15 Ahab looked over the commandos of the regional chiefs; he counted 232. Then he assessed the available troops—7,000.

16-17 At noon they set out after Ben-Hadad who, with his allies, the thirty-two sheiks, was busy at serious drinking in the field shelters. The commandos of the regional chiefs made up the vanguard.

A report was brought to Ben-Hadad: "Men are on their way from Samaria."

18 He said, "If they've come in peace, take them alive as hostages; if they've come to fight, the same—take them alive as hostages."

19-20 The commandos poured out of the city with the full army behind them. They hit hard in hand-to-hand combat. The Arameans scattered from the field, with Israel hard on their heels. But Ben-Hadad king of Aram got away on horseback, along with his cavalry.

21 The king of Israel cut down both horses and chariots—an enormous defeat for Aram.

22 Sometime later the prophet came to the king of Israel and said, "On the alert now—build up your army, assess your capabilities, and see what has to be done. Before the year is out, the king of Aram will be back in force."

NEW KING JAMES VERSION

THE SYRIANS AGAIN DEFEATED

23Then the servants of the king of Syria said
to him, "Their gods *are* gods of the hills. There-
fore they were stronger than we; but if we fight
against them in the plain, surely we will be
stronger than they. 24So do this thing: Dismiss
the kings, each from his position, and put cap-
tains in their places; 25and you shall muster an
army like the army that you have lost, horse for
horse and chariot for chariot. Then we will fight
against them in the plain; surely we will be
stronger than they."

And he listened to their voice and did so.

26So it was, in the spring of the year, that
Ben-Hadad mustered the Syrians and went up
to Aphek to fight against Israel. 27And the chil-
dren of Israel were mustered and given provi-
sions, and they went against them. Now the chil-
dren of Israel encamped before them like two
little flocks of goats, while the Syrians filled the
countryside.

28Then a man of God came and spoke to the
king of Israel, and said, "Thus says the LORD:
'Because the Syrians have said, "The LORD *is*
God of the hills, but He *is* not God of the val-
leys," therefore I will deliver all this great multi-
tude into your hand, and you shall know that I
am the LORD.' " 29And they encamped opposite
each other for seven days. So it was that on the
seventh day the battle was joined; and the chil-
dren of Israel killed one hundred thousand foot
soldiers *of* the Syrians in one day. 30But the rest
fled to Aphek, into the city; then a wall fell on
twenty-seven thousand of the men *who were*
left.

And Ben-Hadad fled and went into the city,
into an inner chamber.

AHAB'S TREATY WITH BEN-HADAD

31Then his servants said to him, "Look now,
we have heard that the kings of the house of Is-
rael *are* merciful kings. Please, let us put sack-
cloth around our waists and ropes around our
heads, and go out to the king of Israel; perhaps
he will spare your life." 32So they wore sackcloth
around their waists and *put* ropes around their
heads, and came to the king of Israel and said,
"Your servant Ben-Hadad says, 'Please let me
live.' "

And he said, "*Is* he still alive? He *is* my
brother."

33Now the men were watching closely to see
whether *any sign of mercy would come* from
him; and they quickly grasped *at this word* and
said, "Your brother Ben-Hadad."

So he said, "Go, bring him." Then Ben-Hadad
came out to him; and he had him come up into
the chariot.

34So *Ben-Hadad* said to him, "The cities
which my father took from your father I will re-
store; and you may set up marketplaces for
yourself in Damascus, as my father did in
Samaria."

Then *Ahab said*, "I will send you away with
this treaty." So he made a treaty with him and
sent him away.

THE MESSAGE

23-25 Meanwhile the advisors to the king of
Aram said, "Their god is a god of the moun-
tains—we don't stand a chance against
them there. So let's engage them on the
plain where we'll have the advantage.
Here's the strategy: Remove each sheik
from his place of leadership and replace
him with a seasoned officer. Then recruit a
fighting force equivalent in size to the army
that deserted earlier—horse for horse, char-
iot for chariot. And we'll fight them on the
plain—we're sure to prove stronger than
they are."

It sounded good to the king; he did what
they advised.

26-27 As the new year approached, Ben-Hadad
rallied Aram and they went up to Aphek to
make war on Israel. The Israelite army pre-
pared to fight and took the field to meet
Aram. They moved into battle formation
before Aram in two camps, like two flocks
of goats. The plain was seething with
Arameans.

28 Just then a holy man approached the
king of Israel saying, "This is GOD's word:
Because Aram said, 'GOD is a god of the
mountains and not a god of the valleys,' I'll
hand over this huge mob of an army to you.
Then you'll know that I am GOD."

29-30 The two armies were poised in a standoff
for seven days. On the seventh day fighting
broke out. The Israelites killed 100,000 of
the Aramean infantry in one day. The rest of
the army ran for their lives back to the city,
Aphek, only to have the city wall fall on
27,000 of the survivors.

30-31 Ben-Hadad escaped into the city and hid
in a closet. Then his advisors told him,
"Look, we've heard that the kings of Israel
play by the rules; let's dress in old gunny-
sacks, carry a white flag of truce, and pre-
sent ourselves to the king of Israel on the
chance that he'll let you live."

32 So that's what they did. They dressed in
old gunnysacks and carried a white flag,
and came to the king of Israel saying, "Your
servant Ben-Hadad said, 'Please let me
live.' "

Ahab said, "You mean to tell me that he's
still alive? If he's alive, he's my brother."

33 The men took this as a good sign and
concluded that everything was going to be
all right: "Ben-Hadad is most certainly your
brother!"

The king said, "Go and get him." They
went and brought him back by chariot.

34 Ahab said, "I am prepared to return the
cities that my father took from your father.
And you can set up your headquarters in
Damascus just as my father did in Samaria;
I'll send you home under safe conduct."
Then he made a covenant with him and sent
him off.

NEW KING JAMES VERSION

AHAB CONDEMNED

35Now a certain man of the sons of the
prophets said to his neighbor by the word of the
LORD, "Strike me, please." And the man refused
to strike him. 36Then he said to him, "Because
you have not obeyed the voice of the LORD,
surely, as soon as you depart from me, a lion
shall kill you." And as soon as he left him, a lion
found him and killed him.

37And he found another man, and said,
"Strike me, please." So the man struck him, in-
flicting a wound. 38Then the prophet departed
and waited for the king by the road, and dis-
guised himself with a bandage over his eyes.
39Now as the king passed by, he cried out to the
king and said, "Your servant went out into the
midst of the battle; and there, a man came over
and brought a man to me, and said, 'Guard this
man; if by any means he is missing, your life
shall be for his life, or else you shall pay a talent
of silver.' 40While your servant was busy here
and there, he was gone."

Then the king of Israel said to him, "So *shall*
your judgment *be;* you yourself have decided *it.*"
41And he hastened to take the bandage away
from his eyes; and the king of Israel recognized
him as one of the prophets. 42Then he said to
him, "Thus says the LORD: 'Because you have let
slip out of *your* hand a man whom I appointed
to utter destruction, therefore your life shall go
for his life, and your people for his people.' "

43So the king of Israel went to his house
sullen and displeased, and came to Samaria.

NABOTH IS MURDERED FOR HIS VINEYARD

21 And it came to pass after these things *that*
Naboth the Jezreelite had a vineyard
which *was* in Jezreel, next to the palace of Ahab
king of Samaria. 2So Ahab spoke to Naboth,
saying, "Give me your vineyard, that I may have
it for a vegetable garden, because it *is* near, next
to my house; and for it I will give you a vineyard
better than it. *Or,* if it seems good to you, I will
give you its worth in money."

3But Naboth said to Ahab, "The LORD forbid
that I should give the inheritance of my fathers
to you!"

4So Ahab went into his house sullen and dis-
pleased because of the word which Naboth the
Jezreelite had spoken to him; for he had said, "I
will not give you the inheritance of my fathers."
And he lay down on his bed, and turned away
his face, and would eat no food. 5But Jezebel his
wife came to him, and said to him, "Why is your
spirit so sullen that you eat no food?"

6He said to her, "Because I spoke to Naboth
the Jezreelite, and said to him, 'Give me your
vineyard for money; or else, if it pleases you, I
will give you *another* vineyard for it.' And he an-
swered, 'I will not give you my vineyard.' "

7Then Jezebel his wife said to him, "You now
exercise authority over Israel! Arise, eat food,
and let your heart be cheerful; I will give you the
vineyard of Naboth the Jezreelite."

8And she wrote letters in Ahab's name,
sealed *them* with his seal, and sent the letters to
the elders and the nobles who *were* dwelling in
the city with Naboth. 9She wrote in the letters,
saying,

THE MESSAGE

35 A man who was one of the prophets said to a bystander, "Hit me; wound me. Do it for GOD's sake—it's his command. Hit me; wound me." But the man wouldn't do it.

36 So he told him, "Because you wouldn't obey GOD's orders, as soon as you leave me a lion will attack you." No sooner had the man left his side than a lion met him and attacked.

37 He then found another man and said, "Hit me; wound me." That man did it—hit him hard in the face, drawing blood.

38-40 Then the prophet went and took a position along the road, with a bandage over his eyes, waiting for the king. It wasn't long before the king happened by. The man cried out to the king, "Your servant was in the thick of the battle when a man showed up and turned over a prisoner to me, saying, 'Guard this man with your life; if he turns up missing you'll pay dearly.' But I got busy doing one thing after another and the next time I looked he was gone."

The king of Israel said, "You've just pronounced your own verdict."

41 At that, the man ripped the bandage off his eyes and the king recognized who he was—one of the prophets!

42 The man said to the king, "GOD's word: Because you let a man go who was under sentence by GOD, it's now your life for his, your people for his."

43 The king of Israel went home in a sulk. He arrived in Samaria in a very bad mood.

1-2 21 And then, to top it off, came this: Naboth the Jezreelite owned a vineyard in Jezreel that bordered the palace of Ahab king of Samaria. One day Ahab spoke to Naboth, saying, "Give me your vineyard so I can use it as a kitchen garden; it's right next to my house—so convenient. In exchange I'll give you a far better vineyard, or if you'd prefer I'll pay you money for it."

3-4 But Naboth told Ahab, "Not on your life! So help me GOD, I'd never sell the family farm to you!" Ahab went home in a black mood, sulking over Naboth the Jezreelite's words, "I'll never turn over my family inheritance to you." He went to bed, stuffed his face in his pillow, and refused to eat.

5 Jezebel his wife came to him. She said, "What's going on? Why are you so out of sorts and refusing to eat?"

6 He told her, "Because I spoke to Naboth the Jezreelite. I said, 'Give me your vineyard—I'll pay you for it or, if you'd rather, I'll give you another vineyard in exchange.' And he said, 'I'll never give you my vineyard.' "

7 Jezebel said, "Is this any way for a king of Israel to act? Aren't you the boss? On your feet! Eat! Cheer up! I'll take care of this; I'll get the vineyard of this Naboth the Jezreelite for you."

8-10 She wrote letters over Ahab's signature, stamped them with his official seal, and sent them to the elders in Naboth's city and to the civic leaders. She wrote "Call for a fast

NEW KING JAMES VERSION

Proclaim a fast, and seat Naboth with high
honor among the people; 10and seat two
men, scoundrels, before him to bear witness
against him, saying, "You have blasphemed
God and the king." *Then* take him out, and
stone him, that he may die.
11So the men of his city, the elders and nobles
who were inhabitants of his city, did as Jezebel
had sent to them, as it *was* written in the letters
which she had sent to them. 12They proclaimed a
fast, and seated Naboth with high honor among
the people. 13And two men, scoundrels, came in
and sat before him; and the scoundrels wit-
nessed against him, against Naboth, in the pres-
ence of the people, saying, "Naboth has blas-
phemed God and the king!" Then they took him
outside the city and stoned him with stones, so
that he died. 14Then they sent to Jezebel, saying,
"Naboth has been stoned and is dead."
15And it came to pass, when Jezebel heard
that Naboth had been stoned and was dead, that
Jezebel said to Ahab, "Arise, take possession of
the vineyard of Naboth the Jezreelite, which he
refused to give you for money; for Naboth is not
alive, but dead." 16So it was, when Ahab heard
that Naboth was dead, that Ahab got up and
went down to take possession of the vineyard of
Naboth the Jezreelite.

THE LORD CONDEMNS AHAB

17Then the word of the LORD came to Elijah
the Tishbite, saying, 18"Arise, go down to meet
Ahab king of Israel, who *lives* in Samaria. There
he is, in the vineyard of Naboth, where he has
gone down to take possession of it. 19You shall
speak to him, saying, 'Thus says the LORD:
"Have you murdered and also taken posses-
sion?" ' And you shall speak to him, saying,
'Thus says the LORD: "In the place where dogs
licked the blood of Naboth, dogs shall lick your
blood, even yours." ' "
20So Ahab said to Elijah, "Have you found
me, O my enemy?"
And he answered, "I have found *you,* be-
cause you have sold yourself to do evil in the
sight of the LORD: 21'Behold, I will bring
calamity on you. I will take away your posterity,
and will cut off from Ahab every male in Israel,
both bond and free. 22I will make your house
like the house of Jeroboam the son of Nebat,
and like the house of Baasha the son of Ahijah,
because of the provocation with which you have
provoked *Me* to anger, and made Israel sin.'
23And concerning Jezebel the LORD also spoke,
saying, 'The dogs shall eat Jezebel by the wall[a]
of Jezreel.' 24The dogs shall eat whoever belongs
to Ahab and dies in the city, and the birds of the
air shall eat whoever dies in the field."
25But there was no one like Ahab who sold
himself to do wickedness in the sight of the
LORD, because Jezebel his wife stirred him up.
26And he behaved very abominably in following
idols, according to all *that* the Amorites had
done, whom the LORD had cast out before the
children of Israel.

21:23 [a]Following Masoretic Text and Septuagint; some Hebrew manuscripts, Syriac, Targum, and Vulgate read *plot of ground* (compare 2 Kings 9:36).

THE MESSAGE

day and put Naboth at the head table. Then seat a couple of stool pigeons across from him who, in front of everybody will say, 'You! You blasphemed God and the king!' Then they'll throw him out and stone him to death."

11-14 And they did it. The men of the city—the elders and civic leaders—followed Jezebel's instructions that she wrote in the letters sent to them. They called for a fast day and seated Naboth at the head table. Then they brought in two stool pigeons and seated them opposite Naboth. In front of everybody the two degenerates accused him, "He blasphemed God and the king!" The company threw him out in the street, stoned him mercilessly, and he died.

15 When Jezebel got word that Naboth had been stoned to death, she told Ahab, "Go for it, Ahab—take the vineyard of Naboth the Jezreelite for your own, the vineyard he refused to sell you. Naboth is no more; Naboth is dead."

16 The minute Ahab heard that Naboth was dead, he set out for the vineyard of Naboth the Jezreelite and claimed it for his own.

17-19 Then GOD stepped in and spoke to Elijah the Tishbite, "On your feet; go down and confront Ahab of Samaria, king of Israel. You'll find him in the vineyard of Naboth; he's gone there to claim it as his own. Say this to him: 'GOD's word: What's going on here? First murder, then theft?' Then tell him, 'GOD's verdict: The very spot where the dogs lapped up Naboth's blood, they'll lap up your blood—that's right, *your* blood.' "

20-22 Ahab answered Elijah, "My enemy! So, you've run me down!"

"Yes, I've found you out," said Elijah. "And because you've bought into the business of evil, defying GOD. 'I will most certainly bring doom upon you, make mincemeat of your descendants, kill off every sorry male wretch who's even remotely connected with the name Ahab. And I'll bring down on you the same fate that fell on Jeroboam son of Nebat and Baasha son of Ahijah—you've made me *that* angry by making Israel sin.' "

23-24 As for Jezebel, GOD said, "Dogs will fight over the flesh of Jezebel all over Jezreel. Anyone tainted by Ahab who dies in the city will be eaten by stray dogs; corpses in the country will be eaten by carrion crows."

25-26 Ahab, pushed by his wife Jezebel and in open defiance of GOD, set an all-time record in making big business of evil. He indulged in outrageous obscenities in the world of idols, copying the Amorites whom GOD had earlier kicked out of Israelite territory.

NEW KING JAMES VERSION

27So it was, when Ahab heard those words,
that he tore his clothes and put sackcloth on his
body, and fasted and lay in sackcloth, and went
about mourning.
28And the word of the LORD came to Elijah
the Tishbite, saying, 29"See how Ahab has hum-
bled himself before Me? Because he has hum-
bled himself before Me, I will not bring the
calamity in his days. In the days of his son I will
bring the calamity on his house."

MICAIAH WARNS AHAB

22 Now three years passed without war be-
tween Syria and Israel. 2Then it came to
pass, in the third year, that Jehoshaphat the king
of Judah went down to *visit* the king of Israel.
3And the king of Israel said to his servants,
"Do you know that Ramoth in Gilead *is* ours, but
we hesitate to take it out of the hand of the king
of Syria?" 4So he said to Jehoshaphat, "Will you
go with me to fight at Ramoth Gilead?"
Jehoshaphat said to the king of Israel, "I *am*
as you *are*, my people as your people, my horses
as your horses." 5Also Jehoshaphat said to the
king of Israel, "Please inquire for the word of
the LORD today."
6Then the king of Israel gathered the
prophets together, about four hundred men, and
said to them, "Shall I go against Ramoth Gilead
to fight, or shall I refrain?"
So they said, "Go up, for the Lord will deliver
it into the hand of the king."
7And Jehoshaphat said, "*Is there* not still a
prophet of the LORD here, that we may inquire of
Him?"[a]
8So the king of Israel said to Jehoshaphat,
"*There is* still one man, Micaiah the son of Im-
lah, by whom we may inquire of the LORD; but I
hate him, because he does not prophesy good
concerning me, but evil."
And Jehoshaphat said, "Let not the king say
such things!"
9Then the king of Israel called an officer and
said, "Bring Micaiah the son of Imlah quickly!"
10The king of Israel and Jehoshaphat the
king of Judah, having put on *their* robes, sat
each on his throne, at a threshing floor at the en-
trance of the gate of Samaria; and all the
prophets prophesied before them. 11Now
Zedekiah the son of Chenaanah had made
horns of iron for himself; and he said, "Thus
says the LORD: 'With these you shall gore the
Syrians until they are destroyed.' " 12And all the
prophets prophesied so, saying, "Go up to
Ramoth Gilead and prosper, for the LORD will
deliver *it* into the king's hand."
13Then the messenger who had gone to call
Micaiah spoke to him, saying, "Now listen, the
words of the prophets with one accord encour-
age the king. Please, let your word be like the
word of one of them, and speak encourage-
ment."
14And Micaiah said, "*As* the LORD lives,
whatever the LORD says to me, that I will speak."
15Then he came to the king; and the king said
to him, "Micaiah, shall we go to war against
Ramoth Gilead, or shall we refrain?"

22:7 [a]Or *him*

THE MESSAGE

27 When Ahab heard what Elijah had to say,
he ripped his clothes to shreds, dressed in
penitential rough burlap, and fasted. He
even slept in coarse burlap pajamas. He tip-
toed around, quiet as a mouse.
28-29 Then GOD spoke to Elijah the Tishbite:
"Do you see how penitently submissive
Ahab has become to me? Because of his re-
pentance I'll not bring the doom during his
lifetime; Ahab's son, though, will get it."

1-3 22 They enjoyed three years of peace—no
fighting between Aram and Israel. In
the third year, Jehoshaphat king of Judah
had a meeting with the king of Israel. Is-
rael's king remarked to his aides, "Do you
realize that Ramoth Gilead belongs to us,
and we're sitting around on our hands in-
stead of taking it back from the king of
Aram?"
4-5 He turned to Jehoshaphat and said, "Will
you join me in fighting for Ramoth Gilead?"
Jehoshaphat said, "You bet. I'm with you
all the way—my troops are your troops, my
horses are your horses." He then continued,
"But before you do anything, ask GOD for
guidance."
6 The king of Israel got the prophets to-
gether—all four hundred of them—and put
the question to them: "Should I attack
Ramoth Gilead? Or should I hold back?"
"Go for it," they said. "GOD will hand it
over to the king."
7 But Jehoshaphat dragged his heels: "Is
there still another prophet of GOD around
here we can consult?"
8 The king of Israel told Jehoshaphat, "As a
matter of fact, there is still one such man.
But I hate him. He never preaches anything
good to me, only doom, doom, doom—
Micaiah son of Imlah."
"The king shouldn't talk about a prophet
like that," said Jehoshaphat.
9 So the king of Israel ordered one of his
men, "On the double! Get Micaiah son of
Imlah."
10-12 Meanwhile, the king of Israel and Je-
hoshaphat were seated on their thrones,
dressed in their royal robes, resplendent in
front of the Samaria city gates. All the
prophets were staging a prophecy-perfor-
mance for their benefit. Zedekiah son of Ke-
naanah had even made a set of iron horns,
and brandishing them called out, "GOD's
word! With these horns you'll gore Aram un-
til there's nothing left of him!" All the
prophets chimed in, "Yes! Go for Ramoth
Gilead! An easy victory! GOD's gift to the
king!"
13 The messenger who went to get Micaiah
said, "The prophets have all said Yes to the
king. Make it unanimous—vote Yes!"
14 But Micaiah said, "As surely as GOD lives,
what GOD says, I'll say."
15 With Micaiah before him, the king asked
him, "So Micaiah—do we attack Ramoth
Gilead, or do we hold back?"

NEW KING JAMES VERSION

And he answered him, "Go and prosper, for
the LORD will deliver *it* into the hand of the
king!"
16So the king said to him, "How many times
shall I make you swear that you tell me nothing
but the truth in the name of the LORD?"
17Then he said, "I saw all Israel scattered on
the mountains, as sheep that have no shepherd.
And the LORD said, 'These have no master. Let
each return to his house in peace.' "
18And the king of Israel said to Jehoshaphat,
"Did I not tell you he would not prophesy good
concerning me, but evil?"
19Then *Micaiah* said, "Therefore hear the
word of the LORD: I saw the LORD sitting on His
throne, and all the host of heaven standing by,
on His right hand and on His left. 20And the
LORD said, 'Who will persuade Ahab to go up,
that he may fall at Ramoth Gilead?' So one
spoke in this manner, and another spoke in that
manner. 21Then a spirit came forward and stood
before the LORD, and said, 'I will persuade him.'
22The LORD said to him, 'In what way?' So he
said, 'I will go out and be a lying spirit in the
mouth of all his prophets.' And the LORD said,
'You shall persuade *him,* and also prevail. Go
out and do so.' 23Therefore look! The LORD has
put a lying spirit in the mouth of all these
prophets of yours, and the LORD has declared
disaster against you."
24Now Zedekiah the son of Chenaanah went
near and struck Micaiah on the cheek, and said,
"Which way did the spirit from the LORD go
from me to speak to you?"
25And Micaiah said, "Indeed, you shall see on
that day when you go into an inner chamber to
hide!"
26So the king of Israel said, "Take Micaiah,
and return him to Amon the governor of the city
and to Joash the king's son; 27and say, 'Thus
says the king: "Put this *fellow* in prison, and
feed him with bread of affliction and water of
affliction, until I come in peace." ' "
28But Micaiah said, "If you ever return in
peace, the LORD has not spoken by me." And he
said, "Take heed, all you people!"

AHAB DIES IN BATTLE

29So the king of Israel and Jehoshaphat the
king of Judah went up to Ramoth Gilead. 30And
the king of Israel said to Jehoshaphat, "I will
disguise myself and go into battle; but you put
on your robes." So the king of Israel disguised
himself and went into battle.
31Now the king of Syria had commanded the
thirty-two captains of his chariots, saying,

THE MESSAGE

"Go ahead," he said. "An easy victory. GOD's gift to the king."

16 "Not so fast," said the king. "How many times have I made you promise under oath to tell me the truth and nothing but the truth?"

17 "All right," said Micaiah, "since you insist.

I saw all of Israel scattered over the hills,
sheep with no shepherd.
Then GOD spoke: 'These poor people
have no one to tell them what to do.
Let them go home and do
the best they can for themselves.' "

18 Then the king of Israel turned to Jehoshaphat, "See! What did I tell you? He never has a good word for me from GOD, only doom."

19-23 Micaiah kept on: "I'm not done yet; listen to GOD's word:

I saw GOD enthroned,
and all the angel armies of heaven
Standing at attention
ranged on his right and his left.
And GOD said, 'How can we seduce Ahab
into attacking Ramoth Gilead?'
Some said this,
and some said that.
Then a bold angel stepped out,
stood before GOD, and said,
'I'll seduce him.'
'And how will you do it?' said GOD.
'Easy,' said the angel,
'I'll get all the prophets to lie.'
'That should do it,' said GOD.
'On your way—seduce him!'

"And that's what has happened. GOD filled the mouths of your puppet prophets with seductive lies. GOD has pronounced your doom."

24 Just then Zedekiah son of Kenaanah came up and punched Micaiah in the nose, saying, "Since when did the Spirit of GOD leave me and take up with you?"

25 Micaiah said, "You'll know soon enough; you'll know it when you're frantically and futilely looking for a place to hide."

26-27 The king of Israel had heard enough: "Get Micaiah out of here! Turn him over to Amon the city magistrate and to Joash the king's son with this message, 'King's orders: Lock him up in jail; keep him on bread and water until I'm back in one piece.' "

28 Micaiah said, "If you ever get back in one piece, I'm no prophet of GOD."

He added,"When it happens, O people, remember where you heard it!"

29-30 The king of Israel and Jehoshaphat king of Judah attacked Ramoth Gilead. The king of Israel said to Jehoshaphat, "Wear my kingly robe; I'm going into battle disguised." So the king of Israel entered the battle in disguise.

31 Meanwhile, the king of Aram had ordered his chariot commanders (there were

NEW KING JAMES VERSION

"Fight with no one small or great, but only with the king of Israel." 32 So it was, when the captains of the chariots saw Jehoshaphat, that they said, "Surely it *is* the king of Israel!" Therefore they turned aside to fight against him, and Jehoshaphat cried out. 33 And it happened, when the captains of the chariots saw that it *was* not the king of Israel, that they turned back from pursuing him. 34 Now a *certain* man drew a bow at random, and struck the king of Israel between the joints of his armor. So he said to the driver of his chariot, "Turn around and take me out of the battle, for I am wounded."

35 The battle increased that day; and the king was propped up in his chariot, facing the Syrians, and died at evening. The blood ran out from the wound onto the floor of the chariot. 36 Then, as the sun was going down, a shout went throughout the army, saying, "Every man to his city, and every man to his own country!"

37 So the king died, and was brought to Samaria. And they buried the king in Samaria. 38 Then *someone* washed the chariot at a pool in Samaria, and the dogs licked up his blood while the harlots bathed,[a] according to the word of the LORD which He had spoken.

39 Now the rest of the acts of Ahab, and all that he did, the ivory house which he built and all the cities that he built, *are* they not written in the book of the chronicles of the kings of Israel? 40 So Ahab rested with his fathers. Then Ahaziah his son reigned in his place.

JEHOSHAPHAT REIGNS IN JUDAH

41 Jehoshaphat the son of Asa had become king over Judah in the fourth year of Ahab king of Israel. 42 Jehoshaphat *was* thirty-five years old when he became king, and he reigned twenty-five years in Jerusalem. His mother's name *was* Azubah the daughter of Shilhi. 43 And he walked in all the ways of his father Asa. He did not turn aside from them, doing *what was* right in the eyes of the LORD. Nevertheless the high places were not taken away, *for* the people offered sacrifices and burned incense on the high places. 44 Also Jehoshaphat made peace with the king of Israel.

45 Now the rest of the acts of Jehoshaphat, the might that he showed, and how he made war, *are* they not written in the book of the chronicles of the kings of Judah? 46 And the rest of the perverted persons,[a] who remained in the days of his father Asa, he banished from the land. 47 *There was* then no king in Edom, only a deputy of the king.

48 Jehoshaphat made merchant ships[a] to go to Ophir for gold; but they never sailed, for the ships were wrecked at Ezion Geber. 49 Then Ahaziah the son of Ahab said to Jehoshaphat, "Let my servants go with your servants in the ships." But Jehoshaphat would not.

50 And Jehoshaphat rested with his fathers, and was buried with his fathers in the City of David his father. Then Jehoram his son reigned in his place.

22:38 [a]Syriac and Targum read *they washed his armor.* **22:46** [a]Hebrew *qadesh*, that is, one practicing sodomy and prostitution in religious rituals **22:48** [a]Or *ships of Tarshish*

THE MESSAGE

thirty-two of them): "Don't bother with anyone, whether small or great; go after the king of Israel and him only."

32-33 When the chariot commanders saw Jehoshaphat they said, "There he is! The king of Israel!" and took after him. Jehoshaphat yelled out, and the chariot commanders realized they had the wrong man—it wasn't the king of Israel after all. They let him go.

34 Just then someone, without aiming, shot an arrow randomly into the crowd and hit the king of Israel in the chink of his armor. The king told his charioteer, "Turn back! Get me out of here—I'm wounded."

35-37 All day the fighting continued, hot and heavy. Propped up in his chariot, the king watched from the sidelines. He died that evening. Blood from his wound pooled in the chariot. As the sun went down, shouts reverberated through the ranks, "Abandon camp! Head for home! The king is dead!"

37-38 The king was brought to Samaria and there they buried him. They washed down the chariot at the pool of Samaria where the town whores bathed, and the dogs lapped up the blood, just as GOD's word had said.

39-40 The rest of Ahab's life—everything he did, the ivory palace he built, the towns he founded, and the defense system he built up—is all written up in *The Chronicles of the Kings of Israel*. He was buried in the family cemetery and his son Ahaziah was the next king.

JEHOSHAPHAT OF JUDAH

41-44 Jehoshaphat son of Asa became king of Judah in the fourth year of Ahab king of Israel. Jehoshaphat was thirty-five years old when he became king and he ruled for twenty-five years in Jerusalem. His mother was Azubah daughter of Shilhi. He continued the kind of life characteristic of his father Asa—no detours, no dead ends—pleasing GOD with his life. But he failed to get rid of the neighborhood sex-and-religion shrines. People continued to pray and worship at these idolatrous shrines. And he kept on good terms with the king of Israel.

45-46 The rest of Jehoshaphat's life, his achievements and his battles, is all written in *The Chronicles of the Kings of Judah*. Also, he got rid of the sacred prostitutes left over from the days of his father Asa.

47 Edom was kingless during his reign; a deputy was in charge.

48-49 Jehoshaphat built ocean-going ships to sail to Ophir for gold. But they never made it; they shipwrecked at Ezion Geber. During that time Ahaziah son of Ahab proposed a joint shipping venture, but Jehoshaphat wouldn't go in with him.

50 Then Jehoshaphat died and was buried in the family cemetery in the City of David his ancestor. Jehoram his son was the next king.

NEW KING JAMES VERSION

AHAZIAH REIGNS IN ISRAEL

51 Ahaziah the son of Ahab became king over
Israel in Samaria in the seventeenth year of Je-
hoshaphat king of Judah, and reigned two years
over Israel. 52 He did evil in the sight of the LORD,
and walked in the way of his father and in the
way of his mother and in the way of Jeroboam
the son of Nebat, who had made Israel sin; 53 for
he served Baal and worshiped him, and pro-
voked the LORD God of Israel to anger, accord-
ing to all that his father had done.

THE MESSAGE

AHAZIAH OF ISRAEL

51-53 Ahaziah son of Ahab became king over Israel in Samaria in the seventeenth year of Jehoshaphat king of Judah. He ruled Israel for two years. As far as GOD was concerned, he lived an evil life, reproducing the bad life of his father and mother, repeating the pattern set down by Jeroboam son of Nebat, who led Israel into a life of sin. Worshiping at the Baal shrines, he made GOD, the God of Israel, angry, oh, so angry. If anything, he was worse than his father.

2 KINGS

NEW KING JAMES VERSION

GOD JUDGES AHAZIAH

1 Moab rebelled against Israel after the death of Ahab.

[2]Now Ahaziah fell through the lattice of his upper room in Samaria, and was injured; so he sent messengers and said to them, "Go, inquire of Baal-Zebub, the god of Ekron, whether I shall recover from this injury." [3]But the angel[a] of the LORD said to Elijah the Tishbite, "Arise, go up to meet the messengers of the king of Samaria, and say to them, '*Is it* because *there is* no God in Israel *that* you are going to inquire of Baal-Zebub, the god of Ekron?' [4]Now therefore, thus says the LORD: 'You shall not come down from the bed to which you have gone up, but you shall surely die.' " So Elijah departed.

[5]And when the messengers returned to him, he said to them, "Why have you come back?"

[6]So they said to him, "A man came up to meet us, and said to us, 'Go, return to the king who sent you, and say to him, "Thus says the LORD: '*Is it* because *there is* no God in Israel *that* you are sending to inquire of Baal-Zebub, the god of Ekron? Therefore you shall not come down from the bed to which you have gone up, but you shall surely die.' " ' "

[7]Then he said to them, "What kind of man *was it* who came up to meet you and told you these words?"

[8]So they answered him, "A hairy man wearing a leather belt around his waist."

And he said, "It *is* Elijah the Tishbite."

[9]Then the king sent to him a captain of fifty with his fifty men. So he went up to him; and there he was, sitting on the top of a hill. And he spoke to him: "Man of God, the king has said, 'Come down!' "

[10]So Elijah answered and said to the captain of fifty, "If I *am* a man of God, then let fire come down from heaven and consume you and your fifty men." And fire came down from heaven and consumed him and his fifty. [11]Then he sent to him another captain of fifty with his fifty men.

And he answered and said to him: "Man of God, thus has the king said, 'Come down quickly!' "

[12]So Elijah answered and said to them, "If I *am* a man of God, let fire come down from heaven and consume you and your fifty men." And the fire of God came down from heaven and consumed him and his fifty.

[13]Again, he sent a third captain of fifty with his fifty men. And the third captain of fifty went up, and came and fell on his knees before Elijah, and pleaded with him, and said to him: "Man of God, please let my life and the life of these fifty servants of yours be precious in your sight. [14]Look, fire has come down from heaven and burned up the first two captains of fifties with their fifties. But let my life now be precious in your sight."

[15]And the angel[a] of the LORD said to Elijah, "Go down with him; do not be afraid of him." So

1:3 [a]Or *Angel* **1:15** [a]Or *Angel*

THE MESSAGE

1 **1** After Ahab died, Moab rebelled against Israel.

2 One day Ahaziah fell through the balcony railing on the rooftop of his house in Samaria and was injured. He sent messengers off to consult Baal-Zebub, the god of Ekron, "Am I going to recover from this accident?"

3-4 GOD's angel spoke to Elijah the Tishbite: "Up on your feet! Go out and meet the messengers of the king of Samaria with this word, 'Is it because there's no God in Israel that you're running off to consult Baal-Zebub god of Ekron?' Here's a message from the GOD you've tried to bypass: 'You're not going to get out of that bed you're in—you're as good as dead already.' " Elijah delivered the message and was gone.

5 The messengers went back. The king said, "So why are you back so soon—what's going on?"

6 They told him, "A man met us and said, 'Turn around and go back to the king who sent you; tell him, GOD's message: Is it because there's no God in Israel that you're running off to consult Baal-Zebub god of Ekron? You needn't bother. You're not going to get out of that bed you're in—you're as good as dead already.' "

7 The king said, "Tell me more about this man who met you and said these things to you. What was he like?"

8 "Shaggy," they said, "and wearing a leather belt."

He said, "That has to be Elijah the Tishbite!"

9 The king sent a captain with fifty men to Elijah. Meanwhile Elijah was sitting, big as life, on top of a hill. The captain said, "O Holy Man! King's orders: Come down!"

10 Elijah answered the captain of the fifty, "If it's true that I'm a 'holy man,' lightning strike you and your fifty men!" Out of the blue lightning struck and incinerated the captain and his fifty.

11 The king sent another captain with his fifty men, "O Holy Man! King's orders: Come down. And right now!"

12 Elijah answered, "If it's true that I'm a 'holy man,' lightning strike you and your fifty men!" Immediately a divine lightning bolt struck and incinerated the captain and his fifty.

13-14 The king then sent a third captain with his fifty men. For a third time, a captain with his fifty approached Elijah. This one fell on his knees in supplication: "O Holy Man, have respect for my life and the souls of these fifty men! Twice now lightning from out of the blue has struck and incinerated captains with their fifty men; please, I beg you, respect my life!"

15 The angel of GOD told Elijah, "Go ahead; and don't be afraid." Elijah got up and went

NEW KING JAMES VERSION

he arose and went down with him to the king.
16Then he said to him, "Thus says the LORD: 'Be-
cause you have sent messengers to inquire of
Baal-Zebub, the god of Ekron, *is it* because
there is no God in Israel to inquire of His word?
Therefore you shall not come down from the
bed to which you have gone up, but you shall
surely die.' "
17So *Ahaziah* died according to the word of
the LORD which Elijah had spoken. Because he
had no son, Jehoram[a] became king in his place,
in the second year of Jehoram the son of Je-
hoshaphat, king of Judah.
18Now the rest of the acts of Ahaziah which
he did, *are* they not written in the book of the
chronicles of the kings of Israel?

ELIJAH ASCENDS TO HEAVEN

2 And it came to pass, when the LORD was
about to take up Elijah into heaven by a
whirlwind, that Elijah went with Elisha from
Gilgal. 2Then Elijah said to Elisha, "Stay here,
please, for the LORD has sent me on to Bethel."
But Elisha said, "*As* the LORD lives, and *as*
your soul lives, I will not leave you!" So they
went down to Bethel.
3Now the sons of the prophets who *were* at
Bethel came out to Elisha, and said to him, "Do
you know that the LORD will take away your
master from over you today?"
And he said, "Yes, I know; keep silent!"
4Then Elijah said to him, "Elisha, stay here,
please, for the LORD has sent me on to Jericho."
But he said, "*As* the LORD lives, and *as* your
soul lives, I will not leave you!" So they came to
Jericho.
5Now the sons of the prophets who *were* at
Jericho came to Elisha and said to him, "Do you
know that the LORD will take away your master
from over you today?"
So he answered, "Yes, I know; keep silent!"
6Then Elijah said to him, "Stay here, please,
for the LORD has sent me on to the Jordan."
But he said, "*As* the LORD lives, and *as* your
soul lives, I will not leave you!" So the two of
them went on. 7And fifty men of the sons of the
prophets went and stood facing *them* at a dis-
tance, while the two of them stood by the Jor-
dan. 8Now Elijah took his mantle, rolled *it* up,
and struck the water; and it was divided this
way and that, so that the two of them crossed
over on dry ground.
9And so it was, when they had crossed over,
that Elijah said to Elisha, "Ask! What may I do
for you, before I am taken away from you?"
Elisha said, "Please let a double portion of
your spirit be upon me."
10So he said, "You have asked a hard thing.
Nevertheless, if you see me *when I am* taken
from you, it shall be so for you; but if not, it shall
not be *so.*" 11Then it happened, as they contin-
ued on and talked, that suddenly a chariot of
fire *appeared* with horses of fire, and separated
the two of them; and Elijah went up by a whirl-
wind into heaven.

1:17 [a]The son of Ahab king of Israel (compare 3:1)

THE MESSAGE

down with him to the king.
16 Elijah told him, "GOD's word: Because
you sent messengers to consult Baal-Zebub
the god of Ekron, as if there were no God in
Israel to whom you could pray, you'll never
get out of that bed alive—already you're as
good as dead."
17 And he died, exactly as GOD's word spo-
ken by Elijah had said.
Because Ahaziah had no son, his brother
Joram became the next king. The succes-
sion took place in the second year of the
reign of Jehoram son of Jehoshaphat king
of Judah.
18 The rest of Ahaziah's life is recorded in
The Chronicles of the Kings of Israel.

1-2 2 Just before GOD took Elijah to heaven in
a whirlwind, Elijah and Elisha were on a
walk out of Gilgal. Elijah said to Elisha,
"Stay here. GOD has sent me on an errand to
Bethel."
Elisha said, "Not on your life! I'm not let-
ting you out of my sight!" So they both went
to Bethel.
3 The guild of prophets at Bethel met Eli-
sha and said, "Did you know that GOD is go-
ing to take your master away from you to-
day?"
"Yes," he said, "I know it. But keep it
quiet."
4 Then Elijah said to Elisha, "Stay here.
GOD has sent me on an errand to Jericho."
Elisha said, "Not on your life! I'm not let-
ting you out of my sight!" So they both went
to Jericho.
5 The guild of prophets at Jericho came to
Elisha and said, "Did you know that GOD is
going to take your master away from you to-
day?"
"Yes," he said, "I know it. But keep it
quiet."
6 Then Elijah said to Elisha, "Stay here.
GOD has sent me on an errand to the Jor-
dan."
Elisha said, "Not on your life! I'm not let-
ting you out of my sight!" And so the two of
them went their way together.
7 Meanwhile, fifty men from the guild of
prophets gathered some distance away
while the two of them stood at the Jordan.
8 Elijah took his cloak, rolled it up, and hit
the water with it. The river divided and the
two men walked through on dry land.
9 When they reached the other side, Elijah
said to Elisha, "What can I do for you before
I'm taken from you? Ask anything."
Elisha said, "Your life repeated in my life.
I want to be a holy man just like you."
10 "That's a hard one!" said Elijah. "But if
you're watching when I'm taken from you,
you'll get what you've asked for. But only if
you're watching."
11-14 And so it happened. They were walking
along and talking. Suddenly a chariot and
horses of fire came between them and Elijah
went up in a whirlwind to heaven. Elisha

New King James Version

12And Elisha saw *it*, and he cried out, "My fa-
ther, my father, the chariot of Israel and its
horsemen!" So he saw him no more. And he
took hold of his own clothes and tore them into
two pieces. 13He also took up the mantle of Eli-
jah that had fallen from him, and went back and
stood by the bank of the Jordan. 14Then he took
the mantle of Elijah that had fallen from him,
and struck the water, and said, "Where *is* the
LORD God of Elijah?" And when he also had
struck the water, it was divided this way and
that; and Elisha crossed over.
15Now when the sons of the prophets who
were from Jericho saw him, they said, "The
spirit of Elijah rests on Elisha." And they came
to meet him, and bowed to the ground before
him. 16Then they said to him, "Look now, there
are fifty strong men with your servants. Please
let them go and search for your master, lest per-
haps the Spirit of the LORD has taken him up
and cast him upon some mountain or into some
valley."
And he said, "You shall not send anyone."
17But when they urged him till he was
ashamed, he said, "Send *them!*" Therefore they
sent fifty men, and they searched for three days
but did not find him. 18And when they came
back to him, for he had stayed in Jericho, he
said to them, "Did I not say to you, 'Do not go'?"

Elisha Performs Miracles

19Then the men of the city said to Elisha,
"Please notice, the situation of this city *is* pleas-
ant, as my lord sees; but the water *is* bad, and
the ground barren."
20And he said, "Bring me a new bowl, and
put salt in it." So they brought *it* to him. 21Then
he went out to the source of the water, and cast
in the salt there, and said, "Thus says the LORD:
'I have healed this water; from it there shall be
no more death or barrenness.' " 22So the water
remains healed to this day, according to the
word of Elisha which he spoke.
23Then he went up from there to Bethel; and
as he was going up the road, some youths came
from the city and mocked him, and said to him,
"Go up, you baldhead! Go up, you baldhead!"
24So he turned around and looked at them,
and pronounced a curse on them in the name of
the LORD. And two female bears came out of the
woods and mauled forty-two of the youths.
25Then he went from there to Mount Carmel,
and from there he returned to Samaria.

Moab Rebels Against Israel

3 Now Jehoram the son of Ahab became king
over Israel at Samaria in the eighteenth year
of Jehoshaphat king of Judah, and reigned
twelve years. 2And he did evil in the sight of the
LORD, but not like his father and mother; for he
put away the *sacred* pillar of Baal that his father
had made. 3Nevertheless he persisted in the sins
of Jeroboam the son of Nebat, who had made Is-
rael sin; he did not depart from them.

The Message

saw it all and shouted, "My father, my fa-
ther! You—the chariot and cavalry of Israel!"
When he could no longer see anything, he
grabbed his robe and ripped it to pieces.
Then he picked up Elijah's cloak that had
fallen from him, returned to the shore of the
Jordan, and stood there. He took Elijah's
cloak—all that was left of Elijah!—and hit
the river with it, saying, "Now where is the
GOD of Elijah? Where is he?"
When he struck the water, the river di-
vided and Elisha walked through.
15 The guild of prophets from Jericho saw
the whole thing from where they were
standing. They said, "The spirit of Elijah
lives in Elisha!" They welcomed and hon-
ored him.
16 They then said, "We're at your service. We
have fifty reliable men here; let's send them
out to look for your master. Maybe GOD's
spirit has swept him off to some mountain
or dropped him into a remote ravine."
Elisha said, "No. Don't send them."
17 But they pestered him until he caved in:
"Go ahead then. Send them."
So they sent the fifty men off. For three
days they looked, searching high and low.
Nothing.
18 Finally, they returned to Elisha in Jericho.
He told them, "So there—didn't I tell you?"

19 One day the men of the city said to Eli-
sha, "You can see for yourself, master, how
well our city is located. But the water is pol-
luted and nothing grows."
20 He said, "Bring me a brand-new bowl and
put some salt in it." They brought it to him.
21-22 He then went to the spring, sprinkled the
salt into it, and proclaimed, "GOD's word:
I've healed this water. It will no longer kill
you or poison your land." And sure enough,
the water was healed—and remains so to
this day, just as Elisha said.

23 Another time, Elisha was on his way to
Bethel and some little kids came out from
the town and taunted him, "What's up, old
baldhead! Out of our way, skinhead!"
24 Elisha turned, took one look at them, and
cursed them in the name of GOD. Two bears
charged out of the underbrush and knocked
them about, ripping them limb from limb—
forty-two children in all!
25 Elisha went on to Mount Carmel, and
then returned to Samaria.

Joram of Israel

1-3 3 Joram son of Ahab began his rule over Is-
rael in Samaria in the eighteenth year of
Jehoshaphat king of Judah. He was king for
twelve years. In GOD's sight he was a bad
king. But he wasn't as bad as his father and
mother—to his credit he destroyed the ob-
scene Baal stone that his father had made.
But he hung on to the sinful practices of Jer-
oboam son of Nebat, the ones that had cor-
rupted Israel for so long. He wasn't about to
give them up.

NEW KING JAMES VERSION

[4]Now Mesha king of Moab was a sheep-
breeder, and he regularly paid the king of Israel
one hundred thousand lambs and the wool of
one hundred thousand rams. [5]But it happened,
when Ahab died, that the king of Moab rebelled
against the king of Israel.

[6]So King Jehoram went out of Samaria at
that time and mustered all Israel. [7]Then he went
and sent to Jehoshaphat king of Judah, saying,
"The king of Moab has rebelled against me. Will
you go with me to fight against Moab?"

And he said, "I will go up; I *am* as you *are*,
my people as your people, my horses as your
horses." [8]Then he said, "Which way shall we go
up?"

And he answered, "By way of the Wilderness
of Edom."

[9]So the king of Israel went with the king of
Judah and the king of Edom, and they marched
on that roundabout route seven days; and there
was no water for the army, nor for the animals
that followed them. [10]And the king of Israel said,
"Alas! For the LORD has called these three kings
together to deliver them into the hand of Moab."

[11]But Jehoshaphat said, "*Is there* no prophet
of the LORD here, that we may inquire of the
LORD by him?"

So one of the servants of the king of Israel
answered and said, "Elisha the son of Shaphat *is*
here, who poured water on the hands of Elijah."

[12]And Jehoshaphat said, "The word of the
LORD is with him." So the king of Israel and Je-
hoshaphat and the king of Edom went down to
him.

[13]Then Elisha said to the king of Israel,
"What have I to do with you? Go to the prophets
of your father and the prophets of your mother."

But the king of Israel said to him, "No, for the
LORD has called these three kings *together* to
deliver them into the hand of Moab."

[14]And Elisha said, "*As* the LORD of hosts
lives, before whom I stand, surely were it not
that I regard the presence of Jehoshaphat king
of Judah, I would not look at you, nor see you.
[15]But now bring me a musician."

Then it happened, when the musician
played, that the hand of the LORD came upon
him. [16]And he said, "Thus says the LORD: 'Make
this valley full of ditches.' [17]For thus says the
LORD: 'You shall not see wind, nor shall you see
rain; yet that valley shall be filled with water, so
that you, your cattle, and your animals may
drink.' [18]And this is a simple matter in the sight
of the LORD; He will also deliver the Moabites
into your hand. [19]Also you shall attack every
fortified city and every choice city, and shall cut
down every good tree, and stop up every spring
of water, and ruin every good piece of land with
stones."

[20]Now it happened in the morning, when the
grain offering was offered, that suddenly water
came by way of Edom, and the land was filled
with water.

[21]And when all the Moabites heard that the
kings had come up to fight against them, all
who were able to bear arms and older were
gathered; and they stood at the border. [22]Then

THE MESSAGE

4-7 King Mesha of Moab raised sheep. He
was forced to give the king of Israel 100,000
lambs and another 100,000 rams. When
Ahab died, the king of Moab rebelled
against the king of Israel. So King Joram set
out from Samaria and prepared Israel for
war. His first move was to send a message to
Jehoshaphat king of Judah: "The king of
Moab has rebelled against me. Would you
join me and fight him?"

7-8 "I'm with you all the way," said Je-
hoshaphat. "My troops are your troops, my
horses are your horses. Which route shall
we take?"

"Through the badlands of Edom."

9 The king of Israel, the king of Judah, and
the king of Edom started out on what
proved to be a looping detour. After seven
days they had run out of water for both
army and animals.

10 The king of Israel said, "Bad news! GOD
has gotten us three kings out here to dump
us into the hand of Moab."

11 But Jehoshaphat said, "Isn't there a
prophet of GOD anywhere around through
whom we can consult GOD?"

One of the servants of the king of Israel
said, "Elisha son of Shaphat is around
somewhere—the one who was Elijah's
right-hand man."

12 Jehoshaphat said, "Good! A man we can
trust!" So the three of them—the king of Is-
rael, Jehoshaphat, and the king of Edom—
went to meet him.

13 Elisha addressed the king of Israel,
"What do you and I have in common? Go
consult the puppet-prophets of your father
and mother."

"Never!" said the king of Israel. "It's GOD
who has gotten us into this fix, dumping all
three of us kings into the hand of Moab."

14-15 Elisha said, "As GOD-of-the-Angel-
Armies lives, and before whom I stand
ready to serve, if it weren't for the respect I
have for Jehoshaphat king of Judah, I
wouldn't give you the time of day. But con-
sidering—bring me a minstrel." (When a
minstrel played, the power of GOD came on
Elisha.)

16-19 He then said, "GOD's word: Dig ditches all
over this valley. Here's what will happen—
you won't hear the wind, you won't see the
rain, but this valley is going to fill up with
water and your army and your animals will
drink their fill. This is easy for GOD to do; he
will also hand over Moab to you. You will
ravage the country: Knock out its fortifica-
tions, level the key villages, clear-cut the or-
chards, clog the springs, and litter the culti-
vated fields with stones."

20 In the morning—it was at the hour of
morning sacrifice—the water had arrived,
water pouring in from the west, from Edom,
a flash flood filling the valley with water.

21-22 By this time everyone in Moab had heard
that the kings had come up to make war
against them. Everyone who was able to
handle a sword was called into service and
took a stand at the border. They were up and

NEW KING JAMES VERSION

they rose up early in the morning, and the sun
was shining on the water; and the Moabites saw
the water on the other side *as* red as blood.
23 And they said, "This is blood; the kings have
surely struck swords and have killed one an-
other; now therefore, Moab, to the spoil!"
24 So when they came to the camp of Israel,
Israel rose up and attacked the Moabites, so that
they fled before them; and they entered *their*
land, killing the Moabites. 25 Then they de-
stroyed the cities, and each man threw a stone
on every good piece of land and filled it; and
they stopped up all the springs of water and cut
down all the good trees. But they left the stones
of Kir Haraseth *intact.* However the slingers
surrounded and attacked it.
26 And when the king of Moab saw that the
battle was too fierce for him, he took with him
seven hundred men who drew swords, to break
through to the king of Edom, but they could not.
27 Then he took his eldest son who would have
reigned in his place, and offered him *as* a burnt
offering upon the wall; and there was great in-
dignation against Israel. So they departed from
him and returned to *their own* land.

ELISHA AND THE WIDOW'S OIL

4 A certain woman of the wives of the sons of
the prophets cried out to Elisha, saying, "Your
servant my husband is dead, and you know that
your servant feared the LORD. And the creditor
is coming to take my two sons to be his slaves."
2 So Elisha said to her, "What shall I do for
you? Tell me, what do you have in the house?"
And she said, "Your maidservant has nothing in
the house but a jar of oil."
3 Then he said, "Go, borrow vessels from
everywhere, from all your neighbors—empty
vessels; do not gather just a few. 4 And when you
have come in, you shall shut the door behind
you and your sons; then pour it into all those
vessels, and set aside the full ones."
5 So she went from him and shut the door be-
hind her and her sons, who brought *the vessels*
to her; and she poured *it* out. 6 Now it came to
pass, when the vessels were full, that she said to
her son, "Bring me another vessel."
And he said to her, "*There is* not another ves-
sel." So the oil ceased. 7 Then she came and told
the man of God. And he said, "Go, sell the oil
and pay your debt; and you *and* your sons live
on the rest."

ELISHA RAISES THE SHUNAMMITE'S SON

8 Now it happened one day that Elisha went
to Shunem, where there *was* a notable woman,
and she persuaded him to eat some food. So it
was, as often as he passed by, he would turn in
there to eat some food. 9 And she said to her hus-
band, "Look now, I know that this *is* a holy man
of God, who passes by us regularly. 10 Please, let

THE MESSAGE

ready early in the morning when the sun rose over the water. From where the Moabites stood, the water reflecting the sun looked red, like blood.

23 "Blood! Look at the blood!" they said. "The kings must have fought each other—a bloody massacre! Go for the loot, Moab!"

24-25 When Moab entered the camp of Israel, the Israelites were up on their feet killing Moabites right and left, the Moabites running for their lives, Israelites relentless in pursuit—a slaughter. They leveled the towns, littered the cultivated fields with rocks, clogged the springs, and clear-cut the orchards. Only the capital, Kir Hareseth, was left intact, and that not for long; it too was surrounded and attacked with thrown and flung rocks.

26-27 When the king of Moab realized that he was fighting a losing battle, he took seven hundred swordsmen to hack a corridor past the king of Edom, but they didn't make it. Then he took his son, his firstborn who would succeed him as king, and sacrificed him on the city wall. That set off furious anger against Israel. Israel pulled back and returned home.

1 4 One day the wife of a man from the guild of prophets called out to Elisha, "Your servant my husband is dead. You well know what a good man he was, devoted to GOD. And now the man to whom he was in debt is on his way to collect by taking my two children as slaves."

2 Elisha said, "I wonder how I can be of help. Tell me, what do you have in your house?"

"Nothing," she said. "Well, I do have a little oil."

3-4 "Here's what you do," said Elisha. "Go up and down the street and borrow jugs and bowls from all your neighbors. And not just a few—all you can get. Then come home and lock the door behind you, you and your sons. Pour oil into each container; when each is full, set it aside."

5-6 She did what he said. She locked the door behind her and her sons; as they brought the containers to her, she filled them. When all the jugs and bowls were full, she said to one of her sons, "Another jug, please."

He said, "That's it. There are no more jugs."

Then the oil stopped.

7 She went and told the story to the man of God. He said, "Go sell the oil and make good on your debts. Live, both you and your sons, on what's left."

8 One day Elisha passed through Shunem. A leading lady of the town talked him into stopping for a meal. And then it became his custom: Whenever he passed through, he stopped by for a meal.

9-10 "I'm certain," said the woman to her husband, "that this man who stops by with us all the time is a holy man of God. Why don't

NEW KING JAMES VERSION

us make a small upper room on the wall; and let us put a bed for him there, and a table and a chair and a lampstand; so it will be, whenever he comes to us, he can turn in there."

[11]And it happened one day that he came there, and he turned in to the upper room and lay down there. [12]Then he said to Gehazi his servant, "Call this Shunammite woman." When he had called her, she stood before him. [13]And he said to him, "Say now to her, 'Look, you have been concerned for us with all this care. What *can I* do for you? Do you want me to speak on your behalf to the king or to the commander of the army?' "

She answered, "I dwell among my own people."

[14]So he said, "What then *is* to be done for her?"

And Gehazi answered, "Actually, she has no son, and her husband is old."

[15]So he said, "Call her." When he had called her, she stood in the doorway. [16]Then he said, "About this time next year you shall embrace a son."

And she said, "No, my lord. Man of God, do not lie to your maidservant!"

[17]But the woman conceived, and bore a son when the appointed time had come, of which Elisha had told her.

[18]And the child grew. Now it happened one day that he went out to his father, to the reapers. [19]And he said to his father, "My head, my head!"

So he said to a servant, "Carry him to his mother." [20]When he had taken him and brought him to his mother, he sat on her knees till noon, and *then* died. [21]And she went up and laid him on the bed of the man of God, shut *the door* upon him, and went out. [22]Then she called to her husband, and said, "Please send me one of the young men and one of the donkeys, that I may run to the man of God and come back."

[23]So he said, "Why are you going to him today? *It is* neither the New Moon nor the Sabbath."

And she said, "*It is* well." [24]Then she saddled a donkey, and said to her servant, "Drive, and go forward; do not slacken the pace for me unless I tell you." [25]And so she departed, and went to the man of God at Mount Carmel.

So it was, when the man of God saw her afar off, that he said to his servant Gehazi, "Look, the Shunammite woman! [26]Please run now to meet her, and say to her, '*Is it* well with you? *Is it* well with your husband? *Is it* well with the child?' "

And she answered, "*It is* well." [27]Now when she came to the man of God at the hill, she caught him by the feet, but Gehazi came near to push her away. But the man of God said, "Let her alone; for her soul *is* in deep distress, and the LORD has hidden *it* from me, and has not told me."

[28]So she said, "Did I ask a son of my lord? Did I not say, 'Do not deceive me'?"

THE MESSAGE

we add on a small room upstairs and furnish it with a bed and desk, chair and lamp, so that when he comes by he can stay with us?"

11 And so it happened that the next time Elisha came by he went to the room and lay down for a nap.

12 Then he said to his servant Gehazi, "Tell the Shunammite woman I want to see her." He called her and she came to him.

13 Through Gehazi Elisha said, "You've gone far beyond the call of duty in taking care of us; what can we do for you? Do you have a request we can bring to the king or to the commander of the army?"

She replied, "Nothing. I'm secure and satisfied in my family."

14 Elisha conferred with Gehazi: "There's got to be something we can do for her. But what?"

Gehazi said, "Well, she has no son, and her husband is an old man."

15 "Call her in," said Elisha. He called her and she stood at the open door.

16 Elisha said to her, "This time next year you're going to be nursing an infant son."

"O my master, O Holy Man," she said, "don't play games with me, teasing me with such fantasies!"

17 The woman conceived. A year later, just as Elisha had said, she had a son.

18-19 The child grew up. One day he went to his father, who was working with the harvest hands, complaining, "My head, my head!"

His father ordered a servant, "Carry him to his mother."

20 The servant took him in his arms and carried him to his mother. He lay on her lap until noon and died.

21 She took him up and laid him on the bed of the man of God, shut him in alone, and left.

22 She then called her husband, "Get me a servant and a donkey so I can go to the Holy Man; I'll be back as soon as I can."

23 "But why today? This isn't a holy day—it's neither New Moon nor Sabbath."

She said, "Don't ask questions; I need to go right now. Trust me."

24-25 She went ahead and saddled the donkey, ordering her servant, "Take the lead—and go as fast as you can; I'll tell you if you're going too fast." And so off she went. She came to the Holy Man at Mount Carmel.

25-26 The Holy Man, spotting her while she was still a long way off, said to his servant Gehazi, "Look out there; why, it's the Shunammite woman! Quickly now. Ask her, 'Is something wrong? Are you all right? Your husband? Your child?' "

She said, "Everything's fine."

27 But when she reached the Holy Man at the mountain, she threw herself at his feet and held tightly to him.

Gehazi came up to pull her away, but the Holy Man said, "Leave her alone—can't you see that she's in distress? But GOD hasn't let me in on why; I'm completely in the dark."

28 Then she spoke up: "Did I ask for a son, master? Didn't I tell you, 'Don't tease me with false hopes'?"

NEW KING JAMES VERSION

29 Then he said to Gehazi, "Get yourself
ready, and take my staff in your hand, and be on
your way. If you meet anyone, do not greet him;
and if anyone greets you, do not answer him;
but lay my staff on the face of the child."
30 And the mother of the child said, "*As* the
LORD lives, and *as* your soul lives, I will not
leave you." So he arose and followed her. 31 Now
Gehazi went on ahead of them, and laid the staff
on the face of the child; but *there was* neither
voice nor hearing. Therefore he went back to
meet him, and told him, saying, "The child has
not awakened."
32 When Elisha came into the house, there
was the child, lying dead on his bed. 33 He went
in therefore, shut the door behind the two of
them, and prayed to the LORD. 34 And he went up
and lay on the child, and put his mouth on his
mouth, his eyes on his eyes, and his hands on
his hands; and he stretched himself out on the
child, and the flesh of the child became warm.
35 He returned and walked back and forth in the
house, and again went up and stretched himself
out on him; then the child sneezed seven times,
and the child opened his eyes. 36 And he called
Gehazi and said, "Call this Shunammite
woman." So he called her. And when she came
in to him, he said, "Pick up your son." 37 So she
went in, fell at his feet, and bowed to the ground;
then she picked up her son and went out.

ELISHA PURIFIES THE POT OF STEW

38 And Elisha returned to Gilgal, and *there
was* a famine in the land. Now the sons of the
prophets *were* sitting before him; and he said to
his servant, "Put on the large pot, and boil stew
for the sons of the prophets." 39 So one went out
into the field to gather herbs, and found a wild
vine, and gathered from it a lapful of wild
gourds, and came and sliced *them* into the pot
of stew, though they did not know *what they
were*. 40 Then they served it to the men to eat.
Now it happened, as they were eating the stew,
that they cried out and said, "Man of God, *there
is* death in the pot!" And they could not eat *it*.
41 So he said, "Then bring some flour." And he
put *it* into the pot, and said, "Serve *it* to the peo-
ple, that they may eat." And there was nothing
harmful in the pot.

ELISHA FEEDS ONE HUNDRED MEN

42 Then a man came from Baal Shalisha, and
brought the man of God bread of the firstfruits,
twenty loaves of barley bread, and newly
ripened grain in his knapsack. And he said,
"Give *it* to the people, that they may eat."
43 But his servant said, "What? Shall I set this
before one hundred men?"
He said again, "Give it to the people, that
they may eat; for thus says the LORD: 'They shall
eat and have *some* left over.' " 44 So he set *it* be-
fore them; and they ate and had *some* left over,
according to the word of the LORD.

THE MESSAGE

29 He ordered Gehazi, "Don't lose a minute—grab my staff and run as fast as you can. If you meet anyone, don't even take time to greet him, and if anyone greets you, don't even answer. Lay my staff across the boy's face."

30 The boy's mother said, "As sure as GOD lives and you live, you're not leaving me behind." And so Gehazi let her take the lead, and followed behind.

31 But Gehazi arrived first and laid the staff across the boy's face. But there was no sound—no sign of life. Gehazi went back to meet Elisha and said, "The boy hasn't stirred."

32-35 Elisha entered the house and found the boy stretched out on the bed dead. He went into the room and locked the door—just the two of them in the room—and prayed to GOD. He then got into bed with the boy and covered him with his body, mouth on mouth, eyes on eyes, hands on hands. As he was stretched out over him like that, the boy's body became warm. Elisha got up and paced back and forth in the room. Then he went back and stretched himself upon the boy again. The boy started sneezing—seven times he sneezed!—and opened his eyes.

36 He called Gehazi and said, "Get the Shunammite woman in here!" He called her and she came in.

Elisha said, "Embrace your son!"

37 She fell at Elisha's feet, face to the ground in reverent awe. Then she embraced her son and went out with him.

38 Elisha went back down to Gilgal. There was a famine there. While he was consulting with the guild of prophets, he told his servant, "Put a large pot on the fire and cook up some stew for the prophets."

39-40 One of the men went out into the field to get some herbs; he came across a wild vine and picked gourds from it, filling his gunnysack. He brought them back, sliced them up, and put them in the stew, even though no one knew what kind of plant it was. The stew was then served up for the men to eat. They started to eat, and then exclaimed, "Death in the pot, O man of God! Death in the pot!" Nobody could eat it.

Elisha ordered, "Get me some meal." Then he sprinkled it into the stew pot.

41 "Now serve it up to the men," he said. They ate it, and it was just fine—nothing wrong with *that* stew!

42 One day a man arrived from Baal Shalishah. He brought the man of God twenty loaves of fresh-baked bread from the early harvest, along with a few apples from the orchard.

Elisha said, "Pass it around to the people to eat."

43 His servant said, "For a hundred men? There's not nearly enough!"

Elisha said, "Just go ahead and do it. GOD says there's plenty."

44 And sure enough, there was. He passed around what he had—they not only ate, but had leftovers.

NEW KING JAMES VERSION

NAAMAN'S LEPROSY HEALED

5 Now Naaman, commander of the army of the king of Syria, was a great and honorable man in the eyes of his master, because by him the LORD had given victory to Syria. He was also a mighty man of valor, *but* a leper. 2And the Syrians had gone out on raids, and had brought back captive a young girl from the land of Israel. She waited on Naaman's wife. 3Then she said to her mistress, "If only my master *were* with the prophet who *is* in Samaria! For he would heal him of his leprosy." 4And *Naaman* went in and told his master, saying, "Thus and thus said the girl who *is* from the land of Israel."

5Then the king of Syria said, "Go now, and I will send a letter to the king of Israel."

So he departed and took with him ten talents of silver, six thousand *shekels* of gold, and ten changes of clothing. 6Then he brought the letter to the king of Israel, which said,

> Now be advised, when this letter comes to you, that I have sent Naaman my servant to you, that you may heal him of his leprosy.

7And it happened, when the king of Israel read the letter, that he tore his clothes and said, "*Am* I God, to kill and make alive, that this man sends a man to me to heal him of his leprosy? Therefore please consider, and see how he seeks a quarrel with me."

8So it was, when Elisha the man of God heard that the king of Israel had torn his clothes, that he sent to the king, saying, "Why have you torn your clothes? Please let him come to me, and he shall know that there is a prophet in Israel."

9Then Naaman went with his horses and chariot, and he stood at the door of Elisha's house. 10And Elisha sent a messenger to him, saying, "Go and wash in the Jordan seven times, and your flesh shall be restored to you, and *you shall* be clean." 11But Naaman became furious, and went away and said, "Indeed, I said to myself, 'He will surely come out *to me,* and stand and call on the name of the LORD his God, and wave his hand over the place, and heal the leprosy.' 12*Are* not the Abanah[a] and the Pharpar, the rivers of Damascus, better than all the waters of Israel? Could I not wash in them and be clean?" So he turned and went away in a rage. 13And his servants came near and spoke to him, and said, "My father, *if* the prophet had told you *to do* something great, would you not have done *it*? How much more then, when he says to you, 'Wash, and be clean'?" 14So he went down and dipped seven times in the Jordan, according to the saying of the man of God; and his flesh was restored like the flesh of a little child, and he was clean.

15And he returned to the man of God, he and all his aides, and came and stood before him; and he said, "Indeed, now I know that *there is* no God in all the earth, except in Israel; now therefore, please take a gift from your servant."

5:12 [a]Following Kethib, Septuagint, and Vulgate; Qere, Syriac, and Targum read *Amanah*.

THE MESSAGE

1-3 5 Naaman was general of the army under
the king of Aram. He was important to his
master, who held him in the highest esteem
because it was by him that GOD had given
victory to Aram: a truly great man, but af-
flicted with a grievous skin disease. It so hap-
pened that Aram, on one of its raiding expe-
ditions against Israel, captured a young girl
who became a maid to Naaman's wife. One
day she said to her mistress, "Oh, if only my
master could meet the prophet of Samaria,
he would be healed of his skin disease."
4 Naaman went straight to his master and
reported what the girl from Israel had said.
5 "Well then, go," said the king of Aram.
"And I'll send a letter of introduction to the
king of Israel."
So he went off, taking with him about 750
pounds of silver, 150 pounds of gold, and ten
sets of clothes.
6 Naaman delivered the letter to the king
of Israel. The letter read, "When you get this
letter, you'll know that I've personally sent
my servant Naaman to you; heal him of his
skin disease."
7 When the king of Israel read the letter, he
was terribly upset, ripping his robe to pieces.
He said, "Am I a god with the power to bring
death or life that I get orders to heal this man
from his disease? What's going on here? That
king's trying to pick a fight, that's what!"
8 Elisha the man of God heard what had
happened, that the king of Israel was so dis-
tressed that he'd ripped his robe to shreds. He
sent word to the king, "Why are you so upset,
ripping your robe like this? Send him to me
so he'll learn that there's a prophet in Israel."
9 So Naaman with his horses and chariots
arrived in style and stopped at Elisha's door.
10 Elisha sent out a servant to meet him
with this message: "Go to the River Jordan
and immerse yourself seven times. Your skin
will be healed and you'll be as good as new."
11-12 Naaman lost his temper. He turned on his
heel saying, "I thought he'd personally come
out and meet me, call on the name of GOD,
wave his hand over the diseased spot, and
get rid of the disease. The Damascus rivers,
Abana and Pharpar, are cleaner by far than
any of the rivers in Israel. Why not bathe in
them? I'd at least get clean." He stomped off,
mad as a hornet.
13 But his servants caught up with him and
said, "Father, if the prophet had asked you to
do something hard and heroic, wouldn't you
have done it? So why not this simple 'wash
and be clean'?"
14 So he did it. He went down and immersed
himself in the Jordan seven times, following
the orders of the Holy Man. His skin was
healed; it was like the skin of a little baby.
He was as good as new.
15 He then went back to the Holy Man, he
and his entourage, stood before him, and
said, "I now know beyond a shadow of a
doubt that there is no God anywhere on
earth other than the God of Israel. In grati-
tude let me give you a gift."

New King James Version

[16]But he said, "*As* the LORD lives, before whom I stand, I will receive nothing." And he urged him to take *it*, but he refused.

[17]So Naaman said, "Then, if not, please let your servant be given two mule-loads of earth; for your servant will no longer offer either burnt offering or sacrifice to other gods, but to the LORD. [18]Yet in this thing may the LORD pardon your servant: when my master goes into the temple of Rimmon to worship there, and he leans on my hand, and I bow down in the temple of Rimmon—when I bow down in the temple of Rimmon, may the LORD please pardon your servant in this thing."

[19]Then he said to him, "Go in peace." So he departed from him a short distance.

Gehazi's Greed

[20]But Gehazi, the servant of Elisha the man of God, said, "Look, my master has spared Naaman this Syrian, while not receiving from his hands what he brought; but *as* the LORD lives, I will run after him and take something from him." [21]So Gehazi pursued Naaman. When Naaman saw *him* running after him, he got down from the chariot to meet him, and said, "*Is* all well?"

[22]And he said, "All *is* well. My master has sent me, saying, 'Indeed, just now two young men of the sons of the prophets have come to me from the mountains of Ephraim. Please give them a talent of silver and two changes of garments.' "

[23]So Naaman said, "Please, take two talents." And he urged him, and bound two talents of silver in two bags, with two changes of garments, and handed *them* to two of his servants; and they carried *them* on ahead of him. [24]When he came to the citadel, he took *them* from their hand, and stored *them* away in the house; then he let the men go, and they departed. [25]Now he went in and stood before his master. Elisha said to him, "Where *did you go,* Gehazi?"

And he said, "Your servant did not go anywhere."

[26]Then he said to him, "Did not my heart go *with you* when the man turned back from his chariot to meet you? *Is it* time to receive money and to receive clothing, olive groves and vineyards, sheep and oxen, male and female servants? [27]Therefore the leprosy of Naaman shall cling to you and your descendants forever." And he went out from his presence leprous, *as white* as snow.

The Floating Ax Head

6 And the sons of the prophets said to Elisha, "See now, the place where we dwell with you is too small for us. [2]Please, let us go to the Jordan, and let every man take a beam from there, and let us make there a place where we may dwell."

So he answered, "Go."

[3]Then one said, "Please consent to go with your servants."

And he answered, "I will go."

The Message

16 "As GOD lives," Elisha replied, "the God whom I serve, I'll take nothing from you." Naaman tried his best to get him to take something, but he wouldn't do it.

17-18 "If you won't take anything," said Naaman, "let me ask you for something: Give me a load of dirt, as much as a team of donkeys can carry, because I'm never again going to worship any god other than GOD. But there's one thing for which I need GOD's pardon: When my master, leaning on my arm, enters the shrine of Rimmon and worships there, and I'm with him there, worshiping Rimmon, may you see to it that GOD forgive me for this."

19-21 Elisha said, "Everything will be all right. Go in peace."

But he hadn't gone far when Gehazi, servant to Elisha the Holy Man, said to himself, "My master has let this Aramean Naaman slip through his fingers without so much as a thank-you. By the living GOD, I'm going after him to get something or other from him!" And Gehazi took off after Naaman.

Naaman saw him running after him and jumped down from his chariot to greet him, "Is something wrong?"

22 "Nothing's wrong, but something's come up. My master sent me to tell you: 'Two young men just showed up from the hill country of Ephraim, brothers from the guild of the prophets. Supply their needs with a gift of 75 pounds of silver and a couple of sets of clothes.' "

23 Naaman said, "Of course, how about a 150 pounds?" Naaman insisted. He tied up the money in two sacks and gave him the two sets of clothes; he even gave him two servants to carry the gifts back with him.

24 When they got to the fort on the hill, Gehazi took the gifts from the servants, stored them inside, then sent the servants back.

25 He returned and stood before his master. Elisha said, "So what have you been up to, Gehazi?"

"Nothing much," he said.

26-27 Elisha said, "Didn't you know I was with you in spirit when that man stepped down from his chariot to greet you? Tell me, is this a time to look after yourself, lining your pockets with gifts? Naaman's skin disease will now infect you and your family, with no relief in sight."

Gehazi walked away, his skin flaky and white like snow.

1-2 6 One day the guild of prophets came to Elisha and said, "You can see that this place where we're living under your leadership is getting cramped—we have no elbow room. Give us permission to go down to the Jordan where each of us will get a log. We'll build a roomier place."

Elisha said, "Go ahead."

3 One of them then said, "Please! Come along with us!"

He said, "Certainly."

NEW KING JAMES VERSION

4So he went with them. And when they came to
the Jordan, they cut down trees. 5But as one was
cutting down a tree, the iron *ax head* fell into
the water; and he cried out and said, "Alas, mas-
ter! For it was borrowed."
6So the man of God said, "Where did it fall?"
And he showed him the place. So he cut off a
stick, and threw *it* in there; and he made the
iron float. 7Therefore he said, "Pick *it* up for
yourself." So he reached out his hand and took
it.

THE BLINDED SYRIANS CAPTURED

8Now the king of Syria was making war
against Israel; and he consulted with his ser-
vants, saying, "My camp *will be* in such and
such a place." 9And the man of God sent to the
king of Israel, saying, "Beware that you do not
pass this place, for the Syrians are coming down
there." 10Then the king of Israel sent *someone* to
the place of which the man of God had told him.
Thus he warned him, and he was watchful there,
not just once or twice.
11Therefore the heart of the king of Syria
was greatly troubled by this thing; and he called
his servants and said to them, "Will you not
show me which of us *is* for the king of Israel?"
12And one of his servants said, "None, my
lord, O king; but Elisha, the prophet who *is* in Is-
rael, tells the king of Israel the words that you
speak in your bedroom."
13So he said, "Go and see where he *is*, that I
may send and get him."
And it was told him, saying, "Surely *he is* in
Dothan."
14Therefore he sent horses and chariots and
a great army there, and they came by night and
surrounded the city. 15And when the servant of
the man of God arose early and went out, there
was an army, surrounding the city with horses
and chariots. And his servant said to him, "Alas,
my master! What shall we do?"
16So he answered, "Do not fear, for those
who *are* with us *are* more than those who *are*
with them." 17And Elisha prayed, and said,
"LORD, I pray, open his eyes that he may see."
Then the LORD opened the eyes of the young
man, and he saw. And behold, the mountain *was*
full of horses and chariots of fire all around Eli-
sha. 18So when *the Syrians* came down to him,
Elisha prayed to the LORD, and said, "Strike this
people, I pray, with blindness." And He struck
them with blindness according to the word of
Elisha.
19Now Elisha said to them, "This *is* not the
way, nor *is* this the city. Follow me, and I will
bring you to the man whom you seek." But he
led them to Samaria.
20So it was, when they had come to Samaria,
that Elisha said, "LORD, open the eyes of these
men, that they may see." And the LORD opened
their eyes, and they saw; and there *they were*,
inside Samaria!
21Now when the king of Israel saw them, he
said to Elisha, "My father, shall I kill *them*?
Shall I kill *them*?"

THE MESSAGE

4-5 He went with them. They came to the Jor-
dan and started chopping down trees. As
one of them was felling a timber, his axhead
flew off and sank in the river.
"Oh no, master!" he cried out. "And it was
borrowed!"
6 The Holy Man said, "Where did it sink?"
The man showed him the place.
He cut off a branch and tossed it at the
spot. The axhead floated up.
7 "Grab it," he said. The man reached out
and took it.

8 One time when the king of Aram was at
war with Israel, after consulting with his of-
ficers, he said, "At such and such a place I
want an ambush set."
9 The Holy Man sent a message to the king
of Israel: "Watch out when you're passing
this place, because Aram has set an ambush
there."
10 So the king of Israel sent word concern-
ing the place of which the Holy Man had
warned him.
This kind of thing happened all the time.
11 The king of Aram was furious over all
this. He called his officers together and said,
"Tell me, who is leaking information to the
king of Israel? Who is the spy in our ranks?"
12 But one of his men said, "No, my master,
dear king. It's not any of us. It's Elisha the
prophet in Israel. He tells the king of Israel
everything you say, even what you whisper
in your bedroom."
13 The king said, "Go and find out where he
is. I'll send someone and capture him."
The report came back, "He's in Dothan."
14 Then he dispatched horses and chariots,
an impressive fighting force. They came by
night and surrounded the city.
15 Early in the morning a servant of the
Holy Man got up and went out. Surprise!
Horses and chariots surrounding the city!
The young man exclaimed, "Oh, master!
What shall we do?"
16 He said, "Don't worry about it—there are
more on our side than on their side."
17 Then Elisha prayed, "O GOD, open his
eyes and let him see."
The eyes of the young man were opened
and he saw. A wonder! The whole mountain-
side full of horses and chariots of fire sur-
rounding Elisha!
18 When the Arameans attacked, Elisha
prayed to GOD, "Strike these people blind!"
And GOD struck them blind, just as Elisha
said.
19 Then Elisha called out to them, "Not that
way! Not this city! Follow me and I'll lead
you to the man you're looking for." And he
led them into Samaria.
20 As they entered the city, Elisha prayed,
"O GOD, open their eyes so they can see
where they are." GOD opened their eyes.
They looked around—they were trapped in
Samaria!
21 When the king of Israel saw them, he said
to Elisha, "Father, shall I massacre the lot?"

NEW KING JAMES VERSION

22 But he answered, "You shall not kill *them*.
Would you kill those whom you have taken cap-
tive with your sword and your bow? Set food
and water before them, that they may eat and
drink and go to their master." 23 Then he pre-
pared a great feast for them; and after they ate
and drank, he sent them away and they went to
their master. So the bands of Syrian *raiders*
came no more into the land of Israel.

SYRIA BESIEGES SAMARIA IN FAMINE

24 And it happened after this that Ben-Hadad
king of Syria gathered all his army, and went up
and besieged Samaria. 25 And there was a great
famine in Samaria; and indeed they besieged it
until a donkey's head was *sold* for eighty
shekels of silver, and one-fourth of a kab of dove
droppings for five *shekels* of silver.
26 Then, as the king of Israel was passing by
on the wall, a woman cried out to him, saying,
"Help, my lord, O king!"
27 And he said, "If the LORD does not help you,
where can I find help for you? From the thresh-
ing floor or from the winepress?" 28 Then the
king said to her, "What is troubling you?"
And she answered, "This woman said to me,
'Give your son, that we may eat him today, and
we will eat my son tomorrow.' 29 So we boiled my
son, and ate him. And I said to her on the next
day, 'Give your son, that we may eat him'; but
she has hidden her son."
30 Now it happened, when the king heard the
words of the woman, that he tore his clothes;
and as he passed by on the wall, the people
looked, and there underneath *he had* sackcloth
on his body. 31 Then he said, "God do so to me
and more also, if the head of Elisha the son of
Shaphat remains on him today!"
32 But Elisha was sitting in his house, and the
elders were sitting with him. And *the king* sent
a man ahead of him, but before the messenger
came to him, he said to the elders, "Do you see
how this son of a murderer has sent someone to
take away my head? Look, when the messenger
comes, shut the door, and hold him fast at the
door. *Is* not the sound of his master's feet behind
him?" 33 And while he was still talking with
them, there was the messenger, coming down to
him; and then *the king* said, "Surely this
calamity *is* from the LORD; why should I wait for
the LORD any longer?"

7 Then Elisha said, "Hear the word of the LORD.
Thus says the LORD: 'Tomorrow about this
time a seah of fine flour *shall be sold* for a
shekel, and two seahs of barley for a shekel, at
the gate of Samaria.' "
2 So an officer on whose hand the king
leaned answered the man of God and said,
"Look, *if* the LORD would make windows in
heaven, could this thing be?"
And he said, "In fact, you shall see *it* with
your eyes, but you shall not eat of it."

THE SYRIANS FLEE

3 Now there were four leprous men at the en-
trance of the gate; and they said to one another,

THE MESSAGE

22 "Not on your life!" said Elisha. "You didn't
lift a hand to capture them, and now you're
going to kill them? No sir, make a feast for
them and send them back to their master."
23 So he prepared a huge feast for them. Af-
ter they ate and drank their fill he dismissed
them. Then they returned home to their
master. The raiding bands of Aram didn't
bother Israel anymore.

24-25 At a later time, this: Ben-Hadad king of
Aram pulled together his troops and
launched a siege on Samaria. This brought
on a terrible famine, so bad that food prices
soared astronomically. Eighty shekels for a
donkey's head! Five shekels for a bowl of
field greens!
26 One day the king of Israel was walking
along the city wall. A woman cried out,
"Help! Your majesty!"
27 He answered, "If GOD won't help you,
where on earth can *I* go for help? To the
granary? To the dairy?"
28-29 The king continued, "Tell me your story."
She said, "This woman came to me and
said, 'Give up your son and we'll have him
for today's supper; tomorrow we'll eat my
son.' So we cooked my son and ate him. The
next day I told her, 'Your turn—bring your
son so we can have him for supper.' But she
had hidden her son away."
30-31 When the king heard the woman's story
he ripped apart his robe. Since he was walk-
ing on the city wall, everyone saw that next
to his skin he was wearing coarse burlap.
And he called out, "God do his worst to
me—and more—if Elisha son of Shaphat
still has a head on his shoulders at this day's
end."
32 Elisha was sitting at home, the elders sit-
ting with him. The king had already dis-
patched an executioner, but before the man
arrived Elisha spoke to the elders: "Do you
know that this murderer has just now sent a
man to take off my head? Look, when the
executioner arrives, shut the door and lock
it. Don't I even now hear the footsteps of his
master behind him?"
33 While he was giving his instructions, the
king showed up, accusing, "This trouble is
directly from GOD! And what's next? I'm fed
up with GOD!"

1 7 Elisha said, "Listen! GOD's word! The
famine's over. This time tomorrow food
will be plentiful—a handful of meal for a
shekel; two handfuls of grain for a shekel.
The market at the city gate will be buzzing."
2 The attendant on whom the king leaned
for support said to the Holy Man, "You ex-
pect us to believe that? Trapdoors opening
in the sky and food tumbling out?"
"You'll watch it with your own eyes," he
said, "but *you* will not eat so much as a
mouthful!"
3-4 It happened that four lepers were sitting
just outside the city gate. They said to one

NEW KING JAMES VERSION

"Why are we sitting here until we die? 4If we say,
'We will enter the city,' the famine *is* in the city,
and we shall die there. And if we sit here, we die
also. Now therefore, come, let us surrender to
the army of the Syrians. If they keep us alive, we
shall live; and if they kill us, we shall only die."
5And they rose at twilight to go to the camp of
the Syrians; and when they had come to the out-
skirts of the Syrian camp, to their surprise no
one *was* there. 6For the LORD had caused the
army of the Syrians to hear the noise of chariots
and the noise of horses—the noise of a great
army; so they said to one another, "Look, the
king of Israel has hired against us the kings of
the Hittites and the kings of the Egyptians to at-
tack us!" 7Therefore they arose and fled at twi-
light, and left the camp intact—their tents, their
horses, and their donkeys—and they fled for
their lives. 8And when these lepers came to the
outskirts of the camp, they went into one tent
and ate and drank, and carried from it silver and
gold and clothing, and went and hid *them;* then
they came back and entered another tent, and
carried *some* from there *also*, and went and hid
it.

9Then they said to one another, "We are not
doing right. This day *is* a day of good news, and
we remain silent. If we wait until morning light,
some punishment will come upon us. Now
therefore, come, let us go and tell the king's
household." 10So they went and called to the
gatekeepers of the city, and told them, saying,
"We went to the Syrian camp, and surprisingly
no one *was* there, not a human sound—only
horses and donkeys tied, and the tents intact."
11And the gatekeepers called out, and they told
it to the king's household inside.

12So the king arose in the night and said to
his servants, "Let me now tell you what the Syr-
ians have done to us. They know that we *are*
hungry; therefore they have gone out of the
camp to hide themselves in the field, saying,
'When they come out of the city, we shall catch
them alive, and get into the city.' "

13And one of his servants answered and said,
"Please, let several *men* take five of the remain-
ing horses which are left in the city. Look, they
may either become like all the multitude of Is-
rael that are left in it; or indeed, *I say,* they *may
become* like all the multitude of Israel left from
those who are consumed; so let us send them
and see." 14Therefore they took two chariots
with horses; and the king sent them in the direc-
tion of the Syrian army, saying, "Go and see."
15And they went after them to the Jordan; and
indeed all the road *was* full of garments and
weapons which the Syrians had thrown away in
their haste. So the messengers returned and told
the king. 16Then the people went out and plun-
dered the tents of the Syrians. So a seah of fine
flour was *sold* for a shekel, and two seahs of
barley for a shekel, according to the word of the
LORD.

17Now the king had appointed the officer on
whose hand he leaned to have charge of the
gate. But the people trampled him in the gate,
and he died, just as the man of God had said,

THE MESSAGE

another, "What are we doing sitting here at death's door? If we enter the famine-struck city we'll die; if we stay here we'll die. So let's take our chances in the camp of Aram and throw ourselves on their mercy. If they receive us we'll live, if they kill us we'll die. We've got nothing to lose."

5-8 So after the sun went down they got up and went to the camp of Aram. When they got to the edge of the camp, surprise! Not a man in the camp! The Master had made the army of Aram hear the sound of horses and a mighty army on the march. They told one another, "The king of Israel hired the kings of the Hittites and the kings of Egypt to attack us!" Panicked, they ran for their lives through the darkness, abandoning tents, horses, donkeys—the whole camp just as it was—running for dear life. These four lepers entered the camp and went into a tent. First they ate and drank. Then they grabbed silver, gold, and clothing, and went off and hid it. They came back, entered another tent, and looted it, again hiding their plunder.

9 Finally they said to one another, "We shouldn't be doing this! This is a day of good news and we're making it into a private party! If we wait around until morning we'll get caught and punished. Come on! Let's go tell the news to the king's palace!"

10 So they went and called out at the city gate, telling what had happened: "We went to the camp of Aram and, surprise!—the place was deserted. Not a soul, not a sound! Horses and donkeys left tethered and tents abandoned just as they were."

11-12 The gatekeepers got the word to the royal palace, giving them the whole story. Roused in the middle of the night, the king told his servants, "Let me tell you what Aram has done. They knew that we were starving, so they left camp and have hid in the field, thinking, 'When they come out of the city, we'll capture them alive and take the city.' "

13 One of his advisors answered, "Let some men go and take five of the horses left behind. The worst that can happen is no worse than what could happen to the whole city. Let's send them and find out what's happened."

14 They took two chariots with horses. The king sent them after the army of Aram with the orders, "Scout them out; find out what happened."

15 They went after them all the way to the Jordan. The whole way was strewn with clothes and equipment that Aram had dumped in their panicked flight. The scouts came back and reported to the king.

16 The people then looted the camp of Aram. Food prices dropped overnight—a handful of meal for a shekel; two handfuls of grain for a shekel—GOD's word to the letter!

17 The king ordered his attendant, the one he leaned on for support, to be in charge of the city gate. The people, turned into a mob, poured through the gate, trampling him to

NEW KING JAMES VERSION

who spoke when the king came down to him.
18So it happened just as the man of God had
spoken to the king, saying, "Two seahs of barley
for a shekel, and a seah of fine flour for a
shekel, shall be *sold* tomorrow about this time in
the gate of Samaria."
19Then that officer had answered the man of
God, and said, "Now look, *if* the LORD would
make windows in heaven, could such a thing
be?"

And he had said, "In fact, you shall see *it*
with your eyes, but you shall not eat of it." 20And
so it happened to him, for the people trampled
him in the gate, and he died.

THE KING RESTORES THE SHUNAMMITE'S LAND

8 Then Elisha spoke to the woman whose son
he had restored to life, saying, "Arise and go,
you and your household, and stay wherever you
can; for the LORD has called for a famine, and
furthermore, it will come upon the land for
seven years." 2So the woman arose and did ac-
cording to the saying of the man of God, and she
went with her household and dwelt in the land
of the Philistines seven years.
3It came to pass, at the end of seven years,
that the woman returned from the land of the
Philistines; and she went to make an appeal to
the king for her house and for her land. 4Then
the king talked with Gehazi, the servant of the
man of God, saying, "Tell me, please, all the
great things Elisha has done." 5Now it hap-
pened, as he was telling the king how he had re-
stored the dead to life, that there was the
woman whose son he had restored to life, ap-
pealing to the king for her house and for her
land. And Gehazi said, "My lord, O king, this *is*
the woman, and this *is* her son whom Elisha re-
stored to life." 6And when the king asked the
woman, she told him.

So the king appointed a certain officer for
her, saying, "Restore all that *was* hers, and all
the proceeds of the field from the day that she
left the land until now."

DEATH OF BEN-HADAD

7Then Elisha went to Damascus, and Ben-
Hadad king of Syria was sick; and it was told
him, saying, "The man of God has come here."
8And the king said to Hazael, "Take a present
in your hand, and go to meet the man of God,
and inquire of the LORD by him, saying, 'Shall I
recover from this disease?' " 9So Hazael went
to meet him and took a present with him, of
every good thing of Damascus, forty camel-
loads; and he came and stood before him, and
said, "Your son Ben-Hadad king of Syria has
sent me to you, saying, 'Shall I recover from
this disease?' "
10And Elisha said to him, "Go, say to him,
'You shall certainly recover.' However the LORD
has shown me that he will really die." 11Then he
set his countenance in a stare until he was
ashamed; and the man of God wept. 12And Haz-
ael said, "Why is my lord weeping?"

THE MESSAGE

death. It was exactly what the Holy Man
had said when the king had come to see
him.

18-20 Every word of the Holy Man to the king—
"A handful of meal for a shekel, two hand-
fuls of grain for a shekel this time tomorrow
in the gate of Samaria," with the attendant's
sarcastic reply to the Holy Man, "You expect
us to believe that? Trapdoors opening in the
sky and food tumbling out?" followed by the
response, "You'll watch it with your own
eyes, but you won't eat so much as a mouth-
ful"—proved true. The final stroke came
when the people trampled the man to death
at the city gate.

1-3 8 Years before, Elisha had told the woman
whose son he had brought to life, "Leave
here and go, you and your family, and live
someplace else. GOD has ordered a famine
in the land; it will last for seven years." The
woman did what the Holy Man told her and
left. She and her family lived as aliens in the
country of Philistia for seven years. Then,
when the seven years were up, the woman
and her family came back. She went di-
rectly to the king and asked for her home
and farm.

4-5 The king was talking with Gehazi, ser-
vant to the Holy Man, saying, "Tell me some
stories of the great things Elisha did." It so
happened that as he was telling the king the
story of the dead person brought back to
life, the woman whose son was brought to
life showed up asking for her home and
farm.

Gehazi said, "My master the king, this is
the woman! And this is her son whom Eli-
sha brought back to life!"

6 The king wanted to know all about it, and
so she told him the story. The king assigned
an officer to take care of her, saying, "Make
sure she gets everything back that's hers,
plus all profits from the farm from the time
she left until now."

7 Elisha traveled to Damascus. Ben-Hadad,
king of Aram, was sick at the time. He was
told, "The Holy Man is in town."

8 The king ordered Hazael, "Take a gift
with you and go meet the Holy Man. Ask
GOD through him, 'Am I going to recover
from this sickness?' "

9 Hazael went and met with Elisha. He
brought with him every choice thing he
could think of from Damascus—forty
camel-loads of items! When he arrived he
stood before Elisha and said, "Your son Ben-
Hadad, king of Aram, sent me here to ask
you, 'Am I going to recover from this sick-
ness?' "

10-11 Elisha answered, "Go and tell him, 'Don't
worry; you'll live.' The fact is, though—GOD
showed me—that he's doomed to die." Eli-
sha then stared hard at Hazael, reading his
heart. Hazael felt exposed and dropped his
eyes. Then the Holy Man wept.

12 Hazael said, "Why does my master weep?"

New King James Version

He answered, "Because I know the evil that
you will do to the children of Israel: Their
strongholds you will set on fire, and their young
men you will kill with the sword; and you will
dash their children, and rip open their women
with child."
13So Hazael said, "But what *is* your servant—
a dog, that he should do this gross thing?"
And Elisha answered, "The LORD has shown
me that you *will become* king over Syria."
14Then he departed from Elisha, and came to
his master, who said to him, "What did Elisha
say to you?" And he answered, "He told me you
would surely recover." 15But it happened on the
next day that he took a thick cloth and dipped *it*
in water, and spread *it* over his face so that he
died; and Hazael reigned in his place.

Jehoram Reigns in Judah

16Now in the fifth year of Joram the son of
Ahab, king of Israel, Jehoshaphat *having been*
king of Judah, Jehoram the son of Jehoshaphat
began to reign as king of Judah. 17He was thirty-
two years old when he became king, and he
reigned eight years in Jerusalem. 18And he
walked in the way of the kings of Israel, just as
the house of Ahab had done, for the daughter of
Ahab was his wife; and he did evil in the sight of
the LORD. 19Yet the LORD would not destroy Ju-
dah, for the sake of His servant David, as He
promised him to give a lamp to him *and* his sons
forever.
20In his days Edom revolted against Judah's
authority, and made a king over themselves.
21So Joram[a] went to Zair, and all his chariots
with him. Then he rose by night and attacked
the Edomites who had surrounded him and the
captains of the chariots; and the troops fled to
their tents. 22Thus Edom has been in revolt
against Judah's authority to this day. And Lib-
nah revolted at that time.
23Now the rest of the acts of Joram, and all
that he did, *are* they not written in the book of
the chronicles of the kings of Judah? 24So Joram
rested with his fathers, and was buried with his
fathers in the City of David. Then Ahaziah his
son reigned in his place.

Ahaziah Reigns in Judah

25In the twelfth year of Joram the son of
Ahab, king of Israel, Ahaziah the son of Jeho-
ram, king of Judah, began to reign. 26Ahaziah
was twenty-two years old when he became
king, and he reigned one year in Jerusalem. His
mother's name *was* Athaliah the granddaughter
of Omri, king of Israel. 27And he walked in the
way of the house of Ahab, and did evil in the
sight of the LORD, like the house of Ahab, for he
was the son-in-law of the house of Ahab.
28Now he went with Joram the son of Ahab
to war against Hazael king of Syria at Ramoth
Gilead; and the Syrians wounded Joram. 29Then
King Joram went back to Jezreel to recover
from the wounds which the Syrians had in-
flicted on him at Ramah, when he fought

8:21 [a]Spelled *Jehoram* in verse 16

The Message

"Because," said Elisha, "I know what you're going to do to the children of Israel:

burn down their forts,
murder their youth,
smash their babies,
rip open their pregnant women."

13 Hazael said, "Am I a mongrel dog that I'd do such a horrible thing?"

"GOD showed me," said Elisha, "that you'll be king of Aram."

14 Hazael left Elisha and returned to his master, who asked, "So, what did Elisha tell you?"

"He told me, 'Don't worry; you'll live.' "

15 But the very next day, someone took a heavy quilt, soaked it in water, covered the king's face, and suffocated him.

Now Hazael was king.

Jehoram of Judah

16-19 In the fifth year of the reign of Joram son of Ahab king of Israel, Jehoram son of Jehoshaphat king of Judah became king. He was thirty-two years old when he began his rule, and was king for eight years in Jerusalem. He copied the way of life of the kings of Israel, marrying into the Ahab family and continuing the Ahab line of sin—from GOD's point of view, an evil man living an evil life. But despite that, because of his servant David, GOD was not ready to destroy Judah. He had, after all, promised to keep a lamp burning through David's descendants.

20-21 During Jehoram's reign, Edom revolted against Judah's rule and set up their own king. Jehoram responded by taking his army of chariots to Zair.

Edom surrounded him, but in the middle of the night he and his charioteers broke through the lines and hit Edom hard. But his infantry deserted him.

22 Edom continues in revolt against Judah right up to the present. Even little Libnah revolted at that time.

23-24 The rest of the life and times of Jehoram, the record of his rule, is written in *The Chronicles of the Kings of Judah*. Jehoram died and was buried in the family grave in the City of David. His son Ahaziah succeeded him as king.

Ahaziah of Judah

25-27 In the twelfth year of the reign of Joram son of Ahab king of Israel, Ahaziah son of Jehoram king of Judah began his reign. Ahaziah was twenty-two years old when he became king; he ruled only a year in Jerusalem. His mother was Athaliah, granddaughter of Omri king of Israel. He lived and ruled just like the Ahab family had done, continuing the same evil-in-GOD's-sight line of sin, related by both marriage and sin to the Ahab clan.

28-29 He joined Joram son of Ahab king of Israel in a war against Hazael king of Aram at Ramoth Gilead. The archers wounded Joram. Joram pulled back to Jezreel to convalesce from the injuries he had received in

NEW KING JAMES VERSION

against Hazael king of Syria. And Ahaziah the
son of Jehoram, king of Judah, went down to see
Joram the son of Ahab in Jezreel, because he
was sick.

JEHU ANOINTED KING OF ISRAEL

9 And Elisha the prophet called one of the sons
of the prophets, and said to him, "Get your-
self ready, take this flask of oil in your hand, and
go to Ramoth Gilead. 2Now when you arrive at
that place, look there for Jehu the son of Je-
hoshaphat, the son of Nimshi, and go in and
make him rise up from among his associates,
and take him to an inner room. 3Then take the
flask of oil, and pour *it* on his head, and say,
'Thus says the LORD: "I have anointed you king
over Israel." ' Then open the door and flee, and
do not delay."
4So the young man, the servant of the
prophet, went to Ramoth Gilead. 5And when he
arrived, there *were* the captains of the army sit-
ting; and he said, "I have a message for you,
Commander."
Jehu said, "For which *one* of us?"
And he said, "For you, Commander." 6Then
he arose and went into the house. And he poured
the oil on his head, and said to him, "Thus says
the LORD God of Israel: 'I have anointed you king
over the people of the LORD, over Israel. 7You
shall strike down the house of Ahab your master,
that I may avenge the blood of My servants the
prophets, and the blood of all the servants of the
LORD, at the hand of Jezebel. 8For the whole
house of Ahab shall perish; and I will cut off
from Ahab all the males in Israel, both bond and
free. 9So I will make the house of Ahab like the
house of Jeroboam the son of Nebat, and like the
house of Baasha the son of Ahijah. 10The dogs
shall eat Jezebel on the plot *of ground* at Jezreel,
and *there shall be* none to bury *her.*' " And he
opened the door and fled.
11Then Jehu came out to the servants of his
master, and *one* said to him, "*Is* all well? Why
did this madman come to you?"
And he said to them, "You know the man and
his babble."
12And they said, "A lie! Tell us now."
So he said, "Thus and thus he spoke to me,
saying, 'Thus says the LORD: "I have anointed
you king over Israel." ' "
13Then each man hastened to take his gar-
ment and put *it* under him on the top of the
steps; and they blew trumpets, saying, "Jehu is
king!"

JORAM OF ISRAEL KILLED

14So Jehu the son of Jehoshaphat, the son of
Nimshi, conspired against Joram. (Now Joram
had been defending Ramoth Gilead, he and all
Israel, against Hazael king of Syria. 15But King
Joram had returned to Jezreel to recover from
the wounds which the Syrians had inflicted on
him when he fought with Hazael king of Syria.)
And Jehu said, "If you are so minded, let no one
leave *or* escape from the city to go and tell *it* in
Jezreel." 16So Jehu rode in a chariot and went to

THE MESSAGE

the fight with Hazael. Ahaziah son of Jeho-
ram king of Judah paid a visit to Joram son
of Ahab on his sickbed in Jezreel.

JEHU OF ISRAEL

1-3 9 One day Elisha the prophet ordered a
member of the guild of prophets, "Get
yourself ready, take a flask of oil, and go to
Ramoth Gilead. Look for Jehu son of Je-
hoshaphat son of Nimshi. When you find
him, get him away from his companions and
take him to a back room. Take your flask of
oil and pour it over his head and say, 'GOD's
word: I anoint you king over Israel.' Then
open the door and get out of there as fast as
you can. Don't wait around."
4-5 The young prophet went to Ramoth
Gilead. On arrival he found the army offi-
cers all sitting around. He said, "I have a
matter of business with you, officer."
Jehu said, "Which one of us?"
"With you, officer."
6-10 He got up and went inside the building.
The young prophet poured the oil on his
head and said, "GOD's word, the God of Is-
rael: I've anointed you to be king over the
people of GOD, over Israel. Your assignment
is to attack the regime of Ahab your master.
I am avenging the massacre of my servants
the prophets—yes, the Jezebel-massacre of
all the prophets of GOD. The entire line of
Ahab is doomed. I'm wiping out the entire
bunch of that sad lot. I'll see to it that the
family of Ahab experiences the same fate as
the family of Jeroboam son of Nebat and the
family of Baasha son of Ahijah. As for
Jezebel, the dogs will eat her carcass in the
open fields of Jezreel. No burial for her!"
Then he opened the door and made a run for
it.
11 Jehu went back out to his master's offi-
cers. They asked, "Is everything all right?
What did that crazy fool want with you?"
He said, "You know that kind of man—all
talk."
12 "That's a lie!" they said. "Tell us what's
going on."
He said, "He told me this and this and
this—in effect, 'GOD's word: I anoint you
king of Israel!' "
13 They sprang into action. Each man
grabbed his robe; they piled them at the top
of the steps for a makeshift throne. Then
they blew the trumpet and declared, "Jehu is
king!"
14-15 That ignited the conspiracy of Jehu son
of Jehoshaphat son of Nimshi against Jo-
ram.
Meanwhile, Joram and the entire army
were defending Ramoth Gilead against
Hazael king of Aram. Except that Joram
had pulled back to Jezreel to convalesce
from the injuries he got from the Arameans
in the battle with Hazael king of Aram.
Jehu said, "If you really want me as king,
don't let anyone sneak out of the city and
blab the news in Jezreel."
16 Then Jehu mounted a chariot and rode to

NEW KING JAMES VERSION

Jezreel, for Joram was laid up there; and Ahaziah king of Judah had come down to see Joram.

17 Now a watchman stood on the tower in Jezreel, and he saw the company of Jehu as he came, and said, "I see a company of men."

And Joram said, "Get a horseman and send him to meet them, and let him say, '*Is it* peace?' "

18 So the horseman went to meet him, and said, "Thus says the king: '*Is it* peace?' "

And Jehu said, "What have you to do with peace? Turn around and follow me."

So the watchman reported, saying, "The messenger went to them, but is not coming back."

19 Then he sent out a second horseman who came to them, and said, "Thus says the king: '*Is it* peace?' "

And Jehu answered, "What have you to do with peace? Turn around and follow me."

20 So the watchman reported, saying, "He went up to them and is not coming back; and the driving *is* like the driving of Jehu the son of Nimshi, for he drives furiously!"

21 Then Joram said, "Make ready." And his chariot was made ready. Then Joram king of Israel and Ahaziah king of Judah went out, each in his chariot; and they went out to meet Jehu, and met him on the property of Naboth the Jezreelite. 22 Now it happened, when Joram saw Jehu, that he said, "*Is it* peace, Jehu?"

So he answered, "What peace, as long as the harlotries of your mother Jezebel and her witchcraft *are so* many?"

23 Then Joram turned around and fled, and said to Ahaziah, "Treachery, Ahaziah!" 24 Now Jehu drew his bow with full strength and shot Jehoram between his arms; and the arrow came out at his heart, and he sank down in his chariot. 25 Then *Jehu* said to Bidkar his captain, "Pick *him* up, *and* throw him into the tract of the field of Naboth the Jezreelite; for remember, when you and I were riding together behind Ahab his father, that the LORD laid this burden upon him: 26 'Surely I saw yesterday the blood of Naboth and the blood of his sons,' says the LORD, 'and I will repay you in this plot,' says the LORD. Now therefore, take *and* throw him on the plot *of ground,* according to the word of the LORD."

AHAZIAH OF JUDAH KILLED

27 But when Ahaziah king of Judah saw *this,* he fled by the road to Beth Haggan.[a] So Jehu pursued him, and said, "Shoot him also in the chariot." *And they shot him* at the Ascent of Gur, which is by Ibleam. Then he fled to Megiddo, and died there. 28 And his servants carried him in the chariot to Jerusalem, and buried him in his tomb with his fathers in the City of David. 29 In the eleventh year of Joram the son of Ahab, Ahaziah had become king over Judah.

9:27 [a]Literally *The Garden House*

THE MESSAGE

Jezreel, where Joram was in bed, resting.
King Ahaziah of Judah had come down to
visit Joram.
17 A sentry standing duty on the watch-
tower in Jezreel saw the company of Jehu
arrive. He said, "I see a band of men."
Joram said, "Get a horseman and send
him out to meet them and inquire, 'Is any-
thing wrong?' "
18 The horseman rode out to meet Jehu and
said, "The king wants to know if there's any-
thing wrong."
Jehu said, "What's it to you whether
things are right or wrong? Fall in behind
me."
The sentry said, "The messenger reached
them, but he's not returning."
19 The king then sent a second horseman.
When he reached them he said, "The king
wants to know if there's anything wrong."
Jehu said, "What's it to you whether things
are right or wrong? Fall in behind me."
20 The sentry said, "The messenger reached
them, but he's not returning. The driving is
like the driving of Jehu son of Nimshi—
crazy!"
21 Joram ordered, "Get my chariot ready!"
They hitched up his chariot. Joram king of
Israel and Ahaziah king of Judah, each in
his own chariot, drove out to meet Jehu.
They met in the field of Naboth of Jezreel.
22 When Joram saw Jehu he called out,
"Good day, Jehu!"
Jehu answered, "What's good about it?
How can there be anything good about it as
long as the promiscuous whoring and sor-
ceries of your mother Jezebel pollute the
country?"
23 Joram wheeled his chariot around and
fled, yelling to Ahaziah, "It's a trap, Ahaziah!"
24 Jehu pulled on his bow and released an
arrow; it hit Joram between the shoulder
blades and went right through his heart. He
slumped to his knees in his chariot.
25-26 Jehu ordered Bidkar, his lieutenant,
"Quick—throw him into the field of Naboth
of Jezreel. Remember when you and I were
driving our chariots behind Ahab his fa-
ther? That's when GOD pronounced this
doom upon him: 'As surely as I saw the
blood of murdered Naboth and his sons yes-
terday, you'll pay for it on this exact piece of
ground. GOD's word!' So take him and throw
him out in the field. GOD's instructions car-
ried out to the letter!"
27 Ahaziah king of Judah saw what was go-
ing on and made his escape on the road to-
ward Beth Haggan. Jehu chased him, yelling
out, "Get him, too!" Jehu's troops shot and
wounded him in his chariot on the hill up to
Gur, near Ibleam. He was able to make it as
far as Megiddo; there he died.
28 His aides drove on to Jerusalem. They
buried him in the family plot in the City of
David.

29 In the eleventh year of the reign of Joram
son of Ahab, Ahaziah had become king of
Judah.

NEW KING JAMES VERSION

JEZEBEL'S VIOLENT DEATH

30 Now when Jehu had come to Jezreel, Jezebel heard *of it;* and she put paint on her eyes and adorned her head, and looked through a window. 31 Then, as Jehu entered at the gate, she said, "*Is it* peace, Zimri, murderer of your master?"

32 And he looked up at the window, and said, "Who *is* on my side? Who?" So two *or* three eunuchs looked out at him. 33 Then he said, "Throw her down." So they threw her down, and *some* of her blood spattered on the wall and on the horses; and he trampled her underfoot. 34 And when he had gone in, he ate and drank. Then he said, "Go now, see to this accursed *woman,* and bury her, for she was a king's daughter." 35 So they went to bury her, but they found no more of her than the skull and the feet and the palms of *her* hands. 36 Therefore they came back and told him. And he said, "This *is* the word of the LORD, which He spoke by His servant Elijah the Tishbite, saying, 'On the plot *of ground* at Jezreel dogs shall eat the flesh of Jezebel;[a] 37 and the corpse of Jezebel shall be as refuse on the surface of the field, in the plot at Jezreel, so that they shall not say, "Here *lies* Jezebel." ' "

AHAB'S SEVENTY SONS KILLED

10 Now Ahab had seventy sons in Samaria. And Jehu wrote and sent letters to Samaria, to the rulers of Jezreel,[a] to the elders, and to those who reared Ahab's *sons,* saying:

> 2 Now as soon as this letter comes to you, since your master's sons *are* with you, and you have chariots and horses, a fortified city also, and weapons, 3 choose the best qualified of your master's sons, set *him* on his father's throne, and fight for your master's house.

4 But they were exceedingly afraid, and said, "Look, two kings could not stand up to him; how then can we stand?" 5 And he who *was* in charge of the house, and he who *was* in charge of the city, the elders also, and those who reared *the sons,* sent to Jehu, saying, "We *are* your servants, we will do all you tell us; but we will not make anyone king. Do *what is* good in your sight." 6 Then he wrote a second letter to them, saying:

> If you *are* for me and will obey my voice, take the heads of the men, your master's sons, and come to me at Jezreel by this time tomorrow.

Now the king's sons, seventy persons, *were* with the great men of the city, *who* were rearing them. 7 So it was, when the letter came to them, that they took the king's sons and slaughtered

9:36 [a]1 Kings 21:23 **10:1** [a]Following Masoretic Text, Syriac, and Targum; Septuagint reads *Samaria;* Vulgate reads *city.*

THE MESSAGE

30-31 When Jezebel heard that Jehu had arrived in Jezreel, she made herself up—put on eyeshadow and arranged her hair—and posed seductively at the window. When Jehu came through the city gate, she called down, "So, how are things, 'Zimri,' you dashing king-killer?"

32 Jehu looked up at the window and called, "Is there anybody up there on my side?" Two or three palace eunuchs looked out.

33 He ordered, "Throw her down!" They threw her out the window. Her blood spattered the wall and the horses, and Jehu trampled her under his horse's hooves.

34 Then Jehu went inside and ate his lunch. During lunch he gave orders, "Take care of that damned woman; give her a decent burial—she is, after all, a king's daughter."

35-36 They went out to bury her, but there was nothing left of her but skull, feet, and hands. They came back and told Jehu. He said, "It's GOD's word, the word spoken by Elijah the Tishbite:

In the field of Jezreel,
dogs will eat Jezebel;
37 The body of Jezebel will be like
dog-droppings on the ground in
Jezreel.
Old friends and lovers will say,
'I wonder, is *this* Jezebel?' "

1-2 10 Ahab had seventy sons still living in Samaria. Jehu wrote letters addressed to the officers of Jezreel, the city elders, and those in charge of Ahab's sons, and posted them to Samaria. The letters read:

> 2-3 This letter is fair warning. You're in charge of your master's children, chariots, horses, fortifications, and weapons. Pick the best and most capable of your master's sons and put him on the throne. Prepare to fight for your master's position.

4 They were absolutely terrified at the letter. They said, "Two kings have already been wiped out by him; what hope do we have?"

5 So they sent the warden of the palace, the mayor of the city, the elders, and the guardians to Jehu with this message: "We are your servants. Whatever you say, we'll do. We're not making anyone king here. You're in charge—do what you think best."

6-7 Then Jehu wrote a second letter:

> If you are on my side and are willing to follow my orders, here's what you do: Decapitate the sons of your master and bring the heads to me by this time tomorrow in Jezreel.

The king's sons numbered seventy. The leaders of the city had taken responsibility for them. When they got the letter, they took the king's sons and killed all seventy. Then

NEW KING JAMES VERSION

seventy persons, put their heads in baskets and
sent *them* to him at Jezreel.
8 Then a messenger came and told him, say-
ing, "They have brought the heads of the king's
sons."
And he said, "Lay them in two heaps at the
entrance of the gate until morning."
9 So it was, in the morning, that he went out
and stood, and said to all the people, "You *are*
righteous. Indeed I conspired against my master
and killed him; but who killed all these? 10 Know
now that nothing shall fall to the earth of the
word of the LORD which the LORD spoke con-
cerning the house of Ahab; for the LORD has
done what He spoke by His servant Elijah." 11 So
Jehu killed all who remained of the house of
Ahab in Jezreel, and all his great men and his
close acquaintances and his priests, until he left
him none remaining.

AHAZIAH'S FORTY-TWO BROTHERS KILLED

12 And he arose and departed and went to
Samaria. On the way, at Beth Eked[a] of the Shep-
herds, 13 Jehu met with the brothers of Ahaziah
king of Judah, and said, "Who *are* you?"
So they answered, "We *are* the brothers of
Ahaziah; we have come down to greet the sons
of the king and the sons of the queen mother."
14 And he said, "Take them alive!" So they
took them alive, and killed them at the well of
Beth Eked, forty-two men; and he left none of
them.

THE REST OF AHAB'S FAMILY KILLED

15 Now when he departed from there, he met
Jehonadab the son of Rechab, *coming* to meet
him; and he greeted him and said to him, "Is
your heart right, as my heart *is* toward your
heart?"
And Jehonadab answered, "It is."
Jehu said, "If it is, give *me* your hand." So he
gave *him* his hand, and he took him up to him
into the chariot. 16 Then he said, "Come with me,
and see my zeal for the LORD." So they had him
ride in his chariot. 17 And when he came to
Samaria, he killed all who remained to Ahab in
Samaria, till he had destroyed them, according
to the word of the LORD which He spoke to Eli-
jah.

WORSHIPERS OF BAAL KILLED

18 Then Jehu gathered all the people together,
and said to them, "Ahab served Baal a little,
Jehu will serve him much. 19 Now therefore, call
to me all the prophets of Baal, all his servants,
and all his priests. Let no one be missing, for I
have a great sacrifice for Baal. Whoever is miss-
ing shall not live." But Jehu acted deceptively,
with the intent of destroying the worshipers of
Baal. 20 And Jehu said, "Proclaim a solemn as-
sembly for Baal." So they proclaimed *it.* 21 Then
Jehu sent throughout all Israel; and all the wor-
shipers of Baal came, so that there was not a
man left who did not come. So they came into

10:12 [a]Or *The Shearing House*

THE MESSAGE

they put the heads in baskets and sent them to Jehu in Jezreel.

8 A messenger reported to Jehu: "They've delivered the heads of the king's sons."

He said, "Stack them in two piles at the city gate until morning."

9-10 In the morning Jehu came out, stood before the people, and addressed them formally: "Do you realize that this very day you are participants in GOD's righteous workings? True, I am the one who conspired against my master and assassinated him. But who, do you suppose, is responsible for this pile of skulls? Know this for certain: Not a single syllable that GOD spoke in judgment on the family of Ahab is canceled; you're seeing it with your own eyes—GOD doing what, through Elijah, he said he'd do."

11 Then Jehu proceeded to kill everyone who had anything to do with Ahab's family in Jezreel—leaders, friends, priests. He wiped out the entire lot.

12-13 That done, he brushed himself off and set out for Samaria. Along the way, at Beth Eked (Binding House) of the Shepherds, he met up with some relatives of Ahaziah king of Judah.

Jehu said, "Who are you?"

They said, "We're relatives of Ahaziah and we've come down to a reunion of the royal family."

14 "Grab them!" ordered Jehu. They were taken and then massacred at the well of Beth Eked. Forty-two of them—no survivors.

15 He went on from there and came upon Jehonadab the Recabite who was on his way to meet him. Greeting him, he said, "Are we together and of one mind in this?"

Jehonadab said, "We are—count on me."

"Then give me your hand," said Jehu.

They shook hands on it and Jehonadab stepped up into the chariot with Jehu.

16 "Come along with me," said Jehu, "and witness my zeal for GOD." Together they proceeded in the chariot.

17 When they arrived in Samaria, Jehu massacred everyone left in Samaria who was in any way connected with Ahab—a mass execution, just as GOD had told Elijah.

18-19 Next, Jehu got all the people together and addressed them:

> Ahab served Baal small-time;
> Jehu will serve him big-time.

"Get all the prophets of Baal here—everyone who served him, all his priests. Get everyone here; don't leave anyone out. I have a great sacrifice to offer Baal. If you don't show up, you won't live to tell about it." (Jehu was lying, of course. He planned to destroy all the worshipers of Baal.)

20 Jehu ordered, "Make preparation for a holy convocation for Baal." They did and posted the date.

21 Jehu then summoned everyone in Israel. They came in droves—every worshiper of Baal in the country. Nobody stayed home.

NEW KING JAMES VERSION

the temple[a] of Baal, and the temple of Baal was full from one end to the other. 22And he said to the one in charge of the wardrobe, "Bring out vestments for all the worshipers of Baal." So he brought out vestments for them. 23Then Jehu and Jehonadab the son of Rechab went into the temple of Baal, and said to the worshipers of Baal, "Search and see that no servants of the LORD are here with you, but only the worshipers of Baal." 24So they went in to offer sacrifices and burnt offerings. Now Jehu had appointed for himself eighty men on the outside, and had said, "*If* any of the men whom I have brought into your hands escapes, *whoever lets him escape, it shall be* his life for the life of the other."

25Now it happened, as soon as he had made an end of offering the burnt offering, that Jehu said to the guard and to the captains, "Go in *and* kill them; let no one come out!" And they killed them with the edge of the sword; then the guards and the officers threw *them* out, and went into the inner room of the temple of Baal. 26And they brought the *sacred* pillars out of the temple of Baal and burned them. 27Then they broke down the *sacred* pillar of Baal, and tore down the temple of Baal and made it a refuse dump to this day. 28Thus Jehu destroyed Baal from Israel.

29However Jehu did not turn away from the sins of Jeroboam the son of Nebat, who had made Israel sin, *that is*, from the golden calves that *were* at Bethel and Dan. 30And the LORD said to Jehu, "Because you have done well in doing *what is* right in My sight, *and* have done to the house of Ahab all that *was* in My heart, your sons shall sit on the throne of Israel to the fourth *generation*." 31But Jehu took no heed to walk in the law of the LORD God of Israel with all his heart; for he did not depart from the sins of Jeroboam, who had made Israel sin.

DEATH OF JEHU

32In those days the LORD began to cut off *parts* of Israel; and Hazael conquered them in all the territory of Israel 33from the Jordan eastward: all the land of Gilead—Gad, Reuben, and Manasseh—from Aroer, which *is* by the River Arnon, including Gilead and Bashan.

34Now the rest of the acts of Jehu, all that he did, and all his might, *are* they not written in the book of the chronicles of the kings of Israel? 35So Jehu rested with his fathers, and they buried him in Samaria. Then Jehoahaz his son reigned in his place. 36And the period that Jehu reigned over Israel in Samaria *was* twenty-eight years.

ATHALIAH REIGNS IN JUDAH

11 When Athaliah the mother of Ahaziah saw that her son was dead, she arose and destroyed all the royal heirs. 2But Jehosheba, the daughter of King Joram, sister of Ahaziah, took Joash the son of Ahaziah, and stole him away from among the king's sons *who were* being

10:21 [a]Literally *house*, and so elsewhere in this chapter

THE MESSAGE

They came and packed the temple of Baal to capacity.

22 Jehu directed the keeper of the wardrobe, "Get robes for all the servants of Baal." He brought out their robes.

23-24 Jehu and Jehonadab the Recabite now entered the temple of Baal and said, "Double-check and make sure that there are no worshipers of GOD in here; only Baal-worshipers are allowed." Then they launched the worship, making the sacrifices and burnt offerings.

Meanwhile, Jehu had stationed eighty men outside with orders: "Don't let a single person escape; if you do, it's your life for his life."

25-27 When Jehu had finished with the sacrificial solemnities, he signaled to the officers and guards, "Enter and kill! No survivors!"

And the bloody slaughter began. The officers and guards threw the corpses outside and cleared the way to enter the inner shrine of Baal. They hauled out the sacred phallic stone from the temple of Baal and pulverized it. They smashed the Baal altars and tore down the Baal temple. It's been a public toilet ever since.

28 And that's the story of Jehu's wasting of Baal in Israel.

29 But for all that, Jehu didn't turn back from the sins of Jeroboam son of Nebat, the sins that had dragged Israel into a life of sin—the golden calves in Bethel and Dan stayed.

30 GOD commended Jehu: "You did well to do what I saw was best. You did what I ordered against the family of Ahab. As reward, your sons will occupy the throne of Israel for four generations."

31 Even then, though, Jehu wasn't careful to walk in GOD's ways and honor the God of Israel from an undivided heart. He didn't turn back from the sins of Jeroboam son of Nebat, who led Israel into a life of sin.

32-33 It was about this time that GOD began to shrink Israel. Hazael hacked away at the borders of Israel from the Jordan to the east—all the territory of Gilead, Gad, Reuben, and Manasseh from Aroer near the Brook Arnon. In effect, all Gilead and Bashan.

34-36 The rest of the life and times of Jehu, his accomplishments and fame, are written in *The Chronicles of the Kings of Israel*. Jehu died and was buried in the family plot in Samaria. His son Jehoahaz was the next king. Jehu ruled Israel from Samaria for twenty-eight years.

ATHALIAH OF JUDAH

1-3 11 Athaliah was the mother of Ahaziah. When she saw that her son was dead, she took over. She began by massacring the entire royal family. But Jehosheba, daughter of King Joram and sister of Ahaziah, took Ahaziah's son Joash and kidnapped him from among the king's sons slated for

NEW KING JAMES VERSION

murdered; and they hid him and his nurse in the
bedroom, from Athaliah, so that he was not
killed. 3So he was hidden with her in the house
of the LORD for six years, while Athaliah reigned
over the land.

JOASH CROWNED KING OF JUDAH

4In the seventh year Jehoiada sent and
brought the captains of hundreds—of the body-
guards and the escorts—and brought them into
the house of the LORD to him. And he made a
covenant with them and took an oath from them
in the house of the LORD, and showed them the
king's son. 5Then he commanded them, saying,
"This *is* what you shall do: One-third of you who
come on duty on the Sabbath shall be keeping
watch over the king's house, 6one-third *shall be*
at the gate of Sur, and one-third at the gate be-
hind the escorts. You shall keep the watch of the
house, lest it be broken down. 7The two contin-
gents of you who go off duty on the Sabbath
shall keep the watch of the house of the LORD
for the king. 8But you shall surround the king on
all sides, every man with his weapons in his
hand; and whoever comes within range, let him
be put to death. You are to be with the king as he
goes out and as he comes in."

9So the captains of the hundreds did accord-
ing to all that Jehoiada the priest commanded.
Each of them took his men who were to be on
duty on the Sabbath, with those who were going
off duty on the Sabbath, and came to Jehoiada
the priest. 10And the priest gave the captains of
hundreds the spears and shields which *had be-
longed* to King David, that were in the temple of
the LORD. 11Then the escorts stood, every man
with his weapons in his hand, all around the king,
from the right side of the temple to the left side of
the temple, by the altar and the house. 12And he
brought out the king's son, put the crown on him,
and *gave him* the Testimony;[a] they made him
king and anointed him, and they clapped their
hands and said, "Long live the king!"

DEATH OF ATHALIAH

13Now when Athaliah heard the noise of the
escorts *and* the people, she came to the people
in the temple of the LORD. 14When she looked,
there was the king standing by a pillar accord-
ing to custom; and the leaders and the trum-
peters were by the king. All the people of the
land were rejoicing and blowing trumpets. So
Athaliah tore her clothes and cried out, "Trea-
son! Treason!"

15And Jehoiada the priest commanded the
captains of the hundreds, the officers of the
army, and said to them, "Take her outside under
guard, and slay with the sword whoever follows
her." For the priest had said, "Do not let her be
killed in the house of the LORD." 16So they seized
her; and she went by way of the horses' entrance
into the king's house, and there she was killed.

17Then Jehoiada made a covenant between
the LORD, the king, and the people, that they
should be the LORD's people, and *also* between
the king and the people.

11:12 [a]That is, the Law (compare Exodus 25:16, 21 and Deuteronomy 31:9)

THE MESSAGE

slaughter. She hid him and his nurse in a
private room away from Athaliah. He didn't
get killed. He was there with her, hidden
away for six years in The Temple of GOD.
Athaliah, oblivious to his existence, ruled
the country.

4 In the seventh year Jehoiada sent for the
captains of the bodyguards and the Palace
Security Force. They met him in The Temple
of GOD. He made a covenant with them,
swore them to secrecy, and only then
showed them the young prince.

5-8 Then he commanded them, "These are
your instructions: Those of you who come
on duty on the Sabbath and guard the
palace, and those of you who go off duty on
the Sabbath and guard The Temple of GOD,
are to join forces at the time of the changing
of the guard and form a ring around the
young king, weapons at the ready. Kill any-
one who tries to break through your ranks.
Your job is to stay with the king at all times
and places, coming and going."

9-11 The captains obeyed the orders of Je-
hoiada the priest. Each took his men, those
who came on duty on the Sabbath and those
who went off duty on the Sabbath, and pre-
sented them to Jehoiada the priest. The
priest armed the officers with spears and
shields originally belonging to King David,
stored in The Temple of GOD. Well-armed,
the guards took up their assigned positions
for protecting the king, from one end of The
Temple to the other, surrounding both Altar
and Temple.

12 Then the priest brought the prince into
view, crowned him, handed him the scroll of
God's covenant, and made him king. As they
anointed him, everyone applauded and
shouted, "Long live the king!"

13-14 Athaliah heard the shouting of guards
and people and came to the crowd gathered
at The Temple of GOD. Astonished, she saw
the king standing beside the throne, flanked
by the captains and heralds, with everybody
beside themselves with joy, trumpets blar-
ing. Athaliah ripped her robes in dismay
and shouted, "Treason! Treason!"

15-16 Jehoiada the priest ordered the military
officers, "Drag her outside and kill anyone
who tries to follow her!" (The priest had
said, "Don't kill her inside The Temple of
GOD.") So they dragged her out to the
palace's horse corral; there they killed her.

17 Jehoiada now made a covenant between
GOD and the king and the people: They were
GOD's people. Another covenant was made
between the king and the people.

NEW KING JAMES VERSION

[18]And all the people of the land went to the tem-
ple of Baal, and tore it down. They thoroughly
broke in pieces its altars and images, and killed
Mattan the priest of Baal before the altars. And
the priest appointed officers over the house of
the LORD. [19]Then he took the captains of hun-
dreds, the bodyguards, the escorts, and all the
people of the land; and they brought the king
down from the house of the LORD, and went by
way of the gate of the escorts to the king's
house. Then he sat on the throne of the kings.
[20]So all the people of the land rejoiced; and the
city was quiet, for they had slain Athaliah with
the sword *in* the king's house. [21]Jehoash *was*
seven years old when he became king.

JEHOASH REPAIRS THE TEMPLE

12 In the seventh year of Jehu, Jehoash[a] be-
came king, and he reigned forty years in
Jerusalem. His mother's name *was* Zibiah of
Beersheba. [2]Jehoash did *what was* right in the
sight of the LORD all the days in which Jehoiada
the priest instructed him. [3]But the high places
were not taken away; the people still sacrificed
and burned incense on the high places.
[4]And Jehoash said to the priests, "All the
money of the dedicated gifts that are brought
into the house of the LORD—each man's census
money, each man's assessment money[a]—*and* all
the money that a man purposes in his heart to
bring into the house of the LORD, [5]let the priests
take *it* themselves, each from his constituency;
and let them repair the damages of the temple,
wherever any dilapidation is found."
[6]Now it was so, by the twenty-third year of
King Jehoash, *that* the priests had not repaired
the damages of the temple. [7]So King Jehoash
called Jehoiada the priest and the *other* priests,
and said to them, "Why have you not repaired
the damages of the temple? Now therefore, do
not take *more* money from your constituency,
but deliver it for repairing the damages of the
temple." [8]And the priests agreed that they would
neither receive *more* money from the people,
nor repair the damages of the temple.
[9]Then Jehoiada the priest took a chest, bored
a hole in its lid, and set it beside the altar, on the
right side as one comes into the house of the
LORD; and the priests who kept the door put
there all the money brought into the house of
the LORD. [10]So it was, whenever they saw that
there was much money in the chest, that the
king's scribe and the high priest came up and
put it in bags, and counted the money that was
found in the house of the LORD. [11]Then they gave
the money, which had been apportioned, into
the hands of those who did the work, who had
the oversight of the house of the LORD; and they
paid it out to the carpenters and builders who
worked on the house of the LORD, [12]and to ma-
sons and stonecutters, and for buying timber
and hewn stone, to repair the damage of the
house of the LORD, and for all that was paid out
to repair the temple. [13]However there were not
made for the house of the LORD basins of silver,
trimmers, sprinkling-bowls, trumpets, any arti-

12:1 [a]Spelled *Joash* in 11:2ff **12:4** [a]Compare Leviticus 27:2ff

THE MESSAGE

18-20 The people poured into the temple of
Baal and tore it down, smashing altar and
images to smithereens. They killed Mattan
the priest in front of the altar.
Jehoiada then stationed sentries in The
Temple of GOD. He arranged for the officers
of the bodyguard and the palace security,
along with the people themselves, to escort
the king down from The Temple of GOD
through the Gate of the Guards and into the
palace. There he sat on the royal throne.
Everybody celebrated the event. And the
city was safe and undisturbed—they had
killed Athaliah with the royal sword.
21 Joash was seven years old when he be-
came king.

JOASH OF JUDAH

1 **12** In the seventh year of Jehu, Joash be-
gan his kingly rule. He was king for
forty years in Jerusalem. His mother's name
was Gazelle. She was from Beersheba.
2-3 Taught and trained by Jehoiada the
priest, Joash did what pleased GOD for as
long as he lived. (Even so, he didn't get rid
of the sacred fertility shrines—people still
frequented them, sacrificing and burning in-
cense.)
4-5 Joash instructed the priests: "Take the
money that is brought into The Temple of
GOD for holy offerings—both mandatory of-
ferings and freewill offerings—and, keeping
a careful accounting, use them to renovate
The Temple wherever it has fallen into dis-
repair."
6 But by the twenty-third year of Joash's
rule, the priests hadn't done one thing—The
Temple was as dilapidated as ever.
7 King Joash called Jehoiada the priest and
the company of priests and said, "Why
haven't you renovated this sorry-looking
Temple? You are forbidden to take any more
money for Temple repairs—from now on,
hand over everything you get."
8 The priests agreed not to take any more
money or to be involved in The Temple ren-
ovation.
9-16 Then Jehoiada took a single chest and
bored a hole in the lid and placed it to the
right of the main entrance into The Temple
of GOD. All the offerings that were brought
to The Temple of GOD were placed in the
chest by the priests who guarded the en-
trance. When they saw that a large sum of
money had accumulated in the chest, the
king's secretary and the chief priest would
empty the chest and count the offerings.
They would give the money accounted for to
the managers of The Temple project; they in
turn would pay the carpenters, construction
workers, masons, stoneworkers, and the
buyers of timber and quarried stone for the
repair and renovation of The Temple of
GOD—any expenses connected with fixing
up The Temple. But none of the money
brought into The Temple of GOD was used
for liturgical "extras" (silver chalices, candle

NEW KING JAMES VERSION

cles of gold or articles of silver, from the money brought into the house of the LORD. 14But they gave that to the workmen, and they repaired the house of the LORD with it. 15Moreover they did not require an account from the men into whose hand they delivered the money to be paid to workmen, for they dealt faithfully. 16The money from the trespass offerings and the money from the sin offerings was not brought into the house of the LORD. It belonged to the priests.

HAZAEL THREATENS JERUSALEM

17Hazael king of Syria went up and fought against Gath, and took it; then Hazael set his face to go up to Jerusalem. 18And Jehoash king of Judah took all the sacred things that his fathers, Jehoshaphat and Jehoram and Ahaziah, kings of Judah, had dedicated, and his own sacred things, and all the gold found in the treasuries of the house of the LORD and in the king's house, and sent *them* to Hazael king of Syria. Then he went away from Jerusalem.

DEATH OF JOASH

19Now the rest of the acts of Joash,[a] and all that he did, *are* they not written in the book of the chronicles of the kings of Judah?

20And his servants arose and formed a conspiracy, and killed Joash in the house of the Millo,[a] which goes down to Silla. 21For Jozachar[a] the son of Shimeath and Jehozabad the son of Shomer,[b] his servants, struck him. So he died, and they buried him with his fathers in the City of David. Then Amaziah his son reigned in his place.

JEHOAHAZ REIGNS IN ISRAEL

13 In the twenty-third year of Joash[a] the son of Ahaziah, king of Judah, Jehoahaz the son of Jehu became king over Israel in Samaria, *and reigned* seventeen years. 2And he did evil in the sight of the LORD, and followed the sins of Jeroboam the son of Nebat, who had made Israel sin. He did not depart from them.

3Then the anger of the LORD was aroused against Israel, and He delivered them into the hand of Hazael king of Syria, and into the hand of Ben-Hadad the son of Hazael, all *their* days. 4So Jehoahaz pleaded with the LORD, and the LORD listened to him; for He saw the oppression of Israel, because the king of Syria oppressed them. 5Then the LORD gave Israel a deliverer, so that they escaped from under the hand of the Syrians; and the children of Israel dwelt in their tents as before. 6Nevertheless they did not depart from the sins of the house of Jeroboam, who had made Israel sin, *but* walked in them; and the wooden image[a] also remained in Samaria. 7For He left of the army of Jehoahaz only fifty horsemen, ten chariots, and ten thousand foot soldiers; for the king of Syria had destroyed them and made them like the dust at threshing.

12:19 [a]Spelled *Jehoash* in 12:1ff **12:20** [a]Literally *The Landfill* **12:21** [a]Called *Zabad* in 2 Chronicles 24:26 [b]Called *Shimrith* in 2 Chronicles 24:26 **13:1** [a]Spelled *Jehoash* in 12:1ff **13:6** [a]Hebrew *Asherah*, a Canaanite goddess

THE MESSAGE

snuffers, trumpets, various gold and silver vessels, etc.). It was given to the workmen to pay for their repairing GOD's Temple. And no one even had to check on the men who handled the money given for the project—they were honest men. Offerings designated for Compensation Offerings and Absolution Offerings didn't go into the building project—those went directly to the priests.

17-18 Around this time Hazael king of Aram ventured out and attacked Gath, and he captured it. Then he decided to try for Jerusalem. Joash king of Judah countered by gathering up all the sacred memorials—gifts dedicated for holy use by his ancestors, the kings of Judah, Jehoshaphat, Jehoram, and Ahaziah, along with the holy memorials he himself had received, plus all the gold that he could find in the temple and palace storerooms—and sent it to Hazael king of Aram. Appeased, Hazael went on his way and didn't bother Jerusalem.

19-21 The rest of the life and times of Joash and all that he did are written in *The Chronicles of the Kings of Judah*. At the last his palace staff formed a conspiracy and assassinated Joash as he was strolling along the ramp of the fortified outside city wall. Jozabad son of Shimeath and Jehozabad son of Shomer were the assassins. And so Joash died and was buried in the family plot in the City of David. His son Amaziah was king after him.

JEHOAHAZ OF ISRAEL

1-3 13 In the twenty-third year of Joash son of Ahaziah king of Judah, Jehoahaz son of Jehu became king of Israel in Samaria—a rule of seventeen years. He lived an evil life before GOD, walking step for step in the tracks of Jeroboam son of Nebat who led Israel into a life of sin, swerving neither left or right. Exasperated, GOD was furious with Israel and turned them over to Hazael king of Aram and Ben-Hadad son of Hazael. This domination went on for a long time.

4-6 Then Jehoahaz prayed for a softening of GOD's anger, and GOD listened. He realized how wretched Israel had become under the brutalities of the king of Aram. So GOD provided a savior for Israel who brought them out from under Aram's oppression. The children of Israel were again able to live at peace in their own homes. But it didn't make any difference: They didn't change their lives, didn't turn away from the Jeroboam-sins that now characterized Israel, including the sex-and-religion shrines of Asherah still flourishing in Samaria.

7 Nothing was left of Jehoahaz's army after Hazael's oppression except for fifty cavalry, ten chariots, and ten thousand infantry. The king of Aram had decimated the rest, leaving behind him mostly chaff.

NEW KING JAMES VERSION

8 Now the rest of the acts of Jehoahaz, all that
he did, and his might, *are* they not written in the
book of the chronicles of the kings of Israel? 9 So
Jehoahaz rested with his fathers, and they
buried him in Samaria. Then Joash his son
reigned in his place.

JEHOASH REIGNS IN ISRAEL

10 In the thirty-seventh year of Joash king of
Judah, Jehoash[a] the son of Jehoahaz became
king over Israel in Samaria, *and reigned* sixteen
years. 11 And he did evil in the sight of the LORD.
He did not depart from all the sins of Jeroboam
the son of Nebat, who made Israel sin, *but*
walked in them.

12 Now the rest of the acts of Joash, all that he
did, and his might with which he fought against
Amaziah king of Judah, *are* they not written in
the book of the chronicles of the kings of Israel?
13 So Joash rested with his fathers. Then Jer-
oboam sat on his throne. And Joash was buried
in Samaria with the kings of Israel.

DEATH OF ELISHA

14 Elisha had become sick with the illness of
which he would die. Then Joash the king of Is-
rael came down to him, and wept over his face,
and said, "O my father, my father, the chariots of
Israel and their horsemen!"

15 And Elisha said to him, "Take a bow and
some arrows." So he took himself a bow and
some arrows. 16 Then he said to the king of Is-
rael, "Put your hand on the bow." So he put his
hand *on it*, and Elisha put his hands on the
king's hands. 17 And he said, "Open the east win-
dow"; and he opened *it*. Then Elisha said,
"Shoot"; and he shot. And he said, "The arrow of
the LORD's deliverance and the arrow of deliver-
ance from Syria; for you must strike the Syrians
at Aphek till you have destroyed *them*." 18 Then
he said, "Take the arrows"; so he took *them*.
And he said to the king of Israel, "Strike the
ground"; so he struck three times, and stopped.
19 And the man of God was angry with him, and
said, "You should have struck five or six times;
then you would have struck Syria till you had
destroyed *it!* But now you will strike Syria *only*
three times."

20 Then Elisha died, and they buried him. And
the *raiding* bands from Moab invaded the land
in the spring of the year. 21 So it was, as they
were burying a man, that suddenly they spied a
band *of raiders;* and they put the man in the
tomb of Elisha; and when the man was let down
and touched the bones of Elisha, he revived and
stood on his feet.

ISRAEL RECAPTURES CITIES FROM SYRIA

22 And Hazael king of Syria oppressed Israel
all the days of Jehoahaz. 23 But the LORD was
gracious to them, had compassion on them, and

13:10 [a]Spelled *Joash* in verse 9

THE MESSAGE

8-9 The rest of the life and times of Jehoahaz, the record of his accomplishments, are written in *The Chronicles of the Kings of Israel.* Jehoahaz died and was buried with his ancestors in Samaria. His son Jehoash succeeded him as king.

JEHOASH OF ISRAEL

10-11 In the thirty-seventh year of Joash king of Judah, Jehoash son of Jehoahaz became king of Israel in Samaria—a reign of sixteen years. In GOD's eyes he lived an evil life. He didn't deviate one bit from the sins of Jeroboam son of Nebat, who led Israel into a life of sin. He plodded along in the same tracks, step after step.

12-13 The rest of the life and times of Jehoash, the record of his accomplishments and his war against Amaziah king of Judah, are written in *The Chronicles of the Kings of Israel.* Jehoash died and joined his ancestors. Jeroboam took over his throne. Jehoash was buried in Samaria in the royal cemetery.

14 Elisha came down sick. It was the sickness of which he would soon die. Jehoash king of Israel paid him a visit. When he saw him he wept openly, crying, "My father, my father! Chariot and horsemen of Israel!"

15 Elisha told him, "Go and get a bow and some arrows." The king brought him the bow and arrows.

16 Then he told the king, "Put your hand on the bow." He put his hand on the bow. Then Elisha put his hand over the hand of the king.

17 Elisha said, "Now open the east window." He opened it.

Then he said, "Shoot!" And he shot.

"The arrow of GOD's salvation!" exclaimed Elisha. "The arrow of deliverance from Aram! You will do battle against Aram until there's nothing left of it."

18 "Now pick up the other arrows," said Elisha. He picked them up.

Then he said to the king of Israel, "Strike the ground."

The king struck the ground three times and then quit.

19 The Holy Man became angry with him: "Why didn't you hit the ground five or six times? Then you would beat Aram until he was finished. As it is, you'll defeat him three times only."

20-21 Then Elisha died and they buried him.

Some time later, raiding bands of Moabites, as they often did, invaded the country. One day, some men were burying a man and spotted the raiders. They threw the man into Elisha's tomb and got away. When the body touched Elisha's bones, the man came alive, stood up, and walked out on his own two feet.

22-24 Hazael king of Aram badgered and bedeviled Israel all through the reign of Jehoahaz. But GOD was gracious and showed mercy to them. He stuck with them out of re-

NEW KING JAMES VERSION

regarded them, because of His covenant with Abraham, Isaac, and Jacob, and would not yet destroy them or cast them from His presence.

24Now Hazael king of Syria died. Then Ben-Hadad his son reigned in his place. 25And Jehoash[a] the son of Jehoahaz recaptured from the hand of Ben-Hadad, the son of Hazael, the cities which he had taken out of the hand of Jehoahaz his father by war. Three times Joash defeated him and recaptured the cities of Israel.

AMAZIAH REIGNS IN JUDAH

14 In the second year of Joash the son of Jehoahaz, king of Israel, Amaziah the son of Joash, king of Judah, became king. 2He was twenty-five years old when he became king, and he reigned twenty-nine years in Jerusalem. His mother's name was Jehoaddan of Jerusalem. 3And he did *what was* right in the sight of the LORD, yet not like his father David; he did everything as his father Joash had done. 4However the high places were not taken away, and the people still sacrificed and burned incense on the high places.

5Now it happened, as soon as the kingdom was established in his hand, that he executed his servants who had murdered his father the king. 6But the children of the murderers he did not execute, according to what is written in the Book of the Law of Moses, in which the LORD commanded, saying, "Fathers shall not be put to death for their children, nor shall children be put to death for their fathers; but a person shall be put to death for his own sin."[a]

7He killed ten thousand Edomites in the Valley of Salt, and took Sela by war, and called its name Joktheel to this day.

8Then Amaziah sent messengers to Jehoash[a] the son of Jehoahaz, the son of Jehu, king of Israel, saying, "Come, let us face one another *in battle.*" 9And Jehoash king of Israel sent to Amaziah king of Judah, saying, "The thistle that *was* in Lebanon sent to the cedar that *was* in Lebanon, saying, 'Give your daughter to my son as wife'; and a wild beast that *was* in Lebanon passed by and trampled the thistle. 10You have indeed defeated Edom, and your heart has lifted you up. Glory *in that*, and stay at home; for why should you meddle with trouble so that you fall—you and Judah with you?"

11But Amaziah would not heed. Therefore Jehoash king of Israel went out; so he and Amaziah king of Judah faced one another at Beth Shemesh, which *belongs* to Judah. 12And Judah was defeated by Israel, and every man fled to his tent.

13:25 [a]Spelled *Joash* in verses 12–14, 25 **14:6** [a]Deuteronomy 24:16 **14:8** [a]Spelled *Joash* in 13:12ff and 2 Chronicles 25:17ff

THE MESSAGE

spect for his covenant with Abraham, Isaac, and Jacob. He never gave up on them, never even considered discarding them, even to this day. Hazael king of Aram died. His son Ben-Hadad was the next king.

25 Jehoash son of Jehoahaz turned things around and took back the cities that Ben-Hadad son of Hazael had taken from his father Jehoahaz. Jehoash went to war three times and defeated him each time, recapturing the cities of Israel.

AMAZIAH OF JUDAH

1-2 14 In the second year of Jehoash son of Jehoahaz king of Israel, Amaziah son of Joash became king of Judah. He was twenty-five years old when he became king and he reigned for twenty-nine years in Jerusalem. His mother's name was Jehoaddin. She was from Jerusalem.

3-4 He lived the way GOD wanted and did the right thing. But he didn't come up to the standards of his ancestor David; instead he lived pretty much as his father Joash had; the local sex-and-religion shrines continued to stay in business with people frequenting them.

5-6 When he had the affairs of the kingdom well in hand, he executed the palace guard that had assassinated his father the king. But he didn't kill the sons of the assassins. He was obedient to what GOD commanded, written in the Word revealed to Moses, that parents shouldn't be executed for their children's sins, nor children for those of their parents. We each pay personally for our sins.

7 Amaziah roundly defeated Edom in the Valley of Salt to the tune of ten thousand dead. In another battle he took The Rock and renamed it Joktheel, the name it still bears.

8 One day Amaziah sent envoys to Jehoash son of Jehoahaz, the son of Jehu, king of Israel, challenging him to a fight: "Come and meet with me—dare you. Let's have it out face-to-face!"

9-10 Jehoash king of Israel replied to Amaziah king of Judah, "One day a thistle in Lebanon sent word to a cedar in Lebanon, 'Give your daughter to my son in marriage.' But then a wild animal of Lebanon passed by and stepped on the thistle, crushing it. Just because you've defeated Edom in battle, you now think you're a big shot. Go ahead and be proud, but stay home. Why press your luck? Why bring defeat on yourself and Judah?"

11 Amaziah wouldn't take No for an answer. So Jehoash king of Israel gave in and agreed to a battle between him and Amaziah king of Judah. They met at Beth Shemesh, a town of Judah.

12 Judah was thoroughly beaten by Israel—all their soldiers ran home in defeat.

New King James Version

13 Then Jehoash king of Israel captured Amaziah
king of Judah, the son of Jehoash, the son of
Ahaziah, at Beth Shemesh; and he went to
Jerusalem, and broke down the wall of Jerusa-
lem from the Gate of Ephraim to the Corner
Gate—four hundred cubits. 14 And he took all the
gold and silver, all the articles that were found
in the house of the LORD and in the treasuries of
the king's house, and hostages, and returned to
Samaria.
15 Now the rest of the acts of Jehoash which
he did—his might, and how he fought with
Amaziah king of Judah—*are* they not written in
the book of the chronicles of the kings of Israel?
16 So Jehoash rested with his fathers, and was
buried in Samaria with the kings of Israel. Then
Jeroboam his son reigned in his place.
17 Amaziah the son of Joash, king of Judah,
lived fifteen years after the death of Jehoash the
son of Jehoahaz, king of Israel. 18 Now the rest of
the acts of Amaziah, *are* they not written in the
book of the chronicles of the kings of Judah?
19 And they formed a conspiracy against him in
Jerusalem, and he fled to Lachish; but they sent
after him to Lachish and killed him there.
20 Then they brought him on horses, and he was
buried at Jerusalem with his fathers in the City
of David.
21 And all the people of Judah took Azariah,[a]
who *was* sixteen years old, and made him king
instead of his father Amaziah. 22 He built Elath
and restored it to Judah, after the king rested
with his fathers.

Jeroboam II Reigns in Israel

23 In the fifteenth year of Amaziah the son of
Joash, king of Judah, Jeroboam the son of
Joash, king of Israel, became king in Samaria,
and reigned forty-one years. 24 And he did evil in
the sight of the LORD; he did not depart from all
the sins of Jeroboam the son of Nebat, who had
made Israel sin. 25 He restored the territory of Is-
rael from the entrance of Hamath to the Sea of
the Arabah, according to the word of the LORD
God of Israel, which He had spoken through His
servant Jonah the son of Amittai, the prophet
who *was* from Gath Hepher. 26 For the LORD saw
that the affliction of Israel *was* very bitter; and
whether bond or free, there was no helper for Is-
rael. 27 And the LORD did not say that He would
blot out the name of Israel from under heaven;
but He saved them by the hand of Jeroboam the
son of Joash.
28 Now the rest of the acts of Jeroboam, and
all that he did—his might, how he made war,
and how he recaptured for Israel, from Damas-
cus and Hamath, *what had belonged* to Judah—
are they not written in the book of the chroni-
cles of the kings of Israel? 29 So Jeroboam rested
with his fathers, the kings of Israel. Then
Zechariah his son reigned in his place.

14:21 [a]Called *Uzziah* in 2 Chronicles 26:1ff, Isaiah 6:1, and elsewhere

The Message

13-14 Jehoash king of Israel captured Amaziah king of Judah, the son of Joash, the son of Ahaziah, at Beth Shemesh. But Jehoash didn't stop there; he went on to attack Jerusalem. He demolished the wall of Jerusalem all the way from the Ephraim Gate to the Corner Gate—a stretch of about six hundred feet. He looted the gold, silver, and furnishings—anything he found that was worth taking—from both the palace and The Temple of GOD. And, for good measure, he took hostages. Then he returned to Samaria.

15-16 The rest of the life and times of Jehoash, his significant accomplishments and the fight with Amaziah king of Judah, are all written in *The Chronicles of the Kings of Israel.* Jehoash died and was buried in Samaria in the cemetery of the kings of Israel. His son Jeroboam became the next king.

17-18 Amaziah son of Joash king of Judah continued as king fifteen years after the death of Jehoash son of Jehoahaz king of Israel. The rest of the life and times of Amaziah is written in *The Chronicles of the Kings of Judah.*

19-20 At the last they cooked up a plot against Amaziah in Jerusalem and he had to flee to Lachish. But they tracked him down in Lachish and killed him there. They brought him back on horseback and buried him in Jerusalem, with his ancestors in the City of David.

21-22 Azariah—he was only sixteen years old at the time—was the unanimous choice of the people of Judah to succeed his father Amaziah as king. Following his father's death, he rebuilt and restored Elath to Judah.

Jeroboam II of Israel

23-25 In the fifteenth year of Amaziah son of Joash king of Judah, Jeroboam son of Jehoash became king of Israel in Samaria. He ruled for forty-one years. As far as GOD was concerned he lived an evil life, never deviating an inch from all the sin of Jeroboam son of Nebat, who led Israel into a life of sin. But he did restore the borders of Israel to Lebo Hamath in the far north and to the Dead Sea in the south, matching what GOD, the God of Israel, had pronounced through his servant Jonah son of Amittai, the prophet from Gath Hepher.

26-27 GOD was fully aware of the trouble in Israel, its bitterly hard times. No one was exempt, whether slave or citizen, and no hope of help anywhere was in sight. But GOD wasn't yet ready to blot out the name of Israel from history, so he used Jeroboam son of Jehoash to save them.

28-29 The rest of the life and times of Jeroboam, his victories in battle and how he recovered for Israel both Damascus and Hamath which had belonged to Judah, these are all written in *The Chronicles of the Kings of Israel.* Jeroboam died and was buried with his ancestors in the royal cemetery. His son Zechariah became the next king.

New King James Version

Azariah Reigns in Judah

15 In the twenty-seventh year of Jeroboam king of Israel, Azariah the son of Amaziah, king of Judah, became king. 2He was sixteen years old when he became king, and he reigned fifty-two years in Jerusalem. His mother's name *was* Jecholiah of Jerusalem. 3And he did *what was* right in the sight of the LORD, according to all that his father Amaziah had done, 4except that the high places were not removed; the people still sacrificed and burned incense on the high places. 5Then the LORD struck the king, so that he was a leper until the day of his death; so he dwelt in an isolated house. And Jotham the king's son *was* over the *royal* house, judging the people of the land.

6Now the rest of the acts of Azariah, and all that he did, *are* they not written in the book of the chronicles of the kings of Judah? 7So Azariah rested with his fathers, and they buried him with his fathers in the City of David. Then Jotham his son reigned in his place.

Zechariah Reigns in Israel

8In the thirty-eighth year of Azariah king of Judah, Zechariah the son of Jeroboam reigned over Israel in Samaria six months. 9And he did evil in the sight of the LORD, as his fathers had done; he did not depart from the sins of Jeroboam the son of Nebat, who had made Israel sin. 10Then Shallum the son of Jabesh conspired against him, and struck and killed him in front of the people; and he reigned in his place.

11Now the rest of the acts of Zechariah, indeed they *are* written in the book of the chronicles of the kings of Israel.

12This *was* the word of the LORD which He spoke to Jehu, saying, "Your sons shall sit on the throne of Israel to the fourth *generation*."[a] And so it was.

Shallum Reigns in Israel

13Shallum the son of Jabesh became king in the thirty-ninth year of Uzziah[a] king of Judah; and he reigned a full month in Samaria. 14For Menahem the son of Gadi went up from Tirzah, came to Samaria, and struck Shallum the son of Jabesh in Samaria and killed him; and he reigned in his place.

15Now the rest of the acts of Shallum, and the conspiracy which he led, indeed they *are* written in the book of the chronicles of the kings of Israel. 16Then from Tirzah, Menahem attacked Tiphsah, all who *were* there, and its territory. Because they did not surrender, therefore he attacked *it*. All the women there who were with child he ripped open.

Menahem Reigns in Israel

17In the thirty-ninth year of Azariah king of Judah, Menahem the son of Gadi became king over Israel, *and reigned* ten years in Samaria. 18And he did evil in the sight of the LORD; he did not depart all his days from the sins of Jer-

15:12 [a]2 Kings 10:30 15:13 [a]Called *Azariah* in 14:21ff and 15:1ff

The Message

Azariah (Uzziah) of Judah

1-5 15 In the twenty-seventh year of Jer-
oboam king of Israel, Azariah son of
Amaziah became king in Judah. He was six-
teen years old when he began his rule and
he was king for fifty-two years in Jerusalem.
His mother's name was Jecoliah. She was
from Jerusalem. He did well in the eyes of
GOD, following in the footsteps of his father
Amaziah. But he also failed to get rid of the
local sex-and-religion shrines; they contin-
ued to be popular with the people. GOD af-
flicted the king with a bad skin disease un-
til the day of his death. He lived in the
palace but no longer acted as king; his son
Jotham ran the government and ruled the
country.
6-7 The rest of the life and times of Azariah,
everything he accomplished, is written in
The Chronicles of the Kings of Judah.
Azariah died and was buried with his ances-
tors in the City of David. Jotham his son was
king after him.

Zechariah of Israel

8-9 In the thirty-eighth year of Azariah king of
Judah, Zechariah son of Jeroboam became
king over Israel in Samaria. He lasted only
six months. He lived a bad life before GOD,
no different from his ancestors. He contin-
ued in the line of Jeroboam son of Nebat
who led Israel into a life of sin.
10 Shallum son of Jabesh conspired against
him, assassinated him in public view, and
took over as king.
11-12 The rest of the life and times of Zech-
ariah is written plainly in *The Chronicles of
the Kings of Israel*. That completed the word
of GOD that was given to Jehu, namely, "For
four generations your sons will sit on the
throne of Israel." Zechariah was the fourth.

Shallum of Israel

13 Shallum son of Jabesh became king in the
thirty-ninth year of Azariah king of Judah.
He was king in Samaria for only a month.
14 Menahem son of Gadi came up from
Tirzah to Samaria. He attacked Shallum son
of Jabesh and killed him. He then became
king.
15 The rest of the life and times of Shallum
and the account of the conspiracy are writ-
ten in *The Chronicles of the Kings of Israel*.

Menahem of Israel

16 Using Tirzah as his base, Menahem opened
his reign by smashing Tiphsah, devastating
both the town and its suburbs because they
didn't welcome him with open arms. He sav-
agely ripped open all the pregnant women.
17-18 In the thirty-ninth year of Azariah king of
Judah, Menahem son of Gadi became king
over Israel. He ruled from Samaria for ten
years. As far as GOD was concerned he lived
an evil life. Sin for sin, he repeated the sins

NEW KING JAMES VERSION

oboam the son of Nebat, who had made Israel
sin. [19]Pul[a] king of Assyria came against the
land; and Menahem gave Pul a thousand talents
of silver, that his hand might be with him to
strengthen the kingdom under his control.
[20]And Menahem exacted the money from Israel,
from all the very wealthy, from each man fifty
shekels of silver, to give to the king of Assyria.
So the king of Assyria turned back, and did not
stay there in the land.
[21]Now the rest of the acts of Menahem, and
all that he did, *are* they not written in the book
of the chronicles of the kings of Israel? [22]So
Menahem rested with his fathers. Then
Pekahiah his son reigned in his place.

PEKAHIAH REIGNS IN ISRAEL

[23]In the fiftieth year of Azariah king of Judah,
Pekahiah the son of Menahem became king over
Israel in Samaria, *and reigned* two years. [24]And
he did evil in the sight of the LORD; he did not de-
part from the sins of Jeroboam the son of Nebat,
who had made Israel sin. [25]Then Pekah the son
of Remaliah, an officer of his, conspired against
him and killed him in Samaria, in the citadel of
the king's house, along with Argob and Arieh;
and with him were fifty men of Gilead. He killed
him and reigned in his place.
[26]Now the rest of the acts of Pekahiah, and
all that he did, indeed they *are* written in the
book of the chronicles of the kings of Israel.

PEKAH REIGNS IN ISRAEL

[27]In the fifty-second year of Azariah king of
Judah, Pekah the son of Remaliah became king
over Israel in Samaria, *and reigned* twenty
years. [28]And he did evil in the sight of the LORD;
he did not depart from the sins of Jeroboam the
son of Nebat, who had made Israel sin. [29]In the
days of Pekah king of Israel, Tiglath-Pileser
king of Assyria came and took Ijon, Abel Beth
Maachah, Janoah, Kedesh, Hazor, Gilead, and
Galilee, all the land of Naphtali; and he carried
them captive to Assyria. [30]Then Hoshea the son
of Elah led a conspiracy against Pekah the son
of Remaliah, and struck and killed him; so he
reigned in his place in the twentieth year of
Jotham the son of Uzziah.
[31]Now the rest of the acts of Pekah, and all
that he did, indeed they *are* written in the book
of the chronicles of the kings of Israel.

JOTHAM REIGNS IN JUDAH

[32]In the second year of Pekah the son of Rem-
aliah, king of Israel, Jotham the son of Uzziah,
king of Judah, began to reign. [33]He was twenty-
five years old when he became king, and he
reigned sixteen years in Jerusalem. His
mother's name *was* Jerusha[a] the daughter of
Zadok. [34]And he did *what was* right in the sight
of the LORD; he did according to all that his fa-
ther Uzziah had done. [35]However the high
places were not removed; the people still sacri-
ficed and burned incense on the high places. He
built the Upper Gate of the house of the LORD.

15:19 [a]That is, Tiglath-Pileser III (compare verse 29)
15:33 [a]Spelled *Jerushah* in 2 Chronicles 27:1

THE MESSAGE

of Jeroboam son of Nebat, who led Israel
into a life of sin.

19-20 Then Tiglath-Pileser III king of Assyria showed up and attacked the country. But Menahem made a deal with him: He bought his support by handing over about thirty-seven tons of silver. He raised the money by making every landowner in Israel pay fifty shekels to the king of Assyria. That satisfied the king of Assyria, and he left the country.

21-22 The rest of the life and times of Menahem, everything he did, is written in *The Chronicles of the Kings of Israel.* Menahem died and joined his ancestors. His son Pekahiah became the next king.

PEKAHIAH OF ISRAEL

23-24 In the fiftieth year of Azariah king of Judah, Pekahiah son of Menahem became king of Israel. He ruled in Samaria for two years. In GOD's eyes he lived an evil life. He stuck to the old sin tracks of Jeroboam son of Nebat, who led Israel into a life of sin.

25 And then his military aide Pekah son of Remaliah conspired against him—killed him in cold blood while he was in his private quarters in the royal palace in Samaria. He also killed Argob and Arieh. Fifty Gadites were in on the conspiracy with him. After the murder he became the next king.

26 The rest of the life and times of Pekahiah, everything he did, is written in *The Chronicles of the Kings of Israel.*

PEKAH OF ISRAEL

27-28 In the fifty-second year of Azariah king of Judah, Pekah son of Remaliah became king of Israel in Samaria. He ruled for twenty years. In GOD's view he lived an evil life; he didn't deviate so much as a hair's breadth from the path laid down by Jeroboam son of Nebat, who led Israel into a life of sin.

29 During the reign of Pekah king of Israel, Tiglath-Pileser III king of Assyria invaded the country. He captured Ijon, Abel Beth Maacah, Janoah, Kedesh, Hazor, Gilead, Galilee—the whole country of Naphtali—and took everyone captive to Assyria.

30 But then Hoshea son of Elah mounted a conspiracy against Pekah son of Remaliah. He assassinated him and took over as king. This was in the twentieth year of Jotham son of Uzziah.

31 The rest of the life and times of Pekah, everything he did, is written in *The Chronicles of the Kings of Israel.*

JOTHAM OF JUDAH

32-35 In the second year of Pekah son of Remaliah king of Israel, Jotham son of Uzziah became king in Judah. He was twenty-five years old when he became king and reigned sixteen years in Jerusalem. His mother's name was Jerusha daughter of Zadok. He acted well in GOD's eyes, following in the steps of his father Uzziah. But he didn't interfere with the traffic to the neighborhood sex-and-religion shrines; they continued, as popular as ever. The construction of the High Gate to The Temple of GOD was his work.

NEW KING JAMES VERSION

36Now the rest of the acts of Jotham, and all
that he did, *are* they not written in the book of
the chronicles of the kings of Judah? 37In those
days the LORD began to send Rezin king of Syria
and Pekah the son of Remaliah against Judah.
38So Jotham rested with his fathers, and was
buried with his fathers in the City of David his
father. Then Ahaz his son reigned in his place.

AHAZ REIGNS IN JUDAH

16 In the seventeenth year of Pekah the son of
Remaliah, Ahaz the son of Jotham, king of
Judah, began to reign. 2Ahaz *was* twenty years
old when he became king, and he reigned six-
teen years in Jerusalem; and he did not do *what*
was right in the sight of the LORD his God, as his
father David *had done.* 3But he walked in the
way of the kings of Israel; indeed he made his
son pass through the fire, according to the
abominations of the nations whom the LORD
had cast out from before the children of Israel.
4And he sacrificed and burned incense on the
high places, on the hills, and under every green
tree.
5Then Rezin king of Syria and Pekah the son
of Remaliah, king of Israel, came up to Jerusa-
lem to *make* war; and they besieged Ahaz but
could not overcome *him.* 6At that time Rezin
king of Syria captured Elath for Syria, and
drove the men of Judah from Elath. Then the
Edomites[a] went to Elath, and dwell there to this
day.
7So Ahaz sent messengers to Tiglath-Pileser
king of Assyria, saying, "I *am* your servant and
your son. Come up and save me from the hand
of the king of Syria and from the hand of the
king of Israel, who rise up against me." 8And
Ahaz took the silver and gold that was found in
the house of the LORD, and in the treasuries of
the king's house, and sent *it as* a present to the
king of Assyria. 9So the king of Assyria heeded
him; for the king of Assyria went up against
Damascus and took it, carried *its people* captive
to Kir, and killed Rezin.
10Now King Ahaz went to Damascus to meet
Tiglath-Pileser king of Assyria, and saw an altar
that *was* at Damascus; and King Ahaz sent to
Urijah the priest the design of the altar and its
pattern, according to all its workmanship.
11Then Urijah the priest built an altar according
to all that King Ahaz had sent from Damascus.
So Urijah the priest made *it* before King Ahaz
came back from Damascus. 12And when the
king came back from Damascus, the king saw
the altar; and the king approached the altar and
made offerings on it. 13So he burned his burnt
offering and his grain offering; and he poured
his drink offering and sprinkled the blood of his
peace offerings on the altar. 14He also brought
the bronze altar which *was* before the LORD,
from the front of the temple—from between the
new altar and the house of the LORD—and put it
on the north side of the *new* altar.

16:6 [a]Some ancient authorities read *Syrians.*

THE MESSAGE

36-38 The rest of the life and times of Jotham, the record of his work, is written in *The Chronicles of the Kings of Judah.* It was during these years that GOD began sending Rezin king of Aram and Pekah son of Remaliah to attack Judah. Jotham died and joined his ancestors. They buried him in the family cemetery in the City of David. His son Ahaz was the next king.

AHAZ OF JUDAH

1-4 16 In the seventeenth year of Pekah son of Remaliah, Ahaz son of Jotham became king of Judah. Ahaz was twenty years old when he became king and he ruled for sixteen years in Jerusalem. He didn't behave in the eyes of his GOD; he wasn't at all like his ancestor David. Instead he followed in the track of the kings of Israel. He even indulged in the outrageous practice of "passing his son through the fire"—a truly abominable act he picked up from the pagans GOD had earlier thrown out of the country. He also participated in the activities of the neighborhood sex-and-religion shrines that flourished all over the place.

5 Then Rezin king of Aram and Pekah son of Remaliah king of Israel ganged up against Jerusalem, throwing a siege around the city, but they couldn't make further headway against Ahaz.

6 At about this same time and on another front, the king of Edom recovered the port of Elath and expelled the men of Judah. The Edomites occupied Elath and have been there ever since.

7-8 Ahaz sent envoys to Tiglath-Pileser king of Assyria with this message: "I'm your servant and your son. Come and save me from the heavy-handed invasion of the king of Aram and the king of Israel. They're attacking me right now." Then Ahaz robbed the treasuries of the palace and The Temple of GOD of their gold and silver and sent them to the king of Assyria as a bribe.

9 The king of Assyria responded to him. He attacked and captured Damascus. He deported the people to Nineveh as exiles. Rezin he killed.

10-11 King Ahaz went to meet Tiglath-Pileser king of Assyria in Damascus. The altar in Damascus made a great impression on him. He sent back to Uriah the priest a drawing and set of blueprints of the altar. Uriah the priest built the altar to the specifications that King Ahaz had sent from Damascus. By the time the king returned from Damascus, Uriah had completed the altar.

12-14 The minute the king saw the altar he approached it with reverence and arranged a service of worship with a full course of offerings: Whole-Burnt-Offerings with billows of smoke, Grain-Offerings, libations of Drink-Offerings, the sprinkling of blood from the Peace-Offerings—the works. But the old bronze Altar that signaled the presence of GOD he displaced from its central place and pushed it off to the side of his new altar.

NEW KING JAMES VERSION

15Then King Ahaz commanded Urijah the priest,
saying, "On the great *new* altar burn the morn-
ing burnt offering, the evening grain offering,
the king's burnt sacrifice, and his grain offering,
with the burnt offering of all the people of the
land, their grain offering, and their drink offer-
ings; and sprinkle on it all the blood of the burnt
offering and all the blood of the sacrifice. And
the bronze altar shall be for me to inquire *by*."
16Thus did Urijah the priest, according to all that
King Ahaz commanded.
17And King Ahaz cut off the panels of the
carts, and removed the lavers from them; and he
took down the Sea from the bronze oxen that
were under it, and put it on a pavement of
stones. 18Also he removed the Sabbath pavilion
which they had built in the temple, and he re-
moved the king's outer entrance from the house
of the LORD, on account of the king of Assyria.
19Now the rest of the acts of Ahaz which he
did, *are* they not written in the book of the
chronicles of the kings of Judah? 20So Ahaz
rested with his fathers, and was buried with his
fathers in the City of David. Then Hezekiah his
son reigned in his place.

HOSHEA REIGNS IN ISRAEL

17 In the twelfth year of Ahaz king of Judah,
Hoshea the son of Elah became king of Is-
rael in Samaria, *and he reigned* nine years. 2And
he did evil in the sight of the LORD, but not as the
kings of Israel who were before him. 3Shal-
maneser king of Assyria came up against him;
and Hoshea became his vassal, and paid him
tribute money. 4And the king of Assyria uncov-
ered a conspiracy by Hoshea; for he had sent
messengers to So, king of Egypt, and brought no
tribute to the king of Assyria, as *he had done*
year by year. Therefore the king of Assyria shut
him up, and bound him in prison.

ISRAEL CARRIED CAPTIVE TO ASSYRIA

5Now the king of Assyria went throughout
all the land, and went up to Samaria and be-
sieged it for three years. 6In the ninth year of
Hoshea, the king of Assyria took Samaria and
carried Israel away to Assyria, and placed them
in Halah and by the Habor, the River of Gozan,
and in the cities of the Medes.
7For so it was that the children of Israel had
sinned against the LORD their God, who had
brought them up out of the land of Egypt, from
under the hand of Pharaoh king of Egypt; and
they had feared other gods, 8and had walked in
the statutes of the nations whom the LORD had
cast out from before the children of Israel, and
of the kings of Israel, which they had made.
9Also the children of Israel secretly did against
the LORD their God things that *were* not right,
and they built for themselves high places in all
their cities, from watchtower to fortified city.
10They set up for themselves *sacred* pillars and
wooden images[a] on every high hill and under

17:10 [a]Hebrew *Asherim*, Canaanite deities

THE MESSAGE

15 Then King Ahaz ordered Uriah the priest:
"From now on offer all the sacrifices on the
new altar, the great altar: morning Whole-
Burnt-Offerings, evening Grain-Offerings,
the king's Whole-Burnt-Offerings and
Grain-Offerings, the people's Whole-Burnt-
Offerings and Grain-Offerings, and also
their Drink-Offerings. Splash all the blood
from the burnt offerings and sacrifices
against this altar. The old bronze Altar will
be for my personal use.
16 The priest Uriah followed King Ahaz's
orders to the letter.
17-18 Then King Ahaz proceeded to plunder
The Temple furniture of all its bronze. He
stripped the bronze from The Temple fur-
nishings, even salvaged the four bronze
oxen that supported the huge basin, The
Sea, and set The Sea unceremoniously on
the stone pavement. Finally, he removed any
distinctive features from within The Temple
that were offensive to the king of Assyria.
19-20 The rest of the life and times of Ahaz is
written in *The Chronicles of the Kings of Ju-
dah*. Ahaz died and was buried with his an-
cestors in the City of David. His son
Hezekiah became the next king.

HOSHEA OF ISRAEL

1-2 17 In the twelfth year of Ahaz king of Ju-
dah, Hoshea son of Elah became king
of Israel. He ruled in Samaria for nine years.
As far as GOD was concerned, he lived a bad
life, but not nearly as bad as the kings who
had preceded him.
3-5 Then Shalmaneser king of Assyria at-
tacked. Hoshea was already a puppet of the
Assyrian king and regularly sent him trib-
ute, but Shalmaneser discovered that
Hoshea had been operating traitorously be-
hind his back—having worked out a deal
with King So of Egypt. And, adding insult to
injury, Hoshea was way behind on his an-
nual payments of tribute to Assyria. So the
king of Assyria arrested him and threw him
in prison, then proceeded to invade the en-
tire country. He attacked Samaria and threw
up a siege against it. The siege lasted three
years.
6 In the ninth year of Hoshea's reign the
king of Assyria captured Samaria and took
the people into exile in Assyria. He relo-
cated them in Halah, in Gozan along the Ha-
bor River, and in the towns of the Medes.
7-12 The exile came about because of sin: The
children of Israel sinned against GOD, their
God, who had delivered them from Egypt
and the brutal oppression of Pharaoh king
of Egypt. They took up with other gods, fell
in with the ways of life of the pagan nations
GOD had chased off, and went along with
whatever their kings did. They did all kinds
of things on the sly, things offensive to their
GOD, then openly and shamelessly built lo-
cal sex-and-religion shrines at every avail-
able site. They set up their sex-and-religion
symbols at practically every crossroads.
Everywhere you looked there was smoke
from their pagan offerings to the deities—

New King James Version

every green tree. 11 There they burned incense on all the high places, like the nations whom the LORD had carried away before them; and they did wicked things to provoke the LORD to anger, 12 for they served idols, of which the LORD had said to them, "You shall not do this thing."

13 Yet the LORD testified against Israel and against Judah, by all of His prophets, every seer, saying, "Turn from your evil ways, and keep My commandments *and* My statutes, according to all the law which I commanded your fathers, and which I sent to you by My servants the prophets." 14 Nevertheless they would not hear, but stiffened their necks, like the necks of their fathers, who did not believe in the LORD their God. 15 And they rejected His statutes and His covenant that He had made with their fathers, and His testimonies which He had testified against them; they followed idols, became idolaters, and *went* after the nations who *were* all around them, *concerning* whom the LORD had charged them that they should not do like them. 16 So they left all the commandments of the LORD their God, made for themselves a molded image *and* two calves, made a wooden image and worshiped all the host of heaven, and served Baal. 17 And they caused their sons and daughters to pass through the fire, practiced witchcraft and soothsaying, and sold themselves to do evil in the sight of the LORD, to provoke Him to anger. 18 Therefore the LORD was very angry with Israel, and removed them from His sight; there was none left but the tribe of Judah alone.

19 Also Judah did not keep the commandments of the LORD their God, but walked in the statutes of Israel which they made. 20 And the LORD rejected all the descendants of Israel, afflicted them, and delivered them into the hand of plunderers, until He had cast them from His sight. 21 For He tore Israel from the house of David, and they made Jeroboam the son of Nebat king. Then Jeroboam drove Israel from following the LORD, and made them commit a great sin. 22 For the children of Israel walked in all the sins of Jeroboam which he did; they did not depart from them, 23 until the LORD removed Israel out of His sight, as He had said by all His servants the prophets. So Israel was carried away from their own land to Assyria, *as it is* to this day.

Assyria Resettles Samaria

24 Then the king of Assyria brought *people* from Babylon, Cuthah, Ava, Hamath, and from Sepharvaim, and placed *them* in the cities of Samaria instead of the children of Israel; and

The Message

the identical offerings that had gotten the pagan nations off into exile. They had accumulated a long list of evil actions and GOD was fed up, fed up with their persistent worship of gods carved out of deadwood or shaped out of clay, even though GOD had plainly said, "Don't do this—ever!"

13 GOD had taken a stand against Israel and Judah, speaking clearly through countless holy prophets and seers time and time again, "Turn away from your evil way of life. Do what I tell you and have been telling you in The Revelation I gave your ancestors and of which I've kept reminding you ever since through my servants the prophets."

14-15 But they wouldn't listen. If anything, they were even more bullheaded than their stubborn ancestors, if that's possible. They were contemptuous of his instructions, the solemn and holy covenant he had made with their ancestors, and of his repeated reminders and warnings. They lived a "nothing" life and became "nothings"—just like the pagan peoples all around them. They were well-warned: GOD said, "Don't!" but they did it anyway.

16-17 They threw out everything GOD, their God, had told them, and replaced him with two statue-gods shaped like bull-calves and then a phallic pole for the whore goddess Asherah. They worshiped cosmic forces—sky gods and goddesses—and frequented the sex-and-religion shrines of Baal. They even sank so low as to offer their own sons and daughters as sacrificial burnt offerings! They indulged in all the black arts of magic and sorcery. In short, they prostituted themselves to every kind of evil available to them. And GOD had had enough.

18-20 GOD was so thoroughly angry that he got rid of them, got them out of the country for good until only one tribe was left—Judah. (Judah, actually, wasn't much better, for Judah also failed to keep GOD's commands, falling into the same way of life that Israel had adopted.) GOD rejected everyone connected with Israel, made life hard for them, and permitted anyone with a mind to exploit them to do so. And then this final No as he threw them out of his sight.

21-23 Back at the time that God ripped Israel out of their place in the family of David, they had made Jeroboam son of Nebat king. Jeroboam debauched Israel—turned them away from serving GOD and led them into a life of total sin. The children of Israel went along with all the sins that Jeroboam did, never murmured so much as a word of protest. In the end, GOD spoke a final No to Israel and turned his back on them. He had given them fair warning, and plenty of time, through the preaching of all his servants the prophets. Then he exiled Israel from her land to Assyria. And that's where they are now.

24-25 The king of Assyria brought in people from Babylon, Cuthah, Avva, Hamath, and Sepharvaim, and relocated them in the towns of Samaria, replacing the exiled Is-

New King James Version

they took possession of Samaria and dwelt in its cities. 25And it was so, at the beginning of their dwelling there, *that* they did not fear the LORD; therefore the LORD sent lions among them, which killed *some* of them. 26So they spoke to the king of Assyria, saying, "The nations whom you have removed and placed in the cities of Samaria do not know the rituals of the God of the land; therefore He has sent lions among them, and indeed, they are killing them because they do not know the rituals of the God of the land." 27Then the king of Assyria commanded, saying, "Send there one of the priests whom you brought from there; let him go and dwell there, and let him teach them the rituals of the God of the land." 28Then one of the priests whom they had carried away from Samaria came and dwelt in Bethel, and taught them how they should fear the LORD.

29However every nation continued to make gods of its own, and put *them* in the shrines on the high places which the Samaritans had made, *every* nation in the cities where they dwelt. 30The men of Babylon made Succoth Benoth, the men of Cuth made Nergal, the men of Hamath made Ashima, 31and the Avites made Nibhaz and Tartak; and the Sepharvites burned their children in fire to Adrammelech and Anammelech, the gods of Sepharvaim. 32So they feared the LORD, and from every class they appointed for themselves priests of the high places, who sacrificed for them in the shrines of the high places. 33They feared the LORD, yet served their own gods—according to the rituals of the nations from among whom they were carried away.

34To this day they continue practicing the former rituals; they do not fear the LORD, nor do they follow their statutes or their ordinances, or the law and commandment which the LORD had commanded the children of Jacob, whom He named Israel, 35with whom the LORD had made a covenant and charged them, saying: "You shall not fear other gods, nor bow down to them nor serve them nor sacrifice to them; 36but the LORD, who brought you up from the land of Egypt with great power and an outstretched arm, Him you shall fear, Him you shall worship, and to Him you shall offer sacrifice. 37And the statutes, the ordinances, the law, and the commandment which He wrote for you, you shall be careful to observe forever; you shall not fear other gods. 38And the covenant that I have made with you, you shall not forget, nor shall you fear other gods. 39But the LORD your God you shall fear; and He will deliver you from the hand of all your enemies."

The Message

raelites. They moved in as if they owned the place and made themselves at home. When the Assyrians first moved in, GOD was just another god to them; they neither honored nor worshiped him. Then GOD sent lions among them and people were mauled and killed.

26 This message was then sent back to the king of Assyria: "The people you brought in to occupy the towns of Samaria don't know what's expected of them from the god of the land, and now he's sent lions and they're killing people right and left because nobody knows what the god of the land expects of them."

27 The king of Assyria ordered, "Send back some priests who were taken into exile from there. They can go back and live there and instruct the people in what the god of the land expects of them."

28 One of the priests who had been exiled from Samaria came back and moved into Bethel. He taught them how to honor and worship GOD.

29-31 But each people that Assyria had settled went ahead anyway making its own gods and setting them up in the neighborhood sex-and-religion shrines that the citizens of Samaria had left behind—a local custom-made god for each people:

for Babylon, Succoth Benoth;
for Cuthah, Nergal;
for Hamath, Ashima;
for Avva, Nibhaz and Tartak;
for Sepharvaim, Adrammelech and
Anammelech (people
burned their children in sacrificial
offerings to these gods!).

32-33 They honored and worshiped GOD, but not exclusively—they also appointed all sorts of priests, regardless of qualification, to conduct a variety of rites at the local fertility shrines. They honored and worshiped GOD, but they also kept up their devotions to the old gods of the places they had come from.

34-39 And they're still doing it, still worshiping any old god that has nostalgic appeal to them. They don't really worship GOD—they don't take seriously what he says regarding how to behave and what to believe, what he revealed to the children of Jacob whom he named Israel. GOD made a covenant with his people and ordered them, "Don't honor other gods: Don't worship them, don't serve them, don't offer sacrifices to them. Worship GOD, the God who delivered you from Egypt in great and personal power. Reverence and fear him. Worship him. Sacrifice to him. And only him! All the things he had written down for you, directing you in what to believe and how to behave—well, do them for as long as you live. And whatever you do, *don't worship other gods!* And the covenant he made with you, don't forget your part in that. *And don't worship other gods!* Worship GOD, and GOD only—he's the one who will save you from enemy oppression."

New King James Version

40However they did not obey, but they followed their former rituals. 41So these nations feared the LORD, yet served their carved images; also their children and their children's children have continued doing as their fathers did, even to this day.

Hezekiah Reigns in Judah

18 Now it came to pass in the third year of Hoshea the son of Elah, king of Israel, *that* Hezekiah the son of Ahaz, king of Judah, began to reign. 2He was twenty-five years old when he became king, and he reigned twenty-nine years in Jerusalem. His mother's name *was* Abi[a] the daughter of Zechariah. 3And he did *what was* right in the sight of the LORD, according to all that his father David had done.

4He removed the high places and broke the *sacred* pillars, cut down the wooden image[a] and broke in pieces the bronze serpent that Moses had made; for until those days the children of Israel burned incense to it, and called it Nehushtan.[b] 5He trusted in the LORD God of Israel, so that after him was none like him among all the kings of Judah, nor who were before him. 6For he held fast to the LORD; he did not depart from following Him, but kept His commandments, which the LORD had commanded Moses. 7The LORD was with him; he prospered wherever he went. And he rebelled against the king of Assyria and did not serve him. 8He subdued the Philistines, as far as Gaza and its territory, from watchtower to fortified city.

9Now it came to pass in the fourth year of King Hezekiah, which *was* the seventh year of Hoshea the son of Elah, king of Israel, *that* Shalmaneser king of Assyria came up against Samaria and besieged it. 10And at the end of three years they took it. In the sixth year of Hezekiah, that *is,* the ninth year of Hoshea king of Israel, Samaria was taken. 11Then the king of Assyria carried Israel away captive to Assyria, and put them in Halah and by the Habor, the River of Gozan, and in the cities of the Medes, 12because they did not obey the voice of the LORD their God, but transgressed His covenant *and* all that Moses the servant of the LORD had commanded; and they would neither hear nor do *them.*

13And in the fourteenth year of King Hezekiah, Sennacherib king of Assyria came up against all the fortified cities of Judah and took them. 14Then Hezekiah king of Judah sent to the king of Assyria at Lachish, saying, "I have done wrong; turn away from me; whatever you impose on me I will pay." And the king of Assyria assessed Hezekiah king of Judah three hundred talents of silver and thirty talents of gold. 15So Hezekiah gave *him* all the silver that was found in the house of the LORD and in the treasuries of the king's house. 16At that time Hezekiah stripped *the gold from* the doors of the temple of the LORD, and *from* the pillars which Hezekiah king of Judah had overlaid, and gave it to the king of Assyria.

18:2 [a]Called *Abijah* in 2 Chronicles 29:1ff **18:4** [a]Hebrew *Asherah,* a Canaanite goddess [b]Literally *Bronze Thing*

The Message

40-41 But they didn't pay any attention. They kept doing what they'd always done. As it turned out, all the time these people were putting on a front of worshiping GOD, they were at the same time involved with their local idols. And they're still doing it. Like father, like son.

Hezekiah of Judah

1-4 18 In the third year of Hoshea son of Elah king of Israel, Hezekiah son of Ahaz began his rule over Judah. He was twenty-five years old when he became king and he ruled for twenty-nine years in Jerusalem. His mother's name was Abijah daughter of Zechariah. In GOD's opinion he was a good king; he kept to the standards of his ancestor David. He got rid of the local fertility shrines, smashed the phallic stone monuments, and cut down the sex-and-religion Asherah groves. As a final stroke he pulverized the ancient bronze serpent that Moses had made; at that time the Israelites had taken up the practice of sacrificing to it—they had even dignified it with a name, Nehushtan (The Old Serpent).

5-6 Hezekiah put his whole trust in the GOD of Israel. There was no king quite like him, either before or after. He held fast to GOD—never loosened his grip—and obeyed to the letter everything GOD had commanded Moses. And GOD, for his part, held fast to him through all his adventures.

7-8 He revolted against the king of Assyria; he refused to serve him one more day. And he drove back the Philistines, whether in sentry outposts or fortress cities, all the way to Gaza and its borders.

9-11 In the fourth year of Hezekiah and the seventh year of Hoshea son of Elah king of Israel, Shalmaneser king of Assyria attacked Samaria. He threw a siege around it and after three years captured it. It was in the sixth year of Hezekiah and the ninth year of Hoshea that Samaria fell to Assyria. The king of Assyria took Israel into exile and relocated them in Halah, in Gozan on the Habor River, and in towns of the Medes.

12 All this happened because they wouldn't listen to the voice of their GOD and treated his covenant with careless contempt. They refused either to listen or do a word of what Moses, the servant of GOD, commanded.

13-14 In the fourteenth year of King Hezekiah, Sennacherib king of Assyria attacked all the outlying fortress cities of Judah and captured them. King Hezekiah sent a message to the king of Assyria at his headquarters in Lachish: "I've done wrong; I admit it. Pull back your army; I'll pay whatever tribute you set."

14-16 The king of Assyria demanded tribute from Hezekiah king of Judah—eleven tons of silver and a ton of gold. Hezekiah turned over all the silver he could find in The Temple of GOD and in the palace treasuries. Hezekiah even took down the doors of The Temple of GOD and the doorposts that he had overlaid with gold and gave them to the king of Assyria.

NEW KING JAMES VERSION

SENNACHERIB BOASTS AGAINST THE LORD

17Then the king of Assyria sent *the* Tartan,[a]
the Rabsaris,[b] *and the* Rabshakeh[c] from
Lachish, with a great army against Jerusalem,
to King Hezekiah. And they went up and came
to Jerusalem. When they had come up, they
went and stood by the aqueduct from the upper
pool, which *was* on the highway to the Fuller's
Field. 18And when they had called to the king,
Eliakim the son of Hilkiah, who *was* over the
household, Shebna the scribe, and Joah the son
of Asaph, the recorder, came out to them. 19Then
the Rabshakeh said to them, "Say now to
Hezekiah, 'Thus says the great king, the king of
Assyria: "What confidence *is* this in which you
trust? 20You speak of *having* plans and power
for war; but *they are* mere words. And in whom
do you trust, that you rebel against me? 21Now
look! You are trusting in the staff of this broken
reed, Egypt, on which if a man leans, it will go
into his hand and pierce it. So *is* Pharaoh king
of Egypt to all who trust in him. 22But if you say
to me, 'We trust in the LORD our God,' *is* it not He
whose high places and whose altars Hezekiah
has taken away, and said to Judah and Jerusa-
lem, 'You shall worship before this altar in
Jerusalem'?" ' 23Now therefore, I urge you, give
a pledge to my master the king of Assyria, and I
will give you two thousand horses—if you are
able on your part to put riders on them! 24How
then will you repel one captain of the least of
my master's servants, and put your trust in
Egypt for chariots and horsemen? 25Have I now
come up without the LORD against this place to
destroy it? The LORD said to me, 'Go up against
this land, and destroy it.' "

26Then Eliakim the son of Hilkiah, Shebna,
and Joah said to *the* Rabshakeh, "Please speak
to your servants in Aramaic, for we understand
it; and do not speak to us in Hebrew[a] in the
hearing of the people who *are* on the wall."

27But *the* Rabshakeh said to them, "Has my
master sent me to your master and to you to
speak these words, and not to the men who sit
on the wall, who will eat and drink their own
waste with you?"

28Then *the* Rabshakeh stood and called out
with a loud voice in Hebrew, and spoke, saying,
"Hear the word of the great king, the king of As-
syria! 29Thus says the king: 'Do not let Hezekiah
deceive you, for he shall not be able to deliver
you from his hand; 30nor let Hezekiah make you
trust in the LORD, saying, "The LORD will surely
deliver us; this city shall not be given into the
hand of the king of Assyria." ' 31Do not listen to
Hezekiah; for thus says the king of Assyria:
'Make *peace* with me by a present and come out

18:17 [a]A title, probably *Commander in Chief* [b]A title, probably *Chief Officer* [c]A title, probably *Chief of Staff* or *Governor*
18:26 [a]Literally *Judean*

THE MESSAGE

17 So the king of Assyria sent his top three military chiefs (the Tartan, the Rabsaris, and the Rabshakeh) from Lachish with a strong military force to King Hezekiah in Jerusalem. When they arrived at Jerusalem, they stopped at the aqueduct of the Upper Pool on the road to the laundry commons.

18 They called loudly for the king. Eliakim son of Hilkiah who was in charge of the palace, Shebna the royal secretary, and Joah son of Asaph the court historian went out to meet them.

19-22 The third officer, the Rabshakeh, was spokesman. He said, "Tell Hezekiah: A message from The Great King, the king of Assyria: You're living in a world of make-believe, of pious fantasy. Do you think that mere words are any substitute for military strategy and troops? Now that you've revolted against me, who can you expect to help you? You thought Egypt would, but Egypt's nothing but a paper tiger—one puff of wind and she collapses; Pharaoh king of Egypt is nothing but bluff and bluster. Or are you going to tell me, 'We rely on GOD'? But Hezekiah has just eliminated most of the people's access to God by getting rid of all the local God-shrines, ordering everyone in Judah and Jerusalem, 'You must worship at the Jerusalem altar only.'

23-24 "So be reasonable. Make a deal with my master, the king of Assyria. I'll give you two thousand horses if you think you can provide riders for them. You can't do it? Well, then, how do you think you're going to turn back even one raw buck private from my master's troops? How long are you going to hold on to that figment of your imagination, these hoped-for Egyptian chariots and horses?

25 "Do you think I've come up here to destroy this country without the express approval of GOD? The fact is that GOD expressly ordered me, 'Attack and destroy this country!' "

26 Eliakim son of Hilkiah and Shebna and Joah said to the Rabshakeh, "Please, speak to us in the Aramaic language. We understand Aramaic. Don't speak in Hebrew—everyone crowded on the city wall can hear you."

27 But the Rabshakeh said, "We weren't sent with a private message to your master and you; this is public—a message to everyone within earshot. After all, they're involved in this as well as you; if you don't come to terms, they'll be eating their own turds and drinking their own pee right along with you."

28-32 Then he stepped forward and spoke in Hebrew loud enough for everyone to hear, "Listen carefully to the words of The Great King, the king of Assyria: Don't let Hezekiah fool you; he can't save you. And don't let Hezekiah give you that line about trusting in GOD, telling you, 'GOD will save us—this city will never be abandoned to the king of Assyria.' Don't listen to Hezekiah—he doesn't know what he's talking about.

NEW KING JAMES VERSION

to me; and every one of you eat from his own vine and every one from his own fig tree, and every one of you drink the waters of his own cistern; 32until I come and take you away to a land like your own land, a land of grain and new wine, a land of bread and vineyards, a land of olive groves and honey, that you may live and not die. But do not listen to Hezekiah, lest he persuade you, saying, "The LORD will deliver us." 33Has any of the gods of the nations at all delivered its land from the hand of the king of Assyria? 34Where *are* the gods of Hamath and Arpad? Where *are* the gods of Sepharvaim and Hena and Ivah? Indeed, have they delivered Samaria from my hand? 35Who among all the gods of the lands have delivered their countries from my hand, that the LORD should deliver Jerusalem from my hand?' "

36But the people held their peace and answered him not a word; for the king's commandment was, "Do not answer him." 37Then Eliakim the son of Hilkiah, who *was* over the household, Shebna the scribe, and Joah the son of Asaph, the recorder, came to Hezekiah with *their* clothes torn, and told him the words of *the* Rabshakeh.

ISAIAH ASSURES DELIVERANCE

19 And so it was, when King Hezekiah heard *it*, that he tore his clothes, covered himself with sackcloth, and went into the house of the LORD. 2Then he sent Eliakim, who *was* over the household, Shebna the scribe, and the elders of the priests, covered with sackcloth, to Isaiah the prophet, the son of Amoz. 3And they said to him, "Thus says Hezekiah: 'This day *is* a day of trouble, and rebuke, and blasphemy; for the children have come to birth, but *there is* no strength to bring them forth. 4It may be that the LORD your God will hear all the words of *the* Rabshakeh, whom his master the king of Assyria has sent to reproach the living God, and will rebuke the words which the LORD your God has heard. Therefore lift up *your* prayer for the remnant that is left.' "

5So the servants of King Hezekiah came to Isaiah. 6And Isaiah said to them, "Thus you shall say to your master, 'Thus says the LORD: "Do not be afraid of the words which you have heard, with which the servants of the king of Assyria have blasphemed Me. 7Surely I will send a spirit upon him, and he shall hear a rumor and return to his own land; and I will cause him to fall by the sword in his own land." ' "

SENNACHERIB'S THREAT AND HEZEKIAH'S PRAYER

8Then *the* Rabshakeh returned and found the king of Assyria warring against Libnah, for he heard that he had departed from Lachish. 9And the king heard concerning Tirhakah king of Ethiopia, "Look, he has come out to make war with you." So he again sent messengers to Hezekiah, saying, 10"Thus you shall speak to Hezekiah king of Judah, saying: 'Do not let your God in whom you trust deceive you, saying,

THE MESSAGE

Listen to the king of Assyria—deal with me
and live the good life; I'll guarantee every-
one your own plot of ground—a garden and
a well! I'll take you to a land sweeter by far
than this one, a land of grain and wine,
bread and vineyards, olive orchards and
honey. You only live once—so live, really
live!
32-35 "No. Don't listen to Hezekiah. Don't lis-
ten to his lies, telling you 'GOD will save us.'
Has there ever been a god anywhere who
delivered anyone from the king of Assyria?
Where are the gods of Hamath and Arpad?
Where are the gods of Sepharvaim, Hena,
and Ivvah? And Samaria—did their gods
save them? Can you name a god who saved
anyone anywhere from me, the king of As-
syria? So what makes you think that GOD
can save Jerusalem from me?"
36 The people were silent. No one spoke a
word for the king had ordered, "Don't any-
one say a word—not one word!"
37 Then Eliakim son of Hilkiah, the palace
administrator, and Shebna the royal secre-
tary, and Joah son of Asaph the court histo-
rian went back to Hezekiah. They had
ripped their robes in despair; they reported
to Hezekiah the speech of the Rabshakeh.

1-3 19 When Hezekiah heard it all, he too
ripped his robes apart and dressed
himself in rough burlap. Then he went into
The Temple of GOD. He sent Eliakim, who
was in charge of the palace, Shebna the sec-
retary, and the senior priests, all of them
dressed in rough burlap, to the prophet
Isaiah son of Amoz. They said to him, "A
message from Hezekiah: 'This is a black
day, a terrible day—doomsday!

> Babies poised to be born,
> No strength to birth them.

4 " 'Maybe GOD, your God, has been listen-
ing to the blasphemous speech of the Rab-
shakeh who was sent by the king of Assyria,
his master, to humiliate the living God;
maybe GOD, your God, won't let him get by
with such talk; and you, maybe you will lift
up prayers for what's left of these people.' "
5 That's the message King Hezekiah's ser-
vants delivered to Isaiah.
6-7 Isaiah answered them, "Tell your master,
'GOD's word: Don't be at all concerned
about what you've heard from the king of
Assyria's bootlicking errand boys—these
outrageous blasphemies. Here's what I'm
going to do: Afflict him with self-doubt. He's
going to hear a rumor and, frightened for
his life, retreat to his own country. Once
there, I'll see to it that he gets killed.' "
8-13 The Rabshakeh left and found that the
king of Assyria had pulled up stakes from
Lachish and was now fighting against Lib-
nah. Then Sennacherib heard that Tirhakah
king of Cush was on his way to fight against
him. So he sent another envoy with orders
to deliver this message to Hezekiah king of
Judah: "Don't let that god that you think so

NEW KING JAMES VERSION

"Jerusalem shall not be given into the hand of
the king of Assyria." [11]Look! You have heard
what the kings of Assyria have done to all lands
by utterly destroying them; and shall you be de-
livered? [12]Have the gods of the nations delivered
those whom my fathers have destroyed, Gozan
and Haran and Rezeph, and the people of Eden
who *were* in Telassar? [13]Where *is* the king of
Hamath, the king of Arpad, and the king of the
city of Sepharvaim, Hena, and Ivah?' "

[14]And Hezekiah received the letter from the
hand of the messengers, and read it; and
Hezekiah went up to the house of the LORD, and
spread it before the LORD. [15]Then Hezekiah
prayed before the LORD, and said: "O LORD God
of Israel, *the One* who dwells *between* the
cherubim, You are God, You alone, of all the
kingdoms of the earth. You have made heaven
and earth. [16]Incline Your ear, O LORD, and hear;
open Your eyes, O LORD, and see; and hear the
words of Sennacherib, which he has sent to re-
proach the living God. [17]Truly, LORD, the kings
of Assyria have laid waste the nations and their
lands, [18]and have cast their gods into the fire; for
they *were* not gods, but the work of men's
hands—wood and stone. Therefore they de-
stroyed them. [19]Now therefore, O LORD our God,
I pray, save us from his hand, that all the king-
doms of the earth may know that You *are* the
LORD God, You alone."

THE WORD OF THE LORD CONCERNING SENNACHERIB

[20]Then Isaiah the son of Amoz sent to
Hezekiah, saying, "Thus says the LORD God of
Israel: 'Because you have prayed to Me against
Sennacherib king of Assyria, I have heard.'
[21]This *is* the word which the LORD has spoken
concerning him:

'The virgin, the daughter of Zion,
Has despised you, laughed you to scorn;
The daughter of Jerusalem
Has shaken *her* head behind your back!

[22]'Whom have you reproached and
blasphemed?
Against whom have you raised *your* voice,
And lifted up your eyes on high?
Against the Holy *One* of Israel.
[23]By your messengers you have reproached
the Lord,
And said: "By the multitude of my chariots
I have come up to the height of the
mountains,
To the limits of Lebanon;
I will cut down its tall cedars
And its choice cypress trees;
I will enter the extremity of its borders,
To its fruitful forest.

THE MESSAGE

much of keep stringing you along with the
line, 'Jerusalem will never fall to the king of
Assyria.' That's a barefaced lie. You know
the track record of the kings of Assyria—
country after country laid waste, devas-
tated. And what makes you think you'll be
an exception? Take a good look at these
wasted nations, destroyed by my ancestors;
did their gods do them any good? Look at
Gozan, Haran, Rezeph, the people of Eden
at Tel Assar. Ruins. And what's left of the
king of Hamath, the king of Arpad, the king
of Sepharvaim, of Hena, of Ivvah? Bones."

14-15 Hezekiah took the letter from the envoy
and read it. He went to The Temple of GOD
and spread it out before GOD. And Hezekiah
prayed—oh, how he prayed!

GOD, God of Israel, seated
in majesty on the cherubim-throne.
You are the one and only God,
sovereign over all kingdoms on earth,
Maker of heaven,
maker of earth.
16 Open your ears, GOD, and listen,
open your eyes and look.
Look at this letter Sennacherib has sent,
a brazen insult to the living God!
17 The facts are true, O GOD: The kings of
Assyria
have laid waste countries and
kingdoms.
18 Huge bonfires they made of their gods,
their
no-gods hand-made from wood and
stone.
19 But now O GOD, *our* God,
save us from raw Assyrian power;
Make all the kingdoms on earth know
that you are GOD, the one and only God.

20-21 It wasn't long before Isaiah son of Amoz
sent word to Hezekiah:

GOD's word: You've prayed to me regarding
Sennacherib king of Assyria; I've heard
your prayer. This is my response to him:

The Virgin Daughter of Zion
holds you in utter contempt;
Daughter Jerusalem
thinks you're nothing but scum.
22 Who do you think it is you've insulted?
Who do you think you've been
bad-mouthing?
Before whom do you suppose you've
been strutting?
The Holy One of Israel, that's who!
23 You dispatched your errand boys
to humiliate the Master.
You bragged, "With my army of chariots
I've climbed the highest mountains,
snow-peaked alpine Lebanon
mountains!
I've cut down its giant cedars,
chopped down its prize pine trees.
I've traveled the world,
visited the finest forest retreats.

NEW KING JAMES VERSION

24I have dug and drunk strange water,
And with the soles of my feet I have dried up
All the brooks of defense."

25'Did you not hear long ago
How I made it,
From ancient times that I formed it?
Now I have brought it to pass,
That you should be
For crushing fortified cities *into* heaps of ruins.
26Therefore their inhabitants had little power;
They were dismayed and confounded;
They were *as* the grass of the field
And the green herb,
As the grass on the housetops
And *grain* blighted before it is grown.

27'But I know your dwelling place,
Your going out and your coming in,
And your rage against Me.
28Because your rage against Me and your tumult
Have come up to My ears,
Therefore I will put My hook in your nose
And My bridle in your lips,
And I will turn you back
By the way which you came.

29'This *shall be* a sign to you:

You shall eat this year such as grows of itself,
And in the second year what springs from the same;
Also in the third year sow and reap,
Plant vineyards and eat the fruit of them.
30And the remnant who have escaped of the house of Judah
Shall again take root downward,
And bear fruit upward.
31For out of Jerusalem shall go a remnant,
And those who escape from Mount Zion.
The zeal of the LORD of hosts[a] will do this.'

32"Therefore thus says the LORD concerning the king of Assyria:

'He shall not come into this city,
Nor shoot an arrow there,
Nor come before it with shield,
Nor build a siege mound against it.
33By the way that he came,
By the same shall he return;
And he shall not come into this city,'
Says the LORD.
34'For I will defend this city, to save it
For My own sake and for My servant David's sake.'"

SENNACHERIB'S DEFEAT AND DEATH

35And it came to pass on a certain night that
the angel[a] of the LORD went out, and killed in the
camp of the Assyrians one hundred and eighty-

19:31 [a]Following many Hebrew manuscripts and ancient versions (compare Isaiah 37:32); Masoretic Text omits *of hosts*.
19:35 [a]Or *Angel*

THE MESSAGE

24 I've dug wells in faraway places
and drunk their exotic waters;
I've waded and splashed barefoot
in the rivers of Egypt."

25 Did it never occur to you
that I'm behind all this?
Long, long ago I drew up the plans,
and now I've gone into action,
Using you as a doomsday weapon,
reducing proud cities to piles of rubble,
26 Leaving their people dispirited,
slumped shoulders, limp souls.
Useless as weeds, fragile as grass,
insubstantial as wind-blown chaff.
27 I know when you sit down, when you come
and when you go;
And, yes, I've marked every one
of your temper tantrums against me.
28 It's because of your temper,
your blasphemous foul temper,
That I'm putting my hook in your nose
and my bit in your mouth
And turning you back
to where you came from.

29 And this, Hezekiah, will be for you the confirming sign:

This year you'll eat the gleanings, next year
whatever you can beg, borrow, or steal;
But the third year you'll sow and harvest,
plant vineyards and eat grapes.
30 A remnant of the family of Judah yet again
will sink down roots and raise up fruit.
31 The remnant will come from Jerusalem,
the survivors from Mount Zion.
The Zeal of GOD
will make it happen.

32 To sum up, this is what GOD says regarding the king of Assyria:

He won't enter this city,
nor shoot so much as a single arrow there;
Won't brandish a shield,
won't even begin to set siege;
33 He'll go home by the same road he came;
he won't enter this city. GOD's word!
34 I'll shield this city, I'll save this city,
for my sake and for David's sake.

35 And it so happened that that very night
an angel of GOD came and massacred
185,000 Assyrians. When the people of

NEW KING JAMES VERSION

five thousand; and when *people* arose early in the morning, there were the corpses—all dead. 36 So Sennacherib king of Assyria departed and went away, returned *home,* and remained at Nineveh. 37 Now it came to pass, as he was worshiping in the temple of Nisroch his god, that his sons Adrammelech and Sharezer struck him down with the sword; and they escaped into the land of Ararat. Then Esarhaddon his son reigned in his place.

HEZEKIAH'S LIFE EXTENDED

20 In those days Hezekiah was sick and near death. And Isaiah the prophet, the son of Amoz, went to him and said to him, "Thus says the LORD: 'Set your house in order, for you shall die, and not live.' "

2 Then he turned his face toward the wall, and prayed to the LORD, saying, 3 "Remember now, O LORD, I pray, how I have walked before You in truth and with a loyal heart, and have done *what was* good in Your sight." And Hezekiah wept bitterly.

4 And it happened, before Isaiah had gone out into the middle court, that the word of the LORD came to him, saying, 5 "Return and tell Hezekiah the leader of My people, 'Thus says the LORD, the God of David your father: "I have heard your prayer, I have seen your tears; surely I will heal you. On the third day you shall go up to the house of the LORD. 6 And I will add to your days fifteen years. I will deliver you and this city from the hand of the king of Assyria; and I will defend this city for My own sake, and for the sake of My servant David." ' "

7 Then Isaiah said, "Take a lump of figs." So they took and laid *it* on the boil, and he recovered.

8 And Hezekiah said to Isaiah, "What *is* the sign that the LORD will heal me, and that I shall go up to the house of the LORD the third day?"

9 Then Isaiah said, "This is the sign to you from the LORD, that the LORD will do the thing which He has spoken: *shall* the shadow go forward ten degrees or go backward ten degrees?"

10 And Hezekiah answered, "It is an easy thing for the shadow to go down ten degrees; no, but let the shadow go backward ten degrees."

11 So Isaiah the prophet cried out to the LORD, and He brought the shadow ten degrees backward, by which it had gone down on the sundial of Ahaz.

THE MESSAGE

Jerusalem got up next morning, there it was—a whole camp of corpses!

36-37 Sennacherib king of Assyria got out of there fast, headed straight home for Nineveh, and stayed put. One day when he was worshiping in the temple of his god Nisroch, his sons Adrammelech and Sharezer murdered him and then escaped to the land of Ararat. His son Esarhaddon became the next king.

1 20 Some time later Hezekiah became deathly sick. The prophet Isaiah son of Amoz paid him a visit and said, "Put your affairs in order; you're about to die—you haven't long to live."

2-3 Hezekiah turned from Isaiah and faced GOD, praying:

Remember, O GOD, who I am, what I've done!
I've lived an honest life before you,
My heart's been true and steady,
I've lived to please you; lived for your approval.

And then the tears flowed. Hezekiah wept.

4-6 Isaiah, leaving, was not halfway across the courtyard when the word of GOD stopped him: "Go back and tell Hezekiah, prince of my people, 'GOD's word, Hezekiah! From the God of your ancestor David: I've listened to your prayer and I've observed your tears. I'm going to heal you. In three days you will walk on your own legs into The Temple of GOD. I've just added fifteen years to your life; I'm saving you from the king of Assyria, and I'm covering this city with my shield—for my sake and my servant David's sake.' "

7 Isaiah then said, "Prepare a plaster of figs."

They prepared the plaster, applied it to the boil, and Hezekiah was on his way to recovery.

8 Hezekiah said to Isaiah, "How do I know whether this is of GOD and not just the fig plaster? What confirming sign is there that GOD is healing me and that in three days I'll walk into The Temple of GOD on my own legs?"

9 "This will be your sign from GOD," said Isaiah, "that GOD is doing what he said he'd do: Do you want the shadow to advance ten degrees on the sundial or go back ten degrees? You choose."

10 Hezekiah said, "It would be easy to make the sun's shadow advance ten degrees. Make it go back ten degrees."

11 So Isaiah called out in prayer to GOD, and the shadow went back ten degrees on Ahaz's sundial.

NEW KING JAMES VERSION

THE BABYLONIAN ENVOYS

[12]At that time Berodach-Baladan[a] the son of Baladan, king of Babylon, sent letters and a present to Hezekiah, for he heard that Hezekiah had been sick. [13]And Hezekiah was attentive to them, and showed them all the house of his treasures—the silver and gold, the spices and precious ointment, and all[a] his armory—all that was found among his treasures. There was nothing in his house or in all his dominion that Hezekiah did not show them.

[14]Then Isaiah the prophet went to King Hezekiah, and said to him, "What did these men say, and from where did they come to you?"

So Hezekiah said, "They came from a far country, from Babylon."

[15]And he said, "What have they seen in your house?"

So Hezekiah answered, "They have seen all that *is* in my house; there is nothing among my treasures that I have not shown them."

[16]Then Isaiah said to Hezekiah, "Hear the word of the LORD: [17]'Behold, the days are coming when all that *is* in your house, and what your fathers have accumulated until this day, shall be carried to Babylon; nothing shall be left,' says the LORD. [18]'And they shall take away some of your sons who will descend from you, whom you will beget; and they shall be eunuchs in the palace of the king of Babylon.' "

[19]So Hezekiah said to Isaiah, "The word of the LORD which you have spoken *is* good!" For he said, "Will there not be peace and truth at least in my days?"

DEATH OF HEZEKIAH

[20]Now the rest of the acts of Hezekiah—all his might, and how he made a pool and a tunnel and brought water into the city—*are* they not written in the book of the chronicles of the kings of Judah? [21]So Hezekiah rested with his fathers. Then Manasseh his son reigned in his place.

MANASSEH REIGNS IN JUDAH

21 Manasseh *was* twelve years old when he became king, and he reigned fifty-five years in Jerusalem. His mother's name *was* Hephzibah. [2]And he did evil in the sight of the LORD, according to the abominations of the nations whom the LORD had cast out before the children of Israel. [3]For he rebuilt the high places which Hezekiah his father had destroyed; he raised up altars for Baal, and made a wooden image,[a] as Ahab king of Israel had done; and he worshiped all the host of heaven[b] and served them. [4]He also built altars in the house of the LORD, of which the LORD had said, "In Jerusalem I will put My name." [5]And he built altars for all the host of heaven in the two courts of the house of the LORD. [6]Also he made his son pass through

20:12 [a]Spelled *Merodach-Baladan* in Isaiah 39:1 **20:13** [a]Following many Hebrew manuscripts, Syriac, and Targum; Masoretic Text omits *all.* **21:3** [a]Hebrew *Asherah,* a Canaanite goddess [b]The gods of the Assryians

THE MESSAGE

12-13 Shortly after this, Merodach-Baladan, the
son of Baladan king of Babylon, having
heard that the king was sick, sent a get-well
card and a gift to Hezekiah. Hezekiah was
pleased and showed the messengers around
the place—silver, gold, spices, aromatic oils,
his stockpile of weapons—a guided tour of
all his prized possessions. There wasn't a
thing in his palace or kingdom that
Hezekiah didn't show them.

14 And then Isaiah the prophet showed up:
"And just what were these men doing here?
Where did they come from and why?"

Hezekiah said, "They came from far
away—from Babylon."

15 "And what did they see in your palace?"

"Everything," said Hezekiah. "There isn't
anything I didn't show them—I gave them
the grand tour."

16-18 Then Isaiah spoke to Hezekiah, "Listen to
what GOD has to say about this: The day is
coming when everything you own and
everything your ancestors have passed
down to you, right down to the last cup and
saucer, will be cleaned out of here—plundered and packed off to Babylon. GOD's
word! Worse yet, your sons, the progeny of
sons you've begotten, will end up as eunuchs in the palace of the king of Babylon."

19 Hezekiah said to Isaiah, "If GOD says it, it
must be good." But he was thinking to himself, "It won't happen during my lifetime—
I'll enjoy peace and security as long as I
live."

20-21 The rest of the life and times of Hezekiah,
along with his projects, especially the way
he engineered the Upper Pool and brought
water into the city, are written in *The Chronicles of the Kings of Judah.* Hezekiah died
and was buried with his ancestors. His son
Manasseh became the next king.

MANASSEH OF JUDAH

1-6 **21** Manasseh was twelve years old when
he became king. He ruled for fifty-five
years in Jerusalem. His mother's name was
Hephzibah. In GOD's judgment he was a bad
king—an evil king. He reintroduced all the
moral rot and spiritual corruption that had
been scoured from the country when GOD
dispossessed the pagan nations in favor of
the children of Israel. He rebuilt all the
sex-and-religion shrines that his father
Hezekiah had torn down, and he built altars
and phallic images for the sex god Baal and
sex goddess Asherah, exactly what Ahaz
king of Israel had done. He worshiped the
cosmic powers, taking orders from the constellations. He even built these pagan altars
in The Temple of GOD, the very Jerusalem
Temple dedicated exclusively by GOD's decree ("in Jerusalem I place my Name") to
GOD's Name. And he built shrines to the cosmic powers and placed them in both courtyards of The Temple of GOD. He burned his
own son in a sacrificial offering. He prac-

NEW KING JAMES VERSION

the fire, practiced soothsaying, used witchcraft, and consulted spiritists and mediums. He did much evil in the sight of the LORD, to provoke *Him* to anger. 7He even set a carved image of Asherah[a] that he had made, in the house of which the LORD had said to David and to Solomon his son, "In this house and in Jerusalem, which I have chosen out of all the tribes of Israel, I will put My name forever; 8and I will not make the feet of Israel wander anymore from the land which I gave their fathers—only if they are careful to do according to all that I have commanded them, and according to all the law that My servant Moses commanded them." 9But they paid no attention, and Manasseh seduced them to do more evil than the nations whom the LORD had destroyed before the children of Israel.

10And the LORD spoke by His servants the prophets, saying, 11"Because Manasseh king of Judah has done these abominations (he has acted more wickedly than all the Amorites who *were* before him, and has also made Judah sin with his idols), 12therefore thus says the LORD God of Israel: 'Behold, *I* am bringing *such* calamity upon Jerusalem and Judah, that whoever hears of it, both his ears will tingle. 13And I will stretch over Jerusalem the measuring line of Samaria and the plummet of the house of Ahab; I will wipe Jerusalem as *one* wipes a dish, wiping *it* and turning *it* upside down. 14So I will forsake the remnant of My inheritance and deliver them into the hand of their enemies; and they shall become victims of plunder to all their enemies, 15because they have done evil in My sight, and have provoked Me to anger since the day their fathers came out of Egypt, even to this day.' "

16Moreover Manasseh shed very much innocent blood, till he had filled Jerusalem from one end to another, besides his sin by which he made Judah sin, in doing evil in the sight of the LORD.

17Now the rest of the acts of Manasseh—all that he did, and the sin that he committed—*are* they not written in the book of the chronicles of the kings of Judah? 18So Manasseh rested with his fathers, and was buried in the garden of his own house, in the garden of Uzza. Then his son Amon reigned in his place.

AMON'S REIGN AND DEATH

19Amon *was* twenty-two years old when he became king, and he reigned two years in Jerusalem. His mother's name *was* Meshullemeth the daughter of Haruz of Jotbah. 20And he did evil in the sight of the LORD, as his father Manasseh had done. 21So he walked in all the ways that his father had walked; and he served the idols that his father had served, and wor-

21:7 [a]A Canaanite goddess

THE MESSAGE

ticed black magic and fortunetelling. He held séances and consulted spirits from the underworld. Much evil—in GOD's judgment, a career in evil. And GOD was angry.

7-8 As a last straw he placed the carved image of the sex goddess Asherah in The Temple of GOD, a flagrant and provocative violation of GOD's well-known statement to both David and Solomon, "In this Temple and in this city Jerusalem, my choice out of all the tribes of Israel, I place my Name—exclusively and forever. Never again will I let my people Israel wander off from this land I gave to their ancestors. But here's the condition: They must keep everything I've commanded in the instructions my servant Moses passed on to them."

9 But the people didn't listen. Manasseh led them off the beaten path into practices of evil even exceeding the evil of the pagan nations that GOD had earlier destroyed.

10-12 GOD, thoroughly fed up, sent word through his servants the prophets: "Because Manasseh king of Judah has committed these outrageous sins, eclipsing the sin-performance of the Amorites before him, setting new records in evil, using foul idols to debase Judah into a nation of sinners, this is my judgment, GOD's verdict: I, the God of Israel, will visit catastrophe on Jerusalem and Judah, a doom so terrible that when people hear of it they'll shake their heads in disbelief, saying, 'I can't believe it!'

13-15 "I'll visit the fate of Samaria on Jerusalem, a rerun of Ahab's doom. I'll wipe out Jerusalem as you would wipe out a dish, wiping it out and turning it over to dry. I'll get rid of what's left of my inheritance, dumping them on their enemies. If their enemies can salvage anything from them, they're welcome to it. They've been nothing but trouble to me from the day their ancestors left Egypt until now. They pushed me to my limit; I won't put up with their evil any longer."

16 The final word on Manasseh was that he was an indiscriminate murderer. He drenched Jerusalem with the innocent blood of his victims. That's on top of all the sins in which he involved his people. As far as GOD was concerned, he'd turned them into a nation of sinners.

17-18 The rest of the life and times of Manasseh, everything he did and his sorry record of sin, is written in *The Chronicles of the Kings of Judah*. Manasseh died and joined his ancestors. He was buried in the palace garden, the Garden of Uzza. His son Amon became the next king.

AMON OF JUDAH

19-22 Amon was twenty-two years old when he became king. He was king for two years in Jerusalem. His mother's name was Meshullemeth, the daughter of Haruz. She was from Jotbah. In GOD's opinion he lived an evil life, just like his father Manasseh. He followed in the footsteps of his father, serving and worshiping the same foul gods his

NEW KING JAMES VERSION

shiped them. 22He forsook the LORD God of his
fathers, and did not walk in the way of the LORD.
23Then the servants of Amon conspired
against him, and killed the king in his own
house. 24But the people of the land executed all
those who had conspired against King Amon.
Then the people of the land made his son Josiah
king in his place.
25Now the rest of the acts of Amon which he
did, *are* they not written in the book of the
chronicles of the kings of Judah? 26And he was
buried in his tomb in the garden of Uzza. Then
Josiah his son reigned in his place.

JOSIAH REIGNS IN JUDAH

22 Josiah *was* eight years old when he became king, and he reigned thirty-one years
in Jerusalem. His mother's name *was* Jedidah
the daughter of Adaiah of Bozkath. 2And he did
what was right in the sight of the LORD, and
walked in all the ways of his father David; he
did not turn aside to the right hand or to the left.

HILKIAH FINDS THE BOOK OF THE LAW

3Now it came to pass, in the eighteenth year
of King Josiah, *that* the king sent Shaphan the
scribe, the son of Azaliah, the son of Meshullam,
to the house of the LORD, saying: 4"Go up to
Hilkiah the high priest, that he may count the
money which has been brought into the house of
the LORD, which the doorkeepers have gathered
from the people. 5And let them deliver it into the
hand of those doing the work, who are the overseers in the house of the LORD; let them give it to
those who *are* in the house of the LORD doing the
work, to repair the damages of the house— 6to
carpenters and builders and masons—and to
buy timber and hewn stone to repair the house.
7However there need be no accounting made
with them of the money delivered into their
hand, because they deal faithfully."
8Then Hilkiah the high priest said to
Shaphan the scribe, "I have found the Book of
the Law in the house of the LORD." And Hilkiah
gave the book to Shaphan, and he read it. 9So
Shaphan the scribe went to the king, bringing
the king word, saying, "Your servants have gathered the money that was found in the house, and
have delivered it into the hand of those who do
the work, who oversee the house of the LORD."
10Then Shaphan the scribe showed the king,
saying, "Hilkiah the priest has given me a book."
And Shaphan read it before the king.
11Now it happened, when the king heard the
words of the Book of the Law, that he tore his
clothes. 12Then the king commanded Hilkiah the
priest, Ahikam the son of Shaphan, Achbor[a] the
son of Michaiah, Shaphan the scribe, and Asaiah
a servant of the king, saying, 13"Go, inquire of the
LORD for me, for the people and for all Judah,
concerning the words of this book that has been
found; for great *is* the wrath of the LORD that is
aroused against us, because our fathers have not
obeyed the words of this book, to do according to
all that is written concerning us."

22:12 [a]*Abdon the son of Micah* in 2 Chronicles 34:20

THE MESSAGE

father had served. He totally deserted the GOD of his ancestors; he did not live GOD's way.

23-24 Amon's servants revolted and assassinated him, killing the king right in his own palace. But the people, in their turn, killed the conspirators against King Amon and then crowned Josiah, Amon's son, as king.

25-26 The rest of the life and times of Amon is written in *The Chronicles of the Kings of Judah*. They buried Amon in his burial plot in the Garden of Uzza. His son Josiah became the next king.

JOSIAH OF JUDAH

1-2 22 Josiah was eight years old when he became king. He ruled for thirty-one years in Jerusalem. His mother's name was Jedidah daughter of Adaiah; she was from Bozkath. He lived the way GOD wanted. He kept straight on the path blazed by his ancestor David, not one step to either left or right.

3-7 One day in the eighteenth year of his kingship, King Josiah sent the royal secretary Shaphan son of Azaliah, the son of Meshullam, to The Temple of GOD with instructions: "Go to Hilkiah the high priest and have him count the money that has been brought to The Temple of GOD that the doormen have collected from the people. Have them turn it over to the foremen who are managing the work on The Temple of GOD so they can pay the workers who are repairing GOD's Temple, all the carpenters, construction workers, and masons. Also, authorize them to buy the lumber and dressed stone for The Temple repairs. You don't need to get a receipt for the money you give them—they're all honest men."

8 The high priest Hilkiah reported to Shaphan the royal secretary, "I've just found the Book of GOD's Revelation, instructing us in GOD's ways. I found it in The Temple!" He gave it to Shaphan and Shaphan read it.

9 Then Shaphan the royal secretary came back to the king and gave him an account of what had gone on: "Your servants have bagged up the money that has been collected for The Temple; they have given it to the foremen to pay The Temple workers."

10 Then Shaphan the royal secretary told the king, "Hilkiah the priest gave me a book." Shaphan proceeded to read it to the king.

11-13 When the king heard what was written in the book, God's Revelation, he ripped his robes in dismay. And then he called for Hilkiah the priest, Ahikam son of Shaphan, Acbor son of Micaiah, Shaphan the royal secretary, and Asaiah the king's personal aide. He ordered them all: "Go and pray to GOD for me and for this people—for all Judah! Find out what we must do in response to what is written in this book that has just been found! GOD's anger must be burning furiously against us—our ancestors haven't obeyed a thing written in this book, followed none of the instructions directed to us."

NEW KING JAMES VERSION

14So Hilkiah the priest, Ahikam, Achbor, Shaphan, and Asaiah went to Huldah the prophetess, the wife of Shallum the son of Tikvah, the son of Harhas, keeper of the wardrobe. (She dwelt in Jerusalem in the Second Quarter.) And they spoke with her. 15Then she said to them, "Thus says the LORD God of Israel, 'Tell the man who sent you to Me, 16"Thus says the LORD: 'Behold, I will bring calamity on this place and on its inhabitants—all the words of the book which the king of Judah has read— 17because they have forsaken Me and burned incense to other gods, that they might provoke Me to anger with all the works of their hands. Therefore My wrath shall be aroused against this place and shall not be quenched.' " ' 18But as for the king of Judah, who sent you to inquire of the LORD, in this manner you shall speak to him, 'Thus says the LORD God of Israel: "*Concerning* the words which you have heard— 19because your heart was tender, and you humbled yourself before the LORD when you heard what I spoke against this place and against its inhabitants, that they would become a desolation and a curse, and you tore your clothes and wept before Me, I also have heard *you*," says the LORD. 20"Surely, therefore, I will gather you to your fathers, and you shall be gathered to your grave in peace; and your eyes shall not see all the calamity which I will bring on this place." ' " So they brought back word to the king.

JOSIAH RESTORES TRUE WORSHIP

23 Now the king sent them to gather all the elders of Judah and Jerusalem to him. 2The king went up to the house of the LORD with all the men of Judah, and with him all the inhabitants of Jerusalem—the priests and the prophets and all the people, both small and great. And he read in their hearing all the words of the Book of the Covenant which had been found in the house of the LORD.

3Then the king stood by a pillar and made a covenant before the LORD, to follow the LORD and to keep His commandments and His testimonies and His statutes, with all *his* heart and all *his* soul, to perform the words of this covenant that were written in this book. And all the people took a stand for the covenant. 4And the king commanded Hilkiah the high priest, the priests of the second order, and the doorkeepers, to bring out of the temple of the LORD all the articles that were made for Baal, for Asherah,[a] and for all the host of heaven;[b] and he burned them outside Jerusalem in the fields of Kidron, and carried their ashes to Bethel. 5Then he removed the idolatrous priests whom the kings of Judah had ordained to burn incense on the high places in the cities of Judah and in the places all around Jerusalem, and those who burned incense to Baal, to the sun, to the moon, to the constellations, and to all the host of heaven. 6And he brought out the wooden image[a] from the house of the LORD, to the Brook Kidron outside Jerusalem, burned it at the Brook Kidron and ground *it* to ashes, and threw its ashes on the graves of the

23:4 [a]A Canaanite goddess [b]The gods of the Assyrians
23:6 [a]Hebrew *Asherah,* a Canaanite goddess

THE MESSAGE

14-17 Hilkiah the priest, Ahikam, Acbor, Shaphan, and Asaiah went straight to Huldah the prophetess. She was the wife of Shallum son of Tikvah, the son of Harhas, who was in charge of the palace wardrobe. She lived in Jerusalem in the Second Quarter. The five men consulted with her. In response to them she said, "GOD's word, the God of Israel: Tell the man who sent you here that I'm on my way to bring the doom of judgment on this place and this people. Every word written in the book read by the king of Judah will happen. And why? Because they've deserted me and taken up with other gods, made me thoroughly angry by setting up their god-making businesses. My anger is raging white-hot against this place and nobody is going to put it out.

18-20 "And also tell the king of Judah, since he sent you to ask GOD for direction; tell him this, GOD's comment on what he read in the book: 'Because you took seriously the doom of judgment I spoke against this place and people, and because you responded in humble repentance, tearing your robe in dismay and weeping before me, I'm taking you seriously. GOD's word: I'll take care of you. You'll have a quiet death and be buried in peace. You won't be around to see the doom that I'm going to bring upon this place.' "

The men took her message back to the king.

1-3 23 The king acted immediately, assembling all the elders of Judah and Jerusalem. Then the king proceeded to The Temple of GOD, bringing everyone in his train—priests and prophets and people ranging from the famous to the unknown. Then he read out publicly everything written in the Book of the Covenant that was found in The Temple of GOD. The king stood by the pillar and before GOD solemnly committed them all to the covenant: to follow GOD believingly and obediently; to follow his instructions, heart and soul, on what to believe and do; to put into practice the entire covenant, all that was written in the book. The people stood in affirmation; their commitment was unanimous.

4-9 Then the king ordered Hilkiah the high priest, his associate priest, and The Temple sentries to clean house—to get rid of everything in The Temple of GOD that had been made for worshiping Baal and Asherah and the cosmic powers. He had them burned outside Jerusalem in the fields of Kidron and then disposed of the ashes in Bethel. He fired the pagan priests whom the kings of Judah had hired to supervise the local sex-and-religion shrines in the towns of Judah and neighborhoods of Jerusalem. In a stroke he swept the country clean of the polluting stench of the round-the-clock worship of Baal, sun and moon, stars—all the so-called cosmic powers. He took the obscene phallic Asherah pole from The Temple of GOD to the Valley of Kidron outside Jerusalem, burned it up, then ground up the

NEW KING JAMES VERSION

common people. [7]Then he tore down the *ritual* booths of the perverted persons[a] that *were* in the house of the LORD, where the women wove hangings for the wooden image. [8]And he brought all the priests from the cities of Judah, and defiled the high places where the priests had burned incense, from Geba to Beersheba; also he broke down the high places at the gates which *were* at the entrance of the Gate of Joshua the governor of the city, which *were* to the left of the city gate. [9]Nevertheless the priests of the high places did not come up to the altar of the LORD in Jerusalem, but they ate unleavened bread among their brethren.

[10]And he defiled Topheth, which *is* in the Valley of the Son[a] of Hinnom, that no man might make his son or his daughter pass through the fire to Molech. [11]Then he removed the horses that the kings of Judah had dedicated to the sun, at the entrance to the house of the LORD, by the chamber of Nathan-Melech, the officer who *was* in the court; and he burned the chariots of the sun with fire. [12]The altars that *were* on the roof, the upper chamber of Ahaz, which the kings of Judah had made, and the altars which Manasseh had made in the two courts of the house of the LORD, the king broke down and pulverized there, and threw their dust into the Brook Kidron. [13]Then the king defiled the high places that *were* east of Jerusalem, which *were* on the south of the Mount of Corruption, which Solomon king of Israel had built for Ashtoreth the abomination of the Sidonians, for Chemosh the abomination of the Moabites, and for Milcom the abomination of the people of Ammon. [14]And he broke in pieces the *sacred* pillars and cut down the wooden images, and filled their places with the bones of men.

[15]Moreover the altar that *was* at Bethel, *and* the high place which Jeroboam the son of Nebat, who made Israel sin, had made, both that altar and the high place he broke down; and he burned the high place *and* crushed *it* to powder, and burned the wooden image. [16]As Josiah turned, he saw the tombs that *were* there on the mountain. And he sent and took the bones out of the tombs and burned *them* on the altar, and defiled it according to the word of the LORD which the man of God proclaimed, who proclaimed these words. [17]Then he said, "What gravestone *is* this that I see?"

So the men of the city told him, "*It is* the tomb of the man of God who came from Judah and proclaimed these things which you have done against the altar of Bethel."

[18]And he said, "Let him alone; let no one move his bones." So they let his bones alone, with the bones of the prophet who came from Samaria.

23:7 [a]Hebrew *qedeshim,* that is, those practicing sodomy and prostitution in religious rituals **23:10** [a]Kethib reads *Sons.*

THE MESSAGE

ashes and scattered them in the cemetery. He tore out the rooms of the male sacred prostitutes that had been set up in The Temple of GOD; women also used these rooms for weavings for Asherah. He swept the outlying towns of Judah clean of priests and smashed the sex-and-religion shrines where they worked their trade from one end of the country to the other—all the way from Geba to Beersheba. He smashed the sex-and-religion shrine that had been set up just to the left of the city gate for the private use of Joshua, the city mayor. Even though these sex-and-religion priests did not defile the Altar in The Temple itself, they were part of the general priestly corruption and had to go.

10-11 Then Josiah demolished the Topheth, the iron furnace griddle set up in the Valley of Ben Hinnom for sacrificing children in the fire. No longer could anyone burn son or daughter to the god Molech. He hauled off the horse statues honoring the sun god that the kings of Judah had set up near the entrance to The Temple. They were in the courtyard next to the office of Nathan-Melech, the warden. He burned up the sun-chariots as so much rubbish.

12-15 The king smashed all the altars to smithereens—the altar on the roof shrine of Ahaz, the various altars the kings of Judah had made, the altars of Manasseh that littered the courtyard of The Temple—he smashed them all, pulverized the fragments, and scattered their dust in the Valley of Kidron. The king proceeded to make a clean sweep of all the sex-and-religion shrines that had proliferated east of Jerusalem on the south slope of Abomination Hill, the ones Solomon king of Israel had built to the obscene Sidonian sex goddess Ashtoreth, to Chemosh the dirty-old-god of the Moabites, and to Milcom the depraved god of the Ammonites. He tore apart the altars, chopped down the phallic Asherah-poles, and scattered old bones over the sites. Next, he took care of the altar at the shrine in Bethel that Jeroboam son of Nebat had built—the same Jeroboam who had led Israel into a life of sin. He tore apart the altar, burned down the shrine leaving it in ashes, and then lit fire to the phallic Asherah-pole.

16 As Josiah looked over the scene, he noticed the tombs on the hillside. He ordered the bones removed from the tombs and had them cremated on the ruined altars, desacralizing the evil altars. This was a fulfillment of the word of GOD spoken by the Holy Man years before when Jeroboam had stood by the altar at the sacred convocation.

17 Then the king said, "And *that* memorial stone—whose is that?"

The men from the city said, "That's the grave of the Holy Man who spoke the message against the altar at Bethel that you have just fulfilled."

18 Josiah said, "Don't trouble his bones." So they left his bones undisturbed, along with the bones of the prophet from Samaria.

NEW KING JAMES VERSION

19Now Josiah also took away all the shrines
of the high places that *were* in the cities of
Samaria, which the kings of Israel had made to
provoke the LORD[a] to anger; and he did to them
according to all the deeds he had done in Bethel.
20He executed all the priests of the high places
who *were* there, on the altars, and burned men's
bones on them; and he returned to Jerusalem.
21Then the king commanded all the people,
saying, "Keep the Passover to the LORD your God,
as *it is* written in this Book of the Covenant."
22Such a Passover surely had never been held
since the days of the judges who judged Israel,
nor in all the days of the kings of Israel and the
kings of Judah. 23But in the eighteenth year of
King Josiah this Passover was held before the
LORD in Jerusalem. 24Moreover Josiah put away
those who consulted mediums and spiritists, the
household gods and idols, all the abominations
that were seen in the land of Judah and in Jerusa-
lem, that he might perform the words of the law
which were written in the book that Hilkiah the
priest found in the house of the LORD. 25Now be-
fore him there was no king like him, who turned
to the LORD with all his heart, with all his soul,
and with all his might, according to all the Law of
Moses; nor after him did *any* arise like him.

IMPENDING JUDGMENT ON JUDAH

26Nevertheless the LORD did not turn from
the fierceness of His great wrath, with which
His anger was aroused against Judah, because
of all the provocations with which Manasseh
had provoked Him. 27And the LORD said, "I will
also remove Judah from My sight, as I have re-
moved Israel, and will cast off this city Jerusa-
lem which I have chosen, and the house of
which I said, 'My name shall be there.' "[a]

JOSIAH DIES IN BATTLE

28Now the rest of the acts of Josiah, and all
that he did, *are* they not written in the book of
the chronicles of the kings of Judah? 29In his
days Pharaoh Necho king of Egypt went to the
aid of the king of Assyria, to the River Eu-
phrates; and King Josiah went against him. And
Pharaoh Necho killed him at Megiddo when he
confronted him. 30Then his servants moved his
body in a chariot from Megiddo, brought him to
Jerusalem, and buried him in his own tomb. And
the people of the land took Jehoahaz the son of
Josiah, anointed him, and made him king in his
father's place.

THE REIGN AND CAPTIVITY OF JEHOAHAZ

31Jehoahaz *was* twenty-three years old when
he became king, and he reigned three months in
Jerusalem. His mother's name *was* Hamutal the
daughter of Jeremiah of Libnah. 32And he did
evil in the sight of the LORD, according to all that
his fathers had done.

23:19 [a]Following Septuagint, Syriac, and Vulgate; Masoretic Text and Targum omit *the LORD*. **23:27** [a]1 Kings 8:29

THE MESSAGE

19-20 But Josiah hadn't finished. He now moved through all the towns of Samaria where the kings of Israel had built neighborhood sex-and-religion shrines, shrines that had so angered GOD. He tore the shrines down and left them in ruins—just as at Bethel. He killed all the priests who had conducted the sacrifices and cremated them on their own altars, thus desacralizing the altars. Only then did Josiah return to Jerusalem.

21 The king now commanded the people, "Celebrate the Passover to GOD, your God, exactly as directed in this Book of the Covenant."

22-23 This commanded Passover had not been celebrated since the days that the judges judged Israel—none of the kings of Israel and Judah had celebrated it. But in the eighteenth year of the rule of King Josiah this very Passover was celebrated to GOD in Jerusalem.

24 Josiah scrubbed the place clean and trashed spirit-mediums, sorcerers, domestic gods, and carved figures—all the vast accumulation of foul and obscene relics and images on display everywhere you looked in Judah and Jerusalem. Josiah did this in obedience to the words of GOD's Revelation written in the book that Hilkiah the priest found in The Temple of GOD.

25 There was no king to compare with Josiah—neither before nor after—a king who turned in total and repentant obedience to GOD, heart and mind and strength, following the instructions revealed to and written by Moses. The world would never again see a king like Josiah.

26-27 But despite Josiah, GOD's hot anger did not cool; the raging anger ignited by Manasseh burned unchecked. And GOD, not swerving in his judgment, gave sentence: "I'll remove Judah from my presence in the same way I removed Israel. I'll turn my back on this city, Jerusalem, that I chose, and even from this Temple of which I said, 'My Name lives here.' "

28-30 The rest of the life and times of Josiah is written in *The Chronicles of the Kings of Judah*. Josiah's death came about when Pharaoh Neco king of Egypt marched out to join forces with the king of Assyria at the Euphrates River. When King Josiah intercepted him at the Plain of Megiddo, Neco killed him. Josiah's servants took his body in a chariot, returned him to Jerusalem, and buried him in his own tomb. By popular choice Jehoahaz son of Josiah was anointed and succeeded his father as king.

JEHOAHAZ OF JUDAH

31 Jehoahaz was twenty-three years old when he began to rule. He was king in Jerusalem for a mere three months. His mother's name was Hamutal daughter of Jeremiah. She came from Libnah.

32 In GOD's opinion, he was an evil king, reverting to the evil ways of his ancestors.

NEW KING JAMES VERSION

33 Now Pharaoh Necho put him in prison at Rib-
lah in the land of Hamath, that he might not
reign in Jerusalem; and he imposed on the land
a tribute of one hundred talents of silver and a
talent of gold. 34 Then Pharaoh Necho made Eli-
akim the son of Josiah king in place of his father
Josiah, and changed his name to Jehoiakim. And
Pharaoh took Jehoahaz and went to Egypt, and
he[a] died there.

JEHOIAKIM REIGNS IN JUDAH

35 So Jehoiakim gave the silver and gold to
Pharaoh; but he taxed the land to give money
according to the command of Pharaoh; he ex-
acted the silver and gold from the people of the
land, from every one according to his assess-
ment, to give *it* to Pharaoh Necho. 36 Jehoiakim
was twenty-five years old when he became
king, and he reigned eleven years in Jerusalem.
His mother's name *was* Zebudah the daughter
of Pedaiah of Rumah. 37 And he did evil in the
sight of the LORD, according to all that his fa-
thers had done.

JUDAH OVERRUN BY ENEMIES

24 In his days Nebuchadnezzar king of Bab-
ylon came up, and Jehoiakim became his
vassal *for* three years. Then he turned and re-
belled against him. 2 And the LORD sent against
him *raiding* bands of Chaldeans, bands of Syri-
ans, bands of Moabites, and bands of the people
of Ammon; He sent them against Judah to de-
stroy it, according to the word of the LORD
which He had spoken by His servants the
prophets. 3 Surely at the commandment of the
LORD *this* came upon Judah, to remove *them*
from His sight because of the sins of Manasseh,
according to all that he had done, 4 and also be-
cause of the innocent blood that he had shed;
for he had filled Jerusalem with innocent blood,
which the LORD would not pardon.

5 Now the rest of the acts of Jehoiakim, and
all that he did, *are* they not written in the book
of the chronicles of the kings of Judah? 6 So Je-
hoiakim rested with his fathers. Then Je-
hoiachin his son reigned in his place.

7 And the king of Egypt did not come out of
his land anymore, for the king of Babylon had
taken all that belonged to the king of Egypt
from the Brook of Egypt to the River Euphrates.

THE REIGN AND CAPTIVITY OF JEHOIACHIN

8 Jehoiachin *was* eighteen years old when he
became king, and he reigned in Jerusalem three
months. His mother's name *was* Nehushta the
daughter of Elnathan of Jerusalem. 9 And he did
evil in the sight of the LORD, according to all that
his father had done.

10 At that time the servants of Nebuchadnez-
zar king of Babylon came up against Jerusalem,
and the city was besieged. 11 And Nebu-
chadnezzar king of Babylon came against the

23:34 [a]That is, Jehoahaz

THE MESSAGE

33-34 Pharaoh Neco captured Jehoahaz at Riblah in the country of Hamath and put him in chains, preventing him from ruling in Jerusalem. He demanded that Judah pay tribute of nearly four tons of silver and seventy-five pounds of gold. Then Pharaoh Neco made Eliakim son of Josiah the successor to Josiah, but changed his name to Jehoiakim. Jehoahaz was carted off to Egypt and eventually died there.

35 Meanwhile Jehoiakim, like a good puppet, dutifully paid out the silver and gold demanded by Pharaoh. He scraped up the money by gouging the people, making everyone pay an assessed tax.

JEHOIAKIM OF JUDAH

36-37 Jehoiakim was twenty-five years old when he began to rule; he was king for eleven years in Jerusalem. His mother's name was Zebidah daughter of Pedaiah. She had come from Rumah. In GOD's opinion he was an evil king, picking up on the evil ways of his ancestors.

1 24 It was during his reign that Nebuchadnezzar king of Babylon invaded the country. Jehoiakim became his puppet. But after three years he had had enough and revolted.

2-4 GOD dispatched a succession of raiding bands against him: Babylonian, Aramean, Moabite, and Ammonite. The strategy was to destroy Judah. Through the preaching of his servants and prophets, GOD had said he would do this, and now he was doing it. None of this was by chance—it was GOD's judgment as he turned his back on Judah because of the enormity of the sins of Manasseh—Manasseh, the killer-king, who made the Jerusalem streets flow with the innocent blood of his victims. GOD wasn't about to overlook such crimes.

5-6 The rest of the life and times of Jehoiakim is written in *The Chronicles of the Kings of Judah.* Jehoiakim died and was buried with his ancestors. His son Jehoiachin became the next king.

7 The threat from Egypt was now over—no more invasions by the king of Egypt—for by this time the king of Babylon had captured all the land between the Brook of Egypt and the Euphrates River, land formerly controlled by the king of Egypt.

JEHOIACHIN OF JUDAH

8-9 Jehoiachin was eighteen years old when he became king. His rule in Jerusalem lasted only three months. His mother's name was Nehushta daughter of Elnathan; she was from Jerusalem. In GOD's opinion he also was an evil king, no different from his father.

10-12 The next thing to happen was that the officers of Nebuchadnezzar king of Babylon attacked Jerusalem and put it under siege. While his officers were laying siege to the city, Nebuchadnezzar king of Babylon paid

New King James Version

city, as his servants were besieging it. 12Then Je-
hoiachin king of Judah, his mother, his servants,
his princes, and his officers went out to the king
of Babylon; and the king of Babylon, in the
eighth year of his reign, took him prisoner.

The Captivity of Jerusalem

13And he carried out from there all the treas-
ures of the house of the LORD and the treasures
of the king's house, and he cut in pieces all the
articles of gold which Solomon king of Israel
had made in the temple of the LORD, as the LORD
had said. 14Also he carried into captivity all
Jerusalem: all the captains and all the mighty
men of valor, ten thousand captives, and all the
craftsmen and smiths. None remained except
the poorest people of the land. 15And he carried
Jehoiachin captive to Babylon. The king's
mother, the king's wives, his officers, and the
mighty of the land he carried into captivity from
Jerusalem to Babylon. 16All the valiant men,
seven thousand, and craftsmen and smiths, one
thousand, all *who were* strong *and* fit for war,
these the king of Babylon brought captive to
Babylon.

Zedekiah Reigns in Judah

17Then the king of Babylon made Mattaniah,
Jehoiachin's[a] uncle, king in his place, and
changed his name to Zedekiah.
18Zedekiah *was* twenty-one years old when
he became king, and he reigned eleven years in
Jerusalem. His mother's name *was* Hamutal the
daughter of Jeremiah of Libnah. 19He also did
evil in the sight of the LORD, according to all that
Jehoiakim had done. 20For because of the anger
of the LORD *this* happened in Jerusalem and Ju-
dah, that He finally cast them out from His pres-
ence. Then Zedekiah rebelled against the king
of Babylon.

The Fall and Captivity of Judah

25 Now it came to pass in the ninth year of
his reign, in the tenth month, on the tenth
day of the month, *that* Nebuchadnezzar king of
Babylon and all his army came against Jerusa-
lem and encamped against it; and they built a
siege wall against it all around. 2So the city was
besieged until the eleventh year of King
Zedekiah. 3By the ninth *day* of the *fourth* month
the famine had become so severe in the city that
there was no food for the people of the land.
4Then the city wall was broken through, and
all the men of war *fled* at night by way of the
gate between two walls, which was by the king's
garden, even though the Chaldeans *were* still
encamped all around against the city. And *the
king*[a] went by way of the plain.[b] 5But the army of
the Chaldeans pursued the king, and they over-
took him in the plains of Jericho. All his army
was scattered from him. 6So they took the king
and brought him up to the king of Babylon at
Riblah, and they pronounced judgment on him.

24:17 [a]Literally *his* **25:4** [a]Literally *he* [b]Or *Arabah,* that is, the Jordan Valley

The Message

a personal visit. And Jehoiachin king of Ju-
dah, along with his mother, officers, advi-
sors, and government leaders, surrendered.
12-14 In the eighth year of his reign Jehoiachin
was taken prisoner by the king of Babylon.
Nebuchadnezzar emptied the treasuries of
both The Temple of GOD and the royal
palace and confiscated all the gold furnish-
ings that Solomon king of Israel had made
for The Temple of GOD. This should have
been no surprise—GOD had said it would
happen. And then he emptied Jerusalem of
people—all its leaders and soldiers, all its
craftsmen and artisans. He took them into
exile, something like ten thousand of them!
The only ones he left were the very poor.
15-16 He took Jehoiachin into exile to Babylon.
With him he took the king's mother, his
wives, his chief officers, the community
leaders, anyone who was anybody—in
round numbers, seven thousand soldiers
plus another thousand or so craftsmen and
artisans, all herded off into exile in Babylon.
17 Then the king of Babylon made Je-
hoiachin's uncle, Mattaniah, his puppet
king, but changed his name to Zedekiah.

Zedekiah of Judah

18 Zedekiah was twenty-one years old when
he started out as king. He was king in
Jerusalem for eleven years. His mother's
name was Hamutal the daughter of Jere-
miah. Her hometown was Libnah.
19 As far as GOD was concerned Zedekiah
was just one more evil king, a carbon copy
of Jehoiakim.
20 The source of all this doom to Jerusalem
and Judah was GOD's anger—GOD turned
his back on them as an act of judgment. And
then Zedekiah revolted against the king of
Babylon.

1-7 25 The revolt dates from the ninth year
and tenth month of Zedekiah's reign.
Nebuchadnezzar set out for Jerusalem im-
mediately with a full army. He set up camp
and sealed off the city by building siege
mounds around it. The city was under siege
for nineteen months (until the eleventh year
of Zedekiah). By the fourth month of
Zedekiah's eleventh year, on the ninth day
of the month, the famine was so bad that
there wasn't so much as a crumb of bread
for anyone. Then there was a breakthrough.
At night, under cover of darkness, the entire
army escaped through an opening in the
wall (it was the gate between the two walls
above the King's Garden). They slipped
through the lines of the Babylonians who
surrounded the city and headed for the Jor-
dan on the Arabah Valley road. But the
Babylonians were in pursuit of the king and
they caught up with him in the Plains of
Jericho. By then Zedekiah's army had de-
serted and was scattered. The Babylonians
took Zedekiah prisoner and marched him
off to the king of Babylon at Riblah, then
tried and sentenced him on the spot.

NEW KING JAMES VERSION

[7]Then they killed the sons of Zedekiah before his eyes, put out the eyes of Zedekiah, bound him with bronze fetters, and took him to Babylon.

[8]And in the fifth month, on the seventh *day* of the month (which *was* the nineteenth year of King Nebuchadnezzar king of Babylon), Nebuzaradan the captain of the guard, a servant of the king of Babylon, came to Jerusalem. [9]He burned the house of the LORD and the king's house; all the houses of Jerusalem, that is, all the houses of the great, he burned with fire. [10]And all the army of the Chaldeans who *were with* the captain of the guard broke down the walls of Jerusalem all around.

[11]Then Nebuzaradan the captain of the guard carried away captive the rest of the people *who* remained in the city and the defectors who had deserted to the king of Babylon, with the rest of the multitude. [12]But the captain of the guard left *some* of the poor of the land as vinedressers and farmers. [13]The bronze pillars that *were* in the house of the LORD, and the carts and the bronze Sea that *were* in the house of the LORD, the Chaldeans broke in pieces, and carried their bronze to Babylon. [14]They also took away the pots, the shovels, the trimmers, the spoons, and all the bronze utensils with which the priests ministered. [15]The firepans and the basins, the things of solid gold and solid silver, the captain of the guard took away. [16]The two pillars, one Sea, and the carts, which Solomon had made for the house of the LORD, the bronze of all these articles was beyond measure. [17]The height of one pillar *was* eighteen cubits, and the capital on it *was* of bronze. The height of the capital was three cubits, and the network and pomegranates all around the capital were all of bronze. The second pillar was the same, with a network.

[18]And the captain of the guard took Seraiah the chief priest, Zephaniah the second priest, and the three doorkeepers. [19]He also took out of the city an officer who had charge of the men of war, five men of the king's close associates who were found in the city, the chief recruiting officer of the army, who mustered the people of the land, and sixty men of the people of the land *who were* found in the city. [20]So Nebuzaradan, captain of the guard, took these and brought them to the king of Babylon at Riblah. [21]Then the king of Babylon struck them and put them to death at Riblah in the land of Hamath. Thus Judah was carried away captive from its own land.

GEDALIAH MADE GOVERNOR OF JUDAH

[22]Then he made Gedaliah the son of Ahikam, the son of Shaphan, governor over the people who remained in the land of Judah, whom Nebuchadnezzar king of Babylon had left. [23]Now when all the captains of the armies, they and *their* men, heard that the king of Babylon had made Gedaliah governor, they came to Gedaliah at Mizpah—Ishmael the son of Nethaniah, Johanan the son of Careah, Seraiah the son of Tanhumeth the Netophathite, and Jaazaniah[a]

25:23 [a]Spelled *Jezaniah* in Jeremiah 40:8

THE MESSAGE

Zedekiah's sons were executed right before his eyes; the summary murder of his sons was the last thing he saw, for they then blinded him. Securely handcuffed, he was hauled off to Babylon.

8-12 In the nineteenth year of Nebuchadnezzar king of Babylon, on the seventh day of the fifth month, Nebuzaradan, the king of Babylon's chief deputy, arrived in Jerusalem. He burned The Temple of GOD to the ground, went on to the royal palace, and then finished off the city—burned the whole place down. He put the Babylonian troops he had with him to work knocking down the city walls. Finally, he rounded up everyone left in the city, including those who had earlier deserted to the king of Babylon, and took them off into exile. He left a few poor dirt farmers behind to tend the vineyards and what was left of the fields.

13-15 The Babylonians broke up the bronze pillars, the bronze washstands, and the huge bronze basin (the Sea) that were in The Temple of GOD and hauled the bronze off to Babylon. They also took the various bronze-crafted liturgical accessories used in the services of Temple worship, as well as the gold and silver censers and sprinkling bowls. The king's deputy didn't miss a thing—he took every scrap of precious metal he could find.

16-17 The amount of bronze they got from the two pillars, the Sea, and all the washstands that Solomon had made for The Temple of GOD was enormous—they couldn't weigh it all! Each pillar stood twenty-seven feet high, plus another four and a half feet for an ornate capital of bronze filigree and decorative fruit.

18-21 The king's deputy took a number of special prisoners: Seraiah the chief priest, Zephaniah the associate priest, three wardens, the chief remaining army officer, five of the king's counselors, the accountant, the chief recruiting officer for the army, and sixty men of standing from among the people. Nebuzaradan the king's deputy marched them all off to the king of Babylon at Riblah. And there at Riblah, in the land of Hamath, the king of Babylon killed the lot of them in cold blood.

Judah went into exile, orphaned from her land.

22-23 Regarding the common people who were left behind in Judah, this: Nebuchadnezzar king of Babylon appointed Gedaliah son of Ahikam, the son of Shaphan, as their governor. When veteran army officers among the people heard that the king of Babylon had appointed Gedaliah, they came to Gedaliah at Mizpah. Among them were Ishmael son of Nethaniah, Johanan son of Kareah, Seraiah son of Tanhumeth the Netophathite,

NEW KING JAMES VERSION

the son of a Maachathite, they and their men.
24And Gedaliah took an oath before them and
their men, and said to them, "Do not be afraid of
the servants of the Chaldeans. Dwell in the land
and serve the king of Babylon, and it shall be
well with you."
25But it happened in the seventh month that
Ishmael the son of Nethaniah, the son of Elish-
ama, of the royal family, came with ten men and
struck and killed Gedaliah, the Jews, as well as
the Chaldeans who were with him at Mizpah.
26And all the people, small and great, and the
captains of the armies, arose and went to Egypt;
for they were afraid of the Chaldeans.

JEHOIACHIN RELEASED FROM PRISON

27Now it came to pass in the thirty-seventh
year of the captivity of Jehoiachin king of Ju-
dah, in the twelfth month, on the twenty-seventh
day of the month, *that* Evil-Merodach[a] king of
Babylon, in the year that he began to reign, re-
leased Jehoiachin king of Judah from prison.
28He spoke kindly to him, and gave him a more
prominent seat than those of the kings who
were with him in Babylon. 29So Jehoiachin
changed from his prison garments, and he ate
bread regularly before the king all the days of
his life. 30And as for his provisions, *there was* a
regular ration given him by the king, a portion
for each day, all the days of his life.

25:27 [a]Literally *Man of Marduk*

THE MESSAGE

Jaazaniah the son of the Maacathite, and some of their followers.

24 Gedaliah assured the officers and their men, giving them his word, "Don't be afraid of the Babylonian officials. Go back to your farms and families and respect the king of Babylon. Trust me, everything is going to be all right."

25 Some time later—it was in the seventh month—Ishmael son of Nethaniah, the son of Elishama (he had royal blood in him), came back with ten men and killed Gedaliah, the traitor Jews, and the Babylonian officials who were stationed at Mizpah—a bloody massacre.

26 But then, afraid of what the Babylonians would do, they all took off for Egypt, leaders and people, small and great.

27-30 When Jehoiachin king of Judah had been in exile for thirty-seven years, Evil-Merodach became king in Babylon and let Jehoiachin out of prison. This release took place on the twenty-seventh day of the twelfth month. The king treated him most courteously and gave him preferential treatment beyond anything experienced by the other political prisoners held in Babylon. Jehoiachin took off his prison garb and for the rest of his life ate his meals in company with the king. The king provided everything he needed to live comfortably.

1 CHRONICLES

NEW KING JAMES VERSION

THE FAMILY OF ADAM—SETH TO ABRAHAM

1 Adam, Seth, Enosh, 2Cainan,[a] Mahalalel, Jared, 3Enoch, Methuselah, Lamech, 4Noah,[a] Shem, Ham, and Japheth.

5The sons of Japheth *were* Gomer, Magog, Madai, Javan, Tubal, Meshech, and Tiras. 6The sons of Gomer *were* Ashkenaz, Diphath,[a] and Togarmah. 7The sons of Javan *were* Elishah, Tarshishah,[a] Kittim, and Rodanim.[b]

8The sons of Ham *were* Cush, Mizraim, Put, and Canaan. 9The sons of Cush *were* Seba, Havilah, Sabta,[a] Raama,[b] and Sabtecha. The sons of Raama *were* Sheba and Dedan. 10Cush begot Nimrod; he began to be a mighty one on the earth. 11Mizraim begot Ludim, Anamim, Lehabim, Naphtuhim, 12Pathrusim, Casluhim (from whom came the Philistines and the Caphtorim). 13Canaan begot Sidon, his firstborn, and Heth; 14the Jebusite, the Amorite, and the Girgashite; 15the Hivite, the Arkite, and the Sinite; 16the Arvadite, the Zemarite, and the Hamathite.

17The sons of Shem *were* Elam, Asshur, Arphaxad, Lud, Aram, Uz, Hul, Gether, and Meshech.[a] 18Arphaxad begot Shelah, and Shelah begot Eber. 19To Eber were born two sons: the name of one *was* Peleg,[a] for in his days the earth was divided; and his brother's name *was* Joktan. 20Joktan begot Almodad, Sheleph, Hazarmaveth, Jerah, 21Hadoram, Uzal, Diklah, 22Ebal,[a] Abimael, Sheba, 23Ophir, Havilah, and Jobab. All these *were* the sons of Joktan.

24Shem, Arphaxad, Shelah, 25Eber, Peleg, Reu, 26Serug, Nahor, Terah, 27and Abram, who *is* Abraham. 28The sons of Abraham *were* Isaac and Ishmael.

THE FAMILY OF ISHMAEL

29These *are* their genealogies: The firstborn of Ishmael *was* Nebajoth; then Kedar, Adbeel, Mibsam, 30Mishma, Dumah, Massa, Hadad,[a] Tema, 31Jetur, Naphish, and Kedemah. These *were* the sons of Ishmael.

THE FAMILY OF KETURAH

32Now the sons born to Keturah, Abraham's concubine, *were* Zimran, Jokshan, Medan, Midian, Ishbak, and Shuah. The sons of Jokshan *were* Sheba and Dedan. 33The sons of Midian *were* Ephah, Epher, Hanoch, Abida, and Eldaah. All these were the children of Keturah.

1:2 [a]Hebrew *Qenan* **1:4** [a]Following Masoretic Text and Vulgate; Septuagint adds *the sons of Noah.* **1:6** [a]Spelled *Riphath* in Genesis 10:3 **1:7** [a]Spelled *Tarshish* in Genesis 10:4 [b]Spelled *Dodanim* in Genesis 10:4 **1:9** [a]Spelled *Sabtah* in Genesis 10:7 [b]Spelled *Raamah* in Genesis 10:7 **1:17** [a]Spelled *Mash* in Genesis 10:23 **1:19** [a]Literally *Division* **1:22** [a]Spelled *Obal* in Genesis 10:28 **1:30** [a]Spelled *Hadar* in Genesis 25:15

THE MESSAGE

ISRAEL'S FAMILY TREE: THE TRUNK

1-4 1 Adam
Seth
Enosh
Kenan
Mahalalel
Jared
Enoch
Methuselah
Lamech
Noah
Shem, Ham, and Japheth.

THE JAPHETH BRANCH

5 Japheth had Gomer, Magog, Madai, Javan, Tubal, Meshech, and Tiras.

6 Gomer had Ashkenaz, Riphath, and Togarmah.

7 Javan had Elisha, Tarshish, Kittim, and Rodanim.

THE HAM BRANCH

8 Ham had Cush, Mizraim, Put, and Canaan.

9 Cush had Seba, Havilah, Sabta, Raamah, and Sabteca.

Raamah had Sheba and Dedan.

10 Cush had Nimrod, the first great hero on earth.

11-12 Mizraim was ancestor to the Ludim, the Anamim, the Lehabim, the Naphtuhim, the Pathrusim, the Casluhim, and the Caphtorim from whom the Philistines descended.

13-16 Canaan had Sidon (his firstborn) and Heth, and was ancestor to the Jebusites, the Amorites, the Girgashites, the Hivites, the Arkites, the Sinites, the Arvadites, the Zemarites, and the Hamathites.

THE SHEM BRANCH

17 Shem had Elam, Asshur, Arphaxad, Lud, Aram, Uz, Hul, Gether, and Meshech.

18-19 Arphaxad had Shelah and Shelah had Eber. Eber had two sons: Peleg (Division) because in his time the earth was divided up; his brother was Joktan.

20-23 Joktan had Almodad, Sheleph, Hazarmaveth, Jerah, Hadoram, Uzal, Diklah, Ebal, Abimael, Sheba, Ophir, Havilah, and Jobab—all sons of Joktan.

24-28 The three main branches in summary: Shem, Arphaxad, Shelah, Eber, Peleg, Reu, Serug, Nahor, Terah, and Abram (Abraham). And Abraham had Isaac and Ishmael.

THE FAMILY OF ABRAHAM

29-31 Abraham's family tree developed along these lines: Ishmael had Nebaioth (his firstborn), then Kedar, Adbeel, Mibsam, Mishma, Dumah, Massa, Hadad, Tema, Jetur, Naphish, and Kedemah—the Ishmael branch.

32-33 Keturah, Abraham's concubine, gave birth to Zimran, Jokshan, Medan, Midian, Ishbak, and Shuah. Then Jokshan had Sheba and Dedan. And Midian had Ephah, Epher, Hanoch, Abida, and Eldaah. These made up the Keturah branch.

NEW KING JAMES VERSION

THE FAMILY OF ISAAC

34And Abraham begot Isaac. The sons of
Isaac *were* Esau and Israel. 35The sons of Esau
were Eliphaz, Reuel, Jeush, Jaalam, and Korah.
36And the sons of Eliphaz *were* Teman, Omar,
Zephi,[a] Gatam, *and* Kenaz; and *by* Timna,[b]
Amalek. 37The sons of Reuel *were* Nahath,
Zerah, Shammah, and Mizzah.

THE FAMILY OF SEIR

38The sons of Seir *were* Lotan, Shobal,
Zibeon, Anah, Dishon, Ezer, and Dishan. 39And
the sons of Lotan *were* Hori and Homam;
Lotan's sister *was* Timna. 40The sons of Shobal
were Alian,[a] Manahath, Ebal, Shephi,[b] and
Onam. The sons of Zibeon *were* Ajah and Anah.
41The son of Anah *was* Dishon. The sons of Di-
shon *were* Hamran,[a] Eshban, Ithran, and Cheran.
42The sons of Ezer *were* Bilhan, Zaavan, *and*
Jaakan.[a] The sons of Dishan *were* Uz and Aran.

THE KINGS OF EDOM

43Now these *were* the kings who reigned in
the land of Edom before a king reigned over the
children of Israel: Bela the son of Beor, and the
name of his city was Dinhabah. 44And when
Bela died, Jobab the son of Zerah of Bozrah
reigned in his place. 45When Jobab died,
Husham of the land of the Temanites reigned in
his place. 46And when Husham died, Hadad the
son of Bedad, who attacked Midian in the field
of Moab, reigned in his place. The name of his
city *was* Avith. 47When Hadad died, Samlah of
Masrekah reigned in his place. 48And when
Samlah died, Saul of Rehoboth-by-the-River
reigned in his place. 49When Saul died, Baal-
Hanan the son of Achbor reigned in his place.
50And when Baal-Hanan died, Hadad[a] reigned
in his place; and the name of his city was Pai.[b]
His wife's name was Mehetabel the daughter of
Matred, the daughter of Mezahab. 51Hadad died
also. And the chiefs of Edom were Chief Tim-
nah, Chief Aliah,[a] Chief Jetheth, 52Chief Aho-
libamah, Chief Elah, Chief Pinon, 53Chief Kenaz,
Chief Teman, Chief Mibzar, 54Chief Magdiel,
and Chief Iram. These *were* the chiefs of Edom.

THE FAMILY OF ISRAEL

2 These *were* the sons of Israel: Reuben,
Simeon, Levi, Judah, Issachar, Zebulun, 2Dan,
Joseph, Benjamin, Naphtali, Gad, and Asher.

FROM JUDAH TO DAVID

3The sons of Judah *were* Er, Onan, and She-
lah. *These* three were born to him by the daugh-
ter of Shua, the Canaanitess. Er, the firstborn of
Judah, was wicked in the sight of the LORD; so
He killed him. 4And Tamar, his daughter-in-law,
bore him Perez and Zerah. All the sons of Judah
were five.

5The sons of Perez *were* Hezron and Hamul.

1:36 [a]Spelled *Zepho* in Genesis 36:11 [b]Compare Genesis 36:12
1:40 [a]Spelled *Alvan* in Genesis 36:23 [b]Spelled *Shepho* in Genesis
36:23 **1:41** [a]Spelled *Hemdan* in Genesis 36:26 **1:42** [a]Spelled
Akan in Genesis 36:27 **1:50** [a]Spelled *Hadar* in Genesis 36:39
[b]Spelled *Pau* in Genesis 36:39 **1:51** [a]Spelled *Alvah* in Genesis
36:40

THE MESSAGE

34-37 Abraham had Isaac, and Isaac had Esau
and Israel (Jacob). Esau had Eliphaz, Reuel,
Jeush, Jalam, and Korah. Eliphaz had Te-
man, Omar, Zepho, Gatam, Kenaz, Timna,
and Amalek. And Reuel had Nahath, Zerah,
Shammah, and Mizzah.

38-42 Seir then had Lotan, Shobal, Zibeon,
Anah, Dishon, Ezer, and Dishan. Lotan had
Hori and Homam. Timna was Lotan's sister.
Shobal had Alian, Manahath, Ebal, Shepho,
and Onam. Zibeon had Aiah and Anah.
Anah had Dishon. Dishon had Hemdan, Esh-
ban, Ithran, and Keran. Ezer had Bilhan, Za-
avan, and Akan. And Dishan had Uz and
Aran.

THE EDOMITE KING LIST

43-51 A list of the kings who ruled in the country
of Edom before Israel had a king:

Bela son of Beor; his city was Dinhabah.

Bela died; Jobab son of Zerah from
Bozrah was the next king.

Jobab died; Husham from the country of
the Temanites was the next king.

Husham died; Hadad son of Bedad, who
defeated Midian in the country of Moab,
was the next king; his city was Avith.

Hadad died; Samlah from Masrekah was
the next king.

Samlah died; Shaul from Rehoboth-by-
the-River was the next king.

Shaul died; Baal-Hanan son of Acbor
was the next king.

Baal-Hanan died; Hadad was the next
king; his city was Pau and his wife was
Mehetabel daughter of Matred, the daugh-
ter of Me-Zahab.

Last of all Hadad died.

51-54 The chieftains of Edom after that were
Chief Timna, Chief Alvah, Chief Jetheth,
Chief Oholibamah, Chief Elah, Chief Pinon,
Chief Kenaz, Chief Teman, Chief Mibzar,
Chief Magdiel, and Chief Iram. These were
the chieftains of Edom.

THE FAMILY OF ISRAEL (JACOB)

1-2 2 Israel's (that is, Jacob's) sons: Reuben,
Simeon, Levi, Judah, Issachar, Zebulun,
Dan, Joseph, Benjamin, Naphtali, Gad, and
Asher.

3-9 Judah had Er, Onan, and Shelah; their
mother was Bathshua the Canaanite. Er, Ju-
dah's firstborn, was so bad before GOD that
GOD killed him. Judah also had Perez and
Zerah by his daughter-in-law Tamar—a total
of five sons. Perez had Hezron and Hamul;

NEW KING JAMES VERSION

6The sons of Zerah *were* Zimri, Ethan, Heman,
Calcol, and Dara—five of them in all.
7The son of Carmi *was* Achar,[a] the troubler
of Israel, who transgressed in the accursed
thing.
8The son of Ethan *was* Azariah.
9Also the sons of Hezron who were born to
him *were* Jerahmeel, Ram, and Chelubai.[a]
10Ram begot Amminadab, and Amminadab be-
got Nahshon, leader of the children of Judah;
11Nahshon begot Salma,[a] and Salma begot
Boaz; 12Boaz begot Obed, and Obed begot Jesse;
13Jesse begot Eliab his firstborn, Abinadab the
second, Shimea[a] the third, 14Nethanel the
fourth, Raddai the fifth, 15Ozem the sixth, *and*
David the seventh.
16Now their sisters *were* Zeruiah and Abi-
gail. And the sons of Zeruiah *were* Abishai,
Joab, and Asahel—three. 17Abigail bore Amasa;
and the father of Amasa *was* Jether the Ish-
maelite.[a]

THE FAMILY OF HEZRON

18Caleb the son of Hezron had children by
Azubah, *his* wife, and by Jerioth. Now these
were her sons: Jesher, Shobab, and Ardon.
19When Azubah died, Caleb took Ephrath[a] as
his wife, who bore him Hur. 20And Hur begot
Uri, and Uri begot Bezalel.
21Now afterward Hezron went in to the
daughter of Machir the father of Gilead, whom
he married when he *was* sixty years old; and
she bore him Segub. 22Segub begot Jair, who
had twenty-three cities in the land of Gilead.
23(Geshur and Syria took from them the towns
of Jair, with Kenath and its towns—sixty towns.)
All these *belonged to* the sons of Machir the fa-
ther of Gilead. 24After Hezron died in Caleb
Ephrathah, Hezron's wife Abijah bore him Ash-
hur the father of Tekoa.

THE FAMILY OF JERAHMEEL

25The sons of Jerahmeel, the firstborn of
Hezron, *were* Ram, the firstborn, and Bunah,
Oren, Ozem, *and* Ahijah. 26Jerahmeel had an-
other wife, whose name was Atarah; she was the
mother of Onam. 27The sons of Ram, the first-
born of Jerahmeel, were Maaz, Jamin, and Eker.
28The sons of Onam were Shammai and Jada.
The sons of Shammai *were* Nadab and Abishur.
29And the name of the wife of Abishur *was*
Abihail, and she bore him Ahban and Molid.
30The sons of Nadab *were* Seled and Appaim;
Seled died without children. 31The son of Ap-
paim *was* Ishi, the son of Ishi *was* Sheshan, and
Sheshan's son *was* Ahlai. 32The sons of Jada, the
brother of Shammai, *were* Jether and Jonathan;
Jether died without children. 33The sons of
Jonathan *were* Peleth and Zaza. These were the
sons of Jerahmeel.
34Now Sheshan had no sons, only daughters.
And Sheshan had an Egyptian servant whose

2:7 [a]Spelled *Achan* in Joshua 7:1 and elsewhere 2:9 [a]Spelled *Caleb* in 2:18, 42 2:11 [a]Spelled *Salmon* in Ruth 4:21 and Luke 3:32 2:13 [a]Spelled *Shammah* in 1 Samuel 16:9 and elsewhere 2:17 [a]Compare 2 Samuel 17:25 2:19 [a]Spelled *Ephrathah* elsewhere

THE MESSAGE

Zerah had Zimri, Ethan, Heman, Calcol, and
Darda—five sons. Carmi had Achar, who
brought doom on Israel when he violated a
holy ban. Ethan's son was Azariah. And
Hezron had Jerahmeel, Ram, and Chelubai.
10-17 Ram had Amminadab and Amminadab
had Nahshon, a prominent leader in the Ju-
dah family. Nahshon had Salmon and
Salmon had Boaz. Boaz had Obed and Obed
had Jesse. Jesse's firstborn was Eliab, fol-
lowed by Abinadab, Shimea, Nethanel, Rad-
dai, Ozem, and finally David; David was the
seventh. Their sisters were Zeruiah and Abi-
gail. Zeruiah gave birth to three sons:
Abishai, Joab, and Asahel; Abigail was the
mother of Amasa (the father was Jether the
Ishmaelite).

THE FAMILY OF CALEB

18-24 Caleb son of Hezron had children by his
wife Azubah and also by Jerioth. Azubah's
sons were Jesher, Shobab, and Ardon. After
Azubah died, Caleb married Ephrath, who
gave birth to Hur. Hur had Uri and Uri had
Bezalel. Some time later Hezron married
the daughter of Makir the father of Gilead;
he was sixty years old when he married her;
she gave birth to Segub. Then Segub had
Jair who owned twenty-three cities in the
land of Gilead. Geshur and Aram captured
the nomadic villages of Jair and Kenath and
their satellite settlements—sixty towns.
These all belonged to Makir the father of
Gilead. After the death of Hezron, Caleb
married Ephrathah the wife of his father
Hezron; she then gave birth to Ashhur the
father of Tekoa.

THE FAMILY OF JERAHMEEL

25-26 The sons of Jerahmeel, Hezron's firstborn:
Ram his firstborn, followed by Bunah, Oren,
Ozem, and Ahijah. Jerahmeel had another
wife whose name was Atarah; she gave
birth to Onam.
27 The sons of Ram, Jerahmeel's firstborn:
Maaz, Jamin, and Eker.
28-29 The sons of Onam: Shammai and Jada.
The sons of Shammai: Nadab and
Abishur. Abishur's wife was Abihail; she
gave birth to Ahban and Molid.
30 Nadab had Seled and Appaim. Seled died
leaving no sons.
31 Appaim had Ishi; Ishi had Sheshan; and
Sheshan had Ahlai.
32 Jada, Shammai's brother, had Jether and
Jonathan. Jether died leaving no sons.
33 Jonathan had Peleth and Zaza.
This is the family tree of the sons of Je-
rahmeel.

34-41 Sheshan had no sons, only daughters. But
Sheshan had an Egyptian servant, Jarha.

NEW KING JAMES VERSION

name *was* Jarha. 35Sheshan gave his daughter to
Jarha his servant as wife, and she bore him Attai.
36Attai begot Nathan, and Nathan begot Zabad;
37Zabad begot Ephlal, and Ephlal begot Obed;
38Obed begot Jehu, and Jehu begot Azariah;
39Azariah begot Helez, and Helez begot Eleasah;
40Eleasah begot Sismai, and Sismai begot Shal-
lum; 41Shallum begot Jekamiah, and Jekamiah
begot Elishama.

THE FAMILY OF CALEB

42The descendants of Caleb the brother of
Jerahmeel *were* Mesha, his firstborn, who was
the father of Ziph, and the sons of Mareshah the
father of Hebron. 43The sons of Hebron *were* Ko-
rah, Tappuah, Rekem, and Shema. 44Shema be-
got Raham the father of Jorkoam, and Rekem
begot Shammai. 45And the son of Shammai *was*
Maon, and Maon *was* the father of Beth Zur.

46Ephah, Caleb's concubine, bore Haran,
Moza, and Gazez; and Haran begot Gazez.
47And the sons of Jahdai *were* Regem, Jotham,
Geshan, Pelet, Ephah, and Shaaph.

48Maachah, Caleb's concubine, bore Sheber
and Tirhanah. 49She also bore Shaaph the father
of Madmannah, Sheva the father of Machbenah
and the father of Gibea. And the daughter of
Caleb *was* Achsah.

50These were the descendants of Caleb: The
sons of Hur, the firstborn of Ephrathah, *were*
Shobal the father of Kirjath Jearim, 51Salma the
father of Bethlehem, *and* Hareph the father of
Beth Gader.

52And Shobal the father of Kirjath Jearim
had descendants: Haroeh, *and* half of the *fami-
lies of* Manuhoth.[a] 53The families of Kirjath
Jearim *were* the Ithrites, the Puthites, the Shu-
mathites, and the Mishraites. From these came
the Zorathites and the Eshtaolites.

54The sons of Salma *were* Bethlehem, the Ne-
tophathites, Atroth Beth Joab, half of the Mana-
hethites, and the Zorites.

55And the families of the scribes who dwelt
at Jabez *were* the Tirathites, the Shimeathites,
and the Suchathites. These *were* the Kenites
who came from Hammath, the father of the
house of Rechab.

THE FAMILY OF DAVID

3 Now these were the sons of David who were
born to him in Hebron: The firstborn *was*
Amnon, by Ahinoam the Jezreelitess; the sec-
ond, Daniel,[a] by Abigail the Carmelitess; 2the
third, Absalom the son of Maacah, the daughter
of Talmai, king of Geshur; the fourth, Adonijah
the son of Haggith; 3the fifth, Shephatiah, by
Abital; the sixth, Ithream, by his wife Eglah.

4*These* six were born to him in Hebron.
There he reigned seven years and six months,
and in Jerusalem he reigned thirty-three years.
5And these were born to him in Jerusalem:
Shimea,[a] Shobab, Nathan, and Solomon—four
by Bathshua[b] the daughter of Ammiel.[c] 6Also

2:52 [a]Same as *the Manahethites,* verse 54 3:1 [a]Called *Chileab* in 2 Samuel 3:3 3:5 [a]Spelled *Shammua* in 14:4 and 2 Samuel 5:14 [b]Spelled *Bathsheba* in 2 Samuel 11:3 [c]Called *Eliam* in 2 Samuel 11:3

THE MESSAGE

Sheshan married his daughter to Jarha and she gave birth to Attai. Attai had Nathan, Nathan had Zabad, Zabad had Ephlal, Ephlal had Obed, Obed had Jehu, Jehu had Azariah, Azariah had Helez, Helez had Eleasah, Eleasah had Sismai, Sismai had Shallum, Shallum had Jekamiah, and Jekamiah had Elishama.

42 Jerahmeel's brother Caleb had a son, his firstborn, named Mesha; Mesha had Ziph; Ziph's son was Mareshah the father of Hebron.

43-44 The sons of Hebron: Korah, Tappuah, Rekem, and Shema. Shema had Raham the father of Jorkeam; Rekem had Shammai.

45 Shammai's son was Maon and Maon was the father of Beth Zur.

46 Caleb's concubine Ephah gave birth to Haran, Moza, and Gazez; Haran had Gazez.

47 The sons of Jahdai: Regem, Jotham, Geshan, Pelet, Ephah, and Shaaph.

48-50 Another concubine of Caleb, Maacah, gave birth to Sheber and Tirhanah. She also bore Shaaph the father of Madmannah and Sheva the father of Macbenah and Gibea. Caleb's daughter was Acsah. These made up the Caleb branch of the family tree.

50-51 The sons of Hur, Ephrathah's firstborn: Shobal who had Kiriath Jearim, Salma who had Bethlehem, and Hareph father of Beth Gader.

52-53 The family of Shobal, father of Kiriath Jearim: Haroeh, half of the population of Manahath, the families of Kiriath Jearim, the Ithrites, the Puthites, the Shumathites, and the Mishraites. The Zorathites and Eshtaolites also came from this line.

54-55 The sons of Salma: Bethlehem, the Netophathites, Atroth Beth Joab, half of the Manahathites, the Zorites, and the families of Sopherim who lived at Jabez—the Tirathites, the Shimeathites, and the Sucathites. They made up the Kenites who came from Hammath the father of the house of Recab.

THE FAMILY OF DAVID

1-3 3 These are the sons that David had while he lived at Hebron:

His firstborn was Amnon by Ahinoam of Jezreel;

second, Daniel by Abigail of Carmel;

third, Absalom born of Maacah, daughter of Talmai king of Geshur;

fourth, Adonijah born of Haggith;

fifth, Shephatiah born of Abital;

sixth, Ithream born of his wife Eglah.

4-9 He had these six sons while he was in Hebron; he was king there for seven years and six months.

He went on to be king in Jerusalem for another thirty-three years. These are the sons he had in Jerusalem: first Shammua, then Shobab, Nathan, and Solomon. Bathsheba daughter of Ammiel was the mother of these four. And then there were

New King James Version

there were Ibhar, Elishama,[a] Eliphelet,[b] 7Nogah, Nepheg, Japhia, 8Elishama, Eliada,[a] and Eliphelet—nine *in all.* 9*These were* all the sons of David, besides the sons of the concubines, and Tamar their sister.

The Family of Solomon

10Solomon's son *was* Rehoboam; Abijah[a] *was* his son, Asa his son, Jehoshaphat his son, 11Joram[a] his son, Ahaziah his son, Joash[b] his son, 12Amaziah his son, Azariah[a] his son, Jotham his son, 13Ahaz his son, Hezekiah his son, Manasseh his son, 14Amon his son, *and* Josiah his son. 15The sons of Josiah *were* Johanan the firstborn, the second Jehoiakim, the third Zedekiah, and the fourth Shallum.[a] 16The sons of Jehoiakim *were* Jeconiah his son *and* Zedekiah[a] his son.

The Family of Jeconiah

17And the sons of Jeconiah[a] *were* Assir,[b] Shealtiel his son, 18*and* Malchiram, Pedaiah, Shenazzar, Jecamiah, Hoshama, and Nedabiah. 19The sons of Pedaiah *were* Zerubbabel and Shimei. The sons of Zerubbabel *were* Meshullam, Hananiah, Shelomith their sister, 20and Hashubah, Ohel, Berechiah, Hasadiah, and Jushab-Hesed—five *in all.*

21The sons of Hananiah *were* Pelatiah and Jeshaiah, the sons of Rephaiah, the sons of Arnan, the sons of Obadiah, and the sons of Shechaniah. 22The son of Shechaniah was Shemaiah. The sons of Shemaiah *were* Hattush, Igal, Bariah, Neariah, and Shaphat—six *in all.* 23The sons of Neariah *were* Elioenai, Hezekiah, and Azrikam—three *in all.* 24The sons of Elioenai *were* Hodaviah, Eliashib, Pelaiah, Akkub, Johanan, Delaiah, and Anani—seven *in all.*

The Family of Judah

4 The sons of Judah *were* Perez, Hezron, Carmi, Hur, and Shobal. 2And Reaiah the son of Shobal begot Jahath, and Jahath begot Ahumai and Lahad. These *were* the families of the Zorathites. 3These *were* the sons *of the father* of Etam: Jezreel, Ishma, and Idbash; and the name of their sister *was* Hazelelponi; 4and Penuel *was* the father of Gedor, and Ezer *was the* father of Hushah.

These *were* the sons of Hur, the firstborn of Ephrathah the father of Bethlehem.

5And Ashhur the father of Tekoa had two wives, Helah and Naarah. 6Naarah bore him Ahuzzam, Hepher, Temeni, and Haahashtari. These *were* the sons of Naarah. 7The sons of Helah *were* Zereth, Zohar, and Ethnan; 8and Koz begot Anub, Zobebah, and the families of Aharhel the son of Harum.

9Now Jabez was more honorable than his brothers, and his mother called his name Jabez,[a] saying, "Because I bore *him* in pain."

3:6 [a]Spelled *Elishua* in 14:5 and 2 Samuel 5:15 [b]Spelled *Elpelet* in 14:5 **3:8** [a]Spelled *Beeliada* in 14:7 **3:10** [a]Spelled *Abijam* in 1 Kings 15:1 **3:11** [a]Spelled *Jehoram* in 2 Kings 1:17 and 8:16 [b]Spelled *Jehoash* in 2 Kings 12:1 **3:12** [a]Called *Uzziah* in Isaiah 6:1 **3:15** [a]Called *Jehoahaz* in 2 Kings 23:31 **3:16** [a]Compare 2 Kings 24:17 **3:17** [a]Also called *Coniah* in Jeremiah 22:24 and *Jehoiachin* in 2 Kings 24:8 [b]Or *Jeconiah the captive were* **4:9** [a]Literally *He Will Cause Pain*

The Message

another nine sons: Ibhar, Elishua, Eliphelet, Nogah, Nepheg, Japhia, Elishama, Eliada, Eliphelet—David's sons, plus Tamar their sister. There were other sons by his concubines.

10-14 In the next generation Solomon had Rehoboam, who had Abijah, who had Asa, who had Jehoshaphat, who had Jehoram, who had Ahaziah, who had Joash, who had Amaziah, who had Azariah, who had Jotham, who had Ahaz, who had Hezekiah, who had Manasseh, who had Amon, who had Josiah.

15 Josiah's firstborn was Johanan, followed by Jehoiakim, then Zedekiah, and finally Shallum.

16 Jehoiakim's sons were Jeconiah (Jehoiachin) and Zedekiah.

17-18 The sons of Jeconiah born while he was captive in Babylon: Shealtiel, Malkiram, Pedaiah, Shenazzar, Jekamiah, Hoshama, and Nedabiah.

19-20 Pedaiah had Zerubbabel and Shimei; Zerubbabel had Meshullam and Hananiah. Shelomith was their sister. And then five more—Hashubah, Ohel, Berekiah, Hasadiah, and Jushab-Hesed.

21 Hananiah's sons were Pelatiah and Jeshaiah. There were also sons of Rephaiah, sons of Arnan, sons of Obadiah, and sons of Shecaniah.

22 Shecaniah had Shemaiah who in his turn had Hattush, Igal, Bariah, Neariah, and Shaphat—six of them.

23 Neariah had three sons: Elioenai, Hizkiah, and Azrikam.

24 And Elioenai had seven sons: Hodaviah, Eliashib, Pelaiah, Akkub, Johanan, Delaiah, and Anani.

An Appendix to the Family of Judah

1-2 4 Sons of Judah: Perez, Hezron, Carmi, Hur, and Shobal. Reaiah, Shobal's son, had Jahath; and Jahath had Ahumai and Lahad. These made up the families of the Zorathites.

3-4 Sons of Etam: Jezreel, Ishma, and Idbash. Their sister was named Hazzelelponi. Penuel had Gedor and Ezer had Hushah. These were the sons of Hur, firstborn son of Ephrathah, who was the father of Bethlehem.

5-8 Ashhur the father of Tekoa had two wives, Helah and Naarah. Naarah gave birth to Ahuzzam, Hepher, Temeni, and Haahashtari—Naarah's children. Helah's sons were Zereth, Zohar, Ethnan, and Koz, who had Anub, Hazzobebah, and the families of Aharhel son of Harum.

9-10 Jabez was a better man than his brothers, a man of honor. His mother had named him Jabez (Oh, the pain!), saying, "A painful

NEW KING JAMES VERSION

[10]And Jabez called on the God of Israel saying,
"Oh, that You would bless me indeed, and en-
large my territory, that Your hand would be with
me, and that You would keep *me* from evil, that
I may not cause pain!" So God granted him what
he requested.
[11]Chelub the brother of Shuhah begot Mehir,
who *was* the father of Eshton. [12]And Eshton be-
got Beth-Rapha, Paseah, and Tehinnah the fa-
ther of Ir-Nahash. These *were* the men of
Rechah.
[13]The sons of Kenaz *were* Othniel and Se-
raiah. The sons of Othniel *were* Hathath,[a] [14]and
Meonothai *who* begot Ophrah. Seraiah begot
Joab the father of Ge Harashim,[a] for they were
craftsmen. [15]The sons of Caleb the son of Je-
phunneh *were* Iru, Elah, and Naam. The son of
Elah *was* Kenaz. [16]The sons of Jehallelel *were*
Ziph, Ziphah, Tiria, and Asarel. [17]The sons of
Ezrah *were* Jether, Mered, Epher, and Jalon.
And *Mered's wife*[a] bore Miriam, Shammai, and
Ishbah the father of Eshtemoa. [18](His wife Je-
hudijah[a] bore Jered the father of Gedor, Heber
the father of Sochoh, and Jekuthiel the father of
Zanoah.) And these were the sons of Bithiah the
daughter of Pharaoh, whom Mered took.
[19]The sons of Hodiah's wife, the sister of Na-
ham, *were* the fathers of Keilah the Garmite and
of Eshtemoa the Maachathite. [20]And the sons of
Shimon *were* Amnon, Rinnah, Ben-Hanan, and
Tilon. And the sons of Ishi *were* Zoheth and
Ben-Zoheth.
[21]The sons of Shelah the son of Judah *were*
Er the father of Lecah, Laadah the father of
Mareshah, and the families of the house of the
linen workers of the house of Ashbea; [22]also
Jokim, the men of Chozeba, and Joash; Saraph,
who ruled in Moab, and Jashubi-Lehem. Now
the records are ancient. [23]These *were* the potters
and those who dwell at Netaim[a] and Gederah;[b]
there they dwelt with the king for his work.

THE FAMILY OF SIMEON

[24]The sons of Simeon *were* Nemuel, Jamin,
Jarib,[a] Zerah,[b] *and* Shaul, [25]Shallum his son,
Mibsam his son, and Mishma his son. [26]And the
sons of Mishma *were* Hamuel his son, Zacchur
his son, and Shimei his son. [27]Shimei had six-
teen sons and six daughters; but his brothers
did not have many children, nor did any of their
families multiply as much as the children of Ju-
dah.
[28]They dwelt at Beersheba, Moladah, Ha-
zar Shual, [29]Bilhah, Ezem, Tolad, [30]Bethuel,
Hormah, Ziklag, [31]Beth Marcaboth, Hazar
Susim, Beth Biri, and at Shaaraim. These *were*
their cities until the reign of David. [32]And their
villages *were* Etam, Ain, Rimmon, Tochen, and
Ashan—five cities— [33]and all the villages that
were around these cities as far as Baal.[a] These
were their dwelling places, and they maintained
their genealogy: [34]Meshobab, Jamlech, and
Joshah the son of Amaziah; [35]Joel, and Jehu the

4:13 [a]Septuagint and Vulgate add *and Meonothai.* **4:14** [a]Literally *Valley of Craftsmen* **4:17** [a]Literally *she* **4:18** [a]Or *His Judean wife* **4:23** [a]Literally *Plants* [b]Literally *Hedges* **4:24** [a]Called *Jachin* in Genesis 46:10 [b]Called *Zohar* in Genesis 46:10 **4:33** [a]Or *Baalath Beer* (compare Joshua 19:8)

THE MESSAGE

birth! I bore him in great pain!" Jabez
prayed to the God of Israel: "Bless me, O
bless me! Give me land, large tracts of land.
And provide your personal protection—
don't let evil hurt me." God gave him what
he asked.

11-12 Kelub, Shuhah's brother, had Mehir; Mehir
had Eshton; Eshton had Beth Rapha,
Paseah, and Tehinnah, who founded Ir Na-
hash (City of Smiths). These were known as
the men of Recah.
13 The sons of Kenaz: Othniel and Seraiah.
The sons of Othniel: Hathath and Me-
onothai.
14 Meonothai had Ophrah; Seraiah had
Joab, the founder of Ge Harashim (Colony
of Artisans).
15 The sons of Caleb son of Jephunneh: Iru,
Elah, and Naam.
The son of Elah: Kenaz.
16 The sons of Jehallelel: Ziph, Ziphah,
Tiria, and Asarel.
17-18 The sons of Ezrah: Jether, Mered, Epher,
and Jalon. One of Mered's wives, Pharaoh's
daughter Bithiah, gave birth to Miriam,
Shammai, and Ishbah the father of Eshte-
moa. His Judean wife gave birth to Jered fa-
ther of Gedor, Heber father of Soco, and
Jekuthiel father of Zanoah.
19 The sons of Hodiah's wife, Naham's sister:
the father of Keilah the Garmite, and Esh-
temoa the Maacathite.
20 The sons of Shimon: Amnon, Rinnah,
Ben-Hanan, and Tilon.
The sons of Ishi: Zoheth and Ben-Zoheth.
21-23 The sons of Shelah son of Judah: Er the
father of Lecah, Laadah the father of Mare-
shah and the family of linen workers at Beth
Ashbea, Jokim, the men of Cozeba, and
Joash and Saraph, who ruled in Moab and
Jashubi Lehem. (These records are from
very old traditions.) They were the potters
who lived at Netaim and Gederah, resident
potters who worked for the king.

THE FAMILY OF SIMEON

24-25 The Simeon family tree: Nemuel, Jamin,
Jarib, Zerah, and Shaul; Shaul had Shallum,
Shallum had Mibsam, and Mibsam had
Mishma.
26 The sons of Mishma: Hammuel had Zac-
cur and Zaccur had Shimei.
27-33 Shimei had sixteen sons and six daugh-
ters, but his brothers were not nearly as pro-
lific and never became a large family like Ju-
dah. They lived in Beersheba, Moladah,
Hazar Shual, Bilhah, Ezem, Tolad, Bethuel,
Hormah, Ziklag, Beth Marcaboth, Hazar
Susim, Beth Biri, and Shaaraim. They lived in
these towns until David became king. Other
settlements in the vicinity were the five
towns of Etam, Ain, Rimmon, Token, and
Ashan, and all the villages around these
towns as far as Baalath. These were their set-
tlements. And they kept good family records.
34-40 Meshobab; Jamlech; Joshah the son of
Amaziah; Joel; Jehu the son of Joshibiah,

NEW KING JAMES VERSION

son of Joshibiah, the son of Seraiah, the son of Asiel; [36]Elioenai, Jaakobah, Jeshohaiah, Asaiah, Adiel, Jesimiel, and Benaiah; [37]Ziza the son of Shiphi, the son of Allon, the son of Jedaiah, the son of Shimri, the son of Shemaiah— [38]these mentioned by name *were* leaders in their families, and their father's house increased greatly.

[39]So they went to the entrance of Gedor, as far as the east side of the valley, to seek pasture for their flocks. [40]And they found rich, good pasture, and the land *was* broad, quiet, and peaceful; for some Hamites formerly lived there.

[41]These recorded by name came in the days of Hezekiah king of Judah; and they attacked their tents and the Meunites who were found there, and utterly destroyed them, as it is to this day. So they dwelt in their place, because *there was* pasture for their flocks there. [42]Now *some* of them, five hundred men of the sons of Simeon, went to Mount Seir, having as their captains Pelatiah, Neariah, Rephaiah, and Uzziel, the sons of Ishi. [43]And they defeated the rest of the Amalekites who had escaped. They have dwelt there to this day.

THE FAMILY OF REUBEN

5 Now the sons of Reuben the firstborn of Israel—he *was* indeed the firstborn, but because he defiled his father's bed, his birthright was given to the sons of Joseph, the son of Israel, so that the genealogy is not listed according to the birthright; [2]yet Judah prevailed over his brothers, and from him *came* a ruler, although the birthright was Joseph's— [3]the sons of Reuben the firstborn of Israel were Hanoch, Pallu, Hezron, and Carmi.

[4]The sons of Joel *were* Shemaiah his son, Gog his son, Shimei his son, [5]Micah his son, Reaiah his son, Baal his son, [6]and Beerah his son, whom Tiglath-Pileser[a] king of Assyria carried into captivity. He *was* leader of the Reubenites. [7]And his brethren by their families, when the genealogy of their generations was registered: the chief, Jeiel, and Zechariah, [8]and Bela the son of Azaz, the son of Shema, the son of Joel, who dwelt in Aroer, as far as Nebo and Baal Meon. [9]Eastward they settled as far as the entrance of the wilderness this side of the River Euphrates, because their cattle had multiplied in the land of Gilead.

[10]Now in the days of Saul they made war with the Hagrites, who fell by their hand; and they dwelt in their tents throughout the entire *area* east of Gilead.

THE FAMILY OF GAD

[11]And the children of Gad dwelt next to them in the land of Bashan as far as Salcah: [12]Joel *was* the chief, Shapham the next, then Jaanai and Shaphat in Bashan, [13]and their brethren of their father's house: Michael, Meshullam, Sheba, Jorai, Jachan, Zia, and Eber—seven *in all.* [14]These *were* the children of Abihail the son of Huri, the son of Jaroah, the son of Gilead, the son of Michael, the son of Jeshishai, the son of

5:6 [a]Hebrew *Tilgath-Pilneser*

THE MESSAGE

the son of Seraiah, the son of Asiel; Elioenai; Jaakobah; Jeshohaiah; Asaiah; Adiel; Jesimiel; Benaiah; and Ziza the son of Shiphi, the son of Allon, the son of Jedaiah, the son of Shimri, the son of Shemaiah—all these were the leaders in their families. They prospered and increased in numbers so that they had to go as far as Gedor (Gerar) to the east of the valley looking for pasture for their flocks. And they found it—lush pasture, lots of elbow room, peaceful and quiet.

40-43 Some Hamites had lived there in former times. But the men in these family trees came when Hezekiah was king of Judah and attacked the Hamites, tearing down their tents and houses. There was nothing left of them, as you can see today. Then they moved in and took over because of the great pastureland. Five hundred of these Simeonites went on and invaded the hill country of Seir, led by Pelatiah, Neariah, Rephaiah, and Uzziel, the sons of Ishi. They killed all the escaped Amalekites who were still around. And they still live there.

THE FAMILY OF REUBEN

1-2 5 The family of Reuben the firstborn of Israel: Though Reuben was Israel's firstborn, after he slept with his father's concubine, a defiling act, his rights as the firstborn were passed on to the sons of Joseph son of Israel. He lost his "firstborn" place in the family tree. And even though Judah became the strongest of his brothers and King David eventually came from that family, the firstborn rights stayed with Joseph.

3 The sons of Reuben, firstborn of Israel: Hanoch, Pallu, Hezron, and Carmi.

4-6 The descendants of Joel: Shemaiah his son, Gog his son, Shimei his son, Micah his son, Reaiah his son, Baal his son, and Beerah his son, whom Tiglath-Pileser king of Assyria took into exile. Beerah was the prince of the Reubenites.

7-10 Beerah's brothers are listed in the family tree by families: first Jeiel, followed by Zechariah: then Bela son of Azaz, the son of Shema, the son of Joel. Joel lived in the area from Aroer to Nebo and Baal Meon. His family occupied the land up to the edge of the desert that goes all the way to the Euphrates River, since their growing herds of livestock spilled out of Gilead. During Saul's reign they fought and defeated the Hagrites; they then took over their tents and lived in them on the eastern frontier of Gilead.

11-12 The family of Gad were their neighbors in Bashan, as far as Salecah: Joel was the chief, Shapham the second-in-command, and then Janai, the judge in Bashan.

13-15 Their brothers, by families, were Michael, Meshullam, Sheba, Jorai, Jacan, Zia, and Eber—seven in all. These were the sons of Abihail son of Huri, the son of Jaroah, the son of Gilead, the son of Michael, the son of

NEW KING JAMES VERSION

Jahdo, the son of Buz; 15Ahi the son of Abdiel,
the son of Guni, *was* chief of their father's house.
16And *the Gadites* dwelt in Gilead, in Bashan
and in its villages, and in all the common-lands
of Sharon within their borders. 17All these were
registered by genealogies in the days of Jotham
king of Judah, and in the days of Jeroboam king
of Israel.

18The sons of Reuben, the Gadites, and half
the tribe of Manasseh *had* forty-four thousand
seven hundred and sixty valiant men, men able
to bear shield and sword, to shoot with the bow,
and skillful in war, who went to war. 19They
made war with the Hagrites, Jetur, Naphish, and
Nodab. 20And they were helped against them,
and the Hagrites were delivered into their hand,
and all who *were* with them, for they cried out
to God in the battle. He heeded their prayer, be-
cause they put their trust in Him. 21Then they
took away their livestock—fifty thousand of
their camels, two hundred and fifty thousand of
their sheep, and two thousand of their don-
keys—also one hundred thousand of their men;
22for many fell dead, because the war *was*
God's. And they dwelt in their place until the
captivity.

THE FAMILY OF MANASSEH (EAST)

23So the children of the half-tribe of Ma-
nasseh dwelt in the land. Their *numbers* in-
creased from Bashan to Baal Hermon, that is, to
Senir, or Mount Hermon. 24These *were* the
heads of their fathers' houses: Epher, Ishi, Eliel,
Azriel, Jeremiah, Hodaviah, and Jahdiel. They
were mighty men of valor, famous men, *and*
heads of their fathers' houses.

25And they were unfaithful to the God of
their fathers, and played the harlot after the
gods of the peoples of the land, whom God had
destroyed before them. 26So the God of Israel
stirred up the spirit of Pul king of Assyria, that
is, Tiglath-Pileser[a] king of Assyria. He carried
the Reubenites, the Gadites, and the half-tribe of
Manasseh into captivity. He took them to Halah,
Habor, Hara, and the river of Gozan to this day.

THE FAMILY OF LEVI

6 The sons of Levi *were* Gershon, Kohath, and
Merari. 2The sons of Kohath *were* Amram,
Izhar, Hebron, and Uzziel. 3The children of Am-
ram *were* Aaron, Moses, and Miriam. And the
sons of Aaron *were* Nadab, Abihu, Eleazar, and
Ithamar. 4Eleazar begot Phinehas, *and* Phinehas
begot Abishua; 5Abishua begot Bukki, and
Bukki begot Uzzi; 6Uzzi begot Zerahiah, and
Zerahiah begot Meraioth; 7Meraioth begot
Amariah, and Amariah begot Ahitub; 8Ahitub
begot Zadok, and Zadok begot Ahimaaz; 9Ahim-
aaz begot Azariah, and Azariah begot Johanan;
10Johanan begot Azariah (it was he who minis-
tered as priest in the temple that Solomon built
in Jerusalem); 11Azariah begot Amariah, and
Amariah begot Ahitub; 12Ahitub begot Zadok,
and Zadok begot Shallum; 13Shallum begot
Hilkiah, and Hilkiah begot Azariah; 14Azariah
begot Seraiah, and Seraiah begot Jehozadak.

5:26 [a]Hebrew *Tilgath-Pilneser*

THE MESSAGE

Jeshishai, the son of Jahdo, the son of Buz. Ahi son of Abdiel, the son of Guni, was head of their family.

16 The family of Gad lived in Gilead and Bashan, including the outlying villages and extending as far as the pastures of Sharon.

17 They were all written into the official family tree during the reigns of Jotham king of Judah and Jeroboam king of Israel.

18-22 The families of Reuben, Gad, and the half-tribe of Manasseh had 44,760 men trained for war—physically fit and skilled in handling shield, sword, and bow. They fought against the Hagrites, Jetur, Naphish, and Nodab. God helped them as they fought. God handed the Hagrites and all their allies over to them, because they cried out to him during the battle. God answered their prayers because they trusted him. They plundered the Hagrite herds and flocks: 50,000 camels, 250,000 sheep, and 2,000 donkeys. They also captured 100,000 people. Many were killed, because the battle was God's. They lived in that country until the exile.

23-26 The half-tribe of Manasseh had a large population. They occupied the land from Bashan to Baal Hermon, that is, to Senir (Mount Hermon). The heads of their families were Epher, Ishi, Eliel, Azriel, Jeremiah, Hodaviah, and Jahdiel—brave warriors, famous, and heads of their families. But they were not faithful to the God of their ancestors. They took up with the ungodly gods of the peoples of the land whom God had gotten rid of before they arrived. So the God of Israel stirred up the spirit of Pul king of Assyria (Tiglath-Pileser king of Assyria) to take the families of Reuben, Gad, and the half-tribe of Manasseh into exile. He deported them to Halah, Habor, Hara, and the river of Gozan. They've been there ever since.

THE FAMILY OF LEVI

1-14 6 The sons of Levi were Gershon, Kohath, and Merari. The sons of Kohath were Amram, Izhar, Hebron, and Uzziel. The children of Amram were Aaron, Moses, and Miriam. The sons of Aaron were Nadab, Abihu, Eleazar, and Ithamar. Eleazar had Phinehas, Phinehas had Abishua, Abishua had Bukki, Bukki had Uzzi, Uzzi had Zerahiah, Zerahiah had Meraioth, Meraioth had Amariah, Amariah had Ahitub, Ahitub had Zadok, Zadok had Ahimaaz, Ahimaaz had Azariah, Azariah had Johanan, and Johanan had Azariah (who served as priest in the temple Solomon built in Jerusalem). Azariah had Amariah, Amariah had Ahitub, Ahitub had Zadok, Zadok had Shallum, Shallum had Hilkiah, Hilkiah had Azariah, Azariah had Seraiah, and Seraiah had Jehozadak.

NEW KING JAMES VERSION

15 Jehozadak went *into captivity* when the LORD carried Judah and Jerusalem into captivity by the hand of Nebuchadnezzar.

16 The sons of Levi *were* Gershon,[a] Kohath, and Merari. 17 These are the names of the sons of Gershon: Libni and Shimei. 18 The sons of Kohath *were* Amram, Izhar, Hebron, and Uzziel. 19 The sons of Merari *were* Mahli and Mushi. Now these *are* the families of the Levites according to their fathers: 20 Of Gershon *were* Libni his son, Jahath his son, Zimmah his son, 21 Joah his son, Iddo his son, Zerah his son, *and* Jeatherai his son. 22 The sons of Kohath *were* Amminadab his son, Korah his son, Assir his son, 23 Elkanah his son, Ebiasaph his son, Assir his son, 24 Tahath his son, Uriel his son, Uzziah his son, and Shaul his son. 25 The sons of Elkanah *were* Amasai and Ahimoth. 26 *As for* Elkanah,[a] the sons of Elkanah *were* Zophai[b] his son, Nahath[c] his son, 27 Eliab[a] his son, Jeroham his son, *and* Elkanah his son. 28 The sons of Samuel *were Joel*[a] the firstborn, and Abijah the second.[b] 29 The sons of Merari *were* Mahli, Libni his son, Shimei his son, Uzzah his son, 30 Shimea his son, Haggiah his son, *and* Asaiah his son.

MUSICIANS IN THE HOUSE OF THE LORD

31 Now these are the men whom David appointed over the service of song in the house of the LORD, after the ark came to rest. 32 They were ministering with music before the dwelling place of the tabernacle of meeting, until Solomon had built the house of the LORD in Jerusalem, and they served in their office according to their order.

33 And these *are* the ones who ministered with their sons: Of the sons of the Kohathites *were* Heman the singer, the son of Joel, the son of Samuel, 34 the son of Elkanah, the son of Jeroham, the son of Eliel,[a] the son of Toah,[b] 35 the son of Zuph, the son of Elkanah, the son of Mahath, the son of Amasai, 36 the son of Elkanah, the son of Joel, the son of Azariah, the son of Zephaniah, 37 the son of Tahath, the son of Assir, the son of Ebiasaph, the son of Korah, 38 the son of Izhar, the son of Kohath, the son of Levi, the son of Israel. 39 And his brother Asaph, who stood at his right hand, *was* Asaph the son of Berachiah, the son of Shimea, 40 the son of Michael, the son of Baaseiah, the son of Malchijah, 41 the son of Ethni, the son of Zerah, the son of Adaiah, 42 the son of Ethan, the son of Zimmah, the son of Shimei, 43 the son of Jahath, the son of Gershon, the son of Levi.

44 Their brethren, the sons of Merari, on the left hand, *were* Ethan the son of Kishi, the son of Abdi, the son of Malluch, 45 the son of Hashabiah, the son of Amaziah, the son of Hilkiah, 46 the son of Amzi, the son of Bani, the son of Shamer, 47 the son of Mahli, the son of Mushi, the son of Merari, the son of Levi.

6:16 [a]Hebrew *Gershom* (alternate spelling of *Gershon*, as in verses 1, 17, 20, 43, 62, and 71) **6:26** [a]Compare verse 35 [b]Spelled *Zuph* in verse 35 and 1 Samuel 1:1 [c]Compare verse 34 **6:27** [a]Compare verse 34 **6:28** [a]Following Septuagint, Syriac, and Arabic (compare verse 33 and 1 Samuel 8:2) [b]Hebrew *Vasheni* **6:34** [a]Spelled *Elihu* in 1 Samuel 1:1 [b]Spelled *Tohu* in 1 Samuel 1:1

THE MESSAGE

15 Jehozadak went off to exile when GOD used Nebuchadnezzar to take Judah and Jerusalem into exile.

16-30 The sons of Levi were Gershon, Kohath, and Merari. These are the names of the sons of Gershon: Libni and Shimei. The sons of Kohath were Amram, Izhar, Hebron, and Uzziel. The sons of Merari were Mahli and Mushi. These are the Levitical clans according to families: the sons of Gershon were Libni his son, Jehath his son, Zimmah his son, Joah his son, Iddo his son, Zerah his son, and Jeatherai his son. The sons of Kohath were Amminadab his son, Korah his son, Assir his son, Elkanah his son, Ebiasaph his son, Assir his son, Tahath his son, Uriel his son, Uzziah his son, and Shaul his son. The sons of Elkanah were Amasai and Ahimoth, Elkanah his son, Zophai his son, Nahath his son, Eliab his son, Jeroham his son, and Elkanah his son. The sons of Samuel were Joel his firstborn son and Abijah his second. The sons of Merari were Mahli, Libni his son, Shimei his son, Uzzah his son, Shimea his son, Haggiah his son, and Asaiah his son.

DAVID'S WORSHIP LEADERS

31-32 These are the persons David appointed to lead the singing in the house of GOD after the Chest was placed there. They were the ministers of music in the place of worship, which was the Tent of Meeting until Solomon built The Temple of GOD in Jerusalem. As they carried out their work, they followed the instructions given to them.

33-38 These are the persons, together with their sons, who served by preparing for and directing worship: from the family of the Kohathites was Heman the choirmaster, the son of Joel, the son of Samuel, the son of Elkanah, the son of Jeroham, the son of Eliel, the son of Toah, the son of Zuph, the son of Elkanah, the son of Mahath, the son of Amasai, the son of Elkanah, the son of Joel, the son of Azariah, the son of Zephaniah, the son of Tahath, the son of Assir, the son of Ebiasaph, the son of Korah, the son of Izhar, the son of Kohath, the son of Levi, the son of Israel.

39-43 Heman's associate Asaph stood at his right hand. Asaph was the son of Berekiah, the son of Shimea, the son of Michael, the son of Baaseiah, the son of Malkijah, the son of Ethni, the son of Zerah, the son of Adaiah, the son of Ethan, the son of Zimmah, the son of Shimei, the son of Jahath, the son of Gershon, the son of Levi.

44-47 Of the sons of Merari, the associates who stood at his left hand, was Ethan the son of Kishi, the son of Abdi, the son of Malluch, the son of Hashabiah, the son of Amaziah, the son of Hilkiah, the son of Amzi, the son of Bani, the son of Shemer, the son of Mahli, the son of Mushi, the son of Merari, the son of Levi.

NEW KING JAMES VERSION

[48]And their brethren, the Levites, *were* appointed to every kind of service of the tabernacle of the house of God.

THE FAMILY OF AARON

[49]But Aaron and his sons offered sacrifices on the altar of burnt offering and on the altar of incense, for all the work of the Most Holy *Place*, and to make atonement for Israel, according to all that Moses the servant of God had commanded. [50]Now these *are* the sons of Aaron: Eleazar his son, Phinehas his son, Abishua his son, [51]Bukki his son, Uzzi his son, Zerahiah his son, [52]Meraioth his son, Amariah his son, Ahitub his son, [53]Zadok his son, *and* Ahimaaz his son.

DWELLING PLACES OF THE LEVITES

[54]Now these *are* their dwelling places throughout their settlements in their territory, for they were *given* by lot to the sons of Aaron, of the family of the Kohathites: [55]They gave them Hebron in the land of Judah, with its surrounding common-lands. [56]But the fields of the city and its villages they gave to Caleb the son of Jephunneh. [57]And to the sons of Aaron they gave *one of* the cities of refuge, Hebron; also Libnah with its common-lands, Jattir, Eshtemoa with its common-lands, [58]Hilen[a] with its common-lands, Debir with its common-lands, [59]Ashan[a] with its common-lands, and Beth Shemesh with its common-lands. [60]And from the tribe of Benjamin: Geba with its common-lands, Alemeth[a] with its common-lands, and Anathoth with its common-lands. All their cities among their families *were* thirteen.

[61]To the rest of the family of the tribe of the Kohathites *they gave* by lot ten cities from half the tribe of Manasseh. [62]And to the sons of Gershon, throughout their families, *they gave* thirteen cities from the tribe of Issachar, from the tribe of Asher, from the tribe of Naphtali, and from the tribe of Manasseh in Bashan. [63]To the sons of Merari, throughout their families, *they gave* twelve cities from the tribe of Reuben, from the tribe of Gad, and from the tribe of Zebulun. [64]So the children of Israel gave *these* cities with their common-lands to the Levites. [65]And they gave by lot from the tribe of the children of Judah, from the tribe of the children of Simeon, and from the tribe of the children of Benjamin these cities which are called by *their* names.

[66]Now some of the families of the sons of Kohath *were given* cities as their territory from the tribe of Ephraim. [67]And they gave them *one of* the cities of refuge, Shechem with its common-lands, in the mountains of Ephraim, also Gezer with its common-lands, [68]Jokmeam with its common-lands, Beth Horon with its common-lands, [69]Aijalon with its common-lands, and Gath Rimmon with its common-lands. [70]And from the half-tribe of Manasseh: Aner with its common-lands and Bileam with its common-lands, for the rest of the family of the sons of Kohath.

6:58 [a]Spelled *Holon* in Joshua 21:15 **6:59** [a]Spelled *Ain* in Joshua 21:16 **6:60** [a]Spelled *Almon* in Joshua 21:18

THE MESSAGE

48 The rest of the Levites were assigned to all the other work in the place of worship, the house of God.

49 Aaron and his sons offered the sacrifices on the Altar of Burnt Offering and the Altar of Incense; they were in charge of all the work surrounding the Holy of Holies. They made atonement for Israel following the instructions commanded by Moses, servant of God.

50-53 These are the sons of Aaron: Eleazar his son, Phinehas his son, Abishua his son, Bukki his son, Uzzi his son, Zerahiah his son, Meraioth his son, Amariah his son, Ahitub his son, Zadok his son, and Ahimaaz his son.

THE PRIESTLY CITIES

54-81 And these are the places where the priestly families were assigned to live. The first assignment went by lot to the sons of Aaron of the Kohathite family; they were given Hebron in the land of Judah and all the neighboring pastures. Caleb the son of Jephunneh got the fields and villages around the city. The family of Aaron was also given the cities of refuge, with pastures included: Hebron, Libnah, Jattir, Eshtemoa, Hilen, Debir, Ashan, and Beth Shemesh. They were also given Geba from the tribe of Benjamin, Alemeth, and Anathoth, all with pastures included. In all, thirteen cities were distributed among the Kohathite families. The rest of the Kohathites were given another ten cities, distributed by lot from the half-tribe of Manasseh. The sons of Gershon were given, family by family, thirteen cities from the tribes of Issachar, Asher, Naphtali, and Manasseh in Bashan. The sons of Merari, family by family, were assigned by lot twelve cities from the tribes of Reuben, Gad, and Zebulun. The sons of Israel gave the Levites both the cities and their pastures. They also distributed by lot cities from the tribes of Judah, Simeon, and Benjamin. Some of the Kohath families were given their cities from the tribe of Ephraim, cities of refuge: Shechem in the hill country of Ephraim, Gezer, Jokmeam, Beth Horon, Aijalon, and Gath Rimmon—all with their pastures. The rest of the sons of Kohath were given Aner and Bileam with their pastures from the half-tribe of Manasseh. The sons of

NEW KING JAMES VERSION

71From the family of the half-tribe of Manasseh the sons of Gershon *were given* Golan in Bashan with its common-lands and Ashtaroth with its common-lands. 72And from the tribe of Issachar: Kedesh with its common-lands, Daberath with its common-lands, 73Ramoth with its common-lands, and Anem with its common-lands. 74And from the tribe of Asher: Mashal with its common-lands, Abdon with its common-lands, 75Hukok with its common-lands, and Rehob with its common-lands. 76And from the tribe of Naphtali: Kedesh in Galilee with its common-lands, Hammon with its common-lands, and Kirjathaim with its common-lands.

77From the tribe of Zebulun the rest of the children of Merari *were given* Rimmon[a] with its common-lands and Tabor with its common-lands. 78And on the other side of the Jordan, across from Jericho, on the east side of the Jordan, *they were given* from the tribe of Reuben: Bezer in the wilderness with its common-lands, Jahzah with its common-lands, 79Kedemoth with its common-lands, and Mephaath with its common-lands. 80And from the tribe of Gad: Ramoth in Gilead with its common-lands, Mahanaim with its common-lands, 81Heshbon with its common-lands, and Jazer with its common-lands.

THE FAMILY OF ISSACHAR

7 The sons of Issachar *were* Tola, Puah,[a] Jashub, and Shimron—four *in all.* 2The sons of Tola *were* Uzzi, Rephaiah, Jeriel, Jahmai, Jibsam, and Shemuel, heads of their father's house. *The sons* of Tola *were* mighty men of valor in their generations; their number in the days of David *was* twenty-two thousand six hundred. 3The son of Uzzi *was* Izrahiah, and the sons of Izrahiah *were* Michael, Obadiah, Joel, and Ishiah. All five of them *were* chief men. 4And with them, by their generations, according to their fathers' houses, *were* thirty-six thousand troops ready for war; for they had many wives and sons.

5Now their brethren among all the families of Issachar *were* mighty men of valor, listed by their genealogies, eighty-seven thousand in all.

THE FAMILY OF BENJAMIN

6*The sons* of Benjamin *were* Bela, Becher, and Jediael—three *in all.* 7The sons of Bela were Ezbon, Uzzi, Uzziel, Jerimoth, and Iri—five *in all.* They *were* heads of *their* fathers' houses, and they were listed by their genealogies, twenty-two thousand and thirty-four mighty men of valor.

8The sons of Becher *were* Zemirah, Joash, Eliezer, Elioenai, Omri, Jerimoth, Abijah, Anathoth, and Alemeth. All these *are* the sons of Becher. 9And they were recorded by genealogy according to their generations, heads of their fathers' houses, twenty thousand two hundred mighty men of valor. 10The son of Jediael *was* Bilhan, and the sons of Bilhan *were* Jeush, Ben-

6:77 [a]Hebrew *Rimmono,* alternate spelling of *Rimmon;* see 4:32
7:1 [a]Spelled *Puvah* in Genesis 46:13

THE MESSAGE

Gershon were given, family by family, from the half-tribe of Manasseh, Golan in Bashan and Ashtaroth; from the tribe of Issachar, Kedesh, Daberath, Ramoth, and Anem; from the tribe of Asher, Mashal, Abdon, Hukok, and Rehob; from the tribe of Naphtali, Kedesh in Galilee, Hammon, and Kiriathaim. The rest of the sons of Merari got Rimmono and Tabor from the tribe of Zebulun; Bezer in the desert, Jahzah, Kedemoth, and Mephaath from the tribe of Reuben to the east of the Jordan; and Ramoth in Gilead, Mahanaim, Heshbon, and Jazer from the tribe of Gad. Pastures were included in all these towns.

THE FAMILY OF ISSACHAR

1-5 7 The sons of Issachar were Tola, Puah, Jashub, and Shimron—four sons. The sons of Tola were Uzzi, Rephaiah, Jeriel, Jahmai, Ibsam, and Samuel—the chiefs of their families. During David's reign, the Tola family counted 22,600 warriors in their lineage. The son of Uzzi was Izrahiah; the sons of Izrahiah were Michael, Obadiah, Joel, and Isshiah—five sons and all of them chiefs. They counted 36,000 warriors in their lineage because they had more wives and sons than their brothers. The extended families of Issachar accounted for 87,000 warriors—all of them listed in the family tree.

THE FAMILY OF BENJAMIN

6-12 Benjamin had three sons: Bela, Beker, and Jediael. Bela had five: Ezbon, Uzzi, Uzziel, Jerimoth, and Iri, all of them chiefs and warriors. They counted 22,034 names in their family tree. Beker's sons were Zemirah, Joash, Eliezer, Elioenai, Omri, Jeremoth, Abijah, Anathoth, and Alemeth. Through these chiefs their family tree listed 20,200 warriors. Jediael's son was Bilhan and the sons of Bilhan were Jeush, Benjamin, Ehud,

NEW KING JAMES VERSION

jamin, Ehud, Chenaanah, Zethan, Tharshish, and Ahishahar.
11All these sons of Jediael *were* heads of their fathers' houses; *there were* seventeen thousand two hundred mighty men of valor fit to go out for war *and* battle. 12Shuppim and Huppim[a] *were* the sons of Ir, *and* Hushim *was* the son of Aher.

THE FAMILY OF NAPHTALI

13The sons of Naphtali *were* Jahziel,[a] Guni, Jezer, and Shallum,[b] the sons of Bilhah.

THE FAMILY OF MANASSEH (WEST)

14The descendants of Manasseh: his Syrian concubine bore him Machir the father of Gilead, the father of Asriel.[a] 15Machir took as his wife *the sister* of Huppim and Shuppim,[a] whose name *was* Maachah. The name of *Gilead's* grandson[b] *was* Zelophehad,[c] but Zelophehad begot only daughters. 16(Maachah the wife of Machir bore a son, and she called his name Peresh. The name of his brother *was* Sheresh, and his sons *were* Ulam and Rakem. 17The son of Ulam *was* Bedan.) These *were* the descendants of Gilead the son of Machir, the son of Manasseh.
18His sister Hammoleketh bore Ishhod, Abiezer, and Mahlah.
19And the sons of Shemida were Ahian, Shechem, Likhi, and Aniam.

THE FAMILY OF EPHRAIM

20The sons of Ephraim *were* Shuthelah, Bered his son, Tahath his son, Eladah his son, Tahath his son, 21Zabad his son, Shuthelah his son, and Ezer and Elead. The men of Gath who were born in *that* land killed *them* because they came down to take away their cattle. 22Then Ephraim their father mourned many days, and his brethren came to comfort him.
23And when he went in to his wife, she conceived and bore a son; and he called his name Beriah,[a] because tragedy had come upon his house. 24Now his daughter *was* Sheerah, who built Lower and Upper Beth Horon and Uzzen Sheerah; 25and Rephah *was* his son, *as well* as Resheph, and Telah his son, Tahan his son, 26Laadan his son, Ammihud his son, Elishama his son, 27Nun[a] his son, and Joshua his son.
28Now their possessions and dwelling places *were* Bethel and its towns: to the east Naaran, to the west Gezer and its towns, and Shechem and its towns, as far as Ayyah[a] and its towns; 29and by the borders of the children of Manasseh *were* Beth Shean and its towns, Taanach and its towns, Megiddo and its towns, Dor and its towns. In these dwelt the children of Joseph, the son of Israel.

7:12 [a]Called *Hupham* in Numbers 26:39 **7:13** [a]Spelled *Jahzeel* in Genesis 46:24 [b]Spelled *Shillem* in Genesis 46:24 **7:14** [a]The son of Gilead (compare Numbers 26:30, 31) **7:15** [a]Compare verse 12 [b]Literally *the second* [c]Compare Numbers 26:30–33 **7:23** [a]Literally *In Tragedy* **7:27** [a]Hebrew *Non* **7:28** [a]Many Hebrew manuscripts, Bomberg, Septuagint, Targum, and Vulgate read *Gazza.*

THE MESSAGE

Kenaanah, Zethan, Tarshish, and Ahishahar—all sons of Jediael and family chiefs; they counted 17,200 combat-ready warriors. Shuppim and Huppim were the sons of Ir; Hushim were from the family of Aher.

THE FAMILY OF NAPHTALI

13 The sons of Naphtali were Jahziel, Guni, Jezer, and Shallum; they are listed under the maternal line of Bilhah, their grandfather's concubine.

THE FAMILY OF MANASSEH

14-19 Manasseh's sons, born of his Aramean concubine, were Asriel and Makir the father of Gilead. Makir got his wife from the Huppites and Shuppites. His sister's name was Maacah. Another son, Zelophehad, had only daughters. Makir's wife Maacah bore a son whom she named Peresh; his brother's name was Sheresh and his sons were Ulam and Rakem. Ulam's son was Bedan. This accounts for the sons of Gilead son of Makir, the son of Manasseh. His sister Hammoleketh gave birth to Ishdod, Abiezer, and Mahlah. The sons of Shemida were Ahian, Shechem, Likhi, and Aniam.

THE FAMILY OF EPHRAIM

20-24 The sons of Ephraim were Shuthelah, Bered his son, Tahath his son, Eleadah his son, Tahath his son, Zabad his son, Shuthelah his son, and Ezer and Elead, cattle-rustlers, killed on one of their raids by the natives of Gath. Their father Ephraim grieved a long time and his family gathered to give him comfort. Then he slept with his wife again. She conceived and produced a son. He named him Beriah (Unlucky), because of the bad luck that had come to his family. His daughter was Sheerah. She built Lower and Upper Beth Horon and Uzzen Sheerah.

25-29 Rephah was Ephraim's son and also Resheph; Telah was his son, Tahan his son, Ladan his son, Ammihud his son, Elishama his son, Nun his son, and Joshua his son. They occupied Bethel and the neighboring country from Naaran on the east to Gezer and its villages on the west, along with Shechem and its villages, and extending as far as Ayyah and its villages. Stretched along the borders of Manasseh were Beth Shan, Taanach, Megiddo, and Dor, together with their satellite villages. The families descended from Joseph son of Israel lived in all these places.

NEW KING JAMES VERSION

THE FAMILY OF ASHER

30The sons of Asher *were* Imnah, Ishvah,
Ishvi, Beriah, and their sister Serah. 31The sons
of Beriah *were* Heber and Malchiel, who was
the father of Birzaith.[a] 32And Heber begot
Japhlet, Shomer,[a] Hotham,[b] and their sister
Shua. 33The sons of Japhlet *were* Pasach,
Bimhal, and Ashvath. These *were* the children
of Japhlet. 34The sons of Shemer *were* Ahi, Roh-
gah, Jehubbah, and Aram. 35And the sons of his
brother Helem *were* Zophah, Imna, Shelesh,
and Amal. 36The sons of Zophah *were* Suah,
Harnepher, Shual, Beri, Imrah, 37Bezer, Hod,
Shamma, Shilshah, Jithran,[a] and Beera. 38The
sons of Jether *were* Jephunneh, Pispah, and
Ara. 39The sons of Ulla *were* Arah, Haniel, and
Rizia.
40All these *were* the children of Asher, heads
of *their* fathers' houses, choice men, mighty
men of valor, chief leaders. And they were
recorded by genealogies among the army fit for
battle; their number *was* twenty-six thousand.

THE FAMILY TREE OF KING SAUL OF BENJAMIN

8 Now Benjamin begot Bela his firstborn, Ash-
bel the second, Aharah[a] the third, 2Nohah the
fourth, and Rapha the fifth. 3The sons of Bela
were Addar,[a] Gera, Abihud, 4Abishua, Naaman,
Ahoah, 5Gera, Shephuphan, and Huram.
6These *are* the sons of Ehud, who were the
heads of the fathers' *houses* of the inhabitants
of Geba, and who forced them to move to Man-
ahath: 7Naaman, Ahijah, and Gera who forced
them to move. He begot Uzza and Ahihud.
8Also Shaharaim had children in the country
of Moab, after he had sent away Hushim and
Baara his wives. 9By Hodesh his wife he begot
Jobab, Zibia, Mesha, Malcam, 10Jeuz, Sachiah,
and Mirmah. These *were* his sons, heads of their
fathers' *houses*.
11And by Hushim he begot Abitub and El-
paal. 12The sons of Elpaal *were* Eber, Misham,
and Shemed, who built Ono and Lod with its
towns; 13and Beriah and Shema, who *were*
heads of their fathers' *houses* of the inhabitants
of Aijalon, who drove out the inhabitants of
Gath. 14Ahio, Shashak, Jeremoth, 15Zebadiah,
Arad, Eder, 16Michael, Ispah, and Joha *were* the
sons of Beriah. 17Zebadiah, Meshullam, Hizki,
Heber, 18Ishmerai, Jizliah, and Jobab *were* the
sons of Elpaal. 19Jakim, Zichri, Zabdi, 20Elienai,
Zillethai, Eliel, 21Adaiah, Beraiah, and Shimrath
were the sons of Shimei. 22Ishpan, Eber, Eliel,
23Abdon, Zichri, Hanan, 24Hananiah, Elam, An-
tothijah, 25Iphdeiah, and Penuel *were* the sons of
Shashak. 26Shamsherai, Shehariah, Athaliah,
27Jaareshiah, Elijah, and Zichri *were* the sons of
Jeroham.
28These *were* heads of the fathers' *houses* by
their generations, chief men. These dwelt in
Jerusalem.
29Now the father of Gibeon, whose wife's
name *was* Maacah, dwelt at Gibeon. 30And his
firstborn son *was* Abdon, then Zur, Kish, Baal,

7:31 [a]Or *Birzavith* or *Birzoth* **7:32** [a]Spelled *Shemer* in verse 34 [b]Spelled *Helem* in verse 35 **7:37** [a]Spelled *Jether* in verse 38 **8:1** [a]Spelled *Ahiram* in Numbers 26:38 **8:3** [a]Called *Ard* in Numbers 26:40

THE MESSAGE

THE FAMILY OF ASHER

30-32 The sons of Asher were Imnah, Ishvah,
Ishvi, and Beriah; Serah was their sister.
The sons of Beriah were Heber and Malkiel,
who had Birzaith. Heber had Japhlet,
Shomer, Hotham, and Shua their sister.
33-40 Japhlet had Pasach, Bimhal, and Ash-
vath. His brother Shomer had Rohgah, Hub-
bah, and Aram. His brother Helem had
Zophah, Imna, Shelesh, and Amal. Zophah
had Suah, Harnepher, Shual, Beri, Imrah,
Bezer, Hod, Shamma, Shilshah, Ithran, and
Beera. Jether had Jephunneh, Pispah, and
Ara. Ulla had Arah, Hanniel, and Rizia.
These were Asher's sons, all of them re-
sponsible, excellent in character, and brave
in battle—good leaders. They listed 26,000
combat-ready men in their family tree.

THE FAMILY OF BENJAMIN (CONTINUED)

1-5 8 Benjamin's firstborn son was Bela, fol-
lowed by Ashbel, Aharah, Nohah, and
Rapha—five in all. Bela's sons were Addar,
Gera, Abihud, Abishua, Naaman, Ahoah,
Gera, Shephuphan, and Huram.
6-7 These are the families of Ehud that lived
in Geba and were exiled to Manahath: Naa-
man, Ahijah, and Gera, who led them to ex-
ile and had Uzza and Ahihud.
8-12 In the land of Moab, Shaharaim had chil-
dren after he divorced his wives Hushim
and Baara. From his new wife Hodesh he
had Jobab, Zibia, Mesha, Malcam, Jeuz,
Sakia, and Mirmah—sons who became
heads of families. From his earlier wife
Hushim he had Abitub and Elpaal. Elpaal's
sons were Eber, Misham, and Shemed, who
built Ono and Lod with all their villages.
13-28 Beriah and Shema were family chiefs
who lived at Aijalon. They drove out the cit-
izens of Gath. Their brothers were Shashak
and Jeremoth. The sons of Beriah were Zeb-
adiah, Arad, Eder, Michael, Ishpah, and
Joha. The sons of Elpaal were Zebadiah,
Meshullam, Hizki, Heber, Ishmerai, Izliah,
and Jobab. The sons of Shimei were Jakim,
Zicri, Zabdi, Elienai, Zillethai, Eliel, Adaiah,
Beraiah, and Shimrath. The sons of
Shashak were Ishpan, Eber, Eliel, Abdon,
Zicri, Hanan, Hananiah, Elam, Anthothijah,
Iphdeiah, and Penuel. The sons of Jeroham
were Shamsherai, Shehariah, Athaliah,
Jaareshiah, Elijah, and Zicri. These were the
chiefs of the families as listed in their family
tree. They lived in Jerusalem.
29-32 Jeiel the father of Gibeon lived in Gibeon.
His wife's name was Maacah. Abdon was
his firstborn son, followed by Zur, Kish,

NEW KING JAMES VERSION

Nadab, [31]Gedor, Ahio, Zecher, [32]and Mikloth, *who* begot Shimeah.[a] They also dwelt alongside their relatives in Jerusalem, with their brethren. [33]Ner[a] begot Kish, Kish begot Saul, and Saul begot Jonathan, Malchishua, Abinadab,[b] and Esh-Baal.[c] [34]The son of Jonathan *was* Merib-Baal,[a] and Merib-Baal begot Micah. [35]The sons of Micah *were* Pithon, Melech, Tarea, and Ahaz. [36]And Ahaz begot Jehoaddah;[a] Jehoaddah begot Alemeth, Azmaveth, and Zimri; and Zimri begot Moza. [37]Moza begot Binea, Raphah[a] his son, Eleasah his son, *and* Azel his son.

[38]Azel had six sons whose names *were* these: Azrikam, Bocheru, Ishmael, Sheariah, Obadiah, and Hanan. All these *were* the sons of Azel. [39]And the sons of Eshek his brother *were* Ulam his firstborn, Jeush the second, and Eliphelet the third.

[40]The sons of Ulam were mighty men of valor—archers. *They* had many sons and grandsons, one hundred and fifty *in all.* These *were* all sons of Benjamin.

9 So all Israel was recorded by genealogies, and indeed, they *were* inscribed in the book of the kings of Israel. But Judah was carried away captive to Babylon because of their unfaithfulness. [2]And the first inhabitants who *dwelt* in their possessions in their cities *were* Israelites, priests, Levites, and the Nethinim.

DWELLERS IN JERUSALEM

[3]Now in Jerusalem the children of Judah dwelt, and some of the children of Benjamin, and of the children of Ephraim and Manasseh: [4]Uthai the son of Ammihud, the son of Omri, the son of Imri, the son of Bani, of the descendants of Perez, the son of Judah. [5]Of the Shilonites: Asaiah the firstborn and his sons. [6]Of the sons of Zerah: Jeuel, and their brethren—six hundred and ninety. [7]Of the sons of Benjamin: Sallu the son of Meshullam, the son of Hodaviah, the son of Hassenuah; [8]Ibneiah the son of Jeroham; Elah the son of Uzzi, the son of Michri; Meshullam the son of Shephatiah, the son of Reuel, the son of Ibnijah; [9]and their brethren, according to their generations—nine hundred and fifty-six. All these men *were* heads of a father's *house* in their fathers' houses.

THE PRIESTS AT JERUSALEM

[10]Of the priests: Jedaiah, Jehoiarib, and Jachin; [11]Azariah the son of Hilkiah, the son of Meshullam, the son of Zadok, the son of Meraioth, the son of Ahitub, the officer over the house of God; [12]Adaiah the son of Jeroham, the son of Pashur, the son of Malchijah; Maasai the son of Adiel, the son of Jahzerah, the son of Meshullam, the son of Meshillemith, the son of Immer; [13]and their brethren, heads of their fathers' houses—one thousand seven hundred and sixty. *They were* very able men for the work of the service of the house of God.

8:32 [a]Spelled *Shimeam* in 9:38 **8:33** [a]Also the son of Gibeon (compare 9:36, 39) [b]Called *Jishui* in 1 Samuel 14:49 [c]Called *Ishbosheth* in 2 Samuel 2:8 and elsewhere **8:34** [a]Called *Mephibosheth* in 2 Samuel 4:4 **8:36** [a]Spelled *Jarah* in 9:42 **8:37** [a]Spelled *Rephaiah* in 9:43

THE MESSAGE

Baal, Nadab, Gedor, Ahio, Zeker, and Mikloth. Mikloth had Shimeah. They lived in the neighborhood of their extended families in Jerusalem.

33-40 Ner had Kish, Kish had Saul, and Saul had Jonathan, Malki-Shua, Abinadab, and Esh-Baal. Jonathan had Merib-Baal, and Merib-Baal had Micah. Micah's sons were Pithon, Melech, Tarea, and Ahaz. Ahaz had Jehoaddah and Jehoaddah had Alemeth, Azmaveth, and Zimri. Zimri had Moza and Moza had Binea. Raphah was his son, Eleasah his son, and Azel his son. Azel had six sons named Azrikam, Bokeru, Ishmael, Sheariah, Obadiah, and Hanan. His brother Eshek's sons were Ulam his firstborn, followed by Jeush and Eliphelet. Ulam's sons were warriors well known as archers. They had lots of sons and grandsons—at least 150. These were all in Benjamin's family tree.

1 9 This is the complete family tree for all Israel, recorded in the *Royal Annals of the Kings of Israel and Judah* at the time they were exiled to Babylon because of their unbelieving and disobedient lives.

THE BACK-FROM-EXILE COMMUNITY IN JERUSALEM

2 The first Israelites to return from exile to their homes and cities were the priests, the Levites, and the temple support staff.

3-6 Returning to Jerusalem from the families of Judah, Benjamin, Ephraim, and Manasseh were the following: Uthai son of Ammihud, the son of Omri, the son of Imri, the son of Bani, from the line of Perez son of Judah; from the Shilonites were Asaiah the firstborn and his sons; from the family of Zerah there was Jeuel. There were 690 in the Judah group.

7-9 From the family of Benjamin were Sallu son of Meshullam, the son of Hodaviah, the son of Hassenuah, and Ibneiah son of Jeroham, and Elah son of Uzzi, the son of Micri, and Meshullam son of Shephatiah, the son of Reuel, the son of Ibnijah. There were 956 in the Benjamin group. All these named were heads of families.

10-13 From the company of priests there were Jedaiah; Jehoiarib; Jakin; Azariah son of Hilkiah, the son of Meshullam, the son of Zadok, the son of Meraioth, the son of Ahitub, who was in charge of taking care of the house of God; Adaiah son of Jeroham, the son of Pashhur, the son of Malkijah; also Maasai son of Adiel, the son of Jahzerah, the son of Meshullam, the son of Meshillemith, the son of Immer. The priests, all of them heads of families, numbered 1,760, skilled and seasoned servants in the work of worshiping God.

NEW KING JAMES VERSION

THE LEVITES AT JERUSALEM

14Of the Levites: Shemaiah the son of Hasshub, the son of Azrikam, the son of Hashabiah, of the sons of Merari; 15Bakbakkar, Heresh, Galal, and Mattaniah the son of Micah, the son of Zichri, the son of Asaph; 16Obadiah the son of Shemaiah, the son of Galal, the son of Jeduthun; and Berechiah the son of Asa, the son of Elkanah, who lived in the villages of the Netophathites.

THE LEVITE GATEKEEPERS

17And the gatekeepers *were* Shallum, Akkub, Talmon, Ahiman, and their brethren. Shallum *was* the chief. 18Until then *they had been* gatekeepers for the camps of the children of Levi at the King's Gate on the east.

19Shallum the son of Kore, the son of Ebiasaph, the son of Korah, and his brethren, from his father's house, the Korahites, *were* in charge of the work of the service, gatekeepers of the tabernacle. Their fathers had been keepers of the entrance to the camp of the LORD. 20And Phinehas the son of Eleazar had been the officer over them in time past; the LORD *was* with him. 21Zechariah the son of Meshelemiah *was* keeper of the door of the tabernacle of meeting.

22All those chosen as gatekeepers *were* two hundred and twelve. They were recorded by their genealogy, in their villages. David and Samuel the seer had appointed them to their trusted office. 23So they and their children *were* in charge of the gates of the house of the LORD, the house of the tabernacle, by assignment. 24The gatekeepers were assigned to the four directions: the east, west, north, and south. 25And their brethren in their villages *had* to come with them from time to time for seven days. 26For in this trusted office *were* four chief gatekeepers; they were Levites. And they had charge over the chambers and treasuries of the house of God. 27And they lodged *all* around the house of God because they *had* the responsibility, and they *were* in charge of opening *it* every morning.

OTHER LEVITE RESPONSIBILITIES

28Now *some* of them were in charge of the serving vessels, for they brought them in and took them out by count. 29*Some* of them *were* appointed over the furnishings and over all the implements of the sanctuary, and over the fine flour and the wine and the oil and the incense and the spices. 30And *some* of the sons of the priests made the ointment of the spices.

31Mattithiah of the Levites, the firstborn of Shallum the Korahite, had the trusted office over the things that were baked in the pans. 32And some of their brethren of the sons of the Kohathites *were* in charge of preparing the showbread for every Sabbath.

33These are the singers, heads of the fathers' *houses* of the Levites, *who lodged* in the chambers, *and were* free *from other duties;* for they were employed in *that* work day and night. 34These heads of the fathers' *houses* of the Levites *were* heads throughout their generations. They dwelt at Jerusalem.

THE MESSAGE

14-16 From the Levites were Shemaiah son of Hasshub, the son of Azrikam, the son of Hashabiah, a Merarite; then Bakbakkar, Heresh, Galal, Mattaniah son of Mica, the son of Zicri, the son of Asaph; also Obadiah son of Shemaiah, the son of Galal, the son of Jeduthun; and finally Berekiah son of Asa, the son of Elkanah, who lived in the villages of the Netophathites.

17-18 The security guards were Shallum, Akkub, Talmon, Ahiman, and their brothers. Shallum was the chief and up to now the security guard at the King's Gate on the east. They also served as security guards at the camps of Levite families.

19-25 Shallum son of Kore, the son of Ebiasaph, the son of Korah, along with his brothers in the Korahite family, were in charge of the services of worship as doorkeepers of the Tent, as their ancestors had guarded the entrance to the camp of God. In the early days, Phinehas son of Eleazar was in charge of the security guards—God be with him! Now Zechariah son of Meshelemiah was the security guard at the entrance of the Tent of Meeting. The number of those who had been chosen to be security guards was 212—they were officially registered in their own camps. David and Samuel the seer handpicked them for their dependability. They and their sons had the permanent responsibility for guarding the gates of God's house, the house of worship; the main security guards were posted at the four entrances, east, west, north, and south; their brothers in the villages were scheduled to give them relief weekly—the four main security guards were responsible for round-the-clock surveillance.

26-32 Being Levites, they were responsible for the security of all supplies and valuables in the house of God. They kept watch all through the night and had the key to open the doors each morning. Some were in charge of the articles used in The Temple worship—they counted them both when they brought them in and when they took them out. Others were in charge of supplies in the sanctuary—flour, wine, oil, incense, and spices. And some of the priests were assigned to mixing the oils for the perfume. The Levite Mattithiah, the firstborn son of Shallum the Korahite, was responsible for baking the bread for the services of worship. Some of the brothers, sons of the Kohathites, were assigned to preparing the bread set out on the table each Sabbath.

33-34 And then there were the musicians, all heads of Levite families. They had permanent living quarters in The Temple; because they were on twenty-four-hour duty, they were exempt from all other duties. These were the heads of Levite families as designated in their family tree. They lived in Jerusalem.

NEW KING JAMES VERSION

THE FAMILY OF KING SAUL

35Jeiel the father of Gibeon, whose wife's name *was* Maacah, dwelt at Gibeon. 36His firstborn son *was* Abdon, then Zur, Kish, Baal, Ner, Nadab, 37Gedor, Ahio, Zechariah,[a] and Mikloth. 38And Mikloth begot Shimeam.[a] They also dwelt alongside their relatives in Jerusalem, with their brethren. 39Ner begot Kish, Kish begot Saul, and Saul begot Jonathan, Malchishua, Abinadab, and Esh-Baal. 40The son of Jonathan *was* Merib-Baal, and Merib-Baal begot Micah. 41The sons of Micah *were* Pithon, Melech, Tahrea,[a] and Ahaz.[b] 42And Ahaz begot Jarah;[a] Jarah begot Alemeth, Azmaveth, and Zimri; and Zimri begot Moza; 43Moza begot Binea, Rephaiah[a] his son, Eleasah his son, and Azel his son.

44And Azel had six sons whose names *were* these: Azrikam, Bocheru, Ishmael, Sheariah, Obadiah, and Hanan; these *were* the sons of Azel.

TRAGIC END OF SAUL AND HIS SONS

10 Now the Philistines fought against Israel; and the men of Israel fled from before the Philistines, and fell slain on Mount Gilboa. 2Then the Philistines followed hard after Saul and his sons. And the Philistines killed Jonathan, Abinadab, and Malchishua, Saul's sons. 3The battle became fierce against Saul. The archers hit him, and he was wounded by the archers. 4Then Saul said to his armorbearer, "Draw your sword, and thrust me through with it, lest these uncircumcised men come and abuse me." But his armorbearer would not, for he was greatly afraid. Therefore Saul took a sword and fell on it. 5And when his armorbearer saw that Saul was dead, he also fell on his sword and died. 6So Saul and his three sons died, and all his house died together. 7And when all the men of Israel who *were* in the valley saw that they had fled and that Saul and his sons were dead, they forsook their cities and fled; then the Philistines came and dwelt in them.

8So it happened the next day, when the Philistines came to strip the slain, that they found Saul and his sons fallen on Mount Gilboa. 9And they stripped him and took his head and his armor, and sent word throughout the land of the Philistines to proclaim the news *in the temple* of their idols and among the people. 10Then they put his armor in the temple of their gods, and fastened his head in the temple of Dagon.

11And when all Jabesh Gilead heard all that the Philistines had done to Saul, 12all the valiant men arose and took the body of Saul and the bodies of his sons; and they brought them to Jabesh, and buried their bones under the tamarisk tree at Jabesh, and fasted seven days.

13So Saul died for his unfaithfulness which he had committed against the LORD, because he did not keep the word of the LORD, and also because he consulted a medium for guidance. 14But *he* did not inquire of the LORD; therefore He killed him, and turned the kingdom over to David the son of Jesse.

9:37 [a]Called *Zecher* in 8:31 **9:38** [a]Spelled *Shimeah* in 8:32 **9:41** [a]Spelled *Tarea* in 8:35 [b]Following Arabic, Syriac, Targum, and Vulgate (compare 8:35); Masoretic Text and Septuagint omit *and Ahaz.* **9:42** [a]Spelled *Jehoaddah* in 8:36 **9:43** [a]Spelled *Raphah* in 8:37

THE MESSAGE

THE FAMILY OF SAUL

35-38 Jeiel the father of Gibeon lived at Gibeon; his wife was Maacah. His firstborn son was Abdon, followed by Zur, Kish, Baal, Ner, Nadab, Gedor, Ahio, Zechariah, and Mikloth. Mikloth had Shimeam. They lived in the same neighborhood as their relatives in Jerusalem.

39-44 Ner had Kish, Kish had Saul, Saul had Jonathan, Malki-Shua, Abinadab, and Esh-Baal. Merib-Baal was the son of Jonathan and Merib-Baal had Micah. Micah's sons were Pithon, Melech, and Tahrea. Ahaz had Jarah, Jarah had Alemeth, Azmaveth, and Zimri; Zimri had Moza, Moza had Binea, Rephaiah was his son, Eleasah was his son, and Azel was his son. Azel had six sons: Azrikam, Bokeru, Ishmael, Sheariah, Obadiah, and Hanan—the sons of Azel.

1-5 10 The Philistines went to war against Israel; the Israelites ran for their lives from the Philistines but fell, slaughtered on Mount Gilboa. The Philistines zeroed in on Saul and his sons and killed his sons Jonathan, Abinadab, and Malki-Shua. The battle went hard against Saul—the archers found him and wounded him. Saul said to his armor bearer, "Draw your sword and finish me off before these pagan pigs get to me and make a sport of my body." But his armor bearer, restrained by both reverence and fear, wouldn't do it. So Saul took his own sword and killed himself. The armor bearer, panicked because Saul was dead, then killed himself.

6-7 So Saul and his three sons—all four the same day—died. When all the Israelites in the valley saw that the army had fled and that Saul and his sons were dead, they abandoned their cities and ran off; the Philistines came and moved in.

8-10 The next day the Philistines came to plunder the dead bodies and found Saul and his sons dead on Mount Gilboa. They stripped Saul, removed his head and his armor, and put them on exhibit throughout Philistia, reporting the victory news to their idols and the people. Then they put Saul's armor on display in the temple of their gods and placed his skull as a trophy in the temple of their god Dagon.

11-12 The people of Jabesh Gilead heard what the Philistines had done to Saul. All of their fighting men went into action—retrieved the bodies of Saul and his sons and brought them to Jabesh, gave them a dignified burial under the oak at Jabesh, and mourned their deaths for seven days.

13-14 Saul died in disobedience, disobedient to GOD. He didn't obey GOD's words. Instead of praying, he went to a witch to seek guidance. Because he didn't go to GOD for help, GOD took his life and turned the kingdom over to David son of Jesse.

NEW KING JAMES VERSION

DAVID MADE KING OVER ALL ISRAEL

11 Then all Israel came together to David at Hebron, saying, "Indeed we *are* your bone and your flesh. 2 Also, in time past, even when Saul was king, you *were* the one who led Israel out and brought them in; and the LORD your God said to you, 'You shall shepherd My people Israel, and be ruler over My people Israel.' " 3 Therefore all the elders of Israel came to the king at Hebron, and David made a covenant with them at Hebron before the LORD. And they anointed David king over Israel, according to the word of the LORD by Samuel.

THE CITY OF DAVID

4 And David and all Israel went to Jerusalem, which is Jebus, where the Jebusites *were*, the inhabitants of the land. 5 But the inhabitants of Jebus said to David, "You shall not come in here!" Nevertheless David took the stronghold of Zion (that is, the City of David). 6 Now David said, "Whoever attacks the Jebusites first shall be chief and captain." And Joab the son of Zeruiah went up first, and became chief. 7 Then David dwelt in the stronghold; therefore they called it the City of David. 8 And he built the city around it, from the Millo[a] to the surrounding area. Joab repaired the rest of the city. 9 So David went on and became great, and the LORD of hosts *was* with him.

THE MIGHTY MEN OF DAVID

10 Now these *were* the heads of the mighty men whom David had, who strengthened themselves with him in his kingdom, with all Israel, to make him king, according to the word of the LORD concerning Israel.

11 And this *is* the number of the mighty men whom David had: Jashobeam the son of a Hachmonite, chief of the captains;[a] he had lifted up his spear against three hundred, killed *by him* at one time.

12 After him *was* Eleazar the son of Dodo, the Ahohite, who *was one* of the three mighty men. 13 He was with David at Pasdammim. Now there the Philistines were gathered for battle, and there was a piece of ground full of barley. So the people fled from the Philistines. 14 But they stationed themselves in the middle of *that* field, defended it, and killed the Philistines. So the LORD brought about a great victory.

15 Now three of the thirty chief men went down to the rock to David, into the cave of Adullam; and the army of the Philistines encamped in the Valley of Rephaim. 16 David *was* then in the stronghold, and the garrison of the Philistines *was* then in Bethlehem. 17 And David said with longing, "Oh, that someone would give me a drink of water from the well of Bethlehem, which is by the gate!" 18 So the three broke through the camp of the Philistines, drew water from the well of Bethlehem that *was* by the gate, and took *it* and brought *it* to David. Nevertheless David would not drink it, but poured it out to the LORD. 19 And he said, "Far be it from me, O

11:8 [a]Literally *The Landfill* 11:11 [a]Following Qere; Kethib, Septuagint, and Vulgate read *the thirty* (compare 2 Samuel 23:8).

THE MESSAGE

KING DAVID

1-3 11 Then all Israel assembled before David at Hebron. "Look at us," they said. "We're your very flesh and blood. In the past, yes, even while Saul was king, you were the real leader of Israel. GOD told you, 'You will shepherd my people Israel; you are to be the ruler of my people Israel.' " When all the elders of Israel came to the king at Hebron, David made a covenant with them in the presence of GOD at Hebron. Then they anointed David king over Israel exactly as GOD had commanded through Samuel.

4-6 David and all Israel went to Jerusalem (it was the old Jebus, where the Jebusites lived). The citizens of Jebus told David, "No trespassing—you can't come here." David came on anyway and captured the fortress of Zion, the City of David. David had said, "The first person to kill a Jebusite will be commander-in-chief." Joab son of Zeruiah was the first; and he became the chief.

7-9 David took up residence in the fortress city; that's how it got its name, "City of David." David fortified the city all the way around, both the outer bulwarks (the Millo) and the outside wall. Joab rebuilt the city gates. David's stride became longer, his embrace larger—yes, GOD-of-the-Angel-Armies was with him!

DAVID'S MIGHTY MEN

10-11 These are the chiefs of David's Mighty Men, the ones who linked arms with him as he took up his kingship, with all Israel joining in, helping him become king in just the way GOD had spoken regarding Israel. The list of David's Mighty Men:

Jashobeam son of Hacmoni was chief of the Thirty. Singlehandedly he killed three hundred men, killed them all in one skirmish.

12-14 Next was Eleazar son of Dodai the Ahohite, one of the Big Three of the Mighty Men. He was with David at Pas Dammim, where the Philistines had mustered their troops for battle. It was an area where there was a field of barley. The army started to flee from the Philistines and then took its stand right in that field—and turned the tide! They slaughtered the Philistines, GOD helping them—a huge victory.

15-19 The Big Three from the Thirty made a rocky descent to David at the Cave of Adullam while a company of Philistines was camped in the Valley of Rephaim. David was holed up in the Cave while the Philistines were prepared for battle at Bethlehem. David had a sudden craving: "What I wouldn't give for a drink of water from the well in Bethlehem, the one at the gate!" The Three penetrated the Philistine camp, drew water from the well at the Bethlehem gate, shouldered it, and brought it to David. And then David wouldn't drink it! He poured it out as a sacred offering to GOD, saying, "I'd rather be damned by God than drink this! It would be

NEW KING JAMES VERSION

my God, that I should do this! Shall I drink the blood of these men *who have put* their lives *in jeopardy?* For at the risk of their lives they brought it." Therefore he would not drink it. These things were done by the three mighty men.

20 Abishai the brother of Joab was chief of *another* three.[a] He had lifted up his spear against three hundred *men,* killed *them,* and won a name among *these* three. 21 Of the three he was more honored than the other two men. Therefore he became their captain. However he did not attain to the *first* three.

22 Benaiah was the son of Jehoiada, the son of a valiant man from Kabzeel, who had done many deeds. He had killed two lion-like heroes of Moab. He also had gone down and killed a lion in the midst of a pit on a snowy day. 23 And he killed an Egyptian, a man of *great* height, five cubits tall. In the Egyptian's hand *there was* a spear like a weaver's beam; and he went down to him with a staff, wrested the spear out of the Egyptian's hand, and killed him with his own spear. 24 These *things* Benaiah the son of Jehoiada did, and won a name among three mighty men. 25 Indeed he was more honored than the thirty, but he did not attain to the *first* three. And David appointed him over his guard.

26 Also the mighty warriors *were* Asahel the brother of Joab, Elhanan the son of Dodo of Bethlehem, 27 Shammoth the Harorite,[a] Helez the Pelonite,[b] 28 Ira the son of Ikkesh the Tekoite, Abiezer the Anathothite, 29 Sibbechai the Hushathite, Ilai the Ahohite, 30 Maharai the Netophathite, Heled[a] the son of Baanah the Netophathite, 31 Ithai[a] the son of Ribai of Gibeah, of the sons of Benjamin, Benaiah the Pirathonite, 32 Hurai[a] of the brooks of Gaash, Abiel[b] the Arbathite, 33 Azmaveth the Baharumite,[a] Eliahba the Shaalbonite, 34 the sons of Hashem the Gizonite, Jonathan the son of Shageh the Hararite, 35 Ahiam the son of Sacar the Hararite, Eliphal the son of Ur, 36 Hepher the Mecherathite, Ahijah the Pelonite, 37 Hezro the Carmelite, Naarai the son of Ezbai, 38 Joel the brother of Nathan, Mibhar the son of Hagri, 39 Zelek the Ammonite, Naharai the Berothite[a] (the armorbearer of Joab the son of Zeruiah), 40 Ira the Ithrite, Gareb the Ithrite, 41 Uriah the Hittite, Zabad the son of Ahlai, 42 Adina the son of Shiza the Reubenite (a chief of the Reubenites) and thirty with him, 43 Hanan the son of Maachah, Joshaphat the Mithnite, 44 Uzzia the Ashterathite, Shama and Jeiel the sons of Hotham the Aroerite, 45 Jediael the son of Shimri, and Joha his brother, the Tizite, 46 Eliel the Mahavite, Jeribai and Joshaviah the sons of Elnaam, Ithmah the Moabite, 47 Eliel, Obed, and Jaasiel the Mezobaite.

11:20 [a]Following Masoretic Text, Septuagint, and Vulgate; Syriac reads *thirty.* **11:27** [a]Spelled *Harodite* in 2 Samuel 23:25 [b]Called *Paltite* in 2 Samuel 23:26 **11:30** [a]Spelled *Heleb* in 2 Samuel 23:29 and *Heldai* in 1 Chronicles 27:15 **11:31** [a]Spelled *Ittai* in 2 Samuel 23:29 **11:32** [a]Spelled *Hiddai* in 2 Samuel 23:30 [b]Spelled *Abi-Albon* in 2 Samuel 23:31 **11:33** [a]Spelled *Barhumite* in 2 Samuel 23:31 **11:39** [a]Spelled *Beerothite* in 2 Samuel 23:37

THE MESSAGE

like drinking the lifeblood of these men—they risked their lives to bring it." So he refused to drink it. These are the kinds of things that the Big Three of the Mighty Men did.

20-21 Abishai brother of Joab was the chief of the Thirty. Singlehandedly he fought three hundred men, and killed the lot, but he never made it into the circle of the Three. He was highly honored by the Thirty—he was their chief—still, he didn't measure up to the Three.

22-25 Benaiah son of Jehoiada was a Mighty Man from Kabzeel with many exploits to his credit: he killed two famous Moabites; he climbed down into a pit and killed a lion on a snowy day; and he killed an Egyptian, a giant seven and a half feet tall. The Egyptian had a spear like a ship's boom but Benaiah went at him with a mere club, tore the spear from the Egyptian's hand, and killed him with it. These are some of the things Benaiah son of Jehoiada did. But he was never included with the Three. He was highly honored among the Thirty, but didn't measure up to the Three. David put him in charge of his personal bodyguard.

26-47 The Mighty Men of the military were Asahel brother of Joab, Elhanan son of Dodo of Bethlehem, Shammoth the Harorite, Helez the Pelonite, Ira son of Ikkesh the Tekoite, Abiezer the Anathothite, Sibbecai the Hushathite, Ilai the Ahohite, Maharai the Netophathite, Heled son of Baanah the Netophathite, Ithai son of Ribai from Gibeah of the Benjaminite, Benaiah the Pirathonite, Hurai from the ravines of Gaash, Abiel the Arbathite, Azmaveth the Baharumite, Eliahba the Shaalbonite, the sons of Hashem the Gizonite, Jonathan son of Shagee the Hararite, Ahiam son of Sacar the Haranite, Eliphal son of Ur, Hepher the Mekerathite, Ahijah the Pelonite, Hezro the Carmelite, Naarai son of Ezbai, Joel brother of Nathan, Mibhar son of Hagri, Zelek the Ammonite, Naharai the Berothite, the armor bearer of Joab son of Zeruiah, Ira the Ithrite, Gareb the Ithrite, Uriah the Hittite, Zabad son of Ahlai, Adina son of Shiza the Reubenite, the Reubenite chief of the Thirty, Hanan son of Maacah, Joshaphat the Mithnite, Uzzia the Ashterathite, Shama and Jeiel the sons of Hotham the Aroerite, Jediael son of Shimri, Joha the Tizite his brother, Eliel the Mahavite, Jeribai and Joshaviah the sons of Elnaam, Ithmah the Moabite, Eliel, Obed, and Jaasiel the Mezobaite.

NEW KING JAMES VERSION

THE GROWTH OF DAVID'S ARMY

12 Now these *were* the men who came to
David at Ziklag while he was still a fugi-
tive from Saul the son of Kish; and they *were*
among the mighty men, helpers in the war,
2armed with bows, using both the right hand
and the left in *hurling* stones and *shooting* ar-
rows with the bow. *They were* of Benjamin,
Saul's brethren.
3The chief *was* Ahiezer, then Joash, the sons
of Shemaah the Gibeathite; Jeziel and Pelet the
sons of Azmaveth; Berachah, and Jehu the
Anathothite; 4Ishmaiah the Gibeonite, a mighty
man among the thirty, and over the thirty; Jere-
miah, Jahaziel, Johanan, and Jozabad the Ge-
derathite; 5Eluzai, Jerimoth, Bealiah, Shem-
ariah, and Shephatiah the Haruphite; 6Elkanah,
Jisshiah, Azarel, Joezer, and Jashobeam, the
Korahites; 7and Joelah and Zebadiah the sons of
Jeroham of Gedor.
8*Some* Gadites joined David at the strong-
hold in the wilderness, mighty men of valor,
men trained for battle, who could handle shield
and spear, whose faces *were like* the faces of li-
ons, and *were* as swift as gazelles on the moun-
tains: 9Ezer the first, Obadiah the second, Eliab
the third, 10Mishmannah the fourth, Jeremiah
the fifth, 11Attai the sixth, Eliel the seventh, 12Jo-
hanan the eighth, Elzabad the ninth, 13Jeremiah
the tenth, and Machbanai the eleventh. 14These
were from the sons of Gad, captains of the army;
the least was over a hundred, and the greatest
was over a thousand. 15These *are* the ones who
crossed the Jordan in the first month, when it
had overflowed all its banks; and they put to
flight all *those* in the valleys, to the east and to
the west.
16Then some of the sons of Benjamin and Ju-
dah came to David at the stronghold. 17And
David went out to meet them, and answered and
said to them, "If you have come peaceably to me
to help me, my heart will be united with you; but
if to betray me to my enemies, since *there is* no
wrong in my hands, may the God of our fathers
look and bring judgment." 18Then the Spirit
came upon Amasai, chief of the captains, *and he
said:*

"*We are* yours, O David;
We *are* on your side, O son of Jesse!
Peace, peace to you,
And peace to your helpers!
For your God helps you."

So David received them, and made them cap-
tains of the troop.
19And *some* from Manasseh defected to David
when he was going with the Philistines to battle
against Saul; but they did not help them, for the
lords of the Philistines sent him away by agree-
ment, saying, "He may defect to his master Saul
and endanger our heads." 20When he went to
Ziklag, those of Manasseh who defected to him
were Adnah, Jozabad, Jediael, Michael, Joz-

THE MESSAGE

1-2 12 These are the men who joined David in
Ziklag; it was during the time he was
banished by Saul the son of Kish; they were
among the Mighty Men, good fighters. They
were armed with bows and could sling
stones and shoot arrows either right- or left-
handed. They hailed from Saul's tribe, Ben-
jamin.
3-7 The first was Ahiezer; then Joash son of
Shemaah the Gibeathite; Jeziel and Pelet
the sons of Azmaveth; Beracah; Jehu the
Anathothite; Ishmaiah the Gibeonite, a
Mighty Man among the Thirty, a leader of
the Thirty; Jeremiah; Jahaziel; Johanan;
Jozabad the Gederathite; Eluzai; Jerimoth;
Bealiah; Shemariah; Shephatiah the
Haruphite; Elkanah; Isshiah; Azarel; Joezer;
Jashobeam; the Korahites; and Joelah and
Zebadiah, the sons of Jeroham from Gedor.
8-15 There were some Gadites there who had
defected to David at his wilderness fortress;
they were seasoned and eager fighters who
knew how to handle shield and spear. They
were wild in appearance, like lions, but as
agile as gazelles racing across the hills. Ezer
was the first, then Obadiah, Eliab, Mish-
mannah, Jeremiah, Attai, Eliel, Johanan,
Elzabad, Jeremiah, and Macbannai—eleven
of them. These Gadites were the cream of
the crop—any one of them was worth a hun-
dred lesser men, and the best of them were
worth a thousand. They were the ones who
crossed the Jordan when it was at flood
stage in the first month, and put everyone in
the lowlands to flight, both east and west.
16-17 There were also men from the tribes of
Benjamin and Judah who joined David in
his wilderness fortress. When David went
out to meet them, this is what he said: "If
you have come in peace and to help me, you
are most welcome to join this company; but
if you have come to betray me to my ene-
mies, innocent as I am, the God of our an-
cestors will see through you and bring judg-
ment on you."
18 Just then Amasai chief of the Thirty,
moved by God's Spirit, said,

We're on your side, O David,
We're committed, O son of Jesse;
All is well, yes, all is well with you,
And all's well with whoever helps
you.
Yes, for your God has helped and does
help you.

So David took them on and assigned
them a place under the chiefs of the raiders.
19 Some from the tribe of Manasseh also de-
fected to David when he started out with the
Philistines to go to war against Saul. In
the end, they didn't actually fight because
the Philistine leaders, after talking it over,
sent them home, saying, "We can't trust
them with our lives—they'll betray us to
their master Saul."
20-22 The men from Manasseh who defected to
David at Ziklag were Adnah, Jozabad, Jedi-

NEW KING JAMES VERSION

abad, Elihu, and Zillethai, captains of the thou-
sands who *were* from Manasseh. 21And they
helped David against the bands *of raiders*, for
they *were* all mighty men of valor, and they
were captains in the army. 22For at *that* time
they came to David day by day to help him, un-
til *it was* a great army, like the army of God.

DAVID'S ARMY AT HEBRON

23Now these *were* the numbers of the divi-
sions *that were* equipped for war, *and* came to
David at Hebron to turn *over* the kingdom of
Saul to him, according to the word of the LORD:
24of the sons of Judah bearing shield and spear,
six thousand eight hundred armed for war; 25of
the sons of Simeon, mighty men of valor fit for
war, seven thousand one hundred; 26of the sons
of Levi four thousand six hundred; 27Jehoiada,
the leader of the Aaronites, and with him three
thousand seven hundred; 28Zadok, a young
man, a valiant warrior, and from his father's
house twenty-two captains; 29of the sons of Ben-
jamin, relatives of Saul, three thousand (until
then the greatest part of them had remained
loyal to the house of Saul); 30of the sons of
Ephraim twenty thousand eight hundred,
mighty men of valor, famous men throughout
their father's house; 31of the half-tribe of Ma-
nasseh eighteen thousand, who were designated
by name to come and make David king; 32of the
sons of Issachar who had understanding of the
times, to know what Israel ought to do, their
chiefs were two hundred; and all their brethren
were at their command; 33of Zebulun there were
fifty thousand who went out to battle, expert in
war with all weapons of war, stouthearted men
who could keep ranks; 34of Naphtali one thou-
sand captains, and with them thirty-seven thou-
sand with shield and spear; 35of the Danites who
could keep battle formation, twenty-eight thou-
sand six hundred; 36of Asher, those who could
go out to war, able to keep battle formation,
forty thousand; 37of the Reubenites and the
Gadites and the half-tribe of Manasseh, from
the other side of the Jordan, one hundred and
twenty thousand armed for battle with every
kind of weapon of war.

38All these men of war, who could keep
ranks, came to Hebron with a loyal heart, to
make David king over all Israel; and all the rest
of Israel *were* of one mind to make David king.
39And they were there with David three days,
eating and drinking, for their brethren had pre-
pared for them. 40Moreover those who were
near to them, from as far away as Issachar and
Zebulun and Naphtali, were bringing food on
donkeys and camels, on mules and oxen—provi-
sions of flour and cakes of figs and cakes of
raisins, wine and oil and oxen and sheep abun-
dantly, for *there was* joy in Israel.

THE ARK BROUGHT FROM KIRJATH JEARIM

13 Then David consulted with the captains of
thousands and hundreds, *and* with every
leader. 2And David said to all the assembly of Is-
rael, "If *it seems* good to you, and if it is of the
LORD our God, let us send out to our brethren
everywhere *who are* left in all the land of Israel,

THE MESSAGE

ael, Michael, Jozabad, Elihu, and Zillethai, all leaders among the families of Manasseh. They helped David in his raids against the desert bandits; they were all stalwart fighters and good leaders among his raiders. Hardly a day went by without men showing up to help—it wasn't long before his band seemed as large as God's own army!

23-37 Here are the statistics on the battle-seasoned warriors who came down from the north to David at Hebron to hand over Saul's kingdom, in accord with GOD's word: from Judah, carrying shield and spear, 6,800 battle-ready; from Simeon, 7,100 stalwart fighters; from Levi, 4,600, which included Jehoiada leader of the family of Aaron, bringing 3,700 men and the young and stalwart Zadok with twenty-two leaders from his family; from Benjamin, Saul's family, 3,000, most of whom had stuck it out with Saul until now; from Ephraim, 20,800, fierce fighters and famous in their hometowns; from the half-tribe of Manasseh, 18,000 elected to come and make David king; from Issachar, men who understood both the times and Israel's duties, 200 leaders with their families; from Zebulun, 50,000 well-equipped veteran warriors, unswervingly loyal; from Naphtali, 1,000 chiefs leading 37,000 men heavily armed; from Dan, 28,600 battle-ready men; from Asher, 40,000 veterans, battle-ready; and from East of Jordan, men from Reuben, Gad, and the half-tribe of Manasseh, heavily armed, 120,000.

38-40 All these soldiers came to David at Hebron, ready to fight if necessary; they were both united and determined to make David king over all Israel. And everyone else in Israel was of the same mind—"Make David king!" They were with David for three days of feasting celebration, with food and drink supplied by their families. Neighbors ranging from as far north as Issachar, Zebulun, and Naphtali arrived with donkeys, camels, mules, and oxen loaded down with food for the party: flour, fig cakes, raisin cakes, wine, oil, cattle, and sheep—joy in Israel!

DAVID GOES TO GET THE CHEST OF GOD

1-14 13 David consulted with all of his leaders, the commanders of thousands and of hundreds. Then David addressed the entire assembly of Israel, "If it seems right to you, and it is GOD's will, let's invite all our relatives wherever they are throughout Israel,

NEW KING JAMES VERSION

and with them to the priests and Levites *who are* in their cities *and* their common-lands, that they may gather together to us; 3and let us bring the ark of our God back to us, for we have not inquired at it since the days of Saul." 4Then all the assembly said that they would do so, for the thing was right in the eyes of all the people.

5So David gathered all Israel together, from Shihor in Egypt to as far as the entrance of Hamath, to bring the ark of God from Kirjath Jearim. 6And David and all Israel went up to Baalah,[a] to Kirjath Jearim, which belonged to Judah, to bring up from there the ark of God the LORD, who dwells *between* the cherubim, where *His* name is proclaimed. 7So they carried the ark of God on a new cart from the house of Abinadab, and Uzza and Ahio drove the cart. 8Then David and all Israel played *music* before God with all *their* might, with singing, on harps, on stringed instruments, on tambourines, on cymbals, and with trumpets.

9And when they came to Chidon's[a] threshing floor, Uzza put out his hand to hold the ark, for the oxen stumbled. 10Then the anger of the LORD was aroused against Uzza, and He struck him because he put his hand to the ark; and he died there before God. 11And David became angry because of the LORD's outbreak against Uzza; therefore that place is called Perez Uzza[a] to this day. 12David was afraid of God that day, saying, "How can I bring the ark of God to me?"

13So David would not move the ark with him into the City of David, but took it aside into the house of Obed-Edom the Gittite. 14The ark of God remained with the family of Obed-Edom in his house three months. And the LORD blessed the house of Obed-Edom and all that he had.

DAVID ESTABLISHED AT JERUSALEM

14 Now Hiram king of Tyre sent messengers to David, and cedar trees, with masons and carpenters, to build him a house. 2So David knew that the LORD had established him as king over Israel, for his kingdom was highly exalted for the sake of His people Israel.

3Then David took more wives in Jerusalem, and David begot more sons and daughters. 4And these are the names of his children whom he had in Jerusalem: Shammua,[a] Shobab, Nathan, Solomon, 5Ibhar, Elishua,[a] Elpelet,[b] 6Nogah, Nepheg, Japhia, 7Elishama, Beeliada,[a] and Eliphelet.

THE PHILISTINES DEFEATED

8Now when the Philistines heard that David had been anointed king over all Israel, all the Philistines went up to search for David. And David heard *of it* and went out against them. 9Then the Philistines went and made a raid on the Valley of Rephaim. 10And David inquired of God, saying, "Shall I go up against the Philistines? Will You deliver them into my hand?"

13:6 [a]Called *Baale Judah* in 2 Samuel 6:2 **13:9** [a]Called *Nachon* in 2 Samuel 6:6 **13:11** [a]Literally *Outburst Against Uzza* **14:4** [a]Spelled *Shimea* in 3:5 **14:5** [a]Spelled *Elishama* in 3:6 [b]Spelled *Eliphelet* in 3:6 **14:7** [a]Spelled *Eliada* in 3:8

THE MESSAGE

along with their relatives, including their priests and Levites from their cities and surrounding pastures, to join us. And let's bring the Chest of our God back—the Chest that was out of sight, out of mind during the days of Saul." The entire assembly of Israel agreed—everybody agreed that it was the right thing to do. So David gathered all Israel together, from Egypt's Pond of Horus in the southwest to the Pass of Hamath in the northeast, to go and get the Chest of God from Kiriath Jearim. Then David and all Israel went to Baalah (Kiriath Jearim) in Judah to bring back the Chest of God, the "Cherubim-Throne-of-GOD," where GOD's Name is invoked. They moved the Chest of God on a brand-new cart from the house of Abinadab with Uzzah and Ahio in charge. In procession with the Chest of God, David and all Israel worshiped exuberantly in song and dance, with a marching band of all kinds of instruments. When they were at the threshing floor of Kidon, the oxen stumbled and Uzzah grabbed the Chest to keep it from falling off. GOD erupted in anger against Uzzah and killed him because he grabbed the Chest. He died on the spot—in the presence of God. David lost his temper, angry because GOD exploded against Uzzah; the place is still called Perez Uzzah (Exploded Uzzah). David was terrified of God that day; he said, "How can I possibly continue this parade with the Chest of God?" So David called off the parade of the Chest to the City of David; instead he stored it in the house of Obed-Edom the Gittite. The Chest of God was in storage in the house of Obed-Edom for three months. GOD blessed the family of Obed-Edom and everything around him.

DAVID BUILDS

1-7 14 King Hiram of Tyre sent an envoy to David, along with cedar lumber, masons, and carpenters to build him a royal palace. Then David knew for sure that GOD had confirmed him as king over Israel, because of the rising reputation that GOD was giving his kingdom for the benefit of his people Israel. David married more wives and had more children in Jerusalem. His children born in Jerusalem were Shammua, Shobab, Nathan, Solomon, Ibhar, Elishua, Elpelet, Nogah, Nepheg, Japhia, Elishama, Beeliada, and Eliphelet.

8-9 The minute the Philistines heard that David had been made king over a united Israel, they went out in force to capture David. When David got the report, he marched out to confront them. On their way, the Philistines stopped off to plunder the Valley of Rephaim.

10 David prayed to God: "Is this the right time to attack the Philistines? Will you give me the victory?"

NEW KING JAMES VERSION

The LORD said to him, "Go up, for I will de-
liver them into your hand."
11So they went up to Baal Perazim, and
David defeated them there. Then David said,
"God has broken through my enemies by my
hand like a breakthrough of water." Therefore
they called the name of that place Baal Pe-
razim.[a] 12And when they left their gods there,
David gave a commandment, and they were
burned with fire.
13Then the Philistines once again made a
raid on the valley. 14Therefore David inquired
again of God, and God said to him, "You shall
not go up after them; circle around them, and
come upon them in front of the mulberry trees.
15And it shall be, when you hear a sound of
marching in the tops of the mulberry trees, then
you shall go out to battle, for God has gone out
before you to strike the camp of the Philistines."
16So David did as God commanded him, and
they drove back the army of the Philistines from
Gibeon as far as Gezer. 17Then the fame of
David went out into all lands, and the LORD
brought the fear of him upon all nations.

THE ARK BROUGHT TO JERUSALEM

15 *David* built houses for himself in the City
of David; and he prepared a place for the
ark of God, and pitched a tent for it. 2Then
David said, "No one may carry the ark of God
but the Levites, for the LORD has chosen them to
carry the ark of God and to minister before Him
forever." 3And David gathered all Israel together
at Jerusalem, to bring up the ark of the LORD to
its place, which he had prepared for it. 4Then
David assembled the children of Aaron and the
Levites: 5of the sons of Kohath, Uriel the chief,
and one hundred and twenty of his brethren; 6of
the sons of Merari, Asaiah the chief, and two
hundred and twenty of his brethren; 7of the sons
of Gershom, Joel the chief, and one hundred and
thirty of his brethren; 8of the sons of Elizaphan,
Shemaiah the chief, and two hundred of his
brethren; 9of the sons of Hebron, Eliel the chief,
and eighty of his brethren; 10of the sons of
Uzziel, Amminadab the chief, and one hundred
and twelve of his brethren.
11And David called for Zadok and Abiathar
the priests, and for the Levites: for Uriel, Asaiah,
Joel, Shemaiah, Eliel, and Amminadab. 12He said
to them, "You *are* the heads of the fathers' *houses*
of the Levites; sanctify yourselves, you and your
brethren, that you may bring up the ark of the
LORD God of Israel to *the place* I have prepared
for it. 13For because you *did* not *do it* the first *time*,
the LORD our God broke out against us, because
we did not consult Him about the proper order."
14So the priests and the Levites sanctified
themselves to bring up the ark of the LORD God
of Israel. 15And the children of the Levites bore
the ark of God on their shoulders, by its poles,
as Moses had commanded according to the
word of the LORD.
16Then David spoke to the leaders of the
Levites to appoint their brethren *to be* the
singers accompanied by instruments of music,
stringed instruments, harps, and cymbals, by
raising the voice with resounding joy.

14:11 [a]Literally *Master of Breakthroughs*

THE MESSAGE

GOD answered, "Attack; I'll give you the victory."

11-12 David attacked at Baal Perazim and slaughtered them. David said, "God exploded my enemies, as water explodes from a burst pipe." That's how the place got its name, Baal Perazim (Baal-Explosion). The Philistines left their gods behind and David ordered that they be burned up.

13-15 And then the Philistines were back at it again, plundering in the valley. David again prayed to God. God answered, "This time don't attack head-on; circle around and come at them out of the balsam grove. When you hear a sound like shuffling feet in the tops of the balsams, attack; God will be two steps ahead of you, slaughtering the Philistines."

16 David did exactly as God commanded, slaughtering Philistines all the way from Gibeon to Gezer.

17 David was soon famous all over the place, far and near; and GOD put the fear of God into the godless nations.

DAVID WORSHIPS

1-2 15 After David built houses for himself in the City of David, he cleared a place for the Chest and pitched a tent for it. Then David gave orders: "No one carries the Chest of God except the Levites; GOD designated them and them only to carry the Chest of GOD and be available full time for service in the work of worship."

3-10 David then called everyone in Israel to assemble in Jerusalem to bring up the Chest of GOD to its specially prepared place. David also called in the family of Aaron and the Levites. From the family of Kohath, Uriel the head with 120 relatives; from the family of Merari, Asaiah the head with 220 relatives; from the family of Gershon, Joel the head with 130 relatives; from the family of Elizaphan, Shemaiah the head with 200 relatives; from the family of Hebron, Eliel the head with 80 relatives; from the family of Uzziel, Amminadab the head with 112 relatives.

11-13 Then David called in Zadok and Abiathar the priests, and Uriel, Asaiah, Joel, Shemaiah, Eliel, and Amminadab the Levites. He said, "You are responsible for the Levitical families; now consecrate yourselves, both you and your relatives, and bring up the Chest of the GOD of Israel to the place I have set aside for it. The first time we did this, you Levites did not carry it properly, and GOD exploded in anger at us because we didn't make proper preparation and follow instructions."

14-15 So the priests and Levites consecrated themselves to bring up the Chest of the GOD of Israel. The Levites carried the Chest of God exactly as Moses, instructed by GOD, commanded—carried it with poles on their shoulders, careful not to touch it with their hands.

16 David ordered the heads of the Levites to assign their relatives to sing in the choir, accompanied by a well-equipped marching band, and fill the air with joyful sound.

New King James Version

17 So the Levites appointed Heman the son of Joel; and of his brethren, Asaph the son of Berechiah; and of their brethren, the sons of Merari, Ethan the son of Kushaiah; 18 and with them their brethren of the second *rank:* Zechariah, Ben,[a] Jaaziel, Shemiramoth, Jehiel, Unni, Eliab, Benaiah, Maaseiah, Mattithiah, Elipheleh, Mikneiah, Obed-Edom, and Jeiel, the gatekeepers; 19 the singers, Heman, Asaph, and Ethan, *were* to sound the cymbals of bronze; 20 Zechariah, Aziel, Shemiramoth, Jehiel, Unni, Eliab, Maaseiah, and Benaiah, with strings according to Alamoth; 21 Mattithiah, Elipheleh, Mikneiah, Obed-Edom, Jeiel, and Azaziah, to direct with harps on the Sheminith; 22 Chenaniah, leader of the Levites, was instructor *in charge of* the music, because he *was* skillful; 23 Berechiah and Elkanah *were* doorkeepers for the ark; 24 Shebaniah, Joshaphat, Nethanel, Amasai, Zechariah, Benaiah, and Eliezer, the priests, were to blow the trumpets before the ark of God; and Obed-Edom and Jehiah, doorkeepers for the ark.

25 So David, the elders of Israel, and the captains over thousands went to bring up the ark of the covenant of the LORD from the house of Obed-Edom with joy. 26 And so it was, when God helped the Levites who bore the ark of the covenant of the LORD, that they offered seven bulls and seven rams. 27 David was clothed with a robe of fine linen, as were all the Levites who bore the ark, the singers, and Chenaniah the music master *with* the singers. David also wore a linen ephod. 28 Thus all Israel brought up the ark of the covenant of the LORD with shouting and with the sound of the horn, with trumpets and with cymbals, making music with stringed instruments and harps.

29 And it happened, *as* the ark of the covenant of the LORD came to the City of David, that Michal, Saul's daughter, looked through a window and saw King David whirling and playing music; and she despised him in her heart.

The Ark Placed in the Tabernacle

16 So they brought the ark of God, and set it in the midst of the tabernacle that David had erected for it. Then they offered burnt offerings and peace offerings before God. 2 And when David had finished offering the burnt offerings and the peace offerings, he blessed the people in the name of the LORD. 3 Then he distributed to everyone of Israel, both man and woman, to everyone a loaf of bread, a piece *of meat,* and a cake of raisins.

4 And he appointed some of the Levites to minister before the ark of the LORD, to commemorate, to thank, and to praise the LORD God of Israel: 5 Asaph the chief, and next to him Zechariah, *then* Jeiel, Shemiramoth, Jehiel, Mattithiah, Eliab, Benaiah, and Obed-Edom: Jeiel with stringed instruments and harps, but

15:18 [a]Following Masoretic Text and Vulgate; Septuagint omits *Ben.*

The Message

17-18 The Levites assigned Heman son of Joel, and from his family, Asaph son of Berekiah, then Ethan son of Kushaiah from the family of Merari, and after them in the second rank their brothers Zechariah, Jaaziel, Shemiramoth, Jehiel, Unni, Eliab, Benaiah, Maaseiah, Mattithiah, Eliphelehu, Mikneiah, Obed-Edom, and Jeiel as security guards.

19-22 The members of the choir and marching band were: Heman, Asaph, and Ethan with bronze cymbals; Zechariah, Aziel, Shemiramoth, Jehiel, Unni, Eliab, Maaseiah, and Benaiah with lyres carrying the melody; Mattithiah, Eliphelehu, Mikneiah, Obed-Edom, Jeiel, and Azaziah with harps filling in the harmony; Kenaniah, the Levite in charge of music, a very gifted musician, was music director.

23-24 Berekiah and Elkanah were porters for the Chest. The priests Shebaniah, Joshaphat, Nethanel, Amasai, Zechariah, Benaiah, and Eliezer blew the trumpets before the Chest of God. Obed-Edom and Jehiah were also porters for the Chest.

25-28 Now they were ready. David, the elders of Israel, and the commanders of thousands started out to get the Chest of the Covenant of GOD and bring it up from the house of Obed-Edom. And they went rejoicing. Because God helped the Levites, strengthening them as they carried the Chest of the Covenant of GOD, they paused to worship by sacrificing seven bulls and seven rams. They were all dressed in elegant linen—David, the Levites carrying the Chest, the choir and band, and Kenaniah who was directing the music. David also wore a linen prayer shawl (called an ephod). On they came, all Israel on parade bringing up the Chest of the Covenant of GOD, shouting and cheering, playing every kind of brass and percussion and string instrument.

29 When the Chest of the Covenant of GOD entered the City of David, Michal, Saul's daughter, was watching from a window. When she saw King David dancing ecstatically she was filled with contempt.

1-3 16 They brought the Chest of God and placed it right in the center of the tent that David had pitched for it; then they worshiped by presenting burnt offerings and peace offerings to God. When David had completed the offerings of worship, he blessed the people in the name of GOD. Then he passed around to every one there, men and women alike, a loaf of bread, a slice of barbecue, and a raisin cake.

4-6 Then David assigned some of the Levites to the Chest of GOD to lead worship—to intercede, give thanks, and praise the GOD of Israel. Asaph was in charge; under him were Zechariah, Jeiel, Shemiramoth, Jehiel, Mattithiah, Eliab, Benaiah, Obed-Edom, and Jeiel, who played the musical instruments.

NEW KING JAMES VERSION

Asaph made music with cymbals; [6]Benaiah and Jahaziel the priests regularly *blew* the trumpets before the ark of the covenant of God.

DAVID'S SONG OF THANKSGIVING

[7]On that day David first delivered *this psalm* into the hand of Asaph and his brethren, to thank the LORD:

[8]Oh, give thanks to the LORD!
Call upon His name;
Make known His deeds among the peoples!
[9]Sing to Him, sing psalms to Him;
Talk of all His wondrous works!
[10]Glory in His holy name;
Let the hearts of those rejoice who seek the LORD!
[11]Seek the LORD and His strength;
Seek His face evermore!
[12]Remember His marvelous works which He has done,
His wonders, and the judgments of His mouth,
[13]O seed of Israel His servant,
You children of Jacob, His chosen ones!

[14]He *is* the LORD our God;
His judgments *are* in all the earth.
[15]Remember His covenant forever,
The word which He commanded, for a thousand generations,
[16]*The covenant which* He made with Abraham,
And His oath to Isaac,
[17]And confirmed it to Jacob for a statute,
To Israel *for* an everlasting covenant,
[18]Saying, "To you I will give the land of Canaan
As the allotment of your inheritance,"
[19]When you were few in number,
Indeed very few, and strangers in it.

[20]When they went from one nation to another,
And from *one* kingdom to another people,
[21]He permitted no man to do them wrong;
Yes, He rebuked kings for their sakes,
[22]*Saying*, "Do not touch My anointed ones,
And do My prophets no harm."[a]

[23]Sing to the LORD, all the earth;
Proclaim the good news of His salvation from day to day.
[24]Declare His glory among the nations,
His wonders among all peoples.
[25]For the LORD *is* great and greatly to be praised;
He *is* also to be feared above all gods.
[26]For all the gods of the peoples *are* idols,
But the LORD made the heavens.
[27]Honor and majesty *are* before Him;
Strength and gladness are in His place.
[28]Give to the LORD, O families of the peoples,
Give to the LORD glory and strength.
[29]Give to the LORD the glory *due* His name;

16:22 [a]Compare verses 8–22 with Psalm 105:1–15

THE MESSAGE

Asaph was on percussion. The priests Benaiah and Jahaziel blew the trumpets before the Chest of the Covenant of God at set times through the day.

7 That was the day that David inaugurated regular worship of praise to GOD, led by Asaph and his company.

8-19 Thank GOD! Call out his Name!
Tell the whole world who he is and what he's done!
Sing to him! Play songs for him!
Broadcast all his wonders!
Revel in his holy Name,
GOD-seekers, be jubilant!
Study GOD and his strength,
seek his presence day and night;
Remember all the wonders he performed,
the miracles and judgments that came out of his mouth.
Seed of Israel his servant!
Children of Jacob, his first choice!
He is GOD, *our* God;
wherever you go you come on his judgments and decisions.
He keeps his commitments across thousands
of generations, the covenant he commanded,
The same one he made with Abraham,
the very one he swore to Isaac;
He posted it in big block letters to Jacob,
this eternal covenant with Israel:
"I give you the land of Canaan,
this is your inheritance;
Even though you're not much to look at,
a few straggling strangers."

20-22 They wandered from country to country,
camped out in one kingdom after another;
But he didn't let anyone push them around,
he stood up for them against bully-kings:
"Don't you dare touch my anointed ones,
don't lay a hand on my prophets."

23-27 Sing to GOD, everyone and everything!
Get out his salvation news every day!
Publish his glory among the godless nations,
his wonders to all races and religions.
And why? Because GOD is great—well worth praising!
No god or goddess comes close in honor.
All the popular gods are stuff and nonsense,
but GOD made the cosmos!
Splendor and majesty flow out of him,
strength and joy fill his place.

28-29 Shout Bravo! to GOD, families of the peoples,
in awe of the Glory, in awe of the Strength: Bravo!

NEW KING JAMES VERSION

Bring an offering, and come before Him.
Oh, worship the LORD in the beauty of
holiness!
30Tremble before Him, all the earth.
The world also is firmly established,
It shall not be moved.

31Let the heavens rejoice, and let the earth be
glad;
And let them say among the nations, "The
LORD reigns."
32Let the sea roar, and all its fullness;
Let the field rejoice, and all that *is* in it.
33Then the trees of the woods shall rejoice
before the LORD,
For He is coming to judge the earth.[a]

34Oh, give thanks to the LORD, for *He is* good!
For His mercy *endures* forever.[a]
35And say, "Save us, O God of our salvation;
Gather us together, and deliver us from the
Gentiles,
To give thanks to Your holy name,
To triumph in Your praise."
36Blessed *be* the LORD God of Israel
From everlasting to everlasting![a]

And all the people said, "Amen!" and praised the
LORD.

REGULAR WORSHIP MAINTAINED

37So he left Asaph and his brothers there be-
fore the ark of the covenant of the LORD to min-
ister before the ark regularly, as every day's
work required; 38and Obed-Edom with his sixty-
eight brethren, including Obed-Edom the son of
Jeduthun, and Hosah, *to be* gatekeepers; 39and
Zadok the priest and his brethren the priests,
before the tabernacle of the LORD at the high
place that *was* at Gibeon, 40to offer burnt offer-
ings to the LORD on the altar of burnt offering
regularly morning and evening, and *to do* ac-
cording to all that is written in the Law of the
LORD which He commanded Israel; 41and with
them Heman and Jeduthun and the rest who
were chosen, who were designated by name, to
give thanks to the LORD, because His mercy *en-
dures* forever; 42and with them Heman and Je-
duthun, to sound aloud with trumpets and cym-
bals and the musical instruments of God. Now
the sons of Jeduthun *were* gatekeepers.
43Then all the people departed, every man to
his house; and David returned to bless his
house.

16:33 [a]Compare verses 23–33 with Psalm 96:1–13 **16:34** [a]Compare verse 34 with Psalm 106:1 **16:36** [a]Compare verses 35, 36 with Psalm 106:47, 48

THE MESSAGE

Shout Bravo! to his famous Name,
lift high an offering and enter his
presence!
Stand resplendent in his robes of
holiness!

30-33 God is serious business, take him
seriously;
he's put the earth in place and it's not
moving.
So let Heaven rejoice, let Earth be
jubilant,
and pass the word among the nations,
"GOD reigns!"
Let Ocean, all teeming with life, bellow,
let Field and all its creatures shake
the rafters;
Then the trees in the forest will add their
applause
to all who are pleased and present
before GOD
—he's on his way to set things right!

34-36 Give thanks to GOD—he is good
and his love never quits.
Say, "Save us, Savior God,
round us up and get us out of these
godless places,
So we can give thanks to your holy
Name,
and bask in your life of praise."
Blessed be GOD, the God of Israel,
from everlasting to everlasting.

Then everybody said, "Yes! Amen!" and "Praise GOD!"

37-42 David left Asaph and his coworkers with the Chest of the Covenant of GOD and in charge of the work of worship; they were responsible for the needs of worship around the clock. He also assigned Obed-Edom and his sixty-eight relatives to help them. Obed-Edom son of Jeduthun and Hosah were in charge of the security guards. The priest Zadok and his family of priests were assigned to the Tent of GOD at the sacred mound at Gibeon to make sure that the services of morning and evening worship were conducted daily, complete with Whole-Burnt-Offerings offered on the Altar of Burnt Offering, as ordered in the Law of GOD, which was the norm for Israel. With them were Heman, Jeduthun, and others specifically named, with the job description: "Give thanks to GOD, for his love never quits!" Heman and Jeduthun were also well equipped with trumpets, cymbals, and other instruments for accompanying sacred songs. The sons of Jeduthun formed the security guard.

43 Arrangements completed, the people all left for home. And David went home to bless his family.

NEW KING JAMES VERSION

GOD'S COVENANT WITH DAVID

17 Now it came to pass, when David was
dwelling in his house, that David said to
Nathan the prophet, "See now, I dwell in a house
of cedar, but the ark of the covenant of the LORD
is under tent curtains."
2 Then Nathan said to David, "Do all that *is* in
your heart, for God *is* with you."
3 But it happened that night that the word of
God came to Nathan, saying, 4 "Go and tell My
servant David, 'Thus says the LORD: "You shall
not build Me a house to dwell in. 5 For I have not
dwelt in a house since the time that I brought up
Israel, even to this day, but have gone from tent
to tent, and from *one* tabernacle *to another.*
6 Wherever I have moved about with all Israel,
have I ever spoken a word to any of the judges
of Israel, whom I commanded to shepherd My
people, saying, 'Why have you not built Me a
house of cedar?' " ' 7 Now therefore, thus shall
you say to My servant David, 'Thus says the
LORD of hosts: "I took you from the sheepfold,
from following the sheep, to be ruler over My
people Israel. 8 And I have been with you wher-
ever you have gone, and have cut off all your en-
emies from before you, and have made you a
name like the name of the great men who *are* on
the earth. 9 Moreover I will appoint a place for
My people Israel, and will plant them, that they
may dwell in a place of their own and move no
more; nor shall the sons of wickedness oppress
them anymore, as previously, 10 since the time
that I commanded judges *to be* over My people
Israel. Also I will subdue all your enemies. Fur-
thermore I tell you that the LORD will build you
a house.[a] 11 And it shall be, when your days are
fulfilled, when you must go *to be* with your fa-
thers, that I will set up your seed after you, who
will be of your sons; and I will establish his
kingdom. 12 He shall build Me a house, and I will
establish his throne forever. 13 I will be his Fa-
ther, and he shall be My son; and I will not take
My mercy away from him, as I took *it* from *him*
who was before you. 14 And I will establish him
in My house and in My kingdom forever; and
his throne shall be established forever." ' "
15 According to all these words and according
to all this vision, so Nathan spoke to David.
16 Then King David went in and sat before the
LORD; and he said: "Who *am* I, O LORD God?
And what is my house, that You have brought
me this far? 17 And *yet* this was a small thing in
Your sight, O God; and You have *also* spoken of
Your servant's house for a great while to come,
and have regarded me according to the rank of
a man of high degree, O LORD God. 18 What more
can David *say* to You for the honor of Your ser-
vant? For You know Your servant. 19 O LORD, for
Your servant's sake, and according to Your own
heart, You have done all this greatness, in mak-

17:10 [a]That is, a royal dynasty

THE MESSAGE

DAVID SUBMITS AND PRAYS

1 17 After the king had made himself at home, he said to Nathan the prophet, "Look at this: Here I am comfortable in a luxurious palace of cedar and the Chest of the Covenant of GOD sits under a tent."

2 Nathan told David, "Whatever is on your heart, go and do it; God is with you."

3-6 But that night, the word of God came to Nathan, saying, "Go and tell my servant David, This is GOD's word on the matter: You will not build me a 'house' to live in. Why, I haven't lived in a 'house' from the time I brought up the children of Israel from Egypt till now; I've gone from one tent and makeshift shelter to another. In all my travels with all Israel, did I ever say to any of the leaders I commanded to shepherd Israel, 'Why haven't you built me a house of cedar?'

7-10 "So here is what you are to tell my servant David: The GOD-of-the-Angel-Armies has this word for you: I took you from the pasture, tagging after sheep, and made you prince over my people Israel. I was with you everywhere you went and mowed your enemies down before you; and now I'm about to make you famous, ranked with the great names on earth. I'm going to set aside a place for my people Israel and plant them there so they'll have their own home and not be knocked around anymore; nor will evil nations afflict them as they always have, even during the days I set judges over my people Israel. And finally, I'm going to conquer all your enemies.

10-14 "And now I'm telling you this: GOD himself will build *you* a house! When your life is complete and you're buried with your ancestors, then I'll raise up your child to succeed you, a child from your own body, and I'll firmly establish his rule. *He* will build a house to honor me, and I will guarantee his kingdom's rule forever. I'll be a father to him, and he'll be a son to me. I will never remove my gracious love from him as I did from the one who preceded you. I will set him over my house and my kingdom forever; his throne will always be there, rock solid."

15 Nathan gave David a complete and accurate report of everything he heard and saw in the vision.

16-27 King David went in, took his place before GOD, and prayed:

> Who am I, my Master GOD, and what is my family, that you have brought me to this place in life? But that's nothing compared to what's coming, for you've also spoken of my family far into the future, given me a glimpse into tomorrow and looked on me, Master GOD, as a Somebody. What's left for David to say to this—to your honoring your servant, even though you know me, just as I am? O GOD, out of the goodness of your heart, you've taken your servant to do this great

NEW KING JAMES VERSION

ing known all these great things. 20O LORD, *there is* none like You, nor *is there any* God besides You, according to all that we have heard with our ears. 21And who *is* like Your people Israel, the one nation on the earth whom God went to redeem for Himself *as* a people—to make for Yourself a name by great and awesome deeds, by driving out nations from before Your people whom You redeemed from Egypt? 22For You have made Your people Israel Your very own people forever; and You, LORD, have become their God.

23"And now, O LORD, the word which You have spoken concerning Your servant and concerning his house, *let it* be established forever, and do as You have said. 24So let it be established, that Your name may be magnified forever, saying, 'The LORD of hosts, the God of Israel, *is* Israel's God.' And let the house of Your servant David be established before You. 25For You, O my God, have revealed to Your servant that You will build him a house. Therefore Your servant has found it *in his heart* to pray before You. 26And now, LORD, You are God, and have promised this goodness to Your servant. 27Now You have been pleased to bless the house of Your servant, that it may continue before You forever; for You have blessed it, O LORD, and *it shall be* blessed forever."

DAVID'S FURTHER CONQUESTS

18 After this it came to pass that David attacked the Philistines, subdued them, and took Gath and its towns from the hand of the Philistines. 2Then he defeated Moab, and the Moabites became David's servants, *and* brought tribute.

3And David defeated Hadadezer[a] king of Zobah *as far as* Hamath, as he went to establish his power by the River Euphrates. 4David took from him one thousand chariots, seven thousand[a] horsemen, and twenty thousand foot soldiers. Also David hamstrung all the chariot *horses*, except that he spared enough of them for one hundred chariots.

5When the Syrians of Damascus came to help Hadadezer king of Zobah, David killed twenty-two thousand of the Syrians. 6Then David put *garrisons* in Syria of Damascus; and the Syrians became David's servants, *and* brought tribute. So the LORD preserved David wherever he went. 7And David took the shields of gold that were on the servants of Hadadezer, and brought them to Jerusalem. 8Also from Tibhath[a] and from Chun, cities of Hadadezer, David brought a large amount of bronze, with which Solomon made the bronze Sea, the pillars, and the articles of bronze.

18:3 [a]Hebrew *Hadarezer*, and so throughout chapters 18 and 19 **18:4** [a]Or *seven hundred* (compare 2 Samuel 8:4) **18:8** [a]Spelled *Betah* in 2 Samuel 8:8

THE MESSAGE

thing and put your great work on display. There's none like you, GOD, no *God* but you, nothing to compare with what we've heard with our own ears. And who is like your people, like Israel, a nation unique on earth, whom God set out to redeem as his own people (and became most famous for it), performing great and fearsome acts, throwing out nations and their gods left and right as you saved your people from Egypt? You established for yourself a people—your very own Israel!—your people forever. And you, GOD, became their God.

So now, great GOD, this word that you have spoken to me and my family, guarantee it forever! Do exactly what you've promised! Then your reputation will be confirmed and flourish always as people exclaim, "The GOD-of-the-Angel-Armies, the God over Israel, is Israel's God!" And the house of your servant David will remain rock solid under your watchful presence. You, my God, have told me plainly, "I will build you a house." That's how I was able to find the courage to pray this prayer to you. GOD, being the God you are, you have spoken all these wonderful words to me. As if that weren't enough, you've blessed my family so that it will continue in your presence always. Because you have blessed it, GOD, it's *really* blessed—blessed for good!

DAVID FIGHTS

1 **18** In the days that followed, David struck hard at the Philistines, bringing them to their knees, captured Gath, and took control of the surrounding countryside.

2 He also fought and defeated Moab. The Moabites came under David's rule and paid regular tribute.

3-4 On his way to restore his sovereignty at the Euphrates River, David defeated Hadadezer king of Zobah (over toward Hamath). David captured a thousand chariots, seven thousand cavalry, and twenty thousand infantry from him. He hamstrung all the chariot horses, but saved back a hundred.

5-6 When the Arameans from Damascus came to the aid of Hadadezer king of Zobah, David killed twenty-two thousand of them. David set up a puppet government in Aram-Damascus. The Arameans became subjects of David and were forced to bring tribute. GOD gave victory to David wherever he marched.

7-8 David plundered the gold shields that belonged to the servants of Hadadezer and brought them to Jerusalem. He also looted Tebah and Cun, cities of Hadadezer, of a huge quantity of bronze that Solomon later used to make the Great Bronze Sea, the Pillars, and bronze equipment in The Temple.

NEW KING JAMES VERSION

9 Now when Tou[a] king of Hamath heard that David had defeated all the army of Hadadezer king of Zobah, 10 he sent Hadoram[a] his son to King David, to greet him and bless him, because he had fought against Hadadezer and defeated him (for Hadadezer had been at war with Tou); and *Hadoram brought with him* all kinds of articles of gold, silver, and bronze. 11 King David also dedicated these to the LORD, along with the silver and gold that he had brought from all *these* nations—from Edom, from Moab, from the people of Ammon, from the Philistines, and from Amalek.

12 Moreover Abishai the son of Zeruiah killed eighteen thousand Edomites[a] in the Valley of Salt. 13 He also put garrisons in Edom, and all the Edomites became David's servants. And the LORD preserved David wherever he went.

DAVID'S ADMINISTRATION

14 So David reigned over all Israel, and administered judgment and justice to all his people. 15 Joab the son of Zeruiah *was* over the army; Jehoshaphat the son of Ahilud *was* recorder; 16 Zadok the son of Ahitub and Abimelech the son of Abiathar *were* the priests; Shavsha[a] *was* the scribe; 17 Benaiah the son of Jehoiada *was* over the Cherethites and the Pelethites; and David's sons *were* chief ministers at the king's side.

THE AMMONITES AND SYRIANS DEFEATED

19 It happened after this that Nahash the king of the people of Ammon died, and his son reigned in his place. 2 Then David said, "I will show kindness to Hanun the son of Nahash, because his father showed kindness to me." So David sent messengers to comfort him concerning his father. And David's servants came to Hanun in the land of the people of Ammon to comfort him.

3 And the princes of the people of Ammon said to Hanun, "Do you think that David really honors your father because he has sent comforters to you? Did his servants not come to you to search and to overthrow and to spy out the land?"

4 Therefore Hanun took David's servants, shaved them, and cut off their garments in the middle, at their buttocks, and sent them away. 5 Then *some* went and told David about the men; and he sent to meet them, because the men were greatly ashamed. And the king said, "Wait at Jericho until your beards have grown, and *then* return."

6 When the people of Ammon saw that they had made themselves repulsive to David, Hanun and the people of Ammon sent a thousand talents of silver to hire for themselves chariots and horsemen from Mesopotamia,[a] from Syrian Maacah, and from Zobah.[b] 7 So they hired for

18:9 [a]Spelled *Toi* in 2 Samuel 8:9, 10 **18:10** [a]Spelled *Joram* in 2 Samuel 8:10 **18:12** [a]Or *Syrians* (compare 2 Samuel 8:13) **18:16** [a]Spelled *Seraiah* in 2 Samuel 8:17 **19:6** [a]Hebrew *Aram Naharaim* [b]Spelled *Zoba* in 2 Samuel 10:6

THE MESSAGE

9-11 Tou king of Hamath heard that David had struck down the entire army of Hadadezer king of Zobah. He sent his son Hadoram to King David to greet and congratulate him for fighting and defeating Hadadezer. Tou and Hadadezer were old enemies. Hadoram brought David various things made of silver, gold, and bronze. King David consecrated these things along with the silver and gold that he had plundered from other nations: Edom, Moab, the Ammonites, the Philistines, and Amalek.

12-13 Abishai son of Zeruiah fought and defeated the Edomites in the Valley of Salt—eighteen thousand of them. He set up a puppet government in Edom and the Edomites became subjects under David.

GOD gave David victory wherever he marched.

14-17 Thus David ruled over all of Israel. He ruled well, fair and evenhanded in all his duties and relationships.

Joab son of Zeruiah was head of the army;
Jehoshaphat son of Ahilud was in charge of public records;
Zadok son of Ahitub and Abimelech son of Abiathar were priests;
Shavsha was secretary;
Benaiah son of Jehoiada was over the special forces, the Kerethites and Pelethites;
And David's sons held high positions, close to the king.

1-2 19 Some time after this Nahash king of the Ammonites died and his son succeeded him as king. David said, "I'd like to show some kindness to Hanun son of Nahash—treat him as well and as kindly as his father treated me." So David sent condolences about his father's death.

2-3 But when David's servants arrived in Ammonite country and came to Hanun to bring condolences, the Ammonite leaders warned Hanun, "Do you for a minute suppose that David is honoring your father by sending you comforters? Don't you know that he's sent these men to snoop around the city and size it up so that he can capture it?"

4 So Hanun seized David's men, shaved them clean, cut off their robes half way up their buttocks, and sent them packing.

5 When this was all reported to David, he sent someone to meet them, for they were seriously humiliated. The king told them, "Stay in Jericho until your beards grow out; only then come back."

6-7 When it dawned on the Ammonites that as far as David was concerned, they stank to high heaven, they hired, at a cost of a thousand talents of silver (thirty-seven and a half tons!), chariots and horsemen from the Arameans of Naharaim, Maacah, and Zobah—thirty-two thousand chariots and

NEW KING JAMES VERSION

themselves thirty-two thousand chariots, with the king of Maacah and his people, who came and encamped before Medeba. Also the people of Ammon gathered together from their cities, and came to battle.

8Now when David heard *of it,* he sent Joab and all the army of the mighty men. 9Then the people of Ammon came out and put themselves in battle array before the gate of the city, and the kings who had come *were* by themselves in the field.

10When Joab saw that the battle line was against him before and behind, he chose some of Israel's best, and put *them* in battle array against the Syrians. 11And the rest of the people he put under the command of Abishai his brother, and they set *themselves* in battle array against the people of Ammon. 12Then he said, "If the Syrians are too strong for me, then you shall help me; but if the people of Ammon are too strong for you, then I will help you. 13Be of good courage, and let us be strong for our people and for the cities of our God. And may the LORD do *what is* good in His sight."

14So Joab and the people who *were* with him drew near for the battle against the Syrians, and they fled before him. 15When the people of Ammon saw that the Syrians were fleeing, they also fled before Abishai his brother, and entered the city. So Joab went to Jerusalem.

16Now when the Syrians saw that they had been defeated by Israel, they sent messengers and brought the Syrians who were beyond the River,[a] and Shophach[b] the commander of Hadadezer's army *went* before them. 17When it was told David, he gathered all Israel, crossed over the Jordan and came upon them, and set up in *battle* array against them. So when David had set up in battle array against the Syrians, they fought with him. 18Then the Syrians fled before Israel; and David killed seven thousand[a] charioteers and forty thousand foot soldiers[b] of the Syrians, and killed Shophach the commander of the army. 19And when the servants of Hadadezer saw that they were defeated by Israel, they made peace with David and became his servants. So the Syrians were not willing to help the people of Ammon anymore.

RABBAH IS CONQUERED

20 It happened in the spring of the year, at the time kings go out *to battle,* that Joab led out the armed forces and ravaged the country of the people of Ammon, and came and besieged Rabbah. But David stayed at Jerusalem. And Joab defeated Rabbah and overthrew it. 2Then David took their king's crown from his head, and found it to weigh a talent of gold, and *there were* precious stones in it. And it was set on David's head. Also he brought out the spoil of the city in great abundance. 3And he brought out the people who *were* in it, and put *them* to work[a] with saws, with iron picks, and with axes.

19:16 [a]That is, the Euphrates [b]Spelled *Shobach* in 2 Samuel 10:16 **19:18** [a]Or *seven hundred* (compare 2 Samuel 10:18) [b]Or *horsemen* (compare 2 Samuel 10:18) **20:3** [a]Septuagint reads *cut them.*

THE MESSAGE

drivers; plus the king of Maacah with his
troops who came and set up camp at
Medeba; the Ammonites, too, were mobilized
from their cities and got ready for battle.
8 When David heard this, he dispatched
Joab with his strongest fighters in full force.
9-13 The Ammonites marched out and spread
out in battle formation at the city gate; the
kings who had come as allies took up a po-
sition in the open fields. When Joab saw that
he had two fronts to fight, before and be-
hind, he took his pick of the best of Israel
and deployed them to confront the
Arameans. The rest of the army he put un-
der the command of Abishai, his brother,
and deployed them to deal with the Am-
monites. Then he said, "If the Arameans are
too much for me, you help me; and if the
Ammonites prove too much for you, I'll
come and help you. Courage! We'll fight
might and main for our people and for the
cities of our God. And GOD will do whatever
he sees needs doing!"
14-15 But when Joab and his soldiers moved in
to fight the Arameans, they ran off in full re-
treat. Then the Ammonites, seeing the
Arameans run for dear life, took to their
heels and ran from Abishai into the city.
So Joab withdrew from the Ammonites
and returned to Jerusalem.
16 When the Arameans saw how badly
they'd been beaten by Israel, they picked
up the pieces and regrouped; they sent for
the Arameans who were across the river;
Shophach, commander of Hadadezer's
army, led them.
17-19 When all this was reported to David, he
mustered all Israel, crossed the Jordan, ad-
vanced, and prepared to fight. The Arameans
went into battle formation, ready for David,
and the fight was on. But the Arameans
again scattered before Israel. David killed
seven thousand chariot drivers and forty
thousand infantry. He also killed Shophach,
the army commander. When all the kings
who were vassals of Hadadezer saw that they
had been routed by Israel, they made peace
with David and served him. The Arameans
were afraid to help the Ammonites ever
again.

1-3 20 That spring, the time when kings usu-
ally go off to war, Joab led the army
out and ravaged the Ammonites. He then set
siege to Rabbah. David meanwhile was
back in Jerusalem. Joab hit Rabbah hard
and left it in ruins. David took the crown off
the head of their king. Its weight was found
to be a talent of gold and set with a precious
stone. It was placed on David's head. He
hauled great quantities of loot from the city
and put the people to hard labor with saws
and picks and axes. This is what he did to all

NEW KING JAMES VERSION

So David did to all the cities of the people of Ammon. Then David and all the people returned *to* Jerusalem.

PHILISTINE GIANTS DESTROYED

4Now it happened afterward that war broke out at Gezer with the Philistines, at which time Sibbechai the Hushathite killed Sippai,[a] *who was one* of the sons of the giant. And they were subdued.

5Again there was war with the Philistines, and Elhanan the son of Jair[a] killed Lahmi the brother of Goliath the Gittite, the shaft of whose spear *was* like a weaver's beam.

6Yet again there was war at Gath, where there was a man of *great* stature, with twenty-four fingers and toes, six *on each hand* and six *on each foot;* and he also was born to the giant. 7So when he defied Israel, Jonathan the son of Shimea,[a] David's brother, killed him.

8These were born to the giant in Gath, and they fell by the hand of David and by the hand of his servants.

THE CENSUS OF ISRAEL AND JUDAH

21 Now Satan stood up against Israel, and moved David to number Israel. 2So David said to Joab and to the leaders of the people, "Go, number Israel from Beersheba to Dan, and bring the number of them to me that I may know *it.*"

3And Joab answered, "May the LORD make His people a hundred times more than they are. But, my lord the king, *are* they not all my lord's servants? Why then does my lord require this thing? Why should he be a cause of guilt in Israel?"

4Nevertheless the king's word prevailed against Joab. Therefore Joab departed and went throughout all Israel and came to Jerusalem. 5Then Joab gave the sum of the number of the people to David. All Israel *had* one million one hundred thousand men who drew the sword, and Judah *had* four hundred and seventy thousand men who drew the sword. 6But he did not count Levi and Benjamin among them, for the king's word was abominable to Joab.

7And God was displeased with this thing; therefore He struck Israel. 8So David said to God, "I have sinned greatly, because I have done this thing; but now, I pray, take away the iniquity of Your servant, for I have done very foolishly."

9Then the LORD spoke to Gad, David's seer, saying, 10"Go and tell David, saying, 'Thus says the LORD: "I offer you three *things;* choose one of them for yourself, that I may do *it* to you." ' "

11So Gad came to David and said to him, "Thus says the LORD: 'Choose for yourself, 12either three[a] years of famine, or three months to be defeated by your foes with the sword of your enemies overtaking *you,* or else for three days the sword of the LORD—the plague in the land, with the angel[b] of the LORD destroying through-

20:4 [a]Spelled *Saph* in 2 Samuel 21:18 **20:5** [a]Spelled *Jaare-Oregim* in 2 Samuel 21:19 **20:7** [a]Spelled *Shimeah* in 2 Samuel 21:21 and *Shammah* in 1 Samuel 16:9 **21:12** [a]Or *seven* (compare 2 Samuel 24:13) [b]Or *Angel,* and so elsewhere in this chapter

THE MESSAGE

the Ammonites. Then David and his army
returned to Jerusalem.
4-8 Later war broke out with the Philistines
at Gezer. That was the time Sibbecai the
Hushathite killed Sippai of the clan of gi-
ants. The Philistines had to eat crow. In an-
other war with the Philistines, Elhanan son
of Jair killed Lahmi, the brother of Goliath
the Gittite whose spear was like a ship's
boom. And then there was the war at Gath
that featured a hulking giant who had
twenty-four fingers and toes, six on each
hand and foot—yet another from the clan of
giants. When he mocked Israel, Jonathan
son of Shimea, David's brother, killed him.
These came from the clan of giants and
were killed by David and his men.

DAVID, SATAN, AND ARAUNAH

1-2 **21** Now Satan entered the scene and se-
duced David into taking a census of Is-
rael. David gave orders to Joab and the
army officers under him, "Canvass all the
tribes of Israel, from Dan to Beersheba, and
get a count of the population. I want to
know the number."
3 Joab resisted: "May GOD multiply his
people by hundreds! Don't they all belong to
my master the king? But why on earth
would you do a thing like this—why risk
getting Israel into trouble with God?"
4-7 But David wouldn't take no for an an-
swer, so Joab went off and did it—canvassed
the country and then came back to
Jerusalem and reported the results of the
census: There were 1,100,000 fighting men;
of that total, Judah accounted for 470,000.
Joab, disgusted by the command—it, in fact,
turned his stomach!—protested by leaving
Levi and Benjamin out of the census-taking.
And God, offended by the whole thing, pun-
ished Israel.
8 Then David prayed, "I have sinned badly
in what I have just done, substituting statis-
tics for trust; forgive my sin—I've been re-
ally stupid."
9-10 GOD answered by speaking to Gad,
David's pastor: "Go and give David this
message: 'GOD's word: You have your choice
of three punishments; choose one and I'll do
the rest.' "
11-12 Gad delivered the message to David: "Do
you want three years of famine, three
months of running from your enemies while
they chase you down, or three days of the
sword of GOD—an epidemic unleashed on
the country by an angel of GOD? Think it

New King James Version

out all the territory of Israel.' Now consider what answer I should take back to Him who sent me."

13And David said to Gad, "I am in great distress. Please let me fall into the hand of the LORD, for His mercies *are* very great; but do not let me fall into the hand of man."

14So the LORD sent a plague upon Israel, and seventy thousand men of Israel fell. 15And God sent an angel to Jerusalem to destroy it. As he[a] was destroying, the LORD looked and relented of the disaster, and said to the angel who was destroying, "It is enough; now restrain your[b] hand." And the angel of the LORD stood by the threshing floor of Ornan[c] the Jebusite.

16Then David lifted his eyes and saw the angel of the LORD standing between earth and heaven, having in his hand a drawn sword stretched out over Jerusalem. So David and the elders, clothed in sackcloth, fell on their faces. 17And David said to God, "Was it not I who commanded the people to be numbered? I am the one who has sinned and done evil indeed; but these sheep, what have they done? Let Your hand, I pray, O LORD my God, be against me and my father's house, but not against Your people that they should be plagued."

18Therefore, the angel of the LORD commanded Gad to say to David that David should go and erect an altar to the LORD on the threshing floor of Ornan the Jebusite. 19So David went up at the word of Gad, which he had spoken in the name of the LORD. 20Now Ornan turned and saw the angel; and his four sons *who were* with him hid themselves, but Ornan continued threshing wheat. 21So David came to Ornan, and Ornan looked and saw David. And he went out from the threshing floor, and bowed before David with *his* face to the ground. 22Then David said to Ornan, "Grant me the place of *this* threshing floor, that I may build an altar on it to the LORD. You shall grant it to me at the full price, that the plague may be withdrawn from the people."

23But Ornan said to David, "Take *it* to yourself, and let my lord the king do *what is* good in his eyes. Look, I *also* give *you* the oxen for burnt offerings, the threshing implements for wood, and the wheat for the grain offering; I give *it* all."

24Then King David said to Ornan, "No, but I will surely buy *it* for the full price, for I will not take what is yours for the LORD, nor offer burnt offerings with *that which* costs *me* nothing." 25So David gave Ornan six hundred shekels of gold by weight for the place. 26And David built there an altar to the LORD, and offered burnt offerings and peace offerings, and called on the LORD; and He answered him from heaven by fire on the altar of burnt offering.

27So the LORD commanded the angel, and he returned his sword to its sheath.

28At that time, when David saw that the LORD had answered him on the threshing floor of Ornan the Jebusite, he sacrificed there. 29For the tabernacle of the LORD and the altar of the burnt offering, which Moses had made in the wilderness, *were* at that time at the high place in

21:15 [a]Or *He* [b]Or *Your* [c]Spelled *Araunah* in 2 Samuel 24:16

The Message

over and make up your mind. What shall I tell the One who sent me?"

13 David told Gad, "They're all terrible! But I'd rather be punished by GOD whose mercy is great, than fall into human hands."

14-15 So GOD unleashed an epidemic in Israel—seventy thousand Israelites died. God then sent the angel to Jerusalem but when he saw the destruction about to begin, he compassionately changed his mind and ordered the death angel, "Enough's enough! Pull back!"

15-16 The angel of GOD had just reached the threshing floor of Araunah the Jebusite. David looked up and saw the angel hovering between earth and sky, sword drawn and about to strike Jerusalem. David and the elders bowed in prayer and covered themselves with rough burlap.

17 David prayed, "Please! I'm the one who sinned; I'm the one at fault. But these sheep, what did they do wrong? Punish me, not them, me and my family; don't take it out on them."

18-19 The angel of GOD ordered Gad to tell David to go and build an altar to GOD on the threshing floor of Araunah the Jebusite. David did what Gad told him in obedience to GOD's command.

20-21 Meanwhile Araunah had quit threshing the wheat and was watching the angel; his four sons took cover and hid. David came up to Araunah. When Araunah saw David, he left the threshing floor and bowed deeply before David, honoring the king.

22 David said to Araunah, "Give me the site of the threshing floor so I can build an altar to GOD. Charge me the market price; we're going to put an end to this disaster."

23 "O Master, my king," said Araunah, "just take it; do whatever you want with it! Look, here's an ox for the burnt offering and threshing paddles for the fuel and wheat for the meal offering—it's all yours!"

24-27 David replied to Araunah, "No. I'm *buying* it from you, and at the full market price. I'm not going to offer GOD sacrifices that are no sacrifice." So David bought the place from Araunah for six hundred shekels of gold. He built an altar to GOD there and sacrificed Whole-Burnt-Offerings and Peace-Offerings. He called out to GOD and GOD answered by striking the altar of Whole-Burnt-Offering with lightning. Then GOD told the angel to put his sword back into its scabbard.

28 And that's the story of what happened when David saw that GOD answered him on the threshing floor of Araunah the Jebusite at the time he offered the sacrifice.

29-1 At this time the Tabernacle that Moses had constructed in the desert, and with it the Altar of Burnt Offering, were set up at the worship center at Gibeon. But David, terrified by the angel's sword, wouldn't go there to pray to God anymore. So David declared,

NEW KING JAMES VERSION

Gibeon. 30But David could not go before it to inquire of God, for he was afraid of the sword of the angel of the LORD.

DAVID PREPARES TO BUILD THE TEMPLE

22 Then David said, "This *is* the house of the LORD God, and this *is* the altar of burnt offering for Israel." 2So David commanded to gather the aliens who *were* in the land of Israel; and he appointed masons to cut hewn stones to build the house of God. 3And David prepared iron in abundance for the nails of the doors of the gates and for the joints, and bronze in abundance beyond measure, 4and cedar trees in abundance; for the Sidonians and those from Tyre brought much cedar wood to David.

5Now David said, "Solomon my son *is* young and inexperienced, and the house to be built for the LORD *must be* exceedingly magnificent, famous and glorious throughout all countries. I will now make preparation for it." So David made abundant preparations before his death.

6Then he called for his son Solomon, and charged him to build a house for the LORD God of Israel. 7And David said to Solomon: "My son, as for me, it was in my mind to build a house to the name of the LORD my God; 8but the word of the LORD came to me, saying, 'You have shed much blood and have made great wars; you shall not build a house for My name, because you have shed much blood on the earth in My sight. 9Behold, a son shall be born to you, who shall be a man of rest; and I will give him rest from all his enemies all around. His name shall be Solomon,[a] for I will give peace and quietness to Israel in his days. 10He shall build a house for My name, and he shall be My son, and I *will be* his Father; and I will establish the throne of his kingdom over Israel forever.' 11Now, my son, may the LORD be with you; and may you prosper, and build the house of the LORD your God, as He has said to you. 12Only may the LORD give you wisdom and understanding, and give you charge concerning Israel, that you may keep the law of the LORD your God. 13Then you will prosper, if you take care to fulfill the statutes and judgments with which the LORD charged Moses concerning Israel. Be strong and of good courage; do not fear nor be dismayed. 14Indeed I have taken much trouble to prepare for the house of the LORD one hundred thousand talents of gold and one million talents of silver, and bronze and iron beyond measure, for it is so abundant. I have prepared timber and stone also, and you may add to them. 15Moreover *there are* workmen with you in abundance: woodsmen and stonecutters, and all types of skillful men for every kind of work. 16Of gold and silver and bronze and iron *there is* no limit. Arise and begin working, and the LORD be with you."

17David also commanded all the leaders of Israel to help Solomon his son, *saying*, 18"*Is* not the LORD your God with you? And has He *not* given you rest on every side? For He has given the inhabitants of the land into my hand, and the land is subdued before the LORD and before

22:9 [a]Literally *Peaceful*

THE MESSAGE

"From now on, *this* is the site for the worship of GOD; *this* is the place for Israel's Altar of Burnt Offering."

DAVID CHARGES SOLOMON TO BUILD THE TEMPLE

2-4 22 David ordered all the resident aliens in the land to come together; he sent them to the stone quarries to cut dressed stone to build The Temple of God. He also stockpiled a huge quantity of iron for nails and bracings for the doors of the gates, more bronze than could be weighed, and cedar logs past counting (the Sidonians and Tyrians shipped in huge loads of cedar logs for David).

5-6 David was thinking, "My son Solomon is too young to plan ahead for this. But the sanctuary that is to be built for GOD has to be the greatest, the talk of all the nations; so I'll get the construction materials together." That's why David prepared this huge stockpile of building materials before he died. Then he called in Solomon his son and commanded him to build a sanctuary for the GOD of Israel.

7-10 David said to Solomon, "I wanted in the worst way to build a sanctuary to honor my GOD. But GOD prevented me, saying, 'You've killed too many people, fought too many wars. You are not the one to honor me by building a sanctuary—you've been responsible for too much killing, too much bloodshed. But you are going to have a son and he will be a quiet and peaceful man, and I will calm his enemies down on all sides. His very name will speak peace—that is, Solomon, which means Peace—and I'll give peace and rest under his rule. He will be the one to build a sanctuary in my honor. He'll be my royal adopted son and I'll be his father; and I'll make sure that the authority of his kingdom over Israel lasts forever.'

11-16 "So now, son, GOD be with you. GOD-speed as you build the sanctuary for your GOD, the job God has given you. And may GOD also give you discernment and understanding when he puts you in charge of Israel so that you will rule in reverent obedience under GOD's Revelation. That's what will make you successful, following the directions and doing the things that GOD commanded Moses for Israel. Courage! Take charge! Don't be timid; don't hold back. Look at this—I've gone to a lot of trouble to stockpile materials for the sanctuary of GOD: a hundred thousand talents (3,775 tons) of gold, a million talents (37,750 tons) of silver, tons of bronze and iron—too much to weigh—and all this timber and stone. And you're free to add more. And workers both plentiful and prepared: stonecutters, masons, carpenters, artisans in gold and silver, bronze and iron. You're all set—get to work! And GOD-speed!"

17-19 David gave orders to all of Israel's leaders to help his son Solomon, saying, "Isn't it obvious that your GOD is present with you; that he has given you peaceful relations with everyone around? My part in this was to put down the enemies, subdue the land to

NEW KING JAMES VERSION

His people. [19]Now set your heart and your soul to seek the LORD your God. Therefore arise and build the sanctuary of the LORD God, to bring the ark of the covenant of the LORD and the holy articles of God into the house that is to be built for the name of the LORD."

THE DIVISIONS OF THE LEVITES

23 So when David was old and full of days, he made his son Solomon king over Israel.

[2]And he gathered together all the leaders of Israel, with the priests and the Levites. [3]Now the Levites were numbered from the age of thirty years and above; and the number of individual males was thirty-eight thousand. [4]Of these, twenty-four thousand *were* to look after the work of the house of the LORD, six thousand *were* officers and judges, [5]four thousand *were* gatekeepers, and four thousand praised the LORD with *musical* instruments, "which I made," *said David,* "for giving praise."

[6]Also David separated them into divisions among the sons of Levi: Gershon, Kohath, and Merari.

[7]Of the Gershonites: Laadan[a] and Shimei. [8]The sons of Laadan: the first Jehiel, then Zetham and Joel—three *in all.* [9]The sons of Shimei: Shelomith, Haziel, and Haran—three *in all.* These were the heads of the fathers' *houses* of Laadan. [10]And the sons of Shimei: Jahath, Zina,[a] Jeush, and Beriah. These *were* the four sons of Shimei. [11]Jahath was the first and Zizah the second. But Jeush and Beriah did not have many sons; therefore they were assigned as one father's house.

[12]The sons of Kohath: Amram, Izhar, Hebron, and Uzziel—four *in all.* [13]The sons of Amram: Aaron and Moses; and Aaron was set apart, he and his sons forever, that he should sanctify the most holy things, to burn incense before the LORD, to minister to Him, and to give the blessing in His name forever. [14]Now the sons of Moses the man of God were reckoned to the tribe of Levi. [15]The sons of Moses *were* Gershon[a] and Eliezer. [16]Of the sons of Gershon, Shebuel[a] *was* the first. [17]Of the descendants of Eliezer, Rehabiah was the first. And Eliezer had no other sons, but the sons of Rehabiah were very many. [18]Of the sons of Izhar, Shelomith *was* the first. [19]Of the sons of Hebron, Jeriah *was* the first, Amariah the second, Jahaziel the third, and Jekameam the fourth. [20]Of the sons of Uzziel, Michah *was* the first and Jesshiah the second.

[21]The sons of Merari *were* Mahli and Mushi. The sons of Mahli *were* Eleazar and Kish. [22]And Eleazar died, and had no sons, but only daughters; and their brethren, the sons of Kish, took them *as wives.* [23]The sons of Mushi *were* Mahli, Eder, and Jeremoth—three *in all.*

[24]These *were* the sons of Levi by their fathers' houses—the heads of the fathers' *houses* as they were counted individually by the number of their names, who did the work for the service of the house of the LORD, from the age of twenty years and above.

23:7 [a]Spelled *Libni* in Exodus 6:17 **23:10** [a]Septuagint and Vulgate read *Zizah* (compare verse 11). **23:15** [a]Hebrew *Gershom* (compare 6:16) **23:16** [a]Spelled *Shubael* in 24:20

THE MESSAGE

GOD and his people; your part is to give
yourselves, heart and soul, to praying to
your GOD. So get moving—build the sacred
house of worship to GOD! Then bring the
Chest of the Covenant of GOD and all the
holy furnishings for the worship of God into
the sanctuary built in honor of GOD."

PREPARATIONS FOR WORSHIP

1 **23** When David got to be an old man, he
made his son Solomon king over Israel.
2-5 At the same time he brought together
all the leaders of Israel, the priests, and the
Levites. The Levites thirty years and older
were counted; the total was thirty-eight
thousand. David sorted them into work
groups: "Twenty-four thousand are in
charge of administering worship in the
sanctuary; six thousand are officials and
judges; four thousand are security guards;
and four thousand are to serve in the orchestra,
praising GOD with instruments that
I have provided for praise."
6 David then divided the Levites into
groupings named after the sons of Levi:
Gershon, Kohath, and Merari.
7-11 The Gershonites: Ladan and Shimei. The
three sons of Ladan: Jehiel, Zetham, and
Joel. The three sons of Shimei: Shelomoth,
Haziel, and Haran, all heads of the families
of Ladan. The four sons of Shimei: Jahath,
Ziza, Jeush, and Beriah. Jahath came first,
followed by Ziza. Jeush and Beriah did not
have many sons so they were counted as
one family with one task.
12-14 The four sons of Kohath: Amram, Izhar,
Hebron, and Uzziel. The sons of Amram:
Aaron and Moses. Aaron was especially ordained
to work in the Holy of Holies, to burn
incense before GOD, to serve God and bless
his Name always. This was a permanent appointment
for Aaron and his sons. Moses
and his sons were counted in the tribe of
Levi.
15-17 The sons of Moses: Gershom and Eliezer.
Shubael was the first son of Gershom. Rehabiah
was the first and only son of Eliezer;
but though Eliezer had no other sons, Rehabiah
had many sons.
18-23 Shelomith was the first son of Izhar. Hebron
had four sons: Jeriah, Amariah, Jahaziel,
and Jekameam. Uzziel had two sons:
Micah and Isshiah. The sons of Merari:
Mahli and Mushi. The sons of Mahli:
Eleazar and Kish. Eleazar died without any
sons, only daughters. Their cousins, the
sons of Kish, married the daughters. Mushi
had three sons: Mahli, Eder, and Jerimoth.
24 These are the sons of Levi twenty years
and older, divided up according to families
and heads of families and listed in the work
groups that took care of the worship in the
sanctuary of GOD.

NEW KING JAMES VERSION

25For David said, "The LORD God of Israel
has given rest to His people, that they may
dwell in Jerusalem forever"; 26and also to the
Levites, "They shall no longer carry the taber-
nacle, or any of the articles for its service." 27For
by the last words of David the Levites *were*
numbered from twenty years old and above;
28because their duty *was* to help the sons of
Aaron in the service of the house of the LORD,
in the courts and in the chambers, in the purify-
ing of all holy things and the work of the serv-
ice of the house of God, 29both with the show-
bread and the fine flour for the grain offering,
with the unleavened cakes and *what is baked in*
the pan, with what is mixed and with all kinds
of measures and sizes; 30to stand every morning
to thank and praise the LORD, and likewise at
evening; 31and at every presentation of a burnt
offering to the LORD on the Sabbaths and on the
New Moons and on the set feasts, by number
according to the ordinance governing them,
regularly before the LORD; 32and that they
should attend to the needs of the tabernacle of
meeting, the needs of the holy *place*, and the
needs of the sons of Aaron their brethren in the
work of the house of the LORD.

THE DIVISIONS OF THE PRIESTS

24 Now *these are* the divisions of the sons of
Aaron. The sons of Aaron *were* Nadab,
Abihu, Eleazar, and Ithamar. 2And Nadab and
Abihu died before their father, and had no chil-
dren; therefore Eleazar and Ithamar ministered
as priests. 3Then David with Zadok of the sons
of Eleazar, and Ahimelech of the sons of
Ithamar, divided them according to the schedule
of their service.
4There were more leaders found of the sons
of Eleazar than of the sons of Ithamar, and *thus*
they were divided. Among the sons of Eleazar
were sixteen heads of *their* fathers' houses, and
eight heads of their fathers' houses among the
sons of Ithamar. 5Thus they were divided by lot,
one group as another, for there were officials of
the sanctuary and officials *of the house* of God,
from the sons of Eleazar and from the sons of
Ithamar. 6And the scribe, Shemaiah the son of
Nethanel, *one of* the Levites, wrote them down
before the king, the leaders, Zadok the priest,
Ahimelech the son of Abiathar, and the heads of
the fathers' *houses* of the priests and Levites,
one father's house taken for Eleazar and *one* for
Ithamar.
7Now the first lot fell to Jehoiarib, the second
to Jedaiah, 8the third to Harim, the fourth to Se-
orim, 9the fifth to Malchijah, the sixth to
Mijamin, 10the seventh to Hakkoz, the eighth to
Abijah, 11the ninth to Jeshua, the tenth to Sheca-
niah, 12the eleventh to Eliashib, the twelfth to

THE MESSAGE

25-27 David said, "Now that the GOD of Israel has given rest to his people and made Jerusalem his permanent home, the Levites no longer have to carry the Tabernacle and all the furniture required for the work of worship." These last words of David referred only to Levites twenty years old and above.

28-31 From now on the assigned work of the Levites was to assist Aaron's sons in the work of worship in GOD's house: maintain courtyards and closets, keep the furniture and utensils of worship clean, take care of any extra work needed in the work of worship, and provide bread for the table and flour for the Meal Offerings and the unraised wafers—all baking and mixing, all measuring and weighing. Also they were to be present for morning prayers, thanking and praising GOD, for evening prayers, and at the service of Whole-Burnt-Offerings to GOD on Sabbath, at New Moons, and at all festivals. They were on regular duty to serve GOD according to their assignment and the required number.

32 In short, the Levites, with the sons of Aaron as their companions in the ministry of holy worship, were responsible for everything that had to do with worship: the place and times and ordering of worship.

1-5 24 The family of Aaron was grouped as follows: Aaron's sons were Nadab, Abihu, Eleazar, and Ithamar. Nadab and Abihu died before their father and left no sons. So Eleazar and Ithamar filled the office of priest. David assigned Zadok from the family of Eleazar and Ahimelech from the family of Ithamar and assigned them to separate divisions for carrying out their appointed ministries. It turned out that there were more leaders in Eleazar's family than in Ithamar's and so they divided them proportionately: sixteen clan leaders from Eleazar's family and eight clan leaders from Ithamar's family. They assigned the leaders by lot, treating both families alike, for there were officials of the sanctuary and officials of God among both the Eleazar and Ithamar families.

6 The secretary Shemaiah son of Nethanel, a Levite, wrote down their names in the presence of the king, the officials, Zadok the priest, Ahimelech son of Abiathar, and the leaders of the priestly and Levitical families. They took turns: One family was selected from Eleazar and then one from Ithamar.

7-18 The first lot fell to Jehoiarib,
the second to Jedaiah,
the third to Harim,
the fourth to Seorim,
the fifth to Malkijah,
the sixth to Mijamin,
the seventh to Hakkoz,
the eighth to Abijah,
the ninth to Jeshua,
the tenth to Shecaniah,
the eleventh to Eliashib,

NEW KING JAMES VERSION

Jakim, 13 the thirteenth to Huppah, the four-
teenth to Jeshebeab, 14 the fifteenth to Bilgah,
the sixteenth to Immer, 15 the seventeenth to
Hezir, the eighteenth to Happizzez,[a] 16 the nine-
teenth to Pethahiah, the twentieth to Jehezekel,[a]
17 the twenty-first to Jachin, the twenty-second
to Gamul, 18 the twenty-third to Delaiah, the
twenty-fourth to Maaziah.
19 This *was* the schedule of their service for
coming into the house of the LORD according to
their ordinance by the hand of Aaron their fa-
ther, as the LORD God of Israel had commanded
him.

OTHER LEVITES

20 And the rest of the sons of Levi: of the sons
of Amram, Shubael;[a] of the sons of Shubael,
Jehdeiah. 21 Concerning Rehabiah, of the sons of
Rehabiah, the first *was* Isshiah. 22 Of the
Izharites, Shelomoth;[a] of the sons of Shelomoth,
Jahath. 23 Of the sons *of Hebron,*[a] Jeriah *was the
first,*[b] Amariah the second, Jahaziel the third,
and Jekameam the fourth. 24 *Of* the sons of
Uzziel, Michah; of the sons of Michah, Shamir.
25 The brother of Michah, Isshiah; of the sons of
Isshiah, Zechariah. 26 The sons of Merari *were*
Mahli and Mushi; the son of Jaaziah, Beno.
27 The sons of Merari by Jaaziah *were* Beno,
Shoham, Zaccur, and Ibri. 28 Of Mahli: Eleazar,
who had no sons. 29 Of Kish: the son of Kish, Je-
rahmeel.
30 Also the sons of Mushi *were* Mahli, Eder,
and Jerimoth. These *were* the sons of the
Levites according to their fathers' houses.
31 These also cast lots just as their brothers
the sons of Aaron did, in the presence of King
David, Zadok, Ahimelech, and the heads of the
fathers' *houses* of the priests and Levites. The
chief fathers *did* just as their younger brethren.

THE MUSICIANS

25 Moreover David and the captains of the
army separated for the service *some* of the
sons of Asaph, of Heman, and of Jeduthun, who
should prophesy with harps, stringed instru-
ments, and cymbals. And the number of the
skilled men performing their service was: 2 Of
the sons of Asaph: Zaccur, Joseph, Nethaniah,
and Asharelah;[a] the sons of Asaph *were* under
the direction of Asaph, who prophesied accord-
ing to the order of the king. 3 Of Jeduthun, the

24:15 [a]Septuagint and Vulgate read *Aphses.* **24:16** [a]Masoretic Text reads *Jehezkel.* **24:20** [a]Spelled *Shebuel* in 23:16 **24:22** [a]Spelled *Shelomith* in 23:18 **24:23** [a]Supplied from 23:19 (following some Hebrew manuscripts and Septuagint manuscripts) [b]Supplied from 23:19 (following some Hebrew manuscripts and Septuagint manuscripts) **25:2** [a]Spelled *Jesharelah* in verse 14

THE MESSAGE

the twelfth to Jakim,
the thirteenth to Huppah,
the fourteenth to Jeshebeab,
the fifteenth to Bilgah,
the sixteenth to Immer,
the seventeenth to Hezir,
the eighteenth to Happizzez,
the nineteenth to Pethahiah,
the twentieth to Jehezkel,
the twenty-first to Jakin,
the twenty-second to Gamul,
the twenty-third to Delaiah,
and the twenty-fourth to Maaziah.

19 They served in this appointed order when
they entered The Temple of GOD, following
the procedures laid down by their ancestor
Aaron as GOD, the God of Israel, had com-
manded him.
20 The rest of the Levites are as follows:
From the sons of Amram: Shubael; from
the sons of Shubael: Jehdeiah.
21 Concerning Rehabiah: from his sons, Is-
shiah was the first.
22 From the Izharites: Shelomoth; from the
sons of Shelomoth: Jahath.
23 The sons of Hebron: Jeriah the first,
Amariah the second, Jahaziel the third, and
Jekameam the fourth.
24-25 The son of Uzziel: Micah, and from the
sons of Micah: Shamir. The brother of
Micah was Isshiah, and from the sons of Is-
shiah: Zechariah.
26-27 The sons of Merari: Mahli and Mushi.
The son of Jaaziah: Beno. The sons of Mer-
ari from Jaaziah: Beno, Shoham, Zaccur,
and Ibri.
28 From Mahli: Eleazar, who had no sons.
29 From Kish: Jerahmeel, the son of Kish.
30-31 And from the sons of Mushi: Mahli, Eder,
and Jerimoth.

These were the Levites by their families.
They also cast lots, the same as their kin-
dred the sons of Aaron had done, in the
presence of David the king, Zadok, Ahim-
elech, and the leaders of the priestly and
Levitical families. The families of the oldest
and youngest brothers were treated the
same.

THE MUSICIANS FOR WORSHIP

1-7 **25** Next David and the worship leaders se-
lected some from the family of Asaph,
Heman, and Jeduthun for special service in
preaching and music. Here is the roster of
names and assignments: From the family of
Asaph: Zaccur, Joseph, Nethaniah, and
Asarelah; they were supervised by Asaph,
who spoke for GOD backed up by the king's
authority. From the family of Jeduthun there

New King James Version

sons of Jeduthun: Gedaliah, Zeri,[a] Jeshaiah, Shimei, Hashabiah, and Mattithiah, six,[b] under the direction of their father Jeduthun, who prophesied with a harp to give thanks and to praise the LORD. 4Of Heman, the sons of Heman: Bukkiah, Mattaniah, Uzziel,[a] Shebuel,[b] Jerimoth,[c] Hananiah, Hanani, Eliathah, Giddalti, Romamti-Ezer, Joshbekashah, Mallothi, Hothir, *and* Mahazioth. 5All these *were* the sons of Heman the king's seer in the words of God, to exalt his horn.[a] For God gave Heman fourteen sons and three daughters.

6All these *were* under the direction of their father for the music *in* the house of the LORD, with cymbals, stringed instruments, and harps, for the service of the house of God. Asaph, Jeduthun, and Heman *were* under the authority of the king. 7So the number of them, with their brethren who were instructed in the songs of the LORD, all who were skillful, *was* two hundred and eighty-eight.

8And they cast lots for their duty, the small as well as the great, the teacher with the student.

9Now the first lot for Asaph came out for Joseph; the second for Gedaliah, him with his brethren and sons, twelve; 10the third for Zaccur, his sons and his brethren, twelve; 11the fourth for Jizri,[a] his sons and his brethren, twelve; 12the fifth for Nethaniah, his sons and his brethren, twelve; 13the sixth for Bukkiah, his sons and his brethren, twelve; 14the seventh for Jesharelah,[a] his sons and his brethren, twelve; 15the eighth for Jeshaiah, his sons and his brethren, twelve; 16the ninth for Mattaniah, his sons and his brethren, twelve; 17the tenth for Shimei, his sons and his brethren, twelve; 18the eleventh for Azarel,[a] his sons and his brethren, twelve; 19the twelfth for Hashabiah, his sons and his brethren, twelve; 20the thirteenth for Shubael,[a] his sons and his brethren, twelve; 21the fourteenth for Mattithiah, his sons and his brethren, twelve; 22the fifteenth for Jeremoth,[a] his sons and his brethren, twelve; 23the sixteenth for Hananiah, his sons and his brethren, twelve; 24the seventeenth for Joshbekashah, his sons and his brethren, twelve; 25the eighteenth for Hanani, his sons and his brethren, twelve; 26the nineteenth for Mallothi, his sons and his brethren, twelve; 27the twentieth for Eliathah, his sons and his brethren, twelve; 28the twenty-first for Hothir, his sons and his brethren, twelve; 29the twenty-second for Giddalti, his sons and his brethren, twelve; 30the twenty-third for Mahazioth, his sons and his brethren, twelve; 31the twenty-fourth for Romamti-Ezer, his sons and his brethren, twelve.

The Gatekeepers

26 Concerning the divisions of the gatekeepers: of the Korahites, Meshelemiah the son of Kore, of the sons of Asaph. 2And the sons of

25:3 [a]Spelled *Jizri* in verse 11 [b]*Shimei,* appearing in one Hebrew and several Septuagint manuscripts, completes the total of six sons (compare verse 17). 25:4 [a]Spelled *Azarel* in verse 18 [b]Spelled *Shubael* in verse 20 [c]Spelled *Jeremoth* in verse 22 25:5 [a]That is, to increase his power or influence 25:11 [a]Spelled *Zeri* in verse 3 25:14 [a]Spelled *Asharelah* in verse 2 25:18 [a]Spelled *Uzziel* in verse 4 25:20 [a]Spelled *Shebuel* in verse 4 25:22 [a]Spelled *Jerimoth* in verse 4

The Message

were six sons: Gedaliah, Zeri, Jeshaiah, Shimei, Hashabiah, and Mattithiah; they were supervised by their father Jeduthun, who preached and accompanied himself with the zither—he was responsible for leading the thanks and praise to GOD. From the family of Heman: Bukkiah, Mattaniah, Uzziel, Shubael, Jerimoth, Hananiah, Hanani, Eliathah, Giddalti, Romamti-Ezer, Joshbekashah, Mallothi, Hothir, and Mahazioth. These were the sons of Heman the king's seer; they supported and assisted him in his divinely appointed work. God gave Heman fourteen sons and three daughters. Under their father's supervision they were in charge of leading the singing and providing musical accompaniment in the work of worship in the sanctuary of God (Asaph, Jeduthun, and Heman took their orders directly from the king). They were well-trained in the sacred music, all of them masters. There were 288 of them.

8 They drew names at random to see who would do what. Nobody, whether young or old, teacher or student, was given preference or advantage over another.

9-31 The first name from Asaph's family was Joseph and his twelve sons and brothers; second, Gedaliah and his twelve sons and brothers; third, Zaccur and his twelve sons and brothers; fourth, Izri and his twelve sons and brothers; fifth, Nethaniah and his twelve sons and brothers; sixth, Bukkiah and his twelve sons and brothers; seventh, Jesarelah and his twelve sons and brothers; eighth, Jeshaiah and his twelve sons and brothers; ninth, Mattaniah and his twelve sons and brothers; tenth, Shimei and his twelve sons and brothers; eleventh, Azarel and his twelve sons and brothers; twelfth, Hashabiah and his twelve sons and brothers; thirteenth, Shubael and his twelve sons and brothers; fourteenth, Mattithiah and his twelve sons and brothers; fifteenth, Jerimoth and his twelve sons and brothers; sixteenth, Hananiah and his twelve sons and brothers; seventeenth, Joshbekashah and his twelve sons and brothers; eighteenth, Hanani and his twelve sons and brothers; nineteenth, Mallothi and his twelve sons and brothers; twentieth, Eliathah and his twelve sons and brothers; twenty-first, Hothir and his twelve sons and brothers; twenty-second, Giddalti and his twelve sons and brothers; twenty-third, Mahazioth and his twelve sons and brothers; twenty-fourth, Romamti-Ezer and his twelve sons and brothers.

The Security Guards

1-11 26 The teams of security guards were from the family of Korah: Meshelemiah son of Kore (one of the sons of Asaph).

NEW KING JAMES VERSION

Meshelemiah *were* Zechariah the firstborn, Je-
diael the second, Zebadiah the third, Jathniel
the fourth, [3]Elam the fifth, Jehohanan the sixth,
Eliehoenai the seventh.
[4]Moreover the sons of Obed-Edom *were* She-
maiah the firstborn, Jehozabad the second, Joah
the third, Sacar the fourth, Nethanel the fifth,
[5]Ammiel the sixth, Issachar the seventh,
Peulthai the eighth; for God blessed him.
[6]Also to Shemaiah his son were sons born
who governed their fathers' houses, because
they *were* men of great ability. [7]The sons of She-
maiah *were* Othni, Rephael, Obed, and Elzabad,
whose brothers Elihu and Semachiah *were* able
men.
[8]All these *were* of the sons of Obed-Edom,
they and their sons and their brethren, able men
with strength for the work: sixty-two of Obed-
Edom.
[9]And Meshelemiah had sons and brethren,
eighteen able men.
[10]Also Hosah, of the children of Merari, had
sons: Shimri the first (for *though* he was not the
firstborn, his father made him the first),
[11]Hilkiah the second, Tebaliah the third,
Zechariah the fourth; all the sons and brethren
of Hosah *were* thirteen.
[12]Among these *were* the divisions of the
gatekeepers, among the chief men, *having* du-
ties just like their brethren, to serve in the house
of the LORD. [13]And they cast lots for each gate,
the small as well as the great, according to their
father's house. [14]The lot for the East *Gate* fell to
Shelemiah. Then they cast lots *for* his son
Zechariah, a wise counselor, and his lot came
out for the North Gate; [15]to Obed-Edom the
South Gate, and to his sons the storehouse.[a] [16]To
Shuppim and Hosah *the lot came out* for the
West Gate, with the Shallecheth Gate on the as-
cending highway—watchman opposite watch-
man. [17]On the east *were* six Levites, on the north
four each day, on the south four each day, and
for the storehouse[a] two by two. [18]As for the Par-
bar[a] on the west, *there were* four on the high-
way *and* two at the Parbar. [19]These were the di-
visions of the gatekeepers among the sons of
Korah and among the sons of Merari.

THE TREASURIES AND OTHER DUTIES

[20]Of the Levites, Ahijah *was* over the treasur-
ies of the house of God and over the treasuries
of the dedicated things. [21]The sons of Laadan,
the descendants of the Gershonites of Laadan,
heads of their fathers' *houses,* of Laadan the
Gershonite: Jehieli. [22]The sons of Jehieli,
Zetham and Joel his brother, *were* over the
treasuries of the house of the LORD. [23]Of the Am-
ramites, the Izharites, the Hebronites, and the
Uzzielites: [24]Shebuel the son of Gershom, the
son of Moses, *was* overseer of the treasuries.
[25]And his brethren by Eliezer *were* Rehabiah his
son, Jeshaiah his son, Joram his son, Zichri his
son, and Shelomith his son.
[26]This Shelomith and his brethren *were* over
all the treasuries of the dedicated things which
King David and the heads of fathers' *houses,* the

26:15 [a]Hebrew *asuppim* **26:17** [a]Hebrew *asuppim* **26:18** [a]Probably a court or colonnade extending west of the temple

THE MESSAGE

Meshelemiah's sons were Zechariah, the firstborn, followed by Jediael, Zebadiah, Jathniel, Elam, Jehohanan, and Eliehoenai—seven sons. Obed-Edom's sons were Shemaiah, the firstborn, followed by Jehozabad, Joah, Sacar, Nethanel, Ammiel, Issachar, and Peullethai—God blessed him with eight sons. His son Shemaiah had sons who provided outstanding leadership in the family: Othni, Rephael, Obed, and Elzabad; his relatives Elihu and Semakiah were also exceptional. These all came from the line of Obed-Edom—all of them outstanding and strong. There were sixty-two of them. Meshelemiah had eighteen sons and relatives who were outstanding. The sons of Hosah the Merarite were Shimri (he was not the firstborn but his father made him first), then Hilkiah, followed by Tabaliah and Zechariah. Hosah accounted for thirteen.

12-16 These teams of security guards, supervised by their leaders, kept order in The Temple of GOD, keeping up the traditions of their ancestors. They were all assigned to their posts by the same method regardless of the prominence of their families—each picked his gate assignment from a hat. Shelemiah was assigned to the East Gate; his son Zechariah, a shrewd counselor, got the North Gate. Obed-Edom got the South Gate; and his sons pulled duty at the storehouse. Shuppim and Hosah were posted to the West Gate and the Shalleketh Gate on the high road.

16-18 The guards stood shoulder to shoulder: six Levites per day on the east, four per day on the north and on the south, and two at a time at the storehouse. At the open court to the west, four guards were posted on the road and two at the court.

19 These are the teams of security guards from the sons of Korah and Merari.

FINANCIAL AFFAIRS: ACCOUNTANTS AND BOOKKEEPERS

20-22 Other Levites were put in charge of the financial affairs of The Temple of God. From the family of Ladan (all Gershonites) came Jehieli, and the sons of Jehieli, Zetham and his brother Joel. They supervised the finances of the sanctuary of GOD.

23-28 From the Amramites, the Izharites, the Hebronites, and the Uzzielites: Shubael, descended from Gershom the son of Moses, was the chief financial officer. His relatives through Eliezer: his son Rehabiah, his son Jeshaiah, his son Joram, his son Zicri, and his son Shelomith. Shelomith and his relatives were in charge of valuables consecrated by David the king, family heads, and

NEW KING JAMES VERSION

captains over thousands and hundreds, and the captains of the army, had dedicated. [27]Some of the spoils won in battles they dedicated to maintain the house of the LORD. [28]And all that Samuel the seer, Saul the son of Kish, Abner the son of Ner, and Joab the son of Zeruiah had dedicated, every dedicated *thing,* was under the hand of Shelomith and his brethren.

[29]Of the Izharites, Chenaniah and his sons *performed* duties as officials and judges over Israel outside Jerusalem.

[30]Of the Hebronites, Hashabiah and his brethren, one thousand seven hundred able men, had the oversight of Israel on the west side of the Jordan for all the business of the LORD, and in the service of the king. [31]Among the Hebronites, Jerijah *was* head of the Hebronites according to his genealogy of the fathers. In the fortieth year of the reign of David they were sought, and there were found among them capable men at Jazer of Gilead. [32]And his brethren *were* two thousand seven hundred able men, heads of fathers' *houses,* whom King David made officials over the Reubenites, the Gadites, and the half-tribe of Manasseh, for every matter pertaining to God and the affairs of the king.

THE MILITARY DIVISIONS

27 And the children of Israel, according to their number, the heads of fathers' *houses,* the captains of thousands and hundreds and their officers, served the king in every matter of the *military* divisions. *These divisions* came in and went out month by month throughout all the months of the year, each division *having* twenty-four thousand.

[2]Over the first division for the first month *was* Jashobeam the son of Zabdiel, and in his division *were* twenty-four thousand; [3]*he was* of the children of Perez, and the chief of all the captains of the army for the first month. [4]Over the division of the second month *was* Dodai[a] an Ahohite, and of his division Mikloth also *was* the leader; in his division *were* twenty-four thousand. [5]The third captain of the army for the third month *was* Benaiah, the son of Jehoiada the priest, who was chief; in his division *were* twenty-four thousand. [6]This was the Benaiah *who was* mighty *among* the thirty, and was over the thirty; in his division *was* Ammizabad his son. [7]The fourth *captain* for the fourth month *was* Asahel the brother of Joab, and Zebadiah his son after him; in his division *were* twenty-four thousand. [8]The fifth captain for the fifth month *was* Shamhuth[a] the Izrahite; in his division were twenty-four thousand. [9]The sixth *captain* for the sixth month *was* Ira the son of Ikkesh the Tekoite; in his division *were* twenty-four thousand.

27:4 [a]Hebrew *Dodai,* usually spelled *Dodo* (compare 2 Samuel 23:9) **27:8** [a]Spelled *Shammoth* in 11:27 and *Shammah* in 2 Samuel 23:11

THE MESSAGE

various generals and commanders from the army. They dedicated the plunder that they had gotten in war to the work of the worship of GOD. In addition, everything that had been dedicated by Samuel the seer, Saul son of Kish, Abner son of Ner, and Joab son of Zeruiah—anything that had been dedicated, ever, was the responsibility of Shelomith and his family.

29-30 From the family of the Izharites, Kenaniah and sons were appointed as officials and judges responsible for affairs outside the work of worship and sanctuary. From the family of the Hebronites, Hashabiah and his relatives—1,700 well-qualified men—were responsible for administration of matters related to the worship of GOD and the king's work in the territory west of the Jordan.

31-32 According to the family tree of the Hebronites, Jeriah held pride of place. In the fortieth year of David's reign (his last), the Hebron family tree was researched and outstanding men were found at Jazer in Gilead, namely, Jeriah and 2,700 men of his extended family: David the king made them responsible for administration of matters related to the worship of God and the work of the king in the territory east of the Jordan—the Reubenites, the Gadites, and the half-tribe of Manasseh.

MILITARY ORGANIZATION

1 **27** Here is the listing of the sons of Israel by family heads, commanders and captains, and other officers who served the king in everything military. Army divisions were on duty a month at a time for the twelve months of the year. Each division comprised 24,000 men.

2-3 First division, first month: Jashobeam son of Zabdiel was in charge with 24,000 men. He came from the line of Perez. He was over all the army officers during the first month.

4 The division for the second month: Dodai the Ahohite was in charge: 24,000 men; Mikloth was the leader of his division.

5-6 Commander for the third month: Benaiah son of Jehoiada the priest with 24,000 men. This was the same Benaiah who was a Mighty Man among the Thirty and their chief. His son Ammizabad was in charge of the division.

7 Fourth division for the fourth month: Asahel brother of Joab; his son Zebadiah succeeded him: 24,000 men.

8 Fifth division, fifth month: commander Shamhuth the Izrahite: 24,000 men.

9 Sixth division, sixth month: Ira son of Ikkesh the Tekoite: 24,000 men.

NEW KING JAMES VERSION

10The seventh *captain* for the seventh month
was Helez the Pelonite, of the children of
Ephraim; in his division *were* twenty-four thou-
sand. 11The eighth *captain* for the eighth month
was Sibbechai the Hushathite, of the Zarhites;
in his division *were* twenty-four thousand. 12The
ninth *captain* for the ninth month *was* Abiezer
the Anathothite, of the Benjamites; in his divi-
sion *were* twenty-four thousand. 13The tenth
captain for the tenth month *was* Maharai the
Netophathite, of the Zarhites; in his division
were twenty-four thousand. 14The eleventh *cap-
tain* for the eleventh month *was* Benaiah the Pir-
athonite, of the children of Ephraim; in his divi-
sion *were* twenty-four thousand. 15The twelfth
captain for the twelfth month *was* Heldai[a] the
Netophathite, of Othniel; in his division *were*
twenty-four thousand.

LEADERS OF TRIBES

16Furthermore, over the tribes of Israel: the
officer over the Reubenites *was* Eliezer the son
of Zichri; over the Simeonites, Shephatiah the
son of Maachah; 17*over* the Levites, Hashabiah
the son of Kemuel; over the Aaronites, Zadok;
18*over* Judah, Elihu, *one* of David's brothers;
over Issachar, Omri the son of Michael; 19*over*
Zebulun, Ishmaiah the son of Obadiah; *over*
Naphtali, Jerimoth the son of Azriel; 20*over* the
children of Ephraim, Hoshea the son of
Azaziah; *over* the half-tribe of Manasseh, Joel
the son of Pedaiah; 21*over* the half-*tribe* of Ma-
nasseh in Gilead, Iddo the son of Zechariah;
over Benjamin, Jaasiel the son of Abner; 22*over*
Dan, Azarel the son of Jeroham. These *were* the
leaders of the tribes of Israel.

23But David did not take the number of those
twenty years old and under, because the LORD
had said He would multiply Israel like the stars
of the heavens. 24Joab the son of Zeruiah began
a census, but he did not finish, for wrath came
upon Israel because of this census; nor was the
number recorded in the account of the chroni-
cles of King David.

OTHER STATE OFFICIALS

25And Azmaveth the son of Adiel *was* over the
king's treasuries; and Jehonathan the son of
Uzziah was over the storehouses in the field, in
the cities, in the villages, and in the fortresses.
26Ezri the son of Chelub was over those who did
the work of the field for tilling the ground. 27And
Shimei the Ramathite *was* over the vineyards,
and Zabdi the Shiphmite was over the produce of
the vineyards for the supply of wine. 28Baal-
Hanan the Gederite was over the olive trees and
the sycamore trees that *were* in the lowlands, and
Joash *was* over the store of oil. 29And Shitrai the
Sharonite *was* over the herds that fed in Sharon,
and Shaphat the son of Adlai was over the
herds *that were* in the valleys. 30Obil the Ish-
maelite *was* over the camels, Jehdeiah the
Meronothite *was* over the donkeys, 31and Jaziz
the Hagrite *was* over the flocks. All these *were*
the officials over King David's property.

27:15 [a]Spelled *Heled* in 11:30 and *Heleb* in 2 Samuel 23:29

THE MESSAGE

10 Seventh division, seventh month: Helez the Pelonite, an Ephraimite: 24,000 men.

11 Eighth division, eighth month: Sibbecai the Hushathite, a Zerahite: 24,000 men.

12 Ninth division, ninth month: Abiezer the Anathothite, a Benjaminite: 24,000 men.

13 Tenth division, tenth month: Maharai the Netophathite, a Zerahite: 24,000 men.

14 Eleventh division, eleventh month: Benaiah the Pirathomite, an Ephraimite: 24,000 men.

15 Twelfth division, twelfth month: Heldai the Netophathite from the family of Othniel: 24,000 men.

TRIBAL ADMINISTRATORS

16-22 Administrators of the affairs of the tribes:
for Reuben: Eliezer son of Zicri;
for Simeon: Shephatiah son of Maacah;
for Levi: Hashabiah son of Kemuel;
for Aaron: Zadok;
for Judah: Elihu, David's brother;
for Issachar: Omri son of Michael;
for Zebulun: Ishmaiah son of Obadiah;
for Naphtali: Jerimoth son of Azriel;
for Ephraim: Hoshea son of Azaziah;
for one half-tribe of Manasseh: Joel son of Pedaiah;
for the half-tribe of Manasseh in Gilead: Iddo son of Zechariah;
for Benjamin: Jaasiel son of Abner;
for Dan: Azarel son of Jeroham.

These are the administrative officers assigned to the tribes of Israel.

23-24 David didn't keep a count of men under the age of twenty, because GOD had promised to give Israel a population as numerous as the stars in the sky. Joab son of Zeruiah started out counting the men, but he never finished. God's anger broke out on Israel because of the counting. As it turned out, the numbers were never entered into the court records of King David.

SUPPLY OFFICERS

25 The king's storage facilities were supervised by Azmaveth son of Adiel. Jonathan son of Uzziah was responsible for the warehouses in the outlying areas.

26 Ezri son of Kelub was in charge of the field workers on the farms.

27 Shimei the Ramathite was in charge of the vineyards and Zabdi the Shiphmite was in charge of grapes for the wine vats.

28 Baal-Hanan the Gederite was in charge of the olive and sycamore-fig trees in the western hills, and Joash was in charge of the olive oil.

29 Shitrai the Sharonite was in charge of herds grazing in Sharon and Shaphat son of Adlai was in charge of herds in the valley.

30-31 Obil the Ismaelite was in charge of the camels, Jehdeiah the Meronothite was in charge of the donkeys, and Jaziz the Hagrite was in charge of the flocks.

These were the ones responsible for taking care of King David's property.

NEW KING JAMES VERSION

32 Also Jehonathan, David's uncle, *was* a
counselor, a wise man, and a scribe; and Jehiel
the son of Hachmoni *was* with the king's sons.
33 Ahithophel *was* the king's counselor, and
Hushai the Archite *was* the king's companion.
34 After Ahithophel *was* Jehoiada the son of Be-
naiah, then Abiathar. And the general of the
king's army *was* Joab.

SOLOMON INSTRUCTED TO BUILD THE TEMPLE

28 Now David assembled at Jerusalem all the
leaders of Israel: the officers of the tribes
and the captains of the divisions who served the
king, the captains over thousands and captains
over hundreds, and the stewards over all the
substance and possessions of the king and of his
sons, with the officials, the valiant men, and all
the mighty men of valor.
2 Then King David rose to his feet and said,
"Hear me, my brethren and my people: I *had* it
in my heart to build a house of rest for the ark
of the covenant of the LORD, and for the foot-
stool of our God, and had made preparations to
build it. 3 But God said to me, 'You shall not build
a house for My name, because you *have been* a
man of war and have shed blood.' 4 However the
LORD God of Israel chose me above all the house
of my father to be king over Israel forever, for
He has chosen Judah *to be* the ruler. And of the
house of Judah, the house of my father, and
among the sons of my father, He was pleased
with me to make *me* king over all Israel. 5 And of
all my sons (for the LORD has given me many
sons) He has chosen my son Solomon to sit on
the throne of the kingdom of the LORD over Is-
rael. 6 Now He said to me, 'It is your son
Solomon *who* shall build My house and My
courts; for I have chosen him *to be* My son, and
I will be his Father. 7 Moreover I will establish his
kingdom forever, if he is steadfast to observe
My commandments and My judgments, as it is
this day.' 8 Now therefore, in the sight of all Is-
rael, the assembly of the LORD, and in the hear-
ing of our God, be careful to seek out all the
commandments of the LORD your God, that you
may possess this good land, and leave *it* as an
inheritance for your children after you forever.
9 "As for you, my son Solomon, know the God
of your father, and serve Him with a loyal heart
and with a willing mind; for the LORD searches
all hearts and understands all the intent of the
thoughts. If you seek Him, He will be found by
you; but if you forsake Him, He will cast you off
forever. 10 Consider now, for the LORD has cho-
sen you to build a house for the sanctuary; be
strong, and do it."
11 Then David gave his son Solomon the
plans for the vestibule, its houses, its treasuries,
its upper chambers, its inner chambers, and the
place of the mercy seat; 12 and the plans for all
that he had by the Spirit, of the courts of the
house of the LORD, of all the chambers all
around, of the treasuries of the house of God,
and of the treasuries for the dedicated things;
13 also for the division of the priests and the
Levites, for all the work of the service of the
house of the LORD, and for all the articles of
service in the house of the LORD. 14 *He gave* gold

THE MESSAGE

DAVID'S COUNSELORS

32 Jonathan, David's uncle, a wise and literate
counselor, and Jehiel son of Hacmoni, were
responsible for rearing the king's sons.
33-34 Ahithophel was the king's counselor;
Hushai the Arkite was the king's friend.
Ahithophel was later replaced by Jehoiada
son of Benaiah and by Abiathar.
Joab was commander of the king's army.

DAVID'S VALEDICTORY ADDRESS

1 28 David called together all the leaders of
Israel—tribal administrators, heads of
various governmental operations, military
commanders and captains, stewards in
charge of the property and livestock belong-
ing to the king and his sons—everyone who
held responsible positions in the kingdom.
2-7 King David stood tall and spoke: "Listen
to me, my people: I fully intended to build a
permanent structure for the Chest of the
Covenant of GOD, God's footstool. But when
I got ready to build it, God said to me, 'You
may not build a house to honor me—you've
done too much fighting—killed too many
people.' GOD chose me out of my family to
be king over Israel forever. First he chose
Judah as the lead tribe, then he narrowed it
down to my family, and finally he picked me
from my father's sons, pleased to make me
the king over all Israel. And then from all
my sons—and GOD gave me many!—he
chose my son Solomon to sit on the throne
of GOD's rule over Israel. He went on to say,
'Your son Solomon will build my house and
my courts: I have chosen him to be my royal
adopted son; and I will be to him a father. I
will guarantee that his kingdom will last if
he continues to be as strong-minded in do-
ing what I command and carrying out my
decisions as he is doing now.'
8 "And now, in this public place, all Israel
looking on and God listening in, as GOD's
people, obey and study every last one of the
commandments of your GOD so that you can
make the most of living in this good land
and pass it on intact to your children, insur-
ing a good future.
9-10 "And you, Solomon my son, get to know
well your father's God; serve him with a
whole heart and eager mind, for GOD exam-
ines every heart and sees through every mo-
tive. If you seek him, he'll make sure you
find him, but if you abandon him, he'll leave
you for good. Look sharp now! GOD has cho-
sen *you* to build his holy house. Be brave,
determined! And do it!"
11-19 Then David presented his son Solomon
with the plans for The Temple complex:
porch, storerooms, meeting rooms, and the
place for atoning sacrifice. He turned over
the plans for everything that God's Spirit
had brought to his mind: the design of the
courtyards, the arrangements of rooms, and
the closets for storing all the holy things. He
gave him his plan for organizing the Levites
and priests in their work of leading and or-
dering worship in the house of God, and for
caring for the liturgical furnishings. He pro-

NEW KING JAMES VERSION

by weight for *things* of gold, for all articles used in every kind of service; also *silver* for all articles of silver by weight, for all articles used in every kind of service; [15]the weight for the lampstands of gold, and their lamps of gold, by weight for each lampstand and its lamps; for the lampstands of silver by weight, for the lampstand and its lamps, according to the use of each lampstand. [16]And by weight *he gave* gold for the tables of the showbread, for each table, and silver for the tables of silver; [17]also pure gold for the forks, the basins, the pitchers of pure gold, and the golden bowls—*he gave gold* by weight for every bowl; and for the silver bowls, *silver* by weight for every bowl; [18]and refined gold by weight for the altar of incense, and for the construction of the chariot, that is, the gold cherubim that spread *their wings* and overshadowed the ark of the covenant of the LORD. [19]"All *this,*" *said David,* "the LORD made me understand in writing, by *His* hand upon me, all the works of these plans."

[20]And David said to his son Solomon, "Be strong and of good courage, and do *it;* do not fear nor be dismayed, for the LORD God—my God—*will be* with you. He will not leave you nor forsake you, until you have finished all the work for the service of the house of the LORD. [21]*Here are* the divisions of the priests and the Levites for all the service of the house of God; and every willing craftsman *will be* with you for all manner of workmanship, for every kind of service; also the leaders and all the people *will be* completely at your command."

OFFERINGS FOR BUILDING THE TEMPLE

29 Furthermore King David said to all the assembly: "My son Solomon, whom alone God has chosen, *is* young and inexperienced; and the work *is* great, because the temple[a] *is* not for man but for the LORD God. [2]Now for the house of my God I have prepared with all my might: gold for *things to be made of* gold, silver for *things of* silver, bronze for *things of* bronze, iron for *things of* iron, wood for *things of* wood, onyx stones, *stones* to be set, glistening stones of various colors, all kinds of precious stones, and marble slabs in abundance. [3]Moreover, because I have set my affection on the house of my God, I have given to the house of my God, over and above all that I have prepared for the holy house, my own special treasure of gold and silver: [4]three thousand talents of gold, of the gold of Ophir, and seven thousand talents of refined silver, to overlay the walls of the houses; [5]the gold for *things of* gold and the silver for *things of* silver, and for all kinds of work *to be done* by the hands of craftsmen. Who *then* is willing to consecrate himself this day to the LORD?"

[6]Then the leaders of the fathers' *houses,* leaders of the tribes of Israel, the captains of thousands and of hundreds, with the officers over the king's work, offered willingly. [7]They gave for the work of the house of God five thousand talents and ten thousand darics of gold, ten thousand talents of silver, eighteen thousand talents of bronze, and one hundred thousand

29:1 [a]Literally *palace*

THE MESSAGE

vided exact specifications for how much gold and silver was needed for each article used in the services of worship: the gold and silver Lampstands and lamps, the gold tables for consecrated bread, the silver tables, the gold forks, the bowls and the jars, and the Incense Altar. And he gave him the plan for sculpting the cherubs with their wings outstretched over the Chest of the Covenant of GOD—the cherubim throne. "Here are the blueprints for the whole project as GOD gave me to understand it," David said.

20-21 David continued to address Solomon: "Take charge! Take heart! Don't be anxious or get discouraged. GOD, my God, is with you in this; he won't walk off and leave you in the lurch. He's at your side until every last detail is completed for conducting the worship of GOD. You have all the priests and Levites standing ready to pitch in, and skillful craftsmen and artisans of every kind ready to go to work. Both leaders and people are ready. Just say the word."

THEY GET READY TO BUILD

1-5 **29** Then David the king addressed the congregation: "My son Solomon was singled out and chosen by God to do this. But he's young and untested and the work is huge—this is not just a place for people to meet each other, but a house for GOD to meet us. I've done my best to get everything together for building this house for my God, all the materials necessary: gold, silver, bronze, iron, lumber, precious and varicolored stones, and building stones—vast stockpiles. Furthermore, because my heart is in this, in addition to and beyond what I have gathered, I'm turning over my personal fortune of gold and silver for making this place of worship for my God: 3,000 talents (about 113 tons) of gold—all from Ophir, the best—and 7,000 talents (214 tons) of silver for covering the walls of the buildings, and for the gold and silver work by craftsmen and artisans.

"And now, how about you? Who among you is ready and willing to join in the giving?"

6-8 Ready and willing, the heads of families, leaders of the tribes of Israel, commanders and captains in the army, stewards of the king's affairs, stepped forward and gave willingly. They gave 5,000 talents (188 tons) and 10,000 darics (185 pounds) of gold, 10,000 talents of silver (377 tons), 18,000 talents of bronze (679 tons), and 100,000 tal-

NEW KING JAMES VERSION

talents of iron. 8And whoever had *precious*
stones gave *them* to the treasury of the house of
the LORD, into the hand of Jehiel[a] the Gershon-
ite. 9Then the people rejoiced, for they had of-
fered willingly, because with a loyal heart they
had offered willingly to the LORD; and King
David also rejoiced greatly.

DAVID'S PRAISE TO GOD

10Therefore David blessed the LORD before
all the assembly; and David said:

"Blessed are You, LORD God of Israel, our
Father, forever and ever.
11Yours, O LORD, *is* the greatness,
The power and the glory,
The victory and the majesty;
For all *that is* in heaven and in earth *is*
Yours;
Yours *is* the kingdom, O LORD,
And You are exalted as head over all.
12Both riches and honor *come* from You,
And You reign over all.
In Your hand *is* power and might;
In Your hand *it is* to make great
And to give strength to all.

13"Now therefore, our God,
We thank You
And praise Your glorious name.
14But who *am* I, and who *are* my people,
That we should be able to offer so willingly
as this?
For all things *come* from You,
And of Your own we have given You.
15For we *are* aliens and pilgrims before You,
As *were* all our fathers;
Our days on earth *are* as a shadow,
And without hope.

16"O LORD our God, all this abundance that
we have prepared to build You a house for Your
holy name is from Your hand, and *is* all Your
own. 17I know also, my God, that You test the
heart and have pleasure in uprightness. As for
me, in the uprightness of my heart I have will-
ingly offered all these *things;* and now with joy
I have seen Your people, who are present here to
offer willingly to You. 18O LORD God of Abra-
ham, Isaac, and Israel, our fathers, keep this for-
ever in the intent of the thoughts of the heart of
Your people, and fix their heart toward You.
19And give my son Solomon a loyal heart to
keep Your commandments and Your testimonies
and Your statutes, to do all *these things*, and to
build the temple[a] for which I have made provi-
sion."

20Then David said to all the assembly, "Now
bless the LORD your God." So all the assembly
blessed the LORD God of their fathers, and
bowed their heads and prostrated themselves
before the LORD and the king.

SOLOMON ANOINTED KING

21And they made sacrifices to the LORD and
offered burnt offerings to the LORD on the next

29:8 [a]Possibly the same as *Jehieli* (compare 26:21, 22) **29:19** [a]Literally *palace*

THE MESSAGE

ents (3,775 tons) of iron. Anyone who had
precious jewels put them in the treasury for
the building of The Temple of GOD in the
custody of Jehiel the Gershonite.
9 And the people were full of a sense of cel-
ebration—all that giving! And all given will-
ingly, freely! King David was exuberant.
10-13 David blessed GOD in full view of the en-
tire congregation:

Blessed are you, GOD of Israel, our father
from of old and forever.
To you, O GOD, belong the greatness and
the might,
the glory, the victory, the majesty, the
splendor;
Yes! Everything in heaven, everything on
earth;
the kingdom all yours! You've raised
yourself high over all.
Riches and glory come from you,
you're ruler over all;
You hold strength and power in the palm
of your hand
to build up and strengthen all.
And here we are, O God, our God, giving
thanks to you,
praising your splendid Name.

14-19 "But me—who am I, and who are these
my people, that we should presume to be
giving something to you? Everything comes
from you; all we're doing is giving back
what we've been given from your generous
hand. As far as you're concerned, we're
homeless, shiftless wanderers like our an-
cestors, our lives mere shadows, hardly any-
thing to us. GOD, our God, all these materi-
als—these piles of stuff for building a house
of worship for you, honoring your Holy
Name—it all came from you! It was all yours
in the first place! I know, dear God, that you
care nothing for the surface—you want *us*,
our true selves—and so I have given from
the heart, honestly and happily. And now
see all these people doing the same, giving
freely, willingly—what a joy! O GOD, God of
our fathers Abraham, Isaac, and Israel, keep
this generous spirit alive forever in these
people always, keep their hearts set firmly
in you. And give my son Solomon an unclut-
tered and focused heart so that he can obey
what you command, live by your directions
and counsel, and carry through with build-
ing The Temple for which I have provided."
20 David then addressed the congregation:
"Bless GOD, your God!" And they did it,
blessed GOD, the God of their ancestors, and
worshiped reverently in the presence of
GOD and the king.
21-22 The very next day they butchered the sac-
rificial animals and offered in the worship

NEW KING JAMES VERSION

day: a thousand bulls, a thousand rams, a thou-
sand lambs, with their drink offerings, and sac-
rifices in abundance for all Israel. 22So they ate
and drank before the LORD with great gladness
on that day. And they made Solomon the son of
David king the second time, and anointed *him*
before the LORD *to be* the leader, and Zadok *to*
be priest. 23Then Solomon sat on the throne of
the LORD as king instead of David his father, and
prospered; and all Israel obeyed him. 24All the
leaders and the mighty men, and also all the
sons of King David, submitted themselves to
King Solomon. 25So the LORD exalted Solomon
exceedingly in the sight of all Israel, and be-
stowed on him *such* royal majesty as had not
been on any king before him in Israel.

THE CLOSE OF DAVID'S REIGN

26Thus David the son of Jesse reigned over
all Israel. 27And the period that he reigned over
Israel *was* forty years; seven years he reigned in
Hebron, and thirty-three *years* he reigned in
Jerusalem. 28So he died in a good old age, full of
days and riches and honor; and Solomon his
son reigned in his place. 29Now the acts of King
David, first and last, indeed they *are* written in
the book of Samuel the seer, in the book of
Nathan the prophet, and in the book of Gad the
seer, 30with all his reign and his might, and the
events that happened to him, to Israel, and to all
the kingdoms of the lands.

THE MESSAGE

of Israel to GOD a thousand bulls, a thou-
sand rams, a thousand sheep, and in addi-
tion drink offerings and many other sacri-
fices. They feasted all day, eating and
drinking before GOD, exuberant with joy.

22-25 Then they ceremonially reenacted
Solomon's coronation, anointing David's
son before GOD as their leader, and Zadok
as priest. Solomon sat on the throne of GOD
as king in place of David his father. And
everything went well; all Israel obeyed him.
All the leaders of the people, including all
the sons of King David, accepted Solomon
as their king and promised their loyalty.
Solomon rode high on a crest of popular ac-
claim—it was all GOD's doing. GOD gave him
position and honor beyond any king in Is-
rael before him.

26-30 David son of Jesse ruled over all Israel. He
was king for forty years. He ruled from He-
bron seven years and from Jerusalem thirty-
three. He died at a ripe old age, full of days,
wealth, and glory. His son Solomon ruled af-
ter him. The history of David the king, from
start to finish, is written in the chronicles of
Samuel the seer, Nathan the prophet, and
Gad the seer, including a full account of his
rule, his exploits, and the times through
which he and Israel and the surrounding
kingdoms passed.

2 CHRONICLES

New King James Version

Solomon Requests Wisdom

1 Now Solomon the son of David was strengthened in his kingdom, and the LORD his God *was* with him and exalted him exceedingly.

2And Solomon spoke to all Israel, to the captains of thousands and of hundreds, to the judges, and to every leader in all Israel, the heads of the fathers' *houses.* 3Then Solomon, and all the assembly with him, went to the high place that *was* at Gibeon; for the tabernacle of meeting with God was there, which Moses the servant of the LORD had made in the wilderness. 4But David had brought up the ark of God from Kirjath Jearim to *the place* David had prepared for it, for he had pitched a tent for it at Jerusalem. 5Now the bronze altar that Bezalel the son of Uri, the son of Hur, had made, he put[a] before the tabernacle of the LORD; Solomon and the assembly sought Him *there.* 6And Solomon went up there to the bronze altar before the LORD, which *was* at the tabernacle of meeting, and offered a thousand burnt offerings on it.

7On that night God appeared to Solomon, and said to him, "Ask! What shall I give you?"

8And Solomon said to God: "You have shown great mercy to David my father, and have made me king in his place. 9Now, O LORD God, let Your promise to David my father be established, for You have made me king over a people like the dust of the earth in multitude. 10Now give me wisdom and knowledge, that I may go out and come in before this people; for who can judge this great people of Yours?"

11Then God said to Solomon: "Because this was in your heart, and you have not asked riches or wealth or honor or the life of your enemies, nor have you asked long life—but have asked wisdom and knowledge for yourself, that you may judge My people over whom I have made you king— 12wisdom and knowledge *are* granted to you; and I will give you riches and wealth and honor, such as none of the kings have had who *were* before you, nor shall any after you have the like."

Solomon's Military and Economic Power

13So Solomon came to Jerusalem from the high place that *was* at Gibeon, from before the tabernacle of meeting, and reigned over Israel. 14And Solomon gathered chariots and horsemen; he had one thousand four hundred chariots and twelve thousand horsemen, whom he stationed in the chariot cities and with the king in Jerusalem. 15Also the king made silver and gold as common in Jerusalem as stones, and he made cedars as abundant as the sycamores which *are* in the lowland. 16And Solomon had horses imported from Egypt and Keveh; the king's merchants bought them in Keveh at the *current* price. 17They also acquired and imported from Egypt a chariot for six hundred *shekels* of silver, and a horse for one hundred

1:5 [a]Some authorities read *it was there.*

The Message

King Solomon

1-6 1 Solomon son of David took a firm grip on the reins of his kingdom. GOD was with him and gave him much help. Solomon addressed all Israel—the commanders and captains, the judges, every leader, and all the heads of families. Then Solomon and the entire company went to the worship center at Gibeon—that's where the Tent of Meeting of God was, the one that Moses the servant of GOD had made in the wilderness. The Chest of God, though, was in Jerusalem—David had brought it up from Kiriath Jearim, prepared a special place for it, and pitched a tent for it. But the Bronze Altar that Bezalel son of Uri, the son of Hur, had made was in Gibeon, in its place before the Tabernacle of GOD; and that is where Solomon and the congregation gathered to pray. Solomon worshiped GOD at the Bronze Altar in front of the Tent of Meeting; he sacrificed a thousand Whole-Burnt-Offerings on it.

7 That night God appeared to Solomon. God said, "What do you want from me? Ask."

8-10 Solomon answered, "You were extravagantly generous with David my father, and now you have made me king in his place. Establish, GOD, the words you spoke to my father, for you've given me a staggering task, ruling this mob of people. Yes, give me wisdom and knowledge as I come and go among this people—for who on his own is capable of leading these, your glorious people?"

11-12 God answered Solomon, "This is what has come out of your heart: You didn't grasp for money, wealth, fame, and the doom of your enemies; you didn't even ask for a long life. You asked for wisdom and knowledge so you could govern well my people over whom I've made you king. Because of this, you get what you asked for—wisdom and knowledge. And I'm presenting you the rest as a bonus—money, wealth, and fame beyond anything the kings before or after you had or will have."

13 Then Solomon left the worship center at Gibeon and the Tent of Meeting and went to Jerusalem. He set to work as king of Israel.

14-17 Solomon collected chariots and horses: fourteen hundred chariots and twelve thousand horses! He stabled them in the special chariot-cities as well as in Jerusalem. The king made silver and gold as common as rocks, and cedar as common as the fig trees in the lowland hills. His horses were brought in from Egypt and Cilicia, specially acquired by the king's agents. Chariots from Egypt went for fifteen pounds of silver and a horse for about three and three-quarters

NEW KING JAMES VERSION

and fifty; thus, through their agents,[a] they exported them to all the kings of the Hittites and the kings of Syria.

SOLOMON PREPARES TO BUILD THE TEMPLE

2 Then Solomon determined to build a temple for the name of the LORD, and a royal house for himself. 2Solomon selected seventy thousand men to bear burdens, eighty thousand to quarry *stone* in the mountains, and three thousand six hundred to oversee them.

3Then Solomon sent to Hiram[a] king of Tyre, saying:

> As you have dealt with David my father, and sent him cedars to build himself a house to dwell in, *so deal with me.* 4Behold, I am building a temple for the name of the LORD my God, to dedicate *it* to Him, to burn before Him sweet incense, for the continual showbread, for the burnt offerings morning and evening, on the Sabbaths, on the New Moons, and on the set feasts of the LORD our God. This *is an ordinance* forever to Israel.
>
> 5And the temple which I build *will be* great, for our God is greater than all gods. 6But who is able to build Him a temple, since heaven and the heaven of heavens cannot contain Him? Who *am* I then, that I should build Him a temple, except to burn sacrifice before Him?
>
> 7Therefore send me at once a man skillful to work in gold and silver, in bronze and iron, in purple and crimson and blue, who has skill to engrave with the skillful men who are with me in Judah and Jerusalem, whom David my father provided. 8Also send me cedar and cypress and algum logs from Lebanon, for I know that your servants have skill to cut timber in Lebanon; and indeed my servants *will be* with your servants, 9to prepare timber for me in abundance, for the temple which I am about to build *shall be* great and wonderful.
>
> 10And indeed I will give to your servants, the woodsmen who cut timber, twenty thousand kors of ground wheat, twenty thousand kors of barley, twenty thousand baths of wine, and twenty thousand baths of oil.

11Then Hiram king of Tyre answered in writing, which he sent to Solomon:

> Because the LORD loves His people, He has made you king over them.

12Hiram[a] also said:

> Blessed *be* the LORD God of Israel, who made heaven and earth, for He has given King David a wise son, endowed with prudence and understanding, who will build a temple for the LORD and a royal house for himself!

1:17 [a]Literally *by their hands* **2:3** [a]Hebrew *Huram* (compare 1 Kings 5:1) **2:12** [a]Hebrew *Huram* (compare 1 Kings 5:1)

THE MESSAGE

of a pound of silver. Solomon carried on a
brisk horse-trading business with the Hittite
and Aramean royal houses.

THE TEMPLE CONSTRUCTION BEGINS

1 2 Solomon gave orders to begin construc-
tion on the house of worship in honor of
GOD and a palace for himself.
2 Solomon assigned seventy thousand
common laborers, eighty thousand to work
the quarries in the mountains, and thirty-six
hundred foremen to manage the workforce.
3-4 Then Solomon sent this message to King
Hiram of Tyre: "Send me cedar logs, the
same kind you sent David my father for
building his palace. I'm about to build a
house of worship in honor of GOD, a holy
place for burning perfumed incense, for set-
ting out holy bread, for making Whole-
Burnt-Offerings at morning and evening
worship, and for Sabbath, New Moon, and
Holy Day services of worship—the acts of
worship required of Israel.
5-10 "The house I am building has to be the
best, for our God is the best, far better than
competing gods. But who is capable of
building such a structure? Why, the skies—
the entire cosmos!—can't begin to contain
him. And me, who am I to think I can build
a house adequate for God—burning incense
to him is about all I'm good for! I need your
help: Send me a master artisan in gold, sil-
ver, bronze, iron, textiles of purple, crimson,
and violet, and who knows the craft of en-
graving; he will supervise the trained crafts-
men in Judah and Jerusalem that my father
provided. Also send cedar, cypress, and al-
gum logs from Lebanon; I know you have
lumberjacks experienced in the Lebanon
forests. I'll send workers to join your crews
to cut plenty of timber—I'm going to need a
lot, for this house I'm building is going to be
absolutely stunning—a showcase temple!
I'll provide all the food necessary for your
crew of lumberjacks and loggers: 130,000
bushels of wheat, 120,000 gallons of wine,
and 120,000 gallons of olive oil."
11 Hiram king of Tyre wrote Solomon in re-
ply: "It's plain that GOD loves his people—he
made you king over them!"
12-14 He wrote on, "Blessed be the GOD of Is-
rael, who made heaven and earth, and who
gave King David a son so wise, so knowl-
edgeable and shrewd, to build a temple for
GOD and a palace for himself. I've sent you

NEW KING JAMES VERSION

13 And now I have sent a skillful man, endowed with understanding, Huram[a] my master[b] *craftsman* 14 (the son of a woman of the daughters of Dan, and his father was a man of Tyre), skilled to work in gold and silver, bronze and iron, stone and wood, purple and blue, fine linen and crimson, and to make any engraving and to accomplish any plan which may be given to him, with your skillful men and with the skillful men of my lord David your father.

15 Now therefore, the wheat, the barley, the oil, and the wine which my lord has spoken of, let him send to his servants. 16 And we will cut wood from Lebanon, as much as you need; we will bring it to you in rafts by sea to Joppa, and you will carry it up to Jerusalem.

17 Then Solomon numbered all the aliens who *were* in the land of Israel, after the census in which David his father had numbered them; and there were found to be one hundred and fifty-three thousand six hundred. 18 And he made seventy thousand of them bearers of burdens, eighty thousand stonecutters in the mountain, and three thousand six hundred overseers to make the people work.

SOLOMON BUILDS THE TEMPLE

3 Now Solomon began to build the house of the LORD at Jerusalem on Mount Moriah, where *the* LORD[a] had appeared to his father David, at the place that David had prepared on the threshing floor of Ornan[b] the Jebusite. 2 And he began to build on the second *day* of the second month in the fourth year of his reign.

3 This is the foundation which Solomon laid for building the house of God: The length *was* sixty cubits (by cubits according to the former measure) and the width twenty cubits. 4 And the vestibule that *was* in front *of the sanctuary*[a] was twenty cubits long across the width of the house, and the height *was* one hundred and[b] twenty. He overlaid the inside with pure gold. 5 The larger room[a] he paneled with cypress which he overlaid with fine gold, and he carved palm trees and chainwork on it. 6 And he decorated the house with precious stones for beauty, and the gold *was* gold from Parvaim. 7 He also overlaid the house—the beams and doorposts, its walls and doors—with gold; and he carved cherubim on the walls.

8 And he made the Most Holy Place. Its length was according to the width of the house, twenty cubits, and its width twenty cubits. He overlaid it with six hundred talents of fine gold. 9 The weight of the nails *was* fifty shekels of gold; and he overlaid the upper area with gold. 10 In the Most Holy Place he made two cherubim,

2:13 [a]Spelled *Hiram* in 1 Kings 7:13 [b]Literally *father* (compare 1 Kings 7:13, 14) **3:1** [a]Literally *He*, following Masoretic Text and Vulgate; Septuagint reads *the LORD;* Targum reads *the Angel of the LORD.* [b]Spelled *Araunah* in 2 Samuel 24:16ff **3:4** [a]The main room of the temple; elsewhere called the holy place (compare 1 Kings 6:3) [b]Following Masoretic Text, Septuagint, and Vulgate; Arabic, some manuscripts of the Septuagint, and Syriac omit *one hundred and.* **3:5** [a]Literally *house*

THE MESSAGE

Huram-Abi—he's already on his way—he knows the construction business inside and out. His mother is from Dan and his father from Tyre. He knows how to work in gold, silver, bronze, iron, stone, and wood, in purple, violet, linen, and crimson textiles; he is also an expert engraver and competent to work out designs with your artists and architects, and those of my master David, your father.

15-16 "Go ahead and send the wheat, barley, olive oil, and wine you promised for my work crews. We'll log the trees you need from the Lebanon forests and raft them down to Joppa. You'll have to get the timber up to Jerusalem yourself."

17-18 Solomon then took a census of all the foreigners living in Israel, using the same census-taking method employed by his father. They numbered 153,600. He assigned 70,000 of them as common laborers, 80,000 to work the quarries in the mountains, and 3,600 as foremen to manage the work crews.

1-4 3 So Solomon broke ground, launched construction of the house of GOD in Jerusalem on Mount Moriah, the place where GOD had appeared to his father David. The precise site, the threshing floor of Araunah the Jebusite, had been designated by David. He broke ground on the second day in the second month of the fourth year of his rule. These are the dimensions that Solomon set for the construction of the house of God: ninety feet long and thirty feet wide. The porch in front stretched the width of the building, that is, thirty feet; and it was thirty feet high.

4-7 The interior was gold-plated. He paneled the main hall with cypress and veneered it with fine gold engraved with palm tree and chain designs. He decorated the building with precious stones and gold from Parvaim. Everything was coated with gold veneer: rafters, doorframes, walls, and doors. Cherubim were engraved on the walls.

8-9 He made the Holy of Holies a cube, thirty feet wide, long, and high. It was veneered with six hundred talents (something over twenty-two tons) of gold. The gold nails weighed fifty shekels (a little over a pound). The upper rooms were also veneered in gold.

10-13 He made two sculptures of cherubim, gi-

New King James Version

fashioned by carving, and overlaid them with gold. 11The wings of the cherubim *were* twenty cubits in *overall* length: one wing *of the one cherub was* five cubits, touching the wall of the room, and the other wing *was* five cubits, touching the wing of the other cherub; 12*one* wing of the other cherub *was* five cubits, touching the wall of the room, and the other wing *also was* five cubits, touching the wing of the other cherub. 13The wings of these cherubim spanned twenty cubits overall. They stood on their feet, and they faced inward. 14And he made the veil of blue, purple, crimson, and fine linen, and wove cherubim into it.

15Also he made in front of the temple[a] two pillars thirty-five[b] cubits high, and the capital that *was* on the top of each of *them* was five cubits. 16He made wreaths of chainwork, as in the inner sanctuary, and put *them* on top of the pillars; and he made one hundred pomegranates, and put *them* on the wreaths of chainwork. 17Then he set up the pillars before the temple, one on the right hand and the other on the left; he called the name of the one on the right hand Jachin, and the name of the one on the left Boaz.

Furnishings of the Temple

4 Moreover he made a bronze altar: twenty cubits was its length, twenty cubits its width, and ten cubits its height.

2Then he made the Sea of cast *bronze,* ten cubits from one brim to the other; *it was* completely round. Its height *was* five cubits, and a line of thirty cubits measured its circumference. 3And under it *was* the likeness of oxen encircling it all around, ten to a cubit, all the way around the Sea. The oxen *were* cast in two rows, when it was cast. 4It stood on twelve oxen: three looking toward the north, three looking toward the west, three looking toward the south, and three looking toward the east; the Sea *was set* upon them, and all their back parts *pointed* inward. 5It *was* a handbreadth thick; and its brim was shaped like the brim of a cup, *like* a lily blossom. It contained three thousand[a] baths.

6He also made ten lavers, and put five on the right side and five on the left, to wash in them; such things as they offered for the burnt offering they would wash in them, but the Sea *was* for the priests to wash in. 7And he made ten lampstands of gold according to their design, and set *them* in the temple, five on the right side and five on the left. 8He also made ten tables, and placed *them* in the temple, five on the right side and five on the left. And he made one hundred bowls of gold.

9Furthermore he made the court of the priests, and the great court and doors for the court; and he overlaid these doors with bronze. 10He set the Sea on the right side, toward the southeast.

11Then Huram made the pots and the shovels and the bowls. So Huram finished doing the work that he was to do for King Solomon for the house of God: 12the two pillars and the bowl-shaped capitals *that were* on top of the two pil-

3:15 [a]Literally *house* [b]Or *eighteen* (compare 1 Kings 7:15; 2 Kings 25:17; and Jeremiah 52:21) **4:5** [a]Or *two thousand* (compare 1 Kings 7:26)

The Message

gantic angel-like figures, for the Holy of Holies, both veneered with gold. The combined wingspread of the side-by-side cherubim (each wing measuring seven and a half feet) stretched from wall to wall, thirty feet. They stood erect facing the main hall.

14 He fashioned the curtain of violet, purple, and crimson fabric and worked a cherub design into it.

15-17 He made two huge free-standing pillars, each fifty-two feet tall, their capitals extending another seven and a half feet. The top of each pillar was set off with an elaborate filigree of chains, like necklaces, from which hung a hundred pomegranates. He placed the pillars in front of The Temple, one on the right, and the other on the left. The right pillar he named Jakin (Security) and the left pillar he named Boaz (Stability).

Temple Furnishings

1 4 He made the Bronze Altar thirty feet long, thirty feet wide, and ten feet high.

2-5 He made a Sea—an immense round basin of cast metal fifteen feet in diameter, seven and a half feet high, and forty-five feet in circumference. Just under the rim, there were two parallel bands of something like bulls, ten to each foot and a half. The figures were cast in one piece with the Sea. The Sea was set on twelve bulls, three facing north, three facing west, three facing south, and three facing east. All the bulls faced outward and supported the Sea on their hindquarters. The Sea was three inches thick and flared at the rim like a cup, or a lily. It held about 18,000 gallons.

6 He made ten Washbasins, five set on the right and five on the left, for rinsing the things used for the Whole-Burnt-Offerings. The priests washed themselves in the Sea.

7 He made ten gold Lampstands, following the specified pattern, and placed five on the right and five on the left.

8 He made ten tables and set five on the right and five on the left. He also made a hundred gold bowls.

9 He built a Courtyard especially for the priests and then the great court and doors for the court. The doors were covered with bronze.

10 He placed the Sea on the right side of The Temple at the southeast corner.

11-16 He also made ash buckets, shovels, and bowls.

And that about wrapped it up: Huram completed the work he had contracted to do for King Solomon:

two pillars;
two bowl-shaped capitals for the tops of
the pillars;

NEW KING JAMES VERSION

lars; the two networks covering the two bowl-shaped capitals which *were* on top of the pillars; 13four hundred pomegranates for the two networks (two rows of pomegranates for each network, to cover the two bowl-shaped capitals that *were* on the pillars); 14he also made carts and the lavers on the carts; 15one Sea and twelve oxen under it; 16also the pots, the shovels, the forks—and all their articles Huram his master[a] *craftsman* made of burnished bronze for King Solomon for the house of the LORD.

17In the plain of Jordan the king had them cast in clay molds, between Succoth and Zeredah.[a] 18And Solomon had all these articles made in such great abundance that the weight of the bronze was not determined.

19Thus Solomon had all the furnishings made for the house of God: the altar of gold and the tables on which *was* the showbread; 20the lampstands with their lamps of pure gold, to burn in the prescribed manner in front of the inner sanctuary, 21with the flowers and the lamps and the wick-trimmers of gold, of purest gold; 22the trimmers, the bowls, the ladles, and the censers of pure gold. As for the entry of the sanctuary, its inner doors to the Most Holy *Place*, and the doors of the main hall of the temple, *were* gold.

5 So all the work that Solomon had done for the house of the LORD was finished; and Solomon brought in the things which his father David had dedicated: the silver and the gold and all the furnishings. And he put *them* in the treasuries of the house of God.

THE ARK BROUGHT INTO THE TEMPLE

2Now Solomon assembled the elders of Israel and all the heads of the tribes, the chief fathers of the children of Israel, in Jerusalem, that they might bring the ark of the covenant of the LORD up from the City of David, which *is* Zion. 3Therefore all the men of Israel assembled with the king at the feast, which *was* in the seventh month. 4So all the elders of Israel came, and the Levites took up the ark. 5Then they brought up the ark, the tabernacle of meeting, and all the holy furnishings that *were* in the tabernacle. The priests and the Levites brought them up. 6Also King Solomon, and all the congregation of Israel who were assembled with him before the ark, were sacrificing sheep and oxen that could not be counted or numbered for multitude. 7Then the priests brought in the ark of the covenant of the LORD to its place, into the inner sanctuary of the temple,[a] to the Most Holy *Place*, under the wings of the cherubim. 8For the cherubim spread *their* wings over the place of

4:16 [a]Literally *father* 4:17 [a]Spelled *Zaretan* in 1 Kings 7:46
5:7 [a]Literally *house*

THE MESSAGE

two decorative filigrees for the capitals;
four hundred pomegranates for the
filigrees (a double row of
pomegranates for each filigree);
ten washstands with their basins;
one Sea and the twelve bulls under it;
miscellaneous buckets, forks, shovels,
and bowls.

16-18 All these artifacts that Huram-Abi made for King Solomon for The Temple of GOD were made of burnished bronze. The king had them cast in clay in a foundry on the Jordan plain between Succoth and Zarethan. These artifacts were never weighed—there were far too many! Nobody has any idea how much bronze was used.

19-22 Solomon was also responsible for the furniture and accessories in The Temple of God:

the gold Altar;
the tables that held the Bread of the
Presence;
the Lampstands of pure gold with their
lamps, to be lighted
before the Inner Sanctuary, the Holy
of Holies;
the gold flowers, lamps, and tongs (all
solid gold);
the gold wick trimmers, bowls, ladles,
and censers;
the gold doors of The Temple, doors to
the Holy of Holies, and the doors
to the main sanctuary.

1 5 That completed the work King Solomon did on The Temple of GOD. He then brought in the holy offerings of his father David, the silver and the gold and the artifacts. He placed them all in the treasury of God's Temple.

INSTALLING THE CHEST

2-3 Bringing all this to a climax, Solomon got all the leaders together in Jerusalem—all the chiefs of tribes and the family patriarchs—to move the Chest of the Covenant of GOD from Zion and install it in The Temple. All the men of Israel assembled before the king on the feast day of the seventh month, the Feast of Booths.

4-6 When all the leaders of Israel were ready, the Levites took up the Chest. They carried the Chest, the Tent of Meeting, and all the sacred things in the Tent used in worship. The priests, all Levites, carried them. King Solomon and the entire congregation of Israel were there before the Chest, worshiping and sacrificing huge numbers of sheep and cattle—so many that no one could keep track.

7-10 The priests brought the Chest of the Covenant of GOD to its place in the Inner Sanctuary, the Holy of Holies, under the wings of the cherubim. The outspread wings of the cherubim formed a canopy over the

NEW KING JAMES VERSION

the ark, and the cherubim overshadowed the ark and its poles. 9The poles extended so that the ends of the poles of the ark could be seen from *the holy place,* in front of the inner sanctuary; but they could not be seen from outside. And they are there to this day. 10Nothing was in the ark except the two tablets which Moses put *there* at Horeb, when the LORD made *a covenant* with the children of Israel, when they had come out of Egypt.

11And it came to pass when the priests came out of the *Most* Holy *Place* (for all the priests who *were* present had sanctified themselves, without keeping to their divisions), 12and the Levites *who were* the singers, all those of Asaph and Heman and Jeduthun, with their sons and their brethren, stood at the east end of the altar, clothed in white linen, having cymbals, stringed instruments and harps, and with them one hundred and twenty priests sounding with trumpets— 13indeed it came to pass, when the trumpeters and singers *were* as one, to make one sound to be heard in praising and thanking the LORD, and when they lifted up their voice with the trumpets and cymbals and instruments of music, and praised the LORD, *saying:*

"*For He is* good,
For His mercy *endures* forever,"[a]

that the house, the house of the LORD, was filled with a cloud, 14so that the priests could not continue ministering because of the cloud; for the glory of the LORD filled the house of God.

6 Then Solomon spoke:

"The LORD said He would dwell in the dark cloud.
2I have surely built You an exalted house,
And a place for You to dwell in forever."

SOLOMON'S SPEECH UPON COMPLETION OF THE WORK

3Then the king turned around and blessed the whole assembly of Israel, while all the assembly of Israel was standing. 4And he said: "Blessed *be* the LORD God of Israel, who has fulfilled with His hands *what* He spoke with His mouth to my father David, saying, 5'Since the day that I brought My people out of the land of Egypt, I have chosen no city from any tribe of Israel *in which* to build a house, that My name might be there, nor did I choose any man to be a ruler over My people Israel. 6Yet I have chosen Jerusalem, that My name may be there, and I have chosen David to be over My people Israel.' 7Now it was in the heart of my father David to build a temple[a] for the name of the LORD God of Israel. 8But the LORD said to my father David, 'Whereas it was in your heart to build a temple for My name, you did well in that it was in your heart. 9Nevertheless you shall not build the temple, but your son who will come from your body, he shall build the temple for My name.' 10So the LORD has fulfilled His word which He spoke, and I have filled the position of my father David,

5:13 [a]Compare Psalm 106:1 **6:7** [a]Literally *house,* and so in verses 8–10

THE MESSAGE

Chest and its poles. The ends of the poles were so long that they stuck out from the entrance of the Inner Sanctuary, but were not noticeable further out—they're still there today. There was nothing in the Chest itself but the two stone tablets that Moses had placed in it at Horeb where GOD made a covenant with Israel after bringing them up from Egypt.

11-13 The priests then left the Holy Place. All
the priests there were consecrated, regard-
less of rank or assignment; and all the
Levites who were musicians were there—
Asaph, Heman, Jeduthun, and their fami-
lies, dressed in their worship robes; the
choir and orchestra assembled on the east
side of the Altar and were joined by 120
priests blowing trumpets. The choir and
trumpets made one voice of praise and
thanks to GOD—orchestra and choir in per-
fect harmony singing and playing praise to
GOD:

Yes! God is good!
His loyal love goes on forever!

13-14 Then a billowing cloud filled The Temple
of GOD. The priests couldn't even carry out
their duties because of the cloud—the glory
of GOD!—that filled The Temple of God.

SOLOMON'S DEDICATION AND PRAYER

1-2 6 Then Solomon said,

GOD said he would dwell in a cloud,
But I've built a temple most splendid,
A place for you to live in forever.

3 The king then turned to face the congre-
gation that had come together and blessed
them:
4-6 "Blessed be GOD, the God of Israel, who
spoke personally to my father David. Now
he has done what he promised when he
said, 'From the day I brought my people Is-
rael up from Egypt, I haven't set apart one
city among the tribes of Israel in which to
build a temple to honor my Name, or chosen
one person to be the leader. But now I have
chosen both a city and a person: Jerusalem
for honoring my Name and David to lead
my people Israel.'
7-9 "My father David very much wanted to
build a temple honoring the Name of GOD,
the God of Israel, but GOD told him, 'It was
good that you wanted to build a temple in
my honor—most commendable! But you are
not the one to do it. Your son, who will carry
on your dynasty, will build it for my Name.'
10-11 "And now you see the promise com-
pleted. GOD has done what he said he would
do; I have succeeded David my father and

NEW KING JAMES VERSION

and sit on the throne of Israel, as the LORD promised; and I have built the temple for the name of the LORD God of Israel. 11And there I have put the ark, in which *is* the covenant of the LORD which He made with the children of Israel."

SOLOMON'S PRAYER OF DEDICATION

12Then *Solomon*[a] stood before the altar of the LORD in the presence of all the assembly of Israel, and spread out his hands 13(for Solomon had made a bronze platform five cubits long, five cubits wide, and three cubits high, and had set it in the midst of the court; and he stood on it, knelt down on his knees before all the assembly of Israel, and spread out his hands toward heaven); 14and he said: "LORD God of Israel, *there is* no God in heaven or on earth like You, who keep *Your* covenant and mercy with Your servants who walk before You with all their hearts. 15You have kept what You promised Your servant David my father; You have both spoken with Your mouth and fulfilled *it* with Your hand, as *it is* this day. 16Therefore, LORD God of Israel, now keep what You promised Your servant David my father, saying, 'You shall not fail to have a man sit before Me on the throne of Israel, only if your sons take heed to their way, that they walk in My law as you have walked before Me.' 17And now, O LORD God of Israel, let Your word come true, which You have spoken to Your servant David.

18"But will God indeed dwell with men on the earth? Behold, heaven and the heaven of heavens cannot contain You. How much less this temple[a] which I have built! 19Yet regard the prayer of Your servant and his supplication, O LORD my God, and listen to the cry and the prayer which Your servant is praying before You: 20that Your eyes may be open toward this temple day and night, toward the place where *You* said *You would* put Your name, that You may hear the prayer which Your servant makes toward this place. 21And may You hear the supplications of Your servant and of Your people Israel, when they pray toward this place. Hear from heaven Your dwelling place, and when You hear, forgive.

22"If anyone sins against his neighbor, and is forced to take an oath, and comes *and* takes an oath before Your altar in this temple, 23then hear from heaven, and act, and judge Your servants, bringing retribution on the wicked by bringing his way on his own head, and justifying the righteous by giving him according to his righteousness.

6:12 [a]Literally *he* (compare 1 Kings 8:22) **6:18** [a]Literally *house*

THE MESSAGE

now rule Israel; and I have built a temple to honor GOD, the God of Israel, and have secured a place for the Chest that holds the Covenant of GOD, the covenant he made with the people of Israel."

12-16 Before the entire congregation of Israel, Solomon took his position at the Altar of GOD and stretched out his hands. Solomon had made a bronze dais seven and a half feet square and four and a half feet high and placed it inside the court; that's where he now stood. Then he knelt in full view of the whole congregation, stretched his hands to heaven, and prayed:

GOD, O God of Israel, there is no God like you in the skies above or on the earth below, who unswervingly keeps covenant with his servants and unfailingly loves them while they sincerely live in obedience to your way. You kept your word to David my father, your promise. You did exactly what you promised—every detail. The proof is before us today!

Keep it up, GOD, O God of Israel! Continue to keep the promises you made to David my father when you said, "You'll always have a descendant to represent my rule on Israel's throne, on the one condition that your sons are as careful to live obediently in my presence as you have."

17 O GOD, God of Israel, let this all happen—
confirm and establish it!

18-21 Can it be that God will actually move into our neighborhood? Why, the cosmos itself isn't large enough to give you breathing room, let alone this Temple I've built. Even so, I'm bold to ask: Pay attention to these my prayers, both intercessory and personal, O GOD, my God. Listen to my prayers, energetic and devout, that I'm setting before you right now. Keep your eyes open to this Temple day and night, this place you promised to dignify with your Name. And listen to the prayers that I pray in this place. And listen to your people Israel when they pray at this place.

Listen from your home in heaven
and when you hear, forgive.

22 When someone hurts a neighbor and promises to make things right, and then comes and repeats the promise before your Altar in this Temple,

23 Listen from heaven and act;
judge your servants, making the
offender pay for the offense
And set the offended free,
dismissing all charges.

NEW KING JAMES VERSION

24 “Or if Your people Israel are defeated be-
fore an enemy because they have sinned against
You, and return and confess Your name, and
pray and make supplication before You in this
temple, 25 then hear from heaven and forgive the
sin of Your people Israel, and bring them back to
the land which You gave to them and their fa-
thers.
26 “When the heavens are shut up and there is
no rain because they have sinned against You,
when they pray toward this place and confess
Your name, and turn from their sin because You
afflict them, 27 then hear *in* heaven, and forgive
the sin of Your servants, Your people Israel, that
You may teach them the good way in which they
should walk; and send rain on Your land which
You have given to Your people as an inheritance.
28 “When there is famine in the land, pesti-
lence or blight or mildew, locusts or grasshop-
pers; when their enemies besiege them in the
land of their cities; whatever plague or whatever
sickness *there is;* 29 whatever prayer, whatever
supplication is *made* by anyone, or by all Your
people Israel, when each one knows his own
burden and his own grief, and spreads out his
hands to this temple: 30 then hear from heaven
Your dwelling place, and forgive, and give to
everyone according to all his ways, whose heart
You know (for You alone know the hearts of the
sons of men), 31 that they may fear You, to walk
in Your ways as long as they live in the land
which You gave to our fathers.
32 “Moreover, concerning a foreigner, who is
not of Your people Israel, but has come from a
far country for the sake of Your great name and
Your mighty hand and Your outstretched arm,
when they come and pray in this temple; 33 then
hear from heaven Your dwelling place, and do
according to all for which the foreigner calls to
You, that all peoples of the earth may know Your
name and fear You, as *do* Your people Israel, and

THE MESSAGE

24-25 When your people Israel are beaten by an enemy because they've sinned against you, but then turn to you and acknowledge your rule in prayers desperate and devout in this Temple,

Listen from your home in heaven;
forgive the sin of your people Israel,
return them to the land you gave
to them and their ancestors.

26-27 When the skies shrivel up and there is no rain because your people have sinned against you, but then they pray at this place, acknowledging your rule and quit their sins because you have scourged them,

Listen from your home in heaven,
forgive the sins of your servants,
your people Israel.
Then start over with them;
train them to live right and well;
Send rain on the land
you gave as inheritance to your
people.

28-31 When disasters strike, famine or catastrophe, crop failure or disease, locust or beetle, or when an enemy attacks their defenses—calamity of any sort—any prayer that's prayed from anyone at all among your people Israel, their hearts penetrated by disaster, hands and arms thrown out for help to this Temple,

Listen from your home in heaven,
forgive and reward us:
reward each life and
circumstance,
For you know each life from the inside,
(you're the only one with such
inside knowledge!),
So they'll live before you in lifelong
reverence and believing
obedience on this land you gave
our ancestors.

32 And don't forget the foreigner who is not a member of your people Israel but has come from a far country because of your reputation—people are going to be attracted here by your great reputation, your wonderworking power—and who come to pray to this Temple.

33 Listen from your home in heaven
and honor the prayers of the
foreigner,
So that people all over the world
will know who you are and what
you're like,
And live in reverent obedience before
you,
just as your own people Israel do,

NEW KING JAMES VERSION

that they may know that this temple which I have built is called by Your name.

34“When Your people go out to battle against their enemies, wherever You send them, and when they pray to You toward this city which You have chosen and the temple which I have built for Your name, 35then hear from heaven their prayer and their supplication, and maintain their cause.

36“When they sin against You (for *there is* no one who does not sin), and You become angry with them and deliver them to the enemy, and they take them captive to a land far or near; 37*yet* when they come to themselves in the land where they were carried captive, and repent, and make supplication to You in the land of their captivity, saying, ‘We have sinned, we have done wrong, and have committed wickedness’; 38and *when* they return to You with all their heart and with all their soul in the land of their captivity, where they have been carried captive, and pray toward their land which You gave to their fathers, the city which You have chosen, and toward the temple which I have built for Your name: 39then hear from heaven Your dwelling place their prayer and their supplications, and maintain their cause, and forgive Your people who have sinned against You. 40Now, my God, I pray, let Your eyes be open and *let* Your ears *be* attentive to the prayer *made* in this place.

41“Now therefore,
Arise, O LORD God, to Your resting place,
You and the ark of Your strength.
Let Your priests, O LORD God, be clothed
with salvation,
And let Your saints rejoice in goodness.

42“O LORD God, do not turn away the face of
Your Anointed;
Remember the mercies of Your servant
David.”[a]

SOLOMON DEDICATES THE TEMPLE

7 When Solomon had finished praying, fire came down from heaven and consumed the burnt offering and the sacrifices; and the glory of the LORD filled the temple.[a] 2And the priests could not enter the house of the LORD, because the glory of the LORD had filled the LORD’s house. 3When all the children of Israel saw how the fire came down, and the glory of the LORD on the temple, they bowed their faces to the ground on the pavement, and worshiped and praised the LORD, *saying:*

6:42 [a]Compare Psalm 132:8–10 **7:1** [a]Literally *house*

THE MESSAGE

So they’ll know that you personally
make this Temple that I’ve built
what it is.

34-35 When your people go to war against their enemies at the time and place you send them and they pray to GOD toward the city you chose and The Temple I’ve built to honor your Name,

Listen from heaven to what they pray
and ask for
and do what is right for them.

36-39 When they sin against you—and they certainly will; there’s no one without sin!—and in anger you turn them over to the enemy and they are taken captive to the enemy’s land, whether far or near, but repent in the country of their captivity and pray with changed hearts in their exile, “We’ve sinned; we’ve done wrong; we’ve been most wicked,” and turn back to you heart and soul in the land of the enemy who conquered them, and pray to you toward their homeland, the land you gave their ancestors, toward the city you chose, and this Temple I have built to the honor of your Name,

Listen from your home in heaven
to their prayers desperate and devout;
Do what is best for them.
Forgive your people who have sinned
against you.

40 And now, dear God, be alert and attentive to prayer, all prayer, offered in this place.

41-42 Up, GOD, enjoy your new place of quiet
repose,
you and your mighty covenant Chest;
Dress your priests up in salvation clothes,
let your holy people celebrate
goodness.
And don’t, GOD, back out on your
anointed ones,
keep in mind the love promised to
David your servant.

THE TEMPLE DEDICATION

1-3 7 When Solomon finished praying, a bolt of lightning out of heaven struck the Whole-Burnt-Offering and sacrifices and the Glory of GOD filled The Temple. The Glory was so dense that the priests couldn’t get in—GOD so filled The Temple that there was no room for the priests! When all Israel saw the fire fall from heaven and the Glory of GOD fill The Temple, they fell on their knees, bowed their heads, and worshiped, thanking GOD:

NEW KING JAMES VERSION

"For *He is* good,
For His mercy *endures* forever."[a]

4Then the king and all the people offered
sacrifices before the LORD. 5King Solomon of-
fered a sacrifice of twenty-two thousand bulls
and one hundred and twenty thousand sheep.
So the king and all the people dedicated the
house of God. 6And the priests attended to their
services; the Levites also with instruments of
the music of the LORD, which King David had
made to praise the LORD, saying, "For His mercy
endures forever,"[a] whenever David offered
praise by their ministry. The priests sounded
trumpets opposite them, while all Israel stood.
7Furthermore Solomon consecrated the mid-
dle of the court that *was* in front of the house of
the LORD; for there he offered burnt offerings
and the fat of the peace offerings, because the
bronze altar which Solomon had made was not
able to receive the burnt offerings, the grain of-
ferings, and the fat.
8At that time Solomon kept the feast seven
days, and all Israel with him, a very great as-
sembly from the entrance of Hamath to the
Brook of Egypt.[a] 9And on the eighth day they
held a sacred assembly, for they observed the
dedication of the altar seven days, and the feast
seven days. 10On the twenty-third day of the sev-
enth month he sent the people away to their
tents, joyful and glad of heart for the good that
the LORD had done for David, for Solomon, and
for His people Israel. 11Thus Solomon finished
the house of the LORD and the king's house; and
Solomon successfully accomplished all that
came into his heart to make in the house of the
LORD and in his own house.

GOD'S SECOND APPEARANCE TO SOLOMON

12Then the LORD appeared to Solomon by
night, and said to him: "I have heard your
prayer, and have chosen this place for Myself as
a house of sacrifice. 13When I shut up heaven
and there is no rain, or command the locusts to
devour the land, or send pestilence among My
people, 14if My people who are called by My
name will humble themselves, and pray and
seek My face, and turn from their wicked ways,
then I will hear from heaven, and will forgive
their sin and heal their land. 15Now My eyes will
be open and My ears attentive to prayer *made* in
this place. 16For now I have chosen and sancti-
fied this house, that My name may be there for-
ever; and My eyes and My heart will be there
perpetually. 17As for you, if you walk before Me
as your father David walked, and do according
to all that I have commanded you, and if you
keep My statutes and My judgments, 18then I
will establish the throne of your kingdom, as I
covenanted with David your father, saying, 'You
shall not fail *to have* a man as ruler in Israel.'
19"But if you turn away and forsake My
statutes and My commandments which I have

7:3 [a]Compare Psalm 106:1 **7:6** [a]Compare Psalm 106:1 **7:8** [a]That is, the Shihor (compare 1 Chronicles 13:5)

THE MESSAGE

Yes! God is good!
His love never quits!

4-6 Then the king and all Israel worshiped, offering sacrifices to GOD. King Solomon worshiped by sacrificing 22,000 cattle and 120,000 sheep at the dedication of The Temple. The priests were all on duty; the choir and orchestra of Levites that David had provided for singing and playing anthems to the praise and love of GOD were all there; across the courtyard the priests blew trumpets. All Israelites were on their feet.

7-10 Solomon set apart the central area of the courtyard in front of GOD's Temple for sacred use and there sacrificed the Whole-Burnt-Offerings, Grain-Offerings, and fat from the Peace-Offerings—the Bronze Altar was too small to handle all these offerings. This is how Solomon kept the great autumn Feast of Booths. For seven days there were people there all the way from the far northeast (the Entrance to Hamath) to the far southwest (the Brook of Egypt)—a huge congregation. They started out celebrating for seven days, and then did it for another seven days, a week for dedicating the Altar and another for the Feast itself—two solid weeks of celebration! On the twenty-third day of the seventh month Solomon dismissed his congregation. They left rejoicing, exuberant over all the good GOD had done for David and Solomon and his people Israel.

GOD'S CONFIRMATION

11 Solomon completed building The Temple of GOD and the royal palace—the projects he had set his heart on doing. Everything was done—success! Satisfaction!

12-18 GOD appeared to Solomon that very night and said, "I accept your prayer; yes, I have chosen this place as a temple for sacrifice, a house of worship. If I ever shut off the supply of rain from the skies or order the locusts to eat the crops or send a plague on my people, and my people, my God-defined people, respond by humbling themselves, praying, seeking my presence, and turning their backs on their wicked lives, I'll be there ready for you: I'll listen from heaven, forgive their sins, and restore their land to health. From now on I'm alert day and night to the prayers offered at this place. Believe me, I've chosen and sanctified this Temple that you have built: My Name is stamped on it forever; my eyes are on it and my heart in it always. As for you, if you live in my presence as your father David lived, pure in heart and action, living the life I've set out for you, attentively obedient to my guidance and judgments, then I'll back your kingly rule over Israel—make it a sure thing on a sure foundation. The same covenant guarantee I gave to David your father I'm giving to you, namely, 'You can count on always having a descendant on Israel's throne.'

19-22 "But if you or your sons betray me, ignoring my guidance and judgments, taking up

NEW KING JAMES VERSION

set before you, and go and serve other gods, and worship them, 20then I will uproot them from My land which I have given them; and this house which I have sanctified for My name I will cast out of My sight, and will make it a proverb and a byword among all peoples.

21"And *as for* this house, which is exalted, everyone who passes by it will be astonished and say, 'Why has the LORD done thus to this land and this house?' 22Then they will answer, 'Because they forsook the LORD God of their fathers, who brought them out of the land of Egypt, and embraced other gods, and worshiped them and served them; therefore He has brought all this calamity on them.' "

SOLOMON'S ADDITIONAL ACHIEVEMENTS

8 It came to pass at the end of twenty years, when Solomon had built the house of the LORD and his own house, 2that the cities which Hiram[a] had given to Solomon, Solomon built them; and he settled the children of Israel there. 3And Solomon went to Hamath Zobah and seized it. 4He also built Tadmor in the wilderness, and all the storage cities which he built in Hamath. 5He built Upper Beth Horon and Lower Beth Horon, fortified cities *with* walls, gates, and bars, 6also Baalath and all the storage cities that Solomon had, and all the chariot cities and the cities of the cavalry, and all that Solomon desired to build in Jerusalem, in Lebanon, and in all the land of his dominion.

7All the people *who were* left of the Hittites, Amorites, Perizzites, Hivites, and Jebusites, who *were* not of Israel— 8that is, their descendants who were left in the land after them, whom the children of Israel did not destroy—from these Solomon raised forced labor, as it is to this day. 9But Solomon did not make the children of Israel servants for his work. Some *were* men of war, captains of his officers, captains of his chariots, and his cavalry. 10And others *were* chiefs of the officials of King Solomon: two hundred and fifty, who ruled over the people.

11Now Solomon brought the daughter of Pharaoh up from the City of David to the house he had built for her, for he said, "My wife shall not dwell in the house of David king of Israel, because *the places* to which the ark of the LORD has come are holy."

12Then Solomon offered burnt offerings to the LORD on the altar of the LORD which he had built before the vestibule, 13according to the daily rate, offering according to the commandment of Moses, for the Sabbaths, the New Moons, and the three appointed yearly feasts—the Feast of Unleavened Bread, the Feast of Weeks, and the Feast of Tabernacles. 14And, according to the order of David his father, he ap-

8:2 [a]Hebrew *Huram* (compare 2 Chronicles 2:3)

THE MESSAGE

with alien gods by serving and worshiping them, then the guarantee is off: I'll wipe Israel right off the map and repudiate this Temple I've just sanctified to honor my Name. And Israel will be nothing but a bad joke among the peoples of the world. And this Temple, splendid as it now is, will become an object of contempt; tourists will shake their heads, saying, 'What happened here? What's the story behind these ruins?' Then they'll be told, 'The people who used to live here betrayed their GOD, the very God who rescued their ancestors from Egypt; they took up with alien gods, worshiping and serving them. That's what's behind this God-visited devastation.' "

MORE ON SOLOMON

1-6 8 At the end of twenty years, Solomon had quite a list of accomplishments. He had:

built The Temple of GOD and his own palace;
rebuilt the cities that Hiram had given him and colonized them with Israelites;
marched on Hamath Zobah and took it;
fortified Tadmor in the desert and all the store-cities he had founded in Hamath;
built the fortress cities Upper Beth Horon and Lower Beth Horon, complete with walls, gates, and bars;
built Baalath and store-cities;
built chariot-cities for his horses.

Solomon built impulsively and extravagantly—whenever a whim took him. And in Jerusalem, in Lebanon—wherever he fancied.

7-10 The remnants from the original inhabitants of the land (Hittites, Amorites, Perizzites, Hivites, Jebusites—all non-Israelites), survivors of the holy wars, were rounded up by Solomon for his gangs of slave labor. The policy is in effect today. But true Israelites were not treated this way; they were used in his army and administration—government leaders and commanders of his chariots and charioteers. They were also the project managers responsible for Solomon's building operations—250 in all in charge of the workforce.

11 Solomon brought Pharaoh's daughter from the City of David to a house built especially for her, "Because," he said, "my wife cannot live in the house of David king of Israel, for the areas in which the Chest of GOD has entered are sacred."

12-13 Then Solomon offered Whole-Burnt-Offerings to GOD on the Altar of GOD that he had built in front of The Temple porch. He kept to the regular schedule of worship set down by Moses: Sabbaths, New Moons, and the three annual feasts of Unraised Bread (Passover), Weeks (Pentecost), and Booths.

14-15 He followed the practice of his father David in setting up groups of priests carry-

NEW KING JAMES VERSION

pointed the divisions of the priests for their service, the Levites for their duties (to praise and serve before the priests) as the duty of each day required, and the gatekeepers by their divisions at each gate; for so David the man of God had commanded. [15]They did not depart from the command of the king to the priests and Levites concerning any matter or concerning the treasuries.

[16]Now all the work of Solomon was well-ordered from[a] the day of the foundation of the house of the LORD until it was finished. So the house of the LORD was completed.

[17]Then Solomon went to Ezion Geber and Elath[a] on the seacoast, in the land of Edom. [18]And Hiram sent him ships by the hand of his servants, and servants who knew the sea. They went with the servants of Solomon to Ophir, and acquired four hundred and fifty talents of gold from there, and brought it to King Solomon.

THE QUEEN OF SHEBA'S PRAISE OF SOLOMON

9 Now when the queen of Sheba heard of the fame of Solomon, she came to Jerusalem to test Solomon with hard questions, *having* a very great retinue, camels that bore spices, gold in abundance, and precious stones; and when she came to Solomon, she spoke with him about all that was in her heart. [2]So Solomon answered all her questions; there was nothing so difficult for Solomon that he could not explain it to her. [3]And when the queen of Sheba had seen the wisdom of Solomon, the house that he had built, [4]the food on his table, the seating of his servants, the service of his waiters and their apparel, his cupbearers and their apparel, and his entryway by which he went up to the house of the LORD, there was no more spirit in her.

[5]Then she said to the king: "*It was* a true report which I heard in my own land about your words and your wisdom. [6]However I did not believe their words until I came and saw with my own eyes; and indeed the half of the greatness of your wisdom was not told me. You exceed the fame of which I heard. [7]Happy *are* your men and happy *are* these your servants, who stand continually before you and hear your wisdom! [8]Blessed be the LORD your God, who delighted in you, setting you on His throne *to be* king for the LORD your God! Because your God has loved Israel, to establish them forever, therefore He made you king over them, to do justice and righteousness."

[9]And she gave the king one hundred and twenty talents of gold, spices in great abundance, and precious stones; there never were any spices such as those the queen of Sheba gave to King Solomon.

[10]Also, the servants of Hiram and the servants of Solomon, who brought gold from Ophir, brought algum[a] wood and precious stones. [11]And the king made walkways *of* the algum[a] wood for the house of the LORD and for the

8:16 [a]Following Septuagint, Syriac, and Vulgate; Masoretic Text reads *as far as.* 8:17 [a]Hebrew *Eloth* (compare 2 Kings 14:22) 9:10 [a]Or *almug* (compare 1 Kings 10:11, 12) 9:11 [a]Or *almug* (compare 1 Kings 10:11, 12)

THE MESSAGE

ing out the work of worship, with the
Levites assigned to lead the sacred music
for praising God and to assist the priests in
the daily worship; he assigned security
guards to be on duty at each gate—that's
what David the man of God had ordered.
The king's directions to the priests and
Levites and financial stewards were kept
right down to the fine print—no innova-
tions—including the treasuries.
16 All that Solomon set out to do, from the
groundbreaking of The Temple of GOD to its
finish, was now complete.
17-18 Then Solomon went to Ezion Geber and
Elath on the coast of Edom. Hiram sent him
ships and with them veteran sailors. Joined
by Solomon's men they sailed to Ophir (in
east Africa), loaded on fifteen tons of gold,
and brought it back to King Solomon.

1-4 9 The queen of Sheba heard of Solomon's
reputation and came to Jerusalem to put
his reputation to the test, asking all the
tough questions. She made a showy en-
trance—an impressive retinue of attendants
and camels loaded with perfume and much
gold and precious stones. She emptied her
heart to Solomon, talking over everything
she cared about. And Solomon answered
everything she put to him—nothing
stumped him. When the queen of Sheba
experienced for herself Solomon's wisdom
and saw with her own eyes the palace he
had built, the meals that were served, the
impressive array of court officials, the
sharply dressed waiters, the cupbearers,
and then the elaborate worship extravagant
with Whole-Burnt-Offerings at The Temple
of GOD, it all took her breath away.
5-8 She said to the king, "It's all true! Your
reputation for accomplishment and wisdom
that reached all the way to my country is
confirmed. I wouldn't have believed it if I
hadn't seen it for myself; they didn't exag-
gerate! Such wisdom and elegance—far
more than I could ever have imagined.
Lucky the men and women who work for
you, getting to be around you every day and
hear your wise words firsthand! And
blessed be your GOD who has taken such a
liking to you, making you king. Clearly,
GOD's love for Israel is behind this, making
you king to keep a just order and nurture a
God-pleasing people."
9-11 She then gave the king four and a half
tons of gold and sack after sack of spices
and precious stones. There hasn't been a
cargo of spices like the shipload the queen
of Sheba brought to King Solomon. The
ships of Hiram also imported gold from
Ophir along with fragrant sandalwood and
expensive gems. The king used the sandal-
wood for fine cabinetry in The Temple of
GOD and the royal palace, and for making

NEW KING JAMES VERSION

king's house, also harps and stringed instru-
ments for singers; and there were none such *as*
these seen before in the land of Judah.
12Now King Solomon gave to the queen of
Sheba all she desired, whatever she asked,
much more than she had brought to the king. So
she turned and went to her own country, she
and her servants.

SOLOMON'S GREAT WEALTH

13The weight of gold that came to Solomon
yearly was six hundred and sixty-six talents of
gold, 14besides *what* the traveling merchants
and traders brought. And all the kings of Arabia
and governors of the country brought gold and
silver to Solomon. 15And King Solomon made
two hundred large shields of hammered gold;
six hundred *shekels* of hammered gold went
into each shield. 16*He* also *made* three hundred
shields of hammered gold; three hundred
shekels[a] of gold went into each shield. The king
put them in the House of the Forest of Lebanon.
17Moreover the king made a great throne of
ivory, and overlaid it with pure gold. 18The
throne *had* six steps, with a footstool of gold,
which were fastened to the throne; there were
armrests on either side of the place of the seat,
and two lions stood beside the armrests.
19Twelve lions stood there, one on each side of
the six steps; nothing like *this* had been made
for any *other* kingdom.
20All King Solomon's drinking vessels *were*
gold, and all the vessels of the House of the For-
est of Lebanon *were* pure gold. Not *one was* sil-
ver, for this was accounted as nothing in the
days of Solomon. 21For the king's ships went to
Tarshish with the servants of Hiram.[a] Once
every three years the merchant ships[b] came,
bringing gold, silver, ivory, apes, and monkeys.[c]
22So King Solomon surpassed all the kings of
the earth in riches and wisdom. 23And all the
kings of the earth sought the presence of
Solomon to hear his wisdom, which God had
put in his heart. 24Each man brought his present:
articles of silver and gold, garments, armor,
spices, horses, and mules, at a set rate year by
year.
25Solomon had four thousand stalls for
horses and chariots, and twelve thousand horse-
men whom he stationed in the chariot cities and
with the king at Jerusalem.
26So he reigned over all the kings from the
River[a] to the land of the Philistines, as far as the
border of Egypt. 27The king made silver *as com-*
mon in Jerusalem as stones, and he made cedar
trees as abundant as the sycamores which *are* in
the lowland. 28And they brought horses to
Solomon from Egypt and from all lands.

DEATH OF SOLOMON

29Now the rest of the acts of Solomon, first
and last, *are* they not written in the book of
Nathan the prophet, in the prophecy of Ahijah
the Shilonite, and in the visions of Iddo the
seer concerning Jeroboam the son of Nebat?

9:16 [a]Or *three minas* (compare 1 Kings 10:17) **9:21** [a]Hebrew *Huram* (compare 1 Kings 10:22) [b]Literally *ships of Tarshish* (deep-sea vessels) [c]Or *peacocks* **9:26** [a]That is, the Euphrates

THE MESSAGE

harps and dulcimers for the musicians.
Nothing like that shipment of sandalwood
has been seen since.
12 King Solomon, for his part, gave the
queen of Sheba all her heart's desire—
everything she asked for. She took away
more than she brought. Satisfied, she re-
turned home with her train of servants.

13-14 Solomon received twenty-five tons of gold
annually. This was above and beyond the
taxes and profit on trade with merchants and
traders. All kings of Arabia and various
and assorted governors also brought silver
and gold to Solomon.
15-16 King Solomon crafted two hundred body-
length shields of hammered gold—about fif-
teen pounds of gold to each shield—and
about three hundred small shields about
half that size. He stored the shields in the
House of the Forest of Lebanon.
17-19 The king made a massive throne of ivory
with a veneer of gold. The throne had six
steps leading up to it with an attached foot-
stool of gold. The armrests on each side
were flanked by lions. Lions, twelve of
them, were placed at either end of the six
steps. There was no throne like it in any
other kingdom.
20 King Solomon's chalices and tankards
were made of gold, and all the dinnerware
and serving utensils in the House of the For-
est of Lebanon were pure gold. Nothing was
made of silver; silver was considered com-
mon and cheap in the time of Solomon.
21 The king's ships, manned by Hiram's
sailors, made a round trip to Tarshish every
three years, returning with a cargo of gold,
silver, and ivory, apes and peacocks.
22-24 King Solomon was richer and wiser than
all the kings of the earth—he surpassed
them all. Kings came from all over the world
to be with Solomon and get in on the wis-
dom God had given him. Everyone who
came brought gifts—artifacts of gold and
silver, fashionable robes and gowns, the lat-
est in weapons, exotic spices, horses, and
mules—parades of visitors, year after year.
25-28 Solomon collected horses and chariots.
He had four thousand stalls for horses and
chariots, and twelve thousand horsemen in
barracks in the chariot-cities and in Jerusa-
lem. He ruled over all the kings from the
River Euphrates in the east, throughout
the Philistine country, and as far west as the
border of Egypt. The king made silver as
common as rocks and cedar as common as
the fig trees in the lowland hills. He carried
on a brisk horse-trading business with
Egypt and other places.

29-31 The rest of Solomon's life and rule, from start
to finish, one can read in the records of
Nathan the prophet, the prophecy of Ahijah
of Shiloh, and in the visions of Iddo the seer
concerning Jeroboam son of Nebat. Solomon

NEW KING JAMES VERSION

[30]Solomon reigned in Jerusalem over all Israel forty years. [31]Then Solomon rested with his fathers, and was buried in the City of David his father. And Rehoboam his son reigned in his place.

THE REVOLT AGAINST REHOBOAM

10 And Rehoboam went to Shechem, for all Israel had gone to Shechem to make him king. [2]So it happened, when Jeroboam the son of Nebat heard *it* (he was in Egypt, where he had fled from the presence of King Solomon), that Jeroboam returned from Egypt. [3]Then they sent for him and called him. And Jeroboam and all Israel came and spoke to Rehoboam, saying, [4]"Your father made our yoke heavy; now therefore, lighten the burdensome service of your father and his heavy yoke which he put on us, and we will serve you."

[5]So he said to them, "Come back to me after three days." And the people departed.

[6]Then King Rehoboam consulted the elders who stood before his father Solomon while he still lived, saying, "How do you advise *me* to answer these people?"

[7]And they spoke to him, saying, "If you are kind to these people, and please them, and speak good words to them, they will be your servants forever."

[8]But he rejected the advice which the elders had given him, and consulted the young men who had grown up with him, who stood before him. [9]And he said to them, "What advice do you give? How should we answer this people who have spoken to me, saying, 'Lighten the yoke which your father put on us'?"

[10]Then the young men who had grown up with him spoke to him, saying, "Thus you should speak to the people who have spoken to you, saying, 'Your father made our yoke heavy, but you make *it* lighter on us'—thus you shall say to them: 'My little *finger* shall be thicker than my father's waist! [11]And now, whereas my father put a heavy yoke on you, I will add to your yoke; my father chastised you with whips, but I *will chastise you* with scourges!' "[a]

[12]So Jeroboam and all the people came to Rehoboam on the third day, as the king had directed, saying, "Come back to me the third day." [13]Then the king answered them roughly. King Rehoboam rejected the advice of the elders, [14]and he spoke to them according to the advice of the young men, saying, "My father[a] made your yoke heavy, but I will add to it; my father chastised you with whips, but I *will chastise you* with scourges!"[b] [15]So the king did not listen to the people; for the turn *of events* was from God, that the LORD might fulfill His word, which He had spoken by the hand of Ahijah the Shilonite to Jeroboam the son of Nebat.

[16]Now when all Israel *saw* that the king did not listen to them, the people answered the king, saying:

"What share have we in David?
We have no inheritance in the son of Jesse.

10:11 [a]Literally *scorpions* **10:14** [a]Following many Hebrew manuscripts, Septuagint, Syriac, and Vulgate (compare verse 10 and 1 Kings 12:14); Masoretic Text reads *I.* [b]Literally *scorpions*

THE MESSAGE

ruled in Jerusalem over all Israel for forty years. Solomon died and was buried in the City of David his father. His son Rehoboam was the next king.

KING REHOBOAM

1-2 10 Rehoboam traveled to Shechem where all Israel had gathered to inaugurate him as king. Jeroboam was then in Egypt, where he had taken asylum from King Solomon; when he got the report of Solomon's death, he came back.

3-4 Summoned by Israel, Jeroboam and all Israel went to Rehoboam and said, "Your father made life hard for us—worked our fingers to the bone. Give us a break; lighten up on us and we'll willingly serve you."

5 "Give me," said Rehoboam, "three days to think it over; then come back." So the people left.

6 King Rehoboam talked it over with the elders who had advised his father when he was alive: "What's your counsel? How do you suggest that I answer the people?"

7 They said, "If you will be a servant to this people, be considerate of their needs and respond with compassion, work things out with them, they'll end up doing anything for you."

8-9 But he rejected the counsel of the elders and asked the young men he'd grown up with who were now currying his favor, "What do you think? What should I say to these people who are saying, 'Give us a break from your father's harsh ways—lighten up on us'?"

10-11 The young turks he'd grown up with said, "These people who complain, 'Your father was too hard on us; lighten up'—well, tell them this: 'My little finger is thicker than my father's waist. If you think life under my father was hard, you haven't seen the half of it. My father thrashed you with whips; I'll beat you bloody with chains!' "

12-14 Three days later Jeroboam and the people showed up, just as Rehoboam had directed when he said, "Give me three days to think it over; then come back." The king's answer was harsh and rude. He spurned the counsel of the elders and went with the advice of the younger set: "If you think life under my father was hard, you haven't seen the half of it: my father thrashed you with whips; I'll beat you bloody with chains!"

15 Rehoboam turned a deaf ear to the people. God was behind all this, confirming the message that he had given to Jeroboam son of Nebat through Ahijah of Shiloh.

16-17 When all Israel realized that the king hadn't listened to a word they'd said, they stood up to him and said,

Get lost, David!
We've had it with you, son of Jesse!

New King James Version

Every man to your tents, O Israel!
Now see to your own house, O David!"

So all Israel departed to their tents. 17But Rehoboam reigned over the children of Israel who dwelt in the cities of Judah.

18Then King Rehoboam sent Hadoram, who *was* in charge of revenue; but the children of Israel stoned him with stones, and he died. Therefore King Rehoboam mounted *his* chariot in haste to flee to Jerusalem. 19So Israel has been in rebellion against the house of David to this day.

11 Now when Rehoboam came to Jerusalem, he assembled from the house of Judah and Benjamin one hundred and eighty thousand chosen *men* who were warriors, to fight against Israel, that he might restore the kingdom to Rehoboam.

2But the word of the LORD came to Shemaiah the man of God, saying, 3"Speak to Rehoboam the son of Solomon, king of Judah, and to all Israel in Judah and Benjamin, saying, 4'Thus says the LORD: "You shall not go up or fight against your brethren! Let every man return to his house, for this thing is from Me." ' " Therefore they obeyed the words of the LORD, and turned back from attacking Jeroboam.

Rehoboam Fortifies the Cities

5So Rehoboam dwelt in Jerusalem, and built cities for defense in Judah. 6And he built Bethlehem, Etam, Tekoa, 7Beth Zur, Sochoh, Adullam, 8Gath, Mareshah, Ziph, 9Adoraim, Lachish, Azekah, 10Zorah, Aijalon, and Hebron, which are in Judah and Benjamin, fortified cities. 11And he fortified the strongholds, and put captains in them, and stores of food, oil, and wine. 12Also in every city *he put* shields and spears, and made them very strong, having Judah and Benjamin on his side.

Priests and Levites Move to Judah

13And from all their territories the priests and the Levites who *were* in all Israel took their stand with him. 14For the Levites left their common-lands and their possessions and came to Judah and Jerusalem, for Jeroboam and his sons had rejected them from serving as priests to the LORD. 15Then he appointed for himself priests for the high places, for the demons, and the calf idols which he had made. 16And after *the Levites left,*[a] those from all the tribes of Israel, such as set their heart to seek the LORD God of Israel, came to Jerusalem to sacrifice to the LORD God of their fathers. 17So they strengthened the kingdom of Judah, and made Rehoboam the son of Solomon strong for three years, because they walked in the way of David and Solomon for three years.

11:16 [a]Literally *after them*

The Message

Let's get out of here, Israel, and fast!
From now on, David, mind your own business.

And with that they left. Rehoboam continued to rule only those who lived in the towns of Judah.

18-19 When King Rehoboam next sent out Adoniram, head of the workforce, the Israelites ganged up on him, pelted him with stones, and killed him. King Rehoboam jumped in his chariot and escaped to Jerusalem as fast as he could. Israel has been in rebellion against the Davidic dynasty ever since.

1 11 When Rehoboam got back to Jerusalem he called up the men of the tribes of Judah and Benjamin, 180,000 of their best soldiers, to go to war against Israel and recover the kingdom.

2-4 At the same time the word of GOD came to Shemaiah, a holy man, "Tell this to Rehoboam son of Solomon, king of Judah, along with all the Israelites in Judah and Benjamin, This is GOD's word: Don't march out; don't fight against your brothers the Israelites. Go back home, every last one of you; *I'm* in charge here." And they did it; they did what GOD said and went home.

5-12 Rehoboam continued to live in Jerusalem but built up a defense system for Judah all around: in Bethlehem, Etam, Tekoa, Beth Zur, Soco, Adullam, Gath, Mareshah, Ziph, Adoraim, Lachish, Azekah, Zorah, Aijalon, and Hebron—a line of defense protecting Judah and Benjamin. He beefed up the fortifications, appointed commanders, and put in supplies of food, olive oil, and wine. He installed arms—large shields and spears—in all the forts, making them very strong. So Judah and Benjamin were secure for the time.

13-17 The priests and Levites from all over Israel came and made themselves available to Rehoboam. The Levites left their pastures and properties and moved to Judah and Jerusalem because Jeroboam and his sons had dismissed them from the priesthood of GOD and replaced them with his own priests to preside over the worship centers at which he had installed goat and calf demon-idols. Everyone from all the tribes of Israel who determined to seek the GOD of Israel migrated with the priests and Levites to Jerusalem to worship there, sacrificing to the GOD of their ancestors. That gave a tremendous boost to the kingdom of Judah. They stuck with Rehoboam son of Solomon for three years, loyal to the ways of David and Solomon for this period.

NEW KING JAMES VERSION

THE FAMILY OF REHOBOAM

[18]Then Rehoboam took for himself as wife Mahalath the daughter of Jerimoth the son of David, *and of* Abihail the daughter of Eliah the son of Jesse. [19]And she bore him children: Jeush, Shamariah, and Zaham. [20]After her he took Maachah the granddaughter[a] of Absalom; and she bore him Abijah, Attai, Ziza, and Shelomith. [21]Now Rehoboam loved Maachah the granddaughter of Absalom more than all his wives and his concubines; for he took eighteen wives and sixty concubines, and begot twenty-eight sons and sixty daughters. [22]And Rehoboam appointed Abijah the son of Maachah as chief, *to be* leader among his brothers; for he *intended* to make him king. [23]He dealt wisely, and dispersed some of his sons throughout all the territories of Judah and Benjamin, to every fortified city; and he gave them provisions in abundance. He also sought many wives *for them.*

EGYPT ATTACKS JUDAH

12 Now it came to pass, when Rehoboam had established the kingdom and had strengthened himself, that he forsook the law of the LORD, and all Israel along with him. [2]And it happened in the fifth year of King Rehoboam *that* Shishak king of Egypt came up against Jerusalem, because they had transgressed against the LORD, [3]with twelve hundred chariots, sixty thousand horsemen, and people without number who came with him out of Egypt—the Lubim and the Sukkiim and the Ethiopians. [4]And he took the fortified cities of Judah and came to Jerusalem.

[5]Then Shemaiah the prophet came to Rehoboam and the leaders of Judah, who were gathered together in Jerusalem because of Shishak, and said to them, "Thus says the LORD: 'You have forsaken Me, and therefore I also have left you in the hand of Shishak.' "

[6]So the leaders of Israel and the king humbled themselves; and they said, "The LORD *is* righteous."

[7]Now when the LORD saw that they humbled themselves, the word of the LORD came to Shemaiah, saying, "They have humbled themselves; *therefore* I will not destroy them, but I will grant them some deliverance. My wrath shall not be poured out on Jerusalem by the hand of Shishak. [8]Nevertheless they will be his servants, that they may distinguish My service from the service of the kingdoms of the nations."

[9]So Shishak king of Egypt came up against Jerusalem, and took away the treasures of the house of the LORD and the treasures of the king's house; he took everything. He also carried away the gold shields which Solomon had made. [10]Then King Rehoboam made bronze shields in their place, and committed *them* to the hands of the captains of the guard, who guarded the doorway of the king's house. [11]And whenever the king entered the house of the LORD, the guard would go and bring them out; then they would take them back into the guardroom.

11:20 [a]Literally *daughter,* but in the broader sense of granddaughter (compare 2 Chronicles 13:2)

THE MESSAGE

18-21 Rehoboam married Mahalath daughter of Jerimoth, David's son, and Abihail daughter of Eliab, Jesse's son. Mahalath bore him Jeush, Shemariah, and Zaham. Then he married Maacah, Absalom's daughter, and she bore him Abijah, Attai, Ziza, and Shelomith. Maacah was Rehoboam's favorite wife; he loved her more than all his other wives and concubines put together (and he had a lot—eighteen wives and sixty concubines who produced twenty-eight sons and sixty daughters!).

22-23 Rehoboam designated Abijah son of Maacah as the "first son" and leader of the brothers—he intended to make him the next king. He was shrewd in deploying his sons in all the fortress cities that made up his defense system in Judah and Benjamin; he kept them happy with much food and many wives.

1 12 By the time Rehoboam had secured his kingdom and was strong again, he, and all Israel with him, had virtually abandoned GOD and his ways.

2-4 In Rehoboam's fifth year, because he and the people were unfaithful to GOD, Shishak king of Egypt invaded as far as Jerusalem. He came with twelve hundred chariots and sixty thousand cavalry, and soldiers from all over—the Egyptian army included Libyans, Sukkites, and Ethiopians. They took the fortress cities of Judah and advanced as far as Jerusalem itself.

5 Then the prophet Shemaiah, accompanied by the leaders of Judah who had retreated to Jerusalem before Shishak, came to Rehoboam and said, "GOD's word: You abandoned me; now I abandon you to Shishak."

6 The leaders of Israel and the king were repentant and said, "GOD is right."

7-8 When GOD saw that they were humbly repentant, the word of GOD came to Shemaiah: "Because they are humble, I'll not destroy them—I'll give them a break; I won't use Shishak to express my wrath against Jerusalem. What I will do, though, is make them Shishak's subjects—they'll learn the difference between serving me and serving human kings."

9 Then Shishak king of Egypt attacked Jerusalem. He plundered the treasury of The Temple of GOD and the treasury of the royal palace—he took everything he could lay his hands on. He even took the gold shields that Solomon had made.

10-11 King Rehoboam replaced the gold shields with bronze shields and gave them to the guards who were posted at the entrance to the royal palace. Whenever the king went to GOD's Temple, the guards went with him carrying the shields, but they always returned them to the guardroom.

NEW KING JAMES VERSION

12When he humbled himself, the wrath of the LORD turned from him, so as not to destroy *him* completely; and things also went well in Judah.

THE END OF REHOBOAM'S REIGN

13Thus King Rehoboam strengthened himself in Jerusalem and reigned. Now Rehoboam *was* forty-one years old when he became king; and he reigned seventeen years in Jerusalem, the city which the LORD had chosen out of all the tribes of Israel, to put His name there. His mother's name *was* Naamah, an Ammonitess. 14And he did evil, because he did not prepare his heart to seek the LORD.

15The acts of Rehoboam, first and last, *are* they not written in the book of Shemaiah the prophet, and of Iddo the seer concerning genealogies? And *there were* wars between Rehoboam and Jeroboam all their days. 16So Rehoboam rested with his fathers, and was buried in the City of David. Then Abijah[a] his son reigned in his place.

ABIJAH REIGNS IN JUDAH

13 In the eighteenth year of King Jeroboam, Abijah became king over Judah. 2He reigned three years in Jerusalem. His mother's name *was* Michaiah[a] the daughter of Uriel of Gibeah.

And there was war between Abijah and Jeroboam. 3Abijah set the battle in order with an army of valiant warriors, four hundred thousand choice men. Jeroboam also drew up in battle formation against him with eight hundred thousand choice men, mighty men of valor.

4Then Abijah stood on Mount Zemaraim, which *is* in the mountains of Ephraim, and said, "Hear me, Jeroboam and all Israel: 5Should you not know that the LORD God of Israel gave the dominion over Israel to David forever, to him and his sons, by a covenant of salt? 6Yet Jeroboam the son of Nebat, the servant of Solomon the son of David, rose up and rebelled against his lord. 7Then worthless rogues gathered to him, and strengthened themselves against Rehoboam the son of Solomon, when Rehoboam was young and inexperienced and could not withstand them. 8And now you think to withstand the kingdom of the LORD, which is in the hand of the sons of David; and you *are* a great multitude, and with you are the gold calves which Jeroboam made for you as gods. 9Have you not cast out the priests of the LORD, the sons of Aaron, and the Levites, and made for yourselves priests, like the peoples of *other* lands, so that whoever comes to consecrate himself with a young bull and seven rams may be a priest of *things that are* not gods? 10But as for us, the LORD *is* our God, and we have not forsaken Him; and the priests who minister to the LORD *are* the sons of Aaron, and the Levites *attend* to *their* duties. 11And they burn to the LORD every morning and every evening burnt sacrifices and sweet incense; *they* also *set* the show-

12:16 [a]Spelled *Abijam* in 1 Kings 14:31 **13:2** [a]Spelled *Maachah* in 11:20, 21 and 1 Kings 15:2

THE MESSAGE

12 Because Rehoboam was repentant, GOD's
anger was blunted, so he wasn't totally destroyed. The picture wasn't entirely bleak—
there were some good things going on in Judah.
13-14 King Rehoboam regrouped and reestablished his rule in Jerusalem. He was forty-
one years old when he became king and
continued as king for seventeen years in
Jerusalem, the city GOD chose out of all the
tribes of Israel as the special presence of his
Name. His mother was Naamah from Ammon. But the final verdict on Rehoboam was
that he was a bad king—GOD was not important to him; his heart neither cared for nor
sought after GOD.
15-16 The history of Rehoboam, from start to
finish, is written in the memoirs of Shemaiah the prophet and Iddo the seer that contain the family trees. There was war between Rehoboam and Jeroboam the whole
time. Rehoboam died and was buried with
his ancestors in the City of David. His son
Abijah ruled after him.

KING ABIJAH

1-2 13 In the eighteenth year of the rule of
King Jeroboam, Abijah took over the
throne of Judah. He ruled in Jerusalem
three years. His mother was Maacah daughter of Uriel of Gibeah.
2-3 War broke out between Abijah and Jeroboam. Abijah started out with 400,000 of
his best soldiers; Jeroboam countered with
800,000 of his best.
4-7 Abijah took a prominent position on
Mount Zemaraim in the hill country of
Ephraim and gave this speech: "Listen, Jeroboam and all Israel! Don't you realize that
GOD, the one and only God of Israel, established David and his sons as the permanent
rulers of Israel, ratified by a 'covenant of
salt'—GOD's kingdom ruled by GOD's king?
And what happened? Jeroboam, the son of
Solomon's slave Nebat, rebelled against his
master. All the riffraff joined his cause and
were too much for Rehoboam, Solomon's
true heir. Rehoboam didn't know his way
around—besides he was a real wimp; he
couldn't stand up against them.
8-9 "Taking advantage of that weakness, you
are asserting yourself against the very rule of
GOD that is delegated to David's descendants—you think you are so big with your
huge army backed up by the golden-calf
idols that Jeroboam made for you as gods!
But just look at what you've done—you threw
out the priests of GOD, the sons of Aaron, and
the Levites, and made priests to suit yourselves, priests just like the pagans have. Anyone who shows up with enough money to
pay for it can be a priest! A priest of No-God!
10-11 "But for the rest of us in Judah, we're
sticking with GOD. We have not traded him
in for the latest model—we're keeping the
tried-and-true priests of Aaron to lead us to
GOD and the Levites to lead us in worship by
sacrificing Whole-Burnt-Offerings and aromatic incense to GOD at the daily morning

NEW KING JAMES VERSION

bread *in order on* the pure *gold* table, and the lampstand of gold with its lamps to burn every evening; for we keep the command of the LORD our God, but you have forsaken Him. [12]Now look, God Himself is with us as *our* head, and His priests with sounding trumpets to sound the alarm against you. O children of Israel, do not fight against the LORD God of your fathers, for you shall not prosper!"

[13]But Jeroboam caused an ambush to go around behind them; so they were in front of Judah, and the ambush *was* behind them. [14]And when Judah looked around, to their surprise the battle line *was* at both front and rear; and they cried out to the LORD, and the priests sounded the trumpets. [15]Then the men of Judah gave a shout; and as the men of Judah shouted, it happened that God struck Jeroboam and all Israel before Abijah and Judah. [16]And the children of Israel fled before Judah, and God delivered them into their hand. [17]Then Abijah and his people struck them with a great slaughter; so five hundred thousand choice men of Israel fell slain. [18]Thus the children of Israel were subdued at that time; and the children of Judah prevailed, because they relied on the LORD God of their fathers.

[19]And Abijah pursued Jeroboam and took cities from him: Bethel with its villages, Jeshanah with its villages, and Ephrain[a] with its villages. [20]So Jeroboam did not recover strength again in the days of Abijah; and the LORD struck him, and he died.

[21]But Abijah grew mighty, married fourteen wives, and begot twenty-two sons and sixteen daughters. [22]Now the rest of the acts of Abijah, his ways, and his sayings *are* written in the annals of the prophet Iddo.

14 So Abijah rested with his fathers, and they buried him in the City of David. Then Asa his son reigned in his place. In his days the land was quiet for ten years.

ASA REIGNS IN JUDAH

[2]Asa did *what was* good and right in the eyes of the LORD his God, [3]for he removed the altars of the foreign *gods* and the high places, and broke down the *sacred* pillars and cut down the wooden images. [4]He commanded Judah to seek the LORD God of their fathers, and to observe the law and the commandment. [5]He also removed the high places and the incense altars from all the cities of Judah, and the kingdom was quiet under him. [6]And he built fortified cities in Judah, for the land had rest; he had no war in those years, because the LORD had given him rest. [7]Therefore he said to Judah, "Let us build these cities and make walls around *them*, and towers, gates, and bars, *while* the land *is* yet before us, because we have sought the LORD our God; we have sought *Him*, and He has given us

13:19 [a]Or *Ephron*

THE MESSAGE

and evening prayers, setting out fresh holy
bread on a clean table, and lighting the lamps
on the golden Lampstand every night. We
continue doing what GOD told us to in the
way he told us to do it; but you have rid your-
selves of him.
12 "Can't you see the obvious? God is on our
side; he's our leader. And his priests with
trumpets are all ready to blow the signal to
battle. O Israel—don't fight against GOD, the
God of your ancestors. You will not win this
battle."
13-18 While Abijah was speaking, Jeroboam
had sent men around to take them by sur-
prise from the rear: Jeroboam in front of Ju-
dah and the ambush behind. When Judah
looked back, they saw they were attacked
front and back. They prayed desperately to
GOD, the priests blew their trumpets, and the
soldiers of Judah shouted their battle cry. At
the battle cry, God routed Jeroboam and all
Israel before Abijah and Judah. The army of
Israel scattered before Judah; God gave
them the victory. Abijah and his troops
slaughtered them—500,000 of Israel's best
fighters were killed that day. The army of Is-
rael fell flat on its face—a humiliating de-
feat. The army of Judah won hands down
because they trusted GOD, the God of their
ancestors.
19-21 Abijah followed up his victory by pursu-
ing Jeroboam, taking the towns of Bethel,
Jeshanah, and Ephron with their surround-
ing villages. Jeroboam never did recover
from his defeat while Abijah lived. Later on
GOD struck him down and he died. Mean-
while Abijah flourished; he married four-
teen wives and ended up with a family of
twenty-two sons and sixteen daughters.
22 The rest of the history of Abijah, what he
did and said, is written in the study written
by Iddo the prophet.

KING ASA

1 **14** Abijah died and was buried with his
ancestors in the City of David. His son
Asa became the next king.
For ten years into Asa's reign the country
was at peace.
2-6 Asa was a good king. He did things right
in GOD's eyes. He cleaned house: got rid of
the pagan altars and shrines, smashed the
sacred stone pillars, and chopped down the
sex-and-religion groves (Asherim). He told
Judah to center their lives in GOD, the God
of their fathers, to do what the law said, and
to follow the commandments. Because he
got rid of all the pagan shrines and altars in
the cities of Judah, his kingdom was at
peace. Because the land was quiet and there
was no war, he was able to build up a good
defense system in Judah. GOD kept the
peace.
7 Asa said to his people, "While we have
the chance and the land is quiet, let's build a
solid defense system, fortifying our cities
with walls, towers, gates, and bars. We have
this peaceful land because we sought GOD;

NEW KING JAMES VERSION

rest on every side." So they built and prospered. 8And Asa had an army of three hundred thousand from Judah who carried shields and spears, and from Benjamin two hundred and eighty thousand men who carried shields and drew bows; all these *were* mighty men of valor.

9Then Zerah the Ethiopian came out against them with an army of a million men and three hundred chariots, and he came to Mareshah. 10So Asa went out against him, and they set the troops in battle array in the Valley of Zephathah at Mareshah. 11And Asa cried out to the LORD his God, and said, "LORD, *it is* nothing for You to help, whether with many or with those who have no power; help us, O LORD our God, for we rest on You, and in Your name we go against this multitude. O LORD, You *are* our God; do not let man prevail against You!"

12So the LORD struck the Ethiopians before Asa and Judah, and the Ethiopians fled. 13And Asa and the people who *were* with him pursued them to Gerar. So the Ethiopians were overthrown, and they could not recover, for they were broken before the LORD and His army. And they carried away very much spoil. 14Then they defeated all the cities around Gerar, for the fear of the LORD came upon them; and they plundered all the cities, for there was exceedingly much spoil in them. 15They also attacked the livestock enclosures, and carried off sheep and camels in abundance, and returned to Jerusalem.

THE REFORMS OF ASA

15 Now the Spirit of God came upon Azariah the son of Oded. 2And he went out to meet Asa, and said to him: "Hear me, Asa, and all Judah and Benjamin. The LORD *is* with you while you are with Him. If you seek Him, He will be found by you; but if you forsake Him, He will forsake you. 3For a long time Israel *has been* without the true God, without a teaching priest, and without law; 4but when in their trouble they turned to the LORD God of Israel, and sought Him, He was found by them. 5And in those times *there was* no peace to the one who went out, nor to the one who came in, but great turmoil *was* on all the inhabitants of the lands. 6So nation was destroyed by nation, and city by city, for God troubled them with every adversity. 7But you, be strong and do not let your hands be weak, for your work shall be rewarded!"

8And when Asa heard these words and the prophecy of Oded[a] the prophet, he took courage, and removed the abominable idols from all the land of Judah and Benjamin and from the cities which he had taken in the mountains of Ephraim; and he restored the altar of the LORD that *was* before the vestibule of the LORD. 9Then he gathered all Judah and Benjamin, and those who dwelt with them from Ephraim, Manasseh, and Simeon, for they came over to him in great numbers from Israel when they saw that the LORD his God was with him.

15:8 [a]Following Masoretic Text and Septuagint; Syriac and Vulgate read *Azariah the son of Oded* (compare verse 1).

THE MESSAGE

he has given us rest from all troubles." So
they built and enjoyed prosperity.
8 Asa had an army of 300,000 Judeans,
equipped with shields and spears, and another 280,000 Benjaminites who were shield
bearers and archers. They were all courageous warriors.
9-11 Zerah the Ethiopian went to war against
Asa with an army of a million plus three
hundred chariots and got as far as Mareshah. Asa met him there and prepared to
fight from the Valley of Zephathah near
Mareshah. Then Asa prayed to GOD, "O
GOD, you aren't impressed by numbers or
intimidated by a show of force once you decide to help: Help us, O GOD; we have come
out to meet this huge army because we trust
in you and who you are. Don't let mere mortals stand against you!"
12-15 GOD defeated the Ethiopians before Asa
and Judah; the Ethiopians ran for their
lives. Asa and his men chased them as far as
Gerar; so many of the Ethiopians were
killed that there was no fight left in them—
a massacre before GOD and his troops; Judah carted off loads of plunder. They devastated all the towns around Gerar whose
people were helpless, paralyzed by the fear
of GOD, and looted the country. They also attacked herdsmen and brought back a lot of
sheep and camels to Jerusalem.

1-6 15 Then Azariah son of Obed, moved by
the Spirit of God, went out to meet
Asa. He said, "Listen carefully, Asa, and listen Judah and Benjamin: GOD will stick with
you as long as you stick with him. If you
look for him he will let himself be found; but
if you leave him he'll leave you. For a long
time Israel didn't have the real God, nor did
they have the help of priest or teacher or
book. But when they were in trouble and got
serious, and decided to seek GOD, the God of
Israel, GOD let himself be found. At that time
it was a dog-eat-dog world; life was constantly up for grabs—no one, regardless of
country, knew what the next day might
bring. Nation battered nation, city pummeled city. God let loose every kind of trouble among them.
7 "But it's different with you: Be strong.
Take heart. Payday is coming!"
8-9 Asa heard the prophecy of Azariah son of
Obed, took a deep breath, then rolled up his
sleeves, and went to work: He cleaned out
the obscene and polluting sacred shrines
from the whole country of Judah and Benjamin and from the towns he had taken in
the hill country of Ephraim. He spruced up
the Altar of GOD that was in front of The
Temple porch. Then he called an assembly
for all Judah and Benjamin, including those
from Ephraim, Manasseh, and Simeon who
were living there at the time (for many from
Israel had left their homes and joined forces
with Asa when they saw that GOD was on
his side).

NEW KING JAMES VERSION

10So they gathered together at Jerusalem in the third month, in the fifteenth year of the reign of Asa. 11And they offered to the LORD at that time seven hundred bulls and seven thousand sheep from the spoil they had brought. 12Then they entered into a covenant to seek the LORD God of their fathers with all their heart and with all their soul; 13and whoever would not seek the LORD God of Israel was to be put to death, whether small or great, whether man or woman. 14Then they took an oath before the LORD with a loud voice, with shouting and trumpets and rams' horns. 15And all Judah rejoiced at the oath, for they had sworn with all their heart and sought Him with all their soul; and He was found by them, and the LORD gave them rest all around.

16Also he removed Maachah, the mother of Asa the king, from *being* queen mother, because she had made an obscene image of Asherah;[a] and Asa cut down her obscene image, then crushed and burned *it* by the Brook Kidron. 17But the high places were not removed from Israel. Nevertheless the heart of Asa was loyal all his days.

18He also brought into the house of God the things that his father had dedicated and that he himself had dedicated: silver and gold and utensils. 19And there was no war until the thirty-fifth year of the reign of Asa.

ASA'S TREATY WITH SYRIA

16 In the thirty-sixth year of the reign of Asa, Baasha king of Israel came up against Judah and built Ramah, that he might let none go out or come in to Asa king of Judah. 2Then Asa brought silver and gold from the treasuries of the house of the LORD and of the king's house, and sent to Ben-Hadad king of Syria, who dwelt in Damascus, saying, 3"*Let there be* a treaty between you and me, as there was between my father and your father. See, I have sent you silver and gold; come, break your treaty with Baasha king of Israel, so that he will withdraw from me."

4So Ben-Hadad heeded King Asa, and sent the captains of his armies against the cities of Israel. They attacked Ijon, Dan, Abel Maim, and all the storage cities of Naphtali. 5Now it happened, when Baasha heard *it*, that he stopped building Ramah and ceased his work. 6Then King Asa took all Judah, and they carried away the stones and timber of Ramah, which Baasha had used for building; and with them he built Geba and Mizpah.

HANANI'S MESSAGE TO ASA

7And at that time Hanani the seer came to Asa king of Judah, and said to him: "Because you have relied on the king of Syria, and have not relied on the LORD your God, therefore the army of the king of Syria has escaped from your hand. 8Were the Ethiopians and the Lubim not a

15:16 [a]A Canaanite deity

THE MESSAGE

10-15 They all arrived in Jerusalem in the third month of the fifteenth year of Asa's reign for a great assembly of worship. From their earlier plunder they offered sacrifices of seven hundred oxen and seven thousand sheep for the worship. Then they bound themselves in a covenant to seek GOD, the God of their fathers, wholeheartedly, holding nothing back. And they agreed that anyone who refused to seek GOD, the God of Israel, should be killed, no matter who it was, young or old, man or woman. They shouted out their promise to GOD, a joyful sound accompanied with blasts from trumpets and rams' horns. The whole country felt good about the covenant promise—they had given their promise joyfully from the heart. Anticipating the best, they had sought God—and he showed up, ready to be found. GOD gave them peace within and without—a most peaceable kingdom!

16-19 In his cleanup of the country, Asa went so far as to remove his mother, Queen Maacah, from her throne because she had built a shockingly obscene image of the sex goddess Asherah. Asa tore it down, smashed it, and burned it up in the Kidron Valley. Unfortunately he didn't get rid of the local sex-and-religion shrines. But he was well-intentioned—his heart was in the right place, loyal to GOD. All the gold and silver vessels and artifacts that he and his father had consecrated for holy use he installed in The Temple of God. There wasn't a trace of war up to the thirty-fifth year of Asa's reign.

1 16 But in the thirty-sixth year of Asa's reign, Baasha king of Israel attacked. He started it by building a fort at Ramah and closing the border between Israel and Judah to keep Asa king of Judah from leaving or entering.

2-3 Asa took silver and gold from the treasuries of The Temple of GOD and the royal palace and sent it to Ben-Hadad, king of Aram who lived in Damascus, with this message: "Let's make a treaty like the one between our fathers. I'm showing my good faith with this gift of silver and gold. Break your deal with Baasha king of Israel so he'll quit fighting against me."

4-5 Ben-Hadad went along with King Asa and sent his troops against the towns of Israel. They sacked Ijon, Dan, Abel Maim, and all the store-cities of Naphtali. When Baasha got the report, he quit fortifying Ramah.

6 Then King Asa issued orders to his people in Judah to haul away the logs and stones Baasha had used in the fortification of Ramah and used them himself to fortify Geba and Mizpah.

7-9 Just after that, Hanani the seer came to Asa king of Judah and said, "Because you went for help to the king of Aram and didn't ask GOD for help, you've lost a victory over the army of the king of Aram. Didn't the Ethiopians and Libyans come against you

NEW KING JAMES VERSION

huge army with very many chariots and horsemen? Yet, because you relied on the LORD, He delivered them into your hand. 9For the eyes of the LORD run to and fro throughout the whole earth, to show Himself strong on behalf of *those* whose heart *is* loyal to Him. In this you have done foolishly; therefore from now on you shall have wars." 10Then Asa was angry with the seer, and put him in prison, for *he was* enraged at him because of this. And Asa oppressed *some* of the people at that time.

ILLNESS AND DEATH OF ASA

11Note that the acts of Asa, first and last, are indeed written in the book of the kings of Judah and Israel. 12And in the thirty-ninth year of his reign, Asa became diseased in his feet, and his malady was severe; yet in his disease he did not seek the LORD, but the physicians.

13So Asa rested with his fathers; he died in the forty-first year of his reign. 14They buried him in his own tomb, which he had made for himself in the City of David; and they laid him in the bed which was filled with spices and various ingredients prepared in a mixture of ointments. They made a very great burning for him.

JEHOSHAPHAT REIGNS IN JUDAH

17 Then Jehoshaphat his son reigned in his place, and strengthened himself against Israel. 2And he placed troops in all the fortified cities of Judah, and set garrisons in the land of Judah and in the cities of Ephraim which Asa his father had taken. 3Now the LORD was with Jehoshaphat, because he walked in the former ways of his father David; he did not seek the Baals, 4but sought the God[a] of his father, and walked in His commandments and not according to the acts of Israel. 5Therefore the LORD established the kingdom in his hand; and all Judah gave presents to Jehoshaphat, and he had riches and honor in abundance. 6And his heart took delight in the ways of the LORD; moreover he removed the high places and wooden images from Judah.

7Also in the third year of his reign he sent his leaders, Ben-Hail, Obadiah, Zechariah, Nethanel, and Michaiah, to teach in the cities of Judah. 8And with them *he sent* Levites: Shemaiah, Nethaniah, Zebadiah, Asahel, Shemiramoth, Jehonathan, Adonijah, Tobijah, and Tobadonijah—the Levites; and with them Elishama and Jehoram, the priests. 9So they taught in Judah, and *had* the Book of the Law of the LORD with them; they went throughout all the cities of Judah and taught the people.

10And the fear of the LORD fell on all the kingdoms of the lands that *were* around Judah, so that they did not make war against Jehoshaphat. 11Also *some* of the Philistines brought Jehoshaphat presents and silver as tribute; and the Arabians brought him flocks, seven thousand seven hundred rams and seven thousand seven hundred male goats.

12So Jehoshaphat became increasingly powerful, and he built fortresses and storage cities

17:4 [a]Septuagint reads *LORD God*.

THE MESSAGE

with superior forces, completely outclassing you with their chariots and cavalry? But you asked GOD for help and he gave you the victory. GOD is always on the alert, constantly on the lookout for people who are totally committed to him. You were foolish to go for human help when you could have had God's help. Now you're in trouble—one round of war after another."

10 At that, Asa lost his temper. Angry, he put
Hanani in the stocks. At the same time Asa
started abusing some of the people.

11-14 A full account of Asa is written in *The
Chronicles of the Kings of Judah.* In the
thirty-ninth year of his reign Asa came
down with a severe case of foot infection.
He didn't ask GOD for help, but went instead
to the doctors. Then Asa died; he died in the
forty-first year of his reign. They buried him
in a mausoleum that he had built for himself
in the City of David. They laid him in a crypt
full of aromatic oils and spices. Then they
had a huge bonfire in his memory.

JEHOSHAPHAT OF JUDAH

1-6 17 Asa's son Jehoshaphat was the next
king; he started out by working on his
defense system against Israel. He put troops
in all the fortress cities of Judah and deployed garrisons throughout Judah and in the towns of Ephraim that his father Asa had captured. GOD was on Jehoshaphat's side because he stuck to the ways of his father Asa's early years. He didn't fool around with the popular Baal religion—he was a seeker and follower of the God of his father and was obedient to him; he wasn't like Israel. And GOD secured the kingdom under his rule, gave him a firm grip on it. And everyone in Judah showed their appreciation by bringing gifts. Jehoshaphat ended up very rich and much honored. He was single-minded in following GOD; and he got rid of the local sex-and-religion shrines.

7-9 In the third year of his reign he sent his
officials—excellent men, every one of them—Ben-Hail, Obadiah, Zechariah, Nethanel, and Micaiah on a teaching mission to the cities of Judah. They were accompanied by Levites—Shemaiah, Nethaniah, Zebadiah, Asahel, Shemiramoth, Jehonathan, Adonijah, Tobijah, and Tob-Adonijah; the priests Elishama and Jehoram were also in the company. They made a circuit of the towns of Judah, teaching the people and using the Book of The Revelation of GOD as their text.

10-12 There was a strong sense of the fear of
GOD in all the kingdoms around Judah—they didn't dare go to war against Jehoshaphat. Some Philistines even brought gifts and a load of silver to Jehoshaphat, and the desert bedouin brought flocks—7,700 rams and 7,700 goats. So Jehoshaphat became stronger by the day, and con-

NEW KING JAMES VERSION

in Judah. 13He had much property in the cities of Judah; and the men of war, mighty men of valor, *were* in Jerusalem.

14These *are* their numbers, according to their fathers' houses. Of Judah, the captains of thousands: Adnah the captain, and with him three hundred thousand mighty men of valor; 15and next to him *was* Jehohanan the captain, and with him two hundred and eighty thousand; 16and next to him *was* Amasiah the son of Zichri, who willingly offered himself to the LORD, and with him two hundred thousand mighty men of valor. 17Of Benjamin: Eliada a mighty man of valor, and with him two hundred thousand men armed with bow and shield; 18and next to him *was* Jehozabad, and with him one hundred and eighty thousand prepared for war. 19These served the king, besides those the king put in the fortified cities throughout all Judah.

MICAIAH WARNS AHAB

18 Jehoshaphat had riches and honor in abundance; and by marriage he allied himself with Ahab. 2After some years he went down to *visit* Ahab in Samaria; and Ahab killed sheep and oxen in abundance for him and the people who were with him, and persuaded him to go up *with him* to Ramoth Gilead. 3So Ahab king of Israel said to Jehoshaphat king of Judah, "Will you go with me *against* Ramoth Gilead?"

And he answered him, "I *am* as you *are,* and my people as your people; *we will be* with you in the war."

4Also Jehoshaphat said to the king of Israel, "Please inquire for the word of the LORD today."

5Then the king of Israel gathered the prophets together, four hundred men, and said to them, "Shall we go to war against Ramoth Gilead, or shall I refrain?"

So they said, "Go up, for God will deliver it into the king's hand."

6But Jehoshaphat said, "*Is there* not still a prophet of the LORD here, that we may inquire of Him?"[a]

7So the king of Israel said to Jehoshaphat, "*There is* still one man by whom we may inquire of the LORD; but I hate him, because he never prophesies good concerning me, but always evil. He *is* Micaiah the son of Imla."

And Jehoshaphat said, "Let not the king say such things!"

8Then the king of Israel called one *of his* officers and said, "Bring Micaiah the son of Imla quickly!"

9The king of Israel and Jehoshaphat king of Judah, clothed in *their* robes, sat each on his throne; and they sat at a threshing floor at the entrance of the gate of Samaria; and all the prophets prophesied before them. 10Now Zedekiah the son of Chenaanah had made horns of iron for himself; and he said, "Thus says the LORD: 'With these you shall gore the Syrians until they are destroyed.' "

11And all the prophets prophesied so, saying, "Go up to Ramoth Gilead and prosper, for the LORD will deliver *it* into the king's hand."

18:6 [a]Or *him*

THE MESSAGE

structed more and more forts and store-
cities—an age of prosperity for Judah!
13-19 He also had excellent fighting men sta-
tioned in Jerusalem. The captains of the mil-
itary units of Judah, classified according to
families, were: Captain Adnah with 300,000
soldiers; his associate Captain Jehohanan
with 280,000; his associate Amasiah son of
Zicri, a volunteer for GOD, with 200,000. Of-
ficer Eliada represented Benjamin with
200,000 fully equipped with bow and shield;
and his associate was Jehozabad with
180,000 armed and ready for battle. These
were under the direct command of the king;
in addition there were the troops assigned
to the fortress cities spread all over Judah.

1-3 18 But even though Jehoshaphat was
very rich and much honored, he made
a marriage alliance with Ahab of Israel.
Some time later he paid a visit to Ahab at
Samaria. Ahab celebrated his visit with a
feast—a huge barbecue with all the lamb
and beef you could eat. But Ahab had a hid-
den agenda; he wanted Jehoshaphat's sup-
port in attacking Ramoth Gilead. Then Ahab
brought it into the open: "Will you join me in
attacking Ramoth Gilead?" Jehoshaphat
said, "You bet. I'm with you all the way; you
can count on me and my troops."
4 Then Jehoshaphat said, "But before you
do anything, ask GOD for guidance."
5 The king of Israel got the prophets to-
gether—all four hundred of them—and put
the question to them: "Should I attack
Ramoth Gilead or should I hold back?"
"Go for it," they said. "God will hand it
over to the king."
6 But Jehoshaphat dragged his feet, "Is
there another prophet of GOD around here
we can consult? Let's get a second opinion."
7 The king of Israel told Jehoshaphat, "As a
matter of fact, there is another. But I hate
him. He never preaches anything good to
me, only doom, doom, doom—Micaiah son
of Imlah."
"The king shouldn't talk about a prophet
like that!" said Jehoshaphat.
8 So the king of Israel ordered one of his
men, "Quickly, get Micaiah son of Imlah."
9-11 Meanwhile, the king of Israel and Je-
hoshaphat were seated on their thrones,
dressed in their royal robes, resplendent in
front of the Samaria city gates. All the
prophets were staging a prophecy-perform-
ance for their benefit. Zedekiah son of Ke-
naanah had even made a set of iron horns,
and brandishing them, called out, "GOD's
word! With these horns you'll gore Aram un-
til there's nothing left of them!" All the
prophets chimed in, "Yes! Go for Ramoth
Gilead! An easy victory! GOD's gift to the
king!"

NEW KING JAMES VERSION

12Then the messenger who had gone to call
Micaiah spoke to him, saying, "Now listen, the
words of the prophets with one accord encour-
age the king. Therefore please let your word be
like *the word of* one of them, and speak encour-
agement."
13And Micaiah said, "*As* the LORD lives,
whatever my God says, that I will speak."
14Then he came to the king; and the king said
to him, "Micaiah, shall we go to war against
Ramoth Gilead, or shall I refrain?"
And he said, "Go and prosper, and they shall
be delivered into your hand!"
15So the king said to him, "How many times
shall I make you swear that you tell me nothing
but the truth in the name of the LORD?"
16Then he said, "I saw all Israel scattered on
the mountains, as sheep that have no shepherd.
And the LORD said, 'These have no master. Let
each return to his house in peace.' "
17And the king of Israel said to Jehoshaphat,
"Did I not tell you he would not prophesy good
concerning me, but evil?"
18Then *Micaiah* said, "Therefore hear the
word of the LORD: I saw the LORD sitting on His
throne, and all the host of heaven standing on
His right hand and His left. 19And the LORD said,
'Who will persuade Ahab king of Israel to go up,
that he may fall at Ramoth Gilead?' So one
spoke in this manner, and another spoke in that
manner. 20Then a spirit came forward and stood
before the LORD, and said, 'I will persuade him.'
The LORD said to him, 'In what way?' 21So he
said, 'I will go out and be a lying spirit in the
mouth of all his prophets.' And *the LORD* said,
'You shall persuade *him* and also prevail; go out
and do so.' 22Therefore look! The LORD has put a
lying spirit in the mouth of these prophets of
yours, and the LORD has declared disaster
against you."
23Then Zedekiah the son of Chenaanah went
near and struck Micaiah on the cheek, and said,
"Which way did the spirit from the LORD go
from me to speak to you?"
24And Micaiah said, "Indeed you shall see on
that day when you go into an inner chamber to
hide!"
25Then the king of Israel said, "Take Micaiah,
and return him to Amon the governor of the city
and to Joash the king's son; 26and say, 'Thus
says the king: "Put this *fellow* in prison, and
feed him with bread of affliction and water of
affliction, until I return in peace." ' "

THE MESSAGE

12 The messenger who went to get Micaiah told him, "The prophets have all said Yes to the king. Make it unanimous—vote Yes!"

13 But Micaiah said, "As sure as GOD lives, what God says, I'll say."

14 With Micaiah before him, the king asked him, "So, Micaiah—do we attack Ramoth Gilead? Or do we hold back?"

"Go ahead," he said, "an easy victory! God's gift to the king."

15 "Not so fast," said the king. "How many times have I made you promise under oath to tell me the truth and nothing but the truth?"

16 "All right," said Micaiah, "since you insist . . .

I saw all of Israel scattered over the hills,
sheep with no shepherd.
Then GOD spoke, 'These poor people
have no one to tell them what to do.
Let them go home and do
the best they can for themselves.' "

17 The king of Israel turned to Jehoshaphat, "See! What did I tell you? He never has a good word for me from GOD, only doom."

18-21 Micaiah kept on, "I'm not done yet; listen to GOD's word:

I saw GOD enthroned,
and all the Angel Armies of heaven
standing at attention,
ranged on his right and his left.
And GOD said, "How can we seduce Ahab
into attacking Ramoth Gilead?"
Some said this,
and some said that.
Then a bold angel stepped out,
stood before GOD, and said,
"I'll seduce him."
"And how will you do it?" said GOD.
"Easy," said the angel,
"I'll get all the prophets to lie."
"That should do it," said GOD;
"On your way—seduce him!"

22 "And that's what has happened. GOD filled the mouths of your puppet prophets with seductive lies. GOD has pronounced your doom."

23 Just then Zedekiah son of Kenaanah came up and slapped Micaiah in the face, saying, "Since when did the Spirit of GOD leave me and take up with you?"

24 Micaiah said, "You'll know soon enough; you'll know it when you're frantically and futilely looking for a place to hide."

25-26 The king of Israel had heard enough: "Get Micaiah out of here! Turn him over to Amon the city magistrate and to Joash the king's son with this message: 'King's orders! Lock him up in jail; keep him on bread and water until I'm back in one piece.' "

NEW KING JAMES VERSION

27But Micaiah said, "If you ever return in
peace, the LORD has not spoken by me." And he
said, "Take heed, all you people!"

AHAB DIES IN BATTLE

28So the king of Israel and Jehoshaphat the
king of Judah went up to Ramoth Gilead. 29And
the king of Israel said to Jehoshaphat, "I will
disguise myself and go into battle; but you put
on your robes." So the king of Israel disguised
himself, and they went into battle.
30Now the king of Syria had commanded the
captains of the chariots who *were* with him, say-
ing, "Fight with no one small or great, but only
with the king of Israel."
31So it was, when the captains of the chariots
saw Jehoshaphat, that they said, "It *is* the king
of Israel!" Therefore they surrounded him to at-
tack; but Jehoshaphat cried out, and the LORD
helped him, and God diverted them from him.
32For so it was, when the captains of the chariots
saw that it was not the king of Israel, that they
turned back from pursuing him. 33Now a certain
man drew a bow at random, and struck the king
of Israel between the joints of his armor. So he
said to the driver of his chariot, "Turn around
and take me out of the battle, for I am
wounded." 34The battle increased that day, and
the king of Israel propped *himself* up in *his* char-
iot facing the Syrians until evening; and about
the time of sunset he died.

19 Then Jehoshaphat the king of Judah re-
turned safely to his house in Jerusalem.
2And Jehu the son of Hanani the seer went out
to meet him, and said to King Jehoshaphat,
"Should you help the wicked and love those who
hate the LORD? Therefore the wrath of the LORD
is upon you. 3Nevertheless good things are
found in you, in that you have removed the
wooden images from the land, and have pre-
pared your heart to seek God."

THE REFORMS OF JEHOSHAPHAT

4So Jehoshaphat dwelt at Jerusalem; and he
went out again among the people from Beer-
sheba to the mountains of Ephraim, and
brought them back to the LORD God of their fa-
thers. 5Then he set judges in the land through-
out all the fortified cities of Judah, city by city,
6and said to the judges, "Take heed to what you
are doing, for you do not judge for man but for
the LORD, who *is* with you in the judgment. 7Now
therefore, let the fear of the LORD be upon you;
take care and do *it*, for *there is* no iniquity with
the LORD our God, no partiality, nor taking of
bribes."
8Moreover in Jerusalem, for the judgment of
the LORD and for controversies, Jehoshaphat ap-
pointed some of the Levites and priests, and
some of the chief fathers of Israel, when they re-

THE MESSAGE

27 Micaiah said,

If you ever get back in one piece,
I'm no prophet of GOD.

He added,

When it happens, O people,
remember where you heard it!

28-29 So the king of Israel and Jehoshaphat king of Judah went ahead and attacked Ramoth Gilead. The king of Israel said to Jehoshaphat, "Wear my kingly robe; I'm going into battle disguised." So the king of Israel entered the battle in disguise.

30 Meanwhile, the king of Aram had ordered his chariot commanders (there were thirty-two of them), "Don't bother with anyone whether small or great; go after the king of Israel and him only."

31-32 When the chariot commanders saw Jehoshaphat, they said, "There he is! The king of Israel!" and took after him. Jehoshaphat yelled out, and the chariot commanders realized they had the wrong man—it wasn't the king of Israel after all. God intervened and they let him go.

33 Just then someone, without aiming, shot an arrow into the crowd and hit the king of Israel in the chink of his armor. The king told his charioteer, "Turn back! Get me out of here—I'm wounded."

34 All day the fighting continued, hot and heavy. Propped up in his chariot, the king watched from the sidelines. He died that evening.

1-3 19 But Jehoshaphat king of Judah got home safe and sound. Jehu, son of Hanani the seer, confronted King Jehoshaphat: "You have no business helping evil, cozying up to GOD-haters. Because you did this, GOD is good and angry with you. But you're not all bad—you made a clean sweep of the polluting sex-and-religion shrines; and you were single-minded in seeking God."

4 Jehoshaphat kept his residence in Jerusalem but made a regular round of visits among the people, from Beersheba in the south to Mount Ephraim in the north, urging them to return to GOD, the God of their ancestors.

5-7 And he was diligent in appointing judges in the land—each of the fortress cities had its judge. He charged the judges: "This is serious work; do it carefully. You are not merely judging between men and women; these are GOD's judgments that you are passing on. Live in the fear of GOD—be most careful, for GOD hates dishonesty, partiality, and bribery."

8-10 In Jerusalem Jehoshaphat also appointed Levites, priests, and family heads to decide on matters that had to do with worship and mediating local differences. He charged

NEW KING JAMES VERSION

turned to Jerusalem.[a] 9And he commanded them, saying, "Thus you shall act in the fear of the LORD, faithfully and with a loyal heart: 10Whatever case comes to you from your brethren who dwell in their cities, whether of bloodshed or offenses against law or commandment, against statutes or ordinances, you shall warn them, lest they trespass against the LORD and wrath come upon you and your brethren. Do this, and you will not be guilty. 11And take notice: Amariah the chief priest *is* over you in all matters of the LORD; and Zebadiah the son of Ishmael, the ruler of the house of Judah, for all the king's matters; also the Levites *will be* officials before you. Behave courageously, and the LORD will be with the good."

AMMON, MOAB, AND MOUNT SEIR DEFEATED

20 It happened after this *that* the people of Moab with the people of Ammon, and *others* with them besides the Ammonites,[a] came to battle against Jehoshaphat. 2Then some came and told Jehoshaphat, saying, "A great multitude is coming against you from beyond the sea, from Syria;[a] and they are in Hazazon Tamar" (which *is* En Gedi). 3And Jehoshaphat feared, and set himself to seek the LORD, and proclaimed a fast throughout all Judah. 4So Judah gathered together to ask *help* from the LORD; and from all the cities of Judah they came to seek the LORD.

5Then Jehoshaphat stood in the assembly of Judah and Jerusalem, in the house of the LORD, before the new court, 6and said: "O LORD God of our fathers, *are* You not God in heaven, and do You *not* rule over all the kingdoms of the nations, and in Your hand *is there not* power and might, so that no one is able to withstand You? 7*Are* You not our God, *who* drove out the inhabitants of this land before Your people Israel, and gave it to the descendants of Abraham Your friend forever? 8And they dwell in it, and have built You a sanctuary in it for Your name, saying, 9'If disaster comes upon us—sword, judgment, pestilence, or famine—we will stand before this temple and in Your presence (for Your name *is* in this temple), and cry out to You in our affliction, and You will hear and save.' 10And now, here are the people of Ammon, Moab, and Mount Seir—whom You would not let Israel invade when they came out of the land of Egypt, but they turned from them and did not destroy them— 11here they are, rewarding us by coming to throw us out of Your possession which You have given us to inherit. 12O our God, will You not judge them? For we have no power against this great multitude that is coming against us; nor do we know what to do, but our eyes *are* upon You."

13Now all Judah, with their little ones, their wives, and their children, stood before the LORD.

14Then the Spirit of the LORD came upon Jahaziel the son of Zechariah, the son of Benaiah,

19:8 [a]Septuagint and Vulgate read *for the inhabitants of Jerusalem.* **20:1** [a]Following Masoretic Text and Vulgate; Septuagint reads *Meunites* (compare 26:7). **20:2** [a]Following Masoretic Text, Septuagint, and Vulgate; some Hebrew manuscripts and Old Latin read *Edom.*

THE MESSAGE

them: "Do your work in the fear of GOD; be dependable and honest in your duties. When a case comes before you involving any of your fellow citizens, whether it seems large (like murder) or small (like matters of interpretation of the law), you are responsible for warning them that they are dealing with GOD. Make that explicit, otherwise both you and they are going to be dealing with GOD's wrath. Do your work well or you'll end up being as guilty as they are.

11 "Amariah the chief priest is in charge of
all cases regarding the worship of GOD; Zebadiah son of Ishmael, the leader of the tribe of Judah, is in charge of all civil cases; the Levites will keep order in the courts. Be bold and diligent. And GOD be with you as you do your best."

1-2 20 Some time later the Moabites and Ammonites, accompanied by Meunites,
joined forces to make war on Jeoshahphat.
Jehoshaphat received this intelligence report: "A huge force is on its way from beyond the Dead Sea to fight you. There's no time to waste—they're already at Hazazon
Tamar, the oasis of En Gedi."
3-4 Shaken, Jehoshaphat prayed. He went to
GOD for help and ordered a nationwide fast. The country of Judah united in seeking GOD's help—they came from all the cities of
Judah to pray to GOD.
5-9 Then Jehoshaphat took a position before
the assembled people of Judah and Jerusalem at The Temple of GOD in front of the new courtyard and said, "O GOD, God of our ancestors, are you not God in heaven above and ruler of all kingdoms below? You hold all power and might in your fist—no one stands a chance against you! And didn't you make the natives of this land leave as you brought your people Israel in, turning it over permanently to your people Israel, the descendants of Abraham your friend? They have lived here and built a holy house of worship to honor you, saying, 'When the worst happens—whether war or flood or disease or famine—and we take our place before this Temple (we know you are personally present in this place!) and pray out our pain and trouble, we know that you will
listen and give victory.'
10-12 "And now it's happened: men from Am-
mon, Moab, and Mount Seir have shown up. You didn't let Israel touch them when we got here at first—we detoured around them and didn't lay a hand on them. And now they've come to kick us out of the country you gave us. O dear God, won't you take care of them? We're helpless before this vandal horde ready to attack us. We don't know
what to do; we're looking to you."
13 Everyone in Judah was there—little chil-
dren, wives, sons—all present and attentive
to GOD.
14-17 Then Jahaziel was moved by the Spirit of
GOD to speak from the midst of the congregation. (Jahaziel was the son of Zechariah, the son of Benaiah, the son of Jeiel, the son

NEW KING JAMES VERSION

the son of Jeiel, the son of Mattaniah, a Levite of the sons of Asaph, in the midst of the assembly. [15]And he said, "Listen, all you of Judah and you inhabitants of Jerusalem, and you, King Jehoshaphat! Thus says the LORD to you: 'Do not be afraid nor dismayed because of this great multitude, for the battle *is* not yours, but God's. [16]Tomorrow go down against them. They will surely come up by the Ascent of Ziz, and you will find them at the end of the brook before the Wilderness of Jeruel. [17]You will not *need* to fight in this *battle.* Position yourselves, stand still and see the salvation of the LORD, who is with you, O Judah and Jerusalem!' Do not fear or be dismayed; tomorrow go out against them, for the LORD *is* with you."

[18]And Jehoshaphat bowed his head with *his* face to the ground, and all Judah and the inhabitants of Jerusalem bowed before the LORD, worshiping the LORD. [19]Then the Levites of the children of the Kohathites and of the children of the Korahites stood up to praise the LORD God of Israel with voices loud and high.

[20]So they rose early in the morning and went out into the Wilderness of Tekoa; and as they went out, Jehoshaphat stood and said, "Hear me, O Judah and you inhabitants of Jerusalem: Believe in the LORD your God, and you shall be established; believe His prophets, and you shall prosper." [21]And when he had consulted with the people, he appointed those who should sing to the LORD, and who should praise the beauty of holiness, as they went out before the army and were saying:

"Praise the LORD,
For His mercy *endures* forever."[a]

[22]Now when they began to sing and to praise, the LORD set ambushes against the people of Ammon, Moab, and Mount Seir, who had come against Judah; and they were defeated. [23]For the people of Ammon and Moab stood up against the inhabitants of Mount Seir to utterly kill and destroy *them.* And when they had made an end of the inhabitants of Seir, they helped to destroy one another.

[24]So when Judah came to a place overlooking the wilderness, they looked toward the multitude; and there *were* their dead bodies, fallen on the earth. No one had escaped.

[25]When Jehoshaphat and his people came to take away their spoil, they found among them an abundance of valuables on the dead bodies,[a] and precious jewelry, which they stripped off for themselves, more than they could carry away; and they were three days gathering the spoil because there was so much. [26]And on the fourth day they assembled in the Valley of Berachah, for there they blessed the LORD; therefore the name of that place was called The Valley of Berachah[a] until this day. [27]Then they returned, every man of Judah and Jerusalem, with Jehoshaphat in front of them, to go back to Jerusalem with joy, for the LORD had made them rejoice over their enemies. [28]So they came to Jerusalem, with stringed instruments and harps and trumpets, to the house of the LORD.

20:21 [a]Compare Psalm 106:1 **20:25** [a]A few Hebrew manuscripts, Old Latin, and Vulgate read *garments;* Septuagint reads *armor.* **20:26** [a]Literally *Blessing*

THE MESSAGE

of Mattaniah the Levite of the Asaph clan.)
He said, "Attention everyone—all of you
from out of town, all you from Jerusalem,
and you King Jehoshaphat—GOD's word:
Don't be afraid; don't pay any mind to this
vandal horde. This is God's war, not yours.
Tomorrow you'll go after them; see, they're
already on their way up the slopes of Ziz;
you'll meet them at the end of the ravine
near the wilderness of Jeruel. You won't
have to lift a hand in this battle; just stand
firm, Judah and Jerusalem, and watch GOD's
saving work for you take shape. Don't be
afraid, don't waver. March out boldly tomorrow—GOD is with you."
18-19 Then Jehoshaphat knelt down, bowing
with his face to the ground. All Judah and
Jerusalem did the same, worshiping GOD.
The Levites (both Kohathites and Korahites)
stood to their feet to praise GOD, the God of
Israel; they praised at the top of their lungs!
20 They were up early in the morning, ready
to march into the wilderness of Tekoa. As
they were leaving, Jehoshaphat stood up
and said, "Listen Judah and Jerusalem! Listen to what I have to say! Believe firmly in
GOD, your God, and your lives will be firm!
Believe in your prophets and you'll come
out on top!"
21 After talking it over with the people, Jehoshaphat appointed a choir for GOD;
dressed in holy robes, they were to march
ahead of the troops, singing,

Give thanks to GOD,
His love never quits.

22-23 As soon as they started shouting and
praising, GOD set ambushes against the men
of Ammon, Moab, and Mount Seir as they
were attacking Judah, and they all ended up
dead. The Ammonites and Moabites mistakenly attacked those from Mount Seir and
massacred them. Then, further confused,
they went at each other, and all ended up
killed.
24 As Judah came up over the rise, looking
into the wilderness for the horde of barbarians, they looked on a killing field of dead
bodies—not a living soul among them.
25-26 When Jehoshaphat and his people came
to carry off the plunder they found more
loot than they could carry off—equipment,
clothing, valuables. It took three days to cart
it away! On the fourth day they came together at the Valley of Blessing (Beracah)
and blessed GOD (that's how it got the name,
Valley of Blessing).
27-28 Jehoshaphat then led all the men of Judah and Jerusalem back to Jerusalem—an
exuberant parade. GOD had given them joyful relief from their enemies! They entered
Jerusalem and came to The Temple of GOD
with all the instruments of the band playing.

NEW KING JAMES VERSION

29 And the fear of God was on all the kingdoms of *those* countries when they heard that the LORD had fought against the enemies of Israel. 30 Then the realm of Jehoshaphat was quiet, for his God gave him rest all around.

THE END OF JEHOSHAPHAT'S REIGN

31 So Jehoshaphat was king over Judah. *He was* thirty-five years old when he became king, and he reigned twenty-five years in Jerusalem. His mother's name *was* Azubah the daughter of Shilhi. 32 And he walked in the way of his father Asa, and did not turn aside from it, doing *what was* right in the sight of the LORD. 33 Nevertheless the high places were not taken away, for as yet the people had not directed their hearts to the God of their fathers.

34 Now the rest of the acts of Jehoshaphat, first and last, indeed they *are* written in the book of Jehu the son of Hanani, which *is* mentioned in the book of the kings of Israel.

35 After this Jehoshaphat king of Judah allied himself with Ahaziah king of Israel, who acted very wickedly. 36 And he allied himself with him to make ships to go to Tarshish, and they made the ships in Ezion Geber. 37 But Eliezer the son of Dodavah of Mareshah prophesied against Jehoshaphat, saying, "Because you have allied yourself with Ahaziah, the LORD has destroyed your works." Then the ships were wrecked, so that they were not able to go to Tarshish.

JEHORAM REIGNS IN JUDAH

21 And Jehoshaphat rested with his fathers, and was buried with his fathers in the City of David. Then Jehoram his son reigned in his place. 2 He had brothers, the sons of Jehoshaphat: Azariah, Jehiel, Zechariah, Azaryahu, Michael, and Shephatiah; all these *were* the sons of Jehoshaphat king of Israel. 3 Their father gave them great gifts of silver and gold and precious things, with fortified cities in Judah; but he gave the kingdom to Jehoram, because he *was* the firstborn.

4 Now when Jehoram was established over the kingdom of his father, he strengthened himself and killed all his brothers with the sword, and also *others* of the princes of Israel.

5 Jehoram *was* thirty-two years old when he became king, and he reigned eight years in Jerusalem. 6 And he walked in the way of the kings of Israel, just as the house of Ahab had done, for he had the daughter of Ahab as a wife; and he did evil in the sight of the LORD. 7 Yet the LORD would not destroy the house of David, because of the covenant that He had made with David, and since He had promised to give a lamp to him and to his sons forever.

8 In his days Edom revolted against Judah's authority, and made a king over themselves. 9 So Jehoram went out with his officers, and all his chariots with him. And he rose by night and attacked the Edomites who had surrounded him and the captains of the chariots. 10 Thus Edom has been in revolt against Judah's authority to this day. At that time Libnah revolted against his

THE MESSAGE

29-30 When the surrounding kingdoms got word that GOD had fought Israel's enemies, the fear of God descended on them. Jehoshaphat heard no more from them; as long as Jehoshaphat reigned, peace reigned.

31-33 That about sums up Jehoshaphat's reign over Judah. He was thirty-five years old when he became king and ruled as king in Jerusalem for twenty-five years. His mother was Azubah daughter of Shilhi. He continued the kind of life characteristic of his father Asa—no detours, no dead-ends—pleasing GOD with his life. But he failed to get rid of the neighborhood sex-and-religion shrines—people continued to pray and worship at these idolatrous god shops.

34 The rest of Jehoshaphat's life, from start to finish, is written in the memoirs of Jehu son of Hanani, which are included in the *Royal Annals of Israel's Kings*.

35-37 Late in life Jehoshaphat formed a trading syndicate with Ahaziah king of Israel—which was very wrong of him to do. He went in as partner with him to build ocean-going ships at Ezion Geber to trade with Tarshish. Eliezer son of Dodavahu of Mareshah preached against Jehoshaphat's venture: "Because you joined forces with Ahaziah, GOD has shipwrecked your work." The ships were smashed and nothing ever came of the trade partnership.

1 21 Jehoshaphat died and was buried in the family cemetery in the City of David. Jehoram his son was the next king.

KING JEHORAM

2-4 Jehoram's brothers were Azariah, Jehiel, Zechariah, Azariahu, Michael, and Shephatiah—the sons of Jehoshaphat king of Judah. Their father had lavished them with gifts—silver, gold, and other valuables, plus the fortress cities in Judah. But Jehoram was his firstborn son and he gave him the kingdom of Judah. But when Jehoram had taken over his father's kingdom and had secured his position, he killed all his brothers along with some of the government officials.

5-7 Jehoram was thirty-two years old when he became king and ruled in Jerusalem for eight years. He imitated Israel's kings and married into the Ahab dynasty. GOD considered him an evil man. But despite that, because of his covenant with David, GOD was not yet ready to destroy the descendants of David; he had, after all, promised to keep a light burning for David and his sons.

8-9 During Jehoram's reign, Edom revolted from Judah's rule and set up their own king. Jehoram responded by setting out with his officers and chariots. Edom surrounded him, but in the middle of the night he and his charioteers broke through the lines and hit Edom hard.

10-11 Edom continues in revolt against Judah right up to the present. Even little Libnah re-

NEW KING JAMES VERSION

rule, because he had forsaken the LORD God of his fathers. 11 Moreover he made high places in the mountains of Judah, and caused the inhabitants of Jerusalem to commit harlotry, and led Judah astray.

12 And a letter came to him from Elijah the prophet, saying,

> Thus says the LORD God of your father David:
> Because you have not walked in the ways of Jehoshaphat your father, or in the ways of Asa king of Judah, 13 but have walked in the way of the kings of Israel, and have made Judah and the inhabitants of Jerusalem to play the harlot like the harlotry of the house of Ahab, and also have killed your brothers, those of your father's household, *who were* better than yourself, 14 behold, the LORD will strike your people with a serious affliction—your children, your wives, and all your possessions; 15 and you *will become* very sick with a disease of your intestines, until your intestines come out by reason of the sickness, day by day.

16 Moreover the LORD stirred up against Jehoram the spirit of the Philistines and the Arabians who *were* near the Ethiopians. 17 And they came up into Judah and invaded it, and carried away all the possessions that were found in the king's house, and also his sons and his wives, so that there was not a son left to him except Jehoahaz,[a] the youngest of his sons.

18 After all this the LORD struck him in his intestines with an incurable disease. 19 Then it happened in the course of time, after the end of two years, that his intestines came out because of his sickness; so he died in severe pain. And his people made no burning for him, like the burning for his fathers.

20 He was thirty-two years old when he became king. He reigned in Jerusalem eight years and, to no one's sorrow, departed. However they buried him in the City of David, but not in the tombs of the kings.

AHAZIAH REIGNS IN JUDAH

22 Then the inhabitants of Jerusalem made Ahaziah his youngest son king in his place, for the raiders who came with the Arabians into the camp had killed all the older *sons*. So Ahaziah the son of Jehoram, king of Judah, reigned. 2 Ahaziah *was* forty-two[a] years old when he became king, and he reigned one year in Jerusalem. His mother's name *was* Athaliah the granddaughter of Omri. 3 He also walked in the ways of the house of Ahab, for his mother advised him to do wickedly. 4 Therefore he did evil in the sight of the LORD, like the house of Ahab; for they were his counselors after the death of his father, to his destruction. 5 He also followed their advice, and went with Jehoram[a] the son of Ahab king of Israel to war against Hazael king of Syria at Ramoth Gilead; and the

21:17 [a]Elsewhere called *Ahaziah* (compare 2 Chronicles 22:1) **22:2** [a]Or *twenty-two* (compare 2 Kings 8:26) **22:5** [a]Also spelled *Joram* (compare verses 5 and 7; 2 Kings 8:28; and elsewhere)

THE MESSAGE

volted at that time. The evidence accumu-
lated: Since Jehoram had abandoned GOD,
the God of his ancestors, God was abandon-
ing him. He even went so far as to build pa-
gan sacred shrines in the mountains of Ju-
dah. He brazenly led Jerusalem away from
God, seducing the whole country.

12-15 One day he got a letter from Elijah the
prophet. It read, "From GOD, the God of your
ancestor David—a message: Because you
have not kept to the ways of Jehoshaphat
your father and Asa your grandfather, kings
of Judah, but have taken up with the ways of
the kings of Israel in the north, leading Ju-
dah and Jerusalem away from God, going
step by step down the apostate path of Ahab
and his crew—why, you even killed your
own brothers, all of them better men than
you!—GOD is going to afflict your people,
your wives, your sons, and everything you
have with a terrible plague. And you are go-
ing to come down with a terrible disease of
the colon, painful and humiliating."

16-20 The trouble started with an invasion. GOD
incited the Philistines and the Arabs who
lived near the Ethiopians to attack Jehoram.
They came to the borders of Judah, forced
their way in, and plundered the place—rob-
bing the royal palace of everything in it in-
cluding his wives and sons. One son, his
youngest, Ahaziah, was left behind. The ter-
rible and fatal disease in his colon followed.
After about two years he was totally incon-
tinent and died writhing in pain. His people
didn't honor him by lighting a great bonfire,
as was customary with his ancestors. He
was thirty-two years old when he became
king and reigned for eight years in Jerusa-
lem. There were no tears shed when he
died—it was good riddance!—and they
buried him in the City of David, but not in
the royal cemetery.

KING AHAZIAH

1-6 22 The people of Jerusalem made Aha-
ziah, Jehoram's youngest son, king.
Raiders from the desert, who had come with
the Arabs against the settlement, had killed
all the older sons. That's how Ahaziah son
of Jehoram king of Judah became king.
Ahaziah was twenty-two years old when he
became king, but reigned only one year in
Jerusalem. His mother was Athaliah, grand-
daughter of Omri. He lived and ruled just
like the Ahab family had done, his mother
training him in evil ways. GOD also consid-
ered him evil, related by both marriage and
sin to the Ahab clan. After the death of his
father, he attended the sin school of Ahab,
and graduated with a degree in doom. He
did what they taught him, went with Joram
son of Ahab king of Israel in the war against
Hazael king of Aram at Ramoth Gilead. Jo-

NEW KING JAMES VERSION

Syrians wounded Joram. 6Then he returned to Jezreel to recover from the wounds which he had received at Ramah, when he fought against Hazael king of Syria. And Azariah[a] the son of Jehoram, king of Judah, went down to see Jehoram the son of Ahab in Jezreel, because he was sick.

7His going to Joram was God's occasion for Ahaziah's downfall; for when he arrived, he went out with Jehoram against Jehu the son of Nimshi, whom the LORD had anointed to cut off the house of Ahab. 8And it happened, when Jehu was executing judgment on the house of Ahab, and found the princes of Judah and the sons of Ahaziah's brothers who served Ahaziah, that he killed them. 9Then he searched for Ahaziah; and they caught him (he was hiding in Samaria), and brought him to Jehu. When they had killed him, they buried him, "because," they said, "he is the son of Jehoshaphat, who sought the LORD with all his heart."

So the house of Ahaziah had no one to assume power over the kingdom.

ATHALIAH REIGNS IN JUDAH

10Now when Athaliah the mother of Ahaziah saw that her son was dead, she arose and destroyed all the royal heirs of the house of Judah. 11But Jehoshabeath,[a] the daughter of the king, took Joash the son of Ahaziah, and stole him away from among the king's sons who were being murdered, and put him and his nurse in a bedroom. So Jehoshabeath, the daughter of King Jehoram, the wife of Jehoiada the priest (for she was the sister of Ahaziah), hid him from Athaliah so that she did not kill him. 12And he was hidden with them in the house of God for six years, while Athaliah reigned over the land.

JOASH CROWNED KING OF JUDAH

23 In the seventh year Jehoiada strengthened himself, *and made a* covenant with the captains of hundreds: Azariah the son of Jeroham, Ishmael the son of Jehohanan, Azariah the son of Obed, Maaseiah the son of Adaiah, and Elishaphat the son of Zichri. 2And they went throughout Judah and gathered the Levites from all the cities of Judah, and the chief fathers of Israel, and they came to Jerusalem.

3Then all the assembly made a covenant with the king in the house of God. And he said to them, "Behold, the king's son shall reign, as the LORD has said of the sons of David. 4This *is* what you shall do: One-third of you entering on the Sabbath, of the priests and the Levites, *shall be* keeping watch over the doors; 5one-third *shall be* at the king's house; and one-third at the Gate of the Foundation. All the people *shall be* in the courts of the house of the LORD. 6But let no one come into the house of the LORD except the priests and those of the Levites who serve.

22:6 [a]Some Hebrew manuscripts, Septuagint, Syriac, Vulgate, and 2 Kings 8:29 read *Ahaziah.* **22:11** [a]Spelled *Jehosheba* in 2 Kings 11:2

THE MESSAGE

ram, wounded by the Arameans, retreated
to Jezreel to recover from the wounds he re-
ceived in Ramah in his war with Hazael
king of Aram. Ahaziah son of Jehoram king
of Judah paid a visit to Joram son of Ahab
on his sickbed at Jezreel.
7-9 The fate of Ahaziah when he went to visit
was God's judgment on him. When Ahaziah
arrived at Jezreel, he and Joram met with
Jehu son of Nimshi, whom GOD had already
authorized to destroy the dynasty of Ahab.
Jehu, already at work, executing doom on
the dynasty of Ahab, came upon the cap-
tains of Judah and Ahaziah's nephews, part
of the Ahaziah delegation, and killed them
outright. Then he sent out a search party
looking for Ahaziah himself. They found
him hiding out in Samaria and hauled him
back to Jehu. And Jehu killed him.
They didn't, though, just leave his body
there. Out of respect for his grandfather Je-
hoshaphat, famous as a sincere seeker after
GOD, they gave him a decent burial. But
there was no one left in Ahaziah's family ca-
pable of ruling the kingdom.

QUEEN ATHALIAH

10-12 When Ahaziah's mother Athaliah saw that
her son was dead, she took over. She began
by massacring the entire royal family. Je-
hosheba, daughter of King Jehoram, took
Ahaziah's son Joash, and kidnapped him
from among the king's sons slated for
slaughter. She hid him and his nurse in a
private room away from Athaliah. So Je-
hosheba, daughter of King Jehoram and
Ahaziah's sister—she was also the wife of
Jehoiada the priest—saved Joash from the
murderous Queen Athaliah. He was there
with her, hidden away for six years in The
Temple of God. Athaliah, oblivious to his ex-
istence, ruled the country.

1-3 23 In the seventh year the priest Jehoiada
decided to make his move and worked
out a strategy with certain influential offi-
cers in the army. He picked Azariah son of
Jeroham, Ishmael son of Jehohanan, Aza-
riah son of Obed, Maaseiah son of Adaiah,
and Elishaphat son of Zicri as his associ-
ates. They dispersed throughout Judah and
called in the Levites from all the towns in
Judah along with the heads of families.
They met in Jerusalem. The gathering met
in The Temple of God. They made a cove-
nant there in The Temple.
3-7 The priest Jehoiada showed them the
young prince and addressed them: "Here he
is—the son of the king. He is going to rule
just as GOD promised regarding the sons of
David. Now this is what you must do: A
third of you priests and Levites who come
on duty on the Sabbath are to be posted as
security guards at the gates; another third
will guard the palace; and the other third
will guard the foundation gate. All the peo-
ple will gather in the courtyards of The Tem-
ple of GOD. No one may enter The Temple of
GOD except the priests and designated

NEW KING JAMES VERSION

They may go in, for they *are* holy; but all the
people shall keep the watch of the LORD. 7And
the Levites shall surround the king on all sides,
every man with his weapons in his hand; and
whoever comes into the house, let him be put to
death. You are to be with the king when he
comes in and when he goes out."
8So the Levites and all Judah did according
to all that Jehoiada the priest commanded. And
each man took his men who were to be on duty
on the Sabbath, with those who were going *off
duty* on the Sabbath; for Jehoiada the priest had
not dismissed the divisions. 9And Jehoiada the
priest gave to the captains of hundreds the
spears and the large and small shields which
had belonged to King David, that *were* in the
temple of God. 10Then he set all the people,
every man with his weapon in his hand, from
the right side of the temple to the left side of the
temple, along by the altar and by the temple, all
around the king. 11And they brought out the
king's son, put the crown on him, *gave him* the
Testimony,[a] and made him king. Then Jehoiada
and his sons anointed him, and said, "*Long* live
the king!"

DEATH OF ATHALIAH

12Now when Athaliah heard the noise of the
people running and praising the king, she came
to the people *in* the temple of the LORD. 13*When*
she looked, there was the king standing by his
pillar at the entrance; and the leaders and the
trumpeters *were* by the king. All the people of
the land were rejoicing and blowing trumpets,
also the singers with musical instruments, and
those who led in praise. So Athaliah tore her
clothes and said, "Treason! Treason!"
14And Jehoiada the priest brought out the
captains of hundreds who were set over the
army, and said to them, "Take her outside under
guard, and slay with the sword whoever follows
her." For the priest had said, "Do not kill her in
the house of the LORD."
15So they seized her; and she went by way of
the entrance of the Horse Gate *into* the king's
house, and they killed her there.
16Then Jehoiada made a covenant between
himself, the people, and the king, that they
should be the LORD's people. 17And all the peo-
ple went to the temple[a] of Baal, and tore it
down. They broke in pieces its altars and im-
ages, and killed Mattan the priest of Baal before
the altars. 18Also Jehoiada appointed the over-
sight of the house of the LORD to the hand of the
priests, the Levites, whom David had assigned
in the house of the LORD, to offer the burnt offer-
ings of the LORD, as *it is* written in the Law of
Moses, with rejoicing and with singing, *as it
was established* by David. 19And he set the gate-
keepers at the gates of the house of the LORD, so
that no one *who was* in any way unclean should
enter.
20Then he took the captains of hundreds, the
nobles, the governors of the people, and all the
people of the land, and brought the king down
from the house of the LORD; and they went

23:11 [a]That is, the Law (compare Exodus 25:16, 21; 31:18)
23:17 [a]Literally *house*

THE MESSAGE

Levites—they are permitted in because they've been consecrated, but all the people must do the work assigned them. The Levites are to form a ring around the young king, weapons at the ready. Kill anyone who tries to break through your ranks. Your job is to stay with the king at all times and places, coming and going."

8-10 All the Levites and officers obeyed the orders of Jehoiada the priest. Each took charge of his men, both those who came on duty on the Sabbath and those who went off duty on the Sabbath, for Jehoiada the priest hadn't exempted any of them from duty. Then the priest armed the officers with spears and the large and small shields originally belonging to King David that were stored in The Temple of God. Well-armed, the guards took up their assigned positions for protecting the king, from one end of The Temple to the other, surrounding both Altar and Temple.

11 Then the priest brought the prince into view, crowned him, handed him the scroll of God's covenant, and made him king. As Jehoiada and his sons anointed him they shouted, "Long live the king!"

12-13 Athaliah, hearing all the commotion, the people running around and praising the king, came to The Temple to see what was going on. Astonished, she saw the young king standing at the entrance flanked by the captains and heralds, with everybody beside themselves with joy, trumpets blaring, the choir and orchestra leading the praise. Athaliah ripped her robes in dismay and shouted, "Treason! Treason!"

14-15 Jehoiada the priest ordered the military officers, "Drag her outside—and kill anyone who tries to follow her!" (The priest had said, "Don't kill her inside The Temple of GOD.") So they dragged her out to the palace's horse corral and there they killed her.

16 Jehoiada now made a covenant between himself and the king and the people: they were to be GOD's special people.

17 The people poured into the temple of Baal and tore it down, smashing altar and images to smithereens. They killed Mattan the priest of Baal in front of the altar.

18-21 Jehoiada turned the care of GOD's Temple over to the priests and Levites, the way David had directed originally. They were to offer the Whole-Burnt-Offerings of GOD as set out in The Revelation of Moses, and with praise and song as directed by David. He also assigned security guards at the gates of GOD's Temple so that no one who was unprepared could enter. Then he got everyone together—officers, nobles, governors, and the people themselves—and escorted the king down from The Temple of GOD, through the

NEW KING JAMES VERSION

through the Upper Gate to the king's house, and set the king on the throne of the kingdom. [21]So all the people of the land rejoiced; and the city was quiet, for they had slain Athaliah with the sword.

JOASH REPAIRS THE TEMPLE

24 Joash *was* seven years old when he became king, and he reigned forty years in Jerusalem. His mother's name *was* Zibiah of Beersheba. [2]Joash did *what was* right in the sight of the LORD all the days of Jehoiada the priest. [3]And Jehoiada took two wives for him, and he had sons and daughters.

[4]Now it happened after this *that* Joash set his heart on repairing the house of the LORD. [5]Then he gathered the priests and the Levites, and said to them, "Go out to the cities of Judah, and gather from all Israel money to repair the house of your God from year to year, and see that you do it quickly."

However the Levites did not do it quickly. [6]So the king called Jehoiada the chief *priest*, and said to him, "Why have you not required the Levites to bring in from Judah and from Jerusalem the collection, *according to the commandment* of Moses the servant of the LORD and of the assembly of Israel, for the tabernacle of witness?" [7]For the sons of Athaliah, that wicked woman, had broken into the house of God, and had also presented all the dedicated things of the house of the LORD to the Baals.

[8]Then at the king's command they made a chest, and set it outside at the gate of the house of the LORD. [9]And they made a proclamation throughout Judah and Jerusalem to bring to the LORD the collection *that* Moses the servant of God *had imposed* on Israel in the wilderness. [10]Then all the leaders and all the people rejoiced, brought their contributions, and put *them* into the chest until all had given. [11]So it was, at that time, when the chest was brought to the king's official by the hand of the Levites, and when they saw that *there was* much money, that the king's scribe and the high priest's officer came and emptied the chest, and took it and returned it to its place. Thus they did day by day, and gathered money in abundance.

[12]The king and Jehoiada gave it to those who did the work of the service of the house of the LORD; and they hired masons and carpenters to repair the house of the LORD, and also those who worked in iron and bronze to restore the house of the LORD. [13]So the workmen labored, and the work was completed by them; they restored the house of God to its original condition and reinforced it. [14]When they had finished, they brought the rest of the money before the king and Jehoiada; they made from it articles for the house of the LORD, articles for serving and offering, spoons and vessels of gold and silver. And they offered burnt offerings in the house of the LORD continually all the days of Jehoiada.

APOSTASY OF JOASH

[15]But Jehoiada grew old and was full of days, and he died; *he was* one hundred and thirty years old when he died. [16]And they buried him in the City of David among the kings, because

THE MESSAGE

Upper Gate, and placed him on the royal throne. Everybody celebrated the event. And the city was safe and undisturbed—Athaliah had been killed; no more Athaliah terror.

KING JOASH

1 **24** Joash was seven years old when he became king; he was king for forty years in Jerusalem. His mother's name was Gazelle (Zibiah). She was from Beersheba.

2-3 Taught and trained by Jehoiada the priest, Joash did what pleased GOD throughout Jehoiada's lifetime. Jehoiada picked out two wives for him; he had a family of both sons and daughters.

4-6 The time came when Joash determined to renovate The Temple of GOD. He got the priests and Levites together and said, "Circulate through the towns of Judah every year and collect money from the people to repair The Temple of your God. You are in charge of carrying this out." But the Levites dragged their feet and didn't do anything.

7 Then the king called in Jehoiada the chief priest and said, "Why haven't you made the Levites bring in from Judah and Jerusalem the tax Moses, servant of GOD and the congregation, set for the upkeep of the place of worship? You can see how bad things are—wicked Queen Athaliah and her sons let The Temple of God go to ruin and took all its sacred artifacts for use in Baal worship."

8-9 Following the king's orders, they made a chest and placed it at the entrance to The Temple of GOD. Then they sent out a tax notice throughout Judah and Jerusalem: "Pay the tax that Moses the servant of GOD set when Israel was in the wilderness."

10 The people and their leaders were glad to do it and cheerfully brought their money until the chest was full.

11-14 Whenever the Levites brought the chest in for a royal audit and found it to be full, the king's secretary and the official of the chief priest would empty the chest and put it back in its place. Day after day they did this and collected a lot of money. The king and Jehoiada gave the money to the managers of The Temple project; they in turn paid the masons and carpenters for the repair work on The Temple of GOD. The construction workers kept at their jobs steadily until the restoration was complete—the house of GOD as good as new! When they had finished the work, they returned the surplus money to the king and Jehoiada, who used the money for making sacred vessels for Temple worship, vessels for the daily worship, for the Whole-Burnt-Offerings, bowls, and other gold and silver liturgical artifacts.

14-16 Whole-Burnt-Offerings were made regularly in The Temple of GOD throughout Jehoiada's lifetime. He died at a ripe old age—130 years old! They buried him in the royal cemetery because he had such a distin-

NEW KING JAMES VERSION

he had done good in Israel, both toward God and His house.

[17]Now after the death of Jehoiada the leaders of Judah came and bowed down to the king. And the king listened to them. [18]Therefore they left the house of the LORD God of their fathers, and served wooden images and idols; and wrath came upon Judah and Jerusalem because of their trespass. [19]Yet He sent prophets to them, to bring them back to the LORD; and they testified against them, but they would not listen.

[20]Then the Spirit of God came upon Zechariah the son of Jehoiada the priest, who stood above the people, and said to them, "Thus says God: 'Why do you transgress the commandments of the LORD, so that you cannot prosper? Because you have forsaken the LORD, He also has forsaken you.'" [21]So they conspired against him, and at the command of the king they stoned him with stones in the court of the house of the LORD. [22]Thus Joash the king did not remember the kindness which Jehoiada his father had done to him, but killed his son; and as he died, he said, "The LORD look on *it*, and repay!"

DEATH OF JOASH

[23]So it happened in the spring of the year *that* the army of Syria came up against him; and they came to Judah and Jerusalem, and destroyed all the leaders of the people from among the people, and sent all their spoil to the king of Damascus. [24]For the army of the Syrians came with a small company of men; but the LORD delivered a very great army into their hand, because they had forsaken the LORD God of their fathers. So they executed judgment against Joash. [25]And when they had withdrawn from him (for they left him severely wounded), his own servants conspired against him because of the blood of the sons[a] of Jehoiada the priest, and killed him on his bed. So he died. And they buried him in the City of David, but they did not bury him in the tombs of the kings.

[26]These are the ones who conspired against him: Zabad[a] the son of Shimeath the Ammonitess, and Jehozabad the son of Shimrith[b] the Moabitess. [27]Now *concerning* his sons, and the many oracles about him, and the repairing of the house of God, indeed they *are* written in the annals of the book of the kings. Then Amaziah his son reigned in his place.

AMAZIAH REIGNS IN JUDAH

25 Amaziah *was* twenty-five years old *when* he became king, and he reigned twenty-nine years in Jerusalem. His mother's name *was* Jehoaddan of Jerusalem. [2]And he did *what was* right in the sight of the LORD, but not with a loyal heart.

[3]Now it happened, as soon as the kingdom was established for him, that he executed his servants who had murdered his father the king. [4]However he did not execute their children, but

24:25 [a]Septuagint and Vulgate read *son* (compare verses 20–22).
24:26 [a]Or *Jozachar* (compare 2 Kings 12:21) [b]Or *Shomer* (compare 2 Kings 12:21)

THE MESSAGE

guished life of service to Israel and God and God's Temple.

17-19 But after the death of Jehoiada things fell
apart. The leaders of Judah made a formal
presentation to the king and he went along
with them. Things went from bad to worse;
they deserted The Temple of GOD and took
up with the cult of sex goddesses. An angry
cloud hovered over Judah and Jerusalem
because of this sin. GOD sent prophets to
straighten them out, warning of judgment.
But nobody paid attention.
20 Then the Spirit of God moved Zechariah
son of Jehoiada the priest to speak up:
"God's word: Why have you deliberately
walked away from GOD's commandments?
You can't live this way! If you walk out on
GOD, he'll walk out on you."
21-22 But they worked out a plot against
Zechariah, and with the complicity of the
king—he actually gave the order!—they
murdered him, pelting him with rocks, right
in the court of The Temple of GOD. That's the
thanks King Joash showed the loyal Je-
hoiada, the priest who had made him king.
He murdered Jehoiada's son. Zechariah's
last words were, "Look, GOD! Make them
pay for this!"
23-24 A year or so later Aramean troops at-
tacked Joash. They invaded Judah and
Jerusalem, massacred the leaders, and
shipped all their plunder back to the king in
Damascus. The Aramean army was quite
small, but GOD used them to wipe out
Joash's large army—their punishment for
deserting GOD, the God of their ancestors.
Arameans implemented God's judgment
against Joash.
25-27 They left Joash badly wounded and his
own servants finished him off—it was a
palace conspiracy, avenging the murder of
the son of Jehoiada the priest. They killed
him in his bed. Afterward they buried him in
the City of David, but he was not honored
with a grave in the royal cemetery. The tem-
ple conspirators were Zabad, whose mother
was Shimeath from Ammon, and Jehoz-
abad, whose mother was Shimrith from
Moab. The story of his sons, the many ser-
mons preached to Joash, and the account of
his repairs on The Temple of God can be
found contained in the commentary on the
royal history.

Amaziah, Joash's son, was the next king.

KING AMAZIAH

1-4 **25** Amaziah was twenty-five years old
when he became king and reigned
twenty-nine years in Jerusalem. His mother
was Jehoaddin from Jerusalem. He lived
well before GOD, doing the right thing for
the most part. But he wasn't wholeheartedly
devoted to God. When he had the affairs of
the kingdom well in hand, he executed the
palace guard who had assassinated his fa-
ther the king. But he didn't kill the sons of

NEW KING JAMES VERSION

did as *it is* written in the Law in the Book of Moses, where the LORD commanded, saying, "The fathers shall not be put to death for their children, nor shall the children be put to death for their fathers; but a person shall die for his own sin."[a]

THE WAR AGAINST EDOM

5 Moreover Amaziah gathered Judah together and set over them captains of thousands and captains of hundreds, according to *their* fathers' houses, throughout all Judah and Benjamin; and he numbered them from twenty years old and above, and found them to be three hundred thousand choice *men, able* to go to war, who could handle spear and shield. 6 He also hired one hundred thousand mighty men of valor from Israel for one hundred talents of silver. 7 But a man of God came to him, saying, "O king, do not let the army of Israel go with you, for the LORD *is* not with Israel—*not with* any of the children of Ephraim. 8 But if you go, be gone! Be strong in battle! *Even so,* God shall make you fall before the enemy; for God has power to help and to overthrow."

9 Then Amaziah said to the man of God, "But what *shall we* do about the hundred talents which I have given to the troops of Israel?"

And the man of God answered, "The LORD is able to give you much more than this." 10 So Amaziah discharged the troops that had come to him from Ephraim, to go back home. Therefore their anger was greatly aroused against Judah, and they returned home in great anger.

11 Then Amaziah strengthened himself, and leading his people, he went to the Valley of Salt and killed ten thousand of the people of Seir. 12 Also the children of Judah took captive ten thousand alive, brought them to the top of the rock, and cast them down from the top of the rock, so that they all were dashed in pieces.

13 But as for the soldiers of the army which Amaziah had discharged, so that they would not go with him to battle, they raided the cities of Judah from Samaria to Beth Horon, killed three thousand in them, and took much spoil.

14 Now it was so, after Amaziah came from the slaughter of the Edomites, that he brought the gods of the people of Seir, set them up *to be* his gods, and bowed down before them and burned incense to them. 15 Therefore the anger of the LORD was aroused against Amaziah, and He sent him a prophet who said to him, "Why have you sought the gods of the people, which could not rescue their own people from your hand?"

16 So it was, as he talked with him, that *the king* said to him, "Have we made you the king's counselor? Cease! Why should you be killed?"

Then the prophet ceased, and said, "I know that God has determined to destroy you, because you have done this and have not heeded my advice."

ISRAEL DEFEATS JUDAH

17 Now Amaziah king of Judah asked advice and sent to Joash[a] the son of Jehoahaz, the son

25:4 [a]Deuteronomy 24:16 **25:17** [a]Spelled *Jehoash* in 2 Kings 14:8ff

THE MESSAGE

the assassins—he was mindful of what GOD commanded in The Revelation of Moses, that parents shouldn't be executed for their childrens' sins, nor children for their parents'. We each pay personally for our sins.

5-6 Amaziah organized Judah and sorted out Judah and Benjamin by families and by military units. Men twenty years and older had to register—they ended up with 300,000 judged capable of military service. In addition he hired 100,000 soldiers from Israel in the north at a cost of about four and a half tons of silver.

7-8 A holy man showed up and said, "No, O King—don't let those northern Israelite soldiers into your army; GOD is not on their side, nor with any of the Ephraimites. Instead, you go by yourself and be strong. God and God only has the power to help or hurt your cause."

9 But Amaziah said to the holy man, "But what about all this money—these tons of silver I have already paid out to hire these men?"

"GOD's help is worth far more to you than that," said the holy man.

10 So Amaziah fired the soldiers he had hired from the north and sent them home. They were very angry at losing their jobs and went home seething.

11-12 But Amaziah was optimistic. He led his troops into the Valley of Salt and killed ten thousand men of Seir. They took another ten thousand as prisoners, led them to the top of the Rock, and pushed them off a cliff. They all died in the fall, smashed on the rocks.

13 But the troops Amaziah had dismissed from his army, angry over their lost opportunity for plunder, rampaged through the towns of Judah all the way from Samaria to Beth Horon, killing three thousand people and taking much plunder.

14-15 On his return from the destruction of the Edomites, Amaziah brought back the gods of the men of Seir and installed them as his own gods, worshiping them and burning incense to them. *That* ignited GOD's anger; a fiery blast of GOD's wrath put into words by a God-sent prophet: "What is this? Why on earth would you pray to inferior gods who couldn't so much as help their own people from you—gods weaker than Amaziah?"

16 Amaziah interrupted him, "Did I ask for your opinion? Shut up or get thrown out!"

The prophet quit speaking, but not before he got in one last word: "I have it on good authority: God has made up his mind to throw *you* out because of what you've done, and because you wouldn't listen to me."

17 One day Amaziah sent envoys to Jehoash son of Jehoahaz, the son of Jehu, king of Israel, challenging him to a fight: "Come and

NEW KING JAMES VERSION

of Jehu, king of Israel, saying, "Come, let us face
one another *in battle.*"
18And Joash king of Israel sent to Amaziah
king of Judah, saying, "The thistle that *was* in
Lebanon sent to the cedar that was in Lebanon,
saying, 'Give your daughter to my son as wife';
and a wild beast that *was* in Lebanon passed by
and trampled the thistle. 19Indeed you say that
you have defeated the Edomites, and your heart
is lifted up to boast. Stay at home now; why
should you meddle with trouble, that you should
fall—you and Judah with you?"
20But Amaziah would not heed, for it *came*
from God, that He might give them into the
hand *of their enemies,* because they sought the
gods of Edom. 21So Joash king of Israel went
out; and he and Amaziah king of Judah faced
one another at Beth Shemesh, which *belongs* to
Judah. 22And Judah was defeated by Israel, and
every man fled to his tent. 23Then Joash the king
of Israel captured Amaziah king of Judah, the
son of Joash, the son of Jehoahaz, at Beth
Shemesh; and he brought him to Jerusalem, and
broke down the wall of Jerusalem from the Gate
of Ephraim to the Corner Gate—four hundred
cubits. 24And *he took* all the gold and silver, all
the articles that were found in the house of God
with Obed-Edom, the treasures of the king's
house, and hostages, and returned to Samaria.

DEATH OF AMAZIAH

25Amaziah the son of Joash, king of Judah,
lived fifteen years after the death of Joash the
son of Jehoahaz, king of Israel. 26Now the rest of
the acts of Amaziah, from first to last, indeed
are they not written in the book of the kings of
Judah and Israel? 27After the time that Amaziah
turned away from following the LORD, they
made a conspiracy against him in Jerusalem,
and he fled to Lachish; but they sent after him to
Lachish and killed him there. 28Then they
brought him on horses and buried him with his
fathers in the City of Judah.

UZZIAH REIGNS IN JUDAH

26 Now all the people of Judah took Uzziah,[a]
who *was* sixteen years old, and made him
king instead of his father Amaziah. 2He built
Elath[a] and restored it to Judah, after the king
rested with his fathers.
3Uzziah *was* sixteen years old when he be-
came king, and he reigned fifty-two years in
Jerusalem. His mother's name was Jecholiah of
Jerusalem. 4And he did *what was* right in the
sight of the LORD, according to all that his father
Amaziah had done. 5He sought God in the days
of Zechariah, who had understanding in the vi-
sions[a] of God; and as long as he sought the
LORD, God made him prosper.

26:1 [a]Called *Azariah* in 2 Kings 14:21ff **26:2** [a]Hebrew *Eloth*
26:5 [a]Several Hebrew manuscripts, Septuagint, Syriac, Targum, and Arabic read *fear.*

THE MESSAGE

meet with me, I dare you. Let's have it out
face-to-face!"
18-19 Jehoash king of Israel replied to Amaziah
king of Judah, "One day a thistle in Lebanon
sent word to a cedar in Lebanon, 'Give your
daughter to my son in marriage.' But then a
wild animal of Lebanon passed by and
stepped on the thistle, crushing it. Just be-
cause you've defeated Edom in battle, you
now think you're a big shot. Go ahead and
be proud, but stay home. Why press your
luck? Why bring defeat on yourself and Ju-
dah?"
20-22 Amaziah wouldn't take no for an an-
swer—God had already decided to let Je-
hoash defeat him because he had defected
to the gods of Edom. So Jehoash king of Is-
rael came on ahead and confronted Ama-
ziah king of Judah. They met at Beth
Shemesh, a town of Judah. Judah was thor-
oughly beaten by Israel—all the soldiers
straggled home in defeat.
23-24 Jehoash king of Israel captured Amaziah
king of Judah, the son of Joash, the son of
Ahaziah, at Beth Shemesh. But Jehoash didn't
stop at that; he went on to attack Jerusalem.
He demolished the Wall of Jerusalem all the
way from the Ephraim Gate to the Corner
Gate—a stretch of about six hundred feet.
He looted the gold, silver, and furnishings—
anything he found that was worth taking—
from both the palace and The Temple of
God—and, for good measure, he took
hostages. Then he returned to Samaria.
25-26 Amaziah son of Joash king of Judah con-
tinued as king fifteen years after the death
of Jehoash son of Jehoahaz king of Israel.
The rest of the life and times of Amaziah
from start to finish is written in the *Royal*
Annals of the Kings of Judah and Israel.
27-28 During those last days, after Amaziah
had defected from GOD, they cooked up a
plot against Amaziah in Jerusalem, and he
had to flee to Lachish. But they tracked him
down in Lachish and killed him there. They
brought him back on horseback and buried
him in Jerusalem with his ancestors in the
City of David.

KING UZZIAH

1-2 26 The people of Judah then took Uzziah,
who was only sixteen years old, and
made him king in place of his father
Amaziah. The first thing he did after his fa-
ther was dead and buried was to recover
Elath for Judah and rebuild it.
3-5 Uzziah was sixteen years old when he be-
came king and reigned for fifty-two years in
Jerusalem. His mother was Jecoliah from
Jerusalem. He behaved well in the eyes of
GOD, following in the footsteps of his father
Amaziah. He was a loyal seeker of God. He
was well trained by his pastor and teacher
Zechariah to live in reverent obedience be-
fore God, and for as long as Zechariah lived,
Uzziah lived a godly life. And God pros-
pered him.

New King James Version

[6]Now he went out and made war against the Philistines, and broke down the wall of Gath, the wall of Jabneh, and the wall of Ashdod; and he built cities *around* Ashdod and among the Philistines. [7]God helped him against the Philistines, against the Arabians who lived in Gur Baal, and against the Meunites. [8]Also the Ammonites brought tribute to Uzziah. His fame spread as far as the entrance of Egypt, for he became exceedingly strong.

[9]And Uzziah built towers in Jerusalem at the Corner Gate, at the Valley Gate, and at the corner buttress of the wall; then he fortified them. [10]Also he built towers in the desert. He dug many wells, for he had much livestock, both in the lowlands and in the plains; *he also had* farmers and vinedressers in the mountains and in Carmel, for he loved the soil.

[11]Moreover Uzziah had an army of fighting men who went out to war by companies, according to the number on their roll as prepared by Jeiel the scribe and Maaseiah the officer, under the hand of Hananiah, *one* of the king's captains. [12]The total number of chief officers[a] of the mighty men of valor *was* two thousand six hundred. [13]And under their authority *was* an army of three hundred and seven thousand five hundred, that made war with mighty power, to help the king against the enemy. [14]Then Uzziah prepared for them, for the entire army, shields, spears, helmets, body armor, bows, and slings *to cast* stones. [15]And he made devices in Jerusalem, invented by skillful men, to be on the towers and the corners, to shoot arrows and large stones. So his fame spread far and wide, for he was marvelously helped till he became strong.

The Penalty for Uzziah's Pride

[16]But when he was strong his heart was lifted up, to *his* destruction, for he transgressed against the LORD his God by entering the temple of the LORD to burn incense on the altar of incense. [17]So Azariah the priest went in after him, and with him were eighty priests of the LORD—valiant men. [18]And they withstood King Uzziah, and said to him, "*It is* not for you, Uzziah, to burn incense to the LORD, but for the priests, the sons of Aaron, who are consecrated to burn incense. Get out of the sanctuary, for you have trespassed! You *shall have* no honor from the LORD God."

[19]Then Uzziah became furious; and he *had* a censer in his hand to burn incense. And while he was angry with the priests, leprosy broke out on his forehead, before the priests in the house of the LORD, beside the incense altar. [20]And Azariah the chief priest and all the priests looked at him, and there, on his forehead, he *was* leprous; so they thrust him out of that place. Indeed he also hurried to get out, because the LORD had struck him.

[21]King Uzziah was a leper until the day of his death. He dwelt in an isolated house, because he was a leper; for he was cut off from the house of the LORD. Then Jotham his son *was* over the king's house, judging the people of the land.

26:12 [a]Literally *chief fathers*

The Message

6-8 He ventured out and fought the Philistines, breaking into the fortress cities of Gath, Jabneh, and Ashdod. He also built settlements around Ashdod and other Philistine areas. God helped him in his wars with the Philistines, the Arabs in Gur Baal, and the Meunites. The Ammonites also paid tribute. Uzziah became famous, his reputation extending all the way to Egypt. He became quite powerful.

9-10 Uzziah constructed defense towers in Jerusalem at the Corner Gate, the Valley Gate, and at the corner of the wall. He also built towers and dug cisterns out in the country. He had herds of cattle down in the foothills and out on the plains, had farmers and vinedressers at work in the hills and fields—he loved growing things.

11-15 On the military side, Uzziah had a well-prepared army ready to fight. They were organized by companies under the direction of Jeiel the secretary, Maaseiah the field captain, and Hananiah of the general staff. The roster of family leaders over the fighting men accounted for 2,600. Under them were reinforcement troops numbering 307,000, with 500 of them on constant alert—a strong royal defense against any attack. Uzziah had them well-armed with shields, spears, helmets, armor, bows, and slingshots. He also installed the latest in military technology on the towers and corners of Jerusalem for shooting arrows and hurling stones. He became well known for all this—a famous king. Everything seemed to go his way.

16-18 But then the strength and success went to his head. Arrogant and proud, he fell. One day, contemptuous of GOD, he walked into The Temple of GOD like he owned it and took over, burning incense on the Incense Altar. The priest Azariah, backed up by eighty brave priests of GOD, tried to prevent him. They confronted Uzziah: "You must not, you *cannot* do this, Uzziah—only the Aaronite priests, especially consecrated for the work, are permitted to burn incense. Get out of God's Temple; you are unfaithful and a disgrace!"

19-21 But Uzziah, censer in hand, was already in the middle of doing it and angrily rebuffed the priests. He lost his temper; angry words were exchanged—and then, even as they quarreled, a skin disease appeared on his forehead. As soon as they saw it, the chief priest Azariah and the other priests got him out of there as fast as they could. He hurried out—he knew that GOD then and there had given him the disease. Uzziah had his skin disease for the rest of his life and had to live in quarantine; he was not permitted to set foot in The Temple of GOD. His son Jotham, who managed the royal palace, took over the government of the country.

NEW KING JAMES VERSION

22Now the rest of the acts of Uzziah, from first to last, the prophet Isaiah the son of Amoz wrote. 23So Uzziah rested with his fathers, and they buried him with his fathers in the field of burial which *belonged* to the kings, for they said, "He is a leper." Then Jotham his son reigned in his place.

JOTHAM REIGNS IN JUDAH

27 Jotham *was* twenty-five years old when he became king, and he reigned sixteen years in Jerusalem. His mother's name *was* Jerushah[a] the daughter of Zadok. 2And he did *what was* right in the sight of the LORD, according to all that his father Uzziah had done (although he did not enter the temple of the LORD). But still the people acted corruptly.

3He built the Upper Gate of the house of the LORD, and he built extensively on the wall of Ophel. 4Moreover he built cities in the mountains of Judah, and in the forests he built fortresses and towers. 5He also fought with the king of the Ammonites and defeated them. And the people of Ammon gave him in that year one hundred talents of silver, ten thousand kors of wheat, and ten thousand of barley. The people of Ammon paid this to him in the second and third years also. 6So Jotham became mighty, because he prepared his ways before the LORD his God.

7Now the rest of the acts of Jotham, and all his wars and his ways, indeed they *are* written in the book of the kings of Israel and Judah. 8He was twenty-five years old when he became king, and he reigned sixteen years in Jerusalem. 9So Jotham rested with his fathers, and they buried him in the City of David. Then Ahaz his son reigned in his place.

AHAZ REIGNS IN JUDAH

28 Ahaz *was* twenty years old when he became king, and he reigned sixteen years in Jerusalem; and he did not do *what was* right in the sight of the LORD, as his father David *had done*. 2For he walked in the ways of the kings of Israel, and made molded images for the Baals. 3He burned incense in the Valley of the Son of Hinnom, and burned his children in the fire, according to the abominations of the nations whom the LORD had cast out before the children of Israel. 4And he sacrificed and burned incense on the high places, on the hills, and under every green tree.

SYRIA AND ISRAEL DEFEAT JUDAH

5Therefore the LORD his God delivered him into the hand of the king of Syria. They defeated him, and carried away a great multitude of them as captives, and brought *them* to Damascus. Then he was also delivered into the hand of the king of Israel, who defeated him with a great slaughter. 6For Pekah the son of Remaliah killed one hundred and twenty thousand in Judah in one day, all valiant men, because they had forsaken the LORD God of their fathers. 7Zichri, a mighty man of Ephraim, killed Maaseiah the

27:1 [a]Spelled *Jerusha* in 2 Kings 15:33

THE MESSAGE

22-23 The rest of the history of Uzziah, from start to finish, was written by the prophet Isaiah son of Amoz. When Uzziah died, they buried him with his ancestors in a field next to the royal cemetery. His skin disease disqualified him from burial in the royal cemetery. His son Jotham became the next king.

KING JOTHAM

1-2 27 Jotham was twenty-five years old when he became king; he reigned sixteen years at Jerusalem. His mother was Jerusha the daughter of Zadok. In GOD's eyes he lived a good life, following the path marked out by his father Uzziah. Unlike his father, though, he didn't desecrate The Temple of GOD. But the people pushed right on in their lives of corruption.

3-6 Jotham constructed the Upper Gate of The Temple of GOD, considerably extended the Wall of the Ophel, and built cities in the high country of Judah and forts and towers down in the forests. He fought and beat the king of the Ammonites—that year the Ammonites turned over three and a quarter tons of silver and about 65,000 bushels of wheat, and another 65,000 bushels of barley. They repeated this for the next two years. Jotham's strength was rooted in his steady and determined life of obedience to GOD.

7-9 The rest of the history of Jotham, including his wars and achievements, are all written in the *Royal Annals of the Kings of Israel and Judah*. He was twenty-five years old when he became king; he reigned for sixteen years at Jerusalem. Jotham died and was buried in the City of David. His son Ahaz became the next king.

KING AHAZ

1-4 28 Ahaz was twenty years old when he became king and reigned sixteen years years in Jerusalem. He didn't live right in the eyes of GOD; he wasn't at all like his ancestor David. Instead he followed in the track of Israel in the north, even casting metal figurines for worshiping the pagan Baal gods. He participated in the outlawed burning of incense in the Valley of Ben Hinnom and—incredibly!—indulged in the outrageous practice of "passing his sons through the fire," a truly abominable thing he picked up from the pagans GOD had earlier thrown out of the country. He also joined in the activities of the neighborhood sex-and-religion shrines that flourished all over the place.

5-8 GOD, fed up, handed him over to the king of Aram, who beat him badly and took many prisoners to Damascus. God also let the king of Israel loose on him and that resulted in a terrible slaughter: Pekah son of Remaliah killed 120,000 in one day, all of them first-class soldiers, and all because they had deserted GOD, the God of their ancestors. Furthermore, Zicri, an Ephraimite

NEW KING JAMES VERSION

king's son, Azrikam the officer over the house, and Elkanah *who was* second to the king. 8And the children of Israel carried away captive of their brethren two hundred thousand women, sons, and daughters; and they also took away much spoil from them, and brought the spoil to Samaria.

ISRAEL RETURNS THE CAPTIVES

9But a prophet of the LORD was there, whose name *was* Oded; and he went out before the army that came to Samaria, and said to them: "Look, because the LORD God of your fathers was angry with Judah, He has delivered them into your hand; but you have killed them in a rage *that* reaches up to heaven. 10And now you propose to force the children of Judah and Jerusalem to be your male and female slaves; *but are* you not also guilty before the LORD your God? 11Now hear me, therefore, and return the captives, whom you have taken captive from your brethren, for the fierce wrath of the LORD *is* upon you."

12Then some of the heads of the children of Ephraim, Azariah the son of Johanan, Berechiah the son of Meshillemoth, Jehizkiah the son of Shallum, and Amasa the son of Hadlai, stood up against those who came from the war, 13and said to them, "You shall not bring the captives here, for we *already* have offended the LORD. You intend to add to our sins and to our guilt; for our guilt is great, and *there is* fierce wrath against Israel." 14So the armed men left the captives and the spoil before the leaders and all the assembly. 15Then the men who were designated by name rose up and took the captives, and from the spoil they clothed all who were naked among them, dressed them and gave them sandals, gave them food and drink, and anointed them; and they let all the feeble ones ride on donkeys. So they brought them to their brethren at Jericho, the city of palm trees. Then they returned to Samaria.

ASSYRIA REFUSES TO HELP JUDAH

16At the same time King Ahaz sent to the kings[a] of Assyria to help him. 17For again the Edomites had come, attacked Judah, and carried away captives. 18The Philistines also had invaded the cities of the lowland and of the South of Judah, and had taken Beth Shemesh, Aijalon, Gederoth, Sochoh with its villages, Timnah with its villages, and Gimzo with its villages; and they dwelt there. 19For the LORD brought Judah low because of Ahaz king of Israel, for he had encouraged moral decline in Judah and had been continually unfaithful to the LORD. 20Also Tiglath-Pileser[a] king of Assyria came to him and distressed him, and did not assist him. 21For Ahaz took part *of the treasures* from the house of the LORD, from the house of the king, and from the leaders, and he gave *it* to the king of Assyria; but he did not help him.

28:16 [a]Septuagint, Syriac, and Vulgate read *king* (compare verse 20). **28:20** [a]Hebrew *Tilgath-Pilneser*

THE MESSAGE

hero, killed the king's son Maaseiah, Azrikam the palace steward, and Elkanah, second in command to the king. And that wasn't the end of it—the Israelites captured 200,000 men, women, and children, besides huge cartloads of plunder that they took to Samaria.

9-11 GOD's prophet Oded was in the neighborhood. He met the army when it entered Samaria and said, "Stop right where you are and listen! GOD, the God of your ancestors, was angry with Judah and used you to punish them; but you took things into your own hands and used *your* anger, uncalled for and irrational, to turn your brothers and sisters from Judah and Jerusalem into slaves. Don't you see that this is a terrible sin against your GOD? Careful now; do exactly what I say—return these captives, every last one of them. If you don't, you'll find out how real anger, GOD's anger, works."

12-13 Some of their Ephraimite leaders—Azariah son of Jehohanan, Berekiah son of Meshillemoth, Jehizkiah son of Shallum, and Amasa son of Hadlai—stood up against the returning army and said, "Don't bring the captives here! We've already sinned against GOD; and now you are about to compound our sin and guilt. We're guilty enough as it is, enough to set off an explosion of divine anger."

14-15 So the soldiers turned over both the captives and the plunder to the leaders and the people. Personally designated men gathered the captives together, dressed the ones who were naked using clothing from the stores of plunder, put shoes on their feet, gave them all a square meal, provided first aid to the injured, put the weak ones on donkeys, and then escorted them to Jericho, the City of Palms, restoring them to their families. Then they went back to Samaria.

16-21 At about that time King Ahaz sent to the king of Assyria asking for personal help. The Edomites had come back and given Judah a bad beating, taking off a bunch of captives. Adding insult to injury the Philistines raided the cities in the foothills to the west and the southern desert and captured Beth Shemesh, Aijalon, and Gederoth, along with Soco, Timnah, and Gimzo, with their surrounding villages, and moved in, making themselves at home. Arrogant King Ahaz, acting as if he could do without God's help, had unleashed an epidemic of depravity. Judah, brought to its knees by GOD, was now reduced to begging for a handout. But the king of Assyria, Tiglath-Pileser, wouldn't help—he came instead and humiliated Ahaz even more by attacking and bullying him. Desperate, Ahaz ransacked The Temple of GOD, the royal palace, and every other place he could think of, scraping together everything he could, and gave it to the king of Assyria—and got nothing in return, not a bit of help.

New King James Version

Apostasy and Death of Ahaz

22Now in the time of his distress King Ahaz
became increasingly unfaithful to the LORD.
This *is that* King Ahaz. 23For he sacrificed to the
gods of Damascus which had defeated him, say-
ing, "Because the gods of the kings of Syria help
them, I will sacrifice to them that they may help
me." But they were the ruin of him and of all Is-
rael. 24So Ahaz gathered the articles of the
house of God, cut in pieces the articles of the
house of God, shut up the doors of the house of
the LORD, and made for himself altars in every
corner of Jerusalem. 25And in every single city
of Judah he made high places to burn incense to
other gods, and provoked to anger the LORD
God of his fathers.

26Now the rest of his acts and all his ways,
from first to last, indeed they *are* written in the
book of the kings of Judah and Israel. 27So Ahaz
rested with his fathers, and they buried him in
the city, in Jerusalem; but they did not bring him
into the tombs of the kings of Israel. Then
Hezekiah his son reigned in his place.

Hezekiah Reigns in Judah

29 Hezekiah became king *when he was*
twenty-five years old, and he reigned
twenty-nine years in Jerusalem. His mother's
name *was* Abijah[a] the daughter of Zechariah.
2And he did *what was* right in the sight of the
LORD, according to all that his father David had
done.

Hezekiah Cleanses the Temple

3In the first year of his reign, in the first
month, he opened the doors of the house of the
LORD and repaired them. 4Then he brought in
the priests and the Levites, and gathered them
in the East Square, 5and said to them: "Hear me,
Levites! Now sanctify yourselves, sanctify the
house of the LORD God of your fathers, and
carry out the rubbish from the holy *place*. 6For
our fathers have trespassed and done evil in the
eyes of the LORD our God; they have forsaken
Him, have turned their faces away from the
dwelling place of the LORD, and turned *their*
backs *on Him*. 7They have also shut up the doors
of the vestibule, put out the lamps, and have not
burned incense or offered burnt offerings in the
holy *place* to the God of Israel. 8Therefore the
wrath of the LORD fell upon Judah and
Jerusalem, and He has given them up to trouble,
to desolation, and to jeering, as you see with
your eyes. 9For indeed, because of this our fa-
thers have fallen by the sword; and our sons, our
daughters, and our wives *are* in captivity.

10"Now *it is* in my heart to make a covenant
with the LORD God of Israel, that His fierce
wrath may turn away from us. 11My sons, do not
be negligent now, for the LORD has chosen you
to stand before Him, to serve Him, and that you
should minister to Him and burn incense."

12Then these Levites arose: Mahath the son
of Amasai and Joel the son of Azariah, of the

29:1 [a]Spelled *Abi* in 2 Kings 18:2

The Message

22-25 But King Ahaz didn't learn his lesson—at the very time that everyone was turning against him, he continued to be against GOD! He offered sacrifices to the gods of Damascus. He had just been defeated by Damascus; he thought, "If I worship the gods who helped Damascus, those gods just might help me, too." But things only went from bad to worse: first Ahaz in ruins and then the country. He cleaned out The Temple of God of everything useful and valuable, boarded up the doors of The Temple, and then went out and set up pagan shrines for his own use all over Jerusalem. And not only in Jerusalem, but all over Judah—neighborhood shrines for worshiping any and every god on sale. And was GOD ever angry!

26-27 The rest of Ahaz's infamous life, all that he did from start to finish, is written in the *Royal Annals of the Kings of Judah and Israel*. When Ahaz died, they buried him in Jerusalem, but he was not honored with a burial in the cemetery of the kings. His son Hezekiah was the next king.

King Hezekiah

1-2 29 Hezekiah became king when he was twenty-five years old and was king in Jerusalem for twenty-nine years. His mother was Abijah daughter of Zechariah. In GOD's opinion he was a good king; he kept to the standards of his ancestor David.

3-9 In the first month of the first year of his reign, Hezekiah, having first repaired the doors of The Temple of GOD, threw them open to the public. He assembled the priests and Levites in the court on the east side and said, "Levites, listen! Consecrate yourselves and consecrate The Temple of GOD—give this much-defiled place a good housecleaning. Our ancestors went wrong and lived badly before GOD—they discarded him, turned away from this house where we meet with GOD, and walked off. They boarded up the doors, turned out the lights, and canceled all the acts of worship of the GOD of Israel in the holy Temple. And because of that, GOD's anger flared up and he turned those people into a public exhibit of disaster, a moral history lesson—look and read! This is why our ancestors were killed, and this is why our wives and sons and daughters were taken prisoner and made slaves.

10-11 "I have decided to make a covenant with the GOD of Israel and turn history around so that GOD will no longer be angry with us. Children, don't drag your feet in this! GOD has chosen you to take your place before him to serve in conducting and leading worship—*this* is your life work; make sure you do it and do it well."

12-17 The Levites stood at attention: Mahath son of Amasai and Joel son of Azariah from

NEW KING JAMES VERSION

sons of the Kohathites; of the sons of Merari,
Kish the son of Abdi and Azariah the son of Je-
hallelel; of the Gershonites, Joah the son of
Zimmah and Eden the son of Joah; 13of the sons
of Elizaphan, Shimri and Jeiel; of the sons of As-
aph, Zechariah and Mattaniah; 14of the sons of
Heman, Jehiel and Shimei; and of the sons of Je-
duthun, Shemaiah and Uzziel.
15And they gathered their brethren, sancti-
fied themselves, and went according to the com-
mandment of the king, at the words of the LORD,
to cleanse the house of the LORD. 16Then the
priests went into the inner part of the house of
the LORD to cleanse *it*, and brought out all the
debris that they found in the temple of the LORD
to the court of the house of the LORD. And the
Levites took *it* out and carried *it* to the Brook
Kidron.
17Now they began to sanctify on the first *day*
of the first month, and on the eighth day of the
month they came to the vestibule of the LORD.
So they sanctified the house of the LORD in eight
days, and on the sixteenth day of the first month
they finished.
18Then they went in to King Hezekiah and
said, "We have cleansed all the house of the
LORD, the altar of burnt offerings with all its ar-
ticles, and the table of the showbread with all its
articles. 19Moreover all the articles which King
Ahaz in his reign had cast aside in his trans-
gression we have prepared and sanctified; and
there they *are*, before the altar of the LORD."

HEZEKIAH RESTORES TEMPLE WORSHIP

20Then King Hezekiah rose early, gathered
the rulers of the city, and went up to the house
of the LORD. 21And they brought seven bulls,
seven rams, seven lambs, and seven male goats
for a sin offering for the kingdom, for the sanc-
tuary, and for Judah. Then he commanded the
priests, the sons of Aaron, to offer *them* on the
altar of the LORD. 22So they killed the bulls, and
the priests received the blood and sprinkled *it*
on the altar. Likewise they killed the rams and
sprinkled the blood on the altar. They also killed
the lambs and sprinkled the blood on the altar.
23Then they brought out the male goats *for* the
sin offering before the king and the assembly,
and they laid their hands on them. 24And the
priests killed them; and they presented their
blood on the altar as a sin offering to make an
atonement for all Israel, for the king com-
manded *that* the burnt offering and the sin of-
fering *be made* for all Israel.
25And he stationed the Levites in the house
of the LORD with cymbals, with stringed instru-
ments, and with harps, according to the com-
mandment of David, of Gad the king's seer, and
of Nathan the prophet; for thus *was* the com-
mandment of the LORD by His prophets. 26The
Levites stood with the instruments of David,
and the priests with the trumpets. 27Then
Hezekiah commanded *them* to offer the burnt
offering on the altar. And when the burnt offer-
ing began, the song of the LORD *also* began, with
the trumpets and with the instruments of David
king of Israel. 28So all the assembly worshiped,
the singers sang, and the trumpeters sounded;
all *this continued* until the burnt offering was

THE MESSAGE

the Kohathites; Kish son of Abdi and Azariah son of Jehallelel from the Merarites; Joah son of Zimmah and Eden son of Joah from the Gershonites; Shimri and Jeiel sons of Elizaphan; Zechariah and Mattaniah sons of Asaph; Jehiel and Shimei of the family of Heman; Shemaiah and Uzziel of the family of Jeduthun. They presented themselves and their brothers, consecrated themselves, and set to work cleaning up The Temple of GOD as the king had directed—as GOD directed! The priests started from the inside and worked out; they emptied the place of the accumulation of defiling junk—pagan rubbish that had no business in that holy place—and the Levites hauled it off to the Kidron Valley. They began the Temple cleaning on the first day of the first month and by the eighth day they had worked their way out to the porch—eight days it took them to clean and consecrate The Temple itself, and in eight more days they had finished with the entire Temple complex.

18-19 Then they reported to Hezekiah the king, "We have cleaned up the entire Temple of GOD, including the Altar of Whole-Burnt-Offering and the Table of the Bread of the Presence with their furnishings. We have also cleaned up and consecrated all the vessels which King Ahaz had gotten rid of during his misrule. Take a look; we have repaired them. They're all there in front of the Altar of GOD."

20-24 Then Hezekiah the king went to work: He got all the leaders of the city together and marched to The Temple of GOD. They brought with them seven bulls, seven rams, seven lambs, and seven he-goats to sacrifice as an Absolution-Offering for the royal family, for the Sanctuary, and for Judah as a whole; he directed the Aaronite priests to sacrifice them on the Altar of GOD. The priests butchered the bulls and then took the blood and sprinkled it on the Altar, and then the same with the rams and lambs. Finally they brought the goats up; the king and congregation laid their hands upon them. The priests butchered them and made an Absolution-Offering with their blood at the Altar to atone for the sin of all Israel—the king had ordered that the Whole-Burnt-Offering and the Absolution-Offering be for all Israel.

25-26 The king ordered the Levites to take their places in The Temple of GOD with their musical instruments—cymbals, harps, zithers—following the original instructions of David, Gad the king's seer, and Nathan the prophet; this was GOD's command conveyed by his prophets. The Levites formed the orchestra of David, while the priests took up the trumpets.

27-30 Then Hezekiah gave the signal to begin: The Whole-Burnt-Offering was offered on the Altar; at the same time the sacred choir began singing, backed up by the trumpets and the David orchestra while the entire congregation worshiped. The singers sang and the trumpeters played all during the sacrifice of the Whole-Burnt-Offering. When

NEW KING JAMES VERSION

finished. 29And when they had finished offering,
the king and all who were present with him
bowed and worshiped. 30Moreover King
Hezekiah and the leaders commanded the
Levites to sing praise to the LORD with the
words of David and of Asaph the seer. So they
sang praises with gladness, and they bowed
their heads and worshiped.
31Then Hezekiah answered and said, "Now
that you have consecrated yourselves to the
LORD, come near, and bring sacrifices and thank
offerings into the house of the LORD." So the as-
sembly brought in sacrifices and thank offer-
ings, and as many as were of a willing heart
brought burnt offerings. 32And the number of
the burnt offerings which the assembly brought
was seventy bulls, one hundred rams, *and* two
hundred lambs; all these *were* for a burnt offer-
ing to the LORD. 33The consecrated things *were*
six hundred bulls and three thousand sheep.
34But the priests were too few, so that they could
not skin all the burnt offerings; therefore their
brethren the Levites helped them until the work
was ended and until the *other* priests had sanc-
tified themselves, for the Levites were more dili-
gent in sanctifying themselves than the priests.
35Also the burnt offerings *were* in abundance,
with the fat of the peace offerings and *with* the
drink offerings for *every* burnt offering.
So the service of the house of the LORD was
set in order. 36Then Hezekiah and all the people
rejoiced that God had prepared the people,
since the events took place so suddenly.

HEZEKIAH KEEPS THE PASSOVER

30 And Hezekiah sent to all Israel and Judah,
and also wrote letters to Ephraim and Ma-
nasseh, that they should come to the house of
the LORD at Jerusalem, to keep the Passover to
the LORD God of Israel. 2For the king and his
leaders and all the assembly in Jerusalem had
agreed to keep the Passover in the second
month. 3For they could not keep it at the regular
time,[a] because a sufficient number of priests
had not consecrated themselves, nor had the
people gathered together at Jerusalem. 4And the
matter pleased the king and all the assembly.
5So they resolved to make a proclamation
throughout all Israel, from Beersheba to Dan,
that they should come to keep the Passover to
the LORD God of Israel at Jerusalem, since they
had not done *it* for a long *time* in the *prescribed*
manner.
6Then the runners went throughout all Israel
and Judah with the letters from the king and his
leaders, and spoke according to the command of
the king: "Children of Israel, return to the LORD
God of Abraham, Isaac, and Israel; then He will
return to the remnant of you who have escaped

30:3 [a]That is, the first month (compare Leviticus 23:5); literally *at that time*

THE MESSAGE

the offering of the sacrifice was completed,
the king and everyone there knelt to the
ground and worshiped. Then Hezekiah the
king and the leaders told the Levites to fin-
ish things off with anthems of praise to GOD
using lyrics by David and Asaph the seer.
They sang their praises with joy and rever-
ence, kneeling in worship.
31-35 Hezekiah then made this response: "The
dedication is complete—you're consecrated
to GOD. Now you're ready: Come forward
and bring your sacrifices and Thank-Offer-
ings to The Temple of GOD."
And come they did. Everyone in the con-
gregation brought sacrifices and Thank-
Offerings and some, overflowing with gen-
erosity, even brought Whole-Burnt-Offer-
ings, a generosity expressed in seventy bulls,
a hundred rams, and two hundred lambs—
all for Whole-Burnt-Offerings for GOD! The
total number of animals consecrated for sac-
rifice that day amounted to six hundred bulls
and three thousand sheep. They ran out of
priests qualified to slaughter all the Whole-
Burnt-Offerings so their brother Levites
stepped in and helped out while other priests
consecrated themselves for the work. It
turned out that the Levites had been more
responsible in making sure they were prop-
erly consecrated than the priests had been.
Besides the overflow of Whole-Burnt-Offer-
ings there were also choice pieces for the
Peace-Offerings and lavish libations that
went with the Whole-Burnt-Offerings. The
worship in The Temple of GOD was on a firm
footing again!
36 Hezekiah and the congregation cele-
brated: God had established a firm founda-
tion for the lives of the people—and so
quickly!

1-5 30 Then Hezekiah invited all of Israel and
Judah, with personal letters to Ephraim
and Manasseh, to come to The Temple of
GOD in Jerusalem to celebrate the Passover
to Israel's God. The king and his officials
and the congregation in Jerusalem had de-
cided to celebrate Passover in the second
month. They hadn't been able to celebrate it
at the regular time because not enough of
the priests were yet personally prepared
and the people hadn't had time to gather in
Jerusalem. Under these circumstances, the
revised date was approved by both king and
people and they sent out the invitation from
one end of the country to the other, from
Beersheba in the south to Dan in the north:
"Come and celebrate the Passover to Israel's
God in Jerusalem." No one living had ever
celebrated it properly.
6-9 The king gave the orders, and the couri-
ers delivered the invitations from the king
and his leaders throughout Israel and Ju-
dah. The invitation read: "O Israelites!
Come back to GOD, the God of Abraham,
Isaac, and Israel, so that he can return to
you who have survived the predations of the

NEW KING JAMES VERSION

from the hand of the kings of Assyria. 7And do
not be like your fathers and your brethren, who
trespassed against the LORD God of their fathers,
so that He gave them up to desolation, as you
see. 8Now do not be stiff-necked, as your fathers
were, but yield yourselves to the LORD; and enter
His sanctuary, which He has sanctified forever,
and serve the LORD your God, that the fierceness
of His wrath may turn away from you. 9For if you
return to the LORD, your brethren and your chil-
dren *will be treated* with compassion by those
who lead them captive, so that they may come
back to this land; for the LORD your God *is* gra-
cious and merciful, and will not turn *His* face
from you if you return to Him."

10So the runners passed from city to city
through the country of Ephraim and Manasseh,
as far as Zebulun; but they laughed at them and
mocked them. 11Nevertheless some from Asher,
Manasseh, and Zebulun humbled themselves
and came to Jerusalem. 12Also the hand of God
was on Judah to give them singleness of heart to
obey the command of the king and the leaders,
at the word of the LORD.

13Now many people, a very great assembly,
gathered at Jerusalem to keep the Feast of Un-
leavened Bread in the second month. 14They
arose and took away the altars that *were* in
Jerusalem, and they took away all the incense
altars and cast *them* into the Brook Kidron.
15Then they slaughtered the Passover *lambs* on
the fourteenth *day* of the second month. The
priests and the Levites were ashamed, and sanc-
tified themselves, and brought the burnt offer-
ings to the house of the LORD. 16They stood in
their place according to their custom, according
to the Law of Moses the man of God; the priests
sprinkled the blood *received* from the hand of
the Levites. 17For *there were* many in the assem-
bly who had not sanctified themselves; there-
fore the Levites had charge of the slaughter of
the Passover *lambs* for everyone *who was* not
clean, to sanctify *them* to the LORD. 18For a mul-
titude of the people, many from Ephraim, Ma-
nasseh, Issachar, and Zebulun, had not cleansed
themselves, yet they ate the Passover contrary
to what was written. But Hezekiah prayed for
them, saying, "May the good LORD provide
atonement for everyone 19*who* prepares his
heart to seek God, the LORD God of his fathers,
though *he is* not *cleansed* according to the pu-
rification of the sanctuary." 20And the LORD lis-
tened to Hezekiah and healed the people.

21So the children of Israel who were present
at Jerusalem kept the Feast of Unleavened
Bread seven days with great gladness; and the
Levites and the priests praised the LORD day by
day, *singing* to the LORD, accompanied by loud
instruments. 22And Hezekiah gave encourage-
ment to all the Levites who taught the good
knowledge of the LORD; and they ate throughout

THE MESSAGE

kings of Assyria. Don't repeat the sins of your ancestors who turned their backs on GOD, the God of their ancestors who then brought them to ruin—you can see the ruins all around you. Don't be pigheaded as your ancestors were. Clasp GOD's outstretched hand. Come to his Temple of holy worship, consecrated for all time. Serve GOD, *your* God. You'll no longer be in danger of his hot anger. If you come back to GOD, your captive relatives and children will be treated compassionately and allowed to come home. Your GOD is gracious and kind and won't snub you—come back and he'll welcome you with open arms."

10-12 So the couriers set out, going from city to city through the country of Ephraim and Manasseh, as far north as Zebulun. But the people poked fun at them, treated them as a joke. But not all; some from Asher, Manasseh, and Zebulun weren't too proud to accept the invitation and come to Jerusalem. It was better in Judah—God worked powerfully among them to make it unanimous, responding to the orders sent out by the king and his officials, orders backed up by the word of GOD.

13-17 It turned out that there was a tremendous crowd of people when the time came in the second month to celebrate the Passover (sometimes called the Feast of Unraised Bread). First they went to work and got rid of all the pagan altars that were in Jerusalem—hauled them off and dumped them in the Kidron Valley. Then, on the fourteenth day of the second month, they slaughtered the Passover lambs. The priests and Levites weren't ready; but now, embarrassed in their laziness, they consecrated themselves and brought Whole-Burnt-Offerings to The Temple of GOD. Ready now, they stood at their posts as designated by The Revelation of Moses the holy man; the priests sprinkled the blood the Levites handed to them. Because so many in the congregation had not properly prepared themselves by consecration and so were not qualified, the Levites took charge of the slaughter of the Passover lambs so that they would be properly consecrated to GOD.

18-19 There were a lot of people, especially those from Ephraim, Manasseh, Issachar, and Zebulun, who did not eat the Passover meal because they had not prepared themselves adequately. Hezekiah prayed for these as follows: "May GOD who is all good, pardon and forgive everyone who sincerely desires GOD, the God of our ancestors. Even—especially!—these who do not meet the literal conditions stated for access to The Temple."

20 GOD responded to Hezekiah's prayer and healed the people.

21-22 All the Israelites present in Jerusalem celebrated the Passover (Feast of Unraised Bread) for seven days, celebrated exuberantly. The Levites and priests praised GOD day after day, filling the air with praise sounds of percussion and brass. Hezekiah commended the Levites for the superb way in which they had led the people in the worship of GOD.

NEW KING JAMES VERSION

the feast seven days, offering peace offerings and making confession to the LORD God of their fathers.

23Then the whole assembly agreed to keep *the feast* another seven days, and they kept it *another* seven days with gladness. 24For Hezekiah king of Judah gave to the assembly a thousand bulls and seven thousand sheep, and the leaders gave to the assembly a thousand bulls and ten thousand sheep; and a great number of priests sanctified themselves. 25The whole assembly of Judah rejoiced, also the priests and Levites, all the assembly that came from Israel, the sojourners who came from the land of Israel, and those who dwelt in Judah. 26So there was great joy in Jerusalem, for since the time of Solomon the son of David, king of Israel, *there had* been nothing like this in Jerusalem. 27Then the priests, the Levites, arose and blessed the people, and their voice was heard; and their prayer came *up* to His holy dwelling place, to heaven.

THE REFORMS OF HEZEKIAH

31 Now when all this was finished, all Israel who were present went out to the cities of Judah and broke the sacred pillars in pieces, cut down the wooden images, and threw down the high places and the altars—from all Judah, Benjamin, Ephraim, and Manasseh—until they had utterly destroyed them all. Then all the children of Israel returned to their own cities, every man to his possession.

2And Hezekiah appointed the divisions of the priests and the Levites according to their divisions, each man according to his service, the priests and Levites for burnt offerings and peace offerings, to serve, to give thanks, and to praise in the gates of the camp[a] of the LORD. 3The king also *appointed* a portion of his possessions for the burnt offerings: for the morning and evening burnt offerings, the burnt offerings for the Sabbaths and the New Moons and the set feasts, as *it is* written in the Law of the LORD. 4Moreover he commanded the people who dwelt in Jerusalem to contribute support for the priests and the Levites, that they might devote themselves to the Law of the LORD.

5As soon as the commandment was circulated, the children of Israel brought in abundance the firstfruits of grain and wine, oil and honey, and of all the produce of the field; and they brought in abundantly the tithe of everything. 6And the children of Israel and Judah, who dwelt in the cities of Judah, brought the tithe of oxen and sheep; also the tithe of holy things which were consecrated to the LORD their God they laid in heaps.

7In the third month they began laying them in heaps, and they finished in the seventh month.

31:2 [a]That is, the temple

THE MESSAGE

22-23 When the feast and festival—that glorious seven days of worship, the making of offerings, and the praising of GOD, the God of their ancestors—were over, the tables cleared and the floors swept, they all decided to keep going for another seven days! So they just kept on celebrating, and as joyfully as they began.

24-26 Hezekiah king of Judah gave one thousand bulls and seven thousand sheep for the congregation's worship; the officials gave an additional one thousand bulls and ten thousand sheep. And there turned out to be plenty of consecrated priests—qualified and well-prepared. The whole congregation of Judah, the priests and Levites, the congregation that came in from Israel, and the resident aliens from both Israel and Judah, were all in on the joyous celebration. Jerusalem was bursting with joy—nothing like this had taken place in Jerusalem since Solomon son of David king of Israel had built and dedicated The Temple.

27 The priests and Levites had the last word: they stood and blessed the people. And God listened, listened as the ascending sound of their prayers entered his holy heaven.

1 31 After the Passover celebration, they all took off for the cities of Judah and smashed the phallic stone monuments, chopped down the sacred Asherah groves, and demolished the neighborhood sex-and-religion shrines and local god shops. They didn't stop until they had been all through Judah, Benjamin, Ephraim, and Manasseh. Then they all went back home and resumed their everyday lives.

2 Hezekiah organized the groups of priests and Levites for their respective tasks, handing out job descriptions for conducting the services of worship: making the various offerings, and making sure that thanks and praise took place wherever and whenever GOD was worshiped.

3 He also designated his personal contribution for the Whole-Burnt-Offerings for the morning and evening worship, for Sabbaths, for New Moon festivals, and for the special worship days set down in The Revelation of GOD.

4 In addition, he asked the people who lived in Jerusalem to be responsible for providing for the priests and Levites so they, without distraction or concern, could give themselves totally to The Revelation of GOD.

5-7 As soon as Hezekiah's orders had gone out, the Israelites responded generously: firstfruits of the grain harvest, new wine, oil, honey—everything they grew. They didn't hold back, turning over a tithe of everything. They also brought in a tithe of their cattle, sheep, and anything else they owned that had been dedicated to GOD. Everything was sorted and piled in mounds. They started doing this in the third month and didn't finish until the seventh month.

NEW KING JAMES VERSION

8And when Hezekiah and the leaders came and
saw the heaps, they blessed the LORD and His
people Israel. 9Then Hezekiah questioned the
priests and the Levites concerning the heaps.
10And Azariah the chief priest, from the house
of Zadok, answered him and said, "Since *the
people* began to bring the offerings into the
house of the LORD, we have had enough to eat
and have plenty left, for the LORD has blessed
His people; and what is left *is* this great abun-
dance."
11Now Hezekiah commanded *them* to pre-
pare rooms in the house of the LORD, and they
prepared them. 12Then they faithfully brought in
the offerings, the tithes, and the dedicated things;
Cononiah the Levite had charge of them, and
Shimei his brother *was* the next. 13Jehiel,
Azaziah, Nahath, Asahel, Jerimoth, Jozabad,
Eliel, Ismachiah, Mahath, and Benaiah *were*
overseers under the hand of Cononiah and
Shimei his brother, at the commandment of
Hezekiah the king and Azariah the ruler of the
house of God. 14Kore the son of Imnah the Levite,
the keeper of the East Gate, *was* over the freewill
offerings to God, to distribute the offerings of the
LORD and the most holy things. 15And under him
were Eden, Miniamin, Jeshua, Shemaiah,
Amariah, and Shecaniah, *his* faithful assistants
in the cities of the priests, to distribute allotments
to their brethren by divisions, to the great as well
as the small.
16Besides those males from three years old
and up who were written in the genealogy, they
distributed to everyone who entered the house
of the LORD his daily portion for the work of his
service, by his division, 17and to the priests who
were written in the genealogy according to their
father's house, and to the Levites from twenty
years old and up according to their work, by
their divisions, 18and to all who were written in
the genealogy—their little ones and their wives,
their sons and daughters, the whole company of
them—for in their faithfulness they sanctified
themselves in holiness.
19Also for the sons of Aaron the priests, *who
were* in the fields of the common-lands of their
cities, in every single city, *there were* men who
were designated by name to distribute portions
to all the males among the priests and to all who
were listed by genealogies among the Levites.
20Thus Hezekiah did throughout all Judah,
and he did what *was* good and right and true be-
fore the LORD his God. 21And in every work that
he began in the service of the house of God, in
the law and in the commandment, to seek his
God, he did *it* with all his heart. So he pros-
pered.

SENNACHERIB BOASTS AGAINST THE LORD

32 After these deeds of faithfulness, Sen-
nacherib king of Assyria came and en-
tered Judah; he encamped against the fortified
cities, thinking to win them over to himself.
2And when Hezekiah saw that Sennacherib had
come, and that his purpose was to make war
against Jerusalem, 3he consulted with his lead-

THE MESSAGE

8-9 When Hezekiah and his leaders came and saw the extent of the mounds of gifts, they praised GOD and commended God's people Israel. Hezekiah then consulted the priests and Levites on how to handle the abundance of offerings.

10 Azariah, chief priest of the family of Zadok, answered, "From the moment of this huge outpouring of gifts to The Temple of GOD, there has been plenty to eat for everyone with food left over. GOD has blessed his people—just look at the evidence!"

11-18 Hezekiah then ordered storerooms to be prepared in The Temple of GOD. When they were ready, they brought in all the offerings of tithes and sacred gifts. They put Conaniah the Levite in charge with his brother Shimei as assistant. Jehiel, Azaziah, Nahath, Asahel, Jerimoth, Jozabad, Eliel, Ismakiah, Mahath, and Benaiah were project managers under the direction of Conaniah and Shimei, carrying out the orders of King Hezekiah and Azariah the chief priest of The Temple of God. Kore son of Imnah the Levite, security guard of the East Gate, was in charge of the Freewill-Offerings of God and responsible for distributing the offerings and sacred gifts. Faithful support out in the priestly cities was provided by Eden, Miniamin, Jeshua, Shemaiah, Amariah, and Shecaniah. They were even-handed in their distributions to their coworkers (all males thirty years and older) in each of their respective divisions as they entered The Temple of GOD each day to do their assigned work (their work was all organized by divisions). The divisions comprised officially registered priests by family and Levites twenty years and older by job description. The official family tree included everyone in the entire congregation—their small children, wives, sons, and daughters. The ardent dedication they showed in bringing themselves and their gifts to worship was total—no one was left out.

19 The Aaronites, the priests who lived out on the pastures that belonged to the priest-cities, had reputable men on hand to distribute regular rations to every priest—everyone listed in the official family tree of the Levites.

20-21 Hezekiah carried out this work and kept it up everywhere in Judah. He was the very best—good, right, and true before his GOD. Everything he took up, whether it had to do with worship in God's Temple or the carrying out of God's Law and Commandments, he did well in a spirit of prayerful worship. He was a great success.

1 32 And then, after this exemplary track record, this: Sennacherib king of Assyria came and attacked Judah. He put the fortified cities under siege, determined to take them.

2-4 When Hezekiah realized that Sennacherib's strategy was to take Jerusalem, he talked to his advisors and military lead-

NEW KING JAMES VERSION

ers and commanders[a] to stop the water from the springs which *were* outside the city; and they helped him. 4Thus many people gathered together who stopped all the springs and the brook that ran through the land, saying, "Why should the kings[a] of Assyria come and find much water?" 5And he strengthened himself, built up all the wall that was broken, raised *it* up to the towers, and *built* another wall outside; also he repaired the Millo[a] *in* the City of David, and made weapons and shields in abundance. 6Then he set military captains over the people, gathered them together to him in the open square of the city gate, and gave them encouragement, saying, 7"Be strong and courageous; do not be afraid nor dismayed before the king of Assyria, nor before all the multitude that *is* with him; for *there are* more with us than with him. 8With him *is* an arm of flesh; but with us *is* the LORD our God, to help us and to fight our battles." And the people were strengthened by the words of Hezekiah king of Judah.

9After this Sennacherib king of Assyria sent his servants to Jerusalem (but he and all the forces with him *laid siege* against Lachish), to Hezekiah king of Judah, and to all Judah who *were* in Jerusalem, saying, 10"Thus says Sennacherib king of Assyria: 'In what do you trust, that you remain under siege in Jerusalem? 11Does not Hezekiah persuade you to give yourselves over to die by famine and by thirst, saying, "The LORD our God will deliver us from the hand of the king of Assyria"? 12Has not the same Hezekiah taken away His high places and His altars, and commanded Judah and Jerusalem, saying, "You shall worship before one altar and burn incense on it"? 13Do you not know what I and my fathers have done to all the peoples of *other* lands? Were the gods of the nations of those lands in any way able to deliver their lands out of my hand? 14Who *was there* among all the gods of those nations that my fathers utterly destroyed that could deliver his people from my hand, that your God should be able to deliver you from my hand? 15Now therefore, do not let Hezekiah deceive you or persuade you like this, and do not believe him; for no god of any nation or kingdom was able to deliver his people from my hand or the hand of my fathers. How much less will your God deliver you from my hand?' "

16Furthermore, his servants spoke against the LORD God and against His servant Hezekiah.

17He also wrote letters to revile the LORD God of Israel, and to speak against Him, saying, "As the gods of the nations of *other* lands have not delivered their people from my hand, so the God of Hezekiah will not deliver His people from my hand." 18Then they called out with a loud voice in Hebrew[a] to the people of Jerusalem who *were* on the wall, to frighten them and trouble them, that they might take the city. 19And they spoke against the God of Jerusalem, as against the gods of the people of the earth—the work of men's hands.

32:3 [a]Literally *mighty men* **32:4** [a]Following Masoretic Text and Vulgate; Arabic, Septuagint, and Syriac read *king.* **32:5** [a]Literally *The Landfill* **32:18** [a]Literally *Judean*

THE MESSAGE

ers about eliminating all the water supplies outside the city; they thought it was a good idea. There was a great turnout of people to plug the springs and tear down the aqueduct. They said, "Why should the kings of Assyria march in and be furnished with running water?"

5-6 Hezekiah also went to work repairing every part of the city wall that was damaged, built defensive towers on it, built another wall of defense further out, and reinforced the defensive rampart (the Millo) of the old City of David. He also built up a large store of armaments—spears and shields. He then appointed military officers to be responsible for the people and got them all together at the public square in front of the city gate.

6-8 Hezekiah rallied the people, saying, "Be strong! Take courage! Don't be intimidated by the king of Assyria and his troops—there are more on our side than on their side. He only has a bunch of mere men; we have our GOD to help us and fight for us!"

Morale surged. Hezekiah's words put steel in their spines.

9-15 Later on, Sennacherib, who had set up camp a few miles away at Lachish, sent messengers to Jerusalem, addressing Judah through Hezekiah: "A proclamation of Sennacherib king of Assyria: You poor people—do you think you're safe in that so-called fortress of Jerusalem? You're sitting ducks. Do you think Hezekiah will save you? Don't be stupid—Hezekiah has fed you a pack of lies. When he says, 'GOD will save us from the power of the king of Assyria,' he's lying—you're all going to end up dead. Wasn't it Hezekiah who cleared out all the neighborhood worship shrines and told you, 'There is only one legitimate place to worship'? Do you have any idea what I and my ancestors have done to all the countries around here? Has there been a single god anywhere strong enough to stand up against me? Can you name one god among all the nations that either I or my ancestors have ravaged that so much as lifted a finger against me? So what makes you think you'll make out any better with your god? Don't let Hezekiah fool you; don't let him get by with his barefaced lies; don't trust him. No god of any country or kingdom ever has been one bit of help against me or my ancestors—what kind of odds does that give your god?"

16 The messengers felt free to throw in their personal comments, putting down both GOD and God's servant Hezekiah.

17 Sennacherib continued to send letters insulting the GOD of Israel: "The gods of the nations were powerless to help their people; the god of Hezekiah is no better, probably worse."

18-19 The messengers would come up to the wall of Jerusalem and shout up to the people standing on the wall, shouting their propaganda in Hebrew, trying to scare them into demoralized submission. They contemptuously lumped the God of Jerusalem in with the handmade gods of other peoples.

New King James Version

Sennacherib's Defeat and Death

20Now because of this King Hezekiah and
the prophet Isaiah, the son of Amoz, prayed and
cried out to heaven. 21Then the LORD sent an an-
gel who cut down every mighty man of valor,
leader, and captain in the camp of the king of
Assyria. So he returned shamefaced to his own
land. And when he had gone into the temple of
his god, some of his own offspring struck him
down with the sword there.
22Thus the LORD saved Hezekiah and the in-
habitants of Jerusalem from the hand of Sen-
nacherib the king of Assyria, and from the hand
of all *others,* and guided them[a] on every side.
23And many brought gifts to the LORD at
Jerusalem, and presents to Hezekiah king of Ju-
dah, so that he was exalted in the sight of all na-
tions thereafter.

Hezekiah Humbles Himself

24In those days Hezekiah was sick and near
death, and he prayed to the LORD; and He spoke
to him and gave him a sign. 25But Hezekiah did
not repay according to the favor *shown* him, for
his heart was lifted up; therefore wrath was
looming over him and over Judah and Jerusa-
lem. 26Then Hezekiah humbled himself for the
pride of his heart, he and the inhabitants of
Jerusalem, so that the wrath of the LORD did not
come upon them in the days of Hezekiah.

Hezekiah's Wealth and Honor

27Hezekiah had very great riches and honor.
And he made himself treasuries for silver, for
gold, for precious stones, for spices, for shields,
and for all kinds of desirable items; 28store-
houses for the harvest of grain, wine, and oil;
and stalls for all kinds of livestock, and folds for
flocks.[a] 29Moreover he provided cities for him-
self, and possessions of flocks and herds in
abundance; for God had given him very much
property. 30This same Hezekiah also stopped the
water outlet of Upper Gihon, and brought the
water by tunnel[a] to the west side of the City of
David. Hezekiah prospered in all his works.
31However, *regarding* the ambassadors of the
princes of Babylon, whom they sent to him to in-
quire about the wonder that was *done* in the
land, God withdrew from him, in order to test
him, that He might know all *that was* in his
heart.

Death of Hezekiah

32Now the rest of the acts of Hezekiah, and
his goodness, indeed they *are* written in the vi-
sion of Isaiah the prophet, the son of Amoz, *and*
in the book of the kings of Judah and Israel. 33So
Hezekiah rested with his fathers, and they
buried him in the upper tombs of the sons of
David; and all Judah and the inhabitants of
Jerusalem honored him at his death. Then Ma-
nasseh his son reigned in his place.

32:22 [a]Septuagint reads *gave them rest;* Vulgate reads *gave them treasures.* **32:28** [a]Following Septuagint and Vulgate; Arabic and Syriac omit *folds for flocks;* Masoretic Text reads *flocks for sheepfolds.* **32:30** [a]Literally *brought it straight* (compare 2 Kings 20:20)

The Message

20-21 King Hezekiah, joined by the prophet Isaiah son of Amoz, responded by praying, calling up to heaven. GOD answered by sending an angel who wiped out everyone in the Assyrian camp, both warriors and officers. Sennacherib was forced to return home in disgrace, tail between his legs. When he went into the temple of his god, his own sons killed him.

22-23 GOD saved Hezekiah and the citizens of Jerusalem from Sennacherib king of Assyria and everyone else. And he continued to take good care of them. People streamed into Jerusalem bringing offerings for the worship of GOD and expensive presents to Hezekiah king of Judah. All the surrounding nations were impressed—Hezekiah's stock soared.

24 Some time later Hezekiah became deathly sick. He prayed to GOD and was given a reassuring sign.

25-26 But the sign, instead of making Hezekiah grateful, made him arrogant. This made GOD angry, and his anger spilled over on Judah and Jerusalem. But then Hezekiah, and Jerusalem with him, repented of his arrogance, and GOD withdrew his anger while Hezekiah lived.

27-31 Hezekiah ended up very wealthy and much honored. He built treasuries for all his silver, gold, precious stones, spices, shields, and valuables, barns for the grain, new wine, and olive oil, stalls for his various breeds of cattle, and pens for his flocks. He founded royal cities for himself and built up huge stocks of sheep and cattle. God saw to it that he was extravagantly rich. Hezekiah was also responsible for diverting the upper outlet of the Gihon spring and rerouting the water to the west side of the City of David. Hezekiah succeeded in everything he did. But when the rulers of Babylon sent emissaries to find out about the sign from God that had taken place earlier, God left him on his own to see what he would do; he wanted to test his heart.

32-33 The rest of the history of Hezekiah and his life of loyal service, you can read for yourself—it's written in the vision of the prophet Isaiah son of Amoz in the *Royal Annals of the Kings of Judah and Israel.* When Hezekiah died, they buried him in the upper part of the King David cemetery. Everyone in Judah and Jerusalem came to the funeral. He was buried in great honor.

Manasseh his son was the next king.

NEW KING JAMES VERSION

MANASSEH REIGNS IN JUDAH

33 Manasseh *was* twelve years old when he
became king, and he reigned fifty-five
years in Jerusalem. [2]But he did evil in the sight
of the LORD, according to the abominations of
the nations whom the LORD had cast out before
the children of Israel. [3]For he rebuilt the high
places which Hezekiah his father had broken
down; he raised up altars for the Baals, and
made wooden images; and he worshiped all the
host of heaven[a] and served them. [4]He also built
altars in the house of the LORD, of which the
LORD had said, "In Jerusalem shall My name be
forever." [5]And he built altars for all the host of
heaven in the two courts of the house of the
LORD. [6]Also he caused his sons to pass through
the fire in the Valley of the Son of Hinnom; he
practiced soothsaying, used witchcraft and sor-
cery, and consulted mediums and spiritists. He
did much evil in the sight of the LORD, to pro-
voke Him to anger. [7]He even set a carved image,
the idol which he had made, in the house of
God, of which God had said to David and to
Solomon his son, "In this house and in
Jerusalem, which I have chosen out of all the
tribes of Israel, I will put My name forever; [8]and
I will not again remove the foot of Israel from
the land which I have appointed for your fa-
thers—only if they are careful to do all that I
have commanded them, according to the whole
law and the statutes and the ordinances by the
hand of Moses." [9]So Manasseh seduced Judah
and the inhabitants of Jerusalem to do more evil
than the nations whom the LORD had destroyed
before the children of Israel.

MANASSEH RESTORED AFTER REPENTANCE

[10]And the LORD spoke to Manasseh and his
people, but they would not listen. [11]Therefore
the LORD brought upon them the captains of the
army of the king of Assyria, who took Manasseh
with hooks,[a] bound him with bronze *fetters*,
and carried him off to Babylon. [12]Now when he
was in affliction, he implored the LORD his God,
and humbled himself greatly before the God of
his fathers, [13]and prayed to Him; and He re-
ceived his entreaty, heard his supplication, and
brought him back to Jerusalem into his king-
dom. Then Manasseh knew that the LORD *was*
God.

[14]After this he built a wall outside the City of
David on the west side of Gihon, in the valley, as
far as the entrance of the Fish Gate; and *it* en-
closed Ophel, and he raised it to a very great
height. Then he put military captains in all the
fortified cities of Judah. [15]He took away the for-
eign gods and the idol from the house of the
LORD, and all the altars that he had built in the
mount of the house of the LORD and in
Jerusalem; and he cast *them* out of the city. [16]He

33:3 [a]The gods of the Assyrians 33:11 [a]That is, nose hooks (compare 2 Kings 19:28)

THE MESSAGE

KING MANASSEH

1-6 33 Manasseh was twelve years old when
he became king. He ruled for fifty-five
years in Jerusalem. In GOD's opinion he was
a bad king—an evil king. He reintroduced
all the moral rot and spiritual corruption
that had been scoured from the country
when GOD dispossessed the pagan nations
in favor of the children of Israel. He rebuilt
the sex-and-religion shrines that his father
Hezekiah had torn down, he built altars and
phallic images for the sex god Baal and the
sex goddess Asherah and worshiped the
cosmic powers, taking orders from the con-
stellations. He built shrines to the cosmic
powers and placed them in both courtyards
of The Temple of GOD, the very Jerusalem
Temple dedicated exclusively by GOD's de-
cree to GOD's Name ("in Jerusalem I place
my Name"). He burned his own sons in a
sacrificial rite in the Valley of Ben Hinnom.
He practiced witchcraft and fortunetelling.
He held séances and consulted spirits from
the underworld. Much evil—in GOD's view a
career in evil. And GOD was angry.
7-8 As a last straw he placed a carved image
of the sex goddess Asherah that he had
commissioned in The Temple of God, a fla-
grant and provocative violation of God's
well-known command to both David and
Solomon, "In this Temple and in this city
Jerusalem, my choice out of all the tribes of
Israel, I place my Name—exclusively and
forever." He had promised, "Never again
will I let my people Israel wander off from
this land I've given to their ancestors. But on
this condition, that they keep everything
I've commanded in the instructions my ser-
vant Moses passed on to them."
9-10 But Manasseh led Judah and the citizens
of Jerusalem off the beaten path into prac-
tices of evil exceeding even the evil of the
pagan nations that GOD had earlier de-
stroyed. When GOD spoke to Manasseh and
his people about this, they ignored him.
11-13 Then GOD directed the leaders of the
troops of the king of Assyria to come after
Manasseh. They put a hook in his nose,
shackles on his feet, and took him off to
Babylon. Now that he was in trouble, he
went to his knees in prayer asking for
help—total repentance before the God of his
ancestors. As he prayed, GOD was touched;
GOD listened and brought him back to
Jerusalem as king. That convinced Ma-
nasseh that GOD was in control.
14-17 After that Manasseh rebuilt the outside
defensive wall of the City of David to the
west of the Gihon spring in the valley. It
went from the Fish Gate and around the hill
of Ophel. He also increased its height. He
tightened up the defense system by posting
army captains in all the fortress cities of Ju-
dah. He also did a good spring cleaning on
The Temple, carting out the pagan idols and
the goddess statue. He took all the altars he
had set up on The Temple hill and through-
out Jerusalem and dumped them outside the
city. He put the Altar of GOD back in work-

NEW KING JAMES VERSION

also repaired the altar of the LORD, sacrificed
peace offerings and thank offerings on it, and
commanded Judah to serve the LORD God of Is-
rael. [17]Nevertheless the people still sacrificed on
the high places, *but* only to the LORD their God.

DEATH OF MANASSEH

[18]Now the rest of the acts of Manasseh, his
prayer to his God, and the words of the seers
who spoke to him in the name of the LORD God
of Israel, indeed they *are written* in the book[a] of
the kings of Israel. [19]Also his prayer and *how*
God received his entreaty, and all his sin and
trespass, and the sites where he built high places
and set up wooden images and carved images,
before he was humbled, indeed they *are* written
among the sayings of Hozai.[a] [20]So Manasseh
rested with his fathers, and they buried him in
his own house. Then his son Amon reigned in his
place.

AMON'S REIGN AND DEATH

[21]Amon *was* twenty-two years old when he
became king, and he reigned two years in
Jerusalem. [22]But he did evil in the sight of the
LORD, as his father Manasseh had done; for
Amon sacrificed to all the carved images which
his father Manasseh had made, and served
them. [23]And he did not humble himself before
the LORD, as his father Manasseh had humbled
himself; but Amon trespassed more and more.

[24]Then his servants conspired against him,
and killed him in his own house. [25]But the peo-
ple of the land executed all those who had con-
spired against King Amon. Then the people of
the land made his son Josiah king in his place.

JOSIAH REIGNS IN JUDAH

34 Josiah *was* eight years old when he be-
came king, and he reigned thirty-one years
in Jerusalem. [2]And he did *what was* right in the
sight of the LORD, and walked in the ways of his
father David; *he* did *not* turn aside to the right
hand or to the left.

[3]For in the eighth year of his reign, while he
was still young, he began to seek the God of his
father David; and in the twelfth year he began to
purge Judah and Jerusalem of the high places,
the wooden images, the carved images, and the
molded images. [4]They broke down the altars of
the Baals in his presence, and the incense altars
which *were* above them he cut down; and the
wooden images, the carved images, and the
molded images he broke in pieces, and made
dust of them and scattered *it* on the graves of
those who had sacrificed to them. [5]He also
burned the bones of the priests on their altars,
and cleansed Judah and Jerusalem. [6]And *so he*
did in the cities of Manasseh, Ephraim, and
Simeon, as far as Naphtali and all around, with
axes.[a] [7]When he had broken down the altars
and the wooden images, had beaten the carved
images into powder, and cut down all the in-

33:18 [a]Literally *words* **33:19** [a]Septuagint reads *the seers.*
34:6 [a]Literally *swords*

THE MESSAGE

ing order and restored worship, sacrificing
Peace-Offerings and Thank-Offerings. He
issued orders to the people: "You shall serve
and worship GOD, the God of Israel." But the
people didn't take him seriously—they used
the name "GOD" but kept on going to the old
pagan neighborhood shrines and doing the
same old things.

18-19 The rest of the history of Manasseh—his
prayer to his God, and the sermons the
prophets personally delivered by authority
of GOD, the God of Israel—this is all written
in *The Chronicles of the Kings of Israel.* His
prayer and how God was touched by his
prayer, a list of all his sins and the things he
did wrong, the actual places where he built
the pagan shrines, the installation of the
sex-goddess Asherah sites, and the idola-
trous images that he worshiped previous to
his conversion—this is all described in the
records of the prophets.

20 When Manasseh died, they buried him in
the palace garden. His son Amon was the
next king.

KING AMON

21-23 Amon was twenty-two years old when he
became king. He was king for two years in
Jerusalem. In GOD's opinion he lived an evil
life, just like his father Manasseh, but he
never did repent to GOD as Manasseh re-
pented. He just kept at it, going from one
thing to another.

24-25 In the end Amon's servants revolted and
assassinated him—killed the king right in
his own palace. The citizens in their turn
then killed the king's assassins. The citizens
then crowned Josiah, Amon's son, as king.

KING JOSIAH

1-2 34 Josiah was eight years old when he be-
came king. He ruled for thirty-one
years in Jerusalem. He behaved well before
GOD. He kept straight on the path blazed by
his ancestor David, not one step to the left
or right.

3-7 When he had been king for eight years—
he was still only a teenager—he began to
seek the God of David his ancestor. Four
years later, the twelfth year of his reign, he
set out to cleanse the neighborhood of sex-
and-religion shrines, and get rid of the sa-
cred Asherah groves and the god and god-
dess figurines, whether carved or cast, from
Judah. He wrecked the Baal shrines, tore
down the altars connected with them, and
scattered the debris and ashes over the
graves of those who had worshiped at them.
He burned the bones of the priests on the
same altars they had used when alive. He
scrubbed the place clean, Judah and
Jerusalem, clean inside and out. The
cleanup campaign ranged outward to the
cities of Manasseh, Ephraim, Simeon, and
the surrounding neighborhoods—as far
north as Naphtali. Throughout Israel he de-
molished the altars and Asherah groves,
pulverized the god and goddess figures,
chopped up the neighborhood shrines into

NEW KING JAMES VERSION

cense altars throughout all the land of Israel, he returned to Jerusalem.

HILKIAH FINDS THE BOOK OF THE LAW

8In the eighteenth year of his reign, when he had purged the land and the temple,[a] he sent Shaphan the son of Azaliah, Maaseiah the governor of the city, and Joah the son of Joahaz the recorder, to repair the house of the LORD his God. 9When they came to Hilkiah the high priest, they delivered the money that was brought into the house of God, which the Levites who kept the doors had gathered from the hand of Manasseh and Ephraim, from all the remnant of Israel, from all Judah and Benjamin, and *which* they had brought back to Jerusalem. 10Then they put *it* in the hand of the foremen who had the oversight of the house of the LORD; and they gave it to the workmen who worked in the house of the LORD, to repair and restore the house. 11They gave *it* to the craftsmen and builders to buy hewn stone and timber for beams, and to floor the houses which the kings of Judah had destroyed. 12And the men did the work faithfully. Their overseers *were* Jahath and Obadiah the Levites, of the sons of Merari, and Zechariah and Meshullam, of the sons of the Kohathites, to supervise. *Others of* the Levites, all of whom were skillful with instruments of music, 13*were* over the burden bearers and *were* overseers of all who did work in any kind of service. And *some* of the Levites *were* scribes, officers, and gatekeepers.

14Now when they brought out the money that was brought into the house of the LORD, Hilkiah the priest found the Book of the Law of the LORD *given* by Moses. 15Then Hilkiah answered and said to Shaphan the scribe, "I have found the Book of the Law in the house of the LORD." And Hilkiah gave the book to Shaphan. 16So Shaphan carried the book to the king, bringing the king word, saying, "All that was committed to your servants they are doing. 17And they have gathered the money that was found in the house of the LORD, and have delivered it into the hand of the overseers and the workmen." 18Then Shaphan the scribe told the king, saying, "Hilkiah the priest has given me a book." And Shaphan read it before the king.

19Thus it happened, when the king heard the words of the Law, that he tore his clothes. 20Then the king commanded Hilkiah, Ahikam the son of Shaphan, Abdon[a] the son of Micah, Shaphan the scribe, and Asaiah a servant of the king, saying, 21"Go, inquire of the LORD for me, and for those who are left in Israel and Judah, concerning the words of the book that is found; for great *is* the wrath of the LORD that is poured out on us, because our fathers have not kept the word of the LORD, to do according to all that is written in this book."

22So Hilkiah and those the king *had appointed* went to Huldah the prophetess, the wife of Shallum the son of Tokhath,[a] the son of Hasrah,[b] keeper of the wardrobe. (She dwelt in

34:8 [a]Literally *house* **34:20** [a]*Achbor the son of Michaiah* in 2 Kings 22:12 **34:22** [a]Spelled *Tikvah* in 2 Kings 22:14 [b]Spelled *Harhas* in 2 Kings 22:14

THE MESSAGE

firewood. With Israel once more intact, he returned to Jerusalem.

8-13 One day in the eighteenth year of his kingship, with the cleanup of country and Temple complete, King Josiah sent Shaphan son of Azaliah, Maaseiah the mayor of the city, and Joah son of Joahaz the historian to renovate The Temple of GOD. First they turned over to Hilkiah the high priest all the money collected by the Levitical security guards from Manasseh and Ephraim and the rest of Israel, and from Judah and Benjamin and the citizens of Jerusalem. It was then put into the hands of the foremen managing the work on The Temple of GOD who then passed it on to the workers repairing GOD'S Temple—the carpenters, construction workers, and masons—so they could buy the lumber and dressed stone for rebuilding the foundations the kings of Judah had allowed to fall to pieces. The workmen were honest and diligent. Their foremen were Jahath and Obadiah, the Merarite Levites, and Zechariah and Meshullam from the Kohathites—these managed the project. The Levites—they were all skilled musicians—were in charge of the common laborers and supervised the workers as they went from job to job. The Levites also served as accountants, managers, and security guards.

14-17 While the money that had been given for The Temple of GOD was being received and dispersed, Hilkiah the high priest found a copy of The Revelation of Moses. He reported to Shaphan the royal secretary, "I've just found the Book of GOD'S Revelation, instructing us in GOD'S way—found it in The Temple!" He gave it to Shaphan, who then gave it to the king. And along with the book, he gave this report: "The job is complete—everything you ordered done is done. They took all the money that was collected in The Temple of GOD and handed it over to the managers and workers."

18 And then Shaphan told the king, "Hilkiah the priest gave me a book." Shaphan proceeded to read it out to the king.

19-21 When the king heard what was written in the book, GOD'S Revelation, he ripped his robes in dismay. And then he called for Hilkiah, Ahikam son of Shaphan, Abdon son of Micah, Shaphan the royal secretary, and Asaiah the king's personal aide. He ordered them all: "Go and pray to GOD for me and what's left of Israel and Judah. Find out what we must do in response to what is written in this book that has just been found! GOD'S anger must be burning furiously against us—our ancestors haven't obeyed a thing written in this book of GOD, followed none of the instructions directed to us."

22-25 Hilkiah and those picked by the king went straight to Huldah the prophetess. She was the wife of Shallum son of Tokhath, the son of Hasrah, who was in charge of the

NEW KING JAMES VERSION

Jerusalem in the Second Quarter.) And they
spoke to her to that *effect*.
23Then she answered them, "Thus says the
LORD God of Israel, 'Tell the man who sent you
to Me, 24"Thus says the LORD: 'Behold, I will
bring calamity on this place and on its inhabi-
tants, all the curses that are written in the book
which they have read before the king of Judah,
25because they have forsaken Me and burned in-
cense to other gods, that they might provoke Me
to anger with all the works of their hands.
Therefore My wrath will be poured out on this
place, and not be quenched.' " ' 26But as for the
king of Judah, who sent you to inquire of the
LORD, in this manner you shall speak to him,
'Thus says the LORD God of Israel: "*Concerning*
the words which you have heard— 27because
your heart was tender, and you humbled your-
self before God when you heard His words
against this place and against its inhabitants,
and you humbled yourself before Me, and you
tore your clothes and wept before Me, I also
have heard *you*," says the LORD. 28"Surely I will
gather you to your fathers, and you shall be
gathered to your grave in peace; and your eyes
shall not see all the calamity which I will bring
on this place and its inhabitants." ' " So they
brought back word to the king.

JOSIAH RESTORES TRUE WORSHIP

29Then the king sent and gathered all the eld-
ers of Judah and Jerusalem. 30The king went up
to the house of the LORD, with all the men of Ju-
dah and the inhabitants of Jerusalem—the
priests and the Levites, and all the people, great
and small. And he read in their hearing all the
words of the Book of the Covenant which had
been found in the house of the LORD. 31Then the
king stood in his place and made a covenant be-
fore the LORD, to follow the LORD, and to keep
His commandments and His testimonies and
His statutes with all his heart and all his soul, to
perform the words of the covenant that were
written in this book. 32And he made all who
were present in Jerusalem and Benjamin take a
stand. So the inhabitants of Jerusalem did ac-
cording to the covenant of God, the God of their
fathers. 33Thus Josiah removed all the abomina-
tions from all the country that *belonged* to the
children of Israel, and made all who were pres-
ent in Israel diligently serve the LORD their God.
All his days they did not depart from following
the LORD God of their fathers.

JOSIAH KEEPS THE PASSOVER

35 Now Josiah kept a Passover to the LORD
in Jerusalem, and they slaughtered the
Passover *lambs* on the fourteenth *day* of the first
month. 2And he set the priests in their duties
and encouraged them for the service of the
house of the LORD. 3Then he said to the Levites
who taught all Israel, who were holy to the
LORD: "Put the holy ark in the house which
Solomon the son of David, king of Israel, built.
It shall no longer *be* a burden on *your* shoul-

THE MESSAGE

palace wardrobe. She lived in Jerusalem in
the Second Quarter. The men consulted with
her. In response to them she said, "GOD's
word, the God of Israel: Tell the man who
sent you here, 'GOD has spoken, I'm on my
way to bring the doom of judgment on this
place and this people. Every word written in
the book read by the king of Judah will hap-
pen. And why? Because they've deserted me
and taken up with other gods; they've made
me thoroughly angry by setting up their
god-making businesses. My anger is raging
white-hot against this place and nobody is
going to put it out.'
26-28 "And also tell the king of Judah, since he
sent you to ask GOD for direction, GOD's
comment on what he read in the book: 'Be-
cause you took seriously the doom of judg-
ment I spoke against this place and people,
and because you responded in humble re-
pentance, tearing your robe in dismay and
weeping before me, I'm taking you seri-
ously. GOD's word. I'll take care of you;
you'll have a quiet death and be buried in
peace. You won't be around to see the doom
that I'm going to bring upon this place and
people.' "
The men took her message back to the
king.
29-31 The king acted immediately, assembling
all the elders of Judah and Jerusalem, and
then proceeding to The Temple of GOD
bringing everyone in his train—priests and
prophets and people ranging from the least
to the greatest. Then he read out publicly
everything written in the Book of the
Covenant that was found in The Temple of
GOD. The king stood by his pillar and before
GOD solemnly committed himself to the
covenant: to follow GOD believingly and
obediently; to follow his instructions, heart
and soul, on what to believe and do; to con-
firm with his life the entire covenant, all that
was written in the book.
32 Then he made everyone in Jerusalem and
Benjamin commit themselves. And they did
it. They committed themselves to the
covenant of God, the God of their ancestors.
33 Josiah did a thorough job of cleaning up
the pollution that had spread throughout Is-
raelite territory and got everyone started
fresh again, serving and worshiping their
GOD. All through Josiah's life the people
kept to the straight and narrow, obediently
following GOD, the God of their ancestors.

1-4 35 Josiah celebrated the Passover to GOD
in Jerusalem. They killed the Passover
lambs on the fourteenth day of the first
month. He gave the priests detailed instruc-
tions and encouraged them in the work of
leading worship in The Temple of GOD. He
also told the Levites who were in charge of
teaching and guiding Israel in all matters of
worship (they were especially consecrated
for this), "Place the sacred Chest in The
Temple that Solomon son of David, the king
of Israel, built. You don't have to carry it

NEW KING JAMES VERSION

ders. Now serve the LORD your God and His people Israel. 4Prepare *yourselves* according to your fathers' houses, according to your divisions, following the written instruction of David king of Israel and the written instruction of Solomon his son. 5And stand in the holy *place* according to the divisions of the fathers' houses of your brethren the *lay* people, and *according to* the division of the father's house of the Levites. 6So slaughter the Passover *offerings*, consecrate yourselves, and prepare *them* for your brethren, that *they* may do according to the word of the LORD by the hand of Moses."

7Then Josiah gave the *lay* people lambs and young goats from the flock, all for Passover *offerings* for all who were present, to the number of thirty thousand, as well as three thousand cattle; these *were* from the king's possessions. 8And his leaders gave willingly to the people, to the priests, and to the Levites. Hilkiah, Zechariah, and Jehiel, rulers of the house of God, gave to the priests for the Passover *offerings* two thousand six hundred *from the flock*, and three hundred cattle. 9Also Conaniah, his brothers Shemaiah and Nethanel, and Hashabiah and Jeiel and Jozabad, chief of the Levites, gave to the Levites for Passover *offerings* five thousand *from the flock* and five hundred cattle.

10So the service was prepared, and the priests stood in their places, and the Levites in their divisions, according to the king's command. 11And they slaughtered the Passover *offerings;* and the priests sprinkled *the blood* with their hands, while the Levites skinned *the animals.* 12Then they removed the burnt offerings that *they* might give them to the divisions of the fathers' houses of the *lay* people, to offer to the LORD, as *it is* written in the Book of Moses. And so *they did* with the cattle. 13Also they roasted the Passover *offerings* with fire according to the ordinance; but the *other* holy *offerings* they boiled in pots, in caldrons, and in pans, and divided *them* quickly among all the *lay* people. 14Then afterward they prepared portions for themselves and for the priests, because the priests, the sons of Aaron, *were busy* in offering burnt offerings and fat until night; therefore the Levites prepared portions for themselves and for the priests, the sons of Aaron. 15And the singers, the sons of Asaph, *were* in their places, according to the command of David, Asaph, Heman, and Jeduthun the king's seer. Also the gatekeepers were at each gate; they did not have to leave their position, because their brethren the Levites prepared portions for them.

16So all the service of the LORD was prepared the same day, to keep the Passover and to offer burnt offerings on the altar of the LORD, according to the command of King Josiah. 17And the children of Israel who were present kept the Passover at that time, and the Feast of Unleavened Bread for seven days. 18There had been no Passover kept in Israel like that since the days of Samuel the prophet; and none of the kings of Israel had kept such a Passover as Josiah kept, with the priests and the Levites, all Judah and Israel who were present, and the inhabitants of

THE MESSAGE

around on your shoulders any longer! Serve
GOD and God's people Israel. Organize
yourselves by families for your respective
responsibilities, following the instructions
left by David king of Israel and Solomon his
son.
5-6 "Take your place in the sanctuary—a
team of Levites for every grouping of your
fellow citizens, the laity. Your job is to kill
the Passover lambs, then consecrate your-
selves and prepare the lambs so that every-
one will be able to keep the Passover ex-
actly as GOD commanded through Moses."
7-9 Josiah personally donated thirty thou-
sand sheep, lambs, and goats and three
thousand bulls—everything needed for the
Passover celebration was there. His officials
also pitched in on behalf of the people, in-
cluding the priests and the Levites. Hilkiah,
Zechariah, and Jehiel, leaders in The Tem-
ple of God, gave twenty-six hundred lambs
and three hundred bulls to the priests for
the Passover offerings. Conaniah, his broth-
ers Shemaiah and Nethanel, along with the
Levitical chiefs Hashabiah, Jeiel, and Joz-
abad, donated five thousand lambs and five
hundred bulls to the Levites for the
Passover offerings.
10-13 Preparations were complete for the serv-
ice of worship; the priests took up their po-
sitions and the Levites were at their posts as
instructed by the king. They killed the
Passover lambs, and while the priests sprin-
kled the blood from the lambs, the Levites
skinned them out. Then they set aside the
Whole-Burnt-Offering for presentation to
the family groupings of the people so that
each group could offer it to GOD following
the instructions in the Book of Moses. They
did the same with the cattle. They roasted
the Passover lamb according to the instruc-
tions and boiled the consecrated offerings in
pots and kettles and pans and promptly
served the people.
14 After the people had eaten the holy meal,
the Levites served themselves and the Aa-
ronite priests—the priests were busy late
into the night making the offerings at the
Altar.
15 The Asaph singers were all in their places
following the instructions of David, Asaph,
Heman, and Jeduthun the king's seer. The
security guards were on duty at each gate—
the Levites also served them because they
couldn't leave their posts.
16-19 Everything went without a hitch in the
worship of GOD that day as they celebrated
the Passover and the offering of the Whole-
Burnt-Offering on the Altar of GOD. It went
just as Josiah had ordered. The Israelites
celebrated the Passover, also known as the
Feast of Unraised Bread, for seven days. The
Passover hadn't been celebrated like this
since the days of Samuel the prophet. None
of the kings had done it. But Josiah, the
priests, the Levites, all Judah and Israel who
were there that week, plus the citizens of
Jerusalem—*they* did it. In the eighteenth

NEW KING JAMES VERSION

Jerusalem. 19In the eighteenth year of the reign
of Josiah this Passover was kept.

JOSIAH DIES IN BATTLE

20After all this, when Josiah had prepared
the temple, Necho king of Egypt came up to
fight against Carchemish by the Euphrates; and
Josiah went out against him. 21But he sent mes-
sengers to him, saying, "What have I to do with
you, king of Judah? *I have* not *come* against you
this day, but against the house with which I have
war; for God commanded me to make haste. Re-
frain *from meddling with* God, who *is* with me,
lest He destroy you." 22Nevertheless Josiah
would not turn his face from him, but disguised
himself so that he might fight with him, and did
not heed the words of Necho from the mouth of
God. So he came to fight in the Valley of
Megiddo.
23And the archers shot King Josiah; and the
king said to his servants, "Take me away, for I
am severely wounded." 24His servants therefore
took him out of that chariot and put him in the
second chariot that he had, and they brought
him to Jerusalem. So he died, and was buried in
one of the tombs of his fathers. And all Judah
and Jerusalem mourned for Josiah.
25Jeremiah also lamented for Josiah. And to
this day all the singing men and the singing
women speak of Josiah in their lamentations.
They made it a custom in Israel; and indeed they
are written in the Laments.
26Now the rest of the acts of Josiah and his
goodness, according to *what was* written in the
Law of the LORD, 27and his deeds from first to
last, indeed they *are* written in the book of the
kings of Israel and Judah.

THE REIGN AND CAPTIVITY OF JEHOAHAZ

36 Then the people of the land took Jehoahaz
the son of Josiah, and made him king in
his father's place in Jerusalem. 2Jehoahaz[a] *was*
twenty-three years old when he became king,
and he reigned three months in Jerusalem.
3Now the king of Egypt deposed him at
Jerusalem; and he imposed on the land a tribute
of one hundred talents of silver and a talent of
gold. 4Then the king of Egypt made *Jehoahaz's*[a]
brother Eliakim king over Judah and Jerusalem,
and changed his name to Jehoiakim. And Necho
took Jehoahaz[b] his brother and carried him off
to Egypt.

THE REIGN AND CAPTIVITY OF JEHOIAKIM

5Jehoiakim *was* twenty-five years old when
he became king, and he reigned eleven years in
Jerusalem. And he did evil in the sight of the
LORD his God. 6Nebuchadnezzar king of Baby-
lon came up against him, and bound him in
bronze *fetters* to carry him off to Babylon. 7Neb-

36:2 [a]Masoretic Text reads *Joahaz*. **36:4** [a]Literally *his* [b]Masoretic Text reads *Joahaz*.

THE MESSAGE

year of the rule of King Josiah, this Passover was celebrated.

20 Some time later, after Josiah's reformation of The Temple, Neco king of Egypt marched out toward Carchemish on the Euphrates River on his way to war. Josiah went out to fight him.

21 Neco sent messengers to Josiah saying, "What do we have against each other, O King of Judah? I haven't come to fight against you but against the country with whom I'm at war. God commanded me to hurry, so don't get in my way; you'll only interfere with God, who is on my side in this, and he'll destroy you."

22-23 But Josiah was spoiling for a fight and wouldn't listen to a thing Neco said (in actuality it was God who said it). Though King Josiah disguised himself when they met on the plain of Megiddo, archers shot him anyway.

The king said to his servants, "Get me out of here—I'm badly wounded."

24-25 So his servants took him out of his chariot and laid him down in an ambulance chariot and drove him back to Jerusalem. He died there and was buried in the family cemetery. Everybody in Judah and Jerusalem attended the funeral. Jeremiah composed an anthem of lament for Josiah. The anthem is still sung by the choirs of Israel to this day. The anthem is written in the Laments.

26-1 The rest of the history of Josiah, his exemplary and devout life, conformed to The Revelation of GOD. The whole story, from start to finish, is written in the *Royal Annals of the Kings of Israel and Judah*. By popular choice, Jehoahaz son of Josiah was made king at Jerusalem, succeeding his father.

KING JEHOAHAZ

2-3 36 Jehoahaz was twenty-three years old when he began to rule. He was king in Jerusalem for a mere three months. The king of Egypt dethroned him and forced the country to pay him nearly four tons of silver and seventy-five pounds of gold.

KING JEHOIAKIM

4 Neco king of Egypt then made Eliakim, Jehoahaz's brother, king of Judah and Jerusalem, but changed his name to Jehoiakim; then he took Jehoahaz back with him to Egypt.

5 Jehoiakim was twenty-five years old when he began to rule; he was king for eleven years in Jerusalem. In GOD's opinion he was an evil king.

6-7 Nebuchadnezzar king of Babylon made war against him, and bound him in bronze chains, intending to take him prisoner to Babylon. Nebuchadnezzar also took things

NEW KING JAMES VERSION

uchadnezzar also carried off *some* of the arti-
cles from the house of the LORD to Babylon, and
put them in his temple at Babylon. 8Now the rest
of the acts of Jehoiakim, the abominations
which he did, and what was found against him,
indeed they *are* written in the book of the kings
of Israel and Judah. Then Jehoiachin his son
reigned in his place.

THE REIGN AND CAPTIVITY OF JEHOIACHIN

9Jehoiachin *was* eight[a] years old when he be-
came king, and he reigned in Jerusalem three
months and ten days. And he did evil in the
sight of the LORD. 10At the turn of the year King
Nebuchadnezzar summoned *him* and took him
to Babylon, with the costly articles from the
house of the LORD, and made Zedekiah, *Je-
hoiakim's*[a] brother, king over Judah and
Jerusalem.

ZEDEKIAH REIGNS IN JUDAH

11Zedekiah *was* twenty-one years old when
he became king, and he reigned eleven years in
Jerusalem. 12He did evil in the sight of the LORD
his God, *and* did not humble himself before Je-
remiah the prophet, *who spoke* from the mouth
of the LORD. 13And he also rebelled against King
Nebuchadnezzar, who had made him swear *an
oath* by God; but he stiffened his neck and hard-
ened his heart against turning to the LORD God
of Israel. 14Moreover all the leaders of the
priests and the people transgressed more and
more, *according* to all the abominations of the
nations, and defiled the house of the LORD
which He had consecrated in Jerusalem.

THE FALL OF JERUSALEM

15And the LORD God of their fathers sent
warnings to them by His messengers, rising up
early and sending *them*, because He had com-
passion on His people and on His dwelling
place. 16But they mocked the messengers of
God, despised His words, and scoffed at His
prophets, until the wrath of the LORD arose
against His people, till *there was* no remedy.
17Therefore He brought against them the
king of the Chaldeans, who killed their young
men with the sword in the house of their sanctu-
ary, and had no compassion on young man or
virgin, on the aged or the weak; He gave *them*
all into his hand. 18And all the articles from the
house of God, great and small, the treasures of
the house of the LORD, and the treasures of the
king and of his leaders, all *these* he took to
Babylon. 19Then they burned the house of God,
broke down the wall of Jerusalem, burned all its
palaces with fire, and destroyed all its precious
possessions. 20And those who escaped from the
sword he carried away to Babylon, where they
became servants to him and his sons until the
rule of the kingdom of Persia,

36:9 [a]Some Hebrew manuscripts, Septuagint, Syriac, and 2 Kings 24:8 read *eighteen.* **36:10** [a]Literally *his* (compare 2 Kings 24:17)

THE MESSAGE

from The Temple of GOD to Babylon and put
them in his royal palace.
8 The rest of the history of Jehoiakim, the
outrageous sacrilege he committed and
what happened to him as a consequence, is
all written in the *Royal Annals of the Kings
of Israel and Judah.*
Jehoiachin his son became the next king.

KING JEHOIACHIN

9-10 Jehoiachin was eighteen years old when he
became king. But he ruled for only three
months and ten days in Jerusalem. In GOD's
opinion he was an evil king. In the spring
King Nebuchadnezzar ordered him brought
to Babylon along with the valuables remain-
ing in The Temple of GOD. Then he made his
uncle Zedekiah a puppet king over Judah
and Jerusalem.

KING ZEDEKIAH

11-13 Zedekiah was twenty-one years old when
he started out as king. He was king in
Jerusalem for eleven years. As far as GOD
was concerned, he was just one more evil
king; there wasn't a trace of contrition in
him when the prophet Jeremiah preached
GOD's word to him. Then he compounded
his troubles by rebelling against King Neb-
uchadnezzar, who earlier had made him
swear in God's name that he would be loyal.
He became set in his own stubborn ways—
he never gave GOD a thought; repentance
never entered his mind.
14 The evil mindset spread to the leaders
and priests and filtered down to the peo-
ple—it kicked off an epidemic of evil, re-
peating the abominations of the pagans and
polluting The Temple of GOD so recently
consecrated in Jerusalem.
15-17 GOD, the God of their ancestors, repeat-
edly sent warning messages to them. Out of
compassion for both his people and his
Temple he wanted to give them every
chance possible. But they wouldn't listen;
they poked fun at God's messengers, de-
spised the message itself, and in general
treated the prophets like idiots. GOD became
more and more angry until there was no
turning back—GOD called in Nebuchadnez-
zar king of Babylon, who came and killed
indiscriminately—and right in The Temple
itself; it was a ruthless massacre: young
men and virgins, the elderly and weak—
they were all the same to him.
18-20 And then he plundered The Temple of
everything valuable, cleaned it out com-
pletely; he emptied the treasuries of The
Temple of God, the treasuries of the king
and his officials, and hauled it all, people
and possessions, off to Babylon. He burned
The Temple of God to the ground, knocked
down the wall of Jerusalem, and set fire to
all the buildings—everything valuable was
burned up. Any survivor was taken prisoner
into exile in Babylon and made a slave to
Nebuchadnezzar and his family. The exile
and slavery lasted until the kingdom of Per-
sia took over.

NEW KING JAMES VERSION

[21]to fulfill the word of the LORD by the mouth of Jeremiah, until the land had enjoyed her Sabbaths. As long as she lay desolate she kept Sabbath, to fulfill seventy years.

THE PROCLAMATION OF CYRUS

[22]Now in the first year of Cyrus king of Persia, that the word of the LORD by the mouth of Jeremiah might be fulfilled, the LORD stirred up the spirit of Cyrus king of Persia, so that he made a proclamation throughout all his kingdom, and also *put it* in writing, saying,

[23]Thus says Cyrus king of Persia:
All the kingdoms of the earth the LORD God of heaven has given me. And He has commanded me to build Him a house at Jerusalem which is in Judah. Who *is* among you of all His people? May the LORD his God *be* with him, and let him go up!

THE MESSAGE

21 This is exactly the message of GOD that Jeremiah had preached: the desolate land put to an extended sabbath rest, a seventy-year Sabbath rest making up for all the unkept Sabbaths.

KING CYRUS

22-23 In the first year of Cyrus king of Persia—this fulfilled the message of GOD preached by Jeremiah—GOD moved Cyrus king of Persia to make an official announcement throughout his kingdom; he wrote it out as follows: "From Cyrus king of Persia a proclamation: GOD, the God of the heavens, has given me all the kingdoms of the earth. He has also assigned me to build him a Temple of worship at Jerusalem in Judah. All who belong to GOD's people are urged to return—and may your GOD be with you! Move forward!"

EZRA

New King James Version

End of the Babylonian Captivity

1 Now in the first year of Cyrus king of Persia, that the word of the LORD by the mouth of Jeremiah might be fulfilled, the LORD stirred up the spirit of Cyrus king of Persia, so that he made a proclamation throughout all his kingdom, and also *put it* in writing, saying,

> 2 Thus says Cyrus king of Persia:
> All the kingdoms of the earth the LORD God of heaven has given me. And He has commanded me to build Him a house at Jerusalem which *is* in Judah. 3 Who *is* among you of all His people? May his God be with him, and let him go up to Jerusalem which *is* in Judah, and build the house of the LORD God of Israel (He *is* God), which *is* in Jerusalem. 4 And whoever is left in any place where he dwells, let the men of his place help him with silver and gold, with goods and livestock, besides the freewill offerings for the house of God which *is* in Jerusalem.

5 Then the heads of the fathers' *houses* of Judah and Benjamin, and the priests and the Levites, with all whose spirits God had moved, arose to go up and build the house of the LORD which *is* in Jerusalem. 6 And all those who *were* around them encouraged them with articles of silver and gold, with goods and livestock, and with precious things, besides all *that* was willingly offered.

7 King Cyrus also brought out the articles of the house of the LORD, which Nebuchadnezzar had taken from Jerusalem and put in the temple of his gods; 8 and Cyrus king of Persia brought them out by the hand of Mithredath the treasurer, and counted them out to Sheshbazzar the prince of Judah. 9 This *is* the number of them: thirty gold platters, one thousand silver platters, twenty-nine knives, 10 thirty gold basins, four hundred and ten silver basins of a similar *kind, and* one thousand other articles. 11 All the articles of gold and silver *were* five thousand four hundred. All *these* Sheshbazzar took with the captives who were brought from Babylon to Jerusalem.

The Captives Who Returned to Jerusalem

2 Now[a] these *are* the people of the province who came back from the captivity, of those who had been carried away, whom Nebuchadnezzar the king of Babylon had carried away to Babylon, and who returned to Jerusalem and Judah, everyone to his *own* city.

2 *Those* who came with Zerubbabel *were*

2:1 [a]Compare this chapter with Nehemiah 7:6–73.

The Message

Cyrus King of Persia: "Build The Temple of God!"

1-4 1 In the first year of Cyrus king of Persia—this fulfilled the Message of God preached by Jeremiah—GOD prodded Cyrus king of Persia to make an official announcement throughout his kingdom. He wrote it out as follows:

> From Cyrus king of Persia, a Proclamation: GOD, the God of the heavens, has given me all the kingdoms of the earth. He has also assigned me to build him a Temple of worship in Jerusalem, Judah. Who among you belongs to his people? God be with you! Go to Jerusalem which is in Judah and build The Temple of GOD, the God of Israel, Jerusalem's God. Those who stay behind, wherever they happen to live, will support them with silver, gold, tools, and pack animals, along with Freewill-Offerings for The Temple of God in Jerusalem.

5-6 The heads of the families of Judah and Benjamin, along with the priests and Levites—everyone, in fact, God prodded—set out to build The Temple of GOD in Jerusalem. Their neighbors rallied behind them enthusiastically with silver, gold, tools, pack animals, expensive gifts, and, over and above these, Freewill-Offerings.

7-10 Also, King Cyrus turned over to them all the vessels and utensils from The Temple of GOD that Nebuchadnezzar had hauled from Jerusalem and put in the temple of his gods. Cyrus king of Persia put Mithredath the treasurer in charge of the transfer; he provided a full inventory for Sheshbazzar the prince of Judah, including the following:

> 30 gold dishes
> 1,000 silver dishes
> 29 silver pans
> 30 gold bowls
> 410 duplicate silver bowls
> 1,000 miscellaneous items.

11 All told, there were 5,400 gold and silver articles that Sheshbazzar took with him when he brought the exiles back from Babylon to Jerusalem.

1-58 2 These are the people from the province who now returned from the captivity, exiles whom Nebuchadnezzar king of Babylon had carried off captive. They returned to Jerusalem and Judah, each to his hometown. They came in company with Zerubba-

NEW KING JAMES VERSION

Jeshua, Nehemiah, Seraiah, Reelaiah, Mordecai,
Bilshan, Mispar,[a] Bigvai, Rehum,[b] *and* Baanah.
The number of the men of the people of Israel:
3the people of Parosh, two thousand one hun-
dred and seventy-two; 4the people of Shepha-
tiah, three hundred and seventy-two; 5the peo-
ple of Arah, seven hundred and seventy-five;
6the people of Pahath-Moab, of the people of
Jeshua *and* Joab, two thousand eight hundred
and twelve; 7the people of Elam, one thousand
two hundred and fifty-four; 8the people of Zattu,
nine hundred and forty-five; 9the people of Zac-
cai, seven hundred and sixty; 10the people of
Bani,[a] six hundred and forty-two; 11the people of
Bebai, six hundred and twenty-three; 12the peo-
ple of Azgad, one thousand two hundred and
twenty-two; 13the people of Adonikam, six hun-
dred and sixty-six; 14the people of Bigvai, two
thousand and fifty-six; 15the people of Adin, four
hundred and fifty-four; 16the people of Ater of
Hezekiah, ninety-eight; 17the people of Bezai,
three hundred and twenty-three; 18the people of
Jorah,[a] one hundred and twelve; 19the people of
Hashum, two hundred and twenty-three; 20the
people of Gibbar,[a] ninety-five; 21the people of
Bethlehem, one hundred and twenty-three; 22the
men of Netophah, fifty-six; 23the men of
Anathoth, one hundred and twenty-eight; 24the
people of Azmaveth,[a] forty-two; 25the people of
Kirjath Arim,[a] Chephirah, and Beeroth, seven
hundred and forty-three; 26the people of Ramah
and Geba, six hundred and twenty-one; 27the
men of Michmas, one hundred and twenty-two;
28the men of Bethel and Ai, two hundred and
twenty-three; 29the people of Nebo, fifty-two;
30the people of Magbish, one hundred and fifty-
six; 31the people of the other Elam, one thou-
sand two hundred and fifty-four; 32the people of
Harim, three hundred and twenty; 33the people
of Lod, Hadid, and Ono, seven hundred and
twenty-five; 34the people of Jericho, three hun-
dred and forty-five; 35the people of Senaah,
three thousand six hundred and thirty.

36The priests: the sons of Jedaiah, of the
house of Jeshua, nine hundred and seventy-
three; 37the sons of Immer, one thousand and
fifty-two; 38the sons of Pashhur, one thousand
two hundred and forty-seven; 39the sons of
Harim, one thousand and seventeen.

40The Levites: the sons of Jeshua and Kad-
miel, of the sons of Hodaviah,[a] seventy-four.

41The singers: the sons of Asaph, one hun-
dred and twenty-eight.

42The sons of the gatekeepers: the sons of
Shallum, the sons of Ater, the sons of Talmon,
the sons of Akkub, the sons of Hatita, and the
sons of Shobai, one hundred and thirty-nine *in*
all.

43The Nethinim: the sons of Ziha, the sons of
Hasupha, the sons of Tabbaoth, 44the sons of
Keros, the sons of Siaha,[a] the sons of Padon,
45the sons of Lebanah, the sons of Hagabah, the
sons of Akkub, 46the sons of Hagab, the sons of

2:2 [a]Spelled *Mispereth* in Nehemiah 7:7 [b]Spelled *Nehum* in Nehemiah 7:7 **2:10** [a]Spelled *Binnui* in Nehemiah 7:15 **2:18** [a]Called *Hariph* in Nehemiah 7:24 **2:20** [a]Called *Gibeon* in Nehemiah 7:25 **2:24** [a]Called *Beth Azmaveth* in Nehemiah 7:28 **2:25** [a]Called *Kirjath Jearim* in Nehemiah 7:29 **2:40** [a]Spelled *Hodevah* in Nehemiah 7:43 **2:44** [a]Spelled *Sia* in Nehemiah 7:47

THE MESSAGE

bel, Jeshua, Nehemiah, Seraiah, Reelaiah, Mordecai, Bilshan, Mispar, Bigvai, Rehum, and Baanah.

The numbers of the returning Israelites by families of origin were as follows:

Parosh, 2,172
Shephatiah, 372
Arah, 775
Pahath-Moab (sons of Jeshua and Joab), 2,812
Elam, 1,254
Zattu, 945
Zaccai, 760
Bani, 642
Bebai, 623
Azgad, 1,222
Adonikam, 666
Bigvai, 2,056
Adin, 454
Ater (sons of Hezekiah), 98
Bezai, 323
Jorah, 112
Hashum, 223
Gibbar, 95.

Israelites identified by place of origin were as follows:

Bethlehem, 123
Netophah, 56
Anathoth, 128
Azmaveth, 42
Kiriath Jearim, Kephirah, and Beeroth, 743
Ramah and Geba, 621
Micmash, 122
Bethel and Ai, 223
Nebo, 52
Magbish, 156
Elam (the other one), 1,254
Harim, 320
Lod, Hadid, and Ono, 725
Jericho, 345
Senaah, 3,630.

Priestly families:
Jedaiah (sons of Jeshua), 973
Immer, 1,052
Pashhur, 1,247
Harim, 1,017.

Levitical families:
Jeshua and Kadmiel (sons of Hodaviah), 74.

Singers:
Asaph's family line, 128.

Security guard families:
Shallum, Ater, Talmon, Akkub, Hatita, and Shobai, 139.

Families of temple support staff:
Ziha, Hasupha, Tabbaoth,
Keros, Siaha, Padon,
Lebanah, Hagabah, Akkub,
Hagab, Shalmai, Hanan,

NEW KING JAMES VERSION

Shalmai, the sons of Hanan, 47the sons of Giddel, the sons of Gahar, the sons of Reaiah, 48the sons of Rezin, the sons of Nekoda, the sons of Gazzam, 49the sons of Uzza, the sons of Paseah, the sons of Besai, 50the sons of Asnah, the sons of Meunim, the sons of Nephusim,[a] 51the sons of Bakbuk, the sons of Hakupha, the sons of Harhur, 52the sons of Bazluth,[a] the sons of Mehida, the sons of Harsha, 53the sons of Barkos, the sons of Sisera, the sons of Tamah, 54the sons of Neziah, and the sons of Hatipha.

55The sons of Solomon's servants: the sons of Sotai, the sons of Sophereth, the sons of Peruda,[a] 56the sons of Jaala, the sons of Darkon, the sons of Giddel, 57the sons of Shephatiah, the sons of Hattil, the sons of Pochereth of Zebaim, and the sons of Ami.[a] 58All the Nethinim and the children of Solomon's servants were three hundred and ninety-two.

59And these *were* the ones who came up from Tel Melah, Tel Harsha, Cherub, Addan,[a] and Immer; but they could not identify their father's house or their genealogy,[b] whether they *were* of Israel: 60the sons of Delaiah, the sons of Tobiah, and the sons of Nekoda, six hundred and fifty-two; 61and of the sons of the priests: the sons of Habaiah, the sons of Koz,[a] and the sons of Barzillai, who took a wife of the daughters of Barzillai the Gileadite, and was called by their name. 62These sought their listing *among* those who were registered by genealogy, but they were not found; therefore they *were excluded* from the priesthood as defiled. 63And the governor[a] said to them that they should not eat of the most holy things till a priest could consult with the Urim and Thummim.

64The whole assembly together *was* forty-two thousand three hundred *and* sixty, 65besides their male and female servants, of whom *there were* seven thousand three hundred and thirty-seven; and they had two hundred men and women singers. 66Their horses *were* seven hundred and thirty-six, their mules two hundred and forty-five, 67their camels four hundred and thirty-five, and *their* donkeys six thousand seven hundred and twenty.

68*Some* of the heads of the fathers' *houses*, when they came to the house of the LORD which *is* in Jerusalem, offered freely for the house of God, to erect it in its place: 69According to their ability, they gave to the treasury for the work sixty-one thousand gold drachmas, five thousand minas of silver, and one hundred priestly garments.

70So the priests and the Levites, *some* of the people, the singers, the gatekeepers, and the Nethinim, dwelt in their cities, and all Israel in their cities.

WORSHIP RESTORED AT JERUSALEM

3 And when the seventh month had come, and the children of Israel *were* in the cities, the people gathered together as one man to Jerusalem. 2Then Jeshua the son of Jozadak[a]

2:50 [a]Spelled *Nephishesim* in Nehemiah 7:52 **2:52** [a]Spelled *Bazlith* in Nehemiah 7:54 **2:55** [a]Spelled *Perida* in Nehemiah 7:57 **2:57** [a]Spelled *Amon* in Nehemiah 7:59 **2:59** [a]Spelled *Addon* in Nehemiah 7:61 [b]Literally *seed* **2:61** [a]Or *Hakkoz* **2:63** [a]Hebrew *Tirshatha* **3:2** [a]Spelled *Jehozadak* in 1 Chronicles 6:14

THE MESSAGE

Giddel, Gahar, Reaiah,
Rezin, Nekoda, Gazzam,
Uzza, Paseah, Besai,
Asnah, Meunim, Nephussim,
Bakbuk, Hakupha, Harhur,
Bazluth, Mehida, Harsha,
Barkos, Sisera, Temah,
Neziah, and Hatipha.

Families of Solomon's servants:
Sotai, Hassophereth, Peruda,
Jaala, Darkon, Giddel,
Shephatiah, Hattil, Pokereth-Hazzebaim, and Ami.

Temple support staff and Solomon's servants added up to 392.

59-60 These are those who came from Tel Melah, Tel Harsha, Kerub, Addon, and Immer. They weren't able to prove their ancestry, whether they were true Israelites or not:

61 Delaiah, Tobiah, and Nekoda, 652 in all.

Likewise with these priestly families:
Hobaiah, Hakkoz, and Barzillai, who had married a daughter of Barzillai the Gileadite and took that name.

62-63 They had thoroughly searched for their family records but couldn't find them. And so they were barred from priestly work as ritually unclean. The governor ruled that they could not eat from the holy food until a priest could determine their status with the Urim and Thummim.

64-67 The total count for the congregation was 42,360. That did not include the male and female slaves, which numbered 7,337. There were also 200 male and female singers, and they had 736 horses, 245 mules, 435 camels, and 6,720 donkeys.

68-69 Some of the heads of families, on arriving at The Temple of GOD in Jerusalem, made Freewill-Offerings toward the rebuilding of The Temple of God on its site. They gave to the building fund as they were able, about 1,100 pounds of gold, about three tons of silver, and 100 priestly robes.

70 The priests, Levites, and some of the people lived in Jerusalem. The singers, security guards, and temple support staff found places in their hometowns. All the Israelites found a place to live.

THE BUILDING BEGUN: "THE FOUNDATION OF THE TEMPLE WAS LAID"

1-2 3 When the seventh month came and the Israelites had settled into their towns, the people assembled together in Jerusalem. Jeshua son of Jozadak and his brother

NEW KING JAMES VERSION

and his brethren the priests, and Zerubbabel the
son of Shealtiel and his brethren, arose and built
the altar of the God of Israel, to offer burnt offer-
ings on it, as *it is* written in the Law of Moses the
man of God. 3Though fear *had come* upon them
because of the people of those countries, they set
the altar on its bases; and they offered burnt of-
ferings on it to the LORD, *both* the morning and
evening burnt offerings. 4They also kept the
Feast of Tabernacles, as *it is* written, and *offered*
the daily burnt offerings in the number required
by ordinance for each day. 5Afterwards *they of-*
fered the regular burnt offering, and *those* for
New Moons and for all the appointed feasts of
the LORD that were consecrated, and *those* of
everyone who willingly offered a freewill offer-
ing to the LORD. 6From the first day of the sev-
enth month they began to offer burnt offerings
to the LORD, although the foundation of the tem-
ple of the LORD had not been laid. 7They also
gave money to the masons and the carpenters,
and food, drink, and oil to the people of Sidon
and Tyre to bring cedar logs from Lebanon to the
sea, to Joppa, according to the permission which
they had from Cyrus king of Persia.

RESTORATION OF THE TEMPLE BEGINS

8Now in the second month of the second year
of their coming to the house of God at
Jerusalem, Zerubbabel the son of Shealtiel,
Jeshua the son of Jozadak,[a] and the rest of their
brethren the priests and the Levites, and all
those who had come out of the captivity to
Jerusalem, began *work* and appointed the
Levites from twenty years old and above to
oversee the work of the house of the LORD.
9Then Jeshua *with* his sons and brothers, Kad-
miel *with* his sons, and the sons of Judah,[a] arose
as one to oversee those working on the house of
God: the sons of Henadad *with* their sons and
their brethren the Levites.
10When the builders laid the foundation of
the temple of the LORD, the priests stood[a] in
their apparel with trumpets, and the Levites, the
sons of Asaph, with cymbals, to praise the LORD,
according to the ordinance of David king of Is-
rael. 11And they sang responsively, praising and
giving thanks to the LORD:

"For *He is* good,
For His mercy *endures* forever toward Israel."[a]

Then all the people shouted with a great shout,
when they praised the LORD, because the foun-
dation of the house of the LORD was laid.
12But many of the priests and Levites and
heads of the fathers' *houses,* old men who had
seen the first temple, wept with a loud voice
when the foundation of this temple was laid be-
fore their eyes. Yet many shouted aloud for joy,
13so that the people could not discern the noise
of the shout of joy from the noise of the weeping
of the people, for the people shouted with a loud
shout, and the sound was heard afar off.

3:8 [a]Spelled *Jehozadak* in 1 Chronicles 6:14 **3:9** [a]Or *Hodaviah* (compare 2:40) **3:10** [a]Following Septuagint, Syriac, and Vulgate; Masoretic Text reads *they stationed the priests.* **3:11** [a]Compare Psalm 136:1

THE MESSAGE

priests, along with Zerubbabel, the son of Shealtiel, and his relatives, went to work and built the Altar of the God of Israel to offer Whole-Burnt-Offerings on it as written in The Revelation of Moses the man of God.

3-5 Even though they were afraid of what their non-Israelite neighbors might do, they went ahead anyway and set up the Altar on its foundations and offered Whole-Burnt-Offerings on it morning and evening. They also celebrated the Festival of Booths as prescribed and the daily Whole-Burnt-Offerings set for each day. And they presented the regular Whole-Burnt-Offerings for Sabbaths, New Moons, and GOD's Holy Festivals, as well as Freewill-Offerings for GOD.

6 They began offering Whole-Burnt-Offerings to GOD from the very first day of the seventh month, even though The Temple of GOD's foundation had not yet been laid.

7 They gave money to hire masons and carpenters. They gave food, drink, and oil to the Sidonians and Tyrians in exchange for the cedar lumber they had brought by sea from Lebanon to Joppa, a shipment authorized by Cyrus the king of Persia.

8-9 In the second month of the second year after their arrival at The Temple of God in Jerusalem, Zerubbabel son of Shealtiel, and Jeshua son of Jozadak, in company with their brother priests and Levites and everyone else who had come back to Jerusalem from captivity, got started. They appointed the Levites twenty years of age and older to direct the rebuilding of The Temple of GOD. Jeshua and his family joined Kadmiel, Binnui, and Hodaviah, along with the extended family of Henadad—all Levites—to direct the work crew on The Temple of God.

10-11 When the workers laid the foundation of The Temple of GOD, the priests in their robes stood up with trumpets, and the Levites, sons of Asaph, with cymbals, to praise GOD in the tradition of David king of Israel. They sang antiphonally praise and thanksgiving to GOD:

Yes! GOD is good!
Oh yes—he'll never quit loving Israel!

11-13 All the people boomed out hurrahs, praising GOD as the foundation of The Temple of GOD was laid. As many were noisily shouting with joy, many of the older priests, Levites, and family heads who had seen the first Temple, when they saw the foundations of this Temple laid, wept loudly for joy. People couldn't distinguish the shouting from the weeping. The sound of their voices reverberated for miles around.

New King James Version

Resistance to Rebuilding the Temple

4 Now when the adversaries of Judah and Ben-
jamin heard that the descendants of the cap-
tivity were building the temple of the LORD God
of Israel, 2they came to Zerubbabel and the
heads of the fathers' *houses,* and said to them,
"Let us build with you, for we seek your God as
you *do;* and we have sacrificed to Him since the
days of Esarhaddon king of Assyria, who
brought us here." 3But Zerubbabel and Jeshua
and the rest of the heads of the fathers' *houses*
of Israel said to them, "You may do nothing with
us to build a house for our God; but we alone
will build to the LORD God of Israel, as King
Cyrus the king of Persia has commanded us."
4Then the people of the land tried to discourage
the people of Judah. They troubled them in
building, 5and hired counselors against them to
frustrate their purpose all the days of Cyrus
king of Persia, even until the reign of Darius
king of Persia.

Rebuilding of Jerusalem Opposed

6In the reign of Ahasuerus, in the beginning of his reign, they wrote an accusation against the inhabitants of Judah and Jerusalem.

7In the days of Artaxerxes also, Bishlam,
Mithredath, Tabel, and the rest of their compan-
ions wrote to Artaxerxes king of Persia; and the
letter *was* written in Aramaic script, and trans-
lated into the Aramaic language. 8Rehum[a] the
commander and Shimshai the scribe wrote a
letter against Jerusalem to King Artaxerxes in
this fashion:

> 9From[a] Rehum the commander, Shimshai
> the scribe, and the rest of their
> companions—*representatives* of the
> Dinaites, the Apharsathchites, the
> Tarpelites, the people of Persia and Erech
> and Babylon and Shushan,[b] the Dehavites,
> the Elamites, 10and the rest of the nations
> whom the great and noble Osnapper took
> captive and settled in the cities of Samaria
> and the remainder beyond the River[a]—and
> so forth.[b]

11(This *is* a copy of the letter that they sent him)

> To King Artaxerxes from your servants, the men *of the region* beyond the River, and so forth:[a]
>
> 12Let it be known to the king that the Jews
> who came up from you have come to us at
> Jerusalem, and are building the rebellious
> and evil city, and are finishing *its* walls and
> repairing the foundations. 13Let it now be
> known to the king that, if this city is built
> and the walls completed, they will not pay
> tax, tribute, or custom, and the king's
> treasury will be diminished. 14Now because
> we receive support from the palace, it was
> not proper for us to see the king's
> dishonor; therefore we have sent and

4:8 [a]The original language of Ezra 4:8 through 6:18 is Aramaic. 4:9 [a]Literally *Then* [b]Or *Susa* 4:10 [a]That is, the Euphrates [b]Literally *and now* 4:11 [a]Literally *and now*

The Message

The Building Stopped: Cease Rebuilding in That City

1-2 4 Old enemies of Judah and Benjamin heard that the exiles were building The Temple of the GOD of Israel. They came to Zerubbabel and the family heads and said, "We'll help you build. We worship your God the same as you. We've been offering sacrifices to him since Esarhaddon king of Assyria brought us here."

3 Zerubbabel, Jeshua, and the rest of the family heads of Israel said to them, "Nothing doing. Building The Temple of our God is not the same thing to you as to us. We alone will build for the GOD of Israel. We're the ones King Cyrus of Persia commanded to do it."

4-5 So these people started beating down the morale of the people of Judah, harassing them as they built. They even hired propagandists to sap their resolve. They kept this up for about fifteen years, throughout the lifetime of Cyrus king of Persia and on into the reign of Darius king of Persia.

6 In fact, in the reign of Xerxes, at the beginning of his reign, they wrote an accusation against those living in Judah and Jerusalem.

7 Again later, in the time of Artaxerxes, Bishlam, Mithredath, Tabeel, and their associates wrote regarding the Jerusalem business to Artaxerxes king of Persia. The letter was written in Aramaic and translated. (What follows is written in Aramaic.)

8-16 Rehum the commanding officer and Shimshai the secretary wrote a letter against Jerusalem to Artaxerxes the king as follows:

> From: Rehum the commanding officer and Shimshai the secretary, backed by the rest of their associates, the judges and officials over the people from Tripolis, Persia, Erech, and Babylon, Elamites of Susa, and all the others whom the great and honorable Ashurbanipal deported and settled in the city of Samaria and other places in the land across the Euphrates.

(This is the copy of the letter they sent to him.)

> To: King Artaxerxes from your servants from the land across the Euphrates.
>
> We are here to inform the king that the Jews who came from you to us have arrived in Jerusalem and have set about rebuilding that rebellious and evil city. They are busy at work finishing the walls and rebuilding the foundations. The king needs to know that once that city is rebuilt and the wall completed they will no longer pay a penny of tribute, tax, or duty. The royal treasury will feel the loss. We're loyal to the king and cannot sit idly by while our king is being in-

NEW KING JAMES VERSION

informed the king, 15 that search may be
made in the book of the records of your
fathers. And you will find in the book of
the records and know that this city *is* a
rebellious city, harmful to kings and
provinces, and that they have incited
sedition within the city in former times, for
which cause this city was destroyed.

16 We inform the king that if this city is
rebuilt and its walls are completed, the
result will be that you will have no
dominion beyond the River.

17 The king sent an answer:

To Rehum the commander, *to* Shimshai the
scribe, *to* the rest of their companions who
dwell in Samaria, and *to* the remainder
beyond the River:

Peace, and so forth.[a]

18 The letter which you sent to us has been
clearly read before me. 19 And I gave the
command, and a search has been made,
and it was found that this city in former
times has revolted against kings, and
rebellion and sedition have been fostered
in it. 20 There have also been mighty kings
over Jerusalem, who have ruled over all
the region beyond the River; and tax,
tribute, and custom were paid to them.
21 Now give the command to make these
men cease, that this city may not be built
until the command is given by me.

22 Take heed now that you do not fail to do
this. Why should damage increase to the
hurt of the kings?

23 Now when the copy of King Artaxerxes'
letter *was* read before Rehum, Shimshai the
scribe, and their companions, they went up in
haste to Jerusalem against the Jews, and by
force of arms made them cease. 24 Thus the work
of the house of God which *is* at Jerusalem
ceased, and it was discontinued until the second
year of the reign of Darius king of Persia.

RESTORATION OF THE TEMPLE RESUMED

5 Then the prophet Haggai and Zechariah the
son of Iddo, prophets, prophesied to the Jews
who *were* in Judah and Jerusalem, in the name of
the God of Israel, *who was* over them. 2 So Zerub-
babel the son of Shealtiel and Jeshua the son of
Jozadak[a] rose up and began to build the house
of God which *is* in Jerusalem; and the prophets of
God *were* with them, helping them.
3 At the same time Tattenai the governor of *the
region* beyond the River[a] and Shethar-Boznai
and their companions came to them and spoke
thus to them: "Who has commanded you to build
this temple and finish this wall?" 4 Then, accord-
ingly, we told them the names of the men who
were constructing this building.

4:17 [a]Literally *and now* **5:2** [a]Spelled *Jehozadak* in 1 Chronicles 6:14 **5:3** [a]That is, the Euphrates

THE MESSAGE

sulted—that's why we are passing this information on. We suggest that you look into the court records of your ancestors; you'll learn from those books that that city is a rebellious city, a thorn in the side to kings and provinces, a historic center of unrest and revolt. That's why the city was wiped out. We are letting the king know that if that city gets rebuilt and its walls restored, you'll end up with nothing in your province beyond the Euphrates.

17-22 The king sent his reply to Rehum the commanding officer, Shimshai the secretary, and the rest of their associates who lived in Samaria and other places beyond the Euphrates.

Peace be with you. The letter that you sent has been translated and read to me. I gave orders to search the records, and sure enough it turns out that this city has revolted against kings time and again—rebellion is an old story there. I find that they've had their share of strong kings who have taken over beyond the Euphrates and exacted taxes, tribute, and duty. So do this: Order these men to stop work immediately—not a lick of rebuilding in that city unless I order it. Act quickly and firmly; they've done enough damage to kings!

23 The letter of King Artaxerxes was read to Rehum and Shimshai the secretary and their associates. They lost no time. They went to the Jews in Jerusalem and made them quit work.
24 That put a stop to the work on The Temple of God in Jerusalem. Nothing more was done until the second year of the reign of Darius king of Persia.

THE BUILDING RESUMED: "HELP THE LEADERS IN THE REBUILDING"

1-2 5 Meanwhile the prophets Haggai and Zechariah son of Iddo were preaching to the Jews in Judah and Jerusalem in the authority of the God of Israel who ruled them. And so Zerubbabel son of Shealtiel and Jeshua son of Jozadak started again, rebuilding The Temple of God in Jerusalem. The prophets of God were right there helping them.
3-4 Tattenai was governor of the land beyond the Euphrates at this time. Tattenai, Shethar-Bozenai, and their associates came to the Israelites and asked, "Who issued you a permit to rebuild this Temple and restore it to use?" Then we told them the names of the men responsible for this construction work.

NEW KING JAMES VERSION

5 But the eye of their God was upon the elders of the Jews, so that they could not make them cease till a report could go to Darius. Then a written answer was returned concerning this *matter.*
6 This is a copy of the letter that Tattenai sent:

The governor of *the region* beyond the River, and Shethar-Boznai, and his companions, the Persians who *were in the region* beyond the River, to Darius the king.

7 (They sent a letter to him, in which was written thus)

To Darius the king:

All peace.

8 Let it be known to the king that we went into the province of Judea, to the temple of the great God, which is being built with heavy stones, and timber is being laid in the walls; and this work goes on diligently and prospers in their hands.

9 Then we asked those elders, *and* spoke thus to them: "Who commanded you to build this temple and to finish these walls?"
10 We also asked them their names to inform you, that we might write the names of the men who *were* chief among them.

11 And thus they returned us an answer, saying: "We are the servants of the God of heaven and earth, and we are rebuilding the temple that was built many years ago, which a great king of Israel built and
completed. 12 But because our fathers provoked the God of heaven to wrath, He gave them into the hand of Nebuchadnezzar king of Babylon, the Chaldean, *who* destroyed this temple and carried the
people away to Babylon. 13 However, in the first year of Cyrus king of Babylon, King Cyrus issued a decree to build this house of
God. 14 Also, the gold and silver articles of the house of God, which Nebuchadnezzar had taken from the temple that *was* in Jerusalem and carried into the temple of Babylon—those King Cyrus took from the temple of Babylon, and they were given to one named Sheshbazzar, whom he had
made governor. 15 And he said to him, 'Take these articles; go, carry them to the temple *site* that *is* in Jerusalem, and let the house of
God be rebuilt on its former site.' 16 Then the same Sheshbazzar came *and* laid the foundation of the house of God which *is* in Jerusalem; but from that time even until now it has been under construction, and it is not finished."

17 Now therefore, if *it seems* good to the king, let a search be made in the king's treasure house, which *is* there in Babylon, whether it is *so* that a decree was issued by King Cyrus to build this house of God at Jerusalem, and let the king send us his pleasure concerning this *matter.*

THE MESSAGE

5 But God had his eye on the leaders of the Jews, and the work wasn't stopped until a report could reach Darius and an official reply be returned.

6-7 Tattenai, governor of the land beyond the Euphrates, and Shethar-Bozenai and his associates—the officials of that land—sent a letter to Darius the king. This is what they wrote to him:

To Darius the king. Peace and blessing!

8 We want to report to the king that we went to the province of Judah, to The Temple of the great God that is being rebuilt with large stones. Timbers are being fitted into the walls; the work is going on with great energy and in good time.

9-10 We asked the leaders, "Who issued you the permit to rebuild this Temple and restore it to use?" We also asked for their names so we could pass them on to you and have a record of the men at the head of the construction work.

11-12 This is what they told us: "We are servants of the God of the heavens and the earth. We are rebuilding The Temple that was built a long time ago. A great king of Israel built it, the entire structure. But our ancestors made the God of the heavens really angry and he turned them over to Nebuchadnezzar, king of Babylon, the Chaldean, who knocked this Temple down and took the people to Babylon in exile.

13-16 "But when Cyrus became king of Babylon, in his first year he issued a building permit to rebuild this Temple of God. He also gave back the gold and silver vessels of The Temple of God that Nebuchadnezzar had carted off and put in the Babylon temple. Cyrus the king removed them from the temple of Babylon and turned them over to Sheshbazzar, the man he had appointed governor. He told him, 'Take these vessels and place them in The Temple of Jerusalem and rebuild The Temple of God on its original site.' And Sheshbazzar did it. He laid the foundation of The Temple of God in Jerusalem. It has been under construction ever since but it is not yet finished."

17 So now, if it please the king, look up the records in the royal archives in Babylon and see if it is indeed a fact that Cyrus the king issued an official building permit authorizing the rebuilding of The Temple of God in Jerusalem. And then send the king's ruling on this matter to us.

NEW KING JAMES VERSION

THE DECREE OF DARIUS

6 Then King Darius issued a decree, and a search was made in the archives,[a] where the treasures were stored in Babylon. 2 And at Achmetha,[a] in the palace that *is* in the province of Media, a scroll was found, and in it a record *was* written thus:

> 3 In the first year of King Cyrus, King Cyrus issued a decree *concerning* the house of God at Jerusalem: "Let the house be rebuilt, the place where they offered sacrifices; and let the foundations of it be firmly laid, its height sixty cubits *and* its width sixty cubits, 4 *with* three rows of heavy stones and one row of new timber. Let the expenses be paid from the king's treasury. 5 Also let the gold and silver articles of the house of God, which Nebuchadnezzar took from the temple which *is* in Jerusalem and brought to Babylon, be restored and taken back to the temple which *is* in Jerusalem, *each* to its place; and deposit *them* in the house of God"—
>
> 6 Now *therefore,* Tattenai, governor of *the region* beyond the River, and Shethar-Boznai, and your companions the Persians who *are* beyond the River, keep yourselves far from there. 7 Let the work of this house of God alone; let the governor of the Jews and the elders of the Jews build this house of God on its site.
>
> 8 Moreover I issue a decree *as to* what you shall do for the elders of these Jews, for the building of this house of God: Let the cost be paid at the king's expense from taxes *on the region* beyond the River; this is to be given immediately to these men, so that they are not hindered. 9 And whatever they need—young bulls, rams, and lambs for the burnt offerings of the God of heaven, wheat, salt, wine, and oil, according to the request of the priests who *are* in Jerusalem—let it be given them day by day without fail, 10 that they may offer sacrifices of sweet aroma to the God of heaven, and pray for the life of the king and his sons.
>
> 11 Also I issue a decree that whoever alters this edict, let a timber be pulled from his house and erected, and let him be hanged on it; and let his house be made a refuse heap because of this. 12 And may the God who causes His name to dwell there destroy any king or people who put their hand to alter it, or to destroy this house of God which is in Jerusalem. I Darius issue a decree; let it be done diligently.

THE TEMPLE COMPLETED AND DEDICATED

13 Then Tattenai, governor of *the region* beyond the River, Shethar-Boznai, and their companions diligently did according to what King Darius had sent.

6:1 [a]Literally *house of the scrolls* **6:2** [a]Probably *Ecbatana,* the ancient capital of Media

THE MESSAGE

1-3 6 So King Darius ordered a search through the records in the archives in Babylon. Eventually a scroll was turned up in the fortress of Ecbatana over in the province of Media, with this writing on it:

> Memorandum
>
> In his first year as king, Cyrus issued an official decree regarding The Temple of God in Jerusalem, as follows:
>
> 3-5 The Temple where sacrifices are offered is to be rebuilt on new foundations. It is to be ninety feet high and ninety feet wide with three courses of large stones topped with one course of timber. The cost is to be paid from the royal bank. The gold and silver vessels from The Temple of God that Nebuchadnezzar carried to Babylon are to be returned to The Temple at Jerusalem, each to its proper place; place them in The Temple of God.
>
> 6-7 Now listen, Tattenai governor of the land beyond the Euphrates, Shethar-Bozenai, associates, and all officials of that land: Stay out of their way. Leave the governor and leaders of the Jews alone so they can work on that Temple of God as they rebuild it.
>
> 8-10 I hereby give official orders on how you are to help the leaders of the Jews in the rebuilding of that Temple of God:
>
> 1. All construction costs are to be paid to these men from the royal bank out of the taxes coming in from the land beyond the Euphrates. And pay them on time, without delays.
>
> 2. Whatever is required for their worship—young bulls, rams, and lambs for Whole-Burnt-Offerings to the God-of-Heaven; and whatever wheat, salt, wine, and anointing oil the priests of Jerusalem request—is to be given to them daily without delay so that they may make sacrifices to the God-of-Heaven and pray for the life of the king and his sons.
>
> 11-12 I've issued an official decree that anyone who violates this order is to be impaled on a timber torn out of his own house, and the house itself made a manure pit. And may the God who put his Name on that place wipe out any king or people who dares to defy this decree and destroy The Temple of God at Jerusalem.
>
> I, Darius, have issued an official decree. Carry it out precisely and promptly.

13 Tattenai governor of the land across the Euphrates, Shethar-Bozenai, and their associates did it: They carried out the decree of Darius precisely and promptly.

NEW KING JAMES VERSION

14 So the elders of the Jews built, and they prospered through the prophesying of Haggai the prophet and Zechariah the son of Iddo. And they built and finished *it*, according to the commandment of the God of Israel, and according to the command of Cyrus, Darius, and Artaxerxes king of Persia. 15 Now the temple was finished on the third day of the month of Adar, which was in the sixth year of the reign of King Darius. 16 Then the children of Israel, the priests and the Levites and the rest of the descendants of the captivity, celebrated the dedication of this house of God with joy. 17 And they offered sacrifices at the dedication of this house of God, one hundred bulls, two hundred rams, four hundred lambs, and as a sin offering for all Israel twelve male goats, according to the number of the tribes of Israel. 18 They assigned the priests to their divisions and the Levites to their divisions, over the service of God in Jerusalem, as it is written in the Book of Moses.

THE PASSOVER CELEBRATED

19 And the descendants of the captivity kept the Passover on the fourteenth *day* of the first month. 20 For the priests and the Levites had purified themselves; all of them *were ritually* clean. And they slaughtered the Passover *lambs* for all the descendants of the captivity, for their brethren the priests, and for themselves. 21 Then the children of Israel who had returned from the captivity ate together with all who had separated themselves from the filth of the nations of the land in order to seek the LORD God of Israel. 22 And they kept the Feast of Unleavened Bread seven days with joy; for the LORD made them joyful, and turned the heart of the king of Assyria toward them, to strengthen their hands in the work of the house of God, the God of Israel.

THE ARRIVAL OF EZRA

7 Now after these things, in the reign of Artaxerxes king of Persia, Ezra the son of Seraiah, the son of Azariah, the son of Hilkiah, 2 the son of Shallum, the son of Zadok, the son of Ahitub, 3 the son of Amariah, the son of Azariah, the son of Meraioth, 4 the son of Zerahiah, the son of Uzzi, the son of Bukki, 5 the son of Abishua, the son of Phinehas, the son of Eleazar, the son of Aaron the chief priest— 6 this Ezra came up from Babylon; and he *was* a skilled scribe in the Law of Moses, which the LORD God of Israel had given. The king granted him all his request, according to the hand of the LORD his God upon him. 7 *Some* of the children of Israel, the priests, the Levites, the singers, the gatekeepers, and the Nethinim came up to Jerusalem in the seventh year of King Artaxerxes. 8 And Ezra came to Jerusalem in the fifth month, which *was* in the seventh year of the king. 9 On the first *day* of the first month he began *his* journey from Babylon, and on the first *day* of the fifth month he came to Jerusalem, according to the good hand of his God upon him. 10 For Ezra had prepared his heart to seek the

THE MESSAGE

THE BUILDING COMPLETED: "EXUBERANTLY CELEBRATED THE DEDICATION"

14-15 So the leaders of the Jews continued to
build; the work went well under the preaching of the prophets Haggai and Zechariah son of Iddo. They completed the rebuilding under orders of the God of Israel and authorization by Cyrus, Darius, and Artaxerxes, kings of Persia. The Temple was completed on the third day of the month Adar in the sixth year of the reign of King Darius.
16-18 And then the Israelites celebrated—
priests, Levites, every last exile, exuberantly celebrated the dedication of The Temple of God. At the dedication of this Temple of God they sacrificed a hundred bulls, two hundred rams, and four hundred lambs—and, as an Absolution-Offering for all Israel, twelve he-goats, one for each of the twelve tribes of Israel. They placed the priests in their divisions and the Levites in their places for the service of God at Jerusalem—all as written out in the Book of Moses.

19 On the fourteenth day of the first month, the
exiles celebrated the Passover.
20 All the priests and Levites had purified
themselves—all, no exceptions. They were all ritually clean. The Levites slaughtered the Passover lamb for the exiles, their brother priests, and themselves.
21-22 Then the Israelites who had returned
from exile, along with everyone who had removed themselves from the defilements of the nations to join them and seek GOD, the God of Israel, ate the Passover. With great joy they celebrated the Feast of Unraised Bread for seven days. GOD had plunged them into a sea of joy; he had changed the mind of the king of Assyria to back them in rebuilding The Temple of God, the God of Israel.

EZRA ARRIVES

1-5 7 After all this, Ezra. It was during the reign
of Artaxerxes king of Persia. Ezra was the son of Seraiah, son of Azariah, son of Hilkiah, son of Shallum, son of Zadok, son of Ahitub, son of Amariah, son of Azariah, son of Meraioth, son of Zerahiah, son of Uzzi, son of Bukki, son of Abishua, son of Phinehas, son of Eleazar, son of Aaron the high priest.
6-7 That's Ezra. He arrived from Babylon, a
scholar well-practiced in the Revelation of Moses that the GOD of Israel had given. Because GOD's hand was on Ezra, the king gave him everything he asked for. Some of the Israelites—priests, Levites, singers, temple security guards, and temple slaves—went with him to Jerusalem. It was in the seventh year of Artaxerxes the king.
8-10 They arrived at Jerusalem in the fifth
month of the seventh year of the king's reign. Ezra had scheduled their departure from Babylon on the first day of the first month; they arrived in Jerusalem on the first day of the fifth month under the generous guidance of his God. Ezra had commit-

NEW KING JAMES VERSION

Law of the LORD, and to do *it,* and to teach
statutes and ordinances in Israel.

THE LETTER OF ARTAXERXES TO EZRA

11 This *is* a copy of the letter that King Arta-
xerxes gave Ezra the priest, the scribe, expert in
the words of the commandments of the LORD,
and of His statutes to Israel:

12 Artaxerxes,[a] king of kings,

To Ezra the priest, a scribe of the Law of
the God of heaven:

Perfect *peace,* and so forth.[b]

13 I issue a decree that all those of the people
of Israel and the priests and Levites in my
realm, who volunteer to go up to
Jerusalem, may go with you. 14 And
whereas you are being sent by the king
and his seven counselors to inquire
concerning Judah and Jerusalem, with
regard to the Law of your God which *is* in
your hand; 15 and *whereas you are* to carry
the silver and gold which the king and his
counselors have freely offered to the God
of Israel, whose dwelling *is* in Jerusalem;
16 and *whereas* all the silver and gold that
you may find in all the province of
Babylon, along with the freewill offering of
the people and the priests, *are to be* freely
offered for the house of their God in
Jerusalem— 17 now therefore, be careful to
buy with this money bulls, rams, and
lambs, with their grain offerings and their
drink offerings, and offer them on the altar
of the house of your God in Jerusalem.

18 And whatever seems good to you and your
brethren to do with the rest of the silver
and the gold, do it according to the will of
your God. 19 Also the articles that are given
to you for the service of the house of your
God, deliver in full before the God of
Jerusalem. 20 And whatever more may be
needed for the house of your God, which
you may have occasion to provide, pay *for
it* from the king's treasury.

21 And I, *even* I, Artaxerxes the king, issue a
decree to all the treasurers who *are in the
region* beyond the River, that whatever
Ezra the priest, the scribe of the Law of the
God of heaven, may require of you, let it be
done diligently, 22 up to one hundred talents
of silver, one hundred kors of wheat, one
hundred baths of wine, one hundred baths
of oil, and salt without prescribed limit.
23 Whatever is commanded by the God of
heaven, let it diligently be done for the
house of the God of heaven. For why
should there be wrath against the realm of
the king and his sons?

7:12 [a]The original language of Ezra 7:12–26 is Aramaic. [b]Literally *and now*

THE MESSAGE

ted himself to studying the Revelation of GOD, to living it, and to teaching Israel to live its truths and ways.

11 What follows is the letter that King Artaxerxes gave Ezra, priest and scholar, expert in matters involving the truths and ways of GOD concerning Israel:

12-20 Artaxerxes, King of Kings, to Ezra the priest, a scholar of the Teaching of the God-of-Heaven.

Peace. I hereby decree that any of the people of Israel living in my kingdom who want to go to Jerusalem, including their priests and Levites, may go with you. You are being sent by the king and his seven advisors to carry out an investigation of Judah and Jerusalem in relation to the Teaching of your God that you are carrying with you. You are also authorized to take the silver and gold that the king and his advisors are giving for the God of Israel, whose residence is in Jerusalem, along with all the silver and gold that has been collected from the generously donated offerings all over Babylon, including that from the people and the priests, for The Temple of their God in Jerusalem. Use this money carefully to buy bulls, rams, lambs, and the ingredients for Grain-Offerings and Drink-Offerings and then offer them on the Altar of The Temple of your God in Jerusalem. You are free to use whatever is left over from the silver and gold for what you and your brothers decide is in keeping with the will of your God. Deliver to the God of Jerusalem the vessels given to you for the services of worship in The Temple of your God. Whatever else you need for The Temple of your God you may pay for out of the royal bank.

21-23 I, Artaxerxes the king, have formally authorized and ordered all the treasurers of the land across the Euphrates to give Ezra the priest, scholar of the Teaching of the God-of-Heaven, the full amount of whatever he asks for up to 100 talents of silver, 650 bushels of wheat, and 607 gallons each of wine and olive oil. There is no limit on the salt. Everything the God-of-Heaven requires for The Temple of God must be given without hesitation. Why would the king and his sons risk stirring up his wrath?

NEW KING JAMES VERSION

24 Also we inform you that it shall not be
lawful to impose tax, tribute, or custom *on*
any of the priests, Levites, singers,
gatekeepers, Nethinim, or servants of this
house of God. 25 And you, Ezra, according
to your God-given wisdom, set magistrates
and judges who may judge all the people
who *are in the region* beyond the River, all
such as know the laws of your God; and
teach those who do not know *them*.
26 Whoever will not observe the law of your
God and the law of the king, let judgment
be executed speedily on him, whether *it be*
death, or banishment, or confiscation of
goods, or imprisonment.

27 Blessed *be* the LORD God of our fathers,
who has put *such a thing* as this in the king's
heart, to beautify the house of the LORD which *is*
in Jerusalem, 28 and has extended mercy to me
before the king and his counselors, and before
all the king's mighty princes.
So I was encouraged, as the hand of the
LORD my God *was* upon me; and I gathered
leading men of Israel to go up with me.

HEADS OF FAMILIES WHO RETURNED WITH EZRA

8 These *are* the heads of their fathers' *houses*,
and *this is* the genealogy of those who went
up with me from Babylon, in the reign of King
Artaxerxes: 2 of the sons of Phinehas, Gershom;
of the sons of Ithamar, Daniel; of the sons of
David, Hattush; 3 of the sons of Shecaniah, of the
sons of Parosh, Zechariah; and registered with
him *were* one hundred and fifty males; 4 of the
sons of Pahath-Moab, Eliehoenai the son of Zer-
ahiah, and with him two hundred males; 5 of the
sons of Shechaniah,[a] Ben-Jahaziel, and with
him three hundred males; 6 of the sons of Adin,
Ebed the son of Jonathan, and with him fifty
males; 7 of the sons of Elam, Jeshaiah the son of
Athaliah, and with him seventy males; 8 of the
sons of Shephatiah, Zebadiah the son of
Michael, and with him eighty males; 9 of the sons
of Joab, Obadiah the son of Jehiel, and with him
two hundred and eighteen males; 10 of the sons
of Shelomith,[a] Ben-Josiphiah, and with him one
hundred and sixty males; 11 of the sons of Bebai,
Zechariah the son of Bebai, and with him
twenty-eight males; 12 of the sons of Azgad, Jo-
hanan the son of Hakkatan, and with him one
hundred and ten males; 13 of the last sons of
Adonikam, whose names *are* these—Eliphelet,
Jeiel, and Shemaiah—and with them sixty
males; 14 also of the sons of Bigvai, Uthai and
Zabbud, and with them seventy males.

SERVANTS FOR THE TEMPLE

15 Now I gathered them by the river that flows
to Ahava, and we camped there three days. And
I looked among the people and the priests, and

8:5 [a]Following Masoretic Text and Vulgate; Septuagint reads *the sons of Zatho, Shechaniah.* **8:10** [a]Following Masoretic Text and Vulgate; Septuagint reads *the sons of Banni, Shelomith.*

THE MESSAGE

24 Also, let it be clear that no one is permitted to impose tribute, tax, or duty on any priest, Levite, singer, temple security guard, temple servant, or any other worker connected with The Temple of God.

25 I authorize you, Ezra, exercising the wisdom of God that you have in your hands, to appoint magistrates and judges so they can administer justice among all the people of the land across the Euphrates who live by the Teaching of your God. Anyone who does not know the Teaching, you teach them.

26 Anyone who does not obey the Teaching of your God and the king must be tried and sentenced at once—death, banishment, a fine, prison, whatever.

EZRA: "I WAS READY TO GO"

27-28 Blessed be GOD, the God-of-Our-Fathers, who put it in the mind of the king to beautify The Temple of GOD in Jerusalem! Not only that, he caused the king and all his advisors and influential officials actually to like me and back me. My God was on my side and I was ready to go. And I organized all the leaders of Israel to go with me.

1-14 8 These are the family heads and those who signed up to go up with me from Babylon in the reign of Artaxerxes the king:

From the family of Phinehas: Gershom
Family of Ithamar: Daniel
Family of David: Hattush
Family of Shecaniah
Family of Parosh: Zechariah, and with him 150 men signed up
Family of Pahath-Moab: Eliehoenai son of Zerahiah, and 200 men
Family of Zattu: Shecaniah son of Jahaziel, and 300 men
Family of Adin: Ebed son of Jonathan, and 50 men
Family of Elam: Jeshaiah son of Athaliah, and 70 men
Family of Shephatiah: Zebadiah son of Michael, and 80 men
Family of Joab: Obadiah son of Jehiel, and 218 men
Family of Bani: Shelomith son of Josiphiah, and 160 men
Family of Bebai: Zechariah son of Bebai, and 28 men
Family of Azgad: Johanan son of Hakkatan, and 110 men
Family of Adonikam (bringing up the rear): their names were Eliphelet, Jeuel, Shemaiah, and 60 men
Family of Bigvai: Uthai and Zaccur, and 70 men.

15-17 I gathered them together at the canal that runs to Ahava. We camped there three days. I looked them over and found that they were all laymen and priests but no Levites. So I

New King James Version

found none of the sons of Levi there. [16]Then I
sent for Eliezer, Ariel, Shemaiah, Elnathan,
Jarib, Elnathan, Nathan, Zechariah, and Meshul-
lam, leaders; also for Joiarib and Elnathan, men
of understanding. [17]And I gave them a command
for Iddo the chief man at the place Casiphia, and
I told them what they should say to Iddo *and* his
brethren[a] the Nethinim at the place Casiphia—
that they should bring us servants for the house
of our God. [18]Then, by the good hand of our God
upon us, they brought us a man of understand-
ing, of the sons of Mahli the son of Levi, the son
of Israel, namely Sherebiah, with his sons and
brothers, eighteen men; [19]and Hashabiah, and
with him Jeshaiah of the sons of Merari, his
brothers and their sons, twenty men; [20]also of
the Nethinim, whom David and the leaders had
appointed for the service of the Levites, two hun-
dred and twenty Nethinim. All of them were des-
ignated by name.

Fasting and Prayer for Protection

[21]Then I proclaimed a fast there at the river
of Ahava, that we might humble ourselves be-
fore our God, to seek from Him the right way for
us and our little ones and all our possessions.
[22]For I was ashamed to request of the king an es-
cort of soldiers and horsemen to help us against
the enemy on the road, because we had spoken
to the king, saying, "The hand of our God *is*
upon all those for good who seek Him, but His
power and His wrath *are* against all those who
forsake Him." [23]So we fasted and entreated our
God for this, and He answered our prayer.

Gifts for the Temple

[24]And I separated twelve of the leaders of the
priests—Sherebiah, Hashabiah, and ten of their
brethren with them— [25]and weighed out to them
the silver, the gold, and the articles, the offering
for the house of our God which the king and his
counselors and his princes, and all Israel *who
were* present, had offered. [26]I weighed into their
hand six hundred and fifty talents of silver, sil-
ver articles *weighing* one hundred talents, one
hundred talents of gold, [27]twenty gold basins
worth a thousand drachmas, and two vessels of
fine polished bronze, precious as gold. [28]And I
said to them, "You *are* holy to the LORD; the ar-
ticles *are* holy also; and the silver and the gold
are a freewill offering to the LORD God of your
fathers. [29]Watch and keep *them* until you weigh
them before the leaders of the priests and the
Levites and heads of the fathers' *houses* of Is-
rael in Jerusalem, *in* the chambers of the house
of the LORD." [30]So the priests and the Levites re-
ceived the silver and the gold and the articles by
weight, to bring *them* to Jerusalem to the house
of our God.

The Return to Jerusalem

[31]Then we departed from the river of Ahava
on the twelfth *day* of the first month, to go to
Jerusalem. And the hand of our God was upon
us, and He delivered us from the hand of the en-
emy and from ambush along the road.

8:17 [a]Following Vulgate; Masoretic Text reads *to Iddo his brother;* Septuagint reads *to their brethren.*

The Message

sent for the leaders Eliezer, Ariel, Shemaiah, Elnathan, Jarib, Elnathan, Nathan, Zechariah, and Meshullam, and for the teachers Joiarib and Elnathan. I then sent them to Iddo, who is head of the town of Casiphia, and told them what to say to Iddo and his relatives who lived there in Casiphia: "Send us ministers for The Temple of God."

18-20 Well, the generous hand of our God was on us, and they brought back to us a wise man from the family of Mahli son of Levi, the son of Israel. His name was Sherebiah. With sons and brothers they numbered eighteen. They also brought Hashabiah and Jeshaiah of the family of Merari, with brothers and their sons, another twenty. And then there were 220 temple servants, descendants of the temple servants that David and the princes had assigned to help the Levites in their work. They were all signed up by name.

21-22 I proclaimed a fast there beside the Ahava Canal, a fast to humble ourselves before our God and pray for wise guidance for our journey—all our people and possessions. I was embarrassed to ask the king for a cavalry bodyguard to protect us from bandits on the road. We had just told the king, "Our God lovingly looks after all those who seek him, but turns away in disgust from those who leave him."

23 So we fasted and prayed about these concerns. And he listened.

24-27 Then I picked twelve of the leading priests—Sherebiah and Hashabiah with ten of their brothers. I weighed out for them the silver, the gold, the vessels, and the offerings for The Temple of our God that the king, his advisors, and all the Israelites had given:

25 tons of silver
100 vessels of silver valued at three and three-quarter tons of gold
20 gold bowls weighing eighteen and a half pounds
2 vessels of bright red copper, as valuable as gold.

28-29 I said to them, "You are holy to GOD and these vessels are holy. The silver and gold are Freewill-Offerings to the GOD of your ancestors. Guard them with your lives until you're able to weigh them out in a secure place in The Temple of our God for the priests and Levites and family heads who are in charge in Jerusalem."

30 The priests and Levites took charge of all that had been weighed out to them, and prepared to deliver it to Jerusalem to The Temple of our God.

31 We left the Ahava Canal on the twelfth day of the first month to travel to Jerusalem. God was with us all the way and kept us safe from bandits and highwaymen.

NEW KING JAMES VERSION

[32]So we came to Jerusalem, and stayed there
three days.
[33]Now on the fourth day the silver and the
gold and the articles were weighed in the house
of our God by the hand of Meremoth the son of
Uriah the priest, and with him *was* Eleazar the
son of Phinehas; with them *were* the Levites,
Jozabad the son of Jeshua and Noadiah the son
of Binnui, [34]with the number *and* weight of
everything. All the weight was written down at
that time.
[35]The children of those who had been carried
away captive, who had come from the captivity,
offered burnt offerings to the God of Israel:
twelve bulls for all Israel, ninety-six rams, sev-
enty-seven lambs, and twelve male goats *as* a
sin offering. All *this was* a burnt offering to the
LORD.
[36]And they delivered the king's orders to the
king's satraps and the governors *in the region*
beyond the River. So they gave support to the
people and the house of God.

INTERMARRIAGE WITH PAGANS

9 When these things were done, the leaders
came to me, saying, "The people of Israel and
the priests and the Levites have not separated
themselves from the peoples of the lands, with
respect to the abominations of the Canaanites,
the Hittites, the Perizzites, the Jebusites, the
Ammonites, the Moabites, the Egyptians, and
the Amorites. [2]For they have taken some of their
daughters *as wives* for themselves and their
sons, so that the holy seed is mixed with the
peoples of *those* lands. Indeed, the hand of the
leaders and rulers has been foremost in this
trespass." [3]So when I heard this thing, I tore my
garment and my robe, and plucked out some of
the hair of my head and beard, and sat down as-
tonished. [4]Then everyone who trembled at the
words of the God of Israel assembled to me, be-
cause of the transgression of those who had
been carried away captive, and I sat astonished
until the evening sacrifice.
[5]At the evening sacrifice I arose from my
fasting; and having torn my garment and my
robe, I fell on my knees and spread out my hands
to the LORD my God. [6]And I said: "O my God, I
am too ashamed and humiliated to lift up my
face to You, my God; for our iniquities have risen
higher than *our* heads, and our guilt has grown
up to the heavens. [7]Since the days of our fathers
to this day we *have been* very guilty, and for our
iniquities we, our kings, *and* our priests have
been delivered into the hand of the kings of the
lands, to the sword, to captivity, to plunder, and
to humiliation, as *it is* this day. [8]And now for a
little while grace has been *shown* from the LORD
our God, to leave us a remnant to escape, and to
give us a peg in His holy place, that our God

THE MESSAGE

32-34 We arrived in Jerusalem and waited there three days. On the fourth day the silver and gold and vessels were weighed out in The Temple of our God into the hands of Meremoth son of Uriah, the priest. Eleazar son of Phinehas was there with him, also the Levites Jozabad son of Jeshua and Noadiah son of Binnui. Everything was counted and weighed and the totals recorded.

35 When they arrived, the exiles, now returned from captivity, offered Whole-Burnt-Offerings to the God of Israel:

12 bulls, representing all Israel
96 rams
77 lambs
12 he-goats as an Absolution-Offering.

All of this was sacrificed as a Whole-Burnt-Offering to GOD.

36 They also delivered the king's orders to the king's provincial administration assigned to the land beyond the Euphrates. They, in turn, gave their support to the people and The Temple of God.

EZRA PRAYS: "LOOK AT US . . . GUILTY BEFORE YOU"

1-2 9 After all this was done, the leaders came to me and said, "The People of Israel, priests and Levites included, have not kept themselves separate from the neighboring people around here with all their vulgar obscenities—Canaanites, Hittites, Perizzites, Jebusites, Ammonites, Moabites, Egyptians, Amorites. They have given some of their daughters in marriage to them and have taken some of their daughters for marriage to their sons. The holy seed is now all mixed in with these other peoples. And our leaders have led the way in this betrayal."

3 When I heard all this, I ripped my clothes and my cape; I pulled hair from my head and out of my beard; I slumped to the ground, appalled.

4-6 Many were in fear and trembling because of what God was saying about the betrayal by the exiles. They gathered around me as I sat there in despair, waiting for the evening sacrifice. At the evening sacrifice I picked myself up from my utter devastation, and in my ripped clothes and cape fell to my knees and stretched out my hands to GOD, my God. And I prayed:

6-7 "My dear God, I'm so totally ashamed, I can't bear to face you. O my God—our iniquities are piled up so high that we can't see out; our guilt touches the skies. We've been stuck in a muck of guilt since the time of our ancestors until right now; we and our kings and priests, because of our sins, have been turned over to foreign kings, to killing, to captivity, to looting, and to public shame—just as you see us now.

8-9 "Now for a brief time GOD, our God, has allowed us, this battered band, to get a firm foothold in his holy place so that our God

NEW KING JAMES VERSION

may enlighten our eyes and give us a measure of revival in our bondage. 9 For we *were* slaves. Yet our God did not forsake us in our bondage; but He extended mercy to us in the sight of the kings of Persia, to revive us, to repair the house of our God, to rebuild its ruins, and to give us a wall in Judah and Jerusalem. 10 And now, O our God, what shall we say after this? For we have forsaken Your commandments, 11 which You commanded by Your servants the prophets, saying, 'The land which you are entering to possess is an unclean land, with the uncleanness of the peoples of the lands, with their abominations which have filled it from one end to another with their impurity. 12 Now therefore, do not give your daughters as wives for their sons, nor take their daughters to your sons; and never seek their peace or prosperity, that you may be strong and eat the good of the land, and leave *it* as an inheritance to your children forever.' 13 And after all that has come upon us for our evil deeds and for our great guilt, since You our God have punished us less than our iniquities *deserve,* and have given us *such* deliverance as this, 14 should we again break Your commandments, and join in marriage with the people *committing* these abominations? Would You not be angry with us until You had consumed *us,* so that *there would be* no remnant or survivor? 15 O LORD God of Israel, You *are* righteous, for we are left as a remnant, as *it is* this day. Here we *are* before You, in our guilt, though no one can stand before You because of this!"

CONFESSION OF IMPROPER MARRIAGES

10 Now while Ezra was praying, and while he was confessing, weeping, and bowing down before the house of God, a very large assembly of men, women, and children gathered to him from Israel; for the people wept very bitterly. 2 And Shechaniah the son of Jehiel, *one* of the sons of Elam, spoke up and said to Ezra, "We have trespassed against our God, and have taken pagan wives from the peoples of the land; yet now there is hope in Israel in spite of this. 3 Now therefore, let us make a covenant with our God to put away all these wives and those who have been born to them, according to the advice of my master and of those who tremble at the commandment of our God; and let it be done according to the law. 4 Arise, for *this* matter *is* your *responsibility.* We also *are* with you. Be of good courage, and do *it.*"

5 Then Ezra arose, and made the leaders of the priests, the Levites, and all Israel swear an oath that they would do according to this word. So they swore an oath. 6 Then Ezra rose up from before the house of God, and went into the chamber of Jehohanan the son of Eliashib; and *when* he came there, he ate no bread and drank no water, for he mourned because of the guilt of those from the captivity.

THE MESSAGE

may brighten our eyes and lighten our burdens as we serve out this hard sentence. We were slaves; yet even as slaves, our God didn't abandon us. He has put us in the good graces of the kings of Persia and given us the heart to build The Temple of our God, restore its ruins, and construct a defensive wall in Judah and Jerusalem.

10-12 "And now, our God, after all this what can we say for ourselves? For we have thrown your commands to the wind, the commands you gave us through your servants the prophets. They told us, 'The land you're taking over is a polluted land, polluted with the obscene vulgarities of the people who live there; they've filled it with their moral rot from one end to the other. Whatever you do, don't give your daughters in marriage to their sons nor marry your sons to their daughters. Don't cultivate their good opinion; don't make over them and get them to like you so you can make a lot of money and build up a tidy estate to hand down to your children.'

13-15 "And now this, on top of all we've already suffered because of our evil ways and accumulated guilt, even though you, dear God, punished us far less than we deserved and even went ahead and gave us this present escape. Yet here we are, at it again, breaking your commandments by intermarrying with the people who practice all these obscenities! Are you angry to the point of wiping us out completely, without even a few stragglers, with no way out at all? You are the righteous GOD of Israel. We are, right now, a small band of escapees. Look at us, openly standing here, guilty before you. No one can last long like this."

EZRA TAKES CHARGE

1 10 Ezra wept, prostrate in front of The Temple of God. As he prayed and confessed, a huge number of the men, women, and children of Israel gathered around him. All the people were now weeping as if their hearts would break.

2-3 Shecaniah son of Jehiel of the family of Elam, acting as spokesman, said to Ezra: "We betrayed our God by marrying foreign wives from the people around here. But all is not lost; there is still hope for Israel. Let's make a covenant right now with our God, agreeing to get rid of all these wives and their children, just as my master and those who honor God's commandment are saying. It's what The Revelation says, so let's do it.

4 "Now get up, Ezra. Take charge—we're behind you. Don't back down."

5 So Ezra stood up and had the leaders of the priests, the Levites, and all Israel solemnly swear to do what Shecaniah proposed. And they did it.

6 Then Ezra left the plaza in front of The Temple of God and went to the home of Jehohanan son of Eliashib where he stayed, still fasting from food and drink, continuing his mourning over the betrayal by the exiles.

NEW KING JAMES VERSION

[7]And they issued a proclamation throughout Judah and Jerusalem to all the descendants of the captivity, that they must gather at Jerusalem, [8]and that whoever would not come within three days, according to the instructions of the leaders and elders, all his property would be confiscated, and he himself would be separated from the assembly of those from the captivity.

[9]So all the men of Judah and Benjamin gathered at Jerusalem within three days. It *was* the ninth month, on the twentieth of the month; and all the people sat in the open square of the house of God, trembling because of *this* matter and because of heavy rain. [10]Then Ezra the priest stood up and said to them, "You have transgressed and have taken pagan wives, adding to the guilt of Israel. [11]Now therefore, make confession to the LORD God of your fathers, and do His will; separate yourselves from the peoples of the land, and from the pagan wives."

[12]Then all the assembly answered and said with a loud voice, "Yes! As you have said, so we must do. [13]But *there are* many people; *it is* the season for heavy rain, and we are not able to stand outside. Nor *is this* the work of one or two days, for *there are* many of us who have transgressed in this matter. [14]Please, let the leaders of our entire assembly stand; and let all those in our cities who have taken pagan wives come at appointed times, together with the elders and judges of their cities, until the fierce wrath of our God is turned away from us in this matter." [15]Only Jonathan the son of Asahel and Jahaziah the son of Tikvah opposed this, and Meshullam and Shabbethai the Levite gave them support.

[16]Then the descendants of the captivity did so. And Ezra the priest, *with* certain heads of the fathers' *households*, were set apart by the fathers' *households*, each of them by name; and they sat down on the first day of the tenth month to examine the matter. [17]By the first day of the first month they finished *questioning* all the men who had taken pagan wives.

PAGAN WIVES PUT AWAY

[18]And among the sons of the priests who had taken pagan wives *the following* were found of the sons of Jeshua the son of Jozadak,[a] and his brothers: Maaseiah, Eliezer, Jarib, and Gedaliah. [19]And they gave their promise that they would put away their wives; and *being* guilty, *they presented* a ram of the flock as their trespass offering.

[20]Also of the sons of Immer: Hanani and Zebadiah; [21]of the sons of Harim: Maaseiah, Elijah, Shemaiah, Jehiel, and Uzziah; [22]of the sons of Pashhur: Elioenai, Maaseiah, Ishmael, Nethanel, Jozabad, and Elasah.

[23]Also of the Levites: Jozabad, Shimei, Kelaiah (the same *is* Kelita), Pethahiah, Judah, and Eliezer.

10:18 [a]Spelled *Jehozadak* in 1 Chronicles 6:14

THE MESSAGE

7-8 A notice was then sent throughout Judah and Jerusalem ordering all the exiles to meet in Jerusalem. Anyone who failed to show up in three days, in compliance with the ruling of the leaders and elders, would have all his possessions confiscated and be thrown out of the congregation of the returned exiles.

9 All the men of Judah and Benjamin met in Jerusalem within the three days. It was the twentieth day of the ninth month. They all sat down in the plaza in front of The Temple of God. Because of the business before them, and aggravated by the buckets of rain coming down on them, they were restless, uneasy, and anxious.

10-11 Ezra the priest stood up and spoke: "You've broken trust. You've married foreign wives. You've piled guilt on Israel. Now make your confession to GOD, the God of your ancestors, and do what he wants you to do: Separate yourselves from the people of the land and from your foreign wives."

12 The whole congregation responded with a shout, "Yes, we'll do it—just the way you said it!"

13-14 They also said, "But look, do you see how many people there are out here? And it's the rainy season; you can't expect us to stand out here soaking wet until this is done—why, it will take days! A lot of us are deeply involved in this transgression. Let our leaders act on behalf of the whole congregation. Have everybody who lives in cities and who has married a foreign wife come at an appointed time, accompanied by the elders and judges of each city. We'll keep at this until the hot anger of our God over this thing is turned away."

15-17 Only Jonathan son of Asahel and Jahzeiah son of Tikvah, supported by Meshullam and Shabbethai the Levite, opposed this. So the exiles went ahead with the plan. Ezra the priest picked men who were family heads, each one by name. They sat down together on the first day of the tenth month to pursue the matter. By the first day of the first month they had finished dealing with every man who had married a foreign wife.

18-19 Among the families of priests, the following were found to have married foreign wives:

The family of Jeshua son of Jozadak and his brothers: Maaseiah, Eliezer, Jarib, and Gedaliah. They all promised to divorce their wives and sealed it with a handshake. For their guilt they brought a ram from the flock as a Compensation-Offering.

20 The family of Immer: Hanani and Zebadiah.

21 The family of Harim: Maaseiah, Elijah, Shemaiah, Jehiel, and Uzziah.

22 The family of Pashhur: Elioenai, Maaseiah, Ishmael, Nethanel, Jozabad, and Elasah.

23 From the Levites: Jozabad, Shimei, Kelaiah—that is, Kelita—Pethahiah, Judah, and Eliezer.

New King James Version

24 Also of the singers: Eliashib; and of the
gatekeepers: Shallum, Telem, and Uri.
25 And others of Israel: of the sons of Parosh:
Ramiah, Jeziah, Malchiah, Mijamin, Eleazar,
Malchijah, and Benaiah; 26 of the sons of Elam:
Mattaniah, Zechariah, Jehiel, Abdi, Jeremoth,
and Eliah; 27 of the sons of Zattu: Elioenai,
Eliashib, Mattaniah, Jeremoth, Zabad, and
Aziza; 28 of the sons of Bebai: Jehohanan, Hana-
niah, Zabbai, *and* Athlai; 29 of the sons of Bani:
Meshullam, Malluch, Adaiah, Jashub, Sheal,
and Ramoth;[a] 30 of the sons of Pahath-Moab:
Adna, Chelal, Benaiah, Maaseiah, Mattaniah,
Bezalel, Binnui, and Manasseh; 31 *of* the sons of
Harim: Eliezer, Ishijah, Malchijah, Shemaiah,
Shimeon, 32 Benjamin, Malluch, *and* Shemariah;
33 of the sons of Hashum: Mattenai, Mattattah,
Zabad, Eliphelet, Jeremai, Manasseh, *and*
Shimei; 34 of the sons of Bani: Maadai, Amram,
Uel, 35 Benaiah, Bedeiah, Cheluh,[a] 36 Vaniah, Mer-
emoth, Eliashib, 37 Mattaniah, Mattenai, Jaasai,[a]
38 Bani, Binnui, Shimei, 39 Shelemiah, Nathan,
Adaiah, 40 Machnadebai, Shashai, Sharai, 41 Az-
arel, Shelemiah, Shemariah, 42 Shallum, Ama-
riah, *and* Joseph; 43 of the sons of Nebo: Jeiel,
Mattithiah, Zabad, Zebina, Jaddai,[a] Joel, *and*
Benaiah.
44 All these had taken pagan wives, and *some*
of them had wives *by whom* they had children.

10:29 [a]Or *Jeremoth* **10:35** [a]Or *Cheluhi,* or *Cheluhu* **10:37** [a]Or *Jaasu* **10:43** [a]Or *Jaddu*

The Message

24 From the singers: Eliashib.
From the temple security guards: Shallum, Telem, and Uri.

25 And from the other Israelites:
The family of Parosh: Ramiah, Izziah, Malkijah, Mijamin, Eleazar, Malkijah, and Benaiah.

26 The family of Elam: Mattaniah, Zechariah, Jehiel, Abdi, Jeremoth, and Elijah.

27 The family of Zattu: Elioenai, Eliashib, Mattaniah, Jeremoth, Zabad, and Aziza.

28 The family of Bebai: Jehohanan, Hananiah, Zabbai, and Athlai.

29 The family of Bani: Meshullam, Malluch, Adaiah, Jashub, Sheal, and Jeremoth.

30 The family of Pahath-Moab: Adna, Kelal, Benaiah, Maaseiah, Mattaniah, Bezalel, Binnui, and Manasseh.

31-32 The family of Harim: Eliezer, Ishijah, Malkijah, Shemaiah, Shimeon, Benjamin, Malluch, and Shemariah.

33 The family of Hashum: Mattenai, Mattattah, Zabad, Eliphelet, Jeremai, Manasseh, and Shimei.

34-37 The family of Bani: Maadai, Amram, Uel, Benaiah, Bedeiah, Keluhi, Vaniah, Meremoth, Eliashib, Mattaniah, Mattenai, and Jaasu.

38-42 The family of Binnui: Shimei, Shelemiah, Nathan, Adaiah, Macnadebai, Shashai, Sharai, Azarel, Shelemiah, Shemariah, Shallum, Amariah, and Joseph.

43 The family of Nebo: Jeiel, Mattithiah, Zabad, Zebina, Jaddai, Joel, and Benaiah.

44 All these had married foreign wives and some had also had children by them.

NEHEMIAH

New King James Version

Nehemiah Prays for His People

1 The words of Nehemiah the son of Hachaliah. It came to pass in the month of Chislev, *in* the twentieth year, as I was in Shushan[a] the citadel, [2]that Hanani one of my brethren came with men from Judah; and I asked them concerning the Jews who had escaped, who had survived the captivity, and concerning Jerusalem. [3]And they said to me, "The survivors who are left from the captivity in the province *are* there in great distress and reproach. The wall of Jerusalem *is* also broken down, and its gates are burned with fire."

[4]So it was, when I heard these words, that I sat down and wept, and mourned *for many* days; I was fasting and praying before the God of heaven.

[5]And I said: "I pray, LORD God of heaven, O great and awesome God, *You* who keep *Your* covenant and mercy with those who love You[a] and observe Your[b] commandments, [6]please let Your ear be attentive and Your eyes open, that You may hear the prayer of Your servant which I pray before You now, day and night, for the children of Israel Your servants, and confess the sins of the children of Israel which we have sinned against You. Both my father's house and I have sinned. [7]We have acted very corruptly against You, and have not kept the commandments, the statutes, nor the ordinances which You commanded Your servant Moses. [8]Remember, I pray, the word that You commanded Your servant Moses, saying, '*If* you are unfaithful, I will scatter you among the nations;[a] [9]but *if* you return to Me, and keep My commandments and do them, though some of you were cast out to the farthest part of the heavens, *yet* I will gather them from there, and bring them to the place which I have chosen as a dwelling for My name.'[a] [10]Now these *are* Your servants and Your people, whom You have redeemed by Your great power, and by Your strong hand. [11]O Lord, I pray, please let Your ear be attentive to the prayer of Your servant, and to the prayer of Your servants who desire to fear Your name; and let Your servant prosper this day, I pray, and grant him mercy in the sight of this man."

For I was the king's cupbearer.

Nehemiah Sent to Judah

2 And it came to pass in the month of Nisan, in the twentieth year of King Artaxerxes, *when* wine *was* before him, that I took the wine and gave it to the king. Now I had never been sad in his presence before. [2]Therefore the king said to me, "Why *is* your face sad, since you *are* not sick? This *is* nothing but sorrow of heart."

So I became dreadfully afraid, [3]and said to the king, "May the king live forever! Why should my face not be sad, when the city, the place of my fathers' tombs, *lies* waste, and its gates are burned with fire?"

1:1 [a]Or *Susa* 1:5 [a]Literally *Him* [b]Literally *His* 1:8 [a]Leviticus 26:33 1:9 [a]Deuteronomy 30:2–5

The Message

1-2 1 The memoirs of Nehemiah son of Hacaliah.
It was the month of Kislev in the twen-
tieth year. At the time I was in the palace
complex at Susa. Hanani, one of my broth-
ers, had just arrived from Judah with some
fellow Jews. I asked them about the condi-
tions among the Jews there who had sur-
vived the exile, and about Jerusalem.
3 They told me, "The exile survivors who
are left there in the province are in bad
shape. Conditions are appalling. The wall of
Jerusalem is still rubble; the city gates are
still cinders."
4 When I heard this, I sat down and wept. I
mourned for days, fasting and praying be-
fore the God-of-Heaven.

5-6 I said, "GOD, God-of-Heaven, the great
and awesome God, loyal to his covenant and
faithful to those who love him and obey his
commands: Look at me, listen to me. Pay at-
tention to this prayer of your servant that
I'm praying day and night in intercession
for your servants, the People of Israel, con-
fessing the sins of the People of Israel. And
I'm including myself, I and my ancestors,
among those who have sinned against you.
7-9 "We've treated you like dirt: We haven't
done what you told us, haven't followed
your commands, and haven't respected the
decisions you gave to Moses your servant.
All the same, remember the warning you
posted to your servant Moses: 'If you betray
me, I'll scatter you to the four winds, but if
you come back to me and do what I tell you,
I'll gather up all these scattered peoples
from wherever they ended up and put them
back in the place I chose to mark with my
Name.'
10-11 "Well, there they are—your servants,
your people whom you so powerfully and
impressively redeemed. O Master, listen to
me, listen to your servant's prayer—and yes,
to all your servants who delight in honoring
you—and make me successful today so that
I get what I want from the king."
I was cupbearer to the king.

1-2 2 It was the month of Nisan in the twenti-
eth year of Artaxerxes the king. At the
hour for serving wine I brought it in and
gave it to the king. I had never been hang-
dog in his presence before, so he asked me,
"Why the long face? You're not sick are you?
Or are you depressed?"
2-3 That made me all the more agitated. I
said, "Long live the king! And why shouldn't
I be depressed when the city, the city where
all my family is buried, is in ruins and the
city gates have been reduced to cinders?"

New King James Version

4Then the king said to me, "What do you request?"

So I prayed to the God of heaven. 5And I said to the king, "If it pleases the king, and if your servant has found favor in your sight, I ask that you send me to Judah, to the city of my fathers' tombs, that I may rebuild it."

6Then the king said to me (the queen also sitting beside him), "How long will your journey be? And when will you return?" So it pleased the king to send me; and I set him a time.

7Furthermore I said to the king, "If it pleases the king, let letters be given to me for the governors *of the region* beyond the River,[a] that they must permit me to pass through till I come to Judah, 8and a letter to Asaph the keeper of the king's forest, that he must give me timber to make beams for the gates of the citadel which *pertains* to the temple,[a] for the city wall, and for the house that I will occupy." And the king granted *them* to me according to the good hand of my God upon me.

9Then I went to the governors *in the region* beyond the River, and gave them the king's letters. Now the king had sent captains of the army and horsemen with me. 10When Sanballat the Horonite and Tobiah the Ammonite official[a] heard *of it,* they were deeply disturbed that a man had come to seek the well-being of the children of Israel.

Nehemiah Views the Wall of Jerusalem

11So I came to Jerusalem and was there three days. 12Then I arose in the night, I and a few men with me; I told no one what my God had put in my heart to do at Jerusalem; nor was there any animal with me, except the one on which I rode. 13And I went out by night through the Valley Gate to the Serpent Well and the Refuse Gate, and viewed the walls of Jerusalem which were broken down and its gates which were burned with fire. 14Then I went on to the Fountain Gate and to the King's Pool, but *there was* no room for the animal under me to pass. 15So I went up in the night by the valley, and viewed the wall; then I turned back and entered by the Valley Gate, and so returned. 16And the officials did not know where I had gone or what I had done; I had not yet told the Jews, the priests, the nobles, the officials, or the others who did the work.

17Then I said to them, "You see the distress that we *are* in, how Jerusalem *lies* waste, and its gates are burned with fire. Come and let us build the wall of Jerusalem, that we may no longer be a reproach." 18And I told them of the hand of my God which had been good upon me, and also of the king's words that he had spoken to me.

So they said, "Let us rise up and build." Then they set their hands to *this* good *work.*

19But when Sanballat the Horonite, Tobiah the Ammonite official, and Geshem the Arab heard *of it,* they laughed at us and despised us, and said, "What *is* this thing that you are doing? Will you rebel against the king?"

2:7 [a]That is, the Euphrates, and so elsewhere in this book **2:8** [a]Literally *house* **2:10** [a]Literally *servant,* and so elsewhere in this book

The Message

4-5 The king then asked me, "So what do you want?"

Praying under my breath to the God-of-Heaven, I said, "If it please the king, and if the king thinks well of me, send me to Judah, to the city where my family is buried, so that I can rebuild it."

6 The king, with the queen sitting alongside him, said, "How long will your work take and when would you expect to return?"

I gave him a time, and the king gave his approval to send me.

7-8 Then I said, "If it please the king, provide me with letters to the governors across the Euphrates that authorize my travel through to Judah; and also an order to Asaph, keeper of the king's forest, to supply me with timber for the beams of The Temple fortress, the wall of the city, and the house where I'll be living."

8-9 The generous hand of my God was with me in this and the king gave them to me. When I met the governors across The River (the Euphrates) I showed them the king's letters. The king even sent along a cavalry escort.

10 When Sanballat the Horonite and Tobiah the Ammonite official heard about this, they were very upset, angry that anyone would come to look after the interests of the People of Israel.

"Come—Let's Build the Wall of Jerusalem"

11-12 And so I arrived in Jerusalem. After I had been there three days, I got up in the middle of the night, I and a few men who were with me. I hadn't told anyone what my God had put in my heart to do for Jerusalem. The only animal with us was the one I was riding.

13-16 Under cover of night I went past the Valley Gate toward the Dragon's Fountain to the Dung Gate looking over the walls of Jerusalem, which had been broken through and whose gates had been burned up. I then crossed to the Fountain Gate and headed for the King's Pool but there wasn't enough room for the donkey I was riding to get through. So I went up the valley in the dark continuing my inspection of the wall. I came back in through the Valley Gate. The local officials had no idea where I'd gone or what I was doing—I hadn't breathed a word to the Jews, priests, nobles, local officials, or anyone else who would be working on the job.

17-18 Then I gave them my report: "Face it: we're in a bad way here. Jerusalem is a wreck; its gates are burned up. Come—let's build the wall of Jerusalem and not live with this disgrace any longer." I told them how God was supporting me and how the king was backing me up.

They said, "We're with you. Let's get started." They rolled up their sleeves, ready for the good work.

19 When Sanballat the Horonite, Tobiah the Ammonite official, and Geshem the Arab heard about it, they laughed at us, mocking, "Ha! What do you think you're doing? Do you think you can cross the king?"

NEW KING JAMES VERSION

20 So I answered them, and said to them, "The God of heaven Himself will prosper us; therefore we His servants will arise and build, but you have no heritage or right or memorial in Jerusalem."

REBUILDING THE WALL

3 Then Eliashib the high priest rose up with his brethren the priests and built the Sheep Gate; they consecrated it and hung its doors. They built as far as the Tower of the Hundred,[a] *and* consecrated it, then as far as the Tower of Hananel. 2 Next to *Eliashib*[a] the men of Jericho built. And next to them Zaccur the son of Imri built.

3 Also the sons of Hassenaah built the Fish Gate; they laid its beams and hung its doors with its bolts and bars. 4 And next to them Meremoth the son of Urijah, the son of Koz,[a] made repairs. Next to them Meshullam the son of Berechiah, the son of Meshezabel, made repairs. Next to them Zadok the son of Baana made repairs. 5 Next to them the Tekoites made repairs; but their nobles did not put their shoulders[a] to the work of their Lord.

6 Moreover Jehoiada the son of Paseah and Meshullam the son of Besodeiah repaired the Old Gate; they laid its beams and hung its doors, with its bolts and bars. 7 And next to them Melatiah the Gibeonite, Jadon the Meronothite, the men of Gibeon and Mizpah, repaired the residence[a] of the governor *of the region* beyond the River. 8 Next to him Uzziel the son of Harhaiah, one of the goldsmiths, made repairs. Also next to him Hananiah, one[a] of the perfumers, made repairs; and they fortified Jerusalem as far as the Broad Wall. 9 And next to them Rephaiah the son of Hur, leader of half the district of Jerusalem, made repairs. 10 Next to them Jedaiah the son of Harumaph made repairs in front of his house. And next to him Hattush the son of Hashabniah made repairs.

11 Malchijah the son of Harim and Hashub the son of Pahath-Moab repaired another section, as well as the Tower of the Ovens. 12 And next to him was Shallum the son of Hallohesh, leader of half the district of Jerusalem; he and his daughters made repairs.

13 Hanun and the inhabitants of Zanoah repaired the Valley Gate. They built it, hung its doors with its bolts and bars, and *repaired* a thousand cubits of the wall as far as the Refuse Gate.

14 Malchijah the son of Rechab, leader of the district of Beth Haccerem, repaired the Refuse Gate; he built it and hung its doors with its bolts and bars.

15 Shallun the son of Col-Hozeh, leader of the district of Mizpah, repaired the Fountain Gate; he built it, covered it, hung its doors with its bolts and bars, and repaired the wall of the Pool of Shelah by the King's Garden, as far as the stairs that go down from the City of David. 16 After him Nehemiah the son of Azbuk, leader of half the district of Beth Zur, made repairs as far as *the place* in front of the tombs[a] of David, to the man-made pool, and as far as the House of the Mighty.

3:1 [a]Hebrew *Hammeah,* also at 12:39 **3:2** [a]Literally *On his hand* **3:4** [a]Or *Hakkoz* **3:5** [a]Literally *necks* **3:7** [a]Literally *throne* **3:8** [a]Literally *the son* **3:16** [a]Septuagint, Syriac, and Vulgate read *tomb.*

THE MESSAGE

20 I shot back, "The God-of-Heaven will make sure we succeed. We're his servants and we're going to work, rebuilding. You can keep your nose out of it. You get no say in this—Jerusalem's none of your business!"

1-2 3 The high priest Eliashib and his fellow priests were up and at it: They went to work on the Sheep Gate; they repaired it and hung its doors, continuing on as far as the Tower of the Hundred and the Tower of Hananel. The men of Jericho worked alongside them; and next to them, Zaccur son of Imri.

3-5 The Fish Gate was built by the Hassenaah brothers; they repaired it, hung its doors, and installed its bolts and bars. Meremoth son of Uriah, the son of Hakkoz, worked; next to him Meshullam son of Berekiah, the son of Meshezabel; next to him Zadok son of Baana; and next to him the Tekoites (except for their nobles, who wouldn't work with their master and refused to get their hands dirty with such work).

6-8 The Jeshanah Gate was rebuilt by Joiada son of Paseah and Meshullam son of Besodeiah; they repaired it, hung its doors, and installed its bolts and bars. Melatiah the Gibeonite, Jadon the Meronothite, and the men of Gibeon and Mizpah, which was under the rule of the governor from across the Euphrates, worked alongside them. Uzziel son of Harhaiah of the goldsmiths' guild worked next to him, and next to him Hananiah, one of the perfumers. They rebuilt the wall of Jerusalem as far as the Broad Wall.

9-10 The next section was worked on by Rephaiah son of Hur, mayor of a half-district of Jerusalem. Next to him Jedaiah son of Harumaph rebuilt the front of his house; Hattush son of Hashabneiah worked next to him.

11-12 Malkijah son of Harim and Hasshub son of Pahath-Moab rebuilt another section that included the Tower of Furnaces. Working next to him was Shallum son of Hallohesh, mayor of the other half-district of Jerusalem, along with his daughters.

13 The Valley Gate was rebuilt by Hanun and villagers of Zanoah; they repaired it, hung its doors, and installed its bolts and bars. They went on to repair 1,500 feet of the wall, as far as the Dung Gate.

14 The Dung Gate itself was rebuilt by Malkijah son of Recab, the mayor of the district of Beth Hakkerem; he repaired it, hung its doors, and installed its bolts and bars.

15 The Fountain Gate was rebuilt by Shallun son of Col-Hozeh, mayor of the Mizpah district; he repaired it, roofed it, hung its doors, and installed its bolts and bars. He also rebuilt the wall of the Pool of Siloam at the King's Garden as far as the steps that go down from the City of David.

16 After him came Nehemiah son of Azbuk, mayor of half the district of Beth Zur. He worked from just in front of the Tomb of David as far as the Pool and the House of Heroes.

New King James Version

17After him the Levites, *under* Rehum the son of Bani, made repairs. Next to him Hashabiah, leader of half the district of Keilah, made repairs for his district. 18After him their brethren, *under* Bavai[a] the son of Henadad, leader of the *other* half of the district of Keilah, made repairs. 19And next to him Ezer the son of Jeshua, the leader of Mizpah, repaired another section in front of the Ascent to the Armory at the buttress. 20After him Baruch the son of Zabbai[a] carefully repaired the other section, from the buttress to the door of the house of Eliashib the high priest. 21After him Meremoth the son of Urijah, the son of Koz,[a] repaired another section, from the door of the house of Eliashib to the end of the house of Eliashib.

22And after him the priests, the men of the plain, made repairs. 23After him Benjamin and Hasshub made repairs opposite their house. After them Azariah the son of Maaseiah, the son of Ananiah, made repairs by his house. 24After him Binnui the son of Henadad repaired another section, from the house of Azariah to the buttress, even as far as the corner. 25Palal the son of Uzai *made repairs* opposite the buttress, and on the tower which projects from the king's upper house that *was* by the court of the prison. After him Pedaiah the son of Parosh *made repairs*.

26Moreover the Nethinim who dwelt in Ophel *made repairs* as far as *the place* in front of the Water Gate toward the east, and on the projecting tower. 27After them the Tekoites repaired another section, next to the great projecting tower, and as far as the wall of Ophel.

28Beyond the Horse Gate the priests made repairs, each in front of his *own* house. 29After them Zadok the son of Immer made repairs in front of his *own* house. After him Shemaiah the son of Shechaniah, the keeper of the East Gate, made repairs. 30After him Hananiah the son of Shelemiah, and Hanun, the sixth son of Zalaph, repaired another section. After him Meshullam the son of Berechiah made repairs in front of his dwelling. 31After him Malchijah, one of the goldsmiths, made repairs as far as the house of the Nethinim and of the merchants, in front of the Miphkad[a] Gate, and as far as the upper room at the corner. 32And between the upper room at the corner, as far as the Sheep Gate, the goldsmiths and the merchants made repairs.

The Wall Defended Against Enemies

4 But it so happened, when Sanballat heard that we were rebuilding the wall, that he was furious and very indignant, and mocked the Jews. 2And he spoke before his brethren and the army of Samaria, and said, "What are these feeble Jews doing? Will they fortify themselves? Will they offer sacrifices? Will they complete it in a day? Will they revive the stones from the heaps of rubbish—*stones* that are burned?"

3Now Tobiah the Ammonite *was* beside him, and he said, "Whatever they build, if even a fox goes up *on it,* he will break down their stone wall."

3:18 [a]Following Masoretic Text and Vulgate; some Hebrew manuscripts, Septuagint, and Syriac read *Binnui* (compare verse 24). **3:20** [a]A few Hebrew manuscripts, Syriac, and Vulgate read *Zaccai.* **3:21** [a]Or *Hakkoz* **3:31** [a]Literally *Inspection* or *Recruiting*

The Message

17-18 Levites under Rehum son of Bani were next in line. Alongside them, Hashabiah, mayor of half the district of Keilah, represented his district in the rebuilding. Next to him their brothers continued the rebuilding under Binnui son of Henadad, mayor of the other half-district of Keilah.

19-23 The section from in front of the Ascent to the Armory as far as the Angle was rebuilt by Ezer son of Jeshua, the mayor of Mizpah. From the Angle to the door of the house of Eliashib the high priest was done by Baruch son of Zabbai. Meremoth son of Uriah, the son of Hakkoz, took it from the door of Eliashib's house to the end of Eliashib's house. Priests from the neighborhood went on from there. Benjamin and Hasshub worked on the wall in front of their house, and Azariah son of Maaseiah, the son of Ananiah, did the work alongside his house.

24-27 The section from the house of Azariah to the Angle at the Corner was rebuilt by Binnui son of Henadad. Palal son of Uzai worked opposite the Angle and the tower that projects from the Upper Palace of the king near the Court of the Guard. Next to him Pedaiah son of Parosh and The Temple support staff who lived on the hill of Ophel worked up to the point opposite the Water Gate eastward and the projecting tower. The men of Tekoa did the section from the great projecting tower as far as the wall of Ophel.

28-30 Above the Horse Gate the priests worked, each priest repairing the wall in front of his own house. After them Zadok son of Immer rebuilt in front of his house and after him Shemaiah son of Shecaniah, the keeper of the East Gate; then Hananiah son of Shelemiah and Hanun, the sixth son of Zalaph; then Meshullam son of Berekiah rebuilt the wall in front of his storage shed.

31-32 Malkijah the goldsmith repaired the wall as far as the house of The Temple support staff and merchants, up to the Inspection Gate, and the Upper Room at the Corner. The goldsmiths and the merchants made the repairs between the Upper Room at the Corner and the Sheep Gate.

"I Stationed Armed Guards"

1-2 4 When Sanballat heard that we were rebuilding the wall he exploded in anger, vilifying the Jews. In the company of his Samaritan cronies and military he let loose: "What are these miserable Jews doing? Do they think they can get everything back to normal overnight? Make building stones out of make-believe?"

3 At his side, Tobiah the Ammonite jumped in and said, "That's right! What do they think they're building? Why, if a fox climbed that wall, it would fall to pieces under his weight."

NEW KING JAMES VERSION

4Hear, O our God, for we are despised; turn
their reproach on their own heads, and give
them as plunder to a land of captivity! 5Do not
cover their iniquity, and do not let their sin be
blotted out from before You; for they have pro-
voked *You* to anger before the builders.
6So we built the wall, and the entire wall was
joined together up to half its *height*, for the peo-
ple had a mind to work.
7Now it happened, when Sanballat, Tobiah,
the Arabs, the Ammonites, and the Ashdodites
heard that the walls of Jerusalem were being re-
stored and the gaps were beginning to be
closed, that they became very angry, 8and all of
them conspired together to come *and* attack
Jerusalem and create confusion. 9Nevertheless
we made our prayer to our God, and because of
them we set a watch against them day and
night.
10Then Judah said, "The strength of the la-
borers is failing, and *there is* so much rubbish
that we are not able to build the wall."
11And our adversaries said, "They will nei-
ther know nor see anything, till we come into
their midst and kill them and cause the work to
cease."
12So it was, when the Jews who dwelt near
them came, that they told us ten times, "From
whatever place you turn, *they will be* upon us."
13Therefore I positioned *men* behind the
lower parts of the wall, at the openings; and I set
the people according to their families, with their
swords, their spears, and their bows. 14And I
looked, and arose and said to the nobles, to the
leaders, and to the rest of the people, "Do not be
afraid of them. Remember the Lord, great and
awesome, and fight for your brethren, your
sons, your daughters, your wives, and your
houses."
15And it happened, when our enemies heard
that it was known to us, and *that* God had
brought their plot to nothing, that all of us re-
turned to the wall, everyone to his work. 16So it
was, from that time on, *that* half of my servants
worked at construction, while the other half
held the spears, the shields, the bows, and *wore*
armor; and the leaders *were* behind all the
house of Judah. 17Those who built on the wall,
and those who carried burdens, loaded them-
selves so that with one hand they worked at
construction, and with the other held a weapon.
18Every one of the builders had his sword girded
at his side as he built. And the one who sounded
the trumpet *was* beside me.
19Then I said to the nobles, the rulers, and
the rest of the people, "The work *is* great and ex-
tensive, and we are separated far from one an-
other on the wall. 20Wherever you hear the
sound of the trumpet, rally to us there. Our God
will fight for us."
21So we labored in the work, and half of *the*
men[a] held the spears from daybreak until the
stars appeared. 22At the same time I also said to
the people, "Let each man and his servant stay
at night in Jerusalem, that they may be our
guard by night and a working party by day."

4:21 [a]Literally *them*

THE MESSAGE

4-5 Nehemiah prayed, "Oh listen to us, dear God. We're so despised: Boomerang their ridicule on their heads; have their enemies cart them off as war trophies to a land of no return; don't forgive their iniquity, don't wipe away their sin—they've insulted the builders!"

6 We kept at it, repairing and rebuilding the wall. The whole wall was soon joined together and halfway to its intended height because the people had a heart for the work.

7-9 When Sanballat, Tobiah, the Arabs, the Ammonites, and the Ashdodites heard that the repairs of the walls of Jerusalem were going so well—that the breaks in the wall were being fixed—they were absolutely furious. They put their heads together and decided to fight against Jerusalem and create as much trouble as they could. We countered with prayer to our God and set a round-the-clock guard against them.

10 But soon word was going around in Judah,

The builders are pooped,
  the rubbish piles up;
We're in over our heads,
  we can't build this wall.

11-12 And all this time our enemies were saying, "They won't know what hit them. Before they know it we'll be at their throats, killing them right and left. *That* will put a stop to the work!" The Jews who were their neighbors kept reporting, "They have us surrounded; they're going to attack!" If we heard it once, we heard it ten times.

13-14 So I stationed armed guards at the most vulnerable places of the wall and assigned people by families with their swords, lances, and bows. After looking things over I stood up and spoke to the nobles, officials, and everyone else: "Don't be afraid of them. Put your minds on the Master, great and awesome, and then fight for your brothers, your sons, your daughters, your wives, and your homes."

15-18 Our enemies learned that we knew all about their plan and that God had frustrated it. And we went back to the wall and went to work. From then on half of my young men worked while the other half stood guard with lances, shields, bows, and mail armor. Military officers served as backup for everyone in Judah who was at work rebuilding the wall. The common laborers held a tool in one hand and a spear in the other. Each of the builders had a sword strapped to his side as he worked. I kept the trumpeter at my side to sound the alert.

19-20 Then I spoke to the nobles and officials and everyone else: "There's a lot of work going on and we are spread out all along the wall, separated from each other. When you hear the trumpet call, join us there; our God will fight for us."

21 And so we kept working, from first light until the stars came out, half of us holding lances.

22 I also instructed the people, "Each person and his helper is to stay inside Jerusalem—guards by night and workmen by day."

NEW KING JAMES VERSION

[23]So neither I, my brethren, my servants, nor the men of the guard who followed me took off our clothes, *except* that everyone took them off for washing.

NEHEMIAH DEALS WITH OPPRESSION

5 And there was a great outcry of the people and their wives against their Jewish brethren. [2]For there were those who said, "We, our sons, and our daughters *are* many; therefore let us get grain, that we may eat and live."

[3]There were also *some* who said, "We have mortgaged our lands and vineyards and houses, that we might buy grain because of the famine."

[4]There were also those who said, "We have borrowed money for the king's tax *on* our lands and vineyards. [5]Yet now our flesh *is* as the flesh of our brethren, our children as their children; and indeed we are forcing our sons and our daughters to be slaves, and *some* of our daughters have been brought into slavery. *It is* not in our power *to redeem them,* for other men have our lands and vineyards."

[6]And I became very angry when I heard their outcry and these words. [7]After serious thought, I rebuked the nobles and rulers, and said to them, "Each of you is exacting usury from his brother." So I called a great assembly against them. [8]And I said to them, "According to our ability we have redeemed our Jewish brethren who were sold to the nations. Now indeed, will you even sell your brethren? Or should they be sold to us?"

Then they were silenced and found nothing *to say.* [9]Then I said, "What you are doing *is* not good. Should you not walk in the fear of our God because of the reproach of the nations, our enemies? [10]I also, *with* my brethren and my servants, am lending them money and grain. Please, let us stop this usury! [11]Restore now to them, even this day, their lands, their vineyards, their olive groves, and their houses, also a hundredth of the money and the grain, the new wine and the oil, that you have charged them."

[12]So they said, "We will restore *it,* and will require nothing from them; we will do as you say."

Then I called the priests, and required an oath from them that they would do according to this promise. [13]Then I shook out the fold of my garment[a] and said, "So may God shake out each man from his house, and from his property, who does not perform this promise. Even thus may he be shaken out and emptied."

And all the assembly said, "Amen!" and praised the LORD. Then the people did according to this promise.

THE GENEROSITY OF NEHEMIAH

[14]Moreover, from the time that I was appointed to be their governor in the land of Judah, from the twentieth year until the thirty-second year of King Artaxerxes, twelve years, neither I nor my brothers ate the governor's provisions. [15]But the former governors who *were*

5:13 [a]Literally *my lap*

THE MESSAGE

23 We all slept in our clothes—I, my broth-
ers, my workmen, and the guards backing
me up. And each one kept his spear in his
hand, even when getting water.

THE "GREAT PROTEST"

1-2 5 A great protest was mounted by the people,
including the wives, against their fellow
Jews. Some said, "We have big families, and
we need food just to survive."
3 Others said, "We're having to mortgage
our fields and vineyards and homes to get
enough grain to keep from starving."
4-5 And others said, "We're having to borrow
money to pay the royal tax on our fields and
vineyards. Look: We're the same flesh and
blood as our brothers here; our children are
just as good as theirs. Yet here we are having
to sell our children off as slaves—some of
our daughters have already been sold—and
we can't do anything about it because our
fields and vineyards are owned by some-
body else."
6-7 I got really angry when I heard their
protest and complaints. After thinking it
over, I called the nobles and officials on the
carpet. I said, "Each one of you is gouging
his brother."
7-8 Then I called a big meeting to deal with
them. I told them, "We did everything we
could to buy back our Jewish brothers who
had to sell themselves as slaves to foreign-
ers. And now you're selling these same
brothers back into debt slavery! Does that
mean that we have to buy them back
again?"
They said nothing. What could they say?
9 "What you're doing is wrong. Is there no
fear of God left in you? Don't you care what
the nations around here, our enemies, think
of you?
10-11 "I and my brothers and the people work-
ing for me have also loaned them money.
But this gouging them with interest has to
stop. Give them back their foreclosed fields,
vineyards, olive groves, and homes right
now. And forgive your claims on their
money, grain, new wine, and olive oil."
12-13 They said, "We'll give it all back. We
won't make any more demands on them.
We'll do everything you say."
Then I called the priests together and
made them promise to keep their word.
Then I emptied my pockets, turning them in-
side out, and said, "So may God empty the
pockets and house of everyone who doesn't
keep this promise—turned inside out and
emptied."
Everyone gave a wholehearted "Yes, we'll
do it!" and praised GOD. And the people did
what they promised.

"REMEMBER IN MY FAVOR, O MY GOD"

14-16 From the time King Artaxerxes appointed
me as their governor in the land of Judah—
from the twentieth to the thirty-second year
of his reign, twelve years—neither I nor my
brothers used the governor's food al-
lowance. Governors who had preceded me

NEW KING JAMES VERSION

before me laid burdens on the people, and took from them bread and wine, besides forty shekels of silver. Yes, even their servants bore rule over the people, but I did not do so, because of the fear of God. [16]Indeed, I also continued the work on this wall, and we[a] did not buy any land. All my servants *were* gathered there for the work.

[17]And at my table *were* one hundred and fifty Jews and rulers, besides those who came to us from the nations around us. [18]Now *that* which was prepared daily *was* one ox *and* six choice sheep. Also fowl were prepared for me, and once every ten days an abundance of all kinds of wine. Yet in spite of this I did not demand the governor's provisions, because the bondage was heavy on this people.

[19]Remember me, my God, for good, *according to* all that I have done for this people.

CONSPIRACY AGAINST NEHEMIAH

6 Now it happened when Sanballat, Tobiah, Geshem the Arab, and the rest of our enemies heard that I had rebuilt the wall, and *that* there were no breaks left in it (though at that time I had not hung the doors in the gates), [2]that Sanballat and Geshem sent to me, saying, "Come, let us meet together among the villages in the plain of Ono." But they thought to do me harm.

[3]So I sent messengers to them, saying, "I *am* doing a great work, so that I cannot come down. Why should the work cease while I leave it and go down to you?"

[4]But they sent me this message four times, and I answered them in the same manner.

[5]Then Sanballat sent his servant to me as before, the fifth time, with an open letter in his hand. [6]In it *was* written:

> It is reported among the nations, and Geshem[a] says, *that* you and the Jews plan to rebel; therefore, according to these rumors, you are rebuilding the wall, that you may be their king. [7]And you have also appointed prophets to proclaim concerning you at Jerusalem, saying, *"There is* a king in Judah!" Now these matters will be reported to the king. So come, therefore, and let us consult together.

[8]Then I sent to him, saying, "No such things as you say are being done, but you invent them in your own heart."

[9]For they all *were trying to* make us afraid, saying, "Their hands will be weakened in the work, and it will not be done."

Now therefore, *O God,* strengthen my hands.

[10]Afterward I came to the house of Shemaiah the son of Delaiah, the son of Mehetabel, who *was* a secret informer; and he said, "Let us meet together in the house of God, within the temple, and let us close the doors of the temple, for they are coming to kill you; indeed, at night they will come to kill you."

5:16 [a]Following Masoretic Text; Septuagint, Syriac, and Vulgate read *I.* **6:6** [a]Hebrew *Gashmu*

THE MESSAGE

had oppressed the people by taxing them forty shekels of silver (about a pound) a day for food and wine while their underlings bullied the people unmercifully. But out of fear of God I did none of that. I had work to do; I worked on this wall. All my men were on the job to do the work. We didn't have time to line our own pockets.

17-18 I fed 150 Jews and officials at my table in addition to those who showed up from the surrounding nations. One ox, six choice sheep, and some chickens were prepared for me daily, and every ten days a large supply of wine was delivered. Even so, I didn't use the food allowance provided for the governor—the people had it hard enough as it was.

19 Remember in my favor, O my God,
Everything I've done for these people.

"I'M DOING A GREAT WORK; I CAN'T COME DOWN"

1-2 **6** When Sanballat, Tobiah, Geshem the Arab, and the rest of our enemies heard that I had rebuilt the wall and that there were no more breaks in it—even though I hadn't yet installed the gates—Sanballat and Geshem sent this message: "Come and meet with us at Kephirim in the valley of Ono."

2-3 I knew they were scheming to hurt me so I sent messengers back with this: "I'm doing a great work; I can't come down. Why should the work come to a standstill just so I can come down to see you?"

4 Four times they sent this message and four times I gave them my answer.

5-6 The fifth time—same messenger, same message—Sanballat sent an unsealed letter with this message:

6-7 "The word is out among the nations—and Geshem says it's true—that you and the Jews are planning to rebel. That's why you are rebuilding the wall. The word is that you want to be king and that you have appointed prophets to announce in Jerusalem, 'There's a king in Judah!' The king is going to be told all this—don't you think we should sit down and have a talk?"

8 I sent him back this: "There's nothing to what you're saying. You've made it all up."

9 They were trying to intimidate us into quitting. They thought, "They'll give up; they'll never finish it."

I prayed, "Give me strength."

10 Then I met secretly with Shemaiah son of Delaiah, the son of Mehetabel, at his house. He said:

> Let's meet at the house of God,
> inside The Temple;
> Let's find safety behind locked doors
> because they're coming to kill you,
> Yes, coming by night to kill you.

NEW KING JAMES VERSION

11And I said, "Should such a man as I flee?
And who *is there* such as I who would go into
the temple to save his life? I will not go in!"
12Then I perceived that God had not sent him at
all, but that he pronounced *this* prophecy
against me because Tobiah and Sanballat had
hired him. 13For this reason he *was* hired, that I
should be afraid and act that way and sin, so
that they might have *cause* for an evil report,
that they might reproach me.
14My God, remember Tobiah and Sanballat,
according to these their works, and the prophet-
ess Noadiah and the rest of the prophets who
would have made me afraid.

THE WALL COMPLETED

15So the wall was finished on the twenty-fifth
day of Elul, in fifty-two days. 16And it happened,
when all our enemies heard *of it,* and all the na-
tions around us saw *these things,* that they were
very disheartened in their own eyes; for they
perceived that this work was done by our God.
17Also in those days the nobles of Judah sent
many letters to Tobiah, and *the letters of* Tobiah
came to them. 18For many in Judah were
pledged to him, because he was the son-in-law
of Shechaniah the son of Arah, and his son Je-
hohanan had married the daughter of Meshul-
lam the son of Berechiah. 19Also they reported
his good deeds before me, and reported my
words to him. Tobiah sent letters to frighten me.

7Then it was, when the wall was built and I
had hung the doors, when the gatekeepers,
the singers, and the Levites had been appointed,
2that I gave the charge of Jerusalem to my
brother Hanani, and Hananiah the leader of the
citadel, for he *was* a faithful man and feared
God more than many.
3And I said to them, "Do not let the gates of
Jerusalem be opened until the sun is hot; and
while they stand *guard,* let them shut and bar
the doors; and appoint guards from among the
inhabitants of Jerusalem, one at his watch sta-
tion and another in front of his own house."

THE CAPTIVES WHO RETURNED TO JERUSALEM

4Now the city *was* large and spacious, but
the people in it *were* few, and the houses *were*
not rebuilt. 5Then my God put it into my heart to
gather the nobles, the rulers, and the people,
that they might be registered by genealogy. And
I found a register of the genealogy of those who
had come up in the first *return,* and found writ-
ten in it:

> 6These[a] *are* the people of the province who
> came back from the captivity, of those who
> had been carried away, whom
> Nebuchadnezzar the king of Babylon had
> carried away, and who returned to
> Jerusalem and Judah, everyone to his city.

7:6 [a]Compare verses 6–72 with Ezra 2:1–70

THE MESSAGE

11 I said, "Why would a man like me run for
cover? And why would a man like me use
The Temple as a hideout? I won't do it."
12-13 I sensed that God hadn't sent this man.
The so-called prophecy he spoke to me was
the work of Tobiah and Sanballat; they had
hired him. He had been hired to scare me
off—trick me—a layman, into desecrating
The Temple and ruining my good reputation
so they could accuse me.
14 "O my God, don't let Tobiah and Sanbal-
lat get by with all the mischief they've done.
And the same goes for the prophetess Noa-
diah and the other prophets who have been
trying to undermine my confidence."

15-16 The wall was finished on the twenty-fifth
day of Elul. It had taken fifty-two days.
When all our enemies heard the news and
all the surrounding nations saw it, our ene-
mies totally lost their nerve. They knew that
God was behind this work.
17-19 All during this time letters were going
back and forth constantly between the no-
bles of Judah and Tobiah. Many of the no-
bles had ties to him because he was son-in-
law to Shecaniah son of Arah and his son
Jehohanan had married the daughter of
Meshullam son of Berekiah. They kept
telling me all the good things he did and
then would report back to him anything I
would say. And then Tobiah would send let-
ters to intimidate me.

THE WALL REBUILT: NAMES AND NUMBERS

1-2 7After the wall was rebuilt and I had in-
stalled the doors, and the security guards,
the singers, and the Levites were appointed,
I put my brother Hanani, along with Hana-
niah the captain of the citadel, in charge of
Jerusalem because he was an honest man
and feared God more than most men.
3 I gave them this order: "Don't open the
gates of Jerusalem until the sun is up. And
shut and bar the gates while the guards are
still on duty. Appoint the guards from the
citizens of Jerusalem and assign them to
posts in front of their own homes."
4 The city was large and spacious with
only a few people in it and the houses not
yet rebuilt.
5 God put it in my heart to gather the no-
bles, the officials, and the people in general
to be registered. I found the genealogical
record of those who were in the first return
from exile. This is the record I found:

> 6-60 These are the people of the province
> who returned from the captivity of the
> Exile, the ones Nebuchadnezzar king
> of Babylon had carried off captive; they
> came back to Jerusalem and Judah,
> each going to his own town. They came

NEW KING JAMES VERSION

7 Those who came with Zerubbabel *were*
Jeshua, Nehemiah, Azariah, Raamiah,
Nahamani, Mordecai, Bilshan, Mispereth,[a]
Bigvai, Nehum, and Baanah.

The number of the men of the people of
Israel: 8 the sons of Parosh, two thousand
one hundred and seventy-two;
9 the sons of Shephatiah, three hundred and
seventy-two;
10 the sons of Arah, six hundred and fifty-
two;
11 the sons of Pahath-Moab, of the sons of
Jeshua and Joab, two thousand eight
hundred and eighteen;
12 the sons of Elam, one thousand two
hundred and fifty-four;
13 the sons of Zattu, eight hundred and forty-
five;
14 the sons of Zaccai, seven hundred and
sixty;
15 the sons of Binnui,[a] six hundred and forty-
eight;
16 the sons of Bebai, six hundred and twenty-
eight;
17 the sons of Azgad, two thousand three
hundred and twenty-two;
18 the sons of Adonikam, six hundred and
sixty-seven;
19 the sons of Bigvai, two thousand and sixty-
seven;
20 the sons of Adin, six hundred and fifty-
five;
21 the sons of Ater of Hezekiah, ninety-eight;
22 the sons of Hashum, three hundred and
twenty-eight;
23 the sons of Bezai, three hundred and
twenty-four;
24 the sons of Hariph,[a] one hundred and
twelve;
25 the sons of Gibeon,[a] ninety-five;
26 the men of Bethlehem and Netophah, one
hundred and eighty-eight;
27 the men of Anathoth, one hundred and
twenty-eight;
28 the men of Beth Azmaveth,[a] forty-two;
29 the men of Kirjath Jearim, Chephirah, and
Beeroth, seven hundred and forty-three;
30 the men of Ramah and Geba, six hundred
and twenty-one;
31 the men of Michmas, one hundred and
twenty-two;
32 the men of Bethel and Ai, one hundred and
twenty-three;
33 the men of the other Nebo, fifty-two;
34 the sons of the other Elam, one thousand
two hundred and fifty-four;
35 the sons of Harim, three hundred and
twenty;
36 the sons of Jericho, three hundred and
forty-five;
37 the sons of Lod, Hadid, and Ono, seven
hundred and twenty-one;
38 the sons of Senaah, three thousand nine
hundred and thirty.

7:7 [a]Spelled *Mispar* in Ezra 2:2 **7:15** [a]Spelled *Bani* in Ezra 2:10 **7:24** [a]Called *Jorah* in Ezra 2:18 **7:25** [a]Called *Gibbar* in Ezra 2:20 **7:28** [a]Called *Azmaveth* in Ezra 2:24

THE MESSAGE

back in the company of Zerubbabel, Jeshua, Nehemiah, Azariah, Raamiah, Nahamani, Mordecai, Bilshan, Mispereth, Bigvai, Nehum, and Baanah.

The numbers of the men of the People of Israel by families of origin:

Parosh, 2,172
Shephatiah, 372
Arah, 652
Pahath-Moab (sons of Jeshua and Joab), 2,818
Elam, 1,254
Zattu, 845
Zaccai, 760
Binnui, 648
Bebai, 628
Azgad, 2,322
Adonikam, 667
Bigvai, 2,067
Adin, 655
Ater (sons of Hezekiah), 98
Hashum, 328
Bezai, 324
Hariph, 112
Gibeon, 95.

Israelites identified by place of origin:

Bethlehem and Netophah, 188
Anathoth, 128
Beth Azmaveth, 42
Kiriath Jearim, Kephirah, and Beeroth, 743
Ramah and Geba, 621
Micmash, 122
Bethel and Ai, 123
Nebo (the other one), 52
Elam (the other one), 1,254
Harim, 320
Jericho, 345
Lod, Hadid, and Ono, 721
Senaah, 3,930.

NEW KING JAMES VERSION

[39]The priests: the sons of Jedaiah, of the
house of Jeshua, nine hundred and seventy-
three;
[40]the sons of Immer, one thousand and fifty-
two;
[41]the sons of Pashhur, one thousand two
hundred and forty-seven;
[42]the sons of Harim, one thousand and
seventeen.

[43]The Levites: the sons of Jeshua, of Kadmiel,
and of the sons of Hodevah,[a] seventy-four.

[44]The singers: the sons of Asaph, one
hundred and forty-eight.

[45]The gatekeepers: the sons of Shallum,
the sons of Ater,
the sons of Talmon,
the sons of Akkub,
the sons of Hatita,
the sons of Shobai, one hundred and thirty-
eight.

[46]The Nethinim: the sons of Ziha,
the sons of Hasupha,
the sons of Tabbaoth,
[47]the sons of Keros,
the sons of Sia,[a]
the sons of Padon,
[48]the sons of Lebana,[a]
the sons of Hagaba,[b]
the sons of Salmai,[c]
[49]the sons of Hanan,
the sons of Giddel,
the sons of Gahar,
[50]the sons of Reaiah,
the sons of Rezin,
the sons of Nekoda,
[51]the sons of Gazzam,
the sons of Uzza,
the sons of Paseah,
[52]the sons of Besai,
the sons of Meunim,
the sons of Nephishesim,[a]
[53]the sons of Bakbuk,
the sons of Hakupha,
the sons of Harhur,
[54]the sons of Bazlith,[a]
the sons of Mehida,
the sons of Harsha,
[55]the sons of Barkos,
the sons of Sisera,
the sons of Tamah,
[56]the sons of Neziah,
and the sons of Hatipha.

[57]The sons of Solomon's servants: the sons of
Sotai,
the sons of Sophereth,
the sons of Perida,[a]
[58]the sons of Jaala,
the sons of Darkon,
the sons of Giddel,

7:43 [a]Spelled *Hodaviah* in Ezra 2:40 **7:47** [a]Spelled *Siaha* in Ezra 2:44 **7:48** [a]Masoretic Text reads *Lebanah.* [b]Masoretic Text reads *Hogabah.* [c]Or *Shalmai,* or *Shamlai* **7:52** [a]Spelled *Nephusim* in Ezra 2:50 **7:54** [a]Spelled *Bazluth* in Ezra 2:52 **7:57** [a]Spelled *Peruda* in Ezra 2:55

THE MESSAGE

Priestly families:
Jedaiah (sons of Jeshua), 973
Immer, 1,052
Pashhur, 1,247
Harim, 1,017.
Levitical families:
Jeshua (sons of Kadmiel and of Hodaviah), 74.
Singers:
Asaph's family line, 148.
Security guard families:
Shallum, Ater, Talmon, Akkub, Hatita, and Shobai, 138.
Families of support staff:
Ziha, Hasupha, Tabbaoth,
Keros, Sia, Padon,
Lebana, Hagaba, Shalmai,
Hanan, Giddel, Gahar,
Reaiah, Rezin, Nekoda,
Gazzam, Uzza, Paseah,
Besai, Meunim, Nephussim,
Bakbuk, Hakupha, Harhur,
Bazluth, Mehida, Harsha,
Barkos, Sisera, Temah,
Neziah, and Hatipha.
Families of Solomon's servants:
Sotai, Sophereth, Perida,
Jaala, Darkon, Giddel,

NEW KING JAMES VERSION

[59]the sons of Shephatiah,
the sons of Hattil,
the sons of Pochereth of Zebaim,
and the sons of Amon.[a]
[60]All the Nethinim, and the sons of
Solomon's servants, *were* three hundred
and ninety-two.

[61]And these *were* the ones who came up from
Tel Melah, Tel Harsha, Cherub, Addon,[a] and
Immer, but they could not identify their
father's house nor their lineage, whether
they *were* of Israel: [62]the sons of Delaiah,
the sons of Tobiah,
the sons of Nekoda, six hundred and forty-two;
[63]and of the priests: the sons of Habaiah,
the sons of Koz,[a]
the sons of Barzillai, who took a wife of the
daughters of Barzillai the Gileadite, and was
called by their name.
[64]These sought their listing *among* those
who were registered by genealogy, but it was
not found; therefore they were excluded
from the priesthood as defiled. [65]And the
governor[a] said to them that they should not
eat of the most holy things till a priest could
consult with the Urim and Thummim.

[66]Altogether the whole assembly *was* forty-two thousand three hundred and sixty,
[67]besides their male and female servants, of
whom *there were* seven thousand three
hundred and thirty-seven; and they had two
hundred and forty-five men and women
singers. [68]Their horses were seven hundred
and thirty-six, their mules two hundred and
forty-five, [69]*their* camels four hundred and
thirty-five, *and* donkeys six thousand seven
hundred and twenty.

[70]And some of the heads of the fathers'
houses gave to the work. The governor[a]
gave to the treasury one thousand gold
drachmas, fifty basins, and five hundred
and thirty priestly garments. [71]Some of the
heads of the fathers' *houses* gave to the
treasury of the work twenty thousand gold
drachmas, and two thousand two hundred
silver minas. [72]And that which the rest of
the people gave *was* twenty thousand gold
drachmas, two thousand silver minas, and
sixty-seven priestly garments.

[73]So the priests, the Levites, the gatekeepers, the singers, *some* of the people, the Nethinim, and all Israel dwelt in their cities.

EZRA READS THE LAW

When the seventh month came, the children of Israel *were* in their cities.

8 Now all the people gathered together as one man in the open square that *was* in front of the Water Gate; and they told Ezra the scribe to

7:59 [a]Spelled *Ami* in Ezra 2:57 **7:61** [a]Spelled *Addan* in Ezra 2:59 **7:63** [a]Or *Hakkoz* **7:65** [a]Hebrew *Tirshatha* **7:70** [a]Hebrew *Tirshatha*

THE MESSAGE

Shephatiah, Hattil, Pokereth-Hazzebaim, and Amon.
The Temple support staff and
Solomon's servants added up
to 392.

61-63 These are those who came from Tel Melah, Tel Harsha, Kerub, Addon, and Immer. They weren't able to prove their ancestry, whether they were true Israelites or not:

The sons of Delaiah, Tobiah, and
Nekoda, 642.
Likewise with these priestly families:
The sons of Hobaiah, Hakkoz, and
Barzillai, who had married a
daughter of Barzillai the Gileadite
and took that name.

64-65 They looked high and low for their family records but couldn't find them. And so they were barred from priestly work as ritually unclean. The governor ruled that they could not eat from the holy food until a priest could determine their status by using the Urim and Thummim.

66-69 The total count for the congregation was 42,360. That did not include the male and female slaves who numbered 7,337. There were also 245 male and female singers. And there were 736 horses, 245 mules, 435 camels, and 6,720 donkeys.

70-72 Some of the heads of families made voluntary offerings for the work. The governor made a gift to the treasury of 1,000 drachmas of gold (about nineteen pounds), 50 bowls, and 530 garments for the priests. Some of the heads of the families made gifts to the treasury for the work; it came to 20,000 drachmas of gold and 2,200 minas of silver (about one and a third tons). Gifts from the rest of the people totaled 20,000 drachmas of gold (about 375 pounds), 2,000 minas of silver, and 67 garments for the priests.

73 The priests, Levites, security guards, singers, and Temple support staff, along with some others, and the rest of the People of Israel, all found a place to live in their own towns.

EZRA AND THE REVELATION

1 8 By the time the seventh month arrived, the People of Israel were settled in their towns. Then all the people gathered as one person in the town square in front of the Water Gate and asked the scholar Ezra to

NEW KING JAMES VERSION

bring the Book of the Law of Moses, which the LORD had commanded Israel. 2So Ezra the priest brought the Law before the assembly of men and women and all who *could* hear with understanding on the first day of the seventh month. 3Then he read from it in the open square that *was* in front of the Water Gate from morning until midday, before the men and women and those who could understand; and the ears of all the people *were attentive* to the Book of the Law.

4So Ezra the scribe stood on a platform of wood which they had made for the purpose; and beside him, at his right hand, stood Mattithiah, Shema, Anaiah, Urijah, Hilkiah, and Maaseiah; and at his left hand Pedaiah, Mishael, Malchijah, Hashum, Hashbadana, Zechariah, *and* Meshullam. 5And Ezra opened the book in the sight of all the people, for he was *standing* above all the people; and when he opened it, all the people stood up. 6And Ezra blessed the LORD, the great God.

Then all the people answered, "Amen, Amen!" while lifting up their hands. And they bowed their heads and worshiped the LORD with *their* faces to the ground.

7Also Jeshua, Bani, Sherebiah, Jamin, Akkub, Shabbethai, Hodijah, Maaseiah, Kelita, Azariah, Jozabad, Hanan, Pelaiah, and the Levites, helped the people to understand the Law; and the people *stood* in their place. 8So they read distinctly from the book, in the Law of God; and they gave the sense, and helped *them* to understand the reading.

9And Nehemiah, who *was* the governor,[a] Ezra the priest *and* scribe, and the Levites who taught the people said to all the people, "This day *is* holy to the LORD your God; do not mourn nor weep." For all the people wept, when they heard the words of the Law.

10Then he said to them, "Go your way, eat the fat, drink the sweet, and send portions to those for whom nothing is prepared; for *this* day *is* holy to our Lord. Do not sorrow, for the joy of the LORD is your strength."

11So the Levites quieted all the people, saying, "Be still, for the day *is* holy; do not be grieved." 12And all the people went their way to eat and drink, to send portions and rejoice greatly, because they understood the words that were declared to them.

THE FEAST OF TABERNACLES

13Now on the second day the heads of the fathers' *houses* of all the people, with the priests and Levites, were gathered to Ezra the scribe, in order to understand the words of the Law. 14And they found written in the Law, which the LORD had commanded by Moses, that the children of Israel should dwell in booths during the feast of the seventh month, 15and that they should announce and proclaim in all their cities and in Jerusalem, saying, "Go out to the mountain, and bring olive branches, branches of oil trees, myrtle branches, palm branches, and branches of leafy trees, to make booths, as *it is* written."

8:9 [a]Hebrew *Tirshatha*

THE MESSAGE

bring the Book of The Revelation of Moses that GOD had commanded for Israel.

2-3 So Ezra the priest brought The Revelation to the congregation, which was made up of both men and women—everyone capable of understanding. It was the first day of the seventh month. He read it facing the town square at the Water Gate from early dawn until noon in the hearing of the men and women, all who could understand it. And all the people listened—they were all ears—to the Book of The Revelation.

4 The scholar Ezra stood on a wooden platform constructed for the occasion. He was flanked on the right by Mattithiah, Shema, Anaiah, Uriah, Hilkiah, and Maaseiah, and on the left by Pedaiah, Mishael, Malkijah, Hashum, Hashbaddanah, Zechariah, and Meshullam.

5-6 Ezra opened the book. Every eye was on him (he was standing on the raised platform) and as he opened the book everyone stood. Then Ezra praised GOD, the great God, and all the people responded, "Oh Yes! Yes!" with hands raised high. And then they fell to their knees in worship of GOD, their faces to the ground.

7-8 Jeshua, Bani, Sherebiah, Jamin, Akkub, Shabbethai, Hodiah, Maaseiah, Kelita, Azariah, Jozabad, Hanan, and Pelaiah, all Levites, explained The Revelation while people stood, listening respectfully. They translated the Book of The Revelation of God so the people could understand it and then explained the reading.

9 Nehemiah the governor, along with Ezra the priest and scholar and the Levites who were teaching the people, said to all the people, "This day is holy to GOD, your God. Don't weep and carry on." They said this because all the people were weeping as they heard the words of The Revelation.

10 He continued, "Go home and prepare a feast, holiday food and drink; and share it with those who don't have anything: This day is holy to God. Don't feel bad. The joy of GOD is your strength!"

11 The Levites calmed the people, "Quiet now. This is a holy day. Don't be upset."

12 So the people went off to feast, eating and drinking and including the poor in a great celebration. Now they got it; they understood the reading that had been given to them.

13-15 On the second day of the month the family heads of all the people, the priests, and the Levites gathered around Ezra the scholar to get a deeper understanding of the words of The Revelation. They found written in The Revelation that GOD commanded through Moses that the People of Israel are to live in booths during the festival of the seventh month. So they published this decree and had it posted in all their cities and in Jerusalem: "Go into the hills and collect olive branches, pine branches, myrtle branches, palm branches, and any other leafy branches to make booths, as it is written."

New King James Version

16Then the people went out and brought *them* and made themselves booths, each one on the roof of his house, or in their courtyards or the courts of the house of God, and in the open square of the Water Gate and in the open square of the Gate of Ephraim. 17So the whole assembly of those who had returned from the captivity made booths and sat under the booths; for since the days of Joshua the son of Nun until that day the children of Israel had not done so. And there was very great gladness. 18Also day by day, from the first day until the last day, he read from the Book of the Law of God. And they kept the feast seven days; and on the eighth day *there was* a sacred assembly, according to the *prescribed* manner.

The People Confess Their Sins

9 Now on the twenty-fourth day of this month the children of Israel were assembled with fasting, in sackcloth, and with dust on their heads.[a] 2Then those of Israelite lineage separated themselves from all foreigners; and they stood and confessed their sins and the iniquities of their fathers. 3And they stood up in their place and read from the Book of the Law of the LORD their God *for one*-fourth of the day; and *for another* fourth they confessed and worshiped the LORD their God.

4Then Jeshua, Bani, Kadmiel, Shebaniah, Bunni, Sherebiah, Bani, *and* Chenani stood on the stairs of the Levites and cried out with a loud voice to the LORD their God. 5And the Levites, Jeshua, Kadmiel, Bani, Hashabniah, Sherebiah, Hodijah, Shebaniah, *and* Pethahiah, said:

"Stand up *and* bless the LORD your God
Forever and ever!

"Blessed be Your glorious name,
Which is exalted above all blessing and
praise!
6You alone *are* the LORD;
You have made heaven,
The heaven of heavens, with all their host,
The earth and everything on it,
The seas and all that is in them,
And You preserve them all.
The host of heaven worships You.

7"You *are* the LORD God,
Who chose Abram,
And brought him out of Ur of the
Chaldeans,
And gave him the name Abraham;
8You found his heart faithful before You,
And made a covenant with him
To give the land of the Canaanites,
The Hittites, the Amorites,
The Perizzites, the Jebusites,
And the Girgashites—
To give *it* to his descendants.
You have performed Your words,
For You *are* righteous.

9:1 [a]Literally *earth on them*

The Message

16-17 So the people went out, brought in
branches, and made themselves booths on
their roofs, courtyards, the courtyards of
The Temple of God, the Water Gate plaza,
and the Ephraim Gate plaza. The entire congregation that had come back from exile
made booths and lived in them. The People
of Israel hadn't done this from the time of
Joshua son of Nun until that very day—a
terrific day! Great joy!
18 Ezra read from the Book of The Revelation of God each day, from the first to the
last day—they celebrated the feast for seven
days. On the eighth day they held a solemn
assembly in accordance with the decree.

1-3 9 Then on the twenty-fourth day of this
month, the People of Israel gathered for a
fast, wearing burlap and faces smudged
with dirt as signs of repentance. The Israelites broke off all relations with foreigners, stood up, and confessed their sins and
the iniquities of their parents. While they
stood there in their places, they read from
the Book of The Revelation of GOD, their
God, for a quarter of the day. For another
quarter of the day they confessed and worshiped their GOD.
4-5 A group of Levites—Jeshua, Bani, Kadmiel, Shebaniah, Bunni, Sherebiah, Bani,
and Kenani—stood on the platform and
cried out to GOD, their God, in a loud voice.
The Levites Jeshua, Kadmiel, Bani, Hashabneiah, Sherebiah, Hodiah, Shebaniah, and
Pethahiah said, "On your feet! Bless GOD,
your God, for ever and ever!"

5-6 Blessed be your glorious name,
exalted above all blessing and praise!
You're the one,
GOD, you alone;
You made the heavens,
the heavens of heavens, and all angels;
The earth and everything on it,
the seas and everything in them;
You keep them all alive;
heaven's angels worship you!

7-8 You're the one, GOD, *the* God
who chose Abram
And brought him from Ur of the Chaldees
and changed his name to Abraham.
You found his heart to be steady and true to
you
and signed a covenant with him,
A covenant to give him the land of the
Canaanites,
the Hittites, and the Amorites,
The Perizzites, Jebusites, and Girgashites,
—to give it to his descendants.
And you kept your word
because you are righteous.

New King James Version

9"You saw the affliction of our fathers in
Egypt,
And heard their cry by the Red Sea.
10You showed signs and wonders against
Pharaoh,
Against all his servants,
And against all the people of his land.
For You knew that they acted proudly
against them.
So You made a name for Yourself, as *it is* this
day.
11And You divided the sea before them,
So that they went through the midst of the
sea on the dry land;
And their persecutors You threw into the
deep,
As a stone into the mighty waters.
12Moreover You led them by day with a cloudy
pillar,
And by night with a pillar of fire,
To give them light on the road
Which they should travel.
13"You came down also on Mount Sinai,
And spoke with them from heaven,
And gave them just ordinances and true laws,
Good statutes and commandments.
14You made known to them Your holy
Sabbath,
And commanded them precepts, statutes
and laws,
By the hand of Moses Your servant.
15You gave them bread from heaven for their
hunger,
And brought them water out of the rock for
their thirst,
And told them to go in to possess the land
Which You had sworn to give them.

16"But they and our fathers acted proudly,
Hardened their necks,
And did not heed Your commandments.
17They refused to obey,
And they were not mindful of Your wonders
That You did among them.
But they hardened their necks,
And in their rebellion[a]
They appointed a leader
To return to their bondage.
But You *are* God,
Ready to pardon,
Gracious and merciful,
Slow to anger,
Abundant in kindness,
And did not forsake them.

18"Even when they made a molded calf for
themselves,
And said, 'This *is* your god
That brought you up out of Egypt,'
And worked great provocations,
19Yet in Your manifold mercies
You did not forsake them in the wilderness.
The pillar of the cloud did not depart from
them by day,
To lead them on the road;

9:17 [a]Following Masoretic Text and Vulgate; Septuagint reads *in Egypt*.

The Message

9-15 You saw the anguish of our parents in
Egypt.
You heard their cries at the Red Sea;
You amazed Pharaoh, his servants, and the
people of his land
with wonders and miracle-signs.
You knew their bullying arrogance against
your people;
you made a name for yourself that lasts
to this day.
You split the sea before them;
they crossed through and never got their
feet wet;
You pitched their pursuers into the deep;
they sank like a rock in the storm-tossed
sea.
By day you led them with a Pillar of Cloud,
and by night with a Pillar of Fire
To show them the way
they were to travel.
You came down onto Mount Sinai,
you spoke to them out of heaven;
You gave them instructions on how to live
well,
true teaching, sound rules and
commands;
You introduced them
to your Holy Sabbath;
Through your servant Moses you decreed
commands, rules, and instruction.
You gave bread from heaven for their
hunger,
you sent water from the rock for their
thirst.
You told them to enter and take the land,
which you promised to give them.

16-19 But they, our ancestors, were arrogant;
bullheaded, they wouldn't obey your
commands.
They turned a deaf ear, they refused
to remember the miracles you had done
for them;
They turned stubborn, got it into their heads
to return to their Egyptian slavery.
And you, a forgiving God,
gracious and compassionate,
Incredibly patient, with tons of love—
you didn't dump them.
Yes, even when they cast a sculpted calf
and said, "This is your god
Who brought you out of Egypt,"
and continued from bad to worse,
You in your amazing compassion
didn't walk off and leave them in the
desert.
The Pillar of Cloud didn't leave them;
daily it continued to show them their
route;

New King James Version

Nor the pillar of fire by night,
To show them light,
And the way they should go.
20You also gave Your good Spirit to instruct them,
And did not withhold Your manna from their mouth,
And gave them water for their thirst.
21Forty years You sustained them in the wilderness;
They lacked nothing;
Their clothes did not wear out[a]
And their feet did not swell.

22"Moreover You gave them kingdoms and nations,
And divided them into districts.[a]
So they took possession of the land of Sihon,
The land of[b] the king of Heshbon,
And the land of Og king of Bashan.
23You also multiplied their children as the stars of heaven,
And brought them into the land
Which You had told their fathers
To go in and possess.
24So the people went in
And possessed the land;
You subdued before them the inhabitants of the land,
The Canaanites,
And gave them into their hands,
With their kings
And the people of the land,
That they might do with them as they wished.
25And they took strong cities and a rich land,
And possessed houses full of all goods,
Cisterns *already* dug, vineyards, olive groves,
And fruit trees in abundance.
So they ate and were filled and grew fat,
And delighted themselves in Your great goodness.

26"Nevertheless they were disobedient
And rebelled against You,
Cast Your law behind their backs
And killed Your prophets, who testified against them
To turn them to Yourself;
And they worked great provocations.
27Therefore You delivered them into the hand of their enemies,
Who oppressed them;
And in the time of their trouble,
When they cried to You,
You heard from heaven;
And according to Your abundant mercies
You gave them deliverers who saved them
From the hand of their enemies.

28"But after they had rest,
They again did evil before You.
Therefore You left them in the hand of their enemies,
So that they had dominion over them;

9:21 [a]Compare Deuteronomy 29:5 **9:22** [a]Literally *corners* [b]Following Masoretic Text and Vulgate; Septuagint omits *The land of.*

The Message

The Pillar of Fire did the same by night,
showed them the right way to go.

20-23 You gave them your good Spirit
to teach them to live wisely.
You never stinted with your manna,
gave them plenty of water to drink.
You supported them forty years in that desert;
they had everything they needed;
Their clothes didn't wear out
and their feet never blistered.
You gave them kingdoms and peoples,
establishing generous boundaries.
They took over the country of Sihon king of Heshbon
and the country of Og king of Bashan.
You multiplied children for them,
rivaling the stars in the night skies,
And you brought them into the land
that you promised their ancestors
they would get and own.

24-25 Well, they entered all right,
they took it and settled in.
The Canaanites who lived there
you brought to their knees before them.
You turned over their land, kings, and peoples
to do with as they pleased.
They took strong cities and fertile fields,
they took over well-furnished houses,
Cisterns, vineyards, olive groves,
and lush, extensive orchards.
And they ate, grew fat on the fat of the land;
they reveled in your bountiful goodness.

26-31 But then they mutinied, rebelled against you,
threw out your laws and killed your prophets,
The very prophets who tried to get them back on your side—
and then things went from bad to worse.
You turned them over to their enemies,
who made life rough for them.
But when they called out for help in their troubles
you listened from heaven;
And in keeping with your bottomless compassion
you gave them saviors:
Saviors who saved them
from the cruel abuse of their enemies.
But as soon as they had it easy again
they were right back at it—more evil.
So you turned away and left them again to their fate,
to the enemies who came right back.

New King James Version

Yet when they returned and cried out to You,
You heard from heaven;
And many times You delivered them
according to Your mercies,
29And testified against them,
That You might bring them back to Your law.
Yet they acted proudly,
And did not heed Your commandments,
But sinned against Your judgments,
'Which if a man does, he shall live by them.'[a]
And they shrugged their shoulders,
Stiffened their necks,
And would not hear.
30Yet for many years You had patience with them,
And testified against them by Your Spirit in Your prophets.
Yet they would not listen;
Therefore You gave them into the hand of the peoples of the lands.
31Nevertheless in Your great mercy
You did not utterly consume them nor forsake them;
For You *are* God, gracious and merciful.

32"Now therefore, our God,
The great, the mighty, and awesome God,
Who keeps covenant and mercy:
Do not let all the trouble seem small before You
That has come upon us,
Our kings and our princes,
Our priests and our prophets,
Our fathers and on all Your people,
From the days of the kings of Assyria until this day.
33However You *are* just in all that has befallen us;
For You have dealt faithfully,
But we have done wickedly.
34Neither our kings nor our princes,
Our priests nor our fathers,
Have kept Your law,
Nor heeded Your commandments and Your testimonies,
With which You testified against them.
35For they have not served You in their kingdom,
Or in the many good *things* that You gave them,
Or in the large and rich land which You set before them;
Nor did they turn from their wicked works.

36"Here we *are*, servants today!
And the land that You gave to our fathers,
To eat its fruit and its bounty,
Here we *are*, servants in it!
37And it yields much increase to the kings
You have set over us,
Because of our sins;
Also they have dominion over our bodies and our cattle
At their pleasure;
And we *are* in great distress.

9:29 [a]Leviticus 18:5

The Message

They cried out to you again; in your great compassion
you heard and helped them again.
This went on over and over and over.
You warned them to return to your Revelation,
they responded with haughty arrogance:
They flouted your commands, spurned your rules
—the very words by which men and women live!
They set their jaws in defiance,
they turned their backs on you and didn't listen.
You put up with them year after year
and warned them by your spirit through your prophets;
But when they refused to listen
you abandoned them to foreigners.
Still, because of your great compassion,
you didn't make a total end to them.
You didn't walk out and leave them for good;
yes, you *are* a God of grace and compassion.

32-37 And now, our God, the great God,
God majestic and terrible, loyal in covenant and love,
Don't treat lightly the trouble that has come to us,
to our kings and princes, our priests and prophets,
Our ancestors, and all your people from the time
of the Assyrian kings right down to today.
You are not to blame
for all that has come down on us;
You did everything right,
we did everything wrong.
None of our kings, princes, priests, or ancestors
followed your Revelation;
They ignored your commands,
dismissed the warnings you gave them.
Even when they had their own kingdom
and were enjoying your generous goodness,
Living in that spacious and fertile land
that you spread out before them,
They didn't serve you
or turn their backs on the practice of evil.
And here we are, slaves again today;
and here's the land you gave our ancestors
So they could eat well and enjoy a good life,
and now look at us—no better than slaves on this land.
Its wonderful crops go to the kings
you put over us because of our sins;
They act like they own our bodies
and do whatever they like with our cattle.
We're in deep trouble.

NEW KING JAMES VERSION

38"And because of all this,
We make a sure *covenant* and write *it;*
Our leaders, our Levites, *and* our priests seal
it."

THE PEOPLE WHO SEALED THE COVENANT

10 Now those who placed *their* seal on *the*
document were:
Nehemiah the governor, the son of
Hacaliah, and Zedekiah, 2Seraiah, Azariah,
Jeremiah, 3Pashhur, Amariah, Malchijah,
4Hattush, Shebaniah, Malluch, 5Harim,
Meremoth, Obadiah, 6Daniel, Ginnethon,
Baruch, 7Meshullam, Abijah, Mijamin,
8Maaziah, Bilgai, *and* Shemaiah. These *were*
the priests.

9The Levites: Jeshua the son of Azaniah,
Binnui of the sons of Henadad, *and*
Kadmiel.

10Their brethren: Shebaniah, Hodijah, Kelita,
Pelaiah, Hanan, 11Micha, Rehob, Hashabiah,
12Zaccur, Sherebiah, Shebaniah, 13Hodijah,
Bani, *and* Beninu.

14The leaders of the people: Parosh, Pahath-
Moab, Elam, Zattu, Bani, 15Bunni, Azgad,
Bebai, 16Adonijah, Bigvai, Adin, 17Ater,
Hezekiah, Azzur, 18Hodijah, Hashum, Bezai,
19Hariph, Anathoth, Nebai, 20Magpiash,
Meshullam, Hezir, 21Meshezabel, Zadok,
Jaddua, 22Pelatiah, Hanan, Anaiah,
23Hoshea, Hananiah, Hasshub, 24Hallohesh,
Pilha, Shobek, 25Rehum, Hashabnah,
Maaseiah, 26Ahijah, Hanan, Anan,
27Malluch, Harim, *and* Baanah.

THE COVENANT THAT WAS SEALED

28Now the rest of the people—the priests, the
Levites, the gatekeepers, the singers, the
Nethinim, and all those who had separated
themselves from the peoples of the lands to the
Law of God, their wives, their sons, and their
daughters, everyone who had knowledge and
understanding— 29these joined with their
brethren, their nobles, and entered into a curse
and an oath to walk in God's Law, which was
given by Moses the servant of God, and to ob-
serve and do all the commandments of the LORD
our Lord, and His ordinances and His statutes:
30We would not give our daughters as wives to
the peoples of the land, nor take their daughters
for our sons; 31*if* the peoples of the land brought
wares or any grain to sell on the Sabbath day,
we would not buy it from them on the Sabbath,
or on a holy day; and we would forego the sev-
enth year's *produce* and the exacting of every
debt.
32Also we made ordinances for ourselves, to
exact from ourselves yearly one-third of a
shekel for the service of the house of our God:

THE MESSAGE

38 "Because of all this we are drawing up a binding pledge, a sealed document signed by our princes, our Levites, and our priests."

1-8 10 The sealed document bore these signatures: Nehemiah the governor, son of Hacaliah, Zedekiah, Seraiah, Azariah, Jeremiah,

Pashhur, Amariah, Malkijah,
Hattush, Shebaniah, Malluch,
Harim, Meremoth, Obadiah,
Daniel, Ginnethon, Baruch,
Meshullam, Abijah, Mijamin,
Maaziah, Bilgai, and Shemaiah.

These were the priests.

9-13 The Levites:
Jeshua son of Azaniah, Binnui of the sons of Henadad, Kadmiel,
and their kinsmen: Shebaniah, Hodiah, Kelita, Pelaiah, Hanan,
Mica, Rehob, Hashabiah,
Zaccur, Sherebiah, Shebaniah,
Hodiah, Bani, and Beninu.

14-27 The heads of the people:
Parosh, Pahath-Moab, Elam, Zattu, Bani,
Bunni, Azgad, Bebai,
Adonijah, Bigvai, Adin,
Ater, Hezekiah, Azzur,
Hodiah, Hashum, Bezai,
Hariph, Anathoth, Nebai,
Magpiash, Meshullam, Hezir,
Meshezabel, Zadok, Jaddua,
Pelatiah, Hanan, Anaiah,
Hoshea, Hananiah, Hasshub,
Hallohesh, Pilha, Shobek,
Rehum, Hashabnah, Maaseiah,
Ahiah, Hanan, Anan,
Malluch, Harim, and Baanah.

28-30 The rest of the people, priests, Levites, security guards, singers, Temple staff, and all who separated themselves from the foreign neighbors to keep The Revelation of God, together with their wives, sons, daughters—everyone old enough to understand—all joined their noble kinsmen in a binding oath to follow The Revelation of God given through Moses the servant of God, to keep and carry out all the commandments of GOD our Master, all his decisions and standards. Thus:

We will not marry our daughters to our foreign neighbors nor let our sons marry their daughters.

31 When the foreign neighbors bring goods or grain to sell on the Sabbath we won't trade with them—not on the Sabbath or any other holy day.

Every seventh year we will leave the land fallow and cancel all debts.

32-33 We accept the responsibility for paying an annual tax of one-third of a shekel (about an eighth ounce) for providing The Temple of our God with

New King James Version

33for the showbread, for the regular grain offering, for the regular burnt offering of the Sabbaths, the New Moons, and the set feasts; for the holy things, for the sin offerings to make atonement for Israel, and all the work of the house of our God. 34We cast lots among the priests, the Levites, and the people, for *bringing* the wood offering into the house of our God, according to our fathers' houses, at the appointed times year by year, to burn on the altar of the LORD our God as *it is* written in the Law.

35And *we made ordinances* to bring the firstfruits of our ground and the firstfruits of all fruit of all trees, year by year, to the house of the LORD; 36to bring the firstborn of our sons and our cattle, as *it is* written in the Law, and the firstborn of our herds and our flocks, to the house of our God, to the priests who minister in the house of our God; 37to bring the firstfruits of our dough, our offerings, the fruit from all kinds of trees, *the* new wine and oil, to the priests, to the storerooms of the house of our God; and to bring the tithes of our land to the Levites, for the Levites should receive the tithes in all our farming communities. 38And the priest, the descendant of Aaron, shall be with the Levites when the Levites receive tithes; and the Levites shall bring up a tenth of the tithes to the house of our God, to the rooms of the storehouse.

39For the children of Israel and the children of Levi shall bring the offering of the grain, of the new wine and the oil, to the storerooms where the articles of the sanctuary *are, where* the priests who minister and the gatekeepers and the singers *are;* and we will not neglect the house of our God.

The People Dwelling in Jerusalem

11 Now the leaders of the people dwelt at Jerusalem; the rest of the people cast lots to bring one out of ten to dwell in Jerusalem, the holy city, and nine-tenths *were to dwell* in *other* cities. 2And the people blessed all the men who willingly offered themselves to dwell at Jerusalem.

3These *are* the heads of the province who dwelt in Jerusalem. (But in the cities of Judah everyone dwelt in his own possession in their cities—Israelites, priests, Levites, Nethinim, and descendants of Solomon's servants.) 4Also in Jerusalem dwelt *some* of the children of Judah and of the children of Benjamin.

The children of Judah: Athaiah the son of Uzziah, the son of Zechariah, the son of Amariah, the son of Shephatiah, the son of Mahalalel, of the children of Perez; 5and Maaseiah the son of Baruch, the son of Col-Hozeh, the son of Hazaiah, the son of Adaiah, the son of Joiarib, the son of Zechariah, the son of Shiloni. 6All the sons of Perez who dwelt at

The Message

bread for the Table
regular Grain-Offerings
regular Whole-Burnt-Offerings
offerings for the Sabbaths, New Moons, and appointed feasts
Dedication-Offerings
Absolution-Offerings to atone for Israel
maintenance of The Temple of our God.

34 We—priests, Levites, and the people—have cast lots to see when each of our families will bring wood for burning on the Altar of our God, following the yearly schedule set down in The Revelation.

35-36 We take responsibility for delivering annually to The Temple of God the firstfruits of our crops and our orchards, our firstborn sons and cattle, and the firstborn from our herds and flocks for the priests who serve in The Temple of our God—just as it is set down in The Revelation.

37-39 We will bring the best of our grain, of our contributions, of the fruit of every tree, of wine, and of oil to the priests in the storerooms of The Temple of our God.

We will bring the tithes from our fields to the Levites, since the Levites are appointed to collect the tithes in the towns where we work. We'll see to it that a priest descended from Aaron will supervise the Levites as they collect the tithes and make sure that they take a tenth of the tithes to the treasury in The Temple of our God. We'll see to it that the People of Israel and Levites bring the grain, wine, and oil to the storage rooms where the vessels of the Sanctuary are kept and where the priests who serve, the security guards, and the choir meet.

We will not neglect The Temple of our God.

1-2 11 The leaders of the people were already living in Jerusalem, so the rest of the people drew lots to get one out of ten to move to Jerusalem, the holy city, while the other nine remained in their towns. The people applauded those who voluntarily offered to live in Jerusalem.

3-4 These are the leaders in the province who resided in Jerusalem (some Israelites, priests, Levites, Temple staff, and descendants of Solomon's slaves lived in the towns of Judah on their own property in various towns; others from both Judah and Benjamin lived in Jerusalem):

4-6 From the family of Judah:

Athaiah son of Uzziah, the son of Zechariah, the son of Amariah, the son of Shephatiah, the son of Mahalalel, from the family line of Perez; Maaseiah son of Baruch, the son of Col-Hozeh, the son of Hazaiah, the son of Adaiah, the son of Joiarib, the son of Zechariah, the son of the Shilonite. The de-

New King James Version

Jerusalem *were* four hundred and sixty-eight valiant men.

7 And these are the sons of Benjamin: Sallu the son of Meshullam, the son of Joed, the son of Pedaiah, the son of Kolaiah, the son of Maaseiah, the son of Ithiel, the son of Jeshaiah; 8 and after him Gabbai *and* Sallai, nine hundred and twenty-eight. 9 Joel the son of Zichri *was* their overseer, and Judah the son of Senuah[a] *was* second over the city.

10 Of the priests: Jedaiah the son of Joiarib, and Jachin; 11 Seraiah the son of Hilkiah, the son of Meshullam, the son of Zadok, the son of Meraioth, the son of Ahitub, *was* the leader of the house of God. 12 Their brethren who did the work of the house *were* eight hundred and twenty-two; and Adaiah the son of Jeroham, the son of Pelaliah, the son of Amzi, the son of Zechariah, the son of Pashhur, the son of Malchijah, 13 and his brethren, heads of the fathers' *houses, were* two hundred and forty-two; and Amashai the son of Azarel, the son of Ahzai, the son of Meshillemoth, the son of Immer, 14 and their brethren, mighty men of valor, *were* one hundred and twenty-eight. Their overseer *was* Zabdiel the son of *one of* the great men.[a]

15 Also of the Levites: Shemaiah the son of Hasshub, the son of Azrikam, the son of Hashabiah, the son of Bunni; 16 Shabbethai and Jozabad, of the heads of the Levites, *had* the oversight of the business outside of the house of God; 17 Mattaniah the son of Micha,[a] the son of Zabdi, the son of Asaph, the leader *who* began the thanksgiving with prayer; Bakbukiah, the second among his brethren; and Abda the son of Shammua, the son of Galal, the son of Jeduthun. 18 All the Levites in the holy city *were* two hundred and eighty-four.

19 Moreover the gatekeepers, Akkub, Talmon, and their brethren who kept the gates, *were* one hundred and seventy-two.

20 And the rest of Israel, of the priests *and* Levites, *were* in all the cities of Judah, everyone in his inheritance. 21 But the Nethinim dwelt in Ophel. And Ziha and Gishpa *were* over the Nethinim.

22 Also the overseer of the Levites at Jerusalem *was* Uzzi the son of Bani, the son of Hashabiah, the son of Mattaniah, the son of Micha, of the sons of Asaph, the singers in charge of the service of the house of God. 23 For *it was* the king's command concerning them that a certain portion should be for the singers, a quota day by day. 24 Pethahiah the son of Meshezabel, of the children of Zerah the son of Judah, *was* the king's deputy[a] in all matters concerning the people.

The People Dwelling Outside Jerusalem

25 And as for the villages with their fields, *some* of the children of Judah dwelt in Kirjath Arba and its villages, Dibon and its villages, Jekabzeel and its villages; 26 in Jeshua, Moladah, Beth Pelet, 27 Hazar Shual, and Beersheba and its villages; 28 in Ziklag and Meconah and its vil-

11:9 [a]Or *Hassenuah* **11:14** [a]Or *the son of Haggedolim* **11:17** [a]Or *Michah* **11:24** [a]Literally *at the king's hand*

The Message

scendants of Perez who lived in Jerusalem numbered 468 valiant men.

7-9 From the family of Benjamin:

Sallu son of Meshullam, the son of Joed, the son of Pedaiah, the son of Kolaiah, the son of Maaseiah, the son of Ithiel, the son of Jeshaiah, and his brothers Gabbai and Sallai: 928 men. Joel son of Zicri was their chief and Judah son of Hassenuah was second in command over the city.

10-14 From the priests:

Jedaiah son of Joiarib; Jakin; Seraiah son of Hilkiah, the son of Meshullam, the son of Zadok, the son of Meraioth, the son of Ahitub, supervisor of The Temple of God, along with their associates responsible for work in The Temple: 822 men. Also Adaiah son of Jeroham, the son of Pelaliah, the son of Amzi, the son of Zechariah, the son of Pashhur, the son of Malkijah, and his associates who were heads of families: 242 men; Amashsai son of Azarel, the son of Ahzai, the son of Meshillemoth, the son of Immer, and his associates, all valiant men: 128 men. Their commander was Zabdiel son of Haggedolim.

15-18 From the Levites:

Shemaiah son of Hasshub, the son of Azrikam, the son of Hashabiah, the son of Bunni; Shabbethai and Jozabad, two of the leaders of the Levites who were in charge of the outside work of The Temple of God; Mattaniah son of Mica, the son of Zabdi, the son of Asaph, the director who led in thanksgiving and prayer; Bakbukiah, second among his associates; and Abda son of Shammua, the son of Galal, the son of Jeduthun. The Levites in the holy city totaled 284.

19 From the security guards:

Akkub, Talmon, and their associates who kept watch over the gates: 172 men.

20 The rest of the Israelites, priests, and Levites were in all the towns of Judah, each on his own family property.

21 The Temple staff lived on the hill Ophel. Ziha and Gishpa were responsible for them.

22-23 The chief officer over the Levites in Jerusalem was Uzzi son of Bani, the son of Hashabiah, the son of Mattaniah, the son of Mica. Uzzi was one of Asaph's descendants, singers who led worship in The Temple of God. The singers got their orders from the king, who drew up their daily schedule.

24 Pethahiah son of Meshezabel, a descendant of Zerah son of Judah, represented the people's concerns at the royal court.

25-30 Some of the Judeans lived in the villages near their farms:

Kiriath Arba (Hebron) and suburbs
Dibon and suburbs
Jekabzeel and suburbs
Jeshua
Moladah
Beth Pelet
Hazar Shual
Beersheba and suburbs
Ziklag

NEW KING JAMES VERSION

lages; [29]in En Rimmon, Zorah, Jarmuth,
[30]Zanoah, Adullam, and their villages; in
Lachish and its fields; in Azekah and its vil-
lages. They dwelt from Beersheba to the Valley
of Hinnom.
[31]Also the children of Benjamin from Geba
dwelt in Michmash, Aija, and Bethel, and their
villages; [32]in Anathoth, Nob, Ananiah; [33]in Ha-
zor, Ramah, Gittaim; [34]in Hadid, Zeboim, Nebal-
lat; [35]in Lod, Ono, *and* the Valley of Craftsmen.
[36]Some of the Judean divisions of Levites *were*
in Benjamin.

THE PRIESTS AND LEVITES

12 Now these *are* the priests and the Levites
who came up with Zerubbabel the son of
Shealtiel, and Jeshua: Seraiah, Jeremiah, Ezra,
[2]Amariah, Malluch, Hattush, [3]Shechaniah, Re-
hum, Meremoth, [4]Iddo, Ginnethoi,[a] Abijah, [5]Mij-
amin, Maadiah, Bilgah, [6]Shemaiah, Joiarib,
Jedaiah, [7]Sallu, Amok, Hilkiah, *and* Jedaiah.
These *were* the heads of the priests and their
brethren in the days of Jeshua.
[8]Moreover the Levites *were* Jeshua, Binnui,
Kadmiel, Sherebiah, Judah, *and* Mattaniah *who
led* the thanksgiving *psalms*, he and his
brethren. [9]Also Bakbukiah and Unni, their
brethren, *stood* across from them in *their* du-
ties.
[10]Jeshua begot Joiakim, Joiakim begot
Eliashib, Eliashib begot Joiada, [11]Joiada begot
Jonathan, and Jonathan begot Jaddua.
[12]Now in the days of Joiakim, the priests, the
heads of the fathers' *houses were:* of Seraiah,
Meraiah; of Jeremiah, Hananiah; [13]of Ezra,
Meshullam; of Amariah, Jehohanan; [14]of
Melichu,[a] Jonathan; of Shebaniah,[b] Joseph; [15]of
Harim,[a] Adna; of Meraioth,[b] Helkai; [16]of Iddo,
Zechariah; of Ginnethon, Meshullam; [17]of Abi-
jah, Zichri; *the son* of Minjamin;[a] of Moadiah,[b]
Piltai; [18]of Bilgah, Shammua; of Shemaiah, Je-
honathan; [19]of Joiarib, Mattenai; of Jedaiah,

12:4 [a]Or *Ginnethon* (compare verse 16) **12:14** [a]Or *Malluch* (compare verse 2) [b]Or *Shechaniah* (compare verse 3) **12:15** [a]Or *Rehum* (compare verse 3) [b]Or *Meremoth* (compare verse 3) **12:17** [a]Or *Mijamin* (compare verse 5) [b]Or *Maadiah* (compare verse 5)

THE MESSAGE

Meconah and suburbs
En Rimmon
Zorah
Jarmuth
Zanoah
Adullam and their towns
Lachish and its fields
Azekah and suburbs.

They were living all the way from Beersheba to the Valley of Hinnom.

31-36 The Benjaminites from Geba lived in:

Micmash
Aijah
Bethel and its suburbs
Anathoth
Nob and Ananiah
Hazor
Ramah and Gittaim
Hadid, Zeboim, and Neballat
Lod and Ono and the Valley of the Craftsmen.

Also some of the Levitical groups of Judah were assigned to Benjamin.

1-7 12 These are the priests and Levites who came up with Zerubbabel son of Shealtiel and with Jeshua:

Seraiah, Jeremiah, Ezra,
Amariah, Malluch, Hattush,
Shecaniah, Rehum, Meremoth,
Iddo, Ginnethon, Abijah,
Mijamin, Moadiah, Bilgah,
Shemaiah, Joiarib, Jedaiah,
Sallu, Amok, Hilkiah, and Jedaiah.

These were the leaders of the priests during the time of Jeshua.

8-9 And the Levites:

Jeshua, Binnui, Kadmiel, Sherebiah, Judah;
Mattaniah, with his brothers, was in charge of songs of praise, and their brothers Bakbukiah and Unni stood opposite them in the services of worship.

10-11 Jeshua fathered Joiakim,
Joiakim fathered Eliashib,
Eliashib fathered Joiada,
Joiada fathered Jonathan,
and Jonathan fathered Jaddua.

12-21 During the time of Joiakim, these were the heads of the priestly families:

of the family of Seraiah, Meraiah;
of Jeremiah, Hananiah;
of Ezra, Meshullam;
of Amariah, Jehohanan;
of Malluch, Jonathan;
of Shecaniah, Joseph;
of Harim, Adna;
of Meremoth, Helkai;
of Iddo, Zechariah;
of Ginnethon, Meshullam;
of Abijah, Zicri;
of Miniamin and Moadiah, Piltai;
of Bilgah, Shammua;
of Shemaiah, Jehonathan;
of Joiarib, Mattenai;

NEW KING JAMES VERSION

Uzzi; [20]of Sallai,[a] Kallai; of Amok, Eber; [21]of Hilkiah, Hashabiah; *and* of Jedaiah, Nethanel.

[22]During the reign of Darius the Persian, a record *was also kept* of the Levites and priests *who had been* heads of their fathers' *houses* in the days of Eliashib, Joiada, Johanan, and Jaddua. [23]The sons of Levi, the heads of the fathers' *houses* until the days of Johanan the son of Eliashib, *were* written in the book of the chronicles.

[24]And the heads of the Levites *were* Hashabiah, Sherebiah, and Jeshua the son of Kadmiel, with their brothers across from them, to praise *and* give thanks, group alternating with group, according to the command of David the man of God. [25]Mattaniah, Bakbukiah, Obadiah, Meshullam, Talmon, and Akkub *were* gatekeepers keeping the watch at the storerooms of the gates. [26]These *lived* in the days of Joiakim the son of Jeshua, the son of Jozadak,[a] and in the days of Nehemiah the governor, and of Ezra the priest, the scribe.

NEHEMIAH DEDICATES THE WALL

[27]Now at the dedication of the wall of Jerusalem they sought out the Levites in all their places, to bring them to Jerusalem to celebrate the dedication with gladness, both with thanksgivings and singing, *with* cymbals and stringed instruments and harps. [28]And the sons of the singers gathered together from the countryside around Jerusalem, from the villages of the Netophathites, [29]from the house of Gilgal, and from the fields of Geba and Azmaveth; for the singers had built themselves villages all around Jerusalem. [30]Then the priests and Levites purified themselves, and purified the people, the gates, and the wall.

[31]So I brought the leaders of Judah up on the wall, and appointed two large thanksgiving choirs. *One* went to the right hand on the wall toward the Refuse Gate. [32]After them went Hoshaiah and half of the leaders of Judah, [33]and Azariah, Ezra, Meshullam, [34]Judah, Benjamin, Shemaiah, Jeremiah, [35]and some of the priests' sons with trumpets—Zechariah the son of Jonathan, the son of Shemaiah, the son of Mattaniah, the son of Michaiah, the son of Zaccur, the son of Asaph, [36]and his brethren, Shemaiah, Azarel, Milalai, Gilalai, Maai, Nethanel, Judah, *and* Hanani, with the musical instruments of David the man of God. And Ezra the scribe *went* before them. [37]By the Fountain Gate, in front of them, they went up the stairs of the City of David, on the stairway of the wall, beyond the house of David, as far as the Water Gate eastward.

12:20 [a]Or *Sallu* (compare verse 7) **12:26** [a]Spelled *Jehozadak* in 1 Chronicles 6:14

THE MESSAGE

of Jedaiah, Uzzi;
of Sallu, Kallai;
of Amok, Eber;
of Hilkiah, Hashabiah;
and of Jedaiah, Nethanel.

22 During the time of Eliashib, Joiada, Johanan, and Jaddua, the Levites were registered as heads of families. During the reign of Darius the Persian, the priests were registered.

23-24 The Levites who were heads of families were registered in the Book of the Chronicles until the time of Johanan son of Eliashib. These were:

Hashabiah,
Sherebiah,
and Jeshua son of Kadmiel.

Their brothers stood opposite them to give praise and thanksgiving, one side responding to the other, as had been directed by David the man of God.

25-26 The security guards included:

Mattaniah,
Bakbukiah,
Obadiah,
Meshullam,
Talmon,
and Akkub.

They guarded the storerooms at the gates. They lived during the time of Joiakim son of Jeshua, the son of Jozadak, the time of Nehemiah the governor and of Ezra the priest and scholar.

DEDICATION OF THE WALL

27-29 When it came time for the dedication of the wall, they tracked down and brought in the Levites from all their homes in Jerusalem to carry out the dedication exuberantly: thanksgiving hymns, songs, cymbals, harps, and lutes. The singers assembled from all around Jerusalem, from the villages of the Netophathites, from Beth Gilgal, from the farms at Geba and Azmaveth—the singers had built villages for themselves all around Jerusalem.

30 The priests and Levites ceremonially purified themselves; then they did the same for the people, the gates, and the wall.

31-36 I had the leaders of Judah come up on the wall, and I appointed two large choirs. One proceeded on the wall to the right toward the Dung Gate. Hashaiah and half the leaders of Judah followed them, including Azariah, Ezra, Meshullam, Judah, Benjamin, Shemaiah, and Jeremiah. Some of the young priests had trumpets. Next, playing the musical instruments of David the man of God, came Zechariah son of Jonathan, the son of Shemaiah, the son of Mattaniah, the son of Micaiah, the son of Zaccur, the son of Asaph, and his brothers Shemaiah, Azarel, Milalai, Gilalai, Maai, Nethanel, Judah, and Hanani. Ezra the scholar led them.

37 At the Fountain Gate they went straight ahead, up the steps of the City of David using the wall stairway above the house of David to the Water Gate on the east.

NEW KING JAMES VERSION

38 The other thanksgiving choir went the op-
posite *way*, and I *was* behind them with half of
the people on the wall, going past the Tower
of the Ovens as far as the Broad Wall, 39 and
above the Gate of Ephraim, above the Old Gate,
above the Fish Gate, the Tower of Hananel, the
Tower of the Hundred, as far as the Sheep Gate;
and they stopped by the Gate of the Prison.
40 So the two thanksgiving choirs stood in the
house of God, likewise I and the half of the
rulers with me; 41 and the priests, Eliakim,
Maaseiah, Minjamin,[a] Michaiah, Elioenai,
Zechariah, *and* Hananiah, with trumpets; 42 also
Maaseiah, Shemaiah, Eleazar, Uzzi, Jehohanan,
Malchijah, Elam, and Ezer. The singers sang
loudly with Jezrahiah the director.
43 Also that day they offered great sacrifices,
and rejoiced, for God had made them rejoice
with great joy; the women and the children also
rejoiced, so that the joy of Jerusalem was heard
afar off.

TEMPLE RESPONSIBILITIES

44 And at the same time some were appointed
over the rooms of the storehouse for the offer-
ings, the firstfruits, and the tithes, to gather into
them from the fields of the cities the portions
specified by the Law for the priests and Levites;
for Judah rejoiced over the priests and Levites
who ministered. 45 Both the singers and the gate-
keepers kept the charge of their God and the
charge of the purification, according to the com-
mand of David *and* Solomon his son. 46 For in the
days of David and Asaph of old *there were*
chiefs of the singers, and songs of praise and
thanksgiving to God. 47 In the days of Zerubba-
bel and in the days of Nehemiah all Israel gave
the portions for the singers and the gatekeepers,
a portion for each day. They also consecrated
holy things for the Levites, and the Levites con-
secrated *them* for the children of Aaron.

PRINCIPLES OF SEPARATION

13 On that day they read from the Book of
Moses in the hearing of the people, and in
it was found written that no Ammonite or
Moabite should ever come into the assembly of
God, 2 because they had not met the children of
Israel with bread and water, but hired Balaam
against them to curse them. However, our God
turned the curse into a blessing. 3 So it was,
when they had heard the Law, that they sepa-
rated all the mixed multitude from Israel.

THE REFORMS OF NEHEMIAH

4 Now before this, Eliashib the priest, having
authority over the storerooms of the house of

12:41 [a]Or *Mijamin* (compare verse 5)

THE MESSAGE

38-39 The other choir proceeded to the left. I and half of the people followed them on the wall from the Tower of Furnaces to the Broad Wall, over the Ephraim Gate, the Jeshanah Gate, the Fish Gate, the Tower of Hananel, and the Tower of the Hundred as far as the Sheep Gate, stopping at the Prison Gate.

40-42 The two choirs then took their places in The Temple of God. I was there with half of the officials, along with the priests Eliakim, Maaseiah, Miniamin, Micaiah, Elioenai, Zechariah, and Hananiah with their trumpets. Also Maaseiah, Shemaiah, Eleazar, Uzzi, Jehohanan, Malkijah, Elam, and Ezer. The singers, directed by Jezrahiah, made the rafters ring.

43 That day they offered great sacrifices, an exuberant celebration because God had filled them with great joy. The women and children raised their happy voices with all the rest. Jerusalem's jubilation was heard far and wide.

44-46 That same day men were appointed to be responsible for the storerooms for the offerings, the firstfruits, and the tithes. They saw to it that the portion directed by The Revelation for the priests and Levites was brought in from the farms connected to the towns. Judah was so appreciative of the priests and Levites and their service; they, along with the singers and security guards, had done everything so well, conducted the worship of their God and the ritual of ceremonial cleansing in a way that would have made David and his son Solomon proud. That's the way it was done in the olden days, the days of David and Asaph, when they had choir directors for singing songs of praise and thanksgiving to God.

47 During the time of Zerubbabel and Nehemiah, all Israel contributed the daily allowances for the singers and security guards. They also set aside what was dedicated to the Levites, and the Levites did the same for the Aaronites.

1-3 13 Also on that same day there was a reading from the Book of Moses in the hearing of the people. It was found written there that no Ammonite or Moabite was permitted to enter the congregation of God, because they hadn't welcomed the People of Israel with food and drink; they even hired Balaam to work against them by cursing them, but our God turned the curse into a blessing. When they heard the reading of The Revelation, they excluded all foreigners from Israel.

4-5 Some time before this, Eliashib the priest had been put in charge of the storerooms of

New King James Version

our God, *was* allied with Tobiah. 5And he had prepared for him a large room, where previously they had stored the grain offerings, the frankincense, the articles, the tithes of grain, the new wine and oil, which were commanded *to be given* to the Levites and singers and gatekeepers, and the offerings for the priests. 6But during all this I was not in Jerusalem, for in the thirty-second year of Artaxerxes king of Babylon I had returned to the king. Then after certain days I obtained leave from the king, 7and I came to Jerusalem and discovered the evil that Eliashib had done for Tobiah, in preparing a room for him in the courts of the house of God. 8And it grieved me bitterly; therefore I threw all the household goods of Tobiah out of the room. 9Then I commanded them to cleanse the rooms; and I brought back into them the articles of the house of God, with the grain offering and the frankincense.

10I also realized that the portions for the Levites had not been given *them;* for each of the Levites and the singers who did the work had gone back to his field. 11So I contended with the rulers, and said, "Why is the house of God forsaken?" And I gathered them together and set them in their place. 12Then all Judah brought the tithe of the grain and the new wine and the oil to the storehouse. 13And I appointed as treasurers over the storehouse Shelemiah the priest and Zadok the scribe, and of the Levites, Pedaiah; and next to them *was* Hanan the son of Zaccur, the son of Mattaniah; for they were considered faithful, and their task *was* to distribute to their brethren.

14Remember me, O my God, concerning this, and do not wipe out my good deeds that I have done for the house of my God, and for its services!

15In those days I saw *people* in Judah treading wine presses on the Sabbath, and bringing in sheaves, and loading donkeys with wine, grapes, figs, and all *kinds of* burdens, which they brought into Jerusalem on the Sabbath day. And I warned *them* about the day on which they were selling provisions. 16Men of Tyre dwelt there also, who brought in fish and all kinds of goods, and sold *them* on the Sabbath to the children of Judah, and in Jerusalem.

17Then I contended with the nobles of Judah, and said to them, "What evil thing *is* this that you do, by which you profane the Sabbath day? 18Did not your fathers do thus, and did not our God bring all this disaster on us and on this city? Yet you bring added wrath on Israel by profaning the Sabbath."

19So it was, at the gates of Jerusalem, as it began to be dark before the Sabbath, that I commanded the gates to be shut, and charged that they must not be opened till after the Sabbath. Then I posted *some* of my servants at the gates, *so that* no burdens would be brought in on the Sabbath day.

The Message

The Temple of God. He was close to Tobiah and had made available to him a large storeroom that had been used to store Grain-Offerings, incense, worship vessels, and the tithes of grain, wine, and oil for the Levites, singers, and security guards, and the offerings for the priests.

6-9 When this was going on I wasn't there in Jerusalem; in the thirty-second year of Artaxerxes king of Babylon, I had traveled back to the king. But later I asked for his permission to leave again. I arrived in Jerusalem and learned of the wrong that Eliashib had done in turning over to him a room in the courts of The Temple of God. I was angry, really angry, and threw everything in the room out into the street, all of Tobiah's stuff. Then I ordered that they ceremonially cleanse the room. Only then did I put back the worship vessels of The Temple of God, along with the Grain-Offerings and the incense.

10-13 And then I learned that the Levites hadn't been given their regular food allotments. So the Levites and singers who led the services of worship had all left and gone back to their farms. I called the officials on the carpet, "Why has The Temple of God been abandoned?" I got everyone back again and put them back on their jobs so that all Judah was again bringing in the tithe of grain, wine, and oil to the storerooms. I put Shelemiah the priest, Zadok the scribe, and a Levite named Pedaiah in charge of the storerooms. I made Hanan son of Zaccur, the son of Mattaniah, their right-hand man. These men had a reputation for honesty and hard work. They were responsible for distributing the rations to their brothers.

14 Remember me, O my God, for this.
Don't ever forget the devoted work I
have done for The Temple of God and
its worship.

15-16 During those days, while back in Judah, I also noticed that people treaded wine presses, brought in sacks of grain, and loaded up their donkeys on the Sabbath. They brought wine, grapes, figs, and all kinds of stuff to sell on the Sabbath. So I spoke up and warned them about selling food on that day. Tyrians living there brought in fish and whatever else, selling it to Judeans—*in Jerusalem,* mind you!—on the Sabbath.

17-18 I confronted the leaders of Judah: "What's going on here? This evil! Profaning the Sabbath! Isn't this exactly what your ancestors did? And because of it didn't God bring down on us and this city all this misery? And here you are adding to it—accumulating more wrath on Jerusalem by profaning the Sabbath."

19 As the gates of Jerusalem were darkened by the shadows of the approaching Sabbath, I ordered the doors shut and not to be opened until the Sabbath was over. I placed some of my servants at the gates to make sure that nothing to be sold would get in on the Sabbath day.

New King James Version

20Now the merchants and sellers of all kinds of
wares lodged outside Jerusalem once or twice.
21Then I warned them, and said to them,
"Why do you spend the night around the wall? If
you do *so* again, I will lay hands on you!" From
that time on they came no *more* on the Sabbath.
22And I commanded the Levites that they should
cleanse themselves, and that they should go and
guard the gates, to sanctify the Sabbath day.

Remember me, O my God, *concerning* this
also, and spare me according to the greatness of
Your mercy!

23In those days I also saw Jews *who* had mar-
ried women of Ashdod, Ammon, *and* Moab.
24And half of their children spoke the language
of Ashdod, and could not speak the language of
Judah, but spoke according to the language of
one or the other people.
25So I contended with them and cursed them,
struck some of them and pulled out their hair,
and made them swear by God, *saying*, "You
shall not give your daughters as wives to their
sons, nor take their daughters for your sons or
yourselves. 26Did not Solomon king of Israel sin
by these things? Yet among many nations there
was no king like him, who was beloved of his
God; and God made him king over all Israel.
Nevertheless pagan women caused even him to
sin. 27Should we then hear of your doing all this
great evil, transgressing against our God by
marrying pagan women?"
28And *one* of the sons of Joiada, the son of
Eliashib the high priest, *was* a son-in-law of
Sanballat the Horonite; therefore I drove him
from me.
29Remember them, O my God, because they
have defiled the priesthood and the covenant of
the priesthood and the Levites.
30Thus I cleansed them of everything pagan.
I also assigned duties to the priests and the
Levites, each to his service, 31and *to bringing* the
wood offering and the firstfruits at appointed
times.

Remember me, O my God, for good!

The Message

20-21 Traders and dealers in various goods camped outside the gates once or twice. But I took them to task. I said, "You have no business camping out here by the wall. If I find you here again, I'll use force to drive you off."

And that did it; they didn't come back on the Sabbath.

22 Then I directed the Levites to ceremonially cleanse themselves and take over as guards at the gates to keep the sanctity of the Sabbath day.

Remember me also for this, my God.
Treat me with mercy according to
your great and steadfast love.

23-27 Also in those days I saw Jews who had married women from Ashdod, Ammon, and Moab. Half the children couldn't even speak the language of Judah; all they knew was the language of Ashdod or some other tongue. So I took those men to task, gave them a piece of my mind, even slapped some of them and jerked them by the hair. I made them swear to God: "Don't marry your daughters to their sons; and don't let their daughters marry your sons—and don't you yourselves marry them! Didn't Solomon the king of Israel sin because of women just like these? Even though there was no king quite like him, and God loved him and made him king over all Israel, foreign women were his downfall. Do you call this obedience—engaging in this extensive evil, showing yourselves faithless to God by marrying foreign wives?"

28 One of the sons of Joiada, the son of Eliashib the high priest, was a son-in-law of Sanballat the Horonite; I drove him out of my presence.

29 Remember them, O my God, how they
defiled the priesthood and the
covenant of the priests and Levites.

30-31 All in all I cleansed them from everything foreign. I organized the orders of service for the priests and Levites so that each man knew his job. I arranged for a regular supply of altar wood at the appointed times and for the firstfruits.

Remember me, O my God, for good.

ESTHER

New King James Version

The King Dethrones Queen Vashti

1 Now it came to pass in the days of Ahasuerus[a] (this *was* the Ahasuerus who reigned over one hundred and twenty-seven provinces, from India to Ethiopia), 2in those days when King Ahasuerus sat on the throne of his kingdom, which *was* in Shushan[a] the citadel, 3*that* in the third year of his reign he made a feast for all his officials and servants—the powers of Persia and Media, the nobles, and the princes of the provinces *being* before him— 4when he showed the riches of his glorious kingdom and the splendor of his excellent majesty for many days, one hundred and eighty days *in all.*

5And when these days were completed, the king made a feast lasting seven days for all the people who were present in Shushan the citadel, from great to small, in the court of the garden of the king's palace. 6*There were* white and blue linen *curtains* fastened with cords of fine linen and purple on silver rods and marble pillars; *and the* couches *were* of gold and silver on a *mosaic* pavement of alabaster, turquoise, and white and black marble. 7And they served drinks in golden vessels, each vessel being different from the other, with royal wine in abundance, according to the generosity of the king. 8In accordance with the law, the drinking was not compulsory; for so the king had ordered all the officers of his household, that they should do according to each man's pleasure.

9Queen Vashti also made a feast for the women *in* the royal palace which *belonged* to King Ahasuerus.

10On the seventh day, when the heart of the king was merry with wine, he commanded Mehuman, Biztha, Harbona, Bigtha, Abagtha, Zethar, and Carcas, seven eunuchs who served in the presence of King Ahasuerus, 11to bring Queen Vashti before the king, *wearing* her royal crown, in order to show her beauty to the people and the officials, for she *was* beautiful to behold. 12But Queen Vashti refused to come at the king's command *brought* by *his* eunuchs; therefore the king was furious, and his anger burned within him.

13Then the king said to the wise men who understood the times (for this *was* the king's manner toward all who knew law and justice, 14those closest to him *being* Carshena, Shethar, Admatha, Tarshish, Meres, Marsena, and Memucan, the seven princes of Persia and Media, who had access to the king's presence, *and* who ranked highest in the kingdom): 15"What *shall we* do to Queen Vashti, according to law, because she did not obey the command of King Ahasuerus *brought to her* by the eunuchs?"

16And Memucan answered before the king and the princes: "Queen Vashti has not only wronged the king, but also all the princes, and all the people who *are* in all the provinces of King Ahasuerus. 17For the queen's behavior will

1:1 [a]Generally identified with Xerxes I (485–464 B.C.) **1:2** [a]Or *Susa,* and so throughout this book

The Message

1-3 **1** This is the story of something that hap-
pened in the time of Xerxes, the Xerxes
who ruled from India to Ethiopia—127
provinces in all. King Xerxes ruled from his
royal throne in the palace complex of Susa.
In the third year of his reign he gave a ban-
quet for all his officials and ministers. The
military brass of Persia and Media were also
there, along with the princes and governors
of the provinces.
4-7 For six months he put on exhibit the huge
wealth of his empire and its stunningly
beautiful royal splendors. At the conclusion
of the exhibit, the king threw a weeklong
party for everyone living in Susa, the capi-
tal—important and unimportant alike. The
party was in the garden courtyard of the
king's summer house. The courtyard was
elaborately decorated with white and blue
cotton curtains tied with linen and purple
cords to silver rings on marble columns. Sil-
ver and gold couches were arranged on a
mosaic pavement of porphyry, marble,
mother-of-pearl, and colored stones. Drinks
were served in gold chalices, each chalice
one-of-a-kind. The royal wine flowed
freely—a generous king!
8-9 The guests could drink as much as they
liked—king's orders!—with waiters at their
elbows to refill the drinks. Meanwhile,
Queen Vashti was throwing a separate party
for women inside King Xerxes' royal palace.
10-11 On the seventh day of the party, the king,
high on the wine, ordered the seven eunuchs
who were his personal servants (Mehuman,
Biztha, Harbona, Bigtha, Abagtha, Zethar,
and Carcas) to bring him Queen Vashti re-
splendent in her royal crown. He wanted to
show off her beauty to the guests and offi-
cials. She was extremely good-looking.
12-15 But Queen Vashti refused to come, re-
fused the summons delivered by the eu-
nuchs. The king lost his temper. Seething
with anger over her insolence, the king
called in his counselors, all experts in legal
matters. It was the king's practice to consult
his expert advisors. Those closest to him
were Carshena, Shethar, Admatha, Tar-
shish, Meres, Marsena, and Memucan, the
seven highest-ranking princes of Persia and
Media, the inner circle with access to the
king's ear. He asked them what legal re-
course they had against Queen Vashti for
not obeying King Xerxes' summons deliv-
ered by the eunuchs.
16-18 Memucan spoke up in the council of the
king and princes: "It's not only the king
Queen Vashti has insulted, it's all of us, lead-
ers and people alike in every last one of
King Xerxes' provinces. The word's going to

NEW KING JAMES VERSION

become known to all women, so that they will
despise their husbands in their eyes, when they
report, 'King Ahasuerus commanded Queen
Vashti to be brought in before him, but she did
not come.' 18This very day the *noble* ladies of
Persia and Media will say to all the king's offi-
cials that they have heard of the behavior of the
queen. Thus *there will be* excessive contempt
and wrath. 19If it pleases the king, let a royal de-
cree go out from him, and let it be recorded in
the laws of the Persians and the Medes, so that
it will not be altered, that Vashti shall come no
more before King Ahasuerus; and let the king
give her royal position to another who is better
than she. 20When the king's decree which he
will make is proclaimed throughout all his em-
pire (for it is great), all wives will honor their
husbands, both great and small."
21And the reply pleased the king and the
princes, and the king did according to the word
of Memucan. 22Then he sent letters to all the
king's provinces, to each province in its own
script, and to every people in their own lan-
guage, that each man should be master in his
own house, and speak in the language of his
own people.

ESTHER BECOMES QUEEN

2 After these things, when the wrath of King
Ahasuerus subsided, he remembered Vashti,
what she had done, and what had been decreed
against her. 2Then the king's servants who at-
tended him said: "Let beautiful young virgins be
sought for the king; 3and let the king appoint of-
ficers in all the provinces of his kingdom, that
they may gather all the beautiful young virgins
to Shushan the citadel, into the women's quar-
ters, under the custody of Hegai[a] the king's eu-
nuch, custodian of the women. And let beauty
preparations be given *them.* 4Then let the young
woman who pleases the king be queen instead
of Vashti."
This thing pleased the king, and he did so.
5In Shushan the citadel there was a certain
Jew whose name *was* Mordecai the son of Jair,
the son of Shimei, the son of Kish, a Benjamite.
6*Kish*[a] had been carried away from Jerusalem
with the captives who had been captured with
Jeconiah[b] king of Judah, whom Nebuchad-
nezzar the king of Babylon had carried away.
7And *Mordecai* had brought up Hadassah, that
is, Esther, his uncle's daughter, for she had nei-
ther father nor mother. The young woman *was*
lovely and beautiful. When her father and
mother died, Mordecai took her as his own
daughter.
8So it was, when the king's command and
decree were heard, and when many young
women were gathered at Shushan the citadel,
under the custody of Hegai, that Esther also was
taken to the king's palace, into the care of Hegai
the custodian of the women. 9Now the young
woman pleased him, and she obtained his favor;
so he readily gave beauty preparations to her,

2:3 [a]Hebrew *Hege* **2:6** [a]Literally *Who* [b]Same as *Jehoiachin,* 2 Kings 24:6 and elsewhere

THE MESSAGE

get out: 'Did you hear the latest about
Queen Vashti? King Xerxes ordered her to
be brought before him and she wouldn't do
it!' When the women hear it, they'll start
treating their husbands with contempt. The
day the wives of the Persian and Mede offi-
cials get wind of the queen's insolence,
they'll be out of control. Is that what we
want, a country of angry women who don't
know their place?
19-20 "So, if the king agrees, let him pronounce
a royal ruling and have it recorded in the
laws of the Persians and Medes so that it
cannot be revoked, that Vashti is perma-
nently banned from King Xerxes' presence.
And then let the king give her royal position
to a woman who knows her place. When the
king's ruling becomes public knowledge
throughout the kingdom, extensive as it is,
every woman, regardless of her social posi-
tion, will show proper respect to her hus-
band."
21-22 The king and the princes liked this. The
king did what Memucan proposed. He sent
bulletins to every part of the kingdom, to
each province in its own script, to each peo-
ple in their own language: "Every man is
master of his own house; whatever he says,
goes."

1-4 2 Later, when King Xerxes' anger had
cooled and he was having second thoughts
about what Vashti had done and what he had
ordered against her, the king's young atten-
dants stepped in and got the ball rolling:
"Let's begin a search for beautiful young
virgins for the king. Let the king appoint of-
ficials in every province of his kingdom to
bring every beautiful young virgin to the
palace complex of Susa and to the harem
run by Hegai, the king's eunuch who over-
sees the women; he will put them through
their beauty treatments. Then let the girl
who best pleases the king be made queen in
place of Vashti."
The king liked this advice and took it.

5-7 Now there was a Jew who lived in the
palace complex in Susa. His name was
Mordecai the son of Jair, the son of Shimei,
the son of Kish—a Benjaminite. His ances-
tors had been taken from Jerusalem with
the exiles and carried off with King Je-
hoiachin of Judah by King Nebuchadnezzar
of Babylon into exile. Mordecai had reared
his cousin Hadassah, otherwise known as
Esther, since she had no father or mother.
The girl had a good figure and a beautiful
face. After her parents died, Mordecai had
adopted her.
8 When the king's order had been publicly
posted, many young girls were brought to
the palace complex of Susa and given over
to Hegai who was overseer of the women.
Esther was among them.
9-10 Hegai liked Esther and took a special in-
terest in her. Right off he started her beauty
treatments, ordered special food, assigned

New King James Version

besides her allowance. Then seven choice maid-
servants were provided for her from the king's
palace, and he moved her and her maidservants
to the best *place* in the house of the women.
10 Esther had not revealed her people or fam-
ily, for Mordecai had charged her not to reveal
it. 11 And every day Mordecai paced in front of
the court of the women's quarters, to learn of
Esther's welfare and what was happening to
her.
12 Each young woman's turn came to go in to
King Ahasuerus after she had completed twelve
months' preparation, according to the regula-
tions for the women, for thus were the days of
their preparation apportioned: six months with
oil of myrrh, and six months with perfumes and
preparations for beautifying women. 13 Thus *pre-*
pared, each young woman went to the king, and
she was given whatever she desired to take with
her from the women's quarters to the king's
palace. 14 In the evening she went, and in the
morning she returned to the second house of the
women, to the custody of Shaashgaz, the king's
eunuch who kept the concubines. She would not
go in to the king again unless the king delighted
in her and called for her by name.
15 Now when the turn came for Esther the
daughter of Abihail the uncle of Mordecai, who
had taken her as his daughter, to go in to the
king, she requested nothing but what Hegai the
king's eunuch, the custodian of the women, ad-
vised. And Esther obtained favor in the sight of
all who saw her. 16 So Esther was taken to King
Ahasuerus, into his royal palace, in the tenth
month, which *is* the month of Tebeth, in the sev-
enth year of his reign. 17 The king loved Esther
more than all the *other* women, and she ob-
tained grace and favor in his sight more than all
the virgins; so he set the royal crown upon her
head and made her queen instead of Vashti.
18 Then the king made a great feast, the Feast of
Esther, for all his officials and servants; and he
proclaimed a holiday in the provinces and gave
gifts according to the generosity of a king.

Mordecai Discovers a Plot

19 When virgins were gathered together a
second time, Mordecai sat within the king's
gate. 20 *Now* Esther had not revealed her family
and her people, just as Mordecai had charged
her, for Esther obeyed the command of Morde-
cai as when she was brought up by him.
21 In those days, while Mordecai sat within
the king's gate, two of the king's eunuchs,
Bigthan and Teresh, doorkeepers, became furi-
ous and sought to lay hands on King Ahasuerus.
22 So the matter became known to Mordecai,
who told Queen Esther, and Esther informed the
king in Mordecai's name. 23 And when an in-
quiry was made into the matter, it was con-
firmed, and both were hanged on a gallows; and
it was written in the book of the chronicles in
the presence of the king.

The Message

her seven personal maids from the palace,
and put her and her maids in the best rooms
in the harem. Esther didn't say anything
about her family and racial background be-
cause Mordecai had told her not to.
11 Every day Mordecai strolled beside the
court of the harem to find out how Esther
was and get news of what she was doing.
12-14 Each girl's turn came to go in to King
Xerxes after she had completed the twelve
months of prescribed beauty treatments—
six months' treatment with oil of myrrh fol-
lowed by six months with perfumes and var-
ious cosmetics. When it was time for the girl
to go to the king, she was given whatever
she wanted to take with her when she left
the harem for the king's quarters. She
would go there in the evening; in the morn-
ing she would return to a second harem
overseen by Shaashgaz, the king's eunuch
in charge of the concubines. She never
again went back to the king unless the king
took a special liking to her and asked for
her by name.
15 When it was Esther's turn to go to the
king (Esther the daughter of Abihail the un-
cle of Mordecai, who had adopted her as his
daughter), she asked for nothing other than
what Hegai, the king's eunuch in charge of
the harem, had recommended. Esther, just
as she was, won the admiration of everyone
who saw her.
16 She was taken to King Xerxes in the
royal palace in the tenth month, the month
of Tebeth, in the seventh year of the king's
reign.
17-18 The king fell in love with Esther far more
than with any of his other women or any of
the other virgins—he was totally smitten by
her. He placed a royal crown on her head
and made her queen in place of Vashti. Then
the king gave a great banquet for all his no-
bles and officials—"Esther's Banquet." He
proclaimed a holiday for all the provinces
and handed out gifts with royal generosity.

19-20 On one of the occasions when the virgins
were being gathered together, Mordecai was
sitting at the King's Gate. All this time, Es-
ther had kept her family background and
race a secret as Mordecai had ordered; Es-
ther still did what Mordecai told her, just as
when she was being raised by him.
21-23 On this day, with Mordecai sitting at the
King's Gate, Bigthana and Teresh, two of the
king's eunuchs who guarded the entrance,
had it in for the king and were making plans
to kill King Xerxes. But Mordecai learned of
the plot and told Queen Esther, who then
told King Xerxes, giving credit to Mordecai.
When the thing was investigated and con-
firmed as true, the two men were hanged on
a gallows. This was all written down in a
logbook kept for the king's use.

NEW KING JAMES VERSION

HAMAN'S CONSPIRACY AGAINST THE JEWS

3 After these things King Ahasuerus promoted Haman, the son of Hammedatha the Agagite, and advanced him and set his seat above all the princes who *were* with him. 2 And all the king's servants who *were* within the king's gate bowed and paid homage to Haman, for so the king had commanded concerning him. But Mordecai would not bow or pay homage. 3 Then the king's servants who *were* within the king's gate said to Mordecai, "Why do you transgress the king's command?" 4 Now it happened, when they spoke to him daily and he would not listen to them, that they told *it* to Haman, to see whether Mordecai's words would stand; for *Mordecai* had told them that he *was* a Jew. 5 When Haman saw that Mordecai did not bow or pay him homage, Haman was filled with wrath. 6 But he disdained to lay hands on Mordecai alone, for they had told him of the people of Mordecai. Instead, Haman sought to destroy all the Jews who *were* throughout the whole kingdom of Ahasuerus—the people of Mordecai.

7 In the first month, which is the month of Nisan, in the twelfth year of King Ahasuerus, they cast Pur (that *is,* the lot), before Haman to determine the day and the month,[a] until *it fell on the* twelfth *month,*[b] which *is* the month of Adar.

8 Then Haman said to King Ahasuerus, "There is a certain people scattered and dispersed among the people in all the provinces of your kingdom; their laws *are* different from all *other* people's, and they do not keep the king's laws. Therefore it *is* not fitting for the king to let them remain. 9 If it pleases the king, let *a decree* be written that they be destroyed, and I will pay ten thousand talents of silver into the hands of those who do the work, to bring *it* into the king's treasuries."

10 So the king took his signet ring from his hand and gave it to Haman, the son of Hammedatha the Agagite, the enemy of the Jews. 11 And the king said to Haman, "The money and the people *are* given to you, to do with them as seems good to you."

12 Then the king's scribes were called on the thirteenth day of the first month, and *a decree* was written according to all that Haman commanded—to the king's satraps, to the governors who *were* over each province, to the officials of all people, to every province according to its script, and to every people in their language. In the name of King Ahasuerus it was written, and sealed with the king's signet ring. 13 And the letters were sent by couriers into all the king's provinces, to destroy, to kill, and to annihilate all the Jews, both young and old, little children and women, in one day, on the thirteenth *day* of the twelfth *month,* which *is* the month of Adar, and to plunder their possessions.[a] 14 A copy of the document was to be issued as law in every province, being published for all people, that they should be ready for that day.

3:7 [a]Septuagint adds *to destroy the people of Mordecai in one day;* Vulgate adds *the nation of the Jews should be destroyed.* [b]Following Masoretic Text and Vulgate; Septuagint reads *and the lot fell on the fourteenth of the month.* **3:13** [a]Septuagint adds the text of the letter here.

THE MESSAGE

1-2 3 Some time later, King Xerxes promoted Haman son of Hammedatha the Agagite, making him the highest-ranking official in the government. All the king's servants at the King's Gate used to honor him by bowing down and kneeling before Haman—that's what the king had commanded.

2-4 Except Mordecai. Mordecai wouldn't do it, wouldn't bow down and kneel. The king's servants at the King's Gate asked Mordecai about it: "Why do you cross the king's command?" Day after day they spoke to him about this but he wouldn't listen, so they went to Haman to see whether something shouldn't be done about it. Mordecai had told them that he was a Jew.

5-6 When Haman saw for himself that Mordecai didn't bow down and kneel before him, he was outraged. Meanwhile, having learned that Mordecai was a Jew, Haman hated to waste his fury on just one Jew; he looked for a way to eliminate not just Mordecai but all Jews throughout the whole kingdom of Xerxes.

7 In the first month, the month of Nisan, of the twelfth year of Xerxes, the *pur*—that is, the lot—was cast under Haman's charge to determine the propitious day and month. The lot turned up the thirteenth day of the twelfth month, which is the month of Adar.

8-9 Haman then spoke with King Xerxes: "There is an odd set of people scattered through the provinces of your kingdom who don't fit in. Their customs and ways are different from those of everybody else. Worse, they disregard the king's laws. They're an affront; the king shouldn't put up with them. If it please the king, let orders be given that they be destroyed. I'll pay for it myself. I'll deposit 375 tons of silver in the royal bank to finance the operation."

10 The king slipped his signet ring from his hand and gave it to Haman son of Hammedatha the Agagite, archenemy of the Jews.

11 "Go ahead," the king said to Haman. "It's your money—do whatever you want with those people."

12 The king's secretaries were brought in on the thirteenth day of the first month. The orders were written out word for word as Haman had addressed them to the king's satraps, the governors of every province, and the officials of every people. They were written in the script of each province and the language of each people in the name of King Xerxes and sealed with the royal signet ring.

13-14 Bulletins were sent out by couriers to all the king's provinces with orders to massacre, kill, and eliminate all the Jews—youngsters and old men, women and babies—on a single day, the thirteenth day of the twelfth month, the month Adar, and to plunder their goods. Copies of the bulletin were to be posted in each province, publicly available to all peoples, to get them ready for that day.

NEW KING JAMES VERSION

15 The couriers went out, hastened by the king's command; and the decree was proclaimed in Shushan the citadel. So the king and Haman sat down to drink, but the city of Shushan was perplexed.

ESTHER AGREES TO HELP THE JEWS

4 When Mordecai learned all that had happened, he tore his clothes and put on sackcloth and ashes, and went out into the midst of the city. He cried out with a loud and bitter cry. 2 He went as far as the front of the king's gate, for no one *might* enter the king's gate clothed with sackcloth. 3 And in every province where the king's command and decree arrived, *there was* great mourning among the Jews, with fasting, weeping, and wailing; and many lay in sackcloth and ashes.

4 So Esther's maids and eunuchs came and told her, and the queen was deeply distressed. Then she sent garments to clothe Mordecai and take his sackcloth away from him, but he would not accept *them.* 5 Then Esther called Hathach, *one* of the king's eunuchs whom he had appointed to attend her, and she gave him a command concerning Mordecai, to learn what and why this *was.* 6 So Hathach went out to Mordecai in the city square that *was* in front of the king's gate. 7 And Mordecai told him all that had happened to him, and the sum of money that Haman had promised to pay into the king's treasuries to destroy the Jews. 8 He also gave him a copy of the written decree for their destruction, which was given at Shushan, that he might show it to Esther and explain it to her, and that he might command her to go in to the king to make supplication to him and plead before him for her people. 9 So Hathach returned and told Esther the words of Mordecai.

10 Then Esther spoke to Hathach, and gave him a command for Mordecai: 11 "All the king's servants and the people of the king's provinces know that any man or woman who goes into the inner court to the king, who has not been called, *he has* but one law: put *all* to death, except the one to whom the king holds out the golden scepter, that he may live. Yet I myself have not been called to go in to the king these thirty days." 12 So they told Mordecai Esther's words.

13 And Mordecai told *them* to answer Esther: "Do not think in your heart that you will escape in the king's palace any more than all the other Jews. 14 For if you remain completely silent at this time, relief and deliverance will arise for the Jews from another place, but you and your father's house will perish. Yet who knows whether you have come to the kingdom for *such* a time as this?"

15 Then Esther told *them* to reply to Mordecai: 16 "Go, gather all the Jews who are present in Shushan, and fast for me; neither eat nor drink for three days, night or day. My maids and I will fast likewise. And so I will go to the king, which *is* against the law; and if I perish, I perish!"

THE MESSAGE

15 At the king's command, the couriers took
off; the order was also posted in the palace
complex of Susa. The king and Haman sat
back and had a drink while the city of Susa
reeled from the news.

1-3 4 When Mordecai learned what had been
done, he ripped his clothes to shreds and
put on sackcloth and ashes. Then he went
out in the streets of the city crying out in
loud and bitter cries. He came only as far as
the King's Gate, for no one dressed in sack-
cloth was allowed to enter the King's Gate.
As the king's order was posted in every
province, there was loud lament among the
Jews—fasting, weeping, wailing. And most
of them stretched out on sackcloth and
ashes.
4-8 Esther's maids and eunuchs came and
told her. The queen was stunned. She sent
fresh clothes to Mordecai so he could take
off his sackcloth but he wouldn't accept
them. Esther called for Hathach, one of the
royal eunuchs whom the king had assigned
to wait on her, and told him to go to Morde-
cai and get the full story of what was hap-
pening. So Hathach went to Mordecai in the
town square in front of the King's Gate.
Mordecai told him everything that had hap-
pened to him. He also told him the exact
amount of money that Haman had promised
to deposit in the royal bank to finance the
massacre of the Jews. Mordecai also gave
him a copy of the bulletin that had been
posted in Susa ordering the massacre so he
could show it to Esther when he reported
back with instructions to go to the king and
intercede and plead with him for her people.
9-11 Hathach came back and told Esther
everything Mordecai had said. Esther talked
it over with Hathach and then sent him back
to Mordecai with this message: "Everyone
who works for the king here, and even the
people out in the provinces, knows that
there is a single fate for every man or
woman who approaches the king without
being invited: death. The one exception is if
the king extends his gold scepter; then he or
she may live. And it's been thirty days now
since I've been invited to come to the king."
12-14 When Hathach told Mordecai what Es-
ther had said, Mordecai sent her this mes-
sage: "Don't think that just because you live
in the king's house you're the one Jew who
will get out of this alive. If you persist in
staying silent at a time like this, help and de-
liverance will arrive for the Jews from
someplace else; but you and your family
will be wiped out. Who knows? Maybe you
were made queen for just such a time as
this."
15-16 Esther sent back her answer to Mordecai:
"Go and get all the Jews living in Susa to-
gether. Fast for me. Don't eat or drink for
three days, either day or night. I and my
maids will fast with you. If you will do this,
I'll go to the king, even though it's forbid-
den. If I die, I die."

NEW KING JAMES VERSION

17So Mordecai went his way and did accord-
ing to all that Esther commanded him.[a]

ESTHER'S BANQUET

5 Now it happened on the third day that Esther
put on *her* royal *robes* and stood in the inner
court of the king's palace, across from the king's
house, while the king sat on his royal throne in
the royal house, facing the entrance of the
house.[a] 2So it was, when the king saw Queen Es-
ther standing in the court, *that* she found favor
in his sight, and the king held out to Esther the
golden scepter that *was* in his hand. Then Es-
ther went near and touched the top of the
scepter.
3And the king said to her, "What do you
wish, Queen Esther? What *is* your request? It
shall be given to you—up to half the kingdom!"
4So Esther answered, "If it pleases the king,
let the king and Haman come today to the ban-
quet that I have prepared for him."
5Then the king said, "Bring Haman quickly,
that he may do as Esther has said." So the king
and Haman went to the banquet that Esther had
prepared.
6At the banquet of wine the king said to Es-
ther, "What *is* your petition? It shall be granted
you. What *is* your request, up to half the king-
dom? It shall be done!"
7Then Esther answered and said, "My peti-
tion and request *is this:* 8If I have found favor in
the sight of the king, and if it pleases the king to
grant my petition and fulfill my request, then let
the king and Haman come to the banquet which
I will prepare for them, and tomorrow I will do
as the king has said."

HAMAN'S PLOT AGAINST MORDECAI

9So Haman went out that day joyful and with
a glad heart; but when Haman saw Mordecai in
the king's gate, and that he did not stand or
tremble before him, he was filled with indigna-
tion against Mordecai. 10Nevertheless Haman
restrained himself and went home, and he sent
and called for his friends and his wife Zeresh.
11Then Haman told them of his great riches, the
multitude of his children, everything in which
the king had promoted him, and how he had ad-
vanced him above the officials and servants of
the king.
12Moreover Haman said, "Besides, Queen Es-
ther invited no one but me to come in with the
king to the banquet that she prepared; and to-
morrow I am again invited by her, along with
the king. 13Yet all this avails me nothing, so long
as I see Mordecai the Jew sitting at the king's
gate."
14Then his wife Zeresh and all his friends
said to him, "Let a gallows be made, fifty cubits
high, and in the morning suggest to the king
that Mordecai be hanged on it; then go merrily
with the king to the banquet."
And the thing pleased Haman; so he had the
gallows made.

4:17 [a]Septuagint adds a prayer of Mordecai here. **5:1** [a]Septuagint adds many extra details in verses 1 and 2.

THE MESSAGE

17 Mordecai left and carried out Esther's instructions.

1-3 5 Three days later Esther dressed in her royal robes and took up a position in the inner court of the palace in front of the king's throne room. The king was on his throne facing the entrance. When he noticed Queen Esther standing in the court, he was pleased to see her; the king extended the gold scepter in his hand. Esther approached and touched the tip of the scepter. The king asked, "And what's your desire, Queen Esther? What do you want? Ask and it's yours—even if it's half my kingdom!"

4 "If it please the king," said Esther, "let the king come with Haman to a dinner I've prepared for him."

5-6 "Get Haman at once," said the king, "so we can go to dinner with Esther."

So the king and Haman joined Esther at the dinner she had arranged. As they were drinking the wine, the king said, "Now, what is it you want? Half of my kingdom isn't too much to ask! Just ask."

7-8 Esther answered, "Here's what I want. If the king favors me and is pleased to do what I desire and ask, let the king and Haman come again tomorrow to the dinner that I will fix for them. Then I'll give a straight answer to the king's question."

9-13 Haman left the palace that day happy, beaming. And then he saw Mordecai sitting at the King's Gate ignoring him, oblivious to him. Haman was furious with Mordecai. But he held himself in and went on home. He got his friends together with his wife Zeresh and started bragging about how much money he had, his many sons, all the times the king had honored him, and his promotion to the highest position in the government. "On top of all that," Haman continued, "Queen Esther invited me to a private dinner she gave for the king, just the three of us. And she's invited me to another one tomorrow. But I can't enjoy any of it when I see Mordecai the Jew sitting at the King's Gate."

14 His wife Zeresh and all his friends said, "Build a gallows seventy-five feet high. First thing in the morning speak with the king; get him to order Mordecai hanged on it. Then happily go with the king to dinner."

Haman liked that. He had the gallows built.

NEW KING JAMES VERSION

THE KING HONORS MORDECAI

6 That night the king could not sleep. So one
was commanded to bring the book of the
records of the chronicles; and they were read
before the king. 2And it was found written that
Mordecai had told of Bigthana and Teresh, two
of the king's eunuchs, the doorkeepers who had
sought to lay hands on King Ahasuerus. 3Then
the king said, "What honor or dignity has been
bestowed on Mordecai for this?"
And the king's servants who attended him
said, "Nothing has been done for him."
4So the king said, "Who *is* in the court?" Now
Haman had *just* entered the outer court of the
king's palace to suggest that the king hang
Mordecai on the gallows that he had prepared
for him.
5The king's servants said to him, "Haman is
there, standing in the court."
And the king said, "Let him come in."
6So Haman came in, and the king asked him,
"What shall be done for the man whom the king
delights to honor?"
Now Haman thought in his heart, "Whom
would the king delight to honor more than me?"
7And Haman answered the king, "*For* the man
whom the king delights to honor, 8let a royal
robe be brought which the king has worn, and a
horse on which the king has ridden, which has
a royal crest placed on its head. 9Then let this
robe and horse be delivered to the hand of one
of the king's most noble princes, that he may ar-
ray the man whom the king delights to honor.
Then parade him on horseback through the city
square, and proclaim before him: 'Thus shall it
be done to the man whom the king delights to
honor!' "
10Then the king said to Haman, "Hurry, take
the robe and the horse, as you have suggested,
and do so for Mordecai the Jew who sits within
the king's gate! Leave nothing undone of all that
you have spoken."
11So Haman took the robe and the horse, ar-
rayed Mordecai and led him on horseback
through the city square, and proclaimed before
him, "Thus shall it be done to the man whom the
king delights to honor!"
12Afterward Mordecai went back to the
king's gate. But Haman hurried to his house,
mourning and with his head covered. 13When
Haman told his wife Zeresh and all his friends
everything that had happened to him, his wise
men and his wife Zeresh said to him, "If Morde-
cai, before whom you have begun to fall, is of
Jewish descent, you will not prevail against him
but will surely fall before him."
14While they *were* still talking with him, the
king's eunuchs came, and hastened to bring
Haman to the banquet which Esther had pre-
pared.

HAMAN HANGED INSTEAD OF MORDECAI

7 So the king and Haman went to dine with
Queen Esther. 2And on the second day, at the
banquet of wine, the king again said to Esther,

THE MESSAGE

1-2 6 That night the king couldn't sleep. He ordered the record book, the day-by-day journal of events, to be brought and read to him. They came across the story there about the time that Mordecai had exposed the plot of Bigthana and Teresh—the two royal eunuchs who guarded the entrance and who had conspired to assassinate King Xerxes.

3 The king asked, "What great honor was given to Mordecai for this?"

"Nothing," replied the king's servants who were in attendance. "Nothing has been done for him."

4 The king said, "Is there anybody out in the court?"

Now Haman had just come into the outer court of the king's palace to talk to the king about hanging Mordecai on the gallows he had built for him.

5 The king's servants said, "Haman is out there, waiting in the court."

"Bring him in," said the king.

6-9 When Haman entered, the king said, "What would be appropriate for the man the king especially wants to honor?"

Haman thought to himself, "He must be talking about honoring me—who else?" So he answered the king, "For the man the king delights to honor, do this: Bring a royal robe that the king has worn and a horse the king has ridden, one with a royal crown on its head. Then give the robe and the horse to one of the king's most noble princes. Have him robe the man whom the king especially wants to honor; have the prince lead him on horseback through the city square, proclaiming before him, 'This is what is done for the man whom the king especially wants to honor!' "

10 "Go and do it," the king said to Haman. "Don't waste another minute. Take the robe and horse and do what you have proposed to Mordecai the Jew who sits at the King's Gate. Don't leave out a single detail of your plan."

11 So Haman took the robe and horse; he robed Mordecai and led him through the city square, proclaiming before him, "This is what is done for the man whom the king especially wants to honor!"

12-13 Then Mordecai returned to the King's Gate, but Haman fled to his house, thoroughly mortified, hiding his face. When Haman had finished telling his wife Zeresh and all his friends everything that had happened to him, his knowledgeable friends who were there and his wife Zeresh said, "If this Mordecai is in fact a Jew, your bad luck has only begun. You don't stand a chance against him—you're as good as ruined."

14 While they were still talking, the king's eunuchs arrived and hurried Haman off to the dinner that Esther had prepared.

1-2 7 So the king and Haman went to dinner with Queen Esther. At this second dinner, while they were drinking wine the king

NEW KING JAMES VERSION

"What *is* your petition, Queen Esther? It shall be
granted you. And what *is* your request, up to
half the kingdom? It shall be done!"
3Then Queen Esther answered and said, "If I
have found favor in your sight, O king, and if it
pleases the king, let my life be given me at my
petition, and my people at my request. 4For we
have been sold, my people and I, to be de-
stroyed, to be killed, and to be annihilated. Had
we been sold as male and female slaves, I would
have held my tongue, although the enemy could
never compensate for the king's loss."
5So King Ahasuerus answered and said to
Queen Esther, "Who is he, and where is he, who
would dare presume in his heart to do such a
thing?"
6And Esther said, "The adversary and enemy
is this wicked Haman!"
So Haman was terrified before the king and
queen.
7Then the king arose in his wrath from the
banquet of wine *and went* into the palace gar-
den; but Haman stood before Queen Esther,
pleading for his life, for he saw that evil was de-
termined against him by the king. 8When the
king returned from the palace garden to the
place of the banquet of wine, Haman had fallen
across the couch where Esther *was*. Then the
king said, "Will he also assault the queen while
I *am* in the house?"
As the word left the king's mouth, they cov-
ered Haman's face. 9Now Harbonah, one of the
eunuchs, said to the king, "Look! The gallows,
fifty cubits high, which Haman made for Morde-
cai, who spoke good on the king's behalf, is
standing at the house of Haman."
Then the king said, "Hang him on it!"
10So they hanged Haman on the gallows that
he had prepared for Mordecai. Then the king's
wrath subsided.

ESTHER SAVES THE JEWS

8 On that day King Ahasuerus gave Queen Es-
ther the house of Haman, the enemy of the
Jews. And Mordecai came before the king, for
Esther had told how he *was related* to her. 2So
the king took off his signet ring, which he had
taken from Haman, and gave it to Mordecai; and
Esther appointed Mordecai over the house of
Haman.
3Now Esther spoke again to the king, fell
down at his feet, and implored him with tears to
counteract the evil of Haman the Agagite, and
the scheme which he had devised against the
Jews. 4And the king held out the golden scepter
toward Esther. So Esther arose and stood before
the king, 5and said, "If it pleases the king, and if
I have found favor in his sight and the thing
seems right to the king and I am pleasing in his
eyes, let it be written to revoke the letters de-
vised by Haman, the son of Hammedatha the
Agagite, which he wrote to annihilate the Jews
who *are* in all the king's provinces. 6For how can
I endure to see the evil that will come to my peo-
ple? Or how can I endure to see the destruction
of my countrymen?"

THE MESSAGE

again asked, "Queen Esther, what would
you like? Half of my kingdom! Just ask and
it's yours."
3 Queen Esther answered, "If I have found
favor in your eyes, O King, and if it please
the king, give me my life, and give my peo-
ple their lives.
4 "We've been sold, I and my people, to be
destroyed—sold to be massacred, elimi-
nated. If we had just been sold off into slav-
ery, I wouldn't even have brought it up; our
troubles wouldn't have been worth bother-
ing the king over."
5 King Xerxes exploded, "Who? Where is
he? This is monstrous!"
6 "An enemy. An adversary. This evil
Haman," said Esther.
Haman was terror-stricken before the
king and queen.
7-8 The king, raging, left his wine and
stalked out into the palace garden.
Haman stood there pleading with Queen
Esther for his life—he could see that the
king was finished with him and that he was
doomed. As the king came back from the
palace garden into the banquet hall, Haman
was groveling at the couch on which Esther
reclined. The king roared out, "Will he even
molest the queen while I'm just around the
corner?"
When that word left the king's mouth, all
the blood drained from Haman's face.
9 Harbona, one of the eunuchs attending
the king, spoke up: "Look over there!
There's the gallows that Haman had built
for Mordecai, who saved the king's life. It's
right next to Haman's house—seventy-five
feet high!"
The king said, "Hang him on it!"
10 So Haman was hanged on the very gal-
lows that he had built for Mordecai. And the
king's hot anger cooled.

1-2 8 That same day King Xerxes gave Queen
Esther the estate of Haman, archenemy
of the Jews. And Mordecai came before the
king because Esther had explained their re-
lationship. The king took off his signet ring,
which he had taken back from Haman, and
gave it to Mordecai. Esther appointed
Mordecai over Haman's estate.
3-6 Then Esther again spoke to the king,
falling at his feet, begging with tears to
counter the evil of Haman the Agagite and
revoke the plan that he had plotted against
the Jews. The king extended his gold
scepter to Esther. She got to her feet and
stood before the king. She said, "If it please
the king and he regards me with favor and
thinks this is right, and if he has any affec-
tion for me at all, let an order be written that
cancels the bulletins authorizing the plan of
Haman son of Hammedatha the Agagite to
annihilate the Jews in all the king's
provinces. How can I stand to see this catas-
trophe wipe out my people? How can I bear
to stand by and watch the massacre of my
own relatives?"

NEW KING JAMES VERSION

7Then King Ahasuerus said to Queen Esther
and Mordecai the Jew, "Indeed, I have given Es-
ther the house of Haman, and they have hanged
him on the gallows because he *tried to* lay his
hand on the Jews. 8You yourselves write *a de-
cree* concerning the Jews, as you please, in the
king's name, and seal *it* with the king's signet
ring; for whatever is written in the king's name
and sealed with the king's signet ring no one
can revoke."
9So the king's scribes were called at that
time, in the third month, which *is* the month of
Sivan, on the twenty-third *day;* and it was writ-
ten, according to all that Mordecai commanded,
to the Jews, the satraps, the governors, and the
princes of the provinces from India to Ethiopia,
one hundred and twenty-seven provinces *in all,*
to every province in its own script, to every peo-
ple in their own language, and to the Jews in
their own script and language. 10And he wrote
in the name of King Ahasuerus, sealed *it* with
the king's signet ring, and sent letters by couri-
ers on horseback, riding on royal horses bred
from swift steeds.[a]
11By these letters the king permitted the
Jews who *were* in every city to gather together
and protect their lives—to destroy, kill, and an-
nihilate all the forces of any people or province
that would assault them, *both* little children and
women, and to plunder their possessions, 12on
one day in all the provinces of King Ahasuerus,
on the thirteenth *day* of the twelfth month,
which *is* the month of Adar.[a] 13A copy of the
document was to be issued as a decree in every
province and published for all people, so that
the Jews would be ready on that day to avenge
themselves on their enemies. 14The couriers who
rode on royal horses went out, hastened and
pressed on by the king's command. And the de-
cree was issued in Shushan the citadel.
15So Mordecai went out from the presence of
the king in royal apparel of blue and white, with
a great crown of gold and a garment of fine
linen and purple; and the city of Shushan re-
joiced and was glad. 16The Jews had light and
gladness, joy and honor. 17And in every province
and city, wherever the king's command and de-
cree came, the Jews had joy and gladness, a
feast and a holiday. Then many of the people of
the land became Jews, because fear of the Jews
fell upon them.

THE JEWS DESTROY THEIR TORMENTORS

9 Now in the twelfth month, that *is,* the month
of Adar, on the thirteenth day, *the time* came
for the king's command and his decree to be ex-
ecuted. On the day that the enemies of the Jews
had hoped to overpower them, the opposite oc-
curred, in that the Jews themselves overpow-
ered those who hated them. 2The Jews gathered
together in their cities throughout all the
provinces of King Ahasuerus to lay hands on
those who sought their harm. And no one could
withstand them, because fear of them fell upon

8:10 [a]Literally *sons of the swift horses* **8:12** [a]Septuagint adds the text of the letter here.

THE MESSAGE

7-8 King Xerxes said to Queen Esther and
Mordecai the Jew: "I've given Haman's es-
tate to Esther and he's been hanged on the
gallows because he attacked the Jews. So go
ahead now and write whatever you decide
on behalf of the Jews; then seal it with the
signet ring." (An order written in the king's
name and sealed with his signet ring is ir-
revocable.)
9 So the king's secretaries were brought in
on the twenty-third day of the third month,
the month of Sivan, and the order regarding
the Jews was written word for word as
Mordecai dictated and was addressed to the
satraps, governors, and officials of the
provinces from India to Ethiopia, 127
provinces in all, to each province in its own
script and each people in their own lan-
guage, including the Jews in their script and
language.
10 He wrote under the name of King Xerxes
and sealed the order with the royal signet
ring; he sent out the bulletins by couriers on
horseback, riding the fastest royal steeds
bred from the royal stud.
11-13 The king's order authorized the Jews in
every city to arm and defend themselves to
the death, killing anyone who threatened
them or their women and children, and con-
fiscating for themselves anything owned by
their enemies. The day set for this in all
King Xerxes' provinces was the thirteenth
day of the twelfth month, the month of Adar.
The order was posted in public places in
each province so everyone could read it, au-
thorizing the Jews to be prepared on that
day to avenge themselves on their enemies.
14 The couriers, fired up by the king's order,
raced off on their royal horses. At the same
time, the order was posted in the palace
complex of Susa.
15-17 Mordecai walked out of the king's pres-
ence wearing a royal robe of violet and
white, a huge gold crown, and a purple cape
of fine linen. The city of Susa exploded with
joy. For Jews it was all sunshine and laugh-
ter: they celebrated, they were honored. It
was that way all over the country, in every
province, every city when the king's bulletin
was posted: the Jews took to the streets in
celebration, cheering, and feasting. Not only
that, but many non-Jews became Jews—
now it was dangerous *not* to be a Jew!

1-4 9 On the thirteenth day of the twelfth
month, the month of Adar, the king's order
came into effect. This was the very day that
the enemies of the Jews had planned to
overpower them, but the tables were now
turned: the Jews overpowered those who
hated them! The Jews had gathered in the
cities throughout King Xerxes' provinces to
lay hands on those who were seeking their
ruin. Not one man was able to stand up
against them—fear made cowards of them

New King James Version

all people. [3]And all the officials of the provinces,
the satraps, the governors, and all those doing
the king's work, helped the Jews, because the
fear of Mordecai fell upon them. [4]For Mordecai
was great in the king's palace, and his fame
spread throughout all the provinces; for this
man Mordecai became increasingly prominent.
[5]Thus the Jews defeated all their enemies with
the stroke of the sword, with slaughter and de-
struction, and did what they pleased with those
who hated them.

[6]And in Shushan the citadel the Jews killed
and destroyed five hundred men. [7]Also Parshan-
datha, Dalphon, Aspatha, [8]Poratha, Adalia, Ari-
datha, [9]Parmashta, Arisai, Aridai, and Vajeza-
tha— [10]the ten sons of Haman the son of
Hammedatha, the enemy of the Jews—they
killed; but they did not lay a hand on the plun-
der.

[11]On that day the number of those who were
killed in Shushan the citadel was brought to the
king. [12]And the king said to Queen Esther, "The
Jews have killed and destroyed five hundred
men in Shushan the citadel, and the ten sons of
Haman. What have they done in the rest of the
king's provinces? Now what *is* your petition? It
shall be granted to you. Or what *is* your further
request? It shall be done."

[13]Then Esther said, "If it pleases the king, let
it be granted to the Jews who *are* in Shushan to
do again tomorrow according to today's decree,
and let Haman's ten sons be hanged on the gal-
lows."

[14]So the king commanded this to be done;
the decree was issued in Shushan, and they
hanged Haman's ten sons.

[15]And the Jews who *were* in Shushan gath-
ered together again on the fourteenth day of the
month of Adar and killed three hundred men at
Shushan; but they did not lay a hand on the
plunder.

[16]The remainder of the Jews in the king's
provinces gathered together and protected their
lives, had rest from their enemies, and killed
seventy-five thousand of their enemies; but they
did not lay a hand on the plunder. [17]*This was* on
the thirteenth day of the month of Adar. And on
the fourteenth of *the month*[a] they rested and
made it a day of feasting and gladness.

The Feast of Purim

[18]But the Jews who *were* at Shushan assem-
bled together on the thirteenth *day*, as well as on
the fourteenth; and on the fifteenth of *the
month*[a] they rested, and made it a day of feast-
ing and gladness. [19]Therefore the Jews of the
villages who dwelt in the unwalled towns cele-
brated the fourteenth day of the month of Adar
with gladness and feasting, as a holiday, and for
sending presents to one another.

[20]And Mordecai wrote these things and sent
letters to all the Jews, near and far, who *were* in
all the provinces of King Ahasuerus, [21]to estab-
lish among them that they should celebrate
yearly the fourteenth and fifteenth days of the
month of Adar, [22]as the days on which the Jews

9:17 [a]Literally *it* **9:18** [a]Literally *it*

The Message

all. What's more, all the government officials,
satraps, governors—everyone who worked
for the king—actually helped the Jews be-
cause of Mordecai; they were afraid of him.
Mordecai by now was a power in the palace.
As Mordecai became more and more power-
ful, his reputation had grown in all the
provinces.

5-9 So the Jews finished off all their enemies
with the sword, slaughtering them right and
left, and did as they pleased to those who
hated them. In the palace complex of Susa
the Jews massacred five hundred men. They
also killed the ten sons of Haman son of
Hammedatha, the archenemy of the Jews:

Parshandatha — Dalphon
Aspatha — Poratha
Adalia — Aridatha
Parmashta — Arisai
Aridai — Vaizatha

10-12 But they took no plunder. That day, when
it was all over, the number of those killed in
the palace complex was given to the king.
The king told Queen Esther, "In the palace
complex alone here in Susa the Jews have
killed five hundred men, plus Haman's ten
sons. Think of the killing that must have
been done in the rest of the provinces! What
else do you want? Name it and it's yours.
Your wish is my command."

13 "If it please the king," Queen Esther re-
sponded, "give the Jews of Susa permission
to extend the terms of the order another day.
And have the bodies of Haman's ten sons
hanged in public display on the gallows."

14 The king commanded it: The order was
extended; the bodies of Haman's ten sons
were publicly hanged.

15 The Jews in Susa went at it again. On the
fourteenth day of Adar they killed another
three hundred men in Susa. But again they
took no plunder.

16-19 Meanwhile in the rest of the king's
provinces, the Jews had organized and de-
fended themselves, freeing themselves from
oppression. On the thirteenth day of the
month of Adar, they killed seventy-five
thousand of those who hated them but did
not take any plunder. The next day, the four-
teenth, they took it easy and celebrated with
much food and laughter. But in Susa, since
the Jews had banded together on both the
thirteenth and fourteenth days, they made
the fifteenth their holiday for laughing and
feasting. (This accounts for why Jews living
out in the country in the rural villages re-
member the fourteenth day of Adar for cel-
ebration, their day for parties and the ex-
change of gifts.)

20-22 Mordecai wrote all this down and sent
copies to all the Jews in all King Xerxes'
provinces, regardless of distance, calling for
an annual celebration on the fourteenth and
fifteenth days of Adar as the occasion when

New King James Version

had rest from their enemies, as the month which was turned from sorrow to joy for them, and from mourning to a holiday; that they should make them days of feasting and joy, of sending presents to one another and gifts to the poor.
23 So the Jews accepted the custom which they had begun, as Mordecai had written to them,
24 because Haman, the son of Hammedatha the Agagite, the enemy of all the Jews, had plotted against the Jews to annihilate them, and had cast Pur (that *is*, the lot), to consume them and destroy them; 25 but when *Esther*[a] came before the king, he commanded by letter that this[b] wicked plot which *Haman* had devised against the Jews should return on his own head, and that he and his sons should be hanged on the gallows.

26 So they called these days Purim, after the name Pur. Therefore, because of all the words of this letter, what they had seen concerning this matter, and what had happened to them, 27 the Jews established and imposed it upon themselves and their descendants and all who would join them, that without fail they should celebrate these two days every year, according to the written *instructions* and according to the *prescribed* time, 28 *that* these days *should be* remembered and kept throughout every generation, every family, every province, and every city, that these days of Purim should not fail *to be observed* among the Jews, and *that* the memory of them should not perish among their descendants.

29 Then Queen Esther, the daughter of Abihail, with Mordecai the Jew, wrote with full authority to confirm this second letter about Purim. 30 And *Mordecai* sent letters to all the Jews, to the one hundred and twenty-seven provinces of the kingdom of Ahasuerus, *with* words of peace and truth, 31 to confirm these days of Purim at their *appointed* time, as Mordecai the Jew and Queen Esther had prescribed for them, and as they had decreed for themselves and their descendants concerning matters of their fasting and lamenting. 32 So the decree of Esther confirmed these matters of Purim, and it was written in the book.

Mordecai's Advancement

10 And King Ahasuerus imposed tribute on the land and *on* the islands of the sea. 2 Now all the acts of his power and his might, and the account of the greatness of Mordecai, to which the king advanced him, *are* they not written in the book of the chronicles of the kings of Media and Persia? 3 For Mordecai the Jew *was* second to King Ahasuerus, and was great among the Jews and well received by the multitude of his brethren, seeking the good of his people and speaking peace to all his countrymen.[a]

9:25 [a]Literally *she* or *it* [b]Literally *his* **10:3** [a]Literally *seed.* Septuagint and Vulgate add a dream of Mordecai here; Vulgate adds six more chapters.

The Message

Jews got relief from their enemies, the month in which their sorrow turned to joy, mourning somersaulted into a holiday for parties and fun and laughter, the sending and receiving of presents and of giving gifts to the poor.

23 And they did it. What started then became a tradition, continuing the practice of what Mordecai had written to them.

24-26 Haman son of Hammedatha, the Agagite, the archenemy of all Jews, had schemed to destroy all Jews. He had cast the *pur* (the lot) to throw them into a panic and destroy them. But when Queen Esther intervened with the king, he gave written orders that the evil scheme that Haman had worked out should boomerang back on his own head. He and his sons were hanged on the gallows. That's why these days are called "Purim," from the word *pur* or "lot."

26-28 Therefore, because of everything written in this letter and because of all that they had been through, the Jews agreed to continue. It became a tradition for them, their children, and all future converts to remember these two days every year on the specified dates set down in the letter. These days are to be remembered and kept by every single generation, every last family, every province and city. These days of Purim must never be neglected among the Jews; the memory of them must never die out among their descendants.

29-32 Queen Esther, the daughter of Abihail, backed Mordecai the Jew, using her full queenly authority in this second Purim letter to endorse and ratify what he wrote. Calming and reassuring letters went out to all the Jews throughout the 127 provinces of Xerxes' kingdom to fix these days of Purim their assigned place on the calendar, dates set by Mordecai the Jew—what they had agreed to for themselves and their descendants regarding their fasting and mourning. Esther's word confirmed the tradition of Purim and was written in the book.

1-2 **10** King Xerxes imposed taxes from one end of his empire to the other. For the rest of it, King Xerxes' extensive accomplishments, along with a detailed account of the brilliance of Mordecai, whom the king had promoted, that's all written in *The Chronicles of the Kings of Media and Persia.*

3 Mordecai the Jew ranked second in command to King Xerxes. He was popular among the Jews and greatly respected by them. He worked hard for the good of his people; he cared for the peace and prosperity of his race.

JOB

New King James Version

Job and His Family in Uz

1 There was a man in the land of Uz, whose name *was* Job; and that man was blameless and upright, and one who feared God and shunned evil. 2And seven sons and three daughters were born to him. 3Also, his possessions were seven thousand sheep, three thousand camels, five hundred yoke of oxen, five hundred female donkeys, and a very large household, so that this man was the greatest of all the people of the East.

4And his sons would go and feast *in their* houses, each on his *appointed* day, and would send and invite their three sisters to eat and drink with them. 5So it was, when the days of feasting had run their course, that Job would send and sanctify them, and he would rise early in the morning and offer burnt offerings *according to* the number of them all. For Job said, "It may be that my sons have sinned and cursed[a] God in their hearts." Thus Job did regularly.

Satan Attacks Job's Character

6Now there was a day when the sons of God came to present themselves before the LORD, and Satan[a] also came among them. 7And the LORD said to Satan, "From where do you come?"

So Satan answered the LORD and said, "From going to and fro on the earth, and from walking back and forth on it."

8Then the LORD said to Satan, "Have you considered My servant Job, that *there is* none like him on the earth, a blameless and upright man, one who fears God and shuns evil?"

9So Satan answered the LORD and said, "Does Job fear God for nothing? 10Have You not made a hedge around him, around his household, and around all that he has on every side? You have blessed the work of his hands, and his possessions have increased in the land. 11But now, stretch out Your hand and touch all that he has, and he will surely curse You to Your face!"

12And the LORD said to Satan, "Behold, all that he has *is* in your power; only do not lay a hand on his *person.*"

So Satan went out from the presence of the LORD.

Job Loses His Property and Children

13Now there was a day when his sons and daughters *were* eating and drinking wine in their oldest brother's house; 14and a messenger came to Job and said, "The oxen were plowing and the donkeys feeding beside them, 15when the Sabeans[a] raided *them* and took them away—indeed they have killed the servants with the edge of the sword; and I alone have escaped to tell you!"

16While he *was* still speaking, another also came and said, "The fire of God fell from heaven and burned up the sheep and the servants, and consumed them; and I alone have escaped to tell you!"

1:5 [a]Literally *blessed,* but used here in the evil sense, and so in verse 11 and 2:5, 9 **1:6** [a]Literally *the Adversary,* and so throughout this book **1:15** [a]Literally *Sheba* (compare 6:19)

The Message

1-3 1 Job was a man who lived in Uz. He was honest inside and out, a man of his word, who was totally devoted to God and hated evil with a passion. He had seven sons and three daughters. He was also very wealthy—seven thousand head of sheep, three thousand camels, five hundred teams of oxen, five hundred donkeys, and a huge staff of servants—the most influential man in all the East!

4-5 His sons used to take turns hosting parties in their homes, always inviting their three sisters to join them in their merrymaking. When the parties were over, Job would get up early in the morning and sacrifice a burnt offering for each of his children, thinking, "Maybe one of them sinned by defying God inwardly." Job made a habit of this sacrificial atonement, just in case they'd sinned.

The First Test: Family and Fortune

6-7 One day when the angels came to report to GOD, Satan, who was the Designated Accuser, came along with them. GOD singled out Satan and said, "What have you been up to?"

Satan answered GOD, "Going here and there, checking things out on earth."

8 GOD said to Satan, "Have you noticed my friend Job? There's no one quite like him—honest and true to his word, totally devoted to God and hating evil."

9-10 Satan retorted, "So do you think Job does all that out of the sheer goodness of his heart? Why, no one ever had it so good! You pamper him like a pet, make sure nothing bad ever happens to him or his family or his possessions, bless everything he does—he can't lose!

11 "But what do you think would happen if you reached down and took away everything that is his? He'd curse you right to your face, that's what."

12 GOD replied, "We'll see. Go ahead—do what you want with all that is his. Just don't hurt *him.*" Then Satan left the presence of GOD.

13-15 Sometime later, while Job's children were having one of their parties at the home of the oldest son, a messenger came to Job and said, "The oxen were plowing and the donkeys grazing in the field next to us when Sabeans attacked. They stole the animals and killed the field hands. I'm the only one to get out alive and tell you what happened."

16 While he was still talking, another messenger arrived and said, "Bolts of lightning struck the sheep and the shepherds and fried them—burned them to a crisp. I'm the only one to get out alive and tell you what happened."

NEW KING JAMES VERSION

17 While he *was* still speaking, another also
came and said, "The Chaldeans formed three
bands, raided the camels and took them away,
yes, and killed the servants with the edge of the
sword; and I alone have escaped to tell you!"
18 While he *was* still speaking, another also
came and said, "Your sons and daughters *were*
eating and drinking wine in their oldest
brother's house, 19 and suddenly a great wind
came from across[a] the wilderness and struck
the four corners of the house, and it fell on the
young people, and they are dead; and I alone
have escaped to tell you!"
20 Then Job arose, tore his robe, and shaved
his head; and he fell to the ground and wor-
shiped. 21 And he said:

"Naked I came from my mother's womb,
And naked shall I return there.
The LORD gave, and the LORD has taken
away;
Blessed be the name of the LORD."

22 In all this Job did not sin nor charge God
with wrong.

SATAN ATTACKS JOB'S HEALTH

2 Again there was a day when the sons of God
came to present themselves before the LORD,
and Satan came also among them to present
himself before the LORD. 2 And the LORD said to
Satan, "From where do you come?"
Satan answered the LORD and said, "From
going to and fro on the earth, and from walking
back and forth on it."
3 Then the LORD said to Satan, "Have you con-
sidered My servant Job, that *there is* none like
him on the earth, a blameless and upright man,
one who fears God and shuns evil? And still he
holds fast to his integrity, although you incited
Me against him, to destroy him without cause."
4 So Satan answered the LORD and said, "Skin
for skin! Yes, all that a man has he will give for
his life. 5 But stretch out Your hand now, and
touch his bone and his flesh, and he will surely
curse You to Your face!"
6 And the LORD said to Satan, "Behold, he *is*
in your hand, but spare his life."
7 So Satan went out from the presence of the
LORD, and struck Job with painful boils from the
sole of his foot to the crown of his head. 8 And he
took for himself a potsherd with which to scrape
himself while he sat in the midst of the ashes.
9 Then his wife said to him, "Do you still hold
fast to your integrity? Curse God and die!"
10 But he said to her, "You speak as one of the
foolish women speaks. Shall we indeed accept
good from God, and shall we not accept adver-
sity?" In all this Job did not sin with his lips.

JOB'S THREE FRIENDS

11 Now when Job's three friends heard of all
this adversity that had come upon him, each one
came from his own place—Eliphaz the Teman-
ite, Bildad the Shuhite, and Zophar the Naa-

1:19 [a]Septuagint omits *across*.

THE MESSAGE

17 While he was still talking, another messenger arrived and said, "Chaldeans coming from three directions raided the camels and massacred the camel drivers. I'm the only one to get out alive and tell you what happened."

18-19 While he was still talking, another messenger arrived and said, "Your children were having a party at the home of the oldest brother when a tornado swept in off the desert and struck the house. It collapsed on the young people and they died. I'm the only one to get out alive and tell you what happened."

20 Job got to his feet, ripped his robe, shaved his head, then fell to the ground and worshiped:

21 Naked I came from my mother's womb,
naked I'll return to the womb of the
earth.
GOD gives, GOD takes.
God's name be ever blessed.

22 Not once through all this did Job sin; not once did he blame God.

THE SECOND TEST: HEALTH

1-3 2 One day when the angels came to report to GOD, Satan also showed up. GOD singled out Satan, saying, "And what have you been up to?" Satan answered GOD, "Oh, going here and there, checking things out." Then GOD said to Satan, "Have you noticed my friend Job? There's no one quite like him, is there—honest and true to his word, totally devoted to God and hating evil? He still has a firm grip on his integrity! You tried to trick me into destroying him, but it didn't work."

4-5 Satan answered, "A human would do anything to save his life. But what do you think would happen if you reached down and took away his health? He'd curse you to your face, that's what."

6 GOD said, "All right. Go ahead—you can do what you like with him. But mind you, don't kill him."

7-8 Satan left GOD and struck Job with terrible sores. Job was ulcers and scabs from head to foot. They itched and oozed so badly that he took a piece of broken pottery to scrape himself, then went and sat on a trash heap, among the ashes.

9 His wife said, "Still holding on to your precious integrity, are you? Curse God and be done with it!"

10 He told her, "You're talking like an empty-headed fool. We take the good days from God—why not also the bad days?"

Not once through all this did Job sin. He said nothing against God.

JOB'S THREE FRIENDS

11-13 Three of Job's friends heard of all the trouble that had fallen on him. Each traveled from his own country—Eliphaz from Teman, Bildad from Shuhah, Zophar from

NEW KING JAMES VERSION

mathite. For they had made an appointment to-
gether to come and mourn with him, and to
comfort him. 12And when they raised their eyes
from afar, and did not recognize him, they lifted
their voices and wept; and each one tore his
robe and sprinkled dust on his head toward
heaven. 13So they sat down with him on the
ground seven days and seven nights, and no one
spoke a word to him, for they saw that *his* grief
was very great.

JOB DEPLORES HIS BIRTH

3 After this Job opened his mouth and cursed
the day of his *birth*. 2And Job spoke, and said:

3"May the day perish on which I was born,
And the night *in which* it was said,
'A male child is conceived.'
4May that day be darkness;
May God above not seek it,
Nor the light shine upon it.
5May darkness and the shadow of death
claim it;
May a cloud settle on it;
May the blackness of the day terrify it.
6*As for* that night, may darkness seize it;
May it not rejoice[a] among the days of the
year,
May it not come into the number of the
months.
7Oh, may that night be barren!
May no joyful shout come into it!
8May those curse it who curse the day,
Those who are ready to arouse Leviathan.
9May the stars of its morning be dark;
May it look for light, but *have* none,
And not see the dawning of the day;
10Because it did not shut up the doors of my
mother's womb,
Nor hide sorrow from my eyes.

11"Why did I not die at birth?
Why did I *not* perish when I came from the
womb?
12Why did the knees receive me?
Or why the breasts, that I should nurse?
13For now I would have lain still and been
quiet,
I would have been asleep;
Then I would have been at rest
14With kings and counselors of the earth,
Who built ruins for themselves,
15Or with princes who had gold,
Who filled their houses *with* silver;
16Or *why* was I not hidden like a stillborn
child,
Like infants who never saw light?
17There the wicked cease *from* troubling,
And there the weary are at rest.
18*There* the prisoners rest together;
They do not hear the voice of the oppressor.
19The small and great are there,
And the servant *is* free from his master.

20"Why is light given to him who is in misery,
And life to the bitter of soul,

3:6 [a]Septuagint, Syriac, Targum, and Vulgate read *be joined.*

THE MESSAGE

Naamath—and went together to Job to keep
him company and comfort him. When they
first caught sight of him, they couldn't believe
what they saw—they hardly recognized him!
They cried out in lament, ripped their robes,
and dumped dirt on their heads as a sign of
their grief. Then they sat with him on the
ground. Seven days and nights they sat there
without saying a word. They could see how
rotten he felt, how deeply he was suffering.

JOB CRIES OUT
WHAT'S THE POINT OF LIFE?

1-2 3 Then Job broke the silence. He spoke up
and cursed his fate:

3-10 "Obliterate the day I was born.
Blank out the night I was conceived!
Let it be a black hole in space.
May God above forget it ever happened.
Erase it from the books!
May the day of my birth be buried in deep
darkness,
shrouded by the fog,
swallowed by the night.
And the night of my conception—the devil
take it!
Rip the date off the calendar,
delete it from the almanac.
Oh, turn that night into pure nothingness—
no sounds of pleasure from that night,
ever!
May those who are good at cursing curse
that day.
Unleash the sea beast, Leviathan, on it.
May its morning stars turn to black
cinders,
waiting for a daylight that never comes,
never once seeing the first light of dawn.
And why? Because it released me from my
mother's womb
into a life with so much trouble.

11-19 "Why didn't I die at birth,
my first breath out of the womb my last?
Why were there arms to rock me,
and breasts for me to drink from?
I could be resting in peace right now,
asleep forever, feeling no pain,
In the company of kings and statesmen
in their royal ruins,
Or with princes resplendent
in their gold and silver tombs.
Why wasn't I stillborn and buried
with all the babies who never saw light,
Where the wicked no longer trouble
anyone
and bone-weary people get a
long-deserved rest?
Prisoners sleep undisturbed,
never again to wake up to the bark of the
guards.
The small and the great are equals in that
place,
and slaves are free from their masters.

20-23 "Why does God bother giving light to the
miserable,
why bother keeping bitter people alive,

NEW KING JAMES VERSION

21Who long for death, but it does not *come*,
And search for it more than hidden treasures;
22Who rejoice exceedingly,
And are glad when they can find the grave?
23*Why is light given* to a man whose way is hidden,
And whom God has hedged in?
24For my sighing comes before I eat,[a]
And my groanings pour out like water.
25For the thing I greatly feared has come upon me,
And what I dreaded has happened to me.
26I am not at ease, nor am I quiet;
I have no rest, for trouble comes."

ELIPHAZ: JOB HAS SINNED

4 Then Eliphaz the Temanite answered and said:

2"If one attempts a word with you, will you become weary?
But who can withhold himself from speaking?
3Surely you have instructed many,
And you have strengthened weak hands.
4Your words have upheld him who was stumbling,
And you have strengthened the feeble knees;
5But now it comes upon you, and you are weary;
It touches you, and you are troubled.
6*Is* not your reverence your confidence?
And the integrity of your ways your hope?

7"Remember now, who *ever* perished being innocent?
Or where were the upright *ever* cut off?
8Even as I have seen,
Those who plow iniquity
And sow trouble reap the same.
9By the blast of God they perish,
And by the breath of His anger they are consumed.
10The roaring of the lion,
The voice of the fierce lion,
And the teeth of the young lions are broken.
11The old lion perishes for lack of prey,
And the cubs of the lioness are scattered.

12"Now a word was secretly brought to me,
And my ear received a whisper of it.
13In disquieting thoughts from the visions of the night,
When deep sleep falls on men,

3:24 [a]Literally *my bread*

THE MESSAGE

Those who want in the worst way to die, and can't,
who can't imagine anything better than death,
Who count the day of their death and burial
the happiest day of their life?
What's the point of life when it doesn't make sense,
when God blocks all the roads to meaning?

24-26 "Instead of bread I get groans for my supper,
then leave the table and vomit my anguish.
The worst of my fears has come true,
what I've dreaded most has happened.
My repose is shattered, my peace destroyed.
No rest for me, ever—death has invaded life."

ELIPHAZ SPEAKS OUT

NOW *YOU'RE* THE ONE IN TROUBLE

1-6 4 Then Eliphaz from Teman spoke up:

"Would you mind if I said something to you?
Under the circumstances it's hard to keep quiet.
You yourself have done this plenty of times, spoken words
that clarify, encouraged those who were about to quit.
Your words have put stumbling people on their feet,
put fresh hope in people about to collapse.
But now *you're* the one in trouble—you're hurting!
You've been hit hard and you're reeling from the blow.
But shouldn't your devout life give you confidence now?
Shouldn't your exemplary life give you hope?

7-11 "Think! Has a truly innocent person ever ended up on the scrap heap?
Do genuinely upright people ever lose out in the end?
It's my observation that those who plow evil
and sow trouble reap evil and trouble.
One breath from God and they fall apart,
one blast of his anger and there's nothing left of them.
The mighty lion, king of the beasts, roars mightily,
but when he's toothless he's useless—
No teeth, no prey—and the cubs
wander off to fend for themselves.

12-16 "A word came to me in secret—
a mere whisper of a word, but I heard it clearly.
It came in a scary dream one night,
after I had fallen into a deep, deep sleep.

NEW KING JAMES VERSION

14Fear came upon me, and trembling,
Which made all my bones shake.
15Then a spirit passed before my face;
The hair on my body stood up.
16It stood still,
But I could not discern its appearance.
A form *was* before my eyes;
There was silence;
Then I heard a voice *saying:*
17'Can a mortal be more righteous than God?
Can a man be more pure than his Maker?
18If He puts no trust in His servants,
If He charges His angels with error,
19How much more those who dwell in houses of clay,
Whose foundation is in the dust,
Who are crushed before a moth?
20They are broken in pieces from morning till evening;
They perish forever, with no one regarding.
21Does not their own excellence go away?
They die, even without wisdom.'

ELIPHAZ: JOB IS CHASTENED BY GOD

5 "Call out now;
Is there anyone who will answer you?
And to which of the holy ones will you turn?
2For wrath kills a foolish man,
And envy slays a simple one.
3I have seen the foolish taking root,
But suddenly I cursed his dwelling place.
4His sons are far from safety,
They are crushed in the gate,
And *there is* no deliverer.
5Because the hungry eat up his harvest,
Taking it even from the thorns,[a]
And a snare snatches their substance.[b]
6For affliction does not come from the dust,
Nor does trouble spring from the ground;
7Yet man is born to trouble,
As the sparks fly upward.

8"But as for me, I would seek God,
And to God I would commit my cause—
9Who does great things, and unsearchable,
Marvelous things without number.
10He gives rain on the earth,
And sends waters on the fields.
11He sets on high those who are lowly,
And those who mourn are lifted to safety.

5:5 [a]Septuagint reads *They shall not be taken from evil men;* Vulgate reads *And the armed man shall take him by violence.* [b]Septuagint reads *The might shall draw them off;* Vulgate reads *And the thirsty shall drink up their riches.*

THE MESSAGE

Dread stared me in the face, and Terror.
I was scared to death—I shook from head to foot.
A spirit glided right in front of me—
the hair on my head stood on end.
I couldn't tell what it was that appeared there—
a blur . . . and then I heard a muffled voice:

17-21 " 'How can mere mortals be more righteous than God?
How can humans be purer than their Creator?
Why, God doesn't even trust his own servants,
doesn't even cheer his angels,
So how much less these bodies composed of mud,
fragile as moths?
These bodies of ours are here today and gone tomorrow,
and no one even notices—gone without a trace.
When the tent stakes are ripped up, the tent collapses—
we die and are never the wiser for having lived.' "

DON'T BLAME FATE WHEN THINGS GO WRONG

1-7 5 "Call for help, Job, if you think anyone will answer!
To which of the holy angels will you turn?
The hot temper of a fool eventually kills him,
the jealous anger of a simpleton does her in.
I've seen it myself—seen fools putting down roots,
and then, suddenly, their houses are cursed.
Their children out in the cold, abused and exploited,
with no one to stick up for them.
Hungry people off the street plunder their harvests,
cleaning them out completely, taking thorns and all,
insatiable for everything they have.
Don't blame fate when things go wrong—
trouble doesn't come from nowhere.
It's human! Mortals are born and bred for trouble,
as certainly as sparks fly upward.

WHAT A BLESSING WHEN GOD CORRECTS YOU!

8-16 "If I were in your shoes, I'd go straight to God,
I'd throw myself on the mercy of God.
After all, he's famous for great and unexpected acts;
there's no end to his surprises.
He gives rain, for instance, across the wide earth,
sends water to irrigate the fields.
He raises up the down-and-out,
gives firm footing to those sinking in grief.

NEW KING JAMES VERSION

12He frustrates the devices of the crafty,
So that their hands cannot carry out their plans.
13He catches the wise in their own craftiness,
And the counsel of the cunning comes quickly upon them.
14They meet with darkness in the daytime,
And grope at noontime as in the night.
15But He saves the needy from the sword,
From the mouth of the mighty,
And from their hand.
16So the poor have hope,
And injustice shuts her mouth.

17"Behold, happy *is* the man whom God corrects;
Therefore do not despise the chastening of the Almighty.
18For He bruises, but He binds up;
He wounds, but His hands make whole.
19He shall deliver you in six troubles,
Yes, in seven no evil shall touch you.
20In famine He shall redeem you from death,
And in war from the power of the sword.
21You shall be hidden from the scourge of the tongue,
And you shall not be afraid of destruction when it comes.
22You shall laugh at destruction and famine,
And you shall not be afraid of the beasts of the earth.
23For you shall have a covenant with the stones of the field,
And the beasts of the field shall be at peace with you.
24You shall know that your tent *is* in peace;
You shall visit your dwelling and find nothing amiss.
25You shall also know that your descendants *shall be* many,
And your offspring like the grass of the earth.
26You shall come to the grave at a full age,
As a sheaf of grain ripens in its season.
27Behold, this we have searched out;
It *is* true.
Hear it, and know for yourself."

JOB: MY COMPLAINT IS JUST

6 Then Job answered and said:

2"Oh, that my grief were fully weighed,
And my calamity laid with it on the scales!
3For then it would be heavier than the sand of the sea—
Therefore my words have been rash.
4For the arrows of the Almighty *are* within me;
My spirit drinks in their poison;
The terrors of God are arrayed against me.
5Does the wild donkey bray when it has grass,

THE MESSAGE

He aborts the schemes of conniving crooks,
so that none of their plots come to term.
He catches the know-it-alls in their conspiracies—
all that intricate intrigue swept out with the trash!
Suddenly they're disoriented, plunged into darkness;
they can't see to put one foot in front of the other.
But the downtrodden are saved by God,
saved from the murderous plots, saved from the iron fist.
And so the poor continue to hope,
while injustice is bound and gagged.

17-19 "So, what a blessing when God steps in and corrects you!
Mind you, don't despise the discipline of Almighty God!
True, he wounds, but he also dresses the wound;
the same hand that hurts you, heals you.
From one disaster after another he delivers you;
no matter what the calamity, the evil can't touch you—

20-26 "In famine, he'll keep you from starving,
in war, from being gutted by the sword.
You'll be protected from vicious gossip
and live fearless through any catastrophe.
You'll shrug off disaster and famine,
and stroll fearlessly among wild animals.
You'll be on good terms with rocks and mountains;
wild animals will become your good friends.
You'll know that your place on earth is safe,
you'll look over your goods and find nothing amiss.
You'll see your children grow up,
your family lovely and lissome as orchard grass.
You'll arrive at your grave ripe with many good years,
like sheaves of golden grain at harvest.

27 "Yes, this is the way things are—my word of honor!
Take it to heart and you won't go wrong."

JOB REPLIES TO ELIPHAZ

GOD HAS DUMPED THE WORKS ON ME

1-7 6 Job answered:

"If my misery could be weighed,
if you could pile the whole bitter load on the scales,
It would be heavier than all the sand of the sea!
Is it any wonder that I'm screaming like a caged cat?
The arrows of God Almighty are in me,
poison arrows—and I'm poisoned all through!
God has dumped the whole works on me.
Donkeys bray and cows moo when they run out of pasture—

NEW KING JAMES VERSION

Or does the ox low over its fodder?
6Can flavorless food be eaten without salt?
Or is there *any* taste in the white of an egg?
7My soul refuses to touch them;
They *are* as loathsome food to me.

8"Oh, that I might have my request,
That God would grant *me* the thing that I long for!
9That it would please God to crush me,
That He would loose His hand and cut me off!
10Then I would still have comfort;
Though in anguish I would exult,
He will not spare;
For I have not concealed the words of the Holy One.

11"What strength do I have, that I should hope?
And what *is* my end, that I should prolong my life?
12*Is* my strength the strength of stones?
Or is my flesh bronze?
13*Is* my help not within me?
And is success driven from me?

14"To him who is afflicted, kindness *should be shown* by his friend,
Even though he forsakes the fear of the Almighty.
15My brothers have dealt deceitfully like a brook,
Like the streams of the brooks that pass away,
16Which are dark because of the ice,
And into which the snow vanishes.
17When it is warm, they cease to flow;
When it is hot, they vanish from their place.
18The paths of their way turn aside,
They go nowhere and perish.
19The caravans of Tema look,
The travelers of Sheba hope for them.
20They are disappointed because they were confident;
They come there and are confused.
21For now you are nothing,
You see terror and are afraid.
22Did I ever say, 'Bring *something* to me'?
Or, 'Offer a bribe for me from your wealth'?
23Or, 'Deliver me from the enemy's hand'?
Or, 'Redeem me from the hand of oppressors'?

24"Teach me, and I will hold my tongue;
Cause me to understand wherein I have erred.
25How forceful are right words!
But what does your arguing prove?
26Do you intend to rebuke *my* words,
And the speeches of a desperate one, *which are* as wind?
27Yes, you overwhelm the fatherless,
And you undermine your friend.

THE MESSAGE

so don't expect me to keep quiet in this.
Do you see what God has dished out for me?
It's enough to turn anyone's stomach!
Everything in me is repulsed by it—
it makes me sick.

PRESSED PAST THE LIMITS

8-13 "All I want is an answer to one prayer,
a last request to be honored:
Let God step on me—squash me like a bug,
and be done with me for good.
I'd at least have the satisfaction
of not having blasphemed the Holy God,
before being pressed past the limits.
Where's the strength to keep my hopes up?
What future do I have to keep me going?
Do you think I have nerves of steel?
Do you think I'm made of iron?
Do you think I can pull myself up by my bootstraps?
Why, I don't even have any boots!

MY SO-CALLED FRIENDS

14-23 "When desperate people give up on God Almighty,
their friends, at least, should stick with them.
But my brothers are fickle as a gulch in the desert—
one day they're gushing with water
From melting ice and snow
cascading out of the mountains,
But by midsummer they're dry,
gullies baked dry in the sun.
Travelers who spot them and go out of their way for a drink
end up in a waterless gulch and die of thirst.
Merchant caravans from Tema see them and expect water,
tourists from Sheba hope for a cool drink.
They arrive so confident—but what a disappointment!
They get there, and their faces fall!
And you, my so-called friends, are no better—there's nothing to you!
One look at a hard scene and you shrink in fear.
It's not as though I asked you for anything—
I didn't ask you for one red cent—
Nor did I beg you to go out on a limb for me.
So why all this dodging and shuffling?

24-27 "Confront me with the truth and I'll shut up,
show me where I've gone off the track.
Honest words never hurt anyone,
but what's the point of all this pious bluster?
You pretend to tell me what's wrong with my life,
but treat my words of anguish as so much hot air.
Are people mere things to you?
Are friends just items of profit and loss?

NEW KING JAMES VERSION

28Now therefore, be pleased to look at me;
For I would never lie to your face.
29Yield now, let there be no injustice!
Yes, concede, my righteousness still stands!
30Is there injustice on my tongue?
Cannot my taste discern the unsavory?

JOB: MY SUFFERING IS COMFORTLESS

7 "*Is there* not a time of hard service for man on earth?
Are not his days also like the days of a hired man?
2Like a servant who earnestly desires the shade,
And like a hired man who eagerly looks for his wages,
3So I have been allotted months of futility,
And wearisome nights have been appointed to me.
4When I lie down, I say, 'When shall I arise,
And the night be ended?'
For I have had my fill of tossing till dawn.
5My flesh is caked with worms and dust,
My skin is cracked and breaks out afresh.

6"My days are swifter than a weaver's shuttle,
And are spent without hope.
7Oh, remember that my life *is* a breath!
My eye will never again see good.
8The eye of him who sees me will see me no *more;*
While your *eyes* are upon me, I shall no longer *be.*
9*As* the cloud disappears and vanishes away,
So he who goes down to the grave does not come up.
10He shall never return to his house,
Nor shall his place know him anymore.

11"Therefore I will not restrain my mouth;
I will speak in the anguish of my spirit;
I will complain in the bitterness of my soul.
12*Am* I a sea, or a sea serpent,
That You set a guard over me?
13When I say, 'My bed will comfort me,
My couch will ease my complaint,'
14Then You scare me with dreams
And terrify me with visions,
15So that my soul chooses strangling
And death rather than my body.[a]
16I loathe *my life;*
I would not live forever.
Let me alone,
For my days *are but* a breath.

17"What *is* man, that You should exalt him,
That You should set Your heart on him,
18That You should visit him every morning,
And test him every moment?
19How long?
Will You not look away from me,
And let me alone till I swallow my saliva?

7:15 [a]Literally *my bones*

THE MESSAGE

28-30 "Look me in the eyes!
Do you think I'd lie to your face?
Think it over—no double-talk!
Think carefully—my integrity is on the line!
Can you detect anything false in what I say?
Don't you trust me to discern good from evil?"

THERE'S NOTHING TO MY LIFE

1-6 7 "Human life is a struggle, isn't it?
It's a life sentence to hard labor.
Like field hands longing for quitting time
and working stiffs with nothing to hope for but payday,
I'm given a life that meanders and goes nowhere—
months of aimlessness, nights of misery!
I go to bed and think, 'How long till I can get up?'
I toss and turn as the night drags on—and I'm fed up!
I'm covered with maggots and scabs.
My skin gets scaly and hard, then oozes with pus.
My days come and go swifter than the click of knitting needles,
and then the yarn runs out—an unfinished life!

7-10 "God, don't forget that I'm only a puff of air!
These eyes have had their last look at goodness.
And your eyes have seen the last of me;
even while you're looking, there'll be nothing left to look at.
When a cloud evaporates, it's gone for good;
those who go to the grave never come back.
They don't return to visit their families;
never again will friends drop in for coffee.

11-16 "And so I'm not keeping one bit of this quiet,
I'm laying it all out on the table;
my complaining to high heaven is bitter, but honest.
Are you going to put a muzzle on me,
the way you quiet the sea and still the storm?
If I say, 'I'm going to bed, then I'll feel better.
A little nap will lift my spirits,'
You come and so scare me with nightmares
and frighten me with ghosts
That I'd rather strangle in the bedclothes
than face this kind of life any longer.
I hate this life! Who needs any more of this?
Let me alone! There's nothing to my life—it's nothing but smoke.

17-21 "What are mortals anyway, that you bother with them,
that you even give them the time of day?
That you check up on them every morning,
looking in on them to see how they're doing?
Let up on me, will you?
Can't you even let me spit in peace?

NEW KING JAMES VERSION

20Have I sinned?
What have I done to You, O watcher of men?
Why have You set me as Your target,
So that I am a burden to myself?[a]
21Why then do You not pardon my
transgression,
And take away my iniquity?
For now I will lie down in the dust,
And You will seek me diligently,
But I *will* no longer *be*."

BILDAD: JOB SHOULD REPENT

8 Then Bildad the Shuhite answered and said:

2"How long will you speak these *things*,
And the words of your mouth *be like* a
strong wind?
3Does God subvert judgment?
Or does the Almighty pervert justice?
4If your sons have sinned against Him,
He has cast them away for their
transgression.
5If you would earnestly seek God
And make your supplication to the
Almighty,
6If you *were* pure and upright,
Surely now He would awake for you,
And prosper your rightful dwelling place.
7Though your beginning was small,
Yet your latter end would increase
abundantly.

8"For inquire, please, of the former age,
And consider the things discovered by their
fathers;
9For we *were born* yesterday, and know
nothing,
Because our days on earth *are* a shadow.
10Will they not teach you and tell you,
And utter words from their heart?

11"Can the papyrus grow up without a marsh?
Can the reeds flourish without water?
12While it *is* yet green *and* not cut down,
It withers before any *other* plant.
13So *are* the paths of all who forget God;
And the hope of the hypocrite shall perish,
14Whose confidence shall be cut off,
And whose trust *is* a spider's web.
15He leans on his house, but it does not stand.
He holds it fast, but it does not endure.
16He grows green in the sun,
And his branches spread out in his garden.

7:20 [a]Following Masoretic Text, Targum, and Vulgate; Septuagint and Jewish tradition read *to You.*

THE MESSAGE

Even suppose I'd sinned—how would that
hurt you?
You're responsible for every human
being.
Don't you have better things to do than
pick on me?
Why make a federal case out of me?
Why don't you just forgive my sins
and start me off with a clean slate?
The way things are going, I'll soon be dead.
You'll look high and low, but I won't be
around."

BILDAD'S RESPONSE

DOES GOD MESS UP?

1-7 8 Bildad from Shuhah was next to speak:

"How can you keep on talking like this?
You're talking nonsense, and noisy
nonsense at that.
Does God mess up?
Does God Almighty ever get things
backward?
It's plain that your children sinned against
him—
otherwise, why would God have
punished them?
Here's what you must do—and don't put it
off any longer:
Get down on your knees before God
Almighty.
If you're as innocent and upright as you
say,
it's not too late—he'll come running;
he'll set everything right again,
reestablish your fortunes.
Even though you're not much right now,
you'll end up better than ever.

TO HANG YOUR LIFE FROM ONE THIN THREAD

8-19 "Put the question to our ancestors,
study what they learned from their
ancestors.
For we're newcomers at this, with a lot to
learn,
and not too long to learn it.
So why not let the ancients teach you, tell
you what's what,
instruct you in what they knew from
experience?
Can mighty pine trees grow tall without
soil?
Can luscious tomatoes flourish without
water?
Blossoming flowers look great before
they're cut or picked,
but without soil or water they wither
more quickly than grass.
That's what happens to all who forget
God—
all their hopes come to nothing.
They hang their life from one thin thread,
they hitch their fate to a spider web.
One jiggle and the thread breaks,
one jab and the web collapses.
Or they're like weeds springing up in the
sunshine,
invading the garden,

NEW KING JAMES VERSION

17His roots wrap around the rock heap,
And look for a place in the stones.
18If he is destroyed from his place,
Then *it* will deny him, *saying*, 'I have not seen you.'

19"Behold, this is the joy of His way,
And out of the earth others will grow.
20Behold, God will not cast away the blameless,
Nor will He uphold the evildoers.
21He will yet fill your mouth with laughing,
And your lips with rejoicing.
22Those who hate you will be clothed with shame,
And the dwelling place of the wicked will come to nothing."[a]

JOB: THERE IS NO MEDIATOR

9 Then Job answered and said:

2"Truly I know *it is* so,
But how can a man be righteous before God?
3If one wished to contend with Him,
He could not answer Him one time out of a thousand.
4*God is* wise in heart and mighty in strength.
Who has hardened *himself* against Him and prospered?
5He removes the mountains, and they do not know
When He overturns them in His anger;
6He shakes the earth out of its place,
And its pillars tremble;
7He commands the sun, and it does not rise;
He seals off the stars;
8He alone spreads out the heavens,
And treads on the waves of the sea;
9He made the Bear, Orion, and the Pleiades,
And the chambers of the south;
10He does great things past finding out,
Yes, wonders without number.
11If He goes by me, I do not see *Him;*
If He moves past, I do not perceive Him;
12If He takes away, who can hinder Him?
Who can say to Him, 'What are You doing?'
13God will not withdraw His anger,
The allies of the proud[a] lie prostrate beneath Him.

14"How then can I answer Him,
And choose my words *to reason* with Him?
15For though I were righteous, I could not answer Him;
I would beg mercy of my Judge.
16If I called and He answered me,
I would not believe that He was listening to my voice.

8:22 [a]Literally *will not be* 9:13 [a]Hebrew *rahab*

THE MESSAGE

Spreading everywhere, overtaking the flowers,
getting a foothold even in the rocks.
But when the gardener rips them out by the roots,
the garden doesn't miss them one bit.
The sooner the godless are gone, the better;
then good plants can grow in their place.

20-22 "There's no way that God will reject a good person,
and there is no way he'll help a bad one.
God will let you laugh again;
you'll raise the roof with shouts of joy,
With your enemies thoroughly discredited,
their house of cards collapsed."

JOB CONTINUES

HOW CAN MERE MORTALS GET RIGHT WITH GOD?

1-13 9 Job continued by saying:

"So what's new? I know all this.
The question is, 'How can mere mortals get right with God?'
If we wanted to bring our case before him,
what chance would we have? Not one in a thousand!
God's wisdom is so deep, God's power so immense,
who could take him on and come out in one piece?
He moves mountains before they know what's happened,
flips them on their heads on a whim.
He gives the earth a good shaking up,
rocks it down to its very foundations.
He tells the sun, 'Don't shine,' and it doesn't;
he pulls the blinds on the stars.
All by himself he stretches out the heavens
and strides on the waves of the sea.
He designed the Big Dipper and Orion,
the Pleiades and Alpha Centauri.
We'll never comprehend all the great things he does;
his miracle-surprises can't be counted.
Somehow, though he moves right in front of me, I don't see him;
quietly but surely he's active, and I miss it.
If he steals you blind, who can stop him?
Who's going to say, 'Hey, what are you doing?'
God doesn't hold back on his anger;
even dragon-bred monsters cringe before him.

14-20 "So how could I ever argue with him,
construct a defense that would influence God?
Even though I'm innocent I could never prove it;
I can only throw myself on the Judge's mercy.
If I called on God and he himself answered me,
then, and only then, would I believe that he'd heard me.

NEW KING JAMES VERSION

[17]For He crushes me with a tempest,
And multiplies my wounds without cause.
[18]He will not allow me to catch my breath,
But fills me with bitterness.
[19]If *it is a matter* of strength, indeed *He is* strong;
And if of justice, who will appoint my day *in court?*
[20]Though I were righteous, my own mouth would condemn me;
Though I *were* blameless, it would prove me perverse.

[21]"I am blameless, yet I do not know myself;
I despise my life.
[22]It *is* all one *thing;*
Therefore I say, 'He destroys the blameless and the wicked.'
[23]If the scourge slays suddenly,
He laughs at the plight of the innocent.
[24]The earth is given into the hand of the wicked.
He covers the faces of its judges.
If it is not *He,* who else could it be?

[25]"Now my days are swifter than a runner;
They flee away, they see no good.
[26]They pass by like swift ships,
Like an eagle swooping on its prey.
[27]If I say, 'I will forget my complaint,
I will put off my sad face and wear a smile,'
[28]I am afraid of all my sufferings;
I know that You will not hold me innocent.
[29]*If* I am condemned,
Why then do I labor in vain?
[30]If I wash myself with snow water,
And cleanse my hands with soap,
[31]Yet You will plunge me into the pit,
And my own clothes will abhor me.

[32]"For *He is* not a man, as I *am,*
That I may answer Him,
And that we should go to court together.
[33]Nor is there any mediator between us,
Who may lay his hand on us both.
[34]Let Him take His rod away from me,
And do not let dread of Him terrify me.
[35]*Then* I would speak and not fear Him,
But it is not so with me.

THE MESSAGE

As it is, he knocks me about from pillar to post,
beating me up, black-and-blue, for no good reason.
He won't even let me catch my breath,
piles bitterness upon bitterness.
If it's a question of who's stronger, he wins, hands down!
If it's a question of justice, who'll serve him the subpoena?
Even though innocent, anything I say incriminates me;
blameless as I am, my defense just makes me sound worse.

IF GOD'S NOT RESPONSIBLE, WHO IS?

21-24 "Believe me, I'm blameless.
I don't understand what's going on.
I hate my life!
Since either way it ends up the same, I can only conclude
that God destroys the good right along with the bad.
When calamity hits and brings sudden death,
he folds his arms, aloof from the despair of the innocent.
He lets the wicked take over running the world,
he installs judges who can't tell right from wrong.
If he's not responsible, who is?

25-31 "My time is short—what's left of my life races off
too fast for me to even glimpse the good.
My life is going fast, like a ship under full sail,
like an eagle plummeting to its prey.
Even if I say, 'I'll put all this behind me,
I'll look on the bright side and force a smile,'
All these troubles would still be like grit in my gut
since it's clear you're not going to let up.
The verdict has already been handed down—'Guilty!'—
so what's the use of protests or appeals?
Even if I scrub myself all over
and wash myself with the strongest soap I can find,
It wouldn't last—you'd push me into a pigpen, or worse,
so nobody could stand me for the stink.

32-35 "God and I are not equals; I can't bring a case against him.
We'll never enter a courtroom as peers.
How I wish we had an arbitrator
to step in and let me get on with life—
To break God's death grip on me,
to free me from this terror so I could breathe again.
Then I'd speak up and state my case boldly.
As things stand, there is no way I can do it."

New King James Version

Job: I Would Plead with God

10 "My soul loathes my life;
I will give free course to my complaint,
I will speak in the bitterness of my soul.
2 I will say to God, 'Do not condemn me;
Show me why You contend with me.
3 *Does it* seem good to You that You should oppress,
That You should despise the work of Your hands,
And smile on the counsel of the wicked?
4 Do You have eyes of flesh?
Or do You see as man sees?
5 *Are* Your days like the days of a mortal man?
Are Your years like the days of a mighty man,
6 That You should seek for my iniquity
And search out my sin,
7 Although You know that I am not wicked,
And *there is* no one who can deliver from Your hand?

8 'Your hands have made me and fashioned me,
An intricate unity;
Yet You would destroy me.
9 Remember, I pray, that You have made me like clay.
And will You turn me into dust again?
10 Did You not pour me out like milk,
And curdle me like cheese,
11 Clothe me with skin and flesh,
And knit me together with bones and sinews?
12 You have granted me life and favor,
And Your care has preserved my spirit.

13 'And these *things* You have hidden in Your heart;
I know that this *was* with You:
14 If I sin, then You mark me,
And will not acquit me of my iniquity.
15 If I am wicked, woe to me;
Even *if* I am righteous, I cannot lift up my head.
I am full of disgrace;
See my misery!
16 If *my head* is exalted,
You hunt me like a fierce lion,
And again You show Yourself awesome against me.
17 You renew Your witnesses against me,
And increase Your indignation toward me;
Changes and war are *ever* with me.

18 'Why then have You brought me out of the womb?
Oh, that I had perished and no eye had seen me!

The Message

To Find Some Skeleton in My Closet

1 10 "I can't stand my life—I hate it!
I'm putting it all out on the table,
all the bitterness of my life—I'm holding back nothing."

2-7 Job prayed:

"Here's what I want to say:
Don't, God, bring in a verdict of guilty
without letting me know the charges you're bringing.
How does this fit into what you once called 'good'—
giving me a hard time, spurning me,
a life you shaped by your very own hands,
and then blessing the plots of the wicked?
You don't look at things the way we mortals do.
You're not taken in by appearances, are you?
Unlike us, you're not working against a deadline.
You have all eternity to work things out.
So what's this all about, anyway—this compulsion
to dig up some dirt, to find some skeleton in my closet?
You know good and well I'm not guilty.
You also know no one can help me.

8-12 "You made me like a handcrafted piece of pottery—
and now are you going to smash me to pieces?
Don't you remember how beautifully you worked my clay?
Will you reduce me now to a mud pie?
Oh, that marvel of conception as you stirred together
semen and ovum—
What a miracle of skin and bone,
muscle and brain!
You gave me life itself, and incredible love.
You watched and guarded every breath I took.

13-17 "But you never told me about this part.
I should have known that there was more to it—
That if I so much as missed a step, you'd notice and pounce,
wouldn't let me get by with a thing.
If I'm truly guilty, I'm doomed.
But if I'm innocent, it's no better—
I'm still doomed.
My belly is full of bitterness.
I'm up to my ears in a swamp of affliction.
I try to make the best of it, try to brave it out,
but you're too much for me,
relentless, like a lion on the prowl.
You line up fresh witnesses against me.
You compound your anger
and pile on the grief and pain!

18-22 "So why did you have me born?
I wish no one had ever laid eyes on me!

NEW KING JAMES VERSION

19I would have been as though I had not been.
I would have been carried from the womb to the grave.
20Are not my days few?
Cease! Leave me alone, that I may take a little comfort,
21Before I go *to the place from which* I shall not return,
To the land of darkness and the shadow of death,
22A land as dark as darkness *itself*,
As the shadow of death, without any order,
Where even the light *is* like darkness.' "

ZOPHAR URGES JOB TO REPENT

11 Then Zophar the Naamathite answered and said:

2"Should not the multitude of words be answered?
And should a man full of talk be vindicated?
3Should your empty talk make men hold their peace?
And when you mock, should no one rebuke you?
4For you have said,
"My doctrine *is* pure,
And I am clean in your eyes.'
5But oh, that God would speak,
And open His lips against you,
6That He would show you the secrets of wisdom!
For *they would* double *your* prudence.
Know therefore that God exacts from you
Less than your iniquity *deserves*.

7"Can you search out the deep things of God?
Can you find out the limits of the Almighty?
8*They are* higher than heaven—what can you do?
Deeper than Sheol—what can you know?
9Their measure *is* longer than the earth
And broader than the sea.

10"If He passes by, imprisons, and gathers *to judgment*,
Then who can hinder Him?
11For He knows deceitful men;
He sees wickedness also.
Will He not then consider *it*?
12For an empty-headed man will be wise,
When a wild donkey's colt is born a man.

13"If you would prepare your heart,
And stretch out your hands toward Him;
14If iniquity *were* in your hand, *and you* put it far away,
And would not let wickedness dwell in your tents;
15Then surely you could lift up your face without spot;
Yes, you could be steadfast, and not fear;
16Because you would forget *your* misery,
And remember *it* as waters *that have* passed away,
17And *your* life would be brighter than noonday.
Though you were dark, you would be like the morning.

THE MESSAGE

I wish I'd never lived—a stillborn,
buried without ever having breathed.
Isn't it time to call it quits on my life?
Can't you let up, and let me smile just once
Before I die and am buried,
before I'm nailed into my coffin, sealed in the ground,
And banished for good to the land of the dead,
blind in the final dark?"

ZOPHAR'S COUNSEL

HOW WISDOM LOOKS FROM THE INSIDE

1-6 11 Now it was the turn of Zophar from Naamath:

"What a flood of words! Shouldn't we put a stop to it?
Should this kind of loose talk be permitted?
Job, do you think you can carry on like this and we'll say nothing?
That we'll let you rail and mock and not step in?
You claim, 'My doctrine is sound
and my conduct impeccable.'
How I wish God would give you a piece of his mind,
tell you what's what!
I wish he'd show you how wisdom looks from the inside,
for true wisdom is mostly 'inside.'
But you can be sure of this,
you haven't gotten half of what you deserve.

7-12 "Do you think you can explain the mystery of God?
Do you think you can diagram God Almighty?
God is far higher than you can imagine,
far deeper than you can comprehend,
Stretching farther than earth's horizons,
far wider than the endless ocean.
If he happens along, throws you in jail
then hauls you into court, can you do anything about it?
He sees through vain pretensions,
spots evil a long way off—
no one pulls the wool over *his* eyes!
Hollow men, hollow women, will wise up
about the same time mules learn to talk.

REACH OUT TO GOD

13-20 "Still, if you set your heart on God
and reach out to him,
If you scrub your hands of sin
and refuse to entertain evil in your home,
You'll be able to face the world unashamed
and keep a firm grip on life, guiltless and fearless.
You'll forget your troubles;
they'll be like old, faded photographs.
Your world will be washed in sunshine,
every shadow dispersed by dayspring.

NEW KING JAMES VERSION

[18]And you would be secure, because there is hope;
Yes, you would dig *around you, and* take your rest in safety.
[19]You would also lie down, and no one would make *you* afraid;
Yes, many would court your favor.
[20]But the eyes of the wicked will fail,
And they shall not escape,
And their hope—loss of life!"

JOB ANSWERS HIS CRITICS

12 Then Job answered and said:

[2]"No doubt you *are* the people,
And wisdom will die with you!
[3]But I have understanding as well as you;
I *am* not inferior to you.
Indeed, who does not *know* such things as these?

[4]"I am one mocked by his friends,
Who called on God, and He answered him,
The just and blameless *who is* ridiculed.
[5]A lamp[a] is despised in the thought of one who is at ease;
It is made ready for those whose feet slip.
[6]The tents of robbers prosper,
And those who provoke God are secure—
In what God provides by His hand.

[7]"But now ask the beasts, and they will teach you;
And the birds of the air, and they will tell you;
[8]Or speak to the earth, and it will teach you;
And the fish of the sea will explain to you.
[9]Who among all these does not know
That the hand of the LORD has done this,
[10]In whose hand *is* the life of every living thing,
And the breath of all mankind?
[11]Does not the ear test words
And the mouth taste its food?
[12]Wisdom *is* with aged men,
And with length of days, understanding.

[13]"With Him *are* wisdom and strength,
He has counsel and understanding.
[14]If He breaks *a thing* down, it cannot be rebuilt;
If He imprisons a man, there can be no release.
[15]If He withholds the waters, they dry up;
If He sends them out, they overwhelm the earth.
[16]With Him *are* strength and prudence.
The deceived and the deceiver *are* His.

12:5 [a]Or *disaster*

THE MESSAGE

Full of hope, you'll relax, confident again;
you'll look around, sit back, and take it easy.
Expansive, without a care in the world,
you'll be hunted out by many for your blessing.
But the wicked will see none of this.
They're headed down a dead-end road
with nothing to look forward to—nothing."

JOB ANSWERS ZOPHAR

PUT YOUR EAR TO THE EARTH

1-3 **12** Job answered:

"I'm sure you speak for all the experts,
and when you die there'll be no one left to tell us how to live.
But don't forget that I also have a brain—
I don't intend to play second fiddle to you.
It doesn't take an expert to know these things.

4-6 "I'm ridiculed by my friends:
'So that's the man who had conversations with God!'
Ridiculed without mercy:
'Look at the man who never did wrong!'
It's easy for the well-to-do to point their fingers in blame,
for the well-fixed to pour scorn on the strugglers.
Crooks reside safely in high-security houses,
insolent blasphemers live in luxury;
they've bought and paid for a god who'll protect them.

7-12 "But ask the animals what they think—let them teach you;
let the birds tell you what's going on.
Put your ear to the earth—learn the basics.
Listen—the fish in the ocean will tell you their stories.
Isn't it clear that they all know and agree
that GOD is sovereign, that he holds all things in his hand—
Every living soul, yes,
every breathing creature?
Isn't this all just common sense,
as common as the sense of taste?
Do you think the elderly have a corner on wisdom,
that you have to grow old before you understand life?

FROM GOD WE LEARN HOW TO LIVE

13-25 "True wisdom and real power belong to God;
from him we learn how to live,
and also what to live for.
If he tears something down, it's down for good;
if he locks people up, they're locked up for good.
If he holds back the rain, there's a drought;
if he lets it loose, there's a flood.
Strength and success belong to God;
both deceived and deceiver must answer to him.

NEW KING JAMES VERSION

17He leads counselors away plundered,
And makes fools of the judges.
18He loosens the bonds of kings,
And binds their waist with a belt.
19He leads princes[a] away plundered,
And overthrows the mighty.
20He deprives the trusted ones of speech,
And takes away the discernment of the elders.
21He pours contempt on princes,
And disarms the mighty.
22He uncovers deep things out of darkness,
And brings the shadow of death to light.
23He makes nations great, and destroys them;
He enlarges nations, and guides them.
24He takes away the understanding[a] of the chiefs of the people of the earth,
And makes them wander in a pathless wilderness.
25They grope in the dark without light,
And He makes them stagger like a drunken *man.*

13 "Behold, my eye has seen all *this,*
My ear has heard and understood it.
2What you know, I also know;
I *am* not inferior to you.
3But I would speak to the Almighty,
And I desire to reason with God.
4But you forgers of lies,
You *are* all worthless physicians.
5Oh, that you would be silent,
And it would be your wisdom!
6Now hear my reasoning,
And heed the pleadings of my lips.
7Will you speak wickedly for God,
And talk deceitfully for Him?
8Will you show partiality for Him?
Will you contend for God?
9Will it be well when He searches you out?
Or can you mock Him as one mocks a man?
10He will surely rebuke you
If you secretly show partiality.
11Will not His excellence make you afraid,
And the dread of Him fall upon you?
12Your platitudes *are* proverbs of ashes,
Your defenses are defenses of clay.

13"Hold your peace with me, and let me speak,
Then let come on me what *may!*
14Why do I take my flesh in my teeth,
And put my life in my hands?
15Though He slay me, yet will I trust Him.
Even so, I will defend my own ways before Him.
16He also *shall* be my salvation,

12:19 [a]Literally *priests,* but not in a technical sense **12:24** [a]Literally *heart*

THE MESSAGE

He strips experts of their vaunted credentials,
exposes judges as witless fools.
He divests kings of their royal garments,
then ties a rag around their waists.
He strips priests of their robes,
and fires high officials from their jobs.
He forces trusted sages to keep silence,
deprives elders of their good sense and wisdom.
He dumps contempt on famous people,
disarms the strong and mighty.
He shines a spotlight into caves of darkness,
hauls deepest darkness into the noonday sun.
He makes nations rise and then fall,
builds up some and abandons others.
He robs world leaders of their reason,
and sends them off into no-man's-land.
They grope in the dark without a clue,
lurching and staggering like drunks."

I'M TAKING MY CASE TO GOD

1-5 13 "Yes, I've seen all this with my own eyes,
heard and understood it with my very own ears.
Everything you know, I know,
so I'm not taking a backseat to any of you.
I'm taking my case straight to God Almighty;
I've had it with you—I'm going directly to God.
You graffiti my life with lies.
You're a bunch of pompous quacks!
I wish you'd shut your mouths—
silence is your only claim to wisdom.

6-12 "Listen now while I make my case,
consider my side of things for a change.
Or are you going to keep on lying 'to do God a service'?
to make up stories 'to get him off the hook'?
Why do you always take his side?
Do you think he needs a lawyer to defend himself?
How would you fare if you were in the dock?
Your lies might convince a jury—but would they convince *God*?
He'd reprimand you on the spot
if he detected a bias in your witness.
Doesn't his splendor put you in awe?
Aren't you afraid to speak cheap lies before him?
Your wise sayings are knickknack wisdom,
good for nothing but gathering dust.

13-19 "So hold your tongue while I have my say,
then I'll take whatever I have coming to me.
Why do I go out on a limb like this
and take my life in my hands?
Because even if he killed me, I'd keep on hoping.
I'd defend my innocence to the very end.
Just wait, this is going to work out for the best—my salvation!

NEW KING JAMES VERSION

For a hypocrite could not come before Him.
17Listen carefully to my speech,
And to my declaration with your ears.
18See now, I have prepared *my* case,
I know that I shall be vindicated.
19Who *is* he *who* will contend with me?
If now I hold my tongue, I perish.

JOB'S DESPONDENT PRAYER

20"Only two *things* do not do to me,
Then I will not hide myself from You:
21Withdraw Your hand far from me,
And let not the dread of You make me afraid.
22Then call, and I will answer;
Or let me speak, then You respond to me.
23How many *are* my iniquities and sins?
Make me know my transgression and my sin.
24Why do You hide Your face,
And regard me as Your enemy?
25Will You frighten a leaf driven to and fro?
And will You pursue dry stubble?
26For You write bitter things against me,
And make me inherit the iniquities of my youth.
27You put my feet in the stocks,
And watch closely all my paths.
You set a limit[a] for the soles of my feet.

28"*Man*[a] decays like a rotten thing,
Like a garment that is moth-eaten.

14 "Man *who is* born of woman
Is of few days and full of trouble.
2He comes forth like a flower and fades away;
He flees like a shadow and does not continue.
3And do You open Your eyes on such a one,
And bring me[a] to judgment with Yourself?
4Who can bring a clean *thing* out of an unclean?
No one!
5Since his days *are* determined,
The number of his months *is* with You;
You have appointed his limits, so that he cannot pass.
6Look away from him that he may rest,
Till like a hired man he finishes his day.

7"For there is hope for a tree,
If it is cut down, that it will sprout again,
And that its tender shoots will not cease.
8Though its root may grow old in the earth,
And its stump may die in the ground,
9*Yet* at the scent of water it will bud
And bring forth branches like a plant.

13:27 [a]Literally *inscribe a print* 13:28 [a]Literally *He* 14:3 [a]Septuagint, Syriac, and Vulgate read *him.*

THE MESSAGE

If I were guilt-stricken do you think I'd be doing this—
laying myself on the line before God?
You'd better pay attention to what I'm telling you,
listen carefully with both ears.
Now that I've laid out my defense,
I'm sure that I'll be acquitted.
Can anyone prove charges against me?
I've said my piece. I rest my case.

WHY DOES GOD STAY HIDDEN AND SILENT?

20-27 "Please, God, I have two requests;
grant them so I'll know I count with you:
First, lay off the afflictions;
the terror is too much for me.
Second, address me directly so I can answer you,
or let me speak and then you answer me.
How many sins have been charged against me?
Show me the list—how bad is it?
Why do you stay hidden and silent?
Why treat me like I'm your enemy?
Why kick me around like an old tin can?
Why beat a dead horse?
You compile a long list of mean things about me,
even hold me accountable for the sins of my youth.
You hobble me so I can't move about.
You watch every move I make,
and brand me as a dangerous character.

28 "Like something rotten, human life fast decomposes,
like a moth-eaten shirt or a mildewed blouse."

IF WE DIE, WILL WE LIVE AGAIN?

1-17 14 "We're all adrift in the same boat:
too few days, too many troubles.
We spring up like wildflowers in the desert and then wilt,
transient as the shadow of a cloud.
Do you occupy your time with such fragile wisps?
Why even bother hauling me into court?
There's nothing much to us to start with;
how do you expect us to amount to anything?
Mortals have a limited life span.
You've already decided how long we'll live—
you set the boundary and no one can cross it.
So why not give us a break? Ease up!
Even ditchdiggers get occasional days off.
For a tree there is always hope.
Chop it down and it still has a chance—
its roots can put out fresh sprouts.
Even if its roots are old and gnarled,
its stump long dormant,
At the first whiff of water it comes to life,
buds and grows like a sapling.

NEW KING JAMES VERSION

[10]But man dies and is laid away;
Indeed he breathes his last
And where *is* he?
[11]*As* water disappears from the sea,
And a river becomes parched and dries up,
[12]So man lies down and does not rise.
Till the heavens *are* no more,
They will not awake
Nor be roused from their sleep.

[13]"Oh, that You would hide me in the grave,
That You would conceal me until Your wrath is past,
That You would appoint me a set time, and remember me!
[14]If a man dies, shall he live *again*?
All the days of my hard service I will wait,
Till my change comes.
[15]You shall call, and I will answer You;
You shall desire the work of Your hands.
[16]For now You number my steps,
But do not watch over my sin.
[17]My transgression *is* sealed up in a bag,
And You cover[a] my iniquity.

[18]"But *as* a mountain falls *and* crumbles away,
And *as* a rock is moved from its place;
[19]*As* water wears away stones,
And as torrents wash away the soil of the earth;
So You destroy the hope of man.
[20]You prevail forever against him, and he passes on;
You change his countenance and send him away.
[21]His sons come to honor, and he does not know *it;*
They are brought low, and he does not perceive *it.*
[22]But his flesh will be in pain over it,
And his soul will mourn over it."

ELIPHAZ ACCUSES JOB OF FOLLY

15 Then Eliphaz the Temanite answered and said:

[2]"Should a wise man answer with empty knowledge,
And fill himself with the east wind?
[3]Should he reason with unprofitable talk,
Or by speeches with which he can do no good?
[4]Yes, you cast off fear,
And restrain prayer before God.
[5]For your iniquity teaches your mouth,
And you choose the tongue of the crafty.
[6]Your own mouth condemns you, and not I;
Yes, your own lips testify against you.

[7]"*Are* you the first man *who* was born?
Or were you made before the hills?
[8]Have you heard the counsel of God?
Do you limit wisdom to yourself?

14:17 [a]Literally *plaster over*

THE MESSAGE

But men and women? They die and stay dead.
They breathe their last, and that's it.
Like lakes and rivers that have dried up,
parched reminders of what once was,
So mortals lie down and never get up,
never wake up again—never.
Why don't you just bury me alive,
get me out of the way until your anger cools?
But don't leave me there!
Set a date when you'll see me again.
If we humans die, will we live again?
That's my question.
All through these difficult days I keep hoping,
waiting for the final change—for resurrection!
Homesick with longing for the creature you made,
you'll call—and I'll answer!
You'll watch over every step I take,
but you won't keep track of my missteps.
My sins will be stuffed in a sack
and thrown into the sea—sunk in deep ocean.

18-22 "Meanwhile, mountains wear down
and boulders break up,
Stones wear smooth
and soil erodes,
as you relentlessly grind down our hope.
You're too much for us.
As always, you get the last word.
We don't like it and our faces show it,
but you send us off anyway.
If our children do well for themselves, we never know it;
if they do badly, we're spared the hurt.
Body and soul, that's it for us—
a lifetime of pain, a lifetime of sorrow."

ELIPHAZ ATTACKS AGAIN

YOU TRIVIALIZE RELIGION

1-16 15 Eliphaz of Teman spoke a second time:

"If you were truly wise, would you sound so much like a
windbag, belching hot air?
Would you talk nonsense in the middle of a serious argument,
babbling baloney?
Look at you! You trivialize religion,
turn spiritual conversation into empty gossip.
It's your sin that taught you to talk this way.
You chose an education in fraud.
Your own words have exposed your guilt.
It's nothing I've said—you've incriminated yourself!
Do you think you're the first person to have to deal with these things?
Have you been around as long as the hills?
Were you listening in when God planned all this?
Do you think you're the only one who knows anything?

NEW KING JAMES VERSION

[9]What do you know that we do not know?
What do you understand that *is* not in us?
[10]Both the gray-haired and the aged *are* among us,
Much older than your father.
[11]*Are* the consolations of God too small for you,
And the word *spoken* gently[a] with you?
[12]Why does your heart carry you away,
And what do your eyes wink at,
[13]That you turn your spirit against God,
And let *such* words go out of your mouth?

[14]"What *is* man, that he could be pure?
And *he who is* born of a woman, that he could be righteous?
[15]If *God* puts no trust in His saints,
And the heavens are not pure in His sight,
[16]How much less man, *who is* abominable and filthy,
Who drinks iniquity like water!

[17]"I will tell you, hear me;
What I have seen I will declare,
[18]What wise men have told,
Not hiding *anything received* from their fathers,
[19]To whom alone the land was given,
And no alien passed among them:
[20]The wicked man writhes with pain all *his* days,
And the number of years is hidden from the oppressor.
[21]Dreadful sounds *are* in his ears;
In prosperity the destroyer comes upon him.
[22]He does not believe that he will return from darkness,
For a sword is waiting for him.
[23]He wanders about for bread, *saying,* 'Where *is it?*'
He knows that a day of darkness is ready at his hand.
[24]Trouble and anguish make him afraid;
They overpower him, like a king ready for battle.
[25]For he stretches out his hand against God,
And acts defiantly against the Almighty,
[26]Running stubbornly against Him
With his strong, embossed shield.

[27]"Though he has covered his face with his fatness,
And made *his* waist heavy with fat,
[28]He dwells in desolate cities,
In houses which no one inhabits,
Which are destined to become ruins.
[29]He will not be rich,
Nor will his wealth continue,
Nor will his possessions overspread the earth.
[30]He will not depart from darkness;
The flame will dry out his branches,
And by the breath of His mouth he will go away.

15:11 [a]Septuagint reads *a secret thing.*

THE MESSAGE

What do you know that we don't know?
What insights do you have that we've missed?
Gray beards and white hair back us up—
old folks who've been around a lot longer than you.
Are God's promises not enough for you,
spoken so gently and tenderly?
Why do you let your emotions take over,
lashing out and spitting fire,
Pitting your whole being against God
by letting words like this come out of your mouth?
Do you think it's possible for any mere mortal to be sinless in God's sight,
for anyone born of a human mother to get it all together?
Why, God can't even trust his holy angels.
He sees the flaws in the very heavens themselves,
So how much less we humans, smelly and foul,
who lap up evil like water?

ALWAYS AT ODDS WITH GOD

17-26 "I've a thing or two to tell you, so listen up!
I'm letting you in on my views;
It's what wise men and women have always taught,
holding nothing back from what *they* were taught
By their parents, back in the days
when they had this land all to themselves:
Those who live by their own rules, not God's, can expect nothing but trouble,
and the longer they live, the worse it gets.
Every little sound terrifies them.
Just when they think they have it made, disaster strikes.
They despair of things ever getting better—
they're on the list of people for whom things always turn out for the worst.
They wander here and there,
never knowing where the next meal is coming from—
every day is doomsday!
They live in constant terror,
always with their backs up against the wall
Because they insist on shaking their fists at God,
defying God Almighty to his face,
Always and ever at odds with God,
always on the defensive.

27-35 "Even if they're the picture of health,
trim and fit and youthful,
They'll end up living in a ghost town
sleeping in a hovel not fit for a dog,
a ramshackle shack.
They'll never get ahead,
never amount to a hill of beans.
And then death—don't think they'll escape that!
They'll end up shriveled weeds,
brought down by a puff of God's breath.

NEW KING JAMES VERSION

31Let him not trust in futile *things*, deceiving
himself,
For futility will be his reward.
32It will be accomplished before his time,
And his branch will not be green.
33He will shake off his unripe grape like a
vine,
And cast off his blossom like an olive tree.
34For the company of hypocrites *will be*
barren,
And fire will consume the tents of bribery.
35They conceive trouble and bring forth
futility;
Their womb prepares deceit."

JOB REPROACHES HIS PITILESS FRIENDS

16 Then Job answered and said:

2"I have heard many such things;
Miserable comforters *are* you all!
3Shall words of wind have an end?
Or what provokes you that you answer?
4I also could speak as you *do*,
If your soul were in my soul's place.
I could heap up words against you,
And shake my head at you;
5*But* I would strengthen you with my mouth,
And the comfort of my lips would relieve
your grief.

6"Though I speak, my grief is not relieved;
And *if* I remain silent, how am I eased?
7But now He has worn me out;
You have made desolate all my company.
8You have shriveled me up,
And it is a witness *against me;*
My leanness rises up against me
And bears witness to my face.
9He tears *me* in His wrath, and hates me;
He gnashes at me with His teeth;
My adversary sharpens His gaze on me.
10They gape at me with their mouth,
They strike me reproachfully on the cheek,
They gather together against me.
11God has delivered me to the ungodly,
And turned me over to the hands of the
wicked.
12I was at ease, but He has shattered me;
He also has taken *me* by my neck, and
shaken me to pieces;
He has set me up for His target,
13His archers surround me.
He pierces my heart[a] and does not pity;
He pours out my gall on the ground.
14He breaks me with wound upon wound;
He runs at me like a warrior.[a]

15"I have sewn sackcloth over my skin,
And laid my head[a] in the dust.

16:13 [a]Literally *kidneys* **16:14** [a]Vulgate reads *giant*. **16:15** [a]Literally *horn*

THE MESSAGE

There's a lesson here: Whoever invests in
lies,
gets lies for interest,
Paid in full before the due date.
Some investment!
They'll be like fruit frost-killed before it
ripens,
like buds sheared off before they bloom.
The godless are fruitless—a barren crew;
a life built on bribes goes up in smoke.
They have sex with sin and give birth to
evil.
Their lives are wombs for breeding
deceit."

JOB DEFENDS HIMSELF

IF YOU WERE IN MY SHOES

1-5 16 Then Job defended himself:

"I've had all I can take of your talk.
What a bunch of miserable comforters!
Is there no end to your windbag speeches?
What's your problem that you go on and
on like this?
If you were in my shoes,
I could talk just like you.
I could put together a terrific harangue
and really let you have it.
But I'd never do that. I'd console and
comfort,
make things better, not worse!

6-14 "When I speak up, I feel no better;
if I say nothing, that doesn't help either.
I feel worn down.
God, you have wasted me totally—me
and my family!
You've shriveled me like a dried prune,
showing the world that you're against me.
My gaunt face stares back at me from the
mirror,
a mute witness to your treatment of me.
Your anger tears at me,
your teeth rip me to shreds,
your eyes burn holes in me—God, my
enemy!
People take one look at me and gasp.
Contemptuous, they slap me around
and gang up against me.
And God just stands there and lets them do
it,
lets wicked people do what they want
with me.
I was contentedly minding my business
when God beat me up.
He grabbed me by the neck and threw
me around.
He set me up as his target,
then rounded up archers to shoot at me.
Merciless, they shot me full of arrows;
bitter bile poured from my gut to the
ground.
He burst in on me, onslaught after
onslaught,
charging me like a mad bull.

15-17 "I sewed myself a shroud and wore it like a
shirt;
I lay facedown in the dirt.

NEW KING JAMES VERSION

[16]My face is flushed from weeping,
And on my eyelids *is* the shadow of death;
[17]Although no violence *is* in my hands,
And my prayer *is* pure.

[18]"O earth, do not cover my blood,
And let my cry have no *resting* place!
[19]Surely even now my witness *is* in heaven,
And my evidence *is* on high.
[20]My friends scorn me;
My eyes pour out *tears* to God.
[21]Oh, that one might plead for a man with God,
As a man *pleads* for his neighbor!
[22]For when a few years are finished,
I shall go the way of no return.

JOB PRAYS FOR RELIEF

17 "My spirit is broken,
My days are extinguished,
The grave *is ready* for me.
[2]*Are* not mockers with me?
And does not my eye dwell on their provocation?

[3]"Now put down a pledge for me with Yourself.
Who *is* he *who* will shake hands with me?
[4]For You have hidden their heart from understanding;
Therefore You will not exalt *them.*
[5]He who speaks flattery to *his* friends,
Even the eyes of his children will fail.

[6]"But He has made me a byword of the people,
And I have become one in whose face men spit.
[7]My eye has also grown dim because of sorrow,
And all my members *are* like shadows.
[8]Upright *men* are astonished at this,
And the innocent stirs himself up against the hypocrite.
[9]Yet the righteous will hold to his way,
And he who has clean hands will be stronger and stronger.

[10]"But please, come back again, all of you,[a]
For I shall not find *one* wise *man* among you.
[11]My days are past,
My purposes are broken off,
Even the thoughts of my heart.
[12]They change the night into day;
'The light *is* near,' *they say,* in the face of darkness.
[13]If I wait *for* the grave *as* my house,
If I make my bed in the darkness,

17:10 [a]Following some Hebrew manuscripts, Septuagint, Syriac, and Vulgate; Masoretic Text and Targum read *all of them.*

THE MESSAGE

Now my face is blotched red from weeping;
look at the dark shadows under my eyes,
Even though I've never hurt a soul
and my prayers are sincere!

THE ONE WHO REPRESENTS MORTALS BEFORE GOD

18-22 "O Earth, don't cover up the wrong done to me!
Don't muffle my cry!
There must be Someone in heaven who knows the truth about me,
in highest heaven, some Attorney who can clear my name—
My Champion, my Friend,
while I'm weeping my eyes out before God.
I appeal to the One who represents mortals before God
as a neighbor stands up for a neighbor.

"Only a few years are left
before I set out on the road of no return."

1-2 17 "My spirit is broken,
my days used up,
my grave dug and waiting.
See how these mockers close in on me?
How long do I have to put up with their insolence?

3-5 "O God, pledge your support for me.
Give it to me in writing, with your signature.
You're the only one who can do it!
These people are so useless!
You know firsthand how stupid they can be.
You wouldn't let them have the last word, would you?
Those who betray their own friends
leave a legacy of abuse to their children.

6-8 "God, you've made me the talk of the town—
people spit in my face;
I can hardly see from crying so much;
I'm nothing but skin and bones.
Decent people can't believe what they're seeing;
the good-hearted wake up and insist I've given up on God.

9 "But principled people hold tight, keep a firm grip on life,
sure that their clean, pure hands will get stronger and stronger!

10-16 "Maybe you'd all like to start over,
to try it again, the bunch of you.
So far I haven't come across one scrap
of wisdom in anything you've said.
My life's about over. All my plans are smashed,
all my hopes are snuffed out—
My hope that night would turn into day,
my hope that dawn was about to break.
If all I have to look forward to is a home in the graveyard,
if my only hope for comfort is a well-built coffin,

NEW KING JAMES VERSION

[14]If I say to corruption, 'You *are* my father,'
And to the worm, 'You *are* my mother and my sister,'
[15]Where then *is* my hope?
As for my hope, who can see it?
[16]*Will* they go down to the gates of Sheol?
Shall *we have* rest together in the dust?"

BILDAD: THE WICKED ARE PUNISHED

18 Then Bildad the Shuhite answered and said:

[2]"How long *till* you put an end to words?
Gain understanding, and afterward we will speak.
[3]Why are we counted as beasts,
And regarded as stupid in your sight?
[4]You who tear yourself in anger,
Shall the earth be forsaken for you?
Or shall the rock be removed from its place?

[5]"The light of the wicked indeed goes out,
And the flame of his fire does not shine.
[6]The light is dark in his tent,
And his lamp beside him is put out.
[7]The steps of his strength are shortened,
And his own counsel casts him down.
[8]For he is cast into a net by his own feet,
And he walks into a snare.
[9]The net takes *him* by the heel,
And a snare lays hold of him.
[10]A noose *is* hidden for him on the ground,
And a trap for him in the road.
[11]Terrors frighten him on every side,
And drive him to his feet.
[12]His strength is starved,
And destruction *is* ready at his side.
[13]It devours patches of his skin;
The firstborn of death devours his limbs.
[14]He is uprooted from the shelter of his tent,
And they parade him before the king of terrors.
[15]They dwell in his tent *who are* none of his;
Brimstone is scattered on his dwelling.
[16]His roots are dried out below,
And his branch withers above.
[17]The memory of him perishes from the earth,
And he has no name among the renowned.[a]
[18]He is driven from light into darkness,
And chased out of the world.
[19]He has neither son nor posterity among his people,
Nor any remaining in his dwellings.
[20]Those in the west are astonished at his day,
As those in the east are frightened.
[21]Surely such *are* the dwellings of the wicked,
And this *is* the place *of him who* does not know God."

18:17 [a]Literally *before the outside*, meaning distinguished, famous

THE MESSAGE

If a family reunion means going six feet under,
and the only family that shows up is worms,
Do you call that hope?
Who on earth could find any hope in that?
No. If hope and I are to be buried together,
I suppose you'll all come to the double funeral!"

BILDAD'S SECOND ATTACK

PLUNGED FROM LIGHT INTO DARKNESS

1-4 **18** Bildad from Shuhah chimed in:

"How monotonous these word games are getting!
Get serious! We need to get down to business.
Why do you treat your friends like slow-witted animals?
You look down on us as if we don't know anything.
Why are you working yourself up like this?
Do you want the world redesigned to suit you?
Should reality be suspended to accommodate you?

5-21 "Here's the rule: The light of the wicked is put out.
Their flame dies down and is extinguished.
Their house goes dark—
every lamp in the place goes out.
Their strong strides weaken, falter;
they stumble into their own traps.
They get all tangled up
in their own red tape,
Their feet are grabbed and caught,
their necks in a noose.
They trip on ropes they've hidden,
and fall into pits they've dug themselves.
Terrors come at them from all sides.
They run helter-skelter.
The hungry grave is ready
to gobble them up for supper,
To lay them out for a gourmet meal,
a treat for ravenous Death.
They are snatched from their home sweet home
and marched straight to the death house.
Their lives go up in smoke;
acid rain soaks their ruins.
Their roots rot
and their branches wither.
They'll never again be remembered—
nameless in unmarked graves.
They are plunged from light into darkness,
banished from the world.
And they leave empty-handed—not one single child—
nothing to show for their life on this earth.
Westerners are aghast at their fate,
easterners are horrified:
'Oh no! So this is what happens to perverse people.
This is how the God-ignorant end up!' "

NEW KING JAMES VERSION

JOB TRUSTS IN HIS REDEEMER

19 Then Job answered and said:

2 "How long will you torment my soul,
And break me in pieces with words?
3 These ten times you have reproached me;
You are not ashamed *that* you have wronged me.[a]
4 And if indeed I have erred,
My error remains with me.
5 If indeed you exalt *yourselves* against me,
And plead my disgrace against me,
6 Know then that God has wronged me,
And has surrounded me with His net.

7 "If I cry out concerning wrong, I am not heard.
If I cry aloud, *there is* no justice.
8 He has fenced up my way, so that I cannot pass;
And He has set darkness in my paths.
9 He has stripped me of my glory,
And taken the crown *from* my head.
10 He breaks me down on every side,
And I am gone;
My hope He has uprooted like a tree.
11 He has also kindled His wrath against me,
And He counts me as *one of* His enemies.
12 His troops come together
And build up their road against me;
They encamp all around my tent.

13 "He has removed my brothers far from me,
And my acquaintances are completely estranged from me.
14 My relatives have failed,
And my close friends have forgotten me.
15 Those who dwell in my house, and my maidservants,
Count me as a stranger;
I am an alien in their sight.
16 I call my servant, but he gives no answer;
I beg him with my mouth.
17 My breath is offensive to my wife,
And I am repulsive to the children of my own body.
18 Even young children despise me;
I arise, and they speak against me.
19 All my close friends abhor me,
And those whom I love have turned against me.
20 My bone clings to my skin and to my flesh,
And I have escaped by the skin of my teeth.

21 "Have pity on me, have pity on me, O you my friends,
For the hand of God has struck me!
22 Why do you persecute me as God *does*,
And are not satisfied with my flesh?

23 "Oh, that my words were written!
Oh, that they were inscribed in a book!
24 That they were engraved on a rock
With an iron pen and lead, forever!

19:3 [a]A Jewish tradition reads *make yourselves strange to me.*

THE MESSAGE

JOB ANSWERS BILDAD

I CALL FOR HELP AND NO ONE BOTHERS

1-6 19 Job answered:

"How long are you going to keep battering away at me,
pounding me with these harangues?
Time after time after time you jump all over me.
Do you have no conscience, abusing me like this?
Even if I have, somehow or other, gotten off the track,
what business is that of yours?
Why do you insist on putting me down,
using my troubles as a stick to beat me?
Tell it to God—he's the one behind all this,
he's the one who dragged me into this mess.

7-12 "Look at me—I shout 'Murder!' and I'm ignored;
I call for help and no one bothers to stop.
God threw a barricade across my path—I'm stymied;
he turned out all the lights—I'm stuck in the dark.
He destroyed my reputation,
robbed me of all self-respect.
He tore me apart piece by piece—I'm ruined!
Then he yanked out hope by the roots.
He's angry with me—oh, how he's angry!
He treats me like his worst enemy.
He has launched a major campaign against me,
using every weapon he can think of,
coming at me from all sides at once.

I KNOW THAT GOD LIVES

13-20 "God alienated my family from me;
everyone who knows me avoids me.
My relatives and friends have all left;
houseguests forget I ever existed.
The servant girls treat me like a bum off the street,
look at me like they've never seen me before.
I call my attendant and he ignores me,
ignores me even though I plead with him.
My wife can't stand to be around me anymore.
I'm repulsive to my family.
Even street urchins despise me;
when I come out, they taunt and jeer.
Everyone I've ever been close to abhors me;
my dearest loved ones reject me.
I'm nothing but a bag of bones;
my life hangs by a thread.

21-22 "Oh, friends, dear friends, take pity on me.
God has come down hard on me!
Do you have to be hard on me, too?
Don't you ever tire of abusing me?

23-27 "If only my words were written in a book—
better yet, chiseled in stone!

NEW KING JAMES VERSION

25For I know *that* my Redeemer lives,
And He shall stand at last on the earth;
26And after my skin is destroyed, this *I know,*
That in my flesh I shall see God,
27Whom I shall see for myself,
And my eyes shall behold, and not another.
How my heart yearns within me!
28If you should say, 'How shall we persecute him?'—
Since the root of the matter is found in me,
29Be afraid of the sword for yourselves;
For wrath *brings* the punishment of the sword,
That you may know *there is* a judgment."

ZOPHAR'S SERMON ON THE WICKED MAN

20 Then Zophar the Naamathite answered and said:

2"Therefore my anxious thoughts make me answer,
Because of the turmoil within me.
3I have heard the rebuke that reproaches me,
And the spirit of my understanding causes me to answer.

4"Do you *not* know this of old,
Since man was placed on earth,
5That the triumphing of the wicked is short,
And the joy of the hypocrite is *but* for a moment?
6Though his haughtiness mounts up to the heavens,
And his head reaches to the clouds,
7*Yet* he will perish forever like his own refuse;
Those who have seen him will say, 'Where is he?'
8He will fly away like a dream, and not be found;
Yes, he will be chased away like a vision of the night.
9The eye *that* saw him will *see him* no more,
Nor will his place behold him anymore.
10His children will seek the favor of the poor,
And his hands will restore his wealth.
11His bones are full of his youthful vigor,
But it will lie down with him in the dust.

12"Though evil is sweet in his mouth,
And he hides it under his tongue,
13*Though* he spares it and does not forsake it,
But still keeps it in his mouth,
14*Yet* his food in his stomach turns sour;
It becomes cobra venom within him.
15He swallows down riches
And vomits them up again;
God casts them out of his belly.

THE MESSAGE

Still, I know that God lives—the One who gives me back my life—
and eventually he'll take his stand on earth.
And I'll see him—even though I get skinned alive!—
see God myself, with my very own eyes.
Oh, how I long for that day!

28-29 "If you're thinking, 'How can we get through to him,
get him to see that his trouble is all his own fault?'
Forget it. Start worrying about *yourselves.*
Worry about your own sins and God's coming judgment,
for judgment is most certainly on the way."

ZOPHAR ATTACKS JOB—THE SECOND ROUND

SAVORING EVIL AS A DELICACY

1-3 20 Zophar from Naamath again took his turn:

"I can't believe what I'm hearing!
You've put my teeth on edge, my stomach in a knot.
How dare you insult my intelligence like this!
Well, here's a piece of my mind!

4-11 "Don't you even know the basics,
how things have been since the earliest days,
when Adam and Eve were first placed on earth?
The good times of the wicked are short-lived;
godless joy is only momentary.
The evil might become world famous,
strutting at the head of the celebrity parade,
But still end up in a pile of dung.
Acquaintances look at them with disgust and say, 'What's that?'
They fly off like a dream that can't be remembered,
like a shadowy illusion that vanishes in the light.
Though once notorious public figures, now they're nobodies,
unnoticed, whether they come or go.
Their children will go begging on skid row,
and they'll have to give back their ill-gotten gain.
Right in the prime of life,
and youthful and vigorous, they'll die.

12-19 "They savor evil as a delicacy,
roll it around on their tongues,
Prolong the flavor, a dalliance in decadence—
real gourmets of evil!
But then they get stomach cramps,
a bad case of food poisoning.
They gag on all that rich food;
God makes them vomit it up.

NEW KING JAMES VERSION

16He will suck the poison of cobras;
The viper's tongue will slay him.
17He will not see the streams,
The rivers flowing with honey and cream.
18He will restore that for which he labored,
And will not swallow *it* down;
From the proceeds of business
He will get no enjoyment.
19For he has oppressed *and* forsaken the poor,
He has violently seized a house which he did not build.

20"Because he knows no quietness in his heart,[a]
He will not save anything he desires.
21Nothing is left for him to eat;
Therefore his well-being will not last.
22In his self-sufficiency he will be in distress;
Every hand of misery will come against him.
23*When* he is about to fill his stomach,
God will cast on him the fury of His wrath,
And will rain *it* on him while he is eating.
24He will flee from the iron weapon;
A bronze bow will pierce him through.
25It is drawn, and comes out of the body;
Yes, the glittering *point comes* out of his gall.
Terrors *come* upon him;
26Total darkness *is* reserved for his treasures.
An unfanned fire will consume him;
It shall go ill with him who is left in his tent.
27The heavens will reveal his iniquity,
And the earth will rise up against him.
28The increase of his house will depart,
And his goods will flow away in the day of His wrath.
29This *is* the portion from God for a wicked man,
The heritage appointed to him by God."

JOB'S DISCOURSE ON THE WICKED

21 Then Job answered and said:

2"Listen carefully to my speech,
And let this be your consolation.
3Bear with me that I may speak,
And after I have spoken, keep mocking.

4"As for me, *is* my complaint against man?
And if *it were*, why should I not be impatient?
5Look at me and be astonished;
Put *your* hand over *your* mouth.
6Even when I remember I am terrified,
And trembling takes hold of my flesh.
7Why do the wicked live *and* become old,
Yes, become mighty in power?

20:20 [a]Literally *belly*

THE MESSAGE

They gorge on evil, make a diet of that poison—
a deadly diet—and it kills them.
No quiet picnics for them beside gentle streams
with fresh-baked bread and cheese, and tall, cool drinks.
They spit out their food half-chewed,
unable to relax and enjoy anything they've worked for.
And why? Because they exploited the poor,
took what never belonged to them.

20-29 "Such God-denying people are never content with what they have or who they are;
their greed drives them relentlessly.
They plunder everything
but they can't hold on to any of it.
Just when they think they have it all,
disaster strikes;
they're served up a plate full of misery.
When they've filled their bellies with that,
God gives them a taste of his anger,
and they get to chew on that for a while.
As they run for their lives from one disaster,
they run smack into another.
They're knocked around from pillar to post,
beaten to within an inch of their lives.
They're trapped in a house of horrors,
and see their loot disappear down a black hole.
Their lives are a total loss—
not a penny to their name, not so much as a bean.
God will strip them of their sin-soaked clothes
and hang their dirty laundry out for all to see.
Life is a complete wipeout for them,
nothing surviving God's wrath.
There! That's God's blueprint for the wicked—
what they have to look forward to."

JOB'S RESPONSE
WHY DO THE WICKED HAVE IT SO GOOD?

1-3 21 Job replied:

"Now listen to me carefully, please listen,
at least do me the favor of listening.
Put up with me while I have my say—
then you can mock me later to your heart's content.

4-16 "It's not *you* I'm complaining to—it's *God*.
Is it any wonder I'm getting fed up with his silence?
Take a good look at me. Aren't you appalled by what's happened?
No! Don't say anything. I can do without your comments.
When I look back, I go into shock,
my body is racked with spasms.
Why do the wicked have it so good,
live to a ripe old age and get rich?

NEW KING JAMES VERSION

8Their descendants are established with
them in their sight,
And their offspring before their eyes.
9Their houses *are* safe from fear,
Neither *is* the rod of God upon them.
10Their bull breeds without failure;
Their cow calves without miscarriage.
11They send forth their little ones like a flock,
And their children dance.
12They sing to the tambourine and harp,
And rejoice to the sound of the flute.
13They spend their days in wealth,
And in a moment go down to the grave.[a]
14Yet they say to God, 'Depart from us,
For we do not desire the knowledge of Your
ways.
15Who *is* the Almighty, that we should serve
Him?
And what profit do we have if we pray to
Him?'
16Indeed their prosperity *is* not in their hand;
The counsel of the wicked is far from me.

17"How often is the lamp of the wicked put
out?
How often does their destruction come upon
them,
The sorrows *God* distributes in His anger?
18They are like straw before the wind,
And like chaff that a storm carries away.
19*They say,* 'God lays up one's[a] iniquity for his
children';
Let Him recompense him, that he may know
it.
20Let his eyes see his destruction,
And let him drink of the wrath of the
Almighty.
21For what does he care about his household
after him,
When the number of his months is cut in
half?

22"Can *anyone* teach God knowledge,
Since He judges those on high?
23One dies in his full strength,
Being wholly at ease and secure;
24His pails[a] are full of milk,
And the marrow of his bones is moist.
25Another man dies in the bitterness of his
soul,
Never having eaten with pleasure.
26They lie down alike in the dust,
And worms cover them.

27"Look, I know your thoughts,
And the schemes *with which* you would
wrong me.
28For you say,
'Where *is* the house of the prince?
And where *is* the tent,[a]
The dwelling place of the wicked?'
29Have you not asked those who travel the
road?
And do you not know their signs?

21:13 [a]Or *Sheol* **21:19** [a]Literally *his* **21:24** [a]Septuagint and Vulgate read *bowels;* Syriac reads *sides;* Targum reads *breasts.* **21:28** [a]Vulgate omits *the tent.*

THE MESSAGE

They get to see their children succeed,
get to watch and enjoy their
grandchildren.
Their homes are peaceful and free from fear;
they never experience God's disciplining
rod.
Their bulls breed with great vigor
and their cows calve without fail.
They send their children out to play
and watch them frolic like spring lambs.
They make music with fiddles and flutes,
have good times singing and dancing.
They have a long life on easy street,
and die painlessly in their sleep.
They say to God, 'Get lost!
We've no interest in you or your ways.
Why should we have dealings with God
Almighty?
What's there in it for us?'
But they're wrong, dead wrong—they're
not gods.
It's beyond me how they can carry on
like this!

17-21 "Still, how often does it happen that the
wicked fail,
or disaster strikes,
or they get their just deserts?
How often are they blown away by bad
luck?
Not very often.
You might say, 'God is saving up the
punishment for their children.'
I say, 'Give it to them right now so they'll
know what they've done!'
They deserve to experience the effects of
their evil,
feel the full force of God's wrath
firsthand.
What do they care what happens to their
families
after they're safely tucked away in the
grave?

FANCY FUNERALS WITH ALL THE TRIMMINGS

22-26 "But who are we to tell God how to run his
affairs?
He's dealing with matters that are way
over our heads.
Some people die in the prime of life,
with everything going for them—
fat and sassy.
Others die bitter and bereft,
never getting a taste of happiness.
They're laid out side by side in the cemetery,
where the worms can't tell one from the
other.

27-33 "I'm not deceived. I know what you're up to,
the plans you're cooking up to bring me
down.
Naively you claim that the castles of
tyrants fall to pieces,
that the achievements of the wicked
collapse.
Have you ever asked world travelers how
they see it?
Have you not listened to their stories

NEW KING JAMES VERSION

30For the wicked are reserved for the day of doom;
They shall be brought out on the day of wrath.
31Who condemns his way to his face?
And who repays him *for what* he has done?
32Yet he shall be brought to the grave,
And a vigil kept over the tomb.
33The clods of the valley shall be sweet to him;
Everyone shall follow him,
As countless *have gone* before him.
34How then can you comfort me with empty words,
Since falsehood remains in your answers?"

ELIPHAZ ACCUSES JOB OF WICKEDNESS

22 Then Eliphaz the Temanite answered and said:

2"Can a man be profitable to God,
Though he who is wise may be profitable to himself?
3*Is it* any pleasure to the Almighty that you are righteous?
Or *is it* gain *to Him* that you make your ways blameless?

4"Is it because of your fear of Him that He corrects you,
And enters into judgment with you?
5*Is* not your wickedness great,
And your iniquity without end?
6For you have taken pledges from your brother for no reason,
And stripped the naked of their clothing.
7You have not given the weary water to drink,
And you have withheld bread from the hungry.
8But the mighty man possessed the land,
And the honorable man dwelt in it.
9You have sent widows away empty,
And the strength of the fatherless was crushed.
10Therefore snares *are* all around you,
And sudden fear troubles you,
11Or darkness *so that* you cannot see;
And an abundance of water covers you.

12"Is not God in the height of heaven?
And see the highest stars, how lofty they are!
13And you say, 'What does God know?
Can He judge through the deep darkness?
14Thick clouds cover Him, so that He cannot see,
And He walks above the circle of heaven.'

THE MESSAGE

Of evil men and women who got off scot-free,
who never had to pay for their wickedness?
Did anyone ever confront them with their crimes?
Did they ever have to face the music?
Not likely—they're given fancy funerals
with all the trimmings,
Gently lowered into expensive graves,
with everyone telling lies about how wonderful they were.

34 "So how do you expect me to get any comfort from your nonsense?
Your so-called comfort is a tissue of lies."

ELIPHAZ ATTACKS JOB—THE THIRD ROUND

COME TO TERMS WITH GOD

1-11 22 Once again Eliphaz the Temanite took up his theme:

"Are any of us strong enough to give God a hand,
or smart enough to give him advice?
So what if you were righteous—would God Almighty even notice?
Even if you gave a perfect performance, do you think he'd applaud?
Do you think it's because he cares about your purity
that he's disciplining you, putting you on the spot?
Hardly! It's because you're a first-class moral failure,
because there's no end to your sins.
When people came to you for help,
you took the shirts off their backs,
exploited their helplessness.
You wouldn't so much as give a drink to the thirsty,
or food, not even a scrap, to the hungry.
And there you sat, strong and honored by everyone,
surrounded by immense wealth!
You turned poor widows away from your door;
heartless, you crushed orphans.
Now *you're* the one trapped in terror,
paralyzed by fear.
Suddenly the tables have turned!
How do you like living in the dark,
sightless,
up to your neck in flood waters?

12-14 "You agree, don't you, that God is in charge?
He runs the universe—just look at the stars!
Yet you dare raise questions: 'What does God know?
From that distance and darkness, how can he judge?
He roams the heavens wrapped in clouds,
so how can he see us?'

NEW KING JAMES VERSION

15Will you keep to the old way
Which wicked men have trod,
16Who were cut down before their time,
Whose foundations were swept away by a flood?
17They said to God, 'Depart from us!
What can the Almighty do to them?'[a]
18Yet He filled their houses with good *things;*
But the counsel of the wicked is far from me.

19"The righteous see *it* and are glad,
And the innocent laugh at them:
20'Surely our adversaries[a] are cut down,
And the fire consumes their remnant.'

21"Now acquaint yourself with Him, and be at peace;
Thereby good will come to you.
22Receive, please, instruction from His mouth,
And lay up His words in your heart.
23If you return to the Almighty, you will be built up;
You will remove iniquity far from your tents.
24Then you will lay your gold in the dust,
And the *gold* of Ophir among the stones of the brooks.
25Yes, the Almighty will be your gold[a]
And your precious silver;
26For then you will have your delight in the Almighty,
And lift up your face to God.
27You will make your prayer to Him,
He will hear you,
And you will pay your vows.
28You will also declare a thing,
And it will be established for you;
So light will shine on your ways.
29When they cast *you* down, and you say,
'Exaltation *will come!*'
Then He will save the humble *person.*
30He will *even* deliver one who is not innocent;
Yes, he will be delivered by the purity of your hands."

JOB PROCLAIMS GOD'S RIGHTEOUS JUDGMENTS

23 Then Job answered and said:

2"Even today my complaint is bitter;
My[a] hand is listless because of my groaning.
3Oh, that I knew where I might find Him,
That I might come to His seat!
4I would present *my* case before Him,
And fill my mouth with arguments.
5I would know the words *which* He would answer me,
And understand what He would say to me.
6Would He contend with me in His great power?
No! But He would take *note* of me.
7There the upright could reason with Him,
And I would be delivered forever from my Judge.

22:17 [a]Septuagint and Syriac read *us.* **22:20** [a]Septuagint reads *substance.* **22:25** [a]The ancient versions suggest *defense;* Hebrew reads *gold* as in verse 24. **23:2** [a]Following Masoretic Text, Targum, and Vulgate; Septuagint and Syriac read *His.*

THE MESSAGE

15-18 "Are you going to persist in that tired old line
that wicked men and women have always used?
Where did it get them? They died young,
flash floods sweeping them off to their doom.
They told God, 'Get lost!
What good is God Almighty to us?'
And yet it was God who gave them everything they had.
It's beyond me how they can carry on like this!

19-20 "Good people see bad people crash, and call for a celebration.
Relieved, they crow,
'At last! Our enemies—wiped out.
Everything they had and stood for is up in smoke!'

21-25 "Give in to God, come to terms with him
and everything will turn out just fine.
Let him tell you what to do;
take his words to heart.
Come back to God Almighty
and he'll rebuild your life.
Clean house of everything evil.
Relax your grip on your money
and abandon your gold-plated luxury.
God Almighty will be your treasure,
more wealth than you can imagine.

26-30 "You'll take delight in God, the Mighty One,
and look to him joyfully, boldly.
You'll pray to him and he'll listen;
he'll help you do what you've promised.
You'll decide what you want and it will happen;
your life will be bathed in light.
To those who feel low you'll say, 'Chin up! Be brave!'
and God will save them.
Yes, even the guilty will escape,
escape through God's grace in your life."

JOB'S DEFENSE

I'M COMPLETELY IN THE DARK

1-7 23 Job replied:

"I'm not letting up—I'm standing my ground.
My complaint is legitimate.
God has no right to treat me like this—
it isn't fair!
If I knew where on earth to find him,
I'd go straight to him.
I'd lay my case before him face-to-face,
give him all my arguments firsthand.
I'd find out exactly what he's thinking,
discover what's going on in his head.
Do you think he'd dismiss me or bully me?
No, he'd take me seriously.
He'd see a straight-living man standing before him;
my Judge would acquit me for good of all charges.

NEW KING JAMES VERSION

8"Look, I go forward, but He is not *there,*
And backward, but I cannot perceive Him;
9When He works on the left hand, I cannot behold *Him;*
When He turns to the right hand, I cannot see *Him.*
10But He knows the way that I take;
When He has tested me, I shall come forth as gold.
11My foot has held fast to His steps;
I have kept His way and not turned aside.
12I have not departed from the commandment of His lips;
I have treasured the words of His mouth
More than my necessary *food.*

13"But He *is* unique, and who can make Him change?
And *whatever* His soul desires, *that* He does.
14For He performs *what is* appointed for me,
And many such *things are* with Him.
15Therefore I am terrified at His presence;
When I consider *this,* I am afraid of Him.
16For God made my heart weak,
And the Almighty terrifies me;
17Because I was not cut off from the presence of darkness,
And He did *not* hide deep darkness from my face.

JOB COMPLAINS OF VIOLENCE ON THE EARTH

24 "*Since* times are not hidden from the Almighty,
Why do those who know Him see not His days?

2"*Some* remove landmarks;
They seize flocks violently and feed *on them;*
3They drive away the donkey of the fatherless;
They take the widow's ox as a pledge.
4They push the needy off the road;
All the poor of the land are forced to hide.
5Indeed, *like* wild donkeys in the desert,
They go out to their work, searching for food.
The wilderness *yields* food for them *and* for *their* children.
6They gather their fodder in the field
And glean in the vineyard of the wicked.
7They spend the night naked, without clothing,
And have no covering in the cold.
8They are wet with the showers of the mountains,
And huddle around the rock for want of shelter.

9"*Some* snatch the fatherless from the breast,
And take a pledge from the poor.
10They cause *the poor* to go naked, without clothing;
And they take away the sheaves from the hungry.
11They press out oil within their walls,
And tread winepresses, yet suffer thirst.
12The dying groan in the city,
And the souls of the wounded cry out;
Yet God does not charge *them* with wrong.

THE MESSAGE

8-9 "I travel East looking for him—I find no one;
then West, but not a trace;
I go North, but he's hidden his tracks;
then South, but not even a glimpse.

10-12 "But he knows where I am and what I've done.
He can cross-examine me all he wants,
and I'll pass the test with honors.
I've followed him closely, my feet in his footprints,
not once swerving from his way.
I've obeyed every word he's spoken,
and not just obeyed his advice—I've *treasured* it.

13-17 "But he is singular and sovereign. Who can argue with him?
He does what he wants, when he wants to.
He'll complete in detail what he's decided about me,
and whatever else he determines to do.
Is it any wonder that I dread meeting him?
Whenever I think about it, I get scared all over again.
God makes my heart sink!
God Almighty gives me the shudders!
I'm completely in the dark,
I can't see my hand in front of my face."

AN ILLUSION OF SECURITY

1-12 24 "But if Judgment Day isn't hidden from the Almighty,
why are we kept in the dark?
There are people out there getting by with murder—
stealing and lying and cheating.
They rip off the poor
and exploit the unfortunate,
Push the helpless into the ditch,
bully the weak so that they fear for their lives.
The poor, like stray dogs and cats,
scavenge for food in back alleys.
They sort through the garbage of the rich,
eke out survival on handouts.
Homeless, they shiver through cold nights on the street;
they've no place to lay their heads.
Exposed to the weather, wet and frozen,
they huddle in makeshift shelters.
Nursing mothers have their babies snatched from them;
the infants of the poor are kidnapped and sold.
They go about patched and threadbare;
even the hard workers go hungry.
No matter how backbreaking their labor,
they can never make ends meet.
People are dying right and left, groaning in torment.
The wretched cry out for help
and God does nothing, acts like nothing's wrong!

NEW KING JAMES VERSION

13"There are those who rebel against the light;
They do not know its ways
Nor abide in its paths.
14The murderer rises with the light;
He kills the poor and needy;
And in the night he is like a thief.
15The eye of the adulterer waits for the twilight,
Saying, 'No eye will see me';
And he disguises *his* face.
16In the dark they break into houses
Which they marked for themselves in the daytime;
They do not know the light.
17For the morning is the same to them as the shadow of death;
If *someone* recognizes *them,*
They are in the terrors of the shadow of death.

18"They *should be* swift on the face of the waters,
Their portion *should be* cursed in the earth,
So that no *one would* turn into the way of their vineyards.
19As drought and heat consume the snow waters,
So the grave[a] *consumes those who* have sinned.
20The womb *should* forget him,
The worm *should* feed sweetly on him;
He *should* be remembered no more,
And wickedness *should* be broken like a tree.
21For he preys on the barren *who* do not bear,
And does no good for the widow.

22"But *God* draws the mighty away with His power;
He rises up, but no *man* is sure of life.
23He gives them security, and they rely *on it;*
Yet His eyes *are* on their ways.
24They are exalted for a little while,
Then they are gone.
They are brought low;
They are taken out of the way like all *others;*
They dry out like the heads of grain.

25"Now if *it is* not *so,* who will prove me a liar,
And make my speech worth nothing?"

BILDAD: HOW CAN MAN BE RIGHTEOUS?

25 Then Bildad the Shuhite answered and said:

2"Dominion and fear *belong* to Him;
He makes peace in His high places.
3Is there any number to His armies?
Upon whom does His light not rise?
4How then can man be righteous before God?
Or how can he be pure *who is* born of a woman?
5If even the moon does not shine,
And the stars are not pure in His sight,
6How much less man, *who is* a maggot,
And a son of man, *who is* a worm?"

24:19 [a]Or *Sheol*

THE MESSAGE

13-17 "Then there are those who avoid light at all costs,
who scorn the light-filled path.
When the sun goes down, the murderer gets up—
kills the poor and robs the defenseless.
Sexual predators can't wait for nightfall,
thinking, 'No one can see us now.'
Burglars do their work at night,
but keep well out of sight through the day.
They want nothing to do with light.
Deep darkness is morning for that bunch;
they make the terrors of darkness their companions in crime.

18-25 "They are scraps of wood floating on the water—
useless, cursed junk, good for nothing.
As surely as snow melts under the hot, summer sun,
sinners disappear in the grave.
The womb has forgotten them, worms have relished them—
nothing that is evil lasts.
Unscrupulous,
they prey on those less fortunate.
However much they strut and flex their muscles,
there's nothing to them. They're hollow.
They may have an illusion of security,
but God has his eye on them.
They may get their brief successes,
but then it's over, nothing to show for it.
Like yesterday's newspaper,
they're used to wrap up the garbage.
You're free to try to prove me a liar,
but you won't be able to do it."

BILDAD'S THIRD ATTACK

EVEN THE STARS AREN'T PERFECT IN GOD'S EYES

1-6 25 Bildad the Shuhite again attacked Job:

"God is sovereign, God is fearsome—
everything in the cosmos fits and works in his plan.
Can anyone count his angel armies?
Is there any place where his light doesn't shine?
How can a mere mortal presume to stand up to God?
How can an ordinary person pretend to be guiltless?
Why, even the moon has its flaws,
even the stars aren't perfect in God's eyes,
So how much less, plain men and women—
slugs and maggots by comparison!"

NEW KING JAMES VERSION

JOB: MAN'S FRAILTY AND GOD'S MAJESTY

26 But Job answered and said:

2 "How have you helped *him who is* without
power?
How have you saved the arm *that has* no
strength?
3 How have you counseled *one who has* no
wisdom?
And *how* have you declared sound advice to
many?
4 To whom have you uttered words?
And whose spirit came from you?

5 "The dead tremble,
Those under the waters and those
inhabiting them.
6 Sheol *is* naked before Him,
And Destruction has no covering.
7 He stretches out the north over empty
space;
He hangs the earth on nothing.
8 He binds up the water in His thick clouds,
Yet the clouds are not broken under it.
9 He covers the face of *His* throne,
And spreads His cloud over it.
10 He drew a circular horizon on the face of
the waters,
At the boundary of light and darkness.
11 The pillars of heaven tremble,
And are astonished at His rebuke.
12 He stirs up the sea with His power,
And by His understanding He breaks up the
storm.
13 By His Spirit He adorned the heavens;
His hand pierced the fleeing serpent.
14 Indeed these *are* the mere edges of His
ways,
And how small a whisper we hear of Him!
But the thunder of His power who can
understand?"

JOB MAINTAINS HIS INTEGRITY

27 Moreover Job continued his discourse, and
said:

2 "*As* God lives, *who* has taken away my
justice,
And the Almighty, *who* has made my soul
bitter,
3 As long as my breath *is* in me,
And the breath of God in my nostrils,
4 My lips will not speak wickedness,
Nor my tongue utter deceit.
5 Far be it from me
That I should say you are right;
Till I die I will not put away my integrity
from me.
6 My righteousness I hold fast, and will not let
it go;
My heart shall not reproach *me* as long as I
live.

7 "May my enemy be like the wicked,
And he who rises up against me like the
unrighteous.

THE MESSAGE

JOB'S DEFENSE

GOD SETS A BOUNDARY BETWEEN LIGHT AND DARKNESS

1-4 26 Job answered:

"Well, you've certainly been a great help to
a helpless man!
You came to the rescue just in the nick of
time!
What wonderful advice you've given to a
mixed-up man!
What amazing insights you've provided!
Where in the world did you learn all this?
How did you become so inspired?

5-14 "All the buried dead are in torment,
and all who've been drowned in the
deep, deep sea.
Hell is ripped open before God,
graveyards dug up and exposed.
He spreads the skies over unformed space,
hangs the earth out in empty space.
He pours water into cumulus cloud-bags
and the bags don't burst.
He makes the moon wax and wane,
putting it through its phases.
He draws the horizon out over the ocean,
sets a boundary between light and
darkness.
Thunder crashes and rumbles in the skies.
Listen! It's God raising his voice!
By his power he stills sea storms,
by his wisdom he tames sea monsters.
With one breath he clears the sky,
with one finger he crushes the sea
serpent.
And this is only the beginning,
a mere whisper of his rule.
Whatever would we do if he *really* raised
his voice!"

NO PLACE TO HIDE

1-6 27 Having waited for Zophar, Job now
resumed his defense:

"God-Alive! He's denied me justice!
God Almighty! He's ruined my life!
But for as long as I draw breath,
and for as long as God breathes life into
me,
I refuse to say one word that isn't true.
I refuse to confess to any charge that's
false.
There is no way I'll ever agree to your
accusations.
I'll not deny my integrity even if it costs
me my life.
I'm holding fast to my integrity and not
loosening my grip—
and, believe me, I'll never regret it.

7-10 "Let my enemy be exposed as wicked!
Let my adversary be proven guilty!

NEW KING JAMES VERSION

8For what is the hope of the hypocrite,
Though he may gain *much*,
If God takes away his life?
9Will God hear his cry
When trouble comes upon him?
10Will he delight himself in the Almighty?
Will he always call on God?

11"I will teach you about the hand of God;
What *is* with the Almighty I will not
conceal.
12Surely all of you have seen *it*;
Why then do you behave with complete
nonsense?

13"This is the portion of a wicked man with
God,
And the heritage of oppressors, received
from the Almighty:
14If his children are multiplied, *it is* for the
sword;
And his offspring shall not be satisfied with
bread.
15Those who survive him shall be buried in
death,
And their[a] widows shall not weep,
16Though he heaps up silver like dust,
And piles up clothing like clay—
17He may pile *it* up, but the just will wear *it*,
And the innocent will divide the silver.
18He builds his house like a moth,[a]
Like a booth *which* a watchman makes.
19The rich man will lie down,
But not be gathered *up*;[a]
He opens his eyes,
And he *is* no more.
20Terrors overtake him like a flood;
A tempest steals him away in the night.
21The east wind carries him away, and he is
gone;
It sweeps him out of his place.
22It hurls against him and does not spare;
He flees desperately from its power.
23*Men* shall clap their hands at him,
And shall hiss him out of his place.

JOB'S DISCOURSE ON WISDOM

28 "Surely there is a mine for silver,
And a place *where* gold is refined.
2Iron is taken from the earth,
And copper *is* smelted *from* ore.
3*Man* puts an end to darkness,
And searches every recess
For ore in the darkness and the shadow of
death.

27:15 [a]Literally *his* **27:18** [a]Following Masoretic Text and Vulgate; Septuagint and Syriac read *spider* (compare 8:14); Targum reads *decay*. **27:19** [a]Following Masoretic Text and Targum; Septuagint and Syriac read *But shall not add* (that is, do it again); Vulgate reads *But take away nothing*.

THE MESSAGE

What hope do people without God have
when life is cut short?
when God puts an end to life?
Do you think God will listen to their cry
for help
when disaster hits?
What interest have they ever shown in the
Almighty?
Have they ever been known to pray
before?

11-12 "I've given you a clear account of God in
action,
suppressed nothing regarding God
Almighty.
The evidence is right before you. You can
all see it for yourselves,
so why do you keep talking nonsense?

13-23 "I'll quote your own words back to you:

" 'This is how God treats the wicked,
this is what evil people can expect from
God Almighty:
Their children—all of them—will die
violent deaths;
they'll never have enough bread to put
on the table.
They'll be wiped out by the plague,
and none of the widows will shed a tear
when they're gone.
Even if they make a lot of money
and are resplendent in the latest
fashions,
It's the good who will end up wearing the
clothes
and the decent who will divide up the
money.
They build elaborate houses
that won't survive a single winter.
They go to bed wealthy
and wake up poor.
Terrors pour in on them like flash floods—
a tornado snatches them away in the
middle of the night,
A cyclone sweeps them up—gone!
Not a trace of them left, not even a
footprint.
Catastrophes relentlessly pursue them;
they run this way and that, but there's no
place to hide—
Pummeled by the weather,
blown to kingdom come by the storm.' "

WHERE DOES WISDOM COME FROM?

1-11 28 "We all know how silver seams the
rocks,
we've seen the stuff from which gold is
refined,
We're aware of how iron is dug out of the
ground
and copper is smelted from rock.
Miners penetrate the earth's darkness,
searching the roots of the mountains for
ore,
digging away in the suffocating
darkness.

NEW KING JAMES VERSION

4He breaks open a shaft away from people;
In places forgotten by feet
They hang far away from men;
They swing to and fro.
5*As for* the earth, from it comes bread,
But underneath it is turned up as by fire;
6Its stones *are* the source of sapphires,
And it contains gold dust.
7*That* path no bird knows,
Nor has the falcon's eye seen it.
8The proud lions[a] have not trodden it,
Nor has the fierce lion passed over it.
9He puts his hand on the flint;
He overturns the mountains at the roots.
10He cuts out channels in the rocks,
And his eye sees every precious thing.
11He dams up the streams from trickling;
What is hidden he brings forth to light.

12"But where can wisdom be found?
And where *is* the place of understanding?
13Man does not know its value,
Nor is it found in the land of the living.
14The deep says, '*It is* not in me';
And the sea says, '*It is* not with me.'
15It cannot be purchased for gold,
Nor can silver be weighed *for* its price.
16It cannot be valued in the gold of Ophir,
In precious onyx or sapphire.
17Neither gold nor crystal can equal it,
Nor can it be exchanged for jewelry of fine gold.
18No mention shall be made of coral or quartz,
For the price of wisdom *is* above rubies.
19The topaz of Ethiopia cannot equal it,
Nor can it be valued in pure gold.

20"From where then does wisdom come?
And where *is* the place of understanding?
21It is hidden from the eyes of all living,
And concealed from the birds of the air.
22Destruction and Death say,
'We have heard a report about it with our ears.'
23God understands its way,
And He knows its place.
24For He looks to the ends of the earth,
And sees under the whole heavens,
25To establish a weight for the wind,
And apportion the waters by measure.
26When He made a law for the rain,
And a path for the thunderbolt,
27Then He saw *wisdom*[a] and declared it;
He prepared it, indeed, He searched it out.
28And to man He said,
'Behold, the fear of the Lord, that *is* wisdom,
And to depart from evil *is* understanding.' "

28:8 [a]Literally *sons of pride,* figurative of the great lions
28:27 [a]Literally *it*

THE MESSAGE

Far from civilization, far from the traffic,
they cut a shaft,
and are lowered into it by ropes.
Earth's surface is a field for grain,
but its depths are a forge
Firing sapphires from stones
and chiseling gold from rocks.
Vultures are blind to its riches,
hawks never lay eyes on it.
Wild animals are oblivious to it,
lions don't know it's there.
Miners hammer away at the rock,
they uproot the mountains.
They tunnel through the rock
and find all kinds of beautiful gems.
They discover the origins of rivers,
and bring earth's secrets to light.

12-19 "But where, oh where, will they find Wisdom?
Where does Insight hide?
Mortals don't have a clue,
haven't the slightest idea where to look.
Earth's depths say, 'It's not here';
ocean deeps echo, 'Never heard of it.'
It can't be bought with the finest gold;
no amount of silver can get it.
Even famous Ophir gold can't buy it,
not even diamonds and sapphires.
Neither gold nor emeralds are comparable;
extravagant jewelry can't touch it.
Pearl necklaces and ruby bracelets—why bother?
None of this is even a down payment on Wisdom!
Pile gold and African diamonds as high as you will,
they can't hold a candle to Wisdom.

20-22 "So where does Wisdom come from?
And where does Insight live?
It can't be found by looking, no matter how deep you dig, no matter how high you fly.
If you search through the graveyard and question the dead,
they say, 'We've only heard rumors of it.'

23-28 "God alone knows the way to Wisdom,
he knows the exact place to find it.
He knows where everything is on earth,
he sees everything under heaven.
After he commanded the winds to blow
and measured out the waters,
Arranged for the rain
and set off explosions of thunder and lightning,
He focused on Wisdom,
made sure it was all set and tested and ready.
Then he addressed the human race: 'Here it is!
Fear-of-the-Lord—that's Wisdom,
and Insight means shunning evil.' "

NEW KING JAMES VERSION

JOB'S SUMMARY DEFENSE

29 Job further continued his discourse, and said:

2"Oh, that I were as *in* months past,
As *in* the days *when* God watched over me;
3When His lamp shone upon my head,
And when by His light I walked *through* darkness;
4Just as I was in the days of my prime,
When the friendly counsel of God *was* over my tent;
5When the Almighty *was* yet with me,
When my children *were* around me;
6When my steps were bathed with cream,[a]
And the rock poured out rivers of oil for me!

7"When I went out to the gate by the city,
When I took my seat in the open square,
8The young men saw me and hid,
And the aged arose *and* stood;
9The princes refrained from talking,
And put *their* hand on their mouth;
10The voice of nobles was hushed,
And their tongue stuck to the roof of their mouth.
11When the ear heard, then it blessed me,
And when the eye saw, then it approved me;
12Because I delivered the poor who cried out,
The fatherless and *the one who* had no helper.
13The blessing of a perishing *man* came upon me,
And I caused the widow's heart to sing for joy.
14I put on righteousness, and it clothed me;
My justice *was* like a robe and a turban.
15I *was* eyes to the blind,
And I *was* feet to the lame.
16I *was* a father to the poor,
And I searched out the case *that* I did not know.
17I broke the fangs of the wicked,
And plucked the victim from his teeth.

18"Then I said, 'I shall die in my nest,
And multiply *my* days as the sand.
19My root *is* spread out to the waters,
And the dew lies all night on my branch.
20My glory *is* fresh within me,
And my bow is renewed in my hand.'

21"*Men* listened to me and waited,
And kept silence for my counsel.
22After my words they did not speak again,
And my speech settled on them *as dew.*
23They waited for me *as* for the rain,
And they opened their mouth wide *as* for the spring rain.
24*If* I mocked at them, they did not believe *it,*
And the light of my countenance they did not cast down.
25I chose the way for them, and sat as chief;
So I dwelt as a king in the army,
As one *who* comforts mourners.

29:6 [a]Masoretic Text reads *wrath;* ancient versions and some Hebrew manuscripts read *cream* (compare 20:17).

THE MESSAGE

WHEN GOD WAS STILL BY MY SIDE

1-6 29 Job now resumed his response:

"Oh, how I long for the good old days,
when God took such very good care of me.
He always held a lamp before me
and I walked through the dark by its light.
Oh, how I miss those golden years
when God's friendship graced my home,
When the Mighty One was still by my side
and my children were all around me,
When everything was going my way,
and nothing seemed too difficult.

7-20 "When I walked downtown
and sat with my friends in the public square,
Young and old greeted me with respect;
I was honored by everyone in town.
When I spoke, everyone listened;
they hung on my every word.
People who knew me spoke well of me;
my reputation went ahead of me.
I was known for helping people in trouble
and standing up for those who were down on their luck.
The dying blessed me,
and the bereaved were cheered by my visits.
All my dealings with people were good.
I was known for being fair to everyone I met.
I was eyes to the blind
and feet to the lame,
Father to the needy,
and champion of abused aliens.
I grabbed street thieves by the scruff of the neck
and made them give back what they'd stolen.
I thought, 'I'll die peacefully in my own bed,
grateful for a long and full life,
A life deep-rooted and well-watered,
a life limber and dew-fresh,
My soul suffused with glory
and my body robust until the day I die.'

21-25 "Men and women listened when I spoke,
hung expectantly on my every word.
After I spoke, they'd be quiet,
taking it all in.
They welcomed my counsel like spring rain,
drinking it all in.
When I smiled at them, they could hardly believe it;
their faces lit up, their troubles took wing!
I was their leader, establishing the mood
and setting the pace by which they lived.
Where I led, they followed."

NEW KING JAMES VERSION

30 "But now they mock at me, *men* younger than I,
Whose fathers I disdained to put with the dogs of my flock.
2 Indeed, what *profit* is the strength of their hands to me?
Their vigor has perished.
3 *They are* gaunt from want and famine,
Fleeing late to the wilderness, desolate and waste,
4 Who pluck mallow by the bushes,
And broom tree roots *for* their food.
5 They were driven out from among *men*,
They shouted at them as *at* a thief.
6 *They had* to live in the clefts of the valleys,
In caves of the earth and the rocks.
7 Among the bushes they brayed,
Under the nettles they nestled.
8 *They were* sons of fools,
Yes, sons of vile men;
They were scourged from the land.

9 "And now I am their taunting song;
Yes, I am their byword.
10 They abhor me, they keep far from me;
They do not hesitate to spit in my face.
11 Because He has loosed my[a] bowstring and afflicted me,
They have cast off restraint before me.
12 At *my* right *hand* the rabble arises;
They push away my feet,
And they raise against me their ways of destruction.
13 They break up my path,
They promote my calamity;
They have no helper.
14 They come as broad breakers;
Under the ruinous storm they roll along.
15 Terrors are turned upon me;
They pursue my honor as the wind,
And my prosperity has passed like a cloud.

16 "And now my soul is poured out because of my *plight;*
The days of affliction take hold of me.
17 My bones are pierced in me at night,
And my gnawing pains take no rest.
18 By great force my garment is disfigured;
It binds me about as the collar of my coat.
19 He has cast me into the mire,
And I have become like dust and ashes.

20 "I cry out to You, but You do not answer me;
I stand up, and You regard me.
21 *But* You have become cruel to me;
With the strength of Your hand You oppose me.
22 You lift me up to the wind and cause me to ride *on it;*
You spoil my success.
23 For I know *that* You will bring me *to* death,
And *to* the house appointed for all living.

30:11 [a]Following Masoretic Text, Syriac, and Targum; Septuagint and Vulgate read *His*.

THE MESSAGE

THE PAIN NEVER LETS UP

1-8 30 "But no longer. Now I'm the butt of their jokes—
young ruffians! whippersnappers!
Why, I considered their fathers
mere inexperienced pups.
But they are worse than dogs—good for nothing,
stray, mangy animals,
Half-starved, scavenging the back alleys,
howling at the moon;
Homeless guttersnipes
chewing on old bones and licking old tin cans;
Outcasts from the community,
cursed as dangerous delinquents.
Nobody would put up with them;
they were driven from the neighborhood.
You could hear them out there at the edge of town,
yelping and barking, huddled in junkyards,
A gang of beggars and no-names,
thrown out on their ears.

9-15 "But now I'm the one they're after,
mistreating me, taunting and mocking.
They abhor me, they abuse me.
How dare those scoundrels—they spit in my face!
Now that God has undone me and left me in a heap,
they hold nothing back. Anything goes.
They come at me from my blind side,
trip me up, then jump on me while I'm down.
They throw every kind of obstacle in my path,
determined to ruin me—
and no one lifts a finger to help me!
They violate my broken body,
trample through the rubble of my ruined life.
Terrors assault me—
my dignity in shreds,
salvation up in smoke.

16-19 "And now my life drains out,
as suffering seizes and grips me hard.
Night gnaws at my bones;
the pain never lets up.
I am tied hand and foot, my neck in a noose.
I twist and turn.
Thrown facedown in the muck,
I'm a muddy mess, inside and out.

WHAT DID I DO TO DESERVE THIS?

20-23 "I shout for help, God, and get nothing, no answer!
I stand to face you in protest, and you give me a blank stare!
You've turned into my tormenter—
you slap me around, knock me about.
You raised me up so I was riding high
and then dropped me, and I crashed.
I know you're determined to kill me,
to put me six feet under.

NEW KING JAMES VERSION

24"Surely He would not stretch out *His* hand
against a heap of ruins,
If they cry out when He destroys *it*.
25Have I not wept for him who was in trouble?
Has *not* my soul grieved for the poor?
26But when I looked for good, evil came *to me;*
And when I waited for light, then came darkness.
27My heart is in turmoil and cannot rest;
Days of affliction confront me.
28I go about mourning, but not in the sun;
I stand up in the assembly *and* cry out for help.
29I am a brother of jackals,
And a companion of ostriches.
30My skin grows black and falls from me;
My bones burn with fever.
31My harp is *turned* to mourning,
And my flute to the voice of those who weep.

31 "I have made a covenant with my eyes;
Why then should I look upon a young woman?
2For what *is* the allotment of God from above,
And the inheritance of the Almighty from on high?
3*Is* it not destruction for the wicked,
And disaster for the workers of iniquity?
4Does He not see my ways,
And count all my steps?

5"If I have walked with falsehood,
Or if my foot has hastened to deceit,
6Let me be weighed on honest scales,
That God may know my integrity.
7If my step has turned from the way,
Or my heart walked after my eyes,
Or if any spot adheres to my hands,
8*Then* let me sow, and another eat;
Yes, let my harvest be rooted out.

9"If my heart has been enticed by a woman,
Or *if* I have lurked at my neighbor's door,
10*Then* let my wife grind for another,
And let others bow down over her.
11For that *would be* wickedness;
Yes, it *would be* iniquity *deserving of* judgment.
12For that *would be* a fire *that* consumes to destruction,
And would root out all my increase.

13"If I have despised the cause of my male or female servant
When they complained against me,
14What then shall I do when God rises up?
When He punishes, how shall I answer Him?
15Did not He who made me in the womb make them?
Did not the same One fashion us in the womb?

THE MESSAGE

24-31 "What did I do to deserve this?
Did I ever hit anyone who was calling for help?
Haven't I wept for those who live a hard life,
been heartsick over the lot of the poor?
But where did it get me?
I expected good but evil showed up.
I looked for light but darkness fell.
My stomach's in a constant churning,
never settles down.
Each day confronts me with more suffering.
I walk under a black cloud. The sun is gone.
I stand in the congregation and protest.
I howl with the jackals,
I hoot with the owls.
I'm black-and-blue all over,
burning up with fever.
My fiddle plays nothing but the blues;
my mouth harp wails laments."

WHAT CAN I EXPECT FROM GOD?

1-4 31 "I made a solemn pact with myself
never to undress a girl with my eyes.
So what can I expect from God?
What do I deserve from God Almighty above?
Isn't calamity reserved for the wicked?
Isn't disaster supposed to strike those who do wrong?
Isn't God looking, observing how I live?
Doesn't he mark every step I take?

5-8 "Have I walked hand in hand with falsehood,
or hung out in the company of deceit?
Weigh me on a set of honest scales
so God has proof of my integrity.
If I've strayed off the straight and narrow,
wanted things I had no right to,
messed around with sin,
Go ahead, then—
give my portion to someone who deserves it.

9-12 "If I've let myself be seduced by a woman
and conspired to go to bed with her,
Fine, my wife has every right to go ahead
and sleep with anyone she wants to.
For disgusting behavior like that,
I'd deserve the worst punishment you could hand out.
Adultery is a fire that burns the house down;
I wouldn't expect anything I count dear to survive it.

13-15 "Have I ever been unfair to my employees
when they brought a complaint to me?
What, then, will I do when God confronts me?
When God examines my books, what can I say?
Didn't the same God who made me, make them?
Aren't we all made of the same stuff,
equals before God?

NEW KING JAMES VERSION

16"If I have kept the poor from *their* desire,
Or caused the eyes of the widow to fail,
17Or eaten my morsel by myself,
So that the fatherless could not eat of it
18(But from my youth I reared him as a father,
And from my mother's womb I guided *the widow*[a]);
19If I have seen anyone perish for lack of clothing,
Or any poor *man* without covering;
20If his heart[a] has not blessed me,
And *if* he was *not* warmed with the fleece of my sheep;
21If I have raised my hand against the fatherless,
When I saw I had help in the gate;
22*Then* let my arm fall from my shoulder,
Let my arm be torn from the socket.
23For destruction *from* God *is* a terror to me,
And because of His magnificence I cannot endure.

24"If I have made gold my hope,
Or said to fine gold, '*You are* my confidence';
25If I have rejoiced because my wealth *was* great,
And because my hand had gained much;
26If I have observed the sun[a] when it shines,
Or the moon moving *in* brightness,
27So that my heart has been secretly enticed,
And my mouth has kissed my hand;
28This also *would be* an iniquity *deserving of* judgment,
For I would have denied God *who is* above.

29"If I have rejoiced at the destruction of him who hated me,
Or lifted myself up when evil found him
30(Indeed I have not allowed my mouth to sin
By asking for a curse on his soul);
31If the men of my tent have not said,
"Who is there that has not been satisfied with his meat?'
32(*But* no sojourner had to lodge in the street,
For I have opened my doors to the traveler[a]);
33If I have covered my transgressions as Adam,
By hiding my iniquity in my bosom,
34Because I feared the great multitude,
And dreaded the contempt of families,
So that I kept silence
And did not go out of the door—
35Oh, that I had one to hear me!
Here is my mark.
Oh, that the Almighty would answer me,
That my Prosecutor had written a book!
36Surely I would carry it on my shoulder,
And bind it on me *like* a crown;

31:18 [a]Literally *her* (compare verse 16) 31:20 [a]Literally *loins*
31:26 [a]Literally *light* 31:32 [a]Following Septuagint, Syriac, Targum, and Vulgate; Masoretic Text reads *road*.

THE MESSAGE

16-18 "Have I ignored the needs of the poor,
turned my back on the indigent,
Taken care of my own needs and fed my own face
while they languished?
Wasn't my home always open to them?
Weren't they always welcome at my table?

19-20 "Have I ever left a poor family shivering in the cold
when they had no warm clothes?
Didn't the poor bless me when they saw me coming,
knowing I'd brought coats from my closet?

21-23 "If I've ever used my strength and influence
to take advantage of the unfortunate,
Go ahead, break both my arms,
cut off all my fingers!
The fear of God has kept me from these things—
how else could I ever face him?

IF ONLY SOMEONE WOULD GIVE ME A HEARING!

24-28 "Did I set my heart on making big money
or worship at the bank?
Did I boast about my wealth,
show off because I was well-off?
Was I ever so awed by the sun's brilliance
and moved by the moon's beauty
That I let myself become seduced by them
and worshiped them on the sly?
If so, I would deserve the worst of punishments,
for I would be betraying God himself.

29-30 "Did I ever crow over my enemy's ruin?
Or gloat over my rival's bad luck?
No, I never said a word of detraction,
never cursed them, even under my breath.

31-34 "Didn't those who worked for me say,
'He fed us well. There were always second helpings'?
And no stranger ever had to spend a night in the street;
my doors were always open to travelers.
Did I hide my sin the way Adam did,
or conceal my guilt behind closed doors
Because I was afraid what people would say,
fearing the gossip of the neighbors so much
That I turned myself into a recluse?
You know good and well that I didn't.

35-37 "Oh, if only someone would give me a hearing!
I've signed my name to my defense—let the Almighty One answer!
I want to see my indictment in writing.
Anyone's welcome to read my defense;
I'll write it on a poster and carry it around town.

NEW KING JAMES VERSION

37I would declare to Him the number of my
steps;
Like a prince I would approach Him.

38"If my land cries out against me,
And its furrows weep together;
39If I have eaten its fruit[a] without money,
Or caused its owners to lose their lives;
40*Then* let thistles grow instead of wheat,
And weeds instead of barley."

The words of Job are ended.

ELIHU CONTRADICTS JOB'S FRIENDS

32 So these three men ceased answering Job,
because he *was* righteous in his own eyes.
2Then the wrath of Elihu, the son of Barachel
the Buzite, of the family of Ram, was aroused
against Job; his wrath was aroused because he
justified himself rather than God. 3Also against
his three friends his wrath was aroused, be-
cause they had found no answer, and *yet* had
condemned Job.
4Now because they *were* years older than he,
Elihu had waited to speak to Job.[a] 5When Elihu
saw that *there was* no answer in the mouth of
these three men, his wrath was aroused.
6So Elihu, the son of Barachel the Buzite, an-
swered and said:

"I *am* young in years, and you *are* very old;
Therefore I was afraid,
And dared not declare my opinion to you.
7I said, 'Age[a] should speak,
And multitude of years should teach
wisdom.'
8But *there is* a spirit in man,
And the breath of the Almighty gives him
understanding.
9Great men[a] are not *always* wise,
Nor do the aged *always* understand justice.

10"Therefore I say, 'Listen to me,
I also will declare my opinion.'
11Indeed I waited for your words,
I listened to your reasonings, while you
searched out what to say.
12I paid close attention to you;
And surely not one of you convinced Job,
Or answered his words—
13Lest you say,
'We have found wisdom';
God will vanquish him, not man.
14Now he has not directed *his* words against
me;
So I will not answer him with your words.

31:39 [a]Literally *its strength* 32:4 [a]Vulgate reads *till Job had spoken.* 32:7 [a]Literally *Days,* that is, years 32:9 [a]Or *Men of many years*

THE MESSAGE

I'm prepared to account for every move
I've ever made—
to anyone and everyone, prince or
pauper.

38-40 "If the very ground that I farm accuses me,
if even the furrows fill with tears from
my abuse,
If I've ever raped the earth for my own
profit
or dispossessed its rightful owners,
Then curse it with thistles instead of
wheat,
curse it with weeds instead of barley."

The words of Job to his three friends
were finished.

ELIHU SPEAKS
GOD'S SPIRIT MAKES WISDOM POSSIBLE

1-5 32 Job's three friends now fell silent.
They were talked out, stymied because
Job wouldn't budge an inch—wouldn't ad-
mit to an ounce of guilt. Then Elihu lost his
temper. (Elihu was the son of Barakel the
Buzite from the clan of Ram.) He blazed out
in anger against Job for pitting his right-
eousness against God's. He was also angry
with the three friends because they had nei-
ther come up with an answer nor proved
Job wrong. Elihu had waited with Job while
they spoke because they were all older than
he. But when he saw that the three other
men had exhausted their arguments, he ex-
ploded with pent-up anger.
6-10 This is what Elihu, son of Barakel the
Buzite, said:

"I'm a young man,
and you are all old and experienced.
That's why I kept quiet
and held back from joining the
discussion.
I kept thinking, 'Experience will tell.
The longer you live, the wiser you
become.'
But I see I was wrong—it's God's Spirit in
a person,
the breath of the Almighty One, that
makes wise human insight possible.
The experts have no corner on wisdom;
getting old doesn't guarantee good
sense.
So I've decided to speak up. Listen well!
I'm going to tell you exactly what I think.

11-14 "I hung on your words while you spoke,
listened carefully to your arguments.
While you searched for the right words,
I was all ears.
And now what have you proved? Nothing.
Nothing you say has even touched Job.
And don't excuse yourselves by saying,
'We've done our best.
Now it's up to God to talk sense into
him.'
Job has yet to contend with me.
And rest assured, I won't be using *your*
arguments!

NEW KING JAMES VERSION

15"They are dismayed and answer no more;
Words escape them.
16And I have waited, because they did not speak,
Because they stood still *and* answered no more.
17I also will answer my part,
I too will declare my opinion.
18For I am full of words;
The spirit within me compels me.
19Indeed my belly *is* like wine *that* has no vent;
It is ready to burst like new wineskins.
20I will speak, that I may find relief;
I must open my lips and answer.
21Let me not, I pray, show partiality to anyone;
Nor let me flatter any man.
22For I do not know how to flatter,
Else my Maker would soon take me away.

ELIHU CONTRADICTS JOB

33 "But please, Job, hear my speech,
And listen to all my words.
2Now, I open my mouth;
My tongue speaks in my mouth.
3My words *come* from my upright heart;
My lips utter pure knowledge.
4The Spirit of God has made me,
And the breath of the Almighty gives me life.
5If you can answer me,
Set *your words* in order before me;
Take your stand.
6Truly I *am* as your spokesman[a] before God;
I also have been formed out of clay.
7Surely no fear of me will terrify you,
Nor will my hand be heavy on you.

8"Surely you have spoken in my hearing,
And I have heard the sound of *your* words, *saying*,
9'I *am* pure, without transgression;
I *am* innocent, and *there is* no iniquity in me.
10Yet He finds occasions against me,
He counts me as His enemy;
11He puts my feet in the stocks,
He watches all my paths.'

12"Look, *in* this you are not righteous.
I will answer you,
For God is greater than man.
13Why do you contend with Him?
For He does not give an accounting of any of His words.
14For God may speak in one way, or in another,
Yet man does not perceive it.
15In a dream, in a vision of the night,
When deep sleep falls upon men,
While slumbering on their beds,

33:6 [a]Literally *as your mouth*

THE MESSAGE

15-22 "Do you three have nothing else to say?
Of *course* you don't! You're total frauds!
Why should I wait any longer,
now that you're stopped dead in your tracks?
I'm ready to speak my piece. That's right!
It's my turn—and it's about time!
I've got a lot to say,
and I'm bursting to say it.
The pressure has built up, like lava beneath the earth.
I'm a volcano ready to blow.
I *have* to speak—I have no choice.
I have to say what's on my heart,
And I'm going to say it straight—
the truth, the whole truth, and nothing but the truth.
I was never any good at bootlicking;
my Maker would make short work of me if I started in now!"

1-4 33 "So please, Job, hear me out,
honor me by listening to me.
What I'm about to say
has been carefully thought out.
I have no ulterior motives in this;
I'm speaking honestly from my heart.
The Spirit of God made me what I am,
the breath of God Almighty gave me life!

GOD ALWAYS ANSWERS, ONE WAY OR ANOTHER

5-7 "And if you think you can prove me wrong, do it.
Lay out your arguments. Stand up for yourself!
Look, I'm human—no better than you;
we're both made of the same kind of mud.
So let's work this through together;
don't let my aggressiveness overwhelm you.

8-11 "Here's what you said.
I heard you say it with my own ears.
You said, 'I'm pure—I've done nothing wrong.
Believe me, I'm clean—my conscience is clear.
But God keeps picking on me;
he treats me like I'm his enemy.
He's thrown me in jail;
he keeps me under constant surveillance.'

12-14 "But let me tell you, Job, you're wrong, dead wrong!
God is far greater than any human.
So how dare you haul him into court,
and then complain that he won't answer your charges?
God always answers, one way or another,
even when people don't recognize his presence.

15-18 "In a dream, for instance, a vision at night,
when men and women are deep in sleep,
fast asleep in their beds—

NEW KING JAMES VERSION

16Then He opens the ears of men,
And seals their instruction.
17In order to turn man *from his* deed,
And conceal pride from man,
18He keeps back his soul from the Pit,
And his life from perishing by the sword.

19"*Man* is also chastened with pain on his bed,
And with strong *pain* in many of his bones,
20So that his life abhors bread,
And his soul succulent food.
21His flesh wastes away from sight,
And his bones stick out *which once* were not seen.
22Yes, his soul draws near the Pit,
And his life to the executioners.

23"If there is a messenger for him,
A mediator, one among a thousand,
To show man His uprightness,
24Then He is gracious to him, and says,
'Deliver him from going down to the Pit;
I have found a ransom';
25His flesh shall be young like a child's,
He shall return to the days of his youth.
26He shall pray to God, and He will delight in him,
He shall see His face with joy,
For He restores to man His righteousness.
27Then he looks at men and says,
'I have sinned, and perverted *what was* right,
And it did not profit me.'
28He will redeem his[a] soul from going down to the Pit,
And his[b] life shall see the light.

29"Behold, God works all these *things,*
Twice, *in fact,* three *times* with a man,
30To bring back his soul from the Pit,
That he may be enlightened with the light of life.

31"Give ear, Job, listen to me;
Hold your peace, and I will speak.
32If you have anything to say, answer me;
Speak, for I desire to justify you.
33If not, listen to me;
Hold your peace, and I will teach you wisdom."

ELIHU PROCLAIMS GOD'S JUSTICE

34 Elihu further answered and said:
2"Hear my words, you wise *men;*
Give ear to me, you who have knowledge.
3For the ear tests words
As the palate tastes food.

33:28 [a]Or *my* (Kethib) [b]Or *my* (Kethib)

THE MESSAGE

God opens their ears
and impresses them with warnings
To turn them back from something bad they're planning,
from some reckless choice,
And keep them from an early grave,
from the river of no return.

19-22 "Or, God might get their attention through pain,
by throwing them on a bed of suffering,
So they can't stand the sight of food,
have no appetite for their favorite treats.
They lose weight, wasting away to nothing,
reduced to a bag of bones.
They hang on the cliff-edge of death,
knowing the next breath may be their last.

23-25 "But even then an angel could come,
a champion—there are thousands of them!—
to take up your cause,
A messenger who would mercifully intervene,
canceling the death sentence with the words:
'I've come up with the ransom!'
Before you know it, you're healed,
the very picture of health!

26-28 "Or, you may fall on your knees and pray—to God's delight!
You'll see God's smile and celebrate,
finding yourself set right with God.
You'll sing God's praises to everyone you meet,
testifying, 'I messed up my life—
and let me tell you, it wasn't worth it.
But God stepped in and saved me from certain death.
I'm alive again! Once more I see the light!'

29-30 "This is the way God works.
Over and over again
He pulls our souls back from certain destruction
so we'll see the light—and *live* in the light!

31-33 "Keep listening, Job.
Don't interrupt—I'm not finished yet.
But if you think of anything I should know, tell me.
There's nothing I'd like better than to see your name cleared.
Meanwhile, keep listening. Don't distract me with interruptions.
I'm going to teach you the basics of wisdom."

ELIHU'S SECOND SPEECH

IT'S IMPOSSIBLE FOR GOD TO DO EVIL

1-4 34 Elihu continued:

"So, my fine friends—listen to me,
and see what you think of this.
Isn't it just common sense—
as common as the sense of taste—

NEW KING JAMES VERSION

4Let us choose justice for ourselves;
Let us know among ourselves what *is* good.

5"For Job has said, 'I am righteous,
But God has taken away my justice;
6Should I lie concerning my right?
My wound *is* incurable, *though I am* without transgression.'
7What man *is* like Job,
Who drinks scorn like water,
8Who goes in company with the workers of iniquity,
And walks with wicked men?
9For he has said, 'It profits a man nothing
That he should delight in God.'

10"Therefore listen to me, you men of understanding:
Far be it from God *to do* wickedness,
And *from* the Almighty to *commit* iniquity.
11For He repays man *according to* his work,
And makes man to find a reward according to *his* way.
12Surely God will never do wickedly,
Nor will the Almighty pervert justice.
13Who gave Him charge over the earth?
Or who appointed *Him over* the whole world?
14If He should set His heart on it,
If He should gather to Himself His Spirit and His breath,
15All flesh would perish together,
And man would return to dust.

16"If *you have* understanding, hear this;
Listen to the sound of my words:
17Should one who hates justice govern?
Will you condemn *Him who is* most just?
18*Is it fitting* to say to a king, '*You are* worthless,'
And to nobles, '*You are* wicked'?
19Yet He is not partial to princes,
Nor does He regard the rich more than the poor;
For they *are* all the work of His hands.
20In a moment they die, in the middle of the night;
The people are shaken and pass away;
The mighty are taken away without a hand.

21"For His eyes *are* on the ways of man,
And He sees all his steps.
22There is no darkness nor shadow of death
Where the workers of iniquity may hide themselves.
23For He need not further consider a man,
That he should go before God in judgment.
24He breaks in pieces mighty men without inquiry,
And sets others in their place.
25Therefore He knows their works;
He overthrows *them* in the night,
And they are crushed.

THE MESSAGE

To put our heads together
and figure out what's going on here?

5-9 "We've all heard Job say, 'I'm in the right,
but God won't give me a fair trial.
When I defend myself, I'm called a liar to my face.
I've done nothing wrong, and I get punished anyway.'
Have you ever heard anything to beat this?
Does nothing faze this man Job?
Do you think he's spent too much time in bad company,
hanging out with the wrong crowd,
So that now he's parroting their line:
'It doesn't pay to try to please God'?

10-15 "You're veterans in dealing with these matters;
certainly we're of one mind on this.
It's impossible for God to do anything evil;
no way can the Mighty One do wrong.
He makes us pay for exactly what we've done—no more, no less.
Our chickens always come home to roost.
It's impossible for God to do anything wicked,
for the Mighty One to subvert justice.
He's the one who runs the earth!
He cradles the whole world in his hand!
If he decided to hold his breath,
every man, woman, and child would die for lack of air.

GOD IS WORKING BEHIND THE SCENES

16-20 "So, Job, use your head;
this is all pretty obvious.
Can someone who hates order, keep order?
Do you dare condemn the righteous, mighty God?
Doesn't God always tell it like it is,
exposing corrupt rulers as scoundrels and criminals?
Does he play favorites with the rich and famous and slight the poor?
Isn't he equally responsible to everybody?
Don't people who deserve it die without notice?
Don't wicked rulers tumble to their doom?
When the so-called great ones are wiped out,
we know God is working behind the scenes.

21-28 "He has his eyes on every man and woman.
He doesn't miss a trick.
There is no night dark enough, no shadow deep enough,
to hide those who do evil.
God doesn't need to gather any more evidence;
their sin is an open-and-shut case.
He deposes the so-called high and mighty without asking questions,
and replaces them at once with others.
Nobody gets by with anything; overnight,
judgment is signed, sealed, and delivered.

NEW KING JAMES VERSION

26 He strikes them as wicked *men*
In the open sight of others,
27 Because they turned back from Him,
And would not consider any of His ways,
28 So that they caused the cry of the poor to come to Him;
For He hears the cry of the afflicted.
29 When He gives quietness, who then can make trouble?
And when He hides *His* face, who then can see Him,
Whether *it is* against a nation or a man alone?—
30 That the hypocrite should not reign,
Lest the people be ensnared.
31 "For has *anyone* said to God,
'I have borne *chastening;*
I will offend no more;
32 Teach me *what* I do not see;
If I have done iniquity, I will do no more'?
33 Should He repay *it* according to your *terms,*
Just because you disavow it?
You must choose, and not I;
Therefore speak what you know.

34 "Men of understanding say to me,
Wise men who listen to me:
35 'Job speaks without knowledge,
His words *are* without wisdom.'
36 Oh, that Job were tried to the utmost,
Because *his* answers *are like* those of wicked men!
37 For he adds rebellion to his sin;
He claps *his hands* among us,
And multiplies his words against God."

ELIHU CONDEMNS SELF-RIGHTEOUSNESS

35 Moreover Elihu answered and said:

2 "Do you think this is right?
Do you say,
'My righteousness is more than God's'?
3 For you say,
'What advantage will it be to You?
What profit shall I have, more than *if* I had sinned?'

4 "I will answer you,
And your companions with you.
5 Look to the heavens and see;
And behold the clouds—
They are higher than you.
6 If you sin, what do you accomplish against Him?
Or, *if* your transgressions are multiplied,
what do you do to Him?

THE MESSAGE

He punishes the wicked for their wickedness
out in the open where everyone can see it,
Because they quit following him,
no longer even thought about him or his ways.
Their apostasy was announced by the cry of the poor;
the cry of the afflicted got God's attention.

BECAUSE YOU REFUSE TO LIVE ON GOD'S TERMS

29-30 "If God is silent, what's that to you?
If he turns his face away, what can you do about it?
But whether silent or hidden, he's there, ruling,
so that those who hate God won't take over
and ruin people's lives.

31-33 "So why don't you simply confess to God?
Say, 'I sinned, but I'll sin no more.
Teach me to see what I still don't see.
Whatever evil I've done, I'll do it no more.'
Just because you refuse to live on God's terms,
do you think he should start living on yours?
You choose. I can't do it for you.
Tell me what you decide.

34-37 "All right-thinking people say—
and the wise who have listened to me concur—
'Job is an ignoramus.
He talks utter nonsense.'
Job, you need to be pushed to the wall and called to account
for wickedly talking back to God the way you have.
You've compounded your original sin
by rebelling against God's discipline,
Defiantly shaking your fist at God,
piling up indictments against the Almighty One."

ELIHU'S THIRD SPEECH

WHEN GOD MAKES CREATION A CLASSROOM

1-3 35 Elihu lit into Job again:

"Does this kind of thing make any sense?
First you say, 'I'm perfectly innocent before God.'
And then you say, 'It doesn't make a bit of difference
whether I've sinned or not.'

4-8 "Well, I'm going to show you
that you don't know what you're talking about,
neither you nor your friends.
Look up at the sky. Take a long hard look.
See those clouds towering above you?
If you sin, what difference could that make to God?
No matter how much you sin, will it matter to him?

NEW KING JAMES VERSION

[7]If you are righteous, what do you give Him?
Or what does He receive from your hand?
[8]Your wickedness affects a man such as you,
And your righteousness a son of man.

[9]"Because of the multitude of oppressions
they cry out;
They cry out for help because of the arm of
the mighty.
[10]But no one says, 'Where *is* God my Maker,
Who gives songs in the night,
[11]Who teaches us more than the beasts of the
earth,
And makes us wiser than the birds of
heaven?'
[12]There they cry out, but He does not answer,
Because of the pride of evil men.
[13]Surely God will not listen to empty *talk*,
Nor will the Almighty regard it.
[14]Although you say you do not see Him,
Yet justice *is* before Him, and you must wait
for Him.
[15]And now, because He has not punished in
His anger,
Nor taken much notice of folly,
[16]Therefore Job opens his mouth in vain;
He multiplies words without knowledge."

ELIHU PROCLAIMS GOD'S GOODNESS

36 Elihu also proceeded and said:

[2]"Bear with me a little, and I will show you
That *there are* yet words to speak on God's
behalf.
[3]I will fetch my knowledge from afar;
I will ascribe righteousness to my Maker.
[4]For truly my words *are* not false;
One who is perfect in knowledge *is* with
you.

[5]"Behold, God *is* mighty, but despises *no one;*
He is mighty in strength of understanding.
[6]He does not preserve the life of the wicked,
But gives justice to the oppressed.
[7]He does not withdraw His eyes from the
righteous;
But *they are* on the throne with kings,
For He has seated them forever,
And they are exalted.
[8]And if *they are* bound in fetters,
Held in the cords of affliction,
[9]Then He tells them their work and their
transgressions—
That they have acted defiantly.
[10]He also opens their ear to instruction,
And commands that they turn from iniquity.

THE MESSAGE

Even if you're good, what would God get
out of that?
Do you think he's dependent on your
accomplishments?
The only ones who care whether you're
good or bad
are your family and friends and
neighbors.
God's not dependent on your behavior.

9-15 "When times get bad, people cry out for
help.
They cry for relief from being kicked
around,
But never give God a thought when things
go well,
when God puts spontaneous songs in
their hearts,
When God sets out the entire creation as a
science classroom,
using birds and beasts to teach wisdom.
People are arrogantly indifferent to God—
until, of course, they're in trouble,
and then God is indifferent to them.
There's nothing behind such prayers
except panic;
the Almighty pays them no mind.
So why would he notice you
just because you say you're tired of
waiting to be heard,
Or waiting for him to get good and angry
and do something about the world's
problems?

16 "Job, you talk sheer nonsense—
nonstop nonsense!"

THOSE WHO LEARN FROM THEIR SUFFERING

1-4 36 Here Elihu took a deep breath, but kept
going:

"Stay with me a little longer. I'll convince
you.
There's still more to be said on God's
side.
I learned all this firsthand from the Source;
everything I know about justice I owe to
my Maker himself.
Trust me, I'm giving you undiluted truth;
believe me, I know these things inside
and out.

5-15 "It's true that God is all-powerful,
but he doesn't bully innocent people.
For the wicked, though, it's a different
story—
he doesn't give them the time of day,
but champions the rights of their victims.
He never takes his eyes off the righteous;
he honors them lavishly, promotes them
endlessly.
When things go badly,
when affliction and suffering descend,
God tells them where they've gone wrong,
shows them how their pride has caused
their trouble.
He forces them to heed his warning,
tells them they must repent of their bad
life.

NEW KING JAMES VERSION

11If they obey and serve *Him,*
They shall spend their days in prosperity,
And their years in pleasures.
12But if they do not obey,
They shall perish by the sword,
And they shall die without knowledge.[a]

13"But the hypocrites in heart store up wrath;
They do not cry for help when He binds
them.
14They die in youth,
And their life *ends* among the perverted
persons.[a]
15He delivers the poor in their affliction,
And opens their ears in oppression.

16"Indeed He would have brought you out of
dire distress,
Into a broad place where *there is* no
restraint;
And what is set on your table *would be* full
of richness.
17But you are filled with the judgment due the
wicked;
Judgment and justice take hold *of you.*
18Because *there is* wrath, *beware* lest He take
you away with *one* blow;
For a large ransom would not help you
avoid *it.*
19Will your riches,
Or all the mighty forces,
Keep you from distress?
20Do not desire the night,
When people are cut off in their place.
21Take heed, do not turn to iniquity,
For you have chosen this rather than
affliction.

22"Behold, God is exalted by His power;
Who teaches like Him?
23Who has assigned Him His way,
Or who has said, 'You have done wrong'?

ELIHU PROCLAIMS GOD'S MAJESTY

24"Remember to magnify His work,
Of which men have sung.
25Everyone has seen it;
Man looks on *it* from afar.

26"Behold, God *is* great, and we do not know
Him;
Nor can the number of His years *be*
discovered.
27For He draws up drops of water,
Which distill as rain from the mist,
28Which the clouds drop down
And pour abundantly on man.
29Indeed, can *anyone* understand the
spreading of clouds,
The thunder from His canopy?
30Look, He scatters His light upon it,
And covers the depths of the sea.

36:12 [a]Masoretic Text reads *as one without knowledge.* **36:14** [a]Hebrew *qedeshim,* that is, those practicing sodomy and prostitution in religious rituals

THE MESSAGE

If they obey and serve him,
they'll have a good, long life on easy
street.
But if they disobey, they'll be cut down in
their prime
and never know the first thing about life.
Angry people without God pile grievance
upon grievance,
always blaming others for their troubles.
Living it up in sexual excesses,
virility wasted, they die young.
But those who learn from their suffering,
God delivers from their suffering.

OBSESSED WITH PUTTING THE BLAME ON GOD

16-21 "Oh, Job, don't you see how God's wooing
you
from the jaws of danger?
How he's drawing you into wide-open
places—
inviting you to feast at a table laden with
blessings?
And here you are laden with the guilt of
the wicked,
obsessed with putting the blame on *God!*
Don't let your great riches mislead you;
don't think you can bribe your way out
of this.
Did you plan to buy your way out of this?
Not on your life!
And don't think that night,
when people sleep off their troubles,
will bring you any relief.
Above all, don't make things worse with
more evil—
that's what's behind your suffering as it is!

22-25 "Do you have any idea how powerful God is?
Have you ever heard of a teacher like
him?
Has anyone ever had to tell him what to do,
or correct him, saying, 'You did that all
wrong!'?
Remember, then, to praise his
workmanship,
which is so often celebrated in song.
Everybody sees it;
nobody is too far away to see it.

NO ONE CAN ESCAPE FROM GOD

26 "Take a long, hard look. See how great he
is—infinite,
greater than anything you could ever
imagine or figure out!

27-33 "He pulls water up out of the sea,
distills it, and fills up his rain-cloud
cisterns.
Then the skies open up
and pour out soaking showers on
everyone.
Does anyone have the slightest idea how
this happens?
How he arranges the clouds, how he
speaks in thunder?
Just look at that lightning, his sky-filling
light show
illumining the dark depths of the sea!

NEW KING JAMES VERSION

31 For by these He judges the peoples;
He gives food in abundance.
32 He covers *His* hands with lightning,
And commands it to strike.
33 His thunder declares it,
The cattle also, concerning the rising *storm.*

37 "At this also my heart trembles,
And leaps from its place.
2 Hear attentively the thunder of His voice,
And the rumbling *that* comes from His
mouth.
3 He sends it forth under the whole heaven,
His lightning to the ends of the earth.
4 After it a voice roars;
He thunders with His majestic voice,
And He does not restrain them when His
voice is heard.
5 God thunders marvelously with His voice;
He does great things which we cannot
comprehend.
6 For He says to the snow, 'Fall *on* the earth';
Likewise to the gentle rain and the heavy
rain of His strength.
7 He seals the hand of every man,
That all men may know His work.
8 The beasts go into dens,
And remain in their lairs.
9 From the chamber *of the south* comes the
whirlwind,
And cold from the scattering winds *of the
north.*
10 By the breath of God ice is given,
And the broad waters are frozen.
11 Also with moisture He saturates the thick
clouds;
He scatters His bright clouds.
12 And they swirl about, being turned by His
guidance,
That they may do whatever He commands
them
On the face of the whole earth.[a]
13 He causes it to come,
Whether for correction,
Or for His land,
Or for mercy.

14 "Listen to this, O Job;
Stand still and consider the wondrous
works of God.
15 Do you know when God dispatches them,
And causes the light of His cloud to shine?
16 Do you know how the clouds are balanced,
Those wondrous works of Him who is
perfect in knowledge?
17 Why *are* your garments hot,
When He quiets the earth by the south
wind?
18 With Him, have you spread out the skies,
Strong as a cast metal mirror?

19 "Teach us what we should say to Him,
For we can prepare nothing because of the
darkness.

37:12 [a]Literally *the world of the earth*

THE MESSAGE

These are the symbols of his sovereignty,
his generosity, his loving care.
He hurls arrows of light,
taking sure and accurate aim.
The High God roars in the thunder,
angry against evil."

1-13 37 "Whenever this happens, my heart
stops—
I'm stunned, I can't catch my breath.
Listen to it! Listen to his thunder,
the rolling, rumbling thunder of his
voice.
He lets loose his lightnings from horizon to
horizon,
lighting up the earth from pole to pole.
In their wake, the thunder echoes his voice,
powerful and majestic.
He lets out all the stops, he holds nothing
back.
No one can mistake that voice—
His word thundering so wondrously,
his mighty acts staggering our
understanding.
He orders the snow, 'Blanket the earth!'
and the rain, 'Soak the whole
countryside!'
No one can escape the weather—it's *there.*
And no one can escape from God.
Wild animals take shelter,
crawling into their dens,
When blizzards roar out of the north
and freezing rain crusts the land.
It's God's breath that forms the ice,
it's God's breath that turns lakes and
rivers solid.
And yes, it's God who fills clouds with
rainwater
and hurls lightning from them every
which way.
He puts them through their paces—first
this way, then that—
commands them to do what he says all
over the world.
Whether for discipline or grace or
extravagant love,
he makes sure they make their mark.

A TERRIBLE BEAUTY STREAMS FROM GOD

14-18 "Job, are you listening? Have you noticed all
this?
Stop in your tracks! Take in God's
miracle-wonders!
Do you have any idea how God does it all,
how he makes bright lightning from
dark storms,
How he piles up the cumulus clouds—
all these miracle-wonders of a perfect
Mind?
Why, you don't even know how to keep
cool
on a sweltering hot day,
So how could you even dream
of making a dent in that hot-tin-roof sky?

19-22 "If you're so smart, give us a lesson in how
to address God.
We're in the dark and can't figure it out.

NEW KING JAMES VERSION

20Should He be told that I *wish to* speak?
If a man were to speak, surely he would be swallowed up.
21Even now *men* cannot look at the light *when it is* bright in the skies,
When the wind has passed and cleared them.
22He comes from the north *as* golden *splendor;*
With God *is* awesome majesty.
23*As for* the Almighty, we cannot find Him;
He is excellent in power,
In judgment and abundant justice;
He does not oppress.
24Therefore men fear Him;
He shows no partiality to any *who are* wise of heart."

THE LORD REVEALS HIS OMNIPOTENCE TO JOB

38 Then the LORD answered Job out of the whirlwind, and said:

2"Who *is* this who darkens counsel
By words without knowledge?
3Now prepare yourself like a man;
I will question you, and you shall answer Me.

4"Where were you when I laid the foundations of the earth?
Tell *Me,* if you have understanding.
5Who determined its measurements?
Surely you know!
Or who stretched the line upon it?
6To what were its foundations fastened?
Or who laid its cornerstone,
7When the morning stars sang together,
And all the sons of God shouted for joy?

8"Or *who* shut in the sea with doors,
When it burst forth *and* issued from the womb;
9When I made the clouds its garment,
And thick darkness its swaddling band;
10When I fixed My limit for it,
And set bars and doors;
11When I said,
'This far you may come, but no farther,
And here your proud waves must stop!'

12"Have you commanded the morning since your days *began,*
And caused the dawn to know its place,
13That it might take hold of the ends of the earth,
And the wicked be shaken out of it?
14It takes on form like clay *under* a seal,
And stands out like a garment.
15From the wicked their light is withheld,
And the upraised arm is broken.

16"Have you entered the springs of the sea?
Or have you walked in search of the depths?
17Have the gates of death been revealed to you?
Or have you seen the doors of the shadow of death?

THE MESSAGE

Do you think I'm dumb enough to challenge God?
Wouldn't that just be asking for trouble?
No one in his right mind stares straight at the sun
on a clear and cloudless day.
As gold comes from the northern mountains,
so a terrible beauty streams from God.

23-24 "Mighty God! Far beyond our reach!
Unsurpassable in power and justice!
It's unthinkable that he'd treat anyone unfairly.
So bow to him in deep reverence, one and all!
If you're wise, you'll most certainly worship him."

GOD CONFRONTS JOB

HAVE YOU GOTTEN TO THE BOTTOM OF THINGS?

1 38 And now, finally, GOD answered Job from the eye of a violent storm. He said:

2-11 "Why do you confuse the issue?
Why do you talk without knowing what you're talking about?
Pull yourself together, Job!
Up on your feet! Stand tall!
I have some questions for you,
and I want some straight answers.
Where were you when I created the earth?
Tell me, since you know so much!
Who decided on its size? Certainly you'll know that!
Who came up with the blueprints and measurements?
How was its foundation poured,
and who set the cornerstone,
While the morning stars sang in chorus
and all the angels shouted praise?
And who took charge of the ocean
when it gushed forth like a baby from the womb?
That was me! I wrapped it in soft clouds,
and tucked it in safely at night.
Then I made a playpen for it,
a strong playpen so it couldn't run loose,
And said, 'Stay here, this is your place.
Your wild tantrums are confined to this place.'

12-15 "And have you ever ordered Morning, 'Get up!'
told Dawn, 'Get to work!'
So you could seize Earth like a blanket
and shake out the wicked like cockroaches?
As the sun brings everything to light,
brings out all the colors and shapes,
The cover of darkness is snatched from the wicked—
they're caught in the very act!

16-18 "Have you ever gotten to the true bottom of things,
explored the labyrinthine caves of deep ocean?
Do you know the first thing about death?
Do you have one clue regarding death's dark mysteries?

NEW KING JAMES VERSION

[18]Have you comprehended the breadth of the earth?
Tell *Me,* if you know all this.

[19]"Where *is* the way *to* the dwelling of light?
And darkness, where *is* its place,
[20]That you may take it to its territory,
That you may know the paths *to* its home?
[21]Do you know *it,* because you were born then,
Or *because* the number of your days *is* great?

[22]"Have you entered the treasury of snow,
Or have you seen the treasury of hail,
[23]Which I have reserved for the time of trouble,
For the day of battle and war?
[24]By what way is light diffused,
Or the east wind scattered over the earth?

[25]"Who has divided a channel for the overflowing *water,*
Or a path for the thunderbolt,
[26]To cause it to rain on a land *where there is* no one,
A wilderness in which *there is* no man;
[27]To satisfy the desolate waste,
And cause to spring forth the growth of tender grass?
[28]Has the rain a father?
Or who has begotten the drops of dew?
[29]From whose womb comes the ice?
And the frost of heaven, who gives it birth?
[30]The waters harden like stone,
And the surface of the deep is frozen.

[31]"Can you bind the cluster of the Pleiades,
Or loose the belt of Orion?
[32]Can you bring out Mazzaroth[a] in its season?
Or can you guide the Great Bear with its cubs?
[33]Do you know the ordinances of the heavens?
Can you set their dominion over the earth?

[34]"Can you lift up your voice to the clouds,
That an abundance of water may cover you?
[35]Can you send out lightnings, that they may go,
And say to you, 'Here we *are!*'?
[36]Who has put wisdom in the mind?[a]
Or who has given understanding to the heart?
[37]Who can number the clouds by wisdom?
Or who can pour out the bottles of heaven,
[38]When the dust hardens in clumps,
And the clods cling together?

[39]"Can you hunt the prey for the lion,
Or satisfy the appetite of the young lions,
[40]When they crouch in *their* dens,
Or lurk in their lairs to lie in wait?

38:32 [a]Literally *Constellations* **38:36** [a]Literally *inward parts*

THE MESSAGE

And do you have any idea how large this earth is?
Speak up if you have even the beginning of an answer.

19-21 "Do you know where Light comes from
and where Darkness lives
So you can take them by the hand
and lead them home when they get lost?
Why, of *course* you know that.
You've known them all your life,
grown up in the same neighborhood with them!

22-30 "Have you ever traveled to where snow is made,
seen the vault where hail is stockpiled,
The arsenals of hail and snow that I keep in readiness
for times of trouble and battle and war?
Can you find your way to where lightning is launched,
or to the place from which the wind blows?
Who do you suppose carves canyons
for the downpours of rain, and charts the route of thunderstorms
That bring water to unvisited fields,
deserts no one ever lays eyes on,
Drenching the useless wastelands
so they're carpeted with wildflowers and grass?
And who do you think is the father of rain and dew,
the mother of ice and frost?
You don't for a minute imagine
these marvels of weather just happen, do you?

31-33 "Can you catch the eye of the beautiful Pleiades sisters,
or distract Orion from his hunt?
Can you get Venus to look your way,
or get the Great Bear and her cubs to come out and play?
Do you know the first thing about the sky's constellations
and how they affect things on Earth?

34-35 "Can you get the attention of the clouds,
and commission a shower of rain?
Can you take charge of the lightning bolts
and have them report to you for orders?

WHAT DO YOU HAVE TO SAY FOR YOURSELF?

36-38 "Who do you think gave weather-wisdom to the ibis,
and storm-savvy to the rooster?
Does anyone know enough to number all the clouds
or tip over the rain barrels of heaven
When the earth is cracked and dry,
the ground baked hard as a brick?

39-41 "Can you teach the lioness to stalk her prey
and satisfy the appetite of her cubs
As they crouch in their den,
waiting hungrily in their cave?

NEW KING JAMES VERSION

[41]Who provides food for the raven,
When its young ones cry to God,
And wander about for lack of food?

39 "Do you know the time when the wild mountain goats bear young?
Or can you mark when the deer gives birth?
[2]Can you number the months *that* they fulfill?
Or do you know the time when they bear young?
[3]They bow down,
They bring forth their young,
They deliver their offspring.[a]
[4]Their young ones are healthy,
They grow strong with grain;
They depart and do not return to them.

[5]"Who set the wild donkey free?
Who loosed the bonds of the onager,
[6]Whose home I have made the wilderness,
And the barren land his dwelling?
[7]He scorns the tumult of the city;
He does not heed the shouts of the driver.
[8]The range of the mountains *is* his pasture,
And he searches after every green thing.

[9]"Will the wild ox be willing to serve you?
Will he bed by your manger?
[10]Can you bind the wild ox in the furrow with ropes?
Or will he plow the valleys behind you?
[11]Will you trust him because his strength *is* great?
Or will you leave your labor to him?
[12]Will you trust him to bring home your grain,
And gather it to your threshing floor?

[13]"The wings of the ostrich wave proudly,
But are her wings and pinions *like the* kindly stork's?
[14]For she leaves her eggs on the ground,
And warms them in the dust;
[15]She forgets that a foot may crush them,
Or that a wild beast may break them.
[16]She treats her young harshly, as though *they were* not hers;
Her labor is in vain, without concern,
[17]Because God deprived her of wisdom,
And did not endow her with understanding.
[18]When she lifts herself on high,
She scorns the horse and its rider.

[19]"Have you given the horse strength?
Have you clothed his neck with thunder?[a]
[20]Can you frighten him like a locust?
His majestic snorting strikes terror.
[21]He paws in the valley, and rejoices in *his* strength;
He gallops into the clash of arms.

39:3 [a]Literally *pangs*, figurative of offspring **39:19** [a]Or *a mane*

THE MESSAGE

And who sets out food for the ravens
when their young cry to God,
fluttering about because they have no food?"

1-4 39 "Do you know the month when mountain goats give birth?
Have you ever watched a doe bear her fawn?
Do you know how many months she is pregnant?
Do you know the season of her delivery,
when she crouches down and drops her offspring?
Her young ones flourish and are soon on their own;
they leave and don't come back.

5-8 "Who do you think set the wild donkey free,
opened the corral gates and let him go?
I gave him the whole wilderness to roam in,
the rolling plains and wide-open places.
He laughs at his city cousins, who are harnessed and harried.
He's oblivious to the cries of teamsters.
He grazes freely through the hills,
nibbling anything that's green.

9-12 "Will the wild buffalo condescend to serve you,
volunteer to spend the night in your barn?
Can you imagine hitching your plow to a buffalo
and getting him to till your fields?
He's hugely strong, yes, but could you trust him,
would you dare turn the job over to him?
You wouldn't for a minute depend on him, would you,
to do what you said when you said it?

13-18 "The ostrich flaps her wings futilely—
all those beautiful feathers, but useless!
She lays her eggs on the hard ground,
leaves them there in the dirt, exposed to the weather,
Not caring that they might get stepped on and cracked
or trampled by some wild animal.
She's negligent with her young, as if they weren't even hers.
She cares nothing about anything.
She wasn't created very smart, that's for sure,
wasn't given her share of good sense.
But when she runs, oh, how she runs,
laughing, leaving horse and rider in the dust.

19-25 "Are you the one who gave the horse his prowess
and adorned him with a shimmering mane?
Did you create him to prance proudly
and strike terror with his royal snorts?
He paws the ground fiercely, eager and spirited,
then charges into the fray.

NEW KING JAMES VERSION

22He mocks at fear, and is not frightened;
Nor does he turn back from the sword.
23The quiver rattles against him,
The glittering spear and javelin.
24He devours the distance with fierceness and rage;
Nor does he come to a halt because the trumpet *has* sounded.
25At *the blast of* the trumpet he says, 'Aha!'
He smells the battle from afar,
The thunder of captains and shouting.

26"Does the hawk fly by your wisdom,
And spread its wings toward the south?
27Does the eagle mount up at your command,
And make its nest on high?
28On the rock it dwells and resides,
On the crag of the rock and the stronghold.
29From there it spies out the prey;
Its eyes observe from afar.
30Its young ones suck up blood;
And where the slain *are*, there it *is*."

40 Moreover the LORD answered Job, and said:

2"Shall the one who contends with the Almighty correct *Him*?
He who rebukes God, let him answer it."

JOB'S RESPONSE TO GOD

3Then Job answered the LORD and said:

4"Behold, I am vile;
What shall I answer You?
I lay my hand over my mouth.
5Once I have spoken, but I will not answer;
Yes, twice, but I will proceed no further."

GOD'S CHALLENGE TO JOB

6Then the LORD answered Job out of the whirlwind, and said:

7"Now prepare yourself like a man;
I will question you, and you shall answer Me:

8"Would you indeed annul My judgment?
Would you condemn Me that you may be justified?
9Have you an arm like God?
Or can you thunder with a voice like His?
10Then adorn yourself *with* majesty and splendor,
And array yourself with glory and beauty.
11Disperse the rage of your wrath;
Look on everyone *who is* proud, and humble him.
12Look on everyone *who is* proud, *and* bring him low;
Tread down the wicked in their place.
13Hide them in the dust together,
Bind their faces in hidden *darkness*.

THE MESSAGE

He laughs at danger, fearless,
doesn't shy away from the sword.
The banging and clanging
of quiver and lance don't faze him.
He quivers with excitement, and at the trumpet blast
races off at a gallop.
At the sound of the trumpet he neighs mightily,
smelling the excitement of battle from a long way off,
catching the rolling thunder of the war cries.

26-30 "Was it through your know-how that the hawk learned to fly,
soaring effortlessly on thermal updrafts?
Did you command the eagle's flight,
and teach her to build her nest in the heights,
Perfectly at home on the high cliff face,
invulnerable on pinnacle and crag?
From her perch she searches for prey,
spies it at a great distance.
Her young gorge themselves on carrion;
wherever there's a roadkill, you'll see her circling."

1-2 40 GOD then confronted Job directly:

"Now what do you have to say for yourself?
Are you going to haul me, the Mighty One, into court and press charges?"

JOB ANSWERS GOD

I'M READY TO SHUT UP AND LISTEN

3-5 Job answered:

"I'm speechless, in awe—words fail me.
I should never have opened my mouth!
I've talked too much, way too much.
I'm ready to shut up and listen."

GOD'S SECOND SET OF QUESTIONS

I WANT STRAIGHT ANSWERS

6-7 GOD addressed Job next from the eye of the storm, and this is what he said:

"I have some more questions for you,
and I want straight answers.

8-14 "Do you presume to tell me what I'm doing wrong?
Are you calling me a sinner so you can be a saint?
Do you have an arm like my arm?
Can you shout in thunder the way I can?
Go ahead, show your stuff.
Let's see what you're made of, what you can do.
Unleash your outrage.
Target the arrogant and lay them flat.
Target the arrogant and bring them to their knees.
Stop the wicked in their tracks—make mincemeat of them!
Dig a mass grave and dump them in it—
faceless corpses in an unmarked grave.

NEW KING JAMES VERSION

14Then I will also confess to you
That your own right hand can save you.
15"Look now at the behemoth,[a] which I made
along with you;
He eats grass like an ox.
16See now, his strength *is* in his hips,
And his power *is* in his stomach muscles.
17He moves his tail like a cedar;
The sinews of his thighs are tightly knit.
18His bones *are like* beams of bronze,
His ribs like bars of iron.
19He *is* the first of the ways of God;
Only He who made him can bring near His
sword.
20Surely the mountains yield food for him,
And all the beasts of the field play there.
21He lies under the lotus trees,
In a covert of reeds and marsh.
22The lotus trees cover him *with* their shade;
The willows by the brook surround him.
23Indeed the river may rage,
Yet he is not disturbed;
He is confident, though the Jordan gushes
into his mouth,
24*Though* he takes it in his eyes,
Or one pierces *his* nose with a snare.

41 "Can you draw out Leviathan[a] with a
hook,
Or *snare* his tongue with a line *which* you
lower?
2Can you put a reed through his nose,
Or pierce his jaw with a hook?
3Will he make many supplications to you?
Will he speak softly to you?
4Will he make a covenant with you?
Will you take him as a servant forever?
5Will you play with him as *with* a bird,
Or will you leash him for your maidens?
6Will *your* companions make a banquet[a] of
him?
Will they apportion him among the
merchants?
7Can you fill his skin with harpoons,
Or his head with fishing spears?
8Lay your hand on him;
Remember the battle—
Never do it again!
9Indeed, *any* hope of *overcoming* him is false;
Shall *one not* be overwhelmed at the sight
of him?
10No one *is so* fierce that he would dare stir
him up.
Who then is able to stand against Me?
11Who has preceded Me, that I should pay
him?
Everything under heaven is Mine.

12"I will not conceal[a] his limbs,
His mighty power, or his graceful proportions.
13Who can remove his outer coat?
Who can approach *him* with a double
bridle?

40:15 [a]A large animal, exact identity unknown 41:1 [a]A large sea creature, exact identity unknown 41:6 [a]Or *bargain over him* 41:12 [a]Literally *keep silent about*

THE MESSAGE

I'll gladly step aside and hand things over
to you—
you can surely save yourself with no
help from me!

15-24 "Look at the land beast, Behemoth. I
created him as well as you.
Grazing on grass, docile as a cow—
Just look at the strength of his back,
the powerful muscles of his belly.
His tail sways like a cedar in the wind;
his huge legs are like beech trees.
His skeleton is made of steel,
every bone in his body hard as steel.
Most magnificent of all my creatures,
but I still lead him around like a lamb!
The grass-covered hills serve him meals,
while field mice frolic in his shadow.
He takes afternoon naps under shade trees,
cools himself in the reedy swamps,
Lazily cool in the leafy shadows
as the breeze moves through the willows.
And when the river rages he doesn't
budge,
stolid and unperturbed even when the
Jordan goes wild.
But you'd never want him for a pet—
you'd never be able to housebreak him!"

I RUN THIS UNIVERSE

1-11 41 "Or can you pull in the sea beast,
Leviathan, with a fly rod
and stuff him in your creel?
Can you lasso him with a rope,
or snag him with an anchor?
Will he beg you over and over for mercy,
or flatter you with flowery speech?
Will he apply for a job with you
to run errands and serve you the rest of
your life?
Will you play with him as if he were a pet
goldfish?
Will you make him the mascot of the
neighborhood children?
Will you put him on display in the market
and have shoppers haggle over the
price?
Could you shoot him full of arrows like a
pin cushion,
or drive harpoons into his huge head?
If you so much as lay a hand on him,
you won't live to tell the story.
What hope would you have with such a
creature?
Why, one look at him would do you in!
If you can't hold your own against his
glowering visage,
how, then, do you expect to stand up to
me?
Who could confront me and get by with it?
I'm *in charge* of all this—I *run* this
universe!

12-17 "But I've more to say about Leviathan, the
sea beast,
his enormous bulk, his beautiful shape.
Who would even dream of piercing that
tough skin
or putting those jaws into bit and bridle?

NEW KING JAMES VERSION

14Who can open the doors of his face,
With his terrible teeth all around?
15*His* rows of scales are *his* pride,
Shut up tightly *as with* a seal;
16One is so near another
That no air can come between them;
17They are joined one to another,
They stick together and cannot be parted.
18His sneezings flash forth light,
And his eyes *are* like the eyelids of the morning.
19Out of his mouth go burning lights;
Sparks of fire shoot out.
20Smoke goes out of his nostrils,
As *from* a boiling pot and burning rushes.
21His breath kindles coals,
And a flame goes out of his mouth.
22Strength dwells in his neck,
And sorrow dances before him.
23The folds of his flesh are joined together;
They are firm on him and cannot be moved.
24His heart is as hard as stone,
Even as hard as the lower *millstone*.
25When he raises himself up, the mighty are afraid;
Because of his crashings they are beside[a] themselves.
26*Though* the sword reaches him, it cannot avail;
Nor does spear, dart, or javelin.
27He regards iron as straw,
And bronze as rotten wood.
28The arrow cannot make him flee;
Slingstones become like stubble to him.
29Darts are regarded as straw;
He laughs at the threat of javelins.
30His undersides *are* like sharp potsherds;
He spreads pointed *marks* in the mire.
31He makes the deep boil like a pot;
He makes the sea like a pot of ointment.
32He leaves a shining wake behind him;
One would think the deep had white hair.
33On earth there is nothing like him,
Which is made without fear.
34He beholds every high *thing*;
He *is* king over all the children of pride."

JOB'S REPENTANCE AND RESTORATION

42 Then Job answered the LORD and said:

2"I know that You can do everything,
And that no purpose *of Yours* can be withheld from You.
3*You asked,* 'Who *is* this who hides counsel without knowledge?'

41:25 [a]Or *purify themselves*

THE MESSAGE

And who would dare knock at the door of his mouth
filled with row upon row of fierce teeth?
His pride is invincible;
nothing can make a dent in that pride.
Nothing can get through that proud skin—
impervious to weapons and weather,
The thickest and toughest of hides,
impenetrable!

18-34 "He snorts and the world lights up with fire,
he blinks and the dawn breaks.
Comets pour out of his mouth,
fireworks arc and branch.
Smoke erupts from his nostrils
like steam from a boiling pot.
He blows and fires blaze;
flames of fire stream from his mouth.
All muscle he is—sheer and seamless muscle.
To meet him is to dance with death.
Sinewy and lithe,
there's not a soft spot in his entire body—
As tough inside as out,
rock-hard, invulnerable.
Even angels run for cover when he surfaces,
cowering before his tail-thrashing turbulence.
Javelins bounce harmlessly off his hide,
harpoons ricochet wildly.
Iron bars are so much straw to him,
bronze weapons beneath notice.
Arrows don't even make him blink;
bullets make no more impression than raindrops.
A battle ax is nothing but a splinter of kindling;
he treats a brandished harpoon as a joke.
His belly is armor-plated, inexorable—
unstoppable as a barge.
He roils deep ocean the way you'd boil water,
he whips the sea like you'd whip an egg into batter.
With a luminous trail stretching out behind him,
you might think Ocean had grown a gray beard!
There's nothing on this earth quite like him,
not an ounce of fear in *that* creature!
He surveys all the high and mighty—
king of the ocean, king of the deep!"

JOB WORSHIPS GOD

I BABBLED ON ABOUT THINGS FAR BEYOND ME

1-6 42 Job answered GOD:

"I'm convinced: You can do anything and everything.
Nothing and no one can upset your plans.
You asked, 'Who is this muddying the water,
ignorantly confusing the issue,
second-guessing my purposes?'

New King James Version

Therefore I have uttered what I did not
understand,
Things too wonderful for me, which I did
not know.
4 Listen, please, and let me speak;
You said, 'I will question you, and you shall
answer Me.'

5 "I have heard of You by the hearing of the ear,
But now my eye sees You.
6 Therefore I abhor *myself,*
And repent in dust and ashes."

7 And so it was, after the LORD had spoken
these words to Job, that the LORD said to Eliphaz
the Temanite, "My wrath is aroused against you
and your two friends, for you have not spoken of
Me *what is* right, as My servant Job *has.* 8 Now
therefore, take for yourselves seven bulls and
seven rams, go to My servant Job, and offer up
for yourselves a burnt offering; and My servant
Job shall pray for you. For I will accept him, lest
I deal with you *according to your* folly; because
you have not spoken of Me *what is* right, as My
servant Job *has.*"
9 So Eliphaz the Temanite and Bildad the
Shuhite *and* Zophar the Naamathite went and
did as the LORD commanded them; for the LORD
had accepted Job. 10 And the LORD restored Job's
losses[a] when he prayed for his friends. Indeed
the LORD gave Job twice as much as he had be-
fore. 11 Then all his brothers, all his sisters, and
all those who had been his acquaintances be-
fore, came to him and ate food with him in his
house; and they consoled him and comforted
him for all the adversity that the LORD had
brought upon him. Each one gave him a piece of
silver and each a ring of gold.
12 Now the LORD blessed the latter *days* of Job
more than his beginning; for he had fourteen
thousand sheep, six thousand camels, one thou-
sand yoke of oxen, and one thousand female
donkeys. 13 He also had seven sons and three
daughters. 14 And he called the name of the first
Jemimah, the name of the second Keziah, and
the name of the third Keren-Happuch. 15 In all
the land were found no women *so* beautiful as
the daughters of Job; and their father gave them
an inheritance among their brothers.
16 After this Job lived one hundred and forty
years, and saw his children and grandchildren
for four generations. 17 So Job died, old and full
of days.

42:10 [a]Literally *Job's captivity,* that is, what was captured from Job

The Message

I admit it. I was the one. I babbled on about
things far beyond me,
made small talk about wonders way over
my head.
You told me, 'Listen, and let me do the
talking.
Let me ask the questions. *You* give the
answers.'
I admit I once lived by rumors of you;
now I have it all firsthand—from my own
eyes and ears!
I'm sorry—forgive me. I'll never do that
again, I promise!
I'll never again live on crusts of hearsay,
crumbs of rumor."

GOD RESTORES JOB

I Will Accept His Prayer

7-8 After GOD had finished addressing Job, he turned to Eliphaz the Temanite and said, "I've had it with you and your two friends. I'm fed up! You haven't been honest either with me or about me—not the way my friend Job has. So here's what you must do. Take seven bulls and seven rams, and go to my friend Job. Sacrifice a burnt offering on your own behalf. My friend Job will pray for you, and I will accept his prayer. He will ask me not to treat you as you deserve for talking nonsense about me, and for not being honest with me, as he has."

9 They did it. Eliphaz the Temanite, Bildad the Shuhite, and Zophar the Naamathite did what God commanded. And God accepted Job's prayer.

10-11 After Job had interceded for his friends, God restored his fortune—and then doubled it! All his brothers and sisters and friends came to his house and celebrated. They told him how sorry they were, and consoled him for all the trouble God had brought him. Each of them brought generous housewarming gifts.

12-15 GOD blessed Job's later life even more than his earlier life. He ended up with fourteen thousand sheep, six thousand camels, one thousand teams of oxen, and one thousand donkeys. He also had seven sons and three daughters. He named the first daughter Dove, the second, Cinnamon, and the third, Darkeyes. There was not a woman in that country as beautiful as Job's daughters. Their father treated them as equals with their brothers, providing the same inheritance.

16-17 Job lived on another 140 years, living to see his children and grandchildren—four generations of them! Then he died—an old man, a full life.

PSALMS

NEW KING JAMES VERSION

Book One: Psalms 1—41

PSALM 1

THE WAY OF THE RIGHTEOUS AND THE END OF THE UNGODLY

[1]Blessed *is* the man
Who walks not in the counsel of the ungodly,
Nor stands in the path of sinners,
Nor sits in the seat of the scornful;
[2]But his delight *is* in the law of the LORD,
And in His law he meditates day and night.
[3]He shall be like a tree
Planted by the rivers of water,
That brings forth its fruit in its season,
Whose leaf also shall not wither;
And whatever he does shall prosper.

[4]The ungodly *are* not so,
But *are* like the chaff which the wind drives away.
[5]Therefore the ungodly shall not stand in the judgment,
Nor sinners in the congregation of the righteous.

[6]For the LORD knows the way of the righteous,
But the way of the ungodly shall perish.

PSALM 2

THE MESSIAH'S TRIUMPH AND KINGDOM

[1]Why do the nations rage,
And the people plot a vain thing?
[2]The kings of the earth set themselves,
And the rulers take counsel together,
Against the LORD and against His Anointed, *saying*,
[3]"Let us break Their bonds in pieces
And cast away Their cords from us."

[4]He who sits in the heavens shall laugh;
The Lord shall hold them in derision.
[5]Then He shall speak to them in His wrath,
And distress them in His deep displeasure:
[6]"Yet I have set My King
On My holy hill of Zion."

[7]"I will declare the decree:
The LORD has said to Me,
'You *are* My Son,
Today I have begotten You.
[8]Ask of Me, and I will give *You*
The nations *for* Your inheritance,
And the ends of the earth *for* Your possession.
[9]You shall break[a] them with a rod of iron;
You shall dash them to pieces like a potter's vessel.' "

2:9 [a]Following Masoretic Text and Targum; Septuagint, Syriac, and Vulgate read *rule* (compare Revelation 2:27).

THE MESSAGE

1 **1** How well God must like you—
you don't hang out at Sin Saloon,
you don't slink along Dead-End Road,
you don't go to Smart-Mouth College.

2-3 Instead you thrill to GOD's Word,
you chew on Scripture day and night.
You're a tree replanted in Eden,
bearing fresh fruit every month,
Never dropping a leaf,
always in blossom.

4-5 You're not at all like the wicked,
who are mere windblown dust—
Without defense in court,
unfit company for innocent people.

6 GOD charts the road you take.
The road *they* take is Skid Row.

1-6 **2** Why the big noise, nations?
Why the mean plots, peoples?
Earth-leaders push for position,
Demagogues and delegates meet for summit talks,
The God-deniers, the Messiah-defiers:
"Let's get free of God!
Cast loose from Messiah!"
Heaven-throned God breaks out laughing.
At first he's amused at their presumption;
Then he gets good and angry.
Furiously, he shuts them up:
"Don't you know there's a King in Zion? A coronation banquet
Is spread for him on the holy summit."

7-9 Let me tell you what GOD said next.
He said, "You're my son,
And today is your birthday.
What do you want? Name it:
Nations as a present? continents as a prize?
You can command them all to dance for you,
Or throw them out with tomorrow's trash."

NEW KING JAMES VERSION

[10]Now therefore, be wise, O kings;
Be instructed, you judges of the earth.
[11]Serve the LORD with fear,
And rejoice with trembling.
[12]Kiss the Son,[a] lest He[b] be angry,
And you perish *in* the way,
When His wrath is kindled but a little.
Blessed *are* all those who put their trust in Him.

PSALM 3

THE LORD HELPS HIS TROUBLED PEOPLE

A Psalm of David when he fled from Absalom his son.

[1]LORD, how they have increased who trouble me!
Many *are* they who rise up against me.
[2]Many *are* they who say of me,
"*There is* no help for him in God." *Selah*

[3]But You, O LORD, *are* a shield for me,
My glory and the One who lifts up my head.
[4]I cried to the LORD with my voice,
And He heard me from His holy hill. *Selah*

[5]I lay down and slept;
I awoke, for the LORD sustained me.
[6]I will not be afraid of ten thousands of people
Who have set *themselves* against me all around.

[7]Arise, O LORD;
Save me, O my God!
For You have struck all my enemies on the cheekbone;
You have broken the teeth of the ungodly.
[8]Salvation *belongs* to the LORD.
Your blessing *is* upon Your people. *Selah*

PSALM 4

THE SAFETY OF THE FAITHFUL

To the Chief Musician. With stringed instruments. A Psalm of David.

[1]Hear me when I call, O God of my righteousness!
You have relieved me in *my* distress;
Have mercy on me, and hear my prayer.

[2]How long, O you sons of men,
Will you turn my glory to shame?
How long will you love worthlessness
And seek falsehood? *Selah*
[3]But know that the LORD has set apart[a] for Himself him who is godly;
The LORD will hear when I call to Him.
[4]Be angry, and do not sin.
Meditate within your heart on your bed, and be still. *Selah*
[5]Offer the sacrifices of righteousness,
And put your trust in the LORD.

2:12 [a]Septuagint and Vulgate read *Embrace discipline;* Targum reads *Receive instruction.* [b]Septuagint reads *the LORD.*
4:3 [a]Many Hebrew manuscripts, Septuagint, Targum, and Vulgate read *made wonderful.*

THE MESSAGE

10-12 So, rebel-kings, use your heads;
Upstart-judges, learn your lesson:
Worship GOD in adoring embrace,
Celebrate in trembling awe. Kiss Messiah!
Your very lives are in danger, you know;
His anger is about to explode,
But if you make a run for God—you won't regret it!

A DAVID PSALM, WHEN HE ESCAPED FOR HIS LIFE FROM ABSALOM, HIS SON

1-2 3 GOD! Look! Enemies past counting!
Enemies sprouting like mushrooms,
Mobs of them all around me, roaring their mockery:
"Hah! No help for *him* from God!"

3-4 But you, GOD, shield me on all sides;
You ground my feet, you lift my head high;
With all my might I shout up to GOD,
His answers thunder from the holy mountain.

5-6 I stretch myself out. I sleep.
Then I'm up again—rested, tall and steady,
Fearless before the enemy mobs
Coming at me from all sides.

7 Up, GOD! My God, help me!
Slap their faces,
First this cheek, then the other,
Your fist hard in their teeth!

8 Real help comes from GOD.
Your blessing clothes your people!

A DAVID PSALM

1 4 When I call, give me answers. God, take my side!
Once, in a tight place, you gave me room;
Now I'm in trouble again: grace me! hear me!

2 You rabble—how long do I put up with your scorn?
How long will you lust after lies?
How long will you live crazed by illusion?

3 Look at this: look
Who got picked by GOD!
He listens the split second I call to him.

4-5 Complain if you must, but don't lash out.
Keep your mouth shut, and let your heart do the talking.
Build your case before God and wait for his verdict.

NEW KING JAMES VERSION

6*There are* many who say,
"Who will show us *any* good?"
LORD, lift up the light of Your countenance
upon us.
7You have put gladness in my heart,
More than in the season that their grain and
wine increased.
8I will both lie down in peace, and sleep;
For You alone, O LORD, make me dwell in
safety.

PSALM 5

A PRAYER FOR GUIDANCE

To the Chief Musician. With flutes.[a] A Psalm of David.

1Give ear to my words, O LORD,
Consider my meditation.
2Give heed to the voice of my cry,
My King and my God,
For to You I will pray.
3My voice You shall hear in the morning,
O LORD;
In the morning I will direct *it* to You,
And I will look up.

4For You *are* not a God who takes pleasure in
wickedness,
Nor shall evil dwell with You.
5The boastful shall not stand in Your sight;
You hate all workers of iniquity.
6You shall destroy those who speak
falsehood;
The LORD abhors the bloodthirsty and
deceitful man.

7But as for me, I will come into Your house in
the multitude of Your mercy;
In fear of You I will worship toward Your
holy temple.
8Lead me, O LORD, in Your righteousness
because of my enemies;
Make Your way straight before my face.

9For *there is* no faithfulness in their mouth;
Their inward part *is* destruction;
Their throat *is* an open tomb;
They flatter with their tongue.
10Pronounce them guilty, O God!
Let them fall by their own counsels;
Cast them out in the multitude of their
transgressions,
For they have rebelled against You.

11But let all those rejoice who put their trust
in You;
Let them ever shout for joy, because You
defend them;
Let those also who love Your name
Be joyful in You.
12For You, O LORD, will bless the righteous;
With favor You will surround him as *with* a
shield.

5:title [a]Hebrew *nehiloth*

THE MESSAGE

6-7 Why is everyone hungry for *more*? "More,
more," they say.
"More, more."
I have God's more-than-enough,
More joy in one ordinary day

7-8 Than they get in all their shopping sprees.
At day's end I'm ready for sound sleep,
For you, GOD, have put my life back
together.

A DAVID PSALM

1-3 5 Listen, GOD! Please, pay attention!
Can you make sense of these ramblings,
my groans and cries?
King-God, I need your help.
Every morning
you'll hear me at it again.
Every morning
I lay out the pieces of my life
on your altar
and watch for fire to descend.

4-6 You don't socialize with Wicked,
or invite Evil over as your houseguest.
Hot-Air-Boaster collapses in front of you;
you shake your head over
Mischief-Maker.
GOD destroys Lie-Speaker;
Blood-Thirsty and Truth-Bender disgust
you.

7-8 And here I am, your invited guest—
it's incredible!
I enter your house; here I am,
prostrate in your inner sanctum,
Waiting for directions
to get me safely through enemy lines.

9-10 Every word they speak is a land mine;
their lungs breathe out poison gas.
Their throats are gaping graves,
their tongues slick as mudslides.
Pile on the guilt, God!
Let their so-called wisdom wreck them.
Kick them out! They've had their chance.

11-12 But you'll welcome us with open arms
when we run for cover to you.
Let the party last all night!
Stand guard over our celebration.
You are famous, GOD, for welcoming
God-seekers,
for decking us out in delight.

NEW KING JAMES VERSION

PSALM 6

A PRAYER OF FAITH IN TIME OF DISTRESS

To the Chief Musician. With stringed instruments. On an eight-stringed harp.[a] A Psalm of David.

1O LORD, do not rebuke me in Your anger,
Nor chasten me in Your hot displeasure.
2Have mercy on me, O LORD, for I *am* weak;
O LORD, heal me, for my bones are troubled.
3My soul also is greatly troubled;
But You, O LORD—how long?

4Return, O LORD, deliver me!
Oh, save me for Your mercies' sake!
5For in death *there is* no remembrance of You;
In the grave who will give You thanks?

6I am weary with my groaning;
All night I make my bed swim;
I drench my couch with my tears.
7My eye wastes away because of grief;
It grows old because of all my enemies.

8Depart from me, all you workers of iniquity;
For the LORD has heard the voice of my weeping.
9The LORD has heard my supplication;
The LORD will receive my prayer.
10Let all my enemies be ashamed and greatly troubled;
Let them turn back *and* be ashamed suddenly.

PSALM 7

PRAYER AND PRAISE FOR DELIVERANCE FROM ENEMIES

A Meditation[a] of David, which he sang to the LORD concerning the words of Cush, a Benjamite.

1O LORD my God, in You I put my trust;
Save me from all those who persecute me;
And deliver me,
2Lest they tear me like a lion,
Rending *me* in pieces, while *there is* none to deliver.

3O LORD my God, if I have done this:
If there is iniquity in my hands,
4If I have repaid evil to him who was at peace with me,
Or have plundered my enemy without cause,
5Let the enemy pursue me and overtake *me;*
Yes, let him trample my life to the earth,
And lay my honor in the dust. *Selah*

6Arise, O LORD, in Your anger;
Lift Yourself up because of the rage of my enemies;
Rise up for me[a] *to* the judgment You have commanded!
7So the congregation of the peoples shall surround You;
For their sakes, therefore, return on high.

6:title [a]Hebrew *sheminith* **7:title** [a]Hebrew *Shiggaion* **7:6** [a]Following Masoretic Text, Targum, and Vulgate; Septuagint reads *O LORD my God.*

THE MESSAGE

A DAVID PSALM

1-2 **6** Please, GOD, no more yelling,
no more trips to the woodshed.
Treat me nice for a change;
I'm so starved for affection.

2-3 Can't you see I'm black-and-blue,
beat up badly in bones and soul?
GOD, how long will it take
for you to let up?

4-5 Break in, GOD, and break up this fight;
if you love me at all, get me out of here.
I'm no good to you dead, am I?
I can't sing in your choir if I'm buried in some tomb!

6-7 I'm tired of all this—so tired. My bed
has been floating forty days and nights
On the flood of my tears.
My mattress is soaked, soggy with tears.
The sockets of my eyes are black holes;
nearly blind, I squint and grope.

8-9 Get out of here, you Devil's crew:
at last GOD has heard my sobs.
My requests have all been granted,
my prayers are answered.

10 Cowards, my enemies disappear.
Disgraced, they turn tail and run.

A DAVID PSALM

1-2 **7** GOD! God! I am running to you for dear life;
the chase is wild.
If they catch me, I'm finished:
ripped to shreds by foes fierce as lions,
dragged into the forest and left
unlooked for, unremembered.

3-5 GOD, if I've done what they say—
betrayed my friends,
ripped off my enemies—
If my hands are really that dirty,
let them get me, walk all over me,
leave me flat on my face in the dirt.

6-8 Stand up, GOD; pit your holy fury
against my furious enemies.
Wake up, God. My accusers have packed
the courtroom; it's judgment time.

NEW KING JAMES VERSION

8The LORD shall judge the peoples;
Judge me, O LORD, according to my
righteousness,
And according to my integrity within me.

9Oh, let the wickedness of the wicked come
to an end,
But establish the just;
For the righteous God tests the hearts and
minds.
10My defense *is* of God,
Who saves the upright in heart.

11God *is* a just judge,
And God is angry *with the wicked* every
day.
12If he does not turn back,
He will sharpen His sword;
He bends His bow and makes it ready.
13He also prepares for Himself instruments of
death;
He makes His arrows into fiery shafts.

14Behold, *the wicked* brings forth iniquity;
Yes, he conceives trouble and brings forth
falsehood.
15He made a pit and dug it out,
And has fallen into the ditch *which* he
made.
16His trouble shall return upon his own head,
And his violent dealing shall come down on
his own crown.

17I will praise the LORD according to His
righteousness,
And will sing praise to the name of the LORD
Most High.

PSALM 8

THE GLORY OF THE LORD IN CREATION

To the Chief Musician. On the instrument of Gath.[a]
A Psalm of David.

1O LORD, our Lord,
How excellent *is* Your name in all the earth,
Who have set Your glory above the heavens!

2Out of the mouth of babes and nursing
infants
You have ordained strength,
Because of Your enemies,
That You may silence the enemy and the
avenger.

3When I consider Your heavens, the work of
Your fingers,
The moon and the stars, which You have
ordained,
4What is man that You are mindful of him,
And the son of man that You visit him?

8:title [a]Hebrew *Al Gittith*

THE MESSAGE

Take your place on the bench, reach for
your gavel,
throw out the false charges against me.
I'm ready, confident in your verdict:
"Innocent."

9-11 Close the book on Evil, GOD,
but publish your mandate for us.
You get us ready for life:
you probe for our soft spots,
you knock off our rough edges.
And I'm feeling so fit, so safe:
made right, kept right.
God in solemn honor does things right,
but his nerves are sandpapered raw.

11-13 Nobody gets by with anything.
God is already in action—
Sword honed on his whetstone,
bow strung, arrow on the string,
Lethal weapons in hand,
each arrow a flaming missile.

14 Look at that guy!
He had sex with sin,
he's pregnant with evil.
Oh, look! He's having
the baby—a Lie-Baby!

15-16 See that man shoveling day after day,
digging, then concealing, his man-trap
down that lonely stretch of road?
Go back and look again—you'll see him in
it headfirst,
legs waving in the breeze.
That's what happens:
mischief backfires;
violence boomerangs.

17 I'm thanking God, who makes things right.
I'm singing the fame of heaven-high GOD.

A DAVID PSALM

1 8 GOD, brilliant Lord,
yours is a household name.

2 Nursing infants gurgle choruses about you;
toddlers shout the songs
That drown out enemy talk,
and silence atheist babble.

3-4 I look up at your macro-skies, dark and
enormous,
your handmade sky-jewelry,
Moon and stars mounted in their settings.
Then I look at my micro-self and wonder,
Why do you bother with us?
Why take a second look our way?

NEW KING JAMES VERSION

5For You have made him a little lower than the angels,[a]
And You have crowned him with glory and honor.

6You have made him to have dominion over the works of Your hands;
You have put all *things* under his feet,
7All sheep and oxen—
Even the beasts of the field,
8The birds of the air,
And the fish of the sea
That pass through the paths of the seas.

9O LORD, our Lord,
How excellent *is* Your name in all the earth!

PSALM 9

PRAYER AND THANKSGIVING FOR THE LORD'S RIGHTEOUS JUDGMENTS

To the Chief Musician. To *the tune of* "Death of the Son."[a] A Psalm of David.

1I will praise *You*, O LORD, with my whole heart;
I will tell of all Your marvelous works.
2I will be glad and rejoice in You;
I will sing praise to Your name, O Most High.

3When my enemies turn back,
They shall fall and perish at Your presence.
4For You have maintained my right and my cause;
You sat on the throne judging in righteousness.
5You have rebuked the nations,
You have destroyed the wicked;
You have blotted out their name forever and ever.

6O enemy, destructions are finished forever!
And you have destroyed cities;
Even their memory has perished.
7But the LORD shall endure forever;
He has prepared His throne for judgment.
8He shall judge the world in righteousness,
And He shall administer judgment for the peoples in uprightness.

9The LORD also will be a refuge for the oppressed,
A refuge in times of trouble.
10And those who know Your name will put their trust in You;
For You, LORD, have not forsaken those who seek You.

11Sing praises to the LORD, who dwells in Zion!
Declare His deeds among the people.
12When He avenges blood, He remembers them;
He does not forget the cry of the humble.

8:5 [a]Hebrew *Elohim, God;* Septuagint, Syriac, Targum, and Jewish tradition translate as *angels.* **9:title** [a]Hebrew *Muth Labben*

THE MESSAGE

5-8 Yet we've so narrowly missed being gods,
bright with Eden's dawn light.
You put us in charge of your handcrafted world,
repeated to us your Genesis-charge,
Made us lords of sheep and cattle,
even animals out in the wild,
Birds flying and fish swimming,
whales singing in the ocean deeps.

9 GOD, brilliant Lord,
your name echoes around the world.

A DAVID PSALM

1-2 9 I'm thanking you, GOD, from a full heart,
I'm writing the book on your wonders.
I'm whistling, laughing, and jumping for joy;
I'm singing your song, High God.

3-4 The day my enemies turned tail and ran,
they stumbled on you and fell on their faces.
You took over and set everything right;
when I needed you, you were there, taking charge.

5-6 You blow the whistle on godless nations;
you throw dirty players out of the game,
wipe their names right off the roster.
Enemies disappear from the sidelines,
their reputation trashed,
their names erased from the halls of fame.

7-8 GOD holds the high center,
he sees and sets the world's mess right.
He decides what is right for us earthlings,
gives people their just deserts.

9-10 GOD's a safe-house for the battered,
a sanctuary during bad times.
The moment you arrive, you relax;
you're never sorry you knocked.

11-12 Sing your songs to Zion-dwelling GOD,
tell his stories to everyone you meet:
How he tracks down killers
yet keeps his eye on us,
registers every whimper and moan.

New King James Version

13Have mercy on me, O Lord!
Consider my trouble from those who hate me,
You who lift me up from the gates of death,
14That I may tell of all Your praise
In the gates of the daughter of Zion.
I will rejoice in Your salvation.

15The nations have sunk down in the pit *which* they made;
In the net which they hid, their own foot is caught.
16The Lord is known *by* the judgment He executes;
The wicked is snared in the work of his own hands.
Meditation.[a] *Selah*

17The wicked shall be turned into hell,
And all the nations that forget God.
18For the needy shall not always be forgotten;
The expectation of the poor shall *not* perish forever.

19Arise, O Lord,
Do not let man prevail;
Let the nations be judged in Your sight.
20Put them in fear, O Lord,
That the nations may know themselves *to be but* men. *Selah*

PSALM 10

A Song of Confidence in God's Triumph over Evil

1Why do You stand afar off, O Lord?
Why do You hide in times of trouble?
2The wicked in *his* pride persecutes the poor;
Let them be caught in the plots which they have devised.

3For the wicked boasts of his heart's desire;
He blesses the greedy *and* renounces the Lord.
4The wicked in his proud countenance does not seek *God;*
God *is* in none of his thoughts.

5His ways are always prospering;
Your judgments *are* far above, out of his sight;
As for all his enemies, he sneers at them.
6He has said in his heart, "I shall not be moved;
I shall never be in adversity."
7His mouth is full of cursing and deceit and oppression;
Under his tongue *is* trouble and iniquity.

8He sits in the lurking places of the villages;
In the secret places he murders the innocent;
His eyes are secretly fixed on the helpless.
9He lies in wait secretly, as a lion in his den;
He lies in wait to catch the poor;
He catches the poor when he draws him into his net.

9:16 [a]Hebrew *Higgaion*

The Message

13-14 Be kind to me, God;
I've been kicked around long enough.
Once you've pulled me back
from the gates of death,
I'll write the book on Hallelujahs;
on the corner of Main and First
I'll hold a street meeting;
I'll be the song leader; we'll fill the air
with salvation songs.

15-16 They're trapped, those godless countries,
in the very snares they set,
Their feet all tangled
in the net they spread.
They have no excuse;
the way God works is well-known.
The cunning machinery made by the wicked
has maimed their own hands.

17-20 The wicked bought a one-way
ticket to hell.
No longer will the poor be nameless—
no more humiliation for the humble.
Up, God! Aren't you fed up with their
empty strutting?
Expose these grand pretensions!
Shake them up, God!
Show them how silly they look.

1-2 **10** God, are you avoiding me?
Where are you when I need you?
Full of hot air, the wicked
are hot on the trail of the poor.
Trip them up, tangle them up
in their fine-tuned plots.

3-4 The wicked are windbags,
the swindlers have foul breath.
The wicked snub God,
their noses stuck high in the air.
Their graffiti are scrawled on the walls:
"Catch us if you can!" "God is dead."

5-6 They care nothing for what you think;
if you get in their way, they blow you off.
They live (they think) a charmed life:
"We can't go wrong. This is our lucky year!"

7-8 They carry a mouthful of hexes,
their tongues spit venom like adders.
They hide behind ordinary people,
then pounce on their victims.

9 They mark the luckless,
then wait like a hunter in a blind;
When the poor wretch wanders too close,
they stab him in the back.

New King James Version

10So he crouches, he lies low,
That the helpless may fall by his strength.
11He has said in his heart,
"God has forgotten;
He hides His face;
He will never see."

12Arise, O Lord!
O God, lift up Your hand!
Do not forget the humble.
13Why do the wicked renounce God?
He has said in his heart,
"You will not require *an account*."

14But You have seen, for You observe trouble and grief,
To repay *it* by Your hand.
The helpless commits himself to You;
You are the helper of the fatherless.
15Break the arm of the wicked and the evil *man;*
Seek out his wickedness *until* You find none.

16The Lord *is* King forever and ever;
The nations have perished out of His land.
17Lord, You have heard the desire of the humble;
You will prepare their heart;
You will cause Your ear to hear,
18To do justice to the fatherless and the oppressed,
That the man of the earth may oppress no more.

PSALM 11

Faith in the Lord's Righteousness
To the Chief Musician. *A Psalm* of David.

1In the Lord I put my trust;
How can you say to my soul,
"Flee *as* a bird to your mountain"?
2For look! The wicked bend *their* bow,
They make ready their arrow on the string,
That they may shoot secretly at the upright in heart.
3If the foundations are destroyed,
What can the righteous do?

4The Lord *is* in His holy temple,
The Lord's throne *is* in heaven;
His eyes behold,
His eyelids test the sons of men.
5The Lord tests the righteous,
But the wicked and the one who loves violence His soul hates.
6Upon the wicked He will rain coals;
Fire and brimstone and a burning wind
Shall be the portion of their cup.

7For the Lord *is* righteous,
He loves righteousness;
His countenance beholds the upright.[a]

11:7 [a]Or *The upright beholds His countenance*

The Message

10-11 The hapless fool is kicked to the ground,
the unlucky victim is brutally axed.
He thinks God has dumped him,
he's sure that God is indifferent to his plight.

12-13 Time to get up, God—get moving.
The luckless think they're Godforsaken.
They wonder why the wicked scorn God
and get away with it,
Why the wicked are so cocksure
they'll never come up for audit.

14 But you know all about it—
the contempt, the abuse.
I dare to believe that the luckless
will get lucky someday in you.
You won't let them down:
orphans won't be orphans forever.

15-16 Break the wicked right arms,
break all the evil left arms.
Search and destroy
every sign of crime.
God's grace and order wins;
godlessness loses.

17-18 The victim's faint pulse picks up;
the hearts of the hopeless pump red blood
as you put your ear to their lips.
Orphans get parents,
the homeless get homes.
The reign of terror is over,
the rule of the gang lords is ended.

A David Psalm

1-3 **11** I've already run for dear life
straight to the arms of God.
So why would I run away now
when you say,

"Run to the mountains; the evil
bows are bent, the wicked arrows
Aimed to shoot under cover of darkness
at every heart open to God.
The bottom's dropped out of the country;
good people don't have a chance"?

4-6 But God hasn't moved to the mountains;
his holy address hasn't changed.
He's in charge, as always, his eyes
taking everything in, his eyelids
Unblinking, examining Adam's unruly brood
inside and out, not missing a thing.
He tests the good and the bad alike;
if anyone cheats, God's outraged.
Fail the test and you're out,
out in a hail of firestones,
Drinking from a canteen
filled with hot desert wind.

7 God's business is putting things right;
he loves getting the lines straight,
Setting us straight. Once we're standing tall,
we can look him straight in the eye.

NEW KING JAMES VERSION

PSALM 12

MAN'S TREACHERY AND GOD'S CONSTANCY

To the Chief Musician. On an eight-stringed harp.[a] A Psalm of David.

1Help, LORD, for the godly man ceases!
For the faithful disappear from among the sons of men.
2They speak idly everyone with his neighbor;
With flattering lips *and* a double heart they speak.

3May the LORD cut off all flattering lips,
And the tongue that speaks proud things,
4Who have said,
"With our tongue we will prevail;
Our lips *are* our own;
Who *is* lord over us?"

5"For the oppression of the poor, for the sighing of the needy,
Now I will arise," says the LORD;
"I will set *him* in the safety for which he yearns."

6The words of the LORD *are* pure words,
Like silver tried in a furnace of earth,
Purified seven times.
7You shall keep them, O LORD,
You shall preserve them from this generation forever.

8The wicked prowl on every side,
When vileness is exalted among the sons of men.

PSALM 13

TRUST IN THE SALVATION OF THE LORD

To the Chief Musician. A Psalm of David.

1How long, O LORD? Will You forget me forever?
How long will You hide Your face from me?
2How long shall I take counsel in my soul,
Having sorrow in my heart daily?
How long will my enemy be exalted over me?

3Consider *and* hear me, O LORD my God;
Enlighten my eyes,
Lest I sleep the *sleep of* death;
4Lest my enemy say,
"I have prevailed against him";
Lest those who trouble me rejoice when I am moved.

5But I have trusted in Your mercy;
My heart shall rejoice in Your salvation.
6I will sing to the LORD,
Because He has dealt bountifully with me.

12:title [a]Hebrew *sheminith*

THE MESSAGE

A DAVID PSALM

1-2 **12** Quick, GOD, I need your helping hand!
The last decent person just went down,
All the friends I depended on gone.
Everyone talks in lie language;
Lies slide off their oily lips.
They doubletalk with forked tongues.

3-4 Slice their lips off their faces! Pull
The braggart tongues from their mouths!
I'm tired of hearing, "We can talk anyone into anything!
Our lips manage the world."

5 Into the hovels of the poor,
Into the dark streets where the homeless groan, God speaks:
"I've had enough; I'm on my way
To heal the ache in the heart of the wretched."

6-8 God's words are pure words,
Pure silver words refined seven times
In the fires of his word-kiln,
Pure on earth as well as in heaven.
GOD, keep us safe from their lies,
From the wicked who stalk us with lies,
From the wicked who collect honors
For their wonderful lies.

A DAVID PSALM

1-2 **13** Long enough, GOD—
you've ignored me long enough.
I've looked at the back of your head
long enough. Long enough
I've carried this ton of trouble,
lived with a stomach full of pain.
Long enough my arrogant enemies
have looked down their noses at me.

3-4 Take a good look at me, GOD, my God;
I want to look life in the eye,
So no enemy can get the best of me
or laugh when I fall on my face.

5-6 I've thrown myself headlong into your arms—
I'm celebrating your rescue.
I'm singing at the top of my lungs,
I'm so full of answered prayers.

NEW KING JAMES VERSION

PSALM 14

FOLLY OF THE GODLESS, AND GOD'S FINAL TRIUMPH

To the Chief Musician. *A Psalm* of David.

1The fool has said in his heart,
"*There is* no God."
They are corrupt,
They have done abominable works,
There is none who does good.

2The LORD looks down from heaven upon the children of men,
To see if there are any who understand, who seek God.
3They have all turned aside,
They have together become corrupt;
There is none who does good,
No, not one.

4Have all the workers of iniquity no knowledge,
Who eat up my people *as* they eat bread,
And do not call on the LORD?
5There they are in great fear,
For God *is* with the generation of the righteous.
6You shame the counsel of the poor,
But the LORD *is* his refuge.

7Oh, that the salvation of Israel *would come* out of Zion!
When the LORD brings back the captivity of His people,
Let Jacob rejoice *and* Israel be glad.

PSALM 15

THE CHARACTER OF THOSE WHO MAY DWELL WITH THE LORD

A Psalm of David.

1LORD, who may abide in Your tabernacle?
Who may dwell in Your holy hill?

2He who walks uprightly,
And works righteousness,
And speaks the truth in his heart;
3He *who* does not backbite with his tongue,
Nor does evil to his neighbor,
Nor does he take up a reproach against his friend;
4In whose eyes a vile person is despised,
But he honors those who fear the LORD;
He *who* swears to his own hurt and does not change;
5He *who* does not put out his money at usury,
Nor does he take a bribe against the innocent.

He who does these *things* shall never be moved.

THE MESSAGE

A DAVID PSALM

1 **14** Bilious and bloated, they gas,
"God is gone."
Their words are poison gas,
fouling the air; they poison
Rivers and skies;
thistles are their cash crop.

2 GOD sticks his head out of heaven.
He looks around.
He's looking for someone not stupid—
one man, even, God-expectant,
just one God-ready woman.

3 He comes up empty. A string
of zeros. Useless, unshepherded
Sheep, taking turns pretending
to be Shepherd.
The ninety and nine
follow their fellow.

4 Don't they know anything,
all these impostors?
Don't they know
they can't get away with this—
Treating people like a fast-food meal
over which they're too busy to pray?

5-6 Night is coming for them, and nightmares,
for God takes the side of victims.
Do you think you can mess
with the dreams of the poor?
You can't, for God
makes their dreams come true.

7 Is there anyone around to save Israel?
Yes. God is around; GOD turns life around.
Turned-around Jacob skips rope,
turned-around Israel sings laughter.

A DAVID PSALM

1 **15** GOD, who gets invited
to dinner at your place?
How do we get on your guest list?

2 "Walk straight,
act right,
tell the truth.

3-4 "Don't hurt your friend,
don't blame your neighbor;
despise the despicable.

5 "Keep your word even when it costs you,
make an honest living,
never take a bribe.

"You'll never get
blacklisted
if you live like this."

NEW KING JAMES VERSION

PSALM 16

THE HOPE OF THE FAITHFUL, AND THE MESSIAH'S VICTORY

A Michtam of David.

1Preserve me, O God, for in You I put my
trust.

2*O my soul,* you have said to the LORD,
"You *are* my Lord,
My goodness is nothing apart from You."
3As for the saints who *are* on the earth,
"They are the excellent ones, in whom is all
my delight."

4Their sorrows shall be multiplied who
hasten *after* another *god;*
Their drink offerings of blood I will not
offer,
Nor take up their names on my lips.

5O LORD, *You are* the portion of my
inheritance and my cup;
You maintain my lot.
6The lines have fallen to me in pleasant
places;
Yes, I have a good inheritance.

7I will bless the LORD who has given me
counsel;
My heart also instructs me in the night
seasons.
8I have set the LORD always before me;
Because *He is* at my right hand I shall not
be moved.

9Therefore my heart is glad, and my glory
rejoices;
My flesh also will rest in hope.
10For You will not leave my soul in Sheol,
Nor will You allow Your Holy One to see
corruption.
11You will show me the path of life;
In Your presence *is* fullness of joy;
At Your right hand *are* pleasures
forevermore.

PSALM 17

PRAYER WITH CONFIDENCE IN FINAL SALVATION

A Prayer of David.

1Hear a just cause, O LORD,
Attend to my cry;
Give ear to my prayer *which is* not from
deceitful lips.
2Let my vindication come from Your
presence;
Let Your eyes look on the things that are
upright.

3You have tested my heart;
You have visited *me* in the night;
You have tried me and have found nothing;
I have purposed that my mouth shall not
transgress.
4Concerning the works of men,
By the word of Your lips,

THE MESSAGE

A DAVID SONG

1-2 16 Keep me safe, O God,
I've run for dear life to you.
I say to GOD, "Be my Lord!"
Without you, nothing makes sense.

3 And these God-chosen lives all around—
what splendid friends they make!

4 Don't just go shopping for a god.
Gods are not for sale.
I swear I'll never treat god-names
like brand-names.

5-6 My choice is you, GOD, first and only.
And now I find I'm *your* choice!
You set me up with a house and yard.
And then you made me your heir!

7-8 The wise counsel GOD gives when I'm
awake
is confirmed by my sleeping heart.
Day and night I'll stick with GOD;
I've got a good thing going and I'm not
letting go.

9-10 I'm happy from the inside out,
and from the outside in, I'm firmly
formed.
You canceled my ticket to hell—
that's not my destination!

11 Now you've got my feet on the life path,
all radiant from the shining of your face.
Ever since you took my hand,
I'm on the right way.

A DAVID PRAYER

1-2 17 Listen while I build my case, GOD,
the most honest prayer you'll ever
hear.
Show the world I'm innocent—
in your heart you know I am.

3 Go ahead, examine me from inside out,
surprise me in the middle of the night—
You'll find I'm just what I say I am.
My words don't run loose.

4-5 I'm not trying to get my way
in the world's way.
I'm trying to get *your* way,
your Word's way.

NEW KING JAMES VERSION

I have kept away from the paths of the
destroyer.
5Uphold my steps in Your paths,
That my footsteps may not slip.

6I have called upon You, for You will hear me,
O God;
Incline Your ear to me, *and* hear my speech.
7Show Your marvelous lovingkindness by
Your right hand,
O You who save those who trust *in You*
From those who rise up *against them.*
8Keep me as the apple of Your eye;
Hide me under the shadow of Your wings,
9From the wicked who oppress me,
From my deadly enemies who surround me.

10They have closed up their fat *hearts;*
With their mouths they speak proudly.
11They have now surrounded us in our steps;
They have set their eyes, crouching down to
the earth,
12As a lion is eager to tear his prey,
And like a young lion lurking in secret
places.

13Arise, O LORD,
Confront him, cast him down;
Deliver my life from the wicked with Your
sword,
14With Your hand from men, O LORD,
From men of the world *who have* their
portion in *this* life,
And whose belly You fill with Your hidden
treasure.
They are satisfied with children,
And leave the rest of their *possession* for
their babes.

15As for me, I will see Your face in
righteousness;
I shall be satisfied when I awake in Your
likeness.

PSALM 18

GOD THE SOVEREIGN SAVIOR

To the Chief Musician. *A Psalm* of David the servant of the LORD, who spoke to the LORD the words of this song on the day that the LORD delivered him from the hand of all his enemies and from the hand of Saul. And he said:

1I will love You, O LORD, my strength.
2The LORD is my rock and my fortress and
my deliverer;
My God, my strength, in whom I will trust;
My shield and the horn of my salvation, my
stronghold.
3I will call upon the LORD, *who is worthy* to
be praised;
So shall I be saved from my enemies.

4The pangs of death surrounded me,
And the floods of ungodliness made me
afraid.
5The sorrows of Sheol surrounded me;
The snares of death confronted me.

THE MESSAGE

I'm staying on your trail;
I'm putting one foot
In front of the other.
I'm not giving up.

6-7 I call to you, God, because I'm sure of an
answer.
So—answer! bend your ear! listen sharp!
Paint grace-graffiti on the fences;
take in your frightened children who
Are running from the neighborhood bullies
straight to you.

8-9 Keep your eye on me;
hide me under your cool wing feathers
From the wicked who are out to get me,
from mortal enemies closing in.

10-14 Their hearts are hard as nails,
their mouths blast hot air.
They are after me, nipping my heels,
determined to bring me down,
Lions ready to rip me apart,
young lions poised to pounce.
Up, GOD: beard them! break them!
By your sword, free me from their
clutches;
Barehanded, GOD, break these mortals,
these flat-earth people who can't think
beyond today.

I'd like to see their bellies
swollen with famine food,
The weeds they've sown
harvested and baked into famine bread,
With second helpings for their children
and crusts for their babies to chew on.

15 And me? I plan on looking
you full in the face. When I get up,
I'll see your full stature
and live heaven on earth.

A DAVID SONG, WHICH HE SANG TO GOD AFTER BEING SAVED FROM ALL HIS ENEMIES AND FROM SAUL

1-2 **18** I love you, GOD—
you make me strong.
GOD is bedrock under my feet,
the castle in which I live,
my rescuing knight.
My God—the high crag
where I run for dear life,
hiding behind the boulders,
safe in the granite hideout.

3 I sing to GOD, the Praise-Lofty,
and find myself safe and saved.

4-5 The hangman's noose was tight at my
throat;
devil waters rushed over me.
Hell's ropes cinched me tight;
death traps barred every exit.

NEW KING JAMES VERSION

6 In my distress I called upon the LORD,
And cried out to my God;
He heard my voice from His temple,
And my cry came before Him, *even* to His ears.

7 Then the earth shook and trembled;
The foundations of the hills also quaked and were shaken,
Because He was angry.
8 Smoke went up from His nostrils,
And devouring fire from His mouth;
Coals were kindled by it.
9 He bowed the heavens also, and came down
With darkness under His feet.
10 And He rode upon a cherub, and flew;
He flew upon the wings of the wind.
11 He made darkness His secret place;
His canopy around Him *was* dark waters
And thick clouds of the skies.
12 From the brightness before Him,
His thick clouds passed with hailstones and coals of fire.

13 The LORD thundered from heaven,
And the Most High uttered His voice,
Hailstones and coals of fire.[a]
14 He sent out His arrows and scattered the foe,
Lightnings in abundance, and He vanquished them.
15 Then the channels of the sea were seen,
The foundations of the world were uncovered
At Your rebuke, O LORD,
At the blast of the breath of Your nostrils.

16 He sent from above, He took me;
He drew me out of many waters.
17 He delivered me from my strong enemy,
From those who hated me,
For they were too strong for me.
18 They confronted me in the day of my calamity,
But the LORD was my support.
19 He also brought me out into a broad place;
He delivered me because He delighted in me.

20 The LORD rewarded me according to my righteousness;
According to the cleanness of my hands
He has recompensed me.
21 For I have kept the ways of the LORD,
And have not wickedly departed from my God.
22 For all His judgments *were* before me,
And I did not put away His statutes from me.
23 I was also blameless before Him,
And I kept myself from my iniquity.
24 Therefore the LORD has recompensed me according to my righteousness,
According to the cleanness of my hands in His sight.

18:13 [a]Following Masoretic Text, Targum, and Vulgate; a few Hebrew manuscripts and Septuagint omit *Hailstones and coals of fire.*

THE MESSAGE

6 A hostile world! I call to GOD,
I cry to God to help me.
From his palace he hears my call;
my cry brings me right into his presence—
a private audience!

7-15 Earth wobbles and lurches;
huge mountains shake like leaves,
Quake like aspen leaves
because of his rage.
His nostrils flare, bellowing smoke;
his mouth spits fire.
Tongues of fire dart in and out;
he lowers the sky.
He steps down;
under his feet an abyss opens up.
He's riding a winged creature,
swift on wind-wings.
Now he's wrapped himself
in a trenchcoat of black-cloud darkness.
But his cloud-brightness bursts through,
spraying hailstones and fireballs.
Then GOD thundered out of heaven;
the High God gave a great shout,
spraying hailstones and fireballs.
God shoots his arrows—pandemonium!
He hurls his lightnings—a rout!
The secret sources of ocean are exposed,
the hidden depths of earth lie uncovered
The moment you roar in protest,
let loose your hurricane anger.

16-19 But me he caught—reached all the way
from sky to sea; he pulled me out
Of that ocean of hate, that enemy chaos,
the void in which I was drowning.
They hit me when I was down,
but GOD stuck by me.
He stood me up on a wide-open field;
I stood there saved—surprised to be loved!

20-24 GOD made my life complete
when I placed all the pieces before him.
When I got my act together,
he gave me a fresh start.
Now I'm alert to GOD's ways;
I don't take God for granted.
Every day I review the ways he works;
I try not to miss a trick.
I feel put back together,
and I'm watching my step.
GOD rewrote the text of my life
when I opened the book of my heart to his eyes.

NEW KING JAMES VERSION

25With the merciful You will show Yourself
merciful;
With a blameless man You will show
Yourself blameless;
26With the pure You will show Yourself pure;
And with the devious You will show Yourself
shrewd.
27For You will save the humble people,
But will bring down haughty looks.

28For You will light my lamp;
The LORD my God will enlighten my
darkness.
29For by You I can run against a troop,
By my God I can leap over a wall.
30*As for* God, His way *is* perfect;
The word of the LORD is proven;
He *is* a shield to all who trust in Him.

31For who *is* God, except the LORD?
And who *is* a rock, except our God?
32*It is* God who arms me with strength,
And makes my way perfect.
33He makes my feet like the *feet of* deer,
And sets me on my high places.
34He teaches my hands to make war,
So that my arms can bend a bow of bronze.

35You have also given me the shield of Your
salvation;
Your right hand has held me up,
Your gentleness has made me great.
36You enlarged my path under me,
So my feet did not slip.

37I have pursued my enemies and overtaken
them;
Neither did I turn back again till they were
destroyed.
38I have wounded them,
So that they could not rise;
They have fallen under my feet.
39For You have armed me with strength for the
battle;
You have subdued under me those who rose
up against me.
40You have also given me the necks of my
enemies,
So that I destroyed those who hated me.
41They cried out, but *there was* none to save;
Even to the LORD, but He did not answer
them.
42Then I beat them as fine as the dust before
the wind;
I cast them out like dirt in the streets.

43You have delivered me from the strivings of
the people;
You have made me the head of the nations;
A people I have not known shall serve me.
44As soon as they hear of me they obey me;
The foreigners submit to me.
45The foreigners fade away,
And come frightened from their hideouts.

46The LORD lives!
Blessed *be* my Rock!
Let the God of my salvation be exalted.
47*It is* God who avenges me,
And subdues the peoples under me;

THE MESSAGE

25-27 The good people taste your goodness,
The whole people taste your health,
The true people taste your truth,
The bad ones can't figure you out.
You take the side of the down-and-out,
But the stuck-up you take down a peg.

28-29 Suddenly, GOD, you floodlight my life;
I'm blazing with glory, God's glory!
I smash the bands of marauders,
I vault the highest fences.

30 What a God! His road
stretches straight and smooth.
Every GOD-direction is road-tested.
Everyone who runs toward him
Makes it.

31-42 Is there any god like GOD?
Are we not at bedrock?
Is not this the God who armed me,
then aimed me in the right direction?
Now I run like a deer;
I'm king of the mountain.
He shows me how to fight;
I can bend a bronze bow!
You protect me with salvation-armor;
you hold me up with a firm hand,
caress me with your gentle ways.
You cleared the ground under me
so my footing was firm.
When I chased my enemies I caught them;
I didn't let go till they were dead men.
I nailed them; they were down for good;
then I walked all over them.
You armed me well for this fight,
you smashed the upstarts.
You made my enemies turn tail,
and I wiped out the haters.
They cried "uncle"
but Uncle didn't come;
They yelled for GOD
and got no for an answer.
I ground them to dust; they gusted in the
wind.
I threw them out, like garbage in the
gutter.

43-45 You rescued me from a squabbling people;
you made me a leader of nations.
People I'd never heard of served me;
the moment they got wind of me they
listened.
The foreign devils gave up; they came
on their bellies, crawling from their
hideouts.

46-48 Live, GOD! Blessings from my Rock,
my free and freeing God, towering!
This God set things right for me
and shut up the people who talked back.

NEW KING JAMES VERSION

48He delivers me from my enemies.
You also lift me up above those who rise against me;
You have delivered me from the violent man.
49Therefore I will give thanks to You, O LORD, among the Gentiles,
And sing praises to Your name.

50Great deliverance He gives to His king,
And shows mercy to His anointed,
To David and his descendants forevermore.

PSALM 19

THE PERFECT REVELATION OF THE LORD

To the Chief Musician. A Psalm of David.

1The heavens declare the glory of God;
And the firmament shows His handiwork.
2Day unto day utters speech,
And night unto night reveals knowledge.
3*There is* no speech nor language
Where their voice is not heard.
4Their line[a] has gone out through all the earth,
And their words to the end of the world.

In them He has set a tabernacle for the sun,
5Which *is* like a bridegroom coming out of his chamber,
And rejoices like a strong man to run its race.
6Its rising *is* from one end of heaven,
And its circuit to the other end;
And there is nothing hidden from its heat.

7The law of the LORD *is* perfect, converting the soul;
The testimony of the LORD *is* sure, making wise the simple;
8The statutes of the LORD *are* right, rejoicing the heart;
The commandment of the LORD *is* pure, enlightening the eyes;
9The fear of the LORD *is* clean, enduring forever;
The judgments of the LORD *are* true *and* righteous altogether.
10More to be desired *are they* than gold,
Yea, than much fine gold;
Sweeter also than honey and the honeycomb.
11Moreover by them Your servant is warned,
And in keeping them *there is* great reward.

12Who can understand *his* errors?
Cleanse me from secret *faults*.
13Keep back Your servant also from presumptuous *sins;*
Let them not have dominion over me.
Then I shall be blameless,
And I shall be innocent of great transgression.

19:4 [a]Septuagint, Syriac, and Vulgate read *sound;* Targum reads *business*.

THE MESSAGE

He rescued me from enemy anger,
he pulled me from the grip of upstarts,
He saved me from the bullies.

49-50 That's why I'm thanking you, GOD,
all over the world.
That's why I'm singing songs
that rhyme your name.
God's king takes the trophy;
God's chosen is beloved.
I mean David and all his children—
always.

A DAVID PSALM

1-2 19 God's glory is on tour in the skies,
God-craft on exhibit across the horizon.
Madame Day holds classes every morning,
Professor Night lectures each evening.

3-4 Their words aren't heard,
their voices aren't recorded,
But their silence fills the earth:
unspoken truth is spoken everywhere.

4-5 God makes a huge dome
for the sun—a superdome!
The morning sun's a new husband
leaping from his honeymoon bed,
The daybreaking sun an athlete
racing to the tape.

6 That's how God's Word vaults across the skies
from sunrise to sunset,
Melting ice, scorching deserts,
warming hearts to faith.

7-9 The revelation of GOD is whole
and pulls our lives together.
The signposts of GOD are clear
and point out the right road.
The life-maps of GOD are right,
showing the way to joy.
The directions of GOD are plain
and easy on the eyes.
GOD's reputation is twenty-four-carat gold,
with a lifetime guarantee.
The decisions of GOD are accurate
down to the nth degree.

10 God's Word is better than a diamond,
better than a diamond set between emeralds.
You'll like it better than strawberries in spring,
better than red, ripe strawberries.

11-14 There's more: God's Word warns us of danger
and directs us to hidden treasure.
Otherwise how will we find our way?
Or know when we play the fool?
Clean the slate, God, so we can start the day fresh!
Keep me from stupid sins,
from thinking I can take over your work;
Then I can start this day sun-washed,
scrubbed clean of the grime of sin.

NEW KING JAMES VERSION

14 Let the words of my mouth and the
meditation of my heart
Be acceptable in Your sight,
O LORD, my strength and my Redeemer.

PSALM 20

THE ASSURANCE OF GOD'S SAVING WORK

To the Chief Musician. A Psalm of David.

1 May the LORD answer you in the day of
trouble;
May the name of the God of Jacob defend
you;
2 May He send you help from the sanctuary,
And strengthen you out of Zion;
3 May He remember all your offerings,
And accept your burnt sacrifice. *Selah*

4 May He grant you according to your heart's
desire,
And fulfill all your purpose.
5 We will rejoice in your salvation,
And in the name of our God we will set up
our banners!
May the LORD fulfill all your petitions.

6 Now I know that the LORD saves His
anointed;
He will answer him from His holy heaven
With the saving strength of His right hand.

7 Some *trust* in chariots, and some in horses;
But we will remember the name of the LORD
our God.
8 They have bowed down and fallen;
But we have risen and stand upright.

9 Save, LORD!
May the King answer us when we call.

PSALM 21

JOY IN THE SALVATION OF THE LORD

To the Chief Musician. A Psalm of David.

1 The king shall have joy in Your strength,
O LORD;
And in Your salvation how greatly shall he
rejoice!
2 You have given him his heart's desire,
And have not withheld the request of his
lips. *Selah*

3 For You meet him with the blessings of
goodness;
You set a crown of pure gold upon his head.
4 He asked life from You, *and* You gave *it* to
him—
Length of days forever and ever.
5 His glory *is* great in Your salvation;
Honor and majesty You have placed upon
him.
6 For You have made him most blessed
forever;
You have made him exceedingly glad with
Your presence.

THE MESSAGE

These are the words in my mouth;
these are what I chew on and pray.
Accept them when I place them
on the morning altar,
O God, my Altar-Rock,
God, Priest-of-My-Altar.

A DAVID PSALM

1-4 **20** GOD answer you on the day you crash,
The name God-of-Jacob put you out of
harm's reach,
Send reinforcements from Holy Hill,
Dispatch from Zion fresh supplies,
Exclaim over your offerings,
Celebrate your sacrifices,
Give you what your heart desires,
Accomplish your plans.

5 When you win, we plan to raise the roof
and lead the parade with our banners.
May all your wishes come true!

6 That clinches it—help's coming,
an answer's on the way,
everything's going to work out.

7-8 See those people polishing their chariots,
and those others grooming their horses?
But we're making garlands for GOD our
God.
The chariots will rust,
those horses pull up lame—
and we'll be on our feet, standing tall.

9 Make the king a winner, GOD;
the day we call, give us your answer.

A DAVID PSALM

1-7 **21** Your strength, GOD, is the king's
strength.
Helped, he's hollering Hosannas.
You gave him exactly what he wanted;
you didn't hold back.
You filled his arms with gifts;
you gave him a right royal welcome.
He wanted a good life; you gave it to him,
and then made it a *long* life as a bonus.
You lifted him high and bright as a cumulus
cloud,
then dressed him in rainbow colors.
You pile blessings on him;
you make him glad when you smile.

NEW KING JAMES VERSION

7For the king trusts in the LORD,
And through the mercy of the Most High he shall not be moved.

8Your hand will find all Your enemies;
Your right hand will find those who hate You.
9You shall make them as a fiery oven in the time of Your anger;
The LORD shall swallow them up in His wrath,
And the fire shall devour them.
10Their offspring You shall destroy from the earth,
And their descendants from among the sons of men.
11For they intended evil against You;
They devised a plot *which* they are not able *to perform*.
12Therefore You will make them turn their back;
You will make ready *Your arrows* on Your string toward their faces.

13Be exalted, O LORD, in Your own strength!
We will sing and praise Your power.

PSALM 22

THE SUFFERING, PRAISE, AND POSTERITY OF THE MESSIAH

To the Chief Musician. Set to "The Deer of the Dawn."[a] A Psalm of David.

1My God, My God, why have You forsaken Me?
Why are You so far from helping Me,
And from the words of My groaning?
2O My God, I cry in the daytime, but You do not hear;
And in the night season, and am not silent.

3But You *are* holy,
Enthroned in the praises of Israel.
4Our fathers trusted in You;
They trusted, and You delivered them.
5They cried to You, and were delivered;
They trusted in You, and were not ashamed.

6But I *am* a worm, and no man;
A reproach of men, and despised by the people.
7All those who see Me ridicule Me;
They shoot out the lip, they shake the head, *saying*,
8"He trusted[a] in the LORD, let Him rescue Him;
Let Him deliver Him, since He delights in Him!"

9But You *are* He who took Me out of the womb;
You made Me trust *while* on My mother's breasts.
10I was cast upon You from birth.
From My mother's womb
You *have been* My God.

22:title [a]Hebrew *Aijeleth Hashahar* **22:8** [a]Septuagint, Syriac, and Vulgate read *hoped;* Targum reads *praised.*

THE MESSAGE

Is it any wonder the king loves GOD?
that he's sticking with the Best?

8-12 With a fistful of enemies in one hand
and a fistful of haters in the other,
You radiate with such brilliance
that they cringe as before a furnace.
Now the furnace swallows them whole,
the fire eats them alive!
You purge the earth of their progeny,
you wipe the slate clean.
All their evil schemes, the plots they cook up,
have fizzled—every one.
You sent them packing;
they couldn't face you.

13 Show your strength, GOD, so no one can miss it.
We are out singing the good news!

A DAVID PSALM

1-2 **22** God, God . . . my God!
Why did you dump me
miles from nowhere?
Doubled up with pain, I call to God
all the day long. No answer. Nothing.
I keep at it all night, tossing and turning.

3-5 And you! Are you indifferent, above it all,
leaning back on the cushions of Israel's praise?
We know you were there for our parents:
they cried for your help and you gave it;
they trusted and lived a good life.

6-8 And here I am, a nothing—an earthworm,
something to step on, to squash.
Everyone pokes fun at me;
they make faces at me, they shake their heads:
"Let's see how GOD handles this one;
since God likes him so much, let *him* help him!"

9-11 And to think you were midwife at my birth,
setting me at my mother's breasts!
When I left the womb you cradled me;
since the moment of birth you've been my God.

NEW KING JAMES VERSION

11Be not far from Me,
For trouble *is* near;
For *there is* none to help.

12Many bulls have surrounded Me;
Strong *bulls* of Bashan have encircled Me.
13They gape at Me *with* their mouths,
Like a raging and roaring lion.

14I am poured out like water,
And all My bones are out of joint;
My heart is like wax;
It has melted within Me.
15My strength is dried up like a potsherd,
And My tongue clings to My jaws;
You have brought Me to the dust of death.

16For dogs have surrounded Me;
The congregation of the wicked has enclosed Me.
They pierced[a] My hands and My feet;
17I can count all My bones.
They look *and* stare at Me.
18They divide My garments among them,
And for My clothing they cast lots.

19But You, O LORD, do not be far from Me;
O My Strength, hasten to help Me!
20Deliver Me from the sword,
My precious *life* from the power of the dog.
21Save Me from the lion's mouth
And from the horns of the wild oxen!

You have answered Me.

22I will declare Your name to My brethren;
In the midst of the assembly I will praise You.
23You who fear the LORD, praise Him!
All you descendants of Jacob, glorify Him,
And fear Him, all you offspring of Israel!
24For He has not despised nor abhorred the affliction of the afflicted;
Nor has He hidden His face from Him;
But when He cried to Him, He heard.

25My praise *shall be* of You in the great assembly;
I will pay My vows before those who fear Him.
26The poor shall eat and be satisfied;
Those who seek Him will praise the LORD.
Let your heart live forever!

27All the ends of the world
Shall remember and turn to the LORD,
And all the families of the nations
Shall worship before You.[a]
28For the kingdom *is* the LORD's,
And He rules over the nations.

22:16 [a]Following some Hebrew manuscripts, Septuagint, Syriac, Vulgate; Masoretic Text reads *Like a lion*. **22:27** [a]Following Masoretic Text, Septuagint, and Targum; Arabic, Syriac, and Vulgate read *Him*.

THE MESSAGE

Then you moved far away
and trouble moved in next door.
I need a neighbor.

12-13 Herds of bulls come at me,
the raging bulls stampede,
Horns lowered, nostrils flaring,
like a herd of buffalo on the move.

14-15 I'm a bucket kicked over and spilled,
every joint in my body has been pulled apart.
My heart is a blob
of melted wax in my gut.
I'm dry as a bone,
my tongue black and swollen.
They have laid me out for burial
in the dirt.

16-18 Now packs of wild dogs come at me;
thugs gang up on me.
They pin me down hand and foot,
and lock me in a cage—a bag
Of bones in a cage, stared at
by every passerby.
They take my wallet and the shirt off my back,
and then throw dice for my clothes.

19-21 You, GOD—don't put off my rescue!
Hurry and help me!
Don't let them cut my throat;
don't let those mongrels devour me.
If you don't show up soon,
I'm done for—gored by the bulls,
meat for the lions.

22-24 Here's the story I'll tell my friends when they come to worship,
and punctuate it with Hallelujahs:
Shout Hallelujah, you God-worshipers;
give glory, you sons of Jacob;
adore him, you daughters of Israel.
He has never let you down,
never looked the other way
when you were being kicked around.
He has never wandered off to do his own thing;
he has been right there, listening.

25-26 Here in this great gathering for worship
I have discovered this praise-life.
And I'll do what I promised right here
in front of the God-worshipers.
Down-and-outers sit at GOD's table
and eat their fill.
Everyone on the hunt for God
is here, praising him.
"Live it up, from head to toe.
Don't ever quit!"

27-28 From the four corners of the earth
people are coming to their senses,
are running back to GOD.
Long-lost families
are falling on their faces before him.
GOD has taken charge;
from now on he has the last word.

NEW KING JAMES VERSION

29All the prosperous of the earth
Shall eat and worship;
All those who go down to the dust
Shall bow before Him,
Even he who cannot keep himself alive.

30A posterity shall serve Him.
It will be recounted of the Lord to the *next*
generation,
31They will come and declare His
righteousness to a people who will be
born,
That He has done *this*.

PSALM 23

THE LORD THE SHEPHERD OF HIS PEOPLE

A Psalm of David.

1The LORD *is* my shepherd;
I shall not want.
2He makes me to lie down in green pastures;
He leads me beside the still waters.
3He restores my soul;
He leads me in the paths of righteousness
For His name's sake.

4Yea, though I walk through the valley of the
shadow of death,
I will fear no evil;
For You *are* with me;
Your rod and Your staff, they comfort me.

5You prepare a table before me in the
presence of my enemies;
You anoint my head with oil;
My cup runs over.
6Surely goodness and mercy shall follow me
All the days of my life;
And I will dwell[a] in the house of the LORD
Forever.

PSALM 24

THE KING OF GLORY AND HIS KINGDOM

A Psalm of David.

1The earth *is* the LORD's, and all its fullness,
The world and those who dwell therein.
2For He has founded it upon the seas,
And established it upon the waters.

3Who may ascend into the hill of the LORD?
Or who may stand in His holy place?
4He who has clean hands and a pure heart,
Who has not lifted up his soul to an idol,
Nor sworn deceitfully.
5He shall receive blessing from the LORD,
And righteousness from the God of his
salvation.
6This *is* Jacob, the generation of those who
seek Him,
Who seek Your face. *Selah*

7Lift up your heads, O you gates!
And be lifted up, you everlasting doors!
And the King of glory shall come in.

23:6 [a]Following Septuagint, Syriac, Targum, and Vulgate; Masoretic Text reads *return*.

THE MESSAGE

29 All the power-mongers are before him
—worshiping!
All the poor and powerless, too
—worshiping!
Along with those who never got it together
—worshiping!

30-31 Our children and their children
will get in on this
As the word is passed along
from parent to child.
Babies not yet conceived
will hear the good news—
that God does what he says.

A DAVID PSALM

1-3 **23** GOD, my shepherd!
I don't need a thing.
You have bedded me down in lush
meadows,
you find me quiet pools to drink from.
True to your word,
you let me catch my breath
and send me in the right direction.

4 Even when the way goes through
Death Valley,
I'm not afraid
when you walk at my side.
Your trusty shepherd's crook
makes me feel secure.

5 You serve me a six-course dinner
right in front of my enemies.
You revive my drooping head;
my cup brims with blessing.

6 Your beauty and love chase after me
every day of my life.
I'm back home in the house of GOD
for the rest of my life.

A DAVID PSALM

1-2 **24** GOD claims Earth and everything in it,
GOD claims World and all who live
on it.
He built it on Ocean foundations,
laid it out on River girders.

3-4 Who can climb Mount GOD?
Who can scale the holy north-face?
Only the clean-handed,
only the pure-hearted;
Men who won't cheat,
women who won't seduce.

5-6 GOD is at their side;
with GOD's help they make it.
This, Jacob, is what happens
to God-seekers, God-questers.

7 Wake up, you sleepyhead city!
Wake up, you sleepyhead people!
King-Glory is ready to enter.

NEW KING JAMES VERSION

8Who *is* this King of glory?
The LORD strong and mighty,
The LORD mighty in battle.
9Lift up your heads, O you gates!
Lift up, you everlasting doors!
And the King of glory shall come in.
10Who is this King of glory?
The LORD of hosts,
He *is* the King of glory. *Selah*

PSALM 25

A PLEA FOR DELIVERANCE AND FORGIVENESS

A Psalm of David.

1To You, O LORD, I lift up my soul.
2O my God, I trust in You;
Let me not be ashamed;
Let not my enemies triumph over me.
3Indeed, let no one who waits on You be
ashamed;
Let those be ashamed who deal
treacherously without cause.

4Show me Your ways, O LORD;
Teach me Your paths.
5Lead me in Your truth and teach me,
For You *are* the God of my salvation;
On You I wait all the day.

6Remember, O LORD, Your tender mercies and
Your lovingkindnesses,
For they *are* from of old.
7Do not remember the sins of my youth, nor
my transgressions;
According to Your mercy remember me,
For Your goodness' sake, O LORD.

8Good and upright *is* the LORD;
Therefore He teaches sinners in the way.
9The humble He guides in justice,
And the humble He teaches His way.
10All the paths of the LORD *are* mercy and
truth,
To such as keep His covenant and His
testimonies.
11For Your name's sake, O LORD,
Pardon my iniquity, for it *is* great.

12Who *is* the man that fears the LORD?
Him shall He[a] teach in the way He[b] chooses.
13He himself shall dwell in prosperity,
And his descendants shall inherit the earth.
14The secret of the LORD *is* with those who
fear Him,
And He will show them His covenant.
15My eyes *are* ever toward the LORD,
For He shall pluck my feet out of the net.

25:12 [a]Or *he* [b]Or *he*

THE MESSAGE

8 Who is this King-Glory?
GOD, armed
and battle-ready.

9 Wake up, you sleepyhead city!
Wake up, you sleepyhead people!
King-Glory is ready to enter.

10 Who is this King-Glory?
GOD-of-the-Angel-Armies:
he is King-Glory.

A DAVID PSALM

1-2 25 My head is high, GOD, held high;
I'm looking to you, GOD;
No hangdog skulking for me.

3 I've thrown in my lot with you;
You won't embarrass me, will you?
Or let my enemies get the best of me?

Don't embarrass any of us
Who went out on a limb for you.
It's the traitors who should be humiliated.

4 Show me how you work, GOD;
School me in your ways.

5 Take me by the hand;
Lead me down the path of truth.
You are my Savior, aren't you?

6 Mark the milestones of your mercy and
love, GOD;
Rebuild the ancient landmarks!

7 Forget that I sowed wild oats;
Mark me with your sign of love.
Plan only the best for me, GOD!

8 GOD is fair and just;
He corrects the misdirected,
Sends them in the right direction.

9 He gives the rejects his hand,
And leads them step-by-step.

10 From now on every road you travel
Will take you to GOD.
Follow the Covenant signs;
Read the charted directions.

11 Keep up your reputation, GOD;
Forgive my bad life;
It's been a very bad life.

12 My question: What are God-worshipers
like?
Your answer: Arrows aimed at God's
bull's-eye.

13 They settle down in a promising place;
Their kids inherit a prosperous farm.

14 God-friendship is for God-worshipers;
They are the ones he confides in.

15 If I keep my eyes on GOD,
I won't trip over my own feet.

NEW KING JAMES VERSION

16Turn Yourself to me, and have mercy on me,
For I *am* desolate and afflicted.
17The troubles of my heart have enlarged;
Bring me out of my distresses!
18Look on my affliction and my pain,
And forgive all my sins.
19Consider my enemies, for they are many;
And they hate me with cruel hatred.
20Keep my soul, and deliver me;
Let me not be ashamed, for I put my trust in
You.
21Let integrity and uprightness preserve me,
For I wait for You.

22Redeem Israel, O God,
Out of all their troubles!

PSALM 26

A PRAYER FOR DIVINE SCRUTINY AND REDEMPTION
A Psalm of David.

1Vindicate me, O LORD,
For I have walked in my integrity.
I have also trusted in the LORD;
I shall not slip.
2Examine me, O LORD, and prove me;
Try my mind and my heart.
3For Your lovingkindness *is* before my eyes,
And I have walked in Your truth.
4I have not sat with idolatrous mortals,
Nor will I go in with hypocrites.
5I have hated the assembly of evildoers,
And will not sit with the wicked.

6I will wash my hands in innocence;
So I will go about Your altar, O LORD,
7That I may proclaim with the voice of
thanksgiving,
And tell of all Your wondrous works.
8LORD, I have loved the habitation of Your
house,
And the place where Your glory dwells.

9Do not gather my soul with sinners,
Nor my life with bloodthirsty men,
10In whose hands *is* a sinister scheme,
And whose right hand is full of bribes.

11But as for me, I will walk in my integrity;
Redeem me and be merciful to me.
12My foot stands in an even place;
In the congregations I will bless the LORD.

THE MESSAGE

16 Look at me and help me!
I'm all alone and in big trouble.

17 My heart and kidneys are fighting each
other;
Call a truce to this civil war.

18 Take a hard look at my life of hard labor,
Then lift this ton of sin.

19 Do you see how many people
Have it in for me?
How viciously they hate me?

20 Keep watch over me and keep me out of
trouble;
Don't let me down when I run to you.

21 Use all your skill to put me together;
I wait to see your finished product.

22 GOD, give your people a break
From this run of bad luck.

A DAVID PSALM

1 26 Clear my name, GOD;
I've kept an honest shop.
I've thrown in my lot with you, GOD, and
I'm not budging.

2 Examine me, GOD, from head to foot,
order your battery of tests.
Make sure I'm fit
inside and out

3 So I never lose
sight of your love,
But keep in step with you,
never missing a beat.

4-5 I don't hang out with tricksters,
I don't pal around with thugs;
I hate that pack of gangsters,
I don't deal with double-dealers.

6-7 I scrub my hands with purest soap,
then join hands with the others in the
great circle,
dancing around your altar, GOD,
Singing God-songs at the top of my lungs,
telling God-stories.

8-10 GOD, I love living with you;
your house glows with your glory.
When it's time for spring cleaning,
don't sweep me out with the quacks and
crooks,
Men with bags of dirty tricks,
women with purses stuffed with
bribe-money.

11-12 You know I've been aboveboard with you;
now be aboveboard with me.
I'm on the level with you, GOD;
I bless you every chance I get.

NEW KING JAMES VERSION

PSALM 27

AN EXUBERANT DECLARATION OF FAITH

A Psalm of David.

1The LORD *is* my light and my salvation;
Whom shall I fear?
The LORD *is* the strength of my life;
Of whom shall I be afraid?
2When the wicked came against me
To eat up my flesh,
My enemies and foes,
They stumbled and fell.
3Though an army may encamp against me,
My heart shall not fear;
Though war may rise against me,
In this I *will be* confident.

4One *thing* I have desired of the LORD,
That will I seek:
That I may dwell in the house of the LORD
All the days of my life,
To behold the beauty of the LORD,
And to inquire in His temple.
5For in the time of trouble
He shall hide me in His pavilion;
In the secret place of His tabernacle
He shall hide me;
He shall set me high upon a rock.

6And now my head shall be lifted up above my enemies all around me;
Therefore I will offer sacrifices of joy in His tabernacle;
I will sing, yes, I will sing praises to the LORD.

7Hear, O LORD, *when* I cry with my voice!
Have mercy also upon me, and answer me.
8*When You said,* "Seek My face,"
My heart said to You, "Your face, LORD, I will seek."
9Do not hide Your face from me;
Do not turn Your servant away in anger;
You have been my help;
Do not leave me nor forsake me,
O God of my salvation.
10When my father and my mother forsake me,
Then the LORD will take care of me.

11Teach me Your way, O LORD,
And lead me in a smooth path, because of my enemies.
12Do not deliver me to the will of my adversaries;
For false witnesses have risen against me,
And such as breathe out violence.
13*I would have lost heart,* unless I had believed
That I would see the goodness of the LORD
In the land of the living.

14Wait on the LORD;
Be of good courage,
And He shall strengthen your heart;
Wait, I say, on the LORD!

THE MESSAGE

A DAVID PSALM

1 27 Light, space, zest—
that's GOD!
So, with him on my side I'm fearless,
afraid of no one and nothing.

2 When vandal hordes ride down
ready to eat me alive,
Those bullies and toughs
fall flat on their faces.

3 When besieged,
I'm calm as a baby.
When all hell breaks loose,
I'm collected and cool.

4 I'm asking GOD for one thing,
only one thing:
To live with him in his house
my whole life long.
I'll contemplate his beauty;
I'll study at his feet.

5 That's the only quiet, secure place
in a noisy world,
The perfect getaway,
far from the buzz of traffic.

6 God holds me head and shoulders
above all who try to pull me down.
I'm headed for his place to offer anthems
that will raise the roof!
Already I'm singing God-songs;
I'm making music to GOD.

7-9 Listen, GOD, I'm calling at the top of my lungs:
"Be good to me! Answer me!"
When my heart whispered, "Seek God,"
my whole being replied,
"I'm seeking him!"
Don't hide from me now!

9-10 You've always been right there for me;
don't turn your back on me now.
Don't throw me out, don't abandon me;
you've always kept the door open.
My father and mother walked out and left me,
but GOD took me in.

11-12 Point me down your highway, GOD;
direct me along a well-lighted street;
show my enemies whose side you're on.
Don't throw me to the dogs,
those liars who are out to get me,
filling the air with their threats.

13-14 I'm sure now I'll see God's goodness
in the exuberant earth.
Stay with GOD!
Take heart. Don't quit.
I'll say it again:
Stay with GOD.

NEW KING JAMES VERSION

PSALM 28

REJOICING IN ANSWERED PRAYER
A Psalm of David.

1To You I will cry, O LORD my Rock:
Do not be silent to me,
Lest, if You *are* silent to me,
I become like those who go down to the pit.
2Hear the voice of my supplications
When I cry to You,
When I lift up my hands toward Your holy sanctuary.

3Do not take me away with the wicked
And with the workers of iniquity,
Who speak peace to their neighbors,
But evil *is* in their hearts.
4Give them according to their deeds,
And according to the wickedness of their endeavors;
Give them according to the work of their hands;
Render to them what they deserve.
5Because they do not regard the works of the LORD,
Nor the operation of His hands,
He shall destroy them
And not build them up.

6Blessed *be* the LORD,
Because He has heard the voice of my supplications!
7The LORD *is* my strength and my shield;
My heart trusted in Him, and I am helped;
Therefore my heart greatly rejoices,
And with my song I will praise Him.

8The LORD *is* their strength,[a]
And He *is* the saving refuge of His anointed.
9Save Your people,
And bless Your inheritance;
Shepherd them also,
And bear them up forever.

PSALM 29

PRAISE TO GOD IN HIS HOLINESS AND MAJESTY
A Psalm of David.

1Give unto the LORD, O you mighty ones,
Give unto the LORD glory and strength.
2Give unto the LORD the glory due to His name;
Worship the LORD in the beauty of holiness.

3The voice of the LORD *is* over the waters;
The God of glory thunders;
The LORD *is* over many waters.
4The voice of the LORD *is* powerful;
The voice of the LORD *is* full of majesty.

5The voice of the LORD breaks the cedars,
Yes, the LORD splinters the cedars of Lebanon.

28:8 [a]Following Masoretic Text and Targum; Septuagint, Syriac, and Vulgate read *the strength of His people.*

THE MESSAGE

A DAVID PSALM

1 **28** Don't turn a deaf ear
when I call you, GOD.
If all I get from you is
deafening silence,
I'd be better off
in the Black Hole.

2 I'm letting you know what I need,
calling out for help
And lifting my arms
toward your inner sanctum.

3-4 Don't shove me into
the same jail cell with those crooks,
With those who are
full-time employees of evil.
They talk a good line of "peace,"
then moonlight for the Devil.

Pay them back for what they've done,
for how bad they've been.
Pay them back for their long hours
in the Devil's workshop;
Then cap it with a huge bonus.

5 Because they have no idea how God works
or what he is up to,
God will smash them to smithereens
and walk away from the ruins.

6-7 Blessed be GOD—
he heard me praying.
He proved he's on my side;
I've thrown my lot in with him.

Now I'm jumping for joy,
and shouting and singing my thanks to him.

8-9 GOD is all strength for his people,
ample refuge for his chosen leader;
Save your people
and bless your heritage.
Care for them;
carry them like a good shepherd.

A DAVID PSALM

1-2 **29** Bravo, GOD, bravo!
Gods and all angels shout, "Encore!"
In awe before the glory,
in awe before God's visible power.
Stand at attention!
Dress your best to honor him!

3 GOD thunders across the waters,
Brilliant, his voice and his face, streaming brightness—
GOD, across the flood waters.

4 GOD's thunder tympanic,
GOD's thunder symphonic.

5 GOD's thunder smashes cedars,
GOD topples the northern cedars.

NEW KING JAMES VERSION

6He makes them also skip like a calf,
Lebanon and Sirion like a young wild ox.
7The voice of the LORD divides the flames of fire.

8The voice of the LORD shakes the wilderness;
The LORD shakes the Wilderness of Kadesh.
9The voice of the LORD makes the deer give birth,
And strips the forests bare;
And in His temple everyone says, "Glory!"

10The LORD sat *enthroned* at the Flood,
And the LORD sits as King forever.
11The LORD will give strength to His people;
The LORD will bless His people with peace.

PSALM 30

THE BLESSEDNESS OF ANSWERED PRAYER

A Psalm. A Song at the dedication of the house of David.

1I will extol You, O LORD, for You have lifted me up,
And have not let my foes rejoice over me.
2O LORD my God, I cried out to You,
And You healed me.
3O LORD, You brought my soul up from the grave;
You have kept me alive, that I should not go down to the pit.[a]

4Sing praise to the LORD, you saints of His,
And give thanks at the remembrance of His holy name.[a]
5For His anger *is but for* a moment,
His favor *is for* life;
Weeping may endure for a night,
But joy *comes* in the morning.

6Now in my prosperity I said,
"I shall never be moved."
7LORD, by Your favor You have made my mountain stand strong;
You hid Your face, *and* I was troubled.

8I cried out to You, O LORD;
And to the LORD I made supplication:
9"What profit *is there* in my blood,
When I go down to the pit?
Will the dust praise You?
Will it declare Your truth?
10Hear, O LORD, and have mercy on me;
LORD, be my helper!"

11You have turned for me my mourning into dancing;
You have put off my sackcloth and clothed me with gladness,
12To the end that *my* glory may sing praise to You and not be silent.
O LORD my God, I will give thanks to You forever.

30:3 [a]Following Qere and Targum; Kethib, Septuagint, Syriac, and Vulgate read *from those who descend to the pit.* **30:4** [a]Or *His holiness*

THE MESSAGE

6 The mountain ranges skip like spring colts,
The high ridges jump like wild kid goats.

7-8 GOD's thunder spits fire.
GOD thunders, the wilderness quakes;
He makes the desert of Kadesh shake.

9 GOD's thunder sets the oak trees dancing
A wild dance, whirling; the pelting rain strips their branches.
We fall to our knees—we call out, "Glory!"

10 Above the floodwaters is GOD's throne
from which his power flows,
from which he rules the world.

11 GOD makes his people strong.
GOD gives his people peace.

A DAVID PSALM

1 30 I give you all the credit, GOD—
you got me out of that mess,
you didn't let my foes gloat.

2-3 GOD, my God, I yelled for help
and you put me together.
GOD, you pulled me out of the grave,
gave me another chance at life
when I was down-and-out.

4-5 All you saints! Sing your hearts out to GOD!
Thank him to his face!
He gets angry once in a while, but across a lifetime there is only love.
The nights of crying your eyes out
give way to days of laughter.

6-7 When things were going great
I crowed, "I've got it made.
I'm GOD's favorite.
He made me king of the mountain."
Then you looked the other way
and I fell to pieces.

8-10 I called out to you, GOD;
I laid my case before you:
"Can you sell me for a profit when I'm dead?
auction me off at a cemetery yard sale?
When I'm 'dust to dust' my songs
and stories of you won't sell.
So listen! and be kind!
Help me out of this!"

11-12 You did it: you changed wild lament
into whirling dance;
You ripped off my black mourning band
and decked me with wildflowers.
I'm about to burst with song;
I can't keep quiet about you.
GOD, my God,
I can't thank you enough.

NEW KING JAMES VERSION

PSALM 31

THE LORD A FORTRESS IN ADVERSITY

To the Chief Musician. A Psalm of David.

1 In You, O LORD, I put my trust;
Let me never be ashamed;
Deliver me in Your righteousness.
2 Bow down Your ear to me,
Deliver me speedily;
Be my rock of refuge,
A fortress of defense to save me.

3 For You *are* my rock and my fortress;
Therefore, for Your name's sake,
Lead me and guide me.
4 Pull me out of the net which they have
secretly laid for me,
For You *are* my strength.
5 Into Your hand I commit my spirit;
You have redeemed me, O LORD God of
truth.

6 I have hated those who regard useless idols;
But I trust in the LORD.
7 I will be glad and rejoice in Your mercy,
For You have considered my trouble;
You have known my soul in adversities,
8 And have not shut me up into the hand of
the enemy;
You have set my feet in a wide place.

9 Have mercy on me, O LORD, for I am in
trouble;
My eye wastes away with grief,
Yes, my soul and my body!
10 For my life is spent with grief,
And my years with sighing;
My strength fails because of my iniquity,
And my bones waste away.
11 I am a reproach among all my enemies,
But especially among my neighbors,
And *am* repulsive to my acquaintances;
Those who see me outside flee from me.
12 I am forgotten like a dead man, out of mind;
I am like a broken vessel.
13 For I hear the slander of many;
Fear *is* on every side;
While they take counsel together against me,
They scheme to take away my life.

14 But as for me, I trust in You, O LORD;
I say, "You *are* my God."
15 My times *are* in Your hand;
Deliver me from the hand of my enemies,
And from those who persecute me.
16 Make Your face shine upon Your servant;
Save me for Your mercies' sake.
17 Do not let me be ashamed, O LORD, for I
have called upon You;
Let the wicked be ashamed;
Let them be silent in the grave.
18 Let the lying lips be put to silence,
Which speak insolent things proudly and
contemptuously against the righteous.

19 Oh, how great *is* Your goodness,
Which You have laid up for those who fear
You,

THE MESSAGE

A DAVID PSALM

1-2 **31** I run to you, GOD; I run for dear life.
Don't let me down!
Take me seriously this time!
Get down on my level and listen,
and please—no procrastination!
Your granite cave a hiding place,
your high cliff aerie a place of safety.

3-5 You're my cave to hide in,
my cliff to climb.
Be my safe leader,
be my true mountain guide.
Free me from hidden traps;
I want to hide in you.
I've put my life in your hands.
You won't drop me,
you'll never let me down.

6-13 I hate all this silly religion,
but you, GOD, I trust.
I'm leaping and singing in the circle of your
love;
you saw my pain,
you disarmed my tormentors,
You didn't leave me in their clutches
but gave me room to breathe.
Be kind to me, GOD—
I'm in deep, deep trouble again.
I've cried my eyes out;
I feel hollow inside.
My life leaks away, groan by groan;
my years fade out in sighs.
My troubles have worn me out,
turned my bones to powder.
To my enemies I'm a monster;
I'm ridiculed by the neighbors.
My friends are horrified;
they cross the street to avoid me.
They want to blot me from memory,
forget me like a corpse in a grave,
discard me like a broken dish in the
trash.
The street-talk gossip has me
"criminally insane"!
Behind locked doors they plot
how to ruin me for good.

14-18 Desperate, I throw myself on you:
you are my God!
Hour by hour I place my days in your hand,
safe from the hands out to get me.
Warm me, your servant, with a smile;
save me because you love me.
Don't embarrass me by not showing up;
I've given you plenty of notice.
Embarrass the wicked, stand them up,
leave them stupidly shaking their heads
as they drift down to hell.
Gag those loudmouthed liars
who heckle me, your follower,
with jeers and catcalls.

19-22 What a stack of blessing you have piled up
for those who worship you,

NEW KING JAMES VERSION

Which You have prepared for those who
trust in You
In the presence of the sons of men!
20You shall hide them in the secret place of
Your presence
From the plots of man;
You shall keep them secretly in a pavilion
From the strife of tongues.

21Blessed *be* the LORD,
For He has shown me His marvelous
kindness in a strong city!
22For I said in my haste,
"I am cut off from before Your eyes";
Nevertheless You heard the voice of my
supplications
When I cried out to You.

23Oh, love the LORD, all you His saints!
For the LORD preserves the faithful,
And fully repays the proud person.
24Be of good courage,
And He shall strengthen your heart,
All you who hope in the LORD.

PSALM 32

THE JOY OF FORGIVENESS

A Psalm of David. A Contemplation.[a]

1Blessed *is he whose* transgression *is*
forgiven,
Whose sin *is* covered.
2Blessed *is* the man to whom the LORD does
not impute iniquity,
And in whose spirit *there is* no deceit.

3When I kept silent, my bones grew old
Through my groaning all the day long.
4For day and night Your hand was heavy
upon me;
My vitality was turned into the drought of
summer. *Selah*
5I acknowledged my sin to You,
And my iniquity I have not hidden.
I said, "I will confess my transgressions to
the LORD,"
And You forgave the iniquity of my sin. *Selah*

6For this cause everyone who is godly shall
pray to You
In a time when You may be found;
Surely in a flood of great waters
They shall not come near him.
7You *are* my hiding place;
You shall preserve me from trouble;
You shall surround me with songs of
deliverance. *Selah*

8I will instruct you and teach you in the way
you should go;
I will guide you with My eye.
9Do not be like the horse *or* like the mule,
Which have no understanding,
Which must be harnessed with bit and
bridle,
Else they will not come near you.

32:title [a]Hebrew *Maschil*

THE MESSAGE

Ready and waiting for all who run to you
to escape an unkind world.
You hide them safely away
from the opposition.
As you slam the door on those oily,
mocking faces,
you silence the poisonous gossip.
Blessed GOD!
His love is the wonder of the world.
Trapped by a siege, I panicked.
"Out of sight, out of mind," I said.
But you heard me say it,
you heard and listened.

23 Love GOD, all you saints;
GOD takes care of all who stay close to
him,
But he pays back in full
those arrogant enough to go it alone.

24 Be brave. Be strong. Don't give up.
Expect GOD to get here soon.

A DAVID PSALM

1 **32** Count yourself lucky, how happy you
must be—
you get a fresh start,
your slate's wiped clean.

2 Count yourself lucky—
GOD holds nothing against you
and you're holding nothing back from
him.

3 When I kept it all inside,
my bones turned to powder,
my words became daylong groans.

4 The pressure never let up;
all the juices of my life dried up.

5 Then I let it all out;
I said, "I'll make a clean breast of my
failures to GOD."

Suddenly the pressure was gone—
my guilt dissolved,
my sin disappeared.

6 These things add up. Every one of us needs
to pray;
when all hell breaks loose and the dam
bursts
we'll be on high ground, untouched.

7 GOD's my island hideaway,
keeps danger far from the shore,
throws garlands of hosannas around my
neck.

8 Let me give you some good advice;
I'm looking you in the eye
and giving it to you straight:

9 "Don't be ornery like a horse or mule
that needs bit and bridle
to stay on track."

NEW KING JAMES VERSION

[10]Many sorrows *shall be* to the wicked;
But he who trusts in the LORD, mercy shall surround him.
[11]Be glad in the LORD and rejoice, you righteous;
And shout for joy, all *you* upright in heart!

PSALM 33

THE SOVEREIGNTY OF THE LORD IN CREATION AND HISTORY

[1]Rejoice in the LORD, O you righteous!
For praise from the upright is beautiful.
[2]Praise the LORD with the harp;
Make melody to Him with an instrument of ten strings.
[3]Sing to Him a new song;
Play skillfully with a shout of joy.

[4]For the word of the LORD *is* right,
And all His work *is done* in truth.
[5]He loves righteousness and justice;
The earth is full of the goodness of the LORD.

[6]By the word of the LORD the heavens were made,
And all the host of them by the breath of His mouth.
[7]He gathers the waters of the sea together as a heap;[a]
He lays up the deep in storehouses.

[8]Let all the earth fear the LORD;
Let all the inhabitants of the world stand in awe of Him.
[9]For He spoke, and it was *done;*
He commanded, and it stood fast.

[10]The LORD brings the counsel of the nations to nothing;
He makes the plans of the peoples of no effect.
[11]The counsel of the LORD stands forever,
The plans of His heart to all generations.
[12]Blessed *is* the nation whose God *is* the LORD,
The people He has chosen as His own inheritance.

[13]The LORD looks from heaven;
He sees all the sons of men.
[14]From the place of His dwelling He looks
On all the inhabitants of the earth;
[15]He fashions their hearts individually;
He considers all their works.

[16]No king *is* saved by the multitude of an army;
A mighty man is not delivered by great strength.
[17]A horse *is* a vain hope for safety;
Neither shall it deliver *any* by its great strength.

[18]Behold, the eye of the LORD *is* on those who fear Him,
On those who hope in His mercy,

33:7 [a]Septuagint, Targum, and Vulgate read *in a vessel.*

THE MESSAGE

10 God-defiers are always in trouble;
GOD-affirmers find themselves loved
every time they turn around.

11 Celebrate GOD.
Sing together—everyone!
All you honest hearts, raise the roof!

1-3 **33** Good people, cheer GOD!
Right-living people sound best when praising.
Use guitars to reinforce your Hallelujahs!
Play his praise on a grand piano!
Invent your own new song to him;
give him a trumpet fanfare.

4-5 For GOD's Word is solid to the core;
everything he makes is sound inside and out.
He loves it when everything fits,
when his world is in plumb-line true.
Earth is drenched
in GOD's affectionate satisfaction.

6-7 The skies were made by GOD's command;
he breathed the word and the stars popped out.
He scooped Sea into his jug,
put Ocean in his keg.

8-9 Earth-creatures, bow before GOD;
world-dwellers—down on your knees!
Here's why: he spoke and there it was,
in place the moment he said so.

10-12 GOD takes the wind out of Babel pretense,
he shoots down the world's power-schemes.
GOD's plan for the world stands up,
all his designs are made to last.
Blessed is the country with GOD for God;
blessed are the people he's put in his will.

13-15 From high in the skies GOD looks around,
he sees all Adam's brood.
From where he sits
he overlooks all us earth-dwellers.
He has shaped each person in turn;
now he watches everything we do.

16-17 No king succeeds with a big army alone,
no warrior wins by brute strength.
Horsepower is not the answer;
no one gets by on muscle alone.

18-19 Watch this: God's eye is on those who respect him,
the ones who are looking for his love.

NEW KING JAMES VERSION

19To deliver their soul from death,
And to keep them alive in famine.

20Our soul waits for the LORD;
He *is* our help and our shield.
21For our heart shall rejoice in Him,
Because we have trusted in His holy name.
22Let Your mercy, O LORD, be upon us,
Just as we hope in You.

PSALM 34

THE HAPPINESS OF THOSE WHO TRUST IN GOD

A Psalm of David when he pretended madness before Abimelech, who drove him away, and he departed.

1I will bless the LORD at all times;
His praise *shall* continually *be* in my mouth.
2My soul shall make its boast in the LORD;
The humble shall hear *of it* and be glad.
3Oh, magnify the LORD with me,
And let us exalt His name together.

4I sought the LORD, and He heard me,
And delivered me from all my fears.
5They looked to Him and were radiant,
And their faces were not ashamed.
6This poor man cried out, and the LORD heard *him*,
And saved him out of all his troubles.
7The angel[a] of the LORD encamps all around those who fear Him,
And delivers them.

8Oh, taste and see that the LORD *is* good;
Blessed *is* the man *who* trusts in Him!
9Oh, fear the LORD, you His saints!
There is no want to those who fear Him.
10The young lions lack and suffer hunger;
But those who seek the LORD shall not lack any good *thing*.

11Come, you children, listen to me;
I will teach you the fear of the LORD.
12Who *is* the man *who* desires life,
And loves *many* days, that he may see good?
13Keep your tongue from evil,
And your lips from speaking deceit.
14Depart from evil and do good;
Seek peace and pursue it.

15The eyes of the LORD *are* on the righteous,
And His ears *are open* to their cry.
16The face of the LORD *is* against those who do evil,
To cut off the remembrance of them from the earth.

17*The righteous* cry out, and the LORD hears,
And delivers them out of all their troubles.

34:7 [a]Or *Angel*

THE MESSAGE

He's ready to come to their rescue in bad times;
in lean times he keeps body and soul together.

20-22 We're depending on GOD;
he's everything we need.
What's more, our hearts brim with joy
since we've taken for our own his holy name.
Love us, GOD, with all you've got—
that's what we're depending on.

A DAVID PSALM, WHEN HE OUTWITTED ABIMELECH AND GOT AWAY

1 34 I bless GOD every chance I get;
my lungs expand with his praise.

2 I live and breathe GOD;
if things aren't going well, hear this and be happy:

3 Join me in spreading the news;
together let's get the word out.

4 GOD met me more than halfway,
he freed me from my anxious fears.

5 Look at him; give him your warmest smile.
Never hide your feelings from him.

6 When I was desperate, I called out,
and GOD got me out of a tight spot.

7 GOD's angel sets up a circle
of protection around us while we pray.

8 Open your mouth and taste, open your eyes and see—
how good GOD is.
Blessed are you who run to him.

9 Worship GOD if you want the best;
worship opens doors to all his goodness.

10 Young lions on the prowl get hungry,
but GOD-seekers are full of God.

11 Come, children, listen closely;
I'll give you a lesson in GOD worship.

12 Who out there has a lust for life?
Can't wait each day to come upon beauty?

13 Guard your tongue from profanity,
and no more lying through your teeth.

14 Turn your back on sin; do something good.
Embrace peace—don't let it get away!

15 GOD keeps an eye on his friends,
his ears pick up every moan and groan.

16 GOD won't put up with rebels;
he'll cull them from the pack.

17 Is anyone crying for help? GOD is listening,
ready to rescue you.

NEW KING JAMES VERSION

18The LORD *is* near to those who have a broken heart,
And saves such as have a contrite spirit.

19Many *are* the afflictions of the righteous,
But the LORD delivers him out of them all.
20He guards all his bones;
Not one of them is broken.
21Evil shall slay the wicked,
And those who hate the righteous shall be condemned.
22The LORD redeems the soul of His servants,
And none of those who trust in Him shall be condemned.

PSALM 35

THE LORD THE AVENGER OF HIS PEOPLE

A Psalm of David.

1Plead *my cause,* O LORD, with those who strive with me;
Fight against those who fight against me.
2Take hold of shield and buckler,
And stand up for my help.
3Also draw out the spear,
And stop those who pursue me.
Say to my soul,
"I *am* your salvation."

4Let those be put to shame and brought to dishonor
Who seek after my life;
Let those be turned back and brought to confusion
Who plot my hurt.
5Let them be like chaff before the wind,
And let the angel[a] of the LORD chase *them.*
6Let their way be dark and slippery,
And let the angel of the LORD pursue them.
7For without cause they have hidden their net for me *in* a pit,
Which they have dug without cause for my life.
8Let destruction come upon him unexpectedly,
And let his net that he has hidden catch himself;
Into that very destruction let him fall.

9And my soul shall be joyful in the LORD;
It shall rejoice in His salvation.
10All my bones shall say,
"LORD, who *is* like You,
Delivering the poor from him who is too strong for him,
Yes, the poor and the needy from him who plunders him?"

11Fierce witnesses rise up;
They ask me *things* that I do not know.
12They reward me evil for good,
To the sorrow of my soul.

35:5 [a]Or *Angel*

THE MESSAGE

18 If your heart is broken, you'll find GOD right there;
if you're kicked in the gut, he'll help you catch your breath.

19 Disciples so often get into trouble;
still, GOD is there every time.

20 He's your bodyguard, shielding every bone;
not even a finger gets broken.

21 The wicked commit slow suicide;
they waste their lives hating the good.

22 GOD pays for each slave's freedom;
no one who runs to him loses out.

A DAVID PSALM

1-3 **35** Harass these hecklers, GOD,
punch these bullies in the nose.
Grab a weapon, anything at hand;
stand up for me!
Get ready to throw the spear, aim the javelin,
at the people who are out to get me.
Reassure me; let me hear you say,
"I'll save you."

4-8 When those thugs try to knife me in the back,
make them look foolish.
Frustrate all those
who are plotting my downfall.
Make them like cinders in a high wind,
with GOD's angel working the bellows.
Make their road lightless and mud-slick,
with GOD's angel on their tails.
Out of sheer cussedness they set a trap to catch me;
for no good reason they dug a ditch to stop me.
Surprise them with your ambush—
catch them in the very trap they set,
the disaster they planned for me.

9-10 But let me run loose and free,
celebrating GOD's great work,
Every bone in my body laughing, singing, "GOD,
there's no one like you.
You put the down-and-out on their feet
and protect the unprotected from bullies!"

11-12 Hostile accusers appear out of nowhere,
they stand up and badger me.
They pay me back misery for mercy,
leaving my soul empty.

NEW KING JAMES VERSION

13But as for me, when they were sick,
My clothing *was* sackcloth;
I humbled myself with fasting;
And my prayer would return to my own heart.
14I paced about as though *he were* my friend *or* brother;
I bowed down heavily, as one who mourns *for his* mother.

15But in my adversity they rejoiced
And gathered together;
Attackers gathered against me,
And I did not know *it;*
They tore *at me* and did not cease;
16With ungodly mockers at feasts
They gnashed at me with their teeth.

17Lord, how long will You look on?
Rescue me from their destructions,
My precious *life* from the lions.
18I will give You thanks in the great assembly;
I will praise You among many people.

19Let them not rejoice over me who are wrongfully my enemies;
Nor let them wink with the eye who hate me without a cause.
20For they do not speak peace,
But they devise deceitful matters
Against *the* quiet ones in the land.
21They also opened their mouth wide against me,
And said, "Aha, aha!
Our eyes have seen *it*."

22*This* You have seen, O LORD;
Do not keep silence.
O Lord, do not be far from me.
23Stir up Yourself, and awake to my vindication,
To my cause, my God and my Lord.
24Vindicate me, O LORD my God, according to Your righteousness;
And let them not rejoice over me.
25Let them not say in their hearts, "Ah, so we would have it!"
Let them not say, "We have swallowed him up."

26Let them be ashamed and brought to mutual confusion
Who rejoice at my hurt;
Let them be clothed with shame and dishonor
Who exalt themselves against me.

27Let them shout for joy and be glad,
Who favor my righteous cause;
And let them say continually,
"Let the LORD be magnified,
Who has pleasure in the prosperity of His servant."
28And my tongue shall speak of Your righteousness
And of Your praise all the day long.

THE MESSAGE

13-14 When they were sick, I dressed in black;
instead of eating, I prayed.
My prayers were like lead in my gut,
like I'd lost my best friend, my brother.
I paced, distraught as a motherless child,
hunched and heavyhearted.

15-16 But when I was down
they threw a party!
All the nameless riffraff of the town came
chanting insults about me.
Like barbarians desecrating a shrine,
they destroyed my reputation.

17-18 GOD, how long are you going
to stand there doing nothing?
Save me from their brutalities;
everything I've got is being thrown to the lions.
I will give you full credit
when everyone gathers for worship;
When the people turn out in force
I will say my Hallelujahs.

19-21 Don't let these liars, my enemies,
have a party at my expense,
Those who hate me for no reason,
winking and rolling their eyes.
No good is going to come
from that crowd;
They spend all their time cooking up gossip
against those who mind their own business.
They open their mouths
in ugly grins,
Mocking, "Ha-ha, ha-ha, thought you'd get away with it?
We've caught you hands down!"

22 Don't you see what they're doing, GOD?
You're not going to let them
Get by with it, are you? Not going to walk off
without *doing* something, are you?

23-26 Please get up—wake up! Tend to my case.
My God, my Lord—my life is on the line.
Do what you think is right, GOD, my God,
but don't make me pay for their good time.
Don't let them say to themselves,
"Ha-ha, we got what we wanted."
Don't let them say,
"We've chewed him up and spit him out."
Let those who are being hilarious
at my expense
Be made to look ridiculous.
Make them wear donkey's ears;
Pin them with the donkey's tail,
who made themselves so high and mighty!

27-28 But those who want
the best for me,
Let them have the last word—a glad shout!—
and say, over and over and over,
"GOD is great—everything works
together for good for his servant."
I'll tell the world how great and good you are,
I'll shout Hallelujah all day, every day.

NEW KING JAMES VERSION

PSALM 36

MAN'S WICKEDNESS AND GOD'S PERFECTIONS

To the Chief Musician. *A Psalm* of David the servant of the LORD.

1An oracle within my heart concerning the transgression of the wicked:
There is no fear of God before his eyes.
2For he flatters himself in his own eyes,
When he finds out his iniquity *and* when he hates.
3The words of his mouth *are* wickedness and deceit;
He has ceased to be wise *and* to do good.
4He devises wickedness on his bed;
He sets himself in a way *that is* not good;
He does not abhor evil.

5Your mercy, O LORD, *is* in the heavens;
Your faithfulness *reaches* to the clouds.
6Your righteousness *is* like the great mountains;
Your judgments *are* a great deep;
O LORD, You preserve man and beast.

7How precious *is* Your lovingkindness, O God!
Therefore the children of men put their trust under the shadow of Your wings.
8They are abundantly satisfied with the fullness of Your house,
And You give them drink from the river of Your pleasures.
9For with You *is* the fountain of life;
In Your light we see light.

10Oh, continue Your lovingkindness to those who know You,
And Your righteousness to the upright in heart.
11Let not the foot of pride come against me,
And let not the hand of the wicked drive me away.
12There the workers of iniquity have fallen;
They have been cast down and are not able to rise.

PSALM 37

THE HERITAGE OF THE RIGHTEOUS AND THE CALAMITY OF THE WICKED

A Psalm of David.

1Do not fret because of evildoers,
Nor be envious of the workers of iniquity.
2For they shall soon be cut down like the grass,
And wither as the green herb.

3Trust in the LORD, and do good;
Dwell in the land, and feed on His faithfulness.
4Delight yourself also in the LORD,
And He shall give you the desires of your heart.

5Commit your way to the LORD,
Trust also in Him,
And He shall bring *it* to pass.

THE MESSAGE

A DAVID PSALM

1-4 **36** The God-rebel tunes in to sedition—
all ears, eager to sin.
He has no regard for God,
he stands insolent before him.
He has smooth-talked himself
into believing
That his evil
will never be noticed.
Words gutter from his mouth,
dishwater dirty.
Can't remember when he
did anything decent.
Every time he goes to bed,
he fathers another evil plot.
When he's loose on the streets,
nobody's safe.
He plays with fire
and doesn't care who gets burned.

5-6 God's love is meteoric,
his loyalty astronomic,
His purpose titanic,
his verdicts oceanic.
Yet in his largeness
nothing gets lost;
Not a man, not a mouse,
slips through the cracks.

7-9 How exquisite your love, O God!
How eager we are to run under your wings,
To eat our fill at the banquet you spread
as you fill our tankards with Eden spring water.
You're a fountain of cascading light,
and you open our eyes to light.

10-12 Keep on loving your friends;
do your work in welcoming hearts.
Don't let the bullies kick me around,
the moral midgets slap me down.
Send the upstarts sprawling
flat on their faces in the mud.

A DAVID PSALM

1-2 **37** Don't bother your head with braggarts
or wish you could succeed like the wicked.
In no time they'll shrivel like grass clippings
and wilt like cut flowers in the sun.

3-4 Get insurance with GOD and do a good deed,
settle down and stick to your last.
Keep company with GOD,
get in on the best.

5-6 Open up before GOD, keep nothing back;
he'll do whatever needs to be done:

NEW KING JAMES VERSION

6He shall bring forth your righteousness as the light,
And your justice as the noonday.

7Rest in the LORD, and wait patiently for Him;
Do not fret because of him who prospers in his way,
Because of the man who brings wicked schemes to pass.
8Cease from anger, and forsake wrath;
Do not fret—*it* only *causes* harm.

9For evildoers shall be cut off;
But those who wait on the LORD,
They shall inherit the earth.
10For yet a little while and the wicked *shall be* no *more;*
Indeed, you will look carefully for his place,
But it *shall be* no *more.*
11But the meek shall inherit the earth,
And shall delight themselves in the abundance of peace.

12The wicked plots against the just,
And gnashes at him with his teeth.
13The Lord laughs at him,
For He sees that his day is coming.
14The wicked have drawn the sword
And have bent their bow,
To cast down the poor and needy,
To slay those who are of upright conduct.
15Their sword shall enter their own heart,
And their bows shall be broken.

16A little that a righteous man has
Is better than the riches of many wicked.
17For the arms of the wicked shall be broken,
But the LORD upholds the righteous.

18The LORD knows the days of the upright,
And their inheritance shall be forever.
19They shall not be ashamed in the evil time,
And in the days of famine they shall be satisfied.
20But the wicked shall perish;
And the enemies of the LORD,
Like the splendor of the meadows, shall vanish.
Into smoke they shall vanish away.

21The wicked borrows and does not repay,
But the righteous shows mercy and gives.
22For *those* blessed by Him shall inherit the earth,
But *those* cursed by Him shall be cut off.

23The steps of a *good* man are ordered by the LORD,
And He delights in his way.
24Though he fall, he shall not be utterly cast down;
For the LORD upholds *him with* His hand.

25I have been young, and *now* am old;
Yet I have not seen the righteous forsaken,
Nor his descendants begging bread.
26*He is* ever merciful, and lends;
And his descendants *are* blessed.

THE MESSAGE

He'll validate your life in the clear light of day
and stamp you with approval at high noon.

7 Quiet down before GOD,
be prayerful before him.
Don't bother with those who climb the ladder,
who elbow their way to the top.

8-9 Bridle your anger, trash your wrath,
cool your pipes—it only makes things worse.
Before long the crooks will be bankrupt;
GOD-investors will soon own the store.

10-11 Before you know it, the wicked will have had it;
you'll stare at his once famous place and—nothing!
Down-to-earth people will move in and take over,
relishing a huge bonanza.

12-13 Bad guys have it in for the good guys,
obsessed with doing them in.
But GOD isn't losing any sleep; to him
they're a joke with no punch line.

14-15 Bullies brandish their swords,
pull back on their bows with a flourish.
They're out to beat up on the harmless,
or mug that nice man out walking his dog.
A banana peel lands them flat on their faces—
slapstick figures in a moral circus.

16-17 Less is more and more is less.
One righteous will outclass fifty wicked,
For the wicked are moral weaklings
but the righteous are GOD-strong.

18-19 GOD keeps track of the decent folk;
what they do won't soon be forgotten.
In hard times, they'll hold their heads high;
when the shelves are bare, they'll be full.

20 God-despisers have had it;
GOD's enemies are finished—
Stripped bare like vineyards at harvest time,
vanished like smoke in thin air.

21-22 Wicked borrows and never returns;
Righteous gives and gives.
Generous gets it all in the end;
Stingy is cut off at the pass.

23-24 Stalwart walks in step with GOD;
his path blazed by GOD, he's happy.
If he stumbles, he's not down for long;
GOD has a grip on his hand.

25-26 I once was young, now I'm a graybeard—
not once have I seen an abandoned believer,
or his kids out roaming the streets.
Every day he's out giving and lending,
his children making him proud.

NEW KING JAMES VERSION

27Depart from evil, and do good;
And dwell forevermore.
28For the LORD loves justice,
And does not forsake His saints;
They are preserved forever,
But the descendants of the wicked shall be cut off.
29The righteous shall inherit the land,
And dwell in it forever.

30The mouth of the righteous speaks wisdom,
And his tongue talks of justice.
31The law of his God *is* in his heart;
None of his steps shall slide.

32The wicked watches the righteous,
And seeks to slay him.
33The LORD will not leave him in his hand,
Nor condemn him when he is judged.

34Wait on the LORD,
And keep His way,
And He shall exalt you to inherit the land;
When the wicked are cut off, you shall see *it.*
35I have seen the wicked in great power,
And spreading himself like a native green tree.
36Yet he passed away,[a] and behold, he *was* no *more;*
Indeed I sought him, but he could not be found.

37Mark the blameless *man,* and observe the upright;
For the future of *that* man *is* peace.
38But the transgressors shall be destroyed together;
The future of the wicked shall be cut off.

39But the salvation of the righteous *is* from the LORD;
He is their strength in the time of trouble.
40And the LORD shall help them and deliver them;
He shall deliver them from the wicked,
And save them,
Because they trust in Him.

PSALM 38

PRAYER IN TIME OF CHASTENING

A Psalm of David. To bring to remembrance.

1O LORD, do not rebuke me in Your wrath,
Nor chasten me in Your hot displeasure!
2For Your arrows pierce me deeply,
And Your hand presses me down.

3*There is* no soundness in my flesh
Because of Your anger,
Nor *any* health in my bones
Because of my sin.
4For my iniquities have gone over my head;
Like a heavy burden they are too heavy for me.
5My wounds are foul *and* festering
Because of my foolishness.

37:36 [a]Following Masoretic Text, Septuagint, and Targum; Syriac and Vulgate read *I passed by.*

THE MESSAGE

27-28 Turn your back on evil,
work for the good and don't quit.
GOD loves this kind of thing,
never turns away from his friends.

28-29 Live this way and you've got it made,
but bad eggs will be tossed out.
The good get planted on good land
and put down healthy roots.

30-31 Righteous chews on wisdom like a dog on a bone,
rolls virtue around on his tongue.
His heart pumps God's Word like blood through his veins;
his feet are as sure as a cat's.

32-33 Wicked sets a watch for Righteous,
he's out for the kill.
GOD, alert, is also on watch—
Wicked won't hurt a hair of his head.

34 Wait passionately for GOD,
don't leave the path.
He'll give you your place in the sun
while you watch the wicked lose it.

35-36 I saw Wicked bloated like a toad,
croaking pretentious nonsense.
The next time I looked there was nothing—
a punctured bladder, vapid and limp.

37-38 Keep your eye on the healthy soul,
scrutinize the straight life;
There's a future
in strenuous wholeness.
But the willful will soon be discarded;
insolent souls are on a dead-end street.

39-40 The spacious, free life is from GOD,
it's also protected and safe.
GOD-strengthened, we're delivered from evil—
when we run to him, he saves us.

A DAVID PSALM

1-2 38 Take a deep breath, GOD; calm down—
don't be so hasty with your punishing rod.
Your sharp-pointed arrows of rebuke draw blood;
my backside smarts from your caning.

3-4 I've lost twenty pounds in two months
because of your accusation.
My bones are brittle as dry sticks
because of my sin.
I'm swamped by my bad behavior,
collapsed under gunnysacks of guilt.

5-8 The cuts in my flesh stink and grow maggots
because I've lived so badly.

NEW KING JAMES VERSION

6I am troubled, I am bowed down greatly;
I go mourning all the day long.
7For my loins are full of inflammation,
And *there is* no soundness in my flesh.
8I am feeble and severely broken;
I groan because of the turmoil of my heart.

9Lord, all my desire *is* before You;
And my sighing is not hidden from You.
10My heart pants, my strength fails me;
As for the light of my eyes, it also has gone from me.

11My loved ones and my friends stand aloof from my plague,
And my relatives stand afar off.
12Those also who seek my life lay snares *for me;*
Those who seek my hurt speak of destruction,
And plan deception all the day long.

13But I, like a deaf *man,* do not hear;
And *I am* like a mute *who* does not open his mouth.
14Thus I am like a man who does not hear,
And in whose mouth *is* no response.

15For in You, O LORD, I hope;
You will hear, O Lord my God.
16For I said, "*Hear me,* lest they rejoice over me,
Lest, when my foot slips, they exalt *themselves* against me."

17For I *am* ready to fall,
And my sorrow *is* continually before me.
18For I will declare my iniquity;
I will be in anguish over my sin.
19But my enemies *are* vigorous, *and* they are strong;
And those who hate me wrongfully have multiplied.
20Those also who render evil for good,
They are my adversaries, because I follow *what is* good.

21Do not forsake me, O LORD;
O my God, be not far from me!
22Make haste to help me,
O Lord, my salvation!

PSALM 39

PRAYER FOR WISDOM AND FORGIVENESS

To the Chief Musician. To Jeduthun. A Psalm of David.

1I said, "I will guard my ways,
Lest I sin with my tongue;
I will restrain my mouth with a muzzle,
While the wicked are before me."
2I was mute with silence,
I held my peace *even* from good;
And my sorrow was stirred up.
3My heart was hot within me;
While I was musing, the fire burned.
Then I spoke with my tongue:

THE MESSAGE

And now I'm flat on my face
feeling sorry for myself morning to night.
All my insides are on fire,
my body is a wreck.
I'm on my last legs; I've had it—
my life is a vomit of groans.

9-16 Lord, my longings are sitting in plain sight,
my groans an old story to you.
My heart's about to break;
I'm a burned-out case.
Cataracts blind me to God and good;
old friends avoid me like the plague.
My cousins never visit,
my neighbors stab me in the back.
My competitors blacken my name,
devoutly they pray for my ruin.
But I'm deaf and mute to it all,
ears shut, mouth shut.
I don't hear a word they say,
don't speak a word in response.
What I do, GOD, is wait for you,
wait for my Lord, my God—you *will* answer!
I wait and pray so they won't laugh me off,
won't smugly strut off when I stumble.

17-20 I'm on the edge of losing it—
the pain in my gut keeps burning.
I'm ready to tell my story of failure,
I'm no longer smug in my sin.
My enemies are alive and in action,
a lynch mob after my neck.
I give out good and get back evil
from God-haters who can't stand a God-lover.

21-22 Don't dump me, GOD;
my God, don't stand me up.
Hurry and help me;
I want some wide-open space in my life!

A DAVID PSALM

1-3 **39** I'm determined to watch steps and tongue
so they won't land me in trouble.
I decided to hold my tongue
as long as Wicked is in the room.
"Mum's the word," I said, and kept quiet.
But the longer I kept silence
The worse it got—
my insides got hotter and hotter.
My thoughts boiled over;
I spilled my guts.

NEW KING JAMES VERSION

4"LORD, make me to know my end,
And what *is* the measure of my days,
That I may know how frail I *am*.
5Indeed, You have made my days *as* handbreadths,
And my age *is* as nothing before You;
Certainly every man at his best state *is* but vapor. *Selah*
6Surely every man walks about like a shadow;
Surely they busy themselves in vain;
He heaps up *riches*,
And does not know who will gather them.

7"And now, Lord, what do I wait for?
My hope *is* in You.
8Deliver me from all my transgressions;
Do not make me the reproach of the foolish.
9I was mute, I did not open my mouth,
Because it was You who did *it*.
10Remove Your plague from me;
I am consumed by the blow of Your hand.
11When with rebukes You correct man for iniquity,
You make his beauty melt away like a moth;
Surely every man *is* vapor. *Selah*

12"Hear my prayer, O LORD,
And give ear to my cry;
Do not be silent at my tears;
For I *am* a stranger with You,
A sojourner, as all my fathers *were*.
13Remove Your gaze from me, that I may regain strength,
Before I go away and am no more."

PSALM 40

FAITH PERSEVERING IN TRIAL

To the Chief Musician. A Psalm of David.

1I waited patiently for the LORD;
And He inclined to me,
And heard my cry.
2He also brought me up out of a horrible pit,
Out of the miry clay,
And set my feet upon a rock,
And established my steps.
3He has put a new song in my mouth—
Praise to our God;
Many will see *it* and fear,
And will trust in the LORD.

4Blessed *is* that man who makes the LORD his trust,
And does not respect the proud, nor such as turn aside to lies.
5Many, O LORD my God, *are* Your wonderful works
Which You have done;
And Your thoughts toward us
Cannot be recounted to You in order;
If I would declare and speak *of them*,
They are more than can be numbered.

6Sacrifice and offering You did not desire;
My ears You have opened.
Burnt offering and sin offering You did not require.

THE MESSAGE

4-6 "Tell me, what's going on, GOD?
How long do I have to live?
Give me the bad news!
You've kept me on pretty short rations;
my life is string too short to be saved.
Oh! we're all puffs of air.
Oh! we're all shadows in a campfire.
Oh! we're just spit in the wind.
We make our pile, and then we leave it.

7-11 "What am I doing in the meantime, Lord?
Hoping, that's what I'm doing—hoping
You'll save me from a rebel life,
save me from the contempt of dunces.
I'll say no more, I'll shut my mouth,
since you, Lord, are behind all this.
But I can't take it much longer.
When you put us through the fire
to purge us from our sin,
our dearest idols go up in smoke.
Are we also nothing but smoke?

12-13 "Ah, GOD, listen to my prayer, my cry—open your ears.
Don't be callous;
just look at these tears of mine.
I'm a stranger here. I don't know my way—
a migrant like my whole family.
Give me a break, cut me some slack
before it's too late and I'm out of here."

A DAVID PSALM

1-3 40 I waited and waited and waited for GOD.
At last he looked; finally he listened.
He lifted me out of the ditch,
pulled me from deep mud.
He stood me up on a solid rock
to make sure I wouldn't slip.
He taught me how to sing the latest God-song,
a praise-song to our God.
More and more people are seeing this:
they enter the mystery,
abandoning themselves to GOD.

4-5 Blessed are you who give yourselves over to GOD,
turn your backs on the world's "sure thing,"
ignore what the world worships;
The world's a huge stockpile
of GOD-wonders and God-thoughts.
Nothing and no one
comes close to you!
I start talking about you, telling what I know,
and quickly run out of words.
Neither numbers nor words
account for you.

6 Doing something for you, bringing something to you—
that's not what you're after.
Being religious, acting pious—
that's not what you're asking for.
You've opened my ears
so I can listen.

NEW KING JAMES VERSION

[7]Then I said, "Behold, I come;
In the scroll of the book *it is* written of me.
[8]I delight to do Your will, O my God,
And Your law *is* within my heart."

[9]I have proclaimed the good news of righteousness
In the great assembly;
Indeed, I do not restrain my lips,
O LORD, You Yourself know.
[10]I have not hidden Your righteousness within my heart;
I have declared Your faithfulness and Your salvation;
I have not concealed Your lovingkindness and Your truth
From the great assembly.

[11]Do not withhold Your tender mercies from me, O LORD;
Let Your lovingkindness and Your truth continually preserve me.
[12]For innumerable evils have surrounded me;
My iniquities have overtaken me, so that I am not able to look up;
They are more than the hairs of my head;
Therefore my heart fails me.

[13]Be pleased, O LORD, to deliver me;
O LORD, make haste to help me!
[14]Let them be ashamed and brought to mutual confusion
Who seek to destroy my life;
Let them be driven backward and brought to dishonor
Who wish me evil.
[15]Let them be confounded because of their shame,
Who say to me, "Aha, aha!"

[16]Let all those who seek You rejoice and be glad in You;
Let such as love Your salvation say continually,
"The LORD be magnified!"
[17]But I *am* poor and needy;
Yet the LORD thinks upon me.
You *are* my help and my deliverer;
Do not delay, O my God.

PSALM 41

THE BLESSING AND SUFFERING OF THE GODLY
To the Chief Musician. A Psalm of David.

[1]Blessed *is* he who considers the poor;
The LORD will deliver him in time of trouble.
[2]The LORD will preserve him and keep him alive,
And he will be blessed on the earth;
You will not deliver him to the will of his enemies.
[3]The LORD will strengthen him on his bed of illness;
You will sustain him on his sickbed.

THE MESSAGE

7-8 So I answered, "I'm coming.
I read in your letter what you wrote about me,
And I'm coming to the party
you're throwing for me."
That's when God's Word entered my life,
became part of my very being.

9-10 I've preached you to the whole congregation,
I've kept back nothing, GOD—you know that.
I didn't keep the news of your ways
a secret, didn't keep it to myself.
I told it all, how dependable you are, how thorough.
I didn't hold back pieces of love and truth
For myself alone. I told it all,
let the congregation know the whole story.

11-12 Now GOD, don't hold out on me,
don't hold back your passion.
Your love and truth
are all that keeps me together.
When troubles ganged up on me,
a mob of sins past counting,
I was so swamped by guilt
I couldn't see my way clear.
More guilt in my heart than hair on my head,
so heavy the guilt that my heart gave out.

13-15 Soften up, GOD, and intervene;
hurry and get me some help,
So those who are trying to kidnap my soul
will be embarrassed and lose face,
So anyone who gets a kick out of making me miserable
will be heckled and disgraced,
So those who pray for my ruin
will be booed and jeered without mercy.

16-17 But all who are hunting for you—
oh, let them sing and be happy.
Let those who know what you're all about
tell the world you're great and not quitting.
And me? I'm a mess. I'm nothing and have nothing:
make something of me.
You can do it; you've got what it takes—
but God, don't put it off.

A DAVID PSALM

1-3 **41** Dignify those who are down on their luck;
you'll feel good—*that's* what GOD does.
GOD looks after us all,
makes us robust with life—
Lucky to be in the land,
we're free from enemy worries.
Whenever we're sick and in bed,
GOD becomes our nurse,
nurses us back to health.

NEW KING JAMES VERSION

4I said, "LORD, be merciful to me;
Heal my soul, for I have sinned against You."
5My enemies speak evil of me:
"When will he die, and his name perish?"
6And if he comes to see *me*, he speaks lies;
His heart gathers iniquity to itself;
When he goes out, he tells *it*.

7All who hate me whisper together against me;
Against me they devise my hurt.
8"An evil disease," *they say*, "clings to him.
And *now* that he lies down, he will rise up no more."
9Even my own familiar friend in whom I trusted,
Who ate my bread,
Has lifted up *his* heel against me.

10But You, O LORD, be merciful to me, and raise me up,
That I may repay them.
11By this I know that You are well pleased with me,
Because my enemy does not triumph over me.
12As for me, You uphold me in my integrity,
And set me before Your face forever.

13Blessed *be* the LORD God of Israel
From everlasting to everlasting!
Amen and Amen.

Book Two: Psalms 42—72

PSALM 42

YEARNING FOR GOD IN THE MIDST OF DISTRESSES

To the Chief Musician. A Contemplation[a] of the sons of Korah.

1As the deer pants for the water brooks,
So pants my soul for You, O God.
2My soul thirsts for God, for the living God.
When shall I come and appear before God?[a]
3My tears have been my food day and night,
While they continually say to me,
"Where *is* your God?"

4When I remember these *things*,
I pour out my soul within me.
For I used to go with the multitude;
I went with them to the house of God,
With the voice of joy and praise,
With a multitude that kept a pilgrim feast.

5Why are you cast down, O my soul?
And *why* are you disquieted within me?
Hope in God, for I shall yet praise Him
For the help of His countenance.[a]

42:title [a]Hebrew *Maschil* **42:2** [a]Following Masoretic Text and Vulgate; some Hebrew manuscripts, Septuagint, Syriac, and Targum read *I see the face of God.* **42:5** [a]Following Masoretic Text and Targum; a few Hebrew manuscripts, Septuagint, Syriac, and Vulgate read *The help of my countenance, my God.*

THE MESSAGE

4-7 I said, "GOD, be gracious!
Put me together again—
my sins have torn me to pieces."
My enemies are wishing the worst for me;
they make bets on what day I will die.
If someone comes to see me,
he mouths empty platitudes,
All the while gathering gossip about me
to entertain the street-corner crowd.
These "friends" who hate me
whisper slanders all over town.
They form committees
to plan misery for me.

8-9 The rumor goes out, "He's got some dirty,
deadly disease. The doctors
have given up on him."
Even my best friend, the one I always told everything
—he ate meals at my house all the time!—
has bitten my hand.

10 GOD, give grace, get me up on my feet.
I'll show them a thing or two.

11-12 Meanwhile, I'm sure you're on my side—
no victory shouts yet from the enemy camp!
You know me inside and out, you hold me together,
you never fail to stand me tall in your presence
so I can look you in the eye.

13 Blessed is GOD, Israel's God,
always, always, always.
Yes. Yes. Yes.

A PSALM OF THE SONS OF KORAH

1-3 42 A white-tailed deer drinks
from the creek;
I want to drink God,
deep draughts of God.
I'm thirsty for God-alive.
I wonder, "Will I ever make it—
arrive and drink in God's presence?"
I'm on a diet of tears—
tears for breakfast, tears for supper.
All day long
people knock at my door,
Pestering,
"Where is this God of yours?"

4 These are the things I go over and over,
emptying out the pockets of my life.
I was always at the head of the worshiping crowd,
right out in front,
Leading them all,
eager to arrive and worship,
Shouting praises, singing thanksgiving—
celebrating, all of us, God's feast!

5 Why are you down in the dumps, dear soul?
Why are you crying the blues?
Fix my eyes on God—
soon I'll be praising again.
He puts a smile on my face.
He's my God.

NEW KING JAMES VERSION

[6]O my God,[a] my soul is cast down within me;
Therefore I will remember You from the land of the Jordan,
And from the heights of Hermon,
From the Hill Mizar.
[7]Deep calls unto deep at the noise of Your waterfalls;
All Your waves and billows have gone over me.
[8]The LORD will command His lovingkindness in the daytime,
And in the night His song *shall be* with me—
A prayer to the God of my life.

[9]I will say to God my Rock,
"Why have You forgotten me?
Why do I go mourning because of the oppression of the enemy?"
[10]*As* with a breaking of my bones,
My enemies reproach me,
While they say to me all day long,
"Where *is* your God?"

[11]Why are you cast down, O my soul?
And why are you disquieted within me?
Hope in God;
For I shall yet praise Him,
The help of my countenance and my God.

PSALM 43

PRAYER TO GOD IN TIME OF TROUBLE

[1]Vindicate me, O God,
And plead my cause against an ungodly nation;
Oh, deliver me from the deceitful and unjust man!
[2]For You *are* the God of my strength;
Why do You cast me off?
Why do I go mourning because of the oppression of the enemy?

[3]Oh, send out Your light and Your truth!
Let them lead me;
Let them bring me to Your holy hill
And to Your tabernacle.
[4]Then I will go to the altar of God,
To God my exceeding joy;
And on the harp I will praise You,
O God, my God.

[5]Why are you cast down, O my soul?
And why are you disquieted within me?
Hope in God;
For I shall yet praise Him,
The help of my countenance and my God.

42:6 [a]Following Masoretic Text and Targum; a few Hebrew manuscripts, Septuagint, Syriac, and Vulgate put *my God* at the end of verse 5.

THE MESSAGE

6-8 When my soul is in the dumps, I rehearse everything I know of you,
From Jordan depths to Hermon heights, including Mount Mizar.
Chaos calls to chaos,
to the tune of whitewater rapids.
Your breaking surf, your thundering breakers
crash and crush me.
Then GOD promises to love me all day,
sing songs all through the night!
My life is God's prayer.

9-10 Sometimes I ask God, my rock-solid God,
"Why did you let me down?
Why am I walking around in tears,
harassed by enemies?"
They're out for the kill, these
tormentors with their obscenities,
Taunting day after day,
"Where is this God of yours?"

11 Why are you down in the dumps, dear soul?
Why are you crying the blues?
Fix my eyes on God—
soon I'll be praising again.
He puts a smile on my face.
He's my God.

1-2 **43** Clear my name, God; stick up for me against these loveless, immoral people.
Get me out of here, away
from these lying degenerates.
I counted on you, God.
Why did you walk out on me?
Why am I pacing the floor, wringing my hands
over these outrageous people?

3-4 Give me your lantern and compass,
give me a map,
So I can find my way to the sacred mountain,
to the place of your presence,
To enter the place of worship,
meet my exuberant God,
Sing my thanks with a harp,
magnificent God, my God.

5 Why are you down in the dumps, dear soul?
Why are you crying the blues?
Fix my eyes on God—
soon I'll be praising again.
He puts a smile on my face.
He's my God.

NEW KING JAMES VERSION

PSALM 44

REDEMPTION REMEMBERED IN PRESENT DISHONOR

To the Chief Musician. A Contemplation[a] of the sons of Korah.

1We have heard with our ears, O God,
Our fathers have told us,
The deeds You did in their days,
In days of old:
2You drove out the nations with Your hand,
But them You planted;
You afflicted the peoples, and cast them out.
3For they did not gain possession of the land
by their own sword,
Nor did their own arm save them;
But it was Your right hand, Your arm, and
the light of Your countenance,
Because You favored them.

4You are my King, O God;[a]
Command[b] victories for Jacob.
5Through You we will push down our
enemies;
Through Your name we will trample those
who rise up against us.
6For I will not trust in my bow,
Nor shall my sword save me.
7But You have saved us from our enemies,
And have put to shame those who hated us.
8In God we boast all day long,
And praise Your name forever. *Selah*

9But You have cast *us* off and put us to
shame,
And You do not go out with our armies.
10You make us turn back from the enemy,
And those who hate us have taken spoil for
themselves.
11You have given us up like sheep *intended*
for food,
And have scattered us among the nations.
12You sell Your people for *next to* nothing,
And are not enriched by selling them.

13You make us a reproach to our neighbors,
A scorn and a derision to those all around
us.
14You make us a byword among the nations,
A shaking of the head among the peoples.
15My dishonor *is* continually before me,
And the shame of my face has covered me,
16Because of the voice of him who reproaches
and reviles,
Because of the enemy and the avenger.

17All this has come upon us;
But we have not forgotten You,
Nor have we dealt falsely with Your
covenant.
18Our heart has not turned back,
Nor have our steps departed from Your way;
19But You have severely broken us in the place
of jackals,
And covered us with the shadow of death.

44:title [a]Hebrew *Maschil* **44:4** [a]Following Masoretic Text and Targum; Septuagint and Vulgate read *and my God.* [b]Following Masoretic Text and Targum; Septuagint, Syriac, and Vulgate read *Who commands.*

THE MESSAGE

A PSALM OF THE SONS OF KORAH

1-3 **44** We've been hearing about this, God,
all our lives.
Our fathers told us the stories
their fathers told them,
How single-handedly you weeded out the
godless
from the fields and planted us,
How you sent those people packing
but gave us a fresh start.
We didn't fight for this land;
we didn't work for it—it was a gift!
You gave it, smiling as you gave it,
delighting as you gave it.

4-8 You're my King, O God—
command victories for Jacob!
With your help we'll wipe out our enemies,
in your name we'll stomp them to dust.
I don't trust in weapons;
my sword won't save me—
But it's you, you who saved us from the
enemy;
you made those who hate us lose face.
All day we parade God's praise—
we thank you by name over and over.

9-12 But now you've walked off and left us,
you've disgraced us and won't fight for
us.
You made us turn tail and run;
those who hate us have cleaned us out.
You delivered us as sheep to the butcher,
you scattered us to the four winds.
You sold your people at a discount—
you made nothing on the sale.

13-16 You made people on the street,
urchins, poke fun and call us names.
You made us a joke among the godless,
a cheap joke among the rabble.
Every day I'm up against it,
my nose rubbed in my shame—
Gossip and ridicule fill the air,
people out to get me crowd the street.

17-19 All this came down on us,
and we've done nothing to deserve it.
We never betrayed your Covenant: our
hearts
were never false, our feet never left your
path.
Do we deserve torture in a den of jackals?
or lockup in a black hole?

NEW KING JAMES VERSION

20If we had forgotten the name of our God,
Or stretched out our hands to a foreign god,
21Would not God search this out?
For He knows the secrets of the heart.
22Yet for Your sake we are killed all day long;
We are accounted as sheep for the slaughter.

23Awake! Why do You sleep, O Lord?
Arise! Do not cast *us* off forever.
24Why do You hide Your face,
And forget our affliction and our oppression?
25For our soul is bowed down to the dust;
Our body clings to the ground.
26Arise for our help,
And redeem us for Your mercies' sake.

PSALM 45

THE GLORIES OF THE MESSIAH AND HIS BRIDE

To the Chief Musician. Set to "The Lilies."[a] A Contemplation[b] of the sons of Korah. A Song of Love.

1My heart is overflowing with a good theme;
I recite my composition concerning the King;
My tongue *is* the pen of a ready writer.

2You are fairer than the sons of men;
Grace is poured upon Your lips;
Therefore God has blessed You forever.
3Gird Your sword upon *Your* thigh, O Mighty One,
With Your glory and Your majesty.
4And in Your majesty ride prosperously because of truth, humility, *and* righteousness;
And Your right hand shall teach You awesome things.
5Your arrows *are* sharp in the heart of the King's enemies;
The peoples fall under You.

6Your throne, O God, *is* forever and ever;
A scepter of righteousness *is* the scepter of Your kingdom.
7You love righteousness and hate wickedness;
Therefore God, Your God, has anointed You
With the oil of gladness more than Your companions.
8All Your garments *are scented* with myrrh and aloes *and* cassia,
Out of the ivory palaces, by which they have made You glad.
9Kings' daughters *are* among Your honorable women;
At Your right hand stands the queen in gold from Ophir.

10Listen, O daughter,
Consider and incline your ear;
Forget your own people also, and your father's house;

45:title [a]Hebrew *Shoshannim* [b]Hebrew *Maschil*

THE MESSAGE

20-22 If we had forgotten to pray to our God
or made fools of ourselves with store-bought gods,
Wouldn't God have figured this out?
We can't hide things from him.
No, you decided to make us martyrs,
lambs assigned for sacrifice each day.

23-26 Get up, GOD! Are you going to sleep all day?
Wake up! Don't you care what happens to us?
Why do you bury your face in the pillow?
Why pretend things are just fine with us?
And here we are—flat on our faces in the dirt,
held down with a boot on our necks.
Get up and come to our rescue.
If you love us so much, *Help us!*

A WEDDING SONG OF THE SONS OF KORAH

1 **45** My heart bursts its banks,
spilling beauty and goodness.
I pour it out in a poem to the king,
shaping the river into words:

2-4 "You're the handsomest of men;
every word from your lips is sheer grace,
and God has blessed you, blessed you so much.
Strap your sword to your side, warrior!
Accept praise! Accept due honor!
Ride majestically! Ride triumphantly!
Ride on the side of truth!
Ride for the righteous meek!

4-5 "Your instructions are glow-in-the-dark;
you shoot sharp arrows
Into enemy hearts; the king's
foes lie down in the dust, beaten.

6-7 "Your throne is God's throne,
ever and always;
The scepter of your royal rule
measures right living.
You love the right
and hate the wrong.
And that is why God, your very own God,
poured fragrant oil on your head,
Marking you out as king
from among your dear companions.

8-9 "Your ozone-drenched garments
are fragrant with mountain breeze.
Chamber music—from the throne room—
makes you want to dance.
Kings' daughters are maids in your court,
the Bride glittering with golden jewelry.

10-12 "Now listen, daughter, don't miss a word:
forget your country, put your home behind you.

New King James Version

[11]So the King will greatly desire your beauty;
Because He *is* your Lord, worship Him.
[12]And the daughter of Tyre *will come* with a gift;
The rich among the people will seek your favor.

[13]The royal daughter *is* all glorious within *the palace;*
Her clothing *is* woven with gold.
[14]She shall be brought to the King in robes of many colors;
The virgins, her companions who follow her, shall be brought to You.
[15]With gladness and rejoicing they shall be brought;
They shall enter the King's palace.

[16]Instead of Your fathers shall be Your sons,
Whom You shall make princes in all the earth.
[17]I will make Your name to be remembered in all generations;
Therefore the people shall praise You forever and ever.

PSALM 46

God the Refuge of His People and Conqueror of the Nations

To the Chief Musician. *A Psalm* of the sons of Korah. A Song for Alamoth.

[1]God *is* our refuge and strength,
A very present help in trouble.
[2]Therefore we will not fear,
Even though the earth be removed,
And though the mountains be carried into the midst of the sea;
[3]*Though* its waters roar *and* be troubled,
Though the mountains shake with its swelling. *Selah*

[4]*There is* a river whose streams shall make glad the city of God,
The holy *place* of the tabernacle of the Most High.
[5]God *is* in the midst of her, she shall not be moved;
God shall help her, just at the break of dawn.
[6]The nations raged, the kingdoms were moved;
He uttered His voice, the earth melted.

[7]The LORD of hosts *is* with us;
The God of Jacob *is* our refuge. *Selah*

[8]Come, behold the works of the LORD,
Who has made desolations in the earth.
[9]He makes wars cease to the end of the earth;
He breaks the bow and cuts the spear in two;
He burns the chariot in the fire.

[10]Be still, and know that I *am* God;
I will be exalted among the nations,
I will be exalted in the earth!

[11]The LORD of hosts *is* with us;
The God of Jacob *is* our refuge. *Selah*

The Message

Be *here*—the king is wild for you.
Since he's your lord, adore him.
Wedding gifts pour in from Tyre;
rich guests shower you with presents."

13-15 (Her wedding dress is dazzling,
lined with gold by the weavers;
All her dresses and robes
are woven with gold.
She is led to the king,
followed by her virgin companions.
A procession of joy and laughter!
a grand entrance to the king's palace!)

16-17 "Set your mind now on sons—
don't dote on father and grandfather.
You'll set your sons up as princes
all over the earth.
I'll make you famous for generations;
you'll be the talk of the town
for a long, long time."

A Song of the Sons of Korah

1-3 **46** God is a safe place to hide,
ready to help when we need him.
We stand fearless at the cliff-edge of doom,
courageous in seastorm and earthquake,
Before the rush and roar of oceans,
the tremors that shift mountains.

Jacob-wrestling God fights for us,
GOD-of-Angel-Armies protects us.

4-6 River fountains splash joy, cooling God's city,
this sacred haunt of the Most High.
God lives here, the streets are safe,
God at your service from crack of dawn.
Godless nations rant and rave, kings and kingdoms threaten,
but Earth does anything he says.

7 Jacob-wrestling God fights for us,
GOD-of-Angel-Armies protects us.

8-10 Attention, all! See the marvels of GOD!
He plants flowers and trees all over the earth,
Bans war from pole to pole,
breaks all the weapons across his knee.
"Step out of the traffic! Take a long,
loving look at me, your High God,
above politics, above everything."

11 Jacob-wrestling God fights for us,
GOD-of-Angel-Armies protects us.

NEW KING JAMES VERSION

PSALM 47

PRAISE TO GOD, THE RULER OF THE EARTH
To the Chief Musician. A Psalm of the sons of Korah.

1 Oh, clap your hands, all you peoples!
Shout to God with the voice of triumph!
2 For the LORD Most High *is* awesome;
He is a great King over all the earth.
3 He will subdue the peoples under us,
And the nations under our feet.
4 He will choose our inheritance for us,
The excellence of Jacob whom He loves. *Selah*

5 God has gone up with a shout,
The LORD with the sound of a trumpet.
6 Sing praises to God, sing praises!
Sing praises to our King, sing praises!
7 For God *is* the King of all the earth;
Sing praises with understanding.

8 God reigns over the nations;
God sits on His holy throne.
9 The princes of the people have gathered together,
The people of the God of Abraham.
For the shields of the earth *belong* to God;
He is greatly exalted.

PSALM 48

THE GLORY OF GOD IN ZION
A Song. A Psalm of the sons of Korah.

1 Great *is* the LORD, and greatly to be praised
In the city of our God,
In His holy mountain.
2 Beautiful in elevation,
The joy of the whole earth,
Is Mount Zion *on* the sides of the north,
The city of the great King.
3 God *is* in her palaces;
He is known as her refuge.

4 For behold, the kings assembled,
They passed by together.
5 They saw *it, and* so they marveled;
They were troubled, they hastened away.
6 Fear took hold of them there,
And pain, as of a woman in birth pangs,
7 *As when* You break the ships of Tarshish
With an east wind.

8 As we have heard,
So we have seen
In the city of the LORD of hosts,
In the city of our God:
God will establish it forever. *Selah*

9 We have thought, O God, on Your lovingkindness,
In the midst of Your temple.
10 According to Your name, O God,
So *is* Your praise to the ends of the earth;
Your right hand is full of righteousness.
11 Let Mount Zion rejoice,
Let the daughters of Judah be glad,
Because of Your judgments.

THE MESSAGE

A PSALM OF THE SONS OF KORAH

1-9 **47** Applause, everyone. Bravo, bravissimo!
Shout God-songs at the top of your lungs!
GOD Most High is stunning,
astride land and ocean.
He crushes hostile people,
puts nations at our feet.
He set us at the head of the line,
prize-winning Jacob, his favorite.
Loud cheers as God climbs the mountain,
a ram's horn blast at the summit.
Sing songs to God, sing out!
Sing to our King, sing praise!
He's Lord over earth,
so sing your best songs to God.
God is Lord of godless nations—
sovereign, he's King of the mountain.
Princes from all over are gathered,
people of Abraham's God.
The powers of earth are God's—
he soars over all.

A PSALM OF THE SONS OF KORAH

1-3 **48** GOD majestic,
praise abounds in our God-city!
His sacred mountain,
breathtaking in its heights—earth's joy.
Zion Mountain looms in the North,
city of the world-King.
God in his citadel peaks
impregnable.

4-6 The kings got together,
they united and came.
They took one look and shook their heads,
they scattered and ran away.
They doubled up in pain
like a woman having a baby.

7-8 You smashed the ships of Tarshish
with a storm out of the East.
We heard about it, then we saw it
with our eyes—
In GOD's city of Angel Armies,
in the city our God
Set on firm foundations,
firm forever.

9-10 We pondered your love-in-action, God,
waiting in your temple:
Your name, God, evokes a train
of Hallelujahs wherever
It is spoken, near and far;
your arms are heaped with
goodness-in-action.

11 Be glad, Zion Mountain;
Dance, Judah's daughters!
He does what he said he'd do!

New King James Version

12Walk about Zion,
And go all around her.
Count her towers;
13Mark well her bulwarks;
Consider her palaces;
That you may tell *it* to the generation following.
14For this *is* God,
Our God forever and ever;
He will be our guide
Even to death.[a]

PSALM 49

The Confidence of the Foolish

To the Chief Musician. A Psalm of the sons of Korah.

1Hear this, all peoples;
Give ear, all inhabitants of the world,
2Both low and high,
Rich and poor together.
3My mouth shall speak wisdom,
And the meditation of my heart *shall give* understanding.
4I will incline my ear to a proverb;
I will disclose my dark saying on the harp.

5Why should I fear in the days of evil,
When the iniquity at my heels surrounds me?
6Those who trust in their wealth
And boast in the multitude of their riches,
7None *of them* can by any means redeem *his* brother,
Nor give to God a ransom for him—
8For the redemption of their souls *is* costly,
And it shall cease forever—
9That he should continue to live eternally,
And not see the Pit.

10For he sees wise men die;
Likewise the fool and the senseless person perish,
And leave their wealth to others.
11Their inner thought *is that* their houses *will last* forever,[a]
Their dwelling places to all generations;
They call *their* lands after their own names.
12Nevertheless man, *though* in honor, does not remain;[a]
He is like the beasts *that* perish.

13This is the way of those who *are* foolish,
And of their posterity who approve their sayings. *Selah*
14Like sheep they are laid in the grave;
Death shall feed on them;
The upright shall have dominion over them in the morning;
And their beauty shall be consumed in the grave, far from their dwelling.
15But God will redeem my soul from the power of the grave,
For He shall receive me. *Selah*

48:14 [a]Following Masoretic Text and Syriac; Septuagint and Vulgate read *Forever.* 49:11 [a]Septuagint, Syriac, Targum, and Vulgate read *Their graves shall be their houses forever.* 49:12 [a]Following Masoretic Text and Targum; Septuagint, Syriac, and Vulgate read *understand* (compare verse 20).

The Message

12-14 Circle Zion, take her measure,
count her fortress peaks,
Gaze long at her sloping bulwark,
climb her citadel heights—
Then you can tell the next generation
detail by detail the story of God,
Our God forever,
who guides us till the end of time.

A Psalm of the Sons of Korah

1-2 **49** Listen, everyone, listen—
earth-dwellers, don't miss this.
All you haves
and have-nots,
All together now: listen.

3-4 I set plainspoken wisdom before you,
my heart-seasoned understandings of life.
I fine-tuned my ear to the sayings of the wise,
I solve life's riddle with the help of a harp.

5-6 So why should I fear in bad times,
hemmed in by enemy malice,
Shoved around by bullies,
demeaned by the arrogant rich?

7-9 Really! There's no such thing as self-rescue,
pulling yourself up by your bootstraps.
The cost of rescue is beyond our means,
and even then it doesn't guarantee
Life forever, or insurance
against the Black Hole.

10-11 Anyone can see that the brightest and best die,
wiped out right along with fools and dunces.
They leave all their prowess behind,
move into their new home, The Coffin,
The cemetery their permanent address.
And to think they named counties after themselves!

12 We aren't immortal. We don't last long.
Like our dogs, we age and weaken. And die.

13-15 This is what happens to those who live for the moment,
who only look out for themselves:
Death herds them like sheep straight to hell;
they disappear down the gullet of the grave;
They waste away to nothing—
nothing left but a marker in a cemetery.
But me? God snatches me from the clutch of death,
he reaches down and grabs me.

NEW KING JAMES VERSION

16Do not be afraid when one becomes rich,
When the glory of his house is increased;
17For when he dies he shall carry nothing away;
His glory shall not descend after him.
18Though while he lives he blesses himself
(For *men* will praise you when you do well for yourself),
19He shall go to the generation of his fathers;
They shall never see light.
20A man *who is* in honor, yet does not understand,
Is like the beasts *that* perish.

PSALM 50

GOD THE RIGHTEOUS JUDGE
A Psalm of Asaph.

1The Mighty One, God the LORD,
Has spoken and called the earth
From the rising of the sun to its going down.
2Out of Zion, the perfection of beauty,
God will shine forth.
3Our God shall come, and shall not keep silent;
A fire shall devour before Him,
And it shall be very tempestuous all around Him.

4He shall call to the heavens from above,
And to the earth, that He may judge His people:
5"Gather My saints together to Me,
Those who have made a covenant with Me by sacrifice."
6Let the heavens declare His righteousness,
For God Himself *is* Judge. *Selah*
7"Hear, O My people, and I will speak,
O Israel, and I will testify against you;
I *am* God, your God!
8I will not rebuke you for your sacrifices
Or your burnt offerings,
Which are continually before Me.
9I will not take a bull from your house,
Nor goats out of your folds.
10For every beast of the forest *is* Mine,
And the cattle on a thousand hills.
11I know all the birds of the mountains,
And the wild beasts of the field *are* Mine.

12"If I were hungry, I would not tell you;
For the world *is* Mine, and all its fullness.
13Will I eat the flesh of bulls,
Or drink the blood of goats?
14Offer to God thanksgiving,
And pay your vows to the Most High.
15Call upon Me in the day of trouble;
I will deliver you, and you shall glorify Me."

16But to the wicked God says:
"What *right* have you to declare My statutes,
Or take My covenant in your mouth,
17Seeing you hate instruction
And cast My words behind you?

THE MESSAGE

16-19 So don't be impressed with those who get rich
and pile up fame and fortune.
They can't take it with them;
fame and fortune all get left behind.
Just when they think they've arrived
and folks praise them because they've made good,
They enter the family burial plot
where they'll never see sunshine again.

20 We aren't immortal. We don't last long.
Like our dogs, we age and weaken. And die.

AN ASAPH PSALM

1-3 **50** The God of gods—it's GOD!—speaks out, shouts, "Earth!"
welcomes the sun in the east,
farewells the disappearing sun in the west.
From the dazzle of Zion,
God blazes into view.
Our God makes his entrance,
he's not shy in his coming.
Starbursts of fireworks precede him.

4-5 He summons heaven and earth as a jury,
he's taking his people to court:
"Round up my saints who swore
on the Bible their loyalty to me."

6 The whole cosmos attests to the fairness of this court,
that here *God* is judge.

7-15 "Are you listening, dear people? I'm getting ready to speak;
Israel, I'm about ready to bring you to trial.
This is God, your God,
speaking to you.
I don't find fault with your acts of worship,
the frequent burnt sacrifices you offer.
But why should I want your blue-ribbon bull,
or more and more goats from your herds?
Every creature in the forest is mine,
the wild animals on all the mountains.
I know every mountain bird by name;
the scampering field mice are my friends.
If I get hungry, do you think I'd tell you?
All creation and its bounty are mine.
Do you think I feast on venison?
or drink draughts of goats' blood?
Spread for me a banquet of praise,
serve High God a feast of kept promises,
And call for help when you're in trouble—
I'll help you, and you'll honor me."

16-21 Next, God calls up the wicked:

"What are you up to, quoting my laws,
talking like we are good friends?
You never answer the door when I call;
you treat my words like garbage.

NEW KING JAMES VERSION

[18]When you saw a thief, you consented[a] with
him,
And have been a partaker with adulterers.
[19]You give your mouth to evil,
And your tongue frames deceit.
[20]You sit *and* speak against your brother;
You slander your own mother's son.
[21]These *things* you have done, and I kept
silent;
You thought that I was altogether like you;
But I will rebuke you,
And set *them* in order before your eyes.

[22]"Now consider this, you who forget God,
Lest I tear *you* in pieces,
And *there be* none to deliver:
[23]Whoever offers praise glorifies Me;
And to him who orders *his* conduct *aright*
I will show the salvation of God."

PSALM 51

A PRAYER OF REPENTANCE

To the Chief Musician. A Psalm of David when Nathan the prophet went to him, after he had gone in to Bathsheba.

[1]Have mercy upon me, O God,
According to Your lovingkindness;
According to the multitude of Your tender
mercies,
Blot out my transgressions.
[2]Wash me thoroughly from my iniquity,
And cleanse me from my sin.

[3]For I acknowledge my transgressions,
And my sin *is* always before me.
[4]Against You, You only, have I sinned,
And done *this* evil in Your sight—
That You may be found just when You
speak,[a]
And blameless when You judge.

[5]Behold, I was brought forth in iniquity,
And in sin my mother conceived me.
[6]Behold, You desire truth in the inward parts,
And in the hidden *part* You will make me to
know wisdom.

[7]Purge me with hyssop, and I shall be clean;
Wash me, and I shall be whiter than snow.
[8]Make me hear joy and gladness,
That the bones You have broken may
rejoice.
[9]Hide Your face from my sins,
And blot out all my iniquities.

[10]Create in me a clean heart, O God,
And renew a steadfast spirit within me.
[11]Do not cast me away from Your presence,
And do not take Your Holy Spirit from me.

50:18 [a]Septuagint, Syriac, Targum, and Vulgate read *ran.*
51:4 [a]Septuagint, Targum, and Vulgate read *in Your words.*

THE MESSAGE

If you find a thief, you make him your
buddy;
adulterers are your friends of choice.
Your mouth drools filth;
lying is a serious art form with you.
You stab your own brother in the back,
rip off your little sister.
I kept a quiet patience while you did these
things;
you thought I went along with your
game.
I'm calling you on the carpet, *now,*
laying your wickedness out in plain
sight.

22-23 "Time's up for playing fast and
loose with me.
I'm ready to pass sentence,
and there's no help in sight!
It's the praising life that honors me.
As soon as you set your foot on the Way,
I'll show you my salvation."

A DAVID PSALM, AFTER HE WAS CONFRONTED BY NATHAN ABOUT THE AFFAIR WITH BATHSHEBA

1-3 **51** Generous in love—God, give grace!
Huge in mercy—wipe out my bad
record.
Scrub away my guilt,
soak out my sins in your laundry.
I know how bad I've been;
my sins are staring me down.

4-6 You're the One I've violated, and you've
seen
it all, seen the full extent of my evil.
You have all the facts before you;
whatever you decide about me is fair.
I've been out of step with you for a long
time,
in the wrong since before I was born.
What you're after is truth from the inside
out.
Enter me, then; conceive a new, true life.

7-15 Soak me in your laundry and I'll come out
clean,
scrub me and I'll have a snow-white life.
Tune me in to foot-tapping songs,
set these once-broken bones to dancing.
Don't look too close for blemishes,
give me a clean bill of health.
God, make a fresh start in me,
shape a Genesis week from the chaos of
my life.
Don't throw me out with the trash,
or fail to breathe holiness in me.

NEW KING JAMES VERSION

12Restore to me the joy of Your salvation,
And uphold me *by Your* generous Spirit.
13*Then* I will teach transgressors Your ways,
And sinners shall be converted to You.

14Deliver me from the guilt of bloodshed, O God,
The God of my salvation,
And my tongue shall sing aloud of Your righteousness.
15O Lord, open my lips,
And my mouth shall show forth Your praise.
16For You do not desire sacrifice, or else I would give *it;*
You do not delight in burnt offering.
17The sacrifices of God *are* a broken spirit,
A broken and a contrite heart—
These, O God, You will not despise.

18Do good in Your good pleasure to Zion;
Build the walls of Jerusalem.
19Then You shall be pleased with the sacrifices of righteousness,
With burnt offering and whole burnt offering;
Then they shall offer bulls on Your altar.

PSALM 52

THE END OF THE WICKED AND THE PEACE OF THE GODLY

To the Chief Musician. A Contemplation[a] of David when Doeg the Edomite went and told Saul, and said to him, "David has gone to the house of Ahimelech."

1Why do you boast in evil, O mighty man?
The goodness of God *endures* continually.
2Your tongue devises destruction,
Like a sharp razor, working deceitfully.
3You love evil more than good,
Lying rather than speaking righteousness. *Selah*
4You love all devouring words,
You deceitful tongue.

5God shall likewise destroy you forever;
He shall take you away, and pluck you out of *your* dwelling place,
And uproot you from the land of the living. *Selah*
6The righteous also shall see and fear,
And shall laugh at him, *saying,*
7"Here is the man *who* did not make God his strength,
But trusted in the abundance of his riches,
And strengthened himself in his wickedness."

8But I *am* like a green olive tree in the house of God;
I trust in the mercy of God forever and ever.
9I will praise You forever,
Because You have done *it;*
And in the presence of Your saints
I will wait on Your name, for *it is* good.

52:title [a]Hebrew *Maschil*

THE MESSAGE

Bring me back from gray exile,
put a fresh wind in my sails!
Give me a job teaching rebels your ways
so the lost can find their way home.
Commute my death sentence, God, my salvation God,
and I'll sing anthems to your life-giving ways.
Unbutton my lips, dear God;
I'll let loose with your praise.

16-17 Going through the motions doesn't please you,
a flawless performance is nothing to you.
I learned God-worship
when my pride was shattered.
Heart-shattered lives ready for love
don't for a moment escape God's notice.

18-19 Make Zion the place you delight in,
repair Jerusalem's broken-down walls.
Then you'll get real worship from us,
acts of worship small and large,
Including all the bulls
they can heave onto your altar!

A DAVID PSALM, WHEN DOEG THE EDOMITE REPORTED TO SAUL, "DAVID'S AT AHIMELECH'S HOUSE"

1-4 **52** Why do you brag of evil, "Big Man"?
God's mercy carries the day.
You scheme catastrophe;
your tongue cuts razor-sharp,
artisan in lies.
You love evil more than good,
you call black white.
You love malicious gossip,
you foul-mouth.

5 God will tear you limb from limb,
sweep you up and throw you out,
Pull you up by the roots
from the land of life.

6-7 Good people will watch and
worship. They'll laugh in relief:
"Big Man bet on the wrong horse,
trusted in big money,
made his living from catastrophe."

8 And I'm an olive tree,
growing green in God's house.
I trusted in the generous mercy
of God then and now.

9 I thank you always
that you went into action.
And I'll stay right here,
your good name my hope,
in company with your faithful friends.

NEW KING JAMES VERSION

PSALM 53

FOLLY OF THE GODLESS, AND THE RESTORATION OF ISRAEL

To the Chief Musician. Set to "Mahalath."
A Contemplation[a] of David.

1The fool has said in his heart,
"*There is* no God."
They are corrupt, and have done
abominable iniquity;
There is none who does good.

2God looks down from heaven upon the
children of men,
To see if there are *any* who understand, who
seek God.
3Every one of them has turned aside;
They have together become corrupt;
There is none who does good,
No, not one.

4Have the workers of iniquity no knowledge,
Who eat up my people *as* they eat bread,
And do not call upon God?
5There they are in great fear
Where no fear was,
For God has scattered the bones of him who
encamps against you;
You have put *them* to shame,
Because God has despised them.

6Oh, that the salvation of Israel would come
out of Zion!
When God brings back the captivity of His
people,
Let Jacob rejoice *and* Israel be glad.

PSALM 54

ANSWERED PRAYER FOR DELIVERANCE FROM ADVERSARIES

To the Chief Musician. With stringed instruments.[a] A Contemplation[b] of David when the Ziphites went and said to Saul, "Is David not hiding with us?"

1Save me, O God, by Your name,
And vindicate me by Your strength.
2Hear my prayer, O God;
Give ear to the words of my mouth.
3For strangers have risen up against me,
And oppressors have sought after my life;
They have not set God before them. *Selah*

4Behold, God *is* my helper;
The Lord *is* with those who uphold my life.
5He will repay my enemies for their evil.
Cut them off in Your truth.

6I will freely sacrifice to You;
I will praise Your name, O LORD, for *it is*
good.
7For He has delivered me out of all trouble;
And my eye has seen *its desire* upon my
enemies.

53:title [a]Hebrew *Maschil* **54:title** [a]Hebrew *neginoth* [b]Hebrew *Maschil*

THE MESSAGE

A DAVID PSALM

1-2 **53** Bilious and bloated, they gas,
"God is gone."
It's poison gas—
they foul themselves, they poison
Rivers and skies;
thistles are their cash crop.
God sticks his head out of heaven.
He looks around.
He's looking for someone not stupid—
one man, even, God-expectant,
just one God-ready woman.

3 He comes up empty. A string
of zeros. Useless, unshepherded
Sheep, taking turns pretending
to be Shepherd.
The ninety and nine
follow the one.

4 Don't they know anything,
all these impostors?
Don't they know
they can't get away with this,
Treating people like a fast-food meal
over which they're too busy to pray?

5 Night is coming for them, and nightmare—
a nightmare they'll never wake up from.
God will make hash of these squatters,
send them packing for good.

6 Is there anyone around to save Israel?
God turns life around.
Turned-around Jacob skips rope,
turned-around Israel sings laughter.

A DAVID PSALM, WHEN THE ZIPHITES REPORTED TO SAUL, "DAVID IS HIDING OUT WITH US"

1-2 **54** God, for your sake, help me!
Use your influence to clear me.
Listen, God—I'm desperate.
Don't be too busy to hear me.

3 Outlaws are out to get me,
hit men are trying to kill me.
Nothing will stop them;
God means nothing to them.

4-5 Oh, look! God's right here helping!
GOD's on my side,
Evil is looping back on my enemies.
Don't let up! Finish them off!

6-7 I'm ready now to worship, so ready.
I thank you, GOD—you're so good.
You got me out of every scrape,
and I saw my enemies get it.

NEW KING JAMES VERSION

PSALM 55

TRUST IN GOD CONCERNING THE TREACHERY OF FRIENDS

To the Chief Musician. With stringed instruments.[a] A Contemplation[b] of David.

1Give ear to my prayer, O God,
And do not hide Yourself from my supplication.
2Attend to me, and hear me;
I am restless in my complaint, and moan noisily,
3Because of the voice of the enemy,
Because of the oppression of the wicked;
For they bring down trouble upon me,
And in wrath they hate me.

4My heart is severely pained within me,
And the terrors of death have fallen upon me.
5Fearfulness and trembling have come upon me,
And horror has overwhelmed me.
6So I said, "Oh, that I had wings like a dove!
I would fly away and be at rest.
7Indeed, I would wander far off,
And remain in the wilderness. *Selah*
8I would hasten my escape
From the windy storm *and* tempest."

9Destroy, O Lord, *and* divide their tongues,
For I have seen violence and strife in the city.
10Day and night they go around it on its walls;
Iniquity and trouble *are* also in the midst of it.
11Destruction *is* in its midst;
Oppression and deceit do not depart from its streets.

12For *it is* not an enemy *who* reproaches me;
Then I could bear *it*.
Nor *is it* one *who* hates me who has exalted *himself* against me;
Then I could hide from him.
13But *it was* you, a man my equal,
My companion and my acquaintance.
14We took sweet counsel together,
And walked to the house of God in the throng.

15Let death seize them;
Let them go down alive into hell,
For wickedness *is* in their dwellings *and* among them.

16As for me, I will call upon God,
And the LORD shall save me.
17Evening and morning and at noon
I will pray, and cry aloud,
And He shall hear my voice.
18He has redeemed my soul in peace from the battle *that was* against me,
For there were many against me.
19God will hear, and afflict them,
Even He who abides from of old. *Selah*
Because they do not change,
Therefore they do not fear God.

55:title [a]Hebrew *neginoth* [b]Hebrew *Maschil*

THE MESSAGE

A DAVID PSALM

1-3 55 Open your ears, God, to my prayer;
don't pretend you don't hear me knocking.
Come close and whisper your answer.
I really need you.
I shudder at the mean voice,
quail before the evil eye,
As they pile on the guilt,
stockpile angry slander.

4-8 My insides are turned inside out;
specters of death have me down.
I shake with fear,
I shudder from head to foot.
"Who will give me wings," I ask—
"wings like a dove?"
Get me out of here on dove wings;
I want some peace and quiet.
I want a walk in the country,
I want a cabin in the woods.
I'm desperate for a change
from rage and stormy weather.

9-11 Come down hard, Lord—slit their tongues.
I'm appalled how they've split the city
Into rival gangs
prowling the alleys
Day and night spoiling for a fight,
trash piled in the streets,
Even shopkeepers gouging and cheating
in broad daylight.

12-14 This isn't the neighborhood bully
mocking me—I could take that.
This isn't a foreign devil spitting
invective—I could tune that out.
It's *you*! We grew up together!
You! My best friend!
Those long hours of leisure as we walked
arm in arm, God a third party to our conversation.

15 Haul my betrayers off alive to hell—let them
experience the horror, let them
feel every desolate detail of a damned life.

16-19 I call to God;
GOD will help me.
At dusk, dawn, and noon I sigh
deep sighs—he hears, he rescues.
My life is well and whole, secure
in the middle of danger
Even while thousands
are lined up against me.
God hears it all, and from his judge's bench
puts them in their place.
But, set in their ways, they won't change;
they pay him no mind.

NEW KING JAMES VERSION

20 He has put forth his hands against those
who were at peace with him;
He has broken his covenant.
21 *The words* of his mouth were smoother than
butter,
But war *was* in his heart;
His words were softer than oil,
Yet they *were* drawn swords.

22 Cast your burden on the LORD,
And He shall sustain you;
He shall never permit the righteous to be
moved.

23 But You, O God, shall bring them down to
the pit of destruction;
Bloodthirsty and deceitful men shall not live
out half their days;
But I will trust in You.

PSALM 56

PRAYER FOR RELIEF FROM TORMENTORS

To the Chief Musician. Set to "The Silent Dove in Distant Lands."[a] A Michtam of David when the Philistines captured him in Gath.

1 Be merciful to me, O God, for man would
swallow me up;
Fighting all day he oppresses me.
2 My enemies would hound *me* all day,
For *there are* many who fight against me,
O Most High.

3 Whenever I am afraid,
I will trust in You.
4 In God (I will praise His word),
In God I have put my trust;
I will not fear.
What can flesh do to me?

5 All day they twist my words;
All their thoughts *are* against me for evil.
6 They gather together,
They hide, they mark my steps,
When they lie in wait for my life.
7 Shall they escape by iniquity?
In anger cast down the peoples, O God!

8 You number my wanderings;
Put my tears into Your bottle;
Are they not in Your book?
9 When I cry out *to You,*
Then my enemies will turn back;
This I know, because God *is* for me.
10 In God (I will praise *His* word),
In the LORD (I will praise *His* word),
11 In God I have put my trust;
I will not be afraid.
What can man do to me?

12 Vows *made* to You *are binding* upon me,
O God;
I will render praises to You,
13 For You have delivered my soul from death.
Have You not *kept* my feet from falling,
That I may walk before God
In the light of the living?

56:title [a]Hebrew *Jonath Elem Rechokim*

THE MESSAGE

20-21 And this, my best friend, betrayed his best
friends;
his life betrayed his word.
All my life I've been charmed by his
speech,
never dreaming he'd turn on me.
His words, which were music to my ears,
turned to daggers in my heart.

22-23 Pile your troubles on GOD's shoulders—
he'll carry your load, he'll help you out.
He'll never let good people
topple into ruin.
But you, God, will throw the others
into a muddy bog,
Cut the lifespan of assassins
and traitors in half.

And I trust in you.

A DAVID PSALM, WHEN HE WAS CAPTURED BY THE PHILISTINES IN GATH

1-4 **56** Take my side, God—I'm getting kicked
around,
stomped on every day.
Not a day goes by
but somebody beats me up;
They make it their duty
to beat me up.
When I get really afraid
I come to you in trust.
I'm proud to praise God;
fearless now, I trust in God.
What can mere mortals do?

5-6 They don't let up—
they smear my reputation
and huddle to plot my collapse.
They gang up,
sneak together through the alleys
To take me by surprise,
wait their chance to get me.

7 Pay them back in evil!
Get angry, God!
Down with these people!

8 You've kept track of my every toss and turn
through the sleepless nights,
Each tear entered in your ledger,
each ache written in your book.

9 If my enemies run away,
turn tail when I yell at them,
Then I'll know
that God is on my side.

10-11 I'm proud to praise God,
proud to praise GOD.
Fearless now, I trust in God;
what can mere mortals do to me?

12-13 God, you did everything you promised,
and I'm thanking you with all my heart.
You pulled me from the brink of death,
my feet from the cliff-edge of doom.
Now I stroll at leisure with God
in the sunlit fields of life.

NEW KING JAMES VERSION

PSALM 57

PRAYER FOR SAFETY FROM ENEMIES

To the Chief Musician. Set to "Do Not Destroy."[a] A Michtam of David when he fled from Saul into the cave.

1 Be merciful to me, O God, be merciful to me!
For my soul trusts in You;
And in the shadow of Your wings I will make my refuge,
Until *these* calamities have passed by.

2 I will cry out to God Most High,
To God who performs *all things* for me.
3 He shall send from heaven and save me;
He reproaches the one who would swallow me up. *Selah*
God shall send forth His mercy and His truth.

4 My soul *is* among lions;
I lie *among* the sons of men
Who are set on fire,
Whose teeth *are* spears and arrows,
And their tongue a sharp sword.
5 Be exalted, O God, above the heavens;
Let Your glory *be* above all the earth.

6 They have prepared a net for my steps;
My soul is bowed down;
They have dug a pit before me;
Into the midst of it they *themselves* have fallen. *Selah*

7 My heart is steadfast, O God, my heart is steadfast;
I will sing and give praise.
8 Awake, my glory!
Awake, lute and harp!
I will awaken the dawn.

9 I will praise You, O Lord, among the peoples;
I will sing to You among the nations.
10 For Your mercy reaches unto the heavens,
And Your truth unto the clouds.

11 Be exalted, O God, above the heavens;
Let Your glory *be* above all the earth.

PSALM 58

THE JUST JUDGMENT OF THE WICKED

To the Chief Musician. Set to "Do Not Destroy."[a] A Michtam of David.

1 Do you indeed speak righteousness, you silent ones?
Do you judge uprightly, you sons of men?
2 No, in heart you work wickedness;
You weigh out the violence of your hands in the earth.

3 The wicked are estranged from the womb;
They go astray as soon as they are born, speaking lies.

57:title [a]Hebrew *Al Tashcheth* 58:title [a]Hebrew *Al Tashcheth*

THE MESSAGE

A DAVID PSALM, WHEN HE HID IN A CAVE FROM SAUL

1-3 **57** Be good to me, God—and now!
I've run to you for dear life.
I'm hiding out under your wings
until the hurricane blows over.
I call out to High God,
the God who holds me together.
He sends orders from heaven and saves me,
he humiliates those who kick me around.
God delivers generous love,
he makes good on his word.

4 I find myself in a pride of lions
who are wild for a taste of human flesh;
Their teeth are lances and arrows,
their tongues are sharp daggers.

5 Soar high in the skies, O God!
Cover the whole earth with your glory!

6 They booby-trapped my path;
I thought I was dead and done for.
They dug a mantrap to catch me,
and fell in headlong themselves.

7-8 I'm ready, God, so ready,
ready from head to toe,
Ready to sing, ready to raise a tune:
"Wake up, soul!
Wake up, harp! wake up, lute!
Wake up, you sleepyhead sun!"

9-10 I'm thanking you, GOD, out loud in the streets,
singing your praises in town and country.
The deeper your love, the higher it goes;
every cloud is a flag to your faithfulness.

11 Soar high in the skies, O God!
Cover the whole earth with your glory!

A DAVID PSALM

1-2 **58** Is this any way to run a country?
Is there an honest politician in the house?
Behind the scenes you brew cauldrons of evil,
behind closed doors you make deals with demons.

3-5 The wicked crawl from the wrong side of the cradle;
their first words out of the womb are lies.

NEW KING JAMES VERSION

[4]Their poison *is* like the poison of a serpent;
They are like the deaf cobra *that* stops its ear,
[5]Which will not heed the voice of charmers,
Charming ever so skillfully.

[6]Break their teeth in their mouth, O God!
Break out the fangs of the young lions, O LORD!
[7]Let them flow away as waters *which* run continually;
When he bends *his bow,*
Let his arrows be as if cut in pieces.
[8]*Let them be* like a snail which melts away as it goes,
Like a stillborn child of a woman, that they may not see the sun.

[9]Before your pots can feel *the burning* thorns,
He shall take them away as with a whirlwind,
As in His living and burning wrath.
[10]The righteous shall rejoice when he sees the vengeance;
He shall wash his feet in the blood of the wicked,
[11]So that men will say,
"Surely *there is* a reward for the righteous;
Surely He is God who judges in the earth."

PSALM 59

THE ASSURED JUDGMENT OF THE WICKED

To the Chief Musician. Set to "Do Not Destroy."[a] A Michtam of David when Saul sent men, and they watched the house in order to kill him.

[1]Deliver me from my enemies, O my God;
Defend me from those who rise up against me.
[2]Deliver me from the workers of iniquity,
And save me from bloodthirsty men.

[3]For look, they lie in wait for my life;
The mighty gather against me,
Not *for* my transgression nor *for* my sin, O LORD.
[4]They run and prepare themselves through no fault *of mine.*

Awake to help me, and behold!
[5]You therefore, O LORD God of hosts, the God of Israel,
Awake to punish all the nations;
Do not be merciful to any wicked transgressors. *Selah*

[6]At evening they return,
They growl like a dog,
And go all around the city.
[7]Indeed, they belch with their mouth;
Swords *are* in their lips;
For *they say,* "Who hears?"

[8]But You, O LORD, shall laugh at them;
You shall have all the nations in derision.
[9]I will wait for You, O You his Strength;[a]
For God *is* my defense.

59:title [a]Hebrew *Al Tashcheth* **59:9** [a]Following Masoretic Text and Syriac; some Hebrew manuscripts, Septuagint, Targum, and Vulgate read *my Strength.*

THE MESSAGE

Poison, lethal rattlesnake poison,
drips from their forked tongues—
Deaf to threats, deaf to charm,
decades of wax built up in their ears.

6-9 God, smash their teeth to bits,
leave them toothless tigers.
Let their lives be buckets of water spilled,
all that's left, a damp stain in the sand.
Let them be trampled grass
worn smooth by the traffic.
Let them dissolve into snail slime,
be a miscarried fetus that never sees sunlight.
Before what they cook up is half-done, God,
throw it out with the garbage!

10-11 The righteous will call up their friends
when they see the wicked get their reward,
Serve up their blood in goblets
as they toast one another,
Everyone cheering, "It's worth it to play by the rules!
God's handing out trophies and tending the earth!"

A DAVID PSALM, WHEN SAUL SET A WATCH ON DAVID'S HOUSE IN ORDER TO KILL HIM

1-2 59 My God! Rescue me from my enemies,
defend me from these mutineers.
Rescue me from their dirty tricks,
save me from their hit men.

3-4 Desperadoes have ganged up on me,
they're hiding in ambush for me.
I did nothing to deserve this, GOD,
crossed no one, wronged no one.
All the same, they're after me,
determined to get me.

4-5 Wake up and see for yourself! You're GOD,
God-of-Angel-Armies, Israel's God!
Get on the job and take care of these pagans,
don't be soft on these hard cases.

6-7 They return when the sun goes down,
They howl like coyotes, ringing the city.
Then suddenly they're all at the gate,
Snarling invective, drawn daggers in their teeth.
They think they'll never get caught.

8-10 But you, GOD, break out laughing;
you treat the godless nations like jokes.
Strong God, I'm watching you do it,
I can always count on you.

NEW KING JAMES VERSION

10My God of mercy[a] shall come to meet me;
God shall let me see *my desire* on my enemies.

11Do not slay them, lest my people forget;
Scatter them by Your power,
And bring them down,
O Lord our shield.
12*For* the sin of their mouth *and* the words of their lips,
Let them even be taken in their pride,
And for the cursing and lying *which* they speak.
13Consume *them* in wrath, consume *them,*
That they *may* not *be;*
And let them know that God rules in Jacob
To the ends of the earth. *Selah*

14And at evening they return,
They growl like a dog,
And go all around the city.
15They wander up and down for food,
And howl[a] if they are not satisfied.

16But I will sing of Your power;
Yes, I will sing aloud of Your mercy in the morning;
For You have been my defense
And refuge in the day of my trouble.
17To You, O my Strength, I will sing praises;
For God *is* my defense,
My God of mercy.

PSALM 60

URGENT PRAYER FOR THE RESTORED FAVOR OF GOD

To the Chief Musician. Set to "Lily of the Testimony."[a] A Michtam of David. For teaching. When he fought against Mesopotamia and Syria of Zobah, and Joab returned and killed twelve thousand Edomites in the Valley of Salt.

1O God, You have cast us off;
You have broken us down;
You have been displeased;
Oh, restore us again!
2You have made the earth tremble;
You have broken it;
Heal its breaches, for it is shaking.
3You have shown Your people hard things;
You have made us drink the wine of confusion.

4You have given a banner to those who fear You,
That it may be displayed because of the truth. *Selah*
5That Your beloved may be delivered,
Save *with* Your right hand, and hear me.

59:10 [a]Following Qere; some Hebrew manuscripts, Septuagint, and Vulgate read *My God, His mercy;* Kethib, some Hebrew manuscripts and Targum read *O God, my mercy;* Syriac reads *O God, Your mercy.* **59:15** [a]Following Septuagint and Vulgate; Masoretic Text, Syriac, and Targum read *spend the night.* **60:title** [a]Hebrew *Shushan Eduth*

THE MESSAGE

God in dependable love shows up on time,
shows me my enemies in ruin.

11-13 Don't make quick work of them, GOD,
lest my people forget.
Bring them down in slow motion,
take them apart piece by piece.
Let all their mean-mouthed arrogance
catch up with them,
Catch them out and bring them down
—every muttered curse
—every barefaced lie.
Finish them off in fine style!
Finish them off for good!
Then all the world will see
that God rules well in Jacob,
everywhere that God's in charge.

14-15 They return when the sun goes down,
They howl like coyotes, ringing the city.
They scavenge for bones,
And bite the hand that feeds them.

16-17 And me? I'm singing your prowess,
shouting at cockcrow your largesse,
For you've been a safe place for me,
a good place to hide.
Strong God, I'm watching you do it,
I can always count on you—
God, my dependable love.

A DAVID PSALM, WHEN HE FOUGHT AGAINST ARAM-NAHARAIM AND ARAM-ZOBAH AND JOAB KILLED TWELVE THOUSAND EDOMITES AT THE VALLEY OF SALT

1-2 **60** God! you walked off and left us,
kicked our defenses to bits
And stalked off angry.
Come back. Oh please, come back!

You shook earth to the foundations,
ripped open huge crevasses.
Heal the breaks! Everything's
coming apart at the seams.

3-5 You made your people look doom in the face,
then gave us cheap wine to drown our troubles.
Then you planted a flag to rally your people,
an unfurled flag to look to for courage.
Now do something quickly, answer right now,
so the one you love best is saved.

NEW KING JAMES VERSION

6God has spoken in His holiness:
"I will rejoice;
I will divide Shechem
And measure out the Valley of Succoth.
7Gilead *is* Mine, and Manasseh *is* Mine;
Ephraim also *is* the helmet for My head;
Judah *is* My lawgiver.
8Moab *is* My washpot;
Over Edom I will cast My shoe;
Philistia, shout in triumph because of Me."

9Who will bring me *to* the strong city?
Who will lead me to Edom?
10*Is it* not You, O God, *who* cast us off?
And You, O God, *who* did not go out with
our armies?
11Give us help from trouble,
For the help of man *is* useless.
12Through God we will do valiantly,
For *it is* He *who* shall tread down our
enemies.[a]

PSALM 61

ASSURANCE OF GOD'S ETERNAL PROTECTION

To the Chief Musician. On a stringed instrument.[a]
A Psalm of David.

1Hear my cry, O God;
Attend to my prayer.
2From the end of the earth I will cry to You,
When my heart is overwhelmed;
Lead me to the rock that is higher than I.

3For You have been a shelter for me,
A strong tower from the enemy.
4I will abide in Your tabernacle forever;
I will trust in the shelter of Your wings. *Selah*

5For You, O God, have heard my vows;
You have given *me* the heritage of those
who fear Your name.
6You will prolong the king's life,
His years as many generations.
7He shall abide before God forever.
Oh, prepare mercy and truth, *which* may
preserve him!

8So I will sing praise to Your name forever,
That I may daily perform my vows.

PSALM 62

A CALM RESOLVE TO WAIT FOR THE SALVATION OF GOD

To the Chief Musician. To Jeduthun. A Psalm of David.

1Truly my soul silently *waits* for God;
From Him *comes* my salvation.
2He only *is* my rock and my salvation;
He is my defense;
I shall not be greatly moved.

3How long will you attack a man?
You shall be slain, all of you,
Like a leaning wall and a tottering fence.

60:12 [a]Compare verses 5–12 with 108:6–13 **61:title** [a]Hebrew *neginah*

THE MESSAGE

6-8 That's when God spoke in holy splendor,
"Bursting with joy,
I make a present of Shechem,
I hand out Succoth Valley as a gift.
Gilead's in my pocket,
to say nothing of Manasseh.
Ephraim's my hard hat,
Judah my hammer;
Moab's a scrub bucket,
I mop the floor with Moab,
Spit on Edom,
rain fireworks all over Philistia."

9-10 Who will take me to the thick of the fight?
Who'll show me the road to Edom?
You aren't giving up on us, are you, God?
refusing to go out with our troops?

11-12 Give us help for the hard task;
human help is worthless.
In God we'll do our very best;
he'll flatten the opposition for good.

A DAVID PSALM

1-2 **61** God, listen to me shout,
bend an ear to my prayer.
When I'm far from anywhere,
down to my last gasp,
I call out, "Guide me
up High Rock Mountain!"

3-5 You've always given me breathing room,
a place to get away from it all,
A lifetime pass to your safe-house,
an open invitation as your guest.
You've always taken me seriously, God,
made me welcome among those who
know and love you.

6-8 Let the days of the king add up
to years and years of good rule.
Set his throne in the full light of God;
post Steady Love and Good Faith as
lookouts,
And I'll be the poet who sings your glory—
and live what I sing every day.

A DAVID PSALM

1-2 **62** God, the one and only—
I'll wait as long as he says.
Everything I need comes from him,
so why not?
He's solid rock under my feet,
breathing room for my soul,
An impregnable castle:
I'm set for life.

3-4 How long will you gang up on me?
How long will you run with the bullies?
There's nothing to you, any of you—
rotten floorboards, worm-eaten rafters,

NEW KING JAMES VERSION

4They only consult to cast *him* down from his high position;
They delight in lies;
They bless with their mouth,
But they curse inwardly. *Selah*

5My soul, wait silently for God alone,
For my expectation *is* from Him.
6He only *is* my rock and my salvation;
He is my defense;
I shall not be moved.
7In God *is* my salvation and my glory;
The rock of my strength,
And my refuge, *is* in God.

8Trust in Him at all times, you people;
Pour out your heart before Him;
God *is* a refuge for us. *Selah*

9Surely men of low degree *are* a vapor,
Men of high degree *are* a lie;
If they are weighed on the scales,
They *are* altogether *lighter* than vapor.
10Do not trust in oppression,
Nor vainly hope in robbery;
If riches increase,
Do not set *your* heart *on them.*

11God has spoken once,
Twice I have heard this:
That power *belongs* to God.
12Also to You, O Lord, *belongs* mercy;
For You render to each one according to his work.

PSALM 63

JOY IN THE FELLOWSHIP OF GOD

A Psalm of David when he was in the wilderness of Judah.

1O God, You *are* my God;
Early will I seek You;
My soul thirsts for You;
My flesh longs for You
In a dry and thirsty land
Where there is no water.
2So I have looked for You in the sanctuary,
To see Your power and Your glory.

3Because Your lovingkindness *is* better than life,
My lips shall praise You.
4Thus I will bless You while I live;
I will lift up my hands in Your name.
5My soul shall be satisfied as with marrow and fatness,
And my mouth shall praise You with joyful lips.

6When I remember You on my bed,
I meditate on You in the *night* watches.
7Because You have been my help,
Therefore in the shadow of Your wings I will rejoice.

THE MESSAGE

Anthills plotting to bring down mountains,
far gone in make-believe.
You talk a good line,
but every "blessing" breathes a curse.

5-6 God, the one and only—
I'll wait as long as he says.
Everything I hope for comes from him,
so why not?
He's solid rock under my feet,
breathing room for my soul,
An impregnable castle:
I'm set for life.

7-8 My help and glory are in God
—granite-strength and safe-harbor-God—
So trust him absolutely, people;
lay your lives on the line for him.
God is a safe place to be.

9 Man as such is smoke,
woman as such, a mirage.
Put them together, they're nothing;
two times nothing is nothing.

10 And a windfall, if it comes—
don't make too much of it.

11 God said this once and for all;
how many times
Have I heard it repeated?
"Strength comes
Straight from God."

12 Love to you, Lord God!
You pay a fair wage for a good day's work!

A DAVID PSALM, WHEN HE WAS OUT IN THE JUDEAN WILDERNESS

1 **63** God—you're my God!
I can't get enough of you!
I've worked up such hunger and thirst for God,
traveling across dry and weary deserts.

2-4 So here I am in the place of worship, eyes open,
drinking in your strength and glory.
In your generous love I am really living at last!
My lips brim praises like fountains.
I bless you every time I take a breath;
My arms wave like banners of praise to you.

5-8 I eat my fill of prime rib and gravy;
I smack my lips. It's time to shout praises!
If I'm sleepless at midnight,
I spend the hours in grateful reflection.
Because you've always stood up for me,
I'm free to run and play.

NEW KING JAMES VERSION

8My soul follows close behind You;
Your right hand upholds me.

9But those *who* seek my life, to destroy *it*,
Shall go into the lower parts of the earth.
10They shall fall by the sword;
They shall be a portion for jackals.

11But the king shall rejoice in God;
Everyone who swears by Him shall glory;
But the mouth of those who speak lies shall be stopped.

PSALM 64

OPPRESSED BY THE WICKED BUT REJOICING IN THE LORD

To the Chief Musician. A Psalm of David.

1Hear my voice, O God, in my meditation;
Preserve my life from fear of the enemy.
2Hide me from the secret plots of the wicked,
From the rebellion of the workers of iniquity,
3Who sharpen their tongue like a sword,
And bend *their bows to shoot* their arrows—bitter words,
4That they may shoot in secret at the blameless;
Suddenly they shoot at him and do not fear.

5They encourage themselves *in* an evil matter;
They talk of laying snares secretly;
They say, "Who will see them?"
6They devise iniquities:
"We have perfected a shrewd scheme."
Both the inward thought and the heart of man are deep.

7But God shall shoot at them *with* an arrow;
Suddenly they shall be wounded.
8So He will make them stumble over their own tongue;
All who see them shall flee away.
9All men shall fear,
And shall declare the work of God;
For they shall wisely consider His doing.

10The righteous shall be glad in the LORD, and trust in Him.
And all the upright in heart shall glory.

PSALM 65

PRAISE TO GOD FOR HIS SALVATION AND PROVIDENCE

To the Chief Musician. A Psalm of David. A Song.

1Praise is awaiting You, O God, in Zion;
And to You the vow shall be performed.
2O You who hear prayer,
To You all flesh will come.
3Iniquities prevail against me;
As for our transgressions,
You will provide atonement for them.

4Blessed *is the man* You choose,
And cause to approach *You*,
That he may dwell in Your courts.

THE MESSAGE

I hold on to you for dear life,
and you hold me steady as a post.

9-11 Those who are out to get me are marked for doom,
marked for death, bound for hell.
They'll die violent deaths;
jackals will tear them limb from limb.
But the king is glad in God;
his true friends spread the joy,
While small-minded gossips
are gagged for good.

A DAVID PSALM

1 **64** Listen and help, O God.
I'm reduced to a whine
And a whimper, obsessed
with feelings of doomsday.

2-6 Don't let them find me—
the conspirators out to get me,
Using their tongues as weapons,
flinging poison words,
poison-tipped arrow-words.
They shoot from ambush,
shoot without warning,
not caring who they hit.
They keep fit doing calisthenics
of evil purpose,
They keep lists of the traps
they've secretly set.
They say to each other,
"No one can catch us,
no one can detect our perfect crime."
The Detective detects the mystery
in the dark of the cellar heart.

7-8 The God of the Arrow shoots!
They double up in pain,
Fall flat on their faces
in full view of the grinning crowd.

9-10 Everyone sees it. God's
work is the talk of the town.
Be glad, good people! Fly to GOD!
Good-hearted people, make praise your habit.

A DAVID PSALM

1-2 **65** Silence is praise to you,
Zion-dwelling God,
And also obedience.
You hear the prayer in it all.

2-8 We all arrive at your doorstep sooner
or later, loaded with guilt,
Our sins too much for us—
but you get rid of them once and for all.
Blessed are the chosen! Blessed the guest
at home in your place!

NEW KING JAMES VERSION

We shall be satisfied with the goodness of
Your house,
Of Your holy temple.

5*By* awesome deeds in righteousness You will
answer us,
O God of our salvation,
You who are the confidence of all the ends
of the earth,
And of the far-off seas;
6Who established the mountains by His
strength,
Being clothed with power;
7You who still the noise of the seas,
The noise of their waves,
And the tumult of the peoples.
8They also who dwell in the farthest parts are
afraid of Your signs;
You make the outgoings of the morning and
evening rejoice.

9You visit the earth and water it,
You greatly enrich it;
The river of God is full of water;
You provide their grain,
For so You have prepared it.
10You water its ridges abundantly,
You settle its furrows;
You make it soft with showers,
You bless its growth.

11You crown the year with Your goodness,
And Your paths drip *with* abundance.
12They drop *on* the pastures of the wilderness,
And the little hills rejoice on every side.
13The pastures are clothed with flocks;
The valleys also are covered with grain;
They shout for joy, they also sing.

PSALM 66

PRAISE TO GOD FOR HIS AWESOME WORKS

To the Chief Musician. A Song. A Psalm.

1Make a joyful shout to God, all the earth!
2Sing out the honor of His name;
Make His praise glorious.
3Say to God,
"How awesome are Your works!
Through the greatness of Your power
Your enemies shall submit themselves to
You.
4All the earth shall worship You
And sing praises to You;
They shall sing praises *to* Your name." *Selah*

5Come and see the works of God;
He is awesome *in His* doing toward the sons
of men.
6He turned the sea into dry *land;*
They went through the river on foot.
There we will rejoice in Him.
7He rules by His power forever;
His eyes observe the nations;
Do not let the rebellious exalt themselves.
Selah

8Oh, bless our God, you peoples!
And make the voice of His praise to be
heard,

THE MESSAGE

We expect our fill of good things
in your house, your heavenly manse.
All your salvation wonders
are on display in your trophy room.
Earth-Tamer, Ocean-Pourer,
Mountain-Maker, Hill-Dresser,
Muzzler of sea storm and wave crash,
of mobs in noisy riot—
Far and wide they'll come to a stop,
they'll stare in awe, in wonder.
Dawn and dusk take turns
calling, "Come and worship."

9-13 Oh, visit the earth,
ask her to join the dance!
Deck her out in spring showers,
fill the God-River with living water.
Paint the wheat fields golden.
Creation was made for this!
Drench the plowed fields,
soak the dirt clods
With rainfall as harrow and rake
bring her to blossom and fruit.
Snow-crown the peaks with splendor,
scatter rose petals down your paths,
All through the wild meadows, rose petals.
Set the hills to dancing,
Dress the canyon walls with live sheep,
a drape of flax across the valleys.
Let them shout, and shout, and shout!
Oh, oh, let them sing!

1-4 **66** All together now—applause for God!
Sing songs to the tune of his glory,
set glory to the rhythms of his praise.
Say of God, "We've never seen anything
like him!"
When your enemies see you in action,
they slink off like scolded dogs.
The whole earth falls to its knees—
it worships you, sings to you,
can't stop enjoying your name and fame.

5-6 Take a good look at God's wonders—
they'll take your breath away.
He converted sea to dry land;
travelers crossed the river on foot.
Now isn't that cause for a song?

7 Ever sovereign in his high tower, he keeps
his eye on the godless nations.
Rebels don't dare
raise a finger against him.

8-12 Bless our God, O peoples!
Give him a thunderous welcome!

New King James Version

9Who keeps our soul among the living,
And does not allow our feet to be moved.
10For You, O God, have tested us;
You have refined us as silver is refined.
11You brought us into the net;
You laid affliction on our backs.
12You have caused men to ride over our heads;
We went through fire and through water;
But You brought us out to rich *fulfillment*.

13I will go into Your house with burnt offerings;
I will pay You my vows,
14Which my lips have uttered
And my mouth has spoken when I was in trouble.
15I will offer You burnt sacrifices of fat animals,
With the sweet aroma of rams;
I will offer bulls with goats. *Selah*

16Come *and* hear, all you who fear God,
And I will declare what He has done for my soul.
17I cried to Him with my mouth,
And He was extolled with my tongue.
18If I regard iniquity in my heart,
The Lord will not hear.
19*But* certainly God has heard *me;*
He has attended to the voice of my prayer.

20Blessed *be* God,
Who has not turned away my prayer,
Nor His mercy from me!

PSALM 67

An Invocation and a Doxology

To the Chief Musician. On stringed instruments.[a] A Psalm. A Song.

1God be merciful to us and bless us,
And cause His face to shine upon us, *Selah*
2That Your way may be known on earth,
Your salvation among all nations.

3Let the peoples praise You, O God;
Let all the peoples praise You.
4Oh, let the nations be glad and sing for joy!
For You shall judge the people righteously,
And govern the nations on earth. *Selah*

5Let the peoples praise You, O God;
Let all the peoples praise You.
6*Then* the earth shall yield her increase;
God, our own God, shall bless us.
7God shall bless us,
And all the ends of the earth shall fear Him.

PSALM 68

The Glory of God in His Goodness to Israel

To the Chief Musician. A Psalm of David. A Song.

1Let God arise,
Let His enemies be scattered;
Let those also who hate Him flee before Him.
2As smoke is driven away,
So drive *them* away;

67:title [a]Hebrew *neginoth*

The Message

Didn't he set us on the road to life?
Didn't he keep us out of the ditch?
He trained us first,
passed us like silver through refining fires,
Brought us into hardscrabble country,
pushed us to our very limit,
Road-tested us inside and out,
took us to hell and back;
Finally he brought us
to this well-watered place.

13-15 I'm bringing my prizes and presents to your house.
I'm doing what I said I'd do,
What I solemnly swore I'd do
that day when I was in so much trouble:
The choicest cuts of meat
for the sacrificial meal;
Even the fragrance
of roasted lamb is like a meal!
Or make it an ox
garnished with goat meat!

16-20 All believers, come here and listen,
let me tell you what God did for me.
I called out to him with my mouth,
my tongue shaped the sounds of music.
If I had been cozy with evil,
the Lord would never have listened.
But he most surely *did* listen,
he came on the double when he heard my prayer.
Blessed be God: he didn't turn a deaf ear,
he stayed with me, loyal in his love.

1-7 67 God, mark us with grace
and blessing! Smile!
The whole country will see how you work,
all the godless nations see how you save.
God! Let people thank and enjoy you.
Let all people thank and enjoy you.
Let all far-flung people become happy
and shout their happiness because
You judge them fair and square,
you tend the far-flung peoples.
God! Let people thank and enjoy you.
Let all people thank and enjoy you.
Earth, display your exuberance!
You mark us with blessing, O God, our God.
You mark us with blessing, O God.
Earth's four corners—honor him!

A David Psalm

1-4 68 Up with God!
Down with his enemies!
Adversaries, run for the hills!
Gone like a puff of smoke,

NEW KING JAMES VERSION

As wax melts before the fire,
So let the wicked perish at the presence of God.
3But let the righteous be glad;
Let them rejoice before God;
Yes, let them rejoice exceedingly.

4Sing to God, sing praises to His name;
Extol Him who rides on the clouds,[a]
By His name YAH,
And rejoice before Him.

5A father of the fatherless, a defender of widows,
Is God in His holy habitation.
6God sets the solitary in families;
He brings out those who are bound into prosperity;
But the rebellious dwell in a dry *land.*

7O God, when You went out before Your people,
When You marched through the wilderness, *Selah*
8The earth shook;
The heavens also dropped *rain* at the presence of God;
Sinai itself *was moved* at the presence of God, the God of Israel.
9You, O God, sent a plentiful rain,
Whereby You confirmed Your inheritance,
When it was weary.
10Your congregation dwelt in it;
You, O God, provided from Your goodness for the poor.

11The Lord gave the word;
Great *was* the company of those who proclaimed *it:*
12"Kings of armies flee, they flee,
And she who remains at home divides the spoil.
13Though you lie down among the sheepfolds,
You will be like the wings of a dove covered with silver,
And her feathers with yellow gold."
14When the Almighty scattered kings in it,
It was *white* as snow in Zalmon.

15A mountain of God *is* the mountain of Bashan;
A mountain *of many* peaks *is* the mountain of Bashan.
16Why do you fume with envy, you mountains of *many* peaks?
This is the mountain *which* God desires to dwell in;
Yes, the LORD will dwell *in it* forever.

17The chariots of God *are* twenty thousand,
Even thousands of thousands;
The Lord is among them *as in* Sinai, in the Holy *Place.*
18You have ascended on high,
You have led captivity captive;
You have received gifts among men,
Even *from* the rebellious,
That the LORD God might dwell *there.*

68:4 [a]Masoretic Text reads *deserts;* Targum reads *heavens* (compare verse 34 and Isaiah 19:1).

THE MESSAGE

like a blob of wax in the fire—
one look at God and the wicked vanish.
When the righteous see God in action
they'll laugh, they'll sing,
they'll laugh and sing for joy.
Sing hymns to God;
all heaven, sing out;
clear the way for the coming of Cloud-Rider.
Enjoy GOD,
cheer when you see him!

5-6 Father of orphans,
champion of widows,
is God in his holy house.
God makes homes for the homeless,
leads prisoners to freedom,
but leaves rebels to rot in hell.

7-10 God, when you took the lead with your people,
when you marched out into the wild,
Earth shook, sky broke out in a sweat;
God was on the march.
Even Sinai trembled at the sight of God on the move,
at the sight of Israel's God.
You pour out rain in buckets, O God;
thorn and cactus become an oasis
For your people to camp in and enjoy.
You set them up in business;
they went from rags to riches.

11-14 The Lord gave the word;
thousands called out the good news:
"Kings of the armies
are on the run, on the run!"
While housewives, safe and sound back home,
divide up the plunder,
the plunder of Canaanite silver and gold.
On that day that Shaddai scattered the kings,
snow fell on Black Mountain.

15-16 You huge mountains, Bashan mountains,
mighty mountains, dragon mountains.
All you mountains not chosen,
sulk now, and feel sorry for yourselves,
For this is the mountain God has chosen to live on;
he'll rule from this mountain forever.

17-18 The chariots of God, twice ten thousand,
and thousands more besides,
The Lord in the lead, riding down Sinai—
straight to the Holy Place!
You climbed to the High Place, captives in tow,
your arms full of booty from rebels,
And now you sit there in state,
GOD, sovereign GOD!

NEW KING JAMES VERSION

19Blessed *be* the Lord,
Who daily loads us *with benefits*,
The God of our salvation! *Selah*
20Our God *is* the God of salvation;
And to GOD the Lord *belong* escapes from death.

21But God will wound the head of His enemies,
The hairy scalp of the one who still goes on in his trespasses.
22The Lord said, "I will bring back from Bashan,
I will bring *them* back from the depths of the sea,
23That your foot may crush *them*[a] in blood,
And the tongues of your dogs *may have* their portion from *your* enemies."

24They have seen Your procession, O God,
The procession of my God, my King, into the sanctuary.
25The singers went before, the players on instruments *followed* after;
Among *them were* the maidens playing timbrels.
26Bless God in the congregations,
The Lord, from the fountain of Israel.
27There *is* little Benjamin, their leader,
The princes of Judah *and* their company,
The princes of Zebulun *and* the princes of Naphtali.

28Your God has commanded[a] your strength;
Strengthen, O God, what You have done for us.
29Because of Your temple at Jerusalem,
Kings will bring presents to You.
30Rebuke the beasts of the reeds,
The herd of bulls with the calves of the peoples,
Till everyone submits himself with pieces of silver.
Scatter the peoples *who* delight in war.
31Envoys will come out of Egypt;
Ethiopia will quickly stretch out her hands to God.

32Sing to God, you kingdoms of the earth;
Oh, sing praises to the Lord, *Selah*
33To Him who rides on the heaven of heavens, *which were* of old!
Indeed, He sends out His voice, a mighty voice.
34Ascribe strength to God;
His excellence *is* over Israel,
And His strength *is* in the clouds.
35O God, *You are* more awesome than Your holy places.
The God of Israel *is* He who gives strength and power to *His* people.

Blessed *be* God!

68:23 [a]Septuagint, Syriac, Targum, and Vulgate read *you may dip your foot.* **68:28** [a]Septuagint, Syriac, Targum, and Vulgate read *Command, O God.*

THE MESSAGE

19-23 Blessed be the Lord—
day after day he carries us along.
He's our Savior, our God, oh yes!
He's God-for-us, he's God-who-saves-us.
Lord GOD knows all
death's ins and outs.
What's more, he made heads roll,
split the skulls of the enemy
As he marched out of heaven,
saying, "I tied up the Dragon in knots,
put a muzzle on the Deep Blue Sea."
You can wade through your enemies' blood,
and your dogs taste of your enemies from your boots.

24-31 See God on parade
to the sanctuary, my God,
my King on the march!
Singers out front, the band behind,
maidens in the middle with castanets.
The whole choir blesses God.
Like a fountain of praise, Israel blesses GOD.
Look—little Benjamin's out
front and leading
Princes of Judah in their royal robes,
princes of Zebulon, princes of Naphtali.
Parade your power, O God,
the power, O God, that made us what we are.
Your temple, High God, is Jerusalem;
kings bring gifts to you.
Rebuke that old crocodile, Egypt,
with her herd of wild bulls and calves,
Rapacious in her lust for silver,
crushing peoples, spoiling for a fight.
Let Egyptian traders bring blue cloth
and Cush come running to God, her hands outstretched.

32-34 Sing, O kings of the earth!
Sing praises to the Lord!
There he is: Sky-Rider,
striding the ancient skies.
Listen—he's calling in thunder,
rumbling, rolling thunder.
Call out "Bravo!" to God,
the High God of Israel.
His splendor and strength
rise huge as thunderheads.

35 A terrible beauty, O God,
streams from your sanctuary.
It's Israel's strong God! He gives
power and might to his people!
O you, his people—bless God!

NEW KING JAMES VERSION

PSALM 69

AN URGENT PLEA FOR HELP IN TROUBLE

To the Chief Musician. Set to "The Lilies."[a] *A Psalm* of David.

1 Save me, O God!
For the waters have come up to *my* neck.
2 I sink in deep mire,
Where *there is* no standing;
I have come into deep waters,
Where the floods overflow me.
3 I am weary with my crying;
My throat is dry;
My eyes fail while I wait for my God.

4 Those who hate me without a cause
Are more than the hairs of my head;
They are mighty who would destroy me,
Being my enemies wrongfully;
Though I have stolen nothing,
I *still* must restore *it*.

5 O God, You know my foolishness;
And my sins are not hidden from You.
6 Let not those who wait for You, O Lord GOD of hosts, be ashamed because of me;
Let not those who seek You be confounded because of me, O God of Israel.
7 Because for Your sake I have borne reproach;
Shame has covered my face.
8 I have become a stranger to my brothers,
And an alien to my mother's children;
9 Because zeal for Your house has eaten me up,
And the reproaches of those who reproach You have fallen on me.
10 When I wept *and chastened* my soul with fasting,
That became my reproach.
11 I also made sackcloth my garment;
I became a byword to them.
12 Those who sit in the gate speak against me,
And I *am* the song of the drunkards.

13 But as for me, my prayer *is* to You,
O LORD, *in* the acceptable time;
O God, in the multitude of Your mercy,
Hear me in the truth of Your salvation.
14 Deliver me out of the mire,
And let me not sink;
Let me be delivered from those who hate me,
And out of the deep waters.
15 Let not the floodwater overflow me,
Nor let the deep swallow me up;
And let not the pit shut its mouth on me.

16 Hear me, O LORD, for Your lovingkindness *is* good;
Turn to me according to the multitude of Your tender mercies.

69:title [a]Hebrew *Shoshannim*

THE MESSAGE

A DAVID PSALM

1 69 God, God, save me!
I'm in over my head,

2 Quicksand under me, swamp water over me;
I'm going down for the third time.

3 I'm hoarse from calling for help,
Bleary-eyed from searching the sky for God.

4 I've got more enemies than hairs on my head;
Sneaks and liars are out to knife me in the back.

What I never stole
Must I now give back?

5 God, you know every sin I've committed;
My life's a wide-open book before you.

6 Don't let those who look to you in hope
Be discouraged by what happens to me,
Dear Lord! GOD of the armies!

Don't let those out looking for you
Come to a dead end by following me—
Please, dear God of Israel!

7 Because of you I look like an idiot,
I walk around ashamed to show my face.

8 My brothers shun me like a bum off the street;
My family treats me like an unwanted guest.

9 I love you more than I can say.
Because I'm madly in love with you,
They blame me for everything they dislike about you.

10 When I poured myself out in prayer and fasting,
All it got me was more contempt.

11 When I put on a sad face,
They treated me like a clown.

12 Now drunks and gluttons
Make up drinking songs about me.

13 And me? I pray.
GOD, it's time for a break!

God, answer in love!
Answer with your sure salvation!

14 Rescue me from the swamp,
Don't let me go under for good,

Pull me out of the clutch of the enemy;
This whirlpool is sucking me down.

15 Don't let the swamp be my grave, the Black Hole
Swallow me, its jaws clenched around me.

16 Now answer me, GOD, because you love me;
Let me see your great mercy full-face.

NEW KING JAMES VERSION

17 And do not hide Your face from Your servant,
For I am in trouble;
Hear me speedily.
18 Draw near to my soul, *and* redeem it;
Deliver me because of my enemies.

19 You know my reproach, my shame, and my dishonor;
My adversaries *are* all before You.
20 Reproach has broken my heart,
And I am full of heaviness;
I looked *for someone* to take pity, but *there was* none;
And for comforters, but I found none.
21 They also gave me gall for my food,
And for my thirst they gave me vinegar to drink.

22 Let their table become a snare before them,
And their well-being a trap.
23 Let their eyes be darkened, so that they do not see;
And make their loins shake continually.
24 Pour out Your indignation upon them,
And let Your wrathful anger take hold of them.
25 Let their dwelling place be desolate;
Let no one live in their tents.
26 For they persecute the *ones* You have struck,
And talk of the grief of those You have wounded.
27 Add iniquity to their iniquity,
And let them not come into Your righteousness.
28 Let them be blotted out of the book of the living,
And not be written with the righteous.

29 But I *am* poor and sorrowful;
Let Your salvation, O God, set me up on high.
30 I will praise the name of God with a song,
And will magnify Him with thanksgiving.
31 *This* also shall please the LORD better than an ox *or* bull,
Which has horns and hooves.
32 The humble shall see *this and* be glad;
And you who seek God, your hearts shall live.
33 For the LORD hears the poor,
And does not despise His prisoners.

34 Let heaven and earth praise Him,
The seas and everything that moves in them.
35 For God will save Zion
And build the cities of Judah,
That they may dwell there and possess it.
36 Also, the descendants of His servants shall inherit it,
And those who love His name shall dwell in it.

THE MESSAGE

17 Don't look the other way; your servant can't take it.
I'm in trouble. Answer right now!

18 Come close, God; get me out of here.
Rescue me from this deathtrap.

19 You know how they kick me around—
Pin on me the donkey's ears, the dunce's cap.

20 I'm broken by their taunts,
Flat on my face, reduced to a nothing.

I looked in vain for one friendly face. Not one.
I couldn't find one shoulder to cry on.

21 They put poison in my soup,
Vinegar in my drink.

22 Let their supper be bait in a trap that snaps shut;
May their best friends be trappers who'll skin them alive.

23 Make them become blind as bats,
Give them the shakes from morning to night.

24 Let them know what you think of them,
Blast them with your red-hot anger.

25 Burn down their houses,
Leave them desolate with nobody at home.

26 They gossiped about the one you disciplined,
Made up stories about anyone wounded by God.

27 Pile on the guilt,
Don't let them off the hook.

28 Strike their names from the list of the living;
No rock-carved honor for them among the righteous.

29 I'm hurt and in pain;
Give me space for healing, and mountain air.

30 Let me shout God's name with a praising song,
Let me tell his greatness in a prayer of thanks.

31 For GOD, this is better than oxen on the altar,
Far better than blue-ribbon bulls.

32 The poor in spirit see and are glad—
Oh, you God-seekers, take heart!

33 For GOD listens to the poor,
He doesn't walk out on the wretched.

34 You heavens, praise him; praise him, earth;
Also ocean and all things that swim in it.

35 For God is out to help Zion,
Rebuilding the wrecked towns of Judah.

Guess who will live there—
The proud owners of the land?

36 No, the children of his servants will get it,
The lovers of his name will live in it.

NEW KING JAMES VERSION

PSALM 70

PRAYER FOR RELIEF FROM ADVERSARIES

To the Chief Musician. *A Psalm* of David. To bring to remembrance.

1*Make haste,* O God, to deliver me!
Make haste to help me, O LORD!

2Let them be ashamed and confounded
Who seek my life;
Let them be turned back[a] and confused
Who desire my hurt.
3Let them be turned back because of their shame,
Who say, "Aha, aha!"

4Let all those who seek You rejoice and be glad in You;
And let those who love Your salvation say continually,
"Let God be magnified!"

5But I *am* poor and needy;
Make haste to me, O God!
You *are* my help and my deliverer;
O LORD, do not delay.

PSALM 71

GOD THE ROCK OF SALVATION

1In You, O LORD, I put my trust;
Let me never be put to shame.
2Deliver me in Your righteousness, and cause me to escape;
Incline Your ear to me, and save me.
3Be my strong refuge,
To which I may resort continually;
You have given the commandment to save me,
For You *are* my rock and my fortress.

4Deliver me, O my God, out of the hand of the wicked,
Out of the hand of the unrighteous and cruel man.
5For You are my hope, O Lord GOD;
You are my trust from my youth.
6By You I have been upheld from birth;
You are He who took me out of my mother's womb.
My praise *shall be* continually of You.

7I have become as a wonder to many,
But You *are* my strong refuge.
8Let my mouth be filled *with* Your praise
And with Your glory all the day.

9Do not cast me off in the time of old age;
Do not forsake me when my strength fails.
10For my enemies speak against me;
And those who lie in wait for my life take counsel together,
11Saying, "God has forsaken him;
Pursue and take him, for *there is* none to deliver *him*."

70:2 [a]Following Masoretic Text, Septuagint, Targum, and Vulgate; some Hebrew manuscripts and Syriac read *be appalled* (compare 40:15).

THE MESSAGE

A DAVID PRAYER

1-3 **70** God! Please hurry to my rescue!
GOD, come quickly to my side!
Those who are out to get me—
let them fall all over themselves.
Those who relish my downfall—
send them down a blind alley.
Give them a taste of their own medicine,
those gossips off clucking their tongues.

4 Let those on the hunt for you
sing and celebrate.
Let all who love your saving way
say over and over, "God is mighty!"

5 But I've lost it. I'm wasted.
God—quickly, quickly!
Quick to my side, quick to my rescue!
GOD, don't lose a minute.

1-3 **71** I run for dear life to GOD,
I'll never live to regret it.
Do what you do so well:
get me out of this mess and up on my feet.
Put your ear to the ground and listen,
give me space for salvation.
Be a guest room where I can retreat;
you said your door was always open!
You're my salvation—my vast, granite fortress.

4-7 My God, free me from the grip of Wicked,
from the clutch of Bad and Bully.
You keep me going when times are tough—
my bedrock, GOD, since my childhood.
I've hung on you from the day of my birth,
the day you took me from the cradle;
I'll never run out of praise.
Many gasp in alarm when they see me,
but you take me in stride.

8-11 Just as each day brims with your beauty,
my mouth brims with praise.
But don't turn me out to pasture when I'm old
or put me on the shelf when I can't pull my weight.
My enemies are talking behind my back,
watching for their chance to knife me.
The gossip is: "God has abandoned him.
Pounce on him now; no one will help him."

NEW KING JAMES VERSION

[12]O God, do not be far from me;
O my God, make haste to help me!
[13]Let them be confounded *and* consumed
Who are adversaries of my life;
Let them be covered *with* reproach and dishonor
Who seek my hurt.

[14]But I will hope continually,
And will praise You yet more and more.
[15]My mouth shall tell of Your righteousness
And Your salvation all the day,
For I do not know *their* limits.
[16]I will go in the strength of the Lord GOD;
I will make mention of Your righteousness, of Yours only.

[17]O God, You have taught me from my youth;
And to this *day* I declare Your wondrous works.
[18]Now also when *I am* old and grayheaded,
O God, do not forsake me,
Until I declare Your strength to *this* generation,
Your power to everyone *who* is to come.

[19]Also Your righteousness, O God, *is* very high,
You who have done great things;
O God, who *is* like You?
[20]*You,* who have shown me great and severe troubles,
Shall revive me again,
And bring me up again from the depths of the earth.
[21]You shall increase my greatness,
And comfort me on every side.

[22]Also with the lute I will praise You—
And Your faithfulness, O my God!
To You I will sing with the harp,
O Holy One of Israel.
[23]My lips shall greatly rejoice when I sing to You,
And my soul, which You have redeemed.
[24]My tongue also shall talk of Your righteousness all the day long;
For they are confounded,
For they are brought to shame
Who seek my hurt.

PSALM 72

GLORY AND UNIVERSALITY OF THE MESSIAH'S REIGN

A Psalm of Solomon.

[1]Give the king Your judgments, O God,
And Your righteousness to the king's Son.
[2]He will judge Your people with righteousness,
And Your poor with justice.
[3]The mountains will bring peace to the people,
And the little hills, by righteousness.
[4]He will bring justice to the poor of the people;
He will save the children of the needy,
And will break in pieces the oppressor.

THE MESSAGE

12-16 God, don't just watch from the sidelines.
Come on! Run to my side!
My accusers—make them lose face.
Those out to get me—make them look
Like idiots, while I stretch out, reaching for you,
and daily add praise to praise.
I'll write the book on your righteousness,
talk up your salvation the livelong day,
never run out of good things to write or say.
I come in the power of the Lord GOD,
I post signs marking his right-of-way.

17-24 You got me when I was an unformed youth,
God, and taught me everything I know.
Now I'm telling the world your wonders;
I'll keep at it until I'm old and gray.
God, don't walk off and leave me
until I get out the news
Of your strong right arm to this world,
news of your power to the world yet to come,
Your famous and righteous
ways, O God.
God, you've done it all!
Who is quite like you?
You, who made me stare trouble in the face,
Turn me around;
Now let me look life in the face.
I've been to the bottom;
Bring me up, streaming with honors;
turn to me, be tender to me,
And I'll take up the lute and thank you
to the tune of your faithfulness, God.
I'll make music for you on a harp,
Holy One of Israel.
When I open up in song to you,
I let out lungsful of praise,
my rescued life a song.
All day long I'm chanting
about you and your righteous ways,
While those who tried to do me in
slink off looking ashamed.

A SOLOMON PSALM

1-8 **72** Give the gift of wise rule to the king, O God,
the gift of just rule to the crown prince.
May he judge your people rightly,
be honorable to your meek and lowly.
Let the mountains give exuberant witness;
shape the hills with the contours of right living.
Please stand up for the poor,
help the children of the needy,
come down hard on the cruel tyrants.

NEW KING JAMES VERSION

5They shall fear You[a]
As long as the sun and moon endure,
Throughout all generations.
6He shall come down like rain upon the grass
before mowing,
Like showers *that* water the earth.
7In His days the righteous shall flourish,
And abundance of peace,
Until the moon is no more.

8He shall have dominion also from sea to sea,
And from the River to the ends of the earth.
9Those who dwell in the wilderness will bow
before Him,
And His enemies will lick the dust.
10The kings of Tarshish and of the isles
Will bring presents;
The kings of Sheba and Seba
Will offer gifts.
11Yes, all kings shall fall down before Him;
All nations shall serve Him.

12For He will deliver the needy when he cries,
The poor also, and *him* who has no helper.
13He will spare the poor and needy,
And will save the souls of the needy.
14He will redeem their life from oppression
and violence;
And precious shall be their blood in His
sight.

15And He shall live;
And the gold of Sheba will be given to Him;
Prayer also will be made for Him
continually,
And daily He shall be praised.

16There will be an abundance of grain in the
earth,
On the top of the mountains;
Its fruit shall wave like Lebanon;
And *those* of the city shall flourish like
grass of the earth.

17His name shall endure forever;
His name shall continue as long as the sun.
And *men* shall be blessed in Him;
All nations shall call Him blessed.

18Blessed *be* the LORD God, the God of Israel,
Who only does wondrous things!
19And blessed *be* His glorious name forever!
And let the whole earth be filled *with* His
glory.
Amen and Amen.

20The prayers of David the son of Jesse are
ended.

72:5 [a]Following Masoretic Text and Targum; Septuagint and Vulgate read *They shall continue.*

THE MESSAGE

Outlast the sun, outlive the moon—
age after age after age.
Be rainfall on cut grass,
earth-refreshing rain showers.
Let righteousness burst into blossom
and peace abound until the moon fades
to nothing.
Rule from sea to sea,
from the River to the Rim.

9-14 Foes will fall on their knees before God,
his enemies lick the dust.
Kings remote and legendary will pay
homage,
kings rich and resplendent will turn over
their wealth.
All kings will fall down and worship,
and godless nations sign up to serve him,
Because he rescues the poor at the first
sign of need,
the destitute who have run out of luck.
He opens a place in his heart for the
down-and-out,
he restores the wretched of the earth.
He frees them from tyranny and torture—
when they bleed, he bleeds;
when they die, he dies.

15-17 And live! Oh, let him live!
Deck him out in Sheba gold.
Offer prayers unceasing to him,
bless him from morning to night.
Fields of golden grain in the land,
cresting the mountains in wild
exuberance,
Cornucopias of praise, praises
springing from the city like grass from
the earth.
May he never be forgotten,
his fame shine on like sunshine.
May all godless people enter his circle of
blessing
and bless the One who blessed them.

18-20 Blessed GOD, Israel's God,
the one and only wonder-working God!
Blessed always his blazing glory!
All earth brims with his glory.
Yes and Yes and Yes.

NEW KING JAMES VERSION

Book Three: Psalms 73—89

PSALM 73

THE TRAGEDY OF THE WICKED, AND THE BLESSEDNESS OF TRUST IN GOD

A Psalm of Asaph.

1 Truly God *is* good to Israel,
To such as are pure in heart.
2 But as for me, my feet had almost stumbled;
My steps had nearly slipped.
3 For I *was* envious of the boastful,
When I saw the prosperity of the wicked.

4 For *there are* no pangs in their death,
But their strength *is* firm.
5 They *are* not in trouble *as other* men,
Nor are they plagued like *other* men.
6 Therefore pride serves as their necklace;
Violence covers them *like* a garment.
7 Their eyes bulge[a] with abundance;
They have more than heart could wish.
8 They scoff and speak wickedly *concerning* oppression;
They speak loftily.
9 They set their mouth against the heavens,
And their tongue walks through the earth.

10 Therefore his people return here,
And waters of a full *cup* are drained by them.
11 And they say, "How does God know?
And is there knowledge in the Most High?"
12 Behold, these *are* the ungodly,
Who are always at ease;
They increase *in* riches.
13 Surely I have cleansed my heart *in* vain,
And washed my hands in innocence.
14 For all day long I have been plagued,
And chastened every morning.

15 If I had said, "I will speak thus,"
Behold, I would have been untrue to the generation of Your children.
16 When I thought *how* to understand this,
It *was* too painful for me—
17 Until I went into the sanctuary of God;
Then I understood their end.

18 Surely You set them in slippery places;
You cast them down to destruction.
19 Oh, how they are *brought* to desolation, as in a moment!
They are utterly consumed with terrors.
20 As a dream when *one* awakes,
So, Lord, when You awake,
You shall despise their image.

21 Thus my heart was grieved,
And I was vexed in my mind.
22 I *was* so foolish and ignorant;
I was *like* a beast before You.
23 Nevertheless I *am* continually with You;
You hold *me* by my right hand.
24 You will guide me with Your counsel,
And afterward receive me *to* glory.

73:7 [a]Targum reads *face bulges;* Septuagint, Syriac, and Vulgate read *iniquity bulges.*

THE MESSAGE

AN ASAPH PSALM

1-5 **73** No doubt about it! God is good—
good to good people, good to the good-hearted.
But I nearly missed it,
missed seeing his goodness.
I was looking the other way,
looking up to the people
At the top,
envying the wicked who have it made,
Who have nothing to worry about,
not a care in the whole wide world.

6-10 Pretentious with arrogance,
they wear the latest fashions in violence,
Pampered and overfed,
decked out in silk bows of silliness.
They jeer, using words to kill;
they bully their way with words.
They're full of hot air,
loudmouths disturbing the peace.
People actually listen to them—can you believe it?
Like thirsty puppies, they lap up their words.

11-14 What's going on here? Is God out to lunch?
Nobody's tending the store.
The wicked get by with everything;
they have it made, piling up riches.
I've been stupid to play by the rules;
what has it gotten me?
A long run of bad luck, that's what—
a slap in the face every time I walk out the door.

15-20 If I'd have given in and talked like this,
I would have betrayed your dear children.
Still, when I tried to figure it out,
all I got was a splitting headache . . .
Until I entered the sanctuary of God.
Then I saw the whole picture:
The slippery road you've put them on,
with a final crash in a ditch of delusions.
In the blink of an eye, disaster!
A blind curve in the dark, and—nightmare!
We wake up and rub our eyes. . . . Nothing.
There's nothing to them. And there never was.

21-24 When I was beleaguered and bitter,
totally consumed by envy,
I was totally ignorant, a dumb ox
in your very presence.
I'm still in your presence,
but you've taken my hand.
You wisely and tenderly lead me,
and then you bless me.

New King James Version

25 Whom have I in heaven *but You?*
And *there is* none upon earth *that* I desire
besides You.
26 My flesh and my heart fail;
But God *is* the strength of my heart and my
portion forever.

27 For indeed, those who are far from You shall
perish;
You have destroyed all those who desert You
for harlotry.
28 But *it is* good for me to draw near to God;
I have put my trust in the Lord GOD,
That I may declare all Your works.

PSALM 74

A Plea for Relief from Oppressors

A Contemplation[a] of Asaph.

1 O God, why have You cast *us* off forever?
Why does Your anger smoke against the
sheep of Your pasture?
2 Remember Your congregation, *which* You
have purchased of old,
The tribe of Your inheritance, *which* You
have redeemed—
This Mount Zion where You have dwelt.
3 Lift up Your feet to the perpetual
desolations.
The enemy has damaged everything in the
sanctuary.
4 Your enemies roar in the midst of Your
meeting place;
They set up their banners *for* signs.
5 They seem like men who lift up
Axes among the thick trees.
6 And now they break down its carved work,
all at once,
With axes and hammers.
7 They have set fire to Your sanctuary;
They have defiled the dwelling place of Your
name to the ground.
8 They said in their hearts,
"Let us destroy them altogether."
They have burned up all the meeting places
of God in the land.

9 We do not see our signs;
There is no longer any prophet;
Nor *is there* any among us who knows how
long.
10 O God, how long will the adversary
reproach?
Will the enemy blaspheme Your name
forever?
11 Why do You withdraw Your hand, even Your
right hand?
Take it out of Your bosom and destroy *them*.
12 For God *is* my King from of old,
Working salvation in the midst of the earth.
13 You divided the sea by Your strength;
You broke the heads of the sea serpents in
the waters.
14 You broke the heads of Leviathan in pieces,
And gave him *as* food to the people
inhabiting the wilderness.
15 You broke open the fountain and the flood;
You dried up mighty rivers.

74:title [a]Hebrew *Maschil*

The Message

25-28 You're all I want in heaven!
You're all I want on earth!
When my skin sags and my bones get
brittle,
GOD is rock-firm and faithful.
Look! Those who left you are falling apart!
Deserters, they'll never be heard from
again.
But I'm in the very presence of God—
oh, how refreshing it is!
I've made Lord GOD my home.
God, I'm telling the world what you do!

An Asaph Psalm

1 **74** You walked off and left us, and never
looked back.
God, how could you do that?
We're your very own sheep;
how can you stomp off in anger?

2-3 Refresh your memory of us—you bought us
a long time ago.
Your most precious tribe—you paid a
good price for us!
Your very own Mount Zion—you
actually lived here once!
Come and visit the site of disaster,
see how they've wrecked the sanctuary.

4-8 While your people were at worship, your
enemies barged in,
brawling and scrawling graffiti.
They set fire to the porch;
axes swinging, they chopped up the
woodwork,
Beat down the doors with sledgehammers,
then split them into kindling.
They burned your holy place to the ground,
violated the place of worship.
They said to themselves, "We'll wipe them
all out,"
and burned down all the places of
worship.

9-17 There's not a sign or symbol of God in
sight,
nor anyone to speak in his name,
no one who knows what's going on.
How long, God, will barbarians blaspheme,
enemies curse and get by with it?
Why don't you do something? How long
are you going
to sit there with your hands folded in
your lap?
God is my King from the very start;
he works salvation in the womb of the
earth.
With one blow you split the sea in two,
you made mincemeat of the dragon
Tannin.
You lopped off the heads of Leviathan,
then served them up in a stew for the
animals.
With your finger you opened up springs
and creeks,
and dried up the wild floodwaters.

NEW KING JAMES VERSION

[16]The day *is* Yours, the night also *is* Yours;
You have prepared the light and the sun.
[17]You have set all the borders of the earth;
You have made summer and winter.

[18]Remember this, *that* the enemy has reproached, O LORD,
And *that* a foolish people has blasphemed Your name.
[19]Oh, do not deliver the life of Your turtledove to the wild beast!
Do not forget the life of Your poor forever.
[20]Have respect to the covenant;
For the dark places of the earth are full of the haunts of cruelty.
[21]Oh, do not let the oppressed return ashamed!
Let the poor and needy praise Your name.

[22]Arise, O God, plead Your own cause;
Remember how the foolish man reproaches You daily.
[23]Do not forget the voice of Your enemies;
The tumult of those who rise up against You increases continually.

PSALM 75

THANKSGIVING FOR GOD'S RIGHTEOUS JUDGMENT

To the Chief Musician. Set to "Do Not Destroy."[a] A Psalm of Asaph. A Song.

[1]We give thanks to You, O God, we give thanks!
For Your wondrous works declare *that* Your name is near.

[2]"When I choose the proper time,
I will judge uprightly.
[3]The earth and all its inhabitants are dissolved;
I set up its pillars firmly. *Selah*

[4]"I said to the boastful, 'Do not deal boastfully,'
And to the wicked, 'Do not lift up the horn.
[5]Do not lift up your horn on high;
Do *not* speak with a stiff neck.' "

[6]For exaltation *comes* neither from the east
Nor from the west nor from the south.
[7]But God *is* the Judge:
He puts down one,
And exalts another.
[8]For in the hand of the LORD *there is* a cup,
And the wine is red;
It is fully mixed, and He pours it out;
Surely its dregs shall all the wicked of the earth
Drain *and* drink down.

[9]But I will declare forever,
I will sing praises to the God of Jacob.

[10]"All the horns of the wicked I will also cut off,
But the horns of the righteous shall be exalted."

75:title [a]Hebrew *Al Tashcheth*

THE MESSAGE

You own the day, you own the night;
you put stars and sun in place.
You laid out the four corners of earth,
shaped the seasons of summer and winter.

18-21 Mark and remember, GOD, all the enemy taunts, each idiot desecration.
Don't throw your lambs to the wolves;
after all we've been through, don't forget us.
Remember your promises;
the city is in darkness, the countryside violent.
Don't leave the victims to rot in the street;
make them a choir that sings your praises.

22-23 On your feet, O God—
stand up for yourself!
Do you hear what they're saying about you,
all the vile obscenities?
Don't tune out their malicious filth,
the brawling invective that never lets up.

AN ASAPH PSALM

1 **75** We thank you, God, we thank you—
your Name is our favorite word;
your mighty works are all we talk about.

2-4 You say, "I'm calling this meeting to order,
I'm ready to set things right.
When the earth goes topsy-turvy
And nobody knows which end is up,
I nail it all down,
I put everything in place again.
I say to the smart alecks, 'That's enough,'
to the bullies, 'Not so fast.' "

5-6 Don't raise your fist against High God.
Don't raise your voice against Rock of Ages.
He's the One from east to west;
from desert to mountains, he's the One.

7-8 God rules: he brings this one down to his knees,
pulls that one up on her feet.
GOD has a cup in his hand,
a bowl of wine, full to the brim.
He draws from it and pours;
it's drained to the dregs.
Earth's wicked ones drink it all,
drink it down to the last bitter drop!

9-10 And I'm telling the story of God Eternal,
singing the praises of Jacob's God.
The fists of the wicked
are bloody stumps,
The arms of the righteous
are lofty green branches.

New King James Version

PSALM 76

The Majesty of God in Judgment
To the Chief Musician. On stringed instruments.[a]
A Psalm of Asaph. A Song.

1In Judah God *is* known;
His name *is* great in Israel.
2In Salem[a] also is His tabernacle,
And His dwelling place in Zion.
3There He broke the arrows of the bow,
The shield and sword of battle. *Selah*

4You *are* more glorious and excellent
Than the mountains of prey.
5The stouthearted were plundered;
They have sunk into their sleep;
And none of the mighty men have found the
use of their hands.
6At Your rebuke, O God of Jacob,
Both the chariot and horse were cast into a
dead sleep.

7You, Yourself, *are* to be feared;
And who may stand in Your presence
When once You are angry?
8You caused judgment to be heard from
heaven;
The earth feared and was still,
9When God arose to judgment,
To deliver all the oppressed of the earth.
Selah
10Surely the wrath of man shall praise You;
With the remainder of wrath You shall gird
Yourself.

11Make vows to the LORD your God, and pay
them;
Let all who are around Him bring presents
to Him who ought to be feared.
12He shall cut off the spirit of princes;
He is awesome to the kings of the earth.

PSALM 77

The Consoling Memory of God's Redemptive Works
To the Chief Musician. To Jeduthun. A Psalm of Asaph.

1I cried out to God with my voice—
To God with my voice;
And He gave ear to me.
2In the day of my trouble I sought the Lord;
My hand was stretched out in the night
without ceasing;
My soul refused to be comforted.
3I remembered God, and was troubled;
I complained, and my spirit was
overwhelmed. *Selah*

4You hold my eyelids *open;*
I am so troubled that I cannot speak.
5I have considered the days of old,
The years of ancient times.
6I call to remembrance my song in the night;
I meditate within my heart,
And my spirit makes diligent search.

76:title [a]Hebrew *neginoth* **76:2** [a]That is, Jerusalem

The Message

An Asaph Psalm
1-3 **76** God is well-known in Judah;
in Israel, he's a household name.
He keeps a house in Salem,
his own suite of rooms in Zion.
That's where, using arrows for kindling,
he made a bonfire of weapons of war.

4-6 Oh, how bright you shine!
Outshining their huge piles of loot!
The warriors were plundered
and left there impotent.
And now there's nothing to them,
nothing to show for their swagger and
threats.
Your sudden roar, God of Jacob,
knocked the wind out of horse and rider.

7-10 Fierce you are, and fearsome!
Who can stand up to your rising anger?
From heaven you thunder judgment;
earth falls to her knees and holds her
breath.
God stands tall and makes things right,
he saves all the wretched on earth.
Instead of smoldering rage—God-praise!
All that sputtering rage—now a garland
for God!

11-12 Do for GOD what you said you'd do—
he is, after all, your God.
Let everyone in town bring offerings
to the One Who Watches our every move.
Nobody gets by with anything,
no one plays fast and loose with him.

An Asaph Psalm
1 **77** I yell out to my God, I yell with all my
might,
I yell at the top of my lungs. He listens.

2-6 I found myself in trouble and went looking
for my Lord;
my life was an open wound that wouldn't
heal.
When friends said, "Everything will turn
out all right,"
I didn't believe a word they said.
I remember God—and shake my head.
I bow my head—then wring my hands.
I'm awake all night—not a wink of sleep;
I can't even say what's bothering me.
I go over the days one by one,
I ponder the years gone by.
I strum my lute all through the night,
wondering how to get my life together.

NEW KING JAMES VERSION

7Will the Lord cast off forever?
And will He be favorable no more?
8Has His mercy ceased forever?
Has *His* promise failed forevermore?
9Has God forgotten to be gracious?
Has He in anger shut up His tender
mercies? *Selah*

10And I said, "This *is* my anguish;
But I will remember the years of the right
hand of the Most High."
11I will remember the works of the LORD;
Surely I will remember Your wonders of old.
12I will also meditate on all Your work,
And talk of Your deeds.
13Your way, O God, *is* in the sanctuary;
Who *is* so great a God as *our* God?
14You *are* the God who does wonders;
You have declared Your strength among the
peoples.
15You have with *Your* arm redeemed Your
people,
The sons of Jacob and Joseph. *Selah*

16The waters saw You, O God;
The waters saw You, they were afraid;
The depths also trembled.
17The clouds poured out water;
The skies sent out a sound;
Your arrows also flashed about.
18The voice of Your thunder *was* in the
whirlwind;
The lightnings lit up the world;
The earth trembled and shook.
19Your way *was* in the sea,
Your path in the great waters,
And Your footsteps were not known.
20You led Your people like a flock
By the hand of Moses and Aaron.

PSALM 78

GOD'S KINDNESS TO REBELLIOUS ISRAEL

A Contemplation[a] of Asaph.

1Give ear, O my people, *to* my law;
Incline your ears to the words of my mouth.
2I will open my mouth in a parable;
I will utter dark sayings of old,
3Which we have heard and known,
And our fathers have told us.
4We will not hide *them* from their children,
Telling to the generation to come the praises
of the LORD,
And His strength and His wonderful works
that He has done.

5For He established a testimony in Jacob,
And appointed a law in Israel,
Which He commanded our fathers,
That they should make them known to their
children;
6That the generation to come might know
them,

78:title [a]Hebrew *Maschil*

THE MESSAGE

7-10 Will the Lord walk off and leave us for
good?
Will he never smile again?
Is his love worn threadbare?
Has his salvation promise burned out?
Has God forgotten his manners?
Has he angrily stalked off and left us?
"Just my luck," I said. "The High God goes
out of business
just the moment I need him."

11-12 Once again I'll go over what GOD has done,
lay out on the table the ancient wonders;
I'll ponder all the things you've
accomplished,
and give a long, loving look at your acts.

13-15 O God! Your way is holy!
No god is great like God!
You're the God who makes things happen;
you showed everyone what you can do—
You pulled your people out of the worst
kind of trouble,
rescued the children of Jacob and
Joseph.

16-19 Ocean saw you in action, God,
saw you and trembled with fear;
Deep Ocean was scared to death.
Clouds belched buckets of rain,
Sky exploded with thunder,
your arrows flashing this way and that.
From Whirlwind came your thundering
voice,
Lightning exposed the world,
Earth reeled and rocked.
You strode right through Ocean,
walked straight through roaring Ocean,
but nobody saw you come or go.

20 Hidden in the hands of Moses and Aaron,
You led your people like a flock of sheep.

AN ASAPH PSALM

1-4 78 Listen, dear friends, to God's truth,
bend your ears to what I tell you.
I'm chewing on the morsel of a proverb;
I'll let you in on the sweet old truths,
Stories we heard from our fathers,
counsel we learned at our mother's knee.
We're not keeping this to ourselves,
we're passing it along to the next
generation—
GOD's fame and fortune,
the marvelous things he has done.

5-8 He planted a witness in Jacob,
set his Word firmly in Israel,
Then commanded our parents
to teach it to their children
So the next generation would know,

NEW KING JAMES VERSION

The children *who* would be born,
That they may arise and declare *them* to their children,
7 That they may set their hope in God,
And not forget the works of God,
But keep His commandments;
8 And may not be like their fathers,
A stubborn and rebellious generation,
A generation *that* did not set its heart aright,
And whose spirit was not faithful to God.

9 The children of Ephraim, *being* armed *and* carrying bows,
Turned back in the day of battle.
10 They did not keep the covenant of God;
They refused to walk in His law,
11 And forgot His works
And His wonders that He had shown them.

12 Marvelous things He did in the sight of their fathers,
In the land of Egypt, *in* the field of Zoan.
13 He divided the sea and caused them to pass through;
And He made the waters stand up like a heap.
14 In the daytime also He led them with the cloud,
And all the night with a light of fire.
15 He split the rocks in the wilderness,
And gave *them* drink in abundance like the depths.
16 He also brought streams out of the rock,
And caused waters to run down like rivers.

17 But they sinned even more against Him
By rebelling against the Most High in the wilderness.
18 And they tested God in their heart
By asking for the food of their fancy.
19 Yes, they spoke against God:
They said, "Can God prepare a table in the wilderness?
20 Behold, He struck the rock,
So that the waters gushed out,
And the streams overflowed.
Can He give bread also?
Can He provide meat for His people?"

21 Therefore the LORD heard *this* and was furious;
So a fire was kindled against Jacob,
And anger also came up against Israel,
22 Because they did not believe in God,
And did not trust in His salvation.
23 Yet He had commanded the clouds above,
And opened the doors of heaven,
24 Had rained down manna on them to eat,
And given them of the bread of heaven.
25 Men ate angels' food;
He sent them food to the full.

26 He caused an east wind to blow in the heavens;
And by His power He brought in the south wind.
27 He also rained meat on them like the dust,
Feathered fowl like the sand of the seas;

THE MESSAGE

and all the generations to come—
Know the truth and tell the stories
so their children can trust in God,
Never forget the works of God
but keep his commands to the letter.
Heaven forbid they should be like their parents,
bullheaded and bad,
A fickle and faithless bunch
who never stayed true to God.

9-16 The Ephraimites, armed to the teeth,
ran off when the battle began.
They were cowards to God's Covenant,
refused to walk by his Word.
They forgot what he had done—
marvels he'd done right before their eyes.
He performed miracles in plain sight of their parents
in Egypt, out on the fields of Zoan.
He split the Sea and they walked right through it;
he piled the waters to the right and the left.
He led them by day with a cloud,
led them all the night long with a fiery torch.
He split rocks in the wilderness,
gave them all they could drink from underground springs;
He made creeks flow out from sheer rock,
and water pour out like a river.

17-20 All they did was sin even more,
rebel in the desert against the High God.
They tried to get their own way with God,
clamored for favors, for special attention.
They whined like spoiled children,
"Why can't God give us a decent meal in this desert?
Sure, he struck the rock and the water flowed,
creeks cascaded from the rock.
But how about some fresh-baked bread?
How about a nice cut of meat?"

21-31 When GOD heard that, he was furious—
his anger flared against Jacob,
he lost his temper with Israel.
It was clear they didn't believe God,
had no intention of trusting in his help.
But God helped them anyway, commanded the clouds
and gave orders that opened the gates of heaven.
He rained down showers of manna to eat,
he gave them the Bread of Heaven.
They ate the bread of the mighty angels;
he sent them all the food they could eat.
He let East Wind break loose from the skies,
gave a strong push to South Wind.
This time it was birds that rained down—
succulent birds, an abundance of birds.

NEW KING JAMES VERSION

28And He let *them* fall in the midst of their
camp,
All around their dwellings.
29So they ate and were well filled,
For He gave them their own desire.
30They were not deprived of their craving;
But while their food *was* still in their
mouths,
31The wrath of God came against them,
And slew the stoutest of them,
And struck down the choice *men* of Israel.

32In spite of this they still sinned,
And did not believe in His wondrous works.
33Therefore their days He consumed in
futility,
And their years in fear.

34When He slew them, then they sought Him;
And they returned and sought earnestly for
God.
35Then they remembered that God *was* their
rock,
And the Most High God their Redeemer.
36Nevertheless they flattered Him with their
mouth,
And they lied to Him with their tongue;
37For their heart was not steadfast with Him,
Nor were they faithful in His covenant.
38But He, *being* full of compassion, forgave
their iniquity,
And did not destroy *them.*
Yes, many a time He turned His anger away,
And did not stir up all His wrath;
39For He remembered that they *were but*
flesh,
A breath that passes away and does not
come again.

40How often they provoked Him in the
wilderness,
And grieved Him in the desert!
41Yes, again and again they tempted God,
And limited the Holy One of Israel.
42They did not remember His power:
The day when He redeemed them from the
enemy,
43When He worked His signs in Egypt,
And His wonders in the field of Zoan;
44Turned their rivers into blood,
And their streams, that they could not drink.
45He sent swarms of flies among them, which
devoured them,
And frogs, which destroyed them.
46He also gave their crops to the caterpillar,
And their labor to the locust.
47He destroyed their vines with hail,
And their sycamore trees with frost.
48He also gave up their cattle to the hail,
And their flocks to fiery lightning.
49He cast on them the fierceness of His anger,
Wrath, indignation, and trouble,
By sending angels of destruction *among*
them.
50He made a path for His anger;
He did not spare their soul from death,
But gave their life over to the plague,
51And destroyed all the firstborn in Egypt,
The first of *their* strength in the tents of Ham.

THE MESSAGE

He aimed them right for the center of their
camp;
all round their tents there were birds.
They ate and had their fill;
he handed them everything they craved
on a platter.
But their greed knew no bounds;
they stuffed their mouths with more and
more.
Finally, God was fed up, his anger
erupted—
he cut down their brightest and best,
he laid low Israel's finest young men.

32-37 And—can you believe it?—they kept right
on sinning;
all those wonders and they still wouldn't
believe!
So their lives dribbled off to nothing—
nothing to show for their lives but a
ghost town.
When he cut them down, they came
running for help;
they turned and pled for mercy.
They gave witness that God was their rock,
that High God was their redeemer,
But they didn't mean a word of it;
they lied through their teeth the whole
time.
They could not have cared less about him,
wanted nothing to do with his Covenant.

38-55 And God? Compassionate!
Forgave the sin! Didn't destroy!
Over and over he reined in his anger,
restrained his considerable wrath.
He knew what they were made of;
he knew there wasn't much to them,
How often in the desert they had spurned
him,
tried his patience in those wilderness
years.
Time and again they pushed him to the
limit,
provoked Israel's Holy God.
How quickly they forgot what he'd done,
forgot their day of rescue from the enemy,
When he did miracles in Egypt,
wonders on the plain of Zoan.
He turned the River and its streams to
blood—
not a drop of water fit to drink.
He sent flies, which ate them alive,
and frogs, which bedeviled them.
He turned their harvest over to caterpillars,
everything they had worked for to the
locusts.
He flattened their grapevines with hail;
a killing frost ruined their orchards.
He pounded their cattle with hail,
let thunderbolts loose on their herds.
His anger flared,
a wild firestorm of havoc,
An advance guard of disease-carrying angels
to clear the ground, preparing the way
before him.
He didn't spare those people,
he let the plague rage through their lives.
He killed all the Egyptian firstborns,
lusty infants, offspring of Ham's virility.

NEW KING JAMES VERSION

52But He made His own people go forth like sheep,
And guided them in the wilderness like a flock;
53And He led them on safely, so that they did not fear;
But the sea overwhelmed their enemies.
54And He brought them to His holy border,
This mountain *which* His right hand had acquired.
55He also drove out the nations before them,
Allotted them an inheritance by survey,
And made the tribes of Israel dwell in their tents.

56Yet they tested and provoked the Most High God,
And did not keep His testimonies,
57But turned back and acted unfaithfully like their fathers;
They were turned aside like a deceitful bow.
58For they provoked Him to anger with their high places,
And moved Him to jealousy with their carved images.
59When God heard *this*, He was furious,
And greatly abhorred Israel,
60So that He forsook the tabernacle of Shiloh,
The tent He had placed among men,
61And delivered His strength into captivity,
And His glory into the enemy's hand.
62He also gave His people over to the sword,
And was furious with His inheritance.
63The fire consumed their young men,
And their maidens were not given in marriage.
64Their priests fell by the sword,
And their widows made no lamentation.

65Then the Lord awoke as *from* sleep,
Like a mighty man who shouts because of wine.
66And He beat back His enemies;
He put them to a perpetual reproach.

67Moreover He rejected the tent of Joseph,
And did not choose the tribe of Ephraim,
68But chose the tribe of Judah,
Mount Zion which He loved.
69And He built His sanctuary like the heights,
Like the earth which He has established forever.
70He also chose David His servant,
And took him from the sheepfolds;
71From following the ewes that had young He brought him,
To shepherd Jacob His people,
And Israel His inheritance.
72So he shepherded them according to the integrity of his heart,
And guided them by the skillfulness of his hands.

THE MESSAGE

Then he led his people out like sheep,
took his flock safely through the wilderness.
He took good care of them; they had nothing to fear.
The Sea took care of their enemies for good.
He brought them into his holy land,
this mountain he claimed for his own.
He scattered everyone who got in their way;
he staked out an inheritance for them—
the tribes of Israel all had their own places.

56-64 But they kept on giving him a hard time,
rebelled against God, the High God,
refused to do anything he told them.
They were worse, if that's possible, than their parents:
traitors—crooked as a corkscrew.
Their pagan orgies provoked God's anger,
their obscene idolatries broke his heart.
When God heard their carryings-on, he was furious;
he posted a huge No over Israel.
He walked off and left Shiloh empty,
abandoned the shrine where he had met with Israel.
He let his pride and joy go to the dogs,
turned his back on the pride of his life.
He turned them loose on fields of battle;
angry, he let them fend for themselves.
Their young men went to war and never came back;
their young women waited in vain.
Their priests were massacred,
and their widows never shed a tear.

65-72 Suddenly the Lord was up on his feet
like someone roused from deep sleep,
shouting like a drunken warrior.
He hit his enemies hard, sent them running,
yelping, not daring to look back.
He disqualified Joseph as leader,
told Ephraim he didn't have what it takes,
And chose the Tribe of Judah instead,
Mount Zion, which he loves so much.
He built his sanctuary there, resplendent,
solid and lasting as the earth itself.
Then he chose David, his servant,
handpicked him from his work in the sheep pens.
One day he was caring for the ewes and their lambs,
the next day God had him shepherding Jacob,
his people Israel, his prize possession.
His good heart made him a good shepherd;
he guided the people wisely and well.

NEW KING JAMES VERSION

PSALM 79

A DIRGE AND A PRAYER FOR ISRAEL, DESTROYED BY ENEMIES

A Psalm of Asaph.

1 O God, the nations have come into Your
inheritance;
Your holy temple they have defiled;
They have laid Jerusalem in heaps.
2 The dead bodies of Your servants
They have given *as* food for the birds of the
heavens,
The flesh of Your saints to the beasts of the
earth.
3 Their blood they have shed like water all
around Jerusalem,
And *there was* no one to bury *them.*
4 We have become a reproach to our
neighbors,
A scorn and derision to those who are
around us.

5 How long, LORD?
Will You be angry forever?
Will Your jealousy burn like fire?
6 Pour out Your wrath on the nations that do
not know You,
And on the kingdoms that do not call on
Your name.
7 For they have devoured Jacob,
And laid waste his dwelling place.

8 Oh, do not remember former iniquities
against us!
Let Your tender mercies come speedily to
meet us,
For we have been brought very low.
9 Help us, O God of our salvation,
For the glory of Your name;
And deliver us, and provide atonement for
our sins,
For Your name's sake!
10 Why should the nations say,
"Where *is* their God?"
Let there be known among the nations in
our sight
The avenging of the blood of Your servants
which has been shed.

11 Let the groaning of the prisoner come
before You;
According to the greatness of Your power
Preserve those who are appointed to die;
12 And return to our neighbors sevenfold into
their bosom
Their reproach with which they have
reproached You, O Lord.

13 So we, Your people and sheep of Your
pasture,
Will give You thanks forever;
We will show forth Your praise to all
generations.

THE MESSAGE

AN ASAPH PSALM

1-4 **79** God! Barbarians have broken into
your home,
violated your holy temple,
left Jerusalem a pile of rubble!
They've served up the corpses of your
servants
as carrion food for birds of prey,
Threw the bones of your holy people
out to the wild animals to gnaw on.
They dumped out their blood
like buckets of water.
All around Jerusalem, their bodies
were left to rot, unburied.
We're nothing but a joke to our neighbors,
graffiti scrawled on the city walls.

5-7 How long do we have to put up with this,
GOD?
Do you have it in for us for good?
Will your smoldering rage never cool
down?
If you're going to be angry, be angry
with the pagans who care nothing about
you,
or your rival kingdoms who ignore you.
They're the ones who ruined Jacob,
who wrecked and looted the place where
he lived.

8-10 Don't blame us for the sins of our parents.
Hurry up and help us; we're at the end of
our rope.
You're famous for helping; God, give *us* a
break.
Your reputation is on the line.
Pull us out of this mess, forgive us our
sins—
do what you're famous for doing!
Don't let the heathen get by with their
sneers:
"Where's your God? Is he out to lunch?"
Go public and show the godless world
that they can't kill your servants and get
by with it.

11-13 Give groaning prisoners a hearing;
pardon those on death row from their
doom—you can do it!
Give our jeering neighbors what they've
got coming to them;
let their God-taunts boomerang and
knock them flat.
Then we, your people, the ones you love
and care for,
will thank you over and over and over.
We'll tell everyone we meet
how wonderful you are, how
praiseworthy you are!

NEW KING JAMES VERSION

PSALM 80

PRAYER FOR ISRAEL'S RESTORATION

To the Chief Musician. Set to "The Lilies."[a]
A Testimony[b] of Asaph. A Psalm.

1Give ear, O Shepherd of Israel,
You who lead Joseph like a flock;
You who dwell *between* the cherubim, shine forth!
2Before Ephraim, Benjamin, and Manasseh,
Stir up Your strength,
And come *and* save us!

3Restore us, O God;
Cause Your face to shine,
And we shall be saved!

4O LORD God of hosts,
How long will You be angry
Against the prayer of Your people?
5You have fed them with the bread of tears,
And given them tears to drink in great measure.
6You have made us a strife to our neighbors,
And our enemies laugh among themselves.

7Restore us, O God of hosts;
Cause Your face to shine,
And we shall be saved!

8You have brought a vine out of Egypt;
You have cast out the nations, and planted it.
9You prepared *room* for it,
And caused it to take deep root,
And it filled the land.
10The hills were covered with its shadow,
And the mighty cedars with its boughs.
11She sent out her boughs to the Sea,[a]
And her branches to the River.[b]

12Why have You broken down her hedges,
So that all who pass by the way pluck her *fruit?*
13The boar out of the woods uproots it,
And the wild beast of the field devours it.

14Return, we beseech You, O God of hosts;
Look down from heaven and see,
And visit this vine
15And the vineyard which Your right hand has planted,
And the branch *that* You made strong for Yourself.
16*It is* burned with fire, *it is* cut down;
They perish at the rebuke of Your countenance.
17Let Your hand be upon the man of Your right hand,
Upon the son of man *whom* You made strong for Yourself.
18Then we will not turn back from You;
Revive us, and we will call upon Your name.

19Restore us, O LORD God of hosts;
Cause Your face to shine,
And we shall be saved!

80:title [a]Hebrew *Shoshannim* [b]Hebrew *Eduth* **80:11** [a]That is, the Mediterranean [b]That is, the Euphrates

THE MESSAGE

AN ASAPH PSALM

1-2 **80** Listen, Shepherd, Israel's Shepherd—
get all your Joseph sheep together.
Throw beams of light
from your dazzling throne
So Ephraim, Benjamin, and Manasseh
can see where they're going.
Get out of bed—you've slept long enough!
Come on the run before it's too late.

3 God, come back!
Smile your blessing smile:
That will be our salvation.

4-6 GOD, God-of-the-Angel-Armies,
how long will you smolder like a sleeping volcano
while your people call for fire and brimstone?
You put us on a diet of tears,
bucket after bucket of salty tears to drink.
You make us look ridiculous to our friends;
our enemies poke fun day after day.

7 God-of-the-Angel-Armies, come back!
Smile your blessing smile:
That will be our salvation.

8-18 Remember how you brought a young vine from Egypt,
cleared out the brambles and briers
and planted your very own vineyard?
You prepared the good earth,
you planted her roots deep;
the vineyard filled the land.
Your vine soared high and shaded the mountains,
even dwarfing the giant cedars.
Your vine ranged west to the Sea,
east to the River.
So why do you no longer protect your vine?
Trespassers pick its grapes at will;
Wild pigs crash through and crush it,
and the mice nibble away at what's left.
God-of-the-Angel-Armies, turn our way!
Take a good look at what's happened
and attend to this vine.
Care for what you once tenderly planted—
the vine you raised from a shoot.
And those who dared to set it on fire—
give them a look that will kill!
Then take the hand of your once-favorite child,
the child you raised to adulthood.
We will never turn our back on you;
breathe life into our lungs so we can shout your name!

19 GOD, God-of-the-Angel-Armies, come back!
Smile your blessing smile:
That will be our salvation.

NEW KING JAMES VERSION

PSALM 81

AN APPEAL FOR ISRAEL'S REPENTANCE

To the Chief Musician. On an instrument of Gath.[a] *A Psalm* of Asaph.

1Sing aloud to God our strength;
Make a joyful shout to the God of Jacob.
2Raise a song and strike the timbrel,
The pleasant harp with the lute.

3Blow the trumpet at the time of the New Moon,
At the full moon, on our solemn feast day.
4For this *is* a statute for Israel,
A law of the God of Jacob.
5This He established in Joseph *as* a testimony,
When He went throughout the land of Egypt,
Where I heard a language I did not understand.

6"I removed his shoulder from the burden;
His hands were freed from the baskets.
7You called in trouble, and I delivered you;
I answered you in the secret place of thunder;
I tested you at the waters of Meribah. *Selah*

8"Hear, O My people, and I will admonish you!
O Israel, if you will listen to Me!
9There shall be no foreign god among you;
Nor shall you worship any foreign god.
10I *am* the LORD your God,
Who brought you out of the land of Egypt;
Open your mouth wide, and I will fill it.

11"But My people would not heed My voice,
And Israel would *have* none of Me.
12So I gave them over to their own stubborn heart,
To walk in their own counsels.

13"Oh, that My people would listen to Me,
That Israel would walk in My ways!
14I would soon subdue their enemies,
And turn My hand against their adversaries.
15The haters of the LORD would pretend submission to Him,
But their fate would endure forever.
16He would have fed them also with the finest of wheat;
And with honey from the rock I would have satisfied you."

PSALM 82

A PLEA FOR JUSTICE

A Psalm of Asaph.

1God stands in the congregation of the mighty;
He judges among the gods.[a]
2How long will you judge unjustly,
And show partiality to the wicked? *Selah*

81:title [a]Hebrew *Al Gittith* **82:1** [a]Hebrew *elohim, mighty ones;* that is, the judges

THE MESSAGE

AN ASAPH PSALM

1-5 **81** A song to our strong God!
a shout to the God of Jacob!
Anthems from the choir, music from the band,
sweet sounds from lute and harp,
Trumpets and trombones and horns:
it's festival day, a feast to God!
A day decreed by God,
solemnly ordered by the God of Jacob.
He commanded Joseph to keep this day
so we'd never forget what he did in Egypt.

I hear this most gentle whisper from One
I never guessed would speak to me:

6-7 "I took the world off your shoulders,
freed you from a life of hard labor.
You called to me in your pain;
I got you out of a bad place.
I answered you from where the thunder hides,
I proved you at Meribah Fountain.

8-10 "Listen, dear ones—get this straight;
O Israel, don't take this lightly.
Don't take up with strange gods,
don't worship the latest in gods.
I'm GOD, your God, the very God
who rescued you from doom in Egypt,
Then fed you all you could eat,
filled your hungry stomachs.

11-12 "But my people didn't listen,
Israel paid no attention;
So I let go of the reins and told them, 'Run!
Do it your own way!'

13-16 "Oh, dear people, will you listen to me now?
Israel, will you follow my map?
I'll make short work of your enemies,
give your foes the back of my hand.
I'll send the GOD-haters cringing like dogs,
never to be heard from again.
You'll feast on my fresh-baked bread
spread with butter and rock-pure honey."

AN ASAPH PSALM

1 **82** God calls the judges into his courtroom,
he puts all the judges in the dock.

2-4 "Enough! You've corrupted justice long enough,
you've let the wicked get away with murder.

NEW KING JAMES VERSION

3Defend the poor and fatherless;
Do justice to the afflicted and needy.
4Deliver the poor and needy;
Free *them* from the hand of the wicked.

5They do not know, nor do they understand;
They walk about in darkness;
All the foundations of the earth are
unstable.

6I said, "You *are* gods,[a]
And all of you *are* children of the Most
High.
7But you shall die like men,
And fall like one of the princes."

8Arise, O God, judge the earth;
For You shall inherit all nations.

PSALM 83

PRAYER TO FRUSTRATE CONSPIRACY AGAINST ISRAEL

A Song. A Psalm of Asaph.

1Do not keep silent, O God!
Do not hold Your peace,
And do not be still, O God!
2For behold, Your enemies make a tumult;
And those who hate You have lifted up their
head.
3They have taken crafty counsel against Your
people,
And consulted together against Your
sheltered ones.
4They have said, "Come, and let us cut them
off from *being* a nation,
That the name of Israel may be remembered
no more."

5For they have consulted together with one
consent;
They form a confederacy against You:
6The tents of Edom and the Ishmaelites;
Moab and the Hagrites;
7Gebal, Ammon, and Amalek;
Philistia with the inhabitants of Tyre;
8Assyria also has joined with them;
They have helped the children of Lot. *Selah*

9Deal with them as *with* Midian,
As *with* Sisera,
As *with* Jabin at the Brook Kishon,
10Who perished at En Dor,
Who became *as* refuse on the earth.
11Make their nobles like Oreb and like Zeeb,
Yes, all their princes like Zebah and
Zalmunna,
12Who said, "Let us take for ourselves
The pastures of God for a possession."

13O my God, make them like the whirling dust,
Like the chaff before the wind!

82:6 [a]Hebrew *elohim, mighty ones;* that is, the judges

THE MESSAGE

You're here to defend the defenseless,
to make sure that underdogs get a fair
break;
Your job is to stand up for the powerless,
and prosecute all those who exploit
them."

5 Ignorant judges! Head-in-the-sand judges!
They haven't a clue to what's going on.
And now everything's falling apart,
the world's coming unglued.

6-7 "I commissioned you judges, each one of
you,
deputies of the High God,
But you've betrayed your commission
and now you're stripped of your rank,
busted."

8 O God, give them their just deserts!
You've got the whole world in your
hands!

AN ASAPH PSALM

1-5 83 GOD, don't shut me out;
don't give me the silent treatment,
O God.
Your enemies are out there whooping it up,
the God-haters are living it up;
They're plotting to do your people in,
conspiring to rob you of your precious
ones.
"Let's wipe this nation from the face of the
earth,"
they say; "scratch Israel's name off the
books."
And now they're putting their heads
together,
making plans to get rid of you.

6-8 Edom and the Ishmaelites,
Moab and the Hagrites,
Gebal and Ammon and Amalek,
Philistia and the Tyrians,
And now Assyria has joined up,
Giving muscle to the gang of Lot.

9-12 Do to them what you did to Midian,
to Sisera and Jabin at Kishon Brook;
They came to a bad end at Endor,
nothing but dung for the garden.
Cut down their leaders as you did Oreb and
Zeeb,
their princes to nothings like Zebah and
Zalmunna,
With their empty brags, "We're grabbing it
all,
grabbing God's gardens for ourselves."

13-18 My God! I've had it with them!
Blow them away!

NEW KING JAMES VERSION

14As the fire burns the woods,
And as the flame sets the mountains on fire,
15So pursue them with Your tempest,
And frighten them with Your storm.
16Fill their faces with shame,
That they may seek Your name, O LORD.
17Let them be confounded and dismayed forever;
Yes, let them be put to shame and perish,
18That they may know that You, whose name alone *is* the LORD,
Are the Most High over all the earth.

PSALM 84

THE BLESSEDNESS OF DWELLING IN THE HOUSE OF GOD

To the Chief Musician. On an instrument of Gath.[a] A Psalm of the sons of Korah.

1How lovely *is* Your tabernacle,
O LORD of hosts!
2My soul longs, yes, even faints
For the courts of the LORD;
My heart and my flesh cry out for the living God.

3Even the sparrow has found a home,
And the swallow a nest for herself,
Where she may lay her young—
Even Your altars, O LORD of hosts,
My King and my God.
4Blessed *are* those who dwell in Your house;
They will still be praising You. *Selah*

5Blessed *is* the man whose strength *is* in You,
Whose heart *is* set on pilgrimage.
6*As they* pass through the Valley of Baca,
They make it a spring;
The rain also covers it with pools.
7They go from strength to strength;
Each one appears before God in Zion.[a]

8O LORD God of hosts, hear my prayer;
Give ear, O God of Jacob! *Selah*
9O God, behold our shield,
And look upon the face of Your anointed.

10For a day in Your courts *is* better than a thousand.
I would rather be a doorkeeper in the house of my God
Than dwell in the tents of wickedness.
11For the LORD God *is* a sun and shield;
The LORD will give grace and glory;
No good *thing* will He withhold
From those who walk uprightly.

12O LORD of hosts,
Blessed *is* the man who trusts in You!

84:title [a]Hebrew *Al Gittith* **84:7** [a]Septuagint, Syriac, and Vulgate read *The God of gods shall be seen.*

THE MESSAGE

Tumbleweeds in the desert waste,
charred sticks in the burned-over ground.
Knock the breath right out of them, so they're gasping
for breath, gasping, "GOD."
Bring them to the end of their rope,
and leave them there dangling, helpless.
Then they'll learn your name: "GOD,"
the one and only High God on earth.

A KORAH PSALM

1-2 **84** What a beautiful home,
GOD-of-the-Angel-Armies!
I've always longed to live in a place like this,
Always dreamed of a room in your house,
where I could sing for joy to God-alive!

3-4 Birds find nooks and crannies in your house,
sparrows and swallows make nests there.
They lay their eggs and raise their young,
singing their songs in the place where we worship.
GOD-of-the-Angel-Armies! King! God!
How blessed they are to live and sing there!

5-7 And how blessed all those in whom you live,
whose lives become roads you travel;
They wind through lonesome valleys, come upon brooks,
discover cool springs and pools brimming with rain!
God-traveled, these roads curve up the mountain, and
at the last turn—Zion! God in full view!

8-9 GOD-of-the-Angel-Armies, listen:
O God of Jacob, open your ears—I'm praying!
Look at our shields, glistening in the sun,
our faces, shining with your gracious anointing.

10-12 One day spent in your house, this beautiful place of worship,
beats thousands spent on Greek island beaches.
I'd rather scrub floors in the house of my God
than be honored as a guest in the palace of sin.
All sunshine and sovereign is GOD,
generous in gifts and glory.
He doesn't scrimp with his traveling companions.
It's smooth sailing all the way with
GOD-of-the-Angel-Armies.

NEW KING JAMES VERSION

PSALM 85

PRAYER THAT THE LORD WILL RESTORE FAVOR TO THE LAND

To the Chief Musician. A Psalm of the sons of Korah.

1 LORD, You have been favorable to Your land;
You have brought back the captivity of Jacob.
2 You have forgiven the iniquity of Your people;
You have covered all their sin. *Selah*
3 You have taken away all Your wrath;
You have turned from the fierceness of Your anger.

4 Restore us, O God of our salvation,
And cause Your anger toward us to cease.
5 Will You be angry with us forever?
Will You prolong Your anger to all generations?
6 Will You not revive us again,
That Your people may rejoice in You?
7 Show us Your mercy, LORD,
And grant us Your salvation.

8 I will hear what God the LORD will speak,
For He will speak peace
To His people and to His saints;
But let them not turn back to folly.
9 Surely His salvation *is* near to those who fear Him,
That glory may dwell in our land.

10 Mercy and truth have met together;
Righteousness and peace have kissed.
11 Truth shall spring out of the earth,
And righteousness shall look down from heaven.
12 Yes, the LORD will give *what is* good;
And our land will yield its increase.
13 Righteousness will go before Him,
And shall make His footsteps *our* pathway.

PSALM 86

PRAYER FOR MERCY, WITH MEDITATION ON THE EXCELLENCIES OF THE LORD

A Prayer of David.

1 Bow down Your ear, O LORD, hear me;
For I *am* poor and needy.
2 Preserve my life, for I *am* holy;
You are my God;
Save Your servant who trusts in You!
3 Be merciful to me, O Lord,
For I cry to You all day long.
4 Rejoice the soul of Your servant,
For to You, O Lord, I lift up my soul.
5 For You, Lord, *are* good, and ready to forgive,
And abundant in mercy to all those who call upon You.

6 Give ear, O LORD, to my prayer;
And attend to the voice of my supplications.
7 In the day of my trouble I will call upon You,
For You will answer me.

THE MESSAGE

A KORAH PSALM

1-3 **85** GOD, you smiled on your good earth!
You brought good times back to Jacob!
You lifted the cloud of guilt from your people,
you put their sins far out of sight.
You took back your sin-provoked threats,
you cooled your hot, righteous anger.

4-7 Help us again, God of our help;
don't hold a grudge against us forever.
You aren't going to keep this up, are you?
scowling and angry, year after year?
Why not help us make a fresh start—
a resurrection life?
Then your people will laugh and sing!
Show us how much you love us, GOD!
Give us the salvation we need!

8-9 I can't wait to hear what he'll say.
GOD's about to pronounce his people well,
The holy people he loves so much,
so they'll never again live like fools.
See how close his salvation is to those who fear him?
Our country is home base for Glory!

10-13 Love and Truth meet in the street,
Right Living and Whole Living embrace and kiss!
Truth sprouts green from the ground,
Right Living pours down from the skies!
Oh yes! GOD gives Goodness and Beauty;
our land responds with Bounty and Blessing.
Right Living strides out before him,
and clears a path for his passage.

A DAVID PSALM

1-7 **86** Bend an ear, GOD; answer me.
I'm one miserable wretch!
Keep me safe—haven't I lived a good life?
Help your servant—I'm depending on you!
You're my God; have mercy on me.
I count on you from morning to night.
Give your servant a happy life;
I put myself in your hands!
You're well-known as good and forgiving,
bighearted to all who ask for help.
Pay attention, GOD, to my prayer;
bend down and listen to my cry for help.
Every time I'm in trouble I call on you,
confident that you'll answer.

NEW KING JAMES VERSION

8 Among the gods *there is* none like You,
O Lord;
Nor *are there any works* like Your works.
9 All nations whom You have made
Shall come and worship before You, O Lord,
And shall glorify Your name.
10 For You *are* great, and do wondrous things;
You alone *are* God.

11 Teach me Your way, O LORD;
I will walk in Your truth;
Unite my heart to fear Your name.
12 I will praise You, O Lord my God, with all
my heart,
And I will glorify Your name forevermore.
13 For great *is* Your mercy toward me,
And You have delivered my soul from the
depths of Sheol.

14 O God, the proud have risen against me,
And a mob of violent *men* have sought my
life,
And have not set You before them.
15 But You, O Lord, *are* a God full of
compassion, and gracious,
Longsuffering and abundant in mercy and
truth.

16 Oh, turn to me, and have mercy on me!
Give Your strength to Your servant,
And save the son of Your maidservant.
17 Show me a sign for good,
That those who hate me may see *it* and be
ashamed,
Because You, LORD, have helped me and
comforted me.

PSALM 87

THE GLORIES OF THE CITY OF GOD

A Psalm of the sons of Korah. A Song.

1 His foundation *is* in the holy mountains.
2 The LORD loves the gates of Zion
More than all the dwellings of Jacob.
3 Glorious things are spoken of you,
O city of God! *Selah*

4 "I will make mention of Rahab and Babylon
to those who know Me;
Behold, O Philistia and Tyre, with Ethiopia:
'This *one* was born there.' "

5 And of Zion it will be said,
"This *one* and that *one* were born in her;
And the Most High Himself shall establish
her."
6 The LORD will record,
When He registers the peoples:
"This *one* was born there." *Selah*

7 Both the singers and the players on
instruments *say*,
"All my springs *are* in you."

THE MESSAGE

8-10 There's no one quite like you among the
gods, O Lord,
and nothing to compare with your
works.
All the nations you made are on their way,
ready to give honor to you, O Lord,
Ready to put your beauty on display,
parading your greatness,
And the great things you do—
God, you're the one, there's no one but
you!

11-17 Train me, GOD, to walk straight;
then I'll follow your true path.
Put me together, one heart and mind;
then, undivided, I'll worship in joyful
fear.
From the bottom of my heart I thank you,
dear Lord;
I've never kept secret what you're up to.
You've always been great toward me—what
love!
You snatched me from the brink of
disaster!
God, these bullies have reared their heads!
A gang of thugs is after me—
and they don't care a thing about you.
But you, O God, are both tender and kind,
not easily angered, immense in love,
and you never, never quit.
So look me in the eye and show kindness,
give your servant the strength to go on,
save your dear, dear child!
Make a show of how much you love me
so the bullies who hate me will stand
there slack-jawed,
As you, GOD, gently and powerfully
put me back on my feet.

A KORAH PSALM

1-3 **87** He founded Zion on the Holy
Mountain—
and oh, how GOD loves his home!
Loves it far better than all
the homes of Jacob put together!
God's hometown—oh!
everyone there is talking about you!

4 I name them off, those among whom I'm
famous:
Egypt and Babylon,
also Philistia,
even Tyre, along with Cush.
Word's getting around; they point them out:
"This one was born again here!"

5 The word's getting out on Zion:
"Men and women, right and left,
get born again in her!"

6 GOD registers their names in his book:
"This one, this one, and this one—
born again, right here."

7 Singers and dancers give credit to Zion:
"All my springs are in you!"

NEW KING JAMES VERSION

PSALM 88

A PRAYER FOR HELP IN DESPONDENCY

A Song. A Psalm of the sons of Korah. To the Chief Musician. Set to "Mahalath Leannoth." A Contemplation[a] of Heman the Ezrahite.

1 O LORD, God of my salvation,
I have cried out day and night before You.
2 Let my prayer come before You;
Incline Your ear to my cry.

3 For my soul is full of troubles,
And my life draws near to the grave.
4 I am counted with those who go down to the pit;
I am like a man *who has* no strength,
5 Adrift among the dead,
Like the slain who lie in the grave,
Whom You remember no more,
And who are cut off from Your hand.

6 You have laid me in the lowest pit,
In darkness, in the depths.
7 Your wrath lies heavy upon me,
And You have afflicted *me* with all Your waves. *Selah*
8 You have put away my acquaintances far from me;
You have made me an abomination to them;
I am shut up, and I cannot get out;
9 My eye wastes away because of affliction.

LORD, I have called daily upon You;
I have stretched out my hands to You.
10 Will You work wonders for the dead?
Shall the dead arise *and* praise You? *Selah*
11 Shall Your lovingkindness be declared in the grave?
Or Your faithfulness in the place of destruction?
12 Shall Your wonders be known in the dark?
And Your righteousness in the land of forgetfulness?

13 But to You I have cried out, O LORD,
And in the morning my prayer comes before You.
14 LORD, why do You cast off my soul?
Why do You hide Your face from me?
15 I *have been* afflicted and ready to die from *my* youth;
I suffer Your terrors;
I am distraught.
16 Your fierce wrath has gone over me;
Your terrors have cut me off.
17 They came around me all day long like water;
They engulfed me altogether.
18 Loved one and friend You have put far from me,
And my acquaintances into darkness.

88:title [a]Hebrew *Maschil*

THE MESSAGE

A KORAH PRAYER OF HEMAN

1-9 **88** GOD, you're my last chance of the day.
I spend the night on my knees before you.
Put me on your salvation agenda;
take notes on the trouble I'm in.
I've had my fill of trouble;
I'm camped on the edge of hell.
I'm written off as a lost cause,
one more statistic, a hopeless case.
Abandoned as already dead,
one more body in a stack of corpses,
And not so much as a gravestone—
I'm a black hole in oblivion.
You've dropped me into a bottomless pit,
sunk me in a pitch-black abyss.
I'm battered senseless by your rage,
relentlessly pounded by your waves of anger.
You turned my friends against me,
made me horrible to them.
I'm caught in a maze and can't find my way out,
blinded by tears of pain and frustration.

9-12 I call to you, GOD; all day I call.
I wring my hands, I plead for help.
Are the dead a live audience for your miracles?
Do ghosts ever join the choirs that praise you?
Does your love make any difference in a graveyard?
Is your faithful presence noticed in the corridors of hell?
Are your marvelous wonders ever seen in the dark,
your righteous ways noticed in the Land of No Memory?

13-18 I'm standing my ground, GOD, shouting for help,
at my prayers every morning, on my knees each daybreak.
Why, GOD, do you turn a deaf ear?
Why do you make yourself scarce?
For as long as I remember I've been hurting;
I've taken the worst you can hand out, and I've had it.
Your wildfire anger has blazed through my life;
I'm bleeding, black-and-blue.
You've attacked me fiercely from every side,
raining down blows till I'm nearly dead.
You made lover and neighbor alike dump me;
the only friend I have left is Darkness.

NEW KING JAMES VERSION

PSALM 89

REMEMBERING THE COVENANT WITH DAVID, AND SORROW FOR LOST BLESSINGS

A Contemplation[a] of Ethan the Ezrahite.

1I will sing of the mercies of the LORD
forever;
With my mouth will I make known Your
faithfulness to all generations.
2For I have said, "Mercy shall be built up
forever;
Your faithfulness You shall establish in the
very heavens."

3"I have made a covenant with My chosen,
I have sworn to My servant David:
4'Your seed I will establish forever,
And build up your throne to all generations.' "
Selah

5And the heavens will praise Your wonders,
O LORD;
Your faithfulness also in the assembly of the
saints.
6For who in the heavens can be compared to
the LORD?
Who among the sons of the mighty can be
likened to the LORD?
7God is greatly to be feared in the assembly
of the saints,
And to be held in reverence by all *those*
around Him.
8O LORD God of hosts,
Who *is* mighty like You, O LORD?
Your faithfulness also surrounds You.
9You rule the raging of the sea;
When its waves rise, You still them.
10You have broken Rahab in pieces, as one
who is slain;
You have scattered Your enemies with Your
mighty arm.

11The heavens *are* Yours, the earth also *is*
Yours;
The world and all its fullness, You have
founded them.
12The north and the south, You have created
them;
Tabor and Hermon rejoice in Your name.
13You have a mighty arm;
Strong is Your hand, *and* high is Your right
hand.
14Righteousness and justice *are* the
foundation of Your throne;
Mercy and truth go before Your face.
15Blessed *are* the people who know the joyful
sound!
They walk, O LORD, in the light of Your
countenance.
16In Your name they rejoice all day long,
And in Your righteousness they are exalted.
17For You *are* the glory of their strength,
And in Your favor our horn is exalted.
18For our shield *belongs* to the LORD,
And our king to the Holy One of Israel.

89:title [a]Hebrew *Maschil*

THE MESSAGE

AN ETHAN PRAYER

1-4 **89** Your love, GOD, is my song, and I'll
sing it!
I'm forever telling everyone how faithful
you are.
I'll never quit telling the story of your
love—
how you built the cosmos
and guaranteed everything in it.
Your love has always been our lives'
foundation,
your fidelity has been the roof over our
world.
You once said, "I joined forces with my
chosen leader,
I pledged my word to my servant, David,
saying,
'Everyone descending from you is
guaranteed life;
I'll make your rule as solid and lasting as
rock.' "

5-18 GOD! Let the cosmos praise your wonderful
ways,
the choir of holy angels sing anthems to
your faithful ways!
Search high and low, scan skies and land,
you'll find nothing and no one quite like
GOD.
The holy angels are in awe before him;
he looms immense and august over
everyone around him.
GOD-of-the-Angel-Armies, who is like you,
powerful and faithful from every angle?
You put the arrogant ocean in its place
and calm its waves when they turn
unruly.
You gave that old hag Egypt the back of
your hand,
you brushed off your enemies with a
flick of your wrist.
You own the cosmos—you made everything
in it,
everything from atom to archangel.
You positioned the North and South Poles;
the mountains Tabor and Hermon sing
duets to you.
With your well-muscled arm and your grip
of steel—
nobody trifles with you!
The Right and Justice are the roots of your
rule;
Love and Truth are its fruits.
Blessed are the people who know the
passwords of praise,
who shout on parade in the bright
presence of GOD.
Delighted, they dance all day long; they
know
who you are, what you do—they can't
keep it quiet!
Your vibrant beauty has gotten inside us—
you've been so good to us! We're walking
on air!
All we are and have we owe to GOD,
Holy God of Israel, our King!

New King James Version

19Then You spoke in a vision to Your holy one,[a]
And said: "I have given help to *one who is* mighty;
I have exalted one chosen from the people.
20I have found My servant David;
With My holy oil I have anointed him,
21With whom My hand shall be established;
Also My arm shall strengthen him.
22The enemy shall not outwit him,
Nor the son of wickedness afflict him.
23I will beat down his foes before his face,
And plague those who hate him.

24"But My faithfulness and My mercy *shall be* with him,
And in My name his horn shall be exalted.
25Also I will set his hand over the sea,
And his right hand over the rivers.
26He shall cry to Me, 'You *are* my Father,
My God, and the rock of my salvation.'
27Also I will make him *My* firstborn,
The highest of the kings of the earth.
28My mercy I will keep for him forever,
And My covenant shall stand firm with him.
29His seed also I will make *to endure* forever,
And his throne as the days of heaven.

30"If his sons forsake My law
And do not walk in My judgments,
31If they break My statutes
And do not keep My commandments,
32Then I will punish their transgression with the rod,
And their iniquity with stripes.
33Nevertheless My lovingkindness I will not utterly take from him,
Nor allow My faithfulness to fail.
34My covenant I will not break,
Nor alter the word that has gone out of My lips.
35Once I have sworn by My holiness;
I will not lie to David:
36His seed shall endure forever,
And his throne as the sun before Me;
37It shall be established forever like the moon,
Even *like* the faithful witness in the sky."
Selah

38But You have cast off and abhorred,
You have been furious with Your anointed.
39You have renounced the covenant of Your servant;
You have profaned his crown *by casting it* to the ground.
40You have broken down all his hedges;
You have brought his strongholds to ruin.
41All who pass by the way plunder him;
He is a reproach to his neighbors.
42You have exalted the right hand of his adversaries;
You have made all his enemies rejoice.
43You have also turned back the edge of his sword,
And have not sustained him in the battle.
44You have made his glory cease,
And cast his throne down to the ground.

89:19 [a]Following many Hebrew manuscripts; Masoretic Text, Septuagint, Targum, and Vulgate read *holy ones*.

The Message

19-37 A long time ago you spoke in a vision,
you spoke to your faithful beloved:
"I've crowned a hero,
I chose the best I could find;
I found David, my servant,
poured holy oil on his head,
And I'll keep my hand steadily on him,
yes, I'll stick with him through thick and thin.
No enemy will get the best of him,
no scoundrel will do him in.
I'll weed out all who oppose him,
I'll clean out all who hate him.
I'm with him for good and I'll love him forever;
I've set him on high—he's riding high!
I've put Ocean in his one hand, River in the other;
he'll call out, 'Oh, my Father—my God,
my Rock of Salvation!'
Yes, I'm setting him apart as the First of the royal line,
High King over all of earth's kings.
I'll preserve him eternally in my love,
I'll faithfully do all I so solemnly promised.
I'll guarantee his family tree
and underwrite his rule.
If his children refuse to do what I tell them,
if they refuse to walk in the way I show them,
If they spit on the directions I give them
and tear up the rules I post for them—
I'll rub their faces in the dirt of their rebellion
and make them face the music.
But I'll never throw them out,
never abandon or disown them.
Do you think I'd withdraw my holy promise?
or take back words I'd already spoken?
I've given my word, my whole and holy word;
do you think I would lie to David?
His family tree is here for good,
his sovereignty as sure as the sun,
Dependable as the phases of the moon,
inescapable as weather."

38-51 But GOD, you did walk off and leave us,
you lost your temper with the one you anointed.
You tore up the promise you made to your servant,
you stomped his crown in the mud.
You blasted his home to kingdom come,
reduced his city to a pile of rubble
Picked clean by wayfaring strangers,
a joke to all the neighbors.
You declared a holiday for all his enemies,
and they're celebrating for all they're worth.
Angry, you opposed him in battle,
refused to fight on his side;
You robbed him of his splendor, humiliated this warrior,
ground his kingly honor in the dirt.

NEW KING JAMES VERSION

[45]The days of his youth You have shortened;
You have covered him with shame. *Selah*

[46]How long, LORD?
Will You hide Yourself forever?
Will Your wrath burn like fire?
[47]Remember how short my time is;
For what futility have You created all the children of men?
[48]What man can live and not see death?
Can he deliver his life from the power of the grave? *Selah*

[49]Lord, where *are* Your former lovingkindnesses,
Which You swore to David in Your truth?
[50]Remember, Lord, the reproach of Your servants—
How I bear in my bosom *the reproach of* all the many peoples,
[51]With which Your enemies have reproached, O LORD,
With which they have reproached the footsteps of Your anointed.

[52]Blessed *be* the LORD forevermore!
Amen and Amen.

Book Four: Psalms 90—106

PSALM 90

THE ETERNITY OF GOD, AND MAN'S FRAILTY

A Prayer of Moses the man of God.

[1]Lord, You have been our dwelling place[a] in all generations.
[2]Before the mountains were brought forth,
Or ever You had formed the earth and the world,
Even from everlasting to everlasting, You *are* God.

[3]You turn man to destruction,
And say, "Return, O children of men."
[4]For a thousand years in Your sight
Are like yesterday when it is past,
And *like* a watch in the night.
[5]You carry them away *like* a flood;
They are like a sleep.
In the morning they are like grass *which* grows up:
[6]In the morning it flourishes and grows up;
In the evening it is cut down and withers.

[7]For we have been consumed by Your anger,
And by Your wrath we are terrified.
[8]You have set our iniquities before You,
Our secret *sins* in the light of Your countenance.
[9]For all our days have passed away in Your wrath;
We finish our years like a sigh.
[10]The days of our lives *are* seventy years;
And if by reason of strength *they are* eighty years,
Yet their boast *is* only labor and sorrow;
For it is soon cut off, and we fly away.
[11]Who knows the power of Your anger?
For as the fear of You, *so is* Your wrath.

90:1 [a]Septuagint, Targum, and Vulgate read *refuge*.

THE MESSAGE

You took the best years of his life
and left him an impotent, ruined husk.
How long do we put up with this, GOD?
Are you gone for good? Will you hold this grudge forever?
Remember my sorrow and how short life is.
Did you create men and women for nothing but this?
We'll see death soon enough. Everyone does.
And there's no back door out of hell.
So where is the love you're so famous for, Lord?
What happened to your promise to David?
Take a good look at your servant, dear Lord;
I'm the butt of the jokes of all nations,
The taunting jokes of your enemies, GOD,
as they dog the steps of your dear anointed.

Blessed be GOD forever and always!
Yes. Oh, yes.

A PRAYER OF MOSES, MAN OF GOD

1-2 **90** God, it seems you've been our home forever;
long before the mountains were born,
Long before you brought earth itself to birth,
from "once upon a time" to "kingdom come"—you are God.

3-11 So don't return us to mud, saying,
"Back to where you came from!"
Patience! You've got all the time in the world—whether
a thousand years or a day, it's all the same to you.
Are we no more to you than a wispy dream,
no more than a blade of grass
That springs up gloriously with the rising sun
and is cut down without a second thought?
Your anger is far and away too much for us;
we're at the end of our rope.
You keep track of all our sins; every misdeed
since we were children is entered in your books.
All we can remember is that frown on your face.
Is that all we're ever going to get?
We live for seventy years or so
(with luck we might make it to eighty),
And what do we have to show for it? Trouble.
Toil and trouble and a marker in the graveyard.
Who can make sense of such rage,
such anger against the very ones who fear you?

NEW KING JAMES VERSION

12So teach *us* to number our days,
That we may gain a heart of wisdom.

13Return, O LORD!
How long?
And have compassion on Your servants.
14Oh, satisfy us early with Your mercy,
That we may rejoice and be glad all our days!
15Make us glad according to the days *in which* You have afflicted us,
The years *in which* we have seen evil.
16Let Your work appear to Your servants,
And Your glory to their children.
17And let the beauty of the LORD our God be upon us,
And establish the work of our hands for us;
Yes, establish the work of our hands.

PSALM 91

SAFETY OF ABIDING IN THE PRESENCE OF GOD

1He who dwells in the secret place of the Most High
Shall abide under the shadow of the Almighty.
2I will say of the LORD, "*He is* my refuge and my fortress;
My God, in Him I will trust."

3Surely He shall deliver you from the snare of the fowler[a]
And from the perilous pestilence.
4He shall cover you with His feathers,
And under His wings you shall take refuge;
His truth *shall be your* shield and buckler.
5You shall not be afraid of the terror by night,
Nor of the arrow *that* flies by day,
6*Nor* of the pestilence *that* walks in darkness,
Nor of the destruction *that* lays waste at noonday.

7A thousand may fall at your side,
And ten thousand at your right hand;
But it shall not come near you.
8Only with your eyes shall you look,
And see the reward of the wicked.

9Because you have made the LORD, *who is* my refuge,
Even the Most High, your dwelling place,
10No evil shall befall you,
Nor shall any plague come near your dwelling;
11For He shall give His angels charge over you,
To keep you in all your ways.
12In *their* hands they shall bear you up,
Lest you dash your foot against a stone.
13You shall tread upon the lion and the cobra,
The young lion and the serpent you shall trample underfoot.

91:3 [a]That is, one who catches birds in a trap or snare

THE MESSAGE

12-17 Oh! Teach us to live well!
Teach us to live wisely and well!
Come back, GOD—how long do we have to wait?—
and treat your servants with kindness for a change.
Surprise us with love at daybreak;
then we'll skip and dance all the day long.
Make up for the bad times with some good times;
we've seen enough evil to last a lifetime.
Let your servants see what you're best at—
the ways you rule and bless your children.
And let the loveliness of our Lord, our God, rest on us,
confirming the work that we do.
Oh, yes. Affirm the work that we do!

1-13 **91** You who sit down in the High God's presence,
spend the night in Shaddai's shadow,
Say this: "GOD, you're my refuge.
I trust in you and I'm safe!"
That's right—he rescues you from hidden traps,
shields you from deadly hazards.
His huge outstretched arms protect you—
under them you're perfectly safe;
his arms fend off all harm.
Fear nothing—not wild wolves in the night,
not flying arrows in the day,
Not disease that prowls through the darkness,
not disaster that erupts at high noon.
Even though others succumb all around,
drop like flies right and left,
no harm will even graze you.
You'll stand untouched, watch it all from a distance,
watch the wicked turn into corpses.
Yes, because GOD's your refuge,
the High God your very own home,
Evil can't get close to you,
harm can't get through the door.
He ordered his angels
to guard you wherever you go.
If you stumble, they'll catch you;
their job is to keep you from falling.
You'll walk unharmed among lions and snakes,
and kick young lions and serpents from the path.

NEW KING JAMES VERSION

[14]"Because he has set his love upon Me,
therefore I will deliver him;
I will set him on high, because he has
known My name.
[15]He shall call upon Me, and I will answer
him;
I *will be* with him in trouble;
I will deliver him and honor him.
[16]With long life I will satisfy him,
And show him My salvation."

PSALM 92

PRAISE TO THE LORD FOR HIS LOVE AND FAITHFULNESS

A Psalm. A Song for the Sabbath day.

[1]*It is* good to give thanks to the LORD,
And to sing praises to Your name, O Most
High;
[2]To declare Your lovingkindness in the
morning,
And Your faithfulness every night,
[3]On an instrument of ten strings,
On the lute,
And on the harp,
With harmonious sound.
[4]For You, LORD, have made me glad through
Your work;
I will triumph in the works of Your hands.

[5]O LORD, how great are Your works!
Your thoughts are very deep.
[6]A senseless man does not know,
Nor does a fool understand this.
[7]When the wicked spring up like grass,
And when all the workers of iniquity
flourish,
It is that they may be destroyed forever.

[8]But You, LORD, *are* on high forevermore.
[9]For behold, Your enemies, O LORD,
For behold, Your enemies shall perish;
All the workers of iniquity shall be
scattered.

[10]But my horn You have exalted like a wild ox;
I have been anointed with fresh oil.
[11]My eye also has seen *my desire* on my
enemies;
My ears hear *my desire* on the wicked
Who rise up against me.

[12]The righteous shall flourish like a palm tree,
He shall grow like a cedar in Lebanon.
[13]Those who are planted in the house of the
LORD
Shall flourish in the courts of our God.
[14]They shall still bear fruit in old age;
They shall be fresh and flourishing,
[15]To declare that the LORD is upright;
He is my rock, and *there is* no
unrighteousness in Him.

THE MESSAGE

14-16 "If you'll hold on to me for dear life," says
GOD,
"I'll get you out of any trouble.
I'll give you the best of care
if you'll only get to know and trust me.
Call me and I'll answer, be at your side in
bad times;
I'll rescue you, then throw you a party.
I'll give you a long life,
give you a long drink of salvation!"

A SABBATH SONG

1-3 **92** What a beautiful thing, GOD, to give
thanks,
to sing an anthem to you, the High God!
To announce your love each daybreak,
sing your faithful presence all through
the night,
Accompanied by dulcimer and harp,
the full-bodied music of strings.

4-9 You made me so happy, GOD
I saw your work and I shouted for joy.
How magnificent your work, GOD!
How profound your thoughts!
Dullards never notice what you do;
fools never do get it.
When the wicked popped up like weeds
and all the evil men and women took
over,
You mowed them down,
finished them off once and for all.
You, GOD, are High and Eternal.
Look at your enemies, GOD!
Look at your enemies—ruined!
Scattered to the winds, all those
hirelings of evil!

10-14 But you've made me strong as a charging
bison,
you've honored me with a festive parade.
The sight of my critics going down is still
fresh,
the rout of my malicious detractors.
My ears are filled with the sounds of
promise:
"Good people will prosper like palm
trees,
Grow tall like Lebanon cedars;
transplanted to GOD's courtyard,
They'll grow tall in the presence of God,
lithe and green, virile still in old age."

15 Such witnesses to upright GOD!
My Mountain, my huge, holy Mountain!

NEW KING JAMES VERSION

PSALM 93

THE ETERNAL REIGN OF THE LORD

1The LORD reigns, He is clothed with majesty;
The LORD is clothed,
He has girded Himself with strength.
Surely the world is established, so that it cannot be moved.
2Your throne *is* established from of old;
You *are* from everlasting.

3The floods have lifted up, O LORD,
The floods have lifted up their voice;
The floods lift up their waves.
4The LORD on high *is* mightier
Than the noise of many waters,
Than the mighty waves of the sea.

5Your testimonies are very sure;
Holiness adorns Your house,
O LORD, forever.

PSALM 94

GOD THE REFUGE OF THE RIGHTEOUS

1O LORD God, to whom vengeance belongs—
O God, to whom vengeance belongs, shine forth!
2Rise up, O Judge of the earth;
Render punishment to the proud.
3LORD, how long will the wicked,
How long will the wicked triumph?

4They utter speech, *and* speak insolent things;
All the workers of iniquity boast in themselves.
5They break in pieces Your people, O LORD,
And afflict Your heritage.
6They slay the widow and the stranger,
And murder the fatherless.
7Yet they say, "The LORD does not see,
Nor does the God of Jacob understand."

8Understand, you senseless among the people;
And *you* fools, when will you be wise?
9He who planted the ear, shall He not hear?
He who formed the eye, shall He not see?
10He who instructs the nations, shall He not correct,
He who teaches man knowledge?
11The LORD knows the thoughts of man,
That they *are* futile.

12Blessed *is* the man whom You instruct, O LORD,
And teach out of Your law,
13That You may give him rest from the days of adversity,
Until the pit is dug for the wicked.
14For the LORD will not cast off His people,
Nor will He forsake His inheritance.
15But judgment will return to righteousness,
And all the upright in heart will follow it.

16Who will rise up for me against the evildoers?
Who will stand up for me against the workers of iniquity?

THE MESSAGE

1-2 **93** GOD is King, robed and ruling,
GOD is robed and surging with strength.

And yes, the world is firm, immovable,
Your throne ever firm—you're Eternal!

3-4 Sea storms are up, GOD,
Sea storms wild and roaring,
Sea storms with thunderous breakers.

Stronger than wild sea storms,
Mightier than sea-storm breakers,
Mighty GOD rules from High Heaven.

5 What you say goes—it always has.
"Beauty" and "Holy" mark your palace rule,
GOD, to the very end of time.

1-2 **94** GOD, put an end to evil;
avenging God, show your colors!
Judge of the earth, take your stand;
throw the book at the arrogant.

3-4 GOD, the wicked get away with murder—
how long will you let this go on?
They brag and boast
and crow about their crimes!

5-7 They walk all over your people, GOD,
exploit and abuse your precious people.
They take out anyone who gets in their way;
if they can't use them, they kill them.
They think, "GOD isn't looking,
Jacob's God is out to lunch."

8-11 Well, think again, you idiots,
fools—how long before you get smart?
Do you think Ear-Maker doesn't hear,
Eye-Shaper doesn't see?
Do you think the trainer of nations doesn't correct,
the teacher of Adam doesn't know?
GOD knows, all right—
knows your stupidity,
sees your shallowness.

12-15 How blessed the man you train, GOD,
the woman you instruct in your Word,
Providing a circle of quiet within the clamor of evil,
while a jail is being built for the wicked.
GOD will never walk away from his people,
never desert his precious people.
Rest assured that justice is on its way
and every good heart put right.

16-19 Who stood up for me against the wicked?
Who took my side against evil workers?

NEW KING JAMES VERSION

17Unless the LORD *had been* my help,
My soul would soon have settled in silence.
18If I say, "My foot slips,"
Your mercy, O LORD, will hold me up.
19In the multitude of my anxieties within me,
Your comforts delight my soul.

20Shall the throne of iniquity, which devises evil by law,
Have fellowship with You?
21They gather together against the life of the righteous,
And condemn innocent blood.
22But the LORD has been my defense,
And my God the rock of my refuge.
23He has brought on them their own iniquity,
And shall cut them off in their own wickedness;
The LORD our God shall cut them off.

PSALM 95

A CALL TO WORSHIP AND OBEDIENCE

1Oh come, let us sing to the LORD!
Let us shout joyfully to the Rock of our salvation.
2Let us come before His presence with thanksgiving;
Let us shout joyfully to Him with psalms.
3For the LORD *is* the great God,
And the great King above all gods.
4In His hand *are* the deep places of the earth;
The heights of the hills *are* His also.
5The sea *is* His, for He made it;
And His hands formed the dry *land.*

6Oh come, let us worship and bow down;
Let us kneel before the LORD our Maker.
7For He *is* our God,
And we *are* the people of His pasture,
And the sheep of His hand.

Today, if you will hear His voice:
8"Do not harden your hearts, as in the rebellion,[a]
As *in* the day of trial[b] in the wilderness,
9When your fathers tested Me;
They tried Me, though they saw My work.
10For forty years I was grieved with *that* generation,
And said, 'It *is* a people who go astray in their hearts,
And they do not know My ways.'
11So I swore in My wrath,
'They shall not enter My rest.' "

95:8 [a]Or *Meribah* [b]Or *Massah*

THE MESSAGE

If GOD hadn't been there for me,
I never would have made it.
The minute I said, "I'm slipping, I'm falling,"
your love, GOD, took hold and held me fast.
When I was upset and beside myself,
you calmed me down and cheered me up.

20-23 Can Misrule have anything in common with you?
Can Troublemaker pretend to be on your side?
They ganged up on good people,
plotted behind the backs of the innocent.
But GOD became my hideout,
God was my high mountain retreat,
Then boomeranged their evil back on them:
for their evil ways he wiped them out,
our GOD cleaned them out for good.

1-2 **95** Come, let's shout praises to GOD,
raise the roof for the Rock who saved us!
Let's march into his presence singing praises,
lifting the rafters with our hymns!

3-5 And why? Because GOD is the best,
High King over all the gods.
In one hand he holds deep caves and caverns,
in the other hand grasps the high mountains.
He made Ocean—he owns it!
His hands sculpted Earth!

6-7 So come, let us worship: bow before him,
on your knees before GOD, who made us!
Oh yes, he's our God,
and we're the people he pastures, the flock he feeds.

7-11 Drop everything and listen, listen as he speaks:
"Don't turn a deaf ear as in the Bitter Uprising,
As on the day of the Wilderness Test,
when your ancestors turned and put *me* to the test.
For forty years they watched me at work among them,
as over and over they tried my patience.
And I was provoked—oh, was I provoked!
'Can't they keep their minds on God for five minutes?
Do they simply refuse to walk down my road?'
Exasperated, I exploded,
'They'll never get where they're headed,
never be able to sit down and rest.' "

NEW KING JAMES VERSION

PSALM 96

A SONG OF PRAISE TO GOD COMING IN JUDGMENT

1 Oh, sing to the LORD a new song!
Sing to the LORD, all the earth.
2 Sing to the LORD, bless His name;
Proclaim the good news of His salvation from day to day.
3 Declare His glory among the nations,
His wonders among all peoples.

4 For the LORD *is* great and greatly to be praised;
He *is* to be feared above all gods.
5 For all the gods of the peoples *are* idols,
But the LORD made the heavens.
6 Honor and majesty *are* before Him;
Strength and beauty *are* in His sanctuary.

7 Give to the LORD, O families of the peoples,
Give to the LORD glory and strength.
8 Give to the LORD the glory *due* His name;
Bring an offering, and come into His courts.
9 Oh, worship the LORD in the beauty of holiness!
Tremble before Him, all the earth.

10 Say among the nations, "The LORD reigns;
The world also is firmly established,
It shall not be moved;
He shall judge the peoples righteously."

11 Let the heavens rejoice, and let the earth be glad;
Let the sea roar, and all its fullness;
12 Let the field be joyful, and all that *is* in it.
Then all the trees of the woods will rejoice before the LORD.
13 For He is coming, for He is coming to judge the earth.
He shall judge the world with righteousness,
And the peoples with His truth.

PSALM 97

A SONG OF PRAISE TO THE SOVEREIGN LORD

1 The LORD reigns;
Let the earth rejoice;
Let the multitude of isles be glad!

2 Clouds and darkness surround Him;
Righteousness and justice *are* the foundation of His throne.
3 A fire goes before Him,
And burns up His enemies round about.
4 His lightnings light the world;
The earth sees and trembles.
5 The mountains melt like wax at the presence of the LORD,
At the presence of the Lord of the whole earth.
6 The heavens declare His righteousness,
And all the peoples see His glory.

THE MESSAGE

1-2 **96** Sing GOD a brand-new song!
Earth and everyone in it, sing!
Sing to GOD—*worship* GOD!

2-3 Shout the news of his victory from sea to sea,
Take the news of his glory to the lost,
News of his wonders to one and all!

4-5 For GOD is great, and worth a thousand Hallelujahs.
His terrible beauty makes the gods look cheap;
Pagan gods are mere tatters and rags.

5-6 GOD made the heavens—
Royal splendor radiates from him,
A powerful beauty sets him apart.

7 Bravo, GOD, Bravo!
Everyone join in the great shout: Encore!
In awe before the beauty, in awe before the might.

8-9 Bring gifts and celebrate,
Bow before the beauty of GOD,
Then to your knees—everyone worship!

10 Get out the message—GOD Rules!
He put the world on a firm foundation;
He treats everyone fair and square.

11 Let's hear it from Sky,
With Earth joining in,
And a huge round of applause from Sea.

12 Let Wilderness turn cartwheels,
Animals, come dance,
Put every tree of the forest in the choir—

13 An extravaganza before GOD as he comes,
As he comes to set everything right on earth,
Set everything right, treat everyone fair.

1 **97** GOD rules: *there's* something to shout over!
On the double, mainlands and islands—celebrate!

2 Bright clouds and storm clouds circle 'round him;
Right and justice anchor his rule.

3 Fire blazes out before him,
Flaming high up the craggy mountains.

4 His lightnings light up the world;
Earth, wide-eyed, trembles in fear.

5 The mountains take one look at GOD
And melt, melt like wax before earth's Lord.

6 The heavens announce that he'll set everything right,
And everyone will see it happen—glorious!

NEW KING JAMES VERSION

7Let all be put to shame who serve carved
images,
Who boast of idols.
Worship Him, all *you* gods.
8Zion hears and is glad,
And the daughters of Judah rejoice
Because of Your judgments, O LORD.
9For You, LORD, *are* most high above all the
earth;
You are exalted far above all gods.

10You who love the LORD, hate evil!
He preserves the souls of His saints;
He delivers them out of the hand of the
wicked.
11Light is sown for the righteous,
And gladness for the upright in heart.
12Rejoice in the LORD, you righteous,
And give thanks at the remembrance of His
holy name.[a]

PSALM 98

A SONG OF PRAISE TO THE LORD FOR HIS SALVATION AND JUDGMENT

A Psalm.

1Oh, sing to the LORD a new song!
For He has done marvelous things;
His right hand and His holy arm have
gained Him the victory.
2The LORD has made known His salvation;
His righteousness He has revealed in the
sight of the nations.
3He has remembered His mercy and His
faithfulness to the house of Israel;
All the ends of the earth have seen the
salvation of our God.

4Shout joyfully to the LORD, all the earth;
Break forth in song, rejoice, and sing
praises.
5Sing to the LORD with the harp,
With the harp and the sound of a psalm,
6With trumpets and the sound of a horn;
Shout joyfully before the LORD, the King.

7Let the sea roar, and all its fullness,
The world and those who dwell in it;
8Let the rivers clap *their* hands;
Let the hills be joyful together before the
LORD,
9For He is coming to judge the earth.
With righteousness He shall judge the
world,
And the peoples with equity.

97:12 [a]Or *His holiness*

THE MESSAGE

7-8 All who serve handcrafted gods will be
sorry—
And they were so proud of their ragamuffin
gods!

On your knees, all you gods—worship him!
And Zion, you listen and take heart!

Daughters of Zion, sing your hearts out:
GOD has done it all, has set everything
right.

9 You, GOD, are High God of the cosmos,
Far, far higher than any of the gods.

10 GOD loves all who hate evil,
And those who love him he keeps safe,
Snatches them from the grip of the wicked.

11 Light-seeds are planted in the souls of
God's people,
Joy-seeds are planted in good heart-soil.

12 So, God's people, shout praise to GOD,
Give thanks to our Holy God!

1 **98** Sing to GOD a brand-new song.
He's made a world of wonders!

He rolled up his sleeves,
He set things right.

2 GOD made history with salvation,
He showed the world what he could do.

3 He remembered to love us, a bonus
To his dear family, Israel—indefatigable
love.

The whole earth comes to attention.
Look—God's work of salvation!

4 Shout your praises to GOD, everybody!
Let loose and sing! Strike up the band!

5 Round up an orchestra to play for GOD,
Add on a hundred-voice choir.

6 Feature trumpets and big trombones,
Fill the air with praises to King GOD.

7 Let the sea and its fish give a round of
applause,
With everything living on earth joining in.

8 Let ocean breakers call out, "Encore!"
And mountains harmonize the finale—

9 A tribute to GOD when he comes,
When he comes to set the earth right.

He'll straighten out the whole world,
He'll put the world right, and everyone
in it.

NEW KING JAMES VERSION

PSALM 99

PRAISE TO THE LORD FOR HIS HOLINESS

[1]The LORD reigns;
Let the peoples tremble!
He dwells *between* the cherubim;
Let the earth be moved!
[2]The LORD *is* great in Zion,
And He *is* high above all the peoples.
[3]Let them praise Your great and awesome name—
He *is* holy.

[4]The King's strength also loves justice;
You have established equity;
You have executed justice and righteousness in Jacob.
[5]Exalt the LORD our God,
And worship at His footstool—
He *is* holy.

[6]Moses and Aaron were among His priests,
And Samuel was among those who called upon His name;
They called upon the LORD, and He answered them.
[7]He spoke to them in the cloudy pillar;
They kept His testimonies and the ordinance He gave them.

[8]You answered them, O LORD our God;
You were to them God-Who-Forgives,
Though You took vengeance on their deeds.
[9]Exalt the LORD our God,
And worship at His holy hill;
For the LORD our God *is* holy.

PSALM 100

A SONG OF PRAISE FOR THE FAITHFULNESS TO HIS PEOPLE

A Psalm of Thanksgiving.

[1]Make a joyful shout to the LORD, all you lands!
[2]Serve the LORD with gladness;
Come before His presence with singing.
[3]Know that the LORD, He *is* God;
It is He *who* has made us, and not we ourselves;[a]
We are His people and the sheep of His pasture.

[4]Enter into His gates with thanksgiving,
And into His courts with praise.
Be thankful to Him, *and* bless His name.
[5]For the LORD *is* good;
His mercy *is* everlasting,
And His truth *endures* to all generations.

PSALM 101

PROMISED FAITHFULNESS TO THE LORD

A Psalm of David.

[1]I will sing of mercy and justice;
To You, O LORD, I will sing praises.

100:3 [a]Following Kethib, Septuagint, and Vulgate; Qere, many Hebrew manuscripts, and Targum read *we are His.*

THE MESSAGE

1-3 **99** GOD rules. On your toes, everybody!
He rules from his angel throne—take notice!
GOD looms majestic in Zion,
He towers in splendor over all the big names.
Great and terrible your beauty: let everyone praise you!
Holy. Yes, holy.

4-5 Strong King, lover of justice,
You laid things out fair and square;
You set down the foundations in Jacob,
Foundation stones of just and right ways.
Honor GOD, our God; worship his rule!
Holy. Yes, holy.

6-9 Moses and Aaron were his priests,
Samuel among those who prayed to him.
They prayed to GOD and he answered them;
He spoke from the pillar of cloud.
And they did what he said; they kept the law he gave them.
And then GOD, our God, answered them
(But you were never soft on their sins).
Lift high GOD, our God; worship at his holy mountain.
Holy. Yes, holy is GOD our God.

A THANKSGIVING PSALM

1-2 **100** On your feet now—applaud GOD!
Bring a gift of laughter,
sing yourselves into his presence.

3 Know this: GOD is God, and God, GOD.
He made us; we didn't make him.
We're his people, his well-tended sheep.

4 Enter with the password: "Thank you!"
Make yourselves at home, talking praise.
Thank him. Worship him.

5 For GOD is sheer beauty,
all-generous in love,
loyal always and ever.

A DAVID PSALM

1-8 **101** My theme song is God's love and justice,
and I'm singing it right to you, GOD.

NEW KING JAMES VERSION

[2]I will behave wisely in a perfect way.
Oh, when will You come to me?
I will walk within my house with a perfect heart.

[3]I will set nothing wicked before my eyes;
I hate the work of those who fall away;
It shall not cling to me.
[4]A perverse heart shall depart from me;
I will not know wickedness.

[5]Whoever secretly slanders his neighbor,
Him I will destroy;
The one who has a haughty look and a proud heart,
Him I will not endure.

[6]My eyes *shall be* on the faithful of the land,
That they may dwell with me;
He who walks in a perfect way,
He shall serve me.
[7]He who works deceit shall not dwell within my house;
He who tells lies shall not continue in my presence.
[8]Early I will destroy all the wicked of the land,
That I may cut off all the evildoers from the city of the LORD.

PSALM 102

THE LORD'S ETERNAL LOVE

A Prayer of the afflicted, when he is overwhelmed and pours out his complaint before the LORD.

[1]Hear my prayer, O LORD,
And let my cry come to You.
[2]Do not hide Your face from me in the day of my trouble;
Incline Your ear to me;
In the day that I call, answer me speedily.

[3]For my days are consumed like smoke,
And my bones are burned like a hearth.
[4]My heart is stricken and withered like grass,
So that I forget to eat my bread.
[5]Because of the sound of my groaning
My bones cling to my skin.
[6]I am like a pelican of the wilderness;
I am like an owl of the desert.
[7]I lie awake,
And am like a sparrow alone on the housetop.

[8]My enemies reproach me all day long;
Those who deride me swear an oath against me.
[9]For I have eaten ashes like bread,
And mingled my drink with weeping,
[10]Because of Your indignation and Your wrath;
For You have lifted me up and cast me away.
[11]My days *are* like a shadow that lengthens,
And I wither away like grass.

THE MESSAGE

I'm finding my way down the road of right living,
but how long before you show up?
I'm doing the very best I can,
and I'm doing it at home, where it counts.
I refuse to take a second look
at corrupting people and degrading things.
I reject made-in-Canaan gods,
stay clear of contamination.
The crooked in heart keep their distance;
I refuse to shake hands with those who plan evil.
I put a gag on the gossip
who bad-mouths his neighbor;
I can't stand
arrogance.
But I have my eye on salt-of-the-earth people—
they're the ones I want working with me;
Men and women on the straight and narrow—
these are the ones I want at my side.
But no one who traffics in lies
gets a job with me; I have no patience with liars.
I've rounded up all the wicked like cattle
and herded them right out of the country.
I purged GOD's city
of all who make a business of evil.

A PRAYER OF ONE WHOSE LIFE IS FALLING TO PIECES, AND WHO LETS GOD KNOW JUST HOW BAD IT IS

1-2 **102** GOD, listen! Listen to my prayer,
listen to the pain in my cries.
Don't turn your back on me
just when I need you so desperately.
Pay attention! This is a cry for *help*!
And hurry—this can't wait!

3-11 I'm wasting away to nothing,
I'm burning up with fever.
I'm a ghost of my former self,
half-consumed already by terminal illness.
My jaws ache from gritting my teeth;
I'm nothing but skin and bones.
I'm like a buzzard in the desert,
a crow perched on the rubble.
Insomniac, I twitter away,
mournful as a sparrow in the gutter.
All day long my enemies taunt me,
while others just curse.
They bring in meals—casseroles of ashes!
I draw drink from a barrel of my tears.
And all because of your furious anger;
you swept me up and threw me out.
There's nothing left of me—
a withered weed, swept clean from the path.

NEW KING JAMES VERSION

12But You, O LORD, shall endure forever,
And the remembrance of Your name to all generations.
13You will arise *and* have mercy on Zion;
For the time to favor her,
Yes, the set time, has come.
14For Your servants take pleasure in her stones,
And show favor to her dust.
15So the nations shall fear the name of the LORD,
And all the kings of the earth Your glory.
16For the LORD shall build up Zion;
He shall appear in His glory.
17He shall regard the prayer of the destitute,
And shall not despise their prayer.

18This will be written for the generation to come,
That a people yet to be created may praise the LORD.
19For He looked down from the height of His sanctuary;
From heaven the LORD viewed the earth,
20To hear the groaning of the prisoner,
To release those appointed to death,
21To declare the name of the LORD in Zion,
And His praise in Jerusalem,
22When the peoples are gathered together,
And the kingdoms, to serve the LORD.

23He weakened my strength in the way;
He shortened my days.
24I said, "O my God,
Do not take me away in the midst of my days;
Your years *are* throughout all generations.
25Of old You laid the foundation of the earth,
And the heavens *are* the work of Your hands.
26They will perish, but You will endure;
Yes, they will all grow old like a garment;
Like a cloak You will change them,
And they will be changed.
27But You *are* the same,
And Your years will have no end.
28The children of Your servants will continue,
And their descendants will be established before You."

PSALM 103

PRAISE FOR THE LORD'S MERCIES

A Psalm of David.

1Bless the LORD, O my soul;
And all that is within me, *bless* His holy name!
2Bless the LORD, O my soul,
And forget not all His benefits:
3Who forgives all your iniquities,
Who heals all your diseases,
4Who redeems your life from destruction,
Who crowns you with lovingkindness and tender mercies,
5Who satisfies your mouth with good *things*,
So that your youth is renewed like the eagle's.

THE MESSAGE

12-17 Yet you, GOD, are sovereign still,
always and ever sovereign.
You'll get up from your throne and help Zion—
it's time for compassionate help.
Oh, how your servants love this city's rubble
and weep with compassion over its dust!
The godless nations will sit up and take notice
—see your glory, worship your name—
When GOD rebuilds Zion,
when he shows up in all his glory,
When he attends to the prayer of the wretched.
He won't dismiss their prayer.

18-22 Write this down for the next generation
so people not yet born will praise GOD:
"GOD looked out from his high holy place;
from heaven he surveyed the earth.
He listened to the groans of the doomed,
he opened the doors of their death cells."
Write it so the story can be told in Zion,
so GOD's praise will be sung in Jerusalem's streets
And wherever people gather together
along with their rulers to worship him.

23-28 GOD sovereignly brought me to my knees,
he cut me down in my prime.
"Oh, don't," I prayed, "please don't let me die.
You have more years than you know what to do with!
You laid earth's foundations a long time ago,
and handcrafted the very heavens;
You'll still be around when they're long gone,
threadbare and discarded like an old suit of clothes.
You'll throw them away like a worn-out coat,
but year after year you're as good as new.
Your servants' children will have a good place to live
and their children will be at home with you."

A DAVID PSALM

1-2 **103** O my soul, bless GOD.
From head to toe, I'll bless his holy name!
O my soul, bless GOD,
don't forget a single blessing!

3-5 He forgives your sins—every one.
He heals your diseases—every one.
He redeems you from hell—saves your life!
He crowns you with love and mercy—
a paradise crown.
He wraps you in goodness—beauty eternal.
He renews your youth—you're always young in his presence.

NEW KING JAMES VERSION

6The LORD executes righteousness
And justice for all who are oppressed.
7He made known His ways to Moses,
His acts to the children of Israel.
8The LORD *is* merciful and gracious,
Slow to anger, and abounding in mercy.
9He will not always strive *with us*,
Nor will He keep *His anger* forever.
10He has not dealt with us according to our sins,
Nor punished us according to our iniquities.

11For as the heavens are high above the earth,
So great is His mercy toward those who fear Him;
12As far as the east is from the west,
So far has He removed our transgressions from us.
13As a father pities *his* children,
So the LORD pities those who fear Him.
14For He knows our frame;
He remembers that we *are* dust.

15*As for* man, his days *are* like grass;
As a flower of the field, so he flourishes.
16For the wind passes over it, and it is gone,
And its place remembers it no more.[a]
17But the mercy of the LORD *is* from everlasting to everlasting
On those who fear Him,
And His righteousness to children's children,
18To such as keep His covenant,
And to those who remember His commandments to do them.

19The LORD has established His throne in heaven,
And His kingdom rules over all.

20Bless the LORD, you His angels,
Who excel in strength, who do His word,
Heeding the voice of His word.
21Bless the LORD, all *you* His hosts,
You ministers of His, who do His pleasure.
22Bless the LORD, all His works,
In all places of His dominion.

Bless the LORD, O my soul!

PSALM 104

PRAISE TO THE SOVEREIGN LORD FOR HIS CREATION AND PROVIDENCE

1Bless the LORD, O my soul!

O LORD my God, You are very great:
You are clothed with honor and majesty,
2Who cover *Yourself* with light as *with* a garment,
Who stretch out the heavens like a curtain.

3He lays the beams of His upper chambers in the waters,
Who makes the clouds His chariot,
Who walks on the wings of the wind,
4Who makes His angels spirits,
His ministers a flame of fire.

103:16 [a]Compare Job 7:10

THE MESSAGE

6-18 GOD makes everything come out right;
he puts victims back on their feet.
He showed Moses how he went about his work,
opened up his plans to all Israel.
GOD is sheer mercy and grace;
not easily angered, he's rich in love.
He doesn't endlessly nag and scold,
nor hold grudges forever.
He doesn't treat us as our sins deserve,
nor pay us back in full for our wrongs.
As high as heaven is over the earth,
so strong is his love to those who fear him.
And as far as sunrise is from sunset,
he has separated us from our sins.
As parents feel for their children,
GOD feels for those who fear him.
He knows us inside and out,
keeps in mind that we're made of mud.
Men and women don't live very long;
like wildflowers they spring up and blossom,
But a storm snuffs them out just as quickly,
leaving nothing to show they were here.
GOD's love, though, is ever and always,
eternally present to all who fear him,
Making everything right for them and their children
as they follow his Covenant ways
and remember to do whatever he said.

19-22 GOD has set his throne in heaven;
he rules over us all. He's the King!
So bless GOD, you angels,
ready and able to fly at his bidding,
quick to hear and do what he says.
Bless GOD, all you armies of angels,
alert to respond to whatever he wills.
Bless GOD, all creatures, wherever you are—
everything and everyone made by GOD.

And you, O my soul, bless GOD!

1-14 **104** O my soul, bless GOD!

GOD, my God, how great you are!
beautifully, gloriously robed,
Dressed up in sunshine,
and all heaven stretched out for your tent.
You built your palace on the ocean deeps,
made a chariot out of clouds and took off on wind-wings.
You commandeered winds as messengers,
appointed fire and flame as ambassadors.

NEW KING JAMES VERSION

5*You who* laid the foundations of the earth,
So *that* it should not be moved forever,
6You covered it with the deep as *with* a
garment;
The waters stood above the mountains.
7At Your rebuke they fled;
At the voice of Your thunder they hastened
away.
8They went up over the mountains;
They went down into the valleys,
To the place which You founded for them.
9You have set a boundary that they may not
pass over,
That they may not return to cover the earth.

10He sends the springs into the valleys;
They flow among the hills.
11They give drink to every beast of the field;
The wild donkeys quench their thirst.
12By them the birds of the heavens have their
home;
They sing among the branches.
13He waters the hills from His upper chambers;
The earth is satisfied with the fruit of Your
works.

14He causes the grass to grow for the cattle,
And vegetation for the service of man,
That he may bring forth food from the
earth,
15And wine *that* makes glad the heart of man,
Oil to make *his* face shine,
And bread *which* strengthens man's heart.
16The trees of the LORD are full *of sap,*
The cedars of Lebanon which He planted,
17Where the birds make their nests;
The stork has her home in the fir trees.
18The high hills *are* for the wild goats;
The cliffs are a refuge for the rock badgers.[a]

19He appointed the moon for seasons;
The sun knows its going down.
20You make darkness, and it is night,
In which all the beasts of the forest creep
about.
21The young lions roar after their prey,
And seek their food from God.
22*When* the sun rises, they gather together
And lie down in their dens.
23Man goes out to his work
And to his labor until the evening.

24O LORD, how manifold are Your works!
In wisdom You have made them all.
The earth is full of Your possessions—
25This great and wide sea,
In which *are* innumerable teeming things,
Living things both small and great.
26There the ships sail about;
There is that Leviathan
Which You have made to play there.

27These all wait for You,
That You may give *them* their food in due
season.
28*What* You give them they gather in;
You open Your hand, they are filled with good.

104:18 [a]Or *rock hyrax* (compare Leviticus 11:5)

THE MESSAGE

You set earth on a firm foundation
so that nothing can shake it, ever.
You blanketed earth with ocean,
covered the mountains with deep waters;
Then you roared and the water ran away—
your thunder crash put it to flight.
Mountains pushed up, valleys spread out
in the places you assigned them.
You set boundaries between earth and sea;
never again will earth be flooded.
You started the springs and rivers,
sent them flowing among the hills.
All the wild animals now drink their fill,
wild donkeys quench their thirst.
Along the riverbanks the birds build nests,
ravens make their voices heard.
You water the mountains from your
heavenly cisterns;
earth is supplied with plenty of water.
You make grass grow for the livestock,
hay for the animals that plow the
ground.

14-23 Oh yes, God brings grain from the land,
wine to make people happy,
Their faces glowing with health,
a people well-fed and hearty.
GOD's trees are well-watered—
the Lebanon cedars he planted.
Birds build their nests in those trees;
look—the stork at home in the treetop.
Mountain goats climb about the cliffs;
badgers burrow among the rocks.
The moon keeps track of the seasons,
the sun is in charge of each day.
When it's dark and night takes over,
all the forest creatures come out.
The young lions roar for their prey,
clamoring to God for their supper.
When the sun comes up, they vanish,
lazily stretched out in their dens.
Meanwhile, men and women go out to
work,
busy at their jobs until evening.

24-30 What a wildly wonderful world, GOD!
You made it all, with Wisdom at your
side,
made earth overflow with your
wonderful creations.
Oh, look—the deep, wide sea,
brimming with fish past counting,
sardines and sharks and salmon.
Ships plow those waters,
and Leviathan, your pet dragon, romps
in them.
All the creatures look expectantly to you
to give them their meals on time.
You come, and they gather around;
you open your hand and they eat from it.

NEW KING JAMES VERSION

29You hide Your face, they are troubled;
You take away their breath, they die and return to their dust.
30You send forth Your Spirit, they are created;
And You renew the face of the earth.

31May the glory of the LORD endure forever;
May the LORD rejoice in His works.
32He looks on the earth, and it trembles;
He touches the hills, and they smoke.

33I will sing to the LORD as long as I live;
I will sing praise to my God while I have my being.
34May my meditation be sweet to Him;
I will be glad in the LORD.
35May sinners be consumed from the earth,
And the wicked be no more.

Bless the LORD, O my soul!
Praise the LORD!

PSALM 105

THE ETERNAL FAITHFULNESS OF THE LORD

1Oh, give thanks to the LORD!
Call upon His name;
Make known His deeds among the peoples!
2Sing to Him, sing psalms to Him;
Talk of all His wondrous works!
3Glory in His holy name;
Let the hearts of those rejoice who seek the LORD!
4Seek the LORD and His strength;
Seek His face evermore!
5Remember His marvelous works which He has done,
His wonders, and the judgments of His mouth,
6O seed of Abraham His servant,
You children of Jacob, His chosen ones!

7He *is* the LORD our God;
His judgments *are* in all the earth.
8He remembers His covenant forever,
The word *which* He commanded, for a thousand generations,
9*The covenant* which He made with Abraham,
And His oath to Isaac,
10And confirmed it to Jacob for a statute,
To Israel *as* an everlasting covenant,
11Saying, "To you I will give the land of Canaan
As the allotment of your inheritance,"
12When they were few in number,
Indeed very few, and strangers in it.

13When they went from one nation to another,
From *one* kingdom to another people,
14He permitted no one to do them wrong;
Yes, He rebuked kings for their sakes,
15*Saying*, "Do not touch My anointed ones,
And do My prophets no harm."

16Moreover He called for a famine in the land;
He destroyed all the provision of bread.

THE MESSAGE

If you turned your back,
they'd die in a minute—
Take back your Spirit and they die,
revert to original mud;
Send out your Spirit and they spring to life—
the whole countryside in bloom and blossom.

31-32 The glory of GOD—let it last forever!
Let GOD enjoy his creation!
He takes one look at earth and triggers an earthquake,
points a finger at the mountains, and volcanoes erupt.

33-35 Oh, let me sing to GOD all my life long,
sing hymns to my God as long as I live!
Oh, let my song please him;
I'm so pleased to be singing to GOD.
But clear the ground of sinners—
no more godless men and women!

O my soul, bless GOD!

1-6 105 Hallelujah!
Thank GOD! Pray to him by name!
Tell everyone you meet what he has done!
Sing him songs, belt out hymns,
translate his wonders into music!
Honor his holy name with Hallelujahs,
you who seek GOD. Live a happy life!
Keep your eyes open for GOD, watch for his works;
be alert for signs of his presence.
Remember the world of wonders he has made,
his miracles, and the verdicts he's rendered—
O seed of Abraham, his servant,
O child of Jacob, his chosen.

7-15 He's GOD, our God,
in charge of the whole earth.
And he remembers, remembers his Covenant—
for a thousand generations he's been as good as his word.
It's the Covenant he made with Abraham,
the same oath he swore to Isaac,
The very statute he established with Jacob,
the eternal Covenant with Israel,
Namely, "I give you the land.
Canaan is your hill-country inheritance."
When they didn't count for much,
a mere handful, and strangers at that,
Wandering from country to country,
drifting from pillar to post,
He permitted no one to abuse them.
He told kings to keep their hands off:
"Don't you dare lay a hand on my anointed,
don't hurt a hair on the heads of my prophets."

16-22 Then he called down a famine on the country,
he broke every last blade of wheat.

NEW KING JAMES VERSION

17He sent a man before them—
Joseph—*who* was sold as a slave.
18They hurt his feet with fetters,
He was laid in irons.
19Until the time that his word came to pass,
The word of the LORD tested him.
20The king sent and released him,
The ruler of the people let him go free.
21He made him lord of his house,
And ruler of all his possessions,
22To bind his princes at his pleasure,
And teach his elders wisdom.

23Israel also came into Egypt,
And Jacob dwelt in the land of Ham.
24He increased His people greatly,
And made them stronger than their enemies.
25He turned their heart to hate His people,
To deal craftily with His servants.

26He sent Moses His servant,
And Aaron whom He had chosen.
27They performed His signs among them,
And wonders in the land of Ham.
28He sent darkness, and made *it* dark;
And they did not rebel against His word.
29He turned their waters into blood,
And killed their fish.
30Their land abounded with frogs,
Even in the chambers of their kings.
31He spoke, and there came swarms of flies,
And lice in all their territory.
32He gave them hail for rain,
And flaming fire in their land.
33He struck their vines also, and their fig trees,
And splintered the trees of their territory.
34He spoke, and locusts came,
Young locusts without number,
35And ate up all the vegetation in their land,
And devoured the fruit of their ground.
36He also destroyed all the firstborn in their land,
The first of all their strength.

37He also brought them out with silver and gold,
And *there was* none feeble among His tribes.
38Egypt was glad when they departed,
For the fear of them had fallen upon them.
39He spread a cloud for a covering,
And fire to give light in the night.
40*The people* asked, and He brought quail,
And satisfied them with the bread of heaven.
41He opened the rock, and water gushed out;
It ran in the dry places *like* a river.

42For He remembered His holy promise,
And Abraham His servant.
43He brought out His people with joy,
His chosen ones with gladness.
44He gave them the lands of the Gentiles,
And they inherited the labor of the nations,
45That they might observe His statutes
And keep His laws.

Praise the LORD!

THE MESSAGE

But he sent a man on ahead:
Joseph, sold as a slave.
They put cruel chains on his ankles,
an iron collar around his neck,
Until God's word came to the Pharaoh,
and GOD confirmed his promise.
God sent the king to release him.
The Pharaoh set Joseph free;
He appointed him master of his palace,
put him in charge of all his business
To personally instruct his princes
and train his advisors in wisdom.

23-42 Then Israel entered Egypt,
Jacob immigrated to the Land of Ham.
God gave his people lots of babies;
soon their numbers alarmed their foes.
He turned the Egyptians against his people;
they abused and cheated God's servants.
Then he sent his servant Moses,
and Aaron, whom he also chose.
They worked marvels in that spiritual wasteland,
miracles in the Land of Ham.
He spoke, "Darkness!" and it turned dark—
they couldn't see what they were doing.
He turned all their water to blood
so that all their fish died;
He made frogs swarm through the land,
even into the king's bedroom;
He gave the word and flies swarmed,
gnats filled the air.
He substituted hail for rain,
he stabbed their land with lightning;
He wasted their vines and fig trees,
smashed their groves of trees to splinters;
With a word he brought in locusts,
millions of locusts, armies of locusts;
They consumed every blade of grass in the country
and picked the ground clean of produce;
He struck down every firstborn in the land,
the first fruits of their virile powers.
He led Israel out, their arms filled with loot,
and not one among his tribes even stumbled.
Egypt was glad to have them go—
they were scared to death of them.
God spread a cloud to keep them cool through the day
and a fire to light their way through the night;
They prayed and he brought quail,
filled them with the bread of heaven;
He opened the rock and water poured out;
it flowed like a river through that desert—
All because he remembered his Covenant,
his promise to Abraham, his servant.

43-45 Remember this! He led his people out singing for joy;
his chosen people marched, singing their hearts out!
He made them a gift of the country they entered,
helped them seize the wealth of the nations
So they could do everything he told them—
could follow his instructions to the letter.
Hallelujah!

NEW KING JAMES VERSION

PSALM 106

JOY IN FORGIVENESS OF ISRAEL'S SINS

1Praise the LORD!

Oh, give thanks to the LORD, for *He is* good!
For His mercy *endures* forever.

2Who can utter the mighty acts of the LORD?
Who can declare all His praise?
3Blessed *are* those who keep justice,
And he who does[a] righteousness at all times!

4Remember me, O LORD, with the favor *You have toward* Your people.
Oh, visit me with Your salvation,
5That I may see the benefit of Your chosen ones,
That I may rejoice in the gladness of Your nation,
That I may glory with Your inheritance.

6We have sinned with our fathers,
We have committed iniquity,
We have done wickedly.
7Our fathers in Egypt did not understand Your wonders;
They did not remember the multitude of Your mercies,
But rebelled by the sea—the Red Sea.

8Nevertheless He saved them for His name's sake,
That He might make His mighty power known.
9He rebuked the Red Sea also, and it dried up;
So He led them through the depths,
As through the wilderness.
10He saved them from the hand of him who hated *them*,
And redeemed them from the hand of the enemy.
11The waters covered their enemies;
There was not one of them left.
12Then they believed His words;
They sang His praise.

13They soon forgot His works;
They did not wait for His counsel,
14But lusted exceedingly in the wilderness,
And tested God in the desert.
15And He gave them their request,
But sent leanness into their soul.

16When they envied Moses in the camp,
And Aaron the saint of the LORD,
17The earth opened up and swallowed Dathan,
And covered the faction of Abiram.
18A fire was kindled in their company;
The flame burned up the wicked.

19They made a calf in Horeb,
And worshiped the molded image.

106:3 [a]Septuagint, Syriac, Targum, and Vulgate read *those who do*.

THE MESSAGE

1-3 **106** Hallelujah!
Thank GOD! And why?
Because he's good, because his love lasts.
But who on earth can do it—
declaim GOD's mighty acts, broadcast all his praises?
You're one happy man when you do what's right,
one happy woman when you form the habit of justice.

4-5 Remember me, GOD, when you enjoy your people;
include me when you save them;
I want to see your chosen succeed,
celebrate with your celebrating nation,
join the Hallelujahs of your pride and joy!

6-12 We've sinned a lot, both we and our parents;
We've fallen short, hurt a lot of people.
After our parents left Egypt,
they took your wonders for granted,
forgot your great and wonderful love.
They were barely beyond the Red Sea
when they defied the High God
—the very place he saved them!
—the place he revealed his amazing power!
He rebuked the Red Sea so that it dried up on the spot
—he paraded them right through!
—no one so much as got wet feet!
He saved them from a life of oppression,
pried them loose from the grip of the enemy.
Then the waters flowed back on their oppressors;
there wasn't a single survivor.
Then they believed his words were true
and broke out in songs of praise.

13-18 But it wasn't long before they forgot the whole thing,
wouldn't wait to be told what to do.
They only cared about pleasing themselves in that desert,
provoked God with their insistent demands.
He gave them exactly what they asked for—
but along with it they got an empty heart.
One day in camp some grew jealous of Moses,
also of Aaron, holy priest of GOD.
The ground opened and swallowed Dathan,
then buried Abiram's gang.
Fire flared against that rebel crew
and torched them to a cinder.

19-22 They cast in metal a bull calf at Horeb
and worshiped the statue they'd made.

NEW KING JAMES VERSION

20Thus they changed their glory
Into the image of an ox that eats grass.
21They forgot God their Savior,
Who had done great things in Egypt,
22Wondrous works in the land of Ham,
Awesome things by the Red Sea.
23Therefore He said that He would destroy them,
Had not Moses His chosen one stood before Him in the breach,
To turn away His wrath, lest He destroy *them.*

24Then they despised the pleasant land;
They did not believe His word,
25But complained in their tents,
And did not heed the voice of the LORD.
26Therefore He raised His hand *in an oath* against them,
To overthrow them in the wilderness,
27To overthrow their descendants among the nations,
And to scatter them in the lands.

28They joined themselves also to Baal of Peor,
And ate sacrifices made to the dead.
29Thus they provoked *Him* to anger with their deeds,
And the plague broke out among them.
30Then Phinehas stood up and intervened,
And the plague was stopped.
31And that was accounted to him for righteousness
To all generations forevermore.

32They angered *Him* also at the waters of strife,[a]
So that it went ill with Moses on account of them;
33Because they rebelled against His Spirit,
So that he spoke rashly with his lips.

34They did not destroy the peoples,
Concerning whom the LORD had commanded them,
35But they mingled with the Gentiles
And learned their works;
36They served their idols,
Which became a snare to them.
37They even sacrificed their sons
And their daughters to demons,
38And shed innocent blood,
The blood of their sons and daughters,
Whom they sacrificed to the idols of Canaan;
And the land was polluted with blood.
39Thus they were defiled by their own works,
And played the harlot by their own deeds.

40Therefore the wrath of the LORD was kindled against His people,
So that He abhorred His own inheritance.
41And He gave them into the hand of the Gentiles,
And those who hated them ruled over them.
42Their enemies also oppressed them,
And they were brought into subjection under their hand.

106:32 [a]Or *Meribah*

THE MESSAGE

They traded the Glory
for a cheap piece of sculpture—
a grass-chewing bull!
They forgot God, their very own Savior,
who turned things around in Egypt,
Who created a world of wonders in the Land of Ham,
who gave that stunning performance at the Red Sea.

23-27 Fed up, God decided to get rid of them—
and except for Moses, his chosen, he would have.
But Moses stood in the gap and deflected God's anger,
prevented it from destroying them utterly.
They went on to reject the Blessed Land,
didn't believe a word of what God promised.
They found fault with the life they had
and turned a deaf ear to GOD's voice.
Exasperated, God swore
that he'd lay them low in the desert,
Scattering their children hither and yon,
strewing them all over the earth.

28-31 Then they linked up with Baal Peor,
attending funeral banquets and eating idol food.
That made God so angry
that a plague spread through their ranks;
Phinehas stood up and pled their case
and the plague was stopped.
This was counted to his credit;
his descendants will never forget it.

32-33 They angered God again at Meribah Springs;
this time Moses got mixed up in their evil;
Because they defied GOD yet again,
Moses exploded and lost his temper.

34-39 They didn't wipe out those godless cultures
as ordered by GOD;
Instead they intermarried with the heathen,
and in time became just like them.
They worshiped their idols,
were caught in the trap of idols.
They sacrificed their sons and daughters
at the altars of demon gods.
They slit the throats of their babies,
murdered their infant girls and boys.
They offered their babies to Canaan's gods;
the blood of their babies stained the land.
Their way of life stank to high heaven;
they lived like whores.

40-43 And GOD was furious—a wildfire anger;
he couldn't stand even to look at his people.
He turned them over to the heathen
so that the people who hated them ruled them.
Their enemies made life hard for them;
they were tyrannized under that rule.

NEW KING JAMES VERSION

43Many times He delivered them;
But they rebelled in their counsel,
And were brought low for their iniquity.

44Nevertheless He regarded their affliction,
When He heard their cry;
45And for their sake He remembered His covenant,
And relented according to the multitude of His mercies.
46He also made them to be pitied
By all those who carried them away captive.

47Save us, O LORD our God,
And gather us from among the Gentiles,
To give thanks to Your holy name,
To triumph in Your praise.

48Blessed *be* the LORD God of Israel
From everlasting to everlasting!
And let all the people say, "Amen!"

Praise the LORD!

Book Five: Psalms 107—150

PSALM 107

THANKSGIVING TO THE LORD FOR HIS GREAT WORKS OF DELIVERANCE

1Oh, give thanks to the LORD, for *He is* good!
For His mercy *endures* forever.
2Let the redeemed of the LORD say *so*,
Whom He has redeemed from the hand of the enemy,
3And gathered out of the lands,
From the east and from the west,
From the north and from the south.

4They wandered in the wilderness in a desolate way;
They found no city to dwell in.
5Hungry and thirsty,
Their soul fainted in them.
6Then they cried out to the LORD in their trouble,
And He delivered them out of their distresses.
7And He led them forth by the right way,
That they might go to a city for a dwelling place.
8Oh, that *men* would give thanks to the LORD *for* His goodness,
And *for* His wonderful works to the children of men!
9For He satisfies the longing soul,
And fills the hungry soul with goodness.

10Those who sat in darkness and in the shadow of death,
Bound in affliction and irons—
11Because they rebelled against the words of God,
And despised the counsel of the Most High,
12Therefore He brought down their heart with labor;
They fell down, and *there was* none to help.
13Then they cried out to the LORD in their trouble,
And He saved them out of their distresses.

THE MESSAGE

Over and over God rescued them, but they never learned—
until finally their sins destroyed them.

44-46 Still, when God saw the trouble they were in
and heard their cries for help,
He remembered his Covenant with them,
and, immense with love, took them by the hand.
He poured out his mercy on them
while their captors looked on, amazed.

47 Save us, GOD, our God!
Gather us back out of exile
So we can give thanks to your holy name
and join in the glory when you are praised!

Blessed be GOD, Israel's God!
Bless now, bless always!
Oh! Let everyone say Amen!
Hallelujah!

1-3 107 Oh, thank GOD—he's so good!
His love never runs out.
All of you set free by GOD, tell the world!
Tell how he freed you from oppression,
Then rounded you up from all over the place,
from the four winds, from the seven seas.

4-9 Some of you wandered for years in the desert,
looking but not finding a good place to live,
Half-starved and parched with thirst,
staggering and stumbling, on the brink of exhaustion.
Then, in your desperate condition, you called out to GOD.
He got you out in the nick of time;
He put your feet on a wonderful road
that took you straight to a good place to live.
So thank GOD for his marvelous love,
for his miracle mercy to the children he loves.
He poured great draughts of water down parched throats;
the starved and hungry got plenty to eat.

10-16 Some of you were locked in a dark cell,
cruelly confined behind bars,
Punished for defying God's Word,
for turning your back on the High God's counsel—
A hard sentence, and your hearts so heavy,
and not a soul in sight to help.
Then you called out to GOD in your desperate condition;
he got you out in the nick of time.

NEW KING JAMES VERSION

14He brought them out of darkness and the
shadow of death,
And broke their chains in pieces.
15Oh, that *men* would give thanks to the LORD
for His goodness,
And *for* His wonderful works to the children
of men!
16For He has broken the gates of bronze,
And cut the bars of iron in two.

17Fools, because of their transgression,
And because of their iniquities, were
afflicted.
18Their soul abhorred all manner of food,
And they drew near to the gates of death.
19Then they cried out to the LORD in their
trouble,
And He saved them out of their distresses.
20He sent His word and healed them,
And delivered *them* from their destructions.
21Oh, that *men* would give thanks to the LORD
for His goodness,
And *for* His wonderful works to the children
of men!
22Let them sacrifice the sacrifices of
thanksgiving,
And declare His works with rejoicing.

23Those who go down to the sea in ships,
Who do business on great waters,
24They see the works of the LORD,
And His wonders in the deep.
25For He commands and raises the stormy
wind,
Which lifts up the waves of the sea.
26They mount up to the heavens,
They go down again to the depths;
Their soul melts because of trouble.
27They reel to and fro, and stagger like a
drunken man,
And are at their wits' end.
28Then they cry out to the LORD in their
trouble,
And He brings them out of their distresses.
29He calms the storm,
So that its waves are still.
30Then they are glad because they are quiet;
So He guides them to their desired haven.
31Oh, that *men* would give thanks to the LORD
for His goodness,
And *for* His wonderful works to the children
of men!
32Let them exalt Him also in the assembly of
the people,
And praise Him in the company of the
elders.

33He turns rivers into a wilderness,
And the watersprings into dry ground;
34A fruitful land into barrenness,
For the wickedness of those who dwell in it.
35He turns a wilderness into pools of water,
And dry land into watersprings.
36There He makes the hungry dwell,
That they may establish a city for a dwelling
place,

THE MESSAGE

He led you out of your dark, dark cell,
broke open the jail and led you out.
So thank GOD for his marvelous love,
for his miracle mercy to the children he
loves;
He shattered the heavy jailhouse doors,
he snapped the prison bars like
matchsticks!

17-22 Some of you were sick because you'd lived
a bad life,
your bodies feeling the effects of your
sin;
You couldn't stand the sight of food,
so miserable you thought you'd be better
off dead.
Then you called out to GOD in your
desperate condition;
he got you out in the nick of time.
He spoke the word that healed you,
that pulled you back from the brink of
death.
So thank GOD for his marvelous love,
for his miracle mercy to the children he
loves;
Offer thanksgiving sacrifices,
tell the world what he's done—sing it
out!

23-32 Some of you set sail in big ships;
you put to sea to do business in faraway
ports.
Out at sea you saw GOD in action,
saw his breathtaking ways with the
ocean:
With a word he called up the wind—
an ocean storm, towering waves!
You shot high in the sky, then the bottom
dropped out;
your hearts were stuck in your throats.
You were spun like a top, you reeled like a
drunk,
you didn't know which end was up.
Then you called out to GOD in your
desperate condition;
he got you out in the nick of time.
He quieted the wind down to a whisper,
put a muzzle on all the big waves.
And you were so glad when the storm died
down,
and he led you safely back to harbor.
So thank GOD for his marvelous love,
for his miracle mercy to the children he
loves.
Lift high your praises when the people
assemble,
shout Hallelujah when the elders meet!

33-41 GOD turned rivers into wasteland,
springs of water into sunbaked mud;
Luscious orchards became alkali flats
because of the evil of the people who
lived there.
Then he changed wasteland into fresh
pools of water,
arid earth into springs of water,
Brought in the hungry and settled them
there;
they moved in—what a great place to live!

NEW KING JAMES VERSION

37And sow fields and plant vineyards,
That they may yield a fruitful harvest.
38He also blesses them, and they multiply greatly;
And He does not let their cattle decrease.

39When they are diminished and brought low
Through oppression, affliction and sorrow,
40He pours contempt on princes,
And causes them to wander in the wilderness *where there is* no way;
41Yet He sets the poor on high, far from affliction,
And makes *their* families like a flock.
42The righteous see *it* and rejoice,
And all iniquity stops its mouth.

43Whoever *is* wise will observe these *things,*
And they will understand the lovingkindness of the LORD.

PSALM 108

ASSURANCE OF GOD'S VICTORY OVER ENEMIES

A Song. A Psalm of David.

1O God, my heart is steadfast;
I will sing and give praise, even with my glory.
2Awake, lute and harp!
I will awaken the dawn.
3I will praise You, O LORD, among the peoples,
And I will sing praises to You among the nations.
4For Your mercy *is* great above the heavens,
And Your truth *reaches* to the clouds.

5Be exalted, O God, above the heavens,
And Your glory above all the earth;
6That Your beloved may be delivered,
Save *with* Your right hand, and hear me.

7God has spoken in His holiness:
"I will rejoice;
I will divide Shechem
And measure out the Valley of Succoth.
8Gilead *is* Mine; Manasseh *is* Mine;
Ephraim also *is* the helmet for My head;
Judah *is* My lawgiver.
9Moab *is* My washpot;
Over Edom I will cast My shoe;
Over Philistia I will triumph."

10Who will bring me *into* the strong city?
Who will lead me to Edom?
11*Is it* not *You,* O God, *who* cast us off?
And *You,* O God, *who* did not go out with our armies?
12Give us help from trouble,
For the help of man is useless.
13Through God we will do valiantly,
For *it is* He *who* shall tread down our enemies.[a]

108:13 [a]Compare verses 6–13 with 60:5–12

THE MESSAGE

They sowed the fields, they planted vineyards,
they reaped a bountiful harvest.
He blessed them and they prospered greatly;
their herds of cattle never decreased.
But abuse and evil and trouble declined
as he heaped scorn on princes and sent them away.
He gave the poor a safe place to live,
treated their clans like well-cared-for sheep.

42-43 Good people see this and are glad;
bad people are speechless, stopped in their tracks.
If you are really wise, you'll think this over—
it's time you appreciated GOD's deep love.

A DAVID PRAYER

1-2 **108** I'm ready, God, so ready,
ready from head to toe.
Ready to sing,
ready to raise a God-song:
"Wake, soul! Wake, lute!
Wake up, you sleepyhead sun!"

3-6 I'm thanking you, GOD, out in the streets,
singing your praises in town and country.
The deeper your love, the higher it goes;
every cloud's a flag to your faithfulness.
Soar high in the skies, O God!
Cover the whole earth with your glory!
And for the sake of the one you love so much,
reach down and help me—answer me!

7-9 That's when God spoke in holy splendor:
"Brimming over with joy,
I make a present of Shechem,
I hand out Succoth Valley as a gift.
Gilead's in my pocket,
to say nothing of Manasseh.
Ephraim's my hard hat,
Judah my hammer.
Moab's a scrub bucket—
I mop the floor with Moab,
Spit on Edom,
rain fireworks all over Philistia."

10-11 Who will take me to the thick of the fight?
Who'll show me the road to Edom?
You aren't giving up on us, are you, God?
refusing to go out with our troops?

12-13 Give us help for the hard task;
human help is worthless.
In God we'll do our very best;
he'll flatten the opposition for good.

NEW KING JAMES VERSION

PSALM 109

PLEA FOR JUDGMENT OF FALSE ACCUSERS

To the Chief Musician. A Psalm of David.

1Do not keep silent,
O God of my praise!
2For the mouth of the wicked and the mouth
of the deceitful
Have opened against me;
They have spoken against me with a lying
tongue.
3They have also surrounded me with words
of hatred,
And fought against me without a cause.
4In return for my love they are my accusers,
But I *give myself to* prayer.
5Thus they have rewarded me evil for good,
And hatred for my love.

6Set a wicked man over him,
And let an accuser[a] stand at his right hand.
7When he is judged, let him be found guilty,
And let his prayer become sin.
8Let his days be few,
And let another take his office.
9Let his children be fatherless,
And his wife a widow.
10Let his children continually be vagabonds,
and beg;
Let them seek *their bread*[a] also from their
desolate places.
11Let the creditor seize all that he has,
And let strangers plunder his labor.
12Let there be none to extend mercy to him,
Nor let there be any to favor his fatherless
children.
13Let his posterity be cut off,
And in the generation following let their
name be blotted out.

14Let the iniquity of his fathers be
remembered before the LORD,
And let not the sin of his mother be blotted
out.
15Let them be continually before the LORD,
That He may cut off the memory of them
from the earth;
16Because he did not remember to show
mercy,
But persecuted the poor and needy man,
That he might even slay the broken in heart.
17As he loved cursing, so let it come to him;
As he did not delight in blessing, so let it be
far from him.
18As he clothed himself with cursing as with
his garment,
So let it enter his body like water,
And like oil into his bones.
19Let it be to him like the garment which
covers him,
And for a belt with which he girds himself
continually.
20*Let* this *be* the LORD's reward to my
accusers,
And to those who speak evil against my
person.

109:6 [a]Hebrew *satan* **109:10** [a]Following Masoretic Text and Targum; Septuagint and Vulgate read *be cast out*.

THE MESSAGE

A DAVID PRAYER

1-5 **109** My God, don't turn a deaf ear to
my hallelujah prayer.
Liars are pouring out invective on me;
Their lying tongues are like a pack of dogs
out to get me,
barking their hate, nipping my heels—
and for no reason!
I loved them and now they slander me—
yes, me!—
and treat my prayer like a crime;
They return my good with evil,
they return my love with hate.

6-20 Send the Evil One to accuse my accusing
judge;
dispatch Satan to prosecute him.
When he's judged, let the verdict be
"Guilty,"
and when he prays, let his prayer turn to
sin.
Give him a short life,
and give his job to somebody else.
Make orphans of his children,
dress his wife in widow's weeds;
Turn his children into begging street
urchins,
evicted from their homes—homeless.
May the bank foreclose and wipe him out,
and strangers, like vultures, pick him
clean.
May there be no one around to help him
out,
no one willing to give his orphans a
break.
Chop down his family tree
so that nobody even remembers his
name.
But erect a memorial to the sin of his
father,
and make sure his mother's name is
there, too—
Their sins recorded forever before GOD,
but they themselves sunk in oblivion.
That's all he deserves since he was never
once kind,
hounded the afflicted and heartbroken to
their graves.
Since he loved cursing so much,
let curses rain down;
Since he had no taste for blessing,
let blessings flee far from him.
He dressed up in curses like a fine suit of
clothes;
he drank curses, took his baths in curses.
So give him a gift—a costume of curses;
he can wear curses every day of the
week!
That's what they'll get, those out to get
me—
an avalanche of just deserts from GOD.

NEW KING JAMES VERSION

21But You, O GOD the Lord,
Deal with me for Your name's sake;
Because Your mercy *is* good, deliver me.
22For I *am* poor and needy,
And my heart is wounded within me.
23I am gone like a shadow when it lengthens;
I am shaken off like a locust.
24My knees are weak through fasting,
And my flesh is feeble from lack of fatness.
25I also have become a reproach to them;
When they look at me, they shake their heads.

26Help me, O LORD my God!
Oh, save me according to Your mercy,
27That they may know that this *is* Your hand—
That You, LORD, have done it!
28Let them curse, but You bless;
When they arise, let them be ashamed,
But let Your servant rejoice.
29Let my accusers be clothed with shame,
And let them cover themselves with their own disgrace as with a mantle.

30I will greatly praise the LORD with my mouth;
Yes, I will praise Him among the multitude.
31For He shall stand at the right hand of the poor,
To save *him* from those who condemn him.

PSALM 110

ANNOUNCEMENT OF THE MESSIAH'S REIGN

A Psalm of David.

1The LORD said to my Lord,
"Sit at My right hand,
Till I make Your enemies Your footstool."
2The LORD shall send the rod of Your strength out of Zion.
Rule in the midst of Your enemies!

3Your people *shall be* volunteers
In the day of Your power;
In the beauties of holiness, from the womb of the morning,
You have the dew of Your youth.
4The LORD has sworn
And will not relent,
"You *are* a priest forever
According to the order of Melchizedek."

5The Lord *is* at Your right hand;
He shall execute kings in the day of His wrath.
6He shall judge among the nations,
He shall fill *the places* with dead bodies,
He shall execute the heads of many countries.
7He shall drink of the brook by the wayside;
Therefore He shall lift up the head.

THE MESSAGE

21-25 Oh, GOD, my Lord, step in;
work a miracle for me—you can do it!
Get me out of here—your love is so great!—
I'm at the end of my rope, my life in ruins.
I'm fading away to nothing, passing away,
my youth gone, old before my time.
I'm weak from hunger and can hardly stand up,
my body a rack of skin and bones.
I'm a joke in poor taste to those who see me;
they take one look and shake their heads.

26-29 Help me, oh help me, GOD, my God,
save me through your wonderful love;
Then they'll know that your hand is in this,
that you, GOD, have been at work.
Let them curse all they want;
you do the blessing.
Let them be jeered by the crowd when they stand up,
followed by cheers for me, your servant.
Dress my accusers in clothes dirty with shame,
discarded and humiliating old ragbag clothes.

30-31 My mouth's full of great praise for GOD,
I'm singing his hallelujahs surrounded by crowds,
For he's always at hand to take the side of the needy,
to rescue a life from the unjust judge.

A DAVID PRAYER

1-3 **110** The word of GOD to my Lord:
"Sit alongside me here on my throne
until I make your enemies a stool for your feet."
You were forged a strong scepter by GOD of Zion;
now rule, though surrounded by enemies!
Your people will freely join you,
resplendent in holy armor
on the great day of your conquest,
Join you at the fresh break of day,
join you with all the vigor of youth.

4-7 GOD gave his word and he won't take it back:
you're the permanent priest, the Melchizedek priest.
The Lord stands true at your side,
crushing kings in his terrible wrath,
Bringing judgment on the nations,
handing out convictions wholesale,
crushing opposition across the wide earth.
The King-Maker put his King on the throne;
the True King rules with head held high!

NEW KING JAMES VERSION

PSALM 111

PRAISE TO GOD FOR HIS FAITHFULNESS AND JUSTICE

1Praise the LORD!

I will praise the LORD with *my* whole heart,
In the assembly of the upright and *in* the congregation.

2The works of the LORD *are* great,
Studied by all who have pleasure in them.
3His work *is* honorable and glorious,
And His righteousness endures forever.
4He has made His wonderful works to be remembered;
The LORD *is* gracious and full of compassion.
5He has given food to those who fear Him;
He will ever be mindful of His covenant.
6He has declared to His people the power of His works,
In giving them the heritage of the nations.

7The works of His hands *are* verity and justice;
All His precepts *are* sure.
8They stand fast forever and ever,
And are done in truth and uprightness.
9He has sent redemption to His people;
He has commanded His covenant forever:
Holy and awesome *is* His name.

10The fear of the LORD *is* the beginning of wisdom;
A good understanding have all those who do *His commandments*.
His praise endures forever.

PSALM 112

THE BLESSED STATE OF THE RIGHTEOUS

1Praise the LORD!

Blessed *is* the man *who* fears the LORD,
Who delights greatly in His commandments.

2His descendants will be mighty on earth;
The generation of the upright will be blessed.
3Wealth and riches *will be* in his house,
And his righteousness endures forever.
4Unto the upright there arises light in the darkness;
He is gracious, and full of compassion, and righteous.
5A good man deals graciously and lends;
He will guide his affairs with discretion.
6Surely he will never be shaken;
The righteous will be in everlasting remembrance.
7He will not be afraid of evil tidings;
His heart is steadfast, trusting in the LORD.
8His heart *is* established;
He will not be afraid,
Until he sees *his desire* upon his enemies.

THE MESSAGE

1-10 **111** Hallelujah!
I give thanks to GOD with everything I've got—
Wherever good people gather, and in the congregation.
GOD's works are so great, worth
A lifetime of study—endless enjoyment!
Splendor and beauty mark his craft;
His generosity never gives out.
His miracles are his memorial—
This GOD of Grace, this GOD of Love.
He gave food to those who fear him,
He remembered to keep his ancient promise.
He proved to his people that he could do what he said:
Hand them the nations on a platter—a gift!
He manufactures truth and justice;
All his products are guaranteed to last—
Never out-of-date, never obsolete, rust-proof.
All that he makes and does is honest and true:
He paid the ransom for his people,
He ordered his Covenant kept forever.
He's so personal and holy, worthy of our respect.
The good life begins in the fear of GOD—
Do that and you'll know the blessing of GOD.
His Hallelujah lasts forever!

1-10 **112** Hallelujah!
Blessed man, blessed woman, who fear GOD,
Who cherish and relish his commandments,
Their children robust on the earth,
And the homes of the upright—how blessed!
Their houses brim with wealth
And a generosity that never runs dry.
Sunrise breaks through the darkness for good people—
God's grace and mercy and justice!
The good person is generous and lends lavishly;
No shuffling or stumbling around for this one,
But a sterling and solid and lasting reputation.
Unfazed by rumor and gossip,
Heart ready, trusting in GOD,
Spirit firm, unperturbed,
Ever blessed, relaxed among enemies,

NEW KING JAMES VERSION

[9]He has dispersed abroad,
He has given to the poor;
His righteousness endures forever;
His horn will be exalted with honor.
[10]The wicked will see *it* and be grieved;
He will gnash his teeth and melt away;
The desire of the wicked shall perish.

PSALM 113

THE MAJESTY AND CONDESCENSION OF GOD

[1]Praise the LORD!

Praise, O servants of the LORD,
Praise the name of the LORD!
[2]Blessed be the name of the LORD
From this time forth and forevermore!
[3]From the rising of the sun to its going down
The LORD's name *is* to be praised.

[4]The LORD *is* high above all nations,
His glory above the heavens.
[5]Who *is* like the LORD our God,
Who dwells on high,
[6]Who humbles Himself to behold
The things that are in the heavens and in the earth?

[7]He raises the poor out of the dust,
And lifts the needy out of the ash heap,
[8]That He may seat *him* with princes—
With the princes of His people.
[9]He grants the barren woman a home,
Like a joyful mother of children.

Praise the LORD!

PSALM 114

THE POWER OF GOD IN HIS DELIVERANCE OF ISRAEL

[1]When Israel went out of Egypt,
The house of Jacob from a people of strange language,
[2]Judah became His sanctuary,
And Israel His dominion.

[3]The sea saw *it* and fled;
Jordan turned back.
[4]The mountains skipped like rams,
The little hills like lambs.
[5]What ails you, O sea, that you fled?
O Jordan, *that* you turned back?
[6]O mountains, *that* you skipped like rams?
O little hills, like lambs?

[7]Tremble, O earth, at the presence of the Lord,
At the presence of the God of Jacob,
[8]Who turned the rock *into* a pool of water,
The flint into a fountain of waters.

PSALM 115

THE FUTILITY OF IDOLS AND THE TRUSTWORTHINESS OF GOD

[1]Not unto us, O LORD, not unto us,
But to Your name give glory,
Because of Your mercy,
Because of Your truth.

THE MESSAGE

They lavish gifts on the poor—
A generosity that goes on, and on, and on.
An honored life! A beautiful life!
Someone wicked takes one look and rages,
Blusters away but ends up speechless.
There's nothing to the dreams of the wicked. Nothing.

1-3 **113** Hallelujah!
You who serve GOD, praise GOD!
Just to speak his name is praise!
Just to remember GOD is a blessing—
now and tomorrow and always.
From east to west, from dawn to dusk,
keep lifting all your praises to GOD!

4-9 GOD is higher than anything and anyone,
outshining everything you can see in the skies.
Who can compare with GOD, our God,
so majestically enthroned,
Surveying his magnificent
heavens and earth?
He picks up the poor from out of the dirt,
rescues the wretched who've been thrown out with the trash,
Seats them among the honored guests,
a place of honor among the brightest and best.
He gives childless couples a family,
gives them joy as the parents of children.
Hallelujah!

1-8 **114** After Israel left Egypt,
the clan of Jacob left those barbarians behind;
Judah became holy land for him,
Israel the place of holy rule.
Sea took one look and ran the other way;
River Jordan turned around and ran off.
The mountains turned playful and skipped like rams,
the hills frolicked like spring lambs.
What's wrong with you, Sea, that you ran away?
and you, River Jordan, that you turned and ran off?
And mountains, why did you skip like rams?
and you, hills, frolic like spring lambs?
Tremble, Earth! You're in the Lord's presence!
in the presence of Jacob's God.
He turned the rock into a pool of cool water,
turned flint into fresh spring water.

1-2 **115** Not for our sake, GOD, no, not for our sake,
but for your name's sake, show your glory.
Do it on account of your merciful love,
do it on account of your faithful ways.

NEW KING JAMES VERSION

2Why should the Gentiles say,
"So where *is* their God?"

3But our God *is* in heaven;
He does whatever He pleases.
4Their idols *are* silver and gold,
The work of men's hands.
5They have mouths, but they do not speak;
Eyes they have, but they do not see;
6They have ears, but they do not hear;
Noses they have, but they do not smell;
7They have hands, but they do not handle;
Feet they have, but they do not walk;
Nor do they mutter through their throat.
8Those who make them are like them;
So is everyone who trusts in them.

9O Israel, trust in the LORD;
He *is* their help and their shield.
10O house of Aaron, trust in the LORD;
He *is* their help and their shield.
11You who fear the LORD, trust in the LORD;
He *is* their help and their shield.

12The LORD has been mindful of *us;*
He will bless us;
He will bless the house of Israel;
He will bless the house of Aaron.
13He will bless those who fear the LORD,
Both small and great.

14May the LORD give you increase more and more,
You and your children.
15*May* you *be* blessed by the LORD,
Who made heaven and earth.

16The heaven, *even* the heavens, *are* the LORD's;
But the earth He has given to the children of men.
17The dead do not praise the LORD,
Nor any who go down into silence.
18But we will bless the LORD
From this time forth and forevermore.

Praise the LORD!

PSALM 116

THANKSGIVING FOR DELIVERANCE FROM DEATH

1I love the LORD, because He has heard
My voice *and* my supplications.
2Because He has inclined His ear to me,
Therefore I will call *upon Him* as long as I live.

3The pains of death surrounded me,
And the pangs of Sheol laid hold of me;
I found trouble and sorrow.
4Then I called upon the name of the LORD:
"O LORD, I implore You, deliver my soul!"

5Gracious *is* the LORD, and righteous;
Yes, our God *is* merciful.
6The LORD preserves the simple;
I was brought low, and He saved me.
7Return to your rest, O my soul,
For the LORD has dealt bountifully with you.

THE MESSAGE

Do it so none of the nations can say,
"Where now, oh where is their God?"

3-8 Our God is in heaven
doing whatever he wants to do.
Their gods are metal and wood,
handmade in a basement shop:
Carved mouths that can't talk,
painted eyes that can't see,
Tin ears that can't hear,
molded noses that can't smell,
Hands that can't grasp, feet that can't walk or run,
throats that never utter a sound.
Those who make them have become just like them,
have become just like the gods they trust.

9-11 But you, Israel: put your trust in GOD!
—trust your Helper! trust your Ruler!
Clan of Aaron, trust in GOD!
—trust your Helper! trust your Ruler!
You who fear GOD, trust in GOD!
—trust your Helper! trust your Ruler!

12-16 O GOD, remember us and bless us,
bless the families of Israel and Aaron.
And let GOD bless all who fear GOD—
bless the small, bless the great.
Oh, let GOD enlarge your families—
giving growth to you, growth to your children.
May you be blessed by GOD,
by GOD, who made heaven and earth.
The heaven of heavens is for GOD,
but he put us in charge of the earth.

17-18 Dead people can't praise GOD—
not a word to be heard from those buried in the ground.
But we bless GOD, oh yes—
we bless him now, we bless him always!
Hallelujah!

1-6 **116** I love GOD because he listened to me,
listened as I begged for mercy.
He listened so intently
as I laid out my case before him.
Death stared me in the face,
hell was hard on my heels.
Up against it, I didn't know which way to turn;
then I called out to GOD for help:
"Please, GOD!" I cried out.
"Save my life!"
GOD is gracious—it is he who makes things right,
our most compassionate God.
GOD takes the side of the helpless;
when I was at the end of my rope, he saved me.

7-8 I said to myself, "Relax and rest.
GOD has showered you with blessings.

NEW KING JAMES VERSION

[8]For You have delivered my soul from death,
My eyes from tears,
And my feet from falling.
[9]I will walk before the LORD
In the land of the living.
[10]I believed, therefore I spoke,
"I am greatly afflicted."
[11]I said in my haste,
"All men *are* liars."

[12]What shall I render to the LORD
For all His benefits toward me?
[13]I will take up the cup of salvation,
And call upon the name of the LORD.
[14]I will pay my vows to the LORD
Now in the presence of all His people.

[15]Precious in the sight of the LORD
Is the death of His saints.

[16]O LORD, truly I *am* Your servant;
I *am* Your servant, the son of Your maidservant;
You have loosed my bonds.
[17]I will offer to You the sacrifice of thanksgiving,
And will call upon the name of the LORD.

[18]I will pay my vows to the LORD
Now in the presence of all His people,
[19]In the courts of the LORD's house,
In the midst of you, O Jerusalem.

Praise the LORD!

PSALM 117

LET ALL PEOPLES PRAISE THE LORD

[1]Praise the LORD, all you Gentiles!
Laud Him, all you peoples!
[2]For His merciful kindness is great toward us,
And the truth of the LORD *endures* forever.

Praise the LORD!

PSALM 118

PRAISE TO GOD FOR HIS EVERLASTING MERCY

[1]Oh, give thanks to the LORD, for *He is* good!
For His mercy *endures* forever.

[2]Let Israel now say,
"His mercy *endures* forever."
[3]Let the house of Aaron now say,
"His mercy *endures* forever."
[4]Let those who fear the LORD now say,
"His mercy *endures* forever."

[5]I called on the LORD in distress;
The LORD answered me *and set me* in a broad place.
[6]The LORD *is* on my side;
I will not fear.
What can man do to me?
[7]The LORD is for me among those who help me;
Therefore I shall see *my desire* on those who hate me.

THE MESSAGE

Soul, you've been rescued from death;
Eye, you've been rescued from tears;
And you, Foot, were kept from stumbling."

9-11 I'm striding in the presence of GOD,
alive in the land of the living!
I stayed faithful, though bedeviled,
and despite a ton of bad luck,
Despite giving up on the human race,
saying, "They're all liars and cheats."

12-19 What can I give back to GOD
for the blessings he's poured out on me?
I'll lift high the cup of salvation—a toast to GOD!
I'll pray in the name of GOD;
I'll complete what I promised GOD I'd do,
and I'll do it together with his people.
When they arrive at the gates of death,
GOD welcomes those who love him.
Oh, GOD, here I am, your servant,
your faithful servant: set me free for your service!
I'm ready to offer the thanksgiving sacrifice
and pray in the name of GOD.
I'll complete what I promised GOD I'd do,
and I'll do it in company with his people,
In the place of worship, in GOD's house,
in Jerusalem, GOD's city.
Hallelujah!

1-2 **117** Praise GOD, everybody!
Applaud GOD, all people!
His love has taken over our lives;
GOD's faithful ways are eternal.
Hallelujah!

1-4 **118** Thank GOD because he's good,
because his love never quits.
Tell the world, Israel,
"His love never quits."
And you, clan of Aaron, tell the world,
"His love never quits."
And you who fear GOD, join in,
"His love never quits."

5-16 Pushed to the wall, I called to GOD;
from the wide open spaces, he answered.
GOD's now at my side and I'm not afraid;
who would dare lay a hand on me?
GOD's my strong champion;
I flick off my enemies like flies.

NEW KING JAMES VERSION

8*It is* better to trust in the LORD
Than to put confidence in man.
9*It is* better to trust in the LORD
Than to put confidence in princes.

10All nations surrounded me,
But in the name of the LORD I will destroy them.
11They surrounded me,
Yes, they surrounded me;
But in the name of the LORD I will destroy them.
12They surrounded me like bees;
They were quenched like a fire of thorns;
For in the name of the LORD I will destroy them.
13You pushed me violently, that I might fall,
But the LORD helped me.
14The LORD *is* my strength and song,
And He has become my salvation.[a]

15The voice of rejoicing and salvation
Is in the tents of the righteous;
The right hand of the LORD does valiantly.
16The right hand of the LORD is exalted;
The right hand of the LORD does valiantly.
17I shall not die, but live,
And declare the works of the LORD.
18The LORD has chastened me severely,
But He has not given me over to death.

19Open to me the gates of righteousness;
I will go through them,
And I will praise the LORD.
20This is the gate of the LORD,
Through which the righteous shall enter.

21I will praise You,
For You have answered me,
And have become my salvation.

22The stone *which* the builders rejected
Has become the chief cornerstone.
23This was the LORD's doing;
It *is* marvelous in our eyes.
24This *is* the day the LORD has made;
We will rejoice and be glad in it.

25Save now, I pray, O LORD;
O LORD, I pray, send now prosperity.
26Blessed *is* he who comes in the name of the LORD!
We have blessed you from the house of the LORD.
27God *is* the LORD,
And He has given us light;
Bind the sacrifice with cords to the horns of the altar.
28You *are* my God, and I will praise You;
You are my God, I will exalt You.

29Oh, give thanks to the LORD, for *He is* good!
For His mercy *endures* forever.

118:14 [a]Compare Exodus 15:2

THE MESSAGE

Far better to take refuge in GOD
than trust in people;
Far better to take refuge in GOD
than trust in celebrities.
Hemmed in by barbarians,
in GOD's name I rubbed their faces in the dirt;
Hemmed in and with no way out,
in GOD's name I rubbed their faces in the dirt;
Like swarming bees, like wild prairie fire,
they hemmed me in;
in GOD's name I rubbed their faces in the dirt.
I was right on the cliff-edge, ready to fall,
when GOD grabbed and held me.
GOD's my strength, he's also my song,
and now he's my salvation.
Hear the shouts, hear the triumph songs
in the camp of the saved?
"The hand of GOD has turned the tide!
The hand of GOD is raised in victory!
The hand of GOD has turned the tide!"

17-20 I didn't die. I *lived*!
And now I'm telling the world what GOD did.
GOD tested me, he pushed me hard,
but he didn't hand me over to Death.
Swing wide the city gates—the *righteous* gates!
I'll walk right through and thank GOD!
This Temple Gate belongs to GOD,
so the victors can enter and praise.

21-25 Thank you for responding to me;
you've truly become my salvation!
The stone the masons discarded as flawed
is now the capstone!
This is GOD's work.
We rub our eyes—we can hardly believe it!
This is the very day GOD acted—
let's celebrate and be festive!
Salvation now, GOD. Salvation now!
Oh yes, GOD—a free and full life!

26-29 Blessed are you who enter in GOD's name—
from GOD's house we bless you!
GOD is God,
he has bathed us in light.
Festoon the shrine with garlands,
hang colored banners above the altar!
You're my God, and I thank you.
O my God, I lift high your praise.
Thank GOD—he's so good.
His love never quits!

NEW KING JAMES VERSION

PSALM 119

MEDITATIONS ON THE EXCELLENCIES OF THE WORD OF GOD

א ALEPH

1Blessed *are* the undefiled in the way,
Who walk in the law of the LORD!
2Blessed *are* those who keep His testimonies,
Who seek Him with the whole heart!
3They also do no iniquity;
They walk in His ways.
4You have commanded *us*
To keep Your precepts diligently.
5Oh, that my ways were directed
To keep Your statutes!
6Then I would not be ashamed,
When I look into all Your commandments.
7I will praise You with uprightness of heart,
When I learn Your righteous judgments.
8I will keep Your statutes;
Oh, do not forsake me utterly!

ב BETH

9How can a young man cleanse his way?
By taking heed according to Your word.
10With my whole heart I have sought You;
Oh, let me not wander from Your
commandments!
11Your word I have hidden in my heart,
That I might not sin against You.
12Blessed *are* You, O LORD!
Teach me Your statutes.
13With my lips I have declared
All the judgments of Your mouth.
14I have rejoiced in the way of Your
testimonies,
As *much as* in all riches.
15I will meditate on Your precepts,
And contemplate Your ways.
16I will delight myself in Your statutes;
I will not forget Your word.

ג GIMEL

17Deal bountifully with Your servant,
That I may live and keep Your word.
18Open my eyes, that I may see
Wondrous things from Your law.
19I *am* a stranger in the earth;
Do not hide Your commandments from me.
20My soul breaks with longing
For Your judgments at all times.
21You rebuke the proud—the cursed,
Who stray from Your commandments.
22Remove from me reproach and contempt,
For I have kept Your testimonies.

THE MESSAGE

1-8 119 You're blessed when you stay on
course,
walking steadily on the road revealed
by GOD.
You're blessed when you follow his
directions,
doing your best to find him.
That's right—you don't go off on your
own;
you walk straight along the road he set.
You, GOD, prescribed the right way to live;
now you expect us to live it.
Oh, that my steps might be steady,
keeping to the course you set;
Then I'd never have any regrets
in comparing my life with your
counsel.
I thank you for speaking straight from
your heart;
I learn the pattern of your righteous
ways.
I'm going to do what you tell me to do;
don't ever walk off and leave me.

9-16 How can a young person live a clean life?
By carefully reading the map of your
Word.
I'm single-minded in pursuit of you;
don't let me miss the road signs you've
posted.
I've banked your promises in the vault of
my heart
so I won't sin myself bankrupt.
Be blessed, GOD;
train me in your ways of wise living.
I'll transfer to my lips
all the counsel that comes from your
mouth;
I delight far more in what you tell me
about living
than in gathering a pile of riches.
I ponder every morsel of wisdom from
you,
I attentively watch how you've done it.
I relish everything you've told me of life,
I won't forget a word of it.

17-24 Be generous with me and I'll live a full life;
not for a minute will I take my eyes off
your road.
Open my eyes so I can see
what you show me of your
miracle-wonders.
I'm a stranger in these parts;
give me clear directions.
My soul is starved and hungry,
ravenous!—
insatiable for your nourishing
commands.
And those who think they know so much,
ignoring everything you tell them—let
them have it!
Don't let them mock and humiliate me;
I've been careful to do just what you
said.

NEW KING JAMES VERSION

23Princes also sit *and* speak against me,
But Your servant meditates on Your statutes.
24Your testimonies also *are* my delight
And my counselors.

ד DALETH

25My soul clings to the dust;
Revive me according to Your word.
26I have declared my ways, and You answered me;
Teach me Your statutes.
27Make me understand the way of Your precepts;
So shall I meditate on Your wonderful works.
28My soul melts from heaviness;
Strengthen me according to Your word.
29Remove from me the way of lying,
And grant me Your law graciously.
30I have chosen the way of truth;
Your judgments I have laid *before me*.
31I cling to Your testimonies;
O LORD, do not put me to shame!
32I will run the course of Your commandments,
For You shall enlarge my heart.

ה HE

33Teach me, O LORD, the way of Your statutes,
And I shall keep it *to* the end.
34Give me understanding, and I shall keep Your law;
Indeed, I shall observe it with *my* whole heart.
35Make me walk in the path of Your commandments,
For I delight in it.
36Incline my heart to Your testimonies,
And not to covetousness.
37Turn away my eyes from looking at worthless things,
And revive me in Your way.[a]
38Establish Your word to Your servant,
Who *is devoted* to fearing You.
39Turn away my reproach which I dread,
For Your judgments *are* good.
40Behold, I long for Your precepts;
Revive me in Your righteousness.

ו WAW

41Let Your mercies come also to me, O LORD—
Your salvation according to Your word.
42So shall I have an answer for him who reproaches me,
For I trust in Your word.
43And take not the word of truth utterly out of my mouth,
For I have hoped in Your ordinances.
44So shall I keep Your law continually,
Forever and ever.
45And I will walk at liberty,
For I seek Your precepts.
46I will speak of Your testimonies also before kings,
And will not be ashamed.
47And I will delight myself in Your commandments,
Which I love.

119:37 [a]Following Masoretic Text, Septuagint, and Vulgate; Targum reads *Your words*.

THE MESSAGE

While bad neighbors maliciously gossip about me,
I'm absorbed in pondering your wise counsel.
Yes, your sayings on life are what give me delight;
I listen to them as to good neighbors!

25-32 I'm feeling terrible—I couldn't feel worse!
Get me on my feet again. You promised, remember?
When I told my story, you responded;
train me well in your deep wisdom.
Help me understand these things inside and out
so I can ponder your miracle-wonders.
My sad life's dilapidated, a falling-down barn;
build me up again by your Word.
Barricade the road that goes Nowhere;
grace me with your clear revelation.
I choose the true road to Somewhere,
I post your road signs at every curve and corner.
I grasp and cling to whatever you tell me;
GOD, don't let me down!
I'll run the course you lay out for me
if you'll just show me how.

33-40 GOD, teach me lessons for living
so I can stay the course.
Give me insight so I can do what you tell me—
my whole life one long, obedient response.
Guide me down the road of your commandments;
I love traveling this freeway!
Give me a bent for your words of wisdom,
and not for piling up loot.
Divert my eyes from toys and trinkets,
invigorate me on the pilgrim way.
Affirm your promises to me—
promises made to all who fear you.
Deflect the harsh words of my critics—
but what you say is always so good.
See how hungry I am for your counsel;
preserve my life through your righteous ways!

41-48 Let your love, GOD, shape my life
with salvation, exactly as you promised;
Then I'll be able to stand up to mockery
because I trusted your Word.
Don't ever deprive me of truth, not ever—
your commandments are what I depend on.
Oh, I'll guard with my life what you've revealed to me,
guard it now, guard it ever;
And I'll stride freely through wide open spaces
as I look for your truth and your wisdom;
Then I'll tell the world what I find,
speak out boldly in public, unembarrassed.

NEW KING JAMES VERSION

48My hands also I will lift up to Your
commandments,
Which I love,
And I will meditate on Your statutes.

ז ZAYIN
49Remember the word to Your servant,
Upon which You have caused me to hope.
50This *is* my comfort in my affliction,
For Your word has given me life.
51The proud have me in great derision,
Yet I do not turn aside from Your law.
52I remembered Your judgments of old,
O LORD,
And have comforted myself.
53Indignation has taken hold of me
Because of the wicked, who forsake Your
law.
54Your statutes have been my songs
In the house of my pilgrimage.
55I remember Your name in the night, O LORD,
And I keep Your law.
56This has become mine,
Because I kept Your precepts.

ח HETH
57*You are* my portion, O LORD;
I have said that I would keep Your words.
58I entreated Your favor with *my* whole heart;
Be merciful to me according to Your word.
59I thought about my ways,
And turned my feet to Your testimonies.
60I made haste, and did not delay
To keep Your commandments.
61The cords of the wicked have bound me,
But I have not forgotten Your law.
62At midnight I will rise to give thanks to You,
Because of Your righteous judgments.
63I *am* a companion of all who fear You,
And of those who keep Your precepts.
64The earth, O LORD, is full of Your mercy;
Teach me Your statutes.

ט TETH
65You have dealt well with Your servant,
O LORD, according to Your word.
66Teach me good judgment and knowledge,
For I believe Your commandments.
67Before I was afflicted I went astray,
But now I keep Your word.
68You *are* good, and do good;
Teach me Your statutes.
69The proud have forged a lie against me,
But I will keep Your precepts with *my* whole
heart.
70Their heart is as fat as grease,
But I delight in Your law.

THE MESSAGE

I cherish your commandments—oh, how I
love them!—
relishing every fragment of your counsel.

49-56 Remember what you said to me, your
servant—
I hang on to these words for dear life!
These words hold me up in bad times;
yes, your promises rejuvenate me.
The insolent ridicule me without mercy,
but I don't budge from your revelation.
I watch for your ancient landmark words,
and know I'm on the right track.
But when I see the wicked ignore your
directions,
I'm beside myself with anger.
I set your instructions to music
and sing them as I walk this pilgrim
way.
I meditate on your name all night, GOD,
treasuring your revelation, O GOD.
Still, I walk through a rain of derision
because I live by your Word and counsel.

57-64 Because you have satisfied me, GOD, I
promise
to do everything you say.
I beg you from the bottom of my heart:
smile,
be gracious to me just as you promised.
When I took a long, careful look at your
ways,
I got my feet back on the trail you
blazed.
I was up at once, didn't drag my feet,
was quick to follow your orders.
The wicked hemmed me in—there was no
way out—
but not for a minute did I forget your
plan for me.
I get up in the middle of the night to thank
you;
your decisions are so right, so true—
I can't wait till morning!
I'm a friend and companion of all who
fear you,
of those committed to living by your
rules.
Your love, GOD, fills the earth!
Train me to live by your counsel.

65-72 Be good to your servant, GOD;
be as good as your Word.
Train me in good common sense;
I'm thoroughly committed to living
your way.
Before I learned to answer you, I
wandered all over the place,
but now I'm in step with your Word.
You are good, and the source of good;
train me in your goodness.
The godless spread lies about me,
but I focus my attention on what you
are saying;
They're bland as a bucket of lard,
while I dance to the tune of your
revelation.

NEW KING JAMES VERSION

71*It is* good for me that I have been afflicted,
That I may learn Your statutes.
72The law of Your mouth *is* better to me
Than thousands of *coins of* gold and silver.

י YOD
73Your hands have made me and fashioned me;
Give me understanding, that I may learn Your commandments.
74Those who fear You will be glad when they see me,
Because I have hoped in Your word.
75I know, O LORD, that Your judgments *are* right,
And *that* in faithfulness You have afflicted me.
76Let, I pray, Your merciful kindness be for my comfort,
According to Your word to Your servant.
77Let Your tender mercies come to me, that I may live;
For Your law *is* my delight.
78Let the proud be ashamed,
For they treated me wrongfully with falsehood;
But I will meditate on Your precepts.
79Let those who fear You turn to me,
Those who know Your testimonies.
80Let my heart be blameless regarding Your statutes,
That I may not be ashamed.

כ KAPH
81My soul faints for Your salvation,
But I hope in Your word.
82My eyes fail *from searching* Your word,
Saying, "When will You comfort me?"
83For I have become like a wineskin in smoke,
Yet I do not forget Your statutes.
84How many *are* the days of Your servant?
When will You execute judgment on those who persecute me?
85The proud have dug pits for me,
Which *is* not according to Your law.
86All Your commandments *are* faithful;
They persecute me wrongfully;
Help me!
87They almost made an end of me on earth,
But I did not forsake Your precepts.
88Revive me according to Your lovingkindness,
So that I may keep the testimony of Your mouth.

ל LAMED
89Forever, O LORD,
Your word is settled in heaven.
90Your faithfulness *endures* to all generations;
You established the earth, and it abides.

THE MESSAGE

My troubles turned out all for the best—
they forced me to learn from your textbook.
Truth from your mouth means more to me
than striking it rich in a gold mine.

73-80 With your very own hands you formed me;
now breathe your wisdom over me so I can understand you.
When they see me waiting, expecting your Word,
those who fear you will take heart and be glad.
I can see now, GOD, that your decisions are right;
your testing has taught me what's true and right.
Oh, love me—and right now!—hold me tight!
just the way you promised.
Now comfort me so I can live, really live;
your revelation is the tune I dance to.
Let the fast-talking tricksters be exposed as frauds;
they tried to sell me a bill of goods,
but I kept my mind fixed on your counsel.
Let those who fear you turn to me
for evidence of your wise guidance.
And let me live whole and holy, soul and body,
so I can always walk with my head held high.

81-88 I'm homesick—longing for your salvation;
I'm waiting for your word of hope.
My eyes grow heavy watching for some sign of your promise;
how long must I wait for your comfort?
There's smoke in my eyes—they burn and water,
but I keep a steady gaze on the instructions you post.
How long do I have to put up with all this?
How long till you haul my tormentors into court?
The arrogant godless try to throw me off track,
ignorant as they are of God and his ways.
Everything you command is a sure thing,
but they harass me with lies. Help!
They've pushed and pushed—they never let up—
but I haven't relaxed my grip on your counsel.
In your great love revive me
so I can alertly obey your every word.

89-96 What you say goes, GOD,
and *stays*, as permanent as the heavens.
Your truth never goes out of fashion;
it's as up-to-date as the earth when the sun comes up.
Your Word and truth are dependable as ever;

NEW KING JAMES VERSION

91They continue this day according to Your ordinances,
For all *are* Your servants.
92Unless Your law *had been* my delight,
I would then have perished in my affliction.
93I will never forget Your precepts,
For by them You have given me life.
94I *am* Yours, save me;
For I have sought Your precepts.
95The wicked wait for me to destroy me,
But I will consider Your testimonies.
96I have seen the consummation of all perfection,
But Your commandment *is* exceedingly broad.

מ MEM

97Oh, how I love Your law!
It *is* my meditation all the day.
98You, through Your commandments, make me wiser than my enemies;
For they *are* ever with me.
99I have more understanding than all my teachers,
For Your testimonies *are* my meditation.
100I understand more than the ancients,
Because I keep Your precepts.
101I have restrained my feet from every evil way,
That I may keep Your word.
102I have not departed from Your judgments,
For You Yourself have taught me.
103How sweet are Your words to my taste,
Sweeter than honey to my mouth!
104Through Your precepts I get understanding;
Therefore I hate every false way.

נ NUN

105Your word *is* a lamp to my feet
And a light to my path.
106I have sworn and confirmed
That I will keep Your righteous judgments.
107I am afflicted very much;
Revive me, O LORD, according to Your word.
108Accept, I pray, the freewill offerings of my mouth, O LORD,
And teach me Your judgments.
109My life *is* continually in my hand,
Yet I do not forget Your law.
110The wicked have laid a snare for me,
Yet I have not strayed from Your precepts.
111Your testimonies I have taken as a heritage forever,
For they *are* the rejoicing of my heart.
112I have inclined my heart to perform Your statutes
Forever, to the very end.

THE MESSAGE

that's what you ordered—you set the earth going.
If your revelation hadn't delighted me so,
I would have given up when the hard times came.
But I'll never forget the advice you gave me;
you saved my life with those wise words.
Save me! I'm all yours.
I look high and low for your words of wisdom.
The wicked lie in ambush to destroy me,
but I'm only concerned with your plans for me.
I see the limits to everything human,
but the horizons can't contain your commands!

97-104 Oh, how I love all you've revealed;
I reverently ponder it all the day long.
Your commands give me an edge on my enemies;
they never become obsolete.
I've even become smarter than my teachers
since I've pondered and absorbed your counsel.
I've become wiser than the wise old sages
simply by doing what you tell me.
I watch my step, avoiding the ditches and ruts of evil
so I can spend all my time keeping your Word.
I never make detours from the route you laid out;
you gave me such good directions.
Your words are so choice, so tasty;
I prefer them to the best home cooking.
With your instruction, I understand life;
that's why I hate false propaganda.

105-112 By your words I can see where I'm going;
they throw a beam of light on my dark path.
I've committed myself and I'll never turn back
from living by your righteous order.
Everything's falling apart on me, GOD;
put me together again with your Word.
Festoon me with your finest sayings, GOD;
teach me your holy rules.
My life is as close as my own hands,
but I don't forget what you have revealed.
The wicked do their best to throw me off track,
but I don't swerve an inch from your course.
I inherited your book on living; it's mine forever—
what a gift! And how happy it makes me!
I concentrate on doing exactly what you say—
I always have and always will.

NEW KING JAMES VERSION

ס SAMEK

113I hate the double-minded,
But I love Your law.
114You *are* my hiding place and my shield;
I hope in Your word.
115Depart from me, you evildoers,
For I will keep the commandments of my God!
116Uphold me according to Your word, that I may live;
And do not let me be ashamed of my hope.
117Hold me up, and I shall be safe,
And I shall observe Your statutes continually.
118You reject all those who stray from Your statutes,
For their deceit *is* falsehood.
119You put away all the wicked of the earth *like* dross;
Therefore I love Your testimonies.
120My flesh trembles for fear of You,
And I am afraid of Your judgments.

ע AYIN

121I have done justice and righteousness;
Do not leave me to my oppressors.
122Be surety for Your servant for good;
Do not let the proud oppress me.
123My eyes fail *from seeking* Your salvation
And Your righteous word.
124Deal with Your servant according to Your mercy,
And teach me Your statutes.
125I *am* Your servant;
Give me understanding,
That I may know Your testimonies.
126*It is* time for *You* to act, O LORD,
For they have regarded Your law as void.
127Therefore I love Your commandments
More than gold, yes, than fine gold!
128Therefore all *Your* precepts *concerning* all *things*
I consider *to be* right;
I hate every false way.

פ PE

129Your testimonies are wonderful;
Therefore my soul keeps them.
130The entrance of Your words gives light;
It gives understanding to the simple.
131I opened my mouth and panted,
For I longed for Your commandments.
132Look upon me and be merciful to me,
As Your custom *is* toward those who love Your name.
133Direct my steps by Your word,
And let no iniquity have dominion over me.
134Redeem me from the oppression of man,
That I may keep Your precepts.
135Make Your face shine upon Your servant,
And teach me Your statutes.
136Rivers of water run down from my eyes,
Because *men* do not keep Your law.

THE MESSAGE

113-120 I hate the two-faced,
but I love your clear-cut revelation.
You're my place of quiet retreat;
I wait for your Word to renew me.
Get out of my life, evildoers,
so I can keep my God's commands.
Take my side as you promised; I'll live then for sure.
Don't disappoint all my grand hopes.
Stick with me and I'll be all right;
I'll give total allegiance to your definitions of life.
Expose all who drift away from your sayings;
their casual idolatry is lethal.
You reject earth's wicked as so much rubbish;
therefore I lovingly embrace everything you say.
I shiver in awe before you;
your decisions leave me speechless with reverence.

121-128 I stood up for justice and the right;
don't leave me to the mercy of my oppressors.
Take the side of your servant, good God;
don't let the godless take advantage of me.
I can't keep my eyes open any longer, waiting for you
to keep your promise to set everything right.
Let your love dictate how you deal with me;
teach me from your textbook on life.
I'm your servant—help me understand what that means,
the inner meaning of your instructions.
It's time to act, GOD;
they've made a shambles of your revelation!
Yea-Saying God, I love what you command,
I love it better than gold and gemstones;
Yea-Saying God, I honor everything you tell me,
I despise every deceitful detour.

129-136 Every word you give me is a miracle word—
how could I help but obey?
Break open your words, let the light shine out,
let ordinary people see the meaning.
Mouth open and panting,
I wanted your commands more than anything.
Turn my way, look kindly on me,
as you always do to those who personally love you.
Steady my steps with your Word of promise
so nothing malign gets the better of me.
Rescue me from the grip of bad men and women
so I can live life your way.
Smile on me, your servant;
teach me the right way to live.
I cry rivers of tears
because nobody's living by your book!

NEW KING JAMES VERSION

צ TSADDE

137Righteous *are* You, O LORD,
And upright *are* Your judgments.
138Your testimonies, *which* You have commanded,
Are righteous and very faithful.
139My zeal has consumed me,
Because my enemies have forgotten Your words.
140Your word *is* very pure;
Therefore Your servant loves it.
141I *am* small and despised,
Yet I do not forget Your precepts.
142Your righteousness *is* an everlasting righteousness,
And Your law *is* truth.
143Trouble and anguish have overtaken me,
Yet Your commandments *are* my delights.
144The righteousness of Your testimonies *is* everlasting;
Give me understanding, and I shall live.

ק QOPH

145I cry out with *my* whole heart;
Hear me, O LORD!
I will keep Your statutes.
146I cry out to You;
Save me, and I will keep Your testimonies.
147I rise before the dawning of the morning,
And cry for help;
I hope in Your word.
148My eyes are awake through the *night* watches,
That I may meditate on Your word.
149Hear my voice according to Your lovingkindness;
O LORD, revive me according to Your justice.
150They draw near who follow after wickedness;
They are far from Your law.
151You *are* near, O LORD,
And all Your commandments *are* truth.
152Concerning Your testimonies,
I have known of old that You have founded them forever.

ר RESH

153Consider my affliction and deliver me,
For I do not forget Your law.
154Plead my cause and redeem me;
Revive me according to Your word.
155Salvation *is* far from the wicked,
For they do not seek Your statutes.
156Great *are* Your tender mercies, O LORD;
Revive me according to Your judgments.
157Many *are* my persecutors and my enemies,
Yet I do not turn from Your testimonies.
158I see the treacherous, and am disgusted,
Because they do not keep Your word.
159Consider how I love Your precepts;
Revive me, O LORD, according to Your lovingkindness.
160The entirety of Your word *is* truth,
And every one of Your righteous judgments *endures* forever.

THE MESSAGE

137-144 You *are* right and you *do* right, GOD;
your decisions are right on target.
You rightly instruct us in how to live
ever faithful to you.
My rivals nearly did me in,
they persistently ignored your commandments.
Your promise has been tested through and through,
and I, your servant, love it dearly.
I'm too young to be important,
but I don't forget what you tell me.
Your righteousness is eternally right,
your revelation is the only truth.
Even though troubles came down on me hard,
your commands always gave me delight.
The way you tell me to live is always right;
help me understand it so I can live to the fullest.

145-152 I call out at the top of my lungs,
"GOD! Answer! I'll do whatever you say."
I called to you, "Save me
so I can carry out all your instructions."
I was up before sunrise,
crying for help, hoping for a word from you.
I stayed awake all night,
prayerfully pondering your promise.
In your love, listen to me;
in your justice, GOD, keep me alive.
As those out to get me come closer and closer,
they go farther and farther from the truth you reveal;
But you're the closest of all to me, GOD,
and all your judgments true.
I've known all along from the evidence of your words
that you meant them to last forever.

153-160 Take a good look at my trouble, and help me—
I haven't forgotten your revelation.
Take my side and get me out of this;
give me back my life, just as you promised.
"Salvation" is only gibberish to the wicked
because they've never looked it up in your dictionary.
Your mercies, GOD, run into the billions;
following your guidelines, revive me.
My antagonists are too many to count,
but I don't swerve from the directions you gave.
I took one look at the quitters and was filled with loathing;
they walked away from your promises so casually!
Take note of how I love what you tell me;
out of your life of love, prolong my life.
Your words all add up to the sum total: Truth.
Your righteous decisions are eternal.

NEW KING JAMES VERSION

ש SHIN
161Princes persecute me without a cause,
But my heart stands in awe of Your word.
162I rejoice at Your word
As one who finds great treasure.
163I hate and abhor lying,
But I love Your law.
164Seven times a day I praise You,
Because of Your righteous judgments.
165Great peace have those who love Your law,
And nothing causes them to stumble.
166LORD, I hope for Your salvation,
And I do Your commandments.
167My soul keeps Your testimonies,
And I love them exceedingly.
168I keep Your precepts and Your testimonies,
For all my ways *are* before You.

ת TAU
169Let my cry come before You, O LORD;
Give me understanding according to Your word.
170Let my supplication come before You;
Deliver me according to Your word.
171My lips shall utter praise,
For You teach me Your statutes.
172My tongue shall speak of Your word,
For all Your commandments *are* righteousness.
173Let Your hand become my help,
For I have chosen Your precepts.
174I long for Your salvation, O LORD,
And Your law *is* my delight.
175Let my soul live, and it shall praise You;
And let Your judgments help me.
176I have gone astray like a lost sheep;
Seek Your servant,
For I do not forget Your commandments.

PSALM 120

PLEA FOR RELIEF FROM BITTER FOES

A Song of Ascents.

1In my distress I cried to the LORD,
And He heard me.
2Deliver my soul, O LORD, from lying lips
And from a deceitful tongue.

3What shall be given to you,
Or what shall be done to you,
You false tongue?
4Sharp arrows of the warrior,
With coals of the broom tree!

5Woe is me, that I dwell in Meshech,
That I dwell among the tents of Kedar!

THE MESSAGE

161-168 I've been slandered unmercifully by the politicians,
but my awe at your words keeps me stable.
I'm ecstatic over what you say,
like one who strikes it rich.
I hate lies—can't stand them!—
but I love what you have revealed.
Seven times each day I stop and shout praises
for the way you keep everything running right.
For those who love what you reveal, everything fits—
no stumbling around in the dark for them.
I wait expectantly for your salvation;
GOD, I do what you tell me.
My soul guards and keeps all your instructions—
oh, how much I love them!
I follow your directions, abide by your counsel;
my life's an open book before you.

169-176 Let my cry come right into your presence, GOD;
provide me with the insight that comes only from your Word.
Give my request your personal attention,
rescue me on the terms of your promise.
Let praise cascade off my lips;
after all, you've taught me the truth about life!
And let your promises ring from my tongue;
every order you've given is right.
Put your hand out and steady me
since I've chosen to live by your counsel.
I'm homesick, GOD, for your salvation;
I love it when you show yourself!
Invigorate my soul so I can praise you well,
use your decrees to put iron in my soul.
And should I wander off like a lost sheep—seek me!
I'll recognize the sound of your voice.

A PILGRIM SONG

1-2 **120** I'm in trouble. I cry to GOD,
desperate for an answer:
"Deliver me from the liars, GOD!
They smile so sweetly but lie through their teeth."

3-4 Do you know what's next, can you see what's coming,
all you barefaced liars?
Pointed arrows and burning coals
will be your reward.

5-7 I'm doomed to live in Meshech,
cursed with a home in Kedar,

NEW KING JAMES VERSION

6My soul has dwelt too long
With one who hates peace.
7I *am for* peace;
But when I speak, they *are* for war.

PSALM 121

GOD THE HELP OF THOSE WHO SEEK HIM
A Song of Ascents.

1I will lift up my eyes to the hills—
From whence comes my help?
2My help *comes* from the LORD,
Who made heaven and earth.

3He will not allow your foot to be moved;
He who keeps you will not slumber.
4Behold, He who keeps Israel
Shall neither slumber nor sleep.

5The LORD *is* your keeper;
The LORD *is* your shade at your right hand.
6The sun shall not strike you by day,
Nor the moon by night.

7The LORD shall preserve you from all evil;
He shall preserve your soul.
8The LORD shall preserve your going out and your coming in
From this time forth, and even forevermore.

PSALM 122

THE JOY OF GOING TO THE HOUSE OF THE LORD
A Song of Ascents. Of David.

1I was glad when they said to me,
"Let us go into the house of the LORD."
2Our feet have been standing
Within your gates, O Jerusalem!

3Jerusalem is built
As a city that is compact together,
4Where the tribes go up,
The tribes of the LORD,
To the Testimony of Israel,
To give thanks to the name of the LORD.
5For thrones are set there for judgment,
The thrones of the house of David.

6Pray for the peace of Jerusalem:
"May they prosper who love you.
7Peace be within your walls,
Prosperity within your palaces."
8For the sake of my brethren and companions,
I will now say, "Peace *be* within you."
9Because of the house of the LORD our God
I will seek your good.

PSALM 123

PRAYER FOR RELIEF FROM CONTEMPT
A Song of Ascents.

1Unto You I lift up my eyes,
O You who dwell in the heavens.
2Behold, as the eyes of servants *look* to the hand of their masters,
As the eyes of a maid to the hand of her mistress,

THE MESSAGE

My whole life lived camping
among quarreling neighbors.
I'm all for peace, but the minute
I tell them so, they go to war!

A PILGRIM SONG

1-2 **121** I look up to the mountains;
does my strength come from mountains?
No, my strength comes from GOD,
who made heaven, and earth, and mountains.

3-4 He won't let you stumble,
your Guardian God won't fall asleep.
Not on your life! Israel's
Guardian will never doze or sleep.

5-6 GOD's your Guardian,
right at your side to protect you—
Shielding you from sunstroke,
sheltering you from moonstroke.

7-8 GOD guards you from every evil,
he guards your very life.
He guards you when you leave and when you return,
he guards you now, he guards you always.

A PILGRIM SONG OF DAVID

1-2 **122** When they said, "Let's go to the house of GOD,"
my heart leaped for joy.
And now we're here, O Jerusalem,
inside Jerusalem's walls!

3-5 Jerusalem, well-built city,
built as a place for worship!
The city to which the tribes ascend,
all GOD's tribes go up to worship,
To give thanks to the name of GOD—
this is what it means to be Israel.
Thrones for righteous judgment
are set there, famous David-thrones.

6-9 Pray for Jerusalem's peace!
Prosperity to all you Jerusalem-lovers!
Friendly insiders, get along!
Hostile outsiders, keep your distance!
For the sake of my family and friends,
I say it again: live in peace!
For the sake of the house of our God, GOD,
I'll do my very best for you.

A PILGRIM SONG

1-4 **123** I look to you, heaven-dwelling God,
look up to you for help.
Like servants, alert to their master's commands,
like a maiden attending her lady,

NEW KING JAMES VERSION

So our eyes *look* to the LORD our God,
Until He has mercy on us.

3Have mercy on us, O LORD, have mercy on us!
For we are exceedingly filled with contempt.
4Our soul is exceedingly filled
With the scorn of those who are at ease,
With the contempt of the proud.

PSALM 124

THE LORD THE DEFENSE OF HIS PEOPLE

A Song of Ascents. Of David.

1"If it had not been the LORD who was on our side,"
Let Israel now say—
2"If it had not been the LORD who was on our side,
When men rose up against us,
3Then they would have swallowed us alive,
When their wrath was kindled against us;
4Then the waters would have overwhelmed us,
The stream would have gone over our soul;
5Then the swollen waters
Would have gone over our soul."

6Blessed *be* the LORD,
Who has not given us *as* prey to their teeth.
7Our soul has escaped as a bird from the snare of the fowlers;[a]
The snare is broken, and we have escaped.
8Our help *is* in the name of the LORD,
Who made heaven and earth.

PSALM 125

THE LORD THE STRENGTH OF HIS PEOPLE

A Song of Ascents.

1Those who trust in the LORD
Are like Mount Zion,
Which cannot be moved, *but* abides forever.
2As the mountains surround Jerusalem,
So the LORD surrounds His people
From this time forth and forever.

3For the scepter of wickedness shall not rest
On the land allotted to the righteous,
Lest the righteous reach out their hands to iniquity.

4Do good, O LORD, to *those who are* good,
And to *those who are* upright in their hearts.

5As for such as turn aside to their crooked ways,
The LORD shall lead them away
With the workers of iniquity.

Peace *be* upon Israel!

124:7 [a]That is, persons who catch birds in a trap or snare

THE MESSAGE

We're watching and waiting, holding our breath,
awaiting your word of mercy.
Mercy, GOD, mercy!
We've been kicked around long enough,
Kicked in the teeth by complacent rich men,
kicked when we're down by arrogant brutes.

A PILGRIM SONG OF DAVID

1-5 **124** If GOD hadn't been for us
—all together now, Israel, sing out!—
If GOD hadn't been for us
when everyone went against us,
We would have been swallowed alive
by their violent anger,
Swept away by the flood of rage,
drowned in the torrent;
We would have lost our lives
in the wild, raging water.

6 Oh, blessed be GOD!
He didn't go off and leave us.
He didn't abandon us defenseless,
helpless as a rabbit in a pack of snarling dogs.

7 We've flown free from their fangs,
free of their traps, free as a bird.
Their grip is broken;
we're free as a bird in flight.

8 GOD's strong name is our help,
the same GOD who made heaven and earth.

A PILGRIM SONG

1-5 **125** Those who trust in GOD
are like Zion Mountain:
Nothing can move it, a rock-solid mountain
you can always depend on.
Mountains encircle Jerusalem,
and GOD encircles his people—
always has and always will.
The fist of the wicked
will never violate
What is due the righteous,
provoking wrongful violence.
Be good to your good people, GOD,
to those whose hearts are right!
GOD will round up the backsliders,
corral them with the incorrigibles.
Peace over Israel!

New King James Version

PSALM 126

A Joyful Return to Zion

A Song of Ascents.

1When the LORD brought back the captivity
of Zion,
We were like those who dream.
2Then our mouth was filled with laughter,
And our tongue with singing.
Then they said among the nations,
"The LORD has done great things for them."
3The LORD has done great things for us,
And we are glad.

4Bring back our captivity, O LORD,
As the streams in the South.

5Those who sow in tears
Shall reap in joy.
6He who continually goes forth weeping,
Bearing seed for sowing,
Shall doubtless come again with rejoicing,
Bringing his sheaves *with him.*

PSALM 127

Laboring and Prospering with the Lord

A Song of Ascents. Of Solomon.

1Unless the LORD builds the house,
They labor in vain who build it;
Unless the LORD guards the city,
The watchman stays awake in vain.
2*It is* vain for you to rise up early,
To sit up late,
To eat the bread of sorrows;
For so He gives His beloved sleep.

3Behold, children *are* a heritage from the
LORD,
The fruit of the womb *is* a reward.
4Like arrows in the hand of a warrior,
So *are* the children of one's youth.
5Happy *is* the man who has his quiver full of
them;
They shall not be ashamed,
But shall speak with their enemies in the
gate.

PSALM 128

Blessings of Those Who Fear the Lord

A Song of Ascents.

1Blessed *is* every one who fears the LORD,
Who walks in His ways.

2When you eat the labor of your hands,
You *shall be* happy, and *it shall be* well with
you.
3Your wife *shall be* like a fruitful vine
In the very heart of your house,
Your children like olive plants
All around your table.
4Behold, thus shall the man be blessed
Who fears the LORD.

The Message

A Pilgrim Song

1-3 **126** It seemed like a dream, too good to
be true,
when GOD returned Zion's exiles.
We laughed, we sang,
we couldn't believe our good fortune.
We were the talk of the nations—
"GOD was wonderful to them!"
GOD *was* wonderful to us;
we are one happy people.

4-6 And now, GOD, do it again—
bring rains to our drought-stricken lives
So those who planted their crops in despair
will shout hurrahs at the harvest,
So those who went off with heavy hearts
will come home laughing, with armloads
of blessing.

A Pilgrim Song of Solomon

1-2 **127** If GOD doesn't build the house,
the builders only build shacks.
If GOD doesn't guard the city,
the night watchman might as well nap.
It's useless to rise early and go to bed late,
and work your worried fingers to the
bone.
Don't you know he enjoys
giving rest to those he loves?

3-5 Don't you see that children are GOD's best
gift?
the fruit of the womb his generous
legacy?
Like a warrior's fistful of arrows
are the children of a vigorous youth.
Oh, how blessed are you parents,
with your quivers full of children!
Your enemies don't stand a chance against
you;
you'll sweep them right off your
doorstep.

A Pilgrim Song

1-2 **128** All you who fear GOD, how blessed
you are!
how happily you walk on his smooth
straight road!
You worked hard and deserve all you've got
coming.
Enjoy the blessing! Revel in the
goodness!

3-4 Your wife will bear children as a vine bears
grapes,
your household lush as a vineyard,
The children around your table
as fresh and promising as young olive
shoots.
Stand in awe of God's Yes.
Oh, how he blesses the one who fears
GOD!

NEW KING JAMES VERSION

5The LORD bless you out of Zion,
And may you see the good of Jerusalem
All the days of your life.
6Yes, may you see your children's children.

Peace *be* upon Israel!

PSALM 129

SONG OF VICTORY OVER ZION'S ENEMIES

A Song of Ascents.

1"Many a time they have afflicted me from my youth,"
Let Israel now say—
2"Many a time they have afflicted me from my youth;
Yet they have not prevailed against me.
3The plowers plowed on my back;
They made their furrows long."
4The LORD *is* righteous;
He has cut in pieces the cords of the wicked.

5Let all those who hate Zion
Be put to shame and turned back.
6Let them be as the grass *on* the housetops,
Which withers before it grows up,
7With which the reaper does not fill his hand,
Nor he who binds sheaves, his arms.
8Neither let those who pass by them say,
"The blessing of the LORD *be* upon you;
We bless you in the name of the LORD!"

PSALM 130

WAITING FOR THE REDEMPTION OF THE LORD

A Song of Ascents.

1Out of the depths I have cried to You,
O LORD;
2Lord, hear my voice!
Let Your ears be attentive
To the voice of my supplications.

3If You, LORD, should mark iniquities,
O Lord, who could stand?
4But *there is* forgiveness with You,
That You may be feared.

5I wait for the LORD, my soul waits,
And in His word I do hope.
6My soul *waits* for the Lord
More than those who watch for the morning—
Yes, more than those who watch for the morning.

7O Israel, hope in the LORD;
For with the LORD *there is* mercy,
And with Him *is* abundant redemption.
8And He shall redeem Israel
From all his iniquities.

PSALM 131

SIMPLE TRUST IN THE LORD

A Song of Ascents. Of David.

1LORD, my heart is not haughty,
Nor my eyes lofty.
Neither do I concern myself with great matters,
Nor with things too profound for me.

THE MESSAGE

5-6 Enjoy the good life in Jerusalem
every day of your life.
And enjoy your grandchildren.
Peace to Israel!

A PILGRIM SONG

1-4 129 "They've kicked me around ever since I was young"
—this is how Israel tells it—
"They've kicked me around ever since I was young,
but they never could keep me down.
Their plowmen plowed long furrows
up and down my back;
Then GOD ripped the harnesses
of the evil plowmen to shreds."

5-8 Oh, let all those who hate Zion
grovel in humiliation;
Let them be like grass in shallow ground
that withers before the harvest,
Before the farmhands can gather it in,
the harvesters get in the crop,
Before the neighbors have a chance to call out,
"Congratulations on your wonderful crop!
We bless you in GOD's name!"

A PILGRIM SONG

1-2 130 Help, GOD—the bottom has fallen out of my life!
Master, hear my cry for help!
Listen hard! Open your ears!
Listen to my cries for mercy.

3-4 If you, GOD, kept records on wrongdoings,
who would stand a chance?
As it turns out, forgiveness is your habit,
and that's why you're worshiped.

5-6 I pray to GOD—my life a prayer—
and wait for what he'll say and do.
My life's on the line before God, my Lord,
waiting and watching till morning,
waiting and watching till morning.

7-8 O Israel, wait and watch for GOD—
with GOD's arrival comes love,
with GOD's arrival comes generous redemption.
No doubt about it—he'll redeem Israel,
buy back Israel from captivity to sin.

A PILGRIM SONG

1 131 GOD, I'm not trying to rule the roost,
I don't want to be king of the mountain.
I haven't meddled where I have no business
or fantasized grandiose plans.

NEW KING JAMES VERSION

2Surely I have calmed and quieted my soul,
Like a weaned child with his mother;
Like a weaned child *is* my soul within me.

3O Israel, hope in the LORD
From this time forth and forever.

PSALM 132

THE ETERNAL DWELLING OF GOD IN ZION
A Song of Ascents.

1LORD, remember David
And all his afflictions;
2How he swore to the LORD,
And vowed to the Mighty One of Jacob:
3"Surely I will not go into the chamber of my house,
Or go up to the comfort of my bed;
4I will not give sleep to my eyes
Or slumber to my eyelids,
5Until I find a place for the LORD,
A dwelling place for the Mighty One of Jacob."

6Behold, we heard of it in Ephrathah;
We found it in the fields of the woods.[a]
7Let us go into His tabernacle;
Let us worship at His footstool.
8Arise, O LORD, to Your resting place,
You and the ark of Your strength.
9Let Your priests be clothed with righteousness,
And let Your saints shout for joy.

10For Your servant David's sake,
Do not turn away the face of Your Anointed.

11The LORD has sworn *in* truth to David;
He will not turn from it:
"I will set upon your throne the fruit of your body.
12If your sons will keep My covenant
And My testimony which I shall teach them,
Their sons also shall sit upon your throne forevermore."

13For the LORD has chosen Zion;
He has desired *it* for His dwelling place:
14"This *is* My resting place forever;
Here I will dwell, for I have desired it.
15I will abundantly bless her provision;
I will satisfy her poor with bread.
16I will also clothe her priests with salvation,
And her saints shall shout aloud for joy.
17There I will make the horn of David grow;
I will prepare a lamp for My Anointed.
18His enemies I will clothe with shame,
But upon Himself His crown shall flourish."

PSALM 133

BLESSED UNITY OF THE PEOPLE OF GOD
A Song of Ascents. Of David.

1Behold, how good and how pleasant *it is*
For brethren to dwell together in unity!

132:6 [a]Hebrew *Jaar*

THE MESSAGE

2 I've kept my feet on the ground,
I've cultivated a quiet heart.
Like a baby content in its mother's arms,
my soul is a baby content.

3 Wait, Israel, for GOD. Wait with hope.
Hope now; hope always!

A PILGRIM SONG

1-5 **132** O GOD, remember David,
remember all his troubles!
And remember how he promised GOD,
made a vow to the Strong God of Jacob,
"I'm not going home,
and I'm not going to bed,
I'm not going to sleep,
not even take time to rest,
Until I find a home for GOD,
a house for the Strong God of Jacob."

6-7 Remember how we got the news in Ephrathah,
learned all about it at Jaar Meadows?
We shouted, "Let's go to the shrine dedication!
Let's worship at God's own footstool!"

8-10 Up, GOD, enjoy your new place of quiet repose,
you and your mighty covenant ark;
Get your priests all dressed up in justice;
prompt your worshipers to sing this prayer:
"Honor your servant David;
don't disdain your anointed one."

11-18 GOD gave David his word,
he won't back out on this promise:
"One of your sons
I will set on your throne;
If your sons stay true to my Covenant
and learn to live the way I teach them,
Their sons will continue the line—
always a son to sit on your throne.
Yes—I, GOD, chose Zion,
the place I wanted for my shrine;
This will always be my home;
this is what I want, and I'm here for good.
I'll shower blessings on the pilgrims who come here,
and give supper to those who arrive hungry;
I'll dress my priests in salvation clothes;
the holy people will sing their hearts out!
Oh, I'll make the place radiant for David!
I'll fill it with light for my anointed!
I'll dress his enemies in dirty rags,
but I'll make his crown sparkle with splendor."

A PILGRIM SONG OF DAVID

1-3 **133** How wonderful, how beautiful,
when brothers and sisters get along!

NEW KING JAMES VERSION

2*It is* like the precious oil upon the head,
Running down on the beard,
The beard of Aaron,

Running down on the edge of his garments.
3*It is* like the dew of Hermon,
Descending upon the mountains of Zion;
For there the LORD commanded the blessing—
Life forevermore.

PSALM 134

PRAISING THE LORD IN HIS HOUSE AT NIGHT
A Song of Ascents.

1Behold, bless the LORD,
All *you* servants of the LORD,
Who by night stand in the house of the LORD!
2Lift up your hands *in* the sanctuary,
And bless the LORD.
3The LORD who made heaven and earth
Bless you from Zion!

PSALM 135

PRAISE TO GOD IN CREATION AND REDEMPTION

1Praise the LORD!

Praise the name of the LORD;
Praise *Him,* O you servants of the LORD!
2You who stand in the house of the LORD,
In the courts of the house of our God,
3Praise the LORD, for the LORD *is* good;
Sing praises to His name, for *it is* pleasant.
4For the LORD has chosen Jacob for Himself,
Israel for His special treasure.

5For I know that the LORD *is* great,
And our Lord *is* above all gods.
6Whatever the LORD pleases He does,
In heaven and in earth,
In the seas and in all deep places.
7He causes the vapors to ascend from the ends of the earth;
He makes lightning for the rain;
He brings the wind out of His treasuries.

8He destroyed the firstborn of Egypt,
Both of man and beast.
9He sent signs and wonders into the midst of you, O Egypt,
Upon Pharaoh and all his servants.
10He defeated many nations
And slew mighty kings—
11Sihon king of the Amorites,
Og king of Bashan,
And all the kingdoms of Canaan—
12And gave their land *as* a heritage,
A heritage to Israel His people.

13Your name, O LORD, *endures* forever,
Your fame, O LORD, throughout all generations.
14For the LORD will judge His people,
And He will have compassion on His servants.

THE MESSAGE

It's like costly anointing oil
flowing down head and beard,
Flowing down Aaron's beard,
flowing down the collar of his priestly robes.
It's like the dew on Mount Hermon
flowing down the slopes of Zion.
Yes, that's where GOD commands the blessing,
ordains eternal life.

A PILGRIM SONG

1-3 **134** Come, bless GOD,
all you servants of GOD!
You priests of GOD, posted to the nightwatch
in GOD's shrine,
Lift your praising hands to the Holy Place,
and bless GOD.
In turn, may GOD of Zion bless you—
GOD who made heaven and earth!

1-4 **135** Hallelujah!
Praise the name of GOD,
praise the works of GOD.
All you priests on duty in GOD's temple,
serving in the sacred halls of our God,
Shout "Hallelujah!" because GOD's so good,
sing anthems to his beautiful name.
And why? Because GOD chose Jacob,
embraced Israel as a prize possession.

5-12 I, too, give witness to the greatness of GOD,
our Lord, high above all other gods.
He does just as he pleases—
however, wherever, whenever.
He makes the weather—clouds and thunder,
lightning and rain, wind pouring out of the north.
He struck down the Egyptian firstborn,
both human and animal firstborn.
He made Egypt sit up and take notice,
confronted Pharaoh and his servants with miracles.
Yes, he struck down great nations,
he slew mighty kings—
Sihon king of the Amorites, also Og of Bashan—
every last one of the Canaanite kings!
Then he turned their land over to Israel,
a gift of good land to his people.

13-18 GOD, your name is eternal,
GOD, you'll never be out-of-date.
GOD stands up for his people,
GOD holds the hands of his people.

NEW KING JAMES VERSION

15The idols of the nations *are* silver and gold,
The work of men's hands.
16They have mouths, but they do not speak;
Eyes they have, but they do not see;
17They have ears, but they do not hear;
Nor is there *any* breath in their mouths.
18Those who make them are like them;
So is everyone who trusts in them.

19Bless the LORD, O house of Israel!
Bless the LORD, O house of Aaron!
20Bless the LORD, O house of Levi!
You who fear the LORD, bless the LORD!
21Blessed be the LORD out of Zion,
Who dwells in Jerusalem!

Praise the LORD!

PSALM 136

THANKSGIVING TO GOD FOR HIS ENDURING MERCY

1Oh, give thanks to the LORD, for *He is* good!
For His mercy *endures* forever.
2Oh, give thanks to the God of gods!
For His mercy *endures* forever.
3Oh, give thanks to the Lord of lords!
For His mercy *endures* forever:

4To Him who alone does great wonders,
For His mercy *endures* forever;
5To Him who by wisdom made the heavens,
For His mercy *endures* forever;
6To Him who laid out the earth above the waters,
For His mercy *endures* forever;
7To Him who made great lights,
For His mercy *endures* forever—
8The sun to rule by day,
For His mercy *endures* forever;
9The moon and stars to rule by night,
For His mercy *endures* forever.

10To Him who struck Egypt in their firstborn,
For His mercy *endures* forever;
11And brought out Israel from among them,
For His mercy *endures* forever;
12With a strong hand, and with an outstretched arm,
For His mercy *endures* forever;
13To Him who divided the Red Sea in two,
For His mercy *endures* forever;
14And made Israel pass through the midst of it,
For His mercy *endures* forever;
15But overthrew Pharaoh and his army in the Red Sea,
For His mercy *endures* forever;
16To Him who led His people through the wilderness,
For His mercy *endures* forever;
17To Him who struck down great kings,
For His mercy *endures* forever;
18And slew famous kings,
For His mercy *endures* forever—
19Sihon king of the Amorites,
For His mercy *endures* forever;
20And Og king of Bashan,
For His mercy *endures* forever—
21And gave their land as a heritage,
For His mercy *endures* forever;

THE MESSAGE

The gods of the godless nations are mere trinkets,
made for quick sale in the markets:
Chiseled mouths that can't talk,
painted eyes that can't see,
Carved ears that can't hear—
dead wood! cold metal!
Those who make and trust them
become like them.

19-21 Family of Israel, bless GOD!
Family of Aaron, bless GOD!
Family of Levi, bless GOD!
You who fear GOD, bless GOD!
Oh, blessed be GOD of Zion,
First Citizen of Jerusalem!
Hallelujah!

1-3 **136** Thank GOD! He deserves your thanks.
His love never quits.
Thank the God of all gods,
His love never quits.
Thank the Lord of all lords.
His love never quits.

4-22 Thank the miracle-working God,
His love never quits.
The God whose skill formed the cosmos,
His love never quits.
The God who laid out earth on ocean foundations,
His love never quits.
The God who filled the skies with light,
His love never quits.
The sun to watch over the day,
His love never quits.
Moon and stars as guardians of the night,
His love never quits.
The God who struck down the Egyptian firstborn,
His love never quits.
And rescued Israel from Egypt's oppression,
His love never quits.
Took Israel in hand with his powerful hand,
His love never quits.
Split the Red Sea right in half,
His love never quits.
Led Israel right through the middle,
His love never quits.
Dumped Pharaoh and his army in the sea,
His love never quits.
The God who marched his people through the desert,
His love never quits.
Smashed huge kingdoms right and left,
His love never quits.
Struck down the famous kings,
His love never quits.
Struck Sihon the Amorite king,
His love never quits.
Struck Og the Bashanite king,
His love never quits.
Then distributed their land as booty,
His love never quits.

NEW KING JAMES VERSION

22A heritage to Israel His servant,
For His mercy *endures* forever.

23Who remembered us in our lowly state,
For His mercy *endures* forever;
24And rescued us from our enemies,
For His mercy *endures* forever;
25Who gives food to all flesh,
For His mercy *endures* forever.

26Oh, give thanks to the God of heaven!
For His mercy *endures* forever.

PSALM 137

LONGING FOR ZION IN A FOREIGN LAND

1By the rivers of Babylon,
There we sat down, yea, we wept
When we remembered Zion.
2We hung our harps
Upon the willows in the midst of it.
3For there those who carried us away captive
asked of us a song,
And those who plundered us *requested*
mirth,
Saying, "Sing us *one* of the songs of Zion!"

4How shall we sing the LORD's song
In a foreign land?
5If I forget you, O Jerusalem,
Let my right hand forget *its skill!*
6If I do not remember you,
Let my tongue cling to the roof of my
mouth—
If I do not exalt Jerusalem
Above my chief joy.

7Remember, O LORD, against the sons of
Edom
The day of Jerusalem,
Who said, "Raze *it*, raze *it*,
To its very foundation!"

8O daughter of Babylon, who are to be
destroyed,
Happy the one who repays you as you have
served us!
9Happy the one who takes and dashes
Your little ones against the rock!

PSALM 138

THE LORD'S GOODNESS TO THE FAITHFUL

A Psalm of David.

1I will praise You with my whole heart;
Before the gods I will sing praises to You.
2I will worship toward Your holy temple,
And praise Your name
For Your lovingkindness and Your truth;
For You have magnified Your word above all
Your name.
3In the day when I cried out, You answered
me,
And made me bold *with* strength in my soul.

4All the kings of the earth shall praise You,
O LORD,
When they hear the words of Your mouth.
5Yes, they shall sing of the ways of the LORD,
For great *is* the glory of the LORD.

THE MESSAGE

Handed the land over to Israel.
His love never quits.

23-26 God remembered us when we were down,
His love never quits.
Rescued us from the trampling boot,
His love never quits.
Takes care of everyone in time of need.
His love never quits.
Thank God, who did it all!
His love never quits!

1-3 **137** Alongside Babylon's rivers
we sat on the banks; we cried
and cried,
remembering the good old days in Zion.
Alongside the quaking aspens
we stacked our unplayed harps;
That's where our captors demanded songs,
sarcastic and mocking:
"Sing us a happy Zion song!"

4-6 Oh, how could we ever sing GOD's song
in this wasteland?
If I ever forget you, Jerusalem,
let my fingers wither and fall off like
leaves.
Let my tongue swell and turn black
if I fail to remember you,
If I fail, O dear Jerusalem,
to honor you as my greatest.

7-9 GOD, remember those Edomites,
and remember the ruin of Jerusalem,
That day they yelled out,
"Wreck it, smash it to bits!"
And you, Babylonians—ravagers!
A reward to whoever gets back at you
for all you've done to us;
Yes, a reward to the one who grabs your
babies
and smashes their heads on the rocks!

A DAVID PSALM

1-3 **138** Thank you! Everything in me says
"Thank you!"
Angels listen as I sing my thanks.
I kneel in worship facing your holy temple
and say it again: "Thank you!"
Thank you for your love,
thank you for your faithfulness;
Most holy is your name,
most holy is your Word.
The moment I called out, you stepped in;
you made my life large with strength.

4-6 When they hear what you have to say, GOD,
all earth's kings will say "Thank you."
They'll sing of what you've done:
"How great the glory of GOD!"

NEW KING JAMES VERSION

6Though the LORD *is* on high,
Yet He regards the lowly;
But the proud He knows from afar.

7Though I walk in the midst of trouble, You will revive me;
You will stretch out Your hand
Against the wrath of my enemies,
And Your right hand will save me.
8The LORD will perfect *that which* concerns me;
Your mercy, O LORD, *endures* forever;
Do not forsake the works of Your hands.

PSALM 139

GOD'S PERFECT KNOWLEDGE OF MAN

For the Chief Musician. A Psalm of David.

1O LORD, You have searched me and known *me*.
2You know my sitting down and my rising up;
You understand my thought afar off.
3You comprehend my path and my lying down,
And are acquainted with all my ways.
4For *there is* not a word on my tongue,
But behold, O LORD, You know it altogether.
5You have hedged me behind and before,
And laid Your hand upon me.
6*Such* knowledge *is* too wonderful for me;
It is high, I cannot *attain* it.

7Where can I go from Your Spirit?
Or where can I flee from Your presence?
8If I ascend into heaven, You *are* there;
If I make my bed in hell, behold, You *are* there.
9*If* I take the wings of the morning,
And dwell in the uttermost parts of the sea,
10Even there Your hand shall lead me,
And Your right hand shall hold me.
11If I say, "Surely the darkness shall fall[a] on me,"
Even the night shall be light about me;
12Indeed, the darkness shall not hide from You,
But the night shines as the day;
The darkness and the light *are* both alike *to You*.

13For You formed my inward parts;
You covered me in my mother's womb.
14I will praise You, for I am fearfully *and* wonderfully made;[a]
Marvelous are Your works,
And *that* my soul knows very well.
15My frame was not hidden from You,
When I was made in secret,
And skillfully wrought in the lowest parts of the earth.
16Your eyes saw my substance, being yet unformed.

139:11 [a]Vulgate and Symmachus read *cover.* **139:14** [a]Following Masoretic Text and Targum; Septuagint, Syriac, and Vulgate read *You are fearfully wonderful.*

THE MESSAGE

And here's why: GOD, high above, sees far below;
no matter the distance, he knows everything about us.

7-8 When I walk into the thick of trouble,
keep me alive in the angry turmoil.
With one hand
strike my foes,
With your other hand
save me.
Finish what you started in me, GOD.
Your love is eternal—don't quit on me now.

A DAVID PSALM

1-6 **139** GOD, investigate my life;
get all the facts firsthand.
I'm an open book to you;
even from a distance, you know what I'm thinking.
You know when I leave and when I get back;
I'm never out of your sight.
You know everything I'm going to say
before I start the first sentence.
I look behind me and you're there,
then up ahead and you're there, too—
your reassuring presence, coming and going.
This is too much, too wonderful—
I can't take it all in!

7-12 Is there anyplace I can go to avoid your Spirit?
to be out of your sight?
If I climb to the sky, you're there!
If I go underground, you're there!
If I flew on morning's wings
to the far western horizon,
You'd find me in a minute—
you're already there waiting!
Then I said to myself, "Oh, he even sees me in the dark!
At night I'm immersed in the light!"
It's a fact: darkness isn't dark to you;
night and day, darkness and light,
they're all the same to you.

13-16 Oh yes, you shaped me first inside, then out;
you formed me in my mother's womb.
I thank you, High God—you're breathtaking!
Body and soul, I am marvelously made!
I worship in adoration—what a creation!
You know me inside and out,
you know every bone in my body;
You know exactly how I was made, bit by bit,
how I was sculpted from nothing into something.
Like an open book, you watched me grow
from conception to birth;

NEW KING JAMES VERSION

And in Your book they all were written,
The days fashioned for me,
When *as yet there were* none of them.

17How precious also are Your thoughts to me, O God!
How great is the sum of them!
18*If* I should count them, they would be more in number than the sand;
When I awake, I am still with You.

19Oh, that You would slay the wicked, O God!
Depart from me, therefore, you bloodthirsty men.
20For they speak against You wickedly;
Your enemies take *Your name* in vain.[a]
21Do I not hate them, O LORD, who hate You?
And do I not loathe those who rise up against You?
22I hate them with perfect hatred;
I count them my enemies.

23Search me, O God, and know my heart;
Try me, and know my anxieties;
24And see if *there is any* wicked way in me,
And lead me in the way everlasting.

PSALM 140

PRAYER FOR DELIVERANCE FROM EVIL MEN
To the Chief Musician. A Psalm of David.

1Deliver me, O LORD, from evil men;
Preserve me from violent men,
2Who plan evil things in *their* hearts;
They continually gather together *for* war.
3They sharpen their tongues like a serpent;
The poison of asps *is* under their lips. *Selah*

4Keep me, O LORD, from the hands of the wicked;
Preserve me from violent men,
Who have purposed to make my steps stumble.
5The proud have hidden a snare for me, and cords;
They have spread a net by the wayside;
They have set traps for me. *Selah*

6I said to the LORD: "You *are* my God;
Hear the voice of my supplications, O LORD.
7O GOD the Lord, the strength of my salvation,
You have covered my head in the day of battle.
8Do not grant, O LORD, the desires of the wicked;
Do not further his *wicked* scheme,
Lest they be exalted. *Selah*

9"*As for* the head of those who surround me,
Let the evil of their lips cover them;

139:20 [a]Septuagint and Vulgate read *They take your cities in vain.*

THE MESSAGE

all the stages of my life were spread out before you,
The days of my life all prepared before I'd even lived one day.

17-22 Your thoughts—how rare, how beautiful!
God, I'll never comprehend them!
I couldn't even begin to count them—
any more than I could count the sand of the sea.
Oh, let me rise in the morning and live always with you!
And please, God, do away with wickedness for good!
And you murderers—out of here!—
all the men and women who belittle you, God,
infatuated with cheap god-imitations.
See how I hate those who hate you, GOD,
see how I loathe all this godless arrogance;
I hate it with pure, unadulterated hatred.
Your enemies are my enemies!

23-24 Investigate my life, O God,
find out everything about me;
Cross-examine and test me,
get a clear picture of what I'm about;
See for yourself whether I've done anything wrong—
then guide me on the road to eternal life.

A DAVID PSALM

1-5 **140** GOD, get me out of here, away from this evil;
protect me from these vicious people.
All they do is think up new ways to be bad;
they spend their days plotting war games.
They practice the sharp rhetoric of hate and hurt,
speak venomous words that maim and kill.
GOD, keep me out of the clutch of these wicked ones,
protect me from these vicious people;
Stuffed with self-importance, they plot ways to trip me up,
determined to bring me down.
These crooks invent traps to catch me
and do their best to incriminate me.

6-8 I prayed, "GOD, you're my God!
Listen, GOD! Mercy!
GOD, my Lord, Strong Savior,
protect me when the fighting breaks out!
Don't let the wicked have their way, GOD,
don't give them an inch!"

9-11 These troublemakers all around me—
let them drown in their own verbal poison.

NEW KING JAMES VERSION

[10]Let burning coals fall upon them;
Let them be cast into the fire,
Into deep pits, that they rise not up again.
[11]Let not a slanderer be established in the earth;
Let evil hunt the violent man to overthrow *him*."

[12]I know that the LORD will maintain
The cause of the afflicted,
And justice for the poor.
[13]Surely the righteous shall give thanks to Your name;
The upright shall dwell in Your presence.

PSALM 141

PRAYER FOR SAFEKEEPING FROM WICKEDNESS

A Psalm of David.

[1]LORD, I cry out to You;
Make haste to me!
Give ear to my voice when I cry out to You.
[2]Let my prayer be set before You *as* incense,
The lifting up of my hands *as* the evening sacrifice.
[3]Set a guard, O LORD, over my mouth;
Keep watch over the door of my lips.
[4]Do not incline my heart to any evil thing,
To practice wicked works
With men who work iniquity;
And do not let me eat of their delicacies.

[5]Let the righteous strike me;
It shall be a kindness.
And let him rebuke me;
It shall be as excellent oil;
Let my head not refuse it.

For still my prayer *is* against the deeds of the wicked.
[6]Their judges are overthrown by the sides of the cliff,
And they hear my words, for they are sweet.
[7]Our bones are scattered at the mouth of the grave,
As when one plows and breaks up the earth.

[8]But my eyes *are* upon You, O GOD the Lord;
In You I take refuge;
Do not leave my soul destitute.
[9]Keep me from the snares they have laid for me,
And from the traps of the workers of iniquity.
[10]Let the wicked fall into their own nets,
While I escape safely.

PSALM 142

A PLEA FOR RELIEF FROM PERSECUTORS

A Contemplation[a] of David. A Prayer when he was in the cave.

[1]I cry out to the LORD with my voice;
With my voice to the LORD I make my supplication.
[2]I pour out my complaint before Him;
I declare before Him my trouble.

142:title [a]Hebrew *Maschil*

THE MESSAGE

Let God pile hellfire on them,
let him bury them alive in crevasses!
These loudmouths—
don't let them be taken seriously;
These savages—
let the Devil hunt them down!

12-13 I know that you, GOD, are on the side of victims,
that you care for the rights of the poor.
And I know that the righteous personally thank you,
that good people are secure in your presence.

A DAVID PSALM

1-2 **141** GOD, come close. Come quickly!
Open your ears—it's my voice you're hearing!
Treat my prayer as sweet incense rising;
my raised hands are my evening prayers.

3-7 Post a guard at my mouth, GOD,
set a watch at the door of my lips.
Don't let me so much as dream of evil
or thoughtlessly fall into bad company.
And these people who only do wrong—
don't let them lure me with their sweet talk!
May the Just One set me straight,
may the Kind One correct me,
Don't let sin anoint my head.
I'm praying hard against their evil ways!
Oh, let their leaders be pushed off a high rock cliff;
make them face the music.
Like a rock pulverized by a maul,
let their bones be scattered at the gates of hell.

8-10 But GOD, dear Lord,
I only have eyes for you.
Since I've run for dear life to you,
take good care of me.
Protect me from their evil scheming,
from all their demonic subterfuge.
Let the wicked fall flat on their faces,
while I walk off without a scratch.

A DAVID PRAYER—WHEN HE WAS IN THE CAVE

1-2 **142** I cry out loudly to GOD,
loudly I plead with GOD for mercy.
I spill out all my complaints before him,
and spell out my troubles in detail:

New King James Version

[3]When my spirit was overwhelmed within me,
Then You knew my path.
In the way in which I walk
They have secretly set a snare for me.
[4]Look on *my* right hand and see,
For *there is* no one who acknowledges me;
Refuge has failed me;
No one cares for my soul.

[5]I cried out to You, O Lord:
I said, "You *are* my refuge,
My portion in the land of the living.
[6]Attend to my cry,
For I am brought very low;
Deliver me from my persecutors,
For they are stronger than I.
[7]Bring my soul out of prison,
That I may praise Your name;
The righteous shall surround me,
For You shall deal bountifully with me."

PSALM 143

An Earnest Appeal for Guidance and Deliverance

A Psalm of David.

[1]Hear my prayer, O Lord,
Give ear to my supplications!
In Your faithfulness answer me,
And in Your righteousness.
[2]Do not enter into judgment with Your servant,
For in Your sight no one living is righteous.

[3]For the enemy has persecuted my soul;
He has crushed my life to the ground;
He has made me dwell in darkness,
Like those who have long been dead.
[4]Therefore my spirit is overwhelmed within me;
My heart within me is distressed.

[5]I remember the days of old;
I meditate on all Your works;
I muse on the work of Your hands.
[6]I spread out my hands to You;
My soul *longs* for You like a thirsty land.
Selah

[7]Answer me speedily, O Lord;
My spirit fails!
Do not hide Your face from me,
Lest I be like those who go down into the pit.
[8]Cause me to hear Your lovingkindness in the morning,
For in You do I trust;
Cause me to know the way in which I should walk,
For I lift up my soul to You.

[9]Deliver me, O Lord, from my enemies;
In You I take shelter.[a]

143:9 [a]Septuagint and Vulgate read *To You I flee.*

The Message

3-7 "As I sink in despair, my spirit ebbing away,
you know how I'm feeling,
Know the danger I'm in,
the traps hidden in my path.
Look right, look left—
there's not a soul who cares what happens!
I'm up against it, with no exit—
bereft, left alone.
I cry out, God, call out:
'You're my last chance, my only hope for life!'
Oh listen, please listen;
I've never been this low.
Rescue me from those who are hunting me down;
I'm no match for them.
Get me out of this dungeon
so I can thank you in public.
Your people will form a circle around me
and you'll bring me showers of blessing!"

A David Psalm

1-2 **143** Listen to this prayer of mine, God;
pay attention to what I'm asking.
Answer me—you're famous for your answers!
Do what's right for me.
But don't, please don't, haul me into court;
not a person alive would be acquitted there.

3-6 The enemy hunted me down;
he kicked me and stomped me within an inch of my life.
He put me in a black hole,
buried me like a corpse in that dungeon.
I sat there in despair, my spirit draining away,
my heart heavy, like lead.
I remembered the old days,
went over all you've done, pondered the ways you've worked,
Stretched out my hands to you,
as thirsty for you as a desert thirsty for rain.

7-10 Hurry with your answer, God!
I'm nearly at the end of my rope.
Don't turn away; don't ignore me!
That would be certain death.
If you wake me each morning with the sound of your loving voice,
I'll go to sleep each night trusting in you.
Point out the road I must travel;
I'm all ears, all eyes before you.
Save me from my enemies, God—
you're my only hope!

NEW KING JAMES VERSION

[10]Teach me to do Your will,
For You *are* my God;
Your Spirit *is* good.
Lead me in the land of uprightness.

[11]Revive me, O LORD, for Your name's sake!
For Your righteousness' sake bring my soul
out of trouble.
[12]In Your mercy cut off my enemies,
And destroy all those who afflict my soul;
For I *am* Your servant.

PSALM 144

A SONG TO THE LORD WHO PRESERVES AND PROSPERS HIS PEOPLE

A Psalm of David.

[1]Blessed *be* the LORD my Rock,
Who trains my hands for war,
And my fingers for battle—
[2]My lovingkindness and my fortress,
My high tower and my deliverer,
My shield and *the One* in whom I take
refuge,
Who subdues my people[a] under me.

[3]LORD, what *is* man, that You take knowledge
of him?
Or the son of man, that You are mindful of
him?
[4]Man is like a breath;
His days *are* like a passing shadow.

[5]Bow down Your heavens, O LORD, and come
down;
Touch the mountains, and they shall smoke.
[6]Flash forth lightning and scatter them;
Shoot out Your arrows and destroy them.
[7]Stretch out Your hand from above;
Rescue me and deliver me out of great
waters,
From the hand of foreigners,
[8]Whose mouth speaks lying words,
And whose right hand *is* a right hand of
falsehood.

[9]I will sing a new song to You, O God;
On a harp of ten strings I will sing praises to
You,
[10]*The One* who gives salvation to kings,
Who delivers David His servant
From the deadly sword.

[11]Rescue me and deliver me from the hand of
foreigners,
Whose mouth speaks lying words,
And whose right hand *is* a right hand of
falsehood—
[12]That our sons *may be* as plants grown up in
their youth;
That our daughters *may be* as pillars,
Sculptured in palace style;
[13]*That* our barns *may be* full,
Supplying all kinds of produce;

144:2 [a]Following Masoretic Text, Septuagint, and Vulgate; Syriac and Targum read *the peoples* (compare 18:47).

THE MESSAGE

Teach me how to live to please you,
because you're my God.
Lead me by your blessed Spirit
into cleared and level pastureland.

11-12 Keep up your reputation, God—give me
life!
In your justice, get me out of this trouble!
In your great love, vanquish my enemies;
make a clean sweep of those who harass
me.
And why? Because I'm your servant.

A DAVID PSALM

1-2 144 Blessed be GOD, my mountain,
who trains me to fight fair and
well.
He's the bedrock on which I stand,
the castle in which I live,
my rescuing knight,
The high crag where I run for dear life,
while he lays my enemies low.

3-4 I wonder why you care, GOD—
why do you bother with us at all?
All we are is a puff of air;
we're like shadows in a campfire.

5-8 Step down out of heaven, GOD;
ignite volcanoes in the hearts of the
mountains.
Hurl your lightnings in every direction;
shoot your arrows this way and that.
Reach all the way from sky to sea:
pull me out of the ocean of hate,
out of the grip of those barbarians
Who lie through their teeth,
who shake your hand
then knife you in the back.

9-10 O God, let me sing a new song to you,
let me play it on a twelve-string guitar—
A song to the God who saved the king,
the God who rescued David, his servant.

11 Rescue me from the enemy sword,
release me from the grip of those
barbarians
Who lie through their teeth,
who shake your hand
then knife you in the back.

12-14 Make our sons in their prime
like sturdy oak trees,
Our daughters as shapely and bright
as fields of wildflowers.
Fill our barns with great harvest,

NEW KING JAMES VERSION

That our sheep may bring forth thousands
And ten thousands in our fields;
14*That* our oxen *may be* well laden;
That there be no breaking in or going out;
That there be no outcry in our streets.
15Happy *are* the people who are in such a state;
Happy *are* the people whose God *is* the LORD!

PSALM 145

A SONG OF GOD'S MAJESTY AND LOVE

A Praise of David.

1I will extol You, my God, O King;
And I will bless Your name forever and ever.
2Every day I will bless You,
And I will praise Your name forever and ever.
3Great *is* the LORD, and greatly to be praised;
And His greatness *is* unsearchable.

4One generation shall praise Your works to another,
And shall declare Your mighty acts.
5I[a] will meditate on the glorious splendor of Your majesty,
And on Your wondrous works.[b]
6*Men* shall speak of the might of Your awesome acts,
And I will declare Your greatness.
7They shall utter the memory of Your great goodness,
And shall sing of Your righteousness.

8The LORD *is* gracious and full of compassion,
Slow to anger and great in mercy.
9The LORD *is* good to all,
And His tender mercies *are* over all His works.

10All Your works shall praise You, O LORD,
And Your saints shall bless You.
11They shall speak of the glory of Your kingdom,
And talk of Your power,
12To make known to the sons of men His mighty acts,
And the glorious majesty of His kingdom.
13Your kingdom *is* an everlasting kingdom,
And Your dominion *endures* throughout all generations.[a]

14The LORD upholds all who fall,
And raises up all *who are* bowed down.
15The eyes of all look expectantly to You,
And You give them their food in due season.
16You open Your hand
And satisfy the desire of every living thing.

145:5 [a]Following Masoretic Text and Targum; Dead Sea Scrolls, Septuagint, Syriac, and Vulgate read *They*. [b]Literally *on the words of Your wondrous works* **145:13** [a]Following Masoretic Text and Targum; Dead Sea Scrolls, Septuagint, Syriac, and Vulgate add *The LORD is faithful in all His words, And holy in all His works.*

THE MESSAGE

fill our fields with huge flocks;
Protect us from invasion and exile—
eliminate the crime in our streets.

15 How blessed the people who have all this!
How blessed the people who have GOD for God!

DAVID'S PRAISE

1 **145** I lift you high in praise, my God, O my King!
and I'll bless your name into eternity.

2 I'll bless you every day,
and keep it up from now to eternity.

3 GOD is magnificent; he can never be praised enough.
There are no boundaries to his greatness.

4 Generation after generation stands in awe of your work;
each one tells stories of your mighty acts.
5 Your beauty and splendor have everyone talking;
I compose songs on your wonders.
6 Your marvelous doings are headline news;
I could write a book full of the details of your greatness.

7 The fame of your goodness spreads across the country;
your righteousness is on everyone's lips.

8 GOD is all mercy and grace—
not quick to anger, is rich in love.
9 GOD is good to one and all;
everything he does is suffused with grace.

10-11 Creation and creatures applaud you, GOD;
your holy people bless you.

They talk about the glories of your rule,
they exclaim over your splendor,
12 Letting the world know of your power for good,
the lavish splendor of your kingdom.
13 Your kingdom is a kingdom eternal;
you never get voted out of office.

GOD always does what he says,
and is gracious in everything he does.

14 GOD gives a hand to those down on their luck,
gives a fresh start to those ready to quit.

15 All eyes are on you, expectant;
you give them their meals on time.

16 Generous to a fault,
you lavish your favor on all creatures.

NEW KING JAMES VERSION

17The LORD *is* righteous in all His ways,
Gracious in all His works.
18The LORD *is* near to all who call upon Him,
To all who call upon Him in truth.
19He will fulfill the desire of those who fear Him;
He also will hear their cry and save them.
20The LORD preserves all who love Him,
But all the wicked He will destroy.
21My mouth shall speak the praise of the LORD,
And all flesh shall bless His holy name
Forever and ever.

PSALM 146

THE HAPPINESS OF THOSE WHOSE HELP IS THE LORD

1Praise the LORD!

Praise the LORD, O my soul!
2While I live I will praise the LORD;
I will sing praises to my God while I have my being.

3Do not put your trust in princes,
Nor in a son of man, in whom *there is* no help.
4His spirit departs, he returns to his earth;
In that very day his plans perish.

5Happy *is he* who *has* the God of Jacob for his help,
Whose hope *is* in the LORD his God,
6Who made heaven and earth,
The sea, and all that *is* in them;
Who keeps truth forever,
7Who executes justice for the oppressed,
Who gives food to the hungry.
The LORD gives freedom to the prisoners.

8The LORD opens *the eyes of* the blind;
The LORD raises those who are bowed down;
The LORD loves the righteous.
9The LORD watches over the strangers;
He relieves the fatherless and widow;
But the way of the wicked He turns upside down.

10The LORD shall reign forever—
Your God, O Zion, to all generations.

Praise the LORD!

PSALM 147

PRAISE TO GOD FOR HIS WORD AND PROVIDENCE

1Praise the LORD!
For *it is* good to sing praises to our God;
For *it is* pleasant, *and* praise is beautiful.

2The LORD builds up Jerusalem;
He gathers together the outcasts of Israel.
3He heals the brokenhearted
And binds up their wounds.

THE MESSAGE

17 Everything GOD does is right—
the trademark on all his works is love.

18 GOD's there, listening for all who pray,
for all who pray and mean it.

19 He does what's best for those who fear him—
hears them call out, and saves them.

20 GOD sticks by all who love him,
but it's all over for those who don't.

21 My mouth is filled with GOD's praise.
Let everything living bless him,
bless his holy name from now to eternity!

1-2 **146** Hallelujah!
O my soul, praise GOD!
All my life long I'll praise GOD,
singing songs to my God as long as I live.

3-9 Don't put your life in the hands of experts
who know nothing of life, of *salvation* life.
Mere humans don't have what it takes;
when they die, their projects die with them.
Instead, get help from the God of Jacob,
put your hope in GOD and know real blessing!
GOD made sky and soil,
sea and all the fish in it.
He always does what he says—
he defends the wronged,
he feeds the hungry.
GOD frees prisoners—
he gives sight to the blind,
he lifts up the fallen.
GOD loves good people, protects strangers,
takes the side of orphans and widows,
but makes short work of the wicked.

10 GOD's in charge—*always*.
Zion's God is God for good!
Hallelujah!

1 **147** Hallelujah!
It's a good thing to sing praise to our God;
praise is beautiful, praise is fitting.

2-6 GOD's the one who rebuilds Jerusalem,
who regathers Israel's scattered exiles.
He heals the heartbroken
and bandages their wounds.

NEW KING JAMES VERSION

4He counts the number of the stars;
He calls them all by name.
5Great *is* our Lord, and mighty in power;
His understanding *is* infinite.
6The LORD lifts up the humble;
He casts the wicked down to the ground.

7Sing to the LORD with thanksgiving;
Sing praises on the harp to our God,
8Who covers the heavens with clouds,
Who prepares rain for the earth,
Who makes grass to grow on the mountains.
9He gives to the beast its food,
And to the young ravens that cry.

10He does not delight in the strength of the horse;
He takes no pleasure in the legs of a man.
11The LORD takes pleasure in those who fear Him,
In those who hope in His mercy.

12Praise the LORD, O Jerusalem!
Praise your God, O Zion!
13For He has strengthened the bars of your gates;
He has blessed your children within you.
14He makes peace *in* your borders,
And fills you with the finest wheat.

15He sends out His command *to the* earth;
His word runs very swiftly.
16He gives snow like wool;
He scatters the frost like ashes;
17He casts out His hail like morsels;
Who can stand before His cold?
18He sends out His word and melts them;
He causes His wind to blow, *and* the waters flow.

19He declares His word to Jacob,
His statutes and His judgments to Israel.
20He has not dealt thus with any nation;
And *as for His* judgments, they have not known them.

Praise the LORD!

PSALM 148

PRAISE TO THE LORD FROM CREATION

1Praise the LORD!

Praise the LORD from the heavens;
Praise Him in the heights!
2Praise Him, all His angels;
Praise Him, all His hosts!
3Praise Him, sun and moon;
Praise Him, all you stars of light!
4Praise Him, you heavens of heavens,
And you waters above the heavens!

5Let them praise the name of the LORD,
For He commanded and they were created.
6He also established them forever and ever;
He made a decree which shall not pass away.

THE MESSAGE

He counts the stars
and assigns each a name.
Our Lord is great, with limitless strength;
we'll never comprehend what he knows and does.
GOD puts the fallen on their feet again
and pushes the wicked into the ditch.

7-11 Sing to GOD a thanksgiving hymn,
play music on your instruments to God,
Who fills the sky with clouds,
preparing rain for the earth,
Then turning the mountains green with grass,
feeding both cattle and crows.
He's not impressed with horsepower;
the size of our muscles means little to him.
Those who fear GOD get GOD's attention;
they can depend on his strength.

12-18 Jerusalem, worship GOD!
Zion, praise your God!
He made your city secure,
he blessed your children among you.
He keeps the peace at your borders,
he puts the best bread on your tables.
He launches his promises earthward—
how swift and sure they come!
He spreads snow like a white fleece,
he scatters frost like ashes,
He broadcasts hail like birdseed—
who can survive his winter?
Then he gives the command and it all melts;
he breathes on winter—suddenly it's spring!

19-20 He speaks the same way to Jacob,
speaks words that work to Israel.
He never did this to the other nations;
they never heard such commands.
Hallelujah!

1-5 **148** Hallelujah!
Praise GOD from heaven,
praise him from the mountaintops;
Praise him, all you his angels,
praise him, all you his warriors,
Praise him, sun and moon,
praise him, you morning stars;
Praise him, high heaven,
praise him, heavenly rain clouds;
Praise, oh let them praise the name of GOD—
he spoke the word, and there they were!

6 He set them in place
from all time to eternity;
He gave his orders,
and that's it!

NEW KING JAMES VERSION

7Praise the LORD from the earth,
You great sea creatures and all the depths;
8Fire and hail, snow and clouds;
Stormy wind, fulfilling His word;
9Mountains and all hills;
Fruitful trees and all cedars;
10Beasts and all cattle;
Creeping things and flying fowl;
11Kings of the earth and all peoples;
Princes and all judges of the earth;
12Both young men and maidens;
Old men and children.

13Let them praise the name of the LORD,
For His name alone is exalted;
His glory *is* above the earth and heaven.
14And He has exalted the horn of His people,
The praise of all His saints—
Of the children of Israel,
A people near to Him.

Praise the LORD!

PSALM 149

PRAISE TO GOD FOR HIS SALVATION AND JUDGMENT

1Praise the LORD!

Sing to the LORD a new song,
And His praise in the assembly of saints.

2Let Israel rejoice in their Maker;
Let the children of Zion be joyful in their
King.
3Let them praise His name with the dance;
Let them sing praises to Him with the
timbrel and harp.
4For the LORD takes pleasure in His people;
He will beautify the humble with salvation.

5Let the saints be joyful in glory;
Let them sing aloud on their beds.
6*Let* the high praises of God *be* in their
mouth,
And a two-edged sword in their hand,
7To execute vengeance on the nations,
And punishments on the peoples;
8To bind their kings with chains,
And their nobles with fetters of iron;
9To execute on them the written judgment—
This honor have all His saints.

Praise the LORD!

PSALM 150

LET ALL THINGS PRAISE THE LORD

1Praise the LORD!

Praise God in His sanctuary;
Praise Him in His mighty firmament!

2Praise Him for His mighty acts;
Praise Him according to His excellent
greatness!

3Praise Him with the sound of the trumpet;
Praise Him with the lute and harp!

THE MESSAGE

7-12 Praise GOD from earth,
you sea dragons, you fathomless ocean
deeps;
Fire and hail, snow and ice,
hurricanes obeying his orders;
Mountains and all hills,
apple orchards and cedar forests;
Wild beasts and herds of cattle,
snakes, and birds in flight;
Earth's kings and all races,
leaders and important people,
Robust men and women in their prime,
and yes, graybeards and little children.

13-14 Let them praise the name of GOD—
it's the only Name worth praising.
His radiance exceeds anything in earth and
sky;
he's built a monument—his very own
people!

Praise from all who love GOD!
Israel's children, intimate friends of GOD.
Hallelujah!

1-4 **149** Hallelujah!
Sing to GOD a brand-new song,
praise him in the company of all who
love him.
Let all Israel celebrate their Sovereign
Creator,
Zion's children exult in their King.
Let them praise his name in dance;
strike up the band and make great
music!
And why? Because GOD delights in his
people,
festoons plain folk with salvation
garlands!

5-9 Let true lovers break out in praise,
sing out from wherever they're sitting,
Shout the high praises of God,
brandish their swords in the wild
sword-dance—
A portent of vengeance on the God-defying
nations,
a signal that punishment's coming,
Their kings chained and hauled off to jail,
their leaders behind bars for good,
The judgment on them carried out to the
letter
—and all who love God in the seat of
honor!
Hallelujah!

1-6 **150** Hallelujah!
Praise God in his holy house of
worship,
praise him under the open skies;
Praise him for his acts of power,
praise him for his magnificent greatness;
Praise with a blast on the trumpet,
praise by strumming soft strings;

NEW KING JAMES VERSION

4 Praise Him with the timbrel and dance;
Praise Him with stringed instruments and flutes!
5 Praise Him with loud cymbals;
Praise Him with clashing cymbals!

6 Let everything that has breath praise the LORD.

Praise the LORD!

THE MESSAGE

Praise him with castanets and dance,
praise him with banjo and flute;
Praise him with cymbals and a big bass drum,
praise him with fiddles and mandolin.
Let every living, breathing creature praise GOD!
Hallelujah!

PROVERBS

NEW KING JAMES VERSION

THE BEGINNING OF KNOWLEDGE

1 The proverbs of Solomon the son of David,
king of Israel:

2 To know wisdom and instruction,
To perceive the words of understanding,
3 To receive the instruction of wisdom,
Justice, judgment, and equity;
4 To give prudence to the simple,
To the young man knowledge and discretion—
5 A wise *man* will hear and increase learning,
And a man of understanding will attain wise counsel,
6 To understand a proverb and an enigma,
The words of the wise and their riddles.

7 The fear of the LORD *is* the beginning of knowledge,
But fools despise wisdom and instruction.

SHUN EVIL COUNSEL

8 My son, hear the instruction of your father,
And do not forsake the law of your mother;
9 For they *will be* a graceful ornament on your head,
And chains about your neck.

10 My son, if sinners entice you,
Do not consent.
11 If they say, "Come with us,
Let us lie in wait to *shed* blood;
Let us lurk secretly for the innocent without cause;
12 Let us swallow them alive like Sheol,[a]
And whole, like those who go down to the Pit;
13 We shall find all *kinds* of precious possessions,
We shall fill our houses with spoil;
14 Cast in your lot among us,
Let us all have one purse"—
15 My son, do not walk in the way with them,
Keep your foot from their path;
16 For their feet run to evil,
And they make haste to shed blood.
17 Surely, in vain the net is spread
In the sight of any bird;
18 But they lie in wait for their *own* blood,
They lurk secretly for their *own* lives.
19 So *are* the ways of everyone who is greedy for gain;
It takes away the life of its owners.

THE CALL OF WISDOM

20 Wisdom calls aloud outside;
She raises her voice in the open squares.
21 She cries out in the chief concourses,[a]
At the openings of the gates in the city
She speaks her words:

1:12 [a]Or *the grave* **1:21** [a]Septuagint, Syriac, and Targum read *top of the walls;* Vulgate reads *the head of multitudes.*

THE MESSAGE

WISE SAYINGS OF SOLOMON

A MANUAL FOR LIVING

1-6 1 These are the wise sayings of Solomon,
David's son, Israel's king—
Written down so we'll know how to live well and right,
to understand what life means and where it's going;
A manual for living,
for learning what's right and just and fair;
To teach the inexperienced the ropes
and give our young people a grasp on reality.
There's something here also for seasoned men and women,
still a thing or two for the experienced to learn—
Fresh wisdom to probe and penetrate,
the rhymes and reasons of wise men and women.

START WITH GOD

7 Start with GOD—the first step in learning is bowing down to GOD;
only fools thumb their noses at such wisdom and learning.

8-19 Pay close attention, friend, to what your father tells you;
never forget what you learned at your mother's knee.
Wear their counsel like flowers in your hair,
like rings on your fingers.
Dear friend, if bad companions tempt you,
don't go along with them.
If they say—"Let's go out and raise some hell.
Let's beat up some old man, mug some old woman.
Let's pick them clean
and get them ready for their funerals.
We'll load up on top-quality loot.
We'll haul it home by the truckload.
Join us for the time of your life!
With us, it's share and share alike!"—
Oh, friend, don't give them a second look;
don't listen to them for a minute.
They're racing to a very bad end,
hurrying to ruin everything they lay hands on.
Nobody robs a bank
with everyone watching,
Yet that's what these people are doing—
they're doing themselves in.
When you grab all you can get, that's what happens:
the more you get, the less you are.

LADY WISDOM

20-21 Lady Wisdom goes out in the street and shouts.
At the town center she makes her speech.
In the middle of the traffic she takes her stand.
At the busiest corner she calls out:

NEW KING JAMES VERSION

22"How long, you simple ones, will you love
simplicity?
For scorners delight in their scorning,
And fools hate knowledge.
23Turn at my rebuke;
Surely I will pour out my spirit on you;
I will make my words known to you.
24Because I have called and you refused,
I have stretched out my hand and no one
regarded,
25Because you disdained all my counsel,
And would have none of my rebuke,
26I also will laugh at your calamity;
I will mock when your terror comes,
27When your terror comes like a storm,
And your destruction comes like a
whirlwind,
When distress and anguish come upon you.
28"Then they will call on me, but I will not
answer;
They will seek me diligently, but they will
not find me.
29Because they hated knowledge
And did not choose the fear of the LORD,
30They would have none of my counsel
And despised my every rebuke.
31Therefore they shall eat the fruit of their
own way,
And be filled to the full with their own
fancies.
32For the turning away of the simple will slay
them,
And the complacency of fools will destroy
them;
33But whoever listens to me will dwell safely,
And will be secure, without fear of evil."

THE VALUE OF WISDOM

2 My son, if you receive my words,
And treasure my commands within you,
2So that you incline your ear to wisdom,
And apply your heart to understanding;
3Yes, if you cry out for discernment,
And lift up your voice for understanding,
4If you seek her as silver,
And search for her as *for* hidden treasures;
5Then you will understand the fear of the
LORD,
And find the knowledge of God.
6For the LORD gives wisdom;
From His mouth *come* knowledge and
understanding;
7He stores up sound wisdom for the upright;

THE MESSAGE

22-24 "Simpletons! How long will you wallow in
ignorance?
Cynics! How long will you feed your
cynicism?
Idiots! How long will you refuse to learn?
About face! I can revise your life.
Look, I'm ready to pour out my spirit on
you;
I'm ready to tell you all I know.
As it is, I've called, but you've turned a deaf
ear;
I've reached out to you, but you've
ignored me.

25-28 "Since you laugh at my counsel
and make a joke of my advice,
How can I take you seriously?
I'll turn the tables and joke about *your*
troubles!
What if the roof falls in,
and your whole life goes to pieces?
What if catastrophe strikes and there's
nothing
to show for your life but rubble and
ashes?
You'll need me then. You'll call for me, but
don't expect an answer.
No matter how hard you look, you won't
find me.

29-33 "Because you hated Knowledge
and had nothing to do with the
Fear-of-GOD,
Because you wouldn't take my advice
and brushed aside all my offers to train
you,
Well, you've made your bed—now lie in it;
you wanted your own way—now, how do
you like it?
Don't you see what happens, you
simpletons, you idiots?
Carelessness kills; complacency is
murder.
First pay attention to me, and then relax.
Now you can take it easy—you're in
good hands."

MAKE INSIGHT YOUR PRIORITY

1-5 2 Good friend, take to heart what I'm telling
you;
collect my counsels and guard them with
your life.
Tune your ears to the world of Wisdom;
set your heart on a life of Understanding.
That's right—if you make Insight your
priority,
and won't take no for an answer,
Searching for it like a prospector panning
for gold,
like an adventurer on a treasure hunt,
Believe me, before you know it Fear-of-GOD
will be yours;
you'll have come upon the Knowledge of
God.

6-8 And here's why: GOD gives out Wisdom free,
is plainspoken in Knowledge and
Understanding.
He's a rich mine of Common Sense for
those who live well,

NEW KING JAMES VERSION

He is a shield to those who walk uprightly;
8He guards the paths of justice,
And preserves the way of His saints.
9Then you will understand righteousness and justice,
Equity *and* every good path.

10When wisdom enters your heart,
And knowledge is pleasant to your soul,
11Discretion will preserve you;
Understanding will keep you,
12To deliver you from the way of evil,
From the man who speaks perverse things,
13From those who leave the paths of uprightness
To walk in the ways of darkness;
14Who rejoice in doing evil,
And delight in the perversity of the wicked;
15Whose ways *are* crooked,
And *who are* devious in their paths;
16To deliver you from the immoral woman,
From the seductress *who* flatters with her words,
17Who forsakes the companion of her youth,
And forgets the covenant of her God.
18For her house leads down to death,
And her paths to the dead;
19None who go to her return,
Nor do they regain the paths of life—
20So you may walk in the way of goodness,
And keep *to* the paths of righteousness.
21For the upright will dwell in the land,
And the blameless will remain in it;
22But the wicked will be cut off from the earth,
And the unfaithful will be uprooted from it.

GUIDANCE FOR THE YOUNG

3 My son, do not forget my law,
But let your heart keep my commands;
2For length of days and long life
And peace they will add to you.

3Let not mercy and truth forsake you;
Bind them around your neck,
Write them on the tablet of your heart,
4*And* so find favor and high esteem
In the sight of God and man.

5Trust in the LORD with all your heart,
And lean not on your own understanding;
6In all your ways acknowledge Him,
And He shall direct[a] your paths.

3:6 [a]Or *make smooth* or *straight*

THE MESSAGE

a personal bodyguard to the candid and sincere.
He keeps his eye on all who live honestly,
and pays special attention to his loyally committed ones.

9-15 So now you can pick out what's true and fair,
find all the good trails!
Lady Wisdom will be your close friend,
and Brother Knowledge your pleasant companion.
Good Sense will scout ahead for danger,
Insight will keep an eye out for you.
They'll keep you from making wrong turns,
or following the bad directions
Of those who are lost themselves
and can't tell a trail from a tumbleweed,
These losers who make a game of evil
and throw parties to celebrate perversity,
Traveling paths that go nowhere,
wandering in a maze of detours and dead ends.

16-19 Wise friends will rescue you from the Temptress—
that smooth-talking Seductress
Who's faithless to the husband she married years ago,
never gave a second thought to her promises before God.
Her whole way of life is doomed;
every step she takes brings her closer to hell.
No one who joins her company ever comes back,
ever sets foot on the path to real living.

20-22 So—join the company of good men and women,
keep your feet on the tried-and-true paths.
It's the men who walk straight who will settle this land,
the women with integrity who will last here.
The corrupt will lose their lives;
the dishonest will be gone for good.

DON'T ASSUME YOU KNOW IT ALL

1-2 3 Good friend, don't forget all I've taught you;
take to heart my commands.
They'll help you live a long, long time,
a long life lived full and well.

3-4 Don't lose your grip on Love and Loyalty.
Tie them around your neck; carve their initials on your heart.
Earn a reputation for living well
in God's eyes and the eyes of the people.

5-12 Trust GOD from the bottom of your heart;
don't try to figure out everything on your own.
Listen for GOD's voice in everything you do,
everywhere you go;
he's the one who will keep you on track.

New King James Version

7Do not be wise in your own eyes;
Fear the LORD and depart from evil.
8It will be health to your flesh,[a]
And strength[b] to your bones.

9Honor the LORD with your possessions,
And with the firstfruits of all your increase;
10So your barns will be filled with plenty,
And your vats will overflow with new wine.

11My son, do not despise the chastening of the LORD,
Nor detest His correction;
12For whom the LORD loves He corrects,
Just as a father the son *in whom* he delights.

13Happy *is* the man *who* finds wisdom,
And the man *who* gains understanding;
14For her proceeds *are* better than the profits of silver,
And her gain than fine gold.
15She *is* more precious than rubies,
And all the things you may desire cannot compare with her.
16Length of days *is* in her right hand,
In her left hand riches and honor.
17Her ways *are* ways of pleasantness,
And all her paths *are* peace.
18She *is* a tree of life to those who take hold of her,
And happy *are all* who retain her.

19The LORD by wisdom founded the earth;
By understanding He established the heavens;
20By His knowledge the depths were broken up,
And clouds drop down the dew.

21My son, let them not depart from your eyes—
Keep sound wisdom and discretion;
22So they will be life to your soul
And grace to your neck.
23Then you will walk safely in your way,
And your foot will not stumble.
24When you lie down, you will not be afraid;
Yes, you will lie down and your sleep will be sweet.
25Do not be afraid of sudden terror,
Nor of trouble from the wicked when it comes;
26For the LORD will be your confidence,
And will keep your foot from being caught.

27Do not withhold good from those to whom it is due,
When it is in the power of your hand to do *so*.
28Do not say to your neighbor,
"Go, and come back,
And tomorrow I will give *it*,"
When *you have* it with you.
29Do not devise evil against your neighbor,
For he dwells by you for safety's sake.

3:8 [a]Literally *navel*, figurative of the body [b]Literally *drink* or *refreshment*

The Message

Don't assume that you know it all.
Run to GOD! Run from evil!
Your body will glow with health,
your very bones will vibrate with life!
Honor GOD with everything you own;
give him the first and the best.
Your barns will burst,
your wine vats will brim over.
But don't, dear friend, resent GOD's discipline;
don't sulk under his loving correction.
It's the child he loves that GOD corrects;
a father's delight is behind all this.

The Very Tree of Life

13-18 You're blessed when you meet Lady Wisdom,
when you make friends with Madame Insight.
She's worth far more than money in the bank;
her friendship is better than a big salary.
Her value exceeds all the trappings of wealth;
nothing you could wish for holds a candle to her.
With one hand she gives long life,
with the other she confers recognition.
Her manner is beautiful,
her life wonderfully complete.
She's the very Tree of Life to those who embrace her.
Hold her tight—and be blessed!

19-20 With Lady Wisdom, GOD formed Earth;
with Madame Insight, he raised Heaven.
They knew when to signal rivers and springs to the surface,
and dew to descend from the night skies.

Never Walk Away

21-26 Dear friend, guard Clear Thinking and Common Sense with your life;
don't for a minute lose sight of them.
They'll keep your soul alive and well,
they'll keep you fit and attractive.
You'll travel safely,
you'll neither tire nor trip.
You'll take afternoon naps without a worry,
you'll enjoy a good night's sleep.
No need to panic over alarms or surprises,
or predictions that doomsday's just around the corner,
Because GOD will be right there with you;
he'll keep you safe and sound.

27-29 Never walk away from someone who deserves help;
your hand is *God's* hand for that person.
Don't tell your neighbor "Maybe some other time"
or "Try me tomorrow"
when the money's right there in your pocket.
Don't figure ways of taking advantage of your neighbor
when he's sitting there trusting and unsuspecting.

NEW KING JAMES VERSION

30Do not strive with a man without cause,
If he has done you no harm.

31Do not envy the oppressor,
And choose none of his ways;
32For the perverse *person is* an abomination
to the LORD,
But His secret counsel *is* with the upright.
33The curse of the LORD *is* on the house of the
wicked,
But He blesses the home of the just.
34Surely He scorns the scornful,
But gives grace to the humble.
35The wise shall inherit glory,
But shame shall be the legacy of fools.

SECURITY IN WISDOM

4 Hear, my children, the instruction of a
father,
And give attention to know understanding;
2For I give you good doctrine:
Do not forsake my law.
3When I was my father's son,
Tender and the only one in the sight of my
mother,
4He also taught me, and said to me:
"Let your heart retain my words;
Keep my commands, and live.
5Get wisdom! Get understanding!
Do not forget, nor turn away from the words
of my mouth.
6Do not forsake her, and she will preserve
you;
Love her, and she will keep you.
7Wisdom *is* the principal thing;
Therefore get wisdom.
And in all your getting, get understanding.
8Exalt her, and she will promote you;
She will bring you honor, when you
embrace her.
9She will place on your head an ornament of
grace;
A crown of glory she will deliver to you."

10Hear, my son, and receive my sayings,
And the years of your life will be many.
11I have taught you in the way of wisdom;
I have led you in right paths.
12When you walk, your steps will not be
hindered,
And when you run, you will not stumble.
13Take firm hold of instruction, do not let go;
Keep her, for she *is* your life.

14Do not enter the path of the wicked,
And do not walk in the way of evil.
15Avoid it, do not travel on it;
Turn away from it and pass on.
16For they do not sleep unless they have done
evil;
And their sleep is taken away unless they
make *someone* fall.

THE MESSAGE

30-32 Don't walk around with a chip on your
shoulder,
always spoiling for a fight.
Don't try to be like those who shoulder
their way through life.
Why be a bully?
"Why not?" you say. Because GOD can't
stand twisted souls.
It's the straightforward who get his
respect.

33-35 GOD's curse blights the house of the
wicked,
but he blesses the home of the righteous.
He gives proud skeptics a cold shoulder,
but if you're down on your luck, he's
right there to help.
Wise living gets rewarded with honor;
stupid living gets the booby prize.

YOUR LIFE IS AT STAKE

1-2 4 Listen, friends, to some fatherly advice;
sit up and take notice so you'll know
how to live.
I'm giving you good counsel;
don't let it go in one ear and out the other.

3-9 When I was a boy at my father's knee,
the pride and joy of my mother,
He would sit me down and drill me:
"Take this to heart. Do what I tell you—
live!
Sell everything and buy Wisdom! Forage
for Understanding!
Don't forget one word! Don't deviate an
inch!
Never walk away from Wisdom—she
guards your life;
love her—she keeps her eye on you.
Above all and before all, do this: Get
Wisdom!
Write this at the top of your list: Get
Understanding!
Throw your arms around her—believe me,
you won't regret it;
never let her go—she'll make your life
glorious.
She'll garland your life with grace,
she'll festoon your days with beauty."

10-15 Dear friend, take my advice;
it will add years to your life.
I'm writing out clear directions to Wisdom
Way,
I'm drawing a map to Righteous Road.
I don't want you ending up in blind alleys,
or wasting time making wrong turns.
Hold tight to good advice; don't relax your
grip.
Guard it well—your life is at stake!
Don't take Wicked Bypass;
don't so much as set foot on that road.
Stay clear of it; give it a wide berth.
Make a detour and be on your way.

16-17 Evil people are restless
unless they're making trouble;
They can't get a good night's sleep
unless they've made life miserable for
somebody.

NEW KING JAMES VERSION

17For they eat the bread of wickedness,
And drink the wine of violence.

18But the path of the just *is* like the shining sun,[a]
That shines ever brighter unto the perfect day.
19The way of the wicked *is* like darkness;
They do not know what makes them stumble.

20My son, give attention to my words;
Incline your ear to my sayings.
21Do not let them depart from your eyes;
Keep them in the midst of your heart;
22For they *are* life to those who find them,
And health to all their flesh.

23Keep your heart with all diligence,
For out of it *spring* the issues of life.
24Put away from you a deceitful mouth,
And put perverse lips far from you.
25Let your eyes look straight ahead,
And your eyelids look right before you.
26Ponder the path of your feet,
And let all your ways be established.
27Do not turn to the right or the left;
Remove your foot from evil.

THE PERIL OF ADULTERY

5 My son, pay attention to my wisdom;
Lend your ear to my understanding,
2That you may preserve discretion,
And your lips may keep knowledge.
3For the lips of an immoral woman drip honey,
And her mouth *is* smoother than oil;
4But in the end she is bitter as wormwood,
Sharp as a two-edged sword.
5Her feet go down to death,
Her steps lay hold of hell.[a]
6Lest you ponder *her* path of life—
Her ways are unstable;
You do not know *them.*

7Therefore hear me now, *my* children,
And do not depart from the words of my mouth.
8Remove your way far from her,
And do not go near the door of her house,
9Lest you give your honor to others,
And your years to the cruel *one;*
10Lest aliens be filled with your wealth,
And your labors *go* to the house of a foreigner;

4:18 [a]Literally *light* **5:5** [a]Or *Sheol*

THE MESSAGE

Perversity is their food and drink,
violence their drug of choice.

18-19 The ways of right-living people glow with light;
the longer they live, the brighter they shine.
But the road of wrongdoing gets darker and darker—
travelers can't see a thing; they fall flat on their faces.

LEARN IT BY HEART

20-22 Dear friend, listen well to my words;
tune your ears to my voice.
Keep my message in plain view at all times.
Concentrate! Learn it by heart!
Those who discover these words live, really live;
body and soul, they're bursting with health.

23-27 Keep vigilant watch over your heart;
that's where life starts.
Don't talk out of both sides of your mouth;
avoid careless banter, white lies, and gossip.
Keep your eyes straight ahead;
ignore all sideshow distractions.
Watch your step,
and the road will stretch out smooth before you.
Look neither right nor left;
leave evil in the dust.

NOTHING BUT SIN AND BONES

1-2 5 Dear friend, pay close attention to this, my wisdom;
listen very closely to the way I see it.
Then you'll acquire a taste for good sense;
what I tell you will keep you out of trouble.

3-6 The lips of a seductive woman are oh so sweet,
her soft words are oh so smooth.
But it won't be long before she's gravel in your mouth,
a pain in your gut, a wound in your heart.
She's dancing down the primrose path to Death;
she's headed straight for Hell and taking you with her.
She hasn't a clue about Real Life,
about who she is or where she's going.

7-14 So, my friend, listen closely;
don't treat my words casually.
Keep your distance from such a woman;
absolutely stay out of her neighborhood.
You don't want to squander your wonderful life,
to waste your precious life among the hardhearted.
Why should you allow strangers to take advantage of you?
Why be exploited by those who care nothing for you?

New King James Version

11And you mourn at last,
When your flesh and your body are consumed,
12And say:
"How I have hated instruction,
And my heart despised correction!
13I have not obeyed the voice of my teachers,
Nor inclined my ear to those who instructed me!
14I was on the verge of total ruin,
In the midst of the assembly and congregation."

15Drink water from your own cistern,
And running water from your own well.
16Should your fountains be dispersed abroad,
Streams of water in the streets?
17Let them be only your own,
And not for strangers with you.
18Let your fountain be blessed,
And rejoice with the wife of your youth.
19*As a* loving deer and a graceful doe,
Let her breasts satisfy you at all times;
And always be enraptured with her love.
20For why should you, my son, be enraptured by an immoral woman,
And be embraced in the arms of a seductress?

21For the ways of man *are* before the eyes of the LORD,
And He ponders all his paths.
22His own iniquities entrap the wicked *man,*
And he is caught in the cords of his sin.
23He shall die for lack of instruction,
And in the greatness of his folly he shall go astray.

Dangerous Promises

6 My son, if you become surety for your friend,
If you have shaken hands in pledge for a stranger,
2You are snared by the words of your mouth;
You are taken by the words of your mouth.
3So do this, my son, and deliver yourself;
For you have come into the hand of your friend:
Go and humble yourself;
Plead with your friend.
4Give no sleep to your eyes,
Nor slumber to your eyelids.
5Deliver yourself like a gazelle from the hand *of the hunter,*
And like a bird from the hand of the fowler.[a]

The Folly of Indolence

6Go to the ant, you sluggard!
Consider her ways and be wise,
7Which, having no captain,
Overseer or ruler,

6:5 [a]That is, one who catches birds in a trap or snare

The Message

You don't want to end your life full of regrets,
nothing but sin and bones,
Saying, "Oh, why didn't I do what they told me?
Why did I reject a disciplined life?
Why didn't I listen to my mentors,
or take my teachers seriously?
My life is ruined!
I haven't one blessed thing to show for my life!"

Never Take Love for Granted

15-16 Do you know the saying, "Drink from your own rain barrel,
draw water from your own spring-fed well"?
It's true. Otherwise, you may one day come home
and find your barrel empty and your well polluted.

17-20 Your spring water is for you and you only,
not to be passed around among strangers.
Bless your fresh-flowing fountain!
Enjoy the wife you married as a young man!
Lovely as an angel, beautiful as a rose—
don't ever quit taking delight in her body.
Never take her love for granted!
Why would you trade enduring intimacies
for cheap thrills with a whore?
for dalliance with a promiscuous stranger?

21-23 Mark well that GOD doesn't miss a move you make;
he's aware of every step you take.
The shadow of your sin will overtake you;
you'll find yourself stumbling all over yourself in the dark.
Death is the reward of an undisciplined life;
your foolish decisions trap you in a dead end.

Like a Deer from the Hunter

1-5 6 Dear friend, if you've gone into hock with your neighbor
or locked yourself into a deal with a stranger,
If you've impulsively promised the shirt off your back
and now find yourself shivering out in the cold,
Friend, don't waste a minute, get yourself out of that mess.
You're in that man's clutches!
Go, put on a long face; act desperate.
Don't procrastinate—
there's no time to lose.
Run like a deer from the hunter,
fly like a bird from the trapper!

A Lesson from the Ant

6-11 You lazy fool, look at an ant.
Watch it closely; let it teach you a thing or two.
Nobody has to tell it what to do.

NEW KING JAMES VERSION

8Provides her supplies in the summer,
And gathers her food in the harvest.
9How long will you slumber, O sluggard?
When will you rise from your sleep?
10A little sleep, a little slumber,
A little folding of the hands to sleep—
11So shall your poverty come on you like a prowler,
And your need like an armed man.

THE WICKED MAN

12A worthless person, a wicked man,
Walks with a perverse mouth;
13He winks with his eyes,
He shuffles his feet,
He points with his fingers;
14Perversity *is* in his heart,
He devises evil continually,
He sows discord.
15Therefore his calamity shall come suddenly;
Suddenly he shall be broken without remedy.

16These six *things* the LORD hates,
Yes, seven *are* an abomination to Him:
17A proud look,
A lying tongue,
Hands that shed innocent blood,
18A heart that devises wicked plans,
Feet that are swift in running to evil,
19A false witness *who* speaks lies,
And one who sows discord among brethren.

BEWARE OF ADULTERY

20My son, keep your father's command,
And do not forsake the law of your mother.
21Bind them continually upon your heart;
Tie them around your neck.
22When you roam, they[a] will lead you;
When you sleep, they will keep you;
And *when* you awake, they will speak with you.
23For the commandment *is* a lamp,
And the law a light;
Reproofs of instruction *are* the way of life,
24To keep you from the evil woman,
From the flattering tongue of a seductress.
25Do not lust after her beauty in your heart,
Nor let her allure you with her eyelids.
26For by means of a harlot
A man is reduced to a crust of bread;
And an adulteress[a] will prey upon his precious life.
27Can a man take fire to his bosom,
And his clothes not be burned?
28Can one walk on hot coals,
And his feet not be seared?

6:22 [a]Literally *it* 6:26 [a]Literally *a man's wife,* that is, of another

THE MESSAGE

All summer it stores up food;
at harvest it stockpiles provisions.
So how long are you going to laze around doing nothing?
How long before you get out of bed?
A nap here, a nap there, a day off here, a day off there,
sit back, take it easy—do you know what comes next?
Just this: You can look forward to a dirt-poor life,
poverty your permanent houseguest!

ALWAYS COOKING UP SOMETHING NASTY

12-15 Riffraff and rascals
talk out of both sides of their mouths.
They wink at each other, they shuffle their feet,
they cross their fingers behind their backs.
Their perverse minds are always cooking up something nasty,
always stirring up trouble.
Catastrophe is just around the corner for them,
a total smashup, their lives ruined beyond repair.

SEVEN THINGS GOD HATES

16-19 Here are six things GOD hates,
and one more that he loathes with a passion:

eyes that are arrogant,
a tongue that lies,
hands that murder the innocent,
a heart that hatches evil plots,
feet that race down a wicked track,
a mouth that lies under oath,
a troublemaker in the family.

WARNING ON ADULTERY

20-23 Good friend, follow your father's good advice;
don't wander off from your mother's teachings.
Wrap yourself in them from head to foot;
wear them like a scarf around your neck.
Wherever you walk, they'll guide you;
whenever you rest, they'll guard you;
when you wake up, they'll tell you what's next.
For sound advice is a beacon,
good teaching is a light,
moral discipline is a life path.

24-35 They'll protect you from wanton women,
from the seductive talk of some temptress.
Don't lustfully fantasize on her beauty,
nor be taken in by her bedroom eyes.
You can buy an hour with a whore for a loaf of bread,
but a wanton woman may well eat *you* alive.
Can you build a fire in your lap
and not burn your pants?
Can you walk barefoot on hot coals
and not get blisters?

NEW KING JAMES VERSION

29So *is* he who goes in to his neighbor's wife;
Whoever touches her shall not be innocent.

30*People* do not despise a thief
If he steals to satisfy himself when he is starving.
31Yet *when* he is found, he must restore sevenfold;
He may have to give up all the substance of his house.
32Whoever commits adultery with a woman lacks understanding;
He *who* does so destroys his own soul.
33Wounds and dishonor he will get,
And his reproach will not be wiped away.
34For jealousy *is* a husband's fury;
Therefore he will not spare in the day of vengeance.
35He will accept no recompense,
Nor will he be appeased though you give many gifts.

7 My son, keep my words,
And treasure my commands within you.
2Keep my commands and live,
And my law as the apple of your eye.
3Bind them on your fingers;
Write them on the tablet of your heart.
4Say to wisdom, "You *are* my sister,"
And call understanding *your* nearest kin,
5That they may keep you from the immoral woman,
From the seductress *who* flatters with her words.

THE CRAFTY HARLOT

6For at the window of my house
I looked through my lattice,
7And saw among the simple,
I perceived among the youths,
A young man devoid of understanding,
8Passing along the street near her corner;
And he took the path to her house
9In the twilight, in the evening,
In the black and dark night.

10And there a woman met him,
With the attire of a harlot, and a crafty heart.
11She *was* loud and rebellious,
Her feet would not stay at home.
12At times *she was* outside, at times in the open square,
Lurking at every corner.
13So she caught him and kissed him;
With an impudent face she said to him:
14"*I have* peace offerings with me;
Today I have paid my vows.
15So I came out to meet you,
Diligently to seek your face,
And I have found you.
16I have spread my bed with tapestry,
Colored coverings of Egyptian linen.
17I have perfumed my bed
With myrrh, aloes, and cinnamon.
18Come, let us take our fill of love until morning;
Let us delight ourselves with love.

THE MESSAGE

It's the same when you have sex with your neighbor's wife:
Touch her and you'll pay for it. No excuses.
Hunger is no excuse
for a thief to steal;
When he's caught he has to pay it back,
even if he has to put his whole house in hock.
Adultery is a brainless act,
soul-destroying, self-destructive;
Expect a bloody nose, a black eye,
and a reputation ruined for good.
For jealousy detonates rage in a cheated husband;
wild for revenge, he won't make allowances.
Nothing you say or pay will make it all right;
neither bribes nor reason will satisfy him.

DRESSED TO SEDUCE

1-5 7 Dear friend, do what I tell you;
treasure my careful instructions.
Do what I say and you'll live well.
My teaching is as precious as your eyesight—guard it!
Write it out on the back of your hands;
etch it on the chambers of your heart.
Talk to Wisdom as to a sister.
Treat Insight as your companion.
They'll be with you to fend off the Temptress—
that smooth-talking, honey-tongued Seductress.

6-12 As I stood at the window of my house
looking out through the shutters,
Watching the mindless crowd stroll by,
I spotted a young man without any sense
Arriving at the corner of the street where she lived,
then turning up the path to her house.
It was dusk, the evening coming on,
the darkness thickening into night.
Just then, a woman met him—
she'd been lying in wait for him, dressed to seduce him.
Brazen and brash she was,
restless and roaming, never at home,
Walking the streets, loitering in the mall,
hanging out at every corner in town.

13-20 She threw her arms around him and kissed him,
boldly took his arm and said,
"I've got all the makings for a feast—
today I made my offerings, my vows are all paid,
So now I've come to find you,
hoping to catch sight of your face—and here you are!
I've spread fresh, clean sheets on my bed,
colorful imported linens.
My bed is aromatic with spices
and exotic fragrances.
Come, let's make love all night,
spend the night in ecstatic lovemaking!

NEW KING JAMES VERSION

[19]For my husband *is* not at home;
He has gone on a long journey;
[20]He has taken a bag of money with him,
And will come home on the appointed day."

[21]With her enticing speech she caused him to yield,
With her flattering lips she seduced him.
[22]Immediately he went after her, as an ox goes to the slaughter,
Or as a fool to the correction of the stocks,[a]
[23]Till an arrow struck his liver.
As a bird hastens to the snare,
He did not know it *would cost* his life.

[24]Now therefore, listen to me, *my* children;
Pay attention to the words of my mouth:
[25]Do not let your heart turn aside to her ways,
Do not stray into her paths;
[26]For she has cast down many wounded,
And all who were slain by her were strong *men*.
[27]Her house *is* the way to hell,[a]
Descending to the chambers of death.

THE EXCELLENCE OF WISDOM

8 Does not wisdom cry out,
And understanding lift up her voice?
[2]She takes her stand on the top of the high hill,
Beside the way, where the paths meet.
[3]She cries out by the gates, at the entry of the city,
At the entrance of the doors:
[4]"To you, O men, I call,
And my voice *is* to the sons of men.
[5]O you simple ones, understand prudence,
And you fools, be of an understanding heart.
[6]Listen, for I will speak of excellent things,
And from the opening of my lips *will come* right things;
[7]For my mouth will speak truth;
Wickedness *is* an abomination to my lips.
[8]All the words of my mouth *are* with righteousness;
Nothing crooked or perverse *is* in them.
[9]They *are* all plain to him who understands,
And right to those who find knowledge.
[10]Receive my instruction, and not silver,
And knowledge rather than choice gold;
[11]For wisdom *is* better than rubies,
And all the things one may desire cannot be compared with her.

[12]"I, wisdom, dwell with prudence,
And find out knowledge *and* discretion.
[13]The fear of the LORD *is* to hate evil;
Pride and arrogance and the evil way
And the perverse mouth I hate.
[14]Counsel *is* mine, and sound wisdom;
I *am* understanding, I have strength.

7:22 [a]Septuagint, Syriac, and Targum read *as a dog to bonds;* Vulgate reads *as a lamb . . . to bonds.* **7:27** [a]Or *Sheol*

THE MESSAGE

My husband's not home; he's away on business,
and he won't be back for a month."

21-23 Soon she has him eating out of her hand,
bewitched by her honeyed speech.
Before you know it, he's trotting behind her,
like a calf led to the butcher shop,
Like a stag lured into ambush
and then shot with an arrow,
Like a bird flying into a net
not knowing that its flying life is over.

24-27 So, friends, listen to me,
take these words of mine most seriously.
Don't fool around with a woman like that;
don't even stroll through her neighborhood.
Countless victims come under her spell;
she's the death of many a poor man.
She runs a halfway house to hell,
fits you out with a shroud and a coffin.

LADY WISDOM CALLS OUT

1-11 8 Do you hear Lady Wisdom calling?
Can you hear Madame Insight raising her voice?
She's taken her stand at First and Main,
at the busiest intersection.
Right in the city square
where the traffic is thickest, she shouts,
"You—I'm talking to all of you,
everyone out here on the streets!
Listen, you idiots—learn good sense!
You blockheads—shape up!
Don't miss a word of this—I'm telling you how to live well,
I'm telling you how to live at your best.
My mouth chews and savors and relishes truth—
I can't stand the taste of evil!
You'll only hear true and right words from my mouth;
not one syllable will be twisted or skewed.
You'll recognize this as true—you with open minds;
truth-ready minds will see it at once.
Prefer my life-disciplines over chasing after money,
and God-knowledge over a lucrative career.
For Wisdom is better than all the trappings of wealth;
nothing you could wish for holds a candle to her.

12-21 "I am Lady Wisdom, and I live next to Sanity;
Knowledge and Discretion live just down the street.
The Fear-of-GOD means hating Evil,
whose ways I hate with a passion—
pride and arrogance and crooked talk.
Good counsel and common sense are my characteristics;
I am both Insight and the Virtue to live it out.

NEW KING JAMES VERSION

15By me kings reign,
And rulers decree justice.
16By me princes rule, and nobles,
All the judges of the earth.[a]
17I love those who love me,
And those who seek me diligently will find me.
18Riches and honor *are* with me,
Enduring riches and righteousness.
19My fruit *is* better than gold, yes, than fine gold,
And my revenue than choice silver.
20I traverse the way of righteousness,
In the midst of the paths of justice,
21That I may cause those who love me to inherit wealth,
That I may fill their treasuries.

22"The LORD possessed me at the beginning of His way,
Before His works of old.
23I have been established from everlasting,
From the beginning, before there was ever an earth.
24When *there were* no depths I was brought forth,
When *there were* no fountains abounding with water.
25Before the mountains were settled,
Before the hills, I was brought forth;
26While as yet He had not made the earth or the fields,
Or the primal dust of the world.
27When He prepared the heavens, I *was* there,
When He drew a circle on the face of the deep,
28When He established the clouds above,
When He strengthened the fountains of the deep,
29When He assigned to the sea its limit,
So that the waters would not transgress His command,
When He marked out the foundations of the earth,
30Then I was beside Him *as* a master craftsman;[a]
And I was daily *His* delight,
Rejoicing always before Him,
31Rejoicing in His inhabited world,
And my delight *was* with the sons of men.

32"Now therefore, listen to me, *my* children,
For blessed *are those who* keep my ways.
33Hear instruction and be wise,
And do not disdain *it*.
34Blessed is the man who listens to me,
Watching daily at my gates,
Waiting at the posts of my doors.
35For whoever finds me finds life,
And obtains favor from the LORD;
36But he who sins against me wrongs his own soul;
All those who hate me love death."

8:16 [a]Masoretic Text, Syriac, Targum, and Vulgate read *righteousness;* Septuagint, Bomberg, and some manuscripts and editions read *earth.* **8:30** [a]A Jewish tradition reads *one brought up.*

THE MESSAGE

With my help, leaders rule,
and lawmakers legislate fairly;
With my help, governors govern,
along with all in legitimate authority.
I love those who love me;
those who look for me find me.
Wealth and Glory accompany me—
also substantial Honor and a Good Name.
My benefits are worth more than a big salary, even a *very* big salary;
the returns on me exceed any imaginable bonus.
You can find me on Righteous Road—that's where I walk—
at the intersection of Justice Avenue,
Handing out life to those who love me,
filling their arms with life—armloads of life!

22-31 "GOD sovereignly made me—the first, the basic—
before he did anything else.
I was brought into being a long time ago,
well before Earth got its start.
I arrived on the scene before Ocean,
yes, even before Springs and Rivers and Lakes.
Before Mountains were sculpted and Hills took shape,
I was already there, newborn;
Long before GOD stretched out Earth's Horizons,
and tended to the minute details of Soil and Weather,
And set Sky firmly in place,
I was there.
When he mapped and gave borders to wild Ocean,
built the vast vault of Heaven,
and installed the fountains that fed Ocean,
When he drew a boundary for Sea,
posted a sign that said NO TRESPASSING,
And then staked out Earth's Foundations,
I was right there with him, making sure everything fit.
Day after day I was there, with my joyful applause,
always enjoying his company,
Delighted with the world of things and creatures,
happily celebrating the human family.

32-36 "So, my dear friends, listen carefully;
those who embrace these my ways are most blessed.
Mark a life of discipline and live wisely;
don't squander your precious life.
Blessed the man, blessed the woman, who listens to me,
awake and ready for me each morning,
alert and responsive as I start my day's work.
When you find me, you find life, real life,
to say nothing of GOD's good pleasure.
But if you wrong me, you damage your very soul;
when you reject me, you're flirting with death."

NEW KING JAMES VERSION

THE WAY OF WISDOM

9 Wisdom has built her house,
She has hewn out her seven pillars;
2She has slaughtered her meat,
She has mixed her wine,
She has also furnished her table.
3She has sent out her maidens,
She cries out from the highest places of the city,
4"Whoever *is* simple, let him turn in here!"
As for him who lacks understanding, she says to him,
5"Come, eat of my bread
And drink of the wine I have mixed.
6Forsake foolishness and live,
And go in the way of understanding.

7"He who corrects a scoffer gets shame for himself,
And he who rebukes a wicked *man only* harms himself.
8Do not correct a scoffer, lest he hate you;
Rebuke a wise *man*, and he will love you.
9Give *instruction* to a wise *man*, and he will be still wiser;
Teach a just *man*, and he will increase in learning.

10"The fear of the LORD *is* the beginning of wisdom,
And the knowledge of the Holy One *is* understanding.
11For by me your days will be multiplied,
And years of life will be added to you.
12If you are wise, you are wise for yourself,
And *if* you scoff, you will bear *it* alone."

THE WAY OF FOLLY

13A foolish woman is clamorous;
She is simple, and knows nothing.
14For she sits at the door of her house,
On a seat *by* the highest places of the city,
15To call to those who pass by,
Who go straight on their way:
16"Whoever *is* simple, let him turn in here";
And *as for* him who lacks understanding, she says to him,
17"Stolen water is sweet,
And bread *eaten* in secret is pleasant."
18But he does not know that the dead *are* there,
That her guests *are* in the depths of hell.[a]

9:18 [a]Or *Sheol*

THE MESSAGE

LADY WISDOM GIVES A DINNER PARTY

1-6 9 Lady Wisdom has built and furnished her home;
it's supported by seven hewn timbers.
The banquet meal is ready to be served:
lamb roasted,
wine poured out, table set with silver and flowers.
Having dismissed her serving maids,
Lady Wisdom goes to town, stands in a prominent place,
and invites everyone within sound of her voice:
"Are you confused about life, don't know what's going on?
Come with me, oh come, have dinner with me!
I've prepared a wonderful spread—
fresh-baked bread,
roast lamb, carefully selected wines.
Leave your impoverished confusion and *live*!
Walk up the street to a life with meaning."

7-12 If you reason with an arrogant cynic, you'll get slapped in the face;
confront bad behavior and get a kick in the shins.
So don't waste your time on a scoffer;
all you'll get for your pains is abuse.
But if you correct those who care about life,
that's different—they'll love you for it!
Save your breath for the wise—they'll be wiser for it;
tell good people what you know—they'll profit from it.
Skilled living gets its start in the Fear-of-GOD,
insight into life from knowing a Holy God.
It's through me, Lady Wisdom, that your life deepens,
and the years of your life ripen.
Live wisely and wisdom will permeate your life;
mock life and life will mock you.

MADAME WHORE CALLS OUT, TOO

13-18 Then there's this other woman, Madame Whore—
brazen, empty-headed, frivolous.
She sits on the front porch
of her house on Main Street,
And as people walk by minding
their own business, calls out,
"Are you confused about life, don't know what's going on?
Steal off with me, I'll show you a good time!
No one will ever know—I'll give you the time of your life."
But they don't know about all the skeletons in her closet,
that all her guests end up in hell.

NEW KING JAMES VERSION

WISE SAYINGS OF SOLOMON

10 The proverbs of Solomon:

A wise son makes a glad father,
But a foolish son *is* the grief of his mother.
2 Treasures of wickedness profit nothing,
But righteousness delivers from death.
3 The LORD will not allow the righteous soul to famish,
But He casts away the desire of the wicked.

4 He who has a slack hand becomes poor,
But the hand of the diligent makes rich.
5 He who gathers in summer *is* a wise son;
He who sleeps in harvest *is* a son who causes shame.

6 Blessings *are* on the head of the righteous,
But violence covers the mouth of the wicked.
7 The memory of the righteous *is* blessed,
But the name of the wicked will rot.

8 The wise in heart will receive commands,
But a prating fool will fall.

9 He who walks with integrity walks securely,
But he who perverts his ways will become known.

10 He who winks with the eye causes trouble,
But a prating fool will fall.

11 The mouth of the righteous *is* a well of life,
But violence covers the mouth of the wicked.

12 Hatred stirs up strife,
But love covers all sins.

13 Wisdom is found on the lips of him who has understanding,
But a rod *is* for the back of him who is devoid of understanding.

14 Wise *people* store up knowledge,
But the mouth of the foolish *is* near destruction.
15 The rich man's wealth *is* his strong city;
The destruction of the poor *is* their poverty.

16 The labor of the righteous *leads* to life,
The wages of the wicked to sin.

17 He who keeps instruction *is in* the way of life,
But he who refuses correction goes astray.

18 Whoever hides hatred *has* lying lips,
And whoever spreads slander *is* a fool.

19 In the multitude of words sin is not lacking,
But he who restrains his lips *is* wise.

THE MESSAGE

THE WISE SAYINGS OF SOLOMON

AN HONEST LIFE IS IMMORTAL

1 10 Wise son, glad father;
stupid son, sad mother.

2 Ill-gotten gain gets you nowhere;
an honest life is immortal.

3 GOD won't starve an honest soul,
but he frustrates the appetites of the wicked.

4 Sloth makes you poor;
diligence brings wealth.

5 Make hay while the sun shines—that's smart;
go fishing during harvest—that's stupid.

6 Blessings accrue on a good and honest life,
but the mouth of the wicked is a dark cave of abuse.

7 A good and honest life is a blessed memorial;
a wicked life leaves a rotten stench.

8 A wise heart takes orders;
an empty head will come unglued.

9 Honesty lives confident and carefree,
but Shifty is sure to be exposed.

10 An evasive eye is a sign of trouble ahead,
but an open, face-to-face meeting results in peace.

11 The mouth of a good person is a deep, life-giving well,
but the mouth of the wicked is a dark cave of abuse.

12 Hatred starts fights,
but love pulls a quilt over the bickering.

13 You'll find wisdom on the lips of a person of insight,
but the shortsighted needs a slap in the face.

14 The wise accumulate knowledge—a true treasure;
know-it-alls talk too much—a sheer waste.

THE ROAD TO LIFE IS A DISCIPLINED LIFE

15 The wealth of the rich is their bastion;
the poverty of the indigent is their ruin.

16 The wage of a good person is exuberant life;
an evil person ends up with nothing but sin.

17 The road to life is a disciplined life;
ignore correction and you're lost for good.

18 Liars secretly hoard hatred;
fools openly spread slander.

19 The more talk, the less truth;
the wise measure their words.

New King James Version

20The tongue of the righteous *is* choice silver;
The heart of the wicked *is worth* little.
21The lips of the righteous feed many,
But fools die for lack of wisdom.[a]

22The blessing of the LORD makes *one* rich,
And He adds no sorrow with it.

23To do evil *is* like sport to a fool,
But a man of understanding has wisdom.
24The fear of the wicked will come upon him,
And the desire of the righteous will be granted.
25When the whirlwind passes by, the wicked *is* no *more*,
But the righteous *has* an everlasting foundation.

26As vinegar to the teeth and smoke to the eyes,
So *is* the lazy *man* to those who send him.

27The fear of the LORD prolongs days,
But the years of the wicked will be shortened.
28The hope of the righteous *will be* gladness,
But the expectation of the wicked will perish.
29The way of the LORD *is* strength for the upright,
But destruction *will come* to the workers of iniquity.

30The righteous will never be removed,
But the wicked will not inhabit the earth.
31The mouth of the righteous brings forth wisdom,
But the perverse tongue will be cut out.
32The lips of the righteous know what is acceptable,
But the mouth of the wicked *what is* perverse.

11 Dishonest scales *are* an abomination to the LORD,
But a just weight *is* His delight.

2When pride comes, then comes shame;
But with the humble *is* wisdom.

3The integrity of the upright will guide them,
But the perversity of the unfaithful will destroy them.
4Riches do not profit in the day of wrath,
But righteousness delivers from death.
5The righteousness of the blameless will direct[a] his way aright,
But the wicked will fall by his own wickedness.

10:21 [a]Literally *heart* 11:5 [a]Or *make smooth* or *straight*

The Message

20 The speech of a good person is worth waiting for;
the blabber of the wicked is worthless.

21 The talk of a good person is rich fare for many,
but chatterboxes die of an empty heart.

Fear-of-God Expands Your Life

22 GOD's blessing makes life rich;
nothing we do can improve on God.

23 An empty-head thinks mischief is fun,
but a mindful person relishes wisdom.

24 The nightmares of the wicked come true;
what the good people desire, they get.

25 When the storm is over, there's nothing left of the wicked;
good people, firm on their rock foundation, aren't even fazed.

26 A lazy employee will give you nothing but trouble;
it's vinegar in the mouth, smoke in the eyes.

27 The Fear-of-GOD expands your life;
a wicked life is a puny life.

28 The aspirations of good people end in celebration;
the ambitions of bad people crash.

29 GOD is solid backing to a well-lived life,
but he calls into question a shabby performance.

30 Good people *last*—they can't be moved;
the wicked are here today, gone tomorrow.

31 A good person's mouth is a clear fountain of wisdom;
a foul mouth is a stagnant swamp.

32 The speech of a good person clears the air;
the words of the wicked pollute it.

Without Good Direction, People Lose Their Way

1 11 GOD hates cheating in the marketplace;
he loves it when business is above-board.

2 The stuck-up fall flat on their faces,
but down-to-earth people stand firm.

3 The integrity of the honest keeps them on track;
the deviousness of crooks brings them to ruin.

4 A thick bankroll is no help when life falls apart,
but a principled life can stand up to the worst.

5 Moral character makes for smooth traveling;
an evil life is a hard life.

NEW KING JAMES VERSION

6The righteousness of the upright will deliver them,
But the unfaithful will be caught by *their* lust.

7When a wicked man dies, *his* expectation will perish,
And the hope of the unjust perishes.
8The righteous is delivered from trouble,
And it comes to the wicked instead.
9The hypocrite with *his* mouth destroys his neighbor,
But through knowledge the righteous will be delivered.
10When it goes well with the righteous, the city rejoices;
And when the wicked perish, *there is* jubilation.
11By the blessing of the upright the city is exalted,
But it is overthrown by the mouth of the wicked.

12He who is devoid of wisdom despises his neighbor,
But a man of understanding holds his peace.

13A talebearer reveals secrets,
But he who is of a faithful spirit conceals a matter.

14Where *there is* no counsel, the people fall;
But in the multitude of counselors *there is* safety.

15He who is surety for a stranger will suffer,
But one who hates being surety is secure.

16A gracious woman retains honor,
But ruthless *men* retain riches.
17The merciful man does good for his own soul,
But *he who is* cruel troubles his own flesh.
18The wicked *man* does deceptive work,
But he who sows righteousness *will have* a sure reward.
19As righteousness *leads* to life,
So he who pursues evil *pursues it* to his own death.
20Those who are of a perverse heart *are* an abomination to the LORD,
But *the* blameless in their ways *are* His delight.
21*Though they join* forces,[a] the wicked will not go unpunished;
But the posterity of the righteous will be delivered.

22*As* a ring of gold in a swine's snout,
So is a lovely woman who lacks discretion.

11:21 [a]Literally *hand to hand*

THE MESSAGE

6 Good character is the best insurance;
crooks get trapped in their sinful lust.

7 When the wicked die, that's it—
the story's over, end of hope.

8 A good person is saved from much trouble;
a bad person runs straight into it.

9 The loose tongue of the godless spreads destruction;
the common sense of the godly preserves them.

10 When it goes well for good people, the whole town cheers;
when it goes badly for bad people, the town celebrates.

11 When right-living people bless the city, it flourishes;
evil talk turns it into a ghost town in no time.

12 Mean-spirited slander is heartless;
quiet discretion accompanies good sense.

13 A gadabout gossip can't be trusted with a secret,
but someone of integrity won't violate a confidence.

14 Without good direction, people lose their way;
the more wise counsel you follow, the better your chances.

15 Whoever makes deals with strangers is sure to get burned;
if you keep a cool head, you'll avoid rash bargains.

16 A woman of gentle grace gets respect,
but men of rough violence grab for loot.

A GOD-SHAPED LIFE

17 When you're kind to others, you help yourself;
when you're cruel to others, you hurt yourself.

18 Bad work gets paid with a bad check;
good work gets solid pay.

19 Take your stand with God's loyal community and live,
or chase after phantoms of evil and die.

20 GOD can't stand deceivers,
but oh how he relishes integrity.

21 Count on this: The wicked won't get off scot-free,
and God's loyal people will triumph.

22 Like a gold ring in a pig's snout
is a beautiful face on an empty head.

NEW KING JAMES VERSION

[23]The desire of the righteous *is* only good,
But the expectation of the wicked *is* wrath.

[24]There is *one* who scatters, yet increases more;
And there is *one* who withholds more than is right,
But it *leads* to poverty.
[25]The generous soul will be made rich,
And he who waters will also be watered himself.
[26]The people will curse him who withholds grain,
But blessing *will be* on the head of him who sells *it*.

[27]He who earnestly seeks good finds favor,
But trouble will come to him who seeks *evil*.

[28]He who trusts in his riches will fall,
But the righteous will flourish like foliage.
[29]He who troubles his own house will inherit the wind,
And the fool *will be* servant to the wise of heart.

[30]The fruit of the righteous *is a* tree of life,
And he who wins souls *is* wise.

[31]If the righteous will be recompensed on the earth,
How much more the ungodly and the sinner.

12 Whoever loves instruction loves knowledge,
But he who hates correction *is* stupid.

[2]A good *man* obtains favor from the LORD,
But a man of wicked intentions He will condemn.

[3]A man is not established by wickedness,
But the root of the righteous cannot be moved.

[4]An excellent[a] wife *is* the crown of her husband,
But she who causes shame *is* like rottenness in his bones.

[5]The thoughts of the righteous *are* right,
But the counsels of the wicked *are* deceitful.
[6]The words of the wicked *are*, "Lie in wait for blood,"
But the mouth of the upright will deliver them.

[7]The wicked are overthrown and *are* no more,
But the house of the righteous will stand.

[8]A man will be commended according to his wisdom,
But he who is of a perverse heart will be despised.

12:4 [a]Literally *A wife of valor*

THE MESSAGE

23 The desires of good people lead straight to the best,
but wicked ambition ends in angry frustration.

24 The world of the generous gets larger and larger;
the world of the stingy gets smaller and smaller.

25 The one who blesses others is abundantly blessed;
those who help others are helped.

26 Curses on those who drive a hard bargain!
Blessings on all who play fair and square!

27 The one who seeks good finds delight;
the student of evil becomes evil.

28 A life devoted to things is a dead life, a stump;
a God-shaped life is a flourishing tree.

29 Exploit or abuse your family, and end up with a fistful of air;
common sense tells you it's a stupid way to live.

30 A good life is a fruit-bearing tree;
a violent life destroys souls.

31 If good people barely make it,
what's in store for the bad!

IF YOU LOVE LEARNING

1 12 If you love learning, you love the discipline that goes with it—
how shortsighted to refuse correction!

2 A good person basks in the delight of GOD,
and he wants nothing to do with devious schemers.

3 You can't find firm footing in a swamp,
but life rooted in God stands firm.

4 A hearty wife invigorates her husband,
but a frigid woman is cancer in the bones.

5 The thinking of principled people makes for justice;
the plots of degenerates corrupt.

6 The words of the wicked kill;
the speech of the upright saves.

7 Wicked people fall to pieces—there's nothing to them;
the homes of good people hold together.

8 A person who talks sense is honored;
airheads are held in contempt.

NEW KING JAMES VERSION

9Better *is the one* who is slighted but has a servant,
Than he who honors himself but lacks bread.

10A righteous *man* regards the life of his animal,
But the tender mercies of the wicked *are* cruel.

11He who tills his land will be satisfied with bread,
But he who follows frivolity *is* devoid of understanding.[a]

12The wicked covet the catch of evil *men*,
But the root of the righteous yields *fruit*.
13The wicked is ensnared by the transgression of *his* lips,
But the righteous will come through trouble.
14A man will be satisfied with good by the fruit of *his* mouth,
And the recompense of a man's hands will be rendered to him.

15The way of a fool *is* right in his own eyes,
But he who heeds counsel *is* wise.
16A fool's wrath is known at once,
But a prudent *man* covers shame.

17He *who* speaks truth declares righteousness,
But a false witness, deceit.
18There is one who speaks like the piercings of a sword,
But the tongue of the wise *promotes* health.
19The truthful lip shall be established forever,
But a lying tongue *is* but for a moment.
20Deceit is in the heart of those who devise evil,
But counselors of peace have joy.
21No grave trouble will overtake the righteous,
But the wicked shall be filled with evil.
22Lying lips *are* an abomination to the LORD,
But those who deal truthfully *are* His delight.

23A prudent man conceals knowledge,
But the heart of fools proclaims foolishness.

24The hand of the diligent will rule,
But the lazy *man* will be put to forced labor.

25Anxiety in the heart of man causes depression,
But a good word makes it glad.

26The righteous should choose his friends carefully,
For the way of the wicked leads them astray.

12:11 [a]Literally *heart*

THE MESSAGE

9 Better to be ordinary and work for a living
than act important and starve in the process.

10 Good people are good to their animals;
the "good-hearted" bad people kick and abuse them.

11 The one who stays on the job has food on the table;
the witless chase whims and fancies.

12 What the wicked construct finally falls into ruin,
while the roots of the righteous give life, and more life.

WISE PEOPLE TAKE ADVICE

13 The gossip of bad people gets them in trouble;
the conversation of good people keeps them out of it.

14 Well-spoken words bring satisfaction;
well-done work has its own reward.

15 Fools are headstrong and do what they like;
wise people take advice.

16 Fools have short fuses and explode all too quickly;
the prudent quietly shrug off insults.

17 Truthful witness by a good person clears the air,
but liars lay down a smoke screen of deceit.

18 Rash language cuts and maims,
but there is healing in the words of the wise.

19 Truth lasts;
lies are here today, gone tomorrow.

20 Evil scheming distorts the schemer;
peace-planning brings joy to the planner.

21 No evil can overwhelm a good person,
but the wicked have their hands full of it.

22 God can't stomach liars;
he loves the company of those who keep their word.

23 Prudent people don't flaunt their knowledge;
talkative fools broadcast their silliness.

24 The diligent find freedom in their work;
the lazy are oppressed by work.

25 Worry weighs us down;
a cheerful word picks us up.

26 A good person survives misfortune,
but a wicked life invites disaster.

NEW KING JAMES VERSION

27The lazy *man* does not roast what he took in
hunting,
But diligence *is* man's precious possession.

28In the way of righteousness *is* life,
And in *its* pathway *there is* no death.

13 A wise son *heeds* his father's instruction,
But a scoffer does not listen to rebuke.

2A man shall eat well by the fruit of *his*
mouth,
But the soul of the unfaithful feeds on
violence.
3He who guards his mouth preserves his life,
But he who opens wide his lips shall have
destruction.

4The soul of a lazy *man* desires, and *has*
nothing;
But the soul of the diligent shall be made
rich.

5A righteous *man* hates lying,
But a wicked *man* is loathsome and comes
to shame.
6Righteousness guards *him whose* way is
blameless,
But wickedness overthrows the sinner.

7There is one who makes himself rich, yet
has nothing;
And one who makes himself poor, yet *has*
great riches.

8The ransom of a man's life *is* his riches,
But the poor does not hear rebuke.

9The light of the righteous rejoices,
But the lamp of the wicked will be put out.

10By pride comes nothing but strife,
But with the well-advised *is* wisdom.

11Wealth *gained by* dishonesty will be
diminished,
But he who gathers by labor will increase.

12Hope deferred makes the heart sick,
But *when* the desire comes, *it is* a tree of
life.

13He who despises the word will be destroyed,
But he who fears the commandment will be
rewarded.
14The law of the wise *is* a fountain of life,
To turn *one* away from the snares of death.

15Good understanding gains favor,
But the way of the unfaithful *is* hard.
16Every prudent *man* acts with knowledge,
But a fool lays open *his* folly.

17A wicked messenger falls into trouble,
But a faithful ambassador *brings* health.

THE MESSAGE

27 A lazy life is an empty life,
but "early to rise" gets the job done.

28 Good men and women travel right into life;
sin's detours take you straight to hell.

WALK WITH THE WISE

1 13 Intelligent children listen to their
parents;
foolish children do their own thing.

2 The good acquire a taste for helpful
conversation;
bullies push and shove their way through
life.

3 Careful words make for a careful life;
careless talk may ruin everything.

4 Indolence wants it all and gets nothing;
the energetic have something to show for
their lives.

5 A good person hates false talk;
a bad person wallows in gibberish.

6 A God-loyal life keeps you on track;
sin dumps the wicked in the ditch.

7 A pretentious, showy life is an empty life;
a plain and simple life is a full life.

8 The rich can be sued for everything they
have,
but the poor are free of such threats.

9 The lives of good people are brightly lit
streets;
the lives of the wicked are dark alleys.

10 Arrogant know-it-alls stir up discord,
but wise men and women listen to each
other's counsel.

11 Easy come, easy go,
but steady diligence pays off.

12 Unrelenting disappointment leaves you
heartsick,
but a sudden good break can turn life
around.

13 Ignore the Word and suffer;
honor God's commands and grow rich.

14 The teaching of the wise is a fountain of life,
so, no more drinking from death-tainted
wells!

15 Sound thinking makes for gracious living,
but liars walk a rough road.

16 A commonsense person *lives* good sense;
fools litter the country with silliness.

17 Irresponsible talk makes a real mess of
things,
but a reliable reporter is a healing
presence.

NEW KING JAMES VERSION

18Poverty and shame *will come* to him who
disdains correction,
But he who regards a rebuke will be
honored.

19A desire accomplished is sweet to the soul,
But *it is* an abomination to fools to depart
from evil.

20He who walks with wise *men* will be wise,
But the companion of fools will be destroyed.

21Evil pursues sinners,
But to the righteous, good shall be repaid.

22A good *man* leaves an inheritance to his
children's children,
But the wealth of the sinner is stored up for
the righteous.

23Much food *is in* the fallow *ground* of the
poor,
And for lack of justice there is waste.[a]

24He who spares his rod hates his son,
But he who loves him disciplines him
promptly.

25The righteous eats to the satisfying of his
soul,
But the stomach of the wicked shall be in
want.

14 The wise woman builds her house,
But the foolish pulls it down with her
hands.

2He who walks in his uprightness fears the
LORD,
But *he who is* perverse in his ways despises
Him.

3In the mouth of a fool *is* a rod of pride,
But the lips of the wise will preserve them.

4Where no oxen *are*, the trough *is* clean;
But much increase *comes* by the strength of
an ox.

5A faithful witness does not lie,
But a false witness will utter lies.

6A scoffer seeks wisdom and does not *find it*,
But knowledge *is* easy to him who
understands.
7Go from the presence of a foolish man,
When you do not perceive *in him* the lips of
knowledge.
8The wisdom of the prudent *is* to understand
his way,
But the folly of fools *is* deceit.

9Fools mock at sin,
But among the upright *there is* favor.

10The heart knows its own bitterness,
And a stranger does not share its joy.

13:23 [a]Literally *what is swept away*

THE MESSAGE

18 Refuse discipline and end up homeless;
embrace correction and live an honored
life.

19 Souls who follow their hearts thrive;
fools bent on evil despise matters of soul.

20 Become wise by walking with the wise;
hang out with fools and watch your life
fall to pieces.

21 Disaster entraps sinners,
but God-loyal people get a good life.

22 A good life gets passed on to the
grandchildren;
ill-gotten wealth ends up with good
people.

23 Banks foreclose on the farms of the poor,
or else the poor lose their shirts to
crooked lawyers.

24 A refusal to correct is a refusal to love;
love your children by disciplining them.

25 An appetite for good brings much
satisfaction,
but the belly of the wicked always wants
more.

A WAY THAT LEADS TO HELL

1 14 Lady Wisdom builds a lovely home;
Sir Fool comes along and tears it
down brick by brick.

2 An honest life shows respect for GOD;
a degenerate life is a slap in his face.

3 Frivolous talk provokes a derisive smile;
wise speech evokes nothing but respect.

4 No cattle, no crops;
a good harvest requires a strong ox for
the plow.

5 A true witness never lies;
a false witness makes a business of it.

6 Cynics look high and low for wisdom—and
never find it;
the open-minded find it right on their
doorstep!

7 Escape quickly from the company of fools;
they're a waste of your time, a waste of
your words.

8 The wisdom of the wise keeps life on track;
the foolishness of fools lands them in the
ditch.

9 The stupid ridicule right and wrong,
but a moral life is a favored life.

10 The person who shuns the bitter moments
of friends
will be an outsider at their celebrations.

NEW KING JAMES VERSION

[11]The house of the wicked will be overthrown,
But the tent of the upright will flourish.

[12]There is a way *that seems* right to a man,
But its end *is* the way of death.
[13]Even in laughter the heart may sorrow,
And the end of mirth *may be* grief.
[14]The backslider in heart will be filled with his own ways,
But a good man *will be satisfied* from above.[a]

[15]The simple believes every word,
But the prudent considers well his steps.
[16]A wise *man* fears and departs from evil,
But a fool rages and is self-confident.
[17]A quick-tempered *man* acts foolishly,
And a man of wicked intentions is hated.
[18]The simple inherit folly,
But the prudent are crowned with knowledge.
[19]The evil will bow before the good,
And the wicked at the gates of the righteous.

[20]The poor *man* is hated even by his own neighbor,
But the rich *has* many friends.
[21]He who despises his neighbor sins;
But he who has mercy on the poor, happy *is* he.
[22]Do they not go astray who devise evil?
But mercy and truth *belong* to those who devise good.

[23]In all labor there is profit,
But idle chatter[a] *leads* only to poverty.

[24]The crown of the wise is their riches,
But the foolishness of fools *is* folly.

[25]A true witness delivers souls,
But a deceitful *witness* speaks lies.

[26]In the fear of the LORD *there is* strong confidence,
And His children will have a place of refuge.
[27]The fear of the LORD *is* a fountain of life,
To turn *one* away from the snares of death.

[28]In a multitude of people *is* a king's honor,
But in the lack of people *is* the downfall of a prince.

[29]*He who is* slow to wrath has great understanding,
But *he who is* impulsive[a] exalts folly.

14:14 [a]Literally *from above himself* 14:23 [a]Literally *talk of the lips* 14:29 [a]Literally *short of spirit*

THE MESSAGE

11 Lives of careless wrongdoing are tumbledown shacks;
holy living builds soaring cathedrals.

12-13 There's a way of life that looks harmless enough;
look again—it leads straight to hell.
Sure, those people appear to be having a good time,
but all that laughter will end in heartbreak.

SIFT AND WEIGH EVERY WORD

14 A mean person gets paid back in meanness,
a gracious person in grace.

15 The gullible believe anything they're told;
the prudent sift and weigh every word.

16 The wise watch their steps and avoid evil;
fools are headstrong and reckless.

17 The hotheaded do things they'll later regret;
the coldhearted get the cold shoulder.

18 Foolish dreamers live in a world of illusion;
wise realists plant their feet on the ground.

19 Eventually, evil will pay tribute to good;
the wicked will respect God-loyal people.

20 An unlucky loser is shunned by all,
but everyone loves a winner.

21 It's criminal to ignore a neighbor in need,
but compassion for the poor—what a blessing!

22 Isn't it obvious that conspirators lose out,
while the thoughtful win love and trust?

23 Hard work always pays off;
mere talk puts no bread on the table.

24 The wise accumulate wisdom;
fools get stupider by the day.

25 Souls are saved by truthful witness
and betrayed by the spread of lies.

26 The Fear-of-GOD builds up confidence,
and makes a world safe for your children.

27 The Fear-of-GOD is a spring of living water
so you won't go off drinking from poisoned wells.

28 The mark of a good leader is loyal followers;
leadership is nothing without a following.

29 Slowness to anger makes for deep understanding;
a quick-tempered person stockpiles stupidity.

NEW KING JAMES VERSION

[30]A sound heart *is* life to the body,
But envy *is* rottenness to the bones.

[31]He who oppresses the poor reproaches his Maker,
But he who honors Him has mercy on the needy.

[32]The wicked is banished in his wickedness,
But the righteous has a refuge in his death.

[33]Wisdom rests in the heart of him who has understanding,
But *what is* in the heart of fools is made known.

[34]Righteousness exalts a nation,
But sin *is* a reproach to *any* people.

[35]The king's favor *is* toward a wise servant,
But his wrath *is against* him who causes shame.

15 A soft answer turns away wrath,
But a harsh word stirs up anger.

[2]The tongue of the wise uses knowledge rightly,
But the mouth of fools pours forth foolishness.

[3]The eyes of the LORD *are* in every place,
Keeping watch on the evil and the good.

[4]A wholesome tongue *is* a tree of life,
But perverseness in it breaks the spirit.

[5]A fool despises his father's instruction,
But he who receives correction is prudent.

[6]*In* the house of the righteous *there is* much treasure,
But in the revenue of the wicked is trouble.

[7]The lips of the wise disperse knowledge,
But the heart of the fool *does* not *do* so.

[8]The sacrifice of the wicked *is* an abomination to the LORD,
But the prayer of the upright *is* His delight.

[9]The way of the wicked *is* an abomination to the LORD,
But He loves him who follows righteousness.

[10]Harsh discipline *is* for him who forsakes the way,
And he who hates correction will die.

[11]Hell[a] and Destruction[b] *are* before the LORD;
So how much more the hearts of the sons of men.

[12]A scoffer does not love one who corrects him,
Nor will he go to the wise.

15:11 [a]Or *Sheol* [b]Hebrew *Abaddon*

THE MESSAGE

30 A sound mind makes for a robust body,
but runaway emotions corrode the bones.

31 You insult your Maker when you exploit the powerless;
when you're kind to the poor, you honor God.

32 The evil of bad people leaves them out in the cold;
the integrity of good people creates a safe place for living.

33 Lady Wisdom is at home in an understanding heart—
fools never even get to say hello.

34 God-devotion makes a country strong;
God-avoidance leaves people weak.

35 Diligent work gets a warm commendation;
shiftless work earns an angry rebuke.

GOD DOESN'T MISS A THING

1 15 A gentle response defuses anger,
but a sharp tongue kindles a temper-fire.

2 Knowledge flows like spring water from the wise;
fools are leaky faucets, dripping nonsense.

3 GOD doesn't miss a thing—
he's alert to good and evil alike.

4 Kind words heal and help;
cutting words wound and maim.

5 Moral dropouts won't listen to their elders;
welcoming correction is a mark of good sense.

6 The lives of God-loyal people flourish;
a misspent life is soon bankrupt.

7 Perceptive words spread knowledge;
fools are hollow—there's nothing to them.

8 GOD can't stand pious poses,
but he delights in genuine prayers.

9 A life frittered away disgusts GOD;
he loves those who run straight for the finish line.

10 It's a school of hard knocks for those who leave God's path,
a dead-end street for those who hate God's rules.

11 Even hell holds no secrets from GOD—
do you think he can't read human hearts?

LIFE ASCENDS TO THE HEIGHTS

12 Know-it-alls don't like being told what to do;
they avoid the company of wise men and women.

NEW KING JAMES VERSION

13A merry heart makes a cheerful countenance,
But by sorrow of the heart the spirit is broken.

14The heart of him who has understanding seeks knowledge,
But the mouth of fools feeds on foolishness.

15All the days of the afflicted *are* evil,
But he who is of a merry heart *has* a continual feast.

16Better *is* a little with the fear of the LORD,
Than great treasure with trouble.
17Better *is* a dinner of herbs[a] where love is,
Than a fatted calf with hatred.

18A wrathful man stirs up strife,
But *he who is* slow to anger allays contention.

19The way of the lazy *man is* like a hedge of thorns,
But the way of the upright *is* a highway.

20A wise son makes a father glad,
But a foolish man despises his mother.

21Folly *is* joy *to him who is* destitute of discernment,
But a man of understanding walks uprightly.

22Without counsel, plans go awry,
But in the multitude of counselors they are established.

23A man has joy by the answer of his mouth,
And a word *spoken* in due season, how good *it is!*

24The way of life *winds* upward for the wise,
That he may turn away from hell[a] below.

25The LORD will destroy the house of the proud,
But He will establish the boundary of the widow.

26The thoughts of the wicked *are* an abomination to the LORD,
But *the words* of the pure *are* pleasant.

27He who is greedy for gain troubles his own house,
But he who hates bribes will live.

28The heart of the righteous studies how to answer,
But the mouth of the wicked pours forth evil.

29The LORD *is* far from the wicked,
But He hears the prayer of the righteous.

15:17 [a]Or *vegetables* **15:24** [a]Or *Sheol*

THE MESSAGE

13 A cheerful heart brings a smile to your face;
a sad heart makes it hard to get through the day.

14 An intelligent person is always eager to take in more truth;
fools feed on fast-food fads and fancies.

15 A miserable heart means a miserable life;
a cheerful heart fills the day with song.

16 A simple life in the Fear-of-GOD
is better than a rich life with a ton of headaches.

17 Better a bread crust shared in love
than a slab of prime rib served in hate.

18 Hot tempers start fights;
a calm, cool spirit keeps the peace.

19 The path of lazy people is overgrown with briers;
the diligent walk down a smooth road.

20 Intelligent children make their parents proud;
lazy students embarrass their parents.

21 The empty-headed treat life as a plaything;
the perceptive grasp its meaning and make a go of it.

22 Refuse good advice and watch your plans fail;
take good counsel and watch them succeed.

23 Congenial conversation—what a pleasure!
The right word at the right time—beautiful!

24 Life ascends to the heights for the thoughtful—
it's a clean about-face from descent into hell.

25 GOD smashes the pretensions of the arrogant;
he stands with those who have no standing.

26 GOD can't stand evil scheming,
but he puts words of grace and beauty on display.

27 A greedy and grasping person destroys community;
those who refuse to exploit live and let live.

28 Prayerful answers come from God-loyal people;
the wicked are sewers of abuse.

29 GOD keeps his distance from the wicked;
he closely attends to the prayers of God-loyal people.

NEW KING JAMES VERSION

30 The light of the eyes rejoices the heart,
And a good report makes the bones
healthy.[a]

31 The ear that hears the rebukes of life
Will abide among the wise.
32 He who disdains instruction despises his
own soul,
But he who heeds rebuke gets
understanding.
33 The fear of the LORD *is* the instruction of
wisdom,
And before honor *is* humility.

16 The preparations of the heart *belong* to
man,
But the answer of the tongue *is* from the
LORD.

2 All the ways of a man *are* pure in his own
eyes,
But the LORD weighs the spirits.
3 Commit your works to the LORD,
And your thoughts will be established.

4 The LORD has made all for Himself,
Yes, even the wicked for the day of doom.

5 Everyone proud in heart *is* an abomination
to the LORD;
Though they join forces,[a] none will go
unpunished.

6 In mercy and truth
Atonement is provided for iniquity;
And by the fear of the LORD *one* departs
from evil.

7 When a man's ways please the LORD,
He makes even his enemies to be at peace
with him.
8 Better *is* a little with righteousness,
Than vast revenues without justice.

9 A man's heart plans his way,
But the LORD directs his steps.
10 Divination *is* on the lips of the king;
His mouth must not transgress in judgment.
11 Honest weights and scales *are* the LORD's;
All the weights in the bag *are* His work.
12 *It is* an abomination for kings to commit
wickedness,
For a throne is established by righteousness.
13 Righteous lips *are* the delight of kings,
And they love him who speaks *what is*
right.
14 As messengers of death *is* the king's wrath,
But a wise man will appease it.

15:30 [a]Literally *fat* **16:5** [a]Literally *hand to hand*

THE MESSAGE

30 A twinkle in the eye means joy in the heart,
and good news makes you feel fit as a
fiddle.

31 Listen to good advice if you want to live
well,
an honored guest among wise men and
women.

32 An undisciplined, self-willed life is puny;
an obedient, God-willed life is spacious.

33 Fear-of-GOD is a school in skilled living—
first you learn humility, then you
experience glory.

EVERYTHING WITH A PLACE AND A PURPOSE

1 16 Mortals make elaborate plans,
but GOD has the last word.

2 Humans are satisfied with whatever looks
good;
GOD probes for what *is* good.

3 Put GOD in charge of your work,
then what you've planned will take
place.

4 GOD made everything with a place and
purpose;
even the wicked are included—but for
judgment.

5 GOD can't stomach arrogance or pretense;
believe me, he'll put those upstarts in
their place.

6 Guilt is banished through love and truth;
Fear-of-GOD deflects evil.

7 When GOD approves of your life,
even your enemies will end up shaking
your hand.

8 Far better to be right and poor
than to be wrong and rich.

9 We plan the way we want to live,
but only GOD makes us able to live it.

IT PAYS TO TAKE LIFE SERIOUSLY

10 A good leader motivates,
doesn't mislead, doesn't exploit.

11 GOD cares about honesty in the workplace;
your business is his business.

12 Good leaders abhor wrongdoing of all kinds;
sound leadership has a moral
foundation.

13 Good leaders cultivate honest speech;
they love advisors who tell them the truth.

14 An intemperate leader wreaks havoc in
lives;
you're smart to stay clear of someone
like that.

New King James Version

[15]In the light of the king's face *is* life,
And his favor *is* like a cloud of the latter rain.

[16]How much better to get wisdom than gold!
And to get understanding is to be chosen rather than silver.

[17]The highway of the upright *is* to depart from evil;
He who keeps his way preserves his soul.

[18]Pride *goes* before destruction,
And a haughty spirit before a fall.
[19]Better *to be* of a humble spirit with the lowly,
Than to divide the spoil with the proud.

[20]He who heeds the word wisely will find good,
And whoever trusts in the LORD, happy *is* he.

[21]The wise in heart will be called prudent,
And sweetness of the lips increases learning.

[22]Understanding *is* a wellspring of life to him who has it.
But the correction of fools *is* folly.

[23]The heart of the wise teaches his mouth,
And adds learning to his lips.

[24]Pleasant words *are like* a honeycomb,
Sweetness to the soul and health to the bones.

[25]There is a way *that seems* right to a man,
But its end *is* the way of death.

[26]The person who labors, labors for himself,
For his *hungry* mouth drives him *on*.

[27]An ungodly man digs up evil,
And *it is* on his lips like a burning fire.
[28]A perverse man sows strife,
And a whisperer separates the best of friends.
[29]A violent man entices his neighbor,
And leads him in a way *that is* not good.
[30]He winks his eye to devise perverse things;
He purses his lips *and* brings about evil.

[31]The silver-haired head *is* a crown of glory,
If it is found in the way of righteousness.

[32]*He who is* slow to anger *is* better than the mighty,
And he who rules his spirit than he who takes a city.

[33]The lot is cast into the lap,
But its every decision *is* from the LORD.

The Message

15 Good-tempered leaders invigorate lives;
they're like spring rain and sunshine.

16 Get wisdom—it's worth more than money;
choose insight over income every time.

17 The road of right living bypasses evil;
watch your step and save your life.

18 First pride, then the crash—
the bigger the ego, the harder the fall.

19 It's better to live humbly among the poor
than to live it up among the rich and famous.

20 It pays to take life seriously;
things work out when you trust in GOD.

21 A wise person gets known for insight;
gracious words add to one's reputation.

22 True intelligence is a spring of fresh water,
while fools sweat it out the hard way.

23 They make a lot of sense, these wise folks;
whenever they speak, their reputation increases.

24 Gracious speech is like clover honey—
good taste to the soul, quick energy for the body.

25 There's a way that looks harmless enough;
look again—it leads straight to hell.

26 Appetite is an incentive to work;
hunger makes you work all the harder.

27 Mean people spread mean gossip;
their words smart and burn.

28 Troublemakers start fights;
gossips break up friendships.

29 Calloused climbers betray their very own friends;
they'd stab their own grandmothers in the back.

30 A shifty eye betrays an evil intention;
a clenched jaw signals trouble ahead.

31 Gray hair is a mark of distinction,
the award for a God-loyal life.

32 Moderation is better than muscle,
self-control better than political power.

33 Make your motions and cast your votes,
but GOD has the final say.

New King James Version

17 Better *is* a dry morsel with quietness,
Than a house full of feasting[a] *with* strife.

2 A wise servant will rule over a son who causes shame,
And will share an inheritance among the brothers.
3 The refining pot *is* for silver and the furnace for gold,
But the LORD tests the hearts.

4 An evildoer gives heed to false lips;
A liar listens eagerly to a spiteful tongue.
5 He who mocks the poor reproaches his Maker;
He who is glad at calamity will not go unpunished.

6 Children's children *are* the crown of old men,
And the glory of children *is* their father.

7 Excellent speech is not becoming to a fool,
Much less lying lips to a prince.

8 A present *is* a precious stone in the eyes of its possessor;
Wherever he turns, he prospers.

9 He who covers a transgression seeks love,
But he who repeats a matter separates friends.

10 Rebuke is more effective for a wise *man*
Than a hundred blows on a fool.
11 An evil *man* seeks only rebellion;
Therefore a cruel messenger will be sent against him.
12 Let a man meet a bear robbed of her cubs,
Rather than a fool in his folly.

13 Whoever rewards evil for good,
Evil will not depart from his house.

14 The beginning of strife *is like* releasing water;
Therefore stop contention before a quarrel starts.
15 He who justifies the wicked, and he who condemns the just,
Both of them alike *are* an abomination to the LORD.
16 Why *is there* in the hand of a fool the purchase price of wisdom,
Since *he has* no heart *for it?*

17 A friend loves at all times,
And a brother is born for adversity.

17:1 [a]Or *sacrificial meals*

The Message

A Whack on the Head of a Fool

1 17 A meal of bread and water in contented peace
is better than a banquet spiced with quarrels.

2 A wise servant takes charge of an unruly child
and is honored as one of the family.

3 As silver in a crucible and gold in a pan,
so our lives are assayed by GOD.

4 Evil people relish malicious conversation;
the ears of liars itch for dirty gossip.

5 Whoever mocks poor people insults their Creator;
gloating over misfortune is a punishable crime.

6 Old people are distinguished by grandchildren;
children take pride in their parents.

7 We don't expect eloquence from fools,
nor do we expect lies from our leaders.

8 Receiving a gift is like getting a rare gemstone;
any way you look at it, you see beauty refracted.

9 Overlook an offense and bond a friendship;
fasten on to a slight and—good-bye, friend!

10 A quiet rebuke to a person of good sense
does more than a whack on the head of a fool.

11 Criminals out looking for nothing but trouble
won't have to wait long—they'll meet it coming and going!

12 Better to meet a grizzly robbed of her cubs
than a fool hellbent on folly.

13 Those who return evil for good
will meet their own evil returning.

14 The start of a quarrel is like a leak in a dam,
so stop it before it bursts.

15 Whitewashing bad people and throwing mud on good people
are equally abhorrent to GOD.

16 What's this? Fools out shopping for wisdom!
They wouldn't recognize it if they saw it!

One Who Knows Much Says Little

17 Friends love through all kinds of weather,
and families stick together in all kinds of trouble.

NEW KING JAMES VERSION

[18]A man devoid of understanding shakes hands in a pledge,
And becomes surety for his friend.

[19]He who loves transgression loves strife,
And he who exalts his gate seeks destruction.

[20]He who has a deceitful heart finds no good,
And he who has a perverse tongue falls into evil.

[21]He who begets a scoffer *does so* to his sorrow,
And the father of a fool has no joy.

[22]A merry heart does good, *like* medicine,[a]
But a broken spirit dries the bones.

[23]A wicked *man* accepts a bribe behind the back[a]
To pervert the ways of justice.

[24]Wisdom *is* in the sight of him who has understanding,
But the eyes of a fool *are* on the ends of the earth.

[25]A foolish son *is* a grief to his father,
And bitterness to her who bore him.

[26]Also, to punish the righteous *is* not good,
Nor to strike princes for *their* uprightness.

[27]He who has knowledge spares his words,
And a man of understanding is of a calm spirit.

[28]Even a fool is counted wise when he holds his peace;
When he shuts his lips, *he is considered* perceptive.

18 A man who isolates himself seeks his own desire;
He rages against all wise judgment.

[2]A fool has no delight in understanding,
But in expressing his own heart.

[3]When the wicked comes, contempt comes also;
And with dishonor *comes* reproach.

[4]The words of a man's mouth *are* deep waters;
The wellspring of wisdom *is* a flowing brook.

[5]*It is* not good to show partiality to the wicked,
Or to overthrow the righteous in judgment.

[6]A fool's lips enter into contention,
And his mouth calls for blows.

[7]A fool's mouth *is* his destruction,
And his lips *are* the snare of his soul.

17:22 [a]Or *makes medicine even better* **17:23** [a]Literally *from the bosom*

THE MESSAGE

[18] It's stupid to try to get something for nothing,
or run up huge bills you can never pay.

[19] The person who courts sin marries trouble;
build a wall, invite a burglar.

[20] A bad motive can't achieve a good end;
double-talk brings you double trouble.

[21] Having a fool for a child is misery;
it's no fun being the parent of a dolt.

[22] A cheerful disposition is good for your health;
gloom and doom leave you bone-tired.

[23] The wicked take bribes under the table;
they show nothing but contempt for justice.

[24] The perceptive find wisdom in their own front yard;
fools look for it everywhere but right here.

[25] A surly, stupid child is sheer pain to a father,
a bitter pill for a mother to swallow.

[26] It's wrong to penalize good behavior,
or make good citizens pay for the crimes of others.

[27] The one who knows much says little;
an understanding person remains calm.

[28] Even dunces who keep quiet are thought to be wise;
as long as they keep their mouths shut, they're smart.

WORDS KILL, WORDS GIVE LIFE

[1] 18 Loners who care only for themselves
spit on the common good.

[2] Fools care nothing for thoughtful discourse;
all they do is run off at the mouth.

[3] When wickedness arrives, shame's not far behind;
contempt for life is contemptible.

[4] Many words rush along like rivers in flood,
but deep wisdom flows up from artesian springs.

[5] It's not right to go easy on the guilty,
or come down hard on the innocent.

[6] The words of a fool start fights;
do him a favor and gag him.

[7] Fools are undone by their big mouths;
their souls are crushed by their words.

NEW KING JAMES VERSION

[8]The words of a talebearer *are* like tasty
trifles,[a]
And they go down into the inmost body.

[9]He who is slothful in his work
Is a brother to him who is a great destroyer.

[10]The name of the LORD *is* a strong tower;
The righteous run to it and are safe.
[11]The rich man's wealth *is* his strong city,
And like a high wall in his own esteem.

[12]Before destruction the heart of a man is
haughty,
And before honor *is* humility.

[13]He who answers a matter before he hears *it*,
It *is* folly and shame to him.
[14]The spirit of a man will sustain him in
sickness,
But who can bear a broken spirit?

[15]The heart of the prudent acquires knowledge,
And the ear of the wise seeks knowledge.

[16]A man's gift makes room for him,
And brings him before great men.

[17]The first *one* to plead his cause *seems* right,
Until his neighbor comes and examines him.

[18]Casting lots causes contentions to cease,
And keeps the mighty apart.

[19]A brother offended *is harder to win* than a
strong city,
And contentions *are* like the bars of a
castle.

[20]A man's stomach shall be satisfied from the
fruit of his mouth;
From the produce of his lips he shall be
filled.

[21]Death and life *are* in the power of the tongue,
And those who love it will eat its fruit.

[22]*He who* finds a wife finds a good *thing*,
And obtains favor from the LORD.

[23]The poor *man* uses entreaties,
But the rich answers roughly.

[24]A man *who has* friends must himself be
friendly,[a]
But there is a friend *who* sticks closer than a
brother.

19 Better *is* the poor who walks in his integrity
Than *one who is* perverse in his lips, and
is a fool.

[2]Also it is not good *for* a soul *to be* without
knowledge,
And he sins who hastens with *his* feet.

18:8 [a]A Jewish tradition reads *wounds*. 18:24 [a]Following Greek manuscripts, Syriac, Targum, and Vulgate; Masoretic Text reads *may come to ruin*.

THE MESSAGE

8 Listening to gossip is like eating cheap
candy;
do you really want junk like that in your
belly?

9 Slack habits and sloppy work
are as bad as vandalism.

10 GOD's name is a place of protection—
good people can run there and be safe.

11 The rich think their wealth protects them;
they imagine themselves safe behind it.

12 Pride first, then the crash,
but humility is precursor to honor.

13 Answering before listening
is both stupid and rude.

14 A healthy spirit conquers adversity,
but what can you do when the spirit is
crushed?

15 Wise men and women are always learning,
always listening for fresh insights.

16 A gift gets attention;
it buys the attention of eminent people.

17 The first speech in a court case is always
convincing—
until the cross-examination starts!

18 You may have to draw straws
when faced with a tough decision.

19 Do a favor and win a friend forever;
nothing can untie that bond.

20 Words satisfy the mind as much as fruit
does the stomach;
good talk is as gratifying as a good
harvest.

21 Words kill, words give life;
they're either poison or fruit—you choose.

22 Find a good spouse, you find a good life—
and even more: the favor of GOD!

23 The poor speak in soft supplications;
the rich bark out answers.

24 Friends come and friends go,
but a true friend sticks by you like
family.

IF YOU QUIT LISTENING

1 19 Better to be poor and honest
than a rich person no one can trust.

2 Ignorant zeal is worthless;
haste makes waste.

NEW KING JAMES VERSION

[3]The foolishness of a man twists his way,
And his heart frets against the LORD.
[4]Wealth makes many friends,
But the poor is separated from his friend.

[5]A false witness will not go unpunished,
And *he who* speaks lies will not escape.

[6]Many entreat the favor of the nobility,
And every man *is* a friend to one who gives gifts.
[7]All the brothers of the poor hate him;
How much more do his friends go far from him!
He may pursue *them with* words, *yet* they abandon *him.*

[8]He who gets wisdom loves his own soul;
He who keeps understanding will find good.

[9]A false witness will not go unpunished,
And *he who* speaks lies shall perish.

[10]Luxury is not fitting for a fool,
Much less for a servant to rule over princes.

[11]The discretion of a man makes him slow to anger,
And his glory *is* to overlook a transgression.
[12]The king's wrath *is* like the roaring of a lion,
But his favor *is* like dew on the grass.

[13]A foolish son *is* the ruin of his father,
And the contentions of a wife *are* a continual dripping.
[14]Houses and riches *are* an inheritance from fathers,
But a prudent wife *is* from the LORD.
[15]Laziness casts *one* into a deep sleep,
And an idle person will suffer hunger.

[16]He who keeps the commandment keeps his soul,
But he who is careless[a] of his ways will die.
[17]He who has pity on the poor lends to the LORD,
And He will pay back what he has given.
[18]Chasten your son while there is hope,
And do not set your heart on his destruction.[a]

[19]*A man of* great wrath will suffer punishment;
For if you rescue *him,* you will have to do it again.

19:16 [a]Literally *despises,* figurative of recklessness or carelessness 19:18 [a]Literally *to put him to death;* a Jewish tradition reads *on his crying.*

THE MESSAGE

[3] People ruin their lives by their own stupidity,
so why does GOD always get blamed?

[4] Wealth attracts friends as honey draws flies,
but poor people are avoided like a plague.

[5] Perjury won't go unpunished.
Would you let a liar go free?

[6] Lots of people flock around a generous person;
everyone's a friend to the philanthropist.

[7] When you're down on your luck, even your family avoids you—
yes, even your best friends wish you'd get lost.
If they see you coming, they look the other way—
out of sight, out of mind.

[8] Grow a wise heart—you'll do yourself a favor;
keep a clear head—you'll find a good life.

[9] The person who tells lies gets caught;
the person who spreads rumors is ruined.

[10] Blockheads shouldn't live on easy street
any more than workers should give orders to their boss.

[11] Smart people know how to hold their tongue;
their grandeur is to forgive and forget.

[12] Mean-tempered leaders are like mad dogs;
the good-natured are like fresh morning dew.

[13] A parent is worn to a frazzle by a stupid child;
a nagging spouse is a leaky faucet.

[14] House and land are handed down from parents,
but a congenial spouse comes straight from GOD.

[15] Life collapses on loafers;
lazybones go hungry.

[16] Keep the rules and keep your life;
careless living kills.

[17] Mercy to the needy is a loan to GOD,
and GOD pays back those loans in full.

[18] Discipline your children while you still have the chance;
indulging them destroys them.

[19] Let angry people endure the backlash of their own anger;
if you try to make it better, you'll only make it worse.

NEW KING JAMES VERSION

20Listen to counsel and receive instruction,
That you may be wise in your latter days.

21There are many plans in a man's heart,
Nevertheless the LORD's counsel—that will stand.

22What is desired in a man is kindness,
And a poor man is better than a liar.

23The fear of the LORD *leads* to life,
And *he who has it* will abide in satisfaction;
He will not be visited with evil.

24A lazy *man* buries his hand in the bowl,[a]
And will not so much as bring it to his mouth again.

25Strike a scoffer, and the simple will become wary;
Rebuke one who has understanding, *and* he will discern knowledge.

26He who mistreats *his* father *and* chases away *his* mother
Is a son who causes shame and brings reproach.

27Cease listening to instruction, my son,
And you will stray from the words of knowledge.

28A disreputable witness scorns justice,
And the mouth of the wicked devours iniquity.

29Judgments are prepared for scoffers,
And beatings for the backs of fools.

20 Wine *is* a mocker,
Strong drink *is* a brawler,
And whoever is led astray by it is not wise.

2The wrath[a] of a king *is* like the roaring of a lion;
Whoever provokes him to anger sins *against* his own life.

3*It is* honorable for a man to stop striving,
Since any fool can start a quarrel.

4The lazy *man* will not plow because of winter;
He will beg during harvest and *have* nothing.

5Counsel in the heart of man *is like* deep water,
But a man of understanding will draw it out.

6Most men will proclaim each his own goodness,
But who can find a faithful man?

7The righteous *man* walks in his integrity;
His children *are* blessed after him.

19:24 [a]Septuagint and Syriac read *bosom;* Targum and Vulgate read *armpit.* **20:2** [a]Literally *fear* or *terror* which is produced by the king's wrath

THE MESSAGE

20 Take good counsel and accept correction—
that's the way to live wisely and well.

21 We humans keep brainstorming options and plans,
but GOD's purpose prevails.

22 It's only human to want to make a buck,
but it's better to be poor than a liar.

23 Fear-of-GOD is life itself,
a full life, and serene—no nasty surprises.

24 Some people dig a fork into the pie
but are too lazy to raise it to their mouth.

25 Punish the insolent—make an example of them.
Who knows? Somebody might learn a good lesson.

26 Kids who lash out against their parents
are an embarrassment and disgrace.

27 If you quit listening, dear child, and strike off on your own,
you'll soon be out of your depth.

28 An unprincipled witness desecrates justice;
the mouths of the wicked spew malice.

29 The irreverent have to learn reverence the hard way;
only a slap in the face brings fools to attention.

DEEP WATER IN THE HEART

1 20 Wine makes you mean, beer makes you quarrelsome—
a staggering drunk is not much fun.

2 Quick-tempered leaders are like mad dogs—
cross them and they bite your head off.

3 It's a mark of good character to avert quarrels,
but fools love to pick fights.

4 A farmer too lazy to plant in the spring
has nothing to harvest in the fall.

5 Knowing what is right is like deep water in the heart;
a wise person draws from the well within.

6 Lots of people claim to be loyal and loving,
but where on earth can you find one?

7 God-loyal people, living honest lives,
make it much easier for their children.

NEW KING JAMES VERSION

8A king who sits on the throne of judgment
Scatters all evil with his eyes.

9Who can say, "I have made my heart clean,
I am pure from my sin"?

10Diverse weights *and* diverse measures,
They *are* both alike, an abomination to the LORD.

11Even a child is known by his deeds,
Whether what he does *is* pure and right.

12The hearing ear and the seeing eye,
The LORD has made them both.

13Do not love sleep, lest you come to poverty;
Open your eyes, *and* you will be satisfied with bread.

14"*It is* good for nothing,"[a] cries the buyer;
But when he has gone his way, then he boasts.

15There is gold and a multitude of rubies,
But the lips of knowledge *are* a precious jewel.

16Take the garment of one who is surety *for* a stranger,
And hold it as a pledge *when it* is for a seductress.

17Bread gained by deceit *is* sweet to a man,
But afterward his mouth will be filled with gravel.

18Plans are established by counsel;
By wise counsel wage war.

19He who goes about *as* a talebearer reveals secrets;
Therefore do not associate with one who flatters with his lips.

20Whoever curses his father or his mother,
His lamp will be put out in deep darkness.

21An inheritance gained hastily at the beginning
Will not be blessed at the end.

22Do not say, "I will recompense evil";
Wait for the LORD, and He will save you.

23Diverse weights *are* an abomination to the LORD,
And dishonest scales *are* not good.

24A man's steps *are* of the LORD;
How then can a man understand his own way?

25*It is* a snare for a man to devote rashly *something as* holy,
And afterward to reconsider *his* vows.

26A wise king sifts out the wicked,
And brings the threshing wheel over them.

20:14 [a]Literally *evil, evil*

THE MESSAGE

8-9 Leaders who know their business and care
keep a sharp eye out for the shoddy and cheap,
For who among us can be trusted
to be always diligent and honest?

10 Switching price tags and padding the expense account
are two things GOD hates.

11 Young people eventually reveal by their actions
if their motives are on the up and up.

DRINKING FROM THE CHALICE OF KNOWLEDGE

12 Ears that hear and eyes that see—
we get our basic equipment from GOD!

13 Don't be too fond of sleep; you'll end up in the poorhouse.
Wake up and get up; then there'll be food on the table.

14 The shopper says, "That's junk—I'll take it off your hands,"
then goes off boasting of the bargain.

15 Drinking from the beautiful chalice of knowledge
is better than adorning oneself with gold and rare gems.

16 Hold tight to collateral on any loan to a stranger;
beware of accepting what a transient has pawned.

17 Stolen bread tastes sweet,
but soon your mouth is full of gravel.

18 Form your purpose by asking for counsel,
then carry it out using all the help you can get.

19 Gossips can't keep secrets,
so never confide in blabbermouths.

20 Anyone who curses father and mother
extinguishes light and exists benighted.

THE VERY STEPS WE TAKE

21 A bonanza at the beginning
is no guarantee of blessing at the end.

22 Don't ever say, "I'll get you for that!"
Wait for GOD; he'll settle the score.

23 GOD hates cheating in the marketplace;
rigged scales are an outrage.

24 The very steps we take come from GOD;
otherwise how would we know where we're going?

25 An impulsive vow is a trap;
later you'll wish you could get out of it.

26 After careful scrutiny, a wise leader
makes a clean sweep of rebels and dolts.

NEW KING JAMES VERSION

27The spirit of a man *is* the lamp of the LORD,
Searching all the inner depths of his heart.[a]

28Mercy and truth preserve the king,
And by lovingkindness he upholds his throne.

29The glory of young men *is* their strength,
And the splendor of old men *is* their gray head.

30Blows that hurt cleanse away evil,
As *do* stripes the inner depths of the heart.[a]

21 The king's heart *is* in the hand of the LORD,
Like the rivers of water; He turns it wherever He wishes.

2Every way of a man *is* right in his own eyes,
But the LORD weighs the hearts.

3To do righteousness and justice
Is more acceptable to the LORD than sacrifice.

4A haughty look, a proud heart,
And the plowing[a] of the wicked *are* sin.

5The plans of the diligent *lead* surely to plenty,
But *those of* everyone *who is* hasty, surely to poverty.

6Getting treasures by a lying tongue
Is the fleeting fantasy of those who seek death.[a]

7The violence of the wicked will destroy them,[a]
Because they refuse to do justice.

8The way of a guilty man *is* perverse;[a]
But *as for* the pure, his work *is* right.

9Better to dwell in a corner of a housetop,
Than in a house shared with a contentious woman.

10The soul of the wicked desires evil;
His neighbor finds no favor in his eyes.

11When the scoffer is punished, the simple is made wise;
But when the wise is instructed, he receives knowledge.

12The righteous *God* wisely considers the house of the wicked,
Overthrowing the wicked for *their* wickedness.

13Whoever shuts his ears to the cry of the poor
Will also cry himself and not be heard.

20:27 [a]Literally *the rooms of the belly* **20:30** [a]Literally *the rooms of the belly* **21:4** [a]Or *lamp* **21:6** [a]Septuagint reads *Pursue vanity on the snares of death;* Vulgate reads *Is vain and foolish, and shall stumble on the snares of death;* Targum reads *They shall be destroyed, and they shall fall who seek death.* **21:7** [a]Literally *drag them away* **21:8** [a]Or *The way of a man is perverse and strange*

THE MESSAGE

27 GOD is in charge of human life,
watching and examining us inside and out.

28 Love and truth form a good leader;
sound leadership is founded on loving integrity.

29 Youth may be admired for vigor,
but gray hair gives prestige to old age.

30 A good thrashing purges evil;
punishment goes deep within us.

GOD EXAMINES OUR MOTIVES

1 21 Good leadership is a channel of water controlled by GOD;
he directs it to whatever ends he chooses.

2 We justify our actions by appearances;
GOD examines our motives.

3 Clean living before God and justice with our neighbors
mean far more to GOD than religious performance.

4 Arrogance and pride—distinguishing marks in the wicked—
are just plain sin.

5 Careful planning puts you ahead in the long run;
hurry and scurry puts you further behind.

6 Make it to the top by lying and cheating;
get paid with smoke and a promotion—to death!

7 The wicked get buried alive by their loot
because they refuse to use it to help others.

8 Mixed motives twist life into tangles;
pure motives take you straight down the road.

DO YOUR BEST, PREPARE FOR THE WORST

9 Better to live alone in a tumbledown shack
than share a mansion with a nagging spouse.

10 Wicked souls love to make trouble;
they feel nothing for friends and neighbors.

11 Simpletons only learn the hard way,
but the wise learn by listening.

12 A God-loyal person will see right through the wicked
and undo the evil they've planned.

13 If you stop your ears to the cries of the poor,
your cries will go unheard, unanswered.

NEW KING JAMES VERSION

[14]A gift in secret pacifies anger,
And a bribe behind the back,[a] strong wrath.

[15]*It is* a joy for the just to do justice,
But destruction *will come* to the workers of iniquity.

[16]A man who wanders from the way of understanding
Will rest in the assembly of the dead.

[17]He who loves pleasure *will be* a poor man;
He who loves wine and oil will not be rich.

[18]The wicked *shall be* a ransom for the righteous,
And the unfaithful for the upright.

[19]Better to dwell in the wilderness,
Than with a contentious and angry woman.

[20]*There is* desirable treasure,
And oil in the dwelling of the wise,
But a foolish man squanders it.

[21]He who follows righteousness and mercy
Finds life, righteousness, and honor.

[22]A wise *man* scales the city of the mighty,
And brings down the trusted stronghold.

[23]Whoever guards his mouth and tongue
Keeps his soul from troubles.

[24]A proud *and* haughty *man*—"Scoffer" *is* his name;
He acts with arrogant pride.

[25]The desire of the lazy *man* kills him,
For his hands refuse to labor.
[26]He covets greedily all day long,
But the righteous gives and does not spare.

[27]The sacrifice of the wicked *is* an abomination;
How much more *when* he brings it with wicked intent!

[28]A false witness shall perish,
But the man who hears *him* will speak endlessly.

[29]A wicked man hardens his face,
But *as for* the upright, he establishes[a] his way.

[30]*There is* no wisdom or understanding
Or counsel against the LORD.

[31]The horse *is* prepared for the day of battle,
But deliverance *is* of the LORD.

21:14 [a]Literally *in the bosom* **21:29** [a]Qere and Septuagint read *understands.*

THE MESSAGE

[14] A quietly given gift soothes an irritable person;
a heartfelt present cools a hot temper.

[15] Good people celebrate when justice triumphs,
but for the workers of evil it's a bad day.

[16] Whoever wanders off the straight and narrow
ends up in a congregation of ghosts.

[17] You're addicted to thrills? What an empty life!
The pursuit of pleasure is never satisfied.

[18] What a bad person plots against the good, boomerangs;
the plotter gets it in the end.

[19] Better to live in a tent in the wild
than with a cross and petulant spouse.

[20] Valuables are safe in a wise person's home;
fools put it all out for yard sales.

[21] Whoever goes hunting for what is right and kind
finds life itself—*glorious* life!

[22] One sage entered a whole city of armed soldiers—
their trusted defenses fell to pieces!

[23] Watch your words and hold your tongue;
you'll save yourself a lot of grief.

[24] You know their names—Brash, Impudent, Blasphemer—
intemperate hotheads, every one.

[25] Lazy people finally die of hunger
because they won't get up and go to work.

[26] Sinners are always wanting what they don't have;
the God-loyal are always giving what they do have.

[27] Religious performance by the wicked stinks;
it's even worse when they use it to get ahead.

[28] A lying witness is unconvincing;
a person who speaks truth is respected.

[29] Unscrupulous people fake it a lot;
honest people are sure of their steps.

[30] Nothing clever, nothing conceived, nothing contrived,
can get the better of GOD.

[31] Do your best, prepare for the worst—
then trust GOD to bring victory.

NEW KING JAMES VERSION

22 A *good* name is to be chosen rather than great riches,
Loving favor rather than silver and gold.

2 The rich and the poor have this in common,
The LORD *is* the maker of them all.

3 A prudent *man* foresees evil and hides himself,
But the simple pass on and are punished.

4 By humility *and* the fear of the LORD
Are riches and honor and life.

5 Thorns *and* snares *are* in the way of the perverse;
He who guards his soul will be far from them.

6 Train up a child in the way he should go,
And when he is old he will not depart from it.

7 The rich rules over the poor,
And the borrower *is* servant to the lender.

8 He who sows iniquity will reap sorrow,
And the rod of his anger will fail.

9 He who has a generous eye will be blessed,
For he gives of his bread to the poor.

10 Cast out the scoffer, and contention will leave;
Yes, strife and reproach will cease.

11 He who loves purity of heart
And has grace on his lips,
The king *will be* his friend.

12 The eyes of the LORD preserve knowledge,
But He overthrows the words of the faithless.

13 The lazy *man* says, "*There is* a lion outside!
I shall be slain in the streets!"

14 The mouth of an immoral woman *is* a deep pit;
He who is abhorred by the LORD will fall there.

15 Foolishness *is* bound up in the heart of a child;
The rod of correction will drive it far from him.

16 He who oppresses the poor to increase his *riches*,
And he who gives to the rich, *will* surely *come* to poverty.

THE MESSAGE

THE CURE COMES THROUGH DISCIPLINE

1 22 A sterling reputation is better than striking it rich;
a gracious spirit is better than money in the bank.

2 The rich and the poor shake hands as equals—
GOD made them both!

3 A prudent person sees trouble coming and ducks;
a simpleton walks in blindly and is clobbered.

4 The payoff for meekness and Fear-of-GOD
is plenty and honor and a satisfying life.

5 The perverse travel a dangerous road, potholed and mud-slick;
if you know what's good for you, stay clear of it.

6 Point your kids in the right direction—
when they're old they won't be lost.

7 The poor are always ruled over by the rich,
so don't borrow and put yourself under their power.

8 Whoever sows sin reaps weeds,
and bullying anger sputters into nothing.

9 Generous hands are blessed hands
because they give bread to the poor.

10 Kick out the troublemakers and things will quiet down;
you need a break from bickering and griping!

11 GOD loves the pure-hearted and well-spoken;
good leaders also delight in their friendship.

12 GOD guards knowledge with a passion,
but he'll have nothing to do with deception.

13 The loafer says, "There's a lion on the loose!
If I go out I'll be eaten alive!"

14 The mouth of a whore is a bottomless pit;
you'll fall in that pit if you're on the outs with GOD.

15 Young people are prone to foolishness and fads;
the cure comes through tough-minded discipline.

16 Exploit the poor or glad-hand the rich—whichever,
you'll end up the poorer for it.

New King James Version

Sayings of the Wise

17Incline your ear and hear the words of the wise,
And apply your heart to my knowledge;
18For *it is* a pleasant thing if you keep them within you;
Let them all be fixed upon your lips,
19So that your trust may be in the LORD;
I have instructed you today, even you.
20Have I not written to you excellent things
Of counsels and knowledge,
21That I may make you know the certainty of the words of truth,
That you may answer words of truth
To those who send to you?

22Do not rob the poor because he *is* poor,
Nor oppress the afflicted at the gate;
23For the LORD will plead their cause,
And plunder the soul of those who plunder them.

24Make no friendship with an angry man,
And with a furious man do not go,
25Lest you learn his ways
And set a snare for your soul.

26Do not be one of those who shakes hands in a pledge,
One of those who is surety for debts;
27If you have nothing *with which* to pay,
Why should he take away your bed from under you?

28Do not remove the ancient landmark
Which your fathers have set.

29Do you see a man *who* excels in his work?
He will stand before kings;
He will not stand before unknown *men.*

23 When you sit down to eat with a ruler,
Consider carefully what *is* before you;
2And put a knife to your throat
If you *are* a man given to appetite.
3Do not desire his delicacies,
For they *are* deceptive food.

4Do not overwork to be rich;
Because of your own understanding, cease!
5Will you set your eyes on that which is not?
For *riches* certainly make themselves wings;
They fly away like an eagle *toward* heaven.

The Message

THE THIRTY PRECEPTS OF THE SAGES

Don't Move Back the Boundary Lines

17-21 Listen carefully to my wisdom;
take to heart what I can teach you.
You'll treasure its sweetness deep within;
you'll give it bold expression in your speech.
To make sure your foundation is trust in GOD,
I'm laying it all out right now just for you.
I'm giving you thirty sterling principles—
tested guidelines to live by.
Believe me—these are truths that work,
and will keep you accountable
to those who sent you.

1

22-23 Don't walk on the poor just because they're poor,
and don't use your position to crush the weak,
Because GOD will come to their defense;
the life you took, he'll take from you and give back to them.

2

24-25 Don't hang out with angry people;
don't keep company with hotheads.
Bad temper is contagious—
don't get infected.

3

26-27 Don't gamble on the pot of gold at the end of the rainbow,
hocking your house against a lucky chance.
The time will come when you have to pay up;
you'll be left with nothing but the shirt on your back.

4

28 Don't stealthily move back the boundary lines
staked out long ago by your ancestors.

5

29 Observe people who are good at their work—
skilled workers are always in demand and admired;
they don't take a backseat to anyone.

Restrain Yourself

6

1-3 23 When you go out to dinner with an influential person,
mind your manners:
Don't gobble your food,
don't talk with your mouth full.
And don't stuff yourself;
bridle your appetite.

7

4-5 Don't wear yourself out trying to get rich;
restrain yourself!
Riches disappear in the blink of an eye;
wealth sprouts wings
and flies off into the wild blue yonder.

NEW KING JAMES VERSION

6Do not eat the bread of a miser,[a]
Nor desire his delicacies;
7For as he thinks in his heart, so *is* he.
"Eat and drink!" he says to you,
But his heart is not with you.
8The morsel you have eaten, you will vomit up,
And waste your pleasant words.

9Do not speak in the hearing of a fool,
For he will despise the wisdom of your words.

10Do not remove the ancient landmark,
Nor enter the fields of the fatherless;
11For their Redeemer *is* mighty;
He will plead their cause against you.

12Apply your heart to instruction,
And your ears to words of knowledge.

13Do not withhold correction from a child,
For *if* you beat him with a rod, he will not die.
14You shall beat him with a rod,
And deliver his soul from hell.[a]

15My son, if your heart is wise,
My heart will rejoice—indeed, I myself;
16Yes, my inmost being will rejoice
When your lips speak right things.

17Do not let your heart envy sinners,
But *be zealous* for the fear of the LORD all the day;
18For surely there is a hereafter,
And your hope will not be cut off.

19Hear, my son, and be wise;
And guide your heart in the way.
20Do not mix with winebibbers,
Or with gluttonous eaters of meat;
21For the drunkard and the glutton will come to poverty,
And drowsiness will clothe *a man* with rags.

22Listen to your father who begot you,
And do not despise your mother when she is old.

23Buy the truth, and do not sell *it*,
Also wisdom and instruction and understanding.
24The father of the righteous will greatly rejoice,
And he who begets a wise *child* will delight in him.
25Let your father and your mother be glad,
And let her who bore you rejoice.

26My son, give me your heart,
And let your eyes observe my ways.

23:6 [a]Literally *one who has an evil eye* **23:14** [a]Or *Sheol*

THE MESSAGE

8
6-8 Don't accept a meal from a tightwad;
don't expect anything special.
He'll be as stingy with you as he is with himself;
he'll say, "Eat! Drink!" but won't mean a word of it.
His miserly serving will turn your stomach
when you realize the meal's a sham.

9
9 Don't bother talking sense to fools;
they'll only poke fun at your words.

10
10-11 Don't stealthily move back the boundary lines
or cheat orphans out of their property,
For they have a powerful Advocate
who will go to bat for them.

11
12 Give yourselves to disciplined instruction;
open your ears to tested knowledge.

12
13-14 Don't be afraid to correct your young ones;
a spanking won't kill them.
A good spanking, in fact, might save them
from something worse than death.

13
15-16 Dear child, if you become wise,
I'll be one happy parent.
My heart will dance and sing
to the tuneful truth you'll speak.

14
17-18 Don't for a minute envy careless rebels;
soak yourself in the Fear-of-GOD—
That's where your future lies.
Then you won't be left with an armload of nothing.

15
19-21 Oh listen, dear child—become wise;
point your life in the right direction.
Don't drink too much wine and get drunk;
don't eat too much food and get fat.
Drunks and gluttons will end up on skid row,
in a stupor and dressed in rags.

BUY WISDOM, EDUCATION, INSIGHT

16
22-25 Listen with respect to the father who raised you,
and when your mother grows old, don't neglect her.
Buy truth—don't sell it for love or money;
buy wisdom, buy education, buy insight.
Parents rejoice when their children turn out well;
wise children become proud parents.
So make your father happy!
Make your mother proud!

17
26 Dear child, I want your full attention;
please do what I show you.

New King James Version

[27]For a harlot *is* a deep pit,
And a seductress *is* a narrow well.
[28]She also lies in wait as *for* a victim,
And increases the unfaithful among men.

[29]Who has woe?
Who has sorrow?
Who has contentions?
Who has complaints?
Who has wounds without cause?
Who has redness of eyes?
[30]Those who linger long at the wine,
Those who go in search of mixed wine.
[31]Do not look on the wine when it is red,
When it sparkles in the cup,
When it swirls around smoothly;
[32]At the last it bites like a serpent,
And stings like a viper.
[33]Your eyes will see strange things,
And your heart will utter perverse things.
[34]Yes, you will be like one who lies down in the midst of the sea,
Or like one who lies at the top of the mast, *saying:*
[35]"They have struck me, *but* I was not hurt;
They have beaten me, but I did not feel *it*.
When shall I awake, that I may seek another *drink*?"

24 Do not be envious of evil men,
Nor desire to be with them;
[2]For their heart devises violence,
And their lips talk of troublemaking.

[3]Through wisdom a house is built,
And by understanding it is established;
[4]By knowledge the rooms are filled
With all precious and pleasant riches.

[5]A wise man *is* strong,
Yes, a man of knowledge increases strength;
[6]For by wise counsel you will wage your own war,
And in a multitude of counselors *there is* safety.

[7]Wisdom *is* too lofty for a fool;
He does not open his mouth in the gate.

[8]He who plots to do evil
Will be called a schemer.
[9]The devising of foolishness *is* sin,
And the scoffer *is* an abomination to men.

[10]*If* you faint in the day of adversity,
Your strength *is* small.

The Message

27-28 A whore is a bottomless pit;
a loose woman can get you in deep trouble fast.
She'll take you for all you've got;
she's worse than a pack of thieves.

18
29-35 Who are the people who are always crying the blues?
Who do you know who reeks of self-pity?
Who keeps getting beat up for no reason at all?
Whose eyes are bleary and bloodshot?
It's those who spend the night with a bottle,
for whom drinking is serious business.
Don't judge wine by its label,
or its bouquet, or its full-bodied flavor.
Judge it rather by the hangover it leaves you with—
the splitting headache, the queasy stomach.
Do you really prefer seeing double,
with your speech all slurred,
Reeling and seasick,
drunk as a sailor?
"They hit me," you'll say, "but it didn't hurt;
they beat on me, but I didn't feel a thing.
When I'm sober enough to manage it,
bring me another drink!"

Intelligence Outranks Muscle

19
1-2 24 Don't envy bad people;
don't even want to be around them.
All they think about is causing a disturbance;
all they talk about is making trouble.

20
3-4 It takes wisdom to build a house,
and understanding to set it on a firm foundation;
It takes knowledge to furnish its rooms
with fine furniture and beautiful draperies.

21
5-6 It's better to be wise than strong;
intelligence outranks muscle any day.
Strategic planning is the key to warfare;
to win, you need a lot of good counsel.

22
7 Wise conversation is way over the head of fools;
in a serious discussion they haven't a clue.

23
8-9 The person who's always cooking up some evil
soon gets a reputation as prince of rogues.
Fools incubate sin;
cynics desecrate beauty.

Rescue the Perishing

24
10 If you fall to pieces in a crisis,
there wasn't much to you in the first place.

NEW KING JAMES VERSION

11Deliver *those who* are drawn toward death,
And hold back *those* stumbling to the slaughter.
12If you say, "Surely we did not know this,"
Does not He who weighs the hearts consider *it?*
He who keeps your soul, does He *not* know *it?*
And will He *not* render to *each* man according to his deeds?

13My son, eat honey because *it is* good,
And the honeycomb *which is* sweet to your taste;
14So *shall* the knowledge of wisdom *be* to your soul;
If you have found *it,* there is a prospect,
And your hope will not be cut off.

15Do not lie in wait, O wicked *man,* against the dwelling of the righteous;
Do not plunder his resting place;
16For a righteous *man* may fall seven times
And rise again,
But the wicked shall fall by calamity.

17Do not rejoice when your enemy falls,
And do not let your heart be glad when he stumbles;
18Lest the LORD see *it,* and it displease Him,
And He turn away His wrath from him.

19Do not fret because of evildoers,
Nor be envious of the wicked;
20For there will be no prospect for the evil *man;*
The lamp of the wicked will be put out.

21My son, fear the LORD and the king;
Do not associate with those given to change;
22For their calamity will rise suddenly,
And who knows the ruin those two can bring?

FURTHER SAYINGS OF THE WISE

23These *things* also *belong* to the wise:

It is not good to show partiality in judgment.
24He who says to the wicked, "You *are* righteous,"
Him the people will curse;
Nations will abhor him.
25But those who rebuke *the wicked* will have delight,
And a good blessing will come upon them.

26He who gives a right answer kisses the lips.

27Prepare your outside work,
Make it fit for yourself in the field;
And afterward build your house.

28Do not be a witness against your neighbor without cause,
For would you deceive[a] with your lips?
29Do not say, "I will do to him just as he has done to me;
I will render to the man according to his work."

24:28 [a]Septuagint and Vulgate read *Do not deceive.*

THE MESSAGE

25
11-12 Rescue the perishing;
don't hesitate to step in and help.
If you say, "Hey, that's none of my business,"
will that get you off the hook?
Someone is watching you closely, you know—
Someone not impressed with weak excuses.

26
13-14 Eat honey, dear child—it's good for you—
and delicacies that melt in your mouth.
Likewise knowledge,
and wisdom for your soul—
Get that and your future's secured,
your hope is on solid rock.

27
15-16 Don't interfere with good people's lives;
don't try to get the best of them.
No matter how many times you trip them up,
God-loyal people don't stay down long;
Soon they're up on their feet,
while the wicked end up flat on their faces.

28
17-18 Don't laugh when your enemy falls;
don't crow over his collapse.
GOD might see, and become very provoked,
and then take pity on his plight.

29
19-20 Don't bother your head with braggarts
or wish you could succeed like the wicked.
Those people have no future at all;
they're headed down a dead-end street.

30
21-22 Fear GOD, dear child—respect your leaders;
don't be defiant or mutinous.
Without warning your life can turn upside down,
and who knows how or when it might happen?

MORE SAYINGS OF THE WISE

AN HONEST ANSWER

23 It's wrong, very wrong,
to go along with injustice.

24-25 Whoever whitewashes the wicked
gets a black mark in the history books,
But whoever exposes the wicked
will be thanked and rewarded.

26 An honest answer
is like a warm hug.

27 First plant your fields;
then build your barn.

28-29 Don't talk about your neighbors behind their backs—
no slander or gossip, please.
Don't say to anyone, "I'll get back at you
for what you did to me.
I'll make you pay for what you did!"

NEW KING JAMES VERSION

30I went by the field of the lazy *man*,
And by the vineyard of the man devoid of understanding;
31And there it was, all overgrown with thorns;
Its surface was covered with nettles;
Its stone wall was broken down.
32When I saw *it*, I considered *it* well;
I looked on *it and* received instruction:
33A little sleep, a little slumber,
A little folding of the hands to rest;
34So shall your poverty come *like* a prowler,
And your need like an armed man.

FURTHER WISE SAYINGS OF SOLOMON

25 These also *are* proverbs of Solomon which the men of Hezekiah king of Judah copied:

2*It is* the glory of God to conceal a matter,
But the glory of kings *is* to search out a matter.

3*As* the heavens for height and the earth for depth,
So the heart of kings *is* unsearchable.

4Take away the dross from silver,
And it will go to the silversmith *for* jewelry.
5Take away the wicked from before the king,
And his throne will be established in righteousness.

6Do not exalt yourself in the presence of the king,
And do not stand in the place of the great;
7For *it is* better that he say to you,
"Come up here,"
Than that you should be put lower in the presence of the prince,
Whom your eyes have seen.

8Do not go hastily to court;
For what will you do in the end,
When your neighbor has put you to shame?
9Debate your case with your neighbor,
And do not disclose the secret to another;
10Lest he who hears *it* expose your shame,
And your reputation be ruined.

11A word fitly spoken *is like* apples of gold
In settings of silver.
12*Like* an earring of gold and an ornament of fine gold
Is a wise rebuker to an obedient ear.

13Like the cold of snow in time of harvest
Is a faithful messenger to those who send him,
For he refreshes the soul of his masters.

14Whoever falsely boasts of giving
Is like clouds and wind without rain.

THE MESSAGE

30-34 One day I walked by the field of an old lazybones,
and then passed the vineyard of a lout;
They were overgrown with weeds,
thick with thistles, all the fences broken down.
I took a long look and pondered what I saw;
the fields preached me a sermon and I listened:
"A nap here, a nap there, a day off here, a day off there,
sit back, take it easy—do you know what comes next?
Just this: You can look forward to a dirt-poor life,
with poverty as your permanent houseguest!"

FURTHER WISE SAYINGS OF SOLOMON

THE RIGHT WORD AT THE RIGHT TIME

1 25 There are also these proverbs of Solomon,
collected by scribes of Hezekiah, king of Judah.

2 God delights in concealing things;
scientists delight in discovering things.

3 Like the horizons for breadth and the ocean for depth,
the understanding of a good leader is broad and deep.

4-5 Remove impurities from the silver
and the silversmith can craft a fine chalice;
Remove the wicked from leadership
and authority will be credible and God-honoring.

6-7 Don't work yourself into the spotlight;
don't push your way into the place of prominence.
It's better to be promoted to a place of honor
than face humiliation by being demoted.

8 Don't jump to conclusions—there may be
a perfectly good explanation for what you just saw.

9-10 In the heat of an argument,
don't betray confidences;
Word is sure to get around,
and no one will trust you.

11-12 The right word at the right time
is like a custom-made piece of jewelry,
And a wise friend's timely reprimand
is like a gold ring slipped on your finger.

13 Reliable friends who do what they say
are like cool drinks in sweltering heat—refreshing!

14 Like billowing clouds that bring no rain
is the person who talks big but never produces.

New King James Version

15By long forbearance a ruler is persuaded,
And a gentle tongue breaks a bone.

16Have you found honey?
Eat only as much as you need,
Lest you be filled with it and vomit.

17Seldom set foot in your neighbor's house,
Lest he become weary of you and hate you.

18A man who bears false witness against his neighbor
Is like a club, a sword, and a sharp arrow.

19Confidence in an unfaithful *man* in time of trouble
Is like a bad tooth and a foot out of joint.

20*Like* one who takes away a garment in cold weather,
And like vinegar on soda,
Is one who sings songs to a heavy heart.

21If your enemy is hungry, give him bread to eat;
And if he is thirsty, give him water to drink;
22For *so* you will heap coals of fire on his head,
And the LORD will reward you.

23The north wind brings forth rain,
And a backbiting tongue an angry countenance.

24*It is* better to dwell in a corner of a housetop,
Than in a house shared with a contentious woman.

25As cold water to a weary soul,
So *is* good news from a far country.

26A righteous *man* who falters before the wicked
Is like a murky spring and a polluted well.

27*It is* not good to eat much honey;
So to seek one's own glory *is not* glory.

28Whoever *has* no rule over his own spirit
Is like a city broken down, without walls.

26 As snow in summer and rain in harvest,
So honor is not fitting for a fool.

2Like a flitting sparrow, like a flying swallow,
So a curse without cause shall not alight.

3A whip for the horse,
A bridle for the donkey,
And a rod for the fool's back.

The Message

15 Patient persistence pierces through indifference;
gentle speech breaks down rigid defenses.

A Person Without Self-Control

16-17 When you're given a box of candy, don't gulp it all down;
eat too much chocolate and you'll make yourself sick;
And when you find a friend, don't outwear your welcome;
show up at all hours and he'll soon get fed up.

18 Anyone who tells lies against the neighbors in court or on the street is a loose cannon.

19 Trusting a double-crosser when you're in trouble
is like biting down on an abscessed tooth.

20 Singing light songs to the heavyhearted
is like pouring salt in their wounds.

21-22 If you see your enemy hungry, go buy him lunch;
if he's thirsty, bring him a drink.
Your generosity will surprise him with goodness,
and GOD will look after you.

23 A north wind brings stormy weather,
and a gossipy tongue stormy looks.

24 Better to live alone in a tumbledown shack
than share a mansion with a nagging spouse.

25 Like a cool drink of water when you're worn out and weary
is a letter from a long-lost friend.

26 A good person who gives in to a bad person
is a muddied spring, a polluted well.

27 It's not smart to stuff yourself with sweets,
nor is glory piled on glory good for you.

28 A person without self-control
is like a house with its doors and windows knocked out.

Fools Recycle Silliness

1 26 We no more give honors to fools
than pray for snow in summer or rain during harvest.

2 You have as little to fear from an undeserved curse
as from the dart of a wren or the swoop of a swallow.

3 A whip for the racehorse, a tiller for the sailboat—
and a stick for the back of fools!

NEW KING JAMES VERSION

[4]Do not answer a fool according to his folly,
Lest you also be like him.
[5]Answer a fool according to his folly,
Lest he be wise in his own eyes.
[6]He who sends a message by the hand of a fool
Cuts off *his own* feet *and* drinks violence.
[7]*Like* the legs of the lame that hang limp
Is a proverb in the mouth of fools.
[8]Like one who binds a stone in a sling
Is he who gives honor to a fool.
[9]*Like* a thorn *that* goes into the hand of a drunkard
Is a proverb in the mouth of fools.
[10]The great *God* who formed everything
Gives the fool *his* hire and the transgressor *his* wages.[a]
[11]As a dog returns to his own vomit,
So a fool repeats his folly.
[12]Do you see a man wise in his own eyes?
There is more hope for a fool than for him.

[13]The lazy *man* says, "*There is* a lion in the road!
A fierce lion *is* in the streets!"
[14]*As* a door turns on its hinges,
So *does* the lazy *man* on his bed.
[15]The lazy *man* buries his hand in the bowl;[a]
It wearies him to bring it back to his mouth.
[16]The lazy *man is* wiser in his own eyes
Than seven men who can answer sensibly.

[17]He who passes by *and* meddles in a quarrel not his own
Is like one who takes a dog by the ears.

[18]Like a madman who throws firebrands, arrows, and death,
[19]*Is* the man *who* deceives his neighbor,
And says, "I was only joking!"

[20]Where *there is* no wood, the fire goes out;
And where *there is* no talebearer, strife ceases.
[21]*As* charcoal *is* to burning coals, and wood to fire,
So *is* a contentious man to kindle strife.
[22]The words of a talebearer *are* like tasty trifles,
And they go down into the inmost body.
[23]Fervent lips with a wicked heart
Are like earthenware covered with silver dross.

26:10 [a]The Hebrew is difficult; ancient and modern translators differ greatly. **26:15** [a]Compare 19:24

THE MESSAGE

4 Don't respond to the stupidity of a fool;
you'll only look foolish yourself.

5 Answer a fool in simple terms
so he doesn't get a swelled head.

6 You're only asking for trouble
when you send a message by a fool.

7 A proverb quoted by fools
is limp as a wet noodle.

8 Putting a fool in a place of honor
is like setting a mud brick on a marble column.

9 To ask a moron to quote a proverb
is like putting a scalpel in the hands of a drunk.

10 Hire a fool or a drunk
and you shoot yourself in the foot.

11 As a dog eats its own vomit,
so fools recycle silliness.

12 See that man who thinks he's so smart?
You can expect far more from a fool than from him.

13 Loafers say, "It's dangerous out there!
Tigers are prowling the streets!"
and then pull the covers back over their heads.

14 Just as a door turns on its hinges,
so a lazybones turns back over in bed.

15 A shiftless sluggard puts his fork in the pie,
but is too lazy to lift it to his mouth.

LIKE GLAZE ON CRACKED POTTERY

16 Dreamers fantasize their self-importance;
they think they are smarter
than a whole college faculty.

17 You grab a mad dog by the ears
when you butt into a quarrel that's none of your business.

18-19 People who shrug off deliberate deceptions,
saying, "I didn't mean it, I was only joking,"
Are worse than careless campers
who walk away from smoldering campfires.

20 When you run out of wood, the fire goes out;
when the gossip ends, the quarrel dies down.

21 A quarrelsome person in a dispute
is like kerosene thrown on a fire.

22 Listening to gossip is like eating cheap candy;
do you want junk like that in your belly?

23 Smooth talk from an evil heart
is like glaze on cracked pottery.

NEW KING JAMES VERSION

24He who hates, disguises *it* with his lips,
And lays up deceit within himself;
25When he speaks kindly, do not believe him,
For *there are* seven abominations in his heart;
26*Though his* hatred is covered by deceit,
His wickedness will be revealed before the assembly.

27Whoever digs a pit will fall into it,
And he who rolls a stone will have it roll back on him.

28A lying tongue hates *those who are* crushed by it,
And a flattering mouth works ruin.

27 Do not boast about tomorrow,
For you do not know what a day may bring forth.

2Let another man praise you, and not your own mouth;
A stranger, and not your own lips.

3A stone *is* heavy and sand *is* weighty,
But a fool's wrath *is* heavier than both of them.

4Wrath *is* cruel and anger a torrent,
But who *is* able to stand before jealousy?

5Open rebuke *is* better
Than love carefully concealed.

6Faithful *are* the wounds of a friend,
But the kisses of an enemy *are* deceitful.

7A satisfied soul loathes the honeycomb,
But to a hungry soul every bitter thing *is* sweet.

8Like a bird that wanders from its nest
Is a man who wanders from his place.

9Ointment and perfume delight the heart,
And the sweetness of a man's friend *gives delight* by hearty counsel.

10Do not forsake your own friend or your father's friend,
Nor go to your brother's house in the day of your calamity;
Better *is* a neighbor nearby than a brother far away.

11My son, be wise, and make my heart glad,
That I may answer him who reproaches me.

THE MESSAGE

24-26 Your enemy shakes hands and greets you like an old friend,
all the while conniving against you.
When he speaks warmly to you, don't believe him for a minute;
he's just waiting for the chance to rip you off.
No matter how cunningly he conceals his malice,
eventually his evil will be exposed in public.

27 Malice backfires;
spite boomerangs.

28 Liars hate their victims;
flatterers sabotage trust.

YOU DON'T KNOW TOMORROW

1 27 Don't brashly announce what you're going to do tomorrow;
you don't know the first thing about tomorrow.

2 Don't call attention to yourself;
let others do that for you.

3 Carrying a log across your shoulders
while you're hefting a boulder with your arms
Is nothing compared to the burden
of putting up with a fool.

4 We're blasted by anger and swamped by rage,
but who can survive jealousy?

5 A spoken reprimand is better
than approval that's never expressed.

6 The wounds from a lover are worth it;
kisses from an enemy do you in.

7 When you've stuffed yourself, you refuse dessert;
when you're starved, you could eat a horse.

8 People who won't settle down, wandering hither and yon,
are like restless birds, flitting to and fro.

9 Just as lotions and fragrance give sensual delight,
a sweet friendship refreshes the soul.

10 Don't leave your friends or your parents' friends
and run home to your family when things get rough;
Better a nearby friend
than a distant family.

11 Become wise, dear child, and make me happy;
then nothing the world throws my way will upset me.

NEW KING JAMES VERSION

12A prudent *man* foresees evil *and* hides himself;
The simple pass on *and* are punished.

13Take the garment of him who is surety for a stranger,
And hold it in pledge *when* he is surety for a seductress.

14He who blesses his friend with a loud voice, rising early in the morning,
It will be counted a curse to him.

15A continual dripping on a very rainy day
And a contentious woman are alike;
16Whoever restrains her restrains the wind,
And grasps oil with his right hand.

17*As* iron sharpens iron,
So a man sharpens the countenance of his friend.

18Whoever keeps the fig tree will eat its fruit;
So he who waits on his master will be honored.

19As in water face *reflects* face,
So a man's heart *reveals* the man.

20Hell[a] and Destruction[b] are never full;
So the eyes of man are never satisfied.

21The refining pot *is* for silver and the furnace for gold,
And a man *is valued* by what others say of him.

22Though you grind a fool in a mortar with a pestle along with crushed grain,
Yet his foolishness will not depart from him.

23Be diligent to know the state of your flocks,
And attend to your herds;
24For riches *are* not forever,
Nor does a crown *endure* to all generations.
25*When* the hay is removed, and the tender grass shows itself,
And the herbs of the mountains are gathered in,
26The lambs *will provide* your clothing,
And the goats the price of a field;
27*You shall have* enough goats' milk for your food,
For the food of your household,
And the nourishment of your maidservants.

28 The wicked flee when no one pursues,
But the righteous are bold as a lion.

2Because of the transgression of a land, many *are* its princes;
But by a man of understanding *and* knowledge
Right will be prolonged.

27:20 [a]Or *Sheol* [b]Hebrew *Abaddon*

THE MESSAGE

12 A prudent person sees trouble coming and ducks;
a simpleton walks in blindly and is clobbered.

13 Hold tight to collateral on any loan to a stranger;
be wary of accepting what a transient has pawned.

14 If you wake your friend in the early morning
by shouting "Rise and shine!"
It will sound to him
more like a curse than a blessing.

15-16 A nagging spouse is like
the drip, drip, drip of a leaky faucet;
You can't turn it off,
and you can't get away from it.

YOUR FACE MIRRORS YOUR HEART

17 You use steel to sharpen steel,
and one friend sharpens another.

18 If you care for your orchard, you'll enjoy its fruit;
if you honor your boss, you'll be honored.

19 Just as water mirrors your face,
so your face mirrors your heart.

20 Hell has a voracious appetite,
and lust just never quits.

21 The purity of silver and gold is tested
by putting them in the fire;
The purity of human hearts is tested
by giving them a little fame.

22 Pound on a fool all you like—
you can't pound out foolishness.

23-27 Know your sheep by name;
carefully attend to your flocks;
(Don't take them for granted;
possessions don't last forever, you know.)
And then, when the crops are in
and the harvest is stored in the barns,
You can knit sweaters from lambs' wool,
and sell your goats for a profit;
There will be plenty of milk and meat
to last your family through the winter.

IF YOU DESERT GOD'S LAW

1 28 The wicked are edgy with guilt, ready to run off
even when no one's after them;
Honest people are relaxed and confident,
bold as lions.

2 When the country is in chaos,
everybody has a plan to fix it—
But it takes a leader of real understanding
to straighten things out.

NEW KING JAMES VERSION

3A poor man who oppresses the poor
Is like a driving rain which leaves no food.

4Those who forsake the law praise the wicked,
But such as keep the law contend with them.

5Evil men do not understand justice,
But those who seek the LORD understand all.

6Better *is* the poor who walks in his integrity
Than one perverse *in his* ways, though he *be* rich.

7Whoever keeps the law *is* a discerning son,
But a companion of gluttons shames his father.

8One who increases his possessions by usury and extortion
Gathers it for him who will pity the poor.

9One who turns away his ear from hearing the law,
Even his prayer *is* an abomination.

10Whoever causes the upright to go astray in an evil way,
He himself will fall into his own pit;
But the blameless will inherit good.

11The rich man *is* wise in his own eyes,
But the poor who has understanding searches him out.

12When the righteous rejoice, *there is* great glory;
But when the wicked arise, men hide themselves.

13He who covers his sins will not prosper,
But whoever confesses and forsakes *them* will have mercy.

14Happy *is* the man who is always reverent,
But he who hardens his heart will fall into calamity.

15*Like* a roaring lion and a charging bear
Is a wicked ruler over poor people.

16A ruler who lacks understanding *is* a great oppressor,
But he who hates covetousness will prolong *his* days.

17A man burdened with bloodshed will flee into a pit;
Let no one help him.

18Whoever walks blamelessly will be saved,
But *he who is* perverse *in his* ways will suddenly fall.

19He who tills his land will have plenty of bread,
But he who follows frivolity will have poverty enough!

THE MESSAGE

3 The wicked who oppress the poor
are like a hailstorm that beats down the harvest.

4 If you desert God's law, you're free to embrace depravity;
if you love God's law, you fight for it tooth and nail.

5 Justice makes no sense to the evilminded;
those who seek GOD know it inside and out.

6 It's better to be poor and direct
than rich and crooked.

7 Practice God's law—get a reputation for wisdom;
hang out with a loose crowd—embarrass your family.

8 Get as rich as you want
through cheating and extortion,
But eventually some friend of the poor
is going to give it all back to them.

9 God has no use for the prayers
of the people who won't listen to him.

10 Lead good people down a wrong path
and you'll come to a bad end;
do good and you'll be rewarded for it.

11 The rich think they know it all,
but the poor can see right through them.

12 When good people are promoted, everything is great,
but when the bad are in charge, watch out!

13 You can't whitewash your sins and get by with it;
you find mercy by admitting and leaving them.

14 A tenderhearted person lives a blessed life;
a hardhearted person lives a hard life.

15 Lions roar and bears charge—
and the wicked lord it over the poor.

16 Among leaders who lack insight, abuse abounds,
but for one who hates corruption, the future is bright.

17 A murderer haunted by guilt
is doomed—there's no helping him.

18 Walk straight—live well and be saved;
a devious life is a doomed life.

DOING GREAT HARM IN SEEMINGLY HARMLESS WAYS

19 Work your garden—you'll end up with plenty of food;
play and party—you'll end up with an empty plate.

NEW KING JAMES VERSION

20A faithful man will abound with blessings,
But he who hastens to be rich will not go unpunished.

21To show partiality *is* not good,
Because for a piece of bread a man will transgress.

22A man with an evil eye hastens after riches,
And does not consider that poverty will come upon him.

23He who rebukes a man will find more favor afterward
Than he who flatters with the tongue.

24Whoever robs his father or his mother,
And says, "*It is* no transgression,"
The same *is* companion to a destroyer.

25He who is of a proud heart stirs up strife,
But he who trusts in the LORD will be prospered.

26He who trusts in his own heart is a fool,
But whoever walks wisely will be delivered.

27He who gives to the poor will not lack,
But he who hides his eyes will have many curses.

28When the wicked arise, men hide themselves;
But when they perish, the righteous increase.

29 He who is often rebuked, *and* hardens *his* neck,
Will suddenly be destroyed, and that without remedy.

2When the righteous are in authority, the people rejoice;
But when a wicked *man* rules, the people groan.

3Whoever loves wisdom makes his father rejoice,
But a companion of harlots wastes *his* wealth.

4The king establishes the land by justice,
But he who receives bribes overthrows it.

5A man who flatters his neighbor
Spreads a net for his feet.

6By transgression an evil man is snared,
But the righteous sings and rejoices.

7The righteous considers the cause of the poor,
But the wicked does not understand *such* knowledge.

THE MESSAGE

20 Committed and persistent work pays off;
get-rich-quick schemes are ripoffs.

21 Playing favorites is always a bad thing;
you can do great harm in seemingly harmless ways.

22 A miser in a hurry to get rich
doesn't know that he'll end up broke.

23 In the end, serious reprimand is appreciated
far more than bootlicking flattery.

24 Anyone who robs father and mother
and says, "So, what's wrong with that?"
is worse than a pirate.

25 A grasping person stirs up trouble,
but trust in GOD brings a sense of well-being.

26 If you think you know it all, you're a fool for sure;
real survivors learn wisdom from others.

27 Be generous to the poor—you'll never go hungry;
shut your eyes to their needs, and run a gauntlet of curses.

28 When corruption takes over, good people go underground,
but when the crooks are thrown out, it's safe to come out.

IF PEOPLE CAN'T SEE WHAT GOD IS DOING

1 29 For people who hate discipline
and only get more stubborn,
There'll come a day when life tumbles in and they break,
but by then it'll be too late to help them.

2 When good people run things, everyone is glad,
but when the ruler is bad, everyone groans.

3 If you love wisdom, you'll delight your parents,
but you'll destroy their trust if you run with whores.

4 A leader of good judgment gives stability;
an exploiting leader leaves a trail of waste.

5 A flattering neighbor is up to no good;
he's probably planning to take advantage of you.

6 Evil people fall into their own traps;
good people run the other way, glad to escape.

7 The good-hearted understand what it's like to be poor;
the hardhearted haven't the faintest idea.

NEW KING JAMES VERSION

8Scoffers set a city aflame,
But wise *men* turn away wrath.

9*If* a wise man contends with a foolish man,
Whether *the fool* rages or laughs, *there is* no peace.

10The bloodthirsty hate the blameless,
But the upright seek his well-being.[a]

11A fool vents all his feelings,[a]
But a wise *man* holds them back.

12If a ruler pays attention to lies,
All his servants *become* wicked.

13The poor *man* and the oppressor have this in common:
The LORD gives light to the eyes of both.

14The king who judges the poor with truth,
His throne will be established forever.

15The rod and rebuke give wisdom,
But a child left *to himself* brings shame to his mother.

16When the wicked are multiplied, transgression increases;
But the righteous will see their fall.

17Correct your son, and he will give you rest;
Yes, he will give delight to your soul.

18Where *there is* no revelation,[a] the people cast off restraint;
But happy *is* he who keeps the law.

19A servant will not be corrected by mere words;
For though he understands, he will not respond.

20Do you see a man hasty in his words?
There is more hope for a fool than for him.

21He who pampers his servant from childhood
Will have him as a son in the end.

22An angry man stirs up strife,
And a furious man abounds in transgression.

23A man's pride will bring him low,
But the humble in spirit will retain honor.

24Whoever is a partner with a thief hates his own life;
He swears to tell the truth,[a] but reveals nothing.

25The fear of man brings a snare,
But whoever trusts in the LORD shall be safe.

29:10 [a]Literally *soul* **29:11** [a]Literally *spirit* **29:18** [a]Or *prophetic vision* **29:24** [a]Literally *hears the adjuration*

THE MESSAGE

8 A gang of cynics can upset a whole city;
a group of sages can calm everyone down.

9 A sage trying to work things out with a fool
gets only scorn and sarcasm for his trouble.

10 Murderers hate honest people;
moral folks encourage them.

11 A fool lets it all hang out;
a sage quietly mulls it over.

12 When a leader listens to malicious gossip,
all the workers get infected with evil.

13 The poor and their abusers have at least something in common:
they can both *see*—their sight, GOD's gift!

14 Leadership gains authority and respect
when the voiceless poor are treated fairly.

15 Wise discipline imparts wisdom;
spoiled adolescents embarrass their parents.

16 When degenerates take charge, crime runs wild,
but the righteous will eventually observe their collapse.

17 Discipline your children; you'll be glad you did—
they'll turn out delightful to live with.

18 If people can't see what God is doing,
they stumble all over themselves;
But when they attend to what he reveals,
they are most blessed.

19 It takes more than talk to keep workers in line;
mere words go in one ear and out the other.

20 Observe the people who always talk before they think—
even simpletons are better off than they are.

21 If you let people treat you like a doormat,
you'll be quite forgotten in the end.

22 Angry people stir up a lot of discord;
the intemperate stir up trouble.

23 Pride lands you flat on your face;
humility prepares you for honors.

24 Befriend an outlaw
and become an enemy to yourself.
When the victims cry out,
you'll be included in their curses
if you're a coward to their cause in court.

25 The fear of human opinion disables;
trusting in GOD protects you from that.

NEW KING JAMES VERSION

26Many seek the ruler's favor,
But justice for man *comes* from the LORD.

27An unjust man *is* an abomination to the righteous,
And *he who is* upright in the way *is* an abomination to the wicked.

THE WISDOM OF AGUR

30 The words of Agur the son of Jakeh, *his* utterance. This man declared to Ithiel—to Ithiel and Ucal:

2Surely I *am* more stupid than *any* man,
And do not have the understanding of a man.
3I neither learned wisdom
Nor have knowledge of the Holy One.

4Who has ascended into heaven, or descended?
Who has gathered the wind in His fists?
Who has bound the waters in a garment?
Who has established all the ends of the earth?
What *is* His name, and what *is* His Son's name,
If you know?

5Every word of God *is* pure;
He *is* a shield to those who put their trust in Him.
6Do not add to His words,
Lest He rebuke you, and you be found a liar.

7Two *things* I request of You
(Deprive me not before I die):
8Remove falsehood and lies far from me;
Give me neither poverty nor riches—
Feed me with the food allotted to me;
9Lest I be full and deny *You*,
And say, "Who *is* the LORD?"
Or lest I be poor and steal,
And profane the name of my God.

10Do not malign a servant to his master,
Lest he curse you, and you be found guilty.

11*There is* a generation *that* curses its father,
And does not bless its mother.
12*There is* a generation *that is* pure in its own eyes,
Yet is not washed from its filthiness.
13*There is* a generation—oh, how lofty are their eyes!
And their eyelids are lifted up.
14*There is* a generation whose teeth *are like* swords,
And whose fangs *are like* knives,
To devour the poor from off the earth,
And the needy from *among* men.

THE MESSAGE

26 Everyone tries to get help from the leader,
but only GOD will give us justice.

27 Good people can't stand the sight of deliberate evil;
the wicked can't stand the sight of well-chosen goodness.

THE WORDS OF AGUR BEN YAKEH

GOD? WHO NEEDS HIM?

1-2 30 The skeptic swore, "There is no God!
No God!—I can do anything I want!
I'm more animal than human;
so-called human intelligence escapes me.

3-4 "I flunked 'wisdom.'
I see no evidence of a holy God.
Has anyone ever seen Anyone
climb into Heaven and take charge?
grab the winds and control them?
gather the rains in his bucket?
stake out the ends of the earth?
Just tell me his name, tell me the names of his sons.
Come on now—tell me!"

5-6 The believer replied, "Every promise of God proves true;
he protects everyone who runs to him for help.
So don't second-guess him;
he might take you to task and show up your lies."

7-9 And then he prayed, "God, I'm asking for two things
before I die; don't refuse me—
Banish lies from my lips
and liars from my presence.
Give me enough food to live on,
neither too much nor too little.
If I'm too full, I might get independent,
saying, 'God? Who needs him?'
If I'm poor, I might steal
and dishonor the name of my God."

10 Don't blow the whistle on your fellow workers behind their backs;
They'll accuse you of being underhanded,
and then *you'll* be the guilty one!

11 Don't curse your father
or fail to bless your mother.

12 Don't imagine yourself to be quite presentable
when you haven't had a bath in weeks.

13 Don't be stuck-up
and think you're better than everyone else.

14 Don't be greedy,
merciless and cruel as wolves,
Tearing into the poor and feasting on them,
shredding the needy to pieces only to discard them.

New King James Version

15The leech has two daughters—
Give *and* Give!
There are three *things that* are never satisfied,
Four never say, "Enough!":
16The grave,[a]
The barren womb,
The earth *that* is not satisfied with water—
And the fire never says, "Enough!"

17The eye *that* mocks *his* father,
And scorns obedience to *his* mother,
The ravens of the valley will pick it out,
And the young eagles will eat it.

18There are three *things which* are too wonderful for me,
Yes, four *which* I do not understand:
19The way of an eagle in the air,
The way of a serpent on a rock,
The way of a ship in the midst of the sea,
And the way of a man with a virgin.

20This *is* the way of an adulterous woman:
She eats and wipes her mouth,
And says, "I have done no wickedness."

21For three *things* the earth is perturbed,
Yes, for four it cannot bear up:
22For a servant when he reigns,
A fool when he is filled with food,
23A hateful *woman* when she is married,
And a maidservant who succeeds her mistress.

24There are four *things which* are little on the earth,
But they *are* exceedingly wise:
25The ants *are* a people not strong,
Yet they prepare their food in the summer;
26The rock badgers[a] are a feeble folk,
Yet they make their homes in the crags;
27The locusts have no king,
Yet they all advance in ranks;
28The spider[a] skillfully grasps with its hands,
And it is in kings' palaces.

29There are three *things which* are majestic in pace,
Yes, four *which* are stately in walk:
30A lion, *which is* mighty among beasts
And does not turn away from any;

30:16 [a]Or *Sheol* **30:26** [a]Or *hyraxes* **30:28** [a]Or *lizard*

The Message

15-16 A leech has twin daughters
named "Gimme" and "Gimme more."

Four Insatiables

Three things are never satisfied,
no, there are four that never say, "That's enough, thank you!"—
hell,
a barren womb,
a parched land,
a forest fire.

17 An eye that disdains a father
and despises a mother—
that eye will be plucked out by wild vultures
and consumed by young eagles.

Four Mysteries

18-19 Three things amaze me,
no, four things I'll never understand—
how an eagle flies so high in the sky,
how a snake glides over a rock,
how a ship navigates the ocean,
why adolescents act the way they do.

20 Here's how a prostitute operates:
she has sex with her client,
Takes a bath,
then asks, "Who's next?"

Four Intolerables

21-23 Three things are too much for even the earth to bear,
yes, four things shake its foundations—
when the janitor becomes the boss,
when a fool gets rich,
when a whore is voted "woman of the year,"
when a "girlfriend" replaces a faithful wife.

Four Small Wonders

24-28 There are four small creatures,
wisest of the wise they are—
ants—frail as they are,
get plenty of food in for the winter;
marmots—vulnerable as they are,
manage to arrange for rock-solid homes;
locusts—leaderless insects,
yet they strip the field like an army regiment;
lizards—easy enough to catch,
but they sneak past vigilant palace guards.

Four Dignitaries

29-31 There are three solemn dignitaries,
four that are impressive in their bearing—
a lion, king of the beasts, deferring to none;

NEW KING JAMES VERSION

31A greyhound,[a]
A male goat also,
And a king *whose* troops *are* with him.[b]

32If you have been foolish in exalting yourself,
Or if you have devised evil, *put your* hand
on *your* mouth.
33For *as* the churning of milk produces butter,
And wringing the nose produces blood,
So the forcing of wrath produces strife.

THE WORDS OF KING LEMUEL'S MOTHER

31 The words of King Lemuel, the utterance which his mother taught him:

2What, my son?
And what, son of my womb?
And what, son of my vows?
3Do not give your strength to women,
Nor your ways to that which destroys kings.

4*It is* not for kings, O Lemuel,
It is not for kings to drink wine,
Nor for princes intoxicating drink;
5Lest they drink and forget the law,
And pervert the justice of all the afflicted.
6Give strong drink to him who is perishing,
And wine to those who are bitter of heart.
7Let him drink and forget his poverty,
And remember his misery no more.

8Open your mouth for the speechless,
In the cause of all *who are* appointed to die.[a]
9Open your mouth, judge righteously,
And plead the cause of the poor and needy.

THE VIRTUOUS WIFE

10Who[a] can find a virtuous[b] wife?
For her worth *is* far above rubies.
11The heart of her husband safely trusts her;
So he will have no lack of gain.
12She does him good and not evil
All the days of her life.
13She seeks wool and flax,
And willingly works with her hands.
14She is like the merchant ships,
She brings her food from afar.
15She also rises while it is yet night,
And provides food for her household,
And a portion for her maidservants.
16She considers a field and buys it;
From her profits she plants a vineyard.
17She girds herself with strength,
And strengthens her arms.
18She perceives that her merchandise *is* good,
And her lamp does not go out by night.

30:31 [a]Exact identity unknown [b]A Jewish tradition reads *a king against whom there is no uprising.* **31:8** [a]Literally *sons of passing away* **31:10** [a]Verses 10 through 31 are an alphabetic acrostic in Hebrew (compare Psalm 119). [b]Literally *a wife of valor,* in the sense of all forms of excellence

THE MESSAGE

a rooster, proud and strutting;
a billy goat;
a head of state in stately procession.

32-33 If you're dumb enough to call attention to yourself
by offending people and making rude gestures,
Don't be surprised if someone bloodies your nose.
Churned milk turns into butter;
riled emotions turn into fist fights.

SPEAK OUT FOR JUSTICE

1 31 The words of King Lemuel,
the strong advice his mother gave him:

2-3 "Oh, son of mine, what can you be thinking of!
Child whom I bore! The son I dedicated to God!
Don't dissipate your virility on fortune-hunting women,
promiscuous women who shipwreck leaders.

4-7 "Leaders can't afford to make fools of themselves,
gulping wine and swilling beer,
Lest, hung over, they don't know right from wrong,
and the people who depend on them are hurt.
Use wine and beer only as sedatives,
to kill the pain and dull the ache
Of the terminally ill,
for whom life is a living death.

8-9 "Speak up for the people who have no voice,
for the rights of all the down-and-outers.
Speak out for justice!
Stand up for the poor and destitute!"

HYMN TO A GOOD WIFE

10-31 A good woman is hard to find,
and worth far more than diamonds.
Her husband trusts her without reserve,
and never has reason to regret it.
Never spiteful, she treats him generously
all her life long.
She shops around for the best yarns and cottons,
and enjoys knitting and sewing.
She's like a trading ship that sails to faraway places
and brings back exotic surprises.
She's up before dawn, preparing breakfast
for her family and organizing her day.
She looks over a field and buys it,
then, with money she's put aside, plants a garden.
First thing in the morning, she dresses for work,
rolls up her sleeves, eager to get started.
She senses the worth of her work,
is in no hurry to call it quits for the day.

NEW KING JAMES VERSION

19She stretches out her hands to the distaff,
And her hand holds the spindle.
20She extends her hand to the poor,
Yes, she reaches out her hands to the needy.
21She is not afraid of snow for her household,
For all her household *is* clothed with scarlet.
22She makes tapestry for herself;
Her clothing *is* fine linen and purple.
23Her husband is known in the gates,
When he sits among the elders of the land.
24She makes linen garments and sells *them*,
And supplies sashes for the merchants.
25Strength and honor *are* her clothing;
She shall rejoice in time to come.
26She opens her mouth with wisdom,
And on her tongue *is* the law of kindness.
27She watches over the ways of her household,
And does not eat the bread of idleness.
28Her children rise up and call her blessed;
Her husband *also*, and he praises her:
29"Many daughters have done well,
But you excel them all."
30Charm *is* deceitful and beauty *is* passing,
But a woman *who* fears the LORD, she shall be praised.
31Give her of the fruit of her hands,
And let her own works praise her in the gates.

THE MESSAGE

She's skilled in the crafts of home and hearth,
diligent in homemaking.
She's quick to assist anyone in need,
reaches out to help the poor.
She doesn't worry about her family when it snows;
their winter clothes are all mended and ready to wear.
She makes her own clothing,
and dresses in colorful linens and silks.
Her husband is greatly respected
when he deliberates with the city fathers.
She designs gowns and sells them,
brings the sweaters she knits to the dress shops.
Her clothes are well-made and elegant,
and she always faces tomorrow with a smile.
When she speaks she has something worthwhile to say,
and she always says it kindly.
She keeps an eye on everyone in her household,
and keeps them all busy and productive.
Her children respect and bless her;
her husband joins in with words of praise:
"Many women have done wonderful things,
but you've outclassed them all!"
Charm can mislead and beauty soon fades.
The woman to be admired and praised
is the woman who lives in the Fear-of-GOD.
Give her everything she deserves!
Festoon her life with praises!

ECCLESIASTES

NEW KING JAMES VERSION

THE VANITY OF LIFE

1 The words of the Preacher, the son of David, king in Jerusalem.

2"Vanity[a] of vanities," says the Preacher;
"Vanity of vanities, all *is* vanity."

3What profit has a man from all his labor
In which he toils under the sun?
4*One* generation passes away, and *another* generation comes;
But the earth abides forever.
5The sun also rises, and the sun goes down,
And hastens to the place where it arose.
6The wind goes toward the south,
And turns around to the north;
The wind whirls about continually,
And comes again on its circuit.
7All the rivers run into the sea,
Yet the sea *is* not full;
To the place from which the rivers come,
There they return again.
8All things *are* full of labor;
Man cannot express *it*.
The eye is not satisfied with seeing,
Nor the ear filled with hearing.

9That which has been *is* what will be,
That which *is* done is what will be done,
And *there is* nothing new under the sun.
10Is there anything of which it may be said,
"See, this *is* new"?
It has already been in ancient times before us.
11*There is* no remembrance of former *things*,
Nor will there be any remembrance of *things* that are to come
By *those* who will come after.

THE GRIEF OF WISDOM

12I, the Preacher, was king over Israel in
Jerusalem. 13And I set my heart to seek and
search out by wisdom concerning all that is
done under heaven; this burdensome task God
has given to the sons of man, by which they may
be exercised. 14I have seen all the works that are
done under the sun; and indeed, all *is* vanity and
grasping for the wind.

15*What is* crooked cannot be made straight,
And what is lacking cannot be numbered.

1:2 [a]Or *Absurdity, Frustration, Futility, Nonsense;* and so throughout this book

THE MESSAGE

THE QUESTER

1 1 These are the words of the Quester, David's son and king in Jerusalem

2-11 Smoke, nothing but smoke. [That's what the Quester says.]
There's nothing to anything—it's all smoke.
What's there to show for a lifetime of work,
a lifetime of working your fingers to the bone?
One generation goes its way, the next one arrives,
but nothing changes—it's business as usual for old planet earth.
The sun comes up and the sun goes down,
then does it again, and again—the same old round.
The wind blows south, the wind blows north.
Around and around and around it blows,
blowing this way, then that—the whirling, erratic wind.
All the rivers flow into the sea,
but the sea never fills up.
The rivers keep flowing to the same old place,
and then start all over and do it again.
Everything's boring, utterly boring—
no one can find any meaning in it.
Boring to the eye,
boring to the ear.
What was will be again,
what happened will happen again.
There's nothing new on this earth.
Year after year it's the same old thing.
Does someone call out, "Hey, *this* is new"?
Don't get excited—it's the same old story.
Nobody remembers what happened yesterday.
And the things that will happen tomorrow?
Nobody'll remember them either.
Don't count on being remembered.

I'VE SEEN IT ALL

12-14 Call me "the Quester." I've been king over Israel in Jerusalem. I looked most carefully into everything, searched out all that is done on this earth. And let me tell you, there's not much to write home about. God hasn't made it easy for us. I've seen it all and it's nothing but smoke—smoke, and spitting into the wind.

15 Life's a corkscrew that can't be straightened,
A minus that won't add up.

NEW KING JAMES VERSION

16 I communed with my heart, saying, "Look,
I have attained greatness, and have gained more
wisdom than all who were before me in
Jerusalem. My heart has understood great wis-
dom and knowledge." 17 And I set my heart to
know wisdom and to know madness and folly. I
perceived that this also is grasping for the wind.

18 For in much wisdom *is* much grief,
And he who increases knowledge increases
sorrow.

THE VANITY OF PLEASURE

2 I said in my heart, "Come now, I will test you
with mirth; therefore enjoy pleasure"; but
surely, this also *was* vanity. 2 I said of laughter—
"Madness!"; and of mirth, "What does it accom-
plish?" 3 I searched in my heart *how* to gratify
my flesh with wine, while guiding my heart with
wisdom, and how to lay hold on folly, till I might
see what *was* good for the sons of men to do un-
der heaven all the days of their lives.
4 I made my works great, I built myself
houses, and planted myself vineyards. 5 I made
myself gardens and orchards, and I planted all
kinds of fruit trees in them. 6 I made myself wa-
ter pools from which to water the growing trees
of the grove. 7 I acquired male and female ser-
vants, and had servants born in my house. Yes, I
had greater possessions of herds and flocks
than all who were in Jerusalem before me. 8 I
also gathered for myself silver and gold and the
special treasures of kings and of the provinces.
I acquired male and female singers, the delights
of the sons of men, *and* musical instruments[a] of
all kinds.
9 So I became great and excelled more than
all who were before me in Jerusalem. Also my
wisdom remained with me.

10 Whatever my eyes desired I did not keep
from them.
I did not withhold my heart from any
pleasure,
For my heart rejoiced in all my labor;
And this was my reward from all my labor.
11 Then I looked on all the works that my
hands had done
And on the labor in which I had toiled;
And indeed all *was* vanity and grasping for
the wind.
There was no profit under the sun.

2:8 [a]Exact meaning unknown

THE MESSAGE

16-17 I said to myself, "I know more and I'm wiser than anyone before me in Jerusalem. I've stockpiled wisdom and knowledge." What I've finally concluded is that so-called wisdom and knowledge are mindless and witless—nothing but spitting into the wind.

18 Much learning earns you much trouble.
The more you know, the more you hurt.

1-3 2 I said to myself, "Let's go for it—experiment with pleasure, have a good time!" But there was nothing to it, nothing but smoke.

What do I think of the fun-filled life?
Insane! Inane!
My verdict on the pursuit of
happiness? Who needs it?
With the help of a bottle of wine
and all the wisdom I could muster,
I tried my level best
to penetrate the absurdity of life.
I wanted to get a handle on anything
useful we mortals might do
during the years we spend on this earth.

I NEVER SAID NO TO MYSELF

4-8 Oh, I did great things:
built houses,
planted vineyards,
designed gardens and parks
and planted a variety of fruit trees
in them,
made pools of water
to irrigate the groves of trees.
I bought slaves, male and female,
who had children, giving me even
more slaves;
then I acquired large herds and
flocks,
larger than any before me in
Jerusalem.
I piled up silver and gold,
loot from kings and kingdoms.
I gathered a chorus of singers to
entertain me with song,
and—most exquisite of all
pleasures—
voluptuous maidens for my bed.

9-10 Oh, how I prospered! I left all my predecessors in Jerusalem far behind, left them behind in the dust. What's more, I kept a clear head through it all. Everything I wanted I took—I never said no to myself. I gave in to every impulse, held back nothing. I sucked the marrow of pleasure out of every task—my reward to myself for a hard day's work!

I HATE LIFE

11 Then I took a good look at everything I'd done, looked at all the sweat and hard work. But when I looked, I saw nothing but smoke. Smoke and spitting into the wind. There was nothing to any of it. Nothing.

NEW KING JAMES VERSION

THE END OF THE WISE AND THE FOOL

12Then I turned myself to consider wisdom
and madness and folly;
For what *can* the man *do* who succeeds the
king?—
Only what he has already done.
13Then I saw that wisdom excels folly
As light excels darkness.
14The wise man's eyes *are* in his head,
But the fool walks in darkness.
Yet I myself perceived
That the same event happens to them all.

15So I said in my heart,
"As it happens to the fool,
It also happens to me,
And why was I then more wise?"
Then I said in my heart,
"This also *is* vanity."
16For *there is* no more remembrance of the
wise than of the fool forever,
Since all that now *is* will be forgotten in the
days to come.
And how does a wise *man* die?
As the fool!

17Therefore I hated life because the work that
was done under the sun *was* distressing to me,
for all *is* vanity and grasping for the wind.
18Then I hated all my labor in which I had
toiled under the sun, because I must leave it to
the man who will come after me. 19And who
knows whether he will be wise or a fool? Yet he
will rule over all my labor in which I toiled and
in which I have shown myself wise under the
sun. This also *is* vanity. 20Therefore I turned my
heart and despaired of all the labor in which I
had toiled under the sun. 21For there is a man
whose labor *is* with wisdom, knowledge, and
skill; yet he must leave his heritage to a man
who has not labored for it. This also *is* vanity
and a great evil. 22For what has man for all his
labor, and for the striving of his heart with
which he has toiled under the sun? 23For all his
days *are* sorrowful, and his work burdensome;
even in the night his heart takes no rest. This
also is vanity.
24Nothing *is* better for a man *than* that he
should eat and drink, and *that* his soul should
enjoy good in his labor. This also, I saw, was
from the hand of God. 25For who can eat, or who
can have enjoyment, more than I?[a] 26For *God*
gives wisdom and knowledge and joy to a man
who *is* good in His sight; but to the sinner He
gives the work of gathering and collecting, that
he may give to *him who is* good before God. This
also *is* vanity and grasping for the wind.

EVERYTHING HAS ITS TIME

3 To everything *there is* a season,
A time for every purpose under heaven:

2A time to be born,
And a time to die;
A time to plant,
And a time to pluck *what is* planted;

2:25 [a]Following Masoretic Text, Targum, and Vulgate; some Hebrew manuscripts, Septuagint, and Syriac read *without Him.*

THE MESSAGE

12-14 And then I took a hard look at what's smart and what's stupid. What's left to do after you've been king? That's a hard act to follow. You just do what you can, and that's it. But I did see that it's better to be smart than stupid, just as light is better than darkness. Even so, though the smart ones see where they're going and the stupid ones grope in the dark, they're all the same in the end. One fate for all—and that's it.

15-16 When I realized that my fate's the same as the fool's, I had to ask myself, "So why bother being wise?" It's all smoke, nothing but smoke. The smart and the stupid both disappear out of sight. In a day or two they're both forgotten. Yes, both the smart and the stupid die, and that's it.

17 I hate life. As far as I can see, what happens on earth is a bad business. It's smoke—and spitting into the wind.

18-19 And I hated everything I'd accomplished and accumulated on this earth. I can't take it with me—no, I have to leave it to whoever comes after me. Whether they're worthy or worthless—and who's to tell?—they'll take over the earthly results of my intense thinking and hard work. Smoke.

20-23 That's when I called it quits, gave up on anything that could be hoped for on this earth. What's the point of working your fingers to the bone if you hand over what you worked for to someone who never lifted a finger for it? Smoke, that's what it is. A bad business from start to finish. So what do you get from a life of hard labor? Pain and grief from dawn to dusk. Never a decent night's rest. Nothing but smoke.

24-26 The best you can do with your life is have a good time and get by the best you can. The way I see it, that's it—divine fate. Whether we feast or fast, it's up to God. God may give wisdom and knowledge and joy to his favorites, but sinners are assigned a life of hard labor, and end up turning their wages over to God's favorites. Nothing but smoke—and spitting into the wind.

THERE'S A RIGHT TIME FOR EVERYTHING

3 1 There's an opportune time to do things, a right time for everything on the earth:

2-8 A right time for birth and another for death,
A right time to plant and another to reap,

NEW KING JAMES VERSION

[3]A time to kill,
And a time to heal;
A time to break down,
And a time to build up;
[4]A time to weep,
And a time to laugh;
A time to mourn,
And a time to dance;
[5]A time to cast away stones,
And a time to gather stones;
A time to embrace,
And a time to refrain from embracing;
[6]A time to gain,
And a time to lose;
A time to keep,
And a time to throw away;
[7]A time to tear,
And a time to sew;
A time to keep silence,
And a time to speak;
[8]A time to love,
And a time to hate;
A time of war,
And a time of peace.

THE GOD-GIVEN TASK

[9]What profit has the worker from that in
which he labors? [10]I have seen the God-given
task with which the sons of men are to be occu-
pied. [11]He has made everything beautiful in its
time. Also He has put eternity in their hearts, ex-
cept that no one can find out the work that God
does from beginning to end.

[12]I know that nothing *is* better for them than
to rejoice, and to do good in their lives, [13]and
also that every man should eat and drink and
enjoy the good of all his labor—it *is* the gift of
God.

[14]I know that whatever God does,
It shall be forever.
Nothing can be added to it,
And nothing taken from it.
God does *it*, that men should fear before
Him.
[15]That which is has already been,
And what is to be has already been;
And God requires an account of what is
past.

INJUSTICE SEEMS TO PREVAIL

[16]Moreover I saw under the sun:

In the place of judgment,
Wickedness *was* there;
And *in* the place of righteousness,
Iniquity *was* there.

[17]I said in my heart,

"God shall judge the righteous and the
wicked,
For *there is* a time there for every purpose
and for every work."

[18]I said in my heart, "Concerning the condi-
tion of the sons of men, God tests them, that they
may see that they themselves are *like* animals."

THE MESSAGE

A right time to kill and another to heal,
A right time to destroy and another to
construct,
A right time to cry and another to laugh,
A right time to lament and another to
cheer,
A right time to make love and another to
abstain,
A right time to embrace and another to
part,
A right time to search and another to
count your losses,
A right time to hold on and another to let
go,
A right time to rip out and another to
mend,
A right time to shut up and another to
speak up,
A right time to love and another to hate,
A right time to wage war and another to
make peace.

9-13 But in the end, does it really make a dif-
ference what anyone does? I've had a good
look at what God has given us to do—busy-
work, mostly. True, God made everything
beautiful in itself and in its time—but he's
left us in the dark, so we can never know
what God is up to, whether he's coming or
going. I've decided that there's nothing bet-
ter to do than go ahead and have a good
time and get the most we can out of life.
That's it—eat, drink, and make the most of
your job. It's God's gift.

14 I've also concluded that whatever God
does, that's the way it's going to be, always.
No addition, no subtraction. God's done it
and that's it. That's so we'll quit asking
questions and simply worship in holy fear.

15 Whatever was, is.
Whatever will be, is.
That's how it always is with God.

GOD'S TESTING US

16-18 I took another good look at what's going
on: The very place of judgment—corrupt!
The place of righteousness—corrupt! I said
to myself, "God will judge righteous and
wicked." There's a right time for every
thing, every deed—and there's no getting
around it. I said to myself regarding the hu-
man race, "God's testing the lot of us, show-
ing us up as nothing but animals."

New King James Version

19 For what happens to the sons of men also hap-
pens to animals; one thing befalls them: as one
dies, so dies the other. Surely, they all have one
breath; man has no advantage over animals, for
all *is* vanity. 20 All go to one place: all are from
the dust, and all return to dust. 21 Who knows the
spirit of the sons of men, which goes upward,
and the spirit of the animal, which goes down to
the earth?[a] 22 So I perceived that nothing *is* bet-
ter than that a man should rejoice in his own
works, for that *is* his heritage. For who can bring
him to see what will happen after him?

4 Then I returned and considered all the op-
pression that is done under the sun:

And look! The tears of the oppressed,
But they have no comforter—
On the side of their oppressors *there is*
power,
But they have no comforter.
2 Therefore I praised the dead who were
already dead,
More than the living who are still alive.
3 Yet, better than both *is he* who has never
existed,
Who has not seen the evil work that is done
under the sun.

The Vanity of Selfish Toil

4 Again, I saw that for all toil and every skill-
ful work a man is envied by his neighbor. This
also *is* vanity and grasping for the wind.

5 The fool folds his hands
And consumes his own flesh.
6 Better a handful *with* quietness
Than both hands full, *together with* toil and
grasping for the wind.

7 Then I returned, and I saw vanity under the
sun:

8 There is one alone, without companion:
He has neither son nor brother.
Yet *there is* no end to all his labors,
Nor is his eye satisfied with riches.
But he never asks,
"For whom do I toil and deprive myself of
good?"
This also *is* vanity and a grave misfortune.

The Value of a Friend

9 Two *are* better than one,
Because they have a good reward for their
labor.
10 For if they fall, one will lift up his
companion.
But woe to him *who is* alone when he falls,
For *he has* no one to help him up.
11 Again, if two lie down together, they will
keep warm;
But how can one be warm *alone?*

3:21 [a]Septuagint, Syriac, Targum, and Vulgate read *Who knows whether the spirit . . . goes upward, and whether . . . goes downward to the earth?*

The Message

19-22 Humans and animals come to the same end—humans die, animals die. We all breathe the same air. So there's really no advantage in being human. None. Everything's smoke. We all end up in the same place—we all came from dust, we all end up as dust. Nobody knows for sure that the human spirit rises to heaven or that the animal spirit sinks into the earth. So I made up my mind that there's nothing better for us men and women than to have a good time in whatever we do—that's our lot. Who knows if there's anything else to life?

Slow Suicide

1-3 4 Next I turned my attention to all the outrageous violence that takes place on this planet—the tears of the victims, no one to comfort them; the iron grip of oppressors, no one to rescue the victims from them. So I congratulated the dead who are already dead instead of the living who are still alive. But luckier than the dead or the living is the person who has never even been, who has never seen the bad business that takes place on this earth.

4 Then I observed all the work and ambition motivated by envy. What a waste! Smoke. And spitting into the wind.

5 The fool sits back and takes it easy,
His sloth is slow suicide.

6 One handful of peaceful repose
Is better than two fistfuls of worried
work—
More spitting into the wind.

Why Am I Working Like a Dog?

7-8 I turned my head and saw yet another wisp of smoke on its way to nothingness: a solitary person, completely alone—no children, no family, no friends—yet working obsessively late into the night, compulsively greedy for more and more, never bothering to ask, "Why am I working like a dog, never having any fun? And who cares?" More smoke. A bad business.

9-10 It's better to have a partner than go it
alone.
Share the work, share the wealth.
And if one falls down, the other helps,
But if there's no one to help, tough!

11 Two in a bed warm each other.
Alone, you shiver all night.

NEW KING JAMES VERSION

[12]Though one may be overpowered by
another, two can withstand him.
And a threefold cord is not quickly broken.

POPULARITY PASSES AWAY

[13]Better a poor and wise youth
Than an old and foolish king who will be
admonished no more.
[14]For he comes out of prison to be king,
Although he was born poor in his kingdom.
[15]I saw all the living who walk under the sun;
They were with the second youth who
stands in his place.
[16]*There was* no end of all the people over
whom he was made king;
Yet those who come afterward will not
rejoice in him.
Surely this also *is* vanity and grasping for
the wind.

FEAR GOD, KEEP YOUR VOWS

5 Walk prudently when you go to the house of
God; and draw near to hear rather than to
give the sacrifice of fools, for they do not know
that they do evil.

[2]Do not be rash with your mouth,
And let not your heart utter anything hastily
before God.
For God *is* in heaven, and you on earth;
Therefore let your words be few.
[3]For a dream comes through much activity,
And a fool's voice *is known* by *his* many
words.

[4]When you make a vow to God, do not delay
to pay it;
For *He has* no pleasure in fools.
Pay what you have vowed—
[5]Better not to vow than to vow and not pay.

[6]Do not let your mouth cause your flesh to sin,
nor say before the messenger *of God* that it *was*
an error. Why should God be angry at your ex-
cuse[a] and destroy the work of your hands? [7]For
in the multitude of dreams and many words
there is also vanity. But fear God.

THE VANITY OF GAIN AND HONOR

[8]If you see the oppression of the poor, and
the violent perversion of justice and righteous-
ness in a province, do not marvel at the matter;
for high official watches over high official, and
higher officials are over them.
[9]Moreover the profit of the land is for all;
even the king is served from the field.

[10]He who loves silver will not be satisfied with
silver;
Nor he who loves abundance, with increase.
This also *is* vanity.

5:6 [a]Literally *voice*

THE MESSAGE

12 By yourself you're unprotected.
With a friend you can face the worst.
Can you round up a third?
A three-stranded rope isn't easily
snapped.

13-16 A poor youngster with some wisdom is bet-
ter off than an old but foolish king who
doesn't know which end is up. I saw a youth
just like this start with nothing and go from
rags to riches, and I saw everyone rally to
the rule of this young successor to the king.
Even so, the excitement died quickly, the
throngs of people soon lost interest. Can't
you see it's only smoke? And spitting into
the wind?

GOD'S IN CHARGE, NOT YOU

1 5 Watch your step when you enter God's
house.
Enter to learn. That's far better than
mindlessly offering a sacrifice,
Doing more harm than good.

2 Don't shoot off your mouth, or speak
before you think.
Don't be too quick to tell God what you
think he wants to hear.
God's in charge, not you—the less you
speak, the better.

3 Overwork makes for restless sleep.
Overtalk shows you up as a fool.

4-5 When you tell God you'll do something,
do it—now.
God takes no pleasure in foolish gabble.
Vow it, then do it.
Far better not to vow in the first place
than to vow and not pay up.

6 Don't let your mouth make a total sinner
of you.
When called to account, you won't get by
with "Sorry, I didn't mean it."
Why risk provoking God to angry
retaliation?

7 But against all illusion and fantasy and
empty talk
There's always this rock foundation:
Fear God!

A SALARY OF SMOKE

8-9 Don't be too upset when you see the poor
kicked around, and justice and right violated
all over the place. Exploitation filters down
from one petty official to another. There's no
end to it, and nothing can be done about it.
But the good earth doesn't cheat anyone—
even a bad king is honestly served by a field.

10 The one who loves money is never
satisfied with money,
Nor the one who loves wealth with big
profits. More smoke.

New King James Version

11When goods increase,
They increase who eat them;
So what profit have the owners
Except to see *them* with their eyes?

12The sleep of a laboring man *is* sweet,
Whether he eats little or much;
But the abundance of the rich will not
permit him to sleep.

13There is a severe evil *which* I have seen
under the sun:
Riches kept for their owner to his hurt.
14But those riches perish through misfortune;
When he begets a son, *there is* nothing in
his hand.
15As he came from his mother's womb, naked
shall he return,
To go as he came;
And he shall take nothing from his labor
Which he may carry away in his hand.
16And this also *is* a severe evil—
Just exactly as he came, so shall he go.
And what profit has he who has labored for
the wind?
17All his days he also eats in darkness,
And *he has* much sorrow and sickness and
anger.

18Here is what I have seen: *It is* good and fit-
ting *for one* to eat and drink, and to enjoy the
good of all his labor in which he toils under the
sun all the days of his life which God gives him;
for it *is* his heritage. 19As for every man to whom
God has given riches and wealth, and given him
power to eat of it, to receive his heritage and re-
joice in his labor—this *is* the gift of God. 20For he
will not dwell unduly on the days of his life, be-
cause God keeps *him* busy with the joy of his
heart.

6 There is an evil which I have seen under the
sun, and it *is* common among men: 2A man to
whom God has given riches and wealth and
honor, so that he lacks nothing for himself of all
he desires; yet God does not give him power to
eat of it, but a foreigner consumes it. This *is* van-
ity, and it *is* an evil affliction.
3If a man begets a hundred *children* and lives
many years, so that the days of his years are
many, but his soul is not satisfied with good-
ness, or indeed he has no burial, I say *that* a
stillborn child *is* better than he— 4for it comes in
vanity and departs in darkness, and its name is
covered with darkness. 5Though it has not seen
the sun or known *anything*, this has more rest
than that man, 6even if he lives a thousand years
twice—but has not seen goodness. Do not all go
to one place?

7All the labor of man *is* for his mouth,
And yet the soul is not satisfied.

The Message

11 The more loot you get, the more looters show up.
And what fun is that—to be robbed in broad daylight?

12 Hard and honest work earns a good night's sleep,
Whether supper is beans or steak.
But a rich man's belly gives him insomnia.

13-17 Here's a piece of bad luck I've seen happen:
A man hoards far more wealth than is good for him
And then loses it all in a bad business deal.
He fathered a child but hasn't a cent left to give him.
He arrived naked from the womb of his mother;
He'll leave in the same condition—with nothing.
This is bad luck, for sure—naked he came, naked he went.
So what was the point of working for a salary of smoke?
All for a miserable life spent in the dark?

Make the Most of What God Gives

18-20 After looking at the way things are on this earth, here's what I've decided is the best way to live: Take care of yourself, have a good time, and make the most of whatever job you have for as long as God gives you life. And that's about it. That's the human lot. Yes, we should make the most of what God gives, both the bounty and the capacity to enjoy it, accepting what's given and delighting in the work. It's God's gift! God deals out joy in the present, the *now*. It's useless to brood over how long we might live.

Things Are Bad

1-2 6 I looked long and hard at what goes on around here, and let me tell you, things are bad. And people feel it. There are people, for instance, on whom God showers everything—money, property, reputation—all they ever wanted or dreamed of. And then God doesn't let them enjoy it. Some stranger comes along and has all the fun. It's more of what I'm calling *smoke*. A bad business.

3-5 Say a couple have scores of children and live a long, long life but never enjoy themselves—even though they end up with a big funeral! I'd say that a stillborn baby gets the better deal. It gets its start in a mist and ends up in the dark—unnamed. It sees nothing and knows nothing, but is better off by far than anyone living.

6 Even if someone lived a thousand years—make it two thousand!—but didn't enjoy anything, what's the point? Doesn't everyone end up in the same place?

7 We work to feed our appetites;
Meanwhile our souls go hungry.

NEW KING JAMES VERSION

8For what more has the wise *man* than the fool?
What does the poor man have,
Who knows *how* to walk before the living?
9Better *is* the sight of the eyes than the wandering of desire.
This also *is* vanity and grasping for the wind.

10Whatever one is, he has been named already,
For it is known that he *is* man;
And he cannot contend with Him who is mightier than he.
11Since there are many things that increase vanity,
How *is* man the better?

12For who knows what *is* good for man in
life, all the days of his vain life which he passes
like a shadow? Who can tell a man what will
happen after him under the sun?

THE VALUE OF PRACTICAL WISDOM

7 A good name is better than precious ointment,
And the day of death than the day of one's birth;
2Better to go to the house of mourning
Than to go to the house of feasting,
For that *is* the end of all men;
And the living will take *it* to heart.
3Sorrow *is* better than laughter,
For by a sad countenance the heart is made better.
4The heart of the wise *is* in the house of mourning,
But the heart of fools *is* in the house of mirth.

5*It is* better to hear the rebuke of the wise
Than for a man to hear the song of fools.
6For like the crackling of thorns under a pot,
So *is* the laughter of the fool.
This also is vanity.
7Surely oppression destroys a wise *man's* reason,
And a bribe debases the heart.
8The end of a thing *is* better than its beginning;
The patient in spirit *is* better than the proud in spirit.
9Do not hasten in your spirit to be angry,
For anger rests in the bosom of fools.
10Do not say,
"Why were the former days better than these?"
For you do not inquire wisely concerning this.

11Wisdom *is* good with an inheritance,
And profitable to those who see the sun.
12For wisdom *is* a defense *as* money *is* a defense,
But the excellence of knowledge *is that* wisdom gives life to those who have it.

THE MESSAGE

8-9 So what advantage has a sage over a fool,
or over some poor wretch who barely gets
by? Just grab whatever you can while you
can; don't assume something better might
turn up by and by. All it amounts to anyway
is smoke. And spitting into the wind.

10 Whatever happens, happens. Its destiny is fixed.
You can't argue with fate.

11-12 The more words that are spoken, the
more smoke there is in the air. And who is
any better off? And who knows what's best
for us as we live out our meager smoke-and-
shadow lives? And who can tell any of us
the next chapter of our lives?

DON'T TAKE ANYTHING FOR GRANTED

1 7 A good reputation is better than a fat bank account.
Your death date tells more than your birth date.

2 You learn more at a funeral than at a feast—
After all, that's where we'll end up. We might discover something from it.

3 Crying is better than laughing.
It blotches the face but it scours the heart.

4 Sages invest themselves in hurt and grieving.
Fools waste their lives in fun and games.

5 You'll get more from the rebuke of a sage
Than from the song and dance of fools.

6 The giggles of fools are like the crackling of twigs
Under the cooking pot. And like smoke.

7 Brutality stupefies even the wise
And destroys the strongest heart.

8 Endings are better than beginnings.
Sticking to it is better than standing out.

9 Don't be quick to fly off the handle.
Anger boomerangs. You can spot a fool by the lumps on his head.

10 Don't always be asking, "Where are the good old days?"
Wise folks don't ask questions like that.

11-12 Wisdom is better when it's paired with money,
Especially if you get both while you're still living.
Double protection: wisdom and wealth!
Plus this bonus: Wisdom energizes its owner.

NEW KING JAMES VERSION

13 Consider the work of God;
For who can make straight what He has made crooked?
14 In the day of prosperity be joyful,
But in the day of adversity consider:
Surely God has appointed the one as well as the other,
So that man can find out nothing *that will come* after him.

15 I have seen everything in my days of vanity:

There is a just *man* who perishes in his righteousness,
And there is a wicked *man* who prolongs *life* in his wickedness.

16 Do not be overly righteous,
Nor be overly wise:
Why should you destroy yourself?
17 Do not be overly wicked,
Nor be foolish:
Why should you die before your time?
18 *It is* good that you grasp this,
And also not remove your hand from the other;
For he who fears God will escape them all.

19 Wisdom strengthens the wise
More than ten rulers of the city.

20 For *there is* not a just man on earth who does good
And does not sin.

21 Also do not take to heart everything people say,
Lest you hear your servant cursing you.
22 For many times, also, your own heart has known
That even you have cursed others.

23 All this I have proved by wisdom.
I said, "I will be wise";
But it *was* far from me.
24 As for that which is far off and exceedingly deep,
Who can find it out?
25 I applied my heart to know,
To search and seek out wisdom and the reason *of things,*
To know the wickedness of folly,
Even of foolishness *and* madness.
26 And I find more bitter than death
The woman whose heart *is* snares and nets,
Whose hands *are* fetters.
He who pleases God shall escape from her,
But the sinner shall be trapped by her.

27 "Here is what I have found," says the Preacher,
"*Adding* one thing to the other to find out the reason,
28 Which my soul still seeks but I cannot find:
One man among a thousand I have found,
But a woman among all these I have not found.
29 Truly, this only I have found:
That God made man upright,
But they have sought out many schemes."

THE MESSAGE

13 Take a good look at God's work.
Who could simplify and reduce
Creation's curves and angles
To a plain straight line?

14 On a good day, enjoy yourself;
On a bad day, examine your conscience.
God arranges for both kinds of days
So that we won't take anything for granted.

STAY IN TOUCH WITH BOTH SIDES

15-17 I've seen it all in my brief and pointless
life—here a good person cut down in the
middle of doing good, there a bad person
living a long life of sheer evil. So don't
knock yourself out being good, and don't go
overboard being wise. Believe me, you won't
get anything out of it. But don't press your
luck by being bad, either. And don't be reck-
less. Why die needlessly?
18 It's best to stay in touch with both sides
of an issue. A person who fears God deals
responsibly with all of reality, not just a
piece of it.

19 Wisdom puts more strength in one wise person
Than ten strong men give to a city.

20 There's not one totally good person on earth,
Not one who is truly pure and sinless.

21-22 Don't eavesdrop on the conversation of others.
What if the gossip's about you and you'd rather not hear it?
You've done that a few times, haven't you—said things
Behind someone's back you wouldn't say to his face?

HOW TO INTERPRET THE MEANING OF LIFE

23-25 I tested everything in my search for wisdom.
I set out to be wise, but it was beyond me,
far beyond me, and deep—oh so deep! Does
anyone ever find it? I concentrated with all
my might, studying and exploring and seek-
ing wisdom—the meaning of life. I also
wanted to identify evil and stupidity, fool-
ishness and craziness.
26-29 One discovery: A woman can be a bitter
pill to swallow, full of seductive scheming
and grasping. The lucky escape her; the
undiscerning get caught. At least this is my
experience—what I, the Quester, have
pieced together as I've tried to make sense
of life. But the wisdom I've looked for I
haven't found. I didn't find one man or
woman in a thousand worth my while. Yet I
did spot one ray of light in this murk: God
made men and women true and upright;
we're the ones who've made a mess of
things.

NEW KING JAMES VERSION

8 Who *is* like a wise *man?*
And who knows the interpretation of a thing?
A man's wisdom makes his face shine,
And the sternness of his face is changed.

OBEY AUTHORITIES FOR GOD'S SAKE

2 I *say,* "Keep the king's commandment for
the sake of your oath to God. 3 Do not be hasty to
go from his presence. Do not take your stand for
an evil thing, for he does whatever pleases him."

4 Where the word of a king *is, there is* power;
And who may say to him, "What are you
doing?"
5 He who keeps his command will experience
nothing harmful;
And a wise man's heart discerns both time
and judgment,
6 Because for every matter there is a time and
judgment,
Though the misery of man increases greatly.
7 For he does not know what will happen;
So who can tell him when it will occur?
8 No one has power over the spirit to retain
the spirit,
And no one has power in the day of death.
There is no release from that war,
And wickedness will not deliver those who
are given to it.

9 All this I have seen, and applied my heart to
every work that is done under the sun: *There is*
a time in which one man rules over another to
his own hurt.

DEATH COMES TO ALL

10 Then I saw the wicked buried, who had
come and gone from the place of holiness, and
they were forgotten[a] in the city where they had
so done. This also *is* vanity. 11 Because the sen-
tence against an evil work is not executed
speedily, therefore the heart of the sons of men
is fully set in them to do evil. 12 Though a sinner
does evil a hundred *times,* and his *days* are pro-
longed, yet I surely know that it will be well with
those who fear God, who fear before Him. 13 But
it will not be well with the wicked; nor will he
prolong *his* days, *which are* as a shadow, be-
cause he does not fear before God.

14 There is a vanity which occurs on earth,
that there are just *men* to whom it happens ac-
cording to the work of the wicked; again, there
are wicked *men* to whom it happens according
to the work of the righteous. I said that this also
is vanity.

15 So I commended enjoyment, because a
man has nothing better under the sun than to
eat, drink, and be merry; for this will remain
with him in his labor *all* the days of his life
which God gives him under the sun.

8:10 [a]Some Hebrew manuscripts, Septuagint, and Vulgate read *praised.*

THE MESSAGE

1 8 There's nothing better than being wise,
Knowing how to interpret the meaning
of life.
Wisdom puts light in the eyes,
And gives gentleness to words and
manners.

NO ONE CAN CONTROL THE WIND

2-7 Do what your king commands; you gave a sacred oath of obedience. Don't worryingly second-guess your orders or try to back out when the task is unpleasant. You're serving his pleasure, not yours. The king has the last word. Who dares say to him, "What are you doing?" Carrying out orders won't hurt you a bit; the wise person obeys promptly and accurately. Yes, there's a right time and way for everything, even though, unfortunately, we miss it for the most part. It's true that no one knows what's going to happen, or when. Who's around to tell us?

8 No one can control the wind or lock it in
a box.
No one has any say-so regarding the day
of death.
No one can stop a battle in its tracks.
No one who does evil can be saved by
evil.

9 All this I observed as I tried my best to understand all that's going on in this world. As long as men and women have the power to hurt each other, this is the way it is.

ONE FATE FOR EVERYBODY

10 One time I saw wicked men given a solemn burial in holy ground. When the people returned to the city, they delivered flowery eulogies—and in the very place where wicked acts were done by those very men! More smoke. Indeed.

11 Because the sentence against evil deeds is so long in coming, people in general think they can get by with murder.

12-13 Even though a person sins and gets by with it hundreds of times throughout a long life, I'm still convinced that the good life is reserved for the person who fears God, who lives reverently in his presence, and that the evil person will not experience a "good" life. No matter how many days he lives, they'll all be as flat and colorless as a shadow—because he doesn't fear God.

14 Here's something that happens all the time and makes no sense at all: Good people get what's coming to the wicked, and bad people get what's coming to the good. I tell you, this makes no sense. It's smoke.

15 So, I'm all for just going ahead and having a good time—the best possible. The only earthly good men and women can look forward to is to eat and drink well and have a good time—compensation for the struggle for survival these few years God gives us on earth.

NEW KING JAMES VERSION

[16]When I applied my heart to know wisdom
and to see the business that is done on earth,
even though one sees no sleep day or night,
[17]then I saw all the work of God, that a man can-
not find out the work that is done under the sun.
For though a man labors to discover *it*, yet he
will not find *it;* moreover, though a wise *man* at-
tempts to know *it*, he will not be able to find *it*.

9 For I considered all this in my heart, so that I
could declare it all: that the righteous and the
wise and their works *are* in the hand of God.
People know neither love nor hatred *by* any-
thing *they see* before them. [2]All things *come*
alike to all:

One event *happens* to the righteous and the wicked;
To the good,[a] the clean, and the unclean;
To him who sacrifices and him who does not sacrifice.
As is the good, so *is* the sinner;
He who takes an oath as *he* who fears an oath.

[3]This *is* an evil in all that is done under the sun:
that one thing *happens* to all. Truly the hearts of
the sons of men are full of evil; madness *is* in
their hearts while they live, and after that *they*
go to the dead. [4]But for him who is joined to all
the living there is hope, for a living dog is better
than a dead lion.

[5]For the living know that they will die;
But the dead know nothing,
And they have no more reward,
For the memory of them is forgotten.
[6]Also their love, their hatred, and their envy
have now perished;
Nevermore will they have a share
In anything done under the sun.

[7]Go, eat your bread with joy,
And drink your wine with a merry heart;
For God has already accepted your works.
[8]Let your garments always be white,
And let your head lack no oil.

[9]Live joyfully with the wife whom you love
all the days of your vain life which He has given
you under the sun, all your days of vanity; for
that *is* your portion in life, and in the labor
which you perform under the sun.
[10]Whatever your hand finds to do, do *it* with
your might; for *there is* no work or device or
knowledge or wisdom in the grave where you
are going.
[11]I returned and saw under the sun that—

The race *is* not to the swift,
Nor the battle to the strong,
Nor bread to the wise,
Nor riches to men of understanding,
Nor favor to men of skill;
But time and chance happen to them all.

9:2 [a]Septuagint, Syriac, and Vulgate read *good and bad*.

THE MESSAGE

16-17 When I determined to load up on wisdom and examine everything taking place on earth, I realized that if you keep your eyes open day and night without even blinking, you'll still never figure out the meaning of what God is doing on this earth. Search as hard as you like, you're not going to make sense of it. No matter how smart you are, you won't get to the bottom of it.

1-3 9 Well, I took all this in and thought it through, inside and out. Here's what I understood: The good, the wise, and all that they do are in God's hands—but, day by day, whether it's love or hate they're dealing with, they don't know.

Anything's possible. It's one fate for everybody—righteous and wicked, good people, bad people, the nice and the nasty, worshipers and nonworshipers, committed and uncommitted. I find this outrageous—the worst thing about living on this earth—that everyone's lumped together in one fate. Is it any wonder that so many people are obsessed with evil? Is it any wonder that people go crazy right and left? Life leads to death. That's it.

SEIZE LIFE!

4-6 Still, anyone selected out for life has hope, for, as they say, "A living dog is better than a dead lion." The living at least know *something*, even if it's only that they're going to die. But the dead know nothing and get nothing. They're a minus that no one remembers. Their loves, their hates, yes, even their dreams, are long gone. There's not a trace of them left in the affairs of this earth.

7-10 Seize life! Eat bread with gusto,
Drink wine with a robust heart.
Oh yes—God takes pleasure in *your* pleasure!
Dress festively every morning.
Don't skimp on colors and scarves.
Relish life with the spouse you love
Each and every day of your precarious life.
Each day is God's gift. It's all you get in exchange
For the hard work of staying alive.
Make the most of each one!
Whatever turns up, grab it and do it. And heartily!
This is your last and only chance at it,
For there's neither work to do nor thoughts to think
In the company of the dead, where you're most certainly headed.

11 I took another walk around the neighborhood and realized that on this earth as it is—

The race is not always to the swift,
Nor the battle to the strong,
Nor satisfaction to the wise,
Nor riches to the smart,
Nor grace to the learned.
Sooner or later bad luck hits us all.

NEW KING JAMES VERSION

[12]For man also does not know his time:
Like fish taken in a cruel net,
Like birds caught in a snare,
So the sons of men *are* snared in an evil time,
When it falls suddenly upon them.

WISDOM SUPERIOR TO FOLLY

[13]This wisdom I have also seen under the
sun, and it *seemed* great to me: [14]*There was* a lit-
tle city with few men in it; and a great king
came against it, besieged it, and built great
snares[a] around it. [15]Now there was found in it a
poor wise man, and he by his wisdom delivered
the city. Yet no one remembered that same poor
man.
[16]Then I said:

"Wisdom *is* better than strength.
Nevertheless the poor man's wisdom *is* despised,
And his words are not heard.
[17]Words of the wise, *spoken* quietly, *should be* heard
Rather than the shout of a ruler of fools.
[18]Wisdom *is* better than weapons of war;
But one sinner destroys much good."

10 Dead flies putrefy[a] the perfumer's ointment,
And cause it to give off a foul odor;
So does a little folly to one respected for wisdom *and* honor.
[2]A wise man's heart *is* at his right hand,
But a fool's heart at his left.
[3]Even when a fool walks along the way,
He lacks wisdom,
And he shows everyone *that* he *is* a fool.
[4]If the spirit of the ruler rises against you,
Do not leave your post;
For conciliation pacifies great offenses.

[5]There is an evil I have seen under the sun,
As an error proceeding from the ruler:
[6]Folly is set in great dignity,
While the rich sit in a lowly place.
[7]I have seen servants on horses,
While princes walk on the ground like servants.

[8]He who digs a pit will fall into it,
And whoever breaks through a wall will be bitten by a serpent.
[9]He who quarries stones may be hurt by them,
And he who splits wood may be endangered by it.

9:14 [a]Septuagint, Syriac, and Vulgate read *bulwarks.* **10:1** [a]Targum and Vulgate omit *putrefy.*

THE MESSAGE

12 No one can predict misfortune.
Like fish caught in a cruel net or birds in a trap,
So men and women are caught
By accidents evil and sudden.

WISDOM IS BETTER THAN MUSCLE

13-15 One day as I was observing how wisdom
fares on this earth, I saw something that
made me sit up and take notice. There was a
small town with only a few people in it. A
strong king came and mounted an attack,
building trenches and attack posts around
it. There was a poor but wise man in that
town whose wisdom saved the town, but he
was promptly forgotten. (He was only a
poor man, after all.)
16 All the same, I still say that wisdom is
better than muscle, even though the wise
poor man was treated with contempt and
soon forgotten.

17 The quiet words of the wise are more effective
Than the ranting of a king of fools.

18 Wisdom is better than warheads,
But one hothead can ruin the good earth.

1 10 Dead flies in perfume make it stink,
And a little foolishness decomposes much wisdom.

2 Wise thinking leads to right living;
Stupid thinking leads to wrong living.

3 Fools on the road have no sense of direction.
The way they walk tells the story: "There goes the fool again!"

4 If a ruler loses his temper against you, don't panic;
A calm disposition quiets intemperate rage.

5-7 Here's a piece of bad business I've seen on this earth,
An error that can be blamed on whoever is in charge:
Immaturity is given a place of prominence,
While maturity is made to take a backseat.
I've seen unproven upstarts riding in style,
While experienced veterans are put out to pasture.

8 Caution: The trap you set might catch you.
Warning: Your accomplice in crime might double-cross you.

9 Safety first: Quarrying stones is dangerous.
Be alert: Felling trees is hazardous.

New King James Version

10If the ax is dull,
And one does not sharpen the edge,
Then he must use more strength;
But wisdom brings success.

11A serpent may bite when *it is* not charmed;
The babbler is no different.
12The words of a wise man's mouth *are*
gracious,
But the lips of a fool shall swallow him up;
13The words of his mouth begin with
foolishness,
And the end of his talk *is* raving madness.
14A fool also multiplies words.
No man knows what is to be;
Who can tell him what will be after him?
15The labor of fools wearies them,
For they do not even know how to go to the
city!

16Woe to you, O land, when your king *is* a child,
And your princes feast in the morning!
17Blessed *are* you, O land, when your king *is*
the son of nobles,
And your princes feast at the proper time—
For strength and not for drunkenness!
18Because of laziness the building decays,
And through idleness of hands the house
leaks.
19A feast is made for laughter,
And wine makes merry;
But money answers everything.

20Do not curse the king, even in your thought;
Do not curse the rich, even in your
bedroom;
For a bird of the air may carry your voice,
And a bird in flight may tell the matter.

The Value of Diligence

11 Cast your bread upon the waters,
For you will find it after many days.
2Give a serving to seven, and also to eight,
For you do not know what evil will be on the
earth.

3If the clouds are full of rain,
They empty *themselves* upon the earth;
And if a tree falls to the south or the north,
In the place where the tree falls, there it
shall lie.
4He who observes the wind will not sow,
And he who regards the clouds will not reap.

5As you do not know what *is* the way of the
wind,[a]
Or how the bones *grow* in the womb of her
who is with child,

11:5 [a]Or *spirit*

The Message

10 Remember: The duller the ax the harder
the work;
Use your head: The more brains, the less
muscle.

11 If the snake bites before it's been charmed,
What's the point in then sending for the
charmer?

12-13 The words of a wise person are gracious.
The talk of a fool self-destructs—
He starts out talking nonsense
And ends up spouting insanity and evil.

14 Fools talk way too much,
Chattering stuff they know nothing about.

15 A decent day's work so fatigues fools
That they can't find their way back to
town.

16-17 Unlucky the land whose king is a young
pup,
And whose princes party all night.
Lucky the land whose king is mature,
Where the princes behave themselves
And don't drink themselves silly.

18 A shiftless man lives in a tumbledown
shack;
A lazy woman ends up with a leaky roof.

19 Laughter and bread go together,
And wine gives sparkle to life—
But it's money that makes the world go
around.

20 Don't bad-mouth your leaders, not even
under your breath,
And don't abuse your betters, even in the
privacy of your home.
Loose talk has a way of getting picked
up and spread around.
Little birds drop the crumbs of your
gossip far and wide.

1 11 Be generous: Invest in acts of charity.
Charity yields high returns.

2 Don't hoard your goods; spread them
around.
Be a blessing to others. This could be
your last night.

3-4 When the clouds are full of water, it
rains.
When the wind blows down a tree, it lies
where it falls.
Don't sit there watching the wind. Do
your own work.
Don't stare at the clouds. Get on with
your life.

5 Just as you'll never understand
the mystery of life forming in a
pregnant woman,

NEW KING JAMES VERSION

So you do not know the works of God who
makes everything.
6In the morning sow your seed,
And in the evening do not withhold your
hand;
For you do not know which will prosper,
Either this or that,
Or whether both alike *will be* good.

7Truly the light is sweet,
And *it is* pleasant for the eyes to behold the
sun;
8But if a man lives many years
And rejoices in them all,
Yet let him remember the days of darkness,
For they will be many.
All that is coming *is* vanity.

SEEK GOD IN EARLY LIFE

9Rejoice, O young man, in your youth,
And let your heart cheer you in the days of
your youth;
Walk in the ways of your heart,
And in the sight of your eyes;
But know that for all these
God will bring you into judgment.
10Therefore remove sorrow from your heart,
And put away evil from your flesh,
For childhood and youth *are* vanity.

12 Remember now your Creator in the days
of your youth,
Before the difficult days come,
And the years draw near when you say,
"I have no pleasure in them":
2While the sun and the light,
The moon and the stars,
Are not darkened,
And the clouds do not return after the rain;
3In the day when the keepers of the house
tremble,
And the strong men bow down;
When the grinders cease because they are
few,
And those that look through the windows
grow dim;
4When the doors are shut in the streets,
And the sound of grinding is low;
When one rises up at the sound of a bird,
And all the daughters of music are brought
low.
5Also they are afraid of height,
And of terrors in the way;
When the almond tree blossoms,
The grasshopper is a burden,
And desire fails.
For man goes to his eternal home,
And the mourners go about the streets.

THE MESSAGE

So you'll never understand
the mystery at work in all that God
does.

6 Go to work in the morning
and stick to it until evening without
watching the clock.
You never know from moment to
moment
how your work will turn out in the
end.

BEFORE THE YEARS TAKE THEIR TOLL

7-8 Oh, how sweet the light of day,
And how wonderful to live in the
sunshine!
Even if you live a long time, don't take a
single day for granted.
Take delight in each light-filled hour,
Remembering that there will also be
many dark days
And that most of what comes your way
is smoke.

9 You who are young, make the most of
your youth.
Relish your youthful vigor.
Follow the impulses of your heart.
If something looks good to you, pursue
it.
But know also that not just anything
goes;
You have to answer to God for every last
bit of it.

10 Live footloose and fancy-free—
You won't be young forever.
Youth lasts about as long as smoke.

1-2 12 Honor and enjoy your Creator while
you're still young,
Before the years take their toll and your
vigor wanes,
Before your vision dims and the
world blurs
And the winter years keep you close to
the fire.

3-5 In old age, your body no longer serves
you so well.
Muscles slacken, grip weakens, joints
stiffen.
The shades are pulled down on the
world.
You can't come and go at will. Things
grind to a halt.
The hum of the household fades away.
You are wakened now by bird-song.
Hikes to the mountains are a thing of the
past.
Even a stroll down the road has its
terrors.
Your hair turns apple-blossom white,
Adorning a fragile and impotent
matchstick body.
Yes, you're well on your way to eternal
rest,
While your friends make plans for your
funeral.

NEW KING JAMES VERSION

[6]*Remember your Creator* before the silver
cord is loosed,[a]
Or the golden bowl is broken,
Or the pitcher shattered at the fountain,
Or the wheel broken at the well.
[7]Then the dust will return to the earth as it
was,
And the spirit will return to God who gave
it.
[8]"Vanity of vanities," says the Preacher,
"All *is* vanity."

THE WHOLE DUTY OF MAN

[9]And moreover, because the Preacher was
wise, he still taught the people knowledge; yes,
he pondered and sought out *and* set in order
many proverbs. [10]The Preacher sought to find
acceptable words; and *what was* written *was*
upright—words of truth. [11]The words of the wise
are like goads, and the words of scholars[a] are
like well-driven nails, given by one Shepherd.
[12]And further, my son, be admonished by these.
Of making many books *there is* no end, and
much study *is* wearisome to the flesh.

[13]Let us hear the conclusion of the whole
matter:

Fear God and keep His commandments,
For this is man's all.
[14]For God will bring every work into
judgment,
Including every secret thing,
Whether good or evil.

12:6 [a]Following Qere and Targum; Kethib reads *removed;* Septuagint and Vulgate read *broken.* **12:11** [a]Literally *masters of the assemblies*

THE MESSAGE

6-7 Life, lovely while it lasts, is soon over.
Life as we know it, precious and
beautiful, ends.
The body is put back in the same ground
it came from.
The spirit returns to God, who first
breathed it.

8 It's all smoke, nothing but smoke.
The Quester says that everything's
smoke.

THE FINAL WORD

9-10 Besides being wise himself, the Quester also taught others knowledge. He weighed, examined, and arranged many proverbs. The Quester did his best to find the right words and write the plain truth.

11 The words of the wise prod us to live
well.
They're like nails hammered home,
holding life together.
They are given by God, the one
Shepherd.

12-13 But regarding anything beyond this, dear friend, go easy. There's no end to the publishing of books, and constant study wears you out so you're no good for anything else. The last and final word is this:

Fear God.
Do what he tells you.

14 And that's it. Eventually God will bring everything that we do out into the open and judge it according to its hidden intent, whether it's good or evil.

SONG OF SOLOMON (SONG OF SONGS)

NEW KING JAMES VERSION

1 The song of songs, which *is* Solomon's.

THE BANQUET

The Shulamite[a]
2Let him kiss me with the kisses of his mouth—
For your[b] love *is* better than wine.
3Because of the fragrance of your good ointments,
Your name *is* ointment poured forth;
Therefore the virgins love you.
4Draw me away!

The Daughters of Jerusalem
We will run after you.[a]

The Shulamite
The king has brought me into his chambers.

The Daughters of Jerusalem
We will be glad and rejoice in you.[b]

We will remember your[c] love more than wine.

The Shulamite
Rightly do they love you.[d]

5I *am* dark, but lovely,
O daughters of Jerusalem,
Like the tents of Kedar,
Like the curtains of Solomon.
6Do not look upon me, because I *am* dark,
Because the sun has tanned me.
My mother's sons were angry with me;
They made me the keeper of the vineyards,
But my own vineyard I have not kept.

(To Her Beloved)
7Tell me, O you whom I love,
Where you feed *your flock*,
Where you make *it* rest at noon.
For why should I be as one who veils herself[a]
By the flocks of your companions?

The Beloved
8If you do not know, O fairest among women,
Follow in the footsteps of the flock,
And feed your little goats
Beside the shepherds' tents.
9I have compared you, my love,
To my filly among Pharaoh's chariots.
10Your cheeks are lovely with ornaments,
Your neck with chains *of gold*.

1:2 [a]A young woman from the town of Shulam or Shunem (compare 6:13). The speaker and audience are identified according to the number, gender, and person of the Hebrew words. Occasionally the identity is not certain. [b]Masculine singular, that is, the Beloved **1:4** [a]Masculine singular, that is, the Beloved [b]Feminine singular, that is, the Shulamite [c]Masculine singular, that is, the Beloved [d]Masculine singular, that is, the Beloved **1:7** [a]Septuagint, Syriac, and Vulgate read *wanders*.

THE MESSAGE

1 1 The Song—best of all songs—Solomon's song!

THE WOMAN

2-3 Kiss me—full on the mouth!
Yes! For your love is better than wine,
headier than your aromatic oils.
The syllables of your name murmur like a meadow brook.
No wonder everyone loves to say your name!

4 Take me away with you! Let's run off together!
An elopement with my King-Lover!
We'll celebrate, we'll sing,
we'll make great music.
Yes! For your love is better than vintage wine.
Everyone loves you—of course! And why not?

5-6 I am weathered but still elegant,
oh, dear sisters in Jerusalem,
Weather-darkened like Kedar desert tents,
time-softened like Solomon's Temple hangings.
Don't look down on me because I'm dark,
darkened by the sun's harsh rays.
My brothers ridiculed me and sent me to work in the fields.
They made me care for the face of the earth,
but I had no time to care for my own face.

7 Tell me where you're working
—I love you so much—
Tell me where you're tending your flocks,
where you let them rest at noontime.
Why should I be the one left out,
outside the orbit of your tender care?

THE MAN

8 If you can't find me, loveliest of all women,
it's all right. Stay with your flocks.
Lead your lambs to good pasture.
Stay with your shepherd neighbors.

9-11 You remind me of Pharaoh's
well-groomed and satiny mares.
Pendant earrings line the elegance of your cheeks;
strands of jewels illumine the curve of your throat.

NEW KING JAMES VERSION

The Daughters of Jerusalem

11We will make you[a] ornaments of gold
With studs of silver.

The Shulamite

12While the king *is* at his table,
My spikenard sends forth its fragrance.
13A bundle of myrrh *is* my beloved to me,
That lies all night between my breasts.
14My beloved *is* to me a cluster of henna *blooms*
In the vineyards of En Gedi.

The Beloved

15Behold, you *are* fair, my love!
Behold, you *are* fair!
You *have* dove's eyes.

The Shulamite

16Behold, you *are* handsome, my beloved!
Yes, pleasant!
Also our bed *is* green.
17The beams of our houses *are* cedar,
And our rafters of fir.

2 I *am* the rose of Sharon,
And the lily of the valleys.

The Beloved

2Like a lily among thorns,
So is my love among the daughters.

The Shulamite

3Like an apple tree among the trees of the woods,
So *is* my beloved among the sons.
I sat down in his shade with great delight,
And his fruit *was* sweet to my taste.

The Shulamite to the Daughters of Jerusalem

4He brought me to the banqueting house,
And his banner over me *was* love.
5Sustain me with cakes of raisins,
Refresh me with apples,
For I *am* lovesick.

6His left hand *is* under my head,
And his right hand embraces me.
7I charge you, O daughters of Jerusalem,
By the gazelles or by the does of the field,
Do not stir up nor awaken love
Until it pleases.

THE BELOVED'S REQUEST

The Shulamite

8The voice of my beloved!
Behold, he comes
Leaping upon the mountains,
Skipping upon the hills.
9My beloved is like a gazelle or a young stag.
Behold, he stands behind our wall;
He is looking through the windows,
Gazing through the lattice.

1:11 [a]Feminine singular, that is, the Shulamite

THE MESSAGE

I'm making jewelry for you, gold and silver jewelry
that will mark and accent your beauty.

THE WOMAN

12-14 When my King-Lover lay down beside me,
my fragrance filled the room.
His head resting between my breasts—
the head of my lover was a sachet of sweet myrrh.
My beloved is a bouquet of wildflowers
picked just for me from the fields of Engedi.

THE MAN

15 Oh, my dear friend! You're so beautiful!
And your eyes so beautiful—like doves!

THE WOMAN

16-17 And you, my dear lover—you're so handsome!
And the bed we share is like a forest glen.
We enjoy a canopy of cedars
enclosed by cypresses, fragrant and green.

1 2 I'm just a wildflower picked from the plains of Sharon,
a lotus blossom from the valley pools.

THE MAN

2 A lotus blossoming in a swamp of weeds—
that's my dear friend among the girls in the village.

THE WOMAN

3-4 As an apricot tree stands out in the forest,
my lover stands above the young men in town.
All I want is to sit in his shade,
to taste and savor his delicious love.
He took me home with him for a festive meal,
but his eyes feasted on *me*!

5-6 Oh! Give me something refreshing to eat—and quickly!
Apricots, raisins—anything. I'm about to faint with love!
His left hand cradles my head,
and his right arm encircles my waist!

7 Oh, let me warn you, sisters in Jerusalem,
by the gazelles, yes, by all the wild deer:
Don't excite love, don't stir it up,
until the time is ripe—and you're ready.

8-10 Look! Listen! There's my lover!
Do you see him coming?
Vaulting the mountains,
leaping the hills.
My lover is like a gazelle, graceful;
like a young stag, virile.
Look at him there, on tiptoe at the gate,
all ears, all eyes—ready!
My lover has arrived
and he's speaking to me!

NEW KING JAMES VERSION

10My beloved spoke, and said to me:
"Rise up, my love, my fair one,
And come away.
11For lo, the winter is past,
The rain is over *and* gone.
12The flowers appear on the earth;
The time of singing has come,
And the voice of the turtledove
Is heard in our land.
13The fig tree puts forth her green figs,
And the vines *with* the tender grapes
Give a good smell.
Rise up, my love, my fair one,
And come away!

14"O my dove, in the clefts of the rock,
In the secret *places* of the cliff,
Let me see your face,
Let me hear your voice;
For your voice *is* sweet,
And your face *is* lovely."

Her Brothers

15Catch us the foxes,
The little foxes that spoil the vines,
For our vines *have* tender grapes.

The Shulamite

16My beloved *is* mine, and I *am* his.
He feeds *his flock* among the lilies.

(To Her Beloved)

17Until the day breaks
And the shadows flee away,
Turn, my beloved,
And be like a gazelle
Or a young stag
Upon the mountains of Bether.[a]

A TROUBLED NIGHT

The Shulamite

3 By night on my bed I sought the one I love;
I sought him, but I did not find him.
2"I will rise now," *I said,*
"And go about the city;
In the streets and in the squares
I will seek the one I love."
I sought him, but I did not find him.
3The watchmen who go about the city found
me;
I said,
"Have you seen the one I love?"

4Scarcely had I passed by them,
When I found the one I love.
I held him and would not let him go,
Until I had brought him to the house of my
mother,
And into the chamber of her who conceived
me.

5I charge you, O daughters of Jerusalem,
By the gazelles or by the does of the field,
Do not stir up nor awaken love
Until it pleases.

2:17 [a]Literally *Separation*

THE MESSAGE

THE MAN

10-14 Get up, my dear friend,
fair and beautiful lover—come to me!
Look around you: Winter is over;
the winter rains are over, gone!
Spring flowers are in blossom all over.
The whole world's a choir—and singing!
Spring warblers are filling the forest
with sweet arpeggios.
Lilacs are exuberantly purple and
perfumed,
and cherry trees fragrant with blossoms.
Oh, get up, dear friend,
my fair and beautiful lover—come to me!
Come, my shy and modest dove—
leave your seclusion, come out in the
open.
Let me see your face,
let me hear your voice.
For your voice is soothing
and your face is ravishing.

THE WOMAN

15 Then you must protect me from the foxes,
foxes on the prowl,
Foxes who would like nothing better
than to get into our flowering garden.

16-17 My lover is mine, and I am his.
Nightly he strolls in our garden,
Delighting in the flowers
until dawn breathes its light and night
slips away.

Turn to me, dear lover.
Come like a gazelle.
Leap like a wild stag
on delectable mountains!

1-4 3 Restless in bed and sleepless through the
night,
I longed for my lover.
I wanted him desperately. His absence
was painful.
So I got up, went out and roved the city,
hunting through streets and down alleys.
I wanted my lover in the worst way!
I looked high and low, and didn't find
him.
And then the night watchmen found me
as they patrolled the darkened city.
"Have you seen my dear lost love?" I
asked.
No sooner had I left them than I found
him,
found my dear lost love.
I threw my arms around him and held him
tight,
wouldn't let him go until I had him home
again,
safe at home beside the fire.

5 Oh, let me warn you, sisters in Jerusalem,
by the gazelles, yes, by all the wild deer:
Don't excite love, don't stir it up,
until the time is ripe—and you're ready.

New King James Version

The Coming of Solomon

The Shulamite

6 Who *is* this coming out of the wilderness
Like pillars of smoke,
Perfumed with myrrh and frankincense,
With all the merchant's fragrant powders?
7 Behold, it *is* Solomon's couch,
With sixty valiant men around it,
Of the valiant of Israel.
8 They all hold swords,
Being expert in war.
Every man *has* his sword on his thigh
Because of fear in the night.

9 Of the wood of Lebanon
Solomon the King
Made himself a palanquin:[a]
10 He made its pillars *of* silver,
Its support *of* gold,
Its seat *of* purple,
Its interior paved *with* love
By the daughters of Jerusalem.
11 Go forth, O daughters of Zion,
And see King Solomon with the crown
With which his mother crowned him
On the day of his wedding,
The day of the gladness of his heart.

The Bridegroom Praises the Bride

The Beloved

4 Behold, you *are* fair, my love!
Behold, you *are* fair!
You *have* dove's eyes behind your veil.
Your hair *is* like a flock of goats,
Going down from Mount Gilead.
2 Your teeth *are* like a flock of shorn *sheep*
Which have come up from the washing,
Every one of which bears twins,
And none *is* barren among them.
3 Your lips *are* like a strand of scarlet,
And your mouth is lovely.
Your temples behind your veil
Are like a piece of pomegranate.
4 Your neck *is* like the tower of David,
Built for an armory,
On which hang a thousand bucklers,
All shields of mighty men.
5 Your two breasts *are* like two fawns,
Twins of a gazelle,
Which feed among the lilies.

6 Until the day breaks
And the shadows flee away,
I will go my way to the mountain of myrrh
And to the hill of frankincense.

7 You *are* all fair, my love,
And *there is* no spot in you.
8 Come with me from Lebanon, *my* spouse,
With me from Lebanon.
Look from the top of Amana,
From the top of Senir and Hermon,
From the lions' dens,
From the mountains of the leopards.

9 You have ravished my heart,
My sister, *my* spouse;
You have ravished my heart

3:9 [a]A portable enclosed chair

The Message

6-10 What's this I see, approaching from the desert,
raising clouds of dust,
Filling the air with sweet smells
and pungent aromatics?
Look! It's Solomon's carriage,
carried and guarded by sixty soldiers,
sixty of Israel's finest,
All of them armed to the teeth,
trained for battle,
ready for anything, anytime.
King Solomon once had a carriage built
from fine-grained Lebanon cedar.
He had it framed with silver and roofed with gold.
The cushions were covered with a purple fabric,
the interior lined with tooled leather.

11 Come and look, sisters in Jerusalem.
Oh, sisters of Zion, don't miss this!
My King-Lover,
dressed and garlanded for his wedding,
his heart full, bursting with joy!

The Man

1-5 4 You're so beautiful, my darling,
so beautiful, and your dove eyes are veiled
By your hair as it flows and shimmers,
like a flock of goats in the distance
streaming down a hillside in the sunshine.
Your smile is generous and full—
expressive and strong and clean.
Your lips are jewel red,
your mouth elegant and inviting,
your veiled cheeks soft and radiant.
The smooth, lithe lines of your neck
command notice—all heads turn in awe and admiration!
Your breasts are like fawns,
twins of a gazelle, grazing among the first spring flowers.

6-7 The sweet, fragrant curves of your body,
the soft, spiced contours of your flesh
Invite me, and I come. I stay
until dawn breathes its light and night slips away.
You're beautiful from head to toe, my dear love,
beautiful beyond compare, absolutely flawless.

8-15 Come with me from Lebanon, my bride.
Leave Lebanon behind, and come.
Leave your high mountain hideaway.
Abandon your wilderness seclusion,
Where you keep company with lions
and panthers guard your safety.
You've captured my heart, dear friend.

NEW KING JAMES VERSION

With one *look* of your eyes,
With one link of your necklace.
10How fair is your love,
My sister, *my* spouse!
How much better than wine is your love,
And the scent of your perfumes
Than all spices!
11Your lips, O *my* spouse,
Drip as the honeycomb;
Honey and milk *are* under your tongue;
And the fragrance of your garments
Is like the fragrance of Lebanon.

12A garden enclosed
Is my sister, *my* spouse,
A spring shut up,
A fountain sealed.
13Your plants *are* an orchard of pomegranates
With pleasant fruits,
Fragrant henna with spikenard,
14Spikenard and saffron,
Calamus and cinnamon,
With all trees of frankincense,
Myrrh and aloes,
With all the chief spices—
15A fountain of gardens,
A well of living waters,
And streams from Lebanon.

The Shulamite
16Awake, O north *wind*,
And come, O south!
Blow upon my garden,
That its spices may flow out.
Let my beloved come to his garden
And eat its pleasant fruits.

The Beloved
5 I have come to my garden, my sister, *my* spouse;
I have gathered my myrrh with my spice;
I have eaten my honeycomb with my honey;
I have drunk my wine with my milk.

(To His Friends)
Eat, O friends!
Drink, yes, drink deeply,
O beloved ones!

THE SHULAMITE'S TROUBLED EVENING
The Shulamite
2I sleep, but my heart is awake;
It is the voice of my beloved!
He knocks, *saying*,
"Open for me, my sister, my love,
My dove, my perfect one;
For my head is covered with dew,
My locks with the drops of the night."

3I have taken off my robe;
How can I put it on *again*?
I have washed my feet;
How can I defile them?
4My beloved put his hand
By the latch *of the door*,
And my heart yearned for him.

THE MESSAGE

You looked at me, and I fell in love.
One look my way and I was hopelessly in love!
How beautiful your love, dear, dear friend—
far more pleasing than a fine, rare wine,
your fragrance more exotic than select spices.
The kisses of your lips are honey, my love,
every syllable you speak a delicacy to savor.
Your clothes smell like the wild outdoors,
the ozone scent of high mountains.
Dear lover and friend, you're a secret garden,
a private and pure fountain.
Body and soul, you are paradise,
a whole orchard of succulent fruits—
Ripe apricots and peaches,
oranges and pears;
Nut trees and cinnamon,
and all scented woods;
Mint and lavender,
and all herbs aromatic;
A garden fountain, sparkling and splashing,
fed by spring waters from the Lebanon mountains.

THE WOMAN
16 Wake up, North Wind,
get moving, South Wind!
Breathe on my garden,
fill the air with spice fragrance.

Oh, let my lover enter his garden!
Yes, let him eat the fine, ripe fruits.

THE MAN
1 5 I went to my garden, dear friend, best lover!
breathed the sweet fragrance.
I ate the fruit and honey,
I drank the nectar and wine.

Celebrate with me, friends!
Raise your glasses—"To life! To love!"

THE WOMAN
2 I was sound asleep, but in my dreams I was wide awake.
Oh, listen! It's the sound of my lover knocking, calling!

THE MAN
"Let me in, dear companion, dearest friend,
my dove, consummate lover!
I'm soaked with the dampness of the night,
drenched with dew, shivering and cold."

THE WOMAN
3 "But I'm in my nightgown—do you expect me to get dressed?
I'm bathed and in bed—do you want me to get dirty?"

4-7 But my lover wouldn't take no for an answer,
and the longer he knocked, the more excited I became.

NEW KING JAMES VERSION

5I arose to open for my beloved,
And my hands dripped *with* myrrh,
My fingers with liquid myrrh,
On the handles of the lock.

6I opened for my beloved,
But my beloved had turned away *and* was gone.
My heart leaped up when he spoke.
I sought him, but I could not find him;
I called him, but he gave me no answer.
7The watchmen who went about the city found me.
They struck me, they wounded me;
The keepers of the walls
Took my veil away from me.
8I charge you, O daughters of Jerusalem,
If you find my beloved,
That you tell him I *am* lovesick!

The Daughters of Jerusalem

9What *is* your beloved
More than *another* beloved,
O fairest among women?
What *is* your beloved
More than *another* beloved,
That you so charge us?

The Shulamite

10My beloved *is* white and ruddy,
Chief among ten thousand.
11His head *is like* the finest gold;
His locks *are* wavy,
And black as a raven.
12His eyes *are* like doves
By the rivers of waters,
Washed with milk,
And fitly set.
13His cheeks *are* like a bed of spices,
Banks of scented herbs.
His lips *are* lilies,
Dripping liquid myrrh.

14His hands *are* rods of gold
Set with beryl.
His body *is* carved ivory
Inlaid *with* sapphires.
15His legs *are* pillars of marble
Set on bases of fine gold.
His countenance *is* like Lebanon,
Excellent as the cedars.
16His mouth *is* most sweet,
Yes, he *is* altogether lovely.
This *is* my beloved,
And this *is* my friend,
O daughters of Jerusalem!

The Daughters of Jerusalem

6 Where has your beloved gone,
O fairest among women?
Where has your beloved turned aside,
That we may seek him with you?

THE MESSAGE

I got up to open the door to my lover,
sweetly ready to receive him,
Desiring and expectant
as I turned the door handle.
But when I opened the door he was gone.
My loved one had tired of waiting and left.
And I died inside—oh, I felt so bad!
I ran out looking for him
But he was nowhere to be found.
I called into the darkness—but no answer.
The night watchmen found me
as they patrolled the streets of the city.
They slapped and beat and bruised me,
ripping off my clothes,
These watchmen,
who were supposed to be guarding the city.

8 I beg you, sisters in Jerusalem—
if you find my lover,
Please tell him I want him,
that I'm heartsick with love for him.

THE CHORUS

9 What's so great about your lover, fair lady?
What's so special about him that you beg for our help?

THE WOMAN

10-16 My dear lover glows with health—
red-blooded, radiant!
He's one in a million.
There's no one quite like him!
My golden one, pure and untarnished,
with raven black curls tumbling across his shoulders.
His eyes are like doves, soft and bright,
but deep-set, brimming with meaning,
like wells of water.
His face is rugged, his beard smells like sage,
His voice, his words, warm and reassuring.
Fine muscles ripple beneath his skin,
quiet and beautiful.
His torso is the work of a sculptor,
hard and smooth as ivory.
He stands tall, like a cedar,
strong and deep-rooted,
A rugged mountain of a man,
aromatic with wood and stone.
His words are kisses, his kisses words.
Everything about him delights me, thrills me
through and through!

That's my lover, that's my man,
dear Jerusalem sisters.

THE CHORUS

1 6 So where has this love of yours gone,
fair one?
Where on earth can he be?
Can we help you look for him?

NEW KING JAMES VERSION

The Shulamite

2My beloved has gone to his garden,
To the beds of spices,
To feed *his flock* in the gardens,
And to gather lilies.
3I *am* my beloved's,
And my beloved *is* mine.
He feeds *his flock* among the lilies.

PRAISE OF THE SHULAMITE'S BEAUTY

The Beloved

4O my love, you *are as* beautiful as Tirzah,
Lovely as Jerusalem,
Awesome as *an army* with banners!
5Turn your eyes away from me,
For they have overcome me.
Your hair *is* like a flock of goats
Going down from Gilead.
6Your teeth *are* like a flock of sheep
Which have come up from the washing;
Every one bears twins,
And none *is* barren among them.
7Like a piece of pomegranate
Are your temples behind your veil.

8There are sixty queens
And eighty concubines,
And virgins without number.
9My dove, my perfect one,
Is the only one,
The only one of her mother,
The favorite of the one who bore her.
The daughters saw her
And called her blessed,
The queens and the concubines,
And they praised her.

10Who is she who looks forth as the morning,
Fair as the moon,
Clear as the sun,
Awesome as *an army* with banners?

The Shulamite

11I went down to the garden of nuts
To see the verdure of the valley,
To see whether the vine had budded
And the pomegranates had bloomed.
12Before I was even aware,
My soul had made me
As the chariots of my noble people.[a]

The Beloved and His Friends

13Return, return, O Shulamite;
Return, return, that we may look upon you!

The Shulamite

What would you see in the Shulamite—
As it were, the dance of the two camps?[a]

EXPRESSIONS OF PRAISE

The Beloved

7 How beautiful are your feet in sandals,
O prince's daughter!
The curves of your thighs *are* like jewels,
The work of the hands of a skillful workman.
2Your navel *is* a rounded goblet;
It lacks no blended beverage.

6:12 [a]Hebrew *Ammi Nadib* **6:13** [a]Hebrew *Mahanaim*

THE MESSAGE

THE WOMAN

2-3 Never mind. My lover is already on his way
to his garden,
to browse among the flowers, touching
the colors and forms.
I am my lover's and my lover is mine.
He caresses the sweet-smelling flowers.

THE MAN

4-7 Dear, dear friend and lover,
you're as beautiful as Tirzah, city of
delights,
Lovely as Jerusalem, city of dreams,
the ravishing visions of my ecstasy.
Your beauty is too much for me—I'm in
over my head.
I'm not used to this! I can't take it in.
Your hair flows and shimmers
like a flock of goats in the distance
streaming down a hillside in the
sunshine.
Your smile is generous and full—
expressive and strong and clean.
Your veiled cheeks
are soft and radiant.

8-9 There's no one like her on earth,
never has been, never will be.
She's a woman beyond compare.
My dove is perfection,
Pure and innocent as the day she was
born,
and cradled in joy by her mother.
Everyone who came by to see her
exclaimed and admired her—
All the fathers and mothers, the neighbors
and friends,
blessed and praised her:

10 "Has anyone ever seen anything like this—
dawn-fresh, moon-lovely, sun-radiant,
ravishing as the night sky with its
galaxies of stars?"

11-12 One day I went strolling through the
orchard,
looking for signs of spring,
Looking for buds about to burst into
flower,
anticipating readiness, ripeness.
Before I knew it my heart was raptured,
carried away by lofty thoughts!

13 Dance, dance, dear Shulammite,
Angel-Princess!
Dance, and we'll feast our eyes on your
grace!
Everyone wants to see the Shulammite
dance
her victory dances of love and peace.

1-9 7 Shapely and graceful your sandaled feet,
and queenly your movement—
Your limbs are lithe and elegant,
the work of a master artist.
Your body is a chalice,
wine-filled.

NEW KING JAMES VERSION

Your waist *is* a heap of wheat
Set about with lilies.
3 Your two breasts *are* like two fawns,
Twins of a gazelle.
4 Your neck *is* like an ivory tower,
Your eyes *like* the pools in Heshbon
By the gate of Bath Rabbim.
Your nose *is* like the tower of Lebanon
Which looks toward Damascus.
5 Your head *crowns* you like *Mount* Carmel,
And the hair of your head *is* like purple;
A king *is* held captive by *your* tresses.

6 How fair and how pleasant you are,
O love, with your delights!
7 This stature of yours is like a palm tree,
And your breasts *like* its clusters.
8 I said, "I will go up to the palm tree,
I will take hold of its branches."
Let now your breasts be like clusters of the vine,
The fragrance of your breath like apples,
9 And the roof of your mouth like the best wine.

The Shulamite

The wine goes *down* smoothly for my beloved,
Moving gently the lips of sleepers.[a]
10 I *am* my beloved's,
And his desire *is* toward me.

11 Come, my beloved,
Let us go forth to the field;
Let us lodge in the villages.
12 Let us get up early to the vineyards;
Let us see if the vine has budded,
Whether the grape blossoms are open,
And the pomegranates are in bloom.
There I will give you my love.
13 The mandrakes give off a fragrance,
And at our gates *are* pleasant *fruits*,
All manner, new and old,
Which I have laid up for you, my beloved.

8 Oh, that you were like my brother,
Who nursed at my mother's breasts!
If I should find you outside,
I would kiss you;
I would not be despised.
2 I would lead you *and* bring you
Into the house of my mother,
She *who* used to instruct me.
I would cause you to drink of spiced wine,
Of the juice of my pomegranate.

7:9 [a]Septuagint, Syriac, and Vulgate read *lips and teeth.*

THE MESSAGE

Your skin is silken and tawny
like a field of wheat touched by the breeze.
Your breasts are like fawns,
twins of a gazelle.
Your neck is carved ivory, curved and slender.
Your eyes are wells of light, deep with mystery.
Quintessentially feminine!
Your profile turns all heads,
commanding attention.
The feelings I get when I see the high mountain ranges
—stirrings of desire, longings for the heights—
Remind me of you,
and I'm spoiled for anyone else!
Your beauty, within and without, is absolute,
dear lover, close companion.
You are tall and supple, like the palm tree,
and your full breasts are like sweet clusters of dates.
I say, "I'm going to climb that palm tree!
I'm going to caress its fruit!"
Oh yes! Your breasts
will be clusters of sweet fruit to me,
Your breath clean and cool like fresh mint,
your tongue and lips like the best wine.

THE WOMAN

9-12 Yes, and yours are, too—my love's kisses
flow from his lips to mine.
I am my lover's.
I'm all he wants. I'm all the world to him!
Come, dear lover—
let's tramp through the countryside.
Let's sleep at some wayside inn,
then rise early and listen to bird-song.
Let's look for wildflowers in bloom,
blackberry bushes blossoming white,
Fruit trees festooned
with cascading flowers.
And there I'll give myself to you,
my love to your love!

13 Love-apples drench us with fragrance,
fertility surrounds, suffuses us,
Fruits fresh and preserved
that I've kept and saved just for you, my love.

1-2 8 I wish you'd been my twin brother,
sharing with me the breasts of my mother,
Playing outside in the street,
kissing in plain view of everyone,
and no one thinking anything of it.
I'd take you by the hand and bring you home
where I was raised by my mother.
You'd drink my wine
and kiss my cheeks.

New King James Version

(To the Daughters of Jerusalem)
3His left hand *is* under my head,
And his right hand embraces me.
4I charge you, O daughters of Jerusalem,
Do not stir up nor awaken love
Until it pleases.

Love Renewed in Lebanon
A Relative
5Who *is* this coming up from the wilderness,
Leaning upon her beloved?

I awakened you under the apple tree.
There your mother brought you forth;
There she *who* bore you brought *you* forth.

The Shulamite to Her Beloved
6Set me as a seal upon your heart,
As a seal upon your arm;
For love *is as* strong as death,
Jealousy *as* cruel as the grave;[a]
Its flames *are* flames of fire,
A most vehement[b] flame.

7Many waters cannot quench love,
Nor can the floods drown it.
If a man would give for love
All the wealth of his house,
It would be utterly despised.

The Shulamite's Brothers
8We have a little sister,
And she has no breasts.
What shall we do for our sister
In the day when she is spoken for?
9If she *is* a wall,
We will build upon her
A battlement of silver;
And if she *is* a door,
We will enclose her
With boards of cedar.

The Shulamite
10I *am* a wall,
And my breasts like towers;
Then I became in his eyes
As one who found peace.
11Solomon had a vineyard at Baal Hamon;
He leased the vineyard to keepers;
Everyone was to bring for its fruit
A thousand silver coins.

(To Solomon)
12My own vineyard *is* before me.
You, O Solomon, *may have* a thousand,
And those who tend its fruit two hundred.

The Beloved
13You who dwell in the gardens,
The companions listen for your voice—
Let me hear it!

The Shulamite
14Make haste, my beloved,
And be like a gazelle
Or a young stag
On the mountains of spices.

8:6 [a]Or *Sheol* [b]Literally *A flame of* YAH (a poetic form of *YHWH, the* LORD)

The Message

3-4 Imagine! His left hand cradling my head,
his right arm around my waist!
Oh, let me warn you, sisters in Jerusalem:
Don't excite love, don't stir it up,
until the time is ripe—and you're ready.

The Chorus
5 Who is this I see coming up from the country,
arm in arm with her lover?

The Man
I found you under the apricot tree,
and woke you up to love.
Your mother went into labor under that tree,
and under that very tree she bore you.

The Woman
6-8 Hang my locket around your neck,
wear my ring on your finger.
Love is invincible facing danger and death.
Passion laughs at the terrors of hell.
The fire of love stops at nothing—
it sweeps everything before it.
Flood waters can't drown love,
torrents of rain can't put it out.
Love can't be bought, love can't be sold—
it's not to be found in the marketplace.
My brothers used to worry about me:

8-9 "Our little sister has no breasts.
What shall we do with our little sister
when men come asking for her?
She's a virgin and vulnerable,
and we'll protect her.
If they think she's a wall, we'll top it with barbed wire.
If they think she's a door, we'll barricade it."

10 Dear brothers, I'm a walled-in virgin still,
but my breasts are full—
And when my lover sees me,
he knows he'll soon be satisfied.

The Man
11-12 King Solomon may have vast vineyards
in lush, fertile country,
Where he hires others to work the ground.
People pay anything to get in on that bounty.
But *my* vineyard is all mine,
and I'm keeping it to myself.
You can have your vast vineyards, Solomon,
you and your greedy guests!

13 Oh, lady of the gardens,
my friends are with me listening.
Let me hear your voice!

The Woman
14 Run to me, dear lover.
Come like a gazelle.
Leap like a wild stag
on the spice mountains.

ISAIAH

NEW KING JAMES VERSION

1 The vision of Isaiah the son of Amoz, which he saw concerning Judah and Jerusalem in the days of Uzziah, Jotham, Ahaz, *and* Hezekiah, kings of Judah.

THE WICKEDNESS OF JUDAH

2Hear, O heavens, and give ear, O earth!
For the LORD has spoken:
"I have nourished and brought up children,
And they have rebelled against Me;
3The ox knows its owner
And the donkey its master's crib;
But Israel does not know,
My people do not consider."

4Alas, sinful nation,
A people laden with iniquity,
A brood of evildoers,
Children who are corrupters!
They have forsaken the LORD,
They have provoked to anger
The Holy One of Israel,
They have turned away backward.

5Why should you be stricken again?
You will revolt more and more.
The whole head is sick,
And the whole heart faints.
6From the sole of the foot even to the head,
There is no soundness in it,
But wounds and bruises and putrefying sores;
They have not been closed or bound up,
Or soothed with ointment.

7Your country *is* desolate,
Your cities *are* burned with fire;
Strangers devour your land in your presence;
And *it is* desolate, as overthrown by strangers.
8So the daughter of Zion is left as a booth in a vineyard,
As a hut in a garden of cucumbers,
As a besieged city.
9Unless the LORD of hosts
Had left to us a very small remnant,
We would have become like Sodom,
We would have been made like Gomorrah.

10Hear the word of the LORD,
You rulers of Sodom;
Give ear to the law of our God,
You people of Gomorrah:
11"To what purpose *is* the multitude of your sacrifices to Me?"
Says the LORD.
"I have had enough of burnt offerings of rams
And the fat of fed cattle.
I do not delight in the blood of bulls,
Or of lambs or goats.

THE MESSAGE

MESSAGES OF JUDGMENT

QUIT YOUR WORSHIP CHARADES

1 1 The vision that Isaiah son of Amoz saw regarding Judah and Jerusalem during the times of the kings of Judah: Uzziah, Jotham, Ahaz, and Hezekiah.

2-4 Heaven and earth, you're the jury.
Listen to GOD's case:
"I had children and raised them well,
and they turned on me.
The ox knows who's boss,
the mule knows the hand that feeds him,
But not Israel.
My people don't know up from down.
Shame! Misguided GOD-dropouts,
staggering under their guilt-baggage,
Gang of miscreants,
band of vandals—
My people have walked out on me, their GOD,
turned their backs on The Holy of Israel,
walked off and never looked back.

5-9 "Why bother even trying to do anything with you
when you just keep to your bullheaded ways?
You keep beating your heads against brick walls.
Everything within you protests against you.
From the bottom of your feet to the top of your head,
nothing's working right.
Wounds and bruises and running sores—
untended, unwashed, unbandaged.
Your country is laid waste,
your cities burned down.
Your land is destroyed by outsiders while you watch,
reduced to rubble by barbarians.
Daughter Zion is deserted—
like a tumbledown shack on a dead-end street,
Like a tarpaper shanty on the wrong side of the tracks,
like a sinking ship abandoned by the rats.
If GOD-of-the-Angel-Armies hadn't left us a few survivors,
we'd be as desolate as Sodom, doomed just like Gomorrah.

10 "Listen to my Message,
you Sodom-schooled leaders.
Receive God's revelation,
you Gomorrah-schooled people.

11-12 "Why this frenzy of sacrifices?"
GOD's asking.
"Don't you think I've had my fill of burnt sacrifices,
rams and plump grain-fed calves?
Don't you think I've had my fill
of blood from bulls, lambs, and goats?

New King James Version

12"When you come to appear before Me,
Who has required this from your hand,
To trample My courts?
13Bring no more futile sacrifices;
Incense is an abomination to Me.
The New Moons, the Sabbaths, and the calling of assemblies—
I cannot endure iniquity and the sacred meeting.
14Your New Moons and your appointed feasts
My soul hates;
They are a trouble to Me,
I am weary of bearing *them.*
15When you spread out your hands,
I will hide My eyes from you;
Even though you make many prayers,
I will not hear.
Your hands are full of blood.

16"Wash yourselves, make yourselves clean;
Put away the evil of your doings from before My eyes.
Cease to do evil,
17Learn to do good;
Seek justice,
Rebuke the oppressor;[a]
Defend the fatherless,
Plead for the widow.

18"Come now, and let us reason together,"
Says the LORD,
"Though your sins are like scarlet,
They shall be as white as snow;
Though they are red like crimson,
They shall be as wool.
19If you are willing and obedient,
You shall eat the good of the land;
20But if you refuse and rebel,
You shall be devoured by the sword";
For the mouth of the LORD has spoken.

The Degenerate City

21How the faithful city has become a harlot!
It was full of justice;
Righteousness lodged in it,
But now murderers.
22Your silver has become dross,
Your wine mixed with water.
23Your princes *are* rebellious,
And companions of thieves;
Everyone loves bribes,
And follows after rewards.
They do not defend the fatherless,
Nor does the cause of the widow come before them.

1:17 [a]Some ancient versions read *the oppressed.*

The Message

When you come before me,
whoever gave you the idea of acting like this,
Running here and there, doing this and that—
all this sheer *commotion* in the place provided for worship?

13-17 "Quit your worship charades.
I can't stand your trivial religious games:
Monthly conferences, weekly Sabbaths, special meetings—
meetings, meetings, meetings—I can't stand one more!
Meetings for this, meetings for that. I hate them!
You've worn me out!
I'm sick of your religion, religion, religion,
while you go right on sinning.
When you put on your next prayer-performance,
I'll be looking the other way.
No matter how long or loud or often you pray,
I'll not be listening.
And do you know why? Because you've been tearing
people to pieces, and your hands are bloody.
Go home and wash up.
Clean up your act.
Sweep your lives clean of your evildoings
so I don't have to look at them any longer.
Say no to wrong.
Learn to do good.
Work for justice.
Help the down-and-out.
Stand up for the homeless.
Go to bat for the defenseless.

Let's Argue This Out

18-20 "Come. Sit down. Let's argue this out."
This is GOD's Message:
"If your sins are blood-red,
they'll be snow-white.
If they're red like crimson,
they'll be like wool.
If you'll willingly obey,
you'll feast like kings.
But if you're willful and stubborn,
you'll die like dogs."
That's right. GOD says so.

Those Who Walk Out on God

21-23 Oh! Can you believe it? The chaste city
has become a whore!
She was once all justice,
everyone living as good neighbors,
And now they're all
at one another's throats.
Your coins are all counterfeits.
Your wine is watered down.
Your leaders are turncoats
who keep company with crooks.
They sell themselves to the highest bidder
and grab anything not nailed down.
They never stand up for the homeless,
never stick up for the defenseless.

NEW KING JAMES VERSION

[24]Therefore the Lord says,
The LORD of hosts, the Mighty One of Israel,
"Ah, I will rid Myself of My adversaries,
And take vengeance on My enemies.
[25]I will turn My hand against you,
And thoroughly purge away your dross,
And take away all your alloy.
[26]I will restore your judges as at the first,
And your counselors as at the beginning.
Afterward you shall be called the city of righteousness, the faithful city."

[27]Zion shall be redeemed with justice,
And her penitents with righteousness.
[28]The destruction of transgressors and of sinners *shall be* together,
And those who forsake the LORD shall be consumed.
[29]For they[a] shall be ashamed of the terebinth trees
Which you have desired;
And you shall be embarrassed because of the gardens
Which you have chosen.
[30]For you shall be as a terebinth whose leaf fades,
And as a garden that has no water.
[31]The strong shall be as tinder,
And the work of it as a spark;
Both will burn together,
And no one shall quench *them*.

THE FUTURE HOUSE OF GOD

2 The word that Isaiah the son of Amoz saw concerning Judah and Jerusalem.

[2]Now it shall come to pass in the latter days
That the mountain of the LORD's house
Shall be established on the top of the mountains,
And shall be exalted above the hills;
And all nations shall flow to it.
[3]Many people shall come and say,
"Come, and let us go up to the mountain of the LORD,
To the house of the God of Jacob;
He will teach us His ways,
And we shall walk in His paths."
For out of Zion shall go forth the law,
And the word of the LORD from Jerusalem.
[4]He shall judge between the nations,
And rebuke many people;
They shall beat their swords into plowshares,
And their spears into pruning hooks;
Nation shall not lift up sword against nation,
Neither shall they learn war anymore.

THE DAY OF THE LORD

[5]O house of Jacob, come and let us walk
In the light of the LORD.

1:29 [a]Following Masoretic Text, Septuagint, and Vulgate; some Hebrew manuscripts and Targum read *you*.

THE MESSAGE

24-31 This Decree, therefore, of the Master,
GOD-of-the-Angel-Armies,
the Strong One of Israel:
"This is it! I'll get my oppressors off my back.
I'll get back at my enemies.
I'll give you the back of my hand,
purge the junk from your life, clean you up.
I'll set honest judges and wise counselors among you
just like it was back in the beginning.
Then you'll be renamed
City-That-Treats-People-Right, the True-Blue City."
GOD's right ways will put Zion right again.
GOD's right actions will restore her penitents.
But it's curtains for rebels and GOD-traitors,
a dead end for those who walk out on GOD.
"Your dalliances in those oak grove shrines
will leave you looking mighty foolish,
All that fooling around in god and goddess gardens
that you thought was the latest thing.
You'll end up like an oak tree
with all its leaves falling off,
Like an unwatered garden,
withered and brown.
'The Big Man' will turn out to be dead bark and twigs,
and his 'work,' the spark that starts the fire
That exposes man and work both
as nothing but cinders and smoke."

CLIMB GOD'S MOUNTAIN

1-5 2 The Message Isaiah got regarding Judah and Jerusalem:

There's a day coming
when the mountain of GOD's House
Will be The Mountain—
solid, towering over all mountains.
All nations will river toward it,
people from all over set out for it.
They'll say, "Come,
let's climb GOD's Mountain,
go to the House of the God of Jacob.
He'll show us the way he works
so we can live the way we're made."
Zion's the source of the revelation.
GOD's Message comes from Jerusalem.
He'll settle things fairly between nations.
He'll make things right between many peoples.
They'll turn their swords into shovels,
their spears into hoes.
No more will nation fight nation;
they won't play war anymore.
Come, family of Jacob,
let's live in the light of GOD.

NEW KING JAMES VERSION

6For You have forsaken Your people, the
house of Jacob,
Because they are filled with eastern ways;
They *are* soothsayers like the Philistines,
And they are pleased with the children of
foreigners.
7Their land is also full of silver and gold,
And there is no end to their treasures;
Their land is also full of horses,
And there is no end to their chariots.
8Their land is also full of idols;
They worship the work of their own hands,
That which their own fingers have made.
9People bow down,
And each man humbles himself;
Therefore do not forgive them.

10Enter into the rock, and hide in the dust,
From the terror of the LORD
And the glory of His majesty.
11The lofty looks of man shall be humbled,
The haughtiness of men shall be bowed
down,
And the LORD alone shall be exalted in that
day.

12For the day of the LORD of hosts
Shall come upon everything proud and lofty,
Upon everything lifted up—
And it shall be brought low—
13Upon all the cedars of Lebanon *that are*
high and lifted up,
And upon all the oaks of Bashan;
14Upon all the high mountains,
And upon all the hills *that are* lifted up;
15Upon every high tower,
And upon every fortified wall;
16Upon all the ships of Tarshish,
And upon all the beautiful sloops.
17The loftiness of man shall be bowed down,
And the haughtiness of men shall be
brought low;
The LORD alone will be exalted in that day,
18But the idols He shall utterly abolish.
19They shall go into the holes of the rocks,
And into the caves of the earth,
From the terror of the LORD
And the glory of His majesty,
When He arises to shake the earth mightily.

20In that day a man will cast away his idols of
silver
And his idols of gold,
Which they made, *each* for himself to
worship,
To the moles and bats,
21To go into the clefts of the rocks,
And into the crags of the rugged rocks,
From the terror of the LORD
And the glory of His majesty,
When He arises to shake the earth mightily.

THE MESSAGE

6-9 GOD, you've walked out on your family
Jacob
because their world is full of hokey
religion,
Philistine witchcraft, and pagan
hocus-pocus,
a world rolling in wealth,
Stuffed with things,
no end to its machines and gadgets,
And gods—gods of all sorts and sizes.
These people make their own gods and
worship what they make.
A degenerate race, facedown in the gutter.
Don't bother with them! They're not
worth forgiving!

PRETENTIOUS EGOS BROUGHT DOWN TO EARTH

10 Head for the hills,
hide in the caves
From the terror of GOD,
from his dazzling presence.

11-17 People with a big head are headed for a
fall,
pretentious egos brought down a peg.
It's GOD alone at front-and-center
on the Day we're talking about,
The Day that GOD-of-the-Angel-Armies
is matched against all big-talking rivals,
against all swaggering big names;
Against all giant sequoias
hugely towering,
and against the expansive chestnut;
Against Kilimanjaro and Annapurna,
against the ranges of Alps and Andes;
Against every soaring skyscraper,
against all proud obelisks and statues;
Against ocean-going luxury liners,
against elegant three-masted schooners.
The swelled big heads will be punctured
bladders,
the pretentious egos brought down to
earth,
Leaving GOD alone at front-and-center
on the Day we're talking about.

18 And all those sticks and stones
dressed up to look like gods
will be gone for good.

19 Clamber into caves in the cliffs,
duck into any hole you can find.
Hide from the terror of GOD,
from his dazzling presence,
When he assumes his full stature on earth,
towering and terrifying.

20-21 On that Day men and women will take
the sticks and stones
They've decked out in gold and silver
to look like gods and then worshiped,
And they will dump them
in any ditch or gully,
Then run for rock caves
and cliff hideouts
To hide from the terror of GOD,
from his dazzling presence,
When he assumes his full stature on earth,
towering and terrifying.

NEW KING JAMES VERSION

22Sever yourselves from such a man,
Whose breath *is* in his nostrils;
For of what account is he?

JUDGMENT ON JUDAH AND JERUSALEM

3 For behold, the Lord, the LORD of hosts,
Takes away from Jerusalem and from Judah
The stock and the store,
The whole supply of bread and the whole supply of water;
2The mighty man and the man of war,
The judge and the prophet,
And the diviner and the elder;
3The captain of fifty and the honorable man,
The counselor and the skillful artisan,
And the expert enchanter.

4"I will give children *to be* their princes,
And babes shall rule over them.
5The people will be oppressed,
Every one by another and every one by his neighbor;
The child will be insolent toward the elder,
And the base toward the honorable."

6When a man takes hold of his brother
In the house of his father, *saying*,
"You have clothing;
You be our ruler,
And *let* these ruins *be* under your power,"[a]
7In that day he will protest, saying,
"I cannot cure *your* ills,
For in my house *is* neither food nor clothing;
Do not make me a ruler of the people."

8For Jerusalem stumbled,
And Judah is fallen,
Because their tongue and their doings
Are against the LORD,
To provoke the eyes of His glory.
9The look on their countenance witnesses against them,
And they declare their sin as Sodom;
They do not hide *it*.
Woe to their soul!
For they have brought evil upon themselves.

10"Say to the righteous that *it shall be* well *with them*,
For they shall eat the fruit of their doings.
11Woe to the wicked! *It shall be* ill *with him*,
For the reward of his hands shall be given him.
12*As for* My people, children *are* their oppressors,
And women rule over them.
O My people! Those who lead you cause *you* to err,
And destroy the way of your paths."

OPPRESSION AND LUXURY CONDEMNED

13The LORD stands up to plead,
And stands to judge the people.
14The LORD will enter into judgment
With the elders of His people
And His princes:

3:6 [a]Literally *hand*

THE MESSAGE

22 Quit scraping and fawning over mere humans,
so full of themselves, so full of hot air!
Can't you see there's nothing to them?

JERUSALEM ON ITS LAST LEGS

1-7 3 The Master, GOD-of-the-Angel-Armies,
is emptying Jerusalem and Judah
Of all the basic necessities,
plain bread and water to begin with.
He's withdrawing police and protection,
judges and courts,
pastors and teachers,
captains and generals,
doctors and nurses,
and, yes, even the repairmen and jacks-of-all-trades.
He says, "I'll put little kids in charge of the city.
Schoolboys and schoolgirls will order everyone around.
People will be at each other's throats,
stabbing one another in the back:
Neighbor against neighbor, young against old,
the no-account against the well-respected.
One brother will grab another and say,
'You look like you've got a head on your shoulders.
Do something!
Get us out of this mess.'
And he'll say, 'Me? Not me! I don't have a clue.
Don't put me in charge of anything.'

8-9 "Jerusalem's on its last legs.
Judah is soon down for the count.
Everything people say and do
is at cross-purposes with GOD,
a slap in my face.
Brazen in their depravity,
they flaunt their sins like degenerate Sodom.
Doom to their eternal souls! They've made their bed;
now they'll sleep in it.

10-11 "Reassure the righteous
that their good living will pay off.
But doom to the wicked! Disaster!
Everything they did will be done to them.

12 "Skinny kids terrorize my people.
Silly girls bully them around.
My dear people! Your leaders are taking you down a blind alley.
They're sending you off on a wild-goose chase."

A CITY BROUGHT TO HER KNEES BY HER SORROWS

13-15 GOD enters the courtroom.
He takes his place at the bench to judge his people.
GOD calls for order in the court,
hauls the leaders of his people into the dock:

NEW KING JAMES VERSION

"For you have eaten up the vineyard;
The plunder of the poor *is* in your houses.
15What do you mean by crushing My people
And grinding the faces of the poor?"
Says the Lord GOD of hosts.

16Moreover the LORD says:

"Because the daughters of Zion are haughty,
And walk with outstretched necks
And wanton eyes,
Walking and mincing *as* they go,
Making a jingling with their feet,
17Therefore the Lord will strike with a scab
The crown of the head of the daughters of Zion,
And the LORD will uncover their secret parts."

18In that day the Lord will take away the finery:
The jingling anklets, the scarves, and the crescents;
19The pendants, the bracelets, and the veils;
20The headdresses, the leg ornaments, and the headbands;
The perfume boxes, the charms,
21and the rings;
The nose jewels,
22the festal apparel, and the mantles;
The outer garments, the purses,
23and the mirrors;
The fine linen, the turbans, and the robes.

24And so it shall be:

Instead of a sweet smell there will be a stench;
Instead of a sash, a rope;
Instead of well-set hair, baldness;
Instead of a rich robe, a girding of sackcloth;
And branding instead of beauty.
25Your men shall fall by the sword,
And your mighty in the war.

26Her gates shall lament and mourn,
And she *being* desolate shall sit on the ground.

4 And in that day seven women shall take hold of one man, saying,
"We will eat our own food and wear our own apparel;
Only let us be called by your name,
To take away our reproach."

THE RENEWAL OF ZION

2In that day the Branch of the LORD shall be beautiful and glorious;
And the fruit of the earth *shall be* excellent and appealing
For those of Israel who have escaped.

3And it shall come to pass that *he who is* left
in Zion and remains in Jerusalem will be called
holy—everyone who is recorded among the liv-
ing in Jerusalem. 4When the Lord has washed
away the filth of the daughters of Zion, and

THE MESSAGE

"You've played havoc with this country.
Your houses are stuffed with what you've stolen from the poor.
What is this anyway? Stomping on my people,
grinding the faces of the poor into the dirt?"
That's what the Master,
GOD-of-the-Angel-Armies, says.

16-17 GOD says, "Zion women are stuck-up,
prancing around in their high heels,
Making eyes at all the men in the street,
swinging their hips,
Tossing their hair,
gaudy and garish in cheap jewelry."
The Master will fix it so those Zion women
will all turn bald—
Scabby, bald-headed women.
The Master will do it.

18-23 The time is coming when the Master will strip them of their fancy baubles—the dangling earrings, anklets and bracelets, combs and mirrors and silk scarves, diamond brooches and pearl necklaces, the rings on their fingers and the rings on their toes, the latest fashions in hats, exotic perfumes and aphrodisiacs, gowns and capes, all the world's finest in fabrics and design.

24 Instead of wearing seductive scents,
these women are going to smell like rotting cabbages;
Instead of modeling flowing gowns,
they'll be sporting rags;
Instead of their stylish hairdos,
scruffy heads;
Instead of beauty marks,
scabs and scars.

25-26 Your finest fighting men will be killed,
your soldiers left dead on the battlefield.
The entrance gate to Zion will be clotted
with people mourning their dead—
A city stooped under the weight of her loss,
brought to her knees by her sorrows.

1 4 That will be the day when seven women
will gang up on one man, saying,
"We'll take care of ourselves,
get our own food and clothes.
Just give us a child. Make us pregnant
so we'll have something to live for!"

GOD'S BRANCH

2-4 And that's when GOD's Branch will sprout green and lush. The produce of the country will give Israel's survivors something to be proud of again. Oh, they'll hold their heads high! Everyone left behind in Zion, all the discards and rejects in Jerusalem, will be reclassified as "holy"—alive and therefore precious. GOD will give Zion's women a

NEW KING JAMES VERSION

purged the blood of Jerusalem from her midst,
by the spirit of judgment and by the spirit of
burning, 5then the LORD will create above every
dwelling place of Mount Zion, and above her as-
semblies, a cloud and smoke by day and the
shining of a flaming fire by night. For over all
the glory there *will be* a covering. 6And there
will be a tabernacle for shade in the daytime
from the heat, for a place of refuge, and for a
shelter from storm and rain.

GOD'S DISAPPOINTING VINEYARD

5 Now let me sing to my Well-beloved
A song of my Beloved regarding His vineyard:

My Well-beloved has a vineyard
On a very fruitful hill.
2He dug it up and cleared out its stones,
And planted it with the choicest vine.
He built a tower in its midst,
And also made a winepress in it;
So He expected *it* to bring forth *good* grapes,
But it brought forth wild grapes.

3"And now, O inhabitants of Jerusalem and men of Judah,
Judge, please, between Me and My vineyard.
4What more could have been done to My vineyard
That I have not done in it?
Why then, when I expected *it* to bring forth *good* grapes,
Did it bring forth wild grapes?
5And now, please let Me tell you what I will do to My vineyard:
I will take away its hedge, and it shall be burned;
And break down its wall, and it shall be trampled down.
6I will lay it waste;
It shall not be pruned or dug,
But there shall come up briers and thorns.
I will also command the clouds
That they rain no rain on it."

7For the vineyard of the LORD of hosts *is* the house of Israel,
And the men of Judah are His pleasant plant.
He looked for justice, but behold, oppression;
For righteousness, but behold, a cry *for help.*

IMPENDING JUDGMENT ON EXCESSES

8Woe to those who join house to house;
They add field to field,
Till *there is* no place
Where they may dwell alone in the midst of the land!
9In my hearing the LORD of hosts *said,*
"Truly, many houses shall be desolate,
Great and beautiful ones, without inhabitant.
10For ten acres of vineyard shall yield one bath,
And a homer of seed shall yield one ephah."

THE MESSAGE

good bath. He'll scrub the bloodstained city of its violence and brutality, purge the place with a firestorm of judgment.

5-6 Then GOD will bring back the ancient pillar of cloud by day and the pillar of fire by night and mark Mount Zion and everyone in it with his glorious presence, his immense, protective presence, shade from the burning sun and shelter from the driving rain.

LOOKING FOR A CROP OF JUSTICE

1-2 5 I'll sing a ballad to the one I love,
a love ballad about his vineyard:
The one I love had a vineyard,
a fine, well-placed vineyard.
He hoed the soil and pulled the weeds,
and planted the very best vines.
He built a lookout, built a winepress,
a vineyard to be proud of.
He looked for a vintage yield of grapes,
but for all his pains he got junk grapes.

3-4 "Now listen to what I'm telling you,
you who live in Jerusalem and Judah.
What do you think is going on
between me and my vineyard?
Can you think of anything I could have done
to my vineyard that I didn't do?
When I expected good grapes,
why did I get bitter grapes?

5-6 "Well now, let me tell you
what I'll do to my vineyard:
I'll tear down its fence
and let it go to ruin.
I'll knock down the gate
and let it be trampled.
I'll turn it into a patch of weeds, untended,
uncared for—
thistles and thorns will take over.
I'll give orders to the clouds:
'Don't rain on that vineyard, ever!' "

7 Do you get it? The vineyard of
GOD-of-the-Angel-Armies
is the country of Israel.
All the men and women of Judah
are the garden he was so proud of.
He looked for a crop of justice
and saw them murdering each other.
He looked for a harvest of righteousness
and heard only the moans of victims.

YOU WHO CALL EVIL GOOD AND GOOD EVIL

8-10 Doom to you who buy up all the houses
and grab all the land for yourselves—
Evicting the old owners,
posting NO TRESPASSING signs,
Taking over the country,
leaving everyone homeless and landless.
I overheard GOD-of-the-Angel-Armies say:
"Those mighty houses will end up empty.
Those extravagant estates will be deserted.
A ten-acre vineyard will produce a pint of wine,
a fifty-pound sack of seed, a quart of grain."

NEW KING JAMES VERSION

11Woe to those who rise early in the morning,
That they may follow intoxicating drink;
Who continue until night, *till* wine inflames them!
12The harp and the strings,
The tambourine and flute,
And wine are in their feasts;
But they do not regard the work of the LORD,
Nor consider the operation of His hands.

13Therefore my people have gone into captivity,
Because *they have* no knowledge;
Their honorable men *are* famished,
And their multitude dried up with thirst.
14Therefore Sheol has enlarged itself
And opened its mouth beyond measure;
Their glory and their multitude and their pomp,
And he who is jubilant, shall descend into it.
15People shall be brought down,
Each man shall be humbled,
And the eyes of the lofty shall be humbled.
16But the LORD of hosts shall be exalted in judgment,
And God who is holy shall be hallowed in righteousness.
17Then the lambs shall feed in their pasture,
And in the waste places of the fat ones strangers shall eat.

18Woe to those who draw iniquity with cords of vanity,
And sin as if with a cart rope;
19That say, "Let Him make speed *and* hasten His work,
That we may see *it;*
And let the counsel of the Holy One of Israel draw near and come,
That we may know *it.*"

20Woe to those who call evil good, and good evil;
Who put darkness for light, and light for darkness;
Who put bitter for sweet, and sweet for bitter!

21Woe to *those who are* wise in their own eyes,
And prudent in their own sight!

22Woe to men mighty at drinking wine,
Woe to men valiant for mixing intoxicating drink,
23Who justify the wicked for a bribe,
And take away justice from the righteous man!

24Therefore, as the fire devours the stubble,
And the flame consumes the chaff,
So their root will be as rottenness,
And their blossom will ascend like dust;
Because they have rejected the law of the LORD of hosts,
And despised the word of the Holy One of Israel.

THE MESSAGE

11-17 Doom to those who get up early
and start drinking booze before breakfast,
Who stay up all hours of the night
drinking themselves into a stupor.
They make sure their banquets are well-furnished
with harps and flutes and plenty of wine,
But they'll have nothing to do with the work of GOD,
pay no mind to what he is doing.
Therefore my people will end up in exile
because they don't know the score.
Their "big men" will starve to death
and the common people die of thirst.
Sheol developed a huge appetite,
swallowing people nonstop!
Big people and little people alike
down that gullet, to say nothing of all the drunks.
The down-and-out on a par
with the high-and-mighty,
Windbag boasters crumpled,
flaccid as a punctured bladder.
But by working justice,
GOD-of-the-Angel-Armies will be a mountain.
By working righteousness,
Holy God will show what "holy" is.
And lambs will graze
as if they owned the place,
Kids and calves
right at home in the ruins.

18-19 Doom to you who use lies to sell evil,
who haul sin to market by the truckload,
Who say, "What's God waiting for?
Let him get a move on so we can see it.
Whatever The Holy of Israel has cooked up,
we'd like to check it out."

20 Doom to you who call evil good
and good evil,
Who put darkness in place of light
and light in place of darkness,
Who substitute bitter for sweet
and sweet for bitter!

21-23 Doom to you who think you're so smart,
who hold such a high opinion of yourselves!
All you're good at is drinking—champion boozers
who collect trophies from drinking bouts
And then line your pockets with bribes from the guilty
while you violate the rights of the innocent.

24 But they won't get by with it. As fire eats stubble
and dry grass goes up in smoke,
Their souls will atrophy,
their achievements crumble into dust,
Because they said no to the revelation
of GOD-of-the-Angel-Armies,
Would have nothing to do
with The Holy of Israel.

NEW KING JAMES VERSION

25Therefore the anger of the LORD is aroused
against His people;
He has stretched out His hand against them
And stricken them,
And the hills trembled.
Their carcasses *were* as refuse in the midst
of the streets.

For all this His anger is not turned away,
But His hand *is* stretched out still.

26He will lift up a banner to the nations from
afar,
And will whistle to them from the end of the
earth;
Surely they shall come with speed, swiftly.
27No one will be weary or stumble among
them,
No one will slumber or sleep;
Nor will the belt on their loins be loosed,
Nor the strap of their sandals be broken;
28Whose arrows *are* sharp,
And all their bows bent;
Their horses' hooves will seem like flint,
And their wheels like a whirlwind.
29Their roaring *will be* like a lion,
They will roar like young lions;
Yes, they will roar
And lay hold of the prey;
They will carry *it* away safely,
And no one will deliver.
30In that day they will roar against them
Like the roaring of the sea.
And if *one* looks to the land,
Behold, darkness *and* sorrow;
And the light is darkened by the clouds.

ISAIAH CALLED TO BE A PROPHET

6In the year that King Uzziah died, I saw the
Lord sitting on a throne, high and lifted up,
and the train of His *robe* filled the temple.
2Above it stood seraphim; each one had six
wings: with two he covered his face, with two he
covered his feet, and with two he flew. 3And one
cried to another and said:

"Holy, holy, holy *is* the LORD of hosts;
The whole earth *is* full of His glory!"

4And the posts of the door were shaken by
the voice of him who cried out, and the house
was filled with smoke.
5So I said:

"Woe *is* me, for I am undone!
Because I *am* a man of unclean lips,
And I dwell in the midst of a people of
unclean lips;
For my eyes have seen the King,
The LORD of hosts."

6Then one of the seraphim flew to me, hav-
ing in his hand a live coal *which* he had taken
with the tongs from the altar. 7And he touched
my mouth *with it,* and said:

THE MESSAGE

25-30 That's why GOD flamed out in anger
against his people,
reached out and knocked them down.
The mountains trembled
as their dead bodies piled up in the
streets.
But even after that, he was still angry,
his fist still raised, ready to hit them
again.
He raises a flag, signaling a distant nation,
whistles for people at the ends of the
earth.
And here they come—
on the run!
None drag their feet, no one stumbles,
no one sleeps or dawdles.
Shirts are on and pants buckled,
every boot is spit-polished and tied.
Their arrows are sharp,
bows strung,
The hooves of their horses shod,
chariot wheels greased.
Roaring like a pride of lions,
the full-throated roars of young lions,
They growl and seize their prey,
dragging it off—no rescue for that one!
They'll roar and roar and roar on that Day,
like the roar of ocean billows.
Look as long and hard as you like at that
land,
you'll see nothing but darkness and
trouble.
Every light in the sky
will be blacked out by the clouds.

HOLY, HOLY, HOLY!

1-8 6In the year that King Uzziah died, I saw
the Master sitting on a throne—high, ex-
alted!—and the train of his robes filled the
Temple. Angel-seraphs hovered above him,
each with six wings. With two wings they
covered their faces, with two their feet, and
with two they flew. And they called back
and forth one to the other,

Holy, Holy, Holy is
GOD-of-the-Angel-Armies.
His bright glory fills the whole earth.

The foundations trembled at the sound of
the angel voices, and then the whole house
filled with smoke. I said,

"Doom! It's Doomsday!
I'm as good as dead!
Every word I've ever spoken is tainted—
blasphemous even!
And the people I live with talk the same
way,
using words that corrupt and desecrate.
And here I've looked God in the face!
The King! GOD-of-the-Angel-Armies!"

Then one of the angel-seraphs flew to me.
He held a live coal that he had taken with
tongs from the altar. He touched my mouth
with the coal and said,

New King James Version

"Behold, this has touched your lips;
Your iniquity is taken away,
And your sin purged."

8Also I heard the voice of the Lord, saying:

"Whom shall I send,
And who will go for Us?"

Then I said, "Here *am* I! Send me."
9And He said, "Go, and tell this people:

'Keep on hearing, but do not understand;
Keep on seeing, but do not perceive.'

10"Make the heart of this people dull,
And their ears heavy,
And shut their eyes;
Lest they see with their eyes,
And hear with their ears,
And understand with their heart,
And return and be healed."
11Then I said, "Lord, how long?"
And He answered:
"Until the cities are laid waste and without inhabitant,
The houses are without a man,
The land is utterly desolate,
12The LORD has removed men far away,
And the forsaken places *are* many in the midst of the land.
13But yet a tenth *will be* in it,
And will return and be for consuming,
As a terebinth tree or as an oak,
Whose stump *remains* when it is cut down.
So the holy seed *shall be* its stump."

Isaiah Sent to King Ahaz

7 Now it came to pass in the days of Ahaz the
son of Jotham, the son of Uzziah, king of Ju-
dah, *that* Rezin king of Syria and Pekah the son
of Remaliah, king of Israel, went up to
Jerusalem to *make* war against it, but could not
prevail against it. 2And it was told to the house
of David, saying, "Syria's forces are deployed in
Ephraim." So his heart and the heart of his peo-
ple were moved as the trees of the woods are
moved with the wind.
3Then the LORD said to Isaiah, "Go out now
to meet Ahaz, you and Shear-Jashub[a] your son,
at the end of the aqueduct from the upper pool,
on the highway to the Fuller's Field, 4and say to
him: 'Take heed, and be quiet; do not fear or be
fainthearted for these two stubs of smoking fire-
brands, for the fierce anger of Rezin and Syria,
and the son of Remaliah. 5Because Syria,
Ephraim, and the son of Remaliah have plotted
evil against you, saying, 6"Let us go up against
Judah and trouble it, and let us make a gap in its
wall for ourselves, and set a king over them, the
son of Tabel"—

7:3 [a]Literally *A Remnant Shall Return*

The Message

"Look. This coal has touched your lips.
Gone your guilt,
your sins wiped out."
And then I heard the voice of the Master:
"Whom shall I send?
Who will go for us?"
I spoke up,
"I'll go.
Send me!"

9-10 He said, "Go and tell this people:

" 'Listen hard, but you aren't going to get it;
look hard, but you won't catch on.'
Make these people blockheads,
with fingers in their ears and blindfolds on their eyes,
So they won't see a thing,
won't hear a word,
So they won't have a clue about what's going on
and, yes, so they won't turn around and be made whole."

11-13 Astonished, I said,
"And Master, how long is this to go on?"
He said, "Until the cities are emptied out,
not a soul left in the cities—
Houses empty of people,
countryside empty of people.
Until I, GOD, get rid of everyone, sending them off,
the land totally empty.
And even if some should survive, say a tenth,
the devastation will start up again.
The country will look like pine and oak forest
with every tree cut down—
Every tree a stump, a huge field of stumps.
But there's a holy seed in those stumps."

A Virgin Will Bear a Son

1-2 7 During the time that Ahaz son of Jotham,
son of Uzziah, was king of Judah, King
Rezin of Aram and King Pekah son of Rem-
aliah of Israel attacked Jerusalem, but the
attack sputtered out. When the Davidic gov-
ernment learned that Aram had joined
forces with Ephraim (that is, Israel), Ahaz
and his people were badly shaken. They
shook like trees in the wind.
3-6 Then GOD told Isaiah, "Go and meet Ahaz.
Take your son Shearjashub (A-Remnant-
Will-Return) with you. Meet him south of the
city at the end of the aqueduct where it emp-
ties into the upper pool on the road to the
public laundry. Tell him, Listen, calm down.
Don't be afraid. And don't panic over these
two burnt-out cases, Rezin of Aram and the
son of Remaliah. They talk big but there's
nothing to them. Aram, along with
Ephraim's son of Remaliah, have plotted to
do you harm. They've conspired against you,
saying, 'Let's go to war against Judah, dis-
member it, take it for ourselves, and set the
son of Tabeel up as a puppet king over it.'

NEW KING JAMES VERSION

7thus says the Lord GOD:

"It shall not stand,
Nor shall it come to pass.
8For the head of Syria *is* Damascus,
And the head of Damascus *is* Rezin.
Within sixty-five years Ephraim will be
broken,
So that it will not *be* a people.
9The head of Ephraim *is* Samaria,
And the head of Samaria *is* Remaliah's son.
If you will not believe,
Surely you shall not be established." ' "

THE IMMANUEL PROPHECY

10Moreover the LORD spoke again to Ahaz,
saying, 11"Ask a sign for yourself from the LORD
your God; ask it either in the depth or in the
height above."

12But Ahaz said, "I will not ask, nor will I test
the LORD!"

13Then he said, "Hear now, O house of David!
Is it a small thing for you to weary men, but will
you weary my God also? 14Therefore the Lord
Himself will give you a sign: Behold, the virgin
shall conceive and bear a Son, and shall call His
name Immanuel.[a] 15Curds and honey He shall
eat, that He may know to refuse the evil and
choose the good. 16For before the Child shall
know to refuse the evil and choose the good, the
land that you dread will be forsaken by both her
kings. 17The LORD will bring the king of Assyria
upon you and your people and your father's
house—days that have not come since the day
that Ephraim departed from Judah."

18And it shall come to pass in that day
That the LORD will whistle for the fly
That *is* in the farthest part of the rivers of
Egypt,
And for the bee that *is* in the land of
Assyria.
19They will come, and all of them will rest
In the desolate valleys and in the clefts of
the rocks,
And on all thorns and in all pastures.

20In the same day the Lord will shave with a
hired razor,
With those from beyond the River,[a] with the
king of Assyria,
The head and the hair of the legs,
And will also remove the beard.

21It shall be in that day
That a man will keep alive a young cow and
two sheep;
22So it shall be, from the abundance of milk
they give,
That he will eat curds;
For curds and honey everyone will eat who
is left in the land.

23It shall happen in that day,
That wherever there could be a thousand
vines
Worth a thousand *shekels* of silver,
It will be for briers and thorns.

7:14 [a]Literally *God-With-Us* **7:20** [a]That is, the Euphrates

THE MESSAGE

7-9 But GOD, the Master, says,

"It won't happen.
Nothing will come of it
Because the capital of Aram is Damascus
and the king of Damascus is a mere
man, Rezin.
As for Ephraim, in sixty-five years
it will be rubble, nothing left of it.
The capital of Ephraim is Samaria,
and the king of Samaria is the mere son
of Remaliah.
If you don't take your stand in faith,
you won't have a leg to stand on."

10-11 GOD spoke again to Ahaz. This time he said,
"Ask for a sign from your GOD. Ask any-
thing. Be extravagant. Ask for the moon!"

12 But Ahaz said, "I'd never do that. I'd never
make demands like that on GOD!"

13-17 So Isaiah told him, "Then listen to this,
government of David! It's bad enough that
you make people tired with your pious,
timid hypocrisies, but now you're making
God tired. So the Master is going to give you
a sign anyway. Watch for this: A girl who is
presently a virgin will get pregnant. She'll
bear a son and name him Immanuel (God-
With-Us). By the time the child is twelve
years old, able to make moral decisions, the
threat of war will be over. Relax, those two
kings that have you so worried will be out of
the picture. But also be warned: GOD will
bring on you and your people and your gov-
ernment a judgment worse than anything
since the time the kingdom split, when
Ephraim left Judah. The king of Assyria is
coming!"

18-19 That's when GOD will whistle for the flies
at the headwaters of Egypt's Nile, and whis-
tle for the bees in the land of Assyria.
They'll come and infest every nook and
cranny of this country. There'll be no getting
away from them.

20 And that's when the Master will take the
razor rented from across the Euphrates—
the king of Assyria no less!—and shave the
hair off your heads and genitals, leaving you
shamed, exposed, and denuded. He'll shave
off your beards while he's at it.

21-22 It will be a time when survivors will
count themselves lucky to have a cow and a
couple of sheep. At least they'll have plenty
of milk! Whoever's left in the land will learn
to make do with the simplest foods—curds,
whey, and honey.

23-25 But that's not the end of it. This country
that used to be covered with fine vine-
yards—thousands of them, worth mil-
lions!—will revert to a weed patch. Weeds

NEW KING JAMES VERSION

24With arrows and bows men will come there,
Because all the land will become briers and thorns.

25And to any hill which could be dug with the hoe,
You will not go there for fear of briers and thorns;
But it will become a range for oxen
And a place for sheep to roam.

ASSYRIA WILL INVADE THE LAND

8 Moreover the LORD said to me, "Take a large
scroll, and write on it with a man's pen con-
cerning Maher-Shalal-Hash-Baz.[a] 2And I will
take for Myself faithful witnesses to record,
Uriah the priest and Zechariah the son of Je-
berechiah."
3Then I went to the prophetess, and she con-
ceived and bore a son. Then the LORD said to
me, "Call his name Maher-Shalal-Hash-Baz; 4for
before the child shall have knowledge to cry
'My father' and 'My mother,' the riches of Da-
mascus and the spoil of Samaria will be taken
away before the king of Assyria."
5The LORD also spoke to me again, saying:

6"Inasmuch as these people refused
The waters of Shiloah that flow softly,
And rejoice in Rezin and in Remaliah's son;
7Now therefore, behold, the Lord brings up over them
The waters of the River,[a] strong and mighty—
The king of Assyria and all his glory;
He will go up over all his channels
And go over all his banks.
8He will pass through Judah,
He will overflow and pass over,
He will reach up to the neck;
And the stretching out of his wings
Will fill the breadth of Your land,
O Immanuel.[a]

9"Be shattered, O you peoples, and be broken in pieces!
Give ear, all you from far countries.
Gird yourselves, but be broken in pieces;
Gird yourselves, but be broken in pieces.
10Take counsel together, but it will come to nothing;
Speak the word, but it will not stand,
For God *is* with us."[a]

FEAR GOD, HEED HIS WORD

11For the LORD spoke thus to me with a
strong hand, and instructed me that I should not
walk in the way of this people, saying:

12"Do not say, 'A conspiracy,'
Concerning all that this people call a conspiracy,
Nor be afraid of their threats, nor be troubled.

8:1 [a]Literally *Speed the Spoil, Hasten the Booty* 8:7 [a]That is, the Euphrates 8:8 [a]Literally *God-With-Us* 8:10 [a]Hebrew *Immanuel*

THE MESSAGE

and thornbushes everywhere! Good for nothing except, perhaps, hunting rabbits. Cattle and sheep will forage as best they can in the fields of weeds—but there won't be a trace of all those fertile and well-tended gardens and fields.

1 8 Then GOD told me, "Get a big sheet of pa-
per and write in indelible ink, 'This be-
longs to Maher-shalal-hash-baz (Spoil-Speeds-
Plunder-Hurries).' "
2-3 I got two honest men, Uriah the priest
and Zechariah son of Jeberekiah, to witness
the document. Then I went home to my wife,
the prophetess. She conceived and gave
birth to a son.
3-4 GOD told me, "Name him Maher-shalal-
hash-baz. Before that baby says 'Daddy' or
'Mamma' the king of Assyria will have plun-
dered the wealth of Damascus and the
riches of Samaria."

5-8 GOD spoke to me again, saying:

"Because this people has turned its back
on the gently flowing stream of Shiloah
And gotten all excited over Rezin
and the son of Remaliah,
I'm stepping in and facing them with
the wild floodwaters of the Euphrates,
The king of Assyria and all his fanfare,
a river in flood, bursting its banks,
Pouring into Judah, sweeping everything before it,
water up to your necks,
A huge wingspan of a raging river,
O Immanuel, spreading across your land."

9-10 But face the facts, all you oppressors, and then wring your hands.
Listen, all of you, far and near.
Prepare for the worst and wring your hands.
Yes, prepare for the worst and wring your hands!
Plan and plot all you want—nothing will come of it.
All your talk is mere talk, empty words,
Because when all is said and done,
the last word is Immanuel—God-With-Us.

A BOULDER BLOCKING YOUR WAY

11-15 GOD spoke strongly to me, grabbed me with
both hands and warned me not to go along
with this people. He said:

"Don't be like this people,
always afraid somebody is plotting against them.
Don't fear what they fear.
Don't take on their worries.

NEW KING JAMES VERSION

13 The LORD of hosts, Him you shall hallow;
Let Him *be* your fear,
And *let* Him *be* your dread.
14 He will be as a sanctuary,
But a stone of stumbling and a rock of offense
To both the houses of Israel,
As a trap and a snare to the inhabitants of Jerusalem.
15 And many among them shall stumble;
They shall fall and be broken,
Be snared and taken."

16 Bind up the testimony,
Seal the law among my disciples.
17 And I will wait on the LORD,
Who hides His face from the house of Jacob;
And I will hope in Him.
18 Here am I and the children whom the LORD has given me!
We are for signs and wonders in Israel
From the LORD of hosts,
Who dwells in Mount Zion.

19 And when they say to you, "Seek those who
are mediums and wizards, who whisper and
mutter," should not a people seek their God?
Should they seek the dead on behalf of the liv-
ing? 20 To the law and to the testimony! If they do
not speak according to this word, *it is* because
there is no light in them.
21 They will pass through it hard-pressed and
hungry; and it shall happen, when they are hun-
gry, that they will be enraged and curse their
king and their God, and look upward. 22 Then
they will look to the earth, and see trouble and
darkness, gloom of anguish; and *they will be*
driven into darkness.

THE GOVERNMENT OF THE PROMISED SON

9 Nevertheless the gloom *will* not *be* upon her who *is* distressed,
As when at first He lightly esteemed
The land of Zebulun and the land of Naphtali,
And afterward more heavily oppressed *her*,
By the way of the sea, beyond the Jordan,
In Galilee of the Gentiles.
2 The people who walked in darkness
Have seen a great light;
Those who dwelt in the land of the shadow of death,
Upon them a light has shined.

3 You have multiplied the nation
And increased its joy;[a]
They rejoice before You
According to the joy of harvest,
As *men* rejoice when they divide the spoil.

9:3 [a]Following Qere and Targum; Kethib and Vulgate read *not increased joy;* Septuagint reads *Most of the people You brought down in Your joy.*

THE MESSAGE

If you're going to worry,
worry about The Holy. Fear
GOD-of-the-Angel-Armies.
The Holy can be either a Hiding Place
or a Boulder blocking your way,
The Rock standing in the willful way
of both houses of Israel,
A barbed-wire Fence preventing trespass
to the citizens of Jerusalem.
Many of them are going to run into that Rock
and get their bones broken,
Get tangled up in that barbed wire
and not get free of it."

16-18 Gather up the testimony,
preserve the teaching for my followers,
While I wait for GOD as long as he remains in hiding,
while I wait and hope for him.
I stand my ground and hope,
I and the children GOD gave me as signs to Israel,
Warning signs and hope signs from
GOD-of-the-Angel-Armies,
who makes his home in Mount Zion.

19-22 When people tell you, "Try out the fortunetellers.
Consult the spiritualists.
Why not tap into the spirit-world,
get in touch with the dead?"
Tell them, "No, we're going to study the Scriptures."
People who try the other ways get
nowhere—a dead end!
Frustrated and famished,
they try one thing after another.
When nothing works out they get angry,
cursing first this god and then that one,
Looking this way and that,
up, down, and sideways—and seeing nothing,
A blank wall, an empty hole.
They end up in the dark with nothing.

A CHILD HAS BEEN BORN—FOR US!

1 9 But there'll be no darkness for those who were in trouble. Earlier he did bring the lands of Zebulun and Naphtali into disrepute, but the time is coming when he'll make that whole area glorious—the road along the Sea, the country past the Jordan, international Galilee.

2-7 The people who walked in darkness
have seen a great light.
For those who lived in a land of deep shadows—
light! sunbursts of light!
You repopulated the nation,
you expanded its joy.
Oh, they're so glad in your presence!
Festival joy!
The joy of a great celebration,
sharing rich gifts and warm greetings.

NEW KING JAMES VERSION

4For You have broken the yoke of his burden
And the staff of his shoulder,
The rod of his oppressor,
As in the day of Midian.
5For every warrior's sandal from the noisy battle,
And garments rolled in blood,
Will be used for burning *and* fuel of fire.

6For unto us a Child is born,
Unto us a Son is given;
And the government will be upon His shoulder.
And His name will be called
Wonderful, Counselor, Mighty God,
Everlasting Father, Prince of Peace.
7Of the increase of *His* government and peace
There will be no end,
Upon the throne of David and over His kingdom,
To order it and establish it with judgment and justice
From that time forward, even forever.
The zeal of the Lord of hosts will perform this.

THE PUNISHMENT OF SAMARIA

8The Lord sent a word against Jacob,
And it has fallen on Israel.
9All the people will know—
Ephraim and the inhabitant of Samaria—
Who say in pride and arrogance of heart:
10"The bricks have fallen down,
But we will rebuild with hewn stones;
The sycamores are cut down,
But we will replace *them* with cedars."
11Therefore the LORD shall set up
The adversaries of Rezin against him,
And spur his enemies on,
12The Syrians before and the Philistines behind;
And they shall devour Israel with an open mouth.

For all this His anger is not turned away,
But His hand *is* stretched out still.

13For the people do not turn to Him who strikes them,
Nor do they seek the LORD of hosts.
14Therefore the LORD will cut off head and tail from Israel,
Palm branch and bulrush in one day.
15The elder and honorable, he *is* the head;
The prophet who teaches lies, he *is* the tail.
16For the leaders of this people cause *them* to err,
And *those who are* led by them are destroyed.
17Therefore the Lord will have no joy in their young men,

THE MESSAGE

The abuse of oppressors and cruelty of tyrants—
all their whips and cudgels and curses—
Is gone, done away with, a deliverance
as surprising and sudden as Gideon's old victory over Midian.
The boots of all those invading troops,
along with their shirts soaked with innocent blood,
Will be piled in a heap and burned,
a fire that will burn for days!
For a child has been born—for us!
the gift of a son—for us!
He'll take over
the running of the world.
His names will be: Amazing Counselor,
Strong God,
Eternal Father,
Prince of Wholeness.
His ruling authority will grow,
and there'll be no limits to the wholeness he brings.
He'll rule from the historic David throne
over that promised kingdom.
He'll put that kingdom on a firm footing
and keep it going
With fair dealing and right living,
beginning now and lasting always.
The zeal of GOD-of-the-Angel-Armies
will do all this.

GOD ANSWERED FIRE WITH FIRE

8-10 The Master sent a message against Jacob.
It landed right on Israel's doorstep.
All the people soon heard the message,
Ephraim and the citizens of Samaria.
But they were a proud and arrogant bunch.
They dismissed the message, saying,
"Things aren't that bad.
We can handle anything that comes.
If our buildings are knocked down,
we'll rebuild them bigger and finer.
If our forests are cut down,
we'll replant them with finer trees."

11-12 So GOD incited their adversaries against them,
stirred up their enemies to attack:
From the east, Arameans; from the west, Philistines.
They made hash of Israel.
But even after that, he was still angry,
his fist still raised, ready to hit them again.

13-17 But the people paid no mind to him who hit them,
didn't seek GOD-of-the-Angel-Armies.
So GOD hacked off Israel's head and tail,
palm branch and reed, both on the same day.
The big-head elders were the head,
the lying prophets were the tail.
Those who were supposed to lead this people
led them down blind alleys,
And those who followed the leaders
ended up lost and confused.
That's why the Master lost interest in the young men,

NEW KING JAMES VERSION

Nor have mercy on their fatherless and widows;
For everyone *is* a hypocrite and an evildoer,
And every mouth speaks folly.

For all this His anger is not turned away,
But His hand *is* stretched out still.

18For wickedness burns as the fire;
It shall devour the briers and thorns,
And kindle in the thickets of the forest;
They shall mount up *like* rising smoke.
19Through the wrath of the LORD of hosts
The land is burned up,
And the people shall be as fuel for the fire;
No man shall spare his brother.
20And he shall snatch on the right hand
And be hungry;
He shall devour on the left hand
And not be satisfied;
Every man shall eat the flesh of his own arm.
21Manasseh *shall devour* Ephraim, and Ephraim Manasseh;
Together they *shall be* against Judah.

For all this His anger is not turned away,
But His hand *is* stretched out still.

10 "Woe to those who decree unrighteous decrees,
Who write misfortune,
Which they have prescribed
2To rob the needy of justice,
And to take what is right from the poor of My people,
That widows may be their prey,
And *that* they may rob the fatherless.
3What will you do in the day of punishment,
And in the desolation *which* will come from afar?
To whom will you flee for help?
And where will you leave your glory?
4Without Me they shall bow down among the prisoners,
And they shall fall among the slain."

For all this His anger is not turned away,
But His hand *is* stretched out still.

ARROGANT ASSYRIA ALSO JUDGED

5"Woe to Assyria, the rod of My anger
And the staff in whose hand is My indignation.
6I will send him against an ungodly nation,
And against the people of My wrath
I will give him charge,
To seize the spoil, to take the prey,
And to tread them down like the mire of the streets.
7Yet he does not mean so,
Nor does his heart think so;
But *it is* in his heart to destroy,
And cut off not a few nations.

THE MESSAGE

had no feeling for their orphans and widows.
All of them were godless and evil,
talking filth and folly.
And even after that, he was still angry,
his fist still raised, ready to hit them again.

18-21 Their wicked lives raged like an out-of-control fire,
the kind that burns everything in its path—
Trees and bushes, weeds and grasses—
filling the skies with smoke.
GOD-of-the-Angel-Armies answered fire with fire,
set the whole country on fire,
Turned the people into consuming fires,
consuming one another in their lusts—
Appetites insatiable, stuffing and gorging
themselves left and right with people and things.
But still they starved. Not even their children
were safe from their rapacious hunger.
Manasseh ate Ephraim, and Ephraim Manasseh,
and then the two ganged up against Judah.
And after that, he was still angry,
his fist still raised, ready to hit them again.

YOU WHO LEGISLATE EVIL

1-4 10 Doom to you who legislate evil,
who make laws that make victims—
Laws that make misery for the poor,
that rob my destitute people of dignity,
Exploiting defenseless widows,
taking advantage of homeless children.
What will you have to say on Judgment Day,
when Doomsday arrives out of the blue?
Who will you get to help you?
What good will your money do you?
A sorry sight you'll be then, huddled with the prisoners,
or just some corpses stacked in the street.
Even after all this, God is still angry,
his fist still raised, ready to hit them again.

DOOM TO ASSYRIA!

5-11 "Doom to Assyria, weapon of my anger.
My wrath is a cudgel in his hands!
I send him against a godless nation,
against the people I'm angry with.
I command him to strip them clean, rob them blind,
and then push their faces in the mud and leave them.
But Assyria has another agenda;
he has something else in mind.
He's out to destroy utterly,
to stamp out as many nations as he can.
Assyria says, 'Aren't my commanders all kings?

NEW KING JAMES VERSION

[8]For he says,
'*Are* not my princes altogether kings?
[9]*Is* not Calno like Carchemish?
Is not Hamath like Arpad?
Is not Samaria like Damascus?
[10]As my hand has found the kingdoms of the idols,
Whose carved images excelled those of Jerusalem and Samaria,
[11]As I have done to Samaria and her idols,
Shall I not do also to Jerusalem and her idols?' "

[12]Therefore it shall come to pass, when the
Lord has performed all His work on Mount Zion
and on Jerusalem, *that He will say,* "I will pun-
ish the fruit of the arrogant heart of the king of
Assyria, and the glory of his haughty looks."
[13]For he says:

"By the strength of my hand I have done *it,*
And by my wisdom, for I am prudent;
Also I have removed the boundaries of the people,
And have robbed their treasuries;
So I have put down the inhabitants like a valiant *man.*
[14]My hand has found like a nest the riches of the people,
And as one gathers eggs *that are* left,
I have gathered all the earth;
And there was no one who moved *his* wing,
Nor opened *his* mouth with even a peep."

[15]Shall the ax boast itself against him who chops with it?
Or shall the saw exalt itself against him who saws with it?
As if a rod could wield *itself* against those who lift it up,
Or as if a staff could lift up, *as if it were* not wood!
[16]Therefore the Lord, the Lord[a] of hosts,
Will send leanness among his fat ones;
And under his glory
He will kindle a burning
Like the burning of a fire.
[17]So the Light of Israel will be for a fire,
And his Holy One for a flame;
It will burn and devour
His thorns and his briers in one day.
[18]And it will consume the glory of his forest and of his fruitful field,
Both soul and body;
And they will be as when a sick man wastes away.
[19]Then the rest of the trees of his forest
Will be so few in number
That a child may write them.

THE RETURNING REMNANT OF ISRAEL

[20]And it shall come to pass in that day
That the remnant of Israel,
And such as have escaped of the house of Jacob,
Will never again depend on him who defeated them,

10:16 [a]Following Bomberg; Masoretic Text and Dead Sea Scrolls read *YHWH* (*the* LORD).

THE MESSAGE

Can't they do whatever they like?
Didn't I destroy Calno as well as Carchemish?
Hamath as well as Arpad? Level Samaria as I did Damascus?
I've eliminated kingdoms full of gods
far more impressive than anything in Jerusalem and Samaria.
So what's to keep me from destroying Jerusalem
in the same way I destroyed Samaria and all her god-idols?' "

12-13 When the Master has finished dealing
with Mount Zion and Jerusalem, he'll say,
"Now it's Assyria's turn. I'll punish the brag-
ging arrogance of the king of Assyria, his
high and mighty posturing, the way he goes
around saying,

13-14 " 'I've done all this by myself.
I know more than anyone.
I've wiped out the boundaries of whole countries.
I've walked in and taken anything I wanted.
I charged in like a bull
and toppled their kings from their thrones.
I reached out my hand and took all that they treasured
as easily as a boy taking a bird's eggs from a nest.
Like a farmer gathering eggs from the henhouse,
I gathered the world in my basket,
And no one so much as fluttered a wing
or squawked or even chirped.' "

15-19 Does an ax take over from the one who swings it?
Does a saw act more important than the sawyer?
As if a shovel did its shoveling by using a ditch digger!
As if a hammer used the carpenter to pound nails!
Therefore the Master,
GOD-of-the-Angel-Armies,
will send a debilitating disease on his robust Assyrian fighters.
Under the canopy of God's bright glory
a fierce fire will break out.
Israel's Light will burst into a conflagration.
The Holy will explode into a firestorm,
And in one day burn to cinders
every last Assyrian thornbush.
GOD will destroy the splendid trees and lush gardens.
The Assyrian body and soul will waste away to nothing
like a disease-ridden invalid.
A child could count what's left of the trees
on the fingers of his two hands.

20-23 And on that Day also, what's left of Israel,
the ragtag survivors of Jacob, will no longer
be fascinated by abusive, battering Assyria.

NEW KING JAMES VERSION

But will depend on the LORD, the Holy One
of Israel, in truth.
21 The remnant will return, the remnant of
Jacob,
To the Mighty God.
22 For though your people, O Israel, be as the
sand of the sea,
A remnant of them will return;
The destruction decreed shall overflow with
righteousness.
23 For the Lord GOD of hosts
Will make a determined end
In the midst of all the land.

24 Therefore thus says the Lord GOD of hosts:
"O My people, who dwell in Zion, do not be
afraid of the Assyrian. He shall strike you with
a rod and lift up his staff against you, in the
manner of Egypt. 25 For yet a very little while and
the indignation will cease, as will My anger in
their destruction." 26 And the LORD of hosts will
stir up a scourge for him like the slaughter of
Midian at the rock of Oreb; *as* His rod was on
the sea, so will He lift it up in the manner of
Egypt.

27 It shall come to pass in that day
That his burden will be taken away from
your shoulder,
And his yoke from your neck,
And the yoke will be destroyed because of
the anointing oil.

28 He has come to Aiath,
He has passed Migron;
At Michmash he has attended to his
equipment.
29 They have gone along the ridge,
They have taken up lodging at Geba.
Ramah is afraid,
Gibeah of Saul has fled.
30 Lift up your voice,
O daughter of Gallim!
Cause it to be heard as far as Laish—
O poor Anathoth![a]
31 Madmenah has fled,
The inhabitants of Gebim seek refuge.
32 As yet he will remain at Nob that day;
He will shake his fist at the mount of the
daughter of Zion,
The hill of Jerusalem.

33 Behold, the Lord,
The LORD of hosts,
Will lop off the bough with terror;
Those of high stature *will be* hewn down,
And the haughty will be humbled.
34 He will cut down the thickets of the forest
with iron,
And Lebanon will fall by the Mighty One.

THE REIGN OF JESSE'S OFFSPRING

11 There shall come forth a Rod from the
stem of Jesse,
And a Branch shall grow out of his roots.
2 The Spirit of the LORD shall rest upon Him,
The Spirit of wisdom and understanding,

10:30 [a]Following Masoretic Text, Targum, and Vulgate; Septuagint and Syriac read *Listen to her, O Anathoth.*

THE MESSAGE

They'll lean on GOD, The Holy—yes, truly. The ragtag remnant—what's left of Jacob—will come back to the Strong God. Your people Israel were once like the sand on the seashore, but only a scattered few will return. Destruction is ordered, brimming over with righteousness. For the Master, GOD-of-the-Angel-Armies, will finish here what he started all over the globe.

24-27 Therefore the Master, GOD-of-the-Angel-Armies, says: "My dear, dear people who live in Zion, don't be terrorized by the Assyrians when they beat you with clubs and threaten you with rods like the Egyptians once did. In just a short time my anger against you will be spent and I'll turn my destroying anger on them. I, GOD-of-the-Angel-Armies, will go after them with a cat-o'-nine-tails and finish them off decisively—as Gideon downed Midian at the rock Oreb, as Moses turned the tables on Egypt. On that day, Assyria will be pulled off your back, and the yoke of slavery lifted from your neck."

27-32 Assyria's on the move: up from Rimmon,
on to Aiath,
through Migron,
with a bivouac at Micmash.
They've crossed the pass,
set camp at Geba for the night.
Ramah trembles with fright.
Gibeah of Saul has run off.
Cry for help, daughter of Gallim!
Listen to her, Laishah!
Do something, Anathoth!
Madmenah takes to the hills.
The people of Gebim flee in panic.
The enemy's soon at Nob—nearly there!
In sight of the city he shakes his fist
At the mount of dear daughter Zion,
the hill of Jerusalem.

33-34 But now watch this: The Master,
GOD-of-the-Angel-Armies,
swings his ax and lops the branches,
Chops down the giant trees,
lays flat the towering
forest-on-the-march.
His ax will make toothpicks of that forest,
that Lebanon-like army reduced to
kindling.

A GREEN SHOOT FROM JESSE'S STUMP

1-5 11 A green Shoot will sprout from Jesse's
stump,
from his roots a budding Branch.
The life-giving Spirit of GOD will hover over
him,
the Spirit that brings wisdom and
understanding,

NEW KING JAMES VERSION

The Spirit of counsel and might,
The Spirit of knowledge and of the fear of the LORD.

3His delight *is* in the fear of the LORD,
And He shall not judge by the sight of His eyes,
Nor decide by the hearing of His ears;
4But with righteousness He shall judge the poor,
And decide with equity for the meek of the earth;
He shall strike the earth with the rod of His mouth,
And with the breath of His lips He shall slay the wicked.
5Righteousness shall be the belt of His loins,
And faithfulness the belt of His waist.

6"The wolf also shall dwell with the lamb,
The leopard shall lie down with the young goat,
The calf and the young lion and the fatling together;
And a little child shall lead them.
7The cow and the bear shall graze;
Their young ones shall lie down together;
And the lion shall eat straw like the ox.
8The nursing child shall play by the cobra's hole,
And the weaned child shall put his hand in the viper's den.
9They shall not hurt nor destroy in all My holy mountain,
For the earth shall be full of the knowledge of the LORD
As the waters cover the sea.

10"And in that day there shall be a Root of Jesse,
Who shall stand as a banner to the people;
For the Gentiles shall seek Him,
And His resting place shall be glorious."

11It shall come to pass in that day
That the Lord shall set His hand again the second time
To recover the remnant of His people who are left,
From Assyria and Egypt,
From Pathros and Cush,
From Elam and Shinar,
From Hamath and the islands of the sea.

12He will set up a banner for the nations,
And will assemble the outcasts of Israel,
And gather together the dispersed of Judah
From the four corners of the earth.
13Also the envy of Ephraim shall depart,
And the adversaries of Judah shall be cut off;
Ephraim shall not envy Judah,
And Judah shall not harass Ephraim.
14But they shall fly down upon the shoulder of the Philistines toward the west;
Together they shall plunder the people of the East;
They shall lay their hand on Edom and Moab;
And the people of Ammon shall obey them.

THE MESSAGE

The Spirit that gives direction and builds strength,
the Spirit that instills knowledge and Fear-of-GOD.
Fear-of-GOD
will be all his joy and delight.
He won't judge by appearances,
won't decide on the basis of hearsay.
He'll judge the needy by what is right,
render decisions on earth's poor with justice.
His words will bring everyone to awed attention.
A mere breath from his lips will topple the wicked.
Each morning he'll pull on sturdy work clothes and boots,
and build righteousness and faithfulness in the land.

A LIVING KNOWLEDGE OF GOD

6-9 The wolf will romp with the lamb,
the leopard sleep with the kid.
Calf and lion will eat from the same trough,
and a little child will tend them.
Cow and bear will graze the same pasture,
their calves and cubs grow up together,
and the lion eat straw like the ox.
The nursing child will crawl over rattlesnake dens,
the toddler stick his hand down the hole of a serpent.
Neither animal nor human will hurt or kill on my holy mountain.
The whole earth will be brimming with knowing God-Alive,
a living knowledge of God ocean-deep, ocean-wide.

10 On that day, Jesse's Root will be raised high,
posted as a rallying banner for the peoples.
The nations will all come to him. His head-
quarters will be glorious.
11 Also on that day, the Master for the sec-
ond time will reach out to bring back what's
left of his scattered people. He'll bring them
back from Assyria, Egypt, Pathros, Ethiopia,
Elam, Sinar, Hamath, and the ocean islands.

12-16 And he'll raise that rallying banner high,
visible to all nations,
gather in all the scattered exiles of Israel,
Pull in all the dispersed refugees of Judah
from the four winds and the seven seas.
The jealousy of Ephraim will dissolve,
the hostility of Judah will vanish—
Ephraim no longer the jealous rival of Judah,
Judah no longer the hostile rival of Ephraim!
Blood brothers united, they'll pounce on the Philistines in the west,
join forces to plunder the people in the east.
They'll attack Edom and Moab.
The Ammonites will fall into line.

NEW KING JAMES VERSION

[15]The LORD will utterly destroy[a] the tongue of the Sea of Egypt;
With His mighty wind He will shake His fist over the River,[b]
And strike it in the seven streams,
And make *men* cross over dryshod.
[16]There will be a highway for the remnant of His people
Who will be left from Assyria,
As it was for Israel
In the day that he came up from the land of Egypt.

A HYMN OF PRAISE

12 And in that day you will say:

"O LORD, I will praise You;
Though You were angry with me,
Your anger is turned away, and You comfort me.
[2]Behold, God *is* my salvation,
I will trust and not be afraid;
'For YAH, the LORD, *is* my strength and song;
He also has become my salvation.' "[a]
[3]Therefore with joy you will draw water
From the wells of salvation.

[4]And in that day you will say:

"Praise the LORD, call upon His name;
Declare His deeds among the peoples,
Make mention that His name is exalted.
[5]Sing to the LORD,
For He has done excellent things;
This *is* known in all the earth.
[6]Cry out and shout, O inhabitant of Zion,
For great *is* the Holy One of Israel in your midst!"

PROCLAMATION AGAINST BABYLON

13 The burden against Babylon which Isaiah the son of Amoz saw.

[2]"Lift up a banner on the high mountain,
Raise your voice to them;
Wave your hand, that they may enter the gates of the nobles.
[3]I have commanded My sanctified ones;
I have also called My mighty ones for My anger—
Those who rejoice in My exaltation."

[4]The noise of a multitude in the mountains,
Like that of many people!
A tumultuous noise of the kingdoms of nations gathered together!
The LORD of hosts musters
The army for battle.
[5]They come from a far country,
From the end of heaven—

11:15 [a]Following Masoretic Text and Vulgate; Septuagint, Syriac, and Targum read *dry up.* [b]That is, the Euphrates **12:2** [a]Exodus 15:2

THE MESSAGE

GOD will once again dry up Egypt's Red Sea,
making for an easy crossing.
He'll send a blistering wind
down on the great River Euphrates,
Reduce it to seven mere trickles.
None even need get their feet wet!
In the end there'll be a highway all the way from Assyria,
easy traveling for what's left of God's people—
A highway just like the one Israel had
when he marched up out of Egypt.

MY STRENGTH AND SONG

1 12 And you will say in that day,
"I thank you, GOD.
You were angry
but your anger wasn't forever.
You withdrew your anger
and moved in and comforted me.

2 "Yes, indeed—God is my salvation.
I trust, I won't be afraid.
GOD—yes GOD!—is my strength and song,
best of all, my salvation!"

3-4 Joyfully you'll pull up buckets of water
from the wells of salvation.
And as you do it, you'll say,
"Give thanks to GOD.
Call out his name.
Ask him anything!
Shout to the nations, tell them what he's done,
spread the news of his great reputation!

5-6 "Sing praise-songs to GOD. He's done it all!
Let the whole earth know what he's done!
Raise the roof! Sing your hearts out, O Zion!
The Greatest lives among you: The Holy of Israel."

BABYLON IS DOOMED!

1 13 The Message on Babylon. Isaiah son of Amoz saw it:

2-3 "Run up a flag on an open hill.
Yell loud. Get their attention.
Wave them into formation.
Direct them to the nerve center of power.
I've taken charge of my special forces,
called up my crack troops.
They're bursting with pride and passion
to carry out my angry judgment."

4-5 Thunder rolls off the mountains
like a mob huge and noisy—
Thunder of kingdoms in an uproar,
nations assembling for war.
GOD-of-the-Angel-Armies is calling
his army into battle formation.
They come from far-off countries,
they pour in across the horizon.

NEW KING JAMES VERSION

The LORD and His weapons of indignation,
To destroy the whole land.

6Wail, for the day of the LORD *is* at hand!
It will come as destruction from the Almighty.
7Therefore all hands will be limp,
Every man's heart will melt,
8And they will be afraid.
Pangs and sorrows will take hold of *them;*
They will be in pain as a woman in childbirth;
They will be amazed at one another;
Their faces *will be like* flames.

9Behold, the day of the LORD comes,
Cruel, with both wrath and fierce anger,
To lay the land desolate;
And He will destroy its sinners from it.
10For the stars of heaven and their constellations
Will not give their light;
The sun will be darkened in its going forth,
And the moon will not cause its light to shine.
11"I will punish the world for *its* evil,
And the wicked for their iniquity;
I will halt the arrogance of the proud,
And will lay low the haughtiness of the terrible.
12I will make a mortal more rare than fine gold,
A man more than the golden wedge of Ophir.
13Therefore I will shake the heavens,
And the earth will move out of her place,
In the wrath of the LORD of hosts
And in the day of His fierce anger.
14It shall be as the hunted gazelle,
And as a sheep that no man takes up;
Every man will turn to his own people,
And everyone will flee to his own land.
15Everyone who is found will be thrust through,
And everyone who is captured will fall by the sword.
16Their children also will be dashed to pieces before their eyes;
Their houses will be plundered
And their wives ravished.

17"Behold, I will stir up the Medes against them,
Who will not regard silver;
And *as for* gold, they will not delight in it.
18Also *their* bows will dash the young men to pieces,
And they will have no pity on the fruit of the womb;
Their eye will not spare children.
19And Babylon, the glory of kingdoms,
The beauty of the Chaldeans' pride,
Will be as when God overthrew Sodom and Gomorrah.
20It will never be inhabited,
Nor will it be settled from generation to generation;
Nor will the Arabian pitch tents there,

THE MESSAGE

It's GOD on the move with the weapons of his wrath,
ready to destroy the whole country.

6-8 Wail! GOD's Day of Judgment is near—
an avalanche crashing down from the Strong God!
Everyone paralyzed in the panic,
hysterical and unstrung,
Doubled up in pain
like a woman giving birth to a baby.
Horrified—everyone they see
is like a face out of a nightmare.

9-16 "Watch now. GOD's Judgment Day comes.
Cruel it is, a day of wrath and anger,
A day to waste the earth
and clean out all the sinners.
The stars in the sky, the great parade of constellations,
will be nothing but black holes.
The sun will come up as a black disk,
and the moon a blank nothing.
I'll put a full stop to the evil on earth,
terminate the dark acts of the wicked.
I'll gag all braggarts and boasters—not a peep anymore from them—
and trip strutting tyrants, leave them flat on their faces.
Proud humanity will disappear from the earth.
I'll make mortals rarer than hens' teeth.
And yes, I'll even make the sky shake,
and the earth quake to its roots
Under the wrath of GOD-of-the-Angel-Armies,
the Judgment Day of his raging anger.
Like a hunted white-tailed deer,
like lost sheep with no shepherd,
People will huddle with a few of their own kind,
run off to some makeshift shelter.
But tough luck to stragglers—they'll be killed on the spot,
throats cut, bellies ripped open,
Babies smashed on the rocks
while mothers and fathers watch,
Houses looted,
wives raped.

17-22 "And now watch this:
Against Babylon, I'm inciting the Medes,
A ruthless bunch indifferent to bribes,
the kind of brutality that no one can blunt.
They massacre the young,
wantonly kick and kill even babies.
And Babylon, most glorious of all kingdoms,
the pride and joy of Chaldeans,
Will end up smoking and stinking like Sodom,
and, yes, like Gomorrah, when God had finished with them.
No one will live there anymore,
generation after generation a ghost town.
Not even Bedouins will pitch tents there.

NEW KING JAMES VERSION

Nor will the shepherds make their
sheepfolds there.
21But wild beasts of the desert will lie there,
And their houses will be full of owls;
Ostriches will dwell there,
And wild goats will caper there.
22The hyenas will howl in their citadels,
And jackals in their pleasant palaces.
Her time *is* near to come,
And her days will not be prolonged."

MERCY ON JACOB

14 For the LORD will have mercy on Jacob,
and will still choose Israel, and settle them
in their own land. The strangers will be joined
with them, and they will cling to the house of Ja-
cob. 2Then people will take them and bring
them to their place, and the house of Israel will
possess them for servants and maids in the land
of the LORD; they will take them captive whose
captives they were, and rule over their oppres-
sors.

FALL OF THE KING OF BABYLON

3It shall come to pass in the day the LORD
gives you rest from your sorrow, and from your
fear and the hard bondage in which you were
made to serve, 4that you will take up this
proverb against the king of Babylon, and say:

"How the oppressor has ceased,
The golden[a] city ceased!
5The LORD has broken the staff of the
wicked,
The scepter of the rulers;
6He who struck the people in wrath with a
continual stroke,
He who ruled the nations in anger,
Is persecuted *and* no one hinders.
7The whole earth is at rest *and* quiet;
They break forth into singing.
8Indeed the cypress trees rejoice over you,
And the cedars of Lebanon,
Saying, 'Since you were cut down,
No woodsman has come up against us.'

9"Hell from beneath is excited about you,
To meet *you* at your coming;
It stirs up the dead for you,
All the chief ones of the earth;
It has raised up from their thrones
All the kings of the nations.
10They all shall speak and say to you:
'Have you also become as weak as we?
Have you become like us?
11Your pomp is brought down to Sheol,
And the sound of your stringed instruments;

14:4 [a]Or *insolent*

THE MESSAGE

Shepherds will give it a wide berth.
But strange and wild animals will like it
just fine,
filling the vacant houses with eerie night
sounds.
Skunks will make it their home,
and unspeakable night hags will haunt
it.
Hyenas will curdle your blood with their
laughing,
and the howling of coyotes will give you
the shivers.

"Babylon is doomed.
It won't be long now."

NOW YOU ARE NOTHING

1-2 14 But not so with Jacob. GOD will have
compassion on Jacob. Once again he'll
choose Israel. He'll establish them in their
own country. Outsiders will be attracted and
throw their lot in with Jacob. The nations
among whom they lived will actually escort
them back home, and then Israel will pay
them back by making slaves of them, men
and women alike, possessing them as slaves
in GOD's country, capturing those who had
captured them, ruling over those who had
abused them.
3-4 When GOD has given you time to recover
from the abuse and trouble and harsh servi-
tude that you had to endure, you can amuse
yourselves by taking up this satire, a taunt
against the king of Babylon:

4-6 Can you believe it? The tyrant is gone!
The tyranny is over!
GOD has broken the rule of the wicked,
the power of the bully-rulers
That crushed many people.
A relentless rain of cruel outrage
Established a violent rule of anger
rife with torture and persecution.

7-10 And now it's over, the whole earth quietly
at rest.
Burst into song! Make the rafters ring!
Ponderosa pine trees are happy,
giant Lebanon cedars are relieved,
saying,
"Since you've been cut down,
there's no one around to cut us down."
And the underworld dead are all excited,
preparing to welcome you when you
come.
Getting ready to greet you are the ghostly
dead,
all the famous names of earth.
All the buried kings of the nations
will stand up on their thrones
With well-prepared speeches,
royal invitations to death:
"Now you are as nothing as we are!
Make yourselves at home with us dead
folks!"

11 This is where your pomp and fine music
led you, Babylon,
to your underworld private chambers,

NEW KING JAMES VERSION

The maggot is spread under you,
And worms cover you.'

THE FALL OF LUCIFER

12"How you are fallen from heaven,
O Lucifer,[a] son of the morning!
How you are cut down to the ground,
You who weakened the nations!
13For you have said in your heart:
'I will ascend into heaven,
I will exalt my throne above the stars of God;
I will also sit on the mount of the congregation
On the farthest sides of the north;
14I will ascend above the heights of the clouds,
I will be like the Most High.'
15Yet you shall be brought down to Sheol,
To the lowest depths of the Pit.

16"Those who see you will gaze at you,
And consider you, *saying*:
'*Is* this the man who made the earth tremble,
Who shook kingdoms,
17Who made the world as a wilderness
And destroyed its cities,
Who did not open the house of his prisoners?'

18"All the kings of the nations,
All of them, sleep in glory,
Everyone in his own house;
19But you are cast out of your grave
Like an abominable branch,
Like the garment of those who are slain,
Thrust through with a sword,
Who go down to the stones of the pit,
Like a corpse trodden underfoot.
20You will not be joined with them in burial,
Because you have destroyed your land
And slain your people.
The brood of evildoers shall never be named.
21Prepare slaughter for his children
Because of the iniquity of their fathers,
Lest they rise up and possess the land,
And fill the face of the world with cities."

BABYLON DESTROYED

22"For I will rise up against them," says the LORD of hosts,
"And cut off from Babylon the name and remnant,
And offspring and posterity," says the LORD.
23"I will also make it a possession for the porcupine,
And marshes of muddy water;
I will sweep it with the broom of destruction," says the LORD of hosts.

ASSYRIA DESTROYED

24The LORD of hosts has sworn, saying,
"Surely, as I have thought, so it shall come to pass,
And as I have purposed, *so* it shall stand:
25That I will break the Assyrian in My land,

14:12 [a]Literally *Day Star*

THE MESSAGE

A king-size mattress of maggots for repose
and a quilt of crawling worms for warmth.

12 What a comedown this, O Babylon!
Daystar! Son of Dawn!
Flat on your face in the underworld mud,
you, famous for flattening nations!

13-14 You said to yourself,
"I'll climb to heaven.
I'll set my throne
over the stars of God.
I'll run the assembly of angels
that meets on sacred Mount Zaphon.
I'll climb to the top of the clouds.
I'll take over as King of the Universe!"

15-17 But you didn't make it, did you?
Instead of climbing up, you came down—
Down with the underground dead,
down to the abyss of the Pit.
People will stare and muse:
"Can this be the one
Who terrorized earth and its kingdoms,
turned earth to a moonscape,
Wasted its cities,
shut up his prisoners to a living death?"

18-20 Other kings get a decent burial,
honored with eulogies and placed in a tomb.
But you're dumped in a ditch unburied,
like a stray dog or cat,
Covered with rotting bodies,
murdered and indigent corpses.
Your dead body desecrated, mutilated—
no state funeral for you!
You've left your land in ruins,
left a legacy of massacre.
The progeny of your evil life
will never be named. Oblivion!

21 Get a place ready to slaughter the sons of the wicked
and wipe out their father's line.
Unthinkable that they should own a square foot of land
or desecrate the face of the world with their cities!

22-23 "I will confront them"—Decree of GOD-of-the-Angel-Armies—"and strip Babylon of name and survivors, children and grandchildren." GOD's Decree. "I'll make it a worthless swamp and give it as a prize to the hedgehog. And then I'll bulldoze it out of existence." Decree of GOD-of-the-Angel-Armies.

WHO COULD EVER CANCEL SUCH PLANS?

24-27 GOD-of-the-Angel-Armies speaks:

"Exactly as I planned,
it will happen.
Following my blueprints,
it will take shape.
I will shatter the Assyrian who trespasses my land

NEW KING JAMES VERSION

And on My mountains tread him underfoot.
Then his yoke shall be removed from them,
And his burden removed from their shoulders.
26This *is* the purpose that is purposed against the whole earth,
And this *is* the hand that is stretched out over all the nations.
27For the LORD of hosts has purposed,
And who will annul *it*?
His hand *is* stretched out,
And who will turn it back?"

PHILISTIA DESTROYED

28This is the burden which came in the year
that King Ahaz died.

29"Do not rejoice, all you of Philistia,
Because the rod that struck you is broken;
For out of the serpent's roots will come forth a viper,
And its offspring *will be* a fiery flying serpent.
30The firstborn of the poor will feed,
And the needy will lie down in safety;
I will kill your roots with famine,
And it will slay your remnant.
31Wail, O gate! Cry, O city!
All you of Philistia *are* dissolved;
For smoke will come from the north,
And no one *will be* alone in his appointed times."
32What will they answer the messengers of the nation?
That the LORD has founded Zion,
And the poor of His people shall take refuge in it.

PROCLAMATION AGAINST MOAB

15 The burden against Moab.

Because in the night Ar of Moab is laid waste
And destroyed,
Because in the night Kir of Moab is laid waste
And destroyed,
2He has gone up to the temple[a] and Dibon,
To the high places to weep.
Moab will wail over Nebo and over Medeba;
On all their heads *will be* baldness,
And every beard cut off.
3In their streets they will clothe themselves with sackcloth;
On the tops of their houses
And in their streets
Everyone will wail, weeping bitterly.
4Heshbon and Elealeh will cry out,
Their voice shall be heard as far as Jahaz;
Therefore the armed soldiers[a] of Moab will cry out;
His life will be burdensome to him.

15:2 [a]Hebrew *bayith*, literally *house* **15:4** [a]Following Masoretic Text, Targum, and Vulgate; Septuagint and Syriac read *loins*.

THE MESSAGE

and stomp him into the dirt on my mountains.
I will ban his taking and making of slaves
and lift the weight of oppression from all shoulders."
This is the plan,
planned for the whole earth,
And this is the hand that will do it,
reaching into every nation.
GOD-of-the-Angel-Armies has planned it.
Who could ever cancel such plans?
His is the hand that's reached out.
Who could brush it aside?

28-31 In the year King Ahaz died, this Message came:

Hold it, Philistines! It's too soon to celebrate
the defeat of your cruel oppressor.
From the death throes of that snake a worse snake will come,
and from that, one even worse.
The poor won't have to worry.
The needy will escape the terror.
But you Philistines will be plunged into famine,
and those who don't starve, God will kill.
Wail and howl, proud city!
Fall prostrate in fear, Philistia!
On the northern horizon, smoke from burned cities,
the wake of a brutal, disciplined destroyer.

32 What does one say to
outsiders who ask questions?
Tell them, "GOD has established Zion.
Those in need and in trouble find refuge in her."

POIGNANT CRIES REVERBERATE THROUGH MOAB

1-4 15 A Message concerning Moab:

Village Ar of Moab is in ruins,
destroyed in a night raid.
Village Kir of Moab is in ruins,
destroyed in a night raid.
Village Dibon climbs to its chapel in the hills,
goes up to lament.
Moab weeps and wails
over Nebo and Medba.
Every head is shaved bald,
every beard shaved clean.
They pour into the streets wearing black,
go up on the roofs, take to the town square,
Everyone in tears,
everyone in grief.
Towns Heshbon and Elealeh cry long and loud.
The sound carries as far as Jahaz.
Moab sobs, shaking in grief.
The soul of Moab trembles.

NEW KING JAMES VERSION

5"My heart will cry out for Moab;
His fugitives *shall flee* to Zoar,
Like a three-year-old heifer.[a]
For by the Ascent of Luhith
They will go up with weeping;
For in the way of Horonaim
They will raise up a cry of destruction,
6For the waters of Nimrim will be desolate,
For the green grass has withered away;
The grass fails, there is nothing green.
7Therefore the abundance they have gained,
And what they have laid up,
They will carry away to the Brook of the Willows.
8For the cry has gone all around the borders of Moab,
Its wailing to Eglaim
And its wailing to Beer Elim.
9For the waters of Dimon[a] will be full of blood;
Because I will bring more upon Dimon,[b]
Lions upon him who escapes from Moab,
And on the remnant of the land."

MOAB DESTROYED

16 Send the lamb to the ruler of the land,
From Sela to the wilderness,
To the mount of the daughter of Zion.
2For it shall be as a wandering bird thrown out of the nest;
So shall be the daughters of Moab at the fords of the Arnon.

3"Take counsel, execute judgment;
Make your shadow like the night in the middle of the day;
Hide the outcasts,
Do not betray him who escapes.
4Let My outcasts dwell with you, O Moab;
Be a shelter to them from the face of the spoiler.
For the extortioner is at an end,
Devastation ceases,
The oppressors are consumed out of the land.
5In mercy the throne will be established;
And One will sit on it in truth, in the tabernacle of David,
Judging and seeking justice and hastening righteousness."

6We have heard of the pride of Moab—
He is very proud—
Of his haughtiness and his pride and his wrath;
But his lies *shall* not *be* so.
7Therefore Moab shall wail for Moab;
Everyone shall wail.
For the foundations of Kir Hareseth you shall mourn;
Surely *they are* stricken.

8For the fields of Heshbon languish,
And the vine of Sibmah;

15:5 [a]Or *The Third Eglath*, an unknown city (compare Jeremiah 48:34) **15:9** [a]Following Masoretic Text and Targum; Dead Sea Scrolls and Vulgate read *Dibon;* Septuagint reads *Rimon.* [b]Following Masoretic Text and Targum; Dead Sea Scrolls and Vulgate read *Dibon;* Septuagint reads *Rimon.*

THE MESSAGE

5-9 Oh, how I grieve for Moab!
Refugees stream to Zoar
and then on to Eglath-shelishiyah.
Up the slopes of Luhith they weep;
on the road to Horonaim they cry their loss.
The springs of Nimrim are dried up—
grass brown, buds stunted, nothing grows.
They leave, carrying all their possessions
on their backs, everything they own,
Making their way as best they can
across Willow Creek to safety.
Poignant cries reverberate
all through Moab,
Gut-wrenching sobs as far as Eglaim,
heart-racking sobs all the way to Beer-elim.
The banks of the Dibon crest with blood,
but God has worse in store for Dibon:
A lion—a lion to finish off the fugitives,
to clean up whoever's left in the land.

A NEW GOVERNMENT IN THE DAVID TRADITION

1-4 16 "Dispatch a gift of lambs," says Moab,
"to the leaders in Jerusalem—
Lambs from Sela sent across the desert
to buy the goodwill of Jerusalem.
The towns and people of Moab
are at a loss,
New-hatched birds knocked from the nest,
fluttering helplessly
At the banks of the Arnon River,
unable to cross:
'Tell us what to do,
help us out!
Protect us,
hide us!
Give the refugees from Moab
sanctuary with you.
Be a safe place for those on the run
from the killing fields.' "

4-5 "When this is all over," Judah answers,
"the tyrant toppled,
The killing at an end,
all signs of these cruelties long gone,
A new government of love will be established
in the venerable David tradition.
A Ruler you can depend upon
will head this government,
A Ruler passionate for justice,
a Ruler quick to set things right."

6-12 We've heard—everyone's heard!—of Moab's pride,
world-famous for pride—
Arrogant, self-important, insufferable,
full of hot air.
So now let Moab lament for a change,
with antiphonal mock-laments from the neighbors!
What a shame! How terrible!
No more fine fruitcakes and Kir-hareseth candies!
All those lush Heshbon fields dried up,
the rich Sibmah vineyards withered!

NEW KING JAMES VERSION

The lords of the nations have broken down its choice plants,
Which have reached to Jazer
And wandered through the wilderness.
Her branches are stretched out,
They are gone over the sea.
9Therefore I will bewail the vine of Sibmah,
With the weeping of Jazer;
I will drench you with my tears,
O Heshbon and Elealeh;
For battle cries have fallen
Over your summer fruits and your harvest.

10Gladness is taken away,
And joy from the plentiful field;
In the vineyards there will be no singing,
Nor will there be shouting;
No treaders will tread out wine in the presses;
I have made their shouting cease.
11Therefore my heart shall resound like a harp for Moab,
And my inner being for Kir Heres.

12And it shall come to pass,
When it is seen that Moab is weary on the high place,
That he will come to his sanctuary to pray;
But he will not prevail.

13This *is* the word which the LORD has spo-
ken concerning Moab since that time. 14But now
the LORD has spoken, saying, "Within three
years, as the years of a hired man, the glory of
Moab will be despised with all that great multi-
tude, and the remnant *will be* very small *and*
feeble."

PROCLAMATION AGAINST SYRIA AND ISRAEL

17 The burden against Damascus.

"Behold, Damascus will cease from *being* a city,
And it will be a ruinous heap.
2The cities of Aroer *are* forsaken;[a]
They will be for flocks
Which lie down, and no one will make *them* afraid.
3The fortress also will cease from Ephraim,
The kingdom from Damascus,
And the remnant of Syria;
They will be as the glory of the children of Israel,"
Says the LORD of hosts.
4"In that day it shall come to pass
That the glory of Jacob will wane,
And the fatness of his flesh grow lean.
5It shall be as when the harvester gathers the grain,
And reaps the heads with his arm;
It shall be as he who gathers heads of grain
In the Valley of Rephaim.
6Yet gleaning grapes will be left in it,
Like the shaking of an olive tree,

17:2 [a]Following Masoretic Text and Vulgate; Septuagint reads *It shall be forsaken forever;* Targum reads *Its cities shall be forsaken and desolate.*

THE MESSAGE

Foreign thugs have crushed and torn out
the famous grapevines
That once reached all the way to Jazer,
right to the edge of the desert,
Ripped out the crops in every direction
as far as the eye can see.
I'll join the weeping. I'll weep right along with Jazer,
weep for the Sibmah vineyards.
And yes, Heshbon and Elealeh,
I'll mingle my tears with your tears!
The joyful shouting at harvest is gone.
Instead of song and celebration, dead silence.
No more boisterous laughter in the orchards,
no more hearty work songs in the vineyards.
Instead of the bustle and sound of good work in the fields,
silence—deathly and deadening silence.
My heartstrings throb like harp strings for Moab,
my soul in sympathy for sad Kir-heres.
When Moab trudges to the shrine to pray,
he wastes both time and energy.
Going to the sanctuary and praying for relief
is useless. Nothing ever happens.

13-14 This is GOD'S earlier Message on Moab.
GOD'S updated Message is, "In three years,
no longer than the term of an enlisted sol-
dier, Moab's impressive presence will be
gone, that splendid hot-air balloon will be
punctured, and instead of a vigorous popu-
lation, just a few shuffling bums cadging
handouts."

DAMASCUS: A PILE OF DUST AND RUBBLE

1-3 17 A Message concerning Damascus:

"Watch this: Damascus undone as a city,
a pile of dust and rubble!
Her towns emptied of people.
The sheep and goats will move in
And take over the towns
as if they owned them—which they will!
Not a sign of a fort is left in Ephraim,
not a trace of government left in Damascus.
What's left of Aram?
The same as what's left of Israel—not much."
Decree of GOD-of-the-Angel-Armies.

THE DAY IS COMING

4-6 "The Day is coming when Jacob's robust splendor goes pale
and his well-fed body turns skinny.
The country will be left empty, picked clean
as a field harvested by field hands.
She'll be like a few stalks of barley left standing
in the lush Valley of Rephaim after harvest,
Or like the couple of ripe olives overlooked
in the top of the olive tree,

NEW KING JAMES VERSION

Two *or* three olives at the top of the uppermost bough,
Four *or* five in its most fruitful branches,"
Says the LORD God of Israel.

7In that day a man will look to his Maker,
And his eyes will have respect for the Holy One of Israel.
8He will not look to the altars,
The work of his hands;
He will not respect what his fingers have made,
Nor the wooden images[a] nor the incense altars.

9In that day his strong cities will be as a forsaken bough[a]
And an uppermost branch,[b]
Which they left because of the children of Israel;
And there will be desolation.

10Because you have forgotten the God of your salvation,
And have not been mindful of the Rock of your stronghold,
Therefore you will plant pleasant plants
And set out foreign seedlings;
11In the day you will make your plant to grow,
And in the morning you will make your seed to flourish;
But the harvest *will be* a heap of ruins
In the day of grief and desperate sorrow.

12Woe to the multitude of many people
Who make a noise like the roar of the seas,
And to the rushing of nations
That make a rushing like the rushing of mighty waters!
13The nations will rush like the rushing of many waters;
But *God* will rebuke them and they will flee far away,
And be chased like the chaff of the mountains before the wind,
Like a rolling thing before the whirlwind.
14Then behold, at eventide, trouble!
And before the morning, he *is* no more.
This *is* the portion of those who plunder us,
And the lot of those who rob us.

PROCLAMATION AGAINST ETHIOPIA

18 Woe to the land shadowed with buzzing wings,
Which *is* beyond the rivers of Ethiopia,
2Which sends ambassadors by sea,
Even in vessels of reed on the waters, *saying,*
"Go, swift messengers, to a nation tall and smooth *of skin,*

17:8 [a]Hebrew *Asherim,* Canaanite deities 17:9 [a]Septuagint reads *Hivites;* Targum reads *laid waste;* Vulgate reads *as the plows.* [b]Septuagint reads *Amorites;* Targum reads *in ruins;* Vulgate reads *corn.*

THE MESSAGE

Or the four or five apples
that the pickers couldn't reach in the orchard."
Decree of the GOD of Israel.

7-8 Yes, the Day is coming when people will
notice The One Who Made Them, take a
long hard look at The Holy of Israel. They'll
lose interest in all the stuff they've made—
altars and monuments and rituals, their
homemade, handmade religion—however
impressive it is.

9 And yes, the Day is coming when their
fortress cities will be abandoned — the very
same cities that the Hivites and Amorites
abandoned when Israel invaded! And the
country will be empty, desolate.

YOU HAVE FORGOTTEN GOD

10-11 And why? Because you have forgotten God-Your-Salvation,
not remembered your Rock-of-Refuge.
And so, even though you are very religious,
planting all sorts of bushes and herbs and trees
to honor and influence your fertility gods,
And even though you make them grow so well,
bursting with buds and sprouts and blossoms,
Nothing will come of them. Instead of a harvest
you'll get nothing but grief and pain, pain, pain.

12-13 Oh my! Thunder! A thundering herd of people!
Thunder like the crashing of ocean waves!
Nations roaring, roaring,
like the roar of a massive waterfall,
Roaring like a deafening Niagara!
But God will silence them with a word,
And then he'll blow them away like dead leaves off a tree,
like down from a thistle.

14 At bedtime, terror fills the air.
By morning it's gone—not a sign of it anywhere!
This is what happens to those who would ruin us,
this is the fate of those out to get us.

PEOPLE MIGHTY AND MERCILESS

1-2 18 Doom to the land of flies and mosquitoes
beyond the Ethiopian rivers,
Shipping emissaries all over the world,
down rivers and across seas.

Go, swift messengers,
go to this people tall and handsome,

NEW KING JAMES VERSION

To a people terrible from their beginning
onward,
A nation powerful and treading down,
Whose land the rivers divide."

3All inhabitants of the world and dwellers on
the earth:
When he lifts up a banner on the mountains,
you see *it;*
And when he blows a trumpet, you hear *it.*
4For so the LORD said to me,
"I will take My rest,
And I will look from My dwelling place
Like clear heat in sunshine,
Like a cloud of dew in the heat of harvest."
5For before the harvest, when the bud is
perfect
And the sour grape is ripening in the flower,
He will both cut off the sprigs with pruning
hooks
And take away *and* cut down the branches.
6They will be left together for the mountain
birds of prey
And for the beasts of the earth;
The birds of prey will summer on them,
And all the beasts of the earth will winter
on them.

7In that time a present will be brought to the
LORD of hosts
From[a] a people tall and smooth *of skin,*
And from a people terrible from their
beginning onward,
A nation powerful and treading down,
Whose land the rivers divide—
To the place of the name of the LORD of
hosts,
To Mount Zion.

PROCLAMATION AGAINST EGYPT

19 The burden against Egypt.

Behold, the LORD rides on a swift cloud,
And will come into Egypt;
The idols of Egypt will totter at His
presence,
And the heart of Egypt will melt in its midst.

2"I will set Egyptians against Egyptians;
Everyone will fight against his brother,
And everyone against his neighbor,
City against city, kingdom against kingdom.
3The spirit of Egypt will fail in its midst;
I will destroy their counsel,
And they will consult the idols and the
charmers,
The mediums and the sorcerers.
4And the Egyptians I will give
Into the hand of a cruel master,
And a fierce king will rule over them,"
Says the Lord, the LORD of hosts.

5The waters will fail from the sea,
And the river will be wasted and dried up.

18:7 [a]Following Dead Sea Scrolls, Septuagint, and Vulgate; Masoretic Text omits *From;* Targum reads *To.*

THE MESSAGE

This people held in respect everywhere,
this people mighty and merciless,
from the land crisscrossed with rivers.

3 Everybody everywhere,
all earth-dwellers:
When you see a flag flying on the
mountain, look!
When you hear the trumpet blown,
listen!

4-6 For here's what GOD told me:

"I'm not going to say anything,
but simply look on from where I live,
Quiet as warmth that comes from the sun,
silent as dew during harvest."
And then, just before harvest, after the
blossom
has turned into a maturing grape,
He'll step in and prune back the new
shoots,
ruthlessly hack off all the growing
branches.
He'll leave them piled on the ground
for birds and animals to feed on—
Fodder for the summering birds,
fodder for the wintering animals.

7 Then tribute will be brought to
GOD-of-the-Angel-Armies,
brought from this people tall and
handsome,
This people once held in respect
everywhere,
this people once mighty and merciless,
From the land crisscrossed with rivers,
to Mount Zion, GOD's place.

ANARCHY AND CHAOS AND KILLING!

1 19 A Message concerning Egypt:
Watch this! GOD riding on a fast-moving
cloud,
moving in on Egypt!
The god-idols of Egypt shudder and shake,
Egyptians paralyzed by panic.

2-4 God says, "I'll make Egyptian fight Egyptian,
brother fight brother, neighbor fight
neighbor,
City fight city, kingdom fight kingdom—
anarchy and chaos and killing!
I'll knock the wind out of the Egyptians.
They won't know coming from going.
They'll go to their god-idols for answers;
they'll conjure ghosts and hold séances,
desperate for answers.
But I'll turn the Egyptians
over to a tyrant most cruel.
I'll put them under the rule of a mean,
merciless king."
Decree of the Master,
GOD-of-the-Angel-Armies.

5-10 The River Nile will dry up,
the riverbed baked dry in the sun.
The canals will become stagnant and stink,
every stream touching the Nile dry up.

NEW KING JAMES VERSION

[6]The rivers will turn foul;
The brooks of defense will be emptied and dried up;
The reeds and rushes will wither.
[7]The papyrus reeds by the River,[a] by the mouth of the River,
And everything sown by the River,
Will wither, be driven away, and be no more.
[8]The fishermen also will mourn;
All those will lament who cast hooks into the River,
And they will languish who spread nets on the waters.
[9]Moreover those who work in fine flax
And those who weave fine fabric will be ashamed;
[10]And its foundations will be broken.
All who make wages *will be* troubled of soul.

[11]Surely the princes of Zoan *are* fools;
Pharaoh's wise counselors give foolish counsel.
How do you say to Pharaoh, "I *am* the son of the wise,
The son of ancient kings?"
[12]Where *are* they?
Where are your wise men?
Let them tell you now,
And let them know what the LORD of hosts has purposed against Egypt.
[13]The princes of Zoan have become fools;
The princes of Noph[a] are deceived;
They have also deluded Egypt,
Those who are the mainstay of its tribes.
[14]The LORD has mingled a perverse spirit in her midst;
And they have caused Egypt to err in all her work,
As a drunken man staggers in his vomit.
[15]Neither will there be *any* work for Egypt,
Which the head or tail,
Palm branch or bulrush, may do.[a]

[16]In that day Egypt will be like women, and
will be afraid and fear because of the waving of
the hand of the LORD of hosts, which He waves
over it. [17]And the land of Judah will be a terror
to Egypt; everyone who makes mention of it will
be afraid in himself, because of the counsel of
the LORD of hosts which He has determined
against it.

EGYPT, ASSYRIA, AND ISRAEL BLESSED

[18]In that day five cities in the land of Egypt
will speak the language of Canaan and swear by
the LORD of hosts; one will be called the City of
Destruction.[a]

[19]In that day there will be an altar to the
LORD in the midst of the land of Egypt, and a pil-
lar to the LORD at its border. [20]And it will be for
a sign and for a witness to the LORD of hosts in
the land of Egypt; for they will cry to the LORD
because of the oppressors, and He will send
them a Savior and a Mighty One, and He will

19:7 [a]That is, the Nile **19:13** [a]That is, ancient Memphis **19:15** [a]Compare Isaiah 9:14–16 **19:18** [a]Some Hebrew manuscripts, Arabic, Dead Sea Scrolls, Targum, and Vulgate read *Sun;* Septuagint reads *Asedek* (literally *Righteousness*).

THE MESSAGE

River vegetation will rot away
the banks of the Nile-baked clay,
The riverbed hard and smooth,
river grasses dried up and gone with the wind.
Fishermen will complain
that the fishing's been ruined.
Textile workers will be out of work, all weavers
and workers in linen and cotton and wool
Dispirited, depressed in their forced idleness—
everyone who works for a living, jobless.

11-15 The princes of Zoan are fools,
the advisors of Pharaoh stupid.
How could any of you dare tell Pharaoh,
"Trust me: I'm wise. I know what's going on.
Why, I'm descended from the old wisdom of Egypt"?
There's not a wise man or woman left in the country.
If there were, one of them would tell you
what GOD-of-the-Angel-Armies has in mind for Egypt.
As it is, the princes of Zoan are all fools
and the princes of Memphis, dunces.
The honored pillars of your society
have led Egypt into detours and dead ends.
GOD has scrambled their brains,
Egypt's become a
falling-down-in-his-own-vomit drunk.
Egypt's hopeless, past helping,
a senile, doddering old fool.

16-17 On that Day, Egyptians will be like hysteri-
cal schoolgirls, screaming at the first hint of
action from GOD-of-the-Angel-Armies. Little
Judah will strike terror in Egyptians! Say
"Judah" to an Egyptian and see panic. The
word triggers fear of the GOD-of-the-Angel-
Armies' plan against Egypt.

18 On that Day, more than one city in Egypt
will learn to speak the language of faith and
promise to follow GOD-of-the-Angel-Armies.
One of these cities will be honored with the
title "City of the Sun."

19-22 On that Day, there will be a place of wor-
ship to GOD in the center of Egypt and a
monument to GOD at its border. It will show
how the GOD-of-the-Angel-Armies has
helped the Egyptians. When they cry out in
prayer to GOD because of oppressors, he'll
send them help, a savior who will keep them

NEW KING JAMES VERSION

deliver them. 21Then the LORD will be known to
Egypt, and the Egyptians will know the LORD in
that day, and will make sacrifice and offering;
yes, they will make a vow to the LORD and per-
form *it*. 22And the LORD will strike Egypt, He
will strike and heal *it;* they will return to the
LORD, and He will be entreated by them and heal
them.

23In that day there will be a highway from
Egypt to Assyria, and the Assyrian will come
into Egypt and the Egyptian into Assyria, and
the Egyptians will serve with the Assyrians.

24In that day Israel will be one of three with
Egypt and Assyria—a blessing in the midst of
the land, 25whom the LORD of hosts shall bless,
saying, "Blessed *is* Egypt My people, and As-
syria the work of My hands, and Israel My in-
heritance."

THE SIGN AGAINST EGYPT AND ETHIOPIA

20 In the year that Tartan[a] came to Ashdod,
when Sargon the king of Assyria sent him,
and he fought against Ashdod and took it, 2at
the same time the LORD spoke by Isaiah the son
of Amoz, saying, "Go, and remove the sackcloth
from your body, and take your sandals off your
feet." And he did so, walking naked and bare-
foot.

3Then the LORD said, "Just as My servant
Isaiah has walked naked and barefoot three
years *for* a sign and a wonder against Egypt and
Ethiopia, 4so shall the king of Assyria lead away
the Egyptians as prisoners and the Ethiopians
as captives, young and old, naked and barefoot,
with their buttocks uncovered, to the shame of
Egypt. 5Then they shall be afraid and ashamed
of Ethiopia their expectation and Egypt their
glory. 6And the inhabitant of this territory will
say in that day, 'Surely such *is* our expectation,
wherever we flee for help to be delivered from
the king of Assyria; and how shall we escape?' "

THE FALL OF BABYLON PROCLAIMED

21 The burden against the Wilderness of the
Sea.

As whirlwinds in the South pass through,
So it comes from the desert, from a terrible
land.
2A distressing vision is declared to me;
The treacherous dealer deals treacherously,
And the plunderer plunders.
Go up, O Elam!
Besiege, O Media!
All its sighing I have made to cease.

3Therefore my loins are filled with pain;
Pangs have taken hold of me, like the pangs
of a woman in labor.

20:1 [a]Or *the Commander in Chief*

THE MESSAGE

safe and take care of them. GOD will openly
show himself to the Egyptians and they'll
get to know him on that Day. They'll wor-
ship him seriously with sacrifices and burnt
offerings. They'll make vows and keep
them. GOD will wound Egypt, first hit and
then heal. Egypt will come back to GOD, and
GOD will listen to their prayers and heal
them, heal them from head to toe.

23 On that Day, there will be a highway all
the way from Egypt to Assyria: Assyrians
will have free range in Egypt and Egyptians
in Assyria. No longer rivals, they'll worship
together, Egyptians and Assyrians!

24-25 On that Day, Israel will take its place
alongside Egypt and Assyria, sharing the
blessing from the center. GOD-of-the-Angel-
Armies, who blessed Israel, will generously
bless them all: "Blessed be Egypt, my peo-
ple! . . . Blessed be Assyria, work of my
hands! . . . Blessed be Israel, my heritage!"

EXPOSED TO MOCKERY AND JEERS

1-2 20 In the year the field commander, sent by
King Sargon of Assyria, came to Ash-
dod and fought and took it, GOD told Isaiah
son of Amoz, "Go, take off your clothes and
sandals," and Isaiah did it, going about
naked and barefooted.

3-6 Then GOD said, "Just as my servant Isaiah
has walked around town naked and bare-
footed for three years as a warning sign to
Egypt and Ethiopia, so the king of Assyria is
going to come and take the Egyptians as
captives and the Ethiopians as exiles. He'll
take young and old alike and march them
out of there naked and barefooted, exposed
to mockery and jeers—the bared buttocks of
Egypt on parade! Everyone who has put
hope in Ethiopia and expected help from
Egypt will be thrown into confusion. Every-
one who lives along this coast will say,
'Look at them! Naked and barefooted, shuf-
fling off to exile! And we thought they were
our best hope, that they'd rescue us from the
king of Assyria. *Now* what's going to hap-
pen to us? How are we going to get out of
this?' "

THE BETRAYER BETRAYED

1-4 21 A Message concerning the desert at the
sea:

As tempests drive through the Negev
Desert,
coming out of the desert, that
terror-filled place,
A hard vision is given me:
The betrayer betrayed, the plunderer
plundered.
Attack, Elam!
Lay siege, Media!
Persians, attack!
Attack, Babylon!
I'll put an end to
all the moaning and groaning.
Because of this news I'm doubled up in pain,
writhing in pain like a woman having a
baby,

NEW KING JAMES VERSION

I was distressed when *I* heard *it;*
I was dismayed when *I* saw *it.*
4My heart wavered, fearfulness frightened me;
The night for which I longed He turned into fear for me.
5Prepare the table,
Set a watchman in the tower,
Eat and drink.
Arise, you princes,
Anoint the shield!

6For thus has the Lord said to me:
"Go, set a watchman,
Let him declare what he sees."
7And he saw a chariot *with* a pair of horsemen,
A chariot of donkeys, *and* a chariot of camels,
And he listened earnestly with great care.
8Then he cried, "A lion,[a] my Lord!
I stand continually on the watchtower in the daytime;
I have sat at my post every night.
9And look, here comes a chariot of men *with* a pair of horsemen!"
Then he answered and said,
"Babylon is fallen, is fallen!
And all the carved images of her gods
He has broken to the ground."

10Oh, my threshing and the grain of my floor!
That which I have heard from the LORD of hosts,
The God of Israel,
I have declared to you.

PROCLAMATION AGAINST EDOM

11The burden against Dumah.

He calls to me out of Seir,
"Watchman, what of the night?
Watchman, what of the night?"
12The watchman said,
"The morning comes, and also the night.
If you will inquire, inquire;
Return! Come back!"

PROCLAMATION AGAINST ARABIA

13The burden against Arabia.

In the forest in Arabia you will lodge,
O you traveling companies of Dedanites.
14O inhabitants of the land of Tema,
Bring water to him who is thirsty;
With their bread they met him who fled.
15For they fled from the swords, from the drawn sword,
From the bent bow, and from the distress of war.

16For thus the LORD has said to me: "Within a
year, according to the year of a hired man, all
the glory of Kedar will fail; 17and the remainder
of the number of archers, the mighty men of the
people of Kedar, will be diminished; for the
LORD God of Israel has spoken *it.*"

21:8 [a]Dead Sea Scrolls read *Then the observer cried.*

THE MESSAGE

Baffled by what I hear,
undone by what I see.
Absolutely stunned,
horror-stricken,
I had hoped for a relaxed evening,
but it has turned into a nightmare.

5 The banquet is spread,
the guests reclining in luxurious ease,
Eating and drinking, having a good time,
and then, "To arms, princes! The fight is on!"

6-9 The Master told me, "Go, post a lookout.
Have him report whatever he spots.
When he sees horses and wagons in battle formation,
lines of donkeys and columns of camels,
Tell him to keep his ear to the ground,
note every whisper, every rumor."
Just then, the lookout shouted,
"I'm at my post, Master,
Sticking to my post day after day
and all through the night!
I watched them come,
the horses and wagons in battle formation.
I heard them call out the war news in headlines:
'Babylon fallen! Fallen!
And all its precious god-idols
smashed to pieces on the ground.'"

10 Dear Israel, you've been through a lot,
you've been put through the mill.
The good news I get from
GOD-of-the-Angel-Armies,
the God of Israel, I now pass on to you.

11-12 A Message concerning Edom:

A voice calls to me
from the Seir mountains in Edom,
"Night watchman! How long till daybreak?
How long will this night last?"
The night watchman calls back,
"Morning's coming,
But for now it's still night.
If you ask me again, I'll give the same answer."

13-15 A Message concerning Arabia:

You'll have to camp out in the desert badlands,
you caravans of Dedanites.
Haul water to the thirsty,
greet fugitives with bread.
Show your desert hospitality,
you who live in Tema.
The desert's swarming with refugees
escaping the horrors of war.

16-17 The Master told me, "Hang on. Within one
year—I'll sign a contract on it!—the arrogant
brutality of Kedar, those hooligans of the
desert, will be over, nothing much left of the
Kedar toughs." The GOD of Israel says so.

NEW KING JAMES VERSION

PROCLAMATION AGAINST JERUSALEM

22 The burden against the Valley of Vision.

What ails you now, that you have all gone
up to the housetops,
2You who are full of noise,
A tumultuous city, a joyous city?
Your slain *men are* not slain with the sword,
Nor dead in battle.
3All your rulers have fled together;
They are captured by the archers.
All who are found in you are bound
together;
They have fled from afar.
4Therefore I said, "Look away from me,
I will weep bitterly;
Do not labor to comfort me
Because of the plundering of the daughter
of my people."

5For *it is* a day of trouble and treading down
and perplexity
By the Lord GOD of hosts
In the Valley of Vision—
Breaking down the walls
And of crying to the mountain.
6Elam bore the quiver
With chariots of men *and* horsemen,
And Kir uncovered the shield.
7It shall come to pass *that* your choicest
valleys
Shall be full of chariots,
And the horsemen shall set themselves in
array at the gate.

8He removed the protection of Judah.
You looked in that day to the armor of the
House of the Forest;
9You also saw the damage to the city of
David,
That it was great;
And you gathered together the waters of the
lower pool.
10You numbered the houses of Jerusalem,
And the houses you broke down
To fortify the wall.
11You also made a reservoir between the two
walls
For the water of the old pool.
But you did not look to its Maker,
Nor did you have respect for Him who
fashioned it long ago.

12And in that day the Lord GOD of hosts
Called for weeping and for mourning,
For baldness and for girding with sackcloth.
13But instead, joy and gladness,
Slaying oxen and killing sheep,
Eating meat and drinking wine:
"Let us eat and drink, for tomorrow we die!"

14Then it was revealed in my hearing by the
LORD of hosts,
"Surely for this iniquity there will be no
atonement for you,

THE MESSAGE

A COUNTRY OF COWARDS

1-3 22 A Message concerning the Valley of
Vision:

What's going on here anyway?
All this partying and noisemaking,
Shouting and cheering in the streets,
the city noisy with celebrations!
You have no brave soldiers to honor,
no combat heroes to be proud of.
Your leaders were all cowards,
captured without even lifting a sword,
A country of cowards
captured escaping the battle.

YOU LOOKED, BUT YOU NEVER LOOKED TO HIM

4-8 In the midst of the shouting, I said, "Let me
alone.
Let me grieve by myself.
Don't tell me it's going to be all right.
These people are doomed. It's *not* all
right."
For the Master, GOD-of-the-Angel-Armies,
is bringing a day noisy with mobs of
people,
Jostling and stampeding in the Valley of
Vision,
knocking down walls
and hollering to the mountains, "Attack!
Attack!"
Old enemies Elam and Kir arrive armed to
the teeth—
weapons and chariots and cavalry.
Your fine valleys are noisy with war,
chariots and cavalry charging this way
and that.
God has left Judah exposed and
defenseless.

8-11 You assessed your defenses that Day, in-
spected your arsenal of weapons in the For-
est Armory. You found the weak places in
the city walls that needed repair. You se-
cured the water supply at the Lower Pool.
You took an inventory of the houses in
Jerusalem and tore down some to get bricks
to fortify the city wall. You built a large cis-
tern to ensure plenty of water.
You looked and looked and looked, but
you never looked to him who gave you this
city, never once consulted the One who has
long had plans for this city.

12-13 The Master, GOD-of-the-Angel-Armies,
called out on that Day,
Called for a day of repentant tears,
called you to dress in somber clothes of
mourning.
But what do *you* do? You throw a party!
Eating and drinking and dancing in the
streets!
You barbecue bulls and sheep, and throw a
huge feast—
slabs of meat, kegs of beer.
"Seize the day! Eat and drink!
Tomorrow we die!"

14 GOD-of-the-Angel-Armies whispered to
me his verdict on this frivolity: "You'll pay

NEW KING JAMES VERSION

Even to your death," says the Lord GOD of
hosts.

THE JUDGMENT ON SHEBNA

15 Thus says the Lord GOD of hosts:

"Go, proceed to this steward,
To Shebna, who *is* over the house, *and say:*
16 'What have you here, and whom have you here,
That you have hewn a sepulcher here,
As he who hews himself a sepulcher on high,
Who carves a tomb for himself in a rock?
17 Indeed, the LORD will throw you away violently,
O mighty man,
And will surely seize you.
18 He will surely turn violently and toss you like a ball
Into a large country;
There you shall die, and there your glorious chariots
Shall be the shame of your master's house.
19 So I will drive you out of your office,
And from your position he will pull you down.[a]

20 'Then it shall be in that day,
That I will call My servant Eliakim the son of Hilkiah;
21 I will clothe him with your robe
And strengthen him with your belt;
I will commit your responsibility into his hand.
He shall be a father to the inhabitants of Jerusalem
And to the house of Judah.
22 The key of the house of David
I will lay on his shoulder;
So he shall open, and no one shall shut;
And he shall shut, and no one shall open.
23 I will fasten him *as* a peg in a secure place,
And he will become a glorious throne to his father's house.

24 'They will hang on him all the glory of his father's house, the offspring and the posterity, all vessels of small quantity, from the cups to all the pitchers. 25 In that day,' says the LORD of hosts, 'the peg that is fastened in the secure place will be removed and be cut down and fall, and the burden that *was* on it will be cut off; for the LORD has spoken.' "

PROCLAMATION AGAINST TYRE

23 The burden against Tyre.

Wail, you ships of Tarshish!
For it is laid waste,
So that there is no house, no harbor;
From the land of Cyprus[a] it is revealed to them.

2 Be still, you inhabitants of the coastland,
You merchants of Sidon,

22:19 [a]Septuagint omits *he will pull you down;* Syriac, Targum, and Vulgate read *I will pull you down.* 23:1 [a]Hebrew *Kittim,* western lands, especially Cyprus

THE MESSAGE

for this outrage until the day you die." The Master, GOD-of-the-Angel-Armies, says so.

THE KEY OF THE DAVIDIC HERITAGE

15-19 The Master, GOD-of-the-Angel-Armies, spoke: "Come. Go to this steward, Shebna, who is in charge of all the king's affairs, and tell him: What's going on here? You're an outsider here and yet you act like you own the place, make a big, fancy tomb for yourself where everyone can see it, making sure everyone will think you're important. GOD is about to sack you, to throw you to the dogs. He'll grab you by the hair, swing you round and round dizzyingly, and then let you go, sailing through the air like a ball, until you're out of sight. Where you'll land, nobody knows. And there you'll die, and all the stuff you've collected heaped on your grave. You've disgraced your master's house! You're fired—and good riddance!

20-24 "On that Day I'll replace Shebna. I will call my servant Eliakim son of Hilkiah. I'll dress him in your robe. I'll put your belt on him. I'll give him your authority. He'll be a father-leader to Jerusalem and the government of Judah. I'll give him the key of the Davidic heritage. He'll have the run of the place—open any door and keep it open, lock any door and keep it locked. I'll pound him like a nail into a solid wall. He'll secure the Davidic tradition. Everything will hang on him—not only the fate of Davidic descendants but also the detailed daily operations of the house, including cups and cutlery.

25 "And then the Day will come," says GOD-of-the-Angel-Armies, "when that nail will come loose and fall out, break loose from that solid wall—and everything hanging on it will go with it." That's what will happen. GOD says so.

IT WAS ALL NUMBERS, DEAD NUMBERS, PROFIT AND LOSS

1-4 23 Wail, ships of Tarshish,
your strong seaports all in ruins!
When the ships returned from Cyprus,
they saw the destruction.
Hold your tongue, you who live on the seacoast,
merchants of Sidon.

NEW KING JAMES VERSION

Whom those who cross the sea have filled.[a]
3And on great waters the grain of Shihor,
The harvest of the River,[a] *is* her revenue;
And she is a marketplace for the nations.

4Be ashamed, O Sidon;
For the sea has spoken,
The strength of the sea, saying,
"I do not labor, nor bring forth children;
Neither do I rear young men,
Nor bring up virgins."
5When the report *reaches* Egypt,
They also will be in agony at the report of Tyre.

6Cross over to Tarshish;
Wail, you inhabitants of the coastland!
7*Is* this your joyous *city*,
Whose antiquity *is* from ancient days,
Whose feet carried her far off to dwell?
8Who has taken this counsel against Tyre, the crowning *city*,
Whose merchants *are* princes,
Whose traders *are* the honorable of the earth?
9The LORD of hosts has purposed it,
To bring to dishonor the pride of all glory,
To bring into contempt all the honorable of the earth.

10Overflow through your land like the River,[a]
O daughter of Tarshish;
There is no more strength.
11He stretched out His hand over the sea,
He shook the kingdoms;
The LORD has given a commandment against Canaan
To destroy its strongholds.
12And He said, "You will rejoice no more,
O you oppressed virgin daughter of Sidon.
Arise, cross over to Cyprus;
There also you will have no rest."

13Behold, the land of the Chaldeans,
This people *which* was not;
Assyria founded it for wild beasts of the desert.
They set up its towers,
They raised up its palaces,
And brought it to ruin.

14Wail, you ships of Tarshish!
For your strength is laid waste.

15Now it shall come to pass in that day that
Tyre will be forgotten seventy years, according
to the days of one king. At the end of seventy
years it will happen to Tyre as *in* the song of the
harlot:

23:2 [a]Following Masoretic Text and Vulgate; Septuagint and Targum read *Passing over the water;* Dead Sea Scrolls read *Your messengers passing over the sea.* 23:3 [a]That is, the Nile 23:10 [a]That is, the Nile

THE MESSAGE

Your people sailed the deep seas,
buying and selling,
Making money on wheat from Shihor,
grown along the Nile—
multinational broker in grains!
Hang your head in shame, Sidon. The Sea speaks up,
the powerhouse of the ocean says,
"I've never had labor pains, never had a baby,
never reared children to adulthood,
Never gave life, never worked with life.
It was all numbers, dead numbers, profit and loss."

5 When Egypt gets the report on Tyre,
what wailing! what wringing of hands!

NOTHING LEFT HERE TO BE PROUD OF

6-12 Visit Tarshish, you who live on the seacoast.
Take a good, long look and wail—yes, cry buckets of tears!
Is this the city you remember as energetic and alive,
bustling with activity, this historic old city,
Expanding throughout the globe,
buying and selling all over the world?
And who is behind the collapse of Tyre,
the Tyre that controlled the world markets?
Tyre's merchants were the business tycoons.
Tyre's traders called all the shots.
GOD-of-the-Angel-Armies ordered the crash
to show the sordid backside of pride
and puncture the inflated reputations.
Sail for home, O ships of Tarshish.
There are no docks left in this harbor.
GOD reached out to the sea and sea traders,
threw the sea kingdoms into turmoil.
GOD ordered the destruction
of the seacoast cities, the centers of commerce.
GOD said, "There's nothing left here to be proud of,
bankrupt and bereft Sidon.
Do you want to make a new start in Cyprus?
Don't count on it. Nothing there will work out for you either."

13 Look at what happened to Babylon:
There's nothing left of it. Assyria turned it
into a desert, into a refuge for wild dogs and
stray cats. They brought in their big siege
engines, tore down the buildings, and left
nothing behind but rubble.

14 Wail, ships of Tarshish,
your strong seaports all in ruins!

15-16 For the next seventy years, a king's lifetime,
Tyre will be forgotten. At the end of the sev-
enty years, Tyre will stage a comeback, but
it will be the comeback of a worn-out
whore, as in the song:

NEW KING JAMES VERSION

16"Take a harp, go about the city,
You forgotten harlot;
Make sweet melody, sing many songs,
That you may be remembered."

17And it shall be, at the end of seventy years,
that the LORD will deal with Tyre. She will return
to her hire, and commit fornication with all the
kingdoms of the world on the face of the earth.
18Her gain and her pay will be set apart for the
LORD; it will not be treasured nor laid up, for her
gain will be for those who dwell before the
LORD, to eat sufficiently, and for fine clothing.

IMPENDING JUDGMENT ON THE EARTH

24 Behold, the LORD makes the earth empty
and makes it waste,
Distorts its surface
And scatters abroad its inhabitants.
2And it shall be:
As with the people, so with the priest;
As with the servant, so with his master;
As with the maid, so with her mistress;
As with the buyer, so with the seller;
As with the lender, so with the borrower;
As with the creditor, so with the debtor.
3The land shall be entirely emptied and
utterly plundered,
For the LORD has spoken this word.

4The earth mourns *and* fades away,
The world languishes *and* fades away;
The haughty people of the earth languish.
5The earth is also defiled under its
inhabitants,
Because they have transgressed the laws,
Changed the ordinance,
Broken the everlasting covenant.
6Therefore the curse has devoured the earth,
And those who dwell in it are desolate.
Therefore the inhabitants of the earth are
burned,
And few men *are* left.

7The new wine fails, the vine languishes,
All the merry-hearted sigh.
8The mirth of the tambourine ceases,
The noise of the jubilant ends,
The joy of the harp ceases.
9They shall not drink wine with a song;
Strong drink is bitter to those who drink it.
10The city of confusion is broken down;
Every house is shut up, so that none may go
in.
11*There is* a cry for wine in the streets,
All joy is darkened,
The mirth of the land is gone.
12In the city desolation is left,
And the gate is stricken with destruction.
13When it shall be thus in the midst of the
land among the people,
It shall be like the shaking of an olive tree,
Like the gleaning of grapes when the
vintage is done.

THE MESSAGE

"Take a harp, circle the city,
unremembered whore.
Sing your old songs, your many old songs.
Maybe someone will remember."

17-18 At the end of the seventy years, GOD will
look in on Tyre. She'll go back to her old
whoring trade, selling herself to the highest
bidder, doing anything with anyone—
promiscuous with all the kingdoms of
earth—for a fee. But everything she gets, all
the money she takes in, will be turned over
to GOD. It will not be put in banks. Her prof-
its will be put to the use of GOD-Aware, GOD-
Serving-People, providing plenty of food
and the best of clothing.

THE LANDSCAPE WILL BE A MOONSCAPE

1-3 24 Danger ahead! GOD's about to ravish
the earth
and leave it in ruins,
Rip everything out by the roots
and send everyone scurrying:
priests and laypeople alike,
owners and workers alike,
celebrities and nobodies alike,
buyers and sellers alike,
bankers and beggars alike,
the haves and have-nots alike.
The landscape will be a moonscape,
totally wasted.
And why? Because GOD says so.
He's issued the orders.

4 The earth turns gaunt and gray,
the world silent and sad,
sky and land lifeless, colorless.

EARTH POLLUTED BY ITS VERY OWN PEOPLE

5-13 Earth is polluted by its very own people,
who have broken its laws,
Disrupted its order,
violated the sacred and eternal covenant.
Therefore a curse, like a cancer,
ravages the earth.
Its people pay the price of their sacrilege.
They dwindle away, dying out one by
one.
No more wine, no more vineyards,
no more songs or singers.
The laughter of castanets is gone,
the shouts of celebrants, gone,
the laughter of fiddles, gone.
No more parties with toasts of champagne.
Serious drinkers gag on their drinks.
The chaotic cities are unlivable. Anarchy
reigns.
Every house is boarded up, condemned.
People riot in the streets for wine,
but the good times are gone forever—
no more joy for this old world.
The city is dead and deserted,
bulldozed into piles of rubble.
That's the way it will be on this earth.
This is the fate of all nations:
An olive tree shaken clean of its olives,
a grapevine picked clean of its grapes.

NEW KING JAMES VERSION

14They shall lift up their voice, they shall sing;
For the majesty of the LORD
They shall cry aloud from the sea.
15Therefore glorify the LORD in the dawning light,
The name of the LORD God of Israel in the coastlands of the sea.
16From the ends of the earth we have heard songs:
"Glory to the righteous!"
But I said, "I am ruined, ruined!
Woe to me!
The treacherous dealers have dealt treacherously,
Indeed, the treacherous dealers have dealt very treacherously."

17Fear and the pit and the snare
Are upon you, O inhabitant of the earth.
18And it shall be
That he who flees from the noise of the fear
Shall fall into the pit,
And he who comes up from the midst of the pit
Shall be caught in the snare;
For the windows from on high are open,
And the foundations of the earth are shaken.

19The earth is violently broken,
The earth is split open,
The earth is shaken exceedingly.
20The earth shall reel to and fro like a drunkard,
And shall totter like a hut;
Its transgression shall be heavy upon it,
And it will fall, and not rise again.

21It shall come to pass in that day
That the LORD will punish on high the host of exalted ones,
And on the earth the kings of the earth.
22They will be gathered together,
As prisoners are gathered in the pit,
And will be shut up in the prison;
After many days they will be punished.
23Then the moon will be disgraced
And the sun ashamed;
For the LORD of hosts will reign
On Mount Zion and in Jerusalem
And before His elders, gloriously.

PRAISE TO GOD

25 O LORD, You *are* my God.
I will exalt You,
I will praise Your name,
For You have done wonderful *things;*
Your counsels of old *are* faithfulness *and* truth.
2For You have made a city a ruin,
A fortified city a ruin,
A palace of foreigners to be a city no more;
It will never be rebuilt.
3Therefore the strong people will glorify You;
The city of the terrible nations will fear You.
4For You have been a strength to the poor,
A strength to the needy in his distress,
A refuge from the storm,
A shade from the heat;

THE MESSAGE

14-16 But there are some who will break into glad song.
Out of the west they'll shout of GOD's majesty.
Yes, from the east GOD's glory will ascend.
Every island of the sea
Will broadcast GOD's fame,
the fame of the God of Israel.
From the four winds and the seven seas we hear the singing:
"All praise to the Righteous One!"

16-20 But I said, "That's all well and good for somebody,
but all I can see is doom, doom, and more doom."
All of them at one another's throats,
yes, all of them at one another's throats.
Terror and pits and booby traps
are everywhere, whoever you are.
If you run from the terror,
you'll fall into the pit.
If you climb out of the pit,
you'll get caught in the trap.
Chaos pours out of the skies.
The foundations of earth are crumbling.
Earth is smashed to pieces,
earth is ripped to shreds,
earth is wobbling out of control,
Earth staggers like a drunk,
sways like a shack in a high wind.
Its piled-up sins are too much for it.
It collapses and won't get up again.

21-23 That's when GOD will call on the carpet
rebel powers in the skies and
Rebel kings on earth.
They'll be rounded up like prisoners in a jail,
Corralled and locked up in a jail,
and then sentenced and put to hard labor.
Shamefaced moon will cower, humiliated,
red-faced sun will skulk, disgraced,
Because GOD-of-the-Angel-Armies will take over,
ruling from Mount Zion and Jerusalem,
Splendid and glorious
before all his leaders.

GOD'S HAND RESTS ON THIS MOUNTAIN

1-5 25 GOD, you are *my* God.
I celebrate you. I praise you.
You've done your share of miracle-wonders,
well-thought-out plans, solid and sure.
Here you've reduced the city to rubble,
the strong city to a pile of stones.
The enemy Big City is a non-city,
never to be a city again.
Superpowers will see it and honor you,
brutal oppressors bow in worshipful reverence.
They'll see that you take care of the poor,
that you take care of poor people in trouble,
Provide a warm, dry place in bad weather,
provide a cool place when it's hot.

NEW KING JAMES VERSION

For the blast of the terrible ones *is* as a
storm *against* the wall.
5 You will reduce the noise of aliens,
As heat in a dry place;
As heat in the shadow of a cloud,
The song of the terrible ones will be
diminished.

6 And in this mountain
The LORD of hosts will make for all people
A feast of choice pieces,
A feast of wines on the lees,
Of fat things full of marrow,
Of well-refined wines on the lees.
7 And He will destroy on this mountain
The surface of the covering cast over all
people,
And the veil that is spread over all nations.
8 He will swallow up death forever,
And the Lord GOD will wipe away tears
from all faces;
The rebuke of His people
He will take away from all the earth;
For the LORD has spoken.

9 And it will be said in that day:
"Behold, this *is* our God;
We have waited for Him, and He will save
us.
This *is* the LORD;
We have waited for Him;
We will be glad and rejoice in His salvation."
10 For on this mountain the hand of the LORD
will rest,
And Moab shall be trampled down under
Him,
As straw is trampled down for the refuse
heap.
11 And He will spread out His hands in their
midst
As a swimmer reaches out to swim,
And He will bring down their pride
Together with the trickery of their hands.
12 The fortress of the high fort of your walls
He will bring down, lay low,
And bring to the ground, down to the dust.

A SONG OF SALVATION

26 In that day this song will be sung in the
land of Judah:

"We have a strong city;
God will appoint salvation *for* walls and
bulwarks.
2 Open the gates,
That the righteous nation which keeps the
truth may enter in.
3 You will keep *him* in perfect peace,
Whose mind *is* stayed *on You,*
Because he trusts in You.
4 Trust in the LORD forever,
For in YAH, the LORD, *is* everlasting strength.[a]
5 For He brings down those who dwell on
high,
The lofty city;
He lays it low,

26:4 [a]Or *Rock of Ages*

THE MESSAGE

Brutal oppressors are like a winter blizzard
and vicious foreigners like high noon in
the desert.
But you, shelter from the storm and shade
from the sun,
shut the mouths of the big-mouthed
bullies.

6-8 But here on this mountain,
GOD-of-the-Angel-Armies
will throw a feast for all the people of the
world,
A feast of the finest foods, a feast with
vintage wines,
a feast of seven courses, a feast lavish
with gourmet desserts.
And here on this mountain, GOD will
banish
the pall of doom hanging over all
peoples,
The shadow of doom darkening all nations.
Yes, he'll banish death forever.
And GOD will wipe the tears from every
face.
He'll remove every sign of disgrace
From his people, wherever they are.
Yes! GOD says so!

9-10 Also at that time, people will say,
"Look at what's happened! This is our
God!
We waited for him and he showed up and
saved us!
This GOD, the one we waited for!
Let's celebrate, sing the joys of his
salvation.
GOD's hand rests on this mountain!"

10-12 As for the Moabites, they'll be treated like
refuse,
waste shoveled into a cesspool.
Thrash away as they will,
like swimmers trying to stay afloat,
They'll sink in the sewage.
Their pride will pull them under.
Their famous fortifications will crumble to
nothing,
those mighty walls reduced to dust.

STRETCH THE BORDERS OF LIFE

1-6 26 At that time, this song
will be sung in the country of Judah:
We have a strong city, Salvation City,
built and fortified with salvation.
Throw wide the gates
so good and true people can enter.
People with their minds set on you,
you keep completely whole,
Steady on their feet,
because they keep at it and don't quit.
Depend on GOD and keep at it
because in the LORD GOD you have a sure
thing.
Those who lived high and mighty
he knocked off their high horse.

NEW KING JAMES VERSION

He lays it low to the ground,
He brings it down to the dust.
6The foot shall tread it down—
The feet of the poor
And the steps of the needy."

7The way of the just *is* uprightness;
O Most Upright,
You weigh the path of the just.
8Yes, in the way of Your judgments,
O LORD, we have waited for You;
The desire of *our* soul *is* for Your name
And for the remembrance of You.
9With my soul I have desired You in the night,
Yes, by my spirit within me I will seek You
early;
For when Your judgments *are* in the earth,
The inhabitants of the world will learn
righteousness.

10Let grace be shown to the wicked,
Yet he will not learn righteousness;
In the land of uprightness he will deal
unjustly,
And will not behold the majesty of the
LORD.
11LORD, *when* Your hand is lifted up, they will
not see.
But they will see and be ashamed
For *their* envy of people;
Yes, the fire of Your enemies shall devour
them.

12LORD, You will establish peace for us,
For You have also done all our works in us.
13O LORD our God, masters besides You
Have had dominion over us;
But by You only we make mention of Your
name.
14*They are* dead, they will not live;
They are deceased, they will not rise.
Therefore You have punished and destroyed
them,
And made all their memory to perish.
15You have increased the nation, O LORD,
You have increased the nation;
You are glorified;
You have expanded all the borders of the land.

16LORD, in trouble they have visited You,
They poured out a prayer *when* Your
chastening *was* upon them.
17As a woman with child
Is in pain and cries out in her pangs,
When she draws near the time of her
delivery,
So have we been in Your sight, O LORD.
18We have been with child, we have been in
pain;
We have, as it were, brought forth wind;
We have not accomplished any deliverance
in the earth,
Nor have the inhabitants of the world fallen.

19Your dead shall live;
Together with my dead body[a] they shall arise.
Awake and sing, you who dwell in dust;

26:19 [a]Following Masoretic Text and Vulgate; Syriac and Targum read *their dead bodies;* Septuagint reads *those in the tombs.*

THE MESSAGE

He used the city built on the hill
as fill for the marshes.
All the exploited and outcast peoples
build their lives on the reclaimed land.

7-10 The path of right-living people is level.
The Leveler evens the road for the
right-living.
We're in no hurry, GOD. We're content to
linger
in the path sign-posted with your
decisions.
Who you are and what you've done
are all we'll ever want.
Through the night my soul longs for you.
Deep from within me my spirit reaches
out to you.
When your decisions are on public display,
everyone learns how to live right.
If the wicked are shown grace,
they don't seem to get it.
In the land of right living, they persist in
wrong living,
blind to the splendor of GOD.

11-15 You hold your hand up high, GOD,
but they don't see it.
Open their eyes to what you do,
to see your zealous love for your people.
Shame them. Light a fire under them.
Get the attention of these enemies of
yours.
GOD, order a peaceful and whole life for us
because everything we've done, you've
done for us.
O GOD, our God, we've had other masters
rule us,
but you're the only Master we've ever
known.
The dead don't talk,
ghosts don't walk,
Because you've said, "Enough—that's all
for you,"
and wiped them off the books.
But the living you make larger than life.
The more life you give, the more glory
you display,
and stretch the borders to accommodate
more living!

16-18 O GOD, they begged you for help when they
were in trouble,
when your discipline was so heavy
they could barely whisper a prayer.
Like a woman having a baby,
writhing in distress, screaming her pain
as the baby is being born,
That's how we were because of you,
O GOD.
We were pregnant full-term.
We writhed in labor but bore no baby.
We gave birth to wind.
Nothing came of our labor.
We produced nothing living.
We couldn't save the world.

19 But friends, your dead will live,
your corpses will get to their feet.
All you dead and buried,
wake up! Sing!

NEW KING JAMES VERSION

For your dew *is like* the dew of herbs,
And the earth shall cast out the dead.

TAKE REFUGE FROM THE COMING JUDGMENT

20Come, my people, enter your chambers,
And shut your doors behind you;
Hide yourself, as it were, for a little moment,
Until the indignation is past.
21For behold, the LORD comes out of His place
To punish the inhabitants of the earth for their iniquity;
The earth will also disclose her blood,
And will no more cover her slain.

27 In that day the LORD with His severe sword, great and strong,
Will punish Leviathan the fleeing serpent,
Leviathan that twisted serpent;
And He will slay the reptile that *is* in the sea.

THE RESTORATION OF ISRAEL

2In that day sing to her,
"A vineyard of red wine![a]
3I, the LORD, keep it,
I water it every moment;
Lest any hurt it,
I keep it night and day.
4Fury *is* not in Me.
Who would set briers *and* thorns
Against Me in battle?
I would go through them,
I would burn them together.
5Or let him take hold of My strength,
That he may make peace with Me;
And he shall make peace with Me."

6Those who come He shall cause to take root in Jacob;
Israel shall blossom and bud,
And fill the face of the world with fruit.

7Has He struck Israel as He struck those who struck him?
Or has He been slain according to the slaughter of those who were slain by Him?
8In measure, by sending it away,
You contended with it.
He removes *it* by His rough wind
In the day of the east wind.
9Therefore by this the iniquity of Jacob will be covered;
And this *is* all the fruit of taking away his sin:
When he makes all the stones of the altar
Like chalkstones that are beaten to dust,
Wooden images[a] and incense altars shall not stand.

27:2 [a]Following Masoretic Text (Kittel's *Biblia Hebraica*), Bomberg, and Vulgate; Masoretic Text (*Biblia Hebraica Stuttgartensia*), some Hebrew manuscripts, and Septuagint read *delight;* Targum reads *choice vineyard.* **27:9** [a]Hebrew *Asherim,* Canaanite deities

THE MESSAGE

Your dew is morning dew
catching the first rays of sun,
The earth bursting with life,
giving birth to the dead.

20-21 Come, my people, go home
and shut yourselves in.
Go into seclusion for a while
until the punishing wrath is past,
Because GOD is sure to come from his place
to punish the wrong of the people on earth.
Earth itself will point out the bloodstains;
it will show where the murdered have been hidden away.

SELECTED GRAIN BY GRAIN

1 27 At that time GOD will unsheathe his sword,
his merciless, massive, mighty sword.
He'll punish the serpent Leviathan as it flees,
the serpent Leviathan thrashing in flight.
He'll kill that old dragon
that lives in the sea.

2-5 "At that same time, a fine vineyard will appear.
There's something to sing about!
I, GOD, tend it.
I keep it well-watered.
I keep careful watch over it
so that no one can damage it.
I'm not angry. I care.
Even if it gives me thistles and thornbushes,
I'll just pull them out
and burn them up.
Let that vine cling to me for safety,
let it find a good and whole life with me,
let it hold on for a good and whole life."

6 The days are coming when Jacob
shall put down roots,
Israel blossom and grow fresh branches,
and fill the world with its fruit.

7-11 Has GOD knocked them to the ground
as he knocked down those who hit them?
Oh, no.
Were they killed
as their killers were killed? Again, no.
He was hard on them all right. The exile was a harsh sentence.
He blew them away on a fierce blast of wind.
But the good news is that through this experience
Jacob's guilt was taken away.
The evidence that his sin is removed will be this:
He will tear down the alien altars,
take them apart stone by stone,
And then crush the stones into gravel
and clean out all the sex-and-religion shrines.

NEW KING JAMES VERSION

10Yet the fortified city *will be* desolate,
The habitation forsaken and left like a wilderness;
There the calf will feed, and there it will lie down
And consume its branches.
11When its boughs are withered, they will be broken off;
The women come *and* set them on fire.
For it *is* a people of no understanding;
Therefore He who made them will not have mercy on them,
And He who formed them will show them no favor.

12And it shall come to pass in that day
That the LORD will thresh,
From the channel of the River[a] to the Brook of Egypt;
And you will be gathered one by one,
O you children of Israel.

13So it shall be in that day:
The great trumpet will be blown;
They will come, who are about to perish in the land of Assyria,
And they who are outcasts in the land of Egypt,
And shall worship the LORD in the holy mount at Jerusalem.

WOE TO EPHRAIM AND JERUSALEM

28 Woe to the crown of pride, to the drunkards of Ephraim,
Whose glorious beauty *is* a fading flower
Which *is* at the head of the verdant valleys,
To those who are overcome with wine!
2Behold, the Lord has a mighty and strong one,
Like a tempest of hail and a destroying storm,
Like a flood of mighty waters overflowing,
Who will bring *them* down to the earth with *His* hand.
3The crown of pride, the drunkards of Ephraim,
Will be trampled underfoot;
4And the glorious beauty is a fading flower
Which *is* at the head of the verdant valley,
Like the first fruit before the summer,
Which an observer sees;
He eats it up while it is still in his hand.

5In that day the LORD of hosts will be
For a crown of glory and a diadem of beauty
To the remnant of His people,
6For a spirit of justice to him who sits in judgment,
And for strength to those who turn back the battle at the gate.

7But they also have erred through wine,
And through intoxicating drink are out of the way;
The priest and the prophet have erred through intoxicating drink,
They are swallowed up by wine,

27:12 [a]That is, the Euphrates

THE MESSAGE

For there's nothing left of that pretentious grandeur.
Nobody lives there anymore. It's unlivable.
But animals do just fine,
browsing and bedding down.
And it's not a bad place to get firewood.
Dry twigs and dead branches are plentiful.
It's the leavings of a people with no sense of God.
So, the God who made them
Will have nothing to do with them.
He who formed them will turn his back on them.

12-13 At that time GOD will thresh
from the River Euphrates to the Brook of Egypt,
And you, people of Israel,
will be selected grain by grain.
At that same time a great trumpet will be blown,
calling home the exiles from Assyria,
Welcoming home the refugees from Egypt
to come and worship GOD on the holy mountain, Jerusalem.

GOD WILL SPEAK IN BABY TALK

1-4 28 Doom to the pretentious drunks of Ephraim,
shabby and washed out and seedy—
Tipsy, sloppy-fat, beer-bellied parodies
of a proud and handsome past.
Watch closely: GOD has someone picked out,
someone tough and strong to flatten them.
Like a hailstorm, like a hurricane, like a flash flood,
one-handed he'll throw them to the ground.
Samaria, the party hat on Israel's head,
will be knocked off with one blow.
It will disappear quicker than
a piece of meat tossed to a dog.

5-6 At that time, GOD-of-the-Angel-Armies will be
the beautiful crown on the head of what's left of his people:
Energy and insights of justice to those who guide and decide,
strength and prowess to those who guard and protect.

7-8 These also, the priest and prophet, stagger from drink,

NEW KING JAMES VERSION

They are out of the way through
intoxicating drink;
They err in vision, they stumble *in*
judgment.
8For all tables are full of vomit *and* filth;
No place *is clean*.

9"Whom will he teach knowledge?
And whom will he make to understand the
message?
Those *just* weaned from milk?
Those *just* drawn from the breasts?
10For precept *must be* upon precept, precept
upon precept,
Line upon line, line upon line,
Here a little, there a little."

11For with stammering lips and another
tongue
He will speak to this people,
12To whom He said, "This *is* the rest *with
which*
You may cause the weary to rest,"
And, "This *is* the refreshing";
Yet they would not hear.
13But the word of the LORD was to them,
"Precept upon precept, precept upon precept,
Line upon line, line upon line,
Here a little, there a little,"
That they might go and fall backward, and
be broken
And snared and caught.

14Therefore hear the word of the LORD, you
scornful men,
Who rule this people who *are* in Jerusalem,
15Because you have said, "We have made a
covenant with death,
And with Sheol we are in agreement.
When the overflowing scourge passes
through,
It will not come to us,
For we have made lies our refuge,
And under falsehood we have hidden
ourselves."

A CORNERSTONE IN ZION

16Therefore thus says the Lord GOD:

"Behold, I lay in Zion a stone for a
foundation,
A tried stone, a precious cornerstone, a sure
foundation;
Whoever believes will not act hastily.
17Also I will make justice the measuring line,
And righteousness the plummet;
The hail will sweep away the refuge of lies,
And the waters will overflow the hiding
place.

THE MESSAGE

weaving, falling-down drunks,
Besotted with wine and whiskey,
can't see straight, can't talk sense.
Every table is covered with vomit.
They *live* in vomit.

9-10 "Is that so? And who do you think you are
to teach us?
Who are you to lord it over us?
We're not babies in diapers
to be talked down to by such as you—
'Da, da, da, da,
blah, blah, blah, blah.
That's a good little girl,
that's a good little boy.' "

11-12 But that's exactly how you will be
addressed.
God will speak to this people
In baby talk, one syllable at a time—
and he'll do it through foreign
oppressors.
He said before, "This is the time and place
to rest,
to give rest to the weary.
This is the place to lay down your burden."
But they won't listen.

13 So GOD will start over with the simple
basics
and address them in baby talk, one
syllable at a time—
"Da, da, da, da,
blah, blah, blah, blah.
That's a good little girl,
that's a good little boy."
And like toddlers, they will get up and fall
down,
get bruised and confused and lost.

14-15 Now listen to GOD's Message, you scoffers,
you who rule this people in Jerusalem.
You say, "We've taken out good life
insurance.
We've hedged all our bets, covered all
our bases.
No disaster can touch us. We've thought of
everything.
We're advised by the experts. We're set."

THE MEANING OF THE STONE

16-17 But the Master, GOD, has something to say
to this:

"Watch closely. I'm laying a foundation in
Zion,
a solid granite foundation, squared and
true.
And this is the meaning of the stone:
A TRUSTING LIFE WON'T TOPPLE.
I'll make justice the measuring stick
and righteousness the plumb line for the
building.
A hailstorm will knock down the
shantytown of lies,
and a flash flood will wash out the
rubble.

NEW KING JAMES VERSION

18Your covenant with death will be annulled,
And your agreement with Sheol will not stand;
When the overflowing scourge passes through,
Then you will be trampled down by it.
19As often as it goes out it will take you;
For morning by morning it will pass over,
And by day and by night;
It will be a terror just to understand the report."

20For the bed is too short to stretch out *on*,
And the covering so narrow that one cannot wrap himself *in it*.
21For the LORD will rise up as *at* Mount Perazim,
He will be angry as in the Valley of Gibeon—
That He may do His work, His awesome work,
And bring to pass His act, His unusual act.
22Now therefore, do not be mockers,
Lest your bonds be made strong;
For I have heard from the Lord GOD of hosts,
A destruction determined even upon the whole earth.

LISTEN TO THE TEACHING OF GOD

23Give ear and hear my voice,
Listen and hear my speech.
24Does the plowman keep plowing all day to sow?
Does he keep turning his soil and breaking the clods?
25When he has leveled its surface,
Does he not sow the black cummin
And scatter the cummin,
Plant the wheat in rows,
The barley in the appointed place,
And the spelt in its place?
26For He instructs him in right judgment,
His God teaches him.

27For the black cummin is not threshed with a threshing sledge,
Nor is a cartwheel rolled over the cummin;
But the black cummin is beaten out with a stick,
And the cummin with a rod.
28Bread *flour* must be ground;
Therefore he does not thresh it forever,
Break *it with* his cartwheel,
Or crush it *with* his horsemen.
29This also comes from the LORD of hosts,
Who is wonderful in counsel *and* excellent in guidance.

WOE TO JERUSALEM

29 "Woe to Ariel,[a] to Ariel, the city *where* David dwelt!
Add year to year;
Let feasts come around.
2Yet I will distress Ariel;
There shall be heaviness and sorrow,
And it shall be to Me as Ariel.
3I will encamp against you all around,
I will lay siege against you with a mound,

29:1 [a]That is, Jerusalem

THE MESSAGE

18-22 "Then you'll see that your precious life insurance policy
wasn't worth the paper it was written on.
Your careful precautions against death
were a pack of illusions and lies.
When the disaster happens,
you'll be crushed by it.
Every time disaster comes, you'll be in on it—
disaster in the morning, disaster at night."
Every report of disaster
will send you cowering in terror.
There will be no place where you can rest,
nothing to hide under.
GOD will rise to full stature,
raging as he did long ago on Mount Perazim
And in the valley of Gibeon against the Philistines.
But this time it's against *you*.
Hard to believe, but true.
Not what you'd expect, but it's coming.
Sober up, friends, and don't scoff.
Scoffing will just make it worse.
I've heard the orders issued for destruction,
orders from
GOD-of-the-Angel-Armies—ending up in an international disaster.

23-26 Listen to me now.
Give me your closest attention.
Do farmers plow and plow and do nothing but plow?
Or harrow and harrow and do nothing but harrow?
After they've prepared the ground, don't they plant?
Don't they scatter dill and spread cumin,
Plant wheat and barley in the fields
and raspberries along the borders?
They know exactly what to do and when to do it.
Their God is their teacher.

27-29 And at the harvest, the delicate herbs and spices,
the dill and cumin, are treated delicately.
On the other hand, wheat is threshed and milled, but still not endlessly.
The farmer knows how to treat each kind of grain.
He's learned it all from
GOD-of-the-Angel-Armies,
who knows everything about when and how and where.

BLIND YOURSELVES SO THAT YOU SEE NOTHING

1-4 29 Doom, Ariel, Ariel,
the city where David set camp!
Let the years add up,
let the festivals run their cycles,
But I'm not letting up on Jerusalem.
The moaning and groaning will continue.
Jerusalem to me is an Ariel.
Like David, I'll set up camp against you.
I'll set siege, build towers,

NEW KING JAMES VERSION

And I will raise siegeworks against you.
4You shall be brought down,
You shall speak out of the ground;
Your speech shall be low, out of the dust;
Your voice shall be like a medium's, out of the ground;
And your speech shall whisper out of the dust.

5"Moreover the multitude of your foes
Shall be like fine dust,
And the multitude of the terrible ones
Like chaff that passes away;
Yes, it shall be in an instant, suddenly.
6You will be punished by the LORD of hosts
With thunder and earthquake and great noise,
With storm and tempest
And the flame of devouring fire.
7The multitude of all the nations who fight against Ariel,
Even all who fight against her and her fortress,
And distress her,
Shall be as a dream of a night vision.
8It shall even be as when a hungry man dreams,
And look—he eats;
But he awakes, and his soul is still empty;
Or as when a thirsty man dreams,
And look—he drinks;
But he awakes, and indeed *he is* faint,
And his soul still craves:
So the multitude of all the nations shall be,
Who fight against Mount Zion."

THE BLINDNESS OF DISOBEDIENCE

9Pause and wonder!
Blind yourselves and be blind!
They are drunk, but not with wine;
They stagger, but not with intoxicating drink.
10For the LORD has poured out on you
The spirit of deep sleep,
And has closed your eyes, namely, the prophets;
And He has covered your heads, *namely,* the seers.

11The whole vision has become to you like
the words of a book that is sealed, which *men*
deliver to one who is literate, saying, "Read this,
please."
And he says, "I cannot, for it *is* sealed."
12Then the book is delivered to one who is il-
literate, saying, "Read this, please."
And he says, "I am not literate."
13Therefore the Lord said:

"Inasmuch as these people draw near with their mouths
And honor Me with their lips,
But have removed their hearts far from Me,
And their fear toward Me is taught by the commandment of men,
14Therefore, behold, I will again do a marvelous work
Among this people,
A marvelous work and a wonder;

THE MESSAGE

bring in siege engines, build siege ramps.
Driven into the ground, you'll speak,
you'll mumble words from the dirt—
Your voice from the ground, like the muttering of a ghost.
Your speech will whisper from the dust.

5-8 But it will be your enemies who are beaten to dust,
the mob of tyrants who will be blown away like chaff.
Because, surprise, as if out of nowhere,
a visit from GOD-of-the-Angel-Armies,
With thunderclaps, earthquakes, and earsplitting noise,
backed up by hurricanes, tornadoes, and lightning strikes,
And the mob of enemies at war with Ariel,
all who trouble and hassle and torment her,
will turn out to be a bad dream, a nightmare.
Like a hungry man dreaming he's eating steak
and wakes up hungry as ever,
Like a thirsty woman dreaming she's drinking iced tea
and wakes up thirsty as ever,
So that mob of nations at war against Mount Zion
will wake up and find they haven't shot an arrow,
haven't killed a single soul.

9-10 Drug yourselves so you feel nothing.
Blind yourselves so you see nothing.
Get drunk, but not on wine.
Black out, but not from whiskey.
For GOD has rocked you into a deep, deep sleep,
put the discerning prophets to sleep,
put the farsighted seers to sleep.

YOU HAVE EVERYTHING BACKWARD

11-12 What you've been shown here is somewhat
like a letter in a sealed envelope. If you give
it to someone who can read and tell her,
"Read this," she'll say, "I can't. The envelope
is sealed." And if you give it to someone who
can't read and tell him, "Read this," he'll say,
"I can't read."

13-14 The Master said:

"These people make a big show of saying the right thing,
but their hearts aren't in it.
Because they act like they're worshiping me
but don't mean it,
I'm going to step in and shock them awake,
astonish them, stand them on their ears.

NEW KING JAMES VERSION

For the wisdom of their wise *men* shall perish,
And the understanding of their prudent *men* shall be hidden."

15 Woe to those who seek deep to hide their counsel far from the LORD,
And their works are in the dark;
They say, "Who sees us?" and, "Who knows us?"
16 Surely you have things turned around!
Shall the potter be esteemed as the clay;
For shall the thing made say of him who made it,
"He did not make me"?
Or shall the thing formed say of him who formed it,
"He has no understanding"?

FUTURE RECOVERY OF WISDOM

17 *Is* it not yet a very little while
Till Lebanon shall be turned into a fruitful field,
And the fruitful field be esteemed as a forest?
18 In that day the deaf shall hear the words of the book,
And the eyes of the blind shall see out of obscurity and out of darkness.
19 The humble also shall increase *their* joy in the LORD,
And the poor among men shall rejoice
In the Holy One of Israel.
20 For the terrible one is brought to nothing,
The scornful one is consumed,
And all who watch for iniquity are cut off—
21 Who make a man an offender by a word,
And lay a snare for him who reproves in the gate,
And turn aside the just by empty words.

22 Therefore thus says the LORD, who re-
deemed Abraham, concerning the house of Ja-
cob:

"Jacob shall not now be ashamed,
Nor shall his face now grow pale;
23 But when he sees his children,
The work of My hands, in his midst,
They will hallow My name,
And hallow the Holy One of Jacob,
And fear the God of Israel.
24 These also who erred in spirit will come to understanding,
And those who complained will learn doctrine."

THE MESSAGE

The wise ones who had it all figured out
will be exposed as fools.
The smart people who thought they knew everything
will turn out to know nothing."

15-16 Doom to you! You pretend to have the inside track.
You shut GOD out and work behind the scenes,
Plotting the future as if you knew everything,
acting mysterious, never showing your hand.
You have everything backward!
You treat the potter as a lump of clay.
Does a book say to its author,
"He didn't write a word of me"?
Does a meal say to the woman who cooked it,
"She had nothing to do with this"?

17-21 And then before you know it,
and without you having anything to do with it,
Wasted Lebanon will be transformed into lush gardens,
and Mount Carmel reforested.
At that time the deaf will hear
word-for-word what's been written.
After a lifetime in the dark,
the blind will see.
The castoffs of society will be laughing and dancing in GOD,
the down-and-outs shouting praise to The Holy of Israel.
For there'll be no more gangs on the street.
Cynical scoffers will be an extinct species.
Those who never missed a chance to hurt or demean
will never be heard of again:
Gone the people who corrupted the courts,
gone the people who cheated the poor,
gone the people who victimized the innocent.

22-24 And finally this, GOD's Message for the family of Jacob,
the same GOD who redeemed Abraham:
"No longer will Jacob hang his head in shame,
no longer grow gaunt and pale with waiting.
For he's going to see his children,
my personal gift to him—lots of children.
And these children will honor me
by living holy lives.
In holy worship they'll honor the Holy One of Jacob
and stand in holy awe of the God of Israel.
Those who got off-track will get back on-track,
and complainers and whiners learn gratitude."

NEW KING JAMES VERSION

FUTILE CONFIDENCE IN EGYPT

30 "Woe to the rebellious children," says the LORD,
"Who take counsel, but not of Me,
And who devise plans, but not of My Spirit,
That they may add sin to sin;
2 Who walk to go down to Egypt,
And have not asked My advice,
To strengthen themselves in the strength of Pharaoh,
And to trust in the shadow of Egypt!
3 Therefore the strength of Pharaoh
Shall be your shame,
And trust in the shadow of Egypt
Shall be *your* humiliation.
4 For his princes were at Zoan,
And his ambassadors came to Hanes.
5 They were all ashamed of a people *who* could not benefit them,
Or be help or benefit,
But a shame and also a reproach."

6 The burden against the beasts of the South.

Through a land of trouble and anguish,
From which *came* the lioness and lion,
The viper and fiery flying serpent,
They will carry their riches on the backs of young donkeys,
And their treasures on the humps of camels,
To a people *who* shall not profit;
7 For the Egyptians shall help in vain and to no purpose.
Therefore I have called her
Rahab-Hem-Shebeth.[a]

A REBELLIOUS PEOPLE

8 Now go, write it before them on a tablet,
And note it on a scroll,
That it may be for time to come,
Forever and ever:
9 That this *is* a rebellious people,
Lying children,
Children *who* will not hear the law of the LORD;
10 Who say to the seers, "Do not see,"
And to the prophets, "Do not prophesy to us right things;
Speak to us smooth things, prophesy deceits.
11 Get out of the way,
Turn aside from the path,
Cause the Holy One of Israel
To cease from before us."

12 Therefore thus says the Holy One of Israel:

"Because you despise this word,
And trust in oppression and perversity,
And rely on them,
13 Therefore this iniquity shall be to you
Like a breach ready to fall,
A bulge in a high wall,
Whose breaking comes suddenly, in an instant.
14 And He shall break it like the breaking of the potter's vessel,
Which is broken in pieces;

30:7 [a]Literally *Rahab Sits Idle*

THE MESSAGE

ALL SHOW, NO SUBSTANCE

1-5 30 "Doom, rebel children!"
GOD's Decree.
"You make plans, but not mine.
You make deals, but not in my Spirit.
You pile sin on sin,
one sin on top of another,
Going off to Egypt
without so much as asking me,
Running off to Pharaoh for protection,
expecting to hide out in Egypt.
Well, some protection Pharaoh will be!
Some hideout, Egypt!
They look big and important, true,
with officials strategically established in
Zoan in the north and Hanes in the south,
but there's nothing to them.
Anyone stupid enough to trust them
will end up looking stupid—
All show, no substance,
an embarrassing farce."

6-7 And this note on the animals of the Negev
encountered on the road to Egypt:
A most dangerous, treacherous route,
menaced by lions and deadly snakes.
And you're going to lug all your stuff down *there*,
your donkeys and camels loaded down with bribes,
Thinking you can buy protection
from that hollow farce of a nation?
Egypt is all show, no substance.
My name for her is Toothless Dragon.

THIS IS A REBEL GENERATION

8-11 So, go now and write all this down.
Put it in a book
So that the record will be there
to instruct the coming generations,
Because this is a rebel generation,
a people who lie,
A people unwilling to listen
to anything GOD tells them.
They tell their spiritual leaders,
"Don't bother us with irrelevancies."
They tell their preachers,
"Don't waste our time on impracticalities.
Tell us what makes us feel better.
Don't bore us with obsolete religion.
That stuff means nothing to us.
Quit hounding us with The Holy of Israel."

12-14 Therefore, The Holy of Israel says this:
"Because you scorn this Message,
Preferring to live by injustice
and shape your lives on lies,
This perverse way of life
will be like a towering, badly built wall
That slowly, slowly tilts and shifts,
and then one day, without warning, collapses—
Smashed to bits like a piece of pottery,

NEW KING JAMES VERSION

He shall not spare.
So there shall not be found among its fragments
A shard to take fire from the hearth,
Or to take water from the cistern."

15For thus says the Lord GOD, the Holy One of Israel:

"In returning and rest you shall be saved;
In quietness and confidence shall be your strength."
But you would not,
16And you said, "No, for we will flee on horses"—
Therefore you shall flee!
And, "We will ride on swift *horses*"—
Therefore those who pursue you shall be swift!

17One thousand *shall flee* at the threat of one,
At the threat of five you shall flee,
Till you are left as a pole on top of a mountain
And as a banner on a hill.

GOD WILL BE GRACIOUS

18Therefore the LORD will wait, that He may be gracious to you;
And therefore He will be exalted, that He may have mercy on you.
For the LORD *is* a God of justice;
Blessed *are* all those who wait for Him.

19For the people shall dwell in Zion at Jerusalem;
You shall weep no more.
He will be very gracious to you at the sound of your cry;
When He hears it, He will answer you.
20And *though* the Lord gives you
The bread of adversity and the water of affliction,
Yet your teachers will not be moved into a corner anymore,
But your eyes shall see your teachers.
21Your ears shall hear a word behind you, saying,
"This *is* the way, walk in it,"
Whenever you turn to the right hand
Or whenever you turn to the left.
22You will also defile the covering of your images of silver,
And the ornament of your molded images of gold.
You will throw them away as an unclean thing;
You will say to them, "Get away!"

23Then He will give the rain for your seed
With which you sow the ground,
And bread of the increase of the earth;
It will be fat and plentiful.
In that day your cattle will feed
In large pastures.
24Likewise the oxen and the young donkeys that work the ground
Will eat cured fodder,
Which has been winnowed with the shovel and fan.

THE MESSAGE

smashed beyond recognition or repair,
Useless, a pile of debris
to be swept up and thrown in the trash."

GOD TAKES THE TIME TO DO EVERYTHING RIGHT

15-17 GOD, the Master, The Holy of Israel,
has this solemn counsel:
"Your salvation requires you to turn back to me
and stop your silly efforts to save yourselves.
Your strength will come from settling down
in complete dependence on me—
The very thing
you've been unwilling to do.
You've said, 'Nothing doing! We'll rush off on horseback!'
You'll rush off, all right! Just not far enough!
You've said, 'We'll ride off on fast horses!'
Do you think your pursuers ride old nags?
Think again: A thousand of you will scatter before one attacker.
Before a mere five you'll all run off.
There'll be nothing left of you—
a flagpole on a hill with no flag,
a signpost on a roadside with the sign torn off."

18 But GOD's not finished. He's waiting
around to be gracious to you.
He's gathering strength to show mercy to you.
GOD takes the time to do everything right—
everything.
Those who wait around for him are the lucky ones.

19-22 Oh yes, people of Zion, citizens of
Jerusalem, your time of tears is over. Cry for
help and you'll find it's grace and more
grace. The moment he hears, he'll answer.
Just as the Master kept you alive during the
hard times, he'll keep your teacher alive and
present among you. Your teacher will be
right there, local and on the job, urging you
on whenever you wander left or right: "This
is the right road. Walk down this road."
You'll scrap your expensive and fashionable
god-images. You'll throw them in the trash
as so much garbage, saying, "Good riddance!"

23-26 God will provide rain for the seeds you
sow. The grain that grows will be abundant.
Your cattle will range far and wide. Oblivious
to war and earthquake, the oxen and
donkeys you use for hauling and plowing
will be fed well near running brooks that

NEW KING JAMES VERSION

[25]There will be on every high mountain
And on every high hill
Rivers *and* streams of waters,
In the day of the great slaughter,
When the towers fall.
[26]Moreover the light of the moon will be as the light of the sun,
And the light of the sun will be sevenfold,
As the light of seven days,
In the day that the LORD binds up the bruise of His people
And heals the stroke of their wound.

JUDGMENT ON ASSYRIA

[27]Behold, the name of the LORD comes from afar,
Burning *with* His anger,
And *His* burden *is* heavy;
His lips are full of indignation,
And His tongue like a devouring fire.
[28]His breath is like an overflowing stream,
Which reaches up to the neck,
To sift the nations with the sieve of futility;
And *there shall be* a bridle in the jaws of the people,
Causing *them* to err.

[29]You shall have a song
As in the night *when* a holy festival is kept,
And gladness of heart as when one goes with a flute,
To come into the mountain of the LORD,
To the Mighty One of Israel.
[30]The LORD will cause His glorious voice to be heard,
And show the descent of His arm,
With the indignation of *His* anger
And the flame of a devouring fire,
With scattering, tempest, and hailstones.
[31]For through the voice of the LORD
Assyria will be beaten down,
As He strikes with the rod.
[32]And *in* every place where the staff of punishment passes,
Which the LORD lays on him,
It will be with tambourines and harps;
And in battles of brandishing He will fight with it.
[33]For Tophet *was* established of old,
Yes, for the king it is prepared.
He has made *it* deep and large;
Its pyre *is* fire with much wood;
The breath of the LORD, like a stream of brimstone,
Kindles it.

THE FOLLY OF NOT TRUSTING GOD

31 Woe to those who go down to Egypt for help,
And rely on horses,
Who trust in chariots because *they are* many,
And in horsemen because they are very strong,
But who do not look to the Holy One of Israel,
Nor seek the LORD!
[2]Yet He also *is* wise and will bring disaster,
And will not call back His words,

THE MESSAGE

flow freely from mountains and hills. Better yet, on the Day GOD heals his people of the wounds and bruises from the time of punishment, moonlight will flare into sunlight, and sunlight, like a whole week of sunshine at once, will flood the land.

27-28 Look, GOD's on his way,
and from a long way off!
Smoking with anger,
immense as he comes into view,
Words steaming from his mouth,
searing, indicting words!
A torrent of words, a flash flood of words
sweeping everyone into the vortex of his words.
He'll shake down the nations in a sieve of destruction,
herd them into a dead end.

29-33 But *you* will sing,
sing through an all-night holy feast!
Your hearts will burst with song,
make music like the sound of flutes on parade,
En route to the mountain of GOD,
on the way to the Rock of Israel.
GOD will sound out in grandiose thunder,
display his hammering arm,
Furiously angry, showering sparks—
cloudburst, storm, hail!
Oh yes, at GOD's thunder
Assyria will cower under the clubbing.
Every blow GOD lands on them with his club
is in time to the music of drums and pipes,
GOD in all-out, two-fisted battle,
fighting against them.
Topheth's fierce fires are well prepared,
ready for the Assyrian king.
The Topheth furnace is deep and wide,
well stoked with hot-burning wood.
GOD's breath, like a river of burning pitch,
starts the fire.

IMPRESSED BY MILITARY MATHEMATICS

1-3 31 Doom to those who go off to Egypt
thinking that horses can help them,
Impressed by military mathematics,
awed by sheer numbers of chariots and riders—
And to The Holy of Israel, not even a glance,
not so much as a prayer to GOD.
Still, he must be reckoned with,
a most wise God who knows what he's doing.
He can call down catastrophe.
He's a God who does what he says.

NEW KING JAMES VERSION

But will arise against the house of evildoers,
And against the help of those who work iniquity.
3Now the Egyptians *are* men, and not God;
And their horses are flesh, and not spirit.
When the LORD stretches out His hand,
Both he who helps will fall,
And he who is helped will fall down;
They all will perish together.

GOD WILL DELIVER JERUSALEM

4For thus the LORD has spoken to me:

"As a lion roars,
And a young lion over his prey
(When a multitude of shepherds is summoned against him,
He will not be afraid of their voice
Nor be disturbed by their noise),
So the LORD of hosts will come down
To fight for Mount Zion and for its hill.
5Like birds flying about,
So will the LORD of hosts defend Jerusalem.
Defending, He will also deliver *it;*
Passing over, He will preserve *it.*"

6Return *to Him* against whom the children of
Israel have deeply revolted. 7For in that day
every man shall throw away his idols of silver
and his idols of gold—sin, which your own
hands have made for yourselves.

8"Then Assyria shall fall by a sword not of man,
And a sword not of mankind shall devour him.
But he shall flee from the sword,
And his young men shall become forced labor.
9He shall cross over to his stronghold for fear,
And his princes shall be afraid of the banner,"
Says the LORD,
Whose fire *is* in Zion
And whose furnace *is* in Jerusalem.

A REIGN OF RIGHTEOUSNESS

32 Behold, a king will reign in righteousness,
And princes will rule with justice.
2A man will be as a hiding place from the wind,
And a cover from the tempest,
As rivers of water in a dry place,
As the shadow of a great rock in a weary land.
3The eyes of those who see will not be dim,
And the ears of those who hear will listen.
4Also the heart of the rash will understand knowledge,
And the tongue of the stammerers will be ready to speak plainly.

5The foolish person will no longer be called generous,
Nor the miser said *to be* bountiful;

THE MESSAGE

He intervenes in the work of those who do wrong,
stands up against interfering evildoers.
Egyptians are mortal, not God,
and their horses are flesh, not Spirit.
When GOD gives the signal, helpers and helped alike
will fall in a heap and share the same dirt grave.

4-5 This is what GOD told me:

"Like a lion, king of the beasts,
that gnaws and chews and worries its prey,
Not fazed in the least by a bunch of shepherds
who arrive to chase it off,
So GOD-of-the-Angel-Armies comes down
to fight on Mount Zion, to make war from its heights.
And like a huge eagle hovering in the sky,
GOD-of-the-Angel-Armies protects Jerusalem.
I'll protect and rescue it.
Yes, I'll hover and deliver."

6-7 Repent, return, dear Israel, to the One
you so cruelly abandoned. On the day you
return, you'll throw away—every last one of
you—the no-gods your sinful hands made
from metal and wood.

8-9 "Assyrians will fall dead,
killed by a sword-thrust but not by a soldier,
laid low by a sword not swung by a mortal.
Assyrians will run from that sword, run for their lives,
and their prize young men made slaves.
Terrorized, that rock-solid people will fall to pieces,
their leaders scatter hysterically."
GOD's Decree on Assyria.
His fire blazes in Zion,
his furnace burns hot in Jerusalem.

SAFE HOUSES, QUIET GARDENS

1-8 32 But look! A king will rule in the right way,
and his leaders will carry out justice.
Each one will stand as a shelter from high winds,
provide safe cover in stormy weather.
Each will be cool running water in parched land,
a huge granite outcrop giving shade in the desert.
Anyone who looks will see,
anyone who listens will hear.
The impulsive will make sound decisions,
the tongue-tied will speak with eloquence.
No more will fools become celebrities,
nor crooks be rewarded with fame.

NEW KING JAMES VERSION

6For the foolish person will speak
foolishness,
And his heart will work iniquity:
To practice ungodliness,
To utter error against the LORD,
To keep the hungry unsatisfied,
And he will cause the drink of the thirsty to
fail.
7Also the schemes of the schemer *are* evil;
He devises wicked plans
To destroy the poor with lying words,
Even when the needy speaks justice.
8But a generous man devises generous
things,
And by generosity he shall stand.

CONSEQUENCES OF COMPLACENCY

9Rise up, you women who are at ease,
Hear my voice;
You complacent daughters,
Give ear to my speech.
10In a year and *some* days
You will be troubled, you complacent
women;
For the vintage will fail,
The gathering will not come.
11Tremble, you *women* who are at ease;
Be troubled, you complacent ones;
Strip yourselves, make yourselves bare,
And gird *sackcloth* on *your* waists.

12People shall mourn upon their breasts
For the pleasant fields, for the fruitful vine.
13On the land of my people will come up
thorns *and* briers,
Yes, on all the happy homes *in* the joyous
city;
14Because the palaces will be forsaken,
The bustling city will be deserted.
The forts and towers will become lairs
forever,
A joy of wild donkeys, a pasture of flocks—
15Until the Spirit is poured upon us from on
high,
And the wilderness becomes a fruitful field,
And the fruitful field is counted as a forest.

THE PEACE OF GOD'S REIGN

16Then justice will dwell in the wilderness,
And righteousness remain in the fruitful
field.
17The work of righteousness will be peace,
And the effect of righteousness, quietness
and assurance forever.
18My people will dwell in a peaceful
habitation,
In secure dwellings, and in quiet resting
places,
19Though hail comes down on the forest,
And the city is brought low in humiliation.

20Blessed *are* you who sow beside all waters,
Who send out freely the feet of the ox and
the donkey.

THE MESSAGE

For fools are fools and that's that,
thinking up new ways to do mischief.
They leave a wake of wrecked lives
and lies about GOD,
Turning their backs on the homeless
hungry,
ignoring those dying of thirst in the
streets.
And the crooks? Underhanded sneaks they
are,
inventive in sin and scandal,
Exploiting the poor with scams and lies,
unmoved by the victimized poor.
But those who are noble make noble plans,
and stand for what is noble.

9-14 Take your stand, indolent women!
Listen to me!
Indulgent, indolent women,
listen closely to what I have to say.
In just a little over a year from now,
you'll be shaken out of your lazy lives.
The grape harvest will fail,
and there'll be no fruit on the trees.
Oh tremble, you indolent women.
Get serious, you pampered dolls!
Strip down and discard your silk fineries.
Put on funeral clothes.
Shed honest tears for the lost harvest,
the failed vintage.
Weep for my people's gardens and farms
that grow nothing but thistles and
thornbushes.
Cry tears, real tears, for the happy homes
no longer happy,
the merry city no longer merry.
The royal palace is deserted,
the bustling city quiet as a morgue,
The emptied parks and playgrounds
taken over by wild animals,
delighted with their new home.

15-20 Yes, weep and grieve until the Spirit is
poured
down on us from above
And the badlands desert grows crops
and the fertile fields become forests.
Justice will move into the badlands desert.
Right will build a home in the fertile
field.
And where there's Right, there'll be Peace
and the progeny of Right: quiet lives and
endless trust.
My people will live in a peaceful
neighborhood—
in safe houses, in quiet gardens.
The forest of your pride will be clear-cut,
the city showing off your power leveled.
But you will enjoy a blessed life,
planting well-watered fields and
gardens,
with your farm animals grazing freely.

NEW KING JAMES VERSION

A PRAYER IN DEEP DISTRESS

33 Woe to you who plunder, though you *have*
not *been* plundered;
And you who deal treacherously, though they
have not dealt treacherously with you!
When you cease plundering,
You will be plundered;
When you make an end of dealing
treacherously,
They will deal treacherously with you.

2 O LORD, be gracious to us;
We have waited for You.
Be their[a] arm every morning,
Our salvation also in the time of trouble.
3 At the noise of the tumult the people shall
flee;
When You lift Yourself up, the nations shall
be scattered;
4 And Your plunder shall be gathered
Like the gathering of the caterpillar;
As the running to and fro of locusts,
He shall run upon them.

5 The LORD is exalted, for He dwells on high;
He has filled Zion with justice and
righteousness.
6 Wisdom and knowledge will be the stability
of your times,
And the strength of salvation;
The fear of the LORD *is* His treasure.

7 Surely their valiant ones shall cry outside,
The ambassadors of peace shall weep
bitterly.
8 The highways lie waste,
The traveling man ceases.
He has broken the covenant,
He has despised the cities,[a]
He regards no man.
9 The earth mourns *and* languishes,
Lebanon is shamed *and* shriveled;
Sharon is like a wilderness,
And Bashan and Carmel shake off *their*
fruits.

IMPENDING JUDGMENT ON ZION

10 "Now I will rise," says the LORD;
"Now I will be exalted,
Now I will lift Myself up.
11 You shall conceive chaff,
You shall bring forth stubble;
Your breath, *as* fire, shall devour you.
12 And the people shall be *like* the burnings of
lime;
Like thorns cut up they shall be burned in
the fire.
13 Hear, you *who are* afar off, what I have done;
And you *who are* near, acknowledge My
might."

14 The sinners in Zion are afraid;
Fearfulness has seized the hypocrites:
"Who among us shall dwell with the
devouring fire?

33:2 [a]Septuagint omits *their;* Syriac, Targum, and Vulgate read *our.* **33:8** [a]Following Masoretic Text and Vulgate; Dead Sea Scrolls read *witnesses;* Septuagint omits *cities;* Targum reads *They have been removed from their cities.*

THE MESSAGE

THE GROUND UNDER OUR FEET MOURNS

1 33 Doom to you, Destroyer,
not yet destroyed;
And doom to you, Betrayer,
not yet betrayed.
When you finish destroying,
your turn will come—destroyed!
When you quit betraying,
your turn will come—betrayed!

2-4 GOD, treat us kindly. You're our only hope.
First thing in the morning, be there for
us!
When things go bad, help us out!
You spoke in thunder and everyone ran.
You showed up and nations scattered.
Your people, for a change, got in on the
loot,
picking the field clean of the enemy
spoils.

5-6 GOD is supremely esteemed. His center
holds.
Zion brims over with all that is just and
right.
GOD keeps your days stable and secure—
salvation, wisdom, and knowledge in
surplus,
and best of all, Zion's treasure,
Fear-of-GOD.

7-9 But look! Listen!
Tough men weep openly.
Peacemaking diplomats are in bitter
tears.
The roads are empty—
not a soul out on the streets.
The peace treaty is broken,
its conditions violated,
its signers reviled.
The very ground under our feet mourns,
the Lebanon mountains hang their
heads,
Flowering Sharon is a weed-choked gully,
and the forests of Bashan and Carmel?
Bare branches.

10-12 "Now I'm stepping in," GOD says.
"From now on, I'm taking over.
The gloves come off. Now see how
mighty I am.
There's nothing to you.
Pregnant with chaff, you produce straw
babies;
full of hot air, you self-destruct.
You're good for nothing but fertilizer and
fuel.
Earth to earth—and the sooner the
better.

13-14 "If you're far away,
get the reports on what I've done,
And if you're in the neighborhood,
pay attention to my record.
The sinners in Zion are rightly terrified;
the godless are at their wit's end:
'Who among us can survive this firestorm?

NEW KING JAMES VERSION

Who among us shall dwell with everlasting burnings?"
15He who walks righteously and speaks uprightly,
He who despises the gain of oppressions,
Who gestures with his hands, refusing bribes,
Who stops his ears from hearing of bloodshed,
And shuts his eyes from seeing evil:
16He will dwell on high;
His place of defense *will be* the fortress of rocks;
Bread will be given him,
His water *will be* sure.

THE LAND OF THE MAJESTIC KING

17Your eyes will see the King in His beauty;
They will see the land that is very far off.
18Your heart will meditate on terror:
"Where *is* the scribe?
Where *is* he who weighs?
Where *is* he who counts the towers?"
19You will not see a fierce people,
A people of obscure speech, beyond perception,
Of a stammering tongue *that you* cannot understand.

20Look upon Zion, the city of our appointed feasts;
Your eyes will see Jerusalem, a quiet home,
A tabernacle *that* will not be taken down;
Not one of its stakes will ever be removed,
Nor will any of its cords be broken.
21But there the majestic LORD *will be* for us
A place of broad rivers *and* streams,
In which no galley with oars will sail,
Nor majestic ships pass by
22(For the LORD *is* our Judge,
The LORD *is* our Lawgiver,
The LORD *is* our King;
He will save us);
23Your tackle is loosed,
They could not strengthen their mast,
They could not spread the sail.

Then the prey of great plunder is divided;
The lame take the prey.
24And the inhabitant will not say, "I am sick";
The people who dwell in it *will be* forgiven *their* iniquity.

JUDGMENT ON THE NATIONS

34 Come near, you nations, to hear;
And heed, you people!
Let the earth hear, and all that is in it,
The world and all things that come forth from it.
2For the indignation of the LORD *is* against all nations,

THE MESSAGE

Who of us can get out of this purge with our lives?'"

15-16 The answer's simple:
Live right,
speak the truth,
despise exploitation,
refuse bribes,
reject violence,
avoid evil amusements.
This is how you raise your standard of living!
A safe and stable way to live.
A nourishing, satisfying way to live.

GOD MAKES ALL THE DECISIONS HERE

17-19 Oh, you'll see the king—a beautiful sight!
And you'll take in the wide vistas of land.
In your mind you'll go over the old terrors:
"What happened to that Assyrian inspector who condemned and confiscated?
And the one who gouged us of taxes?
And that cheating moneychanger?"
Gone! Out of sight forever! Their insolence nothing now but a fading stain on the carpet!
No more putting up with a language you can't understand,
no more sounds of gibberish in your ears.

20-22 Just take a look at Zion, will you?
Centering our worship in festival feasts!
Feast your eyes on Jerusalem,
a quiet and permanent place to live.
No more pulling up stakes and moving on,
no more patched-together lean-tos.
Instead, GOD! GOD majestic, God himself the place
in a country of broad rivers and streams,
But rivers blocked to invading ships,
off-limits to predatory pirates.
For GOD makes all the decisions here. GOD is our king.
GOD runs this place and he'll keep us safe.

23 Ha! Your sails are in shreds,
your mast wobbling,
your hold leaking.
The plunder is free for the taking, free for all—
for weak and strong, insiders and outsiders.

24 No one in Zion will say, "I'm sick."
Best of all, they'll all live guilt-free.

THE FIRES BURNING DAY AND NIGHT

1 34 Draw in close now, nations. Listen carefully,
you people. Pay attention!
Earth, you, too, and everything in you.
World, and all that comes from you.

2-4 And here's why: GOD is angry,
good and angry with all the nations,

NEW KING JAMES VERSION

And *His* fury against all their armies;
He has utterly destroyed them,
He has given them over to the slaughter.
3Also their slain shall be thrown out;
Their stench shall rise from their corpses,
And the mountains shall be melted with their blood.
4All the host of heaven shall be dissolved,
And the heavens shall be rolled up like a scroll;
All their host shall fall down
As the leaf falls from the vine,
And as *fruit* falling from a fig tree.

5"For My sword shall be bathed in heaven;
Indeed it shall come down on Edom,
And on the people of My curse, for judgment.
6The sword of the LORD is filled with blood,
It is made overflowing with fatness,
With the blood of lambs and goats,
With the fat of the kidneys of rams.
For the LORD has a sacrifice in Bozrah,
And a great slaughter in the land of Edom.
7The wild oxen shall come down with them,
And the young bulls with the mighty bulls;
Their land shall be soaked with blood,
And their dust saturated with fatness."

8For *it is* the day of the LORD's vengeance,
The year of recompense for the cause of Zion.
9Its streams shall be turned into pitch,
And its dust into brimstone;
Its land shall become burning pitch.
10It shall not be quenched night or day;
Its smoke shall ascend forever.
From generation to generation it shall lie waste;
No one shall pass through it forever and ever.
11But the pelican and the porcupine shall possess it,
Also the owl and the raven shall dwell in it.
And He shall stretch out over it
The line of confusion and the stones of emptiness.
12They shall call its nobles to the kingdom,
But none *shall be* there, and all its princes shall be nothing.

13And thorns shall come up in its palaces,
Nettles and brambles in its fortresses;
It shall be a habitation of jackals,
A courtyard for ostriches.
14The wild beasts of the desert shall also meet with the jackals,
And the wild goat shall bleat to its companion;
Also the night creature shall rest there,
And find for herself a place of rest.
15There the arrow snake shall make her nest and lay *eggs*
And hatch, and gather *them* under her shadow;
There also shall the hawks be gathered,
Every one with her mate.

THE MESSAGE

So blazingly angry at their arms and armies
that he's going to rid earth of them, wipe them out.
The corpses, thrown in a heap,
will stink like the town dump in midsummer,
Their blood flowing off the mountains
like creeks in spring runoff.
Stars will fall out of the sky
like overripe, rotting fruit in the orchard,
And the sky itself will be folded up like a blanket
and put away in a closet.
All that army of stars, shriveled to nothing,
like leaves and fruit in autumn, dropping and rotting!

5-7 "Once I've finished with earth and sky,
I'll start in on Edom.
I'll come down hard on Edom,
a people I've slated for total termination."
GOD has a sword, thirsty for blood and more blood,
a sword hungry for well-fed flesh,
Lamb and goat blood,
the suet-rich kidneys of rams.
Yes, GOD has scheduled a sacrifice in Bozrah, the capital,
the whole country of Edom a slaughterhouse.
A wholesale slaughter, wild animals
and farm animals alike slaughtered.
The whole country soaked with blood,
all the ground greasy with fat.

8-15 It's GOD's scheduled time for vengeance,
the year all Zion's accounts are settled.
Edom's streams will flow sluggish, thick with pollution,
the soil sterile, poisoned with waste,
The whole country
a smoking, stinking garbage dump—
The fires burning day and night,
the skies black with endless smoke.
Generation after generation of wasteland—
no more travelers through this country!
Vultures and skunks will police the streets;
owls and crows will feel at home there.
God will reverse creation. Chaos!
He will cancel fertility. Emptiness!
Leaders will have no one to lead.
They'll name it No Kingdom There,
A country where all kings
and princes are unemployed.
Thistles will take over, covering the castles,
fortresses conquered by weeds and thornbushes.
Wild dogs will prowl the ruins,
ostriches have the run of the place.
Wildcats and hyenas will hunt together,
demons and devils dance through the night.
The night-demon Lilith, evil and rapacious,
will establish permanent quarters.
Scavenging carrion birds will breed and brood,
infestations of ominous evil.

NEW KING JAMES VERSION

16"Search from the book of the LORD, and read:
Not one of these shall fail;
Not one shall lack her mate.
For My mouth has commanded it, and His
Spirit has gathered them.
17He has cast the lot for them,
And His hand has divided it among them
with a measuring line.
They shall possess it forever;
From generation to generation they shall
dwell in it."

THE FUTURE GLORY OF ZION

35 The wilderness and the wasteland shall
be glad for them,
And the desert shall rejoice and blossom as
the rose;
2It shall blossom abundantly and rejoice,
Even with joy and singing.
The glory of Lebanon shall be given to it,
The excellence of Carmel and Sharon.
They shall see the glory of the LORD,
The excellency of our God.

3Strengthen the weak hands,
And make firm the feeble knees.
4Say to those *who are* fearful-hearted,
"Be strong, do not fear!
Behold, your God will come *with*
vengeance,
With the recompense of God;
He will come and save you."

5Then the eyes of the blind shall be opened,
And the ears of the deaf shall be unstopped.
6Then the lame shall leap like a deer,
And the tongue of the dumb sing.
For waters shall burst forth in the
wilderness,
And streams in the desert.
7The parched ground shall become a pool,
And the thirsty land springs of water;
In the habitation of jackals, where each lay,
There shall be grass with reeds and rushes.

8A highway shall be there, and a road,
And it shall be called the Highway of
Holiness.
The unclean shall not pass over it,
But it *shall be* for others.
Whoever walks the road, although a fool,
Shall not go astray.
9No lion shall be there,
Nor shall *any* ravenous beast go up on it;
It shall not be found there.
But the redeemed shall walk *there,*
10And the ransomed of the LORD shall return,
And come to Zion with singing,
With everlasting joy on their heads.
They shall obtain joy and gladness,
And sorrow and sighing shall flee away.

THE MESSAGE

16-17 Get and read GOD's book:
None of this is going away,
this breeding, brooding evil.
GOD has personally commanded it all.
His Spirit set it in motion.
GOD has assigned them their place,
decreed their fate in detail.
This is permanent—
generation after generation, the same old
thing.

THE VOICELESS BREAK INTO SONG

1-2 35 Wilderness and desert will sing joyously,
the badlands will celebrate and
flower—
Like the crocus in spring, bursting into
blossom,
a symphony of song and color.
Mountain glories of Lebanon—a gift.
Awesome Carmel, stunning Sharon—
gifts.
GOD's resplendent glory, fully on display.
GOD awesome, GOD majestic.

3-4 Energize the limp hands,
strengthen the rubbery knees.
Tell fearful souls,
"Courage! Take heart!
GOD is here, right here,
on his way to put things right
And redress all wrongs.
He's on his way! He'll save you!"

5-7 Blind eyes will be opened,
deaf ears unstopped,
Lame men and women will leap like deer,
the voiceless break into song.
Springs of water will burst out in the
wilderness,
streams flow in the desert.
Hot sands will become a cool oasis,
thirsty ground a splashing fountain.
Even lowly jackals will have water to drink,
and barren grasslands flourish richly.

8-10 There will be a highway
called the Holy Road.
No one rude or rebellious
is permitted on this road.
It's for GOD's people exclusively—
impossible to get lost on this road.
Not even fools can get lost on it.
No lions on this road,
no dangerous wild animals—
Nothing and no one dangerous or
threatening.
Only the redeemed will walk on it.
The people GOD has ransomed
will come back on this road.
They'll sing as they make their way home
to Zion,
unfading halos of joy encircling their
heads,
Welcomed home with gifts of joy and
gladness
as all sorrows and sighs scurry into the
night.

New King James Version

Sennacherib Boasts Against the Lord

36 Now it came to pass in the fourteenth year
of King Hezekiah *that* Sennacherib king
of Assyria came up against all the fortified cities
of Judah and took them. 2 Then the king of As-
syria sent *the* Rabshakeh[a] with a great army
from Lachish to King Hezekiah at Jerusalem.
And he stood by the aqueduct from the upper
pool, on the highway to the Fuller's Field. 3 And
Eliakim the son of Hilkiah, who was over the
household, Shebna the scribe, and Joah the son
of Asaph, the recorder, came out to him.

4 Then *the* Rabshakeh said to them, "Say now
to Hezekiah, 'Thus says the great king, the king
of Assyria: "What confidence is this in which
you trust? 5 I say you speak of having plans and
power for war; but *they are* mere words. Now in
whom do you trust, that you rebel against me?
6 Look! You are trusting in the staff of this bro-
ken reed, Egypt, on which if a man leans, it will
go into his hand and pierce it. So *is* Pharaoh
king of Egypt to all who trust in him.

7 "But if you say to me, 'We trust in the LORD
our God,' *is it* not He whose high places and
whose altars Hezekiah has taken away, and said
to Judah and Jerusalem, 'You shall worship be-
fore this altar'?" ' 8 Now therefore, I urge you,
give a pledge to my master the king of Assyria,
and I will give you two thousand horses—if you
are able on your part to put riders on them!
9 How then will you repel one captain of the least
of my master's servants, and put your trust in
Egypt for chariots and horsemen? 10 Have I now
come up without the LORD against this land to
destroy it? The LORD said to me, 'Go up against
this land, and destroy it.' "

11 Then Eliakim, Shebna, and Joah said to *the*
Rabshakeh, "Please speak to your servants in
Aramaic, for we understand *it;* and do not speak
to us in Hebrew[a] in the hearing of the people
who *are* on the wall."

12 But *the* Rabshakeh said, "Has my master
sent me to your master and to you to speak
these words, and not to the men who sit on the
wall, who will eat and drink their own waste
with you?"

13 Then *the* Rabshakeh stood and called out
with a loud voice in Hebrew, and said, "Hear the
words of the great king, the king of Assyria!
14 Thus says the king: 'Do not let Hezekiah de-
ceive you, for he will not be able to deliver you;
15 nor let Hezekiah make you trust in the LORD,
saying, "The LORD will surely deliver us; this
city will not be given into the hand of the king
of Assyria." ' 16 Do not listen to Hezekiah; for
thus says the king of Assyria: 'Make *peace* with
me *by a* present and come out to me; and every
one of you eat from his own vine and every one
from his own fig tree, and every one of you

36:2 [a]A title, probably *Chief of Staff* or *Governor* **36:11** [a]Literally *Judean*

The Message

It's Their Fate That's at Stake

1-3 **36** In the fourteenth year of King Heze-
kiah, Sennacherib king of Assyria made
war on all the fortress cities of Judah and
took them. Then the king of Assyria sent his
general, the "Rabshekah," accompanied by
a huge army, from Lachish to Jerusalem to
King Hezekiah. The general stopped at the
aqueduct where it empties into the upper
pool on the road to the public laundry. Three
men went out to meet him: Eliakim son of
Hilkiah, in charge of the palace; Shebna the
secretary; and Joah son of Asaph, the offi-
cial historian.

4-7 The Rabshekah said to them, "Tell
Hezekiah that the Great King, the king of
Assyria, says this: 'What kind of backing do
you think you have against me? You're bluff-
ing and I'm calling your bluff. Your words
are no match for my weapons. What kind of
backup do you have now that you've re-
belled against me? Egypt? Don't make me
laugh. Egypt is a rubber crutch. Lean on
Egypt and you'll end up flat on your face.
That's all Pharaoh king of Egypt is to any-
one who leans on him. And if you try to tell
me, "We're leaning on our GOD," isn't it a bit
late? Hasn't Hezekiah just gotten rid of all
the places of worship, telling you, "You've
got to worship at *this* altar"?

8-9 " 'Be reasonable. Face the facts: My mas-
ter the king of Assyria will give you two
thousand horses if you can put riders on
them. You can't do it, can you? So how do
you think, depending on flimsy Egypt's
chariots and riders, you can stand up
against even the lowest-ranking captain in
my master's army?

10 " 'And besides, do you think I came all
this way to destroy this land without first
getting GOD's blessing? It was your GOD
who told me, Make war on this land. De-
stroy it.' "

11 Eliakim, Shebna, and Joah answered the
Rabshekah, "Please talk to us in Aramaic.
We understand Aramaic. Don't talk to us in
Hebrew within earshot of all the people
gathered around."

12 But the Rabshekah replied, "Do you think
my master has sent me to give this message
to your master and you but not also to the
people clustered here? It's their fate that's at
stake. They're the ones who are going to
end up eating their own excrement and
drinking their own urine."

13-15 Then the Rabshekah stood up and called
out loudly in Hebrew, the common lan-
guage, "Listen to the message of the great
king, the king of Assyria! Don't listen to
Hezekiah's lies. He can't save you. And
don't pay any attention to Hezekiah's pious
sermons telling you to lean on GOD, telling
you 'GOD will save us, depend on it. GOD
won't let this city fall to the king of Assyria.'

16-20 "Don't listen to Hezekiah. Listen to the
king of Assyria's offer: 'Make peace with
me. Come and join me. Everyone will end up
with a good life, with plenty of land and wa-
ter, and eventually something far better. I'll

NEW KING JAMES VERSION

drink the waters of his own cistern; [17]until I come and take you away to a land like your own land, a land of grain and new wine, a land of bread and vineyards. [18]*Beware* lest Hezekiah persuade you, saying, "The LORD will deliver us." Has any one of the gods of the nations delivered its land from the hand of the king of Assyria? [19]Where *are* the gods of Hamath and Arpad? Where *are* the gods of Sepharvaim? Indeed, have they delivered Samaria from my hand? [20]Who among all the gods of these lands have delivered their countries from my hand, that the LORD should deliver Jerusalem from my hand?' "

[21]But they held their peace and answered him not a word; for the king's commandment was, "Do not answer him." [22]Then Eliakim the son of Hilkiah, who *was* over the household, Shebna the scribe, and Joah the son of Asaph, the recorder, came to Hezekiah with *their* clothes torn, and told him the words of *the* Rabshakeh.

ISAIAH ASSURES DELIVERANCE

37 And so it was, when King Hezekiah heard *it,* that he tore his clothes, covered himself with sackcloth, and went into the house of the LORD. [2]Then he sent Eliakim, who *was* over the household, Shebna the scribe, and the elders of the priests, covered with sackcloth, to Isaiah the prophet, the son of Amoz. [3]And they said to him, "Thus says Hezekiah: 'This day *is* a day of trouble and rebuke and blasphemy; for the children have come to birth, but *there is* no strength to bring them forth. [4]It may be that the LORD your God will hear the words of *the* Rabshakeh, whom his master the king of Assyria has sent to reproach the living God, and will rebuke the words which the LORD your God has heard. Therefore lift up *your* prayer for the remnant that is left.' "

[5]So the servants of King Hezekiah came to Isaiah. [6]And Isaiah said to them, "Thus you shall say to your master, 'Thus says the LORD: "Do not be afraid of the words which you have heard, with which the servants of the king of Assyria have blasphemed Me. [7]Surely I will send a spirit upon him, and he shall hear a rumor and return to his own land; and I will cause him to fall by the sword in his own land." ' "

SENNACHERIB'S THREAT AND HEZEKIAH'S PRAYER

[8]Then *the* Rabshakeh returned, and found the king of Assyria warring against Libnah, for he heard that he had departed from Lachish. [9]And the king heard concerning Tirhakah king of Ethiopia, "He has come out to make war with you." So when he heard *it,* he sent messengers to Hezekiah, saying, [10]"Thus you shall speak to Hezekiah king of Judah, saying: 'Do not let your God in whom you trust deceive you, saying, "Jerusalem shall not be given into the hand of the king of Assyria." [11]Look! You have heard what the kings of Assyria have done to all lands by utterly destroying them; and shall you be delivered? [12]Have the gods of the nations delivered

THE MESSAGE

turn you loose in wide open spaces, with more than enough fertile and productive land for everyone.' Don't let Hezekiah mislead you with his lies, 'GOD will save us.' Has that ever happened? Has any god in history ever gotten the best of the king of Assyria? Look around you. Where are the gods of Hamath and Arpad? The gods of Sepharvaim? Did the gods do anything for Samaria? Name one god that has ever saved its countries from me. So what makes you think that GOD could save Jerusalem from me?' "

21 The three men were silent. They said
nothing, for the king had already commanded, "Don't answer him."

22 Then Eliakim son of Hilkiah, the palace
administrator, Shebna the secretary, and Joah son of Asaph, the court historian, tearing their clothes in defeat and despair, went back and reported what the Rabshekah had said to Hezekiah.

THE ONLY GOD THERE IS

1-2 37 When King Hezekiah heard the report,
he also tore his clothes and dressed in rough, penitential burlap gunnysacks, and went into the sanctuary of GOD. He sent Eliakim the palace administrator, Shebna the secretary, and the senior priests, all of them also dressed in penitential burlap, to the prophet Isaiah son of Amoz.

3-4 They said to him, "Hezekiah says, 'This is
a black day. We're in crisis. We're like pregnant women without even the strength to have a baby! Do you think your GOD heard what the Rabshekah said, sent by his master the king of Assyria to mock the living God? And do you think your GOD will do anything about it? Pray for us, Isaiah. Pray for those of us left here holding the fort!' "

5-7 Then King Hezekiah's servants came to
Isaiah. Isaiah said, "Tell your master this, 'GOD's Message: Don't be upset by what you've heard, all those words the servants of the Assyrian king have used to mock me. I personally will take care of him. I'll arrange it so that he'll get a rumor of bad news back home and rush home to take care of it. And he'll die there. Killed—a violent death.' "

8 The Rabshekah left and found the king of
Assyria fighting against Libnah. (He had gotten word that the king had left Lachish.)

9-13 Just then the Assyrian king received an
intelligence report on King Tirhakah of Ethiopia: "He is on his way to make war on you."

On hearing that, he sent messengers to Hezekiah with instructions to deliver this message: "Don't let your GOD, on whom you so naively lean, deceive you, promising that Jerusalem won't fall to the king of Assyria. Use your head! Look around at what the kings of Assyria have done all over the world—one country after another devastated! And do you think you're going to get off? Have any of the gods of any of these

NEW KING JAMES VERSION

those whom my fathers have destroyed, Gozan
and Haran and Rezeph, and the people of Eden
who *were* in Telassar? [13]Where *is* the king of
Hamath, the king of Arpad, and the king of the
city of Sepharvaim, Hena, and Ivah?' "
[14]And Hezekiah received the letter from the
hand of the messengers, and read it; and
Hezekiah went up to the house of the LORD, and
spread it before the LORD. [15]Then Hezekiah
prayed to the LORD, saying: [16]"O LORD of hosts,
God of Israel, *the One* who dwells *between* the
cherubim, You *are* God, You alone, of all the
kingdoms of the earth. You have made heaven
and earth. [17]Incline Your ear, O LORD, and hear;
open Your eyes, O LORD, and see; and hear all
the words of Sennacherib, which he has sent to
reproach the living God. [18]Truly, LORD, the kings
of Assyria have laid waste all the nations and
their lands, [19]and have cast their gods into the
fire; for they *were* not gods, but the work of
men's hands—wood and stone. Therefore they
destroyed them. [20]Now therefore, O LORD our
God, save us from his hand, that all the king-
doms of the earth may know that You *are* the
LORD, You alone."

THE WORD OF THE LORD CONCERNING SENNACHERIB

[21]Then Isaiah the son of Amoz sent to
Hezekiah, saying, "Thus says the LORD God of
Israel, 'Because you have prayed to Me against
Sennacherib king of Assyria, [22]this *is* the word
which the LORD has spoken concerning him:

"The virgin, the daughter of Zion,
Has despised you, laughed you to scorn;
The daughter of Jerusalem
Has shaken *her* head behind your back!

[23]"Whom have you reproached and
blasphemed?
Against whom have you raised *your* voice,
And lifted up your eyes on high?
Against the Holy One of Israel.
[24]By your servants you have reproached the
Lord,
And said, 'By the multitude of my chariots
I have come up to the height of the
mountains,
To the limits of Lebanon;
I will cut down its tall cedars
And its choice cypress trees;
I will enter its farthest height,
To its fruitful forest.
[25]I have dug and drunk water,
And with the soles of my feet I have dried
up
All the brooks of defense.'

[26]"Did you not hear long ago
How I made it,
From ancient times that I formed it?
Now I have brought it to pass,

THE MESSAGE

countries ever stepped in and saved them,
even one of these nations my predecessors
destroyed—Gozan, Haran, Rezeph, and the
people of Eden who lived in Telassar? Look
around. Do you see anything left of the king
of Hamath, the king of Arpad, the king of
the city of Sepharvaim, the king of Hena,
the king of Ivvah?"

14 Hezekiah took the letter from the hands
of the messengers and read it. Then he went
into the sanctuary of GOD and spread the
letter out before GOD.

15-20 Then Hezekiah prayed to GOD: "GOD-of-
the-Angel-Armies, enthroned over the
cherubim-angels, you are God, the only God
there is, God of all kingdoms on earth. You
made heaven and earth. Listen, O GOD, and
hear. Look, O GOD, and see. Mark all these
words of Sennacherib that he sent to mock
the living God. It's quite true, O GOD, that
the kings of Assyria have devastated all the
nations and their lands. They've thrown
their gods into the trash and burned them—
no great achievement since they were no-
gods anyway, gods made in workshops,
carved from wood and chiseled from rock.
An end to the no-gods! But now step in, O
GOD, our God. Save us from him. Let all the
kingdoms of earth know that you and you
alone are GOD."

21-25 Then Isaiah son of Amoz sent this word to
Hezekiah: "GOD's Message, the God of Is-
rael: Because you brought King Sen-
nacherib of Assyria to me in prayer, here is
my answer, GOD's answer:

" 'She has no use for you, Sennacherib,
nothing but contempt,
this virgin daughter Zion.
She spits at you and turns on her heel,
this daughter Jerusalem.

" 'Who do you think you've been mocking
and reviling
all these years?
Who do you think you've been jeering
and treating with such utter contempt
All these years?
The Holy of Israel!
You've used your servants to mock the
Master.
You've bragged, "With my fleet of
chariots
I've gone to the highest mountain ranges,
penetrated the far reaches of Lebanon,
Chopped down its giant cedars,
its finest cypresses.
I conquered its highest peak,
explored its deepest forest.
I dug wells
and drank my fill.
I emptied the famous rivers of Egypt
with one kick of my foot.

26-27 " 'Haven't you gotten the news
that I've been behind this all along?
This is a longstanding plan of mine
and I'm just now making it happen,

NEW KING JAMES VERSION

That you should be
For crushing fortified cities *into* heaps of ruins.
27Therefore their inhabitants *had* little power;
They were dismayed and confounded;
They were *as* the grass of the field
And the green herb,
As the grass on the housetops
And grain blighted before it is grown.

28"But I know your dwelling place,
Your going out and your coming in,
And your rage against Me.
29Because your rage against Me and your tumult
Have come up to My ears,
Therefore I will put My hook in your nose
And My bridle in your lips,
And I will turn you back
By the way which you came." '

30"This *shall be* a sign to you:

You shall eat this year such as grows of itself,
And the second year what springs from the same;
Also in the third year sow and reap,
Plant vineyards and eat the fruit of them.
31And the remnant who have escaped of the house of Judah
Shall again take root downward,
And bear fruit upward.
32For out of Jerusalem shall go a remnant,
And those who escape from Mount Zion.
The zeal of the LORD of hosts will do this.

33"Therefore thus says the LORD concerning
the king of Assyria:

'He shall not come into this city,
Nor shoot an arrow there,
Nor come before it with shield,
Nor build a siege mound against it.
34By the way that he came,
By the same shall he return;
And he shall not come into this city,'
Says the LORD.
35'For I will defend this city, to save it
For My own sake and for My servant David's sake.' "

SENNACHERIB'S DEFEAT AND DEATH

36Then the angel[a] of the LORD went out, and
killed in the camp of the Assyrians one hundred
and eighty-five thousand; and when *people*
arose early in the morning, there were the
corpses—all dead. 37So Sennacherib king of As-
syria departed and went away, returned *home*,
and remained at Nineveh. 38Now it came to
pass, as he was worshiping in the house of Nis-
roch his god, that his sons Adrammelech and
Sharezer struck him down with the sword; and
they escaped into the land of Ararat. Then
Esarhaddon his son reigned in his place.

37:36 [a]Or *Angel*

THE MESSAGE

using you to devastate strong cities,
turning them into piles of rubble
and leaving their citizens helpless,
bewildered, and confused,
drooping like unwatered plants,
stunted like withered seedlings.

28-29 " 'I know all about your pretentious poses,
your officious comings and goings,
and, yes, the tantrums you throw against me.
Because of all your wild raging against me,
your unbridled arrogance that I keep hearing of,
I'll put my hook in your nose
and my bit in your mouth.
I'll show you who's boss. I'll turn you around
and take you back to where you came from.

30-32 " 'And this, Hezekiah, will be your confirming sign: This year's crops will be slim pickings, and next year it won't be much better. But in three years, farming will be back to normal, with regular sowing and reaping, planting and harvesting. What's left of the people of Judah will put down roots and make a new start. The people left in Jerusalem will get moving again. Mount Zion survivors will take hold again. The zeal of GOD-of-the-Angel-Armies will do all this.'

33-35 "Finally, this is GOD's verdict on the king of Assyria:

" 'Don't worry, he won't enter this city,
won't let loose a single arrow,
Won't brandish so much as one shield,
let alone build a siege ramp against it.
He'll go back the same way he came.
He won't set a foot in this city.
GOD's Decree.
I've got my hand on this city
to save it,
Save it for my very own sake,
but also for the sake of my David dynasty.' "

36-38 Then the Angel of GOD arrived and struck the Assyrian camp—185,000 Assyrians died. By the time the sun came up, they were all dead—an army of corpses! Sennacherib, king of Assyria, got out of there fast, back home to Nineveh. As he was worshiping in the sanctuary of his god Nisroch, he was murdered by his sons Adrammelech and Sharezer. They escaped to the land of Ararat. His son Esar-haddon became the next king.

New King James Version

Hezekiah's Life Extended

38 In those days Hezekiah was sick and near
death. And Isaiah the prophet, the son of
Amoz, went to him and said to him, "Thus says
the LORD: 'Set your house in order, for you shall
die and not live.' "
2 Then Hezekiah turned his face toward the
wall, and prayed to the LORD, 3 and said, "Re-
member now, O LORD, I pray, how I have walked
before You in truth and with a loyal heart, and
have done *what is* good in Your sight." And
Hezekiah wept bitterly.
4 And the word of the LORD came to Isaiah,
saying, 5 "Go and tell Hezekiah, 'Thus says the
LORD, the God of David your father: "I have
heard your prayer, I have seen your tears; surely
I will add to your days fifteen years. 6 I will de-
liver you and this city from the hand of the king
of Assyria, and I will defend this city." ' 7 And
this *is* the sign to you from the LORD, that the
LORD will do this thing which He has spoken:
8 Behold, I will bring the shadow on the sundial,
which has gone down with the sun on the sun-
dial of Ahaz, ten degrees backward." So the sun
returned ten degrees on the dial by which it had
gone down.
9 This is the writing of Hezekiah king of Ju-
dah, when he had been sick and had recovered
from his sickness:

10 I said,
"In the prime of my life
I shall go to the gates of Sheol;
I am deprived of the remainder of my
years."
11 I said,
"I shall not see YAH,
The LORD[a] in the land of the living;
I shall observe man no more among the
inhabitants of the world.[b]
12 My life span is gone,
Taken from me like a shepherd's tent;
I have cut off my life like a weaver.
He cuts me off from the loom;
From day until night You make an end of
me.
13 I have considered until morning—
Like a lion,
So He breaks all my bones;
From day until night You make an end of
me.
14 Like a crane *or* a swallow, so I chattered;
I mourned like a dove;
My eyes fail *from looking* upward.
O LORD,[a] I am oppressed;
Undertake for me!

15 "What shall I say?
He has both spoken to me,[a]
And He Himself has done *it*.
I shall walk carefully all my years
In the bitterness of my soul.

38:11 [a]Hebrew *YAH, YAH* [b]Following some Hebrew manuscripts; Masoretic Text and Vulgate read *rest;* Septuagint omits *among the inhabitants of the world;* Targum reads *land.* **38:14** [a]Following Bomberg; Masoretic Text and Dead Sea Scrolls read *Lord.* **38:15** [a]Following Masoretic Text and Vulgate; Dead Sea Scrolls and Targum read *And shall I say to Him;* Septuagint omits first half of this verse.

The Message

Time Spent in Death's Waiting Room

1 38 At that time, Hezekiah got sick. He was about to die. The prophet Isaiah son of Amoz visited him and said, "GOD says, 'Prepare your affairs and your family. This is it: You're going to die. You're not going to get well.' "

2-3 Hezekiah turned away from Isaiah and, facing the wall, prayed to GOD: "GOD, please, I beg you: Remember how I've lived my life. I've lived faithfully in your presence, lived out of a heart that was totally yours. You've seen how I've lived, the good that I have done." And Hezekiah wept as he prayed—painful tears.

4-6 Then GOD told Isaiah, "Go and speak with Hezekiah. Give him this Message from me, GOD, the God of your ancestor David: 'I've heard your prayer. I have seen your tears. Here's what I'll do: I'll add fifteen years to your life. And I'll save both you and this city from the king of Assyria. I have my hand on this city.

7-8 " 'And this is your confirming sign, confirming that I, GOD, will do exactly what I have promised. Watch for this: As the sun goes down and the shadow lengthens on the sundial of Ahaz, I'm going to reverse the shadow ten notches on the dial.' " And that's what happened: The declining sun's shadow reversed ten notches on the dial.

9-15 This is what Hezekiah king of Judah wrote after he'd been sick and then recovered from his sickness:

In the very prime of life
I have to leave.
Whatever time I have left
is spent in death's waiting room.
No more glimpses of GOD
in the land of the living,
No more meetings with my neighbors,
no more rubbing shoulders with friends.
This body I inhabit is taken down
and packed away like a camper's tent.
Like a weaver, I've rolled up the carpet of
my life
as God cuts me free of the loom
And at day's end sweeps up the scraps and
pieces.
I cry for help until morning.
Like a lion, God pummels and pounds me,
relentlessly finishing me off.
I squawk like a doomed hen,
moan like a dove.
My eyes ache from looking up for help:
"Master, I'm in trouble! Get me out of
this!"
But what's the use? God himself gave me
the word.
He's done it to me.
I can't sleep—
I'm that upset, that troubled.

NEW KING JAMES VERSION

16O Lord, by these *things men* live;
And in all these *things is* the life of my spirit;
So You will restore me and make me live.
17Indeed *it was* for *my own* peace
That I had great bitterness;
But You have lovingly *delivered* my soul from the pit of corruption,
For You have cast all my sins behind Your back.
18For Sheol cannot thank You,
Death cannot praise You;
Those who go down to the pit cannot hope for Your truth.
19The living, the living man, he shall praise You,
As I *do* this day;
The father shall make known Your truth to the children.

20"The LORD *was ready* to save me;
Therefore we will sing my songs with stringed instruments
All the days of our life, in the house of the LORD."

21Now Isaiah had said, "Let them take a lump
of figs, and apply *it* as a poultice on the boil, and
he shall recover."
22And Hezekiah had said, "What *is* the sign
that I shall go up to the house of the LORD?"

THE BABYLONIAN ENVOYS

39 At that time Merodach-Baladan[a] the son of
Baladan, king of Babylon, sent letters and
a present to Hezekiah, for he heard that he had
been sick and had recovered. 2And Hezekiah
was pleased with them, and showed them the
house of his treasures—the silver and gold, the
spices and precious ointment, and all his armory—all that was found among his treasures.
There was nothing in his house or in all his dominion that Hezekiah did not show them.
3Then Isaiah the prophet went to King
Hezekiah, and said to him, "What did these men
say, and from where did they come to you?"
So Hezekiah said, "They came to me from a
far country, from Babylon."
4And he said, "What have they seen in your
house?"
So Hezekiah answered, "They have seen all
that *is* in my house; there is nothing among my
treasures that I have not shown them."
5Then Isaiah said to Hezekiah, "Hear the
word of the LORD of hosts: 6'Behold, the days are
coming when all that *is* in your house, and what
your fathers have accumulated until this day,

39:1 [a]Spelled *Berodach-Baladan* in 2 Kings 20:12

THE MESSAGE

16-19 O Master, these are the conditions in which people live,
and yes, in these very conditions my spirit is still alive—
fully recovered with a fresh infusion of life!
It seems it was good for me
to go through all those troubles.
Throughout them all you held tight to my lifeline.
You never let me tumble over the edge into nothing.
But my sins you let go of,
threw them over your shoulder—good riddance!
The dead don't thank you,
and choirs don't sing praises from the morgue.
Those buried six feet under
don't witness to your faithful ways.
It's the living—live men, live women—who thank you,
just as I'm doing right now.
Parents give their children
full reports on your faithful ways.

20 GOD saves and will save me.
As fiddles and mandolins strike up the tunes,
We'll sing, oh we'll sing, sing,
for the rest of our lives in the Sanctuary of GOD.

21-22 Isaiah had said, "Prepare a poultice of
figs and put it on the boil so he may recover."
Hezekiah had said, "What is my cue that
it's all right to enter again the Sanctuary of
GOD?"

THERE WILL BE NOTHING LEFT

1 39 Sometime later, King Merodach-baladan son of Baladan of Babylon sent
messengers with greetings and a gift to
Hezekiah. He had heard that Hezekiah had
been sick and was now well.
2 Hezekiah received the messengers
warmly. He took them on a tour of his royal
precincts, proudly showing them all his
treasures: silver, gold, spices, expensive oils,
all his weapons—everything out on display.
There was nothing in his house or kingdom
that Hezekiah didn't show them.
3 Later the prophet Isaiah showed up. He
asked Hezekiah, "What were these men up
to? What did they say? And where did they
come from?"
Hezekiah said, "They came from a long
way off, from Babylon."
4 "And what did they see in your palace?"
"Everything," said Hezekiah. "I showed
them the works, opened all the doors and
impressed them with it all."
5-7 Then Isaiah said to Hezekiah, "Now listen to this Message from GOD-of-the-Angel-Armies: I have to warn you, the time is coming when everything in this palace, along
with everything your ancestors accumu-

NEW KING JAMES VERSION

shall be carried to Babylon; nothing shall be
left,' says the LORD. 7'And they shall take away
some of your sons who will descend from you,
whom you will beget; and they shall be eunuchs
in the palace of the king of Babylon.' "
8So Hezekiah said to Isaiah, "The word of the
LORD which you have spoken *is* good!" For he
said, "At least there will be peace and truth in
my days."

GOD'S PEOPLE ARE COMFORTED

40 "Comfort, yes, comfort My people!"
Says your God.
2"Speak comfort to Jerusalem, and cry out to her,
That her warfare is ended,
That her iniquity is pardoned;
For she has received from the LORD's hand
Double for all her sins."

3The voice of one crying in the wilderness:
"Prepare the way of the LORD;
Make straight in the desert[a]
A highway for our God.
4Every valley shall be exalted
And every mountain and hill brought low;
The crooked places shall be made straight
And the rough places smooth;
5The glory of the LORD shall be revealed,
And all flesh shall see *it* together;
For the mouth of the LORD has spoken."

6The voice said, "Cry out!"
And he[a] said, "What shall I cry?"
"All flesh *is* grass,
And all its loveliness *is* like the flower of the field.
7The grass withers, the flower fades,
Because the breath of the LORD blows upon it;
Surely the people *are* grass.
8The grass withers, the flower fades,
But the word of our God stands forever."

9O Zion,
You who bring good tidings,
Get up into the high mountain;
O Jerusalem,
You who bring good tidings,
Lift up your voice with strength,
Lift *it* up, be not afraid;
Say to the cities of Judah, "Behold your God!"

10Behold, the Lord GOD shall come with a strong *hand*,
And His arm shall rule for Him;
Behold, His reward *is* with Him,
And His work before Him.
11He will feed His flock like a shepherd;
He will gather the lambs with His arm,
And carry *them* in His bosom,
And gently lead those who are with young.

40:3 [a]Following Masoretic Text, Targum, and Vulgate; Septuagint omits *in the desert*. **40:6** [a]Following Masoretic Text and Targum; Dead Sea Scrolls, Septuagint, and Vulgate read *I*.

THE MESSAGE

lated before you, will be hauled off to Babylon. GOD says that there will be nothing left. Nothing. And not only your things but your *sons*. Some of your sons will be taken into exile, ending up as eunuchs in the palace of the king of Babylon."

8 Hezekiah replied to Isaiah, "Good. If GOD says so, it's good." Within himself he was thinking, "But surely nothing bad will happen in my lifetime. I'll enjoy peace and stability as long as I live."

MESSAGES OF COMFORT

PREPARE FOR GOD'S ARRIVAL

1-2 40 "Comfort, oh comfort my people,"
says your God.
"Speak softly and tenderly to Jerusalem,
but also make it very clear
That she has served her sentence,
that her sin is taken care of—forgiven!
She's been punished enough and more than enough,
and now it's over and done with."

3-5 Thunder in the desert!
"Prepare for GOD's arrival!
Make the road straight and smooth,
a highway fit for our God.
Fill in the valleys,
level off the hills,
Smooth out the ruts,
clear out the rocks.
Then GOD's bright glory will shine
and everyone will see it.
Yes. Just as GOD has said."

6-8 A voice says, "Shout!"
I said, "What shall I shout?"

"These people are nothing but grass,
their love fragile as wildflowers.
The grass withers, the wildflowers fade,
if GOD so much as puffs on them.
Aren't these people just so much grass?
True, the grass withers and the wildflowers fade,
but our God's Word stands firm and forever."

9-11 Climb a high mountain, Zion.
You're the preacher of good news.
Raise your voice. Make it good and loud, Jerusalem.
You're the preacher of good news.
Speak loud and clear. Don't be timid!
Tell the cities of Judah,
"Look! Your God!"
Look at him! GOD, the Master, comes in power,
ready to go into action.
He is going to pay back his enemies
and reward those who have loved him.
Like a shepherd, he will care for his flock,
gathering the lambs in his arms,
Hugging them as he carries them,
leading the nursing ewes to good pasture.

NEW KING JAMES VERSION

12Who has measured the waters[a] in the
hollow of His hand,
Measured heaven with a span
And calculated the dust of the earth in a
measure?
Weighed the mountains in scales
And the hills in a balance?
13Who has directed the Spirit of the LORD,
Or *as* His counselor has taught Him?
14With whom did He take counsel, and *who*
instructed Him,
And taught Him in the path of justice?
Who taught Him knowledge,
And showed Him the way of understanding?

15Behold, the nations *are* as a drop in a
bucket,
And are counted as the small dust on the
scales;
Look, He lifts up the isles as a very little
thing.
16And Lebanon *is* not sufficient to burn,
Nor its beasts sufficient for a burnt offering.
17All nations before Him *are* as nothing,
And they are counted by Him less than
nothing and worthless.

18To whom then will you liken God?
Or what likeness will you compare to Him?
19The workman molds an image,
The goldsmith overspreads it with gold,
And the silversmith casts silver chains.
20Whoever *is* too impoverished for *such* a
contribution
Chooses a tree *that* will not rot;
He seeks for himself a skillful workman
To prepare a carved image *that* will not
totter.

21Have you not known?
Have you not heard?
Has it not been told you from the
beginning?
Have you not understood from the
foundations of the earth?
22*It is* He who sits above the circle of the
earth,
And its inhabitants *are* like grasshoppers,
Who stretches out the heavens like a
curtain,
And spreads them out like a tent to dwell in.
23He brings the princes to nothing;
He makes the judges of the earth useless.

24Scarcely shall they be planted,
Scarcely shall they be sown,
Scarcely shall their stock take root in the
earth,
When He will also blow on them,
And they will wither,
And the whirlwind will take them away like
stubble.

25"To whom then will you liken Me,
Or *to whom* shall I be equal?" says the Holy
One.

40:12 [a]Following Masoretic Text, Septuagint, and Vulgate; Dead Sea Scrolls read *waters of the sea;* Targum reads *waters of the world.*

THE MESSAGE

THE CREATOR OF ALL YOU CAN SEE OR IMAGINE

12-17 Who has scooped up the ocean
in his two hands,
or measured the sky between his thumb
and little finger,
Who has put all the earth's dirt in one of
his baskets,
weighed each mountain and hill?
Who could ever have told GOD what to do
or taught him his business?
What expert would he have gone to for
advice,
what school would he attend to learn
justice?
What god do you suppose might have
taught him what he knows,
showed him how things work?
Why, the nations are but a drop in a bucket,
a mere smudge on a window.
Watch him sweep up the islands
like so much dust off the floor!
There aren't enough trees in Lebanon
nor enough animals in those vast forests
to furnish adequate fuel and offerings
for his worship.
All the nations add up to simply nothing
before him—
less than nothing is more like it. A
minus.

18-20 So who even comes close to being like
God?
To whom or what can you compare him?
Some no-god idol? Ridiculous!
It's made in a workshop, cast in bronze,
Given a thin veneer of gold,
and draped with silver filigree.
Or, perhaps someone will select a fine
wood—
olive wood, say—that won't rot,
Then hire a woodcarver to make a no-god,
giving special care to its base so it won't
tip over!

21-24 Have you not been paying attention?
Have you not been listening?
Haven't you heard these stories all your
life?
Don't you understand the foundation of
all things?
God sits high above the round ball of earth.
The people look like mere ants.
He stretches out the skies like a canvas—
yes, like a tent canvas to live under.
He ignores what all the princes say and do.
The rulers of the earth count for nothing.
Princes and rulers don't amount to much.
Like seeds barely rooted, just sprouted,
They shrivel when God blows on them.
Like flecks of chaff, they're gone with
the wind.

25-26 "So—who is like me?
Who holds a candle to me?" says The
Holy.

NEW KING JAMES VERSION

26Lift up your eyes on high,
And see who has created these *things*,
Who brings out their host by number;
He calls them all by name,
By the greatness of His might
And the strength of *His* power;
Not one is missing.

27Why do you say, O Jacob,
And speak, O Israel:
"My way is hidden from the LORD,
And my just claim is passed over by my God"?
28Have you not known?
Have you not heard?
The everlasting God, the LORD,
The Creator of the ends of the earth,
Neither faints nor is weary.
His understanding is unsearchable.
29He gives power to the weak,
And to *those who have* no might He increases strength.
30Even the youths shall faint and be weary,
And the young men shall utterly fall,
31But those who wait on the LORD
Shall renew *their* strength;
They shall mount up with wings like eagles,
They shall run and not be weary,
They shall walk and not faint.

ISRAEL ASSURED OF GOD'S HELP

41 "Keep silence before Me, O coastlands,
And let the people renew *their* strength!
Let them come near, then let them speak;
Let us come near together for judgment.

2"Who raised up one from the east?
Who in righteousness called him to His feet?
Who gave the nations before him,
And made *him* rule over kings?
Who gave *them* as the dust *to* his sword,
As driven stubble to his bow?
3Who pursued them, *and* passed safely
By the way *that* he had not gone with his feet?
4Who has performed and done *it*,
Calling the generations from the beginning?
'I, the LORD, am the first;
And with the last I *am* He.' "

5The coastlands saw *it* and feared,
The ends of the earth were afraid;
They drew near and came.
6Everyone helped his neighbor,
And said to his brother,
"Be of good courage!"
7So the craftsman encouraged the goldsmith;
He who smooths *with* the hammer *inspired* him who strikes the anvil,

THE MESSAGE

Look at the night skies:
Who do you think made all this?
Who marches this army of stars out each night,
counts them off, calls each by name
—so magnificent! so powerful!—
and never overlooks a single one?

27-31 Why would you ever complain, O Jacob,
or, whine, Israel, saying,
"GOD has lost track of me.
He doesn't care what happens to me"?
Don't you know anything? Haven't you been listening?
GOD doesn't come and go. God *lasts*.
He's Creator of all you can see or imagine.
He doesn't get tired out, doesn't pause to catch his breath.
And he knows *everything*, inside and out.
He energizes those who get tired,
gives fresh strength to dropouts.
For even young people tire and drop out,
young folk in their prime stumble and fall.
But those who wait upon GOD get fresh strength.
They spread their wings and soar like eagles,
They run and don't get tired,
they walk and don't lag behind.

DO YOU FEEL LIKE A LOWLY WORM?

1 41 "Quiet down, far-flung ocean islands. Listen!
Sit down and rest, everyone. Recover your strength.
Gather around me. Say what's on your heart.
Together let's decide what's right.

2-3 "Who got things rolling here,
got this champion from the east on the move?
Who recruited him for this job,
then rounded up and corralled the nations
so he could run roughshod over kings?
He's off and running,
pulverizing nations into dust,
leaving only stubble and chaff in his wake.
He chases them and comes through unscathed,
his feet scarcely touching the path.

4 "Who did this? Who made it happen?
Who always gets things started?
I did. GOD. I'm first on the scene.
I'm also the last to leave.

5-7 "Far-flung ocean islands see it and panic.
The ends of the earth are shaken.
Fearfully they huddle together.
They try to help each other out,
making up stories in the dark.
The godmakers in the workshops
go into overtime production, crafting new models of no-gods,

NEW KING JAMES VERSION

Saying, "It *is* ready for the soldering";
Then he fastened it with pegs,
That it might not totter.

8"But you, Israel, *are* My servant,
Jacob whom I have chosen,
The descendants of Abraham My friend.
9*You* whom I have taken from the ends of the earth,
And called from its farthest regions,
And said to you,
'You *are* My servant,
I have chosen you and have not cast you away:
10Fear not, for I *am* with you;
Be not dismayed, for I *am* your God.
I will strengthen you,
Yes, I will help you,
I will uphold you with My righteous right hand.'

11"Behold, all those who were incensed against you
Shall be ashamed and disgraced;
They shall be as nothing,
And those who strive with you shall perish.
12You shall seek them and not find them—
Those who contended with you.
Those who war against you
Shall be as nothing,
As a nonexistent thing.
13For I, the LORD your God, will hold your right hand,
Saying to you, 'Fear not, I will help you.'

14"Fear not, you worm Jacob,
You men of Israel!
I will help you," says the LORD
And your Redeemer, the Holy One of Israel.
15"Behold, I will make you into a new threshing sledge with sharp teeth;
You shall thresh the mountains and beat *them* small,
And make the hills like chaff.
16You shall winnow them, the wind shall carry them away,
And the whirlwind shall scatter them;
You shall rejoice in the LORD,
And glory in the Holy One of Israel.

17"The poor and needy seek water, but *there is* none,
Their tongues fail for thirst.
I, the LORD, will hear them;
I, the God of Israel, will not forsake them.
18I will open rivers in desolate heights,
And fountains in the midst of the valleys;

THE MESSAGE

Urging one another on—'Good job!' 'Great design!'—
pounding in nails at the base
so that the things won't tip over.

8-10 "But you, Israel, are my servant.
You're Jacob, my first choice,
descendants of my good friend Abraham.
I pulled you in from all over the world,
called you in from every dark corner of the earth,
Telling you, 'You're my servant, serving on my side.
I've picked you. I haven't dropped you.'
Don't panic. I'm with you.
There's no need to fear for I'm your God.
I'll give you strength. I'll help you.
I'll hold you steady, keep a firm grip on you.

11-13 "Count on it: Everyone who had it in for you
will end up out in the cold—
real losers.
Those who worked against you
will end up empty-handed—
nothing to show for their lives.
When you go out looking for your old adversaries
you won't find them—
Not a trace of your old enemies,
not even a memory.
That's right. Because I, your GOD,
have a firm grip on you and I'm not letting go.
I'm telling you, 'Don't panic.
I'm right here to help you.'

14-16 "Do you feel like a lowly worm, Jacob?
Don't be afraid.
Feel like a fragile insect, Israel?
I'll help you.
I, GOD, want to reassure you.
The God who buys you back, The Holy of Israel.
I'm transforming you from worm to harrow,
from insect to iron.
As a sharp-toothed harrow you'll smooth out the mountains,
turn those tough old hills into loamy soil.
You'll open the rough ground to the weather,
to the blasts of sun and wind and rain.
But you'll be confident and exuberant,
expansive in The Holy of Israel!

17-20 "The poor and homeless are desperate for water,
their tongues parched and no water to be found.
But *I'm* there to be found, I'm there for them,
and I, God of Israel, will not leave them thirsty.
I'll open up rivers for them on the barren hills,
spout fountains in the valleys.

NEW KING JAMES VERSION

I will make the wilderness a pool of water,
And the dry land springs of water.
19I will plant in the wilderness the cedar and the acacia tree,
The myrtle and the oil tree;
I will set in the desert the cypress tree *and* the pine
And the box tree together,
20That they may see and know,
And consider and understand together,
That the hand of the LORD has done this,
And the Holy One of Israel has created it.

THE FUTILITY OF IDOLS

21"Present your case," says the LORD.
"Bring forth your strong *reasons,*" says the King of Jacob.
22"Let them bring forth and show us what will happen;
Let them show the former things, what they *were,*
That we may consider them,
And know the latter end of them;
Or declare to us things to come.
23Show the things that are to come hereafter,
That we may know that you *are* gods;
Yes, do good or do evil,
That we may be dismayed and see *it* together.
24Indeed you *are* nothing,
And your work *is* nothing;
He who chooses you *is* an abomination.

25"I have raised up one from the north,
And he shall come;
From the rising of the sun he shall call on My name;
And he shall come against princes as *though* mortar,
As the potter treads clay.
26Who has declared from the beginning, that we may know?
And former times, that we may say, '*He is* righteous'?
Surely *there is* no one who shows,
Surely *there is* no one who declares,
Surely *there is* no one who hears your words.
27The first time *I said* to Zion,
'Look, there they are!'
And I will give to Jerusalem one who brings good tidings.
28For I looked, and *there was* no man;
I looked among them, but *there was* no counselor,
Who, when I asked of them, could answer a word.
29Indeed they *are* all worthless;[a]
Their works *are* nothing;
Their molded images *are* wind and confusion.

THE SERVANT OF THE LORD

42 "Behold! My Servant whom I uphold,
My Elect One *in whom* My soul delights!
I have put My Spirit upon Him;

41:29 [a]Following Masoretic Text and Vulgate; Dead Sea Scrolls, Syriac, and Targum read *nothing;* Septuagint omits the first line.

THE MESSAGE

I'll turn the baked-clay badlands into a cool pond,
the waterless waste into splashing creeks.
I'll plant the red cedar in that treeless wasteland,
also acacia, myrtle, and olive.
I'll place the cypress in the desert,
with plenty of oaks and pines.
Everyone will see this. No one can miss it—
unavoidable, indisputable evidence
That I, GOD, personally did this.
It's created and signed by The Holy of Israel.

21-24 "Set out your case for your gods," says GOD.
"Bring your evidence," says the King of Jacob.
"Take the stand on behalf of your idols,
offer arguments,
assemble reasons.
Spread out the facts before us
so that we can assess them ourselves.
Ask them, 'If you are gods, explain what the past means—
or, failing that, tell us what will happen in the future.
Can't do that?
How about doing something—anything!
Good or bad—whatever.
Can you hurt us or help us? Do we need to be afraid?'
They say nothing, because they *are* nothing—
sham gods, no-gods, fool-making gods.

25-29 "I, God, started someone out from the north and he's come.
He was called out of the east by name.
He'll stomp the rulers into the mud
the way a potter works the clay.
Let me ask you, Did anyone guess that this might happen?
Did anyone tell us earlier so we might confirm it
with 'Yes, he's right!'?
No one mentioned it, no one announced it,
no one heard a peep out of you.
But I told Zion all about this beforehand.
I gave Jerusalem a preacher of good news.
But around here there's no one—
no one who knows what's going on.
I ask, but no one can tell me the score.
Nothing here. It's all smoke and hot air—
sham gods, hollow gods, no-gods."

GOD'S SERVANT WILL SET EVERYTHING RIGHT

1-4 42 "Take a good look at my servant.
I'm backing him to the hilt.
He's the one I chose,
and I couldn't be more pleased with him.
I've bathed him with my Spirit, my *life.*

NEW KING JAMES VERSION

He will bring forth justice to the Gentiles.
[2]He will not cry out, nor raise *His voice,*
Nor cause His voice to be heard in the street.
[3]A bruised reed He will not break,
And smoking flax He will not quench;
He will bring forth justice for truth.
[4]He will not fail nor be discouraged,
Till He has established justice in the earth;
And the coastlands shall wait for His law."

[5]Thus says God the LORD,
Who created the heavens and stretched them out,
Who spread forth the earth and that which comes from it,
Who gives breath to the people on it,
And spirit to those who walk on it:
[6]"I, the LORD, have called You in righteousness,
And will hold Your hand;
I will keep You and give You as a covenant to the people,
As a light to the Gentiles,
[7]To open blind eyes,
To bring out prisoners from the prison,
Those who sit in darkness from the prison house.
[8]I *am* the LORD, that *is* My name;
And My glory I will not give to another,
Nor My praise to carved images.
[9]Behold, the former things have come to pass,
And new things I declare;
Before they spring forth I tell you of them."

PRAISE TO THE LORD

[10]Sing to the LORD a new song,
And His praise from the ends of the earth,
You who go down to the sea, and all that is in it,
You coastlands and you inhabitants of them!
[11]Let the wilderness and its cities lift up *their* voice,
The villages *that* Kedar inhabits.
Let the inhabitants of Sela sing,
Let them shout from the top of the mountains.
[12]Let them give glory to the LORD,
And declare His praise in the coastlands.
[13]The LORD shall go forth like a mighty man;
He shall stir up *His* zeal like a man of war.
He shall cry out, yes, shout aloud;
He shall prevail against His enemies.

PROMISE OF THE LORD'S HELP

[14]"I have held My peace a long time,
I have been still and restrained Myself.
Now I will cry like a woman in labor,
I will pant and gasp at once.

THE MESSAGE

He'll set everything right among the nations.
He won't call attention to what he does
with loud speeches or gaudy parades.
He won't brush aside the bruised and the hurt
and he won't disregard the small and insignificant,
but he'll steadily and firmly set things right.
He won't tire out and quit. He won't be stopped
until he's finished his work—to set things right on earth.
Far-flung ocean islands
wait expectantly for his teaching."

THE GOD WHO MAKES US ALIVE WITH HIS OWN LIFE

5-9 GOD's Message,
the God who created the cosmos, stretched out the skies,
laid out the earth and all that grows from it,
Who breathes life into earth's people,
makes them alive with his own life:
"I am GOD. I have called you to live right and well.
I have taken responsibility for you, kept you safe.
I have set you among my people to bind them to me,
and provided you as a lighthouse to the nations,
To make a start at bringing people into the open, into light:
opening blind eyes,
releasing prisoners from dungeons,
emptying the dark prisons.
I am GOD. That's my name.
I don't franchise my glory,
don't endorse the no-god idols.
Take note: The earlier predictions of judgment have been fulfilled.
I'm announcing the new salvation work.
Before it bursts on the scene,
I'm telling you all about it."

10-16 Sing to GOD a brand-new song,
sing his praises all over the world!
Let the sea and its fish give a round of applause,
with all the far-flung islands joining in.
Let the desert and its camps raise a tune,
calling the Kedar nomads to join in.
Let the villagers in Sela round up a choir
and perform from the tops of the mountains.
Make GOD's glory resound;
echo his praises from coast to coast.
GOD steps out like he means business.
You can see he's primed for action.
He shouts, announcing his arrival;
he takes charge and his enemies fall into line:
"I've been quiet long enough.
I've held back, biting my tongue.
But now I'm letting loose, letting go,
like a woman who's having a baby—

NEW KING JAMES VERSION

15I will lay waste the mountains and hills,
And dry up all their vegetation;
I will make the rivers coastlands,
And I will dry up the pools.
16I will bring the blind by a way they did not know;
I will lead them in paths they have not known.
I will make darkness light before them,
And crooked places straight.
These things I will do for them,
And not forsake them.
17They shall be turned back,
They shall be greatly ashamed,
Who trust in carved images,
Who say to the molded images,
'You *are* our gods.'

18"Hear, you deaf;
And look, you blind, that you may see.
19Who *is* blind but My servant,
Or deaf as My messenger *whom* I send?
Who *is* blind as *he who is* perfect,
And blind as the LORD's servant?
20Seeing many things, but you do not observe;
Opening the ears, but he does not hear."

ISRAEL'S OBSTINATE DISOBEDIENCE

21The LORD is well pleased for His righteousness' sake;
He will exalt the law and make *it* honorable.
22But this *is* a people robbed and plundered;
All of them are snared in holes,
And they are hidden in prison houses;
They are for prey, and no one delivers;
For plunder, and no one says, "Restore!"

23Who among you will give ear to this?
Who will listen and hear for the time to come?
24Who gave Jacob for plunder, and Israel to the robbers?
Was it not the LORD,
He against whom we have sinned?
For they would not walk in His ways,
Nor were they obedient to His law.
25Therefore He has poured on him the fury of His anger
And the strength of battle;
It has set him on fire all around,
Yet he did not know;
And it burned him,
Yet he did not take *it* to heart.

THE REDEEMER OF ISRAEL

43 But now, thus says the LORD, who created you, O Jacob,
And He who formed you, O Israel:
"Fear not, for I have redeemed you;
I have called *you* by your name;
You *are* Mine.
2When you pass through the waters, I *will be* with you;
And through the rivers, they shall not overflow you.

THE MESSAGE

Stripping the hills bare,
withering the wildflowers,
Drying up the rivers,
turning lakes into mudflats.
But I'll take the hand of those who don't know the way,
who can't see where they're going.
I'll be a personal guide to them,
directing them through unknown country.
I'll be right there to show them what roads to take,
make sure they don't fall into the ditch.
These are the things I'll be doing for them—
sticking with them, not leaving them for a minute."

17 But those who invested in the no-gods
are bankrupt—dead broke.

YOU'VE SEEN A LOT, BUT LOOKED AT NOTHING

18-25 Pay attention! Are you deaf?
Open your eyes! Are you blind?
You're my servant, and you're not looking!
You're my messenger, and you're not listening!
The very people I depended upon, servants of GOD,
blind as a bat—willfully blind!
You've seen a lot, but looked at nothing.
You've heard everything, but listened to nothing.
GOD intended, out of the goodness of his heart,
to be lavish in his revelation.
But this is a people battered and cowed,
shut up in attics and closets,
Victims licking their wounds,
feeling ignored, abandoned.
But is anyone out there listening?
Is anyone paying attention to what's coming?
Who do you think turned Jacob over to the thugs,
let loose the robbers on Israel?
Wasn't it GOD himself, this God against whom we've sinned—
not doing what he commanded,
not listening to what he said?
Isn't it God's anger that's behind all this,
God's punishing power?
Their whole world collapsed but they still didn't get it;
their life is in ruins but they don't take it to heart.

WHEN YOU'RE BETWEEN A ROCK AND A HARD PLACE

1-4 43 But now, GOD's Message,
the God who made you in the first place, Jacob,
the One who got you started, Israel:
"Don't be afraid, I've redeemed you.
I've called your name. You're mine.
When you're in over your head, I'll be there with you.
When you're in rough waters, you will not go down.

New King James Version

When you walk through the fire, you shall
not be burned,
Nor shall the flame scorch you.
3For I *am* the LORD your God,
The Holy One of Israel, your Savior;
I gave Egypt for your ransom,
Ethiopia and Seba in your place.
4Since you were precious in My sight,
You have been honored,
And I have loved you;
Therefore I will give men for you,
And people for your life.
5Fear not, for I *am* with you;
I will bring your descendants from the east,
And gather you from the west;
6I will say to the north, 'Give them up!'
And to the south, 'Do not keep them back!'
Bring My sons from afar,
And My daughters from the ends of the
earth—
7Everyone who is called by My name,
Whom I have created for My glory;
I have formed him, yes, I have made him."

8Bring out the blind people who have eyes,
And the deaf who have ears.
9Let all the nations be gathered together,
And let the people be assembled.
Who among them can declare this,
And show us former things?
Let them bring out their witnesses, that they
may be justified;
Or let them hear and say, "*It is* truth."
10"You *are* My witnesses," says the LORD,
"And My servant whom I have chosen,
That you may know and believe Me,
And understand that I *am* He.
Before Me there was no God formed,
Nor shall there be after Me.
11I, *even* I, *am* the LORD,
And besides Me *there is* no savior.
12I have declared and saved,
I have proclaimed,
And *there was* no foreign *god* among you;
Therefore you *are* My witnesses,"
Says the LORD, "that I *am* God.
13Indeed before the day *was*, I *am* He;
And *there is* no one who can deliver out of
My hand;
I work, and who will reverse it?"

14Thus says the LORD, your Redeemer,
The Holy One of Israel:
"For your sake I will send to Babylon,
And bring them all down as fugitives—
The Chaldeans, who rejoice in their ships.
15I *am* the LORD, your Holy One,
The Creator of Israel, your King."

The Message

When you're between a rock and a hard
place,
it won't be a dead end—
Because I am GOD, your personal God,
The Holy of Israel, your Savior.
I paid a huge price for you:
all of Egypt, with rich Cush and Seba
thrown in!
That's how much you mean to me!
That's how much I love you!
I'd sell off the whole world to get you back,
trade the creation just for you.

5-7 "So don't be afraid: I'm with you.
I'll round up all your scattered children,
pull them in from east and west.
I'll send orders north and south:
'Send them back.
Return my sons from distant lands,
my daughters from faraway places.
I want them back, every last one who bears
my name,
every man, woman, and child
Whom I created for my glory,
yes, personally formed and made each
one.' "

8-13 Get the blind and deaf out here and ready—
the blind (though there's nothing wrong
with their eyes)
and the deaf (though there's nothing
wrong with their ears).
Then get the other nations out here and
ready.
Let's see what they have to say about this,
how they account for what's happened.
Let them present their expert witnesses
and make their case;
let them try to convince us what they say
is true.
"But *you* are my witnesses." GOD's Decree.
"You're my handpicked servant
So that you'll come to know and trust me,
understand both *that* I am and *who* I am.
Previous to me there was no such thing as
a god,
nor will there be after me.
I, yes I, am GOD.
I'm the only Savior there is.
I spoke, I saved, I told you what existed
long before these upstart gods appeared
on the scene.
And you know it, you're my witnesses,
you're the evidence." GOD's Decree.
"Yes, I am God.
I've always been God
and I always will be God.
No one can take anything from me.
I make; who can unmake it?"

You Didn't Even Do the Minimum

14-15 GOD, your Redeemer,
The Holy of Israel, says:
"Just for you, I will march on Babylon.
I'll turn the tables on the Babylonians.
Instead of whooping it up,
they'll be wailing.
I am GOD, your Holy One,
Creator of Israel, your King."

NEW KING JAMES VERSION

16Thus says the LORD, who makes a way in the sea
And a path through the mighty waters,
17Who brings forth the chariot and horse,
The army and the power
(They shall lie down together, they shall not rise;
They are extinguished, they are quenched like a wick):
18"Do not remember the former things,
Nor consider the things of old.
19Behold, I will do a new thing,
Now it shall spring forth;
Shall you not know it?
I will even make a road in the wilderness
And rivers in the desert.
20The beast of the field will honor Me,
The jackals and the ostriches,
Because I give waters in the wilderness
And rivers in the desert,
To give drink to My people, My chosen.
21This people I have formed for Myself;
They shall declare My praise.

PLEADING WITH UNFAITHFUL ISRAEL

22"But you have not called upon Me, O Jacob;
And you have been weary of Me, O Israel.
23You have not brought Me the sheep for your burnt offerings,
Nor have you honored Me with your sacrifices.
I have not caused you to serve with grain offerings,
Nor wearied you with incense.
24You have bought Me no sweet cane with money,
Nor have you satisfied Me with the fat of your sacrifices;
But you have burdened Me with your sins,
You have wearied Me with your iniquities.

25"I, *even* I, *am* He who blots out your transgressions for My own sake;
And I will not remember your sins.
26Put Me in remembrance;
Let us contend together;
State your *case*, that you may be acquitted.
27Your first father sinned,
And your mediators have transgressed against Me.
28Therefore I will profane the princes of the sanctuary;
I will give Jacob to the curse,
And Israel to reproaches.

GOD'S BLESSING ON ISRAEL

44 "Yet hear me now, O Jacob My servant,
And Israel whom I have chosen.
2Thus says the LORD who made you
And formed you from the womb, *who* will help you:
'Fear not, O Jacob My servant;
And you, Jeshurun, whom I have chosen.
3For I will pour water on him who is thirsty,
And floods on the dry ground;
I will pour My Spirit on your descendants,
And My blessing on your offspring;

THE MESSAGE

16-21 This is what GOD says,
the God who builds a road right through the ocean,
who carves a path through pounding waves,
The God who summons horses and chariots and armies—
they lie down and then can't get up;
they're snuffed out like so many candles:
"Forget about what's happened;
don't keep going over old history.
Be alert, be present. I'm about to do something brand-new.
It's bursting out! Don't you see it?
There it is! I'm making a road through the desert,
rivers in the badlands.
Wild animals will say 'Thank you!'
—the coyotes and the buzzards—
Because I provided water in the desert,
rivers through the sun-baked earth,
Drinking water for the people I chose,
the people I made especially for myself,
a people custom-made to praise me.

22-24 "But you didn't pay a bit of attention to me, Jacob.
You so quickly tired of me, Israel.
You wouldn't even bring sheep for offerings in worship.
You couldn't be bothered with sacrifices.
It wasn't that I asked that much from you.
I didn't expect expensive presents.
But you didn't even do the minimum—
so stingy with me, so closefisted.
Yet you haven't been stingy with your sins.
You've been plenty generous with them—and I'm fed up.

25 "But I, yes I, am the one
who takes care of your sins—that's what I do.
I don't keep a list of your sins.

26-28 "So, make your case against me. Let's have this out.
Make your arguments. Prove you're in the right.
Your original ancestor started the sinning,
and everyone since has joined in.
That's why I had to disqualify the Temple leaders,
repudiate Jacob and discredit Israel."

PROUD TO BE CALLED ISRAEL

1-5 44 "But for now, dear servant Jacob, listen—
yes, you, Israel, my personal choice.
GOD who made you has something to say to you;
the God who formed you in the womb wants to help you.
Don't be afraid, dear servant Jacob,
Jeshurun, the one I chose.
For I will pour water on the thirsty ground
and send streams coursing through the parched earth.
I will pour my Spirit into your descendants
and my blessing on your children.

NEW KING JAMES VERSION

4They will spring up among the grass
Like willows by the watercourses.'
5One will say, 'I *am* the LORD's';
Another will call *himself* by the name of Jacob;
Another will write *with* his hand, 'The LORD's,'
And name *himself* by the name of Israel.

THERE IS NO OTHER GOD

6"Thus says the LORD, the King of Israel,
And his Redeemer, the LORD of hosts:
"I *am* the First and I *am* the Last;
Besides Me *there is* no God.
7And who can proclaim as I do?
Then let him declare it and set it in order for Me,
Since I appointed the ancient people.
And the things that are coming and shall come,
Let them show these to them.
8Do not fear, nor be afraid;
Have I not told you from that time, and declared *it*?
You *are* My witnesses.
Is there a God besides Me?
Indeed *there is* no other Rock;
I know not *one*.' "

IDOLATRY IS FOOLISHNESS

9Those who make an image, all of them *are* useless,
And their precious things shall not profit;
They *are* their own witnesses;
They neither see nor know, that they may be ashamed.
10Who would form a god or mold an image
That profits him nothing?
11Surely all his companions would be ashamed;
And the workmen, they *are* mere men.
Let them all be gathered together,
Let them stand up;
Yet they shall fear,
They shall be ashamed together.

12The blacksmith with the tongs works one in the coals,
Fashions it with hammers,
And works it with the strength of his arms.
Even so, he is hungry, and his strength fails;
He drinks no water and is faint.

13The craftsman stretches out *his* rule,
He marks one out with chalk;
He fashions it with a plane,
He marks it out with the compass,
And makes it like the figure of a man,
According to the beauty of a man, that it may remain in the house.
14He cuts down cedars for himself,
And takes the cypress and the oak;
He secures *it* for himself among the trees of the forest.
He plants a pine, and the rain nourishes *it*.

15Then it shall be for a man to burn,
For he will take some of it and warm himself;

THE MESSAGE

They shall sprout like grass on the prairie,
like willows alongside creeks.
This one will say, 'I am GOD's,'
and another will go by the name Jacob;
That one will write on his hand 'GOD's property'—
and be proud to be called Israel."

6-8 GOD, King of Israel,
your Redeemer, GOD-of-the-Angel-Armies, says:
"I'm first, I'm last, and everything in between.
I'm the only God there is.
Who compares with me?
Speak up. See if you measure up.
From the beginning, who else has always announced what's coming?
So what is coming next? Anybody want to venture a try?
Don't be afraid, and don't worry:
Haven't I always kept you informed, told you what was going on?
You're my eyewitnesses:
Have you ever come across a God, a real God, other than me?
There's no Rock like me that I know of."

LOVER OF EMPTINESS

9-11 All those who make no-god idols don't
amount to a thing, and what they work so
hard at making is nothing. Their little pup-
pet-gods see nothing and know nothing—
they're total embarrassments! Who would
bother making gods that can't do anything,
that can't *"god"*? Watch all the no-god wor-
shipers hide their faces in shame. Watch the
no-god makers slink off humiliated when
their idols fail them. Get them out here in
the open. Make them face God-reality.
12 The blacksmith makes his no-god, works
it over in his forge, hammering it on his
anvil—such hard work! He works away, fa-
tigued with hunger and thirst.
13-17 The woodworker draws up plans for his
no-god, traces it on a block of wood. He
shapes it with chisels and planes into hu-
man shape—a beautiful woman, a hand-
some man, ready to be placed in a chapel.
He first cuts down a cedar, or maybe picks
out a pine or oak, and lets it grow strong in
the forest, nourished by the rain. Then it can
serve a double purpose: Part he uses as fire-
wood for keeping warm and baking bread;

NEW KING JAMES VERSION

Yes, he kindles *it* and bakes bread;
Indeed he makes a god and worships *it;*
He makes it a carved image, and falls down to it.
16He burns half of it in the fire;
With this half he eats meat;
He roasts a roast, and is satisfied.
He even warms *himself* and says,
"Ah! I am warm,
I have seen the fire."
17And the rest of it he makes into a god,
His carved image.
He falls down before it and worships *it,*
Prays to it and says,
"Deliver me, for you *are* my god!"

18They do not know nor understand;
For He has shut their eyes, so that they cannot see,
And their hearts, so that they cannot understand.
19And no one considers in his heart,
Nor *is there* knowledge nor understanding to say,
"I have burned half of it in the fire,
Yes, I have also baked bread on its coals;
I have roasted meat and eaten *it;*
And shall I make the rest of it an abomination?
Shall I fall down before a block of wood?"
20He feeds on ashes;
A deceived heart has turned him aside;
And he cannot deliver his soul,
Nor say, "*Is there* not a lie in my right hand?"

ISRAEL IS NOT FORGOTTEN

21"Remember these, O Jacob,
And Israel, for you *are* My servant;
I have formed you, you *are* My servant;
O Israel, you will not be forgotten by Me!
22I have blotted out, like a thick cloud, your transgressions,
And like a cloud, your sins.
Return to Me, for I have redeemed you."

23Sing, O heavens, for the LORD has done *it!*
Shout, you lower parts of the earth;
Break forth into singing, you mountains,
O forest, and every tree in it!
For the LORD has redeemed Jacob,
And glorified Himself in Israel.

JUDAH WILL BE RESTORED

24Thus says the LORD, your Redeemer,
And He who formed you from the womb:
"I *am* the LORD, who makes all *things,*
Who stretches out the heavens all alone,
Who spreads abroad the earth by Myself;
25Who frustrates the signs of the babblers,
And drives diviners mad;
Who turns wise men backward,
And makes their knowledge foolishness;
26Who confirms the word of His servant,
And performs the counsel of His messengers;
Who says to Jerusalem, 'You shall be inhabited,'
To the cities of Judah, 'You shall be built,'
And I will raise up her waste places;

THE MESSAGE

from the other part he makes a god that he
worships—carves it into a god shape and
prays before it. With half he makes a fire to
warm himself and barbecue his supper. He
eats his fill and sits back satisfied with his
stomach full and his feet warmed by the
fire: "Ah, this is the life." And he still has half
left for a god, made to his personal design—
a handy, convenient no-god to worship
whenever so inclined. Whenever the need
strikes him he prays to it, "Save me. You're
my god."
18-19 Pretty stupid, wouldn't you say? Don't
they have eyes in their heads? Are their
brains working at all? Doesn't it occur to
them to say, "Half of this tree I used for fire-
wood: I baked bread, roasted meat, and en-
joyed a good meal. And now I've used the
rest to make an abominable no-god. Here I
am praying to a stick of wood!"
20 This lover of emptiness, of nothing, is so
out of touch with reality, so far gone, that he
can't even look at what he's doing, can't
even look at the no-god stick of wood in his
hand and say, "This is crazy."

21-22 "Remember these things, O Jacob.
Take it seriously, Israel, that you're my servant.
I made you, *shaped* you: You're my servant.
O Israel, I'll never forget you.
I've wiped the slate of all your wrongdoings.
There's nothing left of your sins.
Come back to me, come back.
I've redeemed you."

23 High heavens, sing!
GOD has done it.
Deep earth, shout!
And you mountains, sing!
A forest choir of oaks and pines and cedars!
GOD has redeemed Jacob.
GOD's glory is on display in Israel.

24 GOD, your Redeemer,
who shaped your life in your mother's womb, says:
"I am GOD. I made all that is.
With no help from you I spread out the skies
and laid out the earth."

25-28 He makes the magicians look ridiculous
and turns fortunetellers into jokes.
He makes the experts look trivial
and their latest knowledge look silly.
But he backs the word of his servant
and confirms the counsel of his messengers.
He says to Jerusalem, "Be inhabited,"
and to the cities of Judah, "Be rebuilt,"
and to the ruins, "I raise you up."

NEW KING JAMES VERSION

27Who says to the deep, 'Be dry!
And I will dry up your rivers';
28Who says of Cyrus, '*He is* My shepherd,
And he shall perform all My pleasure,
Saying to Jerusalem, "You shall be built,"
And to the temple, "Your foundation shall be laid." '

CYRUS, GOD'S INSTRUMENT

45 "Thus says the LORD to His anointed,
To Cyrus, whose right hand I have held—
To subdue nations before him
And loose the armor of kings,
To open before him the double doors,
So that the gates will not be shut:
2'I will go before you
And make the crooked places[a] straight;
I will break in pieces the gates of bronze
And cut the bars of iron.
3I will give you the treasures of darkness
And hidden riches of secret places,
That you may know that I, the LORD,
Who call *you* by your name,
Am the God of Israel.
4For Jacob My servant's sake,
And Israel My elect,
I have even called you by your name;
I have named you, though you have not known Me.
5I *am* the LORD, and *there is* no other;
There is no God besides Me.
I will gird you, though you have not known Me,
6That they may know from the rising of the sun to its setting
That *there is* none besides Me.
I *am* the LORD, and *there is* no other;
7I form the light and create darkness,
I make peace and create calamity;
I, the LORD, do all these *things*.'

8"Rain down, you heavens, from above,
And let the skies pour down righteousness;
Let the earth open, let them bring forth salvation,
And let righteousness spring up together.
I, the LORD, have created it.

9"Woe to him who strives with his Maker!
Let the potsherd *strive* with the potsherds of the earth!
Shall the clay say to him who forms it,
'What are you making?'
Or shall your handiwork *say*, 'He has no hands'?
10Woe to him who says to *his* father, 'What are you begetting?'
Or to the woman, 'What have you brought forth?' "

11Thus says the LORD,
The Holy One of Israel, and his Maker:
"Ask Me of things to come concerning My sons;
And concerning the work of My hands, you command Me.

45:2 [a]Dead Sea Scrolls and Septuagint read *mountains;* Targum reads *I will trample down the walls;* Vulgate reads *I will humble the great ones of the earth.*

THE MESSAGE

He says to Ocean, "Dry up.
I'm drying up your rivers."
He says to Cyrus, "My shepherd—
everything I want, you'll do it."
He says to Jerusalem, "Be built,"
and to the Temple, "Be established."

THE GOD WHO FORMS LIGHT AND DARKNESS

1-7 45 GOD'S Message to his anointed,
to Cyrus, whom he took by the hand
To give the task of taming the nations,
of terrifying their kings—
He gave him free rein,
no restrictions:
"I'll go ahead of you,
clearing and paving the road.
I'll break down bronze city gates,
smash padlocks, kick down barred entrances.
I'll lead you to buried treasures,
secret caches of valuables—
Confirmations that it is, in fact, I, GOD,
the God of Israel, who calls you by your name.
It's because of my dear servant Jacob,
Israel my chosen,
That I've singled you out, called you by name,
and given you this privileged work.
And you don't even know me!
I am GOD, the only God there is.
Besides me there are no real gods.
I'm the one who armed you for this work,
though you don't even know me,
So that everyone, from east to west, will know
that I have no god-rivals.
I am GOD, the only God there is.
I form light and create darkness,
I make harmonies and create discords.
I, GOD, do all these things.

8-10 "Open up, heavens, and rain.
Clouds, pour out buckets of my goodness!
Loosen up, earth, and bloom salvation;
sprout right living.
I, GOD, generate all this.
But doom to you who fight your Maker—
you're a pot at odds with the potter!
Does clay talk back to the potter:
'What are you doing? What clumsy fingers!'
Would a sperm say to a father,
'Who gave you permission to use me to make a baby?'
Or a fetus to a mother,
'Why have you cooped me up in this belly?' "

11-13 Thus GOD, The Holy of Israel, Israel's Maker, says:
"Do you question who or what I'm making?
Are you telling me what I can or cannot do?

NEW KING JAMES VERSION

[12]I have made the earth,
And created man on it.
I—My hands—stretched out the heavens,
And all their host I have commanded.
[13]I have raised him up in righteousness,
And I will direct all his ways;
He shall build My city
And let My exiles go free,
Not for price nor reward,"
Says the LORD of hosts.

THE LORD, THE ONLY SAVIOR

[14]Thus says the LORD:

"The labor of Egypt and merchandise of Cush
And of the Sabeans, men of stature,
Shall come over to you, and they shall be yours;
They shall walk behind you,
They shall come over in chains;
And they shall bow down to you.
They will make supplication to you, *saying*,
'Surely God *is* in you,
And *there is* no other;
There is no other God.' "

[15]Truly You *are* God, who hide Yourself,
O God of Israel, the Savior!
[16]They shall be ashamed
And also disgraced, all of them;
They shall go in confusion together,
Who are makers of idols.
[17]*But* Israel shall be saved by the LORD
With an everlasting salvation;
You shall not be ashamed or disgraced
Forever and ever.

[18]For thus says the LORD,
Who created the heavens,
Who is God,
Who formed the earth and made it,
Who has established it,
Who did not create it in vain,
Who formed it to be inhabited:
"I *am* the LORD, and *there is* no other.
[19]I have not spoken in secret,
In a dark place of the earth;
I did not say to the seed of Jacob,
'Seek Me in vain';
I, the LORD, speak righteousness,
I declare things that are right.

[20]"Assemble yourselves and come;
Draw near together,
You *who have* escaped from the nations.
They have no knowledge,
Who carry the wood of their carved image,
And pray to a god *that* cannot save.

THE MESSAGE

I made earth,
and I created man and woman to live on it.
I handcrafted the skies
and direct all the constellations in their turnings.
And now I've got Cyrus on the move.
I've rolled out the red carpet before him.
He will build my city.
He will bring home my exiles.
I didn't hire him to do this. I *told* him.
I, GOD-of-the-Angel-Armies."

14 GOD says:

"The workers of Egypt, the merchants of Ethiopia,
and those statuesque Sabeans
Will all come over to you—all yours.
Docile in chains, they'll follow you,
Hands folded in reverence, praying before you:
'Amazing! God is with you!
There is no other God—none.' "

LOOK AT THE EVIDENCE

15-17 Clearly, you are a God who works behind the scenes,
God of Israel, Savior God.
Humiliated, all those others
will be ashamed to show their faces in public.
Out of work and at loose ends, the makers of no-god idols
won't know what to do with themselves.
The people of Israel, though, are saved by you, GOD,
saved with an eternal salvation.
They won't be ashamed,
they won't be at loose ends, ever.

18-24 GOD, Creator of the heavens—
he is, remember, *God*.
Maker of earth—
he put it on its foundations, built it from scratch.
He didn't go to all that trouble
to just leave it empty, nothing in it.
He made it to be lived in.

This GOD says:

"I am GOD,
the one and only.
I don't just talk to myself
or mumble under my breath.
I never told Jacob,
'Seek me in emptiness, in dark nothingness.'
I am GOD. I work out in the open,
saying what's right, setting things right.
So gather around, come on in,
all you refugees and castoffs.
They don't seem to know much, do they—
those who carry around their no-god blocks of wood,
praying for help to a dead stick?
So tell me what you think. Look at the evidence.
Put your heads together. Make your case.

NEW KING JAMES VERSION

21Tell and bring forth *your case;*
Yes, let them take counsel together.
Who has declared this from ancient time?
Who has told it from that time?
Have not I, the LORD?
And *there is* no other God besides Me,
A just God and a Savior;
There is none besides Me.

22"Look to Me, and be saved,
All you ends of the earth!
For I *am* God, and *there is* no other.
23I have sworn by Myself;
The word has gone out of My mouth *in*
righteousness,
And shall not return,
That to Me every knee shall bow,
Every tongue shall take an oath.
24He shall say,
"Surely in the LORD I have righteousness and
strength.
To Him *men* shall come,
And all shall be ashamed
Who are incensed against Him.
25In the LORD all the descendants of Israel
Shall be justified, and shall glory.' "

DEAD IDOLS AND THE LIVING GOD

46 Bel bows down, Nebo stoops;
Their idols were on the beasts and on the
cattle.
Your carriages *were* heavily loaded,
A burden to the weary *beast.*
2They stoop, they bow down together;
They could not deliver the burden,
But have themselves gone into captivity.

3"Listen to Me, O house of Jacob,
And all the remnant of the house of Israel,
Who have been upheld *by Me* from birth,
Who have been carried from the womb:
4Even to *your* old age, I *am* He,
And *even* to gray hairs I will carry *you!*
I have made, and I will bear;
Even I will carry, and will deliver *you.*

5"To whom will you liken Me, and make *Me*
equal
And compare Me, that we should be alike?
6They lavish gold out of the bag,
And weigh silver on the scales;
They hire a goldsmith, and he makes it a
god;
They prostrate themselves, yes, they
worship.
7They bear it on the shoulder, they carry it
And set it in its place, and it stands;
From its place it shall not move.
Though *one* cries out to it, yet it cannot
answer
Nor save him out of his trouble.

THE MESSAGE

Who told you, and a long time ago, what's
going on here?
Who made sense of things for you?
Wasn't I the one? GOD?
It had to be me. I'm the only God there
is—
The only God who does things right
and knows how to help.
So turn to me and be helped—saved!—
everyone, whoever and wherever you
are.
I am GOD,
the only God there is, the one and only.
I promise in my own name:
Every word out of my mouth does what
it says.
I never take back what I say.
Everyone is going to end up kneeling
before me.
Everyone is going to end up saying of
me,
'Yes! Salvation and strength are in
GOD!' "

24-25 All who have raged against him
will be brought before him,
disgraced by their unbelief.
And all who are connected with Israel
will have a robust, praising, good life in
GOD!

THIS IS SERIOUS BUSINESS, REBELS

1-2 46 The god Bel falls down, god Nebo
slumps.
The no-god hunks of wood are loaded on
mules
And have to be hauled off,
wearing out the poor mules—
Dead weight, burdens who can't bear
burdens,
hauled off to captivity.

3-4 "Listen to me, family of Jacob,
everyone that's left of the family of
Israel.
I've been carrying you on my back
from the day you were born,
And I'll keep on carrying you when you're
old.
I'll be there, bearing you when you're old
and gray.
I've done it and will keep on doing it,
carrying you on my back, saving you.

5-7 "So to whom will you compare me, the
Incomparable?
Can you picture me without reducing
me?
People with a lot of money
hire craftsmen to make them gods.
The artisan delivers the god,
and they kneel and worship it!
They carry it around in holy parades,
then take it home and put it on a shelf.
And there it sits, day in and day out,
a dependable god, always right where
you put it.
Say anything you want to it, it never talks
back.
Of course, it never *does* anything either!

NEW KING JAMES VERSION

8"Remember this, and show yourselves men;
Recall to mind, O you transgressors.
9Remember the former things of old,
For I *am* God, and *there is* no other;
I am God, and *there is* none like Me,
10Declaring the end from the beginning,
And from ancient times *things* that are not *yet* done,
Saying, 'My counsel shall stand,
And I will do all My pleasure,'
11Calling a bird of prey from the east,
The man who executes My counsel, from a far country.
Indeed I have spoken *it;*
I will also bring it to pass.
I have purposed *it;*
I will also do it.

12"Listen to Me, you stubborn-hearted,
Who *are* far from righteousness:
13I bring My righteousness near, it shall not be far off;
My salvation shall not linger.
And I will place salvation in Zion,
For Israel My glory.

THE HUMILIATION OF BABYLON

47 "Come down and sit in the dust,
O virgin daughter of Babylon;
Sit on the ground without a throne,
O daughter of the Chaldeans!
For you shall no more be called
Tender and delicate.
2Take the millstones and grind meal.
Remove your veil,
Take off the skirt,
Uncover the thigh,
Pass through the rivers.
3Your nakedness shall be uncovered,
Yes, your shame will be seen;
I will take vengeance,
And I will not arbitrate with a man."

4*As for* our Redeemer, the LORD of hosts *is* His name,
The Holy One of Israel.

5"Sit in silence, and go into darkness,
O daughter of the Chaldeans;
For you shall no longer be called
The Lady of Kingdoms.
6I was angry with My people;
I have profaned My inheritance,
And given them into your hand.
You showed them no mercy;
On the elderly you laid your yoke very heavily.
7And you said, 'I shall be a lady forever,'
So that you did not take these *things* to heart,
Nor remember the latter end of them.

8"Therefore hear this now, *you who are* given to pleasures,

THE MESSAGE

8-11 "Think about this. Wrap your minds around it.
This is serious business, rebels. Take it to heart.
Remember your history,
your long and rich history.
I am GOD, the only God you've had or ever will have—
incomparable, irreplaceable—
From the very beginning
telling you what the ending will be,
All along letting you in
on what is going to happen,
Assuring you, 'I'm in this for the long haul,
I'll do exactly what I set out to do,'
Calling that eagle, Cyrus, out of the east,
from a far country the man I chose to help me.
I've said it, and I'll most certainly do it.
I've planned it, so it's as good as done.

12-13 "Now listen to me:
You're a hardheaded bunch and hard to help.
I'm ready to help you right now.
Deliverance is not a long-range plan.
Salvation isn't on hold.
I'm putting salvation to work in Zion now,
and glory in Israel."

THE PARTY'S OVER

1-3 47 "Get off your high horse and sit in the dirt,
virgin daughter of Babylon.
No more throne for you—sit on the ground,
daughter of the Chaldeans.
Nobody will be calling you 'charming'
and 'alluring' anymore. Get used to it.
Get a job, any old job:
Clean gutters, scrub toilets.
Hock your gowns and scarves,
put on overalls—the party's over.
Your nude body will be on public display,
exposed to vulgar taunts.
It's vengeance time, and I'm taking vengeance.
No one gets let off the hook."

YOU'RE ACTING LIKE THE CENTER OF THE UNIVERSE

4-13 Our Redeemer speaks,
named GOD-of-the-Angel-Armies, The Holy of Israel:
"Shut up and get out of the way,
daughter of Chaldeans.
You'll no longer be called
'First Lady of the Kingdoms.'
I was fed up with my people,
thoroughly disgusted with my progeny.
I turned them over to you,
but you had no compassion.
You put old men and women
to cruel, hard labor.
You said, 'I'm the First Lady.
I'll always be the pampered darling.'
You took nothing seriously, took nothing to heart,
never gave tomorrow a thought.
Well, start thinking, playgirl.

NEW KING JAMES VERSION

Who dwell securely,
Who say in your heart, 'I *am*, and *there is* no
one else besides me;
I shall not sit *as* a widow,
Nor shall I know the loss of children';
9But these two *things* shall come to you
In a moment, in one day:
The loss of children, and widowhood.
They shall come upon you in their fullness
Because of the multitude of your sorceries,
For the great abundance of your
enchantments.

10"For you have trusted in your wickedness;
You have said, 'No one sees me';
Your wisdom and your knowledge have
warped you;
And you have said in your heart,
"I *am*, and *there is* no one else besides me.'
11Therefore evil shall come upon you;
You shall not know from where it arises.
And trouble shall fall upon you;
You will not be able to put it off.
And desolation shall come upon you
suddenly,
Which you shall not know.

12"Stand now with your enchantments
And the multitude of your sorceries,
In which you have labored from your
youth—
Perhaps you will be able to profit,
Perhaps you will prevail.
13You are wearied in the multitude of your
counsels;
Let now the astrologers, the stargazers,
And the monthly prognosticators
Stand up and save you
From what shall come upon you.
14Behold, they shall be as stubble,
The fire shall burn them;
They shall not deliver themselves
From the power of the flame;
It shall not *be* a coal to be warmed by,
Nor a fire to sit before!
15Thus shall they be to you
With whom you have labored,
Your merchants from your youth;
They shall wander each one to his quarter.
No one shall save you.

ISRAEL REFINED FOR GOD'S GLORY

48 "Hear this, O house of Jacob,
Who are called by the name of Israel,
And have come forth from the wellsprings
of Judah;
Who swear by the name of the LORD,
And make mention of the God of Israel,
But not in truth or in righteousness;
2For they call themselves after the holy city,
And lean on the God of Israel;
The LORD of hosts *is* His name:

3"I have declared the former things from the
beginning;

THE MESSAGE

You're acting like the center of the
universe,
Smugly saying to yourself, 'I'm Number
One. There's nobody but me.
I'll never be a widow, I'll never lose my
children.'
Those two things are going to hit you both
at once,
suddenly, on the same day:
Spouse and children gone, a total loss,
despite your many enchantments and
charms.
You were so confident and comfortable in
your evil life,
saying, 'No one sees me.'
You thought you knew so much, had
everything figured out.
What delusion!
Smugly telling yourself, 'I'm Number
One. There's nobody but me.'
Ruin descends—
you can't charm it away.
Disaster strikes—
you can't cast it off with spells.
Catastrophe, sudden and total—
and you're totally at sea, totally
bewildered!
But don't give up. From your great
repertoire
of enchantments there must be one you
haven't yet tried.
You've been at this a long time.
Surely *something* will work.
I know you're exhausted trying out
remedies,
but don't give up.
Call in the astrologers and stargazers.
They're good at this. Surely they can
work up something!

14-15 "Fat chance. You'd be grasping at straws
that are already in the fire,
A fire that is even now raging.
Your 'experts' are in it and won't get out.
It's not a fire for cooking venison stew,
not a fire to warm you on a winter night!
That's the fate of your friends in sorcery,
your magician buddies
you've been in cahoots with all your life.
They reel, confused, bumping into one
another.
None of them bother to help you."

TESTED IN THE FURNACE OF AFFLICTION

1-11 48 "And now listen to this, family of Jacob,
you who are called by the name
Israel:
Who got you started in the loins of Judah,
you who use GOD's name to back up
your promises
and pray to the God of Israel?
But do you mean it?
Do you live like it?
You claim to be citizens of the Holy City;
you act as though you lean on the God of
Israel,
named GOD-of-the-Angel-Armies.
For a long time now, I've let you in on the
way I work:

NEW KING JAMES VERSION

They went forth from My mouth, and I caused them to hear it.
Suddenly I did *them*, and they came to pass.
4Because I knew that you *were* obstinate,
And your neck *was* an iron sinew,
And your brow bronze,
5Even from the beginning I have declared *it* to you;
Before it came to pass I proclaimed *it* to you,
Lest you should say, 'My idol has done them,
And my carved image and my molded image
Have commanded them.'

6"You have heard;
See all this.
And will you not declare *it?*
I have made you hear new things from this time,
Even hidden things, and you did not know them.
7They are created now and not from the beginning;
And before this day you have not heard them,
Lest you should say, 'Of course I knew them.'
8Surely you did not hear,
Surely you did not know;
Surely from long ago your ear was not opened.
For I knew that you would deal very treacherously,
And were called a transgressor from the womb.

9"For My name's sake I will defer My anger,
And *for* My praise I will restrain it from you,
So that I do not cut you off.
10Behold, I have refined you, but not as silver;
I have tested you in the furnace of affliction.
11For My own sake, for My own sake, I will do *it;*
For how should *My name* be profaned?
And I will not give My glory to another.

GOD'S ANCIENT PLAN TO REDEEM ISRAEL

12"Listen to Me, O Jacob,
And Israel, My called:
I *am* He, I *am* the First,
I *am* also the Last.
13Indeed My hand has laid the foundation of the earth,
And My right hand has stretched out the heavens;
When I call to them,
They stand up together.

14"All of you, assemble yourselves, and hear!
Who among them has declared these *things?*
The LORD loves him;
He shall do His pleasure on Babylon,
And His arm *shall be against* the Chaldeans.
15I, *even* I, have spoken;
Yes, I have called him,

THE MESSAGE

I told you what I was going to do beforehand,
then I did it and it was done, and that's that.
I know you're a bunch of hardheads,
obstinate and flint-faced,
So I got a running start and began telling you
what was going on before it even happened.
That is why you can't say,
'My god-idol did this.'
'My favorite god-carving commanded this.'
You have all this evidence
confirmed by your own eyes and ears.
Shouldn't you be talking about it?
And that was just the beginning.
I have a lot more to tell you,
things you never knew existed.
This isn't a variation on the same old thing.
This is new, brand-new,
something you'd never guess or dream up.
When you hear this you won't be able to say,
'I knew that all along.'
You've never been good listeners to me.
You have a history of ignoring me,
A sorry track record of fickle attachments—
rebels from the womb.
But out of the sheer goodness of my heart,
because of who I am,
I keep a tight rein on my anger and hold my temper.
I don't wash my hands of you.
Do you see what I've done?
I've refined you, but not without fire.
I've tested you like silver in the furnace of affliction.
Out of myself, simply because of who I am,
I do what I do.
I have my reputation to keep up.
I'm not playing second fiddle to either gods or people.

12-13 "Listen, Jacob. Listen, Israel—
I'm the One who named you!
I'm the One.
I got things started and, yes, I'll wrap them up.
Earth is my work, handmade.
And the skies—I made them, too,
horizon to horizon.
When I speak, they're on their feet, at attention.

14-16 "Come everybody, gather around, listen:
Who among the gods has delivered the news?
I, GOD, love this man Cyrus, and I'm using him
to do what I want with Babylon.
I, yes I, have spoken. I've called him.

NEW KING JAMES VERSION

I have brought him, and his way will
prosper.

16"Come near to Me, hear this:
I have not spoken in secret from the
beginning;
From the time that it was, I *was* there.
And now the Lord GOD and His Spirit
Have[a] sent Me."

17Thus says the LORD, your Redeemer,
The Holy One of Israel:
"I *am* the LORD your God,
Who teaches you to profit,
Who leads you by the way you should go.
18Oh, that you had heeded My
commandments!
Then your peace would have been like a
river,
And your righteousness like the waves of
the sea.
19Your descendants also would have been like
the sand,
And the offspring of your body like the
grains of sand;
His name would not have been cut off
Nor destroyed from before Me."

20Go forth from Babylon!
Flee from the Chaldeans!
With a voice of singing,
Declare, proclaim this,
Utter it to the end of the earth;
Say, "The LORD has redeemed
His servant Jacob!"
21And they did not thirst
When He led them through the deserts;
He caused the waters to flow from the rock
for them;
He also split the rock, and the waters
gushed out.

22"*There is* no peace," says the LORD, "for the
wicked."

THE SERVANT, THE LIGHT TO THE GENTILES

49 "Listen, O coastlands, to Me,
And take heed, you peoples from afar!
The LORD has called Me from the womb;
From the matrix of My mother He has made
mention of My name.
2And He has made My mouth like a sharp
sword;
In the shadow of His hand He has hidden
Me,
And made Me a polished shaft;
In His quiver He has hidden Me."

3"And He said to me,
'You *are* My servant, O Israel,
In whom I will be glorified.'
4Then I said, 'I have labored in vain,
I have spent my strength for nothing and in
vain;
Yet surely my just reward *is* with the LORD,
And my work with my God.' "

48:16 [a]The Hebrew verb is singular.

THE MESSAGE

I've brought him here. He'll be
successful.
Come close, listen carefully:
I've never kept secrets from you.
I've always been present with you."

YOUR PROGENY, LIKE GRAINS OF SAND

16-19 And now, the Master, GOD, sends me and his
Spirit
with this Message from GOD,
your Redeemer, The Holy of Israel:
"I am GOD, your God,
who teaches you how to live right and
well.
I show you what to do, where to go.
If you had listened all along to what I told
you,
your life would have flowed full like a
river,
blessings rolling in like waves from the
sea.
Children and grandchildren are like sand,
your progeny like grains of sand.
There would be no end of them,
no danger of losing touch with me."

20 Get out of Babylon! Run from the
Babylonians!
Shout the news. Broadcast it.
Let the world know, the whole world.
Tell them, "GOD redeemed his dear
servant Jacob!"

21 They weren't thirsty when he led them
through the deserts.
He made water pour out of the rock;
he split the rock and the water gushed.

22 "There is no peace," says GOD, "for the
wicked."

A LIGHT FOR THE NATIONS

1-3 49 Listen, far-flung islands,
pay attention, faraway people:
GOD put me to work from the day I was
born.
The moment I entered the world he
named me.
He gave me speech that would cut and
penetrate.
He kept his hand on me to protect me.
He made me his straight arrow
and hid me in his quiver.
He said to me, "You're my dear servant,
Israel, through whom I'll shine."

4 But I said, "I've worked for nothing.
I've nothing to show for a life of hard
work.
Nevertheless, I'll let GOD have the last
word.
I'll let him pronounce his verdict."

NEW KING JAMES VERSION

5"And now the LORD says,
Who formed Me from the womb *to be* His Servant,
To bring Jacob back to Him,
So that Israel is gathered to Him[a]
(For I shall be glorious in the eyes of the LORD,
And My God shall be My strength),

6Indeed He says,
'It is too small a thing that You should be My Servant
To raise up the tribes of Jacob,
And to restore the preserved ones of Israel;
I will also give You as a light to the Gentiles,
That You should be My salvation to the ends of the earth.' "

7Thus says the LORD,
The Redeemer of Israel, their Holy One,
To Him whom man despises,
To Him whom the nation abhors,
To the Servant of rulers:
"Kings shall see and arise,
Princes also shall worship,
Because of the LORD who is faithful,
The Holy One of Israel;
And He has chosen You."

8Thus says the LORD:

"In an acceptable time I have heard You,
And in the day of salvation I have helped You;
I will preserve You and give You
As a covenant to the people,
To restore the earth,
To cause them to inherit the desolate heritages;
9That You may say to the prisoners, 'Go forth,'
To those who *are* in darkness, 'Show yourselves.'

"They shall feed along the roads,
And their pastures *shall be* on all desolate heights.
10They shall neither hunger nor thirst,
Neither heat nor sun shall strike them;
For He who has mercy on them will lead them,
Even by the springs of water He will guide them.
11I will make each of My mountains a road,
And My highways shall be elevated.
12Surely these shall come from afar;
Look! Those from the north and the west,
And these from the land of Sinim."

13Sing, O heavens!
Be joyful, O earth!
And break out in singing, O mountains!
For the LORD has comforted His people,
And will have mercy on His afflicted.

49:5 [a]Qere, Dead Sea Scrolls, and Septuagint read *is gathered to Him;* Kethib reads *is not gathered.*

THE MESSAGE

5-6 "And now," GOD says,
this God who took me in hand
from the moment of birth to be his servant,
To bring Jacob back home to him,
to set a reunion for Israel—
What an honor for me in GOD's eyes!
That God should be my strength!
He says, "But that's not a big enough job for my servant—
just to recover the tribes of Jacob,
merely to round up the strays of Israel.
I'm setting you up as a light for the *nations*
so that my salvation becomes *global!*"

7 GOD, Redeemer of Israel, The Holy of Israel,
says to the despised one, kicked around by the nations,
slave labor to the ruling class:
"Kings will see, get to their feet—the princes, too—
and then fall on their faces in homage
Because of GOD, who has faithfully kept his word,
The Holy of Israel, who has chosen you."

8-12 GOD also says:

"When the time's ripe, I answer you.
When victory's due, I help you.
I form you and use you
to reconnect the people with me,
To put the land in order,
to resettle families on the ruined properties.
I tell prisoners, 'Come on out. You're free!'
and those huddled in fear, 'It's all right. It's safe now.'
There'll be foodstands along all the roads,
picnics on all the hills—
Nobody hungry, nobody thirsty,
shade from the sun, shelter from the wind,
For the Compassionate One guides them,
takes them to the best springs.
I'll make all my mountains into roads,
turn them into a superhighway.
Look: These coming from far countries,
and those, out of the north,
These streaming in from the west,
and those from all the way down the Nile!"

13 Heavens, raise the roof! Earth, wake the dead!
Mountains, send up cheers!
GOD has comforted his people.
He has tenderly nursed his beaten-up, beaten-down people.

NEW KING JAMES VERSION

GOD WILL REMEMBER ZION

14But Zion said, "The LORD has forsaken me,
And my Lord has forgotten me."

15"Can a woman forget her nursing child,
And not have compassion on the son of her womb?
Surely they may forget,
Yet I will not forget you.
16See, I have inscribed you on the palms *of My hands;*
Your walls *are* continually before Me.
17Your sons[a] shall make haste;
Your destroyers and those who laid you waste
Shall go away from you.
18Lift up your eyes, look around and see;
All these gather together *and* come to you.
As I live," says the LORD,
"You shall surely clothe yourselves with them all as an ornament,
And bind them *on you* as a bride *does.*

19"For your waste and desolate places,
And the land of your destruction,
Will even now be too small for the inhabitants;
And those who swallowed you up will be far away.
20The children you will have,
After you have lost the others,
Will say again in your ears,
'The place *is* too small for me;
Give me a place where I may dwell.'
21Then you will say in your heart,
'Who has begotten these for me,
Since I have lost my children and am desolate,
A captive, and wandering to and fro?
And who has brought these up?
There I was, left alone;
But these, where *were* they?' "

22Thus says the Lord GOD:

"Behold, I will lift My hand in an oath to the nations,
And set up My standard for the peoples;
They shall bring your sons in *their* arms,
And your daughters shall be carried on *their* shoulders;
23Kings shall be your foster fathers,
And their queens your nursing mothers;
They shall bow down to you with *their* faces to the earth,
And lick up the dust of your feet.
Then you will know that I *am* the LORD,
For they shall not be ashamed who wait for Me."

24Shall the prey be taken from the mighty,
Or the captives of the righteous[a] be delivered?

49:17 [a]Dead Sea Scrolls, Septuagint, Targum, and Vulgate read *builders.* **49:24** [a]Following Masoretic Text and Targum; Dead Sea Scrolls, Syriac, and Vulgate read *the mighty;* Septuagint reads *unjustly.*

THE MESSAGE

14 But Zion said, "I don't get it. GOD has left me.
My Master has forgotten I even exist."

15-18 "Can a mother forget the infant at her breast,
walk away from the baby she bore?
But even if mothers forget,
I'd never forget you—never.
Look, I've written your names on the backs of my hands.
The walls you're rebuilding are never out of my sight.
Your builders are faster than your wreckers.
The demolition crews are gone for good.
Look up, look around, look well!
See them all gathering, coming to you?
As sure as I am the living God"—GOD's Decree—
"you're going to put them on like so much jewelry,
you're going to use them to dress up like a bride.

19-21 "And your ruined land?
Your devastated, decimated land?
Filled with more people than you know what to do with!
And your barbarian enemies, a fading memory.
The children born in your exile will be saying,
'It's getting too crowded here. I need more room.'
And you'll say to yourself,
'Where on earth did these children come from?
I lost everything, had nothing, was exiled and penniless.
So who reared these children?
How did these children get here?' "

22-23 The Master, GOD, says:

"Look! I signal to the nations,
I raise my flag to summon the people.
Here they'll come: women carrying your little boys in their arms,
men carrying your little girls on their shoulders.
Kings will be your babysitters,
princesses will be your nursemaids.
They'll offer to do all your drudge work—
scrub your floors, do your laundry.
You'll know then that I am GOD.
No one who hopes in me ever regrets it."

24-26 Can plunder be retrieved from a giant,
prisoners of war gotten back from a tyrant?

NEW KING JAMES VERSION

[25]But thus says the LORD:

"Even the captives of the mighty shall be taken away,
And the prey of the terrible be delivered;
For I will contend with him who contends with you,
And I will save your children.
[26]I will feed those who oppress you with their own flesh,
And they shall be drunk with their own blood as with sweet wine.
All flesh shall know
That I, the LORD, *am* your Savior,
And your Redeemer, the Mighty One of Jacob."

THE SERVANT, ISRAEL'S HOPE

50 Thus says the LORD:

"Where *is* the certificate of your mother's divorce,
Whom I have put away?
Or which of My creditors *is it* to whom I have sold you?
For your iniquities you have sold yourselves,
And for your transgressions your mother has been put away.
[2]Why, when I came, *was there* no man?
Why, when I called, *was there* none to answer?
Is My hand shortened at all that it cannot redeem?
Or have I no power to deliver?
Indeed with My rebuke I dry up the sea,
I make the rivers a wilderness;
Their fish stink because *there is* no water,
And die of thirst.
[3]I clothe the heavens with blackness,
And I make sackcloth their covering."

[4]"The Lord GOD has given Me
The tongue of the learned,
That I should know how to speak
A word in season to *him who is* weary.
He awakens Me morning by morning,
He awakens My ear
To hear as the learned.
[5]The Lord GOD has opened My ear;
And I was not rebellious,
Nor did I turn away.
[6]I gave My back to those who struck *Me,*
And My cheeks to those who plucked out the beard;
I did not hide My face from shame and spitting.

[7]"For the Lord GOD will help Me;
Therefore I will not be disgraced;
Therefore I have set My face like a flint,
And I know that I will not be ashamed.
[8]*He is* near who justifies Me;
Who will contend with Me?
Let us stand together.
Who *is* My adversary?
Let him come near Me.

THE MESSAGE

But GOD says, "Even if a giant grips the plunder
and a tyrant holds my people prisoner,
I'm the one who's on your side,
defending your cause, rescuing your children.
And your enemies, crazed and desperate,
will turn on themselves,
killing each other in a frenzy of self-destruction.
Then everyone will know that I, GOD,
have saved you—I, the Mighty One of Jacob."

WHO OUT THERE FEARS GOD?

1-3 50 GOD says:

"Can you produce your mother's divorce papers
proving I got rid of her?
Can you produce a receipt
proving I sold you?
Of course you can't.
It's your sins that put you here,
your wrongs that got you shipped out.
So why didn't anyone come when I knocked?
Why didn't anyone answer when I called?
Do you think I've forgotten how to help?
Am I so decrepit that I can't deliver?
I'm as powerful as ever,
and can reverse what I once did:
I can dry up the sea with a word,
turn river water into desert sand,
And leave the fish stinking in the sun,
stranded on dry land . . .
Turn all the lights out in the sky
and pull down the curtain."

4-9 The Master, GOD, has given me
a well-taught tongue,
So I know how to encourage tired people.
He wakes me up in the morning,
Wakes me up, opens my ears
to listen as one ready to take orders.
The Master, GOD, opened my ears,
and I didn't go back to sleep,
didn't pull the covers back over my head.
I followed orders,
stood there and took it while they beat me,
held steady while they pulled out my beard,
Didn't dodge their insults,
faced them as they spit in my face.
And the Master, GOD, stays right there and helps me,
so I'm not disgraced.
Therefore I set my face like flint,
confident that I'll never regret this.
My champion is right here.
Let's take our stand together!
Who dares bring suit against me?
Let him try!

NEW KING JAMES VERSION

9Surely the Lord GOD will help Me;
Who *is* he *who* will condemn Me?
Indeed they will all grow old like a garment;
The moth will eat them up.

10"Who among you fears the LORD?
Who obeys the voice of His Servant?
Who walks in darkness
And has no light?
Let him trust in the name of the LORD
And rely upon his God.
11Look, all you who kindle a fire,
Who encircle *yourselves* with sparks:
Walk in the light of your fire and in the sparks you have kindled—
This you shall have from My hand:
You shall lie down in torment.

THE LORD COMFORTS ZION

51 "Listen to Me, you who follow after righteousness,
You who seek the LORD:
Look to the rock *from which* you were hewn,
And to the hole of the pit *from which* you were dug.
2Look to Abraham your father,
And to Sarah *who* bore you;
For I called him alone,
And blessed him and increased him."

3For the LORD will comfort Zion,
He will comfort all her waste places;
He will make her wilderness like Eden,
And her desert like the garden of the LORD;
Joy and gladness will be found in it,
Thanksgiving and the voice of melody.

4"Listen to Me, My people;
And give ear to Me, O My nation:
For law will proceed from Me,
And I will make My justice rest
As a light of the peoples.
5My righteousness *is* near,
My salvation has gone forth,
And My arms will judge the peoples;
The coastlands will wait upon Me,
And on My arm they will trust.
6Lift up your eyes to the heavens,
And look on the earth beneath.
For the heavens will vanish away like smoke,
The earth will grow old like a garment,
And those who dwell in it will die in like manner;
But My salvation will be forever,
And My righteousness will not be abolished.

7"Listen to Me, you who know righteousness,
You people in whose heart *is* My law:
Do not fear the reproach of men,
Nor be afraid of their insults.

THE MESSAGE

Look! the Master, GOD, is right here.
Who would dare call me guilty?
Look! My accusers are a clothes bin of threadbare
socks and shirts, fodder for moths!

10-11 Who out there fears GOD,
actually listens to the voice of his servant?
For anyone out there who doesn't know where you're going,
anyone groping in the dark,
Here's what: Trust in GOD.
Lean on your God!
But if all you're after is making trouble,
playing with fire,
Go ahead and see where it gets you.
Set your fires, stir people up, blow on the flames,
But don't expect me to just stand there and watch.
I'll hold your feet to those flames.

COMMITTED TO SEEKING GOD

1-3 51 "Listen to me, all you who are serious about right living
and committed to seeking GOD.
Ponder the rock from which you were cut,
the quarry from which you were dug.
Yes, ponder Abraham, your father,
and Sarah, who bore you.
Think of it! One solitary man when I called him,
but once I blessed him, he multiplied.
Likewise I, GOD, will comfort Zion,
comfort all her mounds of ruins.
I'll transform her dead ground into Eden,
her moonscape into the garden of GOD,
A place filled with exuberance and laughter,
thankful voices and melodic songs.

4-6 "Pay attention, my people.
Listen to me, nations.
Revelation flows from me.
My decisions light up the world.
My deliverance arrives on the run,
my salvation right on time.
I'll bring justice to the peoples.
Even faraway islands will look to me
and take hope in my saving power.
Look up at the skies,
ponder the earth under your feet.
The skies will fade out like smoke,
the earth will wear out like work pants,
and the people will die off like flies.
But my salvation will last forever,
my setting-things-right will never be obsolete.

7-8 "Listen now, you who know right from wrong,
you who hold my teaching inside you:
Pay no attention to insults, and when mocked
don't let it get you down.

NEW KING JAMES VERSION

8For the moth will eat them up like a
garment,
And the worm will eat them like wool;
But My righteousness will be forever,
And My salvation from generation to
generation."

9Awake, awake, put on strength,
O arm of the LORD!
Awake as in the ancient days,
In the generations of old.
Are You not *the arm* that cut Rahab apart,
And wounded the serpent?

10*Are* You not *the One* who dried up the sea,
The waters of the great deep;
That made the depths of the sea a road
For the redeemed to cross over?
11So the ransomed of the LORD shall return,
And come to Zion with singing,
With everlasting joy on their heads.
They shall obtain joy and gladness;
Sorrow and sighing shall flee away.

12"I, *even* I, *am* He who comforts you.
Who *are* you that you should be afraid
Of a man *who* will die,
And of the son of a man *who* will be made
like grass?
13And you forget the LORD your Maker,
Who stretched out the heavens
And laid the foundations of the earth;
You have feared continually every day
Because of the fury of the oppressor,
When *he has* prepared to destroy.
And where *is* the fury of the oppressor?
14The captive exile hastens, that he may be
loosed,
That he should not die in the pit,
And that his bread should not fail.
15But I *am* the LORD your God,
Who divided the sea whose waves roared—
The LORD of hosts *is* His name.
16And I have put My words in your mouth;
I have covered you with the shadow of My
hand,
That I may plant the heavens,
Lay the foundations of the earth,
And say to Zion, 'You *are* My people.' "

GOD'S FURY REMOVED

17Awake, awake!
Stand up, O Jerusalem,
You who have drunk at the hand of the LORD
The cup of His fury;
You have drunk the dregs of the cup of
trembling,
And drained *it* out.
18*There is* no one to guide her
Among all the sons she has brought forth;
Nor *is there any* who takes her by the hand
Among all the sons she has brought up.
19These two *things* have come to you;
Who will be sorry for you?—
Desolation and destruction, famine and
sword—
By whom will I comfort you?
20Your sons have fainted,
They lie at the head of all the streets,
Like an antelope in a net;

THE MESSAGE

Those insults and mockeries are
moth-eaten,
from brains that are termite-ridden,
But my setting-things-right lasts,
my salvation goes on and on and on."

9-11 Wake up, wake up, flex your muscles, GOD!
Wake up as in the old days, in the long
ago.
Didn't you once make mincemeat of Rahab,
dispatch the old chaos-dragon?
And didn't you once dry up the sea,
the powerful waters of the deep,
And then made the bottom of the ocean a
road
for the redeemed to walk across?
In the same way GOD's ransomed will come
back,
come back to Zion cheering, shouting,
Joy eternal wreathing their heads,
exuberant ecstasies transporting them—
and not a sign of moans or groans.

WHAT ARE YOU AFRAID OF—OR WHO?

12-16 "I, I'm the One comforting you.
What are you afraid of—or who?
Some man or woman who'll soon be dead?
Some poor wretch destined for dust?
You've forgotten me, GOD, who made you,
who unfurled the skies, who founded the
earth.
And here you are, quaking like an aspen
before the tantrums of a tyrant
who thinks he can kick down the world.
But what will come of the tantrums?
The victims will be released before you
know it.
They're not going to die.
They're not even going to go hungry.
For I am GOD, your very own God,
who stirs up the sea and whips up the
waves,
named GOD-of-the-Angel-Armies.
I teach you how to talk, word by word,
and personally watch over you,
Even while I'm unfurling the skies,
setting earth on solid foundations,
and greeting Zion: 'Welcome, my
people!' "

17-20 So wake up! Rub the sleep from your eyes!
Up on your feet, Jerusalem!
You've drunk the cup GOD handed you,
the strong drink of his anger.
You drank it down to the last drop,
staggered and collapsed, dead-drunk.
And nobody to help you home,
no one among your friends or children
to take you by the hand and put you in
bed.
You've been hit with a double dose of
trouble
—does anyone care?
Assault and battery, hunger and death
—will anyone comfort?
Your sons and daughters have passed out,
strewn in the streets like stunned
rabbits,

NEW KING JAMES VERSION

They are full of the fury of the LORD,
The rebuke of your God.

21 Therefore please hear this, you afflicted,
And drunk but not with wine.
22 Thus says your Lord,
The LORD and your God,
Who pleads the cause of His people:
"See, I have taken out of your hand
The cup of trembling,
The dregs of the cup of My fury;
You shall no longer drink it.
23 But I will put it into the hand of those who afflict you,
Who have said to you,[a]
'Lie down, that we may walk over you.'
And you have laid your body like the ground,
And as the street, for those who walk over."

GOD REDEEMS JERUSALEM

52 Awake, awake!
Put on your strength, O Zion;
Put on your beautiful garments,
O Jerusalem, the holy city!
For the uncircumcised and the unclean
Shall no longer come to you.
2 Shake yourself from the dust, arise;
Sit down, O Jerusalem!
Loose yourself from the bonds of your neck,
O captive daughter of Zion!

3 For thus says the LORD:

"You have sold yourselves for nothing,
And you shall be redeemed without money."

4 For thus says the Lord GOD:

"My people went down at first
Into Egypt to dwell there;
Then the Assyrian oppressed them without cause.
5 Now therefore, what have I here," says the LORD,
"That My people are taken away for nothing?
Those who rule over them
Make them wail,"[a] says the LORD,
"And My name *is* blasphemed continually every day.
6 Therefore My people shall know My name;
Therefore *they shall know* in that day
That I *am* He who speaks:
'Behold, *it is* I.' "

7 How beautiful upon the mountains
Are the feet of him who brings good news,
Who proclaims peace,
Who brings glad tidings of good *things*,
Who proclaims salvation,
Who says to Zion,
"Your God reigns!"
8 Your watchmen shall lift up *their* voices,
With their voices they shall sing together;

51:23 [a]Literally *your soul* **52:5** [a]Dead Sea Scrolls read *Mock;* Septuagint reads *Marvel and wail;* Targum reads *Boast themselves;* Vulgate reads *Treat them unjustly.*

THE MESSAGE

Sleeping off the strong drink of GOD's anger,
the rage of your God.

21-23 Therefore listen, please,
you with your splitting headaches,
You who are nursing the hangovers
that didn't come from drinking wine.
Your Master, your GOD, has something to say,
your God has taken up his people's case:
"Look, I've taken back the drink that sent you reeling.
No more drinking from that jug of my anger!
I've passed it over to your abusers to drink,
those who ordered you,
'Down on the ground so we can walk all over you!'
And you had to do it. Flat on the ground,
you were the dirt under their feet."

GOD IS LEADING YOU OUT OF HERE

1-2 52 Wake up, wake up! Pull on your boots, Zion!
Dress up in your Sunday best,
Jerusalem, holy city!
Those who want no part of God have been culled out.
They won't be coming along.
Brush off the dust and get to your feet,
captive Jerusalem!
Throw off your chains, captive daughter of Zion!

3 GOD says, "You were sold for nothing.
You're being bought back for nothing."
4-6 Again, the Master, GOD, says, "Early on,
my people went to Egypt and lived,
strangers in the land. At the other end, As-
syria oppressed them. And now, what have I
here?" GOD's Decree. "My people are hauled
off again for no reason at all. Tyrants on the
warpath, whooping it up, and day after day,
incessantly, my reputation blackened. Now
it's time that my people know who I am,
what I'm made of—yes, that I have some-
thing to say. Here I am!"

7-10 How beautiful on the mountains
are the feet of the messenger bringing good news,
Breaking the news that all's well,
proclaiming good times, announcing salvation,
telling Zion, "Your God reigns!"
Voices! Listen! Your scouts are shouting,
thunderclap shouts,
shouting in joyful unison.

NEW KING JAMES VERSION

For they shall see eye to eye
When the LORD brings back Zion.
9Break forth into joy, sing together,
You waste places of Jerusalem!
For the LORD has comforted His people,
He has redeemed Jerusalem.
10The LORD has made bare His holy arm
In the eyes of all the nations;
And all the ends of the earth shall see
The salvation of our God.

11Depart! Depart! Go out from there,
Touch no unclean *thing;*
Go out from the midst of her,
Be clean,
You who bear the vessels of the LORD.
12For you shall not go out with haste,
Nor go by flight;
For the LORD will go before you,
And the God of Israel *will be* your rear
guard.

THE SIN-BEARING SERVANT
13Behold, My Servant shall deal prudently;
He shall be exalted and extolled and be very
high.
14Just as many were astonished at you,
So His visage was marred more than any
man,
And His form more than the sons of men;
15So shall He sprinkle[a] many nations.
Kings shall shut their mouths at Him;
For what had not been told them they shall
see,
And what they had not heard they shall
consider.

53 Who has believed our report?
And to whom has the arm of the LORD
been revealed?
2For He shall grow up before Him as a tender
plant,
And as a root out of dry ground.
He has no form or comeliness;
And when we see Him,
There is no beauty that we should desire
Him.
3He is despised and rejected by men,
A Man of sorrows and acquainted with
grief.
And we hid, as it were, *our* faces from Him;
He was despised, and we did not esteem
Him.

52:15 [a]Or *startle*

THE MESSAGE

They see with their own eyes
GOD coming back to Zion.
Break into song! Boom it out, ruins of
Jerusalem:
"GOD has comforted his people!
He's redeemed Jerusalem!"
GOD has rolled up his sleeves.
All the nations can see his holy, muscled
arm.
Everyone, from one end of the earth to the
other,
sees him at work, doing his salvation
work.

11-12 Out of here! Out of here! Leave this place!
Don't look back. Don't contaminate
yourselves with plunder.
Just leave, but leave clean. Purify
yourselves
in the process of worship, carrying the
holy vessels of GOD.
But you don't have to be in a hurry.
You're not running from anybody!
GOD is leading you out of here,
and the God of Israel is also your rear
guard.

IT WAS OUR PAINS HE CARRIED
13-15 "Just watch my servant blossom!
Exalted, tall, head and shoulders above
the crowd!
But he didn't begin that way.
At first everyone was appalled.
He didn't even look human—
a ruined face, disfigured past
recognition.
Nations all over the world will be in awe,
taken aback,
kings shocked into silence when they see
him.
For what was unheard of they'll see with
their own eyes,
what was unthinkable they'll have right
before them."

1 53 Who believes what we've heard and
seen?
Who would have thought GOD's saving
power would look like this?

2-6 The servant grew up before God—
a scrawny seedling,
a scrubby plant in a parched field.
There was nothing attractive about him,
nothing to cause us to take a second
look.
He was looked down on and passed over,
a man who suffered, who knew pain
firsthand.
One look at him and people turned away.
We looked down on him, thought he was
scum.
But the fact is, it was *our* pains he carried—
our disfigurements, all the things wrong
with *us.*
We thought he brought it on himself,
that God was punishing him for his own
failures.

NEW KING JAMES VERSION

4Surely He has borne our griefs
And carried our sorrows;
Yet we esteemed Him stricken,
Smitten by God, and afflicted.
5But He *was* wounded for our transgressions,
He was bruised for our iniquities;
The chastisement for our peace *was* upon Him,
And by His stripes we are healed.
6All we like sheep have gone astray;
We have turned, every one, to his own way;
And the LORD has laid on Him the iniquity of us all.

7He was oppressed and He was afflicted,
Yet He opened not His mouth;
He was led as a lamb to the slaughter,
And as a sheep before its shearers is silent,
So He opened not His mouth.
8He was taken from prison and from judgment,
And who will declare His generation?
For He was cut off from the land of the living;
For the transgressions of My people He was stricken.
9And they[a] made His grave with the wicked—
But with the rich at His death,
Because He had done no violence,
Nor *was any* deceit in His mouth.

10Yet it pleased the LORD to bruise Him;
He has put *Him* to grief.
When You make His soul an offering for sin,
He shall see *His* seed, He shall prolong *His* days,
And the pleasure of the LORD shall prosper in His hand.
11He shall see the labor of His soul,[a] *and* be satisfied.
By His knowledge My righteous Servant shall justify many,
For He shall bear their iniquities.
12Therefore I will divide Him a portion with the great,
And He shall divide the spoil with the strong,
Because He poured out His soul unto death,
And He was numbered with the transgressors,
And He bore the sin of many,
And made intercession for the transgressors.

A PERPETUAL COVENANT OF PEACE

54 "Sing, O barren,
You *who* have not borne!
Break forth into singing, and cry aloud,
You *who* have not labored with child!
For more *are* the children of the desolate
Than the children of the married woman,"
says the LORD.

53:9 [a]Literally *he* or *He* **53:11** [a]Following Masoretic Text, Targum, and Vulgate; Dead Sea Scrolls and Septuagint read *From the labor of His soul He shall see light.*

THE MESSAGE

But it was our sins that did that to him,
that ripped and tore and crushed him—
our sins!
He took the punishment, and that made us whole.
Through his bruises we get healed.
We're all like sheep who've wandered off and gotten lost.
We've all done our own thing, gone our own way.
And GOD has piled all our sins, everything we've done wrong,
on him, on him.

7-9 He was beaten, he was tortured,
but he didn't say a word.
Like a lamb taken to be slaughtered
and like a sheep being sheared,
he took it all in silence.
Justice miscarried, and he was led off—
and did anyone really know what was happening?
He died without a thought for his own welfare,
beaten bloody for the sins of my people.
They buried him with the wicked,
threw him in a grave with a rich man,
Even though he'd never hurt a soul
or said one word that wasn't true.

10 Still, it's what GOD had in mind all along,
to crush him with pain.
The plan was that he give himself as an offering for sin
so that he'd see life come from it—life, life, and more life.
And GOD's plan will deeply prosper through him.

11-12 Out of that terrible travail of soul,
he'll see that it's worth it and be glad he did it.
Through what he experienced, my righteous one, my servant,
will make many "righteous ones,"
as he himself carries the burden of their sins.
Therefore I'll reward him extravagantly—
the best of everything, the highest honors—
Because he looked death in the face and didn't flinch,
because he embraced the company of the lowest.
He took on his own shoulders the sin of the many,
he took up the cause of all the black sheep.

SPREAD OUT! THINK BIG!

1-6 **54** "Sing, barren woman, who has never had a baby.
Fill the air with song, you who've never experienced childbirth!
You're ending up with far more children
than all those childbearing women." GOD says so!

NEW KING JAMES VERSION

2 "Enlarge the place of your tent,
And let them stretch out the curtains of your dwellings;
Do not spare;
Lengthen your cords,
And strengthen your stakes.
3 For you shall expand to the right and to the left,
And your descendants will inherit the nations,
And make the desolate cities inhabited.

4 "Do not fear, for you will not be ashamed;
Neither be disgraced, for you will not be put to shame;
For you will forget the shame of your youth,
And will not remember the reproach of your widowhood anymore.
5 For your Maker *is* your husband,
The LORD of hosts *is* His name;
And your Redeemer *is* the Holy One of Israel;
He is called the God of the whole earth.
6 For the LORD has called you
Like a woman forsaken and grieved in spirit,
Like a youthful wife when you were refused,"
Says your God.
7 "For a mere moment I have forsaken you,
But with great mercies I will gather you.
8 With a little wrath I hid My face from you for a moment;
But with everlasting kindness I will have mercy on you,"
Says the LORD, your Redeemer.

9 "For this *is* like the waters of Noah to Me;
For as I have sworn
That the waters of Noah would no longer cover the earth,
So have I sworn
That I would not be angry with you, nor rebuke you.
10 For the mountains shall depart
And the hills be removed,
But My kindness shall not depart from you,
Nor shall My covenant of peace be removed,"
Says the LORD, who has mercy on you.

11 "O you afflicted one,
Tossed with tempest, *and* not comforted,
Behold, I will lay your stones with colorful gems,
And lay your foundations with sapphires.
12 I will make your pinnacles of rubies,
Your gates of crystal,
And all your walls of precious stones.
13 All your children *shall be* taught by the LORD,
And great *shall be* the peace of your children.
14 In righteousness you shall be established;
You shall be far from oppression, for you shall not fear;
And from terror, for it shall not come near you.
15 Indeed they shall surely assemble, *but* not because of Me.

THE MESSAGE

"Clear lots of ground for your tents!
Make your tents large. Spread out! Think big!
Use plenty of rope,
drive the tent pegs deep.
You're going to need lots of elbow room
for your growing family.
You're going to take over whole nations;
you're going to resettle abandoned cities.
Don't be afraid—you're not going to be embarrassed.
Don't hold back—you're not going to come up short.
You'll forget all about the humiliations of your youth,
and the indignities of being a widow will fade from memory.
For your Maker is your bridegroom,
his name, GOD-of-the-Angel-Armies!
Your Redeemer is The Holy of Israel,
known as God of the whole earth.
You were like an abandoned wife,
devastated with grief,
and GOD welcomed you back,
Like a woman married young
and then left," says your God.

7-8 Your Redeemer GOD says:

"I left you, but only for a moment.
Now, with enormous compassion, I'm bringing you back.
In an outburst of anger I turned my back on you—
but only for a moment.
It's with lasting love
that I'm tenderly caring for you.

9-10 "This exile is just like the days of Noah for me:
I promised then that the waters of Noah
would never again flood the earth.
I'm promising now no more anger,
no more dressing you down.
For even if the mountains walk away
and the hills fall to pieces,
My love won't walk away from you,
my covenant commitment of peace won't fall apart."
The GOD who has compassion on you
says so.

11-17 "Afflicted city, storm-battered, unpitied:
I'm about to rebuild you with stones of turquoise,
Lay your foundations with sapphires,
construct your towers with rubies,
Your gates with jewels,
and all your walls with precious stones.
All your children will have GOD for their teacher—
what a mentor for your children!
You'll be built solid, grounded in righteousness,
far from any trouble—nothing to fear!
far from terror—it won't even come close!
If anyone attacks you,
don't for a moment suppose that I sent them,

NEW KING JAMES VERSION

Whoever assembles against you shall fall
for your sake.

16"Behold, I have created the blacksmith
Who blows the coals in the fire,
Who brings forth an instrument for his
work;
And I have created the spoiler to destroy.
17No weapon formed against you shall
prosper,
And every tongue *which* rises against you in
judgment
You shall condemn.
This *is* the heritage of the servants of the
LORD,
And their righteousness *is* from Me,"
Says the LORD.

AN INVITATION TO ABUNDANT LIFE

55 "Ho! Everyone who thirsts,
Come to the waters;
And you who have no money,
Come, buy and eat.
Yes, come, buy wine and milk
Without money and without price.
2Why do you spend money for *what is* not
bread,
And your wages for *what* does not satisfy?
Listen carefully to Me, and eat *what is* good,
And let your soul delight itself in
abundance.
3Incline your ear, and come to Me.
Hear, and your soul shall live;
And I will make an everlasting covenant
with you—
The sure mercies of David.
4Indeed I have given him *as* a witness to the
people,
A leader and commander for the people.
5Surely you shall call a nation you do not
know,
And nations *who* do not know you shall run
to you,
Because of the LORD your God,
And the Holy One of Israel;
For He has glorified you."

6Seek the LORD while He may be found,
Call upon Him while He is near.
7Let the wicked forsake his way,
And the unrighteous man his thoughts;
Let him return to the LORD,
And He will have mercy on him;
And to our God,
For He will abundantly pardon.

8"For My thoughts *are* not your thoughts,
Nor *are* your ways My ways," says the LORD.
9"For *as* the heavens are higher than the
earth,
So are My ways higher than your ways,
And My thoughts than your thoughts.

10"For as the rain comes down, and the snow
from heaven,
And do not return there,
But water the earth,

THE MESSAGE

And if any should attack,
nothing will come of it.
I create the blacksmith
who fires up his forge
and makes a weapon designed to kill.
I also create the destroyer—
but no weapon that can hurt you has
ever been forged.
Any accuser who takes you to court
will be dismissed as a liar.
This is what GOD's servants can expect.
I'll see to it that everything works out for
the best."
GOD's Decree.

BUY WITHOUT MONEY

1-5 55 "Hey there! All who are thirsty,
come to the water!
Are you penniless?
Come anyway—buy and eat!
Come, buy your drinks, buy wine and milk.
Buy without money—everything's free!
Why do you spend your money on junk
food,
your hard-earned cash on cotton candy?
Listen to me, listen well: Eat only the best,
fill yourself with only the finest.
Pay attention, come close now,
listen carefully to my life-giving,
life-nourishing words.
I'm making a lasting covenant commitment
with you,
the same that I made with David: sure,
solid, enduring love.
I set him up as a witness to the nations,
made him a prince and leader of the
nations,
And now I'm doing it to you:
You'll summon nations you've never
heard of,
and nations who've never heard of you
will come running to you
Because of me, your GOD,
because The Holy of Israel has honored
you."

6-7 Seek GOD while he's here to be found,
pray to him while he's close at hand.
Let the wicked abandon their way of life
and the evil their way of thinking.
Let them come back to GOD, who is
merciful,
come back to our God, who is lavish with
forgiveness.

8-11 "I don't think the way you think.
The way you work isn't the way I work."
GOD's Decree.
"For as the sky soars high above earth,
so the way I work surpasses the way you
work,
and the way I think is beyond the way
you think.
Just as rain and snow descend from the
skies
and don't go back until they've watered
the earth,

NEW KING JAMES VERSION

And make it bring forth and bud,
That it may give seed to the sower
And bread to the eater,
11 So shall My word be that goes forth from My mouth;
It shall not return to Me void,
But it shall accomplish what I please,
And it shall prosper *in the thing* for which I sent it.

12 "For you shall go out with joy,
And be led out with peace;
The mountains and the hills
Shall break forth into singing before you,
And all the trees of the field shall clap *their* hands.
13 Instead of the thorn shall come up the cypress tree,
And instead of the brier shall come up the myrtle tree;
And it shall be to the LORD for a name,
For an everlasting sign *that* shall not be cut off."

SALVATION FOR THE GENTILES

56 Thus says the LORD:

"Keep justice, and do righteousness,
For My salvation *is* about to come,
And My righteousness to be revealed.
2 Blessed *is* the man *who* does this,
And the son of man *who* lays hold on it;
Who keeps from defiling the Sabbath,
And keeps his hand from doing any evil."

3 Do not let the son of the foreigner
Who has joined himself to the LORD
Speak, saying,
"The LORD has utterly separated me from His people";
Nor let the eunuch say,
"Here I am, a dry tree."
4 For thus says the LORD:
"To the eunuchs who keep My Sabbaths,
And choose what pleases Me,
And hold fast My covenant,
5 Even to them I will give in My house
And within My walls a place and a name
Better than that of sons and daughters;
I will give them[a] an everlasting name
That shall not be cut off.

6 "Also the sons of the foreigner
Who join themselves to the LORD, to serve Him,
And to love the name of the LORD, to be His servants—

56:5 [a]Literally *him*

THE MESSAGE

Doing their work of making things grow and blossom,
producing seed for farmers and food for the hungry,
So will the words that come out of my mouth
not come back empty-handed.
They'll do the work I sent them to do,
they'll complete the assignment I gave them.

12-13 "So you'll go out in joy,
you'll be led into a whole and complete life.
The mountains and hills will lead the parade,
bursting with song.
All the trees of the forest will join the procession,
exuberant with applause.
No more thistles, but giant sequoias,
no more thornbushes, but stately pines—
Monuments to me, to GOD,
living and lasting evidence of GOD."

MESSAGES OF HOPE

SALVATION IS JUST AROUND THE CORNER

1-3 56 GOD's Message:

"Guard my common good:
Do what's right and do it in the right way,
For salvation is just around the corner,
my setting-things-right is about to go into action.
How blessed are you who enter into these things,
you men and women who embrace them,
Who keep Sabbath and don't defile it,
who watch your step and don't do anything evil!
Make sure no outsider who now follows GOD
ever has occasion to say, 'GOD put me in second-class.
I don't really belong.'
And make sure no physically mutilated person
is ever made to think, 'I'm damaged goods.
I don't really belong.' "

4-5 For GOD says:

"To the mutilated who keep my Sabbaths
and choose what delights me
and keep a firm grip on my covenant,
I'll provide them an honored place
in my family and within my city,
even more honored than that of sons and daughters.
I'll confer permanent honors on them
that will never be revoked.

6-8 "And as for the outsiders who now follow me,
working for me, loving my name,
and wanting to be my servants—

NEW KING JAMES VERSION

Everyone who keeps from defiling the
Sabbath,
And holds fast My covenant—
7Even them I will bring to My holy mountain,
And make them joyful in My house of
prayer.
Their burnt offerings and their sacrifices
Will be accepted on My altar;
For My house shall be called a house of
prayer for all nations."
8The Lord GOD, who gathers the outcasts of
Israel, says,
"Yet I will gather to him
Others besides those who are gathered to
him."

ISRAEL'S IRRESPONSIBLE LEADERS

9All you beasts of the field, come to devour,
All you beasts in the forest.
10His watchmen *are* blind,
They are all ignorant;
They *are* all dumb dogs,
They cannot bark;
Sleeping, lying down, loving to slumber.
11Yes, *they are* greedy dogs
Which never have enough.
And they *are* shepherds
Who cannot understand;
They all look to their own way,
Every one for his own gain,
From his *own* territory.
12"Come," *one says,* "I will bring wine,
And we will fill ourselves with intoxicating
drink;
Tomorrow will be as today,
And much more abundant."

ISRAEL'S FUTILE IDOLATRY

57 The righteous perishes,
And no man takes *it* to heart;
Merciful men *are* taken away,
While no one considers
That the righteous is taken away from evil.
2He shall enter into peace;
They shall rest in their beds,
Each one walking *in* his uprightness.

3"But come here,
You sons of the sorceress,
You offspring of the adulterer and the
harlot!
4Whom do you ridicule?
Against whom do you make a wide mouth
And stick out the tongue?
Are you not children of transgression,
Offspring of falsehood,
5Inflaming yourselves with gods under every
green tree,
Slaying the children in the valleys,
Under the clefts of the rocks?
6Among the smooth *stones* of the stream
Is your portion;
They, they, *are* your lot!
Even to them you have poured a drink
offering,
You have offered a grain offering.
Should I receive comfort in these?

THE MESSAGE

All who keep Sabbath and don't defile it,
holding fast to my covenant—
I'll bring them to my holy mountain
and give them joy in my house of prayer.
They'll be welcome to worship the same as
the 'insiders,'
to bring burnt offerings and sacrifices to
my altar.
Oh yes, my house of worship
will be known as a house of prayer for
all people."
The Decree of the Master, GOD himself,
who gathers in the exiles of Israel:
"I will gather others also,
gather them in with those already
gathered."

9-12 A call to the savage beasts: Come on the run.
Come, devour, beast barbarians!
For Israel's watchmen are blind, the whole
lot of them.
They have no idea what's going on.
They're dogs without sense enough to bark,
lazy dogs, dreaming in the sun—
But hungry dogs, they do know how to eat,
voracious dogs, with never enough.
And these are Israel's shepherds!
They know nothing, understand nothing.
They all look after themselves,
grabbing whatever's not nailed down.
"Come," they say, "let's have a party.
Let's go out and get drunk!"
And tomorrow, more of the same:
"Let's live it up!"

NEVER TIRED OF TRYING NEW RELIGIONS

1-2 57 Meanwhile, right-living people die
and no one gives them a thought.
God-fearing people are carted off
and no one even notices.
The right-living people are out of their
misery,
they're finally at rest.
They lived well and with dignity
and now they're finally at peace.

3-10 "But you, children of a witch, come here!
Sons of a slut, daughters of a whore.
What business do you have taunting,
sneering, and sticking out your tongue?
Do you have any idea what wretches you've
turned out to be?
A race of rebels, a generation of liars.
You satisfy your lust any place you find
some shade
and fornicate at whim.
You kill your children at any convenient
spot—
any cave or crevasse will do.
You take stones from the creek
and set up your sex-and-religion
shrines.
You've chosen your fate.
Your worship will be your doom.

New King James Version

7"On a lofty and high mountain
You have set your bed;
Even there you went up
To offer sacrifice.
8Also behind the doors and their posts
You have set up your remembrance;
For you have uncovered yourself *to those other* than Me,
And have gone up to them;
You have enlarged your bed
And made *a covenant* with them;
You have loved their bed,
Where you saw *their* nudity.[a]
9You went to the king with ointment,
And increased your perfumes;
You sent your messengers far off,
And *even* descended to Sheol.
10You are wearied in the length of your way;
Yet you did not say, 'There is no hope.'
You have found the life of your hand;
Therefore you were not grieved.

11"And of whom have you been afraid, or feared,
That you have lied
And not remembered Me,
Nor taken *it* to your heart?
Is it not because I have held My peace from of old
That you do not fear Me?
12I will declare your righteousness
And your works,
For they will not profit you.
13When you cry out,
Let your collection *of idols* deliver you.
But the wind will carry them all away,
A breath will take *them*.
But he who puts his trust in Me shall possess the land,
And shall inherit My holy mountain."

Healing for the Backslider

14And one shall say,
"Heap it up! Heap it up!
Prepare the way,
Take the stumbling block out of the way of My people."

15For thus says the High and Lofty One
Who inhabits eternity, whose name *is* Holy:
"I dwell in the high and holy *place*,
With him *who* has a contrite and humble spirit,
To revive the spirit of the humble,
And to revive the heart of the contrite ones.
16For I will not contend forever,
Nor will I always be angry;
For the spirit would fail before Me,
And the souls *which* I have made.
17For the iniquity of his covetousness
I was angry and struck him;
I hid and was angry,
And he went on backsliding in the way of his heart.

57:8 [a]Literally *hand*, a euphemism

The Message

You've climbed a high mountain
to practice your foul sex-and-death religion.
Behind closed doors
you assemble your precious gods and goddesses.
Deserting me, you've gone all out, stripped down
and made your bed your place of worship.
You've climbed into bed with the 'sacred' whores
and loved every minute of it,
adoring every curve of their naked bodies.
You anoint your king-god with ointments
and lavish perfumes on yourselves.
You send scouts to search out the latest in religion,
send them all the way to hell and back.
You wear yourselves out trying the new and the different,
and never see what a waste it all is.
You've always found strength for the latest fad,
never got tired of trying new religions.

11-13 "Who talked you into the pursuit of this nonsense,
leaving me high and dry,
forgetting you ever knew me?
Because I don't yell and make a scene
do you think I don't exist?
I'll go over, detail by detail, all your 'righteous' attempts at religion,
and expose the absurdity of it all.
Go ahead, cry for help to your collection of no-gods:
A good wind will blow them away.
They're smoke, nothing but smoke.

"But anyone who runs to me for help
will inherit the land,
will end up owning my holy mountain!"

14 Someone says: "Build, build! Make a road!
Clear the way, remove the rocks
from the road my people will travel."

15-21 A Message from the high and towering God,
who lives in Eternity,
whose name is Holy:
"I live in the high and holy places,
but also with the low-spirited, the spirit-crushed,
And what I do is put new spirit in them,
get them up and on their feet again.
For I'm not going to haul people into court endlessly,
I'm not going to be angry forever.
Otherwise, people would lose heart.
These souls I created would tire out and give up.
I *was* angry, good and angry, because of Israel's sins.
I struck him hard and turned away in anger,
while he kept at his stubborn, willful ways.

New King James Version

18I have seen his ways, and will heal him;
I will also lead him,
And restore comforts to him
And to his mourners.
19"I create the fruit of the lips:
Peace, peace to *him who is* far off and to *him who is* near,"
Says the LORD,
"And I will heal him."
20But the wicked *are* like the troubled sea,
When it cannot rest,
Whose waters cast up mire and dirt.

21"*There is* no peace,"
Says my God, "for the wicked."

Fasting that Pleases God

58 "Cry aloud, spare not;
Lift up your voice like a trumpet;
Tell My people their transgression,
And the house of Jacob their sins.
2Yet they seek Me daily,
And delight to know My ways,
As a nation that did righteousness,
And did not forsake the ordinance of their God.
They ask of Me the ordinances of justice;
They take delight in approaching God.
3'Why have we fasted,' *they say,* 'and You have not seen?
Why have we afflicted our souls, and You take no notice?'

"In fact, in the day of your fast you find pleasure,
And exploit all your laborers.
4Indeed you fast for strife and debate,
And to strike with the fist of wickedness.
You will not fast as *you do* this day,
To make your voice heard on high.
5Is it a fast that I have chosen,
A day for a man to afflict his soul?
Is it to bow down his head like a bulrush,
And to spread out sackcloth and ashes?
Would you call this a fast,
And an acceptable day to the LORD?

6"*Is* this not the fast that I have chosen:
To loose the bonds of wickedness,
To undo the heavy burdens,
To let the oppressed go free,
And that you break every yoke?
7*Is it* not to share your bread with the hungry,
And that you bring to your house the poor who are cast out;
When you see the naked, that you cover him,
And not hide yourself from your own flesh?
8Then your light shall break forth like the morning,
Your healing shall spring forth speedily,

The Message

When I looked again and saw what he was doing,
I decided to heal him, lead him, and comfort him,
creating a new language of praise for the mourners.
Peace to the far-off, peace to the near-at-hand," says GOD—
"and yes, I will heal them.
But the wicked are storm-battered seas
that can't quiet down.
The waves stir up garbage and mud.
There's no peace," God says, "for the wicked."

Your Prayers Won't Get Off the Ground

1-3 58 "Shout! A full-throated shout!
Hold nothing back—
a trumpet-blast shout!
Tell my people what's wrong with their lives,
face my family Jacob with their sins!
They're busy, busy, busy at worship,
and love studying all about me.
To all appearances they're a nation of right-living people—
law-abiding, God-honoring.
They ask me, 'What's the right thing to do?'
and love having me on their side.
But they also complain,
'Why do we fast and you don't look our way?
Why do we humble ourselves and you don't even notice?'

3-5 "Well, here's why:

"The bottom line on your 'fast days' is profit.
You drive your employees much too hard.
You fast, but at the same time you bicker and fight.
You fast, but you swing a mean fist.
The kind of fasting you do
won't get your prayers off the ground.
Do you think this is the kind of fast day I'm after:
a day to show off humility?
To put on a pious long face
and parade around solemnly in black?
Do you call *that* fasting,
a fast day that I, GOD, would like?

6-9 "This is the kind of fast day I'm after:
to break the chains of injustice,
get rid of exploitation in the workplace,
free the oppressed,
cancel debts.
What I'm interested in seeing you do is:
sharing your food with the hungry,
inviting the homeless poor into your homes,
putting clothes on the shivering ill-clad,
being available to your own families.
Do this and the lights will turn on,
and your lives will turn around at once.

NEW KING JAMES VERSION

And your righteousness shall go before you;
The glory of the LORD shall be your rear guard.
9Then you shall call, and the LORD will answer;
You shall cry, and He will say, 'Here I *am*.'

"If you take away the yoke from your midst,
The pointing of the finger, and speaking wickedness,
10*If* you extend your soul to the hungry
And satisfy the afflicted soul,
Then your light shall dawn in the darkness,
And your darkness shall *be* as the noonday.
11The LORD will guide you continually,
And satisfy your soul in drought,
And strengthen your bones;
You shall be like a watered garden,
And like a spring of water, whose waters do not fail.
12Those from among you
Shall build the old waste places;
You shall raise up the foundations of many generations;
And you shall be called the Repairer of the Breach,
The Restorer of Streets to Dwell In.

13"If you turn away your foot from the Sabbath,
From doing your pleasure on My holy day,
And call the Sabbath a delight,
The holy *day* of the LORD honorable,
And shall honor Him, not doing your own ways,
Nor finding your own pleasure,
Nor speaking *your own* words,
14Then you shall delight yourself in the LORD;
And I will cause you to ride on the high hills of the earth,
And feed you with the heritage of Jacob your father.
The mouth of the LORD has spoken."

SEPARATED FROM GOD

59 Behold, the LORD's hand is not shortened,
That it cannot save;
Nor His ear heavy,
That it cannot hear.
2But your iniquities have separated you from your God;
And your sins have hidden *His* face from you,
So that He will not hear.
3For your hands are defiled with blood,
And your fingers with iniquity;
Your lips have spoken lies,
Your tongue has muttered perversity.

4No one calls for justice,
Nor does *any* plead for truth.
They trust in empty words and speak lies;
They conceive evil and bring forth iniquity.

THE MESSAGE

Your righteousness will pave your way.
The GOD of glory will secure your passage.
Then when you pray, GOD will answer.
You'll call out for help and I'll say, 'Here I am.'

A FULL LIFE IN THE EMPTIEST OF PLACES

9-12 "If you get rid of unfair practices,
quit blaming victims,
quit gossiping about other people's sins,
If you are generous with the hungry
and start giving yourselves to the down-and-out,
Your lives will begin to glow in the darkness,
your shadowed lives will be bathed in sunlight.
I will always show you where to go.
I'll give you a full life in the emptiest of places—
firm muscles, strong bones.
You'll be like a well-watered garden,
a gurgling spring that never runs dry.
You'll use the old rubble of past lives to build anew,
rebuild the foundations from out of your past.
You'll be known as those who can fix anything,
restore old ruins, rebuild and renovate,
make the community livable again.

13-14 "If you watch your step on the Sabbath
and don't use my holy day for personal advantage,
If you treat the Sabbath as a day of joy,
GOD's holy day as a celebration,
If you honor it by refusing 'business as usual,'
making money, running here and there—
Then you'll be free to enjoy GOD!
Oh, I'll make you ride high and soar above it all.
I'll make you feast on the inheritance of your ancestor Jacob."
Yes! GOD says so!

WE LONG FOR LIGHT BUT SINK INTO DARKNESS

1-8 59 Look! Listen!
GOD's arm is not amputated—
he can still save.
GOD's ears are not stopped up—he can still hear.
There's nothing wrong with God; the wrong is in *you*.
Your wrongheaded lives caused the split between you and God.
Your sins got between you so that he doesn't hear.
Your hands are drenched in blood,
your fingers dripping with guilt,
Your lips smeared with lies,
your tongue swollen from muttering obscenities.
No one speaks up for the right,
no one deals fairly.
They trust in illusion, they tell lies,
they get pregnant with mischief and have sin-babies.

NEW KING JAMES VERSION

5They hatch vipers' eggs and weave the
spider's web;
He who eats of their eggs dies,
And *from* that which is crushed a viper
breaks out.

6Their webs will not become garments,
Nor will they cover themselves with their
works;
Their works *are* works of iniquity,
And the act of violence *is* in their hands.
7Their feet run to evil,
And they make haste to shed innocent
blood;
Their thoughts *are* thoughts of iniquity;
Wasting and destruction *are* in their paths.
8The way of peace they have not known,
And *there is* no justice in their ways;
They have made themselves crooked paths;
Whoever takes that way shall not know
peace.

SIN CONFESSED

9Therefore justice is far from us,
Nor does righteousness overtake us;
We look for light, but there is darkness!
For brightness, *but* we walk in blackness!
10We grope for the wall like the blind,
And we grope as if *we had* no eyes;
We stumble at noonday as at twilight;
We are as dead *men* in desolate places.
11We all growl like bears,
And moan sadly like doves;
We look for justice, but *there is* none;
For salvation, *but* it is far from us.
12For our transgressions are multiplied before
You,
And our sins testify against us;
For our transgressions *are* with us,
And *as for* our iniquities, we know them:
13In transgressing and lying against the LORD,
And departing from our God,
Speaking oppression and revolt,
Conceiving and uttering from the heart
words of falsehood.
14Justice is turned back,
And righteousness stands afar off;
For truth is fallen in the street,
And equity cannot enter.
15So truth fails,
And he *who* departs from evil makes
himself a prey.

THE REDEEMER OF ZION

Then the LORD saw *it*, and it displeased Him
That *there was* no justice.
16He saw that *there was* no man,
And wondered that *there was* no
intercessor;
Therefore His own arm brought salvation
for Him;
And His own righteousness, it sustained
Him.
17For He put on righteousness as a
breastplate,
And a helmet of salvation on His head;
He put on the garments of vengeance for
clothing,
And was clad with zeal as a cloak.

THE MESSAGE

They hatch snake eggs and weave spider
webs.
Eat an egg and die; break an egg and get
a snake!
The spider webs are no good for shirts or
shawls.
No one can wear these weavings!
They weave wickedness,
they hatch violence.
They compete in the race to do evil
and run to be the first to murder.
They plan and plot evil, think and breathe
evil,
and leave a trail of wrecked lives behind
them.
They know nothing about peace
and less than nothing about justice.
They make tortuously twisted roads.
No peace for the wretch who walks
down those roads!

9-11 Which means that we're a far cry from fair
dealing,
and we're not even close to right living.
We long for light but sink into darkness,
long for brightness but stumble through
the night.
Like the blind, we inch along a wall,
groping eyeless in the dark.
We shuffle our way in broad daylight,
like the dead, but somehow walking.
We're no better off than bears, groaning,
and no worse off than doves, moaning.
We look for justice—not a sign of it;
for salvation—not so much as a hint.

12-15 Our wrongdoings pile up before you, God,
our sins stand up and accuse us.
Our wrongdoings stare us down;
we know in detail what we've done:
Mocking and denying GOD,
not following our God,
Spreading false rumors, inciting sedition,
pregnant with lies, muttering malice.
Justice is beaten back,
Righteousness is banished to the
sidelines,
Truth staggers down the street,
Honesty is nowhere to be found,
Good is missing in action.
Anyone renouncing evil is beaten and
robbed.

15-19 GOD looked and saw evil looming on the
horizon—
so much evil and no sign of Justice.
He couldn't believe what he saw:
not a soul around to correct this awful
situation.
So he did it himself, took on the work of
Salvation,
fueled by his own Righteousness.
He dressed in Righteousness, put it on like
a suit of armor,
with Salvation on his head like a helmet,
Put on Judgment like an overcoat,
and threw a cloak of Passion across his
shoulders.

NEW KING JAMES VERSION

18According to *their* deeds, accordingly He
will repay,
Fury to His adversaries,
Recompense to His enemies;
The coastlands He will fully repay.
19So shall they fear
The name of the LORD from the west,
And His glory from the rising of the sun;
When the enemy comes in like a flood,
The Spirit of the LORD will lift up a standard
against him.

20"The Redeemer will come to Zion,
And to those who turn from transgression in
Jacob,"
Says the LORD.

21"As for Me," says the LORD, "this *is* My cov-
enant with them: My Spirit who *is* upon you,
and My words which I have put in your mouth,
shall not depart from your mouth, nor from the
mouth of your descendants, nor from the mouth
of your descendants' descendants," says the
LORD, "from this time and forevermore."

THE GENTILES BLESS ZION

60 Arise, shine;
For your light has come!
And the glory of the LORD is risen upon you.
2For behold, the darkness shall cover the
earth,
And deep darkness the people;
But the LORD will arise over you,
And His glory will be seen upon you.
3The Gentiles shall come to your light,
And kings to the brightness of your rising.

4"Lift up your eyes all around, and see:
They all gather together, they come to you;
Your sons shall come from afar,
And your daughters shall be nursed at *your*
side.
5Then you shall see and become radiant,
And your heart shall swell with joy;
Because the abundance of the sea shall be
turned to you,
The wealth of the Gentiles shall come to
you.
6The multitude of camels shall cover your
land,
The dromedaries of Midian and Ephah;
All those from Sheba shall come;
They shall bring gold and incense,
And they shall proclaim the praises of the
LORD.
7All the flocks of Kedar shall be gathered
together to you,
The rams of Nebaioth shall minister to you;
They shall ascend with acceptance on My
altar,
And I will glorify the house of My glory.

8"Who *are* these *who* fly like a cloud,
And like doves to their roosts?
9Surely the coastlands shall wait for Me;
And the ships of Tarshish *will come* first,

THE MESSAGE

He'll make everyone pay for what they've
done:
fury for his foes, just deserts for his
enemies.
Even the far-off islands will get paid off
in full.
In the west they'll fear the name of GOD,
in the east they'll fear the glory of GOD,
For he'll arrive like a river in flood stage,
whipped to a torrent by the wind of GOD.

20 "I'll arrive in Zion as Redeemer,
to those in Jacob who leave their sins."
GOD's Decree.

21 "As for me," GOD says, "this is my
covenant with them: My Spirit that I've
placed upon you and the words that I've
given you to speak, they're not going to
leave your mouths nor the mouths of your
children nor the mouths of your grandchil-
dren. You will keep repeating these words
and won't ever stop." GOD's orders.

PEOPLE RETURNING FOR THE REUNION

1-7 60 "Get out of bed, Jerusalem!
Wake up. Put your face in the
sunlight.
GOD's bright glory has risen for you.
The whole earth is wrapped in darkness,
all people sunk in deep darkness,
But GOD rises on you,
his sunrise glory breaks over you.
Nations will come to your light,
kings to your sunburst brightness.
Look up! Look around!
Watch as they gather, watch as they
approach you:
Your sons coming from great distances,
your daughters carried by their nannies.
When you see them coming you'll smile—
big smiles!
Your heart will swell and, yes, burst!
All those people returning by sea for the
reunion,
a rich harvest of exiles gathered in from
the nations!
And then streams of camel caravans as far
as the eye can see,
young camels of nomads in Midian and
Ephah,
Pouring in from the south from Sheba,
loaded with gold and frankincense,
preaching the praises of GOD.
And yes, a great roundup
of flocks from the nomads in Kedar and
Nebaioth,
Welcome gifts for worship at my altar
as I bathe my glorious Temple in
splendor.

WHAT'S THAT WE SEE IN THE DISTANCE?

8-22 "What's that we see in the distance,
a cloud on the horizon, like doves
darkening the sky?
It's ships from the distant islands,
the famous Tarshish ships

NEW KING JAMES VERSION

To bring your sons from afar,
Their silver and their gold with them,
To the name of the LORD your God,
And to the Holy One of Israel,
Because He has glorified you.

10"The sons of foreigners shall build up your walls,
And their kings shall minister to you;
For in My wrath I struck you,
But in My favor I have had mercy on you.
11Therefore your gates shall be open continually;
They shall not be shut day or night,
That *men* may bring to you the wealth of the Gentiles,
And their kings in procession.
12For the nation and kingdom which will not serve you shall perish,
And *those* nations shall be utterly ruined.

13"The glory of Lebanon shall come to you,
The cypress, the pine, and the box tree together,
To beautify the place of My sanctuary;
And I will make the place of My feet glorious.
14Also the sons of those who afflicted you
Shall come bowing to you,
And all those who despised you shall fall prostrate at the soles of your feet;
And they shall call you The City of the LORD,
Zion of the Holy One of Israel.

15"Whereas you have been forsaken and hated,
So that no one went through *you*,
I will make you an eternal excellence,
A joy of many generations.
16You shall drink the milk of the Gentiles,
And milk the breast of kings;
You shall know that I, the LORD, *am* your Savior
And your Redeemer, the Mighty One of Jacob.

17"Instead of bronze I will bring gold,
Instead of iron I will bring silver,
Instead of wood, bronze,
And instead of stones, iron.
I will also make your officers peace,
And your magistrates righteousness.
18Violence shall no longer be heard in your land,
Neither wasting nor destruction within your borders;
But you shall call your walls Salvation,
And your gates Praise.

GOD THE GLORY OF HIS PEOPLE

19"The sun shall no longer be your light by day,
Nor for brightness shall the moon give light to you;
But the LORD will be to you an everlasting light,
And your God your glory.
20Your sun shall no longer go down,
Nor shall your moon withdraw itself;
For the LORD will be your everlasting light,

THE MESSAGE

Returning your children from faraway places,
loaded with riches, with silver and gold,
And backed by the name of your GOD, The Holy of Israel,
showering you with splendor.
Foreigners will rebuild your walls,
and their kings assist you in the conduct of worship.
When I was angry I hit you hard.
It's my desire now to be tender.
Your Jerusalem gates will always be open
—open house day and night!—
Receiving deliveries of wealth from all nations,
and their kings, the delivery boys!
Any nation or kingdom that doesn't deliver will perish;
those nations will be totally wasted.
The rich woods of Lebanon will be delivered
—all that cypress and oak and pine—
To give a splendid elegance to my Sanctuary,
as I make my footstool glorious.
The descendants of your oppressor
will come bowing and scraping to you.
All who looked down at you in contempt
will lick your boots.
They'll confer a title on you: City of GOD,
Zion of The Holy of Israel.
Not long ago you were despised refuse—
out-of-the-way, unvisited, ignored.
But now I've put you on your feet,
towering and grand forever, a joy to look at!
When you suck the milk of nations
and the breasts of royalty,
You'll know that I, GOD, am your Savior,
your Redeemer, Champion of Jacob.
I'll give you only the best—no more hand-me-downs!
Gold instead of bronze, silver instead of iron,
bronze instead of wood, iron instead of stones.
I'll install Peace to run your country,
make Righteousness your boss.
There'll be no more stories of crime in your land,
no more robberies, no more vandalism.
You'll name your main street Salvation Way,
and install Praise Park at the center of town.
You'll have no more need of the sun by day
nor the brightness of the moon at night.
GOD will be your eternal light,
your God will bathe you in splendor.
Your sun will never go down,
your moon will never fade.
I will be your eternal light.

NEW KING JAMES VERSION

And the days of your mourning shall be ended.
21 Also your people *shall* all *be* righteous;
They shall inherit the land forever,
The branch of My planting,
The work of My hands,
That I may be glorified.
22 A little one shall become a thousand,
And a small one a strong nation.
I, the LORD, will hasten it in its time."

THE GOOD NEWS OF SALVATION

61 "The Spirit of the Lord GOD *is* upon Me,
Because the LORD has anointed Me
To preach good tidings to the poor;
He has sent Me to heal the brokenhearted,
To proclaim liberty to the captives,
And the opening of the prison to *those who are* bound;
2 To proclaim the acceptable year of the LORD,
And the day of vengeance of our God;
To comfort all who mourn,
3 To console those who mourn in Zion,
To give them beauty for ashes,
The oil of joy for mourning,
The garment of praise for the spirit of heaviness;
That they may be called trees of righteousness,
The planting of the LORD, that He may be glorified."

4 And they shall rebuild the old ruins,
They shall raise up the former desolations,
And they shall repair the ruined cities,
The desolations of many generations.
5 Strangers shall stand and feed your flocks,
And the sons of the foreigner
Shall be your plowmen and your vinedressers.
6 But you shall be named the priests of the LORD,
They shall call you the servants of our God.
You shall eat the riches of the Gentiles,
And in their glory you shall boast.
7 Instead of your shame *you shall have* double *honor,*
And *instead of* confusion they shall rejoice in their portion.
Therefore in their land they shall possess double;
Everlasting joy shall be theirs.

8 "For I, the LORD, love justice;
I hate robbery for burnt offering;
I will direct their work in truth,
And will make with them an everlasting covenant.
9 Their descendants shall be known among the Gentiles,
And their offspring among the people.
All who see them shall acknowledge them,
That they *are* the posterity *whom* the LORD has blessed."

10 I will greatly rejoice in the LORD,
My soul shall be joyful in my God;
For He has clothed me with the garments of salvation,

THE MESSAGE

Your days of grieving are over.
All your people will live right and well,
in permanent possession of the land.
They're the green shoot that I planted,
planted with my own hands to display my glory.
The runt will become a great tribe,
the weakling become a strong nation.
I am GOD.
At the right time I'll make it happen."

ANNOUNCE FREEDOM TO ALL CAPTIVES

1-7 61 The Spirit of GOD, the Master, is on me
because GOD anointed me.
He sent me to preach good news to the poor,
heal the heartbroken,
Announce freedom to all captives,
pardon all prisoners.
GOD sent me to announce the year of his grace—
a celebration of God's destruction of our enemies—
and to comfort all who mourn,
To care for the needs of all who mourn in Zion,
give them bouquets of roses instead of ashes,
Messages of joy instead of news of doom,
a praising heart instead of a languid spirit.
Rename them "Oaks of Righteousness"
planted by GOD to display his glory.
They'll rebuild the old ruins,
raise a new city out of the wreckage.
They'll start over on the ruined cities,
take the rubble left behind and make it new.
You'll hire outsiders to herd your flocks
and foreigners to work your fields,
But you'll have the title "Priests of GOD,"
honored as ministers of our God.
You'll feast on the bounty of nations,
you'll bask in their glory.
Because you got a double dose of trouble
and more than your share of contempt,
Your inheritance in the land will be doubled
and your joy go on forever.

8-9 "Because I, GOD, love fair dealing
and hate thievery and crime,
I'll pay your wages on time and in full,
and establish my eternal covenant with you.
Your descendants will become well-known all over.
Your children in foreign countries
Will be recognized at once
as the people I have blessed."

10-11 I will sing for joy in GOD,
explode in praise from deep in my soul!
He dressed me up in a suit of salvation,
he outfitted me in a robe of righteousness,

NEW KING JAMES VERSION

He has covered me with the robe of
righteousness,
As a bridegroom decks *himself* with
ornaments,
And as a bride adorns *herself* with her
jewels.
11For as the earth brings forth its bud,
As the garden causes the things that are
sown in it to spring forth,
So the Lord GOD will cause righteousness
and praise to spring forth before all the
nations.

ASSURANCE OF ZION'S SALVATION

62 For Zion's sake I will not hold My peace,
And for Jerusalem's sake I will not rest,
Until her righteousness goes forth as
brightness,
And her salvation as a lamp *that* burns.
2The Gentiles shall see your righteousness,
And all kings your glory.
You shall be called by a new name,
Which the mouth of the LORD will name.
3You shall also be a crown of glory
In the hand of the LORD,
And a royal diadem
In the hand of your God.
4You shall no longer be termed Forsaken,
Nor shall your land any more be termed
Desolate;
But you shall be called Hephzibah,[a] and
your land Beulah;[b]
For the LORD delights in you,
And your land shall be married.
5For *as* a young man marries a virgin,
So shall your sons marry you;
And *as* the bridegroom rejoices over the
bride,
So shall your God rejoice over you.

6I have set watchmen on your walls,
O Jerusalem;
They shall never hold their peace day or
night.
You who make mention of the LORD, do not
keep silent,
7And give Him no rest till He establishes
And till He makes Jerusalem a praise in the
earth.

8The LORD has sworn by His right hand
And by the arm of His strength:
"Surely I will no longer give your grain
As food for your enemies;
And the sons of the foreigner shall not drink
your new wine,
For which you have labored.
9But those who have gathered it shall eat it,
And praise the LORD;
Those who have brought it together shall
drink it in My holy courts."

10Go through,
Go through the gates!
Prepare the way for the people;
Build up,
Build up the highway!

62:4 [a]Literally *My Delight Is in Her* [b]Literally *Married*

THE MESSAGE

As a bridegroom who puts on a tuxedo
and a bride a jeweled tiara.
For as the earth bursts with spring
wildflowers,
and as a garden cascades with blossoms,
So the Master, GOD, brings righteousness
into full bloom
and puts praise on display before the
nations.

LOOK, YOUR SAVIOR COMES!

1-5 62 Regarding Zion, I can't keep my mouth
shut,
regarding Jerusalem, I can't hold my
tongue,
Until her righteousness blazes down like
the sun
and her salvation flames up like a torch.
Foreign countries will see your righteousness,
and world leaders your glory.
You'll get a brand-new name
straight from the mouth of GOD.
You'll be a stunning crown in the palm of
GOD's hand,
a jeweled gold cup held high in the hand
of your God.
No more will anyone call you Rejected,
and your country will no more be called
Ruined.
You'll be called Hephzibah (My Delight),
and your land Beulah (Married),
Because GOD delights in you
and your land will be like a wedding
celebration.
For as a young man marries his virgin bride,
so your builder marries you,
And as a bridegroom is happy in his bride,
so your God is happy with you.

6-7 I've posted watchmen on your walls,
Jerusalem.
Day and night they keep at it, praying,
calling out,
reminding GOD to remember.
They are to give him no peace until he does
what he said,
until he makes Jerusalem famous as the
City of Praise.

8-9 GOD has taken a solemn oath,
an oath he means to keep:
"Never again will I open your grain-filled
barns
to your enemies to loot and eat.
Never again will foreigners drink the wine
that you worked so hard to produce.
No. The farmers who grow the food will eat
the food
and praise GOD for it.
And those who make the wine will drink
the wine
in my holy courtyards."

10-12 Walk out of the gates. Get going!
Get the road ready for the people.
Build the highway. Get at it!

NEW KING JAMES VERSION

Take out the stones,
Lift up a banner for the peoples!

11 Indeed the LORD has proclaimed
To the end of the world:
"Say to the daughter of Zion,
'Surely your salvation is coming;
Behold, His reward *is* with Him,
And His work before Him.' "
12 And they shall call them The Holy People,
The Redeemed of the LORD;
And you shall be called Sought Out,
A City Not Forsaken.

THE LORD IN JUDGMENT AND SALVATION

63 Who *is* this who comes from Edom,
With dyed garments from Bozrah,
This *One who is* glorious in His apparel,
Traveling in the greatness of His strength?—

"I who speak in righteousness, mighty to save."

2 Why *is* Your apparel red,
And Your garments like one who treads in the winepress?

3 "I have trodden the winepress alone,
And from the peoples no one *was* with Me.
For I have trodden them in My anger,
And trampled them in My fury;
Their blood is sprinkled upon My garments,
And I have stained all My robes.
4 For the day of vengeance *is* in My heart,
And the year of My redeemed has come.
5 I looked, but *there was* no one to help,
And I wondered
That *there was* no one to uphold;
Therefore My own arm brought salvation for Me;
And My own fury, it sustained Me.
6 I have trodden down the peoples in My anger,
Made them drunk in My fury,
And brought down their strength to the earth."

GOD'S MERCY REMEMBERED

7 I will mention the lovingkindnesses of the LORD
And the praises of the LORD,
According to all that the LORD has bestowed on us,
And the great goodness toward the house of Israel,
Which He has bestowed on them according to His mercies,
According to the multitude of His lovingkindnesses.
8 For He said, "Surely they *are* My people,
Children *who* will not lie."
So He became their Savior.
9 In all their affliction He was afflicted,
And the Angel of His Presence saved them;
In His love and in His pity He redeemed them;
And He bore them and carried them
All the days of old.

THE MESSAGE

Clear the debris,
hoist high a flag, a signal to all peoples!
Yes! GOD has broadcast to all the world:
"Tell daughter Zion, 'Look! Your Savior comes,
Ready to do what he said he'd do,
prepared to complete what he promised.' "
Zion will be called new names: Holy People, GOD-Redeemed,
Sought-Out, City-Not-Forsaken.

WHO GOES THERE?

1 63 The watchmen call out,
"Who goes there, marching out of Edom,
out of Bozrah in clothes dyed red?
Name yourself, so splendidly dressed,
advancing, bristling with power!"

"It is I: I speak what is right,
I, mighty to save!"

2 "And why are your robes so red,
your clothes dyed red like those who tread grapes?"

3-6 "I've been treading the winepress alone.
No one was there to help me.
Angrily, I stomped the grapes;
raging, I trampled the people.
Their blood spurted all over me—
all my clothes were soaked with blood.
I was set on vengeance.
The time for redemption had arrived.
I looked around for someone to help
—no one.
I couldn't believe it
—not one volunteer.
So I went ahead and did it myself,
fed and fueled by my rage.
I trampled the people in my anger,
crushed them under foot in my wrath,
soaked the earth with their lifeblood."

ALL THE THINGS GOD HAS DONE THAT NEED PRAISING

7-9 I'll make a list of GOD's gracious dealings,
all the things GOD has done that need praising,
All the generous bounties of GOD,
his great goodness to the family of Israel—
Compassion lavished,
love extravagant.
He said, "Without question these are my people,
children who would never betray me."
So he became their Savior.
In all their troubles,
he was troubled, too.
He didn't send someone else to help them.
He did it himself, in person.
Out of his own love and pity
he redeemed them.
He rescued them and carried them along
for a long, long time.

NEW KING JAMES VERSION

10But they rebelled and grieved His Holy Spirit;
So He turned Himself against them as an enemy,
And He fought against them.

11Then he remembered the days of old,
Moses *and* his people, *saying:*
"Where *is* He who brought them up out of the sea
With the shepherd of His flock?
Where *is* He who put His Holy Spirit within them,
12Who led *them* by the right hand of Moses,
With His glorious arm,
Dividing the water before them
To make for Himself an everlasting name,
13Who led them through the deep,
As a horse in the wilderness,
That they might not stumble?"

14As a beast goes down into the valley,
And the Spirit of the LORD causes him to rest,
So You lead Your people,
To make Yourself a glorious name.

A PRAYER OF PENITENCE

15Look down from heaven,
And see from Your habitation, holy and glorious.
Where *are* Your zeal and Your strength,
The yearning of Your heart and Your mercies toward me?
Are they restrained?
16Doubtless You *are* our Father,
Though Abraham was ignorant of us,
And Israel does not acknowledge us.
You, O LORD, *are* our Father;
Our Redeemer from Everlasting *is* Your name.
17O LORD, why have You made us stray from Your ways,
And hardened our heart from Your fear?
Return for Your servants' sake,
The tribes of Your inheritance.
18Your holy people have possessed *it* but a little while;
Our adversaries have trodden down Your sanctuary.
19We have become *like* those of old, over whom You never ruled,
Those who were never called by Your name.

64 Oh, that You would rend the heavens!
That You would come down!
That the mountains might shake at Your presence—
2As fire burns brushwood,
As fire causes water to boil—
To make Your name known to Your adversaries,
That the nations may tremble at Your presence!
3When You did awesome things *for which* we did not look,
You came down,
The mountains shook at Your presence.

THE MESSAGE

10 But they turned on him;
they grieved his Holy Spirit.
So he turned on them,
became their enemy and fought them.

11-14 Then they remembered the old days,
the days of Moses, God's servant:
"Where is he who brought the shepherds of his flock
up and out of the sea?
And what happened to the One who set
his Holy Spirit within them?
Who linked his arm with Moses' right arm,
divided the waters before them,
Making him famous ever after,
and led them through the muddy abyss
as surefooted as horses on hard, level ground?
Like a herd of cattle led to pasture,
the Spirit of GOD gave them rest."

14-19 *That's* how you led your people!
That's how you became so famous!
Look down from heaven, look at us!
Look out the window of your holy and magnificent house!
Whatever happened to your passion,
your famous mighty acts,
Your heartfelt pity, your compassion?
Why are you holding back?
You are our Father.
Abraham and Israel are long dead.
They wouldn't know us from Adam.
But you're our *living* Father,
our Redeemer, famous from eternity!
Why, GOD, did you make us wander from your ways?
Why did you make us cold and stubborn
so that we no longer worshiped you in awe?
Turn back for the sake of your servants.
You own us! We belong to you!
For a while your holy people had it good,
but now our enemies have wrecked your holy place.
For a long time now, you've paid no attention to us.
It's like you never knew us.

CAN WE BE SAVED?

1-7 64 Oh, that you would rip open the heavens
and descend,
make the mountains shudder at your presence—
As when a forest catches fire,
as when fire makes a pot to boil—
To shock your enemies into facing you,
make the nations shake in their boots!
You did terrible things we never expected,
descended and made the mountains
shudder at your presence.

New King James Version

[4]For since the beginning of the world
Men have not heard nor perceived by the ear,
Nor has the eye seen any God besides You,
Who acts for the one who waits for Him.
[5]You meet him who rejoices and does righteousness,
Who remembers You in Your ways.
You are indeed angry, for we have sinned—
In these ways we continue;
And we need to be saved.

[6]But we are all like an unclean *thing*,
And all our righteousnesses *are* like filthy rags;
We all fade as a leaf,
And our iniquities, like the wind,
Have taken us away.
[7]And *there is* no one who calls on Your name,
Who stirs himself up to take hold of You;
For You have hidden Your face from us,
And have consumed us because of our iniquities.

[8]But now, O LORD,
You *are* our Father;
We *are* the clay, and You our potter;
And all we *are* the work of Your hand.
[9]Do not be furious, O LORD,
Nor remember iniquity forever;
Indeed, please look—we all *are* Your people!
[10]Your holy cities are a wilderness,
Zion is a wilderness,
Jerusalem a desolation.
[11]Our holy and beautiful temple,
Where our fathers praised You,
Is burned up with fire;
And all our pleasant things are laid waste.
[12]Will You restrain Yourself because of these *things*, O LORD?
Will You hold Your peace, and afflict us very severely?

The Righteousness of God's Judgment

65 "I was sought by *those who* did not ask *for Me;*
I was found by *those who* did not seek Me.
I said, 'Here I am, here I am,'
To a nation *that* was not called by My name.
[2]I have stretched out My hands all day long to a rebellious people,
Who walk in a way *that is* not good,
According to their own thoughts;
[3]A people who provoke Me to anger continually to My face;
Who sacrifice in gardens,
And burn incense on altars of brick;
[4]Who sit among the graves,
And spend the night in the tombs;
Who eat swine's flesh,
And the broth of abominable things is *in* their vessels;
[5]Who say, 'Keep to yourself,
Do not come near me,
For I am holier than you!'
These *are* smoke in My nostrils,
A fire that burns all the day.

The Message

Since before time began
no one has ever imagined,
No ear heard, no eye seen, a God like you
who works for those who wait for him.
You meet those who happily do what is right,
who keep a good memory of the way you work.
But how angry you've been with us!
We've sinned and kept at it so long!
Is there any hope for us? Can we be saved?
We're all sin-infected, sin-contaminated.
Our best efforts are grease-stained rags.
We dry up like autumn leaves—
sin-dried, we're blown off by the wind.
No one prays to you
or makes the effort to reach out to you
Because you've turned away from us,
left us to stew in our sins.

[8-12] Still, GOD, you are our Father.
We're the clay and you're our potter:
All of us are what you made us.
Don't be too angry with us, O GOD.
Don't keep a permanent account of wrongdoing.
Keep in mind, please, we *are* your people—all of us.
Your holy cities are all ghost towns:
Zion's a ghost town,
Jerusalem's a field of weeds.
Our holy and beautiful Temple,
which our ancestors filled with your praises,
Was burned down by fire,
all our lovely parks and gardens in ruins.
In the face of all this,
are you going to sit there unmoved, GOD?
Aren't you going to say something?
Haven't you made us miserable long enough?

The People Who Bothered to Reach Out to God

[1-7] 65 "I've made myself available
to those who haven't bothered to ask.
I'm here, ready to be found
by those who haven't bothered to look.
I kept saying 'I'm here, I'm right here'
to a nation that ignored me.
I reached out day after day
to a people who turned their backs on me,
People who make wrong turns,
who insist on doing things their own way.
They get on my nerves,
are rude to my face day after day,
Make up their own kitchen religion,
a potluck religious stew.
They spend the night in tombs
to get messages from the dead,
Eat forbidden foods
and drink a witch's brew of potions and charms.
They say, 'Keep your distance.
Don't touch me. I'm holier than thou.'
These people gag me.
I can't stand their stench.

NEW KING JAMES VERSION

6"Behold, *it is* written before Me:
I will not keep silence, but will repay—
Even repay into their bosom—
7Your iniquities and the iniquities of your fathers together,"
Says the LORD,
"Who have burned incense on the mountains
And blasphemed Me on the hills;
Therefore I will measure their former work into their bosom."

8Thus says the LORD:

"As the new wine is found in the cluster,
And *one* says, 'Do not destroy it,
For a blessing *is* in it,'
So will I do for My servants' sake,
That I may not destroy them all.
9I will bring forth descendants from Jacob,
And from Judah an heir of My mountains;
My elect shall inherit it,
And My servants shall dwell there.
10Sharon shall be a fold of flocks,
And the Valley of Achor a place for herds to lie down,
For My people who have sought Me.

11"But you *are* those who forsake the LORD,
Who forget My holy mountain,
Who prepare a table for Gad,[a]
And who furnish a drink offering for Meni.[b]
12Therefore I will number you for the sword,
And you shall all bow down to the slaughter;
Because, when I called, you did not answer;
When I spoke, you did not hear,
But did evil before My eyes,
And chose *that* in which I do not delight."

13Therefore thus says the Lord GOD:

"Behold, My servants shall eat,
But you shall be hungry;
Behold, My servants shall drink,
But you shall be thirsty;
Behold, My servants shall rejoice,
But you shall be ashamed;
14Behold, My servants shall sing for joy of heart,
But you shall cry for sorrow of heart,
And wail for grief of spirit.
15You shall leave your name as a curse to My chosen;
For the Lord GOD will slay you,
And call His servants by another name;
16So that he who blesses himself in the earth
Shall bless himself in the God of truth;
And he who swears in the earth
Shall swear by the God of truth;

65:11 [a]Literally *Troop* or *Fortune*, a pagan deity [b]Literally *Number* or *Destiny*, a pagan deity

THE MESSAGE

Look at this! Their sins are all written out—
I have the list before me.
I'm not putting up with this any longer.
I'll pay them the wages
They have coming for their sins.
And for the sins of their parents lumped in,
a bonus." GOD says so.
"Because they've practiced their blasphemous worship,
mocking me at their hillside shrines,
I'll let loose the consequences
and pay them in full for their actions."

8-10 GOD's Message:

"But just as one bad apple doesn't ruin the whole bushel,
there are still plenty of good apples left.
So I'll preserve those in Israel who obey me.
I won't destroy the whole nation.
I'll bring out my true children from Jacob
and the heirs of my mountains from Judah.
My chosen will inherit the land,
my servants will move in.
The lush valley of Sharon in the west
will be a pasture for flocks,
And in the east, the valley of Achor,
a place for herds to graze.
These will be for the people
who bothered to reach out to me, who wanted me in their lives,
who actually bothered to look for me.

11-12 "But you who abandon me, your GOD,
who forget the holy mountains,
Who hold dinners for Lady Luck
and throw cocktail parties for Sir Fate,
Well, you asked for it. Fate it will be:
your destiny, Death.
For when I invited you, you ignored me;
when I spoke to you, you brushed me off.
You did the very things I exposed as evil;
you chose what I hate."

13-16 Therefore, this is the Message from the Master, GOD:

"My servants will eat,
and you'll go hungry;
My servants will drink,
and you'll go thirsty;
My servants will rejoice,
and you'll hang your heads.
My servants will laugh from full hearts,
and you'll cry out heartbroken,
yes, wail from crushed spirits.
Your legacy to my chosen
will be your name reduced to a cussword.
I, GOD, will put you to death
and give a new name to my servants.
Then whoever prays a blessing in the land
will use my faithful name for the blessing,
And whoever takes an oath in the land
will use my faithful name for the oath,

NEW KING JAMES VERSION

Because the former troubles are forgotten,
And because they are hidden from My eyes.

THE GLORIOUS NEW CREATION

17 "For behold, I create new heavens and a new earth;
And the former shall not be remembered or come to mind.
18 But be glad and rejoice forever in what I create;
For behold, I create Jerusalem *as* a rejoicing,
And her people a joy.
19 I will rejoice in Jerusalem,
And joy in My people;
The voice of weeping shall no longer be heard in her,
Nor the voice of crying.

20 "No more shall an infant from there *live but a few* days,
Nor an old man who has not fulfilled his days;
For the child shall die one hundred years old,
But the sinner *being* one hundred years old shall be accursed.
21 They shall build houses and inhabit *them;*
They shall plant vineyards and eat their fruit.
22 They shall not build and another inhabit;
They shall not plant and another eat;
For as the days of a tree, *so shall be* the days of My people,
And My elect shall long enjoy the work of their hands.
23 They shall not labor in vain,
Nor bring forth children for trouble;
For they *shall be* the descendants of the blessed of the LORD,
And their offspring with them.

24 "It shall come to pass
That before they call, I will answer;
And while they are still speaking, I will hear.
25 The wolf and the lamb shall feed together,
The lion shall eat straw like the ox,
And dust *shall be* the serpent's food.
They shall not hurt nor destroy in all My holy mountain,"
Says the LORD.

TRUE WORSHIP AND FALSE

66 Thus says the LORD:
"Heaven is My throne,
And earth *is* My footstool.
Where *is* the house that you will build Me?
And where *is* the place of My rest?
2 For all those *things* My hand has made,
And all those *things* exist,"
Says the LORD.
"But on this *one* will I look:
On *him who is* poor and of a contrite spirit,
And who trembles at My word.

THE MESSAGE

Because the earlier troubles are gone and forgotten,
banished far from my sight.

NEW HEAVENS AND A NEW EARTH

17-25 "Pay close attention now:
I'm creating new heavens and a new earth.
All the earlier troubles, chaos, and pain
are things of the past, to be forgotten.
Look ahead with joy.
Anticipate what I'm creating:
I'll create Jerusalem as sheer joy,
create my people as pure delight.
I'll take joy in Jerusalem,
take delight in my people:
No more sounds of weeping in the city,
no cries of anguish;
No more babies dying in the cradle,
or old people who don't enjoy a full lifetime;
One-hundredth birthdays will be considered normal—
anything less will seem like a cheat.
They'll build houses
and move in.
They'll plant fields
and eat what they grow.
No more building a house
that some outsider takes over,
No more planting fields
that some enemy confiscates,
For my people will be as long-lived as trees,
my chosen ones will have satisfaction in their work.
They won't work and have nothing come of it,
they won't have children snatched out from under them.
For they themselves are plantings blessed by GOD,
with their children and grandchildren likewise GOD-blessed.
Before they call out, I'll answer.
Before they've finished speaking, I'll have heard.
Wolf and lamb will graze the same meadow,
lion and ox eat straw from the same trough,
but snakes—they'll get a diet of dirt!
Neither animal nor human will hurt or kill
anywhere on my Holy Mountain," says GOD.

LIVING WORSHIP TO GOD

1-2 66 GOD's Message:
"Heaven's my throne,
earth is my footstool.
What sort of house could you build for me?
What holiday spot reserve for me?
I made all this! I own all this!"
GOD's Decree.
"But there *is* something I'm looking for:
a person simple and plain,
reverently responsive to what I say.

NEW KING JAMES VERSION

3"He who kills a bull *is as if* he slays a man;
He who sacrifices a lamb, *as if* he breaks a dog's neck;
He who offers a grain offering, *as if he offers* swine's blood;
He who burns incense, *as if* he blesses an idol.
Just as they have chosen their own ways,
And their soul delights in their abominations,
4So will I choose their delusions,
And bring their fears on them;
Because, when I called, no one answered,
When I spoke they did not hear;
But they did evil before My eyes,
And chose *that* in which I do not delight."

THE LORD VINDICATES ZION

5Hear the word of the LORD,
You who tremble at His word:
"Your brethren who hated you,
Who cast you out for My name's sake, said,
'Let the LORD be glorified,
That we may see your joy.'
But they shall be ashamed."

6The sound of noise from the city!
A voice from the temple!
The voice of the LORD,
Who fully repays His enemies!

7"Before she was in labor, she gave birth;
Before her pain came,
She delivered a male child.
8Who has heard such a thing?
Who has seen such things?
Shall the earth be made to give birth in one day?
Or shall a nation be born at once?
For as soon as Zion was in labor,
She gave birth to her children.
9Shall I bring to the time of birth, and not cause delivery?" says the LORD.
"Shall I who cause delivery shut up *the womb?*" says your God.
10"Rejoice with Jerusalem,
And be glad with her, all you who love her;
Rejoice for joy with her, all you who mourn for her;
11That you may feed and be satisfied
With the consolation of her bosom,
That you may drink deeply and be delighted
With the abundance of her glory."

12For thus says the LORD:

"Behold, I will extend peace to her like a river,
And the glory of the Gentiles like a flowing stream.
Then you shall feed;
On *her* sides shall you be carried,
And be dandled on *her* knees.
13As one whom his mother comforts,
So I will comfort you;
And you shall be comforted in Jerusalem."

THE MESSAGE

3-4 "Your acts of worship
are acts of sin:
Your sacrificial slaughter of the ox
is no different from murdering the neighbor;
Your offerings for worship,
no different from dumping pig's blood on the altar;
Your presentation of memorial gifts,
no different from honoring a no-god idol.
You choose self-serving worship,
you delight in self-centered worship—disgusting!
Well, I choose to expose your nonsense
and let you realize your worst fears,
Because when I invited you, you ignored me;
when I spoke to you, you brushed me off.
You did the very things I exposed as evil,
you chose what I hate."

5 But listen to what GOD has to say
to you who reverently respond to his Word:
"Your own families hate you
and turn you out because of me.
They taunt you, 'Let us see GOD's glory!
If God's so great, why aren't you happy?'
But they're the ones
who are going to end up shamed."

6 Rumbles of thunder from the city!
A voice out of the Temple!
GOD's voice,
handing out judgment to his enemies:

7-9 "Before she went into labor,
she had the baby.
Before the birth pangs hit,
she delivered a son.
Has anyone ever heard of such a thing?
Has anyone seen anything like this?
A country born in a day?
A nation born in a flash?
But Zion was barely in labor
when she had her babies!
Do I open the womb
and not deliver the baby?
Do I, the One who delivers babies,
shut the womb?

10-11 "Rejoice, Jerusalem,
and all who love her, celebrate!
And all you who have shed tears over her,
join in the happy singing.
You newborns can satisfy yourselves
at her nurturing breasts.
Yes, delight yourselves and drink your fill
at her ample bosom."

12-13 GOD's Message:

"I'll pour robust well-being into her like a river,
the glory of nations like a river in flood.
You'll nurse at her breasts,
nestle in her bosom,
and be bounced on her knees.
As a mother comforts her child,
so I'll comfort you.
You will be comforted in Jerusalem."

NEW KING JAMES VERSION

THE REIGN AND INDIGNATION OF GOD

14When you see *this*, your heart shall rejoice,
And your bones shall flourish like grass;
The hand of the LORD shall be known to His servants,
And *His* indignation to His enemies.
15For behold, the LORD will come with fire
And with His chariots, like a whirlwind,
To render His anger with fury,
And His rebuke with flames of fire.
16For by fire and by His sword
The LORD will judge all flesh;
And the slain of the LORD shall be many.

17"Those who sanctify themselves and purify themselves,
To go to the gardens
After an *idol* in the midst,
Eating swine's flesh and the abomination and the mouse,
Shall be consumed together," says the LORD.

18"For I *know* their works and their thoughts.
It shall be that I will gather all nations and
tongues; and they shall come and see My glory.
19I will set a sign among them; and those among
them who escape I will send to the nations: *to*
Tarshish and Pul[a] and Lud, who draw the bow,
and Tubal and Javan, *to* the coastlands afar off
who have not heard My fame nor seen My glory.
And they shall declare My glory among the
Gentiles. 20Then they shall bring all your
brethren for an offering to the LORD out of all
nations, on horses and in chariots and in litters,
on mules and on camels, to My holy mountain
Jerusalem," says the LORD, "as the children of Is-
rael bring an offering in a clean vessel into the
house of the LORD. 21And I will also take some of
them for priests *and* Levites," says the LORD.

22"For as the new heavens and the new earth
Which I will make shall remain before Me," says the LORD,
"So shall your descendants and your name remain.
23And it shall come to pass
That from one New Moon to another,
And from one Sabbath to another,
All flesh shall come to worship before Me," says the LORD.

24"And they shall go forth and look
Upon the corpses of the men
Who have transgressed against Me.
For their worm does not die,
And their fire is not quenched.
They shall be an abhorrence to all flesh."

66:19 [a]Following Masoretic Text and Targum; Septuagint reads *Put* (compare Jeremiah 46:9).

THE MESSAGE

14-16 You'll see all this and burst with joy
—you'll feel ten feet tall—
As it becomes apparent that GOD is on your side
and against his enemies.
For GOD arrives like wildfire
and his chariots like a tornado,
A furious outburst of anger,
a rebuke fierce and fiery.
For it's by fire that GOD brings judgment,
a death sentence on the human race.
Many, oh so many,
are under GOD's sentence of death:

17 "All who enter the sacred groves for initia-
tion in those unholy rituals that climaxed in
that foul and obscene meal of pigs and mice
will eat together and then die together."
GOD's Decree.

18-21 "I know everything they've ever done or
thought. I'm going to come and then gather
everyone—all nations, all languages. They'll
come and see my glory. I'll set up a station
at the center. I'll send the survivors of judg-
ment all over the world: Spain and Africa,
Turkey and Greece, and the far-off islands
that have never heard of me, who know
nothing of what I've done nor who I am. I'll
send them out as missionaries to preach my
glory among the nations. They'll return with
all your long-lost brothers and sisters from
all over the world. They'll bring them back
and offer them in living worship to GOD.
They'll bring them on horses and wagons
and carts, on mules and camels, straight to
my holy mountain Jerusalem," says GOD.
"They'll present them just as Israelites pre-
sent their offerings in a ceremonial vessel in
the Temple of GOD. I'll even take some of
them and make them priests and Levites,"
says GOD.

22-23 "For just as the new heavens and new earth
that I am making will stand firm before me"
—GOD's Decree—
"So will your children
and your reputation stand firm.
Month after month and week by week,
everyone will come to worship me," GOD says.

24 "And then they'll go out and look at what happened
to those who rebelled against me.
Corpses!
Maggots endlessly eating away on them,
an endless supply of fuel for fires.
Everyone who sees what's happened
and smells the stench retches."

JEREMIAH

New King James Version

1 The words of Jeremiah the son of Hilkiah, of
the priests who *were* in Anathoth in the land
of Benjamin, 2to whom the word of the LORD
came in the days of Josiah the son of Amon,
king of Judah, in the thirteenth year of his reign.
3It came also in the days of Jehoiakim the son of
Josiah, king of Judah, until the end of the
eleventh year of Zedekiah the son of Josiah,
king of Judah, until the carrying away of
Jerusalem captive in the fifth month.

The Prophet Is Called

4Then the word of the LORD came to me, saying:

5"Before I formed you in the womb I knew
you;
Before you were born I sanctified you;
I ordained you a prophet to the nations."

6Then said I:

"Ah, Lord GOD!
Behold, I cannot speak, for I *am* a youth."

7But the LORD said to me:

"Do not say, 'I *am* a youth,'
For you shall go to all to whom I send you,
And whatever I command you, you shall
speak.
8Do not be afraid of their faces,
For I *am* with you to deliver you," says the
LORD.

9Then the LORD put forth His hand and
touched my mouth, and the LORD said to me:

"Behold, I have put My words in your mouth.
10See, I have this day set you over the nations
and over the kingdoms,
To root out and to pull down,
To destroy and to throw down,
To build and to plant."

11Moreover the word of the LORD came to
me, saying, "Jeremiah, what do you see?"
And I said, "I see a branch of an almond tree."
12Then the LORD said to me, "You have seen
well, for I am ready to perform My word."
13And the word of the LORD came to me the
second time, saying, "What do you see?"
And I said, "I see a boiling pot, and it is facing away from the north."
14Then the LORD said to me:

"Out of the north calamity shall break forth
On all the inhabitants of the land.
15For behold, I am calling
All the families of the kingdoms of the
north," says the LORD;

The Message

Demolish, and Then Start Over

1-4 1 The Message of Jeremiah son of Hilkiah of
the family of priests who lived in Anathoth
in the country of Benjamin. GOD's Message
began to come to him during the thirteenth
year that Josiah son of Amos reigned over
Judah. It continued to come to him during
the time Jehoiakim son of Josiah reigned
over Judah. And it continued to come to him
clear down to the fifth month of the eleventh
year of the reign of Zedekiah son of Josiah
over Judah, the year that Jerusalem was
taken into exile. This is what GOD said:

5 "Before I shaped you in the womb,
I knew all about you.
Before you saw the light of day,
I had holy plans for you:
A prophet to the nations—
that's what I had in mind for you."

6 But I said, "Hold it, Master GOD! Look at
me.
I don't know anything. I'm only a boy!"

7-8 GOD told me, "Don't say, 'I'm only a boy.'
I'll tell you where to go and you'll go
there.
I'll tell you what to say and you'll say it.
Don't be afraid of a soul.
I'll be right there, looking after you."
GOD's Decree.

9-10 GOD reached out, touched my mouth, and
said,
"Look! I've just put my words in your
mouth—hand-delivered!
See what I've done? I've given you a job to
do
among nations and governments—
a red-letter day!
Your job is to pull up and tear down,
take apart and demolish,
And then start over,
building and planting."

Stand Up and Say Your Piece

11-12 GOD's Message came to me: "What do you
see, Jeremiah?"
I said, "A walking stick—that's all."
And GOD said, "Good eyes! I'm sticking
with you.
I'll make every word I give you come true."

13-15 GOD's Message came again: "So what do
you see now?"
I said, "I see a boiling pot, tipped down
toward us."
Then GOD told me, "Disaster will pour out
of the north
on everyone living in this land.
Watch for this: I'm calling all the kings out
of the north."
GOD's Decree.

NEW KING JAMES VERSION

"They shall come and each one set his throne
At the entrance of the gates of Jerusalem,
Against all its walls all around,
And against all the cities of Judah.
16I will utter My judgments
Against them concerning all their
wickedness,
Because they have forsaken Me,
Burned incense to other gods,
And worshiped the works of their own
hands.

17"Therefore prepare yourself and arise,
And speak to them all that I command you.
Do not be dismayed before their faces,
Lest I dismay you before them.
18For behold, I have made you this day
A fortified city and an iron pillar,
And bronze walls against the whole land—
Against the kings of Judah,
Against its princes,
Against its priests,
And against the people of the land.
19They will fight against you,
But they shall not prevail against you.
For I *am* with you," says the LORD, "to
deliver you."

GOD'S CASE AGAINST ISRAEL

2 Moreover the word of the LORD came to me,
saying, 2"Go and cry in the hearing of Jeru-
salem, saying, 'Thus says the LORD:

"I remember you,
The kindness of your youth,
The love of your betrothal,
When you went after Me in the wilderness,
In a land not sown.
3Israel *was* holiness to the LORD,
The firstfruits of His increase.
All that devour him will offend;
Disaster will come upon them," says the
LORD.' "

4Hear the word of the LORD, O house of Ja-
cob and all the families of the house of Israel.
5Thus says the LORD:

"What injustice have your fathers found in
Me,
That they have gone far from Me,
Have followed idols,
And have become idolaters?
6Neither did they say, 'Where *is* the LORD,
Who brought us up out of the land of Egypt,
Who led us through the wilderness,
Through a land of deserts and pits,
Through a land of drought and the shadow
of death,
Through a land that no one crossed
And where no one dwelt?'

THE MESSAGE

15-16 "They'll come and set up headquarters
facing Jerusalem's gates,
Facing all the city walls,
facing all the villages of Judah.
I'll pronounce my judgment on the people
of Judah
for walking out on me—what a terrible
thing to do!—
And courting other gods with their
offerings,
worshiping as gods sticks they'd carved,
stones they'd painted.

17 "But you—up on your feet and get dressed
for work!
Stand up and say your piece. Say exactly
what I tell you to say.
Don't pull your punches
or I'll pull you out of the lineup.

18-19 "Stand at attention while I prepare you for
your work.
I'm making you as impregnable as a
castle,
Immovable as a steel post,
solid as a concrete block wall.
You're a one-man defense system
against this culture,
Against Judah's kings and princes,
against the priests and local leaders.
They'll fight you, but they won't
even scratch you.
I'll back you up every inch of the way."
GOD's Decree.

ISRAEL WAS GOD'S HOLY CHOICE

1-3 2 GOD's Message came to me. It went like this:
"Get out in the streets and call to
Jerusalem,
'GOD's Message!
I remember your youthful loyalty,
our love as newlyweds.
You stayed with me through the wilderness
years,
stuck with me through all the hard places.
Israel was GOD's holy choice,
the pick of the crop.
Anyone who laid a hand on her
would soon wish he hadn't!' "
GOD's Decree.

4-6 Hear GOD's Message, House of Jacob!
Yes, you—House of Israel!
GOD's Message: "What did your ancestors
find fault with in me
that they drifted so far from me,
Took up with Sir Windbag
and turned into windbags themselves?

It never occurred to them to say, 'Where's
GOD,
the God who got us out of Egypt,
Who took care of us through thick and
thin, those rough-and-tumble
wilderness years of parched deserts and
death valleys,
A land that no one who enters comes out of,
a cruel, inhospitable land?'

NEW KING JAMES VERSION

7I brought you into a bountiful country,
To eat its fruit and its goodness.
But when you entered, you defiled My land
And made My heritage an abomination.
8The priests did not say, 'Where *is* the LORD?'
And those who handle the law did not know Me;
The rulers also transgressed against Me;
The prophets prophesied by Baal,
And walked after *things that* do not profit.

9"Therefore I will yet bring charges against you," says the LORD,
"And against your children's children I will bring charges.
10For pass beyond the coasts of Cyprus[a] and see,
Send to Kedar[b] and consider diligently,
And see if there has been such *a thing*.
11Has a nation changed *its* gods,
Which *are* not gods?
But My people have changed their Glory
For *what* does not profit.
12Be astonished, O heavens, at this,
And be horribly afraid;
Be very desolate," says the LORD.
13"For My people have committed two evils:
They have forsaken Me, the fountain of living waters,
And hewn themselves cisterns—broken cisterns that can hold no water.

14"*Is* Israel a servant?
Is he a homeborn *slave*?
Why is he plundered?
15The young lions roared at him, *and* growled;
They made his land waste;
His cities are burned, without inhabitant.
16Also the people of Noph[a] and Tahpanhes
Have broken the crown of your head.
17Have you not brought this on yourself,
In that you have forsaken the LORD your God
When He led you in the way?
18And now why take the road to Egypt,
To drink the waters of Sihor?
Or why take the road to Assyria,
To drink the waters of the River?[a]
19Your own wickedness will correct you,
And your backslidings will rebuke you.

2:10 [a]Hebrew *Kittim*, western lands, especially Cyprus [b]In the northern Arabian desert, representative of the eastern cultures **2:16** [a]That is, Memphis in ancient Egypt **2:18** [a]That is, the Euphrates

THE MESSAGE

7-8 "I brought you to a garden land
where you could eat lush fruit.
But you barged in and polluted my land,
trashed and defiled my dear land.
The priests never thought to ask, 'Where's GOD?'
The religion experts knew nothing of me.
The rulers defied me.
The prophets preached god Baal
And chased empty god-dreams and silly god-schemes.

9-11 "Because of all this, I'm bringing charges against you"
—GOD's Decree—
"charging you and your children and your grandchildren.
Look around. Have you ever seen anything quite like this?
Sail to the western islands and look.
Travel to the Kedar wilderness and look.
Look closely. Has this ever happened before,
That a nation has traded in its gods
for gods that aren't even close to gods?
But my people have traded my Glory
for empty god-dreams and silly god-schemes.

12-13 "Stand in shock, heavens, at what you see!
Throw up your hands in disbelief—this can't be!"
GOD's Decree.
"My people have committed a compound sin:
they've walked out on me, the fountain
Of fresh flowing waters, and then dug cisterns—
cisterns that leak, cisterns that are no better than sieves.

14-17 "Isn't Israel a valued servant,
born into a family with place and position?
So how did she end up a piece of meat
fought over by snarling and roaring lions?
There's nothing left of her but a few old bones,
her towns trashed and deserted.
Egyptians from the cities of Memphis and Tahpanhes
have broken your skulls.
And why do you think all this has happened?
Isn't it because you walked out on your God
just as he was beginning to lead you in the right way?

18-19 "And now, what do you think you'll get by going off to Egypt?
Maybe a cool drink of Nile River water?
Or what do you think you'll get by going off to Assyria?
Maybe a long drink of Euphrates River water?
Your evil ways will get you a sound thrashing, that's what you'll get.
You'll pay dearly for your disloyal ways.

New King James Version

Know therefore and see that *it is* an evil and
bitter *thing*
That you have forsaken the LORD your God,
And the fear of Me *is* not in you,"
Says the Lord GOD of hosts.

20"For of old I have broken your yoke *and*
burst your bonds;
And you said, 'I will not transgress,'
When on every high hill and under every
green tree
You lay down, playing the harlot.
21Yet I had planted you a noble vine, a seed of
highest quality.
How then have you turned before Me
Into the degenerate plant of an alien vine?
22For though you wash yourself with lye, and
use much soap,
Yet your iniquity is marked before Me," says
the Lord GOD.

23"How can you say, 'I am not polluted,
I have not gone after the Baals'?
See your way in the valley;
Know what you have done:
You are a swift dromedary breaking loose in
her ways,
24A wild donkey used to the wilderness,
That sniffs at the wind in her desire;
In her time of mating, who can turn her
away?
All those who seek her will not weary
themselves;
In her month they will find her.
25Withhold your foot from being unshod, and
your throat from thirst.
But you said, 'There is no hope.
No! For I have loved aliens, and after them I
will go.'

26"As the thief is ashamed when he is found
out,
So is the house of Israel ashamed;
They and their kings and their princes, and
their priests and their prophets,
27Saying to a tree, 'You *are* my father,'
And to a stone, 'You gave birth to me.'
For they have turned *their* back to Me, and
not *their* face.
But in the time of their trouble
They will say, 'Arise and save us.'
28But where *are* your gods that you have
made for yourselves?
Let them arise,
If they can save you in the time of your
trouble;
For *according to* the number of your cities
Are your gods, O Judah.

The Message

Take a long, hard look at what you've done
and its bitter results.
Was it worth it to have walked out on
your God?"
GOD's Decree, Master
GOD-of-the-Angel-Armies.

Addicted to Alien Gods

20-22 "A long time ago you broke out of the harness.
You shook off all restraints.
You said, 'I will not serve!'
and off you went,
Visiting every sex-and-religion shrine on
the way,
like a common whore.
You were a select vine when I planted you
from completely reliable stock.
And look how you've turned out—
a tangle of rancid growth, a poor excuse
for a vine.
Scrub, using the strongest soaps.
Scour your skin raw.
The sin-grease won't come out. I can't
stand to even look at you!"
GOD's Decree, the Master's Decree.

23-24 "How dare you tell me, 'I'm not stained by
sin.
I've never chased after the Baal sex gods'!
Well, look at the tracks you've left behind
in the valley.
How do you account for what is written
in the desert dust—
Tracks of a camel in heat, running this way
and that,
tracks of a wild donkey in rut,
Sniffing the wind for the slightest scent of
sex.
Who could possibly corral her!
On the hunt for sex, sex, and more sex—
insatiable, indiscriminate, promiscuous.

25 "Slow down. Take a deep breath. What's
the hurry?
Why wear yourself out? Just what are
you after anyway?
But you say, 'I can't help it.
I'm addicted to alien gods. I can't quit.'

26-28 "Just as a thief is chagrined, but only when
caught,
so the people of Israel are chagrined,
Caught along with their kings and princes,
their priests and prophets.
They walk up to a tree and say, 'My father!'
They pick up a stone and say, 'My
mother! You bore me!'
All I ever see of them is their backsides.
They never look me in the face.
But when things go badly, they don't
hesitate to come running,
calling out, 'Get a move on! Save us!'
Why not go to your handcrafted gods
you're so fond of?
Rouse them. Let them save you from
your bad times.
You've got more gods, Judah,
than you know what to do with.

NEW KING JAMES VERSION

29"Why will you plead with Me?
You all have transgressed against Me," says the LORD.
30"In vain I have chastened your children;
They received no correction.
Your sword has devoured your prophets
Like a destroying lion.

31"O generation, see the word of the LORD!
Have I been a wilderness to Israel,
Or a land of darkness?
Why do My people say, 'We are lords;
We will come no more to You'?
32Can a virgin forget her ornaments,
Or a bride her attire?
Yet My people have forgotten Me days without number.

33"Why do you beautify your way to seek love?
Therefore you have also taught
The wicked women your ways.
34Also on your skirts is found
The blood of the lives of the poor innocents.
I have not found it by secret search,
But plainly on all these things.
35Yet you say, 'Because I am innocent,
Surely His anger shall turn from me.'
Behold, I will plead My case against you,
Because you say, 'I have not sinned.'
36Why do you gad about so much to change your way?
Also you shall be ashamed of Egypt as you were ashamed of Assyria.
37Indeed you will go forth from him
With your hands on your head;
For the LORD has rejected your trusted allies,
And you will not prosper by them.

ISRAEL IS SHAMELESS

3 "They say, 'If a man divorces his wife,
And she goes from him
And becomes another man's,
May he return to her again?'
Would not that land be greatly polluted?

THE MESSAGE

TRYING OUT ANOTHER SIN-PROJECT

29-30 "What do you have against me,
running off to assert your 'independence'?"
GOD's Decree.
"I've wasted my time trying to train your children.
They've paid no attention to me, ignored my discipline.
And you've gotten rid of your God-messengers,
treating them like dirt and sweeping them away.

31-32 "What a generation you turned out to be!
Didn't I tell you? Didn't I warn you?
Have I let you down, Israel?
Am I nothing but a dead-end street?
Why do my people say, 'Good riddance!
From now on we're on our own'?
Young women don't forget their jewelry, do they?
Brides don't show up without their veils, do they?
But my people forget me.
Day after day after day they never give me a thought.

33-35 "What an impressive start you made
to get the most out of life.
You founded schools of sin,
taught graduate courses in evil!
And now you're sending out graduates,
resplendent in cap and gown—
except the gowns are stained with the blood of your victims!
All that blood convicts you.
You cut and hurt a lot of people to get where you are.
And yet you have the gall to say, 'I've done nothing wrong.
God doesn't mind. He hasn't punished me, has he?'
Don't look now, but judgment's on the way,
aimed at you who say, 'I've done nothing wrong.'

36-37 "You think it's just a small thing, don't you,
to try out another sin-project when the first one fails?
But Egypt will leave you in the lurch
the same way that Assyria did.
You're going to walk away from there
wringing your hands.
I, GOD, have blacklisted those you trusted.
You'll get not a lick of help from them."

YOUR SEX-AND-RELIGION OBSESSIONS

1 3 GOD's Message came to me as follows:

"If a man's wife
walks out on him
And marries another man,
can he take her back as if nothing had happened?
Wouldn't that raise a huge stink
in the land?
And isn't that what you've done—

NEW KING JAMES VERSION

But you have played the harlot with many lovers;
Yet return to Me," says the LORD.

2"Lift up your eyes to the desolate heights and see:
Where have you not lain *with men?*
By the road you have sat for them
Like an Arabian in the wilderness;
And you have polluted the land
With your harlotries and your wickedness.
3Therefore the showers have been withheld,
And there has been no latter rain.
You have had a harlot's forehead;
You refuse to be ashamed.
4Will you not from this time cry to Me,
'My Father, You *are* the guide of my youth?
5Will He remain angry forever?
Will He keep it to the end?'
Behold, you have spoken and done evil things,
As you were able."

A CALL TO REPENTANCE

6The LORD said also to me in the days of
Josiah the king: "Have you seen what backslid-
ing Israel has done? She has gone up on every
high mountain and under every green tree, and
there played the harlot. 7And I said, after she
had done all these *things*, 'Return to Me.' But
she did not return. And her treacherous sister
Judah saw it. 8Then I saw that for all the causes
for which backsliding Israel had committed
adultery, I had put her away and given her a cer-
tificate of divorce; yet her treacherous sister Ju-
dah did not fear, but went and played the harlot
also. 9So it came to pass, through her casual har-
lotry, that she defiled the land and committed
adultery with stones and trees. 10And yet for all
this her treacherous sister Judah has not turned
to Me with her whole heart, but in pretense,"
says the LORD.

11Then the LORD said to me, "Backsliding Is-
rael has shown herself more righteous than
treacherous Judah. 12Go and proclaim these
words toward the north, and say:

'Return, backsliding Israel,' says the LORD;
'I will not cause My anger to fall on you.
For I *am* merciful,' says the LORD;
'I will not remain angry forever.
13Only acknowledge your iniquity,
That you have transgressed against the LORD your God,
And have scattered your charms
To alien deities under every green tree,
And you have not obeyed My voice,' says the LORD.

14"Return, O backsliding children," says the
LORD; "for I am married to you. I will take you,
one from a city and two from a family, and I will

THE MESSAGE

'whored' your way with god after god?
And now you want to come back as if nothing had happened."
GOD's Decree.

2-5 "Look around at the hills.
Where have you *not* had sex?
You've camped out like hunters stalking deer.
You've solicited many lover-gods,
Like a streetwalking whore chasing after other gods.
And so the rain has stopped.
No more rain from the skies!
But it doesn't even faze you. Brazen as whores,
you carry on as if you've done nothing wrong.
Then you have the nerve to call out, 'My father!
You took care of me when I was a child.
Why not now?
Are you going to keep up your anger nonstop?'
That's your line. Meanwhile you keep sinning nonstop."

ADMIT YOUR GOD-DEFIANCE

6-10 GOD spoke to me during the reign of King
Josiah: "You have noticed, haven't you, how
fickle Israel has visited every hill and grove
of trees as a whore at large? I assumed that
after she had gotten it out of her system,
she'd come back, but she didn't. Her flighty
sister, Judah, saw what she did. She also
saw that because of fickle Israel's loose
morals I threw her out, gave her her walking
papers. But that didn't faze flighty sister Ju-
dah. She went out, big as you please, and
took up a whore's life also. She took up
cheap sex-and-religion as a sideline diver-
sion, an indulgent recreation, and used any-
thing and anyone, flouting sanity and sanc-
tity alike, stinking up the country. And not
once in all this did flighty sister Judah even
give me a nod, although she made a show of
it from time to time." GOD's Decree.

11-12 Then GOD told me, "Fickle Israel was a
good sight better than flighty Judah. Go and
preach this message. Face north toward Is-
rael and say:

12-15 " 'Turn back, fickle Israel.
I'm not just hanging back to punish you.
I'm committed in love to you.
My anger doesn't seethe nonstop.
Just admit your guilt.
Admit your God-defiance.
Admit to your promiscuous life with casual partners,
pulling strangers into the sex-and-religion groves
While turning a deaf ear to me.' "
GOD's Decree.
"Come back, wandering children!"
GOD's Decree.
"I, yes I, am your true husband.
I'll pick you out one by one—
This one from the city, these two from the country—

NEW KING JAMES VERSION

bring you to Zion. [15]And I will give you shep-
herds according to My heart, who will feed you
with knowledge and understanding.
16"Then it shall come to pass, when you are
multiplied and increased in the land in those
days," says the LORD, "that they will say no
more, 'The ark of the covenant of the LORD.' It
shall not come to mind, nor shall they remem-
ber it, nor shall they visit *it*, nor shall it be made
anymore.
17"At that time Jerusalem shall be called The
Throne of the LORD, and all the nations shall be
gathered to it, to the name of the LORD, to
Jerusalem. No more shall they follow the dic-
tates of their evil hearts.
18"In those days the house of Judah shall
walk with the house of Israel, and they shall
come together out of the land of the north to the
land that I have given as an inheritance to your
fathers.
19"But I said:

'How can I put you among the children
And give you a pleasant land,
A beautiful heritage of the hosts of nations?'

"And I said:

'You shall call Me, "My Father,"
And not turn away from Me.'
20Surely, *as* a wife treacherously departs from
her husband,
So have you dealt treacherously with Me,
O house of Israel," says the LORD.

21A voice was heard on the desolate heights,
Weeping *and* supplications of the children
of Israel.
For they have perverted their way;
They have forgotten the LORD their God.

22"Return, you backsliding children,
And I will heal your backslidings."

"Indeed we do come to You,
For You are the LORD our God.
23Truly, in vain *is salvation hoped for* from the
hills,
And from the multitude of mountains;
Truly, in the LORD our God
Is the salvation of Israel.
24For shame has devoured
The labor of our fathers from our youth—
Their flocks and their herds,
Their sons and their daughters.
25We lie down in our shame,
And our reproach covers us.
For we have sinned against the LORD our
God,
We and our fathers,
From our youth even to this day,
And have not obeyed the voice of the LORD
our God."

THE MESSAGE

and bring you to Zion.
I'll give you good shepherd-rulers who rule
my way,
who rule you with intelligence and
wisdom.

16 "And this is what will happen: You will in-
crease and prosper in the land. The time will
come"—GOD's Decree!—"when no one will
say any longer, 'Oh, for the good old days!
Remember the Ark of the Covenant?' It
won't even occur to anyone to say it—'the
good old days.' The so-called good old days
of the Ark are gone for good.
17 "Jerusalem will be the new Ark—'GOD's
Throne.' All the godless nations, no longer
stuck in the ruts of their evil ways, will
gather there to honor GOD.
18 "At that time, the House of Judah will join
up with the House of Israel. Holding hands,
they'll leave the north country and come to
the land I willed to your ancestors.

19-20 "I planned what I'd say if you returned to me:
'Good! I'll bring you back into the family.
I'll give you choice land,
land that the godless nations would die
for.'
And I imagined that you would say, 'Dear
father!'
and would never again go off and leave
me.
But no luck. Like a false-hearted woman
walking out on her husband,
you, the whole family of Israel, have
proven false to me."
GOD's Decree.

21-22 The sound of voices comes drifting out of
the hills,
the unhappy sound of Israel's crying,
Israel lamenting the wasted years,
never once giving her God a thought.
"Come back, wandering children!
I can heal your wanderlust!"

22-25 "We're here! We've come back to you.
You're our own true GOD!
All that popular religion was a cheap lie,
duped crowds buying up the latest in gods.
We're back! Back to our true GOD,
the salvation of Israel.
The Fraud picked us clean, swindled us
of what our ancestors bequeathed us,
Gypped us out of our inheritance—
God-blessed flocks and God-given children.
We made our bed and now lie in it,
all tangled up in the dirty sheets of
dishonor.
All because we sinned against our GOD,
we and our fathers and mothers.
From the time we took our first steps, said
our first words,
we've been rebels, disobeying the voice
of our GOD."

NEW KING JAMES VERSION

4 "If you will return, O Israel," says the LORD,
"Return to Me;
And if you will put away your abominations
out of My sight,
Then you shall not be moved.
2And you shall swear, 'The LORD lives,'
In truth, in judgment, and in righteousness;
The nations shall bless themselves in Him,
And in Him they shall glory."

3For thus says the LORD to the men of Judah
and Jerusalem:

"Break up your fallow ground,
And do not sow among thorns.
4Circumcise yourselves to the LORD,
And take away the foreskins of your hearts,
You men of Judah and inhabitants of
Jerusalem,
Lest My fury come forth like fire,
And burn so that no one can quench *it*,
Because of the evil of your doings."

AN IMMINENT INVASION

5Declare in Judah and proclaim in Jeru-
salem, and say:

"Blow the trumpet in the land;
Cry, 'Gather together,'
And say, 'Assemble yourselves,
And let us go into the fortified cities.'
6Set up the standard toward Zion.
Take refuge! Do not delay!
For I will bring disaster from the north,
And great destruction."

7The lion has come up from his thicket,
And the destroyer of nations is on his way.
He has gone forth from his place
To make your land desolate.
Your cities will be laid waste,
Without inhabitant.
8For this, clothe yourself with sackcloth,
Lament and wail.
For the fierce anger of the LORD
Has not turned back from us.

9"And it shall come to pass in that day," says
the LORD,
"*That* the heart of the king shall perish,
And the heart of the princes;
The priests shall be astonished,
And the prophets shall wonder."

10Then I said, "Ah, Lord GOD!
Surely You have greatly deceived this people
and Jerusalem,
Saying, 'You shall have peace,'
Whereas the sword reaches to the heart."

11At that time it will be said
To this people and to Jerusalem,

THE MESSAGE

1-2 4 "If you want to come back, O Israel,
you must really come back to me.
You must get rid of your stinking sin
paraphernalia
and not wander away from me anymore.
Then you can say words like, 'As GOD
lives . . .'
and have them mean something true and
just and right.
And the godless nations will get caught up
in the blessing
and find something in Israel to write
home about."

3-4 Here's another Message from GOD
to the people of Judah and Jerusalem:
"Plow your unplowed fields,
but then don't plant weeds in the soil!
Yes, circumcise your *lives* for God's sake.
Plow your unplowed hearts,
all you people of Judah and Jerusalem.
Prevent fire—the fire of my anger—
for once it starts it can't be put out.
Your wicked ways
are fuel for the fire.

GOD'S SLEDGEHAMMER ANGER

5-8 "Sound the alarm in Judah,
broadcast the news in Jerusalem.
Say, 'Blow the ram's horn trumpet through
the land!'
Shout out—a bullhorn bellow!—
'Close ranks!
Run for your lives to the shelters!'
Send up a flare warning Zion:
'Not a minute to lose! Don't sit on your
hands!'
Disaster's descending from the north. I set
it off!
When it lands, it will shake the
foundations.
Invaders have pounced like a lion from its
cover,
ready to rip nations to shreds,
Leaving your land in wrack and ruin,
your cities in rubble, abandoned.
Dress in funereal black.
Weep and wail,
For GOD's sledgehammer anger
has slammed into us head-on.

9 "When this happens"
—GOD's Decree—
"King and princes will lose heart;
priests will be baffled and prophets
stand dumbfounded."

10 Then I said, "Alas, Master GOD!
You've fed lies to this people, this
Jerusalem.
You assured them, 'All is well, don't worry,'
at the very moment when the sword was
at their throats."

11-12 At that time, this people, yes, this very
Jerusalem,
will be told in plain words:

NEW KING JAMES VERSION

"A dry wind of the desolate heights *blows* in
the wilderness
Toward the daughter of My people—
Not to fan or to cleanse—
12A wind too strong for these will come for
Me;
Now I will also speak judgment against
them."

13"Behold, he shall come up like clouds,
And his chariots like a whirlwind.
His horses are swifter than eagles.
Woe to us, for we are plundered!"

14O Jerusalem, wash your heart from
wickedness,
That you may be saved.
How long shall your evil thoughts lodge
within you?
15For a voice declares from Dan
And proclaims affliction from Mount
Ephraim:
16"Make mention to the nations,
Yes, proclaim against Jerusalem,
That watchers come from a far country
And raise their voice against the cities of
Judah.
17Like keepers of a field they are against her
all around,
Because she has been rebellious against
Me," says the LORD.
18"Your ways and your doings
Have procured these *things* for you.
This *is* your wickedness,
Because it is bitter,
Because it reaches to your heart."

SORROW FOR THE DOOMED NATION

19O my soul, my soul!
I am pained in my very heart!
My heart makes a noise in me;
I cannot hold my peace,
Because you have heard, O my soul,
The sound of the trumpet,
The alarm of war.
20Destruction upon destruction is cried,
For the whole land is plundered.
Suddenly my tents are plundered,
And my curtains in a moment.
21How long will I see the standard,
And hear the sound of the trumpet?

22"For My people *are* foolish,
They have not known Me.
They *are* silly children,
And they have no understanding.
They *are* wise to do evil,
But to do good they have no knowledge."

23I beheld the earth, and indeed *it was*
without form, and void;
And the heavens, they *had* no light.
24I beheld the mountains, and indeed they
trembled,
And all the hills moved back and forth.

THE MESSAGE

"The northern hordes are sweeping in
from the desert steppes—
A wind that's up to no good, a gale-force
wind.
I ordered this wind.
I'm pronouncing
my hurricane judgment on my people."

YOUR EVIL LIFE IS PIERCING YOUR HEART

13-14 Look at them! Like banks of storm clouds,
racing, tumbling, their chariots a
tornado,
Their horses faster than eagles!
Woe to us! We're done for!
Jerusalem! Scrub the evil from your lives
so you'll be fit for salvation.
How much longer will you harbor
devious and malignant designs within
you?

15-17 What's this? A messenger from Dan?
Bad news from Ephraim's hills!
Make the report public.
Broadcast the news to Jerusalem:
"Invaders from far off are
raising war cries against Judah's towns.
They're all over her, like a dog on a bone.
And why? Because she rebelled against
me."
GOD's Decree.

18 "It's the way you've lived
that's brought all this on you.
The bitter taste is from your evil life.
That's what's piercing your heart."

19-21 I'm doubled up with cramps in my belly—
a poker burns in my gut.
My insides are tearing me up,
never a moment's peace.
The ram's horn trumpet blast rings in my
ears,
the signal for all-out war.
Disaster hard on the heels of disaster,
the whole country in ruins!
In one stroke my home is destroyed,
the walls flattened in the blink of an eye.
How long do I have to look at the warning
flares,
listen to the siren of danger?

EXPERTS AT EVIL

22 "What fools my people are!
They have no idea who I am.
A company of half-wits,
dopes and donkeys all!
Experts at evil
but klutzes at good."

23-26 I looked at the earth—
it was back to pre-Genesis chaos and
emptiness.
I looked at the skies,
and not a star to be seen.
I looked at the mountains—
they were trembling like aspen leaves,
And all the hills
rocking back and forth in the wind.

New King James Version

25I beheld, and indeed *there was* no man,
And all the birds of the heavens had fled.
26I beheld, and indeed the fruitful land *was* a wilderness,
And all its cities were broken down
At the presence of the LORD,
By His fierce anger.

27For thus says the LORD:
"The whole land shall be desolate;
Yet I will not make a full end.
28For this shall the earth mourn,
And the heavens above be black,
Because I have spoken.
I have purposed and will not relent,
Nor will I turn back from it.
29The whole city shall flee from the noise of the horsemen and bowmen.
They shall go into thickets and climb up on the rocks.
Every city *shall be* forsaken,
And not a man shall dwell in it.

30"And *when* you *are* plundered,
What will you do?
Though you clothe yourself with crimson,
Though you adorn *yourself* with ornaments of gold,
Though you enlarge your eyes with paint,
In vain you will make yourself fair;
Your lovers will despise you;
They will seek your life.

31"For I have heard a voice as of a woman in labor,
The anguish as of her who brings forth her first child,
The voice of the daughter of Zion bewailing herself;
She spreads her hands, *saying*,
'Woe *is* me now, for my soul is weary
Because of murderers!'

The Justice of God's Judgment

5 "Run to and fro through the streets of Jerusalem;
See now and know;
And seek in her open places
If you can find a man,
If there is *anyone* who executes judgment,
Who seeks the truth,
And I will pardon her.
2Though they say, '*As* the LORD lives,'
Surely they swear falsely."

3O LORD, *are* not Your eyes on the truth?
You have stricken them,
But they have not grieved;
You have consumed them,
But they have refused to receive correction.
They have made their faces harder than rock;
They have refused to return.

4Therefore I said, "Surely these *are* poor.
They are foolish;
For they do not know the way of the LORD,

The Message

I looked—what's this! Not a man or woman in sight,
and not a bird to be seen in the skies.
I looked—this can't be! Every garden and orchard shriveled up.
All the towns were ghost towns.
And all this because of GOD,
because of the blazing anger of GOD.

27-28 Yes, this is GOD's Word on the matter:

"The whole country will be laid waste—
still it won't be the end of the world.
The earth will mourn
and the skies lament
Because I've given my word and won't take it back.
I've decided and won't change my mind."

You're Not Going to Seduce Anyone

29 Someone shouts, "Horsemen and archers!"
and everybody runs for cover.
They hide in ditches,
they climb into caves.
The cities are emptied,
not a person left anywhere.

30-31 And you, what do you think you're up to?
Dressing up in party clothes,
Decking yourselves out in jewelry,
putting on lipstick and rouge and mascara!
Your primping goes for nothing.
You're not going to seduce anyone.
They're out to *kill* you!
And what's that I hear? The cry of a woman in labor,
the screams of a mother giving birth to her firstborn.
It's the cry of Daughter Zion, gasping for breath,
reaching out for help:
"Help, oh help me! I'm dying!
The killers are on me!"

Sins Are Piled Sky-High

1-2 5 "Patrol Jerusalem's streets.
Look around. Take note.
Search the market squares.
See if you can find one man, one woman,
A single soul who does what is right
and tries to live a true life.
I want to forgive that person."
GOD's Decree.
"But if all they do is say, 'As sure as GOD lives . . . ,'
they're nothing but a bunch of liars."

3-6 But you, GOD,
you have an eye for truth, don't you?
You hit them hard, but it didn't faze them.
You disciplined them, but they refused correction.
Hardheaded, harder than rock,
they wouldn't change.
Then I said to myself, "Well, these are just poor people.
They don't know any better.
They were never taught anything about GOD.

NEW KING JAMES VERSION

The judgment of their God.
5I will go to the great men and speak to them,
For they have known the way of the LORD,
The judgment of their God."

But these have altogether broken the yoke
And burst the bonds.
6Therefore a lion from the forest shall slay them,
A wolf of the deserts shall destroy them;
A leopard will watch over their cities.
Everyone who goes out from there shall be torn in pieces,
Because their transgressions are many;
Their backslidings have increased.

7"How shall I pardon you for this?
Your children have forsaken Me
And sworn by *those that are* not gods.
When I had fed them to the full,
Then they committed adultery
And assembled themselves by troops in the harlots' houses.
8They were *like* well-fed lusty stallions;
Every one neighed after his neighbor's wife.
9Shall I not punish *them* for these *things*?"
says the LORD.
"And shall I not avenge Myself on such a nation as this?

10"Go up on her walls and destroy,
But do not make a complete end.
Take away her branches,
For they *are* not the LORD's.
11For the house of Israel and the house of Judah
Have dealt very treacherously with Me,"
says the LORD.

12They have lied about the LORD,
And said, "*It is* not He.
Neither will evil come upon us,
Nor shall we see sword or famine.
13And the prophets become wind,
For the word *is* not in them.
Thus shall it be done to them."

14Therefore thus says the LORD God of hosts:

"Because you speak this word,
Behold, I will make My words in your mouth fire,
And this people wood,
And it shall devour them.
15Behold, I will bring a nation against you from afar,
O house of Israel," says the LORD.
"It *is* a mighty nation,
It *is* an ancient nation,
A nation whose language you do not know,
Nor can you understand what they say.

THE MESSAGE

They never went to prayer meetings.
I'll find some people from the best families.
I'll talk to them.
They'll know what's going on, the way GOD works.
They'll know the score."
But they were no better! Rebels all!
Off doing their own thing.
The invaders are ready to pounce and kill,
like a mountain lion, a wilderness wolf,
Panthers on the prowl.
The streets aren't safe anymore.
And why? Because the people's sins are piled sky-high;
their betrayals are past counting.

7-9 "Why should I even bother with you any longer?
Your children wander off, leaving me,
Taking up with gods
that aren't even gods.
I satisfied their deepest needs, and then
they went off with the 'sacred' whores,
left me for orgies in sex shrines!
A bunch of well-groomed, lusty stallions,
each one pawing and snorting for his neighbor's wife.
Do you think I'm going to stand around
and do nothing?"
GOD's Decree.
"Don't you think I'll take serious measures
against a people like this?

EYES THAT DON'T REALLY LOOK, EARS THAT DON'T REALLY LISTEN

10-11 "Go down the rows of vineyards and rip out the vines,
but not all of them. Leave a few.
Prune back those vines!
That growth didn't come from GOD!
They've betrayed me over and over again,
Judah and Israel both."
GOD's Decree.

12-13 "They've spread lies about GOD.
They've said, 'There's nothing to him.
Nothing bad will happen to us,
neither famine nor war will come our way.
The prophets are all windbags.
They speak nothing but nonsense.' "

14 Therefore, this is what GOD said to me,
GOD-of-the-Angel-Armies:

"Because they have talked this way,
they are going to eat those words.
Watch now! I'm putting my words
as fire in your mouth.
And the people are a pile of kindling
ready to go up in flames.

15-17 "Attention! I'm bringing a far-off nation
against you, O house of Israel."
GOD's Decree.
"A solid nation,
an ancient nation,
A nation that speaks another language.
You won't understand a word they say.

NEW KING JAMES VERSION

16Their quiver *is* like an open tomb;
They *are* all mighty men.
17And they shall eat up your harvest and your bread,
Which your sons and daughters should eat.
They shall eat up your flocks and your herds;
They shall eat up your vines and your fig trees;
They shall destroy your fortified cities,
In which you trust, with the sword.

18"Nevertheless in those days," says the
LORD, "I will not make a complete end of you.
19And it will be when you say, 'Why does the
LORD our God do all these *things* to us?' then
you shall answer them, 'Just as you have for-
saken Me and served foreign gods in your land,
so you shall serve aliens in a land *that is* not
yours.'

20"Declare this in the house of Jacob
And proclaim it in Judah, saying,
21'Hear this now, O foolish people,
Without understanding,
Who have eyes and see not,
And who have ears and hear not:
22Do you not fear Me?' says the LORD.
'Will you not tremble at My presence,
Who have placed the sand as the bound of the sea,
By a perpetual decree, that it cannot pass beyond it?
And though its waves toss to and fro,
Yet they cannot prevail;
Though they roar, yet they cannot pass over it.
23But this people has a defiant and rebellious heart;
They have revolted and departed.
24They do not say in their heart,
"Let us now fear the LORD our God,
Who gives rain, both the former and the latter, in its season.
He reserves for us the appointed weeks of the harvest."
25Your iniquities have turned these *things* away,
And your sins have withheld good from you.

26'For among My people are found wicked *men;*
They lie in wait as one who sets snares;
They set a trap;
They catch men.
27As a cage is full of birds,
So their houses *are* full of deceit.
Therefore they have become great and grown rich.
28They have grown fat, they are sleek;
Yes, they surpass the deeds of the wicked;
They do not plead the cause,
The cause of the fatherless;
Yet they prosper,
And the right of the needy they do not defend.

THE MESSAGE

When they aim their arrows, you're as good as dead.
They're a nation of real fighters!
They'll clean you out of house and home,
rob you of crops and children alike.
They'll feast on your sheep and cattle,
strip your vines and fig trees.
And the fortresses that made you feel so safe—
leveled with a stroke of the sword!

18-19 "Even then, as bad as it will be"—GOD's
Decree!—"it will not be the end of the world
for you. And when people ask, 'Why did our
GOD do all this to us?' you must say to them,
'It's tit for tat. Just as you left me and served
foreign gods in your own country, so now
you must serve foreigners in their own
country.'

20-25 "Tell the house of Jacob this,
put out this bulletin in Judah:
Listen to this,
you scatterbrains, airheads,
With eyes that see but don't really look,
and ears that hear but don't really listen.
Why don't you honor me?
Why aren't you in awe before me?
Yes, *me*, who made the shorelines
to contain the ocean waters.
I drew a line in the sand
that cannot be crossed.
Waves roll in but cannot get through;
breakers crash but that's the end of them.
But this people—what a people!
Uncontrollable, untameable runaways.
It never occurs to them to say,
'How can we honor our GOD with our lives,
The God who gives rain in both spring and autumn
and maintains the rhythm of the seasons,
Who sets aside time each year for harvest
and keeps everything running smoothly for us?'
Of course you don't! Your bad behavior
blinds you to all this.
Your sins keep my blessings at a distance.

TO STAND FOR NOTHING AND STAND UP FOR NO ONE

26-29 "My people are infiltrated by wicked men,
unscrupulous men on the hunt.
They set traps for the unsuspecting.
Their victims are innocent men and women.
Their houses are stuffed with ill-gotten gain,
like a hunter's bag full of birds.
Pretentious and powerful and rich,
hugely obese, oily with rolls of fat.
Worse, they have no conscience.
Right and wrong mean nothing to them.
They stand for nothing, stand up for no one,
throw orphans to the wolves, exploit the poor.

NEW KING JAMES VERSION

29 Shall I not punish *them* for these *things?*'
says the LORD.
'Shall I not avenge Myself on such a nation
as this?'

30 "An astonishing and horrible thing
Has been committed in the land:
31 The prophets prophesy falsely,
And the priests rule by their *own* power;
And My people love *to have it* so.
But what will you do in the end?

IMPENDING DESTRUCTION FROM THE NORTH

6 "O you children of Benjamin,
Gather yourselves to flee from the midst
of Jerusalem!
Blow the trumpet in Tekoa,
And set up a signal-fire in Beth Haccerem;
For disaster appears out of the north,
And great destruction.
2 I have likened the daughter of Zion
To a lovely and delicate woman.
3 The shepherds with their flocks shall come
to her.
They shall pitch *their* tents against her all
around.
Each one shall pasture in his own place."

4 "Prepare war against her;
Arise, and let us go up at noon.
Woe to us, for the day goes away,
For the shadows of the evening are
lengthening.
5 Arise, and let us go by night,
And let us destroy her palaces."

6 For thus has the LORD of hosts said:

"Cut down trees,
And build a mound against Jerusalem.
This *is* the city to be punished.
She *is* full of oppression in her midst.
7 As a fountain wells up with water,
So she wells up with her wickedness.
Violence and plundering are heard in her.
Before Me continually *are* grief and
wounds.
8 Be instructed, O Jerusalem,
Lest My soul depart from you;
Lest I make you desolate,
A land not inhabited."

9 Thus says the LORD of hosts:

"They shall thoroughly glean as a vine the
remnant of Israel;
As a grape-gatherer, put your hand back
into the branches."
10 To whom shall I speak and give warning,
That they may hear?
Indeed their ear *is* uncircumcised,

THE MESSAGE

Do you think I'll stand by and do nothing
about this?"
GOD's Decree.
"Don't you think I'll take serious measures
against a people like this?

30-31 "Unspeakable! Sickening!
What's happened in this country?
Prophets preach lies
and priests hire on as their assistants.
And my people love it. They eat it up!
But what will you do when it's time to
pick up the pieces?"

A CITY FULL OF LIES

1-5 6 "Run for your lives, children of Benjamin!
Get out of Jerusalem, and now!
Give a blast on the ram's horn in Blastville.
Send up smoke signals from
Smoketown.
Doom pours out of the north—
massive terror!
I have likened my dear daughter Zion
to a lovely meadow.
Well, now 'shepherds' from the north have
discovered her
and brought in their flocks of soldiers.
They've pitched camp all around her,
and plan where they'll 'graze.'
And then, 'Prepare to attack! The fight is on!
To arms! We'll strike at noon!
Oh, it's too late? Day is dying?
Evening shadows are upon us?
Well, up anyway! We'll attack by night
and tear apart her defenses stone by
stone.' "

6-8 GOD-of-the-Angel-Armies gave the
orders:

"Chop down her trees.
Build a siege ramp against Jerusalem,
A city full of brutality,
bursting with violence.
Just as a well holds a good supply of water,
she supplies wickedness nonstop.
The streets echo the cries: 'Violence! Rape!'
Victims, bleeding and moaning, lie all
over the place.
You're in deep trouble, Jerusalem.
You've pushed me to the limit.
You're on the brink of being wiped out,
being turned into a ghost town."

9 More orders from GOD-of-the-Angel-
Armies:

"Time's up! Harvest the grapes for
judgment.
Salvage what's left of Israel.
Go back over the vines.
Pick them clean, every last grape.

IS ANYBODY LISTENING?

10-11 "I've got something to say. Is anybody
listening?
I've a warning to post. Will anyone
notice?

NEW KING JAMES VERSION

And they cannot give heed.
Behold, the word of the LORD is a reproach
to them;
They have no delight in it.
11Therefore I am full of the fury of the LORD.
I am weary of holding *it* in.
"I will pour it out on the children outside,
And on the assembly of young men
together;
For even the husband shall be taken with
the wife,
The aged with *him who is* full of days.
12And their houses shall be turned over to
others,
Fields and wives together;
For I will stretch out My hand
Against the inhabitants of the land," says
the LORD.
13"Because from the least of them even to the
greatest of them,
Everyone *is* given to covetousness;
And from the prophet even to the priest,
Everyone deals falsely.
14They have also healed the hurt of My people
slightly,
Saying, 'Peace, peace!'
When *there is* no peace.
15Were they ashamed when they had
committed abomination?
No! They were not at all ashamed;
Nor did they know how to blush.
Therefore they shall fall among those who
fall;
At the time I punish them,
They shall be cast down," says the LORD.

16Thus says the LORD:

"Stand in the ways and see,
And ask for the old paths, where the good
way *is*,
And walk in it;
Then you will find rest for your souls.
But they said, 'We will not walk *in it*.'
17Also, I set watchmen over you, *saying*,
'Listen to the sound of the trumpet!'
But they said, 'We will not listen.'
18Therefore hear, you nations,
And know, O congregation, what *is* among
them.
19Hear, O earth!
Behold, I will certainly bring calamity on
this people—
The fruit of their thoughts,
Because they have not heeded My words
Nor My law, but rejected it.
20For what purpose to Me
Comes frankincense from Sheba,
And sweet cane from a far country?

THE MESSAGE

It's hopeless! Their ears are stuffed with
wax—
deaf as a post, blind as a bat.
It's hopeless! They've tuned out GOD.
They don't want to hear from me.
But I'm bursting with the wrath of GOD.
I can't hold it in much longer.

11-12 "So dump it on the children in the streets.
Let it loose on the gangs of youth.
For no one's exempt: Husbands and wives
will be taken,
the old and those ready to die;
Their homes will be given away—
all they own, even their loved ones—
When I give the signal
against all who live in this country."
GOD's Decree.

13-15 "Everyone's after the dishonest dollar,
little people and big people alike.
Prophets and priests and everyone in
between
twist words and doctor truth.
My people are broken—shattered!—
and they put on Band-Aids,
Saying, 'It's not so bad. You'll be just fine.'
But things are not 'just fine'!
Do you suppose they are embarrassed
over this outrage?
No, they have no shame.
They don't even know how to blush.
There's no hope for them. They've hit
bottom
and there's no getting up.
As far as I'm concerned,
they're finished."
GOD has spoken.

DEATH IS ON THE PROWL

16-20 GOD's Message yet again:

"Go stand at the crossroads and look
around.
Ask for directions to the old road,
The tried-and-true road. Then take it.
Discover the right route for your souls.
But they said, 'Nothing doing.
We aren't going that way.'
I even provided watchmen for them
to warn them, to set off the alarm.
But the people said, 'It's a false alarm.
It doesn't concern us.'
And so I'm calling in the nations as
witnesses:
'Watch, witnesses, what happens to
them!'
And, 'Pay attention, Earth!
Don't miss these bulletins.'
I'm visiting catastrophe on this people, the
end result
of the games they've been playing with
me.
They've ignored everything I've said,
had nothing but contempt for my
teaching.
What would I want with incense brought in
from Sheba,
rare spices from exotic places?

NEW KING JAMES VERSION

Your burnt offerings *are* not acceptable,
Nor your sacrifices sweet to Me."
21Therefore thus says the LORD:

"Behold, I will lay stumbling blocks before this people,
And the fathers and the sons together shall fall on them.
The neighbor and his friend shall perish."

22Thus says the LORD:

"Behold, a people comes from the north country,
And a great nation will be raised from the farthest parts of the earth.
23They will lay hold on bow and spear;
They *are* cruel and have no mercy;
Their voice roars like the sea;
And they ride on horses,
As men of war set in array against you,
O daughter of Zion."
24We have heard the report of it;
Our hands grow feeble.
Anguish has taken hold of us,
Pain as of a woman in labor.
25Do not go out into the field,
Nor walk by the way.
Because of the sword of the enemy,
Fear *is* on every side.
26O daughter of my people,
Dress in sackcloth
And roll about in ashes!
Make mourning *as for* an only son, most bitter lamentation;
For the plunderer will suddenly come upon us.

27"I have set you *as* an assayer *and* a fortress among My people,
That you may know and test their way.
28They *are* all stubborn rebels, walking as slanderers.
They are bronze and iron,
They *are* all corrupters;
29The bellows blow fiercely,
The lead is consumed by the fire;
The smelter refines in vain,
For the wicked are not drawn off.
30*People* will call them rejected silver,
Because the LORD has rejected them."

TRUSTING IN LYING WORDS

7The word that came to Jeremiah from the
LORD, saying, 2"Stand in the gate of the
LORD's house, and proclaim there this word, and
say, 'Hear the word of the LORD, all *you of* Judah
who enter in at these gates to worship the LORD!' "

THE MESSAGE

Your burnt sacrifices in worship give me no pleasure.
Your religious rituals mean nothing to me."

21 So listen to this. Here's GOD's verdict on your way of life:

"Watch out! I'm putting roadblocks and barriers
on the road you're taking.
They'll send you sprawling,
parents and children, neighbors and friends—
and that will be the end of the lot of you."

22-23 And listen to this verdict from GOD:

"Look out! An invasion from the north,
a mighty power on the move from a faraway place:
Armed to the teeth,
vicious and pitiless,
Booming like sea storm and thunder—
tramp, tramp, tramp—
riding hard on war horses,
In battle formation
against you, dear Daughter Zion!"

24-25 We've heard the news,
and we're as limp as wet dishrags.
We're paralyzed with fear.
Terror has a death grip on our throats.
Don't dare go outdoors!
Don't leave the house!
Death is on the prowl.
Danger everywhere!

26 "Dear Daughter Zion: Dress in black.
Blacken your face with ashes.
Weep most bitterly,
as for an only child.
The countdown has begun . . .
six, five, four, three . . .
The Terror is on us!"

27-30 GOD gave me this task:

"I have made you the examiner of my people,
to examine and weigh their lives.
They're a thickheaded, hard-nosed bunch,
rotten to the core, the lot of them.
Refining fires are cranked up to white heat,
but the ore stays a lump, unchanged.
It's useless to keep trying any longer.
Nothing can refine evil out of them.
Men will give up and call them 'slag,'
thrown on the slag heap by me, their GOD."

THE NATION THAT WOULDN'T OBEY GOD

1-2 7The Message from GOD to Jeremiah:
"Stand in the gate of GOD's Temple and
preach this Message.
2-3 "Say, 'Listen, all you people of Judah who
come through these gates to worship GOD.
GOD-of-the-Angel-Armies, Israel's God, has
this to say to you:

New King James Version

3Thus says the LORD of hosts, the God of Israel:
"Amend your ways and your doings, and I will
cause you to dwell in this place. 4Do not trust in
these lying words, saying, 'The temple of the
LORD, the temple of the LORD, the temple of the
LORD *are* these.'

5"For if you thoroughly amend your ways
and your doings, if you thoroughly execute
judgment between a man and his neighbor, 6*if*
you do not oppress the stranger, the fatherless,
and the widow, and do not shed innocent blood
in this place, or walk after other gods to your
hurt, 7then I will cause you to dwell in this place,
in the land that I gave to your fathers forever
and ever.

8"Behold, you trust in lying words that can-
not profit. 9Will you steal, murder, commit adul-
tery, swear falsely, burn incense to Baal, and
walk after other gods whom you do not know,
10and *then* come and stand before Me in this
house which is called by My name, and say, 'We
are delivered to do all these abominations'?
11Has this house, which is called by My name,
become a den of thieves in your eyes? Behold, I,
even I, have seen *it*," says the LORD.

12"But go now to My place which *was* in
Shiloh, where I set My name at the first, and see
what I did to it because of the wickedness of My
people Israel. 13And now, because you have
done all these works," says the LORD, "and I
spoke to you, rising up early and speaking, but
you did not hear, and I called you, but you did
not answer, 14therefore I will do to the house
which is called by My name, in which you trust,
and to this place which I gave to you and your
fathers, as I have done to Shiloh. 15And I will
cast you out of My sight, as I have cast out all
your brethren—the whole posterity of Ephraim.

16"Therefore do not pray for this people, nor
lift up a cry or prayer for them, nor make inter-
cession to Me; for I will not hear you. 17Do you
not see what they do in the cities of Judah and
in the streets of Jerusalem? 18The children
gather wood, the fathers kindle the fire, and the
women knead dough, to make cakes for the
queen of heaven; and *they* pour out drink offer-
ings to other gods, that they may provoke Me to
anger. 19Do they provoke Me to anger?" says the
LORD. "*Do they* not *provoke* themselves, to the
shame of their own faces?"

The Message

3-7 " 'Clean up your act—the way you live, the
things you do—so I can make my home with
you in this place. Don't for a minute believe
the lies being spoken here—"This is GOD's
Temple, GOD's Temple, GOD's Temple!" Total
nonsense! Only if you clean up your act (the
way you live, the things you do), only if you
do a total spring cleaning on the way you live
and treat your neighbors, only if you quit ex-
ploiting the street people and orphans and
widows, no longer taking advantage of inno-
cent people on this very site and no longer
destroying your souls by using this Temple as
a front for other gods—only *then* will I move
into your neighborhood. Only then will this
country I gave your ancestors be my perma-
nent home, my Temple.

8-11 " 'Get smart! Your leaders are handing
you a pack of lies, and you're swallowing
them! Use your heads! Do you think you can
rob and murder, have sex with the neighbor-
hood wives, tell lies nonstop, worship the lo-
cal gods, and buy every novel religious com-
modity on the market—and then march into
this Temple, set apart for my worship, and
say, "We're safe!" thinking that the place it-
self gives you a license to go on with all this
outrageous sacrilege? A cave full of crimi-
nals! Do you think you can turn this Temple,
set apart for my worship, into something
like that? Well, think again. I've got eyes in
my head. I can see what's going on.' " GOD's
Decree!

12 " 'Take a trip down to the place that was
once in Shiloh, where I met my people in the
early days. Take a look at those ruins, what
I did to it because of the evil ways of my
people Israel.

13-15 " 'So now, because of the way you have
lived and failed to listen, even though time
and again I took you aside and talked seri-
ously with you, and because you refused to
change when I called you to repent, I'm go-
ing to do to this Temple, set aside for my
worship, this place you think is going to
keep you safe no matter what, this place I
gave as a gift to your ancestors and you, the
same as I did to Shiloh. And as for you, I'm
going to get rid of you, the same as I got rid
of those old relatives of yours around
Shiloh, your fellow Israelites in that former
kingdom to the north.'

16-18 "And you, Jeremiah, don't waste your
time praying for this people. Don't offer to
make petitions or intercessions. Don't
bother me with them. I'm not listening.
Can't you see what they're doing in all the
villages of Judah and in the Jerusalem
streets? Why, they've got the children gath-
ering wood while the fathers build fires and
the mothers make bread to be offered to 'the
Queen of Heaven'! And as if that weren't
bad enough, they go around pouring out li-
bations to any other gods they come across,
just to hurt me.

19 "But is it me they're hurting?" GOD's De-
cree! "Aren't they just hurting themselves?
Exposing themselves shamefully? Making
themselves ridiculous?

NEW KING JAMES VERSION

20 Therefore thus says the Lord GOD: "Behold, My anger and My fury will be poured out on this place—on man and on beast, on the trees of the field and on the fruit of the ground. And it will burn and not be quenched."

21 Thus says the LORD of hosts, the God of Israel: "Add your burnt offerings to your sacrifices and eat meat. 22 For I did not speak to your fathers, or command them in the day that I brought them out of the land of Egypt, concerning burnt offerings or sacrifices. 23 But this is what I commanded them, saying, 'Obey My voice, and I will be your God, and you shall be My people. And walk in all the ways that I have commanded you, that it may be well with you.' 24 Yet they did not obey or incline their ear, but followed the counsels *and* the dictates of their evil hearts, and went backward and not forward. 25 Since the day that your fathers came out of the land of Egypt until this day, I have even sent to you all My servants the prophets, daily rising up early and sending *them*. 26 Yet they did not obey Me or incline their ear, but stiffened their neck. They did worse than their fathers.

27 "Therefore you shall speak all these words to them, but they will not obey you. You shall also call to them, but they will not answer you.

JUDGMENT ON OBSCENE RELIGION

28 "So you shall say to them, 'This *is* a nation that does not obey the voice of the LORD their God nor receive correction. Truth has perished and has been cut off from their mouth. 29 Cut off your hair and cast *it* away, and take up a lamentation on the desolate heights; for the LORD has rejected and forsaken the generation of His wrath.' 30 For the children of Judah have done evil in My sight," says the LORD. "They have set their abominations in the house which is called by My name, to pollute it. 31 And they have built the high places of Tophet, which *is* in the Valley of the Son of Hinnom, to burn their sons and their daughters in the fire, which I did not command, nor did it come into My heart.

32 "Therefore behold, the days are coming," says the LORD, "when it will no more be called Tophet, or the Valley of the Son of Hinnom, but the Valley of Slaughter; for they will bury in Tophet until there is no room. 33 The corpses of this people will be food for the birds of the heaven and for the beasts of the earth. And no one will frighten *them away*. 34 Then I will cause to cease from the cities of Judah and from the streets of Jerusalem the voice of mirth and the voice of gladness, the voice of the bridegroom and the voice of the bride. For the land shall be desolate.

8 "At that time," says the LORD, "they shall bring out the bones of the kings of Judah, and the bones of its princes, and the bones of the priests, and the bones of the prophets, and the bones of the inhabitants of Jerusalem, out of

THE MESSAGE

20 "Here's what the Master GOD has to say: 'My white-hot anger is about to descend on this country and everything in it—people and animals, trees in the field and vegetables in the garden—a raging wildfire that no one can put out.'

21-23 "The Message from GOD-of-the-Angel-Armies, Israel's God: 'Go ahead! Put your burnt offerings with all your other sacrificial offerings and make a good meal for yourselves. *I* sure don't want them! When I delivered your ancestors out of Egypt, I never said anything to them about wanting burnt offerings and sacrifices as such. But I did say this, *commanded* this: "Obey me. Do what I say and I will be your God and you will be my people. Live the way I tell you. Do what I command so that your lives will go well."

24-26 " 'But do you think they listened? Not a word of it. They did just what they wanted to do, indulged any and every evil whim and got worse day by day. From the time your ancestors left the land of Egypt until now, I've supplied a steady stream of my servants the prophets, but do you think the people listened? Not once. Stubborn as mules and worse than their ancestors!'

27-28 "Tell them all this, but don't expect them to listen. Call out to them, but don't expect an answer. Tell them, 'You are the nation that wouldn't obey GOD, that refused all discipline. Truth has disappeared. There's not a trace of it left in your mouths.

29 " 'So shave your heads.
Go bald to the hills and lament,
For GOD has rejected and left
this generation that has made him so angry.'

30-31 "The people of Judah have lived evil lives while I've stood by and watched." GOD's Decree. "In deliberate insult to me, they've set up their obscene god-images in the very Temple that was built to honor me. They've constructed Topheth altars for burning babies in prominent places all through the valley of Ben-hinnom, altars for burning their sons and daughters alive in the fire—a shocking perversion of all that I am and all I command.

32-34 "But soon, very soon"—GOD's Decree!—"the names Topheth and Benhinnom will no longer be used. They'll call the place what it is: Murder Meadow. Corpses will be stacked up in Topheth because there's no room left to bury them! Corpses abandoned in the open air, fed on by crows and coyotes, who have the run of the place. And I'll empty both smiles and laughter from the villages of Judah and the streets of Jerusalem. No wedding songs, no holiday sounds. *Dead* silence."

1-2 8 "And when the time comes"—GOD's Decree!—"I'll see to it that they dig up the bones of the kings of Judah, the bones of the princes and priests and prophets, and yes, even the bones of the common people.

New King James Version

their graves. [2]They shall spread them before the
sun and the moon and all the host of heaven,
which they have loved and which they have
served and after which they have walked, which
they have sought and which they have wor-
shiped. They shall not be gathered nor buried;
they shall be like refuse on the face of the earth.
[3]Then death shall be chosen rather than life by
all the residue of those who remain of this evil
family, who remain in all the places where I
have driven them," says the LORD of hosts.

The Peril of False Teaching

[4]"Moreover you shall say to them, 'Thus says
the LORD:

"Will they fall and not rise?
Will one turn away and not return?
[5]Why has this people slidden back,
Jerusalem, in a perpetual backsliding?
They hold fast to deceit,
They refuse to return.
[6]I listened and heard,
But they do not speak aright.
No man repented of his wickedness,
Saying, 'What have I done?'
Everyone turned to his own course,
As the horse rushes into the battle.

[7]"Even the stork in the heavens
Knows her appointed times;
And the turtledove, the swift, and the swallow
Observe the time of their coming.
But My people do not know the judgment of the LORD.

[8]"How can you say, 'We *are* wise,
And the law of the LORD *is* with us'?
Look, the false pen of the scribe certainly works falsehood.
[9]The wise men are ashamed,
They are dismayed and taken.
Behold, they have rejected the word of the LORD;
So what wisdom do they have?
[10]Therefore I will give their wives to others,
And their fields to those who will inherit *them;*
Because from the least even to the greatest
Everyone is given to covetousness;
From the prophet even to the priest
Everyone deals falsely.
[11]For they have healed the hurt of the daughter of My people slightly,
Saying, 'Peace, peace!'
When *there is* no peace.
[12]Were they ashamed when they had committed abomination?
No! They were not at all ashamed,
Nor did they know how to blush.
Therefore they shall fall among those who fall;

The Message

They'll dig them up and spread them out like a congregation at worship before sun, moon, and stars, all those sky gods they've been so infatuated with all these years, following their 'lucky stars' in doglike devotion. The bones will be left scattered and exposed, to reenter the soil as fertilizer, like manure.

3 "Everyone left—all from this evil generation unlucky enough to still be alive in whatever godforsaken place I will have driven them to—will wish they were dead." Decree of GOD-of-the-Angel-Armies.

To Know Everything but God's Word

4-7 "Tell them this, GOD's Message:

" 'Do people fall down and not get up?
Or take the wrong road and then just keep going?
So why does this people go backward,
and just keep on going—*backward*!
They stubbornly hold on to their illusions,
refuse to change direction.
I listened carefully
but heard not so much as a whisper.
No one expressed one word of regret.
Not a single "I'm sorry" did I hear.
They just kept at it, blindly and stupidly
banging their heads against a brick wall.
Cranes know when it's time
to move south for winter.
And robins, warblers, and bluebirds
know when it's time to come back again.
But my people? My people know nothing,
not the first thing of GOD and his rule.

8-9 " 'How can you say, "We know the score.
We're the proud owners of GOD's revelation"?
Look where it's gotten you—stuck in illusion.
Your religion experts have taken you for a ride!
Your know-it-alls will be unmasked,
caught and shown up for what they are.
Look at them! They know everything but GOD's Word.
Do you call that "knowing"?

10-12 " 'So here's what will happen to the know-it-alls:
I'll make them wifeless and homeless.
Everyone's after the dishonest dollar,
little people and big people alike.
Prophets and priests and everyone in between
twist words and doctor truth.
My dear Daughter—my people—broken, shattered,
and yet they put on Band-Aids,
Saying, "It's not so bad. You'll be just fine."
But things are not "just fine"!
Do you suppose they are embarrassed over this outrage?
Not really. They have no shame.
They don't even know how to blush.
There's no hope for them. They've hit bottom
and there's no getting up.

NEW KING JAMES VERSION

In the time of their punishment
They shall be cast down," says the LORD.

13"I will surely consume them," says the LORD.
"No grapes *shall be* on the vine,
Nor figs on the fig tree,
And the leaf shall fade;
And *the things* I have given them shall pass away from them." ' "

14"Why do we sit still?
Assemble yourselves,
And let us enter the fortified cities,
And let us be silent there.
For the LORD our God has put us to silence
And given us water of gall to drink,
Because we have sinned against the LORD.

15"*We* looked for peace, but no good *came;*
And for a time of health, and there was trouble!
16The snorting of His horses was heard from Dan.
The whole land trembled at the sound of the neighing of His strong ones;
For they have come and devoured the land and all that is in it,
The city and those who dwell in it."

17"For behold, I will send serpents among you,
Vipers which cannot be charmed,
And they shall bite you," says the LORD.

THE PROPHET MOURNS FOR THE PEOPLE

18I would comfort myself in sorrow;
My heart *is* faint in me.
19Listen! The voice,
The cry of the daughter of my people
From a far country:
"*Is* not the LORD in Zion?
Is not her King in her?"

"Why have they provoked Me to anger
With their carved images—
With foreign idols?"

20"The harvest is past,
The summer is ended,
And we are not saved!"

21For the hurt of the daughter of my people I am hurt.
I am mourning;
Astonishment has taken hold of me.
22*Is there* no balm in Gilead,
Is there no physician there?
Why then is there no recovery
For the health of the daughter of my people?

9 Oh, that my head were waters,
And my eyes a fountain of tears,
That I might weep day and night
For the slain of the daughter of my people!
2Oh, that I had in the wilderness
A lodging place for travelers;

THE MESSAGE

As far as I'm concerned,
they're finished.' " GOD has spoken.

13 " 'I went out to see if I could salvage anything' "
—GOD's Decree—
" 'but found nothing:
Not a grape, not a fig,
just a few withered leaves.
I'm taking back
everything I gave them.' "

14-16 So why are we sitting here, doing nothing?
Let's get organized.
Let's go to the big city
and at least die fighting.
We've gotten GOD's ultimatum:
We're damned if we do and damned if we don't—
damned because of our sin against him.
We hoped things would turn out for the best,
but it didn't happen that way.
We were waiting around for healing—
and terror showed up!
From Dan at the northern borders
we hear the hooves of horses,
Horses galloping, horses neighing.
The ground shudders and quakes.
They're going to swallow up the whole country.
Towns and people alike—fodder for war.

17 " 'What's more, I'm dispatching
poisonous snakes among you,
Snakes that can't be charmed,
snakes that will bite you and kill you.' "
GOD's Decree!

ADVANCING FROM ONE EVIL TO THE NEXT

18-22 I drown in grief.
I'm heartsick.
Oh, listen! Please listen! It's the cry of my dear people
reverberating through the country.
Is GOD no longer in Zion?
Has the King gone away?
Can you tell me why they flaunt their plaything-gods,
their silly, imported no-gods before me?
The crops are in, the summer is over,
but for us nothing's changed.
We're still waiting to be rescued.
For my dear broken people, I'm heartbroken.
I weep, seized by grief.
Are there no healing ointments in Gilead?
Isn't there a doctor in the house?
So why can't something be done
to heal and save my dear, dear people?

1-2 9 I wish my head were a well of water
and my eyes fountains of tears
So I could weep day and night
for casualties among my dear, dear people.
At times I wish I had a wilderness hut,
a backwoods cabin,

NEW KING JAMES VERSION

That I might leave my people,
And go from them!
For they *are* all adulterers,
An assembly of treacherous men.
3"And *like* their bow they have bent their
tongues *for* lies.
They are not valiant for the truth on the
earth.
For they proceed from evil to evil,
And they do not know Me," says the LORD.
4"Everyone take heed to his neighbor,
And do not trust any brother;
For every brother will utterly supplant,
And every neighbor will walk with
slanderers.
5Everyone will deceive his neighbor,
And will not speak the truth;
They have taught their tongue to speak lies;
They weary themselves to commit iniquity.
6Your dwelling place *is* in the midst of deceit;
Through deceit they refuse to know Me,"
says the LORD.

7Therefore thus says the LORD of hosts:

"Behold, I will refine them and try them;
For how shall I deal with the daughter of My
people?
8Their tongue *is* an arrow shot out;
It speaks deceit;
One speaks peaceably to his neighbor with
his mouth,
But in his heart he lies in wait.
9Shall I not punish them for these *things?*"
says the LORD.
"Shall I not avenge Myself on such a nation
as this?"

10I will take up a weeping and wailing for the
mountains,
And for the dwelling places of the
wilderness a lamentation,
Because they are burned up,
So that no one can pass through;
Nor can *men* hear the voice of the cattle.
Both the birds of the heavens and the beasts
have fled;
They are gone.

11"I will make Jerusalem a heap of ruins, a den
of jackals.
I will make the cities of Judah desolate,
without an inhabitant."

12Who *is* the wise man who may understand
this? And *who is he* to whom the mouth of the
LORD has spoken, that he may declare it? Why
does the land perish *and* burn up like a wilder-
ness, so that no one can pass through?

THE MESSAGE

Where I could get away from my people
and never see them again.
They're a faithless, feckless bunch,
a congregation of degenerates.

3-6 "Their tongues shoot out lies
like a bow shoots arrows—
A mighty army of liars,
the sworn enemies of truth.
They advance from one evil to the next,
ignorant of me."
GOD's Decree.
"Be wary of even longtime neighbors.
Don't even trust your grandmother!
Brother schemes against brother,
like old cheating Jacob.
Friend against friend
spreads malicious gossip.
Neighbors gyp neighbors,
never telling the truth.
They've trained their tongues to tell lies,
and now they can't tell the truth.
They pile wrong upon wrong, stack lie
upon lie,
and refuse to know me."
GOD's Decree.

7-9 Therefore, GOD-of-the-Angel-Armies says:

"Watch this! I'll melt them down
and see what they're made of.
What else can I do
with a people this wicked?
Their tongues are poison arrows!
Deadly lies stream from their mouths.
Neighbor greets neighbor with a smile,
'Good morning! How're things?'
while scheming to do away with him.
Do you think I'm going to stand around
and do nothing?"
GOD's Decree.
"Don't you think I'll take serious measures
against a people like this?

10-11 "I'm lamenting the loss of the mountain
pastures.
I'm chanting dirges for the old grazing
grounds.
They've become deserted wastelands too
dangerous for travelers.
No sounds of sheep bleating or cattle
mooing.
Birds and wild animals, all gone.
Nothing stirring, no sounds of life.
I'm going to make Jerusalem a pile of
rubble,
fit for nothing but stray cats and dogs.
I'm going to reduce Judah's towns to piles
of ruins
where no one lives!"

12 I asked, "Is there anyone around bright
enough to tell us what's going on here? Any-
one who has the inside story from GOD and
can let us in on it?
"Why is the country wasted?
"Why no travelers in this desert?"

NEW KING JAMES VERSION

13And the LORD said, "Because they have for-
saken My law which I set before them, and have
not obeyed My voice, nor walked according to
it, 14but they have walked according to the dic-
tates of their own hearts and after the Baals,
which their fathers taught them," 15therefore
thus says the LORD of hosts, the God of Israel:
"Behold, I will feed them, this people, with
wormwood, and give them water of gall to
drink. 16I will scatter them also among the Gen-
tiles, whom neither they nor their fathers have
known. And I will send a sword after them until
I have consumed them."

THE PEOPLE MOURN IN JUDGMENT

17Thus says the LORD of hosts:

"Consider and call for the mourning women,
That they may come;
And send for skillful *wailing* women,
That they may come.
18Let them make haste
And take up a wailing for us,
That our eyes may run with tears,
And our eyelids gush with water.
19For a voice of wailing is heard from Zion:
'How we are plundered!
We are greatly ashamed,
Because we have forsaken the land,
Because we have been cast out of our
dwellings.' "

20Yet hear the word of the LORD, O women,
And let your ear receive the word of His
mouth;
Teach your daughters wailing,
And everyone her neighbor a lamentation.
21For death has come through our windows,
Has entered our palaces,
To kill off the children—*no longer to be*
outside!
And the young men—*no longer* on the
streets!

22Speak, "Thus says the LORD:

'Even the carcasses of men shall fall as
refuse on the open field,
Like cuttings after the harvester,
And no one shall gather *them*.' "

23Thus says the LORD:

"Let not the wise *man* glory in his wisdom,
Let not the mighty *man* glory in his might,
Nor let the rich *man* glory in his riches;
24But let him who glories glory in this,
That he understands and knows Me,
That I *am* the LORD, exercising
lovingkindness, judgment, and
righteousness in the earth.
For in these I delight," says the LORD.

THE MESSAGE

13-15 GOD's answer: "Because they abandoned
my plain teaching. They wouldn't listen to
anything I said, refused to live the way I told
them to. Instead they lived any way they
wanted and took up with the Baal gods, who
they thought would give them what they
wanted—following the example of their par-
ents." And this is the consequence. GOD-of-
the-Angel-Armies says so:

"I'll feed them with pig slop.
"I'll give them poison to drink.
16 "Then I'll scatter them far and wide
among godless peoples that neither they nor
their parents have ever heard of, and I'll
send Death in pursuit until there's nothing
left of them."

A LIFE THAT IS ALL OUTSIDE BUT NO INSIDE

17-19 A Message from GOD-of-the-Angel-Armies:

"Look over the trouble we're in and call for
help.
Send for some singers who can help us
mourn our loss.
Tell them to hurry—
to help us express our loss and lament,
Help us get our tears flowing,
make tearful music of our crying.
Listen to it!
Listen to that torrent of tears out of Zion:
'We're a ruined people,
we're a shamed people!
We've been driven from our homes
and must leave our land!' "

20-21 Mourning women! Oh, listen to GOD's
Message!
Open your ears. Take in what he says.
Teach your daughters songs for the dead
and your friends the songs of
heartbreak.
Death has climbed in through the window,
broken into our bedrooms.
Children on the playgrounds drop dead,
and young men and women collapse at
their games.

22 Speak up! "GOD's Message:

" 'Dead bodies everywhere, scattered at
random
like sheep and goat dung in the fields,
Like wheat cut down by reapers
and left to rot where it falls.' "

23-24 GOD's Message:

"Don't let the wise brag of their wisdom.
Don't let heroes brag of their exploits.
Don't let the rich brag of their riches.
If you brag, brag of this and this only:
That you understand and know me.
I'm GOD, and I act in loyal love.
I do what's right and set things right and fair,
and delight in those who do the same
things.
These are my trademarks."
GOD's Decree.

NEW KING JAMES VERSION

25“Behold, the days are coming,” says the
LORD, “that I will punish all *who are* circumcised
with the uncircumcised— 26Egypt, Judah, Edom,
the people of Ammon, Moab, and all *who are* in
the farthest corners, who dwell in the wilder-
ness. For all *these* nations *are* uncircumcised,
and all the house of Israel *are* uncircumcised in
the heart.”

IDOLS AND THE TRUE GOD

10 Hear the word which the LORD speaks to
you, O house of Israel.
2Thus says the LORD:

“Do not learn the way of the Gentiles;
Do not be dismayed at the signs of heaven,
For the Gentiles are dismayed at them.
3For the customs of the peoples *are* futile;
For *one* cuts a tree from the forest,
The work of the hands of the workman, with
the ax.
4They decorate it with silver and gold;
They fasten it with nails and hammers
So that it will not topple.
5They *are* upright, like a palm tree,
And they cannot speak;
They must be carried,
Because they cannot go *by themselves.*
Do not be afraid of them,
For they cannot do evil,
Nor can they do any good.”

6Inasmuch as *there is* none like You, O LORD
(You *are* great, and Your name *is* great in
might),
7Who would not fear You, O King of the
nations?
For this is Your rightful due.
For among all the wise *men* of the nations,
And in all their kingdoms,
There is none like You.
8But they are altogether dull-hearted and
foolish;
A wooden idol *is* a worthless doctrine.
9Silver is beaten into plates;
It is brought from Tarshish,
And gold from Uphaz,
The work of the craftsman
And of the hands of the metalsmith;
Blue and purple *are* their clothing;
They *are* all the work of skillful *men.*
10But the LORD *is* the true God;
He *is* the living God and the everlasting
King.
At His wrath the earth will tremble,
And the nations will not be able to endure
His indignation.

11Thus you shall say to them: “The gods that
have not made the heavens and the earth shall
perish from the earth and from under these
heavens.”

12He has made the earth by His power,
He has established the world by His
wisdom,
And has stretched out the heavens at His
discretion.

THE MESSAGE

25-26 “Stay alert! It won’t be long now”—
GOD’s Decree!—“when I will personally deal
with everyone whose life is all outside but
no inside: Egypt, Judah, Edom, Ammon,
Moab. All these nations are big on perform-
ance religion—including Israel, who is no
better.”

THE STICK GODS

1-5 10 Listen to the Message that GOD is send-
ing your way, House of Israel. Listen
most carefully:

“Don’t take the godless nations as your
models.
Don’t be impressed by their glamour and
glitz,
no matter how much they’re impressed.
The religion of these peoples
is nothing but smoke.
An idol is nothing but a tree chopped
down,
then shaped by a woodsman’s ax.
They trim it with tinsel and balls,
use hammer and nails to keep it upright.
It’s like a scarecrow in a cabbage patch—
can’t talk!
Dead wood that has to be carried—can’t
walk!
Don’t be impressed by such stuff.
It’s useless for either good or evil.”

6-9 All this is nothing compared to you, O GOD.
You’re wondrously great, famously great.
Who can fail to be impressed by you, King
of the nations?
It’s your very nature to be worshiped!
Look far and wide among the elite of the
nations.
The best they can come up with is
nothing compared to you.
Stupidly, they line them up—a lineup of
sticks,
good for nothing but making smoke.
Gilded with silver foil from Tarshish,
covered with gold from Uphaz,
Hung with violet and purple fabrics—
no matter how fancy the sticks, they’re
still sticks.

10 But GOD is the real thing—
the living God, the eternal King.
When he’s angry, Earth shakes.
Yes, and the godless nations quake.

11-15 “Tell them this, ‘The stick gods
who made nothing, neither sky nor
earth,
Will come to nothing
on the earth and under the sky.’ ”
But it is God whose power made the earth,
whose wisdom gave shape to the world,
who crafted the cosmos.

NEW KING JAMES VERSION

13When He utters His voice,
There is a multitude of waters in the heavens:
"And He causes the vapors to ascend from the ends of the earth.
He makes lightning for the rain,
He brings the wind out of His treasuries."[a]

14Everyone is dull-hearted, without knowledge;
Every metalsmith is put to shame by an image;
For his molded image *is* falsehood,
And *there is* no breath in them.
15They *are* futile, a work of errors;
In the time of their punishment they shall perish.
16The Portion of Jacob *is* not like them,
For He *is* the Maker of all *things*,
And Israel *is* the tribe of His inheritance;
The LORD of hosts *is* His name.

THE COMING CAPTIVITY OF JUDAH

17Gather up your wares from the land,
O inhabitant of the fortress!

18For thus says the LORD:

"Behold, I will throw out at this time
The inhabitants of the land,
And will distress them,
That they may find *it so*."

19Woe is me for my hurt!
My wound is severe.
But I say, "Truly this *is* an infirmity,
And I must bear it."
20My tent is plundered,
And all my cords are broken;
My children have gone from me,
And they *are* no more.
There is no one to pitch my tent anymore,
Or set up my curtains.

21For the shepherds have become dull-hearted,
And have not sought the LORD;
Therefore they shall not prosper,
And all their flocks shall be scattered.
22Behold, the noise of the report has come,
And a great commotion out of the north country,
To make the cities of Judah desolate, a den of jackals.

23O LORD, I know the way of man *is* not in himself;
It is not in man who walks to direct his own steps.
24O LORD, correct me, but with justice;
Not in Your anger, lest You bring me to nothing.
25Pour out Your fury on the Gentiles, who do not know You,
And on the families who do not call on Your name;

10:13 [a]Psalm 135:7

THE MESSAGE

He thunders, and rain pours down.
He sends the clouds soaring.
He embellishes the storm with lightnings,
launches wind from his warehouse.
Stick-god worshipers looking mighty foolish,
god-makers embarrassed by their handmade gods!
Their gods are frauds—dead sticks,
deadwood gods, tasteless jokes.
When the fires of judgment come, they'll be ashes.

16 But the Portion-of-Jacob is the real thing.
He put the whole universe together
And pays special attention to Israel.
His name? GOD-of-the-Angel-Armies!

17-18 Grab your bags,
all you who are under attack.
GOD has given notice:
"Attention! I'm evicting
Everyone who lives here,
And right now—yes, right now!
I'm going to press them to the limit,
squeeze the life right out of them."

19-20 But it's a black day for me!
Hopelessly wounded,
I said, "Why, oh why
did I think I could bear it?"
My house is ruined—
the roof caved in.
Our children are gone—
we'll never see them again.
No one left to help in rebuilding,
no one to make a new start!

21 It's because our leaders are stupid.
They never asked GOD for counsel,
And so nothing worked right.
The people are scattered all over.

22 But listen! Something's coming!
A big commotion from the northern borders!
Judah's towns about to be smashed,
left to all the stray dogs and cats!

23-25 I know, GOD, that mere mortals
can't run their own lives,
That men and women
don't have what it takes to take charge of life.
So correct us, GOD, as you see best.
Don't lose your temper. That would be the end of us.
Vent your anger on the godless nations,
who refuse to acknowledge you,
And on the people
who won't pray to you—

New King James Version

For they have eaten up Jacob,
Devoured him and consumed him,
And made his dwelling place desolate.

The Broken Covenant

11 The word that came to Jeremiah from the
LORD, saying, 2“Hear the words of this
covenant, and speak to the men of Judah and to
the inhabitants of Jerusalem; 3and say to them,
‘Thus says the LORD God of Israel: “Cursed *is*
the man who does not obey the words of this
covenant 4which I commanded your fathers in
the day I brought them out of the land of Egypt,
from the iron furnace, saying, ‘Obey My voice,
and do according to all that I command you; so
shall you be My people, and I will be your God,’
5that I may establish the oath which I have
sworn to your fathers, to give them ‘a land flow-
ing with milk and honey,’[a] as *it is* this day.” ’ ”
And I answered and said, “So be it, LORD.”
6Then the LORD said to me, “Proclaim all
these words in the cities of Judah and in the
streets of Jerusalem, saying: ‘Hear the words of
this covenant and do them. 7For I earnestly ex-
horted your fathers in the day I brought them up
out of the land of Egypt, until this day, rising
early and exhorting, saying, “Obey My voice.”
8Yet they did not obey or incline their ear, but
everyone followed the dictates of his evil heart;
therefore I will bring upon them all the words of
this covenant, which I commanded *them* to do,
but *which* they have not done.’ ”
9And the LORD said to me, “A conspiracy has
been found among the men of Judah and among
the inhabitants of Jerusalem. 10They have
turned back to the iniquities of their forefathers
who refused to hear My words, and they have
gone after other gods to serve them; the house
of Israel and the house of Judah have broken
My covenant which I made with their fathers.”
11Therefore thus says the LORD: “Behold, I
will surely bring calamity on them which they
will not be able to escape; and though they cry
out to Me, I will not listen to them. 12Then the
cities of Judah and the inhabitants of Jerusalem
will go and cry out to the gods to whom they of-
fer incense, but they will not save them at all in
the time of their trouble. 13For *according to* the
number of your cities were your gods, O Judah;
and *according to* the number of the streets of
Jerusalem you have set up altars to *that* shame-
ful thing, altars to burn incense to Baal.
14“So do not pray for this people, or lift up a
cry or prayer for them; for I will not hear *them*
in the time that they cry out to Me because of
their trouble.

15“What has My beloved to do in My house,
Having done lewd deeds with many?
And the holy flesh has passed from you.
When you do evil, then you rejoice.

11:5 [a]Exodus 3:8

The Message

The very ones who’ve made hash out of
Jacob,
yes, made hash
And devoured him whole,
people and pastures alike.

The Terms of This Covenant

1 11 The Message that came to Jeremiah
from GOD:
2-4 “Preach to the people of Judah and citi-
zens of Jerusalem. Tell them this: ‘This is
GOD’s Message, the Message of Israel’s God
to you. Anyone who does not keep the terms
of this covenant is cursed. The terms are
clear. I made them plain to your ancestors
when I delivered them from Egypt, out of
the iron furnace of suffering.
4-5 “ ‘Obey what I tell you. Do exactly what I
command you. Your obedience will close the
deal. You’ll be mine and I’ll be yours. This
will provide the conditions in which I will be
able to do what I promised your ancestors:
to give them a fertile and lush land. And, as
you know, that’s what I did.’ ”
“Yes, GOD,” I replied. “That’s true.”
6-8 GOD continued: “Preach all this in the
towns of Judah and the streets of Jerusalem.
Say, ‘Listen to the terms of this covenant
and carry them out! I warned your ances-
tors when I delivered them from Egypt and
I’ve kept up the warnings. I haven’t quit
warning them for a moment. I warned them
from morning to night: “Obey me or else!”
But they didn’t obey. They paid no attention
to me. They did whatever they wanted to do,
whenever they wanted to do it, until finally I
stepped in and ordered the punishments set
out in the covenant, which, despite all my
warnings, they had ignored.’ ”
9-10 Then GOD said, “There’s a conspiracy
among the people of Judah and the citizens
of Jerusalem. They’ve plotted to reenact the
sins of their ancestors—the ones who dis-
obeyed me and decided to go after other
gods and worship them. Israel and Judah
are in this together, mindlessly breaking the
covenant I made with their ancestors.”
11-13 “Well, your God has something to say
about this: Watch out! I’m about to visit
doom on you, and no one will get out of it.
You’re going to cry for help but I won’t lis-
ten. Then all the people in Judah and
Jerusalem will start praying to the gods
you’ve been sacrificing to all these years,
but it won’t do a bit of good. You’ve got as
many gods as you have villages, Judah! And
you’ve got enough altars for sacrifices to
that impotent sex god Baal to put one on
every street corner in Jerusalem!”
14 “And as for you, Jeremiah, I don’t want you
praying for this people. Nothing! Not a word
of petition. Indeed, I’m not going to listen to a
single syllable of their crisis-prayers.”

Promises and Pious Programs

15-16 “What business do the ones I love have
figuring out
how to get off the hook? And right in the
house of worship!

NEW KING JAMES VERSION

16 The LORD called your name,
Green Olive Tree, Lovely *and* of Good Fruit.
With the noise of a great tumult
He has kindled fire on it,
And its branches are broken.

17 "For the LORD of hosts, who planted you,
has pronounced doom against you for the evil of
the house of Israel and of the house of Judah,
which they have done against themselves to
provoke Me to anger in offering incense to
Baal."

JEREMIAH'S LIFE THREATENED

18 Now the LORD gave me knowledge *of it,*
and I know *it;* for You showed me their doings.
19 But I *was* like a docile lamb brought to the
slaughter; and I did not know that they had de-
vised schemes against me, *saying,* "Let us de-
stroy the tree with its fruit, and let us cut him off
from the land of the living, that his name may be
remembered no more."

20 But, O LORD of hosts,
You who judge righteously,
Testing the mind and the heart,
Let me see Your vengeance on them,
For to You I have revealed my cause.

21 "Therefore thus says the LORD concerning
the men of Anathoth who seek your life, saying,
'Do not prophesy in the name of the LORD, lest
you die by our hand'— 22 therefore thus says the
LORD of hosts: 'Behold, I will punish them. The
young men shall die by the sword, their sons
and their daughters shall die by famine; 23 and
there shall be no remnant of them, for I will
bring catastrophe on the men of Anathoth, *even*
the year of their punishment.' "

JEREMIAH'S QUESTION

12 Righteous *are* You, O LORD, when I plead
with You;
Yet let me talk with You about *Your*
judgments.
Why does the way of the wicked prosper?
Why are those happy who deal so
treacherously?
2 You have planted them, yes, they have taken
root;
They grow, yes, they bear fruit.
You *are* near in their mouth
But far from their mind.

THE MESSAGE

Do you think making promises and
devising pious programs
will save you from doom?
Do you think you can get out of this
by becoming more religious?
A mighty oak tree, majestic and glorious—
that's how I once described you.
But it will only take a clap of thunder and a
bolt of lightning
to leave you a shattered wreck.

17 "I, GOD-of-the-Angel-Armies, who planted
you—yes, I have pronounced doom on you.
Why? Because of the disastrous life you've
lived, Israel and Judah alike, goading me to
anger with your continuous worship and of-
ferings to that sorry god Baal."

18-19 GOD told me what was going on. That's how
I knew.
You, GOD, opened my eyes to their evil
scheming.
I had no idea what was going on—naive as
a lamb
being led to slaughter!
I didn't know they had it in for me,
didn't know of their behind-the-scenes
plots:
"Let's get rid of the preacher.
That will stop the sermons!
Let's get rid of him for good.
He won't be remembered for long."

20 Then I said, "GOD-of-the-Angel-Armies,
you're a fair judge.
You examine and cross-examine
human actions and motives.
I want to see these people shown up and
put down!
I'm an open book before you. Clear my
name."

21-23 That sent a signal to GOD, who spoke up:
"Here's what I'll do to the men of Anathoth
who are trying to murder you, the men who
say, 'Don't preach to us in GOD's name or
we'll kill you.' Yes, it's GOD-of-the-Angel-
Armies speaking. Indeed! I'll call them to
account: Their young people will die in bat-
tle, their children will die of starvation, and
there will be no one left at all, none. I'm vis-
iting the men of Anathoth with doom.
Doomsday!"

WHAT MAKES YOU THINK YOU CAN RACE AGAINST HORSES?

1-4 12 You are right, O GOD, and you set things
right.
I can't argue with that. But I do have
some questions:
Why do bad people have it so good?
Why do con artists make it big?
You planted them and they put down roots.
They flourished and produced fruit.
They talk as if they're old friends with you,
but they couldn't care less about you.

NEW KING JAMES VERSION

3But You, O LORD, know me;
You have seen me,
And You have tested my heart toward You.
Pull them out like sheep for the slaughter,
And prepare them for the day of slaughter.
4How long will the land mourn,
And the herbs of every field wither?
The beasts and birds are consumed,
For the wickedness of those who dwell there,
Because they said, "He will not see our final end."

THE LORD ANSWERS JEREMIAH

5"If you have run with the footmen, and they have wearied you,
Then how can you contend with horses?
And *if* in the land of peace,
In which you trusted, *they wearied you,*
Then how will you do in the floodplain[a] of the Jordan?
6For even your brothers, the house of your father,
Even they have dealt treacherously with you;
Yes, they have called a multitude after you.
Do not believe them,
Even though they speak smooth words to you.

7"I have forsaken My house, I have left My heritage;
I have given the dearly beloved of My soul into the hand of her enemies.
8My heritage is to Me like a lion in the forest;
It cries out against Me;
Therefore I have hated it.
9My heritage *is* to Me *like* a speckled vulture;
The vultures all around *are* against her.
Come, assemble all the beasts of the field,
Bring them to devour!

10"Many rulers[a] have destroyed My vineyard,
They have trodden My portion underfoot;
They have made My pleasant portion a desolate wilderness.
11They have made it desolate;
Desolate, it mourns to Me;
The whole land is made desolate,
Because no one takes *it* to heart.
12The plunderers have come
On all the desolate heights in the wilderness,
For the sword of the LORD shall devour
From *one* end of the land to the *other* end of the land;
No flesh shall have peace.
13They have sown wheat but reaped thorns;
They have put themselves to pain *but* do not profit.
But be ashamed of your harvest
Because of the fierce anger of the LORD."

12:5 [a]Or *thicket* 12:10 [a]Literally *shepherds* or *pastors*

THE MESSAGE

Meanwhile, you know *me* inside and out.
You don't let me get by with a thing!
Make them pay for the way they live,
pay with their lives, like sheep marked for slaughter.
How long do we have to put up with this—
the country depressed, the farms in ruin—
And all because of wickedness, these wicked lives?
Even animals and birds are dying off
Because they'll have nothing to do with God
and think God has nothing to do with them.

5-6 "So, Jeremiah, if you're worn out in this footrace with men,
what makes you think you can race against horses?
And if you can't keep your wits during times of calm,
what's going to happen when troubles break loose like the Jordan in flood?
Those closest to you, your own brothers and cousins,
are working against you.
They're out to get you. They'll stop at nothing.
Don't trust them, especially when they're smiling.

7-11 "I will abandon the House of Israel,
walk away from my beloved people.
I will turn over those I most love
to those who are her enemies.
She's been, this one I held dear,
like a snarling lion in the jungle,
Growling and baring her teeth at me—
and I can't take it anymore.
Has this one I hold dear become a preening peacock?
But isn't she under attack by vultures?
Then invite all the hungry animals at large,
invite them in for a free meal!
Foreign, scavenging shepherds
will loot and trample my fields,
Turn my beautiful, well-cared-for fields
into vacant lots of tin cans and thistles.
They leave them littered with junk—
a ruined land, a land in lament.
The whole countryside is a wasteland,
and no one will really care.

12-13 "The barbarians will invade,
swarm over hills and plains.
The judgment sword of GOD will take its toll
from one end of the land to the other.
Nothing living will be safe.
They will plant wheat and reap weeds.
Nothing they do will work out.
They will look at their meager crops and wring their hands.
All this the result of GOD's fierce anger!"

NEW KING JAMES VERSION

[14]Thus says the LORD: "Against all My evil neighbors who touch the inheritance which I have caused My people Israel to inherit—behold, I will pluck them out of their land and pluck out the house of Judah from among them. [15]Then it shall be, after I have plucked them out, that I will return and have compassion on them and bring them back, everyone to his heritage and everyone to his land. [16]And it shall be, if they will learn carefully the ways of My people, to swear by My name, 'As the LORD lives,' as they taught My people to swear by Baal, then they shall be established in the midst of My people. [17]But if they do not obey, I will utterly pluck up and destroy that nation," says the LORD.

SYMBOL OF THE LINEN SASH

13 Thus the LORD said to me: "Go and get yourself a linen sash, and put it around your waist, but do not put it in water." [2]So I got a sash according to the word of the LORD, and put *it* around my waist.

[3]And the word of the LORD came to me the second time, saying, [4]"Take the sash that you acquired, which *is* around your waist, and arise, go to the Euphrates,[a] and hide it there in a hole in the rock." [5]So I went and hid it by the Euphrates, as the LORD commanded me.

[6]Now it came to pass after many days that the LORD said to me, "Arise, go to the Euphrates, and take from there the sash which I commanded you to hide there." [7]Then I went to the Euphrates and dug, and I took the sash from the place where I had hidden it; and there was the sash, ruined. It was profitable for nothing.

[8]Then the word of the LORD came to me, saying, [9]"Thus says the LORD: 'In this manner I will ruin the pride of Judah and the great pride of Jerusalem. [10]This evil people, who refuse to hear My words, who follow the dictates of their hearts, and walk after other gods to serve them and worship them, shall be just like this sash which is profitable for nothing. [11]For as the sash clings to the waist of a man, so I have caused the whole house of Israel and the whole house of Judah to cling to Me,' says the LORD, 'that they may become My people, for renown, for praise, and for glory; but they would not hear.'

SYMBOL OF THE WINE BOTTLES

[12]"Therefore you shall speak to them this word: 'Thus says the LORD God of Israel: "Every bottle shall be filled with wine." '

"And they will say to you, 'Do we not certainly know that every bottle will be filled with wine?'

[13]"Then you shall say to them, 'Thus says the LORD: "Behold, I will fill all the inhabitants of this land—even the kings who sit on David's throne, the priests, the prophets, and all the inhabitants of Jerusalem—with drunkenness! [14]And I will dash them one against another, even the fathers and the sons together," says the LORD. "I will not pity nor spare nor have mercy, but will destroy them." ' "

13:4 [a]Hebrew *Perath*

THE MESSAGE

14-17 GOD's Message: "Regarding all the bad
neighbors who abused the land I gave to Is-
rael as their inheritance: I'm going to pluck
them out of their lands, and then pluck Ju-
dah out from among them. Once I've pulled
the bad neighbors out, I will relent and take
them tenderly to my heart and put them
back where they belong, put each of them
back in their home country, on their family
farms. Then if they will get serious about
living my way and pray to me as well as
they taught my people to pray to that god
Baal, everything will go well for them. But if
they won't listen, then I'll pull them out of
their land by the roots and cart them off to
the dump. Total destruction!" GOD's Decree.

PEOPLE WHO DO ONLY WHAT THEY WANT TO DO

1-2 13 GOD told me, "Go and buy yourself
some linen shorts. Put them on and
keep them on. Don't even take them off to
wash them." So I bought the shorts as GOD
directed and put them on.
3-5 Then GOD told me, "Take the shorts that
you bought and go straight to Perath and
hide them there in a crack in the rock." So I
did what GOD told me and hid them at
Perath.
6-7 Next, after quite a long time, GOD told
me, "Go back to Perath and get the linen
shorts I told you to hide there." So I went
back to Perath and dug them out of the
place where I had hidden them. The shorts
by then had rotted and were worthless.
8-11 GOD explained, "This is the way I am go-
ing to ruin the pride of Judah and the great
pride of Jerusalem—a wicked bunch of peo-
ple who won't obey me, who do only what
they want to do, who chase after all kinds of
no-gods and worship them. They're going to
turn out as rotten as these old shorts. Just as
shorts clothe and protect, so I kept the
whole family of Israel under my care"—
GOD's Decree—"so that everyone could see
they were my people, a people I could show
off to the world and be proud of. But they re-
fused to do a thing I said.

12 "And then tell them this, 'GOD's Message,
personal from the God of Israel: Every wine
jug should be full of wine.'
"And they'll say, 'Of course. We know
that. Every wine jug should be full of wine!'
13-14 "Then you'll say, 'This is what GOD says:
Watch closely. I'm going to fill every person
who lives in this country—the kings who
rule from David's throne, the priests, the
prophets, the citizens of Jerusalem—with
wine that will make them drunk. And then
I'll smash them, smash the wine-filled
jugs—old and young alike. Nothing will stop
me. Not an ounce of pity or mercy or com-
passion will slow me down. Every last
drunken jug of them will be smashed!' "

NEW KING JAMES VERSION

PRIDE PRECEDES CAPTIVITY

15Hear and give ear:
Do not be proud,
For the LORD has spoken.
16Give glory to the LORD your God
Before He causes darkness,
And before your feet stumble
On the dark mountains,
And while you are looking for light,
He turns it into the shadow of death
And makes *it* dense darkness.
17But if you will not hear it,
My soul will weep in secret for *your* pride;
My eyes will weep bitterly
And run down with tears,
Because the LORD's flock has been taken
captive.

18Say to the king and to the queen mother,
"Humble yourselves;
Sit down,
For your rule shall collapse, the crown of
your glory."
19The cities of the South shall be shut up,
And no one shall open *them;*
Judah shall be carried away captive, all of it;
It shall be wholly carried away captive.

20Lift up your eyes and see
Those who come from the north.
Where *is* the flock *that* was given to you,
Your beautiful sheep?
21What will you say when He punishes you?
For you have taught them
To be chieftains, to be head over you.
Will not pangs seize you,
Like a woman in labor?
22And if you say in your heart,
"Why have these things come upon me?"
For the greatness of your iniquity
Your skirts have been uncovered,
Your heels made bare.
23Can the Ethiopian change his skin or the
leopard its spots?
Then may you also do good who are
accustomed to do evil.

24"Therefore I will scatter them like stubble
That passes away by the wind of the
wilderness.
25This is your lot,
The portion of your measures from Me,"
says the LORD,
"Because you have forgotten Me
And trusted in falsehood.
26Therefore I will uncover your skirts over
your face,
That your shame may appear.
27I have seen your adulteries
And your *lustful* neighings,
The lewdness of your harlotry,

THE MESSAGE

THE LIGHT YOU ALWAYS TOOK FOR GRANTED

15-17 Then I said, Listen. Listen carefully: Don't
stay stuck in your ways!
It's GOD's Message we're dealing with
here.
Let your lives glow bright before GOD
before he turns out the lights,
Before you trip and fall
on the dark mountain paths.
The light you always took for granted will
go out
and the world will turn black.
If you people won't listen,
I'll go off by myself and weep over you,
Weep because of your stubborn arrogance,
bitter, bitter tears,
Rivers of tears from my eyes,
because GOD's sheep will end up in exile.

18-19 Tell the king and the queen-mother,
"Come down off your high horses.
Your dazzling crowns
will tumble off your heads."
The villages in the Negev will be
surrounded,
everyone trapped,
And Judah dragged off to exile,
the whole country dragged to oblivion.

20-22 Look, look, Jerusalem!
Look at the enemies coming out of the
north!
What will become of your flocks of people,
the beautiful flocks in your care?
How are you going to feel when the people
you've played up to, looked up to all
these years
Now look down on you? You didn't expect
this?
Surprise! The pain of a woman having a
baby!
Do I hear you saying,
"What's going on here? Why me?"
The answer's simple: You're guilty,
hugely guilty.
Your guilt has your life endangered,
your guilt has you writhing in pain.

23 Can an African change skin?
Can a leopard get rid of its spots?
So what are the odds on you doing good,
you who are so long-practiced in evil?

24-27 "I'll blow these people away—
like wind-blown leaves.
You have it coming to you.
I've measured it out precisely."
GOD's Decree.
"It's because you forgot me
and embraced the Big Lie,
that so-called god Baal.
I'm the one who will rip off your clothes,
expose and shame you before the
watching world.
Your obsessions with gods, gods, and more
gods,
your goddess affairs, your god-adulteries.

NEW KING JAMES VERSION

Your abominations on the hills in the fields.
Woe to you, O Jerusalem!
Will you still not be made clean?"

SWORD, FAMINE, AND PESTILENCE

14 The word of the LORD that came to Jeremiah concerning the droughts.

2"Judah mourns,
And her gates languish;
They mourn for the land,
And the cry of Jerusalem has gone up.
3Their nobles have sent their lads for water;
They went to the cisterns *and* found no water.
They returned with their vessels empty;
They were ashamed and confounded
And covered their heads.
4Because the ground is parched,
For there was no rain in the land,
The plowmen were ashamed;
They covered their heads.
5Yes, the deer also gave birth in the field,
But left because there was no grass.
6And the wild donkeys stood in the desolate heights;
They sniffed at the wind like jackals;
Their eyes failed because *there was* no grass."

7O LORD, though our iniquities testify against us,
Do it for Your name's sake;
For our backslidings are many,
We have sinned against You.
8O the Hope of Israel, his Savior in time of trouble,
Why should You be like a stranger in the land,
And like a traveler *who* turns aside to tarry for a night?
9Why should You be like a man astonished,
Like a mighty one *who* cannot save?
Yet You, O LORD, *are* in our midst,
And we are called by Your name;
Do not leave us!

10Thus says the LORD to this people:

"Thus they have loved to wander;
They have not restrained their feet.
Therefore the LORD does not accept them;
He will remember their iniquity now,
And punish their sins."

11Then the LORD said to me, "Do not pray for
this people, for *their* good. 12When they fast, I
will not hear their cry; and when they offer

THE MESSAGE

Gods on the hills, gods in the fields—
every time I look you're off with another god.
O Jerusalem, what a sordid life!
Is there any hope for you!"

TIME AND AGAIN WE'VE BETRAYED GOD

1-6 14 GOD's Message that came to Jeremiah regarding the drought:

"Judah weeps,
her cities mourn.
The people fall to the ground, moaning,
while sounds of Jerusalem's sobs rise up, up.
The rich people sent their servants for water.
They went to the cisterns, but the cisterns were dry.
They came back with empty buckets,
wringing their hands, shaking their heads.
All the farm work has stopped.
Not a drop of rain has fallen.
The farmers don't know what to do.
They wring their hands, they shake their heads.
Even the doe abandons her fawn in the field
because there is no grass—
Eyes glazed over, on her last legs,
nothing but skin and bones."

7-9 We know we're guilty. We've lived bad lives—
but do something, GOD. Do it for *your* sake!
Time and time again we've betrayed you.
No doubt about it—we've sinned against you.
Hope of Israel! Our only hope!
Israel's last chance in this trouble!
Why are you acting like a tourist,
taking in the sights, here today and gone tomorrow?
Why do you just stand there and stare,
like someone who doesn't know what to do in a crisis?
But GOD, you are, in fact, *here*, here *with us*!
You know who we are—you named us!
Don't leave us in the lurch.

10 Then GOD said of these people:

"Since they loved to wander this way and that,
never giving a thought to where they were going,
I will now have nothing more to do with them—
except to note their guilt and punish their sins."

THE KILLING FIELDS

11-12 GOD said to me, "Don't pray that everything
will turn out all right for this people. When
they skip their meals in order to pray, I
won't listen to a thing they say. When they

NEW KING JAMES VERSION

burnt offering and grain offering, I will not ac-
cept them. But I will consume them by the
sword, by the famine, and by the pestilence."
13 Then I said, "Ah, Lord GOD! Behold, the
prophets say to them, 'You shall not see the
sword, nor shall you have famine, but I will give
you assured peace in this place.' "
14 And the LORD said to me, "The prophets
prophesy lies in My name. I have not sent them,
commanded them, nor spoken to them; they
prophesy to you a false vision, divination, a
worthless thing, and the deceit of their heart.
15 Therefore thus says the LORD concerning the
prophets who prophesy in My name, whom I did
not send, and who say, 'Sword and famine shall
not be in this land'—'By sword and famine those
prophets shall be consumed! 16 And the people
to whom they prophesy shall be cast out in the
streets of Jerusalem because of the famine and
the sword; they will have no one to bury them—
them nor their wives, their sons nor their daugh-
ters—for I will pour their wickedness on them.'
17 "Therefore you shall say this word to them:

'Let my eyes flow with tears night and day,
And let them not cease;
For the virgin daughter of my people
Has been broken with a mighty stroke, with
a very severe blow.
18 If I go out to the field,
Then behold, those slain with the sword!
And if I enter the city,
Then behold, those sick from famine!
Yes, both prophet and priest go about in a
land they do not know.' "

THE PEOPLE PLEAD FOR MERCY

19 Have You utterly rejected Judah?
Has Your soul loathed Zion?
Why have You stricken us so that *there is* no
healing for us?
We looked for peace, but *there was* no good;
And for the time of healing, and there was
trouble.
20 We acknowledge, O LORD, our wickedness
And the iniquity of our fathers,
For we have sinned against You.
21 Do not abhor *us,* for Your name's sake;
Do not disgrace the throne of Your glory.
Remember, do not break Your covenant with
us.
22 Are there any among the idols of the nations
that can cause rain?
Or can the heavens give showers?
Are You not He, O LORD our God?
Therefore we will wait for You,
Since You have made all these.

THE MESSAGE

redouble their prayers, bringing all kinds of offerings from their herds and crops, I'll not accept them. I'm finishing them off with war and famine and disease."

13 I said, "But Master, GOD! Their preachers have been telling them that everything is going to be all right—no war and no famine—that there's nothing to worry about."

14 Then GOD said, "These preachers are liars, and they use my name to cover their lies. I never sent them, I never commanded them, and I don't talk with them. The sermons they've been handing out are sheer illusion, tissues of lies, whistlings in the dark.

15-16 "So this is my verdict on them: All the preachers who preach using my name as their text, preachers I never sent in the first place, preachers who say, 'War and famine will never come here'—these preachers will die in war and by starvation. And the people to whom they've been preaching will end up as corpses, victims of war and starvation, thrown out in the streets of Jerusalem unburied—no funerals for them or their wives or their children! I'll make sure they get the full brunt of all their evil.

17-18 "And you, Jeremiah, will say this to them:

" 'My eyes pour out tears.
Day and night, the tears never quit.
My dear, dear people are battered and bruised,
hopelessly and cruelly wounded.
I walk out into the fields,
shocked by the killing fields strewn with corpses.
I walk into the city,
shocked by the sight of starving bodies.
And I watch the preachers and priests
going about their business as if nothing's happened!' "

19-22 God, have you said your final No to Judah?
Can you simply not stand Zion any longer?
If not, why have you treated us like this,
beaten us nearly to death?
We hoped for peace—
nothing good came from it;
We looked for healing—
and got kicked in the stomach.
We admit, O GOD, how badly we've lived,
and our ancestors, how bad they were.
We've sinned, they've sinned,
we've all sinned against you!
Your reputation is at stake! Don't quit on us!
Don't walk out and abandon your glorious Temple!
Remember your covenant.
Don't break faith with us!
Can the no-gods of the godless nations cause rain?
Can the sky water the earth by itself?
You're the one, O GOD, who does this.
So you're the one for whom we wait.
You made it all,
you do it all.

NEW KING JAMES VERSION

THE LORD WILL NOT RELENT

15 Then the LORD said to me, "*Even* if Moses
and Samuel stood before Me, My mind
would not *be* favorable toward this people. Cast
them out of My sight, and let them go forth.
2And it shall be, if they say to you, 'Where
should we go?' then you shall tell them, 'Thus
says the LORD:

"Such as *are* for death, to death;
And such as *are* for the sword, to the sword;
And such as *are* for the famine, to the famine;
And such as *are* for the captivity, to the captivity." '

3"And I will appoint over them four forms *of*
destruction," says the LORD: "the sword to slay,
the dogs to drag, the birds of the heavens and the
beasts of the earth to devour and destroy. 4I will
hand them over to trouble, to all kingdoms of the
earth, because of Manasseh the son of Hezekiah,
king of Judah, for what he did in Jerusalem.

5"For who will have pity on you, O Jerusalem?
Or who will bemoan you?
Or who will turn aside to ask how you are doing?
6You have forsaken Me," says the LORD,
"You have gone backward.
Therefore I will stretch out My hand against you and destroy you;
I am weary of relenting!
7And I will winnow them with a winnowing fan in the gates of the land;
I will bereave *them* of children;
I will destroy My people,
Since they do not return from their ways.
8Their widows will be increased to Me more than the sand of the seas;
I will bring against them,
Against the mother of the young men,
A plunderer at noonday;
I will cause anguish and terror to fall on them suddenly.

9"She languishes who has borne seven;
She has breathed her last;
Her sun has gone down
While *it was* yet day;
She has been ashamed and confounded.
And the remnant of them I will deliver to the sword
Before their enemies," says the LORD.

JEREMIAH'S DEJECTION

10Woe is me, my mother,
That you have borne me,
A man of strife and a man of contention to the whole earth!
I have neither lent for interest,
Nor have men lent to me for interest.
Every one of them curses me.

11The LORD said:

"Surely it will be well with your remnant;
Surely I will cause the enemy to intercede with you
In the time of adversity and in the time of affliction.

THE MESSAGE

1-2 15 Then GOD said to me: "Jeremiah, even if
Moses and Samuel stood here and made
their case, I wouldn't feel a thing for this peo-
ple. Get them out of here. Tell them to get
lost! And if they ask you, 'So where do we
go?' tell them GOD says,

" 'If you're assigned to die, go and die;
if assigned to war, go and get killed;
If assigned to starve, go starve;
if assigned to exile, off to exile you go!'

3-4 "I've arranged for four kinds of punish-
ment: death in battle, the corpses dropped
off by killer dogs, the rest picked clean by
vultures, the bones gnawed by hyenas.
They'll be a sight to see, a sight to shock the
whole world—and all because of Manasseh
son of Hezekiah and all he did in Jerusalem.

5 "Who do you think will feel sorry for you, Jerusalem?
Who do you think will waste tears on you?
Who will bother to take the time to ask,
'So, how are things going?'

6-9 "*You* left *me*, remember?" GOD's Decree.
"You turned your back and walked out.
So I will grab you and hit you hard.
I'm tired of letting you off the hook.
I threw you to the four winds
and let the winds scatter you like leaves.
I made sure you'll lose everything,
since nothing makes you change.
I created more widows among you
than grains of sand on the ocean beaches.
At noon mothers will get the news
of their sons killed in action.
Sudden anguish for the mothers—
all those terrible deaths.
A mother of seven falls to the ground,
gasping for breath,
Robbed of her children in their prime.
Her sun sets at high noon!
Then I'll round up any of you that are left alive
and see that you're killed by your enemies."
GOD's Decree.

GIVING EVERYTHING AWAY FOR NOTHING

10-11 Unlucky mother—that you had me as a son,
given the unhappy job of indicting the whole country!
I've never hurt or harmed a soul,
and yet everyone is out to get me.
But, GOD knows, I've done everything I could to help them,
prayed for them and against their enemies.
I've always been on their side, trying to stave off disaster.
God knows how I've tried!

New King James Version

[12]Can anyone break iron,
The northern iron and the bronze?
[13]Your wealth and your treasures
I will give as plunder without price,
Because of all your sins,
Throughout your territories.
[14]And I will make *you* cross over with[a] your enemies
Into a land *which* you do not know;
For a fire is kindled in My anger,
Which shall burn upon you."

[15]O LORD, You know;
Remember me and visit me,
And take vengeance for me on my persecutors.
In Your enduring patience, do not take me away.
Know that for Your sake I have suffered rebuke.
[16]Your words were found, and I ate them,
And Your word was to me the joy and rejoicing of my heart;
For I am called by Your name,
O LORD God of hosts.
[17]I did not sit in the assembly of the mockers,
Nor did I rejoice;
I sat alone because of Your hand,
For You have filled me with indignation.
[18]Why is my pain perpetual
And my wound incurable,
Which refuses to be healed?
Will You surely be to me like an unreliable stream,
As waters *that* fail?

The Lord Reassures Jeremiah

[19]Therefore thus says the LORD:

"If you return,
Then I will bring you back;
You shall stand before Me;
If you take out the precious from the vile,
You shall be as My mouth.
Let them return to you,
But you must not return to them.
[20]And I will make you to this people a fortified bronze wall;
And they will fight against you,
But they shall not prevail against you;
For I *am* with you to save you
And deliver you," says the LORD.
[21]"I will deliver you from the hand of the wicked,
And I will redeem you from the grip of the terrible."

Jeremiah's Life-Style and Message

16 The word of the LORD also came to me,
saying, [2]"You shall not take a wife, nor
shall you have sons or daughters in this place."
[3]For thus says the LORD concerning the sons and
daughters who are born in this place, and con-
cerning their mothers who bore them and their
fathers who begot them in this land: [4]"They
shall die gruesome deaths; they shall not be

15:14 [a]Following Masoretic Text and Vulgate; Septuagint, Syriac, and Targum read *cause you to serve* (compare 17:4).

The Message

12-14 "O Israel, O Judah, what are your chances against the iron juggernaut from the north?
In punishment for your sins, I'm giving away
everything you've got, giving it away for nothing.
I'll make you slaves to your enemies
in a strange and far-off land.
My anger is blazing and fierce,
burning in hot judgment against you."

15-18 You know where I am, GOD! Remember what I'm doing here!
Take my side against my detractors.
Don't stand back while they ruin me.
Just look at the abuse I'm taking!
When your words showed up, I ate them—
swallowed them whole. What a feast!
What delight I took in being yours,
O GOD, GOD-of-the-Angel-Armies!
I never joined the party crowd
in their laughter and their fun.
Led by you, I went off by myself.
You'd filled me with indignation. Their sin had me seething.
But why, why this chronic pain,
this ever worsening wound and no healing in sight?
You're nothing, GOD, but a mirage,
a lovely oasis in the distance—and then nothing!

19-21 This is how GOD answered me:

"Take back those words, and I'll take you back.
Then you'll stand tall before me.
Use words truly and well. Don't stoop to cheap whining.
Then, but only then, you'll speak for me.
Let your words change *them*.
Don't change your words to suit them.
I'll turn you into a steel wall,
a thick steel wall, impregnable.
They'll attack you but won't put a dent in you
because I'm at your side, defending and delivering."
GOD's Decree.
"I'll deliver you from the grip of the wicked.
I'll get you out of the clutch of the ruthless."

Can Mortals Manufacture Gods?

1 16 GOD's Message to me:
2-4 "Jeremiah, don't get married. Don't
raise a family here. I have signed the death
warrant on all the children born in this
country, the mothers who bear them and the
fathers who beget them—an epidemic of
death. Death unlamented, the dead un-

NEW KING JAMES VERSION

lamented nor shall they be buried, *but* they shall be like refuse on the face of the earth. They shall be consumed by the sword and by famine, and their corpses shall be meat for the birds of heaven and for the beasts of the earth."

5 For thus says the LORD: "Do not enter the house of mourning, nor go to lament or bemoan them; for I have taken away My peace from this people," says the LORD, "lovingkindness and mercies. 6 Both the great and the small shall die in this land. They shall not be buried; neither shall men lament for them, cut themselves, nor make themselves bald for them. 7 Nor shall *men* break *bread* in mourning for them, to comfort them for the dead; nor shall *men* give them the cup of consolation to drink for their father or their mother. 8 Also you shall not go into the house of feasting to sit with them, to eat and drink."

9 For thus says the LORD of hosts, the God of Israel: "Behold, I will cause to cease from this place, before your eyes and in your days, the voice of mirth and the voice of gladness, the voice of the bridegroom and the voice of the bride.

10 "And it shall be, when you show this people all these words, and they say to you, 'Why has the LORD pronounced all this great disaster against us? Or what *is* our iniquity? Or what *is* our sin that we have committed against the LORD our God?' 11 then you shall say to them, 'Because your fathers have forsaken Me,' says the LORD; 'they have walked after other gods and have served them and worshiped them, and have forsaken Me and not kept My law. 12 And you have done worse than your fathers, for behold, each one follows the dictates of his own evil heart, so that no one listens to Me. 13 Therefore I will cast you out of this land into a land that you do not know, neither you nor your fathers; and there you shall serve other gods day and night, where I will not show you favor.'

GOD WILL RESTORE ISRAEL

14 "Therefore behold, the days are coming," says the LORD, "that it shall no more be said, 'The LORD lives who brought up the children of Israel from the land of Egypt,' 15 but, 'The LORD lives who brought up the children of Israel from the land of the north and from all the lands where He had driven them.' For I will bring them back into their land which I gave to their fathers.

16 "Behold, I will send for many fishermen," says the LORD, "and they shall fish them; and afterward I will send for many hunters, and they shall hunt them from every mountain and every hill, and out of the holes of the rocks. 17 For My eyes *are* on all their ways; they are not hidden from My face, nor is their iniquity hidden from My eyes. 18 And first I will repay double for their iniquity and their sin, because they have defiled My land; they have filled My inheritance with the carcasses of their detestable and abominable idols."

THE MESSAGE

buried, dead bodies decomposing and stinking like dung, all the killed and starved corpses served up as meals for carrion crows and mongrel dogs!"

5-7 GOD continued: "Don't enter a house where there's mourning. Don't go to the funeral. Don't sympathize. I've quit caring about what happens to this people." GOD's Decree. "No more loyal love on my part, no more compassion. The famous and obscure will die alike here, unlamented and unburied. No funerals will be conducted, no one will give them a second thought, no one will care, no one will say, 'I'm sorry,' no one will so much as offer a cup of tea, not even for the mother or father.

8 "And if there happens to be a feast celebrated, don't go there either to enjoy the festivities."

9 GOD-of-the-Angel-Armies, the God of Israel, says, "Watch this! I'm about to banish smiles and laughter from this place. No more brides and bridegrooms celebrating. And I'm doing it in your lifetime, before your very eyes.

10-13 "When you tell this to the people and they ask, 'Why is GOD talking this way, threatening us with all these calamities? We're not criminals, after all. What have we done to our GOD to be treated like this?' tell them this: 'It's because your ancestors left me, walked off and never looked back. They took up with the no-gods, worshiped and doted on them, and ignored me and wouldn't do a thing I told them. And *you're* even *worse!* Take a good look in the mirror—each of you doing whatever you want, whenever you want, refusing to pay attention to me. And for this I'm getting rid of you, throwing you out in the cold, into a far and strange country. You can worship your precious no-gods there to your heart's content. Rest assured, I won't bother you anymore.'

14-15 "On the other hand, don't miss this: The time is coming when no one will say any longer, 'As sure as GOD lives, the God who delivered Israel from Egypt.' What they'll say is, 'As sure as GOD lives, the God who brought Israel back from the land of the north, brought them back from all the places where he'd scattered them.' That's right, I'm going to bring them back to the land I first gave to their ancestors.

16-17 "Now, watch for what comes next: I'm going to assemble a bunch of fishermen." GOD's Decree! "They'll go fishing for my people and pull them in for judgment. Then I'll send out a party of hunters, and they'll hunt them out in all the mountains, hills, and caves. I'm watching their every move. I haven't lost track of a single one of them, neither them nor their sins.

18 "They won't get by with a thing. They'll pay double for everything they did wrong. They've made a complete mess of things, littering their lives with their obscene no-gods, leaving piles of stinking god-junk all over the place."

NEW KING JAMES VERSION

19O LORD, my strength and my fortress,
My refuge in the day of affliction,
The Gentiles shall come to You
From the ends of the earth and say,
"Surely our fathers have inherited lies,
Worthlessness and unprofitable *things*."
20Will a man make gods for himself,
Which *are* not gods?

21"Therefore behold, I will this once cause
them to know,
I will cause them to know
My hand and My might;
And they shall know that My name *is* the
LORD.

JUDAH'S SIN AND PUNISHMENT

17 "The sin of Judah *is* written with a pen of
iron;
With the point of a diamond *it is* engraved
On the tablet of their heart,
And on the horns of your altars,
2While their children remember
Their altars and their wooden images[a]
By the green trees on the high hills.
3O My mountain in the field,
I will give as plunder your wealth, all your
treasures,
And your high places of sin within all your
borders.
4And you, even yourself,
Shall let go of your heritage which I gave
you;
And I will cause you to serve your enemies
In the land which you do not know;
For you have kindled a fire in My anger
which shall burn forever."

5Thus says the LORD:

"Cursed *is* the man who trusts in man
And makes flesh his strength,
Whose heart departs from the LORD.
6For he shall be like a shrub in the desert,
And shall not see when good comes,
But shall inhabit the parched places in the
wilderness,
In a salt land *which is* not inhabited.

7"Blessed *is* the man who trusts in the LORD,
And whose hope is the LORD.
8For he shall be like a tree planted by the
waters,
Which spreads out its roots by the river,
And will not fear[a] when heat comes;
But its leaf will be green,
And will not be anxious in the year of
drought,
Nor will cease from yielding fruit.

9"The heart *is* deceitful above all *things*,
And desperately wicked;
Who can know it?

17:2 [a]Hebrew *Asherim,* Canaanite deities **17:8** [a]Qere and Targum read *see.*

THE MESSAGE

19-20 GOD, my strength, my stronghold,
my safe retreat when trouble descends:
The godless nations will come
from earth's four corners, saying,
"Our ancestors lived on lies,
useless illusions, all smoke."
Can mortals manufacture gods?
Their factories turn out no-gods!

21 "Watch closely now. I'm going to teach
these wrongheaded people.
Starting right now, I'm going to teach
them
Who I am and what I do,
teach them the meaning of my name,
GOD—'I AM.'"

THE HEART IS HOPELESSLY DARK AND DECEITFUL

1-2 17 "Judah's sin is engraved
with a steel chisel,
A steel chisel with a diamond point—
engraved on their granite hearts,
engraved on the stone corners of their
altars.
The evidence against them is plain to see:
sex-and-religion altars and sacred sex
shrines
Anywhere there's a grove of trees,
anywhere there's an available hill.

3-4 "I'll use your mountains as roadside stands
for giving away everything you have.
All your 'things' will serve as reparations
for your sins all over the country.
You'll lose your gift of land,
The inheritance I gave you.
I'll make you slaves of your enemies
in a far-off and strange land.
My anger is hot and blazing and fierce,
and no one will put it out."

5-6 GOD's Message:

"Cursed is the strong one
who depends on mere humans,
Who thinks he can make it on muscle alone
and sets GOD aside as dead weight.
He's like a tumbleweed on the prairie,
out of touch with the good earth.
He lives rootless and aimless
in a land where nothing grows.

7-8 "But blessed is the man who trusts me,
GOD,
the woman who sticks with GOD.
They're like trees replanted in Eden,
putting down roots near the rivers—
Never a worry through the hottest of
summers,
never dropping a leaf,
Serene and calm through droughts,
bearing fresh fruit every season.

9-10 "The heart is hopelessly dark and deceitful,
a puzzle that no one can figure out.

NEW KING JAMES VERSION

[10]I, the LORD, search the heart,
I test the mind,
Even to give every man according to his ways,
According to the fruit of his doings.

[11]"*As* a partridge that broods but does not hatch,
So is he who gets riches, but not by right;
It will leave him in the midst of his days,
And at his end he will be a fool."

[12]A glorious high throne from the beginning
Is the place of our sanctuary.
[13]O LORD, the hope of Israel,
All who forsake You shall be ashamed.

"Those who depart from Me
Shall be written in the earth,
Because they have forsaken the LORD,
The fountain of living waters."

JEREMIAH PRAYS FOR DELIVERANCE

[14]Heal me, O LORD, and I shall be healed;
Save me, and I shall be saved,
For You *are* my praise.
[15]Indeed they say to me,
"Where *is* the word of the LORD?
Let it come now!"
[16]As for me, I have not hurried away from *being* a shepherd *who* follows You,
Nor have I desired the woeful day;
You know what came out of my lips;
It was right there before You.
[17]Do not be a terror to me;
You *are* my hope in the day of doom.
[18]Let them be ashamed who persecute me,
But do not let me be put to shame;
Let them be dismayed,
But do not let me be dismayed.
Bring on them the day of doom,
And destroy them with double destruction!

HALLOW THE SABBATH DAY

[19]Thus the LORD said to me: "Go and stand in
the gate of the children of the people, by which
the kings of Judah come in and by which they
go out, and in all the gates of Jerusalem; [20]and
say to them, 'Hear the word of the LORD, you
kings of Judah, and all Judah, and all the inhab-
itants of Jerusalem, who enter by these gates.
[21]Thus says the LORD: "Take heed to yourselves,
and bear no burden on the Sabbath day, nor
bring *it* in by the gates of Jerusalem; [22]nor carry
a burden out of your houses on the Sabbath day,
nor do any work, but hallow the Sabbath day, as
I commanded your fathers. [23]But they did not
obey nor incline their ear, but made their neck
stiff, that they might not hear nor receive in-
struction.

[24]"And it shall be, if you heed Me carefully,"
says the LORD, "to bring no burden through the
gates of this city on the Sabbath day, but hallow
the Sabbath day, to do no work in it, [25]then shall
enter the gates of this city kings and princes sit-
ting on the throne of David, riding in chariots

THE MESSAGE

But I, GOD, search the heart
and examine the mind.
I get to the heart of the human.
I get to the root of things.
I treat them as they really are,
not as they pretend to be."

11 Like a cowbird that cheats by laying its eggs in another bird's nest
Is the person who gets rich by cheating.
When the eggs hatch, the deceit is exposed.
What a fool he'll look like then!

12-13 From early on your Sanctuary was set high,
a throne of glory, exalted!
O GOD, you're the hope of Israel.
All who leave you end up as fools,
Deserters with nothing to show for their lives,
who walk off from GOD, fountain of living waters—
and wind up dead!

14-18 GOD, pick up the pieces.
Put me back together again.
You are my praise!
Listen to how they talk about me:
"So where's this 'Word of GOD'?
We'd like to see something happen!"
But it wasn't my idea to call for Doomsday.
I never wanted trouble.
You know what I've said.
It's all out in the open before you.
Don't add to my troubles.
Give me some relief!
Let those who harass me be harassed, not me.
Let *them* be disgraced, not me.
Bring down upon them the day of doom.
Lower the boom. *Boom!*

KEEP THE SABBATH DAY HOLY

19-20 GOD's Message to me: "Go stand in the Peo-
ple's Gate, the one used by Judah's kings as
they come and go, and then proceed in turn
to all the gates of Jerusalem. Tell them, 'Lis-
ten, you kings of Judah, listen to GOD's Mes-
sage—and all you people who go in and out
of these gates, you listen!

21-23 " 'This is GOD's Message. Be careful, if
you care about your lives, not to desecrate
the Sabbath by turning it into just another
workday, lugging stuff here and there. Don't
use the Sabbath to do business as usual.
Keep the Sabbath day holy, as I commanded
your ancestors. They never did it, as you
know. They paid no attention to what I said
and went about their own business, refusing
to be guided or instructed by me.

24-26 " 'But now, take seriously what I tell you.
Quit desecrating the Sabbath by busily go-
ing about your own work, and keep the Sab-
bath day holy by not doing business as
usual. Then kings from the time of David
and their officials will continue to ride

NEW KING JAMES VERSION

and on horses, they and their princes, accompa-
nied by the men of Judah and the inhabitants of
Jerusalem; and this city shall remain forever.
26And they shall come from the cities of Judah
and from the places around Jerusalem, from the
land of Benjamin and from the lowland, from
the mountains and from the South, bringing
burnt offerings and sacrifices, grain offerings
and incense, bringing sacrifices of praise to the
house of the LORD.
27"But if you will not heed Me to hallow the
Sabbath day, such as not carrying a burden
when entering the gates of Jerusalem on the
Sabbath day, then I will kindle a fire in its gates,
and it shall devour the palaces of Jerusalem,
and it shall not be quenched." ' "

THE POTTER AND THE CLAY

18 The word which came to Jeremiah from
the LORD, saying: 2"Arise and go down to
the potter's house, and there I will cause you to
hear My words." 3Then I went down to the pot-
ter's house, and there he was, making some-
thing at the wheel. 4And the vessel that he made
of clay was marred in the hand of the potter; so
he made it again into another vessel, as it
seemed good to the potter to make.
5Then the word of the LORD came to me, say-
ing: 6"O house of Israel, can I not do with you as
this potter?" says the LORD. "Look, as the clay *is*
in the potter's hand, so *are* you in My hand, O
house of Israel! 7The instant I speak concerning
a nation and concerning a kingdom, to pluck up,
to pull down, and to destroy *it*, 8if that nation
against whom I have spoken turns from its evil,
I will relent of the disaster that I thought to
bring upon it. 9And the instant I speak concern-
ing a nation and concerning a kingdom, to build
and to plant *it*, 10if it does evil in My sight so that
it does not obey My voice, then I will relent con-
cerning the good with which I said I would ben-
efit it.
11"Now therefore, speak to the men of Judah
and to the inhabitants of Jerusalem, saying,
'Thus says the LORD: "Behold, I am fashioning a
disaster and devising a plan against you. Return
now every one from his evil way, and make your
ways and your doings good." ' "

GOD'S WARNING REJECTED

12And they said, "That is hopeless! So we will
walk according to our own plans, and we will
every one obey the dictates of his evil heart."
13Therefore thus says the LORD:

"Ask now among the Gentiles,
Who has heard such things?
The virgin of Israel has done a very horrible
thing.
14Will *a man* leave the snow water of
Lebanon,
Which comes from the rock of the field?
Will the cold flowing waters be forsaken for
strange waters?

THE MESSAGE

through these gates on horses or in chariots.
The people of Judah and citizens of
Jerusalem will continue to pass through
them, too. Jerusalem will always be filled
with people. People will stream in from all
over Judah, from the province of Benjamin,
from the Jerusalem suburbs, from foothills
and mountains and deserts. They'll come to
worship, bringing all kinds of offerings—
animals, grains, incense, expressions of
thanks—into the Sanctuary of GOD.
27 " 'But if you won't listen to me, won't
keep the Sabbath holy, won't quit using the
Sabbath for doing your own work, busily
going in and out of the city gates on your
self-important business, then I'll burn the
gates down. In fact, I'll burn the whole city
down, palaces and all, with a fire nobody
will be able to put out!' "

TO WORSHIP THE BIG LIE

1-2 18 GOD told Jeremiah, "Up on your feet!
Go to the potter's house. When you get
there, I'll tell you what I have to say."
3-4 So I went to the potter's house, and sure
enough, the potter was there, working away
at his wheel. Whenever the pot the potter
was working on turned out badly, as some-
times happens when you are working with
clay, the potter would simply start over and
use the same clay to make another pot.
5-10 Then GOD's Message came to me: "Can't
I do just as this potter does, people of Is-
rael?" GOD's Decree! "Watch this potter. In
the same way that this potter works his clay,
I work on you, people of Israel. At any mo-
ment I may decide to pull up a people or a
country by the roots and get rid of them. But
if they repent of their wicked lives, I will
think twice and start over with them. At an-
other time I might decide to plant a people
or country, but if they don't cooperate and
won't listen to me, I will think again and
give up on the plans I had for them.
11 "So, tell the people of Judah and citizens
of Jerusalem my Message: 'Danger! I'm
shaping doom against you, laying plans
against you. Turn back from your doomed
way of life. Straighten out your lives.'
12 "But they'll just say, 'Why should we?
What's the point? We'll live just the way
we've always lived, doom or no doom.' "

13-17 GOD's Message:

"Ask around.
Survey the godless nations.
Has anyone heard the likes of this?
Virgin Israel has become a slut!
Does snow disappear from the Lebanon
peaks?
Do alpine streams run dry?

NEW KING JAMES VERSION

15"Because My people have forgotten Me,
They have burned incense to worthless idols.
And they have caused themselves to stumble in their ways,
From the ancient paths,
To walk in pathways and not on a highway,
16To make their land desolate *and* a perpetual hissing;
Everyone who passes by it will be astonished
And shake his head.
17I will scatter them as with an east wind before the enemy;
I will show them[a] the back and not the face
In the day of their calamity."

JEREMIAH PERSECUTED

18Then they said, "Come and let us devise
plans against Jeremiah; for the law shall not
perish from the priest, nor counsel from the
wise, nor the word from the prophet. Come and
let us attack him with the tongue, and let us not
give heed to any of his words."

19Give heed to me, O LORD,
And listen to the voice of those who contend with me!
20Shall evil be repaid for good?
For they have dug a pit for my life.
Remember that I stood before You
To speak good for them,
To turn away Your wrath from them.
21Therefore deliver up their children to the famine,
And pour out their *blood*
By the force of the sword;
Let their wives *become* widows
And bereaved of their children.
Let their men be put to death,
Their young men *be* slain
By the sword in battle.
22Let a cry be heard from their houses,
When You bring a troop suddenly upon them;
For they have dug a pit to take me,
And hidden snares for my feet.
23Yet, LORD, You know all their counsel
Which is against me, to slay *me*.
Provide no atonement for their iniquity,
Nor blot out their sin from Your sight;
But let them be overthrown before You.
Deal *thus* with them
In the time of Your anger.

THE SIGN OF THE BROKEN FLASK

19 Thus says the LORD: "Go and get a potter's
earthen flask, and *take* some of the elders
of the people and some of the elders of the
priests. 2And go out to the Valley of the Son of
Hinnom, which *is* by the entry of the Potsherd
Gate; and proclaim there the words that I will tell
you, 3and say, 'Hear the word of the LORD, O kings
of Judah and inhabitants of Jerusalem. Thus says
the LORD of hosts, the God of Israel: "Behold, I
will bring such a catastrophe on this place, that
whoever hears of it, his ears will tingle.

18:17 [a]Following Septuagint, Syriac, Targum, and Vulgate; Masoretic Text reads *look them in*.

THE MESSAGE

But my people have left me
to worship the Big Lie.
They've gotten off the track,
the old, well-worn trail,
And now bushwhack through underbrush
in a tangle of roots and vines.
Their land's going to end up a mess—
a fool's memorial to be spit on.
Travelers passing through
will shake their heads in disbelief.
I'll scatter my people before their enemies,
like autumn leaves in a high wind.
On their day of doom, they'll stare at my back as I walk away,
catching not so much as a glimpse of my face."

18 Some of the people said, "Come on, let's
cook up a plot against Jeremiah. We'll still
have the priests to teach us the law, wise
counselors to give us advice, and prophets
to tell us what God has to say. Come on, let's
discredit him so we don't have to put up
with him any longer."

19-23 And I said to GOD:

"GOD, listen to me!
Just listen to what my enemies are saying.
Should I get paid evil for good?
That's what they're doing. They've made plans to kill me!
Remember all the times I stood up for them before you,
speaking up for them,
trying to soften your anger?
But enough! Let their children starve!
Let them be massacred in battle!
Let their wives be childless and widowed,
their friends die and their proud young men be killed.
Let cries of panic sound from their homes
as you surprise them with war parties!
They're all set to lynch me.
The noose is practically around my neck!
But you know all this, GOD.
You know they're determined to kill me.
Don't whitewash their crimes,
don't overlook a single sin!
Round the bunch of them up before you.
Strike while the iron of your anger is hot!"

SMASHING THE CLAY POT

1-2 19 GOD said to me, "Go, buy a clay pot.
Then get a few leaders from the people
and a few of the leading priests and go out
to the Valley of Ben-hinnom, just outside the
Potsherd Gate, and preach there what I tell
you.
3-5 "Say, 'Listen to GOD's Word, you kings of
Judah and people of Jerusalem! This is the
Message from GOD-of-the-Angel-Armies,
the God of Israel. I'm about to bring doom
crashing down on this place. Oh, and will
ears ever ring! Doom—because they've

NEW KING JAMES VERSION

4“Because they have forsaken Me and made this an alien place, because they have burned incense in it to other gods whom neither they, their fathers, nor the kings of Judah have known, and have filled this place with the blood of the innocents 5(they have also built the high places of Baal, to burn their sons with fire *for* burnt offerings to Baal, which I did not command or speak, nor did it come into My mind), 6therefore behold, the days are coming,” says the LORD, “that this place shall no more be called Tophet or the Valley of the Son of Hinnom, but the Valley of Slaughter. 7And I will make void the counsel of Judah and Jerusalem in this place, and I will cause them to fall by the sword before their enemies and by the hands of those who seek their lives; their corpses I will give as meat for the birds of the heaven and for the beasts of the earth. 8I will make this city desolate and a hissing; everyone who passes by it will be astonished and hiss because of all its plagues. 9And I will cause them to eat the flesh of their sons and the flesh of their daughters, and everyone shall eat the flesh of his friend in the siege and in the desperation with which their enemies and those who seek their lives shall drive them to despair.” ’

10“Then you shall break the flask in the sight of the men who go with you, 11and say to them, ‘Thus says the LORD of hosts: “Even so I will break this people and this city, as *one* breaks a potter’s vessel, which cannot be made whole again; and they shall bury *them* in Tophet till *there is* no place to bury. 12Thus I will do to this place,” says the LORD, “and to its inhabitants, and make this city like Tophet. 13And the houses of Jerusalem and the houses of the kings of Judah shall be defiled like the place of Tophet, because of all the houses on whose roofs they have burned incense to all the host of heaven, and poured out drink offerings to other gods.” ’ ”

14Then Jeremiah came from Tophet, where the LORD had sent him to prophesy; and he stood in the court of the Lord’s house and said to all the people, 15“Thus says the LORD of hosts, the God of Israel: ‘Behold, I will bring on this city and on all her towns all the doom that I have pronounced against it, because they have stiffened their necks that they might not hear My words.’ ”

THE WORD OF GOD TO PASHHUR

20 Now Pashhur the son of Immer, the priest who *was* also chief governor in the house of the LORD, heard that Jeremiah prophesied these things. 2Then Pashhur struck Jeremiah the prophet, and put him in the stocks that *were* in the high gate of Benjamin, which *was* by the house of the LORD.

3And it happened on the next day that Pashhur brought Jeremiah out of the stocks. Then Jeremiah said to him, “The LORD has not called your name Pashhur, but Magor-Missabib.[a] 4For thus says the LORD: ‘Behold, I will make you a terror to yourself and to all your friends; and they shall fall by the sword of their enemies, and your eyes shall see *it*. I will give all Judah into

20:3 [a]Literally *Fear on Every Side*

THE MESSAGE

walked off and left me, and made this place
strange by worshiping strange gods, gods
never heard of by them, their parents, or the
old kings of Judah. Doom—because they
have massacred innocent people. Doom—
because they’ve built altars to that no-god
Baal, and burned their own children alive in
the fire as offerings to Baal, an atrocity I
never ordered, never so much as hinted at!
6-9 “ ‘And so it’s payday, and soon’—GOD’s
Decree!—‘this place will no longer be
known as Topheth or Valley of Ben-hinnom,
but Massacre Meadows. I’m canceling all
the plans Judah and Jerusalem had for this
place, and I’ll have them killed by their enemies.
I’ll stack their dead bodies to be eaten
by carrion crows and wild dogs. I’ll turn this
city into such a museum of atrocities that
anyone coming near will be shocked
speechless by the savage brutality. The people
will turn into cannibals. Dehumanized
by the pressure of the enemy siege, they’ll
eat their own children! Yes, they’ll eat one
another, family and friends alike.’
10-13 “Say all this, and then smash the pot in
front of the men who have come with you.
Then say, ‘This is what GOD-of-the-Angel-Armies
says: I’ll smash this people and this
city like a man who smashes a clay pot into
so many pieces it can never be put together
again. They’ll bury bodies here in Topheth
until there’s no more room. And the whole
city will become a Topheth. The city will be
turned by people and kings alike into a center
for worshiping the star gods and goddesses,
turned into an open grave, the whole
city an open grave, stinking like a sewer,
like Topheth.’ ”
14-15 Then Jeremiah left Topheth, where GOD
had sent him to preach the sermon, and
took his stand in the court of GOD’s Temple
and said to the people, “This is the Message
from GOD-of-the-Angel-Armies to you:
‘Warning! Danger! I’m bringing down on
this city and all the surrounding towns the
doom that I have pronounced. They’re set in
their ways and won’t budge. They refuse to
do a thing I say.’ ”

LIFE’S BEEN NOTHING BUT TROUBLE AND TEARS

1-5 20 The priest Pashur son of Immer was the
senior priest in GOD’s Temple. He heard
Jeremiah preach this sermon. He whipped
Jeremiah the prophet and put him in the
stocks at the Upper Benjamin Gate of GOD’s
Temple. The next day Pashur came and let
him go. Jeremiah told him, “GOD has a new
name for you: not Pashur but Danger-Everywhere,
because GOD says, ‘You’re a danger
to yourself and everyone around you. All
your friends are going to get killed in battle
while you stand there and watch. What’s
more, I’m turning all of Judah over to the

NEW KING JAMES VERSION

the hand of the king of Babylon, and he shall
carry them captive to Babylon and slay them
with the sword. 5Moreover I will deliver all the
wealth of this city, all its produce, and all its pre-
cious things; all the treasures of the kings of Ju-
dah I will give into the hand of their enemies,
who will plunder them, seize them, and carry
them to Babylon. 6And you, Pashhur, and all
who dwell in your house, shall go into captivity.
You shall go to Babylon, and there you shall die,
and be buried there, you and all your friends, to
whom you have prophesied lies.' "

JEREMIAH'S UNPOPULAR MINISTRY

7O LORD, You induced me, and I was
persuaded;
You are stronger than I, and have prevailed.
I am in derision daily;
Everyone mocks me.
8For when I spoke, I cried out;
I shouted, "Violence and plunder!"
Because the word of the LORD was made to
me
A reproach and a derision daily.
9Then I said, "I will not make mention of
Him,
Nor speak anymore in His name."
But *His word* was in my heart like a burning
fire
Shut up in my bones;
I was weary of holding *it* back,
And I could not.
10For I heard many mocking:
"Fear on every side!"
"Report," *they say*, "and we will report it!"
All my acquaintances watched for my
stumbling, *saying*,
"Perhaps he can be induced;
Then we will prevail against him,
And we will take our revenge on him."
11But the LORD *is* with me as a mighty,
awesome One.
Therefore my persecutors will stumble, and
will not prevail.
They will be greatly ashamed, for they will
not prosper.
Their everlasting confusion will never be
forgotten.
12But, O LORD of hosts,
You who test the righteous,
And see the mind and heart,
Let me see Your vengeance on them;
For I have pleaded my cause before You.

13Sing to the LORD! Praise the LORD!
For He has delivered the life of the poor
From the hand of evildoers.

14Cursed *be* the day in which I was born!
Let the day not be blessed in which my
mother bore me!
15Let the man *be* cursed
Who brought news to my father, saying,
"A male child has been born to you!"
Making him very glad.
16And let that man be like the cities
Which the LORD overthrew, and did not
relent;

THE MESSAGE

king of Babylon to do whatever he likes
with them—haul them off into exile, kill
them at whim. Everything worth anything in
this city, property and possessions along
with everything in the royal treasury—I'm
handing it all over to the enemy. They'll
rummage through it and take what they
want back to Babylon.

6 " 'And you, Pashur, you and everyone in
your family will be taken prisoner into ex-
ile—that's right, exile in Babylon. You'll die
and be buried there, you and all your
cronies to whom you preached your lies.' "

7-10 You pushed me into this, GOD, and I let you
do it.
You were too much for me.
And now I'm a public joke.
They all poke fun at me.
Every time I open my mouth
I'm shouting, "Murder!" or "Rape!"
And all I get for my GOD-warnings
are insults and contempt.
But if I say, "Forget it!
No more GOD-Messages from me!"
The words are fire in my belly,
a burning in my bones.
I'm worn out trying to hold it in.
I can't do it any longer!
Then I hear whispering behind my back:
"There goes old 'Danger-Everywhere.'
Shut him up! Report him!"
Old friends watch, hoping I'll fall flat on my
face:
"One misstep and we'll have him. We'll
get rid of him for good!"

11 But GOD, a most fierce warrior, is at my
side.
Those who are after me will be sent
sprawling—
Slapstick buffoons falling all over
themselves,
a spectacle of humiliation no one will
ever forget.

12 Oh, GOD-of-the-Angel-Armies, no one fools
you.
You see through everyone, everything.
I want to see you pay them back for what
they've done.
I rest my case with you.

13 Sing to GOD! All praise to GOD!
He saves the weak from the grip of the
wicked.

14-18 Curse the day
I was born!
The day my mother bore me—
a curse on it, I say!
And curse the man who delivered
the news to my father:
"You've got a new baby—a boy baby!"
(How happy it made him.)
Let that birth notice be blacked out,
deleted from the records,

NEW KING JAMES VERSION

Let him hear the cry in the morning
And the shouting at noon,
17Because he did not kill me from the womb,
That my mother might have been my grave,
And her womb always enlarged *with me.*
18Why did I come forth from the womb to see
labor and sorrow,
That my days should be consumed with
shame?

JERUSALEM'S DOOM IS SEALED

21 The word which came to Jeremiah from
the LORD when King Zedekiah sent to him
Pashhur the son of Melchiah, and Zephaniah
the son of Maaseiah, the priest, saying, 2"Please
inquire of the LORD for us, for Nebuchadnezzar[a]
king of Babylon makes war against us. Perhaps
the LORD will deal with us according to all His
wonderful works, that *the king* may go away
from us."
3Then Jeremiah said to them, "Thus you
shall say to Zedekiah, 4'Thus says the LORD God
of Israel: "Behold, I will turn back the weapons
of war that *are* in your hands, with which you
fight against the king of Babylon and the
Chaldeans[a] who besiege you outside the walls;
and I will assemble them in the midst of this
city. 5I Myself will fight against you with an out-
stretched hand and with a strong arm, even in
anger and fury and great wrath. 6I will strike the
inhabitants of this city, both man and beast;
they shall die of a great pestilence. 7And after-
ward," says the LORD, "I will deliver Zedekiah
king of Judah, his servants and the people, and
such as are left in this city from the pestilence
and the sword and the famine, into the hand of
Nebuchadnezzar king of Babylon, into the hand
of their enemies, and into the hand of those who
seek their life; and he shall strike them with the
edge of the sword. He shall not spare them, or
have pity or mercy." '
8"Now you shall say to this people, 'Thus
says the LORD: "Behold, I set before you the way
of life and the way of death. 9He who remains in
this city shall die by the sword, by famine, and
by pestilence; but he who goes out and defects
to the Chaldeans who besiege you, he shall live,
and his life shall be as a prize to him. 10For I
have set My face against this city for adversity
and not for good," says the LORD. "It shall be
given into the hand of the king of Babylon, and
he shall burn it with fire." '

MESSAGE TO THE HOUSE OF DAVID

11"And concerning the house of the king of
Judah, *say,* 'Hear the word of the LORD, 12O
house of David! Thus says the LORD:

"Execute judgment in the morning;
And deliver *him who is* plundered
Out of the hand of the oppressor,
Lest My fury go forth like fire
And burn so that no one can quench *it,*
Because of the evil of your doings.

21:2 [a]Hebrew *Nebuchadrezzar,* and so elsewhere 21:4 [a]Or *Babylonians*

THE MESSAGE

And the man who brought it haunted to his
death
with the bad news he brought.
He should have killed me before I was
born,
with that womb as my tomb,
My mother pregnant for the rest of her life
with a baby dead in her womb.
Why, oh why, did I ever leave that womb?
Life's been nothing but trouble and
tears,
and what's coming is more of the same.

START EACH DAY WITH A SENSE OF JUSTICE

1-2 21 GOD'S Message to Jeremiah when King
Zedekiah sent Pashur son of Malkijah
and the priest Zephaniah son of Maa-
seiah to him with this request: "Nebuchad-
nezzar, king of Babylon, has waged war
against us. Pray to GOD for us. Ask him for
help. Maybe GOD will intervene with one of
his famous miracles and make him leave."
3-7 But Jeremiah said, "Tell Zedekiah: 'This
is the GOD of Israel's Message to you: You
can say good-bye to your army, watch
morale and weapons flushed down the
drain. I'm going to personally lead the king
of Babylon and the Chaldeans, against
whom you're fighting so hard, right into the
city itself. I'm joining *their* side and fighting
against *you,* fighting all-out, holding noth-
ing back. And in fierce anger. I'm prepared
to wipe out the population of this city, peo-
ple and animals alike, in a raging epidemic.
And then I will personally deliver Zedekiah
king of Judah, his princes, and any sur-
vivors left in the city who haven't died from
disease, been killed, or starved. I'll deliver
them to Nebuchadnezzar, king of Babylon—
yes, hand them over to their enemies, who
have come to kill them. He'll kill them ruth-
lessly, showing no mercy.'
8-10 "And then tell the people at large, 'GOD'S
Message to you is this: Listen carefully. I'm
giving you a choice: life or death. Whoever
stays in this city will die—either in battle or
by starvation or disease. But whoever goes
out and surrenders to the Chaldeans who
have surrounded the city will live. You'll lose
everything—but not your life. I'm deter-
mined to see this city destroyed. I'm that an-
gry with this place! GOD'S Decree. I'm going
to give it to the king of Babylon, and he's go-
ing to burn it to the ground.'

11-14 "To the royal house of Judah, listen to GOD'S
Message!
House of David, listen—GOD'S Message
to you:
'Start each day by dealing with justice.
Rescue victims from their exploiters.
Prevent fire—the fire of my anger—
for once it starts, it can't be put out.
Your evil regime
is fuel for my anger.

NEW KING JAMES VERSION

13"Behold, I *am* against you, O inhabitant of
the valley,
And rock of the plain," says the LORD,
"Who say, 'Who shall come down against us?
Or who shall enter our dwellings?'
14But I will punish you according to the fruit
of your doings," says the LORD;
"I will kindle a fire in its forest,
And it shall devour all things around it." ' "

22 Thus says the LORD: "Go down to the
house of the king of Judah, and there
speak this word, 2and say, 'Hear the word of the
LORD, O king of Judah, you who sit on the
throne of David, you and your servants and your
people who enter these gates! 3Thus says the
LORD: "Execute judgment and righteousness,
and deliver the plundered out of the hand of the
oppressor. Do no wrong and do no violence to
the stranger, the fatherless, or the widow, nor
shed innocent blood in this place. 4For if you in-
deed do this thing, then shall enter the gates of
this house, riding on horses and in chariots, ac-
companied by servants and people, kings who
sit on the throne of David. 5But if you will not
hear these words, I swear by Myself," says the
LORD, "that this house shall become a desola-
tion." ' "
6For thus says the LORD to the house of the
king of Judah:

"You *are* Gilead to Me,
The head of Lebanon;
Yet I surely will make you a wilderness,
Cities *which* are not inhabited.
7I will prepare destroyers against you,
Everyone with his weapons;
They shall cut down your choice cedars
And cast *them* into the fire.

8And many nations will pass by this city; and
everyone will say to his neighbor, 'Why has the
LORD done so to this great city?' 9Then they will
answer, 'Because they have forsaken the covenant
of the LORD their God, and worshiped other gods
and served them.' "

10Weep not for the dead, nor bemoan him;
Weep bitterly for him who goes away,
For he shall return no more,
Nor see his native country.

MESSAGE TO THE SONS OF JOSIAH

11For thus says the LORD concerning Shal-
lum[a] the son of Josiah, king of Judah, who
reigned instead of Josiah his father, who went
from this place: "He shall not return here any-
more, 12but he shall die in the place where they
have led him captive, and shall see this land no
more.

22:11 [a]Also called *Jehoahaz*

THE MESSAGE

Don't you realize that I'm against you,
yes, *against* you.
You think you've got it made,
all snug and secure.
You say, "Who can possibly get to us?
Who can crash our party?"
Well, I can—and will!
I'll punish your evil regime.
I'll start a fire that will rage unchecked,
burn everything in sight to cinders.' "

WALKING OUT ON THE COVENANT OF GOD

1-3 22 GOD's orders: "Go to the royal palace
and deliver this Message. Say, 'Listen to
what GOD says, O King of Judah, you who sit
on David's throne—you and your officials
and all the people who go in and out of
these palace gates. This is GOD's Message:
Attend to matters of justice. Set things right
between people. Rescue victims from their
exploiters. Don't take advantage of the
homeless, the orphans, the widows. Stop the
murdering!
4-5 " 'If you obey these commands, then
kings who follow in the line of David will
continue to go in and out of these palace
gates mounted on horses and riding in char-
iots—they and their officials and the citi-
zens of Judah. But if you don't obey these
commands, then I swear—GOD's Decree!—
this palace will end up a heap of rubble.' "

6-7 This is GOD's verdict on Judah's royal palace:

"I number you among my favorite places—
like the lovely hills of Gilead,
like the soaring peaks of Lebanon.
Yet I swear I'll turn you into a wasteland,
as empty as a ghost town.
I'll hire a demolition crew,
well-equipped with sledgehammers and
wrecking bars,
Pound the country to a pulp
and burn it all up.

8-9 "Travelers from all over will come
through here and say to one another, 'Why
would GOD do such a thing to this wonder-
ful city?' They'll be told, 'Because they
walked out on the covenant of their GOD,
took up with other gods and worshiped
them.' "

BUILDING A FINE HOUSE BUT DESTROYING LIVES

10 Don't weep over dead King Josiah.
Don't waste your tears.
Weep for his exiled son:
He's gone for good.
He'll never see home again.
11-12 For this is GOD's Word on Shallum son of
Josiah, who succeeded his father as king of
Judah: "He's gone from here, gone for good.
He'll die in the place they've taken him to.
He'll never see home again."

New King James Version

13"Woe to him who builds his house by
unrighteousness
And his chambers by injustice,
Who uses his neighbor's service without
wages
And gives him nothing for his work,
14Who says, 'I will build myself a wide house
with spacious chambers,
And cut out windows for it,
Paneling *it* with cedar
And painting *it* with vermilion.'

15"Shall you reign because you enclose
yourself in cedar?
Did not your father eat and drink,
And do justice and righteousness?
Then *it was* well with him.
16He judged the cause of the poor and needy;
Then *it was* well.
Was not this knowing Me?" says the LORD.
17"Yet your eyes and your heart *are* for nothing
but your covetousness,
For shedding innocent blood,
And practicing oppression and violence."

18Therefore thus says the LORD concerning
Jehoiakim the son of Josiah, king of Judah:

"They shall not lament for him,
Saying, 'Alas, my brother!' or 'Alas, my
sister!'
They shall not lament for him,
Saying, 'Alas, master!' or 'Alas, his glory!'
19He shall be buried with the burial of a
donkey,
Dragged and cast out beyond the gates of
Jerusalem.

20"Go up to Lebanon, and cry out,
And lift up your voice in Bashan;
Cry from Abarim,
For all your lovers are destroyed.
21I spoke to you in your prosperity,
But you said, 'I will not hear.'
This *has been* your manner from your
youth,
That you did not obey My voice.
22The wind shall eat up all your rulers,
And your lovers shall go into captivity;
Surely then you will be ashamed and
humiliated
For all your wickedness.
23O inhabitant of Lebanon,
Making your nest in the cedars,
How gracious will you be when pangs come
upon you,
Like the pain of a woman in labor?

Message to Coniah

24"*As I* live," says the LORD, "though Coniah[a]
the son of Jehoiakim, king of Judah, were the
signet on My right hand, yet I would pluck you
off; 25and I will give you into the hand of those
who seek your life, and into the hand *of those*
whose face you fear—the hand of Nebu-
chadnezzar king of Babylon and the hand of the
Chaldeans. 26So I will cast you out, and your

22:24 [a]Also called *Jeconiah* and *Jehoiachin*

The Message

13-17 "Doom to him who builds palaces but
bullies people,
who makes a fine house but destroys
lives,
Who cheats his workers
and won't pay them for their work,
Who says, 'I'll build me an elaborate
mansion
with spacious rooms and fancy windows.
I'll bring in rare and expensive woods
and the latest in interior decor.'
So, that makes you a king—
living in a fancy palace?
Your father got along just fine, didn't he?
He did what was right and treated
people fairly,
And things went well with him.
He stuck up for the down-and-out,
And things went well for Judah.
Isn't this what it means to know me?"
GOD's Decree!
"But you're blind and brainless.
All you think about is yourself,
Taking advantage of the weak,
bulldozing your way, bullying victims."

18-19 This is God's epitaph on Jehoiakim son of
Josiah king of Judah:
"Doom to this man!
Nobody will shed tears over him,
'Poor, poor brother!'
Nobody will shed tears over him,
'Poor, poor master!'
They'll give him a donkey's funeral,
drag him out of the city and dump him.

You've Made a Total Mess of Your Life

20-23 "People of Jerusalem, climb a Lebanon peak
and weep,
climb a Bashan mountain and wail,
Climb the Abarim ridge and cry—
you've made a total mess of your life.
I spoke to you when everything was going
your way.
You said, 'I'm not interested.'
You've been that way as long as I've known
you,
never listened to a thing I said.
All your leaders will be blown away,
all your friends end up in exile,
And you'll find yourself in the gutter,
disgraced by your evil life.
You big-city people thought you were so
important,
thought you were 'king of the mountain'!
You're soon going to be doubled up in pain,
pain worse than the pangs of childbirth.

24-26 "As sure as I am the living God"—GOD's De-
cree—"even if you, Jehoiachin son of Je-
hoiakim king of Judah, were the signet ring
on my right hand, I'd pull you off and give
you to those who are out to kill you, to Ne-
buchadnezzar king of Babylon and the
Chaldeans, and then throw you, both you

NEW KING JAMES VERSION

mother who bore you, into another country
where you were not born; and there you shall
die. 27 But to the land to which they desire to re-
turn, there they shall not return.

28 "Is this man Coniah a despised, broken
idol—
A vessel in which *is* no pleasure?
Why are they cast out, he and his
descendants,
And cast into a land which they do not
know?
29 O earth, earth, earth,
Hear the word of the LORD!
30 Thus says the LORD:
'Write this man down as childless,
A man *who* shall not prosper in his days;
For none of his descendants shall prosper,
Sitting on the throne of David,
And ruling anymore in Judah.' "

THE BRANCH OF RIGHTEOUSNESS

23 "Woe to the shepherds who destroy and
scatter the sheep of My pasture!" says the
LORD. 2 Therefore thus says the LORD God of Is-
rael against the shepherds who feed My people:
"You have scattered My flock, driven them
away, and not attended to them. Behold, I will
attend to you for the evil of your doings," says
the LORD. 3 "But I will gather the remnant of My
flock out of all countries where I have driven
them, and bring them back to their folds; and
they shall be fruitful and increase. 4 I will set up
shepherds over them who will feed them; and
they shall fear no more, nor be dismayed, nor
shall they be lacking," says the LORD.

5 "Behold, *the* days are coming," says the
LORD,
"That I will raise to David a Branch of
righteousness;
A King shall reign and prosper,
And execute judgment and righteousness in
the earth.
6 In His days Judah will be saved,
And Israel will dwell safely;
Now this *is* His name by which He will be
called:

THE LORD OUR RIGHTEOUSNESS.[a]

7 "Therefore, behold, *the* days are coming,"
says the LORD, "that they shall no longer say, 'As
the LORD lives who brought up the children of
Israel from the land of Egypt,' 8 but, 'As the LORD
lives who brought up and led the descendants of
the house of Israel from the north country and
from all the countries where I had driven them.'
And they shall dwell in their own land."

FALSE PROPHETS AND EMPTY ORACLES

9 My heart within me is broken
Because of the prophets;
All my bones shake.
I am like a drunken man,
And like a man whom wine has overcome,
Because of the LORD,
And because of His holy words.

23:6 [a]Hebrew *YHWH Tsidkenu*

THE MESSAGE

and your mother, into a foreign country, far
from your place of birth. There you'll both
die.
27 "You'll be homesick, desperately home-
sick, but you'll never get home again."

28-30 Is Jehoiachin a leaky bucket,
a rusted-out pail good for nothing?
Why else would he be thrown away, he and
his children,
thrown away to a foreign place?
O land, land, land,
listen to GOD's Message!
This is GOD's verdict:
"Write this man off as if he were childless,
a man who will never amount to
anything.
Nothing will ever come of his life.
He's the end of the line, the last of the
kings."

AN AUTHENTIC DAVID-BRANCH

1-4 23 "Doom to the shepherd-leaders who
butcher and scatter my sheep!" GOD's
Decree. "So here is what I, GOD, Israel's God,
say to the shepherd-leaders who misled my
people: 'You've scattered my sheep. You've
driven them off. You haven't kept your eye
on them. Well, let me tell you, I'm keeping
my eye on *you*, keeping track of your crimi-
nal behavior. I'll take over and gather what's
left of my sheep, gather them in from all the
lands where I've driven them. I'll bring them
back where they belong, and they'll recover
and flourish. I'll set shepherd-leaders over
them who will take good care of them. They
won't live in fear or panic anymore. All the
lost sheep rounded up!' GOD's Decree."

5-6 "Time's coming"—GOD's Decree—
"when I'll establish a truly righteous
David-Branch,
A ruler who knows how to rule justly.
He'll make sure of justice and keep
people united.
In his time Judah will be secure again
and Israel will live in safety.
This is the name they'll give him:
'GOD-Who-Puts-Everything-Right.'

7-8 "So watch for this. The time's coming"—
GOD's Decree—"when no one will say, 'As
sure as GOD lives, the God who brought the
Israelites out of Egypt,' but, 'As sure as GOD
lives, the God who brought the descendants
of Israel back from the north country and
from the other countries where he'd driven
them, so that they can live on their own
good earth.' "

THE "EVERYTHING WILL TURN OUT FINE" SERMON

9 My head is reeling,
my limbs are limp,
I'm staggering like a drunk,
seeing double from too much wine—
And all because of GOD,
because of his holy words.

NEW KING JAMES VERSION

10For the land is full of adulterers;
For because of a curse the land mourns.
The pleasant places of the wilderness are dried up.
Their course of life is evil,
And their might *is* not right.

11"For both prophet and priest are profane;
Yes, in My house I have found their wickedness," says the LORD.
12"Therefore their way shall be to them
Like slippery *ways;*
In the darkness they shall be driven on
And fall in them;
For I will bring disaster on them,
The year of their punishment," says the LORD.
13"And I have seen folly in the prophets of Samaria:
They prophesied by Baal
And caused My people Israel to err.
14Also I have seen a horrible thing in the prophets of Jerusalem:
They commit adultery and walk in lies;
They also strengthen the hands of evildoers,
So that no one turns back from his wickedness.
All of them are like Sodom to Me,
And her inhabitants like Gomorrah.

15"Therefore thus says the LORD of hosts concerning the prophets:

'Behold, I will feed them with wormwood,
And make them drink the water of gall;
For from the prophets of Jerusalem
Profaneness has gone out into all the land.' "

16Thus says the LORD of hosts:

"Do not listen to the words of the prophets who prophesy to you.
They make you worthless;
They speak a vision of their own heart,
Not from the mouth of the LORD.
17They continually say to those who despise Me,
'The LORD has said, "You shall have peace" ';
And *to* everyone who walks according to the dictates of his own heart, they say,
'No evil shall come upon you.' "

18For who has stood in the counsel of the LORD,

THE MESSAGE

10-12 Now for what GOD says regarding the lying prophets:

"Can you believe it? A country teeming with adulterers!
faithless, promiscuous idolater-adulterers!
They're a curse on the land.
The land's a wasteland.
Their unfaithfulness
is turning the country into a cesspool,
Prophets and priests devoted to desecration.
They have nothing to do with me as their God.
My very own Temple, mind you—
mud-spattered with their crimes." GOD's Decree.
"But they won't get by with it.
They'll find themselves on a slippery slope,
Careening into the darkness,
somersaulting into the pitch-black dark.
I'll make them pay for their crimes.
It will be the Year of Doom." GOD's Decree.

13-14 "Over in Samaria I saw prophets
acting like silly fools—shocking!
They preached using that no-god Baal for a text,
messing with the minds of my people.
And the Jerusalem prophets are even worse—horrible!—
sex-driven, living a lie,
Subsidizing a culture of wickedness,
and never giving it a second thought.
They're as bad as those wretches in old Sodom,
the degenerates of old Gomorrah."

15 So here's the Message to the prophets from GOD-of-the-Angel-Armies:

"I'll cook them a supper of maggoty meat
with after-dinner drinks of strychnine.
The Jerusalem prophets are behind all this.
They're the cause of the godlessness polluting this country."

16-17 A Message from GOD-of-the-Angel-Armies:

"Don't listen to the sermons of the prophets.
It's all hot air. Lies, lies, and more lies.
They make it all up.
Not a word they speak comes from me.
They preach their 'Everything Will Turn Out Fine' sermon
to congregations with no taste for God,
Their 'Nothing Bad Will Ever Happen to You' sermon
to people who are set in their own ways.

18-20 "Have any of these prophets bothered to meet with me, the true GOD?

NEW KING JAMES VERSION

And has perceived and heard His word?
Who has marked His word and heard *it*?
19Behold, a whirlwind of the LORD has gone
forth in fury—
A violent whirlwind!
It will fall violently on the head of the
wicked.
20The anger of the LORD will not turn back
Until He has executed and performed the
thoughts of His heart.
In the latter days you will understand it
perfectly.

21"I have not sent these prophets, yet they ran.
I have not spoken to them, yet they
prophesied.
22But if they had stood in My counsel,
And had caused My people to hear My
words,
Then they would have turned them from
their evil way
And from the evil of their doings.

23"*Am* I a God near at hand," says the LORD,
"And not a God afar off?
24Can anyone hide himself in secret places,
So I shall not see him?" says the LORD;
"Do I not fill heaven and earth?" says the
LORD.

25"I have heard what the prophets have said
who prophesy lies in My name, saying, 'I have
dreamed, I have dreamed!' 26How long will *this*
be in the heart of the prophets who prophesy
lies? Indeed *they are* prophets of the deceit of
their own heart, 27who try to make My people
forget My name by their dreams which every-
one tells his neighbor, as their fathers forgot My
name for Baal.

28"The prophet who has a dream, let him tell a
dream;
And he who has My word, let him speak My
word faithfully.
What *is* the chaff to the wheat?" says the
LORD.
29"*Is* not My word like a fire?" says the LORD,
"And like a hammer *that* breaks the rock in
pieces?

30"Therefore behold, I *am* against the
prophets," says the LORD, "who steal My words
every one from his neighbor. 31Behold, I *am*
against the prophets," says the LORD, "who use
their tongues and say, 'He says.' 32Behold, I *am*
against those who prophesy false dreams," says
the LORD, "and tell them, and cause My people
to err by their lies and by their recklessness.

THE MESSAGE

bothered to take in what *I* have to say?
listened to and then *lived out* my Word?
Look out! GOD's hurricane will be let
loose—
my hurricane blast,
Spinning the heads of the wicked like tops!
God's raging anger won't let up
Until I've made a clean sweep,
completing the job I began.
When the job's done,
you'll see that it's been well done.

QUIT THE "GOD TOLD ME THIS" KIND OF TALK

21-22 "I never sent these prophets,
but they ran anyway.
I never spoke to them,
but they preached away.
If they'd have bothered to sit down and
meet with me,
they'd have preached my Message to my
people.
They'd have gotten them back on the right
track,
gotten them out of their evil ruts.

23-24 "Am I not a God near at hand"—GOD's
Decree—
"and not a God far off?
Can anyone hide out in a corner
where I can't see him?"
GOD's Decree.
"Am I not present everywhere,
whether seen or unseen?"
GOD's Decree.

25-27 "I know what they're saying, all these
prophets who preach lies using me as their
text, saying 'I had this dream! I had this
dream!' How long do I have to put up with
this? Do these prophets give two cents about
me as they preach their lies and spew out
their grandiose delusions? They swap
dreams with one another, feed on each
other's delusive dreams, trying to distract
my people from me just as their ancestors
were distracted by the no-god Baal.

28-29 "You prophets who do nothing but dream—
go ahead and tell your silly dreams.
But you prophets who have a message from
me—
tell it truly and faithfully.
What does straw have in common with
wheat?
Nothing else is like GOD's Decree.
Isn't my Message like fire?" GOD's Decree.
"Isn't it like a sledgehammer busting a
rock?

30-31 "I've had it with the 'prophets' who get all
their sermons secondhand from each other.
Yes, I've had it with them. They make up
stuff and then pretend it's a real sermon.

32 "Oh yes, I've had it with the prophets who
preach the lies they dream up, spreading
them all over the country, ruining the lives of
my people with their cheap and reckless lies.

NEW KING JAMES VERSION

Yet I did not send them or command them; therefore they shall not profit this people at all," says the LORD.

33"So when these people or the prophet or the priest ask you, saying, 'What is the oracle of the LORD?' you shall then say to them, 'What oracle?'[a] I will even forsake you," says the LORD. 34"And *as for* the prophet and the priest and the people who say, 'The oracle of the LORD!' I will even punish that man and his house. 35Thus every one of you shall say to his neighbor, and every one to his brother, 'What has the LORD answered?' and, 'What has the LORD spoken?' 36And the oracle of the LORD you shall mention no more. For every man's word will be his oracle, for you have perverted the words of the living God, the LORD of hosts, our God. 37Thus you shall say to the prophet, 'What has the LORD answered you?' and, 'What has the LORD spoken?' 38But since you say, 'The oracle of the LORD!' therefore thus says the LORD: 'Because you say this word, "The oracle of the LORD!" and I have sent to you, saying, "Do not say, 'The oracle of the LORD!' " 39therefore behold, I, even I, will utterly forget you and forsake you, and the city that I gave you and your fathers, and *will cast you* out of My presence. 40And I will bring an everlasting reproach upon you, and a perpetual shame, which shall not be forgotten.' "

THE SIGN OF TWO BASKETS OF FIGS

24 The LORD showed me, and there were two baskets of figs set before the temple of the LORD, after Nebuchadnezzar king of Babylon had carried away captive Jeconiah the son of Jehoiakim, king of Judah, and the princes of Judah with the craftsmen and smiths, from Jerusalem, and had brought them to Babylon. 2One basket *had* very good figs, like the figs *that are* first ripe; and the other basket *had* very bad figs which could not be eaten, they were so bad. 3Then the LORD said to me, "What do you see, Jeremiah?"

And I said, "Figs, the good figs, very good; and the bad, very bad, which cannot be eaten, they are so bad."

4Again the word of the LORD came to me, saying, 5"Thus says the LORD, the God of Israel: 'Like these good figs, so will I acknowledge those who are carried away captive from Judah, whom I have sent out of this place for *their own* good, into the land of the Chaldeans. 6For I will set My eyes on them for good, and I will bring them back to this land; I will build them and not pull *them* down, and I will plant them and not pluck *them* up. 7Then I will give them a heart to know Me, that I *am* the LORD; and they shall be My people, and I will be their God, for they shall return to Me with their whole heart.

23:33 [a]Septuagint, Targum, and Vulgate read '*You are the burden.*'

THE MESSAGE

"I never sent these prophets, never authorized a single one of them. They do nothing for this people—*nothing!*" GOD's Decree.

33 "And anyone, including prophets and priests, who asks, 'What's GOD got to say about all this, what's troubling him?' tell him, 'You, you're the trouble, and I'm getting rid of you.' " GOD's Decree.

34 "And if anyone, including prophets and priests, goes around saying glibly 'GOD's Message! GOD's Message!' I'll punish him and his family.

35-36 "Instead of claiming to know what GOD says, ask questions of one another, such as 'How do we understand GOD in this?' But don't go around pretending to know it all, saying 'God told me this . . . God told me that. . . .' I don't want to hear it anymore. Only the person I authorize speaks for me. Otherwise, my Message gets twisted, the Message of the living GOD-of-the-Angel-Armies.

37-38 "You can ask the prophets, 'How did GOD answer you? What did he tell you?' But don't pretend that you know all the answers yourselves and talk like you know it all. I'm telling you: Quit the 'God told me this . . . God told me that . . .' kind of talk.

39-40 "Are you paying attention? You'd better, because I'm about to take you in hand and throw you to the ground, you and this entire city that I gave to your ancestors. I've had it with the lot of you. You're never going to live this down. You're going down in history as a disgrace."

TWO BASKETS OF FIGS

1-2 **24** GOD showed me two baskets of figs placed in front of the Temple of GOD. This was after Nebuchadnezzar king of Babylon had taken Jehoiachin son of Jehoiakim king of Judah from Jerusalem into exile in Babylon, along with the leaders of Judah, the craftsmen, and the skilled laborers. In one basket the figs were of the finest quality, ripe and ready to eat. In the other basket the figs were rotten, so rotten they couldn't be eaten.

3 GOD said to me, "Jeremiah, what do you see?"

"Figs," I said. "Excellent figs of the finest quality, and also rotten figs, so rotten they can't be eaten."

4-6 Then GOD told me, "This is the Message from the GOD of Israel: The exiles from here that I've sent off to the land of the Babylonians are like the good figs, and I'll make sure they get good treatment. I'll keep my eye on them so that their lives are good, and I'll bring them back to this land. I'll build them up, not tear them down; I'll plant them, not uproot them.

7 "And I'll give them a heart to know me, GOD. They'll be my people and I'll be their God, for they'll have returned to me with all their hearts.

NEW KING JAMES VERSION

8‘And as the bad figs which cannot be eaten, they are so bad’—surely thus says the LORD—‘so will I give up Zedekiah the king of Judah, his princes, the residue of Jerusalem who remain in this land, and those who dwell in the land of Egypt. 9I will deliver them to trouble into all the kingdoms of the earth, for *their* harm, *to be* a reproach and a byword, a taunt and a curse, in all places where I shall drive them. 10And I will send the sword, the famine, and the pestilence among them, till they are consumed from the land that I gave to them and their fathers.’ ”

SEVENTY YEARS OF DESOLATION

25 The word that came to Jeremiah concerning all the people of Judah, in the fourth year of Jehoiakim the son of Josiah, king of Judah (which *was* the first year of Nebuchadnezzar king of Babylon), 2which Jeremiah the prophet spoke to all the people of Judah and to all the inhabitants of Jerusalem, saying: 3“From the thirteenth year of Josiah the son of Amon, king of Judah, even to this day, this *is* the twenty-third year in which the word of the LORD has come to me; and I have spoken to you, rising early and speaking, but you have not listened. 4And the LORD has sent to you all His servants the prophets, rising early and sending *them,* but you have not listened nor inclined your ear to hear. 5They said, ‘Repent now everyone of his evil way and his evil doings, and dwell in the land that the LORD has given to you and your fathers forever and ever. 6Do not go after other gods to serve them and worship them, and do not provoke Me to anger with the works of your hands; and I will not harm you.’ 7Yet you have not listened to Me,” says the LORD, “that you might provoke Me to anger with the works of your hands to your own hurt.

8“Therefore thus says the LORD of hosts: ‘Because you have not heard My words, 9behold, I will send and take all the families of the north,’ says the LORD, ‘and Nebuchadnezzar the king of Babylon, My servant, and will bring them against this land, against its inhabitants, and against these nations all around, and will utterly destroy them, and make them an astonishment, a hissing, and perpetual desolations. 10Moreover I will take from them the voice of mirth and the voice of gladness, the voice of the bridegroom and the voice of the bride, the sound of the millstones and the light of the lamp. 11And this whole land shall be a desolation *and* an astonishment, and these nations shall serve the king of Babylon seventy years.

12‘Then it will come to pass, when seventy years are completed, *that* I will punish the king of Babylon and that nation, the land of the Chaldeans, for their iniquity,’ says the LORD; ‘and I will make it a perpetual desolation. 13So I will bring on that land all My words which I have pronounced against it, all that is written in this book, which Jeremiah has prophesied concerning all the nations. 14(For many nations and great kings shall be served by them also; and I will repay them according to their deeds and according to the works of their own hands.)’ ”

THE MESSAGE

8-10 “But like the rotten figs, so rotten they can’t be eaten, is Zedekiah king of Judah. Rotten figs—that’s how I’ll treat him and his leaders, along with the survivors here and those down in Egypt. I’ll make them something that the whole world will look on as disgusting—repugnant outcasts, their names used as curse words wherever in the world I drive them. And I’ll make sure they die like flies—from war, starvation, disease, whatever—until the land I once gave to them and their ancestors is completely rid of them.”

DON’T FOLLOW THE GOD-FADS OF THE DAY

1 **25** This is the Message given to Jeremiah for all the people of Judah. It came in the fourth year of Jehoiakim son of Josiah king of Judah. It was the first year of Nebuchadnezzar king of Babylon.

2 Jeremiah the prophet delivered the Message to all the people of Judah and citizens of Jerusalem:

3 From the thirteenth year of Josiah son of Amon king of Judah right up to the present day—twenty-three years it’s been!—GOD’s Word has come to me, and from early each morning to late every night I’ve passed it on to you. And you haven’t listened to a word of it!

4-6 Not only that but GOD also sent a steady stream of prophets to you who were just as persistent as me, and you never listened. They told you, “Turn back—right now, each one of you!—from your evil way of life and bad behavior, and live in the land GOD gave you and your ancestors, the land he intended to give you forever. Don’t follow the god-fads of the day, taking up and worshiping these no-gods. Don’t make me angry with your god-businesses, making and selling gods—a dangerous business!

7 “You refused to listen to any of this, and now I am really angry. These god-making businesses of yours are your doom.”

8-11 The verdict of GOD-of-the-Angel-Armies on all this: “Because you have refused to listen to what I’ve said, I’m stepping in. I’m sending for the armies out of the north headed by Nebuchadnezzar king of Babylon, my servant in this, and I’m setting them on this land and people and even the surrounding countries. I’m devoting the whole works to total destruction—a horror to top all the horrors in history. And I’ll banish every sound of joy—singing, laughter, marriage festivities, genial workmen, candlelit suppers. The whole landscape will be one vast wasteland. These countries will be in subjection to the king of Babylon for seventy years.

12-14 “Once the seventy years is up, I’ll punish the king of Babylon and the whole nation of Babylon for their sin. Then *they’ll* be the wasteland. Everything that I said I’d do to that country, I’ll do—everything that’s written in this book, everything Jeremiah preached against all the godless nations. Many nations and great kings will make slaves of the Babylonians, paying them back for everything they’ve done to others. They won’t get by with anything.” GOD’s Decree.

New King James Version

Judgment on the Nations

15For thus says the LORD God of Israel to me:
"Take this wine cup of fury from My hand, and
cause all the nations, to whom I send you, to
drink it. 16And they will drink and stagger and
go mad because of the sword that I will send
among them."

17Then I took the cup from the LORD's hand,
and made all the nations drink, to whom the
LORD had sent me: 18Jerusalem and the cities of
Judah, its kings and its princes, to make them a
desolation, an astonishment, a hissing, and a
curse, as *it is* this day; 19Pharaoh king of Egypt,
his servants, his princes, and all his people; 20all
the mixed multitude, all the kings of the land of
Uz, all the kings of the land of the Philistines
(namely, Ashkelon, Gaza, Ekron, and the rem-
nant of Ashdod); 21Edom, Moab, and the people
of Ammon; 22all the kings of Tyre, all the kings
of Sidon, and the kings of the coastlands which
are across the sea; 23Dedan, Tema, Buz, and all
who are in the farthest corners; 24all the kings of
Arabia and all the kings of the mixed multitude
who dwell in the desert; 25all the kings of Zimri,
all the kings of Elam, and all the kings of the
Medes; 26all the kings of the north, far and near,
one with another; and all the kingdoms of the
world which *are* on the face of the earth. Also
the king of Sheshach[a] shall drink after them.

27"Therefore you shall say to them, 'Thus
says the LORD of hosts, the God of Israel: "Drink,
be drunk, and vomit! Fall and rise no more, be-
cause of the sword which I will send among
you." ' 28And it shall be, if they refuse to take the
cup from your hand to drink, then you shall say
to them, 'Thus says the LORD of hosts: "You shall
certainly drink! 29For behold, I begin to bring
calamity on the city which is called by My
name, and should you be utterly unpunished?
You shall not be unpunished, for I will call for a
sword on all the inhabitants of the earth," says
the LORD of hosts.'

30"Therefore prophesy against them all these
words, and say to them:

'The LORD will roar from on high,
And utter His voice from His holy
habitation;
He will roar mightily against His fold.
He will give a shout, as those who tread *the*
grapes,
Against all the inhabitants of the earth.
31A noise will come to the ends of the earth—
For the LORD has a controversy with the
nations;
He will plead His case with all flesh.

25:26 [a]A code word for Babylon (compare 51:41)

The Message

God Puts the Human Race on Trial

15-16 This is a Message that the GOD of Israel gave me: "Take this cup filled with the wine of my wrath that I'm handing to you. Make all the nations where I send you drink it down. They'll drink it and get drunk, staggering in delirium because of the killing that I'm going to unleash among them."

17-26 I took the cup from GOD's hand and made them drink it, all the nations to which he sent me:

Jerusalem and the towns of Judah, along with their kings and leaders, turning them into a vast wasteland, a horror to look at, a cussword—which, in fact, they now are;

Pharaoh king of Egypt with his attendants and leaders, plus all his people and the melting pot of foreigners collected there;

All the kings of Uz;

All the kings of the Philistines from Ashkelon, Gaza, Ekron, and what's left of Ashdod;

Edom, Moab, and the Ammonites;

All the kings of Tyre, Sidon, and the coastlands across the sea;

Dedan, Tema, Buz, and the nomads on the fringe of the desert;

All the kings of Arabia and the various Bedouin sheiks and chieftains wandering about in the desert;

All the kings of Zimri, Elam, and the Medes;

All the kings from the north countries near and far, one by one;

All the kingdoms on planet Earth . . .

And the king of Sheshak (that is, Babylon) will be the last to drink.

27 "Tell them, 'These are orders from GOD-of-the-Angel-Armies, the God of Israel: Drink and get drunk and vomit. Fall on your faces and don't get up again. You're slated for a massacre.'

28 "If any of them refuse to take the cup from you and drink it, say to them, 'GOD-of-the-Angel-Armies has ordered you to drink. So drink!

29 " 'Prepare for the worst! I'm starting off the catastrophe in the city that I claim as my own, so don't think you are going to get out of it. No, you're not getting out of anything. It's the sword and nothing but the sword against everyone everywhere!' " The GOD-of-the-Angel-Armies' Decree.

30-31 "Preach it all, Jeremiah. Preach the
entire Message to them. Say:

" 'GOD roars like a lion from high heaven;
thunder rolls out from his holy dwelling—
Ear-splitting bellows against his people,
shouting hurrahs like workers in
harvest.
The noise reverberates all over the earth;
everyone everywhere hears it.
GOD makes his case against the godless
nations.
He's about to put the human race on trial.

NEW KING JAMES VERSION

He will give those *who are* wicked to the
sword,' says the LORD."

32Thus says the LORD of hosts:

"Behold, disaster shall go forth
From nation to nation,
And a great whirlwind shall be raised up
From the farthest parts of the earth.

33"And at that day the slain of the LORD shall
be from *one* end of the earth even to the *other*
end of the earth. They shall not be lamented, or
gathered, or buried; they shall become refuse on
the ground.

34"Wail, shepherds, and cry!
Roll about *in the ashes,*
You leaders of the flock!
For the days of your slaughter and your
dispersions are fulfilled;
You shall fall like a precious vessel.
35And the shepherds will have no way to flee,
Nor the leaders of the flock to escape.
36A voice of the cry of the shepherds,
And a wailing of the leaders to the flock *will
be heard.*
For the LORD has plundered their pasture,
37And the peaceful dwellings are cut down
Because of the fierce anger of the LORD.
38He has left His lair like the lion;
For their land is desolate
Because of the fierceness of the Oppressor,
And because of His fierce anger."

JEREMIAH SAVED FROM DEATH

26 In the beginning of the reign of Jehoiakim
the son of Josiah, king of Judah, this word
came from the LORD, saying, 2"Thus says the
LORD: 'Stand in the court of the LORD's house,
and speak to all the cities of Judah, which come
to worship *in* the LORD's house, all the words
that I command you to speak to them. Do not di-
minish a word. 3Perhaps everyone will listen
and turn from his evil way, that I may relent con-
cerning the calamity which I purpose to bring
on them because of the evil of their doings.'
4And you shall say to them, 'Thus says the LORD:
"If you will not listen to Me, to walk in My law
which I have set before you, 5to heed the words
of My servants the prophets whom I sent to you,
both rising up early and sending *them* (but you
have not heeded), 6then I will make this house
like Shiloh, and will make this city a curse to all
the nations of the earth." ' "
7So the priests and the prophets and all the
people heard Jeremiah speaking these words in
the house of the LORD. 8Now it happened, when
Jeremiah had made an end of speaking all that
the LORD had commanded *him* to speak to all
the people, that the priests and the prophets and
all the people seized him, saying, "You will
surely die! 9Why have you prophesied in the

THE MESSAGE

For the wicked the verdict is clear-cut:
death by the sword.' " GOD's Decree.

32 A Message from GOD-of-the-Angel-Armies:

"Prepare for the worst! Doomsday!
Disaster is spreading from nation to
nation.
A huge storm is about to rage
all across planet Earth."

33 Laid end to end, those killed in GOD's judg-
ment that day will stretch from one end of
the earth to the other. No tears will be shed
and no burials conducted. The bodies will
be left where they fall, like so much horse
dung fertilizing the fields.

34-38 Wail, shepherds! Cry out for help!
Grovel in the dirt, you masters of flocks!
Time's up—you're slated for the
slaughterhouse,
like a choice ram with its throat cut.
There's no way out for the rulers,
no escape for those shepherds.
Hear that? Rulers crying for help,
shepherds of the flock wailing!
GOD is about to ravage their fine pastures.
The peaceful sheepfolds will be silent
with death,
silenced by GOD's deadly anger.
God will come out into the open
like a lion leaping from its cover,
And the country will be torn to pieces,
ripped and ravaged by his anger.

CHANGE THE WAY YOU'RE LIVING

1 26 At the beginning of the reign of Je-
hoiakim son of Josiah king of Judah,
this Message came from GOD to Jeremiah:
2-3 "GOD's Message: Stand in the court of
GOD's Temple and preach to the people who
come from all over Judah to worship in
GOD's Temple. Say everything I tell you to
say to them. Don't hold anything back. Just
maybe they'll listen and turn back from
their bad lives. Then I'll reconsider the dis-
aster that I'm planning to bring on them be-
cause of their evil behavior.
4-6 "Say to them, 'This is GOD's Message: If
you refuse to listen to me and live by my
teaching that I've revealed so plainly to you,
and if you continue to refuse to listen to my
servants the prophets that I tirelessly keep
on sending to you—but you've never lis-
tened! Why would you start now?—then I'll
make this Temple a pile of ruins like Shiloh,
and I'll make this city nothing but a bad
joke worldwide.' "
7-9 Everybody there—priests, prophets, and
people—heard Jeremiah preaching this
Message in the Temple of GOD. When Jer-
emiah had finished his sermon, saying
everything God had commanded him to say,
the priests and prophets and people all
grabbed him, yelling, "Death! You're going
to die for this! How dare you preach—and

New King James Version

name of the LORD, saying, 'This house shall be like Shiloh, and this city shall be desolate, without an inhabitant'?" And all the people were gathered against Jeremiah in the house of the LORD.

10When the princes of Judah heard these things, they came up from the king's house to the house of the LORD and sat down in the entry of the New Gate of the LORD's *house.* 11And the priests and the prophets spoke to the princes and all the people, saying, "This man deserves to die! For he has prophesied against this city, as you have heard with your ears."

12Then Jeremiah spoke to all the princes and all the people, saying: "The LORD sent me to prophesy against this house and against this city with all the words that you have heard. 13Now therefore, amend your ways and your doings, and obey the voice of the LORD your God; then the LORD will relent concerning the doom that He has pronounced against you. 14As for me, here I am, in your hand; do with me as seems good and proper to you. 15But know for certain that if you put me to death, you will surely bring innocent blood on yourselves, on this city, and on its inhabitants; for truly the LORD has sent me to you to speak all these words in your hearing."

16So the princes and all the people said to the priests and the prophets, "This man does not deserve to die. For he has spoken to us in the name of the LORD our God."

17Then certain of the elders of the land rose up and spoke to all the assembly of the people, saying: 18"Micah of Moresheth prophesied in the days of Hezekiah king of Judah, and spoke to all the people of Judah, saying, 'Thus says the LORD of hosts:

"Zion shall be plowed *like* a field,
Jerusalem shall become heaps of ruins,
And the mountain of the temple[a]
Like the bare hills of the forest." '[b]

19Did Hezekiah king of Judah and all Judah ever put him to death? Did he not fear the LORD and seek the LORD's favor? And the LORD relented concerning the doom which He had pronounced against them. But we are doing great evil against ourselves."

20Now there was also a man who prophesied in the name of the LORD, Urijah the son of Shemaiah of Kirjath Jearim, who prophesied against this city and against this land according to all the words of Jeremiah. 21And when Je-

26:18 [a]Literally *house* [b]Compare Micah 3:12

The Message

using GOD's name!—saying that this Temple will become a heap of rubble like Shiloh and this city be wiped out without a soul left in it!"

All the people mobbed Jeremiah right in the Temple itself.

10 Officials from the royal court of Judah were told of this. They left the palace immediately and came to GOD's Temple to investigate. They held court on the spot, at the New Gate entrance to GOD's Temple.

11 The prophets and priests spoke first, addressing the officials, but also the people: "Death to this man! He deserves nothing less than death! He has preached against this city—you've heard the evidence with your own ears."

12-13 Jeremiah spoke next, publicly addressing the officials before the crowd: "GOD sent me to preach against both this Temple and city everything that's been reported to you. So do something about it! Change the way you're living, change your behavior. Listen obediently to the Message of your GOD. Maybe GOD will reconsider the disaster he has threatened.

14-15 "As for me, I'm at your mercy—do whatever you think is best. But take warning: If you kill me, you're killing an innocent man, and you and the city and the people in it will be liable. I didn't say any of this on my own. GOD sent me and told me what to say. You've been listening to GOD speak, not Jeremiah."

16 The court officials, backed by the people, then handed down their ruling to the priests and prophets: "Acquittal. No death sentence for this man. He has spoken to us with the authority of our GOD."

17-18 Then some of the respected leaders stood up and addressed the crowd: "In the reign of Hezekiah king of Judah, Micah of Moresheth preached to the people of Judah this sermon: This is GOD-of-the-Angel-Armies' Message for you:

" 'Because of people like you,
Zion will be turned back into farmland,
Jerusalem end up as a pile of rubble,
and instead of the Temple on the mountain,
a few scraggly scrub pines.'

19 "Did King Hezekiah or anyone else in Judah kill Micah of Moresheth because of that sermon? Didn't Hezekiah honor him and pray for mercy from GOD? And then didn't GOD call off the disaster he had threatened?

"Friends, we're at the brink of bringing a terrible calamity upon ourselves."

20-23 (At another time there had been a man, Uriah son of Shemaiah from Kiriath-jearim, who had preached similarly in the name of GOD. He preached against this same city and country just as Jeremiah did. When

NEW KING JAMES VERSION

hoiakim the king, with all his mighty men and all the princes, heard his words, the king sought to put him to death; but when Urijah heard *it,* he was afraid and fled, and went to Egypt. [22]Then Jehoiakim the king sent men to Egypt: Elnathan the son of Achbor, and *other* men *who went* with him to Egypt. [23]And they brought Urijah from Egypt and brought him to Jehoiakim the king, who killed him with the sword and cast his dead body into the graves of the common people.

[24]Nevertheless the hand of Ahikam the son of Shaphan was with Jeremiah, so that they should not give him into the hand of the people to put him to death.

SYMBOL OF THE BONDS AND YOKES

27 In the beginning of the reign of Jehoiakim[a] the son of Josiah, king of Judah, this word came to Jeremiah from the LORD, saying,[b] [2]"Thus says the LORD to me: 'Make for yourselves bonds and yokes, and put them on your neck, [3]and send them to the king of Edom, the king of Moab, the king of the Ammonites, the king of Tyre, and the king of Sidon, by the hand of the messengers who come to Jerusalem to Zedekiah king of Judah. [4]And command them to say to their masters, "Thus says the LORD of hosts, the God of Israel—thus you shall say to your masters: [5]'I have made the earth, the man and the beast that *are* on the ground, by My great power and by My outstretched arm, and have given it to whom it seemed proper to Me. [6]And now I have given all these lands into the hand of Nebuchadnezzar the king of Babylon, My servant; and the beasts of the field I have also given him to serve him. [7]So all nations shall serve him and his son and his son's son, until the time of his land comes; and then many nations and great kings shall make him serve them. [8]And it shall be, *that* the nation and kingdom which will not serve Nebuchadnezzar the king of Babylon, and which will not put its neck under the yoke of the king of Babylon, that nation I will punish,' says the LORD, 'with the sword, the famine, and the pestilence, until I have consumed them by his hand. [9]Therefore do not listen to your prophets, your diviners, your dreamers, your soothsayers, or your sorcerers, who speak to you, saying, "You shall not serve the king of Babylon." [10]For they prophesy a lie to you, to remove you far from your land; and I will drive you out, and you will perish. [11]But the nations that bring their necks under the yoke of the king of Babylon and serve him, I will let them remain in their own land,' says the LORD, 'and they shall till it and dwell in it.' " ' "

[12]I also spoke to Zedekiah king of Judah according to all these words, saying, "Bring your necks under the yoke of the king of Babylon, and serve him and his people, and live! [13]Why will you die, you and your people, by the sword, by the famine, and by the pestilence, as the LORD has spoken against the nation that will not serve the king of Babylon? [14]Therefore do not listen to the words of the prophets who speak to you, saying, 'You shall not serve the king of

27:1 [a]Following Masoretic Text, Targum, and Vulgate; some Hebrew manuscripts, Arabic, and Syriac read *Zedekiah* (compare 27:3, 12; 28:1). [b]Septuagint omits verse 1.

THE MESSAGE

King Jehoiakim and his royal court heard his sermon, they determined to kill him. Uriah, afraid for his life, went into hiding in Egypt. King Jehoiakim sent Elnathan son of Achbor with a posse of men after him. They brought him back from Egypt and presented him to the king. And the king had him killed. They dumped his body unceremoniously outside the city.

24 But in Jeremiah's case, Ahikam son of Shaphan stepped forward and took his side, preventing the mob from lynching him.)

HARNESS YOURSELVES UP TO THE YOKE

1-4 27 Early in the reign of Zedekiah son of Josiah king of Judah, Jeremiah received this Message from GOD: "Make a harness and a yoke and then harness yourself up. Send a message to the kings of Edom, Moab, Ammon, Tyre, and Sidon. Send it through their ambassadors who have come to Jerusalem to see Zedekiah king of Judah. Give them this charge to take back to their masters: 'This is a Message from GOD-of-the-Angel-Armies, the God of Israel. Tell your masters:

5-8 " 'I'm the one who made the earth, man and woman, and all the animals in the world. I did it on my own without asking anyone's help and I hand it out to whomever I will. Here and now I give all these lands over to my servant Nebuchadnezzar king of Babylon. I have made even the wild animals subject to him. All nations will be under him, then his son, and then his grandson. Then his country's time will be up and the tables will be turned: *Babylon* will be the underdog servant. But until then, any nation or kingdom that won't submit to Nebuchadnezzar king of Babylon must take the yoke of the king of Babylon and harness up. I'll punish that nation with war and starvation and disease until I've got them where I want them.

9-11 " 'So don't for a minute listen to all your prophets and spiritualists and fortunetellers, who claim to know the future and who tell you not to give in to the king of Babylon. They're handing you a line of lies, barefaced lies, that will end up putting you in exile far from home. I myself will drive you out of your lands, and that'll be the end of you. But the nation that accepts the yoke of the king of Babylon and does what he says, I'll let that nation stay right where it is, minding its own business.' "

12-15 Then I gave this same message to Zedekiah king of Judah: "Harness yourself up to the yoke of the king of Babylon. Serve him and his people. Live a long life! Why choose to get killed or starve to death or get sick and die, which is what GOD has threatened to any nation that won't throw its lot in with Babylon? Don't listen to the prophets who are telling you not to submit to the king of

New King James Version

Babylon,' for they prophesy a lie to you; 15for I
have not sent them," says the LORD, "yet they
prophesy a lie in My name, that I may drive you
out, and that you may perish, you and the
prophets who prophesy to you."
16Also I spoke to the priests and to all this
people, saying, "Thus says the LORD: 'Do not lis-
ten to the words of your prophets who prophesy
to you, saying, "Behold, the vessels of the LORD's
house will now shortly be brought back from
Babylon"; for they prophesy a lie to you. 17Do
not listen to them; serve the king of Babylon,
and live! Why should this city be laid waste?
18But if they *are* prophets, and if the word of the
LORD is with them, let them now make interces-
sion to the LORD of hosts, that the vessels which
are left in the house of the LORD, *in* the house of
the king of Judah, and at Jerusalem, do not go to
Babylon.'
19"For thus says the LORD of hosts concern-
ing the pillars, concerning the Sea, concerning
the carts, and concerning the remainder of the
vessels that remain in this city, 20which Ne-
buchadnezzar king of Babylon did not take,
when he carried away captive Jeconiah the son
of Jehoiakim, king of Judah, from Jerusalem to
Babylon, and all the nobles of Judah and
Jerusalem— 21yes, thus says the LORD of hosts,
the God of Israel, concerning the vessels that re-
main in the house of the LORD, and in the house
of the king of Judah and of Jerusalem: 22'They
shall be carried to Babylon, and there they shall
be until the day that I visit them,' says the LORD.
'Then I will bring them up and restore them to
this place.' "

Hananiah's Falsehood and Doom

28 And it happened in the same year, at the
beginning of the reign of Zedekiah king of
Judah, in the fourth year *and* in the fifth month,
that Hananiah the son of Azur the prophet, who
was from Gibeon, spoke to me in the house of
the LORD in the presence of the priests and of all
the people, saying, 2"Thus speaks the LORD of
hosts, the God of Israel, saying: 'I have broken
the yoke of the king of Babylon. 3Within two full
years I will bring back to this place all the ves-
sels of the LORD's house, that Nebuchadnezzar
king of Babylon took away from this place and
carried to Babylon. 4And I will bring back to this
place Jeconiah the son of Jehoiakim, king of Ju-
dah, with all the captives of Judah who went to
Babylon,' says the LORD, 'for I will break the
yoke of the king of Babylon.' "
5Then the prophet Jeremiah spoke to the
prophet Hananiah in the presence of the priests
and in the presence of all the people who stood
in the house of the LORD, 6and the prophet Jere-
miah said, "Amen! The LORD do so; the LORD
perform your words which you have prophe-
sied, to bring back the vessels of the LORD's
house and all who were carried away captive,
from Babylon to this place. 7Nevertheless hear
now this word that I speak in your hearing and
in the hearing of all the people: 8The prophets
who have been before me and before you of old
prophesied against many countries and great

The Message

Babylon. They're telling you lies, *preaching
lies*. GOD's Word on this is, 'I didn't send
those prophets, but they keep preaching
lies, claiming I sent them. If you listen to
them, I'll end up driving you out of here and
that will be the end of you, both you and the
lying prophets.' "
16-22 And finally I spoke to the priests and the
people at large: "This is GOD's Message:
Don't listen to the preaching of the prophets
who keep telling you, 'Trust us: The furnish-
ings, plundered from GOD's Temple, are go-
ing to be returned from Babylon any day
now.' That's a lie. Don't listen to them. Sub-
mit to the king of Babylon and live a long
life. Why do something that will destroy this
city and leave it a heap of rubble? If they are
real prophets and have a Message from
GOD, let them come to GOD-of-the-Angel-
Armies in prayer so that the furnishings that
are still left in GOD's Temple, the king's
palace, and Jerusalem aren't also lost to
Babylon. That's because GOD-of-the-Angel-
Armies has already spoken about the Tem-
ple furnishings that remain—the pillars, the
great bronze basin, the stands, and all the
other bowls and chalices that Nebuchadnez-
zar king of Babylon didn't take when he
took Jehoiachin son of Jehoiakim off to
Babylonian exile along with all the leaders
of Judah and Jerusalem. He said that the
furnishings left behind in the Temple of GOD
and in the royal palace and in Jerusalem
will be taken off to Babylon and stay there
until, in GOD's words, 'I take the matter up
again and bring them back where they be-
long.' "

From a Wooden to an Iron Yoke

1-2 28 Later that same year (it was in the fifth
month of King Zedekiah's fourth year)
Hananiah son of Azzur, a prophet from
Gibeon, confronted Jeremiah in the Temple
of God in front of the priests and all the peo-
ple who were there. Hananiah said:
2-4 "This Message is straight from GOD-of-
the-Angel-Armies, the God of Israel: 'I will
most certainly break the yoke of the king of
Babylon. Before two years are out I'll have
all the furnishings of GOD's Temple back
here, all the things that Nebuchadnezzar
king of Babylon plundered and hauled off to
Babylon. I'll also bring back Jehoiachin son
of Jehoiakim king of Judah and all the ex-
iles who were taken off to Babylon.' GOD's
Decree. 'Yes, I will break the king of Bab-
ylon's yoke. You'll no longer be in harness to
him.' "
5-9 Prophet Jeremiah stood up to prophet
Hananiah in front of the priests and all the
people who were in GOD's Temple that day.
Prophet Jeremiah said, "Wonderful! Would
that it were true—that GOD would validate
your preaching by bringing the Temple fur-
nishings and all the exiles back from Bab-
ylon. But listen to me, listen closely. Listen to
what I tell both you and all the people here
today: The old prophets, the ones before our
time, preached judgment against many

New King James Version

kingdoms—of war and disaster and pestilence.
9As for the prophet who prophesies of peace,
when the word of the prophet comes to pass, the
prophet will be known *as* one whom the LORD
has truly sent."
10Then Hananiah the prophet took the yoke
off the prophet Jeremiah's neck and broke it.
11And Hananiah spoke in the presence of all the
people, saying, "Thus says the LORD: 'Even so I
will break the yoke of Nebuchadnezzar king of
Babylon from the neck of all nations within the
space of two full years.' " And the prophet Jere-
miah went his way.
12Now the word of the LORD came to Jere-
miah, after Hananiah the prophet had broken
the yoke from the neck of the prophet Jeremiah,
saying, 13"Go and tell Hananiah, saying, 'Thus
says the LORD: "You have broken the yokes of
wood, but you have made in their place yokes of
iron." 14For thus says the LORD of hosts, the God
of Israel: "I have put a yoke of iron on the neck
of all these nations, that they may serve Ne-
buchadnezzar king of Babylon; and they shall
serve him. I have given him the beasts of the
field also." ' "
15Then the prophet Jeremiah said to Hana-
niah the prophet, "Hear now, Hananiah, the
LORD has not sent you, but you make this people
trust in a lie. 16Therefore thus says the LORD:
'Behold, I will cast you from the face of the
earth. This year you shall die, because you have
taught rebellion against the LORD.' "
17So Hananiah the prophet died the same
year in the seventh month.

Jeremiah's Letter to the Captives

29 Now these *are* the words of the letter that
Jeremiah the prophet sent from Jerusalem
to the remainder of the elders who were carried
away captive—to the priests, the prophets, and
all the people whom Nebuchadnezzar had car-
ried away captive from Jerusalem to Babylon.
2(This happened after Jeconiah the king, the
queen mother, the eunuchs, the princes of Judah
and Jerusalem, the craftsmen, and the smiths
had departed from Jerusalem.) 3*The letter was
sent* by the hand of Elasah the son of Shaphan,
and Gemariah the son of Hilkiah, whom
Zedekiah king of Judah sent to Babylon, to Ne-
buchadnezzar king of Babylon, saying,

4Thus says the LORD of hosts, the God of
Israel, to all who were carried away
captive, whom I have caused to be carried
away from Jerusalem to Babylon:

5Build houses and dwell *in them;* plant
gardens and eat their fruit. 6Take wives
and beget sons and daughters; and take
wives for your sons and give your
daughters to husbands, so that they may
bear sons and daughters—that you may be
increased there, and not diminished. 7And
seek the peace of the city where I have
caused you to be carried away captive, and
pray to the LORD for it; for in its peace you
will have peace.

The Message

countries and kingdoms, warning of war
and disaster and plague. So any prophet
who preaches that everything is just fine
and there's nothing to worry about stands
out like a sore thumb. We'll wait and see. If
it happens, it happens—and then we'll know
that GOD sent him."
10-11 At that, Hananiah grabbed the yoke from
Jeremiah's shoulders and smashed it. And
then he addressed the people: "This is GOD's
Message: In just this way I will smash the
yoke of the king of Babylon and get him off
the neck of all the nations—and within two
years."
Jeremiah walked out.
12-14 Later, sometime after Hananiah had
smashed the yoke from off his shoulders, Je-
remiah received this Message from GOD:
"Go back to Hananiah and tell him, 'This is
GOD's Message: You smashed the wooden
yoke-bars; now you've got iron yoke-bars.
This is a Message from GOD-of-the-Angel-
Armies, Israel's own God: I've put an iron
yoke on all these nations. They're harnessed
to Nebuchadnezzar king of Babylon. They'll
do just what he tells them. Why, I'm even
putting him in charge of the wild animals.' "
15-16 So prophet Jeremiah told prophet Hana-
niah, "Hold it, Hananiah! GOD never sent
you. You've talked the whole country into
believing a pack of lies! And so GOD says,
'You claim to be sent? I'll send you all
right—right off the face of the earth! Before
the year is out, you'll be dead because you
fomented sedition against GOD.' "
17 Prophet Hananiah died that very year, in
the seventh month.

Plans to Give You the Future You Hope For

1-2 29 This is the letter that the prophet Jere-
miah sent from Jerusalem to what was
left of the elders among the exiles, to the
priests and prophets and all the exiles
whom Nebuchadnezzar had taken to Bab-
ylon from Jerusalem, including King Je-
hoiachin, the queen mother, the government
leaders, and all the skilled laborers and
craftsmen.
3 The letter was carried by Elasah son of
Shaphan and Gemariah son of Hilkiah, whom
Zedekiah king of Judah had sent to Ne-
buchadnezzar king of Babylon. The letter said:

4 This is the Message from GOD-of-the-
Angel-Armies, Israel's God, to all the
exiles I've taken from Jerusalem to
Babylon:
5 "Build houses and make your-
selves at home.
"Put in gardens and eat what
grows in that country.
6 "Marry and have children. Encour-
age your children to marry and have
children so that you'll thrive in that
country and not waste away.
7 "Make yourselves at home there
and work for the country's welfare.
"Pray for Babylon's well-being. If
things go well for Babylon, things will
go well for you."

New King James Version

8 For thus says the LORD of hosts, the God
of Israel: Do not let your prophets and
your diviners who are in your midst
deceive you, nor listen to your dreams
which you cause to be dreamed. 9 For they
prophesy falsely to you in My name; I have
not sent them, says the LORD.

10 For thus says the LORD: After seventy
years are completed at Babylon, I will visit
you and perform My good word toward
you, and cause you to return to this place.
11 For I know the thoughts that I think
toward you, says the LORD, thoughts of
peace and not of evil, to give you a future
and a hope. 12 Then you will call upon Me
and go and pray to Me, and I will listen to
you. 13 And you will seek Me and find *Me,*
when you search for Me with all your
heart. 14 I will be found by you, says the
LORD, and I will bring you back from your
captivity; I will gather you from all the
nations and from all the places where I
have driven you, says the LORD, and I will
bring you to the place from which I cause
you to be carried away captive.

15 Because you have said, "The LORD has
raised up prophets for us in Babylon"—
16 therefore thus says the LORD concerning
the king who sits on the throne of David,
concerning all the people who dwell in this
city, and concerning your brethren who
have not gone out with you into captivity—
17 thus says the LORD of hosts: Behold, I will
send on them the sword, the famine, and
the pestilence, and will make them like
rotten figs that cannot be eaten, they are
so bad. 18 And I will pursue them with the
sword, with famine, and with pestilence;
and I will deliver them to trouble among
all the kingdoms of the earth—to be a
curse, an astonishment, a hissing, and a
reproach among all the nations where I
have driven them, 19 because they have not
heeded My words, says the LORD, which I
sent to them by My servants the prophets,
rising up early and sending *them;* neither
would you heed, says the LORD.
20 Therefore hear the word of the LORD, all
you of the captivity, whom I have sent
from Jerusalem to Babylon.

21 Thus says the LORD of hosts, the God of
Israel, concerning Ahab the son of
Kolaiah, and Zedekiah the son of
Maaseiah, who prophesy a lie to you in My
name: Behold, I will deliver them into the
hand of Nebuchadnezzar king of Babylon,
and he shall slay them before your eyes.
22 And because of them a curse shall be
taken up by all the captivity of Judah who

The Message

8-9 Yes. Believe it or not, this is the
Message from GOD-of-the-Angel-
Armies, Israel's God: "Don't let all
those so-called preachers and know-
it-alls who are all over the place there
take you in with their lies. Don't pay
any attention to the fantasies they
keep coming up with to please you.
They're a bunch of liars preaching
lies—and claiming I sent them! I never
sent them, believe me." GOD's Decree!
10-11 This is GOD's Word on the subject:
"As soon as Babylon's seventy years
are up and not a day before, I'll show
up and take care of you as I promised
and bring you back home. I know
what I'm doing. I have it all planned
out—plans to take care of you, not
abandon you, plans to give you the fu-
ture you hope for.
12 "When you call on me, when you
come and pray to me, I'll listen.
13-14 "When you come looking for me,
you'll find me.
"Yes, when you get serious about
finding me and want it more than any-
thing else, I'll make sure you won't be
disappointed." GOD's Decree.
"I'll turn things around for you. I'll
bring you back from all the countries
into which I drove you"—GOD's De-
cree—"bring you home to the place
from which I sent you off into exile.
You can count on it.
15-19 "But for right now, because you've
taken up with these new-fangled
prophets who set themselves up as
'Babylonian specialists,' spreading
the word 'GOD sent them just for us!'
GOD is setting the record straight: As
for the king still sitting on David's
throne and all the people left in
Jerusalem who didn't go into exile
with you, they're facing bad times.
GOD-of-the-Angel-Armies says, 'Watch
this! Catastrophe is on the way: war,
hunger, disease! They're a barrel of
rotten apples. I'll rid the country of
them through war and hunger and
disease. The whole world is going to
hold its nose at the smell, shut its eyes
at the horrible sight. They'll end up in
slum ghettos because they wouldn't
listen to a thing I said when I sent my
servant-prophets preaching tirelessly
and urgently. No, they wouldn't listen
to a word I said.' " GOD's Decree.
20-23 "And you—you exiles whom I sent
out of Jerusalem to Babylon—listen to
GOD's Message to you. As far as Ahab
son of Kolaiah and Zedekiah son of
Maaseiah are concerned, the 'Bab-
ylonian specialists' who are preaching
lies in my name, I will turn them over
to Nebuchadnezzar king of Babylon,
who will kill them while you watch.
The exiles from Judah will take what
they see at the execution and use it as

NEW KING JAMES VERSION

are in Babylon, saying, "The LORD make you like Zedekiah and Ahab, whom the king of Babylon roasted in the fire";
23because they have done disgraceful things in Israel, have committed adultery with their neighbors' wives, and have spoken lying words in My name, which I have not commanded them. Indeed I know, and *am* a witness, says the LORD.

24You shall also speak to Shemaiah the Nehelamite, saying, 25Thus speaks the LORD of hosts, the God of Israel, saying: You have sent letters in your name to all the people who *are* at Jerusalem, to Zephaniah the son of Maaseiah the priest, and to all the priests, saying, 26"The LORD has made you priest instead of Jehoiada the priest, so that there should be officers *in* the house of the LORD over every man *who* is demented and considers himself a prophet, that you should put him in prison and in the stocks. 27Now therefore, why have you not rebuked Jeremiah of Anathoth who makes himself a prophet to you? 28For he has sent to us *in* Babylon, saying, 'This *captivity is* long; build houses and dwell *in them*, and plant gardens and eat their fruit.' "

29Now Zephaniah the priest read this letter in the hearing of Jeremiah the prophet.
30Then the word of the LORD came to Jeremiah, saying: 31Send to all those in captivity, saying, Thus says the LORD concerning Shemaiah the Nehelamite: Because Shemaiah has prophesied to you, and I have not sent him, and he has caused you to trust in a lie— 32therefore thus says the LORD: Behold, I will punish Shemaiah the Nehelamite and his family: he shall not have anyone to dwell among this people, nor shall he see the good that I will do for My people, says the LORD, because he has taught rebellion against the LORD.

RESTORATION OF ISRAEL AND JUDAH

30 The word that came to Jeremiah from the LORD, saying, 2"Thus speaks the LORD God of Israel, saying: 'Write in a book for yourself all the words that I have spoken to you. 3For behold, the days are coming,' says the LORD, 'that I will bring back from captivity My people Israel and Judah,' says the LORD. 'And I will cause them to return to the land that I gave to their fathers, and they shall possess it.' "
4Now these *are* the words that the LORD spoke concerning Israel and Judah.
5"For thus says the LORD:

'We have heard a voice of trembling,
Of fear, and not of peace.
6Ask now, and see,
Whether a man is ever in labor with child?

THE MESSAGE

a curse: 'GOD fry you to a crisp like the king of Babylon fried Zedekiah and Ahab in the fire!' Those two men, sex predators and prophet-impostors, got what they deserved. They pulled every woman they got their hands on into bed—their neighbors' wives, no less—and preached lies claiming it was my Message. I never sent those men. I've never had anything to do with them." GOD's Decree.
"They won't get away with a thing. I've witnessed it all."

24-26 And this is the Message for Shemaiah the Nehelamite: "GOD-of-the-Angel-Armies, the God of Israel, says: You took it on yourself to send letters to all the people in Jerusalem and to the priest Zephaniah son of Maaseiah and the company of priests. In your letter you told Zephaniah that GOD set you up as priest replacing priest Jehoiadah. He's put you in charge of GOD's Temple and made you responsible for locking up any crazy fellow off the street who takes it into his head to be a prophet.
27-28 "So why haven't you done anything about muzzling Jeremiah of Anathoth, who's going around posing as a prophet? He's gone so far as to write to us in Babylon, 'It's going to be a long exile, so build houses and make yourselves at home. Plant gardens and prepare Babylonian recipes.' "

29 The priest Zephaniah read that letter to the prophet Jeremiah.

30-32 Then GOD told Jeremiah, "Send this Message to the exiles. Tell them what GOD says about Shemaiah the Nehelamite: Shemaiah is preaching lies to you. I didn't send him. He is seducing you into believing lies. So this is GOD's verdict: I will punish Shemaiah the Nehelamite and his whole family. He's going to end up with nothing and no one. No one from his family will be around to see any of the good that I am going to do for my people because he has preached rebellion against me." GOD's Decree.

DON'T DESPAIR, ISRAEL

1-2 30 This is the Message Jeremiah received from GOD: "GOD's Message, the God of Israel: 'Write everything I tell you in a book.
3 " 'Look. The time is coming when I will turn everything around for my people, both Israel and Judah. I, GOD, say so. I'll bring them back to the land I gave their ancestors, and they'll take up ownership again.' "
4 This is the way GOD put it to Israel and Judah:

5-7 "GOD's Message:

" 'Cries of panic are being heard.
The peace has been shattered.
Ask around! Look around!
Can men bear babies?

NEW KING JAMES VERSION

So why do I see every man *with* his hands
on his loins
Like a woman in labor,
And all faces turned pale?
7Alas! For that day *is* great,
So that none *is* like it;
And it *is* the time of Jacob's trouble,
But he shall be saved out of it.

8'For it shall come to pass in that day,'
Says the LORD of hosts,
'*That* I will break his yoke from your neck,
And will burst your bonds;
Foreigners shall no more enslave them.
9But they shall serve the LORD their God,
And David their king,
Whom I will raise up for them.

10"Therefore do not fear, O My servant Jacob,'
says the LORD,
'Nor be dismayed, O Israel;
For behold, I will save you from afar,
And your seed from the land of their
captivity.
Jacob shall return, have rest and be quiet,
And no one shall make *him* afraid.
11For I *am* with you,' says the LORD, 'to save
you;
Though I make a full end of all nations
where I have scattered you,
Yet I will not make a complete end of you.
But I will correct you in justice,
And will not let you go altogether
unpunished.'

12"For thus says the LORD:

'Your affliction *is* incurable,
Your wound *is* severe.
13*There is* no one to plead your cause,
That you may be bound up;
You have no healing medicines.
14All your lovers have forgotten you;
They do not seek you;
For I have wounded you with the wound of
an enemy,
With the chastisement of a cruel one,
For the multitude of your iniquities,
Because your sins have increased.
15Why do you cry about your affliction?
Your sorrow *is* incurable.
Because of the multitude of your iniquities,
Because your sins have increased,
I have done these things to you.

16'Therefore all those who devour you shall be
devoured;
And all your adversaries, every one of them,
shall go into captivity;
Those who plunder you shall become
plunder,
And all who prey upon you I will make a
prey.
17For I will restore health to you
And heal you of your wounds,' says the
LORD,
'Because they called you an outcast *saying*:
"This *is* Zion;
No one seeks her." '

THE MESSAGE

So why do I see all these he-men
holding their bellies like women in labor,
Faces contorted,
pale as death?
The blackest of days,
no day like it ever!
A time of deep trouble for Jacob—
but he'll come out of it alive.

8-9 " 'And then I'll enter the darkness.
I'll break the yoke from their necks,
Cut them loose from the harness.
No more slave labor to foreigners!
They'll serve their GOD
and the David-King I'll establish for
them.

10-11 " 'So fear no more, Jacob, dear servant.
Don't despair, Israel.
Look up! I'll save you out of faraway
places,
I'll bring your children back from exile.
Jacob will come back and find life good,
safe and secure.
I'll be with you. I'll save you.
I'll finish off all the godless nations
Among which I've scattered you,
but I won't finish you off.
I'll punish you, but fairly.
I won't send you off with just a slap on
the wrist.'

12-15 "This is GOD's Message:

" 'You're a burned-out case,
as good as dead.
Everyone has given up on you.
You're hopeless.
All your fair-weather friends have skipped
town
without giving you a second thought.
But I delivered the knockout blow,
a punishment you will never forget,
Because of the enormity of your guilt,
the endless list of your sins.
So why all this self-pity, licking your
wounds?
You deserve all this, and more.
Because of the enormity of your guilt,
the endless list of your sins,
I've done all this to you.

16-17 " 'Everyone who hurt you will be hurt;
your enemies will end up as slaves.
Your plunderers will be plundered;
your looters will become loot.
As for you, I'll come with healing,
curing the incurable,
Because they all gave up on you
and dismissed you as hopeless—
that good-for-nothing Zion.'

NEW KING JAMES VERSION

18"Thus says the LORD:

'Behold, I will bring back the captivity of
Jacob's tents,
And have mercy on his dwelling places;
The city shall be built upon its own mound,
And the palace shall remain according to its
own plan.
19Then out of them shall proceed
thanksgiving
And the voice of those who make merry;
I will multiply them, and they shall not
diminish;
I will also glorify them, and they shall not
be small.
20Their children also shall be as before,
And their congregation shall be established
before Me;
And I will punish all who oppress them.
21Their nobles shall be from among them,
And their governor shall come from their
midst;
Then I will cause him to draw near,
And he shall approach Me;
For who *is* this who pledged his heart to
approach Me?' says the LORD.
22'You shall be My people,
And I will be your God.' "

23Behold, the whirlwind of the LORD
Goes forth with fury,
A continuing whirlwind;
It will fall violently on the head of the
wicked.
24The fierce anger of the LORD will not return
until He has done it,
And until He has performed the intents of
His heart.

In the latter days you will consider it.

THE REMNANT OF ISRAEL SAVED

31 "At the same time," says the LORD, "I will
be the God of all the families of Israel, and
they shall be My people."
2Thus says the LORD:

"The people who survived the sword
Found grace in the wilderness—
Israel, when I went to give him rest."

3The LORD has appeared of old to me, *saying*:
"Yes, I have loved you with an everlasting
love;
Therefore with lovingkindness I have drawn
you.
4Again I will build you, and you shall be
rebuilt,
O virgin of Israel!
You shall again be adorned with your
tambourines,
And shall go forth in the dances of those
who rejoice.

THE MESSAGE

18-21 "Again, GOD's Message:

" 'I'll turn things around for Jacob.
I'll compassionately come in and rebuild
homes.
The town will be rebuilt on its old
foundations;
the mansions will be splendid again.
Thanksgivings will pour out of the
windows;
laughter will spill through the doors.
Things will get better and better.
Depression days are over.
They'll thrive, they'll flourish.
The days of contempt will be over.
They'll look forward to having children
again,
to being a community in which I take
pride.
I'll punish anyone who hurts them,
and their prince will come from their
own ranks.
One of their own people shall be their
leader.
Their ruler will come from their own
ranks.
I'll grant him free and easy access to me.
Would anyone dare to do that on his
own,
to enter my presence uninvited?' GOD's
Decree.

22 " 'And that's it: You'll be my very own
people,
I'll be your very own God.' "

23-24 Look out! GOD's hurricane is let loose,
his hurricane blast,
Spinning the heads of the wicked like dust
devils!
God's raging anger won't let up
Until he's made a clean sweep
completing the job he began.
When the job's done
you'll see it's been well done.

1 31 "And when that happens"—GOD's
Decree—
"it will be plain as the sun at high noon:
I'll be the God of every man, woman, and
child in Israel
and they shall be my very own people."

2-6 This is the way GOD put it:

"They found grace out in the desert,
these people who survived the killing.
Israel, out looking for a place to rest,
met God out looking for them!"
GOD told them, "I've never quit loving you
and never will.
Expect love, love, and more love!
And so now I'll start over with you and
build you up again,
dear virgin Israel.
You'll resume your singing,
grabbing tambourines and joining the
dance.

NEW KING JAMES VERSION

5 You shall yet plant vines on the mountains of Samaria;
The planters shall plant and eat *them* as ordinary food.
6 For there shall be a day
When the watchmen will cry on Mount Ephraim,
'Arise, and let us go up *to* Zion,
To the LORD our God.' "

7 For thus says the LORD:

"Sing with gladness for Jacob,
And shout among the chief of the nations;
Proclaim, give praise, and say,
'O LORD, save Your people,
The remnant of Israel!'
8 Behold, I will bring them from the north country,
And gather them from the ends of the earth,
Among them the blind and the lame,
The woman with child
And the one who labors with child, together;
A great throng shall return there.
9 They shall come with weeping,
And with supplications I will lead them.
I will cause them to walk by the rivers of waters,
In a straight way in which they shall not stumble;
For I am a Father to Israel,
And Ephraim *is* My firstborn.

10 "Hear the word of the LORD, O nations,
And declare *it* in the isles afar off, and say,
'He who scattered Israel will gather him,
And keep him as a shepherd *does* his flock.'
11 For the LORD has redeemed Jacob,
And ransomed him from the hand of one stronger than he.
12 Therefore they shall come and sing in the height of Zion,
Streaming to the goodness of the LORD—
For wheat and new wine and oil,
For the young of the flock and the herd;
Their souls shall be like a well-watered garden,
And they shall sorrow no more at all.

13 "Then shall the virgin rejoice in the dance,
And the young men and the old, together;
For I will turn their mourning to joy,
Will comfort them,
And make them rejoice rather than sorrow.

THE MESSAGE

You'll go back to your old work of planting vineyards
on the Samaritan hillsides,
And sit back and enjoy the fruit—
oh, how you'll enjoy those harvests!
The time's coming when watchmen will call out
from the hilltops of Ephraim:
'On your feet! Let's go to Zion,
go to meet our GOD!' "

7 Oh yes, GOD says so:

"Shout for joy at the top of your lungs for Jacob!
Announce the good news to the number-one nation!
Raise cheers! Sing praises. Say,
'GOD has saved his people,
saved the core of Israel.'

8 "Watch what comes next:

"I'll bring my people back
from the north country
And gather them up from the ends of the earth,
gather those who've gone blind
And those who are lame and limping,
gather pregnant women,
Even the mothers whose birth pangs have started,
bring them all back, a huge crowd!

9 "Watch them come! They'll come weeping for joy
as I take their hands and lead them,
Lead them to fresh flowing brooks,
lead them along smooth, uncluttered paths.
Yes, it's because I'm Israel's Father
and Ephraim's my firstborn son!

10-14 "Hear this, nations! GOD's Message!
Broadcast this all over the world!
Tell them, 'The One who scattered Israel
will gather them together again.
From now on he'll keep a careful eye on them,
like a shepherd with his flock.'
I, GOD, will pay a stiff ransom price for Jacob;
I'll free him from the grip of the Babylonian bully.
The people will climb up Zion's slopes
shouting with joy,
their faces beaming because of GOD's bounty—
Grain and wine and oil,
flocks of sheep, herds of cattle.
Their lives will be like a well-watered garden,
never again left to dry up.
Young women will dance and be happy,
young men and old men will join in.
I'll convert their weeping into laughter,
lavishing comfort, invading their grief with joy.

NEW KING JAMES VERSION

14I will satiate the soul of the priests with abundance,
And My people shall be satisfied with My goodness, says the LORD."

MERCY ON EPHRAIM

15Thus says the LORD:

"A voice was heard in Ramah,
Lamentation *and* bitter weeping,
Rachel weeping for her children,
Refusing to be comforted for her children,
Because they *are* no more."

16Thus says the LORD:

"Refrain your voice from weeping,
And your eyes from tears;
For your work shall be rewarded, says the LORD,
And they shall come back from the land of the enemy.
17There is hope in your future, says the LORD,
That *your* children shall come back to their own border.

18"I have surely heard Ephraim bemoaning himself:
'You have chastised me, and I was chastised,
Like an untrained bull;
Restore me, and I will return,
For You *are* the LORD my God.
19Surely, after my turning, I repented;
And after I was instructed, I struck myself on the thigh;
I was ashamed, yes, even humiliated,
Because I bore the reproach of my youth.'
20*Is* Ephraim My dear son?
Is he a pleasant child?
For though I spoke against him,
I earnestly remember him still;
Therefore My heart yearns for him;
I will surely have mercy on him, says the LORD.

21"Set up signposts,
Make landmarks;
Set your heart toward the highway,
The way in *which* you went.
Turn back, O virgin of Israel,
Turn back to these your cities.
22How long will you gad about,
O you backsliding daughter?
For the LORD has created a new thing in the earth—
A woman shall encompass a man."

FUTURE PROSPERITY OF JUDAH

23Thus says the LORD of hosts, the God of Is-
rael: "They shall again use this speech in the
land of Judah and in its cities, when I bring back
their captivity: 'The LORD bless you, O home of
justice, *and* mountain of holiness!' 24And there
shall dwell in Judah itself, and in all its cities to-
gether, farmers and those going out with flocks.

THE MESSAGE

I'll make sure that their priests get three square meals a day
and that my people have more than enough.' " GOD's Decree.

15-17 Again, GOD's Message:

"Listen to this! Laments coming out of Ramah,
wild and bitter weeping.
It's Rachel weeping for her children,
Rachel refusing all solace.
Her children are gone,
gone—long gone into exile."
But GOD says, "Stop your incessant weeping,
hold back your tears.
Collect wages from your grief work." GOD's Decree.
"They'll be coming back home!
There's hope for your children." GOD's Decree.

18-19 "I've heard the contrition of Ephraim.
Yes, I've heard it clearly, saying,
'You trained me well.
You broke me, a wild yearling horse, to the saddle.
Now put me, trained and obedient, to use.
You are my GOD.
After those years of running loose, I repented.
After you trained me to obedience,
I was ashamed of my past, my wild, unruly past.
Humiliated, I beat on my chest.
Will I ever live this down?'

20 "Oh! Ephraim is my dear, dear son,
my child in whom I take pleasure!
Every time I mention his name,
my heart bursts with longing for him!
Everything in me cries out for him.
Softly and tenderly I wait for him." GOD's Decree.

21-22 "Set up signposts to mark your trip home.
Get a good map.
Study the road conditions.
The road out is the road back.
Come back, dear virgin Israel,
come back to your hometowns.
How long will you flit here and there, indecisive?
How long before you make up your fickle mind?
GOD will create a new thing in this land:
A transformed woman will embrace the transforming GOD!"

23-24 A Message from Israel's GOD-of-the-Angel-
Armies: "When I've turned everything
around and brought my people back, the old
expressions will be heard on the streets:
'GOD bless you!' . . . 'O True Home!' . . . 'O
Holy Mountain!' All Judah's people,
whether in town or country, will get along
just fine with each other.

NEW KING JAMES VERSION

25For I have satiated the weary soul, and I have
replenished every sorrowful soul."
26After this I awoke and looked around, and
my sleep was sweet to me.
27"Behold, the days are coming, says the
LORD, that I will sow the house of Israel and the
house of Judah with the seed of man and the seed
of beast. 28And it shall come to pass, *that* as I
have watched over them to pluck up, to break
down, to throw down, to destroy, and to afflict, so
I will watch over them to build and to plant, says
the LORD. 29In those days they shall say no more:

'The fathers have eaten sour grapes,
And the children's teeth are set on edge.'

30But every one shall die for his own iniquity;
every man who eats the sour grapes, his teeth
shall be set on edge.

A NEW COVENANT

31"Behold, the days are coming, says the
LORD, when I will make a new covenant with
the house of Israel and with the house of Ju-
dah— 32not according to the covenant that I
made with their fathers in the day *that* I took
them by the hand to lead them out of the land
of Egypt, My covenant which they broke,
though I was a husband to them,[a] says the
LORD. 33But this *is* the covenant that I will make
with the house of Israel after those days, says
the LORD: I will put My law in their minds, and
write it on their hearts; and I will be their God,
and they shall be My people. 34No more shall
every man teach his neighbor, and every man
his brother, saying, 'Know the LORD,' for they
all shall know Me, from the least of them to the
greatest of them, says the LORD. For I will for-
give their iniquity, and their sin I will remember
no more."

35Thus says the LORD,
Who gives the sun for a light by day,
The ordinances of the moon and the stars
for a light by night,
Who disturbs the sea,
And its waves roar
(The LORD of hosts *is* His name):

36"If those ordinances depart
From before Me, says the LORD,
Then the seed of Israel shall also cease
From being a nation before Me forever."

37Thus says the LORD:

"If heaven above can be measured,
And the foundations of the earth searched
out beneath,
I will also cast off all the seed of Israel
For all that they have done, says the LORD.

31:32 [a]Following Masoretic Text, Targum, and Vulgate; Septuagint and Syriac read *and I turned away from them.*

THE MESSAGE

25 I'll refresh tired bodies;
I'll restore tired souls.

26 Just then I woke up and looked around—
what a pleasant and satisfying sleep!

27-28 "Be ready. The time's coming"—GOD's De-
cree—"when I will plant people and animals
in Israel and Judah, just as a farmer plants
seed. And in the same way that earlier I re-
lentlessly pulled up and tore down, took
apart and demolished, so now I am sticking
with them as they start over, building and
planting.
29 "When that time comes you won't hear
the old proverb anymore,

Parents ate the green apples,
their children got the stomachache.

30 "No, each person will pay for his own sin.
You eat green apples, you're the one who
gets sick.

31-32 "That's right. The time is coming when I will
make a brand-new covenant with Israel and
Judah. It won't be a repeat of the covenant I
made with their ancestors when I took their
hand to lead them out of the land of Egypt.
They broke that covenant even though I did
my part as their Master." GOD's Decree.
33-34 "This is the brand-new covenant that I
will make with Israel when the time comes.
I will put my law within them—write it on
their hearts!—and be their God. And they
will be my people. They will no longer go
around setting up schools to teach each
other about GOD. They'll know me firsthand,
the dull and the bright, the smart and the
slow. I'll wipe the slate clean for each of
them. I'll forget they ever sinned!" GOD's
Decree.

IF THIS ORDERED COSMOS EVER FELL TO PIECES

35 GOD's Message, from the God who lights up
the day with sun and
brightens the night with moon and stars,
Who whips the ocean into a billowy froth,
whose name is GOD-of-the-Angel-Armies:

36 "If this ordered cosmos ever fell to pieces,
fell into chaos before me"—GOD's
Decree—
"Then and only then might Israel fall apart
and disappear as a nation before me."

37 GOD's Message:

"If the skies could be measured with a
yardstick
and the earth explored to its core,
Then and only then would I turn my back
on Israel,
disgusted with all they've done." GOD's
Decree.

NEW KING JAMES VERSION

38“Behold, the days are coming, says the
LORD, that the city shall be built for the LORD
from the Tower of Hananel to the Corner Gate.
39The surveyor’s line shall again extend straight
forward over the hill Gareb; then it shall turn to-
ward Goath. 40And the whole valley of the dead
bodies and of the ashes, and all the fields as far
as the Brook Kidron, to the corner of the Horse
Gate toward the east, *shall be* holy to the LORD.
It shall not be plucked up or thrown down any-
more forever.”

JEREMIAH BUYS A FIELD

32 The word that came to Jeremiah from the
LORD in the tenth year of Zedekiah king of
Judah, which was the eighteenth year of Ne-
buchadnezzar. 2For then the king of Babylon’s
army besieged Jerusalem, and Jeremiah the
prophet was shut up in the court of the prison,
which *was in* the king of Judah’s house. 3For
Zedekiah king of Judah had shut him up, say-
ing, “Why do you prophesy and say, ‘Thus says
the LORD: “Behold, I will give this city into the
hand of the king of Babylon, and he shall take it;
4and Zedekiah king of Judah shall not escape
from the hand of the Chaldeans, but shall surely
be delivered into the hand of the king of Bab-
ylon, and shall speak with him face to face,[a] and
see him eye to eye; 5then he shall lead Zedekiah
to Babylon, and there he shall be until I visit
him,” says the LORD; “though you fight with the
Chaldeans, you shall not succeed” ’?”
6And Jeremiah said, “The word of the LORD
came to me, saying, 7‘Behold, Hanamel the son
of Shallum your uncle will come to you, saying,
“Buy my field which *is* in Anathoth, for the right
of redemption *is* yours to buy *it*.” ’ 8Then
Hanamel my uncle’s son came to me in the court
of the prison according to the word of the LORD,
and said to me, ‘Please buy my field that *is* in
Anathoth, which *is* in the country of Benjamin;
for the right of inheritance *is* yours, and the re-
demption yours; buy *it* for yourself.’ Then I
knew that this was the word of the LORD. 9So I
bought the field from Hanamel, the son of my
uncle who *was* in Anathoth, and weighed *out to*
him the money—seventeen shekels of silver.
10And I signed the deed and sealed *it*, took wit-
nesses, and weighed the money on the scales.
11So I took the purchase deed, *both* that which
was sealed *according* to the law and custom,
and that which was open; 12and I gave the pur-
chase deed to Baruch the son of Neriah, son of
Mahseiah, in the presence of Hanamel my un-
cle’s *son*, and in the presence of the witnesses
who signed the purchase deed, before all the
Jews who sat in the court of the prison.
13“Then I charged Baruch before them, say-
ing, 14‘Thus says the LORD of hosts, the God of
Israel: “Take these deeds, both this purchase
deed which is sealed and this deed which is
open, and put them in an earthen vessel, that
they may last many days.” 15For thus says the
LORD of hosts, the God of Israel: “Houses and
fields and vineyards shall be possessed again in
this land.” ’

32:4 [a]Literally *mouth to mouth*

THE MESSAGE

38-40 “The time is coming”—it’s GOD’s Decree—
“when GOD’s city will be rebuilt, rebuilt all
the way from the Citadel of Hanamel to the
Corner Gate. The master plan will extend
west to Gareb Hill and then around to
Goath. The whole valley to the south where
incinerated corpses are dumped—a death
valley if there ever was one!—and all the
terraced fields out to the Brook Kidron on
the east as far north as the Horse Gate will
be consecrated to me as a holy place.
“This city will never again be torn down
or destroyed.”

KILLING AND DISEASE ARE ON OUR DOORSTEP

1-5 32 The Message Jeremiah received from
GOD in the tenth year of Zedekiah king
of Judah. It was the eighteenth year of Ne-
buchadnezzar. At that time the army of the
king of Babylon was holding Jerusalem un-
der siege. Jeremiah was shut up in jail in the
royal palace. Zedekiah, king of Judah, had
locked him up, complaining, “How dare you
preach, saying, ‘GOD says, I’m warning you:
I will hand this city over to the king of Bab-
ylon and he will take it over. Zedekiah king of
Judah will be handed over to the Chaldeans
right along with the city. He will be handed
over to the king of Babylon and forced to face
the music. He’ll be hauled off to Babylon
where he’ll stay until I deal with him. GOD’s
Decree. Fight against the Babylonians all you
want—it won’t get you anywhere.’ ”
6-7 Jeremiah said, “GOD’s Message came to
me like this: Prepare yourself! Hanamel,
your uncle Shallum’s son, is on his way to
see you. He is going to say, ‘Buy my field in
Anathoth. You have the legal right to buy it.’
8 “And sure enough, just as GOD had said,
my cousin Hanamel came to me while I was
in jail and said, ‘Buy my field in Anathoth in
the territory of Benjamin, for you have the
legal right to keep it in the family. Buy it.
Take it over.’
“That did it. I knew it was GOD’s Message.
9-12 “So I bought the field at Anathoth from
my cousin Hanamel. I paid him seventeen
silver shekels. I followed all the proper pro-
cedures: In the presence of witnesses I
wrote out the bill of sale, sealed it, and
weighed out the money on the scales. Then
I took the deed of purchase—the sealed
copy that contained the contract and its con-
ditions and also the open copy—and gave
them to Baruch son of Neriah, the son of
Mahseiah. All this took place in the pres-
ence of my cousin Hanamel and the wit-
nesses who had signed the deed, as the Jews
who were at the jail that day looked on.
13-15 “Then, in front of all of them, I told
Baruch, ‘These are orders from GOD-of-the-
Angel-Armies, the God of Israel: Take these
documents—both the sealed and the open
deeds—and put them for safekeeping in a
pottery jar. For GOD-of-the-Angel-Armies,
the God of Israel, says, “Life is going to re-
turn to normal. Homes and fields and vine-
yards are again going to be bought in this
country.” ’

NEW KING JAMES VERSION

JEREMIAH PRAYS FOR UNDERSTANDING

16"Now when I had delivered the purchase deed to Baruch the son of Neriah, I prayed to the LORD, saying: 17'Ah, Lord GOD! Behold, You have made the heavens and the earth by Your great power and outstretched arm. There is nothing too hard for You. 18*You* show lovingkindness to thousands, and repay the iniquity of the fathers into the bosom of their children after them—the Great, the Mighty God, whose name *is* the LORD of hosts. 19*You are* great in counsel and mighty in work, for Your eyes *are* open to all the ways of the sons of men, to give everyone according to his ways and according to the fruit of his doings. 20You have set signs and wonders in the land of Egypt, to this day, and in Israel and among *other* men; and You have made Yourself a name, as it is this day. 21You have brought Your people Israel out of the land of Egypt with signs and wonders, with a strong hand and an outstretched arm, and with great terror; 22You have given them this land, of which You swore to their fathers to give them—"a land flowing with milk and honey."[a] 23And they came in and took possession of it, but they have not obeyed Your voice or walked in Your law. They have done nothing of all that You commanded them to do; therefore You have caused all this calamity to come upon them.

24'Look, the siege mounds! They have come to the city to take it; and the city has been given into the hand of the Chaldeans who fight against it, because of the sword and famine and pestilence. What You have spoken has happened; there You see *it!* 25And You have said to me, O Lord GOD, "Buy the field for money, and take witnesses"!—yet the city has been given into the hand of the Chaldeans.' "

GOD'S ASSURANCE OF THE PEOPLE'S RETURN

26Then the word of the LORD came to Jeremiah, saying, 27"Behold, I *am* the LORD, the God of all flesh. Is there anything too hard for Me? 28Therefore thus says the LORD: 'Behold, I will give this city into the hand of the Chaldeans, into the hand of Nebuchadnezzar king of Babylon, and he shall take it. 29And the Chaldeans who fight against this city shall come and set fire to this city and burn it, with the houses on whose roofs they have offered incense to Baal and poured out drink offerings to other gods, to provoke Me to anger; 30because the children of Israel and the children of Judah have done only evil before Me from their youth. For the children of Israel have provoked Me only to anger with the work of their hands,' says the LORD. 31'For this city has been to Me *a provocation* of My anger and My fury from the day that they built it, even to this day; so I will remove it from before My face 32because of all the evil of the children of Israel and the children of Judah, which they have done to provoke Me to anger—they, their kings, their princes, their priests, their prophets, the men of Judah, and the inhabitants of Jerusalem. 33And they have turned to Me the back, and not the face; though I taught them, rising up early and teaching *them*, yet they have not listened to receive instruction. 34But they set

32:22 [a]Exodus 3:8

THE MESSAGE

16-19 "And then, having handed over the legal documents to Baruch son of Neriah, I prayed to GOD, 'Dear GOD, my Master, you created earth and sky by your great power—by merely stretching out your arm! There is nothing you can't do. You're loyal in your steadfast love to thousands upon thousands—but you also make children live with the fallout from their parents' sins. Great and powerful God, named GOD-of-the-Angel-Armies, determined in purpose and relentless in following through, you see everything that men and women do and respond appropriately to the way they live, to the things they do.

20-23 " 'You performed signs and wonders in the country of Egypt and continue to do so right into the present, right here in Israel and everywhere else, too. You've made a reputation for yourself that doesn't diminish. You brought your people Israel out of Egypt with signs and wonders—a powerful deliverance!—by merely stretching out your arm. You gave them this land and solemnly promised to their ancestors a bountiful and fertile land. But when they entered the land and took it over, they didn't listen to you. They didn't do what you commanded. They wouldn't listen to a thing you told them. And so you brought this disaster on them.

24-25 " 'Oh, look at the siege ramps already set in place to take the city. Killing and starvation and disease are on our doorstep. The Babylonians are attacking! The Word you spoke is coming to pass—it's daily news! And yet you, GOD, the Master, even though it is certain that the city will be turned over to the Babylonians, also told me, Buy the field. Pay for it in cash. And make sure there are witnesses.' "

26-30 Then GOD's Message came again to Jeremiah: "Stay alert! I am GOD, the God of everything living. Is there anything I can't do? So listen to GOD's Message: No doubt about it, I'm handing this city over to the Babylonians and Nebuchadnezzar king of Babylon. He'll take it. The attacking Chaldeans will break through and burn the city down: All those houses whose roofs were used as altars for offerings to Baal and the worship of who knows how many other gods provoked me. It isn't as if this were the first time they had provoked me. The people of Israel and Judah have been doing this for a long time—doing what I hate, making me angry by the way they live." GOD's Decree.

31-35 "This city has made me angry from the day they built it, and now I've had my fill. I'm destroying it. I can't stand to look any longer at the wicked lives of the people of Israel and Judah, deliberately making me angry, the whole lot of them—kings and leaders and priests and preachers, in the country and in the city. They've turned their backs on me—won't even look me in the face!—even though I took great pains to teach them how to live. They refused to listen, refused to be taught. Why, they even set

NEW KING JAMES VERSION

their abominations in the house which is called
by My name, to defile it. 35 And they built the
high places of Baal which *are* in the Valley of the
Son of Hinnom, to cause their sons and their
daughters to pass through *the fire* to Molech,
which I did not command them, nor did it come
into My mind that they should do this abomina-
tion, to cause Judah to sin.'

36 "Now therefore, thus says the LORD, the
God of Israel, concerning this city of which you
say, 'It shall be delivered into the hand of the
king of Babylon by the sword, by the famine,
and by the pestilence: 37 Behold, I will gather
them out of all countries where I have driven
them in My anger, in My fury, and in great
wrath; I will bring them back to this place, and
I will cause them to dwell safely. 38 They shall be
My people, and I will be their God; 39 then I will
give them one heart and one way, that they may
fear Me forever, for the good of them and their
children after them. 40 And I will make an ever-
lasting covenant with them, that I will not turn
away from doing them good; but I will put My
fear in their hearts so that they will not depart
from Me. 41 Yes, I will rejoice over them to do
them good, and I will assuredly plant them in
this land, with all My heart and with all My
soul.'

42 "For thus says the LORD: 'Just as I have
brought all this great calamity on this people, so
I will bring on them all the good that I have
promised them. 43 And fields will be bought in
this land of which you say, "*It is* desolate, with-
out man or beast; it has been given into the
hand of the Chaldeans." 44 Men will buy fields
for money, sign deeds and seal *them,* and take
witnesses, in the land of Benjamin, in the places
around Jerusalem, in the cities of Judah, in the
cities of the mountains, in the cities of the low-
land, and in the cities of the South; for I will
cause their captives to return,' says the LORD."

EXCELLENCE OF THE RESTORED NATION

33 Moreover the word of the LORD came to Jer-
emiah a second time, while he was still
shut up in the court of the prison, saying, 2 "Thus
says the LORD who made it, the LORD who
formed it to establish it (the LORD *is* His name):
3 'Call to Me, and I will answer you, and show
you great and mighty things, which you do not
know.'

4 "For thus says the LORD, the God of Israel,
concerning the houses of this city and the
houses of the kings of Judah, which have been
pulled down *to fortify*[a] against the siege
mounds and the sword: 5 'They come to fight
with the Chaldeans, but *only* to fill their places[a]
with the dead bodies of men whom I will slay in

33:4 [a]Compare Isaiah 22:10 **33:5** [a]Compare 2 Kings 23:14

THE MESSAGE

up obscene god and goddess statues in the Temple built in my honor—an outrageous desecration! And then they went out and built shrines to the god Baal in the valley of Hinnom, where they burned their children in sacrifice to the god Molech—I can hardly conceive of such evil!—turning the whole country into one huge act of sin.

36 "But there is also this Message from me, the GOD of Israel, to this city of which you have said, 'In killing and starvation and disease this city will be delivered up to the king of Babylon':

37-40 " 'Watch for this! I will collect them from all the countries to which I will have driven them in my anger and rage and indignation. Yes, I'll bring them all back to this place and let them live here in peace. They will be my people, I will be their God. I'll make them of one mind and heart, always honoring me, so that they can live good and whole lives, they and their children after them. What's more, I'll make a covenant with them that will last forever, a covenant to stick with them no matter what, and work for their good. I'll fill their hearts with a deep respect for me so they'll not even *think* of turning away from me.

41 " 'Oh how I'll rejoice in them! Oh how I'll delight in doing good things for them! Heart and soul, I'll plant them in this country and keep them here!'

42-44 "Yes, this is GOD's Message: 'I will certainly bring this huge catastrophe on this people, but I will also usher in a wonderful life of prosperity. I promise. Fields are going to be bought here again, yes, in this very country that you assume is going to end up desolate—gone to the dogs, unlivable, wrecked by the Babylonians. Yes, people will buy farms again, and legally, with deeds of purchase, sealed documents, proper witnesses—and right here in the territory of Benjamin, and in the area around Jerusalem, around the villages of Judah and the hill country, the Shephelah and the Negev. I will restore everything that was lost.' GOD's Decree."

THINGS YOU COULD NEVER FIGURE OUT ON YOUR OWN

1 33 While Jeremiah was still locked up in jail, a second Message from GOD was given to him:

2-3 "This is GOD's Message, the God who made earth, made it livable and lasting, known everywhere as *GOD*: 'Call to me and I will answer you. I'll tell you marvelous and wondrous things that you could never figure out on your own.'

4-5 "This is what GOD, the God of Israel, has to say about what's going on in this city, about the homes of both people and kings that have been demolished, about all the ravages of war and the killing by the Chaldeans, and about the streets littered with the dead bodies of those killed because of my raging anger—about all that's hap-

NEW KING JAMES VERSION

My anger and My fury, all for whose wicked-
ness I have hidden My face from this city. 6Be-
hold, I will bring it health and healing; I will
heal them and reveal to them the abundance of
peace and truth. 7And I will cause the captives
of Judah and the captives of Israel to return, and
will rebuild those places as at the first. 8I will
cleanse them from all their iniquity by which
they have sinned against Me, and I will pardon
all their iniquities by which they have sinned
and by which they have transgressed against
Me. 9Then it shall be to Me a name of joy, a
praise, and an honor before all nations of the
earth, who shall hear all the good that I do to
them; they shall fear and tremble for all the
goodness and all the prosperity that I provide
for it.'

10"Thus says the LORD: 'Again there shall be
heard in this place—of which you say, "It *is* des-
olate, without man and without beast"—in the
cities of Judah, in the streets of Jerusalem that
are desolate, without man and without inhabi-
tant and without beast, 11the voice of joy and the
voice of gladness, the voice of the bridegroom
and the voice of the bride, the voice of those
who will say:

"Praise the LORD of hosts,
For the LORD *is* good,
For His mercy *endures* forever"—

and of those *who will* bring the sacrifice of
praise into the house of the LORD. For I will
cause the captives of the land to return as at the
first,' says the LORD.

12"Thus says the LORD of hosts: 'In this place
which is desolate, without man and without
beast, and in all its cities, there shall again be a
dwelling place of shepherds causing *their* flocks
to lie down. 13In the cities of the mountains, in
the cities of the lowland, in the cities of the
South, in the land of Benjamin, in the places
around Jerusalem, and in the cities of Judah, the
flocks shall again pass under the hands of him
who counts *them*,' says the LORD.

14'Behold, the days are coming,' says the
LORD, 'that I will perform that good thing which
I have promised to the house of Israel and to the
house of Judah:

15'In those days and at that time
I will cause to grow up to David
A Branch of righteousness;
He shall execute judgment and
righteousness in the earth.
16In those days Judah will be saved,
And Jerusalem will dwell safely.
And this *is the name* by which she will be
called:

THE LORD OUR RIGHTEOUSNESS.'[a]

17"For thus says the LORD: 'David shall never
lack a man to sit on the throne of the house of Is-
rael; 18nor shall the priests, the Levites, lack a
man to offer burnt offerings before Me, to kindle
grain offerings, and to sacrifice continually.' "

33:16 [a]Compare 23:5, 6

THE MESSAGE

pened because the evil actions in this city
have turned my stomach in disgust.

6-9 "But now take another look. I'm going to
give this city a thorough renovation, work-
ing a true healing inside and out. I'm going
to show them life whole, life brimming with
blessings. I'll restore everything that was
lost to Judah and Jerusalem. I'll build every-
thing back as good as new. I'll scrub them
clean from the dirt they've done against me.
I'll forgive everything they've done wrong,
forgive all their rebellions. And Jerusalem
will be a center of joy and praise and glory
for all the countries on earth. They'll get re-
ports on all the good I'm doing for her.
They'll be in awe of the blessings I am pour-
ing on her.

10-11 "Yes, GOD's Message: 'You're going to
look at this place, these empty and desolate
towns of Judah and streets of Jerusalem,
and say, "A wasteland. Unlivable. Not even a
dog could live here." But the time is coming
when you're going to hear laughter and cel-
ebration, marriage festivities, people ex-
claiming, "Thank GOD-of-the-Angel-Armies.
He's so good! His love never quits," as they
bring thank offerings into GOD's Temple. I'll
restore everything that was lost in this land.
I'll make everything as good as new.' I, GOD,
say so.

12-13 "GOD-of-the-Angel-Armies says: 'This
coming desolation, unfit for even a stray
dog, is once again going to become a pas-
ture for shepherds who care for their flocks.
You'll see flocks everywhere—in the moun-
tains around the towns of the Shephelah
and Negev, all over the territory of Ben-
jamin, around Jerusalem and the towns of
Judah—flocks under the care of shepherds
who keep track of each sheep.' GOD says so.

A FRESH AND TRUE SHOOT FROM THE DAVID-TREE

14-18 " 'Watch for this: The time is coming'—
GOD's Decree—'when I will keep the prom-
ise I made to the families of Israel and Ju-
dah. When that time comes, I will make a
fresh and true shoot sprout from the David-
Tree. He will run this country honestly and
fairly. He will set things right. That's when
Judah will be secure and Jerusalem live in
safety. The motto for the city will be, "GOD
Has Set Things Right for Us." GOD has made
it clear that there will always be a descen-
dant of David ruling the people of Israel and
that there will always be Levitical priests on
hand to offer burnt offerings, present grain
offerings, and carry on the sacrificial wor-
ship in my honor.' "

NEW KING JAMES VERSION

THE PERMANENCE OF GOD'S COVENANT

19And the word of the LORD came to Jere-
miah, saying, 20"Thus says the LORD: 'If you can
break My covenant with the day and My
covenant with the night, so that there will not be
day and night in their season, 21then My
covenant may also be broken with David My
servant, so that he shall not have a son to reign
on his throne, and with the Levites, the priests,
My ministers. 22As the host of heaven cannot be
numbered, nor the sand of the sea measured, so
will I multiply the descendants of David My ser-
vant and the Levites who minister to Me.' "

23Moreover the word of the LORD came to
Jeremiah, saying, 24"Have you not considered
what these people have spoken, saying, 'The two
families which the LORD has chosen, He has also
cast them off'? Thus they have despised My peo-
ple, as if they should no more be a nation before
them.

25"Thus says the LORD: 'If My covenant *is* not
with day and night, *and if* I have not appointed
the ordinances of heaven and earth, 26then I will
cast away the descendants of Jacob and David
My servant, *so* that I will not take *any* of his de-
scendants *to be* rulers over the descendants of
Abraham, Isaac, and Jacob. For I will cause
their captives to return, and will have mercy on
them.' "

ZEDEKIAH WARNED BY GOD

34 The word which came to Jeremiah from
the LORD, when Nebuchadnezzar king of
Babylon and all his army, all the kingdoms of the
earth under his dominion, and all the people,
fought against Jerusalem and all its cities, say-
ing, 2"Thus says the LORD, the God of Israel: 'Go
and speak to Zedekiah king of Judah and tell
him, "Thus says the LORD: 'Behold, I will give
this city into the hand of the king of Babylon,
and he shall burn it with fire. 3And you shall not
escape from his hand, but shall surely be taken
and delivered into his hand; your eyes shall see
the eyes of the king of Babylon, he shall speak
with you face to face,[a] and you shall go to Bab-
ylon.' " ' 4Yet hear the word of the LORD, O
Zedekiah king of Judah! Thus says the LORD
concerning you: 'You shall not die by the sword.
5You shall die in peace; as in the ceremonies of
your fathers, the former kings who were before
you, so they shall burn incense for you and
lament for you, *saying*, "Alas, lord!" For I have
pronounced the word, says the LORD.' "

6Then Jeremiah the prophet spoke all these
words to Zedekiah king of Judah in Jerusalem,
7when the king of Babylon's army fought
against Jerusalem and all the cities of Judah
that were left, against Lachish and Azekah; for
only these fortified cities remained of the cities
of Judah.

34:3 [a]Literally *mouth to mouth*

THE MESSAGE

19-22 GOD's Message to Jeremiah: "GOD says, 'If my covenant with day and my covenant with night ever fell apart so that day and night became haphazard and you never knew which was coming and when, then and only then would my covenant with my servant David fall apart and his descendants no longer rule. The same goes for the Levitical priests who serve me. Just as you can't number the stars in the sky nor measure the sand on the seashore, neither will you be able to account for the descendants of David my servant and the Levites who serve me.' "

23-24 GOD's Message to Jeremiah: "Have you heard the saying that's making the rounds: 'The two families GOD chose, Israel and Judah, he disowned'? And have you noticed that my people are treated with contempt, with rumors afoot that there's nothing to them anymore?

25-26 "Well, here's GOD's response: 'If my covenant with day and night wasn't in working order, if sky and earth weren't functioning the way I set them going, then, but only then, you might think I had disowned the descendants of Jacob and of my servant David, and that I wouldn't set up any of David's descendants over the descendants of Abraham, Isaac, and Jacob. But as it is, I will give them back everything they've lost. The last word is, I will have mercy on them.' "

FREEDOM TO THE SLAVES

1 34 GOD's Message to Jeremiah at the time King Nebuchadnezzar of Babylon mounted an all-out attack on Jerusalem and all the towns around it with his armies and allies and everyone he could muster:

2-3 "I, GOD, the God of Israel, direct you to go and tell Zedekiah king of Judah: 'This is GOD's Message. Listen to me. I am going to hand this city over to the king of Babylon, and he is going to burn it to the ground. And don't think you'll get away. You'll be captured and be his prisoner. You will have a personal confrontation with the king of Babylon and be taken off with him, captive, to Babylon.

4-5 " 'But listen, O Zedekiah king of Judah, to the rest of the Message of GOD. You won't be killed. You'll die a peaceful death. They will honor you with funeral rites as they honored your ancestors, the kings who preceded you. They will properly mourn your death, weeping, "Master, master!" This is a solemn promise. GOD's Decree.' "

6-7 The prophet Jeremiah gave this Message to Zedekiah king of Judah in Jerusalem, gave it to him word for word. It was at the very time that the king of Babylon was mounting his all-out attack on Jerusalem and whatever cities in Judah that were still standing—only Lachish and Azekah, as it turned out (they were the only fortified cities left in Judah).

New King James Version

Treacherous Treatment of Slaves

8*This is* the word that came to Jeremiah from
the Lord, after King Zedekiah had made a
covenant with all the people who *were* at
Jerusalem to proclaim liberty to them: 9that
every man should set free his male and female
slave—a Hebrew man or woman—that no one
should keep a Jewish brother in bondage. 10Now
when all the princes and all the people, who had
entered into the covenant, heard that everyone
should set free his male and female slaves, that
no one should keep them in bondage anymore,
they obeyed and let *them* go. 11But afterward
they changed their minds and made the male
and female slaves return, whom they had set
free, and brought them into subjection as male
and female slaves.

12Therefore the word of the Lord came to Jer-
emiah from the Lord, saying, 13"Thus says the
Lord, the God of Israel: 'I made a covenant with
your fathers in the day that I brought them out
of the land of Egypt, out of the house of
bondage, saying, 14"At the end of seven years let
every man set free his Hebrew brother, who has
been sold to him; and when he has served you
six years, you shall let him go free from you."
But your fathers did not obey Me nor incline
their ear. 15Then you recently turned and did
what was right in My sight—every man pro-
claiming liberty to his neighbor; and you made
a covenant before Me in the house which is
called by My name. 16Then you turned around
and profaned My name, and every one of you
brought back his male and female slaves, whom
you had set at liberty, at their pleasure, and
brought them back into subjection, to be your
male and female slaves.'

17"Therefore thus says the Lord: 'You have
not obeyed Me in proclaiming liberty, every one
to his brother and every one to his neighbor. Be-
hold, I proclaim liberty to you,' says the Lord—
'to the sword, to pestilence, and to famine! And I
will deliver you to trouble among all the king-
doms of the earth. 18And I will give the men who
have transgressed My covenant, who have not
performed the words of the covenant which they
made before Me, when they cut the calf in two
and passed between the parts of it— 19the princes
of Judah, the princes of Jerusalem, the eunuchs,
the priests, and all the people of the land who
passed between the parts of the calf— 20I will
give them into the hand of their enemies and into
the hand of those who seek their life. Their dead
bodies shall be for meat for the birds of the
heaven and the beasts of the earth. 21And I will
give Zedekiah king of Judah and his princes into
the hand of their enemies, into the hand of those
who seek their life, and into the hand of the king
of Babylon's army which has gone back from
you. 22Behold, I will command,' says the Lord,
'and cause them to return to this city. They will
fight against it and take it and burn it with fire;
and I will make the cities of Judah a desolation
without inhabitant.' "

The Obedient Rechabites

35 The word which came to Jeremiah from
the Lord in the days of Jehoiakim the son
of Josiah, king of Judah, saying,

The Message

8-10 God delivered a Message to Jeremiah after King Zedekiah made a covenant with the people of Jerusalem to decree freedom to the slaves who were Hebrews, both men and women. The covenant stipulated that no one in Judah would own a fellow Jew as a slave. All the leaders and people who had signed the covenant set free the slaves, men and women alike.

11 But a little while later, they reneged on the covenant, broke their promise and forced their former slaves to become slaves again.

12-14 Then Jeremiah received this Message from God: "God, the God of Israel, says, 'I made a covenant with your ancestors when I delivered them out of their slavery in Egypt. At the time I made it clear: "At the end of seven years, each of you must free any fellow Hebrew who has had to sell himself to you. After he has served six years, set him free." But your ancestors totally ignored me.

15-16 " 'And now, *you*—what have you done? First you turned back to the right way and did the right thing, decreeing freedom for your brothers and sisters—and you made it official in a solemn covenant in my Temple. And then you turned right around and broke your word, making a mockery of both me and the covenant, and made them all slaves again, these men and women you'd just set free. You forced them back into slavery.

17-20 " 'So here is what I, God, have to say: You have not obeyed me and set your brothers and sisters free. Here is what I'm going to do: I'm going to set *you* free—God's Decree—free to get killed in war or by disease or by starvation. I'll make you a spectacle of horror. People all over the world will take one look at you and shudder. Everyone who violated my covenant, who didn't do what was solemnly promised in the covenant ceremony when they split the young bull into two halves and walked between them, all those people that day who walked between the two halves of the bull—leaders of Judah and Jerusalem, palace officials, priests, and all the rest of the people—I'm handing the lot of them over to their enemies who are out to kill them. Their dead bodies will be carrion food for vultures and stray dogs.

21-22 " 'As for Zedekiah king of Judah and his palace staff, I'll also hand them over to their enemies, who are out to kill them. The army of the king of Babylon has pulled back for a time, but not for long, for I'm going to issue orders that will bring them back to this city. They'll attack and take it and burn it to the ground. The surrounding cities of Judah will fare no better. I'll turn them into ghost towns, unlivable and unlived in.' " God's Decree.

Meeting in God's Temple

1 35 The Message that Jeremiah received from God ten years earlier, during the time of Jehoiakim son of Josiah king of Israel:

NEW KING JAMES VERSION

2“Go to the house of the Rechabites, speak to
them, and bring them into the house of the
LORD, into one of the chambers, and give them
wine to drink.”
3Then I took Jaazaniah the son of Jeremiah,
the son of Habazziniah, his brothers and all his
sons, and the whole house of the Rechabites,
4and I brought them into the house of the LORD,
into the chamber of the sons of Hanan the son
of Igdaliah, a man of God, which *was* by the
chamber of the princes, above the chamber of
Maaseiah the son of Shallum, the keeper of the
door. 5Then I set before the sons of the house of
the Rechabites bowls full of wine, and cups; and
I said to them, “Drink wine.”
6But they said, “We will drink no wine, for
Jonadab the son of Rechab, our father, com-
manded us, saying, ‘You shall drink no wine,
you nor your sons, forever. 7You shall not build
a house, sow seed, plant a vineyard, nor have
any of these; but all your days you shall dwell in
tents, that you may live many days in the land
where you are sojourners.’ 8Thus we have
obeyed the voice of Jonadab the son of Rechab,
our father, in all that he charged us, to drink no
wine all our days, we, our wives, our sons, or our
daughters, 9nor to build ourselves houses to
dwell in; nor do we have vineyard, field, or seed.
10But we have dwelt in tents, and have obeyed
and done according to all that Jonadab our fa-
ther commanded us. 11But it came to pass, when
Nebuchadnezzar king of Babylon came up into
the land, that we said, ‘Come, let us go to
Jerusalem for fear of the army of the Chaldeans
and for fear of the army of the Syrians.’ So we
dwell at Jerusalem.”
12Then came the word of the LORD to Jere-
miah, saying, 13“Thus says the LORD of hosts, the
God of Israel: ‘Go and tell the men of Judah and
the inhabitants of Jerusalem, “Will you not re-
ceive instruction to obey My words?” says the
LORD. 14“The words of Jonadab the son of
Rechab, which he commanded his sons, not to
drink wine, are performed; for to this day they
drink none, and obey their father’s command-
ment. But although I have spoken to you, rising
early and speaking, you did not obey Me. 15I
have also sent to you all My servants the
prophets, rising up early and sending *them,* say-
ing, ‘Turn now everyone from his evil way,
amend your doings, and do not go after other
gods to serve them; then you will dwell in the
land which I have given you and your fathers.’
But you have not inclined your ear, nor obeyed
Me. 16Surely the sons of Jonadab the son of
Rechab have performed the commandment of
their father, which he commanded them, but
this people has not obeyed Me.” ’
17“Therefore thus says the LORD God of
hosts, the God of Israel: ‘Behold, I will bring on

THE MESSAGE

2 “Go visit the Recabite community. Invite
them to meet with you in one of the rooms
in GOD’s Temple. And serve them wine.”
3-4 So I went and got Jaazaniah son of Jere-
miah, son of Habazziniah, along with all his
brothers and sons—the whole community of
the Recabites as it turned out—and brought
them to GOD’s Temple and to the meeting
room of Hanan son of Igdaliah, a man of
God. It was next to the meeting room of the
Temple officials and just over the apartment
of Maaseiah son of Shallum, who was in
charge of Temple affairs.
5 Then I set out chalices and pitchers of
wine for the Recabites and said, “A toast!
Drink up!”
6-7 But they wouldn’t do it. “We don’t drink
wine,” they said. “Our ancestor Jonadab son
of Recab commanded us, ‘You are not to
drink wine, you or your children, ever. Nei-
ther shall you build houses or settle down,
planting fields and gardens and vineyards.
Don’t own property. Live in tents as nomads
so that you will live well and prosper in a
wandering life.’
8-10 “And we’ve done it, done everything Jon-
adab son of Recab commanded. We and our
wives, our sons and daughters, drink no
wine at all. We don’t build houses. We don’t
have vineyards or fields or gardens. We live
in tents as nomads. We’ve listened to our an-
cestor Jonadab and we’ve done everything
he commanded us.
11 “But when Nebuchadnezzar king of
Babylon invaded our land, we said, ‘Let’s go
to Jerusalem and get out of the path of the
Chaldean and Aramean armies, find our-
selves a safe place.’ That’s why we’re living
in Jerusalem right now.”

WHY WON’T YOU LEARN YOUR LESSON?

12-15 Then Jeremiah received this Message from
GOD: “GOD-of-the-Angel-Armies, the God of
Israel, wants you to go tell the people of Ju-
dah and the citizens of Jerusalem that I say,
‘Why won’t you learn your lesson and do
what I tell you?’ GOD’s Decree. ‘The com-
mands of Jonadab son of Recab to his sons
have been carried out to the letter. He told
them not to drink wine, and they haven’t
touched a drop to this very day. They hon-
ored and obeyed their ancestor’s command.
But look at you! I have gone to a lot of trou-
ble to get your attention, and you’ve ignored
me. I sent prophet after prophet to you, all of
them my servants, to tell you from early
morning to late at night to change your life,
make a clean break with your evil past and
do what is right, to not take up with every
Tom, Dick, and Harry of a god that comes
down the pike, but settle down and be faith-
ful in this country I gave your ancestors.
15-16 “ ‘And what do I get from you? Deaf ears.
The descendants of Jonadab son of Recab
carried out to the letter what their ancestor
commanded them, but this people ignores
me.’
17 “So here’s what is going to happen. GOD-
of-the-Angel-Armies, the God of Israel,

NEW KING JAMES VERSION

Judah and on all the inhabitants of Jerusalem all the doom that I have pronounced against them; because I have spoken to them but they have not heard, and I have called to them but they have not answered.' "

18And Jeremiah said to the house of the Rechabites, "Thus says the LORD of hosts, the God of Israel: 'Because you have obeyed the commandment of Jonadab your father, and kept all his precepts and done according to all that he commanded you, 19therefore thus says the LORD of hosts, the God of Israel: "Jonadab the son of Rechab shall not lack a man to stand before Me forever." ' "

THE SCROLL READ IN THE TEMPLE

36 Now it came to pass in the fourth year of Jehoiakim the son of Josiah, king of Judah, *that* this word came to Jeremiah from the LORD, saying: 2"Take a scroll of a book and write on it all the words that I have spoken to you against Israel, against Judah, and against all the nations, from the day I spoke to you, from the days of Josiah even to this day. 3It may be that the house of Judah will hear all the adversities which I purpose to bring upon them, that everyone may turn from his evil way, that I may forgive their iniquity and their sin."

4Then Jeremiah called Baruch the son of Neriah; and Baruch wrote on a scroll of a book, at the instruction of Jeremiah,[a] all the words of the LORD which He had spoken to him. 5And Jeremiah commanded Baruch, saying, "I *am* confined, I cannot go into the house of the LORD. 6You go, therefore, and read from the scroll which you have written at my instruction,[a] the words of the LORD, in the hearing of the people in the LORD's house on the day of fasting. And you shall also read them in the hearing of all Judah who come from their cities. 7It may be that they will present their supplication before the LORD, and everyone will turn from his evil way. For great *is* the anger and the fury that the LORD has pronounced against this people." 8And Baruch the son of Neriah did according to all that Jeremiah the prophet commanded him, reading from the book the words of the LORD in the LORD's house.

9Now it came to pass in the fifth year of Jehoiakim the son of Josiah, king of Judah, in the ninth month, *that* they proclaimed a fast before the LORD to all the people in Jerusalem, and to all the people who came from the cities of Judah to Jerusalem. 10Then Baruch read from the book the words of Jeremiah in the house of the LORD, in the chamber of Gemariah the son of Shaphan the scribe, in the upper court at the entry of the New Gate of the LORD's house, in the hearing of all the people.

THE SCROLL READ IN THE PALACE

11When Michaiah the son of Gemariah, the son of Shaphan, heard all the words of the LORD from the book, 12he then went down to the

36:4 [a]Literally *from Jeremiah's mouth* **36:6** [a]Literally *from my mouth*

THE MESSAGE

says, 'I will bring calamity down on the heads of the people of Judah and Jerusalem—the very calamity I warned you was coming—because you turned a deaf ear when I spoke, turned your backs when I called.' "

18-19 Then, turning to the Recabite community, Jeremiah said, "And this is what GOD-of-the-Angel-Armies, the God of Israel, says to you: Because you have done what Jonadab your ancestor told you, obeyed his commands and followed through on his instructions, receive this Message from GOD-of-the-Angel-Armies, the God of Israel: There will always be a descendant of Jonadab son of Recab at my service! Always!' "

READING GOD'S MESSAGE

1 36 In the fourth year of Jehoiakim son of Josiah king of Judah, Jeremiah received this Message from GOD:

2 "Get a scroll and write down everything I've told you regarding Israel and Judah and all the other nations from the time I first started speaking to you in Josiah's reign right up to the present day.

3 "Maybe the community of Judah will finally get it, finally understand the catastrophe that I'm planning for them, turn back from their bad lives, and let me forgive their perversity and sin."

4 So Jeremiah called in Baruch son of Neriah. Jeremiah dictated and Baruch wrote down on a scroll everything that GOD had said to him.

5-6 Then Jeremiah told Baruch, "I'm blacklisted. I can't go into GOD's Temple, so you'll have to go in my place. Go into the Temple and read everything you've written at my dictation. Wait for a day of fasting when everyone is there to hear you. And make sure that all the people who come from the Judean villages hear you.

7 "Maybe, just maybe, they'll start praying and GOD will hear their prayers. Maybe they'll turn back from their bad lives. This is no light matter. GOD has certainly let them know how angry he is!"

8 Baruch son of Neriah did everything Jeremiah the prophet told him to do. In the Temple of GOD he read the Message of GOD from the scroll.

9 It came about in December of the fifth year of Jehoiakim son of Josiah king of Judah that all the people of Jerusalem, along with all the people from the Judean villages, were there in Jerusalem to observe a fast to GOD.

10 Baruch took the scroll to the Temple and read out publicly the words of Jeremiah. He read from the meeting room of Gemariah son of Shaphan the secretary of state, which was in the upper court right next to the New Gate of GOD's Temple. Everyone could hear him.

11-12 The moment Micaiah the son of Gemariah heard what was being read from the scroll—GOD's Message!—he went straight to

NEW KING JAMES VERSION

king's house, into the scribe's chamber; and
there all the princes were sitting—Elishama the
scribe, Delaiah the son of Shemaiah, Elnathan
the son of Achbor, Gemariah the son of
Shaphan, Zedekiah the son of Hananiah, and all
the princes. 13Then Michaiah declared to them
all the words that he had heard when Baruch
read the book in the hearing of the people.
14Therefore all the princes sent Jehudi the son of
Nethaniah, the son of Shelemiah, the son of
Cushi, to Baruch, saying, "Take in your hand the
scroll from which you have read in the hearing
of the people, and come." So Baruch the son of
Neriah took the scroll in his hand and came to
them. 15And they said to him, "Sit down now,
and read it in our hearing." So Baruch read *it* in
their hearing.
16Now it happened, when they had heard all
the words, that they looked in fear from one to
another, and said to Baruch, "We will surely tell
the king of all these words." 17And they asked
Baruch, saying, "Tell us now, how did you write
all these words—at his instruction?"[a]
18So Baruch answered them, "He proclaimed
with his mouth all these words to me, and I
wrote *them* with ink in the book."
19Then the princes said to Baruch, "Go and
hide, you and Jeremiah; and let no one know
where you are."

THE KING DESTROYS JEREMIAH'S SCROLL

20And they went to the king, into the court;
but they stored the scroll in the chamber of
Elishama the scribe, and told all the words in
the hearing of the king. 21So the king sent Je-
hudi to bring the scroll, and he took it from
Elishama the scribe's chamber. And Jehudi read it
in the hearing of the king and in the hearing of
all the princes who stood beside the king. 22Now
the king was sitting in the winter house in the
ninth month, with *a fire* burning on the hearth
before him. 23And it happened, when Jehudi had
read three or four columns, *that the king* cut it
with the scribe's knife and cast *it* into the fire
that *was* on the hearth, until all the scroll was
consumed in the fire that *was* on the hearth.
24Yet they were not afraid, nor did they tear their
garments, the king nor any of his servants who
heard all these words. 25Nevertheless Elnathan,
Delaiah, and Gemariah implored the king not to
burn the scroll; but he would not listen to them.
26And the king commanded Jerahmeel the
king's[a] son, Seraiah the son of Azriel, and
Shelemiah the son of Abdeel, to seize Baruch
the scribe and Jeremiah the prophet, but the
LORD hid them.

JEREMIAH REWRITES THE SCROLL

27Now after the king had burned the scroll
with the words which Baruch had written at the
instruction of Jeremiah,[a] the word of the LORD
came to Jeremiah, saying: 28"Take yet another
scroll, and write on it all the former words that
were in the first scroll which Jehoiakim the king
of Judah has burned. 29And you shall say to Je-
hoiakim king of Judah, 'Thus says the LORD:
"You have burned this scroll, saying, 'Why have

36:17 [a]Literally *with his mouth* **36:26** [a]Hebrew *Hammelech*
36:27 [a]Literally *from Jeremiah's mouth*

THE MESSAGE

the palace and to the chambers of the secre-
tary of state where all the government offi-
cials were holding a meeting: Elishama the
secretary, Delaiah son of Shemaiah, El-
nathan son of Achbor, Gemariah son of
Shaphan, Zedekiah son of Hananiah, and
all the other government officials.
13 Micaiah reported everything he had
heard Baruch read from the scroll as the of-
ficials listened.
14 Immediately they dispatched Jehudi son
of Nethaniah, son of Semaiah, son of Cushi,
to Baruch, ordering him, "Take the scroll
that you have read to the people and bring it
here." So Baruch went and retrieved the
scroll.
15 The officials told him, "Sit down. Read it
to us, please." Baruch read it.
16 When they had heard it all, they were up-
set. They talked it over. "We've got to tell the
king all this."
17 They asked Baruch, "Tell us, how did you
come to write all this? Was it at Jeremiah's
dictation?"
18 Baruch said, "That's right. Every word
right from his own mouth. And I wrote it
down, word for word, with pen and ink."
19 The government officials told Baruch,
"You need to get out of here. Go into hiding,
you and Jeremiah. Don't let anyone know
where you are!"
20-21 The officials went to the court of the
palace to report to the king, having put the
scroll for safekeeping in the office of
Elishama the secretary of state. The king
sent Jehudi to get the scroll. He brought it
from the office of Elishama the secretary.
Jehudi then read it to the king and the offi-
cials who were in the king's service.
22-23 It was December. The king was sitting in
his winter quarters in front of a charcoal
fire. After Jehudi would read three or four
columns, the king would cut them off the
scroll with his pocketknife and throw them
in the fire. He continued in this way until the
entire scroll had been burned up in the fire.
24-26 Neither the king nor any of his officials
showed the slightest twinge of conscience
as they listened to the messages read. El-
nathan, Delaiah, and Gemariah tried to con-
vince the king not to burn the scroll, but he
brushed them off. He just plowed ahead and
ordered Prince Jerahameel, Seraiah son of
Azriel, and Shelemiah son of Abdeel to ar-
rest Jeremiah the prophet and his secretary
Baruch. But GOD had hidden them away.

27-28 After the king had burned the scroll that
Baruch had written at Jeremiah's dictation,
Jeremiah received this Message from GOD:
"Get another blank scroll and do it all over
again. Write out everything that was in that
first scroll that Jehoiakim king of Judah
burned up.
29 "And send this personal message to Je-
hoiakim king of Judah: 'GOD says, You had
the gall to burn this scroll and then the

NEW KING JAMES VERSION

you written in it that the king of Babylon will
certainly come and destroy this land, and cause
man and beast to cease from here?' " [30]Therefore
thus says the LORD concerning Jehoiakim king
of Judah: "He shall have no one to sit on the
throne of David, and his dead body shall be cast
out to the heat of the day and the frost of the
night. [31]I will punish him, his family, and his ser-
vants for their iniquity; and I will bring on them,
on the inhabitants of Jerusalem, and on the men
of Judah all the doom that I have pronounced
against them; but they did not heed." ' "
[32]Then Jeremiah took another scroll and
gave it to Baruch the scribe, the son of Neriah,
who wrote on it at the instruction of Jeremiah[a]
all the words of the book which Jehoiakim king
of Judah had burned in the fire. And besides,
there were added to them many similar words.

ZEDEKIAH'S VAIN HOPE

37 Now King Zedekiah the son of Josiah
reigned instead of Coniah the son of Je-
hoiakim, whom Nebuchadnezzar king of Bab-
ylon made king in the land of Judah. [2]But nei-
ther he nor his servants nor the people of the
land gave heed to the words of the LORD which
He spoke by the prophet Jeremiah.
[3]And Zedekiah the king sent Jehucal the son
of Shelemiah, and Zephaniah the son of Maa-
seiah, the priest, to the prophet Jeremiah, say-
ing, "Pray now to the LORD our God for us."
[4]Now Jeremiah was coming and going among
the people, for they had not *yet* put him in
prison. [5]Then Pharaoh's army came up from
Egypt; and when the Chaldeans who were be-
sieging Jerusalem heard news of them, they de-
parted from Jerusalem.
[6]Then the word of the LORD came to the
prophet Jeremiah, saying, [7]"Thus says the LORD,
the God of Israel, 'Thus you shall say to the king
of Judah, who sent you to Me to inquire of Me:
"Behold, Pharaoh's army which has come up to
help you will return to Egypt, to their own land.
[8]And the Chaldeans shall come back and fight
against this city, and take it and burn it with
fire." ' [9]Thus says the LORD: 'Do not deceive
yourselves, saying, "The Chaldeans will surely
depart from us," for they will not depart. [10]For
though you had defeated the whole army of the
Chaldeans who fight against you, and there re-
mained *only* wounded men among them, they
would rise up, every man in his tent, and burn
the city with fire.' "

JEREMIAH IMPRISONED

[11]And it happened, when the army of the
Chaldeans left *the siege* of Jerusalem for fear
of Pharaoh's army, [12]that Jeremiah went out of
Jerusalem to go into the land of Benjamin to
claim his property there among the people.

36:32 [a]Literally *from Jeremiah's mouth*

THE MESSAGE

nerve to say, "What kind of nonsense is this
written here—that the king of Babylon will
come and destroy this land and kill every-
thing in it?"
30-31 " 'Well, do you want to know what GOD
says about Jehoiakim king of Judah? This:
No descendant of his will ever rule from
David's throne. His corpse will be thrown in
the street and left unburied, exposed to the
hot sun and the freezing night. I will punish
him and his children and the officials in his
government for their blatant sin. I'll let
loose on them and everyone in Jerusalem
the doomsday disaster of which I warned
them but they spit at.' "
32 So Jeremiah went and got another scroll
and gave it to Baruch son of Neriah, his sec-
retary. At Jeremiah's dictation he again
wrote down everything that Jehoiakim king
of Judah had burned in the fire. There were
also generous additions, but of the same
kind of thing.

IN AN UNDERGROUND DUNGEON

1-2 37 King Zedekiah son of Josiah, a puppet
king set on the throne by Nebuchad-
nezzar king of Babylon in the land of Judah,
was now king in place of Jehoiachin son of
Jehoiakim. But neither he nor his officials
nor the people themselves paid a bit of at-
tention to the Message GOD gave by Jere-
miah the prophet.
3 However, King Zedekiah sent Jehucal
son of Shelemiah, and Zephaniah the priest,
son of Maaseiah, to Jeremiah the prophet,
saying, "Pray for us—pray hard!—to the
Master, our GOD."
4-5 Jeremiah was still moving about freely
among the people in those days. This was
before he had been put in jail. Pharaoh's
army was marching up from Egypt. The
Chaldeans fighting against Jerusalem heard
that the Egyptians were coming and pulled
back.
6-10 Then Jeremiah the prophet received this
Message from GOD: "I, the GOD of Israel,
want you to give this Message to the king of
Judah, who has just sent you to me to find
out what he should do. Tell him, 'Get this:
Pharaoh's army, which is on its way to help
you, isn't going to stick it out. No sooner will
they get here than they'll leave and go home
to Egypt. And then the Babylonians will
come back and resume their attack, capture
this city and burn it to the ground. I, GOD,
am telling you: Don't kid yourselves, reas-
suring one another, "The Babylonians will
leave in a few days." I tell you, they aren't
leaving. Why, even if you defeated the entire
attacking Chaldean army and all that was
left were a few wounded soldiers in their
tents, the wounded would still do the job
and burn this city to the ground.' "

11-13 When the Chaldean army pulled back from
Jerusalem, Jeremiah left Jerusalem to go
over to the territory of Benjamin to take
care of some personal business. When he

NEW KING JAMES VERSION

13And when he was in the Gate of Benjamin, a
captain of the guard *was* there whose name
was Irijah the son of Shelemiah, the son of
Hananiah; and he seized Jeremiah the
prophet, saying, "You are defecting to the
Chaldeans!"
14Then Jeremiah said, "False! I am not de-
fecting to the Chaldeans." But he did not listen
to him.
So Irijah seized Jeremiah and brought him
to the princes. 15Therefore the princes were an-
gry with Jeremiah, and they struck him and put
him in prison in the house of Jonathan the
scribe. For they had made that the prison.
16When Jeremiah entered the dungeon and
the cells, and Jeremiah had remained there
many days, 17then Zedekiah the king sent and
took him *out*. The king asked him secretly in his
house, and said, "Is there *any* word from the
LORD?"
And Jeremiah said, "There is." Then he said,
"You shall be delivered into the hand of the king
of Babylon!"
18Moreover Jeremiah said to King Zedekiah,
"What offense have I committed against you,
against your servants, or against this people,
that you have put me in prison? 19Where now
are your prophets who prophesied to you, say-
ing, 'The king of Babylon will not come against
you or against this land'? 20Therefore please
hear now, O my lord the king. Please, let my pe-
tition be accepted before you, and do not make
me return to the house of Jonathan the scribe,
lest I die there."
21Then Zedekiah the king commanded that
they should commit Jeremiah to the court of the
prison, and that they should give him daily a
piece of bread from the bakers' street, until all
the bread in the city was gone. Thus Jeremiah
remained in the court of the prison.

JEREMIAH IN THE DUNGEON

38Now Shephatiah the son of Mattan,
Gedaliah the son of Pashhur, Jucal[a] the
son of Shelemiah, and Pashhur the son of
Malchiah heard the words that Jeremiah had
spoken to all the people, saying, 2"Thus says the
LORD: 'He who remains in this city shall die by
the sword, by famine, and by pestilence; but he
who goes over to the Chaldeans shall live; his
life shall be as a prize to him, and he shall live.'[a]
3Thus says the LORD: 'This city shall surely be
given into the hand of the king of Babylon's
army, which shall take it.' "
4Therefore the princes said to the king, "Please,
let this man be put to death, for thus he weakens
the hands of the men of war who remain in this
city, and the hands of all the people, by speaking
such words to them. For this man does not seek
the welfare of this people, but their harm."
5Then Zedekiah the king said, "Look, he *is* in
your hand. For the king can *do* nothing against
you." 6So they took Jeremiah and cast him into
the dungeon of Malchiah the king's[a] son, which
was in the court of the prison, and they let Jere-
miah down with ropes. And in the dungeon

38:1 [a]Same as *Jehucal* (compare 37:3) **38:2** [a]Compare 21:9
38:6 [a]Hebrew *Hammelech*

THE MESSAGE

got to the Benjamin Gate, the officer on guard
there, Irijah son of Shelemiah, son of Hana-
niah, grabbed Jeremiah the prophet, accusing
him, "You're deserting to the Chaldeans!"
14-16 "That's a lie," protested Jeremiah. "I
wouldn't think of deserting to the
Chaldeans."
But Irijah wouldn't listen to him. He ar-
rested him and took him to the police. The
police were furious with Jeremiah. They
beat him up and threw him into jail in the
house of Jonathan the secretary of state.
(They were using the house for a prison
cell.) So Jeremiah entered an underground
cell in a cistern turned into a dungeon. He
stayed there a long time.
17 Later King Zedekiah had Jeremiah
brought to him. The king questioned him
privately, "Is there a Message from GOD?"
"There certainly is," said Jeremiah.
"You're going to be turned over to the king
of Babylon."
18-20 Jeremiah continued speaking to King
Zedekiah: "Can you tell me why you threw
me into prison? What crime did I commit
against you or your officials or this people?
And tell me, whatever has become of your
prophets who preached all those sermons
saying that the king of Babylon would never
attack you or this land? Listen to me, please,
my master—my king! Please don't send me
back to that dungeon in the house of
Jonathan the secretary. I'll die there!"
21 So King Zedekiah ordered that Jeremiah
be assigned to the courtyard of the palace
guards. He was given a loaf of bread from
Bakers' Alley every day until all the bread in
the city was gone. And that's where Jere-
miah remained—in the courtyard of the
palace guards.

FROM THE DUNGEON TO THE PALACE

1 38Shaphatiah son of Mattan, Gedaliah son
of Pashur, Jehucal son of Shelemiah,
and Pashur son of Malkijah heard what Jere-
miah was telling the people, namely:
2 "This is GOD's Message: 'Whoever stays
in this town will die—will be killed or starve
to death or get sick and die. But those who
go over to the Babylonians will save their
necks and live.'
3 "And, GOD's sure Word: 'This city is des-
tined to fall to the army of the king of Bab-
ylon. He's going to take it over.' "
4 These officials told the king, "Please, kill
this man. He's got to go! He's ruining the re-
solve of the soldiers who are still left in the
city, as well as the people themselves, by
spreading these words. This man isn't look-
ing after the good of this people. He's trying
to ruin us!"
5 King Zedekiah caved in: "If you say so.
Go ahead, handle it your way. You're too
much for me."
6 So they took Jeremiah and threw him
into the cistern of Malkijah the king's son
that was in the courtyard of the palace
guard. They lowered him down with ropes.

New King James Version

there was no water, but mire. So Jeremiah sank
in the mire.
7Now Ebed-Melech the Ethiopian, one of the
eunuchs, who was in the king's house, heard
that they had put Jeremiah in the dungeon.
When the king was sitting at the Gate of Ben-
jamin, 8Ebed-Melech went out of the king's
house and spoke to the king, saying: 9"My lord
the king, these men have done evil in all that
they have done to Jeremiah the prophet, whom
they have cast into the dungeon, and he is likely
to die from hunger in the place where he is. For
there is no more bread in the city." 10Then the
king commanded Ebed-Melech the Ethiopian,
saying, "Take from here thirty men with you,
and lift Jeremiah the prophet out of the dungeon
before he dies." 11So Ebed-Melech took the men
with him and went into the house of the king un-
der the treasury, and took from there old clothes
and old rags, and let them down by ropes into
the dungeon to Jeremiah. 12Then Ebed-Melech
the Ethiopian said to Jeremiah, "Please put
these old clothes and rags under your armpits,
under the ropes." And Jeremiah did so. 13So they
pulled Jeremiah up with ropes and lifted him
out of the dungeon. And Jeremiah remained in
the court of the prison.

Zedekiah's Fears and Jeremiah's Advice

14Then Zedekiah the king sent and had Jere-
miah the prophet brought to him at the third en-
trance of the house of the Lord. And the king
said to Jeremiah, "I will ask you something.
Hide nothing from me."
15Jeremiah said to Zedekiah, "If I declare *it*
to you, will you not surely put me to death? And
if I give you advice, you will not listen to me."
16So Zedekiah the king swore secretly to Jer-
emiah, saying, "*As* the Lord lives, who made
our very souls, I will not put you to death, nor
will I give you into the hand of these men who
seek your life."
17Then Jeremiah said to Zedekiah, "Thus
says the Lord, the God of hosts, the God of Is-
rael: 'If you surely surrender to the king of
Babylon's princes, then your soul shall live; this
city shall not be burned with fire, and you and
your house shall live. 18But if you do not surren-
der to the king of Babylon's princes, then this
city shall be given into the hand of the
Chaldeans; they shall burn it with fire, and you
shall not escape from their hand.' "
19And Zedekiah the king said to Jeremiah, "I
am afraid of the Jews who have defected to the
Chaldeans, lest they deliver me into their hand,
and they abuse me."
20But Jeremiah said, "They shall not deliver
you. Please, obey the voice of the Lord which I
speak to you. So it shall be well with you, and
your soul shall live. 21But if you refuse to surren-
der, this *is* the word that the Lord has shown
me: 22'Now behold, all the women who are left
in the king of Judah's house *shall be* surren-
dered to the king of Babylon's princes, and
those *women* shall say:

The Message

There wasn't any water in the cistern, only
mud. Jeremiah sank into the mud.
7-9 Ebed-melek the Ethiopian, a court offi-
cial assigned to the royal palace, heard that
they had thrown Jeremiah into the cistern.
While the king was holding court in the
Benjamin Gate, Ebed-melek went immedi-
ately from the palace to the king and said,
"My master, O king—these men are commit-
ting a great crime in what they're doing,
throwing Jeremiah the prophet into the cis-
tern and leaving him there to starve. He's as
good as dead. There isn't a scrap of bread
left in the city."
10 So the king ordered Ebed-melek the
Ethiopian, "Get three men and pull Jere-
miah the prophet out of the cistern before
he dies."
11-12 Ebed-melek got three men and went to
the palace wardrobe and got some scraps of
old clothing, which they tied together and
lowered down with ropes to Jeremiah in the
cistern. Ebed-melek the Ethiopian called
down to Jeremiah, "Put these scraps of old
clothing under your armpits and around the
ropes."
Jeremiah did what he said.
13 And so they pulled Jeremiah up out of the
cistern by the ropes. But he was still con-
fined in the courtyard of the palace guard.
14 Later, King Zedekiah sent for Jeremiah
the prophet and had him brought to the
third entrance of the Temple of God. The
king said to Jeremiah, "I'm going to ask you
something. Don't hold anything back from
me."
15 Jeremiah said, "If I told you the whole
truth, you'd kill me. And no matter what I
said, you wouldn't pay any attention any-
way."
16 Zedekiah swore to Jeremiah right there,
but in secret, "As sure as God lives, who
gives *us* life, I won't kill you, nor will I turn
you over to the men who are trying to kill
you."
17-18 So Jeremiah told Zedekiah, "This is the
Message from God, God-of-the-Angel-
Armies, the God of Israel: 'If you will turn
yourself over to the generals of the king of
Babylon, you will live, this city won't be
burned down, and your family will live. But
if you don't turn yourself over to the gener-
als of the king of Babylon, this city will go
into the hands of the Chaldeans and they'll
burn it down. And don't for a minute think
there's any escape for you.' "
19 King Zedekiah said to Jeremiah, "But I'm
afraid of the Judeans who have already de-
serted to the Chaldeans. If they get hold of
me, they'll rough me up good."
20-22 Jeremiah assured him, "They won't get
hold of you. Listen, please. Listen to God's
voice. I'm telling you this for your own good
so that you'll live. But if you refuse to turn
yourself over, this is what God has shown
me will happen: Picture this in your mind—
all the women still left in the palace of the
king of Judah, led out to the officers of the
king of Babylon, and as they're led out they
are saying:

NEW KING JAMES VERSION

"Your close friends have set upon you
And prevailed against you;
Your feet have sunk in the mire,
And they have turned away again."

23'So they shall surrender all your wives and children to the Chaldeans. You shall not escape from their hand, but shall be taken by the hand of the king of Babylon. And you shall cause this city to be burned with fire.' "

24Then Zedekiah said to Jeremiah, "Let no one know of these words, and you shall not die. 25But if the princes hear that I have talked with you, and they come to you and say to you, 'Declare to us now what you have said to the king, and also what the king said to you; do not hide *it* from us, and we will not put you to death,' 26then you shall say to them, 'I presented my request before the king, that he would not make me return to Jonathan's house to die there.' "

27Then all the princes came to Jeremiah and asked him. And he told them according to all these words that the king had commanded. So they stopped speaking with him, for the conversation had not been heard. 28Now Jeremiah remained in the court of the prison until the day that Jerusalem was taken. And he was *there* when Jerusalem was taken.

THE FALL OF JERUSALEM

39 In the ninth year of Zedekiah king of Judah, in the tenth month, Nebuchadnezzar king of Babylon and all his army came against Jerusalem, and besieged it. 2In the eleventh year of Zedekiah, in the fourth month, on the ninth *day* of the month, the city was penetrated.

3Then all the princes of the king of Babylon came in and sat in the Middle Gate: Nergal-Sharezer, Samgar-Nebo, Sarsechim, Rabsaris,[a] Nergal-Sarezer, Rabmag,[b] with the rest of the princes of the king of Babylon.

4So it was, when Zedekiah the king of Judah and all the men of war saw them, that they fled and went out of the city by night, by way of the king's garden, by the gate between the two walls. And he went out by way of the plain.[a] 5But the Chaldean army pursued them and overtook Zedekiah in the plains of Jericho. And when they had captured him, they brought him up to Nebuchadnezzar king of Babylon, to Riblah in the land of Hamath, where he pronounced judgment on him. 6Then the king of Babylon killed the sons of Zedekiah before his eyes in Riblah; the king of Babylon also killed all the nobles of Judah. 7Moreover he put out Zedekiah's eyes, and bound him with bronze fetters to carry him off to Babylon. 8And the Chaldeans burned the king's house and the houses of the people with fire, and broke down the walls of Jerusalem. 9Then Nebuzaradan the captain of the guard carried away captive to Babylon the remnant of the people who remained in the city and those

39:3 [a]A title, probably *Chief Officer;* also verse 13 [b]A title, probably *Troop Commander;* also verse 13 **39:4** [a]Or *the Arabah,* that is, the Jordan Valley

THE MESSAGE

" 'They lied to you and did you in,
those so-called friends of yours;
And now you're stuck, about knee-deep in mud,
and your "friends," where are they now?'

23 "They'll take all your wives and children and give them to the Chaldeans. And you, don't think you'll get out of this—the king of Babylon will seize you and then burn this city to the ground."

24-26 Zedekiah said to Jeremiah, "Don't let anyone know of this conversation, if you know what's good for you. If the government officials get wind that I've been talking with you, they may come and say, 'Tell us what went on between you and the king, what you said and what he said. Hold nothing back and we won't kill you.' If this happens, tell them, 'I presented my case to the king so that he wouldn't send me back to the dungeon of Jonathan to die there.' "

27 And sure enough, all the officials came to Jeremiah and asked him. He responded as the king had instructed. So they quit asking. No one had overheard the conversation.

28 Jeremiah lived in the courtyard of the palace guards until the day that Jerusalem was captured.

BAD NEWS, NOT GOOD NEWS

1-2 39 In the ninth year and tenth month of Zedekiah king of Judah, Nebuchadnezzar king of Babylon came with his entire army and laid siege to Jerusalem. In the eleventh year and fourth month, on the ninth day of Zedekiah's reign, they broke through into the city.

3 All the officers of the king of Babylon came and set themselves up as a ruling council from the Middle Gate: Nergal-sharezer of Simmagar, Nebushazban the Rabsaris, Nergal-sharezer the Rabmag, along with all the other officials of the king of Babylon.

4-7 When Zedekiah king of Judah and his remaining soldiers saw this, they ran for their lives. They slipped out at night on a path in the king's garden through the gate between two walls and headed for the wilderness, toward the Jordan Valley. The Babylonian army chased them and caught Zedekiah in the wilderness of Jericho. They seized him and took him to Nebuchadnezzar king of Babylon at Riblah in the country of Hamath. Nebuchadnezzar decided his fate. The king of Babylon killed all the sons of Zedekiah in Riblah right before his eyes and then killed all the nobles of Judah. After Zedekiah had seen the slaughter, Nebuchadnezzar blinded him, chained him up, and then took him off to Babylon.

8-10 Meanwhile, the Babylonians burned down the royal palace, the Temple, and all the homes of the people. They leveled the walls of Jerusalem. Nebuzaradan, commander of the king's bodyguard, rounded up everyone left in the city, along with those who had surrendered to him, and herded

New King James Version

who defected to him, with the rest of the people
who remained. [10]But Nebuzaradan the captain
of the guard left in the land of Judah the poor
people, who had nothing, and gave them vine-
yards and fields at the same time.

Jeremiah Goes Free

[11]Now Nebuchadnezzar king of Babylon
gave charge concerning Jeremiah to Ne-
buzaradan the captain of the guard, saying,
[12]"Take him and look after him, and do him no
harm; but do to him just as he says to you." [13]So
Nebuzaradan the captain of the guard sent Ne-
bushasban, Rabsaris, Nergal-Sharezer, Rab-
mag, and all the king of Babylon's chief officers;
[14]then they sent *someone* to take Jeremiah from
the court of the prison, and committed him to
Gedaliah the son of Ahikam, the son of
Shaphan, that he should take him home. So he
dwelt among the people.
[15]Meanwhile the word of the LORD had come
to Jeremiah while he was shut up in the court of
the prison, saying, [16]"Go and speak to Ebed-
Melech the Ethiopian, saying, 'Thus says the
LORD of hosts, the God of Israel: "Behold, I will
bring My words upon this city for adversity and
not for good, and they shall be *performed* in that
day before you. [17]But I will deliver you in that
day," says the LORD, "and you shall not be given
into the hand of the men of whom you *are*
afraid. [18]For I will surely deliver you, and you
shall not fall by the sword; but your life shall be
as a prize to you, because you have put your
trust in Me," says the LORD.' "

Jeremiah with Gedaliah the Governor

40 The word that came to Jeremiah from the
LORD after Nebuzaradan the captain of the
guard had let him go from Ramah, when he had
taken him bound in chains among all who were
carried away captive from Jerusalem and Ju-
dah, who were carried away captive to Babylon.
[2]And the captain of the guard took Jeremiah
and said to him: "The LORD your God has pro-
nounced this doom on this place. [3]Now the LORD
has brought *it*, and has done just as He said. Be-
cause you *people* have sinned against the LORD,
and not obeyed His voice, therefore this thing
has come upon you. [4]And now look, I free you
this day from the chains that *were* on your hand.
If it seems good to you to come with me to Bab-
ylon, come, and I will look after you. But if it
seems wrong for you to come with me to Bab-
ylon, remain here. See, all the land *is* before
you; wherever it seems good and convenient for
you to go, go there."
[5]Now while Jeremiah had not yet gone back,
Nebuzaradan said, "Go back to Gedaliah the son
of Ahikam, the son of Shaphan, whom the king
of Babylon has made governor over the cities of
Judah, and dwell with him among the people. Or
go wherever it seems convenient for you to go."
So the captain of the guard gave him rations
and a gift and let him go.

The Message

them off to exile in Babylon. He didn't
bother taking the few poor people who had
nothing. He left them in the land of Judah to
eke out a living as best they could in the
vineyards and fields.

11-12 Nebuchadnezzar king of Babylon gave Ne-
buzaradan captain of the king's bodyguard
special orders regarding Jeremiah: "Look
out for him. Make sure nothing bad happens
to him. Give him anything he wants."
13-14 So Nebuzaradan, chief of the king's
bodyguard, along with Nebushazban the
Rabsaris, Nergal-sharezer the Rabmag, and
all the chief officers of the king of Babylon,
sent for Jeremiah, taking him from the
courtyard of the royal guards and putting
him under the care of Gedaliah son of
Ahikam, the son of Shaphan, to be taken
home. And so he was able to live with the
people.

15-18 Earlier, while Jeremiah was still in custody
in the courtyard of the royal guards, GOD's
Message came to him: "Go and speak with
Ebed-melek the Ethiopian. Tell him, GOD-of-
the-Angel-Armies, the God of Israel, says,
Listen carefully: I will do exactly what I said
I would do to this city—bad news, not good
news. When it happens, you will be there to
see it. But I'll deliver you on that doomsday.
You won't be handed over to those men
whom you have good reason to fear. Yes, I'll
most certainly save you. You won't be killed.
You'll walk out of there safe and sound be-
cause you trusted me.' " GOD's Decree.

Go and Live Wherever You Wish

1 **40** GOD's Message to Jeremiah after Ne-
buzaradan captain of the bodyguard set
him free at Ramah. When Nebuzaradan
came upon him, he was in chains, along
with all the other captives from Jerusalem
and Judah who were being herded off to ex-
ile in Babylon.
2-3 The captain of the bodyguard singled out
Jeremiah and said to him, "Your GOD pro-
nounced doom on this place. GOD came and
did what he had warned he'd do because
you all sinned against GOD and wouldn't do
what he told you. So now you're all suffer-
ing the consequences.
4-5 "But today, Jeremiah, I'm setting you free,
taking the chains off your hands. If you'd
like to come to Babylon with me, come
along. I'll take good care of you. But if you
don't want to come to Babylon with me,
that's just fine, too. Look, the whole land
stretches out before you. Do what you like.
Go and live wherever you wish. If you want
to stay home, go back to Gedaliah son of
Ahikam, son of Shaphan. The king of Bab-
ylon made him governor of the cities of Ju-
dah. Stay with him and your people. Or go
wherever you'd like. It's up to you."
The captain of the bodyguard gave him
food for the journey and a parting gift, and
sent him off.

NEW KING JAMES VERSION

[6]Then Jeremiah went to Gedaliah the son of
Ahikam, to Mizpah, and dwelt with him among
the people who were left in the land.
[7]And when all the captains of the armies
who *were* in the fields, they and their men,
heard that the king of Babylon had made
Gedaliah the son of Ahikam governor in the
land, and had committed to him men, women,
children, and the poorest of the land who had
not been carried away captive to Babylon, [8]then
they came to Gedaliah at Mizpah—Ishmael the
son of Nethaniah, Johanan and Jonathan the
sons of Kareah, Seraiah the son of Tanhumeth,
the sons of Ephai the Netophathite, and Jez-
aniah[a] the son of a Maachathite, they and their
men. [9]And Gedaliah the son of Ahikam, the son
of Shaphan, took an oath before them and their
men, saying, "Do not be afraid to serve the
Chaldeans. Dwell in the land and serve the king
of Babylon, and it shall be well with you. [10]As
for me, I will indeed dwell at Mizpah and serve
the Chaldeans who come to us. But you, gather
wine and summer fruit and oil, put *them* in your
vessels, and dwell in your cities that you have
taken." [11]Likewise, when all the Jews who *were*
in Moab, among the Ammonites, in Edom, and
who *were* in all the countries, heard that the
king of Babylon had left a remnant of Judah,
and that he had set over them Gedaliah the son
of Ahikam, the son of Shaphan, [12]then all the
Jews returned out of all places where they had
been driven, and came to the land of Judah, to
Gedaliah at Mizpah, and gathered wine and
summer fruit in abundance.
[13]Moreover Johanan the son of Kareah and
all the captains of the forces that *were* in the
fields came to Gedaliah at Mizpah, [14]and said to
him, "Do you certainly know that Baalis the
king of the Ammonites has sent Ishmael the son
of Nethaniah to murder you?" But Gedaliah the
son of Ahikam did not believe them.
[15]Then Johanan the son of Kareah spoke se-
cretly to Gedaliah in Mizpah, saying, "Let me
go, please, and I will kill Ishmael the son of
Nethaniah, and no one will know *it*. Why should
he murder you, so that all the Jews who are
gathered to you would be scattered, and the
remnant in Judah perish?"
[16]But Gedaliah the son of Ahikam said to Jo-
hanan the son of Kareah, "You shall not do this
thing, for you speak falsely concerning Ish-
mael."

INSURRECTION AGAINST GEDALIAH

41 Now it came to pass in the seventh month
that Ishmael the son of Nethaniah, the son
of Elishama, of the royal family and of the offi-
cers of the king, came with ten men to Gedaliah
the son of Ahikam, at Mizpah. And there they

40:8 [a]Spelled *Jaazaniah* in 2 Kings 25:23

THE MESSAGE

6 Jeremiah went to Gedaliah son of
Ahikam at Mizpah and made his home with
him and the people who were left behind in
the land.

TAKE CARE OF THE LAND

7-8 When the army leaders and their men, who
had been hiding out in the fields, heard that
the king of Babylon had appointed Gedaliah
son of Ahikam as governor of the land, putting
him in charge of the men, women, and chil-
dren of the poorest of the poor who hadn't
been taken off to exile in Babylon, they came
to Gedaliah at Mizpah: Ishmael son of Netha-
niah, Johanan and Jonathan the sons of
Kareah, Seraiah son of Tanhumeth, the sons
of Ephai the Netophathite, and Jaazaniah son
of the Maacathite, accompanied by their men.
9 Gedaliah son of Ahikam, the son of
Shaphan, promised them and their men,
"You have nothing to fear from the
Chaldean officials. Stay here on the land. Be
subject to the king of Babylon. You'll get
along just fine.
10 "My job is to stay here in Mizpah and be
your advocate before the Chaldeans when
they show up. Your job is to take care of the
land: Make wine, harvest the summer fruits,
press olive oil. Store it all in pottery jugs and
settle into the towns that you have taken
over."
11-12 The Judeans who had escaped to Moab,
Ammon, Edom, and other countries heard
that the king of Babylon had left a few sur-
vivors in Judah and made Gedaliah son of
Ahikam, son of Shaphan, governor over
them. They all started coming back to Judah
from all the places where they'd been scat-
tered. They came to Judah and to Gedaliah
at Mizpah and went to work gathering in a
huge supply of wine and summer fruits.

13-14 One day Johanan son of Kareah and all the
officers of the army who had been hiding out
in the backcountry came to Gedaliah at Miz-
pah and told him, "You know, don't you, that
Baaliss king of Ammon has sent Ishmael son
of Nethaniah to kill you?" But Gedaliah son
of Ahikam didn't believe them.
15 Then Johanan son of Kareah took
Gedaliah aside privately in Mizpah: "Let me
go and kill Ishmael son of Nethaniah. No one
needs to know about it. Why should we let
him kill you and plunge the land into anar-
chy? Why let everyone you've taken care of be
scattered and what's left of Judah destroyed?"
16 But Gedaliah son of Ahikam told Jo-
hanan son of Kareah, "Don't do it. I forbid it.
You're spreading a false rumor about Ish-
mael."

MURDER

1-3 **41** But in the seventh month, Ishmael son
of Nethaniah, son of Elishama, came.
He had royal blood in his veins and had
been one of the king's high-ranking officers.
He paid a visit to Gedaliah son of Ahikam at
Mizpah with ten of his men. As they were

NEW KING JAMES VERSION

ate bread together in Mizpah. 2Then Ishmael the son of Nethaniah, and the ten men who were with him, arose and struck Gedaliah the son of Ahikam, the son of Shaphan, with the sword, and killed him whom the king of Babylon had made governor over the land. 3Ishmael also struck down all the Jews who were with him, *that is*, with Gedaliah at Mizpah, and the Chaldeans who were found there, the men of war.

4And it happened, on the second day after he had killed Gedaliah, when as yet no one knew *it*, 5that certain men came from Shechem, from Shiloh, and from Samaria, eighty men with their beards shaved and their clothes torn, having cut themselves, with offerings and incense in their hand, to bring *them* to the house of the LORD. 6Now Ishmael the son of Nethaniah went out from Mizpah to meet them, weeping as he went along; and it happened as he met them that he said to them, "Come to Gedaliah the son of Ahikam!" 7So it was, when they came into the midst of the city, that Ishmael the son of Nethaniah killed them *and cast them* into the midst of a pit, he and the men who were with him. 8But ten men were found among them who said to Ishmael, "Do not kill us, for we have treasures of wheat, barley, oil, and honey in the field." So he desisted and did not kill them among their brethren. 9Now the pit into which Ishmael had cast all the dead bodies of the men whom he had slain, because of Gedaliah, *was* the same one Asa the king had made for fear of Baasha king of Israel. Ishmael the son of Nethaniah filled it with *the* slain. 10Then Ishmael carried away captive all the rest of the people who *were* in Mizpah, the king's daughters and all the people who remained in Mizpah, whom Nebuzaradan the captain of the guard had committed to Gedaliah the son of Ahikam. And Ishmael the son of Nethaniah carried them away captive and departed to go over to the Ammonites.

11But when Johanan the son of Kareah and all the captains of the forces that *were* with him heard of all the evil that Ishmael the son of Nethaniah had done, 12they took all the men and went to fight with Ishmael the son of Nethaniah; and they found him by the great pool that *is* in Gibeon. 13So it was, when all the people who *were* with Ishmael saw Johanan the son of Kareah, and all the captains of the forces who *were* with him, that they were glad. 14Then all the people whom Ishmael had carried away captive from Mizpah turned around and came back, and went to Johanan the son of Kareah. 15But Ishmael the son of Nethaniah escaped from Johanan with eight men and went to the Ammonites.

16Then Johanan the son of Kareah, and all the captains of the forces that were with him, took from Mizpah all the rest of the people whom he had recovered from Ishmael the son of Nethaniah after he had murdered Gedaliah the son of Ahikam—the mighty men of war and the women and the children and the eunuchs, whom he had brought back from Gibeon. 17And they departed and dwelt in the habitation of

THE MESSAGE

eating together, Ishmael and his ten men jumped to their feet and knocked Gedaliah down and killed him, killed the man the king of Babylon had appointed governor of the land. Ishmael also killed all the Judeans who were with Gedaliah in Mizpah, as well as the Chaldean soldiers who were stationed there.

4-5 On the second day after the murder of Gedaliah—no one yet knew of it—men arrived from Shechem, Shiloh, and Samaria, eighty of them, with their beards shaved, their clothing ripped, and gashes on their bodies. They were pilgrims carrying grain offerings and incense on their way to worship at the Temple in Jerusalem.

6 Ishmael son of Nethaniah went out from Mizpah to welcome them, weeping ostentatiously. When he greeted them he invited them in: "Come and meet Gedaliah son of Ahikam."

7-8 But as soon as they were inside the city, Ishmael son of Nethaniah and his henchmen slaughtered the pilgrims and dumped the bodies in a cistern. Ten of the men talked their way out of the massacre. They bargained with Ishmael, "Don't kill us. We have a hidden store of wheat, barley, olive oil, and honey out in the fields." So he held back and didn't kill them with their fellow pilgrims.

9 Ishmael's reason for dumping the bodies into a cistern was to cover up the earlier murder of Gedaliah. The cistern had been built by king Asa as a defense against Baasha king of Israel. This was the cistern that Ishmael son of Nethaniah filled with the slaughtered men.

10 Ishmael then took everyone else in Mizpah, including the king's daughters entrusted to the care of Gedaliah son of Ahikam by Nebuzaradan the captain of the bodyguard, as prisoners. Rounding up the prisoners, Ishmael son of Nethaniah proceeded to take them over into the country of Ammon.

11-12 Johanan son of Kareah and all the army officers with him heard about the atrocities committed by Ishmael son of Nethaniah. They set off at once after Ishmael son of Nethaniah. They found him at the large pool at Gibeon.

13-15 When all the prisoners from Mizpah who had been taken by Ishmael saw Johanan son of Kareah and the army officers with him, they couldn't believe their eyes. They were so happy! They all rallied around Johanan son of Kareah and headed back home. But Ishmael son of Nethaniah got away, escaping from Johanan with eight men into the land of Ammon.

16 Then Johanan son of Kareah and the army officers with him gathered together what was left of the people whom Ishmael son of Nethaniah had taken prisoner from Mizpah after the murder of Gedaliah son of Ahikam—men, women, children, eunuchs—and brought them back from Gibeon.

17-18 They set out at once for Egypt to get away from the Chaldeans, stopping on the way at

NEW KING JAMES VERSION

Chimham, which is near Bethlehem, as they
went on their way to Egypt, 18because of the
Chaldeans; for they were afraid of them, be-
cause Ishmael the son of Nethaniah had mur-
dered Gedaliah the son of Ahikam, whom the
king of Babylon had made governor in the land.

THE FLIGHT TO EGYPT FORBIDDEN

42 Now all the captains of the forces, Jo-
hanan the son of Kareah, Jezaniah the son
of Hoshaiah, and all the people, from the least to
the greatest, came near 2and said to Jeremiah
the prophet, "Please, let our petition be accept-
able to you, and pray for us to the LORD your
God, for all this remnant (since we are left *but* a
few of many, as you can see), 3that the LORD
your God may show us the way in which we
should walk and the thing we should do."
4Then Jeremiah the prophet said to them, "I
have heard. Indeed, I will pray to the LORD your
God according to your words, and it shall be,
that whatever the LORD answers you, I will de-
clare *it* to you. I will keep nothing back from
you."
5So they said to Jeremiah, "Let the LORD be a
true and faithful witness between us, if we do
not do according to everything which the LORD
your God sends us by you. 6Whether *it is* pleas-
ing or displeasing, we will obey the voice of the
LORD our God to whom we send you, that it may
be well with us when we obey the voice of the
LORD our God."
7And it happened after ten days that the
word of the LORD came to Jeremiah. 8Then he
called Johanan the son of Kareah, all the cap-
tains of the forces which *were* with him, and all
the people from the least even to the greatest,
9and said to them, "Thus says the LORD, the God
of Israel, to whom you sent me to present your
petition before Him: 10'If you will still remain in
this land, then I will build you and not pull *you*
down, and I will plant you and not pluck *you* up.
For I relent concerning the disaster that I have
brought upon you. 11Do not be afraid of the king
of Babylon, of whom you are afraid; do not be
afraid of him,' says the LORD, 'for I *am* with you,
to save you and deliver you from his hand.
12And I will show you mercy, that he may have
mercy on you and cause you to return to your
own land.'
13"But if you say, 'We will not dwell in this
land,' disobeying the voice of the LORD your
God, 14saying, 'No, but we will go to the land of
Egypt where we shall see no war, nor hear the
sound of the trumpet, nor be hungry for bread,
and there we will dwell'— 15Then hear now the
word of the LORD, O remnant of Judah! Thus
says the LORD of hosts, the God of Israel: 'If you
wholly set your faces to enter Egypt, and go to
dwell there, 16then it shall be *that* the sword
which you feared shall overtake you there in the
land of Egypt; the famine of which you were
afraid shall follow close after you there *in*
Egypt; and there you shall die. 17So shall it be
with all the men who set their faces to go to
Egypt to dwell there. They shall die by the
sword, by famine, and by pestilence. And none
of them shall remain or escape from the disaster
that I will bring upon them.'

THE MESSAGE

Geruth-kimham near Bethlehem. They were
afraid of what the Chaldeans might do in re-
taliation of Ishmael son of Nethaniah's mur-
der of Gedaliah son of Ahikam, whom the
king of Babylon had appointed as governor
of the country.

WHAT YOU FEAR WILL CATCH UP WITH YOU

1-3 42 All the army officers, led by Johanan
son of Kareah and Jezaniah son of
Hoshaiah, accompanied by all the people,
small and great, came to Jeremiah the
prophet and said, "We have a request.
Please listen. Pray to your GOD for us,
what's left of us. You can see for yourself
how few we are! Pray that your GOD will tell
us the way we should go and what we
should do."
4 Jeremiah the prophet said, "I hear your
request. And I will pray to your GOD as you
have asked. Whatever GOD says, I'll pass on
to you. I'll tell you everything, holding noth-
ing back."
5-6 They said to Jeremiah, "Let GOD be our
witness, a true and faithful witness against
us, if we don't do everything that your GOD
directs you to tell us. Whether we like it or
not, we'll do it. We'll obey whatever our GOD
tells us. Yes, count on us. We'll do it."
7-8 Ten days later GOD's Message came to Jer-
emiah. He called together Johanan son of
Kareah and all the army officers with him,
including all the people, regardless of how
much clout they had.
9-12 He then spoke: "This is the Message from
GOD, the God of Israel, to whom you sent me
to present your prayer. He says, 'If you are
ready to stick it out in this land, I will build
you up and not drag you down, I will plant
you and not pull you up like a weed. I feel
deep compassion on account of the doom I
have visited on you. You don't have to fear
the king of Babylon. Your fears are for noth-
ing. I'm on your side, ready to save and de-
liver you from anything he might do. I'll
pour mercy on you. What's more, *he* will
show you mercy! He'll let you come back to
your very own land.'
13-17 "But do not say, 'We're not staying
around this place,' refusing to obey the com-
mand of your GOD and saying instead, 'No!
We're off to Egypt, where things are peace-
ful—no wars, no attacking armies, plenty of
food. We're going to live there.' If what's left
of Judah is headed down that road, then lis-
ten to GOD's Message. This is what GOD-of-
the-Angel-Armies says: 'If you have deter-
mined to go to Egypt and make that your
home, then the very wars you fear will catch
up with you in Egypt and the starvation you
dread will track you down in Egypt. You'll
die there! Every last one of you who is deter-
mined to go to Egypt and make it your home
will either be killed, starve, or get sick and
die. No survivors, not one! No one will es-
cape the doom that I'll bring upon you.'

New King James Version

18“For thus says the LORD of hosts, the God of Israel: ‘As My anger and My fury have been poured out on the inhabitants of Jerusalem, so will My fury be poured out on you when you enter Egypt. And you shall be an oath, an astonishment, a curse, and a reproach; and you shall see this place no more.’

19“The LORD has said concerning you, O remnant of Judah, ‘Do not go to Egypt!’ Know certainly that I have admonished you this day. 20For you were hypocrites in your hearts when you sent me to the LORD your God, saying, ‘Pray for us to the LORD our God, and according to all that the LORD your God says, so declare to us and we will do *it*.’ 21And I have this day declared *it* to you, but you have not obeyed the voice of the LORD your God, or anything which He has sent you by me. 22Now therefore, know certainly that you shall die by the sword, by famine, and by pestilence in the place where you desire to go to dwell.”

Jeremiah Taken to Egypt

43 Now it happened, when Jeremiah had stopped speaking to all the people all the words of the LORD their God, for which the LORD their God had sent him to them, all these words, 2that Azariah the son of Hoshaiah, Johanan the son of Kareah, and all the proud men spoke, saying to Jeremiah, “You speak falsely! The LORD our God has not sent you to say, ‘Do not go to Egypt to dwell there.’ 3But Baruch the son of Neriah has set you against us, to deliver us into the hand of the Chaldeans, that they may put us to death or carry us away captive to Babylon.” 4So Johanan the son of Kareah, all the captains of the forces, and all the people would not obey the voice of the LORD, to remain in the land of Judah. 5But Johanan the son of Kareah and all the captains of the forces took all the remnant of Judah who had returned to dwell in the land of Judah, from all nations where they had been driven— 6men, women, children, the king’s daughters, and every person whom Nebuzaradan the captain of the guard had left with Gedaliah the son of Ahikam, the son of Shaphan, and Jeremiah the prophet and Baruch the son of Neriah. 7So they went to the land of Egypt, for they did not obey the voice of the LORD. And they went as far as Tahpanhes.

8Then the word of the LORD came to Jeremiah in Tahpanhes, saying, 9“Take large stones in your hand, and hide them in the sight of the men of Judah, in the clay in the brick courtyard which *is* at the entrance to Pharaoh’s house in Tahpanhes; 10and say to them, ‘Thus says the LORD of hosts, the God of Israel: “Behold, I will send and bring Nebuchadnezzar the king of Babylon, My servant, and will set his throne above these stones that I have hidden. And he

The Message

18 “This is the Message from GOD-of-the-Angel-Armies, the God of Israel: ‘In the same way that I swept the citizens of Jerusalem away with my anger and wrath, I’ll do the same thing all over again in Egypt. You’ll end up being cursed, reviled, ridiculed, and mocked. And you’ll never see your homeland again.’

19-20 “GOD has plainly told you, you leftovers from Judah, ‘Don’t go to Egypt.’ Could anything be plainer? I warn you this day that you are living out a fantasy. You’re making a fatal mistake.

“Didn’t you just now send me to your GOD, saying, ‘Pray for us to our GOD. Tell us everything that GOD says and we’ll do it all’?

21-22 “Well, now I’ve told you, told you everything he said, and you haven’t obeyed a word of it, not a single word of what your GOD sent me to tell you. So now let me tell you what will happen next: You’ll be killed, you’ll starve to death, you’ll get sick and die in the wonderful country where you’ve determined to go and live.”

Death! Exile! Slaughter!

1-3 43 When Jeremiah finished telling all the people the whole Message that their GOD had sent him to give them—all these words—Azariah son of Hoshaiah and Johanan son of Kareah, backed by all the self-important men, said to Jeremiah, “Liar! Our GOD never sent you with this message telling us not to go to Egypt and live there. Baruch son of Neriah is behind this. He has turned you against us. He’s playing into the hands of the Babylonians so we’ll either end up being killed or taken off to exile in Babylon.”

4 Johanan son of Kareah and the army officers, and the people along with them, wouldn’t listen to GOD’s Message that they stay in the land of Judah and live there.

5-7 Johanan son of Kareah and the army officers gathered up everyone who was left from Judah, who had come back after being scattered all over the place—the men, women, and children, the king’s daughters, all the people that Nebuzaradan captain of the bodyguard had left in the care of Gedaliah son of Ahikam, the son of Shaphan, and last but not least, Jeremiah the prophet and Baruch son of Neriah. They entered the land of Egypt in total disobedience of GOD’s Message and arrived at the city of Tahpanhes.

8-9 While in Tahpanhes, GOD’s Word came to Jeremiah: “Pick up some large stones and cover them with mortar in the vicinity of the pavement that leads up to the building set aside for Pharaoh’s use in Tahpanhes. Make sure some of the men of Judah are watching.

10-13 “Then address them: ‘This is what GOD-of-the-Angel-Armies says: Be on the lookout! I’m sending for and bringing Nebuchadnezzar the king of Babylon—my servant, mind you!—and he’ll set up his throne on these very stones that I’ve had

NEW KING JAMES VERSION

will spread his royal pavilion over them. [11]When he comes, he shall strike the land of Egypt *and deliver* to death *those appointed* for death, and to captivity *those appointed* for captivity, and to the sword *those appointed* for the sword. [12]I[a] will kindle a fire in the houses of the gods of Egypt, and he shall burn them and carry them away captive. And he shall array himself with the land of Egypt, as a shepherd puts on his garment, and he shall go out from there in peace. [13]He shall also break the *sacred* pillars of Beth Shemesh[a] that *are* in the land of Egypt; and the houses of the gods of the Egyptians he shall burn with fire." ' "

ISRAELITES WILL BE PUNISHED IN EGYPT

44 The word that came to Jeremiah concerning all the Jews who dwell in the land of Egypt, who dwell at Migdol, at Tahpanhes, at Noph,[a] and in the country of Pathros, saying, [2]"Thus says the LORD of hosts, the God of Israel: 'You have seen all the calamity that I have brought on Jerusalem and on all the cities of Judah; and behold, this day they *are* a desolation, and no one dwells in them, [3]because of their wickedness which they have committed to provoke Me to anger, in that they went to burn incense *and* to serve other gods whom they did not know, they nor you nor your fathers. [4]However I have sent to you all My servants the prophets, rising early and sending *them,* saying, "Oh, do not do this abominable thing that I hate!" [5]But they did not listen or incline their ear to turn from their wickedness, to burn no incense to other gods. [6]So My fury and My anger were poured out and kindled in the cities of Judah and in the streets of Jerusalem; and they are wasted *and* desolate, as it is this day.'

[7]"Now therefore, thus says the LORD, the God of hosts, the God of Israel: 'Why do you commit *this* great evil against yourselves, to cut off from you man and woman, child and infant, out of Judah, leaving none to remain, [8]in that you provoke Me to wrath with the works of your hands, burning incense to other gods in the land of Egypt where you have gone to dwell, that you may cut yourselves off and be a curse and a reproach among all the nations of the earth? [9]Have you forgotten the wickedness of your fathers, the wickedness of the kings of Judah, the wickedness of their wives, your own wickedness, and the wickedness of your wives, which they committed in the land of Judah and in the streets of Jerusalem? [10]They have not been humbled, to this day, nor have they feared; they have not walked in My law or in My statutes that I set before you and your fathers.'

[11]"Therefore thus says the LORD of hosts, the God of Israel: 'Behold, I will set My face against you for catastrophe and for cutting off all Judah. [12]And I will take the remnant of Judah who have

43:12 [a]Following Masoretic Text and Targum; Septuagint, Syriac, and Vulgate read *He.* **43:13** [a]Literally *House of the Sun,* ancient On; later called Heliopolis **44:1** [a]That is, ancient Memphis

THE MESSAGE

buried here and he'll spread out his canopy over them. He'll come and absolutely smash Egypt, sending each to his assigned fate: death, exile, slaughter. He'll burn down the temples of Egypt's gods. He'll either burn up the gods or haul them off as booty. Like a shepherd who picks lice from his robes, he'll pick Egypt clean. And then he'll walk away without a hand being laid on him. He'll shatter the sacred obelisks at Egypt's House of the Sun and make a huge bonfire of the temples of Egypt's gods.' "

THE SAME FATE WILL FALL UPON ALL

1-6 **44** The Message that Jeremiah received for all the Judeans who lived in the land of Egypt, who had their homes in Migdol, Tahpanhes, Noph, and the land of Pathros: "This is what GOD-of-the-Angel-Armies, the God of Israel, says: 'You saw with your own eyes the terrible doom that I brought down on Jerusalem and the Judean cities. Look at what's left: ghost towns of rubble and smoking ruins, and all because they took up with evil ways, making me angry by going off to offer sacrifices and worship the latest in gods—no-gods that neither they nor you nor your ancestors knew the first thing about. Morning after morning and long into the night I kept after you, sending you all those prophets, my servants, begging you, "Please, please—don't do this, don't fool around in this loathsome gutter of gods that I hate with a passion." But do you think anyone paid the least bit of attention or repented of evil or quit offering sacrifices to the no-gods? Not one. So I let loose with my anger, a firestorm of wrath in the cities of Judah and the streets of Jerusalem, and left them in ruins and wasted. And they're *still* in ruins and wasted.'

7-8 "This is the Message of GOD, GOD-of-the-Angel-Armies, the God of Israel: 'So why are you ruining your lives by amputating yourselves—man, woman, child, and baby—from the life of Judah, leaving yourselves isolated, unconnected? And why do you deliberately make me angry by what you do, offering sacrifices to these no-gods in the land of Egypt where you've come to live? You'll only destroy yourselves and make yourselves an example used in curses and an object of ridicule among all the nations of the earth.

9-11 " 'Have you so soon forgotten the evil lives of your ancestors, the evil lives of the kings of Judah and their wives, to say nothing of your own evil lives, you and your wives, the evil you flaunted in the land of Judah and the streets of Jerusalem? And to this day, there's not a trace of remorse, not a sign of reverence, nobody caring about living by what I tell them or following my instructions that I've set out so plainly before you and your parents! So this is what GOD-of-the-Angel-Armies decrees:

11-14 " 'Watch out! I've decided to bring doom on you and get rid of everyone connected with Judah. I'm going to take what's left of

NEW KING JAMES VERSION

set their faces to go into the land of Egypt to
dwell there, and they shall all be consumed *and*
fall in the land of Egypt. They shall be con-
sumed by the sword *and* by famine. They shall
die, from the least to the greatest, by the sword
and by famine; and they shall be an oath, an as-
tonishment, a curse and a reproach! 13For I will
punish those who dwell in the land of Egypt, as
I have punished Jerusalem, by the sword, by
famine, and by pestilence, 14so that none of the
remnant of Judah who have gone into the land
of Egypt to dwell there shall escape or survive,
lest they return to the land of Judah, to which
they desire to return and dwell. For none shall
return except those who escape.' "

15Then all the men who knew that their
wives had burned incense to other gods, with all
the women who stood by, a great multitude, and
all the people who dwelt in the land of Egypt, in
Pathros, answered Jeremiah, saying: 16"*As for*
the word that you have spoken to us in the name
of the LORD, we will not listen to you! 17But we
will certainly do whatever has gone out of our
own mouth, to burn incense to the queen of
heaven and pour out drink offerings to her, as
we have done, we and our fathers, our kings and
our princes, in the cities of Judah and in the
streets of Jerusalem. For *then* we had plenty of
food, were well-off, and saw no trouble. 18But
since we stopped burning incense to the queen
of heaven and pouring out drink offerings to
her, we have lacked everything and have been
consumed by the sword and by famine."

19*The women also said,* "And when we
burned incense to the queen of heaven and
poured out drink offerings to her, did we make
cakes for her, to worship her, and pour out drink
offerings to her without our husbands' *permis-
sion?*"

20Then Jeremiah spoke to all the people—the
men, the women, and all the people who had
given him *that* answer—saying: 21"The incense
that you burned in the cities of Judah and in the
streets of Jerusalem, you and your fathers, your
kings and your princes, and the people of the
land, did not the LORD remember them, and did
it *not* come into His mind? 22So the LORD could
no longer bear *it*, because of the evil of your do-
ings *and* because of the abominations which
you committed. Therefore your land is a desola-
tion, an astonishment, a curse, and without an
inhabitant, as *it is* this day. 23Because you have
burned incense and because you have sinned
against the LORD, and have not obeyed the voice
of the LORD or walked in His law, in His statutes
or in His testimonies, therefore this calamity
has happened to you, as *at* this day."

24Moreover Jeremiah said to all the people
and to all the women, "Hear the word of the
LORD, all Judah who *are* in the land of Egypt!
25Thus says the LORD of hosts, the God of Israel,
saying: 'You and your wives have spoken with
your mouths and fulfilled with your hands, say-
ing, "We will surely keep our vows that we have

THE MESSAGE

Judah, those who have decided to go to Egypt and live there, and finish them off. In Egypt they will either be killed or starve to death. The same fate will fall upon both the obscure and the important. Regardless of their status, they will either be killed or starve. You'll end up cursed, reviled, ridiculed, and mocked. I'll give those who are in Egypt the same medicine I gave those in Jerusalem: massacre, starvation, and disease. None of those who managed to get out of Judah alive and get away to Egypt are going to make it back to the Judah for which they're so homesick. None will make it back, except maybe a few fugitives.' "

MAKING GODDESS COOKIES

15-18 The men who knew that their wives had been burning sacrifices to the no-gods, joined by a large crowd of women, along with virtually everyone living in Pathros of Egypt, answered Jeremiah: "We're having nothing to do with what you tell us is GOD's Message. We're going to go right on offering sacrifices to the Queen of Heaven and pouring out drink offerings to her, keeping up the traditions set by our ancestors, our kings and government leaders in the cities of Judah and the streets of Jerusalem in the good old days. We had a good life then—lots of food, rising standard of living, and no bad luck. But the moment we quit sacrificing to the Queen of Heaven and pouring out offerings to her, everything fell apart. We've had nothing but massacres and starvation ever since."

19 And then the women chimed in: "Yes! Absolutely! We're going to keep at it, offering sacrifices to the Queen of Heaven and pouring out offerings to her. Aren't our husbands behind us? They like it that we make goddess cookies and pour out our offerings to her."

20-23 Then Jeremiah spoke up, confronting the men and the women, all the people who had answered so insolently. He said, "The sacrifices that you and your parents, your kings, your government officials, and the common people of the land offered up in the cities of Judah and the streets of Jerusalem—don't you think GOD noticed? He noticed, all right. And he got fed up. Finally, he couldn't take your evil behavior and your disgusting acts any longer. Your land became a wasteland, a death valley, a horror story, a ghost town. And it continues to be just that. This doom has come upon you because you kept offering all those sacrifices, and you sinned against GOD! You refused to listen to him, wouldn't live the way he directed, ignored the covenant conditions."

24-25 Jeremiah kept going, but now zeroed in on the women: "Listen, all you who are from Judah and living in Egypt—please, listen to GOD's Word. GOD-of-the-Angel-Armies, the God of Israel, says: 'You women! You said it and then you did it. You said, "We're going to

NEW KING JAMES VERSION

made, to burn incense to the queen of heaven and pour out drink offerings to her." You will surely keep your vows and perform your vows!' 26Therefore hear the word of the LORD, all Judah who dwell in the land of Egypt: 'Behold, I have sworn by My great name,' says the LORD, 'that My name shall no more be named in the mouth of any man of Judah in all the land of Egypt, saying, "The Lord GOD lives." 27Behold, I will watch over them for adversity and not for good. And all the men of Judah who *are* in the land of Egypt shall be consumed by the sword and by famine, until there is an end to them. 28Yet a small number who escape the sword shall return from the land of Egypt to the land of Judah; and all the remnant of Judah, who have gone to the land of Egypt to dwell there, shall know whose words will stand, Mine or theirs. 29And this *shall be* a sign to you,' says the LORD, 'that I will punish you in this place, that you may know that My words will surely stand against you for adversity.'

30"Thus says the LORD: 'Behold, I will give Pharaoh Hophra king of Egypt into the hand of his enemies and into the hand of those who seek his life, as I gave Zedekiah king of Judah into the hand of Nebuchadnezzar king of Babylon, his enemy who sought his life.' "

ASSURANCE TO BARUCH

45 The word that Jeremiah the prophet spoke to Baruch the son of Neriah, when he had written these words in a book at the instruction of Jeremiah,[a] in the fourth year of Jehoiakim the son of Josiah, king of Judah, saying, 2"Thus says the LORD, the God of Israel, to you, O Baruch: 3'You said, "Woe is me now! For the LORD has added grief to my sorrow. I fainted in my sighing, and I find no rest." '

4"Thus you shall say to him, 'Thus says the LORD: "Behold, what I have built I will break down, and what I have planted I will pluck up, that is, this whole land. 5And do you seek great things for yourself? Do not seek *them;* for behold, I will bring adversity on all flesh," says the LORD. "But I will give your life to you as a prize in all places, wherever you go." ' "

JUDGMENT ON EGYPT

46 The word of the LORD which came to Jeremiah the prophet against the nations. 2Against Egypt.

Concerning the army of Pharaoh Necho, king of Egypt, which was by the River Euphrates in Carchemish, and which Nebuchadnezzar king of Babylon defeated in the fourth year of Jehoiakim the son of Josiah, king of Judah:

3"Order the buckler and shield,
And draw near to battle!
4Harness the horses,
And mount up, you horsemen!
Stand forth with *your* helmets,
Polish the spears,
Put on the armor!

45:1 [a]Literally *from Jeremiah's mouth*

THE MESSAGE

keep the vows we made to sacrifice to the Queen of Heaven and pour out offerings to her, and nobody's going to stop us!" '

25-27 "Well, go ahead. Keep your vows. Do it up big. But also listen to what GOD has to say about it, all you who are from Judah but live in Egypt: 'I swear by my great name, backed by everything I am—this is GOD speaking!—that never again shall my name be used in vows, such as "As sure as the Master, GOD, lives!" by anyone in the whole country of Egypt. I've targeted each one of you for doom. The good is gone for good.

27-28 " 'All the Judeans in Egypt will die off by massacre or starvation until they're wiped out. The few who get out of Egypt alive and back to Judah will be *very* few, hardly worth counting. Then that ragtag bunch that left Judah to live in Egypt will know who had the last word.

29-30 " 'And this will be the evidence: I will bring punishment right here, and by this you'll know that the decrees of doom against you are the real thing. Watch for this sign of doom: I will give Pharaoh Hophra king of Egypt over to his enemies, those who are out to kill him, exactly as I gave Zedekiah king of Judah to his enemy Nebuchadnezzar, who was after him.' "

GOD'S PILING ON THE PAIN

1 **45** This is what Jeremiah told Baruch one day in the fourth year of Jehoiakim's reign as he was taking dictation from the prophet:

2-3 "These are the words of GOD, the God of Israel, to you, Baruch. You say, 'These are bad times for me! It's one thing after another. GOD is piling on the pain. I'm worn out and there's no end in sight.'

4-5 "But GOD says, 'Look around. What I've built I'm about to wreck, and what I've planted I'm about to rip up. And I'm doing it everywhere—all over the whole earth! So forget about making any big plans for yourself. Things are going to get worse before they get better. But don't worry. I'll keep you alive through the whole business.' "

YOU VAINLY COLLECT MEDICINES

1 **46** GOD's Messages through the prophet Jeremiah regarding the godless nations.

2-5 The Message to Egypt and the army of Pharaoh Neco king of Egypt at the time it was defeated by Nebuchadnezzar king of Babylon while camped at Carchemish on the Euphrates River in the fourth year of the reign of Jehoiakim king of Judah:

" 'Present arms!
March to the front!
Harness the horses!
Up in the saddles!
Battle formation! Helmets on,
spears sharpened, armor in place!'
But what's this I see?
They're scared out of their wits!
They break ranks and run for cover.
Their soldiers panic.

NEW KING JAMES VERSION

5"Why have I seen them dismayed *and* turned back?
Their mighty ones are beaten down;
They have speedily fled,
And did not look back,
For fear *was* all around," says the LORD.
6"Do not let the swift flee away,
Nor the mighty man escape;
They will stumble and fall
Toward the north, by the River Euphrates.

7"Who *is* this coming up like a flood,
Whose waters move like the rivers?
8Egypt rises up like a flood,
And *its* waters move like the rivers;
And he says, 'I will go up *and* cover the earth,
I will destroy the city and its inhabitants.'
9Come up, O horses, and rage, O chariots!
And let the mighty men come forth:
The Ethiopians and the Libyans who handle the shield,
And the Lydians who handle *and* bend the bow.
10For this *is* the day of the Lord GOD of hosts,
A day of vengeance,
That He may avenge Himself on His adversaries.
The sword shall devour;
It shall be satiated and made drunk with their blood;
For the Lord GOD of hosts has a sacrifice
In the north country by the River Euphrates.

11"Go up to Gilead and take balm,
O virgin, the daughter of Egypt;
In vain you will use many medicines;
You shall not be cured.
12The nations have heard of your shame,
And your cry has filled the land;
For the mighty man has stumbled against the mighty;
They both have fallen together."

BABYLONIA WILL STRIKE EGYPT

13The word that the LORD spoke to Jeremiah
the prophet, how Nebuchadnezzar king of
Babylon would come *and* strike the land of
Egypt.

14"Declare in Egypt, and proclaim in Migdol;
Proclaim in Noph[a] and in Tahpanhes;
Say, 'Stand fast and prepare yourselves,
For the sword devours all around you.'
15Why are your valiant *men* swept away?
They did not stand
Because the LORD drove them away.
16He made many fall;
Yes, one fell upon another.
And they said, 'Arise!
Let us go back to our own people
And to the land of our nativity
From the oppressing sword.'
17They cried there,
'Pharaoh, king of Egypt, *is but* a noise.
He has passed by the appointed time!'

46:14 [a]That is, ancient Memphis

THE MESSAGE

They run this way and that,
stampeding blindly.
It's total chaos, total confusion, danger everywhere!"
GOD's Decree.

6 "The swiftest runners won't get away,
the strongest soldiers won't escape.
In the north country, along the River Euphrates,
they'll stagger, stumble, and fall.

7-9 "Who is this like the Nile in flood?
like its streams torrential?
Why, it's Egypt like the Nile in flood,
like its streams torrential,
Saying, 'I'll take over the world.
I'll wipe out cities and peoples.'
Run, horses!
Roll, chariots!
Advance, soldiers
from Cush and Put with your shields,
Soldiers from Lud,
experts with bow and arrow.

10 "But it's not your day. It's the Master's, me,
GOD-of-the-Angel-Armies—
the day when I have it out with my enemies,
The day when Sword puts an end to my enemies,
when Sword exacts vengeance.
I, the Master, GOD-of-the-Angel-Armies,
will pile them on an altar—a huge sacrifice!—
In the great north country,
along the mighty Euphrates.

11-12 "Oh, virgin Daughter Egypt,
climb into the mountains of Gilead, get healing balm.
You will vainly collect medicines,
for nothing will be able to cure what ails you.
The whole world will hear your anguished cries.
Your wails fill the earth,
As soldier falls against soldier
and they all go down in a heap."

EGYPT'S ARMY SLITHERS LIKE A SNAKE

13 The Message that GOD gave to the prophet Jeremiah when Nebuchadnezzar king of Babylon was on his way to attack Egypt:

14 "Tell Egypt, alert Migdol,
post warnings in Noph and Tahpanhes:
'Wake up! Be prepared!
War's coming!'

15-19 "Why will your bull-god Apis run off?
Because GOD will drive him off.
Your ragtag army will fall to pieces.
The word is passing through the ranks,
'Let's get out of here while we still can.
Let's head for home and save our skins.'
When they get home they'll nickname Pharaoh
'Big-Talk-Bad-Luck.'

NEW KING JAMES VERSION

18"*As* I live," says the King,
Whose name *is* the LORD of hosts,
"Surely as Tabor *is* among the mountains
And as Carmel by the sea, *so* he shall come.
19O you daughter dwelling in Egypt,
Prepare yourself to go into captivity!
For Noph[a] shall be waste and desolate,
without inhabitant.

20"Egypt *is* a very pretty heifer,
But destruction comes, it comes from the north.
21Also her mercenaries are in her midst like fat bulls,
For they also are turned back,
They have fled away together.
They did not stand,
For the day of their calamity had come upon them,
The time of their punishment.
22Her noise shall go like a serpent,
For they shall march with an army
And come against her with axes,
Like those who chop wood.

23"They shall cut down her forest," says the LORD,
"Though it cannot be searched,
Because they *are* innumerable,
And more numerous than grasshoppers.
24The daughter of Egypt shall be ashamed;
She shall be delivered into the hand
Of the people of the north."

25The LORD of hosts, the God of Israel, says:
"Behold, I will bring punishment on Amon[a] of
No,[b] and Pharaoh and Egypt, with their gods
and their kings—Pharaoh and those who trust
in him. 26And I will deliver them into the hand of
those who seek their lives, into the hand of Ne-
buchadnezzar king of Babylon and the hand of
his servants. Afterward it shall be inhabited as
in the days of old," says the LORD.

GOD WILL PRESERVE ISRAEL

27"But do not fear, O My servant Jacob,
And do not be dismayed, O Israel!
For behold, I will save you from afar,
And your offspring from the land of their captivity;
Jacob shall return, have rest and be at ease;
No one shall make *him* afraid.
28Do not fear, O Jacob My servant," says the LORD,
"For I *am* with you;
For I will make a complete end of all the nations
To which I have driven you,
But I will not make a complete end of you.
I will rightly correct you,
For I will not leave you wholly unpunished."

46:19 [a]That is, ancient Memphis 46:25 [a]A sun god [b]That is, ancient Thebes

THE MESSAGE

As sure as I am the living God"
—the King's Decree, GOD-of-the-Angel-Armies is his name—
"A conqueror is coming: like Tabor,
singular among mountains;
like Carmel, jutting up from the sea!
So pack your bags for exile,
you coddled daughters of Egypt,
For Memphis will soon be nothing,
a vacant lot grown over with weeds.

20-21 "Too bad, Egypt, a beautiful sleek heifer
attacked by a horsefly from the north!
All her hired soldiers are stationed to defend her—
like well-fed calves they are.
But when their lives are on the line, they'll run off,
cowards every one.
When the going gets tough,
they'll take the easy way out.

22-24 "Egypt will slither and hiss like a snake
as the enemy army comes in force.
They will rush in, swinging axes
like lumberjacks cutting down trees.
They'll level the country"—GOD's Decree—"nothing
and no one standing for as far as you can see.
The invaders will be a swarm of locusts,
innumerable, past counting.
Daughter Egypt will be ravished,
raped by vandals from the north."

25-26 GOD-of-the-Angel-Armies, the God of Is-
rael, says, "Watch out when I visit doom on
the god Amon of Thebes, Egypt and its gods
and kings, Pharaoh and those who trust in
him. I'll turn them over to those who are out
to kill them, to Nebuchadnezzar and his mil-
itary. Egypt will be set back a thousand
years. Eventually people will live there
again." GOD's Decree.

27-28 "But you, dear Jacob my servant, you have nothing to fear.
Israel, there's no need to worry.
Look up! I'll save you from that far country,
I'll get your children out of the land of exile.
Things are going to be normal again for Jacob,
safe and secure, smooth sailing.
Yes, dear Jacob my servant, you have nothing to fear.
Depend on it, I'm on your side.
I'll finish off all the godless nations
among which I've scattered you,
But I won't finish you off.
I have more work left to do on you.
I'll punish you, but fairly.
No, I'm not finished with you yet."

NEW KING JAMES VERSION

JUDGMENT ON PHILISTIA

47 The word of the LORD that came to Jeremiah the prophet against the Philistines, before Pharaoh attacked Gaza.
2Thus says the LORD:

"Behold, waters rise out of the north,
And shall be an overflowing flood;
They shall overflow the land and all that is in it,
The city and those who dwell within;
Then the men shall cry,
And all the inhabitants of the land shall wail.
3At the noise of the stamping hooves of his strong horses,
At the rushing of his chariots,
At the rumbling of his wheels,
The fathers will not look back for *their* children,
Lacking courage,
4Because of the day that comes to plunder all the Philistines,
To cut off from Tyre and Sidon every helper who remains;
For the LORD shall plunder the Philistines,
The remnant of the country of Caphtor.
5Baldness has come upon Gaza,
Ashkelon is cut off
With the remnant of their valley.
How long will you cut yourself?

6"O you sword of the LORD,
How long until you are quiet?
Put yourself up into your scabbard,
Rest and be still!
7How can it be quiet,
Seeing the LORD has given it a charge
Against Ashkelon and against the seashore?
There He has appointed it."

JUDGMENT ON MOAB

48 Against Moab.
Thus says the LORD of hosts, the God of Israel:

"Woe to Nebo!
For it is plundered,
Kirjathaim is shamed *and* taken;
The high stronghold[a] is shamed and dismayed—
2No more praise of Moab.
In Heshbon they have devised evil against her:
'Come, and let us cut her off as a nation.'
You also shall be cut down, O Madmen![a]
The sword shall pursue you;
3A voice of crying *shall be* from Horonaim:
'Plundering and great destruction!'

4"Moab is destroyed;
Her little ones have caused a cry to be heard;[a]
5For in the Ascent of Luhith they ascend with continual weeping;
For in the descent of Horonaim the enemies have heard a cry of destruction.

48:1 [a]Hebrew *Misgab* 48:2 [a]A city of Moab 48:4 [a]Following Masoretic Text, Targum, and Vulgate; Septuagint reads *Proclaim it in Zoar.*

THE MESSAGE

IT'S DOOMSDAY FOR PHILISTINES

1-5 47 GOD's Message to the prophet Jeremiah regarding the Philistines just before Pharaoh attacked Gaza. This is what GOD says:

"Look out! Water will rise in the north country,
swelling like a river in flood.
The torrent will flood the land,
washing away city and citizen.
Men and women will scream in terror,
wails from every door and window,
As the thunder from the hooves of the horses will be heard,
the clatter of chariots, the banging of wheels.
Fathers, paralyzed by fear,
won't even grab up their babies
Because it will be doomsday for Philistines, one and all,
no hope of help for Tyre and Sidon.
GOD will finish off the Philistines,
what's left of those from the island of Crete.
Gaza will be shaved bald as an egg,
Ashkelon struck dumb as a post.
You're on your last legs.
How long will you keep flailing?

6 "Oh, Sword of GOD,
how long will you keep this up?
Return to your scabbard.
Haven't you had enough? Can't you call it quits?

7 "But how can it quit
when I, GOD, command the action?
I've ordered it to cut down
Ashkelon and the seacoast."

GET OUT WHILE YOU CAN!

1-10 48 The Message on Moab from GOD-of-the-Angel-Armies, the God of Israel:

"Doom to Nebo! Leveled to the ground!
Kiriathaim demeaned and defeated,
The mighty fortress reduced to a molehill,
Moab's glory—dust and ashes.
Conspirators plot Heshbon's doom:
'Come, let's wipe Moab off the map.'
Dungface Dimon will loudly lament,
as killing follows killing.
Listen! A cry out of Horonaim:
'Disaster—doom and more doom!'
Moab will be shattered.
Her cries will be heard clear down in Zoar.
Up the ascent of Luhith
climbers weep,
And down the descent from Horonaim,
cries of loss and devastation.

NEW KING JAMES VERSION

6"Flee, save your lives!
And be like the juniper[a] in the wilderness.
7For because you have trusted in your works and your treasures,
You also shall be taken.
And Chemosh shall go forth into captivity,
His priests and his princes together.
8And the plunderer shall come against every city;
No one shall escape.
The valley also shall perish,
And the plain shall be destroyed,
As the LORD has spoken.

9"Give wings to Moab,
That she may flee and get away;
For her cities shall be desolate,
Without any to dwell in them.
10Cursed *is* he who does the work of the LORD deceitfully,
And cursed *is* he who keeps back his sword from blood.

11"Moab has been at ease from his[a] youth;
He has settled on his dregs,
And has not been emptied from vessel to vessel,
Nor has he gone into captivity.
Therefore his taste remained in him,
And his scent has not changed.

12"Therefore behold, the days are coming,"
says the LORD,
"That I shall send him wine-workers
Who will tip him over
And empty his vessels
And break the bottles.
13Moab shall be ashamed of Chemosh,
As the house of Israel was ashamed of Bethel, their confidence.

14"How can you say, 'We *are* mighty
And strong men for the war'?
15Moab is plundered and gone up *from* her cities;
Her chosen young men have gone down to the slaughter," says the King,
Whose name *is* the LORD of hosts.

16"The calamity of Moab *is* near at hand,
And his affliction comes quickly.
17Bemoan him, all you who are around him;
And all you who know his name,
Say, 'How the strong staff is broken,
The beautiful rod!'

18"O daughter inhabiting Dibon,
Come down from *your* glory,
And sit in thirst;
For the plunderer of Moab has come against you,
He has destroyed your strongholds.
19O inhabitant of Aroer,
Stand by the way and watch;
Ask him who flees
And her who escapes;

48:6 [a]Or *Aroer,* a city of Moab **48:11** [a]The Hebrew uses masculine and feminine pronouns interchangeably in this chapter.

THE MESSAGE

Oh, run for your lives! Get out while you can!
Survive by your wits in the wild!
You trusted in thick walls and big money, yes?
But it won't help you now.
Your big god Chemosh will be hauled off,
his priests and managers with him.
A wrecker will wreck every city.
Not a city will survive.
The valley fields will be ruined,
the plateau pastures destroyed, just as I told you.
Cover the land of Moab with salt.
Make sure nothing ever grows here again.
Her towns will all be ghost towns.
Nobody will ever live here again.
Sloppy work in GOD's name is cursed,
and cursed all halfhearted use of the sword.

11-17 "Moab has always taken it easy—
lazy as a dog in the sun,
Never had to work for a living,
never faced any trouble,
Never had to grow up,
never once worked up a sweat.
But those days are a thing of the past.
I'll put him to work at hard labor.
That will wake him up to the world of hard knocks.
That will smash his illusions.
Moab will be as ashamed of god Chemosh
as Israel was ashamed of her Bethel calf-gods,
the calf-gods she thought were so great.
For how long do you think you'll be saying,
'We're tough.
We can beat anyone anywhere'?
The destruction of Moab has already begun.
Her choice young soldiers are lying dead right now."
The King's Decree—
his full name, GOD-of-the-Angel-Armies.
"Yes. Moab's doom is on countdown,
disaster targeted and launched.
Weep for Moab, friends and neighbors,
all who know how famous he's been.
Lament, 'His mighty scepter snapped in two like a toothpick,
that magnificent royal staff!'

18-20 "Come down from your high horse,
pampered beauty of Dibon.
Sit in dog dung.
The destroyer of Moab will come against you.
He'll wreck your safe, secure houses.
Stand on the roadside,
pampered women of Aroer.
Interview the refugees who are running away.

NEW KING JAMES VERSION

Say, 'What has happened?'
20Moab is shamed, for he is broken down.
Wail and cry!
Tell it in Arnon, that Moab is plundered.

21"And judgment has come on the plain country:
On Holon and Jahzah and Mephaath,
22On Dibon and Nebo and Beth Diblathaim,
23On Kirjathaim and Beth Gamul and Beth Meon,
24On Kerioth and Bozrah,
On all the cities of the land of Moab,
Far or near.
25The horn of Moab is cut off,
And his arm is broken," says the LORD.

26"Make him drunk,
Because he exalted *himself* against the LORD.
Moab shall wallow in his vomit,
And he shall also be in derision.
27For was not Israel a derision to you?
Was he found among thieves?
For whenever you speak of him,
You shake *your head in scorn.*
28You who dwell in Moab,
Leave the cities and dwell in the rock,
And be like the dove *which* makes her nest
In the sides of the cave's mouth.

29"We have heard the pride of Moab
(He *is* exceedingly proud),
Of his loftiness and arrogance and pride,
And of the haughtiness of his heart."

30"I know his wrath," says the LORD,
"But it *is* not right;
His lies have made nothing right.
31Therefore I will wail for Moab,
And I will cry out for all Moab;
I[a] will mourn for the men of Kir Heres.
32O vine of Sibmah! I will weep for you with the weeping of Jazer.
Your plants have gone over the sea,
They reach to the sea of Jazer.
The plunderer has fallen on your summer fruit and your vintage.
33Joy and gladness are taken
From the plentiful field
And from the land of Moab;
I have caused wine to fail from the winepresses;
No one will tread with joyous shouting—
Not joyous shouting!

34"From the cry of Heshbon to Elealeh and to Jahaz
They have uttered their voice,
From Zoar to Horonaim,
Like a three-year-old heifer;[a]
For the waters of Nimrim also shall be desolate.

35"Moreover," says the LORD,
"I will cause to cease in Moab

48:31 [a]Following Dead Sea Scrolls, Septuagint, and Vulgate; Masoretic Text reads *He.* **48:34** [a]Or *The Third Eglath,* an unknown city (compare Isaiah 15:5)

THE MESSAGE

Ask them, 'What's happened? And why?'
Moab will be an embarrassing memory,
nothing left of the place.
Wail and weep your eyes out!
Tell the bad news along the Arnon river.
Tell the world that Moab is no more.

21-24 "My judgment will come to the plateau
cities: on Holon, Jahzah, and Mephaath;
on Dibon, Nebo, and Beth-diblathaim; on
Kiriathaim, Beth-gamul, and Beth-meon; on
Kerioth, Bozrah, and all the cities of Moab,
far and near.

25 "Moab's link to power is severed.
Moab's arm is broken." GOD's Decree.

THE SHEER NOTHINGNESS OF MOAB

26-27 "Turn Moab into a drunken sot, drunk on
the wine of my wrath, a dung-faced drunk,
filling the country with vomit—Moab a
falling-down drunk, a joke in bad taste.
Wasn't it you, Moab, who made crude jokes
over Israel? And when they were caught in
bad company, didn't you cluck and gossip
and snicker?

28 "Leave town! Leave! Look for a home in the cliffs,
you who grew up in Moab.
Try living like a dove
who nests high in the river gorge.

29-33 "We've all heard of Moab's pride,
that legendary pride,
The strutting, bullying, puffed-up pride,
the insufferable arrogance.
I know"—GOD's Decree—"his rooster-crowing pride,
the inflated claims, the sheer nothingness of Moab.
But I will weep for Moab,
yes, I will mourn for the people of Moab.
I will even mourn for the people of Kir-heres.
I'll weep for the grapevines of Sibmah
and join Jazer in her weeping—
Grapevines that once reached the Dead Sea
with tendrils as far as Jazer.
Your summer fruit and your bursting grapes
will be looted by brutal plunderers,
Lush Moab stripped
of song and laughter.
And yes, I'll shut down the winepresses,
stop all the shouts and hurrahs of harvest.

34 "Heshbon and Elealeh will cry out, and
the people in Jahaz will hear the cries. They
will hear them all the way from Zoar to
Horonaim and Eglath-shelishiyah. Even the
waters of Nimrim will be dried up.
35 "I will put a stop in Moab"—GOD's De-

New King James Version

The one who offers *sacrifices* in the high places
And burns incense to his gods.
36Therefore My heart shall wail like flutes for Moab,
And like flutes My heart shall wail
For the men of Kir Heres.
Therefore the riches they have acquired have perished.

37"For every head *shall be* bald, and every beard clipped;
On all the hands *shall be* cuts, and on the loins sackcloth—
38A general lamentation
On all the housetops of Moab,
And in its streets;
For I have broken Moab like a vessel in which *is* no pleasure," says the LORD.
39"They shall wail:
"How she is broken down!
How Moab has turned her back with shame!'
So Moab shall be a derision
And a dismay to all those about her."

40For thus says the LORD:

"Behold, one shall fly like an eagle,
And spread his wings over Moab.
41Kerioth is taken,
And the strongholds are surprised;
The mighty men's hearts in Moab on that day shall be
Like the heart of a woman in birth pangs.
42And Moab shall be destroyed as a people,
Because he exalted *himself* against the LORD.
43Fear and the pit and the snare *shall be* upon you,
O inhabitant of Moab," says the LORD.
44"He who flees from the fear shall fall into the pit,
And he who gets out of the pit shall be caught in the snare.
For upon Moab, upon it I will bring
The year of their punishment," says the LORD.

45"Those who fled stood under the shadow of Heshbon
Because of exhaustion.
But a fire shall come out of Heshbon,
A flame from the midst of Sihon,
And shall devour the brow of Moab,
The crown of the head of the sons of tumult.
46Woe to you, O Moab!
The people of Chemosh perish;
For your sons have been taken captive,
And your daughters captive.

47"Yet I will bring back the captives of Moab
In the latter days," says the LORD.

Thus far *is* the judgment of Moab.

The Message

cree—"to all hiking to the high places to of-
fer burnt sacrifices to the gods.
36 "My heart moans for Moab, for the men
of Kir-heres, like soft flute sounds carried by
the wind. They've lost it all. They've got
nothing.

37 "Everywhere you look are signs of mourning:
heads shaved, beards cut,
Hands scratched and bleeding,
clothes ripped and torn.

38 "In every house in Moab there'll be loud
lamentation, on every street in Moab, loud
lamentation. As with a pottery jug that no
one wants, I'll smash Moab to bits." GOD's
Decree.

39 "Moab ruined!
Moab shamed and ashamed to be seen!
Moab a cruel joke!
The stark horror of Moab!"

40-42 GOD's verdict on Moab. Indeed!

"Look! An eagle is about to swoop down
and spread its wings over Moab.
The towns will be captured,
the fortresses taken.
Brave warriors will double up in pain,
helpless to fight,
like a woman giving birth to a baby.
There'll be nothing left of Moab, nothing at all,
because of his defiant arrogance against me.

43-44 "Terror and pit and trap
are what you have facing you, Moab."
GOD's Decree.
"A man running in terror
will fall into a trap.
A man climbing out of a pit
will be caught in a trap.
This is my agenda for Moab
on doomsday." GOD's Decree.

45-47 "On the outskirts of Heshbon,
refugees will pull up short, worn out.
Fire will flame high from Heshbon,
a firestorm raging from the capital of Sihon's kingdom.
It will burn off Moab's eyebrows,
will scorch the skull of the braggarts.
That's all for you, Moab!
You worshipers of Chemosh will be finished off!
Your sons will be trucked off to prison camps;
your daughters will be herded into exile.
But yet there's a day that's coming
when I'll put things right in Moab.

"For now, that's the judgment on Moab."

NEW KING JAMES VERSION

JUDGMENT ON AMMON

49 Against the Ammonites.
Thus says the LORD:

"Has Israel no sons?
Has he no heir?
Why *then* does Milcom[a] inherit Gad,
And his people dwell in its cities?
2Therefore behold, the days are coming,"
says the LORD,
"That I will cause to be heard an alarm of war
In Rabbah of the Ammonites;
It shall be a desolate mound,
And her villages shall be burned with fire.
Then Israel shall take possession of his inheritance," says the LORD.

3"Wail, O Heshbon, for Ai is plundered!
Cry, you daughters of Rabbah,
Gird yourselves with sackcloth!
Lament and run to and fro by the walls;
For Milcom shall go into captivity
With his priests and his princes together.
4Why do you boast in the valleys,
Your flowing valley, O backsliding daughter?
Who trusted in her treasures, *saying,*
'Who will come against me?'
5Behold, I will bring fear upon you,"
Says the Lord GOD of hosts,
"From all those who are around you;
You shall be driven out, everyone headlong,
And no one will gather those who wander off.
6But afterward I will bring back
The captives of the people of Ammon," says the LORD.

JUDGMENT ON EDOM

7Against Edom.
Thus says the LORD of hosts:

"*Is* wisdom no more in Teman?
Has counsel perished from the prudent?
Has their wisdom vanished?
8Flee, turn back, dwell in the depths,
O inhabitants of Dedan!
For I will bring the calamity of Esau upon him,
The time *that* I will punish him.
9If grape-gatherers came to you,
Would they not leave *some* gleaning grapes?
If thieves by night,
Would they not destroy until they have enough?
10But I have made Esau bare;
I have uncovered his secret places,[a]
And he shall not be able to hide himself.
His descendants are plundered,
His brethren and his neighbors,
And he *is* no more.
11Leave your fatherless children,
I will preserve *them* alive;
And let your widows trust in Me."

49:1 [a]Hebrew *Malcam,* literally *their king,* a god of the Ammonites; also called *Molech* (compare verse 3) 49:10 [a]Compare Obadiah 5, 6

THE MESSAGE

YOU'RE A BROKEN-DOWN HAS-BEEN

1-6 49 GOD's Message on the Ammonites:

"Doesn't Israel have any children,
no one to step into her inheritance?
So why is the god Milcom taking over Gad's land,
his followers moving into its towns?
But not for long! The time's coming"
—GOD's Decree—
"When I'll fill the ears of Rabbah, Ammon's big city,
with battle cries.
She'll end up a pile of rubble,
all her towns burned to the ground.
Then Israel will kick out the invaders.
I, GOD, say so, and it will *be* so.
Wail Heshbon, Ai is in ruins.
Villages of Rabbah, wring your hands!
Dress in mourning, weep buckets of tears.
Go into hysterics, run around in circles!
Your god Milcom will be hauled off to exile,
and all his priests and managers right with him.
Why do you brag of your once-famous strength?
You're a broken-down has-been, a castoff
Who fondles his trophies and dreams of glory days
and vainly thinks, 'No one can lay a hand on me.'
Well, think again. I'll face you with terror from all sides."
Word of the Master,
GOD-of-the-Angel-Armies.
"You'll be stampeded headlong,
with no one to round up the runaways.
Still, the time will come
when I will make things right with Ammon." GOD's Decree.

STRUTTING ACROSS THE STAGE OF HISTORY

7-11 The Message of GOD-of-the-Angel-Armies on Edom:

"Is there nobody wise left in famous Teman?
no one with a sense of reality?
Has their wisdom gone wormy and rotten?
Run for your lives! Get out while you can!
Find a good place to hide,
you who live in Dedan!
I'm bringing doom to Esau.
It's time to settle accounts.
When harvesters work your fields,
don't they leave gleanings?
When burglars break into your house,
don't they take only what they want?
But I'll strip Esau clean.
I'll search out every nook and cranny.
I'll destroy everything connected with him,
children and relatives and neighbors.
There'll be no one left who will be able to say,
'I'll take care of your orphans.
Your widows can depend on me.' "

NEW KING JAMES VERSION

12For thus says the LORD: "Behold, those whose judgment *was* not to drink of the cup have assuredly drunk. And *are* you the one who will altogether go unpunished? You shall not go unpunished, but you shall surely drink *of it*.
13For I have sworn by Myself," says the LORD, "that Bozrah shall become a desolation, a reproach, a waste, and a curse. And all its cities shall be perpetual wastes."

14I have heard a message from the LORD,
And an ambassador has been sent to the nations:
"Gather together, come against her,
And rise up to battle!

15"For indeed, I will make you small among nations,
Despised among men.
16Your fierceness has deceived you,
The pride of your heart,
O you who dwell in the clefts of the rock,
Who hold the height of the hill!
Though you make your nest as high as the eagle,
I will bring you down from there," says the LORD.[a]

17"Edom also shall be an astonishment;
Everyone who goes by it will be astonished
And will hiss at all its plagues.
18As in the overthrow of Sodom and Gomorrah
And their neighbors," says the LORD,
"No one shall remain there,
Nor shall a son of man dwell in it.

19"Behold, he shall come up like a lion from the floodplain[a] of the Jordan
Against the dwelling place of the strong;
But I will suddenly make him run away from her.
And who *is* a chosen *man that* I may appoint over her?
For who *is* like Me?
Who will arraign Me?
And who *is* that shepherd
Who will withstand Me?"

20Therefore hear the counsel of the LORD that He has taken against Edom,
And His purposes that He has proposed against the inhabitants of Teman:
Surely the least of the flock shall draw them out;
Surely He shall make their dwelling places desolate with them.
21The earth shakes at the noise of their fall;
At the cry its noise is heard at the Red Sea.
22Behold, He shall come up and fly like the eagle,
And spread His wings over Bozrah;
The heart of the mighty men of Edom in that day shall be
Like the heart of a woman in birth pangs.

49:16 [a]Compare Obadiah 3, 4 **49:19** [a]Or *thicket*

THE MESSAGE

12-13 Indeed. GOD says, "I tell you, if there are people who have to drink the cup of God's wrath even though they don't deserve it, why would you think you'd get off? You won't get off. You'll drink it. Oh yes, you'll drink every drop. And as for Bozrah, your capital, I swear by all that I am"—GOD's Decree—"that that city will end up a pile of charred ruins, a stinking garbage dump, an obscenity—and all her daughter-cities with her."

14 I've just heard the latest from GOD.
He's sent an envoy to the nations:
"Muster your troops and attack Edom.
Present arms! Go to war!"

15-16 "Ah, Edom, I'm dropping you to last place among nations,
the bottom of the heap, kicked around.
You think you're so great—
strutting across the stage of history,
Living high in the impregnable rocks,
acting like king of the mountain.
You think you're above it all, don't you,
like an eagle in its aerie?
Well, you're headed for a fall.
I'll bring you crashing to the ground."
GOD's Decree.

17-18 "Edom will end up trash. Stinking, despicable trash. A wonder of the world in reverse. She'll join Sodom and Gomorrah and their neighbors in the sewers of history." GOD says so.

"No one will live there,
no mortal soul move in there.

19 "Watch this: Like a lion coming up
from the thick jungle of the Jordan
Looking for prey in the mountain pastures,
I will come upon Edom and pounce.
I'll take my pick of the flock—and who's to stop me?
The shepherds of Edom are helpless before me."

20-22 So, listen to this plan that GOD has worked out against Edom, the blueprint of what he's prepared for those who live in Teman:

"Believe it or not, the young, the vulnerable—
mere lambs and kids—will be dragged off.
Believe it or not, the flock
in shock, helpless to help, will watch it happen.
The very earth will shudder because of their cries,
cries of anguish heard at the distant Red Sea.
Look! An eagle soars, swoops down,
spreads its wings over Bozrah.
Brave warriors will double up in pain,
helpless to fight,
like a woman giving birth to a baby."

NEW KING JAMES VERSION

JUDGMENT ON DAMASCUS

23Against Damascus.

"Hamath and Arpad are shamed,
For they have heard bad news.
They are fainthearted;
There is trouble on the sea;
It cannot be quiet.
24Damascus has grown feeble;
She turns to flee,
And fear has seized *her.*
Anguish and sorrows have taken her like a woman in labor.
25Why is the city of praise not deserted, the city of My joy?
26Therefore her young men shall fall in her streets,
And all the men of war shall be cut off in that day," says the LORD of hosts.
27"I will kindle a fire in the wall of Damascus,
And it shall consume the palaces of Ben-Hadad."[a]

JUDGMENT ON KEDAR AND HAZOR

28Against Kedar and against the kingdoms of
Hazor, which Nebuchadnezzar king of Babylon
shall strike.

Thus says the LORD:

"Arise, go up to Kedar,
And devastate the men of the East!
29Their tents and their flocks they shall take away.
They shall take for themselves their curtains,
All their vessels and their camels;
And they shall cry out to them,
'Fear *is* on every side!'

30"Flee, get far away! Dwell in the depths,
O inhabitants of Hazor!" says the LORD.
"For Nebuchadnezzar king of Babylon has taken counsel against you,
And has conceived a plan against you.

31"Arise, go up to the wealthy nation that dwells securely," says the LORD,
"Which has neither gates nor bars,
Dwelling alone.
32Their camels shall be for booty,
And the multitude of their cattle for plunder.
I will scatter to all winds those in the farthest corners,
And I will bring their calamity from all its sides," says the LORD.
33"Hazor shall be a dwelling for jackals, a desolation forever;
No one shall reside there,
Nor son of man dwell in it."

JUDGMENT ON ELAM

34The word of the LORD that came to Jere-
miah the prophet against Elam, in the beginning
of the reign of Zedekiah king of Judah, saying,
35"Thus says the LORD of hosts:

'Behold, I will break the bow of Elam,
The foremost of their might.

49:27 [a]Compare Amos 1:4

THE MESSAGE

THE BLOOD WILL DRAIN FROM THE FACE OF DAMASCUS

23-27 The Message on Damascus:

"Hamath and Arpad will be in shock
when they hear the bad news.
Their hearts will melt in fear
as they pace back and forth in worry.
The blood will drain from the face of Damascus
as she turns to flee.
Hysterical, she'll fall to pieces,
disabled, like a woman in childbirth.
And now how lonely—bereft, abandoned!
The once famous city, the once happy city.
Her bright young men dead in the streets,
her brave warriors silent as death.
On that day"—Decree of GOD-of-the-Angel-Armies—
"I'll start a fire at the wall of Damascus
that will burn down all of Ben-hadad's forts."

FIND A SAFE PLACE TO HIDE

28-33 The Message on Kedar and the sheikdoms of Hazor who were attacked by Nebuchadnezzar king of Babylon. This is GOD's Message:

"On your feet! Attack Kedar!
Plunder the Bedouin nomads from the east.
Grab their blankets and pots and pans.
Steal their camels.
Traumatize them, shouting, 'Terror! Death! Doom!
Danger everywhere!'
Oh, run for your lives,
You nomads from Hazor." GOD's Decree.
"Find a safe place to hide.
Nebuchadnezzar king of Babylon
has plans to wipe you out,
to go after you with a vengeance:
'After them,' he says. 'Go after these relaxed nomads
who live free and easy in the desert,
Who live in the open with no doors to lock,
who live off by themselves.'
Their camels are there for the taking,
their herds and flocks, easy picking.
I'll scatter them to the four winds,
these defenseless nomads on the fringes of the desert.
I'll bring terror from every direction.
They won't know what hit them." GOD's Decree.
"Jackals will take over the camps of Hazor,
camps abandoned to wind and sand.
No one will live there,
no mortal soul move in there."

THE WINDS WILL BLOW AWAY ELAM

34-39 GOD's Message to the prophet Jeremiah on Elam at the outset of the reign of Zedekiah king of Judah. This is what GOD-of-the-Angel-Armies says:

"Watch this! I'll break Elam's bow,
her weapon of choice, across my knee.

NEW KING JAMES VERSION

36Against Elam I will bring the four winds
From the four quarters of heaven,
And scatter them toward all those winds;
There shall be no nations where the
outcasts of Elam will not go.
37For I will cause Elam to be dismayed before
their enemies
And before those who seek their life.
I will bring disaster upon them,
My fierce anger,' says the LORD;
'And I will send the sword after them
Until I have consumed them.
38I will set My throne in Elam,
And will destroy from there the king and
the princes,' says the LORD.

39'But it shall come to pass in the latter days:
I will bring back the captives of Elam,' says
the LORD."

JUDGMENT ON BABYLON AND BABYLONIA

50 The word that the LORD spoke against
Babylon *and* against the land of the
Chaldeans by Jeremiah the prophet.

2"Declare among the nations,
Proclaim, and set up a standard;
Proclaim—do not conceal *it*—
Say, 'Babylon is taken, Bel is shamed.
Merodach[a] is broken in pieces;
Her idols are humiliated,
Her images are broken in pieces.'
3For out of the north a nation comes up
against her,
Which shall make her land desolate,
And no one shall dwell therein.
They shall move, they shall depart,
Both man and beast.

4"In those days and in that time," says the
LORD,
"The children of Israel shall come,
They and the children of Judah together;
With continual weeping they shall come,
And seek the LORD their God.
5They shall ask the way to Zion,
With their faces toward it, *saying*,
'Come and let us join ourselves to the LORD
In a perpetual covenant
That will not be forgotten.'

6"My people have been lost sheep.
Their shepherds have led them astray;
They have turned them away *on* the
mountains.
They have gone from mountain to hill;
They have forgotten their resting place.
7All who found them have devoured them;
And their adversaries said, 'We have not
offended,
Because they have sinned against the LORD,
the habitation of justice,
The LORD, the hope of their fathers.'

50:2 [a]A Babylonian god; sometimes spelled *Marduk*

THE MESSAGE

Then I'll let four winds loose on Elam,
winds from the four corners of earth.
I'll blow them away in all directions,
landing homeless Elamites in every
country on earth.
They'll live in constant fear and terror
among enemies who want to kill them.
I'll bring doom on them,
my anger-fueled doom.
I'll set murderous hounds on their heels
until there's nothing left of them.
And then I'll set up my throne in Elam,
having thrown out the king and his
henchmen.
But the time will come when I make
everything right for Elam again." GOD's
Decree.

GET OUT OF BABYLON AS FAST AS YOU CAN

1-3 50 The Message of GOD through the
prophet Jeremiah on Babylon, land of
the Chaldeans:

"Get the word out to the nations! Preach it!
Go public with this, broadcast it far and
wide:
Babylon taken, god-Bel hanging his head in
shame,
god-Marduk exposed as a fraud.
All her god-idols shuffling in shame,
all her play-gods exposed as cheap
frauds.
For a nation will come out of the north to
attack her,
reduce her cities to rubble.
Empty of life—no animals, no people—
not a sound, not a movement, not a
breath.

4-5 "In those days, at that time"—GOD's
Decree—
"the people of Israel will come,
And the people of Judah with them.
Walking and weeping, they'll seek me,
their GOD.
They'll ask directions to Zion
and set their faces toward Zion.
They'll come and hold tight to GOD,
bound in a covenant eternal they'll never
forget.

6-7 "My people were lost sheep.
Their shepherds led them astray.
They abandoned them in the mountains
where they wandered aimless through
the hills.
They lost track of home,
couldn't remember where they came
from.
Everyone who met them took advantage of
them.
Their enemies had no qualms:
'Fair game,' they said. 'They walked out on
GOD.
They abandoned the True Pasture, the
hope of their parents.'

NEW KING JAMES VERSION

8"Move from the midst of Babylon,
Go out of the land of the Chaldeans;
And be like the rams before the flocks.
9For behold, I will raise and cause to come up against Babylon
An assembly of great nations from the north country,
And they shall array themselves against her;
From there she shall be captured.
Their arrows *shall be* like *those* of an expert warrior;[a]
None shall return in vain.
10And Chaldea shall become plunder;
All who plunder her shall be satisfied," says the LORD.

11"Because you were glad, because you rejoiced,
You destroyers of My heritage,
Because you have grown fat like a heifer threshing grain,
And you bellow like bulls,
12Your mother shall be deeply ashamed;
She who bore you shall be ashamed.
Behold, the least of the nations *shall be* a wilderness,
A dry land and a desert.
13Because of the wrath of the LORD
She shall not be inhabited,
But she shall be wholly desolate.
Everyone who goes by Babylon shall be horrified
And hiss at all her plagues.

14"Put yourselves in array against Babylon all around,
All you who bend the bow;
Shoot at her, spare no arrows,
For she has sinned against the LORD.
15Shout against her all around;
She has given her hand,
Her foundations have fallen,
Her walls are thrown down;
For it *is* the vengeance of the LORD.
Take vengeance on her.
As she has done, so do to her.
16Cut off the sower from Babylon,
And him who handles the sickle at harvest time.
For fear of the oppressing sword
Everyone shall turn to his own people,
And everyone shall flee to his own land.

17"Israel *is* like scattered sheep;
The lions have driven *him* away.
First the king of Assyria devoured him;
Now at last this Nebuchadnezzar king of Babylon has broken his bones."

18Therefore thus says the LORD of hosts, the God of Israel:

"Behold, I will punish the king of Babylon and his land,

50:9 [a]Following some Hebrew manuscripts, Septuagint, and Syriac; Masoretic Text, Targum, and Vulgate read *a warrior who makes childless.*

THE MESSAGE

8-10 "But now, get out of Babylon as fast as you can.
Be rid of that Babylonian country.
On your way. Good sheepdogs lead, but don't you be led.
Lead the way home!
Do you see what I'm doing?
I'm rallying a host of nations against Babylon.
They'll come out of the north,
attack and take her.
Oh, they know how to fight, these armies.
They never come home empty-handed.
Babylon is ripe for picking!
All her plunderers will fill their bellies!"
GOD's Decree.

11-16 "You Babylonians had a good time while it lasted, didn't you?
You lived it up, exploiting and using my people,
Frisky calves romping in lush pastures,
wild stallions out having a good time!
Well, your mother would hardly be proud of you.
The woman who bore you wouldn't be pleased.
Look at what's come of you! A nothing nation!
Rubble and garbage and weeds!
Emptied of life by my holy anger,
a desert of death and emptiness.
Travelers who pass by Babylon will gasp, appalled,
shaking their heads at such a comedown.
Gang up on Babylon! Pin her down!
Throw everything you have against her.
Hold nothing back. Knock her flat.
She's sinned—oh, how she's sinned, against me!
Shout battle cries from every direction.
All the fight has gone out of her.
Her defenses have been flattened,
her walls smashed.
'Operation GOD's Vengeance.'
Pile on the vengeance!
Do to her as she has done.
Give her a good dose of her own medicine!
Destroy her farms and farmers,
ravage her fields, empty her barns.
And you captives, while the destruction rages,
get out while the getting's good,
get out fast and run for home.

17 "Israel is a scattered flock,
hunted down by lions.
The king of Assyria started the carnage.
The king of Babylon, Nebuchadnezzar,
Has completed the job,
gnawing the bones clean."

18-20 And now this is what
GOD-of-the-Angel-Armies,
the God of Israel, has to say:
"Just watch! I'm bringing doom on the king of Babylon and his land,

New King James Version

As I have punished the king of Assyria.
19But I will bring back Israel to his home,
And he shall feed on Carmel and Bashan;
His soul shall be satisfied on Mount
Ephraim and Gilead.
20In those days and in that time," says the
LORD,
"The iniquity of Israel shall be sought, but
there shall be none;
And the sins of Judah, but they shall not be
found;
For I will pardon those whom I preserve.

21"Go up against the land of Merathaim,
against it,
And against the inhabitants of Pekod.
Waste and utterly destroy them," says the
LORD,
"And do according to all that I have
commanded you.
22A sound of battle *is* in the land,
And of great destruction.
23How the hammer of the whole earth has
been cut apart and broken!
How Babylon has become a desolation
among the nations!
24I have laid a snare for you;
You have indeed been trapped, O Babylon,
And you were not aware;
You have been found and also caught,
Because you have contended against the
LORD.
25The LORD has opened His armory,
And has brought out the weapons of His
indignation;
For this *is* the work of the Lord GOD of hosts
In the land of the Chaldeans.
26Come against her from the farthest border;
Open her storehouses;
Cast her up as heaps of ruins,
And destroy her utterly;
Let nothing of her be left.
27Slay all her bulls,
Let them go down to the slaughter.
Woe to them!
For their day has come, the time of their
punishment.
28The voice of those who flee and escape from
the land of Babylon
Declares in Zion the vengeance of the LORD
our God,
The vengeance of His temple.

29"Call together the archers against Babylon.
All you who bend the bow, encamp against
it all around;
Let none of them escape.[a]
Repay her according to her work;
According to all she has done, do to her;
For she has been proud against the LORD,
Against the Holy One of Israel.
30Therefore her young men shall fall in the
streets,
And all her men of war shall be cut off in
that day," says the LORD.

50:29 [a]Qere, some Hebrew manuscripts, Septuagint, and Targum add *to her.*

The Message

the same doom I brought on the king of
Assyria.
But Israel I'll bring home to good pastures.
He'll graze on the hills of Carmel and
Bashan,
On the slopes of Ephraim and Gilead.
He will eat to his heart's content.
In those days and at that time"—GOD's
Decree—
"they'll look high and low for a sign of
Israel's guilt—nothing;
Search nook and cranny for a trace of
Judah's sin—nothing.
These people that I've saved will start
out with a clean slate.

21 "Attack Merathaim, land of rebels!
Go after Pekod, country of doom!
Hunt them down. Make a clean sweep."
GOD's Decree.
"These are my orders. Do what I tell you.

22-24 "The thunderclap of battle
shakes the foundations!
The Hammer has been hammered,
smashed and splintered,
Babylon pummeled
beyond recognition.
I set out a trap and you were caught in it.
O Babylon, you never knew what hit you,
Caught and held in the steel grip of that
trap!
That's what you get for taking on GOD.

25-28 "I, GOD, opened my arsenal.
I brought out my weapons of wrath.
The Master, GOD-of-the-Angel-Armies,
has a job to do in Babylon.
Come at her from all sides!
Break into her granaries!
Shovel her into piles and burn her up.
Leave nothing! Leave no one!
Kill all her young turks.
Send them to their doom!
Doom to them! Yes, Doomsday!
The clock has finally run out on them.
And here's a surprise:
Runaways and escapees from Babylon
Show up in Zion reporting the news of
GOD's vengeance,
taking vengeance for my own Temple.

29-30 "Call in the troops against Babylon,
anyone who can shoot straight!
Tighten the noose!
Leave no loopholes!
Give her back as good as she gave,
a dose of her own medicine!
Her brazen insolence is an outrage
against GOD, The Holy of Israel.
And now she pays: her young strewn dead
in the streets,
her soldiers dead, silent forever." GOD's
Decree.

NEW KING JAMES VERSION

31"Behold, I *am* against you,
O most haughty one!" says the Lord GOD of hosts;
"For your day has come,
The time *that* I will punish you.[a]
32The most proud shall stumble and fall,
And no one will raise him up;
I will kindle a fire in his cities,
And it will devour all around him."

33Thus says the LORD of hosts:

"The children of Israel *were* oppressed,
Along with the children of Judah;
All who took them captive have held them fast;
They have refused to let them go.
34Their Redeemer *is* strong;
The LORD of hosts *is* His name.
He will thoroughly plead their case,
That He may give rest to the land,
And disquiet the inhabitants of Babylon.

35"A sword *is* against the Chaldeans," says the LORD,
"Against the inhabitants of Babylon,
And against her princes and her wise men.
36A sword *is* against the soothsayers, and they will be fools.
A sword *is* against her mighty men, and they will be dismayed.
37A sword *is* against their horses,
Against their chariots,
And against all the mixed peoples who *are* in her midst;
And they will become like women.
A sword *is* against her treasures, and they will be robbed.
38A drought[a] *is* against her waters, and they will be dried up.
For it *is* the land of carved images,
And they are insane with *their* idols.

39"Therefore the wild desert beasts shall dwell *there* with the jackals,
And the ostriches shall dwell in it.
It shall be inhabited no more forever,
Nor shall it be dwelt in from generation to generation.
40As God overthrew Sodom and Gomorrah
And their neighbors," says the LORD,
"So no one shall reside there,
Nor son of man dwell in it.

41"Behold, a people shall come from the north,
And a great nation and many kings
Shall be raised up from the ends of the earth.
42They shall hold the bow and the lance;
They *are* cruel and shall not show mercy.
Their voice shall roar like the sea;
They shall ride on horses,
Set in array, like a man for the battle,
Against you, O daughter of Babylon.

50:31 [a]Following Masoretic Text and Targum; Septuagint and Vulgate read *The time of your punishment.* **50:38** [a]Following Masoretic Text, Targum, and Vulgate; Syriac reads *sword;* Septuagint omits *A drought is.*

THE MESSAGE

31-32 "Do you get it, Mister Pride? I'm your enemy!"
Decree of the Master,
GOD-of-the-Angel-Armies.
"Time's run out on you:
That's right: It's Doomsday.
Mister Pride will fall flat on his face.
No one will offer him a hand.
I'll set his towns on fire.
The fire will spread wild through the country."

33-34 And here's more from GOD-of-the-Angel-Armies:

"The people of Israel are beaten down,
the people of Judah along with them.
Their oppressors have them in a grip of steel.
They won't let go.
But the Rescuer is strong:
GOD-of-the-Angel-Armies.
Yes, I will take their side,
I'll come to their rescue.
I'll soothe their land,
but rough up the people of Babylon.

35-40 "It's all-out war in Babylon"—GOD's Decree—
"total war against people, leaders, and the wise!
War to the death on her boasting pretenders, fools one and all!
War to the death on her soldiers, cowards to a man!
War to the death on her hired killers, gutless wonders!
War to the death on her banks—looted!
War to the death on her water supply—drained dry!
A land of make-believe gods gone crazy—hobgoblins!
The place will be haunted with jackals and scorpions,
night-owls and vampire bats.
No one will ever live there again.
The land will reek with the stench of death.
It will join Sodom and Gomorrah and their neighbors,
the cities I did away with." GOD's Decree.
"No one will live there again.
No one will again draw breath in that land, ever.

41-43 "And now, watch this! People pouring out of the north, hordes of people,
A mob of kings stirred up
from far-off places.
Flourishing deadly weapons,
barbarians they are, cruel and pitiless.
Roaring and relentless, like ocean breakers,
they come riding fierce stallions,
In battle formation, ready to fight
you, Daughter Babylon!

NEW KING JAMES VERSION

43"The king of Babylon has heard the report
about them,
And his hands grow feeble;
Anguish has taken hold of him,
Pangs as of a woman in childbirth.

44"Behold, he shall come up like a lion from
the floodplain[a] of the Jordan
Against the dwelling place of the strong;
But I will make them suddenly run away
from her.
And who *is* a chosen *man that* I may
appoint over her?
For who *is* like Me?
Who will arraign Me?
And who *is* that shepherd
Who will withstand Me?"

45Therefore hear the counsel of the LORD that
He has taken against Babylon,
And His purposes that He has proposed
against the land of the Chaldeans:
Surely the least of the flock shall draw them
out;
Surely He will make their dwelling place
desolate with them.
46At the noise of the taking of Babylon
The earth trembles,
And the cry is heard among the nations.

THE UTTER DESTRUCTION OF BABYLON

51 Thus says the LORD:
"Behold, I will raise up against Babylon,
Against those who dwell in Leb Kamai,[a]
A destroying wind.
2And I will send winnowers to Babylon,
Who shall winnow her and empty her land.
For in the day of doom
They shall be against her all around.
3Against *her* let the archer bend his bow,
And lift himself up against *her* in his armor.
Do not spare her young men;
Utterly destroy all her army.
4Thus the slain shall fall in the land of the
Chaldeans,
And *those* thrust through in her streets.
5For Israel is not forsaken, nor Judah,
By his God, the LORD of hosts,
Though their land was filled with sin
against the Holy One of Israel."

6Flee from the midst of Babylon,
And every one save his life!
Do not be cut off in her iniquity,
For this *is* the time of the LORD's vengeance;
He shall recompense her.

50:44 [a]Or *thicket* **51:1** [a]A code word for Chaldea (Babylonia); may be translated *The Midst of Those Who Rise Up Against Me*

THE MESSAGE

Babylon's king hears them coming.
He goes white as a ghost, limp as a
dishrag.
Terror-stricken, he doubles up in pain,
helpless to fight,
like a woman giving birth to a baby.

44 "And now watch this: Like a lion coming up
from the thick jungle of the Jordan,
Looking for prey in the mountain
pastures,
I'll take over and pounce.
I'll take my pick of the flock—and who's to
stop me?
All the so-called shepherds are helpless
before me."

45-46 So, listen to this plan that GOD has worked
out against Babylon, the blueprint of what
he's prepared for dealing with Chaldea:

Believe it or not, the young,
the vulnerable—mere lambs and kids—
will be dragged off.
Believe it or not, the flock
in shock, helpless to help, watches it
happen.
When the shout goes up, "Babylon's down!"
the very earth will shudder at the sound.
The news will be heard all over the
world.

HURRICANE PERSIA

1-5 51 There's more. GOD says more:
"Watch this:
I'm whipping up
A death-dealing hurricane against
Babylon—'Hurricane Persia'—
against all who live in that perverse land.
I'm sending a cleanup crew into Babylon.
They'll clean the place out from top to
bottom.
When they get through there'll be nothing
left of her
worth taking or talking about.
They won't miss a thing.
A total and final Doomsday!
Fighters will fight with everything they've
got.
It's no-holds-barred.
They will spare nothing and no one.
It's final and wholesale destruction—
the end!
Babylon littered with the wounded,
streets piled with corpses.
It turns out that Israel and Judah
are not widowed after all.
As their God, GOD-of-the-Angel-Armies, I
am still alive and well,
committed to them even though
They filled their land with sin
against Israel's most Holy God.

6-8 "Get out of Babylon as fast as you can.
Run for your lives! Save your necks!
Don't linger and lose your lives to my
vengeance on her
as I pay her back for her sins.

NEW KING JAMES VERSION

7Babylon *was* a golden cup in the LORD's
hand,
That made all the earth drunk.
The nations drank her wine;
Therefore the nations are deranged.
8Babylon has suddenly fallen and been
destroyed.
Wail for her!
Take balm for her pain;
Perhaps she may be healed.

9We would have healed Babylon,
But she is not healed.
Forsake her, and let us go everyone to his
own country;
For her judgment reaches to heaven and is
lifted up to the skies.
10The LORD has revealed our righteousness.
Come and let us declare in Zion the work of
the LORD our God.

11Make the arrows bright!
Gather the shields!
The LORD has raised up the spirit of the
kings of the Medes.
For His plan *is* against Babylon to destroy it,
Because it *is* the vengeance of the LORD,
The vengeance for His temple.
12Set up the standard on the walls of Babylon;
Make the guard strong,
Set up the watchmen,
Prepare the ambushes.
For the LORD has both devised and done
What He spoke against the inhabitants of
Babylon.
13O you who dwell by many waters,
Abundant in treasures,
Your end has come,
The measure of your covetousness.
14The LORD of hosts has sworn by Himself:
"Surely I will fill you with men, as with
locusts,
And they shall lift up a shout against you."

15He has made the earth by His power;
He has established the world by His
wisdom,
And stretched out the heaven by His
understanding.
16When He utters *His* voice—
There is a multitude of waters in the
heavens:
"He causes the vapors to ascend from the
ends of the earth;
He makes lightnings for the rain;
He brings the wind out of His treasuries."[a]

17Everyone is dull-hearted, without
knowledge;
Every metalsmith is put to shame by the
carved image;
For his molded image *is* falsehood,
And *there is* no breath in them.
18They *are* futile, a work of errors;
In the time of their punishment they shall
perish.

51:16 [a]Psalm 135:7

THE MESSAGE

Babylon was a fancy gold chalice
held in my hand,
Filled with the wine of my anger
to make the whole world drunk.
The nations drank the wine
and they've all gone crazy.
Babylon herself will stagger and crash,
senseless in a drunken stupor—tragic!
Get anointing balm for her wound.
Maybe she can be cured."

9 "We did our best, but she can't be helped.
Babylon is past fixing.
Give her up to her fate.
Go home.
The judgment on her will be vast,
a skyscraper-memorial of vengeance.

YOUR LIFELINE IS CUT

10 "GOD has set everything right for us.
Come! Let's tell the good news
Back home in Zion.
Let's tell what our GOD did to set things
right.

11-13 "Sharpen the arrows!
Fill the quivers!
GOD has stirred up the kings of the Medes,
infecting them with war fever: 'Destroy
Babylon!'
GOD's on the warpath.
He's out to avenge his Temple.
Give the signal to attack Babylon's walls.
Station guards around the clock.
Bring in reinforcements.
Set men in ambush.
GOD will do what he planned,
what he said he'd do to the people of
Babylon.
You have more water than you need,
you have more money than you need—
But your life is over,
your lifeline cut."

14 GOD-of-the-Angel-Armies has solemnly
sworn:
"I'll fill this place with soldiers.
They'll swarm through here like locusts
chanting victory songs over you."

15-19 By his power he made earth.
His wisdom gave shape to the world.
He crafted the cosmos.
He thunders and rain pours down.
He sends the clouds soaring.
He embellishes the storm with lightnings,
launches the wind from his warehouse.
Stick-god worshipers look mighty foolish!
god-makers embarrassed by their
handmade gods!
Their gods are frauds, dead sticks—
deadwood gods, tasteless jokes.
They're nothing but stale smoke.
When the smoke clears, they're gone.

NEW KING JAMES VERSION

19The Portion of Jacob *is* not like them,
For He *is* the Maker of all things;
And *Israel is* the tribe of His inheritance.
The LORD of hosts *is* His name.

20"You *are* My battle-ax *and* weapons of war:
For with you I will break the nation in pieces;
With you I will destroy kingdoms;
21With you I will break in pieces the horse and its rider;
With you I will break in pieces the chariot and its rider;
22With you also I will break in pieces man and woman;
With you I will break in pieces old and young;
With you I will break in pieces the young man and the maiden;
23With you also I will break in pieces the shepherd and his flock;
With you I will break in pieces the farmer and his yoke of oxen;
And with you I will break in pieces governors and rulers.

24"And I will repay Babylon
And all the inhabitants of Chaldea
For all the evil they have done
In Zion in your sight," says the LORD.

25"Behold, I *am* against you, O destroying mountain,
Who destroys all the earth," says the LORD.
"And I will stretch out My hand against you,
Roll you down from the rocks,
And make you a burnt mountain.
26They shall not take from you a stone for a corner
Nor a stone for a foundation,
But you shall be desolate forever," says the LORD.

27Set up a banner in the land,
Blow the trumpet among the nations!
Prepare the nations against her,
Call the kingdoms together against her:
Ararat, Minni, and Ashkenaz.
Appoint a general against her;
Cause the horses to come up like the bristling locusts.
28Prepare against her the nations,
With the kings of the Medes,
Its governors and all its rulers,
All the land of his dominion.
29And the land will tremble and sorrow;
For every purpose of the LORD shall be performed against Babylon,
To make the land of Babylon a desolation without inhabitant.
30The mighty men of Babylon have ceased fighting,
They have remained in their strongholds;
Their might has failed,
They became *like* women;
They have burned her dwelling places,
The bars of her *gate* are broken.
31One runner will run to meet another,
And one messenger to meet another,

THE MESSAGE

But the Portion-of-Jacob is the real thing;
he put the whole universe together,
With special attention to Israel.
His name? GOD-of-the-Angel-Armies!

THEY'LL SLEEP AND NEVER WAKE UP

20-23 God says, "You, Babylon, are my hammer,
my weapon of war.
I'll use you to smash godless nations,
use you to knock kingdoms to bits.
I'll use you to smash horse and rider,
use you to smash chariot and driver.
I'll use you to smash man and woman,
use you to smash the old man and the boy.
I'll use you to smash the young man and young woman,
use you to smash shepherd and sheep.
I'll use you to smash farmer and yoked oxen,
use you to smash governors and senators.

24 "Judeans, you'll see it with your own
eyes. I'll pay Babylon and all the Chaldeans
back for all the evil they did in Zion." GOD's
Decree.

25-26 "I'm your enemy, Babylon, Mount Destroyer,
you ravager of the whole earth.
I'll reach out, I'll take you in my hand,
and I'll crush you till there's no mountain left.
I'll turn you into a gravel pit—
no more cornerstones cut from you,
No more foundation stones quarried from you!
Nothing left of you but gravel." GOD's Decree.

27-28 "Raise the signal in the land,
blow the shofar-trumpet for the nations.
Consecrate the nations for holy work against her.
Call kingdoms into service against her.
Enlist Ararat, Minni, and Ashkenaz.
Appoint a field marshal against her,
and round up horses, locust hordes of horses!
Consecrate the nations for holy work against her—
the king of the Medes, his leaders and people.

29-33 "The very land trembles in terror, writhes in pain,
terrorized by my plans against Babylon,
Plans to turn the country of Babylon
into a lifeless moonscape—a wasteland.
Babylon's soldiers have quit fighting.
They hide out in ruins and caves—
Cowards who've given up without a fight,
exposed as cowering milksops.
Babylon's houses are going up in flames,
the city gates torn off their hinges.
Runner after runner comes racing in,
each on the heels of the last,

NEW KING JAMES VERSION

To show the king of Babylon that his city is
taken on *all* sides;
32 The passages are blocked,
The reeds they have burned with fire,
And the men of war are terrified.

33 For thus says the LORD of hosts, the God of
Israel:

"The daughter of Babylon *is* like a threshing
floor
When it is time to thresh her;
Yet a little while
And the time of her harvest will come."

34 "Nebuchadnezzar the king of Babylon
Has devoured me, he has crushed me;
He has made me an empty vessel,
He has swallowed me up like a monster;
He has filled his stomach with my
delicacies,
He has spit me out.
35 Let the violence *done* to me and my flesh *be*
upon Babylon,"
The inhabitant of Zion will say;
"And my blood be upon the inhabitants of
Chaldea!"
Jerusalem will say.

36 Therefore thus says the LORD:

"Behold, I will plead your case and take
vengeance for you.
I will dry up her sea and make her springs
dry.
37 Babylon shall become a heap,
A dwelling place for jackals,
An astonishment and a hissing,
Without an inhabitant.
38 They shall roar together like lions,
They shall growl like lions' whelps.
39 In their excitement I will prepare their feasts;
I will make them drunk,
That they may rejoice,
And sleep a perpetual sleep
And not awake," says the LORD.
40 "I will bring them down
Like lambs to the slaughter,
Like rams with male goats.

41 "Oh, how Sheshach[a] is taken!
Oh, how the praise of the whole earth is
seized!
How Babylon has become desolate among
the nations!
42 The sea has come up over Babylon;
She is covered with the multitude of its
waves.
43 Her cities are a desolation,
A dry land and a wilderness,
A land where no one dwells,
Through which no son of man passes.
44 I will punish Bel in Babylon,
And I will bring out of his mouth what he
has swallowed;
And the nations shall not stream to him
anymore.
Yes, the wall of Babylon shall fall.

51:41 [a] A code word for Babylon (compare Jeremiah 25:26)

THE MESSAGE

Bringing reports to the king of Babylon
that his city is a lost cause.
The fords of the rivers are all taken.
Wildfire rages through the swamp grass.
Soldiers desert left and right.
I, GOD-of-the-Angel-Armies, said it
would happen:
'Daughter Babylon is a threshing floor
at threshing time.
Soon, oh very soon, her harvest will come
and then the chaff will fly!'

34-37 "Nebuchadnezzar king of Babylon
chewed up my people and spit out the
bones.
He wiped his dish clean, pushed back his
chair,
and belched—a huge gluttonous belch.
Lady Zion says,
'The brutality done to me be done to
Babylon!'
And Jerusalem says,
'The blood spilled from me be charged to
the Chaldeans!'
Then I, GOD, step in and say,
'I'm on your side, taking up your cause.
I'm your Avenger. You'll get your revenge.
I'll dry up her rivers, plug up her springs.
Babylon will be a pile of rubble,
scavenged by stray dogs and cats,
A dumping ground for garbage,
a godforsaken ghost town.'

38-40 "The Babylonians will be like lions and their
cubs,
ravenous, roaring for food.
I'll fix them a meal, all right—a banquet, in
fact.
They'll drink themselves falling-down
drunk.
Dead drunk, they'll sleep—and sleep, and
sleep . . .
and they'll never wake up." GOD's Decree.
"I'll haul these 'lions' off to the
slaughterhouse
like the lambs, rams, and goats,
never to be heard of again.

41-48 "Babylon is finished—
the pride of the whole earth is flat on her
face.
What a comedown for Babylon,
to end up inglorious in the sewer!
Babylon drowned in chaos,
battered by waves of enemy soldiers.
Her towns stink with decay and rot,
the land empty and bare and sterile.
No one lives in these towns anymore.
Travelers give them a wide berth.
I'll bring doom on the glutton god-Bel in
Babylon.
I'll make him vomit up all he gulped
down.
No more visitors stream into this place,
admiring and gawking at the wonders of
Babylon.
The wonders of Babylon are no more.

NEW KING JAMES VERSION

45"My people, go out of the midst of her!
And let everyone deliver himself from the
fierce anger of the LORD.
46And lest your heart faint,
And you fear for the rumor that *will be*
heard in the land
(A rumor will come *one* year,
And after that, in *another* year
A rumor *will come,*
And violence in the land,
Ruler against ruler),
47Therefore behold, the days are coming
That I will bring judgment on the carved
images of Babylon;
Her whole land shall be ashamed,
And all her slain shall fall in her midst.
48Then the heavens and the earth and all that
is in them
Shall sing joyously over Babylon;
For the plunderers shall come to her from
the north," says the LORD.

49As Babylon *has caused* the slain of Israel to
fall,
So at Babylon the slain of all the earth shall
fall.
50You who have escaped the sword,
Get away! Do not stand still!
Remember the LORD afar off,
And let Jerusalem come to your mind.

51We are ashamed because we have heard
reproach.
Shame has covered our faces,
For strangers have come into the
sanctuaries of the LORD's house.

52"Therefore behold, the days are coming,"
says the LORD,
"That I will bring judgment on her carved
images,
And throughout all her land the wounded
shall groan.
53Though Babylon were to mount up to
heaven,
And though she were to fortify the height of
her strength,
Yet from Me plunderers would come to her,"
says the LORD.

54The sound of a cry *comes* from Babylon,
And great destruction from the land of the
Chaldeans,
55Because the LORD is plundering Babylon
And silencing her loud voice,
Though her waves roar like great waters,
And the noise of their voice is uttered,
56Because the plunderer comes against her,
against Babylon,
And her mighty men are taken.
Every one of their bows is broken;
For the LORD *is* the God of recompense,
He will surely repay.

THE MESSAGE

Run for your lives, my dear people!
Run, and don't look back!
Get out of this place while you can,
this place torched by GOD's raging anger.
Don't lose hope. Don't ever give up
when the rumors pour in hot and heavy.
One year it's this, the next year it's that—
rumors of violence, rumors of war.
Trust me, the time is coming
when I'll put the no-gods of Babylon in
their place.
I'll show up the whole country as a
sickening fraud,
with dead bodies strewn all over the
place.
Heaven and earth, angels and people,
will throw a victory party over Babylon
When the avenging armies from the north
descend on her." GOD's Decree!

REMEMBER GOD IN YOUR LONG AND DISTANT EXILE

49-50 "Babylon must fall—
compensation for the war dead in Israel.
Babylonians will be killed
because of all that Babylonian killing.
But you exiles who have escaped a
Babylonian death,
get out! And fast!
Remember GOD in your long and distant
exile.
Keep Jerusalem alive in your memory."
51 How we've been humiliated, taunted and
abused,
kicked around for so long that we hardly
know who we are!
And we hardly know what to think—
our old Sanctuary, GOD's house,
desecrated by strangers.

52-53 "I know, but trust me: The time is coming"
—GOD's Decree—
"When I will bring doom on her no-god
idols,
and all over this land her wounded will
groan.
Even if Babylon climbed a ladder to the
moon
and pulled up the ladder so that no one
could get to her,
That wouldn't stop me.
I'd make sure my avengers would reach
her."
GOD's Decree.

54-56 "But now listen! Do you hear it? A cry out
of Babylon!
An unearthly wail out of Chaldea!
GOD is taking his wrecking bar to Babylon.
We'll be hearing the last of her noise—
Death throes like the crashing of waves,
death rattles like the roar of cataracts.
The avenging destroyer is about to enter
Babylon:
Her soldiers are taken, her weapons are
trashed.
Indeed, GOD is a God who evens things out.
All end up with their just deserts.

NEW KING JAMES VERSION

57“And I will make drunk
Her princes and wise men,
Her governors, her deputies, and her mighty
men.
And they shall sleep a perpetual sleep
And not awake,” says the King,
Whose name *is* the LORD of hosts.

58Thus says the LORD of hosts:

“The broad walls of Babylon shall be utterly
broken,
And her high gates shall be burned with
fire;
The people will labor in vain,
And the nations, because of the fire;
And they shall be weary.”

JEREMIAH'S COMMAND TO SERAIAH

59The word which Jeremiah the prophet
commanded Seraiah the son of Neriah, the son
of Mahseiah, when he went with Zedekiah the
king of Judah to Babylon in the fourth year of
his reign. And Seraiah *was* the quartermaster.
60So Jeremiah wrote in a book all the evil that
would come upon Babylon, all these words that
are written against Babylon. 61And Jeremiah
said to Seraiah, “When you arrive in Babylon
and see it, and read all these words, 62then you
shall say, ‘O LORD, You have spoken against this
place to cut it off, so that none shall remain in it,
neither man nor beast, but it shall be desolate
forever.’ 63Now it shall be, when you have fin-
ished reading this book, *that* you shall tie a
stone to it and throw it out into the Euphrates.
64Then you shall say, ‘Thus Babylon shall sink
and not rise from the catastrophe that I will
bring upon her. And they shall be weary.’ ”
Thus far *are* the words of Jeremiah.

THE FALL OF JERUSALEM REVIEWED

52 Zedekiah *was* twenty-one years old when
he became king, and he reigned eleven
years in Jerusalem. His mother's name *was*
Hamutal the daughter of Jeremiah of Libnah.
2He also did evil in the sight of the LORD, accord-
ing to all that Jehoiakim had done. 3For because
of the anger of the LORD *this* happened in
Jerusalem and Judah, till He finally cast them
out from His presence. Then Zedekiah rebelled
against the king of Babylon.
4Now it came to pass in the ninth year of his
reign, in the tenth month, on the tenth *day* of the
month, *that* Nebuchadnezzar king of Babylon
and all his army came against Jerusalem and
encamped against it; and *they* built a siege wall
against it all around. 5So the city was besieged
until the eleventh year of King Zedekiah. 6By
the fourth month, on the ninth day of the month,
the famine had become so severe in the city that
there was no food for the people of the land.
7Then the city *wall* was broken through, and all
the men of war fled and went out of the city at

THE MESSAGE

57 “I'll get them drunk, the whole lot of
them—
princes, sages, governors, soldiers.
Dead drunk, they'll sleep—and sleep and
sleep . . .
and never wake up.” The King's Decree.
His name? GOD-of-the-Angel-Armies!

58 GOD-of-the-Angel-Armies speaks:

“The city walls of Babylon—those massive
walls!—
will be flattened.
And those city gates—huge gates!—
will be set on fire.
The harder you work at this empty life,
the less you are.
Nothing comes of ambition like this
but ashes.”

59 Jeremiah the prophet gave a job to Seraiah
son of Neriah, son of Mahseiah, when Sera-
iah went with Zedekiah king of Judah to
Babylon. It was in the fourth year of
Zedekiah's reign. Seraiah was in charge of
travel arrangements.
60-62 Jeremiah had written down in a little book-
let all the bad things that would come down
on Babylon. He told Seraiah, “When you get
to Babylon, read this out in public. Read, ‘You,
O GOD, said that you would destroy this place
so that nothing could live here, neither hu-
man nor animal—a wasteland to top all
wastelands, an eternal nothing.’
63-64 “When you've finished reading the page,
tie a stone to it, throw it into the River Eu-
phrates, and watch it sink. Then say, ‘That's
how Babylon will sink to the bottom and
stay there after the disaster I'm going to
bring upon her.’ ”

THE DESTRUCTION OF JERUSALEM AND EXILE OF JUDAH

1 52 Zedekiah was twenty-one years old
when he started out as king. He was
king in Jerusalem for eleven years. His
mother's name was Hamutal, the daughter
of Jeremiah. Her hometown was Libnah.
2 As far as GOD was concerned, Zedekiah
was just one more evil king, a carbon copy
of Jehoiakim.
3-5 The source of all this doom to Jerusalem
and Judah was GOD's anger. GOD turned his
back on them as an act of judgment.
Zedekiah revolted against the king of
Babylon. Nebuchadnezzar set out for
Jerusalem with a full army. He set up camp
and sealed off the city by building siege
mounds around it. He arrived on the ninth
year and tenth month of Zedekiah's reign.
The city was under siege for nineteen months
(until the eleventh year of Zedekiah).
6-8 By the fourth month of Zedekiah's
eleventh year, on the ninth day of the
month, the famine was so bad that there
wasn't so much as a crumb of bread for any-
one. Then the Babylonians broke through
the city walls. Under cover of the night
darkness, the entire Judean army fled

New King James Version

night by way of the gate between the two walls,
which *was* by the king's garden, even though
the Chaldeans *were* near the city all around.
And they went by way of the plain.[a]
8But the army of the Chaldeans pursued the
king, and they overtook Zedekiah in the plains
of Jericho. All his army was scattered from him.
9So they took the king and brought him up to
the king of Babylon at Riblah in the land of
Hamath, and he pronounced judgment on him.
10Then the king of Babylon killed the sons of
Zedekiah before his eyes. And he killed all the
princes of Judah in Riblah. 11He also put out the
eyes of Zedekiah; and the king of Babylon
bound him in bronze fetters, took him to Bab-
ylon, and put him in prison till the day of his
death.

The Temple and City Plundered and Burned

12Now in the fifth month, on the tenth *day* of
the month (which *was* the nineteenth year of
King Nebuchadnezzar king of Babylon), Ne-
buzaradan, the captain of the guard, *who* served
the king of Babylon, came to Jerusalem. 13He
burned the house of the LORD and the king's
house; all the houses of Jerusalem, that is, all
the houses of the great, he burned with fire.
14And all the army of the Chaldeans who *were*
with the captain of the guard broke down all the
walls of Jerusalem all around. 15Then Ne-
buzaradan the captain of the guard carried away
captive *some* of the poor people, the rest of the
people who remained in the city, the defectors
who had deserted to the king of Babylon, and the
rest of the craftsmen. 16But Nebuzaradan the
captain of the guard left *some* of the poor of the
land as vinedressers and farmers.
17The bronze pillars that *were* in the house of
the LORD, and the carts and the bronze Sea that
were in the house of the LORD, the Chaldeans
broke in pieces, and carried all their bronze to
Babylon. 18They also took away the pots, the
shovels, the trimmers, the bowls, the spoons,
and all the bronze utensils with which the
priests ministered. 19The basins, the firepans,
the bowls, the pots, the lampstands, the spoons,
and the cups, whatever *was* solid gold and what-
ever *was* solid silver, the captain of the guard
took away. 20The two pillars, one Sea, the twelve
bronze bulls which *were* under *it, and* the carts,
which King Solomon had made for the house of
the LORD—the bronze of all these articles was
beyond measure. 21Now *concerning* the pillars:
the height of one pillar *was* eighteen cubits, a
measuring line of twelve cubits could measure
its circumference, and its thickness *was* four
fingers; *it was* hollow. 22A capital of bronze *was*
on it; and the height of one capital *was* five cu-
bits, with a network and pomegranates all
around the capital, all of bronze. The second pil-
lar, with pomegranates was the same. 23There
were ninety-six pomegranates on the sides; all
the pomegranates, all around on the network,
were one hundred.

The People Taken Captive to Babylonia

24The captain of the guard took Seraiah the
chief priest, Zephaniah the second priest, and

52:7 [a]Or *the Arabah,* that is, the Jordan Valley

The Message

through an opening in the wall (it was the
gate between the two walls above the King's
Garden). They slipped through the lines of
the Babylonians who surrounded the city
and headed for the Jordan into the Arabah
Valley, but the Babylonians were in full pur-
suit. They caught up with them in the Plains
of Jericho. But by then Zedekiah's army had
deserted and was scattered.
9-11 The Babylonians captured Zedekiah and
marched him off to the king of Babylon at
Riblah in Hamath, who tried and sentenced
him on the spot. The king of Babylon then
killed Zedekiah's sons right before his eyes.
The summary murder of his sons was the
last thing Zedekiah saw, for they then
blinded him. The king of Babylon followed
that up by killing all the officials of Judah.
Securely handcuffed, Zedekiah was hauled
off to Babylon. The king of Babylon threw
him in prison, where he stayed until the day
he died.
12-16 In the nineteenth year of Nebuchadnez-
zar king of Babylon on the seventh day of
the fifth month, Nebuzaradan, the king of
Babylon's chief deputy, arrived in Jeru-
salem. He burned the Temple of GOD to the
ground, went on to the royal palace, and
then finished off the city. He burned the
whole place down. He put the Babylonian
troops he had with him to work knocking
down the city walls. Finally, he rounded up
everyone left in the city, including those
who had earlier deserted to the king of
Babylon, and took them off into exile. He
left a few poor dirt farmers behind to tend
the vineyards and what was left of the fields.
17-19 The Babylonians broke up the bronze pil-
lars, the bronze washstands, and the huge
bronze basin (the Sea) that were in the Tem-
ple of GOD, and hauled the bronze off to
Babylon. They also took the various bronze-
crafted liturgical accessories, as well as the
gold and silver censers and sprinkling
bowls, used in the services of Temple wor-
ship. The king's deputy didn't miss a thing.
He took every scrap of precious metal he
could find.
20-23 The amount of bronze they got from the
two pillars, the Sea, the twelve bronze bulls
that supported the Sea, and the ten wash-
stands that Solomon had made for the Tem-
ple of GOD was enormous. They couldn't
weigh it all! Each pillar stood twenty-seven
feet high with a circumference of eighteen
feet. The pillars were hollow, the bronze a
little less than an inch thick. Each pillar was
topped with an ornate capital of bronze
pomegranates and filigree, which added an-
other seven and a half feet to its height.
There were ninety-six pomegranates evenly
spaced—in all, a hundred pomegranates
worked into the filigree.
24-27 The king's deputy took a number of spe-
cial prisoners: Seraiah the chief priest,
Zephaniah the associate priest, three war-

NEW KING JAMES VERSION

the three doorkeepers. 25He also took out of the
city an officer who had charge of the men of
war, seven men of the king's close associates
who were found in the city, the principal scribe
of the army who mustered the people of the
land, and sixty men of the people of the land
who were found in the midst of the city. 26And
Nebuzaradan the captain of the guard took
these and brought them to the king of Babylon
at Riblah. 27Then the king of Babylon struck
them and put them to death at Riblah in the land
of Hamath. Thus Judah was carried away cap-
tive from its own land.

28These *are* the people whom Nebuchadnez-
zar carried away captive: in the seventh year,
three thousand and twenty-three Jews; 29in the
eighteenth year of Nebuchadnezzar he carried
away captive from Jerusalem eight hundred and
thirty-two persons; 30in the twenty-third year of
Nebuchadnezzar, Nebuzaradan the captain of
the guard carried away captive of the Jews
seven hundred and forty-five persons. All the
persons *were* four thousand six hundred.

JEHOIACHIN RELEASED FROM PRISON

31Now it came to pass in the thirty-seventh
year of the captivity of Jehoiachin king of Ju-
dah, in the twelfth month, on the twenty-fifth
day of the month, *that* Evil-Merodach[a] king of
Babylon, in the *first* year of his reign, lifted up
the head of Jehoiachin king of Judah and
brought him out of prison. 32And he spoke
kindly to him and gave him a more prominent
seat than those of the kings who *were* with him
in Babylon. 33So Jehoiachin changed from his
prison garments, and he ate bread regularly be-
fore the king all the days of his life. 34And as for
his provisions, there was a regular ration given
him by the king of Babylon, a portion for each
day until the day of his death, all the days of his
life.

52:31 [a]Or *Awil-Marduk*

THE MESSAGE

dens, the chief remaining army officer, seven of the king's counselors who happened to be in the city, the chief recruiting officer for the army, and sixty men of standing from among the people who were still there. Nebuzaradan the king's deputy marched them all off to the king of Babylon at Riblah. And there at Riblah, in the land of Hamath, the king of Babylon killed the lot of them in cold blood.

Judah went into exile, orphaned from her land.

28 3,023 men of Judah were taken into exile by Nebuchadnezzar in the seventh year of his reign.

29 832 from Jerusalem were taken in the eighteenth year of his reign.

30 745 men from Judah were taken off by Nebuzaradan, the king's chief deputy, in Nebuchadnezzar's twenty-third year.

The total number of exiles was 4,600.

31-34 When Jehoiachin king of Judah had been in exile for thirty-seven years, Evil-Merodach became king in Babylon and let Jehoiachin out of prison. This release took place on the twenty-fifth day of the twelfth month. The king treated him most courteously and gave him preferential treatment beyond anything experienced by the political prisoners held in Babylon. Jehoiachin took off his prison garb and from then on ate his meals in company with the king. The king provided everything he needed to live comfortably for the rest of his life.

LAMENTATIONS

New King James Version

Jerusalem in Affliction

1 How lonely sits the city
That was full of people!
How like a widow is she,
Who *was* great among the nations!
The princess among the provinces
Has become a slave!

2 She weeps bitterly in the night,
Her tears *are* on her cheeks;
Among all her lovers
She has none to comfort *her.*
All her friends have dealt treacherously with her;
They have become her enemies.

3 Judah has gone into captivity,
Under affliction and hard servitude;
She dwells among the nations,
She finds no rest;
All her persecutors overtake her in dire straits.

4 The roads to Zion mourn
Because no one comes to the set feasts.
All her gates are desolate;
Her priests sigh,
Her virgins are afflicted,
And she *is* in bitterness.

5 Her adversaries have become the master,
Her enemies prosper;
For the LORD has afflicted her
Because of the multitude of her transgressions.
Her children have gone into captivity before the enemy.

6 And from the daughter of Zion
All her splendor has departed.
Her princes have become like deer
That find no pasture,
That flee without strength
Before the pursuer.

7 In the days of her affliction and roaming,
Jerusalem remembers all her pleasant things
That she had in the days of old.
When her people fell into the hand of the enemy,
With no one to help her,
The adversaries saw her
And mocked at her downfall.[a]

8 Jerusalem has sinned gravely,
Therefore she has become vile.[a]
All who honored her despise her
Because they have seen her nakedness;
Yes, she sighs and turns away.

9 Her uncleanness *is* in her skirts;
She did not consider her destiny;

1:7 [a]Vulgate reads *her Sabbaths.* 1:8 [a]Septuagint and Vulgate read *moved* or *removed.*

The Message

Worthless, Cheap, Abject!

1 1 Oh, oh, oh . . .
How empty the city, once teeming with people.
A widow, this city, once in the front rank of nations,
once queen of the ball, she's now a drudge in the kitchen.

2 She cries herself to sleep each night, tears soaking her pillow.
No one's left among her lovers to sit and hold her hand.
Her friends have all dumped her.

3 After years of pain and hard labor, Judah has gone into exile.
She camps out among the nations, never feels at home.
Hunted by all, she's stuck between a rock and a hard place.

4 Zion's roads weep, empty of pilgrims headed to the feasts.
All her city gates are deserted, her priests in despair.
Her virgins are sad. How bitter her fate.

5 Her enemies have become her masters. Her foes are living it up
because GOD laid her low, punishing her repeated rebellions.
Her children, prisoners of the enemy, trudge into exile.

6 All beauty has drained from Daughter Zion's face.
Her princes are like deer famished for food,
chased to exhaustion by hunters.

7 Jerusalem remembers the day she lost everything,
when her people fell into enemy hands, and not a soul there to help.
Enemies looked on and laughed, laughed at her helpless silence.

8 Jerusalem, who outsinned the whole world, is an outcast.
All who admired her despise her now that they see beneath the surface.
Miserable, she groans and turns away in shame.

9 She played fast and loose with life, she never considered tomorrow,

NEW KING JAMES VERSION

Therefore her collapse was awesome;
She had no comforter.
"O LORD, behold my affliction,
For *the* enemy is exalted!"

10 The adversary has spread his hand
Over all her pleasant things;
For she has seen the nations enter her sanctuary,
Those whom You commanded
Not to enter Your assembly.

11 All her people sigh,
They seek bread;
They have given their valuables for food to restore life.
"See, O LORD, and consider,
For I am scorned."

12 "*Is it* nothing to you, all you who pass by?
Behold and see
If there is any sorrow like my sorrow,
Which has been brought on me,
Which the LORD has inflicted
In the day of His fierce anger.

13 "From above He has sent fire into my bones,
And it overpowered them;
He has spread a net for my feet
And turned me back;
He has made me desolate
And faint all the day.

14 "The yoke of my transgressions was bound;[a]
They were woven together by His hands,
And thrust upon my neck.
He made my strength fail;
The Lord delivered me into the hands of *those whom* I am not able to withstand.

15 "The Lord has trampled underfoot all my mighty *men* in my midst;
He has called an assembly against me
To crush my young men;
The Lord trampled *as* in a winepress
The virgin daughter of Judah.

16 "For these *things* I weep;
My eye, my eye overflows with water;
Because the comforter, who should restore my life,
Is far from me.
My children are desolate
Because the enemy prevailed."

17 Zion spreads out her hands,
But no one comforts her;
The LORD has commanded concerning Jacob
That those around him *become* his adversaries;
Jerusalem has become an unclean thing among them.

18 "The LORD is righteous,
For I rebelled against His commandment.
Hear now, all peoples,
And behold my sorrow;

1:14 [a]Following Masoretic Text and Targum; Septuagint, Syriac, and Vulgate read *watched over.*

THE MESSAGE

and now she's crashed royally, with no one to hold her hand:
"Look at my pain, O GOD! And how the enemy cruelly struts."

10 The enemy reached out to take all her favorite things. She watched
as pagans barged into her Sanctuary, those very people for whom
you posted orders: KEEP OUT: THIS ASSEMBLY OFF-LIMITS.

11 All the people groaned, so desperate for food, so desperate to stay alive
that they bartered their favorite things for a bit of breakfast:
"O GOD, look at me! Worthless, cheap, abject!

12 "And you passersby, look at me! Have you ever seen anything like this?
Ever seen pain like my pain, seen what he did to me,
what *GOD* did to me in his rage?

13 "He struck me with lightning, skewered me from head to foot,
then he set traps all around so I could hardly move.
He left me with nothing—left me sick, and sick of living.

14 "He wove my sins into a rope
and harnessed me to captivity's yoke.
I'm goaded by cruel taskmasters.

15 "The Master piled up my best soldiers in a heap,
then called in thugs to break their fine young necks.
The Master crushed the life out of fair virgin Judah.

16 "For all this I weep, weep buckets of tears,
and not a soul within miles around cares for my soul.
My children are wasted, my enemy got his way."

17 Zion reached out for help, but no one helped.
GOD ordered Jacob's enemies to surround him,
and now no one wants anything to do with Jerusalem.

18 "GOD has right on his side. I'm the one who did wrong.
Listen everybody! Look at what I'm going through!

NEW KING JAMES VERSION

My virgins and my young men
Have gone into captivity.

19 "I called for my lovers,
But they deceived me;
My priests and my elders
Breathed their last in the city,
While they sought food
To restore their life.

20 "See, O LORD, that I *am* in distress;
My soul is troubled;
My heart is overturned within me,
For I have been very rebellious.
Outside the sword bereaves,
At home *it is* like death.

21 "They have heard that I sigh,
But no one comforts me.
All my enemies have heard of my trouble;
They are glad that You have done *it*.
Bring on the day You have announced,
That they may become like me.

22 "Let all their wickedness come before You,
And do to them as You have done to me
For all my transgressions;
For my sighs *are* many,
And my heart *is* faint."

GOD'S ANGER WITH JERUSALEM

2 How the Lord has covered the daughter of Zion
With a cloud in His anger!
He cast down from heaven to the earth
The beauty of Israel,
And did not remember His footstool
In the day of His anger.

2 The Lord has swallowed up and has not pitied
All the dwelling places of Jacob.
He has thrown down in His wrath
The strongholds of the daughter of Judah;
He has brought *them* down to the ground;
He has profaned the kingdom and its princes.

3 He has cut off in fierce anger
Every horn of Israel;
He has drawn back His right hand
From before the enemy.
He has blazed against Jacob like a flaming fire
Devouring all around.

4 Standing like an enemy, He has bent His bow;
With His right hand, like an adversary,
He has slain all *who were* pleasing to His eye;
On the tent of the daughter of Zion,
He has poured out His fury like fire.

5 The Lord was like an enemy.
He has swallowed up Israel,
He has swallowed up all her palaces;
He has destroyed her strongholds,
And has increased mourning and lamentation
In the daughter of Judah.

THE MESSAGE

My fair young women, my fine young men, all herded into exile!

19 "I called to my friends; they betrayed me.
My priests and my leaders only looked after themselves,
trying but failing to save their own skins.

20 "O GOD, look at the trouble I'm in! My stomach in knots,
my heart wrecked by a life of rebellion.
Massacres in the streets, starvation in the houses.

21 "Oh, listen to my groans. No one listens, no one cares.
When my enemies heard of the trouble you gave me, they cheered.
Bring on Judgment Day! Let them get what I got!

22 "Take a good look at their evil ways and give it to them!
Give them what you gave me for my sins.
Groaning in pain, body and soul, I've had all I can take."

GOD WALKED AWAY FROM HIS HOLY TEMPLE

1 2 Oh, oh, oh . . .
How the Master has cut down Daughter Zion
from the skies, dashed Israel's glorious city to earth,
in his anger treated his favorite as throwaway junk.

2 The Master, without a second thought, took Israel in one gulp.
Raging, he smashed Judah's defenses,
made hash of her king and princes.

3 His anger blazing, he knocked Israel flat,
broke Israel's arm and turned his back just as the enemy approached,
came on Jacob like a wildfire from every direction.

4 Like an enemy, he aimed his bow, bared his sword,
and killed our young men, our pride and joy.
His anger, like fire, burned down the homes in Zion.

5 The Master became the enemy. He had Israel for supper.
He chewed up and spit out all the defenses.
He left Daughter Judah moaning and groaning.

NEW KING JAMES VERSION

[6]He has done violence to His tabernacle,
As if it were a garden;
He has destroyed His place of assembly;
The LORD has caused
The appointed feasts and Sabbaths to be forgotten in Zion.
In His burning indignation He has spurned the king and the priest.

[7]The Lord has spurned His altar,
He has abandoned His sanctuary;
He has given up the walls of her palaces
Into the hand of the enemy.
They have made a noise in the house of the LORD
As on the day of a set feast.

[8]The LORD has purposed to destroy
The wall of the daughter of Zion.
He has stretched out a line;
He has not withdrawn His hand from destroying;
Therefore He has caused the rampart and wall to lament;
They languished together.

[9]Her gates have sunk into the ground;
He has destroyed and broken her bars.
Her king and her princes *are* among the nations;
The Law *is* no *more,*
And her prophets find no vision from the LORD.

[10]The elders of the daughter of Zion
Sit on the ground *and* keep silence;
They throw dust on their heads
And gird themselves with sackcloth.
The virgins of Jerusalem
Bow their heads to the ground.

[11]My eyes fail with tears,
My heart is troubled;
My bile is poured on the ground
Because of the destruction of the daughter of my people,
Because the children and the infants
Faint in the streets of the city.

[12]They say to their mothers,
"Where *is* grain and wine?"
As they swoon like the wounded
In the streets of the city,
As their life is poured out
In their mothers' bosom.

[13]How shall I console you?
To what shall I liken you,
O daughter of Jerusalem?
What shall I compare with you, that I may comfort you,
O virgin daughter of Zion?
For your ruin *is* spread wide as the sea;
Who can heal you?

[14]Your prophets have seen for you
False and deceptive visions;
They have not uncovered your iniquity,
To bring back your captives,
But have envisioned for you false prophecies and delusions.

THE MESSAGE

6 He plowed up his old trysting place,
trashed his favorite rendezvous.
GOD wiped out Zion's memories of feast days and Sabbaths,
angrily sacked king and priest alike.

7 GOD abandoned his altar, walked away from his holy Temple
and turned the fortifications over to the enemy.
As they cheered in GOD's Temple, you'd have thought it was a feast day!

8 GOD drew up plans to tear down the walls of Daughter Zion.
He assembled his crew, set to work and went at it.
Total demolition! The stones wept!

9 Her city gates, iron bars and all, disappeared in the rubble:
her kings and princes off to exile—no one left to instruct or lead;
her prophets useless—they neither saw nor heard anything from GOD.

10 The elders of Daughter Zion sit silent on the ground.
They throw dust on their heads, dress in rough penitential burlap—
the young virgins of Jerusalem, their faces creased with the dirt.

11 My eyes are blind with tears, my stomach in a knot.
My insides have turned to jelly over my people's fate.
Babies and children are fainting all over the place,

12 Calling to their mothers, "I'm hungry! I'm thirsty!"
then fainting like dying soldiers in the streets,
breathing their last in their mothers' laps.

13 How can I understand your plight, dear Jerusalem?
What can I say to give you comfort, dear Zion?
Who can put you together again? This bust-up is past understanding.

14 Your prophets courted you with sweet talk.
They didn't face you with your sin so that you could repent.
Their sermons were all wishful thinking, deceptive illusions.

NEW KING JAMES VERSION

15All who pass by clap *their* hands at you;
They hiss and shake their heads
At the daughter of Jerusalem:
"*Is* this the city that is called
'The perfection of beauty,
The joy of the whole earth'?"

16All your enemies have opened their mouth against you;
They hiss and gnash *their* teeth.
They say, "We have swallowed *her* up!
Surely this *is* the day we have waited for;
We have found *it*, we have seen *it!*"

17The LORD has done what He purposed;
He has fulfilled His word
Which He commanded in days of old.
He has thrown down and has not pitied,
And He has caused an enemy to rejoice over you;
He has exalted the horn of your adversaries.

18Their heart cried out to the Lord,
"O wall of the daughter of Zion,
Let tears run down like a river day and night;
Give yourself no relief;
Give your eyes no rest.

19"Arise, cry out in the night,
At the beginning of the watches;
Pour out your heart like water before the face of the Lord.
Lift your hands toward Him
For the life of your young children,
Who faint from hunger at the head of every street."

20"See, O LORD, and consider!
To whom have You done this?
Should the women eat their offspring,
The children they have cuddled?[a]
Should the priest and prophet be slain
In the sanctuary of the Lord?

21"Young and old lie
On the ground in the streets;
My virgins and my young men
Have fallen by the sword;
You have slain *them* in the day of Your anger,
You have slaughtered *and* not pitied.

22"You have invited as to a feast day
The terrors that surround me.
In the day of the LORD's anger
There was no refugee or survivor.
Those whom I have borne and brought up
My enemies have destroyed."

THE PROPHET'S ANGUISH AND HOPE

3 I *am* the man *who* has seen affliction by the rod of His wrath.
2He has led me and made *me* walk
In darkness and not *in* light.
3Surely He has turned His hand against me
Time and time again throughout the day.

2:20 [a]Vulgate reads *a span long.*

THE MESSAGE

15 Astonished, passersby can't believe what they see.
They rub their eyes, they shake their heads over Jerusalem.
Is this the city voted "Most Beautiful" and "Best Place to Live"?

16 But now your enemies gape, slack-jawed.
Then they rub their hands in glee:
"We've got them!
We've been waiting for this! Here it is!"

17 GOD did carry out, item by item, exactly what he said he'd do.
He always said he'd do this. Now he's done it—torn the place down.
He's let your enemies walk all over you, declared them world champions!

18 Give out heart-cries to the Master, dear repentant Zion.
Let the tears roll like a river, day and night,
and keep at it—no time-outs. Keep those tears flowing!

19 As each night watch begins, get up and cry out in prayer.
Pour your heart out face-to-face with the Master.
Lift high your hands. Beg for the lives of your children
who are starving to death out on the streets.

20 "Look at us, GOD. Think it over. Have you ever treated *anyone* like this?
Should women eat their own babies, the very children they raised?
Should priests and prophets be murdered in the Master's own Sanctuary?

21 "Boys and old men lie in the gutters of the streets,
my young men and women killed in their prime.
Angry, you killed them in cold blood, cut them down without mercy.

22 "You invited, like friends to a party, men to swoop down in attack
so that on the big day of GOD's wrath no one would get away.
The children I loved and reared—gone, gone, gone."

GOD LOCKED ME UP IN DEEP DARKNESS

1-3 3 I'm the man who has seen trouble,
trouble coming from the lash of GOD's anger.
He took me by the hand and walked me into pitch-black darkness.
Yes, he's given me the back of his hand over and over and over again.

NEW KING JAMES VERSION

4He has aged my flesh and my skin,
And broken my bones.
5He has besieged me
And surrounded *me* with bitterness and woe.
6He has set me in dark places
Like the dead of long ago.

7He has hedged me in so that I cannot get out;
He has made my chain heavy.
8Even when I cry and shout,
He shuts out my prayer.
9He has blocked my ways with hewn stone;
He has made my paths crooked.

10He *has been* to me a bear lying in wait,
Like a lion in ambush.
11He has turned aside my ways and torn me in pieces;
He has made me desolate.
12He has bent His bow
And set me up as a target for the arrow.

13He has caused the arrows of His quiver
To pierce my loins.[a]
14I have become the ridicule of all my people—
Their taunting song all the day.
15He has filled me with bitterness,
He has made me drink wormwood.

16He has also broken my teeth with gravel,
And covered me with ashes.
17You have moved my soul far from peace;
I have forgotten prosperity.
18And I said, "My strength and my hope
Have perished from the LORD."

19Remember my affliction and roaming,
The wormwood and the gall.
20My soul still remembers
And sinks within me.
21This I recall to my mind,
Therefore I have hope.

22*Through* the LORD's mercies we are not consumed,
Because His compassions fail not.
23*They are* new every morning;
Great *is* Your faithfulness.
24"The LORD *is* my portion," says my soul,
"Therefore I hope in Him!"

25The LORD *is* good to those who wait for Him,
To the soul *who* seeks Him.
26*It is* good that *one* should hope and wait quietly
For the salvation of the LORD.
27*It is* good for a man to bear
The yoke in his youth.

28Let him sit alone and keep silent,
Because *God* has laid *it* on him;

3:13 [a]Literally *kidneys*

THE MESSAGE

4-6 He turned me into a scarecrow
of skin and bones, then broke the bones.
He hemmed me in, ganged up on me,
poured on the trouble and hard times.
He locked me up in deep darkness,
like a corpse nailed inside a coffin.

7-9 He shuts me in so I'll never get out,
manacles my hands, shackles my feet.
Even when I cry out and plead for help,
he locks up my prayers and throws away the key.
He sets up blockades with quarried limestone.
He's got me cornered.

10-12 He's a prowling bear tracking me down,
a lion in hiding ready to pounce.
He knocked me from the path and ripped me to pieces.
When he finished, there was nothing left of me.
He took out his bow and arrows
and used me for target practice.

13-15 He shot me in the stomach
with arrows from his quiver.
Everyone took me for a joke,
made me the butt of their mocking ballads.
He forced rotten, stinking food down my throat,
bloated me with vile drinks.

16-18 He ground my face into the gravel.
He pounded me into the mud.
I gave up on life altogether.
I've forgotten what the good life is like.
I said to myself, "This is it. I'm finished.
GOD is a lost cause."

IT'S A GOOD THING TO HOPE FOR HELP FROM GOD

19-21 I'll never forget the trouble, the utter lostness,
the taste of ashes, the poison I've swallowed.
I remember it all—oh, how well I remember—
the feeling of hitting the bottom.
But there's one other thing I remember,
and remembering, I keep a grip on hope:

22-24 GOD's loyal love couldn't have run out,
his merciful love couldn't have dried up.
They're created new every morning.
How great your faithfulness!
I'm sticking with GOD (I say it over and over).
He's all I've got left.

25-27 GOD proves to be good to the man who passionately waits,
to the woman who diligently seeks.
It's a good thing to quietly hope,
quietly hope for help from GOD.
It's a good thing when you're young
to stick it out through the hard times.

28-30 When life is heavy and hard to take,
go off by yourself. Enter the silence.

NEW KING JAMES VERSION

29Let him put his mouth in the dust—
There may yet be hope.
30Let him give *his* cheek to the one who strikes him,
And be full of reproach.

31For the Lord will not cast off forever.
32Though He causes grief,
Yet He will show compassion
According to the multitude of His mercies.
33For He does not afflict willingly,
Nor grieve the children of men.

34To crush under one's feet
All the prisoners of the earth,
35To turn aside the justice *due* a man
Before the face of the Most High,
36Or subvert a man in his cause—
The Lord does not approve.

37Who *is* he *who* speaks and it comes to pass,
When the Lord has not commanded *it?*
38*Is it* not from the mouth of the Most High
That woe and well-being proceed?
39Why should a living man complain,
A man for the punishment of his sins?

40Let us search out and examine our ways,
And turn back to the LORD;
41Let us lift our hearts and hands
To God in heaven.
42We have transgressed and rebelled;
You have not pardoned.

43You have covered *Yourself* with anger
And pursued us;
You have slain *and* not pitied.
44You have covered Yourself with a cloud,
That prayer should not pass through.
45You have made us an offscouring and refuse
In the midst of the peoples.

46All our enemies
Have opened their mouths against us.
47Fear and a snare have come upon us,
Desolation and destruction.
48My eyes overflow with rivers of water
For the destruction of the daughter of my people.

49My eyes flow and do not cease,
Without interruption,
50Till the LORD from heaven
Looks down and sees.
51My eyes bring suffering to my soul
Because of all the daughters of my city.

52My enemies without cause
Hunted me down like a bird.
53They silenced[a] my life in the pit
And threw stones at me.

3:53 [a]Septuagint reads *put to death.*

THE MESSAGE

Bow in prayer. Don't ask questions:
Wait for hope to appear.
Don't run from trouble. Take it full-face.
The "worst" is never the worst.

31-33 Why? Because the Master won't ever
walk out and fail to return.
If he works severely, he also works tenderly.
His stockpiles of loyal love are immense.
He takes no pleasure in making life hard,
in throwing roadblocks in the way:

34-36 Stomping down hard
on luckless prisoners,
Refusing justice to victims
in the court of High God,
Tampering with evidence—
the Master does not approve of such things.

GOD SPEAKS BOTH GOOD THINGS AND HARD THINGS INTO BEING

37-39 Who do you think "spoke and it happened"?
It's the Master who gives such orders.
Doesn't the High God speak everything,
good things and hard things alike, into being?
And why would anyone gifted with life
complain when punished for sin?

40-42 Let's take a good look at the way we're living
and reorder our lives under GOD.
Let's lift our hearts and hands at one and the same time,
praying to God in heaven:
"We've been contrary and willful,
and you haven't forgiven.

43-45 "You lost your temper with us, holding nothing back.
You chased us and cut us down without mercy.
You wrapped yourself in thick blankets of clouds
so no prayers could get through.
You treated us like dirty dishwater,
threw us out in the backyard of the nations.

46-48 "Our enemies shout abuse,
their mouths full of derision, spitting invective.
We've been to hell and back.
We've nowhere to turn, nowhere to go.
Rivers of tears pour from my eyes
at the smashup of my dear people.

49-51 "The tears stream from my eyes,
an artesian well of tears,
Until you, GOD, look down from on high,
look and see my tears.
When I see what's happened to the young women in the city,
the pain breaks my heart.

52-54 "Enemies with no reason to be enemies
hunted me down like a bird.
They threw me into a pit,
then pelted me with stones.

New King James Version

54The waters flowed over my head;
I said, "I am cut off!"

55I called on Your name, O Lord,
From the lowest pit.
56You have heard my voice:
"Do not hide Your ear
From my sighing, from my cry for help."
57You drew near on the day I called on You,
And said, "Do not fear!"

58O Lord, You have pleaded the case for my soul;
You have redeemed my life.
59O Lord, You have seen *how* I am wronged;
Judge my case.
60You have seen all their vengeance,
All their schemes against me.

61You have heard their reproach, O Lord,
All their schemes against me,
62The lips of my enemies
And their whispering against me all the day.
63Look at their sitting down and their rising up;
I *am* their taunting song.

64Repay them, O Lord,
According to the work of their hands.
65Give them a veiled[a] heart;
Your curse *be* upon them!
66In Your anger,
Pursue and destroy them
From under the heavens of the Lord.

The Degradation of Zion

4 How the gold has become dim!
How changed the fine gold!
The stones of the sanctuary are scattered
At the head of every street.
2The precious sons of Zion,
Valuable as fine gold,
How they are regarded as clay pots,
The work of the hands of the potter!

3Even the jackals present their breasts
To nurse their young;
But the daughter of my people *is* cruel,
Like ostriches in the wilderness.

4The tongue of the infant clings
To the roof of its mouth for thirst;
The young children ask for bread,
But no one breaks *it* for them.

5Those who ate delicacies
Are desolate in the streets;
Those who were brought up in scarlet
Embrace ash heaps.

3:65 [a]A Jewish tradition reads *sorrow of.*

The Message

Then the rains came and filled the pit.
The water rose over my head. I said, 'It's all over.'

55-57 "I called out your name, O God,
called from the bottom of the pit.
You listened when I called out, 'Don't shut your ears!
Get me out of here! Save me!'
You came close when I called out.
You said, 'It's going to be all right.'

58-60 "You took my side, Master;
you brought me back alive!
God, you saw the wrongs heaped on me.
Give me my day in court!
Yes, you saw their mean-minded schemes,
their plots to destroy me.

61-63 "You heard, God, their vicious gossip,
their behind-my-back plots to ruin me.
They never quit, these enemies of mine,
dreaming up mischief,
hatching out malice, day after day after day.
Sitting down or standing up—just look at them!—
they mock me with vulgar doggerel.

64-66 "Make them pay for what they've done, God.
Give them their just deserts.
Break their miserable hearts!
Damn their eyes!
Get good and angry. Hunt them down.
Make a total demolition here under your heaven!"

Waking Up with Nothing

1 4 Oh, oh, oh . . .
How gold is treated like dirt,
the finest gold thrown out with the garbage,
Priceless jewels scattered all over,
jewels loose in the gutters.

2 And the people of Zion, once prized,
far surpassing their weight in gold,
Are now treated like cheap pottery,
like everyday pots and bowls
mass-produced by a potter.

3 Even wild jackals nurture their babies,
give them their breasts to suckle.
But my people have turned cruel to their babies,
like an ostrich in the wilderness.

4 Babies have nothing to drink.
Their tongues stick to the roofs of their mouths.
Little children ask for bread
but no one gives them so much as a crust.

5 People used to the finest cuisine
forage for food in the streets.
People used to the latest in fashions
pick through the trash for something to wear.

NEW KING JAMES VERSION

6The punishment of the iniquity of the daughter of my people
Is greater than the punishment of the sin of Sodom,
Which was overthrown in a moment,
With no hand to help her!

7Her Nazirites[a] were brighter than snow
And whiter than milk;
They were more ruddy in body than rubies,
Like sapphire in their appearance.

8*Now* their appearance is blacker than soot;
They go unrecognized in the streets;
Their skin clings to their bones,
It has become as dry as wood.

9*Those* slain by the sword are better off
Than *those* who die of hunger;
For these pine away,
Stricken *for lack* of the fruits of the field.

10The hands of the compassionate women
Have cooked their own children;
They became food for them
In the destruction of the daughter of my people.

11The LORD has fulfilled His fury,
He has poured out His fierce anger.
He kindled a fire in Zion,
And it has devoured its foundations.

12The kings of the earth,
And all inhabitants of the world,
Would not have believed
That the adversary and the enemy
Could enter the gates of Jerusalem—

13Because of the sins of her prophets
And the iniquities of her priests,
Who shed in her midst
The blood of the just.

14They wandered blind in the streets;
They have defiled themselves with blood,
So that no one would touch their garments.

15They cried out to them,
"Go away, unclean!
Go away, go away,
Do not touch us!"
When they fled and wandered,
Those among the nations said,
"They shall no longer dwell *here*."

16The face[a] of the LORD scattered them;
He no longer regards them.
The people do not respect the priests
Nor show favor to the elders.

17Still our eyes failed us,
Watching vainly for our help;
In our watching we watched
For a nation *that* could not save *us*.

18They tracked our steps

4:7 [a]Or *nobles* **4:16** [a]Targum reads *anger*.

THE MESSAGE

6 The evil guilt of my dear people
was worse than the sin of Sodom—
The city was destroyed in a flash,
and no one around to help.

7 The splendid and sacred nobles
once glowed with health.
Their bodies were robust and ruddy,
their beards like carved stone.

8 But now they are smeared with soot,
unrecognizable in the street,
Their bones sticking out,
their skin dried out like old leather.

9 Better to have been killed in battle
than killed by starvation.
Better to have died of battle wounds
than to slowly starve to death.

10 Nice and kindly women
boiled their own children for supper.
This was the only food in town
when my dear people were broken.

11 GOD let all his anger loose, held nothing back.
He poured out his raging wrath.
He set a fire in Zion
that burned it to the ground.

12 The kings of the earth couldn't believe it.
World rulers were in shock,
Watching old enemies march in big as you please,
right through Jerusalem's gates.

13 Because of the sins of her prophets
and the evil of her priests,
Who exploited good and trusting people,
robbing them of their lives,

14 These prophets and priests blindly grope their way through the streets,
grimy and stained from their dirty lives,
Wasted by their wasted lives,
shuffling from fatigue, dressed in rags.

15 People yell at them, "Get out of here, dirty old men!
Get lost, don't touch us, don't infect us!"
They have to leave town. They wander off.
Nobody wants them to stay here.
Everyone knows, wherever they wander,
that they've been kicked out of their own hometown.

16 GOD himself scattered them.
No longer does he look out for them.
He has nothing to do with the priests;
he cares nothing for the elders.

17 We watched and watched,
wore our eyes out looking for help. And nothing.
We mounted our lookouts and looked
for the help that never showed up.

18 They tracked us down, those hunters.

NEW KING JAMES VERSION

So that we could not walk in our streets.
Our end was near;
Our days were over,
For our end had come.

19 Our pursuers were swifter
Than the eagles of the heavens.
They pursued us on the mountains
And lay in wait for us in the wilderness.

20 The breath of our nostrils, the anointed of the LORD,
Was caught in their pits,
Of whom we said, "Under his shadow
We shall live among the nations."

21 Rejoice and be glad, O daughter of Edom,
You who dwell in the land of Uz!
The cup shall also pass over to you
And you shall become drunk and make yourself naked.

22 *The punishment of* your iniquity is accomplished,
O daughter of Zion;
He will no longer send you into captivity.
He will punish your iniquity,
O daughter of Edom;
He will uncover your sins!

A PRAYER FOR RESTORATION

5 Remember, O LORD, what has come upon us;
Look, and behold our reproach!
2 Our inheritance has been turned over to aliens,
And our houses to foreigners.
3 We have become orphans and waifs,
Our mothers *are* like widows.

4 We pay for the water we drink,
And our wood comes at a price.
5 *They* pursue at our heels;[a]
We labor *and* have no rest.
6 We have given our hand *to* the Egyptians
And the Assyrians, to be satisfied with bread.

7 Our fathers sinned *and are* no more,
But we bear their iniquities.
8 Servants rule over us;
There is none to deliver *us* from their hand.
9 We get our bread *at the risk* of our lives,
Because of the sword in the wilderness.

10 Our skin is hot as an oven,
Because of the fever of famine.
11 They ravished the women in Zion,
The maidens in the cities of Judah.
12 Princes were hung up by their hands,
And elders were not respected.
13 Young men ground at the millstones;
Boys staggered under *loads of* wood.
14 The elders have ceased *gathering at* the gate,
And the young men from their music.

5:5 [a]Literally *necks*

THE MESSAGE

It wasn't safe to go out in the street.
Our end was near, our days numbered.
We were doomed.

19 They came after us faster than eagles in flight,
pressed us hard in the mountains,
ambushed us in the desert.

20 Our king, our life's breath, the anointed of GOD,
was caught in their traps—
Our king under whose protection
we always said we'd live.

21 Celebrate while you can, O Edom!
Live it up in Uz!
For it won't be long before you drink this cup, too.
You'll find out what it's like to drink God's wrath,
Get drunk on God's wrath
and wake up with nothing, stripped naked.

22 And that's it for you, Zion. The punishment's complete.
You won't have to go through this exile again.
But Edom, your time is coming:
He'll punish your evil life, put all your sins on display.

GIVE US A FRESH START

1-22 5 "Remember, GOD, all we've been through.
Study our plight, the black mark we've made in history.
Our precious land has been given to outsiders,
our homes to strangers.
Orphans we are, not a father in sight,
and our mothers no better than widows.
We have to pay to drink our own water.
Even our firewood comes at a price.
We're nothing but slaves, bullied and bowed,
worn out and without any rest.
We sold ourselves to Assyria and Egypt
just to get something to eat.
Our parents sinned and are no more,
and now we're paying for the wrongs they did.
Slaves rule over us;
there's no escape from their grip.
We risk our lives to gather food
in the bandit-infested desert.
Our skin has turned black as an oven,
dried out like old leather from the famine.
Our wives were raped in the streets in Zion,
and our virgins in the cities of Judah.
They hanged our princes by their hands,
dishonored our elders.
Strapping young men were put to women's work,
mere boys forced to do men's work.
The city gate is empty of wise elders.
Music from the young is heard no more.

NEW KING JAMES VERSION

15The joy of our heart has ceased;
Our dance has turned into mourning.
16The crown has fallen *from* our head.
Woe to us, for we have sinned!
17Because of this our heart is faint;
Because of these *things* our eyes grow dim;
18Because of Mount Zion which is desolate,
With foxes walking about on it.

19You, O LORD, remain forever;
Your throne from generation to generation.
20Why do You forget us forever,
And forsake us for so long a time?
21Turn us back to You, O LORD, and we will be restored;
Renew our days as of old,
22Unless You have utterly rejected us,
And are very angry with us!

THE MESSAGE

All the joy is gone from our hearts.
Our dances have turned into dirges.
The crown of glory has toppled from our head.
Woe! Woe! Would that we'd never sinned!
Because of all this we're heartsick;
we can't see through the tears.
On Mount Zion, wrecked and ruined,
jackals pace and prowl.
And yet, GOD, you're sovereign still,
your throne intact and eternal.
So why do you keep forgetting us?
Why dump us and leave us like this?
Bring us back to you, GOD—we're ready to come back.
Give us a fresh start.
As it is, you've cruelly disowned us.
You've been so very angry with us."

EZEKIEL

New King James Version

Ezekiel's Vision of God

1 Now it came to pass in the thirtieth year, in the fourth *month,* on the fifth *day* of the month, as I *was* among the captives by the River Chebar, *that* the heavens were opened and I saw visions[a] of God. 2 On the fifth *day* of the month, which *was* in the fifth year of King Jehoiachin's captivity, 3 the word of the LORD came expressly to Ezekiel the priest, the son of Buzi, in the land of the Chaldeans[a] by the River Chebar; and the hand of the LORD was upon him there.

4 Then I looked, and behold, a whirlwind was coming out of the north, a great cloud with raging fire engulfing itself; and brightness *was* all around it and radiating out of its midst like the color of amber, out of the midst of the fire. 5 Also from within it *came* the likeness of four living creatures. And this *was* their appearance: they had the likeness of a man. 6 Each one had four faces, and each one had four wings. 7 Their legs *were* straight, and the soles of their feet *were* like the soles of calves' feet. They sparkled like the color of burnished bronze. 8 The hands of a man *were* under their wings on their four sides; and each of the four had faces and wings. 9 Their wings touched one another. *The creatures* did not turn when they went, but each one went straight forward.

10 As for the likeness of their faces, *each* had the face of a man; each of the four had the face of a lion on the right side, each of the four had the face of an ox on the left side, and each of the four had the face of an eagle. 11 Thus *were* their faces. Their wings stretched upward; two *wings* of each one touched one another, and two covered their bodies. 12 And each one went straight forward; they went wherever the spirit wanted to go, and they did not turn when they went.

13 As for the likeness of the living creatures, their appearance *was* like burning coals of fire, like the appearance of torches going back and forth among the living creatures. The fire was bright, and out of the fire went lightning. 14 And the living creatures ran back and forth, in appearance like a flash of lightning.

15 Now as I looked at the living creatures, behold, a wheel *was* on the earth beside each living creature with its four faces. 16 The appearance of the wheels and their workings *was* like the color of beryl, and all four had the same likeness. The appearance of their workings *was,* as it were, a wheel in the middle of a wheel. 17 When they moved, they went toward any one of four directions; they did not turn aside when they went. 18 As for their rims, they were so high they were awesome; and their rims *were* full of eyes, all around the four of them. 19 When the living creatures went, the wheels went beside them; and when the living creatures were lifted up from the earth, the wheels were lifted up. 20 Wherever the spirit wanted to go, they went,

1:1 [a]Following Masoretic Text, Septuagint, and Vulgate; Syriac and Targum read *a vision.* **1:3** [a]Or *Babylonians,* and so elsewhere in this book

The Message

Wheels Within Wheels, Like a Gyroscope

1 **1** When I was thirty years of age, I was living with the exiles on the Kebar River. On the fifth day of the fourth month, the sky opened up and I saw visions of God.

2-3 (It was the fifth day of the month in the fifth year of the exile of King Jehoiachin that GOD's Word came to Ezekiel the priest, the son of Buzi, on the banks of the Kebar River in the country of Babylon. GOD's hand came upon him that day.)

4-9 I looked: I saw an immense dust storm come from the north, an immense cloud with lightning flashing from it, a huge ball of fire glowing like bronze. Within the fire were what looked like four creatures vibrant with life. Each had the form of a human being, but each also had four faces and four wings. Their legs were as sturdy and straight as columns, but their feet were hoofed like those of a calf and sparkled from the fire like burnished bronze. On all four sides under their wings they had human hands. All four had both faces and wings, with the wings touching one another. They turned neither one way nor the other; they went straight forward.

10-12 Their faces looked like this: In front a human face, on the right side the face of a lion, on the left the face of an ox, and in back the face of an eagle. So much for the faces. The wings were spread out with the tips of one pair touching the creature on either side; the other pair of wings covered its body. Each creature went straight ahead. Wherever the spirit went, they went. They didn't turn as they went.

13-14 The four creatures looked like a blazing fire, or like fiery torches. Tongues of fire shot back and forth between the creatures, and out of the fire, bolts of lightning. The creatures flashed back and forth like strikes of lightning.

15-16 As I watched the four creatures, I saw something that looked like a wheel on the ground beside each of the four-faced creatures. This is what the wheels looked like: They were identical wheels, sparkling like diamonds in the sun. It looked like they were wheels within wheels, like a gyroscope.

17-21 They went in any one of the four directions they faced, but straight, not veering off. The rims were immense, circled with eyes. When the living creatures went, the wheels went; when the living creatures lifted off, the wheels lifted off. Wherever the

NEW KING JAMES VERSION

because there the spirit went; and the wheels
were lifted together with them, for the spirit of
the living creatures[a] *was* in the wheels. 21When
those went, *these* went; when those stood, *these*
stood; and when those were lifted up from the
earth, the wheels were lifted up together with
them, for the spirit of the living creatures[a] *was*
in the wheels.

22The likeness of the firmament above the
heads of the living creatures[a] *was* like the color
of an awesome crystal, stretched out over their
heads. 23And under the firmament their wings
spread out straight, one toward another. Each
one had two which covered one side, and each
one had two which covered the other side of the
body. 24When they went, I heard the noise of
their wings, like the noise of many waters, like
the voice of the Almighty, a tumult like the noise
of an army; and when they stood still, they let
down their wings. 25A voice came from above
the firmament that *was* over their heads; when-
ever they stood, they let down their wings.

26And above the firmament over their heads
was the likeness of a throne, in appearance like
a sapphire stone; on the likeness of the throne
was a likeness with the appearance of a man
high above it. 27Also from the appearance of His
waist and upward I saw, as it were, the color of
amber with the appearance of fire all around
within it; and from the appearance of His waist
and downward I saw, as it were, the appearance
of fire with brightness all around. 28Like the ap-
pearance of a rainbow in a cloud on a rainy day,
so *was* the appearance of the brightness all
around it. This *was* the appearance of the like-
ness of the glory of the LORD.

EZEKIEL SENT TO REBELLIOUS ISRAEL

So when I saw *it*, I fell on my face, and I
heard a voice of One speaking.

2 And He said to me, "Son of man, stand on your
feet, and I will speak to you." 2Then the Spirit
entered me when He spoke to me, and set me on
my feet; and I heard Him who spoke to me. 3And
He said to me: "Son of man, I am sending you to
the children of Israel, to a rebellious nation that
has rebelled against Me; they and their fathers
have transgressed against Me to this very day.
4For *they are* impudent and stubborn children. I
am sending you to them, and you shall say to
them, 'Thus says the Lord GOD.' 5As for them,
whether they hear or whether they refuse—for
they *are* a rebellious house—yet they will know
that a prophet has been among them.

6"And you, son of man, do not be afraid of
them nor be afraid of their words, though briers
and thorns *are* with you and you dwell among
scorpions; do not be afraid of their words or dis-
mayed by their looks, though they *are* a rebel-
lious house. 7You shall speak My words to them,
whether they hear or whether they refuse, for
they *are* rebellious. 8But you, son of man, hear
what I say to you. Do not be rebellious like that
rebellious house; open your mouth and eat what
I give you."

1:20 [a]Literally *living creature;* Septuagint and Vulgate read *spirit of life;* Targum reads *creatures.* **1:21** [a]Literally *living creature;* Septuagint and Vulgate read *spirit of life;* Targum reads *creatures.* **1:22** [a]Following Septuagint, Targum, and Vulgate; Masoretic Text reads *living creature.*

THE MESSAGE

spirit went, they went, the wheels sticking right with them, for the spirit of the living creatures was in the wheels. When the creatures went, the wheels went; when the creatures stopped, the wheels stopped; when the creatures lifted off, the wheels lifted off, because the spirit of the living creatures was in the wheels.

22-24 Over the heads of the living creatures was something like a dome, shimmering like a sky full of cut glass, vaulted over their heads. Under the dome one set of wings was extended toward the others, with another set of wings covering their bodies. When they moved I heard their wings—it was like the roar of a great waterfall, like the voice of The Strong God, like the noise of a battlefield. When they stopped, they folded their wings.

25-28 And then, as they stood with folded wings, there was a voice from above the dome over their heads. Above the dome there was something that looked like a throne, sky-blue like a sapphire, with a humanlike figure towering above the throne. From what I could see, from the waist up he looked like burnished bronze and from the waist down like a blazing fire. Brightness everywhere! The way a rainbow springs out of the sky on a rainy day—that's what it was like. It turned out to be the Glory of GOD!

When I saw all this, I fell to my knees, my face to the ground. Then I heard a voice.

1 2 It said, "Son of man, stand up. I have something to say to you."

2 The moment I heard the voice, the Spirit entered me and put me on my feet. As he spoke to me, I listened.

3-7 He said, "Son of man, I'm sending you to the family of Israel, a rebellious nation if there ever was one. They and their ancestors have fomented rebellion right up to the present. They're a hard case, these people to whom I'm sending you—hardened in their sin. Tell them, 'This is the Message of GOD, the Master.' They are a defiant bunch. Whether or not they listen, at least they'll know that a prophet's been here. But don't be afraid of them, son of man, and don't be afraid of anything they say. Don't be afraid when living among them is like stepping on thorns or finding scorpions in your bed. Don't be afraid of their mean words or their hard looks. They're a bunch of rebels. Your job is to speak to them. Whether they listen is not your concern. They're hardened rebels.

8 "Only take care, son of man, that you don't rebel like these rebels. Open your mouth and eat what I give you."

NEW KING JAMES VERSION

9Now when I looked, there was a hand
stretched out to me; and behold, a scroll of a
book *was* in it. 10Then He spread it before me;
and *there was* writing on the inside and on the
outside, and written on it *were* lamentations and
mourning and woe.

3 Moreover He said to me, "Son of man, eat
what you find; eat this scroll, and go, speak to
the house of Israel." 2So I opened my mouth, and
He caused me to eat that scroll.
3And He said to me, "Son of man, feed your
belly, and fill your stomach with this scroll that
I give you." So I ate, and it was in my mouth like
honey in sweetness.
4Then He said to me: "Son of man, go to the
house of Israel and speak with My words to
them. 5For you *are* not sent to a people of unfa-
miliar speech and of hard language, *but* to the
house of Israel, 6not to many people of unfamil-
iar speech and of hard language, whose words
you cannot understand. Surely, had I sent you to
them, they would have listened to you. 7But the
house of Israel will not listen to you, because
they will not listen to Me; for all the house of Is-
rael *are* impudent and hard-hearted. 8Behold, I
have made your face strong against their faces,
and your forehead strong against their fore-
heads. 9Like adamant stone, harder than flint, I
have made your forehead; do not be afraid of
them, nor be dismayed at their looks, though
they *are* a rebellious house."
10Moreover He said to me: "Son of man, re-
ceive into your heart all My words that I speak
to you, and hear with your ears. 11And go, get to
the captives, to the children of your people, and
speak to them and tell them, 'Thus says the Lord
GOD,' whether they hear, or whether they re-
fuse."
12Then the Spirit lifted me up, and I heard be-
hind me a great thunderous voice: "Blessed *is*
the glory of the LORD from His place!" 13*I also
heard* the noise of the wings of the living crea-
tures that touched one another, and the noise of
the wheels beside them, and a great thunderous
noise. 14So the Spirit lifted me up and took me
away, and I went in bitterness, in the heat of my
spirit; but the hand of the LORD was strong upon
me. 15Then I came to the captives at Tel Abib,
who dwelt by the River Chebar; and I sat where
they sat, and remained there astonished among
them seven days.

EZEKIEL IS A WATCHMAN

16Now it came to pass at the end of seven
days that the word of the LORD came to me, say-
ing, 17"Son of man, I have made you a watchman
for the house of Israel; therefore hear a word
from My mouth, and give them warning from
Me: 18When I say to the wicked, 'You shall
surely die,' and you give him no warning, nor
speak to warn the wicked from his wicked way,
to save his life, that same wicked *man* shall die
in his iniquity; but his blood I will require at
your hand. 19Yet, if you warn the wicked, and he
does not turn from his wickedness, nor from his
wicked way, he shall die in his iniquity; but you
have delivered your soul.
20"Again, when a righteous *man* turns from
his righteousness and commits iniquity, and I

THE MESSAGE

9-10 When I looked he had his hand stretched
out to me, and in the hand a book, a scroll.
He unrolled the scroll. On both sides, front
and back, were written lamentations and
mourning and doom.

WARN THESE PEOPLE

1 3 He told me, "Son of man, eat what you see.
Eat this book. Then go and speak to the
family of Israel."
2-3 As I opened my mouth, he gave me the
scroll to eat, saying, "Son of man, eat this
book that I am giving you. Make a full meal
of it!"
So I ate it. It tasted so good—just like
honey.
4-6 Then he told me, "Son of man, go to the
family of Israel and speak my Message.
Look, I'm not sending you to a people who
speak a hard-to-learn language with words
you can hardly pronounce. If I had sent you
to such people, their ears would have
perked up and they would have listened im-
mediately.
7-9 "But it won't work that way with the fam-
ily of Israel. They won't listen to you be-
cause they won't listen to me. They are, as I
said, a hard case, hardened in their sin. But
I'll make you as hard in your way as they
are in theirs. I'll make your face as hard as
rock, harder than granite. Don't let them in-
timidate you. Don't be afraid of them, even
though they're a bunch of rebels."
10-11 Then he said, "Son of man, get all these
words that I'm giving you inside you. Listen
to them obediently. Make them your own.
And now go. Go to the exiles, your people,
and speak. Tell them, 'This is the Message of
GOD, the Master.' Speak your piece, whether
they listen or not."
12-13 Then the Spirit picked me up. Behind me
I heard a great commotion—"Blessed be the
Glory of GOD in his Sanctuary!"—the wings
of the living creatures beating against each
other, the whirling wheels, the rumble of a
great earthquake.
14-15 The Spirit lifted me and took me away. I
went bitterly and angrily. I didn't want to go.
But GOD had me in his grip. I arrived among
the exiles who lived near the Kebar River at
Tel Aviv. I came to where they were living
and sat there for seven days, appalled.
16 At the end of the seven days, I received
this Message from GOD:
17-19 "Son of man, I've made you a watchman
for the family of Israel. Whenever you hear
me say something, warn them for me. If I
say to the wicked, 'You are going to die,' and
you don't sound the alarm warning them
that it's a matter of life or death, they will
die and it will be your fault. I'll hold you re-
sponsible. But if you warn the wicked and
they keep right on sinning anyway, they'll
most certainly die for their sin, but *you*
won't die. You'll have saved your life.
20-21 "And if the righteous turn back from liv-
ing righteously and take up with evil when I

NEW KING JAMES VERSION

lay a stumbling block before him, he shall die;
because you did not give him warning, he shall
die in his sin, and his righteousness which he
has done shall not be remembered; but his
blood I will require at your hand. 21Nevertheless
if you warn the righteous *man* that the righteous
should not sin, and he does not sin, he shall
surely live because he took warning; also you
will have delivered your soul."

22Then the hand of the LORD was upon me
there, and He said to me, "Arise, go out into the
plain, and there I shall talk with you."

23So I arose and went out into the plain, and
behold, the glory of the LORD stood there, like
the glory which I saw by the River Chebar; and
I fell on my face. 24Then the Spirit entered me
and set me on my feet, and spoke with me and
said to me: "Go, shut yourself inside your house.
25And you, O son of man, surely they will put
ropes on you and bind you with them, so that
you cannot go out among them. 26I will make
your tongue cling to the roof of your mouth, so
that you shall be mute and not be one to rebuke
them, for they *are* a rebellious house. 27But
when I speak with you, I will open your mouth,
and you shall say to them, 'Thus says the Lord
GOD.' He who hears, let him hear; and he who
refuses, let him refuse; for they *are* a rebellious
house.

THE SIEGE OF JERUSALEM PORTRAYED

4 "You also, son of man, take a clay tablet and
lay it before you, and portray on it a city,
Jerusalem. 2Lay siege against it, build a siege
wall against it, and heap up a mound against it;
set camps against it also, and place battering
rams against it all around. 3Moreover take for
yourself an iron plate, and set it *as* an iron wall
between you and the city. Set your face against
it, and it shall be besieged, and you shall lay
siege against it. This *will be* a sign to the house
of Israel.

4"Lie also on your left side, and lay the iniq-
uity of the house of Israel upon it. *According* to
the number of the days that you lie on it, you
shall bear their iniquity. 5For I have laid on you
the years of their iniquity, according to the num-
ber of the days, three hundred and ninety days;
so you shall bear the iniquity of the house of Is-
rael. 6And when you have completed them, lie
again on your right side; then you shall bear the
iniquity of the house of Judah forty days. I have
laid on you a day for each year.

7"Therefore you shall set your face toward
the siege of Jerusalem; your arm *shall be* uncov-
ered, and you shall prophesy against it. 8And
surely I will restrain you so that you cannot turn
from one side to another till you have ended the
days of your siege.

9"Also take for yourself wheat, barley, beans,
lentils, millet, and spelt; put them into one ves-
sel, and make bread of them for yourself. *During*
the number of days that you lie on your side,
three hundred and ninety days, you shall eat it.
10And your food which you eat *shall be* by
weight, twenty shekels a day; from time to time

THE MESSAGE

step in and put them in a hard place, they'll die. If you haven't warned them, they'll die because of their sins, and none of the right things they've done will count for anything—and I'll hold you responsible. But if you warn these righteous people not to sin and they listen to you, they'll live because they took the warning—and again, you'll have saved your life."

22 GOD grabbed me by the shoulder and said, "Get up. Go out on the plain. I want to talk with you."

23 So I got up and went out on the plain. I couldn't believe my eyes: the Glory of GOD! Right there! It was like the Glory I had seen at the Kebar River. I fell to the ground, prostrate.

24-26 Then the Spirit entered me and put me on my feet. He said, "Go home and shut the door behind you." And then something odd: "Son of man: They'll tie you hand and foot with ropes so you can't leave the house. I'll make your tongue stick to the roof of your mouth so you won't be able to talk and tell the people what they're doing wrong, even though they are a bunch of rebels.

27 "But then when the time is ripe, I'll free your tongue and you'll say, 'This is what GOD, the Master, says: . . .' From then on it's up to them. They can listen or not listen, whichever they like. They *are* a bunch of rebels!"

THIS IS WHAT SIN DOES

1-3 4 "Now, son of man, take a brick and place it before you. Draw a picture of the city Jerusalem on it. Then make a model of a military siege against the brick: Build siege walls, construct a ramp, set up army camps, lay in battering rams around it. Then get an iron skillet and place it upright between you and the city—an iron wall. Face the model: The city shall be under siege and you shall be the besieger. This is a sign to the family of Israel.

4-5 "Next lie on your left side and place the sin of the family of Israel on yourself. You will bear their sin for as many days as you lie on your side. The number of days you bear their sin will match the number of years of their sin, namely, 390. For 390 days you will bear the sin of the family of Israel.

6-7 "Then, after you have done this, turn over and lie down on your right side and bear the sin of the family of Judah. Your assignment this time is to lie there for forty days, a day for each year of their sin. Look straight at the siege of Jerusalem. Roll up your sleeve, shake your bare arm, and preach against her.

8 "I will tie you up with ropes, tie you so you can't move or turn over until you have finished the days of the siege.

9-12 "Next I want you to take wheat and barley, beans and lentils, dried millet and spelt, and mix them in a bowl to make a flat bread. This is your food ration for the 390 days you lie on your side. Measure out about half a pound for each day and eat it on schedule. Also measure out your daily ra-

New King James Version

you shall eat it. 11You shall also drink water by
measure, one-sixth of a hin; from time to time
you shall drink. 12And you shall eat it *as* barley
cakes; and bake it using fuel of human waste in
their sight."
13Then the LORD said, "So shall the children
of Israel eat their defiled bread among the Gen-
tiles, where I will drive them."
14So I said, "Ah, Lord GOD! Indeed I have
never defiled myself from my youth till now; I
have never eaten what died of itself or was torn
by beasts, nor has abominable flesh ever come
into my mouth."
15Then He said to me, "See, I am giving you
cow dung instead of human waste, and you shall
prepare your bread over it."
16Moreover He said to me, "Son of man,
surely I will cut off the supply of bread in
Jerusalem; they shall eat bread by weight and
with anxiety, and shall drink water by measure
and with dread, 17that they may lack bread and
water, and be dismayed with one another, and
waste away because of their iniquity.

A Sword Against Jerusalem

5 "And you, son of man, take a sharp sword,
take it as a barber's razor, and pass *it* over
your head and your beard; then take scales to
weigh and divide the hair. 2You shall burn with
fire one-third in the midst of the city, when the
days of the siege are finished; then you shall
take one-third and strike around *it* with the
sword, and one-third you shall scatter in the
wind: I will draw out a sword after them. 3You
shall also take a small number of them and bind
them in the edge of your *garment*. 4Then take
some of them again and throw them into the
midst of the fire, and burn them in the fire. From
there a fire will go out into all the house of
Israel.
5"Thus says the Lord GOD: 'This *is* Jeru-
salem; I have set her in the midst of the nations
and the countries all around her. 6She has re-
belled against My judgments by doing wicked-
ness more than the nations, and against My
statutes more than the countries that *are* all
around her; for they have refused My judg-
ments, and they have not walked in My statutes.'
7Therefore thus says the Lord GOD: 'Because
you have multiplied *disobedience* more than the
nations that *are* all around you, have not walked
in My statutes nor kept My judgments, nor even
done[a] according to the judgments of the nations
that *are* all around you'— 8therefore thus says
the Lord GOD: 'Indeed I, even I, *am* against you
and will execute judgments in your midst in the
sight of the nations. 9And I will do among you
what I have never done, and the like of which I
will never do again, because of all your abomi-
nations. 10Therefore fathers shall eat *their* sons
in your midst, and sons shall eat their fathers;

5:7 [a]Following Masoretic Text, Septuagint, Targum, and Vulgate; many Hebrew manuscripts and Syriac read *but have done* (compare 11:12).

The Message

tion of about a pint of water and drink it on
schedule. Eat the bread as you would a muf-
fin. Bake the muffins out in the open where
everyone can see you, using dried human
dung for fuel."
13 GOD said, "This is what the people of Is-
rael are going to do: Among the pagan na-
tions where I will drive them, they will eat
foods that are strictly taboo to a holy peo-
ple."
14 I said, "GOD, my Master! Never! I've never
contaminated myself with food like that.
Since my youth I've never eaten anything
forbidden by law, nothing found dead or vi-
olated by wild animals. I've never taken a
single bite of forbidden food."
15 "All right," he said. "I'll let you bake your
bread over cow dung instead of human
dung."
16-17 Then he said to me, "Son of man, I'm go-
ing to cut off all food from Jerusalem. The
people will live on starvation rations, worry-
ing where the next meal's coming from,
scrounging for the next drink of water.
Famine conditions. People will look at one
another, see nothing but skin and bones,
and shake their heads. This is what sin
does."

A Jealous God, Not to Be Trifled With

1-2 5 "Now, son of man, take a sharp sword and
use it as a straight razor, shaving your
head and your beard. Then, using a set of
balancing scales, divide the hair into thirds.
When the days of the siege are over, take
one-third of the hair and burn it inside the
city. Take another third, chop it into bits
with the sword and sprinkle it around the
city. The final third you'll throw to the wind.
Then I'll go after them with a sword.
3-4 "Retrieve a few of the hairs and slip them
into your pocket. Take some of them and
throw them into the fire—burn them up.
From them, fire will spread to the whole
family of Israel.
5-6 "This is what GOD, the Master, says: This
means *Jerusalem*. I set her at the center of
the world, all the nations ranged around her.
But she rebelled against my laws and ordi-
nances, rebelled far worse than the nations
ranged around her—sheer wickedness!—
refused my guidance, ignored my directions.
7 "Therefore this is what GOD, the Master,
says: You've been more headstrong and will-
ful than any of the nations around you, re-
fusing my guidance, ignoring my directions.
You've sunk to the gutter level of those
around you.
8-10 "Therefore this is what GOD, the Master,
says: I'm setting myself against you—yes,
against you, Jerusalem. I'm going to punish
you in full sight of the nations. Because of
your disgusting no-god idols, I'm going to
do something to you that I've never done be-
fore and will never do again: turn families
into cannibals—parents eating children,
children eating parents! Punishment in-

NEW KING JAMES VERSION

and I will execute judgments among you, and all
of you who remain I will scatter to all the winds.
11'Therefore, *as* I live,' says the Lord GOD,
'surely, because you have defiled My sanctuary
with all your detestable things and with all your
abominations, therefore I will also diminish
you; My eye will not spare, nor will I have any
pity. 12One-third of you shall die of the pesti-
lence, and be consumed with famine in your
midst; and one-third shall fall by the sword all
around you; and I will scatter another third to
all the winds, and I will draw out a sword after
them.
13'Thus shall My anger be spent, and I will
cause My fury to rest upon them, and I will be
avenged; and they shall know that I, the LORD,
have spoken *it* in My zeal, when I have spent My
fury upon them. 14Moreover I will make you a
waste and a reproach among the nations that
are all around you, in the sight of all who pass
by.
15'So it[a] shall be a reproach, a taunt, a lesson,
and an astonishment to the nations that *are* all
around you, when I execute judgments among
you in anger and in fury and in furious rebukes.
I, the LORD, have spoken. 16When I send against
them the terrible arrows of famine which shall
be for destruction, which I will send to destroy
you, I will increase the famine upon you and cut
off your supply of bread. 17So I will send against
you famine and wild beasts, and they will be-
reave you. Pestilence and blood shall pass
through you, and I will bring the sword against
you. I, the LORD, have spoken.' "

JUDGMENT ON IDOLATROUS ISRAEL

6 Now the word of the LORD came to me,
saying: 2"Son of man, set your face toward
the mountains of Israel, and prophesy against
them, 3and say, 'O mountains of Israel, hear the
word of the Lord GOD! Thus says the Lord GOD
to the mountains, to the hills, to the ravines, and
to the valleys: "Indeed I, *even* I, will bring a
sword against you, and I will destroy your high
places. 4Then your altars shall be desolate, your
incense altars shall be broken, and I will cast
down your slain *men* before your idols. 5And I
will lay the corpses of the children of Israel
before their idols, and I will scatter your bones
all around your altars. 6In all your dwelling
places the cities shall be laid waste, and the high
places shall be desolate, so that your altars may
be laid waste and made desolate, your idols may
be broken and made to cease, your incense
altars may be cut down, and your works may be
abolished. 7The slain shall fall in your midst,
and you shall know that I *am* the LORD.
8"Yet I will leave a remnant, so that you may
have *some* who escape the sword among the na-
tions, when you are scattered through the coun-
tries. 9Then those of you who escape will re-
member Me among the nations where they are
carried captive, because I was crushed by their
adulterous heart which has departed from Me,
and by their eyes which play the harlot after
their idols; they will loathe themselves for the
evils which they committed in all their abomina-
tions. 10And they shall know that I *am* the LORD;

5:15 [a]Septuagint, Syriac, Targum, and Vulgate read *you.*

THE MESSAGE

deed. And whoever's left over I'll throw to
the winds.

11-12 "Therefore, as sure as I am the living God—Decree of GOD, the Master—because you've polluted my Sanctuary with your obscenities and disgusting no-god idols, I'm pulling out. Not an ounce of pity will I show you. A third of your people will die of either disease or hunger inside the city, a third will be killed outside the city, and a third will be thrown to the winds and chased by killers.

13 "Only then will I calm down and let my anger cool. Then you'll know that I was serious about this all along, that I'm a jealous God and not to be trifled with.

14-15 "When I get done with you, you'll be a pile of rubble. Nations who walk by will make coarse jokes. When I finish my angry punishment and searing rebukes, you'll be reduced to an object of ridicule and mockery, turned into a horror story circulating among the surrounding nations. I, GOD, have spoken.

16-17 "When I shoot my lethal famine arrows at you, I'll shoot to kill. Then I'll step up the famine and cut off food supplies. Famine and more famine—and then I'll send in the wild animals to finish off your children. Epidemic disease, unrestrained murder, death—and I will have sent it! I, GOD, have spoken."

TURN ISRAEL INTO WASTELAND

1-7 6 Then the Word of GOD came to me: "Son of man, now turn and face the mountains of Israel and preach against them: 'O Mountains of Israel, listen to the Message of GOD, the Master. GOD, the Master, speaks to the mountains and hills, to the ravines and the valleys: I'm about to destroy your sacred god and goddess shrines. I'll level your altars, bust up your sun-god pillars, and kill your people as they bow down to your no-god idols. I'll stack the dead bodies of Israelites in front of your idols and then scatter your bones around your shrines. Every place where you've lived, the towns will be torn down and the pagan shrines demolished—altars busted up, idols smashed, all your custom-made sun-god pillars in ruins. Corpses everywhere you look! Then you'll know that I am GOD.

8-10 " 'But I'll let a few escape the killing as you are scattered through other lands and nations. In the foreign countries where they're taken as prisoners of war, they'll remember me. They'll realize how devastated I was by their betrayals, by their voracious lust for gratifying themselves in their idolatries. They'll be disgusted with their evil ways, disgusting to God in the way they've lived. They'll know that I am GOD. They'll

NEW KING JAMES VERSION

I have not said in vain that I would bring this
calamity upon them."
[11]"Thus says the Lord GOD: "Pound your fists
and stamp your feet, and say, 'Alas, for all the
evil abominations of the house of Israel! For
they shall fall by the sword, by famine, and by
pestilence. [12]He who is far off shall die by the
pestilence, he who is near shall fall by the
sword, and he who remains and is besieged
shall die by the famine. Thus will I spend My
fury upon them. [13]Then you shall know that I *am*
the LORD, when their slain are among their idols
all around their altars, on every high hill, on all
the mountaintops, under every green tree, and
under every thick oak, wherever they offered
sweet incense to all their idols. [14]So I will stretch
out My hand against them and make the land
desolate, yes, more desolate than the wilderness
toward Diblah, in all their dwelling places. Then
they shall know that I *am* the LORD.' " ' "

JUDGMENT ON ISRAEL IS NEAR

7 Moreover the word of the LORD came to me,
saying, [2]"And you, son of man, thus says the
Lord GOD to the land of Israel:

'An end! The end has come upon the four
corners of the land.
[3]Now the end *has come* upon you,
And I will send My anger against you;
I will judge you according to your ways,
And I will repay you for all your
abominations.
[4]My eye will not spare you,
Nor will I have pity;
But I will repay your ways,
And your abominations will be in your midst;
Then you shall know that I *am* the LORD!'

[5]"Thus says the Lord GOD:

'A disaster, a singular disaster;
Behold, it has come!
[6]An end has come,
The end has come;
It has dawned for you;
Behold, it has come!
[7]Doom has come to you, you who dwell in
the land;
The time has come,
A day of trouble *is* near,
And not of rejoicing in the mountains.
[8]Now upon you I will soon pour out My fury,
And spend My anger upon you;
I will judge you according to your ways,
And I will repay you for all your
abominations.

[9]'My eye will not spare,
Nor will I have pity;
I will repay you according to your ways,
And your abominations will be in your
midst.
Then you shall know that I *am* the LORD
who strikes.

[10]'Behold, the day!
Behold, it has come!

THE MESSAGE

know that my judgment against them was
no empty threat.
11-14 " 'This is what GOD, the Master, says: Clap
your hands, stamp your feet, yell out, "No,
no, no!" because of all the evil obscenities
rife in Israel. They're going to be killed, dy-
ing of hunger, dying of disease—death
everywhere you look, people dropping like
flies, people far away dying, people nearby
dying, and whoever's left in the city starving
to death. Why? Because I'm angry, furiously
angry. They'll realize that I am GOD when
they see their people's corpses strewn over
and around all their ruined sex-and-religion
shrines on the bare hills and in the lush fer-
tility groves, in all the places where they in-
dulged their sensual rites. I'll bring my hand
down hard on them, demolish the country
wherever they live, turn it into wasteland
from one end to the other, from the wilder-
ness to Riblah. Then they'll know that I am
GOD!' "

FATE HAS CAUGHT UP WITH YOU

1-4 **7** GOD's Word came to me, saying, "You, son
of man—GOD, the Master, has this Mes-
sage for the land of Israel:

" 'Endtime.
The end of business as usual for
everyone.
It's all over. The end is upon you.
I've launched my anger against you.
I've issued my verdict on the way you live.
I'll make you pay for your disgusting
obscenities.
I won't look the other way,
I won't feel sorry for you.
I'll make you pay for the way you've lived:
Your disgusting obscenities will
boomerang on you,
and you'll realize that I am GOD.'

5-9 "I, GOD, the Master, say:
'Disaster after disaster! Look, it comes!
Endtime—
the end comes.
The end is ripe. Watch out, it's coming!
This is your fate, you who live in this
land.
Time's up.
It's zero hour.
No dragging of feet now,
no bargaining for more time.
Soon now I'll pour my wrath on you,
pay out my anger against you,
Render my verdict on the way you've lived,
make you pay for your disgusting
obscenities.
I won't look the other way,
I won't feel sorry for you.
I'll make you pay for the way you've lived.
Your disgusting obscenities will
boomerang on you.
Then you'll realize
that it is I, GOD, who have hit you.

10-13 " 'Judgment Day!
Fate has caught up with you.

New King James Version

Doom has gone out;
The rod has blossomed,
Pride has budded.
11 Violence has risen up into a rod of wickedness;
None of them *shall remain,*
None of their multitude,
None of them;
Nor *shall there be* wailing for them.
12 The time has come,
The day draws near.

'Let not the buyer rejoice,
Nor the seller mourn,
For wrath *is* on their whole multitude.
13 For the seller shall not return to what has been sold,
Though he may still be alive;
For the vision concerns the whole multitude,
And it shall not turn back;
No one will strengthen himself
Who lives in iniquity.

14 'They have blown the trumpet and made everyone ready,
But no one goes to battle;
For My wrath *is* on all their multitude.
15 The sword *is* outside,
And the pestilence and famine within.
Whoever *is* in the field
Will die by the sword;
And whoever *is* in the city,
Famine and pestilence will devour him.

16 'Those who survive will escape and be on the mountains
Like doves of the valleys,
All of them mourning,
Each for his iniquity.
17 Every hand will be feeble,
And every knee will be *as* weak *as* water.
18 They will also be girded with sackcloth;
Horror will cover them;
Shame *will be* on every face,
Baldness on all their heads.

19 'They will throw their silver into the streets,
And their gold will be like refuse;
Their silver and their gold will not be able to deliver them
In the day of the wrath of the LORD;
They will not satisfy their souls,
Nor fill their stomachs,
Because it became their stumbling block of iniquity.

20 'As for the beauty of his ornaments,
He set it in majesty;
But they made from it
The images of their abominations—
Their detestable things;
Therefore I have made it
Like refuse to them.
21 I will give it as plunder
Into the hands of strangers,
And to the wicked of the earth as spoil;
And they shall defile it.
22 I will turn My face from them,
And they will defile My secret place;
For robbers shall enter it and defile it.

The Message

The scepter outsized and pretentious,
pride bursting all bounds,
Violence strutting,
brandishing the evil scepter.
But there's nothing to them,
and nothing will be left of them.
Time's up.
Countdown: five, four, three, two . . .
Buyer, don't crow; seller, don't worry:
Judgment wrath has turned the world topsy-turvy.
The bottom has dropped out of buying and selling.
It will never be the same again.
But don't fantasize an upturn in the market.
The country is bankrupt because of its sins,
and it's not going to get any better.

14-16 " 'The trumpet signals the call to battle:
"Present arms!"
But no one marches into battle.
My wrath has them paralyzed!
On the open roads you're killed,
or else you go home and die of hunger and disease.
Either get murdered out in the country
or die of sickness or hunger in town.
Survivors run for the hills.
They moan like doves in the valleys,
Each one moaning
for his own sins.

17-18 " 'Every hand hangs limp,
every knee turns to rubber.
They dress in rough burlap—
sorry scarecrows,
Shifty and shamefaced,
with their heads shaved bald.

19-27 " 'They throw their money into the gutters.
Their hard-earned cash stinks like garbage.
They find that it won't buy a thing
they either want or need on Judgment Day.
They tripped on money
and fell into sin.
Proud and pretentious with their jewels,
they deck out their vile and vulgar no-gods in finery.
I'll make those god-obscenities a stench in their nostrils.
I'll give away their religious junk—
strangers will pick it up for free,
the godless spit on it and make jokes.
I'll turn my face so I won't have to look
as my treasured place and people are violated,
As violent strangers walk in
and desecrate place and people—

NEW KING JAMES VERSION

[23]'Make a chain,
For the land is filled with crimes of blood,
And the city is full of violence.
[24]Therefore I will bring the worst of the Gentiles,
And they will possess their houses;
I will cause the pomp of the strong to cease,
And their holy places shall be defiled.
[25]Destruction comes;
They will seek peace, but *there shall be* none.
[26]Disaster will come upon disaster,
And rumor will be upon rumor.
Then they will seek a vision from a prophet;
But the law will perish from the priest,
And counsel from the elders.

[27]'The king will mourn,
The prince will be clothed with desolation,
And the hands of the common people will tremble.
I will do to them according to their way,
And according to what they deserve I will judge them;
Then they shall know that I *am* the LORD!' "

ABOMINATIONS IN THE TEMPLE

8 And it came to pass in the sixth year, in the
sixth *month,* on the fifth *day* of the month, as
I sat in my house with the elders of Judah sitting
before me, that the hand of the Lord GOD fell
upon me there. [2]Then I looked, and there was a
likeness, like the appearance of fire—from the
appearance of His waist and downward, fire;
and from His waist and upward, like the
appearance of brightness, like the color of
amber. [3]He stretched out the form of a hand, and
took me by a lock of my hair; and the Spirit
lifted me up between earth and heaven, and
brought me in visions of God to Jerusalem, to
the door of the north gate of the inner *court,*
where the seat of the image of jealousy *was,*
which provokes to jealousy. [4]And behold, the
glory of the God of Israel *was* there, like the
vision that I saw in the plain.
[5]Then He said to me, "Son of man, lift your
eyes now toward the north." So I lifted my eyes
toward the north, and there, north of the altar
gate, was this image of jealousy in the entrance.
[6]Furthermore He said to me, "Son of man, do
you see what they are doing, the great abomina-
tions that the house of Israel commits here, to
make Me go far away from My sanctuary? Now
turn again, you will see greater abominations."
[7]So He brought me to the door of the court; and
when I looked, there was a hole in the wall.
[8]Then He said to me, "Son of man, dig into the
wall"; and when I dug into the wall, there was a
door.
[9]And He said to me, "Go in, and see the
wicked abominations which they are doing
there." [10]So I went in and saw, and there—every
sort of creeping thing, abominable beasts, and

THE MESSAGE

A bloody massacre,
as crime and violence fill the city.
I'll bring in the dregs of humanity
to move into their houses.
I'll put a stop to the boasting and strutting
of the high-and-mighty,
And see to it that there'll be nothing holy
left in their holy places.
Catastrophe descends. They look for peace,
but there's no peace to be found—
Disaster on the heels of disaster,
one rumor after another.
They clamor for the prophet to tell them
what's up,
but nobody knows anything.
Priests don't have a clue;
the elders don't know what to say.
The king holds his head in despair;
the prince is devastated.
The common people are paralyzed.
Gripped by fear, they can't move.
I'll deal with them where they are,
judge them on their terms.
They'll know that I am GOD.' "

THE SPIRIT CARRIED ME IN VISIONS

1-4 8 In the sixth year, in the sixth month and
the fifth day, while I was sitting at home
meeting with the leaders of Judah, it hap-
pened that the hand of my Master, GOD,
gripped me. When I looked, I was aston-
ished. What I saw looked like a man—from
the waist down like fire and from the waist
up like highly burnished bronze. He
reached out what looked like a hand and
grabbed me by the hair. The Spirit swept me
high in the air and carried me in visions of
God to Jerusalem, to the entrance of the
north gate of the Temple's inside court
where the image of the sex goddess that
makes God so angry had been set up. Right
before me was the Glory of the God of Is-
rael, exactly like the vision I had seen out on
the plain.
5 He said to me, "Son of man, look north." I
looked north and saw it: Just north of the
entrance loomed the altar of the sex god-
dess, Asherah, that makes God so angry.
6 Then he said, "Son of man, do you see
what they're doing? Outrageous obsceni-
ties! And doing them right here! It's enough
to drive me right out of my own Temple. But
you're going to see worse yet."

7 He brought me to the door of the Temple
court. I looked and saw a gaping hole in the
wall.
8 He said, "Son of man, dig through the
wall."
I dug through the wall and came upon a
door.
9 He said, "Now walk through the door and
take a look at the obscenities they're engag-
ing in."
10-11 I entered and looked. I couldn't believe
my eyes: Painted all over the walls were pic-
tures of reptiles and animals and mon-

NEW KING JAMES VERSION

all the idols of the house of Israel, portrayed all around on the walls. 11And there stood before them seventy men of the elders of the house of Israel, and in their midst stood Jaazaniah the son of Shaphan. Each man had a censer in his hand, and a thick cloud of incense went up. 12Then He said to me, "Son of man, have you seen what the elders of the house of Israel do in the dark, every man in the room of his idols? For they say, 'The LORD does not see us, the LORD has forsaken the land.' "

13And He said to me, "Turn again, *and* you will see greater abominations that they are doing." 14So He brought me to the door of the north gate of the LORD's house; and to my dismay, women were sitting there weeping for Tammuz.

15Then He said to me, "Have you seen *this*, O son of man? Turn again, you will see greater abominations than these." 16So He brought me into the inner court of the LORD's house; and there, at the door of the temple of the LORD, between the porch and the altar, *were* about twenty-five men with their backs toward the temple of the LORD and their faces toward the east, and they were worshiping the sun toward the east.

17And He said to me, "Have you seen *this*, O son of man? Is it a trivial thing to the house of Judah to commit the abominations which they commit here? For they have filled the land with violence; then they have returned to provoke Me to anger. Indeed they put the branch to their nose. 18Therefore I also will act in fury. My eye will not spare nor will I have pity; and though they cry in My ears with a loud voice, I will not hear them."

THE WICKED ARE SLAIN

9 Then He called out in my hearing with a loud voice, saying, "Let those who have charge over the city draw near, each *with* a deadly weapon in his hand." 2And suddenly six men came from the direction of the upper gate, which faces north, each with his battle-ax in his hand. One man among them *was* clothed with linen and had a writer's inkhorn at his side. They went in and stood beside the bronze altar.

3Now the glory of the God of Israel had gone up from the cherub, where it had been, to the threshold of the temple.[a] And He called to the man clothed with linen, who *had* the writer's inkhorn at his side; 4and the LORD said to him, "Go through the midst of the city, through the midst of Jerusalem, and put a mark on the foreheads of the men who sigh and cry over all the abominations that are done within it."

5To the others He said in my hearing, "Go after him through the city and kill; do not let your eye spare, nor have any pity. 6Utterly slay old *and* young men, maidens and little children and women; but do not come near anyone on whom *is* the mark; and begin at My sanctuary." So they began with the elders who *were* before the temple.

9:3 [a]Literally *house*

THE MESSAGE

sters—the whole pantheon of Egyptian gods and goddesses—being worshiped by Israel. In the middle of the room were seventy of the leaders of Israel, with Jaazaniah son of Shaphan standing in the middle. Each held his censer with the incense rising in a fragrant cloud.

12 He said, "Son of man, do you see what the elders are doing here in the dark, each one before his favorite god-picture? They tell themselves, 'GOD doesn't see us. GOD has forsaken the country.' "

13 Then he said, "You're going to see worse yet."

14-15 He took me to the entrance at the north gate of the Temple of GOD. I saw women sitting there, weeping for Tammuz, the Babylonian fertility god. He said, "Have you gotten an eyeful, son of man? You're going to see worse yet."

16 Finally, he took me to the inside court of the Temple of GOD. There between the porch and the altar were about twenty-five men. Their backs were to GOD's Temple. They were facing east, bowing in worship to the sun.

17-18 He said, "Have you seen enough, son of man? Isn't it bad enough that Judah engages in these outrageous obscenities? They fill the country with violence and now provoke me even further with their obscene gestures. That's it. They have an angry God on their hands! From now on, no mercy. They can shout all they want, but I'm not listening."

A MARK ON THE FOREHEAD

1 9 Then I heard him call out loudly, "Executioners, come! And bring your deadly weapons with you."

2 Six men came down the road from the upper gate that faces north, each carrying his lethal weapon. With them was a man dressed in linen with a writing case slung from his shoulder. They entered and stood by the bronze altar.

3-4 The Glory of the God of Israel ascended from his usual place above the cherubim-angels, moved to the threshold of the Temple, and called to the man with the writing case who was dressed in linen: "Go through the streets of Jerusalem and put a mark on the forehead of everyone who is in anguish over the outrageous obscenities being done in the city."

5-6 I listened as he went on to address the executioners: "Follow him through the city and kill. Feel sorry for no one. Show no compassion. Kill old men and women, young men and women, mothers and children. But don't lay a hand on anyone with the mark. Start at my Temple."

They started with the leaders in front of the Temple.

NEW KING JAMES VERSION

7Then He said to them, "Defile the temple, and
fill the courts with the slain. Go out!" And they
went out and killed in the city.
8So it was, that while they were killing them,
I was left *alone;* and I fell on my face and cried
out, and said, "Ah, Lord GOD! Will You destroy all
the remnant of Israel in pouring out Your fury on
Jerusalem?"
9Then He said to me, "The iniquity of the
house of Israel and Judah *is* exceedingly great,
and the land is full of bloodshed, and the city
full of perversity; for they say, 'The LORD has
forsaken the land, and the LORD does not see!'
10And as for Me also, My eye will neither spare,
nor will I have pity, *but* I will recompense their
deeds on their own head."
11Just then, the man clothed with linen, who
had the inkhorn at his side, reported back and
said, "I have done as You commanded me."

THE GLORY DEPARTS FROM THE TEMPLE

10 And I looked, and there in the firmament
that was above the head of the cherubim,
there appeared something like a sapphire stone,
having the appearance of the likeness of a
throne. 2Then He spoke to the man clothed with
linen, and said, "Go in among the wheels, under
the cherub, fill your hands with coals of fire
from among the cherubim, and scatter *them*
over the city." And he went in as I watched.
3Now the cherubim were standing on the
south side of the temple[a] when the man went in,
and the cloud filled the inner court. 4Then the
glory of the LORD went up from the cherub, *and
paused* over the threshold of the temple; and the
house was filled with the cloud, and the court
was full of the brightness of the LORD's glory.
5And the sound of the wings of the cherubim
was heard *even* in the outer court, like the voice
of Almighty God when He speaks.
6Then it happened, when He commanded the
man clothed in linen, saying, "Take fire from
among the wheels, from among the cherubim,"
that he went in and stood beside the wheels. 7And
the cherub stretched out his hand from among
the cherubim to the fire that *was* among the
cherubim, and took *some of it* and put *it* into the
hands of the *man* clothed with linen, who took *it*
and went out. 8The cherubim appeared to have
the form of a man's hand under their wings.
9And when I looked, there were four wheels
by the cherubim, one wheel by one cherub and
another wheel by each other cherub; the wheels
appeared *to have* the color of a beryl stone. 10*As
for* their appearance, all four looked alike—as it
were, a wheel in the middle of a wheel. 11When
they went, they went toward *any of* their four di-
rections; they did not turn aside when they went,
but followed in the direction the head was fac-
ing. They did not turn aside when they went.
12And their whole body, with their back, their
hands, their wings, and the wheels that the four
had, *were* full of eyes all around. 13As for the
wheels, they were called in my hearing, "Wheel."
14Each one had four faces: the first face *was*
the face of a cherub, the second face the face of
a man, the third the face of a lion, and the fourth
the face of an eagle.

10:3 [a]Literally *house,* also in verses 4 and 18

THE MESSAGE

7-8 He told the executioners, "Desecrate the
Temple. Fill it with corpses. Then go out and
continue the killing." So they went out and
struck the city.
While the massacre went forward, I was
left alone. I fell on my face in prayer: "Oh,
oh, GOD, my Master! Are you going to kill
everyone left in Israel in this pouring out of
your anger on Jerusalem?"
9-10 He said, "The guilt of Israel and Judah is
enormous. The land is swollen with murder.
The city is bloated with injustice. They all say,
'GOD has forsaken the country. He doesn't see
anything we do.' Well, I do see, and I'm not
feeling sorry for any of them. They're going
to pay for what they've done."
11 Just then, the man dressed in linen and
carrying the writing case came back and re-
ported, "I've done what you told me."

THE TEMPLE, FILLED WITH THE PRESENCE OF GOD

1 10 When I next looked, oh! Above the
dome over the heads of the cherubim-
angels was what looked like a throne, sky-
blue, like a sapphire!
2-5 GOD said to the man dressed in linen,
"Enter the place of the wheels under the
cherubim-angels. Fill your hands with burn-
ing coals from beneath the cherubim and
scatter them over the city."
I watched as he entered. The cherubim
were standing on the south side of the Tem-
ple when the man entered. A cloud filled the
inside courtyard. Then the Glory of GOD as-
cended from the cherubim and moved to the
threshold of the Temple. The cloud filled the
Temple. Court and Temple were both filled
with the blazing presence of the Glory of
GOD. And the sound! The wings of the
cherubim were audible all the way to the
outer court—the sound of the voice was like
The Strong God in thunder.
6-8 When GOD commanded the man dressed
in linen, "Take fire from among the wheels,
from between the cherubim," he went in and
stood beside a wheel. One of the cherubim
reached into the fire, took some coals, and
put them in the hands of the man dressed in
linen. He took them and went out. Some-
thing that looked like a human hand could
be seen under the wings of the cherubim.
9-13 And then I saw four wheels beside the
cherubim, one beside each cherub. The
wheels radiating were sparkling like dia-
monds in the sun. All four wheels looked
alike, each like a wheel within a wheel.
When they moved, they went in any of the
four directions but in a perfectly straight
line. Where the cherubim went, the wheels
went straight ahead. The cherubim were full
of eyes in their backs, hands, and wings. The
wheels likewise were full of eyes. I heard the
wheels called "wheels within wheels."
14 Each of the cherubim had four faces: the
first, of an angel; the second, a human; the
third, a lion; the fourth, an eagle.

NEW KING JAMES VERSION

15 And the cherubim were lifted up. This *was* the living creature I saw by the River Chebar. 16 When the cherubim went, the wheels went beside them; and when the cherubim lifted their wings to mount up from the earth, the same wheels also did not turn from beside them. 17 When *the cherubim*[a] stood still, *the wheels* stood still, and when *one*[b] was lifted up, *the other*[c] lifted itself up, for the spirit of the living creature *was* in them.

18 Then the glory of the LORD departed from the threshold of the temple and stood over the cherubim. 19 And the cherubim lifted their wings and mounted up from the earth in my sight. When they went out, the wheels *were* beside them; and they stood at the door of the east gate of the LORD's house, and the glory of the God of Israel *was* above them.

20 This *is* the living creature I saw under the God of Israel by the River Chebar, and I knew they *were* cherubim. 21 Each one had four faces and each one four wings, and the likeness of the hands of a man *was* under their wings. 22 And the likeness of their faces *was* the same *as* the faces which I had seen by the River Chebar, their appearance and their persons. They each went straight forward.

JUDGMENT ON WICKED COUNSELORS

11 Then the Spirit lifted me up and brought me to the East Gate of the LORD's house, which faces eastward; and there at the door of the gate were twenty-five men, among whom I saw Jaazaniah the son of Azzur, and Pelatiah the son of Benaiah, princes of the people. 2 And He said to me: "Son of man, these *are* the men who devise iniquity and give wicked counsel in this city, 3 who say, '*The time is* not near to build houses; this *city is* the caldron, and we *are* the meat.' 4 Therefore prophesy against them, prophesy, O son of man!"

5 Then the Spirit of the LORD fell upon me, and said to me, "Speak! 'Thus says the LORD: "Thus you have said, O house of Israel; for I know the things that come into your mind. 6 You have multiplied your slain in this city, and you have filled its streets with the slain." 7 Therefore thus says the Lord GOD: "Your slain whom you have laid in its midst, they *are* the meat, and this *city is* the caldron; but I shall bring you out of the midst of it. 8 You have feared the sword; and I will bring a sword upon you," says the Lord GOD. 9 "And I will bring you out of its midst, and deliver you into the hands of strangers, and execute judgments on you. 10 You shall fall by the sword. I will judge you at the border of Israel. Then you shall know that I *am* the LORD. 11 This *city* shall not be your caldron, nor shall you be the meat in its midst. I will judge you at the border of Israel. 12 And you shall know that I *am* the LORD; for you have not walked in My statutes nor executed My judgments, but have done according to the customs of the Gentiles which *are* all around you." ' "

10:17 [a]Literally *they* [b]Literally *they* [c]Literally *they*

THE MESSAGE

15-17 Then the cherubim ascended. They were the same living creatures I had seen at the Kebar River. When the cherubim moved, the wheels beside them moved. When the cherubim spread their wings to take off from the ground, the wheels stayed right with them. When the cherubim stopped, the wheels stopped. When the cherubim rose, the wheels rose, because the spirit of the living creatures was also in the wheels.

18-19 Then the Glory of GOD left the Temple entrance and hovered over the cherubim. I watched as the cherubim spread their wings and left the ground, the wheels right with them. They stopped at the entrance of the east gate of the Temple. The Glory of the God of Israel was above them.

20-22 These were the same living creatures I had seen previously beneath the God of Israel at the Kebar River. I recognized them as cherubim. Each had four faces and four wings. Under their wings were what looked like human hands. Their faces looked exactly like those I had seen at the Kebar River. Each went straight ahead.

A NEW HEART AND A NEW SPIRIT

1 11 Then the Spirit picked me up and took me to the gate of the Temple that faces east. There were twenty-five men standing at the gate. I recognized the leaders, Jaazaniah son of Azzur and Pelatiah son of Benaiah.

2-3 GOD said, "Son of man, these are the men who draw up blueprints for sin, who think up new programs for evil in this city. They say, 'We can make anything happen here. We're the best. We're the choice pieces of meat in the soup pot.'

4 "Oppose them, son of man. Preach against them."

5-6 Then the Spirit of GOD came upon me and told me what to say: "This is what GOD says: 'That's a fine public speech, Israel, but I know what you are thinking. You've murdered a lot of people in this city. The streets are piled high with corpses.'

7-12 "Therefore this is what GOD, the Master, says: 'The corpses that you've piled in the streets are the meat and this city is the soup pot, and *you're* not even in the pot! I'm throwing you out! You fear war, but war is what you're going to get. I'm bringing war against you. I'm throwing you out of this city, giving you over to foreigners, and punishing you good. You'll be killed in battle. I'll carry out judgment on you at the borders of Israel. Then you'll realize that I am GOD. This city will not be your soup pot and you won't be the choice pieces of meat in it either. Hardly. I will carry out judgment on you at the borders of Israel and you'll realize that I am GOD, for you haven't followed my statutes and ordinances. Instead of following my ways, you've sunk to the level of the laws of the nations around you.' "

New King James Version

13Now it happened, while I was prophesying,
that Pelatiah the son of Benaiah died. Then I fell
on my face and cried with a loud voice, and said,
"Ah, Lord GOD! Will You make a complete end of
the remnant of Israel?"

God Will Restore Israel

14Again the word of the LORD came to me,
saying, 15"Son of man, your brethren, your rela-
tives, your countrymen, and all the house of Is-
rael in its entirety, *are* those about whom the in-
habitants of Jerusalem have said, 'Get far away
from the LORD; this land has been given to us as
a possession.' 16Therefore say, 'Thus says the
Lord GOD: "Although I have cast them far off
among the Gentiles, and although I have scat-
tered them among the countries, yet I shall be a
little sanctuary for them in the countries where
they have gone." ' 17Therefore say, 'Thus says
the Lord GOD: "I will gather you from the peo-
ples, assemble you from the countries where
you have been scattered, and I will give you the
land of Israel." ' 18And they will go there, and
they will take away all its detestable things and
all its abominations from there. 19Then I will
give them one heart, and I will put a new spirit
within them,[a] and take the stony heart out of
their flesh, and give them a heart of flesh, 20that
they may walk in My statutes and keep My
judgments and do them; and they shall be My
people, and I will be their God. 21But *as for those*
whose hearts follow the desire for their de-
testable things and their abominations, I will
recompense their deeds on their own heads,"
says the Lord GOD.

22So the cherubim lifted up their wings, with
the wheels beside them, and the glory of the God
of Israel *was* high above them. 23And the glory of
the LORD went up from the midst of the city and
stood on the mountain, which *is* on the east side
of the city.

24Then the Spirit took me up and brought me
in a vision by the Spirit of God into Chaldea,[a] to
those in captivity. And the vision that I had seen
went up from me. 25So I spoke to those in captiv-
ity of all the things the LORD had shown me.

Judah's Captivity Portrayed

12 Now the word of the LORD came to me,
saying: 2"Son of man, you dwell in the
midst of a rebellious house, which has eyes to
see but does not see, and ears to hear but does
not hear; for they *are* a rebellious house.

3"Therefore, son of man, prepare your be-
longings for captivity, and go into captivity by
day in their sight. You shall go from your place
into captivity to another place in their sight. It
may be that they will consider, though they *are*
a rebellious house. 4By day you shall bring out
your belongings in their sight, as though going
into captivity; and at evening you shall go in
their sight, like those who go into captivity. 5Dig
through the wall in their sight, and carry *your*
belongings out through it. 6In their sight you
shall bear *them* on *your* shoulders *and* carry
them out at twilight; you shall cover your face,

11:19 [a]Literally *you* **11:24** [a]Or *Babylon,* and so elsewhere in this book

The Message

13 Even while I was preaching, Pelatiah son
of Benaiah died. I fell down, face to the
ground, and prayed loudly, "O Master, GOD!
Will you completely wipe out what's left of
Israel?"

14-15 The answer from GOD came back: "Son of
man, your brothers—I mean the whole peo-
ple of Israel who are in exile with you—are
the people of whom the citizens of
Jerusalem are saying, 'They're in the far
country, far from GOD. This land has been
given to us to own.'

16-20 "Well, tell them this, 'This is your Mes-
sage from GOD, the Master. True, I sent you
to the far country and scattered you through
other lands. All the same, I've provided you
a temporary sanctuary in the countries
where you've gone. I will gather you back
from those countries and lands where
you've been scattered and give you back the
land of Israel. You'll come back and clean
house, throw out all the rotten images and
obscene idols. I'll give you a new heart. I'll
put a new spirit in you. I'll cut out your stone
heart and replace it with a red-blooded,
firm-muscled heart. Then you'll obey my
statutes and be careful to obey my com-
mands. You'll be my people! I'll be your God!

21 " 'But not those who are self-willed and
addicted to their rotten images and obscene
idols! I'll see that they're paid in full for
what they've done.' Decree of GOD, the Mas-
ter."

22-23 Then the cherubim spread their wings,
with the wheels beside them and the Glory
of the God of Israel hovering over them. The
Glory of GOD ascended from within the city
and rested on the mountain to the east of
the city.

24-25 Then, still in the vision given me by the
Spirit of God, the Spirit took me and carried
me back to the exiles in Babylon. And then
the vision left me. I told the exiles every-
thing that GOD had shown me.

Put the Bundle on Your Shoulder and Walk into the Night

1-6 **12** GOD's Message came to me: "Son of
man, you're living with a bunch of re-
bellious people. They have eyes but don't
see a thing, they have ears but don't hear a
thing. They're rebels all. So, son of man,
pack up your exile duffel bags. Leave in
broad daylight with everyone watching and
go off, as if into exile. Maybe then they'll un-
derstand what's going on, rebels though
they are. You'll take up your baggage while
they watch, a bundle of the bare necessities
of someone going into exile, and toward
evening leave, just like a person going off
into exile. As they watch, dig through the
wall of the house and carry your bundle
through it. In full sight of the people, put the
bundle on your shoulder and walk out into
the night. Cover your face so you won't have

NEW KING JAMES VERSION

so that you cannot see the ground, for I have made you a sign to the house of Israel."

7So I did as I was commanded. I brought out my belongings by day, as though going into captivity, and at evening I dug through the wall with my hand. I brought *them* out at twilight, *and* I bore *them* on *my* shoulder in their sight.

8And in the morning the word of the LORD came to me, saying, 9"Son of man, has not the house of Israel, the rebellious house, said to you, 'What are you doing?' 10Say to them, 'Thus says the Lord GOD: "This burden *concerns* the prince in Jerusalem and all the house of Israel who are among them." ' 11Say, 'I *am* a sign to you. As I have done, so shall it be done to them; they shall be carried away into captivity.' 12And the prince who *is* among them shall bear *his belongings* on *his* shoulder at twilight and go out. They shall dig through the wall to carry *them* out through it. He shall cover his face, so that he cannot see the ground with *his* eyes. 13I will also spread My net over him, and he shall be caught in My snare. I will bring him to Babylon, *to* the land of the Chaldeans; yet he shall not see it, though he shall die there. 14I will scatter to every wind all who *are* around him to help him, and all his troops; and I will draw out the sword after them.

15"Then they shall know that I *am* the LORD, when I scatter them among the nations and disperse them throughout the countries. 16But I will spare a few of their men from the sword, from famine, and from pestilence, that they may declare all their abominations among the Gentiles wherever they go. Then they shall know that I *am* the LORD."

JUDGMENT NOT POSTPONED

17Moreover the word of the LORD came to me, saying, 18"Son of man, eat your bread with quaking, and drink your water with trembling and anxiety. 19And say to the people of the land, 'Thus says the Lord GOD to the inhabitants of Jerusalem *and* to the land of Israel: "They shall eat their bread with anxiety, and drink their water with dread, so that her land may be emptied of all who are in it, because of the violence of all those who dwell in it. 20Then the cities that are inhabited shall be laid waste, and the land shall become desolate; and you shall know that I *am* the LORD." ' "

21And the word of the LORD came to me, saying, 22"Son of man, what *is* this proverb *that* you *people* have about the land of Israel, which says, 'The days are prolonged, and every vision fails'? 23Tell them therefore, 'Thus says the Lord GOD: "I will lay this proverb to rest, and they shall no more use it as a proverb in Israel." ' But say to them, ' "The days are at hand, and the fulfillment of every vision. 24For no more shall there be any false vision or flattering divination within the house of Israel. 25For I *am* the LORD. I speak, and the word which I speak will come to pass; it will no more be postponed; for in your days, O rebellious house, I will say the word and perform it," says the Lord GOD.' "

THE MESSAGE

to look at what you'll never see again. I'm using you as a sign for the family of Israel."

7 I did exactly as he commanded me. I got my stuff together and brought it out in the street where everyone could see me, bundled it up the way someone being taken off into exile would, and then, as the sun went down, made a hole in the wall of the house with my hands. As it grew dark and as they watched, I left, throwing my bundle across my shoulders.

8-10 The next morning GOD spoke to me: "Son of man, when anyone in Israel, that bunch of rebels, asks you, 'What are you doing?' Tell them, 'GOD, the Master, says that this Message especially concerns the prince in Jerusalem—Zedekiah—but includes all the people of Israel.'

11 "Also tell them, 'I am drawing a picture for you. As I am now doing, it will be done to all the people of Israel. They will go into exile as captives.'

12-15 "The prince will put his bundle on his shoulders in the dark and leave. He'll dig through the wall of the house, covering his face so he won't have to look at the land he'll never see again. But I'll make sure he gets caught and is taken to Babylon. Blinded, he'll never see that land in which he'll die. I'll scatter to the four winds those who helped him escape, along with his troops, and many will die in battle. They'll realize that I am GOD when I scatter them among foreign countries.

16 "I'll permit a few of them to escape the killing, starvation, and deadly sickness so that they can confess among the foreign countries all the disgusting obscenities they've been involved in. They will realize that I am GOD."

17-20 GOD's Message came to me: "Son of man, eat your meals shaking in your boots, drink your water trembling with fear. Tell the people of this land, everyone living in Jerusalem and Israel, GOD's Message: 'You'll eat your meals shaking in your boots and drink your water in terror because your land is going to be stripped bare as punishment for the brutality rampant in it. All the cities and villages will be emptied out and the fields destroyed. Then you'll realize that I am GOD.' "

21-22 GOD's Message came to me: "Son of man, what's this proverb making the rounds in the land of Israel that says, 'Everything goes on the same as ever; all the prophetic warnings are false alarms'?

23-25 "Tell them, 'GOD, the Master, says, This proverb's going to have a short life!'

"Tell them, 'Time's about up. Every warning is about to come true. False alarms and easygoing preaching are a thing of the past in the life of Israel. I, GOD, am doing the speaking. What I say happens. None of what I say is on hold. What I say, I'll do—and soon, you rebels!' Decree of GOD the Master."

NEW KING JAMES VERSION

[26]Again the word of the LORD came to me, saying, [27]"Son of man, look, the house of Israel is saying, 'The vision that he sees *is* for many days *from now,* and he prophesies of times far off.' [28]Therefore say to them, 'Thus says the Lord GOD: "None of My words will be postponed any more, but the word which I speak will be done," says the Lord GOD.' "

WOE TO FOOLISH PROPHETS

13 And the word of the LORD came to me, saying, [2]"Son of man, prophesy against the prophets of Israel who prophesy, and say to those who prophesy out of their own heart, 'Hear the word of the LORD!' "

[3]Thus says the Lord GOD: "Woe to the foolish prophets, who follow their own spirit and have seen nothing! [4]O Israel, your prophets are like foxes in the deserts. [5]You have not gone up into the gaps to build a wall for the house of Israel to stand in battle on the day of the LORD. [6]They have envisioned futility and false divination, saying, 'Thus says the LORD!' But the LORD has not sent them; yet they hope that the word may be confirmed. [7]Have you not seen a futile vision, and have you not spoken false divination? You say, 'The LORD says,' but I have not spoken."

[8]Therefore thus says the Lord GOD: "Because you have spoken nonsense and envisioned lies, therefore I *am* indeed against you," says the Lord GOD. [9]"My hand will be against the prophets who envision futility and who divine lies; they shall not be in the assembly of My people, nor be written in the record of the house of Israel, nor shall they enter into the land of Israel. Then you shall know that I *am* the Lord GOD.

[10]"Because, indeed, because they have seduced My people, saying, 'Peace!' when *there is* no peace—and one builds a wall, and they plaster it with untempered *mortar*— [11]say to those who plaster *it* with untempered *mortar,* that it will fall. There will be flooding rain, and you, O great hailstones, shall fall; and a stormy wind shall tear *it* down. [12]Surely, when the wall has fallen, will it not be said to you, 'Where *is* the mortar with which you plastered *it*?' "

[13]Therefore thus says the Lord GOD: "I will cause a stormy wind to break forth in My fury; and there shall be a flooding rain in My anger, and great hailstones in fury to consume *it.* [14]So I will break down the wall you have plastered with untempered *mortar,* and bring it down to the ground, so that its foundation will be uncovered; it will fall, and you shall be consumed in the midst of it. Then you shall know that I *am* the LORD.

[15]"Thus will I accomplish My wrath on the wall and on those who have plastered it with untempered *mortar;* and I will say to you, 'The wall *is* no *more,* nor those who plastered it, [16]*that is,* the prophets of Israel who prophesy concerning Jerusalem, and who see visions of peace for her when *there is* no peace,' " says the Lord GOD.

THE MESSAGE

26-28 GOD'S Message came to me: "Son of man, do you hear what Israel is saying: that the alarm the prophet raises is for a long time off, that he's preaching about the far-off future? Well, tell them, 'GOD, the Master, says, "Nothing of what I say is on hold. What I say happens." ' Decree of GOD, the Master."

PEOPLE WHO LOVE LISTENING TO LIES

1-2 13 GOD'S Message came to me: "Son of man, preach against the prophets of Israel who are making things up out of their own heads and calling it 'prophesying.'

2-6 "Preach to them the real thing. Tell them, 'Listen to *GOD'S* Message!' GOD, the Master, pronounces doom on the empty-headed prophets who do their own thing and know nothing of what's going on! Your prophets, Israel, are like jackals scavenging through the ruins. They haven't lifted a finger to repair the defenses of the city and have risked nothing to help Israel stand on GOD'S Day of Judgment. All they do is fantasize comforting illusions and preach lying sermons. They say 'GOD says . . .' when GOD hasn't so much as breathed in their direction. And yet they stand around thinking that something they said is going to happen.

7-9 "Haven't you fantasized sheer nonsense? Aren't your sermons tissues of lies, saying 'GOD says . . .' when I've done nothing of the kind? Therefore—and this is the Message of GOD, the Master, remember—I'm dead set against prophets who substitute illusions for visions and use sermons to tell lies. I'm going to ban them from the council of my people, remove them from membership in Israel, and outlaw them from the land of Israel. Then you'll realize that I am GOD, the Master.

10-12 "The fact is that they've lied to my people. They've said, 'No problem; everything's just fine,' when things are not at all fine. When people build a wall, they're right behind them slapping on whitewash. Tell those who are slapping on the whitewash, 'When a torrent of rain comes and the hailstones crash down and the hurricane sweeps in and the wall collapses, what's the good of the whitewash that you slapped on so liberally, making it look so good?'

13-14 "And that's exactly what will happen. I, GOD, the Master, say so: 'I'll let the hurricane of my wrath loose, a torrent of my hailstone-anger. I'll make that wall you've slapped with whitewash collapse. I'll level it to the ground so that only the foundation stones will be left. And in the ruin you'll all die. You'll realize then that I am GOD.

15-16 " 'I'll dump my wrath on that wall, all of it, and on those who plastered it with whitewash. I will say to them, There is no wall, and those who did such a good job of whitewashing it wasted their time, those prophets of Israel who preached to Jerusalem and announced all their visions telling us things were just fine when they weren't at all fine. Decree of GOD, the Master.'

NEW KING JAMES VERSION

17“Likewise, son of man, set your face against the daughters of your people, who prophesy out of their own heart; prophesy against them, 18and say, ‘Thus says the Lord GOD: “Woe to the *women* who sew *magic* charms on their sleeves[a] and make veils for the heads of people of every height to hunt souls! Will you hunt the souls of My people, and keep yourselves alive? 19And will you profane Me among My people for handfuls of barley and for pieces of bread, killing people who should not die, and keeping people alive who should not live, by your lying to My people who listen to lies?”

20‘Therefore thus says the Lord GOD: “Behold, I *am* against your *magic* charms by which you hunt souls there like birds. I will tear them from your arms, and let the souls go, the souls you hunt like birds. 21I will also tear off your veils and deliver My people out of your hand, and they shall no longer be as prey in your hand. Then you shall know that I *am* the LORD.

22“Because with lies you have made the heart of the righteous sad, whom I have not made sad; and you have strengthened the hands of the wicked, so that he does not turn from his wicked way to save his life. 23Therefore you shall no longer envision futility nor practice divination; for I will deliver My people out of your hand, and you shall know that I *am* the LORD.” ’ ”

IDOLATRY WILL BE PUNISHED

14 Now some of the elders of Israel came to me and sat before me. 2And the word of the LORD came to me, saying, 3“Son of man, these men have set up their idols in their hearts, and put before them that which causes them to stumble into iniquity. Should I let Myself be inquired of at all by them?

4“Therefore speak to them, and say to them, ‘Thus says the Lord GOD: “Everyone of the house of Israel who sets up his idols in his heart, and puts before him what causes him to stumble into iniquity, and then comes to the prophet, I the LORD will answer him who comes, according to the multitude of his idols, 5that I may seize the house of Israel by their heart, because they are all estranged from Me by their idols.” ’

6“Therefore say to the house of Israel, ‘Thus says the Lord GOD: “Repent, turn away from your idols, and turn your faces away from all your abominations. 7For anyone of the house of Israel, or of the strangers who dwell in Israel, who separates himself from Me and sets up his idols in his heart and puts before him what causes him to stumble into iniquity, then comes to a prophet to inquire of him concerning Me, I the LORD will answer him by Myself. 8I will set My face against that man and make him a sign and a proverb, and I will cut him off from the midst of My people. Then you shall know that I *am* the LORD.

9“And if the prophet is induced to speak anything, I the LORD have induced that prophet, and

13:18 [a]Literally *over all the joints of My hands;* Vulgate reads *under every elbow;* Septuagint and Targum read *on all elbows of the hands.*

THE MESSAGE

17-19 “And the women prophets—son of man,
take your stand against the women prophets
who make up stuff out of their own minds.
Oppose them. Say ‘Doom’ to the women
who sew magic bracelets and head scarves
to suit every taste, devices to trap souls. Say,
‘Will you kill the souls of my people, use living souls to make yourselves rich and popular? You have profaned me among my people just to get ahead yourselves, used me to make yourselves look good—killing souls who should never have died and coddling souls who shouldn’t live. You’ve lied to people who love listening to lies.’
20-21 “Therefore GOD says, ‘I am against all the
devices and techniques you use to hunt down souls. I’ll rip them out of your hands. I’ll free the souls you’re trying to catch. I’ll rip your magic bracelets and scarves to shreds and deliver my people from your influence so they’ll no longer be victimized by you. That’s how you’ll come to realize that I am GOD.
22-23 “ ‘Because you’ve confounded and con-
fused good people, unsuspecting and innocent people, with your lies, and because you’ve made it easy for others to persist in evil so that it wouldn’t even dawn on them to turn to me so I could save them, as of now you’re finished. No more delusion-mongering from you, no more sermonic lies. I’m going to rescue my people from your clutches. And you’ll realize that I am GOD.’ ”

IDOLS IN THEIR HEARTS

1-5 14 Some of the leaders of Israel ap-
proached me and sat down with me. GOD’s Message came to me: “Son of Man, these people have installed idols in their hearts. They have embraced the wickedness that will ruin them. Why should I even bother with their prayers? Therefore tell them, ‘The Message of GOD, the Master: All in Israel who install idols in their hearts and embrace the wickedness that will ruin them and still have the gall to come to a prophet, be on notice: I, GOD, will step in and personally answer them as they come dragging along their mob of idols. I am ready to go to work on the hearts of the house of Israel, all of whom have left me for their idols.’
6-8 “Therefore, say to the house of Israel:
‘GOD, the Master, says, Repent! Turn your backs on your no-god idols. Turn your backs on all your outrageous obscenities. To every last person from the house of Israel, including any of the resident aliens who live in Israel—all who turn their backs on me and embrace idols, who install the wickedness that will ruin them at the center of their lives and then have the gall to go to the prophet to ask me questions—I, GOD, will step in and give the answer myself. I’ll oppose those people to their faces, make an example of them—a warning lesson—and get rid of them so you will realize that I am GOD.
9-11 “ ‘If a prophet is deceived and tells these
idolaters the lies they want to hear, I, GOD,

NEW KING JAMES VERSION

I will stretch out My hand against him and de-
stroy him from among My people Israel. 10And
they shall bear their iniquity; the punishment of
the prophet shall be the same as the punishment
of the one who inquired, 11that the house of Is-
rael may no longer stray from Me, nor be pro-
faned anymore with all their transgressions, but
that they may be My people and I may be their
God," says the Lord GOD.' "

JUDGMENT ON PERSISTENT UNFAITHFULNESS

12The word of the LORD came again to me,
saying: 13"Son of man, when a land sins against
Me by persistent unfaithfulness, I will stretch
out My hand against it; I will cut off its supply
of bread, send famine on it, and cut off man and
beast from it. 14Even *if* these three men, Noah,
Daniel, and Job, were in it, they would deliver
only themselves by their righteousness," says
the Lord GOD.

15"If I cause wild beasts to pass through the
land, and they empty it, and make it so desolate
that no man may pass through because of the
beasts, 16*even though* these three men *were* in it,
as I live," says the Lord GOD, "they would deliver
neither sons nor daughters; only they would be
delivered, and the land would be desolate.

17"Or *if* I bring a sword on that land, and say,
'Sword, go through the land,' and I cut off man
and beast from it, 18even *though* these three
men *were* in it, *as* I live," says the Lord GOD,
"they would deliver neither sons nor daughters,
but only they themselves would be delivered.

19"Or *if* I send a pestilence into that land and
pour out My fury on it in blood, and cut off from
it man and beast, 20even *though* Noah, Daniel,
and Job *were* in it, *as* I live," says the Lord GOD,
"they would deliver neither son nor daughter;
they would deliver *only* themselves by their
righteousness."

21For thus says the Lord GOD: "How much
more it shall be when I send My four severe
judgments on Jerusalem—the sword and famine
and wild beasts and pestilence—to cut off man
and beast from it? 22Yet behold, there shall be
left in it a remnant who will be brought out,
both sons and daughters; surely they will come
out to you, and you will see their ways and their
doings. Then you will be comforted concerning
the disaster that I have brought upon Jerusalem,
all that I have brought upon it. 23And they will
comfort you, when you see their ways and their
doings; and you shall know that I have done
nothing without cause that I have done in it,"
says the Lord GOD.

THE OUTCAST VINE

15 Then the word of the LORD came to me,
saying: 2"Son of man, how is the wood of
the vine *better* than any other wood, the vine
branch which is among the trees of the forest?
3Is wood taken from it to make any object? Or

THE MESSAGE

get blamed for those lies. He won't get by
with it. I'll grab him by the scruff of the neck
and get him out of there. They'll be equally
guilty, the prophet and the one who goes to
the prophet, so that the house of Israel will
never again wander off my paths and make
themselves filthy in their rebellions, but will
rather be my people, just as I am their God.
Decree of GOD, the Master.' "

12-14 GOD's Message came to me: "Son of man,
when a country sins against me by living
faithlessly and I reach out and destroy its
food supply by bringing on a famine, wiping
out humans and animals alike, even if Noah,
Daniel, and Job—the Big Three—were alive
at the time, it wouldn't do the population
any good. Their righteousness would only
save their own lives." Decree of GOD, the
Master.

15-16 "Or, if I make wild animals go through
the country so that everyone has to leave
and the country becomes wilderness and no
one dares enter it anymore because of the
wild animals, even if these three men were
living there, as sure as I am the living God,
neither their sons nor daughters would be
rescued, but only those three, and the coun-
try would revert to wilderness.

17-18 "Or, if I bring war on that country and
give the order, 'Let the killing begin!' leav-
ing both people and animals dead, even if
those three men were alive at the time, as
sure as I am the living God, neither sons nor
daughters would be rescued, but only these
three.

19-20 "Or, if I visit a deadly disease on that
country, pouring out my lethal anger, killing
both people and animals, and Noah, Daniel,
and Job happened to be alive at the time, as
sure as I am the living God, not a son, not a
daughter, would be rescued. Only these
three would be delivered because of their
righteousness.

21-23 "Now then, that's the picture," says GOD,
the Master, "once I've sent my four cata-
strophic judgments on Jerusalem—war,
famine, wild animals, disease—to kill off
people and animals alike. But look! Believe
it or not, there'll be survivors. Some of their
sons and daughters will be brought out.
When they come out to you and their salva-
tion is right in your face, you'll see for your-
self the life they've been saved from. You'll
know that this severe judgment I brought on
Jerusalem was worth it, that it had to be.
Yes, when you see in detail the kind of lives
they've been living, you'll feel much better.
You'll see the reason behind all that I've
done in Jerusalem." Decree of GOD, the Mas-
ter.

USED AS FUEL FOR THE FIRE

1-3 15 GOD's Message came to me: "Son of
man, how would you compare the wood
of a vine with the branches of any tree you'd
find in the forest? Is vine wood ever used to

NEW KING JAMES VERSION

can *men* make a peg from it to hang any vessel on? 4Instead, it is thrown into the fire for fuel; the fire devours both ends of it, and its middle is burned. Is it useful for *any* work? 5Indeed, when it was whole, no object could be made from it. How much less will it be useful for *any* work when the fire has devoured it, and it is burned?

6"Therefore thus says the Lord GOD: 'Like the wood of the vine among the trees of the forest, which I have given to the fire for fuel, so I will give up the inhabitants of Jerusalem; 7and I will set My face against them. They will go out from *one* fire, but *another* fire shall devour them. Then you shall know that I *am* the LORD, when I set My face against them. 8Thus I will make the land desolate, because they have persisted in unfaithfulness,' says the Lord GOD."

GOD'S LOVE FOR JERUSALEM

16 Again the word of the LORD came to me, saying, 2"Son of man, cause Jerusalem to know her abominations, 3and say, 'Thus says the Lord GOD to Jerusalem: "Your birth and your nativity *are* from the land of Canaan; your father *was* an Amorite and your mother a Hittite. 4*As for* your nativity, on the day you were born your navel cord was not cut, nor were you washed in water to cleanse *you;* you were not rubbed with salt nor wrapped in swaddling cloths. 5No eye pitied you, to do any of these things for you, to have compassion on you; but you were thrown out into the open field, when you yourself were loathed on the day you were born.

6"And when I passed by you and saw you struggling in your own blood, I said to you in your blood, 'Live!' Yes, I said to you in your blood, 'Live!' 7I made you thrive like a plant in the field; and you grew, matured, and became very beautiful. *Your* breasts were formed, your hair grew, but you *were* naked and bare.

8"When I passed by you again and looked upon you, indeed your time *was* the time of love; so I spread My wing over you and covered your nakedness. Yes, I swore an oath to you and entered into a covenant with you, and you became Mine," says the Lord GOD.

9"Then I washed you in water; yes, I thoroughly washed off your blood, and I anointed you with oil. 10I clothed you in embroidered cloth and gave you sandals of badger skin; I clothed you with fine linen and covered you with silk. 11I adorned you with ornaments, put bracelets on your wrists, and a chain on your neck. 12And I put a jewel in your nose, earrings in your ears, and a beautiful crown on your head. 13Thus you were adorned with gold and silver, and your clothing *was of* fine linen, silk, and embroidered cloth. You ate *pastry of* fine flour, honey, and oil. You were exceedingly beautiful, and succeeded to royalty. 14Your fame went out among the nations because of your beauty, for it *was* perfect through My splendor which I had bestowed on you," says the Lord GOD.

THE MESSAGE

make anything? Is it used to make pegs to
hang things from?
4 "I don't think so. At best it's good for fuel.
Look at it: A flimsy piece of vine, thrown in
the fire and then rescued—the ends burned
off and the middle charred. Now is it good
for anything?
5 "Hardly. When it was whole it wasn't
good for anything. Half-burned is no improvement. What's it good for?
6-8 "So here's the Message of GOD, the Master: Like the wood of the vine I selected from
among the trees of the forest and used as
fuel for the fire, just so I'll treat those who
live in Jerusalem. I am dead set against
them. Even though at one time they got out
of the fire charred, the fire's going to burn
them up. When I take my stand against them,
you'll realize that I am GOD. I'll turn this
country into a wilderness because they've
been faithless." Decree of GOD, the Master.

YOUR BEAUTY WENT TO YOUR HEAD

1-3 16 GOD's Message came to me: "Son of
man, confront Jerusalem with her outrageous violations. Say this: 'The Message
of GOD, the Master, to Jerusalem: You were
born and bred among Canaanites. Your father was an Amorite and your mother a Hittite.
4-5 " 'On the day you were born your umbilical cord was not cut, you weren't bathed and
cleaned up, you weren't rubbed with salt,
you weren't wrapped in a baby blanket. No
one cared a fig for you. No one did one thing
to care for you tenderly in these ways. You
were thrown out into a vacant lot and left
there, dirty and unwashed—a newborn nobody wanted.
6-7 " 'And then I came by. I saw you all miserable and bloody. Yes, I said to you, lying
there helpless and filthy, "Live! Grow up like
a plant in the field!" And you did. You grew
up. You grew tall and matured as a woman,
full-breasted, with flowing hair. But you
were naked and vulnerable, fragile and exposed.
8-14 " 'I came by again and saw you, saw that
you were ready for love and a lover. I took
care of you, dressed you and protected you.
I promised you my love and entered the
covenant of marriage with you. I, GOD, the
Master, gave my word. You became mine. I
gave you a good bath, washing off all that
old blood, and anointed you with aromatic
oils. I dressed you in a colorful gown and
put leather sandals on your feet. I gave you
linen blouses and a fashionable wardrobe of
expensive clothing. I adorned you with jewelry: I placed bracelets on your wrists, fitted
you out with a necklace, emerald rings, sapphire earrings, and a diamond tiara. You
were provided with everything precious and
beautiful: with exquisite clothes and elegant
food, garnished with honey and oil. You
were absolutely stunning. You were a queen!
You became world-famous, a legendary
beauty brought to perfection by my adornments. Decree of GOD, the Master.

New King James Version

Jerusalem's Harlotry

15“But you trusted in your own beauty,
played the harlot because of your fame, and
poured out your harlotry on everyone passing
by who *would have* it. 16You took some of your
garments and adorned multicolored high places
for yourself, and played the harlot on them.
Such things should not happen, nor be. 17You
have also taken your beautiful jewelry from My
gold and My silver, which I had given you, and
made for yourself male images and played the
harlot with them. 18You took your embroidered
garments and covered them, and you set My oil
and My incense before them. 19Also My food
which I gave you—the pastry of fine flour, oil,
and honey *which* I fed you—you set it before
them as sweet incense; and *so* it was,” says the
Lord GOD.

20“Moreover you took your sons and your
daughters, whom you bore to Me, and these you
sacrificed to them to be devoured. *Were* your
acts of harlotry a small matter, 21that you have
slain My children and offered them up to them
by causing them to pass through *the fire?* 22And
in all your abominations and acts of harlotry
you did not remember the days of your youth,
when you were naked and bare, struggling in
your blood.

23“Then it was so, after all your wickedness—
‘Woe, woe to you!’ says the Lord GOD— 24*that*
you also built for yourself a shrine, and made a
high place for yourself in every street. 25You
built your high places at the head of every road,
and made your beauty to be abhorred. You of-
fered yourself to everyone who passed by, and
multiplied your acts of harlotry. 26You also com-
mitted harlotry with the Egyptians, your very
fleshly neighbors, and increased your acts of
harlotry to provoke Me to anger.

27“Behold, therefore, I stretched out My hand
against you, diminished your allotment, and
gave you up to the will of those who hate you,
the daughters of the Philistines, who were
ashamed of your lewd behavior. 28You also
played the harlot with the Assyrians, because
you were insatiable; indeed you played the har-
lot with them and still were not satisfied.
29Moreover you multiplied your acts of harlotry
as far as the land of the trader, Chaldea; and
even then you were not satisfied.

30“How degenerate is your heart!” says the
Lord GOD, “seeing you do all these *things*, the
deeds of a brazen harlot.

Jerusalem's Adultery

31“You erected your shrine at the head of
every road, and built your high place in every
street. Yet you were not like a harlot, because
you scorned payment. 32*You are* an adulterous
wife, *who* takes strangers instead of her hus-
band. 33Men make payment to all harlots, but
you made your payments to all your lovers, and
hired them to come to you from all around for
your harlotry. 34You are the opposite of *other*
women in your harlotry, because no one so-
licited you to be a harlot. In that you gave pay-
ment but no payment was given you, therefore
you are the opposite.”

The Message

15-16 “ ‘But your beauty went to your head and you became a common whore, grabbing anyone coming down the street and taking him into your bed. You took your fine dresses and made “tents” of them, using them as brothels in which you practiced your trade. This kind of thing should never happen, never.

What a Sick Soul!

17-19 “ ‘And then you took all that fine jewelry I gave you, my gold and my silver, and made pornographic images of them for your brothels. You decorated your beds with fashionable silks and cottons, and perfumed them with my aromatic oils and incense. And then you set out the wonderful foods I provided—the fresh breads and fruits, with fine herbs and spices, which were my gifts to you—and you served them as delicacies in your whorehouses. That's what happened, says GOD, the Master.

20-21 “ ‘And then you took your sons and your daughters, whom you had given birth to as my children, and you killed them, sacrificing them to idols. Wasn't it bad enough that you had become a whore? And now you're a murderer, killing my children and sacrificing them to idols.

22 “ ‘Not once during these years of outrageous obscenities and whorings did you remember your infancy, when you were naked and exposed, a blood-smeared newborn.

23-24 “ ‘And then to top off all your evil acts, you built your bold brothels in every town square. Doom! Doom to you, says GOD, the Master! At every major intersection you built your bold brothels and exposed your sluttish sex, spreading your legs for everyone who passed by.

25-27 “ ‘And then you went international with your whoring. You fornicated with the Egyptians, seeking them out in their sex orgies. The more promiscuous you became, the angrier I got. Finally, I intervened, reduced your borders and turned you over to the rapacity of your enemies. Even the Philistine women—can you believe it?—were shocked at your sluttish life.

28-29 “ ‘You went on to fornicate with the Assyrians. Your appetite was insatiable. But still you weren't satisfied. You took on the Babylonians, a country of businessmen, and *still* you weren't satisfied.

30-31 “ ‘What a sick soul! Doing all this stuff—the champion whore! You built your bold brothels at every major intersection, opened up your whorehouses in every neighborhood, but you were different from regular whores in that you wouldn't accept a fee.

32-34 “ ‘Wives who are unfaithful to their husbands accept gifts from their lovers. And men commonly pay their whores. But you pay your lovers! You bribe men from all over to come to bed with you! You're just the opposite of the regular whores who get paid for sex. Instead, you pay men for *their* favors! You even pervert whoredom!

NEW KING JAMES VERSION

JERUSALEM'S LOVERS WILL ABUSE HER

35'Now then, O harlot, hear the word of the
LORD! 36Thus says the Lord GOD: "Because your
filthiness was poured out and your nakedness
uncovered in your harlotry with your lovers,
and with all your abominable idols, and because
of the blood of your children which you gave to
them, 37surely, therefore, I will gather all your
lovers with whom you took pleasure, all those
you loved, *and* all those you hated; I will gather
them from all around against you and will un-
cover your nakedness to them, that they may
see all your nakedness. 38And I will judge you as
women who break wedlock or shed blood are
judged; I will bring blood upon you in fury and
jealousy. 39I will also give you into their hand,
and they shall throw down your shrines and
break down your high places. They shall also
strip you of your clothes, take your beautiful
jewelry, and leave you naked and bare.

40"They shall also bring up an assembly
against you, and they shall stone you with
stones and thrust you through with their
swords. 41They shall burn your houses with fire,
and execute judgments on you in the sight of
many women; and I will make you cease playing
the harlot, and you shall no longer hire lovers.
42So I will lay to rest My fury toward you, and
My jealousy shall depart from you. I will be
quiet, and be angry no more. 43Because you did
not remember the days of your youth, but agi-
tated Me[a] with all these *things,* surely I will also
recompense your deeds on *your own* head," says
the Lord GOD. "And you shall not commit lewd-
ness in addition to all your abominations.

MORE WICKED THAN SAMARIA AND SODOM

44"Indeed everyone who quotes proverbs will
use *this* proverb against you: 'Like mother, like
daughter!' 45You *are* your mother's daughter,
loathing husband and children; and you *are* the
sister of your sisters, who loathed their hus-
bands and children; your mother *was* a Hittite
and your father an Amorite.

46"Your elder sister *is* Samaria, who dwells
with her daughters to the north of you; and your
younger sister, who dwells to the south of you, *is*
Sodom and her daughters. 47You did not walk in
their ways nor act according to their abomina-
tions; but, as *if that were* too little, you became
more corrupt than they in all your ways.

48"*As* I live," says the Lord GOD, "neither your
sister Sodom nor her daughters have done as
you and your daughters have done. 49Look, this
was the iniquity of your sister Sodom: She and
her daughter had pride, fullness of food, and
abundance of idleness; neither did she
strengthen the hand of the poor and needy.
50And they were haughty and committed abom-
ination before Me; therefore I took them away
as I saw *fit.*[a]

51"Samaria did not commit half of your sins;
but you have multiplied your abominations
more than they, and have justified your sisters
by all the abominations which you have done.

16:43 [a]Following Septuagint, Syriac, Targum, and Vulgate; Masoretic Text reads *were agitated with Me.* **16:50** [a]Vulgate reads *you saw;* Septuagint reads *he saw;* Targum reads *as was revealed to Me.*

THE MESSAGE

35-38 " 'Therefore, whore, listen to GOD's Message: I, GOD, the Master, say, Because you've been unrestrained in your promiscuity, stripped down for every lover, flaunting your sex, and because of your pornographic idols and all the slaughtered children you offered to them, therefore, because of all this, I'm going to get all your lovers together, all those you've used for your own pleasure, the ones you loved and the ones you loathed. I'll assemble them as a courtroom of spectators around you. In broad daylight I'll strip you naked before them—they'll see what you *really* look like. Then I'll sentence you to the punishment for an adulterous woman and a murderous woman. I'll give you a taste of my wrath!

39-41 " 'I'll gather all your lovers around you and turn you over to them. They'll tear down your bold brothels and sex shrines. They'll rip off your clothes, take your jewels, and leave you naked and exposed. Then they'll call for a mass meeting. The mob will stone you and hack you to pieces with their swords. They'll burn down your houses. A massive judgment—with all the women watching!

41-42 " 'I'll have put a full stop to your whoring life—no more paying lovers to come to your bed! By then my anger will be played out. My jealousy will subside.

43 " 'Because you didn't remember what happened when you were young but made me angry with all this behavior, I'll make you pay for your waywardness. Didn't you just exponentially compound your outrageous obscenities with all your sluttish ways?

44-45 " 'Everyone who likes to use proverbs will use this one: "Like mother, like daughter." You're the daughter of your mother, who couldn't stand her husband and children. And you're a true sister of your sisters, who couldn't stand their husbands and children. Your mother was a Hittite and your father an Amorite.

46-48 " 'Your older sister is Samaria. She lived to the north of you with her daughters. Your younger sister is Sodom, who lived to the south of you with her daughters. Haven't you lived just like they did? Haven't you engaged in outrageous obscenities just like they did? In fact, it didn't take you long to catch up and pass them! As sure as I am the living God!—Decree of GOD, the Master—your sister Sodom and her daughters never even came close to what you and your daughters have done.

49-50 " 'The sin of your sister Sodom was this: She lived with her daughters in the lap of luxury—proud, gluttonous, and lazy. They ignored the oppressed and the poor. They put on airs and lived obscene lives. And you know what happened: I did away with them.

51-52 " 'And Samaria. Samaria didn't sin half as much as you. You've committed far more obscenities than she ever did. Why, you make your two sisters look good in comparison with what you've done! Face it, your sisters

NEW KING JAMES VERSION

52 You who judged your sisters, bear your own
shame also, because the sins which you commit-
ted were more abominable than theirs; they are
more righteous than you. Yes, be disgraced also,
and bear your own shame, because you justified
your sisters.
53 "When I bring back their captives, the cap-
tives of Sodom and her daughters, and the cap-
tives of Samaria and her daughters, then *I will
also bring back* the captives of your captivity
among them, 54 that you may bear your own
shame and be disgraced by all that you did
when you comforted them. 55 When your sisters,
Sodom and her daughters, return to their for-
mer state, and Samaria and her daughters re-
turn to their former state, then you and your
daughters will return to your former state. 56 For
your sister Sodom was not a byword in your
mouth in the days of your pride, 57 before your
wickedness was uncovered. It was like the time
of the reproach of the daughters of Syria[a] and
all *those* around her, and of the daughters of the
Philistines, who despise you everywhere. 58 You
have paid for your lewdness and your abomina-
tions," says the LORD. 59 For thus says the Lord
GOD: "I will deal with you as you have done, who
despised the oath by breaking the covenant.

AN EVERLASTING COVENANT

60 "Nevertheless I will remember My covenant
with you in the days of your youth, and I will es-
tablish an everlasting covenant with you. 61 Then
you will remember your ways and be ashamed,
when you receive your older and your younger
sisters; for I will give them to you for daughters,
but not because of My covenant with you. 62 And
I will establish My covenant with you. Then you
shall know that I *am* the LORD, 63 that you may re-
member and be ashamed, and never open your
mouth anymore because of your shame, when I
provide you an atonement for all you have done,"
says the Lord GOD.' "

THE EAGLES AND THE VINE

17 And the word of the LORD came to me, say-
ing, 2 "Son of man, pose a riddle, and speak
a parable to the house of Israel, 3 and say, 'Thus
says the Lord GOD:

"A great eagle with large wings and long
pinions,
Full of feathers of various colors,
Came to Lebanon
And took from the cedar the highest branch.
4 He cropped off its topmost young twig
And carried it to a land of trade;
He set it in a city of merchants.
5 Then he took some of the seed of the land
And planted it in a fertile field;

16:57 [a]Following Masoretic Text, Septuagint, Targum, and Vulgate; many Hebrew manuscripts and Syriac read *Edom*.

THE MESSAGE

look mighty good compared with you. Because you've outsinned them so completely, you've actually made them look righteous. Aren't you ashamed? But you're going to have to live with it. What a reputation to carry into history: outsinning your two sisters!

53-58 " 'But I'm going to reverse their fortunes, the fortunes of Sodom and her daughters and the fortunes of Samaria and her daughters. And—get this—*your* fortunes right along with them! Still, you're going to have to live with your shame. And by facing and accepting your shame, you're going to provide some comfort to your two sisters. Your sisters, Sodom with her daughters and Samaria with her daughters, will become what they were before, and you will become what you were before. Remember the days when you were putting on airs, acting so high and mighty, looking down on sister Sodom? That was before your evil ways were exposed. And now *you're* the butt of contempt, despised by the Edomite women, the Philistine women, and everybody else around. But you have to face it, to accept the shame of your obscene and vile life. Decree of GOD, the Master.

59-63 " 'GOD, the Master, says, I'll do to you just as you have already done, you who have treated my oath with contempt and broken the covenant. All the same, I'll remember the covenant I made with you when you were young and I'll make a new covenant with you that will last forever. You'll remember your sorry past and be properly contrite when you receive back your sisters, both the older and the younger. I'll give them to you as daughters, but not as participants in your covenant. I'll firmly establish my covenant with you and you'll know that I am GOD. You'll remember your past life and face the shame of it, but when I make atonement for you, make everything right after all you've done, it will leave you speechless.' " Decree of GOD, the Master.

THE GREAT TREE IS MADE SMALL AND THE SMALL TREE GREAT

1-6 17 GOD's Message came to me: "Son of man, make a riddle for the house of Israel. Tell them a story. Say, 'GOD, the Master, says:

" 'A great eagle
with a huge wingspan and long feathers,
In full plumage and bright colors,
came to Lebanon
And took the top off a cedar,
broke off the top branch,
Took it to a land of traders,
and set it down in a city of shopkeepers.
Then he took a cutting from the land

NEW KING JAMES VERSION

He placed *it* by abundant waters
And set it like a willow tree.
6And it grew and became a spreading vine of low stature;
Its branches turned toward him,
But its roots were under it.
So it became a vine,
Brought forth branches,
And put forth shoots.

7"But there was another[a] great eagle with large wings and many feathers;
And behold, this vine bent its roots toward him,
And stretched its branches toward him,
From the garden terrace where it had been planted,
That he might water it.
8It was planted in good soil by many waters,
To bring forth branches, bear fruit,
And become a majestic vine." '

9"Say, 'Thus says the Lord GOD:

"Will it thrive?
Will he not pull up its roots,
Cut off its fruit,
And leave it to wither?
All of its spring leaves will wither,
And no great power or many people
Will be needed to pluck it up by its roots.
10Behold, *it is* planted,
Will it thrive?
Will it not utterly wither when the east wind touches it?
It will wither in the garden terrace where it grew." ' "

11Moreover the word of the LORD came to
me, saying, 12"Say now to the rebellious house:
'Do you not know what these *things mean?*' Tell
them, 'Indeed the king of Babylon went to
Jerusalem and took its king and princes, and led
them with him to Babylon. 13And he took the
king's offspring, made a covenant with him, and
put him under oath. He also took away the
mighty of the land, 14that the kingdom might be
brought low and not lift itself up, *but* that by
keeping his covenant it might stand. 15But he re-
belled against him by sending his ambassadors
to Egypt, that they might give him horses and
many people. Will he prosper? Will he who does
such *things* escape? Can he break a covenant
and still be delivered?
16'*As* I live,' says the Lord GOD, 'surely in the
place *where* the king *dwells* who made him
king, whose oath he despised and whose
covenant he broke—with him in the midst of
Babylon he shall die. 17Nor will Pharaoh with
his mighty army and great company do any-
thing in the war, when they heap up a siege
mound and build a wall to cut off many persons.
18Since he despised the oath by breaking the
covenant, and in fact gave his hand and still did
all these *things,* he shall not escape.' "
19Therefore thus says the Lord GOD: "*As* I
live, surely My oath which he despised, and My

17:7 [a]Following Septuagint, Syriac, and Vulgate; Masoretic Text and Targum read *one.*

THE MESSAGE

and planted it in good, well-watered soil,
like a willow on a riverbank.
It sprouted into a flourishing vine,
low to the ground.
Its branches grew toward the eagle
and the roots became established—
A vine putting out shoots,
developing branches.

7-8 " 'There was another great eagle
with a huge wingspan and thickly feathered.
This vine sent out its roots toward him
from the place where it was planted.
Its branches reached out to him
so he could water it
from a long distance.
It had been planted
in good, well-watered soil,
And it put out branches and bore fruit,
and became a noble vine.

9-10 " 'GOD, the Master, says,
Will it thrive?
Won't he just pull it up by the roots
and leave the grapes to rot
And the branches to shrivel up,
a withered, dead vine?
It won't take much strength
or many hands to pull it up.
Even if it's transplanted,
will it thrive?
When the hot east wind strikes it,
won't it shrivel up?
Won't it dry up and blow away
from the place where it was planted?' "

11-12 GOD's Message came to me: "Tell this house
of rebels, 'Do you get it? Do you know what
this means?'
12-14 "Tell them, 'The king of Babylon came to
Jerusalem and took its king and its leaders
back to Babylon. He took one of the royal
family and made a covenant with him, mak-
ing him swear his loyalty. The king of Bab-
ylon took all the top leaders into exile to
make sure that this kingdom stayed weak—
didn't get any big ideas of itself—and kept
the covenant with him so that it would have
a future.
15 " 'But he rebelled and sent emissaries to
Egypt to recruit horses and a big army. Do
you think that's going to work? Are they go-
ing to get by with this? Does anyone break a
covenant and get off scot-free?
16-18 " 'As sure as I am the living God, this king
who broke his pledge of loyalty and his
covenant will die in that country, in Bab-
ylon. Pharaoh with his big army—all those
soldiers!—won't lift a finger to fight for him
when Babylon sets siege to the city and kills
everyone inside. Because he broke his word
and broke the covenant, even though he
gave his solemn promise, because he went
ahead and did all these things anyway, he
won't escape.
19-21 " 'Therefore, GOD, the Master, says, As
sure as I am the living God, because the

NEW KING JAMES VERSION

covenant which he broke, I will recompense on
his own head. [20]I will spread My net over him,
and he shall be taken in My snare. I will bring
him to Babylon and try him there for the treason
which he committed against Me. [21]All his fugi-
tives[a] with all his troops shall fall by the sword,
and those who remain shall be scattered to
every wind; and you shall know that I, the LORD,
have spoken."

ISRAEL EXALTED AT LAST

[22]Thus says the Lord GOD: "I will take also
one of the highest branches of the high cedar
and set *it* out. I will crop off from the topmost of
its young twigs a tender one, and will plant *it* on
a high and prominent mountain. [23]On the moun-
tain height of Israel I will plant it; and it will
bring forth boughs, and bear fruit, and be a ma-
jestic cedar. Under it will dwell birds of every
sort; in the shadow of its branches they will
dwell. [24]And all the trees of the field shall know
that I, the LORD, have brought down the high
tree and exalted the low tree, dried up the green
tree and made the dry tree flourish; I, the LORD,
have spoken and have done *it*."

A FALSE PROVERB REFUTED

18 The word of the LORD came to me again,
saying, [2]"What do you mean when you use
this proverb concerning the land of Israel, say-
ing:

'The fathers have eaten sour grapes,
And the children's teeth are set on edge'?

[3]"*As I live*," says the Lord GOD, "you shall no
longer use this proverb in Israel.

[4]"Behold, all souls are Mine;
The soul of the father
As well as the soul of the son is Mine;
The soul who sins shall die.
[5]But if a man is just
And does what is lawful and right;
[6]If he has not eaten on the mountains,
Nor lifted up his eyes to the idols of the
house of Israel,
Nor defiled his neighbor's wife,
Nor approached a woman during her
impurity;
[7]If he has not oppressed anyone,
But has restored to the debtor his pledge;
Has robbed no one by violence,
But has given his bread to the hungry
And covered the naked with clothing;
[8]If he has not exacted usury
Nor taken any increase,
But has withdrawn his hand from iniquity
And executed true judgment between man
and man;
[9]*If* he has walked in My statutes
And kept My judgments faithfully—
He *is* just;
He shall surely live!"
Says the Lord GOD.

17:21 [a]Following Masoretic Text and Vulgate; many Hebrew manuscripts and Syriac read *choice men;* Targum reads *mighty men;* Septuagint omits *All his fugitives.*

THE MESSAGE

king despised my oath and broke my
covenant, I'll bring the consequences crash-
ing down on his head. I'll send out a search
party and catch him. I'll take him to Babylon
and have him brought to trial because of his
total disregard for me. All his elite soldiers,
along with the rest of the army, will be killed
in battle, and whoever is left will be scat-
tered to the four winds. Then you'll realize
that I, GOD, have spoken.
22-24 " 'GOD, the Master, says, I personally will
take a shoot from the top of the towering
cedar, a cutting from the crown of the tree,
and plant it on a high and towering moun-
tain, on the high mountain of Israel. It will
grow, putting out branches and fruit—a ma-
jestic cedar. Birds of every sort and kind will
live under it. They'll build nests in the shade
of its branches. All the trees of the field will
recognize that I, GOD, made the great
tree small and the small tree great, made
the green tree turn dry and the dry tree
sprout green branches. I, GOD, said it—and I
did it.' "

JUDGED ACCORDING TO THE WAY YOU LIVE

1-2 18 GOD'S Message to me: "What do you
people mean by going around the coun-
try repeating the saying,

The parents ate green apples,
The children got the stomachache?

3-4 "As sure as I'm the living God, you're not
going to repeat this saying in Israel any
longer. Every soul—man, woman, child—
belongs to me, parent and child alike. You
die for your own sin, not another's.
5-9 "Imagine a person who lives well, treat-
ing others fairly, keeping good relation-
ships—

doesn't eat at the pagan shrines,
doesn't worship the idols so popular
in Israel,
doesn't seduce a neighbor's spouse,
doesn't indulge in casual sex,
doesn't bully anyone,
doesn't pile up bad debts,
doesn't steal,
doesn't refuse food to the hungry,
doesn't refuse clothing to the ill-clad,
doesn't exploit the poor,
doesn't live by impulse and greed,
doesn't treat one person better than
another,
But lives by my statutes and faithfully
honors and obeys my laws.
This person who lives upright and well
shall live a full and true life.
Decree of GOD, the Master.

NEW KING JAMES VERSION

10"If he begets a son *who is* a robber
Or a shedder of blood,
Who does any of these *things*
11And does none of those *duties*,
But has eaten on the mountains
Or defiled his neighbor's wife;
12If he has oppressed the poor and needy,
Robbed by violence,
Not restored the pledge,
Lifted his eyes to the idols,
Or committed abomination;
13If he has exacted usury
Or taken increase—
Shall he then live?
He shall not live!
If he has done any of these abominations,
He shall surely die;
His blood shall be upon him.

14"*If*, however, he begets a son
Who sees all the sins which his father has done,
And considers but does not do likewise;
15*Who* has not eaten on the mountains,
Nor lifted his eyes to the idols of the house of Israel,
Nor defiled his neighbor's wife;
16Has not oppressed anyone,
Nor withheld a pledge,
Nor robbed by violence,
But has given his bread to the hungry
And covered the naked with clothing;
17*Who* has withdrawn his hand from the poor[a]
And not received usury or increase,
But has executed My judgments
And walked in My statutes—
He shall not die for the iniquity of his father;
He shall surely live!

18"*As for* his father,
Because he cruelly oppressed,
Robbed his brother by violence,
And did what *is* not good among his people,
Behold, he shall die for his iniquity.

TURN AND LIVE

19"Yet you say, 'Why should the son not bear
the guilt of the father?' Because the son has
done what is lawful and right, and has kept all
My statutes and observed them, he shall surely
live. 20The soul who sins shall die. The son shall
not bear the guilt of the father, nor the father
bear the guilt of the son. The righteousness of
the righteous shall be upon himself, and the
wickedness of the wicked shall be upon himself.
21"But if a wicked man turns from all his sins
which he has committed, keeps all My statutes,
and does what is lawful and right, he shall
surely live; he shall not die. 22None of the trans-
gressions which he has committed shall be re-
membered against him; because of the righ-
teousness which he has done, he shall live. 23Do
I have any pleasure at all that the wicked should
die?" says the Lord GOD, "*and* not that he should
turn from his ways and live?

18:17 [a]Following Masoretic Text, Targum, and Vulgate; Septuagint reads *iniquity* (compare verse 8).

THE MESSAGE

10-13 "But if this person has a child who turns violent and murders and goes off and does any of these things, even though the parent has done none of them—

eats at the pagan shrines,
seduces his neighbor's spouse,
bullies the weak,
steals,
piles up bad debts,
admires idols,
commits outrageous obscenities,
exploits the poor

"—do you think this person, the child, will live? Not a chance! Because he's done all these vile things, he'll die. And his death will be his own fault.

14-17 "Now look: Suppose that this child has a child who sees all the sins done by his parent. The child sees them, but doesn't follow in the parent's footsteps—

doesn't eat at the pagan shrines,
doesn't worship the popular idols of Israel,
doesn't seduce his neighbor's spouse,
doesn't bully anyone,
doesn't refuse to loan money,
doesn't steal,
doesn't refuse food to the hungry,
doesn't refuse to give clothes to the ill-clad,
doesn't live by impulse and greed,
doesn't exploit the poor.
He does what I say;
he performs my laws and lives by my statutes.

17-18 "This person will not die for the sins of the parent; he will live truly and well. But the parent will die for what the parent did, for the sins of—

oppressing the weak,
robbing brothers and sisters,
doing what is dead wrong in the community.

19-20 "Do you need to ask, 'So why does the child not share the guilt of the parent?'

"Isn't it plain? It's because the child did what is fair and right. Since the child was careful to do what is lawful and right, the child will live truly and well. The soul that sins is the soul that dies. The child does not share the guilt of the parent, nor the parent the guilt of the child. If you live upright and well, you get the credit; if you live a wicked life, you're guilty as charged.

21-23 "But a wicked person who turns his back on that life of sin and keeps all my statutes, living a just and righteous life, he'll live, really live. He won't die. I won't keep a list of all the things he did wrong. He will live. Do you think I take any pleasure in the death of wicked men and women? Isn't it my pleasure that they turn around, no longer living wrong but living right—really living?

NEW KING JAMES VERSION

24“But when a righteous man turns away
from his righteousness and commits iniquity,
and does according to all the abominations that
the wicked *man* does, shall he live? All the righ-
teousness which he has done shall not be re-
membered; because of the unfaithfulness of
which he is guilty and the sin which he has com-
mitted, because of them he shall die.
25“Yet you say, ‘The way of the Lord is not
fair.’ Hear now, O house of Israel, is it not My
way which is fair, and your ways which are not
fair? 26When a righteous *man* turns away from
his righteousness, commits iniquity, and dies in
it, it is because of the iniquity which he has done
that he dies. 27Again, when a wicked *man* turns
away from the wickedness which he committed,
and does what is lawful and right, he preserves
himself alive. 28Because he considers and turns
away from all the transgressions which he com-
mitted, he shall surely live; he shall not die. 29Yet
the house of Israel says, ‘The way of the Lord is
not fair.’ O house of Israel, is it not My ways
which are fair, and your ways which are not
fair?
30“Therefore I will judge you, O house of Is-
rael, every one according to his ways,” says the
Lord GOD. “Repent, and turn from all your trans-
gressions, so that iniquity will not be your ruin.
31Cast away from you all the transgressions
which you have committed, and get yourselves a
new heart and a new spirit. For why should you
die, O house of Israel? 32For I have no pleasure
in the death of one who dies,” says the Lord
GOD. “Therefore turn and live!”

ISRAEL DEGRADED

19 “Moreover take up a lamentation for the
princes of Israel, 2and say:

‘What *is* your mother? A lioness:
She lay down among the lions;
Among the young lions she nourished her
cubs.
3She brought up one of her cubs,
And he became a young lion;
He learned to catch prey,
And he devoured men.
4The nations also heard of him;
He was trapped in their pit,
And they brought him with chains to the
land of Egypt.

5‘When she saw that she waited, *that* her
hope was lost,
She took another of her cubs *and* made him
a young lion.
6He roved among the lions,
And became a young lion;
He learned to catch prey;
He devoured men.
7He knew their desolate places,[a]
And laid waste their cities;
The land with its fullness was desolated
By the noise of his roaring.

19:7 [a]Septuagint reads *He stood in insolence;* Targum reads *He destroyed its palaces;* Vulgate reads *He learned to make widows.*

THE MESSAGE

24 “The same thing goes for a good person
who turns his back on an upright life and
starts sinning, plunging into the same vile
obscenities that the wicked person prac-
tices. Will this person live? I don’t keep a list
of all the things this person did right, like
money in the bank he can draw on. Because
of his defection, because he accumulates
sin, he’ll die.
25-28 “Do I hear you saying, ‘That’s not fair!
God’s not fair!’?
“Listen, Israel. I’m not fair? You’re the
ones who aren’t fair! If a good person turns
away from his good life and takes up sin-
ning, he’ll die for it. He’ll die for his own sin.
Likewise, if a bad person turns away from
his bad life and starts living a good life, a
fair life, he will save his life. Because he
faces up to all the wrongs he’s committed
and puts them behind him, he will live, re-
ally live. He won’t die.
29 “And yet Israel keeps on whining, ‘That’s
not fair! God’s not fair.’
“I’m not fair, Israel? You’re the ones who
aren’t fair.
30-32 “The upshot is this, Israel: I’ll judge each
of you according to the way you live. So turn
around! Turn your backs on your rebellious
living so that sin won’t drag you down.
Clean house. No more rebellions, please.
Get a new heart! Get a new spirit! Why
would you choose to die, Israel? I take no
pleasure in anyone’s death. Decree of GOD,
the Master.
“Make a clean break! Live!”

A STORY OF TWO LIONS

1-4 19 Sing the blues over the princes of Israel.
Say:

What a lioness was your mother
among lions!
She crouched in a pride of young lions.
Her cubs grew large.
She reared one of her cubs to maturity,
a robust young lion.
He learned to hunt.
He ate men.
Nations sounded the alarm.
He was caught in a trap.
They took him with hooks
and dragged him to Egypt.

5-9 When the lioness saw she was luckless,
that her hope for that cub was gone,
She took her other cub
and made him a strong young lion.
He prowled with the lions,
a robust young lion.
He learned to hunt.
He ate men.
He rampaged through their defenses,
left their cities in ruins.
The country and everyone in it
was terrorized by the roars of the lion.

NEW KING JAMES VERSION

8Then the nations set against him from the
provinces on every side,
And spread their net over him;
He was trapped in their pit.
9They put him in a cage with chains,
And brought him to the king of Babylon;
They brought him in nets,
That his voice should no longer be heard on
the mountains of Israel.

10'Your mother *was* like a vine in your
bloodline,[a]
Planted by the waters,
Fruitful and full of branches
Because of many waters.
11She had strong branches for scepters of
rulers.
She towered in stature above the thick
branches,
And was seen in her height amid the dense
foliage.
12But she was plucked up in fury,
She was cast down to the ground,
And the east wind dried her fruit.
Her strong branches were broken and
withered;
The fire consumed them.
13And now she *is* planted in the wilderness,
In a dry and thirsty land.
14Fire has come out from a rod of her
branches
And devoured her fruit,
So that she has no strong branch—
a scepter for ruling.'"

This *is* a lamentation, and has become a
lamentation.

THE REBELLIONS OF ISRAEL

20 It came to pass in the seventh year, in the
fifth *month*, on the tenth *day* of the month,
that certain of the elders of Israel came to in-
quire of the LORD, and sat before me. 2Then the
word of the LORD came to me, saying, 3"Son of
man, speak to the elders of Israel, and say to
them, 'Thus says the Lord GOD: "Have you come
to inquire of Me? *As* I live," says the Lord GOD,
"I will not be inquired of by you." ' 4Will you
judge them, son of man, will you judge *them*?
Then make known to them the abominations of
their fathers.

5"Say to them, 'Thus says the Lord GOD: "On
the day when I chose Israel and raised My hand
in an oath to the descendants of the house of Ja-
cob, and made Myself known to them in the
land of Egypt, I raised My hand in an oath to
them, saying, 'I *am* the LORD your God.' 6On that
day I raised My hand in an oath to them, to
bring them out of the land of Egypt into a land
that I had searched out for them, 'flowing with
milk and honey,'[a] the glory of all lands. 7Then I
said to them, 'Each of you, throw away the
abominations which are before his eyes, and do
not defile yourselves with the idols of Egypt. I
am the LORD your God.'

19:10 [a]Literally *blood,* following Masoretic Text, Syriac, and Vulgate; Septuagint reads *like a flower on a pomegranate tree;* Targum reads *in your likeness.* 20:6 [a]Exodus 3:8

THE MESSAGE

The nations got together to hunt him.
Everyone joined the hunt.
They set out their traps
and caught him.
They put a wooden collar on him
and took him to the king of Babylon.
No more would that voice be heard
disturbing the peace in the mountains of
Israel!

10-14 Here's another way to put it:
Your mother was like a vine in a
vineyard,
transplanted alongside streams of water,
Luxurious in branches and grapes
because of the ample water.
It grew sturdy branches
fit to be carved into a royal scepter.
It grew high, reaching into the clouds.
Its branches filled the horizon,
and everyone could see it.
Then it was ripped up in a rage
and thrown to the ground.
The hot east wind shriveled it up
and stripped its fruit.
The sturdy branches dried out,
fit for nothing but kindling.
Now it's a stick stuck out in the desert,
a bare stick in a desert of death,
Good for nothing but making fires,
campfires in the desert.
Not a hint now of those sturdy branches
fit for use as a royal scepter!

(This is a sad song, a text for singing the
blues.)

GET RID OF ALL THE THINGS YOU'VE BECOME ADDICTED TO

1 20 In the seventh year, the fifth month, on
the tenth day of the month, some of the
leaders of Israel came to ask for guidance
from GOD. They sat down before me.
2-3 Then GOD's Message came to me: "Son of
man, talk with the leaders of Israel. Tell
them, 'GOD, the Master, says, "Have you
come to ask me questions? As sure as I am
the living God, I'll not put up with questions
from you. Decree of GOD, the Master.' "
4-5 "Son of man, why don't *you* do it? Yes, go
ahead. Hold them accountable. Confront
them with the outrageous obscenities of their
parents. Tell them that GOD, the Master, says:
5-6 " 'On the day I chose Israel, I revealed
myself to them in the country of Egypt, rais-
ing my hand in a solemn oath to the people
of Jacob, in which I said, "I am GOD, your
personal God." On the same day that I
raised my hand in the solemn oath, I prom-
ised them that I would take them out of the
country of Egypt and bring them into a
country that I had searched out just for
them, a country flowing with milk and
honey, a jewel of a country.
7 " 'At that time I told them, "Get rid of all
the vile things that you've become addicted
to. Don't make yourselves filthy with the
Egyptian no-god idols. I *alone* am GOD, your
God."

NEW KING JAMES VERSION

8But they rebelled against Me and would not
obey Me. They did not all cast away the abomi-
nations which were before their eyes, nor did
they forsake the idols of Egypt. Then I said, 'I
will pour out My fury on them and fulfill My
anger against them in the midst of the land of
Egypt.' 9But I acted for My name's sake, that it
should not be profaned before the Gentiles
among whom they *were*, in whose sight I had
made Myself known to them, to bring them out
of the land of Egypt.

10"Therefore I made them go out of the land
of Egypt and brought them into the wilderness.
11And I gave them My statutes and showed them
My judgments, 'which, *if* a man does, he shall
live by them.'[a] 12Moreover I also gave them My
Sabbaths, to be a sign between them and Me,
that they might know that I *am* the LORD who
sanctifies them. 13Yet the house of Israel re-
belled against Me in the wilderness; they did not
walk in My statutes; they despised My judg-
ments, 'which, *if* a man does, he shall live by
them';[a] and they greatly defiled My Sabbaths.
Then I said I would pour out My fury on them in
the wilderness, to consume them. 14But I acted
for My name's sake, that it should not be pro-
faned before the Gentiles, in whose sight I had
brought them out. 15So I also raised My hand in
an oath to them in the wilderness, that I would
not bring them into the land which I had given
them, 'flowing with milk and honey,'[a] the glory
of all lands, 16because they despised My judg-
ments and did not walk in My statutes, but pro-
faned My Sabbaths; for their heart went after
their idols. 17Nevertheless My eye spared them
from destruction. I did not make an end of them
in the wilderness.

18"But I said to their children in the wilder-
ness, 'Do not walk in the statutes of your fa-
thers, nor observe their judgments, nor defile
yourselves with their idols. 19I *am* the LORD your
God: Walk in My statutes, keep My judgments,
and do them; 20hallow My Sabbaths, and they
will be a sign between Me and you, that you may
know that I *am* the LORD your God.'

21"Notwithstanding, the children rebelled
against Me; they did not walk in My statutes,
and were not careful to observe My judgments,
'which, *if* a man does, he shall live by them';[a] but
they profaned My Sabbaths. Then I said I would
pour out My fury on them and fulfill My anger
against them in the wilderness. 22Nevertheless I
withdrew My hand and acted for My name's
sake, that it should not be profaned in the sight
of the Gentiles, in whose sight I had brought
them out. 23Also I raised My hand in an oath to
those in the wilderness, that I would scatter
them among the Gentiles and disperse them
throughout the countries, 24because they had
not executed My judgments, but had despised
My statutes, profaned My Sabbaths, and their
eyes were fixed on their fathers' idols.

20:11 [a]Leviticus 18:5 **20:13** [a]Leviticus 18:5 **20:21** [a]Leviticus 18:5 **20:15** [a]Exodus 3:8

THE MESSAGE

8-10 " 'But they rebelled against me, wouldn't listen to a word I said. None got rid of the vile things they were addicted to. They held on to the no-gods of Egypt as if for dear life. I seriously considered inflicting my anger on them in force right there in Egypt. Then I thought better of it. I acted out of who I was, not by how I felt. And I acted in a way that would evoke honor, not blasphemy, from the nations around them, nations who had seen me reveal myself by promising to lead my people out of Egypt. And then I did it: I led them out of Egypt into the desert.

11-12 " 'I gave them laws for living, showed them how to live well and obediently before me. I also gave them my weekly holy rest days, my "Sabbaths," a kind of signpost erected between me and them to show them that I, GOD, am in the business of making them holy.

13-17 " 'But Israel rebelled against me in the desert. They didn't follow my statutes. They despised my laws for living well and obediently in the ways I had set out. And they totally desecrated my holy Sabbaths. I seriously considered unleashing my anger on them right there in the desert. But I thought better of it and acted out of who I was, not by what I felt, so that I might be honored and not blasphemed by the nations who had seen me bring them out. But I did lift my hand in a solemn oath there in the desert and promise them that I would not bring them into the country flowing with milk and honey that I had chosen for them, that jewel among all lands. I canceled my promise because they despised my laws for living obediently, wouldn't follow my statutes, and went ahead and desecrated my holy Sabbaths. They preferred living by their no-god idols. But I didn't go all the way: I didn't wipe them out, didn't finish them off in the desert.

18-20 " 'Then I addressed myself to their children in the desert: "Don't do what your parents did. Don't take up their practices. Don't make yourselves filthy with their no-god idols. I myself am GOD, your God: Keep my statutes and live by my laws. Keep my Sabbaths as holy rest days, signposts between me and you, signaling that I am GOD, *your* God."

21-22 " 'But the children also rebelled against me. They neither followed my statutes nor kept my laws for living upright and well. And they desecrated my Sabbaths. I seriously considered dumping my anger on them, right there in the desert. But I thought better of it and acted out of who I was, not by what I felt, so that I might be honored and not blasphemed by the nations who had seen me bring them out.

23-26 " 'But I did lift my hand in solemn oath there in the desert, and swore that I would scatter them all over the world, disperse them every which way because they didn't keep my laws nor live by my statutes. They desecrated my Sabbaths and remained addicted to the no-god idols of their parents.

NEW KING JAMES VERSION

25"Therefore I also gave them up to statutes *that were* not good, and judgments by which they could not live; 26and I pronounced them unclean because of their ritual gifts, in that they caused all their firstborn to pass through *the fire*, that I might make them desolate and that they might know that I am the LORD." '

27"Therefore, son of man, speak to the house of Israel, and say to them, 'Thus says the Lord GOD: "In this too your fathers have blasphemed Me, by being unfaithful to Me. 28When I brought them into the land *concerning* which I had raised My hand in an oath to give them, and they saw all the high hills and all the thick trees, there they offered their sacrifices and provoked Me with their offerings. There they also sent up their sweet aroma and poured out their drink offerings. 29Then I said to them, 'What *is* this high place to which you go?' So its name is called Bamah[a] to this day." ' 30Therefore say to the house of Israel, 'Thus says the Lord GOD: "Are you defiling yourselves in the manner of your fathers, and committing harlotry according to their abominations? 31For when you offer your gifts and make your sons pass through the fire, you defile yourselves with all your idols, even to this day. So shall I be inquired of by you, O house of Israel? *As* I live," says the Lord GOD, "I will not be inquired of by you. 32What you have in your mind shall never be, when you say, 'We will be like the Gentiles, like the families in other countries, serving wood and stone.'

GOD WILL RESTORE ISRAEL

33"*As* I live," says the Lord GOD, "surely with a mighty hand, with an outstretched arm, and with fury poured out, I will rule over you. 34I will bring you out from the peoples and gather you out of the countries where you are scattered, with a mighty hand, with an outstretched arm, and with fury poured out. 35And I will bring you into the wilderness of the peoples, and there I will plead My case with you face to face. 36Just as I pleaded My case with your fathers in the wilderness of the land of Egypt, so I will plead My case with you," says the Lord GOD.

37"I will make you pass under the rod, and I will bring you into the bond of the covenant; 38I will purge the rebels from among you, and those who transgress against Me; I will bring them out of the country where they dwell, but they shall not enter the land of Israel. Then you will know that I *am* the LORD.

39"As for you, O house of Israel," thus says the Lord GOD: "Go, serve every one of you his idols—and hereafter—if you will not obey Me; but profane My holy name no more with your gifts and your idols. 40For on My holy mountain, on the mountain height of Israel," says the Lord GOD, "there all the house of Israel, all of them in the land, shall serve Me; there I will accept them, and there I will require your offerings and the firstfruits of your sacrifices, together with all your holy things. 41I will accept you as a sweet aroma when I bring you out from the peo-

20:29 [a]Literally *High Place*

THE MESSAGE

Since they were determined to live bad lives, I myself gave them statutes that could not produce goodness and laws that did not produce life. I abandoned them. Filthy in the gutter, they perversely sacrificed their firstborn children in the fire. The very horror should have shocked them into recognizing that I am GOD.'

27-29 "Therefore, speak to Israel, son of man. Tell them that GOD says, 'As if that wasn't enough, your parents further insulted me by betraying me. When I brought them into that land that I had solemnly promised with my upraised hand to give them, every time they saw a hill with a sex-and-religion shrine on it or a grove of trees where the sacred whores practiced, they were there, buying into the whole pagan system. I said to them, "What hill do you go to?" ' (It's still called "Whore Hills.")

30-31 "Therefore, say to Israel, 'The Message of GOD, the Master: You're making your lives filthy by copying the ways of your parents. In repeating their vile practices, you've become whores yourselves. In burning your children as sacrifices, you've become as filthy as your no-god idols—as recently as today!

" 'Am I going to put up with questions from people like you, Israel? As sure as I am the living God, I, GOD, the Master, refuse to be called into question by you!

32 " 'What you're secretly thinking is never going to happen. You're thinking, "We're going to be like everybody else, just like the other nations. We're going to worship gods we can make and control."

33-35 " 'As sure as I am the living God, says GOD, the Master, think again! With a mighty show of strength and a terrifying rush of anger, I will be King over you! I'll bring you back from the nations, collect you out of the countries to which you've been scattered, with a mighty show of strength and a terrifying rush of anger. I'll bring you to the desert of nations and haul you into court, where you'll be face-to-face with judgment.

36-38 " 'As I faced your parents with judgment in the desert of Egypt, so I'll face you with judgment. I'll scrutinize and search every person as you arrive, and I'll bring you under the bond of the covenant. I'll cull out the rebels and traitors. I'll lead them out of their exile, but I won't bring them back to Israel.

" 'Then you'll realize that I am GOD.

39-43 " 'But you, people of Israel, this is the Message of GOD, the Master, to you: Go ahead, serve your no-god idols! But later, you'll think better of it and quit throwing filth and mud on me with your pagan offerings and no-god idols. For on my holy mountain, the high mountain of Israel, I, GOD, the Master, tell you that the entire people of Israel will worship me. I'll receive them there with open arms. I'll demand your best gifts and offerings, all your holy sacrifices. What's more, I'll receive you as the best kind of offerings when I bring you

NEW KING JAMES VERSION

ples and gather you out of the countries where
you have been scattered; and I will be hallowed
in you before the Gentiles. 42 Then you shall
know that I *am* the LORD, when I bring you into
the land of Israel, into the country *for* which I
raised My hand in an oath to give to your fa-
thers. 43 And there you shall remember your
ways and all your doings with which you were
defiled; and you shall loathe yourselves in your
own sight because of all the evils that you have
committed. 44 Then you shall know that I *am* the
LORD, when I have dealt with you for My name's
sake, not according to your wicked ways nor ac-
cording to your corrupt doings, O house of Is-
rael," says the Lord GOD.' "

FIRE IN THE FOREST

45 Furthermore the word of the LORD came to
me, saying, 46 "Son of man, set your face toward
the south; preach against the south and proph-
esy against the forest land, the South,[a] 47 and say
to the forest of the South, 'Hear the word of the
LORD! Thus says the Lord GOD: "Behold, I will
kindle a fire in you, and it shall devour every
green tree and every dry tree in you; the blazing
flame shall not be quenched, and all faces from
the south to the north shall be scorched by it.
48 All flesh shall see that I, the LORD, have kin-
dled it; it shall not be quenched." ' "

49 Then I said, "Ah, Lord GOD! They say of me,
'Does he not speak parables?' "

BABYLON, THE SWORD OF GOD

21 And the word of the LORD came to me, say-
ing, 2 "Son of man, set your face toward
Jerusalem, preach against the holy places, and
prophesy against the land of Israel; 3 and say to
the land of Israel, 'Thus says the LORD: "Behold,
I *am* against you, and I will draw My sword out
of its sheath and cut off both righteous and
wicked from you. 4 Because I will cut off both
righteous and wicked from you, therefore My
sword shall go out of its sheath against all flesh
from south *to* north, 5 that all flesh may know
that I, the LORD, have drawn My sword out of its
sheath; it shall not return anymore." ' 6 Sigh
therefore, son of man, with a breaking heart,
and sigh with bitterness before their eyes. 7 And
it shall be when they say to you, 'Why are you
sighing?' that you shall answer, 'Because of the
news; when it comes, every heart will melt, all
hands will be feeble, every spirit will faint, and
all knees will be weak *as* water. Behold, it is
coming and shall be brought to pass,' says the
Lord GOD."

8 Again the word of the LORD came to me,
saying, 9 "Son of man, prophesy and say, 'Thus
says the LORD!' Say:

'A sword, a sword is sharpened
And also polished!
10 Sharpened to make a dreadful slaughter,
Polished to flash like lightning!
Should we then make mirth?
It despises the scepter of My son,
As it does all wood.
11 And He has given it to be polished,
That it may be handled;

20:46 [a]Hebrew *Negev*

THE MESSAGE

back from all the lands and countries in
which you've been scattered. I'll demon-
strate in the eyes of the world that I am The
Holy. When I return you to the land of Israel,
the land that I solemnly promised with up-
raised arm to give to your parents, you'll re-
alize that I am GOD. Then and there you'll
remember all that you've done, the way
you've lived that has made you so filthy—
and you'll loathe yourselves.

44 " 'But, dear Israel, you'll also realize that
I am GOD when I respond to you out of who
I am, not by what I feel about the evil lives
you've lived, the corrupt history you've com-
piled. Decree of GOD, the Master.' "

NOBODY WILL PUT OUT THE FIRE

45-46 GOD's Message came to me: "Son of man,
face south. Let the Message roll out against
the south. Prophesy against the wilderness
forest of the south.

47-48 "Tell the forest of the south, 'Listen to the
Message of GOD! GOD, the Master, says, I'll
set a fire in you that will burn up every tree,
dead trees and live trees alike. Nobody will
put out the fire. The whole country from
south to north will be blackened by it. Every-
one is going to see that I, GOD, started the
fire and that it's not going to be put out.' "

49 And I said, "O GOD, everyone is saying of
me, 'He just makes up stories.' "

A SWORD! A SWORD!

1-5 21 GOD's Message came to me: "Son of
man, now face Jerusalem and let the
Message roll out against the Sanctuary.
Prophesy against the land of Israel. Say,
'GOD's Message: I'm against you. I'm pulling
my sword from its sheath and killing both
the wicked and the righteous. Because I'm
treating everyone the same, good and bad,
everyone from south to north is going to feel
my sword! Everyone will know that I mean
business.'

6 "So, son of man, groan! Double up in
pain. Make a scene!

7 "When they ask you, 'Why all this groan-
ing, this carrying on?' say, 'Because of the
news that's coming. It'll knock the breath
out of everyone. Hearts will stop cold, knees
turn to rubber. Yes, it's coming. No stopping
it. Decree of GOD, the Master.' "

8-10 GOD's Message to me: "Son of man, proph-
esy. Tell them, 'The Master says:

" 'A sword! A sword!
razor-sharp and polished,
Sharpened to kill,
polished to flash like lightning!

" 'My child, you've despised the scepter of
Judah
by worshiping every tree-idol.

11 " 'The sword is made to glisten,
to be held and brandished.

NEW KING JAMES VERSION

This sword is sharpened, and it is polished
To be given into the hand of the slayer.'

12"Cry and wail, son of man;
For it will be against My people,
Against all the princes of Israel.
Terrors including the sword will be against My people;
Therefore strike *your* thigh.

13"Because *it is* a testing,
And what if *the sword* despises even the scepter?
The scepter shall be no *more*,"

says the Lord GOD.

14"You therefore, son of man, prophesy,
And strike *your* hands together.
The third time let the sword do double *damage*.
It *is* the sword *that* slays,
The sword that slays the great *men*,
That enters their private chambers.
15I have set the point of the sword against all their gates,
That the heart may melt and many may stumble.
Ah! *It is* made bright;
It is grasped for slaughter:

16"Swords at the ready!
Thrust right!
Set your blade!
Thrust left—
Wherever your edge is ordered!

17"I also will beat My fists together,
And I will cause My fury to rest;
I, the LORD, have spoken."

18The word of the LORD came to me again,
saying: 19"And son of man, appoint for yourself
two ways for the sword of the king of Babylon to
go; both of them shall go from the same land.
Make a sign; put *it* at the head of the road to the
city. 20Appoint a road for the sword to go to Rab-
bah of the Ammonites, and to Judah, into forti-
fied Jerusalem. 21For the king of Babylon stands
at the parting of the road, at the fork of the two
roads, to use divination: he shakes the arrows,
he consults the images, he looks at the liver. 22In
his right hand is the divination for Jerusalem: to
set up battering rams, to call for a slaughter, to
lift the voice with shouting, to set battering rams
against the gates, to heap up a *siege* mound, and
to build a wall. 23And it will be to them like a
false divination in the eyes of those who have
sworn oaths with them; but he will bring their in-
iquity to remembrance, that they may be taken.
24"Therefore thus says the Lord GOD: 'Be-
cause you have made your iniquity to be re-
membered, in that your transgressions are un-
covered, so that in all your doings your sins
appear—because you have come to remem-
brance, you shall be taken in hand.
25'Now to you, O profane, wicked prince of
Israel, whose day has come, whose iniquity *shall*
end, 26thus says the Lord GOD:

THE MESSAGE

It's sharpened and polished,
ready to be brandished by the killer.'

12 "Yell out and wail, son of man.
The sword is against my people!
The princes of Israel
and my people—abandoned to the sword!
Wring your hands!
Tear out your hair!

13 " 'Testing comes.
Why have you despised discipline?
You can't get around it.
Decree of GOD, the Master.'

14-17 "So, prophesy, son of man!
Clap your hands. Get their attention.
Tell them that the sword's coming down
once, twice, three times.
It's a sword to kill,
a sword for a massacre,
A sword relentless,
a sword inescapable—
People collapsing right and left,
going down like dominoes.
I've stationed a murderous sword
at every gate in the city,
Flashing like lightning,
brandished murderously.
Cut to the right, thrust to the left,
murderous, sharp-edged sword!
Then I'll clap my hands,
a signal that my anger is spent.
I, GOD, have spoken."

18-22 GOD's Message came to me: "Son of man,
lay out two roads for the sword of the king
of Babylon to take. Start them from the
same place. Place a signpost at the begin-
ning of each road. Post one sign to mark the
road of the sword to Rabbah of the Am-
monites. Post the other to mark the road to
Judah and Fort Jerusalem. The king of
Babylon stands at the fork in the road and
he decides by divination which of the two
roads to take. He draws straws, he throws
god-dice, he examines a goat liver. He opens
his right hand: The omen says, 'Head for
Jerusalem!' So he's on his way with batter-
ing rams, roused to kill, sounding the battle
cry, pounding down city gates, building
siege works.
23 "To the Judah leaders, who themselves
have sworn oaths, it will seem like a false
divination, but he will remind them of their
guilt, and so they'll be captured.
24 "So this is what GOD, the Master, says:
'Because your sin is now out in the open so
everyone can see what you've been doing,
you'll be taken captive.
25-27 " 'O Zedekiah, blasphemous and evil
prince of Israel: Time's up. It's "punishment

NEW KING JAMES VERSION

"Remove the turban, and take off the crown;
Nothing *shall remain* the same.
Exalt the humble, and humble the exalted.
27Overthrown, overthrown,
I will make it overthrown!
It shall be no *longer,*
Until He comes whose right it is,
And I will give it *to Him.*" '

A SWORD AGAINST THE AMMONITES

28"And you, son of man, prophesy and say,
'Thus says the Lord GOD concerning the Ammonites and concerning their reproach,' and say:

'A sword, a sword is drawn,
Polished for slaughter,
For consuming, for flashing—
29While they see false visions for you,
While they divine a lie to you,
To bring you on the necks of the wicked, the slain
Whose day has come,
Whose iniquity *shall* end.

30'Return *it* to its sheath.
I will judge you
In the place where you were created,
In the land of your nativity.
31I will pour out My indignation on you;
I will blow against you with the fire of My wrath,
And deliver you into the hands of brutal men *who are* skillful to destroy.
32You shall be fuel for the fire;
Your blood shall be in the midst of the land.
You shall not be remembered,
For I the LORD have spoken.' "

SINS OF JERUSALEM

22 Moreover the word of the LORD came to
me, saying, 2"Now, son of man, will you
judge, will you judge the bloody city? Yes, show
her all her abominations! 3Then say, 'Thus says
the Lord GOD: "The city sheds blood in her own
midst, that her time may come; and she makes
idols within herself to defile herself. 4You have
become guilty by the blood which you have
shed, and have defiled yourself with the idols
which you have made. You have caused your
days to draw near, and have come to *the end of*
your years; therefore I have made you a reproach to the nations, and a mockery to all
countries. 5*Those* near and *those* far from you
will mock you as infamous *and* full of tumult.
6"Look, the princes of Israel: each one has
used his power to shed blood in you. 7In you
they have made light of father and mother; in
your midst they have oppressed the stranger; in
you they have mistreated the fatherless and the
widow. 8You have despised My holy things and
profaned My Sabbaths. 9In you are men who
slander to cause bloodshed; in you are those
who eat on the mountains; in your midst they
commit lewdness. 10In you men uncover their fathers' nakedness; in you they violate women
who are set apart during their impurity. 11One
commits abomination with his neighbor's wife;
another lewdly defiles his daughter-in-law; and
another in you violates his sister, his father's

THE MESSAGE

payday." GOD says, Take your royal crown off your head. No more "business as usual." The underdog will be promoted and the top dog will be demoted. Ruins, ruins, ruins! I'll turn the whole place into ruins. And ruins it will remain until the one comes who has a right to it. Then I'll give it to him.'

28-32 "But, son of man, your job is to prophesy. Tell them, 'This is the Message from GOD, the Master, against the Ammonites and against their cruel taunts:

" 'A sword! A sword!
Bared to kill,
Sharp as a razor,
flashing like lightning.
Despite false sword propaganda
circulated in Ammon,
The sword will sever Ammonite necks,
for whom it's punishment payday.
Return the sword to the sheath! I'll judge
you in your home country,
in the land where you grew up.
I'll empty out my wrath on you,
breathe hot anger down your neck.
I'll give you to vicious men
skilled in torture.
You'll end up as stove-wood.
Corpses will litter your land.
Not so much as a memory will be left of
you.
I, GOD, have said so.' "

THE SCARECROW OF THE NATIONS

1-5 22 GOD's Message came to me: "Son of man, are you going to judge this bloody city or not? Come now, are you going to judge her? Do it! Face her with all her outrageous obscenities. Tell her, 'This is what GOD, the Master, says: You're a city murderous at the core, just asking for punishment. You're a city obsessed with no-god idols, making yourself filthy. In all your killing, you've piled up guilt. In all your idol-making, you've become filthy. You've forced a premature end to your existence. I'll put you on exhibit as the scarecrow of the nations, the world's worst joke. From far and near they'll deride you as infamous in filth, notorious for chaos.

6-12 " 'Your leaders, the princes of Israel among you, compete in crime. You're a community that's insolent to parents, abusive to outsiders, oppressive against orphans and widows. You treat my holy things with contempt and desecrate my Sabbaths. You have people spreading lies and spilling blood, flocking to the hills to the sex shrines and fornicating unrestrained. Incest is common. Men force themselves on women regardless of whether they're ready or willing. Sex is now anarchy. Anyone is fair game: neighbor, daughter-in-law, sister. Murder is for

NEW KING JAMES VERSION

daughter. [12]In you they take bribes to shed blood; you take usury and increase; you have made profit from your neighbors by extortion, and have forgotten Me," says the Lord GOD.

[13]"Behold, therefore, I beat My fists at the dishonest profit which you have made, and at the bloodshed which has been in your midst. [14]Can your heart endure, or can your hands remain strong, in the days when I shall deal with you? I, the LORD, have spoken, and will do *it*. [15]I will scatter you among the nations, disperse you throughout the countries, and remove your filthiness completely from you. [16]You shall defile yourself in the sight of the nations; then you shall know that I *am* the LORD." ' "

ISRAEL IN THE FURNACE

[17]The word of the LORD came to me, saying, [18]"Son of man, the house of Israel has become dross to Me; they *are* all bronze, tin, iron, and lead, in the midst of a furnace; they have become dross from silver. [19]Therefore thus says the Lord GOD: 'Because you have all become dross, therefore behold, I will gather you into the midst of Jerusalem. [20]*As men* gather silver, bronze, iron, lead, and tin into the midst of a furnace, to blow fire on it, to melt *it;* so I will gather *you* in My anger and in My fury, and I will leave *you there* and melt you. [21]Yes, I will gather you and blow on you with the fire of My wrath, and you shall be melted in its midst. [22]As silver is melted in the midst of a furnace, so shall you be melted in its midst; then you shall know that I, the LORD, have poured out My fury on you.' "

ISRAEL'S WICKED LEADERS

[23]And the word of the LORD came to me, saying, [24]"Son of man, say to her: 'You *are* a land that is not cleansed[a] or rained on in the day of indignation.' [25]The conspiracy of her prophets[a] in her midst is like a roaring lion tearing the prey; they have devoured people; they have taken treasure and precious things; they have made many widows in her midst. [26]Her priests have violated My law and profaned My holy things; they have not distinguished between the holy and unholy, nor have they made known *the difference* between the unclean and the clean; and they have hidden their eyes from My Sabbaths, so that I am profaned among them. [27]Her princes in her midst *are* like wolves tearing the prey, to shed blood, to destroy people, and to get dishonest gain. [28]Her prophets plastered them with untempered *mortar,* seeing false visions, and divining lies for them, saying, 'Thus says the Lord GOD,' when the LORD had not spoken. [29]The people of the land have used oppressions, committed robbery, and mistreated the poor and needy; and they wrongfully oppress the stranger. [30]So I sought for a man among them who would make a wall, and stand in the gap before Me on behalf of the land, that I should not destroy it; but I found no one. [31]Therefore I have poured out My indignation on them; I have consumed them with the fire of My wrath; and I have recompensed their deeds on their own heads," says the Lord GOD.

22:24 [a]Following Masoretic Text, Syriac, and Vulgate; Septuagint reads *showered upon.* **22:25** [a]Following Masoretic Text and Vulgate; Septuagint reads *princes;* Targum reads *scribes.*

THE MESSAGE

hire, usury is rampant, extortion is commonplace.
" 'And you've forgotten *me*. Decree of GOD, the Master.
13-14 " 'Now look! I've clapped my hands, calling everyone's attention to your rapacious
greed and your bloody brutalities. Can you
stick with it? Will you be able to keep at this
once I start dealing with you?
14-16 " 'I, GOD, have spoken. I'll put an end to
this. I'll throw you to the four winds. I'll
scatter you all over the world. I'll put a full
stop to your filthy living. You will be defiled,
spattered with your own mud in the eyes of
the nations. And you'll recognize that I am
GOD.' "

17-22 GOD's Message came to me: "Son of man,
the people of Israel are slag to me, the useless byproduct of refined copper, tin, iron,
and lead left at the smelter—a worthless
slag heap. So tell them, 'GOD, the Master,
has spoken: Because you've all become
worthless slag, you're on notice: I'll assemble you in Jerusalem. As men gather silver,
copper, iron, lead, and tin into a furnace and
blow fire on it to melt it down, so in my
wrath I'll gather you and melt you down. I'll
blow on you with the fire of my wrath to
melt you down in the furnace. As silver is
melted down, you'll be melted down. That
should get through to you. Then you'll recognize that I, GOD, have let my wrath loose
on you.' "

23-25 GOD's Message came to me: "Son of man,
tell her, 'You're a land that during the time I
was angry with you got no rain, not so much
as a spring shower. The leaders among you
became desperate, like roaring, ravaging lions killing indiscriminately. They grabbed
and looted, leaving widows in their wake.
26-29 " 'Your priests violated my law and desecrated my holy things. They can't tell the
difference between sacred and secular. They
tell people there's no difference between
right and wrong. They're contemptuous of
my holy Sabbaths, profaning me by trying
to pull me down to their level. Your politicians are like wolves prowling and killing
and rapaciously taking whatever they want.
Your preachers cover up for the politicians
by pretending to have received visions and
special revelations. They say, "This is what
GOD, the Master, says . . ." when GOD hasn't
said so much as one word. Extortion is rife,
robbery is epidemic, the poor and needy are
abused, outsiders are kicked around at will,
with no access to justice.'
30-31 "I looked for someone to stand up for me
against all this, to repair the defenses of the
city, to take a stand for me and stand in the
gap to protect this land so I wouldn't have to
destroy it. I couldn't find anyone. Not one.
So I'll empty out my wrath on them, burn
them to a crisp with my hot anger, serve
them with the consequences of all they've
done. Decree of GOD, the Master."

NEW KING JAMES VERSION

TWO HARLOT SISTERS

23 The word of the LORD came again to me, saying:

2"Son of man, there were two women,
The daughters of one mother.
3They committed harlotry in Egypt,
They committed harlotry in their youth;
Their breasts were there embraced,
Their virgin bosom was there pressed.
4Their names: Oholah[a] the elder and
Oholibah[b] her sister;
They were Mine,
And they bore sons and daughters.
As for their names,
Samaria *is* Oholah, and Jerusalem *is*
Oholibah.

THE OLDER SISTER, SAMARIA

5"Oholah played the harlot even though she
was Mine;
And she lusted for her lovers, the
neighboring Assyrians,
6*Who were* clothed in purple,
Captains and rulers,
All of them desirable young men,
Horsemen riding on horses.
7Thus she committed her harlotry with them,
All of them choice men of Assyria;
And with all for whom she lusted,
With all their idols, she defiled herself.
8She has never given up her harlotry *brought*
from Egypt,
For in her youth they had lain with her,
Pressed her virgin bosom,
And poured out their immorality upon her.

9"Therefore I have delivered her
Into the hand of her lovers,
Into the hand of the Assyrians,
For whom she lusted.
10They uncovered her nakedness,
Took away her sons and daughters,
And slew her with the sword;
She became a byword among women,
For they had executed judgment on her.

THE YOUNGER SISTER, JERUSALEM

11"Now although her sister Oholibah saw
this, she became more corrupt in her lust than
she, and in her harlotry more corrupt than her
sister's harlotry.

12"She lusted for the neighboring Assyrians,
Captains and rulers,
Clothed most gorgeously,
Horsemen riding on horses,
All of them desirable young men.
13Then I saw that she was defiled;
Both *took* the same way.
14But she increased her harlotry;
She looked at men portrayed on the wall,
Images of Chaldeans portrayed in
vermilion,
15Girded with belts around their waists,
Flowing turbans on their heads,

23:4 [a]Literally *Her Own Tabernacle* [b]Literally *My Tabernacle Is in Her*

THE MESSAGE

WILD WITH LUST

1-4 23 GOD's Message came to me: "Son of
man, there were two women, daughters
of the same mother. They became whores in
Egypt, whores from a young age. Their
breasts were fondled, their young bosoms
caressed. The older sister was named Oho-
lah, the younger was Oholibah. They were
my daughters, and they gave birth to sons
and daughters.
"Oholah is Samaria and Oholibah is
Jerusalem.
5-8 "Oholah started whoring while she was
still mine. She lusted after Assyrians as
lovers: military men smartly uniformed in
blue, ambassadors and governors, good-
looking young men mounted on fine horses.
Her lust was unrestrained. She was a whore
to the Assyrian elite. She compounded her
filth with the idols of those to whom she
gave herself in lust. She never slowed down.
The whoring she began while young in
Egypt she continued, sleeping with men
who played with her breasts and spent their
lust on her.
9-10 "So I left her to her Assyrian lovers, for
whom she was so obsessed with lust. They
ripped off her clothes, took away her chil-
dren, and then, the final indignity, killed her.
Among women her name became Shame—
history's judgment on her.
11-18 "Her sister Oholibah saw all this, but she
became even worse than her sister in lust
and whoring, if you can believe it. She also
went crazy with lust for Assyrians: ambas-
sadors and governors, military men smartly
dressed and mounted on fine horses—the
Assyrian elite. And I saw that she also had
become incredibly filthy. Both women fol-
lowed the same path. But Oholibah sur-
passed her sister. When she saw figures of
Babylonians carved in relief on the walls
and painted red, fancy belts around their
waists, elaborate turbans on their heads, all

NEW KING JAMES VERSION

All of them looking like captains,
In the manner of the Babylonians of Chaldea,
The land of their nativity.
16As soon as her eyes saw them,
She lusted for them
And sent messengers to them in Chaldea.

17"Then the Babylonians came to her, into the bed of love,
And they defiled her with their immorality;
So she was defiled by them, and alienated herself from them.
18She revealed her harlotry and uncovered her nakedness.
Then I alienated Myself from her,
As I had alienated Myself from her sister.

19"Yet she multiplied her harlotry
In calling to remembrance the days of her youth,
When she had played the harlot in the land of Egypt.
20For she lusted for her paramours,
Whose flesh *is like* the flesh of donkeys,
And whose issue *is like* the issue of horses.
21Thus you called to remembrance the lewdness of your youth,
When the Egyptians pressed your bosom
Because of your youthful breasts.

JUDGMENT ON JERUSALEM

22"Therefore, Oholibah, thus says the Lord GOD:

'Behold, I will stir up your lovers against you,
From whom you have alienated yourself,
And I will bring them against you from every side:
23The Babylonians,
All the Chaldeans,
Pekod, Shoa, Koa,
All the Assyrians with them,
All of them desirable young men,
Governors and rulers,
Captains and men of renown,
All of them riding on horses.
24And they shall come against you
With chariots, wagons, and war-horses,
With a horde of people.
They shall array against you
Buckler, shield, and helmet all around.

'I will delegate judgment to them,
And they shall judge you according to their judgments.
25I will set My jealousy against you,
And they shall deal furiously with you;
They shall remove your nose and your ears,
And your remnant shall fall by the sword;
They shall take your sons and your daughters,
And your remnant shall be devoured by fire.
26They shall also strip you of your clothes
And take away your beautiful jewelry.

27'Thus I will make you cease your lewdness and your harlotry

THE MESSAGE

of them looking important—famous Babylonians!—she went wild with lust and sent invitations to them in Babylon. The Babylonians came on the run, fornicated with her, made her dirty inside and out. When they had thoroughly debased her, she lost interest in them. Then she went public with her fornication. She exhibited her sex to the world.

18-21 "I turned my back on her just as I had on her sister. But that didn't slow her down. She went at her whoring harder than ever. She remembered when she was young, just starting out as a whore in Egypt. That whetted her appetite for more virile, vulgar, and violent lovers—stallions obsessive in their lust. She longed for the sexual prowess of her youth back in Egypt, where her firm young breasts were caressed and fondled.

22-27 " 'Therefore, Oholibah, this is the Message from GOD, the Master: I will incite your old lovers against you, lovers you got tired of and left in disgust. I'll bring them against you from every direction, Babylonians and all the Chaldeans, Pekod, Shoa, and Koa, and all Assyrians—good-looking young men, ambassadors and governors, elite officers and celebrities—all of them mounted on fine, spirited horses. They'll come down on you out of the north, armed to the teeth, bringing chariots and troops from all sides. I'll turn over the task of judgment to them. They'll punish you according to their rules. I'll stand totally and relentlessly against you as they rip into you furiously. They'll mutilate you, cutting off your ears and nose, killing at random. They'll enslave your children—and anybody left over will be burned. They'll rip off your clothes and steal your jewelry. I'll put a stop to your sluttish sex, the whoring life you began in Egypt. You won't look on whoring with fondness any-

NEW KING JAMES VERSION

Brought from the land of Egypt,
So that you will not lift your eyes to them,
Nor remember Egypt anymore.'

28"For thus says the Lord GOD: 'Surely I will
deliver you into the hand of those you hate, into
the hand *of those* from whom you alienated
yourself. 29They will deal hatefully with you,
take away all you have worked for, and leave
you naked and bare. The nakedness of your har-
lotry shall be uncovered, both your lewdness
and your harlotry. 30I will do these *things* to you
because you have gone as a harlot after the
Gentiles, because you have become defiled by
their idols. 31You have walked in the way of your
sister; therefore I will put her cup in your hand.'
32"Thus says the Lord GOD:

'You shall drink of your sister's cup,
The deep and wide one;
You shall be laughed to scorn
And held in derision;
It contains much.
33You will be filled with drunkenness and
sorrow,
The cup of horror and desolation,
The cup of your sister Samaria.
34You shall drink and drain it,
You shall break its shards,
And tear at your own breasts;
For I have spoken,'
Says the Lord GOD.

35"Therefore thus says the Lord GOD:

'Because you have forgotten Me and cast Me
behind your back,
Therefore you shall bear the *penalty*
Of your lewdness and your harlotry.' "

BOTH SISTERS JUDGED

36The LORD also said to me: "Son of man, will
you judge Oholah and Oholibah? Then declare
to them their abominations. 37For they have
committed adultery, and blood *is* on their hands.
They have committed adultery with their idols,
and even sacrificed their sons whom they bore
to Me, passing them through *the fire,* to devour
them. 38Moreover they have done this to Me:
They have defiled My sanctuary on the same
day and profaned My Sabbaths. 39For after they
had slain their children for their idols, on the
same day they came into My sanctuary to pro-
fane it; and indeed thus they have done in the
midst of My house.
40"Furthermore you sent for men to come
from afar, to whom a messenger *was* sent; and
there they came. And you washed yourself for
them, painted your eyes, and adorned yourself
with ornaments. 41You sat on a stately couch,
with a table prepared before it, on which you
had set My incense and My oil. 42The sound of a
carefree multitude *was* with her, and Sabeans
were brought from the wilderness with men of
the common sort, who put bracelets on their
wrists and beautiful crowns on their heads.
43Then I said concerning *her who had grown* old
in adulteries, 'Will they commit harlotry with
her now, and she *with them?*' 44Yet they went in

THE MESSAGE

more. You won't think back on Egypt with
stars in your eyes.
28-30 " 'A Message from GOD, the Master: I'm at
the point of abandoning you to those you
hate, to those by whom you're repulsed.
They'll treat you hatefully, leave you pub-
licly naked, your whore's body exposed in
the cruel glare of the sun. Your sluttish lust
will be exposed. Your lust has brought you to
this condition because you whored with pa-
gan nations and made yourself filthy with
their no-god idols.
31-34 " 'You copied the life of your sister. Now
I'll let you drink the cup she drank.

" 'This is the Message of GOD, the Master:
" 'You'll drink your sister's cup,
a cup canyon-deep and ocean-wide.
You'll be shunned and taunted
as you drink from that cup, full to the
brim.
You'll be falling-down-drunk and the tears
will flow
as you drink from that cup titanic with
terror:
It's the cup of your sister Samaria.
You'll drink it dry,
then smash it to bits and eat the pieces,
and end up tearing at your breasts.
I've given the word—
Decree of GOD, the Master.

35 " 'Therefore GOD, the Master, says, Be-
cause you've forgotten all about me, push-
ing me into the background, you now must
pay for what you've done—pay for your
sluttish sex and whoring life.' "

36-39 Then GOD said to me, "Son of man, will
you confront Oholah and Oholibah with
what they've done? Make them face their
outrageous obscenities, obscenities ranging
from adultery to murder. They committed
adultery with their no-god idols, sacrificed
the children they bore me in order to feed
their idols! And there is also this: They've
defiled my holy Sanctuary and desecrated
my holy Sabbaths. The same day that they
sacrificed their children to their idols, they
walked into my Sanctuary and defiled it.
That's what they did—in *my* house!
40-42 "Furthermore, they even sent out invita-
tions by special messenger to men far
away—and, sure enough, they came. They
bathed themselves, put on makeup and
provocative lingerie. They reclined on a
sumptuous bed, aromatic with incense and
oils—*my* incense and oils! The crowd gath-
ered, jostling and pushing, a drunken rab-
ble. They adorned the sisters with bracelets
on their arms and tiaras on their heads.
43-44 "I said, 'She's burned out on sex!' but that
didn't stop them. They kept banging on her
doors night and day as men do when they're

NEW KING JAMES VERSION

to her, as men go in to a woman who plays the
harlot; thus they went in to Oholah and
Oholibah, the lewd women. 45But righteous men
will judge them after the manner of adulter-
esses, and after the manner of women who shed
blood, because they *are* adulteresses, and blood
is on their hands.
46"For thus says the Lord GOD: 'Bring up an
assembly against them, give them up to trouble
and plunder. 47The assembly shall stone them
with stones and execute them with their swords;
they shall slay their sons and their daughters,
and burn their houses with fire. 48Thus I will
cause lewdness to cease from the land, that all
women may be taught not to practice your lewd-
ness. 49They shall repay you for your lewdness,
and you shall pay for your idolatrous sins. Then
you shall know that I *am* the Lord GOD.' "

SYMBOL OF THE COOKING POT

24 Again, in the ninth year, in the tenth
month, on the tenth *day* of the month, the
word of the LORD came to me, saying, 2"Son of
man, write down the name of the day, this very
day—the king of Babylon started his siege
against Jerusalem this very day. 3And utter a
parable to the rebellious house, and say to them,
'Thus says the Lord GOD:

"Put on a pot, set it on,
And also pour water into it.
4Gather pieces *of meat* in it,
Every good piece,
The thigh and the shoulder.
Fill *it* with choice cuts;
5Take the choice of the flock.
Also pile *fuel* bones under it,
Make it boil well,
And let the cuts simmer in it."

6'Therefore thus says the Lord GOD:

"Woe to the bloody city,
To the pot whose scum *is* in it,
And whose scum is not gone from it!
Bring it out piece by piece,
On which no lot has fallen.
7For her blood is in her midst;
She set it on top of a rock;
She did not pour it on the ground,
To cover it with dust.
8That it may raise up fury and take
vengeance,
I have set her blood on top of a rock,
That it may not be covered."

9'Therefore thus says the Lord GOD:

"Woe to the bloody city!
I too will make the pyre great.
10Heap on the wood,
Kindle the fire;
Cook the meat well,
Mix in the spices,
And let the cuts be burned up.

11"Then set the pot empty on the coals,
That it may become hot and its bronze may
burn,

THE MESSAGE

after a whore. That's how they used Oholah
and Oholibah, the worn-out whores.
45 "Righteous men will pronounce judg-
ment on them, giving out sentences for adul-
tery and murder. That was their lifework:
adultery and murder."
46-47 "GOD says, 'Let a mob loose on them: Ter-
ror! Plunder! Let the mob stone them and
hack them to pieces—kill all their children,
burn down their houses!
48-49 " 'I'll put an end to sluttish sex in this
country so that all women will be well
warned and not copy you. You'll pay the
price for all your obsessive sex. You'll pay in
full for your promiscuous affairs with idols.
And you'll realize that I am GOD, the Mas-
ter.' "

BRING THE POT TO A BOIL

1-5 24 The Message of GOD came to me in the
ninth year, the tenth month, and the
tenth day of the month: "Son of man, write
down this date. The king of Babylon has laid
siege to Jerusalem this very day. Tell this
company of rebels a story:

" 'Put on the soup pot.
Fill it with water.
Put chunks of meat into it,
all the choice pieces—loin and brisket.
Pick out the best soup bones
from the best of the sheep in the flock.
Pile wood beneath the pot.
Bring it to a boil
and cook the soup.

6 " 'GOD, the Master, says:

" 'Doom to the city of murder,
to the pot thick with scum,
thick with a filth that can't be scoured.
Empty the pot piece by piece;
don't bother who gets what.

7-8 " 'The blood from murders
has stained the whole city;
Blood runs bold on the street stones,
with no one bothering to wash it off—
Blood out in the open to public view
to provoke my wrath,
to trigger my vengeance.

9-12 " 'Therefore, this is what GOD, the Master,
says:

" 'Doom to the city of murder!
I, too, will pile on the wood.
Stack the wood high,
light the match,
Cook the meat, spice it well, pour out the
broth,
and then burn the bones.
Then I'll set the empty pot on the coals
and heat it red-hot so the bronze glows,

New King James Version

That its filthiness may be melted in it,
That its scum may be consumed.
12She has grown weary with lies,
And her great scum has not gone from her.
Let her scum *be* in the fire!
13In your filthiness *is* lewdness.
Because I have cleansed you, and you were not cleansed,
You will not be cleansed of your filthiness anymore,
Till I have caused My fury to rest upon you.
14I, the LORD, have spoken *it;*
It shall come to pass, and I will do *it;*
I will not hold back,
Nor will I spare,
Nor will I relent;
According to your ways
And according to your deeds
They[a] will judge you,"
Says the Lord GOD.' "

The Prophet's Wife Dies

15Also the word of the LORD came to me, say-
ing, 16"Son of man, behold, I take away from you
the desire of your eyes with one stroke; yet you
shall neither mourn nor weep, nor shall your tears
run down. 17Sigh in silence, make no mourning
for the dead; bind your turban on your head, and
put your sandals on your feet; do not cover *your*
lips, and do not eat man's bread *of sorrow.*"
18So I spoke to the people in the morning,
and at evening my wife died; and the next morn-
ing I did as I was commanded.
19And the people said to me, "Will you not
tell us what these *things signify* to us, that you
behave so?"
20Then I answered them, "The word of the
LORD came to me, saying, 21'Speak to the house of
Israel, "Thus says the Lord GOD: 'Behold, I will
profane My sanctuary, your arrogant boast, the
desire of your eyes, the delight of your soul; and
your sons and daughters whom you left behind
shall fall by the sword. 22And you shall do as I
have done; you shall not cover *your* lips nor eat
man's bread *of sorrow.* 23Your turbans shall be on
your heads and your sandals on your feet; you
shall neither mourn nor weep, but you shall pine
away in your iniquities and mourn with one an-
other. 24Thus Ezekiel is a sign to you; according to
all that he has done you shall do; and when this
comes, you shall know that I *am* the Lord GOD.' "
25'And you, son of man—*will it* not *be* in the
day when I take from them their stronghold, their
joy and their glory, the desire of their eyes, and
that on which they set their minds, their sons and
their daughters: 26*that* on that day one who es-
capes will come to you to let *you* hear *it* with *your*
ears? 27On that day your mouth will be opened to
him who has escaped; you shall speak and no
longer be mute. Thus you will be a sign to them,
and they shall know that I *am* the LORD.' "

Proclamation Against Ammon

25 The word of the LORD came to me, saying,
2"Son of man, set your face against the
Ammonites, and prophesy against them. 3Say to
the Ammonites, 'Hear the word of the Lord GOD!
Thus says the Lord GOD: "Because you said,

24:14 [a]Septuagint, Syriac, Targum, and Vulgate read *I.*

The Message

So the germs are killed
and the corruption is burned off.
But it's hopeless. It's too far gone.
The filth is too thick.

13-14 " 'Your encrusted filth is your filthy sex. I wanted to clean you up, but you wouldn't let me. I'll make no more attempts at cleaning you up until my anger quiets down. I, GOD, have said it, and I'll do it. I'm not holding back. I've run out of compassion. I'm not changing my mind. You're getting exactly what's coming to you. Decree of GOD, the Master.' "

No Tears

15-17 GOD's Message came to me: "Son of man, I'm about to take from you the delight of your life—a real blow, I know. But, please, no tears. Keep your grief to yourself. No public mourning. Get dressed as usual and go about your work—none of the usual funeral rituals."

18 I preached to the people in the morning. That evening my wife died. The next morning I did as I'd been told.

19 The people came to me, saying, "Tell us why you're acting like this. What does it mean, anyway?"

20-21 So I told them, "GOD's Word came to me, saying, 'Tell the family of Israel, This is what GOD, the Master, says: I will desecrate my Sanctuary, your proud impregnable fort, the delight of your life, your heart's desire. The children you left behind will be killed.

22-24 " 'Then you'll do exactly as I've done. You'll perform none of the usual funeral rituals. You'll get dressed as usual and go about your work. No tears. But your sins will eat away at you from within and you'll groan among yourselves. Ezekiel will be your example. The way he did it is the way you'll do it.

" 'When this happens you'll recognize that I am GOD, the Master.' "

25-27 "And you, son of man: The day I take away the people's refuge, their great joy, the delight of their life, what they've most longed for, along with all their children—on that very day a survivor will arrive and tell you what happened to the city. You'll break your silence and start talking again, talking to the survivor. Again, you'll be an example for them. And they'll recognize that I am GOD."

Acts of Vengeance

1-5 25 GOD's Message came to me:

"Son of man, face Ammon and preach against the people: Listen to the Message of GOD, the Master. This is what GOD has to

New King James Version

'Aha!' against My sanctuary when it was profaned, and against the land of Israel when it was desolate, and against the house of Judah when they went into captivity, 4indeed, therefore, I will deliver you as a possession to the men of the East, and they shall set their encampments among you and make their dwellings among you; they shall eat your fruit, and they shall drink your milk. 5And I will make Rabbah a stable for camels and Ammon a resting place for flocks. Then you shall know that I *am* the LORD."

6'For thus says the Lord GOD: "Because you clapped *your* hands, stamped your feet, and rejoiced in heart with all your disdain for the land of Israel, 7indeed, therefore, I will stretch out My hand against you, and give you as plunder to the nations; I will cut you off from the peoples, and I will cause you to perish from the countries; I will destroy you, and you shall know that I *am* the LORD."

Proclamation Against Moab

8'Thus says the Lord GOD: "Because Moab and Seir say, 'Look! The house of Judah *is* like all the nations,' 9therefore, behold, I will clear the territory of Moab of cities, of the cities on its frontier, the glory of the country, Beth Jeshimoth, Baal Meon, and Kirjathaim. 10To the men of the East I will give it as a possession, together with the Ammonites, that the Ammonites may not be remembered among the nations. 11And I will execute judgments upon Moab, and they shall know that I *am* the LORD."

Proclamation Against Edom

12'Thus says the Lord GOD: "Because of what Edom did against the house of Judah by taking vengeance, and has greatly offended by avenging itself on them," 13therefore thus says the Lord GOD: "I will also stretch out My hand against Edom, cut off man and beast from it, and make it desolate from Teman; Dedan shall fall by the sword. 14I will lay My vengeance on Edom by the hand of My people Israel, that they may do in Edom according to My anger and according to My fury; and they shall know My vengeance," says the Lord GOD.

Proclamation Against Philistia

15'Thus says the Lord GOD: "Because the Philistines dealt vengefully and took vengeance with a spiteful heart, to destroy because of the old hatred," 16therefore thus says the Lord GOD: "I will stretch out My hand against the Philistines, and I will cut off the Cherethites and destroy the remnant of the seacoast. 17I will execute great vengeance on them with furious rebukes; and they shall know that I *am* the LORD, when I lay My vengeance upon them." ' "

Proclamation Against Tyre

26 And it came to pass in the eleventh year, on the first *day* of the month, *that* the word of the LORD came to me, saying, 2"Son of man, because Tyre has said against Jerusalem, 'Aha! She is broken who *was* the gateway of the peoples; now she is turned over to me; I shall be filled; she is laid waste.'

The Message

say: Because you cheered when my Sanctuary was desecrated and the land of Judah was devastated and the people of Israel were taken into exile, I'm giving you over to the people of the east. They'll move in and make themselves at home, eating the food right off your tables and drinking your milk. I'll turn your capital, Rabbah, into pasture for camels and all your villages into corrals for flocks. Then you'll realize that I am GOD.

6-7 "GOD, the Master, says, Because you clapped and cheered, venting all your malicious contempt against the land of Israel, I'll step in and hand you out as loot—first come, first served. I'll cross you off the roster of nations. There'll be nothing left of you. And you'll realize that I am GOD."

8-11 "GOD, the Master, says: Because Moab said, 'Look, Judah's nothing special,' I'll lay wide open the flank of Moab by exposing its lovely frontier villages to attack: Beth-jeshimoth, Baal-meon, and Kiriathaim. I'll lump Moab in with Ammon and give them to the people of the east for the taking. Ammon won't be heard from again. I'll punish Moab severely. And they'll realize that I am GOD."

12-14 "GOD, the Master, says: Because Edom reacted against the people of Judah in spiteful revenge and was so criminally vengeful against them, therefore I, GOD, the Master, will oppose Edom and kill the lot of them, people and animals both. I'll waste it—corpses stretched from Teman to Dedan. I'll use my people Israel to bring my vengeance down on Edom. My wrath will fuel their action. And they'll realize it's *my* vengeance. Decree of GOD the Master."

15-17 "GOD, the Master, says: Because the Philistines were so spitefully vengeful—all those centuries of stored-up malice!—and did their best to destroy Judah, therefore I, GOD, the Master, will oppose the Philistines and cut down the Cretans and anybody else left along the seacoast. Huge acts of vengeance, massive punishments! When I bring vengeance, they'll realize that I am GOD."

As the Waves of the Sea, Surging Against the Shore

1-2 26 In the eleventh year, on the first day of the month, GOD's Message came to me: "Son of man, Tyre cheered when they got the news of Jerusalem, exclaiming,

" 'Good! The gateway city is smashed!
Now all her business comes my way.
She's in ruins
and I'm in clover.'

New King James Version

3“Therefore thus says the Lord God: ‘Behold, I *am* against you, O Tyre, and will cause many nations to come up against you, as the sea causes its waves to come up. 4And they shall destroy the walls of Tyre and break down her towers; I will also scrape her dust from her, and make her like the top of a rock. 5It shall be *a place for* spreading nets in the midst of the sea, for I have spoken,’ says the Lord God; ‘it shall become plunder for the nations. 6Also her daughter *villages* which *are* in the fields shall be slain by the sword. Then they shall know that I am the Lord.’

7“For thus says the Lord God: ‘Behold, I will bring against Tyre from the north Nebuchadnezzar[a] king of Babylon, king of kings, with horses, with chariots, and with horsemen, and an army with many people. 8He will slay with the sword your daughter *villages* in the fields; he will heap up a siege mound against you, build a wall against you, and raise a defense against you. 9He will direct his battering rams against your walls, and with his axes he will break down your towers. 10Because of the abundance of his horses, their dust will cover you; your walls will shake at the noise of the horsemen, the wagons, and the chariots, when he enters your gates, as men enter a city that has been breached. 11With the hooves of his horses he will trample all your streets; he will slay your people by the sword, and your strong pillars will fall to the ground. 12They will plunder your riches and pillage your merchandise; they will break down your walls and destroy your pleasant houses; they will lay your stones, your timber, and your soil in the midst of the water. 13I will put an end to the sound of your songs, and the sound of your harps shall be heard no more. 14I will make you like the top of a rock; you shall be *a place for* spreading nets, and you shall never be rebuilt, for I the Lord have spoken,’ says the Lord God.

15“Thus says the Lord God to Tyre: ‘Will the coastlands not shake at the sound of your fall, when the wounded cry, when slaughter is made in the midst of you? 16Then all the princes of the sea will come down from their thrones, lay aside their robes, and take off their embroidered garments; they will clothe themselves with trembling; they will sit on the ground, tremble *every* moment, and be astonished at you. 17And they will take up a lamentation for you, and say to you:

“How you have perished,
O one inhabited by seafaring men,
O renowned city,
Who was strong at sea,
She and her inhabitants,
Who caused their terror *to be* on all her
inhabitants!
18Now the coastlands tremble on the day of
your fall;
Yes, the coastlands by the sea are troubled
at your departure.” ’

26:7 [a]Hebrew *Nebuchadrezzar*, and so elsewhere in this book

The Message

3-6 “Therefore, God, the Master, has this to say:

“ ‘I’m against you, Tyre,
and I’ll bring many nations surging
against you,
as the waves of the sea surging against
the shore.
They’ll smash the city walls of Tyre
and break down her towers.
I’ll wash away the soil
and leave nothing but bare rock.
She’ll be an island of bare rock in the
ocean,
good for nothing but drying fishnets.
Yes, I’ve said so.’ Decree of God, the Master.
‘She’ll be loot, free pickings for the
nations!
Her surrounding villages will be butchered.
Then they’ll realize that I am God.’

7-14 “God, the Master, says: Look! Out of the north I’m bringing Nebuchadnezzar king of Babylon, a king’s king, down on Tyre. He’ll come with chariots and horses and riders—a huge army. He’ll massacre your surrounding villages and lay siege to you. He’ll build siege ramps against your walls. A forest of shields will advance against you! He’ll pummel your walls with his battering rams and shatter your towers with his iron weapons. You’ll be covered with dust from his horde of horses—a thundering herd of war horses pouring through the breaches, pulling chariots. Oh, it will be an earthquake of an army and a city in shock! Horses will stampede through the streets. Your people will be slaughtered and your huge pillars strewn like matchsticks. The invaders will steal and loot—all that wealth, all that stuff! They’ll knock down your fine houses and dump the stone and timber rubble into the sea. And your parties, your famous good-time parties, will be no more. No more songs, no more lutes. I’ll reduce you to an island of bare rock, good for nothing but drying fishnets. You’ll never be rebuilt. I, God, have said so. Decree of God, the Master.

Introduced to the Terrors of Death

15 “This is the Message of God, the Master, to Tyre: Won’t the ocean islands shake at the crash of your collapse, at the groans of your wounded, at your mayhem and massacre?

16-18 “All up and down the coast, the princes will come down from their thrones, take off their royal robes and fancy clothes, and wrap themselves in sheer terror. They’ll sit on the ground, shaken to the core, horrified at you. Then they’ll begin chanting a funeral song over you:

“ ‘Sunk! Sunk to the bottom of the sea,
famous city on the sea!
Power of the seas,
you and your people,
Intimidating everyone
who lived in your shadows.
But now the islands are shaking
at the sound of your crash,
Ocean islands in tremors
from the impact of your fall.’

NEW KING JAMES VERSION

19"For thus says the Lord GOD: 'When I make
you a desolate city, like cities that are not inhab-
ited, when I bring the deep upon you, and great
waters cover you, 20then I will bring you down
with those who descend into the Pit, to the peo-
ple of old, and I will make you dwell in the low-
est part of the earth, in places desolate from an-
tiquity, with those who go down to the Pit, so
that you may never be inhabited; and I shall es-
tablish glory in the land of the living. 21I will
make you a terror, and you *shall be* no *more;*
though you are sought for, you will never be
found again,' says the Lord GOD."

LAMENTATION FOR TYRE

27 The word of the LORD came again to me,
saying, 2"Now, son of man, take up a
lamentation for Tyre, 3and say to Tyre, 'You who
are situated at the entrance of the sea, merchant
of the peoples on many coastlands, thus says the
Lord GOD:

"O Tyre, you have said,
'I *am* perfect in beauty.'
4Your borders *are* in the midst of the seas.
Your builders have perfected your beauty.
5They made all *your* planks of fir trees from
Senir;
They took a cedar from Lebanon to make
you a mast.
6*Of* oaks from Bashan they made your oars;
The company of Ashurites have inlaid your
planks
With ivory from the coasts of Cyprus.[a]
7Fine embroidered linen from Egypt was
what you spread for your sail;
Blue and purple from the coasts of Elishah
was what covered you.

8"Inhabitants of Sidon and Arvad were your
oarsmen;
Your wise men, O Tyre, were in you;
They became your pilots.
9Elders of Gebal and its wise men
Were in you to caulk your seams;
All the ships of the sea
And their oarsmen were in you
To market your merchandise.

10"Those from Persia, Lydia,[a] and Libya[b]
Were in your army as men of war;
They hung shield and helmet in you;
They gave splendor to you.
11Men of Arvad with your army *were* on your
walls *all* around,
And the men of Gammad were in your
towers;
They hung their shields on your walls *all*
around;
They made your beauty perfect.

12"Tarshish *was* your merchant because of
your many luxury goods. They gave you silver,
iron, tin, and lead for your goods. 13Javan, Tubal,
and Meshech *were* your traders. They bartered
human lives and vessels of bronze for your mer-
chandise.

27:6 [a]Hebrew *Kittim,* western lands, especially Cyprus
27:10 [a]Hebrew *Lud* [b]Hebrew *Put*

THE MESSAGE

19-21 "The Message of GOD, the Master: 'When
I turn you into a wasted city, a city empty of
people, a ghost town, and when I bring up
the great ocean deeps and cover you, then
I'll push you down among those who go to
the grave, the long, long dead. I'll make you
live there, in the grave in old ruins, with the
buried dead. You'll never see the land of the
living again. I'll introduce you to the terrors
of death and that'll be the end of you. They'll
send out search parties for you, but you'll
never be found. Decree of GOD, the Master.'
"

TYRE, GATEWAY TO THE SEA

1-9 27 GOD's Message came to me: "You, son
of man, raise a funeral song over Tyre.
Tell Tyre, gateway to the sea, merchant to
the world, trader among the far-off islands,
'This is what GOD, the Master, says:

" 'You boast, Tyre:
"I'm the perfect ship—stately,
handsome."
You ruled the high seas from
a real beauty, crafted to perfection.
Your planking came from
Mount Hermon junipers.
A Lebanon cedar
supplied your mast.
They made your oars
from sturdy Bashan oaks.
Cypress from Cyprus inlaid with ivory
was used for the decks.
Your sail and flag were of colorful
embroidered linen from Egypt.
Your purple deck awnings
also came from Cyprus.
Men of Sidon and Arvad pulled the oars.
Your seasoned seamen, O Tyre, were the
crew.
Ship's carpenters
were old salts from Byblos.
All the ships of the sea and their sailors
clustered around you to barter for your
goods.

10-11 " 'Your army was composed of soldiers
from Paras, Lud, and Put,
Elite troops in uniformed splendor.
They put you on the map!
Your city police were imported from
Arvad, Helech, and Gammad.
They hung their shields from the city walls,
a final, perfect touch to your beauty.

12 " 'Tarshish carried on business with you
because of your great wealth. They worked
for you, trading in silver, iron, tin, and lead
for your products.
13 " 'Greece, Tubal, and Meshech did busi-
ness with you, trading slaves and bronze for
your products.

NEW KING JAMES VERSION

14 Those from the house of Togarmah traded for
your wares with horses, steeds, and mules. 15 The
men of Dedan *were* your traders; many isles
were the market of your hand. They brought
you ivory tusks and ebony as payment. 16 Syria
was your merchant because of the abundance of
goods you made. They gave you for your wares
emeralds, purple, embroidery, fine linen, corals,
and rubies. 17 Judah and the land of Israel *were*
your traders. They traded for your merchandise
wheat of Minnith, millet, honey, oil, and balm.
18 Damascus *was* your merchant because of the
abundance of goods you made, because of your
many luxury items, with the wine of Helbon and
with white wool. 19 Dan and Javan paid for your
wares, traversing back and forth. Wrought iron,
cassia, and cane were among your merchandise.
20 Dedan *was* your merchant in saddlecloths for
riding. 21 Arabia and all the princes of Kedar
were your regular merchants. They traded with
you in lambs, rams, and goats. 22 The merchants
of Sheba and Raamah *were* your merchants.
They traded for your wares the choicest spices,
all kinds of precious stones, and gold. 23 Haran,
Canneh, Eden, the merchants of Sheba, Assyria,
and Chilmad *were* your merchants. 24 These
were your merchants in choice items—in purple
clothes, in embroidered garments, in chests of
multicolored apparel, in sturdy woven cords,
which were in your marketplace.

25 "The ships of Tarshish were carriers of your
merchandise.
You were filled and very glorious in the
midst of the seas.
26 Your oarsmen brought you into many waters,
But the east wind broke you in the midst of
the seas.

27 "Your riches, wares, and merchandise,
Your mariners and pilots,
Your caulkers and merchandisers,
All your men of war who *are* in you,
And the entire company which *is* in your
midst,
Will fall into the midst of the seas on the
day of your ruin.
28 The common-land will shake at the sound of
the cry of your pilots.

29 "All who handle the oar,
The mariners,
All the pilots of the sea
Will come down from their ships *and* stand
on the shore.
30 They will make their voice heard because of
you;
They will cry bitterly and cast dust on their
heads;
They will roll about in ashes;
31 They will shave themselves completely bald
because of you,
Gird themselves with sackcloth,
And weep for you
With bitterness of heart *and* bitter wailing.
32 In their wailing for you
They will take up a lamentation,
And lament for you:
'What *city is* like Tyre,
Destroyed in the midst of the sea?

THE MESSAGE

14 " 'Beth-togarmah traded work horses,
war horses, and mules for your products.
15 " 'The people of Rhodes did business with
you. Many far-off islands traded with you in
ivory and ebony.
16 " 'Edom did business with you because of
all your goods. They traded for your products with agate, purple textiles, embroidered cloth, fine linen, coral, and rubies.
17 " 'Judah and Israel did business with you.
They traded for your products with premium wheat, millet, honey, oil, and balm.
18 " 'Damascus, attracted by your vast array
of products and well-stocked warehouses,
carried on business with you, trading in
wine from Helbon and wool from Zahar.
19 " 'Danites and Greeks from Uzal traded
with you, using wrought iron, cinnamon,
and spices.
20 " 'Dedan traded with you for saddle blankets.
21 " 'Arabia and all the Bedouin sheiks of
Kedar traded lambs, rams, and goats with
you.
22 " 'Traders from Sheba and Raamah in
South Arabia carried on business with you
in premium spices, precious stones, and
gold.
23-24 " 'Haran, Canneh, and Eden from the east
in Assyria and Media traded with you,
bringing elegant clothes, dyed textiles, and
elaborate carpets to your bazaars.
25 " 'The great Tarshish ships were your
freighters, importing and exporting. Oh, it
was big business for you, trafficking the
seaways!

26-32 " 'Your sailors row mightily,
taking you into the high seas.
Then a storm out of the east
shatters your ship in the ocean deep.
Everything sinks—your rich goods and
products,
sailors and crew, ship's carpenters and
soldiers,
Sink to the bottom of the sea.
Total shipwreck.
The cries of your sailors
reverberate on shore.
Sailors everywhere abandon ship.
Veteran seamen swim for dry land.
They cry out in grief,
a choir of bitter lament over you.
They smear their faces with ashes,
shave their heads,
Wear rough burlap,
wildly keening their loss.
They raise their funeral song:
"Who on the high seas is like Tyre!"

NEW KING JAMES VERSION

33'When your wares went out by sea,
You satisfied many people;
You enriched the kings of the earth
With your many luxury goods and your merchandise.
34But you are broken by the seas in the depths of the waters;
Your merchandise and the entire company will fall in your midst.
35All the inhabitants of the isles will be astonished at you;
Their kings will be greatly afraid,
And *their* countenance will be troubled.
36The merchants among the peoples will hiss at you;
You will become a horror, and *be* no more forever.' " ' "

PROCLAMATION AGAINST THE KING OF TYRE

28 The word of the LORD came to me again,
saying, 2"Son of man, say to the prince of
Tyre, 'Thus says the Lord GOD:

"Because your heart *is* lifted up,
And you say, 'I *am* a god,
I sit *in* the seat of gods,
In the midst of the seas,'
Yet you *are* a man, and not a god,
Though you set your heart as the heart of a god
3(Behold, you *are* wiser than Daniel!
There is no secret that can be hidden from you!
4With your wisdom and your understanding
You have gained riches for yourself,
And gathered gold and silver into your treasuries;
5By your great wisdom in trade you have increased your riches,
And your heart is lifted up because of your riches),"

6'Therefore thus says the Lord GOD:

"Because you have set your heart as the heart of a god,
7Behold, therefore, I will bring strangers against you,
The most terrible of the nations;
And they shall draw their swords against the beauty of your wisdom,
And defile your splendor.
8They shall throw you down into the Pit,
And you shall die the death of the slain
In the midst of the seas.

9"Will you still say before him who slays you,
'I *am* a god'?
But you *shall be* a man, and not a god,
In the hand of him who slays you.
10You shall die the death of the uncircumcised
By the hand of aliens;
For I have spoken," says the Lord GOD.' "

LAMENTATION FOR THE KING OF TYRE

11Moreover the word of the LORD came to
me, saying, 12"Son of man, take up a lamenta-
tion for the king of Tyre, and say to him, 'Thus
says the Lord GOD:

THE MESSAGE

33-36 " 'As you crisscrossed the seas with your products,
you satisfied many peoples.
Your worldwide trade
made earth's kings rich.
And now you're battered to bits by the waves,
sunk to the bottom of the sea,
And everything you've bought and sold
has sunk to the bottom with you.
Everyone on shore looks on in terror.
The hair of kings stands on end,
their faces drawn and haggard!
The buyers and sellers of the world
throw up their hands:
This horror can't happen!
Oh, this *has* happened!' "

THE MONEY HAS GONE TO YOUR HEAD

1-5 28 GOD'S Message came to me, "Son of
man, tell the prince of Tyre, 'This is what
GOD, the Master, says:

" 'Your heart is proud,
going around saying, "I'm a god.
I sit on God's divine throne,
ruling the sea"—
You, a mere mortal,
not even close to being a god,
A mere mortal
trying to be a god.
Look, you think you're smarter than Daniel.
No enigmas can stump you.
Your sharp intelligence
made you world-wealthy.
You piled up gold and silver
in your banks.
You used your head well,
worked good deals, made a lot of money.
But the money has gone to your head,
swelled your head—what a big head!

6-11 " 'Therefore, GOD, the Master, says:

" 'Because you're acting like a god,
pretending to *be* a god,
I'm giving fair warning: I'm bringing strangers down on you,
the most vicious of all nations.
They'll pull their swords and make hash
of your reputation for knowing it all.
They'll puncture the balloon
of your god-pretensions.
They'll bring you down from your self-made pedestal
and bury you in the deep blue sea.
Will you protest to your assassins,
"You can't do that! I'm a god"?
To them you're a mere mortal.
They're killing a man, not a god.
You'll die like a stray dog,
killed by strangers—
Because I said so.
Decree of GOD, the Master.' "

11-19 GOD'S Message came to me: "Son of man,
raise a funeral song over the king of Tyre.
Tell him, A Message from GOD, the Master:

NEW KING JAMES VERSION

"You *were* the seal of perfection,
Full of wisdom and perfect in beauty.
13 You were in Eden, the garden of God;
Every precious stone *was* your covering:
The sardius, topaz, and diamond,
Beryl, onyx, and jasper,
Sapphire, turquoise, and emerald with gold.
The workmanship of your timbrels and pipes
Was prepared for you on the day you were created.

14 "You *were* the anointed cherub who covers;
I established you;
You were on the holy mountain of God;
You walked back and forth in the midst of fiery stones.
15 You *were* perfect in your ways from the day you were created,
Till iniquity was found in you.

16 "By the abundance of your trading
You became filled with violence within,
And you sinned;
Therefore I cast you as a profane thing
Out of the mountain of God;
And I destroyed you, O covering cherub,
From the midst of the fiery stones.

17 "Your heart was lifted up because of your beauty;
You corrupted your wisdom for the sake of your splendor;
I cast you to the ground,
I laid you before kings,
That they might gaze at you.

18 "You defiled your sanctuaries
By the multitude of your iniquities,
By the iniquity of your trading;
Therefore I brought fire from your midst;
It devoured you,
And I turned you to ashes upon the earth
In the sight of all who saw you.
19 All who knew you among the peoples are astonished at you;
You have become a horror,
And *shall be* no more forever." ' "

PROCLAMATION AGAINST SIDON

20 Then the word of the LORD came to me, say-
ing, 21 "Son of man, set your face toward Sidon,
and prophesy against her, 22 and say, 'Thus says
the Lord GOD:

"Behold, I *am* against you, O Sidon;
I will be glorified in your midst;
And they shall know that I *am* the LORD,
When I execute judgments in her and am hallowed in her.
23 For I will send pestilence upon her,
And blood in her streets;
The wounded shall be judged in her midst
By the sword against her on every side;
Then they shall know that I *am* the LORD.

24 "And there shall no longer be a pricking
brier or a painful thorn for the house of Israel
from among all *who are* around them, who de-
spise them. Then they shall know that I *am* the
Lord GOD."

THE MESSAGE

"You had everything going for you.
You were in Eden, God's garden.
You were dressed in splendor,
your robe studded with jewels:
Carnelian, peridot, and moonstone,
beryl, onyx, and jasper,
Sapphire, turquoise, and emerald,
all in settings of engraved gold.
A robe was prepared for you
the same day you were created.
You were the anointed cherub.
I placed you on the mountain of God.
You strolled in magnificence
among the stones of fire.
From the day of your creation
you were sheer perfection . . .
and then imperfection—evil!—
was detected in you.
In much buying and selling
you turned violent, you sinned!
I threw you, disgraced, off the mountain of God.
I threw you out—you, the anointed angel-cherub.
No more strolling among the gems of fire for you!
Your beauty went to your head.
You corrupted wisdom
by using it to get worldly fame.
I threw you to the ground,
sent you sprawling before an audience of kings
and let them gloat over your demise.
By sin after sin after sin,
by your corrupt ways of doing business,
you defiled your holy places of worship.
So I set a fire around and within you.
It burned you up. I reduced you to ashes.
All anyone sees now
when they look for you is ashes,
a pitiful mound of ashes.
All who once knew you
now throw up their hands:
'This can't have happened!
This *has* happened!' "

20-23 GOD's Message came to me: "Son of man,
confront Sidon. Preach against it. Say, 'Mes-
sage from GOD, the Master:

" 'Look! I'm against you, Sidon.
I intend to be known for who I truly am among you.'
They'll know that I am GOD
when I set things right
and reveal my holy presence.
I'll order an epidemic of disease there,
along with murder and mayhem in the streets.
People will drop dead right and left,
as war presses in from every side.
Then they'll realize that I mean business,
that I am GOD.

24 "No longer will Israel have to put up with
their thistle-and-thorn neighbors
Who have treated them so contemptuously.
And they also will realize that I am GOD."

NEW KING JAMES VERSION

ISRAEL'S FUTURE BLESSING

25 'Thus says the Lord GOD: "When I have gathered the house of Israel from the peoples among whom they are scattered, and am hallowed in them in the sight of the Gentiles, then they will dwell in their own land which I gave to My servant Jacob. 26 And they will dwell safely there, build houses, and plant vineyards; yes, they will dwell securely, when I execute judgments on all those around them who despise them. Then they shall know that I *am* the LORD their God." ' "

PROCLAMATION AGAINST EGYPT

29 In the tenth year, in the tenth *month,* on the twelfth *day* of the month, the word of the LORD came to me, saying, 2 "Son of man, set your face against Pharaoh king of Egypt, and prophesy against him, and against all Egypt. 3 Speak, and say, 'Thus says the Lord GOD:

"Behold, I *am* against you,
O Pharaoh king of Egypt,
O great monster who lies in the midst of his rivers,
Who has said, 'My River[a] *is* my own;
I have made *it* for myself.'
4 But I will put hooks in your jaws,
And cause the fish of your rivers to stick to your scales;
I will bring you up out of the midst of your rivers,
And all the fish in your rivers will stick to your scales.
5 I will leave you in the wilderness,
You and all the fish of your rivers;
You shall fall on the open field;
You shall not be picked up or gathered.[a]
I have given you as food
To the beasts of the field
And to the birds of the heavens.

6 "Then all the inhabitants of Egypt
Shall know that I *am* the LORD,
Because they have been a staff of reed to the house of Israel.
7 When they took hold of you with the hand,
You broke and tore all their shoulders;[a]
When they leaned on you,
You broke and made all their backs quiver."

8 'Therefore thus says the Lord GOD: "Surely I will bring a sword upon you and cut off from you man and beast. 9 And the land of Egypt shall become desolate and waste; then they will know that I *am* the LORD, because he said, 'The River *is* mine, and I have made *it*.' 10 Indeed, therefore, I *am* against you and against your rivers, and I will make the land of Egypt utterly waste and desolate, from Migdol[a] *to* Syene, as far as the border of Ethiopia. 11 Neither foot of man shall pass through it nor foot of beast pass through it, and it shall be uninhabited forty years. 12 I will make the land of Egypt desolate in the midst of the countries *that are* desolate; and among the

29:3 [a]That is, the Nile **29:5** [a]Following Masoretic Text, Septuagint, and Vulgate; some Hebrew manuscripts and Targum read *buried.* **29:7** [a]Following Masoretic Text and Vulgate; Septuagint and Syriac read *hand.* **29:10** [a]Or *tower*

THE MESSAGE

25-26 GOD, the Master, says, "When I gather Is-
rael from the peoples among whom they've
been scattered and put my holiness on dis-
play among them with all the nations look-
ing on, then they'll live in their own land
that I gave to my servant Jacob. They'll live
there in safety. They'll build houses. They'll
plant vineyards, living in safety. Meanwhile,
I'll bring judgment on all the neighbors who
have treated them with such contempt. And
they'll realize that I am GOD."

NEVER A WORLD POWER AGAIN

1-6 **29** In the tenth year, in the tenth month, on
the twelfth day, GOD's Message came to
me: "Son of man, confront Pharaoh king of
Egypt. Preach against him and all the Egyp-
tians. Tell him, 'GOD, the Master, says:

" 'Watch yourself, Pharaoh, king of Egypt.
I'm dead set against you,
You lumbering old dragon,
lolling and flaccid in the Nile,
Saying, "It's my Nile.
I made it. It's mine."
I'll set hooks in your jaw;
I'll make the fish of the Nile stick to your scales.
I'll pull you out of the Nile,
with all the fish stuck to your scales.
Then I'll drag you out into the desert,
you and all the Nile fish sticking to your scales.
You'll lie there in the open, rotting in the sun,
meat to the wild animals and carrion birds.
Everybody living in Egypt
will realize that I am GOD.

6-9 " 'Because you've been a flimsy reed
crutch to Israel so that when they gripped
you, you splintered and cut their hand, and
when they leaned on you, you broke and
sent them sprawling—Message of GOD, the
Master—I'll bring war against you, do away
with people and animals alike, and turn the
country into an empty desert so they'll real-
ize that I am GOD.
9-11 " 'Because you said, "It's my Nile. I made
it. It's all mine," therefore I am against you
and your rivers. I'll reduce Egypt to an
empty, desolate wasteland all the way from
Migdol in the north to Syene and the border
of Ethiopia in the south. Not a human will
be seen in it, nor will an animal move
through it. It'll be just empty desert, empty
for forty years.
12 " 'I'll make Egypt the most desolate of all
desolations. For forty years I'll make her
cities the most wasted of all wasted cities.

NEW KING JAMES VERSION

cities *that are* laid waste, her cities shall be desolate forty years; and I will scatter the Egyptians among the nations and disperse them throughout the countries."

13"Yet, thus says the Lord GOD: "At the end of forty years I will gather the Egyptians from the peoples among whom they were scattered. 14I will bring back the captives of Egypt and cause them to return to the land of Pathros, to the land of their origin, and there they shall be a lowly kingdom. 15It shall be the lowliest of kingdoms; it shall never again exalt itself above the nations, for I will diminish them so that they will not rule over the nations anymore. 16No longer shall it be the confidence of the house of Israel, but will remind them of *their* iniquity when they turned to follow them. Then they shall know that I *am* the Lord GOD." ' "

BABYLONIA WILL PLUNDER EGYPT

17And it came to pass in the twenty-seventh year, in the first *month*, on the first *day* of the month, *that* the word of the LORD came to me, saying, 18"Son of man, Nebuchadnezzar king of Babylon caused his army to labor strenuously against Tyre; every head *was* made bald, and every shoulder rubbed raw; yet neither he nor his army received wages from Tyre, for the labor which they expended on it. 19Therefore thus says the Lord GOD: 'Surely I will give the land of Egypt to Nebuchadnezzar king of Babylon; he shall take away her wealth, carry off her spoil, and remove her pillage; and that will be the wages for his army. 20I have given him the land of Egypt *for* his labor, because they worked for Me,' says the Lord GOD.

21'In that day I will cause the horn of the house of Israel to spring forth, and I will open your mouth to speak in their midst. Then they shall know that I *am* the LORD.' "

EGYPT AND HER ALLIES WILL FALL

30 The word of the LORD came to me again, saying, 2"Son of man, prophesy and say, 'Thus says the Lord GOD:

"Wail, 'Woe to the day!'
3For the day *is* near,
Even the day of the LORD *is* near;
It will be a day of clouds, the time of the
Gentiles.
4The sword shall come upon Egypt,
And great anguish shall be in Ethiopia,
When the slain fall in Egypt,
And they take away her wealth,
And her foundations are broken down.

5"Ethiopia, Libya,[a] Lydia,[b] all the mingled people, Chub, and the men of the lands who are allied, shall fall with them by the sword."

6'Thus says the LORD:

"Those who uphold Egypt shall fall,
And the pride of her power shall come
down.
From Migdol *to* Syene
Those within her shall fall by the sword,"
Says the Lord GOD.

30:5 [a]Hebrew *Put* [b]Hebrew *Lud*

THE MESSAGE

I'll scatter Egyptians to the four winds, send
them off every which way into exile.
13-16 " 'But,' says GOD, the Master, 'that's not
the end of it. After the forty years, I'll gather
up the Egyptians from all the places where
they've been scattered. I'll put things back
together again for Egypt. I'll bring her back
to Pathros where she got her start long ago.
There she'll start over again from scratch.
She'll take her place at the bottom of the
ladder and there she'll stay, never to climb
that ladder again, never to be a world power
again. Never again will Israel be tempted to
rely on Egypt. All she'll be to Israel is a re-
minder of old sin. Then Egypt will realize
that I am GOD, the Master.' "

17-18 In the twenty-seventh year, in the first
month, on the first day of the month, GOD's
Message came to me: "Son of man, Ne-
buchadnezzar, king of Babylon, has worn
out his army against Tyre. They've worked
their fingers to the bone and have nothing to
show for it.
19-20 "Therefore, GOD, the Master, says, 'I'm
giving Egypt to Nebuchadnezzar king of
Babylon. He'll haul away its wealth, pick the
place clean. He'll pay his army with Egyp-
tian plunder. He's been working for me all
these years without pay. This is his pay:
Egypt. Decree of GOD, the Master.
21 " 'And then I'll stir up fresh hope in Is-
rael—the dawn of deliverance!—and I'll give
you, Ezekiel, bold and confident words to
speak. And they'll realize that I am GOD.' "

EGYPT ON FIRE

1-5 **30** GOD, the Master, spoke to me: "Son of
man, preach. Give them the Message of
GOD, the Master. Wail:

" 'Doomsday!'
Time's up!
GOD's big day of judgment is near.
Thick clouds are rolling in.
It's doomsday for the nations.
Death will rain down on Egypt.
Terror will paralyze Ethiopia
When they see the Egyptians killed,
their wealth hauled off,
their foundations demolished,
And Ethiopia, Put, Lud, Arabia, Libya
—all of Egypt's old allies—
killed right along with them.

6-8 " 'GOD says:

" 'Egypt's allies will fall
and her proud strength will collapse—
From Migdol in the north to Syene in the
south,
a great slaughter in Egypt!
Decree of GOD, the Master.

NEW KING JAMES VERSION

7"They shall be desolate in the midst of the
desolate countries,
And her cities shall be in the midst of the
cities *that are* laid waste.
8Then they will know that I *am* the LORD,
When I have set a fire in Egypt
And all her helpers are destroyed.
9On that day messengers shall go forth from
Me in ships
To make the careless Ethiopians afraid,
And great anguish shall come upon them,
As on the day of Egypt;
For indeed it is coming!"

10'Thus says the Lord GOD:

"I will also make a multitude of Egypt to
cease
By the hand of Nebuchadnezzar king of
Babylon.
11He and his people with him, the most
terrible of the nations,
Shall be brought to destroy the land;
They shall draw their swords against Egypt,
And fill the land with the slain.
12I will make the rivers dry,
And sell the land into the hand of the
wicked;
I will make the land waste, and all that is in
it,
By the hand of aliens.
I, the LORD, have spoken."

13'Thus says the Lord GOD:

"I will also destroy the idols,
And cause the images to cease from Noph;[a]
There shall no longer be princes from the
land of Egypt;
I will put fear in the land of Egypt.
14I will make Pathros desolate,
Set fire to Zoan,
And execute judgments in No.[a]
15I will pour My fury on Sin,[a] the strength of
Egypt;
I will cut off the multitude of No,
16And set a fire in Egypt;
Sin shall have great pain,
No shall be split open,
And Noph *shall be in* distress daily.
17The young men of Aven[a] and Pi Beseth shall
fall by the sword,
And these *cities* shall go into captivity.
18At Tehaphnehes[a] the day shall also be
darkened,[b]
When I break the yokes of Egypt there.
And her arrogant strength shall cease in
her;
As for her, a cloud shall cover her,
And her daughters shall go into captivity.
19Thus I will execute judgments on Egypt,
Then they shall know that I *am* the LORD." ' "

30:13 [a]That is, ancient Memphis **30:14** [a]That is, ancient Thebes **30:15** [a]That is, ancient Pelusium **30:17** [a]That is, ancient On (Heliopolis) **30:18** [a]Spelled *Tahpanhes* in Jeremiah 43:7 and elsewhere [b]Following many Hebrew manuscripts, Bomberg, Septuagint, Syriac, Targum, and Vulgate; Masoretic Text reads *refrained*.

THE MESSAGE

Egypt, most desolate of the desolate,
her cities wasted beyond wasting,
Will realize that I am GOD
when I burn her down
and her helpers are knocked flat.

9 " 'When that happens, I'll send out mes-
sengers by ship to sound the alarm among
the easygoing Ethiopians. They'll be terror-
ized. Egypt's doomed! Judgment's coming!

10-12 " 'GOD, the Master, says:

" 'I'll put a stop to Egypt's arrogance.
I'll use Nebuchadnezzar king of Babylon
to do it.
He and his army, the most brutal of
nations,
shall be used to destroy the country.
They'll brandish their swords
and fill Egypt with corpses.
I'll dry up the Nile
and sell off the land to a bunch of
crooks.
I'll hire outsiders to come in
and waste the country, strip it clean.
I, GOD, have said so.

13-19 " 'And now this is what GOD, the Master,
says:

" 'I'll smash all the no-god idols;
I'll topple all those huge statues in
Memphis.
The prince of Egypt will be gone for good,
and in his place I'll put *fear*—fear
throughout Egypt!
I'll demolish Pathros,
burn Zoan to the ground, and punish
Thebes,
Pour my wrath on Pelusium, Egypt's fort,
and knock Thebes off its proud pedestal.
I'll set Egypt on fire:
Pelusium will writhe in pain,
Thebes blown away,
Memphis raped.
The young warriors of On and Pi-beseth
will be killed and the cities exiled.
A dark day for Tahpanhes
when I shatter Egypt,
When I break Egyptian power
and put an end to her arrogant
oppression!
She'll disappear in a cloud of dust,
her cities hauled off as exiles.
That's how I'll punish Egypt,
and that's how she'll realize that I am
GOD.' "

NEW KING JAMES VERSION

PROCLAMATION AGAINST PHARAOH

20 And it came to pass in the eleventh year, in
the first *month,* on the seventh *day* of the
month, *that* the word of the LORD came to me,
saying, 21 "Son of man, I have broken the arm of
Pharaoh king of Egypt; and see, it has not been
bandaged for healing, nor a splint put on to bind
it, to make it strong enough to hold a sword.
22 Therefore thus says the Lord GOD: 'Surely I
am against Pharaoh king of Egypt, and will
break his arms, both the strong one and the one
that was broken; and I will make the sword fall
out of his hand. 23 I will scatter the Egyptians
among the nations, and disperse them through-
out the countries. 24 I will strengthen the arms of
the king of Babylon and put My sword in his
hand; but I will break Pharaoh's arms, and he
will groan before him with the groanings of a
mortally wounded *man.* 25 Thus I will strengthen
the arms of the king of Babylon, but the arms of
Pharaoh shall fall down; they shall know that I
am the LORD, when I put My sword into the
hand of the king of Babylon and he stretches it
out against the land of Egypt. 26 I will scatter the
Egyptians among the nations and disperse them
throughout the countries. Then they shall know
that I *am* the LORD.' "

EGYPT CUT DOWN LIKE A GREAT TREE

31 Now it came to pass in the eleventh year,
in the third *month,* on the first *day* of the
month, *that* the word of the LORD came to me,
saying, 2 "Son of man, say to Pharaoh king of
Egypt and to his multitude:

'Whom are you like in your greatness?
3 Indeed Assyria *was* a cedar in Lebanon,
With fine branches that shaded the forest,
And of high stature;
And its top was among the thick boughs.
4 The waters made it grow;
Underground waters gave it height,
With their rivers running around the place
where it was planted,
And sent out rivulets to all the trees of the
field.

5 'Therefore its height was exalted above all
the trees of the field;
Its boughs were multiplied,
And its branches became long because of
the abundance of water,
As it sent them out.
6 All the birds of the heavens made their nests
in its boughs;
Under its branches all the beasts of the field
brought forth their young;
And in its shadow all great nations made
their home.
7 'Thus it was beautiful in greatness and in the
length of its branches,
Because its roots reached to abundant
waters.
8 The cedars in the garden of God could not
hide it;
The fir trees were not like its boughs,
And the chestnut[a] trees were not like its
branches;

31:8 [a]Hebrew *armon*

THE MESSAGE

20 In the eleventh year, on the seventh day of the first month, GOD's Message came to me:
21 "Son of man, I've broken the arm of Pharaoh king of Egypt. And look! It hasn't been set. No splint has been put on it so the bones can knit and heal, so he can use a sword again.
22-26 "Therefore, GOD, the Master, says, I am dead set against Pharaoh king of Egypt and will go ahead and break his other arm—both arms broken! There's no way he'll ever swing a sword again. I'll scatter Egyptians all over the world. I'll make the arms of the king of Babylon strong and put my sword in his hand, but I'll break the arms of Pharaoh and he'll groan like one who is mortally wounded. I'll make the arms of the king of Babylon strong, but the arms of Pharaoh shall go limp. The Egyptians will realize that I am GOD when I place my sword in the hand of the king of Babylon. He'll wield it against Egypt and I'll scatter Egyptians all over the world. Then they'll realize that I am GOD."

THE FUNERAL OF THE BIG TREE

1-9 31 In the eleventh year, on the first day of the third month, GOD's Message came to me: "Son of man, tell Pharaoh king of Egypt, that pompous old goat:

" 'Who do you, astride the world,
think you really are?
Look! Assyria was a Big Tree, huge as a
Lebanon cedar,
beautiful limbs offering cool shade,
Skyscraper high,
piercing the clouds.
The waters gave it drink,
the primordial deep lifted it high,
Gushing out rivers around
the place where it was planted,
And then branching out in streams
to all the trees in the forest.
It was immense,
dwarfing all the trees in the forest—
Thick boughs, long limbs,
roots delving deep into earth's waters.
All the birds of the air
nested in its boughs.
All the wild animals
gave birth under its branches.
All the mighty nations
lived in its shade.
It was stunning in its majesty—
the reach of its branches!
the depth of its water-seeking roots!
Not a cedar in God's garden came close to
it.
No pine tree was anything like it.
Mighty oaks looked like bushes
growing alongside it.

NEW KING JAMES VERSION

No tree in the garden of God was like it in
beauty.
9I made it beautiful with a multitude of
branches,
So that all the trees of Eden envied it,
That *were* in the garden of God.’

10“Therefore thus says the Lord GOD: ‘Be-
cause you have increased in height, and it set its
top among the thick boughs, and its heart was
lifted up in its height, 11therefore I will deliver it
into the hand of the mighty one of the nations,
and he shall surely deal with it; I have driven it
out for its wickedness. 12And aliens, the most
terrible of the nations, have cut it down and left
it; its branches have fallen on the mountains
and in all the valleys; its boughs lie broken by
all the rivers of the land; and all the peoples of
the earth have gone from under its shadow and
left it.

13‘On its ruin will remain all the birds of the
heavens,
And all the beasts of the field will come to
its branches—

14‘So that no trees by the waters may ever again
exalt themselves for their height, nor set their
tops among the thick boughs, that no tree which
drinks water may ever be high enough to reach
up to them.

‘For they have all been delivered to death,
To the depths of the earth,
Among the children of men who go down to
the Pit.’

15“Thus says the Lord GOD: ‘In the day when
it went down to hell, I caused mourning. I cov-
ered the deep because of it. I restrained its
rivers, and the great waters were held back. I
caused Lebanon to mourn for it, and all the
trees of the field wilted because of it. 16I made
the nations shake at the sound of its fall, when I
cast it down to hell together with those who de-
scend into the Pit; and all the trees of Eden, the
choice and best of Lebanon, all that drink water,
were comforted in the depths of the earth.
17They also went down to hell with it, with those
slain by the sword; and *those who were* its
strong arm dwelt in its shadows among the na-
tions.
18‘To which of the trees in Eden will you then
be likened in glory and greatness? Yet you shall
be brought down with the trees of Eden to the
depths of the earth; you shall lie in the midst of
the uncircumcised, with *those* slain by the
sword. This *is* Pharaoh and all his multitude,’
says the Lord GOD.”

LAMENTATION FOR PHARAOH AND EGYPT

32 And it came to pass in the twelfth year, in
the twelfth *month,* on the first *day* of the
month, *that* the word of the LORD came to me,
saying, 2“Son of man, take up a lamentation for
Pharaoh king of Egypt, and say to him:

‘You are like a young lion among the
nations,

THE MESSAGE

Not a tree in God’s garden
was in the same class of beauty.
I made it beautiful,
a work of art in limbs and leaves,
The envy of every tree in Eden,
every last tree in God’s garden.’ ”

10-13 Therefore, GOD, the Master, says, “ ‘Be-
cause it skyscrapered upward, piercing the
clouds, swaggering and proud of its stature,
I turned it over to a world-famous leader to
call its evil to account. I’d had enough. Out-
siders, unbelievably brutal, felled it across
the mountain ranges. Its branches were
strewn through all the valleys, its leafy
boughs clogging all the streams and rivers.
Because its shade was gone, everybody
walked off. No longer a tree—just a log. On
that dead log birds perch. Wild animals bur-
row under it.
14 “ ‘That marks the end of the “big tree” na-
tions. No more trees nourished from the
great deep, no more cloud-piercing trees, no
more earthborn trees taking over. They’re
all slated for death—back to earth, right
along with men and women, for whom it’s
“dust to dust.”
15-17 “ ‘The Message of GOD, the Master: On
the day of the funeral of the Big Tree, I
threw the great deep into mourning. I
stopped the flow of its rivers, held back
great seas, and wrapped the Lebanon moun-
tains in black. All the trees of the forest
fainted and fell. I made the whole world
quake when it crashed, and threw it into the
underworld to take its place with all else
that gets buried. All the trees of Eden and
the finest and best trees of Lebanon, well-
watered, were relieved—they had de-
scended to the underworld with it—along
with everyone who had lived in its shade
and all who had been killed.
18 “ ‘Which of the trees of Eden came any-
where close to you in splendor and size? But
you’re slated to be cut down to take your
place in the underworld with the trees of
Eden, to be a dead log stacked with all the
other dead logs, among the other uncircum-
cised who are dead and buried.
“ ‘This means Pharaoh, the pompous old
goat.
“ ‘Decree of GOD, the Master.’ ”

A CLOUD ACROSS THE SUN

1-2 32 In the twelfth year, on the first day of the
twelfth month, GOD’s Message came to
me: “Son of man, sing a funeral lament over
Pharaoh king of Egypt. Tell him:

“ ‘You think you’re a young lion
prowling through the nations.

NEW KING JAMES VERSION

And you *are* like a monster in the seas,
Bursting forth in your rivers,
Troubling the waters with your feet,
And fouling their rivers.

3 'Thus says the Lord GOD:

"I will therefore spread My net over you
with a company of many people,
And they will draw you up in My net.
4 Then I will leave you on the land;
I will cast you out on the open fields,
And cause to settle on you all the birds of
the heavens.
And with you I will fill the beasts of the
whole earth.
5 I will lay your flesh on the mountains,
And fill the valleys with your carcass.

6 "I will also water the land with the flow of
your blood,
Even to the mountains;
And the riverbeds will be full of you.
7 When *I* put out your light,
I will cover the heavens, and make its stars
dark;
I will cover the sun with a cloud,
And the moon shall not give her light.
8 All the bright lights of the heavens I will
make dark over you,
And bring darkness upon your land,"
Says the Lord GOD.

9 'I will also trouble the hearts of many peo-
ples, when I bring your destruction among the
nations, into the countries which you have not
known. 10 Yes, I will make many peoples aston-
ished at you, and their kings shall be horribly
afraid of you when I brandish My sword before
them; and they shall tremble *every* moment,
every man for his own life, in the day of your fall.
11 'For thus says the Lord GOD: "The sword of
the king of Babylon shall come upon you. 12 By
the swords of the mighty warriors, all of them
the most terrible of the nations, I will cause your
multitude to fall.

"They shall plunder the pomp of Egypt,
And all its multitude shall be destroyed.
13 Also I will destroy all its animals
From beside its great waters;
The foot of man shall muddy them no more,
Nor shall the hooves of animals muddy them.
14 Then I will make their waters clear,
And make their rivers run like oil,"
Says the Lord GOD.

15 "When I make the land of Egypt desolate,
And the country is destitute of all that once
filled it,
When I strike all who dwell in it,
Then they shall know that I *am* the LORD.

16 "This *is* the lamentation
With which they shall lament her;
The daughters of the nations shall lament her;
They shall lament for her, for Egypt,
And for all her multitude,"
Says the Lord GOD.'"

THE MESSAGE

You're more like a dragon in the ocean,
snorting and thrashing about.

3-10 " 'GOD, the Master, says:

" 'I'm going to throw my net over you
—many nations will get in on this
operation—
and haul you out with my dragnet.
I'll dump you on the ground
out in an open field
And bring in all the crows and vultures
for a sumptuous carrion lunch.
I'll invite wild animals from all over the
world
to gorge on your guts.
I'll scatter hunks of your meat in the
mountains
and strew your bones in the valleys.
The country, right up to the mountains,
will be drenched with your blood,
your blood filling every ditch and
channel.
When I blot you out,
I'll pull the curtain on the skies
and shut out the stars.
I'll throw a cloud across the sun
and turn off the moonlight.
I'll turn out every light in the sky above you
and put your land in the dark.
Decree of GOD, the Master.
I'll shake up everyone worldwide
when I take you off captive to strange
and far-off countries.
I'll shock people with you.
Kings will take one look and shudder.
I'll shake my sword
and they'll shake in their boots.
On the day you crash, they'll tremble,
thinking, "That could be me!"

TO LAY YOUR PRIDE LOW

11-15 " 'GOD, the Master, says:

" 'The sword of the king of Babylon
is coming against you.
I'll use the swords of champions
to lay your pride low,
Use the most brutal of nations
to knock Egypt off her high horse,
to puncture that hot-air pomposity.
I'll destroy all their livestock
that graze along the river.
Neither human foot nor animal hoof
will muddy those waters anymore.
I'll clear their springs and streams,
make their rivers flow clean and smooth.
Decree of GOD, the Master.
When I turn Egypt back to the wild
and strip her clean of all her abundant
produce,
When I strike dead all who live there,
then they'll realize that I am GOD.

16 "This is a funeral song. Chant it.
Daughters of the nations, chant it.
Chant it over Egypt for the death of its
pomp."
Decree of GOD, the Master.

NEW KING JAMES VERSION

EGYPT AND OTHERS CONSIGNED TO THE PIT

[17]It came to pass also in the twelfth year, on the fifteenth *day* of the month, *that* the word of the LORD came to me, saying:

18"Son of man, wail over the multitude of
Egypt,
And cast them down to the depths of the
earth,
Her and the daughters of the famous
nations,
With those who go down to the Pit:
19'Whom do you surpass in beauty?
Go down, be placed with the
uncircumcised.'

20"They shall fall in the midst of *those* slain by
the sword;
She is delivered to the sword,
Drawing her and all her multitudes.
21The strong among the mighty
Shall speak to him out of the midst of hell
With those who help him:
'They have gone down,
They lie with the uncircumcised, slain by
the sword.'

22"Assyria *is* there, and all her company,
With their graves all around her,
All of them slain, fallen by the sword.
23Her graves are set in the recesses of the Pit,
And her company is all around her grave,
All of them slain, fallen by the sword,
Who caused terror in the land of the living.

24"There *is* Elam and all her multitude,
All around her grave,
All of them slain, fallen by the sword,
Who have gone down uncircumcised to the
lower parts of the earth,
Who caused their terror in the land of the
living;
Now they bear their shame with those who
go down to the Pit.
25They have set her bed in the midst of the
slain,
With all her multitude,
With her graves all around it,
All of them uncircumcised, slain by the
sword;
Though their terror was caused
In the land of the living,
Yet they bear their shame
With those who go down to the Pit;
It was put in the midst of the slain.

26"There *are* Meshech and Tubal and all their
multitudes,
With all their graves around it,
All of them uncircumcised, slain by the
sword,
Though they caused their terror in the land
of the living.
27They do not lie with the mighty
Who are fallen of the uncircumcised,
Who have gone down to hell with their
weapons of war;
They have laid their swords under their
heads,

THE MESSAGE

17-19 In the twelfth year, on the fifteenth day of
the first month, GOD's Message came to me:

"Son of man, lament over Egypt's pompous
ways.
Send her on her way.
Dispatch Egypt
and her proud daughter nations
To the underworld,
down to the country of the dead and
buried.
Say, 'You think you're so high and mighty?
Down! Take your place with the heathen
in that unhallowed grave!'

20-21 "She'll be dumped in with those killed in
battle. The sword is bared. Drag her off in
all her proud pomp! All the big men and
their helpers down among the dead and
buried will greet them: 'Welcome to the
grave of the heathen! Join the ranks of the
victims of war!'
22-23 "Assyria is there and its congregation, the
whole nation a cemetery. Their graves are in
the deepest part of the underworld, a con-
gregation of graves, all killed in battle, these
people who terrorized the land of the living.
24-25 "Elam is there in all her pride, a ceme-
tery—all killed in battle, dumped in her hea-
then grave with the dead and buried, these
people who terrorized the land of the living.
They carry their shame with them, along
with the others in the grave. They turned
Elam into a resort for the pompous dead,
landscaped with heathen graves, slaugh-
tered in battle. They once terrorized the
land of the living. Now they carry their
shame down with the others in deep earth.
They're in the section set aside for the slain
in battle.
26-27 "Meshech-tubal is there in all her pride, a
cemetery in uncircumcised ground, dumped
in with those slaughtered in battle—just
deserts for terrorizing the land of the living.
Now they carry their shame down with the
others in deep earth. They're in the section
set aside for the slain. They're segregated
from the heroes, the old-time giants who en-
tered the grave in full battle dress, their
swords placed under their heads and their

NEW KING JAMES VERSION

But their iniquities will be on their bones,
Because of the terror of the mighty in the
land of the living.
28Yes, you shall be broken in the midst of the
uncircumcised,
And lie with *those* slain by the sword.

29"There *is* Edom,
Her kings and all her princes,
Who despite their might
Are laid beside *those* slain by the sword;
They shall lie with the uncircumcised,
And with those who go down to the Pit.
30There *are* the princes of the north,
All of them, and all the Sidonians,
Who have gone down with the slain
In shame at the terror which they caused by
their might;
They lie uncircumcised with *those* slain by
the sword,
And bear their shame with those who go
down to the Pit.

31"Pharaoh will see them
And be comforted over all his multitude,
Pharaoh and all his army,
Slain by the sword,"
Says the Lord GOD.

32"For I have caused My terror in the land of
the living;
And he shall be placed in the midst of the
uncircumcised
With *those* slain by the sword,
Pharaoh and all his multitude,"
Says the Lord GOD.

THE WATCHMAN AND HIS MESSAGE

33 Again the word of the LORD came to me,
saying, 2"Son of man, speak to the children
of your people, and say to them: 'When I bring
the sword upon a land, and the people of the
land take a man from their territory and make
him their watchman, 3when he sees the sword
coming upon the land, if he blows the trumpet
and warns the people, 4then whoever hears the
sound of the trumpet and does not take warn-
ing, if the sword comes and takes him away, his
blood shall be on his *own* head. 5He heard the
sound of the trumpet, but did not take warning;
his blood shall be upon himself. But he who
takes warning will save his life. 6But if the
watchman sees the sword coming and does not
blow the trumpet, and the people are not
warned, and the sword comes and takes *any*
person from among them, he is taken away in
his iniquity; but his blood I will require at the
watchman's hand.'
7"So you, son of man: I have made you a
watchman for the house of Israel; therefore you
shall hear a word from My mouth and warn
them for Me. 8When I say to the wicked, 'O
wicked *man*, you shall surely die!' and you do
not speak to warn the wicked from his way, that
wicked *man* shall die in his iniquity; but his
blood I will require at your hand. 9Nevertheless
if you warn the wicked to turn from his way, and
he does not turn from his way, he shall die in his
iniquity; but you have delivered your soul.

THE MESSAGE

shields covering their bones, those heroes who spread terror through the land of the living.

28 "And you, Egypt, will be dumped in a heathen grave, along with all the rest, in the section set aside for the slain.

29 "Edom is there, with her kings and princes. In spite of her vaunted greatness, she is dumped in a heathen grave with the others headed for the grave.

30 "The princes of the north are there, the whole lot of them, and all the Sidonians who carry their shame to their graves—all that terror they spread with their brute power!—dumped in unhallowed ground with those killed in battle, carrying their shame with the others headed for deep earth.

31 "Pharaoh will see them all and, pompous old goat that he is, take comfort in the company he'll keep—Pharaoh and his slaughtered army. Decree of GOD, the Master.

32 "I used him to spread terror in the land of the living and now I'm dumping him in heathen ground with those killed by the sword—Pharaoh and all his pomp. Decree of GOD, the Master."

YOU ARE THE WATCHMAN

1-5 33 GOD's Message came to me: "Son of man, speak to your people. Tell them, 'If I bring war on this land and the people take one of their citizens and make him their watchman, and if the watchman sees war coming and blows the trumpet, warning the people, then if anyone hears the sound of the trumpet and ignores it and war comes and takes him off, it's his own fault. He heard the alarm, he ignored it—it's his own fault. If he had listened, he would have saved his life.

6 " 'But if the watchman sees war coming and doesn't blow the trumpet, warning the people, and war comes and takes anyone off, I'll hold the watchman responsible for the bloodshed of any unwarned sinner.'

7-9 "You, son of man, are the watchman. I've made you a watchman for Israel. The minute you hear a message from me, warn them. If I say to the wicked, 'Wicked man, wicked woman, you're on the fast track to death!' and you don't speak up and warn the wicked to change their ways, the wicked will die unwarned in their sins and I'll hold you responsible for their bloodshed. But if you warn the wicked to change their ways and they don't do it, they'll die in their sins well-warned and at least you will have saved your own life.

NEW KING JAMES VERSION

10“Therefore you, O son of man, say to the
house of Israel: ‘Thus you say, “If our transgres-
sions and our sins *lie* upon us, and we pine away
in them, how can we then live?” ’ 11Say to them:
‘*As* I live,’ says the Lord GOD, ‘I have no pleasure
in the death of the wicked, but that the wicked
turn from his way and live. Turn, turn from your
evil ways! For why should you die, O house of Is-
rael?’

THE FAIRNESS OF GOD’S JUDGMENT

12“Therefore you, O son of man, say to the
children of your people: ‘The righteousness of
the righteous man shall not deliver him in the
day of his transgression; as for the wickedness
of the wicked, he shall not fall because of it in
the day that he turns from his wickedness; nor
shall the righteous be able to live because of *his*
righteousness in the day that he sins.’ 13When I
say to the righteous *that* he shall surely live, but
he trusts in his own righteousness and commits
iniquity, none of his righteous works shall be re-
membered; but because of the iniquity that he
has committed, he shall die. 14Again, when I say
to the wicked, ‘You shall surely die,’ if he turns
from his sin and does what is lawful and right,
15*if* the wicked restores the pledge, gives back
what he has stolen, and walks in the statutes of
life without committing iniquity, he shall surely
live; he shall not die. 16None of his sins which he
has committed shall be remembered against
him; he has done what is lawful and right; he
shall surely live.

17“Yet the children of your people say, ‘The
way of the LORD is not fair.’ But it is their way
which is not fair! 18When the righteous turns
from his righteousness and commits iniquity, he
shall die because of it. 19But when the wicked
turns from his wickedness and does what is law-
ful and right, he shall live because of it. 20Yet
you say, ‘The way of the LORD is not fair.’ O
house of Israel, I will judge every one of you ac-
cording to his own ways.”

THE FALL OF JERUSALEM

21And it came to pass in the twelfth year of
our captivity, in the tenth *month*, on the fifth
day of the month, *that* one who had escaped
from Jerusalem came to me and said, “The city
has been captured!”

22Now the hand of the LORD had been upon
me the evening before the man came who had
escaped. And He had opened my mouth; so
when he came to me in the morning, my mouth
was opened, and I was no longer mute.

THE CAUSE OF JUDAH’S RUIN

23Then the word of the LORD came to me, say-
ing: 24“Son of man, they who inhabit those ruins
in the land of Israel are saying, ‘Abraham was
only one, and he inherited the land. But we *are*
many; the land has been given to us as a posses-
sion.’

25“Therefore say to them, ‘Thus says the Lord
GOD: “You eat *meat* with blood, you lift up your
eyes toward your idols, and shed blood. Should
you then possess the land? 26You rely on your
sword, you commit abominations, and you de-
file one another’s wives. Should you then pos-
sess the land?” ’

THE MESSAGE

10 “Son of man, speak to Israel. Tell them, ‘You’ve said, “Our rebellions and sins are weighing us down. We’re wasting away. How can we go on living?” ’

11 “Tell them, ‘As sure as I am the living God, I take no pleasure from the death of the wicked. I want the wicked to change their ways and live. Turn your life around! Reverse your evil ways! Why *die*, Israel?’

12-13 “There’s more, son of man. Tell your people, ‘A good person’s good life won’t save him when he decides to rebel, and a bad person’s bad life won’t prevent him from repenting of his rebellion. A good person who sins can’t expect to live when he chooses to sin. It’s true that I tell good people, “Live! Be alive!” But if they trust in their good deeds and turn to evil, that good life won’t amount to a hill of beans. They’ll die for their evil life.

14-16 “ ‘On the other hand, if I tell a wicked person, “You’ll die for your wicked life,” and he repents of his sin and starts living a righteous and just life—being generous to the down-and-out, restoring what he had stolen, cultivating life-nourishing ways that don’t hurt others—he’ll live. He won’t die. None of his sins will be kept on the books. He’s doing what’s right, living a good life. He’ll live.

17-19 “ ‘Your people say, “The Master’s way isn’t fair.” But it’s the way *they’re* living that isn’t fair. When good people turn back from living good lives and plunge into sin, they’ll die for it. And when a wicked person turns away from his wicked life and starts living a just and righteous life, he’ll come alive.

20 “ ‘Still, you keep on saying, “The Master’s way isn’t fair.” We’ll see, Israel. I’ll decide on each of you exactly according to how you live.’ ”

21 In the twelfth year of our exile, on the fifth day of the tenth month, a survivor from Jerusalem came to me and said, “The city’s fallen.”

22 The evening before the survivor arrived, the hand of GOD had been on me and restored my speech. By the time he arrived in the morning I was able to speak. I could talk again.

23-24 GOD’s Message came to me: “Son of man, those who are living in the ruins back in Israel are saying, ‘Abraham was only one man and he owned the whole country. But there are *lots* of us. Our ownership is even more certain.’

25-26 “So tell them, ‘GOD the Master says, You eat flesh that contains blood, you worship no-god idols, you murder at will—and you expect to own this land? You rely on the sword, you engage in obscenities, you indulge in sex at random—anyone, anytime. And you still expect to own this land?’

New King James Version

27“Say thus to them, ‘Thus says the Lord
GOD: “*As* I live, surely those who *are* in the ru-
ins shall fall by the sword, and the one who *is* in
the open field I will give to the beasts to be de-
voured, and those who *are* in the strongholds
and caves shall die of the pestilence. 28For I will
make the land most desolate, her arrogant
strength shall cease, and the mountains of Israel
shall be so desolate that no one will pass
through. 29Then they shall know that I *am* the
LORD, when I have made the land most desolate
because of all their abominations which they
have committed.” ’

Hearing and Not Doing

30“As for you, son of man, the children of
your people are talking about you beside the
walls and in the doors of the houses; and they
speak to one another, everyone saying to his
brother, ‘Please come and hear what the word is
that comes from the LORD.’ 31So they come to
you as people do, they sit before you *as* My peo-
ple, and they hear your words, but they do not
do them; for with their mouth they show much
love, *but* their hearts pursue their *own* gain.
32Indeed you *are* to them as a very lovely song of
one who has a pleasant voice and can play well
on an instrument; for they hear your words, but
they do not do them. 33And when this comes to
pass—surely it will come—then they will know
that a prophet has been among them.”

Irresponsible Shepherds

34 And the word of the LORD came to me, say-
ing, 2“Son of man, prophesy against the
shepherds of Israel, prophesy and say to them,
‘Thus says the Lord GOD to the shepherds: “Woe
to the shepherds of Israel who feed themselves!
Should not the shepherds feed the flocks? 3You
eat the fat and clothe yourselves with the wool;
you slaughter the fatlings, *but* you do not feed
the flock. 4The weak you have not strengthened,
nor have you healed those who were sick, nor
bound up the broken, nor brought back what
was driven away, nor sought what was lost; but
with force and cruelty you have ruled them. 5So
they were scattered because *there was* no shep-
herd; and they became food for all the beasts of
the field when they were scattered. 6My sheep
wandered through all the mountains, and on
every high hill; yes, My flock was scattered over
the whole face of the earth, and no one was
seeking or searching *for them.*”

7‘Therefore, you shepherds, hear the word of
the LORD: 8“*As* I live,” says the Lord GOD, “surely
because My flock became a prey, and My flock
became food for every beast of the field, be-
cause *there was* no shepherd, nor did My shep-
herds search for My flock, but the shepherds fed
themselves and did not feed My flock”— 9there-
fore, O shepherds, hear the word of the LORD!
10Thus says the Lord GOD: “Behold, I *am* against
the shepherds, and I will require My flock at
their hand; I will cause them to cease feeding
the sheep, and the shepherds shall feed them-
selves no more; for I will deliver My flock from
their mouths, that they may no longer be food
for them.”

The Message

27-28 “Tell them this, Ezekiel: ‘The Message of
GOD, the Master. As sure as I am the living
God, those who are still alive in the ruins
will be killed. Anyone out in the field I’ll
give to wild animals for food. Anyone hiding
out in mountain forts and caves will die of
disease. I’ll make this country an empty
wasteland—no more arrogant bullying! Is-
rael’s mountains will become dangerously
desolate. No one will dare pass through
them.’

29 “They’ll realize that I am GOD when I dev-
astate the country because of all the obscen-
ities they’ve practiced.

30-32 “As for you, son of man, you’ve become
quite the talk of the town. Your people meet
on street corners and in front of their
houses and say, ‘Let’s go hear the latest
news from GOD.’ They show up, as people
tend to do, and sit in your company. They
listen to you speak, but don’t do a thing you
say. They flatter you with compliments, but
all they care about is making money and
getting ahead. To them you’re merely enter-
tainment—a country singer of sad love
songs, playing a guitar. They love to hear
you talk, but nothing comes of it.

33 “But when all this happens—and it is go-
ing to happen!—they’ll realize that a
prophet was among them.”

When the Sheep Get Scattered

1-6 34 GOD’s Message came to me: “Son of
man, prophesy against the shepherd-
leaders of Israel. Yes, prophesy! Tell those
shepherds, ‘GOD, the Master, says: Doom to
you shepherds of Israel, feeding your own
mouths! Aren’t shepherds supposed to feed
sheep? You drink the milk, you make clothes
from the wool, you roast the lambs, but you
don’t feed the sheep. You don’t build up the
weak ones, don’t heal the sick, don’t doctor
the injured, don’t go after the strays, don’t
look for the lost. You bully and badger them.
And now they’re scattered every which way
because there was no shepherd—scattered
and easy pickings for wolves and coyotes.
Scattered—*my sheep!*—exposed and vulner-
able across mountains and hills. My sheep
scattered all over the world, and no one out
looking for them!

7-9 “ ‘Therefore, shepherds, listen to the Mes-
sage of GOD: As sure as I am the living
God—Decree of GOD, the Master—because
my sheep have been turned into mere prey,
into easy meals for wolves because you
shepherds ignored them and only fed your-
selves, listen to what GOD has to say:

10 “ ‘Watch out! I’m coming down on the
shepherds and taking my sheep back.
They’re fired as shepherds of my sheep. No
more shepherds who just feed themselves!
I’ll rescue my sheep from their greed.
They’re not going to feed off my sheep any
longer!

NEW KING JAMES VERSION

GOD, THE TRUE SHEPHERD

11'For thus says the Lord GOD: "Indeed I My-
self will search for My sheep and seek them out.
12As a shepherd seeks out his flock on the day
he is among his scattered sheep, so will I seek
out My sheep and deliver them from all the
places where they were scattered on a cloudy
and dark day. 13And I will bring them out from
the peoples and gather them from the countries,
and will bring them to their own land; I will feed
them on the mountains of Israel, in the valleys
and in all the inhabited places of the country. 14I
will feed them in good pasture, and their fold
shall be on the high mountains of Israel. There
they shall lie down in a good fold and feed in
rich pasture on the mountains of Israel. 15I will
feed My flock, and I will make them lie down,"
says the Lord GOD. 16"I will seek what was lost
and bring back what was driven away, bind up
the broken and strengthen what was sick; but I
will destroy the fat and the strong, and feed
them in judgment."

17'And *as for* you, O My flock, thus says the
Lord GOD: "Behold, I shall judge between sheep
and sheep, between rams and goats. 18*Is it* too
little for you to have eaten up the good pasture,
that you must tread down with your feet the
residue of your pasture—and to have drunk of
the clear waters, that you must foul the residue
with your feet? 19And *as for* My flock, they eat
what you have trampled with your feet, and they
drink what you have fouled with your feet."

20'Therefore thus says the Lord GOD to them:
"Behold, I Myself will judge between the fat and
the lean sheep. 21Because you have pushed with
side and shoulder, butted all the weak ones with
your horns, and scattered them abroad, 22there-
fore I will save My flock, and they shall no
longer be a prey; and I will judge between sheep
and sheep. 23I will establish one shepherd over
them, and he shall feed them—My servant
David. He shall feed them and be their shep-
herd. 24And I, the LORD, will be their God, and
My servant David a prince among them; I, the
LORD, have spoken.

25"I will make a covenant of peace with them,
and cause wild beasts to cease from the land;
and they will dwell safely in the wilderness and
sleep in the woods. 26I will make them and the
places all around My hill a blessing; and I will
cause showers to come down in their season;
there shall be showers of blessing. 27Then the
trees of the field shall yield their fruit, and the
earth shall yield her increase. They shall be safe
in their land; and they shall know that I *am* the
LORD, when I have broken the bands of their
yoke and delivered them from the hand of those
who enslaved them. 28And they shall no longer
be a prey for the nations, nor shall beasts of the
land devour them; but they shall dwell safely,
and no one shall make *them* afraid. 29I will raise
up for them a garden of renown, and they shall
no longer be consumed with hunger in the land,
nor bear the shame of the Gentiles anymore.
30Thus they shall know that I, the LORD their
God, *am* with them, and they, the house of Is-
rael, *are* My people," says the Lord GOD.'

THE MESSAGE

11-16 " 'GOD, the Master, says: From now on, *I
myself* am the shepherd. I'm going looking
for them. As shepherds go after their flocks
when they get scattered, I'm going after my
sheep. I'll rescue them from all the places
they've been scattered to in the storms. I'll
bring them back from foreign peoples,
gather them from foreign countries, and
bring them back to their home country. I'll
feed them on the mountains of Israel, along
the streams, among their own people. I'll
lead them into lush pasture so they can
roam the mountain pastures of Israel, graze
at leisure, feed in the rich pastures on the
mountains of Israel. And I myself will be the
shepherd of my sheep. I myself will make
sure they get plenty of rest. I'll go after the
lost, I'll collect the strays, I'll doctor the in-
jured, I'll build up the weak ones and over-
see the strong ones so they're not exploited.

17-19 " 'And as for you, my dear flock, I'm step-
ping in and judging between one sheep and
another, between rams and goats. Aren't
you satisfied to feed in good pasture without
taking over the whole place? Can't you be
satisfied to drink from the clear stream
without muddying the water with your feet?
Why do the rest of my sheep have to make
do with grass that's trampled down and wa-
ter that's been muddied?

20-22 " 'Therefore, GOD, the Master, says: I my-
self am stepping in and making things right
between the plump sheep and the skinny
sheep. Because you forced your way with
shoulder and rump and butted at all the
weaker animals with your horns till you
scattered them all over the hills, I'll come in
and save my dear flock, no longer let them
be pushed around. I'll step in and set things
right between one sheep and another.

23-24 " 'I'll appoint one shepherd over them all:
my servant David. He'll feed them. He'll be
their shepherd. And I, GOD, will be their
God. My servant David will be their prince.
I, GOD, have spoken.

25-27 " 'I'll make a covenant of peace with
them. I'll banish fierce animals from the
country so the sheep can live safely in the
wilderness and sleep in the forest. I'll make
them and everything around my hill a bless-
ing. I'll send down plenty of rain in season—
showers of blessing! The trees in the or-
chards will bear fruit, the ground will
produce, they'll feel content and safe on
their land, and they'll realize that I am GOD
when I break them out of their slavery and
rescue them from their slave masters.

28-29 " 'No longer will they be exploited by out-
siders and ravaged by fierce beasts. They'll
live safe and sound, fearless and free. I'll
give them rich gardens, lavish in vegeta-
bles—no more living half-starved, no longer
taunted by outsiders.

30-31 " 'They'll know, beyond doubting, that I,
GOD, am their God, that I'm with them and
that they, the people Israel, are my people.
Decree of GOD, the Master:

New King James Version

[31]"You are My flock, the flock of My pasture; you *are* men, *and* I *am* your God," says the Lord GOD.

Judgment on Mount Seir

35 Moreover the word of the LORD came to me, saying, [2]"Son of man, set your face against Mount Seir and prophesy against it, [3]and say to it, 'Thus says the Lord GOD:

"Behold, O Mount Seir, I *am* against you;
I will stretch out My hand against you,
And make you most desolate;
[4]I shall lay your cities waste,
And you shall be desolate.
Then you shall know that I *am* the LORD.

[5]"Because you have had an ancient hatred, and have shed *the blood of* the children of Israel by the power of the sword at the time of their calamity, when their iniquity *came to an* end, [6]therefore, *as* I live," says the Lord GOD, "I will prepare you for blood, and blood shall pursue you; since you have not hated blood, therefore blood shall pursue you. [7]Thus I will make Mount Seir most desolate, and cut off from it the one who leaves and the one who returns. [8]And I will fill its mountains with the slain; on your hills and in your valleys and in all your ravines those who are slain by the sword shall fall. [9]I will make you perpetually desolate, and your cities shall be uninhabited; then you shall know that I *am* the LORD.

[10]"Because you have said, 'These two nations and these two countries shall be mine, and we will possess them,' although the LORD was there, [11]therefore, *as* I live," says the Lord GOD, "I will do according to your anger and according to the envy which you showed in your hatred against them; and I will make Myself known among them when I judge you. [12]Then you shall know that I *am* the LORD. I have heard all your blasphemies which you have spoken against the mountains of Israel, saying, 'They are desolate; they are given to us to consume.' [13]Thus with your mouth you have boasted against Me and multiplied your words against Me; I have heard *them.*"

[14]"Thus says the Lord GOD: "The whole earth will rejoice when I make you desolate. [15]As you rejoiced because the inheritance of the house of Israel was desolate, so I will do to you; you shall be desolate, O Mount Seir, as well as all of Edom—all of it! Then they shall know that I *am* the LORD." '

Blessing on Israel

36 "And you, son of man, prophesy to the mountains of Israel, and say, 'O mountains of Israel, hear the word of the LORD! [2]Thus says the Lord GOD: "Because the enemy has said of you, 'Aha! The ancient heights have become our possession,' " ' [3]therefore prophesy, and say, 'Thus says the Lord GOD: "Because they made *you* desolate and swallowed you up on every side, so that you became the possession of the rest of the nations, and you are taken up by the

The Message

You are my dear flock,
the flock of my pasture, my human flock,
And I am your God.
Decree of GOD, the Master.' "

A Pile of Rubble

1-4 35 GOD's Message came to me: "Son of man, confront Mount Seir. Prophesy against it! Tell them, 'GOD, the Master, says:

" 'I'm coming down hard on you, Mount Seir.
I'm stepping in and turning you to a pile of rubble.
I'll reduce your towns to piles of rocks.
There'll be nothing left of you.
Then you'll realize that I am GOD.

5-9 " 'I'm doing this because you've kept this age-old grudge going against Israel: You viciously attacked them when they were already down, looking their final punishment in the face. Therefore, as sure as I am the living God, I'm lining you up for a real bloodbath. Since you loved blood so much, you'll be chased by rivers of blood. I'll reduce Mount Seir to a heap of rubble. No one will either come or go from that place! I'll blanket your mountains with corpses. Massacred bodies will cover your hills and fill up your valleys and ditches. I'll reduce you to ruins and all your towns will be ghost towns—population zero. Then you'll realize that I am GOD.

10-13 " 'Because you said, "These two nations, these two countries, are mine. I'm taking over" (even though GOD is right there watching, right there listening), I'll turn your hate-bloated anger and rage right back on you. You'll know I mean business when I bring judgment on you. You'll realize then that I, GOD, have overheard all the vile abuse you've poured out against the mountains of Israel, saying, "They're roadkill and we're going to eat them up." You've strutted around, talking so big, insolently pitting yourselves against me. And I've heard it all.

14-15 " 'This is the verdict of GOD, the Master: With the whole earth applauding, I'll demolish you. Since you danced in the streets, thinking it was so wonderful when Israel's inheritance was demolished, I'll give you the same treatment: demolition. Mount Seir demolished—yes, every square inch of Edom. Then they'll realize that I am GOD!' "

Back to Your Own Land

1-5 36 "And now, son of man, prophesy to the mountains of Israel. Say, 'Mountains of Israel, listen to GOD's Message. GOD, the Master, says, Because the enemy crowed over you, "Good! Those old hills are now ours!" now here is a prophecy in the name of GOD, the Master: Because nations came at you from all sides, ripping and plundering, hauling pieces of you off every which way,

NEW KING JAMES VERSION

lips of talkers and slandered by the people"—4therefore, O mountains of Israel, hear the word of the Lord GOD! Thus says the Lord GOD to the mountains, the hills, the rivers, the valleys, the desolate wastes, and the cities that have been forsaken, which became plunder and mockery to the rest of the nations all around—5therefore thus says the Lord GOD: "Surely I have spoken in My burning jealousy against the rest of the nations and against all Edom, who gave My land to themselves as a possession, with wholehearted joy *and* spiteful minds, in order to plunder its open country." '

6"Therefore prophesy concerning the land of Israel, and say to the mountains, the hills, the rivers, and the valleys, 'Thus says the Lord GOD: "Behold, I have spoken in My jealousy and My fury, because you have borne the shame of the nations." 7Therefore thus says the Lord GOD: "I have raised My hand in an oath that surely the nations that *are* around you shall bear their own shame. 8But you, O mountains of Israel, you shall shoot forth your branches and yield your fruit to My people Israel, for they are about to come. 9For indeed I *am* for you, and I will turn to you, and you shall be tilled and sown. 10I will multiply men upon you, all the house of Israel, all of it; and the cities shall be inhabited and the ruins rebuilt. 11I will multiply upon you man and beast; and they shall increase and bear young; I will make you inhabited as in former times, and do better *for you* than at your beginnings. Then you shall know that I *am* the LORD. 12Yes, I will cause men to walk on you, My people Israel; they shall take possession of you, and you shall be their inheritance; no more shall you bereave them *of children.*"

13'Thus says the Lord GOD: "Because they say to you, 'You devour men and bereave your nation *of children,*' 14therefore you shall devour men no more, nor bereave your nation anymore," says the Lord GOD. 15"Nor will I let you hear the taunts of the nations anymore, nor bear the reproach of the peoples anymore, nor shall you cause your nation to stumble anymore," says the Lord GOD.' "

THE RENEWAL OF ISRAEL

16Moreover the word of the LORD came to me, saying: 17"Son of man, when the house of Israel dwelt in their own land, they defiled it by their own ways and deeds; to Me their way was like the uncleanness of a woman in her customary impurity. 18Therefore I poured out My fury on them for the blood they had shed on the land, and for their idols *with which* they had defiled it. 19So I scattered them among the nations, and they were dispersed throughout the countries; I judged them according to their ways and their deeds. 20When they came to the nations, wherever they went, they profaned My holy name—when they said of them, 'These *are* the people of the LORD, *and* yet they have gone out of His land.' 21But I had concern for My holy name, which the house of Israel had profaned among the nations wherever they went.

22"Therefore say to the house of Israel, 'Thus says the Lord GOD: "I do not do *this* for your sake, O house of Israel, but for My holy name's

THE MESSAGE

and you've become the butt of cheap gossip and jokes, therefore, Mountains of Israel, listen to the Message of GOD, the Master. My Message to mountains and hills, to ditches and valleys, to the heaps of rubble and the emptied towns that are looted for plunder and turned into jokes by all the surrounding nations: Therefore, says GOD, the Master, now I'm speaking in a fiery rage against the rest of the nations, but especially against Edom, who in an orgy of violence and shameless insolence robbed me of my land, grabbed it for themselves.'

6-7 "Therefore prophesy over the land of Israel, preach to the mountains and hills, to every ditch and valley: 'The Message of GOD, the Master: Look! Listen! I'm angry—and I care. I'm speaking to you because you've been humiliated among the nations. Therefore I, GOD, the Master, am telling you that I've solemnly sworn that the nations around you are next. It's their turn to be humiliated.

8-12 " 'But you, Mountains of Israel, will burst with new growth, putting out branches and bearing fruit for my people Israel. My people are coming home! Do you see? I'm back again. I'm on your side. You'll be plowed and planted as before! I'll see to it that your population grows all over Israel, that the towns fill up with people, that the ruins are rebuilt. I'll make this place teem with life—human and animal. The country will burst into life, life, and more life, your towns and villages full of people just as in the old days. I'll treat you better than I ever have. And you'll realize that I am GOD. I'll put people over you—my own people Israel! They'll take care of you and you'll be their inheritance. Never again will you be a harsh and unforgiving land to them.

13-15 " 'GOD, the Master, says: Because you have a reputation of being a land that eats people alive and makes women barren, I'm now telling you that you'll never eat people alive again nor make women barren. Decree of GOD, the Master. And I'll never again let the taunts of outsiders be heard over you nor permit nations to look down on you. You'll no longer be a land that makes women barren. Decree of GOD, the Master.' "

16-21 GOD's Message came to me: "Son of man, when the people of Israel lived in their land, they polluted it by the way they lived. I poured out my anger on them because of the polluted blood they poured out on the ground. And so I got thoroughly angry with them polluting the country with their wanton murders and dirty gods. I kicked them out, exiled them to other countries. I sentenced them according to how they had lived. Wherever they went, they gave me a bad name. People said, 'These are GOD's people, but they got kicked off his land.' I suffered much pain over my holy reputation, which the people of Israel blackened in every country they entered.

22-23 "Therefore, tell Israel, 'Message of GOD, the Master: I'm not doing this for you, Israel. I'm doing it for me, to save my character, my

NEW KING JAMES VERSION

sake, which you have profaned among the nations wherever you went. [23]And I will sanctify My great name, which has been profaned among the nations, which you have profaned in their midst; and the nations shall know that I *am* the LORD," says the Lord GOD, "when I am hallowed in you before their eyes. [24]For I will take you from among the nations, gather you out of all countries, and bring you into your own land. [25]Then I will sprinkle clean water on you, and you shall be clean; I will cleanse you from all your filthiness and from all your idols. [26]I will give you a new heart and put a new spirit within you; I will take the heart of stone out of your flesh and give you a heart of flesh. [27]I will put My Spirit within you and cause you to walk in My statutes, and you will keep My judgments and do *them.* [28]Then you shall dwell in the land that I gave to your fathers; you shall be My people, and I will be your God. [29]I will deliver you from all your uncleannesses. I will call for the grain and multiply it, and bring no famine upon you. [30]And I will multiply the fruit of your trees and the increase of your fields, so that you need never again bear the reproach of famine among the nations. [31]Then you will remember your evil ways and your deeds that *were* not good; and you will loathe yourselves in your own sight, for your iniquities and your abominations. [32]Not for your sake do I do *this,*" says the Lord GOD, "let it be known to you. Be ashamed and confounded for your own ways, O house of Israel!"

[33]'Thus says the Lord GOD: "On the day that I cleanse you from all your iniquities, I will also enable *you* to dwell in the cities, and the ruins shall be rebuilt. [34]The desolate land shall be tilled instead of lying desolate in the sight of all who pass by. [35]So they will say, 'This land that was desolate has become like the garden of Eden; and the wasted, desolate, and ruined cities *are now* fortified *and* inhabited.' [36]Then the nations which are left all around you shall know that I, the LORD, have rebuilt the ruined places *and* planted what was desolate. I, the LORD, have spoken *it,* and I will do *it.*"

[37]'Thus says the Lord GOD: "I will also let the house of Israel inquire of Me to do this for them: I will increase their men like a flock. [38]Like a flock *offered as* holy *sacrifices,* like the flock at Jerusalem on its feast days, so shall the ruined cities be filled with flocks of men. Then they shall know that I *am* the LORD." ' "

THE DRY BONES LIVE

37 The hand of the LORD came upon me and brought me out in the Spirit of the LORD, and set me down in the midst of the valley; and it *was* full of bones. [2]Then He caused me to pass by them all around, and behold, *there were* very many in the open valley; and indeed *they were* very dry. [3]And He said to me, "Son of man, can these bones live?"

So I answered, "O Lord GOD, You know."

THE MESSAGE

holy name, which you've blackened in every country where you've gone. I'm going to put my great and holy name on display, the name that has been ruined in so many countries, the name that you blackened wherever you went. Then the nations will realize who I really am, that I am GOD, when I show my holiness through you so that they can see it with their own eyes.

24-28 " 'For here's what I'm going to do: I'm going to take you out of these countries, gather you from all over, and bring you back to your own land. I'll pour pure water over you and scrub you clean. I'll give you a new heart, put a new spirit in you. I'll remove the stone heart from your body and replace it with a heart that's God-willed, not self-willed. I'll put my Spirit in you and make it possible for you to do what I tell you and live by my commands. You'll once again live in the land I gave your ancestors. You'll be my people! I'll be your God!

29-30 " 'I'll pull you out of that stinking pollution. I'll give personal orders to the wheat fields, telling them to grow bumper crops. I'll send no more famines. I'll make sure your fruit trees and field crops flourish. Other nations won't be able to hold you in contempt again because of famine.

31 " 'And then you'll think back over your terrible lives—the evil, the shame—and be thoroughly disgusted with yourselves, realizing how badly you've lived—all those obscenities you've carried out.

32 " 'I'm not doing this for you. Get this through your thick heads! Shame on you. What a mess you made of things, Israel!

33-36 " 'Message of GOD, the Master: On the day I scrub you clean from all your filthy living, I'll also make your cities livable. The ruins will be rebuilt. The neglected land will be worked again, no longer overgrown with weeds and thistles, worthless in the eyes of passersby. People will exclaim, "Why, this weed patch has been turned into a Garden of Eden! And the ruined cities, smashed into oblivion, are now thriving!" The nations around you that are still in existence will realize that I, GOD, rebuild ruins and replant empty waste places. I, GOD, said so, and I'll do it.

37-38 " 'Message of GOD, the Master: Yet again I'm going to do what Israel asks. I'll increase their population as with a flock of sheep. Like the milling flocks of sheep brought for sacrifices in Jerusalem during the appointed feasts, the ruined cities will be filled with flocks of people. And they'll realize that I am GOD.' "

BREATH OF LIFE

1-2 **37** GOD grabbed me. GOD's Spirit took me up and set me down in the middle of an open plain strewn with bones. He led me around and among them—a lot of bones! There were bones all over the plain—dry bones, bleached by the sun.

3 He said to me, "Son of man, can these bones live?"

I said, "Master GOD, only you know that."

NEW KING JAMES VERSION

4Again He said to me, "Prophesy to these
bones, and say to them, 'O dry bones, hear the
word of the LORD! 5Thus says the Lord GOD to
these bones: "Surely I will cause breath to enter
into you, and you shall live. 6I will put sinews on
you and bring flesh upon you, cover you with
skin and put breath in you; and you shall live.
Then you shall know that I *am* the LORD." ' "

7So I prophesied as I was commanded; and
as I prophesied, there was a noise, and suddenly
a rattling; and the bones came together, bone to
bone. 8Indeed, as I looked, the sinews and the
flesh came upon them, and the skin covered
them over; but *there was* no breath in them.

9Also He said to me, "Prophesy to the breath,
prophesy, son of man, and say to the breath,
'Thus says the Lord GOD: "Come from the four
winds, O breath, and breathe on these slain, that
they may live." ' " 10So I prophesied as He com-
manded me, and breath came into them, and
they lived, and stood upon their feet, an exceed-
ingly great army.

11Then He said to me, "Son of man, these
bones are the whole house of Israel. They in-
deed say, 'Our bones are dry, our hope is lost,
and we ourselves are cut off!' 12Therefore
prophesy and say to them, 'Thus says the Lord
GOD: "Behold, O My people, I will open your
graves and cause you to come up from your
graves, and bring you into the land of Israel.
13Then you shall know that I *am* the LORD, when
I have opened your graves, O My people, and
brought you up from your graves. 14I will put My
Spirit in you, and you shall live, and I will place
you in your own land. Then you shall know that
I, the LORD, have spoken *it* and performed *it*,"
says the LORD.' "

ONE KINGDOM, ONE KING

15Again the word of the LORD came to me,
saying, 16"As for you, son of man, take a stick for
yourself and write on it: 'For Judah and for the
children of Israel, his companions.' Then take
another stick and write on it, 'For Joseph, the
stick of Ephraim, and *for* all the house of Israel,
his companions.' 17Then join them one to an-
other for yourself into one stick, and they will
become one in your hand.

18"And when the children of your people
speak to you, saying, 'Will you not show us what
you *mean* by these?'— 19say to them, 'Thus says
the Lord GOD: "Surely I will take the stick of
Joseph, which *is* in the hand of Ephraim, and
the tribes of Israel, his companions; and I will
join them with it, with the stick of Judah, and
make them one stick, and they will be one in My
hand." ' 20And the sticks on which you write will
be in your hand before their eyes.

21"Then say to them, 'Thus says the Lord
GOD: "Surely I will take the children of Israel
from among the nations, wherever they have
gone, and will gather them from every side and
bring them into their own land; 22and I will
make them one nation in the land, on the moun-
tains of Israel; and one king shall be king over
them all; they shall no longer be two nations,
nor shall they ever be divided into two king-
doms again. 23They shall not defile themselves

THE MESSAGE

4 He said to me, "Prophesy over these
bones: 'Dry bones, listen to the Message of
GOD!' "

5-6 GOD, the Master, told the dry bones,
"Watch this: I'm bringing the breath of life
to you and you'll come to life. I'll attach
sinews to you, put meat on your bones,
cover you with skin, and breathe life into
you. You'll come alive and you'll realize that
I am GOD!"

7-8 I prophesied just as I'd been commanded.
As I prophesied, there was a sound and, oh,
rustling! The bones moved and came to-
gether, bone to bone. I kept watching.
Sinews formed, then muscles on the bones,
then skin stretched over them. But they had
no breath in them.

9 He said to me, "Prophesy to the breath.
Prophesy, son of man. Tell the breath, 'GOD,
the Master, says, Come from the four winds.
Come, breath. Breathe on these slain bodies.
Breathe life!' "

10 So I prophesied, just as he commanded
me. The breath entered them and they came
alive! They stood up on their feet, a huge
army.

11 Then God said to me, "Son of man, these
bones are the whole house of Israel. Listen
to what they're saying: 'Our bones are dried
up, our hope is gone, there's nothing left of
us.'

12-14 "Therefore, prophesy. Tell them, 'GOD, the
Master, says: I'll dig up your graves and
bring you out alive—O my people! Then I'll
take you straight to the land of Israel. When
I dig up graves and bring you out as my peo-
ple, you'll realize that I am GOD. I'll breathe
my life into you and you'll live. Then I'll lead
you straight back to your land and you'll re-
alize that I am GOD. I've said it and I'll do it.
GOD's Decree.' "

15-17 GOD's Message came to me: "You, son of
man: Take a stick and write on it, 'For Ju-
dah, with his Israelite companions.' Then
take another stick and write on it, 'For
Joseph—Ephraim's stick, together with all
his Israelite companions.' Then tie the two
sticks together so that you're holding one
stick.

18-19 "When your people ask you, 'Are you go-
ing to tell us what you're doing?' tell them,
'GOD, the Master, says, Watch me! I'll take
the Joseph stick that is in Ephraim's hand,
with the tribes of Israel connected with him,
and lay the Judah stick on it. I'll make them
into one stick. I'm holding one stick.'

20-24 "Then take the sticks you've inscribed
and hold them up so the people can see
them. Tell them, 'GOD, the Master, says,
Watch me! I'm taking the Israelites out of
the nations in which they've been exiled. I'll
gather them in from all directions and bring
them back home. I'll make them one nation
in the land, on the mountains of Israel, and
give them one king—one king over all of
them. Never again will they be divided into
two nations, two kingdoms. Never again will

New King James Version

anymore with their idols, nor with their detestable things, nor with any of their transgressions; but I will deliver them from all their dwelling places in which they have sinned, and will cleanse them. Then they shall be My people, and I will be their God.

24“David My servant *shall be* king over them, and they shall all have one shepherd; they shall also walk in My judgments and observe My statutes, and do them. 25Then they shall dwell in the land that I have given to Jacob My servant, where your fathers dwelt; and they shall dwell there, they, their children, and their children’s children, forever; and My servant David *shall be* their prince forever. 26Moreover I will make a covenant of peace with them, and it shall be an everlasting covenant with them; I will establish them and multiply them, and I will set My sanctuary in their midst forevermore. 27My tabernacle also shall be with them; indeed I will be their God, and they shall be My people. 28The nations also will know that I, the LORD, sanctify Israel, when My sanctuary is in their midst forevermore.” ’ ”

Gog and Allies Attack Israel

38 Now the word of the LORD came to me, saying, 2“Son of man, set your face against Gog, of the land of Magog, the prince of Rosh,[a] Meshech, and Tubal, and prophesy against him, 3and say, ‘Thus says the Lord GOD: “Behold, I *am* against you, O Gog, the prince of Rosh, Meshech, and Tubal. 4I will turn you around, put hooks into your jaws, and lead you out, with all your army, horses, and horsemen, all splendidly clothed, a great company *with* bucklers and shields, all of them handling swords. 5Persia, Ethiopia,[a] and Libya[b] are with them, all of them *with* shield and helmet; 6Gomer and all its troops; the house of Togarmah *from* the far north and all its troops—many people *are* with you.

7“Prepare yourself and be ready, you and all your companies that are gathered about you; and be a guard for them. 8After many days you will be visited. In the latter years you will come into the land of those brought back from the sword *and* gathered from many people on the mountains of Israel, which had long been desolate; they were brought out of the nations, and now all of them dwell safely. 9You will ascend, coming like a storm, covering the land like a cloud, you and all your troops and many peoples with you.”

10‘Thus says the Lord GOD: “On that day it shall come to pass *that* thoughts will arise in your mind, and you will make an evil plan: 11You will say, ‘I will go up against a land of unwalled villages; I will go to a peaceful people, who dwell safely, all of them dwelling without walls, and having neither bars nor gates’— 12to take plunder and to take booty, to stretch out your hand against the waste places *that are again* inhabited, and against a people gathered from the nations, who have acquired livestock and goods, who dwell in the midst of the land. 13Sheba, Dedan, the merchants of Tarshish, and all their

38:2 [a]Targum, Vulgate, and Aquila read *chief prince of* (also verse 3). 38:5 [a]Hebrew *Cush* [b]Hebrew *Put*

The Message

they pollute their lives with their no-god idols and all those vile obscenities and rebellions. I’ll save them out of all their old sinful haunts. I’ll clean them up. They’ll be my people! I’ll be their God! My servant David will be king over them. They’ll all be under one shepherd.

24-27 “ ‘They’ll follow my laws and keep my statutes. They’ll live in the same land I gave my servant Jacob, the land where your ancestors lived. They and their children and their grandchildren will live there forever, and my servant David will be their prince forever. I’ll make a covenant of peace with them that will hold everything together, an everlasting covenant. I’ll make them secure and place my holy place of worship at the center of their lives forever. I’ll live right there with them. I’ll be their God! They’ll be my people!

28 “ ‘The nations will realize that I, GOD, make Israel holy when my holy place of worship is established at the center of their lives forever.’ ”

God Against Gog

1-6 38 GOD’s Message came to me: “Son of man, confront Gog from the country of Magog, head of Meshech and Tubal. Prophesy against him. Say, ‘GOD, the Master, says: Be warned, Gog. I am against you, head of Meshech and Tubal. I’m going to turn you around, put hooks in your jaws, and drag you off with your whole army, your horses and riders in full armor—all those shields and bucklers and swords—fighting men armed to the teeth! Persia and Cush and Put will be in the ranks, also well-armed, as will Gomer and its army and Beth-togarmah out of the north with its army. Many nations will be with you!

7-9 “ ‘Get ready to fight, you and the whole company that’s been called out. Take charge and wait for orders. After a long time, you’ll be given your orders. In the distant future you’ll arrive at a country that has recovered from a devastating war. People from many nations will be gathered there on the mountains of Israel, for a long time now a wasteland. These people have been brought back from many countries and now live safe and secure. You’ll rise like a thunderstorm and roll in like clouds and cover the land, you and the massed troops with you.

10-12 “ ‘Message of GOD, the Master: At that time you’ll start thinking things over and cook up an evil plot. You’ll say, “I’m going to invade a country without defenses, attack an unsuspecting, carefree people going about their business—no gates to their cities, no locks on their doors. And I’m going to plunder the place, march right in and clean them out, this rebuilt country risen from the ashes, these returned exiles and their booming economy centered down at the navel of the earth.”

13 “ ‘Sheba and Dedan and Tarshish, traders all out to make a fast buck, will say, “So!

NEW KING JAMES VERSION

young lions will say to you, ‘Have you come to take plunder? Have you gathered your army to take booty, to carry away silver and gold, to take away livestock and goods, to take great plunder?’ ” ’

14“Therefore, son of man, prophesy and say to Gog, ‘Thus says the Lord GOD: “On that day when My people Israel dwell safely, will you not know *it?* 15Then you will come from your place out of the far north, you and many peoples with you, all of them riding on horses, a great company and a mighty army. 16You will come up against My people Israel like a cloud, to cover the land. It will be in the latter days that I will bring you against My land, so that the nations may know Me, when I am hallowed in you, O Gog, before their eyes.” 17Thus says the Lord GOD: “Are *you* he of whom I have spoken in former days by My servants the prophets of Israel, who prophesied for years in those days that I would bring you against them?

JUDGMENT ON GOG

18“And it will come to pass at the same time, when Gog comes against the land of Israel,” says the Lord GOD, “*that* My fury will show in My face. 19For in My jealousy *and* in the fire of My wrath I have spoken: ‘Surely in that day there shall be a great earthquake in the land of Israel, 20so that the fish of the sea, the birds of the heavens, the beasts of the field, all creeping things that creep on the earth, and all men who *are* on the face of the earth shall shake at My presence. The mountains shall be thrown down, the steep places shall fall, and every wall shall fall to the ground.’ 21I will call for a sword against Gog throughout all My mountains,” says the Lord GOD. “Every man’s sword will be against his brother. 22And I will bring him to judgment with pestilence and bloodshed; I will rain down on him, on his troops, and on the many peoples who *are* with him, flooding rain, great hailstones, fire, and brimstone. 23Thus I will magnify Myself and sanctify Myself, and I will be known in the eyes of many nations. Then they shall know that I *am* the LORD.” ’

GOG’S ARMIES DESTROYED

39 “And you, son of man, prophesy against Gog, and say, ‘Thus says the Lord GOD: “Behold, I *am* against you, O Gog, the prince of Rosh,[a] Meshech, and Tubal; 2and I will turn you around and lead you on, bringing you up from the far north, and bring you against the mountains of Israel. 3Then I will knock the bow out of your left hand, and cause the arrows to fall out of your right hand. 4You shall fall upon the mountains of Israel, you and all your troops and the peoples who *are* with you; I will give you to birds of prey of every sort and *to* the beasts of the field to be devoured. 5You shall fall on the open field; for I have spoken,” says the Lord GOD. 6“And I will send fire on Magog and on those who live in security in the coastlands. Then they shall know that I *am* the LORD. 7So I will make My holy name known in the midst of My people Israel, and I will not *let them* profane

39:1 [a]Targum, Vulgate and Aquila read *chief prince of.*

THE MESSAGE

You’ve opened a new market for plunder!
You’ve brought in your troops to get rich
quick!” ’
14-16 “Therefore, son of man, prophesy! Tell
Gog, ‘A Message from GOD, the Master:
When my people Israel are established securely, will you make your move? Will you come down out of the far north, you and that mob of armies, charging out on your horses like a tidal wave across the land, and invade my people Israel, covering the country like a cloud? When the time’s ripe, I’ll unleash you against my land in such a way that the nations will recognize me, realize that through you, Gog, in full view of the nations, I am putting my holiness on display.

17-22 “ ‘A Message of GOD, the Master: Years ago when I spoke through my servants, the prophets of Israel, wasn’t it you I was talking about? Year after year they prophesied that I would bring you against them. And when the day comes, Gog, you will attack that land of Israel. Decree of GOD, the Master. My raging anger will erupt. Fueled by blazing jealousy, I tell you that then there will be an earthquake that rocks the land of Israel. Fish and birds and wild animals—even ants and beetles!—and every human being will tremble and shake before me. Mountains will disintegrate, terraces will crumble. I’ll order all-out war against you, Gog—Decree of GOD, the Master—Gog killing Gog on all the mountains of Israel. I’ll deluge Gog with judgment: disease and massacre, torrential rain and hail, volcanic lava pouring down on you and your mobs of troops and people.
23 “ ‘I’ll show you how great I am, how holy I am. I’ll make myself known all over the world. Then you’ll realize that I am GOD.’ ”

CALL THE WILD ANIMALS!

1-5 39 “Son of man, prophesy against Gog. Say, ‘A Message of GOD, the Master: I’m against you, Gog, head of Meshech and Tubal. I’m going to turn you around and drag you out, drag you out of the far north and down on the mountains of Israel. Then I’ll knock your bow out of your left hand and your arrows from your right hand. On the mountains of Israel you’ll be slaughtered, you and all your troops and the people with you. I’ll serve you up as a meal to carrion birds and scavenging animals. You’ll be killed in the open field. I’ve given my word. Decree of GOD, the Master.’
6 “I’ll set fire to Magog and the far-off islands, where people are so seemingly secure. And they’ll realize that I am GOD.
7 “I’ll reveal my holy name among my people Israel. Never again will I let my holy name be dragged in the mud. Then the na-

NEW KING JAMES VERSION

My holy name anymore. Then the nations shall
know that *I am* the LORD, the Holy One in Israel.
8Surely it is coming, and it shall be done," says
the Lord GOD. "This *is* the day of which I have
spoken.
9"Then those who dwell in the cities of Israel
will go out and set on fire and burn the
weapons, both the shields and bucklers, the
bows and arrows, the javelins and spears; and
they will make fires with them for seven years.
10They will not take wood from the field nor cut
down *any* from the forests, because they will
make fires with the weapons; and they will
plunder those who plundered them, and pillage
those who pillaged them," says the Lord GOD.

THE BURIAL OF GOG

11"It will come to pass in that day *that* I will
give Gog a burial place there in Israel, the valley
of those who pass by east of the sea; and it will
obstruct travelers, because there they will bury
Gog and all his multitude. Therefore they will
call *it* the Valley of Hamon Gog.[a] 12For seven
months the house of Israel will be burying them,
in order to cleanse the land. 13Indeed all the peo-
ple of the land will be burying, and they will
gain renown for it on the day that I am glori-
fied," says the Lord GOD. 14"They will set apart
men regularly employed, with the help of a
search party,[a] to pass through the land and bury
those bodies remaining on the ground, in order
to cleanse it. At the end of seven months they
will make a search. 15The search party will pass
through the land; and *when anyone* sees a
man's bone, he shall set up a marker by it, till
the buriers have buried it in the Valley of Hamon
Gog. 16*The* name of *the* city *will* also *be* Ha-
monah. Thus they shall cleanse the land." '

A TRIUMPHANT FESTIVAL

17"And as for you, son of man, thus says the
Lord GOD, 'Speak to every sort of bird and to
every beast of the field:

"Assemble yourselves and come;
Gather together from all sides to My
sacrificial meal
Which I am sacrificing for you,
A great sacrificial meal on the mountains of
Israel,
That you may eat flesh and drink blood.
18You shall eat the flesh of the mighty,
Drink the blood of the princes of the earth,
Of rams and lambs,
Of goats and bulls,
All of them fatlings of Bashan.
19You shall eat fat till you are full,
And drink blood till you are drunk,
At My sacrificial meal
Which I am sacrificing for you.
20You shall be filled at My table
With horses and riders,
With mighty men
And with all the men of war," says the Lord
GOD.

39:11 [a]Literally *The Multitude of Gog* **39:14** [a]Literally *those who pass through*

THE MESSAGE

tions will realize that I, GOD, am The Holy in
Israel.
8 "It's coming! Yes, it will happen! This is
the day I've been telling you about.
9-10 "People will come out of the cities of Is-
rael and make a huge bonfire of the
weapons of war, piling on shields large and
small, bows and arrows, clubs and spears, a
fire they'll keep going for seven years. They
won't need to go into the woods to get fuel
for the fire. There'll be plenty of weapons to
keep it going. They'll strip those who
stripped them. They'll rob those who robbed
them. Decree of GOD, the Master.
11 "At that time I'll set aside a burial ground
for Gog in Israel at Traveler's Rest, just east
of the sea. It will obstruct the route of trav-
elers, blocking their way, the mass grave of
Gog and his mob of an army. They'll call the
place Gog's Mob.
12-16 "Israel will bury the corpses in order to
clean up the land. It will take them seven
months. All the people will turn out to help
with the burials. It will be a big day for the
people when it's all done and I'm given my
due. Men will be hired full-time for the
cleanup burial operation and will go
through the country looking for defiling, de-
composing corpses. At the end of seven
months, there'll be an all-out final search.
Anyone who sees a bone will mark the place
with a stick so the buriers can get it and
bury it in the mass burial site, Gog's Mob. (A
town nearby is called Mobville, or Ha-
monah.) That's how they'll clean up the
land.
17-20 "Son of man, GOD, the Master, says: Call
the birds! Call the wild animals! Call out,
'Gather and come, gather around my sacri-
ficial meal that I'm preparing for you on the
mountains of Israel. You'll eat meat and
drink blood. You'll eat off the bodies of great
heroes and drink the blood of famous
princes as if they were so many rams and
lambs, goats and bulls, the choicest grain-
fed animals of Bashan. At the sacrificial
meal I'm fixing for you, you'll eat fat till
you're stuffed and drink blood till you're
drunk. At the table I set for you, you'll stuff
yourselves with horses and riders, heroes
and fighters of every kind.' Decree of GOD,
the Master.

NEW KING JAMES VERSION

ISRAEL RESTORED TO THE LAND

21"I will set My glory among the nations; all the nations shall see My judgment which I have executed, and My hand which I have laid on them. 22So the house of Israel shall know that I *am* the LORD their God from that day forward. 23The Gentiles shall know that the house of Israel went into captivity for their iniquity; because they were unfaithful to Me, therefore I hid My face from them. I gave them into the hand of their enemies, and they all fell by the sword. 24According to their uncleanness and according to their transgressions I have dealt with them, and hidden My face from them." '

25"Therefore thus says the Lord GOD: 'Now I will bring back the captives of Jacob, and have mercy on the whole house of Israel; and I will be jealous for My holy name— 26after they have borne their shame, and all their unfaithfulness in which they were unfaithful to Me, when they dwelt safely in their *own* land and no one made *them* afraid. 27When I have brought them back from the peoples and gathered them out of their enemies' lands, and I am hallowed in them in the sight of many nations, 28then they shall know that I *am* the LORD their God, who sent them into captivity among the nations, but also brought them back to their land, and left none of them captive any longer. 29And I will not hide My face from them anymore; for I shall have poured out My Spirit on the house of Israel,' says the Lord GOD."

A NEW CITY, A NEW TEMPLE

40 In the twenty-fifth year of our captivity, at the beginning of the year, on the tenth *day* of the month, in the fourteenth year after the city was captured, on the very same day the hand of the LORD was upon me; and He took me there. 2In the visions of God He took me into the land of Israel and set me on a very high mountain; on it toward the south *was* something like the structure of a city. 3He took me there, and behold, *there was* a man whose appearance *was* like the appearance of bronze. He had a line of flax and a measuring rod in his hand, and he stood in the gateway.

4And the man said to me, "Son of man, look with your eyes and hear with your ears, and fix your mind on everything I show you; for you *were* brought here so that I might show *them* to you. Declare to the house of Israel everything you see." 5Now there was a wall all around the outside of the temple.[a] In the man's hand was a measuring rod six cubits *long, each being a* cubit and a handbreadth; and he measured the width of the wall structure, one rod; and the height, one rod.

THE EASTERN GATEWAY OF THE TEMPLE

6Then he went to the gateway which faced east; and he went up its stairs and measured the threshold of the gateway, *which was* one rod wide, and the other threshold *was* one rod wide. 7Each gate chamber *was* one rod long and one rod wide; between the gate chambers *was a space of* five cubits; and the threshold of the gateway by the vestibule of the inside gate *was* one rod.

40:5 [a]Literally *house,* and so elsewhere in this book

THE MESSAGE

21-24 "I'll put my glory on display among the
nations and they'll all see the judgment I execute, see me at work handing out judgment. From that day on, Israel will realize that I am their GOD. And the nations will get the message that it was because of their sins that Israel went into exile. They were disloyal to me and I turned away from them. I turned them over to their enemies and they were all killed. I treated them as their polluted and sin-sated lives deserved. I turned away from them, refused to look at them.

25-29 "But now I will return Jacob back from
exile, I'll be compassionate with all the people of Israel, and I'll be zealous for my holy name. Eventually the memory will fade, the memory of their shame over their betrayals of me when they lived securely in their own land, safe and unafraid. Once I've brought them back from foreign parts, gathered them in from enemy territories, I'll use them to demonstrate my holiness with all the nations watching. Then they'll realize for sure that I am their GOD, for even though I sent them off into exile, I will gather them back to their own land, leaving not one soul behind. After I've poured my Spirit on Israel, filled them with my life, I'll no longer turn away. I'll look them full in the face. Decree of GOD, the Master."

MEASURING THE TEMPLE COMPLEX

1-3 40 In the twenty-fifth year of our exile, at
the beginning of the year on the tenth of the month—it was the fourteenth year after the city fell—GOD touched me and brought me here. He brought me in divine vision to the land of Israel and set me down on a high mountain. To the south there were buildings that looked like a city. He took me there and I met a man deeply tanned, like bronze. He stood at the entrance holding a linen cord and a measuring stick.

4 The man said to me, "Son of man, look
and listen carefully. Pay close attention to everything I'm going to show you. That's why you've been brought here. And then tell Israel everything you see."

5 First I saw a wall around the outside of the
Temple complex. The measuring stick in the man's hand was about ten feet long. He measured the thickness of the wall: about ten feet. The height was also about ten feet.

6-7 He went into the gate complex that faced
the east and went up the seven steps. He measured the depth of the outside threshold of the gate complex: ten feet. There were alcoves flanking the gate corridor, each ten feet square, each separated by a wall seven and a half feet thick. The inside threshold of the gate complex that led to the porch facing into the Temple courtyard was ten feet deep.

New King James Version

8He also measured the vestibule of the inside
gate, one rod. 9Then he measured the vestibule
of the gateway, eight cubits; and the gateposts,
two cubits. The vestibule of the gate *was* on the
inside. 10In the eastern gateway *were* three gate
chambers on one side and three on the other;
the three *were* all the same size; also the
gateposts were of the same size on this side and
that side.
11He measured the width of the entrance to
the gateway, ten cubits; *and* the length of the
gate, thirteen cubits. 12*There was* a space in front
of the gate chambers, one cubit *on this side* and
one cubit on that side; the gate chambers *were*
six cubits on this side and six cubits on that side.
13Then he measured the gateway from the roof of
one gate chamber to the roof of the other; the
width *was* twenty-five cubits, as door faces door.
14He measured the gateposts, sixty cubits high,
and the court all around the gateway *extended*
to the gatepost. 15*From* the front of the entrance
gate to the front of the vestibule of the inner gate
was fifty cubits. 16*There were* beveled window
frames in the gate chambers and in their inter-
vening archways on the inside of the gateway all
around, and likewise in the vestibules. *There*
were windows all around on the inside. And on
each gatepost *were* palm trees.

The Outer Court

17Then he brought me into the outer court;
and *there were* chambers and a pavement made
all around the court; thirty chambers faced the
pavement. 18The pavement was by the side of
the gateways, corresponding to the length of the
gateways; *this was* the lower pavement. 19Then
he measured the width from the front of the
lower gateway to the front of the inner court ex-
terior, one hundred cubits toward the east and
the north.

The Northern Gateway

20On the outer court was also a gateway fac-
ing north, and he measured its length and its
width. 21Its gate chambers, three on this side
and three on that side, its gateposts and its
archways, had the same measurements as the
first gate; its length *was* fifty cubits and its
width twenty-five cubits. 22Its windows and
those of its archways, and also its palm trees,
had the same measurements as the gateway
facing east; it was ascended by seven steps,
and its archway *was* in front of it. 23A gate of
the inner court was opposite the northern gate-
way, just as the eastern *gateway;* and he meas-
ured from gateway to gateway, one hundred
cubits.

The Southern Gateway

24After that he brought me toward the south,
and there a gateway was facing south; and he
measured its gateposts and archways according
to these same measurements. 25*There were* win-
dows in it and in its archways all around like
those windows; its length *was* fifty cubits and
its width twenty-five cubits. 26Seven steps led up
to it, and its archway *was* in front of them; and
it had palm trees on its gateposts, one on this
side and one on that side. 27*There was* also a

The Message

8-9 He measured the inside porch of the gate
complex: twelve feet deep, flanked by pillars
three feet thick. The porch opened onto the
Temple courtyard.
10 Inside this east gate complex were three
alcoves on each side. Each room was the
same size and the separating walls were
identical.
11 He measured the outside entrance to the
gate complex: fifteen feet wide and nineteen
and a half feet deep.
12 In front of each alcove was a low wall
eighteen inches high. The alcoves were ten
feet square.
13 He measured the width of the gate com-
plex from the outside edge of the alcove roof
on one side to the outside edge of the alcove
roof on the other: thirty-seven and a half
feet from one top edge to the other.
14 He measured the inside walls of the gate
complex: ninety feet to the porch leading
into the courtyard.
15 The distance from the entrance of the
gate complex to the far end of the porch was
seventy-five feet.
16 The alcoves and their connecting walls
inside the gate complex were topped by nar-
row windows all the way around. The porch
also. All the windows faced inward. The
doorjambs between the alcoves were deco-
rated with palm trees.

17-19 The man then led me to the outside court-
yard and all its rooms. A paved walkway
had been built connecting the courtyard
gates. Thirty rooms lined the courtyard. The
walkway was the same length as the gate-
ways. It flanked them and ran their entire
length. This was the walkway for the out-
side courtyard. He measured the distance
from the front of the entrance gateway
across to the entrance of the inner court:
one hundred fifty feet.

19-23 Then he took me to the north side. Here was
another gate complex facing north, exiting
the outside courtyard. He measured its
length and width. It had three alcoves on
each side. Its gateposts and porch were the
same as in the first gate: eighty-seven and a
half feet by forty-three and three-quarters
feet. The windows and palm trees were
identical to the east gateway. Seven steps
led up to it, and its porch faced inward. Op-
posite this gate complex was a gate complex
to the inside courtyard, on the north as on
the east. The distance between the two was
one hundred seventy-five feet.
24-27 Then he took me to the south side, to the
south gate complex. He measured its
gateposts and its porch. It was the same size
as the others. The porch with its windows
was the same size as those previously men-
tioned. It also had seven steps up to it. Its
porch opened onto the outside courtyard,
with palm trees decorating its gateposts on
both sides. Opposite to it, the gate complex

NEW KING JAMES VERSION

gateway on the inner court, facing south; and he
measured from gateway to gateway toward the
south, one hundred cubits.

GATEWAYS OF THE INNER COURT

28Then he brought me to the inner court
through the southern gateway; he measured the
southern gateway according to these same
measurements. 29Also its gate chambers, its
gateposts, and its archways *were* according to
these same measurements; *there were* windows
in it and in its archways all around; *it was* fifty
cubits long and twenty-five cubits wide. 30*There*
were archways all around, twenty-five cubits
long and five cubits wide. 31Its archways faced
the outer court, palm trees *were* on its gateposts,
and going up to it *were* eight steps.

32And he brought me into the inner court fac-
ing east; he measured the gateway according to
these same measurements. 33Also its gate cham-
bers, its gateposts, and its archways *were* ac-
cording to these same measurements; and *there*
were windows in it and in its archways all
around; *it was* fifty cubits long and twenty-five
cubits wide. 34Its archways faced the outer
court, and palm trees *were* on its gateposts on
this side and on that side; and going up to it
were eight steps.

35Then he brought me to the north gateway
and measured *it* according to these same mea-
surements— 36also its gate chambers, its
gateposts, and its archways. It had windows all
around; its length *was* fifty cubits and its width
twenty-five cubits. 37Its gateposts faced the
outer court, palm trees *were* on its gateposts on
this side and on that side, and going up to it
were eight steps.

WHERE SACRIFICES WERE PREPARED

38*There was* a chamber and its entrance by
the gateposts of the gateway, where they
washed the burnt offering. 39In the vestibule of
the gateway *were* two tables on this side and
two tables on that side, on which to slay the
burnt offering, the sin offering, and the trespass
offering. 40At the outer side of the vestibule, as
one goes up to the entrance of the northern
gateway, *were* two tables; and on the other side
of the vestibule of the gateway *were* two tables.
41Four tables *were* on this side and four tables
on that side, by the side of the gateway, eight ta-
bles on which they slaughtered *the sacrifices.*
42*There were* also four tables of hewn stone for
the burnt offering, one cubit and a half long, one
cubit and a half wide, and one cubit high; on
these they laid the instruments with which they
slaughtered the burnt offering and the sacrifice.
43Inside *were* hooks, a handbreadth wide, fas-
tened all around; and the flesh of the sacrifices
was on the tables.

CHAMBERS FOR SINGERS AND PRIESTS

44Outside the inner gate *were* the chambers
for the singers in the inner court, one facing
south at the side of the northern gateway, and
the other facing north at the side of the south-
ern[a] gateway. 45Then he said to me, "This cham-

40:44 [a]Following Septuagint; Masoretic Text and Vulgate read *eastern.*

THE MESSAGE

for the inner court faced south. He mea-
sured the distance across the courtyard from
gate to gate: one hundred seventy-five feet.

28-31 He led me into the inside courtyard through
the south gate complex. He measured it and
found it the same as the outside ones. Its al-
coves, connecting walls, and vestibule were
the same. The gate complex and porch, win-
dowed all around, measured eighty-seven
and a half by forty-three and three-quarters
feet. The vestibule of each of the gate com-
plexes leading to the inside courtyard was
forty-three and three-quarters by eight and
three-quarters feet. Each vestibule faced the
outside courtyard. Palm trees were carved
on its doorposts. Eight steps led up to it.
32-34 He then took me to the inside courtyard
on the east and measured the gate complex.
It was identical to the others—alcoves, con-
necting walls, and vestibule all the same.
The gate complex and vestibule had win-
dows all around. It measured eighty-seven
and a half by forty-three and three-quarters
feet. Its porch faced the outside courtyard.
There were palm trees on the doorposts on
both sides. And it had eight steps.
35-37 He brought me to the gate complex to the
north and measured it: same measurements.
The alcoves, connecting walls, and vestibule
with its windows: eighty-seven and a half by
forty-three and three-quarters feet. Its porch
faced the outside courtyard. There were
palm trees on its doorposts on both sides.
And it had eight steps.

38-43 There was a room with a door at the
vestibule of the gate complex where the
burnt offerings were cleaned. Two tables
were placed within the vestibule, one on ei-
ther side, on which the animals for burnt of-
ferings, sin offerings, and guilt offerings
were slaughtered. Two tables were also
placed against both outside walls of the
vestibule—four tables inside and four tables
outside, eight tables in all for slaughtering
the sacrificial animals. The four tables used
for the burnt offerings were thirty-one and a
half inches square and twenty-one inches
high. The tools for slaughtering the sacrifi-
cial animals and other sacrifices were kept
there. Meat hooks, three inches long, were
fastened to the walls. The tables were for
the sacrificial animals.

44-46 Right where the inside gate complex opened
onto the inside courtyard there were two
rooms, one at the north gate facing south
and the one at the south gate facing north.
The man told me, "The room facing south is

NEW KING JAMES VERSION

ber which faces south *is* for the priests who
have charge of the temple. 46 The chamber which
faces north *is* for the priests who have charge of
the altar; these *are* the sons of Zadok, from the
sons of Levi, who come near the LORD to minis-
ter to Him."

DIMENSIONS OF THE INNER COURT AND VESTIBULE

47 And he measured the court, one hundred
cubits long and one hundred cubits wide,
foursquare. The altar *was* in front of the temple.
48 Then he brought me to the vestibule of the
temple and measured the doorposts of the
vestibule, five cubits on this side and five cubits
on that side; and the width of the gateway was
three cubits on this side and three cubits on that
side. 49 The length of the vestibule *was* twenty
cubits, and the width eleven cubits; and by the
steps which led up to it *there were* pillars by the
doorposts, one on this side and another on that
side.

DIMENSIONS OF THE SANCTUARY

41 Then he brought me into the sanctuary[a]
and measured the doorposts, six cubits
wide on one side and six cubits wide on the
other side—the width of the tabernacle. 2 The
width of the entryway *was* ten cubits, and the
side walls of the entrance *were* five cubits on
this side and five cubits on the other side; and
he measured its length, forty cubits, and its
width, twenty cubits.

3 Also he went inside and measured the door-
posts, two cubits; and the entrance, six cubits
high; and the width of the entrance, seven cu-
bits. 4 He measured the length, twenty cubits;
and the width, twenty cubits, beyond the sanctu-
ary; and he said to me, "This *is* the Most Holy
Place."

THE SIDE CHAMBERS ON THE WALL

5 Next, he measured the wall of the temple,
six cubits. The width of each side chamber all
around the temple *was* four cubits on every side.
6 The side chambers *were* in three stories, one
above the other, thirty chambers in each story;
they rested on ledges which *were* for the side
chambers all around, that they might be sup-
ported, but not fastened to the wall of the tem-
ple. 7 As one went up from story to story, the side
chambers became wider all around, because
their supporting ledges in the wall of the temple
ascended like steps; therefore the width of the
structure increased as one went up *from* the
lowest *story* to the highest by way of the middle
one. 8 I also saw an elevation all around the tem-
ple; it was the foundation of the side chambers,
a full rod, *that is,* six cubits *high.* 9 The thickness
of the outer wall of the side chambers *was* five
cubits, and so also the remaining terrace by the
place of the side chambers of the temple. 10 And
between *it and* the *wall* chambers was a width
of twenty cubits all around the temple on every
side. 11 The doors of the side chambers opened
on the terrace, one door toward the north and
another toward the south; and the width of the
terrace *was* five cubits all around.

41:1 [a]Hebrew *heykal,* here the main room of the temple, sometimes called the *holy place* (compare Exodus 26:33)

THE MESSAGE

for the priests who are in charge of the Temple. And the room facing north is for the priests who are in charge of the altar. These priests are the sons of Zadok, the only sons of Levi permitted to come near to GOD to serve him."

47 He measured the inside courtyard: a hundred seventy-five feet square. The altar was in front of the Temple.

48-49 He led me to the porch of the Temple and measured the gateposts of the porch: eight and three-quarters feet high on both sides. The entrance to the gate complex was twenty-one feet wide and its connecting walls were four and a half feet thick. The vestibule itself was thirty-five feet wide and twenty-one feet deep. Ten steps led up to the porch. Columns flanked the gateposts.

1-2 41 He brought me into the Temple itself and measured the doorposts on each side. Each was ten and a half feet thick. The entrance was seventeen and a half feet wide. The walls on each side were eight and three-quarters feet thick.

He also measured the Temple Sanctuary: seventy feet by thirty-five feet.

3-4 He went further in and measured the doorposts at the entrance: Each was three and a half feet thick. The entrance itself was ten and a half feet wide, and the entrance walls were twelve and a quarter feet thick. He measured the inside Sanctuary, thirty-five feet square, set at the end of the main Sanctuary. He told me, "This is The Holy of Holies."

5-7 He measured the wall of the Temple. It was ten and a half feet thick. The side rooms around the Temple were seven feet wide. There were three floors of these side rooms, thirty rooms on each of the three floors. There were supporting beams around the Temple wall to hold up the side rooms, but they were freestanding, not attached to the wall itself. The side rooms around the Temple became wider from first floor to second floor to third floor. A staircase went from the bottom floor, through the middle, and then to the top floor.

8-11 I observed that the Temple had a ten-and-a-half-foot-thick raised base around it, which provided a foundation for the side rooms. The outside walls of the side rooms were eight and three-quarters feet thick. The open area between the side rooms of the Temple and the priests' rooms was a thirty-five-foot-wide strip all around the Temple. There were two entrances to the side rooms from the open area, one placed on the north side, the other on the south. There were eight and three-quarters feet of open space all around.

New King James Version

The Building at the Western End

12The building that faced the separating courtyard at its western end *was* seventy cubits wide; the wall of the building *was* five cubits thick all around, and its length ninety cubits.

Dimensions and Design of the Temple Area

13So he measured the temple, one hundred cubits long; and the separating courtyard with the building and its walls *was* one hundred cubits long; 14also the width of the eastern face of the temple, including the separating courtyard, *was* one hundred cubits. 15He measured the length of the building behind it, facing the separating courtyard, with its galleries on the one side and on the other side, one hundred cubits, as well as the inner temple and the porches of the court, 16their doorposts and the beveled window frames. And the galleries all around their three stories opposite the threshold were paneled with wood from the ground to the windows—the windows were covered— 17from the space above the door, even to the inner room,[a] as well as outside, and on every wall all around, inside and outside, by measure.

18And *it was* made with cherubim and palm trees, a palm tree between cherub and cherub. *Each* cherub had two faces, 19so that the face of a man *was* toward a palm tree on one side, and the face of a young lion toward a palm tree on the other side; thus *it was* made throughout the temple all around. 20From the floor to the space above the door, and on the wall of the sanctuary, cherubim and palm trees *were* carved.

21The doorposts of the temple *were* square, *as was* the front of the sanctuary; their appearance was similar. 22The altar *was* of wood, three cubits high, and its length two cubits. Its corners, its length, and its sides *were* of wood; and he said to me, "This *is* the table that *is* before the LORD."

23The temple and the sanctuary had two doors. 24The doors had two panels *apiece*, two folding panels: two *panels* for one door and two panels for the other *door*. 25Cherubim and palm trees *were* carved on the doors of the temple just as they *were* carved on the walls. A wooden canopy *was* on the front of the vestibule outside. 26*There were* beveled window *frames* and palm trees on one side and on the other, on the sides of the vestibule—also on the side chambers of the temple and on the canopies.

The Chambers for the Priests

42 Then he brought me out into the outer court, by the way toward the north; and he brought me into the chamber which *was* opposite the separating courtyard, and which *was* opposite the building toward the north. 2Facing the length, *which was* one hundred cubits (the width was fifty cubits), was the north door. 3Opposite the inner court of twenty *cubits*, and opposite the pavement of the outer court, *was* gallery against gallery in three *stories*. 4In front of the chambers, toward the inside, *was* a walk ten cubits wide, at a distance of one cubit; and their doors faced north. 5Now the upper chambers *were* shorter, because the galleries took

41:17 [a]Literally *house*, here *the Most Holy Place*

The Message

12 The house that faced the Temple courtyard to the west was one hundred twenty-two and a half feet wide, with eight-and-three-quarters-foot-thick walls. The length of the wall and building was one hundred fifty-seven and a half feet.

13-14 He measured the Temple: one hundred seventy-five feet long. The Temple courtyard and the house, including its walls, measured a hundred seventy-five feet. The breadth of the front of the Temple and the open area to the east was a hundred seventy-five feet.

15-18 He measured the length of the house facing the courtyard at the back of the Temple, including the shelters on each side: one hundred seventy-five feet. The main Sanctuary, the inner Sanctuary, and the vestibule facing the courtyard were paneled with wood, and had window frames and door frames in all three sections. From floor to windows the walls were paneled. Above the outside entrance to the inner Sanctuary and on the walls at regular intervals all around the inner Sanctuary and the main Sanctuary, angel-cherubim and palm trees were carved in alternating sequence.

18-20 Each angel-cherub had two faces: a human face toward the palm tree on the right and the face of a lion toward the palm tree on the left. They were carved around the entire Temple. The cherubim–palm tree motif was carved from floor to door height on the wall of the main Sanctuary.

21-22 The main Sanctuary had a rectangular doorframe. In front of the Holy Place was something that looked like an altar of wood, five and a quarter feet high and three and a half feet square. Its corners, base, and sides were of wood. The man said to me, "This is the table that stands before GOD."

23-26 Both the main Sanctuary and the Holy Place had double doors. Each door had two leaves: two hinged leaves for each door, one set swinging inward and the other set outward. The doors of the main Sanctuary were carved with angel-cherubim and palm trees. There was a canopy of wood in front of the vestibule outside. There were narrow windows alternating with carved palm trees on both sides of the porch.

1-9 42 The man led me north into the outside courtyard and brought me to the rooms that are in front of the open space and the house facing north. The length of the house on the north was one hundred seventy-five feet, and its width eighty-seven and a half feet. Across the thirty-five feet that separated the inside courtyard from the paved walkway at the edge of the outside courtyard, the rooms rose level by level for three stories. In front of the rooms on the inside was a hallway seventeen and a half feet wide and one hundred seventy-five feet long. Its entrances were from the north. The upper rooms themselves were narrower,

NEW KING JAMES VERSION

away *space* from them more than from the
lower and middle stories of the building. 6For
they *were* in three *stories* and did not have pil-
lars like the pillars of the courts; therefore *the*
upper level was shortened more than the lower
and middle levels from the ground up. 7And a
wall which *was* outside ran parallel to the
chambers, at the front of the chambers, toward
the outer court; its length *was* fifty cubits. 8The
length of the chambers toward the outer court
was fifty cubits, whereas that facing the temple
was one hundred cubits. 9At the lower chambers
was the entrance on the east side, as one goes
into them from the outer court.

10Also *there were* chambers in the thickness
of the wall of the court toward the east, opposite
the separating courtyard and opposite the build-
ing. 11*There was* a walk in front of them also,
and their appearance *was* like the chambers
which *were* toward the north; they *were* as long
and as wide as the others, and all their exits and
entrances *were* according to plan. 12And
corresponding to the doors of the chambers that
were facing south, as one enters them, *there*
was a door in front of the walk, the way directly
in front of the wall toward the east.

13Then he said to me, "The north chambers
and the south chambers, which *are* opposite the
separating courtyard, *are* the holy chambers
where the priests who approach the LORD shall
eat the most holy offerings. There they shall lay
the most holy offerings—the grain offering, the
sin offering, and the trespass offering—for the
place *is* holy. 14When the priests enter them, they
shall not go out of the holy *chamber* into the
outer court; but there they shall leave their gar-
ments in which they minister, for they *are* holy.
They shall put on other garments; then they may
approach *that* which *is* for the people."

OUTER DIMENSIONS OF THE TEMPLE

15Now when he had finished measuring the
inner temple, he brought me out through the
gateway that faces toward the east, and mea-
sured it all around. 16He measured the east side
with the measuring rod,[a] five hundred rods by
the measuring rod all around. 17He measured the
north side, five hundred rods by the measuring
rod all around. 18He measured the south side,
five hundred rods by the measuring rod. 19He
came around to the west side *and* measured five
hundred rods by the measuring rod. 20He mea-
sured it on the four sides; it had a wall all around,
five hundred *cubits* long and five hundred wide,
to separate the holy areas from the common.

THE TEMPLE, THE LORD'S DWELLING PLACE

43 Afterward he brought me to the gate, the
gate that faces toward the east. 2And be-
hold, the glory of the God of Israel came from
the way of the east. His voice *was* like the sound
of many waters; and the earth shone with His
glory. 3*It was* like the appearance of the vision
which I saw—like the vision which I saw when
I[a] came to destroy the city. The visions *were* like
the vision which I saw by the River Chebar; and
I fell on my face.

42:16 [a]Compare 40:5 43:3 [a]Some Hebrew manuscripts and Vulgate read *He*.

THE MESSAGE

their galleries being wider than on the first and second floors of the building. The rooms on the third floor had no pillars like the pillars in the outside courtyard and were smaller than the rooms on the first and second floors. There was an outside wall parallel to the rooms and the outside courtyard. It fronted the rooms for eighty-seven and a half feet. The row of rooms facing the outside courtyard was eighty-seven and a half feet long. The row on the side nearest the Sanctuary was one hundred seventy-five feet long. The first-floor rooms had their entrance from the east, coming in from the outside courtyard.

10-12 On the south side along the length of the courtyard's outside wall and fronting on the Temple courtyard were rooms with a walkway in front of them. These were just like the rooms on the north—same exits and dimensions—with the main entrance from the east leading to the hallway and the doors to the rooms the same as those on the north side. The design on the south was a mirror image of that on the north.

13-14 Then he said to me, "The north and south rooms adjacent to the open area are holy rooms where the priests who come before GOD eat the holy offerings. There they place the holy offerings—grain offerings, sin offerings, and guilt offerings. These are set-apart rooms, holy space. After the priests have entered the Sanctuary, they must not return to the outside courtyard and mingle among the people until they change the sacred garments in which they minister and put on their regular clothes."

15-16 After he had finished measuring what was inside the Temple area, he took me out the east gate and measured it from the outside. Using his measuring stick, he measured the east side: eight hundred seventy-five feet.

17 He measured the north side: eight hundred seventy-five feet.

18 He measured the south side: eight hundred seventy-five feet.

19 Last of all he went to the west side and measured it: eight hundred seventy-five feet.

20 He measured the wall on all four sides. Each wall was eight hundred seventy-five feet. The walls separated the holy from the ordinary.

THE MEANING OF THE TEMPLE

1-3 **43** The man brought me to the east gate. Oh! The bright Glory of the God of Israel rivered out of the east sounding like the roar of floodwaters, and the earth itself glowed with the bright Glory. It looked just like what I had seen when he came to destroy the city, exactly like what I had seen earlier at the Kebar River. And again I fell, face to the ground.

New King James Version

4And the glory of the LORD came into the temple
by way of the gate which faces toward the east.
5The Spirit lifted me up and brought me into the
inner court; and behold, the glory of the LORD
filled the temple.
6Then I heard *Him* speaking to me from the
temple, while a man stood beside me. 7And He
said to me, "Son of man, *this is* the place of My
throne and the place of the soles of My feet,
where I will dwell in the midst of the children of
Israel forever. No more shall the house of Israel
defile My holy name, they nor their kings, by
their harlotry or with the carcasses of their
kings on their high places. 8When they set their
threshold by My threshold, and their doorpost
by My doorpost, with a wall between them and
Me, they defiled My holy name by the abomina-
tions which they committed; therefore I have
consumed them in My anger. 9Now let them put
their harlotry and the carcasses of their kings
far away from Me, and I will dwell in their midst
forever.
10"Son of man, describe the temple to the
house of Israel, that they may be ashamed of
their iniquities; and let them measure the pat-
tern. 11And if they are ashamed of all that they
have done, make known to them the design of
the temple and its arrangement, its exits and its
entrances, its entire design and all its ordi-
nances, all its forms and all its laws. Write *it*
down in their sight, so that they may keep its
whole design and all its ordinances, and per-
form them. 12This *is* the law of the temple: The
whole area surrounding the mountaintop *is*
most holy. Behold, this *is* the law of the temple.

Dimensions of the Altar

13"These are the measurements of the altar
in cubits (the *cubit is* one cubit and a hand-
breadth): the base one cubit high and one cubit
wide, with a rim all around its edge of one span.
This *is* the height of the altar: 14from the base on
the ground to the lower ledge, two cubits; the
width of the ledge, one cubit; from the smaller
ledge to the larger ledge, four cubits; and the
width of the ledge, *one* cubit. 15The altar hearth
is four cubits high, with four horns extending
upward from the hearth. 16The altar hearth *is*
twelve cubits long, twelve wide, square at its
four corners; 17the ledge, fourteen *cubits* long
and fourteen wide on its four sides, with a rim of
half a cubit around it; its base, one cubit all
around; and its steps face toward the east."

Consecrating the Altar

18And He said to me, "Son of man, thus says
the Lord GOD: 'These *are* the ordinances for the
altar on the day when it is made, for sacrificing
burnt offerings on it, and for sprinkling blood
on it. 19You shall give a young bull for a sin of-
fering to the priests, the Levites, who are of the
seed of Zadok, who approach Me to minister to

The Message

4-5 The bright Glory of GOD poured into the Temple through the east gate. The Spirit put me on my feet and led me to the inside courtyard and—oh! the bright Glory of GOD filled the Temple!

6-9 I heard someone speaking to me from inside the Temple while the man stood beside me. He said, "Son of man, this is the place for my throne, the place I'll plant my feet. This is the place where I'll live with the Israelites forever. Neither the people of Israel nor their kings will ever again drag my holy name through the mud with their whoring and the no-god idols their kings set up at all the wayside shrines. When they set up their worship shrines right alongside mine with only a thin wall between them, they dragged my holy name through the mud with their obscene and vile worship. Is it any wonder that I destroyed them in anger? So let them get rid of their whoring ways and the stinking no-god idols introduced by their kings and I'll move in and live with them forever.

10-11 "Son of man, tell the people of Israel all about the Temple so they'll be dismayed by their wayward lives. Get them to go over the layout. That will bring them up short. Show them the whole plan of the Temple, its ins and outs, the proportions, the regulations, and the laws. Draw a picture so they can see the design and meaning and live by its design and intent.

12 "This is the law of the Temple: As it radiates from the top of the mountain, everything around it becomes holy ground. Yes, this is law, the meaning, of the Temple.

13-14 "These are the dimensions of the altar, using the long (twenty-one-inch) ruler. The gutter at its base is twenty-one inches deep and twenty-one inches wide, with a four-inch lip around its edge.

14-15 "The height of the altar is three and a half feet from the base to the first ledge and twenty inches wide. From the first ledge to the second ledge it is seven feet high and twenty-one inches wide. The altar hearth is another seven feet high. Four horns stick upward from the hearth twenty-one inches high.

16-17 "The top of the altar, the hearth, is square, twenty-one by twenty-one feet. The upper ledge is also square, twenty-four and a half feet on each side, with a ten-and-a-half-inch lip and a twenty-one-inch-wide gutter all the way around.

"The steps of the altar ascend from the east."

18 Then the man said to me, "Son of man, GOD, the Master, says: 'These are the ordinances for conduct at the altar when it is built, for sacrificing burnt offerings and sprinkling blood on it.

19-21 " 'For a sin offering, give a bull to the priests, the Levitical priests who are from the family of Zadok who come into my pres-

NEW KING JAMES VERSION

Me,' says the Lord GOD. [20]'You shall take some of its blood and put *it* on the four horns of the altar, on the four corners of the ledge, and on the rim around it; thus you shall cleanse it and make atonement for it. [21]Then you shall also take the bull of the sin offering, and burn it in the appointed place of the temple, outside the sanctuary. [22]On the second day you shall offer a kid of the goats without blemish for a sin offering; and they shall cleanse the altar, as they cleansed *it* with the bull. [23]When you have finished cleansing *it,* you shall offer a young bull without blemish, and a ram from the flock without blemish. [24]When you offer them before the LORD, the priests shall throw salt on them, and they will offer them up *as* a burnt offering to the LORD. [25]Every day for seven days you shall prepare a goat *for* a sin offering; they shall also prepare a young bull and a ram from the flock, both without blemish. [26]Seven days they shall make atonement for the altar and purify it, and so consecrate *it.* [27]When these days are over it shall be, on the eighth day and thereafter, that the priests shall offer your burnt offerings and your peace offerings on the altar; and I will accept you,' says the Lord GOD."

THE EAST GATE AND THE PRINCE

44 Then He brought me back to the outer gate of the sanctuary which faces toward the east, but it *was* shut. [2]And the LORD said to me, "This gate shall be shut; it shall not be opened, and no man shall enter by it, because the LORD God of Israel has entered by it; therefore it shall be shut. [3]*As for* the prince, *because* he *is* the prince, he may sit in it to eat bread before the LORD; he shall enter by way of the vestibule of the gateway, and go out the same way."

THOSE ADMITTED TO THE TEMPLE

[4]Also He brought me by way of the north gate to the front of the temple; so I looked, and behold, the glory of the LORD filled the house of the LORD; and I fell on my face. [5]And the LORD said to me, "Son of man, mark well, see with your eyes and hear with your ears, all that I say to you concerning all the ordinances of the house of the LORD and all its laws. Mark well who may enter the house and all who go out from the sanctuary.

[6]"Now say to the rebellious, to the house of Israel, 'Thus says the Lord GOD: "O house of Israel, let Us have no more of all your abominations. [7]When you brought in foreigners, uncircumcised in heart and uncircumcised in flesh, to be in My sanctuary to defile it—My house—and when you offered My food, the fat and the blood, then they broke My covenant because of all your abominations. [8]And you have not kept charge of My holy things, but you have set *others* to keep charge of My sanctuary for you." [9]Thus says the Lord GOD: "No foreigner, uncircumcised in heart or uncircumcised in flesh, shall enter My sanctuary, including any foreigner who *is* among the children of Israel.

LAWS GOVERNING PRIESTS

[10]"And the Levites who went far from Me, when Israel went astray, who strayed away from

THE MESSAGE

ence to serve me. Take some of its blood and
smear it on the four horns of the altar that
project from the four corners of the top
ledge and all around the lip. That's to purify
the altar and make it fit for the sacrifice.
Then take the bull for the sin offerings and
burn it in the place set aside for this in the
courtyard outside the Sanctuary.
22-24 " 'On the second day, offer a male goat
without blemish for a sin offering. Purify
the altar the same as you purified it for the
bull. Then, when you have purified it, offer a
bull without blemish and a ram without
blemish from the flock. Present them before
GOD. Sprinkle salt on them and offer them
as a burnt offering to GOD.
25-26 " 'For seven days, prepare a goat for a sin
offering daily, and also a bull and a ram
from the flock, animals without blemish. For
seven days the priests are to get the altar
ready for its work, purifying it. This is how
you dedicate it.
27 " 'After these seven days of dedication,
from the eighth day on, the priests will present your burnt offerings and your peace offerings. And I'll accept you with pleasure,
with delight! Decree of GOD, the Master.' "

SANCTUARY RULES

1 **44** Then the man brought me back to the
outside gate complex of the Sanctuary
that faces east. But it was shut.
2-3 GOD spoke to me: "This gate is shut and
it's to stay shut. No one is to go through it
because GOD, the God of Israel, has gone
through it. It stays shut. Only the prince, because he's the prince, may sit there to eat in
the presence of GOD. He is to enter the gate
complex through the porch and leave by the
same way."
4 The man led me through the north gate to
the front of the Temple. I looked, and—oh!—
the bright Glory of GOD filling the Temple of
GOD! I fell on my face in worship.
5 GOD said to me, "Son of man, get a grip
on yourself. Use your eyes, use your ears,
pay careful attention to everything I tell you
about the ordinances of this Temple of GOD,
the way all the laws work, instructions regarding it and all the entrances and exits of
the Sanctuary.
6-9 "Tell this bunch of rebels, this family Israel, 'Message of GOD, the Master: No more
of these vile obscenities, Israel, dragging irreverent and unrepentant outsiders, uncircumcised in heart and flesh, into my Sanctuary, feeding them the sacrificial offerings as
if it were the food for a neighborhood picnic. With all your vile obscenities, you've
broken trust with me, the solemn covenant I
made with you. You haven't taken care of my
holy things. You've hired out the work to foreigners who care nothing for this place, my
Sanctuary. No irreverent and unrepentant
aliens, uncircumcised in heart or flesh, not
even the ones who live among Israelites, are
to enter my Sanctuary.'
10-14 "The Levites who walked off and left me,
along with everyone else—all Israel—who

NEW KING JAMES VERSION

Me after their idols, they shall bear their iniquity. 11Yet they shall be ministers in My sanctuary, *as* gatekeepers of the house and ministers of the house; they shall slay the burnt offering and the sacrifice for the people, and they shall stand before them to minister to them. 12Because they ministered to them before their idols and caused the house of Israel to fall into iniquity, therefore I have raised My hand in an oath against them," says the Lord GOD, "that they shall bear their iniquity. 13And they shall not come near Me to minister to Me as priest, nor come near any of My holy things, nor into the Most Holy *Place;* but they shall bear their shame and their abominations which they have committed. 14Nevertheless I will make them keep charge of the temple, for all its work, and for all that has to be done in it.

15"But the priests, the Levites, the sons of Zadok, who kept charge of My sanctuary when the children of Israel went astray from Me, they shall come near Me to minister to Me; and they shall stand before Me to offer to Me the fat and the blood," says the Lord GOD. 16"They shall enter My sanctuary, and they shall come near My table to minister to Me, and they shall keep My charge. 17And it shall be, whenever they enter the gates of the inner court, that they shall put on linen garments; no wool shall come upon them while they minister within the gates of the inner court or within the house. 18They shall have linen turbans on their heads and linen trousers on their bodies; they shall not clothe themselves with *anything that causes* sweat. 19When they go out to the outer court, to the outer court to the people, they shall take off their garments in which they have ministered, leave them in the holy chambers, and put on other garments; and in their holy garments they shall not sanctify the people.

20"They shall neither shave their heads, nor let their hair grow long, but they shall keep their hair well trimmed. 21No priest shall drink wine when he enters the inner court. 22They shall not take as wife a widow or a divorced woman, but take virgins of the descendants of the house of Israel, or widows of priests.

23"And they shall teach My people *the difference* between the holy and the unholy, and cause them to discern between the unclean and the clean. 24In controversy they shall stand as judges, *and* judge it according to My judgments. They shall keep My laws and My statutes in all My appointed meetings, and they shall hallow My Sabbaths.

25"They shall not defile *themselves* by coming near a dead person. Only for father or mother, for son or daughter, for brother or unmarried sister may they defile themselves. 26After he is cleansed, they shall count seven days for him. 27And on the day that he goes to the

THE MESSAGE

took up with all the no-god idols, will pay for everything they did wrong. From now on they'll do only the menial work in the Sanctuary: guard the gates and help out with the Temple chores—and also kill the sacrificial animals for the people and serve them. Because they acted as priests to the no-god idols and made my people Israel stumble and fall, I've taken an oath to punish them. Decree of GOD, the Master. Yes, they'll pay for what they've done. They're fired from the priesthood. No longer will they come into my presence and take care of my holy things. No more access to The Holy Place! They'll have to live with what they've done, carry the shame of their vile and obscene lives. From now on, their job is to sweep up and run errands. That's it.

15-16 "But the Levitical priests who descend from Zadok, who faithfully took care of my Sanctuary when everyone else went off and left me, are going to come into my presence and serve me. They are going to carry out the priestly work of offering the solemn sacrifices of worship. Decree of GOD, the Master. They're the only ones permitted to enter my Sanctuary. They're the only ones to approach my table and serve me, accompanying me in my work.

17-19 "When they enter the gate complex of the inside courtyard, they are to dress in linen. No woolens are to be worn while serving at the gate complex of the inside courtyard or inside the Temple itself. They're to wear linen turbans on their heads and linen underclothes—nothing that makes them sweat. When they go out into the outside courtyard where the people gather, they must first change out of the clothes they have been serving in, leaving them in the sacred rooms where they change to their everyday clothes, so that they don't trivialize their holy work by the way they dress.

20 "They are to neither shave their heads nor let their hair become unkempt, but must keep their hair trimmed and neat.

21 "No priest is to drink on the job—no wine while in the inside courtyard.

22 "Priests are not to marry widows or divorcees, but only Israelite virgins or widows of priests.

23 "Their job is to teach my people the difference between the holy and the common, to show them how to discern between unclean and clean.

24 "When there's a difference of opinion, the priests will arbitrate. They'll decide on the basis of my judgments, laws, and statutes. They are in charge of making sure the appointed feasts are honored and my Sabbaths kept holy in the ways I've commanded.

25-27 "A priest must not contaminate himself by going near a corpse. But when the dead person is his father or mother, son or daughter, brother or unmarried sister, he can approach the dead. But after he has been purified, he must wait another seven days. Then, when he returns to the inside courtyard

NEW KING JAMES VERSION

sanctuary to minister in the sanctuary, he must offer his sin offering in the inner court," says the Lord GOD.

28"It shall be, in regard to their inheritance, *that* I *am* their inheritance. You shall give them no possession in Israel, for I *am* their possession. 29They shall eat the grain offering, the sin offering, and the trespass offering; every dedicated thing in Israel shall be theirs. 30The best of all firstfruits of any kind, and every sacrifice of any kind from all your sacrifices, shall be the priest's; also you shall give to the priest the first of your ground meal, to cause a blessing to rest on your house. 31The priests shall not eat anything, bird or beast, that died naturally or was torn *by wild beasts*.

THE HOLY DISTRICT

45 "Moreover, when you divide the land by lot into inheritance, you shall set apart a district for the LORD, a holy section of the land; its length *shall be* twenty-five thousand *cubits*, and the width ten thousand. It *shall be* holy throughout its territory all around. 2Of this there shall be a square plot for the sanctuary, five hundred by five hundred *rods*, with fifty cubits around it for an open space. 3So this is the district you shall measure: twenty-five thousand *cubits* long and ten thousand wide; in it shall be the sanctuary, the Most Holy *Place*. 4It shall be a holy *section* of the land, belonging to the priests, the ministers of the sanctuary, who come near to minister to the LORD; it shall be a place for their houses and a holy place for the sanctuary. 5*An area* twenty-five thousand *cubits* long and ten thousand wide shall belong to the Levites, the ministers of the temple; they shall have twenty chambers as a possession.[a]

PROPERTIES OF THE CITY AND THE PRINCE

6"You shall appoint as the property of the city *an area* five thousand *cubits* wide and twenty-five thousand long, adjacent to the district of the holy *section;* it shall belong to the whole house of Israel.

7"The prince shall have *a section* on one side and the other of the holy district and the city's property; and bordering on the holy district and the city's property, extending westward on the west side and eastward on the east side, the length *shall be* side by side with one of the *tribal* portions, from the west border to the east border. 8The land shall be his possession in Israel; and My princes shall no more oppress My people, but they shall give *the rest of* the land to the house of Israel, according to their tribes."

LAWS GOVERNING THE PRINCE

9'Thus says the Lord GOD: "Enough, O princes of Israel! Remove violence and plundering, execute justice and righteousness, and stop dispossessing My people," says the Lord GOD. 10"You shall have honest scales, an honest ephah, and an honest bath. 11The ephah and the bath shall be of the same measure, so that the

45:5 [a]Following Masoretic Text, Targum, and Vulgate; Septuagint reads *a possession, cities of dwelling.*

THE MESSAGE

of the Sanctuary to do his priestly work in
the Sanctuary, he must first offer a sin offer-
ing for himself. Decree of GOD, the Master.
28-30 "As to priests owning land, I am their in-
heritance. Don't give any land in Israel to
them. *I* am their 'land,' their inheritance.
They'll take their meals from the grain of-
ferings, the sin offerings, and the guilt offer-
ings. Everything in Israel offered to GOD in
worship is theirs. The best of everything
grown, plus all special gifts, comes to the
priests. All that is given in worship to GOD
goes to them. Serve them first. Serve from
your best and your home will be blessed.
31 "Priests are not to eat any meat from bird
or animal unfit for ordinary human con-
sumption, such as carcasses found dead on
the road or in the field."

SACRED SPACE FOR GOD

1-4 45 "When you divide up the inheritance
of the land, you must set aside part of
the land as sacred space for GOD: approxi-
mately seven miles long by six miles wide,
all of it holy ground. Within this rectangle,
reserve a seven-hundred-fifty-foot square
for the Sanctuary with a seventy-five-foot
buffer zone surrounding it. Mark off within
the sacred reserve a section seven miles
long by three miles wide. The Sanctuary
with its Holy of Holies will be placed there.
This is where the priests will live, those who
lead worship in the Sanctuary and serve
GOD there. Their houses will be there along
with The Holy Place.
5 "To the north of the sacred reserve, an
area roughly seven miles long and two and
a quarter miles wide will be set aside as
land for the villages of the Levites who ad-
minister the affairs of worship in the Sanc-
tuary.
6 "To the south of the sacred reserve, mea-
sure off a section seven miles long and
about a mile and a half wide for the city it-
self, an area held in common by the whole
family of Israel.
7-8 "The prince gets the land abutting the
seven-mile east and west borders of the cen-
tral sacred square, extending eastward to-
ward the Jordan and westward toward the
Mediterranean. This is the prince's posses-
sion in Israel. My princes will no longer
bully my people, running roughshod over
them. They'll respect the land as it has been
allotted to the tribes.
9-12 "This is the Message of GOD, the Master:
'I've put up with you long enough, princes of
Israel! Quit bullying and taking advantage
of my people. Do what's just and right for a
change. Use honest scales—honest weights
and honest measures. Every pound must

NEW KING JAMES VERSION

bath contains one-tenth of a homer, and the ephah one-tenth of a homer; their measure shall be according to the homer. 12The shekel *shall be* twenty gerahs; twenty shekels, twenty-five shekels, *and* fifteen shekels shall be your mina.

13"This *is* the offering which you shall offer: you shall give one-sixth of an ephah from a homer of wheat, and one-sixth of an ephah from a homer of barley. 14The ordinance concerning oil, the bath of oil, *is* one-tenth of a bath from a kor. *A kor is* a homer or ten baths, for ten baths *are* a homer. 15And one lamb shall be given from a flock of two hundred, from the rich pastures of Israel. These shall be for grain offerings, burnt offerings, and peace offerings, to make atonement for them," says the Lord GOD. 16"All the people of the land shall give this offering for the prince in Israel. 17Then it shall be the prince's part *to give* burnt offerings, grain offerings, and drink offerings, at the feasts, the New Moons, the Sabbaths, and at all the appointed seasons of the house of Israel. He shall prepare the sin offering, the grain offering, the burnt offering, and the peace offerings to make atonement for the house of Israel."

KEEPING THE FEASTS

18"Thus says the Lord GOD: "In the first *month,* on the first *day* of the month, you shall take a young bull without blemish and cleanse the sanctuary. 19The priest shall take some of the blood of the sin offering and put *it* on the doorposts of the temple, on the four corners of the ledge of the altar, and on the gateposts of the gate of the inner court. 20And so you shall do on the seventh *day* of the month for everyone who has sinned unintentionally or in ignorance. Thus you shall make atonement for the temple.

21"In the first *month,* on the fourteenth day of the month, you shall observe the Passover, a feast of seven days; unleavened bread shall be eaten. 22And on that day the prince shall prepare for himself and for all the people of the land a bull *for* a sin offering. 23On the seven days of the feast he shall prepare a burnt offering to the LORD, seven bulls and seven rams without blemish, daily for seven days, and a kid of the goats daily *for* a sin offering. 24And he shall prepare a grain offering of one ephah for each bull and one ephah for each ram, together with a hin of oil for each ephah.

25"In the seventh *month,* on the fifteenth day of the month, at the feast, he shall do likewise for seven days, according to the sin offering, the burnt offering, the grain offering, and the oil."

THE MANNER OF WORSHIP

46 "Thus says the Lord GOD: "The gateway of the inner court that faces toward the east shall be shut the six working days; but on the Sabbath it shall be opened, and on the day of the New Moon it shall be opened. 2The prince shall enter by way of the vestibule of the gateway from the outside, and stand by the gatepost. The priests shall prepare his burnt offering and his peace offerings. He shall worship at the threshold of the gate. Then he shall go out, but the gate shall not be shut until evening. 3Likewise the

THE MESSAGE

have sixteen ounces. Every gallon must
measure four quarts. The ounce is the basic
measure for both. And your coins must be
honest—no wooden nickels!

EVERYONE IN THE LAND MUST CONTRIBUTE

13-15 " 'These are the prescribed offerings you
are to supply: one-sixtieth part of your
wheat, one-sixtieth part of your barley, one-
hundredth part of your oil, one sheep out of
every two hundred from the lush pastures of
Israel. These will be used for the grain offer-
ings, burnt offerings, and peace offerings
for making the atonement sacrifices for the
people. Decree of GOD, the Master.

16-17 " 'Everyone in the land must contribute to
these special offerings that the prince in Is-
rael will administer. It's the prince's job to
provide the burnt offerings, grain offerings,
and drink offerings at the Holy Festivals, the
New Moons, and the Sabbaths—all the com-
manded feasts among the people of Israel.
Sin offerings, grain offerings, burnt offer-
ings, and peace offerings for making atone-
ment for the people of Israel are his respon-
sibility.

18-20 " 'This is the Message from GOD, the Mas-
ter: On the first day of the first month, take
an unblemished bull calf and purify the
Sanctuary. The priest is to take blood from
the sin offerings and rub it on the doorposts
of the Temple, on the four corners of the
ledge of the altar, and on the gate entrance
to the inside courtyard. Repeat this ritual on
the seventh day of the month for anyone
who sins without knowing it. In this way
you make atonement for the Temple.

21 " 'On the fourteenth day of the first
month, you will observe the Passover, a
feast of seven days. During the feast you
will eat bread made without yeast.

22-23 " 'On Passover, the prince supplies a bull
as a sin offering for himself and all the peo-
ple of the country. Each day for each of the
seven days of the feast, he will supply seven
bulls and seven rams unblemished as a
burnt offering to GOD, and also each day a
male goat.

24 " 'He will supply about five and a half
gallons of grain offering and a gallon of oil
for each bull and each ram.

25 " 'On the fifteenth day of the seventh
month, and on each of the seven days of the
feast, he is to supply the same materials for
sin offerings, burnt offerings, grain offer-
ings, and oil.' "

1-3 46 " 'Message from GOD, the Master: The
gate of the inside courtyard on the east
is to be shut on the six working days, but
open on the Sabbath. It is also to be open on
the New Moon. The prince will enter
through the entrance area of the gate com-
plex and stand at the gateposts as the
priests present his burnt offerings and
peace offerings while he worships there on
the porch. He will then leave, but the gate
won't be shut until evening. On Sabbaths

NEW KING JAMES VERSION

people of the land shall worship at the entrance
to this gateway before the LORD on the Sabbaths
and the New Moons. 4The burnt offering that
the prince offers to the LORD on the Sabbath day
shall be six lambs without blemish, and a ram
without blemish; 5and the grain offering *shall be*
one ephah for a ram, and the grain offering for
the lambs, as much as he wants to give, as well
as a hin of oil with every ephah. 6On the day of
the New Moon *it shall be* a young bull without
blemish, six lambs, and a ram; they shall be
without blemish. 7He shall prepare a grain offer-
ing of an ephah for a bull, an ephah for a ram,
as much as he wants to give for the lambs, and
a hin of oil with every ephah. 8When the prince
enters, he shall go in by way of the vestibule of
the gateway, and go out the same way.
9"But when the people of the land come be-
fore the LORD on the appointed feast days, who-
ever enters by way of the north gate to worship
shall go out by way of the south gate; and who-
ever enters by way of the south gate shall go out
by way of the north gate. He shall not return by
way of the gate through which he came, but
shall go out through the opposite gate. 10The
prince shall then be in their midst. When they go
in, he shall go in; and when they go out, he shall
go out. 11At the festivals and the appointed feast
days the grain offering shall be an ephah for a
bull, an ephah for a ram, as much as he wants to
give for the lambs, and a hin of oil with every
ephah.
12"Now when the prince makes a voluntary
burnt offering or voluntary peace offering to the
LORD, the gate that faces toward the east shall
then be opened for him; and he shall prepare his
burnt offering and his peace offerings as he did
on the Sabbath day. Then he shall go out, and af-
ter he goes out the gate shall be shut.
13"You shall daily make a burnt offering to
the LORD *of* a lamb of the first year without
blemish; you shall prepare it every morning.
14And you shall prepare a grain offering with it
every morning, a sixth of an ephah, and a third
of a hin of oil to moisten the fine flour. This
grain offering is a perpetual ordinance, to be
made regularly to the LORD. 15Thus they shall
prepare the lamb, the grain offering, and the oil,
as a regular burnt offering every morning."

THE PRINCE AND INHERITANCE LAWS

16'Thus says the Lord GOD: "If the prince
gives a gift *of some* of his inheritance to any of
his sons, it shall belong to his sons; it is their
possession by inheritance. 17But if he gives a gift
of some of his inheritance to one of his servants,
it shall be his until the year of liberty, after
which it shall return to the prince. But his inher-
itance shall belong to his sons; it shall become
theirs. 18Moreover the prince shall not take any
of the people's inheritance by evicting them
from their property; he shall provide an inheri-
tance for his sons from his own property, so that
none of My people may be scattered from his
property." ' "

HOW THE OFFERINGS WERE PREPARED

19Now he brought me through the entrance,
which *was* at the side of the gate, into the holy

THE MESSAGE

and New Moons, the people are to worship
before GOD at the outside entrance to that
gate complex.
4-5 " 'The prince supplies for GOD the burnt
offering for the Sabbath—six unblemished
lambs and an unblemished ram. The grain
offering to go with the ram is about five and
a half gallons plus a gallon of oil, and a
handful of grain for each lamb.
6-7 " 'At the New Moon he is to supply a bull
calf, six lambs, and a ram, all without blem-
ish. He will also supply five and a half gal-
lons of grain offering and a gallon of oil for
both ram and bull, and a handful of grain of-
fering for each lamb.
8 " 'When the prince enters, he will go
through the entrance vestibule of the gate
complex and leave the same way.
9-10 " 'But when the people of the land come
to worship GOD at the commanded feasts,
those who enter through the north gate will
exit from the south gate, and those who en-
ter though the south gate will exit from the
north gate. You don't exit the gate through
which you enter, but through the opposite
gate. The prince is to be there, mingling with
them, going in and out with them.
11 " 'At the festivals and the commanded
feasts, the appropriate grain offering is five
and a half gallons, with a gallon of oil for
the bull and ram and a handful of grain for
each lamb.
12 " 'When the prince brings a freewill offer-
ing to GOD, whether a burnt offering or a
peace offering, the east gate is to be opened
for him. He offers his burnt or peace offer-
ing the same as he does on the Sabbath.
Then he leaves, and after he is out, the gate
is shut.
13-15 " 'Every morning you are to bring a year-
ling lamb unblemished for a burnt offering
to GOD. Also, every morning bring a grain
offering of about a gallon of grain with a
quart or so of oil to moisten it. Presenting
this grain offering to GOD is standard proce-
dure. The lamb, the grain offering, and the
oil for the burnt offering are a regular daily
ritual.
16-18 " 'A Message from GOD, the Master: If the
prince deeds a gift from his inheritance to
one of his sons, it stays in the family. But if
he deeds a gift from his inheritance to a ser-
vant, the servant keeps it only until the year
of liberation (the Jubilee year). After that, it
comes back to the prince. His inheritance is
only for his sons. It stays in the family. The
prince must not take the inheritance from
any of the people, dispossessing them of
their land. He can give his sons only what he
himself owns. None of my people are to be
run off their land.' "

19-20 Then the man brought me through the
north gate into the holy chambers assigned

NEW KING JAMES VERSION

chambers of the priests which face toward the
north; and there a place *was* situated at their ex-
treme western end. [20]And he said to me, "This *is*
the place where the priests shall boil the tres-
pass offering and the sin offering, *and* where
they shall bake the grain offering, so that they
do not bring *them* out into the outer court to
sanctify the people."

[21]Then he brought me out into the outer
court and caused me to pass by the four corners
of the court; and in fact, in every corner of the
court *there was another* court. [22]In the four cor-
ners of the court *were* enclosed courts, forty *cu-
bits* long and thirty wide; all four corners *were*
the same size. [23]*There was* a row *of building
stones* all around in them, all around the four of
them; and cooking hearths were made under
the rows of stones all around. [24]And he said to
me, "These *are* the kitchens where the ministers
of the temple shall boil the sacrifices of the peo-
ple."

THE HEALING WATERS AND TREES

47 Then he brought me back to the door of
the temple; and there was water, flowing
from under the threshold of the temple toward
the east, for the front of the temple faced east;
the water was flowing from under the right side
of the temple, south of the altar. [2]He brought me
out by way of the north gate, and led me around
on the outside to the outer gateway that faces
east; and there was water, running out on the
right side.

[3]And when the man went out to the east with
the line in his hand, he measured one thousand
cubits, and he brought me through the waters;
the water *came up to my* ankles. [4]Again he
measured one thousand and brought me
through the waters; the water *came up to my*
knees. Again he measured one thousand and
brought me through; the water *came up to my*
waist. [5]Again he measured one thousand, *and it
was* a river that I could not cross; for the water
was too deep, water in which one must swim, a
river that could not be crossed. [6]He said to me,
"Son of man, have you seen *this*?" Then he
brought me and returned me to the bank of the
river.

[7]When I returned, there, along the bank of
the river, *were* very many trees on one side and
the other. [8]Then he said to me: "This water flows
toward the eastern region, goes down into the
valley, and enters the sea. *When it* reaches the
sea, *its* waters are healed. [9]And it shall be *that*
every living thing that moves, wherever the
rivers go, will live. There will be a very great
multitude of fish, because these waters go there;
for they will be healed, and everything will live
wherever the river goes. [10]It shall be *that* fisher-
men will stand by it from En Gedi to En Eglaim;
they will be *places* for spreading their nets.
Their fish will be of the same kinds as the fish of
the Great Sea, exceedingly many. [11]But its
swamps and marshes will not be healed; they
will be given over to salt. [12]Along the bank of
the river, on this side and that, will grow all
kinds of trees used for food; their leaves will not
wither, and their fruit will not fail. They will
bear fruit every month, because their water

THE MESSAGE

to the priests and showed me a back room to
the west. He said, "This is the kitchen where
the priests will cook the guilt offering and
sin offering and bake the grain offering so
that they won't have to do it in the outside
courtyard and endanger the unprepared
people out there with The Holy."

21-23 He proceeded to take me to the outside
courtyard and around to each of its four cor-
ners. In each corner I observed another
court. In each of the four corners of the out-
side courtyard were smaller courts sixty by
forty-five feet, each the same size. On the in-
side walls of the courts was a stone shelf,
and beneath the shelves, hearths for cook-
ing.

24 He said, "These are the kitchens where
those who serve in the Temple will cook the
sacrifices of the people."

TREES ON BOTH SIDES OF THE RIVER

1-2 **47** Now he brought me back to the en-
trance to the Temple. I saw water pour-
ing out from under the Temple porch to the
east (the Temple faced east). The water
poured from the south side of the Temple,
south of the altar. He then took me out
through the north gate and led me around
the outside to the gate complex on the east.
The water was gushing from under the
south front of the Temple.

3-5 He walked to the east with a measuring
tape and measured off fifteen hundred feet,
leading me through water that was ankle-
deep. He measured off another fifteen hun-
dred feet, leading me through water that
was knee-deep. He measured off another fif-
teen hundred feet, leading me through wa-
ter waist-deep. He measured off another fif-
teen hundred feet. By now it was a river
over my head, water to swim in, water no
one could possibly walk through.

6-7 He said, "Son of man, have you had a
good look?"

Then he took me back to the riverbank.
While sitting on the bank, I noticed a lot of
trees on both sides of the river.

8-10 He told me, "This water flows east, de-
scends to the Arabah and then into the sea,
the sea of stagnant waters. When it empties
into those waters, the sea will become fresh.
Wherever the river flows, life will flourish—
great schools of fish—because the river is
turning the salt sea into fresh water. Where
the river flows, life abounds. Fishermen will
stand shoulder to shoulder along the shore
from En-gedi all the way north to En-
eglaim, casting their nets. The sea will teem
with fish of all kinds, like the fish of the
Great Mediterranean.

11 "The swamps and marshes won't become
fresh. They'll stay salty.

12 "But the river itself, on both banks, will
grow fruit trees of all kinds. Their leaves
won't wither, the fruit won't fail. Every
month they'll bear fresh fruit because the
river from the Sanctuary flows to them.

NEW KING JAMES VERSION

flows from the sanctuary. Their fruit will be for
food, and their leaves for medicine."

BORDERS OF THE LAND

[13]Thus says the Lord GOD: "These *are* the
borders by which you shall divide the land as an
inheritance among the twelve tribes of Israel.
Joseph *shall have two* portions. [14]You shall in-
herit it equally with one another; for I raised My
hand in an oath to give it to your fathers, and
this land shall fall to you as your inheritance.
[15]"This *shall be* the border of the land on the
north: from the Great Sea, *by* the road to
Hethlon, as one goes to Zedad, [16]Hamath,
Berothah, Sibraim (which *is* between the border
of Damascus and the border of Hamath), to
Hazar Hatticon (which *is* on the border of Hau-
ran). [17]Thus the boundary shall be from the Sea
to Hazar Enan, the border of Damascus; and as
for the north, northward, it is the border of
Hamath. *This is* the north side.
[18]"On the east side you shall mark out the
border from between Hauran and Damascus,
and between Gilead and the land of Israel, along
the Jordan, and along the eastern side of the
sea. *This is* the east side.
[19]"The south side, toward the South,[a] *shall be*
from Tamar to the waters of Meribah by
Kadesh, along the brook to the Great Sea. *This
is* the south side, toward the South.
[20]"The west side *shall be* the Great Sea, from
the *southern* boundary until one comes to a
point opposite Hamath. This *is* the west side.
[21]"Thus you shall divide this land among
yourselves according to the tribes of Israel. [22]It
shall be that you will divide it by lot as an inher-
itance for yourselves, and for the strangers who
dwell among you and who bear children among
you. They shall be to you as native-born among
the children of Israel; they shall have an inheri-
tance with you among the tribes of Israel. [23]And
it shall be *that* in whatever tribe the stranger
dwells, there you shall give *him* his inheritance,"
says the Lord GOD.

DIVISION OF THE LAND

48 "Now these *are* the names of the tribes:
From the northern border along the road
to Hethlon at the entrance of Hamath, to Hazar
Enan, the border of Damascus northward, in the
direction of Hamath, *there shall be* one *section
for* Dan from its east to its west side; [2]by the bor-
der of Dan, from the east side to the west, one
section for Asher; [3]by the border of Asher, from
the east side to the west, one *section for* Naph-
tali; [4]by the border of Naphtali, from the east
side to the west, one *section for* Manasseh; [5]by
the border of Manasseh, from the east side to
the west, one *section for* Ephraim; [6]by the bor-
der of Ephraim, from the east side to the west,
one *section for* Reuben; [7]by the border of
Reuben, from the east side to the west, one *sec-
tion for* Judah;

47:19 [a]Hebrew *Negev*

THE MESSAGE

Their fruit will be for food and their leaves
for healing."

DIVIDE UP THIS LAND

13-14 A Message from GOD, the Master: "These
are the boundaries by which you are to di-
vide up the inheritance of the land for the
twelve tribes of Israel, with Joseph getting
two parcels. It is to be divided up equally. I
swore in a solemn oath to give it to your an-
cestors, swore that this land would be your
inheritance.

15-17 "These are the boundaries of the land:
"The northern boundary runs from the
Great Mediterranean Sea along the Hethlon
road to where you turn off to the entrance of
Hamath, Zedad, Berothah, and Sibraim,
which lies between the territory of Damas-
cus and the territory of Hamath, and on to
Hazor-hatticon on the border of Hauran.
The boundary runs from the Sea to Hazor-
enon, with the territories of Damascus and
Hamath to the north. That is the northern
boundary.

18 "The eastern boundary runs between
Damascus and Hauran, down along the Jor-
dan between Gilead and the land of Israel to
the Eastern Sea as far as Tamar. This is the
eastern boundary.

19 "The southern boundary runs west from
Tamar to the waters of Meribah-kadesh,
along the Brook of Egypt, and out to the
Great Mediterranean Sea. This is the south-
ern boundary.

20 "The western boundary is formed by the
Great Mediterranean Sea north to where the
road turns east toward the entrance to
Hamath. This is the western boundary.

21-23 "Divide up this land among the twelve
tribes of Israel. Divide it up as your inheri-
tance, and include in it the resident aliens
who have made themselves at home among
you and now have children. Treat them as if
they were born there, just like yourselves.
They also get an inheritance among the
tribes of Israel. In whatever tribe the resi-
dent alien lives, there he gets his inheri-
tance. Decree of GOD, the Master."

THE SANCTUARY OF GOD AT THE CENTER

1 48 "These are the tribes:
"Dan: one portion, along the north-
ern boundary, following the Hethlon road
that turns off to the entrance of Hamath as
far as Hazor-enon so that the territory of
Damascus lies to the north alongside
Hamath, the northern border stretching
from east to west.

2 "Asher: one portion, bordering Dan from
east to west.

3 "Naphtali: one portion, bordering Asher
from east to west.

4 "Manasseh: one portion, bordering Naph-
tali from east to west.

5 "Ephraim: one portion, bordering Ma-
nasseh from east to west.

6 "Reuben: one portion, bordering Ephraim
from east to west.

7 "Judah: one portion, bordering Reuben
from east to west.

NEW KING JAMES VERSION

8by the border of Judah, from the east side to
the west, shall be the district which you shall set
apart, twenty-five thousand *cubits* in width, and
in length the same as one of the *other* portions,
from the east side to the west, with the sanctu-
ary in the center.
9"The district that you shall set apart for the
LORD *shall be* twenty-five thousand *cubits* in
length and ten thousand in width. 10To these—to
the priests—the holy district shall belong: on the
north twenty-five thousand *cubits in length,* on
the west ten thousand in width, on the east ten
thousand in width, and on the south twenty-five
thousand in length. The sanctuary of the LORD
shall be in the center. 11*It shall be* for the priests
of the sons of Zadok, who are sanctified, who
have kept My charge, who did not go astray
when the children of Israel went astray, as the
Levites went astray. 12And *this* district of land
that is set apart shall be to them a thing most
holy by the border of the Levites.
13"Opposite the border of the priests, the
Levites *shall have an area* twenty-five thousand
cubits in length and ten thousand in width; its
entire length *shall be* twenty-five thousand and
its width ten thousand. 14And they shall not sell
or exchange any of it; they may not alienate this
best *part* of the land, for *it is* holy to the LORD.
15"The five thousand *cubits* in width that re-
main, along the edge of the twenty-five thousand,
shall be for general use by the city, for dwellings
and common-land; and the city shall be in the cen-
ter. 16These *shall be* its measurements: the north
side four thousand five hundred *cubits,* the south
side four thousand five hundred, the east side four
thousand five hundred, and the west side four
thousand five hundred. 17The common-land of the
city shall be: to the north two hundred and fifty *cu-
bits,* to the south two hundred and fifty, to the east
two hundred and fifty, and to the west two hun-
dred and fifty. 18The rest of the length, alongside
the district of the holy *section, shall be* ten thou-
sand *cubits* to the east and ten thousand to the
west. It shall be adjacent to the district of the holy
section, and its produce shall be food for the
workers of the city. 19The workers of the city, from
all the tribes of Israel, shall cultivate it. 20The entire
district *shall be* twenty-five thousand *cubits* by
twenty-five thousand *cubits,* foursquare. You shall
set apart the holy district with the property of the
city.
21"The rest *shall belong* to the prince, on one
side and on the other of the holy district and of
the city's property, next to the twenty-five thou-
sand *cubits* of the *holy* district as far as the east-
ern border, and westward next to the twenty-
five thousand as far as the western border,
adjacent to the *tribal* portions; *it shall belong* to
the prince. It shall be the holy district, and the
sanctuary of the temple *shall be* in the center.
22Moreover, apart from the possession of the
Levites and the possession of the city *which are*
in the midst of what *belongs* to the prince, *the
area* between the border of Judah and the bor-
der of Benjamin shall belong to the prince.
23"As for the rest of the tribes, from the east
side to the west, Benjamin *shall have* one *sec-
tion;* 24by the border of Benjamin, from the east
side to the west, Simeon *shall have* one *section;*

THE MESSAGE

8-9 "Bordering Judah from east to west is the consecrated area that you will set aside as holy: a square approximately seven by seven miles, with the Sanctuary set at the center. The consecrated area reserved for GOD is to be seven miles long and a little less than three miles wide.

10-12 "This is how it will be parceled out. The priest will get the area measuring seven miles on the north and south boundaries, with a width of a little more than three miles at the east and west boundaries. The Sanctuary of GOD will be at the center. This is for the consecrated priests, the Zadokites who stayed true in their service to me and didn't get off track as the Levites did when Israel wandered off the main road. This is their special gift, a gift from the land itself, most holy ground, bordering the section of the Levites.

13-14 "The Levites get a section equal in size to that of the priests, roughly seven by three miles. They are not permitted to sell or trade any of it. It's the choice part of the land, to say nothing of being holy to GOD.

15-19 "What's left of the 'sacred square'—each side measures out at seven miles by a mile and a half—is for ordinary use: the city and its buildings with open country around it, but the city at the center. The north, south, east, and west sides of the city are each about a mile and a half in length. A strip of pasture, one hundred twenty-five yards wide, will border the city on all sides. The remainder of this portion, three miles of countryside to the east and to the west of the sacred precinct, is for farming. It will supply food for the city. Workers from all the tribes of Israel will serve as field hands to farm the land.

20 "This dedicated area, set apart for holy purposes, will be a square, seven miles by seven miles, a 'holy square,' which includes the part set aside for the city.

21-22 "The rest of this land, the country stretching east to the Jordan and west to the Mediterranean from the seven-mile sides of the 'holy square,' belongs to the prince. His land is sandwiched between the tribal portions north and south, and goes out both east and west from the 'sacred square' with its Temple at the center. The land set aside for the Levites on one side and the city on the other is in the middle of the territory assigned to the prince. The 'sacred square' is flanked east and west by the prince's land and bordered on the north and south by the territories of Judah and Benjamin, respectively.

23 "And then the rest of the tribes:

"Benjamin: one portion, stretching from the eastern to the western boundary.

24 "Simeon: one portion, bordering Benjamin from east to west.

NEW KING JAMES VERSION

25 by the border of Simeon, from the east side to
the west, Issachar *shall have* one *section;* 26 by
the border of Issachar, from the east side to the
west, Zebulun *shall have* one *section;* 27 by the
border of Zebulun, from the east side to the west,
Gad *shall have* one *section;* 28 by the border of
Gad, on the south side, toward the South,[a] the
border shall be from Tamar *to* the waters of
Meribah *by* Kadesh, along the brook to the Great
Sea. 29 This *is* the land which you shall divide by
lot as an inheritance among the tribes of Israel,
and these *are* their portions," says the Lord GOD.

THE GATES OF THE CITY AND ITS NAME

30 "These *are* the exits of the city. On the
north side, measuring four thousand five hun-
dred *cubits* 31 (the gates of the city *shall be*
named after the tribes of Israel), the three gates
northward: one gate for Reuben, one gate for
Judah, and one gate for Levi; 32 on the east side,
four thousand five hundred *cubits,* three gates:
one gate for Joseph, one gate for Benjamin, and
one gate for Dan; 33 on the south side, measuring
four thousand five hundred *cubits,* three gates:
one gate for Simeon, one gate for Issachar, and
one gate for Zebulun; 34 on the west side, four
thousand five hundred *cubits* with their three
gates: one gate for Gad, one gate for Asher, and
one gate for Naphtali. 35 All the way around *shall
be* eighteen thousand *cubits;* and the name of
the city from *that* day *shall be:* THE LORD *IS*
THERE."[a]

48:28 [a]Hebrew *Negev* **48:35** [a]Hebrew *YHWH Shammah*

THE MESSAGE

25 "Issachar: one portion, bordering Simeon from east to west.

26 "Zebulun: one portion, bordering Issachar from east to west.

27 "Gad: one portion, bordering Zebulun from east to west.

28 "The southern boundary of Gad will run south from Tamar to the waters of Meribah-kadesh, along the Brook of Egypt and then out to the Great Mediterranean Sea.

29 "This is the land that you are to divide up among the tribes of Israel as their inheritance. These are their portions." Decree of GOD, the Master.

30-31 "These are the gates of the city. On the north side, which is 2,250 yards long (the gates of the city are named after the tribes of Israel), three gates: the gate of Reuben, the gate of Judah, the gate of Levi.

32 "On the east side, measuring 2,250 yards, three gates: the gate of Joseph, the gate of Benjamin, the gate of Dan.

33 "On the south side, measuring 2,250 yards, three gates: the gate of Simeon, the gate of Issachar, the gate of Zebulun.

34 "On the west side, measuring 2,250 yards, three gates: the gate of Gad, the gate of Asher, the gate of Naphtali.

35 "The four sides of the city measure to a total of nearly six miles.

"From now on the name of the city will be
YAHWEH-SHAMMAH:

"GOD-IS-THERE."

DANIEL

New King James Version

Daniel and His Friends Obey God

1 In the third year of the reign of Jehoiakim king of Judah, Nebuchadnezzar king of Babylon came to Jerusalem and besieged it. 2And the Lord gave Jehoiakim king of Judah into his hand, with some of the articles of the house of God, which he carried into the land of Shinar to the house of his god; and he brought the articles into the treasure house of his god.

3Then the king instructed Ashpenaz, the master of his eunuchs, to bring some of the children of Israel and some of the king's descendants and some of the nobles, 4young men in whom *there was* no blemish, but good-looking, gifted in all wisdom, possessing knowledge and quick to understand, who *had* ability to serve in the king's palace, and whom they might teach the language and literature of the Chaldeans. 5And the king appointed for them a daily provision of the king's delicacies and of the wine which he drank, and three years of training for them, so that at the end of *that time* they might serve before the king. 6Now from among those of the sons of Judah were Daniel, Hananiah, Mishael, and Azariah. 7To them the chief of the eunuchs gave names: he gave Daniel *the name* Belteshazzar; to Hananiah, Shadrach; to Mishael, Meshach; and to Azariah, Abed-Nego.

8But Daniel purposed in his heart that he would not defile himself with the portion of the king's delicacies, nor with the wine which he drank; therefore he requested of the chief of the eunuchs that he might not defile himself. 9Now God had brought Daniel into the favor and goodwill of the chief of the eunuchs. 10And the chief of the eunuchs said to Daniel, "I fear my lord the king, who has appointed your food and drink. For why should he see your faces looking worse than the young men who *are* your age? Then you would endanger my head before the king."

11So Daniel said to the steward[a] whom the chief of the eunuchs had set over Daniel, Hananiah, Mishael, and Azariah, 12"Please test your servants for ten days, and let them give us vegetables to eat and water to drink. 13Then let our appearance be examined before you, and the appearance of the young men who eat the portion of the king's delicacies; and as you see fit, *so* deal with your servants." 14So he consented with them in this matter, and tested them ten days.

15And at the end of ten days their features appeared better and fatter in flesh than all the young men who ate the portion of the king's delicacies. 16Thus the steward took away their portion of delicacies and the wine that they were to drink, and gave them vegetables.

17As for these four young men, God gave them knowledge and skill in all literature and wisdom; and Daniel had understanding in all visions and dreams.

18Now at the end of the days, when the king had said that they should be brought in, the

1:11 [a]Hebrew *Melzar,* also in verse 16

The Message

Daniel Was Gifted by God

1-2 1 It was the third year of King Jehoiakim's reign in Judah when King Nebuchadnezzar of Babylon declared war on Jerusalem and besieged the city. The Master handed King Jehoiakim of Judah over to him, along with some of the furnishings from the Temple of God. Nebuchadnezzar took king and furnishings to the country of Babylon, the ancient Shinar. He put the furnishings in the sacred treasury.

3-5 The king told Ashpenaz, head of the palace staff, to get some Israelites from the royal family and nobility—young men who were healthy and handsome, intelligent and well-educated, good prospects for leadership positions in the government, perfect specimens!—and indoctrinate them in the Babylonian language and the lore of magic and fortunetelling. The king then ordered that they be served from the same menu as the royal table—the best food, the finest wine. After three years of training they would be given positions in the king's court.

6-7 Four young men from Judah—Daniel, Hananiah, Mishael, and Azariah—were among those selected. The head of the palace staff gave them Babylonian names: Daniel was named Belteshazzar, Hananiah was named Shadrach, Mishael was named Meshach, Azariah was named Abednego.

8-10 But Daniel determined that he would not defile himself by eating the king's food or drinking his wine, so he asked the head of the palace staff to exempt him from the royal diet. The head of the palace staff, by God's grace, liked Daniel, but he warned him, "I'm afraid of what my master the king will do. He is the one who assigned this diet and if he sees that you are not as healthy as the rest, he'll have my head!"

11-13 But Daniel appealed to a steward who had been assigned by the head of the palace staff to be in charge of Daniel, Hananiah, Mishael, and Azariah: "Try us out for ten days on a simple diet of vegetables and water. Then compare us with the young men who eat from the royal menu. Make your decision on the basis of what you see."

14-16 The steward agreed to do it and fed them vegetables and water for ten days. At the end of the ten days they looked better and more robust than all the others who had been eating from the royal menu. So the steward continued to exempt them from the royal menu of food and drink and served them only vegetables.

17-19 God gave these four young men knowledge and skill in both books and life. In addition, Daniel was gifted in understanding all sorts of visions and dreams. At the end of the time set by the king for their training,

NEW KING JAMES VERSION

chief of the eunuchs brought them in before
Nebuchadnezzar. [19]Then the king interviewed[a]
them, and among them all none was found like
Daniel, Hananiah, Mishael, and Azariah; there-
fore they served before the king. [20]And in all
matters of wisdom *and* understanding about
which the king examined them, he found them
ten times better than all the magicians *and* as-
trologers who *were* in all his realm. [21]Thus
Daniel continued until the first year of King
Cyrus.

NEBUCHADNEZZAR'S DREAM

2 Now in the second year of Nebuchadnezzar's
reign, Nebuchadnezzar had dreams; and his
spirit was *so* troubled that his sleep left him.
[2]Then the king gave the command to call the
magicians, the astrologers, the sorcerers, and
the Chaldeans to tell the king his dreams. So
they came and stood before the king. [3]And the
king said to them, "I have had a dream, and my
spirit is anxious to know the dream."
[4]Then the Chaldeans spoke to the king in
Aramaic,[a] "O king, live forever! Tell your ser-
vants the dream, and we will give the interpre-
tation."
[5]The king answered and said to the
Chaldeans, "My decision is firm: if you do not
make known the dream to me, and its interpre-
tation, you shall be cut in pieces, and your
houses shall be made an ash heap. [6]However, if
you tell the dream and its interpretation, you
shall receive from me gifts, rewards, and great
honor. Therefore tell me the dream and its inter-
pretation."
[7]They answered again and said, "Let the
king tell his servants the dream, and we will
give its interpretation."
[8]The king answered and said, "I know for
certain that you would gain time, because you
see that my decision is firm: [9]if you do not make
known the dream to me, *there is only* one decree
for you! For you have agreed to speak lying and
corrupt words before me till the time has
changed. Therefore tell me the dream, and I
shall know that you can give me its interpreta-
tion."
[10]The Chaldeans answered the king, and
said, "There is not a man on earth who can tell
the king's matter; therefore no king, lord, or
ruler has *ever* asked such things of any magi-
cian, astrologer, or Chaldean. [11]*It is* a difficult
thing that the king requests, and there is no
other who can tell it to the king except the gods,
whose dwelling is not with flesh."
[12]For this reason the king was angry and
very furious, and gave the command to destroy
all the wise *men* of Babylon. [13]So the decree
went out, and they began killing the wise *men;*
and they sought Daniel and his companions, to
kill *them.*

GOD REVEALS NEBUCHADNEZZAR'S DREAM

[14]Then with counsel and wisdom Daniel an-
swered Arioch, the captain of the king's guard,
who had gone out to kill the wise *men* of Babylon;

1:19 [a]Literally *talked with them* **2:4** [a]The original language of Daniel 2:4b through 7:28 is Aramaic.

THE MESSAGE

the head of the royal staff brought them in
to Nebuchadnezzar. When the king inter-
viewed them, he found them far superior to
all the other young men. None were a match
for Daniel, Hananiah, Mishael, and Azariah.
19-20 And so they took their place in the king's
service. Whenever the king consulted them
on anything, on books or on life, he found
them ten times better than all the magicians
and enchanters in his kingdom put together.
21 Daniel continued in the king's service un-
til the first year in the reign of King Cyrus.

KING NEBUCHADNEZZAR'S DREAM

1-3 **2** In the second year of his reign, King Ne-
buchadnezzar started having dreams that
disturbed him deeply. He couldn't sleep. He
called in all the Babylonian magicians, en-
chanters, sorcerers, and fortunetellers to in-
terpret his dreams for him. When they came
and lined up before the king, he said to
them, "I had a dream that I can't get out of
my mind. I can't sleep until I know what it
means."
4 The fortunetellers, speaking in the Ara-
maic language, said, "Long live the king!
Tell us the dream and we will interpret it."
5-6 The king answered the fortunetellers,
"This is my decree: If you can't tell me both
the dream itself and its interpretation, I'll
have you ripped to pieces, limb from limb,
and your homes torn down. But if you tell
me both the dream and its interpretation, I'll
lavish you with gifts and honors. So go to it:
Tell me the dream and its interpretation."
7 They answered, "If it please your majesty,
tell us the dream. We'll give the interpreta-
tion."
8-9 But the king said, "I know what you're up
to—you're just playing for time. You know
you're up a tree. You know that if you can't
tell me my dream, you're doomed. I see right
through you—you're going to cook up some
fancy stories and confuse the issue until I
change my mind. Nothing doing! First tell
me the dream, then I'll know that you're on
the up and up with the interpretation and
not just blowing smoke in my eyes."
10-11 The fortunetellers said, "Nobody any-
where can do what you ask. And no king,
great or small, has ever demanded anything
like this from any magician, enchanter, or
fortuneteller. What you're asking is impossi-
ble unless some god or goddess should re-
veal it—and they don't hang around with
people like us."
12-13 That set the king off. He lost his temper
and ordered the whole company of Bab-
ylonian wise men killed. When the death
warrant was issued, Daniel and his compan-
ions were included. They also were marked
for execution.
14-15 When Arioch, chief of the royal guards,
was making arrangements for the execu-
tion, Daniel wisely took him aside and qui-

NEW KING JAMES VERSION

15he answered and said to Arioch the king's captain, "Why is the decree from the king so urgent?" Then Arioch made the decision known to Daniel.

16So Daniel went in and asked the king to give him time, that he might tell the king the interpretation. 17Then Daniel went to his house, and made the decision known to Hananiah, Mishael, and Azariah, his companions, 18that they might seek mercies from the God of heaven concerning this secret, so that Daniel and his companions might not perish with the rest of the wise *men* of Babylon. 19Then the secret was revealed to Daniel in a night vision. So Daniel blessed the God of heaven.

20Daniel answered and said:

"Blessed be the name of God forever and
ever,
For wisdom and might are His.
21And He changes the times and the seasons;
He removes kings and raises up kings;
He gives wisdom to the wise
And knowledge to those who have
understanding.
22He reveals deep and secret things;
He knows what *is* in the darkness,
And light dwells with Him.

23"I thank You and praise You,
O God of my fathers;
You have given me wisdom and might,
And have now made known to me what we
asked of You,
For You have made known to us the king's
demand."

DANIEL EXPLAINS THE DREAM

24Therefore Daniel went to Arioch, whom the king had appointed to destroy the wise *men* of Babylon. He went and said thus to him: "Do not destroy the wise *men* of Babylon; take me before the king, and I will tell the king the interpretation."

25Then Arioch quickly brought Daniel before the king, and said thus to him, "I have found a man of the captives[a] of Judah, who will make known to the king the interpretation."

26The king answered and said to Daniel, whose name *was* Belteshazzar, "Are you able to make known to me the dream which I have seen, and its interpretation?"

27Daniel answered in the presence of the king, and said, "The secret which the king has demanded, the wise *men,* the astrologers, the magicians, and the soothsayers cannot declare to the king. 28But there is a God in heaven who reveals secrets, and He has made known to King Nebuchadnezzar what will be in the latter days. Your dream, and the visions of your head upon your bed, were these: 29As for you, O king, thoughts came *to* your *mind while* on your bed, *about* what would come to pass after this; and He who reveals secrets has made known to you what will be. 30But as for me, this secret has not been revealed to me because I have more wisdom than anyone living, but for *our* sakes who make known the interpretation to the king, and that you may know the thoughts of your heart.

2:25 [a]Literally *of the sons of the captivity*

THE MESSAGE

etly asked what was going on: "Why this all of a sudden?"

15-16 After Arioch filled in the background, Daniel went to the king and asked for a little time so that he could interpret the dream.

17-18 Daniel then went home and told his companions Hananiah, Mishael, and Azariah what was going on. He asked them to pray to the God of heaven for mercy in solving this mystery so that the four of them wouldn't be killed along with the whole company of Babylonian wise men.

DREAM INTERPRETATION: A STORY OF FIVE KINGDOMS

19-23 That night the answer to the mystery was given to Daniel in a vision. Daniel blessed the God of heaven, saying,

"Blessed be the name of God,
forever and ever.
He knows all, does all:
He changes the seasons and guides
history,
He raises up kings and also brings them
down,
he provides both intelligence and
discernment,
He opens up the depths, tells secrets,
sees in the dark—light spills out of him!
God of all my ancestors, all thanks! all
praise!
You made me wise and strong.
And now you've shown us what we asked
for.
You've solved the king's mystery."

24 So Daniel went back to Arioch, who had been put in charge of the execution. He said, "Call off the execution! Take me to the king and I'll interpret his dream."

25 Arioch didn't lose a minute. He ran to the king, bringing Daniel with him, and said, "I've found a man from the exiles of Judah who can interpret the king's dream!"

26 The king asked Daniel (renamed in Babylonian, Belteshazzar), "Are you sure you can do this—tell me the dream I had and interpret it for me?"

27-28 Daniel answered the king, "No mere human can solve the king's mystery, I don't care who it is—no wise man, enchanter, magician, diviner. But there is a God in heaven who solves mysteries, and he has solved this one. He is letting King Nebuchadnezzar in on what is going to happen in the days ahead. This is the dream you had when you were lying on your bed, the vision that filled your mind:

29-30 "While you were stretched out on your bed, O king, thoughts came to you regarding what is coming in the days ahead. The Revealer of Mysteries showed you what will happen. But the interpretation is given through me, not because I'm any smarter than anyone else in the country, but so that you will know what it means, so that you will understand what you dreamed.

New King James Version

31“You, O king, were watching; and behold, a
great image! This great image, whose splendor
was excellent, stood before you; and its form
was awesome. 32This image’s head *was* of fine
gold, its chest and arms of silver, its belly and
thighs[a] of bronze, 33its legs of iron, its feet partly
of iron and partly of clay.[a] 34You watched while
a stone was cut out without hands, which struck
the image on its feet of iron and clay, and broke
them in pieces. 35Then the iron, the clay, the
bronze, the silver, and the gold were crushed to-
gether, and became like chaff from the summer
threshing floors; the wind carried them away so
that no trace of them was found. And the stone
that struck the image became a great mountain
and filled the whole earth.

36“This *is* the dream. Now we will tell the in-
terpretation of it before the king. 37You, O king,
are a king of kings. For the God of heaven has
given you a kingdom, power, strength, and
glory; 38and wherever the children of men dwell,
or the beasts of the field and the birds of the
heaven, He has given *them* into your hand, and
has made you ruler over them all—you *are* this
head of gold. 39But after you shall arise another
kingdom inferior to yours; then another, a third
kingdom of bronze, which shall rule over all the
earth. 40And the fourth kingdom shall be as
strong as iron, inasmuch as iron breaks in
pieces and shatters everything; and like iron
that crushes, *that kingdom* will break in pieces
and crush all the others. 41Whereas you saw the
feet and toes, partly of potter’s clay and partly
of iron, the kingdom shall be divided; yet the
strength of the iron shall be in it, just as you saw
the iron mixed with ceramic clay. 42And *as* the
toes of the feet *were* partly of iron and partly of
clay, *so* the kingdom shall be partly strong and
partly fragile. 43As you saw iron mixed with ce-
ramic clay, they will mingle with the seed of
men; but they will not adhere to one another,
just as iron does not mix with clay. 44And in the
days of these kings the God of heaven will set
up a kingdom which shall never be destroyed;
and the kingdom shall not be left to other peo-
ple; it shall break in pieces and consume all
these kingdoms, and it shall stand forever.
45Inasmuch as you saw that the stone was cut
out of the mountain without hands, and that it
broke in pieces the iron, the bronze, the clay, the
silver, and the gold—the great God has made
known to the king what will come to pass after
this. The dream is certain, and its interpretation
is sure.”

Daniel and His Friends Promoted

46Then King Nebuchadnezzar fell on his
face, prostrate before Daniel, and commanded
that they should present an offering and incense
to him. 47The king answered Daniel, and said,
“Truly your God *is* the God of gods, the Lord of
kings, and a revealer of secrets, since you could
reveal this secret.” 48Then the king promoted
Daniel and gave him many great gifts; and he
made him ruler over the whole province of
Babylon, and chief administrator over all the
wise *men* of Babylon. 49Also Daniel petitioned

2:32 [a]Or *sides* **2:33** [a]Or *baked clay,* and so in verses 34, 35, and 42

The Message

31-36 “What you saw, O king, was a huge statue standing before you, striking in appearance. And terrifying. The head of the statue was pure gold, the chest and arms were silver, the belly and hips were bronze, the legs were iron, and the feet were an iron-ceramic mixture. While you were looking at this statue, a stone cut out of a mountain by an invisible hand hit the statue, smashing its iron-ceramic feet. Then the whole thing fell to pieces—iron, tile, bronze, silver, and gold, smashed to bits. It was like scraps of old newspapers in a vacant lot in a hot dry summer, blown every which way by the wind, scattered to oblivion. But the stone that hit the statue became a huge mountain, dominating the horizon. This was your dream.

36-40 “And now we’ll interpret it for the king. You, O king, are the most powerful king on earth. The God of heaven has given you the works: rule, power, strength, and glory. He has put you in charge of men and women, wild animals and birds, all over the world—you’re the head ruler, you are the head of gold. But your rule will be taken over by another kingdom, inferior to yours, and that one by a third, a bronze kingdom, but still ruling the whole land, and after that by a fourth kingdom, ironlike in strength. Just as iron smashes things to bits, breaking and pulverizing, it will bust up the previous kingdoms.

41-43 “But then the feet and toes that ended up as a mixture of ceramic and iron will deteriorate into a mongrel kingdom with some remains of iron in it. Just as the toes of the feet were part ceramic and part iron, it will end up a mixed bag of the breakable and unbreakable. That kingdom won’t bond, won’t hold together any more than iron and clay hold together.

44-45 “But throughout the history of these kingdoms, the God of heaven will be building a kingdom that will never be destroyed, nor will this kingdom ever fall under the domination of another. In the end it will crush the other kingdoms and finish them off and come through it all standing strong and eternal. It will be like the stone cut from the mountain by the invisible hand that crushed the iron, the bronze, the ceramic, the silver, and the gold.

“The great God has let the king know what will happen in the years to come. This is an accurate telling of the dream, and the interpretation is also accurate.”

46-47 When Daniel finished, King Nebuchadnezzar fell on his face in awe before Daniel. He ordered the offering of sacrifices and burning of incense in Daniel’s honor. He said to Daniel, “Your God is beyond question the God of all gods, the Master of all kings. And he solves all mysteries, I know, because you’ve solved this mystery.”

48-49 Then the king promoted Daniel to a high position in the kingdom, lavished him with gifts, and made him governor over the entire province of Babylon and the chief in charge of all the Babylonian wise men. At Daniel’s

NEW KING JAMES VERSION

the king, and he set Shadrach, Meshach, and Abed-Nego over the affairs of the province of Babylon; but Daniel *sat* in the gate[a] of the king.

THE IMAGE OF GOLD

3 Nebuchadnezzar the king made an image of gold, whose height *was* sixty cubits *and* its width six cubits. He set it up in the plain of Dura, in the province of Babylon. 2And King Nebuchadnezzar sent *word* to gather together the satraps, the administrators, the governors, the counselors, the treasurers, the judges, the magistrates, and all the officials of the provinces, to come to the dedication of the image which King Nebuchadnezzar had set up. 3So the satraps, the administrators, the governors, the counselors, the treasurers, the judges, the magistrates, and all the officials of the provinces gathered together for the dedication of the image that King Nebuchadnezzar had set up; and they stood before the image that Nebuchadnezzar had set up. 4Then a herald cried aloud: "To you it is commanded, O peoples, nations, and languages, 5*that* at the time you hear the sound of the horn, flute, harp, lyre, *and* psaltery, in symphony with all kinds of music, you shall fall down and worship the gold image that King Nebuchadnezzar has set up; 6and whoever does not fall down and worship shall be cast immediately into the midst of a burning fiery furnace."

7So at that time, when all the people heard the sound of the horn, flute, harp, *and* lyre, in symphony with all kinds of music, all the people, nations, and languages fell down *and* worshiped the gold image which King Nebuchadnezzar had set up.

DANIEL'S FRIENDS DISOBEY THE KING

8Therefore at that time certain Chaldeans came forward and accused the Jews. 9They spoke and said to King Nebuchadnezzar, "O king, live forever! 10You, O king, have made a decree that everyone who hears the sound of the horn, flute, harp, lyre, *and* psaltery, in symphony with all kinds of music, shall fall down and worship the gold image; 11and whoever does not fall down and worship shall be cast into the midst of a burning fiery furnace. 12There are certain Jews whom you have set over the affairs of the province of Babylon: Shadrach, Meshach, and Abed-Nego; these men, O king, have not paid due regard to you. They do not serve your gods or worship the gold image which you have set up."

13Then Nebuchadnezzar, in rage and fury, gave the command to bring Shadrach, Meshach, and Abed-Nego. So they brought these men before the king. 14Nebuchadnezzar spoke, saying to them, "*Is it* true, Shadrach, Meshach, and Abed-Nego, *that* you do not serve my gods or worship the gold image which I have set up? 15Now if you are ready at the time you hear the sound of the horn, flute, harp, lyre, *and* psaltery, in symphony with all kinds of music, and you fall down and worship the image which I have made, *good!* But if you do not worship, you shall be cast immediately into the midst of a burning fiery furnace. And who *is* the god who will deliver you from my hands?"

2:49 [a]That is, the king's court

THE MESSAGE

request the king appointed Shadrach, Meshach, and Abednego to administrative posts throughout Babylon, while Daniel governed from the royal headquarters.

FOUR MEN IN THE FURNACE

1-3 3 King Nebuchadnezzar built a gold statue, ninety feet high and nine feet thick. He set it up on the Dura plain in the province of Babylon. He then ordered all the important leaders in the province, everybody who was anybody, to the dedication ceremony of the statue. They all came for the dedication, all the important people, and took their places before the statue that Nebuchadnezzar had erected.

4-6 A herald then proclaimed in a loud voice: "Attention, everyone! Every race, color, and creed, listen! When you hear the band strike up—all the trumpets and trombones, the tubas and baritones, the drums and cymbals—fall to your knees and worship the gold statue that King Nebuchadnezzar has set up. Anyone who does not kneel and worship shall be thrown immediately into a roaring furnace."

7 The band started to play, a huge band equipped with all the musical instruments of Babylon, and everyone—every race, color, and creed—fell to their knees and worshiped the gold statue that King Nebuchadnezzar had set up.

8-12 Just then, some Babylonian fortunetellers stepped up and accused the Jews. They said to King Nebuchadnezzar, "Long live the king! You gave strict orders, O king, that when the big band started playing, everyone had to fall to their knees and worship the gold statue, and whoever did not go to their knees and worship it had to be pitched into a roaring furnace. Well, there are some Jews here—Shadrach, Meshach, and Abednego—whom you have placed in high positions in the province of Babylon. These men are ignoring you, O king. They don't respect your gods and they won't worship the gold statue you set up."

13-15 Furious, King Nebuchadnezzar ordered Shadrach, Meshach, and Abednego to be brought in. When the men were brought in, Nebuchadnezzar asked, "Is it true, Shadrach, Meshach, and Abednego, that you don't respect my gods and refuse to worship the gold statue that I have set up? I'm giving you a second chance—but from now on, when the big band strikes up you must go to your knees and worship the statue I have made. If you don't worship it, you will be pitched into a roaring furnace, no questions asked. Who is the god who can rescue you from my power?"

NEW KING JAMES VERSION

16 Shadrach, Meshach, and Abed-Nego an-
swered and said to the king, "O Nebuchadnez-
zar, we have no need to answer you in this mat-
ter. 17 If that *is the case,* our God whom we serve
is able to deliver us from the burning fiery fur-
nace, and He will deliver *us* from your hand, O
king. 18 But if not, let it be known to you, O king,
that we do not serve your gods, nor will we wor-
ship the gold image which you have set up."

SAVED IN FIERY TRIAL

19 Then Nebuchadnezzar was full of fury, and
the expression on his face changed toward
Shadrach, Meshach, and Abed-Nego. He spoke
and commanded that they heat the furnace
seven times more than it was usually heated.
20 And he commanded certain mighty men of
valor who *were* in his army to bind Shadrach,
Meshach, and Abed-Nego, *and* cast *them* into
the burning fiery furnace. 21 Then these men
were bound in their coats, their trousers, their
turbans, and their *other* garments, and were
cast into the midst of the burning fiery furnace.
22 Therefore, because the king's command was
urgent, and the furnace exceedingly hot, the
flame of the fire killed those men who took up
Shadrach, Meshach, and Abed-Nego. 23 And
these three men, Shadrach, Meshach, and Abed-
Nego, fell down bound into the midst of the
burning fiery furnace.

24 Then King Nebuchadnezzar was aston-
ished; and he rose in haste *and* spoke, saying to
his counselors, "Did we not cast three men
bound into the midst of the fire?"

They answered and said to the king, "True, O
king."

25 "Look!" he answered, "I see four men loose,
walking in the midst of the fire; and they are not
hurt, and the form of the fourth is like the Son
of God."[a]

NEBUCHADNEZZAR PRAISES GOD

26 Then Nebuchadnezzar went near the
mouth of the burning fiery furnace *and* spoke,
saying, "Shadrach, Meshach, and Abed-Nego,
servants of the Most High God, come out, and
come *here.*" Then Shadrach, Meshach, and
Abed-Nego came from the midst of the fire.
27 And the satraps, administrators, governors,
and the king's counselors gathered together,
and they saw these men on whose bodies the
fire had no power; the hair of their head was not
singed nor were their garments affected, and
the smell of fire was not on them.

28 Nebuchadnezzar spoke, saying, "Blessed
be the God of Shadrach, Meshach, and Abed-
Nego, who sent His Angel[a] and delivered His
servants who trusted in Him, and they have
frustrated the king's word, and yielded their
bodies, that they should not serve nor worship
any god except their own God! 29 Therefore I
make a decree that any people, nation, or lan-
guage which speaks anything amiss against the
God of Shadrach, Meshach, and Abed-Nego
shall be cut in pieces, and their houses shall be
made an ash heap; because there is no other
God who can deliver like this."

3:25 [a]Or *a son of the gods* **3:28** [a]Or *angel*

THE MESSAGE

16-18 Shadrach, Meshach, and Abednego answered King Nebuchadnezzar, "Your threat means nothing to us. If you throw us in the fire, the God we serve can rescue us from your roaring furnace and anything else you might cook up, O king. But even if he doesn't, it wouldn't make a bit of difference, O king. We still wouldn't serve your gods or worship the gold statue you set up."

19-23 Nebuchadnezzar, his face purple with anger, cut off Shadrach, Meshach, and Abednego. He ordered the furnace fired up seven times hotter than usual. He ordered some strong men from the army to tie them up, hands and feet, and throw them into the roaring furnace. Shadrach, Meshach, and Abednego, bound hand and foot, fully dressed from head to toe, were pitched into the roaring fire. Because the king was in such a hurry and the furnace was so hot, flames from the furnace killed the men who carried Shadrach, Meshach, and Abednego to it, while the fire raged around Shadrach, Meshach, and Abednego.

24 Suddenly King Nebuchadnezzar jumped up in alarm and said, "Didn't we throw three men, bound hand and foot, into the fire?"

"That's right, O king," they said.

25 "But look!" he said. "I see four men, walking around freely in the fire, completely unharmed! And the fourth man looks like a son of the gods!"

26 Nebuchadnezzar went to the door of the roaring furnace and called in, "Shadrach, Meshach, and Abednego, servants of the High God, come out here!"

Shadrach, Meshach, and Abednego walked out of the fire.

27 All the important people, the government leaders and king's counselors, gathered around to examine them and discovered that the fire hadn't so much as touched the three men—not a hair singed, not a scorch mark on their clothes, not even the smell of fire on them!

28 Nebuchadnezzar said, "Blessed be the God of Shadrach, Meshach, and Abednego! He sent his angel and rescued his servants who trusted in him! They ignored the king's orders and laid their bodies on the line rather than serve or worship any god but their own.

29 "Therefore I issue this decree: Anyone anywhere, of any race, color, or creed, who says anything against the God of Shadrach, Meshach, and Abednego will be ripped to pieces, limb from limb, and their houses torn down. There has never been a god who can pull off a rescue like this."

NEW KING JAMES VERSION

[30]Then the king promoted Shadrach, Meshach, and Abed-Nego in the province of Babylon.

NEBUCHADNEZZAR'S SECOND DREAM

4 Nebuchadnezzar the king,

To all peoples, nations, and languages that dwell in all the earth:

Peace be multiplied to you.

[2]I thought it good to declare the signs and wonders that the Most High God has worked for me.

[3]How great *are* His signs,
And how mighty His wonders!
His kingdom *is* an everlasting kingdom,
And His dominion *is* from generation to generation.

[4]I, Nebuchadnezzar, was at rest in my house,
and flourishing in my palace. [5]I saw a
dream which made me afraid, and the
thoughts on my bed and the visions of my
head troubled me. [6]Therefore I issued a
decree to bring in all the wise *men* of
Babylon before me, that they might make
known to me the interpretation of the
dream. [7]Then the magicians, the
astrologers, the Chaldeans, and the
soothsayers came in, and I told them the
dream; but they did not make known to me
its interpretation. [8]But at last Daniel came
before me (his name *is* Belteshazzar,
according to the name of my god; in him *is*
the Spirit of the Holy God), and I told the
dream before him, *saying:* [9]"Belteshazzar,
chief of the magicians, because I know that
the Spirit of the Holy God *is* in you, and no
secret troubles you, explain to me the
visions of my dream that I have seen, and
its interpretation.

[10]"These *were* the visions of my head *while* on my bed:

I was looking, and behold,
A tree in the midst of the earth,
And its height was great.
[11]The tree grew and became strong;
Its height reached to the heavens,
And it could be seen to the ends of all the earth.
[12]Its leaves *were* lovely,
Its fruit abundant,
And in it *was* food for all.
The beasts of the field found shade under it,
The birds of the heavens dwelt in its branches,
And all flesh was fed from it.

[13]"I saw in the visions of my head while on my
bed, and there was a watcher, a holy one,
coming down from heaven. [14]He cried aloud
and said thus:

'Chop down the tree and cut off its branches,
Strip off its leaves and scatter its fruit.

THE MESSAGE

30 Then the king promoted Shadrach, Meshach, and Abednego in the province of Babylon.

A DREAM OF A CHOPPED-DOWN TREE

1-2 4 King Nebuchadnezzar to everyone, everywhere—every race, color, and creed: "Peace and prosperity to all! It is my privilege to report to you the gracious miracles that the High God has done for me.

3 "His miracles are staggering,
his wonders are surprising.
His kingdom lasts and lasts,
his sovereign rule goes on forever.

4-7 "I, Nebuchadnezzar, was at home taking
it easy in my palace, without a care in the
world. But as I was stretched out on my bed
I had a dream that scared me—a nightmare
that shook me. I sent for all the wise men of
Babylon so that they could interpret the
dream for me. When they were all assembled—magicians, enchanters, fortunetellers,
witches—I told them the dream. None could
tell me what it meant.
8 "And then Daniel came in. His Babylonian name is Belteshazzar, named after my
god, a man full of the divine Holy Spirit. I
told him my dream.
9 " 'Belteshazzar,' I said, 'chief of the magicians, I know that you are a man full of the
divine Holy Spirit and that there is no mystery that you can't solve. Listen to this
dream that I had and interpret it for me.
10-12 " 'This is what I saw as I was stretched
out on my bed. I saw a big towering tree at
the center of the world. As I watched, the
tree grew huge and strong. Its top reached
the sky and it could be seen from the four
corners of the earth. Its leaves were beautiful, its fruit abundant—enough food for
everyone! Wild animals found shelter under
it, birds nested in its branches, everything
living was fed and sheltered by it.
13-15 " 'And this also is what I saw as I was
stretched out on my bed. I saw a holy watchman descend from heaven, and call out:

Chop down the tree, lop off its branches,
strip its leaves and scatter its fruit.

NEW KING JAMES VERSION

Let the beasts get out from under it,
And the birds from its branches.
15 Nevertheless leave the stump and roots in the earth,
Bound with a band of iron and bronze,
In the tender grass of the field.
Let it be wet with the dew of heaven,
And *let* him graze with the beasts
On the grass of the earth.
16 Let his heart be changed from *that of* a man,
Let him be given the heart of a beast,
And let seven times[a] pass over him.

17 'This decision *is* by the decree of the watchers,
And the sentence by the word of the holy ones,
In order that the living may know
That the Most High rules in the kingdom of men,
Gives it to whomever He will,
And sets over it the lowest of men.'

18 "This dream I, King Nebuchadnezzar, have
seen. Now you, Belteshazzar, declare its
interpretation, since all the wise *men* of my
kingdom are not able to make known to me
the interpretation; but you *are* able, for the
Spirit of the Holy God *is* in you."

DANIEL EXPLAINS THE SECOND DREAM

19 Then Daniel, whose name *was* Belte-
shazzar, was astonished for a time, and his
thoughts troubled him. *So* the king spoke,
and said, "Belteshazzar, do not let the
dream or its interpretation trouble you."
Belteshazzar answered and said, "My lord,
may the dream concern those who hate
you, and its interpretation concern your
enemies!

20 "The tree that you saw, which grew and
became strong, whose height reached to
the heavens and which *could be* seen by all
the earth, 21 whose leaves *were* lovely and
its fruit abundant, in which *was* food for
all, under which the beasts of the field
dwelt, and in whose branches the birds of
the heaven had their home— 22 it *is* you, O
king, who have grown and become strong;
for your greatness has grown and reaches
to the heavens, and your dominion to the
end of the earth.

23 "And inasmuch as the king saw a watcher, a
holy one, coming down from heaven and
saying, 'Chop down the tree and destroy it,
but leave its stump and roots in the earth,
bound with a band of iron and bronze in
the tender grass of the field; let it be wet
with the dew of heaven, and let him graze
with the beasts of the field, till seven times
pass over him'; 24 this is the interpretation,
O king, and this is the decree of the Most
High, which has come upon my lord the
king:

4:16 [a] Possibly *seven years,* and so in verses 23, 25, and 32

THE MESSAGE

Chase the animals from beneath it
and shoo the birds from its branches.
But leave the stump and roots in the ground,
belted with a strap of iron and bronze
in the grassy meadow.

15-16 Let him be soaked in heaven's dew
and take his meals with the animals
that graze.
Let him lose his mind
and get an animal's mind in
exchange,
And let this go on
for seven seasons.

17 The angels announce this decree,
the holy watchmen bring this
sentence,
So that everyone living will know
that the High God rules human
kingdoms.
He arranges kingdom affairs however he
wishes,
and makes leaders out of losers.

18 " 'This is what I, King Nebuchadnezzar,
dreamed. It's your turn, Belteshazzar—in-
terpret it for me. None of the wise men of
Babylon could make heads or tails of it, but
I'm sure you can do it. You're full of the di-
vine Holy Spirit.' "

"YOU WILL GRAZE ON THE GRASS LIKE AN OX"

19 At first Daniel, who had been renamed Bel-
teshazzar in Babylon, was upset. The
thoughts that came swarming into his mind
terrified him.

"Belteshazzar," the king said, "stay calm.
Don't let the dream and its interpretation
scare you."

"My master," said Belteshazzar, "I wish
this dream were about your enemies and its
interpretation for your foes.

20-22 "The tree you saw that grew so large and
sturdy with its top touching the sky, visible
from the four corners of the world; the tree
with the luxuriant foliage and abundant
fruit, enough for everyone; the tree under
which animals took cover and in which
birds built nests—you, O king, are that tree.

"You have grown great and strong. Your
royal majesty reaches sky-high, and your
sovereign rule stretches to the four corners
of the world.

23-25 "But the part about the holy angel de-
scending from heaven and proclaiming,
'Chop down the tree, destroy it, but leave
stump and roots in the ground belted with a
strap of iron and bronze in the grassy
meadow; let him be soaked with heaven's
dew and take his meals with the grazing an-
imals for seven seasons'—this, O king, also
refers to you. It means that the High God
has sentenced my master the king:

NEW KING JAMES VERSION

[25]They shall drive you from men, your dwelling shall be with the beasts of the field, and they shall make you eat grass like oxen. They shall wet you with the dew of heaven, and seven times shall pass over you, till you know that the Most High rules in the kingdom of men, and gives it to whomever He chooses.

[26]"And inasmuch as they gave the command to leave the stump *and* roots of the tree, your kingdom shall be assured to you, after you come to know that Heaven rules.
[27]Therefore, O king, let my advice be acceptable to you; break off your sins by *being* righteous, and your iniquities by showing mercy to *the* poor. Perhaps there may be a lengthening of your prosperity."

NEBUCHADNEZZAR'S HUMILIATION

[28]All *this* came upon King Nebuchadnezzar.
[29]At the end of the twelve months he was walking about the royal palace of Babylon.
[30]The king spoke, saying, "Is not this great Babylon, that I have built for a royal dwelling by my mighty power and for the honor of my majesty?"

[31]While the word *was still* in the king's mouth, a voice fell from heaven: "King Nebuchadnezzar, to you it is spoken: the kingdom has departed from you! [32]And they shall drive you from men, and your dwelling *shall be* with the beasts of the field. They shall make you eat grass like oxen; and seven times shall pass over you, until you know that the Most High rules in the kingdom of men, and gives it to whomever He chooses."

[33]That very hour the word was fulfilled concerning Nebuchadnezzar; he was driven from men and ate grass like oxen; his body was wet with the dew of heaven till his hair had grown like eagles' *feathers* and his nails like birds' *claws*.

NEBUCHADNEZZAR PRAISES GOD

[34]And at the end of the time[a] I, Nebuchadnezzar, lifted my eyes to heaven, and my understanding returned to me; and I blessed the Most High and praised and honored Him who lives forever:

For His dominion *is* an everlasting
dominion,
And His kingdom *is* from generation to
generation.
[35]All the inhabitants of the earth *are* reputed
as nothing;
He does according to His will in the army of
heaven
And *among* the inhabitants of the earth.
No one can restrain His hand
Or say to Him, "What have You done?"

[36]At the same time my reason returned to me, and for the glory of my kingdom, my honor

4:34 [a]Literally *days*

THE MESSAGE

You will be driven away from human company and live with the wild animals. You will graze on grass like an ox. You will be soaked in heaven's dew. This will go on for seven seasons, and you will learn that the High God rules over human kingdoms and that he arranges all kingdom affairs.

26 "The part about the tree stump and roots being left means that your kingdom will still be there for you after you learn that it is heaven that runs things.

27 "So, king, take my advice: Make a clean break with your sins and start living for others. Quit your wicked life and look after the needs of the down-and-out. Then *you* will continue to have a good life."

THE LOSS AND REGAINING OF A MIND AND A KINGDOM

28-30 All this happened to King Nebuchadnezzar. Just twelve months later, he was walking on the balcony of the royal palace in Babylon and boasted, "Look at this, Babylon the great! And I built it all by myself, a royal palace adequate to display my honor and glory!"

31-32 The words were no sooner out of his mouth than a voice out of heaven spoke, "This is the verdict on you, King Nebuchadnezzar: Your kingdom is taken from you. You will be driven out of human company and live with the wild animals. You will eat grass like an ox. The sentence is for seven seasons, enough time to learn that the High God rules human kingdoms and puts whomever he wishes in charge."

33 It happened at once. Nebuchadnezzar was driven out of human company, ate grass like an ox, and was soaked in heaven's dew. His hair grew like the feathers of an eagle and his nails like the claws of a hawk.

34-35 "At the end of the seven years, I, Nebuchadnezzar, looked to heaven. I was given my mind back and I blessed the High God, thanking and glorifying God, who lives forever:

"His sovereign rule lasts and lasts,
his kingdom never declines and falls.
Life on this earth doesn't add up to much,
but God's heavenly army keeps
everything going.
No one can interrupt his work,
no one can call his rule into question.

36-37 "At the same time that I was given back my mind, I was also given back my majesty

NEW KING JAMES VERSION

and splendor returned to me. My counselors and nobles resorted to me, I was restored to my kingdom, and excellent majesty was added to me. 37Now I, Nebuchadnezzar, praise and extol and honor the King of heaven, all of whose works *are* truth, and His ways justice. And those who walk in pride He is able to put down.

BELSHAZZAR'S FEAST

5 Belshazzar the king made a great feast for a thousand of his lords, and drank wine in the presence of the thousand. 2While he tasted the wine, Belshazzar gave the command to bring the gold and silver vessels which his father Nebuchadnezzar had taken from the temple which *had been* in Jerusalem, that the king and his lords, his wives, and his concubines might drink from them. 3Then they brought the gold vessels that had been taken from the temple of the house of God which *had been* in Jerusalem; and the king and his lords, his wives, and his concubines drank from them. 4They drank wine, and praised the gods of gold and silver, bronze and iron, wood and stone.

5In the same hour the fingers of a man's hand appeared and wrote opposite the lampstand on the plaster of the wall of the king's palace; and the king saw the part of the hand that wrote. 6Then the king's countenance changed, and his thoughts troubled him, so that the joints of his hips were loosened and his knees knocked against each other. 7The king cried aloud to bring in the astrologers, the Chaldeans, and the soothsayers. The king spoke, saying to the wise *men* of Babylon, "Whoever reads this writing, and tells me its interpretation, shall be clothed with purple and *have* a chain of gold around his neck; and he shall be the third ruler in the kingdom." 8Now all the king's wise *men* came, but they could not read the writing, or make known to the king its interpretation. 9Then King Belshazzar was greatly troubled, his countenance was changed, and his lords were astonished.

10The queen, because of the words of the king and his lords, came to the banquet hall. The queen spoke, saying, "O king, live forever! Do not let your thoughts trouble you, nor let your countenance change. 11There is a man in your kingdom in whom *is* the Spirit of the Holy God. And in the days of your father, light and understanding and wisdom, like the wisdom of the gods, were found in him; and King Nebuchadnezzar your father—your father the king—made him chief of the magicians, astrologers, Chaldeans, *and* soothsayers. 12Inasmuch as an excellent spirit, knowledge, understanding, interpreting dreams, solving riddles, and explaining enigmas[a] were found in this Daniel, whom the king named Belteshazzar, now let Daniel be called, and he will give the interpretation."

5:12 [a]Literally *untying knots,* and so in verse 16

THE MESSAGE

and splendor, making my kingdom shine. All the leaders and important people came looking for me. I was reestablished as king in my kingdom and became greater than ever. And that's why I'm singing—I, Nebuchadnezzar—singing and praising the King of Heaven:

"Everything he does is right,
and he does it the right way.
He knows how to turn a proud person
into a humble man or woman."

THE WRITING OF A DISEMBODIED HAND

1-4 5 King Belshazzar held a great feast for his one thousand nobles. The wine flowed freely. Belshazzar, heady with the wine, ordered that the gold and silver chalices his father Nebuchadnezzar had stolen from God's Temple of Jerusalem be brought in so that he and his nobles, his wives and concubines, could drink from them. When the gold and silver chalices were brought in, the king and his nobles, his wives and his concubines, drank wine from them. They drank the wine and drunkenly praised their gods made of gold and silver, bronze and iron, wood and stone.

5-7 At that very moment, the fingers of a human hand appeared and began writing on the lamp-illumined, whitewashed wall of the palace. When the king saw the disembodied hand writing away, he went white as a ghost, scared out of his wits. His legs went limp and his knees knocked. He yelled out for the enchanters, the fortunetellers, and the diviners to come. He told these Babylonian magi, "Anyone who can read this writing on the wall and tell me what it means will be famous and rich—purple robe, the great gold chain—and be third-in-command in the kingdom."

8-9 One after the other they tried, but could make no sense of it. They could neither read what was written nor interpret it to the king. So now the king was really frightened. All the blood drained from his face. The nobles were in a panic.

10-12 The queen heard of the hysteria among the king and his nobles and came to the banquet hall. She said, "Long live the king! Don't be upset. Don't sit around looking like ghosts. There is a man in your kingdom who is full of the divine Holy Spirit. During your father's time he was well known for his intellectual brilliance and spiritual wisdom. He was so good that your father, King Nebuchadnezzar, made him the head of all the magicians, enchanters, fortunetellers, and diviners. There was no one quite like him. He could do anything—interpret dreams, solve mysteries, explain puzzles. His name is Daniel, but he was renamed Belteshazzar by the king. Have Daniel called in. He'll tell you what is going on here."

New King James Version

The Writing on the Wall Explained

[13]Then Daniel was brought in before the king. The king spoke, and said to Daniel, "*Are* you that Daniel who is one of the captives[a] from Judah, whom my father the king brought from Judah? [14]I have heard of you, that the Spirit of God *is* in you, and *that* light and understanding and excellent wisdom are found in you. [15]Now the wise *men*, the astrologers, have been brought in before me, that they should read this writing and make known to me its interpretation, but they could not give the interpretation of the thing. [16]And I have heard of you, that you can give interpretations and explain enigmas. Now if you can read the writing and make known to me its interpretation, you shall be clothed with purple and *have* a chain of gold around your neck, and shall be the third ruler in the kingdom."

[17]Then Daniel answered, and said before the king, "Let your gifts be for yourself, and give your rewards to another; yet I will read the writing to the king, and make known to him the interpretation. [18]O king, the Most High God gave Nebuchadnezzar your father a kingdom and majesty, glory and honor. [19]And because of the majesty that He gave him, all peoples, nations, and languages trembled and feared before him. Whomever he wished, he executed; whomever he wished, he kept alive; whomever he wished, he set up; and whomever he wished, he put down. [20]But when his heart was lifted up, and his spirit was hardened in pride, he was deposed from his kingly throne, and they took his glory from him. [21]Then he was driven from the sons of men, his heart was made like the beasts, and his dwelling *was* with the wild donkeys. They fed him with grass like oxen, and his body was wet with the dew of heaven, till he knew that the Most High God rules in the kingdom of men, and appoints over it whomever He chooses.

[22]"But you his son, Belshazzar, have not humbled your heart, although you knew all this. [23]And you have lifted yourself up against the Lord of heaven. They have brought the vessels of His house before you, and you and your lords, your wives and your concubines, have drunk wine from them. And you have praised the gods of silver and gold, bronze and iron, wood and stone, which do not see or hear or know; and the God who *holds* your breath in His hand and owns all your ways, you have not glorified. [24]Then the fingers[a] of the hand were sent from Him, and this writing was written.

[25]"And this is the inscription that was written:

MENE,[a] MENE, TEKEL,[b] UPHARSIN.[c]

[26]This *is* the interpretation of *each* word. MENE: God has numbered your kingdom, and finished it; [27]TEKEL: You have been weighed in the balances, and found wanting; [28]PERES: Your kingdom has been divided, and given to the Medes and Persians."[a]

5:13 [a]Literally *of the sons of the captivity* **5:24** [a]Literally *palm*
5:25 [a]Literally *a mina* (50 shekels) from the verb "to number" [b]Literally *a shekel* from the verb "to weigh" [c]Literally *and half-shekels* from the verb "to divide" **5:28** [a]Aramaic *Paras*, consonant with *Peres*

The Message

13-16 So Daniel was called in. The king asked him, "Are you the Daniel who was one of the Jewish exiles my father brought here from Judah? I've heard about you—that you're full of the Holy Spirit, that you've got a brilliant mind, that you are incredibly wise. The wise men and enchanters were brought in here to read this writing on the wall and interpret it for me. They couldn't figure it out—not a word, not a syllable. But I've heard that you interpret dreams and solve mysteries. So—if you can read the writing and interpret it for me, you'll be rich and famous—a purple robe, the great gold chain around your neck—and third-in-command in the kingdom."

17 Daniel answered the king, "You can keep your gifts, or give them to someone else. But I will read the writing for the king and tell him what it means.

18-21 "Listen, O king! The High God gave your father Nebuchadnezzar a great kingdom and a glorious reputation. Because God made him so famous, people from everywhere, whatever their race, color, and creed, were totally intimidated by him. He killed or spared people on whim. He promoted or humiliated people capriciously. He developed a big head and a hard spirit. Then God knocked him off his high horse and stripped him of his fame. He was thrown out of human company, lost his mind, and lived like a wild animal. He ate grass like an ox and was soaked by heaven's dew until he learned his lesson: that the High God rules human kingdoms and puts anyone he wants in charge.

22-23 "You are his son and have known all this, yet you're as arrogant as he ever was. Look at you, setting yourself up in competition against the Master of heaven! You had the sacred chalices from his Temple brought into your drunken party so that you and your nobles, your wives and your concubines, could drink from them. You used the sacred chalices to toast your gods of silver and gold, bronze and iron, wood and stone—blind, deaf, and imbecile gods. But you treat with contempt the living God who holds your entire life from birth to death in his hand.

24-26 "God sent the hand that wrote on the wall, and this is what is written: MENE, TEQEL, and PERES. This is what the words mean:

"*Mene:* God has numbered the days of your rule and they don't add up.

27 "*Teqel:* You have been weighed on the scales and you don't weigh much.

28 "*Peres:* Your kingdom has been divided up and handed over to the Medes and Persians."

New King James Version

29 Then Belshazzar gave the command, and they clothed Daniel with purple and *put* a chain of gold around his neck, and made a proclamation concerning him that he should be the third ruler in the kingdom.

Belshazzar's Fall

30 That very night Belshazzar, king of the Chaldeans, was slain. 31 And Darius the Mede received the kingdom, *being* about sixty-two years old.

The Plot Against Daniel

6 It pleased Darius to set over the kingdom one hundred and twenty satraps, to be over the whole kingdom; 2 and over these, three governors, of whom Daniel *was* one, that the satraps might give account to them, so that the king would suffer no loss. 3 Then this Daniel distinguished himself above the governors and satraps, because an excellent spirit *was* in him; and the king gave thought to setting him over the whole realm. 4 So the governors and satraps sought to find *some* charge against Daniel concerning the kingdom; but they could find no charge or fault, because he *was* faithful; nor was there any error or fault found in him. 5 Then these men said, "We shall not find any charge against this Daniel unless we find *it* against him concerning the law of his God."

6 So these governors and satraps thronged before the king, and said thus to him: "King Darius, live forever! 7 All the governors of the kingdom, the administrators and satraps, the counselors and advisors, have consulted together to establish a royal statute and to make a firm decree, that whoever petitions any god or man for thirty days, except you, O king, shall be cast into the den of lions. 8 Now, O king, establish the decree and sign the writing, so that it cannot be changed, according to the law of the Medes and Persians, which does not alter." 9 Therefore King Darius signed the written decree.

Daniel in the Lions' Den

10 Now when Daniel knew that the writing was signed, he went home. And in his upper room, with his windows open toward Jerusalem, he knelt down on his knees three times that day, and prayed and gave thanks before his God, as was his custom since early days.

11 Then these men assembled and found Daniel praying and making supplication before his God. 12 And they went before the king, and spoke concerning the king's decree: "Have you not signed a decree that every man who petitions any god or man within thirty days, except you, O king, shall be cast into the den of lions?"

The king answered and said, "The thing *is* true, according to the law of the Medes and Persians, which does not alter."

The Message

29 Belshazzar did what he had promised. He robed Daniel in purple, draped the great gold chain around his neck, and promoted him to third-in-charge in the kingdom.

30-31 That same night the Babylonian king Belshazzar was murdered. Darius the Mede was sixty-two years old when he succeeded him as king.

Daniel in the Lions' Den

1-3 6 Darius reorganized his kingdom. He appointed one hundred twenty governors to administer all the parts of his realm. Over them were three vice-regents, one of whom was Daniel. The governors reported to the vice-regents, who made sure that everything was in order for the king. But Daniel, brimming with spirit and intelligence, so completely outclassed the other vice-regents and governors that the king decided to put him in charge of the whole kingdom.

4-5 The vice-regents and governors got together to find some old scandal or skeleton in Daniel's life that they could use against him, but they couldn't dig up anything. He was totally exemplary and trustworthy. They could find no evidence of negligence or misconduct. So they finally gave up and said, "We're never going to find anything against this Daniel unless we can cook up something religious."

6-7 The vice-regents and governors conspired together and then went to the king and said, "King Darius, live forever! We've convened your vice-regents, governors, and all your leading officials, and have agreed that the king should issue the following decree:

> For the next thirty days no one is to pray to any god or mortal except you, O king. Anyone who disobeys will be thrown into the lions' den.

8 "Issue this decree, O king, and make it unconditional, as if written in stone like all the laws of the Medes and the Persians."

9 King Darius signed the decree.

10 When Daniel learned that the decree had been signed and posted, he continued to pray just as he had always done. His house had windows in the upstairs that opened toward Jerusalem. Three times a day he knelt there in prayer, thanking and praising his God.

11-12 The conspirators came and found him praying, asking God for help. They went straight to the king and reminded him of the royal decree that he had signed. "Did you not," they said, "sign a decree forbidding anyone to pray to any god or man except you for the next thirty days? And anyone caught doing it would be thrown into the lions' den?"

"Absolutely," said the king. "Written in stone, like all the laws of the Medes and Persians."

New King James Version

13So they answered and said before the king,
"That Daniel, who is one of the captives[a] from
Judah, does not show due regard for you, O
king, or for the decree that you have signed, but
makes his petition three times a day."
14And the king, when he heard *these* words,
was greatly displeased with himself, and set *his*
heart on Daniel to deliver him; and he labored
till the going down of the sun to deliver him.
15Then these men approached the king, and said
to the king, "Know, O king, that *it is* the law of
the Medes and Persians that no decree or statute
which the king establishes may be changed."
16So the king gave the command, and they
brought Daniel and cast *him* into the den of li-
ons. *But* the king spoke, saying to Daniel, "Your
God, whom you serve continually, He will de-
liver you." 17Then a stone was brought and laid
on the mouth of the den, and the king sealed it
with his own signet ring and with the signets
of his lords, that the purpose concerning Daniel
might not be changed.

Daniel Saved from the Lions

18Now the king went to his palace and spent
the night fasting; and no musicians[a] were
brought before him. Also his sleep went from
him. 19Then the king arose very early in the
morning and went in haste to the den of lions.
20And when he came to the den, he cried out
with a lamenting voice to Daniel. The king
spoke, saying to Daniel, "Daniel, servant of the
living God, has your God, whom you serve con-
tinually, been able to deliver you from the li-
ons?"
21Then Daniel said to the king, "O king, live
forever! 22My God sent His angel and shut the li-
ons' mouths, so that they have not hurt me, be-
cause I was found innocent before Him; and
also, O king, I have done no wrong before you."
23Now the king was exceedingly glad for
him, and commanded that they should take
Daniel up out of the den. So Daniel was taken
up out of the den, and no injury whatever was
found on him, because he believed in his God.

Darius Honors God

24And the king gave the command, and they
brought those men who had accused Daniel,
and they cast *them* into the den of lions—them,
their children, and their wives; and the lions
overpowered them, and broke all their bones in
pieces before they ever came to the bottom of
the den.
25Then King Darius wrote:

To all peoples, nations, and languages that
dwell in all the earth:

Peace be multiplied to you.

26I make a decree that in every dominion of
my kingdom *men must* tremble and fear
before the God of Daniel.

For He *is* the living God,
And steadfast forever;

6:13 [a]Literally *of the sons of the captivity* 6:18 [a]Exact meaning unknown

The Message

13 Then they said, "Daniel, one of the Jewish
exiles, ignores you, O king, and defies your
decree. Three times a day he prays."
14 At this, the king was very upset and tried
his best to get Daniel out of the fix he'd put
him in. He worked at it the whole day long.
15 But then the conspirators were back: "Re-
member, O king, it's the law of the Medes
and Persians that the king's decree can
never be changed."
16 The king caved in and ordered Daniel
brought and thrown into the lions' den. But
he said to Daniel, "Your God, to whom you
are so loyal, is going to get you out of this."
17 A stone slab was placed over the opening
of the den. The king sealed the cover with
his signet ring and the signet rings of all his
nobles, fixing Daniel's fate.
18 The king then went back to his palace. He
refused supper. He couldn't sleep. He spent
the night fasting.
19-20 At daybreak the king got up and hurried
to the lions' den. As he approached the den,
he called out anxiously, "Daniel, servant of
the living God, has your God, whom you
serve so loyally, saved you from the lions?"
21-22 "O king, live forever!" said Daniel. "My
God sent his angel, who closed the mouths
of the lions so that they would not hurt me.
I've been found innocent before God and
also before you, O king. I've done nothing to
harm you."
23 When the king heard these words, he was
happy. He ordered Daniel taken up out of the
den. When he was hauled up, there wasn't a
scratch on him. He had trusted his God.
24 Then the king commanded that the con-
spirators who had informed on Daniel be
thrown into the lions' den, along with their
wives and children. Before they hit the floor,
the lions had them in their jaws, tearing
them to pieces.
25-27 King Darius published this proclamation
to every race, color, and creed on earth:

Peace to you! Abundant peace!
I decree that Daniel's God shall be
worshiped and feared
in all parts of my kingdom.
He is the living God, world without
end. His kingdom

NEW KING JAMES VERSION

His kingdom *is the one* which shall not be
destroyed,
And His dominion *shall endure* to the end.
27He delivers and rescues,
And He works signs and wonders
In heaven and on earth,
Who has delivered Daniel from the power of
the lions.

28So this Daniel prospered in the reign of
Darius and in the reign of Cyrus the Persian.

VISION OF THE FOUR BEASTS

7In the first year of Belshazzar king of Baby-
lon, Daniel had a dream and visions of his
head *while* on his bed. Then he wrote down the
dream, telling the main facts.[a]
2Daniel spoke, saying, "I saw in my vision by
night, and behold, the four winds of heaven
were stirring up the Great Sea. 3And four great
beasts came up from the sea, each different
from the other. 4The first *was* like a lion, and
had eagle's wings. I watched till its wings were
plucked off; and it was lifted up from the earth
and made to stand on two feet like a man, and a
man's heart was given to it.
5"And suddenly another beast, a second, like
a bear. It was raised up on one side, and *had*
three ribs in its mouth between its teeth. And
they said thus to it: 'Arise, devour much flesh!'
6"After this I looked, and there was another,
like a leopard, which had on its back four wings
of a bird. The beast also had four heads, and do-
minion was given to it.
7"After this I saw in the night visions, and be-
hold, a fourth beast, dreadful and terrible, ex-
ceedingly strong. It had huge iron teeth; it was
devouring, breaking in pieces, and trampling
the residue with its feet. It *was* different from all
the beasts that *were* before it, and it had ten
horns. 8I was considering the horns, and there
was another horn, a little one, coming up among
them, before whom three of the first horns were
plucked out by the roots. And there, in this horn,
were eyes like the eyes of a man, and a mouth
speaking pompous words.

VISION OF THE ANCIENT OF DAYS

9"I watched till thrones were put in place,
And the Ancient of Days was seated;
His garment *was* white as snow,
And the hair of His head *was* like pure
wool.
His throne *was* a fiery flame,
Its wheels a burning fire;
10A fiery stream issued
And came forth from before Him.
A thousand thousands ministered to Him;
Ten thousand times ten thousand stood
before Him.
The court[a] was seated,
And the books were opened.

11"I watched then because of the sound of the
pompous words which the horn was speaking; I

7:1 [a]Literally *the head* (or *chief*) *of the words* 7:10 [a]Or *judgment*

THE MESSAGE

never falls.
His rule continues eternally.
He is a savior and rescuer.
He performs astonishing miracles in
heaven and on earth.
He saved Daniel from the power of
the lions.

28 From then on, Daniel was treated well dur-
ing the reign of Darius, and also in the fol-
lowing reign of Cyrus the Persian.

A VISION OF FOUR ANIMALS

1 7In the first year of the reign of King Bel-
shazzar of Babylon, Daniel had a dream.
What he saw as he slept in his bed terrified
him—a real nightmare. Then he wrote out
his dream:
2-3 "In my dream that night I saw the four
winds of heaven whipping up a great storm
on the sea. Four huge animals, each differ-
ent from the others, ascended out of the sea.
4 "The first animal looked like a lion, but it
had the wings of an eagle. While I watched,
its wings were pulled off. It was then pulled
erect so that it was standing on two feet like
a man. Then a human heart was placed in it.
5 "Then I saw a second animal that looked
like a bear. It lurched from side to side, hold-
ing three ribs in its jaws. It was told, 'Attack!
Devour! Fill your belly!'
6 "Next I saw another animal. This one
looked like a panther. It had four birdlike
wings on its back. This animal had four
heads and was made to rule.
7 "After that, a fourth animal appeared in
my dream. This one was a grisly horror—
hideous. It had huge iron teeth. It crunched
and swallowed its victims. Anything left
over, it trampled into the ground. It was dif-
ferent from the other animals—this one was
a real monster. It had ten horns.
8 "As I was staring at the horns and trying
to figure out what they meant, another horn
sprouted up, a little horn. Three of the origi-
nal horns were pulled out to make room for
it. There were human eyes in this little horn,
and a big mouth speaking arrogantly.
9-10 "As I was watching all this,

"Thrones were set in place
and The Old One sat down.
His robes were white as snow,
his hair was white like wool.
His throne was flaming with fire,
its wheels blazing.
A river of fire
poured out of the throne.
Thousands upon thousands served him,
tens of thousands attended him.
The courtroom was called to order,
and the books were opened.

11-13 "I kept watching. The little horn was
speaking arrogantly. Then, as I watched, the

NEW KING JAMES VERSION

watched till the beast was slain, and its body de-
stroyed and given to the burning flame. 12As for
the rest of the beasts, they had their dominion
taken away, yet their lives were prolonged for a
season and a time.

13"I was watching in the night visions,
And behold, *One* like the Son of Man,
Coming with the clouds of heaven!
He came to the Ancient of Days,
And they brought Him near before Him.
14Then to Him was given dominion and glory
and a kingdom,
That all peoples, nations, and languages
should serve Him.
His dominion *is* an everlasting dominion,
Which shall not pass away,
And His kingdom *the one*
Which shall not be destroyed.

DANIEL'S VISIONS INTERPRETED

15"I, Daniel, was grieved in my spirit within
my body, and the visions of my head troubled
me. 16I came near to one of those who stood by,
and asked him the truth of all this. So he told me
and made known to me the interpretation of
these things: 17'Those great beasts, which are
four, *are* four kings[a] *which* arise out of the earth.
18But the saints of the Most High shall receive
the kingdom, and possess the kingdom forever,
even forever and ever.'

19"Then I wished to know the truth about the
fourth beast, which was different from all the
others, exceedingly dreadful, *with* its teeth of
iron and its nails of bronze, *which* devoured,
broke in pieces, and trampled the residue with
its feet; 20and the ten horns that *were* on its
head, and the other *horn* which came up, before
which three fell, namely, that horn which had
eyes and a mouth which spoke pompous words,
whose appearance *was* greater than his fellows.
21"I was watching; and the same horn was
making war against the saints, and prevailing
against them, 22until the Ancient of Days came,
and a judgment was made *in favor* of the saints
of the Most High, and the time came for the
saints to possess the kingdom.

23"Thus he said:

'The fourth beast shall be
A fourth kingdom on earth,
Which shall be different from all *other*
kingdoms,
And shall devour the whole earth,
Trample it and break it in pieces.
24The ten horns *are* ten kings
Who shall arise from this kingdom.
And another shall rise after them;
He shall be different from the first *ones*,
And shall subdue three kings.
25He shall speak *pompous* words against the
Most High,
Shall persecute[a] the saints of the Most High,
And shall intend to change times and law.
Then *the saints* shall be given into his hand
For a time and times and half a time.

7:17 [a]Representing their kingdoms (compare verse 23)
7:25 [a]Literally *wear out*

THE MESSAGE

monster was killed and its body cremated in
a roaring fire. The other animals lived on for
a limited time, but they didn't really do any-
thing, had no power to rule. My dream con-
tinued.

13-14 "I saw a human form, a son of man,
arriving in a whirl of clouds.
He came to The Old One
and was presented to him.
He was given power to rule—all the glory
of royalty.
Everyone—race, color, and creed—had to
serve him.
His rule would be forever, never ending.
His kingly rule would never be replaced.

15-16 "But as for me, Daniel, I was disturbed.
All these dream-visions had me agitated. So
I went up to one of those standing by and
asked him the meaning of all this. And he
told me, interpreting the dream for me:
17-18 " 'These four huge animals,' he said,
'mean that four kingdoms will appear on
earth. But eventually the holy people of the
High God will be given the kingdom and
have it ever after—yes, forever and ever.'
19-22 "But I wanted to know more. I was curi-
ous about the fourth animal, the one so dif-
ferent from the others, the hideous monster
with the iron teeth and the bronze claws,
gulping down what it ripped to pieces and
trampling the leftovers into the dirt. And I
wanted to know about the ten horns on its
head and the other horn that sprouted up
while three of the original horns were re-
moved. This new horn had eyes and a big
mouth and spoke arrogantly, dominating
the other horns. I watched as this horn was
making war on God's holy people and get-
ting the best of them. But then The Old One
intervened and decided things in favor of
the people of the High God. In the end,
God's holy people took over the kingdom.
23-25 "The bystander continued, telling me
this: 'The fourth animal is a fourth kingdom
that will appear on earth. It will be different
from the first three kingdoms, a monster
kingdom that will chew up everyone in sight
and spit them out. The ten horns are ten
kings, one after another, that will come from
this kingdom. But then another king will ar-
rive. He will be different from the earlier
kings. He will begin by toppling three kings.
Then he will blaspheme the High God, per-
secute the followers of the High God, and
try to get rid of sacred worship and moral
practice. God's holy people will be perse-
cuted by him for a time, two times, half a
time.

NEW KING JAMES VERSION

26‘But the court shall be seated,
And they shall take away his dominion,
To consume and destroy *it* forever.
27Then the kingdom and dominion,
And the greatness of the kingdoms under
the whole heaven,
Shall be given to the people, the saints of
the Most High.
His kingdom *is* an everlasting kingdom,
And all dominions shall serve and obey
Him.’

28“This *is* the end of the account.[a] As for me,
Daniel, my thoughts greatly troubled me, and
my countenance changed; but I kept the matter
in my heart.”

VISION OF A RAM AND A GOAT

8 In the third year of the reign of King Belshaz-
zar a vision appeared *to* me—to me, Daniel—
after the one that appeared to me the first time.
2I saw in the vision, and it so happened while I
was looking, that I *was* in Shushan, the citadel,
which *is* in the province of Elam; and I saw in
the vision that I was by the River Ulai. 3Then I
lifted my eyes and saw, and there, standing be-
side the river, was a ram which had two horns,
and the two horns *were* high; but one *was*
higher than the other, and the higher *one* came
up last. 4I saw the ram pushing westward, north-
ward, and southward, so that no animal could
withstand him; nor *was there any* that could de-
liver from his hand, but he did according to his
will and became great.
5And as I was considering, suddenly a male
goat came from the west, across the surface of
the whole earth, without touching the ground;
and the goat *had* a notable horn between his
eyes. 6Then he came to the ram that had two
horns, which I had seen standing beside the
river, and ran at him with furious power. 7And I
saw him confronting the ram; he was moved
with rage against him, attacked the ram, and
broke his two horns. There was no power in the
ram to withstand him, but he cast him down to
the ground and trampled him; and there was no
one that could deliver the ram from his hand.
8Therefore the male goat grew very great;
but when he became strong, the large horn was
broken, and in place of it four notable ones
came up toward the four winds of heaven. 9And
out of one of them came a little horn which grew
exceedingly great toward the south, toward the
east, and toward the Glorious *Land.* 10And it
grew up to the host of heaven; and it cast down
some of the host and *some* of the stars to the
ground, and trampled them. 11He even exalted
himself as high as the Prince of the host; and by
him the daily *sacrifices* were taken away, and
the place of His sanctuary was cast down. 12Be-
cause of transgression, an army was given over
to the horn to oppose the daily *sacrifices;* and
he cast truth down to the ground. He did *all this*
and prospered.
13Then I heard a holy one speaking; and *an-
other* holy one said to that certain *one* who was

7:28 [a]Literally *the word*

THE MESSAGE

26-27 “ ‘But when the court comes to order, the horn will be stripped of its power and totally destroyed. Then the royal rule and the authority and the glory of all the kingdoms under heaven will be handed over to the people of the High God. Their royal rule will last forever. All other rulers will serve and obey them.’

28 “And there it ended. I, Daniel, was in shock. I was like a man who had seen a ghost. But I kept it all to myself.”

A VISION OF A RAM AND A BILLY GOAT

1 8 “In King Belshazzar’s third year as king, another vision came to me, Daniel. This was now the second vision.

2-4 “In the vision, I saw myself in Susa, the capital city of the province Elam, standing at the Ulai Canal. Looking around, I was surprised to see a ram also standing at the gate. The ram had two huge horns, one bigger than the other, but the bigger horn was the last to appear. I watched as the ram charged: first west, then north, then south. No beast could stand up to him. He did just as he pleased, strutting as if he were king of the beasts.

5-7 “While I was watching this, wondering what it all meant, I saw a billy goat with an immense horn in the middle of its forehead come up out of the west and fly across the whole country, not once touching the ground. The billy goat approached the double-horned ram that I had earlier seen standing at the gate and, enraged, charged it viciously. I watched as, mad with rage, it charged the ram and hit it so hard that it broke off its two horns. The ram didn’t stand a chance against it. The billy goat knocked the ram to the ground and stomped all over it. Nothing could have saved the ram from the goat.

8-12 “Then the billy goat swelled to an enormous size. At the height of its power its immense horn broke off and four other big horns sprouted in its place, pointing to the four points of the compass. And then from one of these big horns another horn sprouted. It started small, but then grew to an enormous size, facing south and east—toward lovely Palestine. The horn grew tall, reaching to the stars, the heavenly army, and threw some of the stars to the earth and stomped on them. It even dared to challenge the power of God, Prince of the Celestial Army! And then it threw out daily worship and desecrated the Sanctuary. As judgment against their sin, the holy people of God got the same treatment as the daily worship. The horn cast God’s Truth aside. High-handed, it took over everything and everyone.

13 “Then I overheard two holy angels talking. One asked, ‘How long is what we see

NEW KING JAMES VERSION

speaking, "How long *will* the vision *be, concerning* the daily *sacrifices* and the transgression of desolation, the giving of both the sanctuary and the host to be trampled underfoot?"
14And he said to me, "For two thousand three hundred days;[a] then the sanctuary shall be cleansed."

GABRIEL INTERPRETS THE VISION

15Then it happened, when I, Daniel, had seen the vision and was seeking the meaning, that suddenly there stood before me one having the appearance of a man.
16And I heard a man's voice between *the banks of* the Ulai, who called, and said, "Gabriel, make this *man* understand the vision."
17So he came near where I stood, and when he came I was afraid and fell on my face; but he said to me, "Understand, son of man, that the vision *refers* to the time of the end."
18Now, as he was speaking with me, I was in a deep sleep with my face to the ground; but he touched me, and stood me upright.
19And he said, "Look, I am making known to you what shall happen in the latter time of the indignation; for at the appointed time the end *shall be.*
20The ram which you saw, having the two horns—*they are* the kings of Media and Persia.
21And the male goat *is* the kingdom[a] of Greece. The large horn that *is* between its eyes *is* the first king.
22As for the broken *horn* and the four that stood up in its place, four kingdoms shall arise out of that nation, but not with its power.

23"And in the latter time of their kingdom,
When the transgressors have reached their fullness,
A king shall arise,
Having fierce features,
Who understands sinister schemes.
24His power shall be mighty, but not by his own power;
He shall destroy fearfully,
And shall prosper and thrive;
He shall destroy the mighty, and *also* the holy people.

25"Through his cunning
He shall cause deceit to prosper under his rule;[a]
And he shall exalt *himself* in his heart.
He shall destroy many in *their* prosperity.
He shall even rise against the Prince of princes;
But he shall be broken without *human* means.[b]

26"And the vision of the evenings and mornings
Which was told is true;
Therefore seal up the vision,
For *it refers* to many days *in the future.*"

27And I, Daniel, fainted and was sick for days; afterward I arose and went about the king's business. I was astonished by the vision, but no one understood it.

8:14 [a]Literally *evening-mornings* **8:21** [a]Literally *king,* representing his kingdom (compare 7:17, 23) **8:25** [a]Literally *hand* [b]Literally *hand*

THE MESSAGE

here going to last—the abolishing of daily worship, this devastating judgment against sin, the kicking around of God's holy people and the Sanctuary?'

14 "The other answered, 'Over the course of 2,300 sacrifices, evening and morning. Then the Sanctuary will be set right again.'

15 "While I, Daniel, was trying to make sense of what I was seeing, suddenly there was a humanlike figure standing before me.

16-17 "Then I heard a man's voice from over by the Ulai Canal calling out, 'Gabriel, tell this man what is going on. Explain the vision to him.' He came up to me, but when he got close I became terrified and fell facedown on the ground.

17-18 "He said, 'Understand that this vision has to do with the time of the end.' As soon as he spoke, I fainted, my face in the dirt. But he picked me up and put me on my feet.

19 "And then he continued, 'I want to tell you what is going to happen as the judgment days of wrath wind down, for there is going to be an end to all this.

20-22 " 'The double-horned ram you saw stands for the two kings of the Medes and Persians. The billy goat stands for the kingdom of the Greeks. The huge horn on its forehead is the first Greek king. The four horns that sprouted after it was broken off are the four kings that come after him, but without his power.

23-26 " 'As their kingdoms cool down
and rebellions heat up,
A king will show up,
hard-faced, a master trickster.
His power will swell enormously.
He'll talk big, high-handedly,
Doing whatever he pleases,
knocking off heroes and holy ones left and right.
He'll plot and scheme to make crime flourish—
and oh, how it will flourish!
He'll think he's invincible
and get rid of anyone who gets in his way.
But when he takes on the Prince of all princes,
he'll be smashed to bits—
but not by human hands.
This vision of the 2,300 sacrifices, evening and morning,
is accurate but confidential.
Keep it to yourself.
It refers to the far future.'

27 "I, Daniel, walked around in a daze, unwell for days. Then I got a grip on myself and went back to work taking care of the king's affairs. But I continued to be upset by the vision. I couldn't make sense of it."

New King James Version

Daniel's Prayer for the People

9 In the first year of Darius the son of Ahasuerus, of the lineage of the Medes, who was made king over the realm of the Chaldeans— [2]in the first year of his reign I, Daniel, understood by the books the number of the years *specified* by the word of the LORD through Jeremiah the prophet, that He would accomplish seventy years in the desolations of Jerusalem.

[3]Then I set my face toward the Lord God to make request by prayer and supplications, with fasting, sackcloth, and ashes. [4]And I prayed to the LORD my God, and made confession, and said, "O Lord, great and awesome God, who keeps His covenant and mercy with those who love Him, and with those who keep His commandments, [5]we have sinned and committed iniquity, we have done wickedly and rebelled, even by departing from Your precepts and Your judgments. [6]Neither have we heeded Your servants the prophets, who spoke in Your name to our kings and our princes, to our fathers and all the people of the land. [7]O Lord, righteousness *belongs* to You, but to us shame of face, as *it is* this day—to the men of Judah, to the inhabitants of Jerusalem and all Israel, those near and those far off in all the countries to which You have driven them, because of the unfaithfulness which they have committed against You.

[8]"O Lord, to us *belongs* shame of face, to our kings, our princes, and our fathers, because we have sinned against You. [9]To the Lord our God *belong* mercy and forgiveness, though we have rebelled against Him. [10]We have not obeyed the voice of the LORD our God, to walk in His laws, which He set before us by His servants the prophets. [11]Yes, all Israel has transgressed Your law, and has departed so as not to obey Your voice; therefore the curse and the oath written in the Law of Moses the servant of God have been poured out on us, because we have sinned against Him. [12]And He has confirmed His words, which He spoke against us and against our judges who judged us, by bringing upon us a great disaster; for under the whole heaven such has never been done as what has been done to Jerusalem.

[13]"As *it is* written in the Law of Moses, all this disaster has come upon us; yet we have not made our prayer before the LORD our God, that we might turn from our iniquities and understand Your truth. [14]Therefore the LORD has kept the disaster in mind, and brought it upon us; for the LORD our God *is* righteous in all the works which He does, though we have not obeyed His voice. [15]And now, O Lord our God, who brought Your people out of the land of Egypt with a mighty hand, and made Yourself a name, as *it is* this day—we have sinned, we have done wickedly!

[16]"O Lord, according to all Your righteousness, I pray, let Your anger and Your fury be turned away from Your city Jerusalem, Your holy mountain; because for our sins, and for the iniquities of our fathers, Jerusalem and Your people

The Message

God's Covenant Commitment

1-4 9 "Darius, son of Ahasuerus, born a Mede, became king over the land of Babylon. In the first year of his reign, I, Daniel, was meditating on the Scriptures that gave, according to the Word of GOD to the prophet Jeremiah, the number of years that Jerusalem had to lie in ruins, namely, seventy. I turned to the Master God, asking for an answer—praying earnestly, fasting from meals, wearing rough penitential burlap, and kneeling in the ashes. I poured out my heart, baring my soul to GOD, my God:

4-8 " 'O Master, great and august God. You never waver in your covenant commitment, never give up on those who love you and do what you say. Yet we have sinned in every way imaginable. We've done evil things, rebelled, dodged and taken detours around your clearly marked paths. We've turned a deaf ear to your servants the prophets, who preached your Word to our kings and leaders, our parents, and all the people in the land. You have done everything right, Master, but all we have to show for our lives is guilt and shame, the whole lot of us—people of Judah, citizens of Jerusalem, Israel at home and Israel in exile in all the places we've been banished to because of our betrayal of you. Oh yes, GOD, we've been exposed in our shame, all of us—our kings, leaders, parents—before the whole world. And deservedly so, because of our sin.

9-12 " 'Compassion is our only hope, the compassion of you, the Master, our God, since in our rebellion we've forfeited our rights. We paid no attention to you when you told us how to live, the clear teaching that came through your servants the prophets. All of us in Israel ignored what you said. We defied your instructions and did what we pleased. And now we're paying for it: The solemn curse written out plainly in the revelation to God's servant Moses is now doing its work among us, the wages of our sin against you. You did to us and our rulers what you said you would do: You brought this catastrophic disaster on us, the worst disaster on record—and in Jerusalem!

13-14 " 'Just as written in God's revelation to Moses, the catastrophe was total. Nothing was held back. We kept at our sinning, never giving you a second thought, oblivious to your clear warning, and so you had no choice but to let the disaster loose on us in full force. You, our GOD, had a perfect right to do this since we persistently and defiantly ignored you.

15-17 " 'Master, you are our God, for you delivered your people from the land of Egypt in a show of power—people are still talking about it! We confess that we have sinned, that we have lived bad lives. Following the lines of what you have always done in setting things right, setting *people* right, please stop being so angry with Jerusalem, your very own city, your holy mountain. We know it's our fault that this has happened, all because of our sins and our parents' sins, and

NEW KING JAMES VERSION

are a reproach to all *those* around us. [17]Now
therefore, our God, hear the prayer of Your ser-
vant, and his supplications, and for the Lord's
sake cause Your face to shine on Your sanctuary,
which is desolate. [18]O my God, incline Your ear
and hear; open Your eyes and see our desola-
tions, and the city which is called by Your name;
for we do not present our supplications before
You because of our righteous deeds, but because
of Your great mercies. [19]O Lord, hear! O Lord,
forgive! O Lord, listen and act! Do not delay for
Your own sake, my God, for Your city and Your
people are called by Your name."

THE SEVENTY-WEEKS PROPHECY

[20]Now while I *was* speaking, praying, and
confessing my sin and the sin of my people Is-
rael, and presenting my supplication before the
LORD my God for the holy mountain of my God,
[21]yes, while I *was* speaking in prayer, the man
Gabriel, whom I had seen in the vision at the be-
ginning, being caused to fly swiftly, reached me
about the time of the evening offering. [22]And he
informed *me*, and talked with me, and said, "O
Daniel, I have now come forth to give you skill
to understand. [23]At the beginning of your sup-
plications the command went out, and I have
come to tell *you*, for you *are* greatly beloved;
therefore consider the matter, and understand
the vision:

[24]"Seventy weeks[a] are determined
For your people and for your holy city,
To finish the transgression,
To make an end of[b] sins,
To make reconciliation for iniquity,
To bring in everlasting righteousness,
To seal up vision and prophecy,
And to anoint the Most Holy.

[25]"Know therefore and understand,
That from the going forth of the command
To restore and build Jerusalem
Until Messiah the Prince,
There shall be seven weeks and sixty-two
weeks;
The street[a] shall be built again, and the wall,[b]
Even in troublesome times.

[26]"And after the sixty-two weeks
Messiah shall be cut off, but not for Himself;
And the people of the prince who is to come
Shall destroy the city and the sanctuary.
The end of it *shall be* with a flood,
And till the end of the war desolations are
determined.
[27]Then he shall confirm a covenant with many
for one week;
But in the middle of the week
He shall bring an end to sacrifice and
offering.
And on the wing of abominations shall be
one who makes desolate,
Even until the consummation, which is
determined,
Is poured out on the desolate."

9:24 [a]Literally *sevens*, and so throughout the chapter [b]Following Qere, Septuagint, Syriac, and Vulgate; Kethib and Theodotion read *To seal up*. **9:25** [a]Or *open square* [b]Or *moat*

THE MESSAGE

now we're an embarrassment to everyone around us. We're a blot on the neighborhood. So listen, God, to this determined prayer of your servant. Have mercy on your ruined Sanctuary. Act out of who you are, not out of what we are.

18 " 'Turn your ears our way, God, and listen. Open your eyes and take a long look at our ruined city, this city named after you. We know that we don't deserve a hearing from you. Our appeal is to your compassion. This prayer is our last and only hope:

19 " 'Master, listen to us!
Master, forgive us!
Master, look at us and do something!
Master, don't put us off!
Your city and your people are named
after you:
You have a stake in us!'

SEVENTY SEVENS

20-21 "While I was pouring out my heart, baring my sins and the sins of my people Israel, praying my life out before my GOD, interceding for the holy mountain of my God—while I was absorbed in this praying, the humanlike Gabriel, the one I had seen in an earlier vision, approached me, flying in like a bird about the time of evening worship.

22-23 "He stood before me and said, 'Daniel, I have come to make things plain to you. You had no sooner started your prayer when the answer was given. And now I'm here to deliver the answer to you. You are much loved! So listen carefully to the answer, the plain meaning of what is revealed:

24 " 'Seventy sevens are set for your people and for your holy city to throttle rebellion, stop sin, wipe out crime, set things right forever, confirm what the prophet saw, and anoint The Holy of Holies.

25-26 " 'Here is what you must understand: From the time the word goes out to rebuild Jerusalem until the coming of the Anointed Leader, there will be seven sevens. The rebuilding will take sixty-two sevens, including building streets and digging a moat. Those will be rough times. After the sixty-two sevens, the Anointed Leader will be killed—the end of him. The city and Sanctuary will be laid in ruins by the army of the newly arriving leader. The end will come in a rush, like a flood. War will rage right up to the end, desolation the order of the day.

27 " 'Then for one seven, he will forge many and strong alliances, but halfway through the seven he will banish worship and prayers. At the place of worship, a desecrating obscenity will be set up and remain until finally the desecrator himself is decisively destroyed.' "

New King James Version

Vision of the Glorious Man

10 In the third year of Cyrus king of Persia a message was revealed to Daniel, whose name was called Belteshazzar. The message *was* true, but the appointed time *was* long;[a] and he understood the message, and had understanding of the vision. [2]In those days I, Daniel, was mourning three full weeks. [3]I ate no pleasant food, no meat or wine came into my mouth, nor did I anoint myself at all, till three whole weeks were fulfilled.

[4]Now on the twenty-fourth day of the first month, as I was by the side of the great river, that *is,* the Tigris,[a] [5]I lifted my eyes and looked, and behold, a certain man clothed in linen, whose waist *was* girded with gold of Uphaz! [6]His body *was* like beryl, his face like the appearance of lightning, his eyes like torches of fire, his arms and feet like burnished bronze in color, and the sound of his words like the voice of a multitude.

[7]And I, Daniel, alone saw the vision, for the men who were with me did not see the vision; but a great terror fell upon them, so that they fled to hide themselves. [8]Therefore I was left alone when I saw this great vision, and no strength remained in me; for my vigor was turned to frailty in me, and I retained no strength. [9]Yet I heard the sound of his words; and while I heard the sound of his words I was in a deep sleep on my face, with my face to the ground.

Prophecies Concerning Persia and Greece

[10]Suddenly, a hand touched me, which made me tremble on my knees and *on* the palms of my hands. [11]And he said to me, "O Daniel, man greatly beloved, understand the words that I speak to you, and stand upright, for I have now been sent to you." While he was speaking this word to me, I stood trembling.

[12]Then he said to me, "Do not fear, Daniel, for from the first day that you set your heart to understand, and to humble yourself before your God, your words were heard; and I have come because of your words. [13]But the prince of the kingdom of Persia withstood me twenty-one days; and behold, Michael, one of the chief princes, came to help me, for I had been left alone there with the kings of Persia. [14]Now I have come to make you understand what will happen to your people in the latter days, for the vision *refers* to *many* days yet *to come.*"

[15]When he had spoken such words to me, I turned my face toward the ground and became speechless. [16]And suddenly, *one* having the likeness of the sons[a] of men touched my lips; then I opened my mouth and spoke, saying to him who stood before me, "My lord, because of the vision my sorrows have overwhelmed me, and I have retained no strength. [17]For how can this servant of my lord talk with you, my lord? As for me, no strength remains in me now, nor is any breath left in me."

10:1 [a]Or *and of great conflict* **10:4** [a]Hebrew *Hiddekel* **10:16** [a]Theodotion and Vulgate read *the son;* Septuagint reads *a hand.*

The Message

A Vision of a Big War

1 10 In the third year of the reign of King Cyrus of Persia, a message was made plain to Daniel, whose Babylonian name was Belteshazzar. The message was true. It dealt with a big war. He understood the message, the understanding coming by revelation:

2-3 "During those days, I, Daniel, went into mourning over Jerusalem for three weeks. I ate only plain and simple food, no seasoning or meat or wine. I neither bathed nor shaved until the three weeks were up.

4-6 "On the twenty-fourth day of the first month I was standing on the bank of the great river, the Tigris. I looked up and to my surprise saw a man dressed in linen with a belt of pure gold around his waist. His body was hard and glistening, as if sculpted from a precious stone, his face radiant, his eyes bright and penetrating like torches, his arms and feet glistening like polished bronze, and his voice, deep and resonant, sounded like a huge choir of voices.

7-8 "I, Daniel, was the only one to see this. The men who were with me, although they didn't see it, were overcome with fear and ran off and hid, fearing the worst. Left alone after the appearance, abandoned by my friends, I went weak in the knees, the blood drained from my face.

9-10 "I heard his voice. At the sound of it I fainted, fell flat on the ground, face in the dirt. A hand touched me and pulled me to my hands and knees.

11 " 'Daniel,' he said, 'man of quality, listen carefully to my message. And get up on your feet. Stand at attention. I've been sent to bring you news.'

"When he had said this, I stood up, but I was still shaking.

12-14 " 'Relax, Daniel,' he continued, 'don't be afraid. From the moment you decided to humble yourself to receive understanding, your prayer was heard, and I set out to come to you. But I was waylaid by the angel-prince of the kingdom of Persia and was delayed for a good three weeks. But then Michael, one of the chief angel-princes, intervened to help me. I left him there with the prince of the kingdom of Persia. And now I'm here to help you understand what will eventually happen to your people. The vision has to do with what's ahead.'

15-17 "While he was saying all this, I looked at the ground and said nothing. Then I was surprised by something like a human hand that touched my lips. I opened my mouth and started talking to the messenger: 'When I saw you, master, I was terror-stricken. My knees turned to water. I couldn't move. How can I, a lowly servant, speak to you, my master? I'm paralyzed. I can hardly breathe!'

NEW KING JAMES VERSION

[18]Then again, *the one* having the likeness of a man touched me and strengthened me. [19]And he said, "O man greatly beloved, fear not! Peace *be* to you; be strong, yes, be strong!"

So when he spoke to me I was strengthened, and said, "Let my lord speak, for you have strengthened me."

[20]Then he said, "Do you know why I have come to you? And now I must return to fight with the prince of Persia; and when I have gone forth, indeed the prince of Greece will come. [21]But I will tell you what is noted in the Scripture of Truth. (No one upholds me against these, except Michael your prince.

11 "Also in the first year of Darius the Mede, I, *even* I, stood up to confirm and strengthen him.) [2]And now I will tell you the truth: Behold, three more kings will arise in Persia, and the fourth shall be far richer than *them* all; by his strength, through his riches, he shall stir up all against the realm of Greece. [3]Then a mighty king shall arise, who shall rule with great dominion, and do according to his will. [4]And when he has arisen, his kingdom shall be broken up and divided toward the four winds of heaven, but not among his posterity nor according to his dominion with which he ruled; for his kingdom shall be uprooted, even for others besides these.

WARRING KINGS OF NORTH AND SOUTH

[5]"Also the king of the South shall become strong, as well as *one* of his princes; and he shall gain power over him and have dominion. His dominion *shall be* a great dominion. [6]And at the end of *some* years they shall join forces, for the daughter of the king of the South shall go to the king of the North to make an agreement; but she shall not retain the power of her authority,[a] and neither he nor his authority[b] shall stand; but she shall be given up, with those who brought her, and with him who begot her, and with him who strengthened her in *those* times. [7]But from a branch of her roots *one* shall arise in his place, who shall come with an army, enter the fortress of the king of the North, and deal with them and prevail. [8]And he shall also carry their gods captive to Egypt, with their princes[a] *and* their precious articles of silver and gold; and he shall continue *more* years than the king of the North.

[9]"Also *the king of the North* shall come to the kingdom of the king of the South, but shall return to his own land. [10]However his sons shall stir up strife, and assemble a multitude of great forces; and *one* shall certainly come and overwhelm and pass through; then he shall return to his fortress and stir up strife.

[11]"And the king of the South shall be moved with rage, and go out and fight with him, with the king of the North, who shall muster a great multitude; but the multitude shall be given into the hand of his *enemy*. [12]When he has taken away the multitude, his heart will be lifted up;

11:6 [a]Literally *arm* [b]Literally *arm* **11:8** [a]Or *molded images*

THE MESSAGE

18-19 "Then this humanlike figure touched me again and gave me strength. He said, 'Don't be afraid, friend. Peace. Everything is going to be all right. Take courage. Be strong.'

"Even as he spoke, courage surged up within me. I said, 'Go ahead, let my master speak. You've given me courage.'

20-21 "He said, 'Do you know why I've come here to you? I now have to go back to fight against the angel-prince of Persia, and when I get him out of the way, the angel-prince of Greece will arrive. But first let me tell you what's written in The True Book. No one helps me in my fight against these beings except Michael, your angel-prince.' "

1 11 " 'And I, in my turn, have been helping him out as best I can ever since the first year in the reign of Darius the Mede.'

THE KINGS OF THE SOUTH AND THE NORTH

2 " 'But now let me tell you the truth of how things stand: Three more kings of Persia will show up, and then a fourth will become richer than all of them. When he senses that he is powerful enough as a result of his wealth, he will go to war against the entire kingdom of Greece.

3-4 " 'Then a powerful king will show up and take over a huge territory and run things just as he pleases. But at the height of his power, with everything seemingly under control, his kingdom will split into four parts, like the four points of the compass. But his heirs won't get in on it. There will be no continuity with his kingship. Others will tear it to pieces and grab whatever they can get for themselves.

5-6 " 'Next the king of the south will grow strong, but one of his princes will grow stronger than he and rule an even larger territory. After a few years, the two of them will make a pact, and the daughter of the king of the south will marry the king of the north to cement the peace agreement. But her influence will weaken and her child will not survive. She and her servants, her child, and her husband will be betrayed.

6-9 " 'Sometime later a member of the royal family will show up and take over. He will take command of his army and invade the defenses of the king of the north and win a resounding victory. He will load up their tin gods and all the gold and silver trinkets that go with them and cart them off to Egypt. Eventually, the king of the north will recover and invade the country of the king of the south, but unsuccessfully. He will have to retreat.

10 " 'But then his sons will raise a huge army and rush down like a flood, a torrential attack, on the defenses of the south.

11-13 " 'Furious, the king of the south will come out and engage the king of the north and his huge army in battle and rout them. As the corpses are cleared from the field, the king, inflamed with bloodlust, will go on a bloodletting rampage, massacring tens of thou-

New King James Version

and he will cast down tens of thousands, but he will not prevail. 13For the king of the North will return and muster a multitude greater than the former, and shall certainly come at the end of some years with a great army and much equipment.

14"Now in those times many shall rise up against the king of the South. Also, violent men[a] of your people shall exalt themselves in fulfillment of the vision, but they shall fall. 15So the king of the North shall come and build a siege mound, and take a fortified city; and the forces[a] of the South shall not withstand *him.* Even his choice troops *shall have* no strength to resist. 16But he who comes against him shall do according to his own will, and no one shall stand against him. He shall stand in the Glorious Land with destruction in his power.[a]

17"He shall also set his face to enter with the strength of his whole kingdom, and upright ones[a] with him; thus shall he do. And he shall give him the daughter of women to destroy it; but she shall not stand *with him,* or be for him. 18After this he shall turn his face to the coastlands, and shall take many. But a ruler shall bring the reproach against them to an end; and with the reproach removed, he shall turn back on him. 19Then he shall turn his face toward the fortress of his own land; but he shall stumble and fall, and not be found.

20"There shall arise in his place one who imposes taxes *on* the glorious kingdom; but within a few days he shall be destroyed, but not in anger or in battle. 21And in his place shall arise a vile person, to whom they will not give the honor of royalty; but he shall come in peaceably, and seize the kingdom by intrigue. 22With the force[a] of a flood they shall be swept away from before him and be broken, and also the prince of the covenant. 23And after the league *is made* with him he shall act deceitfully, for he shall come up and become strong with a small *number of* people. 24He shall enter peaceably, even into the richest places of the province; and he shall do *what* his fathers have not done, nor his forefathers: he shall disperse among them the plunder, spoil, and riches; and he shall devise his plans against the strongholds, but *only* for a time.

25"He shall stir up his power and his courage against the king of the South with a great army. And the king of the South shall be stirred up to battle with a very great and mighty army; but he shall not stand, for they shall devise plans against him. 26Yes, those who eat of the portion of his delicacies shall destroy him; his army shall be swept away, and many shall fall down slain. 27Both these kings' hearts *shall be* bent on evil, and they shall speak lies at the same table; but it shall not prosper, for the end *will* still *be* at the appointed time.

11:14 [a]Or *robbers,* literally *sons of breakage* **11:15** [a]Literally *arms* **11:22** [a]Literally *arms* **11:16** [a]Literally *hand* **11:17** [a]Or *bring equitable terms*

The Message

sands. But his victory won't last long, for the king of the north will put together another army bigger than the last one, and after a few years he'll come back to do battle again with his immense army and endless supplies.

14 " 'In those times, many others will get into the act and go off to fight against the king of the south. Hotheads from your own people, drunk on dreams, will join them. But they'll sputter out.

15-17 " 'When the king of the north arrives, he'll build siege works and capture the outpost fortress city. The armies of the south will fall to pieces before him. Not even their famous commando shock troops will slow down the attacker. He'll march in big as you please, as if he owned the place. He'll take over that beautiful country, Palestine, and make himself at home in it. Then he'll proceed to get everything, lock, stock, and barrel, in his control. He'll cook up a peace treaty and even give his daughter in marriage to the king of the south in a plot to destroy him totally. But the plot will fizzle. It won't succeed.

18-19 " 'Later, he'll turn his attention to the coastal regions and capture a bunch of prisoners, but a general will step in and put a stop to his bullying ways. The bully will be bullied! He'll go back home and tend to his own military affairs. But by then he'll be washed up and soon will be heard of no more.

20 " 'He will be replaced shortly by a real loser, his rule, reputation, and authority already in shreds. And he won't last long. He'll slip out of history quietly, without even a fight.

21-24 " 'His place will be taken by a reject, a man spurned and passed over for advancement. He'll surprise everyone, seemingly coming out of nowhere, and will seize the kingdom. He'll come in like a steamroller, flattening the opposition. Even the Prince of the Covenant will be crushed. After negotiating a cease-fire, he'll betray its terms. With a few henchmen, he'll take total control. Arbitrarily and impulsively, he'll invade the richest provinces. He'll surpass all his ancestors, near and distant, in his rape of the country, grabbing and looting, living with his cronies in corrupt and lavish luxury.

24-26 " 'He will make plans against the fortress cities, but they'll turn out to be shortsighted. He'll get a great army together, all charged up to fight the king of the south. The king of the south in response will get his army—an even greater army—in place, ready to fight. But he won't be able to sustain that intensity for long because of the treacherous intrigue in his own ranks, his court having been honeycombed with vicious plots. His army will be smashed, the battlefield filled with corpses.

27 " 'The two kings, each with evil designs on the other, will sit at the conference table and trade lies. Nothing will come of the treaty, which is nothing but a tissue of lies anyway. But that's not the end of it. There's more to this story.

NEW KING JAMES VERSION

28While returning to his land with great riches, his heart shall be *moved* against the holy covenant; so he shall do *damage* and return to his own land.

THE NORTHERN KING'S BLASPHEMIES

29"At the appointed time he shall return and go toward the south; but it shall not be like the former or the latter. 30For ships from Cyprus[a] shall come against him; therefore he shall be grieved, and return in rage against the holy covenant, and do *damage.*

"So he shall return and show regard for those who forsake the holy covenant. 31And forces[a] shall be mustered by him, and they shall defile the sanctuary fortress; then they shall take away the daily *sacrifices,* and place *there* the abomination of desolation. 32Those who do wickedly against the covenant he shall corrupt with flattery; but the people who know their God shall be strong, and carry out *great exploits.* 33And those of the people who understand shall instruct many; yet *for many* days they shall fall by sword and flame, by captivity and plundering. 34Now when they fall, they shall be aided with a little help; but many shall join with them by intrigue. 35And *some* of those of understanding shall fall, to refine them, purify *them,* and make *them* white, *until* the time of the end; because *it is* still for the appointed time.

36"Then the king shall do according to his own will: he shall exalt and magnify himself above every god, shall speak blasphemies against the God of gods, and shall prosper till the wrath has been accomplished; for what has been determined shall be done. 37He shall regard neither the God[a] of his fathers nor the desire of women, nor regard any god; for he shall exalt himself above *them* all. 38But in their place he shall honor a god of fortresses; and a god which his fathers did not know he shall honor with gold and silver, with precious stones and pleasant things. 39Thus he shall act against the strongest fortresses with a foreign god, which he shall acknowledge, *and* advance *its* glory; and he shall cause them to rule over many, and divide the land for gain.

THE NORTHERN KING'S CONQUESTS

40"At the time of the end the king of the South shall attack him; and the king of the North shall come against him like a whirlwind, with chariots, horsemen, and with many ships; and he shall enter the countries, overwhelm *them,* and pass through. 41He shall also enter the Glorious Land, and many *countries* shall be overthrown; but these shall escape from his hand: Edom, Moab, and the prominent people of Ammon. 42He shall stretch out his hand against the countries, and the land of Egypt shall not escape. 43He shall have power over the treasures of gold and silver, and over all the precious things of Egypt; also the Libyans and Ethiopians *shall follow* at his heels. 44But news from the

11:30 [a]Hebrew *Kittim,* western lands, especially Cyprus
11:31 [a]Literally *arms* **11:37** [a]Or *gods*

THE MESSAGE

28 " 'The king of the north will go home loaded down with plunder, but his mind will be set on destroying the holy covenant as he passes through the country on his way home.

29-32 " 'One year later he will mount a fresh invasion of the south. But the second invasion won't compare to the first. When the Roman ships arrive, he will turn tail and go back home. But as he passes through the country, he will be filled with anger at the holy covenant. He will take up with all those who betray the holy covenant, favoring them. The bodyguards surrounding him will march in and desecrate the Sanctuary and citadel. They'll throw out the daily worship and set up in its place the obscene sacrilege. The king of the north will play up to those who betray the holy covenant, corrupting them even further with his seductive talk, but those who stay courageously loyal to their God will take a strong stand.

33-35 " 'Those who keep their heads on straight will teach the crowds right from wrong by their example. They'll be put to severe testing for a season: some killed, some burned, some exiled, some robbed. When the testing is intense, they'll get some help, but not much. Many of the helpers will be halfhearted at best. The testing will refine, cleanse, and purify those who keep their heads on straight and stay true, for there is still more to come.

36-39 " 'Meanwhile, the king of the north will do whatever he pleases. He'll puff himself up and posture himself as greater than any god. He will even dare to brag and boast in defiance of the God of gods. And he'll get by with it for a while—until this time of wrathful judgment is completed, for what is decreed must be done. He will have no respect for the gods of his ancestors, not even that popular favorite among women, Adonis. Contemptuous of every god and goddess, the king of the north will puff himself up greater than all of them. He'll even stoop to despising the God of the holy ones, and in the place where God is worshiped he will put on exhibit, with a lavish show of silver and gold and jewels, a new god that no one has ever heard of. Marching under the banner of a strange god, he will attack the key fortresses. He will promote everyone who falls into line behind this god, putting them in positions of power and paying them off with grants of land.

40-45 " 'In the final wrap-up of this story, the king of the south will confront him. But the king of the north will come at him like a tornado. Unleashing chariots and horses and an armada of ships, he'll blow away anything in his path. As he enters the beautiful land, people will fall before him like dominoes. Only Edom, Moab, and a few Ammonites will escape. As he reaches out, grabbing country after country, not even Egypt will be exempt. He will confiscate the treasuries of Egyptian gold and silver and other valuables. The Libyans and Ethiopians will fall in with him. Then disturbing reports will come in from

NEW KING JAMES VERSION

east and the north shall trouble him; therefore he shall go out with great fury to destroy and annihilate many. 45And he shall plant the tents of his palace between the seas and the glorious holy mountain; yet he shall come to his end, and no one will help him.

PROPHECY OF THE END TIME

12 "At that time Michael shall stand up,
The great prince who stands *watch* over
the sons of your people;
And there shall be a time of trouble,
Such as never was since there was a nation,
Even to that time.
And at that time your people shall be
delivered,
Every one who is found written in the book.
2And many of those who sleep in the dust of
the earth shall awake,
Some to everlasting life,
Some to shame *and* everlasting contempt.
3Those who are wise shall shine
Like the brightness of the firmament,
And those who turn many to righteousness
Like the stars forever and ever.

4"But you, Daniel, shut up the words, and seal the book until the time of the end; many shall run to and fro, and knowledge shall increase."

5Then I, Daniel, looked; and there stood two others, one on this riverbank and the other on that riverbank. 6And *one* said to the man clothed in linen, who *was* above the waters of the river, "How long shall the fulfillment of these wonders *be*?"

7Then I heard the man clothed in linen, who *was* above the waters of the river, when he held up his right hand and his left hand to heaven, and swore by Him who lives forever, that *it shall be* for a time, times, and half *a time;* and when the power of the holy people has been completely shattered, all these *things* shall be finished.

8Although I heard, I did not understand. Then I said, "My lord, what *shall be* the end of these *things*?"

9And he said, "Go *your way,* Daniel, for the words *are* closed up and sealed till the time of the end. 10Many shall be purified, made white, and refined, but the wicked shall do wickedly; and none of the wicked shall understand, but the wise shall understand.

11"And from the time *that* the daily *sacrifice* is taken away, and the abomination of desolation is set up, *there shall be* one thousand two hundred and ninety days. 12Blessed *is* he who waits, and comes to the one thousand three hundred and thirty-five days.

13"But you, go *your way* till the end; for you shall rest, and will arise to your inheritance at the end of the days."

THE MESSAGE

the north and east that will throw him into a panic. Towering in rage, he'll rush to stamp out the threat. But he'll no sooner have pitched camp between the Mediterranean Sea and the Holy Mountain—all those royal tents!—than he'll meet his end. And not a soul around who can help!' "

THE WORST TROUBLE THE WORLD HAS EVER SEEN

1-2 12 " 'That's when Michael, the great angel-prince, champion of your people, will step in. It will be a time of trouble, the worst trouble the world has ever seen. But your people will be saved from the trouble, every last one found written in the Book. Many who have been long dead and buried will wake up, some to eternal life, others to eternal shame.

3 " 'Men and women who have lived wisely and well will shine brilliantly, like the cloudless, star-strewn night skies. And those who put others on the right path to life will glow like stars forever.

4 " 'This is a confidential report, Daniel, for your eyes and ears only. Keep it secret. Put the book under lock and key until the end. In the interim there is going to be a lot of frantic running around, trying to figure out what's going on.'

5-6 "As I, Daniel, took all this in, two figures appeared, one standing on this bank of the river and one on the other bank. One of them asked a third man who was dressed in linen and who straddled the river, 'How long is this astonishing story to go on?'

7 "The man dressed in linen, who straddled the river, raised both hands to the skies. I heard him solemnly swear by the Eternal One that it would be a time, two times, and half a time, that when the oppressor of the holy people was brought down the story would be complete.

8 "I heard all this plainly enough, but I didn't understand it. So I asked, 'Master, can you explain this to me?'

9-10 " 'Go on about your business, Daniel,' he said. 'The message is confidential and under lock and key until the end, until things are about to be wrapped up. The populace will be washed clean and made like new. But the wicked will just keep on being wicked, without a clue about what is happening. Those who live wisely and well will understand what's going on.'

11 "From the time that the daily worship is banished from the Temple and the obscene desecration is set up in its place, there will be 1,290 days.

12 "Blessed are those who patiently make it through the 1,335 days.

13 "And you? Go about your business without fretting or worrying. Relax. When it's all over, you will be on your feet to receive your reward."

HOSEA

New King James Version

1 The word of the LORD that came to Hosea the son of Beeri, in the days of Uzziah, Jotham, Ahaz, *and* Hezekiah, kings of Judah, and in the days of Jeroboam the son of Joash, king of Israel.

The Family of Hosea

2When the LORD began to speak by Hosea, the LORD said to Hosea:

"Go, take yourself a wife of harlotry
And children of harlotry,
For the land has committed great harlotry
By departing from the LORD."

3So he went and took Gomer the daughter of Diblaim, and she conceived and bore him a son.
4Then the LORD said to him:

"Call his name Jezreel,
For in a little *while*
I will avenge the bloodshed of Jezreel on the house of Jehu,
And bring an end to the kingdom of the house of Israel.
5It shall come to pass in that day
That I will break the bow of Israel in the Valley of Jezreel."

6And she conceived again and bore a daughter. Then *God* said to him:

"Call her name Lo-Ruhamah,[a]
For I will no longer have mercy on the house of Israel,
But I will utterly take them away.[b]
7Yet I will have mercy on the house of Judah,
Will save them by the LORD their God,
And will not save them by bow,
Nor by sword or battle,
By horses or horsemen."

8Now when she had weaned Lo-Ruhamah, she conceived and bore a son. 9Then *God* said:

"Call his name Lo-Ammi,[a]
For you *are* not My people,
And I will not be your *God*.

The Restoration of Israel

10"Yet the number of the children of Israel
Shall be as the sand of the sea,
Which cannot be measured or numbered.
And it shall come to pass
In the place where it was said to them,
'You *are* not My people,'[a]
There it shall be said to them,
'*You are* sons of the living God.'
11Then the children of Judah and the children of Israel
Shall be gathered together,
And appoint for themselves one head;

1:6 [a]Literally *No-Mercy* [b]Or *That I may forgive them at all* **1:9** [a]Literally *Not-My-People* **1:10** [a]Hebrew *lo-ammi* (compare verse 9)

The Message

1 1 This is God's Message to Hosea son of Beeri. It came to him during the royal reigns of Judah's kings Uzziah, Jotham, Ahaz, and Hezekiah. This was also the time that Jeroboam son of Joash was king over Israel.

This Whole Country Has Become a Whorehouse

2 The first time GOD spoke to Hosea he said:

"Find a whore and marry her.
Make this whore the mother of your children.
And here's why: This whole country
has become a whorehouse, unfaithful to me, GOD."

3 Hosea did it. He picked Gomer daughter of Diblaim. She got pregnant and gave him a son.
4-5 Then GOD told him:

"Name him Jezreel. It won't be long now before
I'll make the people of Israel pay for the massacre at Jezreel.
I'm calling it quits on the kingdom of Israel.
Payday is coming! I'm going to chop Israel's bows and arrows
into kindling in the valley of Jezreel."

6-7 Gomer got pregnant again. This time she had a daughter. GOD told Hosea:

"Name this one No-Mercy. I'm fed up with Israel.
I've run out of mercy. There's no more forgiveness.
Judah's another story. I'll continue having mercy on them.
I'll save them. It will be their GOD who saves them,
Not their armaments and armies,
not their horsepower and manpower."

8-9 After Gomer had weaned No-Mercy, she got pregnant yet again and had a son. GOD said:

"Name him Nobody. You've become nobodies to me,
and I, GOD, am a nobody to you.

10-11 "But down the road the population of Israel is going to explode past counting, like sand on the ocean beaches. In the very place where they were once named Nobody, they will be named God's Somebody. Everybody in Judah and everybody in Israel will be assembled as one people. They'll choose a

NEW KING JAMES VERSION

And they shall come out of the land,
For great *will be* the day of Jezreel!

2 Say to your brethren, 'My people,'[a]
And to your sisters, 'Mercy[b] *is shown.*'

GOD'S UNFAITHFUL PEOPLE

2"Bring charges against your mother, bring charges;
For she *is* not My wife, nor *am* I her Husband!
Let her put away her harlotries from her sight,
And her adulteries from between her breasts;
3Lest I strip her naked
And expose her, as in the day she was born,
And make her like a wilderness,
And set her like a dry land,
And slay her with thirst.

4"I will not have mercy on her children,
For they *are* the children of harlotry.
5For their mother has played the harlot;
She who conceived them has behaved shamefully.
For she said, 'I will go after my lovers,
Who give *me* my bread and my water,
My wool and my linen,
My oil and my drink.'

6"Therefore, behold,
I will hedge up your way with thorns,
And wall her in,
So that she cannot find her paths.
7She will chase her lovers,
But not overtake them;
Yes, she will seek them, but not find *them.*
Then she will say,
'I will go and return to my first husband,
For then *it was* better for me than now.'
8For she did not know
That I gave her grain, new wine, and oil,
And multiplied her silver and gold—
Which they prepared for Baal.

9"Therefore I will return and take away
My grain in its time
And My new wine in its season,
And will take back My wool and My linen,
Given to cover her nakedness.
10Now I will uncover her lewdness in the sight of her lovers,
And no one shall deliver her from My hand.
11I will also cause all her mirth to cease,
Her feast days,
Her New Moons,
Her Sabbaths—
All her appointed feasts.

12"And I will destroy her vines and her fig trees,
Of which she has said,
'These *are* my wages that my lovers have given me.'
So I will make them a forest,

2:1 [a]Hebrew *Ammi* (compare 1:9, 10) [b]Hebrew *Ruhamah* (compare 1:6)

THE MESSAGE

single leader. There'll be no stopping them—
a great day in Jezreel!"

1 2 "Rename your brothers 'God's Somebody.'
Rename your sisters 'All Mercy.'

WILD WEEKENDS AND UNHOLY HOLIDAYS

2-13 "Haul your mother into court. Accuse her!
She's no longer my wife.
I'm no longer her husband.
Tell her to quit dressing like a whore,
displaying her breasts for sale.
If she refuses, I'll rip off her clothes
and expose her, naked as a newborn.
I'll turn her skin into dried-out leather,
her body into a badlands landscape,
a rack of bones in the desert.
I'll have nothing to do with her children,
born one and all in a whorehouse.
Face it: Your mother's been a whore,
bringing bastard children into the world.
She said, 'I'm off to see my lovers!
They'll wine and dine me,
Dress and caress me,
perfume and adorn me!'
But I'll fix her: I'll dump her in a field of thistles,
then lose her in a dead-end alley.
She'll go on the hunt for her lovers
but not bring down a single one.
She'll look high and low
but won't find a one. Then she'll say,
'I'm going back to my husband, the one I started out with.
That was a better life by far than this one.'
She didn't know that it was I all along
who wined and dined and adorned her,
That I was the one who dressed her up
in the big-city fashions and jewelry
that she wasted on wild Baal-orgies.
I'm about to bring her up short: No more wining and dining!
Silk lingerie and gowns are a thing of the past.
I'll expose her genitals to the public.
All her fly-by-night lovers will be helpless to help her.
Party time is over. I'm calling a halt to the whole business,
her wild weekends and unholy holidays.
I'll wreck her sumptuous gardens and ornamental fountains,
of which she bragged, 'Whoring paid for all this!'
They will soon be dumping grounds for garbage,
feeding grounds for stray dogs and cats.

NEW KING JAMES VERSION

And the beasts of the field shall eat them.
13I will punish her
For the days of the Baals to which she burned incense.
She decked herself with her earrings and jewelry,
And went after her lovers;
But Me she forgot," says the LORD.

GOD'S MERCY ON HIS PEOPLE

14"Therefore, behold, I will allure her,
Will bring her into the wilderness,
And speak comfort to her.
15I will give her her vineyards from there,
And the Valley of Achor as a door of hope;
She shall sing there,
As in the days of her youth,
As in the day when she came up from the land of Egypt.

16"And it shall be, in that day,"
Says the LORD,
"*That* you will call Me 'My Husband,'[a]
And no longer call Me 'My Master,'[b]
17For I will take from her mouth the names of the Baals,
And they shall be remembered by their name no more.
18In that day I will make a covenant for them
With the beasts of the field,
With the birds of the air,
And *with* the creeping things of the ground.
Bow and sword of battle I will shatter from the earth,
To make them lie down safely.

19"I will betroth you to Me forever;
Yes, I will betroth you to Me
In righteousness and justice,
In lovingkindness and mercy;
20I will betroth you to Me in faithfulness,
And you shall know the LORD.

21"It shall come to pass in that day
That I will answer," says the LORD;
"I will answer the heavens,
And they shall answer the earth.
22The earth shall answer
With grain,
With new wine,
And with oil;
They shall answer Jezreel.[a]
23Then I will sow her for Myself in the earth,
And I will have mercy on *her who had* not obtained mercy;[a]
Then I will say to *those who were* not My people,[b]
'You *are* My people!'
And they shall say, '*You are* my God!' "

ISRAEL WILL RETURN TO GOD

3 Then the LORD said to me, "Go again, love a woman *who is* loved by a lover[a] and is committing adultery, just like the love of the LORD for the children of Israel, who look to other gods and love *the* raisin cakes *of the pagans*."

2:16 [a]Hebrew *Ishi* [b]Hebrew *Baali* **2:22** [a]Literally *God Will Sow* **2:23** [a]Hebrew *lo-ruhamah* [b]Hebrew *lo-ammi* **3:1** [a]Literally *friend* or *husband*

THE MESSAGE

I'll make her pay for her indulgence in promiscuous religion—
all that sensuous Baal worship
And all the promiscuous sex that went with it,
stalking her lovers, dressed to kill,
And not a thought for me."
GOD's Message!

TO START ALL OVER AGAIN

14-15 "And now, here's what I'm going to do:
I'm going to start all over again.
I'm taking her back out into the wilderness
where we had our first date, and I'll court her.
I'll give her bouquets of roses.
I'll turn Heartbreak Valley into Acres of Hope.
She'll respond like she did as a young girl,
those days when she was fresh out of Egypt.

16-20 "At that time"—this is GOD's Message still—
"you'll address me, 'Dear husband!'
Never again will you address me,
'My slave-master!'
I'll wash your mouth out with soap,
get rid of all the dirty false-god names,
not so much as a whisper of those names again.
At the same time I'll make a peace treaty between you
and wild animals and birds and reptiles,
And get rid of all weapons of war.
Think of it! Safe from beasts and bullies!
And then I'll marry you for good—forever!
I'll marry you true and proper, in love and tenderness.
Yes, I'll marry you and neither leave you nor let you go.
You'll know me, GOD, for who I really am.

21-23 "On the very same day, I'll answer"—this is GOD's Message—
"I'll answer the sky, sky will answer earth,
Earth will answer grain and wine and olive oil,
and they'll all answer Jezreel.
I'll plant her in the good earth.
I'll have mercy on No-Mercy.
I'll say to Nobody, 'You're my dear Somebody,'
and he'll say 'You're my God!' "

IN TIME THEY'LL COME BACK

1 3 Then GOD ordered me, "Start all over: Love your wife again, your wife who's in bed with her latest boyfriend, your cheating wife.
Love her the way I, GOD, love the Israelite people,
even as they flirt and party with every god that takes their fancy."

NEW KING JAMES VERSION

2 So I bought her for myself for fifteen *shekels*
of silver, and one and one-half homers of barley.
3 And I said to her, "You shall stay with me many
days; you shall not play the harlot, nor shall you
have a man—so, too, *will* I *be* toward you."
4 For the children of Israel shall abide many
days without king or prince, without sacrifice or
sacred pillar, without ephod or teraphim. 5 After-
ward the children of Israel shall return and seek
the LORD their God and David their king. They
shall fear the LORD and His goodness in the lat-
ter days.

GOD'S CHARGE AGAINST ISRAEL

4 Hear the word of the LORD,
You children of Israel,
For the LORD *brings* a charge against the
inhabitants of the land:

"There is no truth or mercy
Or knowledge of God in the land.
2 *By* swearing and lying,
Killing and stealing and committing
adultery,
They break all restraint,
With bloodshed upon bloodshed.
3 Therefore the land will mourn;
And everyone who dwells there will waste
away
With the beasts of the field
And the birds of the air;
Even the fish of the sea will be taken away.

4 "Now let no man contend, or rebuke another;
For your people *are* like those who contend
with the priest.
5 Therefore you shall stumble in the day;
The prophet also shall stumble with you in
the night;
And I will destroy your mother.
6 My people are destroyed for lack of
knowledge.
Because you have rejected knowledge,
I also will reject you from being priest for
Me;
Because you have forgotten the law of your
God,
I also will forget your children.

7 "The more they increased,
The more they sinned against Me;
I will change[a] their glory[b] into shame.
8 They eat up the sin of My people;
They set their heart on their iniquity.

4:7 [a]Following Masoretic Text, Septuagint, and Vulgate; scribal tradition, Syriac, and Targum read *They will change*. [b]Following Masoretic Text, Septuagint, Syriac, Targum, and Vulgate; scribal tradition reads *My glory*.

THE MESSAGE

2-3 I did it. I paid good money to get her back.
It cost me the price of a slave.
Then I told her, "From now on you're living
with me.
No more whoring, no more sleeping
around.
You're living with me and I'm living with
you."

4-5 The people of Israel are going to live a long
time
stripped of security and protection,
without religion and comfort,
godless and prayerless.
But in time they'll come back, these
Israelites,
come back looking for their GOD and
their David-King.
They'll come back chastened to reverence
before GOD and his good gifts, ready for
the End of the story of his love.

NO ONE IS FAITHFUL

1-3 4 Attention all Israelites! GOD'S Message!
GOD indicts the whole population:
"No one is faithful. No one loves.
No one knows the first thing about God.
All this cussing and lying and killing, theft
and loose sex,
sheer anarchy, one murder after another!
And because of all this, the very land itself
weeps
and everything in it is grief-stricken—
animals in the fields and birds on the wing,
even the fish in the sea are listless,
lifeless.

4-10 "But don't look for someone to blame.
No finger pointing!
You, priest, are the one in the dock.
You stumble around in broad daylight,
And then the prophets take over and
stumble all night.
Your mother is as bad as you.
My people are ruined
because they don't know what's right or
true.
Because you've turned your back on
knowledge,
I've turned my back on you priests.
Because you refuse to recognize the
revelation of God,
I'm no longer recognizing your children.
The more priests, the more sin.
They traded in their glory for shame.
They pig out on my people's sins.
They can't wait for the latest in evil.

NEW KING JAMES VERSION

[9]And it shall be: like people, like priest.
So I will punish them for their ways,
And reward them for their deeds.
[10]For they shall eat, but not have enough;
They shall commit harlotry, but not
increase;
Because they have ceased obeying the LORD.

THE IDOLATRY OF ISRAEL

[11]"Harlotry, wine, and new wine enslave the
heart.
[12]My people ask counsel from their wooden
idols,
And their staff informs them.
For the spirit of harlotry has caused *them* to
stray,
And they have played the harlot against
their God.
[13]They offer sacrifices on the mountaintops,
And burn incense on the hills,
Under oaks, poplars, and terebinths,
Because their shade *is* good.
Therefore your daughters commit harlotry,
And your brides commit adultery.

[14]"I will not punish your daughters when they
commit harlotry,
Nor your brides when they commit adultery;
For *the men* themselves go apart with
harlots,
And offer sacrifices with a ritual harlot.[a]
Therefore people *who* do not understand
will be trampled.

[15]"Though you, Israel, play the harlot,
Let not Judah offend.
Do not come up to Gilgal,
Nor go up to Beth Aven,
Nor swear an oath, *saying*, 'As the LORD
lives'—

[16]"For Israel is stubborn
Like a stubborn calf;
Now the LORD will let them forage
Like a lamb in open country.

[17]"Ephraim *is* joined to idols,
Let him alone.
[18]Their drink is rebellion,
They commit harlotry continually.
Her rulers dearly[a] love dishonor.
[19]The wind has wrapped her up in its wings,
And they shall be ashamed because of their
sacrifices.

IMPENDING JUDGMENT ON ISRAEL AND JUDAH

5 "Hear this, O priests!
Take heed, O house of Israel!
Give ear, O house of the king!
For yours *is* the judgment,
Because you have been a snare to Mizpah
And a net spread on Tabor.

4:14 [a]Compare Deuteronomy 23:18 4:18 [a]Hebrew is difficult; a Jewish tradition reads *Her rulers shamefully love, 'Give!'*

THE MESSAGE

The result: You can't tell the people from
the priests,
the priests from the people.
I'm on my way to make them both pay
and take the consequences of the bad
lives they've lived.
They'll eat and be as hungry as ever,
have sex and get no satisfaction.
They walked out on me, their GOD,
for a life of rutting with whores.

THEY MAKE A PICNIC OUT OF RELIGION

11-14 "Wine and whiskey
leave my people in a stupor.
They ask questions of a dead tree,
expect answers from a sturdy walking
stick.
Drunk on sex, they can't find their way
home.
They've replaced their God with their
genitals.
They worship on the tops of mountains,
make a picnic out of religion.
Under the oaks and elms on the hills
they stretch out and take it easy.
Before you know it, your daughters are
whores
and the wives of your sons are sleeping
around.
But I'm not going after your whoring
daughters
or the adulterous wives of your sons.
It's the men who pick up the whores that
I'm after,
the men who worship at the holy
whorehouses—
a stupid people, ruined by whores!

15-19 "You've ruined your own life, Israel—
but don't drag Judah down with you!
Don't go to the sex shrine at Gilgal,
don't go to that sin city Bethel,
Don't go around saying 'GOD bless you'
and not mean it,
taking God's name in vain.
Israel is stubborn as a mule.
How can GOD lead him like a lamb to
open pasture?
Ephraim is addicted to idols.
Let him go.
When the beer runs out,
it's sex, sex, and more sex.
Bold and sordid debauchery—
how they love it!
The whirlwind has them in its clutches.
Their sex-worship leaves them finally
impotent."

THEY WOULDN'T RECOGNIZE GOD IF THEY SAW HIM

1-2 5 "Listen to this, priests!
Attention, people of Israel!
Royal family—all ears!
You're in charge of justice around here.
But what have you done? Exploited people
at Mizpah,
ripped them off on Tabor,

NEW KING JAMES VERSION

[2]The revolters are deeply involved in slaughter,
Though I rebuke them all.
[3]I know Ephraim,
And Israel is not hidden from Me;
For now, O Ephraim, you commit harlotry;
Israel is defiled.

[4]"They do not direct their deeds
Toward turning to their God,
For the spirit of harlotry is in their midst,
And they do not know the LORD.
[5]The pride of Israel testifies to his face;
Therefore Israel and Ephraim stumble in their iniquity;
Judah also stumbles with them.

[6]"With their flocks and herds
They shall go to seek the LORD,
But they will not find *Him;*
He has withdrawn Himself from them.
[7]They have dealt treacherously with the LORD,
For they have begotten pagan children.
Now a New Moon shall devour them and their heritage.

[8]"Blow the ram's horn in Gibeah,
The trumpet in Ramah!
Cry aloud *at* Beth Aven,
'*Look* behind you, O Benjamin!'
[9]Ephraim shall be desolate in the day of rebuke;
Among the tribes of Israel I make known what is sure.

[10]"The princes of Judah are like those who remove a landmark;
I will pour out My wrath on them like water.
[11]Ephraim is oppressed *and* broken in judgment,
Because he willingly walked by *human* precept.
[12]Therefore I *will be* to Ephraim like a moth,
And to the house of Judah like rottenness.

[13]"When Ephraim saw his sickness,
And Judah *saw* his wound,
Then Ephraim went to Assyria
And sent to King Jareb;
Yet he cannot cure you,
Nor heal you of your wound.
[14]For I *will be* like a lion to Ephraim,
And like a young lion to the house of Judah.
I, *even* I, will tear *them* and go away;
I will take *them* away, and no one shall rescue.
[15]I will return again to My place
Till they acknowledge their offense.
Then they will seek My face;
In their affliction they will earnestly seek Me."

THE MESSAGE

Victimized them at Shittim.
I'm going to punish the lot of you.

3-4 "I know you, Ephraim, inside and out.
Yes, Israel, I see right through you!
Ephraim, you've played your
sex-and-religion games long enough.
All Israel is thoroughly polluted.
They couldn't turn to God if they wanted to.
Their evil life is a bad habit.
Every breath they take is a whore's breath.
They wouldn't recognize GOD if they saw me.

5-7 "Bloated by arrogance, big as a house,
they're a public disgrace,
The lot of them—Israel, Ephraim, Judah—
lurching and weaving down their guilty streets.
When they decide to get their lives together
and go off looking for GOD once again,
They'll find it's too late.
I, GOD, will be long gone.
They've played fast and loose with me for too long,
filling the country with their bastard offspring.
A plague of locusts will
devastate their violated land.

8-9 "Blow the ram's horn shofar in Gibeah,
the bugle in Ramah!
Signal the invasion of Sin City!
Scare the daylights out of Benjamin!
Ephraim will be left wasted,
a lifeless moonscape.
I'm telling it straight, the unvarnished truth,
to the tribes of Israel.

10 "Israel's rulers are crooks and thieves,
cheating the people of their land,
And I'm angry, good and angry.
Every inch of their bodies is going to feel my anger.

11-12 "Brutal Ephraim is himself brutalized—
a taste of his own medicine!
He was so determined
to do it his own worthless way.
Therefore I'm pus to Ephraim,
dry rot in the house of Judah.

13 "When Ephraim saw he was sick
and Judah saw his pus-filled sores,
Ephraim went running to Assyria,
went for help to the big king.
But he can't heal you.
He can't cure your oozing sores.

14-15 "I'm a grizzly charging Ephraim,
a grizzly with cubs charging Judah.
I'll rip them to pieces—yes, I will!
No one can stop me now.
I'll drag them off.
No one can help them.
Then I'll go back to where I came from
until they come to their senses.
When they finally hit rock bottom,
maybe they'll come looking for me."

NEW KING JAMES VERSION

A CALL TO REPENTANCE

6 Come, and let us return to the LORD;
For He has torn, but He will heal us;
He has stricken, but He will bind us up.
2After two days He will revive us;
On the third day He will raise us up,
That we may live in His sight.
3Let us know,
Let us pursue the knowledge of the LORD.
His going forth is established as the morning;
He will come to us like the rain,
Like the latter *and* former rain to the earth.

IMPENITENCE OF ISRAEL AND JUDAH

4"O Ephraim, what shall I do to you?
O Judah, what shall I do to you?
For your faithfulness is like a morning cloud,
And like the early dew it goes away.
5Therefore I have hewn *them* by the prophets,
I have slain them by the words of My mouth;
And your judgments *are like* light *that* goes forth.
6For I desire mercy and not sacrifice,
And the knowledge of God more than burnt offerings.

7"But like men[a] they transgressed the covenant;
There they dealt treacherously with Me.
8Gilead *is* a city of evildoers
And defiled with blood.
9As bands of robbers lie in wait for a man,
So the company of priests murder on the way to Shechem;
Surely they commit lewdness.
10I have seen a horrible thing in the house of Israel:
There *is* the harlotry of Ephraim;
Israel is defiled.
11Also, O Judah, a harvest is appointed for you,
When I return the captives of My people.

7 "When I would have healed Israel,
Then the iniquity of Ephraim was uncovered,
And the wickedness of Samaria.
For they have committed fraud;
A thief comes in;
A band of robbers takes spoil outside.
2They do not consider in their hearts
That I remember all their wickedness;
Now their own deeds have surrounded them;
They are before My face.

6:7 [a]Or *like Adam*

THE MESSAGE

GANGS OF PRIESTS ASSAULTING WORSHIPERS

1-3 6 "Come on, let's go back to GOD.
He hurt us, but he'll heal us.
He hit us hard,
but he'll put us right again.
In a couple of days we'll feel better.
By the third day he'll have made us brand-new,
Alive and on our feet,
fit to face him.
We're ready to study GOD,
eager for God-knowledge.
As sure as dawn breaks,
so sure is his daily arrival.
He comes as rain comes,
as spring rain refreshing the ground."

4-7 "What am I to do with you, Ephraim?
What do I make of you, Judah?
Your declarations of love last no longer
than morning mist and predawn dew.
That's why I use prophets to shake you to attention,
why my words cut you to the quick:
To wake you up to my judgment
blazing like light.
I'm after love that lasts, not more religion.
I want you to know GOD, not go to more prayer meetings.
You broke the covenant—just like Adam!
You broke faith with me—ungrateful wretches!

8-9 "Gilead has become Crime City—
blood on the sidewalks, blood on the streets.
It used to be robbers who mugged pedestrians.
Now it's gangs of priests
Assaulting worshipers on their way to Shechem.
Nothing is sacred to them.

10 "I saw a shocking thing in the country of Israel:
Ephraim worshiping in a religious whorehouse,
and Israel in the mud right there with him.

11 "You're as bad as the worst of them, Judah.
You've been sowing wild oats. Now it's harvest time."

DESPITE ALL THE SIGNS, ISRAEL IGNORES GOD

1-2 7 "Every time I gave Israel a fresh start,
wiped the slate clean and got them going again,
Ephraim soon filled the slate with new sins,
the treachery of Samaria written out in bold print.
Two-faced and double-tongued,
they steal you blind, pick you clean.
It never crosses their mind
that I keep account of their every crime.
They're mud-spattered head to toe with the residue of sin.
I see who they are and what they've done.

NEW KING JAMES VERSION

[3]They make a king glad with their
wickedness,
And princes with their lies.

[4]"They *are* all adulterers.
Like an oven heated by a baker—
He ceases stirring *the fire* after kneading
the dough,
Until it is leavened.
[5]In the day of our king
Princes have made *him* sick, inflamed with
wine;
He stretched out his hand with scoffers.
[6]They prepare their heart like an oven,
While they lie in wait;
Their baker[a] sleeps all night;
In the morning it burns like a flaming fire.
[7]They are all hot, like an oven,
And have devoured their judges;
All their kings have fallen.
None among them calls upon Me.

[8]"Ephraim has mixed himself among the
peoples;
Ephraim is a cake unturned.
[9]Aliens have devoured his strength,
But he does not know *it;*
Yes, gray hairs are here and there on him,
Yet he does not know *it.*
[10]And the pride of Israel testifies to his face,
But they do not return to the LORD their
God,
Nor seek Him for all this.

FUTILE RELIANCE ON THE NATIONS

[11]"Ephraim also is like a silly dove, without
sense—
They call to Egypt,
They go to Assyria.
[12]Wherever they go, I will spread My net on
them;
I will bring them down like birds of the air;
I will chastise them
According to what their congregation has
heard.

[13]"Woe to them, for they have fled from Me!
Destruction to them,
Because they have transgressed against Me!
Though I redeemed them,
Yet they have spoken lies against Me.
[14]They did not cry out to Me with their heart
When they wailed upon their beds.

"They assemble together for[a] grain and new
wine,
They rebel against Me;[b]
[15]Though I disciplined *and* strengthened their
arms,
Yet they devise evil against Me;
[16]They return, *but* not to the Most High;[a]
They are like a treacherous bow.

7:6 [a]Following Masoretic Text and Vulgate; Syriac and Targum read *Their anger;* Septuagint reads *Ephraim.* **7:14** [a]Following Masoretic Text and Targum; Vulgate reads *thought upon;* Septuagint reads *slashed themselves for* (compare 1 Kings 18:28). [b]Following Masoretic Text, Syriac, and Targum; Septuagint omits *They rebel against Me;* Vulgate reads *They departed from Me.* **7:16** [a]Or *upward*

THE MESSAGE

3-7 "They entertain the king with their evil circus,
delight the princes with their acrobatic
lies.
They're a bunch of overheated adulterers,
like an oven that holds its heat
From the kneading of the dough
to the rising of the bread.
On the royal holiday the princes get drunk
on wine and the frenzy of the mocking
mob.
They're like wood stoves,
red-hot with lust.
Through the night their passion is banked;
in the morning it blazes up, flames
hungrily licking.
Murderous and volcanic,
they incinerate their rulers.
Their kings fall one by one,
and no one pays any attention to me.

8-10 "Ephraim mingles with the pagans, dissipating
himself.
Ephraim is half-baked.
Strangers suck him dry
but he doesn't even notice.
His hair has turned gray—
he doesn't notice.
Bloated by arrogance, big as a house,
Israel's a public disgrace.
Israel lumbers along oblivious to GOD,
despite all the signs, ignoring GOD.

11-16 "Ephraim is bird-brained,
mindless, clueless,
First chirping after Egypt,
then fluttering after Assyria.
I'll throw my net over them. I'll clip their
wings.
I'll teach them to mind me!
Doom! They've run away from home.
Now they're *really* in trouble! They've
defied me.
And I'm supposed to help them
while they feed me a line of lies?
Instead of crying out to me in heartfelt
prayer,
they whoop it up in bed with their
whores,
Gash themselves bloody in their sex-and-
religion orgies,
but turn their backs on me.
I'm the one who gave them good minds
and healthy bodies,
and how am I repaid? With evil
scheming!
They turn, but not to me—
turn here, then there, like a weather
vane.

NEW KING JAMES VERSION

Their princes shall fall by the sword
For the cursings of their tongue.
This *shall be* their derision in the land of Egypt.

THE APOSTASY OF ISRAEL

8 "*Set* the trumpet[a] to your mouth!
He shall come like an eagle against the house of the LORD,
Because they have transgressed My covenant
And rebelled against My law.
2Israel will cry to Me,
'My God, we know You!'
3Israel has rejected the good;
The enemy will pursue him.

4"They set up kings, but not by Me;
They made princes, but I did not acknowledge *them*.
From their silver and gold
They made idols for themselves—
That they might be cut off.
5Your calf is rejected, O Samaria!
My anger is aroused against them—
How long until they attain to innocence?
6For from Israel *is* even this:
A workman made it, and it *is* not God;
But the calf of Samaria shall be broken to pieces.

7"They sow the wind,
And reap the whirlwind.
The stalk has no bud;
It shall never produce meal.
If it should produce,
Aliens would swallow it up.
8Israel is swallowed up;
Now they are among the Gentiles
Like a vessel in which *is* no pleasure.
9For they have gone up to Assyria,
Like a wild donkey alone by itself;
Ephraim has hired lovers.
10Yes, though they have hired among the nations,
Now I will gather them;
And they shall sorrow a little,[a]
Because of the burden[b] of the king of princes.

11"Because Ephraim has made many altars for sin,
They have become for him altars for sinning.
12I have written for him the great things of My law,
But they were considered a strange thing.
13*For* the sacrifices of My offerings they sacrifice flesh and eat *it*,
But the LORD does not accept them.
Now He will remember their iniquity and punish their sins.
They shall return to Egypt.

14"For Israel has forgotten his Maker,
And has built temples;[a]

8:1 [a]Hebrew *shophar,* ram's horn 8:10 [a]Or *begin to diminish* [b]Or *oracle* 8:14 [a]Or *palaces*

THE MESSAGE

Their rulers will be cut down, murdered—
just deserts for their mocking blasphemies.
And the final sentence?
Ridicule in the court of world opinion."

ALTARS FOR SINNING

1-3 8 "Blow the trumpet! Sound the alarm!
Vultures are circling over God's people
Who have broken my covenant
and defied my revelation.
Predictably, Israel cries out, 'My God! We know you!'
But they don't act like it.
Israel will have nothing to do with what's good,
and now the enemy is after them.

4-10 "They crown kings, but without asking me.
They set up princes but don't let me in on it.
Instead, they make idols, using silver and gold,
idols that will be their ruin.
Throw that gold calf-god on the trash heap, Samaria!
I'm seething with anger against that rubbish!
How long before they shape up?
And they're Israelites!
A sculptor made that thing—
it's not God.
That Samaritan calf
will be broken to bits.
Look at them! Planting wind-seeds,
they'll harvest tornadoes.
Wheat with no head
produces no flour.
And even if it did,
strangers would gulp it down.
Israel is swallowed up and spit out.
Among the pagans they're a piece of junk.
They trotted off to Assyria:
Why, even wild donkeys stick to their own kind,
but donkey-Ephraim goes out and *pays* to get lovers.
Now, because of their whoring life among the pagans,
I'm going to gather them together and confront them.
They're going to reap the consequences soon,
feel what it's like to be oppressed by the big king.

11-14 "Ephraim has built a lot of altars,
and then uses them for sinning.
Can you believe it? Altars for sinning!
I write out my revelation for them in detail
and they pretend they can't read it.
They offer sacrifices to me
and then they feast on the meat.
GOD is not pleased!
I'm fed up—I'll keep remembering their guilt.
I'll punish their sins
and send them back to Egypt.
Israel has forgotten his Maker
and gotten busy making palaces.

New King James Version

Judah also has multiplied fortified cities;
But I will send fire upon his cities,
And it shall devour his palaces."

Judgment of Israel's Sin

9 Do not rejoice, O Israel, with joy like *other* peoples,
For you have played the harlot against your God.
You have made love *for* hire on every threshing floor.
2The threshing floor and the winepress
Shall not feed them,
And the new wine shall fail in her.

3They shall not dwell in the LORD's land,
But Ephraim shall return to Egypt,
And shall eat unclean *things* in Assyria.
4They shall not offer wine *offerings* to the LORD,
Nor shall their sacrifices be pleasing to Him.
It shall be like bread of mourners to them;
All who eat it shall be defiled.
For their bread *shall be* for their *own* life;
It shall not come into the house of the LORD.

5What will you do in the appointed day,
And in the day of the feast of the LORD?
6For indeed they are gone because of destruction.
Egypt shall gather them up;
Memphis shall bury them.
Nettles shall possess their valuables of silver;
Thorns *shall be* in their tents.

7The days of punishment have come;
The days of recompense have come.
Israel knows!
The prophet *is* a fool,
The spiritual man *is* insane,
Because of the greatness of your iniquity and great enmity.
8The watchman of Ephraim *is* with my God;
But the prophet *is* a fowler's[a] snare in all his ways—
Enmity in the house of his God.
9They are deeply corrupted,
As in the days of Gibeah.
He will remember their iniquity;
He will punish their sins.

10"I found Israel
Like grapes in the wilderness;
I saw your fathers
As the firstfruits on the fig tree in its first season.
But they went to Baal Peor,

9:8 [a]That is, one who catches birds in a trap or snare

The Message

Judah has gone in for a lot of fortress cities.
I'm sending fire on their cities
to burn down their fortifications."

Starved for God

1-6 9 Don't waste your life in wild orgies, Israel.
Don't party away your life with the heathen.
You walk away from your God at the drop of a hat
and like a whore sell yourself promiscuously
at every sex-and-religion party on the street.
All that party food won't fill you up.
You'll end up hungrier than ever.
At this rate you'll not last long in GOD's land:
Some of you are going to end up bankrupt in Egypt.
Some of you will be disillusioned in Assyria.
As refugees in Egypt and Assyria,
you won't have much chance to worship GOD—
Sentenced to rations of bread and water,
and your souls polluted by the spirit-dirty air.
You'll be starved for GOD,
exiled from GOD's own country.
Will you be homesick for the old Holy Days?
Will you miss festival worship of GOD?
Be warned! When you escape from the frying pan of disaster,
you'll fall into the fire of Egypt.
Egypt will give you a fine funeral!
What use will all your god-inspired silver be then
as you eke out a living in a field of weeds?

7-9 Time's up. Doom's at the doorstep.
It's payday!
Did Israel bluster, "The prophet is crazy!
The 'man of the Spirit' is nuts!"?
Think again. Because of your great guilt,
you're in big trouble.
The prophet is looking out for Ephraim,
working under God's orders.
But everyone is trying to trip him up.
He's hated right in God's house, of all places.
The people are going from bad to worse,
rivaling that ancient and unspeakable crime at Gibeah.
God's keeping track of their guilt.
He'll make them pay for their sins.

They Took to Sin Like a Pig to Filth

10-13 "Long ago when I came upon Israel,
it was like finding grapes out in the desert.
When I found your ancestors, it was like finding
a fig tree bearing fruit for the first time.
But when they arrived at Baal-peor, that pagan shrine,

NEW KING JAMES VERSION

And separated themselves *to that* shame;
They became an abomination like the thing
they loved.
11*As for* Ephraim, their glory shall fly away
like a bird—
No birth, no pregnancy, and no conception!
12Though they bring up their children,
Yet I will bereave them to the last man.
Yes, woe to them when I depart from them!
13Just as I saw Ephraim like Tyre, planted in a
pleasant place,
So Ephraim will bring out his children to
the murderer."

14Give them, O LORD—
What will You give?
Give them a miscarrying womb
And dry breasts!

15"All their wickedness *is* in Gilgal,
For there I hated them.
Because of the evil of their deeds
I will drive them from My house;
I will love them no more.
All their princes *are* rebellious.
16Ephraim is stricken,
Their root is dried up;
They shall bear no fruit.
Yes, were they to bear children,
I would kill the darlings of their womb."

17My God will cast them away,
Because they did not obey Him;
And they shall be wanderers among the
nations.

ISRAEL'S SIN AND CAPTIVITY

10 Israel empties *his* vine;
He brings forth fruit for himself.
According to the multitude of his fruit
He has increased the altars;
According to the bounty of his land
They have embellished *his* sacred pillars.
2Their heart is divided;
Now they are held guilty.
He will break down their altars;
He will ruin their sacred pillars.

3For now they say,
"We have no king,
Because we did not fear the LORD.
And as for a king, what would he do for us?"
4They have spoken words,
Swearing falsely in making a covenant.
Thus judgment springs up like hemlock in
the furrows of the field.

5The inhabitants of Samaria fear
Because of the calf[a] of Beth Aven.

10:5 [a]Literally *calves*

THE MESSAGE

they took to sin like a pig to filth,
wallowing in the mud with their
newfound friends.
Ephraim is fickle and scattered, like a flock
of blackbirds,
their beauty dissipated in confusion and
clamor,
Frenetic and noisy, frigid and barren,
and nothing to show for it—neither
conception nor childbirth.
Even if they did give birth, I'd declare them
unfit parents and take away their
children!
Yes indeed—a black day for them
when I turn my back and walk off!
I see Ephraim letting his children run wild.
He might just as well take them and kill
them outright!"

14 Give it to them, GOD! But what?
Give them a dried-up womb and
shriveled breasts.

15-16 "All their evil came out into the open
at the pagan shrine at Gilgal. Oh, how I
hated them there!
Because of their evil practices,
I'll kick them off my land.
I'm wasting no more love on them.
Their leaders are a bunch of rebellious
adolescents.
Ephraim is hit hard—
roots withered, no more fruit.
Even if by some miracle they had children,
the dear babies wouldn't live—I'd make
sure of that!"

17 My God has washed his hands of them.
They wouldn't listen.
They're doomed to be wanderers,
vagabonds among the godless nations.

YOU THOUGHT YOU COULD DO IT ALL ON YOUR OWN

1-2 10 Israel was once a lush vine,
bountiful in grapes.
The more lavish the harvest,
the more promiscuous the worship.
The more money they got,
the more they squandered on
gods-in-their-own-image.
Their sweet smiles are sheer lies.
They're guilty as sin.
God will smash their worship shrines,
pulverize their god-images.

3-4 They go around saying,
"Who needs a king?
We couldn't care less about GOD,
so why bother with a king?
What difference would he make?"
They talk big,
lie through their teeth,
make deals.
But their high-sounding words
turn out to be empty words, litter in the
gutters.

5-6 The people of Samaria travel over to Crime City
to worship the golden calf-god.

NEW KING JAMES VERSION

For its people mourn for it,
And its priests shriek for it—
Because its glory has departed from it.
6*The idol* also shall be carried to Assyria
As a present for King Jareb.
Ephraim shall receive shame,
And Israel shall be ashamed of his own
counsel.

7*As for* Samaria, her king is cut off
Like a twig on the water.
8Also the high places of Aven, the sin of
Israel,
Shall be destroyed.
The thorn and thistle shall grow on their
altars;
They shall say to the mountains, "Cover us!"
And to the hills, "Fall on us!"

9"O Israel, you have sinned from the days of
Gibeah;
There they stood.
The battle in Gibeah against the children of
iniquity[a]
Did not overtake them.
10When *it is* My desire, I will chasten them.
Peoples shall be gathered against them
When I bind them for their two
transgressions.[a]
11Ephraim *is* a trained heifer
That loves to thresh *grain;*
But I harnessed her fair neck,
I will make Ephraim pull *a plow.*
Judah shall plow;
Jacob shall break his clods."

12Sow for yourselves righteousness;
Reap in mercy;
Break up your fallow ground,
For *it is* time to seek the LORD,
Till He comes and rains righteousness on
you.

13You have plowed wickedness;
You have reaped iniquity.
You have eaten the fruit of lies,
Because you trusted in your own way,
In the multitude of your mighty men.
14Therefore tumult shall arise among your
people,
And all your fortresses shall be plundered
As Shalman plundered Beth Arbel in the
day of battle—
A mother dashed in pieces upon *her*
children.
15Thus it shall be done to you, O Bethel,
Because of your great wickedness.
At dawn the king of Israel
Shall be cut off utterly.

GOD'S CONTINUING LOVE FOR ISRAEL

11 "When Israel *was* a child, I loved him,
And out of Egypt I called My son.

10:9 [a]So read many Hebrew manuscripts, Septuagint, and Vulgate; Masoretic Text reads *unruliness.* **10:10** [a]Or *in their two habitations*

THE MESSAGE

They go all out, prancing and hollering,
taken in by their showmen priests.
They act so important around the calf-god,
but are oblivious to the sham, the shame.
They have plans to take it to Assyria,
present it as a gift to the great king.
And so Ephraim makes a fool of himself,
disgraces Israel with his stupid idols.

7-8 Samaria is history. Its king
is a dead branch floating down the river.
Israel's favorite sin centers
will all be torn down.
Thistles and crabgrass
will decorate their ruined altars.
Then they'll say to the mountains, "Bury
us!"
and to the hills, "Fall on us!"

9-10 You got your start in sin at Gibeah—
that ancient, unspeakable, shocking
sin—
And you've been at it ever since.
And Gibeah will mark the end of it
in a war to end all the sinning.
I'll come to teach them a lesson.
Nations will gang up on them,
Making them learn the hard way
the sum of Gibeah plus Gibeah.

11-15 Ephraim was a trained heifer
that loved to thresh.
Passing by and seeing her strong, sleek
neck,
I wanted to harness Ephraim,
Put Ephraim to work in the fields—
Judah plowing, Jacob harrowing:
Sow righteousness,
reap love.
It's time to till the ready earth,
it's time to dig in with GOD,
Until he arrives
with righteousness ripe for harvest.
But instead you plowed wicked ways,
reaped a crop of evil and ate a salad of
lies.
You thought you could do it all on your
own,
flush with weapons and manpower.
But the volcano of war will erupt among
your people.
All your defense posts will be leveled
As viciously as king Shalman
leveled the town of Beth-arba,
When mothers and their babies
were smashed on the rocks.
That's what's ahead for you, you so-called
people of God,
because of your off-the-charts evil.
Some morning you're going to wake up
and find Israel, king and kingdom, a
blank—nothing.

ISRAEL PLAYED AT RELIGION WITH TOY GODS

1-9 **11** "When Israel was only a child, I loved
him.
I called out, 'My son!'—called him out of
Egypt.

NEW KING JAMES VERSION

2*As* they called them,[a]
So they went from them;[b]
They sacrificed to the Baals,
And burned incense to carved images.

3"I taught Ephraim to walk,
Taking them by their arms;[a]
But they did not know that I healed them.
4I drew them with gentle cords,[a]
With bands of love,
And I was to them as those who take the yoke from their neck.[b]
I stooped *and* fed them.

5"He shall not return to the land of Egypt;
But the Assyrian shall be his king,
Because they refused to repent.
6And the sword shall slash in his cities,
Devour his districts,
And consume *them*,
Because of their own counsels.
7My people are bent on backsliding from Me.
Though they call to the Most High,[a]
None at all exalt *Him*.

8"How can I give you up, Ephraim?
How can I hand you over, Israel?
How can I make you like Admah?
How can I set you like Zeboiim?
My heart churns within Me;
My sympathy is stirred.
9I will not execute the fierceness of My anger;
I will not again destroy Ephraim.
For I *am* God, and not man,
The Holy One in your midst;
And I will not come with terror.[a]

10"They shall walk after the LORD.
He will roar like a lion.
When He roars,
Then *His* sons shall come trembling from the west;
11They shall come trembling like a bird from Egypt,
Like a dove from the land of Assyria.
And I will let them dwell in their houses,"
Says the LORD.

GOD'S CHARGE AGAINST EPHRAIM

12"Ephraim has encircled Me with lies,
And the house of Israel with deceit;
But Judah still walks with God,
Even with the Holy One[a] *who is* faithful.

12 "Ephraim feeds on the wind,
And pursues the east wind;
He daily increases lies and desolation.
Also they make a covenant with the Assyrians,
And oil is carried to Egypt.

11:2 [a]Following Masoretic Text and Vulgate; Septuagint reads *Just as I called them;* Targum interprets as *I sent prophets to a thousand of them.* [b]Following Masoretic Text, Targum, and Vulgate; Septuagint reads *from My face.* **11:3** [a]Some Hebrew manuscripts, Septuagint, Syriac, and Vulgate read *My arms.* **11:4** [a]Literally *cords of a man* [b]Literally *jaws* **11:7** [a]Or *upward* **11:9** [a]Or *I will not enter a city* **11:12** [a]Or *holy ones*

THE MESSAGE

But when others called him,
he ran off and left me.
He worshiped the popular sex gods,
he played at religion with toy gods.
Still, I stuck with him. I led Ephraim.
I rescued him from human bondage,
But he never acknowledged my help,
never admitted that I was the one pulling his wagon,
That I lifted him, like a baby, to my cheek,
that I bent down to feed him.
Now he wants to go *back* to Egypt or go over to Assyria—
anything but return to me!
That's why his cities are unsafe—
the murder rate skyrockets
and every plan to improve things falls to pieces.
My people are hell-bent on leaving me.
They pray to god Baal for help.
He doesn't lift a finger to help them.
But how can I give up on you, Ephraim?
How can I turn you loose, Israel?
How can I leave you to be ruined like Admah,
devastated like luckless Zeboim?
I can't bear to even think such thoughts.
My insides churn in protest.
And so I'm not going to act on my anger.
I'm not going to destroy Ephraim.
And why? Because I am God and not a human.
I'm The Holy One and I'm here—in your very midst.

10-12 "The people will end up following GOD.
I will roar like a lion—
Oh, how I'll roar!
My frightened children will come running from the west.
Like frightened birds they'll come from Egypt,
from Assyria like scared doves.
I'll move them back into their homes."
GOD's Word!

SOUL-DESTROYING LIES

Ephraim tells lies right and left.
Not a word of Israel can be trusted.
Judah, meanwhile, is no better,
addicted to cheap gods.

1-5 12 Ephraim, obsessed with god-fantasies,
chases ghosts and phantoms.
He tells lies nonstop,
soul-destroying lies.
Both Ephraim and Judah made deals with Assyria
and tried to get an inside track with Egypt.

NEW KING JAMES VERSION

2"The LORD also *brings* a charge against
Judah,
And will punish Jacob according to his
ways;
According to his deeds He will recompense
him.
3He took his brother by the heel in the womb,
And in his strength he struggled with God.[a]
4Yes, he struggled with the Angel and
prevailed;
He wept, and sought favor from Him.
He found Him *in* Bethel,
And there He spoke to us—
5That is, the LORD God of hosts.
The LORD *is* His memorable name.
6So you, by *the help of* your God, return;
Observe mercy and justice,
And wait on your God continually.

7"A cunning Canaanite!
Deceitful scales *are* in his hand;
He loves to oppress.
8And Ephraim said,
'Surely I have become rich,
I have found wealth for myself;
In all my labors
They shall find in me no iniquity that *is* sin.'

9"But I *am* the LORD your God,
Ever since the land of Egypt;
I will again make you dwell in tents,
As in the days of the appointed feast.
10I have also spoken by the prophets,
And have multiplied visions;
I have given symbols through the witness of
the prophets."

11Though Gilead *has* idols—
Surely they are vanity—
Though they sacrifice bulls in Gilgal,
Indeed their altars *shall be* heaps in the
furrows of the field.

12Jacob fled to the country of Syria;
Israel served for a spouse,
And for a wife he tended *sheep*.
13By a prophet the LORD brought Israel out of
Egypt,
And by a prophet he was preserved.
14Ephraim provoked *Him* to anger most
bitterly;
Therefore his Lord will leave the guilt of his
bloodshed upon him,
And return his reproach upon him.

RELENTLESS JUDGMENT ON ISRAEL

13 When Ephraim spoke, trembling,
He exalted *himself* in Israel;

12:3 [a]Compare Genesis 32:28

THE MESSAGE

GOD is bringing charges against Israel.
Jacob's children are hauled into court to
be punished.
In the womb, that heel, Jacob, got the best
of his brother.
When he grew up, he tried to get the best
of GOD.
But GOD would not be bested.
GOD bested him.
Brought to his knees,
Jacob wept and prayed.
GOD found him at Bethel.
That's where he spoke with him.
GOD is GOD-of-the-Angel-Armies,
GOD-Revealed, GOD-Known.

6 What are you waiting for? Return to your
God!
Commit yourself in love, in justice!
Wait for your God,
and don't give up on him—ever!

7-8 The businessmen engage in wholesale fraud.
They love to rip people off!
Ephraim boasted, "Look, I'm rich!
I've made it big!
And look how well I've covered my tracks:
not a hint of fraud, not a sign of sin!"

9-11 "But not so fast! I'm GOD, *your God!*
Your God from the days in Egypt!
I'm going to put you back to living in tents,
as in the old days when you worshiped
in the wilderness.
I speak through the prophets
to give clear pictures of the way things
are.
Using prophets, I tell revealing stories.
I show Gilead rampant with religious
scandal
and Gilgal teeming with empty-headed
religion.
I expose their worship centers as
stinking piles of garbage in their
gardens."

12-14 Are you going to repeat the life of your
ancestor Jacob?
He ran off guilty to Aram,
Then sold his soul to get ahead,
and made it big through treachery and
deceit.
Your real identity is formed through
God-sent prophets,
who led you out of Egypt and served as
faithful pastors.
As it is, Ephraim has continually
and inexcusably insulted God.
Now he has to pay for his life-destroying
ways.
His Master will do to him what *he* has
done.

RELIGION CUSTOMIZED TO TASTE

1-3 13 God once let loose against Ephraim
a terrifying sentence against Israel:

NEW KING JAMES VERSION

But when he offended through Baal
worship, he died.
2Now they sin more and more,
And have made for themselves molded images,
Idols of their silver, according to their skill;
All of it *is* the work of craftsmen.
They say of them,
"Let the men who sacrifice[a] kiss the calves!"
3Therefore they shall be like the morning cloud
And like the early dew that passes away,
Like chaff blown off from a threshing floor
And like smoke from a chimney.

4"Yet I *am* the LORD your God
Ever since the land of Egypt,
And you shall know no God but Me;
For *there is* no savior besides Me.
5I knew you in the wilderness,
In the land of great drought.
6When they had pasture, they were filled;
They were filled and their heart was exalted;
Therefore they forgot Me.

7"So I will be to them like a lion;
Like a leopard by the road I will lurk;
8I will meet them like a bear deprived *of her cubs;*
I will tear open their rib cage,
And there I will devour them like a lion.
The wild beast shall tear them.

9"O Israel, you are destroyed,[a]
But your help[b] *is* from Me.
10I will be your King;[a]
Where *is any other,*
That he may save you in all your cities?
And your judges to whom you said,
'Give me a king and princes'?
11I gave you a king in My anger,
And took *him* away in My wrath.

12"The iniquity of Ephraim *is* bound up;
His sin *is* stored up.
13The sorrows of a woman in childbirth shall come upon him.
He *is* an unwise son,
For he should not stay long where children are born.

14"I will ransom them from the power of the grave;[a]
I will redeem them from death.

13:2 [a]Or *those who offer human sacrifice* 13:9 [a]Literally *it* or *he destroyed you* [b]Literally *in your help* 13:10 [a]Septuagint, Syriac, Targum, and Vulgate read *Where is your king?* 13:14 [a]Or *Sheol* [b]Septuagint reads *where is your punishment?* [c]Or *Sheol* [d]Septuagint reads *where is your sting?*

THE MESSAGE

Caught and convicted
in the lewd sex-worship of Baal—they died!
And now they're back in the sin business again,
manufacturing god-images they can use,
Religion customized to taste. Professionals see to it:
Anything you want in a god you can get.
Can you believe it? They sacrifice live babies to these dead gods—
kill living babies and kiss golden calves!
And now there's nothing left to these people:
hollow men, desiccated women,
Like scraps of paper blown down the street,
like smoke in a gusty wind.

4-6 "I'm still your GOD,
the God who saved you out of Egypt.
I'm the only real God you've ever known.
I'm the one and only God who delivers.
I took care of you during the wilderness hard times,
those years when you had nothing.
I took care of you, took care of all your needs,
gave you everything you needed.
You were spoiled. You thought you didn't need me.
You forgot me.

7-12 "I'll charge them like a lion,
like a leopard stalking in the brush.
I'll jump them like a sow grizzly robbed of her cubs.
I'll rip out their guts.
Coyotes will make a meal of them.
Crows will clean their bones.
I'm going to destroy you, Israel.
Who is going to stop me?
Where is your trusty king you thought would save you?
Where are all the local leaders you wanted so badly?
All these rulers you insisted on having,
demanding, 'Give me a king! Give me leaders!'?
Well, long ago I gave you a king, but I wasn't happy about it.
Now, fed up, I've gotten rid of him.
I have a detailed record of your infidelities—
Ephraim's sin documented and stored in a safe-deposit box.

13-15 "When birth pangs signaled it was time to be born,
Ephraim was too stupid to come out of the womb.
When the passage into life opened up,
he didn't show.
Shall I intervene and pull them into life?
Shall I snatch them from a certain death?
Who is afraid of you, Death?
Who cares about your threats, Tomb?

New King James Version

O Death, I will be your plagues![b]
O Grave,[c] I will be your destruction![d]
Pity is hidden from My eyes."

15Though he is fruitful among *his* brethren,
An east wind shall come;
The wind of the LORD shall come up from
the wilderness.
Then his spring shall become dry,
And his fountain shall be dried up.
He shall plunder the treasury of every
desirable prize.
16Samaria is held guilty,[a]
For she has rebelled against her God.
They shall fall by the sword,
Their infants shall be dashed in pieces,
And their women with child ripped open.

Israel Restored at Last

14 O Israel, return to the LORD your God,
For you have stumbled because of your
iniquity;
2Take words with you,
And return to the LORD.
Say to Him,
"Take away all iniquity;
Receive *us* graciously,
For we will offer the sacrifices[a] of our lips.
3Assyria shall not save us,
We will not ride on horses,
Nor will we say anymore to the work of our
hands, '*You are* our gods.'
For in You the fatherless finds mercy."

4"I will heal their backsliding,
I will love them freely,
For My anger has turned away from him.
5I will be like the dew to Israel;
He shall grow like the lily,
And lengthen his roots like Lebanon.
6His branches shall spread;
His beauty shall be like an olive tree,
And his fragrance like Lebanon.
7Those who dwell under his shadow shall
return;
They shall be revived *like* grain,
And grow like a vine.
Their scent[a] *shall be* like the wine of
Lebanon.

8"Ephraim *shall say*, 'What have I to do
anymore with idols?'
I have heard and observed him.
I *am* like a green cypress tree;
Your fruit is found in Me."
9Who *is* wise?
Let him understand these things.
Who is prudent?
Let him know them.
For the ways of the LORD *are* right;
The righteous walk in them,
But transgressors stumble in them.

13:16 [a]Septuagint reads *shall be disfigured* 14:2 [a]Literally *bull calves;* Septuagint reads *fruit.* 14:7 [a]Literally *remembrance*

The Message

In the end I'm abolishing regret,
banishing sorrow,
Even though Ephraim ran wild,
the black sheep of the family.

15-16 "GOD's tornado is on its way,
roaring out of the desert.
It will devastate the country,
leaving a trail of ruin and wreckage.
The cities will be gutted,
dear possessions gone for good.
Now Samaria has to face the charges
because she has rebelled against her
God:
Her people will be killed, babies smashed
on the rocks,
pregnant women ripped open."

Come Back! Return to Your God!

1-3 14 O Israel, come back! Return to your GOD!
You're down but you're not out.
Prepare your confession
and come back to GOD.
Pray to him, "Take away our sin,
accept our confession.
Receive as restitution
our repentant prayers.
Assyria won't save us;
horses won't get us where we want to go.
We'll never again say 'our god'
to something we've made or made up.
You're our last hope. Is it not true
that in you the orphan finds mercy?"

4-8 "I will heal their waywardness.
I will love them lavishly. My anger is
played out.
I will make a fresh start with Israel.
He'll burst into bloom like a crocus in
the spring.
He'll put down deep oak tree roots,
he'll become a forest of oaks!
He'll become splendid—like a giant
sequoia,
his fragrance like a grove of cedars!
Those who live near him will be blessed by
him,
be blessed and prosper like golden grain.
Everyone will be talking about them,
spreading their fame as the vintage
children of God.
Ephraim is finished with gods that are
no-gods.
From now on I'm the one who answers
and satisfies him.
I am like a luxuriant fruit tree.
Everything you need is to be found in
me."

9 If you want to live well,
make sure you understand all of this.
If you know what's good for you,
you'll learn this inside and out.
GOD's paths get you where you want to go.
Right-living people walk them easily;
wrong-living people are always tripping
and stumbling.

JOEL

NEW KING JAMES VERSION

1 The word of the LORD that came to Joel the son of Pethuel.

THE LAND LAID WASTE

2 Hear this, you elders,
And give ear, all you inhabitants of the land!
Has *anything like* this happened in your days,
Or even in the days of your fathers?
3 Tell your children about it,
Let your children *tell* their children,
And their children another generation.

4 What the chewing locust[a] left, the swarming locust has eaten;
What the swarming locust left, the crawling locust has eaten;
And what the crawling locust left, the consuming locust has eaten.

5 Awake, you drunkards, and weep;
And wail, all you drinkers of wine,
Because of the new wine,
For it has been cut off from your mouth.
6 For a nation has come up against My land,
Strong, and without number;
His teeth *are* the teeth of a lion,
And he has the fangs of a fierce lion.
7 He has laid waste My vine,
And ruined My fig tree;
He has stripped it bare and thrown *it* away;
Its branches are made white.

8 Lament like a virgin girded with sackcloth
For the husband of her youth.
9 The grain offering and the drink offering
Have been cut off from the house of the LORD;
The priests mourn, who minister to the LORD.
10 The field is wasted,
The land mourns;
For the grain is ruined,
The new wine is dried up,
The oil fails.

11 Be ashamed, you farmers,
Wail, you vinedressers,
For the wheat and the barley;
Because the harvest of the field has perished.
12 The vine has dried up,
And the fig tree has withered;
The pomegranate tree,
The palm tree also,
And the apple tree—
All the trees of the field are withered;
Surely joy has withered away from the sons of men.

MOURNING FOR THE LAND

13 Gird yourselves and lament, you priests;
Wail, you who minister before the altar;
Come, lie all night in sackcloth,

1:4 [a]Exact identity of these locusts is unknown.

THE MESSAGE

GET IN TOUCH WITH REALITY—AND WEEP!

1-3 1 GOD's Message to Joel son of Pethuel:

Attention, elder statesmen! Listen closely,
everyone, whoever and wherever you are!
Have you ever heard of anything like this?
Has anything like this ever happened before—ever?
Make sure you tell your children,
and your children tell their children,
And their children *their* children.
Don't let this message die out.

4 What the chewing locust left,
the gobbling locust ate;
What the gobbling locust left,
the munching locust ate;
What the munching locust left,
the chomping locust ate.

5-7 Sober up, you drunks!
Get in touch with reality—and weep!
Your supply of booze is cut off.
You're on the wagon, like it or not.
My country's being invaded
by an army invincible, past numbering,
Teeth like those of a lion,
fangs like those of a tiger.
It has ruined my vineyards,
stripped my orchards,
And clear-cut the country.
The landscape's a moonscape.

8-10 Weep like a young virgin dressed in black,
mourning the loss of her fiancé.
Without grain and grapes,
worship has been brought to a standstill
in the Sanctuary of GOD.
The priests are at a loss.
GOD's ministers don't know what to do.
The fields are sterile.
The very ground grieves.
The wheat fields are lifeless,
vineyards dried up, olive oil gone.

11-12 Dirt farmers, despair!
Grape growers, wring your hands!
Lament the loss of wheat and barley.
All crops have failed.
Vineyards dried up,
fig trees withered,
Pomegranates, date palms, and apple trees—
deadwood everywhere!
And joy is dried up and withered
in the hearts of the people.

NOTHING'S GOING ON IN THE PLACE OF WORSHIP

13-14 And also you priests,
put on your robes and join the outcry.
You who lead people in worship,
lead them in lament.
Spend the night dressed in gunnysacks,

NEW KING JAMES VERSION

You who minister to my God;
For the grain offering and the drink offering
Are withheld from the house of your God.
14Consecrate a fast,
Call a sacred assembly;
Gather the elders
And all the inhabitants of the land
Into the house of the LORD your God,
And cry out to the LORD.

15Alas for the day!
For the day of the LORD *is* at hand;
It shall come as destruction from the Almighty.
16Is not the food cut off before our eyes,
Joy and gladness from the house of our God?
17The seed shrivels under the clods,
Storehouses are in shambles;
Barns are broken down,
For the grain has withered.
18How the animals groan!
The herds of cattle are restless,
Because they have no pasture;
Even the flocks of sheep suffer punishment.[a]

19O LORD, to You I cry out;
For fire has devoured the open pastures,
And a flame has burned all the trees of the field.
20The beasts of the field also cry out to You,
For the water brooks are dried up,
And fire has devoured the open pastures.

THE DAY OF THE LORD

2 Blow the trumpet in Zion,
And sound an alarm in My holy mountain!
Let all the inhabitants of the land tremble;
For the day of the LORD is coming,
For it is at hand:
2A day of darkness and gloominess,
A day of clouds and thick darkness,
Like the morning *clouds* spread over the mountains.
A people *come*, great and strong,
The like of whom has never been;
Nor will there ever be any *such* after them,
Even for many successive generations.

3A fire devours before them,
And behind them a flame burns;
The land *is* like the Garden of Eden before them,
And behind them a desolate wilderness;
Surely nothing shall escape them.
4Their appearance is like the appearance of horses;
And like swift steeds, so they run.
5With a noise like chariots
Over mountaintops they leap,
Like the noise of a flaming fire that devours the stubble,
Like a strong people set in battle array.
6Before them the people writhe in pain;
All faces are drained of color.[a]

1:18 [a]Septuagint and Vulgate read *are made desolate.* 2:6 [a]Septuagint, Targum, and Vulgate read *gather blackness.*

THE MESSAGE

you servants of my God.
Nothing's going on in the place of worship,
no offerings, no prayers—nothing.
Declare a holy fast, call a special meeting,
get the leaders together,
Round up everyone in the country.
Get them into GOD's Sanctuary for
serious prayer to GOD.

15-18 What a day! Doomsday!
GOD's Judgment Day has come.
The Strong God has arrived.
This is serious business!
Food is just a memory at our tables,
as are joy and singing from God's Sanctuary.
The seeds in the field are dead,
barns deserted,
Grain silos abandoned.
Who needs them? The crops have failed!
The farm animals groan—oh, how they groan!
The cattle mill around.
There's nothing for them to eat.
Not even the sheep find anything.

19-20 GOD! I pray, I cry out to you!
The fields are burning up,
The country is a dust bowl,
forest and prairie fires rage unchecked.
Wild animals, dying of thirst,
look to you for a drink.
Springs and streams are dried up.
The whole country is burning up.

THE LOCUST ARMY

1-3 2 Blow the ram's horn trumpet in Zion!
Trumpet the alarm on my holy mountain!
Shake the country up!
GOD's Judgment's on its way—the Day's almost here!
A black day! A Doomsday!
Clouds with no silver lining!
Like dawn light moving over the mountains,
a huge army is coming.
There's never been anything like it
and never will be again.
Wildfire burns everything before this army
and fire licks up everything in its wake.
Before it arrives, the country is like the Garden of Eden.
When it leaves, it is Death Valley.
Nothing escapes unscathed.

4-6 The locust army seems all horses—
galloping horses, an army of horses.
It sounds like thunder
leaping on mountain ridges,
Or like the roar of wildfire
through grass and brush,
Or like an invincible army shouting for blood,
ready to fight, straining at the bit.
At the sight of this army,
the people panic, faces white with terror.

NEW KING JAMES VERSION

7They run like mighty men,
They climb the wall like men of war;
Every one marches in formation,
And they do not break ranks.
8They do not push one another;
Every one marches in his own column.[a]
Though they lunge between the weapons,
They are not cut down.[b]
9They run to and fro in the city,
They run on the wall;
They climb into the houses,
They enter at the windows like a thief.

10The earth quakes before them,
The heavens tremble;
The sun and moon grow dark,
And the stars diminish their brightness.
11The LORD gives voice before His army,
For His camp is very great;
For strong *is the One* who executes His word.
For the day of the LORD *is* great and very terrible;
Who can endure it?

A CALL TO REPENTANCE

12"Now, therefore," says the LORD,
"Turn to Me with all your heart,
With fasting, with weeping, and with mourning."
13So rend your heart, and not your garments;
Return to the LORD your God,
For He *is* gracious and merciful,
Slow to anger, and of great kindness;
And He relents from doing harm.
14Who knows *if* He will turn and relent,
And leave a blessing behind Him—
A grain offering and a drink offering
For the LORD your God?

15Blow the trumpet in Zion,
Consecrate a fast,
Call a sacred assembly;
16Gather the people,
Sanctify the congregation,
Assemble the elders,
Gather the children and nursing babes;
Let the bridegroom go out from his chamber,
And the bride from her dressing room.
17Let the priests, who minister to the LORD,
Weep between the porch and the altar;
Let them say, "Spare Your people, O LORD,
And do not give Your heritage to reproach,
That the nations should rule over them.
Why should they say among the peoples,
'Where *is* their God?' "

2:8 [a]Literally *his own highway* [b]That is, they are not halted by losses

THE MESSAGE

7-11 The invaders charge.
They climb barricades. Nothing stops them.
Each soldier does what he's told,
so disciplined, so determined.
They don't get in each other's way.
Each one knows his job and does it.
Undaunted and fearless,
unswerving, unstoppable.
They storm the city,
swarm its defenses,
Loot the houses,
breaking down doors, smashing windows.
They arrive like an earthquake,
sweep through like a tornado.
Sun and moon turn out their lights,
stars black out.
GOD himself bellows in thunder
as he commands his forces.
Look at the size of that army!
And the strength of those who obey him!
GOD'S Judgment Day—great and terrible.
Who can possibly survive this?

CHANGE YOUR LIFE

12 But there's also this, it's not too late—
GOD'S personal Message!—
"Come back to me and really mean it!
Come fasting and weeping, sorry for your sins!"

13-14 Change your life, not just your clothes.
Come back to GOD, *your* God.
And here's why: God is kind and merciful.
He takes a deep breath, puts up with a lot,
This most patient God, extravagant in love,
always ready to cancel catastrophe.
Who knows? Maybe he'll do it now,
maybe he'll turn around and show pity.
Maybe, when all's said and done,
there'll be blessings full and robust for your GOD!

15-17 Blow the ram's horn trumpet in Zion!
Declare a day of repentance, a holy fast day.
Call a public meeting.
Get everyone there. Consecrate the congregation.
Make sure the elders come,
but bring in the children, too, even the nursing babies,
Even men and women on their honeymoon—
interrupt them and get them there.
Between Sanctuary entrance and altar,
let the priests, GOD'S servants, weep tears of repentance.
Let them intercede: "Have mercy, GOD, on your people!
Don't abandon your heritage to contempt.
Don't let the pagans take over and rule them
and sneer, 'And so where is this God of theirs?' "

NEW KING JAMES VERSION

THE LAND REFRESHED

18Then the LORD will be zealous for His land,
And pity His people.
19The LORD will answer and say to His people,
"Behold, I will send you grain and new wine and oil,
And you will be satisfied by them;
I will no longer make you a reproach among the nations.

20"But I will remove far from you the northern *army,*
And will drive him away into a barren and desolate land,
With his face toward the eastern sea
And his back toward the western sea;
His stench will come up,
And his foul odor will rise,
Because he has done monstrous things."

21Fear not, O land;
Be glad and rejoice,
For the LORD has done marvelous things!
22Do not be afraid, you beasts of the field;
For the open pastures are springing up,
And the tree bears its fruit;
The fig tree and the vine yield their strength.
23Be glad then, you children of Zion,
And rejoice in the LORD your God;
For He has given you the former rain faithfully,[a]
And He will cause the rain to come down for you—
The former rain,
And the latter rain in the first *month.*
24The threshing floors shall be full of wheat,
And the vats shall overflow with new wine and oil.

25"So I will restore to you the years that the swarming locust has eaten,
The crawling locust,
The consuming locust,
And the chewing locust,[a]
My great army which I sent among you.
26You shall eat in plenty and be satisfied,
And praise the name of the LORD your God,
Who has dealt wondrously with you;
And My people shall never be put to shame.
27Then you shall know that I *am* in the midst of Israel:
I *am* the LORD your God
And there is no other.
My people shall never be put to shame.

GOD'S SPIRIT POURED OUT

28"And it shall come to pass afterward
That I will pour out My Spirit on all flesh;
Your sons and your daughters shall prophesy,
Your old men shall dream dreams,
Your young men shall see visions.
29And also on *My* menservants and on *My* maidservants
I will pour out My Spirit in those days.

2:23 [a]Or *the teacher of righteousness* **2:25** [a]Compare 1:4

THE MESSAGE

18-20 At that, GOD went into action to get his land back.
He took pity on his people.
GOD answered and spoke to his people,
"Look, listen—I'm sending a gift:
Grain and wine and olive oil.
The fast is over—eat your fill!
I won't expose you any longer
to contempt among the pagans.
I'll head off the final enemy coming out of the north
and dump them in a wasteland.
Half of them will end up in the Dead Sea,
the other half in the Mediterranean.
There they'll rot, a stench to high heaven.
The bigger the enemy, the stronger the stench!"

THE TREES ARE BEARING FRUIT AGAIN

21-24 Fear not, Earth! Be glad and celebrate!
GOD has done great things.
Fear not, wild animals!
The fields and meadows are greening up.
The trees are bearing fruit again:
a bumper crop of fig trees and vines!
Children of Zion, celebrate!
Be glad in your GOD.
He's giving you a teacher
to train you how to live right—
Teaching, like rain out of heaven, showers of words
to refresh and nourish your soul, just as he used to do.
And plenty of food for your body—silos full of grain,
casks of wine and barrels of olive oil.

25-27 "I'll make up for the years of the locust,
the great locust devastation—
Locusts savage, locusts deadly,
fierce locusts, locusts of doom,
That great locust invasion
I sent your way.
You'll eat your fill of good food.
You'll be full of praises to your GOD,
The God who has set you back on your heels in wonder.
Never again will my people be despised.
You'll know without question
that I'm in the thick of life with Israel,
That I'm your GOD, yes, *your* GOD,
the one and only real God.
Never again will my people be despised.

THE SUN TURNING BLACK AND THE MOON BLOOD-RED

28-32 "And that's just the beginning: After that—

"I will pour out my Spirit
on every kind of people:
Your sons will prophesy,
also your daughters.
Your old men will dream,
your young men will see visions.
I'll even pour out my Spirit on the servants,
men and women both.

NEW KING JAMES VERSION

30"And I will show wonders in the heavens and
in the earth:
Blood and fire and pillars of smoke.
31The sun shall be turned into darkness,
And the moon into blood,
Before the coming of the great and
awesome day of the LORD.
32And it shall come to pass
That whoever calls on the name of the LORD
Shall be saved.
For in Mount Zion and in Jerusalem there
shall be deliverance,
As the LORD has said,
Among the remnant whom the LORD calls.

GOD JUDGES THE NATIONS

3 "For behold, in those days and at that time,
When I bring back the captives of Judah
and Jerusalem,
2I will also gather all nations,
And bring them down to the Valley of
Jehoshaphat;
And I will enter into judgment with them
there
On account of My people, My heritage
Israel,
Whom they have scattered among the
nations;
They have also divided up My land.
3They have cast lots for My people,
Have given a boy *as payment* for a harlot,
And sold a girl for wine, that they may
drink.

4"Indeed, what have you to do with Me,
O Tyre and Sidon, and all the coasts of
Philistia?
Will you retaliate against Me?
But if you retaliate against Me,
Swiftly and speedily I will return your
retaliation upon your own head;
5Because you have taken My silver and My
gold,
And have carried into your temples My
prized possessions.
6Also the people of Judah and the people of
Jerusalem
You have sold to the Greeks,
That you may remove them far from their
borders.

7"Behold, I will raise them
Out of the place to which you have sold
them,
And will return your retaliation upon your
own head.
8I will sell your sons and your daughters
Into the hand of the people of Judah,
And they will sell them to the Sabeans,[a]
To a people far off;
For the LORD has spoken."

9Proclaim this among the nations:
"Prepare for war!
Wake up the mighty men,
Let all the men of war draw near,
Let them come up.

3:8 [a]Literally *Shebaites* (compare Isaiah 60:6 and Ezekiel 27:22)

THE MESSAGE

I'll set wonders in the sky above
and signs on the earth below:
Blood and fire and billowing smoke,
the sun turning black and the moon
blood-red,
Before the Judgment Day of GOD,
the Day tremendous and awesome.
Whoever calls, 'Help, GOD!'
gets help.
On Mount Zion and in Jerusalem
there will be a great rescue—just as GOD
said.
Included in the survivors
are those that GOD calls."

GOD IS A SAFE HIDING PLACE

1-3 3 "In those days, yes, at that very time
when I put life back together again for
Judah and Jerusalem,
I'll assemble all the godless nations.
I'll lead them down into Judgment Valley
And put them all on trial, and judge them
one and all
because of their treatment of my own
people Israel.
They scattered my people all over the
pagan world
and grabbed my land for themselves.
They threw dice for my people
and used them for barter.
They would trade a boy for a whore,
sell a girl for a bottle of wine when they
wanted a drink.

4-8 "As for you, Tyre and Sidon and Philistia,
why should I bother with you?
Are you trying to get back at me
for something I did to you?
If you are, forget it.
I'll see to it that it boomerangs on you.
You robbed me, cleaned me out of silver
and gold,
carted off everything valuable to furnish
your own temples.
You sold the people of Judah and
Jerusalem
into slavery to the Greeks in faraway
places.
But I'm going to reverse your crime.
I'm going to free those slaves.
I'll have done to you what you did to them:
I'll sell your children as slaves to your
neighbors,
And they'll sell them to the far-off
Sabeans."
GOD's Verdict.

9-11 Announce this to the godless nations:
Prepare for battle!
Soldiers at attention!
Present arms! Advance!
Turn your shovels into swords,

NEW KING JAMES VERSION

10Beat your plowshares into swords
And your pruning hooks into spears;
Let the weak say, 'I *am* strong.'"
11Assemble and come, all you nations,
And gather together all around.
Cause Your mighty ones to go down there,
O LORD.

12"Let the nations be wakened, and come up to
the Valley of Jehoshaphat;
For there I will sit to judge all the
surrounding nations.
13Put in the sickle, for the harvest is ripe.
Come, go down;
For the winepress is full,
The vats overflow—
For their wickedness *is* great."
14Multitudes, multitudes in the valley of
decision!
For the day of the LORD *is* near in the valley
of decision.
15The sun and moon will grow dark,
And the stars will diminish their brightness.
16The LORD also will roar from Zion,
And utter His voice from Jerusalem;
The heavens and earth will shake;
But the LORD will be a shelter for His
people,
And the strength of the children of Israel.

17"So you shall know that I *am* the LORD your
God,
Dwelling in Zion My holy mountain.
Then Jerusalem shall be holy,
And no aliens shall ever pass through her
again."

GOD BLESSES HIS PEOPLE

18And it will come to pass in that day
That the mountains shall drip with new
wine,
The hills shall flow with milk,
And all the brooks of Judah shall be flooded
with water;
A fountain shall flow from the house of the
LORD
And water the Valley of Acacias.

19"Egypt shall be a desolation,
And Edom a desolate wilderness,
Because of violence *against* the people of
Judah,
For they have shed innocent blood in their
land.
20But Judah shall abide forever,
And Jerusalem from generation to
generation.
21For I will acquit them of the guilt of
bloodshed, whom I had not acquitted;
For the LORD dwells in Zion."

THE MESSAGE

turn your hoes into spears.
Let the weak one throw out his chest
and say, "I'm tough, I'm a fighter."
Hurry up, pagans! Wherever you are, get a
move on!
Get your act together.
Prepare to be
shattered by GOD!

12 Let the pagan nations set out
for Judgment Valley.
There I'll take my place at the bench
and judge all the surrounding nations.

13 "Swing the sickle—
the harvest is ready.
Stomp on the grapes—
the winepress is full.
The wine vats are full,
overflowing with vintage evil.

14 "Mass confusion, mob uproar—
in Decision Valley!
GOD'S Judgment Day has arrived
in Decision Valley.

15-17 "The sky turns black,
sun and moon go dark, stars burn out.
GOD roars from Zion, shouts from
Jerusalem.
Earth and sky quake in terror.
But GOD is a safe hiding place,
a granite safe house for the children of
Israel.
Then you'll know for sure
that I'm *your* GOD,
Living in Zion,
my sacred mountain.
Jerusalem will be a sacred city,
posted: 'NO TRESPASSING.'

MILK RIVERING OUT OF THE HILLS

18-21 "What a day!
Wine streaming off the mountains,
Milk rivering out of the hills,
water flowing everywhere in Judah,
A fountain pouring out of GOD'S Sanctuary,
watering all the parks and gardens!
But Egypt will be reduced to weeds in a
vacant lot,
Edom turned into barren badlands,
All because of brutalities to the Judean
people,
the atrocities and murders of helpless
innocents.
Meanwhile, Judah will be filled with
people,
Jerusalem inhabited forever.
The sins I haven't already forgiven, I'll
forgive."
GOD has moved into Zion for good.

AMOS

New King James Version

1 The words of Amos, who was among the sheepbreeders[a] of Tekoa, which he saw con-
cerning Israel in the days of Uzziah king of Ju-
dah, and in the days of Jeroboam the son of
Joash, king of Israel, two years before the earth-
quake.

2And he said:

"The LORD roars from Zion,
And utters His voice from Jerusalem;
The pastures of the shepherds mourn,
And the top of Carmel withers."

Judgment on the Nations

3Thus says the LORD:

"For three transgressions of Damascus, and
for four,
I will not turn away its *punishment*,
Because they have threshed Gilead with
implements of iron.
4But I will send a fire into the house of
Hazael,
Which shall devour the palaces of
Ben-Hadad.
5I will also break the *gate* bar of Damascus,
And cut off the inhabitant from the Valley of
Aven,
And the one who holds the scepter from
Beth Eden.
The people of Syria shall go captive to Kir,"
Says the LORD.

6Thus says the LORD:

"For three transgressions of Gaza, and for
four,
I will not turn away its *punishment*,
Because they took captive the whole
captivity
To deliver *them* up to Edom.
7But I will send a fire upon the wall of Gaza,
Which shall devour its palaces.
8I will cut off the inhabitant from Ashdod,
And the one who holds the scepter from
Ashkelon;
I will turn My hand against Ekron,
And the remnant of the Philistines shall
perish,"
Says the Lord GOD.

9Thus says the LORD:

"For three transgressions of Tyre, and for
four,
I will not turn away its *punishment*,
Because they delivered up the whole
captivity to Edom,
And did not remember the covenant of
brotherhood.
10But I will send a fire upon the wall of Tyre,
Which shall devour its palaces."

1:1 [a]Compare 2 Kings 3:4

The Message

1 1 The Message of Amos, one of the shep-
herds of Tekoa, that he received on behalf
of Israel. It came to him in visions during
the time that Uzziah was king of Judah and
Jeroboam II son of Joash was king of Israel,
two years before the big earthquake.

Swallowing the Same Old Lies

2 The Message:

GOD roars from Zion,
shouts from Jerusalem!
The thunderclap voice withers the pastures
tended by shepherds,
shrivels Mount Carmel's proud peak.

3-5 GOD's Message:

"Because of the three great sins of
Damascus
—make that four—I'm not putting up
with her any longer.
She pounded Gilead to a pulp, pounded her
senseless
with iron hammers and mauls.
For that, I'm setting the palace of Hazael
on fire.
I'm torching Ben-hadad's forts.
I'm going to smash the Damascus gates
and banish the crime king who lives in
Sin Valley,
the vice boss who gives orders from
Paradise Palace.
The people of the land will be sent back
to where they came from—to Kir."
GOD's Decree.

6-8 GOD's Message:

"Because of the three great sins of Gaza
—make that four—I'm not putting up
with her any longer.
She deported whole towns
and then sold the people to Edom.
For that, I'm burning down the walls of
Gaza,
burning up all her forts.
I'll banish the crime king from Ashdod,
the vice boss from Ashkelon.
I'll raise my fist against Ekron,
and what's left of the Philistines will
die."
GOD's Decree.

9-10 GOD's Message:

"Because of the three great sins of Tyre
—make that four—I'm not putting up
with her any longer.
She deported whole towns to Edom,
breaking the treaty she had with her kin.
For that, I'm burning down the walls of
Tyre,
burning up all her forts."

NEW KING JAMES VERSION

11Thus says the LORD:

"For three transgressions of Edom, and for
four,
I will not turn away its *punishment*,
Because he pursued his brother with the
sword,
And cast off all pity;
His anger tore perpetually,
And he kept his wrath forever.
12But I will send a fire upon Teman,
Which shall devour the palaces of Bozrah."

13Thus says the LORD:

"For three transgressions of the people of
Ammon, and for four,
I will not turn away its *punishment*,
Because they ripped open the women with
child in Gilead,
That they might enlarge their territory.
14But I will kindle a fire in the wall of Rabbah,
And it shall devour its palaces,
Amid shouting in the day of battle,
And a tempest in the day of the whirlwind.
15Their king shall go into captivity,
He and his princes together,"
Says the LORD.

2 Thus says the LORD:

"For three transgressions of Moab, and for
four,
I will not turn away its *punishment*,
Because he burned the bones of the king of
Edom to lime.
2But I will send a fire upon Moab,
And it shall devour the palaces of Kerioth;
Moab shall die with tumult,
With shouting *and* trumpet sound.
3And I will cut off the judge from its midst,
And slay all its princes with him,"
Says the LORD.

JUDGMENT ON JUDAH

4Thus says the LORD:

"For three transgressions of Judah, and for
four,
I will not turn away its *punishment*,
Because they have despised the law of the
LORD,
And have not kept His commandments.
Their lies lead them astray,
Lies which their fathers followed.
5But I will send a fire upon Judah,
And it shall devour the palaces of
Jerusalem."

JUDGMENT ON ISRAEL

6Thus says the LORD:

"For three transgressions of Israel, and for
four,
I will not turn away its *punishment*,

THE MESSAGE

11-12 GOD's Message:

"Because of the three great sins of Edom
—make that four—I'm not putting up
with her any longer.
She hunts down her brother to murder
him.
She has no pity, she has no heart.
Her anger rampages day and night.
Her meanness never takes a timeout.
For that, I'm burning down her capital,
Teman,
burning up the forts of Bozrah."

13-15 GOD's Message:

"Because of the three great sins of Ammon
—make that four—I'm not putting up
with her any longer.
She ripped open pregnant women in
Gilead
to get more land for herself.
For that, I'm burning down the walls of her
capital, Rabbah,
burning up her forts.
Battle shouts! War whoops!
with a tornado to finish things off!
The king has been carted off to exile,
the king and his princes with him."
GOD's Decree.

1-3 2 GOD's Message:

"Because of the three great sins of Moab
—make that four—I'm not putting up
with her any longer.
She violated the corpse of Edom's king,
burning it to cinders.
For that, I'm burning down Moab,
burning down the forts of Kerioth.
Moab will die in the shouting,
go out in the blare of war trumpets.
I'll remove the king from the center
and kill all his princes with him."
GOD's Decree.

4-5 GOD's Message:

"Because of the three great sins of Judah
—make that four—I'm not putting up
with them any longer.
They rejected GOD's revelation,
refused to keep my commands.
But they swallowed the same old lies
that got their ancestors onto dead-end
roads.
For that, I'm burning down Judah,
burning down all the forts of Jerusalem."

DESTROYED FROM THE ROOTS UP

6-8 GOD's Message:

"Because of the three great sins of Israel
—make that four—I'm not putting up
with them any longer.

NEW KING JAMES VERSION

Because they sell the righteous for silver,
And the poor for a pair of sandals.
7They pant after[a] the dust of the earth *which*
is on the head of the poor,
And pervert the way of the humble.
A man and his father go in to the *same* girl,
To defile My holy name.
8They lie down by every altar on clothes
taken in pledge,
And drink the wine of the condemned *in* the
house of their god.

9"Yet *it was* I *who* destroyed the Amorite
before them,
Whose height *was* like the height of the
cedars,
And he *was as* strong as the oaks;
Yet I destroyed his fruit above
And his roots beneath.
10Also *it was* I *who* brought you up from the
land of Egypt,
And led you forty years through the
wilderness,
To possess the land of the Amorite.
11I raised up some of your sons as prophets,
And some of your young men as Nazirites.
Is it not so, O you children of Israel?"
Says the LORD.
12"But you gave the Nazirites wine to drink,
And commanded the prophets saying,
'Do not prophesy!'

13"Behold, I am weighed down by you,
As a cart full of sheaves is weighed down.
14Therefore flight shall perish from the swift,
The strong shall not strengthen his power,
Nor shall the mighty deliver himself;
15He shall not stand who handles the bow,
The swift of foot shall not escape,
Nor shall he who rides a horse deliver
himself.
16The most courageous men of might
Shall flee naked in that day,"
Says the LORD.

AUTHORITY OF THE PROPHET'S MESSAGE

3 Hear this word that the LORD has spoken
against you, O children of Israel, against the
whole family which I brought up from the land
of Egypt, saying:

2:7 [a]Or *trample on*

THE MESSAGE

They buy and sell upstanding people.
People for them are only *things*—ways of
making money.
They'd sell a poor man for a pair of shoes.
They'd sell their own grandmother!
They grind the penniless into the dirt,
shove the luckless into the ditch.
Everyone and his brother sleeps with the
'sacred whore'—
a sacrilege against my Holy Name.
Stuff they've extorted from the poor
is piled up at the shrine of their god,
While they sit around drinking wine
they've conned from their victims.

9-11 "In contrast, I was always on your side.
I destroyed the Amorites who confronted
you,
Amorites with the stature of great cedars,
tough as thick oaks.
I destroyed them from the top branches
down.
I destroyed them from the roots up.
And yes, I'm the One who delivered you
from Egypt,
led you safely through the wilderness for
forty years
And then handed you the country of the
Amorites
like a piece of cake on a platter.
I raised up some of your young men to be
prophets,
set aside your best youth for training in
holiness.
Isn't this so, Israel?"
GOD's Decree.

12-13 "But you made the youth-in-training break
training,
and you told the young prophets, 'Don't
prophesy!'
You're too much for me.
I'm hard-pressed—to the breaking point.
I'm like a wagon piled high and over-
loaded,
creaking and groaning.

14-15 "When I go into action, what will you do?
There's no place to run no matter how
fast you run.
The strength of the strong won't count.
Fighters won't make it.
Skilled archers won't make it.
Fast runners won't make it.
Chariot drivers won't make it.
Even the bravest of all your warriors
Won't make it.
He'll run off for dear life, stripped
naked."
GOD's Decree.

THE LION HAS ROARED

1 3 Listen to this, Israel. GOD is calling you to
account—and I mean *all* of you, everyone
connected with the family that he delivered
out of Egypt. Listen!

NEW KING JAMES VERSION

2"You only have I known of all the families of
the earth;
Therefore I will punish you for all your
iniquities."

3Can two walk together, unless they are
agreed?
4Will a lion roar in the forest, when he has no
prey?
Will a young lion cry out of his den, if he
has caught nothing?
5Will a bird fall into a snare on the earth,
where there is no trap for it?
Will a snare spring up from the earth, if it
has caught nothing at all?
6If a trumpet is blown in a city, will not the
people be afraid?
If there is calamity in a city, will not the
LORD have done *it*?

7Surely the Lord GOD does nothing,
Unless He reveals His secret to His servants
the prophets.
8A lion has roared!
Who will not fear?
The Lord GOD has spoken!
Who can but prophesy?

PUNISHMENT OF ISRAEL'S SINS

9"Proclaim in the palaces at Ashdod,[a]
And in the palaces in the land of Egypt, and
say:
'Assemble on the mountains of Samaria;
See great tumults in her midst,
And the oppressed within her.
10For they do not know to do right,'
Says the LORD,
'Who store up violence and robbery in their
palaces.' "

11Therefore thus says the Lord GOD:

"An adversary *shall be* all around the land;
He shall sap your strength from you,
And your palaces shall be plundered."

12Thus says the LORD:

"As a shepherd takes from the mouth of a lion
Two legs or a piece of an ear,
So shall the children of Israel be taken out
Who dwell in Samaria—
In the corner of a bed and on the edge[a] of a
couch!
13Hear and testify against the house of Jacob,"
Says the Lord GOD, the God of hosts,
14"That in the day I punish Israel for their
transgressions,
I will also visit *destruction* on the altars of
Bethel;
And the horns of the altar shall be cut off
And fall to the ground.
15I will destroy the winter house along with
the summer house;
The houses of ivory shall perish,
And the great houses shall have an end,"
Says the LORD.

3:9 [a]Following Masoretic Text; Septuagint reads *Assyria.*
3:12 [a]The Hebrew is uncertain.

THE MESSAGE

2 "Out of all the families on earth,
I picked *you*.
Therefore, because of your special calling,
I'm holding you responsible for all your
sins."

3-7 Do two people walk hand in hand
if they aren't going to the same place?
Does a lion roar in the forest
if there's no carcass to devour?
Does a young lion growl with pleasure
if he hasn't caught his supper?
Does a bird fall to the ground
if it hasn't been hit with a stone?
Does a trap spring shut
if nothing trips it?
When the alarm goes off in the city,
aren't people alarmed?
And when disaster strikes the city,
doesn't GOD stand behind it?
The fact is, GOD, the Master, does nothing
without first telling his prophets the
whole story.

8 The lion has roared—
who isn't frightened?
GOD has spoken—
what prophet can keep quiet?

9-11 Announce to the forts of Assyria,
announce to the forts of Egypt—
Tell them, "Gather on the Samaritan
mountains, take a good, hard look:
what a snake pit of brutality and terror!
They can't—or won't—do one thing right."
GOD said so.
"They stockpile violence and blight.
Therefore"—this is GOD's Word—"an
enemy will surround the country.
He'll strip you of your power and
plunder your forts."

12 GOD's Message:

"In the same way that a shepherd
trying to save a lamb from a lion
Manages to recover
just a pair of legs or the scrap of an ear,
So will little be saved of the Israelites
who live in Samaria—
A couple of old chairs at most,
the broken leg of a table.

13-15 "Listen and bring witness against Jacob's
family"—
this is God's Word, GOD-of-the-Angel-
Armies!
"Note well! The day I make Israel pay for
its sins,
pay for the sin-altars of worship at
Bethel,
The horned altars will all be dehorned
and scattered around.
I'll tear down the winter palace,
smash the summer palace—all your
fancy buildings.
The luxury homes will be demolished,
all those pretentious houses."
GOD's Decree.

NEW KING JAMES VERSION

4 Hear this word, you cows of Bashan, who *are* on the mountain of Samaria,
Who oppress the poor,
Who crush the needy,
Who say to your husbands,[a] "Bring *wine*, let us drink!"
2The Lord GOD has sworn by His holiness:
"Behold, the days shall come upon you
When He will take you away with fishhooks,
And your posterity with fishhooks.
3You will go out *through* broken *walls*,
Each one straight ahead of her,
And you will be cast into Harmon,"
Says the LORD.

4"Come to Bethel and transgress,
At Gilgal multiply transgression;
Bring your sacrifices every morning,
Your tithes every three days.[a]
5Offer a sacrifice of thanksgiving with leaven,
Proclaim *and* announce the freewill offerings;
For this you love,
You children of Israel!"
Says the Lord GOD.

ISRAEL DID NOT ACCEPT CORRECTION

6"Also I gave you cleanness of teeth in all your cities,
And lack of bread in all your places;
Yet you have not returned to Me,"
Says the LORD.

7"I also withheld rain from you,
When *there were* still three months to the harvest.
I made it rain on one city,
I withheld rain from another city.
One part was rained upon,
And where it did not rain the part withered.
8So two *or* three cities wandered to another city to drink water,
But they were not satisfied;
Yet you have not returned to Me,"
Says the LORD.

9"I blasted you with blight and mildew.
When your gardens increased,
Your vineyards,
Your fig trees,
And your olive trees,
The locust devoured *them*;
Yet you have not returned to Me,"
Says the LORD.

10"I sent among you a plague after the manner of Egypt;
Your young men I killed with a sword,
Along with your captive horses;
I made the stench of your camps come up into your nostrils;
Yet you have not returned to Me,"
Says the LORD.

4:1 [a]Literally *their lords* or *their masters* 4:4 [a]Or *years* (compare Deuteronomy 14:28)

THE MESSAGE

YOU NEVER GOT HUNGRY FOR GOD

1 4 "Listen to this, you cows of Bashan
grazing on the slopes of Samaria.
You women! Mean to the poor,
cruel to the down-and-out!
Indolent and pampered, you demand of your husbands,
'Bring us a tall, cool drink!'

2-3 "This is serious—I, GOD, have sworn by my holiness!
Be well warned: Judgment Day is coming!
They're going to rope you up and haul you off,
keep the stragglers in line with cattle prods.
They'll drag you through the ruined city walls,
forcing you out single file,
And kick you to kingdom come."
GOD's Decree.

4-5 "Come along to Bethel and sin!
And then to Gilgal and sin some more!
Bring your sacrifices for morning worship.
Every third day bring your tithe.
Burn pure sacrifices—thank offerings.
Speak up—announce freewill offerings!
That's the sort of religious show
you Israelites just love."
GOD's Decree.

6 "You know, don't you, that I'm the One
who emptied your pantries and cleaned out your cupboards,
Who left you hungry and standing in bread lines?
But you never got hungry for me. You continued to ignore me."
GOD's Decree.

7-8 "Yes, and I'm the One who stopped the rains
three months short of harvest.
I'd make it rain on one village
but not on another.
I'd make it rain on one field
but not on another—and that one would dry up.
People would stagger from village to village
crazed for water and never quenching their thirst.
But you never got thirsty for me.
You ignored me."
GOD's Decree.

9 "I hit your crops with disease
and withered your orchards and gardens.
Locusts devoured your olive and fig trees,
but you continued to ignore me."
GOD's Decree.

10 "I revisited you with the old Egyptian plagues,
killed your choice young men and prize horses.
The stink of rot in your camps was so strong
that you held your noses—
But you didn't notice me.
You continued to ignore me."
GOD's Decree.

NEW KING JAMES VERSION

11"I overthrew *some* of you,
As God overthrew Sodom and Gomorrah,
And you were like a firebrand plucked from the burning;
Yet you have not returned to Me,"
Says the LORD.

12"Therefore thus will I do to you, O Israel;
Because I will do this to you,
Prepare to meet your God, O Israel!"

13For behold,
He who forms mountains,
And creates the wind,
Who declares to man what his[a] thought *is*,
And makes the morning darkness,
Who treads the high places of the earth—
The LORD God of hosts *is* His name.

A LAMENT FOR ISRAEL

5 Hear this word which I take up against you,
a lamentation, O house of Israel:

2The virgin of Israel has fallen;
She will rise no more.
She lies forsaken on her land;
There is no one to raise her up.

3For thus says the Lord GOD:

"The city that goes out by a thousand
Shall have a hundred left,
And that which goes out by a hundred
Shall have ten left to the house of Israel."

A CALL TO REPENTANCE

4For thus says the LORD to the house of Is-
rael:

"Seek Me and live;
5But do not seek Bethel,
Nor enter Gilgal,
Nor pass over to Beersheba;
For Gilgal shall surely go into captivity,
And Bethel shall come to nothing.
6Seek the LORD and live,
Lest He break out like fire *in* the house of Joseph,
And devour *it*,
With no one to quench *it* in Bethel—
7You who turn justice to wormwood,
And lay righteousness to rest in the earth!"

8He made the Pleiades and Orion;
He turns the shadow of death into morning
And makes the day dark as night;
He calls for the waters of the sea
And pours them out on the face of the earth;

4:13 [a]Or *His*

THE MESSAGE

11 "I hit you with earthquake and fire,
left you devastated like Sodom and Gomorrah.
You were like a burning stick
snatched from the flames.
But you never looked my way.
You continued to ignore me."
GOD'S Decree.

12 "All this I have done to you, Israel,
and this is why I have done it.
Time's up, O Israel!
Prepare to meet your God!"

13 Look who's here: Mountain-Shaper! Wind-Maker!
He laid out the whole plot before Adam.
He brings everything out of nothing,
like dawn out of darkness.
He strides across the alpine ridges.
His name is GOD, God-of-the-Angel-Armies.

ALL SHOW, NO SUBSTANCE

1 5 Listen to this, family of Israel,
this Message I'm sending in bold print,
this tragic warning:

2 "Virgin Israel has fallen flat on her face.
She'll never stand up again.
She's been left where she's fallen.
No one offers to help her up."

3 This is the Message, GOD'S Word:

"The city that marches out with a thousand
will end up with a hundred.
The city that marches out with a hundred
will end up with ten. Oh, family of Israel!"

4-5 GOD'S Message to the family of Israel:
"Seek me and live.
Don't fool around at those shrines of Bethel,
Don't waste time taking trips to Gilgal,
and don't bother going down to Beer-sheba.
Gilgal is here today and gone tomorrow
and Bethel is all show, no substance."

6 So seek GOD and live! You don't want to end up
with nothing to show for your life
But a pile of ashes, a house burned to the ground.
For God will send just such a fire,
and the firefighters will show up too late.

RAW TRUTH IS NEVER POPULAR

7-9 Woe to you who turn justice to vinegar
and stomp righteousness into the mud.
Do you realize where you are? You're in a cosmos
star-flung with constellations by God,
A world God wakes up each morning
and puts to bed each night.
God dips water from the ocean
and gives the land a drink.

NEW KING JAMES VERSION

The LORD *is* His name.
9He rains ruin upon the strong,
So that fury comes upon the fortress.

10They hate the one who rebukes in the gate,
And they abhor the one who speaks uprightly.
11Therefore, because you tread down the poor
And take grain taxes from him,
Though you have built houses of hewn stone,
Yet you shall not dwell in them;
You have planted pleasant vineyards,
But you shall not drink wine from them.
12For I know your manifold transgressions
And your mighty sins:
Afflicting the just *and* taking bribes;
Diverting the poor *from justice* at the gate.
13Therefore the prudent keep silent at that time,
For it *is* an evil time.

14Seek good and not evil,
That you may live;
So the LORD God of hosts will be with you,
As you have spoken.
15Hate evil, love good;
Establish justice in the gate.
It may be that the LORD God of hosts
Will be gracious to the remnant of Joseph.

THE DAY OF THE LORD

16Therefore the LORD God of hosts, the Lord,
says this:

"*There shall be* wailing in all streets,
And they shall say in all the highways,
'Alas! Alas!'
They shall call the farmer to mourning,
And skillful lamenters to wailing.
17In all vineyards *there shall be* wailing,
For I will pass through you,"
Says the LORD.

18Woe to you who desire the day of the LORD!
For what good *is* the day of the LORD to you?
It *will be* darkness, and not light.
19It *will be* as though a man fled from a lion,
And a bear met him!
Or *as though* he went into the house,
Leaned his hand on the wall,
And a serpent bit him!

THE MESSAGE

GOD, God-revealed, does all this.
And he can destroy it as easily as make it.
He can turn this vast wonder into total waste.

10-12 People hate this kind of talk.
Raw truth is never popular.
But here it is, bluntly spoken:
Because you run roughshod over the poor
and take the bread right out of their mouths,
You're never going to move into
the luxury homes you have built.
You're never going to drink wine
from the expensive vineyards you've planted.
I know precisely the extent of your violations,
the enormity of your sins. Appalling!
You bully right-living people,
taking bribes right and left and kicking the poor when they're down.

13 Justice is a lost cause. Evil is epidemic.
Decent people throw up their hands.
Protest and rebuke are useless,
a waste of breath.

14 Seek good and not evil—
and live!
You talk about GOD, the God-of-the-Angel-Armies,
being your best friend.
Well, *live like it*,
and maybe it will happen.

15 Hate evil and love good,
then work it out in the public square.
Maybe GOD, the God-of-the-Angel-Armies,
will notice your remnant and be gracious.

16-17 Now again, my Master's Message, GOD,
God-of-the-Angel-Armies:

"Go out into the streets and lament loudly!
Fill the malls and shops with cries of doom!
Weep loudly, 'Not me! Not us, Not now!'
Empty offices, stores, factories, workplaces.
Enlist everyone in the general lament.
I want to hear it loud and clear when I make my visit."
GOD's Decree.

TIME TO FACE HARD REALITY, NOT FANTASY

18-20 Woe to all of you who want GOD's Judgment Day!
Why would you want to see GOD, want him to come?
When GOD comes, it will be bad news before it's good news,
the worst of times, not the best of times.
Here's what it's like: A man runs from a lion
right into the jaws of a bear.
A woman goes home after a hard day's work
and is raped by a neighbor.

NEW KING JAMES VERSION

20*Is* not the day of the LORD darkness, and not light?
Is it not very dark, with no brightness in it?

21"I hate, I despise your feast days,
And I do not savor your sacred assemblies.
22Though you offer Me burnt offerings and your grain offerings,
I will not accept *them,*
Nor will I regard your fattened peace offerings.
23Take away from Me the noise of your songs,
For I will not hear the melody of your stringed instruments.
24But let justice run down like water,
And righteousness like a mighty stream.

25"Did you offer Me sacrifices and offerings
In the wilderness forty years, O house of Israel?
26You also carried Sikkuth[a] your king[b]
And Chiun,[c] your idols,
The star of your gods,
Which you made for yourselves.
27Therefore I will send you into captivity beyond Damascus,"
Says the LORD, whose name *is* the God of hosts.

WARNINGS TO ZION AND SAMARIA

6 Woe to you *who are* at ease in Zion,
And trust in Mount Samaria,
Notable persons in the chief nation,
To whom the house of Israel comes!
2Go over to Calneh and see;
And from there go to Hamath the great;
Then go down to Gath of the Philistines.
Are you better than these kingdoms?
Or is their territory greater than your territory?

3*Woe to* you who put far off the day of doom,
Who cause the seat of violence to come near;
4Who lie on beds of ivory,
Stretch out on your couches,
Eat lambs from the flock
And calves from the midst of the stall;
5Who sing idly to the sound of stringed instruments,
And invent for yourselves musical instruments like David;
6Who drink wine from bowls,
And anoint yourselves with the best ointments,
But are not grieved for the affliction of Joseph.
7Therefore they shall now go captive as the first of the captives,
And those who recline at banquets shall be removed.

5:26 [a]A pagan deity [b]Septuagint and Vulgate read *tabernacle of Moloch.* [c]A pagan deity

THE MESSAGE

At GOD's coming we face hard reality, not fantasy—
a black cloud with no silver lining.

21-24 "I can't stand your religious meetings.
I'm fed up with your conferences and conventions.
I want nothing to do with your religion projects,
your pretentious slogans and goals.
I'm sick of your fund-raising schemes,
your public relations and image making.
I've had all I can take of your noisy ego-music.
When was the last time you sang to *me*?
Do you know what I want?
I want justice—oceans of it.
I want fairness—rivers of it.
That's what I want. That's *all* I want.

25-27 "Didn't you, dear family of Israel, worship me faithfully for forty years in the wilderness, bringing the sacrifices and offerings I commanded? How is it you've stooped to dragging gimcrack statues of your so-called rulers around, hauling the cheap images of all your star-gods here and there? Since you like them so much, you can take them with you when I drive you into exile beyond Damascus." GOD's Message, God-of-the-Angel-Armies.

THOSE WHO LIVE ONLY FOR TODAY

1-2 6 Woe to you who think you live on easy street in Zion,
who think Mount Samaria is the good life.
You assume you're at the top of the heap,
voted the number-one best place to live.
Well, wake up and look around. Get off your pedestal.
Take a look at Calneh.
Go and visit Great Hamath.
Look in on Gath of the Philistines.
Doesn't that take you off your high horse?
Compared to them, you're not much, are you?

3-6 Woe to you who are rushing headlong to disaster!
Catastrophe is just around the corner!
Woe to those who live in luxury
and expect everyone else to serve them!
Woe to those who live only for today,
indifferent to the fate of others!
Woe to the playboys, the playgirls,
who think life is a party held just for them!
Woe to those addicted to feeling good—life without pain!
those obsessed with looking good—life without wrinkles!
They could not care less
about their country going to ruin.

7 But here's what's *really coming:*
a forced march into exile.
They'll leave the country whining,
a rag-tag bunch of good-for-nothings.

NEW KING JAMES VERSION

8 The Lord GOD has sworn by Himself,
The LORD God of hosts says:
"I abhor the pride of Jacob,
And hate his palaces;
Therefore I will deliver up *the* city
And all that is in it."

9 Then it shall come to pass, that if ten men
remain in one house, they shall die. 10 And when
a relative *of the dead,* with one who will burn
the bodies, picks up the bodies[a] to take them out
of the house, he will say to one inside the house,
"*Are there* any more with you?"
Then someone will say, "None."
And he will say, "Hold your tongue! For we
dare not mention the name of the LORD."

11 For behold, the LORD gives a command:
He will break the great house into bits,
And the little house into pieces.

12 Do horses run on rocks?
Does *one* plow *there* with oxen?
Yet you have turned justice into gall,
And the fruit of righteousness into wormwood,
13 You who rejoice over Lo Debar,[a]
Who say, "Have we not taken Karnaim[b] for ourselves
By our own strength?"

14 "But, behold, I will raise up a nation against you,
O house of Israel,"
Says the LORD God of hosts;
"And they will afflict you from the entrance of Hamath
To the Valley of the Arabah."

VISION OF THE LOCUSTS

7 Thus the Lord GOD showed me: Behold, He
formed locust swarms at the beginning of the
late crop; indeed *it was* the late crop after the
king's mowings. 2 And so it was, when they had
finished eating the grass of the land, that I said:

"O Lord GOD, forgive, I pray!
Oh, that Jacob may stand,
For he *is* small!"
3 So the LORD relented concerning this.
"It shall not be," said the LORD.

VISION OF THE FIRE

4 Thus the Lord GOD showed me: Behold, the
Lord GOD called for conflict by fire, and it con-
sumed the great deep and devoured the terri-
tory. 5 Then I said:

"O Lord GOD, cease, I pray!
Oh, that Jacob may stand,
For he *is* small!"
6 So the LORD relented concerning this.
"This also shall not be," said the Lord GOD.

6:10 [a]Literally *bones* **6:13** [a]Literally *Nothing* [b]Literally *Horns,* symbol of strength

THE MESSAGE

YOU'VE MADE A SHAMBLES OF JUSTICE

8 GOD, the Master, has sworn, and solemnly stands by his Word.
The God-of-the-Angel-Armies speaks:

"I hate the arrogance of Jacob.
I have nothing but contempt for his forts.
I'm about to hand over the city
and everyone in it."

9-10 Ten men are in a house, all dead. A relative comes and gets the bodies to prepare them for a decent burial. He discovers a survivor huddled in a closet and asks, "Are there any more?" The answer: "Not a soul. But hush! GOD must not be mentioned in this desecrated place."

11 Note well: God issues the orders.
He'll knock large houses to smithereens.
He'll smash little houses to bits.

12-13 Do you hold a horse race in a field of rocks?
Do you plow the sea with oxen?
You'd cripple the horses
and drown the oxen.
And yet you've made a shambles of justice,
a bloated corpse of righteousness,
Bragging of your trivial pursuits,
beating up on the weak and crowing,
"Look what I've done!"

14 "Enjoy it while you can, you Israelites.
I've got a pagan army on the move against you"
—this is your GOD speaking, God-of-the-Angel-Armies—
"And they'll make hash of you,
from one end of the country to the other."

TO DIE HOMELESS AND FRIENDLESS

1-2 7 GOD, my Master, showed me this vision: He was preparing a locust swarm. The first cutting, which went to the king, was complete, and the second crop was just sprouting. The locusts ate everything green. Not even a blade of grass was left.
I called out, "GOD, my Master! Excuse me, but what's going to come of Jacob? He's so small."
3 GOD gave in.
"It won't happen," he said.

4 GOD showed me this vision: Oh! GOD, my Master GOD was calling up a firestorm. It burned up the ocean. Then it burned up the Promised Land.
5 I said, "GOD, my Master! Hold it—please! What's going to come of Jacob? He's so small."
6 GOD gave in.
"All right, this won't happen either," GOD, my Master, said.

New King James Version

Vision of the Plumb Line

7 Thus He showed me: Behold, the Lord stood
on a wall *made* with a plumb line, with a plumb
line in His hand. 8 And the LORD said to me,
"Amos, what do you see?"

And I said, "A plumb line."
Then the Lord said:

"Behold, I am setting a plumb line
In the midst of My people Israel;
I will not pass by them anymore.
9 The high places of Isaac shall be desolate,
And the sanctuaries of Israel shall be laid
waste.
I will rise with the sword against the house
of Jeroboam."

Amaziah's Complaint

10 Then Amaziah the priest of Bethel sent to
Jeroboam king of Israel, saying, "Amos has con-
spired against you in the midst of the house of
Israel. The land is not able to bear all his words.
11 For thus Amos has said:

'Jeroboam shall die by the sword,
And Israel shall surely be led away captive
From their own land.' "

12 Then Amaziah said to Amos:

"Go, you seer!
Flee to the land of Judah.
There eat bread,
And there prophesy.
13 But never again prophesy at Bethel,
For it *is* the king's sanctuary,
And it *is* the royal residence."

14 Then Amos answered, and said to Amaziah:

"I *was* no prophet,
Nor *was* I a son of a prophet,
But I *was* a sheepbreeder[a]
And a tender of sycamore fruit.
15 Then the LORD took me as I followed the
flock,
And the LORD said to me,
'Go, prophesy to My people Israel.'
16 Now therefore, hear the word of the LORD:
You say, 'Do not prophesy against Israel,
And do not spout against the house of
Isaac.'

17 "Therefore thus says the LORD:

'Your wife shall be a harlot in the city;
Your sons and daughters shall fall by the
sword;
Your land shall be divided by *survey* line;
You shall die in a defiled land;
And Israel shall surely be led away captive
From his own land.' "

Vision of the Summer Fruit

8 Thus the Lord GOD showed me: Behold, a
basket of summer fruit. 2 And He said, "Amos,
what do you see?"

7:14 [a]Compare 2 Kings 3:4

The Message

7 GOD showed me this vision: My Master was
standing beside a wall. In his hand he held a
plumb line.

8-9 GOD said to me, "What do you see, Amos?"
I said, "A plumb line."
Then my Master said, "Look what I've
done. I've hung a plumb line in the midst of
my people Israel. I've spared them for the
last time. This is it!

"Isaac's sex-and-religion shrines will be
smashed,
Israel's unholy shrines will be knocked
to pieces.
I'm raising my sword against the royal
family of Jeroboam."

10 Amaziah, priest at the shrine at Bethel, sent a
message to Jeroboam, king of Israel:
"Amos is plotting to get rid of you; and
he's doing it as an insider, working from
within Israel. His talk will destroy the coun-
try. He's got to be silenced. Do you know
what Amos is saying?

11 'Jeroboam will be killed.
Israel is headed for exile.'

12-13 Then Amaziah confronted Amos: "Seer, be
on your way! Get out of here and go back to Ju-
dah where you came from! Hang out there. Do
your preaching there. But no more preaching at
Bethel! Don't show your face here again. This is
the king's chapel. This is a royal shrine."

14-15 But Amos stood up to Amaziah: "I never
set up to be a preacher, never had plans to
be a preacher. I raised cattle and I pruned
trees. Then GOD took me off the farm and
said, 'Go preach to my people Israel.'

16-17 "So listen to GOD's Word. You tell me,
'Don't preach to Israel. Don't say anything
against the family of Isaac.' But here's what
GOD is telling you:

Your wife will become a whore in town.
Your children will get killed.
Your land will be auctioned off.
You will die homeless and friendless.
And Israel will be hauled off to exile, far
from *home*."

You Who Give Little and Take Much

1 8 My Master GOD showed me this vision: A
bowl of fresh fruit.

2 He said, "What do you see, Amos?"

NEW KING JAMES VERSION

So I said, "A basket of summer fruit."
Then the LORD said to me:

"The end has come upon My people Israel;
I will not pass by them anymore.
3And the songs of the temple
Shall be wailing in that day,"
Says the Lord GOD—
"Many dead bodies everywhere,
They shall be thrown out in silence."

4Hear this, you who swallow up[a] the needy,
And make the poor of the land fail,

5Saying:

"When will the New Moon be past,
That we may sell grain?
And the Sabbath,
That we may trade wheat?
Making the ephah small and the shekel
large,
Falsifying the scales by deceit,
6That we may buy the poor for silver,
And the needy for a pair of sandals—
Even sell the bad wheat?"

7The LORD has sworn by the pride of Jacob:
"Surely I will never forget any of their works.
8Shall the land not tremble for this,
And everyone mourn who dwells in it?
All of it shall swell like the River,[a]
Heave and subside
Like the River of Egypt.

9"And it shall come to pass in that day," says
the Lord GOD,
"That I will make the sun go down at noon,
And I will darken the earth in broad
daylight;
10I will turn your feasts into mourning,
And all your songs into lamentation;
I will bring sackcloth on every waist,
And baldness on every head;
I will make it like mourning for an only *son*,
And its end like a bitter day.

11"Behold, the days are coming," says the Lord
GOD,
"That I will send a famine on the land,
Not a famine of bread,
Nor a thirst for water,
But of hearing the words of the LORD.
12They shall wander from sea to sea,
And from north to east;
They shall run to and fro, seeking the word
of the LORD,
But shall not find *it*.

13"In that day the fair virgins
And strong young men
Shall faint from thirst.

8:4 [a]Or *trample on* (compare 2:7) **8:8** [a]That is, the Nile; some Hebrew manuscripts, Septuagint, Syriac, Targum, and Vulgate read *River;* Masoretic Text reads *the light*.

THE MESSAGE

I said, "A bowl of fresh, ripe fruit."
GOD said, "Right. So, I'm calling it quits with my people Israel. I'm no longer acting as if everything is just fine."

3 "The royal singers will wail when it happens."
My Master GOD said so.
"Corpses will be strewn here, there, and
everywhere.
Hush!"

4-6 Listen to this, you who walk all over the weak,
you who treat poor people as less than
nothing,
Who say, "When's my next paycheck
coming
so I can go out and live it up?
How long till the weekend
when I can go out and have a good
time?"
Who give little and take much,
and never do an honest day's work.
You exploit the poor, using them—
and then, when they're used up, you
discard them.

7-8 GOD swears against the arrogance of Jacob:
"I'm keeping track of their every last
sin."
God's oath will shake earth's foundations,
dissolve the whole world into tears.
God's oath will sweep in like a river that
rises,
flooding houses and lands,
And then recedes,
leaving behind a sea of mud.

9-10 "On Judgment Day, watch out!"
These are the words of GOD, my Master.
"I'll turn off the sun at noon.
In the middle of the day the earth will go
black.
I'll turn your parties into funerals
and make every song you sing a dirge.
Everyone will walk around in rags,
with sunken eyes and bald heads.
Think of the worst that could happen
—your only son, say, murdered.
That's a hint of Judgment Day
—that and much more.

11-12 "Oh yes, Judgment Day is coming!"
These are the words of my Master GOD.
"I'll send a famine through the whole
country.
It won't be food or water that's lacking,
but my Word.
People will drift from one end of the
country to the other,
roam to the north, wander to the east.
They'll go anywhere, listen to anyone,
hoping to hear GOD's Word—but they
won't hear it.

13-14 "On Judgment Day,
lovely young girls will faint of
Word-thirst,
robust young men will faint of
God-thirst,

NEW KING JAMES VERSION

14Those who swear by the sin[a] of Samaria,
Who say,
'As your god lives, O Dan!'
And, 'As the way of Beersheba lives!'
They shall fall and never rise again."

THE DESTRUCTION OF ISRAEL

9 I saw the Lord standing by the altar, and He said:

"Strike the doorposts, that the thresholds may shake,
And break them on the heads of them all.
I will slay the last of them with the sword.
He who flees from them shall not get away,
And he who escapes from them shall not be delivered.

2"Though they dig into hell,[a]
From there My hand shall take them;
Though they climb up to heaven,
From there I will bring them down;
3And though they hide themselves on top of Carmel,
From there I will search and take them;
Though they hide from My sight at the bottom of the sea,
From there I will command the serpent, and it shall bite them;
4Though they go into captivity before their enemies,
From there I will command the sword,
And it shall slay them.
I will set My eyes on them for harm and not for good."

5The Lord GOD of hosts,
He who touches the earth and it melts,
And all who dwell there mourn;
All of it shall swell like the River,[a]
And subside like the River of Egypt.
6He who builds His layers in the sky,
And has founded His strata in the earth;
Who calls for the waters of the sea,
And pours them out on the face of the earth—
The LORD *is* His name.

7"*Are* you not like the people of Ethiopia to Me,
O children of Israel?" says the LORD.
"Did I not bring up Israel from the land of Egypt,
The Philistines from Caphtor,
And the Syrians from Kir?

8"Behold, the eyes of the Lord GOD *are* on the sinful kingdom,
And I will destroy it from the face of the earth;
Yet I will not utterly destroy the house of Jacob,"
Says the LORD.

8:14 [a]Or *Ashima*, a Syrian goddess 9:2 [a]Or *Sheol* 9:5 [a]That is, the Nile

THE MESSAGE

Along with those who take oaths at the Samaria Sin-and-Sex Center,
saying, 'As the lord god of Dan is my witness!'
and 'The lady goddess of Beer-sheba bless you!'
Their lives will fall to pieces.
They'll never put it together again."

ISRAEL THROWN INTO A SIEVE

1-4 9 I saw my Master standing beside the altar at the shrine. He said:

"Hit the tops of the shrine's pillars,
make the floor shake.
The roof's about to fall on the heads of the people,
and whoever's still alive, I'll kill.
No one will get away,
no runaways will make it.
If they dig their way down into the underworld,
I'll find them and bring them up.
If they climb to the stars,
I'll find them and bring them down.
If they hide out at the top of Mount Carmel,
I'll find them and bring them back.
If they dive to the bottom of the ocean,
I'll send Dragon to swallow them up.
If they're captured alive by their enemies,
I'll send Sword to kill them.
I've made up my mind
to hurt them, not help them."

5-6 My Master, God-of-the-Angel-Armies,
touches the earth, a mere touch, and it trembles.
The whole world goes into mourning.
Earth swells like the Nile at flood stage;
then the water subsides, like the great Nile of Egypt.
God builds his palace—towers soaring high in the skies,
foundations set on the rock-firm earth.
He calls ocean waters and they come,
then he ladles them out on the earth.
GOD, your God, does all this.

7-8 "Do you Israelites think you're any better
than the far-off Cushites?" GOD's Decree.
"Am I not involved with all nations? Didn't
I bring Israel up from Egypt, the Philistines
from Caphtor, the Arameans from Qir? But
you can be sure that I, GOD, the Master, have
my eye on the Kingdom of Sin. I'm going to
wipe it off the face of the earth. Still, I won't
totally destroy the family of Jacob." GOD's
Decree.

NEW KING JAMES VERSION

9"For surely I will command,
And will sift the house of Israel among all nations,
As *grain* is sifted in a sieve;
Yet not the smallest grain shall fall to the ground.
10All the sinners of My people shall die by the sword,
Who say, 'The calamity shall not overtake nor confront us.'

ISRAEL WILL BE RESTORED

11"On that day I will raise up
The tabernacle[a] of David, which has fallen down,
And repair its damages;
I will raise up its ruins,
And rebuild it as in the days of old;
12That they may possess the remnant of Edom,[a]
And all the Gentiles who are called by My name,"
Says the LORD who does this thing.

13"Behold, the days are coming," says the LORD,
"When the plowman shall overtake the reaper,
And the treader of grapes him who sows seed;
The mountains shall drip with sweet wine,
And all the hills shall flow *with it.*
14I will bring back the captives of My people Israel;
They shall build the waste cities and inhabit *them;*
They shall plant vineyards and drink wine from them;
They shall also make gardens and eat fruit from them.
15I will plant them in their land,
And no longer shall they be pulled up
From the land I have given them,"
Says the LORD your God.

9:11 [a]Literally *booth,* figure of a deposed dynasty **9:12** [a]Septuagint reads *mankind.*

THE MESSAGE

9-10 "I'm still giving the orders around here. I'm
throwing Israel into a sieve among all the na-
tions and shaking them good, shaking out all the
sin, all the sinners. No real grain will be lost, but
all the sinners will be sifted out and thrown
away, the people who say, 'Nothing bad will ever
happen in our lifetime. It won't even come close.'

BLESSINGS LIKE WINE POURING OFF THE MOUNTAINS

11-12 "But also on that Judgment Day I will re-
store David's house that has fallen to pieces.
I'll repair the holes in the roof, replace the
broken windows, fix it up like new. David's
people will be strong again and seize what's
left of enemy Edom, plus everyone else un-
der my sovereign judgment." GOD's Decree.
He will do this.
13-15 "Yes indeed, it won't be long now." GOD's
Decree.
"Things are going to happen so fast your
head will swim, one thing fast on the heels
of the other. You won't be able to keep up.
Everything will be happening at once—and
everywhere you look, blessings! Blessings
like wine pouring off the mountains and
hills. I'll make everything right again for my
people Israel:

"They'll rebuild their ruined cities.
They'll plant vineyards and drink good wine.
They'll work their gardens and eat fresh vegetables.
And I'll plant *them,* plant them on their own land.
They'll never again be uprooted from the land I've given them."

GOD, your God, says so.

OBADIAH

NEW KING JAMES VERSION

THE COMING JUDGMENT ON EDOM

The vision of Obadiah.

Thus says the Lord GOD concerning Edom
(We have heard a report from the LORD,
And a messenger has been sent among the nations, *saying,*
"Arise, and let us rise up against her for battle"):

2"Behold, I will make you small among the nations;
You shall be greatly despised.
3The pride of your heart has deceived you,
You who dwell in the clefts of the rock,
Whose habitation is high;
You who say in your heart, 'Who will bring me down to the ground?'
4Though you ascend *as* high as the eagle,
And though you set your nest among the stars,
From there I will bring you down," says the LORD.

5"If thieves had come to you,
If robbers by night—
Oh, how you will be cut off!—
Would they not have stolen till they had enough?
If grape-gatherers had come to you,
Would they not have left *some* gleanings?
6"Oh, how Esau shall be searched out!
How his hidden treasures shall be sought after!
7All the men in your confederacy
Shall force you to the border;
The men at peace with you
Shall deceive you *and* prevail against you.
Those who eat your bread shall lay a trap[a] for you.
No one is aware of it.

8"Will I not in that day," says the LORD,
"Even destroy the wise *men* from Edom,
And understanding from the mountains of Esau?
9Then your mighty men, O Teman, shall be dismayed,
To the end that everyone from the mountains of Esau
May be cut off by slaughter.

EDOM MISTREATED HIS BROTHER

10"For violence against your brother Jacob,
Shame shall cover you,
And you shall be cut off forever.
11In the day that you stood on the other side—
In the day that strangers carried captive his forces,
When foreigners entered his gates
And cast lots for Jerusalem—
Even you *were* as one of them.

7 [a]Or *wound,* or *plot*

THE MESSAGE

YOUR WORLD WILL COLLAPSE

1 Obadiah's Message to Edom
from GOD, the Master.
We got the news straight from GOD
by a special messenger sent out to the godless nations:

"On your feet, prepare for battle;
get ready to make war on Edom!"

2-4 "Listen to this, Edom:
I'm turning you to a no-account,
the runt of the godless nations, despised.
You thought you were so great,
perched high among the rocks, king of the mountain,
Thinking to yourself,
'Nobody can get to me! Nobody can touch me!'
Think again. Even if, like an eagle,
you hang out on a high cliff-face,
Even if you build your nest in the stars,
I'll bring you down to earth."
GOD's sure Word.

5-14 "If thieves crept up on you,
they'd rob you blind—isn't that so?
If they mugged you on the streets at night,
they'd pick you clean—isn't that so?
Oh, they'll take Esau apart, piece by piece,
empty his purse and pockets.
All your old partners will drive you to the edge.
Your old friends will lie to your face.
Your old drinking buddies will stab you in the back.
Your world will collapse. You won't know what hit you.
So don't be surprised"—it's GOD's sure Word!—
"when I wipe out all sages from Edom
and rid the Esau mountains of its famous wise men.
Your great heroes will desert you, Teman.
There'll be nobody left in Esau's mountains.
Because of the murderous history compiled against your brother Jacob,
You will be looked down on by everyone.
You'll lose your place in history.
On that day you stood there and didn't do anything.
Strangers took your brother's army into exile.
Godless foreigners invaded and pillaged Jerusalem.
You stood there and watched.
You were as bad as they were.

New King James Version

12“But you should not have gazed on the day of
your brother
In the day of his captivity;[a]
Nor should you have rejoiced over the
children of Judah
In the day of their destruction;
Nor should you have spoken proudly
In the day of distress.
13You should not have entered the gate of My
people
In the day of their calamity.
Indeed, you should not have gazed on their
affliction
In the day of their calamity,
Nor laid *hands* on their substance
In the day of their calamity.
14You should not have stood at the crossroads
To cut off those among them who escaped;
Nor should you have delivered up those
among them who remained
In the day of distress.

15“For the day of the LORD upon all the nations
is near;
As you have done, it shall be done to you;
Your reprisal shall return upon your own
head.
16For as you drank on My holy mountain,
So shall all the nations drink continually;
Yes, they shall drink, and swallow,
And they shall be as though they had never
been.

Israel's Final Triumph

17“But on Mount Zion there shall be
deliverance,
And there shall be holiness;
The house of Jacob shall possess their
possessions.
18The house of Jacob shall be a fire,
And the house of Joseph a flame;
But the house of Esau *shall be* stubble;
They shall kindle them and devour them,
And no survivor shall *remain* of the house
of Esau,”
For the LORD has spoken.

19The South[a] shall possess the mountains of
Esau,
And the Lowland shall possess Philistia.
They shall possess the fields of Ephraim
And the fields of Samaria.
Benjamin *shall possess* Gilead.
20And the captives of this host of the children
of Israel
Shall possess the land of the Canaanites
As far as Zarephath.
The captives of Jerusalem who are in
Sepharad
Shall possess the cities of the South.[a]
21Then saviors[a] shall come to Mount Zion
To judge the mountains of Esau,
And the kingdom shall be the LORD's.

12 [a]Literally *on the day he became a foreigner* **19** [a]Hebrew *Negev* **20** [a]Hebrew *Negev* **21** [a]Or *deliverers*

The Message

You shouldn't have gloated over your
brother
when he was down-and-out.
You shouldn't have laughed and joked at
Judah's sons
when they were facedown in the mud.
You shouldn't have talked so big
when everything was so bad.
You shouldn't have taken advantage of my
people
when their lives had fallen apart.
You of all people should not have been
amused
by their troubles, their wrecked nation.
You shouldn't have taken the shirt off their
back
when they were knocked flat,
defenseless.
And you shouldn't have stood waiting at
the outskirts
and cut off refugees,
And traitorously turned in helpless survivors
who had lost everything.

15-18 “GOD's Judgment Day is near
for all the godless nations.
As you have done, it will be done to you.
What you did will boomerang back
and hit your own head.
Just as you partied on my holy mountain,
all the godless nations will drink God's
wrath.
They'll drink and drink and drink—
they'll drink themselves to death.
But not so on Mount Zion—there's respite
there!
a safe and holy place!
The family of Jacob will take back their
possessions
from those who took them from them.
That's when the family of Jacob will catch
fire,
the family of Joseph become fierce
flame,
while the family of Esau will be straw.
Esau will go up in flames,
nothing left of Esau but a pile of ashes.”
GOD said it, and it is so.

19-21 People from the south will take over the
Esau mountains;
people from the foothills will overrun the
Philistines.
They'll take the farms of Ephraim and
Samaria,
and Benjamin will take Gilead.
Earlier, Israelite exiles will come back
and take Canaanite land to the north at
Zarephath.
Jerusalem exiles from the far northwest in
Sepharad
will come back and take the cities in the
south.
The remnant of the saved in Mount Zion
will go into the mountains of Esau
And rule justly and fairly,
a rule that honors GOD's kingdom.

JONAH

New King James Version

Jonah's Disobedience

1 Now the word of the LORD came to Jonah the son of Amittai, saying, 2"Arise, go to Nineveh, that great city, and cry out against it; for their wickedness has come up before Me." 3But Jonah arose to flee to Tarshish from the presence of the LORD. He went down to Joppa, and found a ship going to Tarshish; so he paid the fare, and went down into it, to go with them to Tarshish from the presence of the LORD.

The Storm at Sea

4But the LORD sent out a great wind on the sea, and there was a mighty tempest on the sea, so that the ship was about to be broken up.

5Then the mariners were afraid; and every man cried out to his god, and threw the cargo that *was* in the ship into the sea, to lighten the load.[a] But Jonah had gone down into the lowest parts of the ship, had lain down, and was fast asleep.

6So the captain came to him, and said to him, "What do you mean, sleeper? Arise, call on your God; perhaps your God will consider us, so that we may not perish."

7And they said to one another, "Come, let us cast lots, that we may know for whose cause this trouble *has come* upon us." So they cast lots, and the lot fell on Jonah. 8Then they said to him, "Please tell us! For whose cause *is* this trouble upon us? What is your occupation? And where do you come from? What is your country? And of what people are you?"

9So he said to them, "I *am* a Hebrew; and I fear the LORD, the God of heaven, who made the sea and the dry *land*."

Jonah Thrown into the Sea

10Then the men were exceedingly afraid, and said to him, "Why have you done this?" For the men knew that he fled from the presence of the LORD, because he had told them. 11Then they said to him, "What shall we do to you that the sea may be calm for us?"—for the sea was growing more tempestuous.

12And he said to them, "Pick me up and throw me into the sea; then the sea will become calm for you. For I know that this great tempest *is* because of me."

13Nevertheless the men rowed hard to return to land, but they could not, for the sea continued to grow more tempestuous against them. 14Therefore they cried out to the LORD and said, "We pray, O LORD, please do not let us perish for this man's life, and do not charge us with innocent blood; for You, O LORD, have done as it pleased You." 15So they picked up Jonah and threw him into the sea, and the sea ceased from its raging. 16Then the men feared the LORD exceedingly, and offered a sacrifice to the LORD and took vows.

1:5 [a]Literally *from upon them*

The Message

Running Away from God

1-2 **1** One day long ago, GOD's Word came to
Jonah, Amittai's son: "Up on your feet and
on your way to the big city of Nineveh!
Preach to them. They're in a bad way and I
can't ignore it any longer."
3 But Jonah got up and went the other di-
rection to Tarshish, running away from GOD.
He went down to the port of Joppa and
found a ship headed for Tarshish. He paid
the fare and went on board, joining those
going to Tarshish—as far away from GOD as
he could get.
4-6 But GOD sent a huge storm at sea, the
waves towering.
The ship was about to break into pieces.
The sailors were terrified. They called out in
desperation to their gods. They threw every-
thing they were carrying overboard to
lighten the ship. Meanwhile, Jonah had
gone down into the hold of the ship to take
a nap. He was sound asleep. The captain
came to him and said, "What's this? Sleep-
ing! Get up! Pray to your god! Maybe your
god will see we're in trouble and rescue us."
7 Then the sailors said to one another,
"Let's get to the bottom of this. Let's draw
straws to identify the culprit on this ship
who's responsible for this disaster."
So they drew straws. Jonah got the short
straw.
8 Then they grilled him: "Confess. Why this
disaster? What is your work? Where do you
come from? What country? What family?"
9 He told them, "I'm a Hebrew. I worship
GOD, the God of heaven who made sea and
land."
10 At that, the men were frightened, really
frightened, and said, "What on earth have
you done!" As Jonah talked, the sailors real-
ized that he was running away from GOD.
11 They said to him, "What are we going to
do with you—to get rid of this storm?" By
this time the sea was wild, totally out of con-
trol.
12 Jonah said, "Throw me overboard, into
the sea. Then the storm will stop. It's all my
fault. I'm the cause of the storm. Get rid of
me and you'll get rid of the storm."
13 But no. The men tried rowing back to
shore. They made no headway. The storm
only got worse and worse, wild and raging.
14 Then they prayed to GOD, "O GOD! Don't
let us drown because of this man's life, and
don't blame us for his death. You are GOD.
Do what you think is best."
15 They took Jonah and threw him over-
board. Immediately the sea was quieted
down.
16 The sailors were impressed, no longer
terrified by the sea, but in awe of GOD. They
worshiped GOD, offered a sacrifice, and
made vows.

New King James Version

Jonah's Prayer and Deliverance

17Now the LORD had prepared a great fish to
swallow Jonah. And Jonah was in the belly of
the fish three days and three nights.

2 Then Jonah prayed to the LORD his God from
the fish's belly. 2And he said:

"I cried out to the LORD because of my
affliction,
And He answered me.

"Out of the belly of Sheol I cried,
And You heard my voice.
3For You cast me into the deep,
Into the heart of the seas,
And the floods surrounded me;
All Your billows and Your waves passed over
me.
4Then I said, 'I have been cast out of Your
sight;
Yet I will look again toward Your holy
temple.'
5The waters surrounded me, *even* to my soul;
The deep closed around me;
Weeds were wrapped around my head.
6I went down to the moorings of the
mountains;
The earth with its bars *closed* behind me
forever;
Yet You have brought up my life from the pit,
O LORD, my God.

7"When my soul fainted within me,
I remembered the LORD;
And my prayer went *up* to You,
Into Your holy temple.

8"Those who regard worthless idols
Forsake their own Mercy.
9But I will sacrifice to You
With the voice of thanksgiving;
I will pay what I have vowed.
Salvation *is* of the LORD."

10So the LORD spoke to the fish, and it vom-
ited Jonah onto dry *land.*

Jonah Preaches at Nineveh

3 Now the word of the LORD came to Jonah the
second time, saying, 2"Arise, go to Nineveh,
that great city, and preach to it the message that
I tell you." 3So Jonah arose and went to Nineveh,
according to the word of the LORD. Now Nin-
eveh was an exceedingly great city, a three-day
journey[a] *in extent.* 4And Jonah began to enter
the city on the first day's walk. Then he cried
out and said, "Yet forty days, and Nineveh shall
be overthrown!"

The People of Nineveh Believe

5So the people of Nineveh believed God, pro-
claimed a fast, and put on sackcloth, from the
greatest to the least of them. 6Then word came
to the king of Nineveh; and he arose from his
throne and laid aside his robe, covered *himself*
with sackcloth and sat in ashes. 7And he caused

3:3 [a]Exact meaning unknown

The Message

17 Then GOD assigned a huge fish to swal-
low Jonah. Jonah was in the fish's belly
three days and nights.

At the Bottom of the Sea

1-9 2 Then Jonah prayed to his God from the
belly of the fish.
He prayed:

"In trouble, deep trouble, I prayed to God.
He answered me.
From the belly of the grave I cried, 'Help!'
You heard my cry.
You threw me into ocean's depths,
into a watery grave,
With ocean waves, ocean breakers
crashing over me.
I said, 'I've been thrown away,
thrown out, out of your sight.
I'll never again lay eyes
on your Holy Temple.'
Ocean gripped me by the throat.
The ancient Abyss grabbed me and held
tight.
My head was all tangled in seaweed
at the bottom of the sea where the
mountains take root.
I was as far down as a body can go,
and the gates were slamming shut
behind me forever—
Yet you pulled me up from that grave alive,
O GOD, my God!
When my life was slipping away,
I remembered GOD,
And my prayer got through to you,
made it all the way to your Holy Temple.
Those who worship hollow gods,
god-frauds,
walk away from their only true love.
But I'm worshiping you, GOD,
calling out in thanksgiving!
And I'll do what I promised I'd do!
Salvation belongs to GOD!"

10 Then GOD spoke to the fish, and it vom-
ited up Jonah on the seashore.

Maybe God Will Change His Mind

1-2 3 Next, GOD spoke to Jonah a second time:
"Up on your feet and on your way to the
big city of Nineveh! Preach to them. They're
in a bad way and I can't ignore it any longer."
3 This time Jonah started off straight for
Nineveh, obeying GOD's orders to the letter.
Nineveh was a big city, very big—it took
three days to walk across it.
4 Jonah entered the city, went one day's
walk and preached, "In forty days Nineveh
will be smashed."
5 The people of Nineveh listened, and
trusted God. They proclaimed a citywide
fast and dressed in burlap to show their re-
pentance. Everyone did it—rich and poor,
famous and obscure, leaders and followers.
6-9 When the message reached the king of
Nineveh, he got up off his throne, threw
down his royal robes, dressed in burlap, and
sat down in the dirt. Then he issued a public

NEW KING JAMES VERSION

it to be proclaimed and published throughout Nineveh by the decree of the king and his nobles, saying,

> Let neither man nor beast, herd nor flock, taste anything; do not let them eat, or drink water. 8But let man and beast be covered with sackcloth, and cry mightily to God; yes, let every one turn from his evil way and from the violence that is in his hands. 9Who can tell *if* God will turn and relent, and turn away from His fierce anger, so that we may not perish?

10Then God saw their works, that they turned from their evil way; and God relented from the disaster that He had said He would bring upon them, and He did not do it.

JONAH'S ANGER AND GOD'S KINDNESS

4 But it displeased Jonah exceedingly, and he became angry. 2So he prayed to the LORD, and said, "Ah, LORD, was not this what I said when I was still in my country? Therefore I fled previously to Tarshish; for I know that You *are* a gracious and merciful God, slow to anger and abundant in lovingkindness, One who relents from doing harm. 3Therefore now, O LORD, please take my life from me, for *it is* better for me to die than to live!"

4Then the LORD said, "*Is it* right for you to be angry?"

5So Jonah went out of the city and sat on the east side of the city. There he made himself a shelter and sat under it in the shade, till he might see what would become of the city. 6And the LORD God prepared a plant[a] and made it come up over Jonah, that it might be shade for his head to deliver him from his misery. So Jonah was very grateful for the plant. 7But as morning dawned the next day God prepared a worm, and it *so* damaged the plant that it withered. 8And it happened, when the sun arose, that God prepared a vehement east wind; and the sun beat on Jonah's head, so that he grew faint. Then he wished death for himself, and said, "*It is* better for me to die than to live."

9Then God said to Jonah, "*Is it* right for you to be angry about the plant?"

And he said, "*It is* right for me to be angry, even to death!"

10But the LORD said, "You have had pity on the plant for which you have not labored, nor made it grow, which came up in a night and perished in a night. 11And should I not pity Nineveh, that great city, in which are more than one hundred and twenty thousand persons who cannot discern between their right hand and their left—and much livestock?"

4:6 [a]Hebrew *kikayon*, exact identity unknown

THE MESSAGE

proclamation throughout Nineveh, authorized by him and his leaders: "Not one drop of water, not one bite of food for man, woman, or animal, including your herds and flocks! Dress them all, both people and animals, in burlap, and send up a cry for help to God. Everyone must turn around, turn back from an evil life and the violent ways that stain their hands. Who knows? Maybe God will turn around and change his mind about us, quit being angry with us and let us live!"

10 God saw what they had done, that they
had turned away from their evil lives. He *did*
change his mind about them. What he said
he would do to them he didn't do.

"I KNEW THIS WAS GOING TO HAPPEN!"

1-2 4 Jonah was furious. He lost his temper. He
yelled at GOD, "GOD! I knew it—when I
was back home, I knew this was going to
happen! That's why I ran off to Tarshish! I
knew you were sheer grace and mercy, not
easily angered, rich in love, and ready at the
drop of a hat to turn your plans of punishment into a program of forgiveness!

3 "So, GOD, if you won't kill them, kill *me*!
I'm better off dead!"

4 GOD said, "What do you have to be angry
about?"

5 But Jonah just left. He went out of the city
to the east and sat down in a sulk. He put together a makeshift shelter of leafy branches
and sat there in the shade to see what would
happen to the city.

6 GOD arranged for a broad-leafed tree to
spring up. It grew over Jonah to cool him off
and get him out of his angry sulk. Jonah was
pleased and enjoyed the shade. Life was
looking up.

7-8 But then God sent a worm. By dawn of
the next day, the worm had bored into the
shade tree and it withered away. The sun
came up and God sent a hot, blistering wind
from the east. The sun beat down on Jonah's
head and he started to faint. He prayed to
die: "I'm better off dead!"

9 Then God said to Jonah, "What right do
you have to get angry about this shade
tree?"

Jonah said, "Plenty of right. It's made me
angry enough to die!"

10-11 GOD said, "What's this? How is it that you
can change your feelings from pleasure to
anger overnight about a mere shade tree
that you did nothing to get? You neither
planted nor watered it. It grew up one night
and died the next night. So, why can't I likewise change what I feel about Nineveh from
anger to pleasure, this big city of more than
120,000 childlike people who don't yet know
right from wrong, to say nothing of all the
innocent animals?"

MICAH

New King James Version

1 The word of the LORD that came to Micah of Moresheth in the days of Jotham, Ahaz, *and* Hezekiah, kings of Judah, which he saw concerning Samaria and Jerusalem.

The Coming Judgment on Israel

2 Hear, all you peoples!
Listen, O earth, and all that is in it!
Let the Lord GOD be a witness against you,
The Lord from His holy temple.

3 For behold, the LORD is coming out of His place;
He will come down
And tread on the high places of the earth.
4 The mountains will melt under Him,
And the valleys will split
Like wax before the fire,
Like waters poured down a steep place.
5 All this is for the transgression of Jacob
And for the sins of the house of Israel.
What *is* the transgression of Jacob?
Is it not Samaria?
And what *are* the high places of Judah?
Are they not Jerusalem?

6 "Therefore I will make Samaria a heap of ruins in the field,
Places for planting a vineyard;
I will pour down her stones into the valley,
And I will uncover her foundations.
7 All her carved images shall be beaten to pieces,
And all her pay as a harlot shall be burned with the fire;
All her idols I will lay desolate,
For she gathered *it* from the pay of a harlot,
And they shall return to the pay of a harlot."

Mourning for Israel and Judah

8 Therefore I will wail and howl,
I will go stripped and naked;
I will make a wailing like the jackals
And a mourning like the ostriches,
9 For her wounds *are* incurable.
For it has come to Judah;
It has come to the gate of My people—
To Jerusalem.

The Message

1 1 GOD's Message as it came to Micah of Moresheth. It came during the reigns of Jotham, Ahaz, and Hezekiah, kings of Judah. It had to do with what was going on in Samaria and Jerusalem.

God Takes the Witness Stand

2 Listen, people—all of you.
Listen, earth, and everyone in it:
The Master, GOD, takes the witness stand against you,
the Master from his Holy Temple.

3-5 Look, here he comes! GOD, from his place!
He comes down and strides across mountains and hills.
Mountains sink under his feet,
valleys split apart;
The rock mountains crumble into gravel,
the river valleys leak like sieves.
All this because of Jacob's sin,
because Israel's family did wrong.
You ask, "So what is Jacob's sin?"
Just look at Samaria—isn't it obvious?
And all the sex-and-religion shrines in Judah—
isn't Jerusalem responsible?

6-7 "I'm turning Samaria into a heap of rubble,
a vacant lot littered with garbage.
I'll dump the stones from her buildings in the valley
and leave her abandoned foundations exposed.
All her carved and cast gods and goddesses
will be sold for stove wood and scrap metal,
All her sacred fertility groves
burned to the ground,
All the sticks and stones she worshiped as gods, destroyed.
These were her earnings from her life as a whore.
This is what happens to the fees of a whore."

8-9 This is why I lament and mourn.
This is why I go around in rags and barefoot.
This is why I howl like a pack of coyotes,
and moan like a mournful owl in the night.
GOD has inflicted punishing wounds;
Judah has been wounded with no healing in sight.
Judgment has marched through the city gates.
Jerusalem must face the charges.

NEW KING JAMES VERSION

10Tell *it* not in Gath,
Weep not at all;
In Beth Aphrah[a]
Roll yourself in the dust.
11Pass by in naked shame, you inhabitant of
Shaphir;
The inhabitant of Zaanan[a] does not go out.
Beth Ezel mourns;
Its place to stand is taken away from you.

12For the inhabitant of Maroth pined[a] for
good,
But disaster came down from the LORD
To the gate of Jerusalem.
13O inhabitant of Lachish,
Harness the chariot to the swift steeds
(She *was* the beginning of sin to the
daughter of Zion),
For the transgressions of Israel were found
in you.

14Therefore you shall give presents to
Moresheth Gath;[a]
The houses of Achzib[b] *shall be* a lie to the
kings of Israel.
15I will yet bring an heir to you, O inhabitant
of Mareshah;[a]
The glory of Israel shall come to Adullam.
16Make yourself bald and cut off your hair,
Because of your precious children;
Enlarge your baldness like an eagle,
For they shall go from you into captivity.

WOE TO EVILDOERS

2 Woe to those who devise iniquity,
And work out evil on their beds!
At morning light they practice it,
Because it is in the power of their hand.
2They covet fields and take *them* by violence,
Also houses, and seize *them*.
So they oppress a man and his house,
A man and his inheritance.

3Therefore thus says the LORD:

"Behold, against this family I am devising
disaster,
From which you cannot remove your necks;
Nor shall you walk haughtily,
For this *is* an evil time.
4In that day *one* shall take up a proverb
against you,
And lament with a bitter lamentation, saying:
'We are utterly destroyed!
He has changed the heritage of my people;
How He has removed *it* from me!
To a turncoat He has divided our fields.' "
5Therefore you will have no one to determine
boundaries[a] by lot
In the assembly of the LORD.

1:10 [a]Literally *House of Dust* **1:11** [a]Literally *Going Out* **1:12** [a]Literally *was sick* **1:14** [a]Literally *Possession of Gath* [b]Literally *Lie* **1:15** [a]Literally *Inheritance* **2:5** [a]Literally *one casting a surveyor's line*

THE MESSAGE

10-16 Don't gossip about this in Telltown.
Don't waste your tears.
In Dustville,
roll in the dust.
In Alarmtown,
the alarm is sounded.
The citizens of Exitburgh
will never get out alive.
Lament, Last-Stand City:
There's nothing in you left standing.
The villagers of Bittertown
wait in vain for sweet peace.
Harsh judgment has come from GOD
and entered Peace City.
All you who live in Chariotville,
get in your chariots for flight.
You led the daughter of Zion
into trusting not God but chariots.
Similar sins in Israel
also got their start in you.
Go ahead and give your good-bye gifts
to Good-byeville.
Miragetown beckoned
but disappointed Israel's kings.
Inheritance City
has lost its inheritance.
Glorytown
has seen its last of glory.
Shave your heads in mourning
over the loss of your precious towns.
Go bald as a goose egg—they've gone
into exile and aren't coming back.

GOD HAS HAD ENOUGH

1-5 2 Doom to those who plot evil,
who go to bed dreaming up crimes!
As soon as it's morning,
they're off, full of energy, doing what
they've planned.
They covet fields and grab them,
find homes and take them.
They bully the neighbor and his family,
see people only for what they can get out
of them.
GOD has had enough. He says,
"I have some plans of my own:
Disaster because of this interbreeding evil!
Your necks are on the line.
You're not walking away from this.
It's doomsday for you.
Mocking ballads will be sung of you,
and you yourselves will sing the blues:
'Our lives are ruined,
our homes and lands auctioned off.
They take everything, leave us nothing!
All is sold to the highest bidder.' "
And there'll be no one to stand up for you,
no one to speak for you before GOD and
his jury.

NEW KING JAMES VERSION

LYING PROPHETS

6"Do not prattle," *you say to those* who
prophesy.
So they shall not prophesy to you;[a]
They shall not return insult for insult.[b]
7*You who are* named the house of Jacob:
"Is the Spirit of the LORD restricted?
Are these His doings?
Do not My words do good
To him who walks uprightly?

8"Lately My people have risen up as an
enemy—
You pull off the robe with the garment
From those who trust *you*, as they pass by,
Like men returned from war.
9The women of My people you cast out
From their pleasant houses;
From their children
You have taken away My glory forever.

10"Arise and depart,
For this *is* not *your* rest;
Because it is defiled, it shall destroy,
Yes, with utter destruction.
11If a man should walk in a false spirit
And speak a lie, *saying*,
'I will prophesy to you of wine and drink,'
Even he would be the prattler of this people.

ISRAEL RESTORED

12"I will surely assemble all of you, O Jacob,
I will surely gather the remnant of Israel;
I will put them together like sheep of the
fold,[a]
Like a flock in the midst of their pasture;
They shall make a loud noise because of *so*
many people.
13The one who breaks open will come up
before them;
They will break out,
Pass through the gate,
And go out by it;
Their king will pass before them,
With the LORD at their head."

WICKED RULERS AND PROPHETS

3 And I said:

"Hear now, O heads of Jacob,
And you rulers of the house of Israel:
Is it not for you to know justice?
2You who hate good and love evil;
Who strip the skin from My people,[a]
And the flesh from their bones;
3Who also eat the flesh of My people,
Flay their skin from them,
Break their bones,
And chop *them* in pieces
Like *meat* for the pot,
Like flesh in the caldron."

2:6 [a]Literally *to these* [b]Vulgate reads *He shall not take shame.*
2:12 [a]Hebrew *Bozrah* **3:2** [a]Literally *them*

THE MESSAGE

6-7 "Don't preach," say the preachers.
"Don't preach such stuff.
Nothing bad will happen to us.
Talk like *this* to the family of Jacob?
Does GOD lose his temper?
Is this the way he acts?
Isn't he on the side of good people?
Doesn't he help those who help
themselves?"

8-11 "What do you mean, 'good people'!
You're the enemy of my people!
You rob unsuspecting people
out for an evening stroll.
You take their coats off their backs
like soldiers who plunder the
defenseless.
You drive the women of my people
out of their ample homes.
You make victims of the children
and leave them vulnerable to violence
and vice.
Get out of here, the lot of you.
You can't take it easy here!
You've polluted this place,
and now *you're* polluted—ruined!
If someone showed up with a good smile
and glib tongue
and told lies from morning to night—
'I'll preach sermons that will tell you
how you can get anything you want from
God:
More money, the best wines . . . you name
it'—
you'd hire him on the spot as your
preacher!

12-13 "I'm calling a meeting, Jacob.
I want everyone back—all the survivors
of Israel.
I'll get them together in one place—
like sheep in a fold, like cattle in a
corral—
a milling throng of homebound people!
Then I, GOD, will burst all confinements
and lead them out into the open.
They'll follow their King.
I will be out in front leading them."

HATERS OF GOOD, LOVERS OF EVIL

1-3 3 Then I said:

"Listen, leaders of Jacob, leaders of
Israel:
Don't you know anything of justice?
Haters of good, lovers of evil:
Isn't justice in your job description?
But you skin my people alive.
You rip the meat off their bones.
You break up the bones, chop the meat,
and throw it in a pot for cannibal stew."

NEW KING JAMES VERSION

4Then they will cry to the LORD,
But He will not hear them;
He will even hide His face from them at that time,
Because they have been evil in their deeds.

5Thus says the LORD concerning the prophets
Who make my people stray;
Who chant "Peace"
While they chew with their teeth,
But who prepare war against him
Who puts nothing into their mouths:
6"Therefore you shall have night without vision,
And you shall have darkness without divination;
The sun shall go down on the prophets,
And the day shall be dark for them.
7So the seers shall be ashamed,
And the diviners abashed;
Indeed they shall all cover their lips;
For *there is* no answer from God."

8But truly I am full of power by the Spirit of the LORD,
And of justice and might,
To declare to Jacob his transgression
And to Israel his sin.
9Now hear this,
You heads of the house of Jacob
And rulers of the house of Israel,
Who abhor justice
And pervert all equity,
10Who build up Zion with bloodshed
And Jerusalem with iniquity:
11Her heads judge for a bribe,
Her priests teach for pay,
And her prophets divine for money.
Yet they lean on the LORD, and say,
"Is not the LORD among us?
No harm can come upon us."
12Therefore because of you
Zion shall be plowed *like* a field,
Jerusalem shall become heaps of ruins,
And the mountain of the temple[a]
Like the bare hills of the forest.

THE LORD'S REIGN IN ZION

4 Now it shall come to pass in the latter days
That the mountain of the LORD's house
Shall be established on the top of the mountains,
And shall be exalted above the hills;
And peoples shall flow to it.
2Many nations shall come and say,

3:12 [a]Literally *house*

THE MESSAGE

4 The time's coming, though, when these same leaders
will cry out for help to GOD, but he won't listen.
He'll turn his face the other way
because of their history of evil.

5-7 Here is GOD's Message to the prophets,
the preachers who lie to my people:
"For as long as they're well paid and well fed,
the prophets preach, 'Isn't life wonderful! Peace to all!'
But if you don't pay up and jump on their bandwagon,
their 'God bless you' turns into 'God damn you.'
Therefore, you're going blind. You'll see nothing.
You'll live in deep shadows and know nothing.
The sun has set on the prophets.
They've had their day; from now on it's night.
Visionaries will be confused,
experts will be all mixed up.
They'll hide behind their reputations and make lame excuses
to cover up their God-ignorance."

8 But me—I'm filled with GOD's power,
filled with GOD's Spirit of justice and strength,
Ready to confront Jacob's crime
and Israel's sin.

9-12 The leaders of Jacob and
the leaders of Israel are
Leaders contemptuous of justice,
who twist and distort right living,
Leaders who build Zion by killing people,
who expand Jerusalem by committing crimes.
Judges sell verdicts to the highest bidder,
priests mass-market their teaching,
prophets preach for high fees,
All the while posturing and pretending
dependence on GOD:
"We've got GOD on our side.
He'll protect us from disaster."
Because of people like you,
Zion will be turned back into farmland,
Jerusalem end up as a pile of rubble,
and instead of the Temple on the mountain,
a few scraggly scrub pines.

THE MAKING OF GOD'S PEOPLE

1-4 4 But when all is said and done,
GOD's Temple on the mountain,
Firmly fixed, will dominate all mountains,
towering above surrounding hills.
People will stream to it
and many nations set out for it,

NEW KING JAMES VERSION

"Come, and let us go up to the mountain of the LORD,
To the house of the God of Jacob;
He will teach us His ways,
And we shall walk in His paths."
For out of Zion the law shall go forth,
And the word of the LORD from Jerusalem.
3He shall judge between many peoples,
And rebuke strong nations afar off;
They shall beat their swords into plowshares,
And their spears into pruning hooks;
Nation shall not lift up sword against nation,
Neither shall they learn war anymore.[a]

4But everyone shall sit under his vine and under his fig tree,
And no one shall make *them* afraid;
For the mouth of the LORD of hosts has spoken.
5For all people walk each in the name of his god,
But we will walk in the name of the LORD our God
Forever and ever.

ZION'S FUTURE TRIUMPH

6"In that day," says the LORD,
"I will assemble the lame,
I will gather the outcast
And those whom I have afflicted;
7I will make the lame a remnant,
And the outcast a strong nation;
So the LORD will reign over them in Mount Zion
From now on, even forever.
8And you, O tower of the flock,
The stronghold of the daughter of Zion,
To you shall it come,
Even the former dominion shall come,
The kingdom of the daughter of Jerusalem."

9Now why do you cry aloud?
Is there no king in your midst?
Has your counselor perished?
For pangs have seized you like a woman in labor.
10Be in pain, and labor to bring forth,
O daughter of Zion,
Like a woman in birth pangs.
For now you shall go forth from the city,
You shall dwell in the field,
And to Babylon you shall go.
There you shall be delivered;
There the LORD will redeem you
From the hand of your enemies.

11Now also many nations have gathered against you,
Who say, "Let her be defiled,
And let our eye look upon Zion."
12But they do not know the thoughts of the LORD,
Nor do they understand His counsel;
For He will gather them like sheaves to the threshing floor.

4:3 [a]Compare Isaiah 2:2–4

THE MESSAGE

Saying, "Come, let's climb GOD's mountain.
Let's go to the Temple of Jacob's God.
He will teach us how to live.
We'll know how to live God's way."
True teaching will issue from Zion,
GOD's revelation from Jerusalem.
He'll establish justice in the rabble of nations
and settle disputes in faraway places.
They'll trade in their swords for shovels,
their spears for rakes and hoes.
Nations will quit fighting each other,
quit learning how to kill one another.
Each man will sit under his own shade tree,
each woman in safety will tend her own garden.
GOD-of-the-Angel-Armies says so,
and he means what he says.

5 Meanwhile, all the other people live
however they wish,
picking and choosing their gods.
But we live honoring GOD,
and we're loyal to our God forever and ever.

6-7 "On that great day," God says,
"I will round up all the hurt and homeless,
everyone I have bruised or banished.
I will transform the battered into a company of the elite.
I will make a strong nation out of the long lost,
A showcase exhibit of GOD's rule in action,
as I rule from Mount Zion, from here to eternity.

8 "And you stragglers around Jerusalem,
eking out a living in shantytowns:
The glory that once was will be again.
Jerusalem's daughter will be the kingdom center."

9-10 So why the doomsday hysterics?
You still have a king, don't you?
But maybe he's not doing his job
and you're panicked like a woman in labor.
Well, go ahead—twist and scream,
Daughter Jerusalem.
You *are* like a woman in childbirth.
You'll soon be out of the city, on your way
and camping in the open country.
And then you'll arrive in Babylon.
What you lost in Jerusalem will be found in Babylon.
GOD will give you new life again.
He'll redeem you from your enemies.

11-12 But for right now, they're ganged up against you,
many godless peoples, saying,
"Kick her when she's down! Violate her!
We want to see Zion grovel in the dirt."
These blasphemers have no idea
what GOD is thinking and doing in this.
They don't know that this is the making of GOD's people,
that they are wheat being threshed, gold being refined.

NEW KING JAMES VERSION

13"Arise and thresh, O daughter of Zion;
For I will make your horn iron,
And I will make your hooves bronze;
You shall beat in pieces many peoples;
I will consecrate their gain to the LORD,
And their substance to the Lord of the whole earth."

5 Now gather yourself in troops,
O daughter of troops;
He has laid siege against us;
They will strike the judge of Israel with a rod on the cheek.

THE COMING MESSIAH

2"But you, Bethlehem Ephrathah,
Though you are little among the thousands of Judah,
Yet out of you shall come forth to Me
The One to be Ruler in Israel,
Whose goings forth *are* from of old,
From everlasting."

3Therefore He shall give them up,
Until the time *that* she who is in labor has given birth;
Then the remnant of His brethren
Shall return to the children of Israel.
4And He shall stand and feed *His flock*
In the strength of the LORD,
In the majesty of the name of the LORD His God;
And they shall abide,
For now He shall be great
To the ends of the earth;
5And this *One* shall be peace.

JUDGMENT ON ISRAEL'S ENEMIES

When the Assyrian comes into our land,
And when he treads in our palaces,
Then we will raise against him
Seven shepherds and eight princely men.
6They shall waste with the sword the land of Assyria,
And the land of Nimrod at its entrances;
Thus He shall deliver *us* from the Assyrian,
When he comes into our land
And when he treads within our borders.

7Then the remnant of Jacob
Shall be in the midst of many peoples,
Like dew from the LORD,
Like showers on the grass,
That tarry for no man
Nor wait for the sons of men.
8And the remnant of Jacob
Shall be among the Gentiles,
In the midst of many peoples,
Like a lion among the beasts of the forest,
Like a young lion among flocks of sheep,
Who, if he passes through,
Both treads down and tears in pieces,
And none can deliver.
9Your hand shall be lifted against your adversaries,
And all your enemies shall be cut off.

THE MESSAGE

13 On your feet, Daughter of Zion! Be threshed of chaff,
be refined of dross.
I'm remaking you into a people invincible,
into God's juggernaut to crush the godless peoples.
You'll bring their plunder as holy offerings to GOD,
their wealth to the Master of the earth.

THE LEADER WHO WILL SHEPHERD-RULE ISRAEL

1 5 But for now, prepare for the worst, victim daughter!
The siege is set against us.
They humiliate Israel's king,
slapping him around like a rag doll.

2-4 But you, Bethlehem, David's country,
the runt of the litter—
From you will come the leader
who will shepherd-rule Israel.
He'll be no upstart, no pretender.
His family tree is ancient and distinguished.
Meanwhile, Israel will be in foster homes
until the birth pangs are over and the child is born,
And the scattered brothers come back
home to the family of Israel.
He will stand tall in his shepherd-rule by GOD's strength,
centered in the majesty of GOD-Revealed.
And the people will have a good and safe home,
for the whole world will hold him in respect—
Peacemaker of the world!

5-6 And if some bullying Assyrian shows up,
invades and violates our land, don't worry.
We'll put him in his place, send him packing,
and watch his every move.
Shepherd-rule will extend as far as needed,
to Assyria and all other Nimrod-bullies.
Our shepherd-ruler will save us from old or new enemies,
from anyone who invades or violates our land.

7 The purged and select company of Jacob will be
like an island in the sea of peoples.
They'll be like dew from GOD,
like summer showers
Not mentioned in the weather forecast,
not subject to calculation or control.

8-9 Yes, the purged and select company of Jacob will be
like an island in the sea of peoples,
Like the king of beasts among wild beasts,
like a young lion loose in a flock of sheep,
Killing and devouring the lambs
and no one able to stop him.
With your arms raised in triumph over your foes,
your enemies will be no more!

NEW KING JAMES VERSION

10"And it shall be in that day," says the LORD,
"That I will cut off your horses from your midst
And destroy your chariots.
11I will cut off the cities of your land
And throw down all your strongholds.
12I will cut off sorceries from your hand,
And you shall have no soothsayers.
13Your carved images I will also cut off,
And your sacred pillars from your midst;
You shall no more worship the work of your hands;
14I will pluck your wooden images[a] from your midst;
Thus I will destroy your cities.
15And I will execute vengeance in anger and fury
On the nations that have not heard."[a]

GOD PLEADS WITH ISRAEL

6 Hear now what the LORD says:

"Arise, plead your case before the mountains,
And let the hills hear your voice.
2Hear, O you mountains, the LORD's complaint,
And you strong foundations of the earth;
For the LORD has a complaint against His people,
And He will contend with Israel.

3"O My people, what have I done to you?
And how have I wearied you?
Testify against Me.
4For I brought you up from the land of Egypt,
I redeemed you from the house of bondage;
And I sent before you Moses, Aaron, and Miriam.
5O My people, remember now
What Balak king of Moab counseled,
And what Balaam the son of Beor answered him,
From Acacia Grove[a] to Gilgal,
That you may know the righteousness of the LORD."

6With what shall I come before the LORD,
And bow myself before the High God?
Shall I come before Him with burnt offerings,
With calves a year old?
7Will the LORD be pleased with thousands of rams,
Ten thousand rivers of oil?
Shall I give my firstborn *for* my transgression,
The fruit of my body *for* the sin of my soul?

8He has shown you, O man, what *is* good;
And what does the LORD require of you
But to do justly,
To love mercy,
And to walk humbly with your God?

5:14 [a]Hebrew *Asherim*, Canaanite deities 5:15 [a]Or *obeyed*
6:5 [a]Hebrew *Shittim* (compare Numbers 25:1; Joshua 2:1; 3:1)

THE MESSAGE

10-15 "The day is coming"
—GOD's Decree—
"When there will be no more war. None.
I'll slaughter your war horses and demolish your chariots.
I'll dismantle military posts
and level your fortifications.
I'll abolish your religious black markets,
your underworld traffic in black magic.
I will smash your carved and cast gods
and chop down your phallic posts.
No more taking control of the world,
worshiping what you do or make.
I'll root out your sacred sex-and-power centers
and destroy the God-defiant.
In raging anger, I'll make a clean sweep
of godless nations who haven't listened."

WHAT GOD IS LOOKING FOR

1-2 6 Listen now, listen to GOD:

"Take your stand in court.
If you have a complaint, tell the mountains;
make your case to the hills.
And now, Mountains, hear GOD's case;
listen, Jury Earth—
For I am bringing charges against my people.
I am building a case against Israel.

3-5 "Dear people, how have I done you wrong?
Have I burdened you, worn you out?
Answer!
I delivered you from a bad life in Egypt;
I paid a good price to get you out of slavery.
I sent Moses to lead you—
and Aaron and Miriam to boot!
Remember what Balak king of Moab tried to pull,
and how Balaam son of Beor turned the tables on him.
Remember all those stories about Shittim and Gilgal.
Keep all GOD's salvation stories fresh and present."

6-7 How can I stand up before God
and show proper respect to the high God?
Should I bring an armload of offerings
topped off with yearling calves?
Would GOD be impressed with thousands of rams,
with buckets and barrels of olive oil?
Would he be moved if I sacrificed my firstborn child,
my precious baby, to cancel my sin?

8 But he's already made it plain how to live, what to do,
what GOD is looking for in men and women.
It's quite simple: Do what is fair and just to your neighbor,
be compassionate and loyal in your love,
And don't take yourself too seriously—
take God seriously.

NEW KING JAMES VERSION

PUNISHMENT OF ISRAEL'S INJUSTICE

9The LORD's voice cries to the city—
Wisdom shall see Your name:

"Hear the rod!
Who has appointed it?
10Are there yet the treasures of wickedness
In the house of the wicked,
And the short measure *that is* an abomination?
11Shall I count pure *those* with the wicked scales,
And with the bag of deceitful weights?
12For her rich men are full of violence,
Her inhabitants have spoken lies,
And their tongue is deceitful in their mouth.

13"Therefore I will also make *you* sick by striking you,
By making *you* desolate because of your sins.
14You shall eat, but not be satisfied;
Hunger[a] *shall be* in your midst.
You may carry *some* away,[b] but shall not save *them;*
And what you do rescue I will give over to the sword.

15"You shall sow, but not reap;
You shall tread the olives, but not anoint yourselves with oil;
And *make* sweet wine, but not drink wine.
16For the statutes of Omri are kept;
All the works of Ahab's house *are done;*
And you walk in their counsels,
That I may make you a desolation,
And your inhabitants a hissing.
Therefore you shall bear the reproach of My people."[a]

SORROW FOR ISRAEL'S SINS

7 Woe is me!
For I am like those who gather summer fruits,
Like those who glean vintage grapes;
There is no cluster to eat
Of the first-ripe fruit *which* my soul desires.
2The faithful *man* has perished from the earth,
And *there is* no one upright among men.
They all lie in wait for blood;
Every man hunts his brother with a net.

3That they may successfully do evil with both hands—
The prince asks *for gifts,*
The judge *seeks* a bribe,
And the great *man* utters his evil desire;
So they scheme together.
4The best of them *is* like a brier;
The most upright *is sharper* than a thorn hedge;
The day of your watchman and your punishment comes;
Now shall be their perplexity.

6:14 [a]Or *Emptiness* or *Humiliation* [b]Targum and Vulgate read *You shall take hold.* **6:16** [a]Following Masoretic Text, Targum, and Vulgate; Septuagint reads of *nations.*

THE MESSAGE

9 Attention! GOD calls out to the city!
If you know what's good for you, you'll listen.
So listen, all of you!
This is serious business.

10-16 "Do you expect me to overlook obscene wealth
you've piled up by cheating and fraud?
Do you think I'll tolerate shady deals
and shifty scheming?
I'm tired of the violent rich
bullying their way with bluffs and lies.
I'm fed up. Beginning now, you're finished.
You'll pay for your sins down to your last cent.
No matter how much you get, it will never be enough—
hollow stomachs, empty hearts.
No matter how hard you work, you'll have nothing to show for it—
bankrupt lives, wasted souls.
You'll plant grass
but never get a lawn.
You'll make jelly
but never spread it on your bread.
You'll press apples
but never drink the cider.
You have lived by the standards of your king, Omri,
the decadent lifestyle of the family of Ahab.
Because you've slavishly followed their fashions,
I'm forcing you into bankruptcy.
Your way of life will be laughed at, a tasteless joke.
Your lives will be derided as futile and fake."

STICK AROUND TO SEE WHAT GOD WILL DO

1-6 7 I'm overwhelmed with sorrow!
sunk in a swamp of despair!
I'm like someone who goes to the garden
to pick cabbages and carrots and corn
And returns empty-handed,
finds nothing for soup or sandwich or salad.
There's not a decent person in sight.
Right-living humans are extinct.
They're all out for one another's blood,
animals preying on each other.
They've all become experts in evil.
Corrupt leaders demand bribes.
The powerful rich
make sure they get what they want.
The best and brightest are thistles.
The top of the line is crabgrass.
But no longer: It's exam time.
Look at them slinking away in disgrace!

NEW KING JAMES VERSION

5Do not trust in a friend;
Do not put your confidence in a companion;
Guard the doors of your mouth
From her who lies in your bosom.
6For son dishonors father,
Daughter rises against her mother,
Daughter-in-law against her mother-in-law;
A man's enemies *are* the men of his own household.
7Therefore I will look to the LORD;
I will wait for the God of my salvation;
My God will hear me.

ISRAEL'S CONFESSION AND COMFORT

8Do not rejoice over me, my enemy;
When I fall, I will arise;
When I sit in darkness,
The LORD *will be* a light to me.
9I will bear the indignation of the LORD,
Because I have sinned against Him,
Until He pleads my case
And executes justice for me.
He will bring me forth to the light;
I will see His righteousness.
10Then *she who is* my enemy will see,
And shame will cover her who said to me,
"Where is the LORD your God?"
My eyes will see her;
Now she will be trampled down
Like mud in the streets.

11*In* the day when your walls are to be built,
In that day the decree shall go far and wide.[a]
12*In* that day they[a] shall come to you
From Assyria and the fortified cities,[b]
From the fortress[c] to the River,[d]
From sea to sea,
And mountain *to* mountain.
13Yet the land shall be desolate
Because of those who dwell in it,
And for the fruit of their deeds.

GOD WILL FORGIVE ISRAEL

14Shepherd Your people with Your staff,
The flock of Your heritage,
Who dwell solitarily *in* a woodland,
In the midst of Carmel;
Let them feed *in* Bashan and Gilead,
As in days of old.

15"As in the days when you came out of the land of Egypt,
I will show them[a] wonders."

16The nations shall see and be ashamed of all their might;

7:11 [a]Or *the boundary shall be extended* **7:12** [a]Literally *he*, collective of the captives [b]Hebrew *arey mazor*, possibly *cities of Egypt* [c]Hebrew *mazor*, possibly *Egypt* [d]That is, the Euphrates **7:15** [a]Literally *him*, collective for the captives

THE MESSAGE

Don't trust your neighbor,
don't confide in your friend.
Watch your words,
even with your spouse.
Neighborhoods and families are falling to pieces.
The closer they are—sons, daughters, in-laws—
The worse they can be.
Your own family is the enemy.

7 But me, I'm not giving up.
I'm sticking around to see what GOD will do.
I'm waiting for God to make things right.
I'm counting on God to listen to me.

SPREADING YOUR WINGS

8-10 Don't, enemy, crow over me.
I'm down, but I'm not out.
I'm sitting in the dark right now,
but GOD is my light.
I can take GOD's punishing rage.
I deserve it—I sinned.
But it's not forever. He's on my side
and is going to get me out of this.
He'll turn on the lights and show me his ways.
I'll see the whole picture and how right he is.
And my enemy will see it, too,
and be discredited—yes, disgraced!
This enemy who kept taunting,
"So where is this GOD of yours?"
I'm going to see it with these, my own eyes—
my enemy disgraced, trash in the gutter.

11-13 Oh, that will be a day! A day for rebuilding your city,
a day for stretching your arms,
spreading your wings!
All your dispersed and scattered people will come back,
old friends and family from faraway places,
From Assyria in the east to Egypt in the west,
from across the seas and out of the mountains.
But there'll be a reversal for everyone else—massive depopulation—
because of the way they lived, the things they did.

14-17 Shepherd, O God, your people with your staff,
your dear and precious flock.
Uniquely yours in a grove of trees,
centered in lotus land.
Let them graze in lush Bashan
as in the old days in green Gilead.
Reproduce the miracle-wonders
of our exodus from Egypt.
And the godless nations: Put them in their place—

NEW KING JAMES VERSION

They shall put *their* hand over *their* mouth;
Their ears shall be deaf.
17They shall lick the dust like a serpent;
They shall crawl from their holes like
snakes of the earth.
They shall be afraid of the LORD our God,
And shall fear because of You.
18Who *is* a God like You,
Pardoning iniquity
And passing over the transgression of the
remnant of His heritage?

He does not retain His anger forever,
Because He delights *in* mercy.
19He will again have compassion on us,
And will subdue our iniquities.

You will cast all our[a] sins
Into the depths of the sea.
20You will give truth to Jacob
And mercy to Abraham,
Which You have sworn to our fathers
From days of old.

7:19 [a]Literally *their*

THE MESSAGE

humiliated in their arrogance, speechless
and clueless.
Make them slink like snakes, crawl like
cockroaches,
come out of their holes from under their
rocks
And face our GOD.
Fill them with holy fear and trembling.

18-20 Where is the god who can compare with
you—
wiping the slate clean of guilt,
Turning a blind eye, a deaf ear,
to the past sins of your purged and
precious people?
You don't nurse your anger and don't stay
angry long,
for mercy is your specialty. That's what
you love most.
And compassion is on its way to us.
You'll stamp out our wrongdoing.
You'll sink our sins
to the bottom of the ocean.
You'll stay true to your word to Father
Jacob
and continue the compassion you
showed Grandfather Abraham—
Everything you promised our ancestors
from a long time ago.

NAHUM

New King James Version

1 The burden[a] against Nineveh. The book of the vision of Nahum the Elkoshite.

God's Wrath on His Enemies

2God *is* jealous, and the LORD avenges;
The LORD avenges and *is* furious.
The LORD will take vengeance on His adversaries,
And He reserves *wrath* for His enemies;
3The LORD *is* slow to anger and great in power,
And will not at all acquit *the wicked.*

The LORD has His way
In the whirlwind and in the storm,
And the clouds *are* the dust of His feet.
4He rebukes the sea and makes it dry,
And dries up all the rivers.
Bashan and Carmel wither,
And the flower of Lebanon wilts.
5The mountains quake before Him,
The hills melt,
And the earth heaves[a] at His presence,
Yes, the world and all who dwell in it.

6Who can stand before His indignation?
And who can endure the fierceness of His anger?
His fury is poured out like fire,
And the rocks are thrown down by Him.

7The LORD *is* good,
A stronghold in the day of trouble;
And He knows those who trust in Him.
8But with an overflowing flood
He will make an utter end of its place,
And darkness will pursue His enemies.

9What do you conspire against the LORD?
He will make an utter end *of it.*
Affliction will not rise up a second time.
10For while tangled *like* thorns,
And while drunken *like* drunkards,
They shall be devoured like stubble fully dried.
11From you comes forth *one*
Who plots evil against the LORD,
A wicked counselor.

12Thus says the LORD:

"Though *they are* safe, and likewise many,
Yet in this manner they will be cut down
When he passes through.
Though I have afflicted you,
I will afflict you no more;
13For now I will break off his yoke from you,
And burst your bonds apart."

1:1 [a]Or *oracle* 1:5 [a]Targum reads *burns.*

The Message

God Is Serious Business

1 1 A report on the problem of Nineveh, the way God gave Nahum of Elkosh to see it:

2-6 GOD is serious business.
He won't be trifled with.
He avenges his foes.
He stands up against his enemies, fierce and raging.
But GOD doesn't lose his temper.
He's powerful, but it's a patient power.
Still, no one gets by with anything.
Sooner or later, everyone pays.
Tornadoes and hurricanes
are the wake of his passage,
Storm clouds are the dust
he shakes off his feet.
He yells at the sea: It dries up.
All the rivers run dry.
The Bashan and Carmel mountains shrivel,
the Lebanon orchards shrivel.
Mountains quake in their roots,
hills dissolve into mud flats.
Earth shakes in fear of GOD.
The whole world's in a panic.
Who can face such towering anger?
Who can stand up to this fierce rage?
His anger spills out like a river of lava,
his fury shatters boulders.

7-10 GOD is good,
a hiding place in tough times.
He recognizes and welcomes
anyone looking for help,
No matter how desperate the trouble.
But cozy islands of escape
He wipes right off the map.
No one gets away from God.
Why waste time conniving against GOD?
He's putting an end to all such scheming.
For troublemakers, no second chances.
Like a pile of dry brush,
Soaked in oil,
they'll go up in flames.

A Think Tank for Lies

11 Nineveh's an anthill
of evil plots against GOD,
A think tank for lies
that seduce and betray.

12-13 And God has something to say about all this:
"Even though you're on top of the world,
With all the applause and all the votes,
you'll be mowed down flat.

"I've afflicted you, Judah, true,
but I won't afflict you again.
From now on I'm taking the yoke from your neck
and splitting it up for kindling.
I'm cutting you free
from the ropes of your bondage."

NEW KING JAMES VERSION

[14]The LORD has given a command concerning you:
"Your name shall be perpetuated no longer.
Out of the house of your gods
I will cut off the carved image and the molded image.
I will dig your grave,
For you are vile."

[15]Behold, on the mountains
The feet of him who brings good tidings,
Who proclaims peace!
O Judah, keep your appointed feasts,
Perform your vows.
For the wicked one shall no more pass through you;
He is utterly cut off.

THE DESTRUCTION OF NINEVEH

2 He who scatters[a] has come up before your face.
Man the fort!
Watch the road!
Strengthen *your* flanks!
Fortify *your* power mightily.

[2]For the LORD will restore the excellence of Jacob
Like the excellence of Israel,
For the emptiers have emptied them out
And ruined their vine branches.

[3]The shields of his mighty men *are* made red,
The valiant men *are* in scarlet.
The chariots *come* with flaming torches
In the day of his preparation,
And the spears are brandished.[a]
[4]The chariots rage in the streets,
They jostle one another in the broad roads;
They seem like torches,
They run like lightning.

[5]He remembers his nobles;
They stumble in their walk;
They make haste to her walls,
And the defense is prepared.
[6]The gates of the rivers are opened,
And the palace is dissolved.
[7]It is decreed:[a]
She shall be led away captive,
She shall be brought up;
And her maidservants shall lead *her* as with the voice of doves,
Beating their breasts.

[8]Though Nineveh of old *was* like a pool of water,
Now they flee away.
"Halt! Halt!" *they cry;*
But no one turns back.
[9]Take spoil of silver!
Take spoil of gold!
There is no end of treasure,
Or wealth of every desirable prize.

2:1 [a]Vulgate reads *He who destroys.* **2:3** [a]Literally *the cypresses are shaken;* Septuagint and Syriac read *the horses rush about;* Vulgate reads *the drivers are stupefied.* **2:7** [a]Hebrew *Huzzab*

THE MESSAGE

14 GOD's orders on Nineveh:

"You're the end of the line.
It's all over with Nineveh.
I'm gutting your temple.
Your gods and goddesses go in the trash.
I'm digging your grave. It's an unmarked grave.
You're nothing—no, you're *less* than nothing!"

15 Look! Striding across the mountains—
a messenger bringing the latest good news: peace!
A holiday, Judah! Celebrate!
Worship and recommit to God!
No more worries about *this enemy.*
This one is history. Close the books.

ISRAEL'S BEEN TO HELL AND BACK

1 2 The juggernaut's coming!
Post guards, lay in supplies.
Get yourselves together,
get ready for the big battle.

2 GOD has restored the Pride of Jacob,
the Pride of Israel.
Israel's lived through hard times.
He's been to hell and back.

3-12 Weapons flash in the sun,
the soldiers splendid in battle dress,
Chariots burnished and glistening,
ready to charge,
A spiked forest of brandished spears,
lethal on the horizon.
The chariots pour into the streets.
They fill the public squares,
Flaming like torches in the sun,
like lightning darting and flashing.
The Assyrian king rallies his men,
but they stagger and stumble.
They run to the ramparts
to stem the tide, but it's too late.
Soldiers pour through the gates.
The palace is demolished.
Soon it's all over:
Nineveh stripped, Nineveh doomed,
Maids and slaves moaning like doves,
beating their breasts.
Nineveh is a tub
from which they've pulled the plug.
Cries go up, "Do something! Do something!"
but it's too late. Nineveh's soon empty—nothing.
Other cries come: "Plunder the silver!
Plunder the gold!
A bonanza of plunder!
Take everything you want!"
Doom! Damnation! Desolation!

NEW KING JAMES VERSION

[10]She is empty, desolate, and waste!
The heart melts, and the knees shake;
Much pain *is* in every side,
And all their faces are drained of color.[a]

[11]Where *is* the dwelling of the lions,
And the feeding place of the young lions,
Where the lion walked, the lioness *and* lion's cub,
And no one made *them* afraid?
[12]The lion tore in pieces enough for his cubs,
Killed for his lionesses,
Filled his caves with prey,
And his dens with flesh.

[13]"Behold, I *am* against you," says the LORD
of hosts, "I will burn your[a] chariots in smoke,
and the sword shall devour your young lions; I
will cut off your prey from the earth, and the
voice of your messengers shall be heard no
more."

THE WOE OF NINEVEH

3 Woe to the bloody city!
It *is* all full of lies *and* robbery.
Its victim never departs.
[2]The noise of a whip
And the noise of rattling wheels,
Of galloping horses,
Of clattering chariots!
[3]Horsemen charge with bright sword and glittering spear.
There is a multitude of slain,
A great number of bodies,
Countless corpses—
They stumble over the corpses—
[4]Because of the multitude of harlotries of the seductive harlot,
The mistress of sorceries,
Who sells nations through her harlotries,
And families through her sorceries.

[5]"Behold, I *am* against you," says the LORD of hosts;
"I will lift your skirts over your face,
I will show the nations your nakedness,
And the kingdoms your shame.
[6]I will cast abominable filth upon you,
Make you vile,
And make you a spectacle.
[7]It shall come to pass *that* all who look upon you
Will flee from you, and say,
'Nineveh is laid waste!
Who will bemoan her?'
Where shall I seek comforters for you?"

[8]Are you better than No Amon[a]
That was situated by the River,[b]

2:10 [a]Compare Joel 2:6 **2:13** [a]Literally *her* **3:8** [a]That is, ancient Thebes; Targum and Vulgate read *populous Alexandria.* [b]Literally *rivers,* that is, the Nile and the surrounding canals

THE MESSAGE

Hearts sink,
knees fold,
stomachs retch,
faces blanch.
So, what happened to the famous
and fierce Assyrian lion
And all those cute Assyrian cubs?
To the lion and lioness
Cozy with their cubs,
fierce and fearless?
To the lion who always returned from the hunt
with fresh kills for lioness and cubs,
The lion lair heaped with bloody meat,
blood and bones for the royal lion feast?

13 "Assyria, I'm your enemy,"
says GOD-of-the-Angel-Armies.
"I'll torch your chariots. They'll go up in smoke.
'Lion Country' will be strewn with carcasses.
The war business is over—you're out of work:
You'll have no more wars to report,
No more victories to announce.
You're out of war work forever."

LET THE NATIONS GET THEIR FILL OF THE UGLY TRUTH

1-4 3 Doom to Murder City—
full of lies, bursting with loot, addicted to violence!
Horns blaring, wheels clattering,
horses rearing, chariots lurching,
Horsemen galloping,
brandishing swords and spears,
Dead bodies rotting in the street,
corpses stacked like cordwood,
Bodies in every gutter and alley,
clogging every intersection!
And whores! Whores without end!
Whore City,
Fatally seductive, you're the Witch of Seduction,
luring nations to their ruin with your evil spells.

5-7 "I'm your enemy, Whore Nineveh—
I, GOD-of-the-Angel-Armies!
I'll strip you of your seductive silk robes
and expose you on the world stage.
I'll let the nations get their fill of the ugly truth
of who you really are and have been all along.
I'll pelt you with dog dung
and place you on a pedestal: 'Slut on Exhibit.'
Everyone who sees you will gag and say,
'Nineveh's a pigsty:
What on earth did we ever see in her?
Who would give her a second look?
Ugh!'"

PAST THE POINT OF NO RETURN

8-13 Do you think you're superior to Egyptian Thebes,
proudly invincible on the River Nile,

New King James Version

That had the waters around her,
Whose rampart *was* the sea,
Whose wall *was* the sea?
9 Ethiopia and Egypt *were* her strength,
And *it was* boundless;
Put and Lubim were your[a] helpers.
10 Yet she *was* carried away,

She went into captivity;
Her young children also were dashed to pieces
At the head of every street;
They cast lots for her honorable men,
And all her great men were bound in chains.
11 You also will be drunk;
You will be hidden;
You also will seek refuge from the enemy.

12 All your strongholds *are* fig trees with ripened figs:
If they are shaken,
They fall into the mouth of the eater.
13 Surely, your people in your midst *are* women!
The gates of your land are wide open for your enemies;
Fire shall devour the bars of your *gates*.

14 Draw your water for the siege!
Fortify your strongholds!
Go into the clay and tread the mortar!
Make strong the brick kiln!
15 There the fire will devour you,
The sword will cut you off;
It will eat you up like a locust.

Make yourself many—like the locust!
Make yourself many— like the *swarming* locusts!
16 You have multiplied your merchants more than the stars of heaven.
The locust plunders and flies away.
17 Your commanders *are* like *swarming* locusts,
And your generals like great grasshoppers,
Which camp in the hedges on a cold day;
When the sun rises they flee away,
And the place where they *are* is not known.

18 Your shepherds slumber, O king of Assyria;
Your nobles rest *in the dust*.
Your people are scattered on the mountains,
And no one gathers them.
19 Your injury *has* no healing,
Your wound is severe.
All who hear news of you
Will clap *their* hands over you,
For upon whom has not your wickedness passed continually?

3:9 [a]Septuagint reads *her*.

The Message

Protected by the great River,
walled in by the River, secure?
Ethiopia stood guard to the south,
Egypt to the north.
Put and Libya, strong friends,
were ready to step in and help.
But you know what happened to her:
The whole city was marched off to a refugee camp,
Her babies smashed to death
in public view on the streets,
Her prize leaders auctioned off,
her celebrities put in chain gangs.
Expect the same treatment, Nineveh.
You'll soon be staggering like a bunch of drunks,
Wondering what hit you,
looking for a place to sleep it off.
All your forts are like peach trees,
the lush peaches ripe, ready for the picking.
One shake of the tree and they fall
straight into hungry mouths.
Face it: Your warriors are wimps.
You're sitting ducks.
Your borders are gaping doors, inviting
your enemies in. And who's to stop them?

14-15 Store up water for the siege.
Shore up your defenses.
Get down to basics: Work the clay
and make bricks.
Sorry. Too late.
Enemy fire will burn you up.
Swords will cut you to pieces.
You'll be chewed up as if by locusts.

15-17 Yes, as if by locusts—a fitting fate,
for you yourselves are a locust plague.
You've multiplied shops and shopkeepers—
more buyers and sellers than stars in the sky!
A plague of locusts, cleaning out the neighborhood
and then flying off.
Your bureaucrats are locusts,
your brokers and bankers are locusts.
Early on, they're all at your service,
full of smiles and promises,
But later when you return with questions or complaints,
you'll find they've flown off and are nowhere to be found.

18-19 King of Assyria! Your shepherd-leaders,
in charge of caring for your people,
Are busy doing everything else but.
They're not doing their job,
And your people are scattered and lost.
There's no one to look after them.
You're past the point of no return.
Your wound is fatal.
When the story of your fate gets out,
the whole world will applaud and cry "Encore!"
Your cruel evil has seeped
into every nook and cranny of the world.
Everyone has felt it and suffered.

HABAKKUK

NEW KING JAMES VERSION

1 The burden[a] which the prophet Habakkuk saw.

THE PROPHET'S QUESTION

2O LORD, how long shall I cry,
And You will not hear?
Even cry out to You, "Violence!"
And You will not save.
3Why do You show me iniquity,
And cause *me* to see trouble?
For plundering and violence *are* before me;
There is strife, and contention arises.
4Therefore the law is powerless,
And justice never goes forth.
For the wicked surround the righteous;
Therefore perverse judgment proceeds.

THE LORD'S REPLY

5"Look among the nations and watch—
Be utterly astounded!
For *I will* work a work in your days
Which you would not believe, though it were told *you*.
6For indeed I am raising up the Chaldeans,
A bitter and hasty nation
Which marches through the breadth of the earth,
To possess dwelling places *that are* not theirs.
7They are terrible and dreadful;
Their judgment and their dignity proceed from themselves.
8Their horses also are swifter than leopards,
And more fierce than evening wolves.
Their chargers charge ahead;
Their cavalry comes from afar;
They fly as the eagle *that* hastens to eat.

9"They all come for violence;
Their faces are set *like* the east wind.
They gather captives like sand.
10They scoff at kings,
And princes are scorned by them.
They deride every stronghold,
For they heap up earthen *mounds* and seize it.
11Then *his* mind[a] changes, and he transgresses;
He commits offense,
Ascribing this power to his god."

THE PROPHET'S SECOND QUESTION

12Are You not from everlasting,
O LORD my God, my Holy One?
We shall not die.
O LORD, You have appointed them for judgment;
O Rock, You have marked them for correction.
13*You are* of purer eyes than to behold evil,
And cannot look on wickedness.
Why do You look on those who deal treacherously,
And hold Your tongue when the wicked devours
A *person* more righteous than he?

1:1 [a]Or *oracle* **1:11** [a]Literally *spirit* or *wind*

THE MESSAGE

JUSTICE IS A JOKE

1-4 1 The problem as God gave Habakkuk to see it:

GOD, how long do I have to cry out for help
before you listen?
How many times do I have to yell, "Help!
Murder! Police!"
before you come to the rescue?
Why do you force me to look at evil,
stare trouble in the face day after day?
Anarchy and violence break out,
quarrels and fights all over the place.
Law and order fall to pieces.
Justice is a joke.
The wicked have the righteous hamstrung
and stand justice on its head.

GOD SAYS, "LOOK!"

5-11 "Look around at the godless nations.
Look long and hard. Brace yourself for a shock.
Something's about to take place
and you're going to find it hard to believe.
I'm about to raise up Babylonians to punish you,
Babylonians, fierce and ferocious—
World-conquering Babylon,
grabbing up nations right and left,
A dreadful and terrible people,
making up its own rules as it goes.
Their horses run like the wind,
attack like bloodthirsty wolves.
A stampede of galloping horses
thunders out of nowhere.
They descend like vultures
circling in on carrion.
They're out to kill. Death is on their minds.
They collect victims like squirrels gathering nuts.
They mock kings,
poke fun at generals,
Spit on forts,
and leave them in the dust.
They'll all be blown away by the wind.
Brazen in sin, they call strength their god."

WHY IS GOD SILENT NOW?

12-13 GOD, you're from eternity, aren't you?
Holy God, we aren't going to die, are we?
GOD, you chose *Babylonians* for your judgment work?
Rock-Solid God, you gave *them* the job of discipline?
But you can't be serious!
You can't condone evil!
So why don't you do something about this?
Why are you silent *now*?
This outrage! Evil men swallow up the righteous
and you stand around and *watch*!

NEW KING JAMES VERSION

14 *Why* do You make men like fish of the sea,
Like creeping things *that have* no ruler over them?

15 They take up all of them with a hook,
They catch them in their net,
And gather them in their dragnet.
Therefore they rejoice and are glad.
16 Therefore they sacrifice to their net,
And burn incense to their dragnet;
Because by them their share *is* sumptuous
And their food plentiful.
17 Shall they therefore empty their net,
And continue to slay nations without pity?

2 I will stand my watch
And set myself on the rampart,
And watch to see what He will say to me,
And what I will answer when I am corrected.

THE JUST LIVE BY FAITH

2 Then the LORD answered me and said:

"Write the vision
And make *it* plain on tablets,
That he may run who reads it.
3 For the vision *is* yet for an appointed time;
But at the end it will speak, and it will not lie.
Though it tarries, wait for it;
Because it will surely come,
It will not tarry.

4 "Behold the proud,
His soul is not upright in him;
But the just shall live by his faith.

WOE TO THE WICKED

5 "Indeed, because he transgresses by wine,
He is a proud man,
And he does not stay at home.
Because he enlarges his desire as hell,[a]
And he *is* like death, and cannot be satisfied,
He gathers to himself all nations
And heaps up for himself all peoples.

6 "Will not all these take up a proverb against him,
And a taunting riddle against him, and say,
'Woe to him who increases
What is not his—how long?
And to him who loads himself with many pledges'?[a]
7 Will not your creditors[a] rise up suddenly?
Will they not awaken who oppress you?
And you will become their booty.

2:5 [a]Or *Sheol* 2:6 [a]Syriac and Vulgate read *thick clay.* 2:7 [a]Literally *those who bite you*

THE MESSAGE

14-16 You're treating men and women
as so many fish in the ocean,
Swimming without direction,
swimming but not getting anywhere.
Then this evil Babylonian arrives and goes fishing.
He pulls in a good catch.
He catches his limit and fills his creel—
a good day of fishing! He's happy!
He praises his rod and reel,
piles his fishing gear on an altar and worships it!
It's made his day,
and he's going to eat well tonight!

17 Are you going to let this go on and on?
Will you let this Babylonian fisherman
Fish like a weekend angler,
killing people as if they're nothing but fish?

1 2 What's God going to say to my questions?
I'm braced for the worst.
I'll climb to the lookout tower and scan the horizon.
I'll wait to see what God says,
how he'll answer my complaint.

FULL OF SELF, BUT SOUL-EMPTY

2-3 And then GOD answered: "Write this.
Write what you see.
Write it out in big block letters
so that it can be read on the run.
This vision-message is a witness
pointing to what's coming.
It aches for the coming—it can hardly wait!
And it doesn't lie.
If it seems slow in coming, wait.
It's on its way. It will come right on time.

4 "Look at that man, bloated by self-importance—
full of himself but soul-empty.
But the person in right standing before God
through loyal and steady believing
is fully alive, *really* alive.

5-6 "Note well: Money deceives.
The arrogant rich don't last.
They are more hungry for wealth
than the grave is for cadavers.
Like death, they always want more,
but the 'more' they get is dead bodies.
They are cemeteries filled with dead nations,
graveyards filled with corpses.
Don't give people like this a second thought.
Soon the whole world will be taunting them:

6-8 " 'Who do you think you are—
getting rich by stealing and extortion?
How long do you think
you can get away with this?'
Indeed, how long before your victims wake up,
stand up and make *you* the victim?

NEW KING JAMES VERSION

8Because you have plundered many nations,
All the remnant of the people shall plunder you,
Because of men's blood
And the violence of the land *and* the city,
And of all who dwell in it.

9"Woe to him who covets evil gain for his house,
That he may set his nest on high,
That he may be delivered from the power of disaster!
10You give shameful counsel to your house,
Cutting off many peoples,
And sin *against* your soul.
11For the stone will cry out from the wall,
And the beam from the timbers will answer it.

12"Woe to him who builds a town with bloodshed,
Who establishes a city by iniquity!
13Behold, *is it* not of the LORD of hosts
That the peoples labor to feed the fire,[a]
And nations weary themselves in vain?
14For the earth will be filled
With the knowledge of the glory of the LORD,
As the waters cover the sea.

15"Woe to him who gives drink to his neighbor,
Pressing[a] *him to* your bottle,
Even to make *him* drunk,
That you may look on his nakedness!
16You are filled with shame instead of glory.
You also—drink!
And be exposed as uncircumcised![a]
The cup of the LORD's right hand *will be* turned against you,
And utter shame will be on your glory.
17For the violence *done to* Lebanon will cover you,
And the plunder of beasts *which* made them afraid,
Because of men's blood
And the violence of the land *and* the city,
And of all who dwell in it.

18"What profit is the image, that its maker should carve it,
The molded image, a teacher of lies,
That the maker of its mold should trust in it,
To make mute idols?
19Woe to him who says to wood, 'Awake!'
To silent stone, 'Arise! It shall teach!'
Behold, it is overlaid with gold and silver,
Yet in it there is no breath at all.

2:13 [a]Literally *for what satisfies fire*, that is, for what is of no lasting value **2:15** [a]Literally *Attaching* or *Joining* **2:16** [a]Dead Sea Scrolls and Septuagint read *And reel!*; Syriac and Vulgate read *And fall fast asleep!*

THE MESSAGE

You've plundered nation after nation.
Now you'll get a taste of your own medicine.
All the survivors are out to plunder you,
a payback for all your murders and massacres.

9-11 "Who do you think you are—
recklessly grabbing and looting,
Living it up, acting like king of the mountain,
acting above it all, above trials and troubles?
You've engineered the ruin of your own house.
In ruining others you've ruined yourself.
You've undermined your foundations,
rotted out your own soul.
The bricks of your house will speak up and accuse you.
The woodwork will step forward with evidence.

12-14 "Who do you think you are—
building a town by murder, a city with crime?
Don't you know that GOD-of-the-Angel-Armies
makes sure nothing comes of that but ashes,
Makes sure the harder you work
at that kind of thing, the less you are?
Meanwhile the earth fills up
with awareness of GOD's glory
as the waters cover the sea.

15-17 "Who do you think you are—
inviting your neighbors to your drunken parties,
Giving them too much to drink,
roping them into your sexual orgies?
You thought you were having the time of your life.
Wrong! It's a time of disgrace.
All the time you were drinking,
you were drinking from the cup of God's wrath.
You'll wake up holding your throbbing head, hung over—
hung over from Lebanon violence,
Hung over from animal massacres,
hung over from murder and mayhem,
From multiple violations
of place and people.

18-19 "What's the use of a carved god
so skillfully carved by its sculptor?
What good is a fancy cast god
when all it tells is lies?
What sense does it make to be a pious god-maker
who makes gods that can't even talk?
Who do you think you are—
saying to a stick of wood, 'Wake up,'
Or to a dumb stone, 'Get up'?
Can they teach you anything about anything?
There's nothing to them but surface.
There's nothing on the inside.

NEW KING JAMES VERSION

20"But the LORD is in His holy temple.
Let all the earth keep silence before Him."

THE PROPHET'S PRAYER

3 A prayer of Habakkuk the prophet, on Shigionoth.[a]

2O LORD, I have heard Your speech *and* was afraid;
O LORD, revive Your work in the midst of the years!
In the midst of the years make *it* known;
In wrath remember mercy.

3God came from Teman,
The Holy One from Mount Paran. *Selah*

His glory covered the heavens,
And the earth was full of His praise.
4*His* brightness was like the light;
He had rays *flashing* from His hand,
And there His power *was* hidden.
5Before Him went pestilence,
And fever followed at His feet.

6He stood and measured the earth;
He looked and startled the nations.
And the everlasting mountains were scattered,
The perpetual hills bowed.
His ways *are* everlasting.
7I saw the tents of Cushan in affliction;
The curtains of the land of Midian trembled.

8O LORD, were *You* displeased with the rivers,
Was Your anger against the rivers,
Was Your wrath against the sea,
That You rode on Your horses,
Your chariots of salvation?
9Your bow was made quite ready;
Oaths were sworn over *Your* arrows.[a] *Selah*

You divided the earth with rivers.
10The mountains saw You *and* trembled;
The overflowing of the water passed by.
The deep uttered its voice,
And lifted its hands on high.
11The sun and moon stood still in their habitation;
At the light of Your arrows they went,
At the shining of Your glittering spear.

12You marched through the land in indignation;
You trampled the nations in anger.
13You went forth for the salvation of Your people,
For salvation with Your Anointed.
You struck the head from the house of the wicked,
By laying bare from foundation to neck. *Selah*

14You thrust through with his own arrows
The head of his villages.
They came out like a whirlwind to scatter me;

3:1 [a]Exact meaning unknown 3:9 [a]Literally *rods* or *tribes* (compare verse 14)

THE MESSAGE

20 "But oh! God is in his holy Temple!
Quiet everyone—a holy silence. Listen!"

GOD RACING ON THE CREST OF THE WAVES

1-2 3 A prayer of the prophet Habakkuk, with orchestra:

GOD, I've heard what our ancestors say about you,
and I'm stopped in my tracks, down on my knees.
Do among us what you did among them.
Work among us as you worked among them.
And as you bring judgment, as you surely must,
remember mercy.

3-7 God's on his way again,
retracing the old salvation route,
Coming up from the south through Teman,
the Holy One from Mount Paran.
Skies are blazing with his splendor,
his praises sounding through the earth,
His cloud-brightness like dawn, exploding, spreading,
forked-lightning shooting from his hand—
what power hidden in that fist!
Plague marches before him,
pestilence at his heels!
He stops. He shakes Earth.
He looks around. Nations tremble.
The age-old mountains fall to pieces;
ancient hills collapse like a spent balloon.
The paths God takes are older
than the oldest mountains and hills.
I saw everyone worried, in a panic:
Old wilderness adversaries,
Cushan and Midian, were terrified,
hoping he wouldn't notice them.

8-16 GOD, is it River you're mad at?
Angry at old River?
Were you raging at Sea when you rode
horse and chariot through to salvation?
You unfurled your bow
and let loose a volley of arrows.
You split Earth with rivers.
Mountains saw what was coming.
They twisted in pain.
Flood Waters poured in.
Ocean roared and reared huge waves.
Sun and Moon stopped in their tracks.
Your flashing arrows stopped them,
your lightning-strike spears impaled them.
Angry, you stomped through Earth.
Furious, you crushed the godless nations.
You were out to save your people,
to save your specially chosen people.
You beat the stuffing
out of King Wicked,
Stripped him naked
from head to toe,
Set his severed head on his own spear
and blew away his army.

NEW KING JAMES VERSION

Their rejoicing was like feasting on the poor
in secret.
15You walked through the sea with Your
horses,
Through the heap of great waters.

16When I heard, my body trembled;
My lips quivered at *the* voice;
Rottenness entered my bones;
And I trembled in myself,
That I might rest in the day of trouble.
When he comes up to the people,
He will invade them with his troops.

A HYMN OF FAITH

17Though the fig tree may not blossom,
Nor fruit be on the vines;
Though the labor of the olive may fail,
And the fields yield no food;
Though the flock may be cut off from the
fold,
And there be no herd in the stalls—
18Yet I will rejoice in the LORD,
I will joy in the God of my salvation.

19The LORD God[a] is my strength;
He will make my feet like deer's *feet*,
And He will make me walk on my high hills.

To the Chief Musician. With my stringed instruments.

3:19 [a]Hebrew *YHWH Adonai*

THE MESSAGE

Scattered they were to the four winds—
and ended up food for the sharks!
You galloped through the Sea on your
horses,
racing on the crest of the waves.
When I heard it, my stomach did flips.
I stammered and stuttered.
My bones turned to water.
I staggered and stumbled.
I sit back and wait for Doomsday
to descend on our attackers.

17-19 Though the cherry trees don't blossom
and the strawberries don't ripen,
Though the apples are worm-eaten
and the wheat fields stunted,
Though the sheep pens are sheepless
and the cattle barns empty,
I'm singing joyful praise to GOD.
I'm turning cartwheels of joy to my
Savior God.
Counting on GOD's Rule to prevail,
I take heart and gain strength.
I run like a deer.
I feel like I'm king of the mountain!

(For congregational use, with a full orchestra.)

ZEPHANIAH

New King James Version

1 The word of the LORD which came to Zephaniah the son of Cushi, the son of Gedaliah, the son of Amariah, the son of Hezekiah, in the days of Josiah the son of Amon, king of Judah.

The Great Day of the Lord

2"I will utterly consume everything
From the face of the land,"
Says the LORD;
3"I will consume man and beast;
I will consume the birds of the heavens,
The fish of the sea,
And the stumbling blocks[a] along with the wicked.
I will cut off man from the face of the land,"
Says the LORD.

4"I will stretch out My hand against Judah,
And against all the inhabitants of Jerusalem.
I will cut off every trace of Baal from this place,
The names of the idolatrous priests[a] with the *pagan* priests—
5Those who worship the host of heaven on the housetops;
Those who worship and swear *oaths* by the LORD,
But who *also* swear by Milcom;[a]
6Those who have turned back from *following* the LORD,
And have not sought the LORD, nor inquired of Him."

7Be silent in the presence of the Lord GOD;
For the day of the LORD *is* at hand,
For the LORD has prepared a sacrifice;
He has invited[a] His guests.

8"And it shall be,
In the day of the LORD's sacrifice,
That I will punish the princes and the king's children,
And all such as are clothed with foreign apparel.
9In the same day I will punish
All those who leap over the threshold,[a]
Who fill their masters' houses with violence and deceit.

10"And there shall be on that day," says the LORD,
"The sound of a mournful cry from the Fish Gate,
A wailing from the Second Quarter,
And a loud crashing from the hills.
11Wail, you inhabitants of Maktesh![a]
For all the merchant people are cut down;
All those who handle money are cut off.

1:3 [a]Figurative of idols **1:4** [a]Hebrew *chemarim* **1:5** [a]Or *Malcam,* an Ammonite god, also called *Molech* (compare Leviticus 18:21) **1:7** [a]Literally *set apart, consecrated* **1:9** [a]Compare 1 Samuel 5:5 **1:11** [a]Literally *Mortar,* a market district of Jerusalem

The Message

No Longer Giving God a Thought or a Prayer

1 1 God's Message to Zephaniah son of Cushi, son of Gedaliah, son of Amariah, son of Hezekiah. It came during the reign of Josiah son of Amon, who was king of Judah:

2 "I'm going to make a clean sweep of the earth,
a thorough housecleaning." GOD's Decree.

3 "Men and women and animals,
including birds and fish—
Anything and everything that causes sin—
will go,
but especially people.

4-6 "I'll start with Judah
and everybody who lives in Jerusalem.
I'll sweep the place clean of every trace
of the sex-and-religion Baal shrines and their priests.
I'll get rid of the people who sneak up to their rooftops at night
to worship the star gods and goddesses;
Also those who continue to worship GOD
but cover their bases by worshiping other king-gods as well;
Not to mention those who've dumped GOD altogether,
no longer giving him a thought or offering a prayer.

7-13 "Quiet now!
Reverent silence before me, GOD, the Master!
Time's up. My Judgment Day is near:
The Holy Day is all set, the invited guests made holy.
On the Holy Day, GOD's Judgment Day,
I will punish the leaders and the royal sons;
I will punish those who dress up like foreign priests and priestesses,
Who introduce pagan prayers and practices;
And I'll punish all who import pagan superstitions
that turn holy places into hellholes.
Judgment Day!" GOD's Decree!
"Cries of panic from the city's Fish Gate,
Cries of terror from the city's Second Quarter,
sounds of great crashing from the hills!
Wail, you shopkeepers on Market Street!
Moneymaking has had its day. The god Money is dead.

NEW KING JAMES VERSION

12"And it shall come to pass at that time
That I will search Jerusalem with lamps,
And punish the men
Who are settled in complacency,[a]
Who say in their heart,
'The LORD will not do good,
Nor will He do evil.'
13Therefore their goods shall become booty,
And their houses a desolation;
They shall build houses, but not inhabit *them;*
They shall plant vineyards, but not drink their wine."

14The great day of the LORD *is* near;
It is near and hastens quickly.
The noise of the day of the LORD is bitter;
There the mighty men shall cry out.
15That day *is* a day of wrath,
A day of trouble and distress,
A day of devastation and desolation,
A day of darkness and gloominess,
A day of clouds and thick darkness,
16A day of trumpet and alarm
Against the fortified cities
And against the high towers.

17"I will bring distress upon men,
And they shall walk like blind men,
Because they have sinned against the LORD;
Their blood shall be poured out like dust,
And their flesh like refuse."

18Neither their silver nor their gold
Shall be able to deliver them
In the day of the LORD's wrath;
But the whole land shall be devoured
By the fire of His jealousy,
For He will make speedy riddance
Of all those who dwell in the land.

A CALL TO REPENTANCE

2 Gather yourselves together, yes, gather together,
O undesirable[a] nation,
2Before the decree is issued,
Or the day passes like chaff,
Before the LORD's fierce anger comes upon you,
Before the day of the LORD's anger comes upon you!
3Seek the LORD, all you meek of the earth,
Who have upheld His justice.
Seek righteousness, seek humility.
It may be that you will be hidden
In the day of the LORD's anger.

1:12 [a]Literally *on their lees,* that is, settled like the dregs of wine **2:1** [a]Or *shameless*

THE MESSAGE

On Judgment Day,
I'll search through every closet and alley in Jerusalem.
I'll find and punish those who are sitting it out, fat and lazy,
amusing themselves and taking it easy,
Who think, 'GOD doesn't do anything, good or bad.
He isn't involved, so neither are we.'
But just wait. They'll lose everything they have,
money and house and land.
They'll build a house and never move in.
They'll plant vineyards and never taste the wine.

A DAY OF DARKNESS AT NOON

14-18 "The Great Judgment Day of GOD is almost here.
It's countdown time: . . . seven, six, five, four . . .
Bitter and noisy cries on my Judgment Day,
even strong men screaming for help.
Judgment Day is payday—my anger paid out:
a day of distress and anguish,
a day of catastrophic doom,
a day of darkness at noon,
a day of black storm clouds,
a day of bloodcurdling war cries,
as forts are assaulted,
as defenses are smashed.
I'll make things so bad they won't know what hit them.
They'll walk around groping like the blind.
They've sinned against GOD!
Their blood will be poured out like old dishwater,
their guts shoveled into slop buckets.
Don't plan on buying your way out.
Your money is worthless for this.
This is the Day of GOD's Judgment—my *wrath!*
I *care* about sin with fiery passion—
A fire to burn up the corrupted world,
a wildfire finish to the corrupting people."

SEEK GOD

1-2 2 So get yourselves together. Shape up!
You're a nation without a clue about what it wants.
Do it before you're blown away
like leaves in a windstorm,
Before GOD's Judgment-anger
sweeps down on you,
Before GOD's Judgment Day wrath
descends with full force.

3 Seek GOD, all you quietly disciplined people
who live by GOD's justice.
Seek GOD's right ways. Seek a quiet and disciplined life.
Perhaps you'll be hidden on the Day of GOD's anger.

New King James Version

Judgment on Nations

4For Gaza shall be forsaken,
And Ashkelon desolate;
They shall drive out Ashdod at noonday,
And Ekron shall be uprooted.
5Woe to the inhabitants of the seacoast,
The nation of the Cherethites!
The word of the LORD *is* against you,
O Canaan, land of the Philistines:
"I will destroy you;
So there shall be no inhabitant."

6The seacoast shall be pastures,
With shelters[a] for shepherds and folds for flocks.
7The coast shall be for the remnant of the house of Judah;
They shall feed *their* flocks there;
In the houses of Ashkelon they shall lie down at evening.
For the LORD their God will intervene for them,
And return their captives.

8"I have heard the reproach of Moab,
And the insults of the people of Ammon,
With which they have reproached My people,
And made arrogant threats against their borders.
9Therefore, as I live,"
Says the LORD of hosts, the God of Israel,
"Surely Moab shall be like Sodom,
And the people of Ammon like Gomorrah—
Overrun with weeds and saltpits,
And a perpetual desolation.
The residue of My people shall plunder them,
And the remnant of My people shall possess them."
10This they shall have for their pride,
Because they have reproached and made arrogant threats
Against the people of the LORD of hosts.
11The LORD *will be* awesome to them,
For He will reduce to nothing all the gods of the earth;
People shall worship Him,
Each one from his place,
Indeed all the shores of the nations.

12"You Ethiopians also,
You shall be slain by My sword."

13And He will stretch out His hand against the north,
Destroy Assyria,
And make Nineveh a desolation,
As dry as the wilderness.
14The herds shall lie down in her midst,
Every beast of the nation.
Both the pelican and the bittern
Shall lodge on the capitals *of her pillars;*
Their voice shall sing in the windows;
Desolation *shall be* at the threshold;

2:6 [a]Literally *excavations,* either underground huts or cisterns

The Message

All Earth-Made Gods Will Blow Away

4-5 Gaza is scheduled for demolition,
Ashdod will be cleaned out by high noon,
Ekron pulled out by the roots.
Doom to the seaside people,
the seafaring people from Crete!
The Word of GOD is bad news for you
who settled Canaan, the Philistine country:
"You're slated for destruction—
no survivors!"

6-7 The lands of the seafarers
will become pastureland,
A country for shepherds and sheep.
What's left of the family of Judah will get it.
Day after day they'll pasture by the sea,
and go home in the evening to Ashkelon to sleep.
Their very own GOD will look out for them.
He'll make things as good as before.

8-12 "I've heard the crude taunts of Moab,
the mockeries flung by Ammon,
The cruel talk they've used to put down my people,
their self-important strutting along Israel's borders.
Therefore, as sure as I am the living God," says
GOD-of-the-Angel-Armies,
Israel's personal God,
"Moab will become a ruin like Sodom,
Ammon a ghost town like Gomorrah,
One a field of rocks, the other a sterile salt flat,
a moonscape forever.
What's left of my people will finish them off,
will pick them clean and take over.
This is what they get for their bloated pride,
their taunts and mockeries of the people of GOD-of-the-Angel-Armies.
GOD will be seen as truly terrible—a Holy Terror.
All earth-made gods will shrivel up and blow away;
And everyone, wherever they are, far or near,
will fall to the ground and worship him.
Also you Ethiopians,
you, too, will die—I'll see to it."

13-15 Then GOD will reach into the north
and destroy Assyria.
He will waste Nineveh,
leave her dry and treeless as a desert.
The ghost town of a city,
the haunt of wild animals,
Nineveh will be home to raccoons and coyotes—
they'll bed down in its ruins.
Owls will hoot in the windows, ravens will croak in the doorways—

NEW KING JAMES VERSION

For He will lay bare the cedar work.
15This is the rejoicing city
That dwelt securely,
That said in her heart,
"I *am it*, and *there is* none besides me."
How has she become a desolation,
A place for beasts to lie down!
Everyone who passes by her
Shall hiss and shake his fist.

THE WICKEDNESS OF JERUSALEM

3 Woe to her who is rebellious and polluted,
To the oppressing city!
2She has not obeyed *His* voice,
She has not received correction;
She has not trusted in the LORD,
She has not drawn near to her God.

3Her princes in her midst *are* roaring lions;
Her judges *are* evening wolves
That leave not a bone till morning.
4Her prophets are insolent, treacherous
people;
Her priests have polluted the sanctuary,
They have done violence to the law.
5The LORD *is* righteous in her midst,
He will do no unrighteousness.
Every morning He brings His justice to
light;
He never fails,
But the unjust knows no shame.

6"I have cut off nations,
Their fortresses are devastated;
I have made their streets desolate,
With none passing by.
Their cities are destroyed;
There is no one, no inhabitant.
7I said, 'Surely you will fear Me,
You will receive instruction'—
So that her dwelling would not be cut off,
Despite everything for which I punished
her.
But they rose early and corrupted all their
deeds.

A FAITHFUL REMNANT

8"Therefore wait for Me," says the LORD,
"Until the day I rise up for plunder;[a]
My determination *is* to gather the nations
To My assembly of kingdoms,
To pour on them My indignation,
All My fierce anger;
All the earth shall be devoured
With the fire of My jealousy.

9"For then I will restore to the peoples a pure
language,

3:8 [a]Septuagint and Syriac read *for witness;* Targum reads *for the day of My revelation for judgment;* Vulgate reads *for the day of My resurrection that is to come.*

THE MESSAGE

all that fancy woodwork now a perch for
birds.
Can this be the famous Fun City
that had it made,
That boasted, "I'm the Number-One City!
I'm King of the Mountain!"
So why is the place deserted,
a lair for wild animals?
Passersby hardly give it a look;
they dismiss it with a gesture.

SEWER CITY

1-5 3 Doom to the rebellious city,
the home of oppressors—Sewer City!
The city that wouldn't take advice,
wouldn't accept correction,
Wouldn't trust GOD,
wouldn't even get close to her own god!
Her very own leaders
are rapacious lions,
Her judges are rapacious timber wolves
out every morning prowling for a fresh
kill.
Her prophets are out for what they can get.
They're opportunists—you can't trust them.
Her priests desecrate the Sanctuary.
They use God's law as a weapon to maim
and kill souls.
Yet GOD remains righteous in her midst,
untouched by the evil.
He stays at it, day after day, meting out
justice.
At evening he's still at it, strong as ever.
But evil men and women, without conscience
and without shame, persist in evil.

6 "So I cut off the godless nations.
I knocked down their defense posts,
Filled her roads with rubble
so no one could get through.
Her cities were bombed-out ruins,
unlivable and unlived in.

7 "I thought, 'Surely she'll honor me now,
accept my discipline and correction,
Find a way of escape from the trouble she's
in,
find relief from the punishment I'm
bringing.'
But it didn't faze her. Bright and early
she was up at it again, doing the same
old things.

8 "Well, if that's what you want, stick around."
GOD's Decree.
"Your day in court is coming,
but remember I'll be there to bring
evidence.
I'll bring all the nations to the courtroom,
round up all the kingdoms,
And let them feel the brunt of my anger,
my raging wrath.
My zeal is a fire
that will purge and purify the earth.

GOD IS IN CHARGE AT THE CENTER

9-13 "In the end I will turn things around for the
people.

NEW KING JAMES VERSION

That they all may call on the name of the
LORD,
To serve Him with one accord.
10From beyond the rivers of Ethiopia
My worshipers,
The daughter of My dispersed ones,
Shall bring My offering.
11In that day you shall not be shamed for any
of your deeds
In which you transgress against Me;
For then I will take away from your midst
Those who rejoice in your pride,
And you shall no longer be haughty
In My holy mountain.
12I will leave in your midst
A meek and humble people,
And they shall trust in the name of the
LORD.
13The remnant of Israel shall do no
unrighteousness
And speak no lies,
Nor shall a deceitful tongue be found in
their mouth;
For they shall feed *their* flocks and lie down,
And no one shall make *them* afraid."

JOY IN GOD'S FAITHFULNESS

14Sing, O daughter of Zion!
Shout, O Israel!
Be glad and rejoice with all *your* heart,
O daughter of Jerusalem!
15The LORD has taken away your judgments,
He has cast out your enemy.
The King of Israel, the LORD, *is* in your
midst;
You shall see[a] disaster no more.

16In that day it shall be said to Jerusalem:
"Do not fear;
Zion, let not your hands be weak.
17The LORD your God in your midst,
The Mighty One, will save;
He will rejoice over you with gladness,
He will quiet *you* with His love,
He will rejoice over you with singing."

18"I will gather those who sorrow over the
appointed assembly,
Who are among you,
To whom its reproach *is* a burden.
19Behold, at that time
I will deal with all who afflict you;
I will save the lame,
And gather those who were driven out;
I will appoint them for praise and fame
In every land where they were put to shame.
20At that time I will bring you back,
Even at the time I gather you;
For I will give you fame and praise
Among all the peoples of the earth,
When I return your captives before your
eyes,"
Says the LORD.

3:15 [a]Some Hebrew manuscripts, Septuagint, and Bomberg read *see;* Masoretic Text and Vulgate read *fear.*

THE MESSAGE

I'll give them a language undistorted,
unpolluted,
Words to address GOD in worship
and, united, to serve me with their
shoulders to the wheel.
They'll come from beyond the Ethiopian
rivers,
they'll come praying—
All my scattered, exiled people
will come home with offerings for worship.
You'll no longer have to be ashamed
of all those acts of rebellion.
I'll have gotten rid of your arrogant leaders.
No more pious strutting on my holy hill!
I'll leave a core of people among you
who are poor in spirit—
What's left of Israel that's really Israel.
They'll make their home in GOD.
This core holy people
will not do wrong.
They won't lie,
won't use words to flatter or seduce.
Content with who they are and where they
are,
unanxious, they'll live at peace."

14-15 So sing, Daughter Zion!
Raise the rafters, Israel!
Daughter Jerusalem,
be happy! celebrate!
GOD has reversed his judgments against you
and sent your enemies off chasing their
tails.
From now on, GOD is Israel's king,
in charge at the center.
There's nothing to fear from evil
ever again!

GOD IS PRESENT AMONG YOU

16-17 Jerusalem will be told:
"Don't be afraid.
Dear Zion,
don't despair.
Your GOD is present among you,
a strong Warrior there to save you.
Happy to have you back, he'll calm you with
his love
and delight you with his songs.

18-20 "The accumulated sorrows of your exile will
dissipate.
I, your God, will get rid of them for you.
You've carried those burdens long enough.
At the same time, I'll get rid of all those
who've made your life miserable.
I'll heal the maimed;
I'll bring home the homeless.
In the very countries where they were hated
they will be venerated.
On Judgment Day
I'll bring you back home—a great family
gathering!
You'll be famous and honored
all over the world.
You'll see it with your own eyes—
all those painful partings turned into
reunions!"
GOD's Promise.

HAGGAI

New King James Version

The Command to Build God's House

1 In the second year of King Darius, in the sixth month, on the first day of the month, the word of the LORD came by Haggai the prophet to Zerubbabel the son of Shealtiel, governor of Judah, and to Joshua the son of Jehozadak, the high priest, saying, 2“Thus speaks the LORD of hosts, saying: ‘This people says, “The time has not come, the time that the LORD's house should be built.” ’ ”

3Then the word of the LORD came by Haggai the prophet, saying, 4“*Is it* time for you yourselves to dwell in your paneled houses, and this temple[a] *to lie* in ruins?” 5Now therefore, thus says the LORD of hosts: “Consider your ways!

6“You have sown much, and bring in little;
You eat, but do not have enough;
You drink, but you are not filled with drink;
You clothe yourselves, but no one is warm;
And he who earns wages,
Earns wages *to put* into a bag with holes.”

7Thus says the LORD of hosts: “Consider your ways! 8Go up to the mountains and bring wood and build the temple, that I may take pleasure in it and be glorified,” says the LORD. 9“*You* looked for much, but indeed *it came to* little; and when you brought it home, I blew it away. Why?” says the LORD of hosts. “Because of My house that *is in* ruins, while every one of you runs to his own house. 10Therefore the heavens above you withhold the dew, and the earth withholds its fruit. 11For I called for a drought on the land and the mountains, on the grain and the new wine and the oil, on whatever the ground brings forth, on men and livestock, and on all the labor of *your* hands.”

1:4 [a]Literally *house*, and so in verse 8

The Message

Caught Up with Taking Care of Your Own Houses

1 **1** On the first day of the sixth month of the second year in the reign of King Darius of Persia, GOD's Message was delivered by the prophet Haggai to the governor of Judah, Zerubbabel son of Shealtiel, and to the high priest, Joshua son of Jehozadak:

2 A Message from GOD-of-the-Angel-Armies: “The people procrastinate. They say this isn't the right time to rebuild my Temple, the Temple of GOD.”

3-4 Shortly after that, GOD said more and Haggai spoke it: “How is it that it's the ‘right time’ for you to live in your fine new homes while the Home, GOD's Temple, is in ruins?”

5-6 And then a little later, GOD-of-the-Angel-Armies spoke out again:

“Take a good, hard look at your life.
Think it over.
You have spent a lot of money,
but you haven't much to show for it.
You keep filling your plates,
but you never get filled up.
You keep drinking and drinking and drinking,
but you're always thirsty.
You put on layer after layer of clothes,
but you can't get warm.
And the people who work for you,
what are they getting out of it?
Not much—
a leaky, rusted-out bucket, that's what.

7 That's why GOD-of-the-Angel-Armies said:

“Take a good, hard look at your life.
Think it over.”

8-9 Then GOD said:

“Here's what I want you to do:
Climb into the hills and cut some timber.
Bring it down and rebuild the Temple.
Do it just for me. Honor me.
You've had great ambitions for yourselves,
but nothing has come of it.
The little you have brought to my Temple
I've blown away—there was nothing to it.

9-11 “And why?” (This is a Message from GOD-of-the-Angel-Armies, remember.) “Because while you've run around, caught up with taking care of your own houses, my Home is in ruins. That's why. Because of your stinginess. And so I've given you a dry summer and a skimpy crop. I've matched your tightfisted stinginess by decreeing a season of drought, drying up fields and hills, withering gardens and orchards, stunting vegetables and fruit. Nothing—not man or woman, not animal or crop—is going to thrive.”

NEW KING JAMES VERSION

THE PEOPLE'S OBEDIENCE

12Then Zerubbabel the son of Shealtiel, and Joshua the son of Jehozadak, the high priest, with all the remnant of the people, obeyed the voice of the LORD their God, and the words of Haggai the prophet, as the LORD their God had sent him; and the people feared the presence of the LORD. 13Then Haggai, the LORD's messenger, spoke the LORD's message to the people, saying, "I *am* with you, says the LORD." 14So the LORD stirred up the spirit of Zerubbabel the son of Shealtiel, governor of Judah, and the spirit of Joshua the son of Jehozadak, the high priest, and the spirit of all the remnant of the people; and they came and worked on the house of the LORD of hosts, their God, 15on the twenty-fourth day of the sixth month, in the second year of King Darius.

THE COMING GLORY OF GOD'S HOUSE

2 In the seventh *month,* on the twenty-first of the month, the word of the LORD came by Haggai the prophet, saying: 2"Speak now to Zerubbabel the son of Shealtiel, governor of Judah, and to Joshua the son of Jehozadak, the high priest, and to the remnant of the people, saying: 3'Who is left among you who saw this temple[a] in its former glory? And how do you see it now? In comparison with it, *is this* not in your eyes as nothing? 4Yet now be strong, Zerubbabel,' says the LORD; 'and be strong, Joshua, son of Jehozadak, the high priest; and be strong, all you people of the land,' says the LORD, 'and work; for I *am* with you,' says the LORD of hosts. 5'*According to* the word that I covenanted with you when you came out of Egypt, so My Spirit remains among you; do not fear!'

6"For thus says the LORD of hosts: 'Once more (it *is* a little while) I will shake heaven and earth, the sea and dry land; 7and I will shake all nations, and they shall come to the Desire of All Nations,[a] and I will fill this temple with glory,' says the LORD of hosts. 8'The silver *is* Mine, and the gold *is* Mine,' says the LORD of hosts. 9'The glory of this latter temple shall be greater than the former,' says the LORD of hosts. 'And in this place I will give peace,' says the LORD of hosts."

THE PEOPLE ARE DEFILED

10On the twenty-fourth *day* of the ninth *month,* in the second year of Darius, the word of the LORD came by Haggai the prophet, saying, 11"Thus says the LORD of hosts: 'Now, ask the priests *concerning the* law, saying, 12"If one carries holy meat in the fold of his garment, and with the edge he touches bread or stew, wine or oil, or any food, will it become holy?" ' "

2:3 [a]Literally *house,* and so in verses 7 and 9 **2:7** [a]Or *the desire of all nations*

THE MESSAGE

12 Then the governor, Zerubbabel son of Shealtiel, and the high priest, Joshua son of Jehozadak, and all the people with them listened, really listened, to the voice of their GOD. When GOD sent the prophet Haggai to them, they paid attention to him. In listening to Haggai, they honored GOD.

13 Then Haggai, GOD's messenger, preached GOD's Message to the people: "I am with you!" GOD's Word.

14-15 This is how GOD got Zerubbabel, Joshua, and all the people moving—got them working on the Temple of GOD-of-the-Angel-Armies. This happened on the twenty-fourth day of the sixth month in the second year of King Darius.

THIS TEMPLE WILL END UP BETTER THAN IT STARTED OUT

1-3 2 On the twenty-first day of the seventh month, the Word of GOD came through the prophet Haggai: "Tell Governor Zerubbabel son of Shealtiel and High Priest Joshua son of Jehozadak and all the people: 'Is there anyone here who saw the Temple the way it used to be, all glorious? And what do you see now? Not much, right?

4-5 " 'So get to work, Zerubbabel!'—GOD is speaking.

" 'Get to work, Joshua son of Jehozadak—high priest!'

" 'Get to work, all you people!'—GOD is speaking.

" 'Yes, get to work! For I am with you.' The GOD-of-the-Angel-Armies is speaking! 'Put into action the word I covenanted with you when you left Egypt. I'm living and breathing among you right now. Don't be timid. Don't hold back.'

6-7 "This is what GOD-of-the-Angel-Armies said: 'Before you know it, I will shake up sky and earth, ocean and fields. And I'll shake down all the godless nations. They'll bring bushels of wealth and I will fill this Temple with splendor.' GOD-of-the-Angel-Armies says so.

8 'I own the silver,
I own the gold.'
Decree of GOD-of-the-Angel-Armies.

9 " 'This Temple is going to end up far better than it started out, a glorious beginning but an even more glorious finish: a place in which I will hand out wholeness and holiness.' Decree of GOD-of-the-Angel-Armies."

10-12 On the twenty-fourth day of the ninth month (again, this was in the second year of Darius), GOD's Message came to Haggai: "GOD-of-the-Angel-Armies speaks: Consult the priests for a ruling. If someone carries a piece of sacred meat in his pocket, meat that is set apart for sacrifice on the altar, and the pocket touches a loaf of bread, a dish of stew, a bottle of wine or oil, or any other food, will these foods be made holy by such contact?"

NEW KING JAMES VERSION

Then the priests answered and said, "No."
13 And Haggai said, "If *one who is* unclean *be-*
cause of a dead body touches any of these, will
it be unclean?"
So the priests answered and said, "It shall be
unclean."
14 Then Haggai answered and said, " 'So is
this people, and so is this nation before Me,'
says the LORD, 'and so is every work of their
hands; and what they offer there is unclean.

PROMISED BLESSING

15 'And now, carefully consider from this day
forward: from before stone was laid upon stone
in the temple of the LORD— 16 since those *days,*
when *one* came to a heap of twenty ephahs,
there were *but* ten; when *one* came to the wine
vat to draw out fifty baths from the press, there
were *but* twenty. 17 I struck you with blight and
mildew and hail in all the labors of your hands;
yet you did not *turn* to Me,' says the LORD.
18 'Consider now from this day forward, from the
twenty-fourth day of the ninth month, from the
day that the foundation of the LORD's temple
was laid—consider it: 19 Is the seed still in the
barn? As yet the vine, the fig tree, the pome-
granate, and the olive tree have not yielded
fruit. But from this day I will bless *you.*' "

ZERUBBABEL CHOSEN AS A SIGNET

20 And again the word of the LORD came to
Haggai on the twenty-fourth day of the month,
saying, 21 "Speak to Zerubbabel, governor of Ju-
dah, saying:

'I will shake heaven and earth.
22 I will overthrow the throne of kingdoms;
I will destroy the strength of the Gentile
kingdoms.
I will overthrow the chariots
And those who ride in them;
The horses and their riders shall come
down,
Every one by the sword of his brother.

23 'In that day,' says the LORD of hosts, 'I will
take you, Zerubbabel My servant, the son of
Shealtiel,' says the LORD, 'and will make you
like a signet *ring;* for I have chosen you,' says
the LORD of hosts."

THE MESSAGE

The priests said, "No."
13 Then Haggai said, "How about someone
who is contaminated by touching a corpse—
if that person touches one of these foods,
will it be contaminated?"
The priests said, "Yes, it will be contami-
nated."
14 Then Haggai said, " 'So, this people is
contaminated. Their nation is contaminated.
Everything they do is contaminated. What-
ever they do for me is contaminated.' GOD
says so.
15-17 " 'Think back. Before you set out to lay
the first foundation stones for the rebuilding
of my Temple, how did it go with you? Isn't
it true that your foot-dragging, halfhearted
efforts at rebuilding the Temple of GOD were
reflected in a sluggish, halfway return on
your crops—half the grain you were used to
getting, half the wine? I hit you with drought
and blight and hail. Everything you were
doing got hit. But it didn't seem to faze you.
You continued to ignore me.' GOD's Decree.
18-19 " 'Now think ahead from this same date—
this twenty-fourth day of the ninth month.
Think ahead from when the Temple rebuild-
ing was launched. Has anything in your
fields—vine, fig tree, pomegranate, olive
tree—failed to flourish? From now on you
can count on a blessing.' "

20-21 GOD's Message came a second time to Hag-
gai on that most memorable day, the twenty-
fourth day of the ninth month: "Speak to
Zerubbabel, the governor of Judah:
21-23 " 'I am about to shake up everything, to
turn everything upside down and start over
from top to bottom—overthrow govern-
ments, destroy foreign powers, dismantle the
world of weapons and armaments, throw
armies into confusion, so that they end up
killing one another. And on that day' "—this
is GOD's Message—" 'I will take you, O
Zerubbabel son of Shealtiel, as my personal
servant and I will set you as a signet ring,
the sign of my sovereign presence and au-
thority. I've looked over the field and chosen
you for this work.' " The Message of GOD-of-
the-Angel-Armies.

ZECHARIAH

NEW KING JAMES VERSION

A CALL TO REPENTANCE

1 In the eighth month of the second year of
Darius, the word of the LORD came to
Zechariah the son of Berechiah, the son of Iddo
the prophet, saying, 2"The LORD has been very
angry with your fathers. 3Therefore say to them,
'Thus says the LORD of hosts: "Return to Me,"
says the LORD of hosts, "and I will return to you,"
says the LORD of hosts. 4"Do not be like your fa-
thers, to whom the former prophets preached,
saying, 'Thus says the LORD of hosts: "Turn now
from your evil ways and your evil deeds." ' But
they did not hear nor heed Me," says the LORD.

5"Your fathers, where *are* they?
And the prophets, do they live forever?
6Yet surely My words and My statutes,
Which I commanded My servants the
prophets,
Did they not overtake your fathers?

"So they returned and said:

'Just as the LORD of hosts determined to do
to us,
According to our ways and according to our
deeds,
So He has dealt with us.' " ' "

VISION OF THE HORSES

7On the twenty-fourth day of the eleventh
month, which is the month Shebat, in the sec-
ond year of Darius, the word of the LORD came
to Zechariah the son of Berechiah, the son of
Iddo the prophet: 8I saw by night, and behold, a
man riding on a red horse, and it stood among
the myrtle trees in the hollow; and behind him
were horses: red, sorrel, and white. 9Then I said,
"My lord, what *are* these?" So the angel who
talked with me said to me, "I will show you what
they *are*."

10And the man who stood among the myrtle
trees answered and said, "These *are the ones*
whom the LORD has sent to walk to and fro
throughout the earth."

11So they answered the Angel of the LORD,
who stood among the myrtle trees, and said,
"We have walked to and fro throughout the
earth, and behold, all the earth is resting qui-
etly."

THE LORD WILL COMFORT ZION

12Then the Angel of the LORD answered and
said, "O LORD of hosts, how long will You not
have mercy on Jerusalem and on the cities of Ju-
dah, against which You were angry these sev-
enty years?"

13And the LORD answered the angel who
talked to me, *with* good *and* comforting words.
14So the angel who spoke with me said to me,
"Proclaim, saying, 'Thus says the LORD of hosts:

"I am zealous for Jerusalem
And for Zion with great zeal.
15I am exceedingly angry with the nations at
ease;

THE MESSAGE

1-4 1 In the eighth month of the second year in
the reign of Darius, GOD's Message came
to the prophet Zechariah son of Berechiah,
son of Iddo: "GOD was very angry with your
ancestors. So give to the people this Mes-
sage from GOD-of-the-Angel-Armies: 'Come
back to me and I'll come back to you. Don't
be like your parents. The old-time prophets
called out to them, "A Message from GOD-of-
the-Angel-Armies: Leave your evil life. Quit
your evil practices." But they ignored every-
thing I said to them, stubbornly refused to
listen.'

5-6 "And where are your ancestors now?
Dead and buried. And the prophets who
preached to them? Also dead and buried.
But the Message that my servants the
prophets spoke, that isn't dead and buried.
That Message did its work on your ances-
tors, did it not? It woke them up and they
came back, saying, 'He did what he said he
would do, sure enough. We didn't get by
with a thing.' "

FIRST VISION: FOUR RIDERS

7 On the twenty-fourth day of the eleventh
month in the second year of the reign of
Darius, the Message of GOD was given to the
prophet Zechariah son of Berechiah, son of
Iddo:

8 One night I looked out and saw a man
astride a red horse. He was in the shadows
in a grove of birches. Behind him were more
horses—a red, a chestnut, and a white.

9 I said, "Sir, what are these horses doing
here? What's the meaning of this?"

The Angel-Messenger said, "Let me show
you."

10 Then the rider in the birch grove spoke
up, "These are the riders that GOD sent to
check things out on earth."

11 They reported their findings to the Angel
of GOD in the birch grove: "We have looked
over the whole earth and all is well. Every-
thing's under control."

12 The Angel of GOD reported back, "O GOD-
of-the-Angel-Armies, how long are you go-
ing to stay angry with Jerusalem and the
cities of Judah? When are you going to let
up? Isn't seventy years long enough?"

13-15 GOD reassured the Angel-Messenger—
good words, comforting words—who then
addressed me: "Tell them this. Tell them that
GOD-of-the-Angel-Armies has spoken. This
is GOD's Message: 'I care deeply for
Jerusalem and Zion. I feel very possessive
of them. But I'm thoroughly angry with the
godless nations that act as if they own the
whole world. I was only moderately angry

NEW KING JAMES VERSION

For I was a little angry,
And they helped—*but* with evil *intent*."

16 'Therefore thus says the LORD:

"I am returning to Jerusalem with mercy;
My house shall be built in it," says the LORD
of hosts,
"And a *surveyor's* line shall be stretched out
over Jerusalem." '

17 "Again proclaim, saying, 'Thus says the
LORD of hosts:

"My cities shall again spread out through
prosperity;
The LORD will again comfort Zion,
And will again choose Jerusalem." ' "

VISION OF THE HORNS

18 Then I raised my eyes and looked, and
there *were* four horns. 19 And I said to the angel
who talked with me, "What *are* these?"
So he answered me, "These *are* the horns
that have scattered Judah, Israel, and Jerusa-
lem."
20 Then the LORD showed me four craftsmen.
21 And I said, "What are these coming to do?"
So he said, "These *are* the horns that scat-
tered Judah, so that no one could lift up his
head; but the craftsmen[a] are coming to terrify
them, to cast out the horns of the nations that
lifted up *their* horn against the land of Judah to
scatter it."

VISION OF THE MEASURING LINE

2 Then I raised my eyes and looked, and be-
hold, a man with a measuring line in his
hand. 2 So I said, "Where are you going?"
And he said to me, "To measure Jerusalem,
to see what *is* its width and what *is* its length."
3 And there *was* the angel who talked with
me, going out; and another angel was coming
out to meet him, 4 who said to him, "Run, speak
to this young man, saying: 'Jerusalem shall be
inhabited *as* towns without walls, because of the
multitude of men and livestock in it. 5 For I,' says
the LORD, 'will be a wall of fire all around her,
and I will be the glory in her midst.' "

FUTURE JOY OF ZION AND MANY NATIONS

6 "Up, up! Flee from the land of the north,"
says the LORD; "for I have spread you abroad
like the four winds of heaven," says the LORD.
7 "Up, Zion! Escape, you who dwell with the
daughter of Babylon."
8 For thus says the LORD of hosts: "He sent Me
after glory, to the nations which plunder you; for

1:21 [a]Literally *these*

THE MESSAGE

earlier, but now they've gone too far. I'm go-
ing into action.

16-17 " 'I've come back to Jerusalem, but with
compassion this time.'
This is GOD speaking.
'I'll see to it that my Temple is rebuilt.'
A Decree of GOD-of-the-Angel-Armies!
'The rebuilding operation is already staked
out.'
Say it again—a Decree of
GOD-of-the-Angel-Armies:
'My cities will prosper again,
GOD will comfort Zion again,
Jerusalem will be back in my favor
again.' "

SECOND VISION: FOUR HORNS AND FOUR BLACKSMITHS

18 I looked up, and was surprised by another
vision: four horns!
19 I asked the Messenger-Angel, "And what's
the meaning of this?"
He said, "These are the powers that have
scattered Judah, Israel, and Jerusalem
abroad."
20 Then GOD expanded the vision to include
four blacksmiths.
21 I asked, "And what are these all about?"
He said, "Since the 'horns' scattered Ju-
dah so badly that no one had any hope left,
these blacksmiths have arrived to combat
the horns. They'll dehorn the godless na-
tions who used their horns to scatter Judah
to the four winds."

THIRD VISION: THE MAN WITH THE TAPE MEASURE

1-5 2 I looked up and was surprised to see
a man holding a tape measure in his
hand.
I said, "What are you up to?"
"I'm on my way," he said, "to survey
Jerusalem,
to measure its width and length."
Just then the Messenger-Angel on his way
out
met another angel coming in and said,
"Run! Tell the Surveyor, 'Jerusalem will
burst its walls—
bursting with people, bursting with
animals.
And I'll be right there with her'—GOD's
Decree—'a wall of fire
around unwalled Jerusalem and a
radiant presence within.' "

6-7 "Up on your feet! Get out of there—and
now!" GOD says so.
"Return from your far exile.
I scattered you to the four winds." GOD's
Decree.
"Escape from Babylon, Zion, and come
home—now!"

8-9 GOD-of-the-Angel-Armies, the One of Glory
who sent me on my mission, commenting on
the godless nations who stripped you and
left you homeless, said, "Anyone who hits

NEW KING JAMES VERSION

he who touches you touches the apple of His
eye. 9For surely I will shake My hand against
them, and they shall become spoil for their ser-
vants. Then you will know that the LORD of
hosts has sent Me.
10“Sing and rejoice, O daughter of Zion! For
behold, I am coming and I will dwell in your
midst,” says the LORD. 11“Many nations shall be
joined to the LORD in that day, and they shall be-
come My people. And I will dwell in your midst.
Then you will know that the LORD of hosts has
sent Me to you. 12And the LORD will take posses-
sion of Judah as His inheritance in the Holy
Land, and will again choose Jerusalem. 13Be
silent, all flesh, before the LORD, for He is
aroused from His holy habitation!”

VISION OF THE HIGH PRIEST

3Then he showed me Joshua the high priest
standing before the Angel of the LORD, and
Satan standing at his right hand to oppose him.
2And the LORD said to Satan, “The LORD rebuke
you, Satan! The LORD who has chosen Jeru-
salem rebuke you! *Is* this not a brand plucked
from the fire?”
3Now Joshua was clothed with filthy gar-
ments, and was standing before the Angel.
4Then He answered and spoke to those who
stood before Him, saying, “Take away the filthy
garments from him.” And to him He said, “See, I
have removed your iniquity from you, and I will
clothe you with rich robes.”
5And I said, “Let them put a clean turban on
his head.”
So they put a clean turban on his head, and
they put the clothes on him. And the Angel of
the LORD stood by.

THE COMING BRANCH

6Then the Angel of the LORD admonished
Joshua, saying, 7“Thus says the LORD of hosts:

‘If you will walk in My ways,
And if you will keep My command,
Then you shall also judge My house,
And likewise have charge of My courts;
I will give you places to walk
Among these who stand here.

8‘Hear, O Joshua, the high priest,
You and your companions who sit before
you,
For they are a wondrous sign;
For behold, I am bringing forth My Servant
the BRANCH.
9For behold, the stone
That I have laid before Joshua:
Upon the stone *are* seven eyes.

THE MESSAGE

you, hits me—bloodies my nose, blackens
my eye. Yes, and at the right time I'll give the
signal and they'll be stripped and thrown
out by their own servants.” Then you'll
know for sure that GOD-of-the-Angel-
Armies sent me on this mission.

10 “Shout and celebrate, Daughter of Zion!
I'm on my way. I'm moving into your
neighborhood!”
GOD'S Decree.

11-12 Many godless nations will be linked up with
GOD at that time. (“They will become my
family! I'll live in their homes!”) And then
you'll know for sure that GOD-of-the-Angel-
Armies sent me on this mission. GOD will re-
claim his Judah inheritance in the Holy
Land. He'll again make clear that Jerusalem
is his choice.

13 Quiet, everyone! Shh! Silence before GOD.
Something's afoot in his holy house. He's on
the move!

FOURTH VISION: JOSHUA'S NEW CLOTHES

1-2 3Next the Messenger-Angel showed me the
high priest Joshua. He was standing be-
fore GOD'S Angel where the Accuser showed
up to accuse him. Then GOD said to the Ac-
cuser, “I, GOD, rebuke you, Accuser! I rebuke
you and choose Jerusalem. Surprise! Every-
thing is going up in flames, but I reach in
and pull out Jerusalem!”
3-4 Joshua, standing before the angel, was
dressed in dirty clothes. The angel spoke to
his attendants, “Get him out of those filthy
clothes,” and then said to Joshua, “Look,
I've stripped you of your sin and dressed
you up in clean clothes.”
5 I spoke up and said, “How about a clean
new turban for his head also?” And they did
it—put a clean new turban on his head.
Then they finished dressing him, with GOD'S
Angel looking on.
6-7 GOD'S Angel then charged Joshua, “Or-
ders from GOD-of-the-Angel-Armies: ‘If you
live the way I tell you and remain obedient
in my service, then you'll make the deci-
sions around here and oversee my affairs.
And all my attendants standing here will be
at your service.
8-9 “ ‘Careful, High Priest Joshua—both you
and your friends sitting here with you, for
your friends are in on this, too! Here's what
I'm doing next: I'm introducing my servant
Branch. And note this: This stone that I'm
placing before Joshua, a single stone with
seven eyes'—Decree of GOD-of-the-Angel-

New King James Version

Behold, I will engrave its inscription,'
Says the LORD of hosts,
'And I will remove the iniquity of that land in
one day.
10In that day,' says the LORD of hosts,
'Everyone will invite his neighbor
Under his vine and under his fig tree.' "

Vision of the Lampstand and Olive Trees

4 Now the angel who talked with me came
back and wakened me, as a man who is wak-
ened out of his sleep. 2And he said to me, "What
do you see?"
So I said, "I am looking, and there *is* a lamp-
stand of solid gold with a bowl on top of it, and
on the *stand* seven lamps with seven pipes to
the seven lamps. 3Two olive trees *are* by it, one
at the right of the bowl and the other at its left."
4So I answered and spoke to the angel who
talked with me, saying, "What *are* these, my
lord?"
5Then the angel who talked with me an-
swered and said to me, "Do you not know what
these are?"
And I said, "No, my lord."
6So he answered and said to me:

"This *is* the word of the LORD to Zerubbabel:
'Not by might nor by power, but by My
Spirit,'
Says the LORD of hosts.
7'Who *are* you, O great mountain?
Before Zerubbabel *you shall become* a
plain!
And he shall bring forth the capstone
With shouts of "Grace, grace to it!" ' "
8Moreover the word of the LORD came to me,
saying:

9"The hands of Zerubbabel
Have laid the foundation of this temple;[a]
His hands shall also finish *it*.
Then you will know
That the LORD of hosts has sent Me to you.
10For who has despised the day of small
things?
For these seven rejoice to see
The plumb line in the hand of Zerubbabel.
They are the eyes of the LORD,
Which scan to and fro throughout the whole
earth."

11Then I answered and said to him, "What
are these two olive trees—at the right of the
lampstand and at its left?" 12And I further an-
swered and said to him, "What *are these* two
olive branches that *drip* into the receptacles[a] of
the two gold pipes from which the golden *oil*
drains?"
13Then he answered me and said, "Do you
not know what these *are*?"
And I said, "No, my lord."
14So he said, "These *are* the two anointed
ones, who stand beside the Lord of the whole
earth."

4:9 [a]Literally *house* **4:12** [a]Literally *into the hands of*

The Message

Armies—'I'll engrave with these words: "I'll strip this land of its filthy sin, all at once, in a single day."

10 " 'At that time, everyone will get along with one another, with friendly visits across the fence, friendly visits on one another's porches.' "

Fifth Vision: A Lampstand and Two Olive Trees

1 4 The Messenger-Angel again called me to attention. It was like being wakened out of deep sleep.

2-3 He said, "What do you see?"

I answered, "I see a lampstand of solid gold with a bowl on top. Seven lamps, each with seven spouts, are set on the bowl. And there are two olive trees, one on either side of the bowl."

4 Then I asked the Messenger-Angel, "What does this mean, sir?"

5-7 The Messenger-Angel said, "Can't you tell?"

"No, sir," I said.

Then he said, "This is GOD's Message to Zerubbabel: 'You can't force these things. They only come about through my Spirit,' says GOD-of-the-Angel-Armies. 'So, big mountain, who do you think you are? Next to Zerubbabel you're nothing but a molehill. He'll proceed to set the Cornerstone in place, accompanied by cheers: Yes! Yes! Do it!' "

8-10 After that, the Word of GOD came to me: "Zerubbabel started rebuilding this Temple and he will complete it. That will be your confirmation that GOD-of-the-Angel-Armies sent me to you. Does anyone dare despise this day of small beginnings? They'll change their tune when they see Zerubbabel setting the last stone in place!"

Going back to the vision, the Messenger-Angel said, "The seven lamps are the eyes of GOD probing the dark corners of the world like searchlights."

11-12 "And the two olive trees on either side of the lampstand?" I asked. "What's the meaning of them? And while you're at it, the two branches of the olive trees that feed oil to the lamps—what do they mean?"

13 He said, "You haven't figured that out?"

I said, "No, sir."

14 He said, "These are the two who stand beside the Master of the whole earth and supply golden lamp oil worldwide."

New King James Version

Vision of the Flying Scroll

5 Then I turned and raised my eyes, and saw
there a flying scroll.
2And he said to me, "What do you see?"
So I answered, "I see a flying scroll. Its
length *is* twenty cubits and its width ten cubits."
3Then he said to me, "This *is* the curse that
goes out over the face of the whole earth: 'Every
thief shall be expelled,' according *to* this side of
the scroll; and, 'Every perjurer shall be ex-
pelled,' according *to* that side of it."

4"I will send out *the curse,*" says the LORD of
hosts;
"It shall enter the house of the thief
And the house of the one who swears
falsely by My name.
It shall remain in the midst of his house
And consume it, with its timber and stones."

Vision of the Woman in a Basket

5Then the angel who talked with me came
out and said to me, "Lift your eyes now, and see
what this *is* that goes forth."
6So I asked, "What *is* it?" And he said, "It *is* a
basket[a] that is going forth."
He also said, "This *is* their resemblance
throughout the earth: 7Here *is* a lead disc lifted
up, and this *is* a woman sitting inside the bas-
ket"; 8then he said, "This *is* Wickedness!" And he
thrust her down into the basket, and threw the
lead cover[a] over its mouth. 9Then I raised my
eyes and looked, and there *were* two women,
coming with the wind in their wings; for they
had wings like the wings of a stork, and they
lifted up the basket between earth and heaven.
10So I said to the angel who talked with me,
"Where are they carrying the basket?"
11And he said to me, "To build a house for it
in the land of Shinar;[a] when it is ready, *the bas-
ket* will be set there on its base."

Vision of the Four Chariots

6 Then I turned and raised my eyes and looked,
and behold, four chariots *were* coming from
between two mountains, and the mountains
were mountains of bronze. 2With the first char-
iot *were* red horses, with the second chariot
black horses, 3with the third chariot white
horses, and with the fourth chariot dappled
horses—strong *steeds.* 4Then I answered and
said to the angel who talked with me, "What *are*
these, my lord?"
5And the angel answered and said to me,
"These *are* four spirits of heaven, who go out
from *their* station before the Lord of all the earth.
6The one with the black horses is going to the
north country, the white are going after them,
and the dappled are going toward the south
country." 7Then the strong *steeds* went out, eager
to go, that they might walk to and fro throughout
the earth. And He said, "Go, walk to and fro
throughout the earth." So they walked to and fro
throughout the earth. 8And He called to me, and
spoke to me, saying, "See, those who go toward
the north country have given rest to My Spirit in
the north country."

5:6 [a]Hebrew *ephah,* a measuring container, and so elsewhere
5:8 [a]Literally *stone* **5:11** [a]That is, Babylon

The Message

Sixth Vision: The Flying Book

1 5 I looked up again and saw—surprise!—a
book on the wing! A book flying!
2 The Messenger-Angel said to me, "What
do you see now?"
I said, "I see a book flying, a huge book—
thirty feet long and fifteen wide!"
3-4 He told me, "This book is the verdict go-
ing out worldwide against thieves and liars.
The first half of the book disposes of every-
one who steals; the second half takes care of
everyone who lies. I launched it"—Decree of
GOD-of-the-Angel-Armies—"and so it will
fly into the house of every thief and every
liar. It will land in each house and tear it
down, timbers and stones."

Seventh Vision: A Woman in a Basket

5 The Messenger-Angel appeared and said,
"Look up. Tell me what you see."
6 I said, "What in the world is that?"
He said, "This is a bushel basket on a
journey. It holds the sin of everyone, every-
where."
7 Then the lid made of lead was removed
from the basket—and there was a woman
sitting in it!
8 He said, "This is Miss Wicked." He
pushed her back down into the basket and
clamped the lead lid over her.
9 Then I looked up and to my surprise saw
two women flying. On outstretched wings
they airlifted the bushel basket into the sky.
10 I said to the Messenger-Angel, "Where
are they taking the bushel basket?"
11 He said, "East to the land of Shinar. They
will build a garage to house it. When it's fin-
ished, the basket will be stored there."

Eighth Vision: Four Chariots

1 6 Once again I looked up—another strange
sight! Four chariots charging out from be-
tween two mountains. The mountains were
bronze.
2-3 The first chariot was drawn by red
horses, the second chariot by black horses,
the third chariot by white horses, and the
fourth chariot by dappled horses. All the
horses were powerful.
4 I asked the Messenger-Angel, "Sir, what's
the meaning here?"
5-7 The angel answered, "These are the four
winds of heaven, which originate with the
Master of the whole earth. The black horses
are headed north with the white ones right
after them. The dappled horses are headed
south." The powerful horses galloped out,
bursting with energy, eager to patrol
through the earth. The Messenger-Angel
commanded: "On your way! Survey the
earth!" and they were off in every direction.
8 Then he called to me and said, "Look at
them go! The ones going north are convey-
ing a sense of my Spirit, serene and secure.
No more trouble from that direction."

New King James Version

The Command to Crown Joshua

9Then the word of the LORD came to me, saying: 10"Receive *the gift* from the captives—from Heldai, Tobijah, and Jedaiah, who have come from Babylon—and go the same day and enter the house of Josiah the son of Zephaniah. 11Take the silver and gold, make an elaborate crown, and set *it* on the head of Joshua the son of Jehozadak, the high priest. 12Then speak to him, saying, 'Thus says the LORD of hosts, saying:

"Behold, the Man whose name *is* the BRANCH!
From His place He shall branch out,
And He shall build the temple of the LORD;
13Yes, He shall build the temple of the LORD.
He shall bear the glory,
And shall sit and rule on His throne;
So He shall be a priest on His throne,
And the counsel of peace shall be between them both." '

14"Now the elaborate crown shall be for a memorial in the temple of the LORD for Helem,[a] Tobijah, Jedaiah, and Hen the son of Zephaniah. 15Even those from afar shall come and build the temple of the LORD. Then you shall know that the LORD of hosts has sent Me to you. And *this* shall come to pass if you diligently obey the voice of the LORD your God."

Obedience Better than Fasting

7 Now in the fourth year of King Darius it came to pass *that* the word of the LORD came to Zechariah, on the fourth *day* of the ninth month, Chislev, 2when *the people*[a] sent Sherezer,[b] with Regem-Melech and his men, *to* the house of God,[c] to pray before the LORD, 3*and* to ask the priests who *were* in the house of the LORD of hosts, and the prophets, saying, "Should I weep in the fifth month and fast as I have done for so many years?"

4Then the word of the LORD of hosts came to me, saying, 5"Say to all the people of the land, and to the priests: 'When you fasted and mourned in the fifth and seventh *months* during those seventy years, did you really fast for Me—for Me? 6When you eat and when you drink, do you not eat and drink *for yourselves?* 7*Should you* not *have obeyed* the words which the LORD proclaimed through the former prophets when Jerusalem and the cities around it were inhabited and prosperous, and the South[a] and the Lowland were inhabited?' "

Disobedience Resulted in Captivity

8Then the word of the LORD came to Zechariah, saying, 9"Thus says the LORD of hosts:

'Execute true justice,
Show mercy and compassion
Everyone to his brother.
10Do not oppress the widow or the fatherless,
The alien or the poor.
Let none of you plan evil in his heart
Against his brother.'

6:14 [a]Following Masoretic Text, Targum, and Vulgate; Syriac reads *for Heldai* (compare verse 10); Septuagint reads *for the patient ones.* **7:2** [a]Literally *they* (compare verse 5) [b]Or *Sar-Ezer* [c]Hebrew *Bethel* **7:7** [a]Hebrew *Negev*

The Message

A Man Named Branch

9-12 Then this Message from GOD came to me: "Take up a collection from the exiles. Target Heldai, Tobiah, and Jedaiah. They've just arrived from Babylon. You'll find them at the home of Josiah son of Zephaniah. Collect silver and gold from them and fashion crowns. Place one on the head of Joshua son of Jehozadak, the high priest, and give him this message:

12-13 " 'A Message from GOD-of-the-Angel-Armies. Be alert. We have a man here whose name is Branch. He will branch out from where he is and build the Temple of GOD. Yes, he's the one. He'll build the Temple of GOD. Then he'll assume the role of royalty, take his place on the throne and rule—a priest sitting on the throne!—showing that king and priest can coexist in harmony.'

14 "The other crown will be in the Temple of GOD as a symbol of royalty, under the custodial care of Helem, Tobiah, Jedaiah, and Hen son of Zephaniah.

15 "People will come from faraway places to pitch in and rebuild the Temple of GOD. This will confirm that GOD-of-the-Angel-Armies did, in fact, send me to you. All this follows as you put your minds to a life of responsive obedience to the voice of your GOD."

"You're Interested in Religion, I'm Interested in People"

1 7 On the fourth day of the ninth month, in the fourth year of the reign of King Darius, GOD's Message again came to Zechariah.

2-3 The town of Bethel had sent a delegation headed by Sarezer and Regem-Melech to pray for GOD's blessing and to confer with the priests of the Temple of GOD-of-the-Angel-Armies, and also with the prophets. They posed this question: "Should we plan for a day of mourning and abstinence next August, the seventieth anniversary of Jerusalem's fall, as we have been doing all these years?"

4-6 GOD-of-the-Angel-Armies gave me this Message for them, for all the people and for the priests: "When you held days of fasting every fifth and seventh month all these seventy years, were you doing it for me? And when you held feasts, was that for me? Hardly. You're interested in religion, I'm interested in people.

7-10 "There's nothing new to say on the subject. Don't you still have the message of the earlier prophets from the time when Jerusalem was still a thriving, bustling city and the outlying countryside, the Negev and Shephelah, was populated? [This is the message that GOD gave Zechariah.] Well, the message hasn't changed. GOD-of-the-Angel-Armies said then and says now:

" 'Treat one another justly.
Love your neighbors.
Be compassionate with each other.
Don't take advantage of widows,
orphans, visitors, and the poor.
Don't plot and scheme against one
another—that's evil.'

NEW KING JAMES VERSION

11“But they refused to heed, shrugged their
shoulders, and stopped their ears so that they
could not hear. 12Yes, they made their hearts like
flint, refusing to hear the law and the words
which the LORD of hosts had sent by His Spirit
through the former prophets. Thus great wrath
came from the LORD of hosts. 13Therefore it hap-
pened, *that* just as He proclaimed and they
would not hear, so they called out and I would
not listen,” says the LORD of hosts. 14“But I scat-
tered them with a whirlwind among all the na-
tions which they had not known. Thus the land
became desolate after them, so that no one
passed through or returned; for they made the
pleasant land desolate.”

JERUSALEM, HOLY CITY OF THE FUTURE

8 Again the word of the LORD of hosts came,
saying, 2“Thus says the LORD of hosts:

‘I am zealous for Zion with great zeal;
With great fervor I am zealous for her.’

3“Thus says the LORD:

‘I will return to Zion,
And dwell in the midst of Jerusalem.
Jerusalem shall be called the City of Truth,
The Mountain of the LORD of hosts,
The Holy Mountain.’

4“Thus says the LORD of hosts:

‘Old men and old women shall again sit
In the streets of Jerusalem,
Each one with his staff in his hand
Because of great age.
5The streets of the city
Shall be full of boys and girls
Playing in its streets.’

6“Thus says the LORD of hosts:

‘If it is marvelous in the eyes of the remnant
of this people in these days,
Will it also be marvelous in My eyes?’
Says the LORD of hosts.

7“Thus says the LORD of hosts:

‘Behold, I will save My people from the land
of the east
And from the land of the west;
8I will bring them *back*,
And they shall dwell in the midst of
Jerusalem.
They shall be My people
And I will be their God,
In truth and righteousness.’

9“Thus says the LORD of hosts:

‘Let your hands be strong,
You who have been hearing in these days
These words by the mouth of the prophets,
Who *spoke* in the day the foundation was laid
For the house of the LORD of hosts,

THE MESSAGE

11-13 “But did your ancestors listen? No, they
set their jaws in defiance. They shut their
ears. They steeled themselves against GOD’s
revelation and the Spirit-filled sermons
preached by the earlier prophets by order of
GOD-of-the-Angel-Armies. And GOD became
angry, really angry, because he told them
everything plainly and they wouldn’t listen
to a word he said.

13-14 “So [this is what GOD-of-the-Angel-
Armies said] if they won’t listen to me, I
won’t listen to them. I scattered them to the
four winds. They ended up strangers wher-
ever they were. Their ‘promised land’ be-
came a vacant lot—weeds and tin cans and
thistles. Not a sign of life. They turned a
dreamland into a wasteland.”

REBUILDING THE TEMPLE

1-2 8 And then these Messages from GOD-of-
the-Angel-Armies:

A Message from GOD-of-the-Angel-Armies:

“I am zealous for Zion—I *care*!
I’m angry about Zion—I’m *involved*!”

GOD’s Message:

3 “I’ve come back to Zion,
I’ve moved back to Jerusalem.
Jerusalem’s new names will be Truth City,
and Mountain of GOD-of-the-Angel-
Armies,
and Mount Holiness.”

4-5 A Message from GOD-of-the-Angel-Armies:
“Old men and old women will come back
to Jerusalem, sit on benches on the streets
and spin tales, move around safely with
their canes—a good city to grow old in. And
boys and girls will fill the public parks,
laughing and playing—a good city to grow
up in.”

6 A Message from GOD-of-the-Angel-Armies:
“Do the problems of returning and re-
building by just a few survivors seem too
much? But is anything too much for me?
Not if I have my say.”

7-8 A Message from GOD-of-the-Angel-Armies:
“I’ll collect my people from countries to
the east and countries to the west. I’ll bring
them back and move them into Jerusalem.
They’ll be my people and I’ll be their God.
I’ll stick with them and do right by them.”

9-10 A Message from GOD-of-the-Angel-Armies:
“Get a grip on things. Hold tight, you who
are listening to what I say through the
preaching of the prophets. The Temple of
GOD-of-the-Angel-Armies has been reestab-

NEW KING JAMES VERSION

That the temple might be built.
10For before these days
There were no wages for man nor any hire
for beast;
There was no peace from the enemy for
whoever went out or came in;
For I set all men, everyone, against his
neighbor.

11But now I *will* not *treat* the remnant of this
people as in the former days,' says the LORD of
hosts.

12'For the seed *shall be* prosperous,
The vine shall give its fruit,
The ground shall give her increase,
And the heavens shall give their dew—
I will cause the remnant of this people
To possess all these.
13And it shall come to pass
That just as you were a curse among the
nations,
O house of Judah and house of Israel,
So I will save you, and you shall be a blessing.
Do not fear,
Let your hands be strong.'

14"For thus says the LORD of hosts:

'Just as I determined to punish you
When your fathers provoked Me to wrath,'
Says the LORD of hosts,
'And I would not relent,
15So again in these days
I am determined to do good
To Jerusalem and to the house of Judah.
Do not fear.
16These *are* the things you shall do:
Speak each man the truth to his neighbor;
Give judgment in your gates for truth,
justice, and peace;
17Let none of you think evil in your[a] heart
against your neighbor;
And do not love a false oath.
For all these *are things* that I hate,'
Says the LORD."

18Then the word of the LORD of hosts came to
me, saying, 19"Thus says the LORD of hosts:

'The fast of the fourth *month*,
The fast of the fifth,
The fast of the seventh,
And the fast of the tenth,
Shall be joy and gladness and cheerful feasts
For the house of Judah.
Therefore love truth and peace.'

20"Thus says the LORD of hosts:

'Peoples shall yet come,
Inhabitants of many cities;
21The inhabitants of one *city* shall go to
another, saying,
"Let us continue to go and pray before the
LORD,
And seek the LORD of hosts.
I myself will go also."

8:17 [a]Literally *his*

THE MESSAGE

lished. The Temple is being rebuilt. We've
come through a hard time: You worked for a
pittance and were lucky to get that; the
streets were dangerous; you could never let
down your guard; I had turned the world
into an armed camp.
11-12 "But things have changed. I'm taking the
side of my core of surviving people:

Sowing and harvesting will resume,
Vines will grow grapes,
Gardens will flourish,
Dew and rain will make everything
green.

12-13 "My core survivors will get everything
they need—and more. You've gotten a repu-
tation as a bad-news people, you people of
Judah and Israel, but I'm coming to save
you. From now on, you're the good-news
people. Don't be afraid. Keep a firm grip on
what I'm doing."

KEEP YOUR LIVES SIMPLE AND HONEST

14-17 A Message from GOD-of-the-Angel-Armies:
"In the same way that I decided to punish
you when your ancestors made me angry,
and didn't pull my punches, at this time I've
decided to bless Jerusalem and the country
of Judah. Don't be afraid. And now here's
what I want you to do: Tell the truth, the
whole truth, when you speak. Do the right
thing by one another, both personally and in
your courts. Don't cook up plans to take un-
fair advantage of others. Don't do or say
what isn't so. I hate all that stuff. Keep your
lives simple and honest." Decree of GOD.

18-19 Again I received a Message from GOD-of-
the-Angel-Armies:
"The days of mourning set for the fourth,
fifth, seventh, and tenth months will be
turned into days of feasting for Judah—cel-
ebration and holiday. Embrace truth! Love
peace!"

20-21 A Message from GOD-of-the-Angel-Armies:
"People and their leaders will come from
all over to see what's going on. The leaders
will confer with one another: 'Shouldn't we
try to get in on this? Get in on GOD's bless-
ings? Pray to GOD-of-the-Angel-Armies?
What's keeping us? Let's go!'

NEW KING JAMES VERSION

22Yes, many peoples and strong nations
Shall come to seek the LORD of hosts in
Jerusalem,
And to pray before the LORD.'

23"Thus says the LORD of hosts: 'In those days
ten men from every language of the nations
shall grasp the sleeve of a Jewish man, saying,
"Let us go with you, for we have heard *that* God
is with you." ' "

ISRAEL DEFENDED AGAINST ENEMIES

9 The burden[a] of the word of the LORD
Against the land of Hadrach,
And Damascus its resting place
(For the eyes of men
And all the tribes of Israel
Are on the LORD);
2Also *against* Hamath, *which* borders on it,
And *against* Tyre and Sidon, though they
are very wise.

3For Tyre built herself a tower,
Heaped up silver like the dust,
And gold like the mire of the streets.
4Behold, the Lord will cast her out;
He will destroy her power in the sea,
And she will be devoured by fire.

5Ashkelon shall see *it* and fear;
Gaza also shall be very sorrowful;
And Ekron, for He dried up her expectation.
The king shall perish from Gaza,
And Ashkelon shall not be inhabited.

6"A mixed race shall settle in Ashdod,
And I will cut off the pride of the Philistines.
7I will take away the blood from his mouth,
And the abominations from between his
teeth.
But he who remains, even he *shall be* for our
God,
And shall be like a leader in Judah,
And Ekron like a Jebusite.
8I will camp around My house
Because of the army,
Because of him who passes by and him who
returns.
No more shall an oppressor pass through
them,
For now I have seen with My eyes.

THE COMING KING

9"Rejoice greatly, O daughter of Zion!
Shout, O daughter of Jerusalem!
Behold, your King is coming to you;
He *is* just and having salvation,
Lowly and riding on a donkey,
A colt, the foal of a donkey.
10I will cut off the chariot from Ephraim
And the horse from Jerusalem;
The battle bow shall be cut off.
He shall speak peace to the nations;
His dominion *shall be* 'from sea to sea,
And from the River to the ends of the
earth.'[a]

9:1 [a]Or *oracle* **9:10** [a]Psalm 72:8

THE MESSAGE

22 "Lots of people, powerful nations—they'll
come to Jerusalem looking for what they
can get from GOD-of-the-Angel-Armies,
looking to get a blessing from GOD."

23 A Message from GOD-of-the-Angel-Armies:
"At that time, ten men speaking a variety
of languages will grab the sleeve of one Jew,
hold tight, and say, 'Let us go with you.
We've heard that God is with you.' "

THE WHOLE WORLD HAS ITS EYES ON GOD

1-6 9 War Bulletin:

GOD's Message challenges the country of
Hadrach.
It will settle on Damascus.
The whole world has its eyes on GOD.
Israel isn't the only one.
That includes Hamath at the border,
and Tyre and Sidon, clever as they think
they are.
Tyre has put together quite a kingdom for
herself;
she has stacked up silver like cordwood,
piled gold high as haystacks.
But God will certainly bankrupt her;
he will dump all that wealth into the
ocean
and burn up what's left in a big fire.
Ashkelon will see it and panic,
Gaza will wring its hands,
Ekron will face a dead end.
Gaza's king will die.
Ashkelon will be emptied out,
And a villain will take over in Ashdod.

6-8 "I'll take proud Philistia down a peg:
I'll make him spit out his bloody booty
and abandon his vile ways."
What's left will be all God's—a core of
survivors,
a family brought together in Judah—
But enemies like Ekron will go the way of
the Jebusites,
into the dustbin of history.
"I will set up camp in my home country
and defend it against invaders.
Nobody is going to hurt my people ever
again.
I'm keeping my eye on them.

A HUMBLE KING RIDING A DONKEY

9-10 "Shout and cheer, Daughter Zion!
Raise the roof, Daughter Jerusalem!
Your king is coming!
a good king who makes all things right,
a humble king riding a donkey,
a mere colt of a donkey.
I've had it with war—no more chariots in
Ephraim,
no more war horses in Jerusalem,
no more swords and spears, bows and
arrows.
He will offer peace to the nations,
a peaceful rule worldwide,
from the four winds to the seven seas.

New King James Version

God Will Save His People

11"As for you also,
Because of the blood of your covenant,
I will set your prisoners free from the waterless pit.
12Return to the stronghold,
You prisoners of hope.
Even today I declare
That I will restore double to you.
13For I have bent Judah, My *bow*,
Fitted the bow with Ephraim,
And raised up your sons, O Zion,
Against your sons, O Greece,
And made you like the sword of a mighty man."

14Then the LORD will be seen over them,
And His arrow will go forth like lightning.
The Lord GOD will blow the trumpet,
And go with whirlwinds from the south.
15The LORD of hosts will defend them;
They shall devour and subdue with slingstones.
They shall drink *and* roar as if with wine;
They shall be filled *with blood* like basins,
Like the corners of the altar.
16The LORD their God will save them in that day,
As the flock of His people.
For they *shall be like* the jewels of a crown,
Lifted like a banner over His land—
17For how great is its[a] goodness
And how great its[b] beauty!
Grain shall make the young men thrive,
And new wine the young women.

Restoration of Judah and Israel

10 Ask the LORD for rain
In the time of the latter rain.[a]
The LORD will make flashing clouds;
He will give them showers of rain,
Grass in the field for everyone.

2For the idols[a] speak delusion;
The diviners envision lies,
And tell false dreams;
They comfort in vain.
Therefore *the people* wend their way like sheep;
They are in trouble because *there is* no shepherd.

3"My anger is kindled against the shepherds,
And I will punish the goatherds.
For the LORD of hosts will visit His flock,
The house of Judah,
And will make them as His royal horse in the battle.
4From him comes the cornerstone,
From him the tent peg,
From him the battle bow,
From him every ruler[a] together.
5They shall be like mighty men,
Who tread down *their enemies*
In the mire of the streets in the battle.
They shall fight because the LORD is with them,
And the riders on horses shall be put to shame.

9:17 [a]Or *His* [b]Or *His* **10:1** [a]That is, spring rain **10:2** [a]Hebrew *teraphim* **10:4** [a]Or *despot*

The Message

11-13 "And you, because of my blood covenant with you,
I'll release your prisoners from their hopeless cells.
Come home, hope-filled prisoners!
This very day I'm declaring a double bonus—
everything you lost returned twice-over!
Judah is now my weapon, the bow I'll pull,
setting Ephraim as an arrow to the string.
I'll wake up your sons, O Zion,
to counter your sons, O Greece.
From now on
people are my swords."

14-17 Then GOD will come into view,
his arrows flashing like lightning!
Master GOD will blast his trumpet
and set out in a whirlwind.
GOD-of-the-Angel-Armies will protect them—
all-out war,
The war to end all wars,
no holds barred.
Their GOD will save the day. He'll rescue them.
They'll become like sheep, gentle and soft,
Or like gemstones in a crown,
catching all the colors of the sun.
Then how they'll shine! shimmer! glow!
the young men robust, the young women lovely!

God's Work of Rebuilding

1 10 Pray to GOD for rain—it's time for the spring rain—to GOD, the rainmaker,
Spring thunderstorm maker,
maker of grain and barley.

2-3 "Store-bought gods babble gibberish.
Religious experts spout rubbish.
They pontificate hot air.
Their prescriptions are nothing but smoke.
And so the people wander like lost sheep,
poor lost sheep without a shepherd.
I'm furious with the so-called shepherds.
They're worse than billy goats, and I'll treat them like goats."

3-5 GOD-of-the-Angel-Armies will step in
and take care of his flock, the people of Judah.
He'll revive their spirits,
make them proud to be on God's side.
God will use them in his work of rebuilding,
use them as foundations and pillars,
Use them as tools and instruments,
use them to oversee his work.
They'll be a workforce to be proud of,
working as one,
their heads held high, striding through swamps and mud,
Courageous and vigorous because GOD is with them,
undeterred by the world's thugs.

NEW KING JAMES VERSION

6"I will strengthen the house of Judah,
And I will save the house of Joseph.
I will bring them back,
Because I have mercy on them.
They shall be as though I had not cast them aside;
For I *am* the LORD their God,
And I will hear them.
7*Those of* Ephraim shall be like a mighty man,
And their heart shall rejoice as if with wine.
Yes, their children shall see *it* and be glad;
Their heart shall rejoice in the LORD.
8I will whistle for them and gather them,
For I will redeem them;
And they shall increase as they once increased.
9"I will sow them among the peoples,
And they shall remember Me in far countries;
They shall live, together with their children,
And they shall return.
10I will also bring them back from the land of Egypt,
And gather them from Assyria.
I will bring them into the land of Gilead and Lebanon,
Until no *more room* is found for them.
11He shall pass through the sea with affliction,
And strike the waves of the sea:
All the depths of the River[a] shall dry up.
Then the pride of Assyria shall be brought down,
And the scepter of Egypt shall depart.
12"So I will strengthen them in the LORD,
And they shall walk up and down in His name,"
Says the LORD.

DESOLATION OF ISRAEL

11 Open your doors, O Lebanon,
That fire may devour your cedars.
2Wail, O cypress, for the cedar has fallen,
Because the mighty *trees* are ruined.
Wail, O oaks of Bashan,
For the thick forest has come down.
3*There is* the sound of wailing shepherds!
For their glory is in ruins.
There is the sound of roaring lions!
For the pride[a] of the Jordan is in ruins.

PROPHECY OF THE SHEPHERDS

4Thus says the LORD my God, "Feed the flock
for slaughter, 5whose owners slaughter them
and feel no guilt; those who sell them say,
'Blessed be the LORD, for I am rich'; and their
shepherds do not pity them.

10:11 [a]That is, the Nile 11:3 [a]Or *floodplain, thicket*

THE MESSAGE

6-12 "I'll put muscle in the people of Judah;
I'll save the people of Joseph.
I know their pain and will make them good as new.
They'll get a fresh start, as if nothing had ever happened.
And why? Because I am their very own GOD,
I'll do what needs to be done for them.
The people of Ephraim will be famous,
their lives brimming with joy.
Their children will get in on it, too—
oh, let them feel blessed by GOD!
I'll whistle and they'll all come running.
I've set them free—oh, how they'll flourish!
Even though I scattered them to the far corners of earth,
they'll remember me in the faraway places.
They'll keep the story alive in their children,
and they will come back.
I'll bring them back from the Egyptian west
and round them up from the Assyrian east.
I'll bring them back to sweet Gilead,
back to leafy Lebanon.
Every square foot of land
will be marked by homecoming.
They'll sail through troubled seas, brush aside brash ocean waves.
Roaring rivers will turn to a trickle.
Gaudy Assyria will be stripped bare,
bully Egypt exposed as a fraud.
But my people—oh, I'll make them strong, GOD-strong!
and they'll live my way." GOD says so!

1-4 11 Open your borders to the immigrants, proud Lebanon!
Your sentinel trees will burn.
Weep, great pine trees! Mourn, you sister cedars!
Your towering trees are cordwood.
Weep Bashan oak trees!
Your thick forest is now a field of stumps.
Do you hear the wailing of shepherds?
They've lost everything they once owned.
Do you hear the outrage of the lions?
The mighty jungle of the Jordan is wasted.
Make room for the returning exiles!

BREAKING THE BEAUTIFUL COVENANT

4-5 GOD commanded me, "Shepherd the sheep
that are soon to be slaughtered. The people
who buy them will butcher them for quick
and easy money. What's worse, they'll get
away with it. The people who sell them will
say, 'Lucky me! God's on my side; I've got it
made!' They have shepherds who couldn't
care less about them."

NEW KING JAMES VERSION

6For I will no longer pity the inhabitants of the land," says the LORD. "But indeed I will give everyone into his neighbor's hand and into the hand of his king. They shall attack the land, and I will not deliver *them* from their hand."

7So I fed the flock for slaughter, in particular the poor of the flock.[a] I took for myself two staffs: the one I called Beauty,[b] and the other I called Bonds;[c] and I fed the flock. 8I dismissed the three shepherds in one month. My soul loathed them, and their soul also abhorred me. 9Then I said, "I will not feed you. Let what is dying die, and what is perishing perish. Let those that are left eat each other's flesh." 10And I took my staff, Beauty, and cut it in two, that I might break the covenant which I had made with all the peoples. 11So it was broken on that day. Thus the poor[a] of the flock, who were watching me, knew that it *was* the word of the LORD. 12Then I said to them, "If it is agreeable to you, give *me* my wages; and if not, refrain." So they weighed out for my wages thirty *pieces* of silver.

13And the LORD said to me, "Throw it to the potter"—that princely price they set on me. So I took the thirty *pieces* of silver and threw them into the house of the LORD for the potter. 14Then I cut in two my other staff, Bonds, that I might break the brotherhood between Judah and Israel.

15And the LORD said to me, "Next, take for yourself the implements of a foolish shepherd. 16For indeed I will raise up a shepherd in the land *who* will not care for those who are cut off, nor seek the young, nor heal those that are broken, nor feed those that still stand. But he will eat the flesh of the fat and tear their hooves in pieces.

17"Woe to the worthless shepherd,
Who leaves the flock!
A sword *shall be* against his arm
And against his right eye;
His arm shall completely wither,
And his right eye shall be totally blinded."

THE COMING DELIVERANCE OF JUDAH

12 The burden[a] of the word of the LORD against Israel. Thus says the LORD, who stretches out the heavens, lays the foundation of the earth, and forms the spirit of man within him: 2"Behold, I will make Jerusalem a cup of drunkenness to all the surrounding peoples, when they lay siege against Judah and Jerusalem. 3And it shall happen in that day that I will make Jerusalem a very heavy stone for all peoples; all who would heave it away will surely be cut in pieces, though all nations of the earth are gathered against it. 4In that day," says the LORD, "I will strike every horse with confusion,

11:7 [a]Following Masoretic Text, Targum, and Vulgate; Septuagint reads *for the Canaanites.* [b]Or *Grace,* and so in verse 10 [c]Or *Unity,* and so in verse 14 **11:11** [a]Following Masoretic Text, Targum, and Vulgate; Septuagint reads *the Canaanites.* **12:1** [a]Or *oracle*

THE MESSAGE

6 GOD's Decree: "I'm washing my hands of the people of this land. From now on they're all on their own. It's dog-eat-dog, survival of the fittest, and the devil take the hindmost. Don't look for help from me."

7-8 So I took over from the crass, money-grubbing owners, and shepherded the sheep marked for slaughter. I got myself two shepherd staffs. I named one Lovely and the other Harmony. Then I went to work shepherding the sheep. Within a month I got rid of the corrupt shepherds. I got tired of putting up with them—and they couldn't stand me.

9 And then I got tired of the sheep and said, "I've had it with you—no more shepherding from me. If you die, you die; if you're attacked, you're attacked. Whoever survives can eat what's left."

10-11 Then I took the staff named Lovely and broke it across my knee, breaking the beautiful covenant I had made with all the peoples. In one stroke, both staff and covenant were broken. The money-hungry owners saw me do it and knew GOD was behind it.

12 Then I addressed them: "Pay me what you think I'm worth." They paid me an insulting sum, counting out thirty silver coins.

13 GOD told me, "Throw it in the poor box." This stingy wage was all they thought of me and my work! So I took the thirty silver coins and threw them into the poor box in GOD's Temple.

14 Then I broke the other staff, Harmony, across my knee, breaking the concord between Judah and Israel.

15-16 GOD then said, "Dress up like a stupid shepherd. I'm going to install just such a shepherd in this land—a shepherd indifferent to victims, who ignores the lost, abandons the injured, and disdains decent citizens. He'll only be in it for what he can get out of it, using and abusing any and all.

17 "Doom to you, useless shepherd,
walking off and leaving the sheep!
A curse on your arm!
A curse on your right eye!
Your arm will hang limp and useless.
Your right eye will go stone blind."

HOME AGAIN IN JERUSALEM

1-2 12 War Bulletin:

GOD's Message concerning Israel, GOD's Decree—the very GOD who threw the skies into space, set earth on a firm foundation, and breathed his own life into men and women: "Watch for this: I'm about to turn Jerusalem into a cup of strong drink that will have the people who have set siege to Judah and Jerusalem staggering in a drunken stupor.

3 "On the Big Day, I'll turn Jerusalem into a huge stone blocking the way for everyone. All who try to lift it will rupture themselves. All the pagan nations will come together and try to get rid of it.

4-5 "On the Big Day"—this is GOD speaking—"I'll throw all the war horses into a crazed

NEW KING JAMES VERSION

and its rider with madness; I will open My eyes
on the house of Judah, and will strike every
horse of the peoples with blindness. 5And the
governors of Judah shall say in their heart, 'The
inhabitants of Jerusalem *are* my strength in the
LORD of hosts, their God.' 6In that day I will
make the governors of Judah like a firepan in
the woodpile, and like a fiery torch in the
sheaves; they shall devour all the surrounding
peoples on the right hand and on the left, but
Jerusalem shall be inhabited again in her own
place—Jerusalem.
7"The LORD will save the tents of Judah first,
so that the glory of the house of David and the
glory of the inhabitants of Jerusalem shall not
become greater than that of Judah. 8In that day
the LORD will defend the inhabitants of
Jerusalem; the one who is feeble among them in
that day shall be like David, and the house of
David *shall be* like God, like the Angel of the
LORD before them. 9It shall be in that day *that* I
will seek to destroy all the nations that come
against Jerusalem.

MOURNING FOR THE PIERCED ONE

10"And I will pour on the house of David and
on the inhabitants of Jerusalem the Spirit of
grace and supplication; then they will look on
Me whom they pierced. Yes, they will mourn for
Him as one mourns for *his* only *son*, and grieve
for Him as one grieves for a firstborn. 11In that
day there shall be a great mourning in
Jerusalem, like the mourning at Hadad Rimmon
in the plain of Megiddo.[a] 12And the land shall
mourn, every family by itself: the family of the
house of David by itself, and their wives by
themselves; the family of the house of Nathan
by itself, and their wives by themselves; 13the
family of the house of Levi by itself, and their
wives by themselves; the family of Shimei by it-
self, and their wives by themselves; 14all the
families that remain, every family by itself, and
their wives by themselves.

IDOLATRY CUT OFF

13 "In that day a fountain shall be opened for
the house of David and for the inhabitants
of Jerusalem, for sin and for uncleanness.
2"It shall be in that day," says the LORD of
hosts, "*that* I will cut off the names of the idols
from the land, and they shall no longer be re-
membered. I will also cause the prophets and
the unclean spirit to depart from the land. 3It
shall come to pass *that* if anyone still prophe-
sies, then his father and mother who begot him

12:11 [a]Hebrew *Megiddon*

THE MESSAGE

panic, and their riders along with them. But
I'll keep my eye on Judah, watching out for
her at the same time that I make the enemy
horses go blind. The families of Judah will
then realize, 'Why, our leaders are strong
and able through GOD-of-the-Angel-Armies,
their personal God.'
6 "On the Big Day, I'll turn the families of
Judah into something like a burning match
in a tinder-dry forest, like a fiercely flaming
torch in a barn full of hay. They'll burn up
everything and everyone in sight—people
to the right, people to the left—while
Jerusalem fills up with people moving in
and making themselves at home—home
again in Jerusalem.
7-8 "I, GOD, will begin by restoring the com-
mon households of Judah so that the glory
of David's family and the leaders in
Jerusalem won't overshadow the ordinary
people in Judah. On the Big Day, I'll look af-
ter everyone who lives in Jerusalem so that
the lowliest, weakest person will be as glori-
ous as David and the family of David itself
will be godlike, like the Angel of GOD lead-
ing the people.
9 "On the Big Day, I'll make a clean sweep
of all the godless nations that fought against
Jerusalem.
10-14 "Next I'll deal with the family of David
and those who live in Jerusalem. I'll pour a
spirit of grace and prayer over them. They'll
then be able to recognize me as the One
they so grievously wounded—that piercing
spear-thrust! And they'll weep—oh, how
they'll weep! Deep mourning as of a parent
grieving the loss of the firstborn child. The
lamentation in Jerusalem that day will be
massive, as famous as the lamentation over
Hadad-Rimmon on the fields of Megiddo:

Everyone will weep and grieve,
    the land and everyone in it:
The family of David off by itself
    and their women off by themselves;
The family of Nathan off by itself
    and their women off by themselves;
The family of Levi off by itself
    and their women off by themselves;
The family of Shimei off by itself
    and their women off by themselves;
And all the rest of the families off by
    themselves
    and their women off by themselves."

WASHING AWAY SINS

1 13 "On the Big Day, a fountain will be
opened for the family of David and all
the leaders of Jerusalem for washing away
their sins, for scrubbing their stained and
soiled lives clean.
2-3 "On the Big Day"—this is GOD-of-the-
Angel-Armies speaking—"I will wipe out the
store-bought gods, erase their names from
memory. People will forget they ever heard
of them. And I'll get rid of the prophets who
polluted the air with their diseased words. If
anyone dares persist in spreading diseased,
polluting words, his very own parents will

NEW KING JAMES VERSION

will say to him, 'You shall not live, because you
have spoken lies in the name of the LORD.' And
his father and mother who begot him shall
thrust him through when he prophesies.
[4]"And it shall be in that day *that* every
prophet will be ashamed of his vision when he
prophesies; they will not wear a robe of coarse
hair to deceive. [5]But he will say, 'I *am* no
prophet, I *am* a farmer; for a man taught me to
keep cattle from my youth.' [6]And *one* will say to
him, 'What are these wounds between your
arms?'[a] Then he will answer, '*Those* with which
I was wounded in the house of my friends.'

THE SHEPHERD SAVIOR

[7]"Awake, O sword, against My Shepherd,
Against the Man who is My Companion,"
Says the LORD of hosts.
"Strike the Shepherd,
And the sheep will be scattered;
Then I will turn My hand against the little ones.
[8]And it shall come to pass in all the land,"
Says the LORD,
"*That* two-thirds in it shall be cut off *and* die,
But *one*-third shall be left in it:
[9]I will bring the *one*-third through the fire,
Will refine them as silver is refined,
And test them as gold is tested.
They will call on My name,
And I will answer them.
I will say, 'This *is* My people';
And each one will say, 'The LORD *is* my God.' "

THE DAY OF THE LORD

14 Behold, the day of the LORD is coming,
And your spoil will be divided in your midst.
[2]For I will gather all the nations to battle against Jerusalem;
The city shall be taken,
The houses rifled,
And the women ravished.
Half of the city shall go into captivity,
But the remnant of the people shall not be cut off from the city.

[3]Then the LORD will go forth
And fight against those nations,
As He fights in the day of battle.
[4]And in that day His feet will stand on the Mount of Olives,
Which faces Jerusalem on the east.
And the Mount of Olives shall be split in two,
From east to west,
Making a very large valley;
Half of the mountain shall move toward the north
And half of it toward the south.

[5]Then you shall flee *through* My mountain valley,
For the mountain valley shall reach to Azal.
Yes, you shall flee
As you fled from the earthquake
In the days of Uzziah king of Judah.

13:6 [a]Or *hands*

THE MESSAGE

step in and say, 'That's it! You're finished!
Your lies about GOD put everyone in danger,'
and then they'll stab him to death in the very
act of prophesying lies about GOD—his own
parents, mind you!
4-6 "On the Big Day, the lying prophets will
be publicly exposed and humiliated. Then
they'll wish they'd never swindled people
with their 'visions.' No more masquerading
in prophet clothes. But they'll deny they've
even heard of such things: 'Me, a prophet?
Not me. I'm a farmer—grew up on the farm.'
And if someone says, 'And so where did you
get that black eye?' they'll say, 'I ran into a
door at a friend's house.'

7-9 "Sword, get moving against my shepherd,
against my close associate!"
Decree of GOD-of-the-Angel-Armies.
"Kill the shepherd! Scatter the sheep!
The back of my hand against even the lambs!
All across the country"—GOD's Decree—
"two-thirds will be devastated
and one-third survive.
I'll deliver the surviving third to the refinery fires.
I'll refine them as silver is refined,
test them for purity as gold is tested.
Then they'll pray to me by name
and I'll answer them personally.
I'll say, 'That's my people.'
They'll say, 'GOD—my God!' "

THE DAY IS COMING

1-2 **14** Note well: GOD's Judgment Day is on the way:
"Plunder will be piled high and handed out.
I'm bringing all the godless nations
to war against Jerusalem—
Houses plundered,
women raped,
Half the city taken into exile,
the other half left behind."

3-5 But then GOD will march out against the
godless nations and fight—a great war!
That's the Day he'll take his stand on the
Mount of Olives, facing Jerusalem from the
east. The Mount of Olives will be split right
down the middle, from east to west, leaving
a wide valley. Half the mountain will shift
north, the other half south. Then you will
run for your lives down the valley, your es-
cape route that will take you all the way to
Azal. You'll run for your lives, just as you
ran on the day of the great earthquake in
the days of Uzziah, king of Judah. Then my

NEW KING JAMES VERSION

Thus the LORD my God will come,
And all the saints with You.[a]

[6]It shall come to pass in that day
That there will be no light;
The lights will diminish.
[7]It shall be one day
Which is known to the LORD—
Neither day nor night.
But at evening time it shall happen
That it will be light.

[8]And in that day it shall be
That living waters shall flow from
Jerusalem,
Half of them toward the eastern sea
And half of them toward the western sea;
In both summer and winter it shall occur.
[9]And the LORD shall be King over all the
earth.
In that day it shall be—
"The LORD *is* one,"[a]
And His name one.

[10]All the land shall be turned into a plain
from Geba to Rimmon south of Jerusalem.
Jerusalem[a] shall be raised up and inhabited in
her place from Benjamin's Gate to the place of
the First Gate and the Corner Gate, and *from* the
Tower of Hananel to the king's winepresses.

[11]*The people* shall dwell in it;
And no longer shall there be utter
destruction,
But Jerusalem shall be safely inhabited.

[12]And this shall be the plague with which the
LORD will strike all the people who fought
against Jerusalem:

Their flesh shall dissolve while they stand
on their feet,
Their eyes shall dissolve in their sockets,
And their tongues shall dissolve in their
mouths.

[13]It shall come to pass in that day
That a great panic from the LORD will be
among them.
Everyone will seize the hand of his
neighbor,
And raise his hand against his neighbor's
hand;
[14]Judah also will fight at Jerusalem.
And the wealth of all the surrounding
nations
Shall be gathered together:
Gold, silver, and apparel in great
abundance.

[15]Such also shall be the plague
On the horse *and* the mule,
On the camel and the donkey,
And on all the cattle that will be in those
camps.
So *shall* this plague *be.*

14:5 [a]Or *you;* Septuagint, Targum, and Vulgate read *Him.*
14:9 [a]Compare Deuteronomy 6:4 **14:10** [a]Literally *She*

THE MESSAGE

GOD will arrive and all the holy angels with
him.
6-7 What a Day that will be! No more cold
nights—in fact, no more nights! The Day is
coming—the timing is GOD's—when it will
be continuous day. Every evening will be a
fresh morning.
8 What a Day that will be! Fresh flowing
rivers out of Jerusalem, half to the eastern
sea, half to the western sea, flowing year-
round, summer and winter!
9 GOD will be king over all the earth, one
GOD and only one. What a Day that will be!

10-11 The land will stretch out spaciously around
Jerusalem—to Geba in the north and Rim-
mon in the south, with Jerusalem towering
at the center, and the commanding city
gates—Gate of Benjamin to First Gate to
Corner Gate to Hananel Tower to the Royal
Winery—ringing the city full of people.
Never again will Jerusalem be totally de-
stroyed. From now on it will be a safe city.
12-14 But this is what will happen to all who
fought against Jerusalem: GOD will visit
them with a terrible plague. People's flesh
will rot off their bones while they are walk-
ing around; their eyes will rot in their sock-
ets and their tongues in their mouths; peo-
ple will be dying on their feet! Mass hysteria
when that happens—total panic! Fellow sol-
diers fighting and killing each other—holy
terror! And then Judah will jump into the
fray!
14-15 Treasures from all the nations will be
piled high—gold, silver, the latest fashions.
The plague will also hit the animals—
horses, mules, camels, donkeys. Everything
alive in the military camps will be hit by the
plague.

NEW KING JAMES VERSION

THE NATIONS WORSHIP THE KING

[16]And it shall come to pass *that* everyone
who is left of all the nations which came against
Jerusalem shall go up from year to year to wor-
ship the King, the LORD of hosts, and to keep the
Feast of Tabernacles. [17]And it shall be *that*
whichever of the families of the earth do not
come up to Jerusalem to worship the King, the
LORD of hosts, on them there will be no rain. [18]If
the family of Egypt will not come up and enter
in, they *shall have* no *rain;* they shall receive the
plague with which the LORD strikes the nations
who do not come up to keep the Feast of Taber-
nacles. [19]This shall be the punishment of Egypt
and the punishment of all the nations that do
not come up to keep the Feast of Tabernacles.
[20]In that day "HOLINESS TO THE LORD"
shall be *engraved* on the bells of the horses. The
pots in the LORD's house shall be like the bowls
before the altar. [21]Yes, every pot in Jerusalem
and Judah shall be holiness to the LORD of
hosts.[a] Everyone who sacrifices shall come and
take them and cook in them. In that day there
shall no longer be a Canaanite in the house of
the LORD of hosts.

14:21 [a]Or *on every pot . . . shall be (engraved) "HOLINESS TO THE LORD OF HOSTS"*

THE MESSAGE

16-19 All the survivors from the godless nations
that fought against Jerusalem will travel to
Jerusalem every year to worship the King,
GOD-of-the-Angel-Armies, and celebrate the
Feast of Booths. If any of these survivors fail
to make the annual pilgrimage to Jerusalem
to worship the King, GOD-of-the-Angel-
Armies, there will be no rain. If the Egyp-
tians don't make the pilgrimage and wor-
ship, there will be no rain for them. Every
nation that does not go up to celebrate the
Feast of Booths will be hit with the plague.
Egypt and any other nation that does not
make pilgrimage to celebrate the Feast of
Booths gets punished.
20-21 On that Day, the Big Day, all the horses'
harness bells will be inscribed "Holy to
GOD." The cooking pots in the Temple of
GOD will be as sacred as chalices and plates
on the altar. In fact, all the pots and pans in
all the kitchens of Jerusalem and Judah will
be holy to GOD-of-the-Angel-Armies. People
who come to worship, preparing meals and
sacrifices, will use them. On that Big Day
there will be no buying or selling in the
Temple of GOD-of-the-Angel-Armies.

MALACHI

New King James Version

1 The burden[a] of the word of the LORD to Israel by Malachi.

Israel Beloved of God

2"I have loved you," says the LORD.
"Yet you say, 'In what way have You loved us?'
Was not Esau Jacob's brother?"
Says the LORD.
"Yet Jacob I have loved;
3But Esau I have hated,
And laid waste his mountains and his heritage
For the jackals of the wilderness."
4Even though Edom has said,
"We have been impoverished,
But we will return and build the desolate places,"
Thus says the LORD of hosts:

"They may build, but I will throw down;
They shall be called the Territory of Wickedness,
And the people against whom the LORD will have indignation forever.
5Your eyes shall see,
And you shall say,
'The LORD is magnified beyond the border of Israel.'

Polluted Offerings

6"A son honors *his* father,
And a servant *his* master.
If then I am the Father,
Where *is* My honor?
And if I *am* a Master,
Where *is* My reverence?
Says the LORD of hosts
To you priests who despise My name.
Yet you say, 'In what way have we despised Your name?'

7"You offer defiled food on My altar,
But say,
'In what way have we defiled You?'
By saying,
'The table of the LORD is contemptible.'
8And when you offer the blind as a sacrifice,
Is it not evil?
And when you offer the lame and sick,
Is it not evil?
Offer it then to your governor!
Would he be pleased with you?
Would he accept you favorably?"
Says the LORD of hosts.

9"But now entreat God's favor,
That He may be gracious to us.
While this is being *done* by your hands,
Will He accept you favorably?"
Says the LORD of hosts.

1:1 [a]Or *oracle*

The Message

No More of This So-Called Worship!

1 1 A Message. GOD'S Word to Israel through
Malachi:
2-3 GOD said, "I love you."
You replied, "Really? How have you loved
us?"
"Look at history" (this is GOD's answer).
"Look at how differently I've treated you,
Jacob, from Esau: I loved Jacob and hated
Esau. I reduced pretentious Esau to a mole-
hill, turned his whole country into a ghost
town."
4 When Edom (Esau) said, "We've been
knocked down, but we'll get up and start
over, good as new," GOD-of-the-Angel-
Armies said, "Just try it and see how far you
get. When I knock you down, you stay down.
People will take one look at you and say,
'Land of Evil!' and 'the GOD-cursed tribe!'
5 "Yes, take a good look. Then you'll see
how faithfully I've loved you and you'll want
even more, saying, 'May GOD be even
greater, beyond the borders of Israel!'

6 "Isn't it true that a son honors his father and
a worker his master? So if I'm your Father,
where's the honor? If I'm your Master,
where's the respect?" GOD-of-the-Angel-
Armies is calling you on the carpet: "You
priests despise me!
"You say, 'Not so! How do we despise
you?'
"By your shoddy, sloppy, defiling wor-
ship.
"You ask, 'What do you mean, "defiling"?
What's defiling about it?'
7-8 "When you say, 'The altar of GOD is not
important anymore; worship of GOD is no
longer a priority,' that's defiling. And when
you offer worthless animals for sacrifices in
worship, animals that you're trying to get
rid of—blind and sick and crippled ani-
mals—isn't that defiling? Try a trick like
that with your banker or your senator—how
far do you think it will get you?" GOD-of-the-
Angel-Armies asks you.
9 "Get on your knees and pray that I will be
gracious to you. You priests have gotten
everyone in trouble. With this kind of con-
duct, do you think I'll pay attention to you?"
GOD-of-the-Angel-Armies asks you.

NEW KING JAMES VERSION

10"Who *is there* even among you who would
shut the doors,
So that you would not kindle fire *on* My
altar in vain?
I have no pleasure in you,"
Says the LORD of hosts,
"Nor will I accept an offering from your
hands.
11For from the rising of the sun, even to its
going down,
My name *shall be* great among the Gentiles;
In every place incense *shall be* offered to
My name,
And a pure offering;
For My name shall be great among the
nations,"
Says the LORD of hosts.

12"But you profane it,
In that you say,
'The table of the LORD[a] is defiled;
And its fruit, its food, *is* contemptible.'
13You also say,
'Oh, what a weariness!'
And you sneer at it,"
Says the LORD of hosts.
"And you bring the stolen, the lame, and the
sick;
Thus you bring an offering!
Should I accept this from your hand?"
Says the LORD.
14"But cursed *be* the deceiver
Who has in his flock a male,
And takes a vow,
But sacrifices to the Lord what is
blemished—
For I *am* a great King,"
Says the LORD of hosts,
"And My name *is to be* feared among the
nations.

CORRUPT PRIESTS

2 "And now, O priests, this commandment is
for you.
2If you will not hear,
And if you will not take *it* to heart,
To give glory to My name,"
Says the LORD of hosts,
"I will send a curse upon you,
And I will curse your blessings.
Yes, I have cursed them already,
Because you do not take *it* to heart.

3"Behold, I will rebuke your descendants
And spread refuse on your faces,
The refuse of your solemn feasts;
And *one* will take you away with it.
4Then you shall know that I have sent this
commandment to you,
That My covenant with Levi may continue,"
Says the LORD of hosts.
5"My covenant was with him, *one* of life and
peace,
And I gave them to him *that he might* fear
Me;
So he feared Me
And was reverent before My name.

1:12 [a]Following Bomberg; Masoretic Text reads *Lord.*

THE MESSAGE

10 "Why doesn't one of you just shut the
Temple doors and lock them? Then none of
you can get in and play at religion with this
silly, empty-headed worship. I am not
pleased. The GOD-of-the-Angel-Armies is
not pleased. And I don't want any more of
this so-called worship!

OFFERING GOD SOMETHING HAND-ME-DOWN, BROKEN, OR USELESS

11 "I am honored all over the world. And there
are people who know how to worship me all
over the world, who honor me by bringing
their best to me. They're saying it every-
where: 'God is greater, this GOD-of-the-
Angel-Armies.'
12-13 "All except you. Instead of honoring me,
you profane me. You profane me when you
say, 'Worship is not important, and what we
bring to worship is of no account,' and when
you say, 'I'm bored—this doesn't do any-
thing for me.' You act so superior, sticking
your noses in the air—act superior to *me*,
GOD-of-the-Angel-Armies! And when you
do offer something to me, it's a hand-me-
down, or broken, or useless. Do you think
I'm going to accept it? This is GOD speaking
to you!
14 "A curse on the person who makes a big
show of doing something great for me—an
expensive sacrifice, say—and then at the
last minute brings in something puny and
worthless! I'm a great king, GOD-of-the-
Angel-Armies, honored far and wide, and
I'll not put up with it!"

DESECRATING THE HOLINESS OF GOD

1-3 2 "And now this indictment, you priests! If
you refuse to obediently listen, and if you
refuse to honor me, GOD-of-the-Angel-
Armies, in worship, then I'll put you under a
curse. I'll exchange all your blessings for
curses. In fact, the curses are already at
work because you're not serious about hon-
oring me. Yes, and the curse will extend to
your children. I'm going to plaster your
faces with rotting garbage, garbage thrown
out from your feasts. That's what you have
to look forward to!
4-6 "Maybe that will wake you up. Maybe
then you'll realize that I'm indicting you in
order to put new life into my covenant with
the priests of Levi, the covenant of GOD-of-
the-Angel-Armies. My covenant with Levi
was to give life and peace. I kept my
covenant with him, and he honored me. He
stood in reverent awe before me. He taught

NEW KING JAMES VERSION

6The law of truth[a] was in his mouth,
And injustice was not found on his lips.
He walked with Me in peace and equity,
And turned many away from iniquity.

7"For the lips of a priest should keep knowledge,
And *people* should seek the law from his mouth;
For he is the messenger of the LORD of hosts.
8But you have departed from the way;
You have caused many to stumble at the law.
You have corrupted the covenant of Levi,"
Says the LORD of hosts.
9"Therefore I also have made you contemptible and base
Before all the people,
Because you have not kept My ways
But have shown partiality in the law."

TREACHERY OF INFIDELITY

10Have we not all one Father?
Has not one God created us?
Why do we deal treacherously with one another
By profaning the covenant of the fathers?
11Judah has dealt treacherously,
And an abomination has been committed in Israel and in Jerusalem,
For Judah has profaned
The LORD's holy *institution* which He loves:
He has married the daughter of a foreign god.
12May the LORD cut off from the tents of Jacob
The man who does this, being awake and aware,[a]
Yet who brings an offering to the LORD of hosts!

13And this is the second thing you do:
You cover the altar of the LORD with tears,
With weeping and crying;
So He does not regard the offering anymore,
Nor receive *it* with goodwill from your hands.
14Yet you say, "For what reason?"
Because the LORD has been witness
Between you and the wife of your youth,
With whom you have dealt treacherously;
Yet she is your companion
And your wife by covenant.
15But did He not make *them* one,
Having a remnant of the Spirit?
And why one?
He seeks godly offspring.
Therefore take heed to your spirit,
And let none deal treacherously with the wife of his youth.

16"For the LORD God of Israel says
That He hates divorce,
For it covers one's garment with violence,"
Says the LORD of hosts.
"Therefore take heed to your spirit,
That you do not deal treacherously."

2:6 [a]Or *true instruction* **2:12** [a]Talmud and Vulgate read *teacher and student.*

THE MESSAGE

the truth and did not lie. He walked with me
in peace and uprightness. He kept many out
of the ditch, kept them on the road.
7-9 "It's the job of priests to teach the truth.
People are supposed to look to them for
guidance. The priest is the messenger of
GOD-of-the-Angel-Armies. But you priests
have abandoned the way of priests. Your
teaching has messed up many lives. You
have corrupted the covenant of priest Levi.
GOD-of-the-Angel-Armies says so. And so I
am showing you up for who you are. Every-
one will be disgusted with you and avoid
you because you don't live the way I told
you to live, and you don't teach my revela-
tion truly and impartially."
10 Don't we all come from one Father?
Aren't we all created by the same God? So
why can't we get along? Why do we dese-
crate the covenant of our ancestors that
binds us together?
11-12 Judah has cheated on GOD—a sickening
violation of trust in Israel and Jerusalem:
Judah has desecrated the holiness of GOD by
falling in love and running off with foreign
women, women who worship alien gods.
GOD's curse on those who do this! Drive
them out of house and home! They're no
longer fit to be part of the community no
matter how many offerings they bring to
GOD-of-the-Angel-Armies.
13-15 And here's a second offense: You fill the
place of worship with your whining and
sniveling because you don't get what you
want from GOD. Do you know why? Simple.
Because GOD was there as a witness when
you spoke your marriage vows to your
young bride, and now you've broken those
vows, broken the faith-bond with your
vowed companion, your covenant wife. GOD,
not you, made marriage. His Spirit inhabits
even the smallest details of marriage. And
what does he want from marriage? Children
of God, that's what. So guard the spirit of
marriage within you. Don't cheat on your
spouse.
16 "I hate divorce," says the GOD of Israel.
GOD-of-the-Angel-Armies says, "I hate the
violent dismembering of the 'one flesh' of
marriage." So watch yourselves. Don't let
your guard down. Don't cheat.

NEW KING JAMES VERSION

17You have wearied the LORD with your words;
Yet you say,
"In what way have we wearied *Him?*"
In that you say,
"Everyone who does evil
Is good in the sight of the LORD,
And He delights in them,"
Or, "Where *is* the God of justice?"

THE COMING MESSENGER

3 "Behold, I send My messenger,
And he will prepare the way before Me.
And the Lord, whom you seek,
Will suddenly come to His temple,
Even the Messenger of the covenant,
In whom you delight.
Behold, He is coming,"
Says the LORD of hosts.

2"But who can endure the day of His coming?
And who can stand when He appears?
For He *is* like a refiner's fire
And like launderers' soap.
3He will sit as a refiner and a purifier of silver;
He will purify the sons of Levi,
And purge them as gold and silver,
That they may offer to the LORD
An offering in righteousness.
4"Then the offering of Judah and Jerusalem
Will be pleasant to the LORD,
As in the days of old,
As in former years.
5And I will come near you for judgment;
I will be a swift witness
Against sorcerers,
Against adulterers,
Against perjurers,
Against those who exploit wage earners and widows and orphans,
And against those who turn away an alien—
Because they do not fear Me,"
Says the LORD of hosts.

6"For I *am* the LORD, I do not change;
Therefore you are not consumed, O sons of Jacob.
7Yet from the days of your fathers
You have gone away from My ordinances
And have not kept *them.*
Return to Me, and I will return to you,"
Says the LORD of hosts.
"But you said,
'In what way shall we return?'

DO NOT ROB GOD

8"Will a man rob God?
Yet you have robbed Me!
But you say,
'In what way have we robbed You?'
In tithes and offerings.
9You are cursed with a curse,
For you have robbed Me,
Even this whole nation.
10Bring all the tithes into the storehouse,
That there may be food in My house,

THE MESSAGE

17 You make GOD tired with all your talk.
"How do we tire him out?" you ask.
By saying, "GOD loves sinners and sin
alike. GOD loves all." And also by saying,
"Judgment? GOD's too nice to judge."

THE MASTER YOU'VE BEEN LOOKING FOR

1 3 "Look! I'm sending my messenger on
ahead to clear the way for me. Suddenly,
out of the blue, the Leader you've been look-
ing for will enter his Temple—yes, the Mes-
senger of the Covenant, the one you've been
waiting for. Look! He's on his way!" A Mes-
sage from the mouth of GOD-of-the-Angel-
Armies.

2-4 But who will be able to stand up to that
coming? Who can survive his appearance?
He'll be like white-hot fire from the
smelter's furnace. He'll be like the strongest
lye soap at the laundry. He'll take his place
as a refiner of silver, as a cleanser of dirty
clothes. He'll scrub the Levite priests clean,
refine them like gold and silver, until they're
fit for GOD, fit to present offerings of righ-
teousness. Then, and only then, will Judah
and Jerusalem be fit and pleasing to GOD, as
they used to be in the years long ago.

5 "Yes, I'm on my way to visit you with Judg-
ment. I'll present compelling evidence
against sorcerers, adulterers, liars, those
who exploit workers, those who take advan-
tage of widows and orphans, those who are
inhospitable to the homeless—anyone and
everyone who doesn't honor me." A Mes-
sage from GOD-of-the-Angel-Armies.

6-7 "I am GOD—yes, I AM. I haven't changed.
And because I haven't changed, you, the de-
scendants of Jacob, haven't been destroyed.
You have a long history of ignoring my com-
mands. You haven't done a thing I've told
you. Return to me so I can return to you,"
says GOD-of-the-Angel-Armies.

"You ask, 'But how do we return?'

8-11 "Begin by being honest. Do honest people
rob God? But you rob me day after day.
"You ask, 'How have we robbed you?'
"The tithe and the offering—that's how!
And now you're under a curse—the whole lot
of you—because you're robbing me. Bring
your full tithe to the Temple treasury so there
will be ample provisions in my Temple. Test

NEW KING JAMES VERSION

And try Me now in this,"
Says the LORD of hosts,
"If I will not open for you the windows of heaven
And pour out for you *such* blessing
That *there will* not *be room* enough *to receive it*.

11"And I will rebuke the devourer for your sakes,
So that he will not destroy the fruit of your ground,
Nor shall the vine fail to bear fruit for you in the field,"
Says the LORD of hosts;
12And all nations will call you blessed,
For you will be a delightful land,"
Says the LORD of hosts.

THE PEOPLE COMPLAIN HARSHLY

13"Your words have been harsh against Me,"
Says the LORD,
"Yet you say,
'What have we spoken against You?'
14You have said,
'It is useless to serve God;
What profit *is it* that we have kept His ordinance,
And that we have walked as mourners
Before the LORD of hosts?
15So now we call the proud blessed,
For those who do wickedness are raised up;
They even tempt God and go free.' "

A BOOK OF REMEMBRANCE

16Then those who feared the LORD spoke to one another,
And the LORD listened and heard *them;*
So a book of remembrance was written before Him
For those who fear the LORD
And who meditate on His name.

17"They shall be Mine," says the LORD of hosts,
"On the day that I make them My jewels.[a]
And I will spare them
As a man spares his own son who serves him."
18Then you shall again discern
Between the righteous and the wicked,
Between one who serves God
And one who does not serve Him.

THE GREAT DAY OF GOD

4 "For behold, the day is coming,
Burning like an oven,
And all the proud, yes, all who do wickedly will be stubble.
And the day which is coming shall burn them up,"
Says the LORD of hosts,
"That will leave them neither root nor branch.
2But to you who fear My name
The Sun of Righteousness shall arise
With healing in His wings;
And you shall go out
And grow fat like stall-fed calves.

3:17 [a]Literally *special treasure*

THE MESSAGE

me in this and see if I don't open up heaven
itself to you and pour out blessings beyond
your wildest dreams. For my part, I will de-
fend you against marauders, protect your
wheat fields and vegetable gardens against
plunderers." The Message of GOD-of-the-
Angel-Armies.
12 "You'll be voted 'Happiest Nation.' You'll
experience what it's like to be a country of
grace." GOD-of-the-Angel-Armies says so.

THE DIFFERENCE BETWEEN SERVING GOD AND NOT SERVING HIM

13 GOD says, "You have spoken hard, rude
words to me.
"You ask, 'When did we ever do that?'
14-15 "When you said, 'It doesn't pay to serve
God. What do we ever get out of it? When we
did what he said and went around with long
faces, serious about GOD-of-the-Angel-
Armies, what difference did it make? Those
who take life into their own hands are the
lucky ones. They break all the rules and get
ahead anyway. They push God to the limit
and get by with it.' "
16 Then those whose lives honored GOD got
together and talked it over. GOD saw what
they were doing and listened in. A book was
opened in God's presence and minutes were
taken of the meeting, with the names of the
GOD-fearers written down, all the names of
those who honored GOD's name.
17-18 GOD-of-the-Angel-Armies said, "They're
mine, all mine. They'll get special treatment
when I go into action. I treat them with the
same consideration and kindness that par-
ents give the child who honors them. Once
more you'll see the difference it makes be-
tween being a person who does the right
thing and one who doesn't, between serving
God and not serving him."

THE SUN OF RIGHTEOUSNESS WILL DAWN

1-3 4 "Count on it: The day is coming, raging
like a forest fire. All the arrogant people
who do evil things will be burned up like
stove wood, burned to a crisp, nothing left
but scorched earth and ash—a black day.
But for you, sunrise! The sun of righteous-
ness will dawn on those who honor my
name, healing radiating from its wings. You
will be bursting with energy, like colts frisky
and frolicking. And you'll tromp on the

NEW KING JAMES VERSION

3 You shall trample the wicked,
For they shall be ashes under the soles of your feet
On the day that I do *this*,"
Says the LORD of hosts.

4 "Remember the Law of Moses, My servant,
Which I commanded him in Horeb for all Israel,
With the statutes and judgments.
5 Behold, I will send you Elijah the prophet
Before the coming of the great and dreadful day of the LORD.
6 And he will turn
The hearts of the fathers to the children,
And the hearts of the children to their fathers,
Lest I come and strike the earth with a curse."

THE MESSAGE

wicked. They'll be nothing but ashes under
your feet on that Day." GOD-of-the-Angel-
Armies says so.
4 "Remember and keep the revelation I
gave through my servant Moses, the revela-
tion I commanded at Horeb for all Israel, all
the rules and procedures for right living.
5-6 "But also look ahead: I'm sending Elijah
the prophet to clear the way for the Big Day
of GOD—the decisive Judgment Day! He will
convince parents to look after their children
and children to look up to their parents. If
they refuse, I'll come and put the land under
a curse."

THE NEW TESTAMENT

MATTHEW

NEW KING JAMES VERSION

THE GENEALOGY OF JESUS CHRIST

1 The book of the genealogy of Jesus Christ,
the Son of David, the Son of Abraham:
2Abraham begot Isaac, Isaac begot Jacob,
and Jacob begot Judah and his brothers. 3Judah
begot Perez and Zerah by Tamar, Perez begot
Hezron, and Hezron begot Ram. 4Ram begot
Amminadab, Amminadab begot Nahshon, and
Nahshon begot Salmon. 5Salmon begot Boaz by
Rahab, Boaz begot Obed by Ruth, Obed begot
Jesse, 6and Jesse begot David the king.

David the king begot Solomon by her *who
had been the wife*[a] of Uriah. 7Solomon begot
Rehoboam, Rehoboam begot Abijah, and Abi-
jah begot Asa.[a] 8Asa begot Jehoshaphat, Je-
hoshaphat begot Joram, and Joram begot
Uzziah. 9Uzziah begot Jotham, Jotham begot
Ahaz, and Ahaz begot Hezekiah. 10Hezekiah be-
got Manasseh, Manasseh begot Amon,[a] and
Amon begot Josiah. 11Josiah begot Jeconiah and
his brothers about the time they were carried
away to Babylon.

12And after they were brought to Babylon,
Jeconiah begot Shealtiel, and Shealtiel begot
Zerubbabel. 13Zerubbabel begot Abiud, Abiud
begot Eliakim, and Eliakim begot Azor. 14Azor
begot Zadok, Zadok begot Achim, and Achim
begot Eliud. 15Eliud begot Eleazar, Eleazar be-
got Matthan, and Matthan begot Jacob. 16And
Jacob begot Joseph the husband of Mary, of
whom was born Jesus who is called Christ.

17So all the generations from Abraham to
David *are* fourteen generations, from David un-
til the captivity in Babylon *are* fourteen genera-
tions, and from the captivity in Babylon until
the Christ *are* fourteen generations.

CHRIST BORN OF MARY

18Now the birth of Jesus Christ was as fol-
lows: After His mother Mary was betrothed to

1:6 [a]Words in italic type have been added for clarity. They are not found in the original Greek. **1:7** [a]NU-Text reads *Asaph.* **1:10** [a]NU-Text reads *Amos.*

THE MESSAGE

1 **1** The family tree of Jesus Christ, David's son, Abraham's son:

2-6 Abraham had Isaac,
Isaac had Jacob,
Jacob had Judah and his brothers,
Judah had Perez and Zerah (the mother was Tamar),
Perez had Hezron,
Hezron had Aram,
Aram had Amminadab,
Amminadab had Nahshon,
Nahshon had Salmon,
Salmon had Boaz (his mother was Rahab),
Boaz had Obed (Ruth was the mother),
Obed had Jesse,
Jesse had David,
and David became king.

6-11 David had Solomon (Uriah's wife was the mother),
Solomon had Rehoboam,
Rehoboam had Abijah,
Abijah had Asa,
Asa had Jehoshaphat,
Jehoshaphat had Joram,
Joram had Uzziah,
Uzziah had Jotham,
Jotham had Ahaz,
Ahaz had Hezekiah,
Hezekiah had Manasseh,
Manasseh had Amon,
Amon had Josiah,
Josiah had Jehoiachin and his brothers,
and then the people were taken into the Babylonian exile.

12-16 When the Babylonian exile ended,
Jeconiah had Shealtiel,
Shealtiel had Zerubbabel,
Zerubbabel had Abiud,
Abiud had Eliakim,
Eliakim had Azor,
Azor had Zadok,
Zadok had Achim,
Achim had Eliud,
Eliud had Eleazar,
Eleazar had Matthan,
Matthan had Jacob,
Jacob had Joseph, Mary's husband,
the Mary who gave birth to Jesus,
the Jesus who was called Christ.

17 There were fourteen generations from Abraham to David,
another fourteen from David to the Babylonian exile,
and yet another fourteen from the Babylonian exile to Christ.

THE BIRTH OF JESUS

18-19 The birth of Jesus took place like this. His mother, Mary, was engaged to be married to

New King James Version

Joseph, before they came together, she was found with child of the Holy Spirit. 19Then Joseph her husband, being a just *man,* and not wanting to make her a public example, was minded to put her away secretly. 20But while he thought about these things, behold, an angel of the Lord appeared to him in a dream, saying, "Joseph, son of David, do not be afraid to take to you Mary your wife, for that which is conceived in her is of the Holy Spirit. 21And she will bring forth a Son, and you shall call His name Jesus, for He will save His people from their sins."

22So all this was done that it might be fulfilled which was spoken by the Lord through the prophet, saying: 23*"Behold, the virgin shall be with child, and bear a Son, and they shall call His name Immanuel,"*[a] which is translated, "God with us."

24Then Joseph, being aroused from sleep, did as the angel of the Lord commanded him and took to him his wife, 25and did not know her till she had brought forth her firstborn Son.[a] And he called His name Jesus.

Wise Men from the East

2 Now after Jesus was born in Bethlehem of Judea in the days of Herod the king, behold, wise men from the East came to Jerusalem, 2saying, "Where is He who has been born King of the Jews? For we have seen His star in the East and have come to worship Him."

3When Herod the king heard *this,* he was troubled, and all Jerusalem with him. 4And when he had gathered all the chief priests and scribes of the people together, he inquired of them where the Christ was to be born.

5So they said to him, "In Bethlehem of Judea, for thus it is written by the prophet:

6*'But you, Bethlehem, in the land of Judah,*
Are not the least among the rulers of Judah;
For out of you shall come a Ruler
Who will shepherd My people Israel.' "[a]

7Then Herod, when he had secretly called the wise men, determined from them what time the star appeared. 8And he sent them to Bethlehem and said, "Go and search carefully for the young Child, and when you have found *Him,* bring back word to me, that I may come and worship Him also."

9When they heard the king, they departed; and behold, the star which they had seen in the East went before them, till it came and stood over where the young Child was. 10When they saw the star, they rejoiced with exceedingly great joy.

1:23 [a]Isaiah 7:14. Words in oblique type in the New Testament are quoted from the Old Testament. **1:25** [a]NU-Text reads *a Son.* **2:6** [a]Micah 5:2

The Message

Joseph. Before they came to the marriage bed, Joseph discovered she was pregnant. (It was by the Holy Spirit, but he didn't know that.) Joseph, chagrined but noble, determined to take care of things quietly so Mary would not be disgraced.

20-23 While he was trying to figure a way out, he had a dream. God's angel spoke in the dream: "Joseph, son of David, don't hesitate to get married. Mary's pregnancy is Spirit-conceived. God's Holy Spirit has made her pregnant. She will bring a son to birth, and when she does, you, Joseph, will name him Jesus—'God saves'—because he will save his people from their sins." This would bring the prophet's embryonic sermon to full term:

Watch for this—a virgin will get
pregnant and bear a son;
They will name him Immanuel (Hebrew
for "God is with us").

24-25 Then Joseph woke up. He did exactly what God's angel commanded in the dream: He married Mary. But he did not consummate the marriage until she had the baby. He named the baby Jesus.

Scholars from the East

1-2 2 After Jesus was born in Bethlehem village, Judah territory—this was during Herod's kingship—a band of scholars arrived in Jerusalem from the East. They asked around, "Where can we find and pay homage to the newborn King of the Jews? We observed a star in the eastern sky that signaled his birth. We're on pilgrimage to worship him."

3-4 When word of their inquiry got to Herod, he was terrified—and not Herod alone, but most of Jerusalem as well. Herod lost no time. He gathered all the high priests and religion scholars in the city together and asked, "Where is the Messiah supposed to be born?"

5-6 They told him, "Bethlehem, Judah territory. The prophet Micah wrote it plainly:

It's you, Bethlehem, in Judah's land,
no longer bringing up the rear.
From you will come the leader
who will shepherd-rule my people,
my Israel."

7-8 Herod then arranged a secret meeting with the scholars from the East. Pretending to be as devout as they were, he got them to tell him exactly when the birth-announcement star appeared. Then he told them the prophecy about Bethlehem, and said, "Go find this child. Leave no stone unturned. As soon as you find him, send word and I'll join you at once in your worship."

9-10 Instructed by the king, they set off. Then the star appeared again, the same star they had seen in the eastern skies. It led them on until it hovered over the place of the child. They could hardly contain themselves: They were in the right place! They had arrived at the right time!

NEW KING JAMES VERSION

11And when they had come into the house, they
saw the young Child with Mary His mother, and
fell down and worshiped Him. And when they
had opened their treasures, they presented gifts
to Him: gold, frankincense, and myrrh.
12Then, being divinely warned in a dream
that they should not return to Herod, they de-
parted for their own country another way.

THE FLIGHT INTO EGYPT

13Now when they had departed, behold, an
angel of the Lord appeared to Joseph in a
dream, saying, "Arise, take the young Child and
His mother, flee to Egypt, and stay there until I
bring you word; for Herod will seek the young
Child to destroy Him."
14When he arose, he took the young Child
and His mother by night and departed for
Egypt, 15and was there until the death of Herod,
that it might be fulfilled which was spoken by
the Lord through the prophet, saying, *"Out of
Egypt I called My Son."* [a]

MASSACRE OF THE INNOCENTS

16Then Herod, when he saw that he was de-
ceived by the wise men, was exceedingly angry;
and he sent forth and put to death all the male
children who were in Bethlehem and in all its
districts, from two years old and under, accord-
ing to the time which he had determined from
the wise men. 17Then was fulfilled what was
spoken by Jeremiah the prophet, saying:

18*"A voice was heard in Ramah,*
Lamentation, weeping, and great mourning,
Rachel weeping for her children,
Refusing to be comforted,
Because they are no more." [a]

THE HOME IN NAZARETH

19Now when Herod was dead, behold, an an-
gel of the Lord appeared in a dream to Joseph in
Egypt, 20saying, "Arise, take the young Child
and His mother, and go to the land of Israel, for
those who sought the young Child's life are
dead." 21Then he arose, took the young Child
and His mother, and came into the land of Is-
rael.
22But when he heard that Archelaus was
reigning over Judea instead of his father Herod,
he was afraid to go there. And being warned by
God in a dream, he turned aside into the region
of Galilee. 23And he came and dwelt in a city
called Nazareth, that it might be fulfilled which
was spoken by the prophets, "He shall be called
a Nazarene."

JOHN THE BAPTIST PREPARES THE WAY

3 In those days John the Baptist came preach-
ing in the wilderness of Judea, 2and saying,
"Repent, for the kingdom of heaven is at hand!"
3For this is he who was spoken of by the prophet
Isaiah, saying:

"The voice of one crying in the wilderness:
'Prepare the way of the Lord;
Make His paths straight.'" [a]

2:15 [a]Hosea 11:1 **2:18** [a]Jeremiah 31:15 **3:3** [a]Isaiah 40:3

THE MESSAGE

11 They entered the house and saw the child in the arms of Mary, his mother. Overcome, they kneeled and worshiped him. Then they opened their luggage and presented gifts: gold, frankincense, myrrh.

12 In a dream, they were warned not to report back to Herod. So they worked out another route, left the territory without being seen, and returned to their own country.

13 After the scholars were gone, God's angel showed up again in Joseph's dream and commanded, "Get up. Take the child and his mother and flee to Egypt. Stay until further notice. Herod is on the hunt for this child, and wants to kill him."

14-15 Joseph obeyed. He got up, took the child and his mother under cover of darkness. They were out of town and well on their way by daylight. They lived in Egypt until Herod's death. This Egyptian exile fulfilled what Hosea had preached: "I called my son out of Egypt."

16-18 Herod, when he realized that the scholars had tricked him, flew into a rage. He commanded the murder of every little boy two years old and under who lived in Bethlehem and its surrounding hills. (He determined that age from information he'd gotten from the scholars.) That's when Jeremiah's sermon was fulfilled:

A sound was heard in Ramah,
  weeping and much lament.
Rachel weeping for her children,
  Rachel refusing all solace,
Her children gone,
  dead and buried.

19-20 Later, when Herod died, God's angel appeared in a dream to Joseph in Egypt: "Up, take the child and his mother and return to Israel. All those out to murder the child are dead."

21-23 Joseph obeyed. He got up, took the child and his mother, and reentered Israel. When he heard, though, that Archelaus had succeeded his father, Herod, as king in Judea, he was afraid to go there. But then Joseph was directed in a dream to go to the hills of Galilee. On arrival, he settled in the village of Nazareth. This move was a fulfillment of the prophetic words, "He shall be called a Nazarene."

THUNDER IN THE DESERT!

1-2 3 While Jesus was living in the Galilean hills, John, called "the Baptizer," was preaching in the desert country of Judea. His message was simple and austere, like his desert surroundings: "Change your life. God's kingdom is here."

3 John and his message were authorized by Isaiah's prophecy:

Thunder in the desert!
Prepare for God's arrival!
Make the road smooth and straight!

New King James Version

4Now John himself was clothed in camel's hair, with a leather belt around his waist; and his food was locusts and wild honey. 5Then Jerusalem, all Judea, and all the region around the Jordan went out to him 6and were baptized by him in the Jordan, confessing their sins.

7But when he saw many of the Pharisees and Sadducees coming to his baptism, he said to them, "Brood of vipers! Who warned you to flee from the wrath to come? 8Therefore bear fruits worthy of repentance, 9and do not think to say to yourselves, 'We have Abraham as *our* father.' For I say to you that God is able to raise up children to Abraham from these stones. 10And even now the ax is laid to the root of the trees. Therefore every tree which does not bear good fruit is cut down and thrown into the fire. 11I indeed baptize you with water unto repentance, but He who is coming after me is mightier than I, whose sandals I am not worthy to carry. He will baptize you with the Holy Spirit and fire.[a] 12His winnowing fan *is* in His hand, and He will thoroughly clean out His threshing floor, and gather His wheat into the barn; but He will burn up the chaff with unquenchable fire."

John Baptizes Jesus

13Then Jesus came from Galilee to John at the Jordan to be baptized by him. 14And John *tried to* prevent Him, saying, "I need to be baptized by You, and are You coming to me?"

15But Jesus answered and said to him, "Permit *it to be so* now, for thus it is fitting for us to fulfill all righteousness." Then he allowed Him.

16When He had been baptized, Jesus came up immediately from the water; and behold, the heavens were opened to Him, and He[a] saw the Spirit of God descending like a dove and alighting upon Him. 17And suddenly a voice *came* from heaven, saying, "This is My beloved Son, in whom I am well pleased."

Satan Tempts Jesus

4 Then Jesus was led up by the Spirit into the wilderness to be tempted by the devil. 2And when He had fasted forty days and forty nights, afterward He was hungry. 3Now when the tempter came to Him, he said, "If You are the Son of God, command that these stones become bread."

4But He answered and said, "It is written, *'Man shall not live by bread alone, but by every word that proceeds from the mouth of God.'* "[a]

3:11 [a]M-Text omits *and fire.* **3:16** [a]Or *he* **4:4** [a]Deuteronomy 8:3

The Message

4-6 John dressed in a camel-hair habit tied at the waist by a leather strap. He lived on a diet of locusts and wild field honey. People poured out of Jerusalem, Judea, and the Jordanian countryside to hear and see him in action. There at the Jordan River those who came to confess their sins were baptized into a changed life.

7-10 When John realized that a lot of Pharisees and Sadducees were showing up for a baptismal experience because it was becoming the popular thing to do, he exploded: "Brood of snakes! What do you think you're doing slithering down here to the river? Do you think a little water on your snakeskins is going to make any difference? It's your life that must change, not your skin! And don't think you can pull rank by claiming Abraham as father. Being a descendant of Abraham is neither here nor there. Descendants of Abraham are a dime a dozen. What counts is your life. Is it green and blossoming? Because if it's deadwood, it goes on the fire.

11-12 "I'm baptizing you here in the river, turning your old life in for a kingdom life. The real action comes next: The main character in this drama—compared to him I'm a mere stagehand—will ignite the kingdom life within you, a fire within you, the Holy Spirit within you, changing you from the inside out. He's going to clean house—make a clean sweep of your lives. He'll place everything true in its proper place before God; everything false he'll put out with the trash to be burned."

13-14 Jesus then appeared, arriving at the Jordan River from Galilee. He wanted John to baptize him. John objected, "I'm the one who needs to be baptized, not *you!*"

15 But Jesus insisted. "Do it. God's work, putting things right all these centuries, is coming together right now in this baptism." So John did it.

16-17 The moment Jesus came up out of the baptismal waters, the skies opened up and he saw God's Spirit—it looked like a dove—descending and landing on him. And along with the Spirit, a voice: "This is my Son, chosen and marked by my love, delight of my life."

The Test

1-3 4 Next Jesus was taken into the wild by the Spirit for the Test. The Devil was ready to give it. Jesus prepared for the Test by fasting forty days and forty nights. That left him, of course, in a state of extreme hunger, which the Devil took advantage of in the first test: "Since you are God's Son, speak the word that will turn these stones into loaves of bread."

4 Jesus answered by quoting Deuteronomy: "It takes more than bread to stay alive. It takes a steady stream of words from God's mouth."

NEW KING JAMES VERSION

5Then the devil took Him up into the holy
city, set Him on the pinnacle of the temple, 6and
said to Him, "If You are the Son of God, throw
Yourself down. For it is written:

'He shall give His angels charge over you,'

and,

'In their hands they shall bear you up,
Lest you dash your foot against a stone.' "[a]

7Jesus said to him, "It is written again, *'You
shall not tempt the Lord your God.' "*[a]
8Again, the devil took Him up on an exceed-
ingly high mountain, and showed Him all the
kingdoms of the world and their glory. 9And he
said to Him, "All these things I will give You if
You will fall down and worship me."
10Then Jesus said to him, "Away with you,[a]
Satan! For it is written, *'You shall worship the
LORD your God, and Him only you shall serve.' "*[b]
11Then the devil left Him, and behold, angels
came and ministered to Him.

JESUS BEGINS HIS GALILEAN MINISTRY

12Now when Jesus heard that John had been
put in prison, He departed to Galilee. 13And
leaving Nazareth, He came and dwelt in Caper-
naum, which is by the sea, in the regions of Zeb-
ulun and Naphtali, 14that it might be fulfilled
which was spoken by Isaiah the prophet, saying:

15*"The land of Zebulun and the land of*
Naphtali,
By the way of the sea, beyond the Jordan,
Galilee of the Gentiles:
16*The people who sat in darkness have seen a*
great light,
And upon those who sat in the region and
shadow of death
Light has dawned."[a]

17From that time Jesus began to preach and
to say, "Repent, for the kingdom of heaven is at
hand."

FOUR FISHERMEN CALLED AS DISCIPLES

18And Jesus, walking by the Sea of Galilee,
saw two brothers, Simon called Peter, and An-
drew his brother, casting a net into the sea; for
they were fishermen. 19Then He said to them,
"Follow Me, and I will make you fishers of men."
20They immediately left *their* nets and followed
Him.
21Going on from there, He saw two other
brothers, James *the son* of Zebedee, and John
his brother, in the boat with Zebedee their fa-
ther, mending their nets. He called them, 22and
immediately they left the boat and their father,
and followed Him.

JESUS HEALS A GREAT MULTITUDE

23And Jesus went about all Galilee, teaching
in their synagogues, preaching the gospel of the
kingdom, and healing all kinds of sickness and

4:6 [a]Psalm 91:11, 12 **4:7** [a]Deuteronomy 6:16 **4:10** [a]M-Text reads *Get behind Me.* [b]Deuteronomy 6:13 **4:16** [a]Isaiah 9:1, 2

THE MESSAGE

5-6 For the second test the Devil took him to
the Holy City. He sat him on top of the Tem-
ple and said, "Since you are God's Son,
jump." The Devil goaded him by quoting
Psalm 91: "He has placed you in the care of
angels. They will catch you so that you
won't so much as stub your toe on a stone."
7 Jesus countered with another citation
from Deuteronomy: "Don't you dare test the
Lord your God."
8-9 For the third test, the Devil took him to
the peak of a huge mountain. He gestured
expansively, pointing out all the earth's
kingdoms, how glorious they all were. Then
he said, "They're yours—lock, stock, and
barrel. Just go down on your knees and wor-
ship me, and they're yours."
10 Jesus' refusal was curt: "Beat it, Satan!"
He backed his rebuke with a third quotation
from Deuteronomy: "Worship the Lord your
God, and only him. Serve him with absolute
single-heartedness."
11 The Test was over. The Devil left. And in
his place, angels! Angels came and took
care of Jesus' needs.

TEACHING AND HEALING

12-17 When Jesus got word that John had been ar-
rested, he returned to Galilee. He moved
from his hometown, Nazareth, to the lake-
side village Capernaum, nestled at the base
of the Zebulun and Naphtali hills. This
move completed Isaiah's sermon:

Land of Zebulun, land of Naphtali,
road to the sea, over Jordan,
Galilee, crossroads for the nations.
People sitting out their lives in the dark
saw a huge light;
Sitting in that dark, dark country of
death,
they watched the sun come up.

This Isaiah-prophesied sermon came to life
in Galilee the moment Jesus started preach-
ing. He picked up where John left off:
"Change your life. God's kingdom is here."
18-20 Walking along the beach of Lake Galilee,
Jesus saw two brothers: Simon (later called
Peter) and Andrew. They were fishing,
throwing their nets into the lake. It was their
regular work. Jesus said to them, "Come
with me. I'll make a new kind of fisherman
out of you. I'll show you how to catch men
and women instead of perch and bass."
They didn't ask questions, but simply
dropped their nets and followed.
21-22 A short distance down the beach they
came upon another pair of brothers, James
and John, Zebedee's sons. These two were
sitting in a boat with their father, Zebedee,
mending their fishnets. Jesus made the
same offer to them, and they were just as
quick to follow, abandoning boat and father.
23-25 From there he went all over Galilee. He
used synagogues for meeting places and
taught people the truth of God. God's king-
dom was his theme—that beginning right

NEW KING JAMES VERSION

all kinds of disease among the people. [24]Then His fame went throughout all Syria; and they brought to Him all sick people who were afflicted with various diseases and torments, and those who were demon-possessed, epileptics, and paralytics; and He healed them. [25]Great multitudes followed Him—from Galilee, and *from* Decapolis, Jerusalem, Judea, and beyond the Jordan.

THE BEATITUDES

5 And seeing the multitudes, He went up on a mountain, and when He was seated His disciples came to Him. [2]Then He opened His mouth and taught them, saying:

[3]"Blessed *are* the poor in spirit,
For theirs is the kingdom of heaven.
[4]Blessed *are* those who mourn,
For they shall be comforted.
[5]Blessed *are* the meek,
For they shall inherit the earth.
[6]Blessed *are* those who hunger and thirst for righteousness,
For they shall be filled.
[7]Blessed *are* the merciful,
For they shall obtain mercy.
[8]Blessed *are* the pure in heart,
For they shall see God.
[9]Blessed *are* the peacemakers,
For they shall be called sons of God.
[10]Blessed *are* those who are persecuted for righteousness' sake,
For theirs is the kingdom of heaven.

[11]"Blessed are you when they revile and persecute you, and say all kinds of evil against you falsely for My sake. [12]Rejoice and be exceedingly glad, for great *is* your reward in heaven, for so they persecuted the prophets who were before you.

BELIEVERS ARE SALT AND LIGHT

[13]"You are the salt of the earth; but if the salt loses its flavor, how shall it be seasoned? It is then good for nothing but to be thrown out and trampled underfoot by men.

[14]"You are the light of the world. A city that is set on a hill cannot be hidden. [15]Nor do they

THE MESSAGE

now they were under God's government, a good government! He also healed people of their diseases and of the bad effects of their bad lives. Word got around the entire Roman province of Syria. People brought anybody with an ailment, whether mental, emotional, or physical. Jesus healed them, one and all. More and more people came, the momentum gathering. Besides those from Galilee, crowds came from the "Ten Towns" across the lake, others up from Jerusalem and Judea, still others from across the Jordan.

YOU'RE BLESSED

1-2 **5** When Jesus saw his ministry drawing huge crowds, he climbed a hillside. Those who were apprenticed to him, the committed, climbed with him. Arriving at a quiet place, he sat down and taught his climbing companions. This is what he said:

3 "You're blessed when you're at the end of your rope. With less of you there is more of God and his rule.

4 "You're blessed when you feel you've lost what is most dear to you. Only then can you be embraced by the One most dear to you.

5 "You're blessed when you're content with just who you are—no more, no less. That's the moment you find yourselves proud owners of everything that can't be bought.

6 "You're blessed when you've worked up a good appetite for God. He's food and drink in the best meal you'll ever eat.

7 "You're blessed when you care. At the moment of being 'care-full,' you find yourselves cared for.

8 "You're blessed when you get your inside world—your mind and heart—put right. Then you can see God in the outside world.

9 "You're blessed when you can show people how to cooperate instead of compete or fight. That's when you discover who you really are, and your place in God's family.

10 "You're blessed when your commitment to God provokes persecution. The persecution drives you even deeper into God's kingdom.

11-12 "Not only that—count yourselves blessed every time people put you down or throw you out or speak lies about you to discredit me. What it means is that the truth is too close for comfort and they are uncomfortable. You can be glad when that happens—give a cheer, even!—for though they don't like it, *I* do! And all heaven applauds. And know that you are in good company. My prophets and witnesses have always gotten into this kind of trouble.

SALT AND LIGHT

13 "Let me tell you why you are here. You're here to be salt-seasoning that brings out the God-flavors of this earth. If you lose your saltiness, how will people taste godliness? You've lost your usefulness and will end up in the garbage.

14-16 "Here's another way to put it: You're here to be light, bringing out the God-colors in the world. God is not a secret to be kept. We're going public with this, as public as a city on a hill. If I make you light-bearers,

NEW KING JAMES VERSION

light a lamp and put it under a basket, but on a
lampstand, and it gives light to all *who are* in
the house. [16]Let your light so shine before men,
that they may see your good works and glorify
your Father in heaven.

CHRIST FULFILLS THE LAW

[17]"Do not think that I came to destroy the
Law or the Prophets. I did not come to destroy
but to fulfill. [18]For assuredly, I say to you, till
heaven and earth pass away, one jot or one tittle
will by no means pass from the law till all is ful-
filled. [19]Whoever therefore breaks one of the
least of these commandments, and teaches men
so, shall be called least in the kingdom of
heaven; but whoever does and teaches *them*, he
shall be called great in the kingdom of heaven.
[20]For I say to you, that unless your righteousness
exceeds *the righteousness* of the scribes and
Pharisees, you will by no means enter the king-
dom of heaven.

MURDER BEGINS IN THE HEART

[21]"You have heard that it was said to those of
old, *'You shall not murder,*[a] and whoever mur-
ders will be in danger of the judgment.' [22]But I
say to you that whoever is angry with his
brother without a cause[a] shall be in danger of
the judgment. And whoever says to his brother,
'Raca!' shall be in danger of the council. But
whoever says, 'You fool!' shall be in danger of
hell fire. [23]Therefore if you bring your gift to the
altar, and there remember that your brother has
something against you, [24]leave your gift there
before the altar, and go your way. First be recon-
ciled to your brother, and then come and offer
your gift. [25]Agree with your adversary quickly,
while you are on the way with him, lest your ad-
versary deliver you to the judge, the judge hand
you over to the officer, and you be thrown into
prison. [26]Assuredly, I say to you, you will by no
means get out of there till you have paid the last
penny.

ADULTERY IN THE HEART

[27]"You have heard that it was said to those of
old,[a] *'You shall not commit adultery.'*[b] [28]But I
say to you that whoever looks at a woman to
lust for her has already committed adultery with
her in his heart. [29]If your right eye causes you to
sin, pluck it out and cast *it* from you; for it is
more profitable for you that one of your mem-
bers perish, than for your whole body to be cast
into hell. [30]And if your right hand causes you to

5:21 [a]Exodus 20:13; Deuteronomy 5:17 **5:22** [a]NU-Text omits *without a cause.* **5:27** [a]NU-Text and M-Text omit *to those of old.* [b]Exodus 20:14; Deuteronomy 5:18

THE MESSAGE

you don't think I'm going to hide you under a bucket, do you? I'm putting you on a light stand. Now that I've put you there on a hill-top, on a light stand—shine! Keep open house; be generous with your lives. By opening up to others, you'll prompt people to open up with God, this generous Father in heaven.

COMPLETING GOD'S LAW

17-18 "Don't suppose for a minute that I have come to demolish the Scriptures—either God's Law or the Prophets. I'm not here to demolish but to complete. I am going to put it all together, pull it all together in a vast panorama. God's Law is more real and lasting than the stars in the sky and the ground at your feet. Long after stars burn out and earth wears out, God's Law will be alive and working.

19-20 "Trivialize even the smallest item in God's Law and you will only have trivialized yourself. But take it seriously, show the way for others, and you will find honor in the kingdom. Unless you do far better than the Pharisees in the matters of right living, you won't know the first thing about entering the kingdom.

MURDER

21-22 "You're familiar with the command to the ancients, 'Do not murder.' I'm telling you that anyone who is so much as angry with a brother or sister is guilty of murder. Carelessly call a brother 'idiot!' and you just might find yourself hauled into court. Thoughtlessly yell 'stupid!' at a sister and you are on the brink of hellfire. The simple moral fact is that words kill.

23-24 "This is how I want you to conduct yourself in these matters. If you enter your place of worship and, about to make an offering, you suddenly remember a grudge a friend has against you, abandon your offering, leave immediately, go to this friend and make things right. Then and only then, come back and work things out with God.

25-26 "Or say you're out on the street and an old enemy accosts you. Don't lose a minute. Make the first move; make things right with him. After all, if you leave the first move to him, knowing his track record, you're likely to end up in court, maybe even jail. If that happens, you won't get out without a stiff fine.

ADULTERY AND DIVORCE

27-28 "You know the next commandment pretty well, too: 'Don't go to bed with another's spouse.' But don't think you've preserved your virtue simply by staying out of bed. Your *heart* can be corrupted by lust even quicker than your *body*. Those leering looks you think nobody notices—they also corrupt.

29-30 "Let's not pretend this is easier than it really is. If you want to live a morally pure life, here's what you have to do: You have to blind your right eye the moment you catch it in a lustful leer. You have to choose to live one-eyed or else be dumped on a moral trash pile. And you have to chop off your

New King James Version

sin, cut it off and cast *it* from you; for it is more
profitable for you that one of your members per-
ish, than for your whole body to be cast into
hell.

Marriage Is Sacred and Binding

31“Furthermore it has been said, ‘Whoever
divorces his wife, let him give her a certificate of
divorce.’ 32But I say to you that whoever di-
vorces his wife for any reason except sexual im-
morality[a] causes her to commit adultery; and
whoever marries a woman who is divorced com-
mits adultery.

Jesus Forbids Oaths

33“Again you have heard that it was said to
those of old, ‘You shall not swear falsely, but
shall perform your oaths to the Lord.’ 34But I say
to you, do not swear at all: neither by heaven, for
it is God’s throne; 35nor by the earth, for it is His
footstool; nor by Jerusalem, for it is the city of
the great King. 36Nor shall you swear by your
head, because you cannot make one hair white
or black. 37But let your ‘Yes’ be ‘Yes,’ and your
‘No,’ ‘No.’ For whatever is more than these is
from the evil one.

Go the Second Mile

38“You have heard that it was said, *‘An eye
for an eye and a tooth for a tooth.’*[a] 39But I tell
you not to resist an evil person. But whoever
slaps you on your right cheek, turn the other to
him also. 40If anyone wants to sue you and take
away your tunic, let him have *your* cloak also.
41And whoever compels you to go one mile, go
with him two. 42Give to him who asks you, and
from him who wants to borrow from you do not
turn away.

Love Your Enemies

43“You have heard that it was said, *‘You shall
love your neighbor*[a] and hate your enemy.’ 44But
I say to you, love your enemies, bless those who
curse you, do good to those who hate you, and
pray for those who spitefully use you and perse-
cute you,[a] 45that you may be sons of your Father
in heaven; for He makes His sun rise on the evil
and on the good, and sends rain on the just and
on the unjust. 46For if you love those who love
you, what reward have you? Do not even the tax
collectors do the same? 47And if you greet your
brethren[a] only, what do you do more *than oth-
ers?* Do not even the tax collectors[b] do so?
48Therefore you shall be perfect, just as your Fa-
ther in heaven is perfect.

5:32 [a]Or *fornication* **5:38** [a]Exodus 21:24; Leviticus 24:20; Deuteronomy 19:21 **5:43** [a]Compare Leviticus 19:18 **5:44** [a]NU-Text omits three clauses from this verse, leaving, *“But I say to you, love your enemies and pray for those who persecute you.”* **5:47** [a]M-Text reads *friends.* [b]NU-Text reads *Gentiles.*

The Message

right hand the moment you notice it raised
threateningly. Better a bloody stump than
your entire being discarded for good in the
dump.

31-32 “Remember the Scripture that says,
‘Whoever divorces his wife, let him do it
legally, giving her divorce papers and her le-
gal rights’? Too many of you are using that
as a cover for selfishness and whim, pre-
tending to be righteous just because you are
‘legal.’ Please, no more pretending. If you
divorce your wife, you’re responsible for
making her an adulteress (unless she has
already made herself that by sexual promis-
cuity). And if you marry such a divorced
adulteress, you’re automatically an adul-
terer yourself. You can’t use legal cover to
mask a moral failure.

Empty Promises

33-37 “And don’t say anything you don’t mean.
This counsel is embedded deep in our tradi-
tions. You only make things worse when you
lay down a smoke screen of pious talk, say-
ing, ‘I’ll pray for you,’ and never doing it, or
saying, ‘God be with you,’ and not meaning
it. You don’t make your words true by embel-
lishing them with religious lace. In making
your speech sound more religious, it be-
comes less true. Just say ‘yes’ and ‘no.’
When you manipulate words to get your
own way, you go wrong.

Love Your Enemies

38-42 “Here’s another old saying that deserves a
second look: ‘Eye for eye, tooth for tooth.’ Is
that going to get us anywhere? Here’s what
I propose: ‘Don’t hit back at all.’ If someone
strikes you, stand there and take it. If some-
one drags you into court and sues for the
shirt off your back, giftwrap your best coat
and make a present of it. And if someone
takes unfair advantage of you, use the occa-
sion to practice the servant life. No more tit-
for-tat stuff. Live generously.

43-47 “You’re familiar with the old written law,
‘Love your friend,’ and its unwritten com-
panion, ‘Hate your enemy.’ I’m challenging
that. I’m telling you to love your enemies.
Let them bring out the best in you, not the
worst. When someone gives you a hard time,
respond with the energies of prayer, for then
you are working out of your true selves,
your God-created selves. This is what God
does. He gives his best—the sun to warm
and the rain to nourish—to everyone, re-
gardless: the good and bad, the nice and
nasty. If all you do is love the lovable, do you
expect a bonus? Anybody can do that. If you
simply say hello to those who greet you, do
you expect a medal? Any run-of-the-mill
sinner does that.

48 “In a word, what I’m saying is, *Grow up.*
You’re kingdom subjects. Now live like it.
Live out your God-created identity. Live
generously and graciously toward others,
the way God lives toward you.”

NEW KING JAMES VERSION

DO GOOD TO PLEASE GOD

6 "Take heed that you do not do your charitable deeds before men, to be seen by them. Otherwise you have no reward from your Father in heaven. [2]Therefore, when you do a charitable deed, do not sound a trumpet before you as the hypocrites do in the synagogues and in the streets, that they may have glory from men. Assuredly, I say to you, they have their reward. [3]But when you do a charitable deed, do not let your left hand know what your right hand is doing, [4]that your charitable deed may be in secret; and your Father who sees in secret will Himself reward you openly.[a]

THE MODEL PRAYER

[5]"And when you pray, you shall not be like the hypocrites. For they love to pray standing in the synagogues and on the corners of the streets, that they may be seen by men. Assuredly, I say to you, they have their reward. [6]But you, when you pray, go into your room, and when you have shut your door, pray to your Father who *is* in the secret *place;* and your Father who sees in secret will reward you openly.[a] [7]And when you pray, do not use vain repetitions as the heathen *do.* For they think that they will be heard for their many words.

[8]"Therefore do not be like them. For your Father knows the things you have need of before you ask Him. [9]In this manner, therefore, pray:

Our Father in heaven,
Hallowed be Your name.
[10]Your kingdom come.
Your will be done
On earth as *it is* in heaven.
[11]Give us this day our daily bread.
[12]And forgive us our debts,
As we forgive our debtors.
[13]And do not lead us into temptation,
But deliver us from the evil one.
For Yours is the kingdom and the power and the glory forever. Amen.[a]

[14]"For if you forgive men their trespasses, your heavenly Father will also forgive you. [15]But if you do not forgive men their trespasses, neither will your Father forgive your trespasses.

FASTING TO BE SEEN ONLY BY GOD

[16]"Moreover, when you fast, do not be like the hypocrites, with a sad countenance. For they disfigure their faces that they may appear to men to be fasting. Assuredly, I say to you, they have their reward. [17]But you, when you fast, anoint your head and wash your face, [18]so that you do not appear to men to be fasting, but to your Father who *is* in the secret *place;* and your

6:4 [a]NU-Text omits *openly.* **6:6** [a]NU-Text omits *openly.*
6:13 [a]NU-Text omits *For Yours* through *Amen.*

THE MESSAGE

THE WORLD IS NOT A STAGE

1 6 "Be especially careful when you are trying
to be good so that you don't make a per-
formance out of it. It might be good theater,
but the God who made you won't be ap-
plauding.
2-4 "When you do something for someone
else, don't call attention to yourself. You've
seen them in action, I'm sure—'playactors' I
call them—treating prayer meeting and
street corner alike as a stage, acting compas-
sionate as long as someone is watching, play-
ing to the crowds. They get applause, true,
but that's all they get. When you help some-
one out, don't think about how it looks. Just
do it—quietly and unobtrusively. That is the
way your God, who conceived you in love,
working behind the scenes, helps you out.

PRAY WITH SIMPLICITY

5 "And when you come before God, don't turn
that into a theatrical production either. All
these people making a regular show out of
their prayers, hoping for stardom! Do you
think God sits in a box seat?
6 "Here's what I want you to do: Find a
quiet, secluded place so you won't be
tempted to role-play before God. Just be
there as simply and honestly as you can
manage. The focus will shift from you to
God, and you will begin to sense his grace.
7-13 "The world is full of so-called prayer war-
riors who are prayer-ignorant. They're full
of formulas and programs and advice, ped-
dling techniques for getting what you want
from God. Don't fall for that nonsense. This
is your Father you are dealing with, and he
knows better than you what you need. With
a God like this loving you, you can pray very
simply. Like this:

Our Father in heaven,
Reveal who you are.
Set the world right;
Do what's best—
as above, so below.
Keep us alive with three square meals.
Keep us forgiven with you and forgiving others.
Keep us safe from ourselves and the Devil.
You're in charge!
You can do anything you want!
You're ablaze in beauty!
Yes. Yes. Yes.

14-15 "In prayer there is a connection between
what God does and what you do. You can't get
forgiveness from God, for instance, without
also forgiving others. If you refuse to do your
part, you cut yourself off from God's part.
16-18 "When you practice some appetite-deny-
ing discipline to better concentrate on God,
don't make a production out of it. It might
turn you into a small-time celebrity but it
won't make you a saint. If you 'go into train-
ing' inwardly, act normal outwardly. Sham-
poo and comb your hair, brush your teeth,
wash your face. God doesn't require atten-

NEW KING JAMES VERSION

Father who sees in secret will reward you openly.[a]

LAY UP TREASURES IN HEAVEN

19“Do not lay up for yourselves treasures on earth, where moth and rust destroy and where thieves break in and steal; 20but lay up for yourselves treasures in heaven, where neither moth nor rust destroys and where thieves do not break in and steal. 21For where your treasure is, there your heart will be also.

THE LAMP OF THE BODY

22“The lamp of the body is the eye. If therefore your eye is good, your whole body will be full of light. 23But if your eye is bad, your whole body will be full of darkness. If therefore the light that is in you is darkness, how great *is* that darkness!

YOU CANNOT SERVE GOD AND RICHES

24“No one can serve two masters; for either he will hate the one and love the other, or else he will be loyal to the one and despise the other. You cannot serve God and mammon.

DO NOT WORRY

25“Therefore I say to you, do not worry about your life, what you will eat or what you will drink; nor about your body, what you will put on. Is not life more than food and the body more than clothing? 26Look at the birds of the air, for they neither sow nor reap nor gather into barns; yet your heavenly Father feeds them. Are you not of more value than they? 27Which of you by worrying can add one cubit to his stature?

28“So why do you worry about clothing? Consider the lilies of the field, how they grow: they neither toil nor spin; 29and yet I say to you that even Solomon in all his glory was not arrayed like one of these. 30Now if God so clothes the grass of the field, which today is, and tomorrow is thrown into the oven, *will He* not much more *clothe* you, O you of little faith?

31“Therefore do not worry, saying, ‘What shall we eat?’ or ‘What shall we drink?’ or ‘What shall we wear?’ 32For after all these things the Gentiles seek. For your heavenly Father knows that you need all these things. 33But seek first the kingdom of God and His righteousness, and all these things shall be added to you. 34Therefore do not worry about tomorrow, for tomorrow will worry about its own things. Sufficient for the day *is* its own trouble.

DO NOT JUDGE

7 “Judge not, that you be not judged. 2For with what judgment you judge, you will be judged; and with the measure you use, it will be measured back to you. 3And why do you look at the speck in your brother’s eye, but do not consider

6:18 [a]NU-Text and M-Text omit *openly.*

THE MESSAGE

tion-getting devices. He won’t overlook what you are doing; he’ll reward you well.

A LIFE OF GOD-WORSHIP

19-21 “Don’t hoard treasure down here where it gets eaten by moths and corroded by rust or—worse!—stolen by burglars. Stockpile treasure in heaven, where it’s safe from moth and rust and burglars. It’s obvious, isn’t it? The place where your treasure is, is the place you will most want to be, and end up being.

22-23 “Your eyes are windows into your body. If you open your eyes wide in wonder and belief, your body fills up with light. If you live squinty-eyed in greed and distrust, your body is a dank cellar. If you pull the blinds on your windows, what a dark life you will have!

24 “You can’t worship two gods at once. Loving one god, you’ll end up hating the other. Adoration of one feeds contempt for the other. You can’t worship God and Money both.

25-26 “If you decide for God, living a life of God-worship, it follows that you don’t fuss about what’s on the table at mealtimes or whether the clothes in your closet are in fashion. There is far more to your life than the food you put in your stomach, more to your outer appearance than the clothes you hang on your body. Look at the birds, free and unfettered, not tied down to a job description, careless in the care of God. And you count far more to him than birds.

27-29 “Has anyone by fussing in front of the mirror ever gotten taller by so much as an inch? All this time and money wasted on fashion—do you think it makes that much difference? Instead of looking at the fashions, walk out into the fields and look at the wildflowers. They never primp or shop, but have you ever seen color and design quite like it? The ten best-dressed men and women in the country look shabby alongside them.

30-33 “If God gives such attention to the appearance of wildflowers—most of which are never even seen—don’t you think he’ll attend to you, take pride in you, do his best for you? What I’m trying to do here is to get you to relax, to not be so preoccupied with *getting,* so you can respond to God’s *giving.* People who don’t know God and the way he works fuss over these things, but you know both God and how he works. Steep your life in God-reality, God-initiative, God-provisions. Don’t worry about missing out. You’ll find all your everyday human concerns will be met.

34 “Give your entire attention to what God is doing right now, and don’t get worked up about what may or may not happen tomorrow. God will help you deal with whatever hard things come up when the time comes.

A SIMPLE GUIDE FOR BEHAVIOR

1-5 7 “Don’t pick on people, jump on their failures, criticize their faults—unless, of course, you want the same treatment. That critical spirit has a way of boomeranging. It’s easy to see a smudge on your neighbor’s face and be oblivious to the ugly sneer on

NEW KING JAMES VERSION

the plank in your own eye? 4Or how can you say
to your brother, 'Let me remove the speck from
your eye'; and look, a plank *is* in your own eye?
5Hypocrite! First remove the plank from your
own eye, and then you will see clearly to remove
the speck from your brother's eye.
6"Do not give what is holy to the dogs; nor
cast your pearls before swine, lest they trample
them under their feet, and turn and tear you in
pieces.

KEEP ASKING, SEEKING, KNOCKING

7"Ask, and it will be given to you; seek, and
you will find; knock, and it will be opened to
you. 8For everyone who asks receives, and he
who seeks finds, and to him who knocks it will
be opened. 9Or what man is there among you
who, if his son asks for bread, will give him a
stone? 10Or if he asks for a fish, will he give him
a serpent? 11If you then, being evil, know how to
give good gifts to your children, how much more
will your Father who is in heaven give good
things to those who ask Him! 12Therefore, what-
ever you want men to do to you, do also to them,
for this is the Law and the Prophets.

THE NARROW WAY

13"Enter by the narrow gate; for wide *is* the
gate and broad *is* the way that leads to destruc-
tion, and there are many who go in by it. 14Be-
cause[a] narrow *is* the gate and difficult *is* the way
which leads to life, and there are few who find
it.

YOU WILL KNOW THEM BY THEIR FRUITS

15"Beware of false prophets, who come to
you in sheep's clothing, but inwardly they are
ravenous wolves. 16You will know them by their
fruits. Do men gather grapes from thornbushes
or figs from thistles? 17Even so, every good tree
bears good fruit, but a bad tree bears bad fruit.
18A good tree cannot bear bad fruit, nor *can* a
bad tree bear good fruit. 19Every tree that does
not bear good fruit is cut down and thrown into
the fire. 20Therefore by their fruits you will
know them.

I NEVER KNEW YOU

21"Not everyone who says to Me, 'Lord,
Lord,' shall enter the kingdom of heaven, but he
who does the will of My Father in heaven.
22Many will say to Me in that day, 'Lord, Lord,
have we not prophesied in Your name, cast out
demons in Your name, and done many wonders
in Your name?' 23And then I will declare to them,
'I never knew you; depart from Me, you who
practice lawlessness!'

BUILD ON THE ROCK

24"Therefore whoever hears these sayings of
Mine, and does them, I will liken him to a wise
man who built his house on the rock: 25and the
rain descended, the floods came, and the winds
blew and beat on that house; and it did not fall,
for it was founded on the rock.

7:14 [a]NU-Text and M-Text read *How . . . !*

THE MESSAGE

your own. Do you have the nerve to say, 'Let
me wash your face for you,' when your own
face is distorted by contempt? It's this whole
traveling road-show mentality all over
again, playing a holier-than-thou part in-
stead of just living your part. Wipe that ugly
sneer off your own face, and you might be
fit to offer a washcloth to your neighbor.

6 "Don't be flip with the sacred. Banter and
silliness give no honor to God. Don't reduce
holy mysteries to slogans. In trying to be rel-
evant, you're only being cute and inviting
sacrilege.

7-11 "Don't bargain with God. Be direct. Ask
for what you need. This isn't a cat-and-
mouse, hide-and-seek game we're in. If your
child asks for bread, do you trick him with
sawdust? If he asks for fish, do you scare
him with a live snake on his plate? As bad as
you are, you wouldn't think of such a thing.
You're at least decent to your own children.
So don't you think the God who conceived
you in love will be even better?

12 "Here is a simple, rule-of-thumb guide for
behavior: Ask yourself what you want peo-
ple to do for you, then grab the initiative and
do it for *them.* Add up God's Law and
Prophets and this is what you get.

BEING AND DOING

13-14 "Don't look for shortcuts to God. The mar-
ket is flooded with surefire, easygoing for-
mulas for a successful life that can be prac-
ticed in your spare time. Don't fall for that
stuff, even though crowds of people do. The
way to life—to God!—is vigorous and re-
quires total attention.

15-20 "Be wary of false preachers who smile a
lot, dripping with practiced sincerity.
Chances are they are out to rip you off some
way or other. Don't be impressed with
charisma; look for character. Who preach-
ers *are* is the main thing, not what they say.
A genuine leader will never exploit your
emotions or your pocketbook. These dis-
eased trees with their bad apples are going
to be chopped down and burned.

21-23 "Knowing the correct password—saying
'Master, Master,' for instance—isn't going to
get you anywhere with me. What is required
is serious obedience—*doing* what my Father
wills. I can see it now—at the Final Judg-
ment thousands strutting up to me and say-
ing, 'Master, we preached the Message, we
bashed the demons, our God-sponsored
projects had everyone talking.' And do you
know what I am going to say? 'You missed
the boat. All you did was use me to make
yourselves important. You don't impress me
one bit. You're out of here.'

24-25 "These words I speak to you are not inci-
dental additions to your life, homeowner
improvements to your standard of living.
They are foundational words, words to build
a life on. If you work these words into your
life, you are like a smart carpenter who built
his house on solid rock. Rain poured down,
the river flooded, a tornado hit—but nothing
moved that house. It was fixed to the rock.

New King James Version

[26]"But everyone who hears these sayings of Mine, and does not do them, will be like a foolish man who built his house on the sand: [27]and the rain descended, the floods came, and the winds blew and beat on that house; and it fell. And great was its fall."

[28]And so it was, when Jesus had ended these sayings, that the people were astonished at His teaching, [29]for He taught them as one having authority, and not as the scribes.

Jesus Cleanses a Leper

8 When He had come down from the mountain, great multitudes followed Him. [2]And behold, a leper came and worshiped Him, saying, "Lord, if You are willing, You can make me clean."

[3]Then Jesus put out *His* hand and touched him, saying, "I am willing; be cleansed." Immediately his leprosy was cleansed.

[4]And Jesus said to him, "See that you tell no one; but go your way, show yourself to the priest, and offer the gift that Moses commanded, as a testimony to them."

Jesus Heals a Centurion's Servant

[5]Now when Jesus had entered Capernaum, a centurion came to Him, pleading with Him, [6]saying, "Lord, my servant is lying at home paralyzed, dreadfully tormented."

[7]And Jesus said to him, "I will come and heal him."

[8]The centurion answered and said, "Lord, I am not worthy that You should come under my roof. But only speak a word, and my servant will be healed. [9]For I also am a man under authority, having soldiers under me. And I say to this *one*, 'Go,' and he goes; and to another, 'Come,' and he comes; and to my servant, 'Do this,' and he does *it*."

[10]When Jesus heard *it*, He marveled, and said to those who followed, "Assuredly, I say to you, I have not found such great faith, not even in Israel! [11]And I say to you that many will come from east and west, and sit down with Abraham, Isaac, and Jacob in the kingdom of heaven. [12]But the sons of the kingdom will be cast out into outer darkness. There will be weeping and gnashing of teeth." [13]Then Jesus said to the centurion, "Go your way; and as you have believed, *so* let it be done for you." And his servant was healed that same hour.

Peter's Mother-in-Law Healed

[14]Now when Jesus had come into Peter's house, He saw his wife's mother lying sick with a fever. [15]So He touched her hand, and the fever left her. And she arose and served them.[a]

Many Healed in the Evening

[16]When evening had come, they brought to Him many who were demon-possessed. And He cast out the spirits with a word, and healed all who were sick, [17]that it might be fulfilled which was spoken by Isaiah the prophet, saying:

8:15 [a]NU-Text and M-Text read *Him.*

The Message

26-27 "But if you just use my words in Bible studies and don't work them into your life, you are like a stupid carpenter who built his house on the sandy beach. When a storm rolled in and the waves came up, it collapsed like a house of cards."

28-29 When Jesus concluded his address, the crowd burst into applause. They had never heard teaching like this. It was apparent that he was living everything he was saying—quite a contrast to their religion teachers! This was the best teaching they had ever heard.

He Carried Our Diseases

1-2 8 Jesus came down the mountain with the cheers of the crowd still ringing in his ears. Then a leper appeared and went to his knees before Jesus, praying, "Master, if you want to, you can heal my body."

3-4 Jesus reached out and touched him, saying, "I want to. Be clean." Then and there, all signs of the leprosy were gone. Jesus said, "Don't talk about this all over town. Just quietly present your healed body to the priest, along with the appropriate expressions of thanks to God. Your cleansed and grateful life, not your words, will bear witness to what I have done."

5-6 As Jesus entered the village of Capernaum, a Roman captain came up in a panic and said, "Master, my servant is sick. He can't walk. He's in terrible pain."

7 Jesus said, "I'll come and heal him."

8-9 "Oh, no," said the captain. "I don't want to put you to all that trouble. Just give the order and my servant will be fine. I'm a man who takes orders and gives orders. I tell one soldier, 'Go,' and he goes; to another, 'Come,' and he comes; to my slave, 'Do this,' and he does it."

10-12 Taken aback, Jesus said, "I've yet to come across this kind of simple trust in Israel, the very people who are supposed to know all about God and how he works. This man is the vanguard of many outsiders who will soon be coming from all directions—streaming in from the east, pouring in from the west, sitting down at God's kingdom banquet alongside Abraham, Isaac, and Jacob. Then those who grew up 'in the faith' but had no faith will find themselves out in the cold, outsiders to grace and wondering what happened."

13 Then Jesus turned to the captain and said, "Go. What you believed could happen has happened." At that moment his servant became well.

14-15 By this time they were in front of Peter's house. On entering, Jesus found Peter's mother-in-law sick in bed, burning up with fever. He touched her hand and the fever was gone. No sooner was she up on her feet than she was fixing dinner for him.

16-17 That evening a lot of demon-afflicted people were brought to him. He relieved the inwardly tormented. He cured the bodily ill. He fulfilled Isaiah's well-known sermon:

NEW KING JAMES VERSION

"He Himself took our infirmities
And bore our sicknesses."[a]

THE COST OF DISCIPLESHIP

18And when Jesus saw great multitudes
about Him, He gave a command to depart to the
other side. 19Then a certain scribe came and said
to Him, "Teacher, I will follow You wherever You
go."

20And Jesus said to him, "Foxes have holes
and birds of the air *have* nests, but the Son of
Man has nowhere to lay *His* head."

21Then another of His disciples said to Him,
"Lord, let me first go and bury my father."

22But Jesus said to him, "Follow Me, and let
the dead bury their own dead."

WIND AND WAVE OBEY JESUS

23Now when He got into a boat, His disciples
followed Him. 24And suddenly a great tempest
arose on the sea, so that the boat was covered
with the waves. But He was asleep. 25Then His
disciples came to *Him* and awoke Him, saying,
"Lord, save us! We are perishing!"

26But He said to them, "Why are you fearful,
O you of little faith?" Then He arose and re-
buked the winds and the sea, and there was a
great calm. 27So the men marveled, saying,
"Who can this be, that even the winds and the
sea obey Him?"

TWO DEMON-POSSESSED MEN HEALED

28When He had come to the other side, to the
country of the Gergesenes,[a] there met Him two
demon-possessed *men,* coming out of the
tombs, exceedingly fierce, so that no one could
pass that way. 29And suddenly they cried out,
saying, "What have we to do with You, Jesus, You
Son of God? Have You come here to torment us
before the time?"

30Now a good way off from them there was a
herd of many swine feeding. 31So the demons
begged Him, saying, "If You cast us out, permit
us to go away[a] into the herd of swine."

32And He said to them, "Go." So when they
had come out, they went into the herd of swine.
And suddenly the whole herd of swine ran vio-
lently down the steep place into the sea, and
perished in the water.

33Then those who kept *them* fled; and they
went away into the city and told everything, in-
cluding what *had happened* to the demon-
possessed *men.* 34And behold, the whole city
came out to meet Jesus. And when they saw
Him, they begged *Him* to depart from their re-
gion.

JESUS FORGIVES AND HEALS A PARALYTIC

9 So He got into a boat, crossed over, and came
to His own city. 2Then behold, they brought to
Him a paralytic lying on a bed. When Jesus saw
their faith, He said to the paralytic, "Son, be of
good cheer; your sins are forgiven you."

3And at once some of the scribes said within
themselves, "This Man blasphemes!"

8:17 [a]Isaiah 53:4 **8:28** [a]NU-Text reads *Gadarenes.* **8:31** [a]NU-Text reads *send us.*

THE MESSAGE

He took our illnesses,
He carried our diseases.

YOUR BUSINESS IS LIFE, NOT DEATH

18-19 When Jesus saw that a curious crowd was
growing by the minute, he told his disciples
to get him out of there to the other side of
the lake. As they left, a religion scholar
asked if he could go along. "I'll go with you,
wherever," he said.

20 Jesus was curt: "Are you ready to rough
it? We're not staying in the best inns, you
know."

21 Another follower said, "Master, excuse
me for a couple of days, please. I have my fa-
ther's funeral to take care of."

22 Jesus refused. "First things first. Your busi-
ness is life, not death. Follow me. Pursue life."

23-25 Then he got in the boat, his disciples with
him. The next thing they knew, they were in
a severe storm. Waves were crashing into
the boat—and he was sound asleep! They
roused him, pleading, "Master, save us!
We're going down!"

26 Jesus reprimanded them. "Why are you
such cowards, such fainthearts?" Then he
stood up and told the wind to be silent, the
sea to quiet down: "Silence!" The sea be-
came smooth as glass.

27 The men rubbed their eyes, astonished.
"What's going on here? Wind and sea come
to heel at his command!"

THE MADMEN AND THE PIGS

28-31 They landed in the country of the Gadarenes
and were met by two madmen, victims of
demons, coming out of the cemetery. The
men had terrorized the region for so long
that no one considered it safe to walk down
that stretch of road anymore. Seeing Jesus,
the madmen screamed out, "What business
do you have giving us a hard time? You're the
Son of God! You weren't supposed to show
up here yet!" Off in the distance a herd of
pigs was browsing and rooting. The evil spir-
its begged Jesus, "If you kick us out of these
men, let us live in the pigs."

32-34 Jesus said, "Go ahead, but get out of
here!" Crazed, the pigs stampeded over a
cliff into the sea and drowned. Scared to
death, the swineherds bolted. They told
everyone back in town what had happened
to the madmen and the pigs. Those who
heard about it were angry about the
drowned pigs. A mob formed and demanded
that Jesus get out and not come back.

WHO NEEDS A DOCTOR?

1-3 9 Back in the boat, Jesus and the disciples
recrossed the sea to Jesus' hometown.
They were hardly out of the boat when some
men carried a paraplegic on a stretcher and
set him down in front of them. Jesus, im-
pressed by their bold belief, said to the para-
plegic, "Cheer up, son. I forgive your sins."
Some religion scholars whispered, "Why,
that's blasphemy!"

NEW KING JAMES VERSION

4But Jesus, knowing their thoughts, said, "Why do you think evil in your hearts? 5For which is easier, to say, '*Your* sins are forgiven you,' or to say, 'Arise and walk'? 6But that you may know that the Son of Man has power on earth to forgive sins"—then He said to the paralytic, "Arise, take up your bed, and go to your house." 7And he arose and departed to his house.

8Now when the multitudes saw *it*, they marveled[a] and glorified God, who had given such power to men.

MATTHEW THE TAX COLLECTOR

9As Jesus passed on from there, He saw a man named Matthew sitting at the tax office. And He said to him, "Follow Me." So he arose and followed Him.

10Now it happened, as Jesus sat at the table in the house, *that* behold, many tax collectors and sinners came and sat down with Him and His disciples. 11And when the Pharisees saw *it*, they said to His disciples, "Why does your Teacher eat with tax collectors and sinners?"

12When Jesus heard *that*, He said to them, "Those who are well have no need of a physician, but those who are sick. 13But go and learn what *this* means: *'I desire mercy and not sacrifice.'*[a] For I did not come to call the righteous, but sinners, to repentance."[b]

JESUS IS QUESTIONED ABOUT FASTING

14Then the disciples of John came to Him, saying, "Why do we and the Pharisees fast often,[a] but Your disciples do not fast?"

15And Jesus said to them, "Can the friends of the bridegroom mourn as long as the bridegroom is with them? But the days will come when the bridegroom will be taken away from them, and then they will fast. 16No one puts a piece of unshrunk cloth on an old garment; for the patch pulls away from the garment, and the tear is made worse. 17Nor do they put new wine into old wineskins, or else the wineskins break, the wine is spilled, and the wineskins are ruined. But they put new wine into new wineskins, and both are preserved."

A GIRL RESTORED TO LIFE AND A WOMAN HEALED

18While He spoke these things to them, behold, a ruler came and worshiped Him, saying, "My daughter has just died, but come and lay Your hand on her and she will live." 19So Jesus arose and followed him, and so *did* His disciples.

20And suddenly, a woman who had a flow of blood for twelve years came from behind and touched the hem of His garment. 21For she said to herself, "If only I may touch His garment, I shall be made well." 22But Jesus turned around, and when He saw her He said, "Be of good cheer, daughter; your faith has made you well." And the woman was made well from that hour.

23When Jesus came into the ruler's house, and saw the flute players and the noisy crowd wailing, 24He said to them, "Make room, for the girl is not dead, but sleeping." And they ridiculed Him. 25But when the crowd was put outside, He went in and took her by the hand,

9:8 [a]NU-Text reads *were afraid.* **9:13** [a]Hosea 6:6 [b]NU-Text omits *to repentance.* **9:14** [a]NU-Text brackets *often* as disputed.

THE MESSAGE

4-8 Jesus knew what they were thinking, and said, "Why this gossipy whispering? Which do you think is simpler: to say, 'I forgive your sins,' or, 'Get up and walk'? Well, just so it's clear that I'm the Son of Man and authorized to do either, or both. . . ." At this he turned to the paraplegic and said, "Get up. Take your bed and go home." And the man did it. The crowd was awestruck, amazed and pleased that God had authorized Jesus to work among them this way.

9 Passing along, Jesus saw a man at his work collecting taxes. His name was Matthew. Jesus said, "Come along with me." Matthew stood up and followed him.

10-11 Later when Jesus was eating supper at Matthew's house with his close followers, a lot of disreputable characters came and joined them. When the Pharisees saw him keeping this kind of company, they had a fit, and lit into Jesus' followers. "What kind of example is this from your Teacher, acting cozy with crooks and riffraff?"

12-13 Jesus, overhearing, shot back, "Who needs a doctor: the healthy or the sick? Go figure out what this Scripture means: 'I'm after mercy, not religion.' I'm here to invite outsiders, not coddle insiders."

KINGDOM COME

14 A little later John's followers approached, asking, "Why is it that we and the Pharisees rigorously discipline body and spirit by fasting, but your followers don't?"

15 Jesus told them, "When you're celebrating a wedding, you don't skimp on the cake and wine. You feast. Later you may need to pull in your belt, but not now. No one throws cold water on a friendly bonfire. This is Kingdom Come!"

16-17 He went on, "No one cuts up a fine silk scarf to patch old work clothes; you want fabrics that match. And you don't put your wine in cracked bottles."

JUST A TOUCH

18-19 As he finished saying this, a local official appeared, bowed politely, and said, "My daughter has just now died. If you come and touch her, she will live." Jesus got up and went with him, his disciples following along.

20-22 Just then a woman who had hemorrhaged for twelve years slipped in from behind and lightly touched his robe. She was thinking to herself, "If I can just put a finger on his robe, I'll get well." Jesus turned—caught her at it. Then he reassured her: "Courage, daughter. You took a risk of faith, and now you're well." The woman was well from then on.

23-26 By now they had arrived at the house of the town official, and pushed their way through the gossips looking for a story and the neighbors bringing in casseroles. Jesus was abrupt: "Clear out! This girl isn't dead. She's sleeping." They told him he didn't know what he was talking about. But when Jesus had gotten rid of the crowd, he went in, took the girl's hand, and pulled her to her

NEW KING JAMES VERSION

and the girl arose. [26]And the report of this went
out into all that land.

TWO BLIND MEN HEALED

[27]When Jesus departed from there, two blind
men followed Him, crying out and saying, "Son
of David, have mercy on us!"
[28]And when He had come into the house, the
blind men came to Him. And Jesus said to them,
"Do you believe that I am able to do this?"
They said to Him, "Yes, Lord."
[29]Then He touched their eyes, saying, "Ac-
cording to your faith let it be to you." [30]And their
eyes were opened. And Jesus sternly warned
them, saying, "See *that* no one knows *it*." [31]But
when they had departed, they spread the news
about Him in all that country.

A MUTE MAN SPEAKS

[32]As they went out, behold, they brought to
Him a man, mute and demon-possessed. [33]And
when the demon was cast out, the mute spoke.
And the multitudes marveled, saying, "It was
never seen like this in Israel!"
[34]But the Pharisees said, "He casts out
demons by the ruler of the demons."

THE COMPASSION OF JESUS

[35]Then Jesus went about all the cities and vil-
lages, teaching in their synagogues, preaching
the gospel of the kingdom, and healing every
sickness and every disease among the people.[a]
[36]But when He saw the multitudes, He was
moved with compassion for them, because they
were weary[a] and scattered, like sheep having no
shepherd. [37]Then He said to His disciples, "The
harvest truly *is* plentiful, but the laborers *are*
few. [38]Therefore pray the Lord of the harvest to
send out laborers into His harvest."

THE TWELVE APOSTLES

10 And when He had called His twelve disci-
ples to *Him*, He gave them power *over* un-
clean spirits, to cast them out, and to heal all
kinds of sickness and all kinds of disease. [2]Now
the names of the twelve apostles are these: first,
Simon, who is called Peter, and Andrew his
brother; James the *son* of Zebedee, and John his
brother; [3]Philip and Bartholomew; Thomas and
Matthew the tax collector; James the *son* of Al-
phaeus, and Lebbaeus, whose surname was[a]
Thaddaeus; [4]Simon the Cananite,[a] and Judas Is-
cariot, who also betrayed Him.

SENDING OUT THE TWELVE

[5]These twelve Jesus sent out and com-
manded them, saying: "Do not go into the way
of the Gentiles, and do not enter a city of the
Samaritans. [6]But go rather to the lost sheep of
the house of Israel. [7]And as you go, preach, say-

9:35 [a]NU-Text omits *among the people.* **9:36** [a]NU-Text and M-Text read *harassed.* **10:3** [a]NU-Text omits *Lebbaeus, whose surname was.* **10:4** [a]NU-Text reads *Cananaean.*

THE MESSAGE

feet—alive. The news was soon out, and
traveled throughout the region.

BECOME WHAT YOU BELIEVE

27-28 As Jesus left the house, he was followed by
two blind men crying out, "Mercy, Son of
David! Mercy on us!" When Jesus got home,
the blind men went in with him. Jesus said
to them, "Do you really believe I can do
this?" They said, "Why, yes, Master!"
29-31 He touched their eyes and said, "Become
what you believe." It happened. They saw.
Then Jesus became very stern. "Don't let a
soul know how this happened." But they
were hardly out the door before they started
blabbing it to everyone they met.
32-33 Right after that, as the blind men were
leaving, a man who had been struck speech-
less by an evil spirit was brought to Jesus.
As soon as Jesus threw the evil tormenting
spirit out, the man talked away just as if he'd
been talking all his life. The people were up
on their feet applauding: "There's never
been anything like this in Israel!"
34 The Pharisees were left sputtering, "Ho-
cus-pocus. It's nothing but hocus-pocus.
He's probably made a pact with the Devil."
35-38 Then Jesus made a circuit of all the towns
and villages. He taught in their meeting
places, reported kingdom news, and healed
their diseased bodies, healed their bruised
and hurt lives. When he looked out over the
crowds, his heart broke. So confused and
aimless they were, like sheep with no shep-
herd. "What a huge harvest!" he said to his
disciples. "How few workers! On your knees
and pray for harvest hands!"

THE TWELVE HARVEST HANDS

1-4 10 The prayer was no sooner prayed than
it was answered. Jesus called twelve of
his followers and sent them into the ripe
fields. He gave them power to kick out the evil
spirits and to tenderly care for the bruised
and hurt lives. This is the list of the twelve he
sent:

Simon (they called him Peter, or "Rock"),
Andrew, his brother,
James, Zebedee's son,
John, his brother,
Philip,
Bartholomew,
Thomas,
Matthew, the tax man,
James, son of Alphaeus,
Thaddaeus,
Simon, the Canaanite,
Judas Iscariot (who later turned on him).

5-8 Jesus sent his twelve harvest hands out
with this charge:
"Don't begin by traveling to some far-off
place to convert unbelievers. And don't try
to be dramatic by tackling some public en-
emy. Go to the lost, confused people right
here in the neighborhood. Tell them that the

New King James Version

ing, 'The kingdom of heaven is at hand.' 8Heal
the sick, cleanse the lepers, raise the dead,[a] cast
out demons. Freely you have received, freely
give. 9Provide neither gold nor silver nor copper
in your money belts, 10nor bag for *your* journey,
nor two tunics, nor sandals, nor staffs; for a
worker is worthy of his food.

11"Now whatever city or town you enter, in-
quire who in it is worthy, and stay there till you
go out. 12And when you go into a household,
greet it. 13If the household is worthy, let your
peace come upon it. But if it is not worthy, let
your peace return to you. 14And whoever will
not receive you nor hear your words, when you
depart from that house or city, shake off the dust
from your feet. 15Assuredly, I say to you, it will
be more tolerable for the land of Sodom and Go-
morrah in the day of judgment than for that
city!

Persecutions Are Coming

16"Behold, I send you out as sheep in the
midst of wolves. Therefore be wise as serpents
and harmless as doves. 17But beware of men, for
they will deliver you up to councils and scourge
you in their synagogues. 18You will be brought
before governors and kings for My sake, as a
testimony to them and to the Gentiles. 19But
when they deliver you up, do not worry about
how or what you should speak. For it will be
given to you in that hour what you should
speak; 20for it is not you who speak, but the
Spirit of your Father who speaks in you.

21"Now brother will deliver up brother to
death, and a father *his* child; and children will
rise up against parents and cause them to be put
to death. 22And you will be hated by all for My
name's sake. But he who endures to the end will
be saved. 23When they persecute you in this city,
flee to another. For assuredly, I say to you, you
will not have gone through the cities of Israel
before the Son of Man comes.

24"A disciple is not above *his* teacher, nor a
servant above his master. 25It is enough for a dis-
ciple that he be like his teacher, and a servant
like his master. If they have called the master of
the house Beelzebub,[a] how much more *will they
call* those of his household! 26Therefore do not
fear them. For there is nothing covered that will
not be revealed, and hidden that will not be
known.

Jesus Teaches the Fear of God

27"Whatever I tell you in the dark, speak in
the light; and what you hear in the ear, preach
on the housetops. 28And do not fear those who
kill the body but cannot kill the soul. But rather
fear Him who is able to destroy both soul and
body in hell. 29Are not two sparrows sold for a
copper coin? And not one of them falls to the

10:8 [a]NU-Text reads *raise the dead, cleanse the lepers;* M-Text omits *raise the dead.* **10:25** [a]NU-Text and M-Text read *Beelzebul.*

The Message

kingdom is here. Bring health to the sick.
Raise the dead. Touch the untouchables.
Kick out the demons. You have been treated
generously, so live generously.

9-10 "Don't think you have to put on a fund-
raising campaign before you start. You don't
need a lot of equipment. *You* are the equip-
ment, and all you need to keep that going is
three meals a day. Travel light.

11 "When you enter a town or village, don't
insist on staying in a luxury inn. Get a mod-
est place with some modest people, and be
content there until you leave.

12-15 "When you knock on a door, be courteous
in your greeting. If they welcome you, be
gentle in your conversation. If they don't
welcome you, quietly withdraw. Don't make
a scene. Shrug your shoulders and be on
your way. You can be sure that on Judgment
Day they'll be mighty sorry—but it's no con-
cern of yours now.

16 "Stay alert. This is hazardous work I'm
assigning you. You're going to be like sheep
running through a wolf pack, so don't call
attention to yourselves. Be as cunning as a
snake, inoffensive as a dove.

17-20 "Don't be naive. Some people will im-
pugn your motives, others will smear your
reputation—just because you believe in me.
Don't be upset when they haul you before
the civil authorities. Without knowing it,
they've done you—and me—a favor, given
you a platform for preaching the kingdom
news! And don't worry about what you'll
say or how you'll say it. The right words will
be there; the Spirit of your Father will sup-
ply the words.

21-23 "When people realize it is the living God
you are presenting and not some idol that
makes them feel good, they are going to
turn on you, even people in your own family.
There is a great irony here: proclaiming so
much love, experiencing so much hate! But
don't quit. Don't cave in. It is all well worth
it in the end. It is not success you are after in
such times but survival. Be survivors! Be-
fore you've run out of options, the Son of
Man will have arrived.

24-25 "A student doesn't get a better desk than
her teacher. A laborer doesn't make more
money than his boss. Be content—pleased,
even—when you, my students, my harvest
hands, get the same treatment I get. If they
call me, the Master, 'Dungface,' what can
the workers expect?

26-27 "Don't be intimidated. Eventually every-
thing is going to be out in the open, and
everyone will know how things really are.
So don't hesitate to go public now.

28 "Don't be bluffed into silence by the
threats of bullies. There's nothing they can
do to your soul, your core being. Save your
fear for God, who holds your entire life—
body and soul—in his hands.

Forget About Yourself

29-31 "What's the price of a pet canary? Some
loose change, right? And God cares what
happens to it even more than you do. He

NEW KING JAMES VERSION

ground apart from your Father's will. 30But the
very hairs of your head are all numbered. 31Do
not fear therefore; you are of more value than
many sparrows.

CONFESS CHRIST BEFORE MEN

32"Therefore whoever confesses Me before
men, him I will also confess before My Father
who is in heaven. 33But whoever denies Me be-
fore men, him I will also deny before My Father
who is in heaven.

CHRIST BRINGS DIVISION

34"Do not think that I came to bring peace on
earth. I did not come to bring peace but a sword.
35For I have come to *'set a man against his fa-
ther, a daughter against her mother, and a
daughter-in-law against her mother-in-law';*
36and *'a man's enemies will be those of his own
household.'*[a] 37He who loves father or mother
more than Me is not worthy of Me. And he who
loves son or daughter more than Me is not wor-
thy of Me. 38And he who does not take his cross
and follow after Me is not worthy of Me. 39He
who finds his life will lose it, and he who loses
his life for My sake will find it.

A CUP OF COLD WATER

40"He who receives you receives Me, and he
who receives Me receives Him who sent Me.
41He who receives a prophet in the name of a
prophet shall receive a prophet's reward. And
he who receives a righteous man in the name of
a righteous man shall receive a righteous man's
reward. 42And whoever gives one of these little
ones only a cup of cold *water* in the name of a
disciple, assuredly, I say to you, he shall by no
means lose his reward."

JOHN THE BAPTIST SENDS MESSENGERS TO JESUS

11 Now it came to pass, when Jesus finished
commanding His twelve disciples, that He
departed from there to teach and to preach in
their cities.

2And when John had heard in prison about
the works of Christ, he sent two of[a] his disciples
3and said to Him, "Are You the Coming One, or
do we look for another?"

4Jesus answered and said to them, "Go and
tell John the things which you hear and see:
5*The* blind see and *the* lame walk; *the* lepers are
cleansed and *the* deaf hear; *the* dead are raised
up and *the* poor have the gospel preached to
them. 6And blessed is he who is not offended be-
cause of Me."

7As they departed, Jesus began to say to the
multitudes concerning John: "What did you go
out into the wilderness to see? A reed shaken by
the wind? 8But what did you go out to see? A
man clothed in soft garments? Indeed, those
who wear soft *clothing* are in kings' houses.
9But what did you go out to see? A prophet? Yes,

10:36 [a]Micah 7:6 **11:2** [a]NU-Text reads *by* for *two of.*

THE MESSAGE

pays even greater attention to you, down to
the last detail—even numbering the hairs on
your head! So don't be intimidated by all
this bully talk. You're worth more than a mil-
lion canaries.

32-33 "Stand up for me against world opinion
and I'll stand up for you before my Father in
heaven. If you turn tail and run, do you
think I'll cover for you?

34-37 "Don't think I've come to make life cozy.
I've come to cut—make a sharp knife-cut
between son and father, daughter and
mother, bride and mother-in-law—cut
through these cozy domestic arrangements
and free you for God. Well-meaning family
members can be your worst enemies. If you
prefer father or mother over me, you don't
deserve me. If you prefer son or daughter
over me, you don't deserve me.

38-39 "If you don't go all the way with me,
through thick and thin, you don't deserve
me. If your first concern is to look after
yourself, you'll never find yourself. But if
you forget about yourself and look to me,
you'll find both yourself and me.

40-42 "We are intimately linked in this harvest
work. Anyone who accepts what you do, ac-
cepts me, the One who sent you. Anyone
who accepts what I do accepts my Father,
who sent me. Accepting a messenger of God
is as good as being God's messenger. Ac-
cepting someone's help is as good as giving
someone help. This is a large work I've
called you into, but don't be overwhelmed
by it. It's best to start small. Give a cool cup
of water to someone who is thirsty, for in-
stance. The smallest act of giving or receiv-
ing makes you a true apprentice. You won't
lose out on a thing."

JOHN THE BAPTIZER

1 11 When Jesus finished placing this charge
before his twelve disciples, he went on
to teach and preach in their villages.

2-3 John, meanwhile, had been locked up in
prison. When he got wind of what Jesus was
doing, he sent his own disciples to ask, "Are
you the One we've been expecting, or are we
still waiting?"

4-6 Jesus told them, "Go back and tell John
what's going on:

The blind see,
The lame walk,
Lepers are cleansed,
The deaf hear,
The dead are raised,
The wretched of the earth learn that God
is on their side.

"Is this what you were expecting? Then
count yourselves most blessed!"

7-10 When John's disciples left to report, Je-
sus started talking to the crowd about John.
"What did you expect when you went out to
see him in the wild? A weekend camper?
Hardly. What then? A sheik in silk pajamas?
Not in the wilderness, not by a long shot.
What then? A prophet? That's right, a

NEW KING JAMES VERSION

I say to you, and more than a prophet. 10For this is *he* of whom it is written:

'Behold, I send My messenger before Your face,
Who will prepare Your way before You.' [a]

11"Assuredly, I say to you, among those born of women there has not risen one greater than John the Baptist; but he who is least in the kingdom of heaven is greater than he. 12And from the days of John the Baptist until now the kingdom of heaven suffers violence, and the violent take it by force. 13For all the prophets and the law prophesied until John. 14And if you are willing to receive *it,* he is Elijah who is to come. 15He who has ears to hear, let him hear!

16"But to what shall I liken this generation? It is like children sitting in the marketplaces and calling to their companions, 17and saying:

'We played the flute for you,
And you did not dance;
We mourned to you,
And you did not lament.'

18For John came neither eating nor drinking, and they say, 'He has a demon.' 19The Son of Man came eating and drinking, and they say, 'Look, a glutton and a winebibber, a friend of tax collectors and sinners!' But wisdom is justified by her children."[a]

Woe to the Impenitent Cities

20Then He began to rebuke the cities in which most of His mighty works had been done, because they did not repent: 21"Woe to you, Chorazin! Woe to you, Bethsaida! For if the mighty works which were done in you had been done in Tyre and Sidon, they would have repented long ago in sackcloth and ashes. 22But I say to you, it will be more tolerable for Tyre and Sidon in the day of judgment than for you. 23And you, Capernaum, who are exalted to heaven, will be[a] brought down to Hades; for if the mighty works which were done in you had been done in Sodom, it would have remained until this day. 24But I say to you that it shall be more tolerable for the land of Sodom in the day of judgment than for you."

Jesus Gives True Rest

25At that time Jesus answered and said, "I thank You, Father, Lord of heaven and earth, that You have hidden these things from *the* wise and prudent and have revealed them to babes. 26Even so, Father, for so it seemed good in Your sight. 27All things have been delivered to Me by My Father, and no one knows the Son except the Father. Nor does anyone know the Father except the Son, and *the one* to whom the Son wills to reveal *Him.* 28Come to Me, all *you* who labor and are heavy laden, and I will give you rest. 29Take My yoke upon you and learn from Me, for I am gentle and lowly in heart, and you will find rest for your souls. 30For My yoke *is* easy and My burden is light."

11:10 [a]Malachi 3:1 **11:19** [a]NU-Text reads *works.* **11:23** [a]NU-Text reads *will you be exalted to heaven? No, you will be.*

THE MESSAGE

prophet! Probably the best prophet you'll ever hear. He is the prophet that Malachi announced when he wrote, 'I'm sending my prophet ahead of you, to make the road smooth for you.'

11-14 "Let me tell you what's going on here: No one in history surpasses John the Baptizer; but in the kingdom he prepared you for, the lowliest person is ahead of him. For a long time now people have tried to force themselves into God's kingdom. But if you read the books of the Prophets and God's Law closely, you will see them culminate in John, teaming up with him in preparing the way for the Messiah of the kingdom. Looked at in this way, John is the 'Elijah' you've all been expecting to arrive and introduce the Messiah.

15 "Are you listening to me? Really listening?

16-19 "How can I account for this generation? The people have been like spoiled children whining to their parents, 'We wanted to skip rope, and you were always too tired; we wanted to talk, but you were always too busy.' John came fasting and they called him crazy. I came feasting and they called me a lush, a friend of the riffraff. Opinion polls don't count for much, do they? The proof of the pudding is in the eating."

The Unforced Rhythms of Grace

20 Next Jesus let fly on the cities where he had worked the hardest but whose people had responded the least, shrugging their shoulders and going their own way.

21-24 "Doom to you, Chorazin! Doom, Bethsaida! If Tyre and Sidon had seen half of the powerful miracles you have seen, they would have been on their knees in a minute. At Judgment Day they'll get off easy compared to you. And Capernaum! With all your peacock strutting, you are going to end up in the abyss. If the people of Sodom had had your chances, the city would still be around. At Judgment Day they'll get off easy compared to you."

25-26 Abruptly Jesus broke into prayer: "Thank you, Father, Lord of heaven and earth. You've concealed your ways from sophisticates and know-it-alls, but spelled them out clearly to ordinary people. Yes, Father, that's the way you like to work."

27 Jesus resumed talking to the people, but now tenderly. "The Father has given me all these things to do and say. This is a unique Father-Son operation, coming out of Father and Son intimacies and knowledge. No one knows the Son the way the Father does, nor the Father the way the Son does. But I'm not keeping it to myself; I'm ready to go over it line by line with anyone willing to listen.

28-30 "Are you tired? Worn out? Burned out on religion? Come to me. Get away with me and you'll recover your life. I'll show you how to take a real rest. Walk with me and work with me—watch how I do it. Learn the unforced rhythms of grace. I won't lay anything heavy or ill-fitting on you. Keep company with me and you'll learn to live freely and lightly."

New King James Version

Jesus Is Lord of the Sabbath

12 At that time Jesus went through the grain-
fields on the Sabbath. And His disciples
were hungry, and began to pluck heads of grain
and to eat. 2And when the Pharisees saw *it,* they
said to Him, "Look, Your disciples are doing
what is not lawful to do on the Sabbath!"
3But He said to them, "Have you not read
what David did when he was hungry, he and
those who were with him: 4how he entered the
house of God and ate the showbread which was
not lawful for him to eat, nor for those who were
with him, but only for the priests? 5Or have you
not read in the law that on the Sabbath the
priests in the temple profane the Sabbath, and
are blameless? 6Yet I say to you that in this place
there is *One* greater than the temple. 7But if you
had known what *this* means, *'I desire mercy and
not sacrifice,'* [a] you would not have condemned
the guiltless. 8For the Son of Man is Lord even[a]
of the Sabbath."

Healing on the Sabbath

9Now when He had departed from there, He
went into their synagogue. 10And behold, there
was a man who had a withered hand. And they
asked Him, saying, "Is it lawful to heal on the
Sabbath?"—that they might accuse Him.
11Then He said to them, "What man is there
among you who has one sheep, and if it falls
into a pit on the Sabbath, will not lay hold of it
and lift *it* out? 12Of how much more value then
is a man than a sheep? Therefore it is lawful to
do good on the Sabbath." 13Then He said to the
man, "Stretch out your hand." And he stretched
it out, and it was restored as whole as the other.
14Then the Pharisees went out and plotted
against Him, how they might destroy Him.

Behold, My Servant

15But when Jesus knew *it,* He withdrew from
there. And great multitudes[a] followed Him, and
He healed them all. 16Yet He warned them not to
make Him known, 17that it might be fulfilled
which was spoken by Isaiah the prophet, saying:

18*"Behold! My Servant whom I have chosen,*
My Beloved in whom My soul is well
pleased!
I will put My Spirit upon Him,
And He will declare justice to the Gentiles.
19*He will not quarrel nor cry out,*
Nor will anyone hear His voice in the
streets.
20*A bruised reed He will not break,*
And smoking flax He will not quench,
Till He sends forth justice to victory;
21*And in His name Gentiles will trust."* [a]

A House Divided Cannot Stand

22Then one was brought to Him who was de-
mon-possessed, blind and mute; and He healed
him, so that the blind and[a] mute man both spoke
and saw. 23And all the multitudes were amazed
and said, "Could this be the Son of David?"

12:7 [a]Hosea 6:6 12:8 [a]NU-Text and M-Text omit *even.* 12:15 [a]NU-Text brackets *multitudes* as disputed. 12:21 [a]Isaiah 42:1–4 12:22 [a]NU-Text omits *blind and.*

The Message

In Charge of the Sabbath

1-2 12 One Sabbath, Jesus was strolling with his disciples through a field of ripe grain. Hungry, the disciples were pulling off the heads of grain and munching on them. Some Pharisees reported them to Jesus: "Your disciples are breaking the Sabbath rules!"

3-5 Jesus said, "Really? Didn't you ever read what David and his companions did when they were hungry, how they entered the sanctuary and ate fresh bread off the altar, bread that no one but priests were allowed to eat? And didn't you ever read in God's Law that priests carrying out their Temple duties break Sabbath rules all the time and it's not held against them?

6-8 "There is far more at stake here than religion. If you had any idea what this Scripture meant—'I prefer a flexible heart to an inflexible ritual'—you wouldn't be nitpicking like this. The Son of Man is no lackey to the Sabbath; he's in charge."

9-10 When Jesus left the field, he entered their meeting place. There was a man there with a crippled hand. They said to Jesus, "Is it legal to heal on the Sabbath?" They were baiting him.

11-14 He replied, "Is there a person here who, finding one of your lambs fallen into a ravine, wouldn't, even though it was a Sabbath, pull it out? Surely kindness to people is as legal as kindness to animals!" Then he said to the man, "Hold out your hand." He held it out and it was healed. The Pharisees walked out furious, sputtering about how they were going to ruin Jesus.

In Charge of Everything

15-21 Jesus, knowing they were out to get him, moved on. A lot of people followed him, and he healed them all. He also cautioned them to keep it quiet, following guidelines set down by Isaiah:

Look well at my handpicked servant;
I love him so much, take such delight
in him.
I've placed my Spirit on him;
he'll decree justice to the nations.
But he won't yell, won't raise his voice;
there'll be no commotion in the
streets.
He won't walk over anyone's feelings,
won't push you into a corner.
Before you know it, his justice will
triumph;
the mere sound of his name will
signal hope, even
among far-off unbelievers.

No Neutral Ground

22-23 Next a poor demon-afflicted wretch, both blind and deaf, was set down before him. Jesus healed him, gave him his sight and hearing. The people who saw it were impressed—"This has to be the Son of David!"

New King James Version

24Now when the Pharisees heard *it* they said, "This *fellow* does not cast out demons except by Beelzebub,[a] the ruler of the demons."

25But Jesus knew their thoughts, and said to them: "Every kingdom divided against itself is brought to desolation, and every city or house divided against itself will not stand. 26If Satan casts out Satan, he is divided against himself. How then will his kingdom stand? 27And if I cast out demons by Beelzebub, by whom do your sons cast *them* out? Therefore they shall be your judges. 28But if I cast out demons by the Spirit of God, surely the kingdom of God has come upon you. 29Or how can one enter a strong man's house and plunder his goods, unless he first binds the strong man? And then he will plunder his house. 30He who is not with Me is against Me, and he who does not gather with Me scatters abroad.

The Unpardonable Sin

31"Therefore I say to you, every sin and blasphemy will be forgiven men, but the blasphemy *against* the Spirit will not be forgiven men. 32Anyone who speaks a word against the Son of Man, it will be forgiven him; but whoever speaks against the Holy Spirit, it will not be forgiven him, either in this age or in the *age* to come.

A Tree Known by Its Fruit

33"Either make the tree good and its fruit good, or else make the tree bad and its fruit bad; for a tree is known by *its* fruit. 34Brood of vipers! How can you, being evil, speak good things? For out of the abundance of the heart the mouth speaks. 35A good man out of the good treasure of his heart[a] brings forth good things, and an evil man out of the evil treasure brings forth evil things. 36But I say to you that for every idle word men may speak, they will give account of it in the day of judgment. 37For by your words you will be justified, and by your words you will be condemned."

The Scribes and Pharisees Ask for a Sign

38Then some of the scribes and Pharisees answered, saying, "Teacher, we want to see a sign from You."

39But He answered and said to them, "An evil and adulterous generation seeks after a sign, and no sign will be given to it except the sign of the prophet Jonah. 40For as Jonah was three days and three nights in the belly of the great fish, so will the Son of Man be three days and three nights in the heart of the earth. 41The men of Nineveh will rise up in the judgment with this

12:24 [a]NU-Text and M-Text read *Beelzebul.* **12:35** [a]NU-Text and M-Text omit *of his heart.*

The Message

24 But the Pharisees, when they heard the report, were cynical. "Black magic," they said. "Some devil trick he's pulled from his sleeve."

25-27 Jesus confronted their slander. "A judge who gives opposite verdicts on the same person cancels himself out; a family that's in a constant squabble disintegrates; if Satan banishes Satan, is there any Satan left? If you're slinging devil mud at me, calling me a devil kicking out devils, doesn't the same mud stick to your own exorcists?

28-29 "But if it's by *God's* power that I am sending the evil spirits packing, then God's kingdom is here for sure. How in the world do you think it's possible in broad daylight to enter the house of an awake, able-bodied man and walk off with his possessions unless you tie him up first? Tie him up, though, and you can clean him out.

30 "This is war, and there is no neutral ground. If you're not on my side, you're the enemy; if you're not helping, you're making things worse.

31-32 "There's nothing done or said that can't be forgiven. But if you deliberately persist in your slanders against God's Spirit, you are repudiating the very One who forgives. If you reject the Son of Man out of some misunderstanding, the Holy Spirit can forgive you, but when you reject the Holy Spirit, you're sawing off the branch on which you're sitting, severing by your own perversity all connection with the One who forgives.

33 "If you grow a healthy tree, you'll pick healthy fruit. If you grow a diseased tree, you'll pick worm-eaten fruit. The fruit tells you about the tree.

34-37 "You have minds like a snake pit! How do you suppose what you say is worth anything when you are so foul-minded? It's your heart, not the dictionary, that gives meaning to your words. A good person produces good deeds and words season after season. An evil person is a blight on the orchard. Let me tell you something: Every one of these careless words is going to come back to haunt you. There will be a time of Reckoning. Words are powerful; take them seriously. Words can be your salvation. Words can also be your damnation."

Jonah-Evidence

38 Later a few religion scholars and Pharisees got on him. "Teacher, we want to see your credentials. Give us some hard evidence that God is in this. How about a miracle?"

39-40 Jesus said, "You're looking for proof, but you're looking for the wrong kind. All you want is something to titillate your curiosity, satisfy your lust for miracles. The only proof you're going to get is what looks like the absence of proof: Jonah-evidence. Like Jonah, three days and nights in the fish's belly, the Son of Man will be gone three days and nights in a deep grave.

41-42 "On Judgment Day, the Ninevites will stand up and give evidence that will con-

NEW KING JAMES VERSION

generation and condemn it, because they re-
pented at the preaching of Jonah; and indeed a
greater than Jonah *is* here. 42The queen of the
South will rise up in the judgment with this gen-
eration and condemn it, for she came from the
ends of the earth to hear the wisdom of
Solomon; and indeed a greater than Solomon *is*
here.

AN UNCLEAN SPIRIT RETURNS

43"When an unclean spirit goes out of a man,
he goes through dry places, seeking rest, and
finds none. 44Then he says, 'I will return to my
house from which I came.' And when he comes,
he finds *it* empty, swept, and put in order. 45Then
he goes and takes with him seven other spirits
more wicked than himself, and they enter and
dwell there; and the last *state* of that man is
worse than the first. So shall it also be with this
wicked generation."

JESUS' MOTHER AND BROTHERS SEND FOR HIM

46While He was still talking to the multi-
tudes, behold, His mother and brothers stood
outside, seeking to speak with Him. 47Then one
said to Him, "Look, Your mother and Your broth-
ers are standing outside, seeking to speak with
You."

48But He answered and said to the one who
told Him, "Who is My mother and who are My
brothers?" 49And He stretched out His hand to-
ward His disciples and said, "Here are My
mother and My brothers! 50For whoever does
the will of My Father in heaven is My brother
and sister and mother."

THE PARABLE OF THE SOWER

13 On the same day Jesus went out of the
house and sat by the sea. 2And great mul-
titudes were gathered together to Him, so that
He got into a boat and sat; and the whole multi-
tude stood on the shore.

3Then He spoke many things to them in
parables, saying: "Behold, a sower went out to
sow. 4And as he sowed, some *seed* fell by the
wayside; and the birds came and devoured
them. 5Some fell on stony places, where they did
not have much earth; and they immediately
sprang up because they had no depth of earth.
6But when the sun was up they were scorched,
and because they had no root they withered
away. 7And some fell among thorns, and the
thorns sprang up and choked them. 8But others
fell on good ground and yielded a crop: some a
hundredfold, some sixty, some thirty. 9He who
has ears to hear, let him hear!"

THE MESSAGE

demn this generation, because when Jonah preached to them they changed their lives. A far greater preacher than Jonah is here, and you squabble about 'proofs.' On Judgment Day, the Queen of Sheba will come forward and bring evidence that will condemn this generation, because she traveled from a far corner of the earth to listen to wise Solomon. Wisdom far greater than Solomon's is right in front of you, and you quibble over 'evidence.'

43-45 "When a defiling evil spirit is expelled from someone, it drifts along through the desert looking for an oasis, some unsuspecting soul it can bedevil. When it doesn't find anyone, it says, 'I'll go back to my old haunt.' On return it finds the person spotlessly clean, but vacant. It then runs out and rounds up seven other spirits more evil than itself and they all move in, whooping it up. That person ends up far worse off than if he'd never gotten cleaned up in the first place.

"That's what this generation is like: You may think you have cleaned out the junk from your lives and gotten ready for God, but you weren't hospitable to my kingdom message, and now all the devils are moving back in."

OBEDIENCE IS THICKER THAN BLOOD

46-47 While he was still talking to the crowd, his mother and brothers showed up. They were outside trying to get a message to him. Someone told Jesus, "Your mother and brothers are out here, wanting to speak with you."

48-50 Jesus didn't respond directly, but said, "Who do you think my mother and brothers are?" He then stretched out his hand toward his disciples. "Look closely. These are my mother and brothers. Obedience is thicker than blood. The person who obeys my heavenly Father's will is my brother and sister and mother."

A HARVEST STORY

1-3 13 At about that same time Jesus left the house and sat on the beach. In no time at all a crowd gathered along the shoreline, forcing him to get into a boat. Using the boat as a pulpit, he addressed his congregation, telling stories.

3-8 "What do you make of this? A farmer planted seed. As he scattered the seed, some of it fell on the road, and birds ate it. Some fell in the gravel; it sprouted quickly but didn't put down roots, so when the sun came up it withered just as quickly. Some fell in the weeds; as it came up, it was strangled by the weeds. Some fell on good earth, and produced a harvest beyond his wildest dreams.

9 "Are you listening to this? Really listening?"

NEW KING JAMES VERSION

THE PURPOSE OF PARABLES

10 And the disciples came and said to Him, "Why do You speak to them in parables?"

11 He answered and said to them, "Because it has been given to you to know the mysteries of the kingdom of heaven, but to them it has not been given. 12 For whoever has, to him more will be given, and he will have abundance; but whoever does not have, even what he has will be taken away from him. 13 Therefore I speak to them in parables, because seeing they do not see, and hearing they do not hear, nor do they understand. 14 And in them the prophecy of Isaiah is fulfilled, which says:

'Hearing you will hear and shall not
understand,
And seeing you will see and not perceive;
15 *For the hearts of this people have grown*
dull.
Their ears are hard of hearing,
And their eyes they have closed,
Lest they should see with their eyes and
hear with their ears,
Lest they should understand with their
hearts and turn,
So that I should [a] *heal them.'* [b]

16 But blessed *are* your eyes for they see, and your ears for they hear; 17 for assuredly, I say to you that many prophets and righteous *men* desired to see what you see, and did not see *it,* and to hear what you hear, and did not hear *it.*

THE PARABLE OF THE SOWER EXPLAINED

18 "Therefore hear the parable of the sower: 19 When anyone hears the word of the kingdom, and does not understand *it,* then the wicked *one* comes and snatches away what was sown in his heart. This is he who received seed by the wayside. 20 But he who received the seed on stony places, this is he who hears the word and immediately receives it with joy; 21 yet he has no root in himself, but endures only for a while. For when tribulation or persecution arises because of the word, immediately he stumbles. 22 Now he who received seed among the thorns is he who hears the word, and the cares of this world and the deceitfulness of riches choke the word, and he becomes unfruitful. 23 But he who received seed on the good ground is he who hears the word and understands *it,* who indeed bears fruit and produces: some a hundredfold, some sixty, some thirty."

THE PARABLE OF THE WHEAT AND THE TARES

24 Another parable He put forth to them, saying: "The kingdom of heaven is like a man who sowed good seed in his field; 25 but while men slept, his enemy came and sowed tares among the wheat and went his way. 26 But when the grain had sprouted and produced a crop, then the tares

13:15 [a]NU-Text and M-Text read *would.* [b]Isaiah 6:9, 10

THE MESSAGE

WHY TELL STORIES?

10 The disciples came up and asked, "Why do you tell stories?"

11-15 He replied, "You've been given insight into God's kingdom. You know how it works. Not everybody has this gift, this insight; it hasn't been given to them. Whenever someone has a ready heart for this, the insights and understandings flow freely. But if there is no readiness, any trace of receptivity soon disappears. That's why I tell stories: to create readiness, to nudge the people toward receptive insight. In their present state they can stare till doomsday and not see it, listen till they're blue in the face and not get it. I don't want Isaiah's forecast repeated all over again:

Your ears are open but you don't hear a
thing.
Your eyes are awake but you don't see
a thing.
The people are blockheads!
They stick their fingers in their ears
so they won't have to listen;
They screw their eyes shut
so they won't have to look,
so they won't have to deal with me
face-to-face
and let me heal them.

16-17 "But you have God-blessed eyes—eyes that see! And God-blessed ears—ears that hear! A lot of people, prophets and humble believers among them, would have given anything to see what you are seeing, to hear what you are hearing, but never had the chance.

THE MEANING OF THE HARVEST STORY

18-19 "Study this story of the farmer planting seed. When anyone hears news of the kingdom and doesn't take it in, it just remains on the surface, and so the Evil One comes along and plucks it right out of that person's heart. This is the seed the farmer scatters on the road.

20-21 "The seed cast in the gravel—this is the person who hears and instantly responds with enthusiasm. But there is no soil of character, and so when the emotions wear off and some difficulty arrives, there is nothing to show for it.

22 "The seed cast in the weeds is the person who hears the kingdom news, but weeds of worry and illusions about getting more and wanting everything under the sun strangle what was heard, and nothing comes of it.

23 "The seed cast on good earth is the person who hears and takes in the News, and then produces a harvest beyond his wildest dreams."

24-26 He told another story. "God's kingdom is like a farmer who planted good seed in his field. That night, while his hired men were asleep, his enemy sowed thistles all through the wheat and slipped away before dawn. When the first green shoots appeared and

NEW KING JAMES VERSION

also appeared. 27So the servants of the owner
came and said to him, 'Sir, did you not sow good
seed in your field? How then does it have tares?'
28He said to them, 'An enemy has done this.' The
servants said to him, 'Do you want us then to go
and gather them up?' 29But he said, 'No, lest while
you gather up the tares you also uproot the wheat
with them. 30Let both grow together until the har-
vest, and at the time of harvest I will say to the
reapers, "First gather together the tares and bind
them in bundles to burn them, but gather the
wheat into my barn." ' "

THE PARABLE OF THE MUSTARD SEED

31Another parable He put forth to them, say-
ing: "The kingdom of heaven is like a mustard
seed, which a man took and sowed in his field,
32which indeed is the least of all the seeds; but
when it is grown it is greater than the herbs and
becomes a tree, so that the birds of the air come
and nest in its branches."

THE PARABLE OF THE LEAVEN

33Another parable He spoke to them: "The
kingdom of heaven is like leaven, which a
woman took and hid in three measures[a] of meal
till it was all leavened."

PROPHECY AND THE PARABLES

34All these things Jesus spoke to the multi-
tude in parables; and without a parable He did
not speak to them, 35that it might be fulfilled
which was spoken by the prophet, saying:

"I will open My mouth in parables;
I will utter things kept secret from the
foundation of the world."[a]

THE PARABLE OF THE TARES EXPLAINED

36Then Jesus sent the multitude away and
went into the house. And His disciples came to
Him, saying, "Explain to us the parable of the
tares of the field."
37He answered and said to them: "He who
sows the good seed is the Son of Man. 38The field
is the world, the good seeds are the sons of the
kingdom, but the tares are the sons of the wicked
one. 39The enemy who sowed them is the devil,
the harvest is the end of the age, and the reapers
are the angels. 40Therefore as the tares are gath-
ered and burned in the fire, so it will be at the end
of this age. 41The Son of Man will send out His
angels, and they will gather out of His kingdom
all things that offend, and those who practice
lawlessness, 42and will cast them into the furnace
of fire. There will be wailing and gnashing of
teeth. 43Then the righteous will shine forth as the
sun in the kingdom of their Father. He who has
ears to hear, let him hear!

THE PARABLE OF THE HIDDEN TREASURE

44"Again, the kingdom of heaven is like trea-
sure hidden in a field, which a man found and
hid; and for joy over it he goes and sells all that
he has and buys that field.

13:33 [a]Greek *sata,* approximately two pecks in all **13:35** [a]Psalm 78:2

THE MESSAGE

the grain began to form, the thistles showed up, too.

27 "The farmhands came to the farmer and said, 'Master, that was clean seed you planted, wasn't it? Where did these thistles come from?'

28 "He answered, 'Some enemy did this.'

"The farmhands asked, 'Should we weed out the thistles?'

29-30 "He said, 'No, if you weed the thistles, you'll pull up the wheat, too. Let them grow together until harvest time. Then I'll instruct the harvesters to pull up the thistles and tie them in bundles for the fire, then gather the wheat and put it in the barn.' "

31-32 Another story. "God's kingdom is like a pine nut that a farmer plants. It is quite small as seeds go, but in the course of years it grows into a huge pine tree, and eagles build nests in it."

33 Another story. "God's kingdom is like yeast that a woman works into the dough for dozens of loaves of barley bread—and waits while the dough rises."

34-35 All Jesus did that day was tell stories—a long storytelling afternoon. His storytelling fulfilled the prophecy:

I will open my mouth and tell stories;
I will bring out into the open
things hidden since the world's first day.

THE CURTAIN OF HISTORY

36 Jesus dismissed the congregation and went into the house. His disciples came in and said, "Explain to us that story of the thistles in the field."

37-39 So he explained. "The farmer who sows the pure seed is the Son of Man. The field is the world, the pure seeds are subjects of the kingdom, the thistles are subjects of the Devil, and the enemy who sows them is the Devil. The harvest is the end of the age, the curtain of history. The harvest hands are angels.

40-43 "The picture of thistles pulled up and burned is a scene from the final act. The Son of Man will send his angels, weed out the thistles from his kingdom, pitch them in the trash, and be done with them. They are going to complain to high heaven, but nobody is going to listen. At the same time, ripe, holy lives will mature and adorn the kingdom of their Father.

"Are you listening to this? Really listening?

44 "God's kingdom is like a treasure hidden in a field for years and then accidentally found by a trespasser. The finder is ecstatic—what a find!—and proceeds to sell everything he owns to raise money and buy that field.

New King James Version

The Parable of the Pearl of Great Price

45"Again, the kingdom of heaven is like a merchant seeking beautiful pearls, 46who, when he had found one pearl of great price, went and sold all that he had and bought it.

The Parable of the Dragnet

47"Again, the kingdom of heaven is like a dragnet that was cast into the sea and gathered some of every kind, 48which, when it was full, they drew to shore; and they sat down and gathered the good into vessels, but threw the bad away. 49So it will be at the end of the age. The angels will come forth, separate the wicked from among the just, 50and cast them into the furnace of fire. There will be wailing and gnashing of teeth."

51Jesus said to them,[a] "Have you understood all these things?"

They said to Him, "Yes, Lord."[b]

52Then He said to them, "Therefore every scribe instructed concerning[a] the kingdom of heaven is like a householder who brings out of his treasure *things* new and old."

Jesus Rejected at Nazareth

53Now it came to pass, when Jesus had finished these parables, that He departed from there. 54When He had come to His own country, He taught them in their synagogue, so that they were astonished and said, "Where did this *Man* get this wisdom and *these* mighty works? 55Is this not the carpenter's son? Is not His mother called Mary? And His brothers James, Joses,[a] Simon, and Judas? 56And His sisters, are they not all with us? Where then did this *Man* get all these things?" 57So they were offended at Him.

But Jesus said to them, "A prophet is not without honor except in his own country and in his own house." 58Now He did not do many mighty works there because of their unbelief.

John the Baptist Beheaded

14 At that time Herod the tetrarch heard the report about Jesus 2and said to his servants, "This is John the Baptist; he is risen from the dead, and therefore these powers are at work in him." 3For Herod had laid hold of John and bound him, and put *him* in prison for the sake of Herodias, his brother Philip's wife. 4Because John had said to him, "It is not lawful for you to have her." 5And although he wanted to put him to death, he feared the multitude, because they counted him as a prophet.

6But when Herod's birthday was celebrated, the daughter of Herodias danced before them and pleased Herod. 7Therefore he promised with an oath to give her whatever she might ask.

8So she, having been prompted by her mother, said, "Give me John the Baptist's head here on a platter."

9And the king was sorry; nevertheless, because of the oaths and because of those who sat with him, he commanded *it* to be given to *her.* 10So he sent and had John beheaded in prison. 11And his head was brought on a platter and given to the girl, and she brought *it* to her

13:51 [a]NU-Text omits *Jesus said to them.* [b]NU-Text omits *Lord.*
13:52 [a]Or *for* **13:55** [a]NU-Text reads *Joseph.*

The Message

45-46 "Or, God's kingdom is like a jewel merchant on the hunt for excellent pearls. Finding one that is flawless, he immediately sells everything and buys it.

47-50 "Or, God's kingdom is like a fishnet cast into the sea, catching all kinds of fish. When it is full, it is hauled onto the beach. The good fish are picked out and put in a tub; those unfit to eat are thrown away. That's how it will be when the curtain comes down on history. The angels will come and cull the bad fish and throw them in the garbage. There will be a lot of desperate complaining, but it won't do any good."

51 Jesus asked, "Are you starting to get a handle on all this?"

They answered, "Yes."

52 He said, "Then you see how every student well-trained in God's kingdom is like the owner of a general store who can put his hands on anything you need, old or new, exactly when you need it."

53-57 When Jesus finished telling these stories, he left there, returned to his hometown, and gave a lecture in the meetinghouse. He made a real hit, impressing everyone. "We had no idea he was this good!" they said. "How did he get so wise, get such ability?" But in the next breath they were cutting him down: "We've known him since he was a kid; he's the carpenter's son. We know his mother, Mary. We know his brothers James and Joseph, Simon and Judas. All his sisters live here. Who does he think he is?" They got their noses all out of joint.

58 But Jesus said, "A prophet is taken for granted in his hometown and his family." He didn't do many miracles there because of their hostile indifference.

The Death of John

1-2 **14** At about this time, Herod, the regional ruler, heard what was being said about Jesus. He said to his servants, "This has to be John the Baptizer come back from the dead. That's why he's able to work miracles!"

3-5 Herod had arrested John, put him in chains, and sent him to prison to placate Herodias, his brother Philip's wife. John had provoked Herod by naming his relationship with Herodias "adultery." Herod wanted to kill him, but he was afraid because so many people revered John as a prophet of God.

6-12 But at his birthday celebration, he got his chance. Herodias's daughter provided the entertainment, dancing for the guests. She swept Herod away. In his drunken enthusiasm, he promised her on oath anything she wanted. Already coached by her mother, she was ready: "Give me, served up on a platter, the head of John the Baptizer." That sobered the king up fast. Unwilling to lose face with his guests, he did it—ordered John's head cut off and presented to the girl on a platter.

NEW KING JAMES VERSION

mother. 12 Then his disciples came and took away the body and buried it, and went and told Jesus.

FEEDING THE FIVE THOUSAND

13 When Jesus heard *it,* He departed from there by boat to a deserted place by Himself. But when the multitudes heard it, they followed Him on foot from the cities. 14 And when Jesus went out He saw a great multitude; and He was moved with compassion for them, and healed their sick. 15 When it was evening, His disciples came to Him, saying, "This is a deserted place, and the hour is already late. Send the multitudes away, that they may go into the villages and buy themselves food."

16 But Jesus said to them, "They do not need to go away. You give them something to eat."

17 And they said to Him, "We have here only five loaves and two fish."

18 He said, "Bring them here to Me." 19 Then He commanded the multitudes to sit down on the grass. And He took the five loaves and the two fish, and looking up to heaven, He blessed and broke and gave the loaves to the disciples; and the disciples gave to the multitudes. 20 So they all ate and were filled, and they took up twelve baskets full of the fragments that remained. 21 Now those who had eaten were about five thousand men, besides women and children.

JESUS WALKS ON THE SEA

22 Immediately Jesus made His disciples get into the boat and go before Him to the other side, while He sent the multitudes away. 23 And when He had sent the multitudes away, He went up on the mountain by Himself to pray. Now when evening came, He was alone there. 24 But the boat was now in the middle of the sea,[a] tossed by the waves, for the wind was contrary.

25 Now in the fourth watch of the night Jesus went to them, walking on the sea. 26 And when the disciples saw Him walking on the sea, they were troubled, saying, "It is a ghost!" And they cried out for fear.

27 But immediately Jesus spoke to them, saying, "Be of good cheer! It is I; do not be afraid."

28 And Peter answered Him and said, "Lord, if it is You, command me to come to You on the water."

29 So He said, "Come." And when Peter had come down out of the boat, he walked on the water to go to Jesus. 30 But when he saw that the wind *was* boisterous,[a] he was afraid; and beginning to sink he cried out, saying, "Lord, save me!"

31 And immediately Jesus stretched out *His* hand and caught him, and said to him, "O you of little faith, why did you doubt?" 32 And when they got into the boat, the wind ceased.

33 Then those who were in the boat came and[a] worshiped Him, saying, "Truly You are the Son of God."

14:24 [a]NU-Text reads *many furlongs away from the land.*
14:30 [a]NU-Text brackets *that* and *boisterous* as disputed.
14:33 [a]NU-Text omits *came and.*

THE MESSAGE

She in turn gave it to her mother. Later, John's disciples got the body, gave it a reverent burial, and reported to Jesus.

SUPPER FOR FIVE THOUSAND

13-14 When Jesus got the news, he slipped away by boat to an out-of-the-way place by himself. But unsuccessfully—someone saw him and the word got around. Soon a lot of people from the nearby villages walked around the lake to where he was. When he saw them coming, he was overcome with pity and healed their sick.

15 Toward evening the disciples approached him. "We're out in the country and it's getting late. Dismiss the people so they can go to the villages and get some supper."

16 But Jesus said, "There is no need to dismiss them. You give them supper."

17 "All we have are five loaves of bread and two fish," they said.

18-21 Jesus said, "Bring them here." Then he had the people sit on the grass. He took the five loaves and two fish, lifted his face to heaven in prayer, blessed, broke, and gave the bread to the disciples. The disciples then gave the food to the congregation. They all ate their fill. They gathered twelve baskets of leftovers. About five thousand were fed.

WALKING ON THE WATER

22-23 As soon as the meal was finished, he insisted that the disciples get in the boat and go on ahead to the other side while he dismissed the people. With the crowd dispersed, he climbed the mountain so he could be by himself and pray. He stayed there alone, late into the night.

24-26 Meanwhile, the boat was far out to sea when the wind came up against them and they were battered by the waves. At about four o'clock in the morning, Jesus came toward them walking on the water. They were scared out of their wits. "A ghost!" they said, crying out in terror.

27 But Jesus was quick to comfort them. "Courage, it's me. Don't be afraid."

28 Peter, suddenly bold, said, "Master, if it's really you, call me to come to you on the water."

29-30 He said, "Come ahead."

Jumping out of the boat, Peter walked on the water to Jesus. But when he looked down at the waves churning beneath his feet, he lost his nerve and started to sink. He cried, "Master, save me!"

31 Jesus didn't hesitate. He reached down and grabbed his hand. Then he said, "Faint-heart, what got into you?"

32-33 The two of them climbed into the boat, and the wind died down. The disciples in the boat, having watched the whole thing, worshiped Jesus, saying, "This is it! You are God's Son for sure!"

NEW KING JAMES VERSION

MANY TOUCH HIM AND ARE MADE WELL

34When they had crossed over, they came to the land of[a] Gennesaret. 35And when the men of that place recognized Him, they sent out into all that surrounding region, brought to Him all who were sick, 36and begged Him that they might only touch the hem of His garment. And as many as touched *it* were made perfectly well.

DEFILEMENT COMES FROM WITHIN

15 Then the scribes and Pharisees who were from Jerusalem came to Jesus, saying, 2"Why do Your disciples transgress the tradition of the elders? For they do not wash their hands when they eat bread."

3He answered and said to them, "Why do you also transgress the commandment of God because of your tradition? 4For God commanded, saying, *'Honor your father and your mother'*;[a] and, *'He who curses father or mother, let him be put to death.'*[b] 5But you say, 'Whoever says to his father or mother, "Whatever profit you might have received from me *is* a gift *to God*"— 6then he need not honor his father or mother.'[a] Thus you have made the commandment[b] of God of no effect by your tradition. 7Hypocrites! Well did Isaiah prophesy about you, saying:

8*'These people draw near to Me with their*
mouth,
And[a] *honor Me with their lips,*
But their heart is far from Me.
9*And in vain they worship Me,*
Teaching as doctrines the commandments
of men.' "[a]

10When He had called the multitude to *Himself,* He said to them, "Hear and understand: 11Not what goes into the mouth defiles a man; but what comes out of the mouth, this defiles a man."

12Then His disciples came and said to Him, "Do You know that the Pharisees were offended when they heard this saying?"

13But He answered and said, "Every plant which My heavenly Father has not planted will be uprooted. 14Let them alone. They are blind leaders of the blind. And if the blind leads the blind, both will fall into a ditch."

15Then Peter answered and said to Him, "Explain this parable to us."

16So Jesus said, "Are you also still without understanding? 17Do you not yet understand that whatever enters the mouth goes into the stomach and is eliminated? 18But those things which proceed out of the mouth come from the heart, and they defile a man. 19For out of the heart proceed evil thoughts, murders, adulteries, fornications, thefts, false witness, blasphemies. 20These are *the things* which defile a man, but to eat with unwashed hands does not defile a man."

A GENTILE SHOWS HER FAITH

21Then Jesus went out from there and departed to the region of Tyre and Sidon. 22And be-

14:34 [a]NU-Text reads *came to land at.* **15:4** [a]Exodus 20:12; Deuteronomy 5:16 [b]Exodus 21:17 **15:6** [a]NU-Text omits *or mother.* [b]NU-Text reads *word.* **15:8** [a]NU-Text omits *draw near to Me with their mouth, And.* **15:9** [a]Isaiah 29:13

THE MESSAGE

34-36 On return, they beached the boat at Gennesaret. When the people got wind that he was back, they sent out word through the neighborhood and rounded up all the sick, who asked for permission to touch the edge of his coat. And whoever touched him was healed.

WHAT POLLUTES YOUR LIFE

1-2 15 After that, Pharisees and religion scholars came to Jesus all the way from Jerusalem, criticizing, "Why do your disciples play fast and loose with the rules?"

3-9 But Jesus put it right back on them. "Why do you use your rules to play fast and loose with God's commands? God clearly says, 'Respect your father and mother,' and, 'Anyone denouncing father or mother should be killed.' But you weasel around that by saying, 'Whoever wants to, can say to father and mother, What I owed to you I've given to God.' That can hardly be called respecting a parent. You cancel God's command by your rules. Frauds! Isaiah's prophecy of you hit the bull's-eye:

These people make a big show of saying
the right thing,
but their heart isn't in it.
They act like they're worshiping me,
but they don't mean it.
They just use me as a cover
for teaching whatever suits their
fancy."

10-11 He then called the crowd together and said, "Listen, and take this to heart. It's not what you swallow that pollutes your life, but what you vomit up."

12 Later his disciples came and told him, "Did you know how upset the Pharisees were when they heard what you said?"

13-14 Jesus shrugged it off. "Every tree that wasn't planted by my Father in heaven will be pulled up by its roots. Forget them. They are blind men leading blind men. When a blind man leads a blind man, they both end up in the ditch."

15 Peter said, "I don't get it. Put it in plain language."

16-20 Jesus replied, "You, too? Are you being willfully stupid? Don't you know that anything that is swallowed works its way through the intestines and is finally defecated? But what comes out of the mouth gets its start in the heart. It's from the heart that we vomit up evil arguments, murders, adulteries, fornications, thefts, lies, and cussing. That's what pollutes. Eating or not eating certain foods, washing or not washing your hands—that's neither here nor there."

HEALING THE PEOPLE

21-22 From there Jesus took a trip to Tyre and Sidon. They had hardly arrived when a

NEW KING JAMES VERSION

hold, a woman of Canaan came from that region
and cried out to Him, saying, "Have mercy on
me, O Lord, Son of David! My daughter is se-
verely demon-possessed."
23 But He answered her not a word.
And His disciples came and urged Him, say-
ing, "Send her away, for she cries out after us."
24 But He answered and said, "I was not sent
except to the lost sheep of the house of Israel."
25 Then she came and worshiped Him, saying,
"Lord, help me!"
26 But He answered and said, "It is not good to
take the children's bread and throw *it* to the lit-
tle dogs."
27 And she said, "Yes, Lord, yet even the little
dogs eat the crumbs which fall from their mas-
ters' table."
28 Then Jesus answered and said to her, "O
woman, great *is* your faith! Let it be to you as
you desire." And her daughter was healed from
that very hour.

JESUS HEALS GREAT MULTITUDES

29 Jesus departed from there, skirted the Sea
of Galilee, and went up on the mountain and sat
down there. 30 Then great multitudes came to
Him, having with them *the* lame, blind, mute,
maimed, and many others; and they laid them
down at Jesus' feet, and He healed them. 31 So
the multitude marveled when they saw *the* mute
speaking, *the* maimed made whole, *the* lame
walking, and *the* blind seeing; and they glorified
the God of Israel.

FEEDING THE FOUR THOUSAND

32 Now Jesus called His disciples to *Himself*
and said, "I have compassion on the multitude,
because they have now continued with Me three
days and have nothing to eat. And I do not want
to send them away hungry, lest they faint on the
way."
33 Then His disciples said to Him, "Where
could we get enough bread in the wilderness to
fill such a great multitude?"
34 Jesus said to them, "How many loaves do
you have?"
And they said, "Seven, and a few little fish."
35 So He commanded the multitude to sit down
on the ground. 36 And He took the seven loaves
and the fish and gave thanks, broke *them* and
gave *them* to His disciples; and the disciples *gave*
to the multitude. 37 So they all ate and were filled,
and they took up seven large baskets full of the
fragments that were left. 38 Now those who ate
were four thousand men, besides women and
children. 39 And He sent away the multitude, got
into the boat, and came to the region of Magdala.[a]

THE PHARISEES AND SADDUCEES SEEK A SIGN

16 Then the Pharisees and Sadducees came,
and testing Him asked that He would show
them a sign from heaven. 2 He answered and
said to them, "When it is evening you say, '*It will
be* fair weather, for the sky is red'; 3 and in the
morning, '*It will be* foul weather today, for the
sky is red and threatening.' Hypocrites![a] You

15:39 [a]NU-Text reads *Magadan*. **16:3** [a]NU-Text omits *Hypocrites*.

THE MESSAGE

Canaanite woman came down from the hills
and pleaded, "Mercy, Master, Son of David!
My daughter is cruelly afflicted by an evil
spirit."
23 Jesus ignored her. The disciples came
and complained, "Now she's bothering us.
Would you please take care of her? She's
driving us crazy."
24 Jesus refused, telling them, "I've got my
hands full dealing with the lost sheep of Is-
rael."
25 Then the woman came back to Jesus,
went to her knees, and begged. "Master,
help me."
26 He said, "It's not right to take bread out
of children's mouths and throw it to dogs."
27 She was quick: "You're right, Master, but
beggar dogs do get scraps from the master's
table."
28 Jesus gave in. "Oh, woman, your faith is
something else. What you want is what you
get!" Right then her daughter became well.
29-31 After Jesus returned, he walked along
Lake Galilee and then climbed a mountain
and took his place, ready to receive visitors.
They came, tons of them, bringing along the
paraplegic, the blind, the maimed, the
mute—all sorts of people in need—and more
or less threw them down at Jesus' feet to see
what he would do with them. He healed
them. When the people saw the mutes speak-
ing, the maimed healthy, the paraplegics
walking around, the blind looking around,
they were astonished and let everyone know
that God was blazingly alive among them.

32 But Jesus wasn't finished with them. He
called his disciples and said, "I hurt for
these people. For three days now they've
been with me, and now they have nothing to
eat. I can't send them away without a meal—
they'd probably collapse on the road."
33 His disciples said, "But where in this de-
serted place are you going to dig up enough
food for a meal?"
34-39 Jesus asked, "How much bread do you
have?"
"Seven loaves," they said, "plus a few
fish." At that, Jesus directed the people to sit
down. He took the seven loaves and the fish.
After giving thanks, he divided it up and
gave it to the people. Everyone ate. They had
all they wanted. It took seven large baskets
to collect the leftovers. Over four thousand
people ate their fill at that meal. After Jesus
sent them away, he climbed in the boat and
crossed over to the Magadan hills.

SOME BAD YEAST

1-4 16 Some Pharisees and Sadducees were on
him again, pressing him to prove him-
self to them. He told them, "You have a saying
that goes, 'Red sky at night, sailor's delight;
red sky at morning, sailors take warning.'
You find it easy enough to forecast the

New King James Version

know how to discern the face of the sky, but you cannot *discern* the signs of the times. 4 A wicked and adulterous generation seeks after a sign, and no sign shall be given to it except the sign of the prophet[a] Jonah." And He left them and departed.

The Leaven of the Pharisees and Sadducees

5 Now when His disciples had come to the other side, they had forgotten to take bread. 6 Then Jesus said to them, "Take heed and beware of the leaven of the Pharisees and the Sadducees."

7 And they reasoned among themselves, saying, "*It is* because we have taken no bread."

8 But Jesus, being aware of *it,* said to them, "O you of little faith, why do you reason among yourselves because you have brought no bread?[a] 9 Do you not yet understand, or remember the five loaves of the five thousand and how many baskets you took up? 10 Nor the seven loaves of the four thousand and how many large baskets you took up? 11 How is it you do not understand that I did not speak to you concerning bread?—*but* to beware of the leaven of the Pharisees and Sadducees." 12 Then they understood that He did not tell *them* to beware of the leaven of bread, but of the doctrine of the Pharisees and Sadducees.

Peter Confesses Jesus as the Christ

13 When Jesus came into the region of Caesarea Philippi, He asked His disciples, saying, "Who do men say that I, the Son of Man, am?"

14 So they said, "Some *say* John the Baptist, some Elijah, and others Jeremiah or one of the prophets."

15 He said to them, "But who do you say that I am?"

16 Simon Peter answered and said, "You are the Christ, the Son of the living God."

17 Jesus answered and said to him, "Blessed are you, Simon Bar-Jonah, for flesh and blood has not revealed *this* to you, but My Father who is in heaven. 18 And I also say to you that you are Peter, and on this rock I will build My church, and the gates of Hades shall not prevail against it. 19 And I will give you the keys of the kingdom of heaven, and whatever you bind on earth will be bound in heaven, and whatever you loose on earth will be loosed[a] in heaven."

20 Then He commanded His disciples that they should tell no one that He was Jesus the Christ.

Jesus Predicts His Death and Resurrection

21 From that time Jesus began to show to His disciples that He must go to Jerusalem, and suffer many things from the elders and chief priests and scribes, and be killed, and be raised the third day.

22 Then Peter took Him aside and began to rebuke Him, saying, "Far be it from You, Lord; this shall not happen to You!"

16:4 [a]NU-Text omits *the prophet.* 16:8 [a]NU-Text reads *you have no bread.* 16:19 [a]Or *will have been bound . . . will have been loosed*

The Message

weather—why can't you read the signs of the times? An evil and wanton generation is always wanting signs and wonders. The only sign you'll get is the Jonah sign." Then he turned on his heel and walked away.

5-6 On their way to the other side of the lake, the disciples discovered they had forgotten to bring along bread. In the meantime, Jesus said to them, "Keep a sharp eye out for Pharisee-Sadducee yeast."

7-12 Thinking he was scolding them for forgetting bread, they discussed in whispers what to do. Jesus knew what they were doing and said, "Why all these worried whispers about forgetting the bread? Runt believers! Haven't you caught on yet? Don't you remember the five loaves of bread and the five thousand people, and how many baskets of fragments you picked up? Or the seven loaves that fed four thousand, and how many baskets of leftovers you collected? Haven't you realized yet that bread isn't the problem? The problem is yeast, Pharisee-Sadducee yeast." Then they got it: that he wasn't concerned about eating, but teaching—the Pharisee-Sadducee kind of teaching.

Son of Man, Son of God

13 When Jesus arrived in the villages of Caesarea Philippi, he asked his disciples, "What are people saying about who the Son of Man is?"

14 They replied, "Some think he is John the Baptizer, some say Elijah, some Jeremiah or one of the other prophets."

15 He pressed them, "And how about you? Who do you say I am?"

16 Simon Peter said, "You're the Christ, the Messiah, the Son of the living God."

17-18 Jesus came back, "God bless you, Simon, son of Jonah! You didn't get that answer out of books or from teachers. My Father in heaven, God himself, let you in on this secret of who I really am. And now I'm going to tell you who you are, *really* are. You are Peter, a rock. This is the rock on which I will put together my church, a church so expansive with energy that not even the gates of hell will be able to keep it out.

19 "And that's not all. You will have complete and free access to God's kingdom, keys to open any and every door: no more barriers between heaven and earth, earth and heaven. A yes on earth is yes in heaven. A no on earth is no in heaven."

20 He swore the disciples to secrecy. He made them promise they would tell no one that he was the Messiah.

You're Not in the Driver's Seat

21-22 Then Jesus made it clear to his disciples that it was now necessary for him to go to Jerusalem, submit to an ordeal of suffering at the hands of the religious leaders, be killed, and then on the third day be raised up alive. Peter took him in hand, protesting, "Impossible, Master! That can never be!"

New King James Version

23But He turned and said to Peter, "Get behind Me, Satan! You are an offense to Me, for you are not mindful of the things of God, but the things of men."

Take Up the Cross and Follow Him

24Then Jesus said to His disciples, "If anyone desires to come after Me, let him deny himself, and take up his cross, and follow Me. 25For whoever desires to save his life will lose it, but whoever loses his life for My sake will find it. 26For what profit is it to a man if he gains the whole world, and loses his own soul? Or what will a man give in exchange for his soul? 27For the Son of Man will come in the glory of His Father with His angels, and then He will reward each according to his works.

Jesus Transfigured on the Mount

28Assuredly, I say to you, there are some standing here who shall not taste death till they see the Son of Man coming in His kingdom."

17 Now after six days Jesus took Peter, James, and John his brother, led them up on a high mountain by themselves; 2and He was transfigured before them. His face shone like the sun, and His clothes became as white as the light. 3And behold, Moses and Elijah appeared to them, talking with Him. 4Then Peter answered and said to Jesus, "Lord, it is good for us to be here; if You wish, let us[a] make here three tabernacles: one for You, one for Moses, and one for Elijah."

5While he was still speaking, behold, a bright cloud overshadowed them; and suddenly a voice came out of the cloud, saying, "This is My beloved Son, in whom I am well pleased. Hear Him!" 6And when the disciples heard *it,* they fell on their faces and were greatly afraid. 7But Jesus came and touched them and said, "Arise, and do not be afraid." 8When they had lifted up their eyes, they saw no one but Jesus only.

9Now as they came down from the mountain, Jesus commanded them, saying, "Tell the vision to no one until the Son of Man is risen from the dead."

10And His disciples asked Him, saying, "Why then do the scribes say that Elijah must come first?"

11Jesus answered and said to them, "Indeed, Elijah is coming first[a] and will restore all things. 12But I say to you that Elijah has come already, and they did not know him but did to him whatever they wished. Likewise the Son of Man is also about to suffer at their hands." 13Then the disciples understood that He spoke to them of John the Baptist.

A Boy Is Healed

14And when they had come to the multitude, a man came to Him, kneeling down to Him and saying, 15"Lord, have mercy on my son, for he is an epileptic[a] and suffers severely; for he often

17:4 [a]NU-Text reads *I will.* **17:11** [a]NU-Text omits *first.* **17:15** [a]Literally *moonstruck*

The Message

23 But Jesus didn't swerve. "Peter, get out of my way. Satan, get lost. You have no idea how God works."

24-26 Then Jesus went to work on his disciples. "Anyone who intends to come with me has to let me lead. You're not in the driver's seat; *I* am. Don't run from suffering; embrace it. Follow me and I'll show you how. Self-help is no help at all. Self-sacrifice is the way, my way, to finding yourself, your true self. What kind of deal is it to get everything you want but lose yourself? What could you ever trade your soul for?

27-28 "Don't be in such a hurry to go into business for yourself. Before you know it the Son of Man will arrive with all the splendor of his Father, accompanied by an army of angels. You'll get everything you have coming to you, a personal gift. This isn't pie in the sky by and by. Some of you standing here are going to see it take place, see the Son of Man in kingdom glory."

Sunlight Poured from His Face

1-3 17 Six days later, three of them saw that glory. Jesus took Peter and the brothers, James and John, and led them up a high mountain. His appearance changed from the inside out, right before their eyes. Sunlight poured from his face. His clothes were filled with light. Then they realized that Moses and Elijah were also there in deep conversation with him.

4 Peter broke in, "Master, this is a great moment! What would you think if I built three memorials here on the mountain—one for you, one for Moses, one for Elijah?"

5 While he was going on like this, babbling, a light-radiant cloud enveloped them, and sounding from deep in the cloud a voice: "This is my Son, marked by my love, focus of my delight. Listen to him."

6-8 When the disciples heard it, they fell flat on their faces, scared to death. But Jesus came over and touched them. "Don't be afraid." When they opened their eyes and looked around all they saw was Jesus, only Jesus.

9 Coming down the mountain, Jesus swore them to secrecy. "Don't breathe a word of what you've seen. After the Son of Man is raised from the dead, you are free to talk."

10 The disciples, meanwhile, were asking questions. "Why do the religion scholars say that Elijah has to come first?"

11-13 Jesus answered, "Elijah does come and get everything ready. I'm telling you, Elijah has already come but they didn't know him when they saw him. They treated him like dirt, the same way they are about to treat the Son of Man." That's when the disciples realized that all along he had been talking about John the Baptizer.

With a Mere Kernel of Faith

14-16 At the bottom of the mountain, they were met by a crowd of waiting people. As they approached, a man came out of the crowd and fell to his knees begging, "Master, have mercy on my son. He goes out of his mind

NEW KING JAMES VERSION

falls into the fire and often into the water. [16]So I brought him to Your disciples, but they could not cure him."

[17]Then Jesus answered and said, "O faithless and perverse generation, how long shall I be with you? How long shall I bear with you? Bring him here to Me." [18]And Jesus rebuked the demon, and it came out of him; and the child was cured from that very hour.

[19]Then the disciples came to Jesus privately and said, "Why could we not cast it out?"

[20]So Jesus said to them, "Because of your unbelief;[a] for assuredly, I say to you, if you have faith as a mustard seed, you will say to this mountain, 'Move from here to there,' and it will move; and nothing will be impossible for you. [21]However, this kind does not go out except by prayer and fasting."[a]

JESUS AGAIN PREDICTS HIS DEATH AND RESURRECTION

[22]Now while they were staying[a] in Galilee, Jesus said to them, "The Son of Man is about to be betrayed into the hands of men, [23]and they will kill Him, and the third day He will be raised up." And they were exceedingly sorrowful.

PETER AND HIS MASTER PAY THEIR TAXES

[24]When they had come to Capernaum,[a] those who received the *temple* tax came to Peter and said, "Does your Teacher not pay the *temple* tax?"

[25]He said, "Yes."

And when he had come into the house, Jesus anticipated him, saying, "What do you think, Simon? From whom do the kings of the earth take customs or taxes, from their sons or from strangers?"

[26]Peter said to Him, "From strangers."

Jesus said to him, "Then the sons are free. [27]Nevertheless, lest we offend them, go to the sea, cast in a hook, and take the fish that comes up first. And when you have opened its mouth, you will find a piece of money;[a] take that and give it to them for Me and you."

WHO IS THE GREATEST?

18 At that time the disciples came to Jesus, saying, "Who then is greatest in the kingdom of heaven?"

[2]Then Jesus called a little child to Him, set him in the midst of them, [3]and said, "Assuredly, I say to you, unless you are converted and become as little children, you will by no means enter the kingdom of heaven. [4]Therefore whoever humbles himself as this little child is the greatest in the kingdom of heaven. [5]Whoever receives one little child like this in My name receives Me.

JESUS WARNS OF OFFENSES

[6]"Whoever causes one of these little ones who believe in Me to sin, it would be better for him if a millstone were hung around his neck, and he were drowned in the depth of the sea.

17:20 [a]NU-Text reads *little faith.* **17:21** [a]NU-Text omits this verse. **17:22** [a]NU-Text reads *gathering together.* **17:24** [a]NU-Text reads *Capharnaum* (here and elsewhere). **17:27** [a]Greek *stater,* the exact amount to pay the temple tax (didrachma) for two

THE MESSAGE

and suffers terribly, falling into seizures. Frequently he is pitched into the fire, other times into the river. I brought him to your disciples, but they could do nothing for him."

17-18 Jesus said, "What a generation! No sense of God! No focus to your lives! How many times do I have to go over these things? How much longer do I have to put up with this? Bring the boy here." He ordered the afflicting demon out—and it was out, gone. From that moment on the boy was well.

19 When the disciples had Jesus off to themselves, they asked, "Why couldn't we throw it out?"

20 "Because you're not yet taking *God* seriously," said Jesus. "The simple truth is that if you had a mere kernel of faith, a poppy seed, say, you would tell this mountain, 'Move!' and it would move. There is nothing you wouldn't be able to tackle."

22-23 As they were regrouping in Galilee, Jesus told them, "The Son of Man is about to be betrayed to some people who want nothing to do with God. They will murder him—and three days later he will be raised alive." The disciples felt terrible.

24 When they arrived at Capernaum, the tax men came to Peter and asked, "Does your teacher pay taxes?"

25 Peter said, "Of course."

But as soon as they were in the house, Jesus confronted him. "Simon, what do you think? When a king levies taxes, who pays—his children or his subjects?"

26-27 He answered, "His subjects."

Jesus said, "Then the children get off free, right? But so we don't upset them needlessly, go down to the lake, cast a hook, and pull in the first fish that bites. Open its mouth and you'll find a coin. Take it and give it to the tax men. It will be enough for both of us."

WHOEVER BECOMES SIMPLE AGAIN

1 18 At about the same time, the disciples came to Jesus asking, "Who gets the highest rank in God's kingdom?"

2-5 For an answer Jesus called over a child, whom he stood in the middle of the room, and said, "I'm telling you, once and for all, that unless you return to square one and start over like children, you're not even going to get a look at the kingdom, let alone get in. Whoever becomes simple and elemental again, like this child, will rank high in God's kingdom. What's more, when you receive the childlike on my account, it's the same as receiving me.

6-7 "But if you give them a hard time, bullying or taking advantage of their simple trust, you'll soon wish you hadn't. You'd be better off dropped in the middle of the lake with a millstone around your neck. Doom to

NEW KING JAMES VERSION

7Woe to the world because of offenses! For offenses must come, but woe to that man by whom the offense comes!

8"If your hand or foot causes you to sin, cut it off and cast *it* from you. It is better for you to enter into life lame or maimed, rather than having two hands or two feet, to be cast into the everlasting fire. 9And if your eye causes you to sin, pluck it out and cast *it* from you. It is better for you to enter into life with one eye, rather than having two eyes, to be cast into hell fire.

THE PARABLE OF THE LOST SHEEP

10"Take heed that you do not despise one of these little ones, for I say to you that in heaven their angels always see the face of My Father who is in heaven. 11For the Son of Man has come to save that which was lost.[a]

12"What do you think? If a man has a hundred sheep, and one of them goes astray, does he not leave the ninety-nine and go to the mountains to seek the one that is straying? 13And if he should find it, assuredly, I say to you, he rejoices more over that *sheep* than over the ninety-nine that did not go astray. 14Even so it is not the will of your Father who is in heaven that one of these little ones should perish.

DEALING WITH A SINNING BROTHER

15"Moreover if your brother sins against you, go and tell him his fault between you and him alone. If he hears you, you have gained your brother. 16But if he will not hear, take with you one or two more, that *'by the mouth of two or three witnesses every word may be established.'*[a] 17And if he refuses to hear them, tell *it* to the church. But if he refuses even to hear the church, let him be to you like a heathen and a tax collector.

18"Assuredly, I say to you, whatever you bind on earth will be bound in heaven, and whatever you loose on earth will be loosed in heaven.

19"Again I say[a] to you that if two of you agree on earth concerning anything that they ask, it will be done for them by My Father in heaven. 20For where two or three are gathered together in My name, I am there in the midst of them."

THE PARABLE OF THE UNFORGIVING SERVANT

21Then Peter came to Him and said, "Lord, how often shall my brother sin against me, and I forgive him? Up to seven times?"

22Jesus said to him, "I do not say to you, up to seven times, but up to seventy times seven. 23Therefore the kingdom of heaven is like a certain king who wanted to settle accounts with his servants. 24And when he had begun to settle accounts, one was brought to him who owed him ten thousand talents. 25But as he was not able to pay, his master commanded that he be sold, with his wife and children and all that he had, and that payment be made. 26The servant therefore fell down before him, saying, 'Master, have patience with me, and I will pay you all.' 27Then the master of that servant was moved with compassion, released him, and forgave him the debt.

18:11 [a]NU-Text omits this verse. **18:16** [a]Deuteronomy 19:15 **18:19** [a]NU-Text and M-Text read *Again, assuredly, I say.*

THE MESSAGE

the world for giving these God-believing children a hard time! Hard times are inevitable, but you don't have to make it worse—and it's doomsday to you if you do.

8-9 "If your hand or your foot gets in the way of God, chop it off and throw it away. You're better off maimed or lame and alive than the proud owners of two hands and two feet, godless in a furnace of eternal fire. And if your eye distracts you from God, pull it out and throw it away. You're better off one-eyed and alive than exercising your twenty-twenty vision from inside the fire of hell.

10 "Watch that you don't treat a single one of these childlike believers arrogantly. You realize, don't you, that their personal angels are constantly in touch with my Father in heaven?

WORK IT OUT BETWEEN YOU

12-14 "Look at it this way. If someone has a hundred sheep and one of them wanders off, doesn't he leave the ninety-nine and go after the one? And if he finds it, doesn't he make far more over it than over the ninety-nine who stay put? Your Father in heaven feels the same way. He doesn't want to lose even one of these simple believers.

15-17 "If a fellow believer hurts you, go and tell him—work it out between the two of you. If he listens, you've made a friend. If he won't listen, take one or two others along so that the presence of witnesses will keep things honest, and try again. If he still won't listen, tell the church. If he won't listen to the church, you'll have to start over from scratch, confront him with the need for repentance, and offer again God's forgiving love.

18-20 "Take this most seriously: A yes on earth is yes in heaven; a no on earth is no in heaven. What you say to one another is eternal. I mean this. When two of you get together on anything at all on earth and make a prayer of it, my Father in heaven goes into action. And when two or three of you are together because of me, you can be sure that I'll be there."

A STORY ABOUT FORGIVENESS

21 At that point Peter got up the nerve to ask, "Master, how many times do I forgive a brother or sister who hurts me? Seven?"

22 Jesus replied, "Seven! Hardly. Try seventy times seven.

23-25 "The kingdom of God is like a king who decided to square accounts with his servants. As he got under way, one servant was brought before him who had run up a debt of a hundred thousand dollars. He couldn't pay up, so the king ordered the man, along with his wife, children, and goods, to be auctioned off at the slave market.

26-27 "The poor wretch threw himself at the king's feet and begged, 'Give me a chance and I'll pay it all back.' Touched by his plea, the king let him off, erasing the debt.

NEW KING JAMES VERSION

28“But that servant went out and found one of his fellow servants who owed him a hundred denarii; and he laid hands on him and took *him* by the throat, saying, ‘Pay me what you owe!’ 29So his fellow servant fell down at his feet[a] and begged him, saying, ‘Have patience with me, and I will pay you all.’[b] 30And he would not, but went and threw him into prison till he should pay the debt. 31So when his fellow servants saw what had been done, they were very grieved, and came and told their master all that had been done. 32Then his master, after he had called him, said to him, ‘You wicked servant! I forgave you all that debt because you begged me. 33Should you not also have had compassion on your fellow servant, just as I had pity on you?’ 34And his master was angry, and delivered him to the torturers until he should pay all that was due to him.

35“So My heavenly Father also will do to you if each of you, from his heart, does not forgive his brother his trespasses.”[a]

MARRIAGE AND DIVORCE

19 Now it came to pass, when Jesus had finished these sayings, *that* He departed from Galilee and came to the region of Judea beyond the Jordan. 2And great multitudes followed Him, and He healed them there.

3The Pharisees also came to Him, testing Him, and saying to Him, “Is it lawful for a man to divorce his wife for *just* any reason?”

4And He answered and said to them, “Have you not read that He who made[a] *them* at the beginning *‘made them male and female,’*[b] 5and said, *‘For this reason a man shall leave his father and mother and be joined to his wife, and the two shall become one flesh’?*[a] 6So then, they are no longer two but one flesh. Therefore what God has joined together, let not man separate.”

7They said to Him, “Why then did Moses command to give a certificate of divorce, and to put her away?”

8He said to them, “Moses, because of the hardness of your hearts, permitted you to divorce your wives, but from the beginning it was not so. 9And I say to you, whoever divorces his wife, except for sexual immorality,[a] and marries another, commits adultery; and whoever marries her who is divorced commits adultery.”

10His disciples said to Him, “If such is the case of the man with *his* wife, it is better not to marry.”

JESUS TEACHES ON CELIBACY

11But He said to them, “All cannot accept this saying, but only *those* to whom it has been given: 12For there are eunuchs who were born thus from *their* mother’s womb, and there are eunuchs who were made eunuchs by men, and there are eunuchs who have made themselves eunuchs for the kingdom of heaven’s sake. He who is able to accept *it,* let him accept *it.*”

18:29 [a]NU-Text omits *at his feet.* [b]NU-Text and M-Text omit *all.* **18:35** [a]NU-Text omits *his trespasses.* **19:4** [a]NU-Text reads *created.* [b]Genesis 1:27; 5:2 **19:5** [a]Genesis 2:24 **19:9** [a]Or *fornication*

THE MESSAGE

28 “The servant was no sooner out of the room when he came upon one of his fellow servants who owed him ten dollars. He seized him by the throat and demanded, ‘Pay up. Now!’

29-31 “The poor wretch threw himself down and begged, ‘Give me a chance and I’ll pay it all back.’ But he wouldn’t do it. He had him arrested and put in jail until the debt was paid. When the other servants saw this going on, they were outraged and brought a detailed report to the king.

32-35 “The king summoned the man and said, ‘You evil servant! I forgave your entire debt when you begged me for mercy. Shouldn’t you be compelled to be merciful to your fellow servant who asked for mercy?’ The king was furious and put the screws to the man until he paid back his entire debt. And that’s exactly what my Father in heaven is going to do to each one of you who doesn’t forgive unconditionally anyone who asks for mercy.”

DIVORCE

1-2 19 When Jesus had completed these teachings, he left Galilee and crossed the region of Judea on the other side of the Jordan. Great crowds followed him there, and he healed them.

3 One day the Pharisees were badgering him: “Is it legal for a man to divorce his wife for any reason?”

4-6 He answered, “Haven’t you read in your Bible that the Creator originally made man and woman for each other, male and female? And because of this, a man leaves father and mother and is firmly bonded to his wife, becoming one flesh—no longer two bodies but one. Because God created this organic union of the two sexes, no one should desecrate his art by cutting them apart.”

7 They shot back in rebuttal, “If that’s so, why did Moses give instructions for divorce papers and divorce procedures?”

8-9 Jesus said, “Moses provided for divorce as a concession to your hard heartedness, but it is not part of God’s original plan. I’m holding you to the original plan, and holding you liable for adultery if you divorce your faithful wife and then marry someone else. I make an exception in cases where the spouse has committed adultery.”

10 Jesus’ disciples objected, “If those are the terms of marriage, we’re stuck. Why get married?”

11-12 But Jesus said, “Not everyone is mature enough to live a married life. It requires a certain aptitude and grace. Marriage isn’t for everyone. Some, from birth seemingly, never give marriage a thought. Others never get asked—or accepted. And some decide not to get married for kingdom reasons. But if you’re capable of growing into the largeness of marriage, do it.”

NEW KING JAMES VERSION

JESUS BLESSES LITTLE CHILDREN

13Then little children were brought to Him that He might put *His* hands on them and pray, but the disciples rebuked them. 14But Jesus said, "Let the little children come to Me, and do not forbid them; for of such is the kingdom of heaven." 15And He laid *His* hands on them and departed from there.

JESUS COUNSELS THE RICH YOUNG RULER

16Now behold, one came and said to Him, "Good[a] Teacher, what good thing shall I do that I may have eternal life?"

17So He said to him, "Why do you call Me good?[a] No one *is* good but One, *that is*, God.[b] But if you want to enter into life, keep the commandments."

18He said to Him, "Which ones?"

Jesus said, " *'You shall not murder,' 'You shall not commit adultery,' 'You shall not steal,' 'You shall not bear false witness,'* 19*'Honor your father and your mother,'*[a] and, *'You shall love your neighbor as yourself.'* "[b]

20The young man said to Him, "All these things I have kept from my youth.[a] What do I still lack?"

21Jesus said to him, "If you want to be perfect, go, sell what you have and give to the poor, and you will have treasure in heaven; and come, follow Me."

22But when the young man heard that saying, he went away sorrowful, for he had great possessions.

WITH GOD ALL THINGS ARE POSSIBLE

23Then Jesus said to His disciples, "Assuredly, I say to you that it is hard for a rich man to enter the kingdom of heaven. 24And again I say to you, it is easier for a camel to go through the eye of a needle than for a rich man to enter the kingdom of God."

25When His disciples heard *it*, they were greatly astonished, saying, "Who then can be saved?"

26But Jesus looked at *them* and said to them, "With men this is impossible, but with God all things are possible."

27Then Peter answered and said to Him, "See, we have left all and followed You. Therefore what shall we have?"

28So Jesus said to them, "Assuredly I say to you, that in the regeneration, when the Son of Man sits on the throne of His glory, you who have followed Me will also sit on twelve thrones, judging the twelve tribes of Israel. 29And everyone who has left houses or brothers or sisters or father or mother or wife[a] or children or lands, for My name's sake, shall receive a hundredfold, and inherit eternal life. 30But many *who are* first will be last, and the last first.

THE PARABLE OF THE WORKERS IN THE VINEYARD

20 "For the kingdom of heaven is like a landowner who went out early in the morning to hire laborers for his vineyard. 2Now when he had agreed with the laborers for a

19:16 [a]NU-Text omits *Good.* **19:17** [a]NU-Text reads *Why do you ask Me about what is good?* [b]NU-Text reads *There is One who is good.* **19:19** [a]Exodus 20:12–16; Deuteronomy 5:16–20 [b]Leviticus 19:18 **19:20** [a]NU-Text omits *from my youth.* **19:29** [a]NU-Text omits *or wife.*

THE MESSAGE

TO ENTER GOD'S KINGDOM

13-15 One day children were brought to Jesus in the hope that he would lay hands on them and pray over them. The disciples shooed them off. But Jesus intervened: "Let the children alone, don't prevent them from coming to me. God's kingdom is made up of people like these." After laying hands on them, he left.

16 Another day, a man stopped Jesus and asked, "Teacher, what good thing must I do to get eternal life?"

17 Jesus said, "Why do you question me about what's good? *God* is the One who is good. If you want to enter the life of God, just do what he tells you."

18-19 The man asked, "What in particular?"

Jesus said, "Don't murder, don't commit adultery, don't steal, don't lie, honor your father and mother, and love your neighbor as you do yourself."

20 The young man said, "I've done all that. What's left?"

21 "If you want to give it all you've got," Jesus replied, "go sell your possessions; give everything to the poor. All your wealth will then be in heaven. Then come follow me."

22 That was the last thing the young man expected to hear. And so, crestfallen, he walked away. He was holding on tight to a lot of things, and he couldn't bear to let go.

23-24 As he watched him go, Jesus told his disciples, "Do you have any idea how difficult it is for the rich to enter God's kingdom? Let me tell you, it's easier to gallop a camel through a needle's eye than for the rich to enter God's kingdom."

25 The disciples were staggered. "Then who has any chance at all?"

26 Jesus looked hard at them and said, "No chance at all if you think you can pull it off yourself. Every chance in the world if you trust God to do it."

27 Then Peter chimed in, "We left everything and followed you. What do we get out of it?"

28-30 Jesus replied, "Yes, you have followed me. In the re-creation of the world, when the Son of Man will rule gloriously, you who have followed me will also rule, starting with the twelve tribes of Israel. And not only you, but anyone who sacrifices home, family, fields—whatever—because of me will get it all back a hundred times over, not to mention the considerable bonus of eternal life. This is the Great Reversal: many of the first ending up last, and the last first."

A STORY ABOUT WORKERS

1-2 20 "God's kingdom is like an estate manager who went out early in the morning to hire workers for his vineyard. They agreed

New King James Version

denarius a day, he sent them into his vineyard. 3And he went out about the third hour and saw others standing idle in the marketplace, 4and said to them, 'You also go into the vineyard, and whatever is right I will give you.' So they went. 5Again he went out about the sixth and the ninth hour, and did likewise. 6And about the eleventh hour he went out and found others standing idle,[a] and said to them, 'Why have you been standing here idle all day?' 7They said to him, 'Because no one hired us.' He said to them, 'You also go into the vineyard, and whatever is right you will receive.'[a]

8"So when evening had come, the owner of the vineyard said to his steward, 'Call the laborers and give them *their* wages, beginning with the last to the first.' 9And when those came who *were hired* about the eleventh hour, they each received a denarius. 10But when the first came, they supposed that they would receive more; and they likewise received each a denarius. 11And when they had received *it,* they complained against the landowner, 12saying, 'These last *men* have worked *only* one hour, and you made them equal to us who have borne the burden and the heat of the day.' 13But he answered one of them and said, 'Friend, I am doing you no wrong. Did you not agree with me for a denarius? 14Take *what is* yours and go your way. I wish to give to this last man *the same* as to you. 15Is it not lawful for me to do what I wish with my own things? Or is your eye evil because I am good?' 16So the last will be first, and the first last. For many are called, but few chosen."[a]

Jesus a Third Time Predicts His Death and Resurrection

17Now Jesus, going up to Jerusalem, took the twelve disciples aside on the road and said to them, 18"Behold, we are going up to Jerusalem, and the Son of Man will be betrayed to the chief priests and to the scribes; and they will condemn Him to death, 19and deliver Him to the Gentiles to mock and to scourge and to crucify. And the third day He will rise again."

Greatness Is Serving

20Then the mother of Zebedee's sons came to Him with her sons, kneeling down and asking something from Him.

21And He said to her, "What do you wish?"

She said to Him, "Grant that these two sons of mine may sit, one on Your right hand and the other on the left, in Your kingdom."

22But Jesus answered and said, "You do not know what you ask. Are you able to drink the cup that I am about to drink, and be baptized with the baptism that I am baptized with?"[a]

They said to Him, "We are able."

23So He said to them, "You will indeed drink My cup, and be baptized with the baptism that I am baptized with;[a] but to sit on My right hand and on My left is not Mine to give, but *it is for those* for whom it is prepared by My Father."

20:6 [a]NU-Text omits *idle.* **20:7** [a]NU-Text omits the last clause of this verse. **20:16** [a]NU-Text omits the last sentence of this verse. **20:22** [a]NU-Text omits *and be baptized with the baptism that I am baptized with.* **20:23** [a]NU-Text omits *and be baptized with the baptism that I am baptized with.*

The Message

on a wage of a dollar a day, and went to work.

3-5 "Later, about nine o'clock, the manager saw some other men hanging around the town square unemployed. He told them to go to work in his vineyard and he would pay them a fair wage. They went.

5-6 "He did the same thing at noon, and again at three o'clock. At five o'clock he went back and found still others standing around. He said, 'Why are you standing around all day doing nothing?'

7 "They said, 'Because no one hired us.'

"He told them to go to work in his vineyard.

8 "When the day's work was over, the owner of the vineyard instructed his foreman, 'Call the workers in and pay them their wages. Start with the last hired and go on to the first.'

9-12 "Those hired at five o'clock came up and were each given a dollar. When those who were hired first saw that, they assumed they would get far more. But they got the same, each of them one dollar. Taking the dollar, they groused angrily to the manager, 'These last workers put in only one easy hour, and you just made them equal to us, who slaved all day under a scorching sun.'

13-15 "He replied to the one speaking for the rest, 'Friend, I haven't been unfair. We agreed on the wage of a dollar, didn't we? So take it and go. I decided to give to the one who came last the same as you. Can't I do what I want with my own money? Are you going to get stingy because I am generous?'

16 "Here it is again, the Great Reversal: many of the first ending up last, and the last first."

To Drink from the Cup

17-19 Jesus, now well on the way up to Jerusalem, took the Twelve off to the side of the road and said, "Listen to me carefully. We are on our way up to Jerusalem. When we get there, the Son of Man will be betrayed to the religious leaders and scholars. They will sentence him to death. They will then hand him over to the Romans for mockery and torture and crucifixion. On the third day he will be raised up alive."

20 It was about that time that the mother of the Zebedee brothers came with her two sons and knelt before Jesus with a request.

21 "What do you want?" Jesus asked.

She said, "Give your word that these two sons of mine will be awarded the highest places of honor in your kingdom, one at your right hand, one at your left hand."

22 Jesus responded, "You have no idea what you're asking." And he said to James and John, "Are you capable of drinking the cup that I'm about to drink?"

They said, "Sure, why not?"

23 Jesus said, "Come to think of it, you *are* going to drink my cup. But as to awarding places of honor, that's not my business. My Father is taking care of that."

NEW KING JAMES VERSION

[24]And when the ten heard *it,* they were greatly displeased with the two brothers. [25]But Jesus called them to *Himself* and said, "You know that the rulers of the Gentiles lord it over them, and those who are great exercise authority over them. [26]Yet it shall not be so among you; but whoever desires to become great among you, let him be your servant. [27]And whoever desires to be first among you, let him be your slave— [28]just as the Son of Man did not come to be served, but to serve, and to give His life a ransom for many."

TWO BLIND MEN RECEIVE THEIR SIGHT

[29]Now as they went out of Jericho, a great multitude followed Him. [30]And behold, two blind men sitting by the road, when they heard that Jesus was passing by, cried out, saying, "Have mercy on us, O Lord, Son of David!"

[31]Then the multitude warned them that they should be quiet; but they cried out all the more, saying, "Have mercy on us, O Lord, Son of David!"

[32]So Jesus stood still and called them, and said, "What do you want Me to do for you?"

[33]They said to Him, "Lord, that our eyes may be opened." [34]So Jesus had compassion and touched their eyes. And immediately their eyes received sight, and they followed Him.

THE TRIUMPHAL ENTRY

21 Now when they drew near Jerusalem, and came to Bethphage,[a] at the Mount of Olives, then Jesus sent two disciples, [2]saying to them, "Go into the village opposite you, and immediately you will find a donkey tied, and a colt with her. Loose *them* and bring *them* to Me. [3]And if anyone says anything to you, you shall say, 'The Lord has need of them,' and immediately he will send them."

[4]All[a] this was done that it might be fulfilled which was spoken by the prophet, saying:

[5]*"Tell the daughter of Zion,*
'Behold, your King is coming to you,
Lowly, and sitting on a donkey,
A colt, the foal of a donkey.' "[a]

[6]So the disciples went and did as Jesus commanded them. [7]They brought the donkey and the colt, laid their clothes on them, and set *Him*[a] on them. [8]And a very great multitude spread their clothes on the road; others cut down branches from the trees and spread *them* on the road. [9]Then the multitudes who went before and those who followed cried out, saying:

"Hosanna to the Son of David!
'Blessed is He who comes in the name of the LORD!'[a]
Hosanna in the highest!"

[10]And when He had come into Jerusalem, all the city was moved, saying, "Who is this?"

21:1 [a]M-Text reads *Bethsphage.* **21:4** [a]NU-Text omits *All.* **21:5**[a]Zechariah 9:9 **21:7**[a]NU-Text reads *and He sat.* **21:9**[a]Psalm 118:26

THE MESSAGE

24-28 When the ten others heard about this, they lost their tempers, thoroughly disgusted with the two brothers. So Jesus got them together to settle things down. He said, "You've observed how godless rulers throw their weight around, how quickly a little power goes to their heads. It's not going to be that way with you. Whoever wants to be great must become a servant. Whoever wants to be first among you must be your slave. That is what the Son of Man has done: He came to serve, not be served—and then to give away his life in exchange for the many who are held hostage."

29-31 As they were leaving Jericho, a huge crowd followed. Suddenly they came upon two blind men sitting alongside the road. When they heard it was Jesus passing, they cried out, "Master, have mercy on us! Mercy, Son of David!" The crowd tried to hush them up, but they got all the louder, crying, "Master, have mercy on us! Mercy, Son of David!"

32 Jesus stopped and called over, "What do you want from me?"

33 They said, "Master, we want our eyes opened. We want to see!"

34 Deeply moved, Jesus touched their eyes. They had their sight back that very instant, and joined the procession.

THE ROYAL WELCOME

1-3 **21** When they neared Jerusalem, having arrived at Bethphage on Mount Olives, Jesus sent two disciples with these instructions: "Go over to the village across from you. You'll find a donkey tethered there, her colt with her. Untie her and bring them to me. If anyone asks what you're doing, say, 'The Master needs them!' He will send them with you."

4-5 This is the full story of what was sketched earlier by the prophet:

Tell Zion's daughter,
"Look, your king's on his way,
poised and ready, mounted
On a donkey, on a colt,
foal of a pack animal."

6-9 The disciples went and did exactly what Jesus told them to do. They led the donkey and colt out, laid some of their clothes on them, and Jesus mounted. Nearly all the people in the crowd threw their garments down on the road, giving him a royal welcome. Others cut branches from the trees and threw them down as a welcome mat. Crowds went ahead and crowds followed, all of them calling out, "Hosanna to David's son!" "Blessed is he who comes in God's name!" "Hosanna in highest heaven!"

10 As he made his entrance into Jerusalem, the whole city was shaken. Unnerved, people were asking, "What's going on here? Who is this?"

NEW KING JAMES VERSION

11So the multitudes said, "This is Jesus, the
prophet from Nazareth of Galilee."

JESUS CLEANSES THE TEMPLE

12Then Jesus went into the temple of God[a]
and drove out all those who bought and sold in
the temple, and overturned the tables of the
money changers and the seats of those who sold
doves. 13And He said to them, "It is written, *'My
house shall be called a house of prayer,'*[a] but
you have made it a *'den of thieves.'* "[b]
14Then *the* blind and *the* lame came to Him
in the temple, and He healed them. 15But when
the chief priests and scribes saw the wonderful
things that He did, and the children crying out
in the temple and saying, "Hosanna to the Son
of David!" they were indignant 16and said to
Him, "Do You hear what these are saying?"
And Jesus said to them, "Yes. Have you
never read,

'Out of the mouth of babes and nursing
infants
You have perfected praise'? "[a]

17Then He left them and went out of the city
to Bethany, and He lodged there.

THE FIG TREE WITHERED

18Now in the morning, as He returned to the
city, He was hungry. 19And seeing a fig tree by
the road, He came to it and found nothing on it
but leaves, and said to it, "Let no fruit grow on
you ever again." Immediately the fig tree with-
ered away.

THE LESSON OF THE WITHERED FIG TREE

20And when the disciples saw *it*, they mar-
veled, saying, "How did the fig tree wither away
so soon?"
21So Jesus answered and said to them, "As-
suredly, I say to you, if you have faith and do not
doubt, you will not only do what was done to the
fig tree, but also if you say to this mountain, 'Be
removed and be cast into the sea,' it will be
done. 22And whatever things you ask in prayer,
believing, you will receive."

JESUS' AUTHORITY QUESTIONED

23Now when He came into the temple, the
chief priests and the elders of the people con-
fronted Him as He was teaching, and said, "By
what authority are You doing these things? And
who gave You this authority?"
24But Jesus answered and said to them, "I
also will ask you one thing, which if you tell Me,
I likewise will tell you by what authority I do
these things: 25The baptism of John—where was
it from? From heaven or from men?"
And they reasoned among themselves, say-
ing, "If we say, 'From heaven,' He will say to us,
'Why then did you not believe him?' 26But if we
say, 'From men,' we fear the multitude, for all

21:12 [a]NU-Text omits *of God.* **21:13** [a]Isaiah 56:7 [b]Jeremiah 7:11 **21:16** [a]Psalm 8:2

THE MESSAGE

11 The parade crowd answered, "This is the prophet Jesus, the one from Nazareth in Galilee."

HE KICKED OVER THE TABLES

12-14 Jesus went straight to the Temple and threw out everyone who had set up shop, buying and selling. He kicked over the tables of loan sharks and the stalls of dove merchants. He quoted this text:

My house was designated a house of
prayer;
You have made it a hangout for thieves.

Now there was room for the blind and crippled to get in. They came to Jesus and he healed them.

15-16 When the religious leaders saw the outrageous things he was doing, and heard all the children running and shouting through the Temple, "Hosanna to David's Son!" they were up in arms and took him to task. "Do you hear what these children are saying?"

Jesus said, "Yes, I hear them. And haven't you read in God's Word, 'From the mouths of children and babies I'll furnish a place of praise'?"

17 Fed up, Jesus turned on his heel and left the city for Bethany, where he spent the night.

THE WITHERED FIG TREE

18-20 Early the next morning Jesus was returning to the city. He was hungry. Seeing a lone fig tree alongside the road, he approached it anticipating a breakfast of figs. When he got to the tree, there was nothing but fig leaves. He said, "No more figs from this tree—ever!" The fig tree withered on the spot, a dry stick. The disciples saw it happen. They rubbed their eyes, saying, "Did we really see this? A leafy tree one minute, a dry stick the next?"

21-22 But Jesus was matter-of-fact: "Yes—and if you embrace this kingdom life and don't doubt God, you'll not only do minor feats like I did to the fig tree, but also triumph over huge obstacles. This mountain, for instance, you'll tell, 'Go jump in the lake,' and it will jump. Absolutely everything, ranging from small to large, as you make it a part of your believing prayer, gets included as you lay hold of God."

TRUE AUTHORITY

23 Then he was back in the Temple, teaching. The high priests and leaders of the people came up and demanded, "Show us your credentials. Who authorized you to teach here?"

24-25 Jesus responded, "First let me ask you a question. You answer my question and I'll answer yours. About the baptism of John—who authorized it: heaven or humans?"

25-27 They were on the spot and knew it. They pulled back into a huddle and whispered, "If we say 'heaven,' he'll ask us why we didn't believe him; if we say 'humans,' we're up against it with the people because they all

NEW KING JAMES VERSION

count John as a prophet." [27]So they answered Jesus and said, "We do not know."

And He said to them, "Neither will I tell you by what authority I do these things.

THE PARABLE OF THE TWO SONS

[28]"But what do you think? A man had two sons, and he came to the first and said, 'Son, go, work today in my vineyard.' [29]He answered and said, 'I will not,' but afterward he regretted it and went. [30]Then he came to the second and said likewise. And he answered and said, 'I *go*, sir,' but he did not go. [31]Which of the two did the will of *his* father?"

They said to Him, "The first."

Jesus said to them, "Assuredly, I say to you that tax collectors and harlots enter the kingdom of God before you. [32]For John came to you in the way of righteousness, and you did not believe him; but tax collectors and harlots believed him; and when you saw *it*, you did not afterward relent and believe him.

THE PARABLE OF THE WICKED VINEDRESSERS

[33]"Hear another parable: There was a certain landowner who planted a vineyard and set a hedge around it, dug a winepress in it and built a tower. And he leased it to vinedressers and went into a far country. [34]Now when vintage-time drew near, he sent his servants to the vinedressers, that they might receive its fruit. [35]And the vinedressers took his servants, beat one, killed one, and stoned another. [36]Again he sent other servants, more than the first, and they did likewise to them. [37]Then last of all he sent his son to them, saying, 'They will respect my son.' [38]But when the vinedressers saw the son, they said among themselves, 'This is the heir. Come, let us kill him and seize his inheritance.' [39]So they took him and cast *him* out of the vineyard and killed *him*.

[40]"Therefore, when the owner of the vineyard comes, what will he do to those vinedressers?"

[41]They said to Him, "He will destroy those wicked men miserably, and lease *his* vineyard to other vinedressers who will render to him the fruits in their seasons."

[42]Jesus said to them, "Have you never read in the Scriptures:

'The stone which the builders rejected
Has become the chief cornerstone.
This was the LORD's doing,
And it is marvelous in our eyes'? [a]

[43]"Therefore I say to you, the kingdom of God will be taken from you and given to a nation bearing the fruits of it. [44]And whoever falls

21:42 [a]Psalm 118:22, 23

THE MESSAGE

hold John up as a prophet." They decided to concede that round to Jesus. "We don't know," they answered.

Jesus said, "Then neither will I answer your question.

THE STORY OF TWO SONS

28 "Tell me what you think of this story: A man had two sons. He went up to the first and said, 'Son, go out for the day and work in the vineyard.'

29 "The son answered, 'I don't want to.' Later on he thought better of it and went.

30 "The father gave the same command to the second son. He answered, 'Sure, glad to.' But he never went.

31-32 "Which of the two sons did what the father asked?"

They said, "The first."

Jesus said, "Yes, and I tell you that crooks and whores are going to precede you into God's kingdom. John came to you showing you the right road. You turned up your noses at him, but the crooks and whores believed him. Even when you saw their changed lives, you didn't care enough to change and believe him.

THE STORY OF THE GREEDY FARMHANDS

33-34 "Here's another story. Listen closely. There was once a man, a wealthy farmer, who planted a vineyard. He fenced it, dug a winepress, put up a watchtower, then turned it over to the farmhands and went off on a trip. When it was time to harvest the grapes, he sent his servants back to collect his profits.

35-37 "The farmhands grabbed the first servant and beat him up. The next one they murdered. They threw stones at the third but he got away. The owner tried again, sending more servants. They got the same treatment. The owner was at the end of his rope. He decided to send his son. 'Surely,' he thought, 'they will respect my son.'

38-39 "But when the farmhands saw the son arrive, they rubbed their hands in greed. 'This is the heir! Let's kill him and have it all for ourselves.' They grabbed him, threw him out, and killed him.

40 "Now, when the owner of the vineyard arrives home from his trip, what do you think he will do to the farmhands?"

41 "He'll kill them—a rotten bunch, and good riddance," they answered. "Then he'll assign the vineyard to farmhands who will hand over the profits when it's time."

42-44 Jesus said, "Right—and you can read it for yourselves in your Bibles:

The stone the masons threw out
is now the cornerstone.
This is God's work;
we rub our eyes, we can hardly
believe it!

"This is the way it is with you. God's kingdom will be taken back from you and handed over to a people who will live out a kingdom life. Whoever stumbles on this

NEW KING JAMES VERSION

on this stone will be broken; but on whomever it falls, it will grind him to powder."

[45]Now when the chief priests and Pharisees heard His parables, they perceived that He was speaking of them. [46]But when they sought to lay hands on Him, they feared the multitudes, because they took Him for a prophet.

THE PARABLE OF THE WEDDING FEAST

22 And Jesus answered and spoke to them again by parables and said: [2]"The kingdom of heaven is like a certain king who arranged a marriage for his son, [3]and sent out his servants to call those who were invited to the wedding; and they were not willing to come. [4]Again, he sent out other servants, saying, 'Tell those who are invited, "See, I have prepared my dinner; my oxen and fatted cattle *are* killed, and all things *are* ready. Come to the wedding." ' [5]But they made light of it and went their ways, one to his own farm, another to his business. [6]And the rest seized his servants, treated *them* spitefully, and killed *them.* [7]But when the king heard *about it,* he was furious. And he sent out his armies, destroyed those murderers, and burned up their city. [8]Then he said to his servants, 'The wedding is ready, but those who were invited were not worthy. [9]Therefore go into the highways, and as many as you find, invite to the wedding.' [10]So those servants went out into the highways and gathered together all whom they found, both bad and good. And the wedding *hall* was filled with guests.

[11]"But when the king came in to see the guests, he saw a man there who did not have on a wedding garment. [12]So he said to him, 'Friend, how did you come in here without a wedding garment?' And he was speechless. [13]Then the king said to the servants, 'Bind him hand and foot, take him away, and[a] cast *him* into outer darkness; there will be weeping and gnashing of teeth.'

[14]"For many are called, but few *are* chosen."

THE PHARISEES: IS IT LAWFUL TO PAY TAXES TO CAESAR?

[15]Then the Pharisees went and plotted how they might entangle Him in *His* talk. [16]And they sent to Him their disciples with the Herodians, saying, "Teacher, we know that You are true, and teach the way of God in truth; nor do You care about anyone, for You do not regard the person of men. [17]Tell us, therefore, what do You think? Is it lawful to pay taxes to Caesar, or not?"

[18]But Jesus perceived their wickedness, and said, "Why do you test Me, *you* hypocrites? [19]Show Me the tax money."

So they brought Him a denarius.

[20]And He said to them, "Whose image and inscription *is* this?"

[21]They said to Him, "Caesar's."

And He said to them, "Render therefore to Caesar the things that are Caesar's, and to God the things that are God's." [22]When they had heard *these words,* they marveled, and left Him and went their way.

22:13 [a]NU-Text omits *take him away, and.*

THE MESSAGE

Stone gets shattered; whoever the Stone
falls on gets smashed."
45-46 When the religious leaders heard this
story, they knew it was aimed at them. They
wanted to arrest Jesus and put him in jail, but,
intimidated by public opinion, they held back.
Most people held him to be a prophet of God.

THE STORY OF THE WEDDING BANQUET

1-3 **22** Jesus responded by telling still more
stories. "God's kingdom," he said, "is
like a king who threw a wedding banquet
for his son. He sent out servants to call in all
the invited guests. And they wouldn't come!
4 "He sent out another round of servants,
instructing them to tell the guests, 'Look,
everything is on the table, the prime rib is
ready for carving. Come to the feast!'
5-7 "They only shrugged their shoulders and
went off, one to weed his garden, another to
work in his shop. The rest, with nothing better to do, beat up on the messengers and
then killed them. The king was outraged
and sent his soldiers to destroy those thugs
and level their city.
8-10 "Then he told his servants, 'We have a
wedding banquet all prepared but no
guests. The ones I invited weren't up to it.
Go out into the busiest intersections in town
and invite anyone you find to the banquet.'
The servants went out on the streets and
rounded up everyone they laid eyes on, good
and bad, regardless. And so the banquet
was on—every place filled.
11-13 "When the king entered and looked over
the scene, he spotted a man who wasn't
properly dressed. He said to him, 'Friend,
how dare you come in here looking like
that!' The man was speechless. Then the
king told his servants, 'Get him out of
here—fast. Tie him up and ship him to hell.
And make sure he doesn't get back in.'
14 "That's what I mean when I say, 'Many
get invited; only a few make it.' "

PAYING TAXES

15-17 That's when the Pharisees plotted a way to
trap him into saying something damaging.
They sent their disciples, with a few of
Herod's followers mixed in, to ask, "Teacher,
we know you have integrity, teach the way
of God accurately, are indifferent to popular
opinion, and don't pander to your students.
So tell us honestly: Is it right to pay taxes to
Caesar or not?"
18-19 Jesus knew they were up to no good. He
said, "Why are you playing these games
with me? Why are you trying to trap me? Do
you have a coin? Let me see it." They
handed him a silver piece.
20 "This engraving—who does it look like?
And whose name is on it?"
21 They said, "Caesar."
"Then give Caesar what is his, and give
God what is his."
22 The Pharisees were speechless. They
went off shaking their heads.

NEW KING JAMES VERSION

THE SADDUCEES: WHAT ABOUT THE RESURRECTION?

23The same day the Sadducees, who say there is no resurrection, came to Him and asked Him, 24saying: "Teacher, Moses said that if a man dies, having no children, his brother shall marry his wife and raise up offspring for his brother. 25Now there were with us seven brothers. The first died after he had married, and having no offspring, left his wife to his brother. 26Likewise the second also, and the third, even to the seventh. 27Last of all the woman died also. 28Therefore, in the resurrection, whose wife of the seven will she be? For they all had her."

29Jesus answered and said to them, "You are mistaken, not knowing the Scriptures nor the power of God. 30For in the resurrection they neither marry nor are given in marriage, but are like angels of God[a] in heaven. 31But concerning the resurrection of the dead, have you not read what was spoken to you by God, saying, 32*'I am the God of Abraham, the God of Isaac, and the God of Jacob'?*[a] God is not the God of the dead, but of the living." 33And when the multitudes heard *this,* they were astonished at His teaching.

THE SCRIBES: WHICH IS THE FIRST COMMANDMENT OF ALL?

34But when the Pharisees heard that He had silenced the Sadducees, they gathered together. 35Then one of them, a lawyer, asked *Him a question,* testing Him, and saying, 36"Teacher, which *is* the great commandment in the law?"

37Jesus said to him, *" 'You shall love the LORD your God with all your heart, with all your soul, and with all your mind.'*[a] 38This is *the* first and great commandment. 39And *the* second *is* like it: *'You shall love your neighbor as yourself.'*[a] 40On these two commandments hang all the Law and the Prophets."

JESUS: HOW CAN DAVID CALL HIS DESCENDANT LORD?

41While the Pharisees were gathered together, Jesus asked them, 42saying, "What do you think about the Christ? Whose Son is He?"

They said to Him, "*The Son* of David."

43He said to them, "How then does David in the Spirit call Him *'Lord,'* saying:

44*'The LORD said to my Lord,*
"Sit at My right hand,
Till I make Your enemies Your
footstool"'?[a]

45If David then calls Him *'Lord,'* how is He his Son?" 46And no one was able to answer Him a word, nor from that day on did anyone dare question Him anymore.

22:30 [a]NU-Text omits *of God.* **22:32** [a]Exodus 3:6, 15 **22:37** [a]Deuteronomy 6:5 **22:39** [a]Leviticus 19:18 **22:44** [a]Psalm 110:1

THE MESSAGE

MARRIAGE AND RESURRECTION

23-28 That same day, Sadducees approached him. This is the party that denies any possibility of resurrection. They asked, "Teacher, Moses said that if a man dies childless, his brother is obligated to marry his widow and get her with child. Here's a case where there were seven brothers. The first brother married and died, leaving no child, and his wife passed to his brother. The second brother also left her childless, then the third—and on and on, all seven. Eventually the wife died. Now here's our question: At the resurrection, whose wife is she? She was a wife to each of them."

29-33 Jesus answered, "You're off base on two counts: You don't know your Bibles, and you don't know how God works. At the resurrection we're beyond marriage. As with the angels, all our ecstasies and intimacies then will be with God. And regarding your speculation on whether the dead are raised or not, don't you read your Bibles? The grammar is clear: God says, 'I am—not *was*—the God of Abraham, the God of Isaac, the God of Jacob.' The living God defines himself not as the God of dead men, but of the *living*." Hearing this exchange the crowd was much impressed.

THE MOST IMPORTANT COMMAND

34-36 When the Pharisees heard how he had bested the Sadducees, they gathered their forces for an assault. One of their religion scholars spoke for them, posing a question they hoped would show him up: "Teacher, which command in God's Law is the most important?"

37-40 Jesus said, " 'Love the Lord your God with all your passion and prayer and intelligence.' This is the most important, the first on any list. But there is a second to set alongside it: 'Love others as well as you love yourself.' These two commands are pegs; everything in God's Law and the Prophets hangs from them."

DAVID'S SON AND MASTER

41-42 As the Pharisees were regrouping, Jesus caught them off balance with his own test question: "What do you think about the Christ? Whose son is he?" They said, "David's son."

43-45 Jesus replied, "Well, if the Christ is David's son, how do you explain that David, under inspiration, named Christ his 'Master'?

God said to my Master,
"Sit here at my right hand
until I make your enemies your
footstool."

"Now if David calls him 'Master,' how can he at the same time be his son?"

46 That stumped them, literalists that they were. Unwilling to risk losing face again in one of these public verbal exchanges, they quit asking questions for good.

NEW KING JAMES VERSION

Woe to the Scribes and Pharisees

23 Then Jesus spoke to the multitudes and to His disciples, 2saying: "The scribes and the Pharisees sit in Moses' seat. 3Therefore whatever they tell you to observe,[a] *that* observe and do, but do not do according to their works; for they say, and do not do. 4For they bind heavy burdens, hard to bear, and lay *them* on men's shoulders; but they *themselves* will not move them with one of their fingers. 5But all their works they do to be seen by men. They make their phylacteries broad and enlarge the borders of their garments. 6They love the best places at feasts, the best seats in the synagogues, 7greetings in the marketplaces, and to be called by men, 'Rabbi, Rabbi.' 8But you, do not be called 'Rabbi'; for One is your Teacher, the Christ,[a] and you are all brethren. 9Do not call anyone on earth your father; for One is your Father, He who is in heaven. 10And do not be called teachers; for One is your Teacher, the Christ. 11But he who is greatest among you shall be your servant. 12And whoever exalts himself will be humbled, and he who humbles himself will be exalted.

13"But woe to you, scribes and Pharisees, hypocrites! For you shut up the kingdom of heaven against men; for you neither go in *yourselves,* nor do you allow those who are entering to go in. 14Woe to you, scribes and Pharisees, hypocrites! For you devour widows' houses, and for a pretense make long prayers. Therefore you will receive greater condemnation.[a]

15"Woe to you, scribes and Pharisees, hypocrites! For you travel land and sea to win one proselyte, and when he is won, you make him twice as much a son of hell as yourselves.

16"Woe to you, blind guides, who say, 'Whoever swears by the temple, it is nothing; but whoever swears by the gold of the temple, he is obliged *to perform it.*' 17Fools and blind! For which is greater, the gold or the temple that sanctifies[a] the gold? 18And, 'Whoever swears by the altar, it is nothing; but whoever swears by the gift that is on it, he is obliged *to perform it.*' 19Fools and blind! For which is greater, the gift or the altar that sanctifies the gift? 20Therefore he who swears by the altar, swears by it and by all things on it. 21He who swears by the temple, swears by it and by Him who dwells[a] in it. 22And he who swears by heaven, swears by the throne of God and by Him who sits on it.

23:3 [a]NU-Text omits *to observe.* **23:8** [a]NU-Text omits *the Christ.* **23:14** [a]NU-Text omits this verse. **23:17** [a]NU-Text reads *sanctified.* **23:21** [a]M-Text reads *dwelt.*

THE MESSAGE

Religious Fashion Shows

1-3 **23** Now Jesus turned to address his disciples, along with the crowd that had gathered with them. "The religion scholars and Pharisees are competent teachers in God's Law. You won't go wrong in following their teachings on Moses. But be careful about following *them.* They talk a good line, but they don't live it. They don't take it into their hearts and live it out in their behavior. It's all spit-and-polish veneer.
4-7 "Instead of giving you God's Law as food and drink by which you can banquet on God, they package it in bundles of rules, loading you down like pack animals. They seem to take pleasure in watching you stagger under these loads, and wouldn't think of lifting a finger to help. Their lives are perpetual fashion shows, embroidered prayer shawls one day and flowery prayers the next. They love to sit at the head table at church dinners, basking in the most prominent positions, preening in the radiance of public flattery, receiving honorary degrees, and getting called 'Doctor' and 'Reverend.'
8-10 "Don't let people do that to *you,* put you on a pedestal like that. You all have a single Teacher, and you are all classmates. Don't set people up as experts over your life, letting them tell you what to do. Save that authority for God; let *him* tell you what to do. No one else should carry the title of 'Father'; you have only one Father, and he's in heaven. And don't let people maneuver you into taking charge of them. There is only one Life-Leader for you and them—Christ.
11-12 "Do you want to stand out? Then step down. Be a servant. If you puff yourself up, you'll get the wind knocked out of you. But if you're content to simply be yourself, your life will count for plenty.

Frauds!

13 "I've had it with you! You're hopeless, you religion scholars, you Pharisees! Frauds! Your lives are roadblocks to God's kingdom. You refuse to enter, and won't let anyone else in either.
15 "You're hopeless, you religion scholars and Pharisees! Frauds! You go halfway around the world to make a convert, but once you get him you make him into a replica of yourselves, double-damned.
16-22 "You're hopeless! What arrogant stupidity! You say, 'If someone makes a promise with his fingers crossed, that's nothing; but if he swears with his hand on the Bible, that's serious.' What ignorance! Does the leather on the Bible carry more weight than the skin on your hands? And what about this piece of trivia: 'If you shake hands on a promise, that's nothing; but if you raise your hand that God is your witness, that's serious'? What ridiculous hairsplitting! What difference does it make whether you shake hands or raise hands? A promise is a promise. What difference does it make if you make your promise inside or outside a house of worship? A promise is a promise. God is present, watching and holding you to account regardless.

New King James Version

23“Woe to you, scribes and Pharisees, hypocrites! For you pay tithe of mint and anise and cummin, and have neglected the weightier *matters* of the law: justice and mercy and faith. These you ought to have done, without leaving the others undone. 24Blind guides, who strain out a gnat and swallow a camel!

25“Woe to you, scribes and Pharisees, hypocrites! For you cleanse the outside of the cup and dish, but inside they are full of extortion and self-indulgence.[a] 26Blind Pharisee, first cleanse the inside of the cup and dish, that the outside of them may be clean also.

27“Woe to you, scribes and Pharisees, hypocrites! For you are like whitewashed tombs which indeed appear beautiful outwardly, but inside are full of dead *men's* bones and all uncleanness. 28Even so you also outwardly appear righteous to men, but inside you are full of hypocrisy and lawlessness.

29“Woe to you, scribes and Pharisees, hypocrites! Because you build the tombs of the prophets and adorn the monuments of the righteous, 30and say, ‘If we had lived in the days of our fathers, we would not have been partakers with them in the blood of the prophets.’

31“Therefore you are witnesses against yourselves that you are sons of those who murdered the prophets. 32Fill up, then, the measure of your fathers' *guilt.* 33Serpents, brood of vipers! How can you escape the condemnation of hell? 34Therefore, indeed, I send you prophets, wise men, and scribes: *some* of them you will kill and crucify, and *some* of them you will scourge in your synagogues and persecute from city to city, 35that on you may come all the righteous blood shed on the earth, from the blood of righteous Abel to the blood of Zechariah, son of Berechiah, whom you murdered between the temple and the altar. 36Assuredly, I say to you, all these things will come upon this generation.

Jesus Laments over Jerusalem

37“O Jerusalem, Jerusalem, the one who kills the prophets and stones those who are sent to her! How often I wanted to gather your children together, as a hen gathers her chicks under *her* wings, but you were not willing! 38See! Your house is left to you desolate; 39for I say to you, you shall see Me no more till you say, *‘Blessed is He who comes in the name of the LORD!’* ”[a]

Jesus Predicts the Destruction of the Temple

24 Then Jesus went out and departed from the temple, and His disciples came up to show Him the buildings of the temple. 2And Jesus said to them, “Do you not see all these things? Assuredly, I say to you, not *one* stone

23:25 [a]M-Text reads *unrighteousness.* **23:39** [a]Psalm 118:26

The Message

23-24 “You're hopeless, you religion scholars and Pharisees! Frauds! You keep meticulous account books, tithing on every nickel and dime you get, but on the meat of God's Law, things like fairness and compassion and commitment—the absolute basics!—you carelessly take it or leave it. Careful bookkeeping is commendable, but the basics are required. Do you have any idea how silly you look, writing a life story that's wrong from start to finish, nitpicking over commas and semicolons?

25-26 “You're hopeless, you religion scholars and Pharisees! Frauds! You burnish the surface of your cups and bowls so they sparkle in the sun, while the insides are maggoty with your greed and gluttony. Stupid Pharisee! Scour the insides, and then the gleaming surface will mean something.

27-28 “You're hopeless, you religion scholars and Pharisees! Frauds! You're like manicured grave plots, grass clipped and the flowers bright, but six feet down it's all rotting bones and worm-eaten flesh. People look at you and think you're saints, but beneath the skin you're total frauds.

29-32 “You're hopeless, you religion scholars and Pharisees! Frauds! You build granite tombs for your prophets and marble monuments for your saints. And you say that if you had lived in the days of your ancestors, no blood would have been on your hands. You protest too much! You're cut from the same cloth as those murderers, and daily add to the death count.

33-34 “Snakes! Reptilian sneaks! Do you think you can worm your way out of this? Never have to pay the piper? It's on account of people like you that I send prophets and wise guides and scholars generation after generation—and generation after generation you treat them like dirt, greeting them with lynch mobs, hounding them with abuse.

35-36 “You can't squirm out of this: Every drop of righteous blood ever spilled on this earth, beginning with the blood of that good man Abel right down to the blood of Zechariah, Barachiah's son, whom you murdered at his prayers, is on your head. All this, I'm telling you, is coming down on you, on your generation.

37-39 “Jerusalem! Jerusalem! Murderer of prophets! Killer of the ones who brought you God's news! How often I've ached to embrace your children, the way a hen gathers her chicks under her wings, and you wouldn't let me. And now you're so desolate, nothing but a ghost town. What is there left to say? Only this: I'm out of here soon. The next time you see me you'll say, ‘Oh, God has blessed him! He's come, bringing God's rule!’ ”

Routine History

1-2 24 Jesus then left the Temple. As he walked away, his disciples pointed out how very impressive the Temple architecture was. Jesus said, “You're not impressed by all this sheer *size,* are you? The truth of the matter is that there's not a stone in that building

NEW KING JAMES VERSION

shall be left here upon another, that shall not be
thrown down."

THE SIGNS OF THE TIMES AND THE END OF THE AGE

[3]Now as He sat on the Mount of Olives, the
disciples came to Him privately, saying, "Tell us,
when will these things be? And what *will be* the
sign of Your coming, and of the end of the age?"
[4]And Jesus answered and said to them:
"Take heed that no one deceives you. [5]For many
will come in My name, saying, 'I am the Christ,'
and will deceive many. [6]And you will hear of
wars and rumors of wars. See that you are not
troubled; for all[a] *these things* must come to
pass, but the end is not yet. [7]For nation will rise
against nation, and kingdom against kingdom.
And there will be famines, pestilences,[a] and
earthquakes in various places. [8]All these *are* the
beginning of sorrows.
[9]"Then they will deliver you up to tribulation
and kill you, and you will be hated by all nations
for My name's sake. [10]And then many will be of-
fended, will betray one another, and will hate
one another. [11]Then many false prophets will
rise up and deceive many. [12]And because law-
lessness will abound, the love of many will grow
cold. [13]But he who endures to the end shall be
saved. [14]And this gospel of the kingdom will be
preached in all the world as a witness to all the
nations, and then the end will come.

THE GREAT TRIBULATION

[15]"Therefore when you see the *'abomination
of desolation,'*[a] spoken of by Daniel the
prophet, standing in the holy place" (whoever
reads, let him understand), [16]"then let those who
are in Judea flee to the mountains. [17]Let him
who is on the housetop not go down to take any-
thing out of his house. [18]And let him who is in
the field not go back to get his clothes. [19]But woe
to those who are pregnant and to those who are
nursing babies in those days! [20]And pray that
your flight may not be in winter or on the Sab-
bath. [21]For then there will be great tribulation,
such as has not been since the beginning of the
world until this time, no, nor ever shall be. [22]And
unless those days were shortened, no flesh
would be saved; but for the elect's sake those
days will be shortened.
[23]"Then if anyone says to you, 'Look, here *is*
the Christ!' or 'There!' do not believe *it*. [24]For
false christs and false prophets will rise and
show great signs and wonders to deceive, if pos-
sible, even the elect. [25]See, I have told you be-
forehand.
[26]"Therefore if they say to you, 'Look, He is
in the desert!' do not go out; *or* 'Look, *He is* in
the inner rooms!' do not believe *it*. [27]For as the

24:6 [a]NU-Text omits *all.* **24:7** [a]NU-Text omits *pestilences.*
24:15 [a]Daniel 11:31; 12:11

THE MESSAGE

that is not going to end up in a pile of rub-
ble."
3 Later as he was sitting on Mount Olives,
his disciples approached and asked him,
"Tell us, when are these things going to hap-
pen? What will be the sign of your coming,
that the time's up?"
4-8 Jesus said, "Watch out for doomsday de-
ceivers. Many leaders are going to show up
with forged identities, claiming, 'I am
Christ, the Messiah.' They will deceive a lot
of people. When reports come in of wars
and rumored wars, keep your head and
don't panic. This is routine history; this is no
sign of the end. Nation will fight nation and
ruler fight ruler, over and over. Famines and
earthquakes will occur in various places.
This is nothing compared to what is coming.
9-10 "They are going to throw you to the
wolves and kill you, everyone hating you be-
cause you carry my name. And then, going
from bad to worse, it will be dog-eat-dog,
everyone at each other's throat, everyone
hating each other.
11-12 "In the confusion, lying preachers will
come forward and deceive a lot of people.
For many others, the overwhelming spread
of evil will do them in—nothing left of their
love but a mound of ashes.
13-14 "Staying with it—that's what God re-
quires. Stay with it to the end. You won't be
sorry, and you'll be saved. All during this
time, the good news—the Message of the
kingdom—will be preached all over the
world, a witness staked out in every country.
And then the end will come.

THE MONSTER OF DESECRATION

15-20 "But be ready to run for it when you see the
monster of desecration set up in the Temple
sanctuary. The prophet Daniel described
this. If you've read Daniel, you'll know what
I'm talking about. If you're living in Judea at
the time, run for the hills; if you're working
in the yard, don't return to the house to get
anything; if you're out in the field, don't go
back and get your coat. Pregnant and nurs-
ing mothers will have it especially hard.
Hope and pray this won't happen during the
winter or on a Sabbath.
21-22 "This is going to be trouble on a scale be-
yond what the world has ever seen, or will
see again. If these days of trouble were left
to run their course, nobody would make it.
But on account of God's chosen people, the
trouble will be cut short.

THE ARRIVAL OF THE SON OF MAN

23-25 "If anyone tries to flag you down, calling out,
'Here's the Messiah!' or points, 'There he is!'
don't fall for it. Fake Messiahs and lying
preachers are going to pop up everywhere.
Their impressive credentials and dazzling
performances will pull the wool over the
eyes of even those who ought to know better.
But I've given you fair warning.
26-28 "So if they say, 'Run to the country and
see him arrive!' or, 'Quick, get downtown,
see him come!' don't give them the time of

NEW KING JAMES VERSION

lightning comes from the east and flashes to the west, so also will the coming of the Son of Man be. [28]For wherever the carcass is, there the eagles will be gathered together.

THE COMING OF THE SON OF MAN

[29]"Immediately after the tribulation of those days the sun will be darkened, and the moon will not give its light; the stars will fall from heaven, and the powers of the heavens will be shaken. [30]Then the sign of the Son of Man will appear in heaven, and then all the tribes of the earth will mourn, and they will see the Son of Man coming on the clouds of heaven with power and great glory. [31]And He will send His angels with a great sound of a trumpet, and they will gather together His elect from the four winds, from one end of heaven to the other.

THE PARABLE OF THE FIG TREE

[32]"Now learn this parable from the fig tree: When its branch has already become tender and puts forth leaves, you know that summer *is* near. [33]So you also, when you see all these things, know that it[a] is near—at the doors! [34]Assuredly, I say to you, this generation will by no means pass away till all these things take place. [35]Heaven and earth will pass away, but My words will by no means pass away.

NO ONE KNOWS THE DAY OR HOUR

[36]"But of that day and hour no one knows, not even the angels of heaven,[a] but My Father only. [37]But as the days of Noah *were*, so also will the coming of the Son of Man be. [38]For as in the days before the flood, they were eating and drinking, marrying and giving in marriage, until the day that Noah entered the ark, [39]and did not know until the flood came and took them all away, so also will the coming of the Son of Man be. [40]Then two *men* will be in the field: one will be taken and the other left. [41]Two *women will be* grinding at the mill: one will be taken and the other left. [42]Watch therefore, for you do not know what hour[a] your Lord is coming. [43]But know this, that if the master of the house had known what hour the thief would come, he would have watched and not allowed his house to be broken into. [44]Therefore you also be ready, for the Son of Man is coming at an hour you do not expect.

THE FAITHFUL SERVANT AND THE EVIL SERVANT

[45]"Who then is a faithful and wise servant, whom his master made ruler over his household, to give them food in due season? [46]Blessed *is* that servant whom his master, when he comes, will find so doing. [47]Assuredly, I say to you that he will make him ruler over all his goods. [48]But if that evil servant says in his heart, 'My master is delaying his coming,'[a] [49]and begins to beat *his* fellow servants, and to eat and drink with the drunkards, [50]the master of that servant will come on a day when he is not look-

24:33 [a]Or *He* **24:36** [a]NU-Text adds *nor the Son.* **24:42** [a]NU-Text reads *day.* **24:48** [a]NU-Text omits *his coming.*

THE MESSAGE

day. The Arrival of the Son of Man isn't
something you go to see. He comes like swift
lightning to you! Whenever you see crowds
gathering, think of carrion vultures circling,
moving in, hovering over a rotting carcass.
You can be quite sure that it's not the living
Son of Man pulling in those crowds.

29 "Following those hard times,

Sun will fade out,
  moon cloud over,
Stars fall out of the sky,
  cosmic powers tremble.

30-31 "Then, the Arrival of the Son of Man! It
will fill the skies—no one will miss it. Unready people all over the world, outsiders to
the splendor and power, will raise a huge
lament as they watch the Son of Man blazing out of heaven. At that same moment,
he'll dispatch his angels with a trumpet-blast summons, pulling in God's chosen
from the four winds, from pole to pole.

32-35 "Take a lesson from the fig tree. From the
moment you notice its buds form, the merest hint of green, you know summer's just
around the corner. So it is with you: When
you see all these things, you'll know he's at
the door. Don't take this lightly. I'm not just
saying this for some future generation, but
for all of you. This age continues until all
these things take place. Sky and earth will
wear out; my words won't wear out.

36 "But the exact day and hour? No one
knows that, not even heaven's angels, not
even the Son. Only the Father knows.

37-39 "The Arrival of the Son of Man will take
place in times like Noah's. Before the great
flood everyone was carrying on as usual,
having a good time right up to the day Noah
boarded the ark. They knew nothing—until
the flood hit and swept everything away.

39-44 "The Son of Man's Arrival will be like
that: Two men will be working in the field—
one will be taken, one left behind; two
women will be grinding at the mill—one will
be taken, one left behind. So stay awake,
alert. You have no idea what day your Master will show up. But you do know this: You
know that if the homeowner had known
what time of night the burglar would arrive,
he would have been there with his dogs to
prevent the break-in. Be vigilant just like
that. You have no idea when the Son of Man
is going to show up.

45-47 "Who here qualifies for the job of overseeing the kitchen? A person the Master can
depend on to feed the workers on time each
day. Someone the Master can drop in on
unannounced and always find him doing his
job. A God-blessed man or woman, I tell
you. It won't be long before the Master will
put this person in charge of the whole operation.

48-51 "But if that person only looks out for himself, and the minute the Master is away does
what he pleases—abusing the help and
throwing drunken parties for his friends—
the Master is going to show up when he

NEW KING JAMES VERSION

ing for *him* and at an hour that he is not aware
of, 51 and will cut him in two and appoint *him* his
portion with the hypocrites. There shall be
weeping and gnashing of teeth.

THE PARABLE OF THE WISE AND FOOLISH VIRGINS

25 "Then the kingdom of heaven shall be
likened to ten virgins who took their lamps
and went out to meet the bridegroom. 2 Now five
of them were wise, and five *were* foolish. 3 Those
who *were* foolish took their lamps and took no
oil with them, 4 but the wise took oil in their ves-
sels with their lamps. 5 But while the bridegroom
was delayed, they all slumbered and slept.
6 "And at midnight a cry was *heard:* 'Behold,
the bridegroom is coming;[a] go out to meet him!'
7 Then all those virgins arose and trimmed their
lamps. 8 And the foolish said to the wise, 'Give us
some of your oil, for our lamps are going out.'
9 But the wise answered, saying, '*No,* lest there
should not be enough for us and you; but go
rather to those who sell, and buy for yourselves.'
10 And while they went to buy, the bridegroom
came, and those who were ready went in with
him to the wedding; and the door was shut.
11 "Afterward the other virgins came also,
saying, 'Lord, Lord, open to us!' 12 But he an-
swered and said, 'Assuredly, I say to you, I do
not know you.'
13 "Watch therefore, for you know neither the
day nor the hour[a] in which the Son of Man is
coming.

THE PARABLE OF THE TALENTS

14 "For *the kingdom of heaven is* like a man
traveling to a far country, *who* called his own
servants and delivered his goods to them. 15 And
to one he gave five talents, to another two, and
to another one, to each according to his own
ability; and immediately he went on a journey.
16 Then he who had received the five talents
went and traded with them, and made another
five talents. 17 And likewise he who *had received*
two gained two more also. 18 But he who had re-
ceived one went and dug in the ground, and hid
his lord's money. 19 After a long time the lord of
those servants came and settled accounts with
them.
20 "So he who had received five talents came
and brought five other talents, saying, 'Lord,
you delivered to me five talents; look, I have
gained five more talents besides them.' 21 His
lord said to him, 'Well *done,* good and faithful
servant; you were faithful over a few things, I
will make you ruler over many things. Enter
into the joy of your lord.' 22 He also who had re-
ceived two talents came and said, 'Lord, you de-
livered to me two talents; look, I have gained
two more talents besides them.' 23 His lord said
to him, 'Well *done,* good and faithful servant;
you have been faithful over a few things, I will
make you ruler over many things. Enter into the
joy of your lord.'
24 "Then he who had received the one talent
came and said, 'Lord, I knew you to be a hard
man, reaping where you have not sown, and
gathering where you have not scattered seed.

25:6 [a]NU-Text omits *is coming.* 25:13 [a]NU-Text omits the rest of this verse.

THE MESSAGE

least expects it and make hash of him. He'll
end up in the dump with the hypocrites, out
in the cold shivering, teeth chattering."

THE STORY OF THE VIRGINS

1-5 25 "God's kingdom is like ten young vir-
gins who took oil lamps and went out to
greet the bridegroom. Five were silly and five
were smart. The silly virgins took lamps, but
no extra oil. The smart virgins took jars of oil
to feed their lamps. The bridegroom didn't
show up when they expected him, and they
all fell asleep.
6 "In the middle of the night someone
yelled out, 'He's here! The bridegroom's
here! Go out and greet him!'
7-8 "The ten virgins got up and got their
lamps ready. The silly virgins said to the
smart ones, 'Our lamps are going out; lend
us some of your oil.'
9 "They answered, 'There might not be
enough to go around; go buy your own.'
10 "They did, but while they were out buying
oil, the bridegroom arrived. When everyone
who was there to greet him had gone into
the wedding feast, the door was locked.
11 "Much later, the other virgins, the silly
ones, showed up and knocked on the door,
saying, 'Master, we're here. Let us in.'
12 "He answered, 'Do I know you? I don't
think I know you.'
13 "So stay alert. You have no idea when he
might arrive.

THE STORY ABOUT INVESTMENT

14-18 "It's also like a man going off on an ex-
tended trip. He called his servants together
and delegated responsibilities. To one he
gave five thousand dollars, to another two
thousand, to a third one thousand, depend-
ing on their abilities. Then he left. Right off,
the first servant went to work and doubled
his master's investment. The second did the
same. But the man with the single thousand
dug a hole and carefully buried his master's
money.
19-21 "After a long absence, the master of those
three servants came back and settled up
with them. The one given five thousand dol-
lars showed him how he had doubled his in-
vestment. His master commended him:
'Good work! You did your job well. From
now on be my partner.'
22-23 "The servant with the two thousand
showed how he also had doubled his mas-
ter's investment. His master commended
him: 'Good work! You did your job well.
From now on be my partner.'
24-25 "The servant given one thousand said,
'Master, I know you have high standards
and hate careless ways, that you demand
the best and make no allowances for error. I
was afraid I might disappoint you, so I

NEW KING JAMES VERSION

25And I was afraid, and went and hid your talent
in the ground. Look, *there* you have *what is*
yours.'
26"But his lord answered and said to him,
'You wicked and lazy servant, you knew that I
reap where I have not sown, and gather where I
have not scattered seed. 27So you ought to have
deposited my money with the bankers, and at
my coming I would have received back my own
with interest. 28So take the talent from him, and
give *it* to him who has ten talents.
29'For to everyone who has, more will be
given, and he will have abundance; but from
him who does not have, even what he has will be
taken away. 30And cast the unprofitable servant
into the outer darkness. There will be weeping
and gnashing of teeth.'

THE SON OF MAN WILL JUDGE THE NATIONS

31"When the Son of Man comes in His glory,
and all the holy[a] angels with Him, then He will
sit on the throne of His glory. 32All the nations
will be gathered before Him, and He will sepa-
rate them one from another, as a shepherd di-
vides *his* sheep from the goats. 33And He will set
the sheep on His right hand, but the goats on the
left. 34Then the King will say to those on His
right hand, 'Come, you blessed of My Father, in-
herit the kingdom prepared for you from the
foundation of the world: 35for I was hungry and
you gave Me food; I was thirsty and you gave
Me drink; I was a stranger and you took Me in;
36I *was* naked and you clothed Me; I was sick
and you visited Me; I was in prison and you
came to Me.'
37"Then the righteous will answer Him, say-
ing, 'Lord, when did we see You hungry and feed
You, or thirsty and give *You* drink? 38When did
we see You a stranger and take *You* in, or naked
and clothe *You*? 39Or when did we see You sick,
or in prison, and come to You?' 40And the King
will answer and say to them, 'Assuredly, I say to
you, inasmuch as you did *it* to one of the least of
these My brethren, you did *it* to Me.'
41"Then He will also say to those on the left
hand, 'Depart from Me, you cursed, into the
everlasting fire prepared for the devil and his
angels: 42for I was hungry and you gave Me no
food; I was thirsty and you gave Me no drink; 43I
was a stranger and you did not take Me in,
naked and you did not clothe Me, sick and in
prison and you did not visit Me.'
44"Then they also will answer Him,[a] saying,
'Lord, when did we see You hungry or thirsty or
a stranger or naked or sick or in prison, and did
not minister to You?' 45Then He will answer
them, saying, 'Assuredly, I say to you, inasmuch
as you did not do *it* to one of the least of these,
you did not do *it* to Me.' 46And these will go
away into everlasting punishment, but the righ-
teous into eternal life."

25:31 [a]NU-Text omits *holy*. **25:44** [a]NU-Text and M-Text omit *Him*.

THE MESSAGE

found a good hiding place and secured your money. Here it is, safe and sound down to the last cent.'

26-27 "The master was furious. 'That's a terrible way to live! It's criminal to live cautiously like that! If you knew I was after the best, why did you do less than the least? The least you could have done would have been to invest the sum with the bankers, where at least I would have gotten a little interest.

28-30 " 'Take the thousand and give it to the one who risked the most. And get rid of this "play-it-safe" who won't go out on a limb. Throw him out into utter darkness.'

THE SHEEP AND THE GOATS

31-33 "When he finally arrives, blazing in beauty and all his angels with him, the Son of Man will take his place on his glorious throne. Then all the nations will be arranged before him and he will sort the people out, much as a shepherd sorts out sheep and goats, putting sheep to his right and goats to his left.

34-36 "Then the King will say to those on his right, 'Enter, you who are blessed by my Father! Take what's coming to you in this kingdom. It's been ready for you since the world's foundation. And here's why:

I was hungry and you fed me,
I was thirsty and you gave me a drink,
I was homeless and you gave me a room,
I was shivering and you gave me clothes,
I was sick and you stopped to visit,
I was in prison and you came to me.'

37-40 "Then those 'sheep' are going to say, 'Master, what are you talking about? When did we ever see you hungry and feed you, thirsty and give you a drink? And when did we ever see you sick or in prison and come to you?' Then the King will say, 'I'm telling the solemn truth: Whenever you did one of these things to someone overlooked or ignored, that was me—you did it to me.'

41-43 "Then he will turn to the 'goats,' the ones on his left, and say, 'Get out, worthless goats! You're good for nothing but the fires of hell. And why? Because—

I was hungry and you gave me no meal,
I was thirsty and you gave me no drink,
I was homeless and you gave me no bed,
I was shivering and you gave me no
clothes,
Sick and in prison, and you never visited.'

44 "Then those 'goats' are going to say, 'Master, what are you talking about? When did we ever see you hungry or thirsty or homeless or shivering or sick or in prison and didn't help?'

45 "He will answer them, 'I'm telling the solemn truth: Whenever you failed to do one of these things to someone who was being overlooked or ignored, that was me—you failed to do it to me.'

46 "Then those 'goats' will be herded to their eternal doom, but the 'sheep' to their eternal reward."

NEW KING JAMES VERSION

THE PLOT TO KILL JESUS

26 Now it came to pass, when Jesus had finished all these sayings, *that* He said to His disciples, 2“You know that after two days is the Passover, and the Son of Man will be delivered up to be crucified.”

3Then the chief priests, the scribes,[a] and the elders of the people assembled at the palace of the high priest, who was called Caiaphas, 4and plotted to take Jesus by trickery and kill *Him.* 5But they said, “Not during the feast, lest there be an uproar among the people.”

THE ANOINTING AT BETHANY

6And when Jesus was in Bethany at the house of Simon the leper, 7a woman came to Him having an alabaster flask of very costly fragrant oil, and she poured *it* on His head as He sat *at the table.* 8But when His disciples saw *it,* they were indignant, saying, “Why this waste? 9For this fragrant oil might have been sold for much and given to *the* poor.”

10But when Jesus was aware of *it,* He said to them, “Why do you trouble the woman? For she has done a good work for Me. 11For you have the poor with you always, but Me you do not have always. 12For in pouring this fragrant oil on My body, she did *it* for My burial. 13Assuredly, I say to you, wherever this gospel is preached in the whole world, what this woman has done will also be told as a memorial to her.”

JUDAS AGREES TO BETRAY JESUS

14Then one of the twelve, called Judas Iscariot, went to the chief priests 15and said, “What are you willing to give me if I deliver Him to you?” And they counted out to him thirty pieces of silver. 16So from that time he sought opportunity to betray Him.

JESUS CELEBRATES PASSOVER WITH HIS DISCIPLES

17Now on the first *day of the Feast* of the Unleavened Bread the disciples came to Jesus, saying to Him, “Where do You want us to prepare for You to eat the Passover?”

18And He said, “Go into the city to a certain man, and say to him, ‘The Teacher says, “My time is at hand; I will keep the Passover at your house with My disciples.” ’ ”

19So the disciples did as Jesus had directed them; and they prepared the Passover.

20When evening had come, He sat down with the twelve. 21Now as they were eating, He said, “Assuredly, I say to you, one of you will betray Me.”

22And they were exceedingly sorrowful, and each of them began to say to Him, “Lord, is it I?”

23He answered and said, “He who dipped *his* hand with Me in the dish will betray Me. 24The Son of Man indeed goes just as it is written of Him, but woe to that man by whom the Son of Man is betrayed! It would have been good for that man if he had not been born.”

25Then Judas, who was betraying Him, answered and said, “Rabbi, is it I?”

He said to him, “You have said it.”

26:3 [a]NU-Text omits *the scribes.*

THE MESSAGE

ANOINTED FOR BURIAL

1-2 **26** When Jesus finished saying these things, he told his disciples, “You know that Passover comes in two days. That’s when the Son of Man will be betrayed and handed over for crucifixion.”

3-5 At that very moment, the party of high priests and religious leaders was meeting in the chambers of the Chief Priest named Caiaphas, conspiring to seize Jesus by stealth and kill him. They agreed that it should not be done during Passover Week. “We don’t want a riot on our hands,” they said.

6-9 When Jesus was at Bethany, a guest of Simon the Leper, a woman came up to him as he was eating dinner and anointed him with a bottle of very expensive perfume. When the disciples saw what was happening, they were furious. “That’s criminal! This could have been sold for a lot and the money handed out to the poor.”

10-13 When Jesus realized what was going on, he intervened. “Why are you giving this woman a hard time? She has just done something wonderfully significant for me. You will have the poor with you every day for the rest of your lives, but not me. When she poured this perfume on my body, what she really did was anoint me for burial. You can be sure that wherever in the whole world the Message is preached, what she has just done is going to be remembered and admired.”

14-16 That is when one of the Twelve, the one named Judas Iscariot, went to the cabal of high priests and said, “What will you give me if I hand him over to you?” They settled on thirty silver pieces. He began looking for just the right moment to hand him over.

THE TRAITOR

17 On the first of the Days of Unleavened Bread, the disciples came to Jesus and said, “Where do you want us to prepare your Passover meal?”

18-19 He said, “Enter the city. Go up to a certain man and say, ‘The Teacher says, My time is near. I and my disciples plan to celebrate the Passover meal at your house.’ ” The disciples followed Jesus’ instructions to the letter, and prepared the Passover meal.

20-21 After sunset, he and the Twelve were sitting around the table. During the meal, he said, “I have something hard but important to say to you: One of you is going to hand me over to the conspirators.”

22 They were stunned, and then began to ask, one after another, “It isn’t me, is it, Master?”

23-24 Jesus answered, “The one who hands me over is someone I eat with daily, one who passes me food at the table. In one sense the Son of Man is entering into a way of treachery well-marked by the Scriptures—no surprises here. In another sense that man who turns him in, turns traitor to the Son of Man—better never to have been born than do this!”

25 Then Judas, already turned traitor, said, “It isn’t me, is it, Rabbi?”

Jesus said, “Don’t play games with me, Judas.”

New King James Version

Jesus Institutes the Lord's Supper

26 And as they were eating, Jesus took bread,
blessed[a] and broke *it,* and gave *it* to the disci-
ples and said, "Take, eat; this is My body."
27 Then He took the cup, and gave thanks,
and gave *it* to them, saying, "Drink from it, all of
you. 28 For this is My blood of the new[a] covenant,
which is shed for many for the remission of sins.
29 But I say to you, I will not drink of this fruit of
the vine from now on until that day when I drink
it new with you in My Father's kingdom."
30 And when they had sung a hymn, they
went out to the Mount of Olives.

Jesus Predicts Peter's Denial

31 Then Jesus said to them, "All of you will be
made to stumble because of Me this night, for it
is written:

'I will strike the Shepherd,
And the sheep of the flock will be
scattered.'[a]

32 But after I have been raised, I will go before
you to Galilee."
33 Peter answered and said to Him, "Even if
all are made to stumble because of You, I will
never be made to stumble."
34 Jesus said to him, "Assuredly, I say to you
that this night, before the rooster crows, you will
deny Me three times."
35 Peter said to Him, "Even if I have to die
with You, I will not deny You!"
And so said all the disciples.

The Prayer in the Garden

36 Then Jesus came with them to a place
called Gethsemane, and said to the disciples,
"Sit here while I go and pray over there." 37 And
He took with Him Peter and the two sons of
Zebedee, and He began to be sorrowful and
deeply distressed. 38 Then He said to them, "My
soul is exceedingly sorrowful, even to death.
Stay here and watch with Me."
39 He went a little farther and fell on His face,
and prayed, saying, "O My Father, if it is possi-
ble, let this cup pass from Me; nevertheless, not
as I will, but as You *will.*"
40 Then He came to the disciples and found
them sleeping, and said to Peter, "What! Could
you not watch with Me one hour? 41 Watch and
pray, lest you enter into temptation. The spirit
indeed *is* willing, but the flesh *is* weak."
42 Again, a second time, He went away and
prayed, saying, "O My Father, if this cup cannot
pass away from Me unless[a] I drink it, Your will
be done." 43 And He came and found them asleep
again, for their eyes were heavy.

26:26 [a]M-Text reads *gave thanks for.* **26:28** [a]NU-Text omits *new.* **26:31** [a]Zechariah 13:7 **26:42** [a]NU-Text reads *if this may not pass away unless.*

The Message

The Bread and the Cup

26-29 During the meal, Jesus took and blessed the
bread, broke it, and gave it to his disciples:

Take, eat.
This is my body.

Taking the cup and thanking God, he gave it
to them:

Drink this, all of you.
This is my blood,
God's new covenant poured out for
many people
for the forgiveness of sins.

"I'll not be drinking wine from this cup
again until that new day when I'll drink with
you in the kingdom of my Father."
30 They sang a hymn and went directly to
Mount Olives.

Gethsemane

31-32 Then Jesus told them, "Before the night's
over, you're going to fall to pieces because
of what happens to me. There is a Scripture
that says,

I'll strike the shepherd;
helter-skelter the sheep will be scattered.

But after I am raised up, I, your Shepherd,
will go ahead of you, leading the way to
Galilee."
33 Peter broke in, "Even if everyone else
falls to pieces on account of you, I won't."
34 "Don't be so sure," Jesus said. "This very
night, before the rooster crows up the dawn,
you will deny me three times."
35 Peter protested, "Even if I had to die with
you, I would never deny you." All the others
said the same thing.
36-38 Then Jesus went with them to a garden
called Gethsemane and told his disciples,
"Stay here while I go over there and pray."
Taking along Peter and the two sons of
Zebedee, he plunged into an agonizing sor-
row. Then he said, "This sorrow is crushing
my life out. Stay here and keep vigil with me."
39 Going a little ahead, he fell on his face,
praying, "My Father, if there is any way, get
me out of this. But please, not what I want.
You, what do *you* want?"
40-41 When he came back to his disciples, he
found them sound asleep. He said to Peter,
"Can't you stick it out with me a single
hour? Stay alert; be in prayer so you don't
wander into temptation without even know-
ing you're in danger. There is a part of you
that is eager, ready for anything in God. But
there's another part that's as lazy as an old
dog sleeping by the fire."
42 He then left them a second time. Again he
prayed, "My Father, if there is no other way
than this, drinking this cup to the dregs, I'm
ready. Do it your way."
43-44 When he came back, he again found
them sound asleep. They simply couldn't
keep their eyes open. This time he let them

NEW KING JAMES VERSION

44 So He left them, went away again, and prayed the third time, saying the same words. 45 Then He came to His disciples and said to them, "Are *you* still sleeping and resting? Behold, the hour is at hand, and the Son of Man is being betrayed into the hands of sinners. 46 Rise, let us be going. See, My betrayer is at hand."

BETRAYAL AND ARREST IN GETHSEMANE

47 And while He was still speaking, behold, Judas, one of the twelve, with a great multitude with swords and clubs, came from the chief priests and elders of the people.

48 Now His betrayer had given them a sign, saying, "Whomever I kiss, He is the One; seize Him." 49 Immediately he went up to Jesus and said, "Greetings, Rabbi!" and kissed Him.

50 But Jesus said to him, "Friend, why have you come?"

Then they came and laid hands on Jesus and took Him. 51 And suddenly, one of those *who were* with Jesus stretched out *his* hand and drew his sword, struck the servant of the high priest, and cut off his ear.

52 But Jesus said to him, "Put your sword in its place, for all who take the sword will perish[a] by the sword. 53 Or do you think that I cannot now pray to My Father, and He will provide Me with more than twelve legions of angels? 54 How then could the Scriptures be fulfilled, that it must happen thus?"

55 In that hour Jesus said to the multitudes, "Have you come out, as against a robber, with swords and clubs to take Me? I sat daily with you, teaching in the temple, and you did not seize Me. 56 But all this was done that the Scriptures of the prophets might be fulfilled."

Then all the disciples forsook Him and fled.

JESUS FACES THE SANHEDRIN

57 And those who had laid hold of Jesus led *Him* away to Caiaphas the high priest, where the scribes and the elders were assembled. 58 But Peter followed Him at a distance to the high priest's courtyard. And he went in and sat with the servants to see the end.

59 Now the chief priests, the elders,[a] and all the council sought false testimony against Jesus to put Him to death, 60 but found none. Even though many false witnesses came forward, they found none.[a] But at last two false witnesses[b] came forward 61 and said, "This *fellow* said, 'I am able to destroy the temple of God and to build it in three days.' "

62 And the high priest arose and said to Him, "Do You answer nothing? What *is it* these men testify against You?" 63 But Jesus kept silent. And the high priest answered and said to Him, "I put You under oath by the living God: Tell us if You are the Christ, the Son of God!"

64 Jesus said to him, "*It is as* you said. Nevertheless, I say to you, hereafter you will see the Son of Man sitting at the right hand of the Power, and coming on the clouds of heaven."

26:52 [a]M-Text reads *die.* **26:59** [a]NU-Text omits *the elders.* **26:60** [a]NU-Text puts a comma after *but found none,* does not capitalize *Even,* and omits *they found none.* [b]NU-Text omits *false witnesses.*

THE MESSAGE

sleep on, and went back a third time to pray, going over the same ground one last time.

45-46 When he came back the next time, he said, "Are you going to sleep on and make a night of it? My time is up, the Son of Man is about to be handed over to the hands of sinners. Get up! Let's get going! My betrayer is here."

WITH SWORDS AND CLUBS

47-49 The words were barely out of his mouth when Judas (the one from the Twelve) showed up, and with him a gang from the high priests and religious leaders brandishing swords and clubs. The betrayer had worked out a sign with them: "The one I kiss, that's the one—seize him." He went straight to Jesus, greeted him, "How are you, Rabbi?" and kissed him.

50-51 Jesus said, "Friend, why this charade?"

Then they came on him—grabbed him and roughed him up. One of those with Jesus pulled his sword and, taking a swing at the Chief Priest's servant, cut off his ear.

52-54 Jesus said, "Put your sword back where it belongs. All who use swords are destroyed by swords. Don't you realize that I am able right now to call to my Father, and twelve companies—more, if I want them—of fighting angels would be here, battle-ready? But if I did that, how would the Scriptures come true that say this is the way it has to be?"

55-56 Then Jesus addressed the mob: "What is this—coming out after me with swords and clubs as if I were a dangerous criminal? Day after day I have been sitting in the Temple teaching, and you never so much as lifted a hand against me. You've done it this way to confirm and fulfill the prophetic writings."

Then all the disciples cut and ran.

FALSE CHARGES

57-58 The gang that had seized Jesus led him before Caiaphas the Chief Priest, where the religion scholars and leaders had assembled. Peter followed at a safe distance until they got to the Chief Priest's courtyard. Then he slipped in and mingled with the servants, watching to see how things would turn out.

59-60 The high priests, conspiring with the Jewish Council, tried to cook up charges against Jesus in order to sentence him to death. But even though many stepped up, making up one false accusation after another, nothing was believable.

60-61 Finally two men came forward with this: "He said, 'I can tear down this Temple of God and after three days rebuild it.' "

62 The Chief Priest stood up and said, "What do you have to say to the accusation?"

63 Jesus kept silent.

Then the Chief Priest said, "I command you by the authority of the living God to say if you are the Messiah, the Son of God."

64 Jesus was curt: "You yourself said it. And that's not all. Soon you'll see it for yourself:

The Son of Man seated at the right hand
of the Mighty One,
Arriving on the clouds of heaven."

NEW KING JAMES VERSION

65 Then the high priest tore his clothes, say-
ing, "He has spoken blasphemy! What further
need do we have of witnesses? Look, now you
have heard His blasphemy! 66 What do you
think?"
They answered and said, "He is deserving of
death."
67 Then they spat in His face and beat Him;
and others struck *Him* with the palms of their
hands, 68 saying, "Prophesy to us, Christ! Who is
the one who struck You?"

PETER DENIES JESUS, AND WEEPS BITTERLY

69 Now Peter sat outside in the courtyard. And
a servant girl came to him, saying, "You also
were with Jesus of Galilee."
70 But he denied it before *them* all, saying, "I
do not know what you are saying."
71 And when he had gone out to the gateway,
another *girl* saw him and said to those *who were*
there, "This *fellow* also was with Jesus of
Nazareth."
72 But again he denied with an oath, "I do not
know the Man!"
73 And a little later those who stood by came
up and said to Peter, "Surely you also are *one* of
them, for your speech betrays you."
74 Then he began to curse and swear, *saying*,
"I do not know the Man!"
Immediately a rooster crowed. 75 And Peter
remembered the word of Jesus who had said to
him, "Before the rooster crows, you will deny
Me three times." So he went out and wept bit-
terly.

JESUS HANDED OVER TO PONTIUS PILATE

27 When morning came, all the chief priests
and elders of the people plotted against Je-
sus to put Him to death. 2 And when they had
bound Him, they led Him away and delivered
Him to Pontius[a] Pilate the governor.

JUDAS HANGS HIMSELF

3 Then Judas, His betrayer, seeing that He
had been condemned, was remorseful and
brought back the thirty pieces of silver to the
chief priests and elders, 4 saying, "I have sinned
by betraying innocent blood."
And they said, "What *is that* to us? You see *to
it!*"
5 Then he threw down the pieces of silver in
the temple and departed, and went and hanged
himself.
6 But the chief priests took the silver pieces
and said, "It is not lawful to put them into the
treasury, because they are the price of blood."
7 And they consulted together and bought with
them the potter's field, to bury strangers in.
8 Therefore that field has been called the Field of
Blood to this day.
9 Then was fulfilled what was spoken by Jere-
miah the prophet, saying, *"And they took the
thirty pieces of silver, the value of Him who was
priced,* whom they of the children of Israel
priced, 10 *and gave them for the potter's field, as
the* LORD *directed me."* [a]

27:2 [a]NU-Text omits *Pontius*. **27:10** [a]Jeremiah 32:6–9

THE MESSAGE

65-66 At that, the Chief Priest lost his temper,
ripping his robes, yelling, "He blasphemed!
Why do we need witnesses to accuse him?
You all heard him blaspheme! Are you go-
ing to stand for such blasphemy?"
They all said, "Death! That seals his
death sentence."
67-68 Then they were spitting in his face and
banging him around. They jeered as they
slapped him: "Prophesy, Messiah: Who hit
you that time?"

DENIAL IN THE COURTYARD

69 All this time, Peter was sitting out in the
courtyard. One servant girl came up to him
and said, "You were with Jesus the Galilean."
70 In front of everybody there, he denied it.
"I don't know what you're talking about."
71 As he moved over toward the gate, some-
one else said to the people there, "This man
was with Jesus the Nazarene."
72 Again he denied it, salting his denial with
an oath: "I swear, I never laid eyes on the
man."
73 Shortly after that, some bystanders ap-
proached Peter. "You've got to be one of
them. Your accent gives you away."
74-75 Then he got really nervous and swore. "I
don't know the man!"
Just then a rooster crowed. Peter remem-
bered what Jesus had said: "Before the roos-
ter crows, you will deny me three times." He
went out and cried and cried and cried.

THIRTY SILVER COINS

1-2 27 In the first light of dawn, all the high
priests and religious leaders met and
put the finishing touches on their plot to kill
Jesus. Then they tied him up and paraded
him to Pilate, the governor.
3-4 Judas, the one who betrayed him, real-
ized that Jesus was doomed. Overcome with
remorse, he gave back the thirty silver coins
to the high priests, saying, "I've sinned. I've
betrayed an innocent man."
They said, "What do we care? That's *your*
problem!"
5 Judas threw the silver coins into the Tem-
ple and left. Then he went out and hung
himself.
6-10 The high priests picked up the silver
pieces, but then didn't know what to do with
them. "It wouldn't be right to give this—a
payment for murder!—as an offering in the
Temple." They decided to get rid of it by
buying the "Potter's Field" and use it as a
burial place for the homeless. That's how
the field got called "Murder Meadow," a
name that has stuck to this day. Then Jere-
miah's words became history:

They took the thirty silver pieces,
The price of the one priced by some sons
of Israel,
And they purchased the potter's field.

And so they unwittingly followed the divine
instructions to the letter.

New King James Version

Jesus Faces Pilate

11 Now Jesus stood before the governor. And
the governor asked Him, saying, "Are You the
King of the Jews?"
Jesus said to him, "*It is as* you say." 12 And
while He was being accused by the chief priests
and elders, He answered nothing.
13 Then Pilate said to Him, "Do You not hear
how many things they testify against You?" 14 But
He answered him not one word, so that the gov-
ernor marveled greatly.

Taking the Place of Barabbas

15 Now at the feast the governor was accus-
tomed to releasing to the multitude one prisoner
whom they wished. 16 And at that time they had
a notorious prisoner called Barabbas.[a] 17 There-
fore, when they had gathered together, Pilate
said to them, "Whom do you want me to release
to you? Barabbas, or Jesus who is called
Christ?" 18 For he knew that they had handed
Him over because of envy.
19 While he was sitting on the judgment seat,
his wife sent to him, saying, "Have nothing to do
with that just Man, for I have suffered many
things today in a dream because of Him."
20 But the chief priests and elders persuaded
the multitudes that they should ask for Barab-
bas and destroy Jesus. 21 The governor answered
and said to them, "Which of the two do you want
me to release to you?"
They said, "Barabbas!"
22 Pilate said to them, "What then shall I do
with Jesus who is called Christ?"
They all said to him, "Let Him be crucified!"
23 Then the governor said, "Why, what evil
has He done?"
But they cried out all the more, saying, "Let
Him be crucified!"
24 When Pilate saw that he could not prevail
at all, but rather *that* a tumult was rising, he
took water and washed *his* hands before the
multitude, saying, "I am innocent of the blood of
this just Person.[a] You see *to it*."
25 And all the people answered and said, "His
blood *be* on us and on our children."
26 Then he released Barabbas to them; and
when he had scourged Jesus, he delivered *Him*
to be crucified.

The Soldiers Mock Jesus

27 Then the soldiers of the governor took Je-
sus into the Praetorium and gathered the whole
garrison around Him. 28 And they stripped Him
and put a scarlet robe on Him. 29 When they had
twisted a crown of thorns, they put *it* on His
head, and a reed in His right hand. And they
bowed the knee before Him and mocked Him,
saying, "Hail, King of the Jews!" 30 Then they
spat on Him, and took the reed and struck Him
on the head. 31 And when they had mocked Him,
they took the robe off Him, put His *own* clothes
on Him, and led Him away to be crucified.

The King on a Cross

32 Now as they came out, they found a man of
Cyrene, Simon by name. Him they compelled to

27:16 [a]NU-Text reads *Jesus Barabbas*. **27:24** [a]NU-Text omits *just*.

The Message

Pilate

11 Jesus was placed before the governor, who
questioned him: "Are you the 'King of the
Jews'?"
Jesus said, "If you say so."
12-14 But when the accusations rained down hot
and heavy from the high priests and religious
leaders, he said nothing. Pilate asked him,
"Do you hear that long list of accusations?
Aren't you going to say something?" Jesus
kept silence—not a word from his mouth. The
governor was impressed, really impressed.
15-18 It was an old custom during the Feast for
the governor to pardon a single prisoner
named by the crowd. At the time, they had
the infamous Jesus Barabbas in prison. With
the crowd before him, Pilate said, "Which
prisoner do you want me to pardon: Jesus
Barabbas, or Jesus the so-called Christ?" He
knew it was through sheer spite that they
had turned Jesus over to him.
19 While court was still in session, Pilate's
wife sent him a message: "Don't get mixed
up in judging this noble man. I've just been
through a long and troubled night because
of a dream about him."
20 Meanwhile, the high priests and religious
leaders had talked the crowd into asking for
the pardon of Barabbas and the execution of
Jesus.
21 The governor asked, "Which of the two
do you want me to pardon?"
They said, "Barabbas!"
22 "Then what do I do with Jesus, the so-
called Christ?"
They all shouted, "Nail him to a cross!"
23 He objected, "But for what crime?"
But they yelled all the louder, "Nail him to
a cross!"
24 When Pilate saw that he was getting
nowhere and that a riot was imminent, he
took a basin of water and washed his hands
in full sight of the crowd, saying, "I'm wash-
ing my hands of responsibility for this
man's death. From now on, it's in your
hands. You're judge and jury."
25 The crowd answered, "We'll take the
blame, we and our children after us."
26 Then he pardoned Barabbas. But he had
Jesus whipped, and then handed over for
crucifixion.

The Crucifixion

27-31 The soldiers assigned to the governor took
Jesus into the governor's palace and got the
entire brigade together for some fun. They
stripped him and dressed him in a red toga.
They plaited a crown from branches of a
thornbush and set it on his head. They put a
stick in his right hand for a scepter. Then
they knelt before him in mocking reverence:
"Bravo, King of the Jews!" they said.
"Bravo!" Then they spit on him and hit him
on the head with the stick. When they had
had their fun, they took off the toga and put
his own clothes back on him. Then they pro-
ceeded out to the crucifixion.
32-34 Along the way they came on a man from
Cyrene named Simon and made him carry

NEW KING JAMES VERSION

bear His cross. 33And when they had come to a place called Golgotha, that is to say, Place of a Skull, 34they gave Him sour[a] wine mingled with gall to drink. But when He had tasted *it,* He would not drink.

35Then they crucified Him, and divided His garments, casting lots,[a] that it might be fulfilled which was spoken by the prophet:

"They divided My garments among them,
And for My clothing they cast lots."[b]

36Sitting down, they kept watch over Him there. 37And they put up over His head the accusation written against Him:

THIS IS JESUS
THE KING OF THE JEWS.

38Then two robbers were crucified with Him, one on the right and another on the left.

39And those who passed by blasphemed Him, wagging their heads 40and saying, "You who destroy the temple and build *it* in three days, save Yourself! If You are the Son of God, come down from the cross."

41Likewise the chief priests also, mocking with the scribes and elders,[a] said, 42"He saved others; Himself He cannot save. If He is the King of Israel,[a] let Him now come down from the cross, and we will believe Him.[b] 43He trusted in God; let Him deliver Him now if He will have Him; for He said, 'I am the Son of God.' "

44Even the robbers who were crucified with Him reviled Him with the same thing.

JESUS DIES ON THE CROSS

45Now from the sixth hour until the ninth hour there was darkness over all the land. 46And about the ninth hour Jesus cried out with a loud voice, saying, "Eli, Eli, lama sabachthani?" that is, *"My God, My God, why have You forsaken Me?"*[a]

47Some of those who stood there, when they heard *that,* said, "This Man is calling for Elijah!" 48Immediately one of them ran and took a sponge, filled *it* with sour wine and put *it* on a reed, and offered it to Him to drink.

49The rest said, "Let Him alone; let us see if Elijah will come to save Him."

50And Jesus cried out again with a loud voice, and yielded up His spirit.

51Then, behold, the veil of the temple was torn in two from top to bottom; and the earth quaked, and the rocks were split, 52and the graves were opened; and many bodies of the saints who had fallen asleep were raised; 53and coming out of the graves after His resurrection, they went into the holy city and appeared to many.

54So when the centurion and those with him, who were guarding Jesus, saw the earthquake and the things that had happened, they feared greatly, saying, "Truly this was the Son of God!"

27:34 [a]NU-Text omits *sour.* **27:35** [a]NU-Text and M-Text omit the rest of this verse. [b]Psalm 22:18 **27:41** [a]M-Text reads *with the scribes, the Pharisees, and the elders.* **27:42** [a]NU-Text reads *He is the King of Israel!* [b]NU-Text and M-Text read *we will believe in Him.* **27:46** [a]Psalm 22:1

THE MESSAGE

Jesus' cross. Arriving at Golgotha, the place
they call "Skull Hill," they offered him a
mild painkiller (a mixture of wine and
myrrh), but when he tasted it he wouldn't
drink it.
35-40 After they had finished nailing him to the
cross and were waiting for him to die, they
whiled away the time by throwing dice for
his clothes. Above his head they had posted
the criminal charge against him: THIS IS
JESUS, THE KING OF THE JEWS. Along with him,
they also crucified two criminals, one to his
right, the other to his left. People passing
along the road jeered, shaking their heads
in mock lament: "You bragged that you
could tear down the Temple and then re-
build it in three days—so show us your stuff!
Save yourself! If you're really God's Son,
come down from that cross!"
41-44 The high priests, along with the religion
scholars and leaders, were right there mix-
ing it up with the rest of them, having a
great time poking fun at him: "He saved oth-
ers—he can't save himself! King of Israel, is
he? Then let him get down from that cross.
We'll *all* become believers then! He was so
sure of God—well, let him rescue his 'Son'
now—if he wants him! He did claim to be
God's Son, didn't he?" Even the two crimi-
nals crucified next to him joined in the
mockery.
45-46 From noon to three, the whole earth was
dark. Around mid-afternoon Jesus groaned
out of the depths, crying loudly, *"Eli, Eli,*
lama sabachthani?" which means, "My God,
my God, why have you abandoned me?"
47-49 Some bystanders who heard him said,
"He's calling for Elijah." One of them ran
and got a sponge soaked in sour wine and
lifted it on a stick so he could drink. The oth-
ers joked, "Don't be in such a hurry. Let's
see if Elijah comes and saves him."
50 But Jesus, again crying out loudly,
breathed his last.
51-53 At that moment, the Temple curtain was
ripped in two, top to bottom. There was an
earthquake, and rocks were split in pieces.
What's more, tombs were opened up, and
many bodies of believers asleep in their
graves were raised. (After Jesus' resurrec-
tion, they left the tombs, entered the holy
city, and appeared to many.)
54 The captain of the guard and those with
him, when they saw the earthquake and
everything else that was happening, were
scared to death. They said, "This has to be
the Son of God!"

NEW KING JAMES VERSION

55And many women who followed Jesus
from Galilee, ministering to Him, were there
looking on from afar, 56among whom were Mary
Magdalene, Mary the mother of James and
Joses,[a] and the mother of Zebedee's sons.

JESUS BURIED IN JOSEPH'S TOMB

57Now when evening had come, there came a
rich man from Arimathea, named Joseph, who
himself had also become a disciple of Jesus.
58This man went to Pilate and asked for the
body of Jesus. Then Pilate commanded the body
to be given to him. 59When Joseph had taken the
body, he wrapped it in a clean linen cloth, 60and
laid it in his new tomb which he had hewn out
of the rock; and he rolled a large stone against
the door of the tomb, and departed. 61And Mary
Magdalene was there, and the other Mary, sit-
ting opposite the tomb.

PILATE SETS A GUARD

62On the next day, which followed the Day of
Preparation, the chief priests and Pharisees
gathered together to Pilate, 63saying, "Sir, we re-
member, while He was still alive, how that de-
ceiver said, 'After three days I will rise.' 64There-
fore command that the tomb be made secure
until the third day, lest His disciples come by
night[a] and steal Him *away,* and say to the peo-
ple, 'He has risen from the dead.' So the last de-
ception will be worse than the first."

65Pilate said to them, "You have a guard; go
your way, make *it* as secure as you know how."
66So they went and made the tomb secure, seal-
ing the stone and setting the guard.

HE IS RISEN

28 Now after the Sabbath, as the first *day* of
the week began to dawn, Mary Magdalene
and the other Mary came to see the tomb. 2And
behold, there was a great earthquake; for an an-
gel of the Lord descended from heaven, and
came and rolled back the stone from the door,[a]
and sat on it. 3His countenance was like light-
ning, and his clothing as white as snow. 4And
the guards shook for fear of him, and became
like dead *men.*

5But the angel answered and said to the
women, "Do not be afraid, for I know that you
seek Jesus who was crucified. 6He is not here;
for He is risen, as He said. Come, see the place
where the Lord lay. 7And go quickly and tell His
disciples that He is risen from the dead, and in-
deed He is going before you into Galilee; there
you will see Him. Behold, I have told you."

8So they went out quickly from the tomb
with fear and great joy, and ran to bring His dis-
ciples word.

THE WOMEN WORSHIP THE RISEN LORD

9And as they went to tell His disciples,[a] be-
hold, Jesus met them, saying, "Rejoice!" So they
came and held Him by the feet and worshiped
Him. 10Then Jesus said to them, "Do not be
afraid. Go *and* tell My brethren to go to Galilee,
and there they will see Me."

27:56 [a]NU-Text reads *Joseph.* **27:64** [a]NU-Text omits *by night.* **28:2** [a]NU-Text omits *from the door.* **28:9** [a]NU-Text omits the first clause of this verse.

THE MESSAGE

55-56 There were also quite a few women watching from a distance, women who had followed Jesus from Galilee in order to serve him. Among them were Mary Magdalene, Mary the mother of James and Joseph, and the mother of the Zebedee brothers.

THE TOMB

57-61 Late in the afternoon a wealthy man from Arimathea, a disciple of Jesus, arrived. His name was Joseph. He went to Pilate and asked for Jesus' body. Pilate granted his request. Joseph took the body and wrapped it in clean linens, put it in his own tomb, a new tomb only recently cut into the rock, and rolled a large stone across the entrance. Then he went off. But Mary Magdalene and the other Mary stayed, sitting in plain view of the tomb.

62-64 After sundown, the high priests and Pharisees arranged a meeting with Pilate. They said, "Sir, we just remembered that that liar announced while he was still alive, 'After three days I will be raised.' We've got to get that tomb sealed until the third day. There's a good chance his disciples will come and steal the corpse and then go around saying, 'He's risen from the dead.' Then we'll be worse off than before, the final deceit surpassing the first."

65-66 Pilate told them, "You will have a guard. Go ahead and secure it the best you can." So they went out and secured the tomb, sealing the stone and posting guards.

RISEN FROM THE DEAD

1-4 28 After the Sabbath, as the first light of the new week dawned, Mary Magdalene and the other Mary came to keep vigil at the tomb. Suddenly the earth reeled and rocked under their feet as God's angel came down from heaven, came right up to where they were standing. He rolled back the stone and then sat on it. Shafts of lightning blazed from him. His garments shimmered snow-white. The guards at the tomb were scared to death. They were so frightened, they couldn't move.

5-6 The angel spoke to the women: "There is nothing to fear here. I know you're looking for Jesus, the One they nailed to the cross. He is not here. He was raised, just as he said. Come and look at the place where he was placed.

7 "Now, get on your way quickly and tell his disciples, 'He is risen from the dead. He is going on ahead of you to Galilee. You will see him there.' That's the message."

8-10 The women, deep in wonder and full of joy, lost no time in leaving the tomb. They ran to tell the disciples. Then Jesus met them, stopping them in their tracks. "Good morning!" he said. They fell to their knees, embraced his feet, and worshiped him. Jesus said, "You're holding on to me for dear life! Don't be frightened like that. Go tell my brothers that they are to go to Galilee, and that I'll meet them there."

NEW KING JAMES VERSION

THE SOLDIERS ARE BRIBED

[11]Now while they were going, behold, some
of the guard came into the city and reported to
the chief priests all the things that had hap-
pened. [12]When they had assembled with the el-
ders and consulted together, they gave a large
sum of money to the soldiers, [13]saying, "Tell
them, 'His disciples came at night and stole Him
away while we slept.' [14]And if this comes to the
governor's ears, we will appease him and make
you secure." [15]So they took the money and did
as they were instructed; and this saying is com-
monly reported among the Jews until this day.

THE GREAT COMMISSION

[16]Then the eleven disciples went away into
Galilee, to the mountain which Jesus had ap-
pointed for them. [17]When they saw Him, they
worshiped Him; but some doubted.
[18]And Jesus came and spoke to them, saying,
"All authority has been given to Me in heaven
and on earth. [19]Go therefore[a] and make disci-
ples of all the nations, baptizing them in the
name of the Father and of the Son and of the
Holy Spirit, [20]teaching them to observe all
things that I have commanded you; and lo, I am
with you always, *even* to the end of the age."
Amen.[a]

28:19 [a]M-Text omits *therefore.* **28:20** [a]NU-Text omits *Amen.*

THE MESSAGE

11-15 Meanwhile, the guards had scattered, but a few of them went into the city and told the high priests everything that had happened. They called a meeting of the religious leaders and came up with a plan: They took a large sum of money and gave it to the soldiers, bribing them to say, "His disciples came in the night and stole the body while we were sleeping." They assured them, "If the governor hears about your sleeping on duty, we will make sure you don't get blamed." The soldiers took the bribe and did as they were told. That story, cooked up in the Jewish High Council, is still going around.

16-17 Meanwhile, the eleven disciples were on their way to Galilee, headed for the mountain Jesus had set for their reunion. The moment they saw him they worshiped him. Some, though, held back, not sure about *worship*, about risking themselves totally.

18-20 Jesus, undeterred, went right ahead and gave his charge: "God authorized and commanded me to commission you: Go out and train everyone you meet, far and near, in this way of life, marking them by baptism in the threefold name: Father, Son, and Holy Spirit. Then instruct them in the practice of all I have commanded you. I'll be with you as you do this, day after day after day, right up to the end of the age."

MARK

New King James Version

John the Baptist Prepares the Way

1 The beginning of the gospel of Jesus Christ, the Son of God. 2As it is written in the Prophets:[a]

"Behold, I send My messenger before Your face,
Who will prepare Your way before You."[b]
3*"The voice of one crying in the wilderness:*
'Prepare the way of the Lord;
Make His paths straight.' "[a]

4John came baptizing in the wilderness and preaching a baptism of repentance for the remission of sins. 5Then all the land of Judea, and those from Jerusalem, went out to him and were all baptized by him in the Jordan River, confessing their sins.

6Now John was clothed with camel's hair and with a leather belt around his waist, and he ate locusts and wild honey. 7And he preached, saying, "There comes One after me who is mightier than I, whose sandal strap I am not worthy to stoop down and loose. 8I indeed baptized you with water, but He will baptize you with the Holy Spirit."

John Baptizes Jesus

9It came to pass in those days *that* Jesus came from Nazareth of Galilee, and was baptized by John in the Jordan. 10And immediately, coming up from[a] the water, He saw the heavens parting and the Spirit descending upon Him like a dove. 11Then a voice came from heaven, "You are My beloved Son, in whom I am well pleased."

Satan Tempts Jesus

12Immediately the Spirit drove Him into the wilderness. 13And He was there in the wilderness forty days, tempted by Satan, and was with the wild beasts; and the angels ministered to Him.

Jesus Begins His Galilean Ministry

14Now after John was put in prison, Jesus came to Galilee, preaching the gospel of the kingdom[a] of God, 15and saying, "The time is fulfilled, and the kingdom of God is at hand. Repent, and believe in the gospel."

Four Fishermen Called as Disciples

16And as He walked by the Sea of Galilee, He saw Simon and Andrew his brother casting a net into the sea; for they were fishermen. 17Then Jesus said to them, "Follow Me, and I will make you become fishers of men." 18They immediately left their nets and followed Him.

19When He had gone a little farther from there, He saw James the *son* of Zebedee, and John his brother, who also *were* in the boat mending their nets. 20And immediately He called them, and they left their father Zebedee in the boat with the hired servants, and went after Him.

1:2 [a]NU-Text reads *Isaiah the prophet.* [b]Malachi 3:1 **1:3** [a]Isaiah 40:3 **1:10** [a]NU-Text reads *out of.* **1:14** [a]NU-Text omits *of the kingdom.*

The Message

John the Baptizer

1-3 1 The good news of Jesus Christ—the Message!—begins here, following to the letter the scroll of the prophet Isaiah.

Watch closely: I'm sending my preacher ahead of you;
He'll make the road smooth for you.
Thunder in the desert!
Prepare for God's arrival!
Make the road smooth and straight!

4-6 John the Baptizer appeared in the wild, preaching a baptism of lifechange that leads to forgiveness of sins. People thronged to him from Judea and Jerusalem and, as they confessed their sins, were baptized by him in the Jordan River into a changed life. John wore a camel-hair habit, tied at the waist with a leather belt. He ate locusts and wild field honey.

7-8 As he preached he said, "The real action comes next: The star in this drama, to whom I'm a mere stagehand, will change your life. I'm baptizing you here in the river, turning your old life in for a kingdom life. His baptism—a holy baptism by the Holy Spirit—will change you from the inside out."

9-11 At this time, Jesus came from Nazareth in Galilee and was baptized by John in the Jordan. The moment he came out of the water, he saw the sky split open and God's Spirit, looking like a dove, come down on him. Along with the Spirit, a voice: "You are my Son, chosen and marked by my love, pride of my life."

God's Kingdom Is Here

12-13 At once, this same Spirit pushed Jesus out into the wild. For forty wilderness days and nights he was tested by Satan. Wild animals were his companions, and angels took care of him.

14-15 After John was arrested, Jesus went to Galilee preaching the Message of God: "Time's up! God's kingdom is here. Change your life and believe the Message."

16-18 Passing along the beach of Lake Galilee, he saw Simon and his brother Andrew netfishing. Fishing was their regular work. Jesus said to them, "Come with me. I'll make a new kind of fisherman out of you. I'll show you how to catch men and women instead of perch and bass." They didn't ask questions. They dropped their nets and followed.

19-20 A dozen yards or so down the beach, he saw the brothers James and John, Zebedee's sons. They were in the boat, mending their fishnets. Right off, he made the same offer. Immediately, they left their father Zebedee, the boat, and the hired hands, and followed.

NEW KING JAMES VERSION

JESUS CASTS OUT AN UNCLEAN SPIRIT

21Then they went into Capernaum, and immediately on the Sabbath He entered the synagogue and taught. 22And they were astonished at His teaching, for He taught them as one having authority, and not as the scribes.

23Now there was a man in their synagogue with an unclean spirit. And he cried out, 24saying, "Let *us* alone! What have we to do with You, Jesus of Nazareth? Did You come to destroy us? I know who You are—the Holy One of God!"

25But Jesus rebuked him, saying, "Be quiet, and come out of him!" 26And when the unclean spirit had convulsed him and cried out with a loud voice, he came out of him. 27Then they were all amazed, so that they questioned among themselves, saying, "What is this? What new doctrine *is* this? For with authority[a] He commands even the unclean spirits, and they obey Him." 28And immediately His fame spread throughout all the region around Galilee.

PETER'S MOTHER-IN-LAW HEALED

29Now as soon as they had come out of the synagogue, they entered the house of Simon and Andrew, with James and John. 30But Simon's wife's mother lay sick with a fever, and they told Him about her at once. 31So He came and took her by the hand and lifted her up, and immediately the fever left her. And she served them.

MANY HEALED AFTER SABBATH SUNSET

32At evening, when the sun had set, they brought to Him all who were sick and those who were demon-possessed. 33And the whole city was gathered together at the door. 34Then He healed many who were sick with various diseases, and cast out many demons; and He did not allow the demons to speak, because they knew Him.

PREACHING IN GALILEE

35Now in the morning, having risen a long while before daylight, He went out and departed to a solitary place; and there He prayed. 36And Simon and those *who were* with Him searched for Him. 37When they found Him, they said to Him, "Everyone is looking for You."

38But He said to them, "Let us go into the next towns, that I may preach there also, because for this purpose I have come forth."

39And He was preaching in their synagogues throughout all Galilee, and casting out demons.

JESUS CLEANSES A LEPER

40Now a leper came to Him, imploring Him, kneeling down to Him and saying to Him, "If You are willing, You can make me clean."

41Then Jesus, moved with compassion, stretched out *His* hand and touched him, and said to him, "I am willing; be cleansed." 42As soon as He had spoken, immediately the leprosy left him, and he was cleansed. 43And He strictly warned him and sent him away at once, 44and said to him, "See that you say nothing to anyone; but go your way, show yourself to the priest, and offer for your cleansing those things

1:27 [a]NU-Text reads *What is this? A new doctrine with authority.*

THE MESSAGE

CONFIDENT TEACHING

21-22 Then they entered Capernaum. When the Sabbath arrived, Jesus lost no time in getting to the meeting place. He spent the day there teaching. They were surprised at his teaching—so forthright, so confident—not quibbling and quoting like the religion scholars.

23-24 Suddenly, while still in the meeting place, he was interrupted by a man who was deeply disturbed and yelling out, "What business do you have here with us, Jesus? Nazarene! I know what you're up to! You're the Holy One of God, and you've come to destroy us!"

25-26 Jesus shut him up: "Quiet! Get out of him!" The afflicting spirit threw the man into spasms, protesting loudly—and got out.

27-28 Everyone there was incredulous, buzzing with curiosity. "What's going on here? A new teaching that does what it says? He shuts up defiling, demonic spirits and sends them packing!" News of this traveled fast and was soon all over Galilee.

29-31 Directly on leaving the meeting place, they came to Simon and Andrew's house, accompanied by James and John. Simon's mother-in-law was sick in bed, burning up with fever. They told Jesus. He went to her, took her hand, and raised her up. No sooner had the fever left than she was up fixing dinner for them.

32-34 That evening, after the sun was down, they brought sick and evil-afflicted people to him, the whole city lined up at his door! He cured their sick bodies and tormented spirits. Because the demons knew his true identity, he didn't let them say a word.

THE LEPER

35-37 While it was still night, way before dawn, he got up and went out to a secluded spot and prayed. Simon and those with him went looking for him. They found him and said, "Everybody's looking for you."

38-39 Jesus said, "Let's go to the rest of the villages so I can preach there also. This is why I've come." He went to their meeting places all through Galilee, preaching and throwing out the demons.

40 A leper came to him, begging on his knees, "If you want to, you can cleanse me."

41-45 Deeply moved, Jesus put out his hand, touched him, and said, "I want to. Be clean." Then and there the leprosy was gone, his skin smooth and healthy. Jesus dismissed him with strict orders: "Say nothing to anyone. Take the offering for cleansing that

New King James Version

which Moses commanded, as a testimony to them."

45 However, he went out and began to proclaim *it* freely, and to spread the matter, so that Jesus could no longer openly enter the city, but was outside in deserted places; and they came to Him from every direction.

Jesus Forgives and Heals a Paralytic

2 And again He entered Capernaum after *some* days, and it was heard that He was in the house. 2 Immediately[a] many gathered together, so that there was no longer room to receive *them,* not even near the door. And He preached the word to them. 3 Then they came to Him, bringing a paralytic who was carried by four *men.* 4 And when they could not come near Him because of the crowd, they uncovered the roof where He was. So when they had broken through, they let down the bed on which the paralytic was lying.

5 When Jesus saw their faith, He said to the paralytic, "Son, your sins are forgiven you."

6 And some of the scribes were sitting there and reasoning in their hearts, 7 "Why does this *Man* speak blasphemies like this? Who can forgive sins but God alone?"

8 But immediately, when Jesus perceived in His spirit that they reasoned thus within themselves, He said to them, "Why do you reason about these things in your hearts? 9 Which is easier, to say to the paralytic, '*Your* sins are forgiven you,' or to say, 'Arise, take up your bed and walk'? 10 But that you may know that the Son of Man has power on earth to forgive sins"—He said to the paralytic, 11 "I say to you, arise, take up your bed, and go to your house." 12 Immediately he arose, took up the bed, and went out in the presence of them all, so that all were amazed and glorified God, saying, "We never saw *anything* like this!"

Matthew the Tax Collector

13 Then He went out again by the sea; and all the multitude came to Him, and He taught them. 14 As He passed by, He saw Levi the *son* of Alphaeus sitting at the tax office. And He said to him, "Follow Me." So he arose and followed Him.

15 Now it happened, as He was dining in *Levi's* house, that many tax collectors and sinners also sat together with Jesus and His disciples; for there were many, and they followed Him. 16 And when the scribes and[a] Pharisees saw Him eating with the tax collectors and sinners, they said to His disciples, "How *is it* that He eats and drinks with tax collectors and sinners?"

17 When Jesus heard *it,* He said to them, "Those who are well have no need of a physician, but those who are sick. I did not come to call *the* righteous, but sinners, to repentance."[a]

2:2 [a]NU-Text omits *Immediately.* **2:16** [a]NU-Text reads *of the.* **2:17** [a]NU-Text omits *to repentance.*

The Message

Moses prescribed and present yourself to the priest. This will validate your healing to the people." But as soon as the man was out of earshot, he told everyone he met what had happened, spreading the news all over town. So Jesus kept to out-of-the-way places, no longer able to move freely in and out of the city. But people found him, and came from all over.

A Paraplegic

1-5 2 After a few days, Jesus returned to Capernaum, and word got around that he was back home. A crowd gathered, jamming the entrance so no one could get in or out. He was teaching the Word. They brought a paraplegic to him, carried by four men. When they weren't able to get in because of the crowd, they removed part of the roof and lowered the paraplegic on his stretcher. Impressed by their bold belief, Jesus said to the paraplegic, "Son, I forgive your sins."

6-7 Some religion scholars sitting there started whispering among themselves, "He can't talk that way! That's blasphemy! God and only God can forgive sins."

8-12 Jesus knew right away what they were thinking, and said, "Why are you so skeptical? Which is simpler: to say to the paraplegic, 'I forgive your sins,' or say, 'Get up, take your stretcher, and start walking'? Well, just so it's clear that I'm the Son of Man and authorized to do either, or both . . ." (he looked now at the paraplegic), "Get up. Pick up your stretcher and go home." And the man did it—got up, grabbed his stretcher, and walked out, with everyone there watching him. They rubbed their eyes, incredulous—and then praised God, saying, "We've never seen anything like this!"

The Tax Collector

13-14 Then Jesus went again to walk alongside the lake. Again a crowd came to him, and he taught them. Strolling along, he saw Levi, son of Alphaeus, at his work collecting taxes. Jesus said, "Come along with me." He came.

15-16 Later Jesus and his disciples were at home having supper with a collection of disreputable guests. Unlikely as it seems, more than a few of them had become followers. The religion scholars and Pharisees saw him keeping this kind of company and lit into his disciples: "What kind of example is this, acting cozy with the riffraff?"

17 Jesus, overhearing, shot back, "Who needs a doctor: the healthy or the sick? I'm here inviting the sin-sick, not the spiritually-fit."

NEW KING JAMES VERSION

JESUS IS QUESTIONED ABOUT FASTING

[18]The disciples of John and of the Pharisees were fasting. Then they came and said to Him, "Why do the disciples of John and of the Pharisees fast, but Your disciples do not fast?"

[19]And Jesus said to them, "Can the friends of the bridegroom fast while the bridegroom is with them? As long as they have the bridegroom with them they cannot fast. [20]But the days will come when the bridegroom will be taken away from them, and then they will fast in those days. [21]No one sews a piece of unshrunk cloth on an old garment; or else the new piece pulls away from the old, and the tear is made worse. [22]And no one puts new wine into old wineskins; or else the new wine bursts the wineskins, the wine is spilled, and the wineskins are ruined. But new wine must be put into new wineskins."

JESUS IS LORD OF THE SABBATH

[23]Now it happened that He went through the grainfields on the Sabbath; and as they went His disciples began to pluck the heads of grain. [24]And the Pharisees said to Him, "Look, why do they do what is not lawful on the Sabbath?"

[25]But He said to them, "Have you never read what David did when he was in need and hungry, he and those with him: [26]how he went into the house of God *in the days* of Abiathar the high priest, and ate the showbread, which is not lawful to eat except for the priests, and also gave some to those who were with him?"

[27]And He said to them, "The Sabbath was made for man, and not man for the Sabbath. [28]Therefore the Son of Man is also Lord of the Sabbath."

HEALING ON THE SABBATH

3 And He entered the synagogue again, and a man was there who had a withered hand. [2]So they watched Him closely, whether He would heal him on the Sabbath, so that they might accuse Him. [3]And He said to the man who had the withered hand, "Step forward." [4]Then He said to them, "Is it lawful on the Sabbath to do good or to do evil, to save life or to kill?" But they kept silent. [5]And when He had looked around at them with anger, being grieved by the hardness of their hearts, He said to the man, "Stretch out your hand." And he stretched *it* out, and his hand was restored as whole as the other.[a] [6]Then the Pharisees went out and immediately plotted with the Herodians against Him, how they might destroy Him.

A GREAT MULTITUDE FOLLOWS JESUS

[7]But Jesus withdrew with His disciples to the sea. And a great multitude from Galilee followed Him, and from Judea [8]and Jerusalem and Idumea and beyond the Jordan; and those from Tyre and Sidon, a great multitude, when they heard how many things He was doing, came to Him. [9]So He told His disciples that a small boat should be kept ready for Him because of the multitude, lest they should crush Him. [10]For He healed many, so that as many as had afflictions pressed about Him to touch Him.

3:5 [a]NU-Text omits *as whole as the other.*

THE MESSAGE

FEASTING OR FASTING?

18 The disciples of John and the disciples of the Pharisees made a practice of fasting. Some people confronted Jesus: "Why do the followers of John and the Pharisees take on the discipline of fasting, but your followers don't?"

19-20 Jesus said, "When you're celebrating a wedding, you don't skimp on the cake and wine. You feast. Later you may need to pull in your belt, but not now. As long as the bride and groom are with you, you have a good time. No one throws cold water on a friendly bonfire. This is Kingdom Come!"

21-22 He went on, "No one cuts up a fine silk scarf to patch old work clothes; you want fabrics that match. And you don't put your wine in cracked bottles."

23-24 One Sabbath day he was walking through a field of ripe grain. As his disciples made a path, they pulled off heads of grain. The Pharisees told on them to Jesus: "Look, your disciples are breaking Sabbath rules!"

25-28 Jesus said, "Really? Haven't you ever read what David did when he was hungry, along with those who were with him? How he entered the sanctuary and ate fresh bread off the altar, with the Chief Priest Abiathar right there watching—holy bread that no one but priests were allowed to eat—and handed it out to his companions?" Then Jesus said, "The Sabbath was made to serve us; we weren't made to serve the Sabbath. The Son of Man is no lackey to the Sabbath. He's in charge!"

DOING GOOD ON THE SABBATH

1-3 3 Then he went back in the meeting place where he found a man with a crippled hand. The Pharisees had their eyes on Jesus to see if he would heal him, hoping to catch him in a Sabbath infraction. He said to the man with the crippled hand, "Stand here where we can see you."

4 Then he spoke to the people: "What kind of action suits the Sabbath best? Doing good or doing evil? Helping people or leaving them helpless?" No one said a word.

5-6 He looked them in the eye, one after another, angry now, furious at their hard-nosed religion. He said to the man, "Hold out your hand." He held it out—it was as good as new! The Pharisees got out as fast as they could, sputtering about how they would join forces with Herod's followers and ruin him.

THE TWELVE APOSTLES

7-10 Jesus went off with his disciples to the sea to get away. But a huge crowd from Galilee trailed after them—also from Judea, Jerusalem, Idumea, across the Jordan, and around Tyre and Sidon—swarms of people who had heard the reports and had come to see for themselves. He told his disciples to get a boat ready so he wouldn't be trampled by the crowd. He had healed many people, and now everyone who had something wrong was pushing and shoving to get near and touch him.

New King James Version

11And the unclean spirits, whenever they saw
Him, fell down before Him and cried out, say-
ing, "You are the Son of God." 12But He sternly
warned them that they should not make Him
known.

The Twelve Apostles

13And He went up on the mountain and
called to *Him* those He Himself wanted. And
they came to Him. 14Then He appointed twelve,[a]
that they might be with Him and that He might
send them out to preach, 15and to have power to
heal sicknesses and[a] to cast out demons: 16Si-
mon,[a] to whom He gave the name Peter; 17James
the *son* of Zebedee and John the brother of
James, to whom He gave the name Boanerges,
that is, "Sons of Thunder"; 18Andrew, Philip,
Bartholomew, Matthew, Thomas, James the *son*
of Alphaeus, Thaddaeus, Simon the Cananite;
19and Judas Iscariot, who also betrayed Him.
And they went into a house.

A House Divided Cannot Stand

20Then the multitude came together again, so
that they could not so much as eat bread. 21But
when His own people heard *about this,* they
went out to lay hold of Him, for they said, "He is
out of His mind."

22And the scribes who came down from
Jerusalem said, "He has Beelzebub," and, "By
the ruler of the demons He casts out demons."

23So He called them to *Himself* and said to
them in parables: "How can Satan cast out Sa-
tan? 24If a kingdom is divided against itself, that
kingdom cannot stand. 25And if a house is di-
vided against itself, that house cannot stand.
26And if Satan has risen up against himself, and
is divided, he cannot stand, but has an end. 27No
one can enter a strong man's house and plunder
his goods, unless he first binds the strong man.
And then he will plunder his house.

The Unpardonable Sin

28"Assuredly, I say to you, all sins will be for-
given the sons of men, and whatever blas-
phemies they may utter; 29but he who blas-
phemes against the Holy Spirit never has
forgiveness, but is subject to eternal condemna-
tion"— 30because they said, "He has an unclean
spirit."

Jesus' Mother and Brothers Send for Him

31Then His brothers and His mother came,
and standing outside they sent to Him, calling
Him. 32And a multitude was sitting around Him;
and they said to Him, "Look, Your mother and
Your brothers[a] are outside seeking You."

3:14 [a]NU-Text adds *whom He also named apostles.* **3:15** [a]NU-Text omits *to heal sicknesses and.* **3:16** [a]NU-Text reads *and He appointed the twelve: Simon. . . .* **3:32** [a]NU-Text and M-Text add *and Your sisters.*

The Message

11-12 Evil spirits, when they recognized him, fell down and cried out, "You are the Son of God!" But Jesus would have none of it. He shut them up, forbidding them to identify him in public.

13-19 He climbed a mountain and invited those he wanted with him. They climbed together. He settled on twelve, and designated them apostles. The plan was that they would be with him, and he would send them out to proclaim the Word and give them authority to banish demons. These are the Twelve:

Simon (Jesus later named him Peter, meaning "Rock"),
James, son of Zebedee,
John, brother of James (Jesus nicknamed the Zebedee brothers Boanerges, meaning "Sons of Thunder"),
Andrew,
Philip,
Bartholomew,
Matthew,
Thomas,
James, son of Alphaeus,
Thaddaeus,
Simon the Canaanite,
Judas Iscariot (who betrayed him).

Satan Fighting Satan?

20-21 Jesus came home and, as usual, a crowd gathered—so many making demands on him that there wasn't even time to eat. His friends heard what was going on and went to rescue him, by force if necessary. They suspected he was getting carried away with himself.

22-27 The religion scholars from Jerusalem came down spreading rumors that he was working black magic, using devil tricks to impress them with spiritual power. Jesus confronted their slander with a story: "Does it make sense to send a devil to catch a devil, to use Satan to get rid of Satan? A constantly squabbling family disintegrates. If Satan were fighting Satan, there soon wouldn't be any Satan left. Do you think it's possible in broad daylight to enter the house of an awake, able-bodied man, and walk off with his possessions unless you tie him up first? Tie him up, though, and you can clean him out.

28-30 "Listen to this carefully. I'm warning you. There's nothing done or said that can't be forgiven. But if you persist in your slanders against God's Holy Spirit, you are repudiating the very One who forgives, sawing off the branch on which you're sitting, severing by your own perversity all connection with the One who forgives." He gave this warning because they were accusing him of being in league with Evil.

Jesus' Mother and Brothers

31-32 Just then his mother and brothers showed up. Standing outside, they relayed a message that they wanted a word with him. He was surrounded by the crowd when he was given the message, "Your mother and brothers and sisters are outside looking for you."

New King James Version

33But He answered them, saying, "Who is My mother, or My brothers?" 34And He looked around in a circle at those who sat about Him, and said, "Here are My mother and My brothers! 35For whoever does the will of God is My brother and My sister and mother."

The Parable of the Sower

4 And again He began to teach by the sea. And a great multitude was gathered to Him, so that He got into a boat and sat *in it* on the sea; and the whole multitude was on the land facing the sea. 2Then He taught them many things by parables, and said to them in His teaching:

3"Listen! Behold, a sower went out to sow. 4And it happened, as he sowed, *that* some *seed* fell by the wayside; and the birds of the air[a] came and devoured it. 5Some fell on stony ground, where it did not have much earth; and immediately it sprang up because it had no depth of earth. 6But when the sun was up it was scorched, and because it had no root it withered away. 7And some *seed* fell among thorns; and the thorns grew up and choked it, and it yielded no crop. 8But other *seed* fell on good ground and yielded a crop that sprang up, increased and produced: some thirtyfold, some sixty, and some a hundred."

9And He said to them,[a] "He who has ears to hear, let him hear!"

The Purpose of Parables

10But when He was alone, those around Him with the twelve asked Him about the parable. 11And He said to them, "To you it has been given to know the mystery of the kingdom of God; but to those who are outside, all things come in parables, 12so that

'Seeing they may see and not perceive,
And hearing they may hear and not
understand;
Lest they should turn,
And their sins be forgiven them.' "[a]

The Parable of the Sower Explained

13And He said to them, "Do you not understand this parable? How then will you understand all the parables? 14The sower sows the word. 15And these are the ones by the wayside where the word is sown. When they hear, Satan comes immediately and takes away the word that was sown in their hearts. 16These likewise are the ones sown on stony ground who, when they hear the word, immediately receive it with gladness; 17and they have no root in themselves, and so endure only for a time. Afterward, when tribulation or persecution arises for the word's sake, immediately they stumble. 18Now these are the ones sown among thorns; *they are* the ones who hear the word, 19and the cares of this world, the deceitfulness of riches, and the desires for other things entering in choke the word, and it becomes unfruitful. 20But these are the ones sown on good ground, those who hear the word, accept *it*, and bear fruit: some thirtyfold, some sixty, and some a hundred."

4:4 [a]NU-Text and M-Text omit *of the air.* 4:9 [a]NU-Text and M-Text omit *to them.* 4:12 [a]Isaiah 6:9, 10

The Message

33-35 Jesus responded, "Who do you think are my mother and brothers?" Looking around, taking in everyone seated around him, he said, "Right here, right in front of you—my mother and my brothers. Obedience is thicker than blood. The person who obeys God's will is my brother and sister and mother."

The Story of the Scattered Seed

1-2 4 He went back to teaching by the sea. A crowd built up to such a great size that he had to get into an offshore boat, using the boat as a pulpit as the people pushed to the water's edge. He taught by using stories, many stories.

3-8 "Listen. What do you make of this? A farmer planted seed. As he scattered the seed, some of it fell on the road and birds ate it. Some fell in the gravel; it sprouted quickly but didn't put down roots, so when the sun came up it withered just as quickly. Some fell in the weeds; as it came up, it was strangled among the weeds and nothing came of it. Some fell on good earth and came up with a flourish, producing a harvest exceeding his wildest dreams.

9 "Are you listening to this? Really listening?"

10-12 When they were off by themselves, those who were close to him, along with the Twelve, asked about the stories. He told them, "You've been given insight into God's kingdom—you know how it works. But to those who can't see it yet, everything comes in stories, creating readiness, nudging them toward receptive insight. These are people—

Whose eyes are open but don't see a thing,
Whose ears are open but don't understand a word,
Who avoid making an about-face and getting forgiven."

13 He continued, "Do you see how this story works? All my stories work this way.

14-15 "The farmer plants the Word. Some people are like the seed that falls on the hardened soil of the road. No sooner do they hear the Word than Satan snatches away what has been planted in them.

16-17 "And some are like the seed that lands in the gravel. When they first hear the Word, they respond with great enthusiasm. But there is such shallow soil of character that when the emotions wear off and some difficulty arrives, there is nothing to show for it.

18-19 "The seed cast in the weeds represents the ones who hear the kingdom news but are overwhelmed with worries about all the things they have to do and all the things they want to get. The stress strangles what they heard, and nothing comes of it.

20 "But the seed planted in the good earth represents those who hear the Word, embrace it, and produce a harvest beyond their wildest dreams."

New King James Version

Light Under a Basket

[21]Also He said to them, "Is a lamp brought to be put under a basket or under a bed? Is it not to be set on a lampstand? [22]For there is nothing hidden which will not be revealed, nor has anything been kept secret but that it should come to light. [23]If anyone has ears to hear, let him hear."

[24]Then He said to them, "Take heed what you hear. With the same measure you use, it will be measured to you; and to you who hear, more will be given. [25]For whoever has, to him more will be given; but whoever does not have, even what he has will be taken away from him."

The Parable of the Growing Seed

[26]And He said, "The kingdom of God is as if a man should scatter seed on the ground, [27]and should sleep by night and rise by day, and the seed should sprout and grow, he himself does not know how. [28]For the earth yields crops by itself: first the blade, then the head, after that the full grain in the head. [29]But when the grain ripens, immediately he puts in the sickle, because the harvest has come."

The Parable of the Mustard Seed

[30]Then He said, "To what shall we liken the kingdom of God? Or with what parable shall we picture it? [31]*It is* like a mustard seed which, when it is sown on the ground, is smaller than all the seeds on earth; [32]but when it is sown, it grows up and becomes greater than all herbs, and shoots out large branches, so that the birds of the air may nest under its shade."

Jesus' Use of Parables

[33]And with many such parables He spoke the word to them as they were able to hear *it.* [34]But without a parable He did not speak to them. And when they were alone, He explained all things to His disciples.

Wind and Wave Obey Jesus

[35]On the same day, when evening had come, He said to them, "Let us cross over to the other side." [36]Now when they had left the multitude, they took Him along in the boat as He was. And other little boats were also with Him. [37]And a great windstorm arose, and the waves beat into the boat, so that it was already filling. [38]But He was in the stern, asleep on a pillow. And they awoke Him and said to Him, "Teacher, do You not care that we are perishing?"

[39]Then He arose and rebuked the wind, and said to the sea, "Peace, be still!" And the wind ceased and there was a great calm. [40]But He said to them, "Why are you so fearful? How *is it* that you have no faith?"[a] [41]And they feared exceedingly, and said to one another, "Who can this be, that even the wind and the sea obey Him!"

A Demon-Possessed Man Healed

5 Then they came to the other side of the sea, to the country of the Gadarenes.[a] [2]And when He had come out of the boat, immediately there met Him out of the tombs a man with an unclean spirit, [3]who had *his* dwelling among the

4:40 [a]NU-Text reads *Have you still no faith?* **5:1** [a]NU-Text reads *Gerasenes.*

The Message

Giving, Not Getting

21-22 Jesus went on: "Does anyone bring a lamp
home and put it under a washtub or beneath
the bed? Don't you put it up on a table or on
the mantel? We're not keeping secrets, we're
telling them; we're not hiding things, we're
bringing them out into the open.

23 "Are you listening to this? Really listen-
ing?

24-25 "Listen carefully to what I am saying—
and be wary of the shrewd advice that tells
you how to get ahead in the world on your
own. Giving, not getting, is the way. Gen-
erosity begets generosity. Stinginess impov-
erishes."

Never Without a Story

26-29 Then Jesus said, "God's kingdom is like
seed thrown on a field by a man who then
goes to bed and forgets about it. The seed
sprouts and grows—he has no idea how it
happens. The earth does it all without his
help: first a green stem of grass, then a bud,
then the ripened grain. When the grain is
fully formed, he reaps—harvest time!

30-32 "How can we picture God's kingdom?
What kind of story can we use? It's like a
pine nut. When it lands on the ground it is
quite small as seeds go, yet once it is planted
it grows into a huge pine tree with thick
branches. Eagles nest in it."

33-34 With many stories like these, he pre-
sented his message to them, fitting the sto-
ries to their experience and maturity. He
was never without a story when he spoke.
When he was alone with his disciples, he
went over everything, sorting out the tan-
gles, untying the knots.

The Wind Ran Out of Breath

35-38 Late that day he said to them, "Let's go
across to the other side." They took him in
the boat as he was. Other boats came along.
A huge storm came up. Waves poured into
the boat, threatening to sink it. And Jesus
was in the stern, head on a pillow, sleeping!
They roused him, saying, "Teacher, is it
nothing to you that we're going down?"

39-40 Awake now, he told the wind to pipe
down and said to the sea, "Quiet! Settle
down!" The wind ran out of breath; the sea
became smooth as glass. Jesus reprimanded
the disciples: "Why are you such cowards?
Don't you have any faith at all?"

41 They were in absolute awe, staggered.
"Who is this, anyway?" they asked. "Wind
and sea at his beck and call!"

The Madman

1-5 **5** They arrived on the other side of the sea in
the country of the Gerasenes. As Jesus got
out of the boat, a madman from the cemetery
came up to him. He lived there among the
tombs and graves. No one could restrain
him—he couldn't be chained, couldn't be

New King James Version

tombs; and no one could bind him,[a] not even with chains, 4because he had often been bound with shackles and chains. And the chains had been pulled apart by him, and the shackles broken in pieces; neither could anyone tame him. 5And always, night and day, he was in the mountains and in the tombs, crying out and cutting himself with stones.

6When he saw Jesus from afar, he ran and worshiped Him. 7And he cried out with a loud voice and said, "What have I to do with You, Jesus, Son of the Most High God? I implore You by God that You do not torment me."

8For He said to him, "Come out of the man, unclean spirit!" 9Then He asked him, "What *is* your name?"

And he answered, saying, "My name *is* Legion; for we are many." 10Also he begged Him earnestly that He would not send them out of the country.

11Now a large herd of swine was feeding there near the mountains. 12So all the demons begged Him, saying, "Send us to the swine, that we may enter them." 13And at once Jesus[a] gave them permission. Then the unclean spirits went out and entered the swine (there were about two thousand); and the herd ran violently down the steep place into the sea, and drowned in the sea.

14So those who fed the swine fled, and they told *it* in the city and in the country. And they went out to see what it was that had happened. 15Then they came to Jesus, and saw the one *who had been* demon-possessed and had the legion, sitting and clothed and in his right mind. And they were afraid. 16And those who saw it told them how it happened to him *who had been* demon-possessed, and about the swine. 17Then they began to plead with Him to depart from their region.

18And when He got into the boat, he who had been demon-possessed begged Him that he might be with Him. 19However, Jesus did not permit him, but said to him, "Go home to your friends, and tell them what great things the Lord has done for you, and how He has had compassion on you." 20And he departed and began to proclaim in Decapolis all that Jesus had done for him; and all marveled.

A Girl Restored to Life and a Woman Healed

21Now when Jesus had crossed over again by boat to the other side, a great multitude gathered to Him; and He was by the sea. 22And behold, one of the rulers of the synagogue came, Jairus by name. And when he saw Him, he fell at His feet 23and begged Him earnestly, saying, "My little daughter lies at the point of death. Come and lay Your hands on her, that she may be healed, and she will live." 24So *Jesus* went with him, and a great multitude followed Him and thronged Him.

25Now a certain woman had a flow of blood for twelve years, 26and had suffered many things from many physicians. She had spent all that she had and was no better, but rather grew worse. 27When she heard about Jesus, she came behind *Him* in the crowd and touched His gar-

5:3 [a]NU-Text adds *anymore.* **5:13** [a]NU-Text reads *And He gave.*

The Message

tied down. He had been tied up many times with chains and ropes, but he broke the chains, snapped the ropes. No one was strong enough to tame him. Night and day he roamed through the graves and the hills, screaming out and slashing himself with sharp stones.

6-8 When he saw Jesus a long way off, he ran and bowed in worship before him—then bellowed in protest, "What business do you have, Jesus, Son of the High God, messing with me? I swear to God, don't give me a hard time!" (Jesus had just commanded the tormenting evil spirit, "Out! Get out of the man!")

9-10 Jesus asked him, "Tell me your name."

He replied, "My name is Mob. I'm a rioting mob." Then he desperately begged Jesus not to banish them from the country.

11-13 A large herd of pigs was browsing and rooting on a nearby hill. The demons begged him, "Send us to the pigs so we can live in them." Jesus gave the order. But it was even worse for the pigs than for the man. Crazed, they stampeded over a cliff into the sea and drowned.

14-15 Those tending the pigs, scared to death, bolted and told their story in town and country. Everyone wanted to see what had happened. They came up to Jesus and saw the madman sitting there wearing decent clothes and making sense, no longer a walking madhouse of a man.

16-17 Those who had seen it told the others what had happened to the demon-possessed man and the pigs. At first they were in awe—and then they were upset, upset over the drowned pigs. They demanded that Jesus leave and not come back.

18-20 As Jesus was getting into the boat, the demon-delivered man begged to go along, but he wouldn't let him. Jesus said, "Go home to your own people. Tell them your story—what the Master did, how he had mercy on you." The man went back and began to preach in the Ten Towns area about what Jesus had done for him. He was the talk of the town.

A Risk of Faith

21-24 After Jesus crossed over by boat, a large crowd met him at the seaside. One of the meeting-place leaders named Jairus came. When he saw Jesus, he fell to his knees, beside himself as he begged, "My dear daughter is at death's door. Come and lay hands on her so she will get well and live." Jesus went with him, the whole crowd tagging along, pushing and jostling him.

25-29 A woman who had suffered a condition of hemorrhaging for twelve years—a long succession of physicians had treated her, and treated her badly, taking all her money and leaving her worse off than before—had heard about Jesus. She slipped in from behind and touched his robe. She was thinking

NEW KING JAMES VERSION

ment. [28]For she said, "If only I may touch His clothes, I shall be made well."

[29]Immediately the fountain of her blood was dried up, and she felt in *her* body that she was healed of the affliction. [30]And Jesus, immediately knowing in Himself that power had gone out of Him, turned around in the crowd and said, "Who touched My clothes?"

[31]But His disciples said to Him, "You see the multitude thronging You, and You say, 'Who touched Me?' "

[32]And He looked around to see her who had done this thing. [33]But the woman, fearing and trembling, knowing what had happened to her, came and fell down before Him and told Him the whole truth. [34]And He said to her, "Daughter, your faith has made you well. Go in peace, and be healed of your affliction."

[35]While He was still speaking, *some* came from the ruler of the synagogue's *house* who said, "Your daughter is dead. Why trouble the Teacher any further?"

[36]As soon as Jesus heard the word that was spoken, He said to the ruler of the synagogue, "Do not be afraid; only believe." [37]And He permitted no one to follow Him except Peter, James, and John the brother of James. [38]Then He came to the house of the ruler of the synagogue, and saw a tumult and those who wept and wailed loudly. [39]When He came in, He said to them, "Why make this commotion and weep? The child is not dead, but sleeping."

[40]And they ridiculed Him. But when He had put them all outside, He took the father and the mother of the child, and those *who were* with Him, and entered where the child was lying. [41]Then He took the child by the hand, and said to her, "Talitha, cumi," which is translated, "Little girl, I say to you, arise." [42]Immediately the girl arose and walked, for she was twelve years *of age.* And they were overcome with great amazement. [43]But He commanded them strictly that no one should know it, and said that *something* should be given her to eat.

JESUS REJECTED AT NAZARETH

6 Then He went out from there and came to His own country, and His disciples followed Him. [2]And when the Sabbath had come, He began to teach in the synagogue. And many hearing *Him* were astonished, saying, "Where *did* this Man *get* these things? And what wisdom *is* this which is given to Him, that such mighty works are performed by His hands! [3]Is this not the carpenter, the Son of Mary, and brother of James, Joses, Judas, and Simon? And are not His sisters here with us?" So they were offended at Him.

THE MESSAGE

to herself, "If I can put a finger on his robe, I can get well." The moment she did it, the flow of blood dried up. She could feel the change and knew her plague was over and done with.

30 At the same moment, Jesus felt energy discharging from him. He turned around to the crowd and asked, "Who touched my robe?"

31 His disciples said, "What are you talking about? With this crowd pushing and jostling you, you're asking, 'Who touched me?' Dozens have touched you!"

32-33 But he went on asking, looking around to see who had done it. The woman, knowing what had happened, knowing she was the one, stepped up in fear and trembling, knelt before him, and gave him the whole story.

34 Jesus said to her, "Daughter, you took a risk of faith, and now you're healed and whole. Live well, live blessed! Be healed of your plague."

35 While he was still talking, some people came from the leader's house and told him, "Your daughter is dead. Why bother the Teacher any more?"

36 Jesus overheard what they were talking about and said to the leader, "Don't listen to them; just trust me."

37-40 He permitted no one to go in with him except Peter, James, and John. They entered the leader's house and pushed their way through the gossips looking for a story and neighbors bringing in casseroles. Jesus was abrupt: "Why all this busybody grief and gossip? This child isn't dead; she's sleeping." Provoked to sarcasm, they told him he didn't know what he was talking about.

40-43 But when he had sent them all out, he took the child's father and mother, along with his companions, and entered the child's room. He clasped the girl's hand and said, "*Talitha koum*," which means, "Little girl, get up." At that, she was up and walking around! This girl was twelve years of age. They, of course, were all beside themselves with joy. He gave them strict orders that no one was to know what had taken place in that room. Then he said, "Give her something to eat."

JUST A CARPENTER

1-2 **6** He left there and returned to his hometown. His disciples came along. On the Sabbath, he gave a lecture in the meeting place. He made a real hit, impressing everyone. "We had no idea he was this good!" they said. "How did he get so wise all of a sudden, get such ability?"

3 But in the next breath they were cutting him down: "He's just a carpenter—Mary's boy. We've known him since he was a kid. We know his brothers, James, Justus, Jude, and Simon, and his sisters. Who does he think he is?" They tripped over what little they knew about him and fell, sprawling. And they never got any further.

NEW KING JAMES VERSION

4But Jesus said to them, "A prophet is not
without honor except in his own country, among
his own relatives, and in his own house." 5Now
He could do no mighty work there, except that
He laid His hands on a few sick people and
healed *them.* 6And He marveled because of
their unbelief. Then He went about the villages
in a circuit, teaching.

SENDING OUT THE TWELVE

7And He called the twelve to *Himself,* and be-
gan to send them out two *by* two, and gave them
power over unclean spirits. 8He commanded
them to take nothing for the journey except a
staff—no bag, no bread, no copper in *their*
money belts— 9but to wear sandals, and not to
put on two tunics.

10Also He said to them, "In whatever place
you enter a house, stay there till you depart
from that place. 11And whoever[a] will not receive
you nor hear you, when you depart from there,
shake off the dust under your feet as a testi-
mony against them.[b] Assuredly, I say to you, it
will be more tolerable for Sodom and Gomorrah
in the day of judgment than for that city!"

12So they went out and preached that *people*
should repent. 13And they cast out many
demons, and anointed with oil many who were
sick, and healed *them.*

JOHN THE BAPTIST BEHEADED

14Now King Herod heard *of Him,* for His
name had become well known. And he said,
"John the Baptist is risen from the dead, and
therefore these powers are at work in him."
15Others said, "It is Elijah."

And others said, "It is the Prophet, or[a] like
one of the prophets."

16But when Herod heard, he said, "This is
John, whom I beheaded; he has been raised
from the dead!" 17For Herod himself had sent
and laid hold of John, and bound him in prison
for the sake of Herodias, his brother Philip's
wife; for he had married her. 18Because John
had said to Herod, "It is not lawful for you to
have your brother's wife."

19Therefore Herodias held it against him and
wanted to kill him, but she could not; 20for
Herod feared John, knowing that he *was* a just
and holy man, and he protected him. And when
he heard him, he did many things, and heard
him gladly.

21Then an opportune day came when Herod
on his birthday gave a feast for his nobles, the
high officers, and the chief *men* of Galilee.
22And when Herodias' daughter herself came in
and danced, and pleased Herod and those who
sat with him, the king said to the girl, "Ask me
whatever you want, and I will give *it* to you."
23He also swore to her, "Whatever you ask me, I
will give you, up to half my kingdom."

24So she went out and said to her mother,
"What shall I ask?"

And she said, "The head of John the Baptist!"
25Immediately she came in with haste to the
king and asked, saying, "I want you to give me at
once the head of John the Baptist on a platter."

6:11 [a]NU-Text reads *whatever place.* [b]NU-Text omits the rest of this verse. **6:15** [a]NU-Text and M-Text omit *or.*

THE MESSAGE

4-6 Jesus told them, "A prophet has little
honor in his hometown, among his relatives,
on the streets he played in as a child." Jesus
wasn't able to do much of anything there—
he laid hands on a few sick people and
healed them, that's all. He couldn't get over
their stubbornness. He left and made a cir-
cuit of the other villages, teaching.

THE TWELVE

7-8 Jesus called the Twelve to him, and sent
them out in pairs. He gave them authority
and power to deal with the evil opposition.
He sent them off with these instructions:

8-9 "Don't think you need a lot of extra
equipment for this. *You* are the equipment.
No special appeals for funds. Keep it simple.

10 "And no luxury inns. Get a modest place
and be content there until you leave.

11 "If you're not welcomed, not listened to,
quietly withdraw. Don't make a scene.
Shrug your shoulders and be on your way."

12-13 Then they were on the road. They
preached with joyful urgency that life can
be radically different; right and left they
sent the demons packing; they brought well-
ness to the sick, anointing their bodies, heal-
ing their spirits.

THE DEATH OF JOHN

14 King Herod heard of all this, for by this time
the name of Jesus was on everyone's lips.
He said, "This has to be John the Baptizer
come back from the dead—that's why he's
able to work miracles!"

15 Others said, "No, it's Elijah."

Others said, "He's a prophet, just like one
of the old-time prophets."

16 But Herod wouldn't budge: "It's John,
sure enough. I cut off his head, and now he's
back, alive."

17-20 Herod was the one who had ordered the ar-
rest of John, put him in chains, and sent him to
prison at the nagging of Herodias, his brother
Philip's wife. For John had provoked Herod by
naming his relationship with Herodias "adul-
tery." Herodias, smoldering with hate, wanted
to kill him, but didn't dare because Herod was
in awe of John. Convinced that he was a holy
man, he gave him special treatment. When-
ever he listened to him he was miserable with
guilt—and yet he couldn't stay away. Some-
thing in John kept pulling him back.

21-22 But a portentous day arrived when Herod
threw a birthday party, inviting all the brass
and bluebloods in Galilee. Herodias's
daughter entered the banquet hall and
danced for the guests. She dazzled Herod
and the guests.

22-23 The king said to the girl, "Ask me any-
thing. I'll give you anything you want." Car-
ried away, he kept on, "I swear, I'll split my
kingdom with you if you say so!"

24 She went back to her mother and said,
"What should I ask for?"

"Ask for the head of John the Baptizer."

25 Excited, she ran back to the king and
said, "I want the head of John the Baptizer
served up on a platter. And I want it now!"

New King James Version

26And the king was exceedingly sorry; *yet,* because of the oaths and because of those who sat with him, he did not want to refuse her. 27Immediately the king sent an executioner and commanded his head to be brought. And he went and beheaded him in prison, 28brought his head on a platter, and gave it to the girl; and the girl gave it to her mother. 29When his disciples heard *of it,* they came and took away his corpse and laid it in a tomb.

Feeding the Five Thousand

30Then the apostles gathered to Jesus and told Him all things, both what they had done and what they had taught. 31And He said to them, "Come aside by yourselves to a deserted place and rest a while." For there were many coming and going, and they did not even have time to eat. 32So they departed to a deserted place in the boat by themselves.

33But the multitudes[a] saw them departing, and many knew Him and ran there on foot from all the cities. They arrived before them and came together to Him. 34And Jesus, when He came out, saw a great multitude and was moved with compassion for them, because they were like sheep not having a shepherd. So He began to teach them many things. 35When the day was now far spent, His disciples came to Him and said, "This is a deserted place, and already the hour *is* late. 36Send them away, that they may go into the surrounding country and villages and buy themselves bread;[a] for they have nothing to eat."

37But He answered and said to them, "You give them something to eat."

And they said to Him, "Shall we go and buy two hundred denarii worth of bread and give them *something* to eat?"

38But He said to them, "How many loaves do you have? Go and see."

And when they found out they said, "Five, and two fish."

39Then He commanded them to make them all sit down in groups on the green grass. 40So they sat down in ranks, in hundreds and in fifties. 41And when He had taken the five loaves and the two fish, He looked up to heaven, blessed and broke the loaves, and gave *them* to His disciples to set before them; and the two fish He divided among *them* all. 42So they all ate and were filled. 43And they took up twelve baskets full of fragments and of the fish. 44Now those who had eaten the loaves were about[a] five thousand men.

Jesus Walks on the Sea

45Immediately He made His disciples get into the boat and go before Him to the other side, to Bethsaida, while He sent the multitude away. 46And when He had sent them away, He departed to the mountain to pray. 47Now when evening came, the boat was in the middle of the sea; and He *was* alone on the land. 48Then He saw them straining at rowing, for the wind was against them. Now about the fourth watch of the

6:33 [a]NU-Text and M-Text read *they.* **6:36** [a]NU-Text reads *something to eat* and omits the rest of this verse. **6:44** [a]NU-Text and M-Text omit *about.*

The Message

26-29 That sobered the king up fast. But unwill-
ing to lose face with his guests, he caved in
and let her have her wish. The king sent the
executioner off to the prison with orders to
bring back John's head. He went, cut off
John's head, brought it back on a platter,
and presented it to the girl, who gave it to
her mother. When John's disciples heard
about this, they came and got the body and
gave it a decent burial.

Supper for Five Thousand

30-31 The apostles then rendezvoused with Jesus
and reported on all that they had done and
taught. Jesus said, "Come off by yourselves;
let's take a break and get a little rest." For
there was constant coming and going. They
didn't even have time to eat.
32-34 So they got in the boat and went off to a
remote place by themselves. Someone saw
them going and the word got around. From
the surrounding towns people went out on
foot, running, and got there ahead of them.
When Jesus arrived, he saw this huge
crowd. At the sight of them, his heart
broke—like sheep with no shepherd they
were. He went right to work teaching them.
35-36 When his disciples thought this had gone
on long enough—it was now quite late in the
day—they interrupted: "We are a long way
out in the country, and it's very late. Pro-
nounce a benediction and send these folks
off so they can get some supper."
37 Jesus said, "You do it. Fix supper for
them."

They replied, "Are you serious? You want
us to go spend a fortune on food for their
supper?"
38 But he was quite serious. "How many
loaves of bread do you have? Take an inven-
tory."

That didn't take long. "Five," they said,
"plus two fish."
39-44 Jesus got them all to sit down in groups
of fifty or a hundred—they looked like a
patchwork quilt of wildflowers spread out
on the green grass! He took the five loaves
and two fish, lifted his face to heaven in
prayer, blessed, broke, and gave the bread to
the disciples, and the disciples in turn gave
it to the people. He did the same with the
fish. They all ate their fill. The disciples
gathered twelve baskets of leftovers. More
than five thousand were at the supper.

Walking on the Sea

45-46 As soon as the meal was finished, Jesus in-
sisted that the disciples get in the boat and
go on ahead across to Bethsaida while he
dismissed the congregation. After sending
them off, he climbed a mountain to pray.
47-49 Late at night, the boat was far out at sea;
Jesus was still by himself on land. He could
see his men struggling with the oars, the
wind having come up against them. At
about four o'clock in the morning, Jesus

NEW KING JAMES VERSION

night He came to them, walking on the sea, and would have passed them by. 49And when they saw Him walking on the sea, they supposed it was a ghost, and cried out; 50for they all saw Him and were troubled. But immediately He talked with them and said to them, "Be of good cheer! It is I; do not be afraid." 51Then He went up into the boat to them, and the wind ceased. And they were greatly amazed in themselves beyond measure, and marveled. 52For they had not understood about the loaves, because their heart was hardened.

MANY TOUCH HIM AND ARE MADE WELL

53When they had crossed over, they came to the land of Gennesaret and anchored there. 54And when they came out of the boat, immediately the people recognized Him, 55ran through that whole surrounding region, and began to carry about on beds those who were sick to wherever they heard He was. 56Wherever He entered, into villages, cities, or the country, they laid the sick in the marketplaces, and begged Him that they might just touch the hem of His garment. And as many as touched Him were made well.

DEFILEMENT COMES FROM WITHIN

7 Then the Pharisees and some of the scribes came together to Him, having come from Jerusalem. 2Now when[a] they saw some of His disciples eat bread with defiled, that is, with unwashed hands, they found fault. 3For the Pharisees and all the Jews do not eat unless they wash *their* hands in a special way, holding the tradition of the elders. 4*When they come* from the marketplace, they do not eat unless they wash. And there are many other things which they have received and hold, *like* the washing of cups, pitchers, copper vessels, and couches.

5Then the Pharisees and scribes asked Him, "Why do Your disciples not walk according to the tradition of the elders, but eat bread with unwashed hands?"

6He answered and said to them, "Well did Isaiah prophesy of you hypocrites, as it is written:

'This people honors Me with their lips,
But their heart is far from Me.
7*And in vain they worship Me,*
Teaching as doctrines the commandments of men.'[a]

8For laying aside the commandment of God, you hold the tradition of men[a]—the washing of pitchers and cups, and many other such things you do."

9He said to them, "*All too* well you reject the commandment of God, that you may keep your tradition. 10For Moses said, *'Honor your father and your mother'*;[a] and, *'He who curses father or mother, let him be put to death.'*[b] 11But you say, 'If a man says to his father or mother, "Whatever profit you might have received from me *is* Corban"—' (that is, a gift *to God*), 12then

7:2 [a]NU-Text omits *when* and *they found fault.* **7:7** [a]Isaiah 29:13 **7:8** [a]NU-Text omits the rest of this verse. **7:10** [a]Exodus 20:12; Deuteronomy 5:16 [b]Exodus 21:17

THE MESSAGE

came toward them, walking on the sea. He intended to go right by them. But when they saw him walking on the sea, they thought it was a ghost and screamed, scared out of their wits.

50-52 Jesus was quick to comfort them: "Courage! It's me. Don't be afraid." As soon as he climbed into the boat, the wind died down. They were stunned, shaking their heads, wondering what was going on. They didn't understand what he had done at the supper. None of this had yet penetrated their hearts.

53-56 They beached the boat at Gennesaret and tied up at the landing. As soon as they got out of the boat, word got around fast. People ran this way and that, bringing their sick on stretchers to where they heard he was. Wherever he went, village or town or country crossroads, they brought their sick to the marketplace and begged him to let them touch the edge of his coat—that's all. And whoever touched him became well.

THE SOURCE OF YOUR POLLUTION

1-4 7 The Pharisees, along with some religion scholars who had come from Jerusalem, gathered around him. They noticed that some of his disciples weren't being careful with ritual washings before meals. The Pharisees—Jews in general, in fact—would never eat a meal without going through the motions of a ritual hand-washing, with an especially vigorous scrubbing if they had just come from the market (to say nothing of the scourings they'd give jugs and pots and pans).

5 The Pharisees and religion scholars asked, "Why do your disciples flout the rules, showing up at meals without washing their hands?"

6-8 Jesus answered, "Isaiah was right about frauds like you, hit the bull's-eye in fact:

These people make a big show of saying
the right thing,
but their heart isn't in it.
They act like they are worshiping me,
but they don't mean it.
They just use me as a cover
for teaching whatever suits their
fancy,
Ditching God's command
and taking up the latest fads."

9-13 He went on, "Well, good for you. You get rid of God's command so you won't be inconvenienced in following the religious fashions! Moses said, 'Respect your father and mother,' and, 'Anyone denouncing father or mother should be killed.' But you weasel out of that by saying that it's perfectly acceptable to say to father or mother, 'Gift! What I owed you I've given as a gift to

NEW KING JAMES VERSION

you no longer let him do anything for his father
or his mother, 13making the word of God of no
effect through your tradition which you have
handed down. And many such things you do."
14When He had called all the multitude to
Himself, He said to them, "Hear Me, everyone,
and understand: 15There is nothing that enters a
man from outside which can defile him; but the
things which come out of him, those are the
things that defile a man. 16If anyone has ears to
hear, let him hear!"[a]
17When He had entered a house away from
the crowd, His disciples asked Him concerning
the parable. 18So He said to them, "Are you thus
without understanding also? Do you not perceive
that whatever enters a man from outside cannot
defile him, 19because it does not enter his heart
but his stomach, and is eliminated, *thus* purifying
all foods?"[a] 20And He said, "What comes out of a
man, that defiles a man. 21For from within, out of
the heart of men, proceed evil thoughts, adulter-
ies, fornications, murders, 22thefts, covetousness,
wickedness, deceit, lewdness, an evil eye, blas-
phemy, pride, foolishness. 23All these evil things
come from within and defile a man."

A GENTILE SHOWS HER FAITH

24From there He arose and went to the region
of Tyre and Sidon.[a] And He entered a house and
wanted no one to know *it,* but He could not be
hidden. 25For a woman whose young daughter
had an unclean spirit heard about Him, and she
came and fell at His feet. 26The woman was a
Greek, a Syro-Phoenician by birth, and she kept
asking Him to cast the demon out of her daugh-
ter. 27But Jesus said to her, "Let the children be
filled first, for it is not good to take the chil-
dren's bread and throw *it* to the little dogs."
28And she answered and said to Him, "Yes,
Lord, yet even the little dogs under the table eat
from the children's crumbs."
29Then He said to her, "For this saying go your
way; the demon has gone out of your daughter."
30And when she had come to her house, she
found the demon gone out, and her daughter ly-
ing on the bed.

JESUS HEALS A DEAF-MUTE

31Again, departing from the region of Tyre
and Sidon, He came through the midst of the re-
gion of Decapolis to the Sea of Galilee. 32Then
they brought to Him one who was deaf and had
an impediment in his speech, and they begged
Him to put His hand on him. 33And He took him
aside from the multitude, and put His fingers in
his ears, and He spat and touched his tongue.
34Then, looking up to heaven, He sighed, and
said to him, "Ephphatha," that is, "Be opened."
35Immediately his ears were opened, and the
impediment of his tongue was loosed, and he
spoke plainly. 36Then He commanded them that
they should tell no one; but the more He com-
manded them, the more widely they proclaimed
it. 37And they were astonished beyond measure,
saying, "He has done all things well. He makes
both the deaf to hear and the mute to speak."

7:16 [a]NU-Text omits this verse. **7:19** [a]NU-Text ends quotation with *eliminated,* setting off the final clause as Mark's comment that Jesus has declared all foods clean. **7:24** [a]NU-Text omits *and Sidon.*

THE MESSAGE

God,' thus relieving yourselves of obligation
to father or mother. You scratch out God's
Word and scrawl a whim in its place. You do
a lot of things like this."
14-15 Jesus called the crowd together again
and said, "Listen now, all of you—take this
to heart. It's not what you swallow that pol-
lutes your life; it's what you vomit—that's
the real pollution."
17 When he was back home after being with
the crowd, his disciples said, "We don't get
it. Put it in plain language."
18-19 Jesus said, "Are you being willfully stu-
pid? Don't you see that what you swallow
can't contaminate you? It doesn't enter your
heart but your stomach, works its way
through the intestines, and is finally
flushed." (That took care of dietary quib-
bling; Jesus was saying that *all* foods are fit
to eat.)
20-23 He went on: "It's what comes out of a per-
son that pollutes: obscenities, lusts, thefts,
murders, adulteries, greed, depravity, decep-
tive dealings, carousing, mean looks, slan-
der, arrogance, foolishness—all these are
vomit from the heart. *There* is the source of
your pollution."

24-26 From there Jesus set out for the vicinity of
Tyre. He entered a house there where he
didn't think he would be found, but he
couldn't escape notice. He was barely inside
when a woman who had a disturbed daugh-
ter heard where he was. She came and knelt
at his feet, begging for help. The woman was
Greek, Syro-Phoenician by birth. She asked
him to cure her daughter.
27 He said, "Stand in line and take your
turn. The children get fed first. If there's any
left over, the dogs get it."
28 She said, "Of course, Master. But don't
dogs under the table get scraps dropped by
the children?"
29-30 Jesus was impressed. "You're right! On
your way! Your daughter is no longer dis-
turbed. The demonic affliction is gone." She
went home and found her daughter relaxed
on the bed, the torment gone for good.
31-35 Then he left the region of Tyre, went
through Sidon back to Galilee Lake and
over to the district of the Ten Towns. Some
people brought a man who could neither
hear nor speak and asked Jesus to lay a
healing hand on him. He took the man off
by himself, put his fingers in the man's ears
and some spit on the man's tongue. Then Je-
sus looked up in prayer, groaned mightily,
and commanded, "*Ephphatha!*—Open up!"
And it happened. The man's hearing was
clear and his speech plain—just like that.
36-37 Jesus urged them to keep it quiet, but
they talked it up all the more, beside them-
selves with excitement. "He's done it all and
done it well. He gives hearing to the deaf,
speech to the speechless."

New King James Version

Feeding the Four Thousand

8 In those days, the multitude being very great and having nothing to eat, Jesus called His disciples *to Him* and said to them, 2"I have compassion on the multitude, because they have now continued with Me three days and have nothing to eat. 3And if I send them away hungry to their own houses, they will faint on the way; for some of them have come from afar."

4Then His disciples answered Him, "How can one satisfy these people with bread here in the wilderness?"

5He asked them, "How many loaves do you have?"

And they said, "Seven."

6So He commanded the multitude to sit down on the ground. And He took the seven loaves and gave thanks, broke *them* and gave *them* to His disciples to set before *them;* and they set *them* before the multitude. 7They also had a few small fish; and having blessed them, He said to set them also before *them.* 8So they ate and were filled, and they took up seven large baskets of leftover fragments. 9Now those who had eaten were about four thousand. And He sent them away, 10immediately got into the boat with His disciples, and came to the region of Dalmanutha.

The Pharisees Seek a Sign

11Then the Pharisees came out and began to dispute with Him, seeking from Him a sign from heaven, testing Him. 12But He sighed deeply in His spirit, and said, "Why does this generation seek a sign? Assuredly, I say to you, no sign shall be given to this generation."

Beware of the Leaven of the Pharisees and Herod

13And He left them, and getting into the boat again, departed to the other side. 14Now the disciples[a] had forgotten to take bread, and they did not have more than one loaf with them in the boat. 15Then He charged them, saying, "Take heed, beware of the leaven of the Pharisees and the leaven of Herod."

16And they reasoned among themselves, saying, "*It is* because we have no bread."

17But Jesus, being aware of *it,* said to them, "Why do you reason because you have no bread? Do you not yet perceive nor understand? Is your heart still[a] hardened? 18Having eyes, do you not see? And having ears, do you not hear? And do you not remember? 19When I broke the five loaves for the five thousand, how many baskets full of fragments did you take up?"

They said to Him, "Twelve."

20"Also, when I broke the seven for the four thousand, how many large baskets full of fragments did you take up?"

And they said, "Seven."

21So He said to them, "How *is it* you do not understand?"

A Blind Man Healed at Bethsaida

22Then He came to Bethsaida; and they brought a blind man to Him, and begged Him to touch him. 23So He took the blind man by the

8:14 [a]NU-Text and M-Text read *they.* **8:17** [a]NU-Text omits *still.*

The Message

A Meal for Four Thousand

1-3 8 At about this same time he again found
himself with a hungry crowd on his hands.
He called his disciples together and said,
"This crowd is breaking my heart. They
have stuck with me for three days, and now
they have nothing to eat. If I send them
home hungry, they'll faint along the way—
some of them have come a long distance."
4 His disciples responded, "What do you
expect us to do about it? Buy food out here
in the desert?"
5 He asked, "How much bread do you
have?"
"Seven loaves," they said.
6-10 So Jesus told the crowd to sit down on
the ground. After giving thanks, he took the
seven bread loaves, broke them into pieces,
and gave them to his disciples so they could
hand them out to the crowd. They also had
a few fish. He pronounced a blessing over
the fish and told his disciples to hand them
out as well. The crowd ate its fill. Seven
sacks of leftovers were collected. There
were well over four thousand at the meal.
Then he sent them home. He himself went
straight to the boat with his disciples and set
out for Dalmanoutha.
11-12 When they arrived, the Pharisees came
out and started in on him, badgering him to
prove himself, pushing him up against the
wall. Provoked, he said, "Why does this gen-
eration clamor for miraculous guarantees?
If I have anything to say about it, you'll not
get so much as a hint of a guarantee."

Contaminating Yeast

13-15 He then left them, got back in the boat, and
headed for the other side. But the disciples
forgot to pack a lunch. Except for a single
loaf of bread, there wasn't a crumb in the
boat. Jesus warned, "Be very careful. Keep a
sharp eye out for the contaminating yeast of
Pharisees and the followers of Herod."
16-19 Meanwhile, the disciples were finding
fault with each other because they had for-
gotten to bring bread. Jesus overheard and
said, "Why are you fussing because you for-
got bread? Don't you see the point of all
this? Don't you get it at all? Remember the
five loaves I broke for the five thousand?
How many baskets of leftovers did you pick
up?"
They said, "Twelve."
20 "And the seven loaves for the four thou-
sand—how many bags full of leftovers did
you get?"
"Seven."
21 He said, "Do you still not get it?"
22-23 They arrived at Bethsaida. Some people
brought a sightless man and begged Jesus
to give him a healing touch. Taking him by

NEW KING JAMES VERSION

hand and led him out of the town. And when He
had spit on his eyes and put His hands on him,
He asked him if he saw anything.
24And he looked up and said, "I see men like
trees, walking."
25Then He put *His* hands on his eyes again
and made him look up. And he was restored and
saw everyone clearly. 26Then He sent him away
to his house, saying, "Neither go into the town,
nor tell anyone in the town."[a]

PETER CONFESSES JESUS AS THE CHRIST

27Now Jesus and His disciples went out to
the towns of Caesarea Philippi; and on the road
He asked His disciples, saying to them, "Who do
men say that I am?"
28So they answered, "John the Baptist; but
some *say,* Elijah; and others, one of the
prophets."
29He said to them, "But who do you say that
I am?"
Peter answered and said to Him, "You are the
Christ."
30Then He strictly warned them that they
should tell no one about Him.

JESUS PREDICTS HIS DEATH AND RESURRECTION

31And He began to teach them that the Son
of Man must suffer many things, and be rejected
by the elders and chief priests and scribes, and
be killed, and after three days rise again. 32He
spoke this word openly. Then Peter took Him
aside and began to rebuke Him. 33But when He
had turned around and looked at His disciples,
He rebuked Peter, saying, "Get behind Me, Sa-
tan! For you are not mindful of the things of
God, but the things of men."

TAKE UP THE CROSS AND FOLLOW HIM

34When He had called the people to *Himself,*
with His disciples also, He said to them, "Who-
ever desires to come after Me, let him deny him-
self, and take up his cross, and follow Me. 35For
whoever desires to save his life will lose it, but
whoever loses his life for My sake and the
gospel's will save it. 36For what will it profit a
man if he gains the whole world, and loses his
own soul? 37Or what will a man give in ex-
change for his soul? 38For whoever is ashamed
of Me and My words in this adulterous and sin-
ful generation, of him the Son of Man also will
be ashamed when He comes in the glory of His
Father with the holy angels."

JESUS TRANSFIGURED ON THE MOUNT

9 And He said to them, "Assuredly, I say to you
that there are some standing here who will
not taste death till they see the kingdom of God
present with power."
2Now after six days Jesus took Peter, James,
and John, and led them up on a high mountain
apart by themselves; and He was transfigured
before them. 3His clothes became shining, ex-
ceedingly white, like snow, such as no launderer
on earth can whiten them. 4And Elijah appeared
to them with Moses, and they were talking with
Jesus.

8:26 [a]NU-Text reads *"Do not even go into the town."*

THE MESSAGE

the hand, he led him out of the village. He
put spit in the man's eyes, laid hands on
him, and asked, "Do you see anything?"
24-26 He looked up. "I see men. They look like
walking trees." So Jesus laid hands on his
eyes again. The man looked hard and real-
ized that he had recovered perfect sight, saw
everything in bright, twenty-twenty focus.
Jesus sent him straight home, telling him,
"Don't enter the village."

THE MESSIAH

27 Jesus and his disciples headed out for the
villages around Caesarea Philippi. As they
walked, he asked, "Who do the people say I
am?"
28 "Some say 'John the Baptizer,'" they
said. "Others say 'Elijah.' Still others say
'one of the prophets.'"
29 He then asked, "And you—what are you
saying about me? Who am I?"
Peter gave the answer: "You are the
Christ, the Messiah."
30-32 Jesus warned them to keep it quiet, not to
breathe a word of it to anyone. He then be-
gan explaining things to them: "It is neces-
sary that the Son of Man proceed to an or-
deal of suffering, be tried and found guilty
by the elders, high priests, and religion
scholars, be killed, and after three days rise
up alive." He said this simply and clearly so
they couldn't miss it.
32-33 But Peter grabbed him in protest. Turning
and seeing his disciples wavering, wonder-
ing what to believe, Jesus confronted Peter.
"Peter, get out of my way! Satan, get lost!
You have no idea how God works."
34-37 Calling the crowd to join his disciples, he
said, "Anyone who intends to come with me
has to let me lead. You're not in the driver's
seat; *I* am. Don't run from suffering; em-
brace it. Follow me and I'll show you how.
Self-help is no help at all. Self-sacrifice is
the way, my way, to saving yourself, your
true self. What good would it do to get every-
thing you want and lose you, the real you?
What could you ever trade your soul for?
38 "If any of you are embarrassed over me
and the way I'm leading you when you get
around your fickle and unfocused friends,
know that you'll be an even greater embar-
rassment to the Son of Man when he arrives
in all the splendor of God, his Father, with
an army of the holy angels."

1 9 Then he drove it home by saying, "This isn't
pie in the sky by and by. Some of you who
are standing here are going to see it happen,
see the kingdom of God arrive in full force."

IN A LIGHT-RADIANT CLOUD

2-4 Six days later, three of them *did* see it. Jesus
took Peter, James, and John and led them up
a high mountain. His appearance changed
from the inside out, right before their eyes.
His clothes shimmered, glistening white,
whiter than any bleach could make them.
Elijah, along with Moses, came into view, in
deep conversation with Jesus.

NEW KING JAMES VERSION

5Then Peter answered and said to Jesus, "Rabbi,
it is good for us to be here; and let us make three
tabernacles: one for You, one for Moses, and one
for Elijah"— 6because he did not know what to
say, for they were greatly afraid.
7And a cloud came and overshadowed them;
and a voice came out of the cloud, saying, "This
is My beloved Son. Hear Him!" 8Suddenly, when
they had looked around, they saw no one any-
more, but only Jesus with themselves.
9Now as they came down from the mountain,
He commanded them that they should tell no
one the things they had seen, till the Son of Man
had risen from the dead. 10So they kept this
word to themselves, questioning what the rising
from the dead meant.
11And they asked Him, saying, "Why do the
scribes say that Elijah must come first?"
12Then He answered and told them, "Indeed,
Elijah is coming first and restores all things.
And how is it written concerning the Son of
Man, that He must suffer many things and be
treated with contempt? 13But I say to you that
Elijah has also come, and they did to him what-
ever they wished, as it is written of him."

A BOY IS HEALED

14And when He came to the disciples, He saw
a great multitude around them, and scribes dis-
puting with them. 15Immediately, when they saw
Him, all the people were greatly amazed, and
running to *Him*, greeted Him. 16And He asked
the scribes, "What are you discussing with
them?"
17Then one of the crowd answered and said,
"Teacher, I brought You my son, who has a mute
spirit. 18And wherever it seizes him, it throws
him down; he foams at the mouth, gnashes his
teeth, and becomes rigid. So I spoke to Your dis-
ciples, that they should cast it out, but they
could not."
19He answered him and said, "O faithless
generation, how long shall I be with you? How
long shall I bear with you? Bring him to Me."
20Then they brought him to Him. And when he
saw Him, immediately the spirit convulsed him,
and he fell on the ground and wallowed, foam-
ing at the mouth.
21So He asked his father, "How long has this
been happening to him?"
And he said, "From childhood. 22And often
he has thrown him both into the fire and into the
water to destroy him. But if You can do anything,
have compassion on us and help us."
23Jesus said to him, "If you can believe,[a] all
things *are* possible to him who believes."
24Immediately the father of the child cried
out and said with tears, "Lord, I believe; help my
unbelief!"
25When Jesus saw that the people came run-
ning together, He rebuked the unclean spirit,
saying to it, "Deaf and dumb spirit, I command
you, come out of him and enter him no more!"

9:23 [a]NU-Text reads "*If You can!' All things. . . .*"

THE MESSAGE

5-6 Peter interrupted, "Rabbi, this is a great moment! Let's build three memorials— one for you, one for Moses, one for Elijah." He blurted this out without thinking, stunned as they all were by what they were seeing.

7 Just then a light-radiant cloud enveloped them, and from deep in the cloud, a voice: "This is my Son, marked by my love. Listen to him."

8 The next minute the disciples were looking around, rubbing their eyes, seeing nothing but Jesus, only Jesus.

9-10 Coming down the mountain, Jesus swore them to secrecy. "Don't tell a soul what you saw. After the Son of Man rises from the dead, you're free to talk." They puzzled over that, wondering what on earth "rising from the dead" meant.

11 Meanwhile they were asking, "Why do the religion scholars say that Elijah has to come first?"

12-13 Jesus replied, "Elijah does come first and get everything ready for the coming of the Son of Man. They treated this Elijah like dirt, much like they will treat the Son of Man, who will, according to Scripture, suffer terribly and be kicked around contemptibly."

THERE ARE NO IFS

14-16 When they came back down the mountain to the other disciples, they saw a huge crowd around them, and the religion scholars cross-examining them. As soon as the people in the crowd saw Jesus, admiring excitement stirred them. They ran and greeted him. He asked, "What's going on? What's all the commotion?"

17-18 A man out of the crowd answered, "Teacher, I brought my mute son, made speechless by a demon, to you. Whenever it seizes him, it throws him to the ground. He foams at the mouth, grinds his teeth, and goes stiff as a board. I told your disciples, hoping they could deliver him, but they couldn't."

19-20 Jesus said, "What a generation! No sense of God! How many times do I have to go over these things? How much longer do I have to put up with this? Bring the boy here." They brought him. When the demon saw Jesus, it threw the boy into a seizure, causing him to writhe on the ground and foam at the mouth.

21-22 He asked the boy's father, "How long has this been going on?"

"Ever since he was a little boy. Many times it pitches him into fire or the river to do away with him. If you can do anything, do it. Have a heart and help us!"

23 Jesus said, "If? There are no 'ifs' among believers. Anything can happen."

24 No sooner were the words out of his mouth than the father cried, "Then I believe. Help me with my doubts!"

25-27 Seeing that the crowd was forming fast, Jesus gave the vile spirit its marching orders: "Dumb and deaf spirit, I command you—Out of him, and stay out!" Screaming,

NEW KING JAMES VERSION

26 Then *the spirit* cried out, convulsed him
greatly, and came out of him. And he became as
one dead, so that many said, "He is dead." 27 But
Jesus took him by the hand and lifted him up,
and he arose.

28 And when He had come into the house, His
disciples asked Him privately, "Why could we
not cast it out?"

29 So He said to them, "This kind can come
out by nothing but prayer and fasting."[a]

JESUS AGAIN PREDICTS HIS DEATH AND RESURRECTION

30 Then they departed from there and passed
through Galilee, and He did not want anyone to
know *it.* 31 For He taught His disciples and said
to them, "The Son of Man is being betrayed into
the hands of men, and they will kill Him. And af-
ter He is killed, He will rise the third day." 32 But
they did not understand this saying, and were
afraid to ask Him.

WHO IS THE GREATEST?

33 Then He came to Capernaum. And when
He was in the house He asked them, "What was
it you disputed among yourselves on the road?"
34 But they kept silent, for on the road they had
disputed among themselves who *would be the*
greatest. 35 And He sat down, called the twelve,
and said to them, "If anyone desires to be first,
he shall be last of all and servant of all." 36 Then
He took a little child and set him in the midst of
them. And when He had taken him in His arms,
He said to them, 37 "Whoever receives one of
these little children in My name receives Me;
and whoever receives Me, receives not Me but
Him who sent Me."

JESUS FORBIDS SECTARIANISM

38 Now John answered Him, saying, "Teacher,
we saw someone who does not follow us casting
out demons in Your name, and we forbade him
because he does not follow us."

39 But Jesus said, "Do not forbid him, for no
one who works a miracle in My name can soon
afterward speak evil of Me. 40 For he who is not
against us is on our[a] side. 41 For whoever gives
you a cup of water to drink in My name, because
you belong to Christ, assuredly, I say to you, he
will by no means lose his reward.

JESUS WARNS OF OFFENSES

42 "But whoever causes one of these little
ones who believe in Me to stumble, it would be
better for him if a millstone were hung around
his neck, and he were thrown into the sea. 43 If
your hand causes you to sin, cut it off. It is bet-
ter for you to enter into life maimed, rather than
having two hands, to go to hell, into the fire that
shall never be quenched— 44 where

'Their worm does not die
And the fire is not quenched.'[a]

45 And if your foot causes you to sin, cut it off. It
is better for you to enter life lame, rather than
having two feet, to be cast into hell, into the fire
that shall never be quenched— 46 where

9:29 [a]NU-Text omits *and fasting.* **9:40** [a]M-Text reads *against you is on your side.* **9:44** [a]NU-Text omits this verse.

THE MESSAGE

and with much thrashing about, it left. The
boy was pale as a corpse, so people started
saying, "He's dead." But Jesus, taking his
hand, raised him. The boy stood up.
28 After arriving back home, his disciples
cornered Jesus and asked, "Why couldn't
we throw the demon out?"
29 He answered, "There is no way to get rid
of this kind of demon except by prayer."
30-32 Leaving there, they went through Galilee.
He didn't want anyone to know their where-
abouts, for he wanted to teach his disciples.
He told them, "The Son of Man is about to
be betrayed to some people who want noth-
ing to do with God. They will murder him.
Three days after his murder, he will rise,
alive." They didn't know what he was talk-
ing about, but were afraid to ask him about
it.

SO YOU WANT FIRST PLACE?

33 They came to Capernaum. When he was
safe at home, he asked them, "What were
you discussing on the road?"
34 The silence was deafening—they had
been arguing with one another over who
among them was greatest.
35 He sat down and summoned the Twelve.
"So you want first place? Then take the last
place. Be the servant of all."
36-37 He put a child in the middle of the room.
Then, cradling the little one in his arms, he
said, "Whoever embraces one of these chil-
dren as I do embraces me, and far more
than me—God who sent me."

38 John spoke up, "Teacher, we saw a man using
your name to expel demons and we stopped
him because he wasn't in our group."
39-41 Jesus wasn't pleased. "Don't stop him. No
one can use my name to do something good
and powerful, and in the next breath cut me
down. If he's not an enemy, he's an ally.
Why, anyone by just giving you a cup of wa-
ter in my name is on our side. Count on it
that God will notice.
42 "On the other hand, if you give one of
these simple, childlike believers a hard time,
bullying or taking advantage of their simple
trust, you'll soon wish you hadn't. You'd be
better off dropped in the middle of the lake
with a millstone around your neck.
43-48 "If your hand or your foot gets in God's
way, chop it off and throw it away. You're
better off maimed or lame and alive than the
proud owner of two hands and two feet,

NEW KING JAMES VERSION

'Their worm does not die
And the fire is not quenched.'[a]

47And if your eye causes you to sin, pluck it out. It is better for you to enter the kingdom of God with one eye, rather than having two eyes, to be cast into hell fire— 48where

'Their worm does not die
And the fire is not quenched.'[a]

TASTELESS SALT IS WORTHLESS

49"For everyone will be seasoned with fire,[a] and every sacrifice will be seasoned with salt. 50Salt *is* good, but if the salt loses its flavor, how will you season it? Have salt in yourselves, and have peace with one another."

MARRIAGE AND DIVORCE

10 Then He arose from there and came to the region of Judea by the other side of the Jordan. And multitudes gathered to Him again, and as He was accustomed, He taught them again.

2The Pharisees came and asked Him, "Is it lawful for a man to divorce *his* wife?" testing Him.

3And He answered and said to them, "What did Moses command you?"

4They said, "Moses permitted *a man* to write a certificate of divorce, and to dismiss *her.*"

5And Jesus answered and said to them, "Because of the hardness of your heart he wrote you this precept. 6But from the beginning of the creation, God *'made them male and female.'*[a] 7*'For this reason a man shall leave his father and mother and be joined to his wife,* 8*and the two shall become one flesh'*;[a] so then they are no longer two, but one flesh. 9Therefore what God has joined together, let not man separate."

10In the house His disciples also asked Him again about the same *matter.* 11So He said to them, "Whoever divorces his wife and marries another commits adultery against her. 12And if a woman divorces her husband and marries another, she commits adultery."

JESUS BLESSES LITTLE CHILDREN

13Then they brought little children to Him, that He might touch them; but the disciples rebuked those who brought *them.* 14But when Jesus saw *it,* He was greatly displeased and said to them, "Let the little children come to Me, and do not forbid them; for of such is the kingdom of God. 15Assuredly, I say to you, whoever does not receive the kingdom of God as a little child will by no means enter it." 16And He took them up in His arms, laid *His* hands on them, and blessed them.

JESUS COUNSELS THE RICH YOUNG RULER

17Now as He was going out on the road, one came running, knelt before Him, and asked Him, "Good Teacher, what shall I do that I may inherit eternal life?"

9:46 [a]NU-Text omits the last clause of verse 45 and all of verse 46. **9:48** [a]Isaiah 66:24 **9:49** [a]NU-Text omits the rest of this verse. **10:6** [a]Genesis 1:27; 5:2 **10:8** [a]Genesis 2:24

THE MESSAGE

godless in a furnace of eternal fire. And if your eye distracts you from God, pull it out and throw it away. You're better off one-eyed and alive than exercising your twenty-twenty vision from inside the fire of hell.

49-50 "Everyone's going through a refining fire sooner or later, but you'll be well-preserved, protected from the *eternal* flames. Be preservatives yourselves. Preserve the peace."

DIVORCE

1-2 10 From there he went to the area of Judea across the Jordan. A crowd of people, as was so often the case, went along, and he, as he so often did, taught them. Pharisees came up, intending to give him a hard time. They asked, "Is it legal for a man to divorce his wife?"

3 Jesus said, "What did Moses command?"

4 They answered, "Moses gave permission to fill out a certificate of dismissal and divorce her."

5-9 Jesus said, "Moses wrote this command only as a concession to your hardhearted ways. In the original creation, God made male and female to be together. Because of this, a man leaves father and mother, and in marriage he becomes one flesh with a woman—no longer two individuals, but forming a new unity. Because God created this organic union of the two sexes, no one should desecrate his art by cutting them apart."

10-12 When they were back home, the disciples brought it up again. Jesus gave it to them straight: "A man who divorces his wife so he can marry someone else commits adultery against her. And a woman who divorces her husband so she can marry someone else commits adultery."

13-16 The people brought children to Jesus, hoping he might touch them. The disciples shooed them off. But Jesus was irate and let them know it: "Don't push these children away. Don't ever get between them and me. These children are at the very center of life in the kingdom. Mark this: Unless you accept God's kingdom in the simplicity of a child, you'll never get in." Then, gathering the children up in his arms, he laid his hands of blessing on them.

TO ENTER GOD'S KINGDOM

17 As he went out into the street, a man came running up, greeted him with great reverence, and asked, "Good Teacher, what must I do to get eternal life?"

New King James Version

18 So Jesus said to him, "Why do you call Me
good? No one *is* good but One, *that is*, God.
19 You know the commandments: *'Do not com-
mit adultery,' 'Do not murder,' 'Do not steal,'
'Do not bear false witness,'* 'Do not defraud,'
'Honor your father and your mother.' "[a]
20 And he answered and said to Him,
"Teacher, all these things I have kept from my
youth."
21 Then Jesus, looking at him, loved him, and
said to him, "One thing you lack: Go your way,
sell whatever you have and give to the poor, and
you will have treasure in heaven; and come,
take up the cross, and follow Me."
22 But he was sad at this word, and went away
sorrowful, for he had great possessions.

With God All Things Are Possible

23 Then Jesus looked around and said to His
disciples, "How hard it is for those who have
riches to enter the kingdom of God!" 24 And the
disciples were astonished at His words. But Je-
sus answered again and said to them, "Children,
how hard it is for those who trust in riches[a] to
enter the kingdom of God! 25 It is easier for a
camel to go through the eye of a needle than for
a rich man to enter the kingdom of God."
26 And they were greatly astonished, saying
among themselves, "Who then can be saved?"
27 But Jesus looked at them and said, "With
men *it is* impossible, but not with God; for with
God all things are possible."
28 Then Peter began to say to Him, "See, we
have left all and followed You."
29 So Jesus answered and said, "Assuredly, I
say to you, there is no one who has left house or
brothers or sisters or father or mother or wife[a]
or children or lands, for My sake and the
gospel's, 30 who shall not receive a hundredfold
now in this time—houses and brothers and sis-
ters and mothers and children and lands, with
persecutions—and in the age to come, eternal
life. 31 But many *who are* first will be last, and
the last first."

Jesus a Third Time Predicts His Death and Resurrection

32 Now they were on the road, going up to
Jerusalem, and Jesus was going before them;
and they were amazed. And as they followed
they were afraid. Then He took the twelve aside
again and began to tell them the things that
would happen to Him: 33 "Behold, we are going
up to Jerusalem, and the Son of Man will be be-
trayed to the chief priests and to the scribes; and
they will condemn Him to death and deliver
Him to the Gentiles; 34 and they will mock Him,
and scourge Him, and spit on Him, and kill Him.
And the third day He will rise again."

Greatness Is Serving

35 Then James and John, the sons of Zebedee,
came to Him, saying, "Teacher, we want You to
do for us whatever we ask."
36 And He said to them, "What do you want
Me to do for you?"

10:19 [a]Exodus 20:12–16; Deuteronomy 5:16–20 **10:24** [a]NU-Text omits *for those who trust in riches.* **10:29** [a]NU-Text omits *or wife.*

The Message

18-19 Jesus said, "Why are you calling me good? No one is good, only God. You know the commandments: Don't murder, don't commit adultery, don't steal, don't lie, don't cheat, honor your father and mother."

20 He said, "Teacher, I have—from my youth—kept them all!"

21 Jesus looked him hard in the eye—and loved him! He said, "There's one thing left: Go sell whatever you own and give it to the poor. All your wealth will then be heavenly wealth. And come follow me."

22 The man's face clouded over. This was the last thing he expected to hear, and he walked off with a heavy heart. He was holding on tight to a lot of things, and not about to let go.

23-25 Looking at his disciples, Jesus said, "Do you have any idea how difficult it is for people who 'have it all' to enter God's kingdom?" The disciples couldn't believe what they were hearing, but Jesus kept on: "You can't imagine how difficult. I'd say it's easier for a camel to go through a needle's eye than for the rich to get into God's kingdom."

26 *That* set the disciples back on their heels. "Then who has any chance at all?" they asked.

27 Jesus was blunt: "No chance at all if you think you can pull it off by yourself. Every chance in the world if you let God do it."

28 Peter tried another angle: "We left everything and followed you."

29-31 Jesus said, "Mark my words, no one who sacrifices house, brothers, sisters, mother, father, children, land—whatever—because of me and the Message will lose out. They'll get it all back, but multiplied many times in homes, brothers, sisters, mothers, children, and land—but also in troubles. And then the bonus of eternal life! This is once again the Great Reversal: Many who are first will end up last, and the last first."

32-34 Back on the road, they set out for Jerusalem. Jesus had a head start on them, and they were following, puzzled and not just a little afraid. He took the Twelve and began again to go over what to expect next. "Listen to me carefully. We're on our way up to Jerusalem. When we get there, the Son of Man will be betrayed to the religious leaders and scholars. They will sentence him to death. Then they will hand him over to the Romans, who will mock and spit on him, give him the third degree, and kill him. After three days he will rise alive."

The Highest Places of Honor

35 James and John, Zebedee's sons, came up to him. "Teacher, we have something we want you to do for us."

36 "What is it? I'll see what I can do."

NEW KING JAMES VERSION

37They said to Him, "Grant us that we may
sit, one on Your right hand and the other on Your
left, in Your glory."
38But Jesus said to them, "You do not know
what you ask. Are you able to drink the cup that
I drink, and be baptized with the baptism that I
am baptized with?"
39They said to Him, "We are able."
So Jesus said to them, "You will indeed drink
the cup that I drink, and with the baptism I am
baptized with you will be baptized; 40but to sit
on My right hand and on My left is not Mine to
give, but *it is for those* for whom it is prepared."
41And when the ten heard *it,* they began to
be greatly displeased with James and John.
42But Jesus called them to *Himself* and said to
them, "You know that those who are considered
rulers over the Gentiles lord it over them, and
their great ones exercise authority over them.
43Yet it shall not be so among you; but whoever
desires to become great among you shall be
your servant. 44And whoever of you desires to
be first shall be slave of all. 45For even the Son
of Man did not come to be served, but to serve,
and to give His life a ransom for many."

JESUS HEALS BLIND BARTIMAEUS

46Now they came to Jericho. As He went out
of Jericho with His disciples and a great multi-
tude, blind Bartimaeus, the son of Timaeus, sat
by the road begging. 47And when he heard that
it was Jesus of Nazareth, he began to cry out
and say, "Jesus, Son of David, have mercy on
me!"
48Then many warned him to be quiet; but he
cried out all the more, "Son of David, have
mercy on me!"
49So Jesus stood still and commanded him to
be called.
Then they called the blind man, saying to
him, "Be of good cheer. Rise, He is calling you."
50And throwing aside his garment, he rose
and came to Jesus.
51So Jesus answered and said to him, "What
do you want Me to do for you?"
The blind man said to Him, "Rabboni, that I
may receive my sight."
52Then Jesus said to him, "Go your way; your
faith has made you well." And immediately he
received his sight and followed Jesus on the
road.

THE TRIUMPHAL ENTRY

11 Now when they drew near Jerusalem, to
Bethphage[a] and Bethany, at the Mount of
Olives, He sent two of His disciples; 2and He
said to them, "Go into the village opposite you;
and as soon as you have entered it you will find
a colt tied, on which no one has sat. Loose it and
bring *it.* 3And if anyone says to you, 'Why are
you doing this?' say, 'The Lord has need of it,'
and immediately he will send it here."
4So they went their way, and found the[a] colt
tied by the door outside on the street, and they
loosed it. 5But some of those who stood there

11:1 [a]M-Text reads *Bethsphage.* **11:4** [a]NU-Text and M-Text read *a.*

THE MESSAGE

37 "Arrange it," they said, "so that we will be
awarded the highest places of honor in your
glory—one of us at your right, the other at
your left."
38 Jesus said, "You have no idea what you're
asking. Are you capable of drinking the cup
I drink, of being baptized in the baptism I'm
about to be plunged into?"
39-40 "Sure," they said. "Why not?"
Jesus said, "Come to think of it, you *will*
drink the cup I drink, and be baptized in my
baptism. But as to awarding places of honor,
that's not my business. There are other
arrangements for that."
41-45 When the other ten heard of this conver-
sation, they lost their tempers with James
and John. Jesus got them together to settle
things down. "You've observed how godless
rulers throw their weight around," he said,
"and when people get a little power how
quickly it goes to their heads. It's not going
to be that way with you. Whoever wants to
be great must become a servant. Whoever
wants to be first among you must be your
slave. That is what the Son of Man has done:
He came to serve, not to be served—and
then to give away his life in exchange for
many who are held hostage."

46-48 They spent some time in Jericho. As Jesus
was leaving town, trailed by his disciples
and a parade of people, a blind beggar by
the name of Bartimaeus, son of Timaeus,
was sitting alongside the road. When he
heard that Jesus the Nazarene was passing
by, he began to cry out, "Son of David, Je-
sus! Mercy, have mercy on me!" Many tried
to hush him up, but he yelled all the louder,
"Son of David! Mercy, have mercy on me!"
49-50 Jesus stopped in his tracks. "Call him
over."
They called him. "It's your lucky day! Get
up! He's calling you to come!" Throwing off
his coat, he was on his feet at once and came
to Jesus.
51 Jesus said, "What can I do for you?"
The blind man said, "Rabbi, I want to
see."
52 "On your way," said Jesus. "Your faith has
saved and healed you."
In that very instant he recovered his sight
and followed Jesus down the road.

ENTERING JERUSALEM ON A COLT

1-3 11 When they were nearing Jerusalem, at
Bethphage and Bethany on Mount
Olives, he sent off two of the disciples with
instructions: "Go to the village across from
you. As soon as you enter, you'll find a colt
tethered, one that has never yet been ridden.
Untie it and bring it. If anyone asks, 'What
are you doing?' say, 'The Master needs him,
and will return him right away.' "
4-7 They went and found a colt tied to a door
at the street corner and untied it. Some of
those standing there said, "What are you do-

NEW KING JAMES VERSION

said to them, "What are you doing, loosing the
colt?"
6And they spoke to them just as Jesus had
commanded. So they let them go. 7Then they
brought the colt to Jesus and threw their clothes
on it, and He sat on it. 8And many spread their
clothes on the road, and others cut down leafy
branches from the trees and spread *them* on the
road. 9Then those who went before and those
who followed cried out, saying:

"Hosanna!
'Blessed is He who comes in the name of the
LORD!'[a]
10Blessed *is* the kingdom of our father David
That comes in the name of the Lord![a]
Hosanna in the highest!"

11And Jesus went into Jerusalem and into the
temple. So when He had looked around at all
things, as the hour was already late, He went out
to Bethany with the twelve.

THE FIG TREE WITHERED

12Now the next day, when they had come out
from Bethany, He was hungry. 13And seeing
from afar a fig tree having leaves, He went to
see if perhaps He would find something on it.
When He came to it, He found nothing but
leaves, for it was not the season for figs. 14In re-
sponse Jesus said to it, "Let no one eat fruit from
you ever again."
And His disciples heard *it*.

JESUS CLEANSES THE TEMPLE

15So they came to Jerusalem. Then Jesus
went into the temple and began to drive out
those who bought and sold in the temple, and
overturned the tables of the money changers
and the seats of those who sold doves. 16And He
would not allow anyone to carry wares through
the temple. 17Then He taught, saying to them, "Is
it not written, *'My house shall be called a house*
of prayer for all nations'?[a] But you have made
it a *'den of thieves.'* "[b]
18And the scribes and chief priests heard it
and sought how they might destroy Him; for
they feared Him, because all the people were as-
tonished at His teaching. 19When evening had
come, He went out of the city.

THE LESSON OF THE WITHERED FIG TREE

20Now in the morning, as they passed by,
they saw the fig tree dried up from the roots.
21And Peter, remembering, said to Him, "Rabbi,
look! The fig tree which You cursed has with-
ered away."
22So Jesus answered and said to them, "Have
faith in God. 23For assuredly, I say to you, who-
ever says to this mountain, 'Be removed and be
cast into the sea,' and does not doubt in his
heart, but believes that those things he says will
be done, he will have whatever he says. 24There-
fore I say to you, whatever things you ask when
you pray, believe that you receive *them*, and you
will have *them*.

11:9 [a]Psalm 118:26 **11:10** [a]NU-Text omits *in the name of the Lord.* **11:17** [a]Isaiah 56:7 [b]Jeremiah 7:11

THE MESSAGE

ing untying that colt?" The disciples replied
exactly as Jesus had instructed them, and
the people let them alone. They brought the
colt to Jesus, spread their coats on it, and he
mounted.

8-10 The people gave him a wonderful wel-
come, some throwing their coats on the
street, others spreading out rushes they had
cut in the fields. Running ahead and follow-
ing after, they were calling out,

Hosanna!
Blessed is he who comes in God's name!
Blessed the coming kingdom of our
father David!
Hosanna in highest heaven!

11 He entered Jerusalem, then entered the
Temple. He looked around, taking it all in.
But by now it was late, so he went back to
Bethany with the Twelve.

THE CURSED FIG TREE

12-14 As they left Bethany the next day, he was
hungry. Off in the distance he saw a fig tree
in full leaf. He came up to it expecting to
find something for breakfast, but found
nothing but fig leaves. (It wasn't yet the sea-
son for figs.) He addressed the tree: "No one
is going to eat fruit from you again—ever!"
And his disciples overheard him.

15-17 They arrived at Jerusalem. Immediately
on entering the Temple Jesus started throw-
ing out everyone who had set up shop there,
buying and selling. He kicked over the ta-
bles of the bankers and the stalls of the pi-
geon merchants. He didn't let anyone even
carry a basket through the Temple. And
then he taught them, quoting this text:

My house was designated a house of
prayer for the nations;
You've turned it into a hangout for
thieves.

18 The high priests and religion scholars
heard what was going on and plotted how
they might get rid of him. They panicked,
for the entire crowd was carried away by his
teaching.

19 At evening, Jesus and his disciples left
the city.

20-21 In the morning, walking along the road,
they saw the fig tree, shriveled to a dry stick.
Peter, remembering what had happened the
previous day, said to him, "Rabbi, look—the
fig tree you cursed is shriveled up!"

22-25 Jesus was matter-of-fact: "Embrace this
God-life. Really embrace it, and nothing will
be too much for you. This mountain, for in-
stance: Just say, 'Go jump in the lake'—no
shuffling or shilly-shallying—and it's as
good as done. That's why I urge you to pray
for absolutely everything, ranging from
small to large. Include everything as you
embrace this God-life, and you'll get God's

NEW KING JAMES VERSION

FORGIVENESS AND PRAYER

25"And whenever you stand praying, if you have anything against anyone, forgive him, that your Father in heaven may also forgive you your trespasses. 26But if you do not forgive, neither will your Father in heaven forgive your trespasses."[a]

JESUS' AUTHORITY QUESTIONED

27Then they came again to Jerusalem. And as He was walking in the temple, the chief priests, the scribes, and the elders came to Him. 28And they said to Him, "By what authority are You doing these things? And who gave You this authority to do these things?"

29But Jesus answered and said to them, "I also will ask you one question; then answer Me, and I will tell you by what authority I do these things: 30The baptism of John—was it from heaven or from men? Answer Me."

31And they reasoned among themselves, saying, "If we say, 'From heaven,' He will say, 'Why then did you not believe him?' 32But if we say, 'From men' "—they feared the people, for all counted John to have been a prophet indeed. 33So they answered and said to Jesus, "We do not know."

And Jesus answered and said to them, "Neither will I tell you by what authority I do these things."

THE PARABLE OF THE WICKED VINEDRESSERS

12 Then He began to speak to them in parables: "A man planted a vineyard and set a hedge around *it*, dug *a place for* the wine vat and built a tower. And he leased it to vinedressers and went into a far country. 2Now at vintage-time he sent a servant to the vinedressers, that he might receive some of the fruit of the vineyard from the vinedressers. 3And they took *him* and beat him and sent *him* away empty-handed. 4Again he sent them another servant, and at him they threw stones,[a] wounded *him* in the head, and sent *him* away shamefully treated. 5And again he sent another, and him they killed; and many others, beating some and killing some. 6Therefore still having one son, his beloved, he also sent him to them last, saying, 'They will respect my son.' 7But those vinedressers said among themselves, 'This is the heir. Come, let us kill him, and the inheritance will be ours.' 8So they took him and killed *him* and cast *him* out of the vineyard.

9"Therefore what will the owner of the vineyard do? He will come and destroy the vinedressers, and give the vineyard to others. 10Have you not even read this Scripture:

'The stone which the builders rejected
Has become the chief cornerstone.
11*This was the LORD's doing,*
And it is marvelous in our eyes'? "[a]

12And they sought to lay hands on Him, but feared the multitude, for they knew He had spoken the parable against them. So they left Him and went away.

11:26 [a]NU-Text omits this verse. **12:4** [a]NU-Text omits *and at him they threw stones.* **12:11** [a]Psalm 118:22, 23

THE MESSAGE

everything. And when you assume the posture of prayer, remember that it's not all *asking*. If you have anything against someone, *forgive*—only then will your heavenly Father be inclined to also wipe your slate clean of sins."

HIS CREDENTIALS

27-28 Then when they were back in Jerusalem once again, as they were walking through the Temple, the high priests, religion scholars, and leaders came up and demanded, "Show us your credentials. Who authorized you to speak and act like this?"

29-30 Jesus responded, "First let me ask you a question. Answer my question and then I'll present my credentials. About the baptism of John—who authorized it: heaven or humans? Tell me."

31-33 They were on the spot, and knew it. They pulled back into a huddle and whispered, "If we say 'heaven,' he'll ask us why we didn't believe John; if we say 'humans,' we'll be up against it with the people because they all hold John up as a prophet." They decided to concede that round to Jesus. "We don't know," they said.

Jesus replied, "Then I won't answer your question either."

THE STORY ABOUT A VINEYARD

1-2 12 Then Jesus started telling them stories. "A man planted a vineyard. He fenced it, dug a winepress, erected a watchtower, turned it over to the farmhands, and went off on a trip. At the time for harvest, he sent a servant back to the farmhands to collect his profits.

3-5 "They grabbed him, beat him up, and sent him off empty-handed. So he sent another servant. That one they tarred and feathered. He sent another and that one they killed. And on and on, many others. Some they beat up, some they killed.

6 "Finally there was only one left: a beloved son. In a last-ditch effort, he sent him, thinking, 'Surely they will respect my son.'

7-8 "But those farmhands saw their chance. They rubbed their hands together in greed and said, 'This is the heir! Let's kill him and have it all for ourselves.' They grabbed him, killed him, and threw him over the fence.

9-11 "What do you think the owner of the vineyard will do? Right. He'll come and clean house. Then he'll assign the care of the vineyard to others. Read it for yourselves in Scripture:

That stone the masons threw out
is now the cornerstone!
This is God's work;
we rub our eyes—we can hardly
believe it!"

12 They wanted to lynch him then and there but, intimidated by public opinion, held back. They knew the story was about them. They got away from there as fast as they could.

New King James Version

The Pharisees: Is It Lawful to Pay Taxes to Caesar?

13Then they sent to Him some of the Phar-
isees and the Herodians, to catch Him in *His*
words. 14When they had come, they said to Him,
"Teacher, we know that You are true, and care
about no one; for You do not regard the person
of men, but teach the way of God in truth. Is it
lawful to pay taxes to Caesar, or not? 15Shall we
pay, or shall we not pay?"
But He, knowing their hypocrisy, said to
them, "Why do you test Me? Bring Me a denar-
ius that I may see *it*." 16So they brought *it*.
And He said to them, "Whose image and in-
scription *is* this?" They said to Him, "Caesar's."
17And Jesus answered and said to them,
"Render to Caesar the things that are Caesar's,
and to God the things that are God's."
And they marveled at Him.

The Sadducees: What About the Resurrection?

18Then *some* Sadducees, who say there is no
resurrection, came to Him; and they asked Him,
saying: 19"Teacher, Moses wrote to us that if a
man's brother dies, and leaves *his* wife behind,
and leaves no children, his brother should take
his wife and raise up offspring for his brother.
20Now there were seven brothers. The first took
a wife; and dying, he left no offspring. 21And the
second took her, and he died; nor did he leave
any offspring. And the third likewise. 22So the
seven had her and left no offspring. Last of all
the woman died also. 23Therefore, in the resur-
rection, when they rise, whose wife will she be?
For all seven had her as wife."
24Jesus answered and said to them, "Are you
not therefore mistaken, because you do not
know the Scriptures nor the power of God?
25For when they rise from the dead, they neither
marry nor are given in marriage, but are like an-
gels in heaven. 26But concerning the dead, that
they rise, have you not read in the book of
Moses, in the *burning* bush *passage*, how God
spoke to him, saying, *'I am the God of Abraham,
the God of Isaac, and the God of Jacob'?*[a] 27He
is not the God of the dead, but the God of the liv-
ing. You are therefore greatly mistaken."

The Scribes: Which Is the First Commandment of All?

28Then one of the scribes came, and having
heard them reasoning together, perceiving[a] that
He had answered them well, asked Him, "Which
is the first commandment of all?"
29Jesus answered him, "The first of all the
commandments *is: 'Hear, O Israel, the Lord our
God, the Lord is one.* 30*And you shall love the
Lord your God with all your heart, with all your
soul, with all your mind, and with all your
strength.'*[a] This *is* the first commandment.[b]
31And the second, like *it, is* this: *'You shall love
your neighbor as yourself.'*[a] There is no other
commandment greater than these."
32So the scribe said to Him, "Well *said*,
Teacher. You have spoken the truth, for there is
one God, and there is no other but He. 33And to
love Him with all the heart, with all the under-

12:26 [a]Exodus 3:6, 15 **12:28** [a]NU-Text reads *seeing*.
12:30 [a]Deuteronomy 6:4, 5 [b]NU-Text omits this sentence.
12:31 [a]Leviticus 19:18

The Message

Paying Taxes to Caesar

13-14 They sent some Pharisees and followers of
Herod to bait him, hoping to catch him say-
ing something incriminating. They came up
and said, "Teacher, we know you have in-
tegrity, that you are indifferent to public
opinion, don't pander to your students, and
teach the way of God accurately. Tell us: Is it
lawful to pay taxes to Caesar or not?"
15-16 He knew it was a trick question, and said,
"Why are you playing these games with me?
Bring me a coin and let me look at it." They
handed him one.
"This engraving—who does it look like?
And whose name is on it?"
"Caesar," they said.
17 Jesus said, "Give Caesar what is his, and
give God what is his."
Their mouths hung open, speechless.

Our Intimacies Will Be with God

18-23 Some Sadducees, the party that denies any
possibility of resurrection, came up and
asked, "Teacher, Moses wrote that if a man
dies and leaves a wife but no child, his
brother is obligated to marry the widow and
have children. Well, there once were seven
brothers. The first took a wife. He died
childless. The second married her. He died,
and still no child. The same with the third.
All seven took their turn, but no child. Fi-
nally the wife died. When they are raised at
the resurrection, whose wife is she? All
seven were her husband."
24-27 Jesus said, "You're way off base, and
here's why: One, you don't know your
Bibles; two, you don't know how God works.
After the dead are raised up, we're past the
marriage business. As it is with angels now,
all our ecstasies and intimacies then will be
with God. And regarding the dead, whether
or not they are raised, don't you ever read
the Bible? How God at the bush said to
Moses, 'I am—not *was*—the God of Abra-
ham, the God of Isaac, and the God of Ja-
cob'? The living God is God of the *living*, not
the dead. You're way, way off base."

The Most Important Commandment

28 One of the religion scholars came up. Hear-
ing the lively exchanges of question and an-
swer and seeing how sharp Jesus was in his
answers, he put in his question: "Which is
most important of all the commandments?"
29-31 Jesus said, "The first in importance is,
'Listen, Israel: The Lord your God is one; so
love the Lord God with all your passion and
prayer and intelligence and energy.' And
here is the second: 'Love others as well as
you love yourself.' There is no other com-
mandment that ranks with these."
32-33 The religion scholar said, "A wonderful
answer, Teacher! So lucid and accurate—
that God is one and there is no other. And
loving him with all passion and intelligence

NEW KING JAMES VERSION

standing, with all the soul,[a] and with all the
strength, and to love one's neighbor as oneself,
is more than all the whole burnt offerings and
sacrifices."
34Now when Jesus saw that he answered
wisely, He said to him, "You are not far from the
kingdom of God."
But after that no one dared question Him.

JESUS: HOW CAN DAVID CALL HIS DESCENDANT LORD?

35Then Jesus answered and said, while He
taught in the temple, "How *is it* that the scribes
say that the Christ is the Son of David? 36For
David himself said by the Holy Spirit:

'The LORD said to my Lord,
"Sit at My right hand,
Till I make Your enemies Your footstool."' [a]

37Therefore David himself calls Him *'Lord'*; how
is He *then* his Son?"
And the common people heard Him gladly.

BEWARE OF THE SCRIBES

38Then He said to them in His teaching, "Be-
ware of the scribes, who desire to go around in
long robes, *love* greetings in the marketplaces,
39the best seats in the synagogues, and the best
places at feasts, 40who devour widows' houses,
and for a pretense make long prayers. These
will receive greater condemnation."

THE WIDOW'S TWO MITES

41Now Jesus sat opposite the treasury and
saw how the people put money into the treasury.
And many *who were* rich put in much. 42Then
one poor widow came and threw in two mites,[a]
which make a quadrans. 43So He called His dis-
ciples to *Himself* and said to them, "Assuredly, I
say to you that this poor widow has put in more
than all those who have given to the treasury;
44for they all put in out of their abundance, but
she out of her poverty put in all that she had, her
whole livelihood."

JESUS PREDICTS THE DESTRUCTION OF THE TEMPLE

13 Then as He went out of the temple, one of
His disciples said to Him, "Teacher, see
what manner of stones and what buildings *are
here!*"
2And Jesus answered and said to him, "Do
you see these great buildings? Not *one* stone
shall be left upon another, that shall not be
thrown down."

THE SIGNS OF THE TIMES AND THE END OF THE AGE

3Now as He sat on the Mount of Olives oppo-
site the temple, Peter, James, John, and Andrew
asked Him privately, 4"Tell us, when will these
things be? And what *will be* the sign when all
these things will be fulfilled?"
5And Jesus, answering them, began to say:
"Take heed that no one deceives you. 6For many

12:33 [a]NU-Text omits *with all the soul.* 12:36 [a]Psalm 110:1
12:42 [a]Greek *lepta,* very small copper coins worth a fraction of
a penny

THE MESSAGE

and energy, and loving others as well as you
love yourself. Why, that's better than all of-
ferings and sacrifices put together!"
34 When Jesus realized how insightful he
was, he said, "You're almost there, right on
the border of God's kingdom."
After that, no one else dared ask a ques-
tion.

35-37 While he was teaching in the Temple, Jesus
asked, "How is it that the religion scholars
say that the Messiah is David's 'son,' when
we all know that David, inspired by the Holy
Spirit, said,

God said to my Master,
"Sit here at my right hand
until I put your enemies under your
feet."

"David here designates the Messiah 'my
Master'—so how can the Messiah also be
his 'son'?"
The large crowd was delighted with what
they heard.
38-40 He continued teaching. "Watch out for
the religion scholars. They love to walk
around in academic gowns, preening in the
radiance of public flattery, basking in
prominent positions, sitting at the head
table at every church function. And all the
time they are exploiting the weak and help-
less. The longer their prayers, the worse
they get. But they'll pay for it in the end."
41-44 Sitting across from the offering box, he
was observing how the crowd tossed money
in for the collection. Many of the rich were
making large contributions. One poor
widow came up and put in two small coins—
a measly two cents. Jesus called his disci-
ples over and said, "The truth is that this
poor widow gave more to the collection
than all the others put together. All the oth-
ers gave what they'll never miss; she gave
extravagantly what she couldn't afford—she
gave her all."

DOOMSDAY DECEIVERS

1 13 As he walked away from the Temple,
one of his disciples said, "Teacher, look
at that stonework! Those buildings!"
2 Jesus said, "You're impressed by this
grandiose architecture? There's not a stone
in the whole works that is not going to end
up in a heap of rubble."
3-4 Later, as he was sitting on Mount Olives
in full view of the Temple, Peter, James,
John, and Andrew got him off by himself
and asked, "Tell us, when is this going to
happen? What sign will we get that things
are coming to a head?"
5-8 Jesus began, "Watch out for doomsday
deceivers. Many leaders are going to show

NEW KING JAMES VERSION

will come in My name, saying, 'I am *He,*' and will deceive many. 7But when you hear of wars and rumors of wars, do not be troubled; for *such things* must happen, but the end *is* not yet. 8For nation will rise against nation, and kingdom against kingdom. And there will be earthquakes in various places, and there will be famines and troubles.[a] These *are* the beginnings of sorrows.

9"But watch out for yourselves, for they will deliver you up to councils, and you will be beaten in the synagogues. You will be brought[a] before rulers and kings for My sake, for a testimony to them. 10And the gospel must first be preached to all the nations. 11But when they arrest *you* and deliver you up, do not worry beforehand, or premeditate[a] what you will speak. But whatever is given you in that hour, speak that; for it is not you who speak, but the Holy Spirit. 12Now brother will betray brother to death, and a father *his* child; and children will rise up against parents and cause them to be put to death. 13And you will be hated by all for My name's sake. But he who endures to the end shall be saved.

THE GREAT TRIBULATION

14"So when you see the *'abomination of desolation,'*[a] spoken of by Daniel the prophet,[b] standing where it ought not" (let the reader understand), "then let those who are in Judea flee to the mountains. 15Let him who is on the housetop not go down into the house, nor enter to take anything out of his house. 16And let him who is in the field not go back to get his clothes. 17But woe to those who are pregnant and to those who are nursing babies in those days! 18And pray that your flight may not be in winter. 19For *in* those days there will be tribulation, such as has not been since the beginning of the creation which God created until this time, nor ever shall be. 20And unless the Lord had shortened those days, no flesh would be saved; but for the elect's sake, whom He chose, He shortened the days.

21"Then if anyone says to you, 'Look, here *is* the Christ!' or, 'Look, *He is* there!' do not believe it. 22For false christs and false prophets will rise and show signs and wonders to deceive, if possible, even the elect. 23But take heed; see, I have told you all things beforehand.

THE COMING OF THE SON OF MAN

24"But in those days, after that tribulation, the sun will be darkened, and the moon will not give its light; 25the stars of heaven will fall, and the powers in the heavens will be shaken. 26Then they will see the Son of Man coming in the clouds with great power and glory. 27And

13:8 [a]NU-Text omits *and troubles.* **13:9** [a]NU-Text and M-Text read *will stand.* **13:11** [a]NU-Text omits *or premeditate.* **13:14** [a]Daniel 11:31; 12:11 [b]NU-Text omits *spoken of by Daniel the prophet.*

THE MESSAGE

up with forged identities claiming, 'I'm the One.' They will deceive a lot of people. When you hear of wars and rumored wars, keep your head and don't panic. This is routine history, and no sign of the end. Nation will fight nation and ruler fight ruler, over and over. Earthquakes will occur in various places. There will be famines. But these things are nothing compared to what's coming.

9-10 "And watch out! They're going to drag you into court. And then it will go from bad to worse, dog-eat-dog, everyone at your throat because you carry my name. You're placed there as sentinels to truth. The Message has to be preached all across the world.

11 "When they bring you, betrayed, into court, don't worry about what you'll say. When the time comes, say what's on your heart—the Holy Spirit will make his witness in and through you.

12-13 "It's going to be brother killing brother, father killing child, children killing parents. There's no telling who will hate you because of me.

"Stay with it—that's what is required. Stay with it to the end. You won't be sorry; you'll be saved.

RUN FOR THE HILLS

14-18 "But be ready to run for it when you see the monster of desecration set up where it should *never* be. You who can read, make sure you understand what I'm talking about. If you're living in Judea at the time, run for the hills; if you're working in the yard, don't go back to the house to get anything; if you're out in the field, don't go back to get your coat. Pregnant and nursing mothers will have it especially hard. Hope and pray this won't happen in the middle of winter.

19-20 "These are going to be hard days—nothing like it from the time God made the world right up to the present. And there'll be nothing like it again. If he let the days of trouble run their course, nobody would make it. But because of God's chosen people, those he personally chose, he has already intervened.

NO ONE KNOWS THE DAY OR HOUR

21-23 "If anyone tries to flag you down, calling out, 'Here's the Messiah!' or points, 'There he is!' don't fall for it. Fake Messiahs and lying preachers are going to pop up everywhere. Their impressive credentials and dazzling performances will pull the wool over the eyes of even those who ought to know better. So watch out. I've given you fair warning.

24-25 "Following those hard times,

Sun will fade out,
    moon cloud over,
Stars fall out of the sky,
    cosmic powers tremble.

26-27 "And then they'll see the Son of Man enter in grand style, his Arrival filling the

NEW KING JAMES VERSION

then He will send His angels, and gather together His elect from the four winds, from the farthest part of earth to the farthest part of heaven.

THE PARABLE OF THE FIG TREE

28“Now learn this parable from the fig tree: When its branch has already become tender, and puts forth leaves, you know that summer is near. 29So you also, when you see these things happening, know that it[a] is near—at the doors! 30Assuredly, I say to you, this generation will by no means pass away till all these things take place. 31Heaven and earth will pass away, but My words will by no means pass away.

NO ONE KNOWS THE DAY OR HOUR

32“But of that day and hour no one knows, not even the angels in heaven, nor the Son, but only the Father. 33Take heed, watch and pray; for you do not know when the time is. 34*It is* like a man going to a far country, who left his house and gave authority to his servants, and to each his work, and commanded the doorkeeper to watch. 35Watch therefore, for you do not know when the master of the house is coming—in the evening, at midnight, at the crowing of the rooster, or in the morning— 36lest, coming suddenly, he find you sleeping. 37And what I say to you, I say to all: Watch!”

THE PLOT TO KILL JESUS

14 After two days it was the Passover and *the Feast* of Unleavened Bread. And the chief priests and the scribes sought how they might take Him by trickery and put *Him* to death. 2But they said, “Not during the feast, lest there be an uproar of the people.”

THE ANOINTING AT BETHANY

3And being in Bethany at the house of Simon the leper, as He sat at the table, a woman came having an alabaster flask of very costly oil of spikenard. Then she broke the flask and poured *it* on His head. 4But there were some who were indignant among themselves, and said, “Why was this fragrant oil wasted? 5For it might have been sold for more than three hundred denarii and given to the poor.” And they criticized her sharply.

6But Jesus said, “Let her alone. Why do you trouble her? She has done a good work for Me. 7For you have the poor with you always, and whenever you wish you may do them good; but Me you do not have always. 8She has done what she could. She has come beforehand to anoint My body for burial. 9Assuredly, I say to you, wherever this gospel is preached in the whole world, what this woman has done will also be told as a memorial to her.”

JUDAS AGREES TO BETRAY JESUS

10Then Judas Iscariot, one of the twelve, went to the chief priests to betray Him to them. 11And when they heard *it*, they were glad, and promised to give him money. So he sought how he might conveniently betray Him.

13:29 [a]Or *He*

THE MESSAGE

sky—no one will miss it! He'll dispatch the
angels; they will pull in the chosen from the
four winds, from pole to pole.
28-31 “Take a lesson from the fig tree. From the
moment you notice its buds form, the merest hint of green, you know summer's just
around the corner. And so it is with you.
When you see all these things, you know he
is at the door. Don't take this lightly. I'm not
just saying this for some future generation,
but for this one, too—these things will happen. Sky and earth will wear out; my words
won't wear out.
32-37 “But the exact day and hour? No one
knows that, not even heaven's angels, not
even the Son. Only the Father. So keep a
sharp lookout, for you don't know the
timetable. It's like a man who takes a trip,
leaving home and putting his servants in
charge, each assigned a task, and commanding the gatekeeper to stand watch. So,
stay at your post, watching. You have no idea
when the homeowner is returning, whether
evening, midnight, cockcrow, or morning.
You don't want him showing up unannounced, with you asleep on the job. I say it
to you, and I'm saying it to all: Stay at your
post. Keep watch.”

ANOINTING HIS HEAD

1-2 14 In only two days the eight-day Festival
of Passover and the Feast of Unleavened
Bread would begin. The high priests and religion scholars were looking for a way they
could seize Jesus by stealth and kill him.
They agreed that it should not be done during Passover Week. “We don't want the
crowds up in arms,” they said.
3-5 Jesus was at Bethany, a guest of Simon
the Leper. While he was eating dinner, a
woman came up carrying a bottle of very
expensive perfume. Opening the bottle, she
poured it on his head. Some of the guests
became furious among themselves. “That's
criminal! A sheer waste! This perfume could
have been sold for well over a year's wages
and handed out to the poor.” They swelled
up in anger, nearly bursting with indignation over her.
6-9 But Jesus said, “Let her alone. Why are
you giving her a hard time? She has just
done something wonderfully significant for
me. You will have the poor with you every
day for the rest of your lives. Whenever you
feel like it, you can do something for them.
Not so with me. She did what she could
when she could—she pre-anointed my body
for burial. And you can be sure that wherever in the whole world the Message is
preached, what she just did is going to be
talked about admiringly.”
10-11 Judas Iscariot, one of the Twelve, went to
the cabal of high priests, determined to betray him. They couldn't believe their ears,
and promised to pay him well. He started
looking for just the right moment to hand
him over.

NEW KING JAMES VERSION

JESUS CELEBRATES THE PASSOVER WITH HIS DISCIPLES

12Now on the first day of Unleavened Bread,
when they killed the Passover *lamb,* His disci-
ples said to Him, "Where do You want us to go
and prepare, that You may eat the Passover?"
13And He sent out two of His disciples and
said to them, "Go into the city, and a man will
meet you carrying a pitcher of water; follow
him. 14Wherever he goes in, say to the master of
the house, 'The Teacher says, "Where is the
guest room in which I may eat the Passover with
My disciples?" ' 15Then he will show you a large
upper room, furnished *and* prepared; there
make ready for us."
16So His disciples went out, and came into
the city, and found it just as He had said to them;
and they prepared the Passover.
17In the evening He came with the twelve.
18Now as they sat and ate, Jesus said, "As-
suredly, I say to you, one of you who eats with
Me will betray Me."
19And they began to be sorrowful, and to say
to Him one by one, "*Is* it I?" And another *said,*
"*Is* it I?"[a]
20He answered and said to them, "*It is* one of
the twelve, who dips with Me in the dish. 21The
Son of Man indeed goes just as it is written of
Him, but woe to that man by whom the Son of
Man is betrayed! It would have been good for
that man if he had never been born."

JESUS INSTITUTES THE LORD'S SUPPER

22And as they were eating, Jesus took bread,
blessed and broke *it,* and gave *it* to them and
said, "Take, eat;[a] this is My body."
23Then He took the cup, and when He had
given thanks He gave *it* to them, and they all
drank from it. 24And He said to them, "This is
My blood of the new[a] covenant, which is shed
for many. 25Assuredly, I say to you, I will no
longer drink of the fruit of the vine until that
day when I drink it new in the kingdom of God."
26And when they had sung a hymn, they
went out to the Mount of Olives.

JESUS PREDICTS PETER'S DENIAL

27Then Jesus said to them, "All of you will be
made to stumble because of Me this night,[a] for it
is written:

'I will strike the Shepherd,
And the sheep will be scattered.'[b]

28"But after I have been raised, I will go be-
fore you to Galilee."
29Peter said to Him, "Even if all are made to
stumble, yet I *will* not *be.*"

14:19 [a]NU-Text omits this sentence. **14:22** [a]NU-Text omits *eat.* **14:24** [a]NU-Text omits *new.* **14:27** [a]NU-Text omits *because of Me this night.* [b]Zechariah 13:7

THE MESSAGE

TRAITOR TO THE SON OF MAN

12 On the first of the Days of Unleavened Bread, the day they prepare the Passover sacrifice, his disciples asked him, "Where do you want us to go and make preparations so you can eat the Passover meal?"

13-15 He directed two of his disciples, "Go into the city. A man carrying a water jug will meet you. Follow him. Ask the owner of whichever house he enters, 'The Teacher wants to know, Where is my guest room where I can eat the Passover meal with my disciples?' He will show you a spacious second-story room, swept and ready. Prepare for us there."

16 The disciples left, came to the city, found everything just as he had told them, and prepared the Passover meal.

17-18 After sunset he came with the Twelve. As they were at the supper table eating, Jesus said, "I have something hard but important to say to you: One of you is going to hand me over to the conspirators, one who at this moment is eating with me."

19 Stunned, they started asking, one after another, "It isn't me, is it?"

20-21 He said, "It's one of the Twelve, one who eats with me out of the same bowl. In one sense, it turns out that the Son of Man is entering into a way of treachery well-marked by the Scriptures—no surprises here. In another sense, the man who turns him in, turns traitor to the Son of Man—better never to have been born than do this!"

"THIS IS MY BODY"

22 In the course of their meal, having taken and blessed the bread, he broke it and gave it to them. Then he said,

Take, this is my body.

23-24 Taking the chalice, he gave it to them, thanking God, and they all drank from it. He said,

This is my blood,
God's new covenant,
Poured out for many people.

25 "I'll not be drinking wine again until the new day when I drink it in the kingdom of God."

26 They sang a hymn and then went directly to Mount Olives.

27-28 Jesus told them, "You're all going to feel that your world is falling apart and that it's my fault. There's a Scripture that says,

I will strike the shepherd;
The sheep will go helter-skelter.

"But after I am raised up, I will go ahead of you, leading the way to Galilee."

29 Peter blurted out, "Even if everyone else is ashamed of you when things fall to pieces, I won't be."

New King James Version

30 Jesus said to him, "Assuredly, I say to you
that today, *even* this night, before the rooster
crows twice, you will deny Me three times."
31 But he spoke more vehemently, "If I have to
die with You, I will not deny You!"
And they all said likewise.

The Prayer in the Garden

32 Then they came to a place which was
named Gethsemane; and He said to His disci-
ples, "Sit here while I pray." 33 And He took Peter,
James, and John with Him, and He began to be
troubled and deeply distressed. 34 Then He said
to them, "My soul is exceedingly sorrowful,
even to death. Stay here and watch."
35 He went a little farther, and fell on the
ground, and prayed that if it were possible, the
hour might pass from Him. 36 And He said,
"Abba, Father, all things *are* possible for You.
Take this cup away from Me; nevertheless, not
what I will, but what You *will*."
37 Then He came and found them sleeping,
and said to Peter, "Simon, are you sleeping?
Could you not watch one hour? 38 Watch and
pray, lest you enter into temptation. The spirit
indeed *is* willing, but the flesh *is* weak."
39 Again He went away and prayed, and
spoke the same words. 40 And when He returned,
He found them asleep again, for their eyes were
heavy; and they did not know what to answer
Him.
41 Then He came the third time and said to
them, "Are you still sleeping and resting? It is
enough! The hour has come; behold, the Son of
Man is being betrayed into the hands of sinners.
42 Rise, let us be going. See, My betrayer is at
hand."

Betrayal and Arrest in Gethsemane

43 And immediately, while He was still speak-
ing, Judas, one of the twelve, with a great multi-
tude with swords and clubs, came from the chief
priests and the scribes and the elders. 44 Now His
betrayer had given them a signal, saying,
"Whomever I kiss, He is the One; seize Him and
lead *Him* away safely."
45 As soon as he had come, immediately he
went up to Him and said to Him, "Rabbi, Rabbi!"
and kissed Him.
46 Then they laid their hands on Him and
took Him. 47 And one of those who stood by drew
his sword and struck the servant of the high
priest, and cut off his ear.
48 Then Jesus answered and said to them,
"Have you come out, as against a robber, with
swords and clubs to take Me? 49 I was daily with
you in the temple teaching, and you did not
seize Me. But the Scriptures must be fulfilled."
50 Then they all forsook Him and fled.

A Young Man Flees Naked

51 Now a certain young man followed Him,
having a linen cloth thrown around *his* naked
body. And the young men laid hold of him, 52 and
he left the linen cloth and fled from them naked.

The Message

30 Jesus said, "Don't be so sure. Today, this
very night in fact, before the rooster crows
twice, you will deny me three times."
31 He blustered in protest, "Even if I have to
die with you, I will never deny you." All the
others said the same thing.

Gethsemane

32-34 They came to an area called Gethsemane.
Jesus told his disciples, "Sit here while I
pray." He took Peter, James, and John with
him. He plunged into a sinkhole of dreadful
agony. He told them, "I feel bad enough
right now to die. Stay here and keep vigil
with me."
35-36 Going a little ahead, he fell to the ground
and prayed for a way out: "Papa, Father, you
can—can't you?—get me out of this. Take
this cup away from me. But please, not what
I want—what do *you* want?"
37-38 He came back and found them sound
asleep. He said to Peter, "Simon, you went to
sleep on me? Can't you stick it out with me
a single hour? Stay alert, be in prayer, so
you don't enter the danger zone without
even knowing it. Don't be naive. Part of you
is eager, ready for anything in God; but an-
other part is as lazy as an old dog sleeping
by the fire."
39-40 He then went back and prayed the same
prayer. Returning, he again found them
sound asleep. They simply couldn't keep
their eyes open, and they didn't have a plau-
sible excuse.
41-42 He came back a third time and said, "Are
you going to sleep all night? No—you've
slept long enough. Time's up. The Son of
Man is about to be betrayed into the hands
of sinners. Get up. Let's get going. My be-
trayer has arrived."

A Gang of Ruffians

43-47 No sooner were the words out of his mouth
when Judas, the one out of the Twelve,
showed up, and with him a gang of ruffians,
sent by the high priests, religion scholars,
and leaders, brandishing swords and clubs.
The betrayer had worked out a signal with
them: "The one I kiss, that's the one—seize
him. Make sure he doesn't get away." He
went straight to Jesus and said, "Rabbi!"
and kissed him. The others then grabbed
him and roughed him up. One of the men
standing there unsheathed his sword,
swung, and came down on the Chief Priest's
servant, lopping off the man's ear.
48-50 Jesus said to them, "What is this, coming
after me with swords and clubs as if I were
a dangerous criminal? Day after day I've
been sitting in the Temple teaching, and you
never so much as lifted a hand against me.
What you in fact have done is confirm the
prophetic writings." All the disciples cut and
ran.
51-52 A young man was following along. All he
had on was a bedsheet. Some of the men
grabbed him but he got away, running off
naked, leaving them holding the sheet.

New King James Version

Jesus Faces the Sanhedrin

53And they led Jesus away to the high priest;
and with him were assembled all the chief
priests, the elders, and the scribes. 54But Peter
followed Him at a distance, right into the court-
yard of the high priest. And he sat with the ser-
vants and warmed himself at the fire.
55Now the chief priests and all the council
sought testimony against Jesus to put Him to
death, but found none. 56For many bore false
witness against Him, but their testimonies did
not agree.
57Then some rose up and bore false witness
against Him, saying, 58"We heard Him say, 'I will
destroy this temple made with hands, and
within three days I will build another made
without hands.' " 59But not even then did their
testimony agree.
60And the high priest stood up in the midst
and asked Jesus, saying, "Do You answer noth-
ing? What *is it* these men testify against You?"
61But He kept silent and answered nothing.
Again the high priest asked Him, saying to
Him, "Are You the Christ, the Son of the
Blessed?"
62Jesus said, "I am. And you will see the Son
of Man sitting at the right hand of the Power,
and coming with the clouds of heaven."
63Then the high priest tore his clothes and
said, "What further need do we have of wit-
nesses? 64You have heard the blasphemy! What
do you think?"
And they all condemned Him to be deserv-
ing of death.
65Then some began to spit on Him, and to
blindfold Him, and to beat Him, and to say to
Him, "Prophesy!" And the officers struck Him
with the palms of their hands.[a]

Peter Denies Jesus, and Weeps

66Now as Peter was below in the courtyard,
one of the servant girls of the high priest came.
67And when she saw Peter warming himself, she
looked at him and said, "You also were with Je-
sus of Nazareth."
68But he denied it, saying, "I neither know
nor understand what you are saying." And he
went out on the porch, and a rooster crowed.
69And the servant girl saw him again, and be-
gan to say to those who stood by, "This is *one* of
them." 70But he denied it again.
And a little later those who stood by said to
Peter again, "Surely you are *one* of them; for
you are a Galilean, and your speech shows *it*."[a]
71Then he began to curse and swear, "I do not
know this Man of whom you speak!"
72A second time *the* rooster crowed. Then Pe-
ter called to mind the word that Jesus had said
to him, "Before the rooster crows twice, you will
deny Me three times." And when he thought
about it, he wept.

14:65 [a]NU-Text reads *received Him with slaps.* **14:70** [a]NU-Text omits *and your speech shows it.*

The Message

Condemned to Death

53-54 They led Jesus to the Chief Priest, where the
high priests, religious leaders, and scholars
had gathered together. Peter followed at a
safe distance until they got to the Chief
Priest's courtyard, where he mingled with
the servants and warmed himself at the fire.

55-59 The high priests conspiring with the Jew-
ish Council looked high and low for evi-
dence against Jesus by which they could
sentence him to death. They found nothing.
Plenty of people were willing to bring in
false charges, but nothing added up, and
they ended up canceling each other out.
Then a few of them stood up and lied: "We
heard him say, 'I am going to tear down this
Temple, built by hard labor, and in three
days build another without lifting a hand.' "
But even they couldn't agree exactly.

60-61 In the middle of this, the Chief Priest
stood up and asked Jesus, "What do you
have to say to the accusation?" Jesus was
silent. He said nothing.
The Chief Priest tried again, this time
asking, "Are you the Messiah, the Son of the
Blessed?"

62 Jesus said, "Yes, I am, and you'll see it
yourself:

The Son of Man seated
At the right hand of the Mighty One,
Arriving on the clouds of heaven."

63-64 The Chief Priest lost his temper. Ripping
his clothes, he yelled, "Did you hear that?
After that do we need witnesses? You heard
the blasphemy. Are you going to stand for
it?"
They condemned him, one and all. The
sentence: death.

65 Some of them started spitting at him.
They blindfolded his eyes, then hit him, say-
ing, "Who hit you? Prophesy!" The guards,
punching and slapping, took him away.

The Rooster Crowed

66-67 While all this was going on, Peter was down
in the courtyard. One of the Chief Priest's
servant girls came in and, seeing Peter
warming himself there, looked hard at him
and said, "You were with the Nazarene, Je-
sus."

68 He denied it: "I don't know what you're
talking about." He went out on the porch. A
rooster crowed.

69-70 The girl spotted him and began telling
the people standing around, "He's one of
them." He denied it again.
After a little while, the bystanders
brought it up again. "You've *got* to be one of
them. You've got 'Galilean' written all over
you."

71-72 Now Peter got really nervous and swore,
"I never laid eyes on this man you're talking
about." Just then the rooster crowed a sec-
ond time. Peter remembered how Jesus had
said, "Before a rooster crows twice, you'll
deny me three times." He collapsed in tears.

NEW KING JAMES VERSION

JESUS FACES PILATE

15 Immediately, in the morning, the chief priests held a consultation with the elders and scribes and the whole council; and they bound Jesus, led *Him* away, and delivered *Him* to Pilate. 2Then Pilate asked Him, "Are You the King of the Jews?"

He answered and said to him, "*It is as* you say."

3And the chief priests accused Him of many things, but He answered nothing. 4Then Pilate asked Him again, saying, "Do You answer nothing? See how many things they testify against You!"[a] 5But Jesus still answered nothing, so that Pilate marveled.

TAKING THE PLACE OF BARABBAS

6Now at the feast he was accustomed to releasing one prisoner to them, whomever they requested. 7And there was one named Barabbas, *who was* chained with his fellow rebels; they had committed murder in the rebellion. 8Then the multitude, crying aloud,[a] began to ask *him to do* just as he had always done for them. 9But Pilate answered them, saying, "Do you want me to release to you the King of the Jews?" 10For he knew that the chief priests had handed Him over because of envy.

11But the chief priests stirred up the crowd, so that he should rather release Barabbas to them. 12Pilate answered and said to them again, "What then do you want me to do *with Him* whom you call the King of the Jews?"

13So they cried out again, "Crucify Him!"

14Then Pilate said to them, "Why, what evil has He done?"

But they cried out all the more, "Crucify Him!"

15So Pilate, wanting to gratify the crowd, released Barabbas to them; and he delivered Jesus, after he had scourged *Him,* to be crucified.

THE SOLDIERS MOCK JESUS

16Then the soldiers led Him away into the hall called Praetorium, and they called together the whole garrison. 17And they clothed Him with purple; and they twisted a crown of thorns, put it on His *head,* 18and began to salute Him, "Hail, King of the Jews!" 19Then they struck Him on the head with a reed and spat on Him; and bowing the knee, they worshiped Him. 20And when they had mocked Him, they took the purple off Him, put His own clothes on Him, and led Him out to crucify Him.

THE KING ON A CROSS

21Then they compelled a certain man, Simon a Cyrenian, the father of Alexander and Rufus, as he was coming out of the country and passing by, to bear His cross. 22And they brought Him to the place Golgotha, which is translated, Place of a Skull. 23Then they gave Him wine mingled with myrrh to drink, but He did not take *it.* 24And when they crucified Him, they divided His garments, casting lots for them to determine what every man should take.

15:4 [a]NU-Text reads *of which they accuse You.* **15:8** [a]NU-Text reads *going up.*

THE MESSAGE

STANDING BEFORE PILATE

1 15 At dawn's first light, the high priests, with the religious leaders and scholars, arranged a conference with the entire Jewish Council. After tying Jesus securely, they took him out and presented him to Pilate.

2-3 Pilate asked him, "Are you the 'King of the Jews'?"

He answered, "If you say so." The high priests let loose a barrage of accusations.

4-5 Pilate asked again, "Aren't you going to answer anything? That's quite a list of accusations." Still, he said nothing. Pilate was impressed, really impressed.

6-10 It was a custom at the Feast to release a prisoner, anyone the people asked for. There was one prisoner called Barabbas, locked up with the insurrectionists who had committed murder during the uprising against Rome. As the crowd came up and began to present its petition for him to release a prisoner, Pilate anticipated them: "Do you want me to release the King of the Jews to you?" Pilate knew by this time that it was through sheer spite that the high priests had turned Jesus over to him.

11-12 But the high priests by then had worked up the crowd to ask for the release of Barabbas. Pilate came back, "So what do I do with this man you call King of the Jews?"

13 They yelled, "Nail him to a cross!"

14 Pilate objected, "But for what crime?"

But they yelled all the louder, "Nail him to a cross!"

15 Pilate gave the crowd what it wanted, set Barabbas free and turned Jesus over for whipping and crucifixion.

16-20 The soldiers took Jesus into the palace (called Praetorium) and called together the entire brigade. They dressed him up in purple and put a crown plaited from a thornbush on his head. Then they began their mockery: "Bravo, King of the Jews!" They banged on his head with a club, spit on him, and knelt down in mock worship. After they had had their fun, they took off the purple cape and put his own clothes back on him. Then they marched out to nail him to the cross.

THE CRUCIFIXION

21 There was a man walking by, coming from work, Simon from Cyrene, the father of Alexander and Rufus. They made him carry Jesus' cross.

22-24 The soldiers brought Jesus to Golgotha, meaning "Skull Hill." They offered him a mild painkiller (wine mixed with myrrh), but he wouldn't take it. And they nailed him to the cross. They divided up his clothes and threw dice to see who would get them.

NEW KING JAMES VERSION

[25]Now it was the third hour, and they crucified Him. [26]And the inscription of His accusation was written above:

THE KING OF THE JEWS.

[27]With Him they also crucified two robbers, one on His right and the other on His left. [28]So the Scripture was fulfilled[a] which says, *"And He was numbered with the transgressors."*[b]

[29]And those who passed by blasphemed Him, wagging their heads and saying, "Aha! *You* who destroy the temple and build *it* in three days, [30]save Yourself, and come down from the cross!"

[31]Likewise the chief priests also, mocking among themselves with the scribes, said, "He saved others; Himself He cannot save. [32]Let the Christ, the King of Israel, descend now from the cross, that we may see and believe."[a]

Even those who were crucified with Him reviled Him.

JESUS DIES ON THE CROSS

[33]Now when the sixth hour had come, there was darkness over the whole land until the ninth hour. [34]And at the ninth hour Jesus cried out with a loud voice, saying, "Eloi, Eloi, lama sabachthani?" which is translated, *"My God, My God, why have You forsaken Me?"*[a]

[35]Some of those who stood by, when they heard *that*, said, "Look, He is calling for Elijah!" [36]Then someone ran and filled a sponge full of sour wine, put *it* on a reed, and offered *it* to Him to drink, saying, "Let Him alone; let us see if Elijah will come to take Him down."

[37]And Jesus cried out with a loud voice, and breathed His last.

[38]Then the veil of the temple was torn in two from top to bottom. [39]So when the centurion, who stood opposite Him, saw that He cried out like this and breathed His last,[a] he said, "Truly this Man was the Son of God!"

[40]There were also women looking on from afar, among whom were Mary Magdalene, Mary the mother of James the Less and of Joses, and Salome, [41]who also followed Him and ministered to Him when He was in Galilee, and many other women who came up with Him to Jerusalem.

JESUS BURIED IN JOSEPH'S TOMB

[42]Now when evening had come, because it was the Preparation Day, that is, the day before the Sabbath, [43]Joseph of Arimathea, a prominent council member, who was himself waiting for the kingdom of God, coming and taking courage, went in to Pilate and asked for the body of Jesus. [44]Pilate marveled that He was already dead; and summoning the centurion, he asked him if He had been dead for some time. [45]So when he found out from the centurion, he granted the body to Joseph. [46]Then he bought fine linen, took Him down, and wrapped Him in the linen. And he laid Him in a tomb which had been hewn out of the rock, and rolled a stone against the door of the tomb. [47]And Mary Magdalene and Mary *the mother* of Joses observed where He was laid.

15:28 [a]Isaiah 53:12 [b]NU-Text omits this verse. **15:32** [a]M-Text reads *believe Him.* **15:34** [a]Psalm 22:1 **15:39** [a]NU-Text reads *that He thus breathed His last.*

THE MESSAGE

25-30 They nailed him up at nine o'clock in the morning. The charge against him—THE KING OF THE JEWS—was printed on a poster. Along with him, they crucified two criminals, one to his right, the other to his left. People passing along the road jeered, shaking their heads in mock lament: "You bragged that you could tear down the Temple and then rebuild it in three days—so show us your stuff! Save yourself! If you're really God's Son, come down from that cross!"

31-32 The high priests, along with the religion scholars, were right there mixing it up with the rest of them, having a great time poking fun at him: "He saved others—but he can't save himself! Messiah, is he? King of Israel? Then let him climb down from that cross. We'll *all* become believers then!" Even the men crucified alongside him joined in the mockery.

33-34 At noon the sky became extremely dark. The darkness lasted three hours. At three o'clock, Jesus groaned out of the depths, crying loudly, *"Eloi, Eloi, lama sabachthani?"* which means, "My God, my God, why have you abandoned me?"

35-36 Some of the bystanders who heard him said, "Listen, he's calling for Elijah." Someone ran off, soaked a sponge in sour wine, put it on a stick, and gave it to him to drink, saying, "Let's see if Elijah comes to take him down."

37-39 But Jesus, with a loud cry, gave his last breath. At that moment the Temple curtain ripped right down the middle. When the Roman captain standing guard in front of him saw that he had quit breathing, he said, "This has to be the Son of God!"

TAKEN TO A TOMB

40-41 There were women watching from a distance, among them Mary Magdalene, Mary the mother of the younger James and Joses, and Salome. When Jesus was in Galilee, these women followed and served him, and had come up with him to Jerusalem.

42-45 Late in the afternoon, since it was the Day of Preparation (that is, Sabbath eve), Joseph of Arimathea, a highly respected member of the Jewish Council, came. He was one who lived expectantly, on the lookout for the kingdom of God. Working up his courage, he went to Pilate and asked for Jesus' body. Pilate questioned whether he could be dead that soon and called for the captain to verify that he was really dead. Assured by the captain, he gave Joseph the corpse.

46-47 Having already purchased a linen shroud, Joseph took him down, wrapped him in the shroud, placed him in a tomb that had been cut into the rock, and rolled a large stone across the opening. Mary Magdalene and Mary, mother of Joses, watched the burial.

NEW KING JAMES VERSION

HE IS RISEN

16 Now when the Sabbath was past, Mary
Magdalene, Mary *the mother* of James,
and Salome bought spices, that they might come
and anoint Him. 2 Very early in the morning, on
the first *day* of the week, they came to the tomb
when the sun had risen. 3 And they said among
themselves, "Who will roll away the stone from
the door of the tomb for us?" 4 But when they
looked up, they saw that the stone had been
rolled away—for it was very large. 5 And enter-
ing the tomb, they saw a young man clothed in
a long white robe sitting on the right side; and
they were alarmed.
6 But he said to them, "Do not be alarmed. You
seek Jesus of Nazareth, who was crucified. He is
risen! He is not here. See the place where they
laid Him. 7 But go, tell His disciples—and Peter—
that He is going before you into Galilee; there
you will see Him, as He said to you."
8 So they went out quickly[a] and fled from the
tomb, for they trembled and were amazed. And
they said nothing to anyone, for they were
afraid.

MARY MAGDALENE SEES THE RISEN LORD

9 Now when *He* rose early on the first *day* of
the week, He appeared first to Mary Magdalene,
out of whom He had cast seven demons. 10 She
went and told those who had been with Him, as
they mourned and wept. 11 And when they heard
that He was alive and had been seen by her, they
did not believe.

JESUS APPEARS TO TWO DISCIPLES

12 After that, He appeared in another form to
two of them as they walked and went into the
country. 13 And they went and told *it* to the rest,
but they did not believe them either.

THE GREAT COMMISSION

14 Later He appeared to the eleven as they sat
at the table; and He rebuked their unbelief and
hardness of heart, because they did not believe
those who had seen Him after He had risen.
15 And He said to them, "Go into all the world
and preach the gospel to every creature. 16 He
who believes and is baptized will be saved; but
he who does not believe will be condemned.
17 And these signs will follow those who believe:
In My name they will cast out demons; they will
speak with new tongues; 18 they[a] will take up
serpents; and if they drink anything deadly, it
will by no means hurt them; they will lay hands
on the sick, and they will recover."

CHRIST ASCENDS TO GOD'S RIGHT HAND

19 So then, after the Lord had spoken to them,
He was received up into heaven, and sat down at
the right hand of God. 20 And they went out and
preached everywhere, the Lord working with
them and confirming the word through the ac-
companying signs. Amen.[a]

16:8 [a]NU-Text and M-Text omit *quickly.* **16:18** [a]NU-Text reads *and in their hands they will.* **16:20** [a]Verses 9–20 are bracketed in NU-Text as not original. They are lacking in Codex Sinaiticus and Codex Vaticanus, although nearly all other manuscripts of Mark contain them.

THE MESSAGE

THE RESURRECTION

1-3 16 When the Sabbath was over, Mary Magdalene, Mary the mother of James, and Salome bought spices so they could embalm him. Very early on Sunday morning, as the sun rose, they went to the tomb. They worried out loud to each other, "Who will roll back the stone from the tomb for us?"

4-5 Then they looked up, saw that it had been rolled back—it was a huge stone—and walked right in. They saw a young man sitting on the right side, dressed all in white. They were completely taken aback, astonished.

6-7 He said, "Don't be afraid. I know you're looking for Jesus the Nazarene, the One they nailed on the cross. He's been raised up; he's here no longer. You can see for yourselves that the place is empty. Now—on your way. Tell his disciples and Peter that he is going on ahead of you to Galilee. You'll see him there, exactly as he said."

8 They got out as fast as they could, beside themselves, their heads swimming. Stunned, they said nothing to anyone.

9-11 [After rising from the dead, Jesus appeared early on Sunday morning to Mary Magdalene, whom he had delivered from seven demons. She went to his former companions, now weeping and carrying on, and told them. When they heard her report that she had seen him alive and well, they didn't believe her.

12-13 Later he appeared, but in a different form, to two of them out walking in the countryside. They went back and told the rest, but they weren't believed either.

14-16 Still later, as the Eleven were eating supper, he appeared and took them to task most severely for their stubborn unbelief, refusing to believe those who had seen him raised up. Then he said, "Go into the world. Go everywhere and announce the Message of God's good news to one and all. Whoever believes and is baptized is saved; whoever refuses to believe is damned.

17-18 "These are some of the signs that will accompany believers: They will throw out demons in my name, they will speak in new tongues, they will take snakes in their hands, they will drink poison and not be hurt, they will lay hands on the sick and make them well."

19-20 Then the Master Jesus, after briefing them, was taken up to heaven, and he sat down beside God in the place of honor. And the disciples went everywhere preaching, the Master working right with them, validating the Message with indisputable evidence.]

Note: Mark 16:9-20 [the portion in brackets] is contained only in later manuscripts.

LUKE

New King James Version

Dedication to Theophilus

1 Inasmuch as many have taken in hand to set in order a narrative of those things which have been fulfilled[a] among us, 2 just as those who from the beginning were eyewitnesses and ministers of the word delivered them to us, 3 it seemed good to me also, having had perfect understanding of all things from the very first, to write to you an orderly account, most excellent Theophilus, 4 that you may know the certainty of those things in which you were instructed.

John's Birth Announced to Zacharias

5 There was in the days of Herod, the king of Judea, a certain priest named Zacharias, of the division of Abijah. His wife *was* of the daughters of Aaron, and her name *was* Elizabeth. 6 And they were both righteous before God, walking in all the commandments and ordinances of the Lord blameless. 7 But they had no child, because Elizabeth was barren, and they were both well advanced in years.

8 So it was, that while he was serving as priest before God in the order of his division, 9 according to the custom of the priesthood, his lot fell to burn incense when he went into the temple of the Lord. 10 And the whole multitude of the people was praying outside at the hour of incense. 11 Then an angel of the Lord appeared to him, standing on the right side of the altar of incense. 12 And when Zacharias saw *him,* he was troubled, and fear fell upon him.

13 But the angel said to him, "Do not be afraid, Zacharias, for your prayer is heard; and your wife Elizabeth will bear you a son, and you shall call his name John. 14 And you will have joy and gladness, and many will rejoice at his birth. 15 For he will be great in the sight of the Lord, and shall drink neither wine nor strong drink. He will also be filled with the Holy Spirit, even from his mother's womb. 16 And he will turn many of the children of Israel to the Lord their God. 17 He will also go before Him in the spirit and power of Elijah, *'to turn the hearts of the fathers to the children,'*[a] and the disobedient to the wisdom of the just, to make ready a people prepared for the Lord."

18 And Zacharias said to the angel, "How shall I know this? For I am an old man, and my wife is well advanced in years."

19 And the angel answered and said to him, "I am Gabriel, who stands in the presence of God, and was sent to speak to you and bring you these glad tidings. 20 But behold, you will be mute and not able to speak until the day these things take place, because you did not believe my words which will be fulfilled in their own time."

21 And the people waited for Zacharias, and marveled that he lingered so long in the temple. 22 But when he came out, he could not speak to

1:1 [a]Or *are most surely believed* **1:17** [a]Malachi 4:5, 6

The Message

1-4 **1** So many others have tried their hand at putting together a story of the wonderful harvest of Scripture and history that took place among us, using reports handed down by the original eyewitnesses who served this Word with their very lives. Since I have investigated all the reports in close detail, starting from the story's beginning, I decided to write it all out for you, most honorable Theophilus, so you can know beyond the shadow of a doubt the reliability of what you were taught.

A Childless Couple Conceives

5-7 During the rule of Herod, King of Judea, there was a priest assigned service in the regiment of Abijah. His name was Zachariah. His wife was descended from the daughters of Aaron. Her name was Elizabeth. Together they lived honorably before God, careful in keeping to the ways of the commandments and enjoying a clear conscience before God. But they were childless because Elizabeth could never conceive, and now they were quite old.

8-12 It so happened that as Zachariah was carrying out his priestly duties before God, working the shift assigned to his regiment, it came his one turn in life to enter the sanctuary of God and burn incense. The congregation was gathered and praying outside the Temple at the hour of the incense offering. Unannounced, an angel of God appeared just to the right of the altar of incense. Zachariah was paralyzed in fear.

13-15 But the angel reassured him, "Don't fear, Zachariah. Your prayer has been heard. Elizabeth, your wife, will bear a son by you. You are to name him John. You're going to leap like a gazelle for joy, and not only you—many will delight in his birth. He'll achieve great stature with God.

15-17 "He'll drink neither wine nor beer. He'll be filled with the Holy Spirit from the moment he leaves his mother's womb. He will turn many sons and daughters of Israel back to their God. He will herald God's arrival in the style and strength of Elijah, soften the hearts of parents to children, and kindle devout understanding among hardened skeptics—he'll get the people ready for God."

18 Zachariah said to the angel, "Do you expect me to believe this? I'm an old man and my wife is an old woman."

19-20 But the angel said, "I am Gabriel, the sentinel of God, sent especially to bring you this glad news. But because you won't believe me, you'll be unable to say a word until the day of your son's birth. Every word I've spoken to you will come true on time—*God's* time."

21-22 Meanwhile, the congregation waiting for Zachariah was getting restless, wondering what was keeping him so long in the sanctuary. When he came out and couldn't speak,

NEW KING JAMES VERSION

them; and they perceived that he had seen a vi-
sion in the temple, for he beckoned to them and
remained speechless.
23So it was, as soon as the days of his service
were completed, that he departed to his own
house. 24Now after those days his wife Elizabeth
conceived; and she hid herself five months, say-
ing, 25"Thus the Lord has dealt with me, in the
days when He looked on *me*, to take away my
reproach among people."

CHRIST'S BIRTH ANNOUNCED TO MARY

26Now in the sixth month the angel Gabriel
was sent by God to a city of Galilee named
Nazareth, 27to a virgin betrothed to a man
whose name was Joseph, of the house of David.
The virgin's name *was* Mary. 28And having
come in, the angel said to her, "Rejoice, highly
favored *one*, the Lord *is* with you; blessed *are*
you among women!"[a]
29But when she saw *him*,[a] she was troubled
at his saying, and considered what manner of
greeting this was. 30Then the angel said to her,
"Do not be afraid, Mary, for you have found fa-
vor with God. 31And behold, you will conceive in
your womb and bring forth a Son, and shall call
His name JESUS. 32He will be great, and will be
called the Son of the Highest; and the Lord God
will give Him the throne of His father David.
33And He will reign over the house of Jacob for-
ever, and of His kingdom there will be no end."
34Then Mary said to the angel, "How can this
be, since I do not know a man?"
35And the angel answered and said to her,
"*The* Holy Spirit will come upon you, and the
power of the Highest will overshadow you;
therefore, also, that Holy One who is to be born
will be called the Son of God. 36Now indeed,
Elizabeth your relative has also conceived a son
in her old age; and this is now the sixth month
for her who was called barren. 37For with God
nothing will be impossible."
38Then Mary said, "Behold the maidservant
of the Lord! Let it be to me according to your
word." And the angel departed from her.

MARY VISITS ELIZABETH

39Now Mary arose in those days and went
into the hill country with haste, to a city of Ju-
dah, 40and entered the house of Zacharias and
greeted Elizabeth. 41And it happened, when
Elizabeth heard the greeting of Mary, that the
babe leaped in her womb; and Elizabeth was
filled with the Holy Spirit. 42Then she spoke out
with a loud voice and said, "Blessed *are* you

1:28 [a]NU-Text omits *blessed are you among women.* 1:29 [a]NU-Text omits *when she saw him.*

THE MESSAGE

they knew he had seen a vision. He contin-
ued speechless and had to use sign lan-
guage with the people.

23-25 When the course of his priestly assign-
ment was completed, he went back home. It
wasn't long before his wife, Elizabeth, con-
ceived. She went off by herself for five
months, relishing her pregnancy. "So, this is
how God acts to remedy my unfortunate
condition!" she said.

A VIRGIN CONCEIVES

26-28 In the sixth month of Elizabeth's pregnancy,
God sent the angel Gabriel to the Galilean
village of Nazareth to a virgin engaged to be
married to a man descended from David. His
name was Joseph, and the virgin's name,
Mary. Upon entering, Gabriel greeted her:

Good morning!
You're beautiful with God's beauty,
Beautiful inside and out!
God be with you.

29-33 She was thoroughly shaken, wondering
what was behind a greeting like that. But
the angel assured her, "Mary, you have noth-
ing to fear. God has a surprise for you: You
will become pregnant and give birth to a
son and call his name Jesus.

He will be great,
be called 'Son of the Highest.'
The Lord God will give him
the throne of his father David;
He will rule Jacob's house forever—
no end, ever, to his kingdom."

34 Mary said to the angel, "But how? I've
never slept with a man."
35 The angel answered,

The Holy Spirit will come upon you,
the power of the Highest hover over
you;
Therefore, the child you bring to birth
will be called Holy, Son of God.

36-38 "And did you know that your cousin Eliz-
abeth conceived a son, old as she is? Every-
one called her barren, and here she is six
months pregnant! Nothing, you see, is im-
possible with God."
And Mary said,

Yes, I see it all now:
I'm the Lord's maid, ready to serve.
Let it be with me
just as you say.

Then the angel left her.

BLESSED AMONG WOMEN

39-45 Mary didn't waste a minute. She got up and
traveled to a town in Judah in the hill coun-
try, straight to Zachariah's house, and
greeted Elizabeth. When Elizabeth heard
Mary's greeting, the baby in her womb
leaped. She was filled with the Holy Spirit,
and sang out exuberantly,

NEW KING JAMES VERSION

among women, and blessed *is* the fruit of your
womb! 43But why *is* this *granted* to me, that the
mother of my Lord should come to me? 44For in-
deed, as soon as the voice of your greeting
sounded in my ears, the babe leaped in my
womb for joy. 45Blessed *is* she who believed, for
there will be a fulfillment of those things which
were told her from the Lord."

THE SONG OF MARY

46And Mary said:

"My soul magnifies the Lord,
47And my spirit has rejoiced in God my
Savior.
48For He has regarded the lowly state of His
maidservant;
For behold, henceforth all generations will
call me blessed.
49For He who is mighty has done great things
for me,
And holy *is* His name.
50And His mercy *is* on those who fear Him
From generation to generation.
51He has shown strength with His arm;
He has scattered *the* proud in the
imagination of their hearts.
52He has put down the mighty from *their*
thrones,
And exalted *the* lowly.
53He has filled *the* hungry with good things,
And *the* rich He has sent away empty.
54He has helped His servant Israel,
In remembrance of *His* mercy,
55As He spoke to our fathers,
To Abraham and to his seed forever."

56And Mary remained with her about three
months, and returned to her house.

BIRTH OF JOHN THE BAPTIST

57Now Elizabeth's full time came for her to
be delivered, and she brought forth a son.
58When her neighbors and relatives heard how
the Lord had shown great mercy to her, they re-
joiced with her.

CIRCUMCISION OF JOHN THE BAPTIST

59So it was, on the eighth day, that they came
to circumcise the child; and they would have
called him by the name of his father, Zacharias.
60His mother answered and said, "No; he shall
be called John."

61But they said to her, "There is no one
among your relatives who is called by this
name." 62So they made signs to his father—what
he would have him called.

63And he asked for a writing tablet, and
wrote, saying, "His name is John." So they all
marveled. 64Immediately his mouth was opened
and his tongue *loosed,* and he spoke, praising
God. 65Then fear came on all who dwelt around
them; and all these sayings were discussed
throughout all the hill country of Judea. 66And
all those who heard *them* kept *them* in their
hearts, saying, "What kind of child will this be?"
And the hand of the Lord was with him.

THE MESSAGE

You're so blessed among women,
and the babe in your womb, also
blessed!
And why am I so blessed that
the mother of my Lord visits me?
The moment the sound of your
greeting entered my ears,
The babe in my womb
skipped like a lamb for sheer joy.
Blessed woman, who believed what God
said,
believed every word would come true!

46-55 And Mary said,

I'm bursting with God-news;
I'm dancing the song of my Savior God.
God took one good look at me, and look
what happened—
I'm the most fortunate woman on
earth!
What God has done for me will never be
forgotten,
the God whose very name is holy, set
apart from all others.
His mercy flows in wave after wave
on those who are in awe before him.
He bared his arm and showed his
strength,
scattered the bluffing braggarts.
He knocked tyrants off their high horses,
pulled victims out of the mud.
The starving poor sat down to a banquet;
the callous rich were left out in the
cold.
He embraced his chosen child, Israel;
he remembered and piled on the
mercies, piled them high.
It's exactly what he promised,
beginning with Abraham and right up
to now.

56 Mary stayed with Elizabeth for three months and then went back to her own home.

THE BIRTH OF JOHN

57-58 When Elizabeth was full-term in her pregnancy, she bore a son. Her neighbors and relatives, seeing that God had overwhelmed her with mercy, celebrated with her.

59-60 On the eighth day, they came to circumcise the child and were calling him Zachariah after his father. But his mother intervened: "No. He is to be called John."

61-62 "But," they said, "no one in your family is named that." They used sign language to ask Zachariah what he wanted him named.

63-64 Asking for a tablet, Zachariah wrote, "His name is to be John." That took everyone by surprise. Surprise followed surprise—Zachariah's mouth was now open, his tongue loose, and he was talking, praising God!

65-66 A deep, reverential fear settled over the neighborhood, and in all that Judean hill country people talked about nothing else. Everyone who heard about it took it to heart, wondering, "What will become of this child? Clearly, God has his hand in this."

New King James Version

Zacharias' Prophecy

67Now his father Zacharias was filled with
the Holy Spirit, and prophesied, saying:

68"Blessed *is* the Lord God of Israel,
For He has visited and redeemed His people,
69And has raised up a horn of salvation for us
In the house of His servant David,
70As He spoke by the mouth of His holy
prophets,
Who *have been* since the world began,
71That we should be saved from our enemies
And from the hand of all who hate us,
72To perform the mercy *promised* to our
fathers
And to remember His holy covenant,
73The oath which He swore to our father
Abraham:
74To grant us that we,
Being delivered from the hand of our
enemies,
Might serve Him without fear,
75In holiness and righteousness before Him
all the days of our life.

76"And you, child, will be called the prophet of
the Highest;
For you will go before the face of the Lord
to prepare His ways,
77To give knowledge of salvation to His
people
By the remission of their sins,
78Through the tender mercy of our God,
With which the Dayspring from on high has
visited[a] us;
79To give light to those who sit in darkness
and the shadow of death,
To guide our feet into the way of peace."

80So the child grew and became strong in
spirit, and was in the deserts till the day of his
manifestation to Israel.

Christ Born of Mary

2 And it came to pass in those days *that* a de-
cree went out from Caesar Augustus that all
the world should be registered. 2This census
first took place while Quirinius was governing
Syria. 3So all went to be registered, everyone to
his own city.

4Joseph also went up from Galilee, out of the
city of Nazareth, into Judea, to the city of David,
which is called Bethlehem, because he was of
the house and lineage of David, 5to be registered
with Mary, his betrothed wife,[a] who was with
child. 6So it was, that while they were there, the
days were completed for her to be delivered.
7And she brought forth her firstborn Son, and
wrapped Him in swaddling cloths, and laid Him
in a manger, because there was no room for
them in the inn.

Glory in the Highest

8Now there were in the same country shep-
herds living out in the fields, keeping watch
over their flock by night. 9And behold,[a] an angel

1:78 [a]NU-Text reads *shall visit.* 2:5 [a]NU-Text omits *wife.* 2:9 [a]NU-Text omits *behold.*

The Message

67-79 Then Zachariah was filled with the Holy
Spirit and prophesied,

Blessed be the Lord, the God of Israel;
he came and set his people free.
He set the power of salvation in the
center of our lives,
and in the very house of David his
servant,
Just as he promised long ago
through the preaching of his holy
prophets:
Deliverance from our enemies
and every hateful hand;
Mercy to our fathers,
as he remembers to do what he said
he'd do,
What he swore to our father Abraham—
a clean rescue from the enemy camp,
So we can worship him without a care in
the world,
made holy before him as long as we
live.

And you, my child, "Prophet of the
Highest,"
will go ahead of the Master to
prepare his ways,
Present the offer of salvation to his
people,
the forgiveness of their sins.
Through the heartfelt mercies of our
God,
God's Sunrise will break in upon us,
Shining on those in the darkness,
those sitting in the shadow of death,
Then showing us the way, one foot at a
time,
down the path of peace.

80 The child grew up, healthy and spirited.
He lived out in the desert until the day he
made his prophetic debut in Israel.

The Birth of Jesus

1-5 2 About that time Caesar Augustus ordered
a census to be taken throughout the Em-
pire. This was the first census when
Quirinius was governor of Syria. Everyone
had to travel to his own ancestral hometown
to be accounted for. So Joseph went from
the Galilean town of Nazareth up to Bethle-
hem in Judah, David's town, for the census.
As a descendant of David, he had to go
there. He went with Mary, his fiancée, who
was pregnant.
6-7 While they were there, the time came for
her to give birth. She gave birth to a son, her
firstborn. She wrapped him in a blanket and
laid him in a manger, because there was no
room in the hostel.

An Event for Everyone

8-12 There were sheepherders camping in the
neighborhood. They had set night watches
over their sheep. Suddenly, God's angel
stood among them and God's glory blazed

NEW KING JAMES VERSION

of the Lord stood before them, and the glory of the Lord shone around them, and they were greatly afraid. [10]Then the angel said to them, "Do not be afraid, for behold, I bring you good tidings of great joy which will be to all people. [11]For there is born to you this day in the city of David a Savior, who is Christ the Lord. [12]And this *will be* the sign to you: You will find a Babe wrapped in swaddling cloths, lying in a manger."

[13]And suddenly there was with the angel a multitude of the heavenly host praising God and saying:

[14]"Glory to God in the highest,
And on earth peace, goodwill toward men!"[a]

[15]So it was, when the angels had gone away from them into heaven, that the shepherds said to one another, "Let us now go to Bethlehem and see this thing that has come to pass, which the Lord has made known to us." [16]And they came with haste and found Mary and Joseph, and the Babe lying in a manger. [17]Now when they had seen *Him*, they made widely[a] known the saying which was told them concerning this Child. [18]And all those who heard *it* marveled at those things which were told them by the shepherds. [19]But Mary kept all these things and pondered *them* in her heart. [20]Then the shepherds returned, glorifying and praising God for all the things that they had heard and seen, as it was told them.

CIRCUMCISION OF JESUS

[21]And when eight days were completed for the circumcision of the Child,[a] His name was called JESUS, the name given by the angel before He was conceived in the womb.

JESUS PRESENTED IN THE TEMPLE

[22]Now when the days of her purification according to the law of Moses were completed, they brought Him to Jerusalem to present *Him* to the Lord [23](as it is written in the law of the Lord, *"Every male who opens the womb shall be called holy to the LORD")*,[a] [24]and to offer a sacrifice according to what is said in the law of the Lord, *"A pair of turtledoves or two young pigeons."*[a]

SIMEON SEES GOD'S SALVATION

[25]And behold, there was a man in Jerusalem whose name *was* Simeon, and this man *was* just and devout, waiting for the Consolation of Israel, and the Holy Spirit was upon him. [26]And it had been revealed to him by the Holy Spirit that he would not see death before he had seen the Lord's Christ. [27]So he came by the Spirit into the temple. And when the parents brought in the Child Jesus, to do for Him according to the custom of the law, [28]he took Him up in his arms and blessed God and said:

[29]"Lord, now You are letting Your servant
depart in peace,
According to Your word;

2:14 [a]NU-Text reads *toward men of goodwill.* **2:17** [a]NU-Text omits *widely.* **2:21** [a]NU-Text reads *for His circumcision.* **2:23** [a]Exodus 13:2, 12, 15 **2:24** [a]Leviticus 12:8

THE MESSAGE

around them. They were terrified. The angel said, "Don't be afraid. I'm here to announce a great and joyful event that is meant for everybody, worldwide: A Savior has just been born in David's town, a Savior who is Messiah and Master. This is what you're to look for: a baby wrapped in a blanket and lying in a manger."

13-14 At once the angel was joined by a huge angelic choir singing God's praises:

Glory to God in the heavenly heights,
Peace to all men and women on earth
who please him.

15-18 As the angel choir withdrew into heaven, the sheepherders talked it over. "Let's get over to Bethlehem as fast as we can and see for ourselves what God has revealed to us." They left, running, and found Mary and Joseph, and the baby lying in the manger. Seeing was believing. They told everyone they met what the angels had said about this child. All who heard the sheepherders were impressed.

19-20 Mary kept all these things to herself, holding them dear, deep within herself. The sheepherders returned and let loose, glorifying and praising God for everything they had heard and seen. It turned out exactly the way they'd been told!

BLESSINGS

21 When the eighth day arrived, the day of circumcision, the child was named Jesus, the name given by the angel before he was conceived.

22-24 Then when the days stipulated by Moses for purification were complete, they took him up to Jerusalem to offer him to God as commanded in God's Law: "Every male who opens the womb shall be a holy offering to God," and also to sacrifice the "pair of doves or two young pigeons" prescribed in God's Law.

25-32 In Jerusalem at the time, there was a man, Simeon by name, a good man, a man who lived in the prayerful expectancy of help for Israel. And the Holy Spirit was on him. The Holy Spirit had shown him that he would see the Messiah of God before he died. Led by the Spirit, he entered the Temple. As the parents of the child Jesus brought him in to carry out the rituals of the Law, Simeon took him into his arms and blessed God:

God, you can now release your servant;
release me in peace as you promised.

NEW KING JAMES VERSION

[30]For my eyes have seen Your salvation
[31]Which You have prepared before the face of
all peoples,
[32]A light to *bring* revelation to the Gentiles,
And the glory of Your people Israel."

[33]And Joseph and His mother[a] marveled at
those things which were spoken of Him. [34]Then
Simeon blessed them, and said to Mary His
mother, "Behold, this *Child* is destined for the
fall and rising of many in Israel, and for a sign
which will be spoken against [35](yes, a sword will
pierce through your own soul also), that the
thoughts of many hearts may be revealed."

ANNA BEARS WITNESS TO THE REDEEMER

[36]Now there was one, Anna, a prophetess,
the daughter of Phanuel, of the tribe of Asher.
She was of a great age, and had lived with a husband seven years from her virginity; [37]and this
woman *was* a widow of about eighty-four
years,[a] who did not depart from the temple, but
served *God* with fastings and prayers night and
day. [38]And coming in that instant she gave
thanks to the Lord,[a] and spoke of Him to all
those who looked for redemption in Jerusalem.

THE FAMILY RETURNS TO NAZARETH

[39]So when they had performed all things according to the law of the Lord, they returned to
Galilee, to their *own* city, Nazareth. [40]And the
Child grew and became strong in spirit,[a] filled
with wisdom; and the grace of God was upon
Him.

THE BOY JESUS AMAZES THE SCHOLARS

[41]His parents went to Jerusalem every year
at the Feast of the Passover. [42]And when He was
twelve years old, they went up to Jerusalem according to the custom of the feast. [43]When they
had finished the days, as they returned, the Boy
Jesus lingered behind in Jerusalem. And Joseph
and His mother[a] did not know *it;* [44]but supposing Him to have been in the company, they went
a day's journey, and sought Him among *their*
relatives and acquaintances. [45]So when they did
not find Him, they returned to Jerusalem, seeking Him. [46]Now so it was *that* after three days
they found Him in the temple, sitting in the
midst of the teachers, both listening to them and
asking them questions. [47]And all who heard
Him were astonished at His understanding and
answers. [48]So when they saw Him, they were
amazed; and His mother said to Him, "Son, why
have You done this to us? Look, Your father and
I have sought You anxiously."

[49]And He said to them, "Why did you seek
Me? Did you not know that I must be about My
Father's business?" [50]But they did not understand the statement which He spoke to them.

JESUS ADVANCES IN WISDOM AND FAVOR

[51]Then He went down with them and came to
Nazareth, and was subject to them, but His
mother kept all these things in her heart. [52]And

2:33 [a]NU-Text reads *And His father and mother.* **2:37** [a]NU-Text reads *a widow until she was eighty-four.* **2:38** [a]NU-Text reads *to God.* **2:40** [a]NU-Text omits *in spirit.* **2:43** [a]NU-Text reads *And His parents.*

THE MESSAGE

With my own eyes I've seen your
salvation;
it's now out in the open for everyone
to see:
A God-revealing light to the non-Jewish
nations,
and of glory for your people Israel.

33-35 Jesus' father and mother were speechless with surprise at these words. Simeon went on to bless them, and said to Mary his mother,

This child marks both the failure and
the recovery of many in Israel,
A figure misunderstood and
contradicted—
the pain of a sword-thrust through
you—
But the rejection will force honesty,
as God reveals who they really are.

36-38 Anna the prophetess was also there, a daughter of Phanuel from the tribe of Asher. She was by now a very old woman. She had been married seven years and a widow for eighty-four. She never left the Temple area, worshiping night and day with her fastings and prayers. At the very time Simeon was praying, she showed up, broke into an anthem of praise to God, and talked about the child to all who were waiting expectantly for the freeing of Jerusalem.

39-40 When they finished everything required by God in the Law, they returned to Galilee and their own town, Nazareth. There the child grew strong in body and wise in spirit. And the grace of God was on him.

THEY FOUND HIM IN THE TEMPLE

41-45 Every year Jesus' parents traveled to Jerusalem for the Feast of Passover. When he was twelve years old, they went up as they always did for the Feast. When it was over and they left for home, the child Jesus stayed behind in Jerusalem, but his parents didn't know it. Thinking he was somewhere in the company of pilgrims, they journeyed for a whole day and then began looking for him among relatives and neighbors. When they didn't find him, they went back to Jerusalem looking for him.

46-48 The next day they found him in the Temple seated among the teachers, listening to them and asking questions. The teachers were all quite taken with him, impressed with the sharpness of his answers. But his parents were not impressed; they were upset and hurt.

His mother said, "Young man, why have you done this to us? Your father and I have been half out of our minds looking for you."

49-50 He said, "Why were you looking for me? Didn't you know that I had to be here, dealing with the things of my Father?" But they had no idea what he was talking about.

51-52 So he went back to Nazareth with them, and lived obediently with them. His mother held these things dearly, deep within herself.

NEW KING JAMES VERSION

Jesus increased in wisdom and stature, and in favor with God and men.

JOHN THE BAPTIST PREPARES THE WAY

3 Now in the fifteenth year of the reign of Tiberius Caesar, Pontius Pilate being governor of Judea, Herod being tetrarch of Galilee, his brother Philip tetrarch of Iturea and the region of Trachonitis, and Lysanias tetrarch of
Abilene, 2while Annas and Caiaphas were high
priests,[a] the word of God came to John the son
of Zacharias in the wilderness. 3And he went
into all the region around the Jordan, preaching
a baptism of repentance for the remission of
sins, 4as it is written in the book of the words of
Isaiah the prophet, saying:

"The voice of one crying in the wilderness:
'Prepare the way of the Lord;
Make His paths straight.
5*Every valley shall be filled*
And every mountain and hill brought low;
The crooked places shall be made straight
And the rough ways smooth;
6*And all flesh shall see the salvation*
of God.' "[a]

JOHN PREACHES TO THE PEOPLE

7Then he said to the multitudes that came out to be baptized by him, "Brood of vipers! Who warned you to flee from the wrath to come?
8Therefore bear fruits worthy of repentance,
and do not begin to say to yourselves, 'We have
Abraham as *our* father.' For I say to you that
God is able to raise up children to Abraham
from these stones. 9And even now the ax is laid
to the root of the trees. Therefore every tree which does not bear good fruit is cut down and thrown into the fire."

10So the people asked him, saying, "What shall we do then?"

11He answered and said to them, "He who has two tunics, let him give to him who has none; and he who has food, let him do likewise."

12Then tax collectors also came to be baptized, and said to him, "Teacher, what shall we do?"

13And he said to them, "Collect no more than what is appointed for you."

14Likewise the soldiers asked him, saying, "And what shall we do?"

So he said to them, "Do not intimidate anyone or accuse falsely, and be content with your wages."

15Now as the people were in expectation, and
all reasoned in their hearts about John, whether
he was the Christ *or* not, 16John answered, say-
ing to all, "I indeed baptize you with water; but
One mightier than I is coming, whose sandal
strap I am not worthy to loose. He will baptize
you with the Holy Spirit and fire. 17His winnow-
ing fan *is* in His hand, and He will thoroughly clean out His threshing floor, and gather the wheat into His barn; but the chaff He will burn with unquenchable fire."

3:2 [a]NU-Text and M-Text read *in the high priesthood of Annas and Caiaphas.* **3:6** [a]Isaiah 40:3–5

THE MESSAGE

And Jesus matured, growing up in both body and spirit, blessed by both God and people.

A BAPTISM OF LIFE-CHANGE

1-6 3 In the fifteenth year of the rule of Caesar Tiberius—it was while Pontius Pilate was governor of Judea; Herod, ruler of Galilee; his brother Philip, ruler of Iturea and Trachonitis; Lysanias, ruler of Abilene; during the Chief-Priesthood of Annas and Caiaphas—John, Zachariah's son, out in the desert at the time, received a message from God. He went all through the country around the Jordan River preaching a baptism of life-change leading to forgiveness of sins, as described in the words of Isaiah the prophet:

Thunder in the desert!
"Prepare God's arrival!
Make the road smooth and straight!
Every ditch will be filled in,
Every bump smoothed out,
The detours straightened out,
All the ruts paved over.
Everyone will be there to see
The parade of God's salvation."

7-9 When crowds of people came out for baptism because it was the popular thing to do, John exploded: "Brood of snakes! What do you think you're doing slithering down here to the river? Do you think a little water on your snakeskins is going to deflect God's judgment? It's your *life* that must change, not your skin. And don't think you can pull rank by claiming Abraham as 'father.' Being a child of Abraham is neither here nor there—children of Abraham are a dime a dozen. God can make children from stones if he wants. What counts is your life. Is it green and blossoming? Because if it's deadwood, it goes on the fire."

10 The crowd asked him, "Then what are we supposed to do?"

11 "If you have two coats, give one away," he said. "Do the same with your food."

12 Tax men also came to be baptized and said, "Teacher, what should we do?"

13 He told them, "No more extortion—collect only what is required by law."

14 Soldiers asked him, "And what should we do?"

He told them, "No shakedowns, no blackmail—and be content with your rations."

15 The interest of the people by now was building. They were all beginning to wonder, "Could this John be the Messiah?"

16-17 But John intervened: "I'm baptizing you here in the river. The main character in this drama, to whom I'm a mere stagehand, will ignite the kingdom life, a fire, the Holy Spirit within you, changing you from the inside out. He's going to clean house—make a clean sweep of your lives. He'll place everything true in its proper place before God; everything false he'll put out with the trash to be burned."

NEW KING JAMES VERSION

18 And with many other exhortations he
preached to the people. 19 But Herod the
tetrarch, being rebuked by him concerning
Herodias, his brother Philip's wife,[a] and for all
the evils which Herod had done, 20 also added
this, above all, that he shut John up in prison.

JOHN BAPTIZES JESUS

21 When all the people were baptized, it came
to pass that Jesus also was baptized; and while
He prayed, the heaven was opened. 22 And the
Holy Spirit descended in bodily form like a dove
upon Him, and a voice came from heaven which
said, "You are My beloved Son; in You I am well
pleased."

THE GENEALOGY OF JESUS CHRIST

23 Now Jesus Himself began *His ministry at*
about thirty years of age, being (as was sup-
posed) *the* son of Joseph, *the son* of Heli, 24 *the*
son of Matthat,[a] *the son* of Levi, *the son* of
Melchi, *the son* of Janna, *the son* of Joseph,
25 *the son* of Mattathiah, *the son* of Amos, *the*
son of Nahum, *the son* of Esli, *the son* of Nag-
gai, 26 *the son* of Maath, *the son* of Mattathiah,
the son of Semei, *the son* of Joseph, *the son* of
Judah, 27 *the son* of Joannas, *the son* of Rhesa,
the son of Zerubbabel, *the son* of Shealtiel, *the*
son of Neri, 28 *the son* of Melchi, *the son* of Addi,
the son of Cosam, *the son* of Elmodam, *the son*
of Er, 29 *the son* of Jose, *the son* of Eliezer, *the*
son of Jorim, *the son* of Matthat, *the son* of Levi,
30 *the son* of Simeon, *the son* of Judah, *the son* of
Joseph, *the son* of Jonan, *the son* of Eliakim,
31 *the son* of Melea, *the son* of Menan, *the son* of
Mattathah, *the son* of Nathan, *the son* of David,
32 *the son* of Jesse, *the son* of Obed, *the son* of
Boaz, *the son* of Salmon, *the son* of Nahshon,
33 *the son* of Amminadab, *the son* of Ram, *the*

3:19 [a]NU-Text reads *his brother's wife.* **3:24** [a]This and several other names in the genealogy are spelled somewhat differently in the NU-Text. Since the New King James Version uses the Old Testament spelling for persons mentioned in the New Testament, these variations, which come from the Greek, have not been footnoted.

THE MESSAGE

18-20 There was a lot more of this—words that gave strength to the people, words that put heart in them. The Message! But Herod, the ruler, stung by John's rebuke in the matter of Herodias, his brother Philip's wife, capped his long string of evil deeds with this outrage: He put John in jail.

21-22 After all the people were baptized, Jesus was baptized. As he was praying, the sky opened up and the Holy Spirit, like a dove descending, came down on him. And along with the Spirit, a voice: "You are my Son, chosen and marked by my love, pride of my life."

SON OF ADAM, SON OF GOD

23-38 When Jesus entered public life he was about thirty years old, the son (in public perception) of Joseph, who was—

son of Heli,
son of Matthat,
son of Levi,
son of Melki,
son of Jannai,
son of Joseph,
son of Mattathias,
son of Amos,
son of Nahum,
son of Esli,
son of Naggai,
son of Maath,
son of Mattathias,
son of Semein,
son of Josech,
son of Joda,
son of Joanan,
son of Rhesa,
son of Zerubbabel,
son of Shealtiel,
son of Neri,
son of Melchi,
son of Addi,
son of Cosam,
son of Elmadam,
son of Er,
son of Joshua,
son of Eliezer,
son of Jorim,
son of Matthat,
son of Levi,
son of Simeon,
son of Judah,
son of Joseph,
son of Jonam,
son of Eliakim,
son of Melea,
son of Menna,
son of Mattatha,
son of Nathan,
son of David,
son of Jesse,
son of Obed,
son of Boaz,
son of Salmon,
son of Nahshon,
son of Amminadab,
son of Admin,
son of Arni,

NEW KING JAMES VERSION

son of Hezron, *the son* of Perez, *the son* of Ju-
dah, 34 *the son* of Jacob, *the son* of Isaac, *the son*
of Abraham, *the son* of Terah, *the son* of Nahor,
35 *the son* of Serug, *the son* of Reu, *the son* of Pe-
leg, *the son* of Eber, *the son* of Shelah, 36 *the son*
of Cainan, *the son* of Arphaxad, *the son* of
Shem, *the son* of Noah, *the son* of Lamech, 37 *the*
son of Methuselah, *the son* of Enoch, *the son* of
Jared, *the son* of Mahalalel, *the son* of Cainan,
38 *the son* of Enosh, *the son* of Seth, *the son* of
Adam, *the son* of God.

SATAN TEMPTS JESUS

4 Then Jesus, being filled with the Holy Spirit,
returned from the Jordan and was led by the
Spirit into[a] the wilderness, 2 being tempted for
forty days by the devil. And in those days He ate
nothing, and afterward, when they had ended,
He was hungry.

3 And the devil said to Him, "If You are the
Son of God, command this stone to become
bread."

4 But Jesus answered him, saying,[a] "It is writ-
ten, *'Man shall not live by bread alone, but by*
every word of God.' "[b]

5 Then the devil, taking Him up on a high
mountain, showed Him[a] all the kingdoms of the
world in a moment of time. 6 And the devil said
to Him, "All this authority I will give You, and
their glory; for *this* has been delivered to me,
and I give it to whomever I wish. 7 Therefore, if
You will worship before me, all will be Yours."

8 And Jesus answered and said to him, "Get
behind Me, Satan![a] For[b] it is written, *'You shall*
worship the Lord your God, and Him only you
shall serve.' "[c]

9 Then he brought Him to Jerusalem, set Him
on the pinnacle of the temple, and said to Him,
"If You are the Son of God, throw Yourself down
from here. 10 For it is written:

'He shall give His angels charge over you,
To keep you,'

11 and,

'In their hands they shall bear you up,
Lest you dash your foot against a stone.' "[a]

4:1 [a]NU-Text reads *in.* **4:4** [a]Deuteronomy 8:3 [b]NU-Text omits *but by every word of God.* **4:5** [a]NU-Text reads *And taking Him up, he showed Him.* **4:8** [a]NU-Text omits *Get behind Me, Satan.* [b]NU-Text and M-Text omit *For.* [c]Deuteronomy 6:13 **4:11** [a]Psalm 91:11, 12

THE MESSAGE

son of Hezron,
son of Perez,
son of Judah,
son of Jacob,
son of Isaac,
son of Abraham,
son of Terah,
son of Nahor,
son of Serug,
son of Reu,
son of Peleg,
son of Eber,
son of Shelah,
son of Kenan,
son of Arphaxad,
son of Shem,
son of Noah,
son of Lamech,
son of Methuselah,
son of Enoch,
son of Jared,
son of Mahalaleel,
son of Kenan,
son of Enos,
son of Seth,
son of Adam,
son of God.

TESTED BY THE DEVIL

1-2 4 Now Jesus, full of the Holy Spirit, left the
Jordan and was led by the Spirit into the
wild. For forty wilderness days and nights
he was tested by the Devil. He ate nothing
during those days, and when the time was
up he was hungry.

3 The Devil, playing on his hunger, gave
the first test: "Since you're God's Son, com-
mand this stone to turn into a loaf of bread."

4 Jesus answered by quoting Deuteron-
omy: "It takes more than bread to really
live."

5-7 For the second test he led him up and
spread out all the kingdoms of the earth on
display at once. Then the Devil said,
"They're yours in all their splendor to serve
your pleasure. I'm in charge of them all and
can turn them over to whomever I wish.
Worship me and they're yours, the whole
works."

8 Jesus refused, again backing his refusal
with Deuteronomy: "Worship the Lord your
God and only the Lord your God. Serve him
with absolute single-heartedness."

9-11 For the third test the Devil took him to
Jerusalem and put him on top of the Temple.
He said, "If you are God's Son, jump. It's
written, isn't it, that 'he has placed you in
the care of angels to protect you; they will
catch you; you won't so much as stub your
toe on a stone'?"

NEW KING JAMES VERSION

12And Jesus answered and said to him, "It
has been said, *'You shall not tempt the LORD
your God.'* "[a]
13Now when the devil had ended every temp-
tation, he departed from Him until an opportune
time.

JESUS BEGINS HIS GALILEAN MINISTRY

14Then Jesus returned in the power of the
Spirit to Galilee, and news of Him went out
through all the surrounding region. 15And He
taught in their synagogues, being glorified by
all.

JESUS REJECTED AT NAZARETH

16So He came to Nazareth, where He had
been brought up. And as His custom was, He
went into the synagogue on the Sabbath day,
and stood up to read. 17And He was handed the
book of the prophet Isaiah. And when He had
opened the book, He found the place where it
was written:

18*"The Spirit of the LORD is upon Me,*
Because He has anointed Me
To preach the gospel to the poor;
He has sent Me to heal the brokenhearted,[a]
To proclaim liberty to the captives
And recovery of sight to the blind,
To set at liberty those who are oppressed;
19*To proclaim the acceptable year of the*
LORD."[a]

20Then He closed the book, and gave *it* back to
the attendant and sat down. And the eyes of all
who were in the synagogue were fixed on Him.
21And He began to say to them, "Today this
Scripture is fulfilled in your hearing." 22So all
bore witness to Him, and marveled at the gra-
cious words which proceeded out of His mouth.
And they said, "Is this not Joseph's son?"
23He said to them, "You will surely say this
proverb to Me, 'Physician, heal yourself! What-
ever we have heard done in Capernaum,[a] do
also here in Your country.' " 24Then He said, "As-
suredly, I say to you, no prophet is accepted in
his own country. 25But I tell you truly, many wid-
ows were in Israel in the days of Elijah, when
the heaven was shut up three years and six
months, and there was a great famine through-
out all the land; 26but to none of them was Elijah
sent except to Zarephath,[a] *in the region* of
Sidon, to a woman *who was* a widow. 27And
many lepers were in Israel in the time of Elisha
the prophet, and none of them was cleansed ex-
cept Naaman the Syrian."
28So all those in the synagogue, when they
heard these things, were filled with wrath, 29and
rose up and thrust Him out of the city; and they
led Him to the brow of the hill on which their
city was built, that they might throw Him down
over the cliff. 30Then passing through the midst
of them, He went His way.

4:12 [a]Deuteronomy 6:16 **4:18** [a]NU-Text omits *to heal the brokenhearted.* **4:19** [a]Isaiah 61:1, 2 **4:23** [a]Here and elsewhere the NU-Text spelling is *Capharnaum.* **4:26** [a]Greek *Sarepta*

THE MESSAGE

12 "Yes," said Jesus, "and it's also written, 'Don't you dare tempt the Lord your God.' "

13 That completed the testing. The Devil retreated temporarily, lying in wait for another opportunity.

TO SET THE BURDENED FREE

14-15 Jesus returned to Galilee powerful in the Spirit. News that he was back spread through the countryside. He taught in their meeting places to everyone's acclaim and pleasure.

16-21 He came to Nazareth where he had been reared. As he always did on the Sabbath, he went to the meeting place. When he stood up to read, he was handed the scroll of the prophet Isaiah. Unrolling the scroll, he found the place where it was written,

God's Spirit is on me;
he's chosen me to preach the
Message of good news to
the poor,
Sent me to announce pardon to
prisoners and
recovery of sight to the blind,
To set the burdened and battered free,
to announce, "This is God's year to
act!"

He rolled up the scroll, handed it back to the assistant, and sat down. Every eye in the place was on him, intent. Then he started in, "You've just heard Scripture make history. It came true just now in this place."

22 All who were there, watching and listening, were surprised at how well he spoke. But they also said, "Isn't this Joseph's son, the one we've known since he was a youngster?"

23-27 He answered, "I suppose you're going to quote the proverb, 'Doctor, go heal yourself. Do here in your hometown what we heard you did in Capernaum.' Well, let me tell you something: No prophet is ever welcomed in his hometown. Isn't it a fact that there were many widows in Israel at the time of Elijah during that three and a half years of drought when famine devastated the land, but the only widow to whom Elijah was sent was in Sarepta in Sidon? And there were many lepers in Israel at the time of the prophet Elisha but the only one cleansed was Naaman the Syrian."

28-30 That set everyone in the meeting place seething with anger. They threw him out, banishing him from the village, then took him to a mountain cliff at the edge of the village to throw him to his doom, but he gave them the slip and was on his way.

NEW KING JAMES VERSION

JESUS CASTS OUT AN UNCLEAN SPIRIT

31Then He went down to Capernaum, a city of Galilee, and was teaching them on the Sabbaths. 32And they were astonished at His teaching, for His word was with authority. 33Now in the synagogue there was a man who had a spirit of an unclean demon. And he cried out with a loud voice, 34saying, "Let *us* alone! What have we to do with You, Jesus of Nazareth? Did You come to destroy us? I know who You are—the Holy One of God!"

35But Jesus rebuked him, saying, "Be quiet, and come out of him!" And when the demon had thrown him in *their* midst, it came out of him and did not hurt him. 36Then they were all amazed and spoke among themselves, saying, "What a word this *is!* For with authority and power He commands the unclean spirits, and they come out." 37And the report about Him went out into every place in the surrounding region.

PETER'S MOTHER-IN-LAW HEALED

38Now He arose from the synagogue and entered Simon's house. But Simon's wife's mother was sick with a high fever, and they made request of Him concerning her. 39So He stood over her and rebuked the fever, and it left her. And immediately she arose and served them.

MANY HEALED AFTER SABBATH SUNSET

40When the sun was setting, all those who had any that were sick with various diseases brought them to Him; and He laid His hands on every one of them and healed them. 41And demons also came out of many, crying out and saying, "You are the Christ,[a] the Son of God!"

And He, rebuking *them,* did not allow them to speak, for they knew that He was the Christ.

JESUS PREACHES IN GALILEE

42Now when it was day, He departed and went into a deserted place. And the crowd sought Him and came to Him, and tried to keep Him from leaving them; 43but He said to them, "I must preach the kingdom of God to the other cities also, because for this purpose I have been sent." 44And He was preaching in the synagogues of Galilee.[a]

FOUR FISHERMEN CALLED AS DISCIPLES

5 So it was, as the multitude pressed about Him to hear the word of God, that He stood by the Lake of Gennesaret, 2and saw two boats standing by the lake; but the fishermen had gone from them and were washing *their* nets. 3Then He got into one of the boats, which was Simon's, and asked him to put out a little from the land. And He sat down and taught the multitudes from the boat.

4When He had stopped speaking, He said to Simon, "Launch out into the deep and let down your nets for a catch."

5But Simon answered and said to Him, "Master, we have toiled all night and caught nothing; nevertheless at Your word I will let down the net." 6And when they had done this, they caught a great number of fish, and their net was break-

4:41 [a]NU-Text omits *the Christ.* **4:44** [a]NU-Text reads *Judea.*

THE MESSAGE

31-32 He went down to Capernaum, a village in
Galilee. He was teaching the people on the
Sabbath. They were surprised and im-
pressed—his teaching was so forthright, so
confident, so authoritative, not the quib-
bling and quoting they were used to.
33-34 In the meeting place that day there was a
man demonically disturbed. He screamed,
"Ho! What business do you have here with
us, Jesus? Nazarene! I know what you're up
to. You're the Holy One of God and you've
come to destroy us!"
35 Jesus shut him up: "Quiet! Get out of
him!" The demonic spirit threw the man
down in front of them all and left. The de-
mon didn't hurt him.
36-37 That set everyone back on their heels,
whispering and wondering, "What's going
on here? Someone whose words make
things happen? Someone who orders de-
monic spirits to get out and they go?" Jesus
was the talk of the town.

HE HEALED THEM ALL

38-39 He left the meeting place and went to Si-
mon's house. Simon's mother-in-law was
running a high fever and they asked him to
do something for her. He stood over her, told
the fever to leave—and it left. Before they
knew it, she was up getting dinner for them.
40-41 When the sun went down, everyone who
had anyone sick with some ailment or other
brought them to him. One by one he placed
his hands on them and healed them.
Demons left in droves, screaming, "Son of
God! You're the Son of God!" But he shut
them up, refusing to let them speak because
they knew too much, knew him to be the
Messiah.
42-44 He left the next day for open country. But
the crowds went looking and, when they
found him, clung to him so he couldn't go
on. He told them, "Don't you realize that
there are yet other villages where I have to
tell the Message of God's kingdom, that this
is the work God sent me to do?" Meanwhile
he continued preaching in the meeting
places of Galilee.

PUSH OUT INTO DEEP WATER

1-3 5 Once when he was standing on the shore
of Lake Gennesaret, the crowd was push-
ing in on him to better hear the Word of
God. He noticed two boats tied up. The fish-
ermen had just left them and were out
scrubbing their nets. He climbed into the
boat that was Simon's and asked him to put
out a little from the shore. Sitting there, us-
ing the boat for a pulpit, he taught the
crowd.
4 When he finished teaching, he said to Si-
mon, "Push out into deep water and let your
nets out for a catch."
5-7 Simon said, "Master, we've been fishing
hard all night and haven't caught even a
minnow. But if you say so, I'll let out the
nets." It was no sooner said than done—a
huge haul of fish, straining the nets past ca-

New King James Version

ing. 7 So they signaled to *their* partners in the other boat to come and help them. And they came and filled both the boats, so that they began to sink. 8 When Simon Peter saw *it*, he fell down at Jesus' knees, saying, "Depart from me, for I am a sinful man, O Lord!"

9 For he and all who were with him were astonished at the catch of fish which they had taken; 10 and so also *were* James and John, the sons of Zebedee, who were partners with Simon. And Jesus said to Simon, "Do not be afraid. From now on you will catch men." 11 So when they had brought their boats to land, they forsook all and followed Him.

Jesus Cleanses a Leper

12 And it happened when He was in a certain city, that behold, a man who was full of leprosy saw Jesus; and he fell on *his* face and implored Him, saying, "Lord, if You are willing, You can make me clean."

13 Then He put out *His* hand and touched him, saying, "I am willing; be cleansed." Immediately the leprosy left him. 14 And He charged him to tell no one, "But go and show yourself to the priest, and make an offering for your cleansing, as a testimony to them, just as Moses commanded."

15 However, the report went around concerning Him all the more; and great multitudes came together to hear, and to be healed by Him of their infirmities. 16 So He Himself *often* withdrew into the wilderness and prayed.

Jesus Forgives and Heals a Paralytic

17 Now it happened on a certain day, as He was teaching, that there were Pharisees and teachers of the law sitting by, who had come out of every town of Galilee, Judea, and Jerusalem. And the power of the Lord was *present* to heal them.[a] 18 Then behold, men brought on a bed a man who was paralyzed, whom they sought to bring in and lay before Him. 19 And when they could not find how they might bring him in, because of the crowd, they went up on the housetop and let him down with *his* bed through the tiling into the midst before Jesus.

20 When He saw their faith, He said to him, "Man, your sins are forgiven you."

21 And the scribes and the Pharisees began to reason, saying, "Who is this who speaks blasphemies? Who can forgive sins but God alone?"

22 But when Jesus perceived their thoughts, He answered and said to them, "Why are you reasoning in your hearts? 23 Which is easier, to say, 'Your sins are forgiven you,' or to say, 'Rise up and walk'? 24 But that you may know that the Son of Man has power on earth to forgive sins"—He said to the man who was paralyzed, "I say to you, arise, take up your bed, and go to your house."

25 Immediately he rose up before them, took up what he had been lying on, and departed to his own house, glorifying God. 26 And they were all amazed, and they glorified God and were filled with fear, saying, "We have seen strange things today!"

5:17 [a]NU-Text reads *present with Him to heal.*

The Message

pacity. They waved to their partners in the other boat to come help them. They filled both boats, nearly swamping them with the catch.

8-10 Simon Peter, when he saw it, fell to his knees before Jesus. "Master, leave. I'm a sinner and can't handle this holiness. Leave me to myself." When they pulled in that catch of fish, awe overwhelmed Simon and everyone with him. It was the same with James and John, Zebedee's sons, coworkers with Simon.

10-11 Jesus said to Simon, "There is nothing to fear. From now on you'll be fishing for men and women." They pulled their boats up on the beach, left them, nets and all, and followed him.

Invitation to a Changed Life

12 One day in one of the villages there was a man covered with leprosy. When he saw Jesus he fell down before him in prayer and said, "If you want to, you can cleanse me."

13 Jesus put out his hand, touched him, and said, "I want to. Be clean." Then and there his skin was smooth, the leprosy gone.

14-16 Jesus instructed him, "Don't talk about this all over town. Just quietly present your healed self to the priest, along with the offering ordered by Moses. Your cleansed and obedient life, not your words, will bear witness to what I have done." But the man couldn't keep it to himself, and the word got out. Soon a large crowd of people had gathered to listen and be healed of their ailments. As often as possible Jesus withdrew to out-of-the-way places for prayer.

17 One day as he was teaching, Pharisees and religion teachers were sitting around. They had come from nearly every village in Galilee and Judea, even as far away as Jerusalem, to be there. The healing power of God was on him.

18-20 Some men arrived carrying a paraplegic on a stretcher. They were looking for a way to get into the house and set him before Jesus. When they couldn't find a way in because of the crowd, they went up on the roof, removed some tiles, and let him down in the middle of everyone, right in front of Jesus. Impressed by their bold belief, he said, "Friend, I forgive your sins."

21 That set the religion scholars and Pharisees buzzing. "Who does he think he is? That's blasphemous talk! God and only God can forgive sins."

22-26 Jesus knew exactly what they were thinking and said, "Why all this gossipy whispering? Which is simpler: to say 'I forgive your sins,' or to say 'Get up and start walking'? Well, just so it's clear that I'm the Son of Man and authorized to do either, or both. . . ." He now spoke directly to the paraplegic: "Get up. Take your bedroll and go home." Without a moment's hesitation, he did it—got up, took his blanket, and left for home, giving glory to God all the way. The people rubbed their eyes, incredulous—and then also gave glory to God. Awestruck, they said, "We've never seen anything like that!"

New King James Version

Matthew the Tax Collector

27After these things He went out and saw a tax collector named Levi, sitting at the tax office. And He said to him, "Follow Me." 28So he left all, rose up, and followed Him.

29Then Levi gave Him a great feast in his own house. And there were a great number of tax collectors and others who sat down with them. 30And their scribes and the Pharisees[a] complained against His disciples, saying, "Why do You eat and drink with tax collectors and sinners?"

31Jesus answered and said to them, "Those who are well have no need of a physician, but those who are sick. 32I have not come to call *the* righteous, but sinners, to repentance."

Jesus Is Questioned About Fasting

33Then they said to Him, "Why do[a] the disciples of John fast often and make prayers, and likewise those of the Pharisees, but Yours eat and drink?"

34And He said to them, "Can you make the friends of the bridegroom fast while the bridegroom is with them? 35But the days will come when the bridegroom will be taken away from them; then they will fast in those days."

36Then He spoke a parable to them: "No one puts a piece from a new garment on an old one;[a] otherwise the new makes a tear, and also the piece that was *taken* out of the new does not match the old. 37And no one puts new wine into old wineskins; or else the new wine will burst the wineskins and be spilled, and the wineskins will be ruined. 38But new wine must be put into new wineskins, and both are preserved.[a] 39And no one, having drunk old *wine,* immediately[a] desires new; for he says, 'The old is better.' "[b]

Jesus Is Lord of the Sabbath

6 Now it happened on the second Sabbath after the first[a] that He went through the grainfields. And His disciples plucked the heads of grain and ate *them,* rubbing *them* in *their* hands. 2And some of the Pharisees said to them, "Why are you doing what is not lawful to do on the Sabbath?"

3But Jesus answering them said, "Have you not even read this, what David did when he was hungry, he and those who were with him: 4how he went into the house of God, took and ate the showbread, and also gave some to those with him, which is not lawful for any but the priests to eat?" 5And He said to them, "The Son of Man is also Lord of the Sabbath."

Healing on the Sabbath

6Now it happened on another Sabbath, also, that He entered the synagogue and taught. And a man was there whose right hand was withered. 7So the scribes and Pharisees watched Him closely, whether He would heal on the Sabbath, that they might find an accusation against Him. 8But He knew their thoughts, and said to

5:30 [a]NU-Text reads *But the Pharisees and their scribes.* **5:33** [a]NU-Text omits *Why do,* making the verse a statement. **5:36** [a]NU-Text reads *No one tears a piece from a new garment and puts it on an old one.* **5:38** [a]NU-Text omits *and both are preserved.* **5:39** [a]NU-Text omits *immediately.* [b]NU-Text reads *good.* **6:1** [a]NU-Text reads *on a Sabbath.*

The Message

27-28 After this he went out and saw a man named Levi at his work collecting taxes. Jesus said, "Come along with me." And he did—walked away from everything and went with him.

29-30 Levi gave a large dinner at his home for Jesus. Everybody was there, tax men and other disreputable characters as guests at the dinner. The Pharisees and their religion scholars came to his disciples greatly offended. "What is he doing eating and drinking with crooks and 'sinners'?"

31-32 Jesus heard about it and spoke up, "Who needs a doctor: the healthy or the sick? I'm here inviting outsiders, not insiders—an invitation to a changed life, changed inside and out."

33 They asked him, "John's disciples are well-known for keeping fasts and saying prayers. Also the Pharisees. But you seem to spend most of your time at parties. Why?"

34-35 Jesus said, "When you're celebrating a wedding, you don't skimp on the cake and wine. You feast. Later you may need to pull in your belt, but this isn't the time. As long as the bride and groom are with you, you have a good time. When the groom is gone, the fasting can begin. No one throws cold water on a friendly bonfire. This is Kingdom Come!

36-39 "No one cuts up a fine silk scarf to patch old work clothes; you want fabrics that match. And you don't put wine in old, cracked bottles; you get strong, clean bottles for your fresh vintage wine. And no one who has ever tasted fine aged wine prefers unaged wine."

In Charge of the Sabbath

1-2 6 On a certain Sabbath Jesus was walking through a field of ripe grain. His disciples were pulling off heads of grain, rubbing them in their hands to get rid of the chaff, and eating them. Some Pharisees said, "Why are you doing that, breaking a Sabbath rule?"

3-4 But Jesus stood up for them. "Have you never read what David and those with him did when they were hungry? How he entered the sanctuary and ate fresh bread off the altar, bread that no one but priests were allowed to eat? He also handed it out to his companions."

5 Then he said, "The Son of Man is no slave to the Sabbath; he's in charge."

6-8 On another Sabbath he went to the meeting place and taught. There was a man there with a crippled right hand. The religion scholars and Pharisees had their eye on Jesus to see if he would heal the man, hoping to catch him in a Sabbath infraction. He knew what they were up to and spoke to the

NEW KING JAMES VERSION

the man who had the withered hand, "Arise and
stand here." And he arose and stood. 9Then Je-
sus said to them, "I will ask you one thing: Is it
lawful on the Sabbath to do good or to do evil,
to save life or to destroy?"[a] 10And when He had
looked around at them all, He said to the man,[a]
"Stretch out your hand." And he did so, and his
hand was restored as whole as the other.[b] 11But
they were filled with rage, and discussed with
one another what they might do to Jesus.

THE TWELVE APOSTLES

12Now it came to pass in those days that He
went out to the mountain to pray, and continued
all night in prayer to God. 13And when it was
day, He called His disciples to *Himself;* and from
them He chose twelve whom He also named
apostles: 14Simon, whom He also named Peter,
and Andrew his brother; James and John; Philip
and Bartholomew; 15Matthew and Thomas;
James the *son* of Alphaeus, and Simon called
the Zealot; 16Judas *the son* of James, and Judas
Iscariot who also became a traitor.

JESUS HEALS A GREAT MULTITUDE

17And He came down with them and stood
on a level place with a crowd of His disciples
and a great multitude of people from all Judea
and Jerusalem, and from the seacoast of Tyre
and Sidon, who came to hear Him and be healed
of their diseases, 18as well as those who were
tormented with unclean spirits. And they were
healed. 19And the whole multitude sought to
touch Him, for power went out from Him and
healed *them* all.

THE BEATITUDES

20Then He lifted up His eyes toward His dis-
ciples, and said:

"Blessed *are you* poor,
For yours is the kingdom of God.
21Blessed *are you* who hunger now,
For you shall be filled.
Blessed *are you* who weep now,
For you shall laugh.
22Blessed are you when men hate you,
And when they exclude you,
And revile *you,* and cast out your name
as evil,
For the Son of Man's sake.
23Rejoice in that day and leap for joy!
For indeed your reward *is* great in
heaven,
For in like manner their fathers did to
the prophets.

6:9 [a]M-Text reads *to kill.* **6:10** [a]NU-Text and M-Text read *to him.* [b]NU-Text omits *as whole as the other.*

THE MESSAGE

man with the crippled hand: "Get up and stand here before us." He did.

9 Then Jesus addressed them, "Let me ask you something: What kind of action suits the Sabbath best? Doing good or doing evil? Helping people or leaving them helpless?"

10-11 He looked around, looked each one in the eye. He said to the man, "Hold out your hand." He held it out—it was as good as new! They were beside themselves with anger, and started plotting how they might get even with him.

THE TWELVE APOSTLES

12-16 At about that same time he climbed a mountain to pray. He was there all night in prayer before God. The next day he summoned his disciples; from them he selected twelve he designated as apostles:

Simon, whom he named Peter,
Andrew, his brother,
James,
John,
Philip,
Bartholomew,
Matthew,
Thomas,
James, son of Alphaeus,
Simon, called the Zealot,
Judas, son of James,
Judas Iscariot, who betrayed him.

YOU'RE BLESSED

17-21 Coming down off the mountain with them, he stood on a plain surrounded by disciples, and was soon joined by a huge congregation from all over Judea and Jerusalem, even from the seaside towns of Tyre and Sidon. They had come both to hear him and to be cured of their ailments. Those disturbed by evil spirits were healed. Everyone was trying to touch him—so much energy surging from him, so many people healed! Then he spoke:

You're blessed when you've lost it all.
God's kingdom is there for the finding.

You're blessed when you're ravenously
hungry.
Then you're ready for the Messianic
meal.

You're blessed when the tears flow
freely.
Joy comes with the morning.

22-23 "Count yourself blessed every time someone cuts you down or throws you out, every time someone smears or blackens your name to discredit me. What it means is that the truth is too close for comfort and that that person is uncomfortable. You can be glad when that happens—skip like a lamb, if you like!—for even though they don't like it, I do . . . and all heaven applauds. And know that you are in good company; my preachers and witnesses have always been treated like this.

New King James Version

Jesus Pronounces Woes

24“But woe to you who are rich,
For you have received your consolation.
25Woe to you who are full,
For you shall hunger.
Woe to you who laugh now,
For you shall mourn and weep.
26Woe to you[a] when all[b] men speak well of you,
For so did their fathers to the false
prophets.

Love Your Enemies

27“But I say to you who hear: Love your ene-
mies, do good to those who hate you, 28bless
those who curse you, and pray for those who
spitefully use you. 29To him who strikes you on
the *one* cheek, offer the other also. And from
him who takes away your cloak, do not with-
hold *your* tunic either. 30Give to everyone who
asks of you. And from him who takes away your
goods do not ask *them* back. 31And just as you
want men to do to you, you also do to them like-
wise.

32“But if you love those who love you, what
credit is that to you? For even sinners love those
who love them. 33And if you do good to those
who do good to you, what credit is that to you?
For even sinners do the same. 34And if you lend
to those from whom you hope to receive back,
what credit is that to you? For even sinners lend
to sinners to receive as much back. 35But love
your enemies, do good, and lend, hoping for
nothing in return; and your reward will be great,
and you will be sons of the Most High. For He is
kind to the unthankful and evil. 36Therefore be
merciful, just as your Father also is merciful.

Do Not Judge

37“Judge not, and you shall not be judged.
Condemn not, and you shall not be condemned.
Forgive, and you will be forgiven. 38Give, and it
will be given to you: good measure, pressed
down, shaken together, and running over will be
put into your bosom. For with the same measure
that you use, it will be measured back to you.”

39And He spoke a parable to them: “Can the
blind lead the blind? Will they not both fall into
the ditch? 40A disciple is not above his teacher,
but everyone who is perfectly trained will be
like his teacher. 41And why do you look at the
speck in your brother’s eye, but do not perceive
the plank in your own eye? 42Or how can you
say to your brother, ‘Brother, let me remove the

6:26 [a]NU-Text and M-Text omit *to you.* [b]M-Text omits *all.*

The Message

Give Away Your Life

24 But it’s trouble ahead if you think you have
it made.
What you have is all you’ll ever get.

25 And it’s trouble ahead if you’re satisfied
with yourself.
Your *self* will not satisfy you for long.

And it’s trouble ahead if you think life’s
all fun and games.
There’s suffering to be met, and you’re
going to meet it.

26 “There’s trouble ahead when you live
only for the approval of others, saying what
flatters them, doing what indulges them.
Popularity contests are not truth contests—
look how many scoundrel preachers were
approved by your ancestors! Your task is to
be true, not popular.

27-30 “To you who are ready for the truth, I say
this: Love your enemies. Let them bring out
the best in you, not the worst. When some-
one gives you a hard time, respond with the
energies of prayer for that person. If some-
one slaps you in the face, stand there and
take it. If someone grabs your shirt, giftwrap
your best coat and make a present of it. If
someone takes unfair advantage of you, use
the occasion to practice the servant life. No
more tit-for-tat stuff. Live generously.

31-34 “Here is a simple rule of thumb for be-
havior: Ask yourself what you want people
to do for you; then grab the initiative and do
it for *them*! If you only love the lovable, do
you expect a pat on the back? Run-of-the-
mill sinners do that. If you only help those
who help you, do you expect a medal?
Garden-variety sinners do that. If you only
give for what you hope to get out of it, do
you think that’s charity? The stingiest of
pawnbrokers does that.

35-36 “I tell you, love your enemies. Help and
give without expecting a return. You’ll
never—I promise—regret it. Live out this
God-created identity the way our Father
lives toward us, generously and graciously,
even when we’re at our worst. Our Father is
kind; you be kind.

37-38 “Don’t pick on people, jump on their fail-
ures, criticize their faults—unless, of course,
you want the same treatment. Don’t con-
demn those who are down; that hardness
can boomerang. Be easy on people; you’ll
find life a lot easier. Give away your life;
you’ll find life given back, but not merely
given back—given back with bonus and
blessing. Giving, not getting, is the way.
Generosity begets generosity.”

39-40 He quoted a proverb: “ ‘Can a blind man
guide a blind man?’ Wouldn’t they both end
up in the ditch? An apprentice doesn’t lec-
ture the master. The point is to be careful
who you follow as your teacher.

41-42 “It’s easy to see a smudge on your neigh-
bor’s face and be oblivious to the ugly sneer
on your own. Do you have the nerve to say,
‘Let me wash your face for you,’ when your

NEW KING JAMES VERSION

speck that *is* in your eye,' when you yourself do not see the plank that *is* in your own eye? Hypocrite! First remove the plank from your own eye, and then you will see clearly to remove the speck that is in your brother's eye.

A TREE IS KNOWN BY ITS FRUIT

43"For a good tree does not bear bad fruit, nor does a bad tree bear good fruit. 44For every tree is known by its own fruit. For *men* do not gather figs from thorns, nor do they gather grapes from a bramble bush. 45A good man out of the good treasure of his heart brings forth good; and an evil man out of the evil treasure of his heart[a] brings forth evil. For out of the abundance of the heart his mouth speaks.

BUILD ON THE ROCK

46"But why do you call Me 'Lord, Lord,' and not do the things which I say? 47Whoever comes to Me, and hears My sayings and does them, I will show you whom he is like: 48He is like a man building a house, who dug deep and laid the foundation on the rock. And when the flood arose, the stream beat vehemently against that house, and could not shake it, for it was founded on the rock.[a] 49But he who heard and did nothing is like a man who built a house on the earth without a foundation, against which the stream beat vehemently; and immediately it fell.[a] And the ruin of that house was great."

JESUS HEALS A CENTURION'S SERVANT

7 Now when He concluded all His sayings in the hearing of the people, He entered Capernaum. 2And a certain centurion's servant, who was dear to him, was sick and ready to die. 3So when he heard about Jesus, he sent elders of the Jews to Him, pleading with Him to come and heal his servant. 4And when they came to Jesus, they begged Him earnestly, saying that the one for whom He should do this was deserving, 5"for he loves our nation, and has built us a synagogue."

6Then Jesus went with them. And when He was already not far from the house, the centurion sent friends to Him, saying to Him, "Lord, do not trouble Yourself, for I am not worthy that You should enter under my roof. 7Therefore I did not even think myself worthy to come to You. But say the word, and my servant will be healed. 8For I also am a man placed under authority, having soldiers under me. And I say to one, 'Go,' and he goes; and to another, 'Come,' and he comes; and to my servant, 'Do this,' and he does *it*."

9When Jesus heard these things, He marveled at him, and turned around and said to the crowd that followed Him, "I say to you, I have not found such great faith, not even in Israel!" 10And those who were sent, returning to the house, found the servant well who had been sick.[a]

6:45 [a]NU-Text omits *treasure of his heart.* **6:48** [a]NU-Text reads *for it was well built.* **6:49** [a]NU-Text reads *collapsed.* **7:10** [a]NU-Text omits *who had been sick.*

THE MESSAGE

own face is distorted by contempt? It's this I-know-better-than-you mentality again, playing a holier-than-thou part instead of just living your own part. Wipe that ugly sneer off your own face and you might be fit to offer a washcloth to your neighbor.

WORK THE WORDS INTO YOUR LIFE

43-45 "You don't get wormy apples off a healthy tree, nor good apples off a diseased tree. The health of the apple tells the health of the tree. You must begin with your own life-giving lives. It's who you are, not what you say and do, that counts. Your true being brims over into true words and deeds.

46-47 "Why are you so polite with me, always saying 'Yes, sir,' and 'That's right, sir,' but never doing a thing I tell you? These words I speak to you are not mere additions to your life, homeowner improvements to your standard of living. They are foundation words, words to build a life on.

48-49 "If you work the words into your life, you are like a smart carpenter who dug deep and laid the foundation of his house on bedrock. When the river burst its banks and crashed against the house, nothing could shake it; it was built to last. But if you just use my words in Bible studies and don't work them into your life, you are like a dumb carpenter who built a house but skipped the foundation. When the swollen river came crashing in, it collapsed like a house of cards. It was a total loss."

A PLACE OF HOLY MYSTERY

1-5 7 When he finished speaking to the people, he entered Capernaum. A Roman captain there had a servant who was on his deathbed. He prized him highly and didn't want to lose him. When he heard Jesus was back, he sent leaders from the Jewish community asking him to come and heal his servant. They came to Jesus and urged him to do it, saying, "He deserves this. He loves our people. He even built our meeting place."

6-8 Jesus went with them. When he was still quite far from the house, the captain sent friends to tell him, "Master, you don't have to go to all this trouble. I'm not that good a person, you know. I'd be embarrassed for you to come to my house, even embarrassed to come to you in person. Just give the order and my servant will get well. I'm a man under orders; I also give orders. I tell one soldier, 'Go,' and he goes; another, 'Come,' and he comes; my slave, 'Do this,' and he does it."

9-10 Taken aback, Jesus addressed the accompanying crowd: "I've yet to come across this kind of simple trust anywhere in Israel, the very people who are supposed to know about God and how he works." When the messengers got back home, they found the servant up and well.

New King James Version

Jesus Raises the Son of the Widow of Nain

11Now it happened, the day after, *that* He
went into a city called Nain; and many of His
disciples went with Him, and a large crowd.
12And when He came near the gate of the city,
behold, a dead man was being carried out, the
only son of his mother; and she was a widow.
And a large crowd from the city was with her.
13When the Lord saw her, He had compassion
on her and said to her, "Do not weep." 14Then He
came and touched the open coffin, and those
who carried *him* stood still. And He said, "Young
man, I say to you, arise." 15So he who was dead
sat up and began to speak. And He presented
him to his mother.

16Then fear came upon all, and they glorified
God, saying, "A great prophet has risen up
among us"; and, "God has visited His people."
17And this report about Him went throughout all
Judea and all the surrounding region.

John the Baptist Sends Messengers to Jesus

18Then the disciples of John reported to him
concerning all these things. 19And John, calling
two of his disciples to *him,* sent *them* to Jesus,[a]
saying, "Are You the Coming One, or do we look
for another?"

20When the men had come to Him, they said,
"John the Baptist has sent us to You, saying, 'Are
You the Coming One, or do we look for an-
other?' " 21And that very hour He cured many of
infirmities, afflictions, and evil spirits; and to
many blind He gave sight.

22Jesus answered and said to them, "Go and
tell John the things you have seen and heard:
that *the* blind see, *the* lame walk, *the* lepers are
cleansed, *the* deaf hear, *the* dead are raised, *the*
poor have the gospel preached to them. 23And
blessed is *he* who is not offended because of
Me."

24When the messengers of John had de-
parted, He began to speak to the multitudes con-
cerning John: "What did you go out into the
wilderness to see? A reed shaken by the wind?
25But what did you go out to see? A man clothed
in soft garments? Indeed those who are gor-
geously appareled and live in luxury are in
kings' courts. 26But what did you go out to see?
A prophet? Yes, I say to you, and more than a
prophet. 27This is *he* of whom it is written:

'Behold, I send My messenger before Your
face,
Who will prepare Your way before You.' [a]

28For I say to you, among those born of women
there is not a greater prophet than John the
Baptist;[a] but he who is least in the kingdom of
God is greater than he."

29And when all the people heard *Him,* even
the tax collectors justified God, having been
baptized with the baptism of John. 30But the

7:19 [a]NU-Text reads *the Lord.* **7:27** [a]Malachi 3:1 **7:28** [a]NU-Text reads *there is none greater than John.*

The Message

11-15 Not long after that, Jesus went to the vil-
lage Nain. His disciples were with him,
along with quite a large crowd. As they ap-
proached the village gate, they met a funeral
procession—a woman's only son was being
carried out for burial. And the mother was a
widow. When Jesus saw her, his heart broke.
He said to her, "Don't cry." Then he went
over and touched the coffin. The pallbearers
stopped. He said, "Young man, I tell you: Get
up." The dead son sat up and began talking.
Jesus presented him to his mother.

16-17 They all realized they were in a place of
holy mystery, that God was at work among
them. They were quietly worshipful—and
then noisily grateful, calling out among
themselves, "God is back, looking to the
needs of his people!" The news of Jesus
spread all through the country.

Is This What You Were Expecting?

18-19 John's disciples reported back to him the
news of all these events taking place. He
sent two of them to the Master to ask the
question, "Are you the One we've been ex-
pecting, or are we still waiting?"

20 The men showed up before Jesus and
said, "John the Baptizer sent us to ask you,
'Are you the One we've been expecting, or
are we still waiting?' "

21-23 In the next two or three hours Jesus
healed many from diseases, distress, and
evil spirits. To many of the blind he gave the
gift of sight. Then he gave his answer: "Go
back and tell John what you have just seen
and heard:

The blind see,
The lame walk,
Lepers are cleansed,
The deaf hear,
The dead are raised,
The wretched of the earth
have God's salvation hospitality
extended to them.

"Is this what you were expecting? Then
count yourselves fortunate!"

24-27 After John's messengers left to make
their report, Jesus said more about John to
the crowd of people. "What did you expect
when you went out to see him in the wild? A
weekend camper? Hardly. What then? A
sheik in silk pajamas? Not in the wilder-
ness, not by a long shot. What then? A mes-
senger from God? That's right, a messenger!
Probably the greatest messenger you'll ever
hear. He is the messenger Malachi an-
nounced when he wrote,

I'm sending my messenger on ahead
To make the road smooth for you.

28-30 "Let me lay it out for you as plainly as I
can: No one in history surpasses John the
Baptizer, but in the kingdom he prepared you
for, the lowliest person is ahead of him. The
ordinary and disreputable people who heard
John, by being baptized by him into the king-

NEW KING JAMES VERSION

Pharisees and lawyers rejected the will of God for themselves, not having been baptized by him.

[31]And the Lord said,[a] "To what then shall I liken the men of this generation, and what are they like? [32]They are like children sitting in the marketplace and calling to one another, saying:

'We played the flute for you,
And you did not dance;
We mourned to you,
And you did not weep.'

[33]For John the Baptist came neither eating bread nor drinking wine, and you say, 'He has a demon.' [34]The Son of Man has come eating and drinking, and you say, 'Look, a glutton and a winebibber, a friend of tax collectors and sinners!' [35]But wisdom is justified by all her children."

A SINFUL WOMAN FORGIVEN

[36]Then one of the Pharisees asked Him to eat with him. And He went to the Pharisee's house, and sat down to eat. [37]And behold, a woman in the city who was a sinner, when she knew that *Jesus* sat at the table in the Pharisee's house, brought an alabaster flask of fragrant oil, [38]and stood at His feet behind *Him* weeping; and she began to wash His feet with her tears, and wiped *them* with the hair of her head; and she kissed His feet and anointed *them* with the fragrant oil. [39]Now when the Pharisee who had invited Him saw *this,* he spoke to himself, saying, "This Man, if He were a prophet, would know who and what manner of woman *this is* who is touching Him, for she is a sinner."

[40]And Jesus answered and said to him, "Simon, I have something to say to you."

So he said, "Teacher, say it."

[41]"There was a certain creditor who had two debtors. One owed five hundred denarii, and the other fifty. [42]And when they had nothing with which to repay, he freely forgave them both. Tell Me, therefore, which of them will love him more?"

[43]Simon answered and said, "I suppose the *one* whom he forgave more."

And He said to him, "You have rightly judged." [44]Then He turned to the woman and said to Simon, "Do you see this woman? I entered your house; you gave Me no water for My feet, but she has washed My feet with her tears and wiped *them* with the hair of her head. [45]You gave Me no kiss, but this woman has not ceased to kiss My feet since the time I came in. [46]You did not anoint My head with oil, but this woman has anointed My feet with fragrant oil. [47]Therefore I say to you, her sins, *which are* many, are forgiven, for she loved much. But to whom little is forgiven, *the same* loves little."

[48]Then He said to her, "Your sins are forgiven."

[49]And those who sat at the table with Him began to say to themselves, "Who is this who even forgives sins?"

[50]Then He said to the woman, "Your faith has saved you. Go in peace."

7:31 [a]NU-Text and M-Text omit *And the Lord said.*

THE MESSAGE

dom, are the clearest evidence; the Pharisees and religious officials would have nothing to do with such a baptism, wouldn't think of giving up their place in line to their inferiors.

31-35 "How can I account for the people of this generation? They're like spoiled children complaining to their parents, 'We wanted to skip rope and you were always too tired; we wanted to talk but you were always too busy.' John the Baptizer came fasting and you called him crazy. The Son of Man came feasting and you called him a lush. Opinion polls don't count for much, do they? The proof of the pudding is in the eating."

ANOINTING HIS FEET

36-39 One of the Pharisees asked him over for a meal. He went to the Pharisee's house and sat down at the dinner table. Just then a woman of the village, the town harlot, having learned that Jesus was a guest in the home of the Pharisee, came with a bottle of very expensive perfume and stood at his feet, weeping, raining tears on his feet. Letting down her hair, she dried his feet, kissed them, and anointed them with the perfume. When the Pharisee who had invited him saw this, he said to himself, "If this man was the prophet I thought he was, he would have known what kind of woman this is who is falling all over him."

40 Jesus said to him, "Simon, I have something to tell you."

"Oh? Tell me."

41-42 "Two men were in debt to a banker. One owed five hundred silver pieces, the other fifty. Neither of them could pay up, and so the banker canceled both debts. Which of the two would be more grateful?"

43-47 Simon answered, "I suppose the one who was forgiven the most."

"That's right," said Jesus. Then turning to the woman, but speaking to Simon, he said, "Do you see this woman? I came to your home; you provided no water for my feet, but she rained tears on my feet and dried them with her hair. You gave me no greeting, but from the time I arrived she hasn't quit kissing my feet. You provided nothing for freshening up, but she has soothed my feet with perfume. Impressive, isn't it? She was forgiven many, many sins, and so she is very, very grateful. If the forgiveness is minimal, the gratitude is minimal."

48 Then he spoke to her: "I forgive your sins."

49 That set the dinner guests talking behind his back: "Who does he think he is, forgiving sins!"

50 He ignored them and said to the woman, "Your faith has saved you. Go in peace."

NEW KING JAMES VERSION

MANY WOMEN MINISTER TO JESUS

8 Now it came to pass, afterward, that He went through every city and village, preaching and bringing the glad tidings of the kingdom of God. And the twelve *were* with Him, [2]and certain women who had been healed of evil spirits and infirmities—Mary called Magdalene, out of whom had come seven demons, [3]and Joanna the wife of Chuza, Herod's steward, and Susanna, and many others who provided for Him[a] from their substance.

THE PARABLE OF THE SOWER

[4]And when a great multitude had gathered, and they had come to Him from every city, He spoke by a parable: [5]"A sower went out to sow his seed. And as he sowed, some fell by the wayside; and it was trampled down, and the birds of the air devoured it. [6]Some fell on rock; and as soon as it sprang up, it withered away because it lacked moisture. [7]And some fell among thorns, and the thorns sprang up with it and choked it. [8]But others fell on good ground, sprang up, and yielded a crop a hundredfold." When He had said these things He cried, "He who has ears to hear, let him hear!"

THE PURPOSE OF PARABLES

[9]Then His disciples asked Him, saying, "What does this parable mean?"

[10]And He said, "To you it has been given to know the mysteries of the kingdom of God, but to the rest *it is given* in parables, that

'Seeing they may not see,
And hearing they may not understand.'[a]

THE PARABLE OF THE SOWER EXPLAINED

[11]"Now the parable is this: The seed is the word of God. [12]Those by the wayside are the ones who hear; then the devil comes and takes away the word out of their hearts, lest they should believe and be saved. [13]But the ones on the rock *are those* who, when they hear, receive the word with joy; and these have no root, who believe for a while and in time of temptation fall away. [14]Now the ones *that* fell among thorns are those who, when they have heard, go out and are choked with cares, riches, and pleasures of life, and bring no fruit to maturity. [15]But the ones *that* fell on the good ground are those who, having heard the word with a noble and good heart, keep *it* and bear fruit with patience.

THE PARABLE OF THE REVEALED LIGHT

[16]"No one, when he has lit a lamp, covers it with a vessel or puts *it* under a bed, but sets *it* on a lampstand, that those who enter may see the light. [17]For nothing is secret that will not be revealed, nor *anything* hidden that will not be known and come to light. [18]Therefore take heed how you hear. For whoever has, to him *more* will be given; and whoever does not have, even what he seems to have will be taken from him."

8:3 [a]NU-Text and M-Text read *them.* **8:10** [a]Isaiah 6:9

THE MESSAGE

1-3 8 He continued according to plan, traveled to town after town, village after village, preaching God's kingdom, spreading the Message. The Twelve were with him. There were also some women in their company who had been healed of various evil afflictions and illnesses: Mary, the one called Magdalene, from whom seven demons had gone out; Joanna, wife of Chuza, Herod's manager; and Susanna—along with many others who used their considerable means to provide for the company.

THE STORY OF THE SEEDS

4-8 As they went from town to town, a lot of people joined in and traveled along. He addressed them, using this story: "A farmer went out to sow his seed. Some of it fell on the road; it was tramped down and the birds ate it. Other seed fell in the gravel; it sprouted, but withered because it didn't have good roots. Other seed fell in the weeds; the weeds grew with it and strangled it. Other seed fell in rich earth and produced a bumper crop.

"Are you listening to this? Really listening?"

9 His disciples asked, "Why did you tell this story?"

10 He said, "You've been given insight into God's kingdom—you know how it works. There are others who need stories. But even with stories some of them aren't going to get it:

Their eyes are open but don't see a thing,
Their ears are open but don't hear a thing.

11-12 "This story is about some of those people. The seed is the Word of God. The seeds on the road are those who hear the Word, but no sooner do they hear it than the Devil snatches it from them so they won't believe and be saved.

13 "The seeds in the gravel are those who hear with enthusiasm, but the enthusiasm doesn't go very deep. It's only another fad, and the moment there's trouble it's gone.

14 "And the seed that fell in the weeds—well, these are the ones who hear, but then the seed is crowded out and nothing comes of it as they go about their lives worrying about tomorrow, making money, and having fun.

15 "But the seed in the good earth—these are the good-hearts who seize the Word and hold on no matter what, sticking with it until there's a harvest.

MISERS OF WHAT YOU HEAR

16-18 "No one lights a lamp and then covers it with a washtub or shoves it under the bed. No, you set it up on a lamp stand so those who enter the room can see their way. We're not keeping secrets; we're telling them. We're not hiding things; we're bringing *everything* out into the open. So be careful that you don't become misers of what you hear. Generosity begets generosity. Stinginess impoverishes."

New King James Version

Jesus' Mother and Brothers Come to Him

19 Then His mother and brothers came to
Him, and could not approach Him because of
the crowd. 20 And it was told Him *by some,* who
said, "Your mother and Your brothers are stand-
ing outside, desiring to see You."
21 But He answered and said to them, "My
mother and My brothers are these who hear the
word of God and do it."

Wind and Wave Obey Jesus

22 Now it happened, on a certain day, that He
got into a boat with His disciples. And He said to
them, "Let us cross over to the other side of the
lake." And they launched out. 23 But as they
sailed He fell asleep. And a windstorm came
down on the lake, and they were filling *with wa-
ter,* and were in jeopardy. 24 And they came to
Him and awoke Him, saying, "Master, Master,
we are perishing!"
Then He arose and rebuked the wind and the
raging of the water. And they ceased, and there
was a calm. 25 But He said to them, "Where is
your faith?"
And they were afraid, and marveled, saying
to one another, "Who can this be? For He com-
mands even the winds and water, and they obey
Him!"

A Demon-Possessed Man Healed

26 Then they sailed to the country of the
Gadarenes,[a] which is opposite Galilee. 27 And
when He stepped out on the land, there met Him
a certain man from the city who had demons for
a long time. And he wore no clothes,[a] nor did he
live in a house but in the tombs. 28 When he saw
Jesus, he cried out, fell down before Him, and
with a loud voice said, "What have I to do with
You, Jesus, Son of the Most High God? I beg You,
do not torment me!" 29 For He had commanded
the unclean spirit to come out of the man. For it
had often seized him, and he was kept under
guard, bound with chains and shackles; and he
broke the bonds and was driven by the demon
into the wilderness.
30 Jesus asked him, saying, "What is your
name?"
And he said, "Legion," because many
demons had entered him. 31 And they begged
Him that He would not command them to go out
into the abyss.
32 Now a herd of many swine was feeding
there on the mountain. So they begged Him that
He would permit them to enter them. And He
permitted them. 33 Then the demons went out of
the man and entered the swine, and the herd ran
violently down the steep place into the lake and
drowned.
34 When those who fed *them* saw what had
happened, they fled and told *it* in the city and in
the country. 35 Then they went out to see what
had happened, and came to Jesus, and found the
man from whom the demons had departed, sit-
ting at the feet of Jesus, clothed and in his right
mind. And they were afraid. 36 They also who
had seen *it* told them by what means he who
had been demon-possessed was healed.

8:26 [a]NU-Text reads *Gerasenes.* **8:27** [a]NU-Text reads *who had demons and for a long time wore no clothes.*

The Message

19-20 His mother and brothers showed up but
couldn't get through to him because of the
crowd. He was given the message, "Your
mother and brothers are standing outside
wanting to see you."
21 He replied, "My mother and brothers are
the ones who hear and do God's Word. Obe-
dience is thicker than blood."
22-24 One day he and his disciples got in a
boat. "Let's cross the lake," he said. And off
they went. It was smooth sailing, and he fell
asleep. A terrific storm came up suddenly
on the lake. Water poured in, and they were
about to capsize. They woke Jesus: "Master,
Master, we're going to drown!"
Getting to his feet, he told the wind, "Si-
lence!" and the waves, "Quiet down!" They
did it. The lake became smooth as glass.
25 Then he said to his disciples, "Why can't
you trust me?"
They were in absolute awe, staggered
and stammering, "Who is this, anyway? He
calls out to the winds and sea, and they do
what he tells them!"

The Madman and the Pigs

26-29 They sailed on to the country of the
Gerasenes, directly opposite Galilee. As he
stepped out onto land, a madman from town
met him; he was a victim of demons. He
hadn't worn clothes for a long time, nor
lived at home; he lived in the cemetery.
When he saw Jesus he screamed, fell before
him, and bellowed, "What business do you
have messing with me? You're Jesus, Son of
the High God, but don't give me a hard
time!" (The man said this because Jesus had
started to order the unclean spirit out of
him.) Time after time the demon threw the
man into convulsions. He had been placed
under constant guard and tied with chains
and shackles, but crazed and driven wild by
the demon, he would shatter the bonds.
30-31 Jesus asked him, "What is your name?"
"Mob. My name is Mob," he said, because
many demons afflicted him. And they
begged Jesus desperately not to order them
to the bottomless pit.
32-33 A large herd of pigs was browsing and
rooting on a nearby hill. The demons
begged Jesus to order them into the pigs. He
gave the order. It was even worse for the
pigs than for the man. Crazed, they stam-
peded over a cliff into the lake and
drowned.
34-36 Those tending the pigs, scared to death,
bolted and told their story in town and
country. People went out to see what had
happened. They came to Jesus and found
the man from whom the demons had been
sent, sitting there at Jesus' feet, wearing de-
cent clothes and making sense. It was a holy
moment, and for a short time they were
more reverent than curious. Then those who
had seen it happen told how the demoniac
had been saved.

New King James Version

[37]Then the whole multitude of the surrounding region of the Gadarenes[a] asked Him to depart from them, for they were seized with great fear. And He got into the boat and returned.

[38]Now the man from whom the demons had departed begged Him that he might be with Him. But Jesus sent him away, saying, [39]"Return to your own house, and tell what great things God has done for you." And he went his way and proclaimed throughout the whole city what great things Jesus had done for him.

A Girl Restored to Life and a Woman Healed

[40]So it was, when Jesus returned, that the multitude welcomed Him, for they were all waiting for Him. [41]And behold, there came a man named Jairus, and he was a ruler of the synagogue. And he fell down at Jesus' feet and begged Him to come to his house, [42]for he had an only daughter about twelve years of age, and she was dying.

But as He went, the multitudes thronged Him. [43]Now a woman, having a flow of blood for twelve years, who had spent all her livelihood on physicians and could not be healed by any, [44]came from behind and touched the border of His garment. And immediately her flow of blood stopped.

[45]And Jesus said, "Who touched Me?"

When all denied it, Peter and those with him[a] said, "Master, the multitudes throng and press You, and You say, 'Who touched Me?' "[b]

[46]But Jesus said, "Somebody touched Me, for I perceived power going out from Me." [47]Now when the woman saw that she was not hidden, she came trembling; and falling down before Him, she declared to Him in the presence of all the people the reason she had touched Him and how she was healed immediately.

[48]And He said to her, "Daughter, be of good cheer;[a] your faith has made you well. Go in peace."

[49]While He was still speaking, someone came from the ruler of the synagogue's *house,* saying to him, "Your daughter is dead. Do not trouble the Teacher."[a]

[50]But when Jesus heard *it,* He answered him, saying, "Do not be afraid; only believe, and she will be made well." [51]When He came into the house, He permitted no one to go in[a] except Peter, James, and John,[b] and the father and mother of the girl. [52]Now all wept and mourned for her; but He said, "Do not weep; she is not dead, but sleeping." [53]And they ridiculed Him, knowing that she was dead.

[54]But He put them all outside,[a] took her by the hand and called, saying, "Little girl, arise." [55]Then her spirit returned, and she arose immediately. And He commanded that she be given *something* to eat. [56]And her parents were astonished, but He charged them to tell no one what had happened.

8:37 [a]NU-Text reads *Gerasenes.* **8:45** [a]NU-Text omits *and those with him.* [b]NU-Text omits *and You say, 'Who touched Me?'* **8:48** [a]NU-Text omits *be of good cheer.* **8:49** [a]NU-Text adds *anymore.* **8:51** [a]NU-Text adds *with Him.* [b]NU-Text and M-Text read *Peter, John, and James.* **8:54** [a]NU-Text omits *put them all outside.*

The Message

37-39 Later, a great many people from the Gerasene countryside got together and asked Jesus to leave—too much change, too fast, and they were scared. So Jesus got back in the boat and set off. The man whom he had delivered from the demons asked to go with him, but he sent him back, saying, "Go home and tell everything God did in you." So he went back and preached all over town everything Jesus had done in him.

His Touch

40-42 On his return, Jesus was welcomed by a crowd. They were all there expecting him. A man came up, Jairus by name. He was president of the meeting place. He fell at Jesus' feet and begged him to come to his home because his twelve-year-old daughter, his only child, was dying. Jesus went with him, making his way through the pushing, jostling crowd.

43-45 In the crowd that day there was a woman who for twelve years had been afflicted with hemorrhages. She had spent every penny she had on doctors but not one had been able to help her. She slipped in from behind and touched the edge of Jesus' robe. At that very moment her hemorrhaging stopped. Jesus said, "Who touched me?"

When no one stepped forward, Peter said, "But Master, we've got crowds of people on our hands. Dozens have touched you."

46 Jesus insisted, "Someone touched me. I felt power discharging from me."

47 When the woman realized that she couldn't remain hidden, she knelt trembling before him. In front of all the people, she blurted out her story—why she touched him and how at that same moment she was healed.

48 Jesus said, "Daughter, you took a risk trusting me, and now you're healed and whole. Live well, live blessed!"

49 While he was still talking, someone from the leader's house came up and told him, "Your daughter died. No need now to bother the Teacher."

50-51 Jesus overheard and said, "Don't be upset. Just trust me and everything will be all right." Going into the house, he wouldn't let anyone enter with him except Peter, John, James, and the child's parents.

52-53 Everyone was crying and carrying on over her. Jesus said, "Don't cry. She didn't die; she's sleeping." They laughed at him. They knew she was dead.

54-56 Then Jesus, gripping her hand, called, "My dear child, get up." She was up in an instant, up and breathing again! He told them to give her something to eat. Her parents were ecstatic, but Jesus warned them to keep quiet. "Don't tell a soul what happened in this room."

NEW KING JAMES VERSION

SENDING OUT THE TWELVE

9 Then He called His twelve disciples together
and gave them power and authority over all
demons, and to cure diseases. 2He sent them to
preach the kingdom of God and to heal the sick.
3And He said to them, "Take nothing for the
journey, neither staffs nor bag nor bread nor
money; and do not have two tunics apiece.
4"Whatever house you enter, stay there, and
from there depart. 5And whoever will not re-
ceive you, when you go out of that city, shake off
the very dust from your feet as a testimony
against them."
6So they departed and went through the
towns, preaching the gospel and healing every-
where.

HEROD SEEKS TO SEE JESUS

7Now Herod the tetrarch heard of all that
was done by Him; and he was perplexed, be-
cause it was said by some that John had risen
from the dead, 8and by some that Elijah had ap-
peared, and by others that one of the old
prophets had risen again. 9Herod said, "John I
have beheaded, but who is this of whom I hear
such things?" So he sought to see Him.

FEEDING THE FIVE THOUSAND

10And the apostles, when they had returned,
told Him all that they had done. Then He took
them and went aside privately into a deserted
place belonging to the city called Bethsaida.
11But when the multitudes knew *it,* they fol-
lowed Him; and He received them and spoke to
them about the kingdom of God, and healed
those who had need of healing. 12When the day
began to wear away, the twelve came and said to
Him, "Send the multitude away, that they may
go into the surrounding towns and country, and
lodge and get provisions; for we are in a de-
serted place here."
13But He said to them, "You give them some-
thing to eat."
And they said, "We have no more than five
loaves and two fish, unless we go and buy food
for all these people." 14For there were about five
thousand men.
Then He said to His disciples, "Make them sit
down in groups of fifty." 15And they did so, and
made them all sit down.
16Then He took the five loaves and the two
fish, and looking up to heaven, He blessed and
broke *them,* and gave *them* to the disciples to
set before the multitude. 17So they all ate and
were filled, and twelve baskets of the leftover
fragments were taken up by them.

PETER CONFESSES JESUS AS THE CHRIST

18And it happened, as He was alone praying,
that His disciples joined Him, and He asked
them, saying, "Who do the crowds say that I
am?"
19So they answered and said, "John the Bap-
tist, but some *say* Elijah; and others *say* that one
of the old prophets has risen again."
20He said to them, "But who do you say that
I am?"
Peter answered and said, "The Christ of
God."

THE MESSAGE

KEEP IT SIMPLE

1-5 9 Jesus now called the Twelve and gave them authority and power to deal with all the demons and cure diseases. He commissioned them to preach the news of God's kingdom and heal the sick. He said, "Don't load yourselves up with equipment. Keep it simple; *you* are the equipment. And no luxury inns—get a modest place and be content there until you leave. If you're not welcomed, leave town. Don't make a scene. Shrug your shoulders and move on."

6 Commissioned, they left. They traveled from town to town telling the latest news of God, the Message, and curing people everywhere they went.

7-9 Herod, the ruler, heard of these goings on and didn't know what to think. There were people saying John had come back from the dead, others that Elijah had appeared, still others that some prophet of long ago had shown up. Herod said, "But I killed John—took off his head. So who is this that I keep hearing about?" Curious, he looked for a chance to see him in action.

10-11 The apostles returned and reported on what they had done. Jesus took them away, off by themselves, near the town called Bethsaida. But the crowds got wind of it and followed. Jesus graciously welcomed them and talked to them about the kingdom of God. Those who needed healing, he healed.

BREAD AND FISH FOR FIVE THOUSAND

12 As the day declined, the Twelve said, "Dismiss the crowd so they can go to the farms or villages around here and get a room for the night and a bite to eat. We're out in the middle of nowhere."

13-14 "You feed them," Jesus said.

They said, "We couldn't scrape up more than five loaves of bread and a couple of fish—unless, of course, you want us to go to town ourselves and buy food for everybody." (There were more than five thousand people in the crowd.)

14-17 But he went ahead and directed his disciples, "Sit them down in groups of about fifty." They did what he said, and soon had everyone seated. He took the five loaves and two fish, lifted his face to heaven in prayer, blessed, broke, and gave the bread and fish to the disciples to hand out to the crowd. After the people had all eaten their fill, twelve baskets of leftovers were gathered up.

DON'T RUN FROM SUFFERING

18 One time when Jesus was off praying by himself, his disciples nearby, he asked them, "What are the crowds saying about me, about who I am?"

19 They said, "John the Baptizer. Others say Elijah. Still others say that one of the prophets from long ago has come back."

20-21 He then asked, "And you—what are you saying about me? Who am I?"

Peter answered, "The Messiah of God."

NEW KING JAMES VERSION

JESUS PREDICTS HIS DEATH AND RESURRECTION

21And He strictly warned and commanded
them to tell this to no one, 22saying, "The Son of
Man must suffer many things, and be rejected
by the elders and chief priests and scribes, and
be killed, and be raised the third day."

TAKE UP THE CROSS AND FOLLOW HIM

23Then He said to *them* all, "If anyone desires
to come after Me, let him deny himself, and take
up his cross daily,[a] and follow Me. 24For who-
ever desires to save his life will lose it, but who-
ever loses his life for My sake will save it. 25For
what profit is it to a man if he gains the whole
world, and is himself destroyed or lost? 26For
whoever is ashamed of Me and My words, of
him the Son of Man will be ashamed when He
comes in His *own* glory, and *in His* Father's, and
of the holy angels.

JESUS TRANSFIGURED ON THE MOUNT

27But I tell you truly, there are some standing
here who shall not taste death till they see the
kingdom of God."

28Now it came to pass, about eight days after
these sayings, that He took Peter, John, and
James and went up on the mountain to pray.
29As He prayed, the appearance of His face was
altered, and His robe *became* white *and* glisten-
ing. 30And behold, two men talked with Him,
who were Moses and Elijah, 31who appeared in
glory and spoke of His decease which He was
about to accomplish at Jerusalem. 32But Peter
and those with him were heavy with sleep; and
when they were fully awake, they saw His glory
and the two men who stood with Him. 33Then it
happened, as they were parting from Him, *that*
Peter said to Jesus, "Master, it is good for us to
be here; and let us make three tabernacles: one
for You, one for Moses, and one for Elijah"—not
knowing what he said.

34While he was saying this, a cloud came and
overshadowed them; and they were fearful as
they entered the cloud. 35And a voice came out
of the cloud, saying, "This is My beloved Son.[a]
Hear Him!" 36When the voice had ceased, Jesus
was found alone. But they kept quiet, and told
no one in those days any of the things they had
seen.

A BOY IS HEALED

37Now it happened on the next day, when
they had come down from the mountain, that a
great multitude met Him. 38Suddenly a man
from the multitude cried out, saying, "Teacher, I
implore You, look on my son, for he is my only

9:23 [a]M-Text omits *daily*. **9:35** [a]NU-Text reads *This is My Son, the Chosen One.*

THE MESSAGE

Jesus then warned them to keep it quiet.
They were to tell no one what Peter had
said.

22 He went on, "It is necessary that the Son
of Man proceed to an ordeal of suffering, be
tried and found guilty by the religious lead-
ers, high priests, and religion scholars, be
killed, and on the third day be raised up
alive."

23-27 Then he told them what they could ex-
pect for themselves: "Anyone who intends to
come with me has to let me lead. You're not
in the driver's seat—I am. Don't run from
suffering; embrace it. Follow me and I'll
show you how. Self-help is no help at all.
Self-sacrifice is the way, *my* way, to finding
yourself, your true self. What good would it
do to get everything you want and lose you,
the real you? If any of you is embarrassed
with me and the way I'm leading you, know
that the Son of Man will be far more embar-
rassed with you when he arrives in all his
splendor in company with the Father and
the holy angels. This isn't, you realize, pie in
the sky by and by. Some who have taken
their stand right here are going to see it hap-
pen, see with their own eyes the kingdom of
God."

JESUS IN HIS GLORY

28-31 About eight days after saying this, he
climbed the mountain to pray, taking Peter,
John, and James along. While he was in
prayer, the appearance of his face changed
and his clothes became blinding white. At
once two men were there talking with him.
They turned out to be Moses and Elijah—
and what a glorious appearance they made!
They talked over his exodus, the one Jesus
was about to complete in Jerusalem.

32-33 Meanwhile, Peter and those with him
were slumped over in sleep. When they
came to, rubbing their eyes, they saw Jesus
in his glory and the two men standing with
him. When Moses and Elijah had left, Peter
said to Jesus, "Master, this is a great mo-
ment! Let's build three memorials: one for
you, one for Moses, and one for Elijah." He
blurted this out without thinking.

34-35 While he was babbling on like this, a
light-radiant cloud enveloped them. As they
found themselves buried in the cloud, they
became deeply aware of God. Then there
was a voice out of the cloud: "This is my
Son, the Chosen! Listen to him."

36 When the sound of the voice died away,
they saw Jesus there alone. They were
speechless. And they continued speechless,
said not one thing to anyone during those
days of what they had seen.

37-40 When they came down off the mountain the
next day, a big crowd was there to meet
them. A man called from out of the crowd,
"Please, please, Teacher, take a look at my

NEW KING JAMES VERSION

child. [39]And behold, a spirit seizes him, and he
suddenly cries out; it convulses him so that he
foams *at the mouth;* and it departs from him
with great difficulty, bruising him. [40]So I im-
plored Your disciples to cast it out, but they
could not."
[41]Then Jesus answered and said, "O faithless
and perverse generation, how long shall I be
with you and bear with you? Bring your son
here." [42]And as he was still coming, the demon
threw him down and convulsed *him.* Then Jesus
rebuked the unclean spirit, healed the child, and
gave him back to his father.

JESUS AGAIN PREDICTS HIS DEATH

[43]And they were all amazed at the majesty of
God.

But while everyone marveled at all the
things which Jesus did, He said to His disciples,
[44]"Let these words sink down into your ears, for
the Son of Man is about to be betrayed into the
hands of men." [45]But they did not understand
this saying, and it was hidden from them so that
they did not perceive it; and they were afraid to
ask Him about this saying.

WHO IS THE GREATEST?

[46]Then a dispute arose among them as to
which of them would be greatest. [47]And Jesus,
perceiving the thought of their heart, took a lit-
tle child and set him by Him, [48]and said to them,
"Whoever receives this little child in My name
receives Me; and whoever receives Me receives
Him who sent Me. For he who is least among
you all will be great."

JESUS FORBIDS SECTARIANISM

[49]Now John answered and said, "Master, we
saw someone casting out demons in Your name,
and we forbade him because he does not follow
with us."
[50]But Jesus said to him, "Do not forbid *him,*
for he who is not against us[a] is on our[b] side."

A SAMARITAN VILLAGE REJECTS THE SAVIOR

[51]Now it came to pass, when the time had
come for Him to be received up, that He stead-
fastly set His face to go to Jerusalem, [52]and sent
messengers before His face. And as they went,
they entered a village of the Samaritans, to pre-
pare for Him. [53]But they did not receive Him, be-
cause His face was *set* for the journey to
Jerusalem. [54]And when His disciples James and
John saw *this,* they said, "Lord, do You want us
to command fire to come down from heaven and
consume them, just as Elijah did?"[a]
[55]But He turned and rebuked them,[a] and
said, "You do not know what manner of spirit
you are of. [56]For the Son of Man did not come to
destroy men's lives but to save *them.*"[a] And they
went to another village.

THE COST OF DISCIPLESHIP

[57]Now it happened as they journeyed on the
road, *that* someone said to Him, "Lord, I will fol-
low You wherever You go."

9:50 [a]NU-Text reads *you.* [b]NU-Text reads *your.* **9:54** [a]NU-Text omits *just as Elijah did.* **9:55** [a]NU-Text omits the rest of this verse. **9:56** [a]NU-Text omits the first sentence of this verse.

THE MESSAGE

son. He's my only child. Often a spirit seizes him. Suddenly he's screaming, thrown into convulsions, his mouth foaming. And then it beats him black-and-blue before it leaves. I asked your disciples to deliver him but they couldn't."

41 Jesus said, "What a generation! No sense of God! No focus to your lives! How many times do I have to go over these things? How much longer do I have to put up with this? Bring your son here."

42-43 While he was coming, the demon slammed him to the ground and threw him into convulsions. Jesus stepped in, ordered the vile spirit gone, healed the boy, and handed him back to his father. They all shook their heads in wonder, astonished at God's greatness, God's majestic greatness.

YOUR BUSINESS IS LIFE

43-44 While they continued to stand around exclaiming over all the things he was doing, Jesus said to his disciples, "Treasure and ponder each of these next words: The Son of Man is about to be betrayed into human hands."

45 They didn't get what he was saying. It was like he was speaking a foreign language and they couldn't make heads or tails of it. But they were embarrassed to ask him what he meant.

46-48 They started arguing over which of them would be most famous. When Jesus realized how much this mattered to them, he brought a child to his side. "Whoever accepts this child as if the child were me, accepts me," he said. "And whoever accepts me, accepts the One who sent me. You become great by accepting, not asserting. Your spirit, not your size, makes the difference."

49 John spoke up, "Master, we saw a man using your name to expel demons and we stopped him because he wasn't of our group."

50 Jesus said, "Don't stop him. If he's not an enemy, he's an ally."

51-54 When it came close to the time for his Ascension, he gathered up his courage and steeled himself for the journey to Jerusalem. He sent messengers on ahead. They came to a Samaritan village to make arrangements for his hospitality. But when the Samaritans learned that his destination was Jerusalem, they refused hospitality. When the disciples James and John learned of it, they said, "Master, do you want us to call a bolt of lightning down out of the sky and incinerate them?"

55-56 Jesus turned on them: "Of course not!" And they traveled on to another village.

57 On the road someone asked if he could go along. "I'll go with you, wherever," he said.

NEW KING JAMES VERSION

58 And Jesus said to him, "Foxes have holes and birds of the air *have* nests, but the Son of Man has nowhere to lay *His* head."

59 Then He said to another, "Follow Me."

But he said, "Lord, let me first go and bury my father."

60 Jesus said to him, "Let the dead bury their own dead, but you go and preach the kingdom of God."

61 And another also said, "Lord, I will follow You, but let me first go *and* bid them farewell who are at my house."

62 But Jesus said to him, "No one, having put his hand to the plow, and looking back, is fit for the kingdom of God."

THE SEVENTY SENT OUT

10 After these things the Lord appointed seventy others also,[a] and sent them two by two before His face into every city and place where He Himself was about to go. 2 Then He said to them, "The harvest truly *is* great, but the laborers *are* few; therefore pray the Lord of the harvest to send out laborers into His harvest. 3 Go your way; behold, I send you out as lambs among wolves. 4 Carry neither money bag, knapsack, nor sandals; and greet no one along the road. 5 But whatever house you enter, first say, 'Peace to this house.' 6 And if a son of peace is there, your peace will rest on it; if not, it will return to you. 7 And remain in the same house, eating and drinking such things as they give, for the laborer is worthy of his wages. Do not go from house to house. 8 Whatever city you enter, and they receive you, eat such things as are set before you. 9 And heal the sick there, and say to them, 'The kingdom of God has come near to you.' 10 But whatever city you enter, and they do not receive you, go out into its streets and say, 11 'The very dust of your city which clings to us[a] we wipe off against you. Nevertheless know this, that the kingdom of God has come near you.' 12 But[a] I say to you that it will be more tolerable in that Day for Sodom than for that city.

WOE TO THE IMPENITENT CITIES

13 "Woe to you, Chorazin! Woe to you, Bethsaida! For if the mighty works which were done in you had been done in Tyre and Sidon, they would have repented long ago, sitting in sackcloth and ashes. 14 But it will be more tolerable for Tyre and Sidon at the judgment than for you. 15 And you, Capernaum, who are exalted to heaven, will be brought down to Hades.[a] 16 He who hears you hears Me, he who rejects you rejects Me, and he who rejects Me rejects Him who sent Me."

THE SEVENTY RETURN WITH JOY

17 Then the seventy[a] returned with joy, saying, "Lord, even the demons are subject to us in Your name."

10:1 [a]NU-Text reads *seventy-two others.* **10:11** [a]NU-Text reads *our feet.* **10:12** [a]NU-Text and M-Text omit *But.* **10:15** [a]NU-Text reads *will you be exalted to heaven? You will be thrust down to Hades!* **10:17** [a]NU-Text reads *seventy-two.*

THE MESSAGE

58 Jesus was curt: "Are you ready to rough it? We're not staying in the best inns, you know."

Jesus said to another, "Follow me."

59 He said, "Certainly, but first excuse me for a couple of days, please. I have to make arrangements for my father's funeral."

60 Jesus refused. "First things first. Your business is life, not death. And life is urgent: Announce God's kingdom!"

61 Then another said, "I'm ready to follow you, Master, but first excuse me while I get things straightened out at home."

62 Jesus said, "No procrastination. No backward looks. You can't put God's kingdom off till tomorrow. Seize the day."

LAMBS IN A WOLF PACK

1-2 10 Later the Master selected seventy and sent them ahead of him in pairs to every town and place where he intended to go. He gave them this charge:

"What a huge harvest! And how few the harvest hands. So on your knees; ask the God of the Harvest to send harvest hands.

3 "On your way! But be careful—this is hazardous work. You're like lambs in a wolf pack.

4 "Travel light. Comb and toothbrush and no extra luggage.

"Don't loiter and make small talk with everyone you meet along the way.

5-6 "When you enter a home, greet the family, 'Peace.' If your greeting is received, then it's a good place to stay. But if it's not received, take it back and get out. Don't impose yourself.

7 "Stay at one home, taking your meals there, for a worker deserves three square meals. Don't move from house to house, looking for the best cook in town.

8-9 "When you enter a town and are received, eat what they set before you, heal anyone who is sick, and tell them, 'God's kingdom is right on your doorstep!'

10-12 "When you enter a town and are not received, go out in the street and say, 'The only thing we got from you is the dirt on our feet, and we're giving it back. Did you have any idea that God's kingdom was right on your doorstep?' Sodom will have it better on Judgment Day than the town that rejects you.

13-14 "Doom, Chorazin! Doom, Bethsaida! If Tyre and Sidon had been given half the chances given you, they'd have been on their knees long ago, repenting and crying for mercy. Tyre and Sidon will have it easy on Judgment Day compared to you.

15 "And you, Capernaum! Do you think you're about to be promoted to heaven? Think again. You're on a mudslide to hell.

16 "The one who listens to you, listens to me. The one who rejects you, rejects me. And rejecting me is the same as rejecting God, who sent me."

17 The seventy came back triumphant. "Master, even the demons danced to your tune!"

NEW KING JAMES VERSION

18And He said to them, "I saw Satan fall like
lightning from heaven. 19Behold, I give you the
authority to trample on serpents and scorpions,
and over all the power of the enemy, and noth-
ing shall by any means hurt you. 20Nevertheless
do not rejoice in this, that the spirits are subject
to you, but rather[a] rejoice because your names
are written in heaven."

JESUS REJOICES IN THE SPIRIT

21In that hour Jesus rejoiced in the Spirit and
said, "I thank You, Father, Lord of heaven and
earth, that You have hidden these things from
the wise and prudent and revealed them to
babes. Even so, Father, for so it seemed good in
Your sight. 22All[a] things have been delivered to
Me by My Father, and no one knows who the
Son is except the Father, and who the Father is
except the Son, and *the one* to whom the Son
wills to reveal *Him.*"

23Then He turned to *His* disciples and said
privately, "Blessed *are* the eyes which see the
things you see; 24for I tell you that many
prophets and kings have desired to see what
you see, and have not seen *it,* and to hear what
you hear, and have not heard *it.*"

THE PARABLE OF THE GOOD SAMARITAN

25And behold, a certain lawyer stood up and
tested Him, saying, "Teacher, what shall I do to
inherit eternal life?"

26He said to him, "What is written in the law?
What is your reading *of it?*"

27So he answered and said, " *'You shall love
the Lord your God with all your heart, with all
your soul, with all your strength, and with all
your mind,'* [a] and *'your neighbor as yourself.'* "[b]

28And He said to him, "You have answered
rightly; do this and you will live."

29But he, wanting to justify himself, said to
Jesus, "And who is my neighbor?"

30Then Jesus answered and said: "A certain
man went down from Jerusalem to Jericho, and
fell among thieves, who stripped him of his
clothing, wounded *him,* and departed, leaving
him half dead. 31Now by chance a certain priest
came down that road. And when he saw him, he
passed by on the other side. 32Likewise a Levite,
when he arrived at the place, came and looked,
and passed by on the other side. 33But a certain
Samaritan, as he journeyed, came where he
was. And when he saw him, he had compassion.
34So he went to *him* and bandaged his wounds,
pouring on oil and wine; and he set him on his
own animal, brought him to an inn, and took
care of him. 35On the next day, when he de-
parted,[a] he took out two denarii, gave *them* to
the innkeeper, and said to him, 'Take care of
him; and whatever more you spend, when I
come again, I will repay you.' 36So which of
these three do you think was neighbor to him
who fell among the thieves?"

37And he said, "He who showed mercy on
him."

Then Jesus said to him, "Go and do likewise."

10:20 [a]NU-Text and M-Text omit *rather.* **10:22** [a]M-Text reads *And turning to the disciples He said, "All . . .* **10:27** [a]Deuteronomy 6:5 [b]Leviticus 19:18 **10:35** [a]NU-Text omits *when he departed.*

THE MESSAGE

18-20 Jesus said, "I know. I saw Satan fall, a
bolt of lightning out of the sky. See what I've
given you? Safe passage as you walk on
snakes and scorpions, and protection from
every assault of the Enemy. No one can put
a hand on you. All the same, the great tri-
umph is not in your authority over evil, but
in God's authority over you and presence
with you. Not what you do for God but what
God does for you—that's the agenda for re-
joicing."

21 At that, Jesus rejoiced, exuberant in the
Holy Spirit. "I thank you, Father, Master of
heaven and earth, that you hid these things
from the know-it-alls and showed them to
these innocent newcomers. Yes, Father, it
pleased you to do it this way.

22 "I've been given it all by my Father! Only
the Father knows who the Son is and only the
Son knows who the Father is. The Son can in-
troduce the Father to anyone he wants to."

23-24 He then turned in a private aside to his
disciples. "Fortunate the eyes that see what
you're seeing! There are plenty of prophets
and kings who would have given their right
arm to see what you are seeing but never
got so much as a glimpse, to hear what you
are hearing but never got so much as a
whisper."

DEFINING "NEIGHBOR"

25 Just then a religion scholar stood up with a
question to test Jesus. "Teacher, what do I
need to do to get eternal life?"

26 He answered, "What's written in God's
Law? How do you interpret it?"

27 He said, "That you love the Lord your
God with all your passion and prayer and
muscle and intelligence—and that you love
your neighbor as well as you do yourself."

28 "Good answer!" said Jesus. "Do it and
you'll live."

29 Looking for a loophole, he asked, "And
just how would you define 'neighbor'?"

30-32 Jesus answered by telling a story. "There
was once a man traveling from Jerusalem to
Jericho. On the way he was attacked by rob-
bers. They took his clothes, beat him up, and
went off leaving him half-dead. Luckily, a
priest was on his way down the same road,
but when he saw him he angled across to
the other side. Then a Levite religious man
showed up; he also avoided the injured man.

33-35 "A Samaritan traveling the road came on
him. When he saw the man's condition, his
heart went out to him. He gave him first aid,
disinfecting and bandaging his wounds.
Then he lifted him onto his donkey, led him
to an inn, and made him comfortable. In the
morning he took out two silver coins and
gave them to the innkeeper, saying, 'Take
good care of him. If it costs any more, put it
on my bill—I'll pay you on my way back.'

36 "What do you think? Which of the three
became a neighbor to the man attacked by
robbers?"

37 "The one who treated him kindly," the re-
ligion scholar responded.

Jesus said, "Go and do the same."

NEW KING JAMES VERSION

MARY AND MARTHA WORSHIP AND SERVE

38Now it happened as they went that He en-
tered a certain village; and a certain woman
named Martha welcomed Him into her house.
39And she had a sister called Mary, who also sat
at Jesus'[a] feet and heard His word. 40But Martha
was distracted with much serving, and she ap-
proached Him and said, "Lord, do You not care
that my sister has left me to serve alone? There-
fore tell her to help me."
41And Jesus[a] answered and said to her,
"Martha, Martha, you are worried and troubled
about many things. 42But one thing is needed,
and Mary has chosen that good part, which will
not be taken away from her."

THE MODEL PRAYER

11 Now it came to pass, as He was praying in
a certain place, when He ceased, *that* one
of His disciples said to Him, "Lord, teach us to
pray, as John also taught his disciples."
2So He said to them, "When you pray, say:

Our Father in heaven,[a]
Hallowed be Your name.
Your kingdom come.[b]
Your will be done
On earth as *it is* in heaven.
3Give us day by day our daily bread.
4And forgive us our sins,
For we also forgive everyone who is
indebted to us.
And do not lead us into temptation,
But deliver us from the evil one."[a]

A FRIEND COMES AT MIDNIGHT

5And He said to them, "Which of you shall
have a friend, and go to him at midnight and say
to him, 'Friend, lend me three loaves; 6for a
friend of mine has come to me on his journey,
and I have nothing to set before him'; 7and he
will answer from within and say, 'Do not trouble
me; the door is now shut, and my children are
with me in bed; I cannot rise and give to you'? 8I
say to you, though he will not rise and give to
him because he is his friend, yet because of his
persistence he will rise and give him as many as
he needs.

KEEP ASKING, SEEKING, KNOCKING

9"So I say to you, ask, and it will be given to
you; seek, and you will find; knock, and it will
be opened to you. 10For everyone who asks re-
ceives, and he who seeks finds, and to him who
knocks it will be opened. 11If a son asks for
bread[a] from any father among you, will he give
him a stone? Or if *he asks* for a fish, will he give
him a serpent instead of a fish? 12Or if he asks
for an egg, will he offer him a scorpion? 13If you
then, being evil, know how to give good gifts to
your children, how much more will *your* heav-
enly Father give the Holy Spirit to those who
ask Him!"

10:39 [a]NU-Text reads *the Lord's.* **10:41** [a]NU-Text reads *the Lord.* **11:2** [a]NU-Text omits *Our* and *in heaven.* [b]NU-Text omits the rest of this verse. **11:4** [a]NU-Text omits *But deliver us from the evil one.* **11:11** [a]NU-Text omits the words from *bread* through *for* in the next sentence.

THE MESSAGE

MARY AND MARTHA

38-40 As they continued their travel, Jesus entered a village. A woman by the name of Martha welcomed him and made him feel quite at home. She had a sister, Mary, who sat before the Master, hanging on every word he said. But Martha was pulled away by all she had to do in the kitchen. Later, she stepped in, interrupting them. "Master, don't you care that my sister has abandoned the kitchen to me? Tell her to lend me a hand."

41-42 The Master said, "Martha, dear Martha, you're fussing far too much and getting yourself worked up over nothing. One thing only is essential, and Mary has chosen it—it's the main course, and won't be taken from her."

ASK FOR WHAT YOU NEED

1 11 One day he was praying in a certain place. When he finished, one of his disciples said, "Master, teach us to pray just as John taught his disciples."

2-4 So he said, "When you pray, say,

Father,
Reveal who you are.
Set the world right.
Keep us alive with three square meals.
Keep us forgiven with you and forgiving
others.
Keep us safe from ourselves and the
Devil."

5-6 Then he said, "Imagine what would happen if you went to a friend in the middle of the night and said, 'Friend, lend me three loaves of bread. An old friend traveling through just showed up, and I don't have a thing on hand.'

7 "The friend answers from his bed, 'Don't bother me. The door's locked; my children are all down for the night; I can't get up to give you anything.'

8 "But let me tell you, even if he won't get up because he's a friend, if you stand your ground, knocking and waking all the neighbors, he'll finally get up and get you whatever you need.

9 "Here's what I'm saying:

Ask and you'll get;
Seek and you'll find;
Knock and the door will open.

10-13 "Don't bargain with God. Be direct. Ask for what you need. This is not a cat-and-mouse, hide-and-seek game we're in. If your little boy asks for a serving of fish, do you scare him with a live snake on his plate? If your little girl asks for an egg, do you trick her with a spider? As bad as you are, you wouldn't think of such a thing—you're at least decent to your own children. And don't you think the Father who conceived you in love will give the Holy Spirit when you ask him?"

NEW KING JAMES VERSION

A House Divided Cannot Stand

14 And He was casting out a demon, and it was mute. So it was, when the demon had gone out, that the mute spoke; and the multitudes marveled. 15 But some of them said, "He casts out demons by Beelzebub,[a] the ruler of the demons."

16 Others, testing *Him,* sought from Him a sign from heaven. 17 But He, knowing their thoughts, said to them: "Every kingdom divided against itself is brought to desolation, and a house *divided* against a house falls. 18 If Satan also is divided against himself, how will his kingdom stand? Because you say I cast out demons by Beelzebub. 19 And if I cast out demons by Beelzebub, by whom do your sons cast *them* out? Therefore they will be your judges. 20 But if I cast out demons with the finger of God, surely the kingdom of God has come upon you. 21 When a strong man, fully armed, guards his own palace, his goods are in peace. 22 But when a stronger than he comes upon him and overcomes him, he takes from him all his armor in which he trusted, and divides his spoils. 23 He who is not with Me is against Me, and he who does not gather with Me scatters.

An Unclean Spirit Returns

24 "When an unclean spirit goes out of a man, he goes through dry places, seeking rest; and finding none, he says, 'I will return to my house from which I came.' 25 And when he comes, he finds *it* swept and put in order. 26 Then he goes and takes with *him* seven other spirits more wicked than himself, and they enter and dwell there; and the last *state* of that man is worse than the first."

Keeping the Word

27 And it happened, as He spoke these things, that a certain woman from the crowd raised her voice and said to Him, "Blessed *is* the womb that bore You, and *the* breasts which nursed You!"

28 But He said, "More than that, blessed *are* those who hear the word of God and keep it!"

Seeking a Sign

29 And while the crowds were thickly gathered together, He began to say, "This is an evil generation. It seeks a sign, and no sign will be given to it except the sign of Jonah the prophet.[a] 30 For as Jonah became a sign to the Ninevites, so also the Son of Man will be to this generation. 31 The queen of the South will rise up in the judgment with the men of this generation and

11:15 [a]NU-Text and M-Text read *Beelzebul.* **11:29** [a]NU-Text omits *the prophet.*

THE MESSAGE

No Neutral Ground

14-16 Jesus delivered a man from a demon that had kept him speechless. The demon gone, the man started talking a blue streak, taking the crowd by complete surprise. But some from the crowd were cynical. "Black magic," they said. "Some devil trick he's pulled from his sleeve." Others were skeptical, waiting around for him to prove himself with a spectacular miracle.

17-20 Jesus knew what they were thinking and said, "Any country in civil war for very long is wasted. A constantly squabbling family falls to pieces. If Satan cancels Satan, is there any Satan left? You accuse me of ganging up with the Devil, the prince of demons, to cast out demons, but if you're slinging devil mud at me, calling me a devil who kicks out devils, doesn't the same mud stick to your own exorcists? But if it's *God's* finger I'm pointing that sends the demons on their way, then God's kingdom is here for sure.

21-22 "When a strong man, armed to the teeth, stands guard in his front yard, his property is safe and sound. But what if a stronger man comes along with superior weapons? Then he's beaten at his own game, the arsenal that gave him such confidence hauled off, and his precious possessions plundered.

23 "This is war, and there is no neutral ground. If you're not on my side, you're the enemy; if you're not helping, you're making things worse.

24-26 "When a corrupting spirit is expelled from someone, it drifts along through the desert looking for an oasis, some unsuspecting soul it can bedevil. When it doesn't find anyone, it says, 'I'll go back to my old haunt.' On return, it finds the person swept and dusted, but vacant. It then runs out and rounds up seven other spirits dirtier than itself and they all move in, whooping it up. That person ends up far worse than if he'd never gotten cleaned up in the first place."

27 While he was saying these things, some woman lifted her voice above the murmur of the crowd: "Blessed the womb that carried you, and the breasts at which you nursed!"

28 Jesus commented, "Even more blessed are those who hear God's Word and guard it with their lives!"

Keep Your Eyes Open

29-30 As the crowd swelled, he took a fresh tack: "The mood of this age is all wrong. Everybody's looking for proof, but you're looking for the wrong kind. All you're looking for is something to titillate your curiosity, satisfy your lust for miracles. But the only proof you're going to get is the Jonah-proof given to the Ninevites, which looks like no proof at all. What Jonah was to Nineveh, the Son of Man is to this age.

32,31 "On Judgment Day the Ninevites will stand up and give evidence that will condemn this generation, because when Jonah preached to them they changed their lives. A far greater preacher than Jonah is here,

NEW KING JAMES VERSION

condemn them, for she came from the ends of the earth to hear the wisdom of Solomon; and indeed a greater than Solomon *is* here. 32The men of Nineveh will rise up in the judgment with this generation and condemn it, for they repented at the preaching of Jonah; and indeed a greater than Jonah *is* here.

THE LAMP OF THE BODY

33"No one, when he has lit a lamp, puts *it* in a secret place or under a basket, but on a lampstand, that those who come in may see the light. 34The lamp of the body is the eye. Therefore, when your eye is good, your whole body also is full of light. But when *your eye* is bad, your body also *is* full of darkness. 35Therefore take heed that the light which is in you is not darkness. 36If then your whole body *is* full of light, having no part dark, *the* whole *body* will be full of light, as when the bright shining of a lamp gives you light."

WOE TO THE PHARISEES AND LAWYERS

37And as He spoke, a certain Pharisee asked Him to dine with him. So He went in and sat down to eat. 38When the Pharisee saw *it*, he marveled that He had not first washed before dinner.

39Then the Lord said to him, "Now you Pharisees make the outside of the cup and dish clean, but your inward part is full of greed and wickedness. 40Foolish ones! Did not He who made the outside make the inside also? 41But rather give alms of such things as you have; then indeed all things are clean to you.

42"But woe to you Pharisees! For you tithe mint and rue and all manner of herbs, and pass by justice and the love of God. These you ought to have done, without leaving the others undone. 43Woe to you Pharisees! For you love the best seats in the synagogues and greetings in the marketplaces. 44Woe to you, scribes and Pharisees, hypocrites![a] For you are like graves which are not seen, and the men who walk over *them* are not aware *of them*."

45Then one of the lawyers answered and said to Him, "Teacher, by saying these things You reproach us also."

46And He said, "Woe to you also, lawyers! For you load men with burdens hard to bear, and you yourselves do not touch the burdens with one of your fingers. 47Woe to you! For you build the tombs of the prophets, and your fathers killed them. 48In fact, you bear witness that you approve the deeds of your fathers; for they indeed killed them, and you build their tombs. 49Therefore the wisdom of God also said, 'I will send them prophets and apostles, and *some* of them they will kill and persecute,' 50that the blood of all the prophets which was shed from the foundation of the world may be required of this generation, 51from the blood of Abel to the blood of Zechariah who perished between the

11:44 [a]NU-Text omits *scribes and Pharisees, hypocrites.*

THE MESSAGE

and you squabble about 'proofs.' On Judgment Day the Queen of Sheba will come forward and bring evidence that condemns this generation, because she traveled from a far corner of the earth to listen to wise Solomon. Wisdom far greater than Solomon's is right in front of you, and you quibble over 'evidence.'

33-36 "No one lights a lamp, then hides it in a drawer. It's put on a lamp stand so those entering the room have light to see where they're going. Your eye is a lamp, lighting up your whole body. If you live wide-eyed in wonder and belief, your body fills up with light. If you live squinty-eyed in greed and distrust, your body is a dank cellar. Keep your eyes open, your lamp burning, so you don't get musty and murky. Keep your life as well-lighted as your best-lighted room."

FRAUDS!

37-41 When he finished that talk, a Pharisee asked him to dinner. He entered his house and sat right down at the table. The Pharisee was shocked and somewhat offended when he saw that Jesus didn't wash up before the meal. But the Master said to him, "I know you Pharisees burnish the surface of your cups and plates so they sparkle in the sun, but I also know your insides are maggoty with greed and secret evil. Stupid Pharisees! Didn't the One who made the outside also make the inside? Turn both your pockets and your hearts inside out and give generously to the poor; then your *lives* will be clean, not just your dishes and your hands.

42 "I've had it with you! You're hopeless, you Pharisees! Frauds! You keep meticulous account books, tithing on every nickel and dime you get, but manage to find loopholes for getting around basic matters of justice and God's love. Careful bookkeeping is commendable, but the basics are required.

43-44 "You're hopeless, you Pharisees! Frauds! You love sitting at the head table at church dinners, love preening yourselves in the radiance of public flattery. Frauds! You're just like unmarked graves: People walk over that nice, grassy surface, never suspecting the rot and corruption that is six feet under."

45 One of the religion scholars spoke up: "Teacher, do you realize that in saying these things you're insulting us?"

46 He said, "Yes, and I can be even more explicit. You're hopeless, you religion scholars! You load people down with rules and regulations, nearly breaking their backs, but never lift even a finger to help.

47-51 "You're hopeless! You build tombs for the prophets your ancestors killed. The tombs you build are monuments to your murdering ancestors more than to the murdered prophets. That accounts for God's Wisdom saying, 'I will send them prophets and apostles, but they'll kill them and run them off.' What it means is that every drop of righteous blood ever spilled from the time earth began until now, from the blood of Abel to the blood of Zechariah, who was struck

NEW KING JAMES VERSION

altar and the temple. Yes, I say to you, it shall be required of this generation.

52 "Woe to you lawyers! For you have taken away the key of knowledge. You did not enter in yourselves, and those who were entering in you hindered."

53 And as He said these things to them,[a] the scribes and the Pharisees began to assail *Him* vehemently, and to cross-examine Him about many things, 54 lying in wait for Him, and seeking to catch Him in something He might say, that they might accuse Him.[a]

BEWARE OF HYPOCRISY

12 In the meantime, when an innumerable multitude of people had gathered together, so that they trampled one another, He began to say to His disciples first *of all,* "Beware of the leaven of the Pharisees, which is hypocrisy. 2 For there is nothing covered that will not be revealed, nor hidden that will not be known. 3 Therefore whatever you have spoken in the dark will be heard in the light, and what you have spoken in the ear in inner rooms will be proclaimed on the housetops.

JESUS TEACHES THE FEAR OF GOD

4 "And I say to you, My friends, do not be afraid of those who kill the body, and after that have no more that they can do. 5 But I will show you whom you should fear: Fear Him who, after He has killed, has power to cast into hell; yes, I say to you, fear Him!

6 "Are not five sparrows sold for two copper coins?[a] And not one of them is forgotten before God. 7 But the very hairs of your head are all numbered. Do not fear therefore; you are of more value than many sparrows.

CONFESS CHRIST BEFORE MEN

8 "Also I say to you, whoever confesses Me before men, him the Son of Man also will confess before the angels of God. 9 But he who denies Me before men will be denied before the angels of God.

10 "And anyone who speaks a word against the Son of Man, it will be forgiven him; but to him who blasphemes against the Holy Spirit, it will not be forgiven.

11 "Now when they bring you to the synagogues and magistrates and authorities, do not worry about how or what you should answer, or what you should say. 12 For the Holy Spirit will teach you in that very hour what you ought to say."

THE PARABLE OF THE RICH FOOL

13 Then one from the crowd said to Him, "Teacher, tell my brother to divide the inheritance with me."

11:53 [a]NU-Text reads *And when He left there.* **11:54** [a]NU-Text omits *and seeking* and *that they might accuse Him.* **12:6** [a]Greek *assarion,* a coin of very small value

THE MESSAGE

down between altar and sanctuary, is on your heads. Yes, it's on the bill of this generation and this generation will pay.

52 "You're hopeless, you religion scholars! You took the key of knowledge, but instead of unlocking doors, you locked them. You won't go in yourself, and won't let anyone else in either."

53-54 As soon as Jesus left the table, the religion scholars and Pharisees went into a rage. They went over and over everything he said, plotting how they could trap him in something from his own mouth.

CAN'T HIDE BEHIND A RELIGIOUS MASK

1-3 12 By this time the crowd, unwieldy and stepping on each other's toes, numbered into the thousands. But Jesus' primary concern was his disciples. He said to them, "Watch yourselves carefully so you don't get contaminated with Pharisee yeast, Pharisee phoniness. You can't keep your true self hidden forever; before long you'll be exposed. You can't hide behind a religious mask forever; sooner or later the mask will slip and your true face will be known. You can't whisper one thing in private and preach the opposite in public; the day's coming when those whispers will be repeated all over town.

4-5 "I'm speaking to you as dear friends. Don't be bluffed into silence or insincerity by the threats of religious bullies. True, they can kill you, but *then* what can they do? There's nothing they can do to your soul, your core being. Save your fear for God, who holds your entire life—body and soul—in his hands.

6-7 "What's the price of two or three pet canaries? Some loose change, right? But God never overlooks a single one. And he pays even greater attention to you, down to the last detail—even numbering the hairs on your head! So don't be intimidated by all this bully talk. You're worth more than a million canaries.

8-9 "Stand up for me among the people you meet and the Son of Man will stand up for you before all God's angels. But if you pretend you don't know me, do you think I'll defend you before God's angels?

10 "If you bad-mouth the Son of Man out of misunderstanding or ignorance, that can be overlooked. But if you're knowingly attacking God himself, taking aim at the Holy Spirit, that won't be overlooked.

11-12 "When they drag you into their meeting places, or into police courts and before judges, don't worry about defending yourselves—what you'll say or how you'll say it. The right words will be there. The Holy Spirit will give you the right words when the time comes."

THE STORY OF THE GREEDY FARMER

13 Someone out of the crowd said, "Teacher, order my brother to give me a fair share of the family inheritance."

NEW KING JAMES VERSION

14But He said to him, "Man, who made Me a
judge or an arbitrator over you?" 15And He said
to them, "Take heed and beware of covetous-
ness,[a] for one's life does not consist in the abun-
dance of the things he possesses."
16Then He spoke a parable to them, saying:
"The ground of a certain rich man yielded plen-
tifully. 17And he thought within himself, saying,
'What shall I do, since I have no room to store
my crops?' 18So he said, 'I will do this: I will pull
down my barns and build greater, and there I
will store all my crops and my goods. 19And I
will say to my soul, "Soul, you have many goods
laid up for many years; take your ease; eat,
drink, *and* be merry." ' 20But God said to him,
'Fool! This night your soul will be required of
you; then whose will those things be which you
have provided?'
21"So *is* he who lays up treasure for himself,
and is not rich toward God."

DO NOT WORRY

22Then He said to His disciples, "Therefore I
say to you, do not worry about your life, what
you will eat; nor about the body, what you will
put on. 23Life is more than food, and the body *is*
more than clothing. 24Consider the ravens, for
they neither sow nor reap, which have neither
storehouse nor barn; and God feeds them. Of
how much more value are you than the birds?
25And which of you by worrying can add one cu-
bit to his stature? 26If you then are not able to do
the least, why are you anxious for the rest?
27Consider the lilies, how they grow: they nei-
ther toil nor spin; and yet I say to you, even
Solomon in all his glory was not arrayed like
one of these. 28If then God so clothes the grass,
which today is in the field and tomorrow is
thrown into the oven, how much more *will He*
clothe you, O *you* of little faith?
29"And do not seek what you should eat or
what you should drink, nor have an anxious
mind. 30For all these things the nations of the
world seek after, and your Father knows that
you need these things. 31But seek the kingdom
of God, and all these things[a] shall be added to
you.
32"Do not fear, little flock, for it is your Fa-
ther's good pleasure to give you the kingdom.
33Sell what you have and give alms; provide
yourselves money bags which do not grow old,
a treasure in the heavens that does not fail,
where no thief approaches nor moth destroys.
34For where your treasure is, there your heart
will be also.

THE FAITHFUL SERVANT AND THE EVIL SERVANT

35"Let your waist be girded and *your* lamps
burning; 36and you yourselves be like men who
wait for their master, when he will return from
the wedding, that when he comes and knocks

12:15 [a]NU-Text reads *all covetousness.* **12:31** [a]NU-Text reads *His kingdom, and these things.*

THE MESSAGE

14 He replied, "Mister, what makes you think it's any of my business to be a judge or mediator for you?"

15 Speaking to the people, he went on, "Take care! Protect yourself against the least bit of greed. Life is not defined by what you have, even when you have a lot."

16-19 Then he told them this story: "The farm of a certain rich man produced a terrific crop. He talked to himself: 'What can I do? My barn isn't big enough for this harvest.' Then he said, 'Here's what I'll do: I'll tear down my barns and build bigger ones. Then I'll gather in all my grain and goods, and I'll say to myself, Self, you've done well! You've got it made and can now retire. Take it easy and have the time of your life!'

20 "Just then God showed up and said, 'Fool! Tonight you die. And your barnful of goods—who gets it?'

21 "That's what happens when you fill your barn with Self and not with God."

STEEP YOURSELF IN GOD-REALITY

22-24 He continued this subject with his disciples. "Don't fuss about what's on the table at mealtimes or if the clothes in your closet are in fashion. There is far more to your inner life than the food you put in your stomach, more to your outer appearance than the clothes you hang on your body. Look at the ravens, free and unfettered, not tied down to a job description, carefree in the care of God. And you count far more.

25-28 "Has anyone by fussing before the mirror ever gotten taller by so much as an inch? If fussing can't even do that, why fuss at all? Walk into the fields and look at the wildflowers. They don't fuss with their appearance—but have you ever seen color and design quite like it? The ten best-dressed men and women in the country look shabby alongside them. If God gives such attention to the wildflowers, most of them never even seen, don't you think he'll attend to you, take pride in you, do his best for you?

29-32 "What I'm trying to do here is get you to relax, not be so preoccupied with *getting* so you can respond to God's *giving*. People who don't know God and the way he works fuss over these things, but you know both God and how he works. Steep yourself in God-reality, God-initiative, God-provisions. You'll find all your everyday human concerns will be met. Don't be afraid of missing out. You're my dearest friends! The Father wants to give you the very kingdom itself.

33-34 "Be generous. Give to the poor. Get yourselves a bank that can't go bankrupt, a bank in heaven far from bankrobbers, safe from embezzlers, a bank you can bank on. It's obvious, isn't it? The place where your treasure is, is the place you will most want to be, and end up being.

WHEN THE MASTER SHOWS UP

35-38 "Keep your shirts on; keep the lights on! Be like house servants waiting for their master to come back from his honeymoon, awake

NEW KING JAMES VERSION

they may open to him immediately. 37 Blessed *are* those servants whom the master, when he comes, will find watching. Assuredly, I say to you that he will gird himself and have them sit down *to eat,* and will come and serve them. 38 And if he should come in the second watch, or come in the third watch, and find *them* so, blessed are those servants. 39 But know this, that if the master of the house had known what hour the thief would come, he would have watched and[a] not allowed his house to be broken into. 40 Therefore you also be ready, for the Son of Man is coming at an hour you do not expect."

41 Then Peter said to Him, "Lord, do You speak this parable *only* to us, or to all *people?*"

42 And the Lord said, "Who then is that faithful and wise steward, whom *his* master will make ruler over his household, to give *them their* portion of food in due season? 43 Blessed *is* that servant whom his master will find so doing when he comes. 44 Truly, I say to you that he will make him ruler over all that he has. 45 But if that servant says in his heart, 'My master is delaying his coming,' and begins to beat the male and female servants, and to eat and drink and be drunk, 46 the master of that servant will come on a day when he is not looking for *him,* and at an hour when he is not aware, and will cut him in two and appoint *him* his portion with the unbelievers. 47 And that servant who knew his master's will, and did not prepare *himself* or do according to his will, shall be beaten with many *stripes.* 48 But he who did not know, yet committed things deserving of stripes, shall be beaten with few. For everyone to whom much is given, from him much will be required; and to whom much has been committed, of him they will ask the more.

CHRIST BRINGS DIVISION

49 "I came to send fire on the earth, and how I wish it were already kindled! 50 But I have a baptism to be baptized with, and how distressed I am till it is accomplished! 51 Do *you* suppose that I came to give peace on earth? I tell you, not at all, but rather division. 52 For from now on five in one house will be divided: three against two, and two against three. 53 Father will be divided against son and son against father, mother against daughter and daughter against mother, mother-in-law against her daughter-in-law and daughter-in-law against her mother-in-law."

DISCERN THE TIME

54 Then He also said to the multitudes, "Whenever you *see* a cloud rising out of the west, immediately you say, 'A shower is coming'; and so it is. 55 And when you see the south wind blow, you say, 'There will be hot weather'; and there is. 56 Hypocrites! You can discern the face of the sky and of the earth, but how *is it* you do not discern this time?

MAKE PEACE WITH YOUR ADVERSARY

57 "Yes, and why, even of yourselves, do you not judge what is right? 58 When you go with your adversary to the magistrate, make every ef-

12:39 [a]NU-Text reads *he would not have allowed.*

THE MESSAGE

and ready to open the door when he arrives and knocks. Lucky the servants whom the master finds on watch! He'll put on an apron, sit them at the table, and serve them a meal, sharing his wedding feast with them. It doesn't matter what time of the night he arrives; they're awake—and so blessed!

39-40 "You know that if the house owner had known what night the burglar was coming, he wouldn't have stayed out late and left the place unlocked. So don't you be slovenly and careless. Just when you don't expect him, the Son of Man will show up."

41 Peter said, "Master, are you telling this story just for us? Or is it for everybody?"

42-46 The Master said, "Let me ask you: Who is the dependable manager, full of common sense, that the master puts in charge of his staff to feed them well and on time? He is a blessed man if when the master shows up he's doing his job. But if he says to himself, 'The master is certainly taking his time,' begins maltreating the servants and maids, throws parties for his friends, and gets drunk, the master will walk in when he least expects it, give him the thrashing of his life, and put him back in the kitchen peeling potatoes.

47-48 "The servant who knows what his master wants and ignores it, or insolently does whatever he pleases, will be thoroughly thrashed. But if he does a poor job through ignorance, he'll get off with a slap on the hand. Great gifts mean great responsibilities; greater gifts, greater responsibilities!

TO START A FIRE

49-53 "I've come to start a fire on this earth—how I wish it were blazing right now! I've come to change everything, turn everything rightside up—how I long for it to be finished! Do you think I came to smooth things over and make everything nice? Not so. I've come to disrupt and confront! From now on, when you find five in a house, it will be—

Three against two,
    and two against three;
Father against son,
    and son against father;
Mother against daughter,
    and daughter against mother;
Mother-in-law against bride,
    and bride against mother-in-law."

54-56 Then he turned to the crowd: "When you see clouds coming in from the west, you say, 'Storm's coming'—and you're right. And when the wind comes out of the south, you say, 'This'll be a hot one'—and you're right. Frauds! You know how to tell a change in the weather, so don't tell me you can't tell a change in the season, the God-season we're in right now.

57-59 "You don't have to be a genius to understand these things. Just use your common sense, the kind you'd use if, while being taken to court, you decided to settle up with

NEW KING JAMES VERSION

fort along the way to settle with him, lest he
drag you to the judge, the judge deliver you to
the officer, and the officer throw you into
prison. 59I tell you, you shall not depart from
there till you have paid the very last mite."

REPENT OR PERISH

13 There were present at that season some
who told Him about the Galileans whose
blood Pilate had mingled with their sacrifices.
2And Jesus answered and said to them, "Do you
suppose that these Galileans were worse sin-
ners than all *other* Galileans, because they suf-
fered such things? 3I tell you, no; but unless you
repent you will all likewise perish. 4Or those
eighteen on whom the tower in Siloam fell and
killed them, do you think that they were worse
sinners than all *other* men who dwelt in
Jerusalem? 5I tell you, no; but unless you repent
you will all likewise perish."

THE PARABLE OF THE BARREN FIG TREE

6He also spoke this parable: "A certain *man*
had a fig tree planted in his vineyard, and he
came seeking fruit on it and found none. 7Then
he said to the keeper of his vineyard, 'Look, for
three years I have come seeking fruit on this fig
tree and find none. Cut it down; why does it use
up the ground?' 8But he answered and said to
him, 'Sir, let it alone this year also, until I dig
around it and fertilize *it*. 9And if it bears fruit,
well. But if not, after that[a] you can cut it down.' "

A SPIRIT OF INFIRMITY

10Now He was teaching in one of the syna-
gogues on the Sabbath. 11And behold, there was
a woman who had a spirit of infirmity eighteen
years, and was bent over and could in no way
raise *herself* up. 12But when Jesus saw her, He
called *her* to *Him* and said to her, "Woman, you
are loosed from your infirmity." 13And He laid
His hands on her, and immediately she was
made straight, and glorified God.

14But the ruler of the synagogue answered
with indignation, because Jesus had healed on
the Sabbath; and he said to the crowd, "There
are six days on which men ought to work; there-
fore come and be healed on them, and not on
the Sabbath day."

15The Lord then answered him and said,
"Hypocrite![a] Does not each one of you on the
Sabbath loose his ox or donkey from the stall,
and lead *it* away to water it? 16So ought not this
woman, being a daughter of Abraham, whom Sa-
tan has bound—think of it—for eighteen years,
be loosed from this bond on the Sabbath?" 17And
when He said these things, all His adversaries
were put to shame; and all the multitude rejoiced
for all the glorious things that were done by Him.

THE PARABLE OF THE MUSTARD SEED

18Then He said, "What is the kingdom of God
like? And to what shall I compare it? 19It is like
a mustard seed, which a man took and put in his
garden; and it grew and became a large[a] tree,
and the birds of the air nested in its branches."

13:9 [a]NU-Text reads *And if it bears fruit after that, well. But if not, you can cut it down.* **13:15** [a]NU-Text and M-Text read *Hypocrites.* **13:19** [a]NU-Text omits *large.*

THE MESSAGE

your accuser on the way, knowing that if the
case went to the judge you'd probably go to
jail and pay every last penny of the fine.
That's the kind of decision I'm asking you to
make."

UNLESS YOU TURN TO GOD

1-5 13 About that time some people came up
and told him about the Galileans Pilate
had killed while they were at worship, mix-
ing their blood with the blood of the sacri-
fices on the altar. Jesus responded, "Do you
think those murdered Galileans were worse
sinners than all other Galileans? Not at all.
Unless you turn to God, you, too, will die.
And those eighteen in Jerusalem the other
day, the ones crushed and killed when the
Tower of Siloam collapsed and fell on them,
do you think they were worse citizens than
all other Jerusalemites? Not at all. Unless
you turn to God, you, too, will die."

6-7 Then he told them a story: "A man had an
apple tree planted in his front yard. He came
to it expecting to find apples, but there
weren't any. He said to his gardener, 'What's
going on here? For three years now I've
come to this tree expecting apples and not
one apple have I found. Chop it down! Why
waste good ground with it any longer?'

8-9 "The gardener said, 'Let's give it another
year. I'll dig around it and fertilize, and
maybe it will produce next year; if it doesn't,
then chop it down.' "

HEALING ON THE SABBATH

10-13 He was teaching in one of the meeting
places on the Sabbath. There was a woman
present, so twisted and bent over with
arthritis that she couldn't even look up. She
had been afflicted with this for eighteen
years. When Jesus saw her, he called her
over. "Woman, you're free!" He laid hands
on her and suddenly she was standing
straight and tall, giving glory to God.

14 The meeting-place president, furious be-
cause Jesus had healed on the Sabbath, said
to the congregation, "Six days have been de-
fined as work days. Come on one of the six
if you want to be healed, but not on the sev-
enth, the Sabbath."

15-16 But Jesus shot back, "You frauds! Each
Sabbath every one of you regularly unties
your cow or donkey from its stall, leads it
out for water, and thinks nothing of it. So
why isn't it all right for me to untie this
daughter of Abraham and lead her from the
stall where Satan has had her tied these
eighteen years?"

17 When he put it that way, his critics were
left looking quite silly and redfaced. The
congregation was delighted and cheered
him on.

THE WAY TO GOD

18-19 Then he said, "How can I picture God's king-
dom for you? What kind of story can I use?
It's like a pine nut that a man plants in his
front yard. It grows into a huge pine tree with
thick branches, and eagles build nests in it."

NEW KING JAMES VERSION

THE PARABLE OF THE LEAVEN

[20]And again He said, "To what shall I liken the kingdom of God? [21]It is like leaven, which a woman took and hid in three measures[a] of meal till it was all leavened."

THE NARROW WAY

[22]And He went through the cities and villages, teaching, and journeying toward Jerusalem. [23]Then one said to Him, "Lord, are there few who are saved?"

And He said to them, [24]"Strive to enter through the narrow gate, for many, I say to you, will seek to enter and will not be able. [25]When once the Master of the house has risen up and shut the door, and you begin to stand outside and knock at the door, saying, 'Lord, Lord, open for us,' and He will answer and say to you, 'I do not know you, where you are from,' [26]then you will begin to say, 'We ate and drank in Your presence, and You taught in our streets.' [27]But He will say, 'I tell you I do not know you, where you are from. Depart from Me, all you workers of iniquity.' [28]There will be weeping and gnashing of teeth, when you see Abraham and Isaac and Jacob and all the prophets in the kingdom of God, and yourselves thrust out. [29]They will come from the east and the west, from the north and the south, and sit down in the kingdom of God. [30]And indeed there are last who will be first, and there are first who will be last."

[31]On that very day[a] some Pharisees came, saying to Him, "Get out and depart from here, for Herod wants to kill You."

[32]And He said to them, "Go, tell that fox, 'Behold, I cast out demons and perform cures today and tomorrow, and the third *day* I shall be perfected.' [33]Nevertheless I must journey today, tomorrow, and the *day* following; for it cannot be that a prophet should perish outside of Jerusalem.

JESUS LAMENTS OVER JERUSALEM

[34]"O Jerusalem, Jerusalem, the one who kills the prophets and stones those who are sent to her! How often I wanted to gather your children together, as a hen *gathers* her brood under *her* wings, but you were not willing! [35]See! Your house is left to you desolate; and assuredly,[a] I say to you, you shall not see Me until *the time* comes when you say, *'Blessed is He who comes in the name of the LORD!'* "[b]

A MAN WITH DROPSY HEALED ON THE SABBATH

14 Now it happened, as He went into the house of one of the rulers of the Pharisees to eat bread on the Sabbath, that they watched

13:21 [a]Greek *sata,* approximately two pecks in all 13:31 [a]NU-Text reads *In that very hour.* 13:35 [a]NU-Text and M-Text omit *assuredly.* [b]Psalm 118:26

THE MESSAGE

20-21 He tried again. "How can I picture God's kingdom? It's like yeast that a woman works into enough dough for three loaves of bread—and waits while the dough rises."

22 He went on teaching from town to village, village to town, but keeping on a steady course toward Jerusalem.

23-25 A bystander said, "Master, will only a few be saved?"

He said, "Whether few or many is none of your business. Put your mind on your life with God. The way to life—to God!—is vigorous and requires your total attention. A lot of you are going to assume that you'll sit down to God's salvation banquet just because you've been hanging around the neighborhood all your lives. Well, one day you're going to be banging on the door, wanting to get in, but you'll find the door locked and the Master saying, 'Sorry, you're not on my guest list.'

26-27 "You'll protest, 'But we've known you all our lives!' only to be interrupted with his abrupt, 'Your kind of knowing can hardly be called knowing. You don't know the first thing about me.'

28-30 "That's when you'll find yourselves out in the cold, strangers to grace. You'll watch Abraham, Isaac, Jacob, and all the prophets march into God's kingdom. You'll watch outsiders stream in from east, west, north, and south and sit down at the table of God's kingdom. And all the time you'll be outside looking in—and wondering what happened. This is the Great Reversal: the last in line put at the head of the line, and the so-called first ending up last."

31 Just then some Pharisees came up and said, "Run for your life! Herod's on the hunt. He's out to kill you!"

32-35 Jesus said, "Tell that fox that I've no time for him right now. Today and tomorrow I'm busy clearing out the demons and healing the sick; the third day I'm wrapping things up. Besides, it's not proper for a prophet to come to a bad end outside Jerusalem.

Jerusalem, Jerusalem, killer of prophets,
abuser of the messengers of God!
How often I've longed to gather your children,
gather your children like a hen,
Her brood safe under her wings—
but you refused and turned away!
And now it's too late: You won't see me again
until the day you say,
'Blessed is he
who comes in
the name of God.' "

1-3 **14** One time when Jesus went for a Sabbath meal with one of the top leaders of the Pharisees, all the guests had their eyes on him, watching his every move. Right be-

NEW KING JAMES VERSION

Him closely. [2]And behold, there was a certain man before Him who had dropsy. [3]And Jesus, answering, spoke to the lawyers and Pharisees, saying, "Is it lawful to heal on the Sabbath?"[a]

[4]But they kept silent. And He took *him* and healed him, and let him go. [5]Then He answered them, saying, "Which of you, having a donkey[a] or an ox that has fallen into a pit, will not immediately pull him out on the Sabbath day?" [6]And they could not answer Him regarding these things.

TAKE THE LOWLY PLACE

[7]So He told a parable to those who were invited, when He noted how they chose the best places, saying to them: [8]"When you are invited by anyone to a wedding feast, do not sit down in the best place, lest one more honorable than you be invited by him; [9]and he who invited you and him come and say to you, 'Give place to this man,' and then you begin with shame to take the lowest place. [10]But when you are invited, go and sit down in the lowest place, so that when he who invited you comes he may say to you, 'Friend, go up higher.' Then you will have glory in the presence of those who sit at the table with you. [11]For whoever exalts himself will be humbled, and he who humbles himself will be exalted."

[12]Then He also said to him who invited Him, "When you give a dinner or a supper, do not ask your friends, your brothers, your relatives, nor rich neighbors, lest they also invite you back, and you be repaid. [13]But when you give a feast, invite *the* poor, *the* maimed, *the* lame, *the* blind. [14]And you will be blessed, because they cannot repay you; for you shall be repaid at the resurrection of the just."

THE PARABLE OF THE GREAT SUPPER

[15]Now when one of those who sat at the table with Him heard these things, he said to Him, "Blessed *is* he who shall eat bread[a] in the kingdom of God!"

[16]Then He said to him, "A certain man gave a great supper and invited many, [17]and sent his servant at supper time to say to those who were invited, 'Come, for all things are now ready.' [18]But they all with one *accord* began to make excuses. The first said to him, 'I have bought a piece of ground, and I must go and see it. I ask you to have me excused.' [19]And another said, 'I have bought five yoke of oxen, and I am going to test them. I ask you to have me excused.' [20]Still another said, 'I have married a wife, and therefore I cannot come.' [21]So that servant came and reported these things to his master. Then the master of the house, being angry, said to his servant, 'Go out quickly into the streets and

14:3 [a]NU-Text adds *or not.* **14:5** [a]NU-Text and M-Text read *son.* **14:15** [a]M-Text reads *dinner.*

THE MESSAGE

fore him there was a man hugely swollen in his joints. So Jesus asked the religion scholars and Pharisees present, "Is it permitted to heal on the Sabbath? Yes or no?"

4-6 They were silent. So he took the man, healed him, and sent him on his way. Then he said, "Is there anyone here who, if a child or animal fell down a well, wouldn't rush to pull him out immediately, not asking whether or not it was the Sabbath?" They were stumped. There was nothing they could say to that.

INVITE THE MISFITS

7-9 He went on to tell a story to the guests around the table. Noticing how each had tried to elbow into the place of honor, he said, "When someone invites you to dinner, don't take the place of honor. Somebody more important than you might have been invited by the host. Then he'll come and call out in front of everybody, 'You're in the wrong place. The place of honor belongs to this man.' Red-faced, you'll have to make your way to the very last table, the only place left.

10-11 "When you're invited to dinner, go and sit at the last place. Then when the host comes he may very well say, 'Friend, come up to the front.' That will give the dinner guests something to talk about! What I'm saying is, If you walk around with your nose in the air, you're going to end up flat on your face. But if you're content to be simply yourself, you will become more than yourself."

12-14 Then he turned to the host. "The next time you put on a dinner, don't just invite your friends and family and rich neighbors, the kind of people who will return the favor. Invite some people who never get invited out, the misfits from the wrong side of the tracks. You'll be—and experience—a blessing. They won't be able to return the favor, but the favor will be returned—oh, how it will be returned!—at the resurrection of God's people."

THE STORY OF THE DINNER PARTY

15 That triggered a response from one of the guests: "How fortunate the one who gets to eat dinner in God's kingdom!"

16-17 Jesus followed up. "Yes. For there was once a man who threw a great dinner party and invited many. When it was time for dinner, he sent out his servant to the invited guests, saying, 'Come on in; the food's on the table.'

18 "Then they all began to beg off, one after another making excuses. The first said, 'I bought a piece of property and need to look it over. Send my regrets.'

19 "Another said, 'I just bought five teams of oxen, and I really need to check them out. Send my regrets.'

20 "And yet another said, 'I just got married and need to get home to my wife.'

21 "The servant went back and told the master what had happened. He was outraged and told the servant, 'Quickly, get out into

NEW KING JAMES VERSION

lanes of the city, and bring in here *the* poor and *the* maimed and *the* lame and *the* blind.' 22And the servant said, 'Master, it is done as you commanded, and still there is room.' 23Then the master said to the servant, 'Go out into the highways and hedges, and compel *them* to come in, that my house may be filled. 24For I say to you that none of those men who were invited shall taste my supper.' "

LEAVING ALL TO FOLLOW CHRIST

25Now great multitudes went with Him. And He turned and said to them, 26"If anyone comes to Me and does not hate his father and mother, wife and children, brothers and sisters, yes, and his own life also, he cannot be My disciple. 27And whoever does not bear his cross and come after Me cannot be My disciple. 28For which of you, intending to build a tower, does not sit down first and count the cost, whether he has *enough* to finish *it*— 29lest, after he has laid the foundation, and is not able to finish, all who see *it* begin to mock him, 30saying, 'This man began to build and was not able to finish'? 31Or what king, going to make war against another king, does not sit down first and consider whether he is able with ten thousand to meet him who comes against him with twenty thousand? 32Or else, while the other is still a great way off, he sends a delegation and asks conditions of peace. 33So likewise, whoever of you does not forsake all that he has cannot be My disciple.

TASTELESS SALT IS WORTHLESS

34"Salt *is* good; but if the salt has lost its flavor, how shall it be seasoned? 35It is neither fit for the land nor for the dunghill, *but* men throw it out. He who has ears to hear, let him hear!"

THE PARABLE OF THE LOST SHEEP

15 Then all the tax collectors and the sinners drew near to Him to hear Him. 2And the Pharisees and scribes complained, saying, "This Man receives sinners and eats with them." 3So He spoke this parable to them, saying:

4"What man of you, having a hundred sheep, if he loses one of them, does not leave the ninety-nine in the wilderness, and go after the one which is lost until he finds it? 5And when he has found *it*, he lays *it* on his shoulders, rejoicing. 6And when he comes home, he calls together *his* friends and neighbors, saying to them, 'Rejoice with me, for I have found my sheep which was lost!' 7I say to you that likewise there will be more joy in heaven over one sinner who repents than over ninety-nine just persons who need no repentance.

THE PARABLE OF THE LOST COIN

8"Or what woman, having ten silver coins,[a] if she loses one coin, does not light a lamp, sweep

15:8 [a]Greek *drachma*, a valuable coin often worn in a ten-piece garland by married women

THE MESSAGE

the city streets and alleys. Collect all who look like they need a square meal, all the misfits and homeless and wretched you can lay your hands on, and bring them here.'

22 "The servant reported back, 'Master, I did what you commanded—and there's still room.'

23-24 "The master said, 'Then go to the country roads. Whoever you find, drag them in. I want my house full! Let me tell you, not one of those originally invited is going to get so much as a bite at my dinner party.' "

FIGURE THE COST

25-27 One day when large groups of people were walking along with him, Jesus turned and told them, "Anyone who comes to me but refuses to let go of father, mother, spouse, children, brothers, sisters—yes, even one's own self!—can't be my disciple. Anyone who won't shoulder his own cross and follow behind me can't be my disciple.

28-30 "Is there anyone here who, planning to build a new house, doesn't first sit down and figure the cost so you'll know if you can complete it? If you only get the foundation laid and then run out of money, you're going to look pretty foolish. Everyone passing by will poke fun at you: 'He started something he couldn't finish.'

31-32 "Or can you imagine a king going into battle against another king without first deciding whether it is possible with his ten thousand troops to face the twenty thousand troops of the other? And if he decides he can't, won't he send an emissary and work out a truce?

33 "Simply put, if you're not willing to take what is dearest to you, whether plans or people, and kiss it good-bye, you can't be my disciple.

34 "Salt is excellent. But if the salt goes flat, it's useless, good for nothing.

"Are you listening to this? Really listening?"

THE STORY OF THE LOST SHEEP

1-3 15 By this time a lot of men and women of doubtful reputation were hanging around Jesus, listening intently. The Pharisees and religion scholars were not pleased, not at all pleased. They growled, "He takes in sinners and eats meals with them, treating them like old friends." Their grumbling triggered this story.

4-7 "Suppose one of you had a hundred sheep and lost one. Wouldn't you leave the ninety-nine in the wilderness and go after the lost one until you found it? When found, you can be sure you would put it across your shoulders, rejoicing, and when you got home call in your friends and neighbors, saying, 'Celebrate with me! I've found my lost sheep!' Count on it—there's more joy in heaven over one sinner's rescued life than over ninety-nine good people in no need of rescue.

THE STORY OF THE LOST COIN

8-10 "Or imagine a woman who has ten coins and loses one. Won't she light a lamp and

NEW KING JAMES VERSION

the house, and search carefully until she finds
it? 9And when she has found *it*, she calls *her*
friends and neighbors together, saying, 'Rejoice
with me, for I have found the piece which I lost!'
10Likewise, I say to you, there is joy in the pres-
ence of the angels of God over one sinner who
repents."

THE PARABLE OF THE LOST SON

11Then He said: "A certain man had two sons.
12And the younger of them said to *his* father, 'Fa-
ther, give me the portion of goods that falls *to*
me.' So he divided to them *his* livelihood. 13And
not many days after, the younger son gathered
all together, journeyed to a far country, and
there wasted his possessions with prodigal liv-
ing. 14But when he had spent all, there arose a
severe famine in that land, and he began to be in
want. 15Then he went and joined himself to a cit-
izen of that country, and he sent him into his
fields to feed swine. 16And he would gladly have
filled his stomach with the pods that the swine
ate, and no one gave him *anything*.
17"But when he came to himself, he said,
'How many of my father's hired servants have
bread enough and to spare, and I perish with
hunger! 18I will arise and go to my father, and
will say to him, "Father, I have sinned against
heaven and before you, 19and I am no longer
worthy to be called your son. Make me like one
of your hired servants." '
20"And he arose and came to his father. But
when he was still a great way off, his father saw
him and had compassion, and ran and fell on his
neck and kissed him. 21And the son said to him,
'Father, I have sinned against heaven and in
your sight, and am no longer worthy to be called
your son.'
22"But the father said to his servants, 'Bring[a]
out the best robe and put *it* on him, and put a
ring on his hand and sandals on *his* feet. 23And
bring the fatted calf here and kill *it*, and let us
eat and be merry; 24for this my son was dead
and is alive again; he was lost and is found.' And
they began to be merry.
25"Now his older son was in the field. And as
he came and drew near to the house, he heard
music and dancing. 26So he called one of the ser-
vants and asked what these things meant. 27And
he said to him, 'Your brother has come, and be-
cause he has received him safe and sound, your
father has killed the fatted calf.'
28"But he was angry and would not go in.
Therefore his father came out and pleaded with
him. 29So he answered and said to *his* father, 'Lo,
these many years I have been serving you; I
never transgressed your commandment at any
time; and yet you never gave me a young goat,
that I might make merry with my friends. 30But
as soon as this son of yours came, who has de-
voured your livelihood with harlots, you killed
the fatted calf for him.'

15:22 [a]NU-Text reads *Quickly bring*.

THE MESSAGE

scour the house, looking in every nook and
cranny until she finds it? And when she
finds it you can be sure she'll call her
friends and neighbors: 'Celebrate with me! I
found my lost coin!' Count on it—that's the
kind of party God's angels throw every time
one lost soul turns to God."

THE STORY OF THE LOST SON

11-12 Then he said, "There was once a man who
had two sons. The younger said to his father,
'Father, I want right now what's coming to
me.'
12-16 "So the father divided the property be-
tween them. It wasn't long before the
younger son packed his bags and left for a
distant country. There, undisciplined and
dissipated, he wasted everything he had. Af-
ter he had gone through all his money, there
was a bad famine all through that country
and he began to hurt. He signed on with a
citizen there who assigned him to his fields
to slop the pigs. He was so hungry he would
have eaten the corncobs in the pig slop, but
no one would give him any.
17-20 "That brought him to his senses. He said,
'All those farmhands working for my father
sit down to three meals a day, and here I am
starving to death. I'm going back to my fa-
ther. I'll say to him, Father, I've sinned
against God, I've sinned before you; I don't
deserve to be called your son. Take me on as
a hired hand.' He got right up and went
home to his father.
20-21 "When he was still a long way off, his fa-
ther saw him. His heart pounding, he ran
out, embraced him, and kissed him. The son
started his speech: 'Father, I've sinned
against God, I've sinned before you; I don't
deserve to be called your son ever again.'
22-24 "But the father wasn't listening. He was
calling to the servants, 'Quick. Bring a clean
set of clothes and dress him. Put the family
ring on his finger and sandals on his feet.
Then get a grain-fed heifer and roast it.
We're going to feast! We're going to have a
wonderful time! My son is here—given up
for dead and now alive! Given up for lost
and now found!' And they began to have a
wonderful time.
25-27 "All this time his older son was out in the
field. When the day's work was done he
came in. As he approached the house, he
heard the music and dancing. Calling over
one of the houseboys, he asked what was
going on. He told him, 'Your brother came
home. Your father has ordered a feast—bar-
becued beef!—because he has him home
safe and sound.'
28-30 "The older brother stalked off in an angry
sulk and refused to join in. His father came
out and tried to talk to him, but he wouldn't
listen. The son said, 'Look how many years
I've stayed here serving you, never giving
you one moment of grief, but have you ever
thrown a party for me and my friends? Then
this son of yours who has thrown away your
money on whores shows up and you go all
out with a feast!'

NEW KING JAMES VERSION

31"And he said to him, 'Son, you are always with me, and all that I have is yours. 32It was right that we should make merry and be glad, for your brother was dead and is alive again, and was lost and is found.' "

THE PARABLE OF THE UNJUST STEWARD

16 He also said to His disciples: "There was a certain rich man who had a steward, and an accusation was brought to him that this man was wasting his goods. 2So he called him and said to him, 'What is this I hear about you? Give an account of your stewardship, for you can no longer be steward.'

3"Then the steward said within himself, 'What shall I do? For my master is taking the stewardship away from me. I cannot dig; I am ashamed to beg. 4I have resolved what to do, that when I am put out of the stewardship, they may receive me into their houses.'

5"So he called every one of his master's debtors to *him*, and said to the first, 'How much do you owe my master?' 6And he said, 'A hundred measures[a] of oil.' So he said to him, 'Take your bill, and sit down quickly and write fifty.' 7Then he said to another, 'And how much do you owe?' So he said, 'A hundred measures[a] of wheat.' And he said to him, 'Take your bill, and write eighty.' 8So the master commended the unjust steward because he had dealt shrewdly. For the sons of this world are more shrewd in their generation than the sons of light.

9"And I say to you, make friends for yourselves by unrighteous mammon, that when you fail,[a] they may receive you into an everlasting home. 10He who *is* faithful in *what is* least is faithful also in much; and he who is unjust in *what is* least is unjust also in much. 11Therefore if you have not been faithful in the unrighteous mammon, who will commit to your trust the true *riches?* 12And if you have not been faithful in what is another man's, who will give you what is your own?

13"No servant can serve two masters; for either he will hate the one and love the other, or else he will be loyal to the one and despise the other. You cannot serve God and mammon."

THE LAW, THE PROPHETS, AND THE KINGDOM

14Now the Pharisees, who were lovers of money, also heard all these things, and they de-

16:6 [a]Greek *batos,* eight or nine gallons each (Old Testament *bath*) 16:7 [a]Greek *koros,* ten or twelve bushels each (Old Testament *kor*) 16:9 [a]NU-Text reads *it fails.*

THE MESSAGE

31-32 "His father said, 'Son, you don't understand. You're with me all the time, and everything that is mine is yours—but this is a wonderful time, and we had to celebrate. This brother of yours was dead, and he's alive! He was lost, and he's found!' "

THE STORY OF THE CROOKED MANAGER

1-2 16 Jesus said to his disciples, "There was once a rich man who had a manager. He got reports that the manager had been taking advantage of his position by running up huge personal expenses. So he called him in and said, 'What's this I hear about you? You're fired. And I want a complete audit of your books.'

3-4 "The manager said to himself, 'What am I going to do? I've lost my job as manager. I'm not strong enough for a laboring job, and I'm too proud to beg. . . . Ah, I've got a plan. Here's what I'll do . . . then when I'm turned out into the street, people will take me into their houses.'

5 "Then he went at it. One after another, he called in the people who were in debt to his master. He said to the first, 'How much do you owe my master?'

6 "He replied, 'A hundred jugs of olive oil.'

"The manager said, 'Here, take your bill, sit down here—quick now—write fifty.'

7 "To the next he said, 'And you, what do you owe?'

"He answered, 'A hundred sacks of wheat.'

"He said, 'Take your bill, write in eighty.'

8-9 "Now here's a surprise: The master praised the crooked manager! And why? Because he knew how to look after himself. Streetwise people are smarter in this regard than law-abiding citizens. They are on constant alert, looking for angles, surviving by their wits. I want you to be smart in the same way—but for what is *right*—using every adversity to stimulate you to creative survival, to concentrate your attention on the bare essentials, so you'll live, really live, and not complacently just get by on good behavior."

GOD SEES BEHIND APPEARANCES

10-13 Jesus went on to make these comments:

If you're honest in small things,
you'll be honest in big things;
If you're a crook in small things,
you'll be a crook in big things.
If you're not honest in small jobs,
who will put you in charge of the
store?
No worker can serve two bosses:
He'll either hate the first and love the
second
Or adore the first and despise the
second.
You can't serve both God and the
Bank.

14-18 When the Pharisees, a money-obsessed bunch, heard him say these things, they

NEW KING JAMES VERSION

rided Him. 15 And He said to them, "You are those who justify yourselves before men, but God knows your hearts. For what is highly esteemed among men is an abomination in the sight of God.

16 "The law and the prophets *were* until John. Since that time the kingdom of God has been preached, and everyone is pressing into it. 17 And it is easier for heaven and earth to pass away than for one tittle of the law to fail.

18 "Whoever divorces his wife and marries another commits adultery; and whoever marries her who is divorced from *her* husband commits adultery.

THE RICH MAN AND LAZARUS

19 "There was a certain rich man who was clothed in purple and fine linen and fared sumptuously every day. 20 But there was a certain beggar named Lazarus, full of sores, who was laid at his gate, 21 desiring to be fed with the crumbs which fell[a] from the rich man's table. Moreover the dogs came and licked his sores. 22 So it was that the beggar died, and was carried by the angels to Abraham's bosom. The rich man also died and was buried. 23 And being in torments in Hades, he lifted up his eyes and saw Abraham afar off, and Lazarus in his bosom.

24 "Then he cried and said, 'Father Abraham, have mercy on me, and send Lazarus that he may dip the tip of his finger in water and cool my tongue; for I am tormented in this flame.' 25 But Abraham said, 'Son, remember that in your lifetime you received your good things, and likewise Lazarus evil things; but now he is comforted and you are tormented. 26 And besides all this, between us and you there is a great gulf fixed, so that those who want to pass from here to you cannot, nor can those from there pass to us.'

27 "Then he said, 'I beg you therefore, father, that you would send him to my father's house, 28 for I have five brothers, that he may testify to them, lest they also come to this place of torment.' 29 Abraham said to him, 'They have Moses and the prophets; let them hear them.' 30 And he said, 'No, father Abraham; but if one goes to them from the dead, they will repent.' 31 But he said to him, 'If they do not hear Moses and the prophets, neither will they be persuaded though one rise from the dead.' "

16:21 [a]NU-Text reads *with what fell.*

THE MESSAGE

rolled their eyes, dismissing him as hopelessly out of touch. So Jesus spoke to them: "You are masters at making yourselves look good in front of others, but God knows what's behind the appearance.

What society sees and calls
monumental,
God sees through and calls
monstrous.
God's Law and the Prophets climaxed in
John;
Now it's all kingdom of God—the glad
news
and compelling invitation to every
man and woman.
The sky will disintegrate and the earth
dissolve
before a single letter of God's Law
wears out.
Using the legalities of divorce
as a cover for lust is adultery;
Using the legalities of marriage
as a cover for lust is adultery.

THE RICH MAN AND LAZARUS

19-21 "There once was a rich man, expensively dressed in the latest fashions, wasting his days in conspicuous consumption. A poor man named Lazarus, covered with sores, had been dumped on his doorstep. All he lived for was to get a meal from scraps off the rich man's table. His best friends were the dogs who came and licked his sores.

22-24 "Then he died, this poor man, and was taken up by the angels to the lap of Abraham. The rich man also died and was buried. In hell and in torment, he looked up and saw Abraham in the distance and Lazarus in his lap. He called out, 'Father Abraham, mercy! Have mercy! Send Lazarus to dip his finger in water to cool my tongue. I'm in agony in this fire.'

25-26 "But Abraham said, 'Child, remember that in your lifetime you got the good things and Lazarus the bad things. It's not like that here. Here he's consoled and you're tormented. Besides, in all these matters there is a huge chasm set between us so that no one can go from us to you even if he wanted to, nor can anyone cross over from you to us.'

27-28 "The rich man said, 'Then let me ask you, Father: Send him to the house of my father where I have five brothers, so he can tell them the score and warn them so they won't end up here in this place of torment.'

29 "Abraham answered, 'They have Moses and the Prophets to tell them the score. Let them listen to them.'

30 " 'I know, Father Abraham,' he said, 'but they're not listening. If someone came back to them from the dead, they would change their ways.'

31 "Abraham replied, 'If they won't listen to Moses and the Prophets, they're not going to be convinced by someone who rises from the dead.' "

NEW KING JAMES VERSION

JESUS WARNS OF OFFENSES

17 Then He said to the disciples, "It is impossible that no offenses should come, but woe *to him* through whom they do come! [2]It would be better for him if a millstone were hung around his neck, and he were thrown into the sea, than that he should offend one of these little ones. [3]Take heed to yourselves. If your brother sins against you,[a] rebuke him; and if he repents, forgive him. [4]And if he sins against you seven times in a day, and seven times in a day returns to you,[a] saying, 'I repent,' you shall forgive him."

FAITH AND DUTY

[5]And the apostles said to the Lord, "Increase our faith."

[6]So the Lord said, "If you have faith as a mustard seed, you can say to this mulberry tree, 'Be pulled up by the roots and be planted in the sea,' and it would obey you. [7]And which of you, having a servant plowing or tending sheep, will say to him when he has come in from the field, 'Come at once and sit down to eat'? [8]But will he not rather say to him, 'Prepare something for my supper, and gird yourself and serve me till I have eaten and drunk, and afterward you will eat and drink'? [9]Does he thank that servant because he did the things that were commanded him? I think not.[a] [10]So likewise you, when you have done all those things which you are commanded, say, 'We are unprofitable servants. We have done what was our duty to do.' "

TEN LEPERS CLEANSED

[11]Now it happened as He went to Jerusalem that He passed through the midst of Samaria and Galilee. [12]Then as He entered a certain village, there met Him ten men who were lepers, who stood afar off. [13]And they lifted up *their* voices and said, "Jesus, Master, have mercy on us!"

[14]So when He saw *them,* He said to them, "Go, show yourselves to the priests." And so it was that as they went, they were cleansed.

[15]And one of them, when he saw that he was healed, returned, and with a loud voice glorified God, [16]and fell down on *his* face at His feet, giving Him thanks. And he was a Samaritan.

[17]So Jesus answered and said, "Were there not ten cleansed? But where *are* the nine? [18]Were there not any found who returned to give glory to God except this foreigner?" [19]And He said to him, "Arise, go your way. Your faith has made you well."

THE COMING OF THE KINGDOM

[20]Now when He was asked by the Pharisees when the kingdom of God would come, He answered them and said, "The kingdom of God does not come with observation; [21]nor will they say, 'See here!' or 'See there!'[a] For indeed, the kingdom of God is within you."

[22]Then He said to the disciples, "The days will come when you will desire to see one of the days of the Son of Man, and you will not see *it.*

17:3 [a]NU-Text omits *against you.* **17:4** [a]M-Text omits *to you.*
17:9 [a]NU-Text ends verse with *commanded;* M-Text omits *him.*
17:21 [a]NU-Text reverses *here* and *there.*

THE MESSAGE

A KERNEL OF FAITH

1-2 **17** He said to his disciples, "Hard trials and
temptations are bound to come, but too
bad for whoever brings them on! Better to
wear a millstone necklace and take a swim
in the deep blue sea than give even one of
these dear little ones a hard time!
3-4 "Be alert. If you see your friend going
wrong, correct him. If he responds, forgive
him. Even if it's personal against you and
repeated seven times through the day, and
seven times he says, 'I'm sorry, I won't do it
again,' forgive him."
5 The apostles came up and said to the
Master, "Give us more faith."
6 But the Master said, "You don't need
more faith. There is no 'more' or 'less' in
faith. If you have a bare kernel of faith, say
the size of a poppy seed, you could say to
this sycamore tree, 'Go jump in the lake,'
and it would do it.
7-10 "Suppose one of you has a servant who
comes in from plowing the field or tending
the sheep. Would you take his coat, set the
table, and say, 'Sit down and eat'? Wouldn't
you be more likely to say, 'Prepare dinner;
change your clothes and wait table for me
until I've finished my coffee; then go to the
kitchen and have your supper'? Does the
servant get special thanks for doing what's
expected of him? It's the same with you.
When you've done everything expected of
you, be matter-of-fact and say, 'The work is
done. What we were told to do, we did.' "
11-13 It happened that as he made his way to-
ward Jerusalem, he crossed over the border
between Samaria and Galilee. As he entered
a village, ten men, all lepers, met him. They
kept their distance but raised their voices,
calling out, "Jesus, Master, have mercy on
us!"
14-16 Taking a good look at them, he said, "Go,
show yourselves to the priests."
They went, and while still on their way,
became clean. One of them, when he real-
ized that he was healed, turned around and
came back, shouting his gratitude, glorify-
ing God. He kneeled at Jesus' feet, so grate-
ful. He couldn't thank him enough—and he
was a Samaritan.
17-19 Jesus said, "Were not ten healed? Where
are the nine? Can none be found to come
back and give glory to God except this out-
sider?" Then he said to him, "Get up. On your
way. Your faith has healed and saved you."

WHEN THE SON OF MAN ARRIVES

20-21 Jesus, grilled by the Pharisees on when the
kingdom of God would come, answered,
"The kingdom of God doesn't come by
counting the days on the calendar. Nor
when someone says, 'Look here!' or, 'There
it is!' And why? Because God's kingdom is
already among you."
22-24 He went on to say to his disciples, "The
days are coming when you are going to be
desperately homesick for just a glimpse of
one of the days of the Son of Man, and you
won't see a thing. And they'll say to you,

NEW KING JAMES VERSION

23And they will say to you, 'Look here!' or 'Look
there!'[a] Do not go after *them* or follow *them*.
24For as the lightning that flashes out of one *part*
under heaven shines to the other *part* under
heaven, so also the Son of Man will be in His
day. 25But first He must suffer many things and
be rejected by this generation. 26And as it was in
the days of Noah, so it will be also in the days of
the Son of Man: 27They ate, they drank, they
married wives, they were given in marriage, un-
til the day that Noah entered the ark, and the
flood came and destroyed them all. 28Likewise
as it was also in the days of Lot: They ate, they
drank, they bought, they sold, they planted, they
built; 29but on the day that Lot went out of
Sodom it rained fire and brimstone from heaven
and destroyed *them* all. 30Even so will it be in
the day when the Son of Man is revealed.
31"In that day, he who is on the housetop, and
his goods *are* in the house, let him not come
down to take them away. And likewise the one
who is in the field, let him not turn back. 32Re-
member Lot's wife. 33Whoever seeks to save his
life will lose it, and whoever loses his life will
preserve it. 34I tell you, in that night there will be
two *men* in one bed: the one will be taken and
the other will be left. 35Two *women* will be grind-
ing together: the one will be taken and the other
left. 36Two *men* will be in the field: the one will
be taken and the other left."[a]
37And they answered and said to Him,
"Where, Lord?"
So He said to them, "Wherever the body is,
there the eagles will be gathered together."

THE PARABLE OF THE PERSISTENT WIDOW

18 Then He spoke a parable to them, that men
always ought to pray and not lose heart,
2saying: "There was in a certain city a judge who
did not fear God nor regard man. 3Now there
was a widow in that city; and she came to him,
saying, 'Get justice for me from my adversary.'
4And he would not for a while; but afterward he
said within himself, 'Though I do not fear God
nor regard man, 5yet because this widow trou-
bles me I will avenge her, lest by her continual
coming she weary me.' "
6Then the Lord said, "Hear what the unjust
judge said. 7And shall God not avenge His own
elect who cry out day and night to Him, though
He bears long with them? 8I tell you that He will
avenge them speedily. Nevertheless, when the
Son of Man comes, will He really find faith on
the earth?"

17:23 [a]NU-Text reverses *here* and *there*. **17:36** [a]NU-Text and M-Text omit verse 36.

THE MESSAGE

'Look over there!' or, 'Look here!' Don't fall
for any of that nonsense. The arrival of the
Son of Man is not something you go out to
see. He simply comes.
24-25 "You know how the whole sky lights up
from a single flash of lightning? That's how
it will be on the Day of the Son of Man. But
first it's necessary that he suffer many
things and be turned down by the people of
today.
26-27 "The time of the Son of Man will be just
like the time of Noah—everyone carrying on
as usual, having a good time right up to the
day Noah boarded the ship. They suspected
nothing until the flood hit and swept every-
thing away.
28-30 "It was the same in the time of Lot—the
people carrying on, having a good time,
business as usual right up to the day Lot
walked out of Sodom and a firestorm swept
down and burned everything to a crisp.
That's how it will be—sudden, total—when
the Son of Man is revealed.
31-33 "When the Day arrives and you're out
working in the yard, don't run into the
house to get anything. And if you're out in
the field, don't go back and get your coat.
Remember what happened to Lot's wife! If
you grasp and cling to life on your terms,
you'll lose it, but if you let that life go, you'll
get life on God's terms.
34-35 "On that Day, two men will be in the same
boat fishing—one taken, the other left. Two
women will be working in the same
kitchen—one taken, the other left."
37 Trying to take all this in, the disciples
said, "Master, where?"
He told them, "Watch for the circling of
the vultures. They'll spot the corpse first.
The action will begin around my dead
body."

THE STORY OF THE PERSISTENT WIDOW

1-3 18 Jesus told them a story showing that it
was necessary for them to pray consis-
tently and never quit. He said, "There was
once a judge in some city who never gave
God a thought and cared nothing for people.
A widow in that city kept after him: 'My
rights are being violated. Protect me!'
4-5 "He never gave her the time of day. But
after this went on and on he said to himself,
'I care nothing what God thinks, even less
what people think. But because this widow
won't quit badgering me, I'd better do some-
thing and see that she gets justice—other-
wise I'm going to end up beaten black-and-
blue by her pounding.' "
6-8 Then the Master said, "Do you hear what
that judge, corrupt as he is, is saying? So
what makes you think God won't step in
and work justice for his chosen people, who
continue to cry out for help? Won't he stick
up for them? I assure you, he will. He will
not drag his feet. But how much of that kind
of persistent faith will the Son of Man find
on the earth when he returns?"

New King James Version

The Parable of the Pharisee and the Tax Collector

9 Also He spoke this parable to some who
trusted in themselves that they were righteous,
and despised others: 10 "Two men went up to the
temple to pray, one a Pharisee and the other a
tax collector. 11 The Pharisee stood and prayed
thus with himself, 'God, I thank You that I am
not like other men—extortioners, unjust, adul-
terers, or even as this tax collector. 12 I fast twice
a week; I give tithes of all that I possess.' 13 And
the tax collector, standing afar off, would not so
much as raise *his* eyes to heaven, but beat his
breast, saying, 'God, be merciful to me a sinner!'
14 I tell you, this man went down to his house jus-
tified *rather* than the other; for everyone who
exalts himself will be humbled, and he who
humbles himself will be exalted."

Jesus Blesses Little Children

15 Then they also brought infants to Him that
He might touch them; but when the disciples
saw *it*, they rebuked them. 16 But Jesus called
them to *Him* and said, "Let the little children
come to Me, and do not forbid them; for of such
is the kingdom of God. 17 Assuredly, I say to you,
whoever does not receive the kingdom of God
as a little child will by no means enter it."

Jesus Counsels the Rich Young Ruler

18 Now a certain ruler asked Him, saying,
"Good Teacher, what shall I do to inherit eternal
life?"
19 So Jesus said to him, "Why do you call Me
good? No one *is* good but One, *that is*, God.
20 You know the commandments: *'Do not com-*
mit adultery,' 'Do not murder,' 'Do not steal,'
'Do not bear false witness,' 'Honor your father
and your mother.' "[a]
21 And he said, "All these things I have kept
from my youth."
22 So when Jesus heard these things, He said
to him, "You still lack one thing. Sell all that you
have and distribute to the poor, and you will
have treasure in heaven; and come, follow Me."
23 But when he heard this, he became very
sorrowful, for he was very rich.

With God All Things Are Possible

24 And when Jesus saw that he became very
sorrowful, He said, "How hard it is for those
who have riches to enter the kingdom of God!
25 For it is easier for a camel to go through the
eye of a needle than for a rich man to enter the
kingdom of God."
26 And those who heard it said, "Who then
can be saved?"
27 But He said, "The things which are impos-
sible with men are possible with God."
28 Then Peter said, "See, we have left all[a] and
followed You."
29 So He said to them, "Assuredly, I say to you,
there is no one who has left house or parents or
brothers or wife or children, for the sake of the

18:20 [a]Exodus 20:12–16; Deuteronomy 5:16–20 **18:28** [a]NU-Text reads *our own.*

The Message

The Story of the Tax Man and the Pharisee

9-12 He told his next story to some who were
complacently pleased with themselves over
their moral performance and looked down
their noses at the common people: "Two
men went up to the Temple to pray, one a
Pharisee, the other a tax man. The Pharisee
posed and prayed like this: 'Oh, God, I thank
you that I am not like other people—rob-
bers, crooks, adulterers, or, heaven forbid,
like this tax man. I fast twice a week and
tithe on all my income.'
13 "Meanwhile the tax man, slumped in the
shadows, his face in his hands, not daring to
look up, said, 'God, give mercy. Forgive me,
a sinner.' "
14 Jesus commented, "This tax man, not the
other, went home made right with God. If
you walk around with your nose in the air,
you're going to end up flat on your face, but
if you're content to be simply yourself, you
will become more than yourself."

15-17 People brought babies to Jesus, hoping he
might touch them. When the disciples saw
it, they shooed them off. Jesus called them
back. "Let these children alone. Don't get
between them and me. These children are
the kingdom's pride and joy. Mark this: Un-
less you accept God's kingdom in the sim-
plicity of a child, you'll never get in."

The Rich Official

18 One day one of the local officials asked him,
"Good Teacher, what must I do to deserve
eternal life?"
19-20 Jesus said, "Why are you calling me
good? No one is good—only God. You know
the commandments, don't you? No illicit
sex, no killing, no stealing, no lying, honor
your father and mother."
21 He said, "I've kept them all for as long as
I can remember."
22 When Jesus heard that, he said, "Then
there's only one thing left to do: Sell every-
thing you own and give it away to the poor.
You will have riches in heaven. Then come,
follow me."
23 This was the last thing the official ex-
pected to hear. He was very rich and became
terribly sad. He was holding on tight to a lot
of things and not about to let them go.
24-25 Seeing his reaction, Jesus said, "Do you
have any idea how difficult it is for people
who have it all to enter God's kingdom? I'd
say it's easier to thread a camel through a
needle's eye than get a rich person into
God's kingdom."
26 "Then who has any chance at all?" the
others asked.
27 "No chance at all," Jesus said, "if you
think you can pull it off by yourself. Every
chance in the world if you trust God to do it."
28 Peter tried to regain some initiative: "We
left everything we owned and followed you,
didn't we?"
29-30 "Yes," said Jesus, "and you won't regret it.
No one who has sacrificed home, spouse,
brothers and sisters, parents, children—

NEW KING JAMES VERSION

kingdom of God, 30who shall not receive many
times more in this present time, and in the age
to come eternal life."

JESUS A THIRD TIME PREDICTS HIS DEATH AND RESURRECTION

31Then He took the twelve aside and said to
them, "Behold, we are going up to Jerusalem,
and all things that are written by the prophets
concerning the Son of Man will be accom-
plished. 32For He will be delivered to the Gen-
tiles and will be mocked and insulted and spit
upon. 33They will scourge *Him* and kill Him.
And the third day He will rise again."

34But they understood none of these things;
this saying was hidden from them, and they did
not know the things which were spoken.

A BLIND MAN RECEIVES HIS SIGHT

35Then it happened, as He was coming near
Jericho, that a certain blind man sat by the road
begging. 36And hearing a multitude passing by,
he asked what it meant. 37So they told him that
Jesus of Nazareth was passing by. 38And he
cried out, saying, "Jesus, Son of David, have
mercy on me!"

39Then those who went before warned him
that he should be quiet; but he cried out all the
more, "Son of David, have mercy on me!"

40So Jesus stood still and commanded him to
be brought to Him. And when he had come near,
He asked him, 41saying, "What do you want Me
to do for you?"

He said, "Lord, that I may receive my sight."

42Then Jesus said to him, "Receive your
sight; your faith has made you well." 43And im-
mediately he received his sight, and followed
Him, glorifying God. And all the people, when
they saw *it*, gave praise to God.

JESUS COMES TO ZACCHAEUS' HOUSE

19 Then *Jesus* entered and passed through
Jericho. 2Now behold, *there was* a man
named Zacchaeus who was a chief tax collector,
and he was rich. 3And he sought to see who Je-
sus was, but could not because of the crowd, for
he was of short stature. 4So he ran ahead and
climbed up into a sycamore tree to see Him, for
He was going to pass that *way*. 5And when Jesus
came to the place, He looked up and saw him,[a]
and said to him, "Zacchaeus, make haste and
come down, for today I must stay at your
house." 6So he made haste and came down, and
received Him joyfully. 7But when they saw *it*,
they all complained, saying, "He has gone to be
a guest with a man who is a sinner."

8Then Zacchaeus stood and said to the Lord,
"Look, Lord, I give half of my goods to the poor;
and if I have taken anything from anyone by
false accusation, I restore fourfold."

9And Jesus said to him, "Today salvation has
come to this house, because he also is a son of
Abraham; 10for the Son of Man has come to
seek and to save that which was lost."

19:5 [a]NU-Text omits *and saw him.*

THE MESSAGE

whatever—will lose out. It will all come back multiplied many times over in your lifetime. And then the bonus of eternal life!"

I WANT TO SEE AGAIN

31-34 Then Jesus took the Twelve off to the side and said, "Listen carefully. We're on our way up to Jerusalem. Everything written in the Prophets about the Son of Man will take place. He will be handed over to the Romans, jeered at, made sport of, and spit on. Then, after giving him the third degree, they will kill him. In three days he will rise, alive." But they didn't get it, could make neither heads nor tails of what he was talking about.

35-37 He came to the outskirts of Jericho. A blind man was sitting beside the road asking for handouts. When he heard the rustle of the crowd, he asked what was going on. They told him, "Jesus the Nazarene is going by."

38 He yelled, "Jesus! Son of David! Mercy, have mercy on me!"

39 Those ahead of Jesus told the man to shut up, but he only yelled all the louder, "Son of David! Mercy, have mercy on me!"

40 Jesus stopped and ordered him to be brought over. When he had come near, Jesus asked, "What do you want from me?"

41 He said, "Master, I want to see again."

42-43 Jesus said, "Go ahead—see again! Your faith has saved and healed you!" The healing was instant: He looked up, seeing—and then followed Jesus, glorifying God. Everyone in the street joined in, shouting praise to God.

ZACCHAEUS

1-4 19 Then Jesus entered and walked through Jericho. There was a man there, his name Zacchaeus, the head tax man and quite rich. He wanted desperately to see Jesus, but the crowd was in his way—he was a short man and couldn't see over the crowd. So he ran on ahead and climbed up in a sycamore tree so he could see Jesus when he came by.

5-7 When Jesus got to the tree, he looked up and said, "Zacchaeus, hurry down. Today is my day to be a guest in your home." Zacchaeus scrambled out of the tree, hardly believing his good luck, delighted to take Jesus home with him. Everyone who saw the incident was indignant and grumped, "What business does he have getting cozy with this crook?"

8 Zacchaeus just stood there, a little stunned. He stammered apologetically, "Master, I give away half my income to the poor—and if I'm caught cheating, I pay four times the damages."

9-10 Jesus said, "Today is salvation day in this home! Here he is: Zacchaeus, son of Abraham! For the Son of Man came to find and restore the lost."

NEW KING JAMES VERSION

THE PARABLE OF THE MINAS

11 Now as they heard these things, He spoke
another parable, because He was near
Jerusalem and because they thought the king-
dom of God would appear immediately. 12 There-
fore He said: "A certain nobleman went into a
far country to receive for himself a kingdom
and to return. 13 So he called ten of his servants,
delivered to them ten minas,[a] and said to them,
'Do business till I come.' 14 But his citizens hated
him, and sent a delegation after him, saying, 'We
will not have this *man* to reign over us.'

15 "And so it was that when he returned, hav-
ing received the kingdom, he then commanded
these servants, to whom he had given the
money, to be called to him, that he might know
how much every man had gained by trading.
16 Then came the first, saying, 'Master, your mina
has earned ten minas.' 17 And he said to him,
'Well *done,* good servant; because you were
faithful in a very little, have authority over ten
cities.' 18 And the second came, saying, 'Master,
your mina has earned five minas.' 19 Likewise he
said to him, 'You also be over five cities.'

20 "Then another came, saying, 'Master, here
is your mina, which I have kept put away in a
handkerchief. 21 For I feared you, because you
are an austere man. You collect what you did not
deposit, and reap what you did not sow.' 22 And
he said to him, 'Out of your own mouth I will
judge you, *you* wicked servant. You knew that I
was an austere man, collecting what I did not
deposit and reaping what I did not sow. 23 Why
then did you not put my money in the bank, that
at my coming I might have collected it with in-
terest?'

24 "And he said to those who stood by, 'Take
the mina from him, and give *it* to him who has
ten minas.' 25 (But they said to him, 'Master, he
has ten minas.') 26 'For I say to you, that to every-
one who has will be given; and from him who
does not have, even what he has will be taken
away from him. 27 But bring here those enemies
of mine, who did not want me to reign over
them, and slay *them* before me.' "

THE TRIUMPHAL ENTRY

28 When He had said this, He went on ahead,
going up to Jerusalem. 29 And it came to pass,
when He drew near to Bethphage[a] and Bethany,
at the mountain called Olivet, *that* He sent two
of His disciples, 30 saying, "Go into the village
opposite *you,* where as you enter you will find a
colt tied, on which no one has ever sat. Loose it
and bring *it here.* 31 And if anyone asks you,
'Why are you loosing *it?*' thus you shall say to
him, 'Because the Lord has need of it.' "

32 So those who were sent went their way and
found *it* just as He had said to them. 33 But as
they were loosing the colt, the owners of it said
to them, "Why are you loosing the colt?"

34 And they said, "The Lord has need of him."

19:13 [a]The *mina* (Greek *mna,* Hebrew *minah*) was worth about three months' salary. **19:29** [a]M-Text reads *Bethsphage.*

THE MESSAGE

THE STORY ABOUT INVESTMENT

11 While he had their attention, and because
they were getting close to Jerusalem by this
time and expectation was building that
God's kingdom would appear any minute,
he told this story:

12-13 "There was once a man descended from a
royal house who needed to make a long trip
back to headquarters to get authorization
for his rule and then return. But first he
called ten servants together, gave them each
a sum of money, and instructed them, 'Oper-
ate with this until I return.'

14 "But the citizens there hated him. So they
sent a commission with a signed petition to
oppose his rule: 'We don't want this man to
rule us.'

15 "When he came back bringing the au-
thorization of his rule, he called those ten
servants to whom he had given the money
to find out how they had done.

16 "The first said, 'Master, I doubled your
money.'

17 "He said, 'Good servant! Great work! Be-
cause you've been trustworthy in this small
job, I'm making you governor of ten towns.'

18 "The second said, 'Master, I made a fifty
percent profit on your money.'

19 "He said, 'I'm putting you in charge of
five towns.'

20-21 "The next servant said, 'Master, here's
your money safe and sound. I kept it hidden
in the cellar. To tell you the truth, I was a lit-
tle afraid. I know you have high standards
and hate sloppiness, and don't suffer fools
gladly.'

22-23 "He said, 'You're right that I don't suffer
fools gladly—and you've acted the fool!
Why didn't you at least invest the money in
securities so I would have gotten a little in-
terest on it?'

24 "Then he said to those standing there,
'Take the money from him and give it to the
servant who doubled my stake.'

25 "They said, 'But Master, he already has
double . . .'

26 "He said, 'That's what I mean: Risk your
life and get more than you ever dreamed of.
Play it safe and end up holding the bag.

27 " 'As for these enemies of mine who peti-
tioned against my rule, clear them out of
here. I don't want to see their faces around
here again.' "

GOD'S PERSONAL VISIT

28-31 After saying these things, Jesus headed
straight up to Jerusalem. When he got near
Bethphage and Bethany at the mountain
called Olives, he sent off two of the disciples
with instructions: "Go to the village across
from you. As soon as you enter, you'll find a
colt tethered, one that has never been rid-
den. Untie it and bring it. If anyone says
anything, asks, 'What are you doing?' say,
'His Master needs him.' "

32-33 The two left and found it just as he said.
As they were untying the colt, its owners
said, "What are you doing untying the colt?"

34 They said, "His Master needs him."

New King James Version

35Then they brought him to Jesus. And they threw their own clothes on the colt, and they set Jesus on him. 36And as He went, *many* spread their clothes on the road.

37Then, as He was now drawing near the descent of the Mount of Olives, the whole multitude of the disciples began to rejoice and praise God with a loud voice for all the mighty works they had seen, 38saying:

" '*Blessed is the King who comes in the name of the LORD!*'[a]
Peace in heaven and glory in the highest!"

39And some of the Pharisees called to Him from the crowd, "Teacher, rebuke Your disciples."

40But He answered and said to them, "I tell you that if these should keep silent, the stones would immediately cry out."

Jesus Weeps over Jerusalem

41Now as He drew near, He saw the city and wept over it, 42saying, "If you had known, even you, especially in this your day, the things *that make* for your peace! But now they are hidden from your eyes. 43For days will come upon you when your enemies will build an embankment around you, surround you and close you in on every side, 44and level you, and your children within you, to the ground; and they will not leave in you one stone upon another, because you did not know the time of your visitation."

Jesus Cleanses the Temple

45Then He went into the temple and began to drive out those who bought and sold in it,[a] 46saying to them, "It is written, '*My house is*[a] *a house of prayer*,'[b] but you have made it a '*den of thieves*.' "[c]

47And He was teaching daily in the temple. But the chief priests, the scribes, and the leaders of the people sought to destroy Him, 48and were unable to do anything; for all the people were very attentive to hear Him.

Jesus' Authority Questioned

20 Now it happened on one of those days, as He taught the people in the temple and preached the gospel, *that* the chief priests and the scribes, together with the elders, confronted *Him* 2and spoke to Him, saying, "Tell us, by what authority are You doing these things? Or who is he who gave You this authority?"

3But He answered and said to them, "I also will ask you one thing, and answer Me: 4The baptism of John—was it from heaven or from men?"

5And they reasoned among themselves, saying, "If we say, 'From heaven,' He will say, 'Why then[a] did you not believe him?' 6But if we say, 'From men,' all the people will stone us, for they are persuaded that John was a prophet." 7So they answered that they did not know where *it was* from.

8And Jesus said to them, "Neither will I tell you by what authority I do these things."

19:38 [a]Psalm 118:26 **19:45** [a]NU-Text reads *those who were selling.* **19:46** [a]NU-Text reads *shall be.* [b]Isaiah 56:7 [c]Jeremiah 7:11 **20:5** [a]NU-Text and M-Text omit *then.*

The Message

35-36 They brought the colt to Jesus. Then, throwing their coats on its back, they helped Jesus get on. As he rode, the people gave him a grand welcome, throwing their coats on the street.

37-38 Right at the crest, where Mount Olives begins its descent, the whole crowd of disciples burst into enthusiastic praise over all the mighty works they had witnessed:

Blessed is he who comes,
the king in God's name!
All's well in heaven!
Glory in the high places!

39 Some Pharisees from the crowd told him, "Teacher, get your disciples under control!"

40 But he said, "If they kept quiet, the stones would do it for them, shouting praise."

41-44 When the city came into view, he wept over it. "If you had only recognized this day, and everything that was good for you! But now it's too late. In the days ahead your enemies are going to bring up their heavy artillery and surround you, pressing in from every side. They'll smash you and your babies on the pavement. Not one stone will be left intact. All this because you didn't recognize and welcome God's personal visit."

45-46 Going into the Temple he began to throw out everyone who had set up shop, selling everything and anything. He said, "It's written in Scripture,

My house is a house of prayer;
You have turned it into a religious bazaar."

47-48 From then on he taught each day in the Temple. The high priests, religion scholars, and the leaders of the people were trying their best to find a way to get rid of him. But with the people hanging on every word he spoke, they couldn't come up with anything.

1-2 20 One day he was teaching the people in the Temple, proclaiming the Message. The high priests, religion scholars, and leaders confronted him and demanded, "Show us your credentials. Who authorized you to speak and act like this?"

3-4 Jesus answered, "First, let me ask you a question: About the baptism of John—who authorized it, heaven or humans?"

5-7 They were on the spot, and knew it. They pulled back into a huddle and whispered, "If we say 'heaven,' he'll ask us why we didn't believe him; if we say 'humans,' the people will tear us limb from limb, convinced as they are that John was God's prophet." They agreed to concede that round to Jesus and said they didn't know.

8 Jesus said, "Then neither will I answer your question."

NEW KING JAMES VERSION

THE PARABLE OF THE WICKED VINEDRESSERS

9 Then He began to tell the people this parable: "A certain man planted a vineyard, leased it to vinedressers, and went into a far country for a long time. 10 Now at vintage-time he sent a servant to the vinedressers, that they might give him some of the fruit of the vineyard. But the vinedressers beat him and sent *him* away empty-handed. 11 Again he sent another servant; and they beat him also, treated *him* shamefully, and sent *him* away empty-handed. 12 And again he sent a third; and they wounded him also and cast *him* out.

13 "Then the owner of the vineyard said, 'What shall I do? I will send my beloved son. Probably they will respect *him* when they see him.' 14 But when the vinedressers saw him, they reasoned among themselves, saying, 'This is the heir. Come, let us kill him, that the inheritance may be ours.' 15 So they cast him out of the vineyard and killed *him*. Therefore what will the owner of the vineyard do to them? 16 He will come and destroy those vinedressers and give the vineyard to others."

And when they heard *it* they said, "Certainly not!"

17 Then He looked at them and said, "What then is this that is written:

'The stone which the builders rejected
Has become the chief cornerstone'?[a]

18 Whoever falls on that stone will be broken; but on whomever it falls, it will grind him to powder."

19 And the chief priests and the scribes that very hour sought to lay hands on Him, but they feared the people[a]—for they knew He had spoken this parable against them.

THE PHARISEES: IS IT LAWFUL TO PAY TAXES TO CAESAR?

20 So they watched *Him*, and sent spies who pretended to be righteous, that they might seize on His words, in order to deliver Him to the power and the authority of the governor.

21 Then they asked Him, saying, "Teacher, we know that You say and teach rightly, and You do not show personal favoritism, but teach the way of God in truth: 22 Is it lawful for us to pay taxes to Caesar or not?"

23 But He perceived their craftiness, and said to them, "Why do you test Me?[a] 24 Show Me a denarius. Whose image and inscription does it have?"

They answered and said, "Caesar's."

25 And He said to them, "Render therefore to Caesar the things that are Caesar's, and to God the things that are God's."

26 But they could not catch Him in His words in the presence of the people. And they marveled at His answer and kept silent.

THE SADDUCEES: WHAT ABOUT THE RESURRECTION?

27 Then some of the Sadducees, who deny that there is a resurrection, came to *Him* and asked Him, 28 saying: "Teacher, Moses wrote to

20:17 [a]Psalm 118:22 **20:19** [a]M-Text reads *but they were afraid.*
20:23 [a]NU-Text omits *Why do you test Me?*

THE MESSAGE

THE STORY OF CORRUPT FARMHANDS

9-12 Jesus told another story to the people: "A
man planted a vineyard. He handed it over
to farmhands and went off on a trip. He was
gone a long time. In time he sent a servant
back to the farmhands to collect the profits,
but they beat him up and sent him off
empty-handed. He decided to try again and
sent another servant. That one they beat
black-and-blue, and sent him off empty-
handed. He tried a third time. They worked
that servant over from head to foot and
dumped him in the street.
13 "Then the owner of the vineyard said, 'I
know what I'll do: I'll send my beloved son.
They're bound to respect my son.'
14-15 "But when the farmhands saw him com-
ing, they quickly put their heads together.
'This is our chance—this is the heir! Let's
kill him and have it all to ourselves.' They
killed him and threw him over the fence.
15-16 "What do you think the owner of the
vineyard will do? Right. He'll come and
clean house. Then he'll assign the care of
the vineyard to others."

Those who were listening said, "Oh, no! He'd never do that!"

17-18 But Jesus didn't back down. "Why, then,
do you think this was written:

That stone the masons threw out—
It's now the cornerstone!?

"Anyone falling over that stone will break every bone in his body; if the stone falls on anyone, it will be a total smashup."

19 The religion scholars and high priests
wanted to lynch him on the spot, but they
were intimidated by public opinion. They
knew the story was about them.

PAYING TAXES

20-22 Watching for a chance to get him, they sent
spies who posed as honest inquirers, hoping
to trick him into saying something that
would get him in trouble with the law. So
they asked him, "Teacher, we know that
you're honest and straightforward when
you teach, that you don't pander to anyone
but teach the way of God accurately. Tell us:
Is it lawful to pay taxes to Caesar or not?"
23-24 He knew they were laying for him and
said, "Show me a coin. Now, this engraving,
who does it look like and what does it say?"
25 "Caesar," they said.

Jesus said, "Then give Caesar what is his and give God what is his."

26 Try as they might, they couldn't trap him
into saying anything incriminating. His an-
swer caught them off guard and left them
speechless.

ALL INTIMACIES WILL BE WITH GOD

27-33 Some Sadducees came up. This is the Jew-
ish party that denies any possibility of res-
urrection. They asked, "Teacher, Moses

NEW KING JAMES VERSION

us *that* if a man's brother dies, having a wife,
and he dies without children, his brother should
take his wife and raise up offspring for his
brother. 29Now there were seven brothers. And
the first took a wife, and died without children.
30And the second[a] took her as wife, and he died
childless. 31Then the third took her, and in like
manner the seven also; and they left no chil-
dren,[a] and died. 32Last of all the woman died
also. 33Therefore, in the resurrection, whose wife
does she become? For all seven had her as wife."
34Jesus answered and said to them, "The sons
of this age marry and are given in marriage.
35But those who are counted worthy to attain
that age, and the resurrection from the dead, nei-
ther marry nor are given in marriage; 36nor can
they die anymore, for they are equal to the an-
gels and are sons of God, being sons of the res-
urrection. 37But even Moses showed in the *burn-
ing* bush *passage* that the dead are raised, when
he called the Lord *'the God of Abraham, the God
of Isaac, and the God of Jacob.'*[a] 38For He is not
the God of the dead but of the living, for all live
to Him."
39Then some of the scribes answered and
said, "Teacher, You have spoken well." 40But after
that they dared not question Him anymore.

JESUS: HOW CAN DAVID CALL HIS DESCENDANT LORD?

41And He said to them, "How can they say
that the Christ is the Son of David? 42Now David
himself said in the Book of Psalms:

'The Lord said to my Lord,
"Sit at My right hand,
43*Till I make Your enemies Your footstool."'*[a]

44Therefore David calls Him *'Lord';* how is
He then his Son?"

BEWARE OF THE SCRIBES

45Then, in the hearing of all the people, He
said to His disciples, 46"Beware of the scribes,
who desire to go around in long robes, love
greetings in the marketplaces, the best seats in
the synagogues, and the best places at feasts,
47who devour widows' houses, and for a pre-
tense make long prayers. These will receive
greater condemnation."

THE WIDOW'S TWO MITES

21 And He looked up and saw the rich putting
their gifts into the treasury, 2and He saw
also a certain poor widow putting in two mites.
3So He said, "Truly I say to you that this poor
widow has put in more than all; 4for all these out
of their abundance have put in offerings for
God,[a] but she out of her poverty put in all the
livelihood that she had."

JESUS PREDICTS THE DESTRUCTION OF THE TEMPLE

5Then, as some spoke of the temple, how it
was adorned with beautiful stones and dona-
tions, He said, 6"These things which you see—the
days will come in which not *one* stone shall be
left upon another that shall not be thrown down."

20:30 [a]NU-Text ends verse 30 here. **20:31** [a]NU-Text and M-Text read *the seven also left no children.* **20:37** [a]Exodus 3:6, 15 **20:43** [a]Psalm 110:1 **21:4** [a]NU-Text omits *for God.*

THE MESSAGE

wrote us that if a man dies and leaves a wife but no child, his brother is obligated to take the widow to wife and get her with child. Well, there once were seven brothers. The first took a wife. He died childless. The second married her and died, then the third, and eventually all seven had their turn, but no child. After all that, the wife died. That wife, now—in the resurrection whose wife is she? All seven married her."

34-38 Jesus said, "Marriage is a major preoccupation here, but not there. Those who are included in the resurrection of the dead will no longer be concerned with marriage nor, of course, with death. They will have better things to think about, if you can believe it. All ecstasies and intimacies then will be with God. Even Moses exclaimed about resurrection at the burning bush, saying, 'God: God of Abraham, God of Isaac, God of Jacob!' God isn't the God of dead men, but of the living. To him all are alive."

39-40 Some of the religion scholars said, "Teacher, that's a great answer!" For a while, anyway, no one dared put questions to him.

41-44 Then he put a question to them: "How is it that they say that the Messiah is David's son? In the Book of Psalms, David clearly says,

God said to my Master,
"Sit here at my right hand
until I put your enemies under your
feet."

"David here designates the Messiah as 'my Master'—so how can the Messiah also be his 'son'?"

45-47 With everybody listening, Jesus spoke to his disciples. "Watch out for the religion scholars. They love to walk around in academic gowns, preen in the radiance of public flattery, bask in prominent positions, sit at the head table at every church function. And all the time they are exploiting the weak and helpless. The longer their prayers, the worse they get. But they'll pay for it in the end."

1-4 21 Just then he looked up and saw the rich people dropping offerings in the collection plate. Then he saw a poor widow put in two pennies. He said, "The plain truth is that this widow has given by far the largest offering today. All these others made offerings that they'll never miss; she gave extravagantly what she couldn't afford—she gave her all!"

WATCH OUT FOR DOOMSDAY DECEIVERS

5-6 One day people were standing around talking about the Temple, remarking how beautiful it was, the splendor of its stonework and memorial gifts. Jesus said, "All this you're admiring so much—the time is coming when every stone in that building will end up in a heap of rubble."

NEW KING JAMES VERSION

THE SIGNS OF THE TIMES AND THE END OF THE AGE

7So they asked Him, saying, "Teacher, but
when will these things be? And what sign *will
there be* when these things are about to take
place?"
8And He said: "Take heed that you not be de-
ceived. For many will come in My name, saying,
'I am *He*,' and, 'The time has drawn near.' There-
fore[a] do not go after them. 9But when you hear
of wars and commotions, do not be terrified; for
these things must come to pass first, but the end
will not *come* immediately."

10Then He said to them, "Nation will rise
against nation, and kingdom against kingdom.
11And there will be great earthquakes in various
places, and famines and pestilences; and there
will be fearful sights and great signs from
heaven. 12But before all these things, they will
lay their hands on you and persecute *you*, deliv-
ering *you* up to the synagogues and prisons. You
will be brought before kings and rulers for My
name's sake. 13But it will turn out for you as an
occasion for testimony. 14Therefore settle *it* in
your hearts not to meditate beforehand on what
you will answer; 15for I will give you a mouth
and wisdom which all your adversaries will not
be able to contradict or resist. 16You will be be-
trayed even by parents and brothers, relatives
and friends; and they will put *some* of you to
death. 17And you will be hated by all for My
name's sake. 18But not a hair of your head shall
be lost. 19By your patience possess your souls.

THE DESTRUCTION OF JERUSALEM

20"But when you see Jerusalem surrounded
by armies, then know that its desolation is near.
21Then let those who are in Judea flee to the
mountains, let those who are in the midst of her
depart, and let not those who are in the country
enter her. 22For these are the days of vengeance,
that all things which are written may be ful-
filled. 23But woe to those who are pregnant and
to those who are nursing babies in those days!
For there will be great distress in the land and
wrath upon this people. 24And they will fall by
the edge of the sword, and be led away captive
into all nations. And Jerusalem will be trampled
by Gentiles until the times of the Gentiles are
fulfilled.

THE COMING OF THE SON OF MAN

25"And there will be signs in the sun, in the
moon, and in the stars; and on the earth distress
of nations, with perplexity, the sea and the
waves roaring; 26men's hearts failing them from
fear and the expectation of those things which
are coming on the earth, for the powers of the
heavens will be shaken. 27Then they will see the
Son of Man coming in a cloud with power and
great glory. 28Now when these things begin to
happen, look up and lift up your heads, because
your redemption draws near."

THE PARABLE OF THE FIG TREE

29Then He spoke to them a parable: "Look at
the fig tree, and all the trees. 30When they are al-
ready budding, you see and know for yourselves
that summer is now near. 31So you also, when

21:8 [a]NU-Text omits *Therefore.*

THE MESSAGE

7 They asked him, "Teacher, when is this
going to happen? What clue will we get that
it's about to take place?"
8-9 He said, "Watch out for the doomsday de-
ceivers. Many leaders are going to show up
with forged identities claiming, 'I'm the
One,' or, 'The end is near.' Don't fall for any
of that. When you hear of wars and upris-
ings, keep your head and don't panic. This is
routine history and no sign of the end."
10-11 He went on, "Nation will fight nation and
ruler fight ruler, over and over. Huge earth-
quakes will occur in various places. There
will be famines. You'll think at times that the
very sky is falling.
12-15 "But before any of this happens, they'll
arrest you, hunt you down, and drag you to
court and jail. It will go from bad to worse,
dog-eat-dog, everyone at your throat be-
cause you carry my name. You'll end up on
the witness stand, called to testify. Make up
your mind right now not to worry about it.
I'll give you the words and wisdom that will
reduce all your accusers to stammers and
stutters.
16-19 "You'll even be turned in by parents,
brothers, relatives, and friends. Some of you
will be killed. There's no telling who will
hate you because of me. Even so, every de-
tail of your body and soul—even the hairs of
your head!—is in my care; nothing of you
will be lost. Staying with it—that's what is
required. Stay with it to the end. You won't
be sorry; you'll be saved.

VENGEANCE DAY

20-24 "When you see soldiers camped all around
Jerusalem, then you'll know that she is
about to be devastated. If you're living in
Judea at the time, run for the hills. If you're
in the city, get out quickly. If you're out in
the fields, don't go home to get your coat.
This is Vengeance Day—everything written
about it will come to a head. Pregnant and
nursing mothers will have it especially hard.
Incredible misery! Torrential rage! People
dropping like flies; people dragged off to
prisons; Jerusalem under the boot of bar-
barians until the nations finish what was
given them to do.
25-26 "It will seem like all hell has broken
loose—sun, moon, stars, earth, sea, in an up-
roar and everyone all over the world in a
panic, the wind knocked out of them by the
threat of doom, the powers-that-be quaking.
27-28 "And then—then!—they'll see the Son of
Man welcomed in grand style—a glorious
welcome! When all this starts to happen, up
on your feet. Stand tall with your heads
high. Help is on the way!"
29-33 He told them a story. "Look at a fig tree.
Any tree for that matter. When the leaves
begin to show, one look tells you that sum-
mer is right around the corner. The same

NEW KING JAMES VERSION

you see these things happening, know that the kingdom of God is near. 32Assuredly, I say to you, this generation will by no means pass away till all things take place. 33Heaven and earth will pass away, but My words will by no means pass away.

THE IMPORTANCE OF WATCHING

34"But take heed to yourselves, lest your hearts be weighed down with carousing, drunkenness, and cares of this life, and that Day come on you unexpectedly. 35For it will come as a snare on all those who dwell on the face of the whole earth. 36Watch therefore, and pray always that you may be counted worthy[a] to escape all these things that will come to pass, and to stand before the Son of Man."

37And in the daytime He was teaching in the temple, but at night He went out and stayed on the mountain called Olivet. 38Then early in the morning all the people came to Him in the temple to hear Him.

THE PLOT TO KILL JESUS

22 Now the Feast of Unleavened Bread drew near, which is called Passover. 2And the chief priests and the scribes sought how they might kill Him, for they feared the people.

3Then Satan entered Judas, surnamed Iscariot, who was numbered among the twelve. 4So he went his way and conferred with the chief priests and captains, how he might betray Him to them. 5And they were glad, and agreed to give him money. 6So he promised and sought opportunity to betray Him to them in the absence of the multitude.

JESUS AND HIS DISCIPLES PREPARE THE PASSOVER

7Then came the Day of Unleavened Bread, when the Passover must be killed. 8And He sent Peter and John, saying, "Go and prepare the Passover for us, that we may eat."

9So they said to Him, "Where do You want us to prepare?"

10And He said to them, "Behold, when you have entered the city, a man will meet you carrying a pitcher of water; follow him into the house which he enters. 11Then you shall say to the master of the house, 'The Teacher says to you, "Where is the guest room where I may eat the Passover with My disciples?" ' 12Then he will show you a large, furnished upper room; there make ready."

13So they went and found it just as He had said to them, and they prepared the Passover.

JESUS INSTITUTES THE LORD'S SUPPER

14When the hour had come, He sat down, and the twelve[a] apostles with Him. 15Then He said to them, "With *fervent* desire I have desired to eat this Passover with you before I suffer; 16for I say to you, I will no longer eat of it until it is fulfilled in the kingdom of God."

17Then He took the cup, and gave thanks, and said, "Take this and divide *it* among yourselves;

21:36 [a]NU-Text reads *may have strength.* **22:14** [a]NU-Text omits *twelve.*

THE MESSAGE

here—when you see these things happen, you know God's kingdom is about here. Don't brush this off: I'm not just saying this for some future generation, but for this one, too—these things will happen. Sky and earth will wear out; my words won't wear out.

34-36 "But be on your guard. Don't let the sharp edge of your expectation get dulled by parties and drinking and shopping. Otherwise, that Day is going to take you by complete surprise, spring on you suddenly like a trap, for it's going to come on everyone, everywhere, at once. So, whatever you do, don't go to sleep at the switch. Pray constantly that you will have the strength and wits to make it through everything that's coming and end up on your feet before the Son of Man."

37-38 He spent his days in the Temple teaching, but his nights out on the mountain called Olives. All the people were up at the crack of dawn to come to the Temple and listen to him.

THE PASSOVER MEAL

1-2 22 The Feast of Unleavened Bread, also called Passover, drew near. The high priests and religion scholars were looking for a way to do away with Jesus but, fearful of the people, they were also looking for a way to cover their tracks.

3-6 That's when Satan entered Judas, the one called Iscariot. He was one of the Twelve. Leaving the others, he conferred with the high priests and the Temple guards about how he might betray Jesus to them. They couldn't believe their good luck and agreed to pay him well. He gave them his word and started looking for a way to betray Jesus, but out of sight of the crowd.

7-8 The Day of Unleavened Bread came, the day the Passover lamb was butchered. Jesus sent Peter and John off, saying, "Go prepare the Passover for us so we can eat it together."

9 They said, "Where do you want us to do this?"

10-12 He said, "Keep your eyes open as you enter the city. A man carrying a water jug will meet you. Follow him home. Then speak with the owner of the house: The Teacher wants to know, 'Where is the guest room where I can eat the Passover meal with my disciples?' He will show you a spacious second-story room, swept and ready. Prepare the meal there."

13 They left, found everything just as he told them, and prepared the Passover meal.

14-16 When it was time, he sat down, all the apostles with him, and said, "You've no idea how much I have looked forward to eating this Passover meal with you before I enter my time of suffering. It's the last one I'll eat until we all eat it together in the kingdom of God."

17-18 Taking the cup, he blessed it, then said, "Take this and pass it among you. As for me,

NEW KING JAMES VERSION

18 for I say to you,[a] I will not drink of the fruit of the vine until the kingdom of God comes."
19 And He took bread, gave thanks and broke *it*, and gave *it* to them, saying, "This is My body which is given for you; do this in remembrance of Me."
20 Likewise He also *took* the cup after supper, saying, "This cup *is* the new covenant in My blood, which is shed for you. 21 But behold, the hand of My betrayer *is* with Me on the table. 22 And truly the Son of Man goes as it has been determined, but woe to that man by whom He is betrayed!"
23 Then they began to question among themselves, which of them it was who would do this thing.

THE DISCIPLES ARGUE ABOUT GREATNESS

24 Now there was also a dispute among them, as to which of them should be considered the greatest. 25 And He said to them, "The kings of the Gentiles exercise lordship over them, and those who exercise authority over them are called 'benefactors.' 26 But not so *among* you; on the contrary, he who is greatest among you, let him be as the younger, and he who governs as he who serves. 27 For who *is* greater, he who sits at the table, or he who serves? *Is* it not he who sits at the table? Yet I am among you as the One who serves.
28 "But you are those who have continued with Me in My trials. 29 And I bestow upon you a kingdom, just as My Father bestowed *one* upon Me, 30 that you may eat and drink at My table in My kingdom, and sit on thrones judging the twelve tribes of Israel."

JESUS PREDICTS PETER'S DENIAL

31 And the Lord said,[a] "Simon, Simon! Indeed, Satan has asked for you, that he may sift *you* as wheat. 32 But I have prayed for you, that your faith should not fail; and when you have returned to *Me*, strengthen your brethren."
33 But he said to Him, "Lord, I am ready to go with You, both to prison and to death."
34 Then He said, "I tell you, Peter, the rooster shall not crow this day before you will deny three times that you know Me."

SUPPLIES FOR THE ROAD

35 And He said to them, "When I sent you without money bag, knapsack, and sandals, did you lack anything?"

So they said, "Nothing."

36 Then He said to them, "But now, he who has a money bag, let him take *it*, and likewise a knapsack; and he who has no sword, let him sell his garment and buy one. 37 For I say to you that this which is written must still be accomplished in Me: *'And He was numbered with the transgressors.'*[a] For the things concerning Me have an end."
38 So they said, "Lord, look, here *are* two swords."

And He said to them, "It is enough."

22:18 [a]NU-Text adds *from now on.* **22:31** [a]NU-Text omits *And the Lord said.* **22:37** [a]Isaiah 53:12

THE MESSAGE

I'll not drink wine again until the kingdom of God arrives."

19 Taking bread, he blessed it, broke it, and gave it to them, saying, "This is my body, given for you. Eat it in my memory."

20 He did the same with the cup after supper, saying, "This cup is the new covenant written in my blood, blood poured out for you.

21-22 "Do you realize that the hand of the one who is betraying me is at this moment on this table? It's true that the Son of Man is going down a path already marked out—no surprises there. But for the one who turns him in, turns traitor to the Son of Man, this is doomsday."

23 They immediately became suspicious of each other and began quizzing one another, wondering who might be about to do this.

GET READY FOR TROUBLE

24-26 Within minutes they were bickering over who of them would end up the greatest. But Jesus intervened: "Kings like to throw their weight around and people in authority like to give themselves fancy titles. It's not going to be that way with you. Let the senior among you become like the junior; let the leader act the part of the servant.

27-30 "Who would you rather be: the one who eats the dinner or the one who serves the dinner? You'd rather eat and be served, right? But I've taken my place among you as the one who serves. And you've stuck with me through thick and thin. Now I confer on you the royal authority my Father conferred on me so you can eat and drink at my table in my kingdom and be strengthened as you take up responsibilities among the congregations of God's people.

31-32 "Simon, stay on your toes. Satan has tried his best to separate all of you from me, like chaff from wheat. Simon, I've prayed for you in particular that you not give in or give out. When you have come through the time of testing, turn to your companions and give them a fresh start."

33 Peter said, "Master, I'm ready for anything with you. I'd go to jail for you. I'd *die* for you!"

34 Jesus said, "I'm sorry to have to tell you this, Peter, but before the rooster crows you will have three times denied that you know me."

35 Then Jesus said, "When I sent you out and told you to travel light, to take only the bare necessities, did you get along all right?"

"Certainly," they said, "we got along just fine."

36-37 He said, "This is different. Get ready for trouble. Look to what you'll need; there are difficult times ahead. Pawn your coat and get a sword. What was written in Scripture, 'He was lumped in with the criminals,' gets its final meaning in me. Everything written about me is now coming to a conclusion."

38 They said, "Look, Master, two swords!"

But he said, "Enough of that; no more sword talk!"

New King James Version

The Prayer in the Garden

39 Coming out, He went to the Mount of Olives, as He was accustomed, and His disciples also followed Him. 40 When He came to the place, He said to them, "Pray that you may not enter into temptation."

41 And He was withdrawn from them about a stone's throw, and He knelt down and prayed, 42 saying, "Father, if it is Your will, take this cup away from Me; nevertheless not My will, but Yours, be done." 43 Then an angel appeared to Him from heaven, strengthening Him. 44 And being in agony, He prayed more earnestly. Then His sweat became like great drops of blood falling down to the ground.[a]

45 When He rose up from prayer, and had come to His disciples, He found them sleeping from sorrow. 46 Then He said to them, "Why do you sleep? Rise and pray, lest you enter into temptation."

Betrayal and Arrest in Gethsemane

47 And while He was still speaking, behold, a multitude; and he who was called Judas, one of the twelve, went before them and drew near to Jesus to kiss Him. 48 But Jesus said to him, "Judas, are you betraying the Son of Man with a kiss?"

49 When those around Him saw what was going to happen, they said to Him, "Lord, shall we strike with the sword?" 50 And one of them struck the servant of the high priest and cut off his right ear.

51 But Jesus answered and said, "Permit even this." And He touched his ear and healed him.

52 Then Jesus said to the chief priests, captains of the temple, and the elders who had come to Him, "Have you come out, as against a robber, with swords and clubs? 53 When I was with you daily in the temple, you did not try to seize Me. But this is your hour, and the power of darkness."

Peter Denies Jesus, and Weeps Bitterly

54 Having arrested Him, they led *Him* and brought Him into the high priest's house. But Peter followed at a distance. 55 Now when they had kindled a fire in the midst of the courtyard and sat down together, Peter sat among them. 56 And a certain servant girl, seeing him as he sat by the fire, looked intently at him and said, "This man was also with Him."

57 But he denied Him,[a] saying, "Woman, I do not know Him."

58 And after a little while another saw him and said, "You also are of them."

But Peter said, "Man, I am not!"

59 Then after about an hour had passed, another confidently affirmed, saying, "Surely this *fellow* also was with Him, for he is a Galilean."

60 But Peter said, "Man, I do not know what you are saying!"

Immediately, while he was still speaking, the rooster[a] crowed. 61 And the Lord turned and looked at Peter. Then Peter remembered the word of the Lord, how He had said to him, "Be-

22:44 [a]NU-Text brackets verses 43 and 44 as not in the original text. 22:57 [a]NU-Text reads *denied it.* 22:60 [a]NU-Text and M-Text read *a rooster.*

The Message

A Dark Night

39-40 Leaving there, he went, as he so often did, to Mount Olives. The disciples followed him. When they arrived at the place, he said, "Pray that you don't give in to temptation."

41-44 He pulled away from them about a stone's throw, knelt down, and prayed, "Father, remove this cup from me. But please, not what I want. What do *you* want?" At once an angel from heaven was at his side, strengthening him. He prayed on all the harder. Sweat, wrung from him like drops of blood, poured off his face.

45-46 He got up from prayer, went back to the disciples and found them asleep, drugged by grief. He said, "What business do you have sleeping? Get up. Pray so you won't give in to temptation."

47-48 No sooner were the words out of his mouth than a crowd showed up, Judas, the one from the Twelve, in the lead. He came right up to Jesus to kiss him. Jesus said, "Judas, you would betray the Son of Man with a kiss?"

49-50 When those with him saw what was happening, they said, "Master, shall we fight?" One of them took a swing at the Chief Priest's servant and cut off his right ear.

51 Jesus said, "Let them be. Even in this." Then, touching the servant's ear, he healed him.

52-53 Jesus spoke to those who had come—high priests, Temple police, religion leaders: "What is this, jumping me with swords and clubs as if I were a dangerous criminal? Day after day I've been with you in the Temple and you've not so much as lifted a hand against me. But do it your way—it's a dark night, a dark hour."

A Rooster Crowed

54-56 Arresting Jesus, they marched him off and took him into the house of the Chief Priest. Peter followed, but at a safe distance. In the middle of the courtyard some people had started a fire and were sitting around it, trying to keep warm. One of the serving maids sitting at the fire noticed him, then took a second look and said, "This man was with him!"

57 He denied it, "Woman, I don't even know him."

58 A short time later, someone else noticed him and said, "You're one of them."

But Peter denied it: "Man, I am not."

59 About an hour later, someone else spoke up, really adamant: "He's got to have been with him! He's got 'Galilean' written all over him."

60-62 Peter said, "Man, I don't know what you're talking about." At that very moment, the last word hardly off his lips, a rooster crowed. Just then, the Master turned and looked at Peter. Peter remembered what the Master had said to him: "Before the rooster

NEW KING JAMES VERSION

fore the rooster crows,[a] you will deny Me three
times." 62So Peter went out and wept bitterly.

JESUS MOCKED AND BEATEN

63Now the men who held Jesus mocked Him
and beat Him. 64And having blindfolded Him,
they struck Him on the face and asked Him,[a] say-
ing, "Prophesy! Who is the one who struck You?"
65And many other things they blasphemously
spoke against Him.

JESUS FACES THE SANHEDRIN

66As soon as it was day, the elders of the peo-
ple, both chief priests and scribes, came to-
gether and led Him into their council, saying,
67"If You are the Christ, tell us."
But He said to them, "If I tell you, you will by
no means believe. 68And if I also ask *you,* you
will by no means answer Me or let *Me* go.[a]
69Hereafter the Son of Man will sit on the right
hand of the power of God."
70Then they all said, "Are You then the Son of
God?"
So He said to them, "You *rightly* say that I
am."
71And they said, "What further testimony do
we need? For we have heard it ourselves from
His own mouth."

JESUS HANDED OVER TO PONTIUS PILATE

23 Then the whole multitude of them arose
and led Him to Pilate. 2And they began to
accuse Him, saying, "We found this *fellow* per-
verting the[a] nation, and forbidding to pay taxes
to Caesar, saying that He Himself is Christ, a
King."
3Then Pilate asked Him, saying, "Are You the
King of the Jews?"
He answered him and said, "*It is as* you say."
4So Pilate said to the chief priests and the
crowd, "I find no fault in this Man."
5But they were the more fierce, saying, "He
stirs up the people, teaching throughout all
Judea, beginning from Galilee to this place."

JESUS FACES HEROD

6When Pilate heard of Galilee,[a] he asked if
the Man were a Galilean. 7And as soon as he
knew that He belonged to Herod's jurisdiction,
he sent Him to Herod, who was also in
Jerusalem at that time. 8Now when Herod saw
Jesus, he was exceedingly glad; for he had de-
sired for a long *time* to see Him, because he had
heard many things about Him, and he hoped to
see some miracle done by Him. 9Then he ques-
tioned Him with many words, but He answered
him nothing. 10And the chief priests and scribes
stood and vehemently accused Him. 11Then
Herod, with his men of war, treated Him with
contempt and mocked *Him,* arrayed Him in a
gorgeous robe, and sent Him back to Pilate.
12That very day Pilate and Herod became
friends with each other, for previously they had
been at enmity with each other.

22:61 [a]NU-Text adds *today.* **22:64** [a]NU-Text reads *And having blindfolded Him, they asked Him.* **22:68** [a]NU-Text omits *also* and *Me or let Me go.* **23:2** [a]NU-Text reads *our.* **23:6** [a]NU-Text omits *of Galilee.*

THE MESSAGE

crows, you will deny me three times." He
went out and cried and cried and cried.

SLAPPING HIM AROUND

63-65 The men in charge of Jesus began poking
fun at him, slapping him around. They put a
blindfold on him and taunted, "Who hit you
that time?" They were having a grand time
with him.
66-67 When it was morning, the religious lead-
ers of the people and the high priests and
scholars all got together and brought him
before their High Council. They said, "Are
you the Messiah?"
67-69 He answered, "If I said yes, you wouldn't
believe me. If I asked what you meant by
your question, you wouldn't answer me. So
here's what I have to say: From here on the
Son of Man takes his place at God's right
hand, the place of power."
70 They all said, "So you admit your claim to
be the Son of God?"
"You're the ones who keep saying it," he
said.
71 But they had made up their minds, "Why
do we need any more evidence? We've all
heard him as good as say it himself."

PILATE

1-2 23 Then they all took Jesus to Pilate and
began to bring up charges against him.
They said, "We found this man undermining
our law and order, forbidding taxes to be paid
to Caesar, setting himself up as Messiah-
King."
3 Pilate asked him, "Is this true that you're
'King of the Jews'?"
"Those are your words, not mine," Jesus
replied.
4 Pilate told the high priests and the ac-
companying crowd, "I find nothing wrong
here. He seems harmless enough to me."
5 But they were vehement. "He's stirring up
unrest among the people with his teaching,
disturbing the peace everywhere, starting in
Galilee and now all through Judea. He's a
dangerous man, endangering the peace."
6-7 When Pilate heard that, he asked, "So,
he's a Galilean?" Realizing that he properly
came under Herod's jurisdiction, he passed
the buck to Herod, who just happened to be
in Jerusalem for a few days.
8-10 Herod was delighted when Jesus showed
up. He had wanted for a long time to see him,
he'd heard so much about him. He hoped to
see him do something spectacular. He pep-
pered him with questions. Jesus didn't an-
swer—not one word. But the high priests and
religion scholars were right there, saying
their piece, strident and shrill in their accu-
sations.
11-12 Mightily offended, Herod turned on Je-
sus. His soldiers joined in, taunting and jeer-
ing. Then they dressed him up in an elabo-
rate king costume and sent him back to
Pilate. That day Herod and Pilate became
thick as thieves. Always before they had
kept their distance.

New King James Version

Taking the Place of Barabbas

13Then Pilate, when he had called together
the chief priests, the rulers, and the people,
14said to them, "You have brought this Man to
me, as one who misleads the people. And in-
deed, having examined *Him* in your presence, I
have found no fault in this Man concerning
those things of which you accuse Him; 15no, nei-
ther did Herod, for I sent you back to him;[a] and
indeed nothing deserving of death has been
done by Him. 16I will therefore chastise Him and
release *Him*" 17(for it was necessary for him to
release one to them at the feast).[a]

18And they all cried out at once, saying, "Away
with this *Man,* and release to us Barabbas"—
19who had been thrown into prison for a certain
rebellion made in the city, and for murder.

20Pilate, therefore, wishing to release Jesus,
again called out to them. 21But they shouted,
saying, "Crucify *Him,* crucify Him!"

22Then he said to them the third time, "Why,
what evil has He done? I have found no reason
for death in Him. I will therefore chastise Him
and let *Him* go."

23But they were insistent, demanding with
loud voices that He be crucified. And the voices
of these men and of the chief priests prevailed.[a]
24So Pilate gave sentence that it should be as
they requested. 25And he released to them[a] the
one they requested, who for rebellion and mur-
der had been thrown into prison; but he deliv-
ered Jesus to their will.

The King on a Cross

26Now as they led Him away, they laid hold
of a certain man, Simon a Cyrenian, who was
coming from the country, and on him they laid
the cross that he might bear *it* after Jesus.

27And a great multitude of the people fol-
lowed Him, and women who also mourned and
lamented Him. 28But Jesus, turning to them,
said, "Daughters of Jerusalem, do not weep for
Me, but weep for yourselves and for your chil-
dren. 29For indeed the days are coming in which
they will say, 'Blessed *are* the barren, wombs
that never bore, and breasts which never
nursed!' 30Then they will begin *'to say to the*
mountains, "Fall on us!" and to the hills, "Cover
us!"' [a] 31For if they do these things in the green
wood, what will be done in the dry?"

32There were also two others, criminals, led
with Him to be put to death. 33And when they
had come to the place called Calvary, there they
crucified Him, and the criminals, one on the
right hand and the other on the left. 34Then Je-
sus said, "Father, forgive them, for they do not
know what they do."[a]

And they divided His garments and cast lots.
35And the people stood looking on. But even the
rulers with them sneered, saying, "He saved oth-
ers; let Him save Himself if He is the Christ, the
chosen of God."

36The soldiers also mocked Him, coming and
offering Him sour wine, 37and saying, "If You are
the King of the Jews, save Yourself."

23:15 [a]NU-Text reads *for he sent Him back to us.* **23:17** [a]NU-Text omits verse 17. **23:23** [a]NU-Text omits *and of the chief priests.* **23:25** [a]NU-Text and M-Text omit *to them.* **23:30** [a]Hosea 10:8 **23:34** [a]NU-Text brackets the first sentence as a later addition.

The Message

13-16 Then Pilate called in the high priests,
rulers, and the others and said, "You
brought this man to me as a disturber of the
peace. I examined him in front of all of you
and found there was nothing to your charge.
And neither did Herod, for he has sent him
back here with a clean bill of health. It's
clear that he's done nothing wrong, let
alone anything deserving death. I'm going
to warn him to watch his step and let him
go."

18-20 At that, the crowd went wild: "Kill him!
Give us Barabbas!" (Barabbas had been
thrown in prison for starting a riot in the
city and for murder.) Pilate still wanted to
let Jesus go, and so spoke out again.

21 But they kept shouting back, "Crucify!
Crucify him!"

22 He tried a third time. "But for what
crime? I've found nothing in him deserving
death. I'm going to warn him to watch his
step and let him go."

23-25 But they kept at it, a shouting mob, de-
manding that he be crucified. And finally
they shouted him down. Pilate caved in and
gave them what they wanted. He released
the man thrown in prison for rioting and
murder, and gave them Jesus to do whatever
they wanted.

Skull Hill

26-31 As they led him off, they made Simon, a man
from Cyrene who happened to be coming in
from the countryside, carry the cross behind
Jesus. A huge crowd of people followed,
along with women weeping and carrying on.
At one point Jesus turned to the women and
said, "Daughters of Jerusalem, don't cry for
me. Cry for yourselves and for your children.
The time is coming when they'll say, 'Lucky
the women who never conceived! Lucky the
wombs that never gave birth! Lucky the
breasts that never gave milk!' Then they'll
start calling to the mountains, 'Fall down on
us!' calling to the hills, 'Cover us up!' If peo-
ple do these things to a live, green tree, can
you imagine what they'll do with dead-
wood?"

32 Two others, both criminals, were taken
along with him for execution.

33 When they got to the place called Skull
Hill, they crucified him, along with the crim-
inals, one on his right, the other on his left.

34-35 Jesus prayed, "Father, forgive them; they
don't know what they're doing."

Dividing up his clothes, they threw dice
for them. The people stood there staring at
Jesus, and the ringleaders made faces,
taunting, "He saved others. Let's see him
save himself! The Messiah of God—ha! The
Chosen—ha!"

36-37 The soldiers also came up and poked fun
at him, making a game of it. They toasted
him with sour wine: "So you're King of the
Jews! Save yourself!"

NEW KING JAMES VERSION

38 And an inscription also was written over
Him in letters of Greek, Latin, and Hebrew:[a]

THIS IS THE KING OF THE JEWS.

39 Then one of the criminals who were
hanged blasphemed Him, saying, "If You are the
Christ,[a] save Yourself and us."
40 But the other, answering, rebuked him, saying, "Do you not even fear God, seeing you are
under the same condemnation? 41 And we in-
deed justly, for we receive the due reward of our
deeds; but this Man has done nothing wrong."
42 Then he said to Jesus, "Lord,[a] remember me
when You come into Your kingdom."
43 And Jesus said to him, "Assuredly, I say to
you, today you will be with Me in Paradise."

JESUS DIES ON THE CROSS

44 Now it was[a] about the sixth hour, and there
was darkness over all the earth until the ninth
hour. 45 Then the sun was darkened,[a] and the veil
of the temple was torn in two. 46 And when Jesus
had cried out with a loud voice, He said, "Father,
'into Your hands I commit My spirit.' "[a] Having
said this, He breathed His last.
47 So when the centurion saw what had hap-
pened, he glorified God, saying, "Certainly this
was a righteous Man!"
48 And the whole crowd who came together
to that sight, seeing what had been done, beat
their breasts and returned. 49 But all His ac-
quaintances, and the women who followed Him
from Galilee, stood at a distance, watching these
things.

JESUS BURIED IN JOSEPH'S TOMB

50 Now behold, *there was* a man named
Joseph, a council member, a good and just man.
51 He had not consented to their decision and
deed. *He was* from Arimathea, a city of the
Jews, who himself was also waiting[a] for the
kingdom of God. 52 This man went to Pilate and
asked for the body of Jesus. 53 Then he took it
down, wrapped it in linen, and laid it in a tomb
that was hewn out of the rock, where no one
had ever lain before. 54 That day was the Prepa-
ration, and the Sabbath drew near.
55 And the women who had come with Him
from Galilee followed after, and they observed
the tomb and how His body was laid. 56 Then
they returned and prepared spices and fragrant
oils. And they rested on the Sabbath according
to the commandment.

HE IS RISEN

24 Now on the first *day* of the week, very early
in the morning, they, and certain *other
women* with them,[a] came to the tomb bringing
the spices which they had prepared. 2 But they
found the stone rolled away from the tomb.
3 Then they went in and did not find the body of
the Lord Jesus. 4 And it happened, as they were
greatly[a] perplexed about this, that behold, two

23:38 [a]NU-Text omits *written* and *in letters of Greek, Latin, and Hebrew.* **23:39** [a]NU-Text reads *Are You not the Christ?* **23:42** [a]NU-Text reads *And he said, "Jesus, remember me.* **23:44** [a]NU-Text adds *already.* **23:45** [a]NU-Text reads *obscured.* **23:46** [a]Psalm 31:5 **23:51** [a]NU-Text reads *who was waiting.* **24:1** [a]NU-Text omits *and certain other women with them.* **24:4** [a]NU-Text omits *greatly.*

THE MESSAGE

38 Printed over him was a sign: THIS IS THE
KING OF THE JEWS.
39 One of the criminals hanging alongside
cursed him: "Some Messiah you are! Save
yourself! Save us!"
40-41 But the other one made him shut up:
"Have you no fear of God? You're getting the
same as him. We deserve this, but not him—
he did nothing to deserve this."
42 Then he said, "Jesus, remember me when
you enter your kingdom."
43 He said, "Don't worry, I will. Today you
will join me in paradise."
44-46 By now it was noon. The whole earth be-
came dark, the darkness lasting three
hours—a total blackout. The Temple curtain
split right down the middle. Jesus called
loudly, "Father, I place my life in your
hands!" Then he breathed his last.

47 When the captain there saw what hap-
pened, he honored God: "This man was in-
nocent! A good man, and innocent!"
48-49 All who had come around as spectators
to watch the show, when they saw what ac-
tually happened, were overcome with grief
and headed home. Those who knew Jesus
well, along with the women who had fol-
lowed him from Galilee, stood at a respect-
ful distance and kept vigil.
50-54 There was a man by the name of Joseph,
a member of the Jewish High Council, a
man of good heart and good character. He
had not gone along with the plans and ac-
tions of the council. His hometown was the
Jewish village of Arimathea. He lived in
alert expectation of the kingdom of God. He
went to Pilate and asked for the body of Je-
sus. Taking him down, he wrapped him in a
linen shroud and placed him in a tomb chis-
eled into the rock, a tomb never yet used. It
was the day before Sabbath, the Sabbath
just about to begin.
55-56 The women who had been companions of
Jesus from Galilee followed along. They saw
the tomb where Jesus' body was placed.
Then they went back to prepare burial
spices and perfumes. They rested quietly on
the Sabbath, as commanded.

LOOKING FOR THE LIVING ONE IN A CEMETERY

1-3 24 At the crack of dawn on Sunday, the
women came to the tomb carrying the
burial spices they had prepared. They found
the entrance stone rolled back from the
tomb, so they walked in. But once inside,
they couldn't find the body of the Master Je-
sus.
4-8 They were puzzled, wondering what to
make of this. Then, out of nowhere it

New King James Version

men stood by them in shining garments. [5]Then, as they were afraid and bowed *their* faces to the earth, they said to them, "Why do you seek the living among the dead? [6]He is not here, but is risen! Remember how He spoke to you when He was still in Galilee, [7]saying, 'The Son of Man must be delivered into the hands of sinful men, and be crucified, and the third day rise again.' "

[8]And they remembered His words. [9]Then they returned from the tomb and told all these things to the eleven and to all the rest. [10]It was Mary Magdalene, Joanna, Mary *the mother* of James, and the other *women* with them, who told these things to the apostles. [11]And their words seemed to them like idle tales, and they did not believe them. [12]But Peter arose and ran to the tomb; and stooping down, he saw the linen cloths lying[a] by themselves; and he departed, marveling to himself at what had happened.

The Road to Emmaus

[13]Now behold, two of them were traveling that same day to a village called Emmaus, which was seven miles[a] from Jerusalem. [14]And they talked together of all these things which had happened. [15]So it was, while they conversed and reasoned, that Jesus Himself drew near and went with them. [16]But their eyes were restrained, so that they did not know Him.

[17]And He said to them, "What kind of conversation *is* this that you have with one another as you walk and are sad?"[a]

[18]Then the one whose name was Cleopas answered and said to Him, "Are You the only stranger in Jerusalem, and have You not known the things which happened there in these days?"

[19]And He said to them, "What things?"

So they said to Him, "The things concerning Jesus of Nazareth, who was a Prophet mighty in deed and word before God and all the people, [20]and how the chief priests and our rulers delivered Him to be condemned to death, and crucified Him. [21]But we were hoping that it was He who was going to redeem Israel. Indeed, besides all this, today is the third day since these things happened. [22]Yes, and certain women of our company, who arrived at the tomb early, astonished us. [23]When they did not find His body, they came saying that they had also seen a vision of angels who said He was alive. [24]And certain of those *who were* with us went to the tomb and found *it* just as the women had said; but Him they did not see."

[25]Then He said to them, "O foolish ones, and slow of heart to believe in all that the prophets have spoken! [26]Ought not the Christ to have suffered these things and to enter into His glory?" [27]And beginning at Moses and all the Prophets, He expounded to them in all the Scriptures the things concerning Himself.

The Disciples' Eyes Opened

[28]Then they drew near to the village where they were going, and He indicated that He would have gone farther. [29]But they constrained Him, saying, "Abide with us, for it is toward

24:12 [a]NU-Text omits *lying.* **24:13** [a]Literally *sixty stadia* **24:17** [a]NU-Text reads *as you walk? And they stood still, looking sad.*

The Message

seemed, two men, light cascading over them, stood there. The women were awestruck and bowed down in worship. The men said, "Why are you looking for the Living One in a cemetery? He is not here, but raised up. Remember how he told you when you were still back in Galilee that he had to be handed over to sinners, be killed on a cross, and in three days rise up?" Then they remembered Jesus' words.

9-11 They left the tomb and broke the news of all this to the Eleven and the rest. Mary Magdalene, Joanna, Mary the mother of James, and the other women with them kept telling these things to the apostles, but the apostles didn't believe a word of it, thought they were making it all up.

12 But Peter jumped to his feet and ran to the tomb. He stooped to look in and saw a few grave clothes, that's all. He walked away puzzled, shaking his head.

The Road to Emmaus

13-16 That same day two of them were walking to the village Emmaus, about seven miles out of Jerusalem. They were deep in conversation, going over all these things that had happened. In the middle of their talk and questions, Jesus came up and walked along with them. But they were not able to recognize who he was.

17-18 He asked, "What's this you're discussing so intently as you walk along?"

They just stood there, long-faced, like they had lost their best friend. Then one of them, his name was Cleopas, said, "Are you the only one in Jerusalem who hasn't heard what's happened during the last few days?"

19-24 He said, "What has happened?"

They said, "The things that happened to Jesus the Nazarene. He was a man of God, a prophet, dynamic in work and word, blessed by both God and all the people. Then our high priests and leaders betrayed him, got him sentenced to death, and crucified him. And we had our hopes up that he was the One, the One about to deliver Israel. And it is now the third day since it happened. But now some of our women have completely confused us. Early this morning they were at the tomb and couldn't find his body. They came back with the story that they had seen a vision of angels who said he was alive. Some of our friends went off to the tomb to check and found it empty just as the women said, but they didn't see Jesus."

25-27 Then he said to them, "So thick-headed! So slow-hearted! Why can't you simply believe all that the prophets said? Don't you see that these things had to happen, that the Messiah had to suffer and only then enter into his glory?" Then he started at the beginning, with the Books of Moses, and went on through all the Prophets, pointing out everything in the Scriptures that referred to him.

28-31 They came to the edge of the village where they were headed. He acted as if he were going on but they pressed him: "Stay and have supper with us. It's nearly evening;

NEW KING JAMES VERSION

evening, and the day is far spent." And He went
in to stay with them.
30 Now it came to pass, as He sat at the table
with them, that He took bread, blessed and
broke *it,* and gave it to them. 31 Then their eyes
were opened and they knew Him; and He van-
ished from their sight.
32 And they said to one another, "Did not our
heart burn within us while He talked with us on
the road, and while He opened the Scriptures to
us?" 33 So they rose up that very hour and re-
turned to Jerusalem, and found the eleven and
those *who were* with them gathered together,
34 saying, "The Lord is risen indeed, and has ap-
peared to Simon!" 35 And they told about the
things *that had happened* on the road, and how
He was known to them in the breaking of bread.

Jesus Appears to His Disciples

36 Now as they said these things, Jesus Him-
self stood in the midst of them, and said to them,
"Peace to you." 37 But they were terrified and
frightened, and supposed they had seen a spirit.
38 And He said to them, "Why are you troubled?
And why do doubts arise in your hearts? 39 Be-
hold My hands and My feet, that it is I Myself.
Handle Me and see, for a spirit does not have
flesh and bones as you see I have."
40 When He had said this, He showed them His
hands and His feet.[a] 41 But while they still did not
believe for joy, and marveled, He said to them,
"Have you any food here?" 42 So they gave Him a
piece of a broiled fish and some honeycomb.[a]
43 And He took *it* and ate in their presence.

The Scriptures Opened

44 Then He said to them, "These *are* the words
which I spoke to you while I was still with you,
that all things must be fulfilled which were writ-
ten in the Law of Moses and *the* Prophets and
the Psalms concerning Me." 45 And He opened
their understanding, that they might compre-
hend the Scriptures.
46 Then He said to them, "Thus it is written,
and thus it was necessary for the Christ to suf-
fer and to rise[a] from the dead the third day,
47 and that repentance and remission of sins
should be preached in His name to all nations,
beginning at Jerusalem. 48 And you are wit-
nesses of these things. 49 Behold, I send the
Promise of My Father upon you; but tarry in the
city of Jerusalem[a] until you are endued with
power from on high."

The Ascension

50 And He led them out as far as Bethany, and
He lifted up His hands and blessed them. 51 Now
it came to pass, while He blessed them, that He
was parted from them and carried up into
heaven. 52 And they worshiped Him, and re-
turned to Jerusalem with great joy, 53 and were
continually in the temple praising and[a] blessing
God. Amen.[b]

24:40 [a]Some printed New Testaments omit this verse. It is found in nearly all Greek manuscripts. **24:42** [a]NU-Text omits *and some honeycomb.* **24:46** [a]NU-Text reads *written, that the Christ should suffer and rise.* **24:49** [a]NU-Text omits *of Jerusalem.* **24:53** [a]NU-Text omits *praising and.* [b]NU-Text omits *Amen.*

THE MESSAGE

the day is done." So he went in with them. And here is what happened: He sat down at the table with them. Taking the bread, he blessed and broke and gave it to them. At that moment, open-eyed, wide-eyed, they recognized him. And then he disappeared.

32 Back and forth they talked. "Didn't we feel on fire as he conversed with us on the road, as he opened up the Scriptures for us?"

A Ghost Doesn't Have Muscle and Bone

33-34 They didn't waste a minute. They were up and on their way back to Jerusalem. They found the Eleven and their friends gathered together, talking away: "It's really happened! The Master has been raised up—Simon saw him!"

35 Then the two went over everything that happened on the road and how they recognized him when he broke the bread.

36-41 While they were saying all this, Jesus appeared to them and said, "Peace be with you." They thought they were seeing a ghost and were scared half to death. He continued with them, "Don't be upset, and don't let all these doubting questions take over. Look at my hands; look at my feet—it's really me. Touch me. Look me over from head to toe. A ghost doesn't have muscle and bone like this." As he said this, he showed them his hands and feet. They still couldn't believe what they were seeing. It was too much; it seemed too good to be true.

41-43 He asked, "Do you have any food here?" They gave him a piece of leftover fish they had cooked. He took it and ate it right before their eyes.

You're the Witnesses

44 Then he said, "Everything I told you while I was with you comes to this: All the things written about me in the Law of Moses, in the Prophets, and in the Psalms have to be fulfilled."

45-49 He went on to open their understanding of the Word of God, showing them how to read their Bibles this way. He said, "You can see now how it is written that the Messiah suffers, rises from the dead on the third day, and then a total life-change through the forgiveness of sins is proclaimed in his name to all nations—starting from here, from Jerusalem! You're the first to hear and see it. You're the witnesses. What comes next is very important: I am sending what my Father promised to you, so stay here in the city until he arrives, until you're equipped with power from on high."

50-51 He then led them out of the city over to Bethany. Raising his hands he blessed them, and while blessing them, took his leave, being carried up to heaven.

52-53 And they were on their knees, worshiping him. They returned to Jerusalem bursting with joy. They spent all their time in the Temple praising God. Yes.

JOHN

New King James Version

The Eternal Word

1 In the beginning was the Word, and the Word was with God, and the Word was God. [2]He was in the beginning with God. [3]All things were made through Him, and without Him nothing was made that was made. [4]In Him was life, and the life was the light of men. [5]And the light shines in the darkness, and the darkness did not comprehend[a] it.

John's Witness: The True Light

[6]There was a man sent from God, whose name *was* John. [7]This man came for a witness, to bear witness of the Light, that all through him might believe. [8]He was not that Light, but *was sent* to bear witness of that Light. [9]That was the true Light which gives light to every man coming into the world.[a]

[10]He was in the world, and the world was made through Him, and the world did not know Him. [11]He came to His own,[a] and His own[b] did not receive Him. [12]But as many as received Him, to them He gave the right to become children of God, to those who believe in His name: [13]who were born, not of blood, nor of the will of the flesh, nor of the will of man, but of God.

The Word Becomes Flesh

[14]And the Word became flesh and dwelt among us, and we beheld His glory, the glory as of the only begotten of the Father, full of grace and truth.

[15]John bore witness of Him and cried out, saying, "This was He of whom I said, 'He who comes after me is preferred before me, for He was before me.' "

[16]And[a] of His fullness we have all received, and grace for grace. [17]For the law was given through Moses, *but* grace and truth came through Jesus Christ.

1:5 [a]Or *overcome* **1:9** [a]Or *That was the true Light which, coming into the world, gives light to every man.* **1:11** [a]That is, His own things or domain [b]That is, His own people **1:16** [a]NU-Text reads *For.*

The Message

The Life-Light

1-2 1 The Word was first,
the Word present to God,
God present to the Word.
The Word was God,
in readiness for God from day one.

3-5 Everything was created through him;
nothing—not one thing!—
came into being without him.
What came into existence was Life,
and the Life was Light to live by.
The Life-Light blazed out of the darkness;
the darkness couldn't put it out.

6-8 There once was a man, his name John, sent by God to point out the way to the Life-Light. He came to show everyone where to look, who to believe in. John was not himself the Light; he was there to show the way to the Light.

9-13 The Life-Light was the real thing:
Every person entering Life
he brings into Light.
He was in the world,
the world was there through him,
and yet the world didn't even notice.
He came to his own people,
but they didn't want him.
But whoever did want him,
who believed he was who he claimed
and would do what he said,
He made to be their true selves,
their child-of-God selves.
These are the God-begotten,
not blood-begotten,
not flesh-begotten,
not sex-begotten.

14 The Word became flesh and blood,
and moved into the neighborhood.
We saw the glory with our own eyes,
the one-of-a-kind glory,
like Father, like Son,
Generous inside and out,
true from start to finish.

15 John pointed him out and called, "This is the One! The One I told you was coming after me but in fact was ahead of me. He has always been ahead of me, has always had the first word."

16-18 We all live off his generous bounty,
gift after gift after gift.
We got the basics from Moses,
and then this exuberant giving and receiving,
This endless knowing and understanding—
all this came through Jesus, the Messiah.

New King James Version

18No one has seen God at any time. The only be-
gotten Son,[a] who is in the bosom of the Father,
He has declared *Him*.

A Voice in the Wilderness

19Now this is the testimony of John, when the
Jews sent priests and Levites from Jerusalem to
ask him, "Who are you?"
20He confessed, and did not deny, but con-
fessed, "I am not the Christ."
21And they asked him, "What then? Are you
Elijah?"
He said, "I am not."
"Are you the Prophet?"
And he answered, "No."
22Then they said to him, "Who are you, that
we may give an answer to those who sent us?
What do you say about yourself?"
23He said: "I *am*

'The voice of one crying in the wilderness:
"Make straight the way of the Lord," ' [a]

as the prophet Isaiah said."
24Now those who were sent were from the
Pharisees. 25And they asked him, saying, "Why
then do you baptize if you are not the Christ, nor
Elijah, nor the Prophet?"
26John answered them, saying, "I baptize
with water, but there stands One among you
whom you do not know. 27It is He who, coming
after me, is preferred before me, whose sandal
strap I am not worthy to loose."
28These things were done in Bethabara[a] be-
yond the Jordan, where John was baptizing.

The Lamb of God

29The next day John saw Jesus coming to-
ward him, and said, "Behold! The Lamb of God
who takes away the sin of the world! 30This is He
of whom I said, 'After me comes a Man who is
preferred before me, for He was before me.' 31I
did not know Him; but that He should be re-
vealed to Israel, therefore I came baptizing with
water."
32And John bore witness, saying, "I saw the
Spirit descending from heaven like a dove, and
He remained upon Him. 33I did not know Him,
but He who sent me to baptize with water said
to me, 'Upon whom you see the Spirit descend-
ing, and remaining on Him, this is He who bap-
tizes with the Holy Spirit.' 34And I have seen and
testified that this is the Son of God."

The First Disciples

35Again, the next day, John stood with two of
his disciples. 36And looking at Jesus as He
walked, he said, "Behold the Lamb of God!"
37The two disciples heard him speak, and
they followed Jesus. 38Then Jesus turned, and
seeing them following, said to them, "What do
you seek?"

1:18 [a]NU-Text reads *only begotten God.* **1:23** [a]Isaiah 40:3
1:28 [a]NU-Text and M-Text read *Bethany.*

The Message

No one has ever seen God,
not so much as a glimpse.
This one-of-a-kind God-Expression,
who exists at the very heart of the Father,
has made him plain as day.

Thunder in the Desert

19-20 When Jews from Jerusalem sent a group of priests and officials to ask John who he was, he was completely honest. He didn't evade the question. He told the plain truth: "I am not the Messiah."

21 They pressed him, "Who, then? Elijah?"
"I am not."
"The Prophet?"
"No."

22 Exasperated, they said, "Who, then? We need an answer for those who sent us. Tell us something—anything!—about yourself."

23 "I'm thunder in the desert: 'Make the road straight for God!' I'm doing what the prophet Isaiah preached."

24-25 Those sent to question him were from the Pharisee party. Now they had a question of their own: "If you're neither the Messiah, nor Elijah, nor the Prophet, why do you baptize?"

26-27 John answered, "I only baptize using water. A person you don't recognize has taken his stand in your midst. He comes after me, but he is not in second place to me. I'm not even worthy to hold his coat for him."

28 These conversations took place in Bethany on the other side of the Jordan, where John was baptizing at the time.

The God-Revealer

29-31 The very next day John saw Jesus coming toward him and yelled out, "Here he is, God's Passover Lamb! He forgives the sins of the world! This is the man I've been talking about, 'the One who comes after me but is really ahead of me.' I knew nothing about who he was—only this: that my task has been to get Israel ready to recognize him as the God-Revealer. That is why I came here baptizing with water, giving you a good bath and scrubbing sins from your life so you can get a fresh start with God."

32-34 John clinched his witness with this: "I watched the Spirit, like a dove flying down out of the sky, making himself at home in him. I repeat, I know nothing about him except this: The One who authorized me to baptize with water told me, 'The One on whom you see the Spirit come down and stay, this One will baptize with the Holy Spirit.' That's exactly what I saw happen, and I'm telling you, there's no question about it: *This* is the Son of God."

Come, See for Yourself

35-36 The next day John was back at his post with two disciples, who were watching. He looked up, saw Jesus walking nearby, and said, "Here he is, God's Passover Lamb."

37-38 The two disciples heard him and went after Jesus. Jesus looked over his shoulder and said to them, "What are you after?"

New King James Version

They said to Him, "Rabbi" (which is to say,
when translated, Teacher), "where are You stay-
ing?"
39He said to them, "Come and see." They
came and saw where He was staying, and re-
mained with Him that day (now it was about the
tenth hour).
40One of the two who heard John *speak,* and
followed Him, was Andrew, Simon Peter's
brother. 41He first found his own brother Simon,
and said to him, "We have found the Messiah"
(which is translated, the Christ). 42And he
brought him to Jesus.
Now when Jesus looked at him, He said,
"You are Simon the son of Jonah.[a] You shall be
called Cephas" (which is translated, A Stone).

Philip and Nathanael

43The following day Jesus wanted to go to
Galilee, and He found Philip and said to him,
"Follow Me." 44Now Philip was from Bethsaida,
the city of Andrew and Peter. 45Philip found
Nathanael and said to him, "We have found Him
of whom Moses in the law, and also the
prophets, wrote—Jesus of Nazareth, the son of
Joseph."
46And Nathanael said to him, "Can anything
good come out of Nazareth?"
Philip said to him, "Come and see."
47Jesus saw Nathanael coming toward Him,
and said of him, "Behold, an Israelite indeed, in
whom is no deceit!"
48Nathanael said to Him, "How do You know
me?"
Jesus answered and said to him, "Before
Philip called you, when you were under the fig
tree, I saw you."
49Nathanael answered and said to Him,
"Rabbi, You are the Son of God! You are the King
of Israel!"
50Jesus answered and said to him, "Because I
said to you, 'I saw you under the fig tree,' do you
believe? You will see greater things than these."
51And He said to him, "Most assuredly, I say to
you, hereafter[a] you shall see heaven open, and
the angels of God ascending and descending
upon the Son of Man."

Water Turned to Wine

2 On the third day there was a wedding in Cana
of Galilee, and the mother of Jesus was there.
2Now both Jesus and His disciples were invited
to the wedding. 3And when they ran out of wine,
the mother of Jesus said to Him, "They have no
wine."
4Jesus said to her, "Woman, what does your
concern have to do with Me? My hour has not
yet come."
5His mother said to the servants, "Whatever
He says to you, do *it.*"
6Now there were set there six waterpots of
stone, according to the manner of purification of
the Jews, containing twenty or thirty gallons
apiece. 7Jesus said to them, "Fill the waterpots
with water." And they filled them up to the brim.
8And He said to them, "Draw *some* out now, and
take *it* to the master of the feast." And they took *it.*

1:42 [a]NU-Text reads *John.* **1:51** [a]NU-Text omits *hereafter.*

The Message

They said, "Rabbi" (which means
"Teacher"), "where are you staying?"
39 He replied, "Come along and see for
yourself."
They came, saw where he was living, and
ended up staying with him for the day. It
was late afternoon when this happened.
40-42 Andrew, Simon Peter's brother, was one
of the two who heard John's witness and
followed Jesus. The first thing he did after
finding where Jesus lived was find his own
brother, Simon, telling him, "We've found
the Messiah" (that is, "Christ"). He immedi-
ately led him to Jesus.
Jesus took one look up and said, "You're
John's son, Simon? From now on your name
is Cephas" (or Peter, which means "Rock").
43-44 The next day Jesus decided to go to
Galilee. When he got there, he ran across
Philip and said, "Come, follow me." (Philip's
hometown was Bethsaida, the same as An-
drew and Peter.)
45-46 Philip went and found Nathanael and
told him, "We've found the One Moses wrote
of in the Law, the One preached by the
prophets. It's *Jesus,* Joseph's son, the one
from Nazareth!" Nathanael said, "Nazareth?
You've got to be kidding."
But Philip said, "Come, see for yourself."
47 When Jesus saw him coming he said,
"There's a real Israelite, not a false bone in
his body."
48 Nathanael said, "Where did you get that
idea? You don't know me."
Jesus answered, "One day, long before
Philip called you here, I saw you under the
fig tree."
49 Nathanael exclaimed, "Rabbi! You are the
Son of God, the King of Israel!"
50-51 Jesus said, "You've become a believer
simply because I say I saw you one day sit-
ting under the fig tree? You haven't seen
anything yet! Before this is over you're go-
ing to see heaven open and God's angels de-
scending to the Son of Man and ascending
again."

From Water to Wine

1-3 2 Three days later there was a wedding in
the village of Cana in Galilee. Jesus'
mother was there. Jesus and his disciples
were guests also. When they started running
low on wine at the wedding banquet, Jesus'
mother told him, "They're just about out of
wine."
4 Jesus said, "Is that any of our business,
Mother—yours or mine? This isn't my time.
Don't push me."
5 She went ahead anyway, telling the ser-
vants, "Whatever he tells you, do it."
6-7 Six stoneware water pots were there,
used by the Jews for ritual washings. Each
held twenty to thirty gallons. Jesus ordered
the servants, "Fill the pots with water." And
they filled them to the brim.
8 "Now fill your pitchers and take them to
the host," Jesus said, and they did.

NEW KING JAMES VERSION

9 When the master of the feast had tasted the water that was made wine, and did not know where it came from (but the servants who had drawn the water knew), the master of the feast called the bridegroom. 10 And he said to him, "Every man at the beginning sets out the good wine, and when the *guests* have well drunk, then the inferior. You have kept the good wine until now!"

11 This beginning of signs Jesus did in Cana of Galilee, and manifested His glory; and His disciples believed in Him.

12 After this He went down to Capernaum, He, His mother, His brothers, and His disciples; and they did not stay there many days.

JESUS CLEANSES THE TEMPLE

13 Now the Passover of the Jews was at hand, and Jesus went up to Jerusalem. 14 And He found in the temple those who sold oxen and sheep and doves, and the money changers doing business. 15 When He had made a whip of cords, He drove them all out of the temple, with the sheep and the oxen, and poured out the changers' money and overturned the tables. 16 And He said to those who sold doves, "Take these things away! Do not make My Father's house a house of merchandise!" 17 Then His disciples remembered that it was written, *"Zeal for Your house has eaten*[a] *Me up."*[b]

18 So the Jews answered and said to Him, "What sign do You show to us, since You do these things?"

19 Jesus answered and said to them, "Destroy this temple, and in three days I will raise it up."

20 Then the Jews said, "It has taken forty-six years to build this temple, and will You raise it up in three days?"

21 But He was speaking of the temple of His body. 22 Therefore, when He had risen from the dead, His disciples remembered that He had said this to them;[a] and they believed the Scripture and the word which Jesus had said.

THE DISCERNER OF HEARTS

23 Now when He was in Jerusalem at the Passover, during the feast, many believed in His name when they saw the signs which He did. 24 But Jesus did not commit Himself to them, because He knew all *men,* 25 and had no need that anyone should testify of man, for He knew what was in man.

THE NEW BIRTH

3 There was a man of the Pharisees named Nicodemus, a ruler of the Jews. 2 This man came to Jesus by night and said to Him, "Rabbi, we know that You are a teacher come from God; for no one can do these signs that You do unless God is with him."

3 Jesus answered and said to him, "Most assuredly, I say to you, unless one is born again, he cannot see the kingdom of God."

2:17 [a]NU-Text and M-Text read *will eat.* [b]Psalm 69:9 **2:22** [a]NU-Text and M-Text omit *to them.*

THE MESSAGE

9-10 When the host tasted the water that had become wine (he didn't know what had just happened but the servants, of course, knew), he called out to the bridegroom, "Everybody I know begins with their finest wines and after the guests have had their fill brings in the cheap stuff. But you've saved the best till now!"

11 This act in Cana of Galilee was the first sign Jesus gave, the first glimpse of his glory. And his disciples believed in him.

12 After this he went down to Capernaum along with his mother, brothers, and disciples, and stayed several days.

TEAR DOWN THIS TEMPLE . . .

13-14 When the Passover Feast, celebrated each spring by the Jews, was about to take place, Jesus traveled up to Jerusalem. He found the Temple teeming with people selling cattle and sheep and doves. The loan sharks were also there in full strength.

15-17 Jesus put together a whip out of strips of leather and chased them out of the Temple, stampeding the sheep and cattle, upending the tables of the loan sharks, spilling coins left and right. He told the dove merchants, "Get your things out of here! Stop turning my Father's house into a shopping mall!" That's when his disciples remembered the Scripture, "Zeal for your house consumes me."

18-19 But the Jews were upset. They asked, "What credentials can you present to justify this?" Jesus answered, "Tear down this Temple and in three days I'll put it back together."

20-22 They were indignant: "It took forty-six years to build this Temple, and you're going to rebuild it in three days?" But Jesus was talking about his body as the Temple. Later, after he was raised from the dead, his disciples remembered he had said this. They then put two and two together and believed both what was written in Scripture and what Jesus had said.

23-25 During the time he was in Jerusalem, those days of the Passover Feast, many people noticed the signs he was displaying and, seeing they pointed straight to God, entrusted their lives to him. But Jesus didn't entrust his life to them. He knew them inside and out, knew how untrustworthy they were. He didn't need any help in seeing right through them.

BORN FROM ABOVE

1-2 3 There was a man of the Pharisee sect, Nicodemus, a prominent leader among the Jews. Late one night he visited Jesus and said, "Rabbi, we all know you're a teacher straight from God. No one could do all the God-pointing, God-revealing acts you do if God weren't in on it."

3 Jesus said, "You're absolutely right. Take it from me: Unless a person is born from above, it's not possible to see what I'm pointing to—to God's kingdom."

New King James Version

4Nicodemus said to Him, “How can a man be born when he is old? Can he enter a second time into his mother’s womb and be born?”

5Jesus answered, “Most assuredly, I say to you, unless one is born of water and the Spirit, he cannot enter the kingdom of God. 6That which is born of the flesh is flesh, and that which is born of the Spirit is spirit. 7Do not marvel that I said to you, ‘You must be born again.’ 8The wind blows where it wishes, and you hear the sound of it, but cannot tell where it comes from and where it goes. So is everyone who is born of the Spirit.”

9Nicodemus answered and said to Him, “How can these things be?”

10Jesus answered and said to him, “Are you the teacher of Israel, and do not know these things? 11Most assuredly, I say to you, We speak what We know and testify what We have seen, and you do not receive Our witness. 12If I have told you earthly things and you do not believe, how will you believe if I tell you heavenly things? 13No one has ascended to heaven but He who came down from heaven, *that is,* the Son of Man who is in heaven.[a] 14And as Moses lifted up the serpent in the wilderness, even so must the Son of Man be lifted up, 15that whoever believes in Him should not perish but[a] have eternal life. 16For God so loved the world that He gave His only begotten Son, that whoever believes in Him should not perish but have everlasting life. 17For God did not send His Son into the world to condemn the world, but that the world through Him might be saved.

18“He who believes in Him is not condemned; but he who does not believe is condemned already, because he has not believed in the name of the only begotten Son of God. 19And this is the condemnation, that the light has come into the world, and men loved darkness rather than light, because their deeds were evil. 20For every-

3:13 [a]NU-Text omits *who is in heaven.* **3:15** [a]NU-Text omits *not perish but.*

The Message

4 “How can anyone,” said Nicodemus, “be born who has already been born and grown up? You can’t re-enter your mother’s womb and be born again. What are you saying with this ‘born-from-above’ talk?”

5-6 Jesus said, “You’re not listening. Let me say it again. Unless a person submits to this original creation—the ‘wind-hovering-over-the-water’ creation, the invisible moving the visible, a baptism into a new life—it’s not possible to enter God’s kingdom. When you look at a baby, it’s just that: a body you can look at and touch. But the person who takes shape within is formed by something you can’t see and touch—the Spirit—and becomes a living spirit.

7-8 “So don’t be so surprised when I tell you that you have to be ‘born from above’—out of this world, so to speak. You know well enough how the wind blows this way and that. You hear it rustling through the trees, but you have no idea where it comes from or where it’s headed next. That’s the way it is with everyone ‘born from above’ by the wind of God, the Spirit of God.”

9 Nicodemus asked, “What do you mean by this? How does this happen?”

10-12 Jesus said, “You’re a respected teacher of Israel and you don’t know these basics? Listen carefully. I’m speaking sober truth to you. I speak only of what I know by experience; I give witness only to what I have seen with my own eyes. There is nothing secondhand here, no hearsay. Yet instead of facing the evidence and accepting it, you procrastinate with questions. If I tell you things that are plain as the hand before your face and you don’t believe me, what use is there in telling you of things you can’t see, the things of God?

13-15 “No one has ever gone up into the presence of God except the One who came down from that Presence, the Son of Man. In the same way that Moses lifted the serpent in the desert so people could have something to see and then believe, it is necessary for the Son of Man to be lifted up—and everyone who looks up to him, trusting and expectant, will gain a real life, eternal life.

16-18 “This is how much God loved the world: He gave his Son, his one and only Son. And this is why: so that no one need be destroyed; by believing in him, anyone can have a whole and lasting life. God didn’t go to all the trouble of sending his Son merely to point an accusing finger, telling the world how bad it was. He came to help, to put the world right again. Anyone who trusts in him is acquitted; anyone who refuses to trust him has long since been under the death sentence without knowing it. And why? Because of that person’s failure to believe in the one-of-a-kind Son of God when introduced to him.

19-21 “This is the crisis we’re in: God-light streamed into the world, but men and women everywhere ran for the darkness. They went for the darkness because they were not really interested in pleasing God.

NEW KING JAMES VERSION

one practicing evil hates the light and does not
come to the light, lest his deeds should be ex-
posed. 21But he who does the truth comes to the
light, that his deeds may be clearly seen, that
they have been done in God."

JOHN THE BAPTIST EXALTS CHRIST

22After these things Jesus and His disciples
came into the land of Judea, and there He re-
mained with them and baptized. 23Now John
also was baptizing in Aenon near Salim, be-
cause there was much water there. And they
came and were baptized. 24For John had not yet
been thrown into prison.

25Then there arose a dispute between *some*
of John's disciples and the Jews about purifica-
tion. 26And they came to John and said to him,
"Rabbi, He who was with you beyond the Jor-
dan, to whom you have testified—behold, He is
baptizing, and all are coming to Him!"

27John answered and said, "A man can re-
ceive nothing unless it has been given to him
from heaven. 28You yourselves bear me witness,
that I said, 'I am not the Christ,' but, 'I have been
sent before Him.' 29He who has the bride is the
bridegroom; but the friend of the bridegroom,
who stands and hears him, rejoices greatly be-
cause of the bridegroom's voice. Therefore this
joy of mine is fulfilled. 30He must increase, but I
must decrease. 31He who comes from above is
above all; he who is of the earth is earthly and
speaks of the earth. He who comes from heaven
is above all. 32And what He has seen and heard,
that He testifies; and no one receives His testi-
mony. 33He who has received His testimony has
certified that God is true. 34For He whom God
has sent speaks the words of God, for God does
not give the Spirit by measure. 35The Father
loves the Son, and has given all things into His
hand. 36He who believes in the Son has everlast-
ing life; and he who does not believe the Son
shall not see life, but the wrath of God abides on
him."

A SAMARITAN WOMAN MEETS HER MESSIAH

4 Therefore, when the Lord knew that the
Pharisees had heard that Jesus made and
baptized more disciples than John 2(though Je-
sus Himself did not baptize, but His disciples),

THE MESSAGE

Everyone who makes a practice of doing evil, addicted to denial and illusion, hates God-light and won't come near it, fearing a painful exposure. But anyone working and living in truth and reality welcomes God-light so the work can be seen for the God-work it is."

THE BRIDEGROOM'S FRIEND

22-26 After this conversation, Jesus went on with his disciples into the Judean countryside and relaxed with them there. He was also baptizing. At the same time, John was baptizing over at Aenon near Salim, where water was abundant. This was before John was thrown into jail. John's disciples got into an argument with the establishment Jews over the nature of baptism. They came to John and said, "Rabbi, you know the one who was with you on the other side of the Jordan? The one you authorized with your witness? Well, he's now competing with us. He's baptizing, too, and everyone's going to him instead of us."

27-29 John answered, "It's not possible for a person to succeed—I'm talking about *eternal* success—without heaven's help. You yourselves were there when I made it public that I was not the Messiah but simply the one sent ahead of him to get things ready. The one who gets the bride is, by definition, the bridegroom. And the bridegroom's friend, his 'best man'—that's me—in place at his side where he can hear every word, is genuinely happy. How could he be jealous when he knows that the wedding is finished and the marriage is off to a good start?

29-30 "That's why my cup is running over. This is the assigned moment for him to move into the center, while I slip off to the sidelines.

31-33 "The One who comes from above is head and shoulders over other messengers from God. The earthborn is earthbound and speaks earth language; the heavenborn is in a league of his own. He sets out the evidence of what he saw and heard in heaven. No one wants to deal with these facts. But anyone who examines this evidence will come to stake his life on this: that God himself is the truth.

34-36 "The One that God sent speaks God's words. And don't think he rations out the Spirit in bits and pieces. The Father loves the Son extravagantly. He turned everything over to him so he could give it away—a lavish distribution of gifts. That is why whoever accepts and trusts the Son gets in on everything, life complete and forever! And that is also why the person who avoids and distrusts the Son is in the dark and doesn't see life. All he experiences of God is darkness, and an angry darkness at that."

THE WOMAN AT THE WELL

1-3 4 Jesus realized that the Pharisees were keeping count of the baptisms that he and John performed (although his disciples, not Jesus, did the actual baptizing). They had posted the score that Jesus was ahead, turning him and John into rivals in the eyes of

NEW KING JAMES VERSION

3 He left Judea and departed again to Galilee.
4 But He needed to go through Samaria.
5 So He came to a city of Samaria which is
called Sychar, near the plot of ground that Jacob
gave to his son Joseph. 6 Now Jacob's well was
there. Jesus therefore, being wearied from *His*
journey, sat thus by the well. It was about the
sixth hour.
7 A woman of Samaria came to draw water.
Jesus said to her, "Give Me a drink." 8 For His
disciples had gone away into the city to buy
food.
9 Then the woman of Samaria said to Him,
"How is it that You, being a Jew, ask a drink
from me, a Samaritan woman?" For Jews have
no dealings with Samaritans.
10 Jesus answered and said to her, "If you
knew the gift of God, and who it is who says to
you, 'Give Me a drink,' you would have asked
Him, and He would have given you living wa-
ter."
11 The woman said to Him, "Sir, You have
nothing to draw with, and the well is deep.
Where then do You get that living water? 12 Are
You greater than our father Jacob, who gave us
the well, and drank from it himself, as well as
his sons and his livestock?"
13 Jesus answered and said to her, "Whoever
drinks of this water will thirst again, 14 but who-
ever drinks of the water that I shall give him will
never thirst. But the water that I shall give him
will become in him a fountain of water spring-
ing up into everlasting life."
15 The woman said to Him, "Sir, give me this
water, that I may not thirst, nor come here to
draw."
16 Jesus said to her, "Go, call your husband,
and come here."
17 The woman answered and said, "I have no
husband."
Jesus said to her, "You have well said, 'I have
no husband,' 18 for you have had five husbands,
and the one whom you now have is not your
husband; in that you spoke truly."
19 The woman said to Him, "Sir, I perceive
that You are a prophet. 20 Our fathers worshiped
on this mountain, and you *Jews* say that in
Jerusalem is the place where one ought to wor-
ship."
21 Jesus said to her, "Woman, believe Me, the
hour is coming when you will neither on this
mountain, nor in Jerusalem, worship the Father.
22 You worship what you do not know; we know
what we worship, for salvation is of the Jews.
23 But the hour is coming, and now is, when the
true worshipers will worship the Father in spirit
and truth; for the Father is seeking such to wor-
ship Him. 24 God *is* Spirit, and those who wor-
ship Him must worship in spirit and truth."

THE MESSAGE

the people. So Jesus left the Judean country-
side and went back to Galilee.
4-6 To get there, he had to pass through
Samaria. He came into Sychar, a Samaritan
village that bordered the field Jacob had
given his son Joseph. Jacob's well was still
there. Jesus, worn out by the trip, sat down
at the well. It was noon.
7-8 A woman, a Samaritan, came to draw wa-
ter. Jesus said, "Would you give me a drink
of water?" (His disciples had gone to the vil-
lage to buy food for lunch.)
9 The Samaritan woman, taken aback,
asked, "How come you, a Jew, are asking
me, a Samaritan woman, for a drink?" (Jews
in those days wouldn't be caught dead talk-
ing to Samaritans.)
10 Jesus answered, "If you knew the gen-
erosity of God and who I am, you would be
asking *me* for a drink, and I would give you
fresh, living water."
11-12 The woman said, "Sir, you don't even
have a bucket to draw with, and this well is
deep. So how are you going to get this 'liv-
ing water'? Are you a better man than our
ancestor Jacob, who dug this well and drank
from it, he and his sons and livestock, and
passed it down to us?"
13-14 Jesus said, "Everyone who drinks this
water will get thirsty again and again. Any-
one who drinks the water I give will never
thirst—not ever. The water I give will be an
artesian spring within, gushing fountains of
endless life."
15 The woman said, "Sir, give me this water
so I won't ever get thirsty, won't ever have to
come back to this well again!"
16 He said, "Go call your husband and then
come back."
17-18 "I have no husband," she said.
"That's nicely put: 'I have no husband.'
You've had five husbands, and the man
you're living with now isn't even your hus-
band. You spoke the truth there, sure
enough."
19-20 "Oh, so you're a prophet! Well, tell me
this: Our ancestors worshiped God at this
mountain, but you Jews insist that
Jerusalem is the only place for worship,
right?"
21-23 "Believe me, woman, the time is coming
when you Samaritans will worship the Fa-
ther neither here at this mountain nor there
in Jerusalem. You worship guessing in the
dark; we Jews worship in the clear light of
day. God's way of salvation is made avail-
able through the Jews. But the time is com-
ing—it has, in fact, come—when what
you're called will not matter and where you
go to worship will not matter.
23-24 "It's who you are and the way you live that
count before God. Your worship must engage
your spirit in the pursuit of truth. That's the
kind of people the Father is out looking for:
those who are simply and honestly *them-
selves* before him in their worship. God is
sheer being itself—Spirit. Those who wor-
ship him must do it out of their very being,
their spirits, their true selves, in adoration."

NEW KING JAMES VERSION

[25]The woman said to Him, "I know that Messiah is coming" (who is called Christ). "When He comes, He will tell us all things."

[26]Jesus said to her, "I who speak to you am *He*."

THE WHITENED HARVEST

[27]And at this *point* His disciples came, and they marveled that He talked with a woman; yet no one said, "What do You seek?" or, "Why are You talking with her?"

[28]The woman then left her waterpot, went her way into the city, and said to the men, [29]"Come, see a Man who told me all things that I ever did. Could this be the Christ?" [30]Then they went out of the city and came to Him.

[31]In the meantime His disciples urged Him, saying, "Rabbi, eat."

[32]But He said to them, "I have food to eat of which you do not know."

[33]Therefore the disciples said to one another, "Has anyone brought Him *anything* to eat?"

[34]Jesus said to them, "My food is to do the will of Him who sent Me, and to finish His work. [35]Do you not say, 'There are still four months and *then* comes the harvest'? Behold, I say to you, lift up your eyes and look at the fields, for they are already white for harvest! [36]And he who reaps receives wages, and gathers fruit for eternal life, that both he who sows and he who reaps may rejoice together. [37]For in this the saying is true: 'One sows and another reaps.' [38]I sent you to reap that for which you have not labored; others have labored, and you have entered into their labors."

THE SAVIOR OF THE WORLD

[39]And many of the Samaritans of that city believed in Him because of the word of the woman who testified, "He told me all that I *ever* did." [40]So when the Samaritans had come to Him, they urged Him to stay with them; and He stayed there two days. [41]And many more believed because of His own word.

[42]Then they said to the woman, "Now we believe, not because of what you said, for we ourselves have heard *Him* and we know that this is indeed the Christ,[a] the Savior of the world."

WELCOME AT GALILEE

[43]Now after the two days He departed from there and went to Galilee. [44]For Jesus Himself testified that a prophet has no honor in his own country. [45]So when He came to Galilee, the Galileans received Him, having seen all the things He did in Jerusalem at the feast; for they also had gone to the feast.

A NOBLEMAN'S SON HEALED

[46]So Jesus came again to Cana of Galilee where He had made the water wine. And there was a certain nobleman whose son was sick at

4:42 [a]NU-Text omits *the Christ.*

THE MESSAGE

25 The woman said, "I don't know about that. I do know that the Messiah is coming. When he arrives, we'll get the whole story."

26 "I am he," said Jesus. "You don't have to wait any longer or look any further."

27 Just then his disciples came back. They were shocked. They couldn't believe he was talking with that kind of a woman. No one said what they were all thinking, but their faces showed it.

28-30 The woman took the hint and left. In her confusion she left her water pot. Back in the village she told the people, "Come see a man who knew all about the things I did, who knows me inside and out. Do you think this could be the Messiah?" And they went out to see for themselves.

IT'S HARVEST TIME

31 In the meantime, the disciples pressed him, "Rabbi, eat. Aren't you going to eat?"

32 He told them, "I have food to eat you know nothing about."

33 The disciples were puzzled. "Who could have brought him food?"

34-35 Jesus said, "The food that keeps me going is that I do the will of the One who sent me, finishing the work he started. As you look around right now, wouldn't you say that in about four months it will be time to harvest? Well, I'm telling you to open your eyes and take a good look at what's right in front of you. These Samaritan fields are ripe. It's harvest time!

36-38 "The Harvester isn't waiting. He's taking his pay, gathering in this grain that's ripe for eternal life. Now the Sower is arm in arm with the Harvester, triumphant. That's the truth of the saying, 'This one sows, that one harvests.' I sent you to harvest a field you never worked. Without lifting a finger, you have walked in on a field worked long and hard by others."

39-42 Many of the Samaritans from that village committed themselves to him because of the woman's witness: "He knew all about the things I did. He knows me inside and out!" They asked him to stay on, so Jesus stayed two days. A lot more people entrusted their lives to him when they heard what he had to say. They said to the woman, "We're no longer taking this on your say-so. We've heard it for ourselves and know it for sure. He's the Savior of the world!"

43-45 After the two days he left for Galilee. Now, Jesus knew well from experience that a prophet is not respected in the place where he grew up. So when he arrived in Galilee, the Galileans welcomed him, but only because they were impressed with what he had done in Jerusalem during the Passover Feast, not that they really had a clue about who he was or what he was up to.

46-48 Now he was back in Cana of Galilee, the place where he made the water into wine. Meanwhile in Capernaum, there was a certain official from the king's court whose son

NEW KING JAMES VERSION

Capernaum. 47When he heard that Jesus had come out of Judea into Galilee, he went to Him and implored Him to come down and heal his son, for he was at the point of death. 48Then Jesus said to him, "Unless you *people* see signs and wonders, you will by no means believe."

49The nobleman said to Him, "Sir, come down before my child dies!"

50Jesus said to him, "Go your way; your son lives." So the man believed the word that Jesus spoke to him, and he went his way. 51And as he was now going down, his servants met him and told *him,* saying, "Your son lives!"

52Then he inquired of them the hour when he got better. And they said to him, "Yesterday at the seventh hour the fever left him." 53So the father knew that *it was* at the same hour in which Jesus said to him, "Your son lives." And he himself believed, and his whole household.

54This again *is* the second sign Jesus did when He had come out of Judea into Galilee.

A MAN HEALED AT THE POOL OF BETHESDA

5 After this there was a feast of the Jews, and Jesus went up to Jerusalem. 2Now there is in Jerusalem by the Sheep *Gate* a pool, which is called in Hebrew, Bethesda,[a] having five porches. 3In these lay a great multitude of sick people, blind, lame, paralyzed, waiting for the moving of the water. 4For an angel went down at a certain time into the pool and stirred up the water; then whoever stepped in first, after the stirring of the water, was made well of whatever disease he had.[a] 5Now a certain man was there who had an infirmity thirty-eight years. 6When Jesus saw him lying there, and knew that he already had been *in that condition* a long time, He said to him, "Do you want to be made well?"

7The sick man answered Him, "Sir, I have no man to put me into the pool when the water is stirred up; but while I am coming, another steps down before me."

8Jesus said to him, "Rise, take up your bed and walk." 9And immediately the man was made well, took up his bed, and walked.

And that day was the Sabbath. 10The Jews therefore said to him who was cured, "It is the Sabbath; it is not lawful for you to carry your bed."

11He answered them, "He who made me well said to me, 'Take up your bed and walk.' "

12Then they asked him, "Who is the Man who said to you, 'Take up your bed and walk'?" 13But the one who was healed did not know who it was, for Jesus had withdrawn, a multitude being in *that* place. 14Afterward Jesus found him in the temple, and said to him, "See, you have been made well. Sin no more, lest a worse thing come upon you."

15The man departed and told the Jews that it was Jesus who had made him well.

HONOR THE FATHER AND THE SON

16For this reason the Jews persecuted Jesus, and sought to kill Him,[a] because He had done these things on the Sabbath.

5:2 [a]NU-Text reads *Bethzatha.* **5:4** [a]NU-Text omits *waiting for the moving of the water* at the end of verse 3, and all of verse 4. **5:16** [a]NU-Text omits *and sought to kill Him.*

THE MESSAGE

was sick. When he heard that Jesus had
come from Judea to Galilee, he went and
asked that he come down and heal his son,
who was on the brink of death. Jesus put
him off: "Unless you people are dazzled by
a miracle, you refuse to believe."
49 But the court official wouldn't be put off.
"Come down! It's life or death for my son."
50-51 Jesus simply replied, "Go home. Your son
lives."
The man believed the bare word Jesus
spoke and headed home. On his way back,
his servants intercepted him and an-
nounced, "Your son lives!"
52-53 He asked them what time he began to get
better. They said, "The fever broke yester-
day afternoon at one o'clock." The father
knew that that was the very moment Jesus
had said, "Your son lives."
53-54 That clinched it. Not only he but his en-
tire household believed. This was now the
second sign Jesus gave after having come
from Judea into Galilee.

EVEN ON THE SABBATH

1-6 5 Soon another Feast came around and Je-
sus was back in Jerusalem. Near the Sheep
Gate in Jerusalem there was a pool, in He-
brew called *Bethesda,* with five alcoves.
Hundreds of sick people—blind, crippled,
paralyzed—were in these alcoves. One man
had been an invalid there for thirty-eight
years. When Jesus saw him stretched out by
the pool and knew how long he had been
there, he said, "Do you want to get well?"
7 The sick man said, "Sir, when the water is
stirred, I don't have anybody to put me in
the pool. By the time I get there, somebody
else is already in."
8-9 Jesus said, "Get up, take your bedroll,
start walking." The man was healed on the
spot. He picked up his bedroll and walked
off.
9-10 That day happened to be the Sabbath.
The Jews stopped the healed man and said,
"It's the Sabbath. You can't carry your
bedroll around. It's against the rules."
11 But he told them, "The man who made
me well told me to. He said, 'Take your
bedroll and start walking.' "
12-13 They asked, "Who gave you the order to
take it up and start walking?" But the healed
man didn't know, for Jesus had slipped
away into the crowd.
14 A little later Jesus found him in the Tem-
ple and said, "You look wonderful! You're
well! Don't return to a sinning life or some-
thing worse might happen."
15-16 The man went back and told the Jews
that it was Jesus who had made him well.
That is why the Jews were out to get Jesus—
because he did this kind of thing on the Sab-
bath.

NEW KING JAMES VERSION

17 But Jesus answered them, "My Father has
been working until now, and I have been work-
ing."
18 Therefore the Jews sought all the more to
kill Him, because He not only broke the Sab-
bath, but also said that God was His Father,
making Himself equal with God. 19 Then Jesus
answered and said to them, "Most assuredly, I
say to you, the Son can do nothing of Himself,
but what He sees the Father do; for whatever He
does, the Son also does in like manner. 20 For the
Father loves the Son, and shows Him all things
that He Himself does; and He will show Him
greater works than these, that you may marvel.
21 For as the Father raises the dead and gives life
to *them,* even so the Son gives life to whom He
will. 22 For the Father judges no one, but has
committed all judgment to the Son, 23 that all
should honor the Son just as they honor the Fa-
ther. He who does not honor the Son does not
honor the Father who sent Him.

LIFE AND JUDGMENT ARE THROUGH THE SON

24 "Most assuredly, I say to you, he who hears
My word and believes in Him who sent Me has
everlasting life, and shall not come into judg-
ment, but has passed from death into life. 25 Most
assuredly, I say to you, the hour is coming, and
now is, when the dead will hear the voice of the
Son of God; and those who hear will live. 26 For
as the Father has life in Himself, so He has
granted the Son to have life in Himself, 27 and
has given Him authority to execute judgment
also, because He is the Son of Man. 28 Do not
marvel at this; for the hour is coming in which
all who are in the graves will hear His voice
29 and come forth—those who have done good, to
the resurrection of life, and those who have
done evil, to the resurrection of condemnation.
30 I can of Myself do nothing. As I hear, I judge;
and My judgment is righteous, because I do not
seek My own will but the will of the Father who
sent Me.

THE FOURFOLD WITNESS

31 "If I bear witness of Myself, My witness is
not true. 32 There is another who bears witness
of Me, and I know that the witness which He
witnesses of Me is true. 33 You have sent to John,
and he has borne witness to the truth. 34 Yet I do
not receive testimony from man, but I say these
things that you may be saved. 35 He was the
burning and shining lamp, and you were willing
for a time to rejoice in his light. 36 But I have a
greater witness than John's; for the works
which the Father has given Me to finish—the

THE MESSAGE

17 But Jesus defended himself. "My Father is
working straight through, even on the Sab-
bath. So am I."

18 That really set them off. The Jews were
now not only out to expose him; they were
out to *kill* him. Not only was he breaking the
Sabbath, but he was calling God his own Fa-
ther, putting himself on a level with God.

WHAT THE FATHER DOES, THE SON DOES

19-20 So Jesus explained himself at length. "I'm
telling you this straight. The Son can't inde-
pendently do a thing, only what he sees the
Father doing. What the Father does, the Son
does. The Father loves the Son and includes
him in everything he is doing.

20-23 "But you haven't seen the half of it yet,
for in the same way that the Father raises
the dead and creates life, so does the Son.
The Son gives life to anyone he chooses.
Neither he nor the Father shuts anyone out.
The Father handed all authority to judge
over to the Son so that the Son will be hon-
ored equally with the Father. Anyone who
dishonors the Son, dishonors the Father, for
it was the Father's decision to put the Son in
the place of honor.

24 "It's urgent that you listen carefully to
this: Anyone here who believes what I am
saying right now and aligns himself with
the Father, who has in fact put me in charge,
has at this very moment the real, lasting life
and is no longer condemned to be an out-
sider. This person has taken a giant step
from the world of the dead to the world of
the living.

25-27 "It's urgent that you get this right: The
time has arrived—I mean right now!—when
dead men and women will hear the voice of
the Son of God and, hearing, will come
alive. Just as the Father has life in himself,
he has conferred on the Son life in himself.
And he has given him the authority, simply
because he is the Son of Man, to decide and
carry out matters of Judgment.

28-29 "Don't act so surprised at all this. The
time is coming when everyone dead and
buried will hear his voice. Those who have
lived the right way will walk out into a res-
urrection Life; those who have lived the
wrong way, into a resurrection Judgment.

30-33 "I can't do a solitary thing on my own: I
listen, then I decide. You can trust my deci-
sion because I'm not out to get my own way
but only to carry out orders. If I were simply
speaking on my own account, it would be an
empty, self-serving witness. But an inde-
pendent witness confirms me, the most reli-
able Witness of all. Furthermore, you all saw
and heard John, and he gave expert and re-
liable testimony about me, didn't he?

34-38 "But my purpose is not to get your vote,
and not to appeal to mere human testimony.
I'm speaking to you this way so that you will
be saved. John was a torch, blazing and
bright, and you were glad enough to dance
for an hour or so in his bright light. But the
witness that really confirms me far exceeds
John's witness. It's the work the Father gave

NEW KING JAMES VERSION

very works that I do—bear witness of Me, that the Father has sent Me. 37And the Father Himself, who sent Me, has testified of Me. You have neither heard His voice at any time, nor seen His form. 38But you do not have His word abiding in you, because whom He sent, Him you do not believe. 39You search the Scriptures, for in them you think you have eternal life; and these are they which testify of Me. 40But you are not willing to come to Me that you may have life.

41"I do not receive honor from men. 42But I know you, that you do not have the love of God in you. 43I have come in My Father's name, and you do not receive Me; if another comes in his own name, him you will receive. 44How can you believe, who receive honor from one another, and do not seek the honor that *comes* from the only God? 45Do not think that I shall accuse you to the Father; there is *one* who accuses you—Moses, in whom you trust. 46For if you believed Moses, you would believe Me; for he wrote about Me. 47But if you do not believe his writings, how will you believe My words?"

FEEDING THE FIVE THOUSAND

6 After these things Jesus went over the Sea of Galilee, which is *the Sea* of Tiberias. 2Then a great multitude followed Him, because they saw His signs which He performed on those who were diseased. 3And Jesus went up on the mountain, and there He sat with His disciples.

4Now the Passover, a feast of the Jews, was near. 5Then Jesus lifted up *His* eyes, and seeing a great multitude coming toward Him, He said to Philip, "Where shall we buy bread, that these may eat?" 6But this He said to test him, for He Himself knew what He would do.

7Philip answered Him, "Two hundred denarii worth of bread is not sufficient for them, that every one of them may have a little."

8One of His disciples, Andrew, Simon Peter's brother, said to Him, 9"There is a lad here who has five barley loaves and two small fish, but what are they among so many?"

10Then Jesus said, "Make the people sit down." Now there was much grass in the place. So the men sat down, in number about five thousand. 11And Jesus took the loaves, and when He had given thanks He distributed *them* to the disciples, and the disciples[a] to those sitting down; and likewise of the fish, as much as they wanted. 12So when they were filled, He said to His disciples, "Gather up the fragments that remain, so that nothing is lost." 13Therefore they

6:11 [a]NU-Text omits *to the disciples, and the disciples.*

THE MESSAGE

me to complete. These very tasks, as I go about completing them, confirm that the Father, in fact, sent me. The Father who sent me, confirmed me. And you missed it. You never heard his voice, you never saw his appearance. There is nothing left in your memory of his Message because you do not take his Messenger seriously.

39-40 "You have your heads in your Bibles constantly because you think you'll find eternal life there. But you miss the forest for the trees. These Scriptures are all about *me!* And here I am, standing right before you, and you aren't willing to receive from me the life you say you want.

41-44 "I'm not interested in crowd approval. And do you know why? Because I know you and your crowds. I know that love, especially God's love, is not on your working agenda. I came with the authority of my Father, and you either dismiss me or avoid me. If another came, acting self-important, you would welcome him with open arms. How do you expect to get anywhere with God when you spend all your time jockeying for position with each other, ranking your rivals and ignoring God?

45-47 "But don't think I'm going to accuse you before my Father. Moses, in whom you put so much stock, is your accuser. If you believed, really believed, what Moses said, you would believe me. He wrote of me. If you won't take seriously what *he* wrote, how can I expect you to take seriously what *I* speak?"

BREAD AND FISH FOR ALL

1-4 6 After this, Jesus went across the Sea of Galilee (some call it Tiberias). A huge crowd followed him, attracted by the miracles they had seen him do among the sick. When he got to the other side, he climbed a hill and sat down, surrounded by his disciples. It was nearly time for the Feast of Passover, kept annually by the Jews.

5-6 When Jesus looked out and saw that a large crowd had arrived, he said to Philip, "Where can we buy bread to feed these people?" He said this to stretch Philip's faith. He already knew what he was going to do.

7 Philip answered, "Two hundred silver pieces wouldn't be enough to buy bread for each person to get a piece."

8-9 One of the disciples—it was Andrew, brother to Simon Peter—said, "There's a little boy here who has five barley loaves and two fish. But that's a drop in the bucket for a crowd like this."

10-11 Jesus said, "Make the people sit down." There was a nice carpet of green grass in this place. They sat down, about five thousand of them. Then Jesus took the bread and, having given thanks, gave it to those who were seated. He did the same with the fish. All ate as much as they wanted.

12-13 When the people had eaten their fill, he said to his disciples, "Gather the leftovers so nothing is wasted." They went to work and

NEW KING JAMES VERSION

gathered *them* up, and filled twelve baskets with the fragments of the five barley loaves which were left over by those who had eaten. [14]Then those men, when they had seen the sign that Jesus did, said, "This is truly the Prophet who is to come into the world."

JESUS WALKS ON THE SEA

[15]Therefore when Jesus perceived that they were about to come and take Him by force to make Him king, He departed again to the mountain by Himself alone.

[16]Now when evening came, His disciples went down to the sea, [17]got into the boat, and went over the sea toward Capernaum. And it was already dark, and Jesus had not come to them. [18]Then the sea arose because a great wind was blowing. [19]So when they had rowed about three or four miles,[a] they saw Jesus walking on the sea and drawing near the boat; and they were afraid. [20]But He said to them, "It is I; do not be afraid." [21]Then they willingly received Him into the boat, and immediately the boat was at the land where they were going.

THE BREAD FROM HEAVEN

[22]On the following day, when the people who were standing on the other side of the sea saw that there was no other boat there, except that one which His disciples had entered,[a] and that Jesus had not entered the boat with His disciples, but His disciples had gone away alone— [23]however, other boats came from Tiberias, near the place where they ate bread after the Lord had given thanks— [24]when the people therefore saw that Jesus was not there, nor His disciples, they also got into boats and came to Capernaum, seeking Jesus. [25]And when they found Him on the other side of the sea, they said to Him, "Rabbi, when did You come here?"

[26]Jesus answered them and said, "Most assuredly, I say to you, you seek Me, not because you saw the signs, but because you ate of the loaves and were filled. [27]Do not labor for the food which perishes, but for the food which endures to everlasting life, which the Son of Man will give you, because God the Father has set His seal on Him."

[28]Then they said to Him, "What shall we do, that we may work the works of God?"

[29]Jesus answered and said to them, "This is the work of God, that you believe in Him whom He sent."

[30]Therefore they said to Him, "What sign will You perform then, that we may see it and believe You? What work will You do? [31]Our fathers ate the manna in the desert; as it is written, *'He gave them bread from heaven to eat.'* "[a]

[32]Then Jesus said to them, "Most assuredly, I say to you, Moses did not give you the bread from heaven, but My Father gives you the true bread from heaven. [33]For the bread of God is He who comes down from heaven and gives life to the world."

[34]Then they said to Him, "Lord, give us this bread always."

6:19 [a]Literally *twenty-five or thirty stadia* **6:22** [a]NU-Text omits *that* and *which His disciples had entered.* **6:31** [a]Exodus 16:4; Nehemiah 9:15; Psalm 78:24

THE MESSAGE

filled twelve large baskets with leftovers from the five barley loaves.

14-15 The people realized that God was at work among them in what Jesus had just done. They said, "This is the Prophet for sure, God's Prophet right here in Galilee!" Jesus saw that in their enthusiasm, they were about to grab him and make him king, so he slipped off and went back up the mountain to be by himself.

16-21 In the evening his disciples went down to the sea, got in the boat, and headed back across the water to Capernaum. It had grown quite dark and Jesus had not yet returned. A huge wind blew up, churning the sea. They were maybe three or four miles out when they saw Jesus walking on the sea, quite near the boat. They were scared senseless, but he reassured them, "It's me. It's all right. Don't be afraid." So they took him on board. In no time they reached land—the exact spot they were headed to.

22-24 The next day the crowd that was left behind realized that there had been only one boat, and that Jesus had not gotten into it with his disciples. They had seen them go off without him. By now boats from Tiberias had pulled up near where they had eaten the bread blessed by the Master. So when the crowd realized he was gone and wasn't coming back, they piled into the Tiberias boats and headed for Capernaum, looking for Jesus.

25 When they found him back across the sea, they said, "Rabbi, when did you get here?"

26 Jesus answered, "You've come looking for me not because you saw God in my actions but because I fed you, filled your stomachs—and for free.

THE BREAD OF LIFE

27 "Don't waste your energy striving for perishable food like that. Work for the food that sticks with you, food that nourishes your lasting life, food the Son of Man provides. He and what he does are guaranteed by God the Father to last."

28 To that they said, "Well, what do we do then to get in on God's works?"

29 Jesus said, "Throw your lot in with the One that God has sent. That kind of a commitment gets you in on God's works."

30-31 They waffled: "Why don't you give us a clue about who you are, just a hint of what's going on? When we see what's up, we'll commit ourselves. Show us what you can do. Moses fed our ancestors with bread in the desert. It says so in the Scriptures: 'He gave them bread from heaven to eat.' "

32-33 Jesus responded, "The real significance of that Scripture is not that Moses gave you bread from heaven but that my Father is right now offering you bread from heaven, the *real* bread. The Bread of God came down out of heaven and is giving life to the world."

34 They jumped at that: "Master, give us this bread, now and forever!"

NEW KING JAMES VERSION

[35]And Jesus said to them, "I am the bread of
life. He who comes to Me shall never hunger,
and he who believes in Me shall never thirst.
[36]But I said to you that you have seen Me and yet
do not believe. [37]All that the Father gives Me will
come to Me, and the one who comes to Me I will
by no means cast out. [38]For I have come down
from heaven, not to do My own will, but the will
of Him who sent Me. [39]This is the will of the Fa-
ther who sent Me, that of all He has given Me I
should lose nothing, but should raise it up at the
last day. [40]And this is the will of Him who sent
Me, that everyone who sees the Son and be-
lieves in Him may have everlasting life; and I
will raise him up at the last day."

REJECTED BY HIS OWN

[41]The Jews then complained about Him, be-
cause He said, "I am the bread which came
down from heaven." [42]And they said, "Is not this
Jesus, the son of Joseph, whose father and
mother we know? How is it then that He says, 'I
have come down from heaven'?"

[43]Jesus therefore answered and said to them,
"Do not murmur among yourselves. [44]No one
can come to Me unless the Father who sent Me
draws him; and I will raise him up at the last
day. [45]It is written in the prophets, *'And they
shall all be taught by God.'* [a] Therefore everyone
who has heard and learned[b] from the Father
comes to Me. [46]Not that anyone has seen the Fa-
ther, except He who is from God; He has seen
the Father. [47]Most assuredly, I say to you, he who
believes in Me[a] has everlasting life. [48]I am the
bread of life. [49]Your fathers ate the manna in the
wilderness, and are dead. [50]This is the bread
which comes down from heaven, that one may
eat of it and not die. [51]I am the living bread
which came down from heaven. If anyone eats
of this bread, he will live forever; and the bread
that I shall give is My flesh, which I shall give
for the life of the world."

[52]The Jews therefore quarreled among them-
selves, saying, "How can this Man give us *His*
flesh to eat?"

[53]Then Jesus said to them, "Most assuredly, I
say to you, unless you eat the flesh of the Son of
Man and drink His blood, you have no life in
you. [54]Whoever eats My flesh and drinks My
blood has eternal life, and I will raise him up at
the last day. [55]For My flesh is food indeed,[a] and
My blood is drink indeed. [56]He who eats My
flesh and drinks My blood abides in Me, and I in

6:45 [a]Isaiah 54:13 [b]M-Text reads *hears and has learned.* **6:47** [a]NU-Text omits *in Me.* **6:55** [a]NU-Text reads *true food* and *true drink.*

THE MESSAGE

35-38 Jesus said, "I am the Bread of Life. The
person who aligns with me hungers no
more and thirsts no more, ever. I have told
you this explicitly because even though you
have seen me in action, you don't really be-
lieve me. Every person the Father gives me
eventually comes running to me. And once
that person is with me, I hold on and don't
let go. I came down from heaven not to fol-
low my own whim but to accomplish the
will of the One who sent me.

39-40 "This, in a nutshell, is that will: that
everything handed over to me by the Father
be completed—not a single detail missed—
and at the wrap-up of time I have everything
and everyone put together, upright and
whole. This is what my Father wants: that
anyone who sees the Son and trusts who he
is and what he does and then aligns with
him will enter *real* life, *eternal* life. My part
is to put them on their feet alive and whole
at the completion of time."

41-42 At this, because he said, "I am the Bread
that came down from heaven," the Jews
started arguing over him: "Isn't this the son
of Joseph? Don't we know his father? Don't
we know his mother? How can he now say,
'I came down out of heaven' and expect any-
one to believe him?"

43-46 Jesus said, "Don't bicker among your-
selves over me. You're not in charge here.
The Father who sent me is in charge. He
draws people to me—that's the only way
you'll ever come. Only then do I do my
work, putting people together, setting them
on their feet, ready for the End. This is what
the prophets meant when they wrote, 'And
then they will all be personally taught by
God.' Anyone who has spent any time at all
listening to the Father, really listening and
therefore learning, comes to me to be taught
personally—to see it with his own eyes, hear
it with his own ears, from me, since I have it
firsthand from the Father. No one has seen
the Father except the One who has his Being
alongside the Father—and you can see *me*.

47-51 "I'm telling you the most solemn and
sober truth now: Whoever believes in me
has real life, eternal life. I am the Bread of
Life. Your ancestors ate the manna bread in
the desert and died. But now here is Bread
that truly comes down out of heaven. Any-
one eating this Bread will not die, ever. I am
the Bread—living Bread!—who came down
out of heaven. Anyone who eats this Bread
will live—and forever! The Bread that I
present to the world so that it can eat and
live is myself, this flesh-and-blood self."

52 At this, the Jews started fighting among
themselves: "How can this man serve up his
flesh for a meal?"

53-58 But Jesus didn't give an inch. "Only inso-
far as you eat and drink flesh and blood, the
flesh and blood of the Son of Man, do you
have life within you. The one who brings a
hearty appetite to this eating and drinking
has eternal life and will be fit and ready for
the Final Day. My flesh is real food and my
blood is real drink. By eating my flesh and
drinking my blood you enter into me and I

NEW KING JAMES VERSION

him. 57As the living Father sent Me, and I live be-
cause of the Father, so he who feeds on Me will
live because of Me. 58This is the bread which
came down from heaven—not as your fathers
ate the manna, and are dead. He who eats this
bread will live forever."

59These things He said in the synagogue as
He taught in Capernaum.

MANY DISCIPLES TURN AWAY

60Therefore many of His disciples, when they
heard *this,* said, "This is a hard saying; who can
understand it?"

61When Jesus knew in Himself that His disci-
ples complained about this, He said to them,
"Does this offend you? 62*What* then if you
should see the Son of Man ascend where He
was before? 63It is the Spirit who gives life; the
flesh profits nothing. The words that I speak to
you are spirit, and *they* are life. 64But there are
some of you who do not believe." For Jesus
knew from the beginning who they were who
did not believe, and who would betray Him.
65And He said, "Therefore I have said to you that
no one can come to Me unless it has been
granted to him by My Father."

66From that *time* many of His disciples went
back and walked with Him no more. 67Then Je-
sus said to the twelve, "Do you also want to go
away?"

68But Simon Peter answered Him, "Lord, to
whom shall we go? You have the words of eter-
nal life. 69Also we have come to believe and
know that You are the Christ, the Son of the liv-
ing God."[a]

70Jesus answered them, "Did I not choose
you, the twelve, and one of you is a devil?" 71He
spoke of Judas Iscariot, *the son* of Simon, for it
was he who would betray Him, being one of the
twelve.

JESUS' BROTHERS DISBELIEVE

7 After these things Jesus walked in Galilee;
for He did not want to walk in Judea, because
the Jews[a] sought to kill Him. 2Now the Jews'
Feast of Tabernacles was at hand. 3His brothers
therefore said to Him, "Depart from here and go
into Judea, that Your disciples also may see the
works that You are doing. 4For no one does any-
thing in secret while he himself seeks to be
known openly. If You do these things, show Your-
self to the world." 5For even His brothers did not
believe in Him.

6Then Jesus said to them, "My time has not
yet come, but your time is always ready. 7The
world cannot hate you, but it hates Me because
I testify of it that its works are evil. 8You go up
to this feast. I am not yet[a] going up to this feast,
for My time has not yet fully come." 9When He
had said these things to them, He remained in
Galilee.

6:69 [a]NU-Text reads *You are the Holy One of God.* **7:1** [a]That is, the ruling authorities **7:8** [a]NU-Text omits *yet.*

THE MESSAGE

into you. In the same way that the fully alive Father sent me here and I live because of him, so the one who makes a meal of me lives because of me. This is the Bread from heaven. Your ancestors ate bread and later died. Whoever eats this Bread will live always."

59 He said these things while teaching in the meeting place in Capernaum.

TOO TOUGH TO SWALLOW

60 Many among his disciples heard this and said, "This is tough teaching, too tough to swallow."

61-65 Jesus sensed that his disciples were having a hard time with this and said, "Does this throw you completely? What would happen if you saw the Son of Man ascending to where he came from? The Spirit can make life. Sheer muscle and willpower don't make anything happen. Every word I've spoken to you is a Spirit-word, and so it is life-making. But some of you are resisting, refusing to have any part in this." (Jesus knew from the start that some weren't going to risk themselves with him. He knew also who would betray him.) He went on to say, "This is why I told you earlier that no one is capable of coming to me on his own. You get to me only as a gift from the Father."

66-67 After this a lot of his disciples left. They no longer wanted to be associated with him. Then Jesus gave the Twelve their chance: "Do you also want to leave?"

68-69 Peter replied, "Master, to whom would we go? You have the words of real life, eternal life. We've already committed ourselves, confident that you are the Holy One of God."

70-71 Jesus responded, "Haven't I handpicked you, the Twelve? Still, one of you is a devil!" He was referring to Judas, son of Simon Iscariot. This man—one from the Twelve!—was even then getting ready to betray him.

1-2 7 Later Jesus was going about his business in Galilee. He didn't want to travel in Judea because the Jews there were looking for a chance to kill him. It was near the time of Tabernacles, a feast observed annually by the Jews.

3-5 His brothers said, "Why don't you leave here and go up to the Feast so your disciples can get a good look at the works you do? No one who intends to be publicly known does everything behind the scenes. If you're serious about what you are doing, come out in the open and show the world." His brothers were pushing him like this because they didn't believe in him either.

6-8 Jesus came back at them, "Don't crowd me. This isn't my time. It's your time—it's *always* your time; you have nothing to lose. The world has nothing against you, but it's up in arms against me. It's against me because I expose the evil behind its pretensions. You go ahead, go up to the Feast. Don't wait for me. I'm not ready. It's not the right time for me."

9-11 He said this and stayed on in Galilee. But later, after his family had gone up to the

New King James Version

The Heavenly Scholar

[10]But when His brothers had gone up, then
He also went up to the feast, not openly, but as
it were in secret. [11]Then the Jews sought Him at
the feast, and said, "Where is He?" [12]And there
was much complaining among the people con-
cerning Him. Some said, "He is good"; others
said, "No, on the contrary, He deceives the peo-
ple." [13]However, no one spoke openly of Him for
fear of the Jews.

[14]Now about the middle of the feast Jesus
went up into the temple and taught. [15]And the
Jews marveled, saying, "How does this Man
know letters, having never studied?"

[16]Jesus[a] answered them and said, "My doc-
trine is not Mine, but His who sent Me. [17]If any-
one wills to do His will, he shall know concern-
ing the doctrine, whether it is from God or
whether I speak on My own *authority*. [18]He who
speaks from himself seeks his own glory; but He
who seeks the glory of the One who sent Him is
true, and no unrighteousness is in Him. [19]Did
not Moses give you the law, yet none of you
keeps the law? Why do you seek to kill Me?"

[20]The people answered and said, "You have a
demon. Who is seeking to kill You?"

[21]Jesus answered and said to them, "I did one
work, and you all marvel. [22]Moses therefore
gave you circumcision (not that it is from Moses,
but from the fathers), and you circumcise a man
on the Sabbath. [23]If a man receives circumcision
on the Sabbath, so that the law of Moses should
not be broken, are you angry with Me because I
made a man completely well on the Sabbath?
[24]Do not judge according to appearance, but
judge with righteous judgment."

Could This Be the Christ?

[25]Now some of them from Jerusalem said, "Is
this not He whom they seek to kill? [26]But look!
He speaks boldly, and they say nothing to Him.
Do the rulers know indeed that this is truly[a] the
Christ? [27]However, we know where this Man is
from; but when the Christ comes, no one knows
where He is from."

[28]Then Jesus cried out, as He taught in the
temple, saying, "You both know Me, and you
know where I am from; and I have not come of
Myself, but He who sent Me is true, whom you
do not know. [29]But[a] I know Him, for I am from
Him, and He sent Me."

[30]Therefore they sought to take Him; but no
one laid a hand on Him, because His hour had
not yet come. [31]And many of the people believed
in Him, and said, "When the Christ comes, will
He do more signs than these which this *Man* has
done?"

7:16 [a]NU-Text and M-Text read *So Jesus*. **7:26** [a]NU-Text omits *truly*. **7:29** [a]NU-Text and M-Text omit *But*.

The Message

Feast, he also went. But he kept out of the way, careful not to draw attention to himself. The Jews were already out looking for him, asking around, "Where is that man?"

12-13 There was a lot of contentious talk about him circulating through the crowds. Some were saying, "He's a good man." But others said, "Not so. He's selling snake oil." This kind of talk went on in guarded whispers because of the intimidating Jewish leaders.

Could It Be the Messiah?

14-15 With the Feast already half over, Jesus showed up in the Temple, teaching. The Jews were impressed, but puzzled: "How does he know so much without being schooled?"

16-19 Jesus said, "I didn't make this up. What I teach comes from the One who sent me. Anyone who wants to do his will can test this teaching and know whether it's from God or whether I'm making it up. A person making things up tries to make himself look good. But someone trying to honor the one who sent him sticks to the facts and doesn't tamper with reality. It was Moses, wasn't it, who gave you God's Law? But none of you are living it. So why are you trying to kill me?"

20 The crowd said, "You're crazy! Who's trying to kill you? You're demon-possessed."

21-24 Jesus said, "I did one miraculous thing a few months ago, and you're still standing around getting all upset, wondering what I'm up to. Moses prescribed circumcision—originally it came not from Moses but from his ancestors—and so you circumcise a man, dealing with one part of his body, even if it's the Sabbath. You do this in order to preserve one item in the Law of Moses. So why are you upset with me because I made a man's whole body well on the Sabbath? Don't be nitpickers; use your head—and heart!—to discern what is right, to test what is authentically right."

25-27 That's when some of the people of Jerusalem said, "Isn't this the one they were out to kill? And here he is out in the open, saying whatever he pleases, and no one is stopping him. Could it be that the rulers know that he is, in fact, the Messiah? And yet we know where this man came from. The Messiah is going to come out of nowhere. Nobody is going to know where he comes from."

28-29 That provoked Jesus, who was teaching in the Temple, to cry out, "Yes, you think you know me and where I'm from, but that's not where I'm from. I didn't set myself up in business. My true origin is in the One who sent me, and you don't know him at all. I come from him—that's how I know him. He sent me here."

30-31 They were looking for a way to arrest him, but not a hand was laid on him because it wasn't yet God's time. Many from the crowd committed themselves in faith to him, saying, "Will the Messiah, when he comes, provide better or more convincing evidence than this?"

NEW KING JAMES VERSION

JESUS AND THE RELIGIOUS LEADERS

32 The Pharisees heard the crowd murmuring these things concerning Him, and the Pharisees and the chief priests sent officers to take Him. 33 Then Jesus said to them,[a] "I shall be with you a little while longer, and *then* I go to Him who sent Me. 34 You will seek Me and not find *Me,* and where I am you cannot come."

35 Then the Jews said among themselves, "Where does He intend to go that we shall not find Him? Does He intend to go to the Dispersion among the Greeks and teach the Greeks? 36 What is this thing that He said, 'You will seek Me and not find Me, and where I am you cannot come'?"

THE PROMISE OF THE HOLY SPIRIT

37 On the last day, that great *day* of the feast, Jesus stood and cried out, saying, "If anyone thirsts, let him come to Me and drink. 38 He who believes in Me, as the Scripture has said, out of his heart will flow rivers of living water." 39 But this He spoke concerning the Spirit, whom those believing[a] in Him would receive; for the Holy[b] Spirit was not yet *given,* because Jesus was not yet glorified.

WHO IS HE?

40 Therefore many[a] from the crowd, when they heard this saying, said, "Truly this is the Prophet." 41 Others said, "This is the Christ."

But some said, "Will the Christ come out of Galilee? 42 Has not the Scripture said that the Christ comes from the seed of David and from the town of Bethlehem, where David was?" 43 So there was a division among the people because of Him. 44 Now some of them wanted to take Him, but no one laid hands on Him.

REJECTED BY THE AUTHORITIES

45 Then the officers came to the chief priests and Pharisees, who said to them, "Why have you not brought Him?"

46 The officers answered, "No man ever spoke like this Man!"

47 Then the Pharisees answered them, "Are you also deceived? 48 Have any of the rulers or the Pharisees believed in Him? 49 But this crowd that does not know the law is accursed."

50 Nicodemus (he who came to Jesus by night,[a] being one of them) said to them, 51 "Does our law judge a man before it hears him and knows what he is doing?"

52 They answered and said to him, "Are you also from Galilee? Search and look, for no prophet has arisen[a] out of Galilee."

AN ADULTERESS FACES THE LIGHT OF THE WORLD

53 And everyone went to his *own* house.[a]

8 But Jesus went to the Mount of Olives. 2 Now early[a] in the morning He came again into the temple, and all the people came to Him; and He sat down and taught them.

7:33 [a]NU-Text and M-Text omit *to them.* 7:39 [a]NU-Text reads *who believed.* [b]NU-Text omits Holy. 7:40 [a]NU-Text reads *some.* 7:50 [a]NU-Text reads *before.* 7:52 [a]NU-Text reads *is to rise.* 7:53 [a]The words *And everyone* through *sin no more* (8:11) are bracketed by NU-Text as not original. They are present in over 900 manuscripts. 8:2 [a]M-Text reads *very early.*

THE MESSAGE

32-34 The Pharisees, alarmed at this seditious
undertow going through the crowd, teamed
up with the high priests and sent their police
to arrest him. Jesus rebuffed them: "I am with
you only a short time. Then I go on to the One
who sent me. You will look for me, but you
won't find me. Where I am, you can't come."
35-36 The Jews put their heads together.
"Where do you think he is going that we
won't be able to find him? Do you think he
is about to travel to the Greek world to teach
the Jews? What is he talking about, anyway:
'You will look for me, but you won't find
me,' and 'Where I am, you can't come'?"
37-39 On the final and climactic day of the
Feast, Jesus took his stand. He cried out, "If
anyone thirsts, let him come to me and
drink. Rivers of living water will brim and
spill out of the depths of anyone who be-
lieves in me this way, just as the Scripture
says." (He said this in regard to the Spirit,
whom those who believed in him were about
to receive. The Spirit had not yet been given
because Jesus had not yet been glorified.)
40-44 Those in the crowd who heard these words
were saying, "This has to be the Prophet."
Others said, "He is the Messiah!" But others
were saying, "The Messiah doesn't come from
Galilee, does he? Don't the Scriptures tell us
that the Messiah comes from David's line and
from Bethlehem, David's village?" So there
was a split in the crowd over him. Some went
so far as wanting to arrest him, but no one
laid a hand on him.
45 That's when the Temple police reported
back to the high priests and Pharisees, who
demanded, "Why didn't you bring him with
you?"
46 The police answered, "Have you heard
the way he talks? We've never heard anyone
speak like this man."
47-49 The Pharisees said, "Are you carried
away like the rest of the rabble? You don't
see any of the leaders believing in him, do
you? Or any from the Pharisees? It's only
this crowd, ignorant of God's Law, that is
taken in by him—and damned."
50-51 Nicodemus, the man who had come to Je-
sus earlier and was both a ruler and a Phar-
isee, spoke up. "Does our Law decide about
a man's guilt without first listening to him
and finding out what he is doing?"
52-53 But they cut him off. "Are you also cam-
paigning for the Galilean? Examine the evi-
dence. See if any prophet ever comes from
Galilee."

Then they all went home.

TO THROW THE STONE

1-2 8 Jesus went across to Mount Olives, but he
was soon back in the Temple again.
Swarms of people came to him. He sat down
and taught them.

New King James Version

3Then the scribes and Pharisees brought to Him
a woman caught in adultery. And when they had
set her in the midst, 4they said to Him, "Teacher,
this woman was caught[a] in adultery, in the very
act. 5Now Moses, in the law, commanded[a] us
that such should be stoned.[b] But what do You
say?"[c] 6This they said, testing Him, that they
might have *something* of which to accuse Him.
But Jesus stooped down and wrote on the
ground with *His* finger, as though He did not
hear.[a]
7So when they continued asking Him, He
raised Himself up[a] and said to them, "He who is
without sin among you, let him throw a stone at
her first." 8And again He stooped down and
wrote on the ground. 9Then those who heard *it*,
being convicted by *their* conscience,[a] went out
one by one, beginning with the oldest *even* to
the last. And Jesus was left alone, and the
woman standing in the midst. 10When Jesus had
raised Himself up and saw no one but the
woman, He said to her,[a] "Woman, where are
those accusers of yours?[b] Has no one con-
demned you?"
11She said, "No one, Lord."
And Jesus said to her, "Neither do I condemn
you; go and[a] sin no more."
12Then Jesus spoke to them again, saying, "I
am the light of the world. He who follows Me
shall not walk in darkness, but have the light of
life."

Jesus Defends His Self-Witness

13The Pharisees therefore said to Him, "You
bear witness of Yourself; Your witness is not
true."
14Jesus answered and said to them, "Even if I
bear witness of Myself, My witness is true, for I
know where I came from and where I am going;
but you do not know where I come from and
where I am going. 15You judge according to the
flesh; I judge no one. 16And yet if I do judge, My
judgment is true; for I am not alone, but I *am*
with the Father who sent Me. 17It is also written
in your law that the testimony of two men is
true. 18I am One who bears witness of Myself,
and the Father who sent Me bears witness of
Me."
19Then they said to Him, "Where is Your Fa-
ther?"
Jesus answered, "You know neither Me nor
My Father. If you had known Me, you would
have known My Father also."
20These words Jesus spoke in the treasury, as
He taught in the temple; and no one laid hands
on Him, for His hour had not yet come.

Jesus Predicts His Departure

21Then Jesus said to them again, "I am going
away, and you will seek Me, and will die in your
sin. Where I go you cannot come."

8:4 [a]M-Text reads *we found this woman.* **8:5** [a]M-Text reads *in our law Moses commanded.* [b]NU-Text and M-Text read *to stone such.* [c]M-Text adds *about her.* **8:6** [a]NU-Text and M-Text omit *as though He did not hear.* **8:7** [a]M-Text reads *He looked up.* **8:9** [a]NU-Text and M-Text omit *being convicted by their conscience.* **8:10** [a]NU-Text omits *and saw no one but the woman;* M-Text reads *He saw her and said.* [b]NU-Text and M-Text omit *of yours.* **8:11** [a]NU-Text and M-Text add *from now on.*

The Message

3-6 The religion scholars and Pharisees led
in a woman who had been caught in an act
of adultery. They stood her in plain sight of
everyone and said, "Teacher, this woman
was caught red-handed in the act of adul-
tery. Moses, in the Law, gives orders to stone
such persons. What do you say?" They were
trying to trap him into saying something in-
criminating so they could bring charges
against him.
6-8 Jesus bent down and wrote with his fin-
ger in the dirt. They kept at him, badgering
him. He straightened up and said, "The sin-
less one among you, go first: Throw the
stone." Bending down again, he wrote some
more in the dirt.
9-10 Hearing that, they walked away, one after
another, beginning with the oldest. The
woman was left alone. Jesus stood up and
spoke to her. "Woman, where are they? Does
no one condemn you?"
11 "No one, Master."
"Neither do I," said Jesus. "Go on your
way. From now on, don't sin."

You're Missing God in All This

12 Jesus once again addressed them: "I am the
world's Light. No one who follows me stum-
bles around in the darkness. I provide
plenty of light to live in."
13 The Pharisees objected, "All we have is
your word on this. We need more than this
to go on."
14-18 Jesus replied, "You're right that you only
have my word. But you can depend on it be-
ing true. I know where I've come from and
where I go next. You don't know where I'm
from or where I'm headed. You decide ac-
cording to what you can see and touch. I
don't make judgments like that. But even if
I did, my judgment would be true because I
wouldn't make it out of the narrowness of
my experience but in the largeness of the
One who sent me, the Father. That fulfills
the conditions set down in God's Law: that
you can count on the testimony of two wit-
nesses. And that is what you have: You have
my word and you have the word of the Fa-
ther who sent me."
19 They said, "Where is this so-called Father
of yours?"
Jesus said, "You're looking right at me
and you don't see me. How do you expect to
see the Father? If you knew me, you would
at the same time know the Father."
20 He gave this speech in the Treasury while
teaching in the Temple. No one arrested him
because his time wasn't yet up.
21 Then he went over the same ground
again. "I'm leaving and you are going to
look for me, but you're missing God in this
and are headed for a dead end. There is no
way you can come with me."

NEW KING JAMES VERSION

22So the Jews said, "Will He kill Himself, be-
cause He says, 'Where I go you cannot come'?"
23And He said to them, "You are from be-
neath; I am from above. You are of this world; I
am not of this world. 24Therefore I said to you
that you will die in your sins; for if you do not
believe that I am *He*, you will die in your sins."
25Then they said to Him, "Who are You?"
And Jesus said to them, "Just what I have
been saying to you from the beginning. 26I have
many things to say and to judge concerning you,
but He who sent Me is true; and I speak to the
world those things which I heard from Him."
27They did not understand that He spoke to
them of the Father.
28Then Jesus said to them, "When you lift up
the Son of Man, then you will know that I am
He, and *that* I do nothing of Myself; but as My
Father taught Me, I speak these things. 29And He
who sent Me is with Me. The Father has not left
Me alone, for I always do those things that
please Him." 30As He spoke these words, many
believed in Him.

THE TRUTH SHALL MAKE YOU FREE

31Then Jesus said to those Jews who believed
Him, "If you abide in My word, you are My dis-
ciples indeed. 32And you shall know the truth,
and the truth shall make you free."
33They answered Him, "We are Abraham's
descendants, and have never been in bondage to
anyone. How *can* You say, 'You will be made
free'?"
34Jesus answered them, "Most assuredly, I
say to you, whoever commits sin is a slave of
sin. 35And a slave does not abide in the house
forever, *but* a son abides forever. 36Therefore if
the Son makes you free, you shall be free in-
deed.

ABRAHAM'S SEED AND SATAN'S

37"I know that you are Abraham's descen-
dants, but you seek to kill Me, because My word
has no place in you. 38I speak what I have seen
with My Father, and you do what you have seen
with[a] your father."
39They answered and said to Him, "Abraham
is our father."
Jesus said to them, "If you were Abraham's
children, you would do the works of Abraham.
40But now you seek to kill Me, a Man who has
told you the truth which I heard from God.
Abraham did not do this. 41You do the deeds of
your father."
Then they said to Him, "We were not born of
fornication; we have one Father—God."
42Jesus said to them, "If God were your Fa-
ther, you would love Me, for I proceeded forth

8:38 [a]NU-Text reads *heard from.*

THE MESSAGE

22 The Jews said, "So, is he going to kill
himself? Is that what he means by 'You can't
come with me'?"
23-24 Jesus said, "You're tied down to the mun-
dane; I'm in touch with what is beyond your
horizons. You live in terms of what you see
and touch. I'm living on other terms. I told
you that you were missing God in all this.
You're at a dead end. If you won't believe I
am who I say I am, you're at the dead end of
sins. You're missing God in your lives."
25-26 They said to him, "Just who are you any-
way?"
Jesus said, "What I've said from the start.
I have so many things to say that concern
you, judgments to make that affect you, but
if you don't accept the trustworthiness of the
One who commanded my words and acts,
none of it matters. That is who you are ques-
tioning—not me but the One who sent me."
27-29 They still didn't get it, didn't realize that
he was referring to the Father. So Jesus tried
again. "When you raise up the Son of Man,
then you will know who I am—that I'm not
making this up, but speaking only what the
Father taught me. The One who sent me
stays with me. He doesn't abandon me. He
sees how much joy I take in pleasing him."
30 When he put it in these terms, many peo-
ple decided to believe.

IF THE SON SETS YOU FREE

31-32 Then Jesus turned to the Jews who had
claimed to believe in him. "If you stick with
this, living out what I tell you, you are my
disciples for sure. Then you will experience
for yourselves the truth, and the truth will
free you."
33 Surprised, they said, "But we're descen-
dants of Abraham. We've never been slaves
to anyone. How can you say, 'The truth will
free you'?"
34-38 Jesus said, "I tell you most solemnly that
anyone who chooses a life of sin is trapped
in a dead-end life and is, in fact, a slave. A
slave is a transient, who can't come and go
at will. The Son, though, has an established
position, the run of the house. So if the Son
sets you free, you are free through and
through. I know you are Abraham's descen-
dants. But I also know that you are trying to
kill me because my message hasn't yet pen-
etrated your thick skulls. I'm talking about
things I have seen while keeping company
with the Father, and you just go on doing
what you have heard from your father."
39-41 They were indignant. "Our father is Abra-
ham!"
Jesus said, "If you were Abraham's chil-
dren, you would have been doing the things
Abraham did. And yet here you are trying to
kill me, a man who has spoken to you the
truth he got straight from God! Abraham
never did that sort of thing. You persist in re-
peating the works of your father."
They said, "We're not bastards. We have a
legitimate father: the one and only God."
42-47 "If God were your father," said Jesus,
"you would love me, for I came from God

NEW KING JAMES VERSION

and came from God; nor have I come of Myself, but He sent Me. [43]Why do you not understand My speech? Because you are not able to listen to My word. [44]You are of *your* father the devil, and the desires of your father you want to do. He was a murderer from the beginning, and does not stand in the truth, because there is no truth in him. When he speaks a lie, he speaks from his own *resources,* for he is a liar and the father of it. [45]But because I tell the truth, you do not believe Me. [46]Which of you convicts Me of sin? And if I tell the truth, why do you not believe Me? [47]He who is of God hears God's words; therefore you do not hear, because you are not of God."

BEFORE ABRAHAM WAS, I AM

[48]Then the Jews answered and said to Him, "Do we not say rightly that You are a Samaritan and have a demon?"

[49]Jesus answered, "I do not have a demon; but I honor My Father, and you dishonor Me. [50]And I do not seek My *own* glory; there is One who seeks and judges. [51]Most assuredly, I say to you, if anyone keeps My word he shall never see death."

[52]Then the Jews said to Him, "Now we know that You have a demon! Abraham is dead, and the prophets; and You say, 'If anyone keeps My word he shall never taste death.' [53]Are You greater than our father Abraham, who is dead? And the prophets are dead. Who do You make Yourself out to be?"

[54]Jesus answered, "If I honor Myself, My honor is nothing. It is My Father who honors Me, of whom you say that He is your[a] God. [55]Yet you have not known Him, but I know Him. And if I say, 'I do not know Him,' I shall be a liar like you; but I do know Him and keep His word. [56]Your father Abraham rejoiced to see My day, and he saw *it* and was glad."

[57]Then the Jews said to Him, "You are not yet fifty years old, and have You seen Abraham?"

[58]Jesus said to them, "Most assuredly, I say to you, before Abraham was, I AM."

[59]Then they took up stones to throw at Him; but Jesus hid Himself and went out of the temple,[a] going through the midst of them, and so passed by.

A MAN BORN BLIND RECEIVES SIGHT

9 Now as *Jesus* passed by, He saw a man who was blind from birth. [2]And His disciples asked Him, saying, "Rabbi, who sinned, this man or his parents, that he was born blind?"

[3]Jesus answered, "Neither this man nor his parents sinned, but that the works of God should be revealed in him. [4]I[a] must work the

8:54 [a]NU-Text and M-Text read *our.* **8:59** [a]NU-Text omits the rest of this verse. **9:4** [a]NU-Text reads *We.*

THE MESSAGE

and arrived here. I didn't come on my own. He sent me. Why can't you understand one word I say? Here's why: You can't handle it. You're from your father, the Devil, and all you want to do is please him. He was a killer from the very start. He couldn't stand the truth because there wasn't a shred of truth in him. When the Liar speaks, he makes it up out of his lying nature and fills the world with lies. I arrive on the scene, tell you the plain truth, and you refuse to have a thing to do with me. Can any one of you convict me of a single misleading word, a single sinful act? But if I'm telling the truth, why don't you believe me? Anyone on God's side listens to God's words. This is why you're not listening—because you're not on God's side."

I AM WHO I AM

48 The Jews then said, "That clinches it. We were right all along when we called you a Samaritan and said you were crazy—demon-possessed!"

49-51 Jesus said, "I'm not crazy. I simply honor my Father, while you dishonor me. I am not trying to get anything for myself. God intends something gloriously grand here and is making the decisions that will bring it about. I say this with absolute confidence. If you practice what I'm telling you, you'll never have to look death in the face."

52-53 At this point the Jews said, "Now we *know* you're crazy. Abraham died. The prophets died. And you show up saying, 'If you practice what I'm telling you, you'll never have to face death, not even a taste.' Are you greater than Abraham, who died? And the prophets died! Who do you think you are!"

54-56 Jesus said, "If I turned the spotlight on myself, it wouldn't amount to anything. But my Father, the same One you say is your Father, put me here at this time and place of splendor. You haven't recognized him in this. But I have. If I, in false modesty, said I didn't know what was going on, I would be as much of a liar as you are. But I do know, and I am doing what he says. Abraham—your 'father'—with jubilant faith looked down the corridors of history and saw my day coming. He saw it and cheered."

57 The Jews said, "You're not even fifty years old—and Abraham saw you?"

58 "Believe me," said Jesus, "*I am who I am* long before Abraham was anything."

59 That did it—pushed them over the edge. They picked up rocks to throw at him. But Jesus slipped away, getting out of the Temple.

TRUE BLINDNESS

1-2 **9** Walking down the street, Jesus saw a man blind from birth. His disciples asked, "Rabbi, who sinned: this man or his parents, causing him to be born blind?"

3-5 Jesus said, "You're asking the wrong question. You're looking for someone to blame. There is no such cause-effect here. Look instead for what God can do. We need to be energetically at work for the One who

NEW KING JAMES VERSION

works of Him who sent Me while it is day; *the* night is coming when no one can work. 5As long as I am in the world, I am the light of the world."

6When He had said these things, He spat on the ground and made clay with the saliva; and He anointed the eyes of the blind man with the clay. 7And He said to him, "Go, wash in the pool of Siloam" (which is translated, Sent). So he went and washed, and came back seeing.

8Therefore the neighbors and those who previously had seen that he was blind[a] said, "Is not this he who sat and begged?"

9Some said, "This is he." Others *said*, "He is like him."[a]

He said, "I am *he*."

10Therefore they said to him, "How were your eyes opened?"

11He answered and said, "A Man called Jesus made clay and anointed my eyes and said to me, 'Go to the pool of[a] Siloam and wash.' So I went and washed, and I received sight."

12Then they said to him, "Where is He?"

He said, "I do not know."

THE PHARISEES EXCOMMUNICATE THE HEALED MAN

13They brought him who formerly was blind to the Pharisees. 14Now it was a Sabbath when Jesus made the clay and opened his eyes. 15Then the Pharisees also asked him again how he had received his sight. He said to them, "He put clay on my eyes, and I washed, and I see."

16Therefore some of the Pharisees said, "This Man is not from God, because He does not keep the Sabbath."

Others said, "How can a man who is a sinner do such signs?" And there was a division among them.

17They said to the blind man again, "What do you say about Him because He opened your eyes?"

He said, "He is a prophet."

18But the Jews did not believe concerning him, that he had been blind and received his sight, until they called the parents of him who had received his sight. 19And they asked them, saying, "Is this your son, who you say was born blind? How then does he now see?"

20His parents answered them and said, "We know that this is our son, and that he was born blind; 21but by what means he now sees we do not know, or who opened his eyes we do not know. He is of age; ask him. He will speak for himself." 22His parents said these *things* because they feared the Jews, for the Jews had agreed already that if anyone confessed *that* He *was* Christ, he would be put out of the synagogue. 23Therefore his parents said, "He is of age; ask him."

24So they again called the man who was blind, and said to him, "Give God the glory! We know that this Man is a sinner."

25He answered and said, "Whether He is a sinner *or not* I do not know. One thing I know: that though I was blind, now I see."

26Then they said to him again, "What did He do to you? How did He open your eyes?"

9:8 [a]NU-Text reads *a beggar.* **9:9** [a]NU-Text reads *"No, but he is like him."* **9:11** [a]NU-Text omits *the pool of.*

THE MESSAGE

sent me here, working while the sun shines. When night falls, the workday is over. For as long as I am in the world, there is plenty of light. I am the world's Light."

6-7 He said this and then spit in the dust, made a clay paste with the saliva, rubbed the paste on the blind man's eyes, and said, "Go, wash at the Pool of Siloam" (Siloam means "Sent"). The man went and washed—and saw.

8 Soon the town was buzzing. His relatives and those who year after year had seen him as a blind man begging were saying, "Why, isn't this the man we knew, who sat here and begged?"

9 Others said, "It's him all right!"

But others objected, "It's not the same man at all. It just looks like him."

He said, "It's me, the very one."

10 They said, "How did your eyes get opened?"

11 "A man named Jesus made a paste and rubbed it on my eyes and told me, 'Go to Siloam and wash.' I did what he said. When I washed, I saw."

12 "So where is he?"

"I don't know."

13-15 They marched the man to the Pharisees. This day when Jesus made the paste and healed his blindness was the Sabbath. The Pharisees grilled him again on how he had come to see. He said, "He put a clay paste on my eyes, and I washed, and now I see."

16 Some of the Pharisees said, "Obviously, this man can't be from God. He doesn't keep the Sabbath."

Others countered, "How can a bad man do miraculous, God-revealing things like this?" There was a split in their ranks.

17 They came back at the blind man, "You're the expert. He opened *your* eyes. What do you say about him?"

He said, "He is a prophet."

18-19 The Jews didn't believe it, didn't believe the man was blind to begin with. So they called the parents of the man now bright-eyed with sight. They asked them, "Is this your son, the one you say was born blind? So how is it that he now sees?"

20-23 His parents said, "We know he is our son, and we know he was born blind. But we don't know how he came to see—haven't a clue about who opened his eyes. Why don't you ask him? He's a grown man and can speak for himself." (His parents were talking like this because they were intimidated by the Jewish leaders, who had already decided that anyone who took a stand that this was the Messiah would be kicked out of the meeting place. That's why his parents said, "Ask him. He's a grown man.")

24 They called the man back a second time—the man who had been blind—and told him, "Give credit to God. We know this man is an impostor."

25 He replied, "I know nothing about that one way or the other. But I know one thing for sure: I was blind . . . I now see."

26 They said, "What did he do to you? How did he open your eyes?"

NEW KING JAMES VERSION

27 He answered them, "I told you already, and you did not listen. Why do you want to hear *it* again? Do you also want to become His disciples?"

28 Then they reviled him and said, "You are His disciple, but we are Moses' disciples. 29 We know that God spoke to Moses; *as for* this *fellow,* we do not know where He is from."

30 The man answered and said to them, "Why, this is a marvelous thing, that you do not know where He is from; yet He has opened my eyes! 31 Now we know that God does not hear sinners; but if anyone is a worshiper of God and does His will, He hears him. 32 Since the world began it has been unheard of that anyone opened the eyes of one who was born blind. 33 If this Man were not from God, He could do nothing."

34 They answered and said to him, "You were completely born in sins, and are you teaching us?" And they cast him out.

TRUE VISION AND TRUE BLINDNESS

35 Jesus heard that they had cast him out; and when He had found him, He said to him, "Do you believe in the Son of God?"[a]

36 He answered and said, "Who is He, Lord, that I may believe in Him?"

37 And Jesus said to him, "You have both seen Him and it is He who is talking with you."

38 Then he said, "Lord, I believe!" And he worshiped Him.

39 And Jesus said, "For judgment I have come into this world, that those who do not see may see, and that those who see may be made blind."

40 Then *some* of the Pharisees who were with Him heard these words, and said to Him, "Are we blind also?"

41 Jesus said to them, "If you were blind, you would have no sin; but now you say, 'We see.' Therefore your sin remains.

JESUS THE TRUE SHEPHERD

10 "Most assuredly, I say to you, he who does not enter the sheepfold by the door, but climbs up some other way, the same is a thief and a robber. 2 But he who enters by the door is the shepherd of the sheep. 3 To him the doorkeeper opens, and the sheep hear his voice; and he calls his own sheep by name and leads them out. 4 And when he brings out his own sheep, he goes before them; and the sheep follow him, for they know his voice. 5 Yet they will by no means follow a stranger, but will flee from him, for they do not know the voice of strangers." 6 Jesus used this illustration, but they did not understand the things which He spoke to them.

JESUS THE GOOD SHEPHERD

7 Then Jesus said to them again, "Most assuredly, I say to you, I am the door of the sheep. 8 All who *ever* came before Me[a] are thieves and robbers, but the sheep did not hear them. 9 I am the door. If anyone enters by Me, he will be saved, and will go in and out and find pasture.

9:35 [a]NU-Text reads *Son of Man.* **10:8** [a]M-Text omits *before Me.*

THE MESSAGE

27 "I've told you over and over and you haven't listened. Why do you want to hear it again? Are you so eager to become his disciples?"

28-29 With that they jumped all over him. "*You* might be a disciple of that man, but we're disciples of Moses. We know for sure that God spoke to Moses, but we have no idea where this man even comes from."

30-33 The man replied, "This is amazing! You claim to know nothing about him, but the fact is, he opened my eyes! It's well known that God isn't at the beck and call of sinners, but listens carefully to anyone who lives in reverence and does his will. That someone opened the eyes of a man born blind has never been heard of—ever. If this man didn't come from God, he wouldn't be able to do anything."

34 They said, "You're nothing but dirt! How dare you take that tone with us!" Then they threw him out in the street.

35 Jesus heard that they had thrown him out, and went and found him. He asked him, "Do you believe in the Son of Man?"

36 The man said, "Point him out to me, sir, so that I can believe in him."

37 Jesus said, "You're looking right at him. Don't you recognize my voice?"

38 "Master, I believe," the man said, and worshiped him.

39 Jesus then said, "I came into the world to bring everything into the clear light of day, making all the distinctions clear, so that those who have never seen will see, and those who have made a great pretense of seeing will be exposed as blind."

40 Some Pharisees overheard him and said, "Does that mean you're calling us blind?"

41 Jesus said, "If you were really blind, you would be blameless, but since you claim to see everything so well, you're accountable for every fault and failure."

HE CALLS HIS SHEEP BY NAME

1-5 10 "Let me set this before you as plainly as I can. If a person climbs over or through the fence of a sheep pen instead of going through the gate, you know he's up to no good—a sheep rustler! The shepherd walks right up to the gate. The gatekeeper opens the gate to him and the sheep recognize his voice. He calls his own sheep by name and leads them out. When he gets them all out, he leads them and they follow because they are familiar with his voice. They won't follow a stranger's voice but will scatter because they aren't used to the sound of it."

6-10 Jesus told this simple story, but they had no idea what he was talking about. So he tried again. "I'll be explicit, then. I am the Gate for the sheep. All those others are up to no good—sheep stealers, every one of them. But the sheep didn't listen to them. I am the Gate. Anyone who goes through me will be cared for—will freely go in and out, and find pas-

NEW KING JAMES VERSION

10 The thief does not come except to steal, and to kill, and to destroy. I have come that they may have life, and that they may have *it* more abundantly.

11 "I am the good shepherd. The good shepherd gives His life for the sheep. 12 But a hireling, *he who is* not the shepherd, one who does not own the sheep, sees the wolf coming and leaves the sheep and flees; and the wolf catches the sheep and scatters them. 13 The hireling flees because he is a hireling and does not care about the sheep. 14 I am the good shepherd; and I know My *sheep*, and am known by My own. 15 As the Father knows Me, even so I know the Father; and I lay down My life for the sheep. 16 And other sheep I have which are not of this fold; them also I must bring, and they will hear My voice; and there will be one flock *and* one shepherd.

17 "Therefore My Father loves Me, because I lay down My life that I may take it again. 18 No one takes it from Me, but I lay it down of Myself. I have power to lay it down, and I have power to take it again. This command I have received from My Father."

19 Therefore there was a division again among the Jews because of these sayings. 20 And many of them said, "He has a demon and is mad. Why do you listen to Him?"

21 Others said, "These are not the words of one who has a demon. Can a demon open the eyes of the blind?"

THE SHEPHERD KNOWS HIS SHEEP

22 Now it was the Feast of Dedication in Jerusalem, and it was winter. 23 And Jesus walked in the temple, in Solomon's porch. 24 Then the Jews surrounded Him and said to Him, "How long do You keep us in doubt? If You are the Christ, tell us plainly."

25 Jesus answered them, "I told you, and you do not believe. The works that I do in My Father's name, they bear witness of Me. 26 But you do not believe, because you are not of My sheep, as I said to you.[a] 27 My sheep hear My voice, and I know them, and they follow Me. 28 And I give them eternal life, and they shall never perish; neither shall anyone snatch them out of My hand. 29 My Father, who has given *them* to Me, is greater than all; and no one is able to snatch *them* out of My Father's hand. 30 I and *My* Father are one."

RENEWED EFFORTS TO STONE JESUS

31 Then the Jews took up stones again to stone Him. 32 Jesus answered them, "Many good works I have shown you from My Father. For which of those works do you stone Me?"

33 The Jews answered Him, saying, "For a good work we do not stone You, but for blasphemy, and because You, being a Man, make Yourself God."

34 Jesus answered them, "Is it not written in your law, *'I said, "You are gods"'*?[a] 35 If He called them gods, to whom the word of God

10:26 [a]NU-Text omits *as I said to you.* **10:34** [a]Psalm 82:6

THE MESSAGE

ture. A thief is only there to steal and kill and destroy. I came so they can have real and eternal life, more and better life than they ever dreamed of.

11-13 "I am the Good Shepherd. The Good Shepherd puts the sheep before himself, sacrifices himself if necessary. A hired man is not a real shepherd. The sheep mean nothing to him. He sees a wolf come and runs for it, leaving the sheep to be ravaged and scattered by the wolf. He's only in it for the money. The sheep don't matter to him.

14-18 "I am the Good Shepherd. I know my own sheep and my own sheep know me. In the same way, the Father knows me and I know the Father. I put the sheep before myself, sacrificing myself if necessary. You need to know that I have other sheep in addition to those in this pen. I need to gather and bring them, too. They'll also recognize my voice. Then it will be one flock, one Shepherd. This is why the Father loves me: because I freely lay down my life. And so I am free to take it up again. No one takes it from me. I lay it down of my own free will. I have the right to lay it down; I also have the right to take it up again. I received this authority personally from my Father."

19-21 This kind of talk caused another split in the Jewish ranks. A lot of them were saying, "He's crazy, a maniac—out of his head completely. Why bother listening to him?" But others weren't so sure: "These aren't the words of a crazy man. Can a 'maniac' open blind eyes?"

22-24 They were celebrating Hanukkah just then in Jerusalem. It was winter. Jesus was strolling in the Temple across Solomon's Porch. The Jews, circling him, said, "How long are you going to keep us guessing? If you're the Messiah, tell us straight out."

25-30 Jesus answered, "I told you, but you don't believe. Everything I have done has been authorized by my Father, actions that speak louder than words. You don't believe because you're not my sheep. My sheep recognize my voice. I know them, and they follow me. I give them real and eternal life. They are protected from the Destroyer for good. No one can steal them from out of my hand. The Father who put them under my care is so much greater than the Destroyer and Thief. No one could ever get them away from him. I and the Father are one heart and mind."

31-32 Again the Jews picked up rocks to throw at him. Jesus said, "I have made a present to you from the Father of a great many good actions. For which of these acts do you stone me?"

33 The Jews said, "We're not stoning you for anything good you did, but for what you said—this blasphemy of calling yourself God."

34-38 Jesus said, "I'm only quoting your inspired Scriptures, where God said, 'I tell you—you are gods.' If God called your an-

NEW KING JAMES VERSION

came (and the Scripture cannot be broken), [36]do you say of Him whom the Father sanctified and sent into the world, 'You are blaspheming,' because I said, 'I am the Son of God'? [37]If I do not do the works of My Father, do not believe Me; [38]but if I do, though you do not believe Me, believe the works, that you may know and believe[a] that the Father *is* in Me, and I in Him." [39]Therefore they sought again to seize Him, but He escaped out of their hand.

THE BELIEVERS BEYOND JORDAN

[40]And He went away again beyond the Jordan to the place where John was baptizing at first, and there He stayed. [41]Then many came to Him and said, "John performed no sign, but all the things that John spoke about this Man were true." [42]And many believed in Him there.

THE DEATH OF LAZARUS

11 Now a certain *man* was sick, Lazarus of Bethany, the town of Mary and her sister Martha. [2]It was *that* Mary who anointed the Lord with fragrant oil and wiped His feet with her hair, whose brother Lazarus was sick. [3]Therefore the sisters sent to Him, saying, "Lord, behold, he whom You love is sick."

[4]When Jesus heard *that*, He said, "This sickness is not unto death, but for the glory of God, that the Son of God may be glorified through it."

[5]Now Jesus loved Martha and her sister and Lazarus. [6]So, when He heard that he was sick, He stayed two more days in the place where He was. [7]Then after this He said to *the* disciples, "Let us go to Judea again."

[8]*The* disciples said to Him, "Rabbi, lately the Jews sought to stone You, and are You going there again?"

[9]Jesus answered, "Are there not twelve hours in the day? If anyone walks in the day, he does not stumble, because he sees the light of this world. [10]But if one walks in the night, he stumbles, because the light is not in him." [11]These things He said, and after that He said to them, "Our friend Lazarus sleeps, but I go that I may wake him up."

[12]Then His disciples said, "Lord, if he sleeps he will get well." [13]However, Jesus spoke of his death, but they thought that He was speaking about taking rest in sleep.

[14]Then Jesus said to them plainly, "Lazarus is dead. [15]And I am glad for your sakes that I was not there, that you may believe. Nevertheless let us go to him."

[16]Then Thomas, who is called the Twin, said to his fellow disciples, "Let us also go, that we may die with Him."

I AM THE RESURRECTION AND THE LIFE

[17]So when Jesus came, He found that he had already been in the tomb four days. [18]Now Bethany was near Jerusalem, about two miles[a]

10:38 [a]NU-Text reads *understand.* **11:18** [a]Literally *fifteen stadia*

THE MESSAGE

cestors 'gods'—and Scripture doesn't lie—why do you yell, 'Blasphemer! Blasphemer!' at the unique One the Father consecrated and sent into the world, just because I said, 'I am the Son of God'? If I don't do the things my Father does, well and good; don't believe me. But if I am doing them, put aside for a moment what you hear me say about myself and just take the evidence of the actions that are right before your eyes. Then perhaps things will come together for you, and you'll see that not only are we doing the same thing, we *are* the same—Father and Son. He is in me; I am in him."

39-42 They tried yet again to arrest him, but he slipped through their fingers. He went back across the Jordan to the place where John first baptized, and stayed there. A lot of people followed him over. They were saying, "John did no miracles, but everything he said about this man has come true." Many believed in him then and there.

THE DEATH OF LAZARUS

1-3 **11** A man was sick, Lazarus of Bethany, the town of Mary and her sister Martha. This was the same Mary who massaged the Lord's feet with aromatic oils and then wiped them with her hair. It was her brother Lazarus who was sick. So the sisters sent word to Jesus, "Master, the one you love so very much is sick."

4 When Jesus got the message, he said, "This sickness is not fatal. It will become an occasion to show God's glory by glorifying God's Son."

5-7 Jesus loved Martha and her sister and Lazarus, but oddly, when he heard that Lazarus was sick, he stayed on where he was for two more days. After the two days, he said to his disciples, "Let's go back to Judea."

8 They said, "Rabbi, you can't do that. The Jews are out to kill you, and you're going back?"

9-10 Jesus replied, "Are there not twelve hours of daylight? Anyone who walks in daylight doesn't stumble because there's plenty of light from the sun. Walking at night, he might very well stumble because he can't see where he's going."

11 He said these things, and then announced, "Our friend Lazarus has fallen asleep. I'm going to wake him up."

12-13 The disciples said, "Master, if he's gone to sleep, he'll get a good rest and wake up feeling fine." Jesus was talking about death, while his disciples thought he was talking about taking a nap.

14-15 Then Jesus became explicit: "Lazarus died. And I am glad for your sakes that I wasn't there. You're about to be given new grounds for believing. Now let's go to him."

16 That's when Thomas, the one called the Twin, said to his companions, "Come along. We might as well die with him."

17-20 When Jesus finally got there, he found Lazarus already four days dead. Bethany was near Jerusalem, only a couple of miles

NEW KING JAMES VERSION

away. 19And many of the Jews had joined the
women around Martha and Mary, to comfort
them concerning their brother.
20Now Martha, as soon as she heard that Je-
sus was coming, went and met Him, but Mary
was sitting in the house. 21Now Martha said to
Jesus, "Lord, if You had been here, my brother
would not have died. 22But even now I know that
whatever You ask of God, God will give You."
23Jesus said to her, "Your brother will rise
again."
24Martha said to Him, "I know that he will
rise again in the resurrection at the last day."
25Jesus said to her, "I am the resurrection
and the life. He who believes in Me, though he
may die, he shall live. 26And whoever lives and
believes in Me shall never die. Do you believe
this?"
27She said to Him, "Yes, Lord, I believe that
You are the Christ, the Son of God, who is to
come into the world."

JESUS AND DEATH, THE LAST ENEMY

28And when she had said these things, she
went her way and secretly called Mary her sis-
ter, saying, "The Teacher has come and is calling
for you." 29As soon as she heard *that,* she arose
quickly and came to Him. 30Now Jesus had not
yet come into the town, but was[a] in the place
where Martha met Him. 31Then the Jews who
were with her in the house, and comforting her,
when they saw that Mary rose up quickly and
went out, followed her, saying, "She is going to
the tomb to weep there."[a]
32Then, when Mary came where Jesus was,
and saw Him, she fell down at His feet, saying to
Him, "Lord, if You had been here, my brother
would not have died."
33Therefore, when Jesus saw her weeping,
and the Jews who came with her weeping, He
groaned in the spirit and was troubled. 34And He
said, "Where have you laid him?"
They said to Him, "Lord, come and see."
35Jesus wept. 36Then the Jews said, "See how
He loved him!"
37And some of them said, "Could not this
Man, who opened the eyes of the blind, also
have kept this man from dying?"

LAZARUS RAISED FROM THE DEAD

38Then Jesus, again groaning in Himself,
came to the tomb. It was a cave, and a stone lay
against it. 39Jesus said, "Take away the stone."
Martha, the sister of him who was dead, said
to Him, "Lord, by this time there is a stench, for
he has been *dead* four days."
40Jesus said to her, "Did I not say to you that
if you would believe you would see the glory of
God?" 41Then they took away the stone *from the
place* where the dead man was lying.[a] And Jesus
lifted up *His* eyes and said, "Father, I thank You
that You have heard Me. 42And I know that You
always hear Me, but because of the people who
are standing by I said *this,* that they may believe
that You sent Me." 43Now when He had said
these things, He cried with a loud voice,

11:30 [a]NU-Text adds *still.* **11:31** [a]NU-Text reads *supposing that she was going to the tomb to weep there.* **11:41** [a]NU-Text omits *from the place where the dead man was lying.*

THE MESSAGE

away, and many of the Jews were visiting Martha and Mary, sympathizing with them over their brother. Martha heard Jesus was coming and went out to meet him. Mary remained in the house.

21-22 Martha said, "Master, if you'd been here, my brother wouldn't have died. Even now, I know that whatever you ask God he will give you."

23 Jesus said, "Your brother will be raised up."

24 Martha replied, "I know that he will be raised up in the resurrection at the end of time."

25-26 "You don't have to wait for the End. I am, right now, Resurrection and Life. The one who believes in me, even though he or she dies, will live. And everyone who lives believing in me does not ultimately die at all. Do you believe this?"

27 "Yes, Master. All along I have believed that you are the Messiah, the Son of God who comes into the world."

28 After saying this, she went to her sister Mary and whispered in her ear, "The Teacher is here and is asking for you."

29-32 The moment she heard that, she jumped up and ran out to him. Jesus had not yet entered the town but was still at the place where Martha had met him. When her sympathizing Jewish friends saw Mary run off, they followed her, thinking she was on her way to the tomb to weep there. Mary came to where Jesus was waiting and fell at his feet, saying, "Master, if only you had been here, my brother would not have died."

33-34 When Jesus saw her sobbing and the Jews with her sobbing, a deep anger welled up within him. He said, "Where did you put him?"

34-35 "Master, come and see," they said. Now Jesus wept.

36 The Jews said, "Look how deeply he loved him."

37 Others among them said, "Well, if he loved him so much, why didn't he do something to keep him from dying? After all, he opened the eyes of a blind man."

38-39 Then Jesus, the anger again welling up within him, arrived at the tomb. It was a simple cave in the hillside with a slab of stone laid against it. Jesus said, "Remove the stone."

The sister of the dead man, Martha, said, "Master, by this time there's a stench. He's been dead four days!"

40 Jesus looked her in the eye. "Didn't I tell you that if you believed, you would see the glory of God?"

41-42 Then, to the others, "Go ahead, take away the stone."

They removed the stone. Jesus raised his eyes to heaven and prayed, "Father, I'm grateful that you have listened to me. I know you always do listen, but on account of this crowd standing here I've spoken so that they might believe that you sent me."

43-44 Then he shouted, "Lazarus, come out!" And he came out, a cadaver, wrapped from

NEW KING JAMES VERSION

"Lazarus, come forth!" [44]And he who had died came out bound hand and foot with graveclothes, and his face was wrapped with a cloth. Jesus said to them, "Loose him, and let him go."

THE PLOT TO KILL JESUS

[45]Then many of the Jews who had come to Mary, and had seen the things Jesus did, believed in Him. [46]But some of them went away to the Pharisees and told them the things Jesus did. [47]Then the chief priests and the Pharisees gathered a council and said, "What shall we do? For this Man works many signs. [48]If we let Him alone like this, everyone will believe in Him, and the Romans will come and take away both our place and nation."

[49]And one of them, Caiaphas, being high priest that year, said to them, "You know nothing at all, [50]nor do you consider that it is expedient for us[a] that one man should die for the people, and not that the whole nation should perish." [51]Now this he did not say on his own *authority;* but being high priest that year he prophesied that Jesus would die for the nation, [52]and not for that nation only, but also that He would gather together in one the children of God who were scattered abroad.

[53]Then, from that day on, they plotted to put Him to death. [54]Therefore Jesus no longer walked openly among the Jews, but went from there into the country near the wilderness, to a city called Ephraim, and there remained with His disciples.

[55]And the Passover of the Jews was near, and many went from the country up to Jerusalem before the Passover, to purify themselves. [56]Then they sought Jesus, and spoke among themselves as they stood in the temple, "What do you think—that He will not come to the feast?" [57]Now both the chief priests and the Pharisees had given a command, that if anyone knew where He was, he should report *it,* that they might seize Him.

THE ANOINTING AT BETHANY

12 Then, six days before the Passover, Jesus came to Bethany, where Lazarus was who had been dead,[a] whom He had raised from the dead. [2]There they made Him a supper; and Martha served, but Lazarus was one of those who sat at the table with Him. [3]Then Mary took a pound of very costly oil of spikenard, anointed the feet of Jesus, and wiped His feet with her hair. And the house was filled with the fragrance of the oil.

[4]But one of His disciples, Judas Iscariot, Simon's *son,* who would betray Him, said, [5]"Why was this fragrant oil not sold for three hundred denarii[a] and given to the poor?" [6]This he said, not that he cared for the poor, but because he was a thief, and had the money box; and he used to take what was put in it.

11:50 [a]NU-Text reads *you.* 12:1 [a]NU-Text omits *who had been dead.* 12:5 [a]About one year's wages for a worker

THE MESSAGE

head to toe, and with a kerchief over his face.

Jesus told them, "Unwrap him and let him loose."

THE MAN WHO CREATES GOD-SIGNS

45-48 That was a turnaround for many of the Jews who were with Mary. They saw what Jesus did, and believed in him. But some went back to the Pharisees and told on Jesus. The high priests and Pharisees called a meeting of the Jewish ruling body. "What do we do now?" they asked. "This man keeps on doing things, creating God-signs. If we let him go on, pretty soon everyone will be believing in him and the Romans will come and remove what little power and privilege we still have."

49-52 Then one of them—it was Caiaphas, the designated Chief Priest that year—spoke up, "Don't you know anything? Can't you see that it's to our advantage that one man dies for the people rather than the whole nation be destroyed?" He didn't say this of his own accord, but as Chief Priest that year he unwittingly prophesied that Jesus was about to die sacrificially for the nation, and not only for the nation but so that all God's exile-scattered children might be gathered together into one people.

53-54 From that day on, they plotted to kill him. So Jesus no longer went out in public among the Jews. He withdrew into the country bordering the desert to a town called Ephraim and secluded himself there with his disciples.

55-56 The Jewish Passover was coming up. Crowds of people were making their way from the country up to Jerusalem to get themselves ready for the Feast. They were curious about Jesus. There was a lot of talk of him among those standing around in the Temple: "What do you think? Do you think he'll show up at the Feast or not?"

57 Meanwhile, the high priests and Pharisees gave out the word that anyone getting wind of him should inform them. They were all set to arrest him.

ANOINTING HIS FEET

1-3 **12** Six days before Passover, Jesus entered Bethany where Lazarus, so recently raised from the dead, was living. Lazarus and his sisters invited Jesus to dinner at their home. Martha served. Lazarus was one of those sitting at the table with them. Mary came in with a jar of very expensive aromatic oils, anointed and massaged Jesus' feet, and then wiped them with her hair. The fragrance of the oils filled the house.

4-6 Judas Iscariot, one of his disciples, even then getting ready to betray him, said, "Why wasn't this oil sold and the money given to the poor? It would have easily brought three hundred silver pieces." He said this not because he cared two cents about the poor but because he was a thief. He was in charge of their common funds, but also embezzled them.

NEW KING JAMES VERSION

[7]But Jesus said, "Let her alone; she has kept[a] this for the day of My burial. [8]For the poor you have with you always, but Me you do not have always."

THE PLOT TO KILL LAZARUS

[9]Now a great many of the Jews knew that He was there; and they came, not for Jesus' sake only, but that they might also see Lazarus, whom He had raised from the dead. [10]But the chief priests plotted to put Lazarus to death also, [11]because on account of him many of the Jews went away and believed in Jesus.

THE TRIUMPHAL ENTRY

[12]The next day a great multitude that had come to the feast, when they heard that Jesus was coming to Jerusalem, [13]took branches of palm trees and went out to meet Him, and cried out:

"Hosanna!
'Blessed is He who comes in the name of the LORD!'[a]
The King of Israel!"

[14]Then Jesus, when He had found a young donkey, sat on it; as it is written:

[15]*"Fear not, daughter of Zion;*
Behold, your King is coming,
Sitting on a donkey's colt."[a]

[16]His disciples did not understand these things at first; but when Jesus was glorified, then they remembered that these things were written about Him and *that* they had done these things to Him.

[17]Therefore the people, who were with Him when He called Lazarus out of his tomb and raised him from the dead, bore witness. [18]For this reason the people also met Him, because they heard that He had done this sign. [19]The Pharisees therefore said among themselves, "You see that you are accomplishing nothing. Look, the world has gone after Him!"

THE FRUITFUL GRAIN OF WHEAT

[20]Now there were certain Greeks among those who came up to worship at the feast. [21]Then they came to Philip, who was from Bethsaida of Galilee, and asked him, saying, "Sir, we wish to see Jesus."

[22]Philip came and told Andrew, and in turn Andrew and Philip told Jesus.

[23]But Jesus answered them, saying, "The hour has come that the Son of Man should be glorified. [24]Most assuredly, I say to you, unless a grain of wheat falls into the ground and dies, it remains alone; but if it dies, it produces much grain. [25]He who loves his life will lose it, and he who hates his life in this world will keep it for eternal life. [26]If anyone serves Me, let him follow Me; and where I am, there My servant will be also. If anyone serves Me, him *My* Father will honor.

12:7 [a]NU-Text reads *that she may keep.* **12:13** [a]Psalm 118:26
12:15 [a]Zechariah 9:9

THE MESSAGE

7-8 Jesus said, "Let her alone. She's anticipating and honoring the day of my burial. You always have the poor with you. You don't always have me."

9-11 Word got out among the Jews that he was back in town. The people came to take a look, not only at Jesus but also at Lazarus, who had been raised from the dead. So the high priests plotted to kill Lazarus because so many of the Jews were going over and believing in Jesus on account of him.

SEE HOW YOUR KING COMES

12-15 The next day the huge crowd that had arrived for the Feast heard that Jesus was entering Jerusalem. They broke off palm branches and went out to meet him. And they cheered:

Hosanna!
Blessed is he who comes in God's name!
Yes! The King of Israel!

Jesus got a young donkey and rode it, just as the Scripture has it:

No fear, Daughter Zion:
See how your king comes,
riding a donkey's colt.

16 The disciples didn't notice the fulfillment of many Scriptures at the time, but after Jesus was glorified, they remembered that what was written about him matched what was done to him.

17-19 The crowd that had been with him when he called Lazarus from the tomb, raising him from the dead, was there giving eyewitness accounts. It was because they had spread the word of this latest God-sign that the crowd swelled to a welcoming parade. The Pharisees took one look and threw up their hands: "It's out of control. The world's in a stampede after him."

A GRAIN OF WHEAT MUST DIE

20-21 There were some Greeks in town who had come up to worship at the Feast. They approached Philip, who was from Bethsaida in Galilee: "Sir, we want to see Jesus. Can you help us?"

22-23 Philip went and told Andrew. Andrew and Philip together told Jesus. Jesus answered, "Time's up. The time has come for the Son of Man to be glorified.

24-25 "Listen carefully: Unless a grain of wheat is buried in the ground, dead to the world, it is never any more than a grain of wheat. But if it is buried, it sprouts and reproduces itself many times over. In the same way, anyone who holds on to life just as it is destroys that life. But if you let it go, reckless in your love, you'll have it forever, real and eternal.

26 "If any of you wants to serve me, then follow me. Then you'll be where I am, ready to serve at a moment's notice. The Father will honor and reward anyone who serves me.

New King James Version

Jesus Predicts His Death on the Cross
27“Now My soul is troubled, and what shall I
say? ‘Father, save Me from this hour’? But for
this purpose I came to this hour. 28Father, glorify
Your name.”
Then a voice came from heaven, *saying,* “I
have both glorified *it* and will glorify *it* again.”
29Therefore the people who stood by and
heard *it* said that it had thundered. Others said,
“An angel has spoken to Him.”
30Jesus answered and said, “This voice did
not come because of Me, but for your sake.
31Now is the judgment of this world; now the
ruler of this world will be cast out. 32And I, if I
am lifted up from the earth, will draw all *peo-*
ples to Myself.” 33This He said, signifying by
what death He would die.
34The people answered Him, “We have heard
from the law that the Christ remains forever;
and how *can* You say, ‘The Son of Man must be
lifted up’? Who is this Son of Man?”
35Then Jesus said to them, “A little while
longer the light is with you. Walk while you have
the light, lest darkness overtake you; he who
walks in darkness does not know where he is
going. 36While you have the light, believe in the
light, that you may become sons of light.” These
things Jesus spoke, and departed, and was hid-
den from them.

Who Has Believed Our Report?
37But although He had done so many signs
before them, they did not believe in Him, 38that
the word of Isaiah the prophet might be ful-
filled, which he spoke:

“Lord, who has believed our report?
And to whom has the arm of the L*ORD* *been*
revealed?” [a]

39Therefore they could not believe, because
Isaiah said again:

40*“He has blinded their eyes and hardened*
their hearts,
Lest they should see with their eyes,
Lest they should understand with their
hearts and turn,
So that I should heal them.” [a]

41These things Isaiah said when[a] he saw His
glory and spoke of Him.

Walk in the Light
42Nevertheless even among the rulers many
believed in Him, but because of the Pharisees
they did not confess *Him,* lest they should be put
out of the synagogue; 43for they loved the praise
of men more than the praise of God.
44Then Jesus cried out and said, “He who be-
lieves in Me, believes not in Me but in Him who
sent Me. 45And he who sees Me sees Him who
sent Me. 46I have come *as* a light into the world,
that whoever believes in Me should not abide in
darkness.

12:38 [a]Isaiah 53:1 **12:40** [a]Isaiah 6:10 **12:41** [a]NU-Text reads *because.*

The Message

27-28 “Right now I am storm-tossed. And what am I going to say? ‘Father, get me out of this’? No, this is why I came in the first place. I’ll say, ‘Father, put your glory on display.’ ”

A voice came out of the sky: “I have glorified it, and I’ll glorify it again.”

29 The listening crowd said, “Thunder!” Others said, “An angel spoke to him!”

30-33 Jesus said, “The voice didn’t come for me but for you. At this moment the world is in crisis. Now Satan, the ruler of this world, will be thrown out. And I, as I am lifted up from the earth, will attract everyone to me and gather them around me.” He put it this way to show how he was going to be put to death.

34 Voices from the crowd answered, “We heard from God’s Law that the Messiah lasts forever. How can it be necessary, as you put it, that the Son of Man ‘be lifted up’? Who is this ‘Son of Man’?”

35-36 Jesus said, “For a brief time still, the light is among you. Walk by the light you have so darkness doesn’t destroy you. If you walk in darkness, you don’t know where you’re going. As you have the light, believe in the light. Then the light will be within you, and shining through your lives. You’ll be children of light.”

Their Eyes Are Blinded

36-40 Jesus said all this, and then went into hiding. All these God-signs he had given them and they still didn’t get it, still wouldn’t trust him. This proved that the prophet Isaiah was right:

God, who believed what we preached?
Who recognized God’s arm, outstretched
and ready to act?

First they wouldn’t believe, then they *couldn’t*—again, just as Isaiah said:

Their eyes are blinded,
their hearts are hardened,
So that they wouldn’t see with their eyes
and perceive with their hearts,
And turn to me, God,
so I could heal them.

41 Isaiah said these things after he got a glimpse of God’s cascading brightness that would pour through the Messiah.

42-43 On the other hand, a considerable number from the ranks of the leaders did believe. But because of the Pharisees, they didn’t come out in the open with it. They were afraid of getting kicked out of the meeting place. When push came to shove they cared more for human approval than for God’s glory.

44-46 Jesus summed it all up when he cried out, “Whoever believes in me, believes not just in me but in the One who sent me. Whoever looks at me is looking, in fact, at the One who sent me. I am Light that has come into the world so that all who believe in me won’t have to stay any longer in the dark.

New King James Version

47And if anyone hears My words and does not believe,[a] I do not judge him; for I did not come to judge the world but to save the world. 48He who rejects Me, and does not receive My words, has that which judges him—the word that I have spoken will judge him in the last day. 49For I have not spoken on My own *authority;* but the Father who sent Me gave Me a command, what I should say and what I should speak. 50And I know that His command is everlasting life. Therefore, whatever I speak, just as the Father has told Me, so I speak."

Jesus Washes the Disciples' Feet

13 Now before the Feast of the Passover, when Jesus knew that His hour had come that He should depart from this world to the Father, having loved His own who were in the world, He loved them to the end.

2And supper being ended,[a] the devil having already put it into the heart of Judas Iscariot, Simon's *son,* to betray Him, 3Jesus, knowing that the Father had given all things into His hands, and that He had come from God and was going to God, 4rose from supper and laid aside His garments, took a towel and girded Himself. 5After that, He poured water into a basin and began to wash the disciples' feet, and to wipe *them* with the towel with which He was girded. 6Then He came to Simon Peter. And *Peter* said to Him, "Lord, are You washing my feet?"

7Jesus answered and said to him, "What I am doing you do not understand now, but you will know after this."

8Peter said to Him, "You shall never wash my feet!"

Jesus answered him, "If I do not wash you, you have no part with Me."

9Simon Peter said to Him, "Lord, not my feet only, but also *my* hands and *my* head!"

10Jesus said to him, "He who is bathed needs only to wash *his* feet, but is completely clean; and you are clean, but not all of you." 11For He knew who would betray Him; therefore He said, "You are not all clean."

12So when He had washed their feet, taken His garments, and sat down again, He said to them, "Do you know what I have done to you? 13You call Me Teacher and Lord, and you say well, for *so* I am. 14If I then, *your* Lord and Teacher, have washed your feet, you also ought to wash one another's feet. 15For I have given you an example, that you should do as I have done to you. 16Most assuredly, I say to you, a servant is not greater than his master; nor is he who is sent greater than he who sent him. 17If you know these things, blessed are you if you do them.

Jesus Identifies His Betrayer

18"I do not speak concerning all of you. I know whom I have chosen; but that the Scrip-

12:47 [a]NU-Text reads *keep them.* **13:2** [a]NU-Text reads *And during supper.*

The Message

47-50 "If anyone hears what I am saying and doesn't take it seriously, I don't reject him. I didn't come to reject the world; I came to save the world. But you need to know that whoever puts me off, refusing to take in what I'm saying, is willfully choosing rejection. The Word, the Word-made-flesh that I have spoken and that I am, *that* Word and no other is the last word. I'm not making any of this up on my own. The Father who sent me gave me orders, told me what to say and how to say it. And I know exactly what his command produces: real and eternal life. That's all I have to say. What the Father told me, I tell you."

Washing His Disciples' Feet

1-2 13 Just before the Passover Feast, Jesus knew that the time had come to leave this world to go to the Father. Having loved his dear companions, he continued to love them right to the end. It was suppertime. The Devil by now had Judas, son of Simon the Iscariot, firmly in his grip, all set for the betrayal.

3-6 Jesus knew that the Father had put him in complete charge of everything, that he came from God and was on his way back to God. So he got up from the supper table, set aside his robe, and put on an apron. Then he poured water into a basin and began to wash the feet of the disciples, drying them with his apron. When he got to Simon Peter, Peter said, "Master, *you* wash *my* feet?"

7 Jesus answered, "You don't understand now what I'm doing, but it will be clear enough to you later."

8 Peter persisted, "You're not going to wash my feet—ever!"

Jesus said, "If I don't wash you, you can't be part of what I'm doing."

9 "Master!" said Peter. "Not only my feet, then. Wash my hands! Wash my head!"

10-12 Jesus said, "If you've had a bath in the morning, you only need your feet washed now and you're clean from head to toe. My concern, you understand, is holiness, not hygiene. So now you're clean. But not every one of you." (He knew who was betraying him. That's why he said, "Not every one of you.") After he had finished washing their feet, he took his robe, put it back on, and went back to his place at the table.

12-17 Then he said, "Do you understand what I have done to you? You address me as 'Teacher' and 'Master,' and rightly so. That is what I am. So if I, the Master and Teacher, washed your feet, you must now wash each other's feet. I've laid down a pattern for you. What I've done, you do. I'm only pointing out the obvious. A servant is not ranked above his master; an employee doesn't give orders to the employer. If you understand what I'm telling you, act like it—and live a blessed life.

The One Who Ate Bread at My Table

18-20 "I'm not including all of you in this. I know precisely whom I've selected, so as not to interfere with the fulfillment of this Scripture:

New King James Version

ture may be fulfilled, *'He who eats bread with
Me*[a] *has lifted up his heel against Me.'*[b] 19Now I
tell you before it comes, that when it does come
to pass, you may believe that I am *He.* 20Most as-
suredly, I say to you, he who receives whomever
I send receives Me; and he who receives Me re-
ceives Him who sent Me."
21When Jesus had said these things, He was
troubled in spirit, and testified and said, "Most
assuredly, I say to you, one of you will betray
Me." 22Then the disciples looked at one another,
perplexed about whom He spoke.
23Now there was leaning on Jesus' bosom
one of His disciples, whom Jesus loved. 24Simon
Peter therefore motioned to him to ask who it
was of whom He spoke.
25Then, leaning back[a] on Jesus' breast, he
said to Him, "Lord, who is it?"
26Jesus answered, "It is he to whom I shall
give a piece of bread when I have dipped *it.*"
And having dipped the bread, He gave *it* to Ju-
das Iscariot, *the son* of Simon. 27Now after the
piece of bread, Satan entered him. Then Jesus
said to him, "What you do, do quickly." 28But no
one at the table knew for what reason He said
this to him. 29For some thought, because Judas
had the money box, that Jesus had said to him,
"Buy *those things* we need for the feast," or that
he should give something to the poor.
30Having received the piece of bread, he then
went out immediately. And it was night.

The New Commandment

31So, when he had gone out, Jesus said, "Now
the Son of Man is glorified, and God is glorified
in Him. 32If God is glorified in Him, God will also
glorify Him in Himself, and glorify Him immedi-
ately. 33Little children, I shall be with you a little
while longer. You will seek Me; and as I said to
the Jews, 'Where I am going, you cannot come,'
so now I say to you. 34A new commandment I
give to you, that you love one another; as I have
loved you, that you also love one another. 35By
this all will know that you are My disciples, if
you have love for one another."

Jesus Predicts Peter's Denial

36Simon Peter said to Him, "Lord, where are
You going?"
Jesus answered him, "Where I am going you
cannot follow Me now, but you shall follow Me
afterward."
37Peter said to Him, "Lord, why can I not fol-
low You now? I will lay down my life for Your
sake."
38Jesus answered him, "Will you lay down
your life for My sake? Most assuredly, I say to
you, the rooster shall not crow till you have de-
nied Me three times.

13:18 [a]NU-Text reads *My bread.* [b]Psalm 41:9 13:25 [a]NU-Text and M-Text add *thus.*

The Message

The one who ate bread at my table
Turned on his heel against me.

"I'm telling you all this ahead of time so that
when it happens you will believe that I am
who I say I am. Make sure you get this right:
Receiving someone I send is the same as re-
ceiving me, just as receiving me is the same
as receiving the One who sent me."
21 After he said these things, Jesus became
visibly upset, and then he told them why.
"One of you is going to betray me."
22-25 The disciples looked around at one an-
other, wondering who on earth he was talk-
ing about. One of the disciples, the one Je-
sus loved dearly, was reclining against him,
his head on his shoulder. Peter motioned to
him to ask who Jesus might be talking
about. So, being the closest, he said, "Mas-
ter, who?"
26-27 Jesus said, "The one to whom I give this
crust of bread after I've dipped it." Then he
dipped the crust and gave it to Judas, son of
Simon the Iscariot. As soon as the bread
was in his hand, Satan entered him.
"What you must do," said Jesus, "do. Do it
and get it over with."
28-29 No one around the supper table knew
why he said this to him. Some thought that
since Judas was their treasurer, Jesus was
telling him to buy what they needed for the
Feast, or that he should give something to
the poor.
30 Judas, with the piece of bread, left. It was
night.

A New Command

31-32 When he had left, Jesus said, "Now the Son
of Man is seen for who he is, and God seen
for who he is in him. The moment God is
seen in him, God's glory will be on display.
In glorifying him, he himself is glorified—
glory all around!
33 "Children, I am with you for only a short
time longer. You are going to look high and
low for me. But just as I told the Jews, I'm
telling you: 'Where I go, you are not able to
come.'
34-35 "Let me give you a new command: Love
one another. In the same way I loved you,
you love one another. This is how everyone
will recognize that you are my disciples—
when they see the love you have for each
other."
36 Simon Peter asked, "Master, just where
are you going?"
Jesus answered, "You can't now follow
me where I'm going. You will follow later."
37 "Master," said Peter, "why can't I follow
now? I'll lay down my life for you!"
38 "Really? You'll lay down your life for me?
The truth is that before the rooster crows,
you'll deny me three times."

New King James Version

The Way, the Truth, and the Life

14 "Let not your heart be troubled; you be-
lieve in God, believe also in Me. 2In My Fa-
ther's house are many mansions;[a] if *it were* not
so, I would have told you. I go to prepare a place
for you.[b] 3And if I go and prepare a place for
you, I will come again and receive you to My-
self; that where I am, *there* you may be also.
4And where I go you know, and the way you
know."
5Thomas said to Him, "Lord, we do not know
where You are going, and how can we know the
way?"
6Jesus said to him, "I am the way, the truth,
and the life. No one comes to the Father except
through Me.

The Father Revealed

7"If you had known Me, you would have
known My Father also; and from now on you
know Him and have seen Him."
8Philip said to Him, "Lord, show us the Fa-
ther, and it is sufficient for us."
9Jesus said to him, "Have I been with you so
long, and yet you have not known Me, Philip? He
who has seen Me has seen the Father; so how
can you say, 'Show us the Father'? 10Do you not
believe that I am in the Father, and the Father in
Me? The words that I speak to you I do not speak
on My own *authority;* but the Father who dwells
in Me does the works. 11Believe Me that I *am* in
the Father and the Father in Me, or else believe
Me for the sake of the works themselves.

The Answered Prayer

12"Most assuredly, I say to you, he who be-
lieves in Me, the works that I do he will do also;
and greater *works* than these he will do, be-
cause I go to My Father. 13And whatever you ask
in My name, that I will do, that the Father may
be glorified in the Son. 14If you ask[a] anything in
My name, I will do *it.*

Jesus Promises Another Helper

15"If you love Me, keep[a] My commandments.
16And I will pray the Father, and He will give you
another Helper, that He may abide with you for-
ever— 17the Spirit of truth, whom the world can-
not receive, because it neither sees Him nor
knows Him; but you know Him, for He dwells
with you and will be in you. 18I will not leave you
orphans; I will come to you.

Indwelling of the Father and the Son

19"A little while longer and the world will see
Me no more, but you will see Me. Because I live,
you will live also. 20At that day you will know
that I *am* in My Father, and you in Me, and I in
you. 21He who has My commandments and
keeps them, it is he who loves Me. And he who
loves Me will be loved by My Father, and I will
love him and manifest Myself to him."
22Judas (not Iscariot) said to Him, "Lord, how
is it that You will manifest Yourself to us, and not
to the world?"

14:2 [a]Literally *dwellings* [b]NU-Text adds a word which would cause the text to read either *if it were not so, would I have told you that I go to prepare a place for you?* or *if it were not so I would have told you; for I go to prepare a place for you.*
14:14 [a]NU-Text adds *Me.* **14:15** [a]NU-Text reads *you will keep.*

The Message

The Road

1-4 14 "Don't let this throw you. You trust God,
don't you? Trust me. There is plenty of
room for you in my Father's home. If that
weren't so, would I have told you that I'm on
my way to get a room ready for you? And if
I'm on my way to get your room ready, I'll
come back and get you so you can live
where I live. And you already know the road
I'm taking."
5 Thomas said, "Master, we have no idea
where you're going. How do you expect us
to know the road?"
6-7 Jesus said, "I am the Road, also the Truth,
also the Life. No one gets to the Father apart
from me. If you really knew me, you would
know my Father as well. From now on, you
do know him. You've even seen him!"
8 Philip said, "Master, show us the Father;
then we'll be content."
9-10 "You've been with me all this time, Philip,
and you still don't understand? To see me is
to see the Father. So how can you ask,
'Where is the Father?' Don't you believe that
I am in the Father and the Father is in me?
The words that I speak to you aren't mere
words. I don't just make them up on my
own. The Father who resides in me crafts
each word into a divine act.
11-14 "Believe me: I am in my Father and my
Father is in me. If you can't believe that, be-
lieve what you see—these works. The per-
son who trusts me will not only do what I'm
doing but even greater things, because I, on
my way to the Father, am giving you the
same work to do that I've been doing. You
can count on it. From now on, whatever you
request along the lines of who I am and
what I am doing, I'll do it. That's how the Fa-
ther will be seen for who he is in the Son. I
mean it. Whatever you request in this way,
I'll do.

The Spirit of Truth

15-17 "If you love me, show it by doing what I've
told you. I will talk to the Father, and he'll
provide you another Friend so that you will
always have someone with you. This Friend
is the Spirit of Truth. The godless world
can't take him in because it doesn't have
eyes to see him, doesn't know what to look
for. But you know him already because he
has been staying with you, and will even be
in you!
18-20 "I will not leave you orphaned. I'm com-
ing back. In just a little while the world will
no longer see me, but you're going to see me
because I am alive and you're about to come
alive. At that moment you will know ab-
solutely that I'm in my Father, and you're in
me, and I'm in you.
21 "The person who knows my command-
ments and keeps them, that's who loves me.
And the person who loves me will be loved
by my Father, and I will love him and make
myself plain to him."
22 Judas (not Iscariot) said, "Master, why is
it that you are about to make yourself plain
to us but not to the world?"

NEW KING JAMES VERSION

23Jesus answered and said to him, “If anyone
loves Me, he will keep My word; and My Father
will love him, and We will come to him and
make Our home with him. 24He who does not
love Me does not keep My words; and the word
which you hear is not Mine but the Father’s who
sent Me.

THE GIFT OF HIS PEACE

25“These things I have spoken to you while
being present with you. 26But the Helper, the
Holy Spirit, whom the Father will send in My
name, He will teach you all things, and bring to
your remembrance all things that I said to you.
27Peace I leave with you, My peace I give to you;
not as the world gives do I give to you. Let not
your heart be troubled, neither let it be afraid.
28You have heard Me say to you, ‘I am going
away and coming *back* to you.’ If you loved Me,
you would rejoice because I said,[a] ‘I am going to
the Father,’ for My Father is greater than I.
29“And now I have told you before it comes,
that when it does come to pass, you may believe.
30I will no longer talk much with you, for the
ruler of this world is coming, and he has noth-
ing in Me. 31But that the world may know that I
love the Father, and as the Father gave Me com-
mandment, so I do. Arise, let us go from here.

THE TRUE VINE

15“I am the true vine, and My Father is the
vinedresser. 2Every branch in Me that does
not bear fruit He takes away;[a] and every *branch*
that bears fruit He prunes, that it may bear more
fruit. 3You are already clean because of the word
which I have spoken to you. 4Abide in Me, and I
in you. As the branch cannot bear fruit of itself,
unless it abides in the vine, neither can you, un-
less you abide in Me.
5“I am the vine, you *are* the branches. He
who abides in Me, and I in him, bears much
fruit; for without Me you can do nothing. 6If any-
one does not abide in Me, he is cast out as a
branch and is withered; and they gather them
and throw *them* into the fire, and they are
burned. 7If you abide in Me, and My words abide
in you, you will[a] ask what you desire, and it
shall be done for you. 8By this My Father is glo-
rified, that you bear much fruit; so you will be
My disciples.

LOVE AND JOY PERFECTED

9“As the Father loved Me, I also have loved
you; abide in My love. 10If you keep My com-
mandments, you will abide in My love, just as I
have kept My Father’s commandments and
abide in His love.
11“These things I have spoken to you, that My
joy may remain in you, and *that* your joy may
be full. 12This is My commandment, that you

14:28 [a]NU-Text omits *I said.* **15:2** [a]Or *lifts up* **15:7** [a]NU-Text omits *you will.*

THE MESSAGE

23-24 “Because a loveless world,” said Jesus, “is
a sightless world. If anyone loves me, he will
carefully keep my word and my Father will
love him—we’ll move right into the neighbor-
hood! Not loving me means not keeping my
words. The message you are hearing isn’t
mine. It’s the message of the Father who sent
me.
25-27 “I’m telling you these things while I’m
still living with you. The Friend, the Holy
Spirit whom the Father will send at my re-
quest, will make everything plain to you. He
will remind you of all the things I have told
you. I’m leaving you well and whole. That’s
my parting gift to you. Peace. I don’t leave
you the way you’re used to being left—feel-
ing abandoned, bereft. So don’t be upset.
Don’t be distraught.
28 “You’ve heard me tell you, ‘I’m going
away, and I’m coming back.’ If you loved
me, you would be glad that I’m on my way
to the Father because the Father is the goal
and purpose of my life.
29-31 “I’ve told you this ahead of time, before it
happens, so that when it does happen, the
confirmation will deepen your belief in me.
I’ll not be talking with you much more like
this because the chief of this godless world
is about to attack. But don’t worry—he has
nothing on me, no claim on me. But so the
world might know how thoroughly I love
the Father, I am carrying out my Father’s in-
structions right down to the last detail.
“Get up. Let’s go. It’s time to leave here.”

THE VINE AND THE BRANCHES

1-3 15“I am the Real Vine and my Father is the
Farmer. He cuts off every branch of me
that doesn’t bear grapes. And every branch
that is grape-bearing he prunes back so it
will bear even more. You are already pruned
back by the message I have spoken.
4 “Live in me. Make your home in me just
as I do in you. In the same way that a branch
can’t bear grapes by itself but only by being
joined to the vine, you can’t bear fruit unless
you are joined with me.
5-8 “I am the Vine, you are the branches.
When you’re joined with me and I with you,
the relation intimate and organic, the har-
vest is sure to be abundant. Separated, you
can’t produce a thing. Anyone who sepa-
rates from me is deadwood, gathered up and
thrown on the bonfire. But if you make
yourselves at home with me and my words
are at home in you, you can be sure that
whatever you ask will be listened to and
acted upon. This is how my Father shows
who he is—when you produce grapes, when
you mature as my disciples.
9-10 “I’ve loved you the way my Father has
loved me. Make yourselves at home in my
love. If you keep my commands, you’ll re-
main intimately at home in my love. That’s
what I’ve done—kept my Father’s com-
mands and made myself at home in his love.
11-15 “I’ve told you these things for a purpose:
that my joy might be your joy, and your joy
wholly mature. This is my command: Love

NEW KING JAMES VERSION

love one another as I have loved you. [13]Greater love has no one than this, than to lay down one's life for his friends. [14]You are My friends if you do whatever I command you. [15]No longer do I call you servants, for a servant does not know what his master is doing; but I have called you friends, for all things that I heard from My Father I have made known to you. [16]You did not choose Me, but I chose you and appointed you that you should go and bear fruit, and *that* your fruit should remain, that whatever you ask the Father in My name He may give you. [17]These things I command you, that you love one another.

THE WORLD'S HATRED

[18]"If the world hates you, you know that it hated Me before *it hated* you. [19]If you were of the world, the world would love its own. Yet because you are not of the world, but I chose you out of the world, therefore the world hates you. [20]Remember the word that I said to you, 'A servant is not greater than his master.' If they persecuted Me, they will also persecute you. If they kept My word, they will keep yours also. [21]But all these things they will do to you for My name's sake, because they do not know Him who sent Me. [22]If I had not come and spoken to them, they would have no sin, but now they have no excuse for their sin. [23]He who hates Me hates My Father also. [24]If I had not done among them the works which no one else did, they would have no sin; but now they have seen and also hated both Me and My Father. [25]But *this happened* that the word might be fulfilled which is written in their law, *'They hated Me without a cause.'*[a]

THE COMING REJECTION

[26]"But when the Helper comes, whom I shall send to you from the Father, the Spirit of truth who proceeds from the Father, He will testify of Me. [27]And you also will bear witness, because you have been with Me from the beginning.

16 "These things I have spoken to you, that you should not be made to stumble. [2]They will put you out of the synagogues; yes, the time is coming that whoever kills you will think that he offers God service. [3]And these things they will do to you[a] because they have not known the Father nor Me. [4]But these things I have told you, that when the[a] time comes, you may remember that I told you of them.

"And these things I did not say to you at the beginning, because I was with you.

THE WORK OF THE HOLY SPIRIT

[5]"But now I go away to Him who sent Me, and none of you asks Me, 'Where are You going?' [6]But because I have said these things to you, sorrow has filled your heart. [7]Nevertheless

15:25 [a]Psalm 69:4 **16:3** [a]NU-Text and M-Text omit *to you.* **16:4** [a]NU-Text reads *their.*

THE MESSAGE

one another the way I loved you. This is the very best way to love. Put your life on the line for your friends. You are my friends when you do the things I command you. I'm no longer calling you servants because servants don't understand what their master is thinking and planning. No, I've named you friends because I've let you in on everything I've heard from the Father.

16 "You didn't choose me, remember; I chose you, and put you in the world to bear fruit, fruit that won't spoil. As fruit bearers, whatever you ask the Father in relation to me, he gives you.

17 "But remember the root command: Love one another.

HATED BY THE WORLD

18-19 "If you find the godless world is hating you, remember it got its start hating me. If you lived on the world's terms, the world would love you as one of its own. But since I picked you to live on God's terms and no longer on the world's terms, the world is going to hate you.

20 "When that happens, remember this: Servants don't get better treatment than their masters. If they beat on me, they will certainly beat on you. If they did what I told them, they will do what you tell them.

21-25 "They are going to do all these things to you because of the way they treated me, because they don't know the One who sent me. If I hadn't come and told them all this in plain language, it wouldn't be so bad. As it is, they have no excuse. Hate me, hate my Father—it's all the same. If I hadn't done what I have done among them, works no one has *ever* done, they wouldn't be to blame. But they saw the God-signs and hated anyway, both me and my Father. Interesting—they have verified the truth of their own Scriptures where it is written, 'They hated me for no good reason.'

26-27 "When the Friend I plan to send you from the Father comes—the Spirit of Truth issuing from the Father—he will confirm everything about me. You, too, from your side must give your confirming evidence, since you are in this with me from the start."

1-4 16 "I've told you these things to prepare you for rough times ahead. They are going to throw you out of the meeting places. There will even come a time when anyone who kills you will think he's doing God a favor. They will do these things because they never really understood the Father. I've told you these things so that when the time comes and they start in on you, you'll be well-warned and ready for them.

THE FRIEND WILL COME

4-7 "I didn't tell you this earlier because I was with you every day. But now I am on my way to the One who sent me. Not one of you has asked, 'Where are you going?' Instead, the longer I've talked, the sadder you've become. So let me say it again, this truth: It's

NEW KING JAMES VERSION

I tell you the truth. It is to your advantage that I
go away; for if I do not go away, the Helper will
not come to you; but if I depart, I will send Him
to you. [8]And when He has come, He will convict
the world of sin, and of righteousness, and of
judgment: [9]of sin, because they do not believe in
Me; [10]of righteousness, because I go to My Fa-
ther and you see Me no more; [11]of judgment, be-
cause the ruler of this world is judged.
[12]"I still have many things to say to you, but
you cannot bear *them* now. [13]However, when
He, the Spirit of truth, has come, He will guide
you into all truth; for He will not speak on His
own *authority*, but whatever He hears He will
speak; and He will tell you things to come. [14]He
will glorify Me, for He will take of what is Mine
and declare *it* to you. [15]All things that the Father
has are Mine. Therefore I said that He will take
of Mine and declare *it* to you.[a]

SORROW WILL TURN TO JOY

[16]"A little while, and you will not see Me; and
again a little while, and you will see Me, because
I go to the Father."
[17]Then *some* of His disciples said among
themselves, "What is this that He says to us, 'A
little while, and you will not see Me; and again a
little while, and you will see Me'; and, 'because
I go to the Father'?" [18]They said therefore,
"What is this that He says, 'A little while'? We do
not know what He is saying."
[19]Now Jesus knew that they desired to ask
Him, and He said to them, "Are you inquiring
among yourselves about what I said, 'A little
while, and you will not see Me; and again a lit-
tle while, and you will see Me'? [20]Most as-
suredly, I say to you that you will weep and
lament, but the world will rejoice; and you will
be sorrowful, but your sorrow will be turned
into joy. [21]A woman, when she is in labor, has
sorrow because her hour has come; but as soon
as she has given birth to the child, she no longer
remembers the anguish, for joy that a human
being has been born into the world. [22]Therefore
you now have sorrow; but I will see you again
and your heart will rejoice, and your joy no one
will take from you.
[23]"And in that day you will ask Me nothing.
Most assuredly, I say to you, whatever you ask
the Father in My name He will give you. [24]Until
now you have asked nothing in My name. Ask,
and you will receive, that your joy may be full.

JESUS CHRIST HAS OVERCOME THE WORLD

[25]"These things I have spoken to you in figu-
rative language; but the time is coming when I
will no longer speak to you in figurative lan-
guage, but I will tell you plainly about the Fa-
ther. [26]In that day you will ask in My name, and

16:15 [a]NU-Text and M-Text read *He takes of Mine and will declare it to you.*

THE MESSAGE

better for you that I leave. If I don't leave, the Friend won't come. But if I go, I'll send him to you.

8-11 "When he comes, he'll expose the error of the godless world's view of sin, righteousness, and judgment: He'll show them that their refusal to believe in me is their basic sin; that righteousness comes from above, where I am with the Father, out of their sight and control; that judgment takes place as the ruler of this godless world is brought to trial and convicted.

12-15 "I still have many things to tell you, but you can't handle them now. But when the Friend comes, the Spirit of the Truth, he will take you by the hand and guide you into all the truth there is. He won't draw attention to himself, but will make sense out of what is about to happen and, indeed, out of all that I have done and said. He will honor me; he will take from me and deliver it to you. Everything the Father has is also mine. That is why I've said, 'He takes from me and delivers to you.'

16 "In a day or so you're not going to see me, but then in another day or so you will see me."

JOY LIKE A RIVER OVERFLOWING

17-18 That stirred up a hornet's nest of questions among the disciples: "What's he talking about: 'In a day or so you're not going to see me, but then in another day or so you will see me'? And, 'Because I'm on my way to the Father'? What is this 'day or so'? We don't know what he's talking about."

19-20 Jesus knew they were dying to ask him what he meant, so he said, "Are you trying to figure out among yourselves what I meant when I said, 'In a day or so you're not going to see me, but then in another day or so you will see me'? Then fix this firmly in your minds: You're going to be in deep mourning while the godless world throws a party. You'll be sad, very sad, but your sadness will develop into gladness.

21-23 "When a woman gives birth, she has a hard time, there's no getting around it. But when the baby is born, there is joy in the birth. This new life in the world wipes out memory of the pain. The sadness you have right now is similar to that pain, but the coming joy is also similar. When I see you again, you'll be full of joy, and it will be a joy no one can rob from you. You'll no longer be so full of questions.

23-24 "This is what I want you to do: Ask the Father for whatever is in keeping with the things I've revealed to you. Ask in my name, according to my will, and he'll most certainly give it to you. Your joy will be a river overflowing its banks!

25-28 "I've used figures of speech in telling you these things. Soon I'll drop the figures and tell you about the Father in plain language. Then you can make your requests directly to him in relation to this life I've revealed to you. I won't continue making requests of the Father on your behalf. I won't need to. Be-

NEW KING JAMES VERSION

I do not say to you that I shall pray the Father
for you; 27for the Father Himself loves you, be-
cause you have loved Me, and have believed that
I came forth from God. 28I came forth from the
Father and have come into the world. Again, I
leave the world and go to the Father."
29His disciples said to Him, "See, now You are
speaking plainly, and using no figure of speech!
30Now we are sure that You know all things, and
have no need that anyone should question You.
By this we believe that You came forth from
God."
31Jesus answered them, "Do you now be-
lieve? 32Indeed the hour is coming, yes, has now
come, that you will be scattered, each to his
own, and will leave Me alone. And yet I am not
alone, because the Father is with Me. 33These
things I have spoken to you, that in Me you may
have peace. In the world you will[a] have tribula-
tion; but be of good cheer, I have overcome the
world."

JESUS PRAYS FOR HIMSELF

17Jesus spoke these words, lifted up His eyes
to heaven, and said: "Father, the hour has
come. Glorify Your Son, that Your Son also may
glorify You, 2as You have given Him authority
over all flesh, that He should[a] give eternal life to
as many as You have given Him. 3And this is
eternal life, that they may know You, the only
true God, and Jesus Christ whom You have sent.
4I have glorified You on the earth. I have finished
the work which You have given Me to do. 5And
now, O Father, glorify Me together with Yourself,
with the glory which I had with You before the
world was.

JESUS PRAYS FOR HIS DISCIPLES

6"I have manifested Your name to the men
whom You have given Me out of the world. They
were Yours, You gave them to Me, and they have
kept Your word. 7Now they have known that all
things which You have given Me are from You.
8For I have given to them the words which You
have given Me; and they have received *them*,
and have known surely that I came forth from
You; and they have believed that You sent Me.
9"I pray for them. I do not pray for the world
but for those whom You have given Me, for they
are Yours. 10And all Mine are Yours, and Yours
are Mine, and I am glorified in them.

16:33 [a]NU-Text and M-Text omit *will*. **17:2** [a]M-Text reads *shall*.

THE MESSAGE

cause you've gone out on a limb, committed yourselves to love and trust in me, believing I came directly from the Father, the Father loves you directly. First, I left the Father and arrived in the world; now I leave the world and travel to the Father."

29-30 His disciples said, "Finally! You're giving it to us straight, in plain talk—no more figures of speech. Now we know that you know everything—it all comes together in you. You won't have to put up with our questions anymore. We're convinced you came from God."

31-33 Jesus answered them, "Do you finally believe? In fact, you're about to make a run for it—saving your own skins and abandoning me. But I'm not abandoned. The Father is with me. I've told you all this so that trusting me, you will be unshakable and assured, deeply at peace. In this godless world you will continue to experience difficulties. But take heart! I've conquered the world."

JESUS' PRAYER FOR HIS FOLLOWERS

1-5 17Jesus said these things. Then, raising his eyes in prayer, he said:

Father, it's time.
Display the bright splendor of your Son
So the Son in turn may show your bright
splendor.
You put him in charge of everything
human
So he might give real and eternal life to
all in his charge.
And this is the real and eternal life:
That they know you,
The one and only true God,
And Jesus Christ, whom you sent.
I glorified you on earth
By completing down to the last detail
What you assigned me to do.
And now, Father, glorify me with your
very own splendor,
The very splendor I had in your presence
Before there was a world.

6-12 I spelled out your character in detail
To the men and women you gave me.
They were yours in the first place;
Then you gave them to me,
And they have now done what you said.
They know now, beyond the shadow of a
doubt,
That everything you gave me is firsthand
from you,
For the message you gave me, I gave
them;
And they took it, and were convinced
That I came from you.
They believed that you sent me.
I pray for them.
I'm not praying for the God-rejecting
world
But for those you gave me,
For they are yours by right.
Everything mine is yours, and yours mine,
And my life is on display in them.

NEW KING JAMES VERSION

11 Now I am no longer in the world, but these are
in the world, and I come to You. Holy Father,
keep through Your name those whom You have
given Me,[a] that they may be one as We *are.*
12 While I was with them in the world,[a] I kept
them in Your name. Those whom You gave Me I
have kept;[b] and none of them is lost except the
son of perdition, that the Scripture might be ful-
filled. 13 But now I come to You, and these things
I speak in the world, that they may have My joy
fulfilled in themselves. 14 I have given them Your
word; and the world has hated them because
they are not of the world, just as I am not of the
world. 15 I do not pray that You should take them
out of the world, but that You should keep them
from the evil one. 16 They are not of the world,
just as I am not of the world. 17 Sanctify them by
Your truth. Your word is truth. 18 As You sent Me
into the world, I also have sent them into the
world. 19 And for their sakes I sanctify Myself,
that they also may be sanctified by the truth.

JESUS PRAYS FOR ALL BELIEVERS

20 "I do not pray for these alone, but also for
those who will[a] believe in Me through their
word; 21 that they all may be one, as You, Father,
are in Me, and I in You; that they also may be
one in Us, that the world may believe that You
sent Me. 22 And the glory which You gave Me I
have given them, that they may be one just as
We are one: 23 I in them, and You in Me; that they
may be made perfect in one, and that the world
may know that You have sent Me, and have
loved them as You have loved Me.

17:11 [a]NU-Text and M-Text read *keep them through Your name which You have given Me.* **17:12** [a]NU-Text omits *in the world.* [b]NU-Text reads *in Your name which You gave Me. And I guarded them;* (or *it;*). **17:20** [a]NU-Text and M-Text omit *will.*

THE MESSAGE

For I'm no longer going to be visible in
  the world;
They'll continue in the world
While I return to you.
Holy Father, guard them as they pursue
  this life
That you conferred as a gift through me,
So they can be one heart and mind
As we are one heart and mind.
As long as I was with them, I guarded
  them
In the pursuit of the life you gave
  through me;
I even posted a night watch.
And not one of them got away,
Except for the rebel bent on destruction
(the exception that proved the rule of
  Scripture).

13-19 Now I'm returning to you.
I'm saying these things in the world's
  hearing
So my people can experience
My joy completed in them.
I gave them your word;
The godless world hated them because
  of it,
Because they didn't join the world's
  ways,
Just as I didn't join the world's ways.
I'm not asking that you take them out of
  the world
But that you guard them from the Evil
  One.
They are no more defined by the world
Than I am defined by the world.
Make them holy—consecrated—with the
  truth;
Your word is consecrating truth.
In the same way that you gave me a
  mission in the world,
I give them a mission in the world.
I'm consecrating myself for their sakes
So they'll be truth-consecrated in their
  mission.

20-23 I'm praying not only for them
But also for those who will believe in me
Because of them and their witness about
  me.
The goal is for all of them to become one
  heart and mind—
Just as you, Father, are in me and I in you,
So they might be one heart and mind
  with us.
Then the world might believe that you, in
  fact, sent me.
The same glory you gave me, I gave them,
So they'll be as unified and together as
  we are—
I in them and you in me.
Then they'll be mature in this oneness,
And give the godless world evidence
That you've sent me and loved them
In the same way you've loved me.

NEW KING JAMES VERSION

24“Father, I desire that they also whom You gave Me may be with Me where I am, that they may behold My glory which You have given Me; for You loved Me before the foundation of the world. 25O righteous Father! The world has not known You, but I have known You; and these have known that You sent Me. 26And I have declared to them Your name, and will declare *it*, that the love with which You loved Me may be in them, and I in them.”

BETRAYAL AND ARREST IN GETHSEMANE

18 When Jesus had spoken these words, He went out with His disciples over the Brook Kidron, where there was a garden, which He and His disciples entered. 2And Judas, who betrayed Him, also knew the place; for Jesus often met there with His disciples. 3Then Judas, having received a detachment *of troops*, and officers from the chief priests and Pharisees, came there with lanterns, torches, and weapons. 4Jesus therefore, knowing all things that would come upon Him, went forward and said to them, “Whom are you seeking?”

5They answered Him, “Jesus of Nazareth.”

Jesus said to them, “I am *He*.” And Judas, who betrayed Him, also stood with them. 6Now when He said to them, “I am *He*,” they drew back and fell to the ground.

7Then He asked them again, “Whom are you seeking?”

And they said, “Jesus of Nazareth.”

8Jesus answered, “I have told you that I am *He*. Therefore, if you seek Me, let these go their way,” 9that the saying might be fulfilled which He spoke, “Of those whom You gave Me I have lost none.”

10Then Simon Peter, having a sword, drew it and struck the high priest’s servant, and cut off his right ear. The servant’s name was Malchus.

11So Jesus said to Peter, “Put your sword into the sheath. Shall I not drink the cup which My Father has given Me?”

BEFORE THE HIGH PRIEST

12Then the detachment *of troops* and the captain and the officers of the Jews arrested Jesus and bound Him. 13And they led Him away to Annas first, for he was the father-in-law of Caiaphas who was high priest that year. 14Now it was Caiaphas who advised the Jews that it was expedient that one man should die for the people.

PETER DENIES JESUS

15And Simon Peter followed Jesus, and so *did* another[a] disciple. Now that disciple was known to the high priest, and went with Jesus into the courtyard of the high priest. 16But Peter stood at the door outside. Then the other disciple, who

18:15 [a]M-Text reads *the other.*

THE MESSAGE

24-26 Father, I want those you gave me
To be with me, right where I am,
So they can see my glory, the splendor
you gave me,
Having loved me
Long before there ever was a world.
Righteous Father, the world has never
known you,
But I have known you, and these
disciples know
That you sent me on this mission.
I have made your very being known to
them—
Who you are and what you do—
And continue to make it known,
So that your love for me
Might be in them
Exactly as I am in them.

SEIZED IN THE GARDEN AT NIGHT

1 18 Jesus, having prayed this prayer, left with his disciples and crossed over the brook Kidron at a place where there was a garden. He and his disciples entered it.

2-4 Judas, his betrayer, knew the place because Jesus and his disciples went there often. So Judas led the way to the garden, and the Roman soldiers and police sent by the high priests and Pharisees followed. They arrived there with lanterns and torches and swords. Jesus, knowing by now everything that was coming down on him, went out and met them. He said, “Who are you after?”

They answered, “Jesus the Nazarene.”

5-6 He said, “That’s me.” The soldiers recoiled, totally taken aback. Judas, his betrayer, stood out like a sore thumb.

7 Jesus asked again, “Who are you after?”

They answered, “Jesus the Nazarene.”

8-9 “I told you,” said Jesus, “that’s me. I’m the one. So if it’s me you’re after, let these others go.” (This validated the words in his prayer, “I didn’t lose one of those you gave.”)

10 Just then Simon Peter, who was carrying a sword, pulled it from its sheath and struck the Chief Priest’s servant, cutting off his right ear. Malchus was the servant’s name.

11 Jesus ordered Peter, “Put back your sword. Do you think for a minute I’m not going to drink this cup the Father gave me?”

12-14 Then the Roman soldiers under their commander, joined by the Jewish police, seized Jesus and tied him up. They took him first to Annas, father-in-law of Caiaphas. Caiaphas was the Chief Priest that year. It was Caiaphas who had advised the Jews that it was to their advantage that one man die for the people.

15-16 Simon Peter and another disciple followed Jesus. That other disciple was known to the Chief Priest, and so he went in with Jesus to the Chief Priest’s courtyard. Peter had to stay outside. Then the other disciple

New King James Version

was known to the high priest, went out and
spoke to her who kept the door, and brought Pe-
ter in. 17Then the servant girl who kept the door
said to Peter, "You are not also *one* of this Man's
disciples, are you?"

He said, "I am not."

18Now the servants and officers who had
made a fire of coals stood there, for it was cold,
and they warmed themselves. And Peter stood
with them and warmed himself.

Jesus Questioned by the High Priest

19The high priest then asked Jesus about His
disciples and His doctrine.

20Jesus answered him, "I spoke openly to the
world. I always taught in synagogues and in the
temple, where the Jews always meet,[a] and in se-
cret I have said nothing. 21Why do you ask Me?
Ask those who have heard Me what I said to
them. Indeed they know what I said."

22And when He had said these things, one of
the officers who stood by struck Jesus with the
palm of his hand, saying, "Do You answer the
high priest like that?"

23Jesus answered him, "If I have spoken evil,
bear witness of the evil; but if well, why do you
strike Me?"

24Then Annas sent Him bound to Caiaphas
the high priest.

Peter Denies Twice More

25Now Simon Peter stood and warmed him-
self. Therefore they said to him, "You are not
also *one* of His disciples, are you?"

He denied *it* and said, "I am not!"

26One of the servants of the high priest, a rel-
ative *of him* whose ear Peter cut off, said, "Did I
not see you in the garden with Him?" 27Peter
then denied again; and immediately a rooster
crowed.

In Pilate's Court

28Then they led Jesus from Caiaphas to the
Praetorium, and it was early morning. But they
themselves did not go into the Praetorium, lest
they should be defiled, but that they might eat
the Passover. 29Pilate then went out to them and
said, "What accusation do you bring against this
Man?"

30They answered and said to him, "If He were
not an evildoer, we would not have delivered
Him up to you."

31Then Pilate said to them, "You take Him
and judge Him according to your law."

Therefore the Jews said to him, "It is not law-
ful for us to put anyone to death," 32that the say-
ing of Jesus might be fulfilled which He spoke,
signifying by what death He would die.

33Then Pilate entered the Praetorium again,
called Jesus, and said to Him, "Are You the King
of the Jews?"

34Jesus answered him, "Are you speaking for
yourself about this, or did others tell you this
concerning Me?"

35Pilate answered, "Am I a Jew? Your own na-
tion and the chief priests have delivered You to
me. What have You done?"

18:20 [a]NU-Text reads *where all the Jews meet.*

The Message

went out, spoke to the doorkeeper, and got Peter in.

17 The young woman who was the doorkeeper said to Peter, "Aren't you one of this man's disciples?"

He said, "No, I'm not."

18 The servants and police had made a fire because of the cold and were huddled there warming themselves. Peter stood with them, trying to get warm.

The Interrogation

19-21 Annas interrogated Jesus regarding his disciples and his teaching. Jesus answered, "I've spoken openly in public. I've taught regularly in meeting places and the Temple, where the Jews all come together. Everything has been out in the open. I've said nothing in secret. So why are you treating me like a conspirator? Question those who have been listening to me. They know well what I have said. My teachings have all been aboveboard."

22 When he said this, one of the policemen standing there slapped Jesus across the face, saying, "How dare you speak to the Chief Priest like that!"

23 Jesus replied, "If I've said something wrong, prove it. But if I've spoken the plain truth, why this slapping around?"

24 Then Annas sent him, still tied up, to the Chief Priest Caiaphas.

25 Meanwhile, Simon Peter was back at the fire, still trying to get warm. The others there said to him, "Aren't you one of his disciples?"

He denied it, "Not me."

26 One of the Chief Priest's servants, a relative of the man whose ear Peter had cut off, said, "Didn't I see you in the garden with him?"

27 Again, Peter denied it. Just then a rooster crowed.

The King of the Jews

28-29 They led Jesus then from Caiaphas to the Roman governor's palace. It was early morning. They themselves didn't enter the palace because they didn't want to be disqualified from eating the Passover. So Pilate came out to them and spoke. "What charge do you bring against this man?"

30 They said, "If he hadn't been doing something evil, do you think we'd be here bothering you?"

31-32 Pilate said, "You take him. Judge him by *your* law."

The Jews said, "We're not allowed to kill anyone." (This would confirm Jesus' word indicating the way he would die.)

33 Pilate went back into the palace and called for Jesus. He said, "Are you the 'King of the Jews'?"

34 Jesus answered, "Are you saying this on your own, or did others tell you this about me?"

35 Pilate said, "Do I look like a Jew? Your people and your high priests turned you over to me. What did you do?"

NEW KING JAMES VERSION

36Jesus answered, "My kingdom is not of this
world. If My kingdom were of this world, My
servants would fight, so that I should not be de-
livered to the Jews; but now My kingdom is not
from here."
37Pilate therefore said to Him, "Are You a
king then?"
Jesus answered, "You say *rightly* that I am a
king. For this cause I was born, and for this
cause I have come into the world, that I should
bear witness to the truth. Everyone who is of the
truth hears My voice."
38Pilate said to Him, "What is truth?" And
when he had said this, he went out again to the
Jews, and said to them, "I find no fault in Him at
all.

TAKING THE PLACE OF BARABBAS

39"But you have a custom that I should re-
lease someone to you at the Passover. Do you
therefore want me to release to you the King of
the Jews?"
40Then they all cried again, saying, "Not this
Man, but Barabbas!" Now Barabbas was a rob-
ber.

THE SOLDIERS MOCK JESUS

19 So then Pilate took Jesus and scourged
Him. 2And the soldiers twisted a crown of
thorns and put *it* on His head, and they put on
Him a purple robe. 3Then they said,[a] "Hail, King
of the Jews!" And they struck Him with their
hands.
4Pilate then went out again, and said to them,
"Behold, I am bringing Him out to you, that you
may know that I find no fault in Him."

PILATE'S DECISION

5Then Jesus came out, wearing the crown of
thorns and the purple robe. And *Pilate* said to
them, "Behold the Man!"
6Therefore, when the chief priests and offi-
cers saw Him, they cried out, saying, "Crucify
Him, crucify *Him!*"
Pilate said to them, "You take Him and cru-
cify *Him,* for I find no fault in Him."
7The Jews answered him, "We have a law,
and according to our[a] law He ought to die, be-
cause He made Himself the Son of God."
8Therefore, when Pilate heard that saying, he
was the more afraid, 9and went again into the
Praetorium, and said to Jesus, "Where are You
from?" But Jesus gave him no answer.
10Then Pilate said to Him, "Are You not
speaking to me? Do You not know that I have
power to crucify You, and power to release You?"
11Jesus answered, "You could have no power
at all against Me unless it had been given you
from above. Therefore the one who delivered
Me to you has the greater sin."
12From then on Pilate sought to release Him,
but the Jews cried out, saying, "If you let this
Man go, you are not Caesar's friend. Whoever
makes himself a king speaks against Caesar."
13When Pilate therefore heard that saying, he
brought Jesus out and sat down in the judgment
seat in a place that is called *The* Pavement, but

19:3 [a]NU-Text reads *And they came up to Him and said.*
19:7 [a]NU-Text reads *the law.*

THE MESSAGE

36 "My kingdom," said Jesus, "doesn't con-
sist of what you see around you. If it did, my
followers would fight so that I wouldn't be
handed over to the Jews. But I'm not that
kind of king, not the world's kind of king."
37 Then Pilate said, "So, are you a king or
not?"
Jesus answered, "You tell me. Because I
am King, I was born and entered the world
so that I could witness to the truth. Every-
one who cares for truth, who has any feeling
for the truth, recognizes my voice."
38-39 Pilate said, "What is truth?"
Then he went back out to the Jews and
told them, "I find nothing wrong in this man.
It's your custom that I pardon one prisoner
at Passover. Do you want me to pardon the
'King of the Jews'?"
40 They shouted back, "Not this one, but
Barabbas!" Barabbas was a Jewish freedom
fighter.

THE THORN CROWN OF THE KING

1-3 19 So Pilate took Jesus and had him
whipped. The soldiers, having braided a
crown from thorns, set it on his head, threw a
purple robe over him, and approached him
with, "Hail, King of the Jews!" Then they
greeted him with slaps in the face.
4-5 Pilate went back out again and said to
them, "I present him to you, but I want you
to know that I do not find him guilty of any
crime." Just then Jesus came out wearing
the thorn crown and purple robe.
Pilate announced, "Here he is: the Man."
6 When the high priests and police saw
him, they shouted in a frenzy, "Crucify! Cru-
cify!"
Pilate told them, "You take him. You cru-
cify him. I find nothing wrong with him."
7 The Jews answered, "We have a law, and
by that law he must die because he claimed
to be the Son of God."
8-9 When Pilate heard this, he became even
more scared. He went back into the palace
and said to Jesus, "Where did you come
from?"
Jesus gave no answer.
10 Pilate said, "You won't talk? Don't you
know that I have the authority to pardon
you, and the authority to—crucify you?"
11 Jesus said, "You haven't a shred of au-
thority over me except what has been given
you from heaven. That's why the one who
betrayed me to you has committed a far
greater fault."
12 At this, Pilate tried his best to pardon
him, but the Jews shouted him down: "If you
pardon this man, you're no friend of Cae-
sar's. Anyone setting himself up as 'king'
defies Caesar."
13-14 When Pilate heard those words, he led Je-
sus outside. He sat down at the judgment
seat in the area designated Stone Court (in

NEW KING JAMES VERSION

in Hebrew, Gabbatha. 14Now it was the Preparation Day of the Passover, and about the sixth hour. And he said to the Jews, "Behold your King!"

15But they cried out, "Away with *Him,* away with *Him!* Crucify Him!"

Pilate said to them, "Shall I crucify your King?"

The chief priests answered, "We have no king but Caesar!"

16Then he delivered Him to them to be crucified. Then they took Jesus and led *Him* away.[a]

THE KING ON A CROSS

17And He, bearing His cross, went out to a place called *the Place* of a Skull, which is called in Hebrew, Golgotha, 18where they crucified Him, and two others with Him, one on either side, and Jesus in the center. 19Now Pilate wrote a title and put *it* on the cross. And the writing was:

JESUS OF NAZARETH,
THE KING OF THE JEWS.

20Then many of the Jews read this title, for the place where Jesus was crucified was near the city; and it was written in Hebrew, Greek, *and* Latin.

21Therefore the chief priests of the Jews said to Pilate, "Do not write, 'The King of the Jews,' but, 'He said, "I am the King of the Jews." ' "

22Pilate answered, "What I have written, I have written."

23Then the soldiers, when they had crucified Jesus, took His garments and made four parts, to each soldier a part, and also the tunic. Now the tunic was without seam, woven from the top in one piece. 24They said therefore among themselves, "Let us not tear it, but cast lots for it, whose it shall be," that the Scripture might be fulfilled which says:

"They divided My garments among them,
And for My clothing they cast lots."[a]

Therefore the soldiers did these things.

BEHOLD YOUR MOTHER

25Now there stood by the cross of Jesus His mother, and His mother's sister, Mary the *wife* of Clopas, and Mary Magdalene. 26When Jesus therefore saw His mother, and the disciple whom He loved standing by, He said to His mother, "Woman, behold your son!" 27Then He said to the disciple, "Behold your mother!" And from that hour that disciple took her to his own *home.*

IT IS FINISHED

28After this, Jesus, knowing[a] that all things were now accomplished, that the Scripture might be fulfilled, said, "I thirst!" 29Now a vessel full of sour wine was sitting there; and they filled a sponge with sour wine, put *it* on hyssop, and put *it* to His mouth. 30So when Jesus had received the sour wine, He said, "It is finished!" And bowing His head, He gave up His spirit.

19:16 [a]NU-Text omits *and led Him away.* **19:24** [a]Psalm 22:18
19:28 [a]M-Text reads *seeing.*

THE MESSAGE

Hebrew, *Gabbatha*). It was the preparation day for Passover. The hour was noon. Pilate said to the Jews, "Here is your king."

15 They shouted back, "Kill him! Kill him! Crucify him!"

Pilate said, "I am to crucify your king?"

The high priests answered, "We have no king except Caesar."

16-19 Pilate caved in to their demand. He turned him over to be crucified.

THE CRUCIFIXION

They took Jesus away. Carrying his cross, Jesus went out to the place called Skull Hill (the name in Hebrew is *Golgotha*), where they crucified him, and with him two others, one on each side, Jesus in the middle. Pilate wrote a sign and had it placed on the cross. It read:

JESUS THE NAZARENE
THE KING OF THE JEWS.

20-21 Many of the Jews read the sign because the place where Jesus was crucified was right next to the city. It was written in Hebrew, Latin, and Greek. The Jewish high priests objected. "Don't write," they said to Pilate, " 'The King of the Jews.' Make it, 'This man said, "I am the King of the Jews." ' "

22 Pilate said, "What I've written, I've written."

23-24 When they crucified him, the Roman soldiers took his clothes and divided them up four ways, to each soldier a fourth. But his robe was seamless, a single piece of weaving, so they said to each other, "Let's not tear it up. Let's throw dice to see who gets it." This confirmed the Scripture that said, "They divided up my clothes among them and threw dice for my coat." (The soldiers validated the Scriptures!)

24-27 While the soldiers were looking after themselves, Jesus' mother, his aunt, Mary the wife of Clopas, and Mary Magdalene stood at the foot of the cross. Jesus saw his mother and the disciple he loved standing near her. He said to his mother, "Woman, here is your son." Then to the disciple, "Here is your mother." From that moment the disciple accepted her as his own mother.

28 Jesus, seeing that everything had been completed so that the Scripture record might also be complete, then said, "I'm thirsty."

29-30 A jug of sour wine was standing by. Someone put a sponge soaked with the wine on a javelin and lifted it to his mouth. After he took the wine, Jesus said, "It's done . . . complete." Bowing his head, he offered up his spirit.

New King James Version

Jesus' Side Is Pierced

31 Therefore, because it was the Preparation *Day*, that the bodies should not remain on the cross on the Sabbath (for that Sabbath was a high day), the Jews asked Pilate that their legs might be broken, and *that* they might be taken away. 32 Then the soldiers came and broke the legs of the first and of the other who was crucified with Him. 33 But when they came to Jesus and saw that He was already dead, they did not break His legs. 34 But one of the soldiers pierced His side with a spear, and immediately blood and water came out. 35 And he who has seen has testified, and his testimony is true; and he knows that he is telling the truth, so that you may believe. 36 For these things were done that the Scripture should be fulfilled, *"Not one of His bones shall be broken."*[a] 37 And again another Scripture says, *"They shall look on Him whom they pierced."*[a]

Jesus Buried in Joseph's Tomb

38 After this, Joseph of Arimathea, being a disciple of Jesus, but secretly, for fear of the Jews, asked Pilate that he might take away the body of Jesus; and Pilate gave *him* permission. So he came and took the body of Jesus. 39 And Nicodemus, who at first came to Jesus by night, also came, bringing a mixture of myrrh and aloes, about a hundred pounds. 40 Then they took the body of Jesus, and bound it in strips of linen with the spices, as the custom of the Jews is to bury. 41 Now in the place where He was crucified there was a garden, and in the garden a new tomb in which no one had yet been laid. 42 So there they laid Jesus, because of the Jews' Preparation *Day*, for the tomb was nearby.

The Empty Tomb

20 Now the first *day* of the week Mary Magdalene went to the tomb early, while it was still dark, and saw *that* the stone had been taken away from the tomb. 2 Then she ran and came to Simon Peter, and to the other disciple, whom Jesus loved, and said to them, "They have taken away the Lord out of the tomb, and we do not know where they have laid Him."

3 Peter therefore went out, and the other disciple, and were going to the tomb. 4 So they both ran together, and the other disciple outran Peter and came to the tomb first. 5 And he, stooping down and looking in, saw the linen cloths lying *there;* yet he did not go in. 6 Then Simon Peter came, following him, and went into the tomb; and he saw the linen cloths lying *there,* 7 and the handkerchief that had been around His head, not lying with the linen cloths, but folded together in a place by itself. 8 Then the other disciple, who came to the tomb first, went in also; and he saw and believed. 9 For as yet they did not know the Scripture, that He must rise again from the dead. 10 Then the disciples went away again to their own homes.

19:36 [a]Exodus 12:46; Numbers 9:12; Psalm 34:20 **19:37** [a]Zechariah 12:10

The Message

31-34 Then the Jews, since it was the day of Sabbath preparation, and so the bodies wouldn't stay on the crosses over the Sabbath (it was a high holy day that year), petitioned Pilate that their legs be broken to speed death, and the bodies taken down. So the soldiers came and broke the legs of the first man crucified with Jesus, and then the other. When they got to Jesus, they saw that he was already dead, so they didn't break his legs. One of the soldiers stabbed him in the side with his spear. Blood and water gushed out.

35 The eyewitness to these things has presented an accurate report. He saw it himself and is telling the truth so that you, also, will believe.

36-37 These things that happened confirmed the Scripture, "Not a bone in his body was broken," and the other Scripture that reads, "They will stare at the one they pierced."

38 After all this, Joseph of Arimathea (he was a disciple of Jesus, but secretly, because he was intimidated by the Jews) petitioned Pilate to take the body of Jesus. Pilate gave permission. So Joseph came and took the body.

39-42 Nicodemus, who had first come to Jesus at night, came now in broad daylight carrying a mixture of myrrh and aloes, about seventy-five pounds. They took Jesus' body and, following the Jewish burial custom, wrapped it in linen with the spices. There was a garden near the place he was crucified, and in the garden a new tomb in which no one had yet been placed. So, because it was Sabbath preparation for the Jews and the tomb was convenient, they placed Jesus in it.

Resurrection!

1-2 **20** Early in the morning on the first day of the week, while it was still dark, Mary Magdalene came to the tomb and saw that the stone was moved away from the entrance. She ran at once to Simon Peter and the other disciple, the one Jesus loved, breathlessly panting, "They took the Master from the tomb. We don't know where they've put him."

3-10 Peter and the other disciple left immediately for the tomb. They ran, neck and neck. The other disciple got to the tomb first, outrunning Peter. Stooping to look in, he saw the pieces of linen cloth lying there, but he didn't go in. Simon Peter arrived after him, entered the tomb, observed the linen cloths lying there, and the kerchief used to cover his head not lying with the linen cloths but separate, neatly folded by itself. Then the other disciple, the one who had gotten there first, went into the tomb, took one look at the evidence, and believed. No one yet knew from the Scripture that he had to rise from the dead. The disciples then went back home.

NEW KING JAMES VERSION

MARY MAGDALENE SEES THE RISEN LORD

11But Mary stood outside by the tomb weep-
ing, and as she wept she stooped down *and*
looked into the tomb. 12And she saw two angels
in white sitting, one at the head and the other at
the feet, where the body of Jesus had lain.
13Then they said to her, "Woman, why are you
weeping?"

She said to them, "Because they have taken
away my Lord, and I do not know where they
have laid Him."

14Now when she had said this, she turned
around and saw Jesus standing *there,* and did
not know that it was Jesus. 15Jesus said to her,
"Woman, why are you weeping? Whom are you
seeking?"

She, supposing Him to be the gardener, said
to Him, "Sir, if You have carried Him away, tell
me where You have laid Him, and I will take Him
away."

16Jesus said to her, "Mary!"

She turned and said to Him,[a] "Rabboni!"
(which is to say, Teacher).

17Jesus said to her, "Do not cling to Me, for I
have not yet ascended to My Father; but go to
My brethren and say to them, 'I am ascending to
My Father and your Father, and *to* My God and
your God.' "

18Mary Magdalene came and told the disci-
ples that she had seen the Lord,[a] and *that* He
had spoken these things to her.

THE APOSTLES COMMISSIONED

19Then, the same day at evening, being the
first *day* of the week, when the doors were shut
where the disciples were assembled,[a] for fear of
the Jews, Jesus came and stood in the midst,
and said to them, "Peace *be* with you." 20When
He had said this, He showed them *His* hands
and His side. Then the disciples were glad when
they saw the Lord.

21So Jesus said to them again, "Peace to you!
As the Father has sent Me, I also send you."
22And when He had said this, He breathed on
them, and said to them, "Receive the Holy
Spirit. 23If you forgive the sins of any, they are
forgiven them; if you retain the *sins* of any, they
are retained."

SEEING AND BELIEVING

24Now Thomas, called the Twin, one of the
twelve, was not with them when Jesus came.
25The other disciples therefore said to him, "We
have seen the Lord."

So he said to them, "Unless I see in His
hands the print of the nails, and put my finger
into the print of the nails, and put my hand into
His side, I will not believe."

26And after eight days His disciples were
again inside, and Thomas with them. Jesus
came, the doors being shut, and stood in the
midst, and said, "Peace to you!" 27Then He said
to Thomas, "Reach your finger here, and look at
My hands; and reach your hand *here,* and put *it*
into My side. Do not be unbelieving, but believ-
ing."

20:16 [a]NU-Text adds *in Hebrew.* **20:18** [a]NU-Text reads *disciples, "I have seen the Lord,"* . . . **20:19** [a]NU-Text omits *assembled.*

THE MESSAGE

11-13 But Mary stood outside the tomb weep-
ing. As she wept, she knelt to look into the
tomb and saw two angels sitting there,
dressed in white, one at the head, the other
at the foot of where Jesus' body had been
laid. They said to her, "Woman, why do you
weep?"

13-14 "They took my Master," she said, "and I
don't know where they put him." After she
said this, she turned away and saw Jesus
standing there. But she didn't recognize
him.

15 Jesus spoke to her, "Woman, why do you
weep? Who are you looking for?"

She, thinking that he was the gardener,
said, "Mister, if you took him, tell me where
you put him so I can care for him."

16 Jesus said, "Mary."

Turning to face him, she said in Hebrew,
"*Rabboni!*" meaning "Teacher!"

17 Jesus said, "Don't cling to me, for I have
not yet ascended to the Father. Go to my
brothers and tell them, 'I ascend to my Fa-
ther and your Father, my God and your
God.' "

18 Mary Magdalene went, telling the news
to the disciples: "I saw the Master!" And she
told them everything he said to her.

TO BELIEVE

19-20 Later on that day, the disciples had gathered
together, but, fearful of the Jews, had locked
all the doors in the house. Jesus entered,
stood among them, and said, "Peace to you."
Then he showed them his hands and side.

20-21 The disciples, seeing the Master with
their own eyes, were exuberant. Jesus re-
peated his greeting: "Peace to you. Just as
the Father sent me, I send you."

22-23 Then he took a deep breath and breathed
into them. "Receive the Holy Spirit," he said.
"If you forgive someone's sins, they're gone
for good. If you don't forgive sins, what are
you going to do with them?"

24-25 But Thomas, sometimes called the Twin,
one of the Twelve, was not with them when
Jesus came. The other disciples told him,
"We saw the Master."

But he said, "Unless I see the nail holes in
his hands, put my finger in the nail holes,
and stick my hand in his side, I won't be-
lieve it."

26 Eight days later, his disciples were again
in the room. This time Thomas was with
them. Jesus came through the locked doors,
stood among them, and said, "Peace to you."

27 Then he focused his attention on
Thomas. "Take your finger and examine my
hands. Take your hand and stick it in my
side. Don't be unbelieving. Believe."

New King James Version

28And Thomas answered and said to Him, "My Lord and my God!"

29Jesus said to him, "Thomas,[a] because you have seen Me, you have believed. Blessed *are* those who have not seen and *yet* have believed."

That You May Believe

30And truly Jesus did many other signs in the presence of His disciples, which are not written in this book; 31but these are written that you may believe that Jesus is the Christ, the Son of God, and that believing you may have life in His name.

Breakfast by the Sea

21 After these things Jesus showed Himself again to the disciples at the Sea of Tiberias, and in this way He showed *Himself:* 2Simon Peter, Thomas called the Twin, Nathanael of Cana in Galilee, the *sons* of Zebedee, and two others of His disciples were together. 3Simon Peter said to them, "I am going fishing."

They said to him, "We are going with you also." They went out and immediately[a] got into the boat, and that night they caught nothing. 4But when the morning had now come, Jesus stood on the shore; yet the disciples did not know that it was Jesus. 5Then Jesus said to them, "Children, have you any food?"

They answered Him, "No."

6And He said to them, "Cast the net on the right side of the boat, and you will find *some.*" So they cast, and now they were not able to draw it in because of the multitude of fish.

7Therefore that disciple whom Jesus loved said to Peter, "It is the Lord!" Now when Simon Peter heard that it was the Lord, he put on *his* outer garment (for he had removed it), and plunged into the sea. 8But the other disciples came in the little boat (for they were not far from land, but about two hundred cubits), dragging the net with fish. 9Then, as soon as they had come to land, they saw a fire of coals there, and fish laid on it, and bread. 10Jesus said to them, "Bring some of the fish which you have just caught."

11Simon Peter went up and dragged the net to land, full of large fish, one hundred and fifty-three; and although there were so many, the net was not broken. 12Jesus said to them, "Come *and* eat breakfast." Yet none of the disciples dared ask Him, "Who are You?"—knowing that it was the Lord. 13Jesus then came and took the bread and gave it to them, and likewise the fish.

14This *is* now the third time Jesus showed Himself to His disciples after He was raised from the dead.

Jesus Restores Peter

15So when they had eaten breakfast, Jesus said to Simon Peter, "Simon, *son* of Jonah,[a] do you love Me more than these?"

He said to Him, "Yes, Lord; You know that I love You."

He said to him, "Feed My lambs."

16He said to him again a second time, "Simon, *son* of Jonah,[a] do you love Me?"

20:29 [a]NU-Text and M-Text omit *Thomas.* **21:3** [a]NU-Text omits *immediately.* **21:15** [a]NU-Text reads *John.* **21:16** [a]NU-Text reads *John.*

The Message

28 Thomas said, "My Master! My God!"

29 Jesus said, "So, you believe because you've seen with your own eyes. Even better blessings are in store for those who believe without seeing."

30-31 Jesus provided far more God-revealing signs than are written down in this book. These are written down so you will believe that Jesus is the Messiah, the Son of God, and in the act of believing, have real and eternal life in the way he personally revealed it.

Fishing

1-3 21 After this, Jesus appeared again to the disciples, this time at the Tiberias Sea (the Sea of Galilee). This is how he did it: Simon Peter, Thomas (nicknamed "Twin"), Nathanael from Cana in Galilee, the brothers Zebedee, and two other disciples were together. Simon Peter announced, "I'm going fishing."

3-4 The rest of them replied, "We're going with you." They went out and got in the boat. They caught nothing that night. When the sun came up, Jesus was standing on the beach, but they didn't recognize him.

5 Jesus spoke to them: "Good morning! Did you catch anything for breakfast?"

They answered, "No."

6 He said, "Throw the net off the right side of the boat and see what happens."

They did what he said. All of a sudden there were so many fish in it, they weren't strong enough to pull it in.

7-9 Then the disciple Jesus loved said to Peter, "It's the Master!"

When Simon Peter realized that it was the Master, he threw on some clothes, for he was stripped for work, and dove into the sea. The other disciples came in by boat for they weren't far from land, a hundred yards or so, pulling along the net full of fish. When they got out of the boat, they saw a fire laid, with fish and bread cooking on it.

10-11 Jesus said, "Bring some of the fish you've just caught." Simon Peter joined them and pulled the net to shore—153 big fish! And even with all those fish, the net didn't rip.

12 Jesus said, "Breakfast is ready." Not one of the disciples dared ask, "Who are you?" They knew it was the Master.

13-14 Jesus then took the bread and gave it to them. He did the same with the fish. This was now the third time Jesus had shown himself alive to the disciples since being raised from the dead.

Do You Love Me?

15 After breakfast, Jesus said to Simon Peter, "Simon, son of John, do you love me more than these?"

"Yes, Master, you know I love you."

Jesus said, "Feed my lambs."

16 He then asked a second time, "Simon, son of John, do you love me?"

NEW KING JAMES VERSION

He said to Him, "Yes, Lord; You know that I love You."

He said to him, "Tend My sheep."

17He said to him the third time, "Simon, *son* of Jonah,[a] do you love Me?" Peter was grieved because He said to him the third time, "Do you love Me?"

And he said to Him, "Lord, You know all things; You know that I love You."

Jesus said to him, "Feed My sheep. 18Most assuredly, I say to you, when you were younger, you girded yourself and walked where you wished; but when you are old, you will stretch out your hands, and another will gird you and carry *you* where you do not wish." 19This He spoke, signifying by what death he would glorify God. And when He had spoken this, He said to him, "Follow Me."

THE BELOVED DISCIPLE AND HIS BOOK

20Then Peter, turning around, saw the disciple whom Jesus loved following, who also had leaned on His breast at the supper, and said, "Lord, who is the one who betrays You?" 21Peter, seeing him, said to Jesus, "But Lord, what *about* this man?"

22Jesus said to him, "If I will that he remain till I come, what *is that* to you? You follow Me."

23Then this saying went out among the brethren that this disciple would not die. Yet Jesus did not say to him that he would not die, but, "If I will that he remain till I come, what *is that* to you?"

24This is the disciple who testifies of these things, and wrote these things; and we know that his testimony is true.

25And there are also many other things that Jesus did, which if they were written one by one, I suppose that even the world itself could not contain the books that would be written. Amen.

21:17 [a]NU-Text reads *John.*

THE MESSAGE

"Yes, Master, you know I love you."
Jesus said, "Shepherd my sheep."
17-19 Then he said it a third time: "Simon, son
of John, do you love me?"
Peter was upset that he asked for the
third time, "Do you love me?" so he answered, "Master, you know everything there
is to know. You've got to know that I love
you."
Jesus said, "Feed my sheep. I'm telling
you the very truth now: When you were
young you dressed yourself and went wherever you wished, but when you get old you'll
have to stretch out your hands while someone else dresses you and takes you where
you don't want to go." He said this to hint at
the kind of death by which Peter would glorify God. And then he commanded, "Follow
me."

20-21 Turning his head, Peter noticed the disciple Jesus loved following right behind.
When Peter noticed him, he asked Jesus,
"Master, what's going to happen to *him*?"
22-23 Jesus said, "If I want him to live until I
come again, what's that to you? You—follow
me." That is how the rumor got out among
the brothers that this disciple wouldn't die.
But that is not what Jesus said. He simply
said, "If I want him to live until I come
again, what's that to you?"
24 This is the same disciple who was eyewitness to all these things and wrote them
down. And we all know that his eyewitness
account is reliable and accurate.
25 There are so many other things Jesus did.
If they were all written down, each of them,
one by one, I can't imagine a world big
enough to hold such a library of books.

ACTS

New King James Version

Prologue

1 The former account I made, O Theophilus, of all that Jesus began both to do and teach, [2]until the day in which He was taken up, after He through the Holy Spirit had given commandments to the apostles whom He had chosen, [3]to whom He also presented Himself alive after His suffering by many infallible proofs, being seen by them during forty days and speaking of the things pertaining to the kingdom of God.

The Holy Spirit Promised

[4]And being assembled together with *them,* He commanded them not to depart from Jerusalem, but to wait for the Promise of the Father, "which," *He said,* "you have heard from Me; [5]for John truly baptized with water, but you shall be baptized with the Holy Spirit not many days from now." [6]Therefore, when they had come together, they asked Him, saying, "Lord, will You at this time restore the kingdom to Israel?" [7]And He said to them, "It is not for you to know times or seasons which the Father has put in His own authority. [8]But you shall receive power when the Holy Spirit has come upon you; and you shall be witnesses to Me[a] in Jerusalem, and in all Judea and Samaria, and to the end of the earth."

Jesus Ascends to Heaven

[9]Now when He had spoken these things, while they watched, He was taken up, and a cloud received Him out of their sight. [10]And while they looked steadfastly toward heaven as He went up, behold, two men stood by them in white apparel, [11]who also said, "Men of Galilee, why do you stand gazing up into heaven? This *same* Jesus, who was taken up from you into heaven, will so come in like manner as you saw Him go into heaven."

The Upper Room Prayer Meeting

[12]Then they returned to Jerusalem from the mount called Olivet, which is near Jerusalem, a Sabbath day's journey. [13]And when they had entered, they went up into the upper room where they were staying: Peter, James, John, and Andrew; Philip and Thomas; Bartholomew and Matthew; James *the son* of Alphaeus and Simon the Zealot; and Judas *the son* of James. [14]These all continued with one accord in prayer and supplication,[a] with the women and Mary the mother of Jesus, and with His brothers.

Matthias Chosen

[15]And in those days Peter stood up in the midst of the disciples[a] (altogether the number of names was about a hundred and twenty), and

1:8 [a]NU-Text reads *My witnesses.* **1:14** [a]NU-Text omits *and supplication.* **1:15** [a]NU-Text reads *brethren.*

The Message

To the Ends of the World

1-5 **1** Dear Theophilus, in the first volume of this book I wrote on everything that Jesus began to do and teach until the day he said good-bye to the apostles, the ones he had chosen through the Holy Spirit, and was taken up to heaven. After his death, he presented himself alive to them in many different settings over a period of forty days. In face-to-face meetings, he talked to them about things concerning the kingdom of God. As they met and ate meals together, he told them that they were on no account to leave Jerusalem but "must wait for what the Father promised: the promise you heard from me. John baptized in water; you will be baptized in the Holy Spirit. And soon."

6 When they were together for the last time they asked, "Master, are you going to restore the kingdom to Israel now? Is this the time?"

7-8 He told them, "You don't get to know the time. Timing is the Father's business. What you'll get is the Holy Spirit. And when the Holy Spirit comes on you, you will be able to be my witnesses in Jerusalem, all over Judea and Samaria, even to the ends of the world."

9-11 These were his last words. As they watched, he was taken up and disappeared in a cloud. They stood there, staring into the empty sky. Suddenly two men appeared—in white robes! They said, "You Galileans!—why do you just stand here looking up at an empty sky? This very Jesus who was taken up from among you to heaven will come as certainly—and mysteriously—as he left."

Returning to Jerusalem

12-13 So they left the mountain called Olives and returned to Jerusalem. It was a little over half a mile. They went to the upper room they had been using as a meeting place:

Peter,
John,
James,
Andrew,
Philip,
Thomas,
Bartholomew,
Matthew,
James, son of Alphaeus,
Simon the Zealot,
Judas, son of James.

14 They agreed they were in this for good, completely together in prayer, the women included. Also Jesus' mother, Mary, and his brothers.

Replacing Judas

15-17 During this time, Peter stood up in the company—there were about 120 of them in the room at the time—and said, "Friends, long

New King James Version

said, 16“Men *and* brethren, this Scripture had to
be fulfilled, which the Holy Spirit spoke before
by the mouth of David concerning Judas, who
became a guide to those who arrested Jesus;
17for he was numbered with us and obtained a
part in this ministry.”
18(Now this man purchased a field with the
wages of iniquity; and falling headlong, he burst
open in the middle and all his entrails gushed
out. 19And it became known to all those dwelling
in Jerusalem; so that field is called in their own
language, Akel Dama, that is, Field of Blood.)
20“For it is written in the Book of Psalms:

‘Let his dwelling place be desolate,
And let no one live in it’;[a]

and,

‘Let[b] *another take his office.’*[c]

21“Therefore, of these men who have accom-
panied us all the time that the Lord Jesus went
in and out among us, 22beginning from the bap-
tism of John to that day when He was taken up
from us, one of these must become a witness
with us of His resurrection.”
23And they proposed two: Joseph called
Barsabas, who was surnamed Justus, and
Matthias. 24And they prayed and said, “You, O
Lord, who know the hearts of all, show which of
these two You have chosen 25to take part in this
ministry and apostleship from which Judas by
transgression fell, that he might go to his own
place.” 26And they cast their lots, and the lot fell
on Matthias. And he was numbered with the
eleven apostles.

Coming of the Holy Spirit

2 When the Day of Pentecost had fully come,
they were all with one accord[a] in one place.
2And suddenly there came a sound from
heaven, as of a rushing mighty wind, and it
filled the whole house where they were sitting.
3Then there appeared to them divided tongues,
as of fire, and *one* sat upon each of them. 4And
they were all filled with the Holy Spirit and be-
gan to speak with other tongues, as the Spirit
gave them utterance.

The Crowd’s Response

5And there were dwelling in Jerusalem Jews,
devout men, from every nation under heaven.
6And when this sound occurred, the multitude
came together, and were confused, because
everyone heard them speak in his own lan-
guage. 7Then they were all amazed and mar-
veled, saying to one another, “Look, are not all
these who speak Galileans? 8And how *is it that*
we hear, each in our own language in which we
were born? 9Parthians and Medes and Elamites,
those dwelling in Mesopotamia, Judea and Cap-
padocia, Pontus and Asia, 10Phrygia and Pam-
phylia, Egypt and the parts of Libya adjoining
Cyrene, visitors from Rome, both Jews and
proselytes,

1:20 [a]Psalm 69:25 [b]Psalm 109:8 [c]Greek *episkopen,* position of overseer **2:1** [a]NU-Text reads *together.*

The Message

ago the Holy Spirit spoke through David regarding Judas, who became the guide to those who arrested Jesus. That Scripture had to be fulfilled, and now has been. Judas was one of us and had his assigned place in this ministry.

18-20 “As you know, he took the evil bribe money and bought a small farm. There he came to a bad end, rupturing his belly and spilling his guts. Everybody in Jerusalem knows this by now; they call the place Murder Meadow. It’s exactly what we find written in the Psalms:

Let his farm become haunted
So no one can ever live there.

“And also what was written later:

Let someone else take over his post.

21-22 “Judas must now be replaced. The replacement must come from the company of men who stayed together with us from the time Jesus was baptized by John up to the day of his ascension, designated along with us as a witness to his resurrection.”

23-26 They nominated two: Joseph Barsabbas, nicknamed Justus, and Matthias. Then they prayed, “You, O God, know every one of us inside and out. Make plain which of these two men you choose to take the place in this ministry and leadership that Judas threw away in order to go his own way.” They then drew straws. Matthias won and was counted in with the eleven apostles.

A Sound Like a Strong Wind

1-4 2 When the Feast of Pentecost came, they were all together in one place. Without warning there was a sound like a strong wind, gale force—no one could tell where it came from. It filled the whole building. Then, like a wildfire, the Holy Spirit spread through their ranks, and they started speaking in a number of different languages as the Spirit prompted them.

5-11 There were many Jews staying in Jerusalem just then, devout pilgrims from all over the world. When they heard the sound, they came on the run. Then when they heard, one after another, their own mother tongues being spoken, they were thunderstruck. They couldn’t for the life of them figure out what was going on, and kept saying, “Aren’t these all Galileans? How come we’re hearing them talk in our various mother tongues?

Parthians, Medes, and Elamites;
Visitors from Mesopotamia, Judea, and
Cappadocia,
Pontus and Asia, Phrygia and
Pamphylia,
Egypt and the parts of Libya
belonging to Cyrene;
Immigrants from Rome, both Jews and
proselytes;

NEW KING JAMES VERSION

[11]Cretans and Arabs—we hear them speaking in our own tongues the wonderful works of God." [12]So they were all amazed and perplexed, saying to one another, "Whatever could this mean?" [13]Others mocking said, "They are full of new wine."

PETER'S SERMON

[14]But Peter, standing up with the eleven, raised his voice and said to them, "Men of Judea and all who dwell in Jerusalem, let this be known to you, and heed my words. [15]For these are not drunk, as you suppose, since it is *only* the third hour of the day. [16]But this is what was spoken by the prophet Joel:

[17]*'And it shall come to pass in the last days, says God,*
That I will pour out of My Spirit on all flesh;
Your sons and your daughters shall prophesy,
Your young men shall see visions,
Your old men shall dream dreams.
[18]*And on My menservants and on My maidservants*
I will pour out My Spirit in those days;
And they shall prophesy.
[19]*I will show wonders in heaven above*
And signs in the earth beneath:
Blood and fire and vapor of smoke.
[20]*The sun shall be turned into darkness,*
And the moon into blood,
Before the coming of the great and awesome day of the LORD.
[21]*And it shall come to pass*
That whoever calls on the name of the LORD
Shall be saved.' [a]

[22]"Men of Israel, hear these words: Jesus of Nazareth, a Man attested by God to you by miracles, wonders, and signs which God did through Him in your midst, as you yourselves also know— [23]Him, being delivered by the determined purpose and foreknowledge of God, you have taken[a] by lawless hands, have crucified, and put to death; [24]whom God raised up, having loosed the pains of death, because it was not possible that He should be held by it. [25]For David says concerning Him:

'I foresaw the LORD always before my face,
For He is at my right hand, that I may not be shaken.
[26]*Therefore my heart rejoiced, and my tongue was glad;*
Moreover my flesh also will rest in hope.
[27]*For You will not leave my soul in Hades,*
Nor will You allow Your Holy One to see corruption.
[28]*You have made known to me the ways of life;*
You will make me full of joy in Your presence.' [a]

2:21 [a]Joel 2:28–32 **2:23** [a]NU-Text omits *have taken.* **2:28** [a]Psalm 16:8–11

THE MESSAGE

Even Cretans and Arabs!

"They're speaking our languages, describing God's mighty works!"

12 Their heads were spinning; they couldn't make head or tail of any of it. They talked back and forth, confused: "What's going on here?"

13 Others joked, "They're drunk on cheap wine."

PETER SPEAKS UP

14-21 That's when Peter stood up and, backed by the other eleven, spoke out with bold urgency: "Fellow Jews, all of you who are visiting Jerusalem, listen carefully and get this story straight. These people aren't drunk as some of you suspect. They haven't had time to get drunk—it's only nine o'clock in the morning. This is what the prophet Joel announced would happen:

"In the Last Days," God says,
"I will pour out my Spirit
on every kind of people:
Your sons will prophesy,
also your daughters;
Your young men will see visions,
your old men dream dreams.
When the time comes,
I'll pour out my Spirit
On those who serve me, men and women both,
and they'll prophesy.
I'll set wonders in the sky above
and signs on the earth below,
Blood and fire and billowing smoke,
the sun turning black and the moon blood-red,
Before the Day of the Lord arrives,
the Day tremendous and marvelous;
And whoever calls out for help
to me, God, will be saved."

22-28 "Fellow Israelites, listen carefully to these words: Jesus the Nazarene, a man thoroughly accredited by God to you—the miracles and wonders and signs that God did through him are common knowledge—this Jesus, following the deliberate and well-thought-out plan of God, was betrayed by men who took the law into their own hands, and was handed over to you. And you pinned him to a cross and killed him. But God untied the death ropes and raised him up. Death was no match for him. David said it all:

I saw God before me for all time.
Nothing can shake me; he's right by my side.
I'm glad from the inside out, ecstatic;
I've pitched my tent in the land of hope.
I know you'll never dump me in Hades;
I'll never even smell the stench of death.
You've got my feet on the life-path,
with your face shining sun-joy all around.

NEW KING JAMES VERSION

29“Men *and* brethren, let *me* speak freely to
you of the patriarch David, that he is both dead
and buried, and his tomb is with us to this day.
30Therefore, being a prophet, and knowing that
God had sworn with an oath to him that of the
fruit of his body, according to the flesh, He
would raise up the Christ to sit on his throne,[a]
31he, foreseeing this, spoke concerning the res-
urrection of the Christ, that His soul was not left
in Hades, nor did His flesh see corruption. 32This
Jesus God has raised up, of which we are all wit-
nesses. 33Therefore being exalted to the right
hand of God, and having received from the Fa-
ther the promise of the Holy Spirit, He poured
out this which you now see and hear.
34“For David did not ascend into the heavens,
but he says himself:

‘The Lord said to my Lord,
“Sit at My right hand,
35*Till I make Your enemies Your footstool.” ’*[a]

36“Therefore let all the house of Israel know
assuredly that God has made this Jesus, whom
you crucified, both Lord and Christ.”
37Now when they heard *this*, they were cut to
the heart, and said to Peter and the rest of the
apostles, “Men *and* brethren, what shall we do?”
38Then Peter said to them, “Repent, and let
every one of you be baptized in the name of Je-
sus Christ for the remission of sins; and you
shall receive the gift of the Holy Spirit. 39For the
promise is to you and to your children, and to all
who are afar off, as many as the Lord our God
will call.”

A VITAL CHURCH GROWS

40And with many other words he testified
and exhorted them, saying, “Be saved from this
perverse generation.” 41Then those who gladly[a]
received his word were baptized; and that day
about three thousand souls were added *to them*.
42And they continued steadfastly in the apostles’
doctrine and fellowship, in the breaking of
bread, and in prayers. 43Then fear came upon
every soul, and many wonders and signs were
done through the apostles. 44Now all who be-
lieved were together, and had all things in com-
mon, 45and sold their possessions and goods,
and divided them among all, as anyone had
need.
46So continuing daily with one accord in the
temple, and breaking bread from house to
house, they ate their food with gladness and
simplicity of heart, 47praising God and having
favor with all the people. And the Lord added to
the church[a] daily those who were being saved.

A LAME MAN HEALED

3 Now Peter and John went up together to the
temple at the hour of prayer, the ninth *hour*.
2And a certain man lame from his mother’s
womb was carried, whom they laid daily at the
gate of the temple which is called Beautiful, to
ask alms from those who entered the temple;

2:30 [a]NU-Text omits *according to the flesh, He would raise up the Christ* and completes the verse with *He would seat one on his throne.* **2:35** [a]Psalm 110:1 **2:41** [a]NU-Text omits *gladly.* **2:47** [a]NU-Text omits *to the church.*

THE MESSAGE

29-36 “Dear friends, let me be completely frank with you. Our ancestor David is dead and buried—his tomb is in plain sight today. But being also a prophet and knowing that God had solemnly sworn that a descendant of his would rule his kingdom, seeing far ahead, he talked of the resurrection of the Messiah—‘no trip to Hades, no stench of death.’ This Jesus, God raised up. And every one of us here is a witness to it. Then, raised to the heights at the right hand of God and receiving the promise of the Holy Spirit from the Father, he poured out the Spirit he had just received. That is what you see and hear. For David himself did not ascend to heaven, but he did say,

God said to my Master, “Sit at my right
hand
Until I make your enemies a stool for
resting your feet.”

“All Israel, then, know this: There’s no longer room for doubt—God made him Master and Messiah, this Jesus whom you killed on a cross.”

37 Cut to the quick, those who were there listening asked Peter and the other apostles, “Brothers! Brothers! So now what do we do?”

38-39 Peter said, “Change your life. Turn to God and be baptized, each of you, in the name of Jesus Christ, so your sins are forgiven. Receive the gift of the Holy Spirit. The promise is targeted to you and your children, but also to all who are far away—whomever, in fact, our Master God invites.”

40 He went on in this vein for a long time, urging them over and over, “Get out while you can; get out of this sick and stupid culture!”

41-42 That day about three thousand took him at his word, were baptized and were signed up. They committed themselves to the teaching of the apostles, the life together, the common meal, and the prayers.

43-45 Everyone around was in awe—all those wonders and signs done through the apostles! And all the believers lived in a wonderful harmony, holding everything in common. They sold whatever they owned and pooled their resources so that each person’s need was met.

46-47 They followed a daily discipline of worship in the Temple followed by meals at home, every meal a celebration, exuberant and joyful, as they praised God. People in general liked what they saw. Every day their number grew as God added those who were saved.

1-5 3 One day at three o’clock in the afternoon, Peter and John were on their way into the Temple for prayer meeting. At the same time there was a man crippled from birth being carried up. Every day he was set down at the Temple gate, the one named Beautiful, to beg from those going into the Temple. When

NEW KING JAMES VERSION

[3]who, seeing Peter and John about to go into the temple, asked for alms. [4]And fixing his eyes on him, with John, Peter said, "Look at us." [5]So he gave them his attention, expecting to receive something from them. [6]Then Peter said, "Silver and gold I do not have, but what I do have I give you: In the name of Jesus Christ of Nazareth, rise up and walk." [7]And he took him by the right hand and lifted *him* up, and immediately his feet and ankle bones received strength. [8]So he, leaping up, stood and walked and entered the temple with them—walking, leaping, and praising God. [9]And all the people saw him walking and praising God. [10]Then they knew that it was he who sat begging alms at the Beautiful Gate of the temple; and they were filled with wonder and amazement at what had happened to him.

PREACHING IN SOLOMON'S PORTICO

[11]Now as the lame man who was healed held on to Peter and John, all the people ran together to them in the porch which is called Solomon's, greatly amazed. [12]So when Peter saw *it*, he responded to the people: "Men of Israel, why do you marvel at this? Or why look so intently at us, as though by our own power or godliness we had made this man walk? [13]The God of Abraham, Isaac, and Jacob, the God of our fathers, glorified His Servant Jesus, whom you delivered up and denied in the presence of Pilate, when he was determined to let *Him* go. [14]But you denied the Holy One and the Just, and asked for a murderer to be granted to you, [15]and killed the Prince of life, whom God raised from the dead, of which we are witnesses. [16]And His name, through faith in His name, has made this man strong, whom you see and know. Yes, the faith which *comes* through Him has given him this perfect soundness in the presence of you all.

[17]"Yet now, brethren, I know that you did *it* in ignorance, as *did* also your rulers. [18]But those things which God foretold by the mouth of all His prophets, that the Christ would suffer, He has thus fulfilled. [19]Repent therefore and be converted, that your sins may be blotted out, so that times of refreshing may come from the presence of the Lord, [20]and that He may send Jesus Christ, who was preached to you before,[a] [21]whom heaven must receive until the times of restoration of all things, which God has spoken by the mouth of all His holy prophets since the world began. [22]For Moses truly said to the fathers, *'The LORD your God will raise up for you a Prophet like me from your brethren. Him you shall hear in all things, whatever He says to you.* [23]*And it shall be that every soul who will not hear that Prophet shall be utterly destroyed from among the people.'*[a] [24]Yes, and all the prophets, from Samuel and those who follow, as many as have spoken, have also foretold[a] these days. [25]You are sons of the prophets, and of the covenant which God made with our fathers, saying to Abraham, *'And in your seed all the fami-*

3:20 [a]NU-Text and M-Text read *Christ Jesus, who was ordained for you before.* **3:23** [a]Deuteronomy 18:15, 18, 19 **3:24** [a]NU-Text and M-Text read *proclaimed.*

THE MESSAGE

he saw Peter and John about to enter the Temple, he asked for a handout. Peter, with John at his side, looked him straight in the eye and said, "Look here." He looked up, expecting to get something from them.

6-8 Peter said, "I don't have a nickel to my name, but what I do have, I give you: In the name of Jesus Christ of Nazareth, walk!" He grabbed him by the right hand and pulled him up. In an instant his feet and ankles became firm. He jumped to his feet and walked.

8-10 The man went into the Temple with them, walking back and forth, dancing and praising God. Everybody there saw him walking around and praising God. They recognized him as the one who sat begging at the Temple's Gate Beautiful and rubbed their eyes, astonished, scarcely believing what they were seeing.

11 The man threw his arms around Peter and John, ecstatic. All the people ran up to where they were at Solomon's Porch to see it for themselves.

TURN TO FACE GOD

12-16 When Peter saw he had a congregation, he addressed the people:

"Oh, Israelites, why does this take you by such complete surprise, and why stare at us as if *our* power or piety made him walk? The God of Abraham and Isaac and Jacob, the God of our ancestors, has glorified his Son Jesus. The very One that Pilate called innocent, you repudiated. You repudiated the Holy One, the Just One, and asked for a murderer in his place. You no sooner killed the Author of Life than God raised him from the dead—and we're the witnesses. Faith in Jesus' name put this man, whose condition you know so well, on his feet—yes, faith and nothing but faith put this man healed and whole right before your eyes.

17-18 "And now, friends, I know you had no idea what you were doing when you killed Jesus, and neither did your leaders. But God, who through the preaching of all the prophets had said all along that his Messiah would be killed, knew exactly what you were doing and used it to fulfill his plans.

19-23 "Now it's time to change your ways! Turn to face God so he can wipe away your sins, pour out showers of blessing to refresh you, and send you the Messiah he prepared for you, namely, Jesus. For the time being he must remain out of sight in heaven until everything is restored to order again just the way God, through the preaching of his holy prophets of old, said it would be. Moses, for instance, said, 'Your God will raise up for you a prophet just like me from your family. Listen to every word he speaks to you. Every last living soul who refuses to listen to that prophet will be wiped out from the people.'

24-26 "All the prophets from Samuel on down said the same thing, said most emphatically that these days would come. These prophets, along with the covenant God made with your ancestors, are your family tree. God's covenant-word to Abraham pro-

NEW KING JAMES VERSION

lies of the earth shall be blessed.' [a] [26]To you first,
God, having raised up His Servant Jesus, sent
Him to bless you, in turning away every one *of*
you from your iniquities."

PETER AND JOHN ARRESTED

4 Now as they spoke to the people, the priests,
the captain of the temple, and the Sadducees
came upon them, [2]being greatly disturbed that
they taught the people and preached in Jesus
the resurrection from the dead. [3]And they laid
hands on them, and put *them* in custody until
the next day, for it was already evening. [4]How-
ever, many of those who heard the word be-
lieved; and the number of the men came to be
about five thousand.

ADDRESSING THE SANHEDRIN

[5]And it came to pass, on the next day, that
their rulers, elders, and scribes, [6]as well as An-
nas the high priest, Caiaphas, John, and Alexan-
der, and as many as were of the family of the
high priest, were gathered together at
Jerusalem. [7]And when they had set them in the
midst, they asked, "By what power or by what
name have you done this?"
[8]Then Peter, filled with the Holy Spirit, said
to them, "Rulers of the people and elders of Is-
rael: [9]If we this day are judged for a good deed
done to a helpless man, by what means he has
been made well, [10]let it be known to you all, and
to all the people of Israel, that by the name of Je-
sus Christ of Nazareth, whom you crucified,
whom God raised from the dead, by Him this
man stands here before you whole. [11]This is the
'stone which was rejected by you builders,
which has become the chief cornerstone.' [a]
[12]Nor is there salvation in any other, for there is
no other name under heaven given among men
by which we must be saved."

THE NAME OF JESUS FORBIDDEN

[13]Now when they saw the boldness of Peter
and John, and perceived that they were unedu-
cated and untrained men, they marveled. And
they realized that they had been with Jesus.
[14]And seeing the man who had been healed
standing with them, they could say nothing
against it. [15]But when they had commanded
them to go aside out of the council, they con-
ferred among themselves, [16]saying, "What shall
we do to these men? For, indeed, that a notable
miracle has been done through them *is* evident
to all who dwell in Jerusalem, and we cannot
deny *it*. [17]But so that it spreads no further
among the people, let us severely threaten them,
that from now on they speak to no man in this
name."
[18]So they called them and commanded them
not to speak at all nor teach in the name of Je-
sus. [19]But Peter and John answered and said to
them, "Whether it is right in the sight of God to
listen to you more than to God, you judge. [20]For
we cannot but speak the things which we have
seen and heard."

3:25 [a]Genesis 22:18; 26:4; 28:14 **4:11** [a]Psalm 118:22

THE MESSAGE

vides the text: 'By your offspring all the families of the earth will be blessed.' But you are first in line: God, having raised up his Son, sent him to bless you as you turn, one by one, from your evil ways."

NOTHING TO HIDE

1-4 4 While Peter and John were addressing the people, the priests, the chief of the Temple police, and some Sadducees came up, indignant that these upstart apostles were instructing the people and proclaiming that the resurrection from the dead had taken place in Jesus. They arrested them and threw them in jail until morning, for by now it was late in the evening. But many of those who listened had already believed the Message—in round numbers about five thousand!

5-7 The next day a meeting was called in Jerusalem. The rulers, religious leaders, religion scholars, Annas the Chief Priest, Caiaphas, John, Alexander—everybody who was anybody was there. They stood Peter and John in the middle of the room and grilled them: "Who put you in charge here? What business do you have doing this?"

8-12 With that, Peter, full of the Holy Spirit, let loose: "Rulers and leaders of the people, if we have been brought to trial today for helping a sick man, put under investigation regarding this healing, I'll be completely frank with you—we have nothing to hide. By the name of Jesus Christ of Nazareth, the One you killed on a cross, the One God raised from the dead, by means of his name this man stands before you healthy and whole. Jesus is 'the stone you masons threw out, which is now the cornerstone.' Salvation comes no other way; no other name has been or will be given to us by which we can be saved, only this one."

13-14 They couldn't take their eyes off them—Peter and John standing there so confident, so sure of themselves! Their fascination deepened when they realized these two were laymen with no training in Scripture or formal education. They recognized them as companions of Jesus, but with the man right before them, seeing him standing there so upright—so healed!—what could they say against that?

15-17 They sent them out of the room so they could work out a plan. They talked it over: "What can we do with these men? By now it's known all over town that a miracle has occurred, and that they are behind it. There is no way we can refute that. But so that it doesn't go any further, let's silence them with threats so they won't dare to use Jesus' name ever again with anyone."

18-20 They called them back and warned them that they were on no account ever again to speak or teach in the name of Jesus. But Peter and John spoke right back, "Whether it's right in God's eyes to listen to you rather than to God, you decide. As for us, there's no question—we can't keep quiet about what we've seen and heard."

NEW KING JAMES VERSION

21So when they had further threatened them,
they let them go, finding no way of punishing
them, because of the people, since they all glori-
fied God for what had been done. 22For the man
was over forty years old on whom this miracle
of healing had been performed.

PRAYER FOR BOLDNESS

23And being let go, they went to their own
companions and reported all that the chief
priests and elders had said to them. 24So when
they heard that, they raised their voice to God
with one accord and said: "Lord, You *are* God,
who made heaven and earth and the sea, and all
that is in them, 25who by the mouth of Your ser-
vant David[a] have said:

'Why did the nations rage,
And the people plot vain things?
26*The kings of the earth took their stand,*
And the rulers were gathered together
Against the LORD and against His Christ.' [a]

27"For truly against Your holy Servant Jesus,
whom You anointed, both Herod and Pontius Pi-
late, with the Gentiles and the people of Israel,
were gathered together 28to do whatever Your
hand and Your purpose determined before to be
done. 29Now, Lord, look on their threats, and
grant to Your servants that with all boldness
they may speak Your word, 30by stretching out
Your hand to heal, and that signs and wonders
may be done through the name of Your holy Ser-
vant Jesus."

31And when they had prayed, the place
where they were assembled together was
shaken; and they were all filled with the Holy
Spirit, and they spoke the word of God with
boldness.

SHARING IN ALL THINGS

32Now the multitude of those who believed
were of one heart and one soul; neither did any-
one say that any of the things he possessed was
his own, but they had all things in common.
33And with great power the apostles gave wit-
ness to the resurrection of the Lord Jesus. And
great grace was upon them all. 34Nor was there
anyone among them who lacked; for all who
were possessors of lands or houses sold them,
and brought the proceeds of the things that
were sold, 35and laid *them* at the apostles' feet;
and they distributed to each as anyone had
need.

36And Joses,[a] who was also named Barnabas
by the apostles (which is translated Son of En-
couragement), a Levite of the country of
Cyprus, 37having land, sold *it*, and brought the
money and laid *it* at the apostles' feet.

LYING TO THE HOLY SPIRIT

5 But a certain man named Ananias, with Sap-
phira his wife, sold a possession. 2And he

4:25 [a]NU-Text reads *who through the Holy Spirit, by the mouth of our father, Your servant David.* **4:26** [a]Psalm 2:1, 2 **4:36** [a]NU-Text reads *Joseph.*

THE MESSAGE

21-22 The religious leaders renewed their
threats, but then released them. They couldn't
come up with a charge that would stick, that
would keep them in jail. The people wouldn't
have stood for it—they were all praising God
over what had happened. The man who had
been miraculously healed was over forty
years old.

ONE HEART, ONE MIND

23-26 As soon as Peter and John were let go, they
went to their friends and told them what the
high priests and religious leaders had said.
Hearing the report, they lifted their voices in
a wonderful harmony in prayer: "Strong
God, you made heaven and earth and sea
and everything in them. By the Holy Spirit
you spoke through the mouth of your ser-
vant and our father, David:

Why the big noise, nations?
Why the mean plots, peoples?
Earth's leaders push for position,
Potentates meet for summit talks,
The God-deniers, the Messiah-defiers!

27-28 "For in fact they did meet—Herod and
Pontius Pilate with nations and peoples,
even Israel itself!—met in this very city to
plot against your holy Son Jesus, the One
you made Messiah, to carry out the plans
you long ago set in motion.

29-30 "And now they're at it again! Take care of
their threats and give your servants fearless
confidence in preaching your Message, as
you stretch out your hand to us in healings
and miracles and wonders done in the name
of your holy servant Jesus."

31 While they were praying, the place where
they were meeting trembled and shook.
They were all filled with the Holy Spirit and
continued to speak God's Word with fear-
less confidence.

32-33 The whole congregation of believers was
united as one—one heart, one mind! They
didn't even claim ownership of their own
possessions. No one said, "That's mine; you
can't have it." They shared everything. The
apostles gave powerful witness to the resur-
rection of the Master Jesus, and grace was
on all of them.

34-35 And so it turned out that not a person
among them was needy. Those who owned
fields or houses sold them and brought the
price of the sale to the apostles and made an
offering of it. The apostles then distributed
it according to each person's need.

36-37 Joseph, called by the apostles "Barnabas"
(which means "Son of Comfort"), a Levite
born in Cyprus, sold a field that he owned,
brought the money, and made an offering of
it to the apostles.

ANANIAS AND SAPPHIRA

1-2 5 But a man named Ananias—his wife, Sap-
phira, conniving in this with him—sold a

NEW KING JAMES VERSION

kept back *part* of the proceeds, his wife also being aware *of it,* and brought a certain part and laid *it* at the apostles' feet. [3]But Peter said, "Ananias, why has Satan filled your heart to lie to the Holy Spirit and keep back *part* of the price of the land for yourself? [4]While it remained, was it not your own? And after it was sold, was it not in your own control? Why have you conceived this thing in your heart? You have not lied to men but to God."

[5]Then Ananias, hearing these words, fell down and breathed his last. So great fear came upon all those who heard these things. [6]And the young men arose and wrapped him up, carried *him* out, and buried *him.*

[7]Now it was about three hours later when his wife came in, not knowing what had happened. [8]And Peter answered her, "Tell me whether you sold the land for so much?"

She said, "Yes, for so much."

[9]Then Peter said to her, "How is it that you have agreed together to test the Spirit of the Lord? Look, the feet of those who have buried your husband *are* at the door, and they will carry you out." [10]Then immediately she fell down at his feet and breathed her last. And the young men came in and found her dead, and carrying *her* out, buried *her* by her husband. [11]So great fear came upon all the church and upon all who heard these things.

CONTINUING POWER IN THE CHURCH

[12]And through the hands of the apostles many signs and wonders were done among the people. And they were all with one accord in Solomon's Porch. [13]Yet none of the rest dared join them, but the people esteemed them highly. [14]And believers were increasingly added to the Lord, multitudes of both men and women, [15]so that they brought the sick out into the streets and laid *them* on beds and couches, that at least the shadow of Peter passing by might fall on some of them. [16]Also a multitude gathered from the surrounding cities to Jerusalem, bringing sick people and those who were tormented by unclean spirits, and they were all healed.

IMPRISONED APOSTLES FREED

[17]Then the high priest rose up, and all those who *were* with him (which is the sect of the Sadducees), and they were filled with indignation, [18]and laid their hands on the apostles and put them in the common prison. [19]But at night an angel of the Lord opened the prison doors and brought them out, and said, [20]"Go, stand in the temple and speak to the people all the words of this life."

[21]And when they heard *that,* they entered the temple early in the morning and taught. But the high priest and those with him came and called the council together, with all the elders of the children of Israel, and sent to the prison to have them brought.

APOSTLES ON TRIAL AGAIN

[22]But when the officers came and did not find them in the prison, they returned and re-

THE MESSAGE

piece of land, secretly kept part of the price for himself, and then brought the rest to the apostles and made an offering of it.

3-4 Peter said, "Ananias, how did Satan get you to lie to the Holy Spirit and secretly keep back part of the price of the field? Before you sold it, it was all yours, and after you sold it, the money was yours to do with as you wished. So what got into you to pull a trick like this? You didn't lie to men but to God."

5-6 Ananias, when he heard those words, fell down dead. *That* put the fear of God into everyone who heard of it. The younger men went right to work and wrapped him up, then carried him out and buried him.

7-8 Not more than three hours later, his wife, knowing nothing of what had happened, came in. Peter said, "Tell me, were you given this price for your field?"

"Yes," she said, "that price."

9-10 Peter responded, "What's going on here that you connived to conspire against the Spirit of the Master? The men who buried your husband are at the door, and you're next." No sooner were the words out of his mouth than she also fell down, dead. When the young men returned they found her body. They carried her out and buried her beside her husband.

11 By this time the whole church and, in fact, everyone who heard of these things had a healthy respect for God. They knew God was not to be trifled with.

THEY ALL MET REGULARLY

12-16 Through the work of the apostles, many God-signs were set up among the people, many wonderful things done. They all met regularly and in remarkable harmony on the Temple porch named after Solomon. But even though people admired them a lot, outsiders were wary about joining them. On the other hand, those who put their trust in the Master were added right and left, men and women both. They even carried the sick out into the streets and laid them on stretchers and bedrolls, hoping they would be touched by Peter's shadow when he walked by. They came from the villages surrounding Jerusalem, throngs of them, bringing the sick and bedeviled. And they all were healed.

TO OBEY GOD RATHER THAN MEN

17-20 Provoked mightily by all this, the Chief Priest and those on his side, mainly the sect of Sadducees, went into action, arrested the apostles and put them in the town jail. But during the night an angel of God opened the jailhouse door and led them out. He said, "Go to the Temple and take your stand. Tell the people everything there is to say about this Life."

Promptly obedient, they entered the Temple at daybreak and went on with their teaching.

21-23 Meanwhile, the Chief Priest and his cronies convened the High Council, Israel's senate, and sent to the jail to have the prisoners brought in. When the police got there, they couldn't find them anywhere in the jail.

NEW KING JAMES VERSION

ported, 23 saying, "Indeed we found the prison shut securely, and the guards standing outside[a] before the doors; but when we opened them, we found no one inside!" 24 Now when the high priest,[a] the captain of the temple, and the chief priests heard these things, they wondered what the outcome would be. 25 So one came and told them, saying,[a] "Look, the men whom you put in prison are standing in the temple and teaching the people!"

26 Then the captain went with the officers and brought them without violence, for they feared the people, lest they should be stoned. 27 And when they had brought them, they set *them* before the council. And the high priest asked them, 28 saying, "Did we not strictly command you not to teach in this name? And look, you have filled Jerusalem with your doctrine, and intend to bring this Man's blood on us!"

29 But Peter and the *other* apostles answered and said: "We ought to obey God rather than men. 30 The God of our fathers raised up Jesus whom you murdered by hanging on a tree. 31 Him God has exalted to His right hand *to be* Prince and Savior, to give repentance to Israel and forgiveness of sins. 32 And we are His witnesses to these things, and *so* also *is* the Holy Spirit whom God has given to those who obey Him."

GAMALIEL'S ADVICE

33 When they heard *this,* they were furious and plotted to kill them. 34 Then one in the council stood up, a Pharisee named Gamaliel, a teacher of the law held in respect by all the people, and commanded them to put the apostles outside for a little while. 35 And he said to them: "Men of Israel, take heed to yourselves what you intend to do regarding these men. 36 For some time ago Theudas rose up, claiming to be somebody. A number of men, about four hundred, joined him. He was slain, and all who obeyed him were scattered and came to nothing. 37 After this man, Judas of Galilee rose up in the days of the census, and drew away many people after him. He also perished, and all who obeyed him were dispersed. 38 And now I say to you, keep away from these men and let them alone; for if this plan or this work is of men, it will come to nothing; 39 but if it is of God, you cannot overthrow it—lest you even be found to fight against God."

40 And they agreed with him, and when they had called for the apostles and beaten *them,* they commanded that they should not speak in the name of Jesus, and let them go. 41 So they departed from the presence of the council, rejoicing that they were counted worthy to suffer shame for His[a] name. 42 And daily in the temple, and in every house, they did not cease teaching and preaching Jesus *as* the Christ.

5:23 [a]NU-Text and M-Text omit *outside.* **5:24** [a]NU-Text omits *the high priest.* **5:25** [a]NU-Text and M-Text omit *saying.* **5:41** [a]NU-Text reads *the name;* M-Text reads *the name of Jesus.*

THE MESSAGE

They went back and reported, "We found the jail locked tight as a drum and the guards posted at the doors, but when we went inside we didn't find a soul."

24 The chief of the Temple police and the high priests were puzzled. "What's going on here anyway?"

25-26 Just then someone showed up and said, "Did you know that the men you put in jail are back in the Temple teaching the people?" The chief and his police went and got them, but they handled them gently, fearful that the people would riot and turn on them.

27-28 Bringing them back, they stood them before the High Council. The Chief Priest said, "Didn't we give you strict orders not to teach in Jesus' name? And here you have filled Jerusalem with your teaching and are trying your best to blame us for the death of this man."

29-32 Peter and the apostles answered, "It's necessary to obey God rather than men. The God of our ancestors raised up Jesus, the One you killed by hanging him on a cross. God set him on high at his side, Prince and Savior, to give Israel the gift of a changed life and sins forgiven. And we are witnesses to these things. The Holy Spirit, whom God gives to those who obey him, corroborates every detail."

33-37 When they heard that, they were furious and wanted to kill them on the spot. But one of the council members stood up, a Pharisee by the name of Gamaliel, a teacher of God's Law who was honored by everyone. He ordered the men taken out of the room for a short time, then said, "Fellow Israelites, be careful what you do to these men. Not long ago Theudas made something of a splash, claiming to be somebody, and got about four hundred men to join him. He was killed, his followers dispersed, and nothing came of it. A little later, at the time of the census, Judas the Galilean appeared and acquired a following. He also fizzled out and the people following him were scattered to the four winds.

38-39 "So I am telling you: Hands off these men! Let them alone. If this program or this work is merely human, it will fall apart, but if it is of God, there is nothing you can do about it—and you better not be found fighting against God!"

40-42 That convinced them. They called the apostles back in. After giving them a thorough whipping, they warned them not to speak in Jesus' name and sent them off. The apostles went out of the High Council overjoyed because they had been given the honor of being dishonored on account of the Name. Every day they were in the Temple and homes, teaching and preaching Christ Jesus, not letting up for a minute.

NEW KING JAMES VERSION

SEVEN CHOSEN TO SERVE

6 Now in those days, when *the number of* the disciples was multiplying, there arose a complaint against the Hebrews by the Hellenists,[a] because their widows were neglected in the daily distribution. 2Then the twelve summoned the multitude of the disciples and said, "It is not desirable that we should leave the word of God and serve tables. 3Therefore, brethren, seek out from among you seven men of *good* reputation, full of the Holy Spirit and wisdom, whom we may appoint over this business; 4but we will give ourselves continually to prayer and to the ministry of the word."

5And the saying pleased the whole multitude. And they chose Stephen, a man full of faith and the Holy Spirit, and Philip, Prochorus, Nicanor, Timon, Parmenas, and Nicolas, a proselyte from Antioch, 6whom they set before the apostles; and when they had prayed, they laid hands on them.

7Then the word of God spread, and the number of the disciples multiplied greatly in Jerusalem, and a great many of the priests were obedient to the faith.

STEPHEN ACCUSED OF BLASPHEMY

8And Stephen, full of faith[a] and power, did great wonders and signs among the people. 9Then there arose some from what is called the Synagogue of the Freedmen (Cyrenians, Alexandrians, and those from Cilicia and Asia), disputing with Stephen. 10And they were not able to resist the wisdom and the Spirit by which he spoke. 11Then they secretly induced men to say, "We have heard him speak blasphemous words against Moses and God." 12And they stirred up the people, the elders, and the scribes; and they came upon *him,* seized him, and brought *him* to the council. 13They also set up false witnesses who said, "This man does not cease to speak blasphemous[a] words against this holy place and the law; 14for we have heard him say that this Jesus of Nazareth will destroy this place and change the customs which Moses delivered to us." 15And all who sat in the council, looking steadfastly at him, saw his face as the face of an angel.

6:1 [a]That is, Greek-speaking Jews **6:8** [a]NU-Text reads *grace.*
6:13 [a]NU-Text omits *blasphemous.*

THE MESSAGE

THE WORD OF GOD PROSPERED

1-4 6 During this time, as the disciples were increasing in numbers by leaps and bounds, hard feelings developed among the Greek-speaking believers—"Hellenists"—toward the Hebrew-speaking believers because their widows were being discriminated against in the daily food lines. So the Twelve called a meeting of the disciples. They said, "It wouldn't be right for us to abandon our responsibilities for preaching and teaching the Word of God to help with the care of the poor. So, friends, choose seven men from among you whom everyone trusts, men full of the Holy Spirit and good sense, and we'll assign them this task. Meanwhile, we'll stick to our assigned tasks of prayer and speaking God's Word."

5-6 The congregation thought this was a great idea. They went ahead and chose—

Stephen, a man full of faith and the Holy Spirit,
Philip,
Procorus,
Nicanor,
Timon,
Parmenas,
Nicolas, a convert from Antioch.

Then they presented them to the apostles. Praying, the apostles laid on hands and commissioned them for their task.

7 The Word of God prospered. The number of disciples in Jerusalem increased dramatically. Not least, a great many priests submitted themselves to the faith.

8-10 Stephen, brimming with God's grace and energy, was doing wonderful things among the people, unmistakable signs that God was among them. But then some men from the meeting place whose membership was made up of freed slaves, Cyrenians, Alexandrians, and some others from Cilicia and Asia, went up against him trying to argue him down. But they were no match for his wisdom and spirit when he spoke.

11 So in secret they bribed men to lie: "We heard him cursing Moses and God."

12-14 That stirred up the people, the religious leaders, and religion scholars. They grabbed Stephen and took him before the High Council. They put forward their bribed witnesses to testify: "This man talks nonstop against this Holy Place and God's Law. We even heard him say that Jesus of Nazareth would tear this place down and throw out all the customs Moses gave us."

15 As all those who sat on the High Council looked at Stephen, they found they couldn't take their eyes off him—his face was like the face of an angel!

New King James Version

Stephen's Address: The Call of Abraham

7 Then the high priest said, "Are these things so?"

2And he said, "Brethren and fathers, listen: The God of glory appeared to our father Abraham when he was in Mesopotamia, before he dwelt in Haran, 3and said to him, *'Get out of your country and from your relatives, and come to a land that I will show you.'*[a] 4Then he came out of the land of the Chaldeans and dwelt in Haran. And from there, when his father was dead, He moved him to this land in which you now dwell. 5And *God* gave him no inheritance in it, not even *enough* to set his foot on. But even when *Abraham* had no child, He promised to give it to him for a possession, and to his descendants after him. 6But God spoke in this way: that his descendants would dwell in a foreign land, and that they would bring them into bondage and oppress *them* four hundred years. 7*'And the nation to whom they will be in bondage I will judge,'*[a] said God, *'and after that they shall come out and serve Me in this place.'*[b] 8Then He gave him the covenant of circumcision; and so *Abraham* begot Isaac and circumcised him on the eighth day; and Isaac *begot* Jacob, and Jacob *begot* the twelve patriarchs.

The Patriarchs in Egypt

9"And the patriarchs, becoming envious, sold Joseph into Egypt. But God was with him 10and delivered him out of all his troubles, and gave him favor and wisdom in the presence of Pharaoh, king of Egypt; and he made him governor over Egypt and all his house. 11Now a famine and great trouble came over all the land of Egypt and Canaan, and our fathers found no sustenance. 12But when Jacob heard that there was grain in Egypt, he sent out our fathers first. 13And the second *time* Joseph was made known to his brothers, and Joseph's family became known to the Pharaoh. 14Then Joseph sent and called his father Jacob and all his relatives to *him,* seventy-five[a] people. 15So Jacob went down to Egypt; and he died, he and our fathers. 16And they were carried back to Shechem and laid in the tomb that Abraham bought for a sum of money from the sons of Hamor, *the father* of Shechem.

God Delivers Israel by Moses

17"But when the time of the promise drew near which God had sworn to Abraham, the people grew and multiplied in Egypt 18till another king arose who did not know Joseph. 19This man dealt treacherously with our people, and oppressed our forefathers, making them expose their babies, so that they might not live. 20At this time Moses was born, and was well pleasing to God; and he was brought up in his

7:3 [a]Genesis 12:1 **7:7** [a]Genesis 15:14 [b]Exodus 3:12 **7:14** [a]Or *seventy* (compare Exodus 1:5)

The Message

Stephen, Full of the Holy Spirit

1 7 Then the Chief Priest said, "What do you have to say for yourself?"

2-3 Stephen replied, "Friends, fathers, and brothers, the God of glory appeared to our father Abraham when he was still in Mesopotamia, before the move to Haran, and told him, 'Leave your country and family and go to the land I'll show you.'

4-7 "So he left the country of the Chaldees and moved to Haran. After the death of his father, he immigrated to this country where you now live, but God gave him nothing, not so much as a foothold. He did promise to give the country to him and his son later on, even though Abraham had no son at the time. God let him know that his offspring would move to an alien country where they would be enslaved and brutalized for four hundred years. 'But,' God said, 'I will step in and take care of those slaveholders and bring my people out so they can worship me in this place.'

8 "Then he made a covenant with him and signed it in Abraham's flesh by circumcision. When Abraham had his son Isaac, within eight days he reproduced the sign of circumcision in him. Isaac became father of Jacob, and Jacob father of twelve 'fathers,' each faithfully passing on the covenant sign.

9-10 "But then those 'fathers,' burning up with jealousy, sent Joseph off to Egypt as a slave. God was right there with him, though—he not only rescued him from all his troubles but brought him to the attention of Pharaoh, king of Egypt. He was so impressed with Joseph that he put him in charge of the whole country, including his own personal affairs.

11-15 "Later a famine descended on that entire region, stretching from Egypt to Canaan, bringing terrific hardship. Our hungry fathers looked high and low for food, but the cupboard was bare. Jacob heard there was food in Egypt and sent our fathers to scout it out. Having confirmed the report, they went back to Egypt a second time to get food. On that visit, Joseph revealed his true identity to his brothers and introduced the Jacob family to Pharaoh. Then Joseph sent for his father, Jacob, and everyone else in the family, seventy-five in all. That's how the Jacob family got to Egypt.

15-16 "Jacob died, and our fathers after him. They were taken to Shechem and buried in the tomb for which Abraham paid a good price to the sons of Hamor.

17-19 "When the four hundred years were nearly up, the time God promised Abraham for deliverance, the population of our people in Egypt had become very large. And there was now a king over Egypt who had never heard of Joseph. He exploited our race mercilessly. He went so far as forcing us to abandon our newborn infants, exposing them to the elements to die a cruel death.

20-22 "In just such a time Moses was born, a most beautiful baby. He was hidden at home

NEW KING JAMES VERSION

father's house for three months. 21But when he was set out, Pharaoh's daughter took him away and brought him up as her own son. 22And Moses was learned in all the wisdom of the Egyptians, and was mighty in words and deeds.

23"Now when he was forty years old, it came into his heart to visit his brethren, the children of Israel. 24And seeing one of *them* suffer wrong, he defended and avenged him who was oppressed, and struck down the Egyptian. 25For he supposed that his brethren would have understood that God would deliver them by his hand, but they did not understand. 26And the next day he appeared to two of them as they were fighting, and *tried to* reconcile them, saying, 'Men, you are brethren; why do you wrong one another?' 27But he who did his neighbor wrong pushed him away, saying, *'Who made you a ruler and a judge over us? 28Do you want to kill me as you did the Egyptian yesterday?'* [a] 29Then, at this saying, Moses fled and became a dweller in the land of Midian, where he had two sons.

30"And when forty years had passed, an Angel of the Lord[a] appeared to him in a flame of fire in a bush, in the wilderness of Mount Sinai. 31When Moses saw *it*, he marveled at the sight; and as he drew near to observe, the voice of the Lord came to him, 32*saying, 'I am the God of your fathers—the God of Abraham, the God of Isaac, and the God of Jacob.'* [a] And Moses trembled and dared not look. 33*'Then the Lord said to him, "Take your sandals off your feet, for the place where you stand is holy ground. 34I have surely seen the oppression of My people who are in Egypt; I have heard their groaning and have come down to deliver them. And now come, I will send you to Egypt." '* [a]

35"This Moses whom they rejected, saying, *'Who made you a ruler and a judge?'* [a] is the one God sent *to be* a ruler and a deliverer by the hand of the Angel who appeared to him in the bush. 36He brought them out, after he had shown wonders and signs in the land of Egypt, and in the Red Sea, and in the wilderness forty years.

ISRAEL REBELS AGAINST GOD

37"This is that Moses who said to the children of Israel,[a] *'The Lord your God will raise up for you a Prophet like me from your brethren. Him you shall hear.'* [b]

38"This is he who was in the congregation in the wilderness with the Angel who spoke to him on Mount Sinai, and *with* our fathers, the one who received the living oracles to give to us, 39whom our fathers would not obey, but rejected. And in their hearts they turned back to Egypt, 40saying to Aaron, *'Make us gods to go before us; as for this Moses who brought us out of the land of Egypt, we do not know what has become of him.'* [a] 41And they made a calf in those days, offered sacrifices to the idol, and rejoiced in the works of their own hands.

7:28 [a]Exodus 2:14 **7:35** [a]Exodus 2:14 **7:30** [a]NU-Text omits *of the Lord.* **7:32** [a]Exodus 3:6, 15 **7:34** [a]Exodus 3:5, 7, 8, 10 **7:37** [a]Deuteronomy 18:15 [b]NU-Text and M-Text omit *Him you shall hear.* **7:40** [a]Exodus 32:1, 23

THE MESSAGE

for three months. When he could be hidden
no longer, he was put outside—and immedi-
ately rescued by Pharaoh's daughter, who
mothered him as her own son. Moses was
educated in the best schools in Egypt. He
was equally impressive as a thinker and an
athlete.
23-26 "When he was forty years old, he won-
dered how everything was going with his
Hebrew kin and went out to look things
over. He saw an Egyptian abusing one of
them and stepped in, avenging his underdog
brother by knocking the Egyptian flat. He
thought his brothers would be glad that he
was on their side, and even see him as an in-
strument of God to deliver them. But they
didn't see it that way. The next day two of
them were fighting and he tried to break it
up, told them to shake hands and get along
with each other: 'Friends, you are brothers,
why are you beating up on each other?'
27-29 "The one who had started the fight said,
'Who put you in charge of us? Are you going
to kill me like you killed that Egyptian yes-
terday?' When Moses heard that, realizing
that the word was out, he ran for his life and
lived in exile over in Midian. During the
years of exile, two sons were born to him.
30-32 "Forty years later, in the wilderness of
Mount Sinai, an angel appeared to him in
the guise of flames of a burning bush.
Moses, not believing his eyes, went up to
take a closer look. He heard God's voice: 'I
am the God of your fathers, the God of
Abraham, Isaac, and Jacob.' Frightened
nearly out of his skin, Moses shut his eyes
and turned away.
33-34 "God said, 'Kneel and pray. You are in a
holy place, on holy ground. I've seen the
agony of my people in Egypt. I've heard
their groans. I've come to help them. So get
yourself ready; I'm sending you back to
Egypt.'
35-39 "This is the same Moses whom they ear-
lier rejected, saying, 'Who put you in charge
of us?' This is the Moses that God, using the
angel flaming in the burning bush, sent
back as ruler and redeemer. He led them out
of their slavery. He did wonderful things,
setting up God-signs all through Egypt,
down at the Red Sea, and out in the wilder-
ness for forty years. This is the Moses who
said to his congregation, 'God will raise up a
prophet just like me from your descen-
dants.' This is the Moses who stood between
the angel speaking at Sinai and your fathers
assembled in the wilderness and took the
life-giving words given to him and handed
them over to us, words our fathers would
have nothing to do with.
39-41 "They craved the old Egyptian ways,
whining to Aaron, 'Make us gods we can see
and follow. This Moses who got us out here
miles from nowhere—who knows what's
happened to him!' That was the time when
they made a calf-idol, brought sacrifices to
it, and congratulated each other on the won-
derful religious program they had put to-
gether.

New King James Version

42 Then God turned and gave them up to worship
the host of heaven, as it is written in the book of
the Prophets:

'Did you offer Me slaughtered animals and
sacrifices during forty years in the
wilderness,
O house of Israel?
43 *You also took up the tabernacle of Moloch,*
And the star of your god Remphan,
Images which you made to worship;
And I will carry you away beyond
Babylon.' [a]

God's True Tabernacle

44 "Our fathers had the tabernacle of witness
in the wilderness, as He appointed, instructing
Moses to make it according to the pattern that
he had seen, 45 which our fathers, having re-
ceived it in turn, also brought with Joshua into
the land possessed by the Gentiles, whom God
drove out before the face of our fathers until the
days of David, 46 who found favor before God
and asked to find a dwelling for the God of Ja-
cob. 47 But Solomon built Him a house.
48 "However, the Most High does not dwell in
temples made with hands, as the prophet says:

49 *'Heaven is My throne,*
And earth is My footstool.
What house will you build for Me? says the
Lord,
Or what is the place of My rest?
50 *Has My hand not made all these things?'* [a]

Israel Resists the Holy Spirit

51 "*You* stiff-necked and uncircumcised in
heart and ears! You always resist the Holy
Spirit; as your fathers *did*, so *do* you. 52 Which of
the prophets did your fathers not persecute?
And they killed those who foretold the coming
of the Just One, of whom you now have become
the betrayers and murderers, 53 who have re-
ceived the law by the direction of angels and
have not kept *it*."

Stephen the Martyr

54 When they heard these things they were
cut to the heart, and they gnashed at him with
their teeth. 55 But he, being full of the Holy Spirit,
gazed into heaven and saw the glory of God,
and Jesus standing at the right hand of God,
56 and said, "Look! I see the heavens opened and
the Son of Man standing at the right hand of
God!"
57 Then they cried out with a loud voice,
stopped their ears, and ran at him with one ac-
cord; 58 and they cast *him* out of the city and
stoned *him*. And the witnesses laid down their
clothes at the feet of a young man named Saul.
59 And they stoned Stephen as he was calling on
God and saying, "Lord Jesus, receive my spirit."
60 Then he knelt down and cried out with a loud
voice, "Lord, do not charge them with this sin."
And when he had said this, he fell asleep.

7:43 [a] Amos 5:25–27 **7:50** [a] Isaiah 66:1, 2

The Message

42-43 "God wasn't at all pleased; but he let them do it their way, worship every new god that came down the pike—and live with the consequences, consequences described by the prophet Amos:

Did you bring me offerings of animals
and grains
those forty wilderness years,
O Israel?
Hardly. You were too busy building
shrines
to war gods, to sex goddesses,
Worshiping them with all your might.
That's why I put you in exile in
Babylon.

44-47 "And all this time our ancestors had a tent shrine for true worship, made to the exact specifications God provided Moses. They had it with them as they followed Joshua, when God cleared the land of pagans, and still had it right down to the time of David. David asked God for a permanent place for worship. But Solomon built it.

48-50 "Yet that doesn't mean that Most High God lives in a building made by carpenters and masons. The prophet Isaiah put it well when he wrote,

"Heaven is my throne room;
I rest my feet on earth.
So what kind of house
will you build me?" says God.
"Where I can get away and relax?
It's already built, and I built it."

51-53 "And you continue, so bullheaded! Calluses on your hearts, flaps on your ears! Deliberately ignoring the Holy Spirit, you're just like your ancestors. Was there ever a prophet who didn't get the same treatment? Your ancestors killed anyone who dared talk about the coming of the Just One. And you've kept up the family tradition—traitors and murderers, all of you. You had God's Law handed to you by angels—gift-wrapped!—and you squandered it!"

54-56 At that point they went wild, a rioting mob of catcalls and whistles and invective. But Stephen, full of the Holy Spirit, hardly noticed—he only had eyes for God, whom he saw in all his glory with Jesus standing at his side. He said, "Oh! I see heaven wide open and the Son of Man standing at God's side!"

57-58 Yelling and hissing, the mob drowned him out. Now in full stampede, they dragged him out of town and pelted him with rocks. The ringleaders took off their coats and asked a young man named Saul to watch them.

59-60 As the rocks rained down, Stephen prayed, "Master Jesus, take my life." Then he knelt down, praying loud enough for everyone to hear, "Master, don't blame them for this sin"—his last words. Then he died.

1 Saul was right there, congratulating the killers.

NEW KING JAMES VERSION

SAUL PERSECUTES THE CHURCH

8 Now Saul was consenting to his death.
At that time a great persecution arose against the church which was at Jerusalem; and they were all scattered throughout the regions of Judea and Samaria, except the apostles. [2]And devout men carried Stephen *to his burial,* and made great lamentation over him.

[3]As for Saul, he made havoc of the church, entering every house, and dragging off men and women, committing *them* to prison.

CHRIST IS PREACHED IN SAMARIA

[4]Therefore those who were scattered went everywhere preaching the word. [5]Then Philip went down to the[a] city of Samaria and preached Christ to them. [6]And the multitudes with one accord heeded the things spoken by Philip, hearing and seeing the miracles which he did. [7]For unclean spirits, crying with a loud voice, came out of many who were possessed; and many who were paralyzed and lame were healed. [8]And there was great joy in that city.

THE SORCERER'S PROFESSION OF FAITH

[9]But there was a certain man called Simon, who previously practiced sorcery in the city and astonished the people of Samaria, claiming that he was someone great, [10]to whom they all gave heed, from the least to the greatest, saying, "This man is the great power of God." [11]And they heeded him because he had astonished them with his sorceries for a long time. [12]But when they believed Philip as he preached the things concerning the kingdom of God and the name of Jesus Christ, both men and women were baptized. [13]Then Simon himself also believed; and when he was baptized he continued with Philip, and was amazed, seeing the miracles and signs which were done.

THE SORCERER'S SIN

[14]Now when the apostles who were at Jerusalem heard that Samaria had received the word of God, they sent Peter and John to them, [15]who, when they had come down, prayed for them that they might receive the Holy Spirit. [16]For as yet He had fallen upon none of them. They had only been baptized in the name of the Lord Jesus. [17]Then they laid hands on them, and they received the Holy Spirit.

[18]And when Simon saw that through the laying on of the apostles' hands the Holy Spirit was given, he offered them money, [19]saying, "Give me this power also, that anyone on whom I lay hands may receive the Holy Spirit."

[20]But Peter said to him, "Your money perish with you, because you thought that the gift of God could be purchased with money! [21]You have neither part nor portion in this matter, for your heart is not right in the sight of God. [22]Repent therefore of this your wickedness, and pray God if perhaps the thought of your heart may be forgiven you. [23]For I see that you are poisoned by bitterness and bound by iniquity."

[24]Then Simon answered and said, "Pray to the Lord for me, that none of the things which you have spoken may come upon me."

8:5 [a]Or *a*

THE MESSAGE

SIMON THE WIZARD

1-2 8 That set off a terrific persecution of the church in Jerusalem. The believers were all scattered throughout Judea and Samaria. All, that is, but the apostles. Good and brave men buried Stephen, giving him a solemn funeral—not many dry eyes that day!

3-8 And Saul just went wild, devastating the church, entering house after house, dragging men and women off to jail. Forced to leave home base, the followers of Jesus all became missionaries. Wherever they were scattered, they preached the Message about Jesus. Going down to a Samaritan city, Philip proclaimed the Message of the Messiah. When the people heard what he had to say and saw the miracles, the clear signs of God's action, they hung on his every word. Many who could neither stand nor walk were healed that day. The evil spirits protested loudly as they were sent on their way. And what joy in the city!

9-11 Previous to Philip's arrival, a certain Simon had practiced magic in the city, posing as a famous man and dazzling all the Samaritans with his wizardry. He had them all, from little children to old men, eating out of his hand. They all thought he had supernatural powers, and called him "the Great Wizard." He had been around a long time and everyone was more or less in awe of him.

12-13 But when Philip came to town announcing the news of God's kingdom and proclaiming the name of Jesus Christ, they forgot Simon and were baptized, becoming believers right and left! Even Simon himself believed and was baptized. From that moment he was like Philip's shadow, so fascinated with all the God-signs and miracles that he wouldn't leave Philip's side.

14-17 When the apostles in Jerusalem received the report that Samaria had accepted God's Message, they sent Peter and John down to pray for them to receive the Holy Spirit. Up to this point they had only been baptized in the name of the Master Jesus; the Holy Spirit hadn't yet fallen on them. Then the apostles laid their hands on them and they did receive the Holy Spirit.

18-19 When Simon saw that the apostles by merely laying on hands conferred the Spirit, he pulled out his money, excited, and said, "Sell me your secret! Show me how you did that! How much do you want? Name your price!"

20-23 Peter said, "To hell with your money! And you along with it. Why, that's unthinkable—trying to buy God's gift! You'll never be part of what God is doing by striking bargains and offering bribes. Change your ways—and now! Ask the Master to forgive you for trying to use God to make money. I can see this is an old habit with you; you reek with money-lust."

24 "Oh!" said Simon, "pray for me! Pray to the Master that nothing like that will ever happen to me!"

NEW KING JAMES VERSION

25So when they had testified and preached the word of the Lord, they returned to Jerusalem, preaching the gospel in many villages of the Samaritans.

CHRIST IS PREACHED TO AN ETHIOPIAN

26Now an angel of the Lord spoke to Philip, saying, "Arise and go toward the south along the road which goes down from Jerusalem to Gaza." This is desert. 27So he arose and went. And behold, a man of Ethiopia, a eunuch of great authority under Candace the queen of the Ethiopians, who had charge of all her treasury, and had come to Jerusalem to worship, 28was returning. And sitting in his chariot, he was reading Isaiah the prophet. 29Then the Spirit said to Philip, "Go near and overtake this chariot."

30So Philip ran to him, and heard him reading the prophet Isaiah, and said, "Do you understand what you are reading?"

31And he said, "How can I, unless someone guides me?" And he asked Philip to come up and sit with him. 32The place in the Scripture which he read was this:

"He was led as a sheep to the slaughter;
And as a lamb before its shearer is silent,
So He opened not His mouth.
33*In His humiliation His justice was taken away,*
And who will declare His generation?
For His life is taken from the earth."[a]

34So the eunuch answered Philip and said, "I ask you, of whom does the prophet say this, of himself or of some other man?" 35Then Philip opened his mouth, and beginning at this Scripture, preached Jesus to him. 36Now as they went down the road, they came to some water. And the eunuch said, "See, *here is* water. What hinders me from being baptized?"

37Then Philip said, "If you believe with all your heart, you may."

And he answered and said, "I believe that Jesus Christ is the Son of God."[a]

38So he commanded the chariot to stand still. And both Philip and the eunuch went down into the water, and he baptized him. 39Now when they came up out of the water, the Spirit of the Lord caught Philip away, so that the eunuch saw him no more; and he went on his way rejoicing. 40But Philip was found at Azotus. And passing through, he preached in all the cities till he came to Caesarea.

THE DAMASCUS ROAD: SAUL CONVERTED

9 Then Saul, still breathing threats and murder against the disciples of the Lord, went to the high priest 2and asked letters from him to the synagogues of Damascus, so that if he found any who were of the Way, whether men or women, he might bring them bound to Jerusalem.

3As he journeyed he came near Damascus, and suddenly a light shone around him from heaven. 4Then he fell to the ground, and heard a

8:33 [a]Isaiah 53:7, 8 **8:37** [a]NU-Text and M-Text omit this verse. It is found in Western texts, including the Latin tradition.

THE MESSAGE

25 And with that, the apostles were on their way, continuing to witness and spread the Message of God's salvation, preaching in every Samaritan town they passed through on their return to Jerusalem.

THE ETHIOPIAN EUNUCH

26-28 Later God's angel spoke to Philip: "At noon today I want you to walk over to that desolate road that goes from Jerusalem down to Gaza." He got up and went. He met an Ethiopian eunuch coming down the road. The eunuch had been on a pilgrimage to Jerusalem and was returning to Ethiopia, where he was minister in charge of all the finances of Candace, queen of the Ethiopians. He was riding in a chariot and reading the prophet Isaiah.

29-30 The Spirit told Philip, "Climb into the chariot." Running up alongside, Philip heard the eunuch reading Isaiah and asked, "Do you understand what you're reading?"

31-33 He answered, "How can I without some help?" and invited Philip into the chariot with him. The passage he was reading was this:

As a sheep led to slaughter,
and quiet as a lamb being sheared,
He was silent, saying nothing.
He was mocked and put down, never
got a fair trial.
But who now can count his kin
since he's been taken from the earth?

34-35 The eunuch said, "Tell me, who is the prophet talking about: himself or some other?" Philip grabbed his chance. Using this passage as his text, he preached Jesus to him.

36-39 As they continued down the road, they came to a stream of water. The eunuch said, "Here's water. Why can't I be baptized?" He ordered the chariot to stop. They both went down to the water, and Philip baptized him on the spot. When they came up out of the water, the Spirit of God suddenly took Philip off, and that was the last the eunuch saw of him. But he didn't mind. He had what he'd come for and went on down the road as happy as he could be.

40 Philip showed up in Azotus and continued north, preaching the Message in all the villages along that route until he arrived at Caesarea.

THE BLINDING OF SAUL

1-2 9 All this time Saul was breathing down the necks of the Master's disciples, out for the kill. He went to the Chief Priest and got arrest warrants to take to the meeting places in Damascus so that if he found anyone there belonging to the Way, whether men or women, he could arrest them and bring them to Jerusalem.

3-4 He set off. When he got to the outskirts of Damascus, he was suddenly dazed by a blinding flash of light. As he fell to the

NEW KING JAMES VERSION

voice saying to him, "Saul, Saul, why are you
persecuting Me?"
5And he said, "Who are You, Lord?"
Then the Lord said, "I am Jesus, whom you
are persecuting.[a] It *is* hard for you to kick
against the goads."
6So he, trembling and astonished, said,
"Lord, what do You want me to do?"
Then the Lord *said* to him, "Arise and go into
the city, and you will be told what you must do."
7And the men who journeyed with him stood
speechless, hearing a voice but seeing no one.
8Then Saul arose from the ground, and when his
eyes were opened he saw no one. But they led
him by the hand and brought *him* into Damas-
cus. 9And he was three days without sight, and
neither ate nor drank.

ANANIAS BAPTIZES SAUL

10Now there was a certain disciple at Damas-
cus named Ananias; and to him the Lord said in
a vision, "Ananias."
And he said, "Here I am, Lord."
11So the Lord *said* to him, "Arise and go to
the street called Straight, and inquire at the
house of Judas for *one* called Saul of Tarsus, for
behold, he is praying. 12And in a vision he has
seen a man named Ananias coming in and put-
ting *his* hand on him, so that he might receive
his sight."
13Then Ananias answered, "Lord, I have
heard from many about this man, how much
harm he has done to Your saints in Jerusalem.
14And here he has authority from the chief
priests to bind all who call on Your name."
15But the Lord said to him, "Go, for he is a
chosen vessel of Mine to bear My name before
Gentiles, kings, and the children of Israel. 16For
I will show him how many things he must suffer
for My name's sake."
17And Ananias went his way and entered the
house; and laying his hands on him he said,
"Brother Saul, the Lord Jesus,[a] who appeared to
you on the road as you came, has sent me that
you may receive your sight and be filled with
the Holy Spirit." 18Immediately there fell from
his eyes *something* like scales, and he received
his sight at once; and he arose and was bap-
tized.
19So when he had received food, he was
strengthened. Then Saul spent some days with
the disciples at Damascus.

SAUL PREACHES CHRIST

20Immediately he preached the Christ[a] in the
synagogues, that He is the Son of God.
21Then all who heard were amazed, and said,
"Is this not he who destroyed those who called
on this name in Jerusalem, and has come here
for that purpose, so that he might bring them
bound to the chief priests?"
22But Saul increased all the more in strength,
and confounded the Jews who dwelt in Damas-
cus, proving that this *Jesus* is the Christ.

9:5 [a]NU-Text and M-Text omit the last sentence of verse 5 and begin verse 6 with *But arise and go.* **9:17** [a]M-Text omits *Jesus.* **9:20** [a]NU-Text reads *Jesus.*

THE MESSAGE

ground, he heard a voice: "Saul, Saul, why are you out to get me?"

5-6 He said, "Who are you, Master?"

"I am Jesus, the One you're hunting down. I want you to get up and enter the city. In the city you'll be told what to do next."

7-9 His companions stood there dumbstruck—they could hear the sound, but couldn't see anyone—while Saul, picking himself up off the ground, found himself stone-blind. They had to take him by the hand and lead him into Damascus. He continued blind for three days. He ate nothing, drank nothing.

10 There was a disciple in Damascus by the name of Ananias. The Master spoke to him in a vision: "Ananias."

"Yes, Master?" he answered.

11-12 "Get up and go over to Straight Avenue. Ask at the house of Judas for a man from Tarsus. His name is Saul. He's there praying. He has just had a dream in which he saw a man named Ananias enter the house and lay hands on him so he could see again."

13-14 Ananias protested, "Master, you can't be serious. Everybody's talking about this man and the terrible things he's been doing, his reign of terror against your people in Jerusalem! And now he's shown up here with papers from the Chief Priest that give him license to do the same to us."

15-16 But the Master said, "Don't argue. Go! I have picked him as my personal representative to non-Jews and kings and Jews. And now I'm about to show him what he's in for —the hard suffering that goes with this job."

17-19 So Ananias went and found the house, placed his hands on blind Saul, and said, "Brother Saul, the Master sent me, the same Jesus you saw on your way here. He sent me so you could see again and be filled with the Holy Spirit." No sooner were the words out of his mouth than something like scales fell from Saul's eyes—he could see again! He got to his feet, was baptized, and sat down with them to a hearty meal.

PLOTS AGAINST SAUL

19-21 Saul spent a few days getting acquainted with the Damascus disciples, but then went right to work, wasting no time, preaching in the meeting places that this Jesus was the Son of God. They were caught off guard by this and, not at all sure they could trust him, they kept saying, "Isn't this the man who wreaked havoc in Jerusalem among the believers? And didn't he come here to do the same thing—arrest us and drag us off to jail in Jerusalem for sentencing by the high priests?"

22 But their suspicions didn't slow Saul down for even a minute. His momentum was up now and he plowed straight into the opposition, disarming the Damascus Jews and trying to show them that this Jesus was the Messiah.

New King James Version

Saul Escapes Death

23Now after many days were past, the Jews
plotted to kill him. 24But their plot became
known to Saul. And they watched the gates day
and night, to kill him. 25Then the disciples took
him by night and let *him* down through the wall
in a large basket.

Saul at Jerusalem

26And when Saul had come to Jerusalem, he
tried to join the disciples; but they were all
afraid of him, and did not believe that he was a
disciple. 27But Barnabas took him and brought
him to the apostles. And he declared to them
how he had seen the Lord on the road, and that
He had spoken to him, and how he had
preached boldly at Damascus in the name of Je-
sus. 28So he was with them at Jerusalem, coming
in and going out. 29And he spoke boldly in the
name of the Lord Jesus and disputed against the
Hellenists, but they attempted to kill him.
30When the brethren found out, they brought
him down to Caesarea and sent him out to Tar-
sus.

The Church Prospers

31Then the churches[a] throughout all Judea,
Galilee, and Samaria had peace and were edi-
fied. And walking in the fear of the Lord and in
the comfort of the Holy Spirit, they were multi-
plied.

Aeneas Healed

32Now it came to pass, as Peter went through
all *parts of the country,* that he also came down
to the saints who dwelt in Lydda. 33There he
found a certain man named Aeneas, who had
been bedridden eight years and was paralyzed.
34And Peter said to him, "Aeneas, Jesus the
Christ heals you. Arise and make your bed."
Then he arose immediately. 35So all who dwelt
at Lydda and Sharon saw him and turned to the
Lord.

Dorcas Restored to Life

36At Joppa there was a certain disciple
named Tabitha, which is translated Dorcas. This
woman was full of good works and charitable
deeds which she did. 37But it happened in those
days that she became sick and died. When they
had washed her, they laid *her* in an upper room.
38And since Lydda was near Joppa, and the dis-
ciples had heard that Peter was there, they sent
two men to him, imploring *him* not to delay in
coming to them. 39Then Peter arose and went
with them. When he had come, they brought
him to the upper room. And all the widows
stood by him weeping, showing the tunics and
garments which Dorcas had made while she
was with them. 40But Peter put them all out, and
knelt down and prayed. And turning to the body
he said, "Tabitha, arise." And she opened her
eyes, and when she saw Peter she sat up. 41Then
he gave her *his* hand and lifted her up; and
when he had called the saints and widows, he
presented her alive.

9:31 [a]NU-Text reads *church . . . was edified.*

The Message

23-25 After this had gone on quite a long time,
some Jews conspired to kill him, but Saul
got wind of it. They were watching the city
gates around the clock so they could kill
him. Then one night the disciples engi-
neered his escape by lowering him over the
wall in a basket.

26-27 Back in Jerusalem he tried to join the dis-
ciples, but they were all afraid of him. They
didn't trust him one bit. Then Barnabas took
him under his wing. He introduced him to
the apostles and stood up for him, told them
how Saul had seen and spoken to the Mas-
ter on the Damascus Road and how in Da-
mascus itself he had laid his life on the line
with his bold preaching in Jesus' name.

28-30 After that he was accepted as one of
them, going in and out of Jerusalem with no
questions asked, uninhibited as he preached
in the Master's name. But then he ran afoul
of a group called Hellenists—he had been
engaged in a running argument with them—
who plotted his murder. When his friends
learned of the plot, they got him out of town,
took him to Caesarea, and then shipped him
off to Tarsus.

31 Things calmed down after that and the
church had smooth sailing for a while. All
over the country—Judea, Samaria, Galilee—
the church grew. They were permeated with
a deep sense of reverence for God. The Holy
Spirit was with them, strengthening them.
They prospered wonderfully.

Tabitha

32-35 Peter went off on a mission to visit all the
churches. In the course of his travels he ar-
rived in Lydda and met with the believers
there. He came across a man—his name was
Aeneas—who had been in bed eight years
paralyzed. Peter said, "Aeneas, Jesus Christ
heals you. Get up and make your bed!" And
he did it—jumped right out of bed. Every-
body who lived in Lydda and Sharon saw
him walking around and woke up to the fact
that God was alive and active among them.

36-37 Down the road a way in Joppa there was
a disciple named Tabitha, "Gazelle" in our
language. She was well-known for doing
good and helping out. During the time Peter
was in the area she became sick and died.
Her friends prepared her body for burial
and put her in a cool room.

38-40 Some of the disciples had heard that Pe-
ter was visiting in nearby Lydda and sent
two men to ask if he would be so kind as to
come over. Peter got right up and went with
them. They took him into the room where
Tabitha's body was laid out. Her old friends,
most of them widows, were in the room
mourning. They showed Peter pieces of
clothing the Gazelle had made while she
was with them. Peter put the widows all out
of the room. He knelt and prayed. Then he
spoke directly to the body: "Tabitha, get up."

40-41 She opened her eyes. When she saw Pe-
ter, she sat up. He took her hand and helped
her up. Then he called in the believers and
widows, and presented her to them alive.

New King James Version

42And it became known throughout all Joppa, and many believed on the Lord. 43So it was that he stayed many days in Joppa with Simon, a tanner.

Cornelius Sends a Delegation

10 There was a certain man in Caesarea called Cornelius, a centurion of what was called the Italian Regiment, 2a devout *man* and one who feared God with all his household, who gave alms generously to the people, and prayed to God always. 3About the ninth hour of the day he saw clearly in a vision an angel of God coming in and saying to him, "Cornelius!"

4And when he observed him, he was afraid, and said, "What is it, lord?"

So he said to him, "Your prayers and your alms have come up for a memorial before God. 5Now send men to Joppa, and send for Simon whose surname is Peter. 6He is lodging with Simon, a tanner, whose house is by the sea.[a] He will tell you what you must do." 7And when the angel who spoke to him had departed, Cornelius called two of his household servants and a devout soldier from among those who waited on him continually. 8So when he had explained all *these* things to them, he sent them to Joppa.

Peter's Vision

9The next day, as they went on their journey and drew near the city, Peter went up on the housetop to pray, about the sixth hour. 10Then he became very hungry and wanted to eat; but while they made ready, he fell into a trance 11and saw heaven opened and an object like a great sheet bound at the four corners, descending to him and let down to the earth. 12In it were all kinds of four-footed animals of the earth, wild beasts, creeping things, and birds of the air. 13And a voice came to him, "Rise, Peter; kill and eat."

14But Peter said, "Not so, Lord! For I have never eaten anything common or unclean."

15And a voice *spoke* to him again the second time, "What God has cleansed you must not call common." 16This was done three times. And the object was taken up into heaven again.

Summoned to Caesarea

17Now while Peter wondered within himself what this vision which he had seen meant, behold, the men who had been sent from Cornelius had made inquiry for Simon's house, and stood before the gate. 18And they called and asked whether Simon, whose surname was Peter, was lodging there.

19While Peter thought about the vision, the Spirit said to him, "Behold, three men are seeking you. 20Arise therefore, go down and go with them, doubting nothing; for I have sent them."

21Then Peter went down to the men who had been sent to him from Cornelius,[a] and said, "Yes, I am he whom you seek. For what reason have you come?"

22And they said, "Cornelius *the* centurion, a just man, one who fears God and has a good

10:6 [a]NU-Text and M-Text omit the last sentence of this verse.
10:21 [a]NU-Text and M-Text omit *who had been sent to him from Cornelius.*

The Message

42-43 When this became known all over Joppa,
many put their trust in the Master. Peter
stayed on a long time in Joppa as a guest of
Simon the Tanner.

Peter's Vision

1-3 **10** There was a man named Cornelius who
lived in Caesarea, captain of the Italian
Guard stationed there. He was a thoroughly
good man. He had led everyone in his house
to live worshipfully before God, was always
helping people in need, and had the habit of
prayer. One day about three o'clock in the
afternoon he had a vision. An angel of God,
as real as his next-door neighbor, came in
and said, "Cornelius."

4-6 Cornelius stared hard, wondering if he
was seeing things. Then he said, "What do
you want, sir?"
The angel said, "Your prayers and neigh-
borly acts have brought you to God's atten-
tion. Here's what you are to do. Send men to
Joppa to get Simon, the one everyone calls
Peter. He is staying with Simon the Tanner,
whose house is down by the sea."

7-8 As soon as the angel was gone, Cornelius
called two servants and one particularly de-
vout soldier from the guard. He went over
with them in great detail everything that
had just happened, and then sent them off to
Joppa.

9-13 The next day as the three travelers were
approaching the town, Peter went out on the
balcony to pray. It was about noon. Peter got
hungry and started thinking about lunch.
While lunch was being prepared, he fell into
a trance. He saw the skies open up. Some-
thing that looked like a huge blanket low-
ered by ropes at its four corners settled on
the ground. Every kind of animal and reptile
and bird you could think of was on it. Then
a voice came: "Go to it, Peter—kill and eat."

14 Peter said, "Oh, no, Lord. I've never so
much as tasted food that was not kosher."

15 The voice came a second time: "If God
says it's okay, it's okay."

16 This happened three times, and then the
blanket was pulled back up into the skies.

17-20 As Peter, puzzled, sat there trying to fig-
ure out what it all meant, the men sent by
Cornelius showed up at Simon's front door.
They called in, asking if there was a Simon,
also called Peter, staying there. Peter, lost in
thought, didn't hear them, so the Spirit
whispered to him, "Three men are knocking
at the door looking for you. Get down there
and go with them. Don't ask any questions.
I sent them to get you."

21 Peter went down and said to the men, "I
think I'm the man you're looking for. What's
up?"

22-23 They said, "Captain Cornelius, a God-
fearing man well-known for his fair play—

NEW KING JAMES VERSION

reputation among all the nation of the Jews, was
divinely instructed by a holy angel to summon
you to his house, and to hear words from you."
[23]Then he invited them in and lodged *them.*
On the next day Peter went away with them,
and some brethren from Joppa accompanied
him.

PETER MEETS CORNELIUS

[24]And the following day they entered Caes-
area. Now Cornelius was waiting for them, and
had called together his relatives and close
friends. [25]As Peter was coming in, Cornelius met
him and fell down at his feet and worshiped
him. [26]But Peter lifted him up, saying, "Stand up;
I myself am also a man." [27]And as he talked with
him, he went in and found many who had come
together. [28]Then he said to them, "You know
how unlawful it is for a Jewish man to keep
company with or go to one of another nation.
But God has shown me that I should not call any
man common or unclean. [29]Therefore I came
without objection as soon as I was sent for. I
ask, then, for what reason have you sent for
me?"
[30]So Cornelius said, "Four days ago I was
fasting until this hour; and at the ninth hour[a] I
prayed in my house, and behold, a man stood
before me in bright clothing, [31]and said, 'Cor-
nelius, your prayer has been heard, and your
alms are remembered in the sight of God.
[32]Send therefore to Joppa and call Simon here,
whose surname is Peter. He is lodging in the
house of Simon, a tanner, by the sea.[a] When he
comes, he will speak to you.' [33]So I sent to you
immediately, and you have done well to come.
Now therefore, we are all present before God, to
hear all the things commanded you by God."

PREACHING TO CORNELIUS' HOUSEHOLD

[34]Then Peter opened *his* mouth and said: "In
truth I perceive that God shows no partiality.
[35]But in every nation whoever fears Him and
works righteousness is accepted by Him. [36]The
word which *God* sent to the children of Israel,
preaching peace through Jesus Christ—He is
Lord of all— [37]that word you know, which was
proclaimed throughout all Judea, and began
from Galilee after the baptism which John
preached: [38]how God anointed Jesus of Naza-
reth with the Holy Spirit and with power, who
went about doing good and healing all who
were oppressed by the devil, for God was with
Him. [39]And we are witnesses of all things which
He did both in the land of the Jews and in
Jerusalem, whom they[a] killed by hanging on a
tree. [40]Him God raised up on the third day, and
showed Him openly, [41]not to all the people, but
to witnesses chosen before by God, *even* to us

10:30 [a]NU-Text reads *Four days ago to this hour, at the ninth hour.* **10:32** [a]NU-Text omits the last sentence of this verse. **10:39** [a]NU-Text and M-Text add *also.*

THE MESSAGE

ask any Jew in this part of the country—was commanded by a holy angel to get you and bring you to his house so he could hear what you had to say." Peter invited them in and made them feel at home.

GOD PLAYS NO FAVORITES

23-26 The next morning he got up and went with them. Some of his friends from Joppa went along. A day later they entered Caesarea. Cornelius was expecting them and had his relatives and close friends waiting with him. The minute Peter came through the door, Cornelius was up on his feet greeting him—and then down on his face worshiping him! Peter pulled him up and said, "None of that—I'm a man and only a man, no different from you."

27-29 Talking things over, they went on into the house, where Cornelius introduced Peter to everyone who had come. Peter addressed them, "You know, I'm sure that this is highly irregular. Jews just don't do this—visit and relax with people of another race. But God has just shown me that no race is better than any other. So the minute I was sent for, I came, no questions asked. But now I'd like to know why you sent for me."

30-32 Cornelius said, "Four days ago at about this time, midafternoon, I was home praying. Suddenly there was a man right in front of me, flooding the room with light. He said, 'Cornelius, your daily prayers and neighborly acts have brought you to God's attention. I want you to send to Joppa to get Simon, the one they call Peter. He's staying with Simon the Tanner down by the sea.'

33 "So I did it—I sent for you. And you've been good enough to come. And now we're all here in God's presence, ready to listen to whatever the Master put in your heart to tell us."

34-36 Peter fairly exploded with his good news: "It's God's own truth, nothing could be plainer: God plays no favorites! It makes no difference who you are or where you're from—if you want God and are ready to do as he says, the door is open. The Message he sent to the children of Israel—that through Jesus Christ everything is being put together again—well, he's doing it everywhere, among everyone.

37-38 "You know the story of what happened in Judea. It began in Galilee after John preached a total life-change. Then Jesus arrived from Nazareth, anointed by God with the Holy Spirit, ready for action. He went through the country helping people and healing everyone who was beaten down by the Devil. He was able to do all this because God was with him.

39-43 "And we saw it, saw it all, everything he did in the land of the Jews and in Jerusalem where they killed him, hung him from a cross. But in three days God had him up, alive, and out where he could be seen. Not everyone saw him—he wasn't put on public display. Witnesses had been carefully handpicked by God beforehand—us! We were the

NEW KING JAMES VERSION

who ate and drank with Him after He arose from the dead. [42]And He commanded us to preach to the people, and to testify that it is He who was ordained by God *to be* Judge of the living and the dead. [43]To Him all the prophets witness that, through His name, whoever believes in Him will receive remission of sins."

THE HOLY SPIRIT FALLS ON THE GENTILES

[44]While Peter was still speaking these words, the Holy Spirit fell upon all those who heard the word. [45]And those of the circumcision who believed were astonished, as many as came with Peter, because the gift of the Holy Spirit had been poured out on the Gentiles also. [46]For they heard them speak with tongues and magnify God.

Then Peter answered, [47]"Can anyone forbid water, that these should not be baptized who have received the Holy Spirit just as we *have?*" [48]And he commanded them to be baptized in the name of the Lord. Then they asked him to stay a few days.

PETER DEFENDS GOD'S GRACE

11 Now the apostles and brethren who were in Judea heard that the Gentiles had also received the word of God. [2]And when Peter came up to Jerusalem, those of the circumcision contended with him, [3]saying, "You went in to uncircumcised men and ate with them!"

[4]But Peter explained *it* to them in order from the beginning, saying: [5]"I was in the city of Joppa praying; and in a trance I saw a vision, an object descending like a great sheet, let down from heaven by four corners; and it came to me. [6]When I observed it intently and considered, I saw four-footed animals of the earth, wild beasts, creeping things, and birds of the air. [7]And I heard a voice saying to me, 'Rise, Peter; kill and eat.' [8]But I said, 'Not so, Lord! For nothing common or unclean has at any time entered my mouth.' [9]But the voice answered me again from heaven, 'What God has cleansed you must not call common.' [10]Now this was done three times, and all were drawn up again into heaven. [11]At that very moment, three men stood before the house where I was, having been sent to me from Caesarea. [12]Then the Spirit told me to go with them, doubting nothing. Moreover these six brethren accompanied me, and we entered the man's house. [13]And he told us how he had seen an angel standing in his house, who said to him, 'Send men to Joppa, and call for Simon whose surname is Peter, [14]who will tell you words by which you and all your household will be saved.' [15]And as I began to speak, the Holy Spirit fell upon them, as upon us at the beginning. [16]Then I remembered the word of the Lord, how He said, 'John indeed baptized with water,

THE MESSAGE

ones, there to eat and drink with him after he came back from the dead. He commissioned us to announce this in public, to bear solemn witness that he is in fact the One whom God destined as Judge of the living and dead. But we're not alone in this. Our witness that he is the means to forgiveness of sins is backed up by the witness of all the prophets."

44-46 No sooner were these words out of Peter's mouth than the Holy Spirit came on the listeners. The believing Jews who had come with Peter couldn't believe it, couldn't believe that the gift of the Holy Spirit was poured out on "outsider" non-Jews, but there it was—they heard them speaking in tongues, heard them praising God.

46-48 Then Peter said, "Do I hear any objections to baptizing these friends with water? They've received the Holy Spirit exactly as we did." Hearing no objections, he ordered that they be baptized in the name of Jesus Christ.

Then they asked Peter to stay on for a few days.

GOD HAS BROKEN THROUGH

1-3 11 The news traveled fast and in no time the leaders and friends back in Jerusalem heard about it—heard that the non-Jewish "outsiders" were now "in." When Peter got back to Jerusalem, some of his old associates, concerned about circumcision, called him on the carpet: "What do you think you're doing rubbing shoulders with that crowd, eating what is prohibited and ruining our good name?"

4-6 So Peter, starting from the beginning, laid it out for them step-by-step: "Recently I was in the town of Joppa praying. I fell into a trance and saw a vision: Something like a huge blanket, lowered by ropes at its four corners, came down out of heaven and settled on the ground in front of me. Milling around on the blanket were farm animals, wild animals, reptiles, birds—you name it, it was there. Fascinated, I took it all in.

7-10 "Then I heard a voice: 'Go to it, Peter—kill and eat.' I said, 'Oh, no, Master. I've never so much as tasted food that wasn't kosher.' The voice spoke again: 'If God says it's okay, it's okay.' This happened three times, and then the blanket was pulled back up into the sky.

11-14 "Just then three men showed up at the house where I was staying, sent from Caesarea to get me. The Spirit told me to go with them, no questions asked. So I went with them, I and six friends, to the man who had sent for me. He told us how he had seen an angel right in his own house, real as his next-door neighbor, saying, 'Send to Joppa and get Simon, the one they call Peter. He'll tell you something that will save your life—in fact, you and everyone you care for.'

15-17 "So I started in, talking. Before I'd spoken half a dozen sentences, the Holy Spirit fell on them just as he did on us the first time. I remembered Jesus' words: 'John baptized with water; you will be baptized with the

New King James Version

but you shall be baptized with the Holy Spirit.'
[17]If therefore God gave them the same gift as *He*
gave us when we believed on the Lord Jesus
Christ, who was I that I could withstand God?"
[18]When they heard these things they became
silent; and they glorified God, saying, "Then
God has also granted to the Gentiles repentance
to life."

Barnabas and Saul at Antioch

[19]Now those who were scattered after the
persecution that arose over Stephen traveled as
far as Phoenicia, Cyprus, and Antioch, preach-
ing the word to no one but the Jews only. [20]But
some of them were men from Cyprus and
Cyrene, who, when they had come to Antioch,
spoke to the Hellenists, preaching the Lord Je-
sus. [21]And the hand of the Lord was with them,
and a great number believed and turned to the
Lord.
[22]Then news of these things came to the ears
of the church in Jerusalem, and they sent out
Barnabas to go as far as Antioch. [23]When he
came and had seen the grace of God, he was
glad, and encouraged them all that with purpose
of heart they should continue with the Lord.
[24]For he was a good man, full of the Holy Spirit
and of faith. And a great many people were
added to the Lord.
[25]Then Barnabas departed for Tarsus to seek
Saul. [26]And when he had found him, he brought
him to Antioch. So it was that for a whole year
they assembled with the church and taught a
great many people. And the disciples were first
called Christians in Antioch.

Relief to Judea

[27]And in these days prophets came from
Jerusalem to Antioch. [28]Then one of them,
named Agabus, stood up and showed by the
Spirit that there was going to be a great famine
throughout all the world, which also happened
in the days of Claudius Caesar. [29]Then the disci-
ples, each according to his ability, determined to
send relief to the brethren dwelling in Judea.
[30]This they also did, and sent it to the elders by
the hands of Barnabas and Saul.

Herod's Violence to the Church

12 Now about that time Herod the king
stretched out *his* hand to harass some
from the church. [2]Then he killed James the
brother of John with the sword. [3]And because
he saw that it pleased the Jews, he proceeded
further to seize Peter also. Now it was *during* the
Days of Unleavened Bread. [4]So when he had ar-
rested him, he put *him* in prison, and delivered
him to four squads of soldiers to keep him, in-
tending to bring him before the people after
Passover.

Peter Freed from Prison

[5]Peter was therefore kept in prison, but con-
stant[a] prayer was offered to God for him by the
church.

12:5 [a]NU-Text reads *constantly* (or *earnestly*).

The Message

Holy Spirit.' So I ask you: If God gave the
same exact gift to them as to us when we be-
lieved in the Master Jesus Christ, how could
I object to God?"
18 Hearing it all laid out like that, they qui-
eted down. And then, as it sank in, they
started praising God. "It's really happened!
God has broken through to the other na-
tions, opened them up to Life!"
19-21 Those who had been scattered by the per-
secution triggered by Stephen's death trav-
eled as far as Phoenicia, Cyprus, and Anti-
och, but they were still only speaking and
dealing with their fellow Jews. Then some
of the men from Cyprus and Cyrene who
had come to Antioch started talking to
Greeks, giving them the Message of the
Master Jesus. God was pleased with what
they were doing and put his stamp of ap-
proval on it—quite a number of the Greeks
believed and turned to the Master.
22-24 When the church in Jerusalem got wind
of this, they sent Barnabas to Antioch to
check on things. As soon as he arrived, he
saw that God was behind and in it all. He
threw himself in with them, got behind
them, urging them to stay with it the rest of
their lives. He was a good man that way, en-
thusiastic and confident in the Holy Spirit's
ways. The community grew large and
strong in the Master.
25-26 Then Barnabas went on to Tarsus to look
for Saul. He found him and brought him
back to Antioch. They were there a whole
year, meeting with the church and teaching
a lot of people. It was in Antioch that the dis-
ciples were for the first time called Chris-
tians.
27-30 It was about this same time that some
prophets came to Antioch from Jerusalem.
One of them named Agabus stood up one
day and, prompted by the Spirit, warned
that a severe famine was about to devastate
the country. (The famine eventually came
during the rule of Claudius.) So the disciples
decided that each of them would send what-
ever they could to their fellow Christians in
Judea to help out. They sent Barnabas and
Saul to deliver the collection to the leaders
in Jerusalem.

Peter Under Heavy Guard

1-4 12 That's when King Herod got it into his
head to go after some of the church
members. He murdered James, John's
brother. When he saw how much it raised
his popularity ratings with the Jews, he ar-
rested Peter—all this during Passover Week,
mind you—and had him thrown in jail, put-
ting four squads of four soldiers each to
guard him. He was planning a public lynch-
ing after Passover.
5 All the time that Peter was under heavy
guard in the jailhouse, the church prayed for
him most strenuously.

NEW KING JAMES VERSION

6And when Herod was about to bring him out,
that night Peter was sleeping, bound with two
chains between two soldiers; and the guards be-
fore the door were keeping the prison. 7Now be-
hold, an angel of the Lord stood by *him*, and a
light shone in the prison; and he struck Peter on
the side and raised him up, saying, "Arise
quickly!" And his chains fell off *his* hands.
8Then the angel said to him, "Gird yourself and
tie on your sandals"; and so he did. And he said
to him, "Put on your garment and follow me."
9So he went out and followed him, and did not
know that what was done by the angel was real,
but thought he was seeing a vision. 10When they
were past the first and the second guard posts,
they came to the iron gate that leads to the city,
which opened to them of its own accord; and
they went out and went down one street, and
immediately the angel departed from him.
11And when Peter had come to himself, he
said, "Now I know for certain that the Lord has
sent His angel, and has delivered me from the
hand of Herod and *from* all the expectation of
the Jewish people."
12So, when he had considered *this*, he came
to the house of Mary, the mother of John whose
surname was Mark, where many were gathered
together praying. 13And as Peter knocked at the
door of the gate, a girl named Rhoda came to
answer. 14When she recognized Peter's voice,
because of *her* gladness she did not open the
gate, but ran in and announced that Peter stood
before the gate. 15But they said to her, "You are
beside yourself!" Yet she kept insisting that it
was so. So they said, "It is his angel."
16Now Peter continued knocking; and when
they opened *the door* and saw him, they were
astonished. 17But motioning to them with his
hand to keep silent, he declared to them how the
Lord had brought him out of the prison. And he
said, "Go, tell these things to James and to the
brethren." And he departed and went to another
place.
18Then, as soon as it was day, there was no
small stir among the soldiers about what had
become of Peter. 19But when Herod had
searched for him and not found him, he exam-
ined the guards and commanded that *they*
should be put to death.
And he went down from Judea to Caesarea,
and stayed *there*.

HEROD'S VIOLENT DEATH

20Now Herod had been very angry with the
people of Tyre and Sidon; but they came to him
with one accord, and having made Blastus the
king's personal aide their friend, they asked for
peace, because their country was supplied with
food by the king's *country*.
21So on a set day Herod, arrayed in royal ap-

THE MESSAGE

6 Then the time came for Herod to bring
him out for the kill. That night, even though
shackled to two soldiers, one on either side,
Peter slept like a baby. And there were
guards at the door keeping their eyes on the
place. Herod was taking no chances!
7-9 Suddenly there was an angel at his side
and light flooding the room. The angel
shook Peter and got him up: "Hurry!" The
handcuffs fell off his wrists. The angel said,
"Get dressed. Put on your shoes." Peter did
it. Then, "Grab your coat and let's get out of
here." Peter followed him, but didn't believe
it was really an angel—he thought he was
dreaming.
10-11 Past the first guard and then the second,
they came to the iron gate that led into the
city. It swung open before them on its own,
and they were out on the street, free as the
breeze. At the first intersection the angel left
him, going his own way. That's when Peter
realized it was no dream. "I can't believe it—
this really happened! The Master sent his
angel and rescued me from Herod's vicious
little production and the spectacle the Jew-
ish mob was looking forward to."
12-14 Still shaking his head, amazed, he went
to Mary's house, the Mary who was John
Mark's mother. The house was packed with
praying friends. When he knocked on the
door to the courtyard, a young woman
named Rhoda came to see who it was. But
when she recognized his voice—Peter's
voice!—she was so excited and eager to tell
everyone Peter was there that she forgot to
open the door and left him standing in the
street.
15-16 But they wouldn't believe her, dismissing
her, dismissing her report. "You're crazy,"
they said. She stuck by her story, insisting.
They still wouldn't believe her and said, "It
must be his angel." All this time poor Peter
was standing out in the street, knocking
away.
16-17 Finally they opened up and saw him—
and went wild! Peter put his hands up and
calmed them down. He described how the
Master had gotten him out of jail, then said,
"Tell James and the brothers what's hap-
pened." He left them and went off to another
place.
18-19 At daybreak the jail was in an uproar.
"Where is Peter? What's happened to Pe-
ter?" When Herod sent for him and they
could neither produce him nor explain why
not, he ordered their execution: "Off with
their heads!" Fed up with Judea and Jews,
he went for a vacation to Caesarea.

THE DEATH OF HEROD

20-22 But things went from bad to worse for
Herod. Now people from Tyre and Sidon put
him on the warpath. But they got Blastus,
King Herod's right-hand man, to put in a
good word for them and got a delegation to-
gether to iron things out. Because they were
dependent on Judea for food supplies, they
couldn't afford to let this go on too long. On
the day set for their meeting, Herod, robed

NEW KING JAMES VERSION

parel, sat on his throne and gave an oration to
them. 22And the people kept shouting, "The
voice of a god and not of a man!" 23Then imme-
diately an angel of the Lord struck him, because
he did not give glory to God. And he was eaten
by worms and died.
24But the word of God grew and multiplied.

BARNABAS AND SAUL APPOINTED

25And Barnabas and Saul returned from[a]
Jerusalem when they had fulfilled *their* min-
istry, and they also took with them John whose
surname was Mark.

13 Now in the church that was at Antioch
there were certain prophets and teachers:
Barnabas, Simeon who was called Niger, Lucius
of Cyrene, Manaen who had been brought up
with Herod the tetrarch, and Saul. 2As they min-
istered to the Lord and fasted, the Holy Spirit
said, "Now separate to Me Barnabas and Saul
for the work to which I have called them."
3Then, having fasted and prayed, and laid hands
on them, they sent *them* away.

PREACHING IN CYPRUS

4So, being sent out by the Holy Spirit, they
went down to Seleucia, and from there they
sailed to Cyprus. 5And when they arrived in
Salamis, they preached the word of God in the
synagogues of the Jews. They also had John as
their assistant.
6Now when they had gone through the is-
land[a] to Paphos, they found a certain sorcerer, a
false prophet, a Jew whose name *was* Bar-Jesus,
7who was with the proconsul, Sergius Paulus, an
intelligent man. This man called for Barnabas
and Saul and sought to hear the word of God.
8But Elymas the sorcerer (for so his name is
translated) withstood them, seeking to turn the
proconsul away from the faith. 9Then Saul, who
also *is called* Paul, filled with the Holy Spirit,
looked intently at him 10and said, "O full of all
deceit and all fraud, *you* son of the devil, *you* en-
emy of all righteousness, will you not cease per-
verting the straight ways of the Lord? 11And
now, indeed, the hand of the Lord *is* upon you,
and you shall be blind, not seeing the sun for a
time."
And immediately a dark mist fell on him,
and he went around seeking someone to lead
him by the hand.

12:25 [a]NU-Text and M-Text read *to.* **13:6** [a]NU-Text reads *the whole island.*

THE MESSAGE

in pomposity, took his place on the throne and regaled them with a lot of hot air. The people played their part to the hilt and shouted flatteries: "The voice of God! The voice of God!"

23 That was the last straw. God had had enough of Herod's arrogance and sent an angel to strike him down. Herod had given God no credit for anything. Down he went. Rotten to the core, a maggoty old man if there ever was one, he died.

24 Meanwhile, the ministry of God's Word grew by leaps and bounds.

25 Barnabas and Saul, once they had delivered the relief offering to the church in Jerusalem, went back to Antioch. This time they took John with them, the one they called Mark.

BARNABAS, SAUL, AND DOCTOR KNOW-IT-ALL

1-2 13 The congregation in Antioch was blessed with a number of prophet-preachers and teachers:

Barnabas,
Simon, nicknamed Niger,
Lucius the Cyrenian,
Manaen, an advisor to the ruler Herod,
Saul.

One day as they were worshiping God—they were also fasting as they waited for guidance—the Holy Spirit spoke: "Take Barnabas and Saul and commission them for the work I have called them to do."

3 So they commissioned them. In that circle of intensity and obedience, of fasting and praying, they laid hands on their heads and sent them off.

4-5 Sent off on their new assignment by the Holy Spirit, Barnabas and Saul went down to Seleucia and caught a ship for Cyprus. The first thing they did when they put in at Salamis was preach God's Word in the Jewish meeting places. They had John along to help out as needed.

6-7 They traveled the length of the island, and at Paphos came upon a Jewish wizard who had worked himself into the confidence of the governor, Sergius Paulus, an intelligent man not easily taken in by charlatans. The wizard's name was Bar-Jesus. He was as crooked as a corkscrew.

7-11 The governor invited Barnabas and Saul in, wanting to hear God's Word firsthand from them. But Dr. Know-It-All (that's the wizard's name in plain English) stirred up a ruckus, trying to divert the governor from becoming a believer. But Saul (or Paul), full of the Holy Spirit and looking him straight in the eye, said, "You bag of wind, you parody of a devil—why, you stay up nights inventing schemes to cheat people out of God. But now you've come up against God himself, and your game is up. You're about to go blind—no sunlight for you for a good long stretch." He was plunged immediately into a shadowy mist and stumbled around, begging people to take his hand and show him the way.

NEW KING JAMES VERSION

12Then the proconsul believed, when he saw
what had been done, being astonished at the
teaching of the Lord.

AT ANTIOCH IN PISIDIA

13Now when Paul and his party set sail from
Paphos, they came to Perga in Pamphylia; and
John, departing from them, returned to
Jerusalem. 14But when they departed from
Perga, they came to Antioch in Pisidia, and went
into the synagogue on the Sabbath day and sat
down. 15And after the reading of the Law and
the Prophets, the rulers of the synagogue sent to
them, saying, "Men *and* brethren, if you have
any word of exhortation for the people, say on."

16Then Paul stood up, and motioning with *his*
hand said, "Men of Israel, and you who fear
God, listen: 17The God of this people Israel[a]
chose our fathers, and exalted the people when
they dwelt as strangers in the land of Egypt, and
with an uplifted arm He brought them out of it.
18Now for a time of about forty years He put up
with their ways in the wilderness. 19And when
He had destroyed seven nations in the land of
Canaan, He distributed their land to them by al-
lotment.

20"After that He gave *them* judges for about
four hundred and fifty years, until Samuel the
prophet. 21And afterward they asked for a king;
so God gave them Saul the son of Kish, a man of
the tribe of Benjamin, for forty years. 22And
when He had removed him, He raised up for
them David as king, to whom also He gave tes-
timony and said, *'I have found David*[a] the *son* of
Jesse, *a man after My own heart, who will do all
My will.'*[b] 23From this man's seed, according to
the promise, God raised up for Israel a Savior—
Jesus—[a] 24after John had first preached, before
His coming, the baptism of repentance to all the
people of Israel. 25And as John was finishing his
course, he said, 'Who do you think I am? I am
not *He.* But behold, there comes One after me,
the sandals of whose feet I am not worthy to
loose.'

26"Men *and* brethren, sons of the family of
Abraham, and those among you who fear God,
to you the word of this salvation has been sent.
27For those who dwell in Jerusalem, and their
rulers, because they did not know Him, nor even
the voices of the Prophets which are read every
Sabbath, have fulfilled *them* in condemning
Him. 28And though they found no cause for
death *in Him,* they asked Pilate that He should
be put to death. 29Now when they had fulfilled
all that was written concerning Him, they took
Him down from the tree and laid *Him* in a tomb.
30But God raised Him from the dead. 31He was

13:17 [a]M-Text omits *Israel.* **13:22** [a]Psalm 89:20 [b]1 Samuel
13:14 **13:23** [a]M-Text reads *for Israel salvation.*

THE MESSAGE

12 When the governor saw what happened,
he became a believer, full of enthusiasm over
what they were saying about the Master.

DON'T TAKE THIS LIGHTLY

13-14 From Paphos, Paul and company put out to
sea, sailing on to Perga in Pamphylia. That's
where John called it quits and went back to
Jerusalem. From Perga the rest of them trav-
eled on to Antioch in Pisidia.

14-15 On the Sabbath they went to the meeting
place and took their places. After the read-
ing of the Scriptures—God's Law and the
Prophets—the president of the meeting
asked them, "Friends, do you have anything
you want to say? A word of encouragement,
perhaps?"

16-20 Paul stood up, paused and took a deep
breath, then said, "Fellow Israelites and
friends of God, listen. God took a special in-
terest in our ancestors, pulled our people
who were beaten down in Egyptian exile to
their feet, and led them out of there in grand
style. He took good care of them for nearly
forty years in that godforsaken wilderness
and then, having wiped out seven enemies
who stood in the way, gave them the land of
Canaan for their very own—a span in all of
about 450 years.

20-22 "Up to the time of Samuel the prophet,
God provided judges to lead them. But then
they asked for a king, and God gave them
Saul, son of Kish, out of the tribe of Ben-
jamin. After Saul had ruled forty years, God
removed him from office and put King David
in his place, with this commendation: 'I've
searched the land and found this David, son
of Jesse. He's a man whose heart beats to my
heart, a man who will do what I tell him.'

23-25 "From out of David's descendants God
produced a Savior for Israel, Jesus, exactly
as he promised—but only after John had
thoroughly alerted the people to his arrival
by preparing them for a total life-change. As
John was finishing up his work, he said, 'Did
you think I was the One? No, I'm not the
One. But the One you've been waiting for all
these years is just around the corner, about
to appear. And I'm about to disappear.'

26-29 "Dear brothers and sisters, children of
Abraham, and friends of God, this message
of salvation has been precisely targeted to
you. The citizens and rulers in Jerusalem
didn't recognize who he was and con-
demned him to death. They couldn't find a
good reason, but demanded that Pilate exe-
cute him anyway. They did just what the
prophets said they would do, but had no
idea they were following to the letter the
script of the prophets, even though those
same prophets are read every Sabbath in
their meeting places.

29-31 "After they had done everything the
prophets said they would do, they took him
down from the cross and buried him. And
then God raised him from death. There is no
disputing that—he appeared over and over
again many times and places to those who
had known him well in the Galilean years,

NEW KING JAMES VERSION

seen for many days by those who came up with
Him from Galilee to Jerusalem, who are His wit-
nesses to the people. 32And we declare to you
glad tidings—that promise which was made to
the fathers. 33God has fulfilled this for us their
children, in that He has raised up Jesus. As it is
also written in the second Psalm:

'You are My Son,
Today I have begotten You.'[a]

34And that He raised Him from the dead, no
more to return to corruption, He has spoken
thus:

'I will give you the sure mercies of David.'[a]

35Therefore He also says in another *Psalm:*

'You will not allow Your Holy One to see
corruption.'[a]

36"For David, after he had served his own
generation by the will of God, fell asleep, was
buried with his fathers, and saw corruption;
37but He whom God raised up saw no corrup-
tion. 38Therefore let it be known to you,
brethren, that through this Man is preached to
you the forgiveness of sins; 39and by Him every-
one who believes is justified from all things
from which you could not be justified by the law
of Moses. 40Beware therefore, lest what has
been spoken in the prophets come upon you:

41*'Behold, you despisers,*
Marvel and perish!
For I work a work in your days,
A work which you will by no means believe,
Though one were to declare it to you.'"[a]

BLESSING AND CONFLICT AT ANTIOCH

42So when the Jews went out of the syna-
gogue,[a] the Gentiles begged that these words
might be preached to them the next Sabbath.
43Now when the congregation had broken up,
many of the Jews and devout proselytes fol-
lowed Paul and Barnabas, who, speaking to
them, persuaded them to continue in the grace
of God.

44On the next Sabbath almost the whole city
came together to hear the word of God. 45But
when the Jews saw the multitudes, they were
filled with envy; and contradicting and blas-
pheming, they opposed the things spoken by
Paul. 46Then Paul and Barnabas grew bold and
said, "It was necessary that the word of God
should be spoken to you first; but since you re-
ject it, and judge yourselves unworthy of ever-
lasting life, behold, we turn to the Gentiles. 47For
so the Lord has commanded us:

'I have set you as a light to the Gentiles,
That you should be for salvation to the ends
of the earth.'"[a]

13:33 [a]Psalm 2:7 **13:34** [a]Isaiah 55:3 **13:35** [a]Psalm 16:10
13:41 [a]Habakkuk 1:5 **13:42** [a]Or *And when they went out of the synagogue of the Jews;* NU-Text reads *And when they went out, they begged.* **13:47** [a]Isaiah 49:6

THE MESSAGE

and these same people continue to give wit-
ness that he is alive.

32-35 "And we're here today bringing you good
news: the Message that what God promised
the fathers has come true for the children—
for us! He raised Jesus, exactly as described
in the second Psalm:

My Son! My very own Son!
Today I celebrate you!

"When he raised him from the dead, he did it
for good—no going back to that rot and de-
cay for him. That's why Isaiah said, 'I'll give
to all of you David's guaranteed blessings.'
So also the psalmist's prayer: 'You'll never
let your Holy One see death's rot and decay.'

36-39 "David, of course, having completed the
work God set out for him, has been in the
grave, dust and ashes, a long time now. But
the One God raised up—no dust and ashes
for him! I want you to know, my very dear
friends, that it is on account of this resur-
rected Jesus that the forgiveness of your
sins can be promised. He accomplishes, in
those who believe, everything that the Law
of Moses could never make good on. But
everyone who believes in this raised-up Je-
sus is declared good and right and whole
before God.

40-41 "Don't take this lightly. You don't want
the prophet's sermon to describe you:

Watch out, cynics;
Look hard—watch your world fall to
pieces.
I'm doing something right before your eyes
That you won't believe, though it's
staring you in the face."

42-43 When the service was over, Paul and
Barnabas were invited back to preach again
the next Sabbath. As the meeting broke up,
a good many Jews and converts to Judaism
went along with Paul and Barnabas, who
urged them in long conversations to stick
with what they'd started, this living in and
by God's grace.

44-45 When the next Sabbath came around,
practically the whole city showed up to hear
the Word of God. Some of the Jews, seeing
the crowds, went wild with jealousy and
tore into Paul, contradicting everything he
was saying, making an ugly scene.

46-47 But Paul and Barnabas didn't back down.
Standing their ground they said, "It was re-
quired that God's Word be spoken first of all
to you, the Jews. But seeing that you want no
part of it—you've made it quite clear that you
have no taste or inclination for eternal life—
the door is open to all the outsiders. And
we're on our way through it, following orders,
doing what God commanded when he said,

I've set you up
as light to all nations.
You'll proclaim salvation
to the four winds and seven seas!"

NEW KING JAMES VERSION

48Now when the Gentiles heard this, they were glad and glorified the word of the Lord. And as many as had been appointed to eternal life believed.

49And the word of the Lord was being spread throughout all the region. 50But the Jews stirred up the devout and prominent women and the chief men of the city, raised up persecution against Paul and Barnabas, and expelled them from their region. 51But they shook off the dust from their feet against them, and came to Iconium. 52And the disciples were filled with joy and with the Holy Spirit.

AT ICONIUM

14 Now it happened in Iconium that they went together to the synagogue of the Jews, and so spoke that a great multitude both of the Jews and of the Greeks believed. 2But the unbelieving Jews stirred up the Gentiles and poisoned their minds against the brethren. 3Therefore they stayed there a long time, speaking boldly in the Lord, who was bearing witness to the word of His grace, granting signs and wonders to be done by their hands.

4But the multitude of the city was divided: part sided with the Jews, and part with the apostles. 5And when a violent attempt was made by both the Gentiles and Jews, with their rulers, to abuse and stone them, 6they became aware of it and fled to Lystra and Derbe, cities of Lycaonia, and to the surrounding region. 7And they were preaching the gospel there.

IDOLATRY AT LYSTRA

8And in Lystra a certain man without strength in his feet was sitting, a cripple from his mother's womb, who had never walked. 9*This* man heard Paul speaking. Paul, observing him intently and seeing that he had faith to be healed, 10said with a loud voice, "Stand up straight on your feet!" And he leaped and walked. 11Now when the people saw what Paul had done, they raised their voices, saying in the Lycaonian *language*, "The gods have come down to us in the likeness of men!" 12And Barnabas they called Zeus, and Paul, Hermes, because he was the chief speaker. 13Then the priest of Zeus, whose temple was in front of their city, brought oxen and garlands to the gates, intending to sacrifice with the multitudes.

14But when the apostles Barnabas and Paul heard this, they tore their clothes and ran in among the multitude, crying out 15and saying, "Men, why are you doing these things? We also are men with the same nature as you, and preach to you that you should turn from these useless things to the living God, who made the

THE MESSAGE

48-49 When the non-Jewish outsiders heard this, they could hardly believe their good fortune. All who were marked out for *real life* put their trust in God—they honored God's Word by receiving that life. And this Message of salvation spread like wildfire all through the region.

50-52 Some of the Jews convinced the most respected women and leading men of the town that their precious way of life was about to be destroyed. Alarmed, they turned on Paul and Barnabas and forced them to leave. Paul and Barnabas shrugged their shoulders and went on to the next town, Iconium, brimming with joy and the Holy Spirit, two happy disciples.

1-3 14 When they got to Iconium they went, as they always did, to the meeting place of the Jews and gave their message. The Message convinced both Jews and non-Jews—and not just a few, either. But the unbelieving Jews worked up a whispering campaign against Paul and Barnabas, sowing mistrust and suspicion in the minds of the people in the street. The two apostles were there a long time, speaking freely, openly, and confidently as they presented the clear evidence of God's gifts, God corroborating their work with miracles and wonders.

4-7 But then there was a split in public opinion, some siding with the Jews, some with the apostles. One day, learning that both the Jews and non-Jews had been organized by their leaders to beat them up, they escaped as best they could to the next towns—Lyconia, Lystra, Derbe, and that neighborhood—but then were right back at it again, getting out the Message.

GODS OR MEN?

8-10 There was a man in Lystra who couldn't walk. He sat there, crippled since the day of his birth. He heard Paul talking, and Paul, looking him in the eye, saw that he was ripe for God's work, ready to believe. So he said, loud enough for everyone to hear, "Up on your feet!" The man was up in a flash—jumped up and walked around as if he'd been walking all his life.

11-13 When the crowd saw what Paul had done, they went wild, calling out in their Lyconian dialect, "The gods have come down! These men are gods!" They called Barnabas "Zeus" and Paul "Hermes" (since Paul did most of the speaking). The priest of the local Zeus shrine got up a parade—bulls and banners and people lined right up to the gates, ready for the ritual of sacrifice.

14-15 When Barnabas and Paul finally realized what was going on, they stopped them. Waving their arms, they interrupted the parade, calling out, "What do you think you're doing! We're not gods! We are men just like you, and we're here to bring you the Message, to persuade you to abandon these silly god-superstitions and embrace God himself, the living God. We don't make God; he

NEW KING JAMES VERSION

heaven, the earth, the sea, and all things that are in them, [16]who in bygone generations allowed all nations to walk in their own ways. [17]Nevertheless He did not leave Himself without witness, in that He did good, gave us rain from heaven and fruitful seasons, filling our hearts with food and gladness." [18]And with these sayings they could scarcely restrain the multitudes from sacrificing to them.

STONING, ESCAPE TO DERBE

[19]Then Jews from Antioch and Iconium came there; and having persuaded the multitudes, they stoned Paul *and* dragged *him* out of the city, supposing him to be dead. [20]However, when the disciples gathered around him, he rose up and went into the city. And the next day he departed with Barnabas to Derbe.

STRENGTHENING THE CONVERTS

[21]And when they had preached the gospel to that city and made many disciples, they returned to Lystra, Iconium, and Antioch, [22]strengthening the souls of the disciples, exhorting *them* to continue in the faith, and *saying*, "We must through many tribulations enter the kingdom of God." [23]So when they had appointed elders in every church, and prayed with fasting, they commended them to the Lord in whom they had believed. [24]And after they had passed through Pisidia, they came to Pamphylia. [25]Now when they had preached the word in Perga, they went down to Attalia. [26]From there they sailed to Antioch, where they had been commended to the grace of God for the work which they had completed.

[27]Now when they had come and gathered the church together, they reported all that God had done with them, and that He had opened the door of faith to the Gentiles. [28]So they stayed there a long time with the disciples.

CONFLICT OVER CIRCUMCISION

15 And certain *men* came down from Judea and taught the brethren, "Unless you are circumcised according to the custom of Moses, you cannot be saved." [2]Therefore, when Paul and Barnabas had no small dissension and dispute with them, they determined that Paul and Barnabas and certain others of them should go up to Jerusalem, to the apostles and elders, about this question.

[3]So, being sent on their way by the church, they passed through Phoenicia and Samaria, describing the conversion of the Gentiles; and they caused great joy to all the brethren. [4]And when they had come to Jerusalem, they were re-

THE MESSAGE

makes us, and all of this—sky, earth, sea, and everything in them.

16-18 "In the generations before us, God let all the different nations go their own way. But even then he didn't leave them without a clue, for he made a good creation, poured down rain and gave bumper crops. When your bellies were full and your hearts happy, there was evidence of good beyond your doing." Talking fast and hard like this, they prevented them from carrying out the sacrifice that would have honored them as gods—but just barely.

19-20 Then some Jews from Antioch and Iconium caught up with them and turned the fickle crowd against them. They beat Paul unconscious, dragged him outside the town and left him for dead. But as the disciples gathered around him, he came to and got up. He went back into town and the next day left with Barnabas for Derbe.

PLENTY OF HARD TIMES

21-22 After proclaiming the Message in Derbe and establishing a strong core of disciples, they retraced their steps to Lystra, then Iconium, and then Antioch, putting muscle and sinew in the lives of the disciples, urging them to stick with what they had begun to believe and not quit, making it clear to them that it wouldn't be easy: "Anyone signing up for the kingdom of God has to go through plenty of hard times."

23-26 Paul and Barnabas handpicked leaders in each church. After praying—their prayers intensified by fasting—they presented these new leaders to the Master to whom they had entrusted their lives. Working their way back through Pisidia, they came to Pamphylia and preached in Perga. Finally, they made it to Attalia and caught a ship back to Antioch, where it had all started—launched by God's grace and now safely home by God's grace. A good piece of work.

27-28 On arrival, they got the church together and reported on their trip, telling in detail how God had used them to throw the door of faith wide open so people of all nations could come streaming in. Then they settled down for a long, leisurely visit with the disciples.

TO LET OUTSIDERS INSIDE

1-2 **15** It wasn't long before some Jews showed up from Judea insisting that everyone be circumcised: "If you're not circumcised in the Mosaic fashion, you can't be saved." Paul and Barnabas were up on their feet at once in fierce protest. The church decided to resolve the matter by sending Paul, Barnabas, and a few others to put it before the apostles and leaders in Jerusalem.

3 After they were sent off and on their way, they told everyone they met as they traveled through Phoenicia and Samaria about the breakthrough to the non-Jewish outsiders. Everyone who heard the news cheered—it was terrific news!

4-5 When they got to Jerusalem, Paul and Barnabas were graciously received by the

NEW KING JAMES VERSION

ceived by the church and the apostles and the
elders; and they reported all things that God
had done with them. 5But some of the sect of the
Pharisees who believed rose up, saying, "It is
necessary to circumcise them, and to command
them to keep the law of Moses."

THE JERUSALEM COUNCIL

6Now the apostles and elders came together
to consider this matter. 7And when there had
been much dispute, Peter rose up *and* said to
them: "Men *and* brethren, you know that a good
while ago God chose among us, that by my
mouth the Gentiles should hear the word of
the gospel and believe. 8So God, who knows the
heart, acknowledged them by giving them the
Holy Spirit, just as *He did* to us, 9and made no
distinction between us and them, purifying their
hearts by faith. 10Now therefore, why do you test
God by putting a yoke on the neck of the disci-
ples which neither our fathers nor we were able
to bear? 11But we believe that through the grace
of the Lord Jesus Christ[a] we shall be saved in
the same manner as they."

12Then all the multitude kept silent and lis-
tened to Barnabas and Paul declaring how
many miracles and wonders God had worked
through them among the Gentiles. 13And after
they had become silent, James answered, say-
ing, "Men *and* brethren, listen to me: 14Simon
has declared how God at the first visited the
Gentiles to take out of them a people for His
name. 15And with this the words of the prophets
agree, just as it is written:

16'*After this I will return*
And will rebuild the tabernacle of David,
which has fallen down;
I will rebuild its ruins,
And I will set it up;
17*So that the rest of mankind may seek the*
LORD,
Even all the Gentiles who are called by My
name,
Says the LORD who does all these things.'[a]

18"Known to God from eternity are all His
works.[a] 19Therefore I judge that we should not
trouble those from among the Gentiles who are
turning to God, 20but that we write to them to
abstain from things polluted by idols, *from* sex-
ual immorality,[a] *from* things strangled, and *from*
blood. 21For Moses has had throughout many
generations those who preach him in every city,
being read in the synagogues every Sabbath."

15:11 [a]NU-Text and M-Text omit *Christ*. **15:17** [a]Amos 9:11, 12
15:18 [a]NU-Text (combining with verse 17) reads *Says the Lord, who makes these things known from eternity (of old)*. **15:20** [a]Or *fornication*

THE MESSAGE

whole church, including the apostles and
leaders. They reported on their recent jour-
ney and how God had used them to open
things up to the outsiders. Some Pharisees
stood up to say their piece. They had become
believers, but continued to hold to the hard
party line of the Pharisees. "You have to cir-
cumcise the pagan converts," they said. "You
must make them keep the Law of Moses."

6-9 The apostles and leaders called a special
meeting to consider the matter. The argu-
ments went on and on, back and forth, get-
ting more and more heated. Then Peter took
the floor: "Friends, you well know that from
early on God made it quite plain that he
wanted the pagans to hear the Message of
this good news and embrace it—and not in
any secondhand or roundabout way, but
firsthand, straight from my mouth. And
God, who can't be fooled by any pretense on
our part but always knows a person's
thoughts, gave them the Holy Spirit exactly
as he gave him to us. He treated the out-
siders exactly as he treated us, beginning at
the very center of who they were and work-
ing from that center outward, cleaning up
their lives as they trusted and believed him.

10-11 "So why are you now trying to out-god
God, loading these new believers down with
rules that crushed our ancestors and
crushed us, too? Don't we believe that we
are saved because the Master Jesus amaz-
ingly and out of sheer generosity moved to
save us just as he did those from beyond our
nation? So what are we arguing about?"

12-13 There was dead silence. No one said a
word. With the room quiet, Barnabas and
Paul reported matter-of-factly on the mira-
cles and wonders God had done among the
other nations through their ministry. The si-
lence deepened; you could hear a pin drop.

13-18 James broke the silence. "Friends, listen.
Simeon has told us the story of how God at
the very outset made sure that racial out-
siders were included. This is in perfect
agreement with the words of the prophets:

After this, I'm coming back;
I'll rebuild David's ruined house;
I'll put all the pieces together again;
I'll make it look like new
So outsiders who seek will find,
so they'll have a place to come to,
All the pagan peoples
included in what I'm doing.

"God said it and now he's doing it. It's no af-
terthought; he's always known he would do
this.

19-21 "So here is my decision: We're not going
to unnecessarily burden non-Jewish people
who turn to the Master. We'll write them a
letter and tell them, 'Be careful to not get in-
volved in activities connected with idols, to
guard the morality of sex and marriage, to
not serve food offensive to Jewish Chris-
tians—blood, for instance.' This is basic wis-
dom from Moses, preached and honored for
centuries now in city after city as we have
met and kept the Sabbath."

NEW KING JAMES VERSION

THE JERUSALEM DECREE

22Then it pleased the apostles and elders,
with the whole church, to send chosen men of
their own company to Antioch with Paul and
Barnabas, *namely,* Judas who was also named
Barsabas,[a] and Silas, leading men among the
brethren.
23They wrote this, *letter* by them:

The apostles, the elders, and the brethren,

To the brethren who are of the Gentiles in
Antioch, Syria, and Cilicia:

Greetings.

24Since we have heard that some who went
out from us have troubled you with words,
unsettling your souls, saying, "*You must* be
circumcised and keep the law"[a]—to whom
we gave no *such* commandment—25it
seemed good to us, being assembled with
one accord, to send chosen men to you with
our beloved Barnabas and Paul, 26men who
have risked their lives for the name of our
Lord Jesus Christ. 27We have therefore sent
Judas and Silas, who will also report the
same things by word of mouth. 28For it
seemed good to the Holy Spirit, and to us,
to lay upon you no greater burden than
these necessary things: 29that you abstain
from things offered to idols, from blood,
from things strangled, and from sexual im-
morality.[a] If you keep yourselves from
these, you will do well.

Farewell.

CONTINUING MINISTRY IN SYRIA

30So when they were sent off, they came to
Antioch; and when they had gathered the multi-
tude together, they delivered the letter. 31When
they had read it, they rejoiced over its encourage-
ment. 32Now Judas and Silas, themselves being
prophets also, exhorted and strengthened the
brethren with many words. 33And after they had
stayed *there* for a time, they were sent back with
greetings from the brethren to the apostles.[a]
34However, it seemed good to Silas to remain
there.[a] 35Paul and Barnabas also remained in
Antioch, teaching and preaching the word of the
Lord, with many others also.

DIVISION OVER JOHN MARK

36Then after some days Paul said to Bar-
nabas, "Let us now go back and visit our
brethren in every city where we have preached
the word of the Lord, *and see* how they are do-
ing." 37Now Barnabas was determined to take
with them John called Mark. 38But Paul insisted
that they should not take with them the one who
had departed from them in Pamphylia, and had
not gone with them to the work. 39Then the con-
tention became so sharp that they parted from
one another. And so Barnabas took Mark and

15:22 [a]NU-Text and M-Text read *Barsabbas.* **15:24** [a]NU-Text omits *saying, "You must be circumcised and keep the law."* **15:29** [a]Or *fornication* **15:33** [a]NU-Text reads *to those who had sent them.* **15:34** [a]NU-Text and M-Text omit this verse.

THE MESSAGE

22-23 Everyone agreed: apostles, leaders, all the people. They picked Judas (nicknamed Barsabbas) and Silas—they both carried considerable weight in the church—and sent them to Antioch with Paul and Barnabas with this letter:

From the apostles and leaders, your friends, to our friends in Antioch, Syria, and Cilicia:

Hello!

24-27 We heard that some men from our church went to you and said things that confused and upset you. Mind you, they had no authority from us; we didn't send them. We have agreed unanimously to pick representatives and send them to you with our good friends Barnabas and Paul. We picked men we knew you could trust, Judas and Silas—they've looked death in the face time and again for the sake of our Master Jesus Christ. We've sent them to confirm in a face-to-face meeting with you what we've written.

28-29 It seemed to the Holy Spirit and to us that you should not be saddled with any crushing burden, but be responsible only for these bare necessities: Be careful not to get involved in activities connected with idols; avoid serving food offensive to Jewish Christians (blood, for instance); and guard the morality of sex and marriage.

These guidelines are sufficient to keep relations congenial between us. And God be with you!

BARNABAS AND PAUL GO THEIR SEPARATE WAYS

30-33 And so off they went to Antioch. On arrival, they gathered the church and read the letter. The people were greatly relieved and pleased. Judas and Silas, good preachers both of them, strengthened their new friends with many words of courage and hope. Then it was time to go home. They were sent off by their new friends with laughter and embraces all around to report back to those who had sent them.

35 Paul and Barnabas stayed on in Antioch, teaching and preaching the Word of God. But they weren't alone. There were a number of teachers and preachers at that time in Antioch.

36 After a few days of this, Paul said to Barnabas, "Let's go back and visit all our friends in each of the towns where we preached the Word of God. Let's see how they're doing."

37-41 Barnabas wanted to take John along, the John nicknamed Mark. But Paul wouldn't have him; he wasn't about to take along a quitter who, as soon as the going got tough, had jumped ship on them in Pamphylia. Tempers flared, and they ended up going their separate ways: Barnabas took Mark

NEW KING JAMES VERSION

sailed to Cyprus; [40]but Paul chose Silas and departed, being commended by the brethren to the grace of God. [41]And he went through Syria and Cilicia, strengthening the churches.

TIMOTHY JOINS PAUL AND SILAS

16 Then he came to Derbe and Lystra. And behold, a certain disciple was there, named Timothy, *the* son of a certain Jewish woman who believed, but his father *was* Greek. [2]He was well spoken of by the brethren who were at Lystra and Iconium. [3]Paul wanted to have him go on with him. And he took *him* and circumcised him because of the Jews who were in that region, for they all knew that his father was Greek. [4]And as they went through the cities, they delivered to them the decrees to keep, which were determined by the apostles and elders at Jerusalem. [5]So the churches were strengthened in the faith, and increased in number daily.

THE MACEDONIAN CALL

[6]Now when they had gone through Phrygia and the region of Galatia, they were forbidden by the Holy Spirit to preach the word in Asia. [7]After they had come to Mysia, they tried to go into Bithynia, but the Spirit[a] did not permit them. [8]So passing by Mysia, they came down to Troas. [9]And a vision appeared to Paul in the night. A man of Macedonia stood and pleaded with him, saying, "Come over to Macedonia and help us." [10]Now after he had seen the vision, immediately we sought to go to Macedonia, concluding that the Lord had called us to preach the gospel to them.

LYDIA BAPTIZED AT PHILIPPI

[11]Therefore, sailing from Troas, we ran a straight course to Samothrace, and the next *day* came to Neapolis, [12]and from there to Philippi, which is the foremost city of that part of Macedonia, a colony. And we were staying in that city for some days. [13]And on the Sabbath day we went out of the city to the riverside, where prayer was customarily made; and we sat down and spoke to the women who met *there*. [14]Now a certain woman named Lydia heard *us*. She was a seller of purple from the city of Thyatira, who worshiped God. The Lord opened her heart to heed the things spoken by Paul. [15]And when she and her household were baptized, she begged *us*, saying, "If you have judged me to be faithful to the Lord, come to my house and stay." So she persuaded us.

PAUL AND SILAS IMPRISONED

[16]Now it happened, as we went to prayer, that a certain slave girl possessed with a spirit of divination met us, who brought her masters much profit by fortune-telling. [17]This girl followed

16:7 [a]NU-Text adds *of Jesus*.

THE MESSAGE

and sailed for Cyprus; Paul chose Silas and, offered up by their friends to the grace of the Master, went to Syria and Cilicia to build up muscle and sinew in those congregations.

A DREAM GAVE PAUL HIS MAP

1-3 **16** Paul came first to Derbe, then Lystra. He found a disciple there by the name of Timothy, son of a devout Jewish mother and Greek father. Friends in Lystra and Iconium all said what a fine young man he was. Paul wanted to recruit him for their mission, but first took him aside and circumcised him so he wouldn't offend the Jews who lived in those parts. They all knew that his father was Greek.

4-5 As they traveled from town to town, they presented the simple guidelines the Jerusalem apostles and leaders had come up with. That turned out to be most helpful. Day after day the congregations became stronger in faith and larger in size.

6-8 They went to Phrygia, and then on through the region of Galatia. Their plan was to turn west into Asia province, but the Holy Spirit blocked that route. So they went to Mysia and tried to go north to Bithynia, but the Spirit of Jesus wouldn't let them go there either. Proceeding on through Mysia, they went down to the seaport Troas.

9-10 That night Paul had a dream: A Macedonian stood on the far shore and called across the sea, "Come over to Macedonia and help us!" The dream gave Paul his map. We went to work at once getting things ready to cross over to Macedonia. All the pieces had come together. We knew now for sure that God had called us to preach the good news to the Europeans.

11-12 Putting out from the harbor at Troas, we made a straight run for Samothrace. The next day we tied up at New City and walked from there to Philippi, the main city in that part of Macedonia and, even more importantly, a Roman colony. We lingered there several days.

13-14 On the Sabbath, we left the city and went down along the river where we had heard there was to be a prayer meeting. We took our place with the women who had gathered there and talked with them. One woman, Lydia, was from Thyatira and a dealer in expensive textiles, known to be a God-fearing woman. As she listened with intensity to what was being said, the Master gave her a trusting heart—and she believed!

15 After she was baptized, along with everyone in her household, she said in a surge of hospitality, "If you're confident that I'm in this with you and believe in the Master truly, come home with me and be my guests." We hesitated, but she wouldn't take no for an answer.

BEAT UP AND THROWN IN JAIL

16-18 One day, on our way to the place of prayer, a slave girl ran into us. She was a psychic and, with her fortunetelling, made a lot of

NEW KING JAMES VERSION

Paul and us, and cried out, saying, "These men
are the servants of the Most High God, who pro-
claim to us the way of salvation." [18]And this she
did for many days.
But Paul, greatly annoyed, turned and said to
the spirit, "I command you in the name of Jesus
Christ to come out of her." And he came out that
very hour. [19]But when her masters saw that their
hope of profit was gone, they seized Paul and
Silas and dragged *them* into the marketplace to
the authorities.
[20]And they brought them to the magistrates,
and said, "These men, being Jews, exceedingly
trouble our city; [21]and they teach customs which
are not lawful for us, being Romans, to receive
or observe." [22]Then the multitude rose up to-
gether against them; and the magistrates tore
off their clothes and commanded *them* to be
beaten with rods. [23]And when they had laid
many stripes on them, they threw *them* into
prison, commanding the jailer to keep them se-
curely. [24]Having received such a charge, he put
them into the inner prison and fastened their
feet in the stocks.

The Philippian Jailer Saved

[25]But at midnight Paul and Silas were pray-
ing and singing hymns to God, and the prison-
ers were listening to them. [26]Suddenly there was
a great earthquake, so that the foundations of
the prison were shaken; and immediately all the
doors were opened and everyone's chains were
loosed. [27]And the keeper of the prison, awaking
from sleep and seeing the prison doors open,
supposing the prisoners had fled, drew his
sword and was about to kill himself. [28]But Paul
called with a loud voice, saying, "Do yourself no
harm, for we are all here."
[29]Then he called for a light, ran in, and fell
down trembling before Paul and Silas. [30]And he
brought them out and said, "Sirs, what must I do
to be saved?"
[31]So they said, "Believe on the Lord Jesus
Christ, and you will be saved, you and your
household." [32]Then they spoke the word of the
Lord to him and to all who were in his house.
[33]And he took them the same hour of the night
and washed *their* stripes. And immediately he
and all his *family* were baptized. [34]Now when he
had brought them into his house, he set food be-
fore them; and he rejoiced, having believed in
God with all his household.

Paul Refuses to Depart Secretly

[35]And when it was day, the magistrates sent
the officers, saying, "Let those men go."
[36]So the keeper of the prison reported these
words to Paul, saying, "The magistrates have
sent to let you go. Now therefore depart, and go
in peace."
[37]But Paul said to them, "They have beaten
us openly, uncondemned Romans, *and* have

THE MESSAGE

money for the people who owned her. She
started following Paul around, calling every-
one's attention to us by yelling out, "These
men are working for the Most High God.
They're laying out the road of salvation for
you!" She did this for a number of days un-
til Paul, finally fed up with her, turned and
commanded the spirit that possessed her,
"Out! In the name of Jesus Christ, get out of
her!" And it was gone, just like that.

19-22 When her owners saw that their lucrative
little business was suddenly bankrupt, they
went after Paul and Silas, roughed them up
and dragged them into the market square.
Then the police arrested them and pulled
them into a court with the accusation,
"These men are disturbing the peace—dan-
gerous Jewish agitators subverting our Ro-
man law and order." By this time the crowd
had turned into a restless mob out for blood.

22-24 The judges went along with the mob, had
Paul and Silas's clothes ripped off and or-
dered a public beating. After beating them
black-and-blue, they threw them into jail,
telling the jailkeeper to put them under
heavy guard so there would be no chance of
escape. He did just that—threw them into
the maximum security cell in the jail and
clamped leg irons on them.

25-26 Along about midnight, Paul and Silas
were at prayer and singing a robust hymn to
God. The other prisoners couldn't believe
their ears. Then, without warning, a huge
earthquake! The jailhouse tottered, every
door flew open, all the prisoners were loose.

27-28 Startled from sleep, the jailer saw all the
doors swinging loose on their hinges. As-
suming that all the prisoners had escaped,
he pulled out his sword and was about to do
himself in, figuring he was as good as dead
anyway, when Paul stopped him: "Don't do
that! We're all still here! Nobody's run
away!"

29-31 The jailer got a torch and ran inside.
Badly shaken, he collapsed in front of Paul
and Silas. He led them out of the jail and
asked, "Sirs, what do I have to do to be
saved, to really live?" They said, "Put your
entire trust in the Master Jesus. Then you'll
live as you were meant to live—and every-
one in your house included!"

32-34 They went on to spell out in detail the
story of the Master—the entire family got in
on this part. They never did get to bed that
night. The jailer made them feel at home,
dressed their wounds, and then—he couldn't
wait till morning!—was baptized, he and
everyone in his family. There in his home, he
had food set out for a festive meal. It was a
night to remember: He and his entire family
had put their trust in God; everyone in the
house was in on the celebration.

35-36 At daybreak, the court judges sent offi-
cers with the instructions, "Release these
men." The jailer gave Paul the message,
"The judges sent word that you're free to go
on your way. Congratulations! Go in peace!"

37 But Paul wouldn't budge. He told the offi-
cers, "They beat us up in public and threw

NEW KING JAMES VERSION

thrown *us* into prison. And now do they put us
out secretly? No indeed! Let them come them-
selves and get us out."
38And the officers told these words to the
magistrates, and they were afraid when they
heard that they were Romans. 39Then they came
and pleaded with them and brought *them* out,
and asked *them* to depart from the city. 40So
they went out of the prison and entered *the
house of* Lydia; and when they had seen the
brethren, they encouraged them and departed.

PREACHING CHRIST AT THESSALONICA

17 Now when they had passed through Am-
phipolis and Apollonia, they came to Thes-
salonica, where there was a synagogue of the
Jews. 2Then Paul, as his custom was, went in to
them, and for three Sabbaths reasoned with
them from the Scriptures, 3explaining and
demonstrating that the Christ had to suffer and
rise again from the dead, and *saying*, "This Je-
sus whom I preach to you is the Christ." 4And
some of them were persuaded; and a great mul-
titude of the devout Greeks, and not a few of the
leading women, joined Paul and Silas.

ASSAULT ON JASON'S HOUSE

5But the Jews who were not persuaded, be-
coming envious,[a] took some of the evil men
from the marketplace, and gathering a mob, set
all the city in an uproar and attacked the house
of Jason, and sought to bring them out to the
people. 6But when they did not find them, they
dragged Jason and some brethren to the rulers
of the city, crying out, "These who have turned
the world upside down have come here too. 7Ja-
son has harbored them, and these are all acting
contrary to the decrees of Caesar, saying there
is another king—Jesus." 8And they troubled the
crowd and the rulers of the city when they
heard these things. 9So when they had taken se-
curity from Jason and the rest, they let them go.

MINISTERING AT BEREA

10Then the brethren immediately sent Paul
and Silas away by night to Berea. When they ar-
rived, they went into the synagogue of the Jews.
11These were more fair-minded than those in
Thessalonica, in that they received the word with
all readiness, and searched the Scriptures daily
to find out whether these things were so. 12There-
fore many of them believed, and also not a few of
the Greeks, prominent women as well as men.

17:5 [a]NU-Text omits *who were not persuaded*; M-Text omits *be-
coming envious.*

THE MESSAGE

us in jail, Roman citizens in good standing!
And now they want to get us out of the way
on the sly without anyone knowing? Noth-
ing doing! If they want us out of here, let
them come themselves and lead us out in
broad daylight."
38-40 When the officers reported this, the
judges panicked. They had no idea that Paul
and Silas were Roman citizens. They hur-
ried over and apologized, personally es-
corted them from the jail, and then asked
them if they wouldn't please leave the city.
Walking out of the jail, Paul and Silas went
straight to Lydia's house, saw their friends
again, encouraged them in the faith, and
only then went on their way.

THESSALONICA

1-3 17 They took the road south through Am-
phipolis and Apollonia to Thessalonica,
where there was a community of Jews. Paul
went to their meeting place, as he usually did
when he came to a town, and for three Sab-
baths running he preached to them from the
Scriptures. He opened up the texts so they
understood what they'd been reading all their
lives: that the Messiah absolutely *had* to be
put to death and raised from the dead—there
were no other options—and that "this Jesus
I'm introducing you to is that Messiah."
4-5 Some of them were won over and joined
ranks with Paul and Silas, among them a
great many God-fearing Greeks and a con-
siderable number of women from the aris-
tocracy. But the hard-line Jews became furi-
ous over the conversions. Mad with
jealousy, they rounded up a bunch of
brawlers off the streets and soon had an
ugly mob terrorizing the city as they hunted
down Paul and Silas.
5-7 They broke into Jason's house, thinking
that Paul and Silas were there. When they
couldn't find them, they collared Jason and
his friends instead and dragged them before
the city fathers, yelling hysterically, "These
people are out to destroy the world, and now
they've shown up on our doorstep, attacking
everything we hold dear! And Jason is hid-
ing them, these traitors and turncoats who
say Jesus is king and Caesar is nothing!"
8-9 The city fathers and the crowd of people
were totally alarmed by what they heard.
They made Jason and his friends post heavy
bail and let them go while they investigated
the charges.

BEREA

10-12 That night, under cover of darkness, their
friends got Paul and Silas out of town as fast
as they could. They sent them to Berea,
where they again met with the Jewish com-
munity. They were treated a lot better there
than in Thessalonica. The Jews received
Paul's message with enthusiasm and met
with him daily, examining the Scriptures to
see if they supported what he said. A lot of
them became believers, including many
Greeks who were prominent in the commu-
nity, women and men of influence.

New King James Version

[13]But when the Jews from Thessalonica learned that the word of God was preached by Paul at Berea, they came there also and stirred up the crowds. [14]Then immediately the brethren sent Paul away, to go to the sea; but both Silas and Timothy remained there. [15]So those who conducted Paul brought him to Athens; and receiving a command for Silas and Timothy to come to him with all speed, they departed.

The Philosophers at Athens

[16]Now while Paul waited for them at Athens, his spirit was provoked within him when he saw that the city was given over to idols. [17]Therefore he reasoned in the synagogue with the Jews and with the *Gentile* worshipers, and in the marketplace daily with those who happened to be there. [18]Then[a] certain Epicurean and Stoic philosophers encountered him. And some said, "What does this babbler want to say?"

Others said, "He seems to be a proclaimer of foreign gods," because he preached to them Jesus and the resurrection.

[19]And they took him and brought him to the Areopagus, saying, "May we know what this new doctrine *is* of which you speak? [20]For you are bringing some strange things to our ears. Therefore we want to know what these things mean." [21]For all the Athenians and the foreigners who were there spent their time in nothing else but either to tell or to hear some new thing.

Addressing the Areopagus

[22]Then Paul stood in the midst of the Areopagus and said, "Men of Athens, I perceive that in all things you are very religious; [23]for as I was passing through and considering the objects of your worship, I even found an altar with this inscription:

TO THE UNKNOWN GOD.

Therefore, the One whom you worship without knowing, Him I proclaim to you: [24]God, who made the world and everything in it, since He is Lord of heaven and earth, does not dwell in temples made with hands. [25]Nor is He worshiped with men's hands, as though He needed anything, since He gives to all life, breath, and all things. [26]And He has made from one blood[a] every nation of men to dwell on all the face of the earth, and has determined their preappointed times and the boundaries of their dwellings, [27]so that they should seek the Lord, in the hope that they might grope for Him and find Him, though He is not far from each one of us; [28]for in Him we live and move and have our being, as also some of your own poets have said, 'For we are also His offspring.' [29]Therefore, since we are the offspring of God, we ought not to think that the Divine Nature is like gold or silver or stone, something shaped by art and man's devising. [30]Truly, these times of ignorance God overlooked, but now commands all men every-

17:18 [a]NU-Text and M-Text add *also.* **17:26** [a]NU-Text omits *blood.*

The Message

13-15 But it wasn't long before reports got back to the Thessalonian hardline Jews that Paul was at it again, preaching the Word of God, this time in Berea. They lost no time responding, and created a mob scene there, too. With the help of his friends, Paul gave them the slip—caught a boat and put out to sea. Silas and Timothy stayed behind. The men who helped Paul escape got him as far as Athens and left him there. Paul sent word back with them to Silas and Timothy: "Come as quickly as you can!"

Athens

16 The longer Paul waited in Athens for Silas and Timothy, the angrier he got—all those idols! The city was a junkyard of idols.

17-18 He discussed it with the Jews and other like-minded people at their meeting place. And every day he went out on the streets and talked with anyone who happened along. He got to know some of the Epicurean and Stoic intellectuals pretty well through these conversations. Some of them dismissed him with sarcasm: "What an airhead!" But others, listening to him go on about Jesus and the resurrection, were intrigued: "That's a new slant on the gods. Tell us more."

19-21 These people got together and asked him to make a public presentation over at the Areopagus, where things were a little quieter. They said, "This is a new one on us. We've never heard anything quite like it. Where did you come up with this anyway? Explain it so we can understand." Downtown Athens was a great place for gossip. There were always people hanging around, natives and tourists alike, waiting for the latest tidbit on most anything.

22-23 So Paul took his stand in the open space at the Areopagus and laid it out for them. "It is plain to see that you Athenians take your religion seriously. When I arrived here the other day, I was fascinated with all the shrines I came across. And then I found one inscribed, TO THE GOD NOBODY KNOWS. I'm here to introduce you to this God so you can worship intelligently, know who you're dealing with.

24-29 "The God who made the world and everything in it, this Master of sky and land, doesn't live in custom-made shrines or need the human race to run errands for him, as if he couldn't take care of himself. He makes the creatures; the creatures don't make him. Starting from scratch, he made the entire human race and made the earth hospitable, with plenty of time and space for living so we could seek after God, and not just grope around in the dark but actually *find* him. He doesn't play hide-and-seek with us. He's not remote; he's *near*. We live and move in him, can't get away from him! One of your poets said it well: 'We're the God-created.' Well, if we are the God-created, it doesn't make a lot of sense to think we could hire a sculptor to chisel a god out of stone for *us*, does it?

30-31 "God overlooks it as long as you don't know any better—but that time is past. The

NEW KING JAMES VERSION

where to repent, [31]because He has appointed a day on which He will judge the world in righteousness by the Man whom He has ordained. He has given assurance of this to all by raising Him from the dead."

[32]And when they heard of the resurrection of the dead, some mocked, while others said, "We will hear you again on this *matter.*" [33]So Paul departed from among them. [34]However, some men joined him and believed, among them Dionysius the Areopagite, a woman named Damaris, and others with them.

MINISTERING AT CORINTH

18 After these things Paul departed from Athens and went to Corinth. [2]And he found a certain Jew named Aquila, born in Pontus, who had recently come from Italy with his wife Priscilla (because Claudius had commanded all the Jews to depart from Rome); and he came to them. [3]So, because he was of the same trade, he stayed with them and worked; for by occupation they were tentmakers. [4]And he reasoned in the synagogue every Sabbath, and persuaded both Jews and Greeks.

[5]When Silas and Timothy had come from Macedonia, Paul was compelled by the Spirit, and testified to the Jews *that* Jesus *is* the Christ. [6]But when they opposed him and blasphemed, he shook *his* garments and said to them, "Your blood *be* upon your *own* heads; I *am* clean. From now on I will go to the Gentiles." [7]And he departed from there and entered the house of a certain *man* named Justus,[a] *one* who worshiped God, whose house was next door to the synagogue. [8]Then Crispus, the ruler of the synagogue, believed on the Lord with all his household. And many of the Corinthians, hearing, believed and were baptized.

[9]Now the Lord spoke to Paul in the night by a vision, "Do not be afraid, but speak, and do not keep silent; [10]for I am with you, and no one will attack you to hurt you; for I have many people in this city." [11]And he continued *there* a year and six months, teaching the word of God among them.

[12]When Gallio was proconsul of Achaia, the Jews with one accord rose up against Paul and brought him to the judgment seat, [13]saying, "This *fellow* persuades men to worship God contrary to the law."

[14]And when Paul was about to open *his* mouth, Gallio said to the Jews, "If it were a matter of wrongdoing or wicked crimes, O Jews,

18:7 [a]NU-Text reads *Titius Justus.*

THE MESSAGE

unknown is now known, and he's calling for
a radical life-change. He has set a day when
the entire human race will be judged and
everything set right. And he has already ap-
pointed the judge, confirming him before
everyone by raising him from the dead."
32-34 At the phrase "raising him from the
dead," the listeners split: Some laughed at
him and walked off making jokes; others
said, "Let's do this again. We want to hear
more." But that was it for the day, and Paul
left. There were still others, it turned out,
who were convinced then and there, and
stuck with Paul—among them Dionysius the
Areopagite and a woman named Damaris.

CORINTH

1-4 **18** After Athens, Paul went to Corinth. That
is where he discovered Aquila, a Jew
born in Pontus, and his wife, Priscilla. They
had just arrived from Italy, part of the gen-
eral expulsion of Jews from Rome ordered
by Claudius. Paul moved in with them, and
they worked together at their common trade
of tentmaking. But every Sabbath he was at
the meeting place, doing his best to con-
vince both Jews and Greeks about Jesus.
5-6 When Silas and Timothy arrived from
Macedonia, Paul was able to give all his
time to preaching and teaching, doing
everything he could to persuade the Jews
that Jesus was in fact God's Messiah. But no
such luck. All they did was argue con-
tentiously and contradict him at every turn.
Totally exasperated, Paul had finally had it
with them and gave it up as a bad job. "Have
it your way, then," he said. "You've made
your bed; now lie in it. From now on I'm
spending my time with the other nations."
7-8 He walked out and went to the home of
Titius Justus, a God-fearing man who lived
right next to the Jews' meeting place. But
Paul's efforts with the Jews weren't a total
loss, for Crispus, the meeting-place presi-
dent, put his trust in the Master. His entire
family believed with him.
8-11 In the course of listening to Paul, a great
many Corinthians believed and were bap-
tized. One night the Master spoke to Paul in
a dream: "Keep it up, and don't let anyone
intimidate or silence you. No matter what
happens, I'm with you and no one is going
to be able to hurt you. You have no idea how
many people I have on my side in this city."
That was all he needed to stick it out. He
stayed another year and a half, faithfully
teaching the Word of God to the Corinthi-
ans.
12-13 But when Gallio was governor of Achaia
province, the Jews got up a campaign
against Paul, hauled him into court, and
filed charges: "This man is seducing people
into acts of worship that are illegal."
14-16 Just as Paul was about to defend himself,
Gallio interrupted and said to the Jews, "If
this was a matter of criminal conduct, I
would gladly hear you out. But it sounds to
me like one more Jewish squabble, another
of your endless hairsplitting quarrels over

NEW KING JAMES VERSION

there would be reason why I should bear with you. 15But if it is a question of words and names and your own law, look *to it* yourselves; for I do not want to be a judge of such *matters*." 16And he drove them from the judgment seat. 17Then all the Greeks[a] took Sosthenes, the ruler of the synagogue, and beat *him* before the judgment seat. But Gallio took no notice of these things.

PAUL RETURNS TO ANTIOCH

18So Paul still remained a good while. Then he took leave of the brethren and sailed for Syria, and Priscilla and Aquila *were* with him. He had *his* hair cut off at Cenchrea, for he had taken a vow. 19And he came to Ephesus, and left them there; but he himself entered the synagogue and reasoned with the Jews. 20When they asked *him* to stay a longer time with them, he did not consent, 21but took leave of them, saying, "I must by all means keep this coming feast in Jerusalem;[a] but I will return again to you, God willing." And he sailed from Ephesus.

22And when he had landed at Caesarea, and gone up and greeted the church, he went down to Antioch. 23After he had spent some time *there,* he departed and went over the region of Galatia and Phrygia in order, strengthening all the disciples.

MINISTRY OF APOLLOS

24Now a certain Jew named Apollos, born at Alexandria, an eloquent man *and* mighty in the Scriptures, came to Ephesus. 25This man had been instructed in the way of the Lord; and being fervent in spirit, he spoke and taught accurately the things of the Lord, though he knew only the baptism of John. 26So he began to speak boldly in the synagogue. When Aquila and Priscilla heard him, they took him aside and explained to him the way of God more accurately. 27And when he desired to cross to Achaia, the brethren wrote, exhorting the disciples to receive him; and when he arrived, he greatly helped those who had believed through grace; 28for he vigorously refuted the Jews publicly, showing from the Scriptures that Jesus is the Christ.

PAUL AT EPHESUS

19 And it happened, while Apollos was at Corinth, that Paul, having passed through the upper regions, came to Ephesus. And finding some disciples 2he said to them, "Did you receive the Holy Spirit when you believed?"

So they said to him, "We have not so much as heard whether there is a Holy Spirit."

18:17 [a]NU-Text reads *they all.* 18:21 [a]NU-Text omits *I must through Jerusalem.*

THE MESSAGE

religion. Take care of it on your own time. I
can't be bothered with this nonsense," and
he cleared them out of the courtroom.
17 Now the street rabble turned on Sos-
thenes, the new meeting-place president,
and beat him up in plain sight of the court.
Gallio didn't raise a finger. He could not
have cared less.

EPHESUS

18 Paul stayed a while longer in Corinth, but
then it was time to take leave of his friends.
Saying his good-byes, he sailed for Syria,
Priscilla and Aquila with him. Before board-
ing the ship in the harbor town of Cenchrea,
he had his head shaved as part of a vow he
had taken.
19-21 They landed in Ephesus, where Priscilla
and Aquila got off and stayed. Paul left the
ship briefly to go to the meeting place and
preach to the Jews. They wanted him to stay
longer, but he said he couldn't. But after say-
ing good-bye, he promised, "I'll be back,
God willing."
21-22 From Ephesus he sailed to Caesarea. He
greeted the church there, and then went on
to Antioch, completing the journey.
23 After spending a considerable time with
the Antioch Christians, Paul set off again for
Galatia and Phrygia, retracing his old
tracks, one town after another, putting fresh
heart into the disciples.
24-26 A man named Apollos came to Ephesus.
He was a Jew, born in Alexandria, Egypt,
and a terrific speaker, eloquent and power-
ful in his preaching of the Scriptures. He
was well-educated in the way of the Master
and fiery in his enthusiasm. Apollos was ac-
curate in everything he taught about Jesus
up to a point, but he only went as far as the
baptism of John. He preached with power in
the meeting place. When Priscilla and
Aquila heard him, they took him aside and
told him the rest of the story.
27-28 When Apollos decided to go on to Achaia
province, his Ephesian friends gave their
blessing and wrote a letter of recommenda-
tion for him, urging the disciples there to
welcome him with open arms. The welcome
paid off: Apollos turned out to be a great
help to those who had become believers
through God's immense generosity. He was
particularly effective in public debate with
the Jews as he brought out proof after con-
vincing proof from the Scriptures that Jesus
was in fact God's Messiah.

1-2 **19** Now, it happened that while Apollos
was away in Corinth, Paul made his way
down through the mountains, came to Eph-
esus, and happened on some disciples there.
The first thing he said was, "Did you receive
the Holy Spirit when you believed? Did you
take God into your mind only, or did you
also embrace him with your heart? Did he
get inside you?"
"We've never even heard of that—a Holy
Spirit? God within us?"

New King James Version

3And he said to them, "Into what then were
you baptized?"
So they said, "Into John's baptism."
4Then Paul said, "John indeed baptized with
a baptism of repentance, saying to the people
that they should believe on Him who would
come after him, that is, on Christ Jesus."
5When they heard *this*, they were baptized in
the name of the Lord Jesus. 6And when Paul had
laid hands on them, the Holy Spirit came upon
them, and they spoke with tongues and prophe-
sied. 7Now the men were about twelve in all.
8And he went into the synagogue and spoke
boldly for three months, reasoning and persuad-
ing concerning the things of the kingdom of
God. 9But when some were hardened and did
not believe, but spoke evil of the Way before the
multitude, he departed from them and withdrew
the disciples, reasoning daily in the school of
Tyrannus. 10And this continued for two years, so
that all who dwelt in Asia heard the word of the
Lord Jesus, both Jews and Greeks.

Miracles Glorify Christ

11Now God worked unusual miracles by the
hands of Paul, 12so that even handkerchiefs or
aprons were brought from his body to the sick,
and the diseases left them and the evil spirits
went out of them. 13Then some of the itinerant
Jewish exorcists took it upon themselves to call
the name of the Lord Jesus over those who had
evil spirits, saying, "We[a] exorcise you by the Je-
sus whom Paul preaches." 14Also there were
seven sons of Sceva, a Jewish chief priest, who
did so.
15And the evil spirit answered and said, "Je-
sus I know, and Paul I know; but who are you?"
16Then the man in whom the evil spirit was
leaped on them, overpowered[a] them, and pre-
vailed against them,[b] so that they fled out of that
house naked and wounded. 17This became
known both to all Jews and Greeks dwelling in
Ephesus; and fear fell on them all, and the name
of the Lord Jesus was magnified. 18And many
who had believed came confessing and telling
their deeds. 19Also, many of those who had prac-
ticed magic brought their books together and
burned *them* in the sight of all. And they
counted up the value of them, and *it* totaled fifty
thousand *pieces* of silver. 20So the word of the
Lord grew mightily and prevailed.

19:13 [a]NU-Text reads *I.* **19:16** [a]M-Text reads *and they over-
powered. [b]NU-Text reads *both of them.*

The Message

3 "How were you baptized, then?" asked
Paul.
"In John's baptism."
4 "That explains it," said Paul. "John
preached a baptism of radical life-change so
that people would be ready to receive the One
coming after him, who turned out to be Jesus.
If you've been baptized in John's baptism,
you're ready now for the real thing, for Jesus."
5-7 And they were. As soon as they heard of
it, they were baptized in the name of the
Master Jesus. Paul put his hands on their
heads and the Holy Spirit entered them.
From that moment on, they were praising
God in tongues and talking about God's ac-
tions. Altogether there were about twelve
people there that day.
8-10 Paul then went straight to the meeting
place. He had the run of the place for three
months, doing his best to make the things of
the kingdom of God real and convincing to
them. But then resistance began to form as
some of them began spreading evil rumors
through the congregation about the Chris-
tian way of life. So Paul left, taking the dis-
ciples with him, and set up shop in the
school of Tyrannus, holding class there
daily. He did this for two years, giving every-
one in the province of Asia, Jews as well as
Greeks, ample opportunity to hear the Mes-
sage of the Master.

Witches Came out of the Woodwork

11-12 God did powerful things through Paul,
things quite out of the ordinary. The word
got around and people started taking pieces
of clothing—handkerchiefs and scarves and
the like—that had touched Paul's skin and
then touching the sick with them. The touch
did it—they were healed and whole.
13-16 Some itinerant Jewish exorcists who hap-
pened to be in town at the time tried their
hand at what they assumed to be Paul's
"game." They pronounced the name of the
Master Jesus over victims of evil spirits, say-
ing, "I command you by the Jesus preached
by Paul!" The seven sons of a certain Sceva,
a Jewish high priest, were trying to do this
on a man when the evil spirit talked back: "I
know Jesus and I've heard of Paul, but who
are you?" Then the possessed man went
berserk—jumped the exorcists, beat them
up, and tore off their clothes. Naked and
bloody, they got away as best they could.
17-20 It was soon news all over Ephesus among
both Jews and Greeks. The realization
spread that God was in and behind this. Cu-
riosity about Paul developed into reverence
for the Master Jesus. Many of those who
thus believed came out of the closet and
made a clean break with their secret sor-
ceries. All kinds of witches and warlocks
came out of the woodwork with their books
of spells and incantations and made a huge
bonfire of them. Someone estimated their
worth at fifty thousand silver coins. In such
ways it became evident that the Word of the
Master was now sovereign and prevailed in
Ephesus.

New King James Version

The Riot at Ephesus

21When these things were accomplished, Paul purposed in the Spirit, when he had passed through Macedonia and Achaia, to go to Jerusalem, saying, "After I have been there, I must also see Rome." 22So he sent into Macedonia two of those who ministered to him, Timothy and Erastus, but he himself stayed in Asia for a time.

23And about that time there arose a great commotion about the Way. 24For a certain man named Demetrius, a silversmith, who made silver shrines of Diana,[a] brought no small profit to the craftsmen. 25He called them together with the workers of similar occupation, and said: "Men, you know that we have our prosperity by this trade. 26Moreover you see and hear that not only at Ephesus, but throughout almost all Asia, this Paul has persuaded and turned away many people, saying that they are not gods which are made with hands. 27So not only is this trade of ours in danger of falling into disrepute, but also the temple of the great goddess Diana may be despised and her magnificence destroyed,[a] whom all Asia and the world worship."

28Now when they heard *this,* they were full of wrath and cried out, saying, "Great *is* Diana of the Ephesians!" 29So the whole city was filled with confusion, and rushed into the theater with one accord, having seized Gaius and Aristarchus, Macedonians, Paul's travel companions. 30And when Paul wanted to go in to the people, the disciples would not allow him. 31Then some of the officials of Asia, who were his friends, sent to him pleading that he would not venture into the theater. 32Some therefore cried one thing and some another, for the assembly was confused, and most of them did not know why they had come together. 33And they drew Alexander out of the multitude, the Jews putting him forward. And Alexander motioned with his hand, and wanted to make his defense to the people. 34But when they found out that he was a Jew, all with one voice cried out for about two hours, "Great *is* Diana of the Ephesians!"

35And when the city clerk had quieted the crowd, he said: "Men of Ephesus, what man is there who does not know that the city of the Ephesians is temple guardian of the great goddess Diana, and of the *image* which fell down from Zeus? 36Therefore, since these things cannot be denied, you ought to be quiet and do nothing rashly. 37For you have brought these men here who are neither robbers of temples nor blasphemers of your[a] goddess. 38Therefore, if Demetrius and his fellow craftsmen have a case against anyone, the courts are open and

19:24 [a]Greek *Artemis* **19:27** [a]NU-Text reads *she be deposed from her magnificence.* **19:37** [a]NU-Text reads *our.*

The Message

The Goddess Artemis

21-22 After all this had come to a head, Paul decided it was time to move on to Macedonia and Achaia provinces, and from there to Jerusalem. "Then," he said, "I'm off to Rome. I've got to see Rome!" He sent two of his assistants, Timothy and Erastus, on to Macedonia and then stayed for a while and wrapped things up in Asia.

23-26 But before he got away, a huge ruckus occurred over what was now being referred to as "the Way." A certain silversmith, Demetrius, conducted a brisk trade in the manufacture of shrines to the goddess Artemis, employing a number of artisans in his business. He rounded up his workers and others similarly employed and said, "Men, you well know that we have a good thing going here—and you've seen how Paul has barged in and discredited what we're doing by telling people that there's no such thing as a god made with hands. A lot of people are going along with him, not only here in Ephesus but all through Asia province.

27 "Not only is our little business in danger of falling apart, but the temple of our famous goddess Artemis will certainly end up a pile of rubble as her glorious reputation fades to nothing. And this is no mere local matter—the whole world worships our Artemis!"

28-31 That set them off in a frenzy. They ran into the street yelling, "Great Artemis of the Ephesians! Great Artemis of the Ephesians!" They put the whole city in an uproar, stampeding into the stadium, and grabbing two of Paul's associates on the way, the Macedonians Gaius and Aristarchus. Paul wanted to go in, too, but the disciples wouldn't let him. Prominent religious leaders in the city who had become friendly to Paul concurred: "By no means go near that mob!"

32-34 Some were yelling one thing, some another. Most of them had no idea what was going on or why they were there. As the Jews pushed Alexander to the front to try to gain control, different factions clamored to get him on their side. But he brushed them off and quieted the mob with an impressive sweep of his arms. But the moment he opened his mouth and they knew he was a Jew, they shouted him down: "Great Artemis of the Ephesians! Great Artemis of the Ephesians!"—on and on and on, for over two hours.

35-37 Finally, the town clerk got the mob quieted down and said, "Fellow citizens, is there anyone anywhere who doesn't know that our dear city Ephesus is protector of glorious Artemis and her sacred stone image that fell straight out of heaven? Since this is beyond contradiction, you had better get hold of yourselves. This is conduct unworthy of Artemis. These men you've dragged in here have done nothing to harm either our temple or our goddess.

38-41 "So if Demetrius and his guild of artisans have a complaint, they can take it to court

NEW KING JAMES VERSION

there are proconsuls. Let them bring charges
against one another. 39But if you have any other
inquiry to make, it shall be determined in the
lawful assembly. 40For we are in danger of being
called in question for today's uproar, there be-
ing no reason which we may give to account for
this disorderly gathering." 41And when he had
said these things, he dismissed the assembly.

JOURNEYS IN GREECE

20 After the uproar had ceased, Paul called
the disciples to *himself*, embraced *them*,
and departed to go to Macedonia. 2Now when
he had gone over that region and encouraged
them with many words, he came to Greece 3and
stayed three months. And when the Jews plotted
against him as he was about to sail to Syria, he
decided to return through Macedonia. 4And
Sopater of Berea accompanied him to Asia—
also Aristarchus and Secundus of the Thessalo-
nians, and Gaius of Derbe, and Timothy, and
Tychicus and Trophimus of Asia. 5These men,
going ahead, waited for us at Troas. 6But we
sailed away from Philippi after the Days of Un-
leavened Bread, and in five days joined them at
Troas, where we stayed seven days.

MINISTERING AT TROAS

7Now on the first *day* of the week, when the
disciples came together to break bread, Paul,
ready to depart the next day, spoke to them and
continued his message until midnight. 8There
were many lamps in the upper room where
they[a] were gathered together. 9And in a window
sat a certain young man named Eutychus, who
was sinking into a deep sleep. He was overcome
by sleep; and as Paul continued speaking, he fell
down from the third story and was taken up
dead. 10But Paul went down, fell on him, and em-
bracing *him* said, "Do not trouble yourselves,
for his life is in him." 11Now when he had come
up, had broken bread and eaten, and talked a
long while, even till daybreak, he departed.
12And they brought the young man in alive, and
they were not a little comforted.

FROM TROAS TO MILETUS

13Then we went ahead to the ship and sailed
to Assos, there intending to take Paul on board;
for so he had given orders, intending himself to
go on foot. 14And when he met us at Assos, we
took him on board and came to Mitylene. 15We
sailed from there, and the next *day* came oppo-
site Chios. The following *day* we arrived at
Samos and stayed at Trogyllium. The next *day*
we came to Miletus. 16For Paul had decided to
sail past Ephesus, so that he would not have to
spend time in Asia; for he was hurrying to be at
Jerusalem, if possible, on the Day of Pentecost.

THE EPHESIAN ELDERS EXHORTED

17From Miletus he sent to Ephesus and called
for the elders of the church. 18And when they
had come to him, he said to them: "You know,

20:8 [a]NU-Text and M-Text read *we*.

THE MESSAGE

and make all the accusations they want. If
anything else is bothering you, bring it to
the regularly scheduled town meeting and
let it be settled there. There is no excuse for
what's happened today. We're putting our
city in serious danger. Rome, remember,
does not look kindly on rioters." With that,
he sent them home.

MACEDONIA AND GREECE

1-2 20 With things back to normal, Paul called
the disciples together and encouraged
them to keep up the good work in Ephesus.
Then, saying his good-byes, he left for
Macedonia. Traveling through the country,
passing from one gathering to another, he
gave constant encouragement, lifting their
spirits and charging them with fresh hope.
2-4 Then he came to Greece and stayed on for
three months. Just as he was about to sail for
Syria, the Jews cooked up a plot against him.
So he went the other way, by land back
through Macedonia, and gave them the slip.
His companions for the journey were Sopa-
ter, son of Pyrrhus, from Berea; Aristarchus
and Secundus, both Thessalonians; Gaius
from Derbe; Timothy; and the two from
western Asia, Tychicus and Trophimus.
5-6 They went on ahead and waited for us in
Troas. Meanwhile, we stayed in Philippi for
Passover Week, and then set sail. Within five
days we were again in Troas and stayed a
week.
7-9 We met on Sunday to worship and cele-
brate the Master's Supper. Paul addressed
the congregation. Our plan was to leave first
thing in the morning, but Paul talked on, way
past midnight. We were meeting in a well-
lighted upper room. A young man named
Eutychus was sitting in an open window. As
Paul went on and on, Eutychus fell sound
asleep and toppled out the third-story win-
dow. When they picked him up, he was dead.
10-12 Paul went down, stretched himself on
him, and hugged him hard. "No more cry-
ing," he said. "There's life in him yet." Then
Paul got up and served the Master's Supper.
And went on telling stories of the faith until
dawn! On that note, they left—Paul going
one way, the congregation another, leading
the boy off alive, and full of life themselves.
13-16 In the meantime, the rest of us had gone
on ahead to the ship and sailed for Assos,
where we planned to pick up Paul. Paul
wanted to walk there, and so had made
these arrangements earlier. Things went ac-
cording to plan: We met him in Assos, took
him on board, and sailed to Mitylene. The
next day we put in opposite Chios, Samos a
day later, and then Miletus. Paul had de-
cided to bypass Ephesus so that he wouldn't
be held up in Asia province. He was in a
hurry to get to Jerusalem in time for the
Feast of Pentecost, if at all possible.

ON TO JERUSALEM

17-21 From Miletus he sent to Ephesus for the
leaders of the congregation. When they ar-
rived, he said, "You know that from day one

NEW KING JAMES VERSION

from the first day that I came to Asia, in what
manner I always lived among you, 19serving the
Lord with all humility, with many tears and tri-
als which happened to me by the plotting of the
Jews; 20how I kept back nothing that was help-
ful, but proclaimed it to you, and taught you
publicly and from house to house, 21testifying to
Jews, and also to Greeks, repentance toward
God and faith toward our Lord Jesus Christ.
22And see, now I go bound in the spirit to
Jerusalem, not knowing the things that will hap-
pen to me there, 23except that the Holy Spirit
testifies in every city, saying that chains and
tribulations await me. 24But none of these things
move me; nor do I count my life dear to myself,[a]
so that I may finish my race with joy, and the
ministry which I received from the Lord Jesus,
to testify to the gospel of the grace of God.

25"And indeed, now I know that you all,
among whom I have gone preaching the king-
dom of God, will see my face no more. 26There-
fore I testify to you this day that I *am* innocent
of the blood of all *men.* 27For I have not shunned
to declare to you the whole counsel of God.
28Therefore take heed to yourselves and to all
the flock, among which the Holy Spirit has
made you overseers, to shepherd the church of
God[a] which He purchased with His own blood.
29For I know this, that after my departure savage
wolves will come in among you, not sparing the
flock. 30Also from among yourselves men will
rise up, speaking perverse things, to draw away
the disciples after themselves. 31Therefore
watch, and remember that for three years I did
not cease to warn everyone night and day with
tears.

32"So now, brethren, I commend you to God
and to the word of His grace, which is able to
build you up and give you an inheritance
among all those who are sanctified. 33I have
coveted no one's silver or gold or apparel.
34Yes,[a] you yourselves know that these hands
have provided for my necessities, and for those
who were with me. 35I have shown you in every
way, by laboring like this, that you must sup-
port the weak. And remember the words of the
Lord Jesus, that He said, 'It is more blessed to
give than to receive.' "

36And when he had said these things, he
knelt down and prayed with them all. 37Then
they all wept freely, and fell on Paul's neck and
kissed him, 38sorrowing most of all for the
words which he spoke, that they would see his
face no more. And they accompanied him to the
ship.

20:24 [a]NU-Text reads *But I do not count my life of any value or dear to myself.* **20:28** [a]M-Text reads *of the Lord and God.* **20:34** [a]NU-Text and M-Text omit *Yes.*

THE MESSAGE

of my arrival in Asia I was with you to-
tally—laying my life on the line, serving the
Master no matter what, putting up with no
end of scheming by Jews who wanted to do
me in. I didn't skimp or trim in any way.
Every truth and encouragement that could
have made a difference to you, you got. I
taught you out in public and I taught you in
your homes, urging Jews and Greeks alike
to a radical life-change before God and an
equally radical trust in our Master Jesus.

22-24 "But there is another urgency before me
now. I feel compelled to go to Jerusalem. I'm
completely in the dark about what will hap-
pen when I get there. I do know that it won't
be any picnic, for the Holy Spirit has let me
know repeatedly and clearly that there are
hard times and imprisonment ahead. But
that matters little. What matters most to me
is to finish what God started: the job the
Master Jesus gave me of letting everyone I
meet know all about this incredibly extrav-
agant generosity of God.

25-27 "And so this is good-bye. You're not going
to see me again, nor I you, you whom I have
gone among for so long proclaiming the
news of God's inaugurated kingdom. I've
done my best for you, given you my all, held
back nothing of God's will for you.

28 "Now it's up to you. Be on your toes—
both for yourselves and your congregation
of sheep. The Holy Spirit has put you in
charge of these people—God's people they
are—to guard and protect them. God him-
self thought they were worth dying for.

29-31 "I know that as soon as I'm gone, vicious
wolves are going to show up and rip into
this flock, men from your very own ranks
twisting words so as to seduce disciples into
following them instead of Jesus. So stay
awake and keep up your guard. Remember
those three years I kept at it with you, never
letting up, pouring my heart out with you,
one after another.

32 "Now I'm turning you over to God, our
marvelous God whose gracious Word can
make you into what he wants you to be and
give you everything you could possibly need
in this community of holy friends.

33-35 "I've never, as you so well know, had any
taste for wealth or fashion. With these bare
hands I took care of my own basic needs
and those who worked with me. In every-
thing I've done, I have demonstrated to you
how necessary it is to work on behalf of the
weak and not exploit them. You'll not likely
go wrong here if you keep remembering
that our Master said, 'You're far happier giv-
ing than getting.' "

36-38 Then Paul went down on his knees, all of
them kneeling with him, and prayed. And
then a river of tears. Much clinging to Paul,
not wanting to let him go. They knew they
would never see him again—he had told
them quite plainly. The pain cut deep. Then,
bravely, they walked him down to the ship.

NEW KING JAMES VERSION

WARNINGS ON THE JOURNEY TO JERUSALEM

21 Now it came to pass, that when we had de-
parted from them and set sail, running a
straight course we came to Cos, the following
day to Rhodes, and from there to Patara. 2And
finding a ship sailing over to Phoenicia, we went
aboard and set sail. 3When we had sighted
Cyprus, we passed it on the left, sailed to Syria,
and landed at Tyre; for there the ship was to un-
load her cargo. 4And finding disciples,[a] we
stayed there seven days. They told Paul through
the Spirit not to go up to Jerusalem. 5When we
had come to the end of those days, we departed
and went on our way; and they all accompanied
us, with wives and children, till *we were* out of
the city. And we knelt down on the shore and
prayed. 6When we had taken our leave of one
another, we boarded the ship, and they returned
home.

7And when we had finished *our* voyage from
Tyre, we came to Ptolemais, greeted the
brethren, and stayed with them one day. 8On the
next *day* we who were Paul's companions[a] de-
parted and came to Caesarea, and entered the
house of Philip the evangelist, who was *one* of
the seven, and stayed with him. 9Now this man
had four virgin daughters who prophesied.
10And as we stayed many days, a certain
prophet named Agabus came down from Judea.
11When he had come to us, he took Paul's belt,
bound his *own* hands and feet, and said, "Thus
says the Holy Spirit, 'So shall the Jews at
Jerusalem bind the man who owns this belt, and
deliver *him* into the hands of the Gentiles.' "

12Now when we heard these things, both we
and those from that place pleaded with him not
to go up to Jerusalem. 13Then Paul answered,
"What do you mean by weeping and breaking
my heart? For I am ready not only to be bound,
but also to die at Jerusalem for the name of the
Lord Jesus."

14So when he would not be persuaded, we
ceased, saying, "The will of the Lord be done."

PAUL URGED TO MAKE PEACE

15And after those days we packed and went
up to Jerusalem. 16Also some of the disciples
from Caesarea went with us and brought with
them a certain Mnason of Cyprus, an early dis-
ciple, with whom we were to lodge.

17And when we had come to Jerusalem, the
brethren received us gladly. 18On the following
day Paul went in with us to James, and all the el-
ders were present. 19When he had greeted them,
he told in detail those things which God had done
among the Gentiles through his ministry.

21:4 [a]NU-Text reads *the disciples.* 21:8 [a]NU-Text omits *who were Paul's companions.*

THE MESSAGE

TYRE AND CAESAREA

1-4 21 And so, with the tearful good-byes behind us, we were on our way. We made a straight run to Cos, the next day reached Rhodes, and then Patara. There we found a ship going direct to Phoenicia, got on board, and set sail. Cyprus came into view on our left, but was soon out of sight as we kept on course for Syria, and eventually docked in the port of Tyre. While the cargo was being unloaded, we looked up the local disciples and stayed with them seven days. Their message to Paul, from insight given by the Spirit, was "Don't go to Jerusalem."

5-6 When our time was up, they escorted us out of the city to the docks. Everyone came along—men, women, children. They made a farewell party of the occasion! We all kneeled together on the beach and prayed. Then, after another round of saying good-bye, we climbed on board the ship while they drifted back to their homes.

7-9 A short run from Tyre to Ptolemais completed the voyage. We greeted our Christian friends there and stayed with them a day. In the morning we went on to Caesarea and stayed with Philip the Evangelist, one of "the Seven." Philip had four virgin daughters who prophesied.

10-11 After several days of visiting, a prophet from Judea by the name of Agabus came down to see us. He went right up to Paul, took Paul's belt, and, in a dramatic gesture, tied himself up, hands and feet. He said, "This is what the Holy Spirit says: The Jews in Jerusalem are going to tie up the man who owns this belt just like this and hand him over to godless unbelievers."

12-13 When we heard that, we and everyone there that day begged Paul not to be stubborn and persist in going to Jerusalem. But Paul wouldn't budge: "Why all this hysteria? Why do you insist on making a scene and making it even harder for me? You're looking at this backward. The issue in Jerusalem is not what they do to me, whether arrest or murder, but what the Master Jesus does through my obedience. Can't you see that?"

14 We saw that we weren't making even a dent in his resolve, and gave up. "It's in God's hands now," we said. "Master, you handle it."

15-16 It wasn't long before we had our luggage together and were on our way to Jerusalem. Some of the disciples from Caesarea went with us and took us to the home of Mnason, who received us warmly as his guests. A native of Cyprus, he had been among the earliest disciples.

JERUSALEM

17-19 In Jerusalem, our friends, glad to see us, received us with open arms. The first thing next morning, we took Paul to see James. All the church leaders were there. After a time of greeting and small talk, Paul told the story, detail by detail, of what God had done among the non-Jewish people through his ministry. They listened with delight and gave God the glory.

NEW KING JAMES VERSION

20 And when they heard *it,* they glorified the Lord. And they said to him, "You see, brother, how many myriads of Jews there are who have believed, and they are all zealous for the law; 21 but they have been informed about you that you teach all the Jews who are among the Gentiles to forsake Moses, saying that they ought not to circumcise *their* children nor to walk according to the customs. 22 What then? The assembly must certainly meet, for they will[a] hear that you have come. 23 Therefore do what we tell you: We have four men who have taken a vow. 24 Take them and be purified with them, and pay their expenses so that they may shave *their* heads, and that all may know that those things of which they were informed concerning you are nothing, but *that* you yourself also walk orderly and keep the law. 25 But concerning the Gentiles who believe, we have written *and* decided that they should observe no such thing, except[a] that they should keep themselves from *things* offered to idols, from blood, from things strangled, and from sexual immorality."

ARRESTED IN THE TEMPLE

26 Then Paul took the men, and the next day, having been purified with them, entered the temple to announce the expiration of the days of purification, at which time an offering should be made for each one of them.

27 Now when the seven days were almost ended, the Jews from Asia, seeing him in the temple, stirred up the whole crowd and laid hands on him, 28 crying out, "Men of Israel, help! This is the man who teaches all *men* everywhere against the people, the law, and this place; and furthermore he also brought Greeks into the temple and has defiled this holy place." 29 (For they had previously[a] seen Trophimus the Ephesian with him in the city, whom they supposed that Paul had brought into the temple.)

30 And all the city was disturbed; and the people ran together, seized Paul, and dragged him out of the temple; and immediately the doors were shut. 31 Now as they were seeking to kill him, news came to the commander of the garrison that all Jerusalem was in an uproar. 32 He immediately took soldiers and centurions, and ran down to them. And when they saw the commander and the soldiers, they stopped beating Paul. 33 Then the commander came near and took him, and commanded *him* to be bound with two chains; and he asked who he was and what

21:22 [a]NU-Text reads *What then is to be done? They will certainly.* **21:25** [a]NU-Text omits *that they should observe no such thing, except.* **21:29** [a]M-Text omits *previously.*

THE MESSAGE

20-21 They had a story to tell, too: "And just look at what's been happening here—thousands upon thousands of God-fearing Jews have become believers in Jesus! But there's also a problem because they are more zealous than ever in observing the laws of Moses. They've been told that you advise believing Jews who live surrounded by unbelieving outsiders to go light on Moses, telling them that they don't need to circumcise their children or keep up the old traditions. This isn't sitting at all well with them.

22-24 "We're worried about what will happen when they discover you're in town. There's bound to be trouble. So here is what we want you to do: There are four men from our company who have taken a vow involving ritual purification, but have no money to pay the expenses. Join these men in their vows and pay their expenses. Then it will become obvious to everyone that there is nothing to the rumors going around about you and that you are in fact scrupulous in your reverence for the laws of Moses.

25 "In asking you to do this, we're not going back on our agreement regarding non-Jews who have become believers. We continue to hold fast to what we wrote in that letter, namely, to be careful not to get involved in activities connected with idols; to avoid serving food offensive to Jewish Christians; to guard the morality of sex and marriage."

26 So Paul did it—took the men, joined them in their vows, and paid their way. The next day he went to the Temple to make it official and stay there until the proper sacrifices had been offered and completed for each of them.

PAUL UNDER ARREST

27-29 When the seven days of their purification were nearly up, some Jews from around Ephesus spotted him in the Temple. At once they turned the place upside-down. They grabbed Paul and started yelling at the top of their lungs, "Help! You Israelites, help! This is the man who is going all over the world telling lies against us and our religion and this place. He's even brought Greeks in here and defiled this holy place." (What had happened was that they had seen Paul and Trophimus, the Ephesian Greek, walking together in the city and had just assumed that he had also taken him to the Temple and shown him around.)

30 Soon the whole city was in an uproar, people running from everywhere to the Temple to get in on the action. They grabbed Paul, dragged him outside, and locked the Temple gates so he couldn't get back in and gain sanctuary.

31-32 As they were trying to kill him, word came to the captain of the guard, "A riot! The whole city's boiling over!" He acted swiftly. His soldiers and centurions ran to the scene at once. As soon as the mob saw the captain and his soldiers, they quit beating Paul.

33-36 The captain came up and put Paul under arrest. He first ordered him handcuffed, and

NEW KING JAMES VERSION

he had done. 34And some among the multitude
cried one thing and some another.
So when he could not ascertain the truth be-
cause of the tumult, he commanded him to be
taken into the barracks. 35When he reached the
stairs, he had to be carried by the soldiers be-
cause of the violence of the mob. 36For the mul-
titude of the people followed after, crying out,
"Away with him!"

ADDRESSING THE JERUSALEM MOB

37Then as Paul was about to be led into the
barracks, he said to the commander, "May I
speak to you?"
He replied, "Can you speak Greek? 38Are you
not the Egyptian who some time ago stirred up
a rebellion and led the four thousand assassins
out into the wilderness?"
39But Paul said, "I am a Jew from Tarsus, in
Cilicia, a citizen of no mean city; and I implore
you, permit me to speak to the people."
40So when he had given him permission, Paul
stood on the stairs and motioned with his hand
to the people. And when there was a great si-
lence, he spoke to *them* in the Hebrew lan-
guage, saying,

22 "Brethren and fathers, hear my defense
before you now." 2And when they heard
that he spoke to them in the Hebrew language,
they kept all the more silent.
Then he said: 3"I am indeed a Jew, born in
Tarsus of Cilicia, but brought up in this city at
the feet of Gamaliel, taught according to the
strictness of our fathers' law, and was zealous
toward God as you all are today. 4I persecuted
this Way to the death, binding and delivering
into prisons both men and women, 5as also the
high priest bears me witness, and all the council
of the elders, from whom I also received letters
to the brethren, and went to Damascus to bring
in chains even those who were there to
Jerusalem to be punished.
6"Now it happened, as I journeyed and came
near Damascus at about noon, suddenly a great
light from heaven shone around me. 7And I fell
to the ground and heard a voice saying to me,
'Saul, Saul, why are you persecuting Me?' 8So I
answered, 'Who are You, Lord?' And He said to
me, 'I am Jesus of Nazareth, whom you are per-
secuting.'
9"And those who were with me indeed saw
the light and were afraid,[a] but they did not hear
the voice of Him who spoke to me. 10So I said,
'What shall I do, Lord?' And the Lord said to me,
'Arise and go into Damascus, and there you will
be told all things which are appointed for you to
do.' 11And since I could not see for the glory of
that light, being led by the hand of those who
were with me, I came into Damascus.

22:9 [a]NU-Text omits *and were afraid.*

THE MESSAGE

then asked who he was and what he had
done. All he got from the crowd were shouts,
one yelling this, another that. It was impossi-
ble to tell one word from another in the mob
hysteria, so the captain ordered Paul taken
to the military barracks. But when they got
to the Temple steps, the mob became so vio-
lent that the soldiers had to carry Paul. As
they carried him away, the crowd followed,
shouting, "Kill him! Kill him!"
37-38 When they got to the barracks and were
about to go in, Paul said to the captain, "Can
I say something to you?"
He answered, "Oh, I didn't know you
spoke Greek. I thought you were the Egyp-
tian who not long ago started a riot here,
and then hid out in the desert with his four
thousand thugs."
39 Paul said, "No, I'm a Jew, born in Tarsus.
And I'm a citizen still of that influential city.
I have a simple request: Let me speak to the
crowd."

PAUL TELLS HIS STORY

40 Standing on the barracks steps, Paul turned
and held his arms up. A hush fell over the
crowd as Paul began to speak. He spoke in
Hebrew.

1-2 22 "My dear brothers and fathers, listen
carefully to what I have to say before
you jump to conclusions about me." When
they heard him speaking Hebrew, they grew
even quieter. No one wanted to miss a word
of this.
2-3 He continued, "I am a good Jew, born in
Tarsus in the province of Cilicia, but edu-
cated here in Jerusalem under the exacting
eye of Rabbi Gamaliel, thoroughly in-
structed in our religious traditions. And I've
always been passionately on God's side, just
as you are right now.
4-5 "I went after anyone connected with this
'Way,' went at them hammer and tongs, ready
to kill for God. I rounded up men and women
right and left and had them thrown in prison.
You can ask the Chief Priest or anyone in the
High Council to verify this; they all knew me
well. Then I went off to our brothers in Da-
mascus, armed with official documents au-
thorizing me to hunt down the followers of
Jesus there, arrest them, and bring them
back to Jerusalem for sentencing.
6-7 "As I arrived on the outskirts of Damascus
about noon, a blinding light blazed out of the
skies and I fell to the ground, dazed. I heard a
voice: 'Saul, Saul, why are you out to get me?'
8-9 " 'Who are you, Master?' I asked.
"He said, 'I am Jesus the Nazarene, the
One you're hunting down.' My companions
saw the light, but they didn't hear the con-
versation.
10-11 "Then I said, 'What do I do now, Master?'
"He said, 'Get to your feet and enter Da-
mascus. There you'll be told everything that's
been set out for you to do.' And so we entered
Damascus, but nothing like the entrance I
had planned—I was blind as a bat and my
companions had to lead me in by the hand.

New King James Version

12"Then a certain Ananias, a devout man according to the law, having a good testimony with all the Jews who dwelt *there,* 13came to me; and he stood and said to me, 'Brother Saul, receive your sight.' And at that same hour I looked up at him. 14Then he said, 'The God of our fathers has chosen you that you should know His will, and see the Just One, and hear the voice of His mouth. 15For you will be His witness to all men of what you have seen and heard. 16And now why are you waiting? Arise and be baptized, and wash away your sins, calling on the name of the Lord.'

17"Now it happened, when I returned to Jerusalem and was praying in the temple, that I was in a trance 18and saw Him saying to me, 'Make haste and get out of Jerusalem quickly, for they will not receive your testimony concerning Me.' 19So I said, 'Lord, they know that in every synagogue I imprisoned and beat those who believe on You. 20And when the blood of Your martyr Stephen was shed, I also was standing by consenting to his death,[a] and guarding the clothes of those who were killing him.' 21Then He said to me, 'Depart, for I will send you far from here to the Gentiles.' "

Paul's Roman Citizenship

22And they listened to him until this word, and *then* they raised their voices and said, "Away with such a *fellow* from the earth, for he is not fit to live!" 23Then, as they cried out and tore off *their* clothes and threw dust into the air, 24the commander ordered him to be brought into the barracks, and said that he should be examined under scourging, so that he might know why they shouted so against him. 25And as they bound him with thongs, Paul said to the centurion who stood by, "Is it lawful for you to scourge a man who is a Roman, and uncondemned?"

26When the centurion heard *that,* he went and told the commander, saying, "Take care what you do, for this man is a Roman."

27Then the commander came and said to him, "Tell me, are you a Roman?"

He said, "Yes."

28The commander answered, "With a large sum I obtained this citizenship."

And Paul said, "But I was born *a citizen.*"

29Then immediately those who were about to examine him withdrew from him; and the commander was also afraid after he found out that

22:20 [a]NU-Text omits *to his death.*

The Message

12-13 "And that's when I met Ananias, a man with a sterling reputation in observing our laws—the Jewish community in Damascus is unanimous on that score. He came and put his arm on my shoulder. 'Look up,' he said. I looked, and found myself looking right into his eyes—I could see again!

14-16 "Then he said, 'The God of our ancestors has handpicked you to be briefed on his plan of action. You've actually seen the Righteous Innocent and heard him speak. You are to be a key witness to everyone you meet of what you've seen and heard. So what are you waiting for? Get up and get yourself baptized, scrubbed clean of those sins and personally acquainted with God.'

17-18 "Well, it happened just as Ananias said. After I was back in Jerusalem and praying one day in the Temple, lost in the presence of God, I saw him, saw God's Righteous Innocent, and heard him say to me, 'Hurry up! Get out of here as quickly as you can. None of the Jews here in Jerusalem are going to accept what you say about me.'

19-20 "At first I objected: 'Who has better credentials? They all know how obsessed I was with hunting out those who believed in you, beating them up in the meeting places and throwing them in jail. And when your witness Stephen was murdered, I was right there, holding the coats of the murderers and cheering them on. And now they see me totally converted. What better qualification could I have?'

21 "But he said, 'Don't argue. Go. I'm sending you on a long journey to outsider non-Jews.' "

A Roman Citizen

22-25 The people in the crowd had listened attentively up to this point, but now they broke loose, shouting out, "Kill him! He's an insect! Stomp on him!" They shook their fists. They filled the air with curses. That's when the captain intervened and ordered Paul taken into the barracks. By now the captain was thoroughly exasperated. He decided to interrogate Paul under torture in order to get to the bottom of this, to find out what he had done that provoked this outraged violence. As they spread-eagled him with thongs, getting him ready for the whip, Paul said to the centurion standing there, "Is this legal: torturing a Roman citizen without a fair trial?"

26 When the centurion heard that, he went directly to the captain. "Do you realize what you've done? This man is a Roman citizen!"

27 The captain came back and took charge. "Is what I hear right? You're a Roman citizen?"

Paul said, "I certainly am."

28 The captain was impressed. "I paid a huge sum for my citizenship. How much did it cost you?"

"Nothing," said Paul. "It cost me nothing. I was free from the day of my birth."

29 That put a stop to the interrogation. And it put the fear of God into the captain. He

NEW KING JAMES VERSION

he was a Roman, and because he had bound
him.

THE SANHEDRIN DIVIDED

30 The next day, because he wanted to know
for certain why he was accused by the Jews, he
released him from *his* bonds, and commanded
the chief priests and all their council to appear,
and brought Paul down and set him before
them.

23 Then Paul, looking earnestly at the coun-
cil, said, "Men *and* brethren, I have lived in
all good conscience before God until this day."
2 And the high priest Ananias commanded those
who stood by him to strike him on the mouth.
3 Then Paul said to him, "God will strike you, *you*
whitewashed wall! For you sit to judge me ac-
cording to the law, and do you command me to
be struck contrary to the law?"
4 And those who stood by said, "Do you revile
God's high priest?"
5 Then Paul said, "I did not know, brethren,
that he was the high priest; for it is written, *'You
shall not speak evil of a ruler of your people.'* "[a]
6 But when Paul perceived that one part were
Sadducees and the other Pharisees, he cried out
in the council, "Men *and* brethren, I am a Phar-
isee, the son of a Pharisee; concerning the hope
and resurrection of the dead I am being judged!"
7 And when he had said this, a dissension
arose between the Pharisees and the Sadducees;
and the assembly was divided. 8 For Sadducees
say that there is no resurrection—and no angel
or spirit; but the Pharisees confess both. 9 Then
there arose a loud outcry. And the scribes of the
Pharisees' party arose and protested, saying,
"We find no evil in this man; but if a spirit or an
angel has spoken to him, let us not fight against
God."[a]
10 Now when there arose a great dissension,
the commander, fearing lest Paul might be
pulled to pieces by them, commanded the sol-
diers to go down and take him by force from
among them, and bring him into the barracks.

THE PLOT AGAINST PAUL

11 But the following night the Lord stood by
him and said, "Be of good cheer, Paul; for as you
have testified for Me in Jerusalem, so you must
also bear witness at Rome."
12 And when it was day, some of the Jews
banded together and bound themselves under
an oath, saying that they would neither eat nor
drink till they had killed Paul. 13 Now there were
more than forty who had formed this conspir-
acy. 14 They came to the chief priests and elders,
and said, "We have bound ourselves under a

23:5 [a]Exodus 22:28 **23:9** [a]NU-Text omits last clause and reads *what if a spirit or an angel has spoken to him?*

THE MESSAGE

had put a Roman citizen in chains and come
within a whisker of putting him under tor-
ture!
30 The next day, determined to get to the
root of the trouble and know for sure what
was behind the Jewish accusation, the cap-
tain released Paul and ordered a meeting of
the high priests and the High Council to see
what they could make of it. Paul was led in
and took his place before them.

BEFORE THE HIGH COUNCIL

1-3 **23** Paul surveyed the members of the coun-
cil with a steady gaze, and then said his
piece: "Friends, I've lived with a clear con-
science before God all my life, up to this very
moment." That set the Chief Priest Ananias
off. He ordered his aides to slap Paul in the
face. Paul shot back, "God will slap you
down! What a fake you are! You sit there and
judge me by the Law and then break the
Law by ordering me slapped around!"
4 The aides were scandalized: "How dare
you talk to God's Chief Priest like that!"
5 Paul acted surprised. "How was I to know
he was Chief Priest? He doesn't act like a
Chief Priest. You're right, the Scripture does
say, 'Don't speak abusively to a ruler of the
people.' Sorry."
6 Paul, knowing some of the council was
made up of Sadducees and others of Phar-
isees and how they hated each other, de-
cided to exploit their antagonism: "Friends,
I am a stalwart Pharisee from a long line of
Pharisees. It's because of my Pharisee con-
victions—the hope and resurrection of the
dead—that I've been hauled into this court."
7-9 The moment he said this, the council split
right down the middle, Pharisees and Sad-
ducees going at each other in heated argu-
ment. Sadducees have nothing to do with a
resurrection or angels or even a spirit. If
they can't see it, they don't believe it. Phar-
isees believe it all. And so a huge and noisy
quarrel broke out. Then some of the religion
scholars on the Pharisee side shouted down
the others: "We don't find anything wrong
with this man! And what if a spirit has spo-
ken to him? Or maybe an angel? What if it
turns out we're fighting against God?"
10 That was fuel on the fire. The quarrel
flamed up and became so violent the cap-
tain was afraid they would tear Paul apart,
limb from limb. He ordered the soldiers to
get him out of there and escort him back to
the safety of the barracks.

A PLOT AGAINST PAUL

11 That night the Master appeared to Paul: "It's
going to be all right. Everything is going to
turn out for the best. You've been a good wit-
ness for me here in Jerusalem. Now you're
going to be my witness in Rome!"
12-15 Next day the Jews worked up a plot
against Paul. They took a solemn oath that
they would neither eat nor drink until they
had killed him. Over forty of them ritually
bound themselves to this murder pact and
presented themselves to the high priests
and religious leaders. "We've bound our-

NEW KING JAMES VERSION

great oath that we will eat nothing until we have
killed Paul. [15]Now you, therefore, together with
the council, suggest to the commander that he
be brought down to you tomorrow,[a] as though
you were going to make further inquiries con-
cerning him; but we are ready to kill him before
he comes near."
[16]So when Paul's sister's son heard of their
ambush, he went and entered the barracks and
told Paul. [17]Then Paul called one of the centuri-
ons to *him* and said, "Take this young man to the
commander, for he has something to tell him."
[18]So he took him and brought *him* to the com-
mander and said, "Paul the prisoner called me
to *him* and asked *me* to bring this young man to
you. He has something to say to you."
[19]Then the commander took him by the
hand, went aside, and asked privately, "What is
it that you have to tell me?"
[20]And he said, "The Jews have agreed to ask
that you bring Paul down to the council tomor-
row, as though they were going to inquire more
fully about him. [21]But do not yield to them, for
more than forty of them lie in wait for him, men
who have bound themselves by an oath that
they will neither eat nor drink till they have
killed him; and now they are ready, waiting for
the promise from you."
[22]So the commander let the young man de-
part, and commanded *him*, "Tell no one that you
have revealed these things to me."

SENT TO FELIX

[23]And he called for two centurions, saying,
"Prepare two hundred soldiers, seventy horse-
men, and two hundred spearmen to go to Caes-
area at the third hour of the night; [24]and provide
mounts to set Paul on, and bring *him* safely to
Felix the governor." [25]He wrote a letter in the fol-
lowing manner:

[26]Claudius Lysias,

To the most excellent governor Felix:

Greetings.

[27]This man was seized by the Jews and was
about to be killed by them. Coming with the
troops I rescued him, having learned that he
was a Roman. [28]And when I wanted to
know the reason they accused him, I
brought him before their council. [29]I found
out that he was accused concerning
questions of their law, but had nothing
charged against him deserving of death or
chains. [30]And when it was told me that the
Jews lay in wait for the man,[a] I sent him
immediately to you, and also commanded
his accusers to state before you the charges
against him.

Farewell.

[31]Then the soldiers, as they were com-
manded, took Paul and brought *him* by night to

23:15 [a]NU-Text omits *tomorrow.* **23:30** [a]NU-Text reads *there would be a plot against the man.*

THE MESSAGE

selves by a solemn oath to eat nothing until
we have killed Paul. But we need your help.
Send a request from the council to the cap-
tain to bring Paul back so that you can in-
vestigate the charges in more detail. We'll
do the rest. Before he gets anywhere near
you, we'll have killed him. You won't be in-
volved."

16-17 Paul's nephew, his sister's son, overheard
them plotting the ambush. He went immedi-
ately to the barracks and told Paul. Paul
called over one of the centurions and said,
"Take this young man to the captain. He has
something important to tell him."

18 The centurion brought him to the captain
and said, "The prisoner Paul asked me to
bring this young man to you. He said he has
something urgent to tell you."

19 The captain took him by the arm and led
him aside privately. "What is it? What do
you have to tell me?"

20-21 Paul's nephew said, "The Jews have
worked up a plot against Paul. They're going
to ask you to bring Paul to the council first
thing in the morning on the pretext that they
want to investigate the charges against him
in more detail. But it's a trick to get him out
of your safekeeping so they can murder him.
Right now there are more than forty men ly-
ing in ambush for him. They've all taken a
vow to neither eat nor drink until they've
killed him. The ambush is set—all they're
waiting for is for you to send him over."

22 The captain dismissed the nephew with a
warning: "Don't breathe a word of this to a
soul."

23-24 The captain called up two centurions.
"Get two hundred soldiers ready to go im-
mediately to Caesarea. Also seventy cavalry
and two hundred light infantry. I want them
ready to march by nine o'clock tonight. And
you'll need a couple of mules for Paul and
his gear. We're going to present this man
safe and sound to Governor Felix."

25-30 Then he wrote this letter:

From Claudius Lysias, to the Most
Honorable Governor Felix:

Greetings!

I rescued this man from a Jewish
mob. They had seized him and were
about to kill him when I learned that
he was a Roman citizen. So I sent in
my soldiers. Wanting to know what he
had done wrong, I had him brought
before their council. It turned out to
be a squabble turned vicious over
some of their religious differences,
but nothing remotely criminal.

The next thing I knew, they had
cooked up a plot to murder him. I de-
cided that for his own safety I'd better
get him out of here in a hurry. So I'm
sending him to you. I'm informing his
accusers that he's now under your ju-
risdiction.

31-33 The soldiers, following orders, took Paul
that same night to safety in Antipatris. In

NEW KING JAMES VERSION

Antipatris. 32The next day they left the horsemen to go on with him, and returned to the barracks. 33When they came to Caesarea and had delivered the letter to the governor, they also presented Paul to him. 34And when the governor had read *it*, he asked what province he was from. And when he understood that *he was* from Cilicia, 35he said, "I will hear you when your accusers also have come." And he commanded him to be kept in Herod's Praetorium.

ACCUSED OF SEDITION

24 Now after five days Ananias the high priest came down with the elders and a certain orator *named* Tertullus. These gave evidence to the governor against Paul.

2And when he was called upon, Tertullus began his accusation, saying: "Seeing that through you we enjoy great peace, and prosperity is being brought to this nation by your foresight, 3we accept *it* always and in all places, most noble Felix, with all thankfulness. 4Nevertheless, not to be tedious to you any further, I beg you to hear, by your courtesy, a few words from us. 5For we have found this man a plague, a creator of dissension among all the Jews throughout the world, and a ringleader of the sect of the Nazarenes. 6He even tried to profane the temple, and we seized him,[a] and wanted to judge him according to our law. 7But the commander Lysias came by and with great violence took *him* out of our hands, 8commanding his accusers to come to you. By examining him yourself you may ascertain all these things of which we accuse him." 9And the Jews also assented,[a] maintaining that these things were so.

THE DEFENSE BEFORE FELIX

10Then Paul, after the governor had nodded to him to speak, answered: "Inasmuch as I know that you have been for many years a judge of this nation, I do the more cheerfully answer for myself, 11because you may ascertain that it is no more than twelve days since I went up to Jerusalem to worship. 12And they neither found me in the temple disputing with anyone nor inciting the crowd, either in the synagogues or in the city. 13Nor can they prove the things of which they now accuse me. 14But this I confess to you, that according to the Way which they call a sect, so I worship the God of my fathers, believing all things which are written in the Law and in the Prophets. 15I have hope in God, which they themselves also accept, that there will be a resurrection of *the* dead,[a] both of *the* just and *the* unjust. 16This *being* so, I myself always strive to have a conscience without offense toward God and men.

24:6 [a]NU-Text ends the sentence here and omits the rest of verse 6, all of verse 7, and the first clause of verse 8. 24:9 [a]NU-Text and M-Text read *joined the attack*. 24:15 [a]NU-Text omits *of the dead*.

THE MESSAGE

the morning the soldiers returned to their
barracks in Jerusalem, sending Paul on to
Caesarea under guard of the cavalry. The
cavalry entered Caesarea and handed Paul
and the letter over to the governor.
34-35 After reading the letter, the governor
asked Paul what province he came from and
was told "Cilicia." Then he said, "I'll take up
your case when your accusers show up." He
ordered him locked up for the meantime in
King Herod's official quarters.

PAUL STATES HIS DEFENSE

1-4 24 Within five days, the Chief Priest Ananias arrived with a contingent of leaders, along with Tertullus, a trial lawyer. They
presented the governor with their case
against Paul. When Paul was called before
the court, Tertullus spoke for the prosecution: "Most Honorable Felix, we are most
grateful in all times and places for your wise
and gentle rule. We are much aware that it is
because of you and you alone that we enjoy
all this peace and gain daily profit from
your reforms. I'm not going to tire you out
with a long speech. I beg your kind indulgence in listening to me. I'll be quite brief.
5-8 "We've found this man time and again
disturbing the peace, stirring up riots
against Jews all over the world, the ringleader of a seditious sect called Nazarenes.
He's a real bad apple, I must say. We caught
him trying to defile our holy Temple and arrested him. You'll be able to verify all these
accusations when you examine him yourself."
9 The Jews joined in: "Hear, hear! That's
right!"
10-13 The governor motioned to Paul that it
was now his turn. Paul said, "I count myself
fortunate to be defending myself before you,
Governor, knowing how fair-minded you've
been in judging us all these years. I've been
back in the country only twelve days—you
can check out these dates easily enough. I
came with the express purpose of worshiping in Jerusalem on Pentecost, and I've been
minding my own business the whole time.
Nobody can say they saw me arguing in the
Temple or working up a crowd in the streets.
Not one of their charges can be backed up
with evidence or witnesses.
14-15 "But I do freely admit this: In regard to
the Way, which they malign as a dead-end
street, I serve and worship the very same
God served and worshiped by all our ancestors and embrace everything written in all
our Scriptures. And I admit to living in
hopeful anticipation that God will raise the
dead, both the good and the bad. If that's my
crime, my accusers are just as guilty as I am.
16-19 "Believe me, I do my level best to keep a
clear conscience before God and my neighbors in everything I do. I've been out of the
country for a number of years and now I'm
back. While I was away, I took up a collection for the poor and brought that with me,
along with offerings for the Temple. It was
while making those offerings that they

NEW KING JAMES VERSION

17"Now after many years I came to bring
alms and offerings to my nation, 18in the midst
of which some Jews from Asia found me puri-
fied in the temple, neither with a mob nor with
tumult. 19They ought to have been here before
you to object if they had anything against me.
20Or else let those who are *here* themselves say
if they found any wrongdoing[a] in me while I
stood before the council, 21unless *it is* for this
one statement which I cried out, standing
among them, 'Concerning the resurrection of
the dead I am being judged by you this day.' "

FELIX PROCRASTINATES

22But when Felix heard these things, having
more accurate knowledge of *the* Way, he ad-
journed the proceedings and said, "When Lysias
the commander comes down, I will make a deci-
sion on your case." 23So he commanded the cen-
turion to keep Paul and to let *him* have liberty,
and told him not to forbid any of his friends to
provide for or visit him.

24And after some days, when Felix came with
his wife Drusilla, who was Jewish, he sent for
Paul and heard him concerning the faith in
Christ. 25Now as he reasoned about righteous-
ness, self-control, and the judgment to come, Fe-
lix was afraid and answered, "Go away for now;
when I have a convenient time I will call for
you." 26Meanwhile he also hoped that money
would be given him by Paul, that he might re-
lease him.[a] Therefore he sent for him more of-
ten and conversed with him.

27But after two years Porcius Festus suc-
ceeded Felix; and Felix, wanting to do the Jews
a favor, left Paul bound.

PAUL APPEALS TO CAESAR

25 Now when Festus had come to the
province, after three days he went up from
Caesarea to Jerusalem. 2Then the high priest[a]
and the chief men of the Jews informed him
against Paul; and they petitioned him, 3asking a
favor against him, that he would summon him to
Jerusalem—while *they* lay in ambush along the
road to kill him. 4But Festus answered that Paul
should be kept at Caesarea, and that he himself
was going *there* shortly. 5"Therefore," he said,
"let those who have authority among you go
down with *me* and accuse this man, to see if
there is any fault in him."

6And when he had remained among them
more than ten days, he went down to Caesarea.
And the next day, sitting on the judgment seat,
he commanded Paul to be brought. 7When he
had come, the Jews who had come down from
Jerusalem stood about and laid many serious
complaints against Paul, which they could not
prove, 8while he answered for himself, "Neither
against the law of the Jews, nor against the tem-
ple, nor against Caesar have I offended in any-
thing at all."

24:20 [a]NU-Text and M-Text read *say what wrongdoing they found.*
24:26 [a]NU-Text omits *that he might release him.* **25:2** [a]NU-Text
reads *chief priests.*

THE MESSAGE

found me quietly at my prayers in the Temple.
There was no crowd, there was no distur-
bance. It was some Jews from around Ephesus
who started all this trouble. And you'll notice
they're not here today. They're cowards, too
cowardly to accuse me in front of you.

20-21 "So ask these others what crime they've
caught me in. Don't let them hide behind
this smooth-talking Tertullus. The only
thing they have on me is that one sentence I
shouted out in the council: 'It's because I be-
lieve in the resurrection that I've been
hauled into this court!' Does that sound to
you like grounds for a criminal case?"

22-23 Felix shilly-shallied. He knew far more
about the Way than he let on, and could have
settled the case then and there. But uncertain
of his best move politically, he played for
time. "When Captain Lysias comes down, I'll
decide your case." He gave orders to the cen-
turion to keep Paul in custody, but to more or
less give him the run of the place and not pre-
vent his friends from helping him.

24-26 A few days later Felix and his wife,
Drusilla, who was Jewish, sent for Paul and
listened to him talk about a life of believing
in Jesus Christ. As Paul continued to insist
on right relations with God and his people,
about a life of moral discipline and the com-
ing Judgment, Felix felt things getting a lit-
tle too close for comfort and dismissed him.
"That's enough for today. I'll call you back
when it's convenient." At the same time he
was secretly hoping that Paul would offer
him a substantial bribe. These conversa-
tions were repeated frequently.

27 After two years of this, Felix was re-
placed by Porcius Festus. Still playing up to
the Jews and ignoring justice, Felix left Paul
in prison.

AN APPEAL TO CAESAR

1-3 25 Three days after Festus arrived in Caes-
area to take up his duties as governor,
he went up to Jerusalem. The high priests
and top leaders renewed their vendetta
against Paul. They asked Festus if he wouldn't
please do them a favor by sending Paul to
Jerusalem to respond to their charges. A lie,
of course—they had revived their old plot to
set an ambush and kill him along the way.

4-5 Festus answered that Caesarea was the
proper jurisdiction for Paul, and that he
himself was going back there in a few days.
"You're perfectly welcome," he said, "to go
back with me then and accuse him of what-
ever you think he's done wrong."

6-7 About eight or ten days later, Festus re-
turned to Caesarea. The next morning he
took his place in the courtroom and had
Paul brought in. The minute he walked in,
the Jews who had come down from
Jerusalem were all over him, hurling the
most extreme accusations, none of which
they could prove.

8 Then Paul took the stand and said simply,
"I've done nothing wrong against the Jewish
religion, or the Temple, or Caesar. Period."

NEW KING JAMES VERSION

9But Festus, wanting to do the Jews a favor,
answered Paul and said, "Are you willing to go
up to Jerusalem and there be judged before me
concerning these things?"
10So Paul said, "I stand at Caesar's judgment
seat, where I ought to be judged. To the Jews I
have done no wrong, as you very well know.
11For if I am an offender, or have committed any-
thing deserving of death, I do not object to dy-
ing; but if there is nothing in these things of
which these men accuse me, no one can deliver
me to them. I appeal to Caesar."
12Then Festus, when he had conferred with
the council, answered, "You have appealed to
Caesar? To Caesar you shall go!"

PAUL BEFORE AGRIPPA

13And after some days King Agrippa and
Bernice came to Caesarea to greet Festus.
14When they had been there many days, Festus
laid Paul's case before the king, saying: "There
is a certain man left a prisoner by Felix, 15about
whom the chief priests and the elders of the
Jews informed *me*, when I was in Jerusalem,
asking for a judgment against him. 16To them I
answered, 'It is not the custom of the Romans to
deliver any man to destruction[a] before the ac-
cused meets the accusers face to face, and has
opportunity to answer for himself concerning
the charge against him.' 17Therefore when they
had come together, without any delay, the next
day I sat on the judgment seat and commanded
the man to be brought in. 18When the accusers
stood up, they brought no accusation against
him of such things as I supposed, 19but had
some questions against him about their own re-
ligion and about a certain Jesus, who had died,
whom Paul affirmed to be alive. 20And because I
was uncertain of such questions, I asked
whether he was willing to go to Jerusalem and
there be judged concerning these matters. 21But
when Paul appealed to be reserved for the deci-
sion of Augustus, I commanded him to be kept
till I could send him to Caesar."
22Then Agrippa said to Festus, "I also would
like to hear the man myself."
"Tomorrow," he said, "you shall hear him."
23So the next day, when Agrippa and Bernice
had come with great pomp, and had entered the
auditorium with the commanders and the
prominent men of the city, at Festus' command
Paul was brought in. 24And Festus said: "King
Agrippa and all the men who are here present
with us, you see this man about whom the whole
assembly of the Jews petitioned me, both at
Jerusalem and here, crying out that he was not
fit to live any longer. 25But when I found that he
had committed nothing deserving of death, and

25:16 [a]NU-Text omits *to destruction*, although it is implied.

THE MESSAGE

9 Festus, though, wanted to get on the good
side of the Jews and so said, "How would
you like to go up to Jerusalem, and let me
conduct your trial there?"
10-11 Paul answered, "I'm standing at this mo-
ment before Caesar's bar of justice, where I
have a perfect right to stand. And I'm going
to keep standing here. I've done nothing
wrong to the Jews, and you know it as well
as I do. If I've committed a crime and de-
serve death, name the day. I can face it. But
if there's nothing to their accusations—and
you know there isn't—nobody can force me
to go along with their nonsense. We've
fooled around here long enough. I appeal to
Caesar."
12 Festus huddled with his advisors briefly
and then gave his verdict: "You've appealed
to Caesar; you'll go to Caesar!"

13-17 A few days later King Agrippa and his wife,
Bernice, visited Caesarea to welcome Festus
to his new post. After several days, Festus
brought up Paul's case to the king. "I have a
man on my hands here, a prisoner left by Fe-
lix. When I was in Jerusalem, the high
priests and Jewish leaders brought a bunch
of accusations against him and wanted me
to sentence him to death. I told them that
wasn't the way we Romans did things. Just
because a man is accused, we don't throw
him out to the dogs. We make sure the ac-
cused has a chance to face his accusers and
defend himself of the charges. So when they
came down here I got right on the case. I
took my place in the courtroom and put the
man on the stand.
18-21 "The accusers came at him from all sides,
but their accusations turned out to be noth-
ing more than arguments about their reli-
gion and a dead man named Jesus, who the
prisoner claimed was alive. Since I'm a new-
comer here and don't understand every-
thing involved in cases like this, I asked if
he'd be willing to go to Jerusalem and be
tried there. Paul refused and demanded a
hearing before His Majesty in our highest
court. So I ordered him returned to custody
until I could send him to Caesar in Rome."
22 Agrippa said, "I'd like to see this man and
hear his story."
"Good," said Festus. "We'll bring him in
first thing in the morning and you'll hear it
for yourself."
23 The next day everybody who was any-
body in Caesarea found his way to the Great
Hall, along with the top military brass.
Agrippa and Bernice made a flourishing
grand entrance and took their places. Festus
then ordered Paul brought in.
24-26 Festus said, "King Agrippa and distin-
guished guests, take a good look at this
man. A bunch of Jews petitioned me first in
Jerusalem, and later here, to do away with
him. They have been most vehement in de-
manding his execution. I looked into it and
decided that he had committed no crime. He
requested a trial before Caesar and I agreed
to send him to Rome. But what am I going to

NEW KING JAMES VERSION

that he himself had appealed to Augustus, I de-
cided to send him. 26I have nothing certain to
write to my lord concerning him. Therefore I
have brought him out before you, and especially
before you, King Agrippa, so that after the ex-
amination has taken place I may have some-
thing to write. 27For it seems to me unreasonable
to send a prisoner and not to specify the charges
against him."

PAUL'S EARLY LIFE

26 Then Agrippa said to Paul, "You are per-
mitted to speak for yourself."
So Paul stretched out his hand and answered
for himself: 2"I think myself happy, King
Agrippa, because today I shall answer for my-
self before you concerning all the things of
which I am accused by the Jews, 3especially be-
cause you are expert in all customs and ques-
tions which have to do with the Jews. Therefore
I beg you to hear me patiently.
4"My manner of life from my youth, which
was spent from the beginning among my own
nation at Jerusalem, all the Jews know. 5They
knew me from the first, if they were willing to
testify, that according to the strictest sect of our
religion I lived a Pharisee. 6And now I stand and
am judged for the hope of the promise made by
God to our fathers. 7To this *promise* our twelve
tribes, earnestly serving *God* night and day,
hope to attain. For this hope's sake, King
Agrippa, I am accused by the Jews. 8Why should
it be thought incredible by you that God raises
the dead?
9"Indeed, I myself thought I must do many
things contrary to the name of Jesus of
Nazareth. 10This I also did in Jerusalem, and
many of the saints I shut up in prison, having re-
ceived authority from the chief priests; and
when they were put to death, I cast my vote
against *them*. 11And I punished them often in
every synagogue and compelled *them* to blas-
pheme; and being exceedingly enraged against
them, I persecuted *them* even to foreign cities.

PAUL RECOUNTS HIS CONVERSION

12"While thus occupied, as I journeyed to
Damascus with authority and commission from
the chief priests, 13at midday, O king, along the
road I saw a light from heaven, brighter than the
sun, shining around me and those who jour-
neyed with me. 14And when we all had fallen to
the ground, I heard a voice speaking to me and
saying in the Hebrew language, 'Saul, Saul, why
are you persecuting Me? *It is* hard for you to
kick against the goads.' 15So I said, 'Who are
You, Lord?' And He said, 'I am Jesus, whom you
are persecuting. 16But rise and stand on your
feet; for I have appeared to you for this purpose,
to make you a minister and a witness both of the
things which you have seen and of the things
which I will yet reveal to you. 17I will deliver you
from the *Jewish* people, as well as *from* the Gen-
tiles, to whom I now[a] send you, 18to open their

26:17 [a]NU-Text and M-Text omit *now*.

THE MESSAGE

write to my master, Caesar? All the charges
made by the Jews were fabrications, and
I've uncovered nothing else.
26-27 "That's why I've brought him before this
company, and especially you, King Agrippa:
so we can come up with something in the
nature of a charge that will hold water. For
it seems to me silly to send a prisoner all
that way for a trial and not be able to docu-
ment what he did wrong."

"I COULDN'T JUST WALK AWAY"

1-3 **26** Agrippa spoke directly to Paul: "Go
ahead—tell us about yourself."
Paul took the stand and told his story. "I
can't think of anyone, King Agrippa, before
whom I'd rather be answering all these Jew-
ish accusations than you, knowing how well
you are acquainted with Jewish ways and
all our family quarrels.
4-8 "From the time of my youth, my life has
been lived among my own people in
Jerusalem. Practically every Jew in town
who watched me grow up—and if they were
willing to stick their necks out they'd tell
you in person—knows that I lived as a strict
Pharisee, the most demanding branch of our
religion. It's because I believed it and took it
seriously, committed myself heart and soul
to what God promised my ancestors—the
identical hope, mind you, that the twelve
tribes have lived for night and day all these
centuries—it's because I have held on to this
tested and tried hope that I'm being called
on the carpet by the Jews. They should be
the ones standing trial here, not me! For the
life of me, I can't see why it's a criminal of-
fense to believe that God raises the dead.
9-11 "I admit that I didn't always hold to this po-
sition. For a time I thought it was my duty to
oppose this Jesus of Nazareth with all my
might. Backed with the full authority of the
high priests, I threw these believers—I had no
idea they were God's people!—into the
Jerusalem jail right and left, and whenever it
came to a vote, I voted for their execution. I
stormed through their meeting places, bully-
ing them into cursing Jesus, a one-man terror
obsessed with obliterating these people. And
then I started on the towns outside Jerusalem.
12-14 "One day on my way to Damascus, armed
as always with papers from the high priests
authorizing my action, right in the middle of
the day a blaze of light, light outshining the
sun, poured out of the sky on me and my com-
panions. Oh, King, it was so bright! We fell flat
on our faces. Then I heard a voice in Hebrew:
'Saul, Saul, why are you out to get me? Why
do you insist on going against the grain?'
15-16 "I said, 'Who are you, Master?'
"The voice answered, 'I am Jesus, the One
you're hunting down like an animal. But
now, up on your feet—I have a job for you.
I've handpicked you to be a servant and wit-
ness to what's happened today, and to what
I am going to show you.
17-18 " 'I'm sending you off to open the eyes of
the outsiders so they can see the difference
between dark and light, and choose light,

NEW KING JAMES VERSION

eyes, *in order* to turn *them* from darkness to light, and *from* the power of Satan to God, that they may receive forgiveness of sins and an inheritance among those who are sanctified by faith in Me.'

PAUL'S POST-CONVERSION LIFE

19"Therefore, King Agrippa, I was not disobedient to the heavenly vision, 20but declared first to those in Damascus and in Jerusalem, and throughout all the region of Judea, and *then* to the Gentiles, that they should repent, turn to God, and do works befitting repentance. 21For these reasons the Jews seized me in the temple and tried to kill *me*. 22Therefore, having obtained help from God, to this day I stand, witnessing both to small and great, saying no other things than those which the prophets and Moses said would come— 23that the Christ would suffer, that He would be the first to rise from the dead, and would proclaim light to the *Jewish* people and to the Gentiles."

AGRIPPA PARRIES PAUL'S CHALLENGE

24Now as he thus made his defense, Festus said with a loud voice, "Paul, you are beside yourself! Much learning is driving you mad!"

25But he said, "I am not mad, most noble Festus, but speak the words of truth and reason. 26For the king, before whom I also speak freely, knows these things; for I am convinced that none of these things escapes his attention, since this thing was not done in a corner. 27King Agrippa, do you believe the prophets? I know that you do believe."

28Then Agrippa said to Paul, "You almost persuade me to become a Christian."

29And Paul said, "I would to God that not only you, but also all who hear me today, might become both almost and altogether such as I am, except for these chains."

30When he had said these things, the king stood up, as well as the governor and Bernice and those who sat with them; 31and when they had gone aside, they talked among themselves, saying, "This man is doing nothing deserving of death or chains."

32Then Agrippa said to Festus, "This man might have been set free if he had not appealed to Caesar."

THE VOYAGE TO ROME BEGINS

27 And when it was decided that we should sail to Italy, they delivered Paul and some other prisoners to *one* named Julius, a centurion of the Augustan Regiment. 2So, entering a ship of Adramyttium, we put to sea, meaning to sail along the coasts of Asia. Aristarchus, a Macedonian of Thessalonica, was with us.

THE MESSAGE

see the difference between Satan and God, and choose God. I'm sending you off to present my offer of sins forgiven, and a place in the family, inviting them into the company of those who begin real living by believing in me.'

19-20 "What could I do, King Agrippa? I couldn't just walk away from a vision like that! I became an obedient believer on the spot. I started preaching this life-change—this radical turn to God and everything it meant in everyday life—right there in Damascus, went on to Jerusalem and the surrounding countryside, and from there to the whole world.

21-23 "It's because of this 'whole world' dimension that the Jews grabbed me in the Temple that day and tried to kill me. They want to keep God for themselves. But God has stood by me, just as he promised, and I'm standing here saying what I've been saying to anyone, whether king or child, who will listen. And everything I'm saying is completely in line with what the prophets and Moses said would happen: One, the Messiah must die; two, raised from the dead, he would be the first rays of God's daylight shining on people far and near, people both godless and God-fearing."

24 That was too much for Festus. He interrupted with a shout: "Paul, you're crazy! You've read too many books, spent too much time staring off into space! Get a grip on yourself, get back in the real world!"

25-27 But Paul stood his ground. "With all respect, Festus, Your Honor, I'm not crazy. I'm both accurate and sane in what I'm saying. The king knows what I'm talking about. I'm sure that nothing of what I've said sounds crazy to him. He's known all about it for a long time. You must realize that this wasn't done behind the scenes. You believe the prophets, don't you, King Agrippa? Don't answer that—I know you believe."

28 But Agrippa did answer: "Keep this up much longer and you'll make a Christian out of me!"

29 Paul, still in chains, said, "That's what I'm praying for, whether now or later, and not only you but everyone listening today, to become like me—except, of course, for this prison jewelry!"

30-31 The king and the governor, along with Bernice and their advisors, got up and went into the next room to talk over what they had heard. They quickly agreed on Paul's innocence, saying, "There's nothing in this man deserving prison, let alone death."

32 Agrippa told Festus, "He could be set free right now if he hadn't requested the hearing before Caesar."

A STORM AT SEA

1-2 27 As soon as arrangements were complete for our sailing to Italy, Paul and a few other prisoners were placed under the supervision of a centurion named Julius, a member of an elite guard. We boarded a ship from Adramyttium that was bound for Ephesus and ports west. Aristarchus, a Macedonian from Thessalonica, went with us.

NEW KING JAMES VERSION

3And the next *day* we landed at Sidon. And Julius treated Paul kindly and gave *him* liberty to go to his friends and receive care. 4When we had put to sea from there, we sailed under *the shelter of* Cyprus, because the winds were contrary. 5And when we had sailed over the sea which is off Cilicia and Pamphylia, we came to Myra, *a city* of Lycia. 6There the centurion found an Alexandrian ship sailing to Italy, and he put us on board.

7When we had sailed slowly many days, and arrived with difficulty off Cnidus, the wind not permitting us to proceed, we sailed under *the shelter of* Crete off Salmone. 8Passing it with difficulty, we came to a place called Fair Havens, near the city of Lasea.

PAUL'S WARNING IGNORED

9Now when much time had been spent, and sailing was now dangerous because the Fast was already over, Paul advised them, 10saying, "Men, I perceive that this voyage will end with disaster and much loss, not only of the cargo and ship, but also our lives." 11Nevertheless the centurion was more persuaded by the helmsman and the owner of the ship than by the things spoken by Paul. 12And because the harbor was not suitable to winter in, the majority advised to set sail from there also, if by any means they could reach Phoenix, a harbor of Crete opening toward the southwest and northwest, *and* winter *there*.

IN THE TEMPEST

13When the south wind blew softly, supposing that they had obtained *their* desire, putting out to sea, they sailed close by Crete. 14But not long after, a tempestuous head wind arose, called Euroclydon.[a] 15So when the ship was caught, and could not head into the wind, we let *her* drive. 16And running under *the shelter of* an island called Clauda,[a] we secured the skiff with difficulty. 17When they had taken it on board, they used cables to undergird the ship; and fearing lest they should run aground on the Syrtis[a] *Sands*, they struck sail and so were driven. 18And because we were exceedingly tempest-tossed, the next *day* they lightened the ship. 19On the third *day* we threw the ship's tackle overboard with our own hands. 20Now when neither sun nor stars appeared for many days, and no small tempest beat on *us*, all hope that we would be saved was finally given up.

21But after long abstinence from food, then Paul stood in the midst of them and said, "Men, you should have listened to me, and not have sailed from Crete and incurred this disaster and loss. 22And now I urge you to take heart, for there will be no loss of life among you, but only of the ship. 23For there stood by me this night an angel of the God to whom I belong and whom I serve, 24saying, 'Do not be afraid, Paul; you must be brought before Caesar; and indeed God has granted you all those who sail with you.' 25Therefore take heart, men, for I believe God that it will be just as it was told me. 26However, we must run aground on a certain island."

27:14 [a]NU-Text reads *Euraquilon.* **27:16** [a]NU-Text reads *Cauda.* **27:17** [a]M-Text reads *Syrtes.*

THE MESSAGE

3 The next day we put in at Sidon. Julius treated Paul most decently—let him get off the ship and enjoy the hospitality of his friends there.

4-8 Out to sea again, we sailed north under the protection of the northeast shore of Cyprus because winds out of the west were against us, and then along the coast westward to the port of Myra. There the centurion found an Egyptian ship headed for Italy and transferred us on board. We ran into bad weather and found it impossible to stay on course. After much difficulty, we finally made it to the southern coast of the island of Crete and docked at Good Harbor (appropriate name!).

9-10 By this time we had lost a lot of time. We had passed the autumn equinox, so it would be stormy weather from now on through the winter, too dangerous for sailing. Paul warned, "I see only disaster ahead for cargo and ship—to say nothing of our lives!—if we put out to sea now."

12,11 But it was not the best harbor for staying the winter. Phoenix, a few miles further on, was more suitable. The centurion set Paul's warning aside and let the ship captain and the shipowner talk him into trying for the next harbor.

13-15 When a gentle southerly breeze came up, they weighed anchor, thinking it would be smooth sailing. But they were no sooner out to sea than a gale-force wind, the infamous nor'easter, struck. They lost all control of the ship. It was a cork in the storm.

16-17 We came under the lee of the small island named Clauda, and managed to get a lifeboat ready and reef the sails. But rocky shoals prevented us from getting close. We only managed to avoid them by throwing out drift anchors.

18-20 Next day, out on the high seas again and badly damaged now by the storm, we dumped the cargo overboard. The third day the sailors lightened the ship further by throwing off all the tackle and provisions. It had been many days since we had seen either sun or stars. Wind and waves were battering us unmercifully, and we lost all hope of rescue.

21-22 With our appetite for both food and life long gone, Paul took his place in our midst and said, "Friends, you really should have listened to me back in Crete. We could have avoided all this trouble and trial. But there's no need to dwell on that now. From now on, things are looking up! I can assure you that there'll not be a single drowning among us, although I can't say as much for the ship—the ship itself is doomed.

23-26 "Last night God's angel stood at my side, an angel of this God I serve, saying to me, 'Don't give up, Paul. You're going to stand before Caesar yet—and everyone sailing with you is also going to make it.' So, dear friends, take heart. I believe God will do exactly what he told me. But we're going to shipwreck on some island or other."

NEW KING JAMES VERSION

27Now when the fourteenth night had come,
as we were driven up and down in the Adriatic
Sea, about midnight the sailors sensed that they
were drawing near some land. 28And they took
soundings and found *it* to be twenty fathoms;
and when they had gone a little farther, they
took soundings again and found *it* to be fifteen
fathoms. 29Then, fearing lest we should run
aground on the rocks, they dropped four an-
chors from the stern, and prayed for day to
come. 30And as the sailors were seeking to es-
cape from the ship, when they had let down the
skiff into the sea, under pretense of putting out
anchors from the prow, 31Paul said to the centu-
rion and the soldiers, "Unless these men stay in
the ship, you cannot be saved." 32Then the sol-
diers cut away the ropes of the skiff and let it
fall off.
33And as day was about to dawn, Paul im-
plored *them* all to take food, saying, "Today is
the fourteenth day you have waited and contin-
ued without food, and eaten nothing. 34There-
fore I urge you to take nourishment, for this is
for your survival, since not a hair will fall from
the head of any of you." 35And when he had said
these things, he took bread and gave thanks to
God in the presence of them all; and when he
had broken *it* he began to eat. 36Then they were
all encouraged, and also took food themselves.
37And in all we were two hundred and seventy-
six persons on the ship. 38So when they had
eaten enough, they lightened the ship and threw
out the wheat into the sea.

SHIPWRECKED ON MALTA

39When it was day, they did not recognize the
land; but they observed a bay with a beach, onto
which they planned to run the ship if possible.
40And they let go the anchors and left *them* in
the sea, meanwhile loosing the rudder ropes;
and they hoisted the mainsail to the wind and
made for shore. 41But striking a place where two
seas met, they ran the ship aground; and the
prow stuck fast and remained immovable, but
the stern was being broken up by the violence of
the waves.
42And the soldiers' plan was to kill the pris-
oners, lest any of them should swim away and
escape. 43But the centurion, wanting to save
Paul, kept them from *their* purpose, and com-
manded that those who could swim should jump
overboard first and get to land, 44and the rest,
some on boards and some on *parts* of the ship.
And so it was that they all escaped safely to
land.

PAUL'S MINISTRY ON MALTA

28 Now when they had escaped, they then
found out that the island was called Malta.
2And the natives showed us unusual kindness;
for they kindled a fire and made us all welcome,
because of the rain that was falling and because
of the cold. 3But when Paul had gathered a bun-
dle of sticks and laid *them* on the fire, a viper
came out because of the heat, and fastened on

THE MESSAGE

27-29 On the fourteenth night, adrift some-
where on the Adriatic Sea, at about mid-
night the sailors sensed that we were ap-
proaching land. Sounding, they measured a
depth of 120 feet, and shortly after that
ninety feet. Afraid that we were about to run
aground, they threw out four anchors and
prayed for daylight.
30-32 Some of the sailors tried to jump ship.
They let down the lifeboat, pretending they
were going to set out more anchors from the
bow. Paul saw through their guise and told
the centurion and his soldiers, "If these
sailors don't stay with the ship, we're all go-
ing down." So the soldiers cut the lines to
the lifeboat and let it drift off.
33-34 With dawn about to break, Paul called
everyone together and proposed breakfast:
"This is the fourteenth day we've gone with-
out food. None of us has felt like eating! But
I urge you to eat something now. You'll need
strength for the rescue ahead. You're going
to come out of this without even a scratch!"
35-38 He broke the bread, gave thanks to God,
passed it around, and they all ate heartily—
276 of us, all told! With the meal finished
and everyone full, the ship was further light-
ened by dumping the grain overboard.
39-41 At daybreak, no one recognized the land—
but then they did notice a bay with a nice
beach. They decided to try to run the ship up
on the beach. They cut the anchors, loosed the
tiller, raised the sail, and ran before the wind
toward the beach. But we didn't make it. Still
far from shore, we hit a reef and the ship be-
gan to break up.
42-44 The soldiers decided to kill the prisoners
so none could escape by swimming, but the
centurion, determined to save Paul, stopped
them. He gave orders for anyone who could
swim to dive in and go for it, and for the rest
to grab a plank. Everyone made it to shore
safely.

1-2 28 Once everyone was accounted for and
we realized we had all made it, we
learned that we were on the island of Malta.
The natives went out of their way to be
friendly to us. The day was rainy and cold
and we were already soaked to the bone, but
they built a huge bonfire and gathered us
around it.
3-6 Paul pitched in and helped. He had gath-
ered up a bundle of sticks, but when he put
it on the fire, a venomous snake, roused
from its torpor by the heat, struck his hand

New King James Version

his hand. 4So when the natives saw the creature
hanging from his hand, they said to one another,
"No doubt this man is a murderer, whom,
though he has escaped the sea, yet justice does
not allow to live." 5But he shook off the creature
into the fire and suffered no harm. 6However,
they were expecting that he would swell up or
suddenly fall down dead. But after they had
looked for a long time and saw no harm come to
him, they changed their minds and said that he
was a god.

7In that region there was an estate of the
leading citizen of the island, whose name was
Publius, who received us and entertained us
courteously for three days. 8And it happened
that the father of Publius lay sick of a fever and
dysentery. Paul went in to him and prayed, and
he laid his hands on him and healed him. 9So
when this was done, the rest of those on the is-
land who had diseases also came and were
healed. 10They also honored us in many ways;
and when we departed, they provided such
things as were necessary.

Arrival at Rome

11After three months we sailed in an Alexan-
drian ship whose figurehead was the Twin
Brothers, which had wintered at the island.
12And landing at Syracuse, we stayed three
days. 13From there we circled round and reached
Rhegium. And after one day the south wind
blew; and the next day we came to Puteoli,
14where we found brethren, and were invited to
stay with them seven days. And so we went to-
ward Rome. 15And from there, when the
brethren heard about us, they came to meet us
as far as Appii Forum and Three Inns. When
Paul saw them, he thanked God and took
courage.

16Now when we came to Rome, the centurion
delivered the prisoners to the captain of the
guard; but Paul was permitted to dwell by him-
self with the soldier who guarded him.

Paul's Ministry at Rome

17And it came to pass after three days that
Paul called the leaders of the Jews together. So
when they had come together, he said to them:
"Men *and* brethren, though I have done nothing
against our people or the customs of our fathers,
yet I was delivered as a prisoner from Jerusalem
into the hands of the Romans, 18who, when they
had examined me, wanted to let *me* go, because
there was no cause for putting me to death.
19But when the Jews[a] spoke against *it*, I was
compelled to appeal to Caesar, not that I had
anything of which to accuse my nation. 20For
this reason therefore I have called for you, to see
you and speak with *you*, because for the hope of
Israel I am bound with this chain."

21Then they said to him, "We neither received
letters from Judea concerning you, nor have any
of the brethren who came reported or spoken
any evil of you. 22But we desire to hear from you
what you think; for concerning this sect, we
know that it is spoken against everywhere."

28:19 [a]That is, the ruling authorities

The Message

and held on. Seeing the snake hanging from Paul's hand like that, the natives jumped to the conclusion that he was a murderer getting his just deserts. Paul shook the snake off into the fire, none the worse for wear. They kept expecting him to drop dead, but when it was obvious he wasn't going to, they jumped to the conclusion that he was a god!

7-9 The head man in that part of the island was Publius. He took us into his home as his guests, drying us out and putting us up in fine style for the next three days. Publius's father was sick at the time, down with a high fever and dysentery. Paul went to the old man's room, and when he laid hands on him and prayed, the man was healed. Word of the healing got around fast, and soon everyone on the island who was sick came and got healed.

Rome

10-11 We spent a wonderful three months on Malta. They treated us royally, took care of all our needs and outfitted us for the rest of the journey. When an Egyptian ship that had wintered there in the harbor prepared to leave for Italy, we got on board. The ship had a carved Gemini for its figurehead: "the Heavenly Twins."

12-14 We put in at Syracuse for three days and then went up the coast to Rhegium. Two days later, with the wind out of the south, we sailed into the Bay of Naples. We found Christian friends there and stayed with them for a week.

14-16 And then we came to Rome. Friends in Rome heard we were on the way and came out to meet us. One group got as far as Appian Court; another group met us at Three Taverns—emotion-packed meetings, as you can well imagine. Paul, brimming over with praise, led us in prayers of thanksgiving. When we actually entered Rome, they let Paul live in his own private quarters with a soldier who had been assigned to guard him.

17-20 Three days later, Paul called the Jewish leaders together for a meeting at his house. He said, "The Jews in Jerusalem arrested me on trumped-up charges, and I was taken into custody by the Romans. I assure you that I did absolutely nothing against Jewish laws or Jewish customs. After the Romans investigated the charges and found there was nothing to them, they wanted to set me free, but the Jews objected so fiercely that I was forced to appeal to Caesar. I did this not to accuse them of any wrongdoing or to get our people in trouble with Rome. We've had enough trouble through the years that way. I did it *for* Israel. I asked you to come and listen to me today to make it clear that I'm on Israel's side, not against her. I'm a hostage here for hope, not doom."

21-22 They said, "Nobody wrote warning us about you. And no one has shown up saying anything bad about you. But we would like very much to hear more. The only thing we know about this Christian sect is that nobody seems to have anything good to say about it."

New King James Version

[23]So when they had appointed him a day,
many came to him at *his* lodging, to whom he
explained and solemnly testified of the kingdom
of God, persuading them concerning Jesus from
both the Law of Moses and the Prophets, from
morning till evening. [24]And some were per-
suaded by the things which were spoken, and
some disbelieved. [25]So when they did not agree
among themselves, they departed after Paul had
said one word: "The Holy Spirit spoke rightly
through Isaiah the prophet to our[a] fathers, [26]say-
ing,

'Go to this people and say:
"Hearing you will hear, and shall not
understand;
And seeing you will see, and not perceive;
[27]*For the hearts of this people have grown*
dull.
Their ears are hard of hearing,
And their eyes they have closed,
Lest they should see with their eyes and
hear with their ears,
Lest they should understand with their
hearts and turn,
So that I should heal them."'[a]

[28]"Therefore let it be known to you that the
salvation of God has been sent to the Gentiles,
and they will hear it!" [29]And when he had said
these words, the Jews departed and had a great
dispute among themselves.[a]
[30]Then Paul dwelt two whole years in his
own rented house, and received all who came to
him, [31]preaching the kingdom of God and teach-
ing the things which concern the Lord Jesus
Christ with all confidence, no one forbidding
him.

28:25 [a]NU-Text reads *your.* **28:27** [a]Isaiah 6:9, 10 **28:29** [a]NU-Text omits this verse.

The Message

23 They agreed on a time. When the day ar-
rived, they came back to his home with a
number of their friends. Paul talked to them
all day, from morning to evening, explaining
everything involved in the kingdom of God,
and trying to persuade them all about Jesus
by pointing out what Moses and the
prophets had written about him.
24-27 Some of them were persuaded by what
he said, but others refused to believe a word
of it. When the unbelievers got cantanker-
ous and started bickering with each other,
Paul interrupted: "I have just one more thing
to say to you. The Holy Spirit sure knew
what he was talking about when he ad-
dressed our ancestors through Isaiah the
prophet:

Go to this people and tell them this:
"You're going to listen with your ears,
but you won't hear a word;
You're going to stare with your eyes,
but you won't see a thing.
These people are blockheads!
They stick their fingers in their ears
so they won't have to listen;
They screw their eyes shut
so they won't have to look,
so they won't have to deal with me
face-to-face
and let me heal them."

28 "You've had your chance. The non-Jewish
outsiders are next on the list. And believe
me, they're going to receive it with open
arms!"
30-31 Paul lived for two years in his rented
house. He welcomed everyone who came to
visit. He urgently presented all matters of
the kingdom of God. He explained every-
thing about Jesus Christ. His door was al-
ways open.

ROMANS

New King James Version

Greeting

1 Paul, a bondservant of Jesus Christ, called *to*
be an apostle, separated to the gospel of God
2which He promised before through His
prophets in the Holy Scriptures, 3concerning
His Son Jesus Christ our Lord, who was born of
the seed of David according to the flesh, 4*and*
declared *to be* the Son of God with power ac-
cording to the Spirit of holiness, by the resurrec-
tion from the dead. 5Through Him we have re-
ceived grace and apostleship for obedience to
the faith among all nations for His name,
6among whom you also are the called of Jesus
Christ;

7To all who are in Rome, beloved of God,
called *to be* saints:

Grace to you and peace from God our Father
and the Lord Jesus Christ.

Desire to Visit Rome

8First, I thank my God through Jesus Christ
for you all, that your faith is spoken of through-
out the whole world. 9For God is my witness,
whom I serve with my spirit in the gospel of His
Son, that without ceasing I make mention of you
always in my prayers, 10making request if, by
some means, now at last I may find a way in the
will of God to come to you. 11For I long to see
you, that I may impart to you some spiritual gift,
so that you may be established— 12that is, that I
may be encouraged together with you by the
mutual faith both of you and me.
13Now I do not want you to be unaware,
brethren, that I often planned to come to you
(but was hindered until now), that I might have
some fruit among you also, just as among the
other Gentiles. 14I am a debtor both to Greeks
and to barbarians, both to wise and to unwise.
15So, as much as is in me, *I am* ready to preach
the gospel to you who are in Rome also.

The Just Live by Faith

16For I am not ashamed of the gospel of
Christ,[a] for it is the power of God to salvation
for everyone who believes, for the Jew first and
also for the Greek. 17For in it the righteousness
of God is revealed from faith to faith; as it is
written, *"The just shall live by faith."* [a]

God's Wrath on Unrighteousness

18For the wrath of God is revealed from
heaven against all ungodliness and unrigh-
teousness of men, who suppress the truth in un-
righteousness, 19because what may be known of
God is manifest in them, for God has shown *it* to

1:16 [a]NU-Text omits *of Christ*. 1:17 [a]Habakkuk 2:4

The Message

1 1 I, Paul, am a devoted slave of Jesus Christ on assignment, authorized as an apostle to proclaim God's words and acts. I write this letter to all the believers in Rome, God's friends.

2-7 The sacred writings contain preliminary reports by the prophets on God's Son. His descent from David roots him in history; his unique identity as Son of God was shown by the Spirit when Jesus was raised from the dead, setting him apart as the Messiah, our Master. Through him we received both the generous gift of his life and the urgent task of passing it on to others who receive it by entering into obedient trust in Jesus. You are who you are through this gift and call of Jesus Christ! And I greet you now with all the generosity of God our Father and our Master Jesus, the Messiah.

8-12 I thank God through Jesus for every one of you. That's first. People everywhere keep telling me about your lives of faith, and every time I hear them, I thank him. And God, whom I so love to worship and serve by spreading the good news of his Son—the Message!—knows that every time I think of you in my prayers, which is practically all the time, I ask him to clear the way for me to come and see you. The longer this waiting goes on, the deeper the ache. I so want to be there to deliver God's gift in person and watch you grow stronger right before my eyes! But don't think I'm not expecting to get something out of this, too! You have as much to give me as I do to you.

13-15 Please don't misinterpret my failure to visit you, friends. You have no idea how many times I've made plans for Rome. I've been determined to get some personal enjoyment out of God's work among you, as I have in so many other non-Jewish towns and communities. But something has always come up and prevented it. Everyone I meet—it matters little whether they're mannered or rude, smart or simple—deepens my sense of interdependence and obligation. And that's why I can't wait to get to you in Rome, preaching this wonderful good news of God.

16-17 It's news I'm most proud to proclaim, this extraordinary Message of God's powerful plan to rescue everyone who trusts him, starting with Jews and then right on to everyone else! God's way of putting people right shows up in the acts of faith, confirming what Scripture has said all along: "The person in right standing before God by trusting him really lives."

Ignoring God Leads to a Downward Spiral

18-23 But God's angry displeasure erupts as acts of human mistrust and wrongdoing and lying accumulate, as people try to put a shroud over truth. But the basic reality of God is

New King James Version

them. [20]For since the creation of the world His invisible *attributes* are clearly seen, being understood by the things that are made, *even* His eternal power and Godhead, so that they are without excuse, [21]because, although they knew God, they did not glorify *Him* as God, nor were thankful, but became futile in their thoughts, and their foolish hearts were darkened. [22]Professing to be wise, they became fools, [23]and changed the glory of the incorruptible God into an image made like corruptible man—and birds and four-footed animals and creeping things.

[24]Therefore God also gave them up to uncleanness, in the lusts of their hearts, to dishonor their bodies among themselves, [25]who exchanged the truth of God for the lie, and worshiped and served the creature rather than the Creator, who is blessed forever. Amen.

[26]For this reason God gave them up to vile passions. For even their women exchanged the natural use for what is against nature. [27]Likewise also the men, leaving the natural use of the woman, burned in their lust for one another, men with men committing what is shameful, and receiving in themselves the penalty of their error which was due.

[28]And even as they did not like to retain God in *their* knowledge, God gave them over to a debased mind, to do those things which are not fitting; [29]being filled with all unrighteousness, sexual immorality,[a] wickedness, covetousness, maliciousness; full of envy, murder, strife, deceit, evil-mindedness; *they are* whisperers, [30]backbiters, haters of God, violent, proud, boasters, inventors of evil things, disobedient to parents, [31]undiscerning, untrustworthy, unloving, unforgiving,[a] unmerciful; [32]who, knowing the righteous judgment of God, that those who practice such things are deserving of death, not only do the same but also approve of those who practice them.

God's Righteous Judgment

2 Therefore you are inexcusable, O man, whoever you are who judge, for in whatever you judge another you condemn yourself; for you who judge practice the same things. [2]But we know that the judgment of God is according to truth against those who practice such things. [3]And do you think this, O man, you who judge those practicing such things, and doing the same, that you will escape the judgment of God?

1:29 [a]NU-Text omits *sexual immorality.* 1:31 [a]NU-Text omits *unforgiving.*

The Message

plain enough. Open your eyes and there it is! By taking a long and thoughtful look at what God has created, people have always been able to see what their eyes as such can't see: eternal power, for instance, and the mystery of his divine being. So nobody has a good excuse. What happened was this: People knew God perfectly well, but when they didn't treat him like God, refusing to worship him, they trivialized themselves into silliness and confusion so that there was neither sense nor direction left in their lives. They pretended to know it all, but were illiterate regarding life. They traded the glory of God who holds the whole world in his hands for cheap figurines you can buy at any roadside stand.

24-25 So God said, in effect, "If that's what you want, that's what you get." It wasn't long before they were living in a pigpen, smeared with filth, filthy inside and out. And all this because they traded the true God for a fake god, and worshiped the god they made instead of the God who made them—the God we bless, the God who blesses *us*. Oh, yes!

26-27 Worse followed. Refusing to know God, they soon didn't know how to be human either—women didn't know how to be women, men didn't know how to be men. Sexually confused, they abused and defiled one another, women with women, men with men—all lust, no love. And then they paid for it, oh, how they paid for it—emptied of God and love, godless and loveless wretches.

28-32 Since they didn't bother to acknowledge God, God quit bothering them and let them run loose. And then all hell broke loose: rampant evil, grabbing and grasping, vicious backstabbing. They made life hell on earth with their envy, wanton killing, bickering, and cheating. Look at them: mean-spirited, venomous, fork-tongued God-bashers. Bullies, swaggerers, insufferable windbags! They keep inventing new ways of wrecking lives. They ditch their parents when they get in the way. Stupid, slimy, cruel, cold-blooded. And it's not as if they don't know better. They know perfectly well they're spitting in God's face. And they don't care—worse, they hand out prizes to those who do the worst things best!

God Is Kind, but Not Soft

1-2 **2** Those people are on a dark spiral downward. But if you think that leaves you on the high ground where you can point your finger at others, think again. Every time you criticize someone, you condemn yourself. It takes one to know one. Judgmental criticism of others is a well-known way of escaping detection in your own crimes and misdemeanors. But God isn't so easily diverted. He sees right through all such smoke screens and holds you to what *you've* done.

3-4 You didn't think, did you, that just by pointing your finger at others you would distract God from seeing all your misdoings and from coming down on you hard? Or did you think that because he's such a nice God,

NEW KING JAMES VERSION

4Or do you despise the riches of His goodness,
forbearance, and longsuffering, not knowing
that the goodness of God leads you to repen-
tance? 5But in accordance with your hardness
and your impenitent heart you are treasuring up
for yourself wrath in the day of wrath and reve-
lation of the righteous judgment of God, 6who
"will render to each one according to his
deeds":[a] 7eternal life to those who by patient
continuance in doing good seek for glory, honor,
and immortality; 8but to those who are self-
seeking and do not obey the truth, but obey
unrighteousness—indignation and wrath,
9tribulation and anguish, on every soul of man
who does evil, of the Jew first and also of the
Greek; 10but glory, honor, and peace to everyone
who works what is good, to the Jew first and
also to the Greek. 11For there is no partiality
with God.

12For as many as have sinned without law
will also perish without law, and as many as
have sinned in the law will be judged by the law
13(for not the hearers of the law *are* just in the
sight of God, but the doers of the law will be jus-
tified; 14for when Gentiles, who do not have the
law, by nature do the things in the law, these, al-
though not having the law, are a law to them-
selves, 15who show the work of the law written
in their hearts, their conscience also bearing
witness, and between themselves *their* thoughts
accusing or else excusing *them*) 16in the day
when God will judge the secrets of men by Jesus
Christ, according to my gospel.

THE JEWS GUILTY AS THE GENTILES

17Indeed[a] you are called a Jew, and rest on
the law, and make your boast in God, 18and
know *His* will, and approve the things that are
excellent, being instructed out of the law, 19and
are confident that you yourself are a guide to
the blind, a light to those who are in darkness,
20an instructor of the foolish, a teacher of babes,
having the form of knowledge and truth in the
law. 21You, therefore, who teach another, do you
not teach yourself? You who preach that a man
should not steal, do you steal? 22You who say,
"Do not commit adultery," do you commit adul-
tery? You who abhor idols, do you rob temples?
23You who make your boast in the law, do you

2:6 [a]Psalm 62:12; Proverbs 24:12 **2:17** [a]NU-Text reads *But if.*

THE MESSAGE

he'd let you off the hook? Better think this one through from the beginning. God is kind, but he's not soft. In kindness he takes us firmly by the hand and leads us into a radical life-change.

5-8 You're not getting by with anything. Every refusal and avoidance of God adds fuel to the fire. The day is coming when it's going to blaze hot and high, God's fiery and righteous judgment. Make no mistake: In the end you get what's coming to you—*Real Life* for those who work on God's side, but to those who insist on getting their own way and take the path of least resistance, *Fire!*

9-11 If you go against the grain, you get splinters, regardless of which neighborhood you're from, what your parents taught you, what schools you attended. But if you embrace the way God does things, there are wonderful payoffs, again without regard to where you are from or how you were brought up. Being a Jew won't give you an automatic stamp of approval. God pays no attention to what others say (or what you think) about you. He makes up his own mind.

12-13 If you sin without knowing what you're doing, God takes that into account. But if you sin knowing full well what you're doing, that's a different story entirely. Merely hearing God's law is a waste of your time if you don't do what he commands. Doing, not hearing, is what makes the difference with God.

14-16 When outsiders who have never heard of God's law follow it more or less by instinct, they confirm its truth by their obedience. They show that God's law is not something alien, imposed on us from without, but woven into the very fabric of our creation. There is something deep within them that echoes God's yes and no, right and wrong. Their response to God's yes and no will become public knowledge on the day God makes his final decision about every man and woman. The Message from God that I proclaim through Jesus Christ takes into account all these differences.

RELIGION CAN'T SAVE YOU

17-24 If you're brought up Jewish, don't assume that you can lean back in the arms of your religion and take it easy, feeling smug because you're an insider to God's revelation, a connoisseur of the best things of God, informed on the latest doctrines! I have a special word of caution for you who are sure that you have it all together yourselves and, because you know God's revealed Word inside and out, feel qualified to guide others through their blind alleys and dark nights and confused emotions to God. While you are guiding others, who is going to guide you? I'm quite serious. While preaching "Don't steal!" are you going to rob people blind? Who would suspect you? The same with adultery. The same with idolatry. You can get by with almost anything if you front it with eloquent talk about God and his law.

NEW KING JAMES VERSION

dishonor God through breaking the law? 24For
*"the name of God is blasphemed among the
Gentiles because of you,"* [a] as it is written.

CIRCUMCISION OF NO AVAIL

25For circumcision is indeed profitable if you
keep the law; but if you are a breaker of the law,
your circumcision has become uncircumcision.
26Therefore, if an uncircumcised man keeps the
righteous requirements of the law, will not his
uncircumcision be counted as circumcision?
27And will not the physically uncircumcised, if
he fulfills the law, judge you who, *even* with
your written *code* and circumcision, *are* a trans-
gressor of the law? 28For he is not a Jew who *is
one* outwardly, nor *is* circumcision that which *is*
outward in the flesh; 29but *he is* a Jew who *is one*
inwardly; and circumcision *is that* of the heart,
in the Spirit, not in the letter; whose praise *is* not
from men but from God.

GOD'S JUDGMENT DEFENDED

3 What advantage then has the Jew, or what *is*
the profit of circumcision? 2Much in every
way! Chiefly because to them were committed
the oracles of God. 3For what if some did not be-
lieve? Will their unbelief make the faithfulness
of God without effect? 4Certainly not! Indeed, let
God be true but every man a liar. As it is written:

"That You may be justified in Your words,
And may overcome when You are judged." [a]

5But if our unrighteousness demonstrates
the righteousness of God, what shall we say? *Is*
God unjust who inflicts wrath? (I speak as a
man.) 6Certainly not! For then how will God
judge the world?
7For if the truth of God has increased
through my lie to His glory, why am I also still
judged as a sinner? 8And *why* not *say,* "Let us do
evil that good may come"?—as we are slander-
ously reported and as some affirm that we say.
Their condemnation is just.

ALL HAVE SINNED

9What then? Are we better *than they?* Not at
all. For we have previously charged both Jews
and Greeks that they are all under sin.
10As it is written:

2:24 [a]Isaiah 52:5; Ezekiel 36:22 **3:4** [a]Psalm 51:4

THE MESSAGE

The line from Scripture, "It's because of you Jews that the outsiders are down on God," shows it's an old problem that isn't going to go away.

25-29 Circumcision, the surgical ritual that marks you as a Jew, is great if you live in accord with God's law. But if you don't, it's worse than not being circumcised. The reverse is also true: The uncircumcised who keep God's ways are as good as the circumcised—in fact, better. Better to keep God's law uncircumcised than break it circumcised. Don't you see: It's not the cut of a knife that makes a Jew. You become a Jew by who you *are*. It's the mark of God on your heart, not of a knife on your skin, that makes a Jew. And recognition comes from God, not legalistic critics.

1-2 3 So what difference does it make who's a Jew and who isn't, who has been trained in God's ways and who hasn't? As it turns out, it makes a lot of difference—but not the difference so many have assumed.

2-6 First, there's the matter of being put in charge of writing down and caring for God's revelation, these Holy Scriptures. So, what if, in the course of doing that, some of those Jews abandoned their post? God didn't abandon them. Do you think their faithlessness cancels out his faithfulness? Not on your life! Depend on it: God keeps his word even when the whole world is lying through its teeth. Scripture says the same:

Your words stand fast and true;
Rejection doesn't faze you.

But if our wrongdoing only underlines and confirms God's rightdoing, shouldn't we be commended for helping out? Since our bad words don't even make a dent in his good words, isn't it wrong of God to back us to the wall and hold us to our word? These questions come up. The answer to such questions is *no,* a most emphatic *No!* How else would things ever get straightened out if *God* didn't do the straightening?

7-8 It's simply perverse to say, "If my lies serve to show off God's truth all the more gloriously, why blame me? I'm doing God a favor." Some people are actually trying to put such words in our mouths, claiming that we go around saying, "The more evil we do, the more good God does, so let's just do it!" That's pure slander, as I'm sure you'll agree.

WE'RE ALL IN THE SAME SINKING BOAT

9-20 So where does that put us? Do we Jews get a better break than the others? Not really. Basically, all of us, whether insiders or outsiders, start out in identical conditions, which is to say that we all start out as sinners. Scripture leaves no doubt about it:

NEW KING JAMES VERSION

"There is none righteous, no, not one;
11*There is none who understands;*
There is none who seeks after God.
12*They have all turned aside;*
They have together become unprofitable;
There is none who does good, no, not one." [a]
13*"Their throat is an open tomb;*
With their tongues they have practiced
deceit"; [a]
"The poison of asps is under their lips"; [b]
14*"Whose mouth is full of cursing and*
bitterness." [a]
15*"Their feet are swift to shed blood;*
16*Destruction and misery are in their ways;*
17*And the way of peace they have not*
known." [a]
18*"There is no fear of God before their eyes."* [a]

19Now we know that whatever the law says,
it says to those who are under the law, that every
mouth may be stopped, and all the world may
become guilty before God. 20Therefore by the
deeds of the law no flesh will be justified in His
sight, for by the law *is* the knowledge of sin.

GOD'S RIGHTEOUSNESS THROUGH FAITH

21But now the righteousness of God apart
from the law is revealed, being witnessed by the
Law and the Prophets, 22even the righteousness
of God, through faith in Jesus Christ, to all and
on all[a] who believe. For there is no difference;
23for all have sinned and fall short of the glory
of God, 24being justified freely by His grace
through the redemption that is in Christ Jesus,
25whom God set forth *as* a propitiation by His
blood, through faith, to demonstrate His righ-
teousness, because in His forbearance God had
passed over the sins that were previously com-
mitted, 26to demonstrate at the present time His
righteousness, that He might be just and the jus-
tifier of the one who has faith in Jesus.

BOASTING EXCLUDED

27Where *is* boasting then? It is excluded. By
what law? Of works? No, but by the law of faith.
28Therefore we conclude that a man is justified
by faith apart from the deeds of the law.

3:12 [a]Psalms 14:1–3; 53:1–3; Ecclesiastes 7:20 **3:13** [a]Psalm 5:9 [b]Psalm 140:3 **3:14** [a]Psalm 10:7 **3:17** [a]Isaiah 59:7, 8 **3:18** [a]Psalm 36:1 **3:22** [a]NU-Text omits *and on all.*

THE MESSAGE

There's nobody living right, not even one,
nobody who knows the score, nobody
alert for God.
They've all taken the wrong turn;
they've all wandered down blind
alleys.
No one's living right;
I can't find a single one.
Their throats are gaping graves,
their tongues slick as mudslides.
Every word they speak is tinged with
poison.
They open their mouths and pollute
the air.
They race for the honor of
sinner-of-the-year,
litter the land with heartbreak and ruin,
Don't know the first thing about living
with others.
They never give God the time of day.

This makes it clear, doesn't it, that whatever is written in these Scriptures is not what God says *about others* but *to us* to whom these Scriptures were addressed in the first place! And it's clear enough, isn't it, that we're sinners, every one of us, in the same sinking boat with everybody else? Our involvement with God's revelation doesn't put us right with God. What it does is force us to face our complicity in everyone else's sin.

GOD HAS SET THINGS RIGHT

21-24 But in our time something new has been added. What Moses and the prophets witnessed to all those years has happened. The God-setting-things-right that we read about has become Jesus-setting-things-right for us. And not only for us, but for everyone who believes in him. For there is no difference between us and them in this. Since we've compiled this long and sorry record as sinners (both us and them) and proved that we are utterly incapable of living the glorious lives God wills for us, God did it for us. Out of sheer generosity he put us in right standing with himself. A pure gift. He got us out of the mess we're in and restored us to where he always wanted us to be. And he did it by means of Jesus Christ.

25-26 God sacrificed Jesus on the altar of the world to clear that world of sin. Having faith in him sets us in the clear. God decided on this course of action in full view of the public—to set the world in the clear with himself through the sacrifice of Jesus, finally taking care of the sins he had so patiently endured. This is not only clear, but it's *now*—this is current history! God sets things right. He also makes it possible for us to live in his rightness.

27-28 So where does that leave our proud Jewish insider claims and counterclaims? Canceled? Yes, canceled. What we've learned is this: God does not respond to what *we* do; we respond to what *God* does. We've finally figured it out. Our lives get in step with God and all others by letting him set the pace, not by proudly or anxiously trying to run the parade.

NEW KING JAMES VERSION

29 Or *is He* the God of the Jews only? *Is He* not also the God of the Gentiles? Yes, of the Gentiles also, 30 since *there is* one God who will justify the circumcised by faith and the uncircumcised through faith. 31 Do we then make void the law through faith? Certainly not! On the contrary, we establish the law.

ABRAHAM JUSTIFIED BY FAITH

4 What then shall we say that Abraham our father has found according to the flesh?[a] 2 For if Abraham was justified by works, he has *something* to boast about, but not before God. 3 For what does the Scripture say? *"Abraham believed God, and it was accounted to him for righteousness."*[a] 4 Now to him who works, the wages are not counted as grace but as debt.

DAVID CELEBRATES THE SAME TRUTH

5 But to him who does not work but believes on Him who justifies the ungodly, his faith is accounted for righteousness, 6 just as David also describes the blessedness of the man to whom God imputes righteousness apart from works:

7 *"Blessed are those whose lawless deeds are*
forgiven,
And whose sins are covered;
8 *Blessed is the man to whom the LORD shall*
not impute sin."[a]

ABRAHAM JUSTIFIED BEFORE CIRCUMCISION

9 *Does* this blessedness then *come* upon the circumcised *only,* or upon the uncircumcised also? For we say that faith was accounted to Abraham for righteousness. 10 How then was it accounted? While he was circumcised, or uncircumcised? Not while circumcised, but while uncircumcised. 11 And he received the sign of circumcision, a seal of the righteousness of the faith which *he had while still* uncircumcised, that he might be the father of all those who believe, though they are uncircumcised, that righteousness might be imputed to them also,

4:1 [a]Or *Abraham our (fore)father according to the flesh has found?* 4:3 [a]Genesis 15:6 4:8 [a]Psalm 32:1, 2

THE MESSAGE

29-30 And where does that leave our proud Jewish claim of having a corner on God? Also canceled. God is the God of outsider non-Jews as well as insider Jews. How could it be otherwise since there is only one God? God sets right all who welcome his action and enter into it, both those who follow our religious system and those who have never heard of our religion.

31 But by shifting our focus from what *we* do to what *God* does, don't we cancel out all our careful keeping of the rules and ways God commanded? Not at all. What happens, in fact, is that by putting that entire way of life in its proper place, we confirm it.

TRUSTING GOD

1-3 4 So how do we fit what we know of Abraham, our first father in the faith, into this new way of looking at things? If Abraham, by what he *did* for God, got God to approve him, he could certainly have taken credit for it. But the story we're given is a God-story, not an Abraham-story. What we read in Scripture is, "Abraham entered into what God was doing for him, and *that* was the turning point. He trusted God to set him right instead of trying to be right on his own."

4-5 If you're a hard worker and do a good job, you deserve your pay; we don't call your wages a gift. But if you see that the job is too big for you, that it's something only *God* can do, and you trust him to do it—you could never do it for yourself no matter how hard and long you worked—well, that trusting-him-to-do-it is what gets you set right with God, *by* God. Sheer gift.

6-9 David confirms this way of looking at it, saying that the one who trusts God to do the putting-everything-right without insisting on having a say in it is one fortunate man:

Fortunate those whose crimes are
carted off,
whose sins are wiped clean from the
slate.
Fortunate the person against
whom the Lord does not keep score.

Do you think for a minute that this blessing is only pronounced over those of us who keep our religious ways and are circumcised? Or do you think it possible that the blessing could be given to those who never even heard of our ways, who were never brought up in the disciplines of God? We all agree, don't we, that it was by embracing what God did for him that Abraham was declared fit before God?

10-11 Now *think*: Was that declaration made before or after he was marked by the covenant rite of circumcision? That's right, *before* he was marked. That means that he underwent circumcision as evidence and confirmation of what God had done long before to bring him into this acceptable standing with himself, an act of God he had embraced with his whole life.

New King James Version

12and the father of circumcision to those who
not only *are* of the circumcision, but who also
walk in the steps of the faith which our father
Abraham *had while still* uncircumcised.

The Promise Granted Through Faith

13For the promise that he would be the heir of
the world *was* not to Abraham or to his seed
through the law, but through the righteousness
of faith. 14For if those who are of the law *are*
heirs, faith is made void and the promise made
of no effect, 15because the law brings about
wrath; for where there is no law *there is* no
transgression.

16Therefore *it is* of faith that *it might be* ac-
cording to grace, so that the promise might be
sure to all the seed, not only to those who are of
the law, but also to those who are of the faith of
Abraham, who is the father of us all 17(as it is
written, *"I have made you a father of many na-
tions"* [a]) in the presence of Him whom he be-
lieved—God, who gives life to the dead and calls
those things which do not exist as though they
did; 18who, contrary to hope, in hope believed, so
that he became the father of many nations, ac-
cording to what was spoken, *"So shall your de-
scendants be."* [a] 19And not being weak in faith,
he did not consider his own body, already dead
(since he was about a hundred years old), and
the deadness of Sarah's womb. 20He did not wa-
ver at the promise of God through unbelief, but
was strengthened in faith, giving glory to God,

4:17 [a]Genesis 17:5 **4:18** [a]Genesis 15:5

The Message

12 And it means further that Abraham is father of *all* people who embrace what God does for them while they are still on the "outs" with God, as yet unidentified as God's, in an "uncircumcised" condition. It is precisely these people in this condition who are called "set right by God and with God"! Abraham is also, of course, father of those who have undergone the religious rite of circumcision *not* just because of the ritual but because they were willing to live in the risky faith-embrace of God's action for them, the way Abraham lived long before he was marked by circumcision.

13-15 That famous promise God gave Abraham—that he and his children would possess the earth—was not given because of something Abraham did or would do. It was based on God's decision to put everything together for him, which Abraham then entered when he believed. If those who get what God gives them only get it by doing everything they are told to do and filling out all the right forms properly signed, that eliminates personal trust completely and turns the promise into an ironclad *contract*! That's not a holy promise; that's a business deal. A contract drawn up by a hard-nosed lawyer and with plenty of fine print only makes sure that you will never be able to collect. But if there is no contract in the first place, simply a *promise*—and God's promise at that—you can't break it.

16 This is why the fulfillment of God's promise depends entirely on trusting God and his way, and then simply embracing him and what he does. God's promise arrives as pure gift. That's the only way everyone can be sure to get in on it, those who keep the religious traditions *and* those who have never heard of them. For Abraham is father of us all. He is not our racial father—that's reading the story backward. He is our *faith* father.

17-18 We call Abraham "father" not because he got God's attention by living like a saint, but because God made something out of Abraham when he was a nobody. Isn't that what we've always read in Scripture, God saying to Abraham, "I set you up as father of many peoples"? Abraham was first named "father" and then *became* a father because he dared to trust God to do what only God could do: raise the dead to life, with a word make something out of nothing. When everything was hopeless, Abraham believed anyway, deciding to live not on the basis of what he saw he *couldn't* do but on what God said he *would* do. And so he was made father of a multitude of peoples. God himself said to him, "You're going to have a big family, Abraham!"

19-25 Abraham didn't focus on his own impotence and say, "It's hopeless. This hundred-year-old body could never father a child." Nor did he survey Sarah's decades of infertility and give up. He didn't tiptoe around God's promise asking cautiously skeptical questions. He plunged into the promise and

NEW KING JAMES VERSION

21and being fully convinced that what He had promised He was also able to perform. 22And therefore *"it was accounted to him for righteousness."*[a]

23Now it was not written for his sake alone that it was imputed to him, 24but also for us. It shall be imputed to us who believe in Him who raised up Jesus our Lord from the dead, 25who was delivered up because of our offenses, and was raised because of our justification.

FAITH TRIUMPHS IN TROUBLE

5 Therefore, having been justified by faith, we have[a] peace with God through our Lord Jesus Christ, 2through whom also we have access by faith into this grace in which we stand, and rejoice in hope of the glory of God. 3And not only *that,* but we also glory in tribulations, knowing that tribulation produces perseverance; 4and perseverance, character; and character, hope. 5Now hope does not disappoint, because the love of God has been poured out in our hearts by the Holy Spirit who was given to us.

CHRIST IN OUR PLACE

6For when we were still without strength, in due time Christ died for the ungodly. 7For scarcely for a righteous man will one die; yet perhaps for a good man someone would even dare to die. 8But God demonstrates His own love toward us, in that while we were still sinners, Christ died for us. 9Much more then, having now been justified by His blood, we shall be saved from wrath through Him. 10For if when we were enemies we were reconciled to God through the death of His Son, much more, having been reconciled, we shall be saved by His life. 11And not only *that,* but we also rejoice in God through our Lord Jesus Christ, through whom we have now received the reconciliation.

DEATH IN ADAM, LIFE IN CHRIST

12Therefore, just as through one man sin entered the world, and death through sin, and thus death spread to all men, because all sinned—

4:22 [a]Genesis 15:6 **5:1** [a]Another ancient reading is, *let us have peace.*

THE MESSAGE

came up strong, ready for God, sure that God would make good on what he had said. That's why it is said, "Abraham was declared fit before God by trusting God to set him right." But it's not just Abraham; it's also us! The same thing gets said about us when we embrace and believe the One who brought Jesus to life when the conditions were equally hopeless. The sacrificed Jesus made us fit for God, set us *right with God.*

DEVELOPING PATIENCE

1-2 5 By entering through faith into what God has always wanted to do for us—set us right with him, make us fit for him—we have it all together with God because of our Master Jesus. And that's not all: We throw open our doors to God and discover at the same moment that he has already thrown open his door to us. We find ourselves standing where we always hoped we might stand—out in the wide open spaces of God's grace and glory, standing tall and shouting our praise.

3-5 There's more to come: We continue to shout our praise even when we're hemmed in with troubles, because we know how troubles can develop passionate patience in us, and how that patience in turn forges the tempered steel of virtue, keeping us alert for whatever God will do next. In alert expectancy such as this, we're never left feeling shortchanged. Quite the contrary—we can't round up enough containers to hold everything God generously pours into our lives through the Holy Spirit!

6-8 Christ arrives right on time to make this happen. He didn't, and doesn't, wait for us to get ready. He presented himself for this sacrificial death when we were far too weak and rebellious to do anything to get ourselves ready. And even if we hadn't been so weak, we wouldn't have known what to do anyway. We can understand someone dying for a person worth dying for, and we can understand how someone good and noble could inspire us to selfless sacrifice. But God put his love on the line for us by offering his Son in sacrificial death while we were of no use whatever to him.

9-11 Now that we are set right with God by means of this sacrificial death, the consummate blood sacrifice, there is no longer a question of being at odds with God in any way. If, when we were at our worst, we were put on friendly terms with God by the sacrificial death of his Son, now that we're at our best, just think of how our lives will expand and deepen by means of his resurrection life! Now that we have actually received this amazing friendship with God, we are no longer content to simply say it in plodding prose. We sing and shout our praises to God through Jesus, the Messiah!

THE DEATH-DEALING SIN, THE LIFE-GIVING GIFT

12-14 You know the story of how Adam landed us in the dilemma we're in—first sin, then death, and no one exempt from either sin or

New King James Version

13(For until the law sin was in the world, but sin is not imputed when there is no law. 14Nevertheless death reigned from Adam to Moses, even over those who had not sinned according to the likeness of the transgression of Adam, who is a type of Him who was to come. 15But the free gift *is* not like the offense. For if by the one man's offense many died, much more the grace of God and the gift by the grace of the one Man, Jesus Christ, abounded to many. 16And the gift *is* not like *that which came* through the one who sinned. For the judgment *which came* from one *offense resulted* in condemnation, but the free gift *which came* from many offenses *resulted* in justification. 17For if by the one man's offense death reigned through the one, much more those who receive abundance of grace and of the gift of righteousness will reign in life through the One, Jesus Christ.)

18Therefore, as through one man's offense *judgment came* to all men, resulting in condemnation, even so through one Man's righteous act *the free gift came* to all men, resulting in justification of life. 19For as by one man's disobedience many were made sinners, so also by one Man's obedience many will be made righteous.

20Moreover the law entered that the offense might abound. But where sin abounded, grace abounded much more, 21so that as sin reigned in death, even so grace might reign through righteousness to eternal life through Jesus Christ our Lord.

Dead to Sin, Alive to God

6 What shall we say then? Shall we continue in sin that grace may abound? 2Certainly not! How shall we who died to sin live any longer in it? 3Or do you not know that as many of us as were baptized into Christ Jesus were baptized into His death? 4Therefore we were buried with Him through baptism into death, that just as Christ was raised from the dead by the glory of the Father, even so we also should walk in newness of life.

5For if we have been united together in the likeness of His death, certainly we also shall be *in the likeness* of *His* resurrection,

The Message

death. That sin disturbed relations with God in everything and everyone, but the extent of the disturbance was not clear until God spelled it out in detail to Moses. So death, this huge abyss separating us from God, dominated the landscape from Adam to Moses. Even those who didn't sin precisely as Adam did by disobeying a specific command of God still had to experience this termination of life, this separation from God. But Adam, who got us into this, also points ahead to the One who will get us out of it.

15-17 Yet the rescuing gift is not exactly parallel to the death-dealing sin. If one man's sin put crowds of people at the dead-end abyss of separation from God, just think what God's gift poured through one man, Jesus Christ, will do! There's no comparison between that death-dealing sin and this generous, life-giving gift. The verdict on that one sin was the death sentence; the verdict on the many sins that followed was this wonderful life sentence. If death got the upper hand through one man's wrongdoing, can you imagine the breathtaking recovery life makes, sovereign life, in those who grasp with both hands this wildly extravagant life-gift, this grand setting-everything-right, that the one man Jesus Christ provides?

18-19 Here it is in a nutshell: Just as one person did it wrong and got us in all this trouble with sin and death, another person did it right and got us out of it. But more than just getting us out of trouble, he got us into life! One man said no to God and put many people in the wrong; one man said yes to God and put many in the right.

20-21 All that passing laws against sin did was produce more lawbreakers. But sin didn't, and doesn't, have a chance in competition with the aggressive forgiveness we call *grace*. When it's sin versus grace, grace wins hands down. All sin can do is threaten us with death, and that's the end of it. Grace, because God is putting everything together again through the Messiah, invites us into life—a life that goes on and on and on, world without end.

When Death Becomes Life

1-3 6 So what do we do? Keep on sinning so God can keep on forgiving? I should hope not! If we've left the country where sin is sovereign, how can we still live in our old house there? Or didn't you realize we packed up and left there for good? That is what happened in baptism. When we went under the water, we left the old country of sin behind; when we came up out of the water, we entered into the new country of grace—a new life in a new land!

3-5 That's what baptism into the life of Jesus means. When we are lowered into the water, it is like the burial of Jesus; when we are raised up out of the water, it is like the resurrection of Jesus. Each of us is raised into a light-filled world by our Father so that we can see where we're going in our new grace-sovereign country.

NEW KING JAMES VERSION

[6]knowing this, that our old man was crucified
with *Him*, that the body of sin might be done
away with, that we should no longer be slaves of
sin. [7]For he who has died has been freed from
sin. [8]Now if we died with Christ, we believe that
we shall also live with Him, [9]knowing that
Christ, having been raised from the dead, dies
no more. Death no longer has dominion over
Him. [10]For *the death* that He died, He died to sin
once for all; but *the life* that He lives, He lives to
God. [11]Likewise you also, reckon yourselves to
be dead indeed to sin, but alive to God in Christ
Jesus our Lord.

[12]Therefore do not let sin reign in your mor-
tal body, that you should obey it in its lusts.
[13]And do not present your members *as* instru-
ments of unrighteousness to sin, but present
yourselves to God as being alive from the dead,
and your members *as* instruments of righteous-
ness to God. [14]For sin shall not have dominion
over you, for you are not under law but under
grace.

FROM SLAVES OF SIN TO SLAVES OF GOD

[15]What then? Shall we sin because we are
not under law but under grace? Certainly not!
[16]Do you not know that to whom you present
yourselves slaves to obey, you are that one's
slaves whom you obey, whether of sin *leading* to
death, or of obedience *leading* to righteousness?
[17]But God be thanked that *though* you were
slaves of sin, yet you obeyed from the heart that
form of doctrine to which you were delivered.
[18]And having been set free from sin, you became
slaves of righteousness. [19]I speak in human
terms because of the weakness of your flesh.
For just as you presented your members *as*
slaves of uncleanness, and of lawlessness *lead-
ing* to *more* lawlessness, so now present your
members *as* slaves *of* righteousness for holi-
ness.

[20]For when you were slaves of sin, you were
free in regard to righteousness. [21]What fruit did
you have then in the things of which you are
now ashamed? For the end of those things *is*
death. [22]But now having been set free from sin,
and having become slaves of God, you have
your fruit to holiness, and the end, everlasting
life. [23]For the wages of sin *is* death, but the gift
of God *is* eternal life in Christ Jesus our Lord.

THE MESSAGE

6-11 Could it be any clearer? Our old way of life was nailed to the cross with Christ, a decisive end to that sin-miserable life—no longer at sin's every beck and call! What we believe is this: If we get included in Christ's sin-conquering death, we also get included in his life-saving resurrection. We know that when Jesus was raised from the dead it was a signal of the end of death-as-the-end. Never again will death have the last word. When Jesus died, he took sin down with him, but alive he brings God down to us. From now on, think of it this way: Sin speaks a dead language that means nothing to you; God speaks your mother tongue, and you hang on every word. You are dead to sin and alive to God. That's what Jesus did.

12-14 That means you must not give sin a vote in the way you conduct your lives. Don't give it the time of day. Don't even run little errands that are connected with that old way of life. Throw yourselves wholeheartedly and full-time—remember, you've been raised from the dead!—into God's way of doing things. Sin can't tell you how to live. After all, you're not living under that old tyranny any longer. You're living in the freedom of God.

WHAT IS TRUE FREEDOM?

15-18 So, since we're out from under the old tyranny, does that mean we can live any old way we want? Since we're free in the freedom of God, can we do anything that comes to mind? Hardly. You know well enough from your own experience that there are some acts of so-called freedom that destroy freedom. Offer yourselves to sin, for instance, and it's your last free act. But offer yourselves to the ways of God and the freedom never quits. All your lives you've let sin tell you what to do. But thank God you've started listening to a new master, one whose commands set you free to live openly in *his* freedom!

19 I'm using this freedom language because it's easy to picture. You can readily recall, can't you, how at one time the more you did just what you felt like doing—not caring about others, not caring about God—the worse your life became and the less freedom you had? And how much different is it now as you live in God's freedom, your lives healed and expansive in holiness?

20-21 As long as you did what you felt like doing, ignoring God, you didn't have to bother with right thinking or right living, or right *anything* for that matter. But do you call that a free life? What did you get out of it? Nothing you're proud of now. Where did it get you? A dead end.

22-23 But now that you've found you don't have to listen to sin tell you what to do, and have discovered the delight of listening to God telling you, what a surprise! A whole, healed, put-together life right now, with more and more of life on the way! Work hard for sin your whole life and your pension is death. But God's gift is *real life*, eternal life, delivered by Jesus, our Master.

New King James Version

Freed from the Law

7 Or do you not know, brethren (for I speak to those who know the law), that the law has dominion over a man as long as he lives? [2]For the woman who has a husband is bound by the law to *her* husband as long as he lives. But if the husband dies, she is released from the law of *her* husband. [3]So then if, while *her* husband lives, she marries another man, she will be called an adulteress; but if her husband dies, she is free from that law, so that she is no adulteress, though she has married another man. [4]Therefore, my brethren, you also have become dead to the law through the body of Christ, that you may be married to another—to Him who was raised from the dead, that we should bear fruit to God. [5]For when we were in the flesh, the sinful passions which were aroused by the law were at work in our members to bear fruit to death. [6]But now we have been delivered from the law, having died to what we were held by, so that we should serve in the newness of the Spirit and not *in* the oldness of the letter.

Sin's Advantage in the Law

[7]What shall we say then? *Is* the law sin? Certainly not! On the contrary, I would not have known sin except through the law. For I would not have known covetousness unless the law had said, *"You shall not covet."* [a] [8]But sin, taking opportunity by the commandment, produced in me all *manner of* evil desire. For apart from the law sin *was* dead. [9]I was alive once without the law, but when the commandment came, sin revived and I died. [10]And the commandment, which *was* to *bring* life, I found to *bring* death. [11]For sin, taking occasion by the commandment, deceived me, and by it killed *me*. [12]Therefore the law *is* holy, and the commandment holy and just and good.

Law Cannot Save from Sin

[13]Has then what is good become death to me? Certainly not! But sin, that it might appear sin, was producing death in me through what is good, so that sin through the commandment might become exceedingly sinful.

7:7 [a]Exodus 20:17; Deuteronomy 5:21

The Message

Torn Between One Way and Another

1-3 7 You shouldn't have any trouble understanding this, friends, for you know all the ins and outs of the law—how it works and how its power touches only the living. For instance, a wife is legally tied to her husband while he lives, but if he dies, she's free. If she lives with another man while her husband is living, she's obviously an adulteress. But if he dies, she is quite free to marry another man in good conscience, with no one's disapproval.

4-6 So, my friends, this is something like what has taken place with you. When Christ died he took that entire rule-dominated way of life down with him and left it in the tomb, leaving you free to "marry" a resurrection life and bear "offspring" of faith for God. For as long as we lived that old way of life, doing whatever we felt we could get away with, sin was calling most of the shots as the old law code hemmed us in. And this made us all the more rebellious. In the end, all we had to show for it was miscarriages and stillbirths. But now that we're no longer shackled to that domineering mate of sin, and out from under all those oppressive regulations and fine print, we're free to live a new life in the freedom of God.

7 But I can hear you say, "If the law code was as bad as all that, it's no better than sin itself." That's certainly not true. The law code had a perfectly legitimate function. Without its clear guidelines for right and wrong, moral behavior would be mostly guesswork. Apart from the succinct, surgical command, "You shall not covet," I could have dressed covetousness up to look like a virtue and ruined my life with it.

8-12 Don't you remember how it was? I do, perfectly well. The law code started out as an excellent piece of work. What happened, though, was that sin found a way to pervert the command into a temptation, making a piece of "forbidden fruit" out of it. The law code, instead of being used to guide me, was used to seduce me. Without all the paraphernalia of the law code, sin looked pretty dull and lifeless, and I went along without paying much attention to it. But once sin got its hands on the law code and decked itself out in all that finery, I was fooled, and fell for it. The very command that was supposed to guide me into life was cleverly used to trip me up, throwing me headlong. So sin was plenty alive, and I was stone dead. But the law code itself is God's good and common sense, each command sane and holy counsel.

13 I can already hear your next question: "Does that mean I can't even trust what is good [that is, the law]? Is good just as dangerous as evil?" No again! Sin simply did what sin is so famous for doing: using the good as a cover to tempt me to do what would finally destroy me. By hiding within God's good commandment, sin did far more mischief than it could ever have accomplished on its own.

New King James Version

14For we know that the law is spiritual, but I am
carnal, sold under sin. 15For what I am doing, I
do not understand. For what I will to do, that I
do not practice; but what I hate, that I do. 16If,
then, I do what I will not to do, I agree with the
law that *it is* good. 17But now, *it is* no longer I
who do it, but sin that dwells in me. 18For I know
that in me (that is, in my flesh) nothing good
dwells; for to will is present with me, but *how* to
perform what is good I do not find. 19For the
good that I will *to do*, I do not do; but the evil I
will not *to do*, that I practice. 20Now if I do what
I will not *to do*, it is no longer I who do it, but sin
that dwells in me.

21I find then a law, that evil is present with
me, the one who wills to do good. 22For I delight
in the law of God according to the inward man.
23But I see another law in my members, warring
against the law of my mind, and bringing me
into captivity to the law of sin which is in my
members. 24O wretched man that I am! Who will
deliver me from this body of death? 25I thank
God—through Jesus Christ our Lord!

So then, with the mind I myself serve the law of God, but with the flesh the law of sin.

Free from Indwelling Sin

8 *There* is therefore now no condemnation to
those who are in Christ Jesus,[a] who do not
walk according to the flesh, but according to the
Spirit. 2For the law of the Spirit of life in Christ
Jesus has made me free from the law of sin and
death. 3For what the law could not do in that it
was weak through the flesh, God *did* by sending
His own Son in the likeness of sinful flesh, on
account of sin: He condemned sin in the flesh,
4that the righteous requirement of the law might
be fulfilled in us who do not walk according to
the flesh but according to the Spirit. 5For those
who live according to the flesh set their minds
on the things of the flesh, but those *who live* ac-
cording to the Spirit, the things of the Spirit.

8:1 [a]NU-Text omits the rest of this verse.

The Message

14-16 I can anticipate the response that is coming: "I know that all God's commands are spiritual, but I'm not. Isn't this also your experience?" Yes. I'm full of myself—after all, I've spent a long time in sin's prison. What I don't understand about myself is that I decide one way, but then I act another, doing things I absolutely despise. So if I can't be trusted to figure out what is best for myself and then do it, it becomes obvious that God's command is necessary.

17-20 But I need something *more*! For if I know the law but still can't keep it, and if the power of sin within me keeps sabotaging my best intentions, I obviously need help! I realize that I don't have what it takes. I can will it, but I can't *do* it. I decide to do good, but I don't *really* do it; I decide not to do bad, but then I do it anyway. My decisions, such as they are, don't result in actions. Something has gone wrong deep within me and gets the better of me every time.

21-23 It happens so regularly that it's predictable. The moment I decide to do good, sin is there to trip me up. I truly delight in God's commands, but it's pretty obvious that not all of me joins in that delight. Parts of me covertly rebel, and just when I least expect it, they take charge.

24 I've tried everything and nothing helps. I'm at the end of my rope. Is there no one who can do anything for me? Isn't that the real question?

25 The answer, thank God, is that Jesus Christ can and does. He acted to set things right in this life of contradictions where I want to serve God with all my heart and mind, but am pulled by the influence of sin to do something totally different.

The Solution Is Life on God's Terms

1-2 8 With the arrival of Jesus, the Messiah, that fateful dilemma is resolved. Those who enter into Christ's being-here-for-us no longer have to live under a continuous, low-lying black cloud. A new power is in operation. The Spirit of life in Christ, like a strong wind, has magnificently cleared the air, freeing you from a fated lifetime of brutal tyranny at the hands of sin and death.

3-4 God went for the jugular when he sent his own Son. He didn't deal with the problem as something remote and unimportant. In his Son, Jesus, he personally took on the human condition, entered the disordered mess of struggling humanity in order to set it right once and for all. The law code, weakened as it always was by fractured human nature, could never have done that.

The law always ended up being used as a Band-Aid on sin instead of a deep healing of it. And now what the law code asked for but we couldn't deliver is accomplished as we, instead of redoubling our own efforts, simply embrace what the Spirit is doing in us.

5-8 Those who think they can do it on their own end up obsessed with measuring their own moral muscle but never get around to exercising it in real life. Those who trust

NEW KING JAMES VERSION

6For to be carnally minded *is* death, but to be
spiritually minded *is* life and peace. 7Because
the carnal mind *is* enmity against God; for it is
not subject to the law of God, nor indeed can be.
8So then, those who are in the flesh cannot
please God.
9But you are not in the flesh but in the Spirit,
if indeed the Spirit of God dwells in you. Now if
anyone does not have the Spirit of Christ, he is
not His. 10And if Christ *is* in you, the body *is*
dead because of sin, but the Spirit *is* life because
of righteousness. 11But if the Spirit of Him who
raised Jesus from the dead dwells in you, He
who raised Christ from the dead will also give
life to your mortal bodies through His Spirit
who dwells in you.

SONSHIP THROUGH THE SPIRIT

12Therefore, brethren, we are debtors—not to
the flesh, to live according to the flesh. 13For if
you live according to the flesh you will die; but
if by the Spirit you put to death the deeds of the
body, you will live. 14For as many as are led by
the Spirit of God, these are sons of God. 15For
you did not receive the spirit of bondage again
to fear, but you received the Spirit of adoption
by whom we cry out, "Abba, Father." 16The Spirit
Himself bears witness with our spirit that we
are children of God, 17and if children, then
heirs—heirs of God and joint heirs with Christ,
if indeed we suffer with *Him,* that we may also
be glorified together.

FROM SUFFERING TO GLORY

18For I consider that the sufferings of this
present time are not worthy *to be compared*
with the glory which shall be revealed in us.
19For the earnest expectation of the creation ea-
gerly waits for the revealing of the sons of God.
20For the creation was subjected to futility, not
willingly, but because of Him who subjected *it*
in hope; 21because the creation itself also will be
delivered from the bondage of corruption into
the glorious liberty of the children of God. 22For
we know that the whole creation groans and
labors with birth pangs together until now. 23Not
only *that,* but we also who have the firstfruits of
the Spirit, even we ourselves groan within our-

THE MESSAGE

God's action in them find that God's Spirit is in them—living and breathing God! Obsession with self in these matters is a dead end; attention to God leads us out into the open, into a spacious, free life. Focusing on the self is the opposite of focusing on God. Anyone completely absorbed in self ignores God, ends up thinking more about self than God. That person ignores who God is and what he is doing. And God isn't pleased at being ignored.

9-11 But if God himself has taken up residence in your life, you can hardly be thinking more of yourself than of him. Anyone, of course, who has not welcomed this invisible but clearly present God, the Spirit of Christ, won't know what we're talking about. But for you who welcome him, in whom he dwells—even though you still experience all the limitations of sin—you yourself experience life on God's terms. It stands to reason, doesn't it, that if the alive-and-present God who raised Jesus from the dead moves into your life, he'll do the same thing in you that he did in Jesus, bringing you alive to himself? When God lives and breathes in you (and he does, as surely as he did in Jesus), you are delivered from that dead life. With his Spirit living in you, your body will be as alive as Christ's!

12-14 So don't you see that we don't owe this old do-it-yourself life one red cent. There's nothing in it for us, nothing at all. The best thing to do is give it a decent burial and get on with your new life. God's Spirit beckons. There are things to do and places to go!

15-17 This resurrection life you received from God is not a timid, gravetending life. It's adventurously expectant, greeting God with a childlike "What's next, Papa?" God's Spirit touches our spirits and confirms who we really are. We know who he is, and we know who we are: Father and children. And we know we are going to get what's coming to us—an unbelievable inheritance! We go through exactly what Christ goes through. If we go through the hard times with him, then we're certainly going to go through the good times with him!

18-21 That's why I don't think there's any comparison between the present hard times and the coming good times. The created world itself can hardly wait for what's coming next. Everything in creation is being more or less held back. God reins it in until both creation and all the creatures are ready and can be released at the same moment into the glorious times ahead. Meanwhile, the joyful anticipation deepens.

22-25 All around us we observe a pregnant creation. The difficult times of pain throughout the world are simply birth pangs. But it's not only around us; it's *within* us. The Spirit of God is arousing us within. We're also feeling the birth pangs. These sterile and barren bodies of ours are yearning for full deliverance. That is why waiting does not diminish

NEW KING JAMES VERSION

selves, eagerly waiting for the adoption, the redemption of our body. 24For we were saved in this hope, but hope that is seen is not hope; for why does one still hope for what he sees? 25But if we hope for what we do not see, we eagerly wait for *it* with perseverance.

26Likewise the Spirit also helps in our weaknesses. For we do not know what we should pray for as we ought, but the Spirit Himself makes intercession for us[a] with groanings which cannot be uttered. 27Now He who searches the hearts knows what the mind of the Spirit *is,* because He makes intercession for the saints according to *the will of* God.

28And we know that all things work together for good to those who love God, to those who are the called according to *His* purpose. 29For whom He foreknew, He also predestined *to be* conformed to the image of His Son, that He might be the firstborn among many brethren. 30Moreover whom He predestined, these He also called; whom He called, these He also justified; and whom He justified, these He also glorified.

GOD'S EVERLASTING LOVE

31What then shall we say to these things? If God *is* for us, who *can be* against us? 32He who did not spare His own Son, but delivered Him up for us all, how shall He not with Him also freely give us all things? 33Who shall bring a charge against God's elect? *It is* God who justifies. 34Who *is* he who condemns? *It is* Christ who died, and furthermore is also risen, who is even at the right hand of God, who also makes intercession for us. 35Who shall separate us from the love of Christ? *Shall* tribulation, or distress, or persecution, or famine, or nakedness, or peril, or sword? 36As it is written:

"For Your sake we are killed all day long;
We are accounted as sheep for the
slaughter."[a]

37Yet in all these things we are more than conquerors through Him who loved us. 38For I am persuaded that neither death nor life, nor angels nor principalities nor powers, nor things present nor things to come, 39nor height nor depth, nor any other created thing, shall be able to separate us from the love of God which is in Christ Jesus our Lord.

ISRAEL'S REJECTION OF CHRIST

9 I tell the truth in Christ, I am not lying, my conscience also bearing me witness in the Holy Spirit, 2that I have great sorrow and continual grief in my heart. 3For I could wish that I myself were accursed from Christ for my

8:26 [a]NU-Text omits *for us.* **8:36** [a]Psalm 44:22

THE MESSAGE

us, any more than waiting diminishes a preg-
nant mother. We are enlarged in the waiting.
We, of course, don't see what is enlarging us.
But the longer we wait, the larger we be-
come, and the more joyful our expectancy.
26-28 Meanwhile, the moment we get tired in
the waiting, God's Spirit is right alongside
helping us along. If we don't know how or
what to pray, it doesn't matter. He does our
praying in and for us, making prayer out of
our wordless sighs, our aching groans. He
knows us far better than we know ourselves,
knows our pregnant condition, and keeps us
present before God. That's why we can be so
sure that every detail in our lives of love for
God is worked into something good.
29-30 God knew what he was doing from the
very beginning. He decided from the outset
to shape the lives of those who love him
along the same lines as the life of his Son.
The Son stands first in the line of humanity
he restored. We see the original and in-
tended shape of our lives there in him. After
God made that decision of what his children
should be like, he followed it up by calling
people by name. After he called them by
name, he set them on a solid basis with him-
self. And then, after getting them estab-
lished, he stayed with them to the end, glori-
ously completing what he had begun.
31-39 So, what do you think? With God on our
side like this, how can we lose? If God didn't
hesitate to put everything on the line for us,
embracing our condition and exposing him-
self to the worst by sending his own Son, is
there anything else he wouldn't gladly and
freely do for us? And who would dare tangle
with God by messing with one of God's cho-
sen? Who would dare even to point a finger?
The One who died for us—who was raised
to life for us!—is in the presence of God at
this very moment sticking up for us. Do you
think anyone is going to be able to drive a
wedge between us and Christ's love for us?
There is no way! Not trouble, not hard
times, not hatred, not hunger, not homeless-
ness, not bullying threats, not backstabbing,
not even the worst sins listed in Scripture:

They kill us in cold blood because they
hate you.
We're sitting ducks; they pick us off one
by one.

None of this fazes us because Jesus loves us. I'm absolutely convinced that nothing—nothing living or dead, angelic or demonic, today or tomorrow, high or low, thinkable or unthinkable—absolutely *nothing* can get between us and God's love because of the way that Jesus our Master has embraced us.

GOD IS CALLING HIS PEOPLE

1-5 9 At the same time, you need to know that I
carry with me at all times a huge sorrow.
It's an enormous pain deep within me, and
I'm never free of it. I'm not exaggerating—
Christ and the Holy Spirit are my witnesses.

NEW KING JAMES VERSION

brethren, my countrymen[a] according to the flesh, [4]who are Israelites, to whom *pertain* the adoption, the glory, the covenants, the giving of the law, the service *of God,* and the promises; [5]of whom *are* the fathers and from whom, according to the flesh, Christ *came,* who is over all, *the* eternally blessed God. Amen.

ISRAEL'S REJECTION AND GOD'S PURPOSE

[6]But it is not that the word of God has taken no effect. For they *are* not all Israel who *are* of Israel, [7]nor *are they* all children because they are the seed of Abraham; but, *"In Isaac your seed shall be called."*[a] [8]That is, those who *are* the children of the flesh, these *are* not the children of God; but the children of the promise are counted as the seed. [9]For this *is* the word of promise: *"At this time I will come and Sarah shall have a son."*[a]

[10]And not only *this,* but when Rebecca also had conceived by one man, *even* by our father Isaac [11](for *the children* not yet being born, nor having done any good or evil, that the purpose of God according to election might stand, not of works but of Him who calls), [12]it was said to her, *"The older shall serve the younger."*[a] [13]As it is written, *"Jacob I have loved, but Esau I have hated."*[a]

ISRAEL'S REJECTION AND GOD'S JUSTICE

[14]What shall we say then? *Is there* unrighteousness with God? Certainly not! [15]For He says to Moses, *"I will have mercy on whomever I will have mercy, and I will have compassion on whomever I will have compassion."*[a] [16]So then *it is* not of him who wills, nor of him who runs, but of God who shows mercy. [17]For the Scripture says to the Pharaoh, *"For this very purpose I have raised you up, that I may show My power in you, and that My name may be declared in all the earth."*[a] [18]Therefore He has mercy on whom He wills, and whom He wills He hardens.

[19]You will say to me then, "Why does He still find fault? For who has resisted His will?" [20]But indeed, O man, who are you to reply against God? Will the thing formed say to him who formed *it,* "Why have you made me like this?" [21]Does not the potter have power over the clay, from the same lump to make one vessel for honor and another for dishonor?

[22]*What* if God, wanting to show *His* wrath and to make His power known, endured with much longsuffering the vessels of wrath prepared for destruction, [23]and that He might make known the riches of His glory on the vessels of mercy, which He had prepared beforehand for glory, [24]even us whom He called, not of the Jews only, but also of the Gentiles?

[25]As He says also in Hosea:

9:3 [a]Or *relatives* **9:7** [a]Genesis 21:12 **9:9** [a]Genesis 18:10, 14
9:12 [a]Genesis 25:23 **9:13** [a]Malachi 1:2, 3 **9:15** [a]Exodus 33:19
9:17 [a]Exodus 9:16

THE MESSAGE

It's the Israelites . . . If there were any way I could be cursed by the Messiah so they could be blessed by him, I'd do it in a minute. They're my family. I grew up with them. They had everything going for them—family, glory, covenants, revelation, worship, promises, to say nothing of being the race that produced the Messiah, the Christ, who is God over everything, always. Oh, yes!

6-9 Don't suppose for a moment, though, that God's Word has malfunctioned in some way or other. The problem goes back a long way. From the outset, not all Israelites of the flesh were Israelites of the spirit. It wasn't Abraham's sperm that gave identity here, but God's *promise.* Remember how it was put: "Your family will be defined by Isaac"? That means that Israelite identity was never racially determined by sexual transmission, but it was *God*-determined by promise. Remember that promise, "When I come back next year at this time, Sarah will have a son"?

10-13 And that's not the only time. To Rebecca, also, a promise was made that took priority over genetics. When she became pregnant by our one-of-a-kind ancestor, Isaac, and her babies were still innocent in the womb—incapable of good or bad—she received a special assurance from God. What God did in this case made it perfectly plain that his purpose is not a hit-or-miss thing dependent on what we do or don't do, but a sure thing determined by his decision, flowing steadily from his initiative. God told Rebecca, "The firstborn of your twins will take second place." Later that was turned into a stark epigram: "I loved Jacob; I hated Esau."

14-18 Is that grounds for complaining that God is unfair? Not so fast, please. God told Moses, "*I'm* in charge of mercy. *I'm* in charge of compassion." Compassion doesn't originate in our bleeding hearts or moral sweat, but in God's mercy. The same point was made when God said to Pharaoh, "I picked you as a bit player in this drama of my salvation power." All we're saying is that God has the first word, initiating the action in which we play our part for good or ill.

19 Are you going to object, "So how can God blame us for anything since he's in charge of everything? If the big decisions are already made, what say do we have in it?"

20-33 Who in the world do you think you are to second-guess God? Do you for one moment suppose any of us knows enough to call God into question? Clay doesn't talk back to the fingers that mold it, saying, "Why did you shape me like this?" Isn't it obvious that a potter has a perfect right to shape one lump of clay into a vase for holding flowers and another into a pot for cooking beans? If God needs one style of pottery especially designed to show his angry displeasure and another style carefully crafted to show his glorious goodness, isn't that all right? Either or both happens to Jews, but it also happens to the other people. Hosea put it well:

NEW KING JAMES VERSION

"I will call them My people, who were not
My people,
And her beloved, who was not beloved."[a]
26*"And it shall come to pass in the place*
where it was said to them,
'You are not My people,'
There they shall be called sons of the living
God."[a]

27Isaiah also cries out concerning Israel:[a]

"Though the number of the children of Israel
be as the sand of the sea,
The remnant will be saved.
28*For He will finish the work and cut it short*
in righteousness,
Because the LORD will make a short work
upon the earth."[a]

29And as Isaiah said before:

"Unless the LORD of Sabaoth[a] *had left us a*
seed,
We would have become like Sodom,
And we would have been made like
Gomorrah."[b]

PRESENT CONDITION OF ISRAEL

30What shall we say then? That Gentiles, who
did not pursue righteousness, have attained to
righteousness, even the righteousness of faith;
31but Israel, pursuing the law of righteousness,
has not attained to the law of righteousness.[a]
32Why? Because *they did* not *seek it* by faith, but
as it were, by the works of the law.[a] For they
stumbled at that stumbling stone. 33As it is writ-
ten:

"Behold, I lay in Zion a stumbling stone and
rock of offense,
And whoever believes on Him will not be
put to shame."[a]

ISRAEL NEEDS THE GOSPEL

10 Brethren, my heart's desire and prayer to
God for Israel[a] is that they may be saved.
2For I bear them witness that they have a zeal
for God, but not according to knowledge. 3For
they being ignorant of God's righteousness, and
seeking to establish their own righteousness,
have not submitted to the righteousness of God.

9:25 [a]Hosea 2:23 **9:26** [a]Hosea 1:10 **9:27** [a]Isaiah 10:22, 23 **9:28** [a]NU-Text reads *For the LORD will finish the work and cut it short upon the earth.* **9:29** [a]Literally, in Hebrew, *Hosts* [b]Isaiah 1:9 **9:31** [a]NU-Text omits of *righteousness.* **9:32** [a]NU-Text reads *by works.* **9:33** [a]Isaiah 8:14; 28:16 **10:1** [a]NU-Text reads *them.*

THE MESSAGE

I'll call nobodies and make them
somebodies;
I'll call the unloved and make them
beloved.
In the place where they yelled out,
"You're nobody!"
they're calling you "God's living
children."

Isaiah maintained this same emphasis:
If each grain of sand on the seashore
were numbered
and the sum labeled "chosen of God,"
They'd be numbers still, not names;
salvation comes by personal
selection.
God doesn't count us; he calls us by
name.
Arithmetic is not his focus.

Isaiah had looked ahead and spoken the truth:
If our powerful God
had not provided us a legacy of living
children,
We would have ended up like ghost
towns,
like Sodom and Gomorrah.

How can we sum this up? All those people who didn't seem interested in what God was doing actually *embraced* what God was doing as he straightened out their lives. And Israel, who seemed so interested in reading and talking about what God was doing, missed it. How could they miss it? Because instead of trusting God, *they* took over. They were absorbed in what they themselves were doing. They were so absorbed in their "God projects" that they didn't notice God right in front of them, like a huge rock in the middle of the road. And so they stumbled into him and went sprawling. Isaiah (again!) gives us the metaphor for pulling this together:

Careful! I've put a huge stone on the
road to Mount Zion,
a stone you can't get around.
But the stone is me! If you're looking
for me,
you'll find me on the way, not in the
way.

ISRAEL REDUCED TO RELIGION

1-3 10 Believe me, friends, all I want for Israel is what's best for Israel: salvation, nothing less. I want it with all my heart and pray to God for it all the time. I readily admit that the Jews are impressively energetic regarding God—but they are doing everything exactly backward. They don't seem to realize that this comprehensive setting-things-right that is salvation is *God's* business, and a most flourishing business it is. Right across the street they set up their own salvation shops and noisily hawk their wares. After all these years of refusing to really deal with God on his terms, insisting instead on making their own deals, they have nothing to show for it.

NEW KING JAMES VERSION

4For Christ *is* the end of the law for righteousness to everyone who believes.

5For Moses writes about the righteousness which is of the law, *"The man who does those things shall live by them."*[a] 6But the righteousness of faith speaks in this way, *"Do not say in your heart, 'Who will ascend into heaven?' "*[a] (that is, to bring Christ down *from above*) 7or, *" 'Who will descend into the abyss?' "*[a] (that is, to bring Christ up from the dead). 8But what does it say? *"The word is near you, in your mouth and in your heart"*[a] (that is, the word of faith which we preach): 9that if you confess with your mouth the Lord Jesus and believe in your heart that God has raised Him from the dead, you will be saved. 10For with the heart one believes unto righteousness, and with the mouth confession is made unto salvation. 11For the Scripture says, *"Whoever believes on Him will not be put to shame."*[a] 12For there is no distinction between Jew and Greek, for the same Lord over all is rich to all who call upon Him. 13For *"whoever calls on the name of the LORD shall be saved."*[a]

ISRAEL REJECTS THE GOSPEL

14How then shall they call on Him in whom they have not believed? And how shall they believe in Him of whom they have not heard? And how shall they hear without a preacher? 15And how shall they preach unless they are sent? As it is written:

"How beautiful are the feet of those who
preach the gospel of peace,[a]
Who bring glad tidings of good things!"[b]

16But they have not all obeyed the gospel. For Isaiah says, *"LORD, who has believed our report?"*[a] 17So then faith *comes* by hearing, and hearing by the word of God.

18But I say, have they not heard? Yes indeed:

"Their sound has gone out to all the earth,
And their words to the ends of the world."[a]

19But I say, did Israel not know? First Moses says:

10:5 [a]Leviticus 18:5 10:6 [a]Deuteronomy 30:12 10:7 [a]Deuteronomy 30:13 10:8 [a]Deuteronomy 30:14 10:11 [a]Isaiah 28:16 10:13 [a]Joel 2:32 10:15 [a]NU-Text omits *preach the gospel of peace, Who.* [b]Isaiah 52:7; Nahum 1:15 10:16 [a]Isaiah 53:1 10:18 [a]Psalm 19:4

THE MESSAGE

4-10 The earlier revelation was intended simply to get us ready for the Messiah, who then puts everything right for those who trust him to do it. Moses wrote that anyone who insists on using the law code to live right before God soon discovers it's not so easy—every detail of life regulated by fine print! But trusting God to shape the right living in us is a different story—no precarious climb up to heaven to recruit the Messiah, no dangerous descent into hell to rescue the Messiah. So what exactly was Moses saying?

The word that saves is right here,
as near as the tongue in your mouth,
as close as the heart in your chest.

It's the word of faith that welcomes God to go to work and set things right for us. This is the core of our preaching. Say the welcoming word to God—"Jesus is my Master"—embracing, body and soul, God's work of doing in us what he did in raising Jesus from the dead. That's it. You're not "doing" anything; you're simply calling out to God, trusting him to do it for you. That's salvation. With your whole being you embrace God setting things right, and then you say it, right out loud: "God has set everything right between him and me!"

11-13 Scripture reassures us, "No one who trusts God like this—heart and soul—will ever regret it." It's exactly the same no matter what a person's religious background may be: the same God for all of us, acting the same incredibly generous way to everyone who calls out for help. "Everyone who calls, 'Help, God!' gets help."

14-17 But how can people call for help if they don't know who to trust? And how can they know who to trust if they haven't heard of the One who can be trusted? And how can they hear if nobody tells them? And how is anyone going to tell them, unless someone is sent to do it? That's why Scripture exclaims,

A sight to take your breath away!
Grand processions of people
telling all the good things of God!

But not everybody is ready for this, ready to see and hear and act. Isaiah asked what we all ask at one time or another: "Does anyone care, God? Is anyone listening and believing a word of it?" The point is: Before you trust, you have to listen. But unless Christ's Word is preached, there's nothing to listen to.

18-21 But haven't there been plenty of opportunities for Israel to listen and understand what's going on? *Plenty*, I'd say.

Preachers' voices have gone 'round the world,
Their message to earth's seven seas.

So the big question is, Why didn't Israel understand that she had no corner on this message? Moses had it right when he predicted,

NEW KING JAMES VERSION

"I will provoke you to jealousy by those who
are not a nation,
I will move you to anger by a foolish
nation." [a]

20But Isaiah is very bold and says:

"I was found by those who did not seek Me;
I was made manifest to those who did not
ask for Me." [a]

21But to Israel he says:

"All day long I have stretched out My hands
To a disobedient and contrary people." [a]

ISRAEL'S REJECTION NOT TOTAL

11 I say then, has God cast away His people?
Certainly not! For I also am an Israelite, of
the seed of Abraham, of the tribe of Benjamin.
2God has not cast away His people whom He
foreknew. Or do you not know what the Scrip-
ture says of Elijah, how he pleads with God
against Israel, saying, 3*"LORD, they have killed*
Your prophets and torn down Your altars, and I
alone am left, and they seek my life"?[a] 4But
what does the divine response say to him? *"I*
have reserved for Myself seven thousand men
who have not bowed the knee to Baal." [a] 5Even
so then, at this present time there is a remnant
according to the election of grace. 6And if by
grace, then *it is* no longer of works; otherwise
grace is no longer grace.[a] But if *it is* of works, it
is no longer grace; otherwise work is no longer
work.
7What then? Israel has not obtained what it
seeks; but the elect have obtained it, and the rest
were blinded. 8Just as it is written:

10:19 [a]Deuteronomy 32:21 **10:20** [a]Isaiah 65:1 **10:21** [a]Isaiah 65:2 **11:3** [a]1 Kings 19:10, 14 **11:4** [a]1 Kings 19:18 **11:6** [a]NU-Text omits the rest of this verse.

THE MESSAGE

When you see God reach out to those
you consider your inferiors—
outsiders!—
you'll become insanely jealous.
When you see God reach out to people
you think are religiously stupid,
you'll throw temper tantrums.

Isaiah dared to speak out these words of God:

People found and welcomed me
who never so much as looked for me.
And I found and welcomed people
who had never even asked about me.

Then he capped it with a damning indictment:

Day after day after day,
I beckoned Israel with open arms,
And got nothing for my trouble
but cold shoulders and icy stares.

THE LOYAL MINORITY

1-2 11 Does this mean, then, that God is so fed
up with Israel that he'll have nothing
more to do with them? Hardly. Remember
that I, the one writing these things, am an Is-
raelite, a descendant of Abraham out of the
tribe of Benjamin. You can't get much more
Semitic than that! So we're not talking
about repudiation. God has been too long
involved with Israel, has too much invested,
to simply wash his hands of them.
2-6 Do you remember that time Elijah was
agonizing over this same Israel and cried
out in prayer?

God, they murdered your prophets,
They trashed your altars;
I'm the only one left and now they're
after me!

And do you remember God's answer?

I still have seven thousand who haven't
quit,
Seven thousand who are loyal to the
finish.

It's the same today. There's a fiercely loyal minority still—not many, perhaps, but probably more than you think. They're holding on, not because of what they think they're going to get out of it, but because they're convinced of God's grace and purpose in choosing them. If they were only thinking of their own immediate self-interest, they would have left long ago.
7-10 And then what happened? Well, when Is-
rael tried to be right with God on her own,
pursuing her own self-interest, she didn't
succeed. The chosen ones of God were those
who let God pursue his interest in them, and
as a result received his stamp of legitimacy.
The "self-interest Israel" became thick-
skinned toward God. Moses and Isaiah both
commented on this:

Fed up with their quarrelsome,
self-centered ways,

NEW KING JAMES VERSION

"God has given them a spirit of stupor,
Eyes that they should not see
And ears that they should not hear,
To this very day." [a]

[9]And David says:

"Let their table become a snare and a trap,
A stumbling block and a recompense to
them.
[10]*Let their eyes be darkened, so that they do*
not see,
And bow down their back always." [a]

ISRAEL'S REJECTION NOT FINAL

[11]I say then, have they stumbled that they
should fall? Certainly not! But through their fall,
to provoke them to jealousy, salvation *has come*
to the Gentiles. [12]Now if their fall *is* riches for
the world, and their failure riches for the Gen-
tiles, how much more their fullness!
[13]For I speak to you Gentiles; inasmuch as I
am an apostle to the Gentiles, I magnify my
ministry, [14]if by any means I may provoke to
jealousy *those who are* my flesh and save some
of them. [15]For if their being cast away *is* the rec-
onciling of the world, what *will* their acceptance
be but life from the dead?
[16]For if the firstfruit *is* holy, the lump *is* also
holy; and if the root *is* holy, so *are* the branches.
[17]And if some of the branches were broken off,
and you, being a wild olive tree, were grafted in
among them, and with them became a partaker
of the root and fatness of the olive tree, [18]do not
boast against the branches. But if you do boast,
remember that you do not support the root, but
the root *supports* you.
[19]You will say then, "Branches were broken
off that I might be grafted in." [20]Well *said.* Be-
cause of unbelief they were broken off, and you
stand by faith. Do not be haughty, but fear. [21]For
if God did not spare the natural branches, He
may not spare you either. [22]Therefore consider
the goodness and severity of God: on those who

11:8 [a]Deuteronomy 29:4; Isaiah 29:10 **11:10** [a]Psalm 69:22, 23

THE MESSAGE

God blurred their eyes and dulled
their ears,
Shut them in on themselves in a hall of
mirrors,
and they're there to this day.

David was upset about the same thing:
I hope they get sick eating self-serving
meals,
break a leg walking their self-serving
ways.
I hope they go blind staring in their
mirrors,
get ulcers from playing at god.

PRUNING AND GRAFTING BRANCHES

11-12 The next question is, "Are they down for the count? Are they out of this for good?" And the answer is a clear-cut *No.* Ironically when they walked out, they left the door open and the outsiders walked in. But the next thing you know, the Jews were starting to wonder if perhaps they had walked out on a good thing. Now, if their leaving triggered this worldwide coming of non-Jewish outsiders to God's kingdom, just imagine the effect of their coming back! What a homecoming!

13-15 But I don't want to go on about them. It's you, the outsiders, that I'm concerned with now. Because my personal assignment is focused on the so-called outsiders, I make as much of this as I can when I'm among my Israelite kin, the so-called *insiders,* hoping they'll realize what they're missing and want to get in on what God is doing. If their falling out initiated this worldwide coming together, their recovery is going to set off something even better: mass homecoming! If the first thing the Jews did, even though it was wrong for them, turned out for your good, just think what's going to happen when they get it right!

16-18 Behind and underneath all this there is a holy, God-planted, God-tended root. If the primary root of the tree is holy, there's bound to be some holy fruit. Some of the tree's branches were pruned and you wild olive shoots were grafted in. Yet the fact that you are now fed by that rich and holy root gives you no cause to crow over the pruned branches. Remember, you aren't feeding the root; the root is feeding you.

19-20 It's certainly possible to say, "Other branches were pruned so that *I* could be grafted in!" Well and good. But they were pruned because they were deadwood, no longer connected by belief and commitment to the root. The only reason you're on the tree is because your graft "took" when you believed, and because you're connected to that belief-nurturing root. So don't get cocky and strut your branch. Be humbly mindful of the root that keeps you lithe and green.

21-22 If God didn't think twice about taking pruning shears to the natural branches, why would he hesitate over you? He wouldn't give it a second thought. Make sure you stay alert to these qualities of gentle kindness

NEW KING JAMES VERSION

fell, severity; but toward you, goodness,[a] if you
continue in *His* goodness. Otherwise you also
will be cut off. 23And they also, if they do not
continue in unbelief, will be grafted in, for God
is able to graft them in again. 24For if you were
cut out of the olive tree which is wild by nature,
and were grafted contrary to nature into a culti-
vated olive tree, how much more will these, who
are natural *branches,* be grafted into their own
olive tree?

25For I do not desire, brethren, that you
should be ignorant of this mystery, lest you
should be wise in your own opinion, that blind-
ness in part has happened to Israel until the full-
ness of the Gentiles has come in. 26And so all Is-
rael will be saved,[a] as it is written:

"The Deliverer will come out of Zion,
And He will turn away ungodliness from
Jacob;
27*For this is My covenant with them,*
When I take away their sins."[a]

28Concerning the gospel *they are* enemies
for your sake, but concerning the election *they*
are beloved for the sake of the fathers. 29For the
gifts and the calling of God *are* irrevocable.
30For as you were once disobedient to God, yet
have now obtained mercy through their disobe-
dience, 31even so these also have now been dis-
obedient, that through the mercy shown you
they also may obtain mercy. 32For God has com-
mitted them all to disobedience, that He might
have mercy on all.

33Oh, the depth of the riches both of the wis-
dom and knowledge of God! How unsearchable
are His judgments and His ways past finding
out!

11:22 [a]NU-Text adds *of God.* 11:26 [a]Or *delivered* 11:27 [a]Isaiah 59:20, 21

THE MESSAGE

and ruthless severity that exist side by side in God—ruthless with the deadwood, gentle with the grafted shoot. But don't presume on this gentleness. The moment you become deadwood, you're out of there.

23-24 And don't get to feeling superior to those pruned branches down on the ground. If they don't persist in remaining deadwood, they could very well get grafted back in. God can do that. He can perform miracle grafts. Why, if he could graft *you*—branches cut from a tree out in the wild—into an orchard tree, he certainly isn't going to have any trouble grafting branches back into the tree they grew from in the first place. Just be glad you're in the tree, and hope for the best for the others.

A COMPLETE ISRAEL

25-29 I want to lay all this out on the table as clearly as I can, friends. This is complicated. It would be easy to misinterpret what's going on and arrogantly assume that you're royalty and they're just rabble, out on their ears for good. But that's not it at all. This hardness on the part of insider Israel toward God is temporary. Its effect is to open things up to all the outsiders so that we end up with a full house. Before it's all over, there will be a complete Israel. As it is written,

A champion will stride down from the
mountain of Zion;
he'll clean house in Jacob.
And this is my commitment to my
people:
removal of their sins.

From your point of view as you hear and embrace the good news of the Message, it looks like the Jews are God's enemies. But looked at from the long-range perspective of God's overall purpose, they remain God's oldest friends. God's gifts and God's call are under full warranty—never canceled, never rescinded.

30-32 There was a time not so long ago when you were on the outs with God. But then the Jews slammed the door on him and things opened up for you. Now *they* are on the outs. But with the door held wide open for you, they have a way back in. In one way or another, God makes sure that we all experience what it means to be outside so that he can personally open the door and welcome us back in.

33-36 Have you ever come on anything quite like this extravagant generosity of God, this deep, deep wisdom? It's way over our heads. We'll never figure it out.

Is there anyone around who can explain
God?
Anyone smart enough to tell him what to
do?
Anyone who has done him such a huge
favor
that God has to ask his advice?

New King James Version

34 *"For who has known the mind of the* LORD*?*
Or who has become His counselor?"[a]
35 *"Or who has first given to Him*
And it shall be repaid to him?"[a]

36 For of Him and through Him and to Him *are* all things, to whom *be* glory forever. Amen.

Living Sacrifices to God

12 I beseech you therefore, brethren, by the mercies of God, that you present your bodies a living sacrifice, holy, acceptable to God, *which is* your reasonable service. 2 And do not be conformed to this world, but be transformed by the renewing of your mind, that you may prove what *is* that good and acceptable and perfect will of God.

Serve God with Spiritual Gifts

3 For I say, through the grace given to me, to everyone who is among you, not to think *of himself* more highly than he ought to think, but to think soberly, as God has dealt to each one a measure of faith. 4 For as we have many members in one body, but all the members do not have the same function, 5 so we, *being* many, are one body in Christ, and individually members of one another. 6 Having then gifts differing according to the grace that is given to us, *let us use them:* if prophecy, *let us prophesy* in proportion to our faith; 7 or ministry, *let us use it* in *our* ministering; he who teaches, in teaching; 8 he who exhorts, in exhortation; he who gives, with liberality; he who leads, with diligence; he who shows mercy, with cheerfulness.

Behave Like a Christian

9 *Let* love *be* without hypocrisy. Abhor what is evil. Cling to what is good. 10 *Be* kindly affectionate to one another with brotherly love, in honor giving preference to one another;

11:34 [a]Isaiah 40:13; Jeremiah 23:18 **11:35** [a]Job 41:11

The Message

Everything comes from him;
Everything happens through him;
Everything ends up in him.
Always glory! Always praise!
Yes. Yes. Yes.

Place Your Life Before God

1-2 **12** So here's what I want you to do, God helping you: Take your everyday, ordinary life—your sleeping, eating, going-to-work, and walking-around life—and place it before God as an offering. Embracing what God does for you is the best thing you can do for him. Don't become so well-adjusted to your culture that you fit into it without even thinking. Instead, fix your attention on God. You'll be changed from the inside out. Readily recognize what he wants from you, and quickly respond to it. Unlike the culture around you, always dragging you down to its level of immaturity, God brings the best out of you, develops well-formed maturity in you.

3 I'm speaking to you out of deep gratitude for all that God has given me, and especially as I have responsibilities in relation to you. Living then, as every one of you does, in pure grace, it's important that you not misinterpret yourselves as people who are bringing this goodness to God. No, God brings it all to you. The only accurate way to understand ourselves is by what God is and by what he does for us, not by what we are and what we do for him.

4-6 In this way we are like the various parts of a human body. Each part gets its meaning from the body as a whole, not the other way around. The body we're talking about is Christ's body of chosen people. Each of us finds our meaning and function as a part of his body. But as a chopped-off finger or cut-off toe we wouldn't amount to much, would we? So since we find ourselves fashioned into all these excellently formed and marvelously functioning parts in Christ's body, let's just go ahead and be what we were made to be, without enviously or pridefully comparing ourselves with each other, or trying to be something we aren't.

6-8 If you preach, just preach God's Message, nothing else; if you help, just help, don't take over; if you teach, stick to your teaching; if you give encouraging guidance, be careful that you don't get bossy; if you're put in charge, don't manipulate; if you're called to give aid to people in distress, keep your eyes open and be quick to respond; if you work with the disadvantaged, don't let yourself get irritated with them or depressed by them. Keep a smile on your face.

9-10 Love from the center of who you are; don't fake it. Run for dear life from evil; hold on for dear life to good. Be good friends who love deeply; practice playing second fiddle.

NEW KING JAMES VERSION

11 not lagging in diligence, fervent in spirit, serving the Lord; 12 rejoicing in hope, patient in tribulation, continuing steadfastly in prayer; 13 distributing to the needs of the saints, given to hospitality.

14 Bless those who persecute you; bless and do not curse. 15 Rejoice with those who rejoice, and weep with those who weep. 16 Be of the same mind toward one another. Do not set your mind on high things, but associate with the humble. Do not be wise in your own opinion.

17 Repay no one evil for evil. Have regard for good things in the sight of all men. 18 If it is possible, as much as depends on you, live peaceably with all men. 19 Beloved, do not avenge yourselves, but *rather* give place to wrath; for it is written, *"Vengeance is Mine, I will repay,"* [a] says the Lord. 20 Therefore

"If your enemy is hungry, feed him;
If he is thirsty, give him a drink;
For in so doing you will heap coals of fire
on his head." [a]

21 Do not be overcome by evil, but overcome evil with good.

SUBMIT TO GOVERNMENT

13 Let every soul be subject to the governing authorities. For there is no authority except from God, and the authorities that exist are appointed by God. 2 Therefore whoever resists the authority resists the ordinance of God, and those who resist will bring judgment on themselves. 3 For rulers are not a terror to good works, but to evil. Do you want to be unafraid of the authority? Do what is good, and you will have praise from the same. 4 For he is God's minister to you for good. But if you do evil, be afraid; for he does not bear the sword in vain; for he is God's minister, an avenger to *execute* wrath on him who practices evil. 5 Therefore *you* must be subject, not only because of wrath but also for conscience' sake. 6 For because of this you also pay taxes, for they are God's ministers attending continually to this very thing. 7 Render therefore to all their due: taxes to whom taxes *are due,* customs to whom customs, fear to whom fear, honor to whom honor.

LOVE YOUR NEIGHBOR

8 Owe no one anything except to love one another, for he who loves another has fulfilled the law. 9 For the commandments, *"You shall not commit adultery," "You shall not murder," "You shall not steal," "You shall not bear false witness,"* [a] *"You shall not covet,"* [b] and if *there is* any other commandment, are *all* summed up in this saying, namely, *"You shall love your neighbor as yourself."* [c] 10 Love does no harm to a neighbor; therefore love *is* the fulfillment of the law.

PUT ON CHRIST

11 And *do* this, knowing the time, that now *it is* high time to awake out of sleep; for now our

12:19 [a]Deuteronomy 32:35 **12:20** [a]Proverbs 25:21, 22 **13:9** [a]NU-Text omits *"You shall not bear false witness."* [b]Exodus 20:13–15, 17; Deuteronomy 5:17–19, 21 [c]Leviticus 19:18

THE MESSAGE

11-13 Don't burn out; keep yourselves fueled and aflame. Be alert servants of the Master, cheerfully expectant. Don't quit in hard times; pray all the harder. Help needy Christians; be inventive in hospitality.

14-16 Bless your enemies; no cursing under your breath. Laugh with your happy friends when they're happy; share tears when they're down. Get along with each other; don't be stuck-up. Make friends with nobodies; don't be the great somebody.

17-19 Don't hit back; discover beauty in everyone. If you've got it in you, get along with everybody. Don't insist on getting even; that's not for you to do. "I'll do the judging," says God. "I'll take care of it."

20-21 Our Scriptures tell us that if you see your enemy hungry, go buy that person lunch, or if he's thirsty, get him a drink. Your generosity will surprise him with goodness. Don't let evil get the best of you; get the best of evil by doing good.

TO BE A RESPONSIBLE CITIZEN

1-3 **13** Be a good citizen. All governments are under God. Insofar as there is peace and order, it's God's order. So live responsibly as a citizen. If you're irresponsible to the state, then you're irresponsible with God, and God will hold you responsible. Duly constituted authorities are only a threat if you're trying to get by with something. Decent citizens should have nothing to fear.

3-5 Do you want to be on good terms with the government? Be a responsible citizen and you'll get on just fine, the government working to your advantage. But if you're breaking the rules right and left, watch out. The police aren't there just to be admired in their uniforms. God also has an interest in keeping order, and he uses them to do it. That's why you must live responsibly—not just to avoid punishment but also because it's the right way to live.

6-7 That's also why you pay taxes—so that an orderly way of life can be maintained. Fulfill your obligations as a citizen. Pay your taxes, pay your bills, respect your leaders.

8-10 Don't run up debts, except for the huge debt of love you owe each other. When you love others, you complete what the law has been after all along. The law code—don't sleep with another person's spouse, don't take someone's life, don't take what isn't yours, don't always be wanting what you don't have, and any other "don't" you can think of—finally adds up to this: Love other people as well as you do yourself. You can't go wrong when you love others. When you add up everything in the law code, the sum total is *love.*

11-14 But make sure that you don't get so absorbed and exhausted in taking care of all

NEW KING JAMES VERSION

salvation *is* nearer than when we *first* believed. [12]The night is far spent, the day is at hand. Therefore let us cast off the works of darkness, and let us put on the armor of light. [13]Let us walk properly, as in the day, not in revelry and drunkenness, not in lewdness and lust, not in strife and envy. [14]But put on the Lord Jesus Christ, and make no provision for the flesh, to *fulfill its* lusts.

THE LAW OF LIBERTY

14 Receive one who is weak in the faith, *but* not to disputes over doubtful things. [2]For one believes he may eat all things, but he who is weak eats *only* vegetables. [3]Let not him who eats despise him who does not eat, and let not him who does not eat judge him who eats; for God has received him. [4]Who are you to judge another's servant? To his own master he stands or falls. Indeed, he will be made to stand, for God is able to make him stand.

[5]One person esteems *one* day above another; another esteems every day *alike*. Let each be fully convinced in his own mind. [6]He who observes the day, observes *it* to the Lord;[a] and he who does not observe the day, to the Lord he does not observe *it*. He who eats, eats to the Lord, for he gives God thanks; and he who does not eat, to the Lord he does not eat, and gives God thanks. [7]For none of us lives to himself, and no one dies to himself. [8]For if we live, we live to the Lord; and if we die, we die to the Lord. Therefore, whether we live or die, we are the Lord's. [9]For to this end Christ died and rose[a] and lived again, that He might be Lord of both the dead and the living. [10]But why do you judge your brother? Or why do you show contempt for your brother? For we shall all stand before the judgment seat of Christ.[a] [11]For it is written:

14:6 [a]NU-Text omits the rest of this sentence. **14:9** [a]NU-Text omits *and rose*. **14:10** [a]NU-Text reads *of God*.

THE MESSAGE

your day-by-day obligations that you lose track of the time and doze off, oblivious to God. The night is about over, dawn is about to break. Be up and awake to what God is doing! God is putting the finishing touches on the salvation work he began when we first believed. We can't afford to waste a minute, must not squander these precious daylight hours in frivolity and indulgence, in sleeping around and dissipation, in bickering and grabbing everything in sight. Get out of bed and get dressed! Don't loiter and linger, waiting until the very last minute. Dress yourselves in Christ, and be up and about!

CULTIVATING GOOD RELATIONSHIPS

1 14 Welcome with open arms fellow believers who don't see things the way you do. And don't jump all over them every time they do or say something you don't agree with—even when it seems that they are strong on opinions but weak in the faith department. Remember, they have their own history to deal with. Treat them gently.

2-4 For instance, a person who has been around for a while might well be convinced that he can eat anything on the table, while another, with a different background, might assume he should only be a vegetarian and eat accordingly. But since both are guests at Christ's table, wouldn't it be terribly rude if they fell to criticizing what the other ate or didn't eat? God, after all, invited them both to the table. Do you have any business crossing people off the guest list or interfering with God's welcome? If there are corrections to be made or manners to be learned, God can handle that without your help.

5 Or, say, one person thinks that some days should be set aside as holy and another thinks that each day is pretty much like any other. There are good reasons either way. So, each person is free to follow the convictions of conscience.

6-9 What's important in all this is that if you keep a holy day, keep it for *God's* sake; if you eat meat, eat it to the glory of God and thank God for prime rib; if you're a vegetarian, eat vegetables to the glory of God and thank God for broccoli. None of us are permitted to insist on our own way in these matters. It's *God* we are answerable to—all the way from life to death and everything in between—not each other. That's why Jesus lived and died and then lived again: so that he could be our Master across the entire range of life and death, and free us from the petty tyrannies of each other.

10-12 So where does that leave you when you criticize a brother? And where does that leave you when you condescend to a sister? I'd say it leaves you looking pretty silly—or worse. Eventually, we're all going to end up kneeling side by side in the place of judgment, facing God. Your critical and condescending ways aren't going to improve your position there one bit. Read it for yourself in Scripture:

New King James Version

"As I live, says the Lord,
Every knee shall bow to Me,
And every tongue shall confess to God."[a]

[12]So then each of us shall give account of himself to God. [13]Therefore let us not judge one another anymore, but rather resolve this, not to put a stumbling block or a cause to fall in *our* brother's way.

The Law of Love

[14]I know and am convinced by the Lord Jesus that *there is* nothing unclean of itself; but to him who considers anything to be unclean, to him *it is* unclean. [15]Yet if your brother is grieved because of *your* food, you are no longer walking in love. Do not destroy with your food the one for whom Christ died. [16]Therefore do not let your good be spoken of as evil; [17]for the kingdom of God is not eating and drinking, but righteousness and peace and joy in the Holy Spirit. [18]For he who serves Christ in these things[a] *is* acceptable to God and approved by men.

[19]Therefore let us pursue the things *which make* for peace and the things by which one may edify another. [20]Do not destroy the work of God for the sake of food. All things indeed *are* pure, but *it is* evil for the man who eats with offense. [21]*It is* good neither to eat meat nor drink wine nor *do anything* by which your brother stumbles or is offended or is made weak.[a] [22]Do you have faith?[a] Have *it* to yourself before God. Happy *is* he who does not condemn himself in what he approves. [23]But he who doubts is condemned if he eats, because *he does* not *eat* from faith; for whatever *is* not from faith is sin.[a]

Bearing Others' Burdens

15 We then who are strong ought to bear with the scruples of the weak, and not to please ourselves. [2]Let each of us please *his* neighbor for *his* good, leading to edification. [3]For even Christ did not please Himself; but as it is written, *"The reproaches of those who reproached*

14:11 [a]Isaiah 45:23 **14:18** [a]NU-Text reads *this.* **14:21** [a]NU-Text omits *or is offended or is made weak.* **14:22** [a]NU-Text reads *The faith which you have—have.* **14:23** [a]M-Text puts Romans 16:25–27 here.

The Message

"As I live and breathe," God says,
"every knee will bow before me;
Every tongue will tell the honest truth
that I and only I am God."

So tend to your knitting. You've got your hands full just taking care of your own life before God.

13-14 Forget about deciding what's right for each other. Here's what you need to be concerned about: that you don't get in the way of someone else, making life more difficult than it already is. I'm convinced—Jesus convinced me!—that everything as it is in itself is holy. We, of course, by the way we treat it or talk about it, can contaminate it.

15-16 If you confuse others by making a big issue over what they eat or don't eat, you're no longer a companion with them in love, are you? These, remember, are persons for whom Christ died. Would you risk sending them to hell over an item in their diet? Don't you dare let a piece of God-blessed food become an occasion of soul-poisoning!

17-18 God's kingdom isn't a matter of what you put in your stomach, for goodness' sake. It's what God does with your life as he sets it right, puts it together, and completes it with joy. Your task is to single-mindedly serve Christ. Do that and you'll kill two birds with one stone: pleasing the God above you and proving your worth to the people around you.

19-21 So let's agree to use all our energy in getting along with each other. Help others with encouraging words; don't drag them down by finding fault. You're certainly not going to permit an argument over what is served or not served at supper to wreck God's work among you, are you? I said it before and I'll say it again: All food is good, but it can turn bad if you use it badly, if you use it to trip others up and send them sprawling. When you sit down to a meal, your primary concern should not be to feed your own face but to share the life of Jesus. So be sensitive and courteous to the others who are eating. Don't eat or say or do things that might interfere with the free exchange of love.

22-23 Cultivate your own relationship with God, but don't impose it on others. You're fortunate if your behavior and your belief are coherent. But if you're not sure, if you notice that you are acting in ways inconsistent with what you believe—some days trying to impose your opinions on others, other days just trying to please them—then you know that you're out of line. If the way you live isn't consistent with what you believe, then it's wrong.

1-2 **15** Those of us who are strong and able in the faith need to step in and lend a hand to those who falter, and not just do what is most convenient for us. Strength is for service, not status. Each one of us needs to look after the good of the people around us, asking ourselves, "How can I help?"

3-6 That's exactly what Jesus did. He didn't make it easy for himself by avoiding people's troubles, but waded right in and helped

NEW KING JAMES VERSION

You fell on Me."[a] [4]For whatever things were written before were written for our learning, that we through the patience and comfort of the Scriptures might have hope. [5]Now may the God of patience and comfort grant you to be like-minded toward one another, according to Christ Jesus, [6]that you may with one mind *and* one mouth glorify the God and Father of our Lord Jesus Christ.

GLORIFY GOD TOGETHER

[7]Therefore receive one another, just as Christ also received us,[a] to the glory of God. [8]Now I say that Jesus Christ has become a servant to the circumcision for the truth of God, to confirm the promises *made* to the fathers, [9]and that the Gentiles might glorify God for *His* mercy, as it is written:

"For this reason I will confess to You among
the Gentiles,
And sing to Your name."[a]

[10]And again he says:

"Rejoice, O Gentiles, with His people!"[a]

[11]And again:

"Praise the LORD, all you Gentiles!
Laud Him, all you peoples!"[a]

[12]And again, Isaiah says:

"There shall be a root of Jesse;
And He who shall rise to reign over the
Gentiles,
In Him the Gentiles shall hope."[a]

[13]Now may the God of hope fill you with all joy and peace in believing, that you may abound in hope by the power of the Holy Spirit.

FROM JERUSALEM TO ILLYRICUM

[14]Now I myself am confident concerning you, my brethren, that you also are full of goodness, filled with all knowledge, able also to admonish one another.[a] [15]Nevertheless, brethren, I have written more boldly to you on *some* points, as reminding you, because of the grace given to me by God, [16]that I might be a minister of Jesus Christ to the Gentiles, ministering the gospel of God, that the offering of the Gentiles might be acceptable, sanctified by the Holy Spirit. [17]Therefore I have reason to glory in Christ Jesus in the things *which pertain* to God. [18]For I will not dare to speak of any of those things

15:3 [a]Psalm 69:9 **15:7** [a]NU-Text and M-Text read *you.* **15:9** [a]2 Samuel 22:50; Psalm 18:49 **15:10** [a]Deuteronomy 32:43 **15:11** [a]Psalm 117:1 **15:12** [a]Isaiah 11:10 **15:14** [a]M-Text reads *others.*

THE MESSAGE

out. "I took on the troubles of the troubled," is the way Scripture puts it. Even if it was written in Scripture long ago, you can be sure it's written for *us*. God wants the combination of his steady, constant calling and warm, personal counsel in Scripture to come to characterize *us*, keeping us alert for whatever he will do next. May our dependably steady and warmly personal God develop maturity in you so that you get along with each other as well as Jesus gets along with us all. Then we'll be a choir—not our voices only, but our very lives singing in harmony in a stunning anthem to the God and Father of our Master Jesus!

7-13 So reach out and welcome one another to God's glory. Jesus did it; now *you* do it! Jesus, staying true to God's purposes, reached out in a special way to the Jewish insiders so that the old ancestral promises would come true for them. As a result, the non-Jewish outsiders have been able to experience mercy and to show appreciation to God. Just think of all the Scriptures that will come true in what we do! For instance:

Then I'll join outsiders in a hymn-sing;
I'll sing to your name!

And this one:

Outsiders and insiders, rejoice together!

And again:

People of all nations, celebrate God!
All colors and races, give hearty praise!

And Isaiah's word:

There's the root of our ancestor Jesse,
breaking through the earth and
growing tree tall,
Tall enough for everyone everywhere to
see and take hope!

Oh! May the God of green hope fill you up with joy, fill you up with peace, so that your believing lives, filled with the life-giving energy of the Holy Spirit, will brim over with hope!

14-16 Personally, I've been completely satisfied with who you are and what you are doing. You seem to me to be well-motivated and well-instructed, quite capable of guiding and advising one another. So, my dear friends, don't take my rather bold and blunt language as criticism. It's not criticism. I'm simply underlining how very much I need your help in carrying out this highly focused assignment God gave me, this priestly and gospel work of serving the spiritual needs of the non-Jewish outsiders so they can be presented as an acceptable offering to God, made whole and holy by God's Holy Spirit.

17-21 Looking back over what has been accomplished and what I have observed, I must say I am most pleased—in the context of Jesus, I'd even say *proud*, but only in that context. I have no interest in giving you a chatty

NEW KING JAMES VERSION

which Christ has not accomplished through me, in word and deed, to make the Gentiles obedient— 19in mighty signs and wonders, by the power of the Spirit of God, so that from Jerusalem and round about to Illyricum I have fully preached the gospel of Christ. 20And so I have made it my aim to preach the gospel, not where Christ was named, lest I should build on another man's foundation, 21but as it is written:

"To whom He was not announced, they shall see;
And those who have not heard shall understand."[a]

PLAN TO VISIT ROME

22For this reason I also have been much hindered from coming to you. 23But now no longer having a place in these parts, and having a great desire these many years to come to you, 24whenever I journey to Spain, I shall come to you.[a] For I hope to see you on my journey, and to be helped on my way there by you, if first I may enjoy your *company* for a while. 25But now I am going to Jerusalem to minister to the saints. 26For it pleased those from Macedonia and Achaia to make a certain contribution for the poor among the saints who are in Jerusalem. 27It pleased them indeed, and they are their debtors. For if the Gentiles have been partakers of their spiritual things, their duty is also to minister to them in material things. 28Therefore, when I have performed this and have sealed to them this fruit, I shall go by way of you to Spain. 29But I know that when I come to you, I shall come in the fullness of the blessing of the gospel[a] of Christ.

30Now I beg you, brethren, through the Lord Jesus Christ, and through the love of the Spirit, that you strive together with me in prayers to God for me, 31that I may be delivered from those in Judea who do not believe, and that my service for Jerusalem may be acceptable to the saints, 32that I may come to you with joy by the will of God, and may be refreshed together with you. 33Now the God of peace *be* with you all. Amen.

SISTER PHOEBE COMMENDED

16 I commend to you Phoebe our sister, who is a servant of the church in Cenchrea, 2that you may receive her in the Lord in a manner worthy of the saints, and assist her in whatever business she has need of you; for indeed she has been a helper of many and of myself also.

15:21 [a]Isaiah 52:15 **15:24** [a]NU-Text omits *I shall come to you* (and joins *Spain* with the next sentence). **15:29** [a]NU-Text omits *of the gospel.*

THE MESSAGE

account of my adventures, only the wondrously powerful and transformingly present words and deeds of Christ in me that triggered a believing response among the outsiders. In such ways I have trailblazed a preaching of the Message of Jesus all the way from Jerusalem far into northwestern Greece. This has all been pioneer work, bringing the Message only into those places where Jesus was not yet known and worshiped. My text has been,

Those who were never told of him—
they'll see him!
Those who've never heard of him—
they'll get the message!

22-24 And that's why it has taken me so long to finally get around to coming to you. But now that there is no more pioneering work to be done in these parts, and since I have looked forward to seeing you for many years, I'm planning my visit. I'm headed for Spain, and expect to stop off on the way to enjoy a good visit with you, and eventually have you send me off with God's blessing.

25-29 First, though, I'm going to Jerusalem to deliver a relief offering to the followers of Jesus there. The Greeks—all the way from the Macedonians in the north to the Achaians in the south—decided they wanted to take up a collection for the poor among the believers in Jerusalem. They were happy to do this, but it was also their duty. Seeing that they got in on all the spiritual gifts that flowed out of the Jerusalem community so generously, it is only right that they do what they can to relieve their poverty. As soon as I have done this—personally handed over this "fruit basket"—I'm off to Spain, with a stopover with you in Rome. My hope is that my visit with you is going to be one of Christ's more extravagant blessings.

30-33 I have one request, dear friends: Pray for me. Pray strenuously with and for me—to God the Father, through the power of our Master Jesus, through the love of the Spirit—that I will be delivered from the lions' den of unbelievers in Judea. Pray also that my relief offering to the Jerusalem believers will be accepted in the spirit in which it is given. Then, God willing, I'll be on my way to you with a light and eager heart, looking forward to being refreshed by your company. God's peace be with all of you. Oh, yes!

1-2 **16** Be sure to welcome our friend Phoebe in the way of the Master, with all the generous hospitality we Christians are famous for. I heartily endorse both her and her work. She's a key representative of the church at Cenchrea. Help her out in whatever she asks. She deserves anything you can do for her. She's helped many a person, including me.

New King James Version

Greeting Roman Saints

3 Greet Priscilla and Aquila, my fellow workers in Christ Jesus, 4 who risked their own necks for my life, to whom not only I give thanks, but also all the churches of the Gentiles. 5 Likewise *greet* the church that is in their house.

Greet my beloved Epaenetus, who is the firstfruits of Achaia[a] to Christ. 6 Greet Mary, who labored much for us. 7 Greet Andronicus and Junia, my countrymen and my fellow prisoners, who are of note among the apostles, who also were in Christ before me.

8 Greet Amplias, my beloved in the Lord. 9 Greet Urbanus, our fellow worker in Christ, and Stachys, my beloved. 10 Greet Apelles, approved in Christ. Greet those who are of the *household* of Aristobulus. 11 Greet Herodion, my countryman.[a] Greet those who are of the *household* of Narcissus who are in the Lord.

12 Greet Tryphena and Tryphosa, who have labored in the Lord. Greet the beloved Persis, who labored much in the Lord. 13 Greet Rufus, chosen in the Lord, and his mother and mine. 14 Greet Asyncritus, Phlegon, Hermas, Patrobas, Hermes, and the brethren who are with them. 15 Greet Philologus and Julia, Nereus and his sister, and Olympas, and all the saints who are with them.

16 Greet one another with a holy kiss. The[a] churches of Christ greet you.

Avoid Divisive Persons

17 Now I urge you, brethren, note those who cause divisions and offenses, contrary to the doctrine which you learned, and avoid them. 18 For those who are such do not serve our Lord Jesus[a] Christ, but their own belly, and by smooth words and flattering speech deceive the hearts of the simple. 19 For your obedience has become known to all. Therefore I am glad on your behalf; but I want you to be wise in what is good, and simple concerning evil. 20 And the God of peace will crush Satan under your feet shortly.

The grace of our Lord Jesus Christ *be* with you. Amen.

Greetings from Paul's Friends

21 Timothy, my fellow worker, and Lucius, Jason, and Sosipater, my countrymen, greet you.

22 I, Tertius, who wrote *this* epistle, greet you in the Lord.

16:5 [a]NU-Text reads *Asia.* **16:11** [a]Or *relative* **16:16** [a]NU-Text reads *All the churches.* **16:18** [a]NU-Text and M-Text omit *Jesus.*

The Message

3-5 Say hello to Priscilla and Aquila, who have worked hand in hand with me in serving Jesus. They once put their lives on the line for me. And I'm not the only one grateful to them. All the non-Jewish gatherings of believers also owe them plenty, to say nothing of the church that meets in their house.

Hello to my dear friend Epenetus. He was the very first follower of Jesus in the province of Asia.

6 Hello to Mary. What a worker she has turned out to be!

7 Hello to my cousins Andronicus and Junias. We once shared a jail cell. They were believers in Christ before I was. Both of them are outstanding leaders.

8 Hello to Ampliatus, my good friend in the family of God.

9 Hello to Urbanus, our companion in Christ's work, and my good friend Stachys.

10 Hello to Apelles, a tried-and-true veteran in following Christ.

Hello to the family of Aristobulus.

11 Hello to my cousin Herodion.

Hello to those who belong to the Lord from the family of Narcissus.

12 Hello to Tryphena and Tryphosa—such diligent women in serving the Master.

Hello to Persis, a dear friend and hard worker in Christ.

13 Hello to Rufus—a good choice by the Master!—and his mother. She has also been a dear mother to me.

14 Hello to Asyncritus, Phlegon, Hermes, Patrobas, Hermas, and also to all of their families.

15 Hello to Philologus, Julia, Nereus and his sister, and Olympas—and all the followers of Jesus who live with them.

16 Holy embraces all around! All the churches of Christ send their warmest greetings!

17-18 One final word of counsel, friends. Keep a sharp eye out for those who take bits and pieces of the teaching that you learned and then use them to make trouble. Give these people a wide berth. They have no intention of living for our Master Christ. They're only in this for what they can get out of it, and aren't above using pious sweet talk to dupe unsuspecting innocents.

19-20 And so while there has never been any question about your honesty in these matters—I couldn't be more proud of you!—I want you also to be smart, making sure every "good" thing is the *real* thing. Don't be gullible in regard to smooth-talking evil. Stay alert like this, and before you know it the God of peace will come down on Satan with both feet, stomping him into the dirt. Enjoy the best of Jesus!

21 And here are some more greetings from our end. Timothy, my partner in this work, Lucius, and my cousins Jason and Sosipater all said to tell you hello.

22 I, Tertius, who wrote this letter at Paul's dictation, send you my personal greetings.

NEW KING JAMES VERSION

[23]Gaius, my host and *the host* of the whole church, greets you. Erastus, the treasurer of the city, greets you, and Quartus, a brother. [24]The grace of our Lord Jesus Christ *be* with you all. Amen.[a]

BENEDICTION

[25]Now to Him who is able to establish you according to my gospel and the preaching of Jesus Christ, according to the revelation of the mystery kept secret since the world began [26]but now made manifest, and by the prophetic Scriptures made known to all nations, according to the commandment of the everlasting God, for obedience to the faith— [27]to God, alone wise, *be* glory through Jesus Christ forever. Amen.[a]

16:24 [a]NU-Text omits this verse. **16:27** [a]M-Text puts Romans 16:25–27 after Romans 14:23.

THE MESSAGE

23 Gaius, who is host here to both me and the whole church, wants to be remembered to you.

Erastus, the city treasurer, and our good friend Quartus send their greetings.

25-26 All of our praise rises to the One who is strong enough to make *you* strong, exactly as preached in Jesus Christ, precisely as revealed in the mystery kept secret for so long but now an open book through the prophetic Scriptures. All the nations of the world can now know the truth and be brought into obedient belief, carrying out the orders of God, who got all this started, down to the very last letter.

27 All our praise is focused through Jesus on this incomparably wise God! Yes!

1 CORINTHIANS

NEW KING JAMES VERSION

GREETING

1 Paul, called *to be* an apostle of Jesus Christ through the will of God, and Sosthenes *our* brother,

2To the church of God which is at Corinth, to those who are sanctified in Christ Jesus, called *to be* saints, with all who in every place call on the name of Jesus Christ our Lord, both theirs and ours:

3Grace to you and peace from God our Father and the Lord Jesus Christ.

SPIRITUAL GIFTS AT CORINTH

4I thank my God always concerning you for the grace of God which was given to you by Christ Jesus, 5that you were enriched in everything by Him in all utterance and all knowledge, 6even as the testimony of Christ was confirmed in you, 7so that you come short in no gift, eagerly waiting for the revelation of our Lord Jesus Christ, 8who will also confirm you to the end, *that you may be* blameless in the day of our Lord Jesus Christ. 9God *is* faithful, by whom you were called into the fellowship of His Son, Jesus Christ our Lord.

SECTARIANISM IS SIN

10Now I plead with you, brethren, by the name of our Lord Jesus Christ, that you all speak the same thing, and *that* there be no divisions among you, but *that* you be perfectly joined together in the same mind and in the same judgment. 11For it has been declared to me concerning you, my brethren, by those of Chloe's *household,* that there are contentions among you. 12Now I say this, that each of you says, "I am of Paul," or "I am of Apollos," or "I am of Cephas," or "I am of Christ." 13Is Christ divided? Was Paul crucified for you? Or were you baptized in the name of Paul?

14I thank God that I baptized none of you except Crispus and Gaius, 15lest anyone should say that I had baptized in my own name. 16Yes, I also baptized the household of Stephanas. Besides, I do not know whether I baptized any other. 17For Christ did not send me to baptize, but to preach the gospel, not with wisdom of words, lest the cross of Christ should be made of no effect.

THE MESSAGE

1-2 I, Paul, have been called and sent by Jesus, the Messiah, according to God's plan, along with my friend Sosthenes. I send this letter to you in God's church at Corinth, believers cleaned up by Jesus and set apart for a God-filled life. I include in my greeting all who call out to Jesus, wherever they live. He's their Master as well as ours!

3 May all the gifts and benefits that come from God our Father, and the Master, Jesus Christ, be yours.

4-6 Every time I think of you—and I think of you often!—I thank God for your lives of free and open access to God, given by Jesus. There's no end to what has happened in you—it's beyond speech, beyond knowledge. The evidence of Christ has been clearly verified in your lives.

7-9 Just think—you don't need a thing, you've got it all! All God's gifts are right in front of you as you wait expectantly for our Master Jesus to arrive on the scene for the Finale. And not only that, but God himself is right alongside to keep you steady and on track until things are all wrapped up by Jesus. God, who got you started in this spiritual adventure, shares with us the life of his Son and our Master Jesus. He will never give up on you. Never forget that.

THE CROSS: THE IRONY OF GOD'S WISDOM

10 I have a serious concern to bring up with you, my friends, using the authority of Jesus, our Master. I'll put it as urgently as I can: You *must* get along with each other. You must learn to be considerate of one another, cultivating a life in common.

11-12 I bring this up because some from Chloe's family brought a most disturbing report to my attention—that you're fighting among yourselves! I'll tell you exactly what I was told: You're all picking sides, going around saying, "I'm on Paul's side," or "I'm for Apollos," or "Peter is my man," or "I'm in the Messiah group."

13-16 I ask you, "Has the Messiah been chopped up in little pieces so we can each have a relic all our own? Was Paul crucified for you? Was a single one of you baptized in Paul's name?" I was not involved with any of your baptisms—except for Crispus and Gaius—and on getting this report, I'm sure glad I wasn't. At least no one can go around saying he was baptized in my name. (Come to think of it, I also baptized Stephanas's family, but as far as I can recall, that's it.)

17 God didn't send me out to collect a following for myself, but to preach the Message of what he has done, collecting a following for him. And he didn't send me to do it with a lot of fancy rhetoric of my own, lest the powerful action at the center—Christ on the Cross—be trivialized into mere words.

New King James Version

Christ the Power and Wisdom of God

18For the message of the cross is foolishness to those who are perishing, but to us who are being saved it is the power of God. 19For it is written:

> *"I will destroy the wisdom of the wise,*
> *And bring to nothing the understanding of the prudent."*[a]

20Where *is* the wise? Where *is* the scribe? Where *is* the disputer of this age? Has not God made foolish the wisdom of this world? 21For since, in the wisdom of God, the world through wisdom did not know God, it pleased God through the foolishness of the message preached to save those who believe. 22For Jews request a sign, and Greeks seek after wisdom; 23but we preach Christ crucified, to the Jews a stumbling block and to the Greeks[a] foolishness, 24but to those who are called, both Jews and Greeks, Christ the power of God and the wisdom of God. 25Because the foolishness of God is wiser than men, and the weakness of God is stronger than men.

Glory Only in the Lord

26For you see your calling, brethren, that not many wise according to the flesh, not many mighty, not many noble, *are called.* 27But God has chosen the foolish things of the world to put to shame the wise, and God has chosen the weak things of the world to put to shame the things which are mighty; 28and the base things of the world and the things which are despised God has chosen, and the things which are not, to bring to nothing the things that are, 29that no flesh should glory in His presence. 30But of Him you are in Christ Jesus, who became for us wisdom from God—and righteousness and sanctification and redemption— 31that, as it is written, *"He who glories, let him glory in the LORD."*[a]

Christ Crucified

2 And I, brethren, when I came to you, did not come with excellence of speech or of wisdom declaring to you the testimony[a] of God. 2For I determined not to know anything among you except Jesus Christ and Him crucified. 3I was with you in weakness, in fear, and in much trembling. 4And my speech and my preaching *were* not with persuasive words of human[a] wisdom, but in demonstration of the Spirit and of power, 5that your faith should not be in the wisdom of men but in the power of God.

Spiritual Wisdom

6However, we speak wisdom among those who are mature, yet not the wisdom of this age,

1:19 [a]Isaiah 29:14 **1:23** [a]NU-Text reads *Gentiles.* **1:31** [a]Jeremiah 9:24 **2:1** [a]NU-Text reads *mystery.* **2:4** [a]NU-Text omits *human.*

The Message

18-21 The Message that points to Christ on the Cross seems like sheer silliness to those hellbent on destruction, but for those on the way of salvation it makes perfect sense. This is the way God works, and most powerfully as it turns out. It's written,

> I'll turn conventional wisdom on its head,
> I'll expose so-called experts as crackpots.

So where can you find someone truly wise, truly educated, truly intelligent in this day and age? Hasn't God exposed it all as pretentious nonsense? Since the world in all its fancy wisdom never had a clue when it came to knowing God, God in his wisdom took delight in using what the world considered dumb—*preaching*, of all things!—to bring those who trust him into the way of salvation.

22-25 While Jews clamor for miraculous demonstrations and Greeks go in for philosophical wisdom, we go right on proclaiming Christ, the Crucified. Jews treat this like an *anti*-miracle—and Greeks pass it off as absurd. But to us who are personally called by God himself—both Jews and Greeks—Christ is God's ultimate miracle and wisdom all wrapped up in one. Human wisdom is so tinny, so impotent, next to the seeming absurdity of God. Human strength can't begin to compete with God's "weakness."

26-31 Take a good look, friends, at who you were when you got called into this life. I don't see many of "the brightest and the best" among you, not many influential, not many from high-society families. Isn't it obvious that God deliberately chose men and women that the culture overlooks and exploits and abuses, chose these "nobodies" to expose the hollow pretensions of the "somebodies"? That makes it quite clear that none of you can get by with blowing your own horn before God. Everything that we have—right thinking and right living, a clean slate and a fresh start—comes from God by way of Jesus Christ. That's why we have the saying, "If you're going to blow a horn, blow a trumpet for God."

1-2 **2** You'll remember, friends, that when I first came to you to let you in on God's master stroke, I didn't try to impress you with polished speeches and the latest philosophy. I deliberately kept it plain and simple: first Jesus and who he is; then Jesus and what he did—Jesus crucified.

3-5 I was unsure of how to go about this, and felt totally inadequate—I was scared to death, if you want the truth of it—and so nothing I said could have impressed you or anyone else. But the Message came through anyway. God's Spirit and God's power did it, which made it clear that your life of faith is a response to God's power, not to some fancy mental or emotional footwork by me or anyone else.

6-10 We, of course, have plenty of wisdom to pass on to you once you get your feet on

NEW KING JAMES VERSION

nor of the rulers of this age, who are coming to
nothing. 7But we speak the wisdom of God in a
mystery, the hidden *wisdom* which God or-
dained before the ages for our glory, 8which
none of the rulers of this age knew; for had they
known, they would not have crucified the Lord
of glory.
9But as it is written:

> *"Eye has not seen, nor ear heard,*
> *Nor have entered into the heart of man*
> *The things which God has prepared for*
> *those who love Him."*[a]

10But God has revealed *them* to us through His
Spirit. For the Spirit searches all things, yes, the
deep things of God. 11For what man knows the
things of a man except the spirit of the man
which is in him? Even so no one knows the
things of God except the Spirit of God. 12Now
we have received, not the spirit of the world, but
the Spirit who is from God, that we might know
the things that have been freely given to us by
God.
13These things we also speak, not in words
which man's wisdom teaches but which the
Holy[a] Spirit teaches, comparing spiritual things
with spiritual. 14But the natural man does not re-
ceive the things of the Spirit of God, for they are
foolishness to him; nor can he know *them*, be-
cause they are spiritually discerned. 15But he
who is spiritual judges all things, yet he himself
is *rightly* judged by no one. 16For *"who has
known the mind of the LORD that he may in-
struct Him?"*[a] But we have the mind of Christ.

SECTARIANISM IS CARNAL

3 And I, brethren, could not speak to you as to
spiritual *people* but as to carnal, as to babes
in Christ. 2I fed you with milk and not with solid
food; for until now you were not able *to receive
it*, and even now you are still not able; 3for you
are still carnal. For where *there are* envy, strife,
and divisions among you, are you not carnal
and behaving like *mere* men? 4For when one
says, "I am of Paul," and another, "I *am* of Apol-
los," are you not carnal?

2:9 [a]Isaiah 64:4 **2:13** [a]NU-Text omits *Holy.* **2:16** [a]Isaiah 40:13

THE MESSAGE

firm spiritual ground, but it's not popular wisdom, the fashionable wisdom of high-priced experts that will be out-of-date in a year or so. God's wisdom is something mysterious that goes deep into the interior of his purposes. You don't find it lying around on the surface. It's not the latest message, but more like the oldest—what God determined as the way to bring out his best in us, long before we ever arrived on the scene. The experts of our day haven't a clue about what this eternal plan is. If they had, they wouldn't have killed the Master of the God-designed life on a cross. That's why we have this Scripture text:

> No one's ever seen or heard anything
> like this,
> Never so much as imagined anything
> quite like it—
> What God has arranged for those who
> love him.

But *you've* seen and heard it because God by his Spirit has brought it all out into the open before you.

10-13 The Spirit, not content to flit around on the surface, dives into the depths of God, and brings out what God planned all along. Who ever knows what you're thinking and planning except you yourself? The same with God—except that he not only knows what he's thinking, but he lets *us* in on it. God offers a full report on the gifts of life and salvation that he is giving us. We don't have to rely on the world's guesses and opinions. We didn't learn this by reading books or going to school; we learned it from God, who taught us person-to-person through Jesus, and we're passing it on to you in the same firsthand, personal way.

14-16 The unspiritual self, just as it is by nature, can't receive the gifts of God's Spirit. There's no capacity for them. They seem like so much silliness. Spirit can be known only by spirit—God's Spirit and our spirits in open communion. Spiritually alive, we have access to everything God's Spirit is doing, and can't be judged by unspiritual critics. Isaiah's question, "Is there anyone around who knows God's Spirit, anyone who knows what he is doing?" has been answered: Christ knows, and we have Christ's Spirit.

1-4 3 But for right now, friends, I'm completely frustrated by your unspiritual dealings with each other and with God. You're acting like infants in relation to Christ, capable of nothing much more than nursing at the breast. Well, then, I'll nurse you since you don't seem capable of anything more. As long as you grab for what makes you feel good or makes you look important, are you really much different than a babe at the breast, content only when everything's going your way? When one of you says, "I'm on Paul's side," and another says, "I'm for Apollos," aren't you being totally infantile?

New King James Version

Watering, Working, Warning

5Who then is Paul, and who *is* Apollos, but ministers through whom you believed, as the Lord gave to each one? 6I planted, Apollos watered, but God gave the increase. 7So then neither he who plants is anything, nor he who waters, but God who gives the increase. 8Now he who plants and he who waters are one, and each one will receive his own reward according to his own labor.

9For we are God's fellow workers; you are God's field, *you are* God's building. 10According to the grace of God which was given to me, as a wise master builder I have laid the foundation, and another builds on it. But let each one take heed how he builds on it. 11For no other foundation can anyone lay than that which is laid, which is Jesus Christ. 12Now if anyone builds on this foundation *with* gold, silver, precious stones, wood, hay, straw, 13each one's work will become clear; for the Day will declare it, because it will be revealed by fire; and the fire will test each one's work, of what sort it is. 14If anyone's work which he has built on *it* endures, he will receive a reward. 15If anyone's work is burned, he will suffer loss; but he himself will be saved, yet so as through fire.

16Do you not know that you are the temple of God and *that* the Spirit of God dwells in you? 17If anyone defiles the temple of God, God will destroy him. For the temple of God is holy, which *temple* you are.

Avoid Worldly Wisdom

18Let no one deceive himself. If anyone among you seems to be wise in this age, let him become a fool that he may become wise. 19For the wisdom of this world is foolishness with God. For it is written, *"He catches the wise in their own craftiness"*;[a] 20and again, *"The LORD knows the thoughts of the wise, that they are futile."*[a] 21Therefore let no one boast in men. For all things are yours: 22whether Paul or Apollos or Cephas, or the world or life or death, or things present or things to come—all are yours. 23And you *are* Christ's, and Christ *is* God's.

Stewards of the Mysteries of God

4 Let a man so consider us, as servants of Christ and stewards of the mysteries of God. 2Moreover it is required in stewards that one be found faithful. 3But with me it is a very small thing that I should be judged by you or by a human court.[a] In fact, I do not even judge myself. 4For I know of nothing against myself, yet I am not justified by this; but He who judges me is the

3:19 [a]Job 5:13 **3:20** [a]Psalm 94:11 **4:3** [a]Literally *day*

The Message

5-9 Who do you think Paul is, anyway? Or Apollos, for that matter? Servants, both of us—servants who waited on you as you gradually learned to entrust your lives to our mutual Master. We each carried out our servant assignment. I planted the seed, Apollos watered the plants, but *God* made you grow. It's not the one who plants or the one who waters who is at the center of this process but God, who makes things grow. Planting and watering are menial servant jobs at minimum wages. What makes them worth doing is the God we are serving. You happen to be God's field in which we are working.

9-15 Or, to put it another way, you are God's house. Using the gift God gave me as a good architect, I designed blueprints; Apollos is putting up the walls. Let each carpenter who comes on the job take care to build on the foundation! Remember, there is only one foundation, the one already laid: Jesus Christ. Take particular care in picking out your building materials. Eventually there is going to be an inspection. If you use cheap or inferior materials, you'll be found out. The inspection will be thorough and rigorous. You won't get by with a thing. If your work passes inspection, fine; if it doesn't, your part of the building will be torn out and started over. But *you* won't be torn out; you'll survive—but just barely.

16-17 You realize, don't you, that you are the temple of God, and God himself is present in you? No one will get by with vandalizing God's temple, you can be sure of that. God's temple is sacred—and you, remember, *are* the temple.

18-20 Don't fool yourself. Don't think that you can be wise merely by being up-to-date with the times. Be God's fool—that's the path to true wisdom. What the world calls smart, God calls stupid. It's written in Scripture,

He exposes the chicanery of the chic.
The Master sees through the smoke screens
of the know-it-alls.

21-23 I don't want to hear any of you bragging about yourself or anyone else. Everything is already yours as a gift—Paul, Apollos, Peter, the world, life, death, the present, the future—all of it is yours, and you are privileged to be in union with Christ, who is in union with God.

1-4 **4** Don't imagine us leaders to be something we aren't. We are servants of Christ, not his masters. We are guides into God's most sublime secrets, not security guards posted to protect them. The requirements for a good guide are reliability and accurate knowledge. It matters very little to me what you think of me, even less where I rank in popular opinion. I don't even rank myself. Comparisons in these matters are pointless. I'm not aware of anything that would disqualify me from being a good guide for you,

NEW KING JAMES VERSION

Lord. 5 Therefore judge nothing before the time, until the Lord comes, who will both bring to light the hidden things of darkness and reveal the counsels of the hearts. Then each one's praise will come from God.

FOOLS FOR CHRIST'S SAKE

6 Now these things, brethren, I have figuratively transferred to myself and Apollos for your sakes, that you may learn in us not to think beyond what is written, that none of you may be puffed up on behalf of one against the other.
7 For who makes you differ *from another*? And what do you have that you did not receive? Now if you did indeed receive *it*, why do you boast as if you had not received *it*?

8 You are already full! You are already rich! You have reigned as kings without us—and indeed I could wish you did reign, that we also
might reign with you! 9 For I think that God has displayed us, the apostles, last, as men condemned to death; for we have been made a spectacle to the world, both to angels and to men.
10 We *are* fools for Christ's sake, but you *are* wise in Christ! We *are* weak, but you *are* strong! You *are* distinguished, but we *are* dishonored! 11 To
the present hour we both hunger and thirst, and we are poorly clothed, and beaten, and homeless. 12 And we labor, working with our own hands. Being reviled, we bless; being persecuted, we endure; 13 being defamed, we entreat.
We have been made as the filth of the world, the offscouring of all things until now.

PAUL'S PATERNAL CARE

14 I do not write these things to shame you, but as my beloved children I warn *you*. 15 For
though you might have ten thousand instructors in Christ, yet *you do* not *have* many fathers; for in Christ Jesus I have begotten you through the gospel. 16 Therefore I urge you, imitate me. 17 For
this reason I have sent Timothy to you, who is my beloved and faithful son in the Lord, who will remind you of my ways in Christ, as I teach everywhere in every church.

THE MESSAGE

but that doesn't mean much. The *Master* makes that judgment.

5 So don't get ahead of the Master and jump to conclusions with your judgments before all the evidence is in. When he comes, he will bring out in the open and place in evidence all kinds of things we never even dreamed of—inner motives and purposes and prayers. Only then will any one of us get to hear the "Well done!" of God.

6 All I'm doing right now, friends, is showing how these things pertain to Apollos and me so that you will learn restraint and not rush into making judgments without knowing all the facts. It's important to look at things from God's point of view. I would rather not see you inflating or deflating reputations based on mere hearsay.

7-8 For who do you know that really knows *you*, knows your heart? And even if they did, is there anything they would discover in you that you could take credit for? Isn't everything you *have* and everything you *are* sheer gifts from God? So what's the point of all this comparing and competing? You already have all you need. You already have more access to God than you can handle. Without bringing either Apollos or me into it, you're sitting on top of the world—at least God's world—and we're right there, sitting alongside you!

9-13 It seems to me that God has put us who bear his Message on stage in a theater in which no one wants to buy a ticket. We're something everyone stands around and stares at, like an accident in the street. We're the Messiah's misfits. You might be sure of yourselves, but we live in the midst of frailties and uncertainties. You might be well-thought-of by others, but we're mostly kicked around. Much of the time we don't have enough to eat, we wear patched and threadbare clothes, we get doors slammed in our faces, and we pick up odd jobs anywhere we can to eke out a living. When they call us names, we say, "God bless you." When they spread rumors about *us*, we put in a good word for *them*. We're treated like garbage, potato peelings from the culture's kitchen. And it's not getting any better.

14-16 I'm not writing all this as a neighborhood scold just to make you feel rotten. I'm writing as a father to you, my children. I love you and want you to grow up well, not spoiled. There are a lot of people around who can't wait to tell you what you've done wrong, but there aren't many fathers willing to take the time and effort to help you grow up. It was as Jesus helped me proclaim God's Message to you that I became your father. I'm not, you know, asking you to do anything I'm not already doing myself.

17 This is why I sent Timothy to you earlier. He is also my dear son, and true to the Master. He will refresh your memory on the instructions I regularly give all the churches on the way of Christ.

New King James Version

18Now some are puffed up, as though I were not coming to you. 19But I will come to you shortly, if the Lord wills, and I will know, not the word of those who are puffed up, but the power. 20For the kingdom of God *is* not in word but in power. 21What do you want? Shall I come to you with a rod, or in love and a spirit of gentleness?

Immorality Defiles the Church

5 It is actually reported *that there is* sexual immorality among you, and such sexual immorality as is not even named[a] among the Gentiles—that a man has his father's wife! 2And you are puffed up, and have not rather mourned, that he who has done this deed might be taken away from among you. 3For I indeed, as absent in body but present in spirit, have already judged (as though I were present) him who has so done this deed. 4In the name of our Lord Jesus Christ, when you are gathered together, along with my spirit, with the power of our Lord Jesus Christ, 5deliver such a one to Satan for the destruction of the flesh, that his spirit may be saved in the day of the Lord Jesus.[a]

6Your glorying *is* not good. Do you not know that a little leaven leavens the whole lump? 7Therefore purge out the old leaven, that you may be a new lump, since you truly are unleavened. For indeed Christ, our Passover, was sacrificed for us.[a] 8Therefore let us keep the feast, not with old leaven, nor with the leaven of malice and wickedness, but with the unleavened *bread* of sincerity and truth.

Immorality Must Be Judged

9I wrote to you in my epistle not to keep company with sexually immoral people. 10Yet *I* certainly *did* not *mean* with the sexually immoral people of this world, or with the covetous, or extortioners, or idolaters, since then you would need to go out of the world. 11But now I have written to you not to keep company with anyone named a brother, who is sexually immoral, or covetous, or an idolater, or a reviler, or a drunk-

5:1 [a]NU-Text omits *named.* **5:5** [a]NU-Text omits *Jesus.* **5:7** [a]NU-Text omits *for us.*

The Message

18-20 I know there are some among you who are so full of themselves they never listen to anyone, let alone me. They don't think I'll ever show up in person. But I'll be there sooner than you think, God willing, and then we'll see if they're full of anything but hot air. God's Way is not a matter of mere talk; it's an empowered life.

21 So how should I prepare to come to you? As a severe disciplinarian who makes you toe the mark? Or as a good friend and counselor who wants to share heart-to-heart with you? You decide.

The Mystery of Sex

1-2 5 I also received a report of scandalous sex within your church family, a kind that wouldn't be tolerated even outside the church: One of your men is sleeping with his stepmother. And you're so above it all that it doesn't even faze you! Shouldn't this break your hearts? Shouldn't it bring you to your knees in tears? Shouldn't this person and his conduct be confronted and dealt with?

3-5 I'll tell you what I would do. Even though I'm not there in person, consider me right there with you, because I can fully see what's going on. I'm telling you that this is wrong. You must not simply look the other way and hope it goes away on its own. Bring it out in the open and deal with it in the authority of Jesus our Master. Assemble the community—I'll be present in spirit with you and our Master Jesus will be present in power. Hold this man's conduct up to public scrutiny. Let him defend it if he can! But if he can't, then out with him! It will be totally devastating to him, of course, and embarrassing to you. But better devastation and embarrassment than damnation. You want him on his feet and forgiven before the Master on the Day of Judgment.

6-8 Your flip and callous arrogance in these things bothers me. You pass it off as a small thing, but it's anything but that. Yeast, too, is a "small thing," but it works its way through a whole batch of bread dough pretty fast. So get rid of this "yeast." Our true identity is flat and plain, not puffed up with the wrong kind of ingredient. The Messiah, our Passover Lamb, has already been sacrificed for the Passover meal, and we are the Unraised Bread part of the Feast. So let's live out our part in the Feast, not as raised bread swollen with the yeast of evil, but as flat bread—simple, genuine, unpretentious.

9-13 I wrote you in my earlier letter that you shouldn't make yourselves at home among the sexually promiscuous. I didn't mean that you should have nothing at all to do with outsiders of that sort. Or with crooks, whether blue- or white-collar. Or with spiritual phonies, for that matter. You'd have to leave the world entirely to do that! But I *am* saying that you shouldn't act as if everything is just fine when a friend who claims to be a Christian is promiscuous or crooked, is flip with God or rude to friends, gets drunk or becomes greedy and predatory.

NEW KING JAMES VERSION

ard, or an extortioner—not even to eat with such a person.

12For what *have* I *to do* with judging those also who are outside? Do you not judge those who are inside? 13But those who are outside God judges. Therefore *"put away from yourselves the evil person."*[a]

DO NOT SUE THE BRETHREN

6 Dare any of you, having a matter against another, go to law before the unrighteous, and not before the saints? 2Do you not know that the saints will judge the world? And if the world will be judged by you, are you unworthy to judge the smallest matters? 3Do you not know that we shall judge angels? How much more, things that pertain to this life? 4If then you have judgments concerning things pertaining to this life, do you appoint those who are least esteemed by the church to judge? 5I say this to your shame. Is it so, that there is not a wise man among you, not even one, who will be able to judge between his brethren? 6But brother goes to law against brother, and that before unbelievers!

7Now therefore, it is already an utter failure for you that you go to law against one another. Why do you not rather accept wrong? Why do you not rather *let yourselves* be cheated? 8No, you yourselves do wrong and cheat, and *you do* these things *to your* brethren! 9Do you not know that the unrighteous will not inherit the kingdom of God? Do not be deceived. Neither fornicators, nor idolaters, nor adulterers, nor homosexuals,[a] nor sodomites, 10nor thieves, nor covetous, nor drunkards, nor revilers, nor extortioners will inherit the kingdom of God. 11And such were some of you. But you were washed, but you were sanctified, but you were justified in the name of the Lord Jesus and by the Spirit of our God.

GLORIFY GOD IN BODY AND SPIRIT

12All things are lawful for me, but all things are not helpful. All things are lawful for me, but I will not be brought under the power of any. 13Foods for the stomach and the stomach for foods, but God will destroy both it and them. Now the body *is* not for sexual immorality but for the Lord, and the Lord for the body. 14And God both raised up the Lord and will also raise us up by His power.

5:13 [a]Deuteronomy 17:7; 19:19; 22:21, 24; 24:7 6:9 [a]That is, catamites

THE MESSAGE

You can't just go along with this, treating it as acceptable behavior. I'm not responsible for what the *outsiders* do, but don't we have some responsibility for those within our community of believers? God decides on the outsiders, but we need to decide when our brothers and sisters are out of line and, if necessary, clean house.

1-4 6 And how dare you take each other to
court! When you think you have been
wronged, does it make any sense to go before
a court that knows nothing of God's ways in-
stead of a family of Christians? The day is
coming when the world is going to stand be-
fore a jury made up of followers of Jesus. If
someday you are going to rule on the world's
fate, wouldn't it be a good idea to practice on
some of these smaller cases? Why, we're
even going to judge angels! So why not these
everyday affairs? As these disagreements
and wrongs surface, why would you ever en-
trust them to the judgment of people you
don't trust in any other way?
5-6 I say this as bluntly as I can to wake you
up to the stupidity of what you're doing. Is it
possible that there isn't one levelheaded
person among you who can make fair deci-
sions when disagreements and disputes
come up? I don't believe it. And here you are
taking each other to court before people
who don't even believe in God! How can
they render justice if they don't believe in
the *God* of justice?
7-8 These court cases are an ugly blot on
your community. Wouldn't it be far better to
just take it, to let yourselves be wronged and
forget it? All you're doing is providing fuel
for more wrong, more injustice, bringing
more hurt to the people of your own spiri-
tual family.
9-11 Don't you realize that this is not the way
to live? Unjust people who don't care about
God will not be joining in his kingdom.
Those who use and abuse each other, use
and abuse sex, use and abuse the earth and
everything in it, don't qualify as citizens in
God's kingdom. A number of you know from
experience what I'm talking about, for not so
long ago you were on that list. Since then,
you've been cleaned up and given a fresh
start by Jesus, our Master, our Messiah, and
by our God present in us, the Spirit.
12 Just because something is technically le-
gal doesn't mean that it's spiritually appro-
priate. If I went around doing whatever I
thought I could get by with, I'd be a slave to
my whims.
13 You know the old saying, "First you eat to
live, and then you live to eat"? Well, it may
be true that the body is only a temporary
thing, but that's no excuse for stuffing your
body with food, or indulging it with sex.
Since the Master honors you with a body,
honor him with your body!
14-15 God honored the Master's body by rais-
ing it from the grave. He'll treat yours with
the same resurrection power. Until that
time, remember that your bodies are created

NEW KING JAMES VERSION

15Do you not know that your bodies are members of Christ? Shall I then take the members of Christ and make *them* members of a harlot? Certainly not! 16Or do you not know that he who is joined to a harlot is one body *with her?* For *"the two,"* He says, *"shall become one flesh."*[a] 17But he who is joined to the Lord is one spirit *with Him.*

18Flee sexual immorality. Every sin that a man does is outside the body, but he who commits sexual immorality sins against his own body. 19Or do you not know that your body is the temple of the Holy Spirit *who is* in you, whom you have from God, and you are not your own? 20For you were bought at a price; therefore glorify God in your body[a] and in your spirit, which are God's.

PRINCIPLES OF MARRIAGE

7 Now concerning the things of which you wrote to me:

It is good for a man not to touch a woman. 2Nevertheless, because of sexual immorality, let each man have his own wife, and let each woman have her own husband. 3Let the husband render to his wife the affection due her, and likewise also the wife to her husband. 4The wife does not have authority over her own body, but the husband *does.* And likewise the husband does not have authority over his own body, but the wife *does.* 5Do not deprive one another except with consent for a time, that you may give yourselves to fasting and prayer; and come together again so that Satan does not tempt you because of your lack of self-control. 6But I say this as a concession, not as a commandment. 7For I wish that all men were even as I myself. But each one has his own gift from God, one in this manner and another in that.

8But I say to the unmarried and to the widows: It is good for them if they remain even as I am; 9but if they cannot exercise self-control, let them marry. For it is better to marry than to burn *with passion.*

KEEP YOUR MARRIAGE VOWS

10Now to the married I command, *yet* not I but the Lord: A wife is not to depart from *her* husband. 11But even if she does depart, let her remain unmarried or be reconciled to *her* husband. And a husband is not to divorce *his* wife.

6:16 [a]Genesis 2:24 **6:20** [a]NU-Text ends the verse at *body.*

THE MESSAGE

with the same dignity as the Master's body. You wouldn't take the Master's body off to a whorehouse, would you? I should hope not.

16-20 There's more to sex than mere skin on skin. Sex is as much spiritual mystery as physical fact. As written in Scripture, "The two become one." Since we want to become spiritually one with the Master, we must not pursue the kind of sex that avoids commitment and intimacy, leaving us more lonely than ever—the kind of sex that can never "become one." There is a sense in which sexual sins are different from all others. In sexual sin we violate the sacredness of our own bodies, these bodies that were made for God-given and God-modeled love, for "becoming one" with another. Or didn't you realize that your body is a sacred place, the place of the Holy Spirit? Don't you see that you can't live however you please, squandering what God paid such a high price for? The physical part of you is not some piece of property belonging to the spiritual part of you. God owns the whole works. So let people see God in and through your body.

TO BE MARRIED, TO BE SINGLE . . .

1 **7** Now, getting down to the questions you asked in your letter to me. First, Is it a good thing to have sexual relations?

2-6 Certainly—but only within a certain context. It's good for a man to have a wife, and for a woman to have a husband. Sexual drives are strong, but marriage is strong enough to contain them and provide for a balanced and fulfilling sexual life in a world of sexual disorder. The marriage bed must be a place of mutuality—the husband seeking to satisfy his wife, the wife seeking to satisfy her husband. Marriage is not a place to "stand up for your rights." Marriage is a decision to serve the other, whether in bed or out. Abstaining from sex is permissible for a period of time if you both agree to it, and if it's for the purposes of prayer and fasting—but only for such times. Then come back together again. Satan has an ingenious way of tempting us when we least expect it. I'm not, understand, commanding these periods of abstinence—only providing my best counsel if you should choose them.

7 Sometimes I wish everyone were single like me—a simpler life in many ways! But celibacy is not for everyone any more than marriage is. God gives the gift of the single life to some, the gift of the married life to others.

8-9 I do, though, tell the unmarried and widows that singleness might well be the best thing for them, as it has been for me. But if they can't manage their desires and emotions, they should by all means go ahead and get married. The difficulties of marriage are preferable by far to a sexually tortured life as a single.

10-11 And if you are married, stay married. This is the Master's command, not mine. If a wife should leave her husband, she must either remain single or else come back and make things right with him. And a husband has no right to get rid of his wife.

New King James Version

12But to the rest I, not the Lord, say: If any
brother has a wife who does not believe, and she
is willing to live with him, let him not divorce
her. 13And a woman who has a husband who
does not believe, if he is willing to live with her,
let her not divorce him. 14For the unbelieving
husband is sanctified by the wife, and the unbe-
lieving wife is sanctified by the husband; other-
wise your children would be unclean, but now
they are holy. 15But if the unbeliever departs, let
him depart; a brother or a sister is not under
bondage in such *cases*. But God has called us to
peace. 16For how do you know, O wife, whether
you will save *your* husband? Or how do you
know, O husband, whether you will save *your*
wife?

Live as You Are Called

17But as God has distributed to each one, as
the Lord has called each one, so let him walk.
And so I ordain in all the churches. 18Was any-
one called while circumcised? Let him not be-
come uncircumcised. Was anyone called while
uncircumcised? Let him not be circumcised.
19Circumcision is nothing and uncircumcision is
nothing, but keeping the commandments of God
is what matters. 20Let each one remain in the
same calling in which he was called. 21Were you
called *while* a slave? Do not be concerned about
it; but if you can be made free, rather use *it*.
22For he who is called in the Lord *while* a slave
is the Lord's freedman. Likewise he who is
called *while* free is Christ's slave. 23You were
bought at a price; do not become slaves of men.
24Brethren, let each one remain with God in that
state in which he was called.

To the Unmarried and Widows

25Now concerning virgins: I have no com-
mandment from the Lord; yet I give judgment as
one whom the Lord in His mercy has made
trustworthy. 26I suppose therefore that this is
good because of the present distress—that *it is*
good for a man to remain as he is: 27Are you
bound to a wife? Do not seek to be loosed. Are
you loosed from a wife? Do not seek a wife.
28But even if you do marry, you have not sinned;
and if a virgin marries, she has not sinned. Nev-
ertheless such will have trouble in the flesh, but
I would spare you.

The Message

12-14 For the rest of you who are in mixed marriages—Christian married to non-Christian—we have no explicit command from the Master. So this is what you must do. If you are a man with a wife who is not a believer but who still wants to live with you, hold on to her. If you are a woman with a husband who is not a believer but he wants to live with you, hold on to him. The unbelieving husband shares to an extent in the holiness of his wife, and the unbelieving wife is likewise touched by the holiness of her husband. Otherwise, your children would be left out; as it is, they also are included in the spiritual purposes of God.

15-16 On the other hand, if the unbelieving spouse walks out, you've got to let him or her go. You don't have to hold on desperately. God has called us to make the best of it, as peacefully as we can. You never know, wife: The way you handle this might bring your husband not only back to you but to God. You never know, husband: The way you handle this might bring your wife not only back to you but to God.

17 And don't be wishing you were someplace else or with someone else. Where you are right now is God's place for you. Live and obey and love and believe right there. God, not your marital status, defines your life. Don't think I'm being harder on you than on the others. I give this same counsel in all the churches.

18-19 Were you Jewish at the time God called you? Don't try to remove the evidence. Were you non-Jewish at the time of your call? Don't become a Jew. Being Jewish isn't the point. The really important thing is obeying God's call, following his commands.

20-22 Stay where you were when God called your name. Were you a slave? Slavery is no roadblock to obeying and believing. I don't mean you're stuck and can't leave. If you have a chance at freedom, go ahead and take it. I'm simply trying to point out that under your new Master you're going to experience a marvelous freedom you would never have dreamed of. On the other hand, if you were free when Christ called you, you'll experience a delightful "enslavement to God" you would never have dreamed of.

23-24 All of you, slave and free both, were once held hostage in a sinful society. Then a huge sum was paid out for your ransom. So please don't, out of old habit, slip back into being or doing what everyone else tells you. Friends, stay where you were called to be. God is there. Hold the high ground with him at your side.

25-28 The Master did not give explicit direction regarding virgins, but as one much experienced in the mercy of the Master and loyal to him all the way, you can trust my counsel. Because of the current pressures on us from all sides, I think it would probably be best to stay just as you are. Are you married? Stay married. Are you unmarried? Don't get married. But there's certainly no sin in getting married, whether you're a virgin or not. All I am saying is that when you marry, you take on additional stress in an already stressful time, and I want to spare you if possible.

New King James Version

29But this I say, brethren, the time *is* short, so
that from now on even those who have wives
should be as though they had none, 30those who
weep as though they did not weep, those who re-
joice as though they did not rejoice, those who
buy as though they did not possess, 31and those
who use this world as not misusing *it*. For the
form of this world is passing away.
32But I want you to be without care. He who
is unmarried cares for the things of the Lord—
how he may please the Lord. 33But he who is
married cares about the things of the world—
how he may please *his* wife. 34There is[a] a differ-
ence between a wife and a virgin. The unmar-
ried woman cares about the things of the Lord,
that she may be holy both in body and in spirit.
But she who is married cares about the things of
the world—how she may please *her* husband.
35And this I say for your own profit, not that I
may put a leash on you, but for what is proper,
and that you may serve the Lord without dis-
traction.
36But if any man thinks he is behaving im-
properly toward his virgin, if she is past the
flower of youth, and thus it must be, let him do
what he wishes. He does not sin; let them marry.
37Nevertheless he who stands steadfast in his
heart, having no necessity, but has power over
his own will, and has so determined in his heart
that he will keep his virgin,[a] does well. 38So then
he who gives *her*[a] in marriage does well, but he
who does not give *her* in marriage does better.
39A wife is bound by law as long as her hus-
band lives; but if her husband dies, she is at lib-
erty to be married to whom she wishes, only in
the Lord. 40But she is happier if she remains as
she is, according to my judgment—and I think I
also have the Spirit of God.

Be Sensitive to Conscience

8 Now concerning things offered to idols: We
know that we all have knowledge. Knowl-
edge puffs up, but love edifies. 2And if anyone
thinks that he knows anything, he knows noth-
ing yet as he ought to know. 3But if anyone loves
God, this one is known by Him.
4Therefore concerning the eating of things
offered to idols, we know that an idol *is* nothing
in the world, and that *there is* no other God but

7:34 [a]M-Text adds *also*. **7:37** [a]Or *virgin daughter* **7:38** [a]NU-Text reads *his own virgin*.

The Message

29-31 I do want to point out, friends, that time is of the essence. There is no time to waste, so don't complicate your lives unnecessarily. Keep it simple—in marriage, grief, joy, whatever. Even in ordinary things—your daily routines of shopping, and so on. Deal as sparingly as possible with the things the world thrusts on you. This world as you see it is on its way out.

32-35 I want you to live as free of complications as possible. When you're unmarried, you're free to concentrate on simply pleasing the Master. Marriage involves you in all the nuts and bolts of domestic life and in wanting to please your spouse, leading to so many more demands on your attention. The time and energy that married people spend on caring for and nurturing each other, the unmarried can spend in becoming whole and holy instruments of God. I'm trying to be helpful and make it as easy as possible for you, not make things harder. All I want is for you to be able to develop a way of life in which you can spend plenty of time together with the Master without a lot of distractions.

36-38 If a man has a woman friend to whom he is loyal but never intended to marry, having decided to serve God as a "single," and then changes his mind, deciding he should marry her, he should go ahead and marry. It's no sin; it's not even a "step down" from celibacy, as some say. On the other hand, if a man is comfortable in his decision for a single life in service to God and it's entirely his own conviction and not imposed on him by others, he ought to stick with it. Marriage is spiritually and morally right and not inferior to singleness in any way, although as I indicated earlier, because of the times we live in, I do have pastoral reasons for encouraging singleness.

39-40 A wife must stay with her husband as long as he lives. If he dies, she is free to marry anyone she chooses. She will, of course, want to marry a believer and have the blessing of the Master. By now you know that I think she'll be better off staying single. The Master, in my opinion, thinks so, too.

Freedom with Responsibility

1-3 8 The question keeps coming up regarding meat that has been offered up to an idol: Should you attend meals where such meat is served, or not? We sometimes tend to think we know all we need to know to answer these kinds of questions—*but* sometimes our humble hearts can help us more than our proud minds. We never really know enough until we recognize that God alone knows it all.

4-6 Some people say, quite rightly, that idols have no actual existence, that there's nothing to them, that there is no God other than our one God, that no matter how many of these so-called gods are named and worshiped they still don't add up to anything but a tall story. They say—again, quite rightly—that there is only one God the Fa-

New King James Version

one. 5For even if there are so-called gods, whether in heaven or on earth (as there are many gods and many lords), 6yet for us *there is* one God, the Father, of whom *are* all things, and we for Him; and one Lord Jesus Christ, through whom *are* all things, and through whom we *live.*
7However, *there is* not in everyone that knowledge; for some, with consciousness of the idol, until now eat *it* as a thing offered to an idol; and their conscience, being weak, is defiled.
8But food does not commend us to God; for neither if we eat are we the better, nor if we do not eat are we the worse.
9But beware lest somehow this liberty of yours become a stumbling block to those who are weak. 10For if anyone sees you who have knowledge eating in an idol's temple, will not the conscience of him who is weak be emboldened to eat those things offered to idols? 11And because of your knowledge shall the weak brother perish, for whom Christ died? 12But when you thus sin against the brethren, and wound their weak conscience, you sin against Christ. 13Therefore, if food makes my brother stumble, I will never again eat meat, lest I make my brother stumble.

A Pattern of Self-Denial

9 Am I not an apostle? Am I not free? Have I not seen Jesus Christ our Lord? Are you not my work in the Lord? 2If I am not an apostle to others, yet doubtless I am to you. For you are the seal of my apostleship in the Lord.
3My defense to those who examine me is this: 4Do we have no right to eat and drink? 5Do we have no right to take along a believing wife,

The Message

ther, that everything comes from him, and
that he wants us to live for him. Also, they
say that there is only one Master—Jesus the
Messiah—and that everything is for his
sake, including us. Yes. It's true.
7 In strict logic, then, nothing happened to
the meat when it was offered up to an idol.
It's just like any other meat. I know that, and
you know that. But knowing isn't every-
thing. If it becomes everything, some people
end up as know-it-alls who treat others as
know-nothings. Real knowledge isn't that
insensitive.

We need to be sensitive to the fact that
we're not all at the same level of under-
standing in this. Some of you have spent
your entire lives eating "idol meat," and are
sure that there's something bad in the meat
that then becomes something bad inside of
you. An imagination and conscience shaped
under those conditions isn't going to change
overnight.
8-9 But fortunately God doesn't grade us on
our diet. We're neither commended when we
clean our plate nor reprimanded when we
just can't stomach it. But God *does* care
when you use your freedom carelessly in a
way that leads a fellow believer still vulner-
able to those old associations to be thrown
off track.
10 For instance, say you flaunt your freedom
by going to a banquet thrown in honor of
idols, where the main course is meat sacri-
ficed to idols. Isn't there great danger if
someone still struggling over this issue,
someone who looks up to you as knowl-
edgeable and mature, sees you go into that
banquet? The danger is that he will become
terribly confused—maybe even to the point
of getting mixed up himself in what his con-
science tells him is wrong.
11-13 Christ gave up his life for that person.
Wouldn't you at least be willing to give up
going to dinner for him—because, as you
say, it doesn't really make any difference?
But it *does* make a difference if you hurt
your friend terribly, risking his eternal ruin!
When you hurt your friend, you hurt Christ.
A free meal here and there isn't worth it at
the cost of even one of these "weak ones."
So, never go to these idol-tainted meals if
there's any chance it will trip up one of your
brothers or sisters.

1-2 9 And don't tell me that I have no authority
to write like this. I'm perfectly free to do
this—isn't that obvious? Haven't I been
given a job to do? Wasn't I commissioned to
this work in a face-to-face meeting with Je-
sus, our Master? Aren't you yourselves
proof of the good work that I've done for the
Master? Even if no one else admits the au-
thority of my commission, *you* can't deny it.
Why, my work with you is living proof of my
authority!
3-7 I'm not shy in standing up to my critics.
We who are on missionary assignments for
God have a right to decent accommoda-

NEW KING JAMES VERSION

as *do* also the other apostles, the brothers of the
Lord, and Cephas? 6Or *is it* only Barnabas and I
who have no right to refrain from working?
7Who ever goes to war at his own expense? Who
plants a vineyard and does not eat of its fruit?
Or who tends a flock and does not drink of the
milk of the flock?
8Do I say these things as a *mere* man? Or
does not the law say the same also? 9For it is
written in the law of Moses, *"You shall not muz-
zle an ox while it treads out the grain."*[a] Is it
oxen God is concerned about? 10Or does He say
it altogether for our sakes? For our sakes, no
doubt, *this* is written, that he who plows should
plow in hope, and he who threshes in hope
should be partaker of his hope. 11If we have
sown spiritual things for you, *is it* a great thing
if we reap your material things? 12If others are
partakers of *this* right over you, *are* we not even
more?
Nevertheless we have not used this right, but
endure all things lest we hinder the gospel of
Christ. 13Do you not know that those who minis-
ter the holy things eat *of the things* of the tem-
ple, and those who serve at the altar partake of
the offerings of the altar? 14Even so the Lord has
commanded that those who preach the gospel
should live from the gospel.
15But I have used none of these things, nor
have I written these things that it should be
done so to me; for it *would be* better for me to
die than that anyone should make my boasting
void. 16For if I preach the gospel, I have nothing
to boast of, for necessity is laid upon me; yes,
woe is me if I do not preach the gospel! 17For if I
do this willingly, I have a reward; but if against
my will, I have been entrusted with a steward-
ship. 18What is my reward then? That when I
preach the gospel, I may present the gospel of
Christ[a] without charge, that I may not abuse my
authority in the gospel.

SERVING ALL MEN

19For though I am free from all *men,* I have
made myself a servant to all, that I might win
the more; 20and to the Jews I became as a Jew,
that I might win Jews; to those *who are* under
the law, as under the law,[a] that I might win those
who are under the law; 21to those *who are* with-
out law, as without law (not being without law
toward God,[a] but under law toward Christ[b]),
that I might win those *who are* without law; 22to
the weak I became as[a] weak, that I might win
the weak. I have become all things to all *men,*
that I might by all means save some. 23Now this
I do for the gospel's sake, that I may be partaker
of it with *you.*

9:9 [a]Deuteronomy 25:4 **9:18** [a]NU-Text omits *of Christ.*
9:20 [a]NU-Text adds *though not being myself under the law.*
9:21 [a]NU-Text reads *God's law.* [b]NU-Text reads *Christ's law.*
9:22 [a]NU-Text omits *as.*

THE MESSAGE

tions, and we have a right to support for us and our families. You don't seem to have raised questions with the other apostles and our Master's brothers and Peter in these matters. So, why me? Is it just Barnabas and I who have to go it alone and pay our own way? Are soldiers self-employed? Are gardeners forbidden to eat vegetables from their own gardens? Don't milkmaids get to drink their fill from the pail?

8-12 I'm not just sounding off because I'm irritated. This is all written in the scriptural law. Moses wrote, "Don't muzzle an ox to keep it from eating the grain when it's threshing." Do you think Moses' primary concern was the care of farm animals? Don't you think his concern extends to us? Of course. Farmers plow and thresh expecting something when the crop comes in. So if we have planted spiritual seed among you, is it out of line to expect a meal or two from you? Others demand plenty from you in these ways. Don't we who have never demanded deserve even more?

12-14 But we're not going to start demanding now what we've always had a perfect right to. Our decision all along has been to put up with anything rather than to get in the way or detract from the Message of Christ. All I'm concerned with right now is that you not use our decision to take advantage of others, depriving them of what is rightly theirs. You know, don't you, that it's always been taken for granted that those who work in the Temple live off the proceeds of the Temple, and that those who offer sacrifices at the altar eat their meals from what has been sacrificed? Along the same lines, the Master directed that those who spread the Message be supported by those who believe the Message.

15-18 Still, I want it made clear that I've never gotten anything out of this for myself, and that I'm not writing now to get something. I'd rather die than give anyone ammunition to discredit me or impugn my motives. If I proclaim the Message, it's not to get something out of it for myself. I'm *compelled* to do it, and doomed if I don't! If this was my own idea of just another way to make a living, I'd expect some pay. But since it's *not* my idea but something solemnly entrusted to me, why would I expect to get paid? So am I getting anything out of it? Yes, as a matter of fact: the pleasure of proclaiming the Message at no cost to you. You don't even have to pay my expenses!

19-23 Even though I am free of the demands and expectations of everyone, I have voluntarily become a servant to any and all in order to reach a wide range of people: religious, nonreligious, meticulous moralists, loose-living immoralists, the defeated, the demoralized—whoever. I didn't take on their way of life. I kept my bearings in Christ—but I entered their world and tried to experience things from their point of view. I've become just about every sort of servant there is in my attempts to lead those I meet into a God-saved life. I did all this because of the Message. I didn't just want to talk about it; I wanted to be *in* on it!

NEW KING JAMES VERSION

STRIVING FOR A CROWN

[24]Do you not know that those who run in a race all run, but one receives the prize? Run in such a way that you may obtain *it.* [25]And everyone who competes *for the prize* is temperate in all things. Now they *do it* to obtain a perishable crown, but we *for* an imperishable *crown.* [26]Therefore I run thus: not with uncertainty. Thus I fight: not as *one who* beats the air. [27]But I discipline my body and bring *it* into subjection, lest, when I have preached to others, I myself should become disqualified.

OLD TESTAMENT EXAMPLES

10 Moreover, brethren, I do not want you to be unaware that all our fathers were under the cloud, all passed through the sea, [2]all were baptized into Moses in the cloud and in the sea, [3]all ate the same spiritual food, [4]and all drank the same spiritual drink. For they drank of that spiritual Rock that followed them, and that Rock was Christ. [5]But with most of them God was not well pleased, for *their bodies* were scattered in the wilderness.

[6]Now these things became our examples, to the intent that we should not lust after evil things as they also lusted. [7]And do not become idolaters as *were* some of them. As it is written, *"The people sat down to eat and drink, and rose up to play."*[a] [8]Nor let us commit sexual immorality, as some of them did, and in one day twenty-three thousand fell; [9]nor let us tempt Christ, as some of them also tempted, and were destroyed by serpents; [10]nor complain, as some of them also complained, and were destroyed by the destroyer. [11]Now all[a] these things happened to them as examples, and they were written for our admonition, upon whom the ends of the ages have come.

[12]Therefore let him who thinks he stands take heed lest he fall. [13]No temptation has overtaken you except such as is common to man; but God *is* faithful, who will not allow you to be tempted beyond what you are able, but with the temptation will also make the way of escape, that you may be able to bear *it.*

FLEE FROM IDOLATRY

[14]Therefore, my beloved, flee from idolatry. [15]I speak as to wise men; judge for yourselves what I say. [16]The cup of blessing which we bless, is it not the communion of the blood of Christ?

10:7 [a]Exodus 32:6 **10:11** [a]NU-Text omits *all.*

THE MESSAGE

24-25 You've all been to the stadium and seen the athletes race. Everyone runs; one wins. Run to win. All good athletes train hard. They do it for a gold medal that tarnishes and fades. You're after one that's gold eternally.

26-27 I don't know about you, but I'm running hard for the finish line. I'm giving it everything I've got. No sloppy living for me! I'm staying alert and in top condition. I'm not going to get caught napping, telling everyone else all about it and then missing out myself.

1-5 **10** Remember our history, friends, and be warned. All our ancestors were led by the providential Cloud and taken miraculously through the Sea. They went through the waters, in a baptism like ours, as Moses led them from enslaving death to salvation life. They all ate and drank identical food and drink, meals provided daily by God. They drank from the Rock, God's fountain for them that stayed with them wherever they were. And the Rock was Christ. But just experiencing God's wonder and grace didn't seem to mean much—most of them were defeated by temptation during the hard times in the desert, and God was not pleased.

6-10 The same thing could happen to us. We must be on guard so that we never get caught up in wanting our own way as they did. And we must not turn our religion into a circus as they did—"First the people partied, then they threw a dance." We must not be sexually promiscuous—they paid for that, remember, with 23,000 deaths in one day! We must never try to get Christ to serve us instead of us serving him; they tried it, and God launched an epidemic of poisonous snakes. We must be careful not to stir up discontent; discontent destroyed them.

11-12 These are all warning markers—DANGER!—in our history books, written down so that we don't repeat their mistakes. Our positions in the story are parallel—they at the beginning, we at the end—and we are just as capable of messing it up as they were. Don't be so naive and self-confident. You're not exempt. You could fall flat on your face as easily as anyone else. Forget about self-confidence; it's useless. Cultivate God-confidence.

13 No test or temptation that comes your way is beyond the course of what others have had to face. All you need to remember is that God will never let you down; he'll never let you be pushed past your limit; he'll always be there to help you come through it.

14 So, my very dear friends, when you see people reducing God to something they can use or control, get out of their company as fast as you can.

15-18 I assume I'm addressing believers now who are mature. Draw your own conclusions: When we drink the cup of blessing, aren't we taking into ourselves the blood, the very life, of Christ? And isn't it the same with the loaf of bread we break and eat? Don't we take into ourselves the body, the

NEW KING JAMES VERSION

The bread which we break, is it not the com-
munion of the body of Christ? 17For we, *though*
many, are one bread *and* one body; for we all
partake of that one bread.
18Observe Israel after the flesh: Are not those
who eat of the sacrifices partakers of the altar?
19What am I saying then? That an idol is any-
thing, or what is offered to idols is anything?
20Rather, that the things which the Gentiles sac-
rifice they sacrifice to demons and not to God,
and I do not want you to have fellowship with
demons. 21You cannot drink the cup of the Lord
and the cup of demons; you cannot partake of
the Lord's table and of the table of demons. 22Or
do we provoke the Lord to jealousy? Are we
stronger than He?

ALL TO THE GLORY OF GOD

23All things are lawful for me,[a] but not all
things are helpful; all things are lawful for me,[b]
but not all things edify. 24Let no one seek his
own, but each one the other's *well-being.*
25Eat whatever is sold in the meat market,
asking no questions for conscience' sake; 26for
"the earth is the LORD'S*, and all its fullness."*[a]
27If any of those who do not believe invites
you *to dinner,* and you desire to go, eat whatever
is set before you, asking no question for con-
science' sake. 28But if anyone says to you, "This
was offered to idols," do not eat it for the sake of
the one who told you, and for conscience' sake;[a]
for *"the earth is the* LORD'S*, and all its full-
ness."*[b] 29"Conscience," I say, not your own, but
that of the other. For why is my liberty judged by
another *man's* conscience? 30But if I partake
with thanks, why am I evil spoken of for *the
food* over which I give thanks?
31Therefore, whether you eat or drink, or
whatever you do, do all to the glory of God.
32Give no offense, either to the Jews or to the
Greeks or to the church of God, 33just as I also
please all *men* in all *things,* not seeking my own
profit, but the *profit* of many, that they may be
saved.

10:23 [a]NU-Text omits *for me.* [b]NU-Text omits *for me.* **10:26** [a]Psalm 24:1 **10:28** [a]NU-Text omits the rest of this verse. [b]Psalm 24:1

THE MESSAGE

very life, of Christ? Because there is one loaf, our many-ness becomes oneness—Christ doesn't become fragmented in us. Rather, we become unified in him. We don't reduce Christ to what we are; he raises us to what he is. That's basically what happened even in old Israel—those who ate the sacrifices offered on God's altar entered into God's action at the altar.

19-22 Do you see the difference? Sacrifices offered to idols are offered to nothing, for what's the idol but a nothing? Or worse than nothing, a minus, a demon! I don't want you to become part of something that reduces you to less than yourself. And you can't have it both ways, banqueting with the Master one day and slumming with demons the next. Besides, the Master won't put up with it. He wants *us*—all or nothing. Do you think you can get off with anything less?

23-24 Looking at it one way, you could say, "Anything goes. Because of God's immense generosity and grace, we don't have to dissect and scrutinize every action to see if it will pass muster." But the point is not to just get by. We want to live well, but our foremost efforts should be to help *others* live well.

25-28 With that as a base to work from, common sense can take you the rest of the way. Eat anything sold at the butcher shop, for instance; you don't have to run an "idolatry test" on every item. "The earth," after all, "is God's, and everything in it." That "everything" certainly includes the leg of lamb in the butcher shop. If a nonbeliever invites you to dinner and you feel like going, go ahead and enjoy yourself; eat everything placed before you. It would be both bad manners and bad spirituality to cross-examine your host on the ethical purity of each course as it is served. On the other hand, if he goes out of his way to tell you that this or that was sacrificed to god or goddess so-and-so, you should pass. Even though you may be indifferent as to where it came from, he isn't, and you don't want to send mixed messages to him about who *you* are worshiping.

29-30 But, except for these special cases, I'm not going to walk around on eggshells worrying about what small-minded people might say; I'm going to stride free and easy, knowing what our large-minded Master has already said. If I eat what is served to me, grateful to God for what is on the table, how can I worry about what someone will say? I thanked God for it and he blessed it!

31-33 So eat your meals heartily, not worrying about what others say about you—you're eating to God's glory, after all, not to please them. As a matter of fact, do everything that way, heartily and freely to God's glory. At the same time, don't be callous in your exercise of freedom, thoughtlessly stepping on the toes of those who aren't as free as you are. I try my best to be considerate of everyone's feelings in all these matters; I hope you will be, too.

NEW KING JAMES VERSION

11 Imitate me, just as I also *imitate* Christ.

HEAD COVERINGS

2 Now I praise you, brethren, that you remem-
ber me in all things and keep the traditions just
as I delivered *them* to you. 3 But I want you to
know that the head of every man is Christ, the
head of woman *is* man, and the head of Christ *is*
God. 4 Every man praying or prophesying, hav-
ing *his* head covered, dishonors his head. 5 But
every woman who prays or prophesies with *her*
head uncovered dishonors her head, for that is
one and the same as if her head were shaved.
6 For if a woman is not covered, let her also be
shorn. But if it is shameful for a woman to be
shorn or shaved, let her be covered. 7 For a man
indeed ought not to cover *his* head, since he is
the image and glory of God; but woman is the
glory of man. 8 For man is not from woman, but
woman from man. 9 Nor was man created for the
woman, but woman for the man. 10 For this rea-
son the woman ought to have *a symbol of* au-
thority on *her* head, because of the angels.
11 Nevertheless, neither *is* man independent of
woman, nor woman independent of man, in the
Lord. 12 For as woman *came* from man, even so
man also *comes* through woman; but all things
are from God.

13 Judge among yourselves. Is it proper for a
woman to pray to God with her head uncov-
ered? 14 Does not even nature itself teach you
that if a man has long hair, it is a dishonor to
him? 15 But if a woman has long hair, it is a glory
to her; for *her* hair is given to her[a] for a cover-
ing. 16 But if anyone seems to be contentious, we
have no such custom, nor *do* the churches of
God.

CONDUCT AT THE LORD'S SUPPER

17 Now in giving these instructions I do not
praise *you,* since you come together not for the
better but for the worse. 18 For first of all, when
you come together as a church, I hear that there
are divisions among you, and in part I believe it.
19 For there must also be factions among you,
that those who are approved may be recognized
among you. 20 Therefore when you come to-
gether in one place, it is not to eat the Lord's
Supper. 21 For in eating, each one takes his own
supper ahead of *others;* and one is hungry and
another is drunk. 22 What! Do you not have
houses to eat and drink in? Or do you despise
the church of God and shame those who have
nothing? What shall I say to you? Shall I praise
you in this? I do not praise *you.*

INSTITUTION OF THE LORD'S SUPPER

23 For I received from the Lord that which I
also delivered to you: that the Lord Jesus on the

11:15 [a]M-Text omits *to her.*

THE MESSAGE

TO HONOR GOD

1-2 **11** It pleases me that you continue to remember and honor me by keeping up the traditions of the faith I taught you. All actual authority stems from Christ.

3-9 In a marriage relationship, there is authority from Christ to husband, and from husband to wife. The authority of Christ is the authority of God. Any man who speaks with God or about God in a way that shows a lack of respect for the authority of Christ, dishonors Christ. In the same way, a wife who speaks with God in a way that shows a lack of respect for the authority of her husband, dishonors her husband. Worse, she dishonors herself—an ugly sight, like a woman with her head shaved. This is basically the origin of these customs we have of women wearing head coverings in worship, while men take their hats off. By these symbolic acts, men and women, who far too often butt heads with each other, submit their "heads" to the Head: God.

10-12 Don't, by the way, read too much into the differences here between men and women. Neither man nor woman can go it alone or claim priority. Man was created first, as a beautiful shining reflection of God—that is true. But the head on a woman's body clearly outshines in beauty the head of her "head," her husband. The first woman came from man, true—but ever since then, every man comes from a woman! And since virtually everything comes from God anyway, let's quit going through these "who's first" routines.

13-16 Don't you agree there is something naturally powerful in the symbolism—a woman, her beautiful hair reminiscent of angels, praying in adoration; a man, his head bared in reverence, praying in submission? I hope you're not going to be argumentative about this. All God's churches see it this way; I don't want you standing out as an exception.

17-19 Regarding this next item, I'm not at all pleased. I am getting the picture that when you meet together it brings out your worst side instead of your best! First, I get this report on your divisiveness, competing with and criticizing each other. I'm reluctant to believe it, but there it is. The best that can be said for it is that the testing process will bring truth into the open and confirm it.

20-22 And then I find that you bring your divisions to worship—you come together, and instead of eating the Lord's Supper, you bring in a lot of food from the outside and make pigs of yourselves. Some are left out, and go home hungry. Others have to be carried out, too drunk to walk. I can't believe it! Don't you have your own homes to eat and drink in? Why would you stoop to desecrating God's church? Why would you actually shame God's poor? I never would have believed you would stoop to this. And I'm not going to stand by and say nothing.

23-26 Let me go over with you again exactly what goes on in the Lord's Supper and why

NEW KING JAMES VERSION

same night in which He was betrayed took
bread; 24and when He had given thanks, He
broke *it* and said, "Take, eat;[a] this is My body
which is broken[b] for you; do this in remem-
brance of Me." 25In the same manner *He* also
took the cup after supper, saying, "This cup is
the new covenant in My blood. This do, as often
as you drink *it,* in remembrance of Me."
26For as often as you eat this bread and drink
this cup, you proclaim the Lord's death till He
comes.

EXAMINE YOURSELF

27Therefore whoever eats this bread or
drinks *this* cup of the Lord in an unworthy man-
ner will be guilty of the body and blood[a] of the
Lord. 28But let a man examine himself, and so let
him eat of the bread and drink of the cup. 29For
he who eats and drinks in an unworthy manner[a]
eats and drinks judgment to himself, not dis-
cerning the Lord's[b] body. 30For this reason many
are weak and sick among you, and many sleep.
31For if we would judge ourselves, we would not
be judged. 32But when we are judged, we are
chastened by the Lord, that we may not be con-
demned with the world.
33Therefore, my brethren, when you come to-
gether to eat, wait for one another. 34But if any-
one is hungry, let him eat at home, lest you come
together for judgment. And the rest I will set in
order when I come.

SPIRITUAL GIFTS: UNITY IN DIVERSITY

12 Now concerning spiritual *gifts,* brethren, I
do not want you to be ignorant: 2You know
that[a] you were Gentiles, carried away to these
dumb idols, however you were led. 3Therefore I
make known to you that no one speaking by the
Spirit of God calls Jesus accursed, and no one
can say that Jesus is Lord except by the Holy
Spirit.

11:24 [a]NU-Text omits *Take, eat.* [b]NU-Text omits *broken.* **11:27** [a]NU-Text and M-Text read *the blood.* **11:29** [a]NU-Text omits *in an unworthy manner.* [b]NU-Text omits *Lord's.* **12:2** [a]NU-Text and M-Text add *when.*

THE MESSAGE

it is so centrally important. I received my instructions from the Master himself and passed them on to you. The Master, Jesus, on the night of his betrayal, took bread. Having given thanks, he broke it and said,

This is my body, broken for you.
Do this to remember me.

After supper, he did the same thing with the cup:

This cup is my blood, my new covenant
with you.
Each time you drink this cup, remember
me.

What you must solemnly realize is that every time you eat this bread and every time you drink this cup, you reenact in your words and actions the death of the Master. You will be drawn back to this meal again and again until the Master returns. You must never let familiarity breed contempt.

27-28 Anyone who eats the bread or drinks the cup of the Master irreverently is like part of the crowd that jeered and spit on him at his death. Is that the kind of "remembrance" you want to be part of? Examine your motives, test your heart, come to this meal in holy awe.

29-32 If you give no thought (or worse, don't care) about the broken body of the Master when you eat and drink, you're running the risk of serious consequences. That's why so many of you even now are listless and sick, and others have gone to an early grave. If we get this straight now, we won't have to be straightened out later on. Better to be confronted by the Master now than to face a fiery confrontation later.

33-34 So, my friends, when you come together to the Lord's Table, be reverent and courteous with one another. If you're so hungry that you can't wait to be served, go home and get a sandwich. But by no means risk turning this Meal into an eating and drinking binge or a family squabble. It is a spiritual meal—a love feast.

The other things you asked about, I'll respond to in person when I make my next visit.

SPIRITUAL GIFTS

1-3 12 What I want to talk about now is the various ways God's Spirit gets worked into our lives. This is complex and often misunderstood, but I want you to be informed and knowledgeable. Remember how you were when you didn't know God, led from one phony god to another, never knowing what you were doing, just doing it because everybody else did it? It's different in this life. God wants us to use our intelligence, to seek to understand as well as we can. For instance, by using your heads, you know perfectly well that the Spirit of God would never prompt anyone to say "Jesus be damned!" Nor would anyone be inclined to say "Jesus is Master!" without the insight of the Holy Spirit.

NEW KING JAMES VERSION

4 There are diversities of gifts, but the same Spirit. 5 There are differences of ministries, but the same Lord. 6 And there are diversities of activities, but it is the same God who works all in all. 7 But the manifestation of the Spirit is given to each one for the profit *of all:* 8 for to one is given the word of wisdom through the Spirit, to another the word of knowledge through the same Spirit, 9 to another faith by the same Spirit, to another gifts of healings by the same[a] Spirit, 10 to another the working of miracles, to another prophecy, to another discerning of spirits, to another *different* kinds of tongues, to another the interpretation of tongues. 11 But one and the same Spirit works all these things, distributing to each one individually as He wills.

UNITY AND DIVERSITY IN ONE BODY

12 For as the body is one and has many members, but all the members of that one body, being many, are one body, so also *is* Christ. 13 For by one Spirit we were all baptized into one body—whether Jews or Greeks, whether slaves or free—and have all been made to drink into[a] one Spirit. 14 For in fact the body is not one member but many.

15 If the foot should say, "Because I am not a hand, I am not of the body," is it therefore not of the body? 16 And if the ear should say, "Because I am not an eye, I am not of the body," is it therefore not of the body? 17 If the whole body *were* an eye, where *would be* the hearing? If the whole *were* hearing, where *would be* the smelling? 18 But now God has set the members, each one of them, in the body just as He pleased. 19 And if they were all one member, where *would* the body *be?*

20 But now indeed *there are* many members, yet one body. 21 And the eye cannot say to the hand, "I have no need of you"; nor again the head to the feet, "I have no need of you." 22 No,

12:9 [a]NU-Text reads *one.* 12:13 [a]NU-Text omits *into.*

THE MESSAGE

4-11 God's various gifts are handed out everywhere; but they all originate in God's Spirit. God's various ministries are carried out everywhere; but they all originate in God's Spirit. God's various expressions of power are in action everywhere; but God himself is behind it all. Each person is given something to do that shows who God is: Everyone gets in on it, everyone benefits. All kinds of things are handed out by the Spirit, and to all kinds of people! The variety is wonderful:

wise counsel
clear understanding
simple trust
healing the sick
miraculous acts
proclamation
distinguishing between spirits
tongues
interpretation of tongues.

All these gifts have a common origin, but are handed out one by one by the one Spirit of God. He decides who gets what, and when.

12-13 You can easily enough see how this kind of thing works by looking no further than your own body. Your body has many parts—limbs, organs, cells—but no matter how many parts you can name, you're still one body. It's exactly the same with Christ. By means of his one Spirit, we all said good-bye to our partial and piecemeal lives. We each used to independently call our own shots, but then we entered into a large and integrated life in which *he* has the final say in everything. (This is what we proclaimed in word and action when we were baptized.) Each of us is now a part of his resurrection body, refreshed and sustained at one fountain—his Spirit—where we all come to drink. The old labels we once used to identify ourselves—labels like Jew or Greek, slave or free—are no longer useful. We need something larger, more comprehensive.

14-18 I want you to think about how all this makes you more significant, not less. A body isn't just a single part blown up into something huge. It's all the different-but-similar parts arranged and functioning together. If Foot said, "I'm not elegant like Hand, embellished with rings; I guess I don't belong to this body," would that make it so? If Ear said, "I'm not beautiful like Eye, limpid and expressive; I don't deserve a place on the head," would you want to remove it from the body? If the body was all eye, how could it hear? If all ear, how could it smell? As it is, we see that God has carefully placed each part of the body right where he wanted it.

19-24 But I also want you to think about how this keeps your significance from getting blown up into self-importance. For no matter how significant you are, it is only because of what you are a *part* of. An enormous eye or a gigantic hand wouldn't be a

NEW KING JAMES VERSION

much rather, those members of the body which seem to be weaker are necessary. 23And those *members* of the body which we think to be less honorable, on these we bestow greater honor; and our unpresentable *parts* have greater modesty, 24but our presentable *parts* have no need. But God composed the body, having given greater honor to that *part* which lacks it, 25that there should be no schism in the body, but *that* the members should have the same care for one another. 26And if one member suffers, all the members suffer with *it;* or if one member is honored, all the members rejoice with *it.*

27Now you are the body of Christ, and members individually. 28And God has appointed these in the church: first apostles, second prophets, third teachers, after that miracles, then gifts of healings, helps, administrations, varieties of tongues. 29*Are* all apostles? *Are* all prophets? *Are* all teachers? *Are* all workers of miracles? 30Do all have gifts of healings? Do all speak with tongues? Do all interpret? 31But earnestly desire the best[a] gifts. And yet I show you a more excellent way.

THE GREATEST GIFT

13 Though I speak with the tongues of men and of angels, but have not love, I have become sounding brass or a clanging cymbal. 2And though I have *the gift of* prophecy, and understand all mysteries and all knowledge, and though I have all faith, so that I could remove mountains, but have not love, I am nothing. 3And though I bestow all my goods to feed *the poor,* and though I give my body to be burned,[a] but have not love, it profits me nothing.

12:31 [a]NU-Text reads *greater.* **13:3** [a]NU-Text reads *so I may boast.*

THE MESSAGE

body, but a monster. What we have is one body with many parts, each its proper size and in its proper place. No part is important on its own. Can you imagine Eye telling Hand, "Get lost; I don't need you"? Or, Head telling Foot, "You're fired; your job has been phased out"? As a matter of fact, in practice it works the other way—the "lower" the part, the more basic, and therefore necessary. You can live without an eye, for instance, but not without a stomach. When it's a part of your own body you are concerned with, it makes *no* difference whether the part is visible or clothed, higher or lower. You give it dignity and honor just as it is, without comparisons. If anything, you have more concern for the lower parts than the higher. If you had to choose, wouldn't you prefer good digestion to full-bodied hair?

25-26 The way God designed our bodies is a model for understanding our lives together as a church: every part dependent on every other part, the parts we mention and the parts we don't, the parts we see and the parts we don't. If one part hurts, every other part is involved in the hurt, and in the healing. If one part flourishes, every other part enters into the exuberance.

27-31 You are Christ's body—that's who you are! You must never forget this. Only as you accept your part of that body does your "part" mean anything. You're familiar with some of the parts that God has formed in his church, which is his "body":

apostles
prophets
teachers
miracle workers
healers
helpers
organizers
those who pray in tongues.

But it's obvious by now, isn't it, that Christ's church is a complete Body and not a gigantic, unidimensional Part? It's not all Apostle, not all Prophet, not all Miracle Worker, not all Healer, not all Prayer in Tongues, not all Interpreter of Tongues. And yet some of you keep competing for so-called "important" parts.

But now I want to lay out a far better way for you.

THE WAY OF LOVE

1 **13** If I speak with human eloquence and angelic ecstasy but don't love, I'm nothing but the creaking of a rusty gate.

2 If I speak God's Word with power, revealing all his mysteries and making everything plain as day, and if I have faith that says to a mountain, "Jump," and it jumps, but I don't love, I'm nothing.

3-7 If I give everything I own to the poor and even go to the stake to be burned as a martyr, but I don't love, I've gotten nowhere. So, no matter what I say, what I believe, and what I do, I'm bankrupt without love.

NEW KING JAMES VERSION

4Love suffers long *and* is kind; love does not
envy; love does not parade itself, is not puffed
up; 5does not behave rudely, does not seek its
own, is not provoked, thinks no evil; 6does not
rejoice in iniquity, but rejoices in the truth;
7bears all things, believes all things, hopes all
things, endures all things.

8Love never fails. But whether *there are*
prophecies, they will fail; whether *there are*
tongues, they will cease; whether *there is*
knowledge, it will vanish away. 9For we know in
part and we prophesy in part. 10But when that
which is perfect has come, then that which is in
part will be done away.

11When I was a child, I spoke as a child, I un-
derstood as a child, I thought as a child; but
when I became a man, I put away childish
things. 12For now we see in a mirror, dimly, but
then face to face. Now I know in part, but then I
shall know just as I also am known.

13And now abide faith, hope, love, these
three; but the greatest of these *is* love.

PROPHECY AND TONGUES

14 Pursue love, and desire spiritual *gifts,* but
especially that you may prophesy. 2For he
who speaks in a tongue does not speak to men
but to God, for no one understands *him;* how-
ever, in the spirit he speaks mysteries. 3But he
who prophesies speaks edification and exhorta-
tion and comfort to men. 4He who speaks in a
tongue edifies himself, but he who prophesies
edifies the church. 5I wish you all spoke with
tongues, but even more that you prophesied;
for[a] he who prophesies *is* greater than he who
speaks with tongues, unless indeed he inter-
prets, that the church may receive edification.

14:5 [a]NU-Text reads *and.*

THE MESSAGE

Love never gives up.
Love cares more for others than for self.
Love doesn't want what it doesn't have.
Love doesn't strut,
Doesn't have a swelled head,
Doesn't force itself on others,
Isn't always "me first,"
Doesn't fly off the handle,
Doesn't keep score of the sins of others,
Doesn't revel when others grovel,
Takes pleasure in the flowering of truth,
Puts up with anything,
Trusts God always,
Always looks for the best,
Never looks back,
But keeps going to the end.

8-10 Love never dies. Inspired speech will be over some day; praying in tongues will end; understanding will reach its limit. We know only a portion of the truth, and what we say about God is always incomplete. But when the Complete arrives, our incompletes will be canceled.

11 When I was an infant at my mother's breast, I gurgled and cooed like any infant. When I grew up, I left those infant ways for good.

12 We don't yet see things clearly. We're squinting in a fog, peering through a mist. But it won't be long before the weather clears and the sun shines bright! We'll see it all then, see it all as clearly as God sees us, knowing him directly just as he knows us!

13 But for right now, until that completeness, we have three things to do to lead us toward that consummation: Trust steadily in God, hope unswervingly, love extravagantly. And the best of the three is love.

PRAYER LANGUAGE

1-3 **14** Go after a life of love as if your life depended on it—because it does. Give yourselves to the gifts God gives you. Most of all, try to proclaim his truth. If you praise him in the private language of tongues, God understands you but no one else does, for you are sharing intimacies just between you and him. But when you proclaim his truth in everyday speech, you're letting *others* in on the truth so that they can grow and be strong and experience his presence with you.

4-5 The one who prays using a private "prayer language" certainly gets a lot out of it, but proclaiming God's truth to the church in its common language brings the whole church into growth and strength. I want all of you to develop intimacies with God in prayer, but please don't stop with that. Go on and proclaim his clear truth to others. It's more important that everyone have access to the knowledge and love of God in language everyone understands than that you go off and cultivate God's presence in a mysterious prayer language—unless, of course, there is someone who can interpret what you are saying for the benefit of all.

New King James Version

Tongues Must Be Interpreted

[6]But now, brethren, if I come to you speaking with tongues, what shall I profit you unless I speak to you either by revelation, by knowledge, by prophesying, or by teaching? [7]Even things without life, whether flute or harp, when they make a sound, unless they make a distinction in the sounds, how will it be known what is piped or played? [8]For if the trumpet makes an uncertain sound, who will prepare for battle? [9]So likewise you, unless you utter by the tongue words easy to understand, how will it be known what is spoken? For you will be speaking into the air. [10]There are, it may be, so many kinds of languages in the world, and none of them *is* without significance. [11]Therefore, if I do not know the meaning of the language, I shall be a foreigner to him who speaks, and he who speaks *will be* a foreigner to me. [12]Even so you, since you are zealous for spiritual *gifts, let it be* for the edification of the church *that* you seek to excel.

[13]Therefore let him who speaks in a tongue pray that he may interpret. [14]For if I pray in a tongue, my spirit prays, but my understanding is unfruitful. [15]What is *the conclusion* then? I will pray with the spirit, and I will also pray with the understanding. I will sing with the spirit, and I will also sing with the understanding. [16]Otherwise, if you bless with the spirit, how will he who occupies the place of the uninformed say "Amen" at your giving of thanks, since he does not understand what you say? [17]For you indeed give thanks well, but the other is not edified.

[18]I thank my God I speak with tongues more than you all; [19]yet in the church I would rather speak five words with my understanding, that I may teach others also, than ten thousand words in a tongue.

Tongues a Sign to Unbelievers

[20]Brethren, do not be children in understanding; however, in malice be babes, but in understanding be mature.

[21]In the law it is written:

"With men of other tongues and other lips
I will speak to this people;
And yet, for all that, they will not hear
Me,"[a]

says the Lord.

14:21 [a]Isaiah 28:11, 12

The Message

6-8 Think, friends: If I come to you and all I do is pray privately to God in a way only he can understand, what are you going to get out of that? If I don't address you plainly with some insight or truth or proclamation or teaching, what help am I to you? If musical instruments—flutes, say, or harps—aren't played so that each note is distinct and in tune, how will anyone be able to catch the melody and enjoy the music? If the trumpet call can't be distinguished, will anyone show up for the battle?

9-12 So if you speak in a way no one can understand, what's the point of opening your mouth? There are many languages in the world and they all mean something to someone. But if *I* don't understand the language, it's not going to do me much good. It's no different with you. Since you're so eager to participate in what God is doing, why don't you concentrate on doing what helps everyone in the church?

13-17 So, when you pray in your private prayer language, don't hoard the experience for yourself. Pray for the insight and ability to bring others into that intimacy. If I pray in tongues, my spirit prays but my mind lies fallow, and all that intelligence is wasted. So what's the solution? The answer is simple enough. Do both. I should be spiritually free and expressive as I pray, but I should also be thoughtful and mindful as I pray. I should sing with my spirit, and sing with my mind. If you give a blessing using your private prayer language, which no one else understands, how can some outsider who has just shown up and has no idea what's going on know when to say "Amen"? Your blessing might be beautiful, but you have very effectively cut that person out of it.

18-19 I'm grateful to God for the gift of praying in tongues that he gives us for praising him, which leads to wonderful intimacies we enjoy with him. I enter into this as much or more than any of you. But when I'm in a church assembled for worship, I'd rather say five words that everyone can understand and learn from than say ten thousand that sound to others like gibberish.

20-25 To be perfectly frank, I'm getting exasperated with your infantile thinking. How long before you grow up and use your head—your *adult* head? It's all right to have a childlike unfamiliarity with evil; a simple *no* is all that's needed there. But there's far more to saying *yes* to something. Only mature and well-exercised intelligence can save you from falling into gullibility. It's written in Scripture that God said,

In strange tongues
  and from the mouths of strangers
I will preach to this people,
  but they'll neither listen nor believe.

So where does it get you, all this speaking in tongues no one understands? It doesn't help believers, and it only gives unbelievers something to gawk at. Plain truth-speaking,

New King James Version

22Therefore tongues are for a sign, not to those who believe but to unbelievers; but prophesying is not for unbelievers but for those who believe. 23Therefore if the whole church comes together in one place, and all speak with tongues, and there come in *those who are* uninformed or unbelievers, will they not say that you are out of your mind? 24But if all prophesy, and an unbeliever or an uninformed person comes in, he is convinced by all, he is convicted by all. 25And thus[a] the secrets of his heart are revealed; and so, falling down on *his* face, he will worship God and report that God is truly among you.

Order in Church Meetings

26How is it then, brethren? Whenever you come together, each of you has a psalm, has a teaching, has a tongue, has a revelation, has an interpretation. Let all things be done for edification. 27If anyone speaks in a tongue, *let there be* two or at the most three, *each* in turn, and let one interpret. 28But if there is no interpreter, let him keep silent in church, and let him speak to himself and to God. 29Let two or three prophets speak, and let the others judge. 30But if *anything* is revealed to another who sits by, let the first keep silent. 31For you can all prophesy one by one, that all may learn and all may be encouraged. 32And the spirits of the prophets are subject to the prophets. 33For God is not *the author* of confusion but of peace, as in all the churches of the saints.

34Let your[a] women keep silent in the churches, for they are not permitted to speak; but *they are* to be submissive, as the law also says. 35And if they want to learn something, let them ask their own husbands at home; for it is shameful for women to speak in church.

36Or did the word of God come *originally* from you? Or *was it* you only that it reached? 37If anyone thinks himself to be a prophet or spiritual, let him acknowledge that the things which I write to you are the commandments of the Lord. 38But if anyone is ignorant, let him be ignorant.[a]

39Therefore, brethren, desire earnestly to prophesy, and do not forbid to speak with tongues. 40Let all things be done decently and in order.

The Risen Christ, Faith's Reality

15 Moreover, brethren, I declare to you the gospel which I preached to you, which also you received and in which you stand, 2by which also you are saved, if you hold fast that word

14:25 [a]NU-Text omits *And thus.* 14:34 [a]NU-Text omits *your.* 14:38 [a]NU-Text reads *if anyone does not recognize this, he is not recognized.*

The Message

on the other hand, goes straight to the heart of believers and doesn't get in the way of unbelievers. If you come together as a congregation and some unbelieving outsiders walk in on you as you're all praying in tongues, unintelligible to each other and to them, won't they assume you've taken leave of your senses and get out of there as fast as they can? But if some unbelieving outsiders walk in on a service where people are speaking out God's truth, the plain words will bring them up against the truth and probe their hearts. Before you know it, they're going to be on their faces before God, recognizing that God is among you.

26-33 So here's what I want you to do. When you gather for worship, each one of you be prepared with something that will be useful for all: Sing a hymn, teach a lesson, tell a story, lead a prayer, provide an insight. If prayers are offered in tongues, two or three's the limit, and then only if someone is present who can interpret what you're saying. Otherwise, keep it between God and yourself. And no more than two or three speakers at a meeting, with the rest of you listening and taking it to heart. Take your turn, no one person taking over. Then each speaker gets a chance to say something special from God, and you all learn from each other. If you choose to speak, you're also responsible for how and when you speak. When we worship the right way, God doesn't stir us up into confusion; he brings us into harmony. This goes for all the churches—no exceptions.

34-36 Wives must not disrupt worship, talking when they should be listening, asking questions that could more appropriately be asked of their husbands at home. God's Book of the law guides our manners and customs here. Wives have no license to use the time of worship for unwarranted speaking. Do you—both women *and* men—imagine that you're a sacred oracle determining what's right and wrong? Do you think everything revolves around you?

37-38 If any one of you thinks God has something for you to say or has inspired you to do something, pay close attention to what I have written. This is the way the Master wants it. If you won't play by these rules, God can't use you. Sorry.

39-40 Three things, then, to sum this up: When you speak forth God's truth, speak your heart out. Don't tell people how they should or shouldn't pray when they're praying in tongues that you don't understand. Be courteous and considerate in everything.

Resurrection

1-2 15 Friends, let me go over the Message with you one final time—this Message that I proclaimed and that you made your own; this Message on which you took your stand and by which your life has been saved. (I'm assuming, now, that your belief was the

NEW KING JAMES VERSION

which I preached to you—unless you believed in
vain.
[3]For I delivered to you first of all that which
I also received: that Christ died for our sins ac-
cording to the Scriptures, [4]and that He was
buried, and that He rose again the third day ac-
cording to the Scriptures, [5]and that He was seen
by Cephas, then by the twelve. [6]After that He
was seen by over five hundred brethren at once,
of whom the greater part remain to the present,
but some have fallen asleep. [7]After that He was
seen by James, then by all the apostles. [8]Then
last of all He was seen by me also, as by one
born out of due time.
[9]For I am the least of the apostles, who am
not worthy to be called an apostle, because I
persecuted the church of God. [10]But by the grace
of God I am what I am, and His grace toward me
was not in vain; but I labored more abundantly
than they all, yet not I, but the grace of God
which was with me. [11]Therefore, whether *it was*
I or they, so we preach and so you believed.

THE RISEN CHRIST, OUR HOPE

[12]Now if Christ is preached that He has been
raised from the dead, how do some among you
say that there is no resurrection of the dead?
[13]But if there is no resurrection of the dead, then
Christ is not risen. [14]And if Christ is not risen,
then our preaching *is* empty and your faith *is*
also empty. [15]Yes, and we are found false wit-
nesses of God, because we have testified of God
that He raised up Christ, whom He did not raise
up—if in fact the dead do not rise. [16]For if *the*
dead do not rise, then Christ is not risen. [17]And
if Christ is not risen, your faith *is* futile; you are
still in your sins! [18]Then also those who have
fallen asleep in Christ have perished. [19]If in this
life only we have hope in Christ, we are of all
men the most pitiable.

THE LAST ENEMY DESTROYED

[20]But now Christ is risen from the dead, *and*
has become the firstfruits of those who have
fallen asleep. [21]For since by man *came* death, by
Man also *came* the resurrection of the dead.
[22]For as in Adam all die, even so in Christ all
shall be made alive. [23]But each one in his own
order: Christ the firstfruits, afterward those *who
are* Christ's at His coming. [24]Then *comes* the
end, when He delivers the kingdom to God the
Father, when He puts an end to all rule and all
authority and power. [25]For He must reign till He
has put all enemies under His feet. [26]The last en-

THE MESSAGE

real thing and not a passing fancy, that you're in this for good and holding fast.)

3-9 The first thing I did was place before you what was placed so emphatically before me: that the Messiah died for our sins, exactly as Scripture tells it; that he was buried; that he was raised from death on the third day, again exactly as Scripture says; that he presented himself alive to Peter, then to his closest followers, and later to more than five hundred of his followers all at the same time, most of them still around (although a few have since died); that he then spent time with James and the rest of those he commissioned to represent him; and that he finally presented himself alive to *me*. It was fitting that I bring up the rear. I don't deserve to be included in that inner circle, as you well know, having spent all those early years trying my best to stamp God's church right out of existence.

10-11 But because God was so gracious, so very generous, here I am. And I'm not about to let his grace go to waste. Haven't I worked hard trying to do more than any of the others? Even then, my work didn't amount to all that much. It was God giving me the work to do, God giving me the energy to do it. So whether you heard it from me or from those others, it's all the same: We spoke God's truth and you entrusted your lives.

12-15 Now, let me ask you something profound yet troubling. If you became believers because you trusted the proclamation that Christ is alive, risen from the dead, how can you let people say that there is no such thing as a resurrection? If there's no resurrection, there's no living Christ. And face it—if there's no resurrection for Christ, everything we've told you is smoke and mirrors, and everything you've staked your life on is smoke and mirrors. Not only that, but we would be guilty of telling a string of barefaced lies about God, all these affidavits we passed on to you verifying that God raised up Christ—sheer fabrications, if there's no resurrection.

16-20 If corpses can't be raised, then Christ wasn't, because he was indeed dead. And if Christ weren't raised, then all you're doing is wandering about in the dark, as lost as ever. It's even worse for those who died hoping in Christ and resurrection, because they're already in their graves. If all we get out of Christ is a little inspiration for a few short years, we're a pretty sorry lot. But the truth is that Christ *has* been raised up, the first in a long legacy of those who are going to leave the cemeteries.

21-28 There is a nice symmetry in this: Death initially came by a man, and resurrection from death came by a man. Everybody dies in Adam; everybody comes alive in Christ. But we have to wait our turn: Christ is first, then those with him at his Coming, the grand consummation when, after crushing the opposition, he hands over his kingdom to God the Father. He won't let up until the last enemy is down—and the very last en-

NEW KING JAMES VERSION

emy *that* will be destroyed *is* death. [27]For *"He has put all things under His feet."* [a] But when He says "all things are put under *Him,*" *it is* evident that He who put all things under Him is excepted. [28]Now when all things are made subject to Him, then the Son Himself will also be subject to Him who put all things under Him, that God may be all in all.

EFFECTS OF DENYING THE RESURRECTION

[29]Otherwise, what will they do who are baptized for the dead, if the dead do not rise at all? Why then are they baptized for the dead? [30]And why do we stand in jeopardy every hour? [31]I affirm, by the boasting in you which I have in Christ Jesus our Lord, I die daily. [32]If, in the manner of men, I have fought with beasts at Ephesus, what advantage *is it* to me? If *the* dead do not rise, *"Let us eat and drink, for tomorrow we die!"* [a]

[33]Do not be deceived: "Evil company corrupts good habits." [34]Awake to righteousness, and do not sin; for some do not have the knowledge of God. I speak *this* to your shame.

A GLORIOUS BODY

[35]But someone will say, "How are the dead raised up? And with what body do they come?" [36]Foolish one, what you sow is not made alive unless it dies. [37]And what you sow, you do not sow that body that shall be, but mere grain—perhaps wheat or some other *grain.* [38]But God gives it a body as He pleases, and to each seed its own body.

[39]All flesh *is* not the same flesh, but *there is* one *kind of* flesh[a] of men, another flesh of animals, another of fish, *and* another of birds.

[40]*There are* also celestial bodies and terrestrial bodies; but the glory of the celestial *is* one, and the *glory* of the terrestrial *is* another. [41]*There is* one glory of the sun, another glory of the moon, and another glory of the stars; for *one* star differs from *another* star in glory.

15:27 [a]Psalm 8:6 **15:32** [a]Isaiah 22:13 **15:39** [a]NU-Text and M-Text omit *of flesh.*

THE MESSAGE

emy is death! As the psalmist said, "He laid them low, one and all; he walked all over them." When Scripture says that "he walked all over them," it's obvious that he couldn't at the same time be walked on. When everything and everyone is finally under God's rule, the Son will step down, taking his place with everyone else, showing that God's rule is absolutely comprehensive—a perfect ending!

29 Why do you think people offer themselves to be baptized for those already in the grave? If there's no chance of resurrection for a corpse, if God's power stops at the cemetery gates, why do we keep doing things that suggest he's going to clean the place out someday, pulling everyone up on their feet alive?

30-33 And why do you think I keep risking my neck in this dangerous work? I look death in the face practically every day I live. Do you think I'd do this if I wasn't convinced of your resurrection and mine as guaranteed by the resurrected Messiah Jesus? Do you think I was just trying to act heroic when I fought the wild beasts at Ephesus, hoping it wouldn't be the end of me? Not on your life! It's resurrection, resurrection, always resurrection, that undergirds what I do and say, the way I live. If there's no resurrection, "We eat, we drink, the next day we die," and that's all there is to it. But don't fool yourselves. Don't let yourselves be poisoned by this anti-resurrection loose talk. "Bad company ruins good manners."

34 Think straight. Awaken to the holiness of life. No more playing fast and loose with resurrection facts. Ignorance of God is a luxury you can't afford in times like these. Aren't you embarrassed that you've let this kind of thing go on as long as you have?

35-38 Some skeptic is sure to ask, "Show me how resurrection works. Give me a diagram; draw me a picture. What does this 'resurrection body' look like?" If you look at this question closely, you realize how absurd it is. There are no diagrams for this kind of thing. We do have a parallel experience in gardening. You plant a "dead" seed; soon there is a flourishing plant. There is no visual likeness between seed and plant. You could never guess what a tomato would look like by looking at a tomato seed. What we plant in the soil and what grows out of it don't look anything alike. The dead body that we bury in the ground and the resurrection body that comes from it will be dramatically different.

39-41 You will notice that the variety of bodies is stunning. Just as there are different kinds of seeds, there are different kinds of bodies—humans, animals, birds, fish— each unprecedented in its form. You get a hint at the diversity of resurrection glory by looking at the diversity of bodies not only on earth but in the skies—sun, moon, stars—all these varieties of beauty and brightness. And we're only looking at pre-resurrection "seeds"—who can imagine what the resurrection "plants" will be like!

New King James Version

42So also *is* the resurrection of the dead. *The
body* is sown in corruption, it is raised in incor-
ruption. 43It is sown in dishonor, it is raised in
glory. It is sown in weakness, it is raised in
power. 44It is sown a natural body, it is raised a
spiritual body. There is a natural body, and there
is a spiritual body. 45And so it is written, *"The
first man Adam became a living being."*[a] The
last Adam *became* a life-giving spirit.
46However, the spiritual is not first, but the
natural, and afterward the spiritual. 47The first
man *was* of the earth, *made* of dust; the second
Man *is* the Lord[a] from heaven. 48As *was* the *man*
of dust, so also *are* those *who are made* of dust;
and as *is* the heavenly *Man*, so also *are* those
who are heavenly. 49And as we have borne the
image of the *man* of dust, we shall also bear[a] the
image of the heavenly *Man*.

Our Final Victory

50Now this I say, brethren, that flesh and blood
cannot inherit the kingdom of God; nor does cor-
ruption inherit incorruption. 51Behold, I tell you a
mystery: We shall not all sleep, but we shall all be
changed— 52in a moment, in the twinkling of an
eye, at the last trumpet. For the trumpet will
sound, and the dead will be raised incorruptible,
and we shall be changed. 53For this corruptible
must put on incorruption, and this mortal *must*
put on immortality. 54So when this corruptible has
put on incorruption, and this mortal has put on
immortality, then shall be brought to pass the say-
ing that is written: *"Death is swallowed up in vic-
tory."*[a]

55*"O Death, where is your sting?*[a]
O Hades, where is your victory?"[b]

56The sting of death *is* sin, and the strength of
sin *is* the law. 57But thanks *be* to God, who gives
us the victory through our Lord Jesus Christ.
58Therefore, my beloved brethren, be stead-
fast, immovable, always abounding in the work
of the Lord, knowing that your labor is not in
vain in the Lord.

Collection for the Saints

16 Now concerning the collection for the
saints, as I have given orders to the

15:45 [a]Genesis 2:7 **15:47** [a]NU-Text omits *the Lord.* **15:49** [a]M-Text reads *let us also bear.* **15:54** [a]Isaiah 25:8 **15:55** [a]Hosea 13:14 [b]NU-Text reads *O Death, where is your victory? O Death, where is your sting?*

The Message

42-44 This image of planting a dead seed and raising a live plant is a mere sketch at best, but perhaps it will help in approaching the mystery of the resurrection body—but only if you keep in mind that when we're raised, we're raised for *good*, alive forever! The corpse that's planted is no beauty, but when it's raised, it's glorious. Put in the ground weak, it comes up powerful. The seed sown is natural; the seed grown is supernatural—same seed, same body, but what a difference from when it goes down in physical mortality to when it is raised up in spiritual immortality!

45-49 We follow this sequence in Scripture: The First Adam received life, the Last Adam is a life-giving Spirit. Physical life comes first, then spiritual—a firm base shaped from the earth, a final completion coming out of heaven. The First Man was made out of earth, and people since then are earthy; the Second Man was made out of heaven, and people now can be heavenly. In the same way that we've worked from our earthy origins, let's embrace our heavenly ends.

50 I need to emphasize, friends, that our natural, earthy lives don't in themselves lead us by their very nature into the kingdom of God. Their very "nature" is to die, so how could they "naturally" end up in the Life kingdom?

51-57 But let me tell you something wonderful, a mystery I'll probably never fully understand. We're not all going to die—*but* we are all going to be changed. You hear a blast to end all blasts from a trumpet, and in the time that you look up and blink your eyes—it's over. On signal from that trumpet from heaven, the dead will be up and out of their graves, beyond the reach of death, never to die again. At the same moment and in the same way, we'll all be changed. In the resurrection scheme of things, this has to happen: everything perishable taken off the shelves and replaced by the imperishable, this mortal replaced by the immortal. Then the saying will come true:

Death swallowed by triumphant Life!
Who got the last word, oh, Death?
Oh, Death, who's afraid of you now?

It was sin that made death so frightening and law-code guilt that gave sin its leverage, its destructive power. But now in a single victorious stroke of Life, all three—sin, guilt, death—are gone, the gift of our Master, Jesus Christ. Thank God!

58 With all this going for us, my dear, dear friends, stand your ground. And don't hold back. Throw yourselves into the work of the Master, confident that nothing you do for him is a waste of time or effort.

Coming to See You

1-4 16 Regarding the relief offering for poor Christians that is being collected, you get the same instructions I gave the

NEW KING JAMES VERSION

churches of Galatia, so you must do also: 2On
the first *day* of the week let each one of you lay
something aside, storing up as he may prosper,
that there be no collections when I come. 3And
when I come, whomever you approve by *your*
letters I will send to bear your gift to Jerusalem.
4But if it is fitting that I go also, they will go with
me.

PERSONAL PLANS

5Now I will come to you when I pass through
Macedonia (for I am passing through Macedo-
nia). 6And it may be that I will remain, or even
spend the winter with you, that you may send
me on my journey, wherever I go. 7For I do not
wish to see you now on the way; but I hope to
stay a while with you, if the Lord permits.

8But I will tarry in Ephesus until Pentecost.
9For a great and effective door has opened to
me, and *there are* many adversaries.

10And if Timothy comes, see that he may be
with you without fear; for he does the work of
the Lord, as I also *do.* 11Therefore let no one de-
spise him. But send him on his journey in peace,
that he may come to me; for I am waiting for
him with the brethren.

12Now concerning *our* brother Apollos, I
strongly urged him to come to you with the
brethren, but he was quite unwilling to come at
this time; however, he will come when he has a
convenient time.

FINAL EXHORTATIONS

13Watch, stand fast in the faith, be brave, be
strong. 14Let all *that* you *do* be done with love.

15I urge you, brethren—you know the house-
hold of Stephanas, that it is the firstfruits of
Achaia, and *that* they have devoted themselves
to the ministry of the saints— 16that you also
submit to such, and to everyone who works and
labors with *us.*

17I am glad about the coming of Stephanas,
Fortunatus, and Achaicus, for what was lacking
on your part they supplied. 18For they refreshed
my spirit and yours. Therefore acknowledge
such men.

GREETINGS AND A SOLEMN FAREWELL

19The churches of Asia greet you. Aquila and
Priscilla greet you heartily in the Lord, with the
church that is in their house. 20All the brethren
greet you.

Greet one another with a holy kiss.

21The salutation with my own hand—Paul's.

22If anyone does not love the Lord Jesus
Christ, let him be accursed.[a] O Lord, come![b]

23The grace of our Lord Jesus Christ *be* with
you. 24My love *be* with you all in Christ Jesus.
Amen.

16:22 [a]Greek *anathema* [b]Aramaic *Maranatha*

THE MESSAGE

churches in Galatia. Every Sunday each of you make an offering and put it in safekeeping. Be as generous as you can. When I get there you'll have it ready, and I won't have to make a special appeal. Then after I arrive, I'll write letters authorizing whomever you delegate, and send them off to Jerusalem to deliver your gift. If you think it best that I go along, I'll be glad to travel with them.

5-9 I plan to visit you after passing through northern Greece. I won't be staying long there, but maybe I can stay awhile with you—maybe even spend the winter? Then you could give me a good send-off, wherever I may be headed next. I don't want to just drop by in between other "primary" destinations. I want a good, long, leisurely visit. If the Master agrees, we'll have it! For the present, I'm staying right here in Ephesus. A huge door of opportunity for good work has opened up here. (There is also mushrooming opposition.)

10-11 If Timothy shows up, take good care of him. Make him feel completely at home among you. He works so hard for the Master, just as I do. Don't let anyone disparage him. After a while, send him on to me with your blessing. Tell him I'm expecting him, and any friends he has with him.

12 About our friend Apollos, I've done my best to get him to pay you a visit, but haven't talked him into it yet. He doesn't think this is the right time. But there will be a "right time."

13-14 Keep your eyes open, hold tight to your convictions, give it all you've got, be resolute, and love without stopping.

15-16 Would you do me a favor, friends, and give special recognition to the family of Stephanas? You know, they were among the first converts in Greece, and they've put themselves out, serving Christians ever since then. I want you to honor and look up to people like that: companions and workers who show us how to do it, giving us something to aspire to.

17-18 I want you to know how delighted I am to have Stephanas, Fortunatus, and Achaicus here with me. They partially make up for your absence! They've refreshed me by keeping me in touch with you. Be proud that you have people like this among you.

19 The churches here in western Asia send greetings.

Aquila, Priscilla, and the church that meets in their house say hello.

20 All the friends here say hello.

Pass the greetings around with holy embraces!

21 And I, Paul—in my own handwriting!—send you my regards.

22 If anyone won't love the Master, throw him out. Make room for the Master!

23 Our Master Jesus has his arms wide open for you.

24 And I love all of you in the Messiah, in Jesus.

2 CORINTHIANS

New King James Version

Greeting

1 Paul, an apostle of Jesus Christ by the will of God, and Timothy *our* brother,

To the church of God which is at Corinth, with all the saints who are in all Achaia:

2 Grace to you and peace from God our Father and the Lord Jesus Christ.

Comfort in Suffering

3 Blessed *be* the God and Father of our Lord Jesus Christ, the Father of mercies and God of all comfort, 4 who comforts us in all our tribulation, that we may be able to comfort those who are in any trouble, with the comfort with which we ourselves are comforted by God. 5 For as the sufferings of Christ abound in us, so our consolation also abounds through Christ. 6 Now if we are afflicted, *it is* for your consolation and salvation, which is effective for enduring the same sufferings which we also suffer. Or if we are comforted, *it is* for your consolation and salvation. 7 And our hope for you *is* steadfast, because we know that as you are partakers of the sufferings, so also *you will partake* of the consolation.

Delivered from Suffering

8 For we do not want you to be ignorant, brethren, of our trouble which came to us in Asia: that we were burdened beyond measure, above strength, so that we despaired even of life. 9 Yes, we had the sentence of death in ourselves, that we should not trust in ourselves but in God who raises the dead, 10 who delivered us from so great a death, and does[a] deliver us; in whom we trust that He will still deliver *us,* 11 you also helping together in prayer for us, that thanks may be given by many persons on our[a] behalf for the gift *granted* to us through many.

Paul's Sincerity

12 For our boasting is this: the testimony of our conscience that we conducted ourselves in the world in simplicity and godly sincerity, not with fleshly wisdom but by the grace of God, and more abundantly toward you. 13 For we are not writing any other things to you than what you read or understand. Now I trust you will understand, even to the end 14 (as also you have understood us in part), that we are your boast as you also *are* ours, in the day of the Lord Jesus.

1:10 [a]NU-Text reads *shall.* **1:11** [a]M-Text reads *your behalf.*

The Message

1-2 **1** I, Paul, have been sent on a special mission by the Messiah, Jesus, planned by God himself. I write this to God's congregation in Corinth, and to believers all over Achaia province. May all the gifts and benefits that come from God our Father and the Master, Jesus Christ, be yours! Timothy, someone you know and trust, joins me in this greeting.

The Rescue

3-5 All praise to the God and Father of our Master, Jesus the Messiah! Father of all mercy! God of all healing counsel! He comes alongside us when we go through hard times, and before you know it, he brings us alongside someone else who is going through hard times so that we can be there for that person just as God was there for us. We have plenty of hard times that come from following the Messiah, but no more so than the good times of his healing comfort—we get a full measure of that, too.

6-7 When we suffer for Jesus, it works out for your healing and salvation. If we are treated well, given a helping hand and encouraging word, that also works to your benefit, spurring you on, face forward, unflinching. Your hard times are also our hard times. When we see that you're just as willing to endure the hard times as to enjoy the good times, we know you're going to make it, no doubt about it.

8-11 We don't want you in the dark, friends, about how hard it was when all this came down on us in Asia province. It was so bad we didn't think we were going to make it. We felt like we'd been sent to death row, that it was all over for us. As it turned out, it was the best thing that could have happened. Instead of trusting in our own strength or wits to get out of it, we were forced to trust God totally—not a bad idea since he's the God who raises the dead! And he did it, rescued us from certain doom. *And* he'll do it again, rescuing us as many times as we need rescuing. You and your prayers are part of the rescue operation—I don't want you in the dark about that either. I can see your faces even now, lifted in praise for God's deliverance of us, a rescue in which your prayers played such a crucial part.

12-14 Now that the worst is over, we're pleased we can report that we've come out of this with conscience and faith intact, and can face the world—and even more importantly, face you with our heads held high. But it wasn't by any fancy footwork on our part. It was *God* who kept us focused on him, uncompromised. Don't try to read between the lines or look for hidden meanings in this letter. We're writing plain, unembellished truth, hoping that you'll now see the whole picture as well as you've seen some of the details. We want you to be as proud of us as we are of you when we stand together before our Master Jesus.

New King James Version

Sparing the Church

15And in this confidence I intended to come to you before, that you might have a second benefit— 16to pass by way of you to Macedonia, to come again from Macedonia to you, and be helped by you on my way to Judea. 17Therefore, when I was planning this, did I do it lightly? Or the things I plan, do I plan according to the flesh, that with me there should be Yes, Yes, and No, No? 18But *as* God *is* faithful, our word to you was not Yes and No. 19For the Son of God, Jesus Christ, who was preached among you by us—by me, Silvanus, and Timothy—was not Yes and No, but in Him was Yes. 20For all the promises of God in Him *are* Yes, and in Him Amen, to the glory of God through us. 21Now He who establishes us with you in Christ and has anointed us *is* God, 22who also has sealed us and given us the Spirit in our hearts as a guarantee.

23Moreover I call God as witness against my soul, that to spare you I came no more to Corinth. 24Not that we have dominion over your faith, but are fellow workers for your joy; for by faith you stand.

2 But I determined this within myself, that I would not come again to you in sorrow. 2For if I make you sorrowful, then who is he who makes me glad but the one who is made sorrowful by me?

Forgive the Offender

3And I wrote this very thing to you, lest, when I came, I should have sorrow over those from whom I ought to have joy, having confidence in you all that my joy is *the joy* of you all. 4For out of much affliction and anguish of heart I wrote to you, with many tears, not that you should be grieved, but that you might know the love which I have so abundantly for you.

5But if anyone has caused grief, he has not grieved me, but all of you to some extent—not to be too severe. 6This punishment which *was inflicted* by the majority *is* sufficient for such a man, 7so that, on the contrary, you *ought* rather to forgive and comfort *him*, lest perhaps such a one be swallowed up with too much sorrow. 8Therefore I urge you to reaffirm *your* love to him.

The Message

15-16 Confident of your welcome, I had originally planned two great visits with you—coming by on my way to Macedonia province, and then again on my return trip. Then we could have had a bon-voyage party as you sent me off to Judea. That was the plan.

17-19 Are you now going to accuse me of being flip with my promises because it didn't work out? Do you think I talk out of both sides of my mouth—a glib *yes* one moment, a glib *no* the next? Well, you're wrong. I try to be as true to my word as God is to his. Our word to you wasn't a careless yes canceled by an indifferent no. How could it be? When Silas and Timothy and I proclaimed the Son of God among you, did you pick up on any yes-and-no, on-again, off-again waffling? Wasn't it a clean, strong Yes?

20-22 Whatever God has promised gets stamped with the Yes of Jesus. In him, this is what we preach and pray, the great Amen, God's Yes and our Yes together, gloriously evident. God affirms us, making us a sure thing in Christ, putting his Yes within us. By his Spirit he has stamped us with his eternal pledge—a sure beginning of what he is destined to complete.

23 Now, are you ready for the real reason I didn't visit you in Corinth? As God is my witness, the only reason I didn't come was to spare you pain. I was being *considerate* of you, not indifferent, not manipulative.

24 We're not in charge of how you live out the faith, looking over your shoulders, suspiciously critical. We're partners, working alongside you, joyfully expectant. I know that you stand by your own faith, not by ours.

1-2 2 That's why I decided not to make another visit that could only be painful to both of us. If by merely showing up I would put you in an embarrassingly painful position, how would you then be free to cheer and refresh me?

3-4 That was my reason for writing a letter instead of coming—so I wouldn't have to spend a miserable time disappointing the very friends I had looked forward to cheering me up. I was convinced at the time I wrote it that what was best for me was also best for you. As it turned out, there was pain enough just in writing that letter, more tears than ink on the parchment. But I didn't write it to cause pain; I wrote it so you would know how much I care—oh, more than care—*love* you!

5-8 Now, regarding the one who started all this—the person in question who caused all this pain—I want you to know that I am not the one injured in this as much as, with a few exceptions, all of you. So I don't want to come down too hard. What the majority of you agreed to as punishment is punishment enough. Now is the time to forgive this man and help him back on his feet. If all you do is pour on the guilt, you could very well drown him in it. My counsel now is to pour on the love.

NEW KING JAMES VERSION

9For to this end I also wrote, that I might put you to the test, whether you are obedient in all things. 10Now whom you forgive anything, I also *forgive.* For if indeed I have forgiven anything, I have forgiven that one[a] for your sakes in the presence of Christ, 11lest Satan should take advantage of us; for we are not ignorant of his devices.

TRIUMPH IN CHRIST

12Furthermore, when I came to Troas to *preach* Christ's gospel, and a door was opened to me by the Lord, 13I had no rest in my spirit, because I did not find Titus my brother; but taking my leave of them, I departed for Macedonia.

14Now thanks *be* to God who always leads us in triumph in Christ, and through us diffuses the fragrance of His knowledge in every place. 15For we are to God the fragrance of Christ among those who are being saved and among those who are perishing. 16To the one *we are* the aroma of death *leading* to death, and to the other the aroma of life *leading* to life. And who *is* sufficient for these things? 17For we are not, as so many,[a] peddling the word of God; but as of sincerity, but as from God, we speak in the sight of God in Christ.

CHRIST'S EPISTLE

3 Do we begin again to commend ourselves? Or do we need, as some *others,* epistles of commendation to you or *letters* of commendation from you? 2You are our epistle written in our hearts, known and read by all men; 3clearly you are an epistle of Christ, ministered by us, written not with ink but by the Spirit of the living God, not on tablets of stone but on tablets of flesh, *that is,* of the heart.

THE SPIRIT, NOT THE LETTER

4And we have such trust through Christ toward God. 5Not that we are sufficient of ourselves to think of anything as *being* from ourselves, but our sufficiency *is* from God, 6who also made us sufficient as ministers of the new covenant, not of the letter but of the Spirit;[a] for the letter kills, but the Spirit gives life.

GLORY OF THE NEW COVENANT

7But if the ministry of death, written *and* engraved on stones, was glorious, so that the children of Israel could not look steadily at the face of Moses because of the glory of his counte-

2:10 [a]NU-Text reads *For indeed, what I have forgiven, if I have forgiven anything, I did it.* **2:17** [a]M-Text reads *the rest.* **3:6** [a]Or *spirit*

THE MESSAGE

9-11 The focus of my letter wasn't on punishing the offender but on getting you to take responsibility for the health of the church. So if you forgive him, I forgive him. Don't think I'm carrying around a list of personal grudges. The fact is that I'm joining in with *your* forgiveness, as Christ is with us, guiding us. After all, we don't want to unwittingly give Satan an opening for yet more mischief—we're not oblivious to his sly ways!

AN OPEN DOOR

12-14 When I arrived in Troas to proclaim the Message of the Messiah, I found the place wide open: God had opened the door; all I had to do was walk through it. But when I didn't find Titus waiting for me with news of your condition, I couldn't relax. Worried about you, I left and came on to Macedonia province looking for Titus and a reassuring word on you. And I got it, thank God!

14-16 In the Messiah, in Christ, God leads us from place to place in one perpetual victory parade. Through us, he brings knowledge of Christ. Everywhere we go, people breathe in the exquisite fragrance. Because of Christ, we give off a sweet scent rising to God, which is recognized by those on the way of salvation—an aroma redolent with life. But those on the way to destruction treat us more like the stench from a rotting corpse.

16-17 This is a terrific responsibility. Is anyone competent to take it on? No—but at least we don't take God's Word, water it down, and then take it to the streets to sell it cheap. We stand in Christ's presence when we speak; God looks us in the face. We get what we say straight from God and say it as honestly as we can.

1-3 3 Does it sound like we're patting ourselves on the back, insisting on our credentials, asserting our authority? Well, we're not. Neither do we need letters of endorsement, either to you or from you. You yourselves are all the endorsement we need. Your very lives are a letter that anyone can read by just looking at you. Christ himself wrote it—not with ink, but with God's living Spirit; not chiseled into stone, but carved into human lives—and we publish it.

4-6 We couldn't be more sure of ourselves in this—that *you,* written by Christ himself for God, are our letter of recommendation. We wouldn't think of writing this kind of letter about ourselves. Only God can write such a letter. His letter authorizes us to help carry out this new plan of action. The plan wasn't written out with ink on paper, with pages and pages of legal footnotes, killing your spirit. It's written with Spirit on spirit, his life on our lives!

LIFTING THE VEIL

7-8 The Government of Death, its constitution chiseled on stone tablets, had a dazzling inaugural. Moses' face as he delivered the tablets was so bright that day (even though it would fade soon enough) that the people of

New King James Version

nance, which *glory* was passing away, [8]how will
the ministry of the Spirit not be more glorious?
[9]For if the ministry of condemnation *had* glory,
the ministry of righteousness exceeds much
more in glory. [10]For even what was made glori-
ous had no glory in this respect, because of the
glory that excels. [11]For if what is passing away
was glorious, what remains *is* much more glori-
ous.

[12]Therefore, since we have such hope, we use
great boldness of speech— [13]unlike Moses, *who*
put a veil over his face so that the children of Is-
rael could not look steadily at the end of what
was passing away. [14]But their minds were
blinded. For until this day the same veil remains
unlifted in the reading of the Old Testament, be-
cause the *veil* is taken away in Christ. [15]But even
to this day, when Moses is read, a veil lies on
their heart. [16]Nevertheless when one turns to the
Lord, the veil is taken away. [17]Now the Lord is
the Spirit; and where the Spirit of the Lord *is*,
there *is* liberty. [18]But we all, with unveiled face,
beholding as in a mirror the glory of the Lord,
are being transformed into the same image from
glory to glory, just as by the Spirit of the Lord.

The Light of Christ's Gospel

4 Therefore, since we have this ministry, as we
have received mercy, we do not lose heart.
[2]But we have renounced the hidden things of
shame, not walking in craftiness nor handling
the word of God deceitfully, but by manifesta-
tion of the truth commending ourselves to every
man's conscience in the sight of God. [3]But even
if our gospel is veiled, it is veiled to those who
are perishing, [4]whose minds the god of this age
has blinded, who do not believe, lest the light of
the gospel of the glory of Christ, who is the im-
age of God, should shine on them. [5]For we do
not preach ourselves, but Christ Jesus the Lord,
and ourselves your bondservants for Jesus'
sake. [6]For it is the God who commanded light to

The Message

Israel could no more look right at him than stare into the sun. How much more dazzling, then, the Government of Living Spirit?

9-11 If the Government of Condemnation was impressive, how about this Government of Affirmation? Bright as that old government was, it would look downright dull alongside this new one. If that makeshift arrangement impressed us, how much more this brightly shining government installed for eternity?

12-15 With that kind of hope to excite us, nothing holds us back. Unlike Moses, we have nothing to hide. Everything is out in the open with us. He wore a veil so the children of Israel wouldn't notice that the glory was fading away—and they *didn't* notice. They didn't notice it then and they don't notice it now, don't notice that there's nothing left behind that veil. Even today when the proclamations of that old, bankrupt government are read out, they can't see through it. Only Christ can get rid of the veil so they can see for themselves that there's nothing there.

16-18 Whenever, though, they turn to face God as Moses did, God removes the veil and there they are—face-to-face! They suddenly recognize that God is a living, personal presence, not a piece of chiseled stone. And when God is personally present, a living Spirit, that old, constricting legislation is recognized as obsolete. We're free of it! All of us! Nothing between us and God, our faces shining with the brightness of his face. And so we are transfigured much like the Messiah, our lives gradually becoming brighter and more beautiful as God enters our lives and we become like him.

Trial and Torture

1-2 4 Since God has so generously let us in on what he is doing, we're not about to throw up our hands and walk off the job just because we run into occasional hard times. We refuse to wear masks and play games. We don't maneuver and manipulate behind the scenes. And we don't twist God's Word to suit ourselves. Rather, we keep everything we do and say out in the open, the whole truth on display, so that those who want to can see and judge for themselves in the presence of God.

3-4 If our Message is obscure to anyone, it's not because we're holding back in any way. No, it's because these other people are looking or going the wrong way and refuse to give it serious attention. All they have eyes for is the fashionable god of darkness. They think he can give them what they want, and that they won't have to bother believing a Truth they can't see. They're stone-blind to the dayspring brightness of the Message that shines with Christ, who gives us the best picture of God we'll ever get.

5-6 Remember, our Message is not about ourselves; we're proclaiming Jesus Christ, the Master. All we are is messengers, errand runners from Jesus for you. It started when

NEW KING JAMES VERSION

shine out of darkness, who has shone in our
hearts to *give* the light of the knowledge of the
glory of God in the face of Jesus Christ.

CAST DOWN BUT UNCONQUERED

7But we have this treasure in earthen vessels,
that the excellence of the power may be of God
and not of us. 8*We are* hard-pressed on every
side, yet not crushed; *we are* perplexed, but not
in despair; 9persecuted, but not forsaken; struck
down, but not destroyed— 10always carrying
about in the body the dying of the Lord Jesus,
that the life of Jesus also may be manifested in
our body. 11For we who live are always delivered
to death for Jesus' sake, that the life of Jesus
also may be manifested in our mortal flesh. 12So
then death is working in us, but life in you.
13And since we have the same spirit of faith,
according to what is written, *"I believed and
therefore I spoke,"*[a] we also believe and there-
fore speak, 14knowing that He who raised up the
Lord Jesus will also raise us up with Jesus, and
will present *us* with you. 15For all things *are* for
your sakes, that grace, having spread through
the many, may cause thanksgiving to abound to
the glory of God.

SEEING THE INVISIBLE

16Therefore we do not lose heart. Even
though our outward man is perishing, yet the in-
ward *man* is being renewed day by day. 17For
our light affliction, which is but for a moment, is
working for us a far more exceeding *and* eternal
weight of glory, 18while we do not look at the
things which are seen, but at the things which
are not seen. For the things which are seen *are*
temporary, but the things which are not seen *are*
eternal.

ASSURANCE OF THE RESURRECTION

5 For we know that if our earthly house, *this*
tent, is destroyed, we have a building from
God, a house not made with hands, eternal in
the heavens. 2For in this we groan, earnestly de-
siring to be clothed with our habitation which is
from heaven, 3if indeed, having been clothed, we
shall not be found naked. 4For we who are in
this tent groan, being burdened, not because we
want to be unclothed, but further clothed, that
mortality may be swallowed up by life. 5Now He
who has prepared us for this very thing *is* God,
who also has given us the Spirit as a guarantee.
6So *we are* always confident, knowing that
while we are at home in the body we are absent
from the Lord. 7For we walk by faith, not by
sight. 8We are confident, yes, well pleased rather
to be absent from the body and to be present
with the Lord.

4:13 [a]Psalm 116:10

THE MESSAGE

God said, "Light up the darkness!" and our lives filled up with light as we saw and understood God in the face of Christ, all bright and beautiful.

7-12 If you only look at *us*, you might well miss the brightness. We carry this precious Message around in the unadorned clay pots of our ordinary lives. That's to prevent anyone from confusing God's incomparable power with us. As it is, there's not much chance of that. You know for yourselves that we're not much to look at. We've been surrounded and battered by troubles, but we're not demoralized; we're not sure what to do, but we know that God knows what to do; we've been spiritually terrorized, but God hasn't left our side; we've been thrown down, but we haven't broken. What they did to Jesus, they do to us—trial and torture, mockery and murder; what Jesus did among them, he does in us—he lives! Our lives are at constant risk for Jesus' sake, which makes Jesus' life all the more evident in us. While we're going through the worst, you're getting in on the best!

13-15 We're not keeping this quiet, not on your life. Just like the psalmist who wrote, "I believed it, so I said it," we say what we believe. And what we believe is that the One who raised up the Master Jesus will just as certainly raise us up with you, alive. Every detail works to your advantage and to God's glory: more and more grace, more and more people, more and more praise!

16-18 So we're not giving up. How could we! Even though on the outside it often looks like things are falling apart on us, on the inside, where God is making new life, not a day goes by without his unfolding grace. These hard times are small potatoes compared to the coming good times, the lavish celebration prepared for us. There's far more here than meets the eye. The things we see now are here today, gone tomorrow. But the things we can't see now will last forever.

1-5 5 For instance, we know that when these bodies of ours are taken down like tents and folded away, they will be replaced by resurrection bodies in heaven—God-made, not handmade—and we'll never have to relocate our "tents" again. Sometimes we can hardly wait to move—and so we cry out in frustration. Compared to what's coming, living conditions around here seem like a stopover in an unfurnished shack, and we're tired of it! We've been given a glimpse of the real thing, our true home, our resurrection bodies! The Spirit of God whets our appetite by giving us a taste of what's ahead. He puts a little of heaven in our hearts so that we'll never settle for less.

6-8 That's why we live with such good cheer. You won't see us drooping our heads or dragging our feet! Cramped conditions here don't get us down. They only remind us of the spacious living conditions ahead. It's what we trust in but don't yet see that keeps us going. Do you suppose a few ruts in the road or rocks in the path are going to stop us? When the time comes, we'll be plenty ready to exchange exile for homecoming.

NEW KING JAMES VERSION

THE JUDGMENT SEAT OF CHRIST
[9]Therefore we make it our aim, whether
present or absent, to be well pleasing to Him.
[10]For we must all appear before the judgment
seat of Christ, that each one may receive the
things *done* in the body, according to what he
has done, whether good or bad. [11]Knowing,
therefore, the terror of the Lord, we persuade
men; but we are well known to God, and I also
trust are well known in your consciences.

BE RECONCILED TO GOD
[12]For we do not commend ourselves again to
you, but give you opportunity to boast on our
behalf, that you may have *an answer* for those
who boast in appearance and not in heart. [13]For
if we are beside ourselves, *it is* for God; or if we
are of sound mind, *it is* for you. [14]For the love of
Christ compels us, because we judge thus: that
if One died for all, then all died; [15]and He died
for all, that those who live should live no longer
for themselves, but for Him who died for them
and rose again.
[16]Therefore, from now on, we regard no one
according to the flesh. Even though we have
known Christ according to the flesh, yet now we
know *Him thus* no longer. [17]Therefore, if anyone
is in Christ, *he is* a new creation; old things have
passed away; behold, all things have become
new. [18]Now all things *are* of God, who has rec-
onciled us to Himself through Jesus Christ, and
has given us the ministry of reconciliation,
[19]that is, that God was in Christ reconciling the
world to Himself, not imputing their trespasses
to them, and has committed to us the word of
reconciliation.
[20]Now then, we are ambassadors for Christ,
as though God were pleading through us: we
implore *you* on Christ's behalf, be reconciled to
God. [21]For He made Him who knew no sin *to be*
sin for us, that we might become the righteous-
ness of God in Him.

MARKS OF THE MINISTRY
6 We then, *as* workers together *with Him* also
plead with *you* not to receive the grace of
God in vain. [2]For He says:

"In an acceptable time I have heard you,
And in the day of salvation I have helped
you." [a]

6:2 [a]Isaiah 49:8

THE MESSAGE

9-10 But neither exile nor homecoming is the
main thing. Cheerfully pleasing God is the
main thing, and that's what we aim to do, re-
gardless of our conditions. Sooner or later
we'll all have to face God, regardless of our
conditions. We will appear before Christ and
take what's coming to us as a result of our
actions, either good or bad.
11-14 *That* keeps us vigilant, you can be sure.
It's no light thing to know that we'll all one
day stand in that place of Judgment. That's
why we work urgently with everyone we
meet to get them ready to face God. God
alone knows how well we do this, but I hope
you realize how much and deeply we care.
We're not saying this to make ourselves
look good to you. We just thought it would
make you feel good, proud even, that we're
on your side and not just nice to your face as
so many people are. If I acted crazy, I did it
for God; if I acted overly serious, I did it for
you. Christ's love has moved me to such ex-
tremes. His love has the first and last word
in everything we do.

A NEW LIFE
14-15 Our firm decision is to work from this fo-
cused center: One man died for everyone.
That puts everyone in the same boat. He in-
cluded everyone in his death so that every-
one could also be included in his life, a res-
urrection life, a far better life than people
ever lived on their own.
16-20 Because of this decision we don't evalu-
ate people by what they have or how they
look. We looked at the Messiah that way
once and got it all wrong, as you know. We
certainly don't look at him that way any-
more. Now we look inside, and what we see
is that anyone united with the Messiah gets
a fresh start, is created new. The old life is
gone; a new life burgeons! Look at it! All
this comes from the God who settled the re-
lationship between us and him, and then
called us to settle our relationships with
each other. God put the world square with
himself through the Messiah, giving the
world a fresh start by offering forgiveness
of sins. God has given us the task of telling
everyone what he is doing. We're Christ's
representatives. God uses us to persuade
men and women to drop their differences
and enter into God's work of making things
right between them. We're speaking for
Christ himself now: Become friends with
God; he's already a friend with you.
21 How? you ask. In Christ. God put the
wrong on him who never did anything
wrong, so we could be put right with God.

STAYING AT OUR POST
1-10 **6** Companions as we are in this work with
you, we beg you, please don't squander
one bit of this marvelous life God has given
us. God reminds us,

I heard your call in the nick of time;
The day you needed me, I was there to
help.

NEW KING JAMES VERSION

Behold, now *is* the accepted time; behold, now *is* the day of salvation.

3We give no offense in anything, that our ministry may not be blamed. 4But in all *things* we commend ourselves as ministers of God: in much patience, in tribulations, in needs, in distresses, 5in stripes, in imprisonments, in tumults, in labors, in sleeplessness, in fastings; 6by purity, by knowledge, by longsuffering, by kindness, by the Holy Spirit, by sincere love, 7by the word of truth, by the power of God, by the armor of righteousness on the right hand and on the left, 8by honor and dishonor, by evil report and good report; as deceivers, and *yet* true; 9as unknown, and *yet* well known; as dying, and behold we live; as chastened, and *yet* not killed; 10as sorrowful, yet always rejoicing; as poor, yet making many rich; as having nothing, and *yet* possessing all things.

BE HOLY

11O Corinthians! We have spoken openly to you, our heart is wide open. 12You are not restricted by us, but you are restricted by your *own* affections. 13Now in return for the same (I speak as to children), you also be open.

14Do not be unequally yoked together with unbelievers. For what fellowship has righteousness with lawlessness? And what communion has light with darkness? 15And what accord has Christ with Belial? Or what part has a believer with an unbeliever? 16And what agreement has the temple of God with idols? For you[a] are the temple of the living God. As God has said:

"I will dwell in them
And walk among them.
I will be their God,
And they shall be My people."[b]

17Therefore

"Come out from among them
And be separate, says the Lord.
Do not touch what is unclean,
And I will receive you."[a]
18*"I will be a Father to you,*
And you shall be My sons and daughters,
Says the LORD Almighty."[a]

7 Therefore, having these promises, beloved, let us cleanse ourselves from all filthiness of the flesh and spirit, perfecting holiness in the fear of God.

THE CORINTHIANS' REPENTANCE

2Open *your hearts* to us. We have wronged no one, we have corrupted no one, we have

6:16 [a]NU-Text reads *we.* [b]Leviticus 26:12; Jeremiah 32:38; Ezekiel 37:27 **6:17** [a]Isaiah 52:11; Ezekiel 20:34, 41 **6:18** [a]2 Samuel 7:14

THE MESSAGE

Well, now is the right time to listen, the day to be helped. Don't put it off; don't frustrate God's work by showing up late, throwing a question mark over everything we're doing. Our work as God's servants gets validated—or not—in the details. People are watching us as we stay at our post, alertly, unswervingly . . . in hard times, tough times, bad times; when we're beaten up, jailed, and mobbed; working hard, working late, working without eating; with pure heart, clear head, steady hand; in gentleness, holiness, and honest love; when we're telling the truth, and when God's showing his power; when we're doing our best setting things right; when we're praised, and when we're blamed; slandered, and honored; true to our word, though distrusted; ignored by the world, but recognized by God; terrifically alive, though rumored to be dead; beaten within an inch of our lives, but refusing to die; immersed in tears, yet always filled with deep joy; living on handouts, yet enriching many; having nothing, having it all.

11-13 Dear, dear Corinthians, I can't tell you how much I long for you to enter this wide-open, spacious life. We didn't fence you in. The smallness you feel comes from within you. Your lives aren't small, but you're living them in a small way. I'm speaking as plainly as I can and with great affection. Open up your lives. Live openly and expansively!

14-18 Don't become partners with those who reject God. How can you make a partnership out of right and wrong? That's not partnership; that's war. Is light best friends with dark? Does Christ go strolling with the Devil? Do trust and mistrust hold hands? Who would think of setting up pagan idols in God's holy Temple? But that is exactly what we are, each of us a temple in whom God lives. God himself put it this way:

"I'll live in them, move into them;
I'll be their God and they'll be my people.
So leave the corruption and compromise;
leave it for good," says God.
"Don't link up with those who will pollute you.
I want you all for myself.
I'll be a Father to you;
you'll be sons and daughters to me."
The Word of the Master, God.

1 7 With promises like this to pull us on, dear friends, let's make a clean break with everything that defiles or distracts us, both within and without. Let's make our entire lives fit and holy temples for the worship of God.

MORE PASSIONATE, MORE RESPONSIBLE

2-4 Trust us. We've never hurt a soul, never exploited or taken advantage of anyone. Don't

NEW KING JAMES VERSION

cheated no one. [3]I do not say *this* to condemn;
for I have said before that you are in our hearts,
to die together and to live together. [4]Great *is* my
boldness of speech toward you, great *is* my
boasting on your behalf. I am filled with com-
fort. I am exceedingly joyful in all our tribula-
tion.
[5]For indeed, when we came to Macedonia,
our bodies had no rest, but we were troubled on
every side. Outside *were* conflicts, inside *were*
fears. [6]Nevertheless God, who comforts the
downcast, comforted us by the coming of Titus,
[7]and not only by his coming, but also by the con-
solation with which he was comforted in you,
when he told us of your earnest desire, your
mourning, your zeal for me, so that I rejoiced
even more.
[8]For even if I made you sorry with my letter,
I do not regret it; though I did regret it. For I per-
ceive that the same epistle made you sorry,
though only for a while. [9]Now I rejoice, not that
you were made sorry, but that your sorrow led
to repentance. For you were made sorry in a
godly manner, that you might suffer loss from
us in nothing. [10]For godly sorrow produces re-
pentance *leading* to salvation, not to be regret-
ted; but the sorrow of the world produces death.
[11]For observe this very thing, that you sorrowed
in a godly manner: What diligence it produced
in you, *what* clearing *of yourselves, what* indig-
nation, *what* fear, *what* vehement desire, *what*
zeal, *what* vindication! In all *things* you proved
yourselves to be clear in this matter. [12]There-
fore, although I wrote to you, *I did* not *do it* for
the sake of him who had done the wrong, nor
for the sake of him who suffered wrong, but that
our care for you in the sight of God might ap-
pear to you.

THE JOY OF TITUS

[13]Therefore we have been comforted in your
comfort. And we rejoiced exceedingly more for
the joy of Titus, because his spirit has been re-
freshed by you all. [14]For if in anything I have
boasted to him about you, I am not ashamed.
But as we spoke all things to you in truth, even
so our boasting to Titus was found true. [15]And
his affections are greater for you as he remem-
bers the obedience of you all, how with fear and
trembling you received him. [16]Therefore I re-
joice that I have confidence in you in every-
thing.

EXCEL IN GIVING

8 Moreover, brethren, we make known to you
the grace of God bestowed on the churches of
Macedonia: [2]that in a great trial of affliction the
abundance of their joy and their deep poverty
abounded in the riches of their liberality. [3]For I
bear witness that according to *their* ability, yes,

THE MESSAGE

think I'm finding fault with you. I told you earlier that I'm with you all the way, no matter what. I have, in fact, the greatest confidence in you. If only you knew how proud I am of you! I am overwhelmed with joy despite all our troubles.

5-7 When we arrived in Macedonia province, we couldn't settle down. The fights in the church and the fears in our hearts kept us on pins and needles. We couldn't relax because we didn't know how it would turn out. Then the God who lifts up the downcast lifted our heads and our hearts with the arrival of Titus. We were glad just to see him, but the true reassurance came in what he told us about you: how much you cared, how much you grieved, how concerned you were for me. I went from worry to tranquility in no time!

8-9 I know I distressed you greatly with my letter. Although I felt awful at the time, I don't feel at all bad now that I see how it turned out. The letter upset you, but only for a while. Now I'm glad—not that you were upset, but that you were jarred into turning things around. You let the distress bring you to God, not drive you from him. The result was all gain, no loss.

10 Distress that drives us to God does that. It turns us around. It gets us back in the way of salvation. We never regret that kind of pain. But those who let distress drive them away from God are full of regrets, end up on a deathbed of regrets.

11-13 And now, isn't it wonderful all the ways in which this distress has goaded you closer to God? You're more alive, more concerned, more sensitive, more reverent, more human, more passionate, more responsible. Looked at from any angle, you've come out of this with purity of heart. And that is what I was hoping for in the first place when I wrote the letter. My primary concern was not for the one who did the wrong or even the one wronged, but for you—that you would realize and act upon the deep, deep ties between us before God. That's what happened—and we felt just great.

13-16 And then, when we saw how Titus felt—his exuberance over your response—our joy doubled. It was wonderful to see how revived and refreshed he was by everything you did. If I went out on a limb in telling Titus how great I thought you were, you didn't cut off that limb. As it turned out, I hadn't exaggerated one bit. Titus saw for himself that everything I had said about you was true. He can't quit talking about it, going over again and again the story of your prompt obedience, and the dignity and sensitivity of your hospitality. He was quite overwhelmed by it all! And I couldn't be more pleased—I'm so confident and proud of you.

THE OFFERING

1-4 8 Now, friends, I want to report on the surprising and generous ways in which God is working in the churches in Macedonia province. Fierce troubles came down on the people of those churches, pushing them to

NEW KING JAMES VERSION

and beyond *their* ability, *they were* freely will-
ing, [4]imploring us with much urgency that we
would receive[a] the gift and the fellowship of the
ministering to the saints. [5]And not *only* as we
had hoped, but they first gave themselves to the
Lord, and *then* to us by the will of God. [6]So we
urged Titus, that as he had begun, so he would
also complete this grace in you as well. [7]But as
you abound in everything—in faith, in speech, in
knowledge, in all diligence, and in your love for
us—*see* that you abound in this grace also.

CHRIST OUR PATTERN

[8]I speak not by commandment, but I am test-
ing the sincerity of your love by the diligence of
others. [9]For you know the grace of our Lord Je-
sus Christ, that though He was rich, yet for your
sakes He became poor, that you through His
poverty might become rich.

[10]And in this I give advice: It is to your ad-
vantage not only to be doing what you began
and were desiring to do a year ago; [11]but now
you also must complete the doing *of it;* that as
there was a readiness to desire *it,* so *there* also
may be a completion out of what *you* have. [12]For
if there is first a willing mind, *it is* accepted ac-
cording to what one has, *and* not according to
what he does not have.

[13]For *I do* not *mean* that others should be
eased and you burdened; [14]but by an equality,
that now at this time your abundance *may sup-
ply* their lack, that their abundance also may
supply your lack—that there may be equality.
[15]As it is written, *"He who gathered much had
nothing left over, and he who gathered little had
no lack."*[a]

COLLECTION FOR THE JUDEAN SAINTS

[16]But thanks *be* to God who puts[a] the same
earnest care for you into the heart of Titus. [17]For
he not only accepted the exhortation, but being
more diligent, he went to you of his own accord.
[18]And we have sent with him the brother whose
praise *is* in the gospel throughout all the
churches, [19]and not only *that,* but who was also
chosen by the churches to travel with us with
this gift, which is administered by us to the
glory of the Lord Himself and *to show* your
ready mind, [20]avoiding this: that anyone should
blame us in this lavish gift which is adminis-
tered by us— [21]providing honorable things, not
only in the sight of the Lord, but also in the sight
of men.

8:4 [a]NU-Text and M-Text omit *that we would receive,* thus chang-
ing text to *urgency for the favor and fellowship. . . .* **8:15** [a]Exo-
dus 16:18 **8:16** [a]NU-Text reads *has put.*

THE MESSAGE

the very limit. The trial exposed their true colors: They were incredibly happy, though desperately poor. The pressure triggered something totally unexpected: an outpouring of pure and generous gifts. I was there and saw it for myself. They gave offerings of whatever they could—far more than they could afford!—pleading for the privilege of helping out in the relief of poor Christians.

5-7 This was totally spontaneous, entirely their own idea, and caught us completely off guard. What explains it was that they had first given themselves unreservedly to God and to us. The other giving simply flowed out of the purposes of God working in their lives. That's what prompted us to ask Titus to bring the relief offering to your attention, so that what was so well begun could be finished up. You do so well in so many things—you trust God, you're articulate, you're insightful, you're passionate, you love us—now, do your best in this, too.

8-9 I'm not trying to order you around against your will. But by bringing in the Macedonians' enthusiasm as a stimulus to your love, I am hoping to bring the best out of you. You are familiar with the generosity of our Master, Jesus Christ. Rich as he was, he gave it all away for us—in one stroke he became poor and we became rich.

10-20 So here's what I think: The best thing you can do right now is to finish what you started last year and not let those good intentions grow stale. Your heart's been in the right place all along. You've got what it takes to finish it up, so go to it. Once the commitment is clear, you do what you can, not what you can't. The heart regulates the hands. This isn't so others can take it easy while you sweat it out. No, you're shoulder to shoulder with them all the way, your surplus matching their deficit, their surplus matching your deficit. In the end you come out even. As it is written,

Nothing left over to the one with the
most,
Nothing lacking to the one with the
least.

I thank God for giving Titus the same devoted concern for you that I have. He was most considerate of how we felt, but his eagerness to go to you and help out with this relief offering is his own idea. We're sending a companion along with him, someone very popular in the churches for his preaching of the Message. But there's far more to him than popularity. He's rock-solid trustworthy. The churches handpicked him to go with us as we travel about doing this work of sharing God's gifts to honor God as well as we can, taking every precaution against scandal.

20-22 We don't want anyone suspecting us of taking one penny of this money for ourselves. We're being as careful in our reputation with the public as in our reputation with God. That's why we're sending another trusted friend along. He's proved his dependability

NEW KING JAMES VERSION

22 And we have sent with them our brother whom we have often proved diligent in many things, but now much more diligent, because of the great confidence which *we have* in you. 23 If *anyone inquires* about Titus, *he is* my partner and fellow worker concerning you. Or if our brethren *are inquired about, they are* messengers of the churches, the glory of Christ. 24 Therefore show to them, and[a] before the churches, the proof of your love and of our boasting on your behalf.

ADMINISTERING THE GIFT

9 Now concerning the ministering to the saints, it is superfluous for me to write to you; 2 for I know your willingness, about which I boast of you to the Macedonians, that Achaia was ready a year ago; and your zeal has stirred up the majority. 3 Yet I have sent the brethren, lest our boasting of you should be in vain in this respect, that, as I said, you may be ready; 4 lest if *some* Macedonians come with me and find you unprepared, we (not to mention you!) should be ashamed of this confident boasting.[a] 5 Therefore I thought it necessary to exhort the brethren to go to you ahead of time, and prepare your generous gift beforehand, which *you had* previously promised, that it may be ready as *a matter of* generosity and not as a grudging obligation.

THE CHEERFUL GIVER

6 But this *I say:* He who sows sparingly will also reap sparingly, and he who sows bountifully will also reap bountifully. 7 *So let* each one *give* as he purposes in his heart, not grudgingly or of necessity; for God loves a cheerful giver. 8 And God *is* able to make all grace abound toward you, that you, always having all sufficiency in all *things,* may have an abundance for every good work. 9 As it is written:

"He has dispersed abroad,
He has given to the poor;
His righteousness endures forever."[a]

10 Now may[a] He who supplies seed to the sower, and bread for food, supply and multiply the seed you have *sown* and increase the fruits of your righteousness, 11 while *you are* enriched in everything for all liberality, which causes thanksgiving through us to God. 12 For the administration of this service not only supplies the needs of the saints, but also is abounding through many thanksgivings to God, 13 while,

8:24 [a]NU-Text and M-Text omit *and.* **9:4** [a]NU-Text reads *this confidence.* **9:9** [a]Psalm 112:9 **9:10** [a]NU-Text reads *Now He who supplies . . . will supply. . . .*

THE MESSAGE

many times over, and carries on as energetically as the day he started. He's heard much about you, and liked what he's heard—so much so that he can't wait to get there.

23-24 I don't need to say anything further about Titus. We've been close associates in this work of serving you for a long time. The brothers who travel with him are delegates from churches, a real credit to Christ. Show them what you're made of, the love I've been talking up in the churches. Let them see it for themselves!

1-2 9 If I wrote any more on this relief offering for the poor Christians, I'd be repeating myself. I know you're on board and ready to go. I've been bragging about you all through Macedonia province, telling them, "Achaia province has been ready to go on this since last year." Your enthusiasm by now has spread to most of them.

3-5 Now I'm sending the brothers to make sure you're ready, as I said you would be, so my bragging won't turn out to be just so much hot air. If some Macedonians and I happened to drop in on you and found you weren't prepared, we'd all be pretty red-faced—you and us—for acting so sure of ourselves. So to make sure there will be no slipup, I've recruited these brothers as an advance team to get you and your promised offering all ready before I get there. I want you to have all the time you need to make this offering in your own way. I don't want anything forced or hurried at the last minute.

6-7 Remember: A stingy planter gets a stingy crop; a lavish planter gets a lavish crop. I want each of you to take plenty of time to think it over, and make up your own mind what you will give. That will protect you against sob stories and arm-twisting. God loves it when the giver delights in the giving.

8-11 God can pour on the blessings in astonishing ways so that you're ready for anything and everything, more than just ready to do what needs to be done. As one psalmist puts it,

He throws caution to the winds,
giving to the needy in reckless abandon.
His right-living, right-giving ways
never run out, never wear out.

This most generous God who gives seed to the farmer that becomes bread for your meals is more than extravagant with you. He gives you something you can then give away, which grows into full-formed lives, robust in God, wealthy in every way, so that you can be generous in every way, producing with us great praise to God.

12-15 Carrying out this social relief work involves far more than helping meet the bare needs of poor Christians. It also produces abundant and bountiful thanksgivings to God. This relief offering is a prod to live at

New King James Version

through the proof of this ministry, they glorify God for the obedience of your confession to the gospel of Christ, and for *your* liberal sharing with them and all *men*, 14and by their prayer for you, who long for you because of the exceeding grace of God in you. 15Thanks *be* to God for His indescribable gift!

The Spiritual War

10 Now I, Paul, myself am pleading with you by the meekness and gentleness of Christ—who in presence *am* lowly among you, but being absent am bold toward you. 2But I beg *you* that when I am present I may not be bold with that confidence by which I intend to be bold against some, who think of us as if we walked according to the flesh. 3For though we walk in the flesh, we do not war according to the flesh. 4For the weapons of our warfare *are* not carnal but mighty in God for pulling down strongholds, 5casting down arguments and every high thing that exalts itself against the knowledge of God, bringing every thought into captivity to the obedience of Christ, 6and being ready to punish all disobedience when your obedience is fulfilled.

Reality of Paul's Authority

7Do you look at things according to the outward appearance? If anyone is convinced in himself that he is Christ's, let him again consider this in himself, that just as he *is* Christ's, even so we *are* Christ's.[a] 8For even if I should boast somewhat more about our authority, which the Lord gave us[a] for edification and not for your destruction, I shall not be ashamed— 9lest I seem to terrify you by letters. 10"For *his* letters," they say, "*are* weighty and powerful, but *his* bodily presence *is* weak, and *his* speech contemptible." 11Let such a person consider this, that what we are in word by letters when we are absent, such *we will* also *be* in deed when we are present.

Limits of Paul's Authority

12For we dare not class ourselves or compare ourselves with those who commend themselves. But they, measuring themselves by themselves, and comparing themselves among themselves, are not wise. 13We, however, will not boast beyond measure, but within the limits of the sphere which God appointed us—a sphere which especially includes you. 14For we are not overextending ourselves (as though *our authority* did not extend to you), for it was to you that we came with the gospel of Christ;

10:7 [a]NU-Text reads *even as we are.* 10:8 [a]NU-Text omits *us.*

The Message

your very best, showing your gratitude to God by being openly obedient to the plain meaning of the Message of Christ. You show your gratitude through your generous offerings to your needy brothers and sisters, and really toward everyone. Meanwhile, moved by the extravagance of God in your lives, they'll respond by praying for you in passionate intercession for whatever you need. Thank God for this gift, his gift. No language can praise it enough!

Tearing Down Barriers

1-2 **10** And now a personal but most urgent
matter; I write in the gentle but firm
spirit of Christ. I hear that I'm being painted
as cringing and wishy-washy when I'm with
you, but harsh and demanding when at a
safe distance writing letters. Please don't
force me to take a hard line when I'm present
with you. Don't think that I'll hesitate a
single minute to stand up to those who say
I'm an unprincipled opportunist. Then
they'll have to eat their words.
3-6 The world is unprincipled. It's dog-eat-dog
out there! The world doesn't fight fair. But we
don't live or fight our battles that way—never
have and never will. The tools of our trade
aren't for marketing or manipulation, but
they are for demolishing that entire massively
corrupt culture. We use our powerful God-tools
for smashing warped philosophies, tearing
down barriers erected against the truth of
God, fitting every loose thought and emotion
and impulse into the structure of life shaped
by Christ. Our tools are ready at hand for
clearing the ground of every obstruction and
building lives of obedience into maturity.
7-8 You stare and stare at the obvious, but
you can't see the forest for the trees. If
you're looking for a clear example of someone
on Christ's side, why do you so quickly
cut me out? Believe me, I am quite sure of
my standing with Christ. You may think I
overstate the authority he gave me, but I'm
not backing off. Every bit of my commitment
is for the purpose of building you up,
after all, not tearing you down.
9-11 And what's this talk about me bullying you
with my letters? "His letters are brawny and
potent, but in person he's a weakling and
mumbles when he talks." Such talk won't survive
scrutiny. What we write when away, we
do when present. We're the exact same people,
absent or present, in letter or in person.
12 We're not, understand, putting ourselves
in a league with those who boast that
they're our superiors. We wouldn't dare do
that. But in all this comparing and grading
and competing, they quite miss the point.
13-14 We aren't making outrageous claims
here. We're sticking to the limits of what
God has set for us. But there can be no question
that those limits reach to and include
you. We're not moving into someone else's
"territory." We were already there with you,
weren't we? We were the first ones to get
there with the Message of Christ, right? So
how can there be any question of overstepping
our bounds by writing or visiting you?

NEW KING JAMES VERSION

15not boasting of things beyond measure, *that is,* in other men's labors, but having hope, *that* as your faith is increased, we shall be greatly enlarged by you in our sphere, 16to preach the gospel in the *regions* beyond you, *and* not to boast in another man's sphere of accomplishment.

17But *"he who glories, let him glory in the LORD."*[a] 18For not he who commends himself is approved, but whom the Lord commends.

CONCERN FOR THEIR FAITHFULNESS

11 Oh, that you would bear with me in a little folly—and indeed you do bear with me. 2For I am jealous for you with godly jealousy. For I have betrothed you to one husband, that I may present *you as* a chaste virgin to Christ. 3But I fear, lest somehow, as the serpent deceived Eve by his craftiness, so your minds may be corrupted from the simplicity[a] that is in Christ. 4For if he who comes preaches another Jesus whom we have not preached, or *if* you receive a different spirit which you have not received, or a different gospel which you have not accepted—you may well put up with it!

PAUL AND FALSE APOSTLES

5For I consider that I am not at all inferior to the most eminent apostles. 6Even though *I am* untrained in speech, yet *I am* not in knowledge. But we have been thoroughly manifested[a] among you in all things.

7Did I commit sin in humbling myself that you might be exalted, because I preached the gospel of God to you free of charge? 8I robbed other churches, taking wages *from them* to minister to you. 9And when I was present with you, and in need, I was a burden to no one, for what I lacked the brethren who came from Macedonia supplied. And in everything I kept myself from being burdensome to you, and so I will keep *myself.* 10As the truth of Christ is in me, no one shall stop me from this boasting in the regions of Achaia. 11Why? Because I do not love you? God knows!

12But what I do, I will also continue to do, that I may cut off the opportunity from those who desire an opportunity to be regarded just as we are in the things of which they boast. 13For such *are* false apostles, deceitful workers, transforming themselves into apostles of Christ. 14And no wonder! For Satan himself transforms himself into an angel of light. 15Therefore *it is* no great thing if his ministers also transform themselves into ministers of righteousness, whose end will be according to their works.

10:17 [a]Jeremiah 9:24 **11:3** [a]NU-Text adds *and purity.* **11:6** [a]NU-Text omits *been.*

THE MESSAGE

15-18 We're not barging in on the rightful work
of others, interfering with their ministries,
demanding a place in the sun with them.
What we're hoping for is that as your lives
grow in faith, you'll play a part within our
expanding work. And we'll all still be within
the limits God sets as we proclaim the Mes-
sage in countries beyond Corinth. But we
have no intention of moving in on what oth-
ers have done and taking credit for it. "If
you want to claim credit, claim it for God."
What you say about yourself means nothing
in God's work. It's what God says about you
that makes the difference.

PSEUDO-SERVANTS OF GOD

1-3 11 Will you put up with a little foolish aside
from me? Please, just for a moment. The
thing that has me so upset is that I care about
you so much—this is the passion of God
burning inside me! I promised your hand in
marriage to Christ, presented you as a pure
virgin to her husband. And now I'm afraid
that exactly as the Snake seduced Eve with
his smooth patter, you are being lured away
from the simple purity of your love for Christ.
4-6 It seems that if someone shows up
preaching quite another Jesus than we
preached—different spirit, different mes-
sage—you put up with him quite nicely. But
if you put up with these big-shot "apostles,"
why can't you put up with simple me? I'm as
good as they are. It's true that I don't have
their voice, haven't mastered that smooth
eloquence that impresses you so much. But
when I do open my mouth, I at least know
what I'm talking about. We haven't kept
anything back. We let you in on everything.
7-12 I wonder, did I make a bad mistake in
proclaiming God's Message to you without
asking for something in return, serving you
free of charge so that you wouldn't be in-
convenienced by me? It turns out that the
other churches paid my way so that you
could have a free ride. Not once during the
time I lived among you did anyone have to
lift a finger to help me out. My needs were
always supplied by the believers from Mace-
donia province. I was careful never to be a
burden to you, and I never will be, you can
count on it. With Christ as my witness, it's a
point of honor with me, and I'm not going to
keep it quiet just to protect you from what
the neighbors will think. It's not that I don't
love you; God knows I do. I'm just trying to
keep things open and honest between us.
12-15 And I'm not changing my position on this.
I'd die before taking your money. I'm giving
nobody grounds for lumping me in with
those money-grubbing "preachers," vaunting
themselves as something special. They're a
sorry bunch—pseudo-apostles, lying preach-
ers, crooked workers—posing as Christ's
agents but sham to the core. And no wonder!
Satan does it all the time, dressing up as a
beautiful angel of light. So it shouldn't sur-
prise us when his servants masquerade as
servants of God. But they're not getting by
with anything. They'll pay for it in the end.

NEW KING JAMES VERSION

RELUCTANT BOASTING

[16]I say again, let no one think me a fool. If
otherwise, at least receive me as a fool, that I
also may boast a little. [17]What I speak, I speak
not according to the Lord, but as it were, fool-
ishly, in this confidence of boasting. [18]Seeing
that many boast according to the flesh, I also
will boast. [19]For you put up with fools gladly,
since you *yourselves* are wise! [20]For you put up
with it if one brings you into bondage, if one de-
vours *you,* if one takes *from you,* if one exalts
himself, if one strikes you on the face. [21]To *our*
shame I say that we were too weak for that! But
in whatever anyone is bold—I speak foolishly—
I am bold also.

SUFFERING FOR CHRIST

[22]Are they Hebrews? So *am* I. Are they Is-
raelites? So *am* I. Are they the seed of Abraham?
So *am* I. [23]Are they ministers of Christ?—I speak
as a fool—I *am* more: in labors more abundant,
in stripes above measure, in prisons more fre-
quently, in deaths often. [24]From the Jews five
times I received forty *stripes* minus one. [25]Three
times I was beaten with rods; once I was stoned;
three times I was shipwrecked; a night and a
day I have been in the deep; [26]*in* journeys often,
in perils of waters, *in* perils of robbers, *in* perils
of *my own* countrymen, *in* perils of the Gentiles,
in perils in the city, *in* perils in the wilderness, *in*
perils in the sea, *in* perils among false brethren;
[27]in weariness and toil, in sleeplessness often, in
hunger and thirst, in fastings often, in cold and
nakedness— [28]besides the other things, what
comes upon me daily: my deep concern for all
the churches. [29]Who is weak, and I am not
weak? Who is made to stumble, and I do not
burn *with indignation*?

[30]If I must boast, I will boast in the things
which concern my infirmity. [31]The God and Fa-
ther of our Lord Jesus Christ, who is blessed for-
ever, knows that I am not lying. [32]In Damascus
the governor, under Aretas the king, was guard-
ing the city of the Damascenes with a garrison,
desiring to arrest me; [33]but I was let down in a
basket through a window in the wall, and es-
caped from his hands.

THE VISION OF PARADISE

12 It is doubtless[a] not profitable for me to
boast. I will come to visions and revela-
tions of the Lord: [2]I know a man in Christ who
fourteen years ago—whether in the body I do

12:1 [a]NU-Text reads *necessary, though not profitable, to boast.*

THE MESSAGE

MANY A LONG AND LONELY NIGHT

16-21 Let me come back to where I started—and
don't hold it against me if I continue to
sound a little foolish. Or if you'd rather, just
accept that I am a fool and let me rant on a
little. I didn't learn this kind of talk from
Christ. Oh, no, it's a bad habit I picked up
from the three-ring preachers that are so
popular these days. Since you sit there in
the judgment seat observing all these
shenanigans, you can afford to humor an
occasional fool who happens along. You
have such admirable tolerance for impos-
tors who rob your freedom, rip you off, steal
you blind, put you down—even slap your
face! I shouldn't admit it to you, but our
stomachs aren't strong enough to tolerate
that kind of stuff.

21-23 Since you admire the egomaniacs of the
pulpit so much (remember, this is your old
friend, the fool, talking), let me try my hand
at it. Do they brag of being Hebrews, Is-
raelites, the pure race of Abraham? I'm their
match. Are they servants of Christ? I can go
them one better. (I can't believe I'm saying
these things. It's crazy to talk this way! But
I started, and I'm going to finish.)

23-27 I've worked much harder, been jailed
more often, beaten up more times than I can
count, and at death's door time after time.
I've been flogged five times with the Jews'
thirty-nine lashes, beaten by Roman rods
three times, pummeled with rocks once. I've
been shipwrecked three times, and im-
mersed in the open sea for a night and a day.
In hard traveling year in and year out, I've
had to ford rivers, fend off robbers, struggle
with friends, struggle with foes. I've been at
risk in the city, at risk in the country, endan-
gered by desert sun and sea storm, and be-
trayed by those I thought were my brothers.
I've known drudgery and hard labor, many
a long and lonely night without sleep, many
a missed meal, blasted by the cold, naked to
the weather.

28-29 And that's not the half of it, when you
throw in the daily pressures and anxieties of
all the churches. When someone gets to the
end of his rope, I feel the desperation in my
bones. When someone is duped into sin, an
angry fire burns in my gut.

30-33 If I have to "brag" about myself, I'll brag
about the humiliations that make me like Je-
sus. The eternal and blessed God and Father
of our Master Jesus knows I'm not lying. Re-
member the time I was in Damascus and the
governor of King Aretas posted guards at
the city gates to arrest me? I crawled
through a window in the wall, was let down
in a basket, and had to run for my life.

STRENGTH FROM WEAKNESS

1-5 **12** You've forced me to talk this way, and I
do it against my better judgment. But
now that we're at it, I may as well bring up
the matter of visions and revelations that
God gave me. For instance, I know a man
who, fourteen years ago, was seized by
Christ and swept in ecstasy to the heights of

NEW KING JAMES VERSION

not know, or whether out of the body I do not know, God knows—such a one was caught up to the third heaven. 3And I know such a man—whether in the body or out of the body I do not know, God knows— 4how he was caught up into Paradise and heard inexpressible words, which it is not lawful for a man to utter. 5Of such a one I will boast; yet of myself I will not boast, except in my infirmities. 6For though I might desire to boast, I will not be a fool; for I will speak the truth. But I refrain, lest anyone should think of me above what he sees me *to be* or hears from me.

THE THORN IN THE FLESH

7And lest I should be exalted above measure by the abundance of the revelations, a thorn in the flesh was given to me, a messenger of Satan to buffet me, lest I be exalted above measure. 8Concerning this thing I pleaded with the Lord three times that it might depart from me. 9And He said to me, "My grace is sufficient for you, for My strength is made perfect in weakness." Therefore most gladly I will rather boast in my infirmities, that the power of Christ may rest upon me. 10Therefore I take pleasure in infirmities, in reproaches, in needs, in persecutions, in distresses, for Christ's sake. For when I am weak, then I am strong.

SIGNS OF AN APOSTLE

11I have become a fool in boasting;[a] you have compelled me. For I ought to have been commended by you; for in nothing was I behind the most eminent apostles, though I am nothing. 12Truly the signs of an apostle were accomplished among you with all perseverance, in signs and wonders and mighty deeds. 13For what is it in which you were inferior to other churches, except that I myself was not burdensome to you? Forgive me this wrong!

LOVE FOR THE CHURCH

14Now *for* the third time I am ready to come to you. And I will not be burdensome to you; for I do not seek yours, but you. For the children ought not to lay up for the parents, but the par-

12:11 [a]NU-Text omits *in boasting.*

THE MESSAGE

heaven. I really don't know if this took place in the body or out of it; only God knows. I also know that this man was hijacked into paradise—again, whether in or out of the body, I don't know; God knows. There he heard the unspeakable spoken, but was forbidden to tell what he heard. This is the man I want to talk about. But about myself, I'm not saying another word apart from the humiliations.

6 If I had a mind to brag a little, I could probably do it without looking ridiculous, and I'd still be speaking plain truth all the way. But I'll spare you. I don't want anyone imagining me as anything other than the fool you'd encounter if you saw me on the street or heard me talk.

7-10 Because of the extravagance of those revelations, and so I wouldn't get a big head, I was given the gift of a handicap to keep me in constant touch with my limitations. Satan's angel did his best to get me down; what he in fact did was push me to my knees. No danger then of walking around high and mighty! At first I didn't think of it as a gift, and begged God to remove it. Three times I did that, and then he told me,

> My grace is enough; it's all you need.
> My strength comes into its own in your weakness.

Once I heard that, I was glad to let it happen. I quit focusing on the handicap and began appreciating the gift. It was a case of Christ's strength moving in on my weakness. Now I take limitations in stride, and with good cheer, these limitations that cut me down to size—abuse, accidents, opposition, bad breaks. I just let Christ take over! And so the weaker I get, the stronger I become.

11-13 Well, now I've done it! I've made a complete fool of myself by going on like this. But it's not all my fault; you put me up to it. You should have been doing this for me, sticking up for me and commending me instead of making me do it for myself. You know from personal experience that even if I'm a nobody, a nothing, I wasn't second-rate compared to those big-shot apostles you're so taken with. All the signs that mark a true apostle were in evidence while I was with you through both good times and bad: signs of portent, signs of wonder, signs of power. Did you get less of me or of God than any of the other churches? The only thing you got less of was less responsibility for my upkeep. Well, I'm sorry. Forgive me for depriving you.

14-15 Everything is in readiness now for this, my third visit to you. But don't worry about it; you won't have to put yourselves out. I'll be no more of a bother to you this time than on the other visits. I have no interest in what you have—only in you. Children shouldn't have to look out for their parents; parents

NEW KING JAMES VERSION

ents for the children. [15]And I will very gladly spend and be spent for your souls; though the more abundantly I love you, the less I am loved.

[16]But be that *as it may,* I did not burden you. Nevertheless, being crafty, I caught you by cunning! [17]Did I take advantage of you by any of those whom I sent to you? [18]I urged Titus, and sent our brother with *him.* Did Titus take advantage of you? Did we not walk in the same spirit? Did *we* not *walk* in the same steps?

[19]Again, do you think[a] that we excuse ourselves to you? We speak before God in Christ. But *we do* all things, beloved, for your edification. [20]For I fear lest, when I come, I shall not find you such as I wish, and *that* I shall be found by you such as you do not wish; lest *there be* contentions, jealousies, outbursts of wrath, selfish ambitions, backbitings, whisperings, conceits, tumults; [21]lest, when I come again, my God will humble me among you, and I shall mourn for many who have sinned before and have not repented of the uncleanness, fornication, and lewdness which they have practiced.

COMING WITH AUTHORITY

13 This *will be* the third *time* I am coming to you. *"By the mouth of two or three witnesses every word shall be established."*[a] [2]I have told you before, and foretell as if I were present the second time, and now being absent I write[a] to those who have sinned before, and to all the rest, that if I come again I will not spare— [3]since you seek a proof of Christ speaking in me, who is not weak toward you, but mighty in you. [4]For though He was crucified in weakness, yet He lives by the power of God. For we also are weak in Him, but we shall live with Him by the power of God toward you.

[5]Examine yourselves *as to* whether you are in the faith. Test yourselves. Do you not know yourselves, that Jesus Christ is in you?—unless indeed you are disqualified. [6]But I trust that you will know that we are not disqualified.

PAUL PREFERS GENTLENESS

[7]Now I[a] pray to God that you do no evil, not that we should appear approved, but that you should do what is honorable, though we may seem disqualified. [8]For we can do nothing against the truth, but for the truth. [9]For we are glad when we are weak and you are strong. And

12:19 [a]NU-Text reads *You have been thinking for a long time. . . .* **13:1** [a]Deuteronomy 19:15 **13:2** [a]NU-Text omits *I write.* **13:7** [a]NU-Text reads *we.*

THE MESSAGE

look out for the children. I'd be most happy to empty my pockets, even mortgage my life, for your good. So how does it happen that the more I love you, the less I'm loved?

16-18 And why is it that I keep coming across these whiffs of gossip about how my self-support was a front behind which I worked an elaborate scam? Where's the evidence? Did I cheat or trick you through anyone I sent? I asked Titus to visit, and sent some brothers along. Did they swindle you out of anything? And haven't we always been just as aboveboard, just as honest?

19 I hope you don't think that all along we've been making our defense before you, the jury. You're not the jury; God is the jury—God revealed in Christ—and we make our case before him. And we've gone to all the trouble of supporting ourselves so that we won't be in the way or get in the way of your growing up.

20-21 I do admit that I have fears that when I come you'll disappoint me and I'll disappoint you, and in frustration with each other everything will fall to pieces—quarrels, jealousy, flaring tempers, taking sides, angry words, vicious rumors, swelled heads, and general bedlam. I don't look forward to a second humiliation by God among you, compounded by hot tears over that crowd that keeps sinning over and over in the same old ways, who refuse to turn away from the pigsty of evil, sexual disorder, and indecency in which they wallow.

HE'S ALIVE NOW!

1-4 **13** Well, this is my third visit coming up. Remember the Scripture that says, "A matter becomes clear after two or three witnesses give evidence"? On my second visit I warned that bunch that keeps sinning over and over in the same old ways that when I came back I wouldn't go easy on them. Now, preparing for the third, I'm saying it again from a distance. If you haven't changed your ways by the time I get there, look out. You who have been demanding proof that Christ speaks through me will get more than you bargained for. You'll get the full force of Christ, don't think you won't. He was sheer weakness and humiliation when he was killed on the cross, but oh, he's alive now—in the mighty power of God! We weren't much to look at, either, when we were humiliated among you, but when we deal with you this next time, we'll be alive in Christ, strengthened by God.

5-9 Test yourselves to make sure you are solid in the faith. Don't drift along taking everything for granted. Give yourselves regular checkups. You need firsthand evidence, not mere hearsay, that Jesus Christ is in you. Test it out. If you fail the test, do something about it. I hope the test won't show that we have failed. But if it comes to that, we'd rather the test showed our failure than yours. We're rooting for the truth to win out in you. We couldn't possibly do otherwise.

New King James Version

this also we pray, that you may be made com-
plete. 10Therefore I write these things being ab-
sent, lest being present I should use sharpness,
according to the authority which the Lord has
given me for edification and not for destruction.

Greetings and Benediction

11Finally, brethren, farewell. Become com-
plete. Be of good comfort, be of one mind, live in
peace; and the God of love and peace will be
with you.
12Greet one another with a holy kiss.
13All the saints greet you.
14The grace of the Lord Jesus Christ, and the
love of God, and the communion of the Holy
Spirit *be* with you all. Amen.

The Message

We don't just put up with our limitations; we celebrate them, and then go on to celebrate every strength, every triumph of the truth in you. We pray hard that it will all come together in your lives.

10 I'm writing this to you now so that when I come I won't have to say another word on the subject. The authority the Master gave me is for putting people together, not taking them apart. I want to get on with it, and not have to spend time on reprimands.

11-13 And that's about it, friends. Be cheerful. Keep things in good repair. Keep your spirits up. Think in harmony. Be agreeable. Do all that, and the God of love and peace will be with you for sure. Greet one another with a holy embrace. All the brothers and sisters here say hello.

14 The amazing grace of the Master, Jesus Christ, the extravagant love of God, the intimate friendship of the Holy Spirit, be with all of you.

GALATIANS

NEW KING JAMES VERSION

GREETING

1 Paul, an apostle (not from men nor through man, but through Jesus Christ and God the Father who raised Him from the dead), 2and all the brethren who are with me,

To the churches of Galatia:

3Grace to you and peace from God the Father and our Lord Jesus Christ, 4who gave Himself for our sins, that He might deliver us from this present evil age, according to the will of our God and Father, 5to whom *be* glory forever and ever. Amen.

ONLY ONE GOSPEL

6I marvel that you are turning away so soon from Him who called you in the grace of Christ, to a different gospel, 7which is not another; but there are some who trouble you and want to pervert the gospel of Christ. 8But even if we, or an angel from heaven, preach any other gospel to you than what we have preached to you, let him be accursed. 9As we have said before, so now I say again, if anyone preaches any other gospel to you than what you have received, let him be accursed.

10For do I now persuade men, or God? Or do I seek to please men? For if I still pleased men, I would not be a bondservant of Christ.

CALL TO APOSTLESHIP

11But I make known to you, brethren, that the gospel which was preached by me is not according to man. 12For I neither received it from man, nor was I taught *it,* but *it came* through the revelation of Jesus Christ.

13For you have heard of my former conduct in Judaism, how I persecuted the church of God beyond measure and *tried to* destroy it. 14And I advanced in Judaism beyond many of my contemporaries in my own nation, being more exceedingly zealous for the traditions of my fathers.

15But when it pleased God, who separated me from my mother's womb and called *me* through His grace, 16to reveal His Son in me, that I might preach Him among the Gentiles, I did not immediately confer with flesh and blood, 17nor did I go up to Jerusalem to those *who were* apostles before me; but I went to Arabia, and returned again to Damascus.

CONTACTS AT JERUSALEM

18Then after three years I went up to Jerusalem to see Peter,[a] and remained with him

1:18 [a]NU-Text reads *Cephas.*

THE MESSAGE

1-5 1 I, Paul, and my companions in faith here,
send greetings to the Galatian churches.
My authority for writing to you does not
come from any popular vote of the people,
nor does it come through the appointment
of some human higher-up. It comes directly
from Jesus the Messiah and God the Father,
who raised him from the dead. I'm God-commissioned. So I greet you with the great
words, grace and peace! We know the meaning of those words because Jesus Christ rescued us from this evil world we're in by offering himself as a sacrifice for our sins.
God's plan is that we all experience that rescue. Glory to God forever! Oh, yes!

THE MESSAGE

6-9 I can't believe your fickleness—how easily
you have turned traitor to him who called
you by the grace of Christ by embracing a
variant message! It is not a minor variation,
you know; it is completely other, an alien
message, a no-message, a lie about God.
Those who are provoking this agitation
among you are turning the Message of
Christ on its head. Let me be blunt: If one of
us—even if an angel from heaven!—were to
preach something other than what we
preached originally, let him be cursed. I said
it once; I'll say it again: If anyone, regardless
of reputation or credentials, preaches something other than what you received originally, let him be cursed.
10-12 Do you think I speak this strongly in order to manipulate crowds? Or curry favor
with God? Or get popular applause? If my
goal was popularity, I wouldn't bother being
Christ's slave. Know this—I am most emphatic here, friends—this great Message I
delivered to you is not mere human optimism. I didn't receive it through the traditions, and I wasn't taught it in some school.
I got it straight from God, received the Message directly from Jesus Christ.
13-16 I'm sure that you've heard the story of my
earlier life when I lived in the Jewish way. In
those days I went all out in persecuting
God's church. I was systematically destroying it. I was so enthusiastic about the traditions of my ancestors that I advanced head
and shoulders above my peers in my career.
Even then God had designs on me. Why,
when I was still in my mother's womb he
chose and called me out of sheer generosity!
Now he has intervened and revealed his Son
to me so that I might joyfully tell non-Jews
about him.
16-20 Immediately after my calling—without
consulting anyone around me and without
going up to Jerusalem to confer with those
who were apostles long before I was—I got
away to Arabia. Later I returned to Damascus, but it was three years before I went up
to Jerusalem to compare stories with Peter.

NEW KING JAMES VERSION

fifteen days. 19But I saw none of the other apos-
tles except James, the Lord's brother. 20(Now
concerning the things which I write to you, in-
deed, before God, I do not lie.)
21Afterward I went into the regions of Syria
and Cilicia. 22And I was unknown by face to the
churches of Judea which *were* in Christ. 23But
they were hearing only, "He who formerly per-
secuted us now preaches the faith which he
once *tried to* destroy." 24And they glorified God
in me.

DEFENDING THE GOSPEL

2Then after fourteen years I went up again to
Jerusalem with Barnabas, and also took Titus
with *me.* 2And I went up by revelation, and com-
municated to them that gospel which I preach
among the Gentiles, but privately to those who
were of reputation, lest by any means I might
run, or had run, in vain. 3Yet not even Titus who
was with me, being a Greek, was compelled to
be circumcised. 4And *this occurred* because of
false brethren secretly brought in (who came in
by stealth to spy out our liberty which we have
in Christ Jesus, that they might bring us into
bondage), 5to whom we did not yield submission
even for an hour, that the truth of the gospel
might continue with you.
6But from those who seemed to be some-
thing—whatever they were, it makes no differ-
ence to me; God shows personal favoritism to
no man—for those who seemed *to be something*
added nothing to me. 7But on the contrary, when
they saw that the gospel for the uncircumcised
had been committed to me, as *the gospel* for the
circumcised *was* to Peter 8(for He who worked
effectively in Peter for the apostleship to the cir-
cumcised also worked effectively in me toward
the Gentiles), 9and when James, Cephas, and
John, who seemed to be pillars, perceived the
grace that had been given to me, they gave me
and Barnabas the right hand of fellowship, that
we *should go* to the Gentiles and they to the cir-
cumcised. 10*They desired* only that we should re-
member the poor, the very thing which I also
was eager to do.

NO RETURN TO THE LAW

11Now when Peter[a] had come to Antioch, I
withstood him to his face, because he was to be
blamed; 12for before certain men came from
James, he would eat with the Gentiles; but when
they came, he withdrew and separated himself,
fearing those who were of the circumcision.
13And the rest of the Jews also played the hyp-
ocrite with him, so that even Barnabas was car-
ried away with their hypocrisy.

2:11 [a]NU-Text reads *Cephas.*

THE MESSAGE

I was there only fifteen days—but what days
they were! Except for our Master's brother
James, I saw no other apostles. (I'm telling
you the absolute truth in this.)
21-24 Then I began my ministry in the regions
of Syria and Cilicia. After all that time and
activity I was still unknown by face among
the Christian churches in Judea. There was
only this report: "That man who once perse-
cuted us is now preaching the very message
he used to try to destroy." Their response
was to recognize and worship *God* because
of *me*!

WHAT IS CENTRAL?

1-5 2Fourteen years after that first visit, Barn-
abas and I went up to Jerusalem and took
Titus with us. I went to clarify with them
what had been revealed to me. At that time
I placed before them exactly what I was
preaching to the non-Jews. I did this in pri-
vate with the leaders, those held in esteem
by the church, so that our concern would
not become a controversial public issue,
marred by ethnic tensions, exposing my
years of work to denigration and endanger-
ing my present ministry. Significantly, Titus,
non-Jewish though he was, was not re-
quired to be circumcised. While we were in
conference we were infiltrated by spies pre-
tending to be Christians, who slipped in to
find out just how free true Christians are.
Their ulterior motive was to reduce us to
their brand of servitude. We didn't give them
the time of day. We were determined to pre-
serve the truth of the Message for you.
6-10 As for those who were considered impor-
tant in the church, their reputation doesn't
concern me. God isn't impressed with mere
appearances, and neither am I. And of course
these leaders were able to add nothing to the
message I had been preaching. It was soon
evident that God had entrusted me with the
same message to the non-Jews as Peter had
been preaching to the Jews. Recognizing that
my calling had been given by God, James, Pe-
ter, and John—the pillars of the church—
shook hands with me and Barnabas, assign-
ing us to a ministry to the non-Jews, while
they continued to be responsible for reaching
out to the Jews. The only additional thing
they asked was that we remember the poor,
and I was already eager to do that.
11-13 Later, when Peter came to Antioch, I had
a face-to-face confrontation with him be-
cause he was clearly out of line. Here's the
situation. Earlier, before certain persons
had come from James, Peter regularly ate
with the non-Jews. But when that conserva-
tive group came from Jerusalem, he cau-
tiously pulled back and put as much dis-
tance as he could manage between himself
and his non-Jewish friends. That's how fear-
ful he was of the conservative Jewish clique
that's been pushing the old system of cir-
cumcision. Unfortunately, the rest of the
Jews in the Antioch church joined in that
hypocrisy so that even Barnabas was swept
along in the charade.

New King James Version

14 But when I saw that they were not straightforward about the truth of the gospel, I said to Peter before *them* all, "If you, being a Jew, live in the manner of Gentiles and not as the Jews, why do you[a] compel Gentiles to live as Jews?[b] 15 We *who are* Jews by nature, and not sinners of the Gentiles, 16 knowing that a man is not justified by the works of the law but by faith in Jesus Christ, even we have believed in Christ Jesus, that we might be justified by faith in Christ and not by the works of the law; for by the works of the law no flesh shall be justified.

17 "But if, while we seek to be justified by Christ, we ourselves also are found sinners, *is* Christ therefore a minister of sin? Certainly not! 18 For if I build again those things which I destroyed, I make myself a transgressor. 19 For I through the law died to the law that I might live to God. 20 I have been crucified with Christ; it is no longer I who live, but Christ lives in me; and the *life* which I now live in the flesh I live by faith in the Son of God, who loved me and gave Himself for me. 21 I do not set aside the grace of God; for if righteousness *comes* through the law, then Christ died in vain."

Justification by Faith

3 O foolish Galatians! Who has bewitched you that you should not obey the truth,[a] before whose eyes Jesus Christ was clearly portrayed among you[b] as crucified? 2 This only I want to learn from you: Did you receive the Spirit by the works of the law, or by the hearing of faith? 3 Are you so foolish? Having begun in the Spirit, are

2:14 [a]NU-Text reads *how can you.* [b]Some interpreters stop the quotation here. **3:1** [a]NU-Text omits *that you should not obey the truth.* [b]NU-Text omits *among you.*

The Message

14 But when I saw that they were not maintaining a steady, straight course according to the Message, I spoke up to Peter in front of them all: "If you, a Jew, live like a non-Jew when you're not being observed by the watchdogs from Jerusalem, what right do you have to require non-Jews to conform to Jewish customs just to make a favorable impression on your old Jerusalem cronies?"

15-16 We Jews know that we have no advantage of birth over "non-Jewish sinners." We know very well that we are not set right with God by rule-keeping but only through personal faith in Jesus Christ. How do we know? We tried it—and we had the best system of rules the world has ever seen! Convinced that no human being can please God by self-improvement, we believed in Jesus as the Messiah so that we might be set right before God by trusting in the Messiah, not by trying to be good.

17-18 Have some of you noticed that we are not yet perfect? (No great surprise, right?) And are you ready to make the accusation that since people like me, who go through Christ in order to get things right with God, aren't perfectly virtuous, Christ must therefore be an accessory to sin? The accusation is frivolous. If I was "trying to be good," I would be rebuilding the same old barn that I tore down. I would be acting as a charlatan.

19-21 What actually took place is this: I tried keeping rules and working my head off to please God, and it didn't work. So I quit being a "law man" so that I could be *God's* man. Christ's life showed me how, and enabled me to do it. I identified myself completely with him. Indeed, I have been crucified with Christ. My ego is no longer central. It is no longer important that I appear righteous before you or have your good opinion, and I am no longer driven to impress God. Christ lives in me. The life you see me living is not "mine," but it is lived by faith in the Son of God, who loved me and gave himself for me. I am not going to go back on that.

Is it not clear to you that to go back to that old rule-keeping, peer-pleasing religion would be an abandonment of everything personal and free in my relationship with God? I refuse to do that, to repudiate God's grace. If a living relationship with God could come by rule-keeping, then Christ died unnecessarily.

Trust in Christ, Not the Law

1 3 You crazy Galatians! Did someone put a hex on you? Have you taken leave of your senses? Something crazy has happened, for it's obvious that you no longer have the crucified Jesus in clear focus in your lives. His sacrifice on the cross was certainly set before you clearly enough.

2-4 Let me put this question to you: How did your new life begin? Was it by working your heads off to please God? Or was it by responding to God's Message to you? Are you going to continue this craziness? For only crazy people would think they could com-

NEW KING JAMES VERSION

you now being made perfect by the flesh? [4]Have
you suffered so many things in vain—if indeed
it was in vain?
[5]Therefore He who supplies the Spirit to you
and works miracles among you, *does He do it* by
the works of the law, or by the hearing of
faith?— [6]just as Abraham *"believed God, and it*
was accounted to him for righteousness." [a]
[7]Therefore know that *only* those who are of
faith are sons of Abraham. [8]And the Scripture,
foreseeing that God would justify the Gentiles
by faith, preached the gospel to Abraham be-
forehand, *saying, "In you all the nations shall be*
blessed." [a] [9]So then those who *are* of faith are
blessed with believing Abraham.

THE LAW BRINGS A CURSE

[10]For as many as are of the works of the law
are under the curse; for it is written, *"Cursed is*
everyone who does not continue in all things
which are written in the book of the law, to do
them." [a] [11]But that no one is justified by the law
in the sight of God *is* evident, for *"the just shall*
live by faith." [a] [12]Yet the law is not of faith, but
"the man who does them shall live by them." [a]
[13]Christ has redeemed us from the curse of
the law, having become a curse for us (for it is
written, *"Cursed is everyone who hangs on a*
tree" [a]), [14]that the blessing of Abraham might
come upon the Gentiles in Christ Jesus, that we
might receive the promise of the Spirit through
faith.

THE CHANGELESS PROMISE

[15]Brethren, I speak in the manner of men:
Though *it is* only a man's covenant, yet *if it is*
confirmed, no one annuls or adds to it. [16]Now to
Abraham and his Seed were the promises made.

3:6 [a]Genesis 15:6 **3:8** [a]Genesis 12:3; 18:18; 22:18; 26:4; 28:14 **3:10** [a]Deuteronomy 27:26 **3:11** [a]Habakkuk 2:4 **3:12** [a]Leviticus 18:5 **3:13** [a]Deuteronomy 21:23

THE MESSAGE

plete by their own efforts what was begun by God. If you weren't smart enough or strong enough to begin it, how do you suppose you could perfect it? Did you go through this whole painful learning process for nothing? It is not yet a total loss, but it certainly will be if you keep this up!

5-6 Answer this question: Does the God who lavishly provides you with his own presence, his Holy Spirit, working things in your lives you could never do for yourselves, does he do these things because of your strenuous moral striving *or* because you trust him to do them in you? Don't these things happen among you just as they happened with Abraham? He believed God, and that act of belief was turned into a life that was right with God.

7-8 Is it not obvious to you that persons who put their trust in Christ (not persons who put their trust in the law!) are like Abraham: children of faith? It was all laid out beforehand in Scripture that God would set things right with non-Jews by *faith.* Scripture anticipated this in the promise to Abraham: "All nations will be blessed in you."

9-10 So those now who live by faith are blessed along with Abraham, who lived by faith—this is no new doctrine! And that means that anyone who tries to live by his own effort, independent of God, is doomed to failure. Scripture backs this up: "Utterly cursed is every person who fails to carry out every detail written in the Book of the law."

11-12 The obvious impossibility of carrying out such a moral program should make it plain that no one can sustain a relationship with God that way. The person who lives in right relationship with God does it by embracing what God arranges for him. Doing things for God is the opposite of entering into what God does for you. Habakkuk had it right: "The person who believes God, is set right by God—and that's the real life." Rule-keeping does not naturally evolve into living by faith, but only perpetuates itself in more and more rule-keeping, a fact observed in Scripture: "The one who does these things [rule-keeping] continues to live by them."

13-14 Christ redeemed us from that self-defeating, cursed life by absorbing it completely into himself. Do you remember the Scripture that says, "Cursed is everyone who hangs on a tree"? That is what happened when Jesus was nailed to the cross: He became a curse, and at the same time dissolved the curse. And now, because of that, the air is cleared and we can see that Abraham's blessing is present and available for non-Jews, too. We are *all* able to receive God's life, his Spirit, in and with us by believing—just the way Abraham received it.

15-18 Friends, let me give you an example from everyday affairs of the free life I am talking about. Once a person's will has been ratified, no one else can annul it or add to it. Now, the promises were made to Abraham

NEW KING JAMES VERSION

He does not say, "And to seeds," as of many, but
as of one, *"And to your Seed,"*[a] who is Christ.
17And this I say, *that* the law, which was four
hundred and thirty years later, cannot annul the
covenant that was confirmed before by God in
Christ,[a] that it should make the promise of no
effect. 18For if the inheritance *is* of the law, *it is*
no longer of promise; but God gave *it* to Abra-
ham by promise.

PURPOSE OF THE LAW

19What purpose then *does* the law *serve?* It
was added because of transgressions, till the
Seed should come to whom the promise was
made; *and it was* appointed through angels by
the hand of a mediator. 20Now a mediator does
not *mediate* for one *only*, but God is one.
21*Is* the law then against the promises of
God? Certainly not! For if there had been a law
given which could have given life, truly righ-
teousness would have been by the law. 22But the
Scripture has confined all under sin, that the
promise by faith in Jesus Christ might be given
to those who believe. 23But before faith came, we
were kept under guard by the law, kept for the
faith which would afterward be revealed.
24Therefore the law was our tutor *to bring us* to
Christ, that we might be justified by faith. 25But
after faith has come, we are no longer under a
tutor.

SONS AND HEIRS

26For you are all sons of God through faith in
Christ Jesus. 27For as many of you as were bap-
tized into Christ have put on Christ. 28There is
neither Jew nor Greek, there is neither slave nor
free, there is neither male nor female; for you
are all one in Christ Jesus. 29And if you *are*
Christ's, then you are Abraham's seed, and heirs
according to the promise.

3:16 [a]Genesis 12:7; 13:15; 24:7 3:17 [a]NU-Text omits *in Christ*.

THE MESSAGE

and to his descendant. You will observe that Scripture, in the careful language of a legal document, does not say "to descendants," referring to everybody in general, but "to your descendant" (the noun, note, is singular), referring to Christ. This is the way I interpret this: A will, earlier ratified by God, is not annulled by an addendum attached 430 years later, thereby negating the promise of the will. No, this addendum, with its instructions and regulations, has nothing to do with the promised inheritance in the will.

18-20 What is the point, then, of the law, the attached addendum? It was a thoughtful addition to the original covenant promises made to Abraham. The purpose of the law was to keep a sinful people in the way of salvation until Christ (the descendant) came, inheriting the promises and distributing them to us. Obviously this law was not a firsthand encounter with God. It was arranged by angelic messengers through a middleman, Moses. But if there is a middleman as there was at Sinai, then the people are not dealing directly with God, are they? But the original promise is the *direct* blessing of God, received by faith.

21-22 If such is the case, is the law, then, an anti-promise, a negation of God's will for us? Not at all. Its purpose was to make obvious to everyone that we are, in ourselves, out of right relationship with God, and therefore to show us the futility of devising some religious system for getting by our own efforts what we can only get by waiting in faith for God to complete his promise. For if any kind of rule-keeping had power to create life in us, we would certainly have gotten it by this time.

23-24 Until the time when we were mature enough to respond freely in faith to the living God, we were carefully surrounded and protected by the Mosaic law. The law was like those Greek tutors, with which you are familiar, who escort children to school and protect them from danger or distraction, making sure the children will really get to the place they set out for.

25-27 But now you have arrived at your destination: By faith in Christ you are in direct relationship with God. Your baptism in Christ was not just washing you up for a fresh start. It also involved dressing you in an adult faith wardrobe—Christ's life, the fulfillment of God's original promise.

IN CHRIST'S FAMILY

28-29 In Christ's family there can be no division into Jew and non-Jew, slave and free, male and female. Among us you are all equal. That is, we are all in a common relationship with Jesus Christ. Also, since you are Christ's family, then you are Abraham's famous "descendant," heirs according to the covenant promises.

New King James Version

4 Now I say *that* the heir, as long as he is a child, does not differ at all from a slave, though he is master of all, [2]but is under guardians and stewards until the time appointed by the father. [3]Even so we, when we were children, were in bondage under the elements of the world. [4]But when the fullness of the time had come, God sent forth His Son, born[a] of a woman, born under the law, [5]to redeem those who were under the law, that we might receive the adoption as sons.

[6]And because you are sons, God has sent forth the Spirit of His Son into your hearts, crying out, "Abba, Father!" [7]Therefore you are no longer a slave but a son, and if a son, then an heir of[a] God through Christ.

Fears for the Church

[8]But then, indeed, when you did not know God, you served those which by nature are not gods. [9]But now after you have known God, or rather are known by God, how *is it that* you turn again to the weak and beggarly elements, to which you desire again to be in bondage? [10]You observe days and months and seasons and years. [11]I am afraid for you, lest I have labored for you in vain.

[12]Brethren, I urge you to become like me, for I *became* like you. You have not injured me at all. [13]You know that because of physical infirmity I preached the gospel to you at the first. [14]And my trial which was in my flesh you did not despise or reject, but you received me as an angel of God, *even* as Christ Jesus. [15]What[a] then was the blessing you *enjoyed*? For I bear you witness that, if possible, you would have plucked out your own eyes and given them to me. [16]Have I therefore become your enemy because I tell you the truth?

[17]They zealously court you, *but* for no good; yes, they want to exclude you, that you may be zealous for them.

4:4 [a]Or *made* **4:7** [a]NU-Text reads *through God* and omits *through Christ.* **4:15** [a]NU-Text reads *Where.*

The Message

1-3 4 Let me show you the implications of this. As long as the heir is a minor, he has no advantage over the slave. Though legally he owns the entire inheritance, he is subject to tutors and administrators until whatever date the father has set for emancipation. That is the way it is with us: When we were minors, we were just like slaves ordered around by simple instructions (the tutors and administrators of this world), with no say in the conduct of our own lives.

4-7 But when the time arrived that was set by God the Father, God sent his Son, born among us of a woman, born under the conditions of the law so that he might redeem those of us who have been kidnapped by the law. Thus we have been set free to experience our rightful heritage. You can tell for sure that you are now fully adopted as his own children because God sent the Spirit of his Son into our lives crying out, "Papa! Father!" Doesn't that privilege of intimate conversation with God make it plain that you are not a slave, but a child? And if you are a child, you're also an heir, with complete access to the inheritance.

8-11 Earlier, before you knew God personally, you were enslaved to so-called gods that had nothing of the divine about them. But now that you know the real God—or rather since God knows you—how can you possibly subject yourselves again to those paper tigers? For that is exactly what you do when you are intimidated into scrupulously observing all the traditions, taboos, and superstitions associated with special days and seasons and years. I am afraid that all my hard work among you has gone up in a puff of smoke!

12-13 My dear friends, what I would really like you to do is try to put yourselves in my shoes to the same extent that I, when I was with you, put myself in yours. You were very sensitive and kind then. You did not come down on me personally. You were well aware that the reason I ended up preaching to you was that I was physically broken, and so, prevented from continuing my journey, I was forced to stop with you. That is how I came to preach to you.

14-16 And don't you remember that even though taking in a sick guest was most troublesome for you, you chose to treat me as well as you would have treated an angel of God—as well as you would have treated Jesus himself if he had visited you? What has happened to the satisfaction you felt at that time? There were some of you then who, if possible, would have given your very eyes to me—that is how deeply you cared! And now have I suddenly become your enemy simply by telling you the truth? I can't believe it.

17 Those heretical teachers go to great lengths to flatter you, but their motives are rotten. They want to shut you out of the free world of God's grace so that you will always depend on them for approval and direction, making them feel important.

New King James Version

18But it is good to be zealous in a good thing al-
ways, and not only when I am present with you.
19My little children, for whom I labor in birth
again until Christ is formed in you, 20I would
like to be present with you now and to change
my tone; for I have doubts about you.

Two Covenants

21Tell me, you who desire to be under the law,
do you not hear the law? 22For it is written that
Abraham had two sons: the one by a bond-
woman, the other by a freewoman. 23But he *who*
was of the bondwoman was born according to
the flesh, and he of the freewoman through
promise, 24which things are symbolic. For these
are the[a] two covenants: the one from Mount
Sinai which gives birth to bondage, which is Ha-
gar— 25for this Hagar is Mount Sinai in Arabia,
and corresponds to Jerusalem which now is,
and is in bondage with her children— 26but the
Jerusalem above is free, which is the mother of
us all. 27For it is written:

"Rejoice, O barren,
You who do not bear!
Break forth and shout,
You who are not in labor!
For the desolate has many more children
Than she who has a husband."[a]

28Now we, brethren, as Isaac *was,* are chil-
dren of promise. 29But, as he who was born ac-
cording to the flesh then persecuted him *who*
was born according to the Spirit, even so *it is*
now. 30Nevertheless what does the Scripture
say? *"Cast out the bondwoman and her son, for*
the son of the bondwoman shall not be heir with
the son of the freewoman."[a] 31So then, brethren,
we are not children of the bondwoman but of
the free.

Christian Liberty

5 Stand fast therefore in the liberty by which
Christ has made us free,[a] and do not be en-
tangled again with a yoke of bondage. 2Indeed I,
Paul, say to you that if you become circumcised,
Christ will profit you nothing. 3And I testify
again to every man who becomes circumcised
that he is a debtor to keep the whole law.

4:24 [a]NU-Text and M-Text omit *the.* **4:27** [a]Isaiah 54:1 **4:30** [a]Genesis 21:10 **5:1** [a]NU-Text reads *For freedom Christ has made us free; stand fast therefore.*

The Message

18-20 It is a good thing to be ardent in doing good, but not just when I am in your presence. Can't you continue the same concern for both my person and my message when I am away from you that you had when I was with you? Do you know how I feel right now, and will feel until Christ's life becomes visible in your lives? Like a mother in the pain of childbirth. Oh, I keep wishing that I was with you. Then I wouldn't be reduced to this blunt, letter-writing language out of sheer frustration.

21-31 Tell me now, you who have become so enamored with the law: Have you paid close attention to that law? Abraham, remember, had *two* sons: one by the slave woman and one by the free woman. The son of the slave woman was born by human connivance; the son of the free woman was born by God's promise. This illustrates the very thing we are dealing with now. The two births represent two ways of being in relationship with God. One is from Mount Sinai in Arabia. It corresponds with what is now going on in Jerusalem—a slave life, producing slaves as offspring. This is the way of Hagar. In contrast to that, there is an invisible Jerusalem, a free Jerusalem, and she is our mother—this is the way of Sarah. Remember what Isaiah wrote:

Rejoice, barren woman who bears no children,
shout and cry out, woman who has no birth pangs,
Because the children of the barren woman
now surpass the children of the chosen woman.

Isn't it clear, friends, that you, like Isaac, are children of promise? In the days of Hagar and Sarah, the child who came from faithless connivance (Ishmael) harassed the child who came—empowered by the Spirit—from the faithful promise (Isaac). Isn't it clear that the harassment you are now experiencing from the Jerusalem heretics follows that old pattern? There is a Scripture that tells us what to do: "Expel the slave mother with her son, for the slave son will not inherit with the free son." Isn't that conclusive? We are not children of the slave woman, but of the free woman.

The Life of Freedom

1 5 Christ has set us free to live a free life. So take your stand! Never again let anyone put a harness of slavery on you.

2-3 I am emphatic about this. The moment any one of you submits to circumcision or any other rule-keeping system, at that same moment Christ's hard-won gift of freedom is squandered. I repeat my warning: The person who accepts the ways of circumcision trades all the advantages of the free life in Christ for the obligations of the slave life of the law.

New King James Version

4 You have become estranged from Christ, you who *attempt to* be justified by law; you have fallen from grace. 5 For we through the Spirit eagerly wait for the hope of righteousness by faith. 6 For in Christ Jesus neither circumcision nor uncircumcision avails anything, but faith working through love.

Love Fulfills the Law

7 You ran well. Who hindered you from obeying the truth? 8 This persuasion does not *come* from Him who calls you. 9 A little leaven leavens the whole lump. 10 I have confidence in you, in the Lord, that you will have no other mind; but he who troubles you shall bear his judgment, whoever he is.

11 And I, brethren, if I still preach circumcision, why do I still suffer persecution? Then the offense of the cross has ceased. 12 I could wish that those who trouble you would even cut themselves off!

13 For you, brethren, have been called to liberty; only do not *use* liberty as an opportunity for the flesh, but through love serve one another. 14 For all the law is fulfilled in one word, *even* in this: *"You shall love your neighbor as yourself."* [a] 15 But if you bite and devour one another, beware lest you be consumed by one another!

Walking in the Spirit

16 I say then: Walk in the Spirit, and you shall not fulfill the lust of the flesh. 17 For the flesh lusts against the Spirit, and the Spirit against the flesh; and these are contrary to one another, so that you do not do the things that you wish. 18 But if you are led by the Spirit, you are not under the law.

19 Now the works of the flesh are evident, which are: adultery,[a] fornication, uncleanness, lewdness, 20 idolatry, sorcery, hatred, contentions, jealousies, outbursts of wrath, selfish

5:14 [a]Leviticus 19:18 **5:19** [a]NU-Text omits *adultery.*

The Message

4-6 I suspect you would never intend this, but
this is what happens. When you attempt to
live by your own religious plans and projects, you are cut off from Christ, you fall out of grace. Meanwhile we expectantly wait for a satisfying relationship with the Spirit. For in Christ, neither our most conscientious religion nor disregard of religion amounts to anything. What matters is something far
more interior: faith expressed in love.
7-10 You were running superbly! Who cut in
on you, deflecting you from the true course of obedience? This detour doesn't come from the One who called you into the race in the first place. And please don't toss this off as insignificant. It only takes a minute amount of yeast, you know, to permeate an entire loaf of bread. Deep down, the Master has given me confidence that you will not defect. But the one who is upsetting you, whoever he is, will bear the divine judgment.
11-12 As for the rumor that I continue to preach
the ways of circumcision (as I did in those pre-Damascus Road days), that is absurd. Why would I still be persecuted, then? If I were preaching that old message, no one would be offended if I mentioned the Cross now and then—it would be so watered-down it wouldn't matter one way or the other. Why don't these agitators, obsessive as they are about circumcision, go all the
way and castrate themselves!
13-15 It is absolutely clear that God has called
you to a free life. Just make sure that you don't use this freedom as an excuse to do whatever you want to do and destroy your freedom. Rather, use your freedom to serve one another in love; that's how freedom grows. For everything we know about God's Word is summed up in a single sentence: Love others as you love yourself. That's an act of true freedom. If you bite and ravage each other, watch out—in no time at all you will be annihilating each other, and where
will your precious freedom be then?
16-18 My counsel is this: Live freely, animated
and motivated by God's Spirit. Then you won't feed the compulsions of selfishness. For there is a root of sinful self-interest in us that is at odds with a free spirit, just as the free spirit is incompatible with selfishness. These two ways of life are antithetical, so that you cannot live at times one way and at times another way according to how you feel on any given day. Why don't you choose to be led by the Spirit and so escape the erratic compulsions of a law-dominated existence?

19-21 It is obvious what kind of life develops out
of trying to get your own way all the time: repetitive, loveless, cheap sex; a stinking accumulation of mental and emotional garbage; frenzied and joyless grabs for happiness; trinket gods; magic-show religion; paranoid loneliness; cutthroat competition; all-consuming-yet-never-satisfied wants; a

NEW KING JAMES VERSION

ambitions, dissensions, heresies, [21]envy, murders,[a] drunkenness, revelries, and the like; of which I tell you beforehand, just as I also told *you* in time past, that those who practice such things will not inherit the kingdom of God.

[22]But the fruit of the Spirit is love, joy, peace, longsuffering, kindness, goodness, faithfulness, [23]gentleness, self-control. Against such there is no law. [24]And those *who are* Christ's have crucified the flesh with its passions and desires. [25]If we live in the Spirit, let us also walk in the Spirit. [26]Let us not become conceited, provoking one another, envying one another.

BEAR AND SHARE THE BURDENS

6 Brethren, if a man is overtaken in any trespass, you who *are* spiritual restore such a one in a spirit of gentleness, considering yourself lest you also be tempted. [2]Bear one another's burdens, and so fulfill the law of Christ. [3]For if anyone thinks himself to be something, when he is nothing, he deceives himself. [4]But let each one examine his own work, and then he will have rejoicing in himself alone, and not in another. [5]For each one shall bear his own load.

BE GENEROUS AND DO GOOD

[6]Let him who is taught the word share in all good things with him who teaches.

[7]Do not be deceived, God is not mocked; for whatever a man sows, that he will also reap. [8]For he who sows to his flesh will of the flesh reap corruption, but he who sows to the Spirit will of the Spirit reap everlasting life.

5:21 [a]NU-Text omits *murders*.

THE MESSAGE

brutal temper; an impotence to love or be loved; divided homes and divided lives; small-minded and lopsided pursuits; the vicious habit of depersonalizing everyone into a rival; uncontrolled and uncontrollable addictions; ugly parodies of community. I could go on.

This isn't the first time I have warned you, you know. If you use your freedom this way, you will not inherit God's kingdom.

22-23 But what happens when we live God's way? He brings gifts into our lives, much the same way that fruit appears in an orchard—things like affection for others, exuberance about life, serenity. We develop a willingness to stick with things, a sense of compassion in the heart, and a conviction that a basic holiness permeates things and people. We find ourselves involved in loyal commitments, not needing to force our way in life, able to marshal and direct our energies wisely.

23-24 Legalism is helpless in bringing this about; it only gets in the way. Among those who belong to Christ, everything connected with getting our own way and mindlessly responding to what everyone else calls necessities is killed off for good—crucified.

25-26 Since this is the kind of life we have chosen, the life of the Spirit, let us make sure that we do not just hold it as an idea in our heads or a sentiment in our hearts, but work out its implications in every detail of our lives. That means we will not compare ourselves with each other as if one of us were better and another worse. We have far more interesting things to do with our lives. Each of us is an original.

NOTHING BUT THE CROSS

1-3 **6** Live creatively, friends. If someone falls into sin, forgivingly restore him, saving your critical comments for yourself. *You* might be needing forgiveness before the day's out. Stoop down and reach out to those who are oppressed. Share their burdens, and so complete Christ's law. If you think you are too good for that, you are badly deceived.

4-5 Make a careful exploration of who you are and the work you have been given, and then sink yourself into that. Don't be impressed with yourself. Don't compare yourself with others. Each of you must take responsibility for doing the creative best you can with your own life.

6 Be very sure now, you who have been trained to a self-sufficient maturity, that you enter into a generous common life with those who have trained you, sharing all the good things that you have and experience.

7-8 Don't be misled: No one makes a fool of God. What a person plants, he will harvest. The person who plants selfishness, ignoring the needs of others—ignoring God!—harvests a crop of weeds. All he'll have to show for his life is weeds! But the one who plants in response to God, letting God's Spirit do the growth work in him, harvests a crop of real life, eternal life.

NEW KING JAMES VERSION

9And let us not grow weary while doing good,
for in due season we shall reap if we do not lose
heart. 10Therefore, as we have opportunity, let us
do good to all, especially to those who are of the
household of faith.

GLORY ONLY IN THE CROSS

11See with what large letters I have written to
you with my own hand! 12As many as desire to
make a good showing in the flesh, these *would*
compel you to be circumcised, only that they
may not suffer persecution for the cross of
Christ. 13For not even those who are circumcised
keep the law, but they desire to have you cir-
cumcised that they may boast in your flesh.
14But God forbid that I should boast except in
the cross of our Lord Jesus Christ, by whom[a] the
world has been crucified to me, and I to the
world. 15For in Christ Jesus neither circumcision
nor uncircumcision avails anything, but a new
creation.

BLESSING AND A PLEA

16And as many as walk according to this
rule, peace and mercy *be* upon them, and upon
the Israel of God.

17From now on let no one trouble me, for I
bear in my body the marks of the Lord Jesus.

18Brethren, the grace of our Lord Jesus
Christ *be* with your spirit. Amen.

6:14 [a]Or *by which* (the cross)

THE MESSAGE

9-10 So let's not allow ourselves to get fa-
tigued doing good. At the right time we will
harvest a good crop if we don't give up, or
quit. Right now, therefore, every time we get
the chance, let us work for the benefit of all,
starting with the people closest to us in the
community of faith.

11-13 Now, in these last sentences, I want to
emphasize in the bold scrawls of my per-
sonal handwriting the immense importance
of what I have written to you. These people
who are attempting to force the ways of cir-
cumcision on you have only one motive:
They want an easy way to look good before
others, lacking the courage to live by a faith
that shares Christ's suffering and death. All
their talk about the law is gas. They *them-
selves* don't keep the law! And they are
highly selective in the laws they *do* observe.
They only want you to be circumcised so
they can boast of their success in recruiting
you to their side. That is contemptible!

14-16 For my part, I am going to boast about
nothing but the Cross of our Master, Jesus
Christ. Because of that Cross, I have been
crucified in relation to the world, set free
from the stifling atmosphere of pleasing
others and fitting into the little patterns that
they dictate. Can't you see the central issue
in all this? It is not what you and I do—sub-
mit to circumcision, reject circumcision. It is
what *God* is doing, and he is creating some-
thing totally new, a free life! All who walk
by this standard are the true Israel of God—
his chosen people. Peace and mercy on
them!

17 Quite frankly, I don't want to be bothered
anymore by these disputes. I have far more
important things to do—the serious living of
this faith. I bear in my body scars from my
service to Jesus.

18 May what our Master Jesus Christ gives
freely be deeply and personally yours, my
friends. Oh, yes!

EPHESIANS

New King James Version

Greeting

1 Paul, an apostle of Jesus Christ by the will of God,

To the saints who are in Ephesus, and faithful in Christ Jesus:

[2]Grace to you and peace from God our Father and the Lord Jesus Christ.

Redemption in Christ

[3]Blessed *be* the God and Father of our Lord Jesus Christ, who has blessed us with every spiritual blessing in the heavenly *places* in Christ, [4]just as He chose us in Him before the foundation of the world, that we should be holy and without blame before Him in love, [5]having predestined us to adoption as sons by Jesus Christ to Himself, according to the good pleasure of His will, [6]to the praise of the glory of His grace, by which He made us accepted in the Beloved.

[7]In Him we have redemption through His blood, the forgiveness of sins, according to the riches of His grace [8]which He made to abound toward us in all wisdom and prudence, [9]having made known to us the mystery of His will, according to His good pleasure which He purposed in Himself, [10]that in the dispensation of the fullness of the times He might gather together in one all things in Christ, both[a] which are in heaven and which are on earth—in Him. [11]In Him also we have obtained an inheritance, being predestined according to the purpose of Him who works all things according to the counsel of His will, [12]that we who first trusted in Christ should be to the praise of His glory.

[13]In Him you also *trusted,* after you heard the word of truth, the gospel of your salvation; in whom also, having believed, you were sealed with the Holy Spirit of promise, [14]who[a] is the guarantee of our inheritance until the redemption of the purchased possession, to the praise of His glory.

Prayer for Spiritual Wisdom

[15]Therefore I also, after I heard of your faith in the Lord Jesus and your love for all the saints, [16]do not cease to give thanks for you, making mention of you in my prayers: [17]that the God of our Lord Jesus Christ, the Father of glory, may give to you the spirit of wisdom and revelation in the knowledge of Him, [18]the eyes of your understanding[a] being enlightened; that you may know what is the hope of His calling, what are the riches of the glory of His inheritance in the saints, [19]and what *is* the exceeding greatness of His power toward us who believe, according to the working of His mighty power

1:10 [a]NU-Text and M-Text omit *both.* **1:14** [a]NU-Text reads *which.* **1:18** [a]NU-Text and M-Text read *hearts.*

The Message

1-2 1 I, Paul, am under God's plan as an apos-
tle, a special agent of Christ Jesus, writing
to you faithful believers in Ephesus. I greet
you with the grace and peace poured into
our lives by God our Father and our Master,
Jesus Christ.

The God of Glory

3-6 How blessed is God! And what a blessing he
is! He's the Father of our Master, Jesus
Christ, and takes us to the high places of
blessing in him. Long before he laid down
earth's foundations, he had us in mind, had
settled on us as the focus of his love, to be
made whole and holy by his love. Long, long
ago he decided to adopt us into his family
through Jesus Christ. (What pleasure he
took in planning this!) He wanted us to en-
ter into the celebration of his lavish gift-
giving by the hand of his beloved Son.

7-10 Because of the sacrifice of the Messiah,
his blood poured out on the altar of the
Cross, we're a free people—free of penalties
and punishments chalked up by all our mis-
deeds. And not just barely free, either.
Abundantly free! He thought of everything,
provided for everything we could possibly
need, letting us in on the plans he took such
delight in making. He set it all out before us
in Christ, a long-range plan in which every-
thing would be brought together and
summed up in him, everything in deepest
heaven, everything on planet earth.

11-12 It's in Christ that we find out who we are
and what we are living for. Long before we
first heard of Christ and got our hopes up,
he had his eye on us, had designs on us for
glorious living, part of the overall purpose
he is working out in everything and every-
one.

13-14 It's in Christ that you, once you heard the
truth and believed it (this Message of your
salvation), found yourselves home free—
signed, sealed, and delivered by the Holy
Spirit. This signet from God is the first in-
stallment on what's coming, a reminder that
we'll get everything God has planned for us,
a praising and glorious life.

15-19 That's why, when I heard of the solid trust
you have in the Master Jesus and your out-
pouring of love to all the followers of Jesus,
I couldn't stop thanking God for you—every
time I prayed, I'd think of you and give
thanks. But I do more than thank. I ask—
ask the God of our Master, Jesus Christ, the
God of glory—to make you intelligent and
discerning in knowing him personally, your
eyes focused and clear, so that you can see
exactly what it is he is calling you to do,
grasp the immensity of this glorious way of
life he has for his followers, oh, the utter ex-
travagance of his work in us who trust
him—endless energy, boundless strength!

New King James Version

[20]which He worked in Christ when He raised
Him from the dead and seated *Him* at His right
hand in the heavenly *places,* [21]far above all prin-
cipality and power and might and dominion,
and every name that is named, not only in this
age but also in that which is to come.
[22]And He put all *things* under His feet, and
gave Him *to be* head over all *things* to the
church, [23]which is His body, the fullness of Him
who fills all in all.

By Grace Through Faith

2 And you *He made alive,* who were dead in
trespasses and sins, [2]in which you once
walked according to the course of this world, ac-
cording to the prince of the power of the air, the
spirit who now works in the sons of disobedi-
ence, [3]among whom also we all once conducted
ourselves in the lusts of our flesh, fulfilling the
desires of the flesh and of the mind, and were by
nature children of wrath, just as the others.
[4]But God, who is rich in mercy, because of
His great love with which He loved us, [5]even
when we were dead in trespasses, made us alive
together with Christ (by grace you have been
saved), [6]and raised *us* up together, and made *us*
sit together in the heavenly *places* in Christ Je-
sus, [7]that in the ages to come He might show the
exceeding riches of His grace in *His* kindness
toward us in Christ Jesus. [8]For by grace you
have been saved through faith, and that not of
yourselves; *it is* the gift of God, [9]not of works,
lest anyone should boast. [10]For we are His work-
manship, created in Christ Jesus for good
works, which God prepared beforehand that we
should walk in them.

Brought Near by His Blood

[11]Therefore remember that you, once Gen-
tiles in the flesh—who are called Uncircumci-
sion by what is called the Circumcision made in
the flesh by hands— [12]that at that time you were
without Christ, being aliens from the common-
wealth of Israel and strangers from the
covenants of promise, having no hope and with-
out God in the world. [13]But now in Christ Jesus
you who once were far off have been brought
near by the blood of Christ.

Christ Our Peace

[14]For He Himself is our peace, who has made
both one, and has broken down the middle wall
of separation, [15]having abolished in His flesh the
enmity, *that is,* the law of commandments *con-
tained* in ordinances, so as to create in Himself
one new man *from* the two, *thus* making peace,

The Message

20-23 All this energy issues from Christ: God raised him from death and set him on a throne in deep heaven, in charge of running the universe, everything from galaxies to governments, no name and no power exempt from his rule. And not just for the time being, but *forever.* He is in charge of it all, has the final word on everything. At the center of all this, Christ rules the church. The church, you see, is not peripheral to the world; the world is peripheral to the church. The church is Christ's body, in which he speaks and acts, by which he fills everything with his presence.

He Tore Down the Wall

1-6 2 It wasn't so long ago that you were mired in that old stagnant life of sin. You let the world, which doesn't know the first thing about living, tell you how to live. You filled your lungs with polluted unbelief, and then exhaled disobedience. We all did it, all of us doing what we felt like doing, when we felt like doing it, all of us in the same boat. It's a wonder God didn't lose his temper and do away with the whole lot of us. Instead, immense in mercy and with an incredible love, he embraced us. He took our sin-dead lives and made us alive in Christ. He did all this on his own, with no help from us! Then he picked us up and set us down in highest heaven in company with Jesus, our Messiah.

7-10 Now God has us where he wants us, with all the time in this world and the next to shower grace and kindness upon us in Christ Jesus. Saving is all his idea, and all his work. All we do is trust him enough to let him do it. It's God's gift from start to finish! We don't play the major role. If we did, we'd probably go around bragging that we'd done the whole thing! No, we neither make nor save ourselves. God does both the making and saving. He creates each of us by Christ Jesus to join him in the work he does, the good work he has gotten ready for us to do, work we had better be doing.

11-13 But don't take any of this for granted. It was only yesterday that you outsiders to God's ways had no idea of any of this, didn't know the first thing about the way God works, hadn't the faintest idea of Christ. You knew nothing of that rich history of God's covenants and promises in Israel, hadn't a clue about what God was doing in the world at large. Now because of Christ—dying that death, shedding that blood—you who were once out of it altogether are in on everything.

14-15 The Messiah has made things up between us so that we're now together on this, both non-Jewish outsiders and Jewish insiders. He tore down the wall we used to keep each other at a distance. He repealed the law code that had become so clogged with fine print and footnotes that it hindered more than it helped. Then he started over. Instead of continuing with two groups of people separated by centuries of animosity and suspicion, he created a new kind of human being, a fresh start for everybody.

NEW KING JAMES VERSION

16and that He might reconcile them both to God in one body through the cross, thereby putting to death the enmity. 17And He came and preached peace to you who were afar off and to those who were near. 18For through Him we both have access by one Spirit to the Father.

CHRIST OUR CORNERSTONE

19Now, therefore, you are no longer strangers and foreigners, but fellow citizens with the saints and members of the household of God, 20having been built on the foundation of the apostles and prophets, Jesus Christ Himself being the chief corner*stone,* 21in whom the whole building, being fitted together, grows into a holy temple in the Lord, 22in whom you also are being built together for a dwelling place of God in the Spirit.

THE MYSTERY REVEALED

3 For this reason I, Paul, the prisoner of Christ Jesus for you Gentiles— 2if indeed you have heard of the dispensation of the grace of God which was given to me for you, 3how that by revelation He made known to me the mystery (as I have briefly written already, 4by which, when you read, you may understand my knowledge in the mystery of Christ), 5which in other ages was not made known to the sons of men, as it has now been revealed by the Spirit to His holy apostles and prophets: 6that the Gentiles should be fellow heirs, of the same body, and partakers of His promise in Christ through the gospel, 7of which I became a minister according to the gift of the grace of God given to me by the effective working of His power.

PURPOSE OF THE MYSTERY

8To me, who am less than the least of all the saints, this grace was given, that I should preach among the Gentiles the unsearchable riches of Christ, 9and to make all see what *is* the fellowship[a] of the mystery, which from the beginning of the ages has been hidden in God who created all things through Jesus Christ;[b] 10to the intent that now the manifold wisdom of God might be made known by the church to the principalities and powers in the heavenly *places,*

3:9 [a]NU-Text and M-Text read *stewardship (dispensation).* [b]NU-Text omits *through Jesus Christ.*

THE MESSAGE

16-18 Christ brought us together through his death on the cross. The Cross got us to embrace, and that was the end of the hostility. Christ came and preached peace to you outsiders and peace to us insiders. He treated us as equals, and so made us equals. Through him we both share the same Spirit and have equal access to the Father.

19-22 That's plain enough, isn't it? You're no longer wandering exiles. This kingdom of faith is now your home country. You're no longer strangers or outsiders. You *belong* here, with as much right to the name Christian as anyone. God is building a home. He's using us all—irrespective of how we got here—in what he is building. He used the apostles and prophets for the foundation. Now he's using you, fitting you in brick by brick, stone by stone, with Christ Jesus as the cornerstone that holds all the parts together. We see it taking shape day after day—a holy temple built by God, all of us built into it, a temple in which God is quite at home.

THE SECRET PLAN OF GOD

1-3 3 This is why I, Paul, am in jail for Christ, having taken up the cause of you outsiders, so-called. I take it that you're familiar with the part I was given in God's plan for including everybody. I got the inside story on this from God himself, as I just wrote you in brief.

4-6 As you read over what I have written to you, you'll be able to see for yourselves into the mystery of Christ. None of our ancestors understood this. Only in our time has it been made clear by God's Spirit through his holy apostles and prophets of this new order. The mystery is that people who have never heard of God and those who have heard of him all their lives (what I've been calling outsiders and insiders) stand on the same ground before God. They get the same offer, same help, same promises in Christ Jesus. The Message is accessible and welcoming to everyone, across the board.

7-8 This is my life work: helping people understand and respond to this Message. It came as a sheer gift to me, a real surprise, God handling all the details. When it came to presenting the Message to people who had no background in God's way, I was the least qualified of any of the available Christians. God saw to it that I was equipped, but you can be sure that it had nothing to do with my natural abilities.

8-10 And so here I am, preaching and writing about things that are way over my head, the inexhaustible riches and generosity of Christ. My task is to bring out in the open and make plain what God, who created all this in the first place, has been doing in secret and behind the scenes all along. Through followers of Jesus like yourselves gathered in churches, this extraordinary plan of God is becoming known and talked about even among the angels!

NEW KING JAMES VERSION

[11]according to the eternal purpose which He ac-
complished in Christ Jesus our Lord, [12]in whom
we have boldness and access with confidence
through faith in Him. [13]Therefore I ask that you
do not lose heart at my tribulations for you,
which is your glory.

APPRECIATION OF THE MYSTERY

[14]For this reason I bow my knees to the Fa-
ther of our Lord Jesus Christ,[a] [15]from whom the
whole family in heaven and earth is named,
[16]that He would grant you, according to the
riches of His glory, to be strengthened with
might through His Spirit in the inner man, [17]that
Christ may dwell in your hearts through faith;
that you, being rooted and grounded in love,
[18]may be able to comprehend with all the saints
what *is* the width and length and depth and
height— [19]to know the love of Christ which
passes knowledge; that you may be filled with
all the fullness of God.

[20]Now to Him who is able to do exceedingly
abundantly above all that we ask or think, ac-
cording to the power that works in us, [21]to Him
be glory in the church by Christ Jesus to all gen-
erations, forever and ever. Amen.

WALK IN UNITY

4 I, therefore, the prisoner of the Lord, beseech
you to walk worthy of the calling with which
you were called, [2]with all lowliness and gentle-
ness, with longsuffering, bearing with one an-
other in love, [3]endeavoring to keep the unity of
the Spirit in the bond of peace. [4]*There is* one
body and one Spirit, just as you were called in
one hope of your calling; [5]one Lord, one faith,
one baptism; [6]one God and Father of all, who *is*
above all, and through all, and in you[a] all.

SPIRITUAL GIFTS

[7]But to each one of us grace was given ac-
cording to the measure of Christ's gift. [8]There-
fore He says:

"When He ascended on high,
He led captivity captive,
And gave gifts to men." [a]

[9](Now this, *"He ascended"*—what does it mean
but that He also first[a] descended into the lower

3:14 [a]NU-Text omits *of our Lord Jesus Christ.* **4:6** [a]NU-Text omits *you;* M-Text reads *us.* **4:8** [a]Psalm 68:18 **4:9** [a]NU-Text omits *first.*

THE MESSAGE

11-13 All this is proceeding along lines planned
all along by God and then executed in
Christ Jesus. When we trust in him, we're
free to say whatever needs to be said, bold
to go wherever we need to go. So don't let
my present trouble on your behalf get you
down. Be proud!

14-19 My response is to get down on my knees be-
fore the Father, this magnificent Father who
parcels out all heaven and earth. I ask him
to strengthen you by his Spirit—not a brute
strength but a glorious inner strength—that
Christ will live in you as you open the door
and invite him in. And I ask him that with
both feet planted firmly on love, you'll be
able to take in with all followers of Jesus the
extravagant dimensions of Christ's love.
Reach out and experience the breadth! Test
its length! Plumb the depths! Rise to the
heights! Live full lives, full in the fullness of
God.

20-21 God can do anything, you know—far
more than you could ever imagine or guess
or request in your wildest dreams! He does
it not by pushing us around but by working
within us, his Spirit deeply and gently
within us.

Glory to God in the church!
Glory to God in the Messiah, in Jesus!
Glory down all the generations!
Glory through all millennia! Oh, yes!

TO BE MATURE

1-3 **4** In light of all this, here's what I want you
to do. While I'm locked up here, a prisoner
for the Master, I want you to get out there
and walk—better yet, run!—on the road God
called you to travel. I don't want any of you
sitting around on your hands. I don't want
anyone strolling off, down some path that
goes nowhere. And mark that you do this
with humility and discipline—not in fits and
starts, but steadily, pouring yourselves out
for each other in acts of love, alert at notic-
ing differences and quick at mending
fences.

4-6 You were all called to travel on the same
road and in the same direction, so stay to-
gether, both outwardly and inwardly. You
have one Master, one faith, one baptism, one
God and Father of all, who rules over all,
works through all, and is present in all.
Everything you are and think and do is per-
meated with Oneness.

7-13 But that doesn't mean you should all look
and speak and act the same. Out of the gen-
erosity of Christ, each of us is given his own
gift. The text for this is,

He climbed the high mountain,
He captured the enemy and seized the
booty,
He handed it all out in gifts to the people.

Is it not true that the One who climbed up
also climbed down, down to the valley of

NEW KING JAMES VERSION

parts of the earth? 10He who descended is also the One who ascended far above all the heavens, that He might fill all things.)

11And He Himself gave some *to be* apostles, some prophets, some evangelists, and some pastors and teachers, 12for the equipping of the saints for the work of ministry, for the edifying of the body of Christ, 13till we all come to the unity of the faith and of the knowledge of the Son of God, to a perfect man, to the measure of the stature of the fullness of Christ; 14that we should no longer be children, tossed to and fro and carried about with every wind of doctrine, by the trickery of men, in the cunning craftiness of deceitful plotting, 15but, speaking the truth in love, may grow up in all things into Him who is the head—Christ— 16from whom the whole body, joined and knit together by what every joint supplies, according to the effective working by which every part does its share, causes growth of the body for the edifying of itself in love.

THE NEW MAN

17This I say, therefore, and testify in the Lord, that you should no longer walk as the rest of[a] the Gentiles walk, in the futility of their mind, 18having their understanding darkened, being alienated from the life of God, because of the ignorance that is in them, because of the blindness of their heart; 19who, being past feeling, have given themselves over to lewdness, to work all uncleanness with greediness.

20But you have not so learned Christ, 21if indeed you have heard Him and have been taught by Him, as the truth is in Jesus: 22that you put off, concerning your former conduct, the old man which grows corrupt according to the deceitful lusts, 23and be renewed in the spirit of your mind, 24and that you put on the new man which was created according to God, in true righteousness and holiness.

DO NOT GRIEVE THE SPIRIT

25Therefore, putting away lying, *"Let each one of you speak truth with his neighbor,"*[a] for we are members of one another. 26*"Be angry, and do not sin"*:[a] do not let the sun go down on your wrath, 27nor give place to the devil. 28Let him who stole steal no longer, but rather let him labor, working with *his* hands what is good, that he may have something to give him who has need. 29Let no corrupt word proceed out of your mouth, but what is good for necessary edification, that it may impart grace to the hearers. 30And do not grieve the Holy Spirit of God, by whom you were sealed for the day of redemption.

4:17[a]NU-Text omits *the rest of.* **4:25**[a]Zechariah 8:16 **4:26**[a]Psalm 4:4

THE MESSAGE

earth? And the One who climbed down is the One who climbed back up, up to highest heaven. He handed out gifts above and below, filled heaven with his gifts, filled earth with his gifts. He handed out gifts of apostle, prophet, evangelist, and pastor-teacher to train Christ's followers in skilled servant work, working within Christ's body, the church, until we're all moving rhythmically and easily with each other, efficient and graceful in response to God's Son, fully mature adults, fully developed within and without, fully alive like Christ.

14-16 No prolonged infancies among us, please. We'll not tolerate babes in the woods, small children who are an easy mark for impostors. God wants us to grow up, to know the whole truth and tell it in love—like Christ in everything. We take our lead from Christ, who is the source of everything we do. He keeps us in step with each other. His very breath and blood flow through us, nourishing us so that we will grow up healthy in God, robust in love.

THE OLD WAY HAS TO GO

17-19 And so I insist—and God backs me up on this—that there be no going along with the crowd, the empty-headed, mindless crowd. They've refused for so long to deal with God that they've lost touch not only with God but with reality itself. They can't think straight anymore. Feeling no pain, they let themselves go in sexual obsession, addicted to every sort of perversion.

20-24 But that's no life for you. You learned Christ! My assumption is that you have paid careful attention to him, been well instructed in the truth precisely as we have it in Jesus. Since, then, we do not have the excuse of ignorance, everything—and I do mean everything—connected with that old way of life has to go. It's rotten through and through. Get rid of it! And then take on an entirely new way of life—a God-fashioned life, a life renewed from the inside and working itself into your conduct as God accurately reproduces his character in you.

25 What this adds up to, then, is this: no more lies, no more pretense. Tell your neighbor the truth. In Christ's body we're all connected to each other, after all. When you lie to others, you end up lying to yourself.

26-27 Go ahead and be angry. You do well to be angry—but don't use your anger as fuel for revenge. And don't stay angry. Don't go to bed angry. Don't give the Devil that kind of foothold in your life.

28 Did you use to make ends meet by stealing? Well, no more! Get an honest job so that you can help others who can't work.

29 Watch the way you talk. Let nothing foul or dirty come out of your mouth. Say only what helps, each word a gift.

30 Don't grieve God. Don't break his heart. His Holy Spirit, moving and breathing in you, is the most intimate part of your life, making you fit for himself. Don't take such a gift for granted.

NEW KING JAMES VERSION

31 Let all bitterness, wrath, anger, clamor, and
evil speaking be put away from you, with all
malice. 32 And be kind to one another, tender-
hearted, forgiving one another, even as God in
Christ forgave you.

WALK IN LOVE

5 Therefore be imitators of God as dear chil-
dren. 2 And walk in love, as Christ also has
loved us and given Himself for us, an offering
and a sacrifice to God for a sweet-smelling
aroma.

3 But fornication and all uncleanness or cov-
etousness, let it not even be named among you,
as is fitting for saints; 4 neither filthiness, nor
foolish talking, nor coarse jesting, which are not
fitting, but rather giving of thanks. 5 For this you
know,[a] that no fornicator, unclean person, nor
covetous man, who is an idolater, has any inher-
itance in the kingdom of Christ and God. 6 Let no
one deceive you with empty words, for because
of these things the wrath of God comes upon the
sons of disobedience. 7 Therefore do not be par-
takers with them.

WALK IN LIGHT

8 For you were once darkness, but now *you
are* light in the Lord. Walk as children of light
9 (for the fruit of the Spirit[a] *is* in all goodness,
righteousness, and truth), 10 finding out what is
acceptable to the Lord. 11 And have no fellow-
ship with the unfruitful works of darkness, but
rather expose *them.* 12 For it is shameful even to
speak of those things which are done by them in
secret. 13 But all things that are exposed are
made manifest by the light, for whatever makes
manifest is light. 14 Therefore He says:

"Awake, you who sleep,
Arise from the dead,
And Christ will give you light."

WALK IN WISDOM

15 See then that you walk circumspectly, not
as fools but as wise, 16 redeeming the time, be-
cause the days are evil.

17 Therefore do not be unwise, but under-
stand what the will of the Lord *is.* 18 And do not
be drunk with wine, in which is dissipation; but
be filled with the Spirit, 19 speaking to one an-
other in psalms and hymns and spiritual songs,
singing and making melody in your heart to the
Lord, 20 giving thanks always for all things to
God the Father in the name of our Lord Jesus
Christ,

5:5 [a]NU-Text reads *For know this.* **5:9** [a]NU-Text reads *light.*

THE MESSAGE

31-32 Make a clean break with all cutting, backbiting, profane talk. Be gentle with one another, sensitive. Forgive one another as quickly and thoroughly as God in Christ forgave you.

WAKE UP FROM YOUR SLEEP

1-2 5 Watch what God does, and then you do it, like children who learn proper behavior from their parents. Mostly what God does is love you. Keep company with him and learn a life of love. Observe how Christ loved us. His love was not cautious but extravagant. He didn't love in order to get something from us but to give everything of himself to us. Love like that.

3-4 Don't allow love to turn into lust, setting off a downhill slide into sexual promiscuity, filthy practices, or bullying greed. Though some tongues just love the taste of gossip, those who follow Jesus have better uses for language than that. Don't talk dirty or silly. That kind of talk doesn't fit our style. Thanksgiving is our dialect.

5 You can be sure that using people or religion or things just for what you can get out of them—the usual variations on idolatry—will get you nowhere, and certainly nowhere near the kingdom of Christ, the kingdom of God.

6-7 Don't let yourselves get taken in by religious smooth talk. God gets furious with people who are full of religious sales talk but want nothing to do with him. Don't even hang around people like that.

8-10 You groped your way through that murk once, but no longer. You're out in the open now. The bright light of Christ makes your way plain. So no more stumbling around. Get on with it! The good, the right, the true—these are the actions appropriate for daylight hours. Figure out what will please Christ, and then do it.

11-16 Don't waste your time on useless work, mere busywork, the barren pursuits of darkness. Expose these things for the sham they are. It's a scandal when people waste their lives on things they must do in the darkness where no one will see. Rip the cover off those frauds and see how attractive they look in the light of Christ.

Wake up from your sleep,
Climb out of your coffins;
Christ will show you the light!

So watch your step. Use your head. Make the most of every chance you get. These are desperate times!

17 Don't live carelessly, unthinkingly. Make sure you understand what the Master wants.

18-20 Don't drink too much wine. That cheapens your life. Drink the Spirit of God, huge draughts of him. Sing hymns instead of drinking songs! Sing songs from your heart to Christ. Sing praises over everything, any excuse for a song to God the Father in the name of our Master, Jesus Christ.

NEW KING JAMES VERSION

21submitting to one another in the fear of God.[a]

MARRIAGE—CHRIST AND THE CHURCH

22Wives, submit to your own husbands, as to
the Lord. 23For the husband is head of the wife,
as also Christ is head of the church; and He is
the Savior of the body. 24Therefore, just as the
church is subject to Christ, so *let* the wives *be* to
their own husbands in everything.

25Husbands, love your wives, just as Christ
also loved the church and gave Himself for her,
26that He might sanctify and cleanse her with
the washing of water by the word, 27that He
might present her to Himself a glorious church,
not having spot or wrinkle or any such thing,
but that she should be holy and without blem-
ish. 28So husbands ought to love their own wives
as their own bodies; he who loves his wife loves
himself. 29For no one ever hated his own flesh,
but nourishes and cherishes it, just as the Lord
does the church. 30For we are members of His
body,[a] of His flesh and of His bones. 31*"For this
reason a man shall leave his father and mother
and be joined to his wife, and the two shall be-
come one flesh."*[a] 32This is a great mystery, but I
speak concerning Christ and the church. 33Nev-
ertheless let each one of you in particular so
love his own wife as himself, and let the wife *see*
that she respects *her* husband.

CHILDREN AND PARENTS

6 Children, obey your parents in the Lord, for
this is right. 2*"Honor your father and
mother,"* which is the first commandment with
promise: 3*"that it may be well with you and you
may live long on the earth."*[a]

4And you, fathers, do not provoke your chil-
dren to wrath, but bring them up in the training
and admonition of the Lord.

BONDSERVANTS AND MASTERS

5Bondservants, be obedient to those who are
your masters according to the flesh, with fear
and trembling, in sincerity of heart, as to Christ;
6not with eyeservice, as men-pleasers, but as
bondservants of Christ, doing the will of God
from the heart, 7with goodwill doing service, as
to the Lord, and not to men, 8knowing that what-
ever good anyone does, he will receive the same
from the Lord, whether *he is* a slave or free.

9And you, masters, do the same things to
them, giving up threatening, knowing that your
own Master also[a] is in heaven, and there is no
partiality with Him.

THE WHOLE ARMOR OF GOD

10Finally, my brethren, be strong in the Lord
and in the power of His might. 11Put on the
whole armor of God, that you may be able to
stand against the wiles of the devil. 12For we do

5:21 [a]NU-Text reads *Christ.* **5:30** [a]NU-Text omits the rest of this verse. **5:31** [a]Genesis 2:24 **6:3** [a]Deuteronomy 5:16 **6:9** [a]NU-Text reads *He who is both their Master and yours.*

THE MESSAGE

RELATIONSHIPS

21 Out of respect for Christ, be courteously reverent to one another.

22-24 Wives, understand and support your husbands in ways that show your support for Christ. The husband provides leadership to his wife the way Christ does to his church, not by domineering but by cherishing. So just as the church submits to Christ as he exercises such leadership, wives should likewise submit to their husbands.

25-28 Husbands, go all out in your love for your wives, exactly as Christ did for the church—a love marked by giving, not getting. Christ's love makes the church whole. His words evoke her beauty. Everything he does and says is designed to bring the best out of her, dressing her in dazzling white silk, radiant with holiness. And that is how husbands ought to love their wives. They're really doing themselves a favor—since they're already "one" in marriage.

29-33 No one abuses his own body, does he? No, he feeds and pampers it. That's how Christ treats us, the church, since we are part of his body. And this is why a man leaves father and mother and cherishes his wife. No longer two, they become "one flesh." This is a huge mystery, and I don't pretend to understand it all. What is clearest to me is the way Christ treats the church. And this provides a good picture of how each husband is to treat his wife, loving himself in loving her, and how each wife is to honor her husband.

1-3 6 Children, do what your parents tell you. This is only right. "Honor your father and mother" is the first commandment that has a promise attached to it, namely, "so you will live well and have a long life."

4 Fathers, don't exasperate your children by coming down hard on them. Take them by the hand and lead them in the way of the Master.

5-8 Servants, respectfully obey your earthly masters but always with an eye to obeying the *real* master, Christ. Don't just do what you have to do to get by, but work heartily, as Christ's servants doing what God wants you to do. And work with a smile on your face, always keeping in mind that no matter who happens to be giving the orders, you're really serving God. Good work will get you good pay from the Master, regardless of whether you are slave or free.

9 Masters, it's the same with you. No abuse, please, and no threats. You and your servants are both under the same Master in heaven. He makes no distinction between you and them.

A FIGHT TO THE FINISH

10-12 And that about wraps it up. God is strong, and he wants you strong. So take everything the Master has set out for you, well-made weapons of the best materials. And put them to use so you will be able to stand up to everything the Devil throws your way. This

New King James Version

not wrestle against flesh and blood, but against
principalities, against powers, against the rulers
of the darkness of this age,[a] against spiritual
hosts of wickedness in the heavenly *places.*
13 Therefore take up the whole armor of God,
that you may be able to withstand in the evil
day, and having done all, to stand.
14 Stand therefore, having girded your waist
with truth, having put on the breastplate of
righteousness, 15 and having shod your feet with
the preparation of the gospel of peace; 16 above
all, taking the shield of faith with which you will
be able to quench all the fiery darts of the
wicked one. 17 And take the helmet of salvation,
and the sword of the Spirit, which is the word of
God; 18 praying always with all prayer and sup-
plication in the Spirit, being watchful to this end
with all perseverance and supplication for all
the saints— 19 and for me, that utterance may be
given to me, that I may open my mouth boldly to
make known the mystery of the gospel, 20 for
which I am an ambassador in chains; that in it I
may speak boldly, as I ought to speak.

A Gracious Greeting

21 But that you also may know my affairs *and*
how I am doing, Tychicus, a beloved brother and
faithful minister in the Lord, will make all
things known to you; 22 whom I have sent to you
for this very purpose, that you may know our af-
fairs, and *that* he may comfort your hearts.
23 Peace to the brethren, and love with faith,
from God the Father and the Lord Jesus Christ.
24 Grace *be* with all those who love our Lord Je-
sus Christ in sincerity. Amen.

6:12 [a]NU-Text reads *rulers of this darkness.*

The Message

is no afternoon athletic contest that we'll
walk away from and forget about in a cou-
ple of hours. This is for keeps, a life-or-death
fight to the finish against the Devil and all
his angels.
13-18 Be prepared. You're up against far more
than you can handle on your own. Take all
the help you can get, every weapon God has
issued, so that when it's all over but the
shouting you'll still be on your feet. Truth,
righteousness, peace, faith, and salvation
are more than words. Learn how to apply
them. You'll need them throughout your life.
God's Word is an *indispensable* weapon. In
the same way, prayer is essential in this on-
going warfare. Pray hard and long. Pray for
your brothers and sisters. Keep your eyes
open. Keep each other's spirits up so that no
one falls behind or drops out.
19-20 And don't forget to pray for me. Pray that
I'll know what to say and have the courage
to say it at the right time, telling the mystery
to one and all, the Message that I, jailbird
preacher that I am, am responsible for get-
ting out.
21-22 Tychicus, my good friend here, will tell
you what I'm doing and how things are go-
ing with me. He is certainly a dependable
servant of the Master! I've sent him not only
to tell you about us but to cheer you on in
your faith.
23-24 Good-bye, friends. Love mixed with faith
be yours from God the Father and from the
Master, Jesus Christ. Pure grace and noth-
ing but grace be with all who love our Mas-
ter, Jesus Christ.

PHILIPPIANS

New King James Version

Greeting

1 Paul and Timothy, bondservants of Jesus Christ,

To all the saints in Christ Jesus who are in Philippi, with the bishops[a] and deacons:

2 Grace to you and peace from God our Father and the Lord Jesus Christ.

Thankfulness and Prayer

3 I thank my God upon every remembrance of you, 4 always in every prayer of mine making request for you all with joy, 5 for your fellowship in the gospel from the first day until now, 6 being confident of this very thing, that He who has begun a good work in you will complete *it* until the day of Jesus Christ; 7 just as it is right for me to think this of you all, because I have you in my heart, inasmuch as both in my chains and in the defense and confirmation of the gospel, you all are partakers with me of grace. 8 For God is my witness, how greatly I long for you all with the affection of Jesus Christ.

9 And this I pray, that your love may abound still more and more in knowledge and all discernment, 10 that you may approve the things that are excellent, that you may be sincere and without offense till the day of Christ, 11 being filled with the fruits of righteousness which *are* by Jesus Christ, to the glory and praise of God.

Christ Is Preached

12 But I want you to know, brethren, that the things *which happened* to me have actually turned out for the furtherance of the gospel, 13 so that it has become evident to the whole palace guard, and to all the rest, that my chains are in Christ; 14 and most of the brethren in the Lord, having become confident by my chains, are much more bold to speak the word without fear.

15 Some indeed preach Christ even from envy and strife, and some also from goodwill: 16 The former[a] preach Christ from selfish ambition, not sincerely, supposing to add affliction to my chains; 17 but the latter out of love, knowing that I am appointed for the defense of the gospel.

1:1 [a]Literally *overseers* 1:16 [a]NU-Text reverses the contents of verses 16 and 17.

The Message

1-2 1 Paul and Timothy, both of us committed
servants of Christ Jesus, write this letter to
all the followers of Jesus in Philippi, pastors
and ministers included. We greet you with
the grace and peace that comes from God
our Father and our Master, Jesus Christ.

A Love That Will Grow

3-6 Every time you cross my mind, I break out
in exclamations of thanks to God. Each ex-
clamation is a trigger to prayer. I find myself
praying for you with a glad heart. I am so
pleased that you have continued on in this
with us, believing and proclaiming God's
Message, from the day you heard it right up
to the present. There has never been the
slightest doubt in my mind that the God who
started this great work in you would keep at
it and bring it to a flourishing finish on the
very day Christ Jesus appears.

7-8 It's not at all fanciful for me to think this
way about you. My prayers and hopes have
deep roots in reality. You have, after all,
stuck with me all the way from the time I
was thrown in jail, put on trial, and came out
of it in one piece. All along you have experi-
enced with me the most generous help from
God. He knows how much I love and miss
you these days. Sometimes I think I feel as
strongly about you as Christ does!

9-11 So this is my prayer: that your love will
flourish and that you will not only love
much but well. Learn to love appropriately.
You need to use your head and test your
feelings so that your love is sincere and in-
telligent, not sentimental gush. Live a
lover's life, circumspect and exemplary, a
life Jesus will be proud of: bountiful in fruits
from the soul, making Jesus Christ attrac-
tive to all, getting everyone involved in the
glory and praise of God.

They Can't Imprison the Message

12-14 I want to report to you, friends, that my im-
prisonment here has had the opposite of its
intended effect. Instead of being squelched,
the Message has actually prospered. All the
soldiers here, and everyone else, too, found
out that I'm in jail because of this Messiah.
That piqued their curiosity, and now they've
learned all about him. Not only that, but
most of the followers of Jesus here have be-
come far more sure of themselves in the
faith than ever, speaking out fearlessly
about God, about the Messiah.

15-17 It's true that some here preach Christ be-
cause with me out of the way, they think
they'll step right into the spotlight. But the
others do it with the best heart in the world.
One group is motivated by pure love, know-
ing that I am here defending the Message,
wanting to help. The others, now that I'm
out of the picture, are merely greedy, hoping

NEW KING JAMES VERSION

18 What then? Only *that* in every way, whether in pretense or in truth, Christ is preached; and in this I rejoice, yes, and will rejoice.

TO LIVE IS CHRIST

19 For I know that this will turn out for my deliverance through your prayer and the supply of the Spirit of Jesus Christ, 20 according to my earnest expectation and hope that in nothing I shall be ashamed, but with all boldness, as always, so now also Christ will be magnified in my body, whether by life or by death. 21 For to me, to live *is* Christ, and to die *is* gain. 22 But if *I* live on in the flesh, this *will mean* fruit from *my* labor; yet what I shall choose I cannot tell. 23 For[a] I am hard-pressed between the two, having a desire to depart and be with Christ, *which is* far better. 24 Nevertheless to remain in the flesh *is* more needful for you. 25 And being confident of this, I know that I shall remain and continue with you all for your progress and joy of faith, 26 that your rejoicing for me may be more abundant in Jesus Christ by my coming to you again.

STRIVING AND SUFFERING FOR CHRIST

27 Only let your conduct be worthy of the gospel of Christ, so that whether I come and see you or am absent, I may hear of your affairs, that you stand fast in one spirit, with one mind striving together for the faith of the gospel, 28 and not in any way terrified by your adversaries, which is to them a proof of perdition, but to you of salvation,[a] and that from God. 29 For to you it has been granted on behalf of Christ, not only to believe in Him, but also to suffer for His sake, 30 having the same conflict which you saw in me and now hear *is* in me.

UNITY THROUGH HUMILITY

2 Therefore if *there is* any consolation in Christ, if any comfort of love, if any fellowship of the Spirit, if any affection and mercy, 2 fulfill my joy by being like-minded, having the same love, *being* of one accord, of one mind. 3 *Let* nothing *be done* through selfish ambition or conceit, but in lowliness of mind let each esteem others better than himself. 4 Let each of you look out not only for his own interests, but also for the interests of others.

1:23 [a]NU-Text and M-Text read *But*. **1:28** [a]NU-Text reads *of your salvation.*

THE MESSAGE

to get something out of it for themselves. Their motives are bad. They see me as their competition, and so the worse it goes for me, the better—they think—for them.

18-21 So how am I to respond? I've decided that I really don't care about their motives, whether mixed, bad, or indifferent. Every time one of them opens his mouth, Christ is proclaimed, so I just cheer them on!

And I'm going to keep that celebration going because I know how it's going to turn out. Through your faithful prayers and the generous response of the Spirit of Jesus Christ, everything he wants to do in and through me will be done. I can hardly wait to continue on my course. I don't expect to be embarrassed in the least. On the contrary, everything happening to me in this jail only serves to make Christ more accurately known, regardless of whether I live or die. They didn't shut me up; they gave me a pulpit! Alive, I'm Christ's messenger; dead, I'm his bounty. Life versus even more life! I can't lose.

22-26 As long as I'm alive in this body, there is good work for me to do. If I had to choose right now, I hardly know which I'd choose. Hard choice! The desire to break camp here and be with Christ is powerful. Some days I can think of nothing better. But most days, because of what you are going through, I am sure that it's better for me to stick it out here. So I plan to be around awhile, companion to you as your growth and joy in this life of trusting God continues. You can start looking forward to a great reunion when I come visit you again. We'll be praising Christ, enjoying each other.

27-30 Meanwhile, live in such a way that you are a credit to the Message of Christ. Let nothing in your conduct hang on whether I come or not. Your conduct must be the same whether I show up to see things for myself or hear of it from a distance. Stand united, singular in vision, contending for people's trust in the Message, the good news, not flinching or dodging in the slightest before the opposition. Your courage and unity will show them what they're up against: defeat for them, victory for you—and both because of God. There's far more to this life than trusting in Christ. There's also suffering for him. And the suffering is as much a gift as the trusting. You're involved in the same kind of struggle you saw me go through, on which you are now getting an updated report in this letter.

HE TOOK ON THE STATUS OF A SLAVE

1-4 **2** If you've gotten anything at all out of following Christ, if his love has made any difference in your life, if being in a community of the Spirit means anything to you, if you have a heart, if you *care*—then do me a favor: Agree with each other, love each other, be deep-spirited friends. Don't push your way to the front; don't sweet-talk your way to the top. Put yourself aside, and help others get ahead. Don't be obsessed with getting your own advantage. Forget yourselves long enough to lend a helping hand.

New King James Version

The Humbled and Exalted Christ

[5]Let this mind be in you which was also in
Christ Jesus, [6]who, being in the form of God, did
not consider it robbery to be equal with God,
[7]but made Himself of no reputation, taking the
form of a bondservant, *and* coming in the like-
ness of men. [8]And being found in appearance as
a man, He humbled Himself and became obedi-
ent to *the point of* death, even the death of the
cross. [9]Therefore God also has highly exalted
Him and given Him the name which is above
every name, [10]that at the name of Jesus every
knee should bow, of those in heaven, and of
those on earth, and of those under the earth,
[11]and *that* every tongue should confess that Je-
sus Christ *is* Lord, to the glory of God the Father.

Light Bearers

[12]Therefore, my beloved, as you have always
obeyed, not as in my presence only, but now
much more in my absence, work out your own
salvation with fear and trembling; [13]for it is God
who works in you both to will and to do for *His*
good pleasure.

[14]Do all things without complaining and dis-
puting, [15]that you may become blameless and
harmless, children of God without fault in the
midst of a crooked and perverse generation,
among whom you shine as lights in the world,
[16]holding fast the word of life, so that I may re-
joice in the day of Christ that I have not run in
vain or labored in vain.

[17]Yes, and if I am being poured out *as a drink
offering* on the sacrifice and service of your
faith, I am glad and rejoice with you all. [18]For
the same reason you also be glad and rejoice
with me.

Timothy Commended

[19]But I trust in the Lord Jesus to send Timo-
thy to you shortly, that I also may be encouraged
when I know your state. [20]For I have no one like-
minded, who will sincerely care for your state.
[21]For all seek their own, not the things which are
of Christ Jesus. [22]But you know his proven char-
acter, that as a son with *his* father he served
with me in the gospel. [23]Therefore I hope to send
him at once, as soon as I see how it goes with
me. [24]But I trust in the Lord that I myself shall
also come shortly.

Epaphroditus Praised

[25]Yet I considered it necessary to send to you
Epaphroditus, my brother, fellow worker, and
fellow soldier, but your messenger and the one
who ministered to my need; [26]since he was long-

The Message

5-8 Think of yourselves the way Christ Jesus
thought of himself. He had equal status with
God but didn't think so much of himself that
he had to cling to the advantages of that status
no matter what. Not at all. When the time
came, he set aside the privileges of deity and
took on the status of a slave, became *human*!
Having become human, he stayed human. It
was an incredibly humbling process. He didn't
claim special privileges. Instead, he lived a
selfless, obedient life and then died a selfless,
obedient death—and the worst kind of death
at that—a crucifixion.

9-11 Because of that obedience, God lifted him
high and honored him far beyond anyone or
anything, ever, so that all created beings in
heaven and on earth—even those long ago
dead and buried—will bow in worship be-
fore this Jesus Christ, and call out in praise
that he is the Master of all, to the glorious
honor of God the Father.

Rejoicing Together

12-13 What I'm getting at, friends, is that you
should simply keep on doing what you've
done from the beginning. When I was living
among you, you lived in responsive obedi-
ence. Now that I'm separated from you,
keep it up. Better yet, redouble your efforts.
Be energetic in your life of salvation, rever-
ent and sensitive before God. That energy is
God's energy, an energy deep within you,
God himself willing and working at what
will give him the most pleasure.

14-16 Do everything readily and cheerfully—no
bickering, no second-guessing allowed! Go
out into the world uncorrupted, a breath of
fresh air in this squalid and polluted society.
Provide people with a glimpse of good living
and of the living God. Carry the light-giving
Message into the night so I'll have good
cause to be proud of you on the day that
Christ returns. You'll be living proof that I
didn't go to all this work for nothing.

17-18 Even if I am executed here and now, I'll
rejoice in being an element in the offering of
your faith that you make on Christ's altar, a
part of your rejoicing. But turnabout's fair
play—you must join me in *my* rejoicing.
Whatever you do, don't feel sorry for me.

19-24 I plan (according to Jesus' plan) to send
Timothy to you very soon so he can bring
back all the news of you he can gather. Oh,
how that will do my heart good! I have no
one quite like Timothy. He is loyal, and gen-
uinely concerned for you. Most people
around here are looking out for themselves,
with little concern for the things of Jesus. But
you know yourselves that Timothy's the real
thing. He's been a devoted son to me as to-
gether we've delivered the Message. As soon
as I see how things are going to fall out for
me here, I plan to send him off. And then I'm
hoping and praying to be right on his heels.

25-27 But for right now, I'm dispatching Epaph-
roditus, my good friend and companion in
my work. You sent him to help me out; now
I'm sending him to help you out. He has
been wanting in the worst way to get back

NEW KING JAMES VERSION

ing for you all, and was distressed because you
had heard that he was sick. [27]For indeed he was
sick almost unto death; but God had mercy on
him, and not only on him but on me also, lest I
should have sorrow upon sorrow. [28]Therefore I
sent him the more eagerly, that when you see
him again you may rejoice, and I may be less
sorrowful. [29]Receive him therefore in the Lord
with all gladness, and hold such men in esteem;
[30]because for the work of Christ he came close
to death, not regarding his life, to supply what
was lacking in your service toward me.

ALL FOR CHRIST

3 Finally, my brethren, rejoice in the Lord. For
me to write the same things to you *is* not te-
dious, but for you *it is* safe.
[2]Beware of dogs, beware of evil workers, be-
ware of the mutilation! [3]For we are the circum-
cision, who worship God in the Spirit,[a] rejoice in
Christ Jesus, and have no confidence in the
flesh, [4]though I also might have confidence in
the flesh. If anyone else thinks he may have con-
fidence in the flesh, I more so: [5]circumcised the
eighth day, of the stock of Israel, *of* the tribe of
Benjamin, a Hebrew of the Hebrews; concern-
ing the law, a Pharisee; [6]concerning zeal, perse-
cuting the church; concerning the righteousness
which is in the law, blameless.
[7]But what things were gain to me, these I
have counted loss for Christ. [8]Yet indeed I also
count all things loss for the excellence of the
knowledge of Christ Jesus my Lord, for whom I
have suffered the loss of all things, and count
them as rubbish, that I may gain Christ [9]and be
found in Him, not having my own righteous-
ness, which *is* from the law, but that which *is*
through faith in Christ, the righteousness which
is from God by faith; [10]that I may know Him and
the power of His resurrection, and the fellow-
ship of His sufferings, being conformed to His
death, [11]if, by any means, I may attain to the res-
urrection from the dead.

3:3 [a]NU-Text and M-Text read *who worship in the Spirit of God.*

THE MESSAGE

with you. Especially since recovering from
the illness you heard about, he's been want-
ing to get back and reassure you that he is
just fine. He nearly died, as you know, but
God had mercy on him. And not only on
him—he had mercy on me, too. His death
would have been one huge grief piled on top
of all the others.
28-30 So you can see why I'm so delighted to
send him on to you. When you see him
again, hale and hearty, how you'll rejoice
and how relieved I'll be. Give him a grand
welcome, a joyful embrace! People like him
deserve the best you can give. Remember
the ministry to me that you started but
weren't able to complete? Well, in the
process of finishing up that work, he put his
life on the line and nearly died doing it.

TO KNOW HIM PERSONALLY

1 3 And that's about it, friends. Be glad in
God!
I don't mind repeating what I have writ-
ten in earlier letters, and I hope you don't
mind hearing it again. Better safe than
sorry—so here goes.
2-6 Steer clear of the barking dogs, those re-
ligious busybodies, all bark and no bite. All
they're interested in is appearances—knife-
happy circumcisers, I call them. The *real* be-
lievers are the ones the Spirit of God leads
to work away at this ministry, filling the air
with Christ's praise as we do it. We couldn't
carry this off by our own efforts, and we
know it—even though we can list what
many might think are impressive creden-
tials. You know my pedigree: a legitimate
birth, circumcised on the eighth day; an Is-
raelite from the elite tribe of Benjamin; a
strict and devout adherent to God's law; a
fiery defender of the purity of my religion,
even to the point of persecuting the church;
a meticulous observer of everything set
down in God's law Book.
7-9 The very credentials these people are
waving around as something special, I'm
tearing up and throwing out with the
trash—along with everything else I used to
take credit for. And why? Because of Christ.
Yes, all the things I once thought were so
important are gone from my life. Compared
to the high privilege of knowing Christ Je-
sus as my Master, firsthand, everything I
once thought I had going for me is insignif-
icant—dog dung. I've dumped it all in the
trash so that I could embrace Christ and be
embraced by him. I didn't want some petty,
inferior brand of righteousness that comes
from keeping a list of rules when I could get
the robust kind that comes from trusting
Christ—*God's* righteousness.
10-11 I gave up all that inferior stuff so I could
know Christ personally, experience his res-
urrection power, be a partner in his suffer-
ing, and go all the way with him to death it-
self. If there was any way to get in on the
resurrection from the dead, I wanted to do
it.

New King James Version

Pressing Toward the Goal

12 Not that I have already attained, or am already perfected; but I press on, that I may lay hold of that for which Christ Jesus has also laid hold of me. 13 Brethren, I do not count myself to have apprehended; but one thing *I do,* forgetting those things which are behind and reaching forward to those things which are ahead, 14 I press toward the goal for the prize of the upward call of God in Christ Jesus.

15 Therefore let us, as many as are mature, have this mind; and if in anything you think otherwise, God will reveal even this to you. 16 Nevertheless, to *the degree* that we have already attained, let us walk by the same rule,[a] let us be of the same mind.

Our Citizenship in Heaven

17 Brethren, join in following my example, and note those who so walk, as you have us for a pattern. 18 For many walk, of whom I have told you often, and now tell you even weeping, *that they are* the enemies of the cross of Christ: 19 whose end *is* destruction, whose god *is their* belly, and *whose* glory *is* in their shame—who set their mind on earthly things. 20 For our citizenship is in heaven, from which we also eagerly wait for the Savior, the Lord Jesus Christ, 21 who will transform our lowly body that it may be conformed to His glorious body, according to the working by which He is able even to subdue all things to Himself.

4 Therefore, my beloved and longed-for brethren, my joy and crown, so stand fast in the Lord, beloved.

Be United, Joyful, and in Prayer

2 I implore Euodia and I implore Syntyche to be of the same mind in the Lord. 3 And[a] I urge you also, true companion, help these women who labored with me in the gospel, with Clement also, and the rest of my fellow workers, whose names *are* in the Book of Life.

4 Rejoice in the Lord always. Again I will say, rejoice!

5 Let your gentleness be known to all men. The Lord *is* at hand.

6 Be anxious for nothing, but in everything by prayer and supplication, with thanksgiving, let your requests be made known to God; 7 and the peace of God, which surpasses all understanding, will guard your hearts and minds through Christ Jesus.

3:16 [a]NU-Text omits *rule* and the rest of the verse. **4:3** [a]NU-Text and M-Text read *Yes.*

The Message

Focused on the Goal

12-14 I'm not saying that I have this all together, that I have it made. But I am well on my way, reaching out for Christ, who has so wondrously reached out for me. Friends, don't get me wrong: By no means do I count myself an expert in all of this, but I've got my eye on the goal, where God is beckoning us onward—to Jesus. I'm off and running, and I'm not turning back.

15-16 So let's keep focused on that goal, those of us who want everything God has for us. If any of you have something else in mind, something less than total commitment, God will clear your blurred vision—you'll see it yet! Now that we're on the right track, let's stay on it.

17-19 Stick with me, friends. Keep track of those you see running this same course, headed for this same goal. There are many out there taking other paths, choosing other goals, and trying to get you to go along with them. I've warned you of them many times; sadly, I'm having to do it again. All they want is easy street. They hate Christ's Cross. But easy street is a dead-end street. Those who live there make their bellies their gods; belches are their praise; all they can think of is their appetites.

20-21 But there's far more to life for us. We're citizens of high heaven! We're waiting the arrival of the Savior, the Master, Jesus Christ, who will transform our earthy bodies into glorious bodies like his own. He'll make us beautiful and whole with the same powerful skill by which he is putting everything as it should be, under and around him.

1 4 My dear, dear friends! I love you so much. I do want the very best for you. You make me feel such joy, fill me with such pride. Don't waver. Stay on track, steady in God.

Pray About Everything

2 I urge Euodia and Syntyche to iron out their differences and make up. God doesn't want his children holding grudges.

3 And, oh, yes, Syzygus, since you're right there to help them work things out, do your best with them. These women worked for the Message hand in hand with Clement and me, and with the other veterans—worked as hard as any of us. Remember, their names are also in the Book of Life.

4-5 Celebrate God all day, every day. I mean, *revel* in him! Make it as clear as you can to all you meet that you're on their side, working with them and not against them. Help them see that the Master is about to arrive. He could show up any minute!

6-7 Don't fret or worry. Instead of worrying, pray. Let petitions and praises shape your worries into prayers, letting God know your concerns. Before you know it, a sense of God's wholeness, everything coming together for good, will come and settle you down. It's wonderful what happens when Christ displaces worry at the center of your life.

New King James Version

Meditate on These Things

8Finally, brethren, whatever things are true, whatever things *are* noble, whatever things *are* just, whatever things *are* pure, whatever things *are* lovely, whatever things *are* of good report, if *there is* any virtue and if *there is* anything praiseworthy—meditate on these things. 9The things which you learned and received and heard and saw in me, these do, and the God of peace will be with you.

Philippian Generosity

10But I rejoiced in the Lord greatly that now at last your care for me has flourished again; though you surely did care, but you lacked opportunity. 11Not that I speak in regard to need, for I have learned in whatever state I am, to be content: 12I know how to be abased, and I know how to abound. Everywhere and in all things I have learned both to be full and to be hungry, both to abound and to suffer need. 13I can do all things through Christ[a] who strengthens me.

14Nevertheless you have done well that you shared in my distress. 15Now you Philippians know also that in the beginning of the gospel, when I departed from Macedonia, no church shared with me concerning giving and receiving but you only. 16For even in Thessalonica you sent *aid* once and again for my necessities. 17Not that I seek the gift, but I seek the fruit that abounds to your account. 18Indeed I have all and abound. I am full, having received from Epaphroditus the things *sent* from you, a sweet-smelling aroma, an acceptable sacrifice, well pleasing to God. 19And my God shall supply all your need according to His riches in glory by Christ Jesus. 20Now to our God and Father *be* glory forever and ever. Amen.

Greeting and Blessing

21Greet every saint in Christ Jesus. The brethren who are with me greet you. 22All the saints greet you, but especially those who are of Caesar's household.

23The grace of our Lord Jesus Christ be with you all.[a] Amen.

4:13 [a]NU-Text reads *Him who.* **4:23** [a]NU-Text reads *your spirit.*

The Message

8-9 Summing it all up, friends, I'd say you'll do best by filling your minds and meditating on things true, noble, reputable, authentic, compelling, gracious—the best, not the worst; the beautiful, not the ugly; things to praise, not things to curse. Put into practice what you learned from me, what you heard and saw and realized. Do that, and God, who makes everything work together, will work you into his most excellent harmonies.

Content Whatever the Circumstances

10-14 I'm glad in God, far happier than you would ever guess—happy that you're again showing such strong concern for me. Not that you ever quit praying and thinking about me. You just had no chance to show it. Actually, I don't have a sense of needing anything personally. I've learned by now to be quite content whatever my circumstances. I'm just as happy with little as with much, with much as with little. I've found the recipe for being happy whether full or hungry, hands full or hands empty. Whatever I have, wherever I am, I can make it through anything in the One who makes me who I am. I don't mean that your help didn't mean a lot to me—it did. It was a beautiful thing that you came alongside me in my troubles.

15-17 You Philippians well know, and you can be sure I'll never forget it, that when I first left Macedonia province, venturing out with the Message, not one church helped out in the give-and-take of this work except you. You were the only one. Even while I was in Thessalonica, you helped out—and not only once, but twice. Not that I'm looking for handouts, but I do want you to experience the blessing that issues from generosity.

18-20 And now I have it all—and keep getting more! The gifts you sent with Epaphroditus were more than enough, like a sweet-smelling sacrifice roasting on the altar, filling the air with fragrance, pleasing God no end. You can be sure that God will take care of everything you need, his generosity exceeding even yours in the glory that pours from Jesus. Our God and Father abounds in glory that just pours out into eternity. Yes.

21-22 Give our regards to every follower of Jesus you meet. Our friends here say hello. All the Christians here, especially the believers who work in the palace of Caesar, want to be remembered to you.

23 Receive and experience the amazing grace of the Master, Jesus Christ, deep, deep within yourselves.

COLOSSIANS

New King James Version

Greeting

1 Paul, an apostle of Jesus Christ by the will of God, and Timothy our brother,

2 To the saints and faithful brethren in Christ *who are* in Colosse:

Grace to you and peace from God our Father and the Lord Jesus Christ.[a]

Their Faith in Christ

3 We give thanks to the God and Father of our Lord Jesus Christ, praying always for you, 4 since we heard of your faith in Christ Jesus and of your love for all the saints; 5 because of the hope which is laid up for you in heaven, of which you heard before in the word of the truth of the gospel, 6 which has come to you, as *it has* also in all the world, and is bringing forth fruit,[a] as *it is* also among you since the day you heard and knew the grace of God in truth; 7 as you also learned from Epaphras, our dear fellow servant, who is a faithful minister of Christ on your behalf, 8 who also declared to us your love in the Spirit.

Preeminence of Christ

9 For this reason we also, since the day we heard it, do not cease to pray for you, and to ask that you may be filled with the knowledge of His will in all wisdom and spiritual understanding; 10 that you may walk worthy of the Lord, fully pleasing *Him,* being fruitful in every good work and increasing in the knowledge of God; 11 strengthened with all might, according to His glorious power, for all patience and longsuffering with joy; 12 giving thanks to the Father who has qualified us to be partakers of the inheritance of the saints in the light. 13 He has delivered us from the power of darkness and conveyed *us* into the kingdom of the Son of His love, 14 in whom we have redemption through His blood,[a] the forgiveness of sins.

15 He is the image of the invisible God, the firstborn over all creation. 16 For by Him all things were created that are in heaven and that are on earth, visible and invisible, whether thrones or dominions or principalities or powers. All things were created through Him and for Him. 17 And He is before all things, and in

1:2 [a]NU-Text omits *and the Lord Jesus Christ.* **1:6** [a]NU-Text and M-Text add *and growing.* **1:14** [a]NU-Text and M-Text omit *through His blood.*

The Message

1-2 **1** I, Paul, have been sent on special assignment by Christ as part of God's master plan. Together with my friend Timothy, I greet the Christians and stalwart followers of Christ who live in Colosse. May everything good from God our Father be yours!

Working in His Orchard

3-5 Our prayers for you are always spilling over into thanksgivings. We can't quit thanking God our Father and Jesus our Messiah for you! We keep getting reports on your steady faith in Christ, our Jesus, and the love you continuously extend to all Christians. The lines of purpose in your lives never grow slack, tightly tied as they are to your future in heaven, kept taut by hope.

5-8 The Message is as true among you today as when you first heard it. It doesn't diminish or weaken over time. It's the same all over the world. The Message bears fruit and gets larger and stronger, just as it has in you. From the very first day you heard and recognized the truth of what God is doing, you've been hungry for more. It's as vigorous in you now as when you learned it from our friend and close associate Epaphras. He is one reliable worker for Christ! I could always depend on him. He's the one who told us how thoroughly love had been worked into your lives by the Spirit.

9-12 Be assured that from the first day we heard of you, we haven't stopped praying for you, asking God to give you wise minds and spirits attuned to his will, and so acquire a thorough understanding of the ways in which God works. We pray that you'll live well for the Master, making him proud of you as you work hard in his orchard. As you learn more and more how God works, you will learn how to do *your* work. We pray that you'll have the strength to stick it out over the long haul—not the grim strength of gritting your teeth but the glory-strength God gives. It is strength that endures the unendurable and spills over into joy, thanking the Father who makes us strong enough to take part in everything bright and beautiful that he has for us.

13-14 God rescued us from dead-end alleys and dark dungeons. He's set us up in the kingdom of the Son he loves so much, the Son who got us out of the pit we were in, got rid of the sins we were doomed to keep repeating.

Christ Holds It All Together

15-18 We look at this Son and see the God who cannot be seen. We look at this Son and see God's original purpose in everything created. For everything, absolutely everything, above and below, visible and invisible, rank after rank after rank of angels—*everything* got started in him and finds its purpose in him. He was there before any of it came into

New King James Version

Him all things consist. [18]And He is the head of
the body, the church, who is the beginning, the
firstborn from the dead, that in all things He
may have the preeminence.

Reconciled in Christ

[19]For it pleased *the Father that* in Him all the
fullness should dwell, [20]and by Him to reconcile
all things to Himself, by Him, whether things on
earth or things in heaven, having made peace
through the blood of His cross.
[21]And you, who once were alienated and en-
emies in your mind by wicked works, yet now
He has reconciled [22]in the body of His flesh
through death, to present you holy, and blame-
less, and above reproach in His sight— [23]if in-
deed you continue in the faith, grounded and
steadfast, and are not moved away from the
hope of the gospel which you heard, which was
preached to every creature under heaven, of
which I, Paul, became a minister.

Sacrificial Service for Christ

[24]I now rejoice in my sufferings for you, and
fill up in my flesh what is lacking in the afflic-
tions of Christ, for the sake of His body, which is
the church, [25]of which I became a minister ac-
cording to the stewardship from God which was
given to me for you, to fulfill the word of God,
[26]the mystery which has been hidden from ages
and from generations, but now has been re-
vealed to His saints. [27]To them God willed to
make known what are the riches of the glory of
this mystery among the Gentiles: which[a] is
Christ in you, the hope of glory. [28]Him we
preach, warning every man and teaching every
man in all wisdom, that we may present every
man perfect in Christ Jesus. [29]To this *end* I also
labor, striving according to His working which
works in me mightily.

Not Philosophy but Christ

2 For I want you to know what a great conflict
I have for you and those in Laodicea, and *for*
as many as have not seen my face in the flesh,
[2]that their hearts may be encouraged, being knit
together in love, and *attaining* to all riches of
the full assurance of understanding, to the

1:27 [a]M-Text reads *who*.

The Message

existence and holds it all together right up to this moment. And when it comes to the church, he organizes and holds it together, like a head does a body.

18-20 He was supreme in the beginning and—leading the resurrection parade—he is supreme in the end. From beginning to end he's there, towering far above everything, everyone. So spacious is he, so roomy, that everything of God finds its proper place in him without crowding. Not only that, but all the broken and dislocated pieces of the universe—people and things, animals and atoms—get properly fixed and fit together in vibrant harmonies, all because of his death, his blood that poured down from the cross.

21-23 You yourselves are a case study of what he does. At one time you all had your backs turned to God, thinking rebellious thoughts of him, giving him trouble every chance you got. But now, by giving himself completely at the Cross, actually *dying* for you, Christ brought you over to God's side and put your lives together, whole and holy in his presence. You don't walk away from a gift like that! You stay grounded and steady in that bond of trust, constantly tuned in to the Message, careful not to be distracted or diverted. There is no other Message—just this one. Every creature under heaven gets this same Message. I, Paul, am a messenger of this Message.

24-25 I want you to know how glad I am that it's me sitting here in this jail and not you. There's a lot of suffering to be entered into in this world—the kind of suffering Christ takes on. I welcome the chance to take my share in the church's part of that suffering. When I became a servant in this church, I experienced this suffering as a sheer gift, God's way of helping me serve you, laying out the whole truth.

26-29 This mystery has been kept in the dark for a long time, but now it's out in the open. God wanted everyone, not just Jews, to know this rich and glorious secret inside and out, regardless of their background, regardless of their religious standing. The mystery in a nutshell is just this: Christ is in you, so therefore you can look forward to sharing in God's glory. It's that simple. That is the substance of our Message. We preach *Christ*, warning people not to add to the Message. We teach in a spirit of profound common sense so that we can bring each person to maturity. To be mature is to be basic. Christ! No more, no less. That's what I'm working so hard at day after day, year after year, doing my best with the energy God so generously gives me.

1 **2** I want you to realize that I continue to work as hard as I know how for you, and also for the Christians over at Laodicea. Not many of you have met me face-to-face, but that doesn't make any difference. Know that I'm on your side, right alongside you. You're not in this alone.

2-4 I want you woven into a tapestry of love, in touch with everything there is to know of

NEW KING JAMES VERSION

knowledge of the mystery of God, both of the
Father and[a] of Christ, 3in whom are hidden all
the treasures of wisdom and knowledge.
4Now this I say lest anyone should deceive
you with persuasive words. 5For though I am ab-
sent in the flesh, yet I am with you in spirit, re-
joicing to see your *good* order and the steadfast-
ness of your faith in Christ.
6As you therefore have received Christ Jesus
the Lord, so walk in Him, 7rooted and built up in
Him and established in the faith, as you have
been taught, abounding in it[a] with thanksgiving.
8Beware lest anyone cheat you through phi-
losophy and empty deceit, according to the tra-
dition of men, according to the basic principles
of the world, and not according to Christ. 9For in
Him dwells all the fullness of the Godhead bod-
ily; 10and you are complete in Him, who is the
head of all principality and power.

NOT LEGALISM BUT CHRIST

11In Him you were also circumcised with the
circumcision made without hands, by putting
off the body of the sins[a] of the flesh, by the cir-
cumcision of Christ, 12buried with Him in bap-
tism, in which you also were raised with *Him*
through faith in the working of God, who raised
Him from the dead. 13And you, being dead in
your trespasses and the uncircumcision of your
flesh, He has made alive together with Him,
having forgiven you all trespasses, 14having
wiped out the handwriting of requirements that
was against us, which was contrary to us. And
He has taken it out of the way, having nailed it
to the cross. 15Having disarmed principalities
and powers, He made a public spectacle of
them, triumphing over them in it.
16So let no one judge you in food or in drink,
or regarding a festival or a new moon or sab-
baths, 17which are a shadow of things to come,
but the substance is of Christ.

2:2 [a]NU-Text omits *both of the Father and.* **2:7** [a]NU-Text omits *in it.* **2:11** [a]NU-Text omits *of the sins.*

THE MESSAGE

God. Then you will have minds confident
and at rest, focused on Christ, God's great
mystery. All the richest treasures of wisdom
and knowledge are embedded in that mys-
tery and nowhere else. And we've been
shown the mystery! I'm telling you this be-
cause I don't want anyone leading you off
on some wild-goose chase, after other so-
called mysteries, or "the Secret."
5 I'm a long way off, true, and you may
never lay eyes on me, but believe me, I'm on
your side, right beside you. I am delighted to
hear of the careful and orderly ways you
conduct your affairs, and impressed with
the solid substance of your faith in Christ.

FROM THE SHADOWS TO THE SUBSTANCE

6-7 My counsel for you is simple and straight-
forward: Just go ahead with what you've
been given. You received Christ Jesus, the
Master; now *live* him. You're deeply rooted
in him. You're well constructed upon him.
You know your way around the faith. Now
do what you've been taught. School's out;
quit studying the subject and start *living* it!
And let your living spill over into thanksgiv-
ing.
8-10 Watch out for people who try to dazzle
you with big words and intellectual double-
talk. They want to drag you off into endless
arguments that never amount to anything.
They spread their ideas through the empty
traditions of human beings and the empty
superstitions of spirit beings. But that's not
the way of Christ. Everything of God gets
expressed in him, so you can see and hear
him clearly. You don't need a telescope, a mi-
croscope, or a horoscope to realize the full-
ness of Christ, and the emptiness of the uni-
verse without him. When you come to him,
that fullness comes together for you, too.
His power extends over everything.
11-15 Entering into this fullness is not some-
thing you figure out or achieve. It's not a
matter of being circumcised or keeping a
long list of laws. No, you're already *in*—in-
siders—not through some secretive initia-
tion rite but rather through what Christ has
already gone through for you, destroying
the power of sin. If it's an initiation ritual
you're after, you've already been through it
by submitting to baptism. Going under the
water was a burial of your old life; coming
up out of it was a resurrection, God raising
you from the dead as he did Christ. When
you were stuck in your old sin-dead life, you
were incapable of responding to God. God
brought you alive—right along with Christ!
Think of it! All sins forgiven, the slate wiped
clean, that old arrest warrant canceled and
nailed to Christ's cross. He stripped all the
spiritual tyrants in the universe of their
sham authority at the Cross and marched
them naked through the streets.
16-17 So don't put up with anyone pressuring
you in details of diet, worship services, or
holy days. All those things are mere shad-
ows cast before what was to come; the sub-
stance is Christ.

NEW KING JAMES VERSION

[18]Let no one cheat you of your reward, taking delight in *false* humility and worship of angels, intruding into those things which he has not[a] seen, vainly puffed up by his fleshly mind, [19]and not holding fast to the Head, from whom all the body, nourished and knit together by joints and ligaments, grows with the increase *that is* from God.

[20]Therefore,[a] if you died with Christ from the basic principles of the world, why, as *though* living in the world, do you subject yourselves to regulations— [21]"Do not touch, do not taste, do not handle," [22]which all concern things which perish with the using—according to the commandments and doctrines of men? [23]These things indeed have an appearance of wisdom in self-imposed religion, *false* humility, and neglect of the body, *but are* of no value against the indulgence of the flesh.

NOT CARNALITY BUT CHRIST

3 If then you were raised with Christ, seek those things which are above, where Christ is, sitting at the right hand of God. [2]Set your mind on things above, not on things on the earth. [3]For you died, and your life is hidden with Christ in God. [4]When Christ *who is* our life appears, then you also will appear with Him in glory.

[5]Therefore put to death your members which are on the earth: fornication, uncleanness, passion, evil desire, and covetousness, which is idolatry. [6]Because of these things the wrath of God is coming upon the sons of disobedience, [7]in which you yourselves once walked when you lived in them.

[8]But now you yourselves are to put off all these: anger, wrath, malice, blasphemy, filthy language out of your mouth. [9]Do not lie to one another, since you have put off the old man with his deeds, [10]and have put on the new *man* who is renewed in knowledge according to the image of Him who created him, [11]where there is neither Greek nor Jew, circumcised nor uncircumcised, barbarian, Scythian, slave *nor* free, but Christ *is* all and in all.

CHARACTER OF THE NEW MAN

[12]Therefore, as *the* elect of God, holy and beloved, put on tender mercies, kindness, humility, meekness, longsuffering; [13]bearing with one another, and forgiving one another, if anyone

2:18 [a]NU-Text omits *not.* **2:20** [a]NU-Text and M-Text omit *Therefore.*

THE MESSAGE

18-19 Don't tolerate people who try to run your life, ordering you to bow and scrape, insisting that you join their obsession with angels and that you seek out visions. They're a lot of hot air, that's all they are. They're completely out of touch with the source of life, Christ, who puts us together in one piece, whose very breath and blood flow through us. He is the Head and we are the body. We can grow up healthy in God only as he nourishes us.

20-23 So, then, if with Christ you've put all that pretentious and infantile religion behind you, why do you let yourselves be bullied by it? "Don't touch this! Don't taste that! Don't go near this!" Do you think things that are here today and gone tomorrow are worth that kind of attention? Such things sound impressive if said in a deep enough voice. They even give the illusion of being pious and humble and ascetic. But they're just another way of showing off, making yourselves look important.

HE IS YOUR LIFE

1-2 3 So if you're serious about living this new resurrection life with Christ, *act* like it. Pursue the things over which Christ presides. Don't shuffle along, eyes to the ground, absorbed with the things right in front of you. Look up, and be alert to what is going on around Christ—that's where the action is. See things from *his* perspective.

3-4 Your old life is dead. Your new life, which is your *real* life—even though invisible to spectators—is with Christ in God. *He* is your life. When Christ (your real life, remember) shows up again on this earth, you'll show up, too—the real you, the glorious you. Meanwhile, be content with obscurity, like Christ.

5-8 And that means killing off everything connected with that way of death: sexual promiscuity, impurity, lust, doing whatever you feel like whenever you feel like it, and grabbing whatever attracts your fancy. That's a life shaped by things and feelings instead of by God. It's because of this kind of thing that God is about to explode in anger. It wasn't long ago that you were doing all that stuff and not knowing any better. But you know better now, so make sure it's all gone for good: bad temper, irritability, meanness, profanity, dirty talk.

9-11 Don't lie to one another. You're done with that old life. It's like a filthy set of ill-fitting clothes you've stripped off and put in the fire. Now you're dressed in a new wardrobe. Every item of your new way of life is custom-made by the Creator, with his label on it. All the old fashions are now obsolete. Words like Jewish and non-Jewish, religious and irreligious, insider and outsider, uncivilized and uncouth, slave and free, mean nothing. From now on everyone is defined by Christ, everyone is included in Christ.

12-14 So, chosen by God for this new life of love, dress in the wardrobe God picked out for you: compassion, kindness, humility, quiet strength, discipline. Be even-tempered,

NEW KING JAMES VERSION

has a complaint against another; even as Christ
forgave you, so you also *must do*. 14But above all
these things put on love, which is the bond of
perfection. 15And let the peace of God rule in
your hearts, to which also you were called in
one body; and be thankful. 16Let the word of
Christ dwell in you richly in all wisdom, teach-
ing and admonishing one another in psalms and
hymns and spiritual songs, singing with grace in
your hearts to the Lord. 17And whatever you do
in word or deed, *do* all in the name of the Lord
Jesus, giving thanks to God the Father through
Him.

THE CHRISTIAN HOME

18Wives, submit to your own husbands, as is
fitting in the Lord.

19Husbands, love your wives and do not be
bitter toward them.

20Children, obey your parents in all things,
for this is well pleasing to the Lord.

21Fathers, do not provoke your children, lest
they become discouraged.

22Bondservants, obey in all things your mas-
ters according to the flesh, not with eyeservice,
as men-pleasers, but in sincerity of heart, fear-
ing God. 23And whatever you do, do it heartily,
as to the Lord and not to men, 24knowing that
from the Lord you will receive the reward of the
inheritance; for[a] you serve the Lord Christ. 25But
he who does wrong will be repaid for what he
has done, and there is no partiality.

4 Masters, give your bondservants what is just
and fair, knowing that you also have a Master
in heaven.

CHRISTIAN GRACES

2Continue earnestly in prayer, being vigilant
in it with thanksgiving; 3meanwhile praying
also for us, that God would open to us a door for
the word, to speak the mystery of Christ, for
which I am also in chains, 4that I may make it
manifest, as I ought to speak.

5Walk in wisdom toward those *who are* out-
side, redeeming the time. 6*Let* your speech al-
ways *be* with grace, seasoned with salt, that you
may know how you ought to answer each one.

FINAL GREETINGS

7Tychicus, a beloved brother, faithful minis-
ter, and fellow servant in the Lord, will tell you
all the news about me. 8I am sending him to you
for this very purpose, that he[a] may know your
circumstances and comfort your hearts, 9with
Onesimus, a faithful and beloved brother, who is
one of you. They will make known to you all
things which *are happening* here.

3:24 [a]NU-Text omits *for.* **4:8** [a]NU-Text reads *you may know our circumstances and he may.*

THE MESSAGE

content with second place, quick to forgive
an offense. Forgive as quickly and com-
pletely as the Master forgave you. And re-
gardless of what else you put on, wear love.
It's your basic, all-purpose garment. Never
be without it.

15-17 Let the peace of Christ keep you in tune
with each other, in step with each other.
None of this going off and doing your own
thing. And cultivate thankfulness. Let the
Word of Christ—the Message—have the run
of the house. Give it plenty of room in your
lives. Instruct and direct one another using
good common sense. And sing, sing your
hearts out to God! Let every detail in your
lives—words, actions, whatever—be done in
the name of the Master, Jesus, thanking God
the Father every step of the way.

18 Wives, understand and support your hus-
bands by submitting to them in ways that
honor the Master.

19 Husbands, go all out in love for your
wives. Don't take advantage of them.

20 Children, do what your parents tell you.
This delights the Master no end.

21 Parents, don't come down too hard on
your children or you'll crush their spirits.

22-25 Servants, do what you're told by your
earthly masters. And don't just do the mini-
mum that will get you by. Do your best. Work
from the heart for your real Master, for God,
confident that you'll get paid in full when you
come into your inheritance. Keep in mind al-
ways that the ultimate Master you're serving
is Christ. The sullen servant who does shoddy
work will be held responsible. Being a fol-
lower of Jesus doesn't cover up bad work.

1 4 And masters, treat your servants consid-
erately. Be fair with them. Don't forget for
a minute that you, too, serve a Master—God
in heaven.

PRAY FOR OPEN DOORS

2-4 Pray diligently. Stay alert, with your eyes
wide open in gratitude. Don't forget to pray
for us, that God will open doors for telling
the mystery of Christ, even while I'm locked
up in this jail. Pray that every time I open
my mouth I'll be able to make Christ plain
as day to them.

5-6 Use your heads as you live and work
among outsiders. Don't miss a trick. Make
the most of every opportunity. Be gracious
in your speech. The goal is to bring out the
best in others in a conversation, not put
them down, not cut them out.

7-9 My good friend Tychicus will tell you all
about me. He's a trusted minister and com-
panion in the service of the Master. I've sent
him to you so that you would know how
things are with us, and so he could encour-
age you in your faith. And I've sent Ones-
imus with him. Onesimus is one of you, and
has become such a trusted and dear brother!
Together they'll bring you up-to-date on
everything that has been going on here.

NEW KING JAMES VERSION

[10]Aristarchus my fellow prisoner greets you,
with Mark the cousin of Barnabas (about whom
you received instructions: if he comes to you,
welcome him), [11]and Jesus who is called Justus.
These *are my* only fellow workers for the king-
dom of God who are of the circumcision; they
have proved to be a comfort to me.
[12]Epaphras, who is *one* of you, a bondservant
of Christ, greets you, always laboring fervently
for you in prayers, that you may stand perfect
and complete[a] in all the will of God. [13]For I bear
him witness that he has a great zeal[a] for you,
and those who are in Laodicea, and those in Hi-
erapolis. [14]Luke the beloved physician and De-
mas greet you. [15]Greet the brethren who are in
Laodicea, and Nymphas and the church that *is*
in his[a] house.

CLOSING EXHORTATIONS AND BLESSING

[16]Now when this epistle is read among you,
see that it is read also in the church of the
Laodiceans, and that you likewise read the *epis-
tle* from Laodicea. [17]And say to Archippus,
"Take heed to the ministry which you have re-
ceived in the Lord, that you may fulfill it."
[18]This salutation by my own hand—Paul. Re-
member my chains. Grace *be* with you. Amen.

4:12 [a]NU-Text reads *fully assured.* **4:13** [a]NU-Text reads *concern.* **4:15** [a]NU-Text reads *Nympha . . . her house.*

THE MESSAGE

10-11 Aristarchus, who is in jail here with me, sends greetings; also Mark, cousin of Barnabas (you received a letter regarding him; if he shows up, welcome him); and also Jesus, the one they call Justus. These are the only ones left from the old crowd who have stuck with me in working for God's kingdom. Don't think they haven't been a big help!

12-13 Epaphras, who is one of you, says hello. What a trooper he has been! He's been tireless in his prayers for you, praying that you'll stand firm, mature and confident in everything God wants you to do. I've watched him closely, and can report on how hard he has worked for you and for those in Laodicea and Hierapolis.

14 Luke, good friend and physician, and Demas both send greetings.

15 Say hello to our friends in Laodicea; also to Nympha and the church that meets in her house.

16 After this letter has been read to you, make sure it gets read also in Laodicea. And get the letter that went to Laodicea and have it read to you.

17 And, oh, yes, tell Archippus, "Do your best in the job you received from the Master. Do your very best."

18 I'm signing off in my own handwriting—Paul. Remember to pray for me in this jail. Grace be with you.

1 THESSALONIANS

New King James Version

Greeting

1 Paul, Silvanus, and Timothy,

To the church of the Thessalonians in God the Father and the Lord Jesus Christ:

Grace to you and peace from God our Father and the Lord Jesus Christ.[a]

Their Good Example

2We give thanks to God always for you all, making mention of you in our prayers, 3remembering without ceasing your work of faith, labor of love, and patience of hope in our Lord Jesus Christ in the sight of our God and Father, 4knowing, beloved brethren, your election by God. 5For our gospel did not come to you in word only, but also in power, and in the Holy Spirit and in much assurance, as you know what kind of men we were among you for your sake.

6And you became followers of us and of the Lord, having received the word in much affliction, with joy of the Holy Spirit, 7so that you became examples to all in Macedonia and Achaia who believe. 8For from you the word of the Lord has sounded forth, not only in Macedonia and Achaia, but also in every place. Your faith toward God has gone out, so that we do not need to say anything. 9For they themselves declare concerning us what manner of entry we had to you, and how you turned to God from idols to serve the living and true God, 10and to wait for His Son from heaven, whom He raised from the dead, *even* Jesus who delivers us from the wrath to come.

Paul's Conduct

2 For you yourselves know, brethren, that our coming to you was not in vain. 2But even[a] after we had suffered before and were spitefully treated at Philippi, as you know, we were bold in our God to speak to you the gospel of God in much conflict.

3For our exhortation *did* not *come* from error or uncleanness, nor *was it* in deceit.

4But as we have been approved by God to be entrusted with the gospel, even so we speak, not as pleasing men, but God who tests our hearts. 5For neither at any time did we use flattering words, as you know, nor a cloak for covetousness—God *is* witness.

1:1 [a]NU-Text omits *from God our Father and the Lord Jesus Christ.* **2:2** [a]NU-Text and M-Text omit *even.*

The Message

1 1 I, Paul, together here with Silas and Tim-
othy, send greetings to the church at Thes-
salonica, Christians assembled by God the
Father and by the Master, Jesus Christ.
God's amazing grace be with you! God's ro-
bust peace!

Convictions of Steel

2-5 Every time we think of you, we thank God
for you. Day and night you're in our prayers
as we call to mind your work of faith, your
labor of love, and your patience of hope in
following our Master, Jesus Christ, before
God our Father. It is clear to us, friends, that
God not only loves you very much but also
has put his hand on you for something spe-
cial. When the Message we preached came
to you, it wasn't just words. Something hap-
pened in you. The Holy Spirit put steel in
your convictions.

5-6 You paid careful attention to the way we
lived among you, and determined to live
that way yourselves. In imitating us, you im-
itated the Master. Although great trouble ac-
companied the Word, you were able to take
great joy from the Holy Spirit!—taking the
trouble with the joy, the joy with the trouble.

7-10 Do you know that all over the provinces
of both Macedonia and Achaia believers
look up to you? The word has gotten
around. Your lives are echoing the Master's
Word, not only in the provinces but all over
the place. The news of your faith in God is
out. We don't even have to say anything any-
more—*you're* the message! People come up
and tell us how you received us with open
arms, how you deserted the dead idols of
your old life so you could embrace and
serve God, the true God. They marvel at
how expectantly you await the arrival of his
Son, whom he raised from the dead—Jesus,
who rescued us from certain doom.

1-2 2 So, friends, it's obvious that our visit to
you was no waste of time. We had just
been given rough treatment in Philippi, as you
know, but that didn't slow us down. We were
sure of ourselves in God, and went right
ahead and said our piece, presenting God's
Message to you, defiant of the opposition.

No Hidden Agendas

3-5 God tested us thoroughly to make sure we
were qualified to be trusted with this Mes-
sage. Be assured that when we speak to you
we're not after crowd approval—only God
approval. Since we've been put through that
battery of tests, you're guaranteed that both
we and the Message are free of error, mixed
motives, or hidden agendas. We never used
words to butter you up. No one knows that
better than you. And God knows we never
used words as a smoke screen to take ad-
vantage of you.

New King James Version

[6]Nor did we seek glory from men, either from you or from others, when we might have made demands as apostles of Christ. [7]But we were gentle among you, just as a nursing *mother* cherishes her own children. [8]So, affectionately longing for you, we were well pleased to impart to you not only the gospel of God, but also our own lives, because you had become dear to us. [9]For you remember, brethren, our labor and toil; for laboring night and day, that we might not be a burden to any of you, we preached to you the gospel of God.

[10]You *are* witnesses, and God *also*, how devoutly and justly and blamelessly we behaved ourselves among you who believe; [11]as you know how we exhorted, and comforted, and charged[a] every one of you, as a father *does* his own children, [12]that you would walk worthy of God who calls you into His own kingdom and glory.

Their Conversion

[13]For this reason we also thank God without ceasing, because when you received the word of God which you heard from us, you welcomed *it* not *as* the word of men, but as it is in truth, the word of God, which also effectively works in you who believe. [14]For you, brethren, became imitators of the churches of God which are in Judea in Christ Jesus. For you also suffered the same things from your own countrymen, just as they *did* from the Judeans, [15]who killed both the Lord Jesus and their own prophets, and have persecuted us; and they do not please God and are contrary to all men, [16]forbidding us to speak to the Gentiles that they may be saved, so as always to fill up *the measure of* their sins; but wrath has come upon them to the uttermost.

Longing to See Them

[17]But we, brethren, having been taken away from you for a short time in presence, not in heart, endeavored more eagerly to see your face with great desire. [18]Therefore we wanted to come to you—even I, Paul, time and again—but Satan hindered us. [19]For what *is* our hope, or joy, or crown of rejoicing? *Is it* not even you in the presence of our Lord Jesus Christ at His coming? [20]For you are our glory and joy.

Concern for Their Faith

3 Therefore, when we could no longer endure it, we thought it good to be left in Athens alone, [2]and sent Timothy, our brother and minister of God, and our fellow laborer in the gospel of Christ, to establish you and encourage you concerning your faith, [3]that no one should be

2:11 [a]NU-Text and M-Text read *implored.*

The Message

6-8 Even though we had some standing as
Christ's apostles, we never threw our weight
around or tried to come across as important,
with you or anyone else. We weren't aloof
with you. We took you just as you were. We
were never patronizing, never condescend-
ing, but we cared for you the way a mother
cares for her children. We loved you dearly.
Not content to just pass on the Message, we
wanted to give you our hearts. And we *did.*
9-12 You remember us in those days, friends,
working our fingers to the bone, up half the
night, moonlighting so you wouldn't have
the burden of supporting us while we pro-
claimed God's Message to you. You saw with
your own eyes how discreet and courteous
we were among you, with keen sensitivity to
you as fellow believers. And God knows we
weren't freeloaders! You experienced it all
firsthand. With each of you we were like a
father with his child, holding your hand,
whispering encouragement, showing you
step-by-step how to live well before God,
who called us into his own kingdom, into
this delightful life.
13 And now we look back on all this and
thank God, an artesian well of thanks!
When you got the Message of God we
preached, you didn't pass it off as just one
more human opinion, but you took it to
heart as God's true word to you, which it is,
God himself at work in you believers!
14-16 Friends, do you realize that you followed
in the exact footsteps of the churches of
God in Judea, those who were the first to
follow in the footsteps of Jesus Christ? You
got the same bad treatment from your
countrymen as they did from theirs, the
Jews who killed the Master Jesus (to say
nothing of the prophets) and followed it up
by running us out of town. They make
themselves offensive to God and everyone
else by trying to keep us from telling people
who've never heard of our God how to be
saved. They've made a career of opposing
God, and have gotten mighty good at it. But
God is fed up, ready to put an end to it.

17-20 Do you have any idea how very homesick
we became for you, dear friends? Even
though it hadn't been that long and it was
only our bodies that were separated from
you, not our hearts, we tried our very best to
get back to see you. You can't imagine how
much we missed you! I, Paul, tried over and
over to get back, but Satan stymied us each
time. Who do you think we're going to be
proud of when our Master Jesus appears if
it's not you? You're our pride and joy!

1-2 3 So when we couldn't stand being sepa-
rated from you any longer and could find
no way to visit you ourselves, we stayed in
Athens and sent Timothy to get you up and
about, cheering you on so you wouldn't be

NEW KING JAMES VERSION

shaken by these afflictions; for you yourselves
know that we are appointed to this. 4For, in fact,
we told you before when we were with you that
we would suffer tribulation, just as it happened,
and you know. 5For this reason, when I could no
longer endure it, I sent to know your faith, lest
by some means the tempter had tempted you,
and our labor might be in vain.

ENCOURAGED BY TIMOTHY

6But now that Timothy has come to us from
you, and brought us good news of your faith and
love, and that you always have good remem-
brance of us, greatly desiring to see us, as we
also *to see* you— 7therefore, brethren, in all our
affliction and distress we were comforted con-
cerning you by your faith. 8For now we live, if
you stand fast in the Lord.

9For what thanks can we render to God for
you, for all the joy with which we rejoice for
your sake before our God, 10night and day pray-
ing exceedingly that we may see your face and
perfect what is lacking in your faith?

PRAYER FOR THE CHURCH

11Now may our God and Father Himself, and
our Lord Jesus Christ, direct our way to you.
12And may the Lord make you increase and
abound in love to one another and to all, just as
we *do* to you, 13so that He may establish your
hearts blameless in holiness before our God and
Father at the coming of our Lord Jesus Christ
with all His saints.

PLEA FOR PURITY

4 Finally then, brethren, we urge and exhort in
the Lord Jesus that you should abound more
and more, just as you received from us how you
ought to walk and to please God; 2for you know
what commandments we gave you through the
Lord Jesus.

3For this is the will of God, your sanctifica-
tion: that you should abstain from sexual im-
morality; 4that each of you should know how to
possess his own vessel in sanctification and
honor, 5not in passion of lust, like the Gentiles
who do not know God; 6that no one should take
advantage of and defraud his brother in this
matter, because the Lord *is* the avenger of all
such, as we also forewarned you and testified.
7For God did not call us to uncleanness, but in
holiness. 8Therefore he who rejects *this* does not
reject man, but God, who has also given[a] us His
Holy Spirit.

A BROTHERLY AND ORDERLY LIFE

9But concerning brotherly love you have no
need that I should write to you, for you your-
selves are taught by God to love one another;

4:8 [a]NU-Text reads *who also gives.*

THE MESSAGE

discouraged by these hard times. He's a
brother and companion in the faith, God's
man in spreading the Message, preaching
Christ.

3-5 Not that the troubles should come as any
surprise to you. You've always known that
we're in for this kind of thing. It's part of our
calling. When we were with you, we made it
quite clear that there was trouble ahead.
And now that it's happened, you know what
it's like. That's why I couldn't quit worrying;
I had to know for myself how you were do-
ing in the faith. I didn't want the Tempter
getting to you and tearing down everything
we had built up together.

6-8 But now that Timothy is back, bringing
this terrific report on your faith and love, we
feel a lot better. It's especially gratifying to
know that you continue to think well of us,
and that you want to see us as much as we
want to see you! In the middle of our trouble
and hard times here, just knowing how
you're doing keeps us going. Knowing that
your faith is alive keeps us alive.

9-10 What would be an adequate thanksgiving
to offer God for all the joy we experience be-
fore him because of you? We do what we
can, praying away, night and day, asking for
the bonus of seeing your faces again and do-
ing what we can to help when your faith fal-
ters.

11-13 May God our Father himself and our
Master Jesus clear the road to you! And may
the Master pour on the love so it fills your
lives and splashes over on everyone around
you, just as it does from us to you. May you
be infused with strength and purity, filled
with confidence in the presence of God our
Father when our Master Jesus arrives with
all his followers.

YOU'RE GOD-TAUGHT

1-3 4 One final word, friends. We ask you—*urge*
is more like it—that you keep on doing
what we told you to do to please God, not in
a dogged religious plod, but in a living, spir-
ited dance. You know the guidelines we laid
out for you from the Master Jesus. God
wants you to live a pure life.

Keep yourselves from sexual promiscu-
ity.

4-5 Learn to appreciate and give dignity to
your body, not abusing it, as is so common
among those who know nothing of God.

6-7 Don't run roughshod over the concerns
of your brothers and sisters. Their concerns
are God's concerns, and *he* will take care of
them. We've warned you about this before.
God hasn't invited us into a disorderly, un-
kempt life but into something holy and
beautiful—as beautiful on the inside as the
outside.

8 If you disregard this advice, you're not of-
fending your neighbors; you're rejecting
God, who is making you a gift of his Holy
Spirit.

9-10 Regarding life together and getting along
with each other, you don't need me to tell
you what to do. You're *God*-taught in these

NEW KING JAMES VERSION

[10]and indeed you do so toward all the brethren who are in all Macedonia. But we urge you, brethren, that you increase more and more; [11]that you also aspire to lead a quiet life, to mind your own business, and to work with your own hands, as we commanded you, [12]that you may walk properly toward those who are outside, and *that* you may lack nothing.

THE COMFORT OF CHRIST'S COMING

[13]But I do not want you to be ignorant, brethren, concerning those who have fallen asleep, lest you sorrow as others who have no hope. [14]For if we believe that Jesus died and rose again, even so God will bring with Him those who sleep in Jesus.[a] [15]For this we say to you by the word of the Lord, that we who are alive *and* remain until the coming of the Lord will by no means precede those who are asleep. [16]For the Lord Himself will descend from heaven with a shout, with the voice of an archangel, and with the trumpet of God. And the dead in Christ will rise first. [17]Then we who are alive *and* remain shall be caught up together with them in the clouds to meet the Lord in the air. And thus we shall always be with the Lord. [18]Therefore comfort one another with these words.

THE DAY OF THE LORD

5 But concerning the times and the seasons, brethren, you have no need that I should write to you. [2]For you yourselves know perfectly that the day of the Lord so comes as a thief in the night. [3]For when they say, "Peace and safety!" then sudden destruction comes upon them, as labor pains upon a pregnant woman. And they shall not escape. [4]But you, brethren, are not in darkness, so that this Day should overtake you as a thief. [5]You are all sons of light and sons of the day. We are not of the night nor of darkness. [6]Therefore let us not sleep, as others *do*, but let us watch and be sober. [7]For those who sleep, sleep at night, and those who get drunk are drunk at night. [8]But let us who are of the day be sober, putting on the breastplate of faith and love, and *as* a helmet the hope of salvation. [9]For God did not appoint us to wrath, but to obtain salvation through our Lord Jesus

4:14 [a]Or *those who through Jesus sleep*

THE MESSAGE

matters. Just love one another! You're already good at it; your friends all over the province of Macedonia are the evidence. Keep it up; get better and better at it.

11-12 Stay calm; mind your own business; do your own job. You've heard all this from us before, but a reminder never hurts. We want you living in a way that will command the respect of outsiders, not lying around sponging off your friends.

THE MASTER'S COMING

13-14 And regarding the question, friends, that has come up about what happens to those already dead and buried, we don't want you in the dark any longer. First off, you must not carry on over them like people who have nothing to look forward to, as if the grave were the last word. Since Jesus died and broke loose from the grave, God will most certainly bring back to life those who died in Jesus.

15-18 And then this: We can tell you with complete confidence—we have the Master's word on it—that when the Master comes again to get us, those of us who are still alive will not get a jump on the dead and leave them behind. In actual fact, they'll be ahead of us. The Master himself will give the command. Archangel thunder! God's trumpet blast! He'll come down from heaven and the dead in Christ will rise—they'll go first. Then the rest of us who are still alive at the time will be caught up with them into the clouds to meet the Master. Oh, we'll be walking on air! And then there will be one huge family reunion with the Master. So reassure one another with these words.

1-3 5 I don't think, friends, that I need to deal with the question of when all this is going to happen. You know as well as I that the day of the Master's coming can't be posted on our calendars. He won't call ahead and make an appointment any more than a burglar would. About the time everybody's walking around complacently, congratulating each other—"We've sure got it made! Now we can take it easy!"—suddenly everything will fall apart. It's going to come as suddenly and inescapably as birth pangs to a pregnant woman.

4-8 But friends, you're not in the dark, so how could you be taken off guard by any of this? You're sons of Light, daughters of Day. We live under wide open skies and know where we stand. So let's not sleepwalk through life like those others. Let's keep our eyes open and be smart. People sleep at night and get drunk at night. But not us! Since we're creatures of Day, let's act like it. Walk out into the daylight sober, dressed up in faith, love, and the hope of salvation.

9-11 God didn't set us up for an angry rejection but for salvation by our Master, Jesus Christ. He died for us, a death that triggered life. Whether we're awake with the living or asleep with the dead, we're *alive* with him! So speak encouraging words to one another.

New King James Version

Christ, 10 who died for us, that whether we wake
or sleep, we should live together with Him.
11 Therefore comfort each other and edify
one another, just as you also are doing.

Various Exhortations

12 And we urge you, brethren, to recognize
those who labor among you, and are over you in
the Lord and admonish you, 13 and to esteem
them very highly in love for their work's sake.
Be at peace among yourselves.
14 Now we exhort you, brethren, warn those
who are unruly, comfort the fainthearted, up-
hold the weak, be patient with all. 15 See that no
one renders evil for evil to anyone, but always
pursue what is good both for yourselves and for
all.
16 Rejoice always, 17 pray without ceasing, 18 in
everything give thanks; for this is the will of
God in Christ Jesus for you.
19 Do not quench the Spirit. 20 Do not despise
prophecies. 21 Test all things; hold fast what is
good. 22 Abstain from every form of evil.

Blessing and Admonition

23 Now may the God of peace Himself sanc-
tify you completely; and may your whole spirit,
soul, and body be preserved blameless at the
coming of our Lord Jesus Christ. 24 He who calls
you *is* faithful, who also will do *it*.
25 Brethren, pray for us.
26 Greet all the brethren with a holy kiss.
27 I charge you by the Lord that this epistle be
read to all the holy[a] brethren.
28 The grace of our Lord Jesus Christ *be* with
you. Amen.

5:27 [a]NU-Text omits *holy*.

The Message

Build up hope so you'll all be together in this, no one left out, no one left behind. I know you're already doing this; just keep on doing it.

The Way He Wants You to Live

12-13 And now, friends, we ask you to honor those leaders who work so hard for you, who have been given the responsibility of urging and guiding you along in your obedience. Overwhelm them with appreciation and love!

13-15 Get along among yourselves, each of you doing your part. Our counsel is that you warn the freeloaders to get a move on. Gently encourage the stragglers, and reach out for the exhausted, pulling them to their feet. Be patient with each person, attentive to individual needs. And be careful that when you get on each other's nerves you don't snap at each other. Look for the best in each other, and always do your best to bring it out.

16-18 Be cheerful no matter what; pray all the time; thank God no matter what happens. This is the way God wants you who belong to Christ Jesus to live.

19-22 Don't suppress the Spirit, and don't stifle those who have a word from the Master. On the other hand, don't be gullible. Check out everything, and keep only what's good. Throw out anything tainted with evil.

23-24 May God himself, the God who makes everything holy and whole, make you holy and whole, put you together—spirit, soul, and body—and keep you fit for the coming of our Master, Jesus Christ. The One who called you is completely dependable. If he said it, he'll do it!

25-27 Friends, keep up your prayers for us. Greet all the followers of Jesus there with a holy embrace. And make sure this letter gets read to all the brothers and sisters. Don't leave anyone out.

28 The amazing grace of Jesus Christ be with you!

2 THESSALONIANS

New King James Version

Greeting

1 Paul, Silvanus, and Timothy,

To the church of the Thessalonians in God our Father and the Lord Jesus Christ:

2 Grace to you and peace from God our Father and the Lord Jesus Christ.

God's Final Judgment and Glory

3 We are bound to thank God always for you, brethren, as it is fitting, because your faith grows exceedingly, and the love of every one of you all abounds toward each other, 4 so that we ourselves boast of you among the churches of God for your patience and faith in all your persecutions and tribulations that you endure, 5 *which is* manifest evidence of the righteous judgment of God, that you may be counted worthy of the kingdom of God, for which you also suffer; 6 since *it is* a righteous thing with God to repay with tribulation those who trouble you, 7 and to *give* you who are troubled rest with us when the Lord Jesus is revealed from heaven with His mighty angels, 8 in flaming fire taking vengeance on those who do not know God, and on those who do not obey the gospel of our Lord Jesus Christ. 9 These shall be punished with everlasting destruction from the presence of the Lord and from the glory of His power, 10 when He comes, in that Day, to be glorified in His saints and to be admired among all those who believe,[a] because our testimony among you was believed.

11 Therefore we also pray always for you that our God would count you worthy of *this* calling, and fulfill all the good pleasure of *His* goodness and the work of faith with power, 12 that the name of our Lord Jesus Christ may be glorified in you, and you in Him, according to the grace of our God and the Lord Jesus Christ.

The Great Apostasy

2 Now, brethren, concerning the coming of our Lord Jesus Christ and our gathering together to Him, we ask you, 2 not to be soon shaken in mind or troubled, either by spirit or by word or by letter, as if from us, as though the day of Christ[a] had come. 3 Let no one deceive you by any means; for *that Day will not come* unless the falling away comes first, and the man of sin[a] is revealed, the son of perdition, 4 who opposes and exalts himself above all that is called God or that is worshiped, so that he sits as God[a] in the temple of God, showing himself that he is God.

1:10 [a]NU-Text and M-Text read *have believed.* **2:2** [a]NU-Text reads *the Lord.* **2:3** [a]NU-Text reads *lawlessness.* **2:4** [a]NU-Text omits *as God.*

The Message

1-2 **1** I, Paul, together with Silas and Timothy, greet the church of the Thessalonian Christians in the name of God our Father and our Master, Jesus Christ. Our God gives you everything you need, makes you everything you're to be.

Justice Is on the Way

3-4 You need to know, friends, that thanking God over and over for you is not only a pleasure; it's a must. We *have* to do it. Your faith is growing phenomenally; your love for each other is developing wonderfully. Why, it's only right that we give thanks. We're so proud of you; you're so steady and determined in your faith despite all the hard times that have come down on you. We tell everyone we meet in the churches all about you.

5-10 All this trouble is a clear sign that God has decided to make you fit for the kingdom. You're suffering now, but justice is on the way. When the Master Jesus appears out of heaven in a blaze of fire with his strong angels, he'll even up the score by settling accounts with those who gave you such a bad time. His coming will be the break we've been waiting for. Those who refuse to know God and refuse to obey the Message will pay for what they've done. Eternal exile from the presence of the Master and his splendid power is their sentence. But on that very same day when he comes, he will be exalted by his followers and celebrated by all who believe—and all because you believed what we told you.

11-12 Because we know that this extraordinary day is just ahead, we pray for you all the time—pray that our God will make you fit for what he's called you to be, pray that he'll fill your good ideas and acts of faith with his own energy so that it all amounts to something. If your life honors the name of Jesus, he will honor you. Grace is behind and through all of this, our God giving himself freely, the Master, Jesus Christ, giving himself freely.

The Anarchist

1-3 **2** Now, friends, read these next words carefully. Slow down and don't go jumping to conclusions regarding the day when our Master, Jesus Christ, will come back and we assemble to welcome him. Don't let anyone shake you up or get you excited over some breathless report or rumored letter from me that the day of the Master's arrival has come and gone. Don't fall for any line like that.

3-5 Before that day comes, a couple of things have to happen. First, the Apostasy. Second, the debut of the Anarchist, a real dog of Satan. He'll defy and then take over every so-called god or altar. Having cleared away the opposition, he'll then set himself up in God's Temple as "God Almighty." Don't you remem-

NEW KING JAMES VERSION

5Do you not remember that when I was still with you I told you these things? 6And now you know what is restraining, that he may be revealed in his own time. 7For the mystery of lawlessness is already at work; only He[a] who now restrains *will do so* until He[b] is taken out of the way. 8And then the lawless one will be revealed, whom the Lord will consume with the breath of His mouth and destroy with the brightness of His coming. 9The coming of the *lawless one* is according to the working of Satan, with all power, signs, and lying wonders, 10and with all unrighteous deception among those who perish, because they did not receive the love of the truth, that they might be saved. 11And for this reason God will send them strong delusion, that they should believe the lie, 12that they all may be condemned who did not believe the truth but had pleasure in unrighteousness.

STAND FAST

13But we are bound to give thanks to God always for you, brethren beloved by the Lord, because God from the beginning chose you for salvation through sanctification by the Spirit and belief in the truth, 14to which He called you by our gospel, for the obtaining of the glory of our Lord Jesus Christ. 15Therefore, brethren, stand fast and hold the traditions which you were taught, whether by word or our epistle.

16Now may our Lord Jesus Christ Himself, and our God and Father, who has loved us and given *us* everlasting consolation and good hope by grace, 17comfort your hearts and establish you in every good word and work.

PRAY FOR US

3 Finally, brethren, pray for us, that the word of the Lord may run *swiftly* and be glorified, just as *it is* with you, 2and that we may be delivered from unreasonable and wicked men; for not all have faith.

3But the Lord is faithful, who will establish you and guard *you* from the evil one. 4And we have confidence in the Lord concerning you, both that you do and will do the things we command you.

5Now may the Lord direct your hearts into the love of God and into the patience of Christ.

WARNING AGAINST IDLENESS

6But we command you, brethren, in the name of our Lord Jesus Christ, that you withdraw from every brother who walks disorderly and not according to the tradition which he[a] received from us. 7For you yourselves know how you ought to follow us, for we were not disorderly among you; 8nor did we eat anyone's bread free of charge, but worked with labor and toil night and day, that we might not be a burden

2:7 [a]Or *he* [b]Or *he* **3:6** [a]NU-Text and M-Text read *they.*

THE MESSAGE

ber me going over all this in detail when I was with you? Are your memories that short?

6-8 You'll also remember that I told you the Anarchist is being held back until just the right time. That doesn't mean that the spirit of anarchy is not now at work. It is, secretly and underground. But the time will come when the Anarchist will no longer be held back, but will be let loose. But don't worry. The Master Jesus will be right on his heels and blow him away. The Master appears and—puff!—the Anarchist is out of there.

9-12 The Anarchist's coming is all Satan's work. All his power and signs and miracles are fake, evil sleight of hand that plays to the gallery of those who hate the truth that could save them. And since they're so obsessed with evil, God rubs their noses in it—gives them what they want. Since they refuse to trust truth, they're banished to their chosen world of lies and illusions.

13-14 Meanwhile, we've got our hands full continually thanking God for you, our good friends—so loved by God! God picked you out as his from the very start. Think of it: included in God's original plan of salvation by the bond of faith in the living truth. This is the life of the Spirit he invited you to through the Message we delivered, in which you get in on the glory of our Master, Jesus Christ.

15-17 So, friends, take a firm stand, feet on the ground and head high. Keep a tight grip on what you were taught, whether in personal conversation or by our letter. May Jesus himself and God our Father, who reached out in love and surprised you with gifts of unending help and confidence, put a fresh heart in you, invigorate your work, enliven your speech.

THOSE WHO ARE LAZY

1-3 3 One more thing, friends: Pray for us. Pray that the Master's Word will simply take off and race through the country to a groundswell of response, just as it did among you. And pray that we'll be rescued from these scoundrels who are trying to do us in. I'm finding that not all "believers" are believers. But the Master never lets us down. He'll stick by you and protect you from evil.

4-5 Because of the *Master,* we have great confidence in *you.* We know you're doing everything we told you and will continue doing it. May the Master take you by the hand and lead you along the path of God's love and Christ's endurance.

6-9 Our orders—backed up by the Master, Jesus—are to refuse to have anything to do with those among you who are lazy and refuse to work the way we taught you. Don't permit them to freeload on the rest. We showed you how to pull your weight when we were with you, so get on with it. We didn't sit around on our hands expecting others to take care of us. In fact, we worked our fingers to the bone, up half the night moonlighting so you wouldn't be burdened with taking care of us. And it wasn't because we didn't

NEW KING JAMES VERSION

to any of you, [9]not because we do not have au-
thority, but to make ourselves an example of
how you should follow us.
[10]For even when we were with you, we com-
manded you this: If anyone will not work, nei-
ther shall he eat. [11]For we hear that there are
some who walk among you in a disorderly man-
ner, not working at all, but are busybodies.
[12]Now those who are such we command and ex-
hort through our Lord Jesus Christ that they
work in quietness and eat their own bread.
[13]But *as for* you, brethren, do not grow weary
in doing good. [14]And if anyone does not obey
our word in this epistle, note that person and do
not keep company with him, that he may be
ashamed. [15]Yet do not count *him* as an enemy,
but admonish *him* as a brother.

BENEDICTION

[16]Now may the Lord of peace Himself give
you peace always in every way. The Lord *be*
with you all.
[17]The salutation of Paul with my own hand,
which is a sign in every epistle; so I write.
[18]The grace of our Lord Jesus Christ *be* with
you all. Amen.

THE MESSAGE

have a right to your support; we did. We simply wanted to provide an example of diligence, hoping it would prove contagious.

10-13 Don't you remember the rule we had when we lived with you? "If you don't work, you don't eat." And now we're getting reports that a bunch of lazy good-for-nothings are taking advantage of you. This must not be tolerated. We command them to get to work immediately—no excuses, no arguments—and earn their own keep. Friends, don't slack off in doing your duty.

14-15 If anyone refuses to obey our clear command written in this letter, don't let him get by with it. Point out such a person and refuse to subsidize his freeloading. Maybe then he'll think twice. But don't treat him as an enemy. Sit him down and talk about the problem as someone who cares.

16 May the Master of Peace himself give you the gift of getting along with each other at all times, in all ways. May the Master be truly among you!

17 I, Paul, bid you good-bye in my own handwriting. I do this in all my letters, so examine my signature as proof that the letter is genuine.

18 The incredible grace of our Master, Jesus Christ, be with all of you!

1 TIMOTHY

New King James Version

Greeting

1 Paul, an apostle of Jesus Christ, by the commandment of God our Savior and the Lord Jesus Christ, our hope,

2To Timothy, a true son in the faith:

Grace, mercy, *and* peace from God our Father and Jesus Christ our Lord.

No Other Doctrine

3As I urged you when I went into Macedonia—remain in Ephesus that you may charge some that they teach no other doctrine, 4nor give heed to fables and endless genealogies, which cause disputes rather than godly edification which is in faith. 5Now the purpose of the commandment is love from a pure heart, *from* a good conscience, and *from* sincere faith, 6from which some, having strayed, have turned aside to idle talk, 7desiring to be teachers of the law, understanding neither what they say nor the things which they affirm.

8But we know that the law *is* good if one uses it lawfully, 9knowing this: that the law is not made for a righteous person, but for *the* lawless and insubordinate, for *the* ungodly and for sinners, for *the* unholy and profane, for murderers of fathers and murderers of mothers, for manslayers, 10for fornicators, for sodomites, for kidnappers, for liars, for perjurers, and if there is any other thing that is contrary to sound doctrine, 11according to the glorious gospel of the blessed God which was committed to my trust.

Glory to God for His Grace

12And I thank Christ Jesus our Lord who has enabled me, because He counted me faithful, putting *me* into the ministry, 13although I was formerly a blasphemer, a persecutor, and an insolent man; but I obtained mercy because I did *it* ignorantly in unbelief. 14And the grace of our Lord was exceedingly abundant, with faith and love which are in Christ Jesus. 15This *is* a faithful saying and worthy of all acceptance, that Christ Jesus came into the world to save sinners, of whom I am chief. 16However, for this reason I obtained mercy, that in me first Jesus Christ might show all longsuffering, as a pattern to those who are going to believe on Him for everlasting life. 17Now to the King eternal, immortal, invisible, to God who alone is wise,[a] *be* honor and glory forever and ever. Amen.

1:17 [a]NU-Text reads *to the only God.*

The Message

1-2 1 I, Paul, am an apostle on special assignment for Christ, our living hope. Under God our Savior's command, I'm writing this to you, Timothy, my son in the faith. All the best from our God and Christ be yours!

Self-Appointed Experts on Life

3-4 On my way to the province of Macedonia, I advised you to stay in Ephesus. Well, I haven't changed my mind. Stay right there on top of things so that the teaching stays on track. Apparently some people have been introducing fantasy stories and fanciful family trees that digress into silliness instead of pulling the people back into the center, deepening faith and obedience.

5-7 The whole point of what we're urging is simply *love*—love uncontaminated by self-interest and counterfeit faith, a life open to God. Those who fail to keep to this point soon wander off into cul-de-sacs of gossip. They set themselves up as experts on religious issues, but haven't the remotest idea of what they're holding forth with such imposing eloquence.

8-11 It's true that moral guidance and counsel need to be given, but the way you say it and to whom you say it are as important as what you say. It's obvious, isn't it, that the law code isn't primarily for people who live responsibly, but for the irresponsible, who defy all authority, riding roughshod over God, life, sex, truth, whatever! They are contemptuous of this great Message I've been put in charge of by this great God.

12-14 I'm so grateful to Christ Jesus for making me adequate to do this work. He went out on a limb, you know, in trusting me with this ministry. The only credentials I brought to it were invective and witch hunts and arrogance. But I was treated mercifully because I didn't know what I was doing—didn't know Who I was doing it against! Grace mixed with faith and love poured over me and into me. And all because of Jesus.

15-19 Here's a word you can take to heart and depend on: Jesus Christ came into the world to save sinners. I'm proof—Public Sinner Number One—of someone who could never have made it apart from sheer mercy. And now he shows me off—evidence of his endless patience—to those who are right on the edge of trusting him forever.

Deep honor and bright glory
to the King of All Time—
One God, Immortal, Invisible,
ever and always. Oh, yes!

I'm passing this work on to you, my son Timothy. The prophetic word that was directed to you prepared us for this. All those

New King James Version

Fight the Good Fight

[18]This charge I commit to you, son Timothy,
according to the prophecies previously made
concerning you, that by them you may wage the
good warfare, [19]having faith and a good con-
science, which some having rejected, concern-
ing the faith have suffered shipwreck, [20]of
whom are Hymenaeus and Alexander, whom I
delivered to Satan that they may learn not to
blaspheme.

Pray for All Men

2 Therefore I exhort first of all that supplica-
tions, prayers, intercessions, *and* giving of
thanks be made for all men, [2]for kings and all
who are in authority, that we may lead a quiet
and peaceable life in all godliness and rever-
ence. [3]For this *is* good and acceptable in the
sight of God our Savior, [4]who desires all men to
be saved and to come to the knowledge of the
truth. [5]For *there is* one God and one Mediator
between God and men, *the* Man Christ Jesus,
[6]who gave Himself a ransom for all, to be testi-
fied in due time, [7]for which I was appointed a
preacher and an apostle—I am speaking the
truth in Christ[a] *and* not lying—a teacher of the
Gentiles in faith and truth.

Men and Women in the Church

[8]I desire therefore that the men pray every-
where, lifting up holy hands, without wrath and
doubting; [9]in like manner also, that the women
adorn themselves in modest apparel, with pro-
priety and moderation, not with braided hair or
gold or pearls or costly clothing, [10]but, which is
proper for women professing godliness, with
good works. [11]Let a woman learn in silence with
all submission. [12]And I do not permit a woman
to teach or to have authority over a man, but to
be in silence. [13]For Adam was formed first, then
Eve. [14]And Adam was not deceived, but the
woman being deceived, fell into transgression.
[15]Nevertheless she will be saved in childbearing
if they continue in faith, love, and holiness, with
self-control.

Qualifications of Overseers

3 This *is* a faithful saying: If a man desires the
position of a bishop,[a] he desires a good work.
[2]A bishop then must be blameless, the husband
of one wife, temperate, sober-minded, of good
behavior, hospitable, able to teach; [3]not given to
wine, not violent, not greedy for money,[a] but
gentle, not quarrelsome, not covetous; [4]one who
rules his own house well, having *his* children in
submission with all reverence [5](for if a man
does not know how to rule his own house, how
will he take care of the church of God?); [6]not a
novice, lest being puffed up with pride he fall
into the *same* condemnation as the devil. [7]More-
over he must have a good testimony among
those who are outside, lest he fall into reproach
and the snare of the devil.

2:7 [a]NU-Text omits *in Christ.* **3:1** [a]Literally *overseer* **3:3** [a]NU-Text omits *not greedy for money.*

The Message

prayers are coming together now so you will
do this well, fearless in your struggle, keep-
ing a firm grip on your faith and on yourself.
After all, this is a fight we're in.
19-20 There are some, you know, who by relax-
ing their grip and thinking anything goes
have made a thorough mess of their faith.
Hymenaeus and Alexander are two of them.
I let them wander off to Satan to be taught a
lesson or two about not blaspheming.

Simple Faith and Plain Truth

1-3 2 The first thing I want you to do is pray.
Pray every way you know how, for every-
one you know. Pray especially for rulers and
their governments to rule well so we can be
quietly about our business of living simply,
in humble contemplation. This is the way
our Savior God wants us to live.
4-7 He wants not only us but *everyone* saved,
you know, everyone to get to know the truth
we've learned: that there's one God and only
one, and one Priest-Mediator between God
and us—Jesus, who offered himself in ex-
change for everyone held captive by sin, to
set them all free. Eventually the news is go-
ing to get out. This and this only has been my
appointed work: getting this news to those
who have never heard of God, and explaining
how it works by simple faith and plain truth.
8-10 Since prayer is at the bottom of all this,
what I want mostly is for men to pray—not
shaking angry fists at enemies but raising
holy hands to God. And I want women to get
in there with the men in humility before God,
not primping before a mirror or chasing the
latest fashions but doing something beautiful
for God and becoming beautiful doing it.
11-15 I don't let women take over and tell the
men what to do. They should study to be
quiet and obedient along with everyone
else. Adam was made first, then Eve;
woman was deceived first—our pioneer in
sin!—with Adam right on her heels. On the
other hand, her childbearing brought about
salvation, reversing Eve. But this salvation
only comes to those who continue in faith,
love, and holiness, gathering it all into matu-
rity. You can depend on this.

Leadership in the Church

1-7 3 If anyone wants to provide leadership in
the church, good! But there are precondi-
tions: A leader must be well-thought-of,
committed to his wife, cool and collected,
accessible, and hospitable. He must know
what he's talking about, not be overfond of
wine, not pushy but gentle, not thin-
skinned, not money-hungry. He must handle
his own affairs well, attentive to his own
children and having their respect. For if
someone is unable to handle his own affairs,
how can he take care of God's church? He
must not be a new believer, lest the position
go to his head and the Devil trip him up.
Outsiders must think well of him, or else the
Devil will figure out a way to lure him into
his trap.

New King James Version

Qualifications of Deacons

[8]Likewise deacons *must be* reverent, not double-tongued, not given to much wine, not greedy for money, [9]holding the mystery of the faith with a pure conscience. [10]But let these also first be tested; then let them serve as deacons, being *found* blameless. [11]Likewise, *their* wives *must be* reverent, not slanderers, temperate, faithful in all things. [12]Let deacons be the husbands of one wife, ruling *their* children and their own houses well. [13]For those who have served well as deacons obtain for themselves a good standing and great boldness in the faith which is in Christ Jesus.

The Great Mystery

[14]These things I write to you, though I hope to come to you shortly; [15]but if I am delayed, *I write* so that you may know how you ought to conduct yourself in the house of God, which is the church of the living God, the pillar and ground of the truth. [16]And without controversy great is the mystery of godliness:

God[a] was manifested in the flesh,
Justified in the Spirit,
Seen by angels,
Preached among the Gentiles,
Believed on in the world,
Received up in glory.

The Great Apostasy

4 Now the Spirit expressly says that in latter times some will depart from the faith, giving heed to deceiving spirits and doctrines of demons, [2]speaking lies in hypocrisy, having their own conscience seared with a hot iron, [3]forbidding to marry, *and commanding* to abstain from foods which God created to be received with thanksgiving by those who believe and know the truth. [4]For every creature of God *is* good, and nothing is to be refused if it is received with thanksgiving; [5]for it is sanctified by the word of God and prayer.

A Good Servant of Jesus Christ

[6]If you instruct the brethren in these things, you will be a good minister of Jesus Christ, nourished in the words of faith and of the good doctrine which you have carefully followed. [7]But reject profane and old wives' fables, and exercise yourself toward godliness. [8]For bodily exercise profits a little, but godliness is profitable for all things, having promise of the life that now is and of that which is to come. [9]This *is* a faithful saying and worthy of all acceptance. [10]For to this *end* we both labor and suffer reproach,[a] because we trust in the living God, who is *the* Savior of all men, especially of those who believe. [11]These things command and teach.

3:16 [a]NU-Text reads *Who*. 4:10 [a]NU-Text reads *we labor and strive*.

The Message

8-13 The same goes for those who want to be servants in the church: serious, not deceitful, not too free with the bottle, not in it for what they can get out of it. They must be reverent before the mystery of the faith, not using their position to try to run things. Let them prove themselves first. If they show they can do it, take them on. No exceptions are to be made for women—same qualifications: serious, dependable, not sharp-tongued, not overfond of wine. Servants in the church are to be committed to their spouses, attentive to their own children, and diligent in looking after their own affairs. Those who do this servant work will come to be highly respected, a real credit to this Jesus-faith.

14-16 I hope to visit you soon, but just in case I'm delayed, I'm writing this letter so you'll know how things ought to go in God's household, this God-alive church, bastion of truth. This Christian life is a great mystery, far exceeding our understanding, but some things are clear enough:

He appeared in a human body,
was proved right by the invisible Spirit,
was seen by angels.
He was proclaimed among all kinds of peoples,
believed in all over the world,
taken up into heavenly glory.

Teach with Your Life

1-5 4 The Spirit makes it clear that as time goes on, some are going to give up on the faith and chase after demonic illusions put forth by professional liars. These liars have lied so well and for so long that they've lost their capacity for truth. They will tell you not to get married. They'll tell you not to eat this or that food—perfectly good food God created to be eaten heartily and with thanksgiving by believers who know better! Everything God created is good, and to be received with thanks. Nothing is to be sneered at and thrown out. God's Word and our prayers make every item in creation holy.

6-10 You've been raised on the Message of the faith and have followed sound teaching. Now pass on this counsel to the followers of Jesus there, and you'll be a good servant of Jesus. Stay clear of silly stories that get dressed up as religion. Exercise daily in God—no spiritual flabbiness, please! Workouts in the gymnasium are useful, but a disciplined life in God is far more so, making you fit both today and forever. You can count on this. Take it to heart. This is why we've thrown ourselves into this venture so totally. We're banking on the living God, Savior of all men and women, especially believers.

11-14 Get the word out. Teach all these things.

New King James Version

Take Heed to Your Ministry

12 Let no one despise your youth, but be an example to the believers in word, in conduct, in love, in spirit,[a] in faith, in purity. 13 Till I come, give attention to reading, to exhortation, to doctrine. 14 Do not neglect the gift that is in you, which was given to you by prophecy with the laying on of the hands of the eldership. 15 Meditate on these things; give yourself entirely to them, that your progress may be evident to all. 16 Take heed to yourself and to the doctrine. Continue in them, for in doing this you will save both yourself and those who hear you.

Treatment of Church Members

5 Do not rebuke an older man, but exhort *him* as a father, younger men as brothers, 2 older women as mothers, younger women as sisters, with all purity.

Honor True Widows

3 Honor widows who are really widows. 4 But if any widow has children or grandchildren, let them first learn to show piety at home and to repay their parents; for this is good and[a] acceptable before God. 5 Now she who is really a widow, and left alone, trusts in God and continues in supplications and prayers night and day. 6 But she who lives in pleasure is dead while she lives. 7 And these things command, that they may be blameless. 8 But if anyone does not provide for his own, and especially for those of his household, he has denied the faith and is worse than an unbeliever.

9 Do not let a widow under sixty years old be taken into the number, *and not unless* she has been the wife of one man, 10 well reported for good works: if she has brought up children, if she has lodged strangers, if she has washed the saints' feet, if she has relieved the afflicted, if she has diligently followed every good work.

11 But refuse *the* younger widows; for when they have begun to grow wanton against Christ, they desire to marry, 12 having condemnation because they have cast off their first faith. 13 And besides they learn *to be* idle, wandering about from house to house, and not only idle but also gossips and busybodies, saying things which they ought not. 14 Therefore I desire that *the* younger *widows* marry, bear children, manage the house, give no opportunity to the adversary to speak reproachfully. 15 For some have already turned aside after Satan. 16 If any believing man or[a] woman has widows, let them relieve them, and do not let the church be burdened, that it may relieve those who are really widows.

Honor the Elders

17 Let the elders who rule well be counted worthy of double honor, especially those who labor in the word and doctrine. 18 For the Scrip-

4:12 [a]NU-Text omits *in spirit.* **5:4** [a]NU-Text and M-Text omit *good and.* **5:16** [a]NU-Text omits *man or.*

The Message

And don't let anyone put you down because you're young. Teach believers with your life: by word, by demeanor, by love, by faith, by integrity. Stay at your post reading Scripture, giving counsel, teaching. And that special gift of ministry you were given when the leaders of the church laid hands on you and prayed—keep that dusted off and in use.

15-16 Cultivate these things. Immerse yourself in them. The people will all see you mature right before their eyes! Keep a firm grasp on both your character and your teaching. Don't be diverted. Just keep at it. Both you and those who hear you will experience salvation.

The Family of Faith

1-2 5 Don't be harsh or impatient with an older man. Talk to him as you would your own father, and to the younger men as your brothers. Reverently honor an older woman as you would your mother, and the younger women as sisters.

3-8 Take care of widows who are destitute. If a widow has family members to take care of her, let them learn that religion begins at their own doorstep and that they should pay back with gratitude some of what they have received. This pleases God immensely. You can tell a legitimate widow by the way she has put all her hope in God, praying to him constantly for the needs of others as well as her own. But a widow who exploits people's emotions and pocketbooks—well, there's nothing to her. Tell these things to the people so that they will do the right thing in their extended family. Anyone who neglects to care for family members in need repudiates the faith. That's worse than refusing to believe in the first place.

9-10 Sign some widows up for the special ministry of offering assistance. They will in turn receive support from the church. They must be over sixty, married only once, and have a reputation for helping out with children, strangers, tired Christians, the hurt and troubled.

11-15 Don't put young widows on this list. No sooner will they get on than they'll want to get off, obsessed with wanting to get a husband rather than serving Christ in this way. By breaking their word, they're liable to go from bad to worse, frittering away their days on empty talk, gossip, and trivialities. No, I'd rather the young widows go ahead and get married in the first place, have children, manage their homes, and not give critics any foothold for finding fault. Some of them have already left and gone after Satan.

16 Any Christian woman who has widows in her family is responsible for them. They shouldn't be dumped on the church. The church has its hands full already with widows who need help.

17-18 Give a bonus to leaders who do a good job, especially the ones who work hard at preaching and teaching. Scripture tells us,

NEW KING JAMES VERSION

ture says, *"You shall not muzzle an ox while it treads out the grain,"*[a] and, "The laborer *is* worthy of his wages."[b] 19 Do not receive an accusation against an elder except from two or three witnesses. 20 Those who are sinning rebuke in the presence of all, that the rest also may fear.

21 I charge *you* before God and the Lord Jesus Christ and the elect angels that you observe these things without prejudice, doing nothing with partiality. 22 Do not lay hands on anyone hastily, nor share in other people's sins; keep yourself pure.

23 No longer drink only water, but use a little wine for your stomach's sake and your frequent infirmities.

24 Some men's sins are clearly evident, preceding *them* to judgment, but those of some *men* follow later. 25 Likewise, the good works *of some* are clearly evident, and those that are otherwise cannot be hidden.

HONOR MASTERS

6 Let as many bondservants as are under the yoke count their own masters worthy of all honor, so that the name of God and *His* doctrine may not be blasphemed. 2 And those who have believing masters, let them not despise *them* because they are brethren, but rather serve *them* because those who are benefited are believers and beloved. Teach and exhort these things.

ERROR AND GREED

3 If anyone teaches otherwise and does not consent to wholesome words, *even* the words of our Lord Jesus Christ, and to the doctrine which accords with godliness, 4 he is proud, knowing nothing, but is obsessed with disputes and arguments over words, from which come envy, strife, reviling, evil suspicions, 5 useless wranglings[a] of men of corrupt minds and destitute of the truth, who suppose that godliness is a *means of* gain. From such withdraw yourself.[b]

6 Now godliness with contentment is great gain. 7 For we brought nothing into *this* world, *and it is* certain[a] we can carry nothing out. 8 And having food and clothing, with these we shall be content. 9 But those who desire to be rich fall into temptation and a snare, and *into* many foolish and harmful lusts which drown men in destruction and perdition. 10 For the love of money is a root of all *kinds of* evil, for which some have strayed from the faith in their greediness, and pierced themselves through with many sorrows.

THE GOOD CONFESSION

11 But you, O man of God, flee these things and pursue righteousness, godliness, faith, love, patience, gentleness. 12 Fight the good fight of faith, lay hold on eternal life, to which you were also called and have confessed the good confession in the presence of many witnesses.

5:18 [a]Deuteronomy 25:4 [b]Luke 10:7 **6:5** [a]NU-Text and M-Text read *constant friction.* [b]NU-Text omits this sentence. **6:7** [a]NU-Text omits *and it is certain.*

THE MESSAGE

"Don't muzzle a working ox" and "A worker deserves his pay."

19 Don't listen to a complaint against a leader that isn't backed up by two or three responsible witnesses.

20 If anyone falls into sin, call that person on the carpet. Those who are inclined that way will know right off they can't get by with it.

21-23 God and Jesus and angels all back me up in these instructions. Carry them out without favoritism, without taking sides. Don't appoint people to church leadership positions too hastily. If a person is involved in some serious sins, you don't want to become an unwitting accomplice. In any event, keep a close check on yourself. And don't worry too much about what the critics will say. Go ahead and drink a little wine, for instance; it's good for your digestion, good medicine for what ails you.

24-25 The sins of some people are blatant and march them right into court. The sins of others don't show up until much later. The same with good deeds. Some you see right off, but none are hidden forever.

1-2 6 Whoever is a slave must make the best of it, giving respect to his master so that outsiders don't blame God and our teaching for his behavior. Slaves with Christian masters all the more so—their masters are really their beloved brothers!

THE LUST FOR MONEY

2-5 These are the things I want you to teach and preach. If you have leaders there who teach otherwise, who refuse the solid words of our Master Jesus and this godly instruction, tag them for what they are: ignorant windbags who infect the air with germs of envy, controversy, bad-mouthing, suspicious rumors. Eventually there's an epidemic of backstabbing, and truth is but a distant memory. They think religion is a way to make a fast buck.

6-8 A devout life does bring wealth, but it's the rich simplicity of being yourself before God. Since we entered the world penniless and will leave it penniless, if we have bread on the table and shoes on our feet, that's enough.

9-10 But if it's only money these leaders are after, they'll self-destruct in no time. Lust for money brings trouble and nothing but trouble. Going down that path, some lose their footing in the faith completely and live to regret it bitterly ever after.

RUNNING HARD

11-12 But you, Timothy, man of God: Run for your life from all this. Pursue a righteous life—a life of wonder, faith, love, steadiness, courtesy. Run hard and fast in the faith. Seize the eternal life, the life you were called to, the life you so fervently embraced in the presence of so many witnesses.

NEW KING JAMES VERSION

[13]I urge you in the sight of God who gives life to
all things, and *before* Christ Jesus who wit-
nessed the good confession before Pontius Pi-
late, [14]that you keep *this* commandment without
spot, blameless until our Lord Jesus Christ's ap-
pearing, [15]which He will manifest in His own
time, *He who is* the blessed and only Potentate,
the King of kings and Lord of lords, [16]who alone
has immortality, dwelling in unapproachable
light, whom no man has seen or can see, to
whom *be* honor and everlasting power. Amen.

INSTRUCTIONS TO THE RICH

[17]Command those who are rich in this pres-
ent age not to be haughty, nor to trust in uncer-
tain riches but in the living God, who gives us
richly all things to enjoy. [18]*Let them* do good,
that they be rich in good works, ready to give,
willing to share, [19]storing up for themselves a
good foundation for the time to come, that they
may lay hold on eternal life.

GUARD THE FAITH

[20]O Timothy! Guard what was committed to
your trust, avoiding the profane *and* idle bab-
blings and contradictions of what is falsely
called knowledge— [21]by professing it some have
strayed concerning the faith.

Grace *be* with you. Amen.

THE MESSAGE

13-16 I'm charging you before the life-giving God and before Christ, who took his stand before Pontius Pilate and didn't give an inch: Keep this command to the letter, and don't slack off. Our Master, Jesus Christ, is on his way. He'll show up right on time, his arrival guaranteed by the Blessed and Undisputed Ruler, High King, High God. He's the only one death can't touch, his light so bright no one can get close. He's never been seen by human eyes—human eyes can't take him in! Honor to him, and eternal rule! Oh, yes.

17-19 Tell those rich in this world's wealth to quit being so full of themselves and so obsessed with money, which is here today and gone tomorrow. Tell them to go after God, who piles on all the riches we could ever manage—to do good, to be rich in helping others, to be extravagantly generous. If they do that, they'll build a treasury that will last, gaining life that is truly life.

20-21 And oh, my dear Timothy, guard the treasure you were given! Guard it with your life. Avoid the talk-show religion and the practiced confusion of the so-called experts. People caught up in a lot of talk can miss the whole point of faith.

Overwhelming grace keep you!

2 TIMOTHY

New King James Version

Greeting

1 Paul, an apostle of Jesus Christ[a] by the will of God, according to the promise of life which is in Christ Jesus,

2To Timothy, a beloved son:

Grace, mercy, *and* peace from God the Father and Christ Jesus our Lord.

Timothy's Faith and Heritage

3I thank God, whom I serve with a pure conscience, as *my* forefathers *did,* as without ceasing I remember you in my prayers night and day, 4greatly desiring to see you, being mindful of your tears, that I may be filled with joy, 5when I call to remembrance the genuine faith that is in you, which dwelt first in your grandmother Lois and your mother Eunice, and I am persuaded is in you also. 6Therefore I remind you to stir up the gift of God which is in you through the laying on of my hands. 7For God has not given us a spirit of fear, but of power and of love and of a sound mind.

Not Ashamed of the Gospel

8Therefore do not be ashamed of the testimony of our Lord, nor of me His prisoner, but share with me in the sufferings for the gospel according to the power of God, 9who has saved us and called *us* with a holy calling, not according to our works, but according to His own purpose and grace which was given to us in Christ Jesus before time began, 10but has now been revealed by the appearing of our Savior Jesus Christ, *who* has abolished death and brought life and immortality to light through the gospel, 11to which I was appointed a preacher, an apostle, and a teacher of the Gentiles.[a] 12For this reason I also suffer these things; nevertheless I am not ashamed, for I know whom I have believed and am persuaded that He is able to keep what I have committed to Him until that Day.

Be Loyal to the Faith

13Hold fast the pattern of sound words which you have heard from me, in faith and love which are in Christ Jesus. 14That good thing which was committed to you, keep by the Holy Spirit who dwells in us.

15This you know, that all those in Asia have turned away from me, among whom are Phygellus and Hermogenes. 16The Lord grant mercy to the household of Onesiphorus, for he often refreshed me, and was not ashamed of my chain; 17but when he arrived in Rome, he sought me out very zealously and found *me.* 18The Lord grant to him that he may find mercy from the Lord in that Day—and you know very well how many ways he ministered *to me*[a] at Ephesus.

1:1 [a]NU-Text and M-Text read *Christ Jesus.* **1:11** [a]NU-Text omits *of the Gentiles.* **1:18** [a]*To me* is from the Vulgate and a few Greek manuscripts.

The Message

1-2 1 I, Paul, am on special assignment for
Christ, carrying out God's plan laid out in
the Message of Life by Jesus. I write this to
you, Timothy, the son I love so much. All the
best from our God and Christ be yours!

To Be Bold with God's Gifts

3-4 Every time I say your name in prayer—
which is practically all the time—I thank
God for you, the God I worship with my
whole life in the tradition of my ancestors. I
miss you a lot, especially when I remember
that last tearful good-bye, and I look forward to a joy-packed reunion.

5-7 That precious memory triggers another:
your honest faith—and what a rich faith it
is, handed down from your grandmother
Lois to your mother Eunice, and now to you!
And the special gift of ministry you received
when I laid hands on you and prayed—keep
that ablaze! God doesn't want us to be shy
with his gifts, but bold and loving and sensible.

8-10 So don't be embarrassed to speak up for
our Master or for me, his prisoner. Take
your share of suffering for the Message
along with the rest of us. We can only keep
on going, after all, by the power of God, who
first saved us and then called us to this holy
work. We had nothing to do with it. It was all
his idea, a gift prepared for us in Jesus long
before we knew anything about it. But we
know it now. Since the appearance of our
Savior, nothing could be plainer: death defeated, life vindicated in a steady blaze of
light, all through the work of Jesus.

11-12 This is the Message I've been set apart to
proclaim as preacher, emissary, and teacher.
It's also the cause of all this trouble I'm in.
But I have no regrets. I couldn't be more
sure of my ground—the One I've trusted in
can take care of what he's trusted me to do
right to the end.

13-14 So keep at your work, this faith and love
rooted in Christ, exactly as I set it out for
you. It's as sound as the day you first heard
it from me. Guard this precious thing placed
in your custody by the Holy Spirit who
works in us.

15-18 I'm sure you know by now that everyone
in the province of Asia deserted me, even
Phygelus and Hermogenes. But God bless
Onesiphorus and his family! Many's the
time I've been refreshed in that house. And
he wasn't embarrassed a bit that I was in
jail. The first thing he did when he got to
Rome was look me up. May God on the Last
Day treat him as well as he treated me. And
then there was all the help he provided in
Ephesus—but you know that better than I.

NEW KING JAMES VERSION

BE STRONG IN GRACE

2 You therefore, my son, be strong in the grace that is in Christ Jesus. 2And the things that you have heard from me among many witnesses, commit these to faithful men who will be able to teach others also. 3You therefore must endure[a] hardship as a good soldier of Jesus Christ. 4No one engaged in warfare entangles himself with the affairs of *this* life, that he may please him who enlisted him as a soldier. 5And also if anyone competes in athletics, he is not crowned unless he competes according to the rules. 6The hardworking farmer must be first to partake of the crops. 7Consider what I say, and may[a] the Lord give you understanding in all things.

8Remember that Jesus Christ, of the seed of David, was raised from the dead according to my gospel, 9for which I suffer trouble as an evildoer, *even* to the point of chains; but the word of God is not chained. 10Therefore I endure all things for the sake of the elect, that they also may obtain the salvation which is in Christ Jesus with eternal glory.

11*This is* a faithful saying:

For if we died with *Him,*
 We shall also live with *Him.*
12If we endure,
 We shall also reign with *Him.*
If we deny *Him,*
 He also will deny us.
13If we are faithless,
 He remains faithful;
He cannot deny Himself.

APPROVED AND DISAPPROVED WORKERS

14Remind *them* of these things, charging *them* before the Lord not to strive about words to no profit, to the ruin of the hearers. 15Be diligent to present yourself approved to God, a worker who does not need to be ashamed, rightly dividing the word of truth. 16But shun profane *and* idle babblings, for they will increase to more ungodliness. 17And their message will spread like cancer. Hymenaeus and Philetus are of this sort, 18who have strayed concerning the truth, saying that the resurrection is already past; and they overthrow the faith of some. 19Nevertheless the solid foundation of God stands, having this seal: "The Lord knows those who are His," and, "Let everyone who names the name of Christ[a] depart from iniquity."

20But in a great house there are not only vessels of gold and silver, but also of wood and clay, some for honor and some for dishonor. 21Therefore if anyone cleanses himself from the latter, he will be a vessel for honor, sanctified and useful for the Master, prepared for every good work. 22Flee also youthful lusts; but pursue righteousness, faith, love, peace with those who call on the Lord out of a pure heart. 23But avoid foolish and ignorant disputes, knowing that they generate strife. 24And a servant of the Lord

2:3 [a]NU-Text reads *You must share.* **2:7** [a]NU-Text reads *the Lord will give you.* **2:19** [a]NU-Text and M-Text read *the Lord.*

THE MESSAGE

DOING YOUR BEST FOR GOD

1-7 2 So, my son, throw yourself into this work for Christ. Pass on what you heard from me—the whole congregation saying Amen!—to reliable leaders who are competent to teach others. When the going gets rough, take it on the chin with the rest of us, the way Jesus did. A soldier on duty doesn't get caught up in making deals at the marketplace. He concentrates on carrying out orders. An athlete who refuses to play by the rules will never get anywhere. It's the diligent farmer who gets the produce. Think it over. God will make it all plain.

8-13 Fix this picture firmly in your mind: Jesus, descended from the line of David, raised from the dead. It's what you've heard from me all along. It's what I'm sitting in jail for right now—but God's Word isn't in jail! That's why I stick it out here—so that everyone God calls will get in on the salvation of Christ in all its glory. This is a sure thing:

If we die with him, we'll live with him;
If we stick it out with him, we'll rule with
 him;
If we turn our backs on him, he'll turn
 his back on us;
If we give up on him, he does not give
 up—
for there's no way he can be false to
 himself.

14-18 Repeat these basic essentials over and over to God's people. Warn them before God against pious nitpicking, which chips away at the faith. It just wears everyone out. Concentrate on doing your best for God, work you won't be ashamed of, laying out the truth plain and simple. Stay clear of pious talk that is only talk. Words are not mere words, you know. If they're not backed by a godly life, they accumulate as poison in the soul. Hymenaeus and Philetus are examples, throwing believers off stride and missing the truth by a mile by saying the resurrection is over and done with.

19 Meanwhile, God's firm foundation is as firm as ever, these sentences engraved on the stones:

GOD KNOWS WHO BELONGS TO HIM.
SPURN EVIL, ALL YOU WHO NAME GOD AS GOD.

20-21 In a well-furnished kitchen there are not only crystal goblets and silver platters, but waste cans and compost buckets—some containers used to serve fine meals, others to take out the garbage. Become the kind of container God can use to present any and every kind of gift to his guests for their blessing.

22-26 Run away from infantile indulgence. Run after mature righteousness—faith, love, peace—joining those who are in honest and serious prayer before God. Refuse to get involved in inane discussions; they always end up in fights. God's servant must not be

NEW KING JAMES VERSION

must not quarrel but be gentle to all, able to
teach, patient, [25]in humility correcting those
who are in opposition, if God perhaps will grant
them repentance, so that they may know the
truth, [26]and *that* they may come to their senses
and escape the snare of the devil, having been
taken captive by him to *do* his will.

PERILOUS TIMES AND PERILOUS MEN

3 But know this, that in the last days perilous
times will come: [2]For men will be lovers of
themselves, lovers of money, boasters, proud,
blasphemers, disobedient to parents, unthank-
ful, unholy, [3]unloving, unforgiving, slanderers,
without self-control, brutal, despisers of good,
[4]traitors, headstrong, haughty, lovers of pleas-
ure rather than lovers of God, [5]having a form of
godliness but denying its power. And from such
people turn away! [6]For of this sort are those who
creep into households and make captives of
gullible women loaded down with sins, led away
by various lusts, [7]always learning and never
able to come to the knowledge of the truth.
[8]Now as Jannes and Jambres resisted Moses, so
do these also resist the truth: men of corrupt
minds, disapproved concerning the faith; [9]but
they will progress no further, for their folly will
be manifest to all, as theirs also was.

THE MAN OF GOD AND THE WORD OF GOD

[10]But you have carefully followed my doc-
trine, manner of life, purpose, faith, longsuffer-
ing, love, perseverance, [11]persecutions, afflic-
tions, which happened to me at Antioch, at
Iconium, at Lystra—what persecutions I en-
dured. And out of *them* all the Lord delivered
me. [12]Yes, and all who desire to live godly in
Christ Jesus will suffer persecution. [13]But evil
men and impostors will grow worse and worse,
deceiving and being deceived. [14]But you must
continue in the things which you have learned
and been assured of, knowing from whom you
have learned *them,* [15]and that from childhood
you have known the Holy Scriptures, which are
able to make you wise for salvation through
faith which is in Christ Jesus.

[16]All Scripture *is* given by inspiration of God,
and *is* profitable for doctrine, for reproof, for
correction, for instruction in righteousness,
[17]that the man of God may be complete, thor-
oughly equipped for every good work.

PREACH THE WORD

4 I charge *you* therefore before God and the
Lord Jesus Christ, who will judge the living
and the dead at[a] His appearing and His king-

4:1 [a]NU-Text omits *therefore* and reads *and by* for *at.*

THE MESSAGE

argumentative, but a gentle listener and a
teacher who keeps cool, working firmly but
patiently with those who refuse to obey. You
never know how or when God might sober
them up with a change of heart and a turn-
ing to the truth, enabling them to escape the
Devil's trap, where they are caught and held
captive, forced to run his errands.

DIFFICULT TIMES AHEAD

1-5 **3** Don't be naive. There are difficult times
ahead. As the end approaches, people are
going to be self-absorbed, money-hungry,
self-promoting, stuck-up, profane, contemp-
tuous of parents, crude, coarse, dog-eat-dog,
unbending, slanderers, impulsively wild,
savage, cynical, treacherous, ruthless,
bloated windbags, addicted to lust, and al-
lergic to God. They'll make a show of reli-
gion, but behind the scenes they're animals.
Stay clear of these people.

6-9 These are the kind of people who
smooth-talk themselves into the homes of
unstable and needy women and take advan-
tage of them; women who, depressed by
their sinfulness, take up with every new re-
ligious fad that calls itself "truth." They get
exploited every time and never really learn.
These men are like those old Egyptian
frauds Jannes and Jambres, who challenged
Moses. They were rejects from the faith,
twisted in their thinking, defying truth itself.
But nothing will come of these latest impos-
tors. Everyone will see through them, just as
people saw through that Egyptian hoax.

KEEP THE MESSAGE ALIVE

10-13 You've been a good apprentice to me, a part
of my teaching, my manner of life, direction,
faith, steadiness, love, patience, troubles,
sufferings—suffering along with me in all
the grief I had to put up with in Antioch, Ico-
nium, and Lystra. And you also well know
that God rescued me! Anyone who wants to
live all out for Christ is in for a lot of trou-
ble; there's no getting around it. Unscrupu-
lous con men will continue to exploit the
faith. They're as deceived as the people they
lead astray. As long as they are out there,
things can only get worse.

14-17 But don't let it faze you. Stick with what
you learned and believed, sure of the in-
tegrity of your teachers—why, you took in
the sacred Scriptures with your mother's
milk! There's nothing like the written Word
of God for showing you the way to salvation
through faith in Christ Jesus. Every part of
Scripture is God-breathed and useful one
way or another —showing us truth, expos-
ing our rebellion, correcting our mistakes,
training us to live God's way. Through the
Word we are put together and shaped up for
the tasks God has for us.

1-2 **4** I can't impress this on you too strongly.
God is looking over your shoulder. Christ
himself is the Judge, with the final say on
everyone, living and dead. He is about to
break into the open with his rule, so pro-

NEW KING JAMES VERSION

dom: 2Preach the word! Be ready in season *and*
out of season. Convince, rebuke, exhort, with all
longsuffering and teaching. 3For the time will
come when they will not endure sound doctrine,
but according to their own desires, *because* they
have itching ears, they will heap up for them-
selves teachers; 4and they will turn *their* ears
away from the truth, and be turned aside to fa-
bles. 5But you be watchful in all things, endure
afflictions, do the work of an evangelist, fulfill
your ministry.

PAUL'S VALEDICTORY

6For I am already being poured out as a
drink offering, and the time of my departure is
at hand. 7I have fought the good fight, I have fin-
ished the race, I have kept the faith. 8Finally,
there is laid up for me the crown of righteous-
ness, which the Lord, the righteous Judge, will
give to me on that Day, and not to me only but
also to all who have loved His appearing.

THE ABANDONED APOSTLE

9Be diligent to come to me quickly; 10for De-
mas has forsaken me, having loved this present
world, and has departed for Thessalonica—
Crescens for Galatia, Titus for Dalmatia. 11Only
Luke is with me. Get Mark and bring him with
you, for he is useful to me for ministry. 12And
Tychicus I have sent to Ephesus. 13Bring the
cloak that I left with Carpus at Troas when you
come—and the books, especially the parch-
ments.
14Alexander the coppersmith did me much
harm. May the Lord repay him according to his
works. 15You also must beware of him, for he
has greatly resisted our words.
16At my first defense no one stood with me,
but all forsook me. May it not be charged
against them.

THE LORD IS FAITHFUL

17But the Lord stood with me and strength-
ened me, so that the message might be preached
fully through me, and *that* all the Gentiles
might hear. Also I was delivered out of the
mouth of the lion. 18And the Lord will deliver me
from every evil work and preserve *me* for His
heavenly kingdom. To Him *be* glory forever and
ever. Amen!

COME BEFORE WINTER

19Greet Prisca and Aquila, and the household
of Onesiphorus. 20Erastus stayed in Corinth, but
Trophimus I have left in Miletus sick.
21Do your utmost to come before winter.
Eubulus greets you, as well as Pudens, Linus,
Claudia, and all the brethren.

FAREWELL

22The Lord Jesus Christ[a] be with your spirit.
Grace be with you. Amen.

4:22 [a]NU-Text omits *Jesus Christ.*

THE MESSAGE

claim the Message with intensity; keep on
your watch. Challenge, warn, and urge your
people. Don't ever quit. Just keep it simple.

3-5 You're going to find that there will be
times when people will have no stomach for
solid teaching, but will fill up on spiritual
junk food—catchy opinions that tickle their
fancy. They'll turn their backs on truth and
chase mirages. But *you*—keep your eye on
what you're doing; accept the hard times
along with the good; keep the Message
alive; do a thorough job as God's servant.

6-8 You take over. I'm about to die, my life an
offering on God's altar. This is the only race
worth running. I've run hard right to the fin-
ish, believed all the way. All that's left now
is the shouting—God's applause! Depend on
it, he's an honest judge. He'll do right not
only by me, but by everyone eager for his
coming.

9-13 Get here as fast as you can. Demas, chasing
fads, went off to Thessalonica and left me
here. Crescens is in Galatia province, Titus
in Dalmatia. Luke is the only one here with
me. Bring Mark with you; he'll be my right-
hand man since I'm sending Tychicus to
Ephesus. Bring the winter coat I left in Troas
with Carpus; also the books and parchment
notebooks.

14-15 Watch out for Alexander the copper-
smith. Fiercely opposed to our Message, he
caused no end of trouble. God will give him
what he's got coming.

16-18 At my preliminary hearing no one stood
by me. They all ran like scared rabbits. But
it doesn't matter—the Master stood by me
and helped me spread the Message loud and
clear to those who had never heard it. I was
snatched from the jaws of the lion! God's
looking after me, keeping me safe in the
kingdom of heaven. All praise to him, praise
forever! Oh, yes!

19-20 Say hello to Priscilla and Aquila; also, the
family of Onesiphorus. Erastus stayed be-
hind in Corinth. I had to leave Trophimus
sick in Miletus.

21 Try hard to get here before winter.
Eubulus, Pudens, Linus, Claudia, and all
your friends here send greetings.

22 God be with you. Grace be with you.

TITUS

New King James Version

Greeting

1 Paul, a bondservant of God and an apostle of Jesus Christ, according to the faith of God's elect and the acknowledgment of the truth which accords with godliness, 2in hope of eternal life which God, who cannot lie, promised before time began, 3but has in due time manifested His word through preaching, which was committed to me according to the commandment of God our Savior;

4To Titus, a true son in *our* common faith:

Grace, mercy, *and* peace from God the Father and the Lord Jesus Christ[a] our Savior.

Qualified Elders

5For this reason I left you in Crete, that you should set in order the things that are lacking, and appoint elders in every city as I commanded you— 6if a man is blameless, the husband of one wife, having faithful children not accused of dissipation or insubordination. 7For a bishop[a] must be blameless, as a steward of God, not self-willed, not quick-tempered, not given to wine, not violent, not greedy for money, 8but hospitable, a lover of what is good, sober-minded, just, holy, self-controlled, 9holding fast the faithful word as he has been taught, that he may be able, by sound doctrine, both to exhort and convict those who contradict.

The Elders' Task

10For there are many insubordinate, both idle talkers and deceivers, especially those of the circumcision, 11whose mouths must be stopped, who subvert whole households, teaching things which they ought not, for the sake of dishonest gain. 12One of them, a prophet of their own, said, "Cretans *are* always liars, evil beasts, lazy gluttons." 13This testimony is true. Therefore rebuke them sharply, that they may be sound in the faith, 14not giving heed to Jewish fables and commandments of men who turn from the truth. 15To the pure all things are pure, but to those who are defiled and unbelieving nothing is pure; but even their mind and conscience are defiled. 16They profess to know God, but in works they deny Him, being abominable, disobedient, and disqualified for every good work.

Qualities of a Sound Church

2 But as for you, speak the things which are proper for sound doctrine: 2that the older men be sober, reverent, temperate, sound in faith, in love, in patience; 3the older women likewise, that they be reverent in behavior, not slanderers, not given to much wine, teachers of good things— 4that they admonish the young women

1:4 [a]NU-Text reads *and Christ Jesus.* 1:7 [a]Literally *overseer*

The Message

1-4 **1** I, Paul, am God's slave and Christ's agent for promoting the faith among God's chosen people, getting out the accurate word on God and how to respond rightly to it. My aim is to raise hopes by pointing the way to life without end. This is the life God promised long ago—and he doesn't break promises! And then when the time was ripe, he went public with his truth. I've been entrusted to proclaim this Message by order of our Savior, God himself. Dear Titus, legitimate son in the faith: Receive everything God our Father and Jesus our Savior give you!

A Good Grip on the Message

5-9 I left you in charge in Crete so you could complete what I left half-done. Appoint leaders in every town according to my instructions. As you select them, ask, "Is this man well-thought-of? Is he committed to his wife? Are his children believers? Do they respect him and stay out of trouble?" It's important that a church leader, responsible for the affairs in God's house, be looked up to—not pushy, not short-tempered, not a drunk, not a bully, not money-hungry. He must welcome people, be helpful, wise, fair, reverent, have a good grip on himself, and have a good grip on the Message, knowing how to use the truth to either spur people on in knowledge or stop them in their tracks if they oppose it.

10-16 For there are a lot of rebels out there, full of loose, confusing, and deceiving talk. Those who were brought up religious and ought to know better are the worst. They've got to be shut up. They're disrupting entire families with their teaching, and all for the sake of a fast buck. One of their own prophets said it best:

> The Cretans are liars from the womb,
> barking dogs, lazy bellies.

He certainly spoke the truth. Get on them right away. Stop that diseased talk of Jewish make-believe and made-up rules so they can recover a robust faith. Everything is clean to the clean-minded; nothing is clean to dirty-minded unbelievers. They leave their dirty fingerprints on every thought and act. They say they know God, but their actions speak louder than their words. They're real creeps, disobedient good-for-nothings.

A God-Filled Life

1-6 **2** Your job is to speak out on the things that make for solid doctrine. Guide older men into lives of temperance, dignity, and wisdom, into healthy faith, love, and endurance. Guide older women into lives of reverence so they end up as neither gossips nor drunks, but models of goodness. By looking at them, the younger women will know how

NEW KING JAMES VERSION

to love their husbands, to love their children, 5to be discreet, chaste, homemakers, good, obedient to their own husbands, that the word of God may not be blasphemed.

6Likewise, exhort the young men to be sober-minded, 7in all things showing yourself *to be* a pattern of good works; in doctrine *showing* integrity, reverence, incorruptibility,[a] 8sound speech that cannot be condemned, that one who is an opponent may be ashamed, having nothing evil to say of you.[a]

9*Exhort* bondservants to be obedient to their own masters, to be well pleasing in all *things*, not answering back, 10not pilfering, but showing all good fidelity, that they may adorn the doctrine of God our Savior in all things.

TRAINED BY SAVING GRACE

11For the grace of God that brings salvation has appeared to all men, 12teaching us that, denying ungodliness and worldly lusts, we should live soberly, righteously, and godly in the present age, 13looking for the blessed hope and glorious appearing of our great God and Savior Jesus Christ, 14who gave Himself for us, that He might redeem us from every lawless deed and purify for Himself *His* own special people, zealous for good works.

15Speak these things, exhort, and rebuke with all authority. Let no one despise you.

GRACES OF THE HEIRS OF GRACE

3 Remind them to be subject to rulers and authorities, to obey, to be ready for every good work, 2to speak evil of no one, to be peaceable, gentle, showing all humility to all men. 3For we ourselves were also once foolish, disobedient, deceived, serving various lusts and pleasures, living in malice and envy, hateful and hating one another. 4But when the kindness and the love of God our Savior toward man appeared, 5not by works of righteousness which we have done, but according to His mercy He saved us, through the washing of regeneration and renewing of the Holy Spirit, 6whom He poured out on us abundantly through Jesus Christ our Savior, 7that having been justified by His grace we should become heirs according to the hope of eternal life.

8This is a faithful saying, and these things I want you to affirm constantly, that those who have believed in God should be careful to maintain good works. These things are good and profitable to men.

AVOID DISSENSION

9But avoid foolish disputes, genealogies, contentions, and strivings about the law; for they are unprofitable and useless. 10Reject a divisive man after the first and second admonition, 11knowing that such a person is warped and sinning, being self-condemned.

2:7 [a]NU-Text omits *incorruptibility.* 2:8 [a]NU-Text and M-Text read *us.*

THE MESSAGE

to love their husbands and children, be virtuous and pure, keep a good house, be good wives. We don't want anyone looking down on God's Message because of their behavior. Also, guide the young men to live disciplined lives.

7-8 But mostly, show them all this by doing it yourself, incorruptible in your teaching, your words solid and sane. Then anyone who is dead set against us, when he finds nothing weird or misguided, might eventually come around.

9-10 Guide slaves into being loyal workers, a bonus to their masters—no back talk, no petty thievery. Then their good character will shine through their actions, adding luster to the teaching of our Savior God.

11-14 God's readiness to give and forgive is now public. Salvation's available for everyone! We're being shown how to turn our backs on a godless, indulgent life, and how to take on a God-filled, God-honoring life. This new life is starting right now, and is whetting our appetites for the glorious day when our great God and Savior, Jesus Christ, appears. He offered himself as a sacrifice to free us from a dark, rebellious life into this good, pure life, making us a people he can be proud of, energetic in goodness.

15 Tell them all this. Build up their courage, and discipline them if they get out of line. You're in charge. Don't let anyone put you down.

HE PUT OUR LIVES TOGETHER

1-2 3 Remind the people to respect the government and be law-abiding, always ready to lend a helping hand. No insults, no fights. God's people should be bighearted and courteous.

3-8 It wasn't so long ago that we ourselves were stupid and stubborn, dupes of sin, ordered every which way by our glands, going around with a chip on our shoulder, hated and hating back. But when God, our kind and loving Savior God, stepped in, he saved us from all that. It was all his doing; we had nothing to do with it. He gave us a good bath, and we came out of it new people, washed inside and out by the Holy Spirit. Our Savior Jesus poured out new life so generously. God's gift has restored our relationship with him and given us back our lives. And there's more life to come—an eternity of life! You can count on this.

8-11 I want you to put your foot down. Take a firm stand on these matters so that those who have put their trust in God will concentrate on the essentials that are good for everyone. Stay away from mindless, pointless quarreling over genealogies and fine print in the law code. That gets you nowhere. Warn a quarrelsome person once or twice, but then be done with him. It's obvious that such a person is out of line, rebellious against God. By persisting in divisiveness he cuts himself off.

NEW KING JAMES VERSION

FINAL MESSAGES

[12]When I send Artemas to you, or Tychicus,
be diligent to come to me at Nicopolis, for I have
decided to spend the winter there. [13]Send Zenas
the lawyer and Apollos on their journey with
haste, that they may lack nothing. [14]And let our
people also learn to maintain good works, to
meet urgent needs, that they may not be unfruitful.

FAREWELL

[15]All who *are* with me greet you. Greet those
who love us in the faith.

Grace *be* with you all. Amen.

THE MESSAGE

12-13 As soon as I send either Artemas or Tychicus to you, come immediately and meet me in Nicopolis. I've decided to spend the winter there. Give Zenas the lawyer and Apollos a hearty send-off. Take good care of them.

14 Our people have to learn to be diligent in their work so that all necessities are met (especially among the needy) and they don't end up with nothing to show for their lives.

15 All here want to be remembered to you. Say hello to our friends in the faith. Grace to all of you.

PHILEMON

New King James Version

Greeting

Paul, a prisoner of Christ Jesus, and Timothy *our* brother,

To Philemon our beloved *friend* and fellow laborer, [2]to the beloved[a] Apphia, Archippus our fellow soldier, and to the church in your house:

[3]Grace to you and peace from God our Father and the Lord Jesus Christ.

Philemon's Love and Faith

[4]I thank my God, making mention of you always in my prayers, [5]hearing of your love and faith which you have toward the Lord Jesus and toward all the saints, [6]that the sharing of your faith may become effective by the acknowledgment of every good thing which is in you[a] in Christ Jesus. [7]For we have[a] great joy[b] and consolation in your love, because the hearts of the saints have been refreshed by you, brother.

The Plea for Onesimus

[8]Therefore, though I might be very bold in Christ to command you what is fitting, [9]*yet* for love's sake I rather appeal *to you*—being such a one as Paul, the aged, and now also a prisoner of Jesus Christ— [10]I appeal to you for my son Onesimus, whom I have begotten *while* in my chains, [11]who once was unprofitable to you, but now is profitable to you and to me.

[12]I am sending him back.[a] You therefore receive him, that is, my own heart, [13]whom I wished to keep with me, that on your behalf he might minister to me in my chains for the gospel. [14]But without your consent I wanted to do nothing, that your good deed might not be by compulsion, as it were, but voluntary.

[15]For perhaps he departed for a while for this *purpose*, that you might receive him forever, [16]no longer as a slave but more than a slave—a beloved brother, especially to me but how much more to you, both in the flesh and in the Lord.

Philemon's Obedience Encouraged

[17]If then you count me as a partner, receive him as *you would* me. [18]But if he has wronged you or owes anything, put that on my account. [19]I, Paul, am writing with my own hand. I will repay—not to mention to you that you owe me even your own self besides. [20]Yes, brother, let me have joy from you in the Lord; refresh my heart in the Lord.

[21]Having confidence in your obedience, I write to you, knowing that you will do even more than I say. [22]But, meanwhile, also prepare a guest room for me, for I trust that through your prayers I shall be granted to you.

Farewell

[23]Epaphras, my fellow prisoner in Christ Jesus, greets you, [24]*as do* Mark, Aristarchus, Demas, Luke, my fellow laborers.

[25]The grace of our Lord Jesus Christ *be* with your spirit. Amen.

2 [a]NU-Text reads *to our sister Apphia.* **6** [a]NU-Text and M-Text read *us.* **7** [a]NU-Text reads *had.* [b]M-Text reads *thanksgiving.* **12** [a]NU-Text reads *back to you in person, that is, my own heart.*

The Message

1-3 I, Paul, am a prisoner for the sake of Christ,
here with my brother Timothy. I write this
letter to you, Philemon, my good friend and
companion in this work—also to our sister
Apphia, to Archippus, a real trooper, and to
the church that meets in your house. God's
best to you! Christ's blessings on you!

4-7 Every time your name comes up in my
prayers, I say, "Oh, thank you, God!" I keep
hearing of the love and faith you have for
the Master Jesus, which brims over to other
believers. And I keep praying that this faith
we hold in common keeps showing up in the
good things we do, and that people recognize Christ in all of it. Friend, you have no
idea how good your love makes me feel,
doubly so when I see your hospitality to fellow believers.

To Call the Slave Your Friend

8-9 In line with all this I have a favor to ask of
you. As Christ's ambassador and now a
prisoner for him, I wouldn't hesitate to command this if I thought it necessary, but I'd
rather make it a personal request.

10-14 While here in jail, I've fathered a child, so
to speak. And here he is, hand-carrying this
letter—Onesimus! He was useless to you before; now he's useful to both of us. I'm sending him back to you, but it feels like I'm cutting off my right arm in doing so. I wanted
in the worst way to keep him here as your
stand-in to help out while I'm in jail for the
Message. But I didn't want to do anything
behind your back, make you do a good deed
that you hadn't willingly agreed to.

15-16 Maybe it's all for the best that you lost
him for a while. You're getting him back
now for good—and no mere slave this time,
but a true Christian brother! That's what he
was to me—he'll be even more than that to
you.

17-20 So if you still consider me a comrade-in-arms, welcome him back as you would me.
If he damaged anything or owes you anything, chalk it up to my account. This is my
personal signature—Paul—and I stand behind it. (I don't need to remind you, do I, that
you owe your very life to me?) Do me this
big favor, friend. You'll be doing it for Christ,
but it will also do my heart good.

21-22 I know you well enough to know you will.
You'll probably go far beyond what I've
written. And by the way, get a room ready
for me. Because of your prayers, I fully expect to be your guest again.

23-25 Epaphras, my cellmate in the cause of
Christ, says hello. Also my coworkers Mark,
Aristarchus, Demas, and Luke. All the best
to you from the Master, Jesus Christ!

HEBREWS

NEW KING JAMES VERSION

GOD'S SUPREME REVELATION

1 God, who at various times and in various
ways spoke in time past to the fathers by the
prophets, 2 has in these last days spoken to us by
His Son, whom He has appointed heir of all
things, through whom also He made the worlds;
3 who being the brightness of *His* glory and the
express image of His person, and upholding all
things by the word of His power, when He had
by Himself[a] purged our[b] sins, sat down at the
right hand of the Majesty on high, 4 having be-
come so much better than the angels, as He has
by inheritance obtained a more excellent name
than they.

THE SON EXALTED ABOVE ANGELS

5 For to which of the angels did He ever say:

"You are My Son,
Today I have begotten You"?[a]

And again:

"I will be to Him a Father,
And He shall be to Me a Son"?[b]

6 But when He again brings the firstborn into
the world, He says:

"Let all the angels of God worship Him."[a]

7 And of the angels He says:

"Who makes His angels spirits
And His ministers a flame of fire."[a]

8 But to the Son *He says:*

"Your throne, O God, is forever and ever;
A scepter of righteousness is the scepter of Your kingdom.
9 *You have loved righteousness and hated lawlessness;*
Therefore God, Your God, has anointed You
With the oil of gladness more than Your companions."[a]

10 And:

"You, LORD, in the beginning laid the foundation of the earth,
And the heavens are the work of Your hands.
11 *They will perish, but You remain;*
And they will all grow old like a garment;
12 *Like a cloak You will fold them up,*
And they will be changed.
But You are the same,
And Your years will not fail."[a]

1:3 [a]NU-Text omits *by Himself.* [b]NU-Text omits *our.* **1:5** [a]Psalm 2:7 [b]2 Samuel 7:14 **1:6** [a]Deuteronomy 32:43 (Septuagint, Dead Sea Scrolls); Psalm 97:7 **1:7** [a]Psalm 104:4 **1:9** [a]Psalm 45:6, 7 **1:12** [a]Psalm 102:25–27

THE MESSAGE

1-3 1 Going through a long line of prophets, God has been adressing our ancestors in different ways for centuries. Recently he spoke to us directly through his Son. By his Son, God created the world in the beginning, and it will all belong to the Son at the end. This Son perfectly mirrors God, and is stamped with God's nature. He holds everything together by what he says—powerful words!

THE SON IS HIGHER THAN ANGELS

3-6 After he finished the sacrifice for sins, the Son took his honored place high in the heavens right alongside God, far higher than any angel in rank and rule. Did God ever say to an angel, "You're my Son; today I celebrate you" or "I'm his Father, he's my Son"? When he presents his honored Son to the world, he says, "All angels must worship him."

7 Regarding angels he says,

The messengers are winds,
the servants are tongues of fire.

8-9 But he says to the Son,
You're God, and on the throne for good;
your rule makes everything right.
You love it when things are right;
you hate it when things are wrong.
That is why God, your God,
poured fragrant oil on your head,
Marking you out as king,
far above your dear companions.

10-12 And again to the Son,
You, Master, started it all, laid earth's foundations,
then crafted the stars in the sky.
Earth and sky will wear out, but not you;
they become threadbare like an old coat;
You'll fold them up like a worn-out cloak,
and lay them away on the shelf.
But you'll stay the same, year after year;
you'll never fade, you'll never wear out.

New King James Version

13 But to which of the angels has He ever said:

"Sit at My right hand,
Till I make Your enemies Your footstool"?[a]

14 Are they not all ministering spirits sent forth to minister for those who will inherit salvation?

Do Not Neglect Salvation

2 Therefore we must give the more earnest heed to the things we have heard, lest we drift away. 2 For if the word spoken through angels proved steadfast, and every transgression and disobedience received a just reward, 3 how shall we escape if we neglect so great a salvation, which at the first began to be spoken by the Lord, and was confirmed to us by those who heard *Him,* 4 God also bearing witness both with signs and wonders, with various miracles, and gifts of the Holy Spirit, according to His own will?

The Son Made Lower than Angels

5 For He has not put the world to come, of which we speak, in subjection to angels. 6 But one testified in a certain place, saying:

"What is man that You are mindful of him,
Or the son of man that You take care of him?
7 *You have made him a little lower than the angels;*
You have crowned him with glory and honor,[a]
And set him over the works of Your hands.
8 *You have put all things in subjection under his feet."*[a]

For in that He put all in subjection under him, He left nothing *that is* not put under him. But now we do not yet see all things put under him. 9 But we see Jesus, who was made a little lower than the angels, for the suffering of death crowned with glory and honor, that He, by the grace of God, might taste death for everyone.

Bringing Many Sons to Glory

10 For it was fitting for Him, for whom *are* all things and by whom *are* all things, in bringing many sons to glory, to make the captain of their salvation perfect through sufferings. 11 For both He who sanctifies and those who are being sanctified *are* all of one, for which reason He is not ashamed to call them brethren, 12 saying:

"I will declare Your name to My brethren;
In the midst of the assembly I will sing praise to You."[a]

13 And again:

"I will put My trust in Him."[a]

1:13 [a]Psalm 110:1 **2:7** [a]NU-Text and M-Text omit the rest of verse 7. **2:8** [a]Psalm 8:4–6 **2:12** [a]Psalm 22:22 **2:13** [a]2 Samuel 22:3; Isaiah 8:17

The Message

13 And did he ever say anything like this to an angel?

Sit alongside me here on my throne
Until I make your enemies a stool for your feet.

14 Isn't it obvious that all angels are sent to help out with those lined up to receive salvation?

1-4 2 It's crucial that we keep a firm grip on what we've heard so that we don't drift off. If the old message delivered by the angels was valid and nobody got away with anything, do you think we can risk neglecting this latest message, this magnificent salvation? First of all, it was delivered in person by the Master, then accurately passed on to us by those who heard it from him. All the while God was validating it with gifts through the Holy Spirit, all sorts of signs and miracles, as he saw fit.

The Salvation Pioneer

5-9 God didn't put angels in charge of this business of salvation that we're dealing with here. It says in Scripture,

What is man and woman that you bother with them;
why take a second look their way?
You made them not quite as high as angels,
bright with Eden's dawn light;
Then you put them in charge
of your entire handcrafted world.

When God put them in charge of everything, nothing was excluded. But we don't see it yet, don't see everything under human jurisdiction. What we do see is Jesus, made "not quite as high as angels," and then, through the experience of death, crowned so much higher than any angel, with a glory "bright with Eden's dawn light." In that death, by God's grace, he fully experienced death in every person's place.

10-13 It makes good sense that the God who got everything started and keeps everything going now completes the work by making the Salvation Pioneer perfect through suffering as he leads all these people to glory. Since the One who saves and those who are saved have a common origin, Jesus doesn't hesitate to treat them as family, saying,

I'll tell my good friends, my brothers and sisters, all I know about you;
I'll join them in worship and praise to you.

Again, he puts himself in the same family circle when he says,
Even *I* live by placing my trust in God.

New King James Version

And again:

> *"Here am I and the children whom God has given Me."* [b]

14Inasmuch then as the children have partaken of flesh and blood, He Himself likewise shared in the same, that through death He might destroy him who had the power of death, that is, the devil, 15and release those who through fear of death were all their lifetime subject to bondage. 16For indeed He does not give aid to angels, but He does give aid to the seed of Abraham. 17Therefore, in all things He had to be made like *His* brethren, that He might be a merciful and faithful High Priest in things *pertaining* to God, to make propitiation for the sins of the people. 18For in that He Himself has suffered, being tempted, He is able to aid those who are tempted.

The Son Was Faithful

3 Therefore, holy brethren, partakers of the heavenly calling, consider the Apostle and High Priest of our confession, Christ Jesus, 2who was faithful to Him who appointed Him, as Moses also *was faithful* in all His house. 3For this One has been counted worthy of more glory than Moses, inasmuch as He who built the house has more honor than the house. 4For every house is built by someone, but He who built all things *is* God. 5And Moses indeed *was* faithful in all His house as a servant, for a testimony of those things which would be spoken *afterward*, 6but Christ as a Son over His own house, whose house we are if we hold fast the confidence and the rejoicing of the hope firm to the end.[a]

Be Faithful

7Therefore, as the Holy Spirit says:

"Today, if you will hear His voice,
8Do not harden your hearts as in the rebellion,
In the day of trial in the wilderness,
9Where your fathers tested Me, tried Me,
And saw My works forty years.
10Therefore I was angry with that generation,
And said, 'They always go astray in their heart,
And they have not known My ways.'
11So I swore in My wrath,
'They shall not enter My rest.' " [a]

12Beware, brethren, lest there be in any of you an evil heart of unbelief in departing from the living God; 13but exhort one another daily, while it is called *"Today,"* lest any of you be hardened through the deceitfulness of sin. 14For we have become partakers of Christ if we hold the beginning of our confidence steadfast to the end, 15while it is said:

"Today, if you will hear His voice,

2:13 [b]Isaiah 8:18 **3:6** [a]NU-Text omits *firm to the end.* **3:11** [a]Psalm 95:7–11

The Message

And yet again,
I'm here with the children God gave me.

14-15 Since the children are made of flesh and blood, it's logical that the Savior took on flesh and blood in order to rescue them by his death. By embracing death, taking it into himself, he destroyed the Devil's hold on death and freed all who cower through life, scared to death of death.

16-18 It's obvious, of course, that he didn't go to all this trouble for angels. It was for people like us, children of Abraham. That's why he had to enter into every detail of human life. Then, when he came before God as high priest to get rid of the people's sins, he would have already experienced it all himself—all the pain, all the testing—and would be able to help where help was needed.

The Centerpiece of All We Believe

1-6 3 So, my dear Christian friends, companions in following this call to the heights, take a good hard look at Jesus. He's the centerpiece of everything we believe, faithful in everything God gave him to do. Moses was also faithful, but Jesus gets far more honor. A builder is more valuable than a building any day. Every house has a builder, but the Builder behind them all is God. Moses did a good job in God's house, but it was all servant work, getting things ready for what was to come. Christ as Son is in charge of the house.

6-11 Now, if we can only keep a firm grip on this bold confidence, we're the house! That's why the Holy Spirit says,

Today, please listen;
don't turn a deaf ear as in "the bitter uprising,"
that time of wilderness testing!
Even though they watched me at work for forty years,
your ancestors refused to let me do it my way;
over and over they tried my patience.
And I was provoked, oh, so provoked!
I said, "They'll never keep their minds on God;
they refuse to walk down my road."
Exasperated, I vowed,
"They'll never get where they're going,
never be able to sit down and rest."

12-14 So watch your step, friends. Make sure there's no evil unbelief lying around that will trip you up and throw you off course, diverting you from the living God. For as long as it's still God's Today, keep each other on your toes so sin doesn't slow down your reflexes. If we can only keep our grip on the sure thing we started out with, we're in this with Christ for the long haul.

These words keep ringing in our ears:

Today, please listen;

NEW KING JAMES VERSION

Do not harden your hearts as in the
rebellion." [a]

FAILURE OF THE WILDERNESS WANDERERS

16For who, having heard, rebelled? Indeed, *was it* not all who came out of Egypt, *led* by Moses? 17Now with whom was He angry forty years? *Was it* not with those who sinned, whose corpses fell in the wilderness? 18And to whom did He swear that they would not enter His rest, but to those who did not obey? 19So we see that they could not enter in because of unbelief.

THE PROMISE OF REST

4 Therefore, since a promise remains of entering His rest, let us fear lest any of you seem to have come short of it. 2For indeed the gospel was preached to us as well as to them; but the word which they heard did not profit them,[a] not being mixed with faith in those who heard *it.* 3For we who have believed do enter that rest, as He has said:

"So I swore in My wrath,
'They shall not enter My rest,' " [a]

although the works were finished from the foundation of the world. 4For He has spoken in a certain place of the seventh *day* in this way: *"And God rested on the seventh day from all His works";*[a] 5and again in this *place: "They shall not enter My rest."* [a]

6Since therefore it remains that some *must* enter it, and those to whom it was first preached did not enter because of disobedience, 7again He designates a certain day, saying in David, *"Today,"* after such a long time, as it has been said:

"Today, if you will hear His voice,
Do not harden your hearts." [a]

8For if Joshua had given them rest, then He would not afterward have spoken of another day. 9There remains therefore a rest for the people of God. 10For he who has entered His rest has himself also ceased from his works as God *did* from His.

THE WORD DISCOVERS OUR CONDITION

11Let us therefore be diligent to enter that rest, lest anyone fall according to the same example of disobedience. 12For the word of God *is* living and powerful, and sharper than any two-edged sword, piercing even to the division of soul and spirit, and of joints and marrow, and is a discerner of the thoughts and intents of the heart. 13And there is no creature hidden from His sight, but all things *are* naked and open to the eyes of Him to whom we *must give* account.

OUR COMPASSIONATE HIGH PRIEST

14Seeing then that we have a great High Priest who has passed through the heavens,

3:15 [a]Psalm 95:7, 8 **4:2** [a]NU-Text and M-Text read *profit them,* since they were not united by faith with those who heeded it. **4:3** [a]Psalm 95:11 **4:4** [a]Genesis 2:2 **4:5** [a]Psalm 95:11 **4:7** [a]Psalm 95:7, 8

THE MESSAGE

don't turn a deaf ear as in the bitter
uprising.

15-19 For who were the people who turned a deaf ear? Weren't they the very ones Moses led out of Egypt? And who was God provoked with for forty years? Wasn't it those who turned a deaf ear and ended up corpses in the wilderness? And when he swore that they'd never get where they were going, wasn't he talking to the ones who turned a deaf ear? They never got there because they never listened, never believed.

WHEN THE PROMISES ARE MIXED WITH FAITH

1-3 4 For as long, then, as that promise of resting in him pulls us on to God's goal for us, we need to be careful that we're not disqualified. We received the same promises as those people in the wilderness, but the promises didn't do them a bit of good because they didn't receive the promises with faith. If we believe, though, we'll experience that state of resting. But not if we don't have faith. Remember that God said,

Exasperated, I vowed,
"They'll never get where they're
going,
never be able to sit down and rest."

3-7 God made that vow, even though he'd finished *his* part before the foundation of the world. Somewhere it's written, "God rested the seventh day, having completed his work," but in this other text he says, "They'll never be able to sit down and rest." So this promise has not yet been fulfilled. Those earlier ones never did get to the place of rest because they were disobedient. God keeps renewing the promise and setting the date as *today,* just as he did in David's psalm, centuries later than the original invitation:

Today, please listen,
don't turn a deaf ear . . .

8-11 And so this is still a live promise. It wasn't canceled at the time of Joshua; otherwise, God wouldn't keep renewing the appointment for "today." The promise of "arrival" and "rest" is still there for God's people. God himself is at rest. And at the end of the journey we'll surely rest with God. So let's keep at it and eventually arrive at the place of rest, not drop out through some sort of disobedience.

12-13 God means what he says. What he says goes. His powerful Word is sharp as a surgeon's scalpel, cutting through everything, whether doubt or defense, laying us open to listen and obey. Nothing and no one is impervious to God's Word. We can't get away from it—no matter what.

THE HIGH PRIEST WHO CRIED OUT IN PAIN

14-16 Now that we know what we have—Jesus, this great High Priest with ready access to

NEW KING JAMES VERSION

Jesus the Son of God, let us hold fast *our* confession. [15]For we do not have a High Priest who cannot sympathize with our weaknesses, but was in all *points* tempted as *we are, yet* without sin. [16]Let us therefore come boldly to the throne of grace, that we may obtain mercy and find grace to help in time of need.

QUALIFICATIONS FOR HIGH PRIESTHOOD

5 For every high priest taken from among men is appointed for men in things *pertaining* to God, that he may offer both gifts and sacrifices for sins. [2]He can have compassion on those who are ignorant and going astray, since he himself is also subject to weakness. [3]Because of this he is required as for the people, so also for himself, to offer *sacrifices* for sins. [4]And no man takes this honor to himself, but he who is called by God, just as Aaron *was.*

A PRIEST FOREVER

[5]So also Christ did not glorify Himself to become High Priest, but *it was* He who said to Him:

"You are My Son,
Today I have begotten You."[a]

[6]As *He* also says in another *place:*

"You are a priest forever
According to the order of Melchizedek";[a]

[7]who, in the days of His flesh, when He had offered up prayers and supplications, with vehement cries and tears to Him who was able to save Him from death, and was heard because of His godly fear, [8]though He was a Son, *yet* He learned obedience by the things which He suffered. [9]And having been perfected, He became the author of eternal salvation to all who obey Him, [10]called by God as High Priest *"according to the order of Melchizedek,"* [11]of whom we have much to say, and hard to explain, since you have become dull of hearing.

SPIRITUAL IMMATURITY

[12]For though by this time you ought to be teachers, you need *someone* to teach you again the first principles of the oracles of God; and you have come to need milk and not solid food. [13]For everyone who partakes *only* of milk *is* unskilled in the word of righteousness, for he is a babe. [14]But solid food belongs to those who are of full age, *that is,* those who by reason of use have their senses exercised to discern both good and evil.

THE PERIL OF NOT PROGRESSING

6 Therefore, leaving the discussion of the elementary *principles* of Christ, let us go on to perfection, not laying again the foundation of repentance from dead works and of faith toward God, [2]of the doctrine of baptisms, of laying on of hands, of resurrection of the dead, and of eternal judgment. [3]And this we will[a] do if God permits.

5:5 [a]Psalm 2:7 5:6 [a]Psalm 110:4 6:3 [a]M-Text reads *let us do.*

THE MESSAGE

God—let's not let it slip through our fingers. We don't have a priest who is out of touch with our reality. He's been through weakness and testing, experienced it all—all but the sin. So let's walk right up to him and get what he is so ready to give. Take the mercy, accept the help.

1-3 **5** Every high priest selected to represent men and women before God and offer sacrifices for their sins should be able to deal gently with their failings, since he knows what it's like from his own experience. But that also means that he has to offer sacrifices for his own sins as well as the peoples'.

4-6 No one elects himself to this honored position. He's called to it by God, as Aaron was. Neither did Christ presume to set himself up as high priest, but was set apart by the One who said to him, "You're my Son; today I celebrate you!" In another place God declares, "You're a priest forever in the royal order of Melchizedek."

7-10 While he lived on earth, anticipating death, Jesus cried out in pain and wept in sorrow as he offered up priestly prayers to God. Because he honored God, God answered him. Though he was God's Son, he learned trusting-obedience by what he suffered, just as we do. Then, having arrived at the full stature of his maturity and having been announced by God as high priest in the order of Melchizedek, he became the source of eternal salvation to all who believingly obey him.

RE-CRUCIFYING JESUS

11-14 I have a lot more to say about this, but it is hard to get it across to you since you've picked up this bad habit of not listening. By this time you ought to be teachers yourselves, yet here I find you need someone to sit down with you and go over the basics on God again, starting from square one—baby's milk, when you should have been on solid food long ago! Milk is for beginners, inexperienced in God's ways; solid food is for the mature, who have some practice in telling right from wrong.

1-3 **6** So come on, let's leave the preschool fingerpainting exercises on Christ and get on with the grand work of art. Grow up in Christ. The basic foundational truths are in place: turning your back on "salvation by self-help" and turning in trust toward God; baptismal instructions; laying on of hands; resurrection of the dead; eternal judgment. God helping us, we'll stay true to all that. But there's so much more. Let's get on with it!

NEW KING JAMES VERSION

4For *it is* impossible for those who were once enlightened, and have tasted the heavenly gift, and have become partakers of the Holy Spirit, 5and have tasted the good word of God and the powers of the age to come, 6if they fall away,[a] to renew them again to repentance, since they crucify again for themselves the Son of God, and put *Him* to an open shame.

7For the earth which drinks in the rain that often comes upon it, and bears herbs useful for those by whom it is cultivated, receives blessing from God; 8but if it bears thorns and briers, *it is* rejected and near to being cursed, whose end *is* to be burned.

A Better Estimate

9But, beloved, we are confident of better things concerning you, yes, things that accompany salvation, though we speak in this manner. 10For God *is* not unjust to forget your work and labor of[a] love which you have shown toward His name, *in that* you have ministered to the saints, and do minister. 11And we desire that each one of you show the same diligence to the full assurance of hope until the end, 12that you do not become sluggish, but imitate those who through faith and patience inherit the promises.

God's Infallible Purpose in Christ

13For when God made a promise to Abraham, because He could swear by no one greater, He swore by Himself, 14saying, *"Surely blessing I will bless you, and multiplying I will multiply you."* [a] 15And so, after he had patiently endured, he obtained the promise. 16For men indeed swear by the greater, and an oath for confirmation *is* for them an end of all dispute. 17Thus God, determining to show more abundantly to the heirs of promise the immutability of His counsel, confirmed *it* by an oath, 18that by two immutable things, in which it *is* impossible for God to lie, we might[a] have strong consolation, who have fled for refuge to lay hold of the hope set before *us*.

19This *hope* we have as an anchor of the soul, both sure and steadfast, and which enters the *Presence* behind the veil, 20where the forerunner has entered for us, *even* Jesus, having become High Priest forever according to the order of Melchizedek.

The King of Righteousness

7 For this Melchizedek, king of Salem, priest of the Most High God, who met Abraham returning from the slaughter of the kings and blessed him, 2to whom also Abraham gave a tenth part of all, first being translated "king of righteousness," and then also king of Salem, meaning "king of peace," 3without father, without mother, without genealogy, having neither beginning of days nor end of life, but made like the Son of God, remains a priest continually.

6:6 [a]Or *and have fallen away* **6:10** [a]NU-Text omits *labor of.*
6:14 [a]Genesis 22:17 **6:18** [a]M-Text omits *might.*

THE MESSAGE

4-8 Once people have seen the light, gotten a taste of heaven and been part of the work of the Holy Spirit, once they've personally experienced the sheer goodness of God's Word and the powers breaking in on us—if then they turn their backs on it, washing their hands of the whole thing, well, they can't start over as if nothing happened. That's impossible. Why, they've re-crucified Jesus! They've repudiated him in public! Parched ground that soaks up the rain and then produces an abundance of carrots and corn for its gardener gets God's "Well done!" But if it produces weeds and thistles, it's more likely to get cussed out. Fields like that are burned, not harvested.

9-12 I'm sure that won't happen to you, friends. I have better things in mind for you—salvation things! God doesn't miss anything. He knows perfectly well all the love you've shown him by helping needy Christians, and that you keep at it. And now I want each of you to extend that same intensity toward a full-bodied hope, and keep at it till the finish. Don't drag your feet. Be like those who stay the course with committed faith and then get everything promised to them.

God Gave His Word

13-18 When God made his promise to Abraham, he backed it to the hilt, putting his own reputation on the line. He said, "I promise that I'll bless you with everything I have—bless and bless and bless!" Abraham stuck it out and got everything that had been promised to him. When people make promises, they guarantee them by appeal to some authority above them so that if there is any question that they'll make good on the promise, the authority will back them up. When God wanted to guarantee his promises, he gave his word, a rock-solid guarantee—God *can't* break his word. And because his word cannot change, the promise is likewise unchangeable.

18-20 We who have run for our very lives to God have every reason to grab the promised hope with both hands and never let go. It's an unbreakable spiritual lifeline, reaching past all appearances right to the very presence of God where Jesus, running on ahead of us, has taken up his permanent post as high priest for us, in the order of Melchizedek.

Melchizedek, Priest of God

1-3 7 Melchizedek was king of Salem and priest of the Highest God. He met Abraham, who was returning from "the royal massacre," and gave him his blessing. Abraham in turn gave him a tenth of the spoils. "Melchizedek" means "King of Righteousness." "Salem" means "Peace." So, he is also "King of Peace." Melchizedek towers out of the past—without record of family ties, no account of beginning or end. In this way he is like the Son of God, one huge priestly presence dominating the landscape always.

NEW KING JAMES VERSION

4 Now consider how great this man *was,* to whom even the patriarch Abraham gave a tenth of the spoils. 5 And indeed those who are of the sons of Levi, who receive the priesthood, have a commandment to receive tithes from the people according to the law, that is, from their brethren, though they have come from the loins of Abraham; 6 but he whose genealogy is not derived from them received tithes from Abraham and blessed him who had the promises. 7 Now beyond all contradiction the lesser is blessed by the better. 8 Here mortal men receive tithes, but there he *receives them,* of whom it is witnessed that he lives. 9 Even Levi, who receives tithes, paid tithes through Abraham, so to speak, 10 for he was still in the loins of his father when Melchizedek met him.

NEED FOR A NEW PRIESTHOOD

11 Therefore, if perfection were through the Levitical priesthood (for under it the people received the law), what further need *was there* that another priest should rise according to the order of Melchizedek, and not be called according to the order of Aaron? 12 For the priesthood being changed, of necessity there is also a change of the law. 13 For He of whom these things are spoken belongs to another tribe, from which no man has officiated at the altar.

14 For *it is* evident that our Lord arose from Judah, of which tribe Moses spoke nothing concerning priesthood.[a] 15 And it is yet far more evident if, in the likeness of Melchizedek, there arises another priest 16 who has come, not according to the law of a fleshly commandment, but according to the power of an endless life. 17 For He testifies:[a]

"You are a priest forever
According to the order of Melchizedek."[b]

18 For on the one hand there is an annulling of the former commandment because of its weakness and unprofitableness, 19 for the law made nothing perfect; on the other hand, *there is the* bringing in of a better hope, through which we draw near to God.

GREATNESS OF THE NEW PRIEST

20 And inasmuch as *He was* not *made priest* without an oath 21 (for they have become priests without an oath, but He with an oath by Him who said to Him:

"The LORD has sworn
And will not relent,
'You are a priest forever[a]
According to the order of Melchizedek' "),[b]

22 by so much more Jesus has become a surety of a better covenant.

23 Also there were many priests, because they were prevented by death from continuing. 24 But He, because He continues forever, has an unchangeable priesthood. 25 Therefore He is also able to save to the uttermost those who come to God through Him, since He always lives to make intercession for them.

7:14 [a]NU-Text reads *priests.* **7:17** [a]NU-Text reads *it is testified.* [b]Psalm 110:4 **7:21** [a]NU-Text ends the quotation here. [b]Psalm 110:4

THE MESSAGE

4-7 You realize just how great Melchizedek is when you see that Father Abraham gave him a tenth of the captured treasure. Priests descended from Levi are commanded by law to collect tithes from the people, even though they are all more or less equals, priests and people, having a common father in Abraham. But this man, a complete outsider, collected tithes from Abraham and blessed him, the one to whom the promises had been given. In acts of blessing, the lesser is blessed by the greater.

8-10 Or look at it this way: We pay our tithes to priests who die, but Abraham paid tithes to a priest who, the Scripture says, "lives." Ultimately you could even say that since Levi descended from Abraham, who paid tithes to Melchizedek, when we pay tithes to the priestly tribe of Levi they end up with Melchizedek.

A PERMANENT PRIESTHOOD

11-14 If the priesthood of Levi and Aaron, which provided the framework for the giving of the law, could really make people perfect, there wouldn't have been need for a new priesthood like that of Melchizedek. But since it didn't get the job done, there was a change of priesthood, which brought with it a radical new kind of law. There is no way of understanding this in terms of the old Levitical priesthood, which is why there is nothing in Jesus' family tree connecting him with that priestly line.

15-19 But the Melchizedek story provides a perfect analogy: Jesus, a priest like Melchizedek, not by genealogical descent but by the sheer force of resurrection life—he lives!—"priest forever in the royal order of Melchizedek." The former way of doing things, a system of commandments that never worked out the way it was supposed to, was set aside; the law brought nothing to maturity. Another way—Jesus!—a way that *does* work, that brings us right into the presence of God, is put in its place.

20-22 The old priesthood of Aaron perpetuated itself automatically, father to son, without explicit confirmation by God. But then God intervened and called this new, permanent priesthood into being with an added promise:

God gave his word;
he won't take it back:
"You're the permanent priest."

This makes Jesus the guarantee of a far better way between us and God—one that really works! A new covenant.

23-25 Earlier there were a lot of priests, for they died and had to be replaced. But Jesus' priesthood is permanent. He's there from now to eternity to save everyone who comes to God through him, always on the job to speak up for them.

New King James Version

[26]For such a High Priest was fitting for us, *who is* holy, harmless, undefiled, separate from sinners, and has become higher than the heavens; [27]who does not need daily, as those high priests, to offer up sacrifices, first for His own sins and then for the people's, for this He did once for all when He offered up Himself. [28]For the law appoints as high priests men who have weakness, but the word of the oath, which came after the law, *appoints* the Son who has been perfected forever.

The New Priestly Service

8 Now *this is* the main point of the things we are saying: We have such a High Priest, who is seated at the right hand of the throne of the Majesty in the heavens, [2]a Minister of the sanctuary and of the true tabernacle which the Lord erected, and not man.

[3]For every high priest is appointed to offer both gifts and sacrifices. Therefore *it is* necessary that this One also have something to offer. [4]For if He were on earth, He would not be a priest, since there are priests who offer the gifts according to the law; [5]who serve the copy and shadow of the heavenly things, as Moses was divinely instructed when he was about to make the tabernacle. For He said, *"See that you make all things according to the pattern shown you on the mountain."*[a] [6]But now He has obtained a more excellent ministry, inasmuch as He is also Mediator of a better covenant, which was established on better promises.

A New Covenant

[7]For if that first *covenant* had been faultless, then no place would have been sought for a second. [8]Because finding fault with them, He says: *"Behold, the days are coming, says the Lord, when I will make a new covenant with the house of Israel and with the house of Judah— [9]not according to the covenant that I made with their fathers in the day when I took them by the hand to lead them out of the land of Egypt; because they did not continue in My covenant, and I disregarded them, says the Lord. [10]For this is the covenant that I will make with the house of Israel after those days, says the Lord: I will put My laws in their mind and write them on their hearts; and I will be their God, and they shall be My people. [11]None of them shall teach his neighbor, and none his brother, saying, 'Know the Lord,' for all shall know Me, from the least of them to the greatest of them. [12]For I will be merciful to their unrighteousness, and their sins and their lawless deeds*[a] *I will remember no more."*[b]

8:5 [a]Exodus 25:40 **8:12** [a]NU-Text omits *and their lawless deeds.* [b]Jeremiah 31:31–34

The Message

26-28 So now we have a high priest who perfectly fits our needs: completely holy, uncompromised by sin, with authority extending as high as God's presence in heaven itself. Unlike the other high priests, he doesn't have to offer sacrifices for his own sins every day before he can get around to us and our sins. He's done it, once and for all: offered up *himself* as the sacrifice. The law appoints as high priests men who are never able to get the job done right. But this intervening command of God, which came later, appoints the Son, who is absolutely, eternally perfect.

A New Plan with Israel

1-2 8 In essence, we have just such a high priest: authoritative right alongside God, conducting worship in the one true sanctuary built by God.

3-5 The assigned task of a high priest is to offer both gifts and sacrifices, and it's no different with the priesthood of Jesus. If he were limited to earth, he wouldn't even be a priest. We wouldn't need him since there are plenty of priests who offer the gifts designated in the law. These priests provide only a hint of what goes on in the true sanctuary of heaven, which Moses caught a glimpse of as he was about to set up the tent-shrine. It was then that God said, "Be careful to do it exactly as you saw it on the Mountain."

6-13 But Jesus' priestly work far surpasses what these other priests do, since he's working from a far better plan. If the first plan—the old covenant—had worked out, a second wouldn't have been needed. But we know the first was found wanting, because God said,

Heads up! The days are coming
when I'll set up a new plan
for dealing with Israel and Judah.
I'll throw out the old plan
I set up with their ancestors
when I led them by the hand out of Egypt.
They didn't keep their part of the bargain,
so I looked away and let it go.
This new plan I'm making with Israel
isn't going to be written on paper,
isn't going to be chiseled in stone;
This time I'm writing out the plan *in* them,
carving it on the lining of their hearts.
I'll be their God,
they'll be my people.
They won't go to school to learn about me,
or buy a book called *God in Five Easy Lessons.*
They'll all get to know me firsthand,
the little and the big, the small and the great.
They'll get to know me by being kindly forgiven,
with the slate of their sins forever wiped clean.

NEW KING JAMES VERSION

13 In that He says, *"A new covenant,"* He has made the first obsolete. Now what is becoming obsolete and growing old is ready to vanish away.

THE EARTHLY SANCTUARY

9 Then indeed, even the first *covenant* had ordinances of divine service and the earthly sanctuary. 2 For a tabernacle was prepared: the first *part,* in which *was* the lampstand, the table, and the showbread, which is called the sanctuary; 3 and behind the second veil, the part of the tabernacle which is called the Holiest of All, 4 which had the golden censer and the ark of the covenant overlaid on all sides with gold, in which *were* the golden pot that had the manna, Aaron's rod that budded, and the tablets of the covenant; 5 and above it were the cherubim of glory overshadowing the mercy seat. Of these things we cannot now speak in detail.

LIMITATIONS OF THE EARTHLY SERVICE

6 Now when these things had been thus prepared, the priests always went into the first part of the tabernacle, performing *the services.* 7 But into the second part the high priest *went* alone once a year, not without blood, which he offered for himself and *for* the people's sins *committed* in ignorance; 8 the Holy Spirit indicating this, that the way into the Holiest of All was not yet made manifest while the first tabernacle was still standing. 9 It *was* symbolic for the present time in which both gifts and sacrifices are offered which cannot make him who performed the service perfect in regard to the conscience— 10 *concerned* only with foods and drinks, various washings, and fleshly ordinances imposed until the time of reformation.

THE HEAVENLY SANCTUARY

11 But Christ came *as* High Priest of the good things to come,[a] with the greater and more perfect tabernacle not made with hands, that is, not of this creation. 12 Not with the blood of goats and calves, but with His own blood He entered the Most Holy Place once for all, having obtained eternal redemption. 13 For if the blood of bulls and goats and the ashes of a heifer, sprinkling the unclean, sanctifies for the purifying of the flesh, 14 how much more shall the blood of Christ, who through the eternal Spirit offered Himself without spot to God, cleanse your conscience from dead works to serve the living God? 15 And for this reason He is the Mediator of the new covenant, by means of death, for the redemption of the transgressions under the first covenant, that those who are called may receive the promise of the eternal inheritance.

THE MEDIATOR'S DEATH NECESSARY

16 For where there *is* a testament, there must also of necessity be the death of the testator. 17 For a testament *is* in force after men are dead, since it has no power at all while the testator lives.

9:11 [a]NU-Text reads *that have come.*

THE MESSAGE

By coming up with a new plan, a new covenant between God and his people, God put the old plan on the shelf. And there it stays, gathering dust.

A VISIBLE PARABLE

1-5 **9** That first plan contained directions for worship, and a specially designed place of worship. A large outer tent was set up. The lampstand, the table, and "the bread of presence" were placed in it. This was called "the Holy Place." Then a curtain was stretched, and behind it a smaller, inside tent set up. This was called "the Holy of Holies." In it were placed the gold incense altar and the gold-covered ark of the covenant containing the gold urn of manna, Aaron's rod that budded, the covenant tablets, and the angel-wing-shadowed mercy seat. But we don't have time to comment on these now.

6-10 After this was set up, the priests went about their duties in the large tent. Only the high priest entered the smaller, inside tent, and then only once a year, offering a blood sacrifice for his own sins and the people's accumulated sins. This was the Holy Spirit's way of showing with a visible parable that as long as the large tent stands, people can't just walk in on God. Under this system, the gifts and sacrifices can't really get to the heart of the matter, can't assuage the conscience of the people, but are limited to matters of ritual and behavior. It's essentially a temporary arrangement until a complete overhaul could be made.

POINTING TO THE REALITIES OF HEAVEN

11-15 But when the Messiah arrived, high priest of the superior things of this new covenant, he bypassed the old tent and its trappings in this created world and went straight into heaven's "tent"—the true Holy Place—once and for all. He also bypassed the sacrifices consisting of goat and calf blood, instead using his own blood as the price to set us free once and for all. If that animal blood and the other rituals of purification were effective in cleaning up certain matters of our religion and behavior, think how much more the blood of Christ cleans up our whole lives, inside and out. Through the Spirit, Christ offered himself as an unblemished sacrifice, freeing us from all those dead-end efforts to make ourselves respectable, so that we can live all out for God.

16-17 Like a will that takes effect when someone dies, the new covenant was put into action at Jesus' death. His death marked the transition from the old plan to the new one, canceling the old obligations and accompanying sins, and summoning the heirs to receive the eternal inheritance that was promised them. He brought together God and his people in this new way.

New King James Version

18Therefore not even the first *covenant* was ded-
icated without blood. 19For when Moses had
spoken every precept to all the people according
to the law, he took the blood of calves and goats,
with water, scarlet wool, and hyssop, and sprin-
kled both the book itself and all the people,
20saying, *"This is the blood of the covenant
which God has commanded you."*[a] 21Then like-
wise he sprinkled with blood both the taberna-
cle and all the vessels of the ministry. 22And ac-
cording to the law almost all things are purified
with blood, and without shedding of blood there
is no remission.

Greatness of Christ's Sacrifice

23Therefore *it was* necessary that the copies
of the things in the heavens should be purified
with these, but the heavenly things themselves
with better sacrifices than these. 24For Christ
has not entered the holy places made with
hands, *which are* copies of the true, but into
heaven itself, now to appear in the presence of
God for us; 25not that He should offer Himself
often, as the high priest enters the Most Holy
Place every year with blood of another— 26He
then would have had to suffer often since the
foundation of the world; but now, once at the
end of the ages, He has appeared to put away
sin by the sacrifice of Himself. 27And as it is ap-
pointed for men to die once, but after this the
judgment, 28so Christ was offered once to bear
the sins of many. To those who eagerly wait for
Him He will appear a second time, apart from
sin, for salvation.

Animal Sacrifices Insufficient

10 For the law, having a shadow of the good
things to come, *and* not the very image of
the things, can never with these same sacrifices,
which they offer continually year by year, make
those who approach perfect. 2For then would
they not have ceased to be offered? For the wor-
shipers, once purified, would have had no more
consciousness of sins. 3But in those *sacrifices
there is* a reminder of sins every year. 4For *it is*
not possible that the blood of bulls and goats
could take away sins.

Christ's Death Fulfills God's Will

5Therefore, when He came into the world, He
said:

"Sacrifice and offering You did not desire,
But a body You have prepared for Me.
6*In burnt offerings and sacrifices for sin*
You had no pleasure.
7*Then I said, 'Behold, I have come—*
In the volume of the book it is written of
Me—
To do Your will, O God.' "[a]

9:20 [a]Exodus 24:8 **10:7** [a]Psalm 40:6–8

The Message

18-22 Even the first plan required a death to set it in motion. After Moses had read out all the terms of the plan of the law—God's "will"—he took the blood of sacrificed animals and, in a solemn ritual, sprinkled the document and the people who were its beneficiaries. And then he attested its validity with the words, "This is the blood of the covenant commanded by God." He did the same thing with the place of worship and its furniture. Moses said to the people, "This is the blood of the covenant God has established with you." Practically everything in a will hinges on a death. That's why blood, the evidence of death, is used so much in our tradition, especially regarding forgiveness of sins.

23-26 That accounts for the prominence of blood and death in all these secondary practices that point to the realities of heaven. It also accounts for why, when the real thing takes place, these animal sacrifices aren't needed anymore, having served their purpose. For Christ didn't enter the earthly version of the Holy Place; he entered the Place Itself, and offered himself to God as the sacrifice for our sins. He doesn't do this every year as the high priests did under the old plan with blood that was not their own; if that had been the case, he would have to sacrifice himself repeatedly throughout the course of history. But instead he sacrificed himself once and for all, summing up all the other sacrifices in this sacrifice of himself, the final solution of sin.

27-28 Everyone has to die once, then face the consequences. Christ's death was also a one-time event, but it was a sacrifice that took care of sins forever. And so, when he next appears, the outcome for those eager to greet him is, precisely, *salvation*.

The Sacrifice of Jesus

1-10 10 The old plan was only a hint of the good things in the new plan. Since that old "law plan" wasn't complete in itself, it couldn't complete those who followed it. No matter how many sacrifices were offered year after year, they never added up to a complete solution. If they had, the worshipers would have gone merrily on their way, no longer dragged down by their sins. But instead of removing awareness of sin, when those animal sacrifices were repeated over and over they actually heightened awareness and guilt. The plain fact is that bull and goat blood can't get rid of sin. That is what is meant by this prophecy, put in the mouth of Christ:

You don't want sacrifices and offerings
year after year;
you've prepared a body for me for a
sacrifice.
It's not fragrance and smoke from the
altar
that whet your appetite.
So I said, "I'm here to do it your way,
O God,
the way it's described in your Book."

NEW KING JAMES VERSION

8Previously saying, *"Sacrifice and offering, burnt offerings, and offerings for sin You did not desire, nor had pleasure in them"* (which are offered according to the law), 9then He said, *"Behold, I have come to do Your will, O God."*[a] He takes away the first that He may establish the second. 10By that will we have been sanctified through the offering of the body of Jesus Christ once *for all.*

CHRIST'S DEATH PERFECTS THE SANCTIFIED

11And every priest stands ministering daily and offering repeatedly the same sacrifices, which can never take away sins. 12But this Man, after He had offered one sacrifice for sins forever, sat down at the right hand of God, 13from that time waiting till His enemies are made His footstool. 14For by one offering He has perfected forever those who are being sanctified.

15But the Holy Spirit also witnesses to us; for after He had said before,

16*"This is the covenant that I will make with them after those days, says the LORD: I will put My laws into their hearts, and in their minds I will write them,"*[a] 17*then He adds, "Their sins and their lawless deeds I will remember no more."*[a] 18Now where there is remission of these, *there is* no longer an offering for sin.

HOLD FAST YOUR CONFESSION

19Therefore, brethren, having boldness to enter the Holiest by the blood of Jesus, 20by a new and living way which He consecrated for us, through the veil, that is, His flesh, 21and *having* a High Priest over the house of God, 22let us draw near with a true heart in full assurance of faith, having our hearts sprinkled from an evil conscience and our bodies washed with pure water. 23Let us hold fast the confession of *our* hope without wavering, for He who promised *is* faithful. 24And let us consider one another in order to stir up love and good works, 25not forsaking the assembling of ourselves together, as *is* the manner of some, but exhorting *one another,* and so much the more as you see the Day approaching.

THE JUST LIVE BY FAITH

26For if we sin willfully after we have received the knowledge of the truth, there no longer remains a sacrifice for sins, 27but a certain fearful expectation of judgment, and fiery indignation which will devour the adversaries. 28Anyone who has rejected Moses' law dies without mercy on the testimony of two or three witnesses. 29Of how much worse punishment, do you suppose, will he be thought worthy who has trampled the Son of God underfoot, counted the blood of the covenant by which he was sanctified a common thing, and insulted the Spirit of grace? 30For we know Him who said, *"Vengeance is Mine, I will repay,"*[a] says the Lord.[b] And again, *"The LORD will judge His people."*[c] 31It is a fearful thing to fall into the hands of the living God.

10:9 [a]NU-Text and M-Text omit *O God.* **10:16** [a]Jeremiah 31:33 **10:17** [a]Jeremiah 31:34 **10:30** [a]Deuteronomy 32:35 [b]NU-Text omits *says the Lord.* [c]Deuteronomy 32:36

THE MESSAGE

When he said, "You don't want sacrifices and offerings," he was referring to practices according to the old plan. When he added, "I'm here to do it your way," he set aside the first in order to enact the new plan—*God's* way—by which we are made fit for God by the once-for-all sacrifice of Jesus.

11-18 Every priest goes to work at the altar each day, offers the same old sacrifices year in, year out, and never makes a dent in the sin problem. As a priest, Christ made a single sacrifice for sins, and that was it! Then he sat down right beside God and waited for his enemies to cave in. It was a perfect sacrifice by a perfect person to perfect some very imperfect people. By that single offering, he did everything that needed to be done for everyone who takes part in the purifying process. The Holy Spirit confirms this:

This new plan I'm making with Israel
isn't going to be written on paper,
isn't going to be chiseled in stone;
This time "I'm writing out the plan *in* them,
carving it on the lining of their hearts."

He concludes,

I'll forever wipe the slate clean of their sins.

Once sins are taken care of for good, there's no longer any need to offer sacrifices for them.

DON'T THROW IT ALL AWAY

19-21 So, friends, we can now—without hesitation—walk right up to God, into "the Holy Place." Jesus has cleared the way by the blood of his sacrifice, acting as our priest before God. The "curtain" into God's presence is his body.

22-25 So let's *do* it—full of belief, confident that we're presentable inside and out. Let's keep a firm grip on the promises that keep us going. He always keeps his word. Let's see how inventive we can be in encouraging love and helping out, not avoiding worshiping together as some do but spurring each other on, especially as we see the big Day approaching.

26-31 If we give up and turn our backs on all we've learned, all we've been given, all the truth we now know, we repudiate Christ's sacrifice and are left on our own to face the Judgment—and a mighty fierce judgment it will be! If the penalty for breaking the law of Moses is physical death, what do you think will happen if you turn on God's Son, spit on the sacrifice that made you whole, and insult this most gracious Spirit? This is no light matter. God has warned us that he'll hold us to account and make us pay. He was quite explicit: "Vengeance is mine, and I won't overlook a thing" and "God will judge his people." Nobody's getting by with anything, believe me.

New King James Version

32But recall the former days in which, after
you were illuminated, you endured a great
struggle with sufferings: 33partly while you were
made a spectacle both by reproaches and tribu-
lations, and partly while you became compan-
ions of those who were so treated; 34for you had
compassion on me[a] in my chains, and joyfully
accepted the plundering of your goods, knowing
that you have a better and an enduring posses-
sion for yourselves in heaven.[b] 35Therefore do
not cast away your confidence, which has great
reward. 36For you have need of endurance, so
that after you have done the will of God, you
may receive the promise:

37*"For yet a little while,*
And He[a] *who is coming will come and will*
not tarry.
38*Now the*[a] *just shall live by faith;*
But if anyone draws back,
My soul has no pleasure in him."[b]

39But we are not of those who draw back to
perdition, but of those who believe to the saving
of the soul.

By Faith We Understand

11 Now faith is the substance of things hoped
for, the evidence of things not seen. 2For by
it the elders obtained a *good* testimony.
3By faith we understand that the worlds
were framed by the word of God, so that the
things which are seen were not made of things
which are visible.

Faith at the Dawn of History

4By faith Abel offered to God a more excel-
lent sacrifice than Cain, through which he ob-
tained witness that he was righteous, God testi-
fying of his gifts; and through it he being dead
still speaks.
5By faith Enoch was taken away so that he
did not see death, *"and was not found, because
God had taken him"*;[a] for before he was taken
he had this testimony, that he pleased God. 6But
without faith *it is* impossible to please *Him,* for
he who comes to God must believe that He is,
and *that* He is a rewarder of those who dili-
gently seek Him.
7By faith Noah, being divinely warned of
things not yet seen, moved with godly fear, pre-
pared an ark for the saving of his household, by
which he condemned the world and became heir
of the righteousness which is according to faith.

Faithful Abraham

8By faith Abraham obeyed when he was
called to go out to the place which he would re-
ceive as an inheritance. And he went out, not
knowing where he was going. 9By faith he dwelt
in the land of promise as *in* a foreign country,

10:34 [a]NU-Text reads *the prisoners* instead of *me in my chains.* [b]NU-Text omits *in heaven.* 10:37 [a]Or *that which* 10:38 [a]NU-Text reads *My just one.* [b]Habakkuk 2:3, 4 11:5 [a]Genesis 5:24

The Message

32-39 Remember those early days after you first saw the light? Those were the hard times! Kicked around in public, targets of every kind of abuse—some days it was you, other days your friends. If some friends went to prison, you stuck by them. If some enemies broke in and seized your goods, you let them go with a smile, knowing they couldn't touch your real treasure. Nothing they did bothered you, nothing set you back. So don't throw it all away now. You were sure of yourselves then. It's *still* a sure thing! But you need to stick it out, staying with God's plan so you'll be there for the promised completion.

It won't be long now, he's on the way;
he'll show up most any minute.
But anyone who is right with me thrives
on loyal trust;
if he cuts and runs, I won't be very
happy.

But we're not quitters who lose out. Oh, no! We'll stay with it and survive, trusting all the way.

Faith in What We Don't See

1-2 11 The fundamental fact of existence is that this trust in God, this faith, is the firm foundation under everything that makes life worth living. It's our handle on what we can't see. The act of faith is what distinguished our ancestors, set them above the crowd.

3 By faith, we see the world called into existence by God's word, what we see created by what we don't see.

4 By an act of faith, Abel brought a better sacrifice to God than Cain. It was what he *believed,* not what he *brought,* that made the difference. That's what God noticed and approved as righteous. After all these centuries, that belief continues to catch our notice.

5-6 By an act of faith, Enoch skipped death completely. "They looked all over and couldn't find him because God had taken him." We know on the basis of reliable testimony that before he was taken "he pleased God." It's impossible to please God apart from faith. And why? Because anyone who wants to approach God must believe both that he exists *and* that he cares enough to respond to those who seek him.

7 By faith, Noah built a ship in the middle of dry land. He was warned about something he couldn't see, and acted on what he was told. The result? His family was saved. His act of faith drew a sharp line between the evil of the unbelieving world and the rightness of the believing world. As a result, Noah became intimate with God.

8-10 By an act of faith, Abraham said yes to God's call to travel to an unknown place that would become his home. When he left he had no idea where he was going. By an act of faith he lived in the country promised him, lived as a stranger camping in tents.

New King James Version

dwelling in tents with Isaac and Jacob, the heirs
with him of the same promise; 10for he waited
for the city which has foundations, whose
builder and maker *is* God.
11By faith Sarah herself also received
strength to conceive seed, and she bore a child[a]
when she was past the age, because she judged
Him faithful who had promised. 12Therefore
from one man, and him as good as dead, were
born *as many* as the stars of the sky in multi-
tude—innumerable as the sand which is by the
seashore.

The Heavenly Hope

13These all died in faith, not having received
the promises, but having seen them afar off
were assured of them,[a] embraced *them* and con-
fessed that they were strangers and pilgrims on
the earth. 14For those who say such things de-
clare plainly that they seek a homeland. 15And
truly if they had called to mind that *country*
from which they had come out, they would have
had opportunity to return. 16But now they desire
a better, that is, a heavenly *country.* Therefore
God is not ashamed to be called their God, for
He has prepared a city for them.

The Faith of the Patriarchs

17By faith Abraham, when he was tested, of-
fered up Isaac, and he who had received the
promises offered up his only begotten *son,* 18of
whom it was said, *"In Isaac your seed shall be
called,"* [a] 19concluding that God *was* able to raise
him up, even from the dead, from which he also
received him in a figurative sense.
20By faith Isaac blessed Jacob and Esau con-
cerning things to come.
21By faith Jacob, when he was dying, blessed
each of the sons of Joseph, and worshiped, *lean-
ing* on the top of his staff.
22By faith Joseph, when he was dying, made
mention of the departure of the children of Is-
rael, and gave instructions concerning his
bones.

The Faith of Moses

23By faith Moses, when he was born, was
hidden three months by his parents, because
they saw *he was* a beautiful child; and they were
not afraid of the king's command.
24By faith Moses, when he became of age, re-
fused to be called the son of Pharaoh's daugh-
ter, 25choosing rather to suffer affliction with the
people of God than to enjoy the passing plea-
sures of sin, 26esteeming the reproach of Christ
greater riches than the treasures in[a] Egypt; for
he looked to the reward.
27By faith he forsook Egypt, not fearing the
wrath of the king; for he endured as seeing Him
who is invisible. 28By faith he kept the Passover
and the sprinkling of blood, lest he who de-
stroyed the firstborn should touch them.
29By faith they passed through the Red Sea
as by dry *land, whereas* the Egyptians, attempt-
ing to do so, were drowned.

11:11 [a]NU-Text omits *she bore a child.* **11:13** [a]NU-Text and M-Text omit *were assured of them.* **11:18** [a]Genesis 21:12 **11:26** [a]NU-Text and M-Text read *of.*

The Message

Isaac and Jacob did the same, living under the same promise. Abraham did it by keeping his eye on an unseen city with real, eternal foundations—the City designed and built by God.

11-12 By faith, barren Sarah was able to become pregnant, old woman as she was at the time, because she believed the One who made a promise would do what he said. That's how it happened that from one man's dead and shriveled loins there are now people numbering into the millions.

13-16 Each one of these people of faith died not yet having in hand what was promised, but still believing. How did they do it? They saw it way off in the distance, waved their greeting, and accepted the fact that they were transients in this world. People who live this way make it plain that they are looking for their true home. If they were homesick for the old country, they could have gone back any time they wanted. But they were after a far better country than that—*heaven* country. You can see why God is so proud of them, and has a City waiting for them.

17-19 By faith, Abraham, at the time of testing, offered Isaac back to God. Acting in faith, he was as ready to return the promised son, his only son, as he had been to receive him—and this after he had already been told, "Your descendants shall come from Isaac." Abraham figured that if God wanted to, he could raise the dead. In a sense, that's what happened when he received Isaac back, alive from off the altar.

20 By an act of faith, Isaac reached into the future as he blessed Jacob and Esau.

21 By an act of faith, Jacob on his deathbed blessed each of Joseph's sons in turn, blessing them with God's blessing, not his own—as he bowed worshipfully upon his staff.

22 By an act of faith, Joseph, while dying, prophesied the exodus of Israel, and made arrangements for his own burial.

23 By an act of faith, Moses' parents hid him away for three months after his birth. They saw the child's beauty, and they braved the king's decree.

24-28 By faith, Moses, when grown, refused the privileges of the Egyptian royal house. He chose a hard life with God's people rather than an opportunistic soft life of sin with the oppressors. He valued suffering in the Messiah's camp far greater than Egyptian wealth because he was looking ahead, anticipating the payoff. By an act of faith, he turned his heel on Egypt, indifferent to the king's blind rage. He had his eye on the One no eye can see, and kept right on going. By an act of faith, he kept the Passover Feast and sprinkled Passover blood on each house so that the destroyer of the firstborn wouldn't touch them.

29 By an act of faith, Israel walked through the Red Sea on dry ground. The Egyptians tried it and drowned.

NEW KING JAMES VERSION

BY FAITH THEY OVERCAME

30By faith the walls of Jericho fell down after
they were encircled for seven days. 31By faith
the harlot Rahab did not perish with those who
did not believe, when she had received the spies
with peace.

32And what more shall I say? For the time
would fail me to tell of Gideon and Barak and
Samson and Jephthah, also *of* David and
Samuel and the prophets: 33who through faith
subdued kingdoms, worked righteousness, ob-
tained promises, stopped the mouths of lions,
34quenched the violence of fire, escaped the
edge of the sword, out of weakness were made
strong, became valiant in battle, turned to flight
the armies of the aliens. 35Women received their
dead raised to life again.

Others were tortured, not accepting deliver-
ance, that they might obtain a better resurrec-
tion. 36Still others had trial of mockings and
scourgings, yes, and of chains and imprison-
ment. 37They were stoned, they were sawn in
two, were tempted,[a] were slain with the sword.
They wandered about in sheepskins and
goatskins, being destitute, afflicted, tor-
mented— 38of whom the world was not worthy.
They wandered in deserts and mountains, *in*
dens and caves of the earth.

39And all these, having obtained a good testi-
mony through faith, did not receive the promise,
40God having provided something better for us,
that they should not be made perfect apart from
us.

THE RACE OF FAITH

12 Therefore we also, since we are sur-
rounded by so great a cloud of witnesses,
let us lay aside every weight, and the sin which
so easily ensnares *us*, and let us run with en-
durance the race that is set before us, 2looking
unto Jesus, the author and finisher of *our* faith,
who for the joy that was set before Him endured
the cross, despising the shame, and has sat
down at the right hand of the throne of God.

THE DISCIPLINE OF GOD

3For consider Him who endured such hostil-
ity from sinners against Himself, lest you be-
come weary and discouraged in your souls. 4You
have not yet resisted to bloodshed, striving
against sin. 5And you have forgotten the exhor-
tation which speaks to you as to sons:

"My son, do not despise the chastening of the
LORD,
Nor be discouraged when you are rebuked
by Him;
6*For whom the LORD loves He chastens,*
And scourges every son whom He
receives."[a]

11:37 [a]NU-Text omits *were tempted.* **12:6** [a]Proverbs 3:11, 12

THE MESSAGE

30 By faith, the Israelites marched around the walls of Jericho for seven days, and the walls fell flat.

31 By an act of faith, Rahab, the Jericho harlot, welcomed the spies and escaped the destruction that came on those who refused to trust God.

32-38 I could go on and on, but I've run out of time. There are so many more—Gideon, Barak, Samson, Jephthah, David, Samuel, the prophets. . . . Through acts of faith, they toppled kingdoms, made justice work, took the promises for themselves. They were protected from lions, fires, and sword thrusts, turned disadvantage to advantage, won battles, routed alien armies. Women received their loved ones back from the dead. There were those who, under torture, refused to give in and go free, preferring something better: resurrection. Others braved abuse and whips, and, yes, chains and dungeons. We have stories of those who were stoned, sawed in two, murdered in cold blood; stories of vagrants wandering the earth in animal skins, homeless, friendless, powerless—the world didn't deserve them!—making their way as best they could on the cruel edges of the world.

39-40 Not one of these people, even though their lives of faith were exemplary, got their hands on what was promised. God had a better plan for us: that their faith and our faith would come together to make one completed whole, their lives of faith not complete apart from ours.

DISCIPLINE IN A LONG-DISTANCE RACE

1-3 12 Do you see what this means—all these pioneers who blazed the way, all these veterans cheering us on? It means we'd better get on with it. Strip down, start running—and never quit! No extra spiritual fat, no parasitic sins. Keep your eyes on *Jesus*, who both began and finished this race we're in. Study how he did it. Because he never lost sight of where he was headed—that exhilarating finish in and with God—he could put up with anything along the way: Cross, shame, whatever. And now he's *there*, in the place of honor, right alongside God. When you find yourselves flagging in your faith, go over that story again, item by item, that long litany of hostility he plowed through. *That* will shoot adrenaline into your souls!

4-11 In this all-out match against sin, others have suffered far worse than you, to say nothing of what Jesus went through—all that bloodshed! So don't feel sorry for yourselves. Or have you forgotten how good parents treat children, and that God regards you as *his* children?

My dear child, don't shrug off God's
discipline,
but don't be crushed by it either.
It's the child he loves that he disciplines;
the child he embraces, he also corrects.

NEW KING JAMES VERSION

7If[a] you endure chastening, God deals with you as with sons; for what son is there whom a father does not chasten? 8But if you are without chastening, of which all have become partakers, then you are illegitimate and not sons. 9Furthermore, we have had human fathers who corrected *us,* and we paid *them* respect. Shall we not much more readily be in subjection to the Father of spirits and live? 10For they indeed for a few days chastened *us* as seemed *best* to them, but He for *our* profit, that *we* may be partakers of His holiness. 11Now no chastening seems to be joyful for the present, but painful; nevertheless, afterward it yields the peaceable fruit of righteousness to those who have been trained by it.

RENEW YOUR SPIRITUAL VITALITY

12Therefore strengthen the hands which hang down, and the feeble knees, 13and make straight paths for your feet, so that what is lame may not be dislocated, but rather be healed.

14Pursue peace with all *people,* and holiness, without which no one will see the Lord: 15looking carefully lest anyone fall short of the grace of God; lest any root of bitterness springing up cause trouble, and by this many become defiled; 16lest there *be* any fornicator or profane person like Esau, who for one morsel of food sold his birthright. 17For you know that afterward, when he wanted to inherit the blessing, he was rejected, for he found no place for repentance, though he sought it diligently with tears.

THE GLORIOUS COMPANY

18For you have not come to the mountain that[a] may be touched and that burned with fire, and to blackness and darkness[b] and tempest, 19and the sound of a trumpet and the voice of words, so that those who heard *it* begged that the word should not be spoken to them anymore. 20(For they could not endure what was commanded: *"And if so much as a beast touches the mountain, it shall be stoned*[a] *or shot with an arrow."*[b] 21And so terrifying was the sight *that* Moses said, *"I am exceedingly afraid* and trembling."[a])

22But you have come to Mount Zion and to the city of the living God, the heavenly Jerusalem, to an innumerable company of angels, 23to the general assembly and church of the firstborn *who are* registered in heaven, to God the Judge of all, to the spirits of just men made perfect, 24to Jesus the Mediator of the new covenant, and to the blood of sprinkling that speaks better things than *that of* Abel.

HEAR THE HEAVENLY VOICE

25See that you do not refuse Him who speaks. For if they did not escape who refused Him who spoke on earth, much more *shall we not escape* if we turn away from Him who *speaks* from heaven, 26whose voice then shook the earth; but now He has promised, saying,

12:7 [a]NU-Text and M-Text read *It is for discipline that you endure; God* . . . . **12:18** [a]NU-Text reads *to that which.* [b]NU-Text reads *gloom.* **12:20** [a]NU-Text and M-Text omit the rest of this verse. [b]Exodus 19:12, 13 **12:21** [a]Deuteronomy 9:19

THE MESSAGE

God is educating you; that's why you must never drop out. He's treating you as dear children. This trouble you're in isn't punishment; it's *training,* the normal experience of children. Only irresponsible parents leave children to fend for themselves. Would you prefer an irresponsible God? We respect our own parents for training and not spoiling us, so why not embrace God's training so we can truly *live?* While we were children, our parents did what *seemed* best to them. But God is doing what *is* best for us, training us to live God's holy best. At the time, discipline isn't much fun. It always feels like it's going against the grain. Later, of course, it pays off handsomely, for it's the well-trained who find themselves mature in their relationship with God.

12-13 So don't sit around on your hands! No more dragging your feet! Clear the path for long-distance runners so no one will trip and fall, so no one will step in a hole and sprain an ankle. Help each other out. And run for it!

14-17 Work at getting along with each other and with God. Otherwise you'll never get so much as a glimpse of God. Make sure no one gets left out of God's generosity. Keep a sharp eye out for weeds of bitter discontent. A thistle or two gone to seed can ruin a whole garden in no time. Watch out for the Esau syndrome: trading away God's lifelong gift in order to satisfy a short-term appetite. You well know how Esau later regretted that impulsive act and wanted God's blessing—but by then it was too late, tears or no tears.

AN UNSHAKABLE KINGDOM

18-21 Unlike your ancestors, you didn't come to Mount Sinai—all that volcanic blaze and earthshaking rumble—to hear God speak. The earsplitting words and soul-shaking message terrified them and they begged him to stop. When they heard the words—"If an animal touches the Mountain, it's as good as dead"—they were afraid to move. Even Moses was terrified.

22-24 No, that's not *your* experience at all. You've come to Mount Zion, the city where the living God resides. The invisible Jerusalem is populated by throngs of festive angels and Christian citizens. It is the city where God is Judge, with judgments that make us just. You've come to Jesus, who presents us with a new covenant, a fresh charter from God. He is the Mediator of this covenant. The murder of Jesus, unlike Abel's—a homicide that cried out for vengeance—became a proclamation of grace.

25-27 So don't turn a deaf ear to these gracious words. If those who ignored earthly warnings didn't get away with it, what will happen to us if we turn our backs on heavenly warnings? His voice that time shook the earth to its foundations; this time—he's told us this quite plainly—he'll also rock the heavens: "One last shaking, from top to bot-

NEW KING JAMES VERSION

"Yet once more I shake[a] *not only the earth, but also heaven."*[b] 27Now this, *"Yet once more,"* indicates the removal of those things that are being shaken, as of things that are made, that the things which cannot be shaken may remain.

28Therefore, since we are receiving a kingdom which cannot be shaken, let us have grace, by which we may[a] serve God acceptably with reverence and godly fear. 29For our God *is* a consuming fire.

CONCLUDING MORAL DIRECTIONS

13 Let brotherly love continue. 2Do not forget to entertain strangers, for by so *doing* some have unwittingly entertained angels. 3Remember the prisoners as if chained with them—those who are mistreated—since you yourselves are in the body also.

4Marriage *is* honorable among all, and the bed undefiled; but fornicators and adulterers God will judge.

5*Let your* conduct *be* without covetousness; *be* content with such things as you have. For He Himself has said, *"I will never leave you nor forsake you."*[a] 6So we may boldly say:

"The LORD is my helper;
I will not fear.
What can man do to me?"[a]

CONCLUDING RELIGIOUS DIRECTIONS

7Remember those who rule over you, who have spoken the word of God to you, whose faith follow, considering the outcome of *their* conduct. 8Jesus Christ *is* the same yesterday, today, and forever. 9Do not be carried about[a] with various and strange doctrines. For *it is* good that the heart be established by grace, not with foods which have not profited those who have been occupied with them.

10We have an altar from which those who serve the tabernacle have no right to eat. 11For the bodies of those animals, whose blood is brought into the sanctuary by the high priest for sin, are burned outside the camp. 12Therefore Jesus also, that He might sanctify the people with His own blood, suffered outside the gate. 13Therefore let us go forth to Him, outside the camp, bearing His reproach. 14For here we have no continuing city, but we seek the one to come. 15Therefore by Him let us continually offer the sacrifice of praise to God, that is, the fruit of *our* lips, giving thanks to His name.

12:26 [a]NU-Text reads *will shake.* [b]Haggai 2:6 **12:28** [a]M-Text omits *may.* **13:5** [a]Deuteronomy 31:6, 8; Joshua 1:5 **13:6** [a]Psalm 118:6 **13:9** [a]NU-Text and M-Text read *away.*

THE MESSAGE

tom, stem to stern." The phrase "one last shaking" means a thorough housecleaning, getting rid of all the historical and religious junk so that the unshakable essentials stand clear and uncluttered.

28-29 Do you see what we've got? An unshakable kingdom! And do you see how thankful we must be? Not only thankful, but brimming with worship, deeply reverent before God. For God is not an indifferent bystander. He's actively cleaning house, torching all that needs to burn, and he won't quit until it's all cleansed. God himself is Fire!

JESUS DOESN'T CHANGE

1-4 13 Stay on good terms with each other, held together by love. Be ready with a meal or a bed when it's needed. Why, some have extended hospitality to angels without ever knowing it! Regard prisoners as if you were in prison with them. Look on victims of abuse as if what happened to them had happened to you. Honor marriage, and guard the sacredness of sexual intimacy between wife and husband. God draws a firm line against casual and illicit sex.

5-6 Don't be obsessed with getting more material things. Be relaxed with what you have. Since God assured us, "I'll never let you down, never walk off and leave you," we can boldly quote,

God is there, ready to help;
I'm fearless no matter what.
Who or what can get to me?

7-8 Appreciate your pastoral leaders who gave you the Word of God. Take a good look at the way they live, and let their faithfulness instruct you, as well as their truthfulness. There should be a consistency that runs through us all. For Jesus doesn't change—yesterday, today, tomorrow, he's always totally himself.

9 Don't be lured away from him by the latest speculations about him. The grace of Christ is the only good ground for life. Products named after Christ don't seem to do much for those who buy them.

10-12 The altar from which God gives us the gift of himself is not for exploitation by insiders who grab and loot. In the old system, the animals are killed and the bodies disposed of outside the camp. The blood is then brought inside to the altar as a sacrifice for sin. It's the same with Jesus. He was crucified outside the city gates—*that* is where he poured out the sacrificial blood that was brought to God's altar to cleanse his people.

13-15 So let's go outside, where Jesus is, where the action is—not trying to be privileged insiders, but taking our share in the abuse of Jesus. This "insider world" is not our home. We have our eyes peeled for the City about to come. Let's take our place outside with Jesus, no longer pouring out the sacrificial blood of animals but pouring out sacrificial praises from our lips to God in Jesus' name.

New King James Version

16But do not forget to do good and to share, for
with such sacrifices God is well pleased.
17Obey those who rule over you, and be sub-
missive, for they watch out for your souls, as
those who must give account. Let them do so
with joy and not with grief, for that would be un-
profitable for you.

Prayer Requested

18Pray for us; for we are confident that we
have a good conscience, in all things desiring to
live honorably. 19But I especially urge *you* to do
this, that I may be restored to you the sooner.

Benediction, Final Exhortation, Farewell

20Now may the God of peace who brought up
our Lord Jesus from the dead, that great Shep-
herd of the sheep, through the blood of the ever-
lasting covenant, 21make you complete in every
good work to do His will, working in you[a] what
is well pleasing in His sight, through Jesus
Christ, to whom *be* glory forever and ever.
Amen.
22And I appeal to you, brethren, bear with
the word of exhortation, for I have written to
you in few words. 23Know that *our* brother Tim-
othy has been set free, with whom I shall see
you if he comes shortly.
24Greet all those who rule over you, and all
the saints. Those from Italy greet you.
25Grace *be* with you all. Amen.

13:21 [a]NU-Text and M-Text read *us.*

The Message

16 Make sure you don't take things for granted and go slack in working for the common good; share what you have with others. God takes particular pleasure in acts of worship—a different kind of "sacrifice"—that take place in kitchen and workplace and on the streets.

17 Be responsive to your pastoral leaders. Listen to their counsel. They are alert to the condition of your lives and work under the strict supervision of God. Contribute to the joy of their leadership, not its drudgery. Why would you want to make things harder for them?

18-21 Pray for us. We have no doubts about what we're doing or why, but it's hard going and we need your prayers. All we care about is living well before God. Pray that we may be together soon.

May God, who puts all things together,
makes all things whole,
Who made a lasting mark through the
sacrifice of Jesus,
the sacrifice of blood that sealed the
eternal covenant,
Who led Jesus, our Great Shepherd,
up and alive from the dead,
Now put you together, provide you
with everything you need to please
him,
Make us into what gives him most
pleasure,
by means of the sacrifice of Jesus, the
Messiah.
All glory to Jesus forever and always!
Oh, yes, yes, yes.

22-23 Friends, please take what I've written most seriously. I've kept this as brief as possible; I haven't piled on a lot of extras. You'll be glad to know that Timothy has been let out of prison. If he leaves soon, I'll come with him and get to see you myself.

24 Say hello to your pastoral leaders and all the congregations. Everyone here in Italy wants to be remembered to you.

25 Grace be with you, every one.

JAMES

New King James Version

Greeting to the Twelve Tribes

1 James, a bondservant of God and of the Lord Jesus Christ,

To the twelve tribes which are scattered abroad:

Greetings.

Profiting from Trials

2My brethren, count it all joy when you fall into various trials, 3knowing that the testing of your faith produces patience. 4But let patience have *its* perfect work, that you may be perfect and complete, lacking nothing. 5If any of you lacks wisdom, let him ask of God, who gives to all liberally and without reproach, and it will be given to him. 6But let him ask in faith, with no doubting, for he who doubts is like a wave of the sea driven and tossed by the wind. 7For let not that man suppose that he will receive anything from the Lord; 8*he is* a double-minded man, unstable in all his ways.

The Perspective of Rich and Poor

9Let the lowly brother glory in his exaltation, 10but the rich in his humiliation, because as a flower of the field he will pass away. 11For no sooner has the sun risen with a burning heat than it withers the grass; its flower falls, and its beautiful appearance perishes. So the rich man also will fade away in his pursuits.

Loving God Under Trials

12Blessed *is* the man who endures temptation; for when he has been approved, he will receive the crown of life which the Lord has promised to those who love Him. 13Let no one say when he is tempted, "I am tempted by God"; for God cannot be tempted by evil, nor does He Himself tempt anyone. 14But each one is tempted when he is drawn away by his own desires and enticed. 15Then, when desire has conceived, it gives birth to sin; and sin, when it is full-grown, brings forth death.

16Do not be deceived, my beloved brethren. 17Every good gift and every perfect gift is from above, and comes down from the Father of lights, with whom there is no variation or shadow of turning. 18Of His own will He brought us forth by the word of truth, that we might be a kind of firstfruits of His creatures.

Qualities Needed in Trials

19So then,[a] my beloved brethren, let every man be swift to hear, slow to speak, slow to wrath; 20for the wrath of man does not produce the righteousness of God.

Doers—Not Hearers Only

21Therefore lay aside all filthiness and overflow of wickedness, and receive with meekness

1:19 [a]NU-Text reads *Know this* or *This you know.*

The Message

1 1 I, James, am a slave of God and the Master Jesus, writing to the twelve tribes scattered to Kingdom Come: Hello!

Faith Under Pressure

2-4 Consider it a sheer gift, friends, when tests and challenges come at you from all sides. You know that under pressure, your faith-life is forced into the open and shows its true colors. So don't try to get out of anything prematurely. Let it do its work so you become mature and well-developed, not deficient in any way.

5-8 If you don't know what you're doing, pray to the Father. He loves to help. You'll get his help, and won't be condescended to when you ask for it. Ask boldly, believingly, without a second thought. People who "worry their prayers" are like wind-whipped waves. Don't think you're going to get anything from the Master that way, adrift at sea, keeping all your options open.

9-11 When down-and-outers get a break, cheer! And when the arrogant rich are brought down to size, cheer! Prosperity is as short-lived as a wildflower, so don't ever count on it. You know that as soon as the sun rises, pouring down its scorching heat, the flower withers. Its petals wilt and, before you know it, that beautiful face is a barren stem. Well, that's a picture of the "prosperous life." At the very moment everyone is looking on in admiration, it fades away to nothing.

12 Anyone who meets a testing challenge head-on and manages to stick it out is mighty fortunate. For such persons loyally in love with God, the reward is life and more life.

13-15 Don't let anyone under pressure to give in to evil say, "God is trying to trip me up." God is impervious to evil, and puts evil in no one's way. The temptation to give in to evil comes from us and only us. We have no one to blame but the leering, seducing flare-up of our own lust. Lust gets pregnant, and has a baby: sin! Sin grows up to adulthood, and becomes a real killer.

16-18 So, my very dear friends, don't get thrown off course. Every desirable and beneficial gift comes out of heaven. The gifts are rivers of light cascading down from the Father of Light. There is nothing deceitful in God, nothing two-faced, nothing fickle. He brought us to life using the true Word, showing us off as the crown of all his creatures.

Act on What You Hear

19-21 Post this at all the intersections, dear friends: Lead with your ears, follow up with your tongue, and let anger straggle along in the rear. God's righteousness doesn't grow from human anger. So throw all spoiled virtue and cancerous evil in the garbage. In

New King James Version

the implanted word, which is able to save your souls.

22 But be doers of the word, and not hearers only, deceiving yourselves. 23 For if anyone is a hearer of the word and not a doer, he is like a man observing his natural face in a mirror; 24 for he observes himself, goes away, and immediately forgets what kind of man he was. 25 But he who looks into the perfect law of liberty and continues *in it*, and is not a forgetful hearer but a doer of the work, this one will be blessed in what he does.

26 If anyone among you[a] thinks he is religious, and does not bridle his tongue but deceives his own heart, this one's religion *is* useless. 27 Pure and undefiled religion before God and the Father is this: to visit orphans and widows in their trouble, *and* to keep oneself unspotted from the world.

Beware of Personal Favoritism

2 My brethren, do not hold the faith of our Lord Jesus Christ, *the Lord* of glory, with partiality. 2 For if there should come into your assembly a man with gold rings, in fine apparel, and there should also come in a poor man in filthy clothes, 3 and you pay attention to the one wearing the fine clothes and say to him, "You sit here in a good place," and say to the poor man, "You stand there," or, "Sit here at my footstool," 4 have you not shown partiality among yourselves, and become judges with evil thoughts?

5 Listen, my beloved brethren: Has God not chosen the poor of this world *to be* rich in faith and heirs of the kingdom which He promised to those who love Him? 6 But you have dishonored the poor man. Do not the rich oppress you and drag you into the courts? 7 Do they not blaspheme that noble name by which you are called?

8 If you really fulfill *the* royal law according to the Scripture, *"You shall love your neighbor as yourself,"*[a] you do well; 9 but if you show partiality, you commit sin, and are convicted by the law as transgressors. 10 For whoever shall keep the whole law, and yet stumble in one *point*, he is guilty of all. 11 For He who said, *"Do not commit adultery,"*[a] also said, *"Do not murder."*[b] Now if you do not commit adultery, but you do murder, you have become a transgressor of the law. 12 So speak and so do as those who will be judged by the law of liberty. 13 For judgment is without mercy to the one who has shown no mercy. Mercy triumphs over judgment.

1:26 [a]NU-Text omits *among you.* **2:8** [a]Leviticus 19:18 **2:11** [a]Exodus 20:14; Deuteronomy 5:18 [b]Exodus 20:13; Deuteronomy 5:17

The Message

simple humility, let our gardener, God, landscape you with the Word, making a salvation-garden of your life.

22-24 Don't fool yourself into thinking that you are a listener when you are anything but, letting the Word go in one ear and out the other. *Act* on what you hear! Those who hear and don't act are like those who glance in the mirror, walk away, and two minutes later have no idea who they are, what they look like.

25 But whoever catches a glimpse of the revealed counsel of God—the free life!—even out of the corner of his eye, and sticks with it, is no distracted scatterbrain but a man or woman of action. That person will find delight and affirmation in the action.

26-27 Anyone who sets himself up as "religious" by talking a good game is self-deceived. This kind of religion is hot air and only hot air. Real religion, the kind that passes muster before God the Father, is this: Reach out to the homeless and loveless in their plight, and guard against corruption from the godless world.

The Royal Rule of Love

1-4 2 My dear friends, don't let public opinion influence how you live out our glorious, Christ-originated faith. If a man enters your church wearing an expensive suit, and a street person wearing rags comes in right after him, and you say to the man in the suit, "Sit here, sir; this is the best seat in the house!" and either ignore the street person or say, "Better sit here in the back row," haven't you segregated God's children and proved that you are judges who can't be trusted?

5-7 Listen, dear friends. Isn't it clear by now that God operates quite differently? He chose the world's down-and-out as the kingdom's first citizens, with full rights and privileges. This kingdom is promised to anyone who loves God. And here you are abusing these same citizens! Isn't it the high and mighty who exploit you, who use the courts to rob you blind? Aren't they the ones who scorn the new name—"Christian"—used in your baptisms?

8-11 You do well when you complete the Royal Rule of the Scriptures: "Love others as you love yourself." But if you play up to these so-called important people, you go against the Rule and stand convicted by it. You can't pick and choose in these things, specializing in keeping one or two things in God's law and ignoring others. The same God who said, "Don't commit adultery," also said, "Don't murder." If you don't commit adultery but go ahead and murder, do you think your non-adultery will cancel out your murder? No, you're a murderer, period.

12-13 Talk and act like a person expecting to be judged by the Rule that sets us free. For if you refuse to act kindly, you can hardly expect to be treated kindly. Kind mercy wins over harsh judgment every time.

New King James Version

Faith Without Works Is Dead

14 What *does it* profit, my brethren, if someone says he has faith but does not have works? Can faith save him? 15 If a brother or sister is naked and destitute of daily food, 16 and one of you says to them, "Depart in peace, be warmed and filled," but you do not give them the things which are needed for the body, what *does it* profit? 17 Thus also faith by itself, if it does not have works, is dead.

18 But someone will say, "You have faith, and I have works." Show me your faith without your[a] works, and I will show you my faith by my[b] works. 19 You believe that there is one God. You do well. Even the demons believe—and tremble! 20 But do you want to know, O foolish man, that faith without works is dead?[a] 21 Was not Abraham our father justified by works when he offered Isaac his son on the altar? 22 Do you see that faith was working together with his works, and by works faith was made perfect? 23 And the Scripture was fulfilled which says, *"Abraham believed God, and it was accounted to him for righteousness."*[a] And he was called the friend of God. 24 You see then that a man is justified by works, and not by faith only.

25 Likewise, was not Rahab the harlot also justified by works when she received the messengers and sent *them* out another way?

26 For as the body without the spirit is dead, so faith without works is dead also.

The Untamable Tongue

3 My brethren, let not many of you become teachers, knowing that we shall receive a stricter judgment. 2 For we all stumble in many things. If anyone does not stumble in word, he *is* a perfect man, able also to bridle the whole body. 3 Indeed,[a] we put bits in horses' mouths that they may obey us, and we turn their whole body. 4 Look also at ships: although they are so large and are driven by fierce winds, they are turned by a very small rudder wherever the pi-

2:18 [a]NU-Text omits *your.* [b]NU-Text omits *my.* **2:20** [a]NU-Text reads *useless.* **2:23** [a]Genesis 15:6 **3:3** [a]NU-Text reads *Now if.*

The Message

Faith in Action

14-17 Dear friends, do you think you'll get anywhere in this if you learn all the right words but never do anything? Does merely talking about faith indicate that a person really has it? For instance, you come upon an old friend dressed in rags and half-starved and say, "Good morning, friend! Be clothed in Christ! Be filled with the Holy Spirit!" and walk off without providing so much as a coat or a cup of soup—where does that get you? Isn't it obvious that God-talk without God-acts is outrageous nonsense?

18 I can already hear one of you agreeing by saying, "Sounds good. You take care of the faith department, I'll handle the works department."

Not so fast. You can no more show me your works apart from your faith than I can show you my faith apart from my works. Faith and works, works and faith, fit together hand in glove.

19-20 Do I hear you professing to believe in the one and only God, but then observe you complacently sitting back as if you had done something wonderful? That's just great. Demons do that, but what good does it do them? Use your heads! Do you suppose for a minute that you can cut faith and works in two and not end up with a corpse on your hands?

21-24 Wasn't our ancestor Abraham "made right with God by works" when he placed his son Isaac on the sacrificial altar? Isn't it obvious that faith and works are yoked partners, that faith expresses itself in works? That the works are "works of faith"? The full meaning of "believe" in the Scripture sentence, "Abraham believed God and was set right with God," includes his action. It's that mesh of believing and acting that got Abraham named "God's friend." Is it not evident that a person is made right with God not by a barren faith but by faith fruitful in works?

25-26 The same with Rahab, the Jericho harlot. Wasn't her action in hiding God's spies and helping them escape—that seamless unity of *believing* and *doing*—what counted with God? The very moment you separate body and spirit, you end up with a corpse. Separate faith and works and you get the same thing: a corpse.

When You Open Your Mouth

1-2 **3** Don't be in any rush to become a teacher, my friends. Teaching is highly responsible work. Teachers are held to the strictest standards. And none of us is perfectly qualified. We get it wrong nearly every time we open our mouths. If you could find someone whose speech was perfectly true, you'd have a perfect person, in perfect control of life.

3-5 A bit in the mouth of a horse controls the whole horse. A small rudder on a huge ship in the hands of a skilled captain sets a course in the face of the strongest winds. A word out of your mouth may seem of no account, but it can accomplish nearly anything—or destroy it!

NEW KING JAMES VERSION

lot desires. 5Even so the tongue is a little mem-
ber and boasts great things.
See how great a forest a little fire kindles!
6And the tongue *is* a fire, a world of iniquity. The
tongue is so set among our members that it de-
files the whole body, and sets on fire the course
of nature; and it is set on fire by hell. 7For every
kind of beast and bird, of reptile and creature of
the sea, is tamed and has been tamed by
mankind. 8But no man can tame the tongue. *It is*
an unruly evil, full of deadly poison. 9With it we
bless our God and Father, and with it we curse
men, who have been made in the similitude of
God. 10Out of the same mouth proceed blessing
and cursing. My brethren, these things ought
not to be so. 11Does a spring send forth fresh
water and bitter from the same opening? 12Can
a fig tree, my brethren, bear olives, or a
grapevine bear figs? Thus no spring yields both
salt water and fresh.[a]

HEAVENLY VERSUS DEMONIC WISDOM

13Who *is* wise and understanding among
you? Let him show by good conduct *that* his
works *are done* in the meekness of wisdom.
14But if you have bitter envy and self-seeking in
your hearts, do not boast and lie against the
truth. 15This wisdom does not descend from
above, but *is* earthly, sensual, demonic. 16For
where envy and self-seeking *exist*, confusion
and every evil thing *are* there. 17But the wisdom
that is from above is first pure, then peaceable,
gentle, willing to yield, full of mercy and good
fruits, without partiality and without hypocrisy.
18Now the fruit of righteousness is sown in
peace by those who make peace.

PRIDE PROMOTES STRIFE

4 Where do wars and fights *come* from among
you? Do *they* not *come* from your *desires for*
pleasure that war in your members? 2You lust
and do not have. You murder and covet and can-
not obtain. You fight and war. Yet[a] you do not
have because you do not ask. 3You ask and do
not receive, because you ask amiss, that you
may spend *it* on your pleasures. 4Adulterers
and[a] adulteresses! Do you not know that friend-
ship with the world is enmity with God? Who-
ever therefore wants to be a friend of the world
makes himself an enemy of God. 5Or do you
think that the Scripture says in vain, "The Spirit
who dwells in us yearns jealously"?

3:12 [a]NU-Text reads *Neither can a salty spring produce fresh water.* **4:2** [a]NU-Text and M-Text omit *Yet.* **4:4** [a]NU-Text omits *Adulterers and.*

THE MESSAGE

5-6 It only takes a spark, remember, to set off
a forest fire. A careless or wrongly placed
word out of your mouth can do that. By our
speech we can ruin the world, turn harmony
to chaos, throw mud on a reputation, send
the whole world up in smoke and go up in
smoke with it, smoke right from the pit of
hell.
7-10 This is scary: You can tame a tiger, but
you can't tame a tongue—it's never been
done. The tongue runs wild, a wanton killer.
With our tongues we bless God our Father;
with the same tongues we curse the very
men and women he made in his image.
Curses and blessings out of the same
mouth!
10-12 My friends, this can't go on. A spring
doesn't gush fresh water one day and brack-
ish the next, does it? Apple trees don't bear
strawberries, do they? Raspberry bushes
don't bear apples, do they? You're not going
to dip into a polluted mud hole and get a cup
of clear, cool water, are you?

LIVE WELL, LIVE WISELY

13-16 Do you want to be counted wise, to build a
reputation for wisdom? Here's what you do:
Live well, live wisely, live humbly. It's the
way you live, not the way you talk, that
counts. Mean-spirited ambition isn't wis-
dom. Boasting that you are wise isn't wis-
dom. Twisting the truth to make yourselves
sound wise isn't wisdom. It's the furthest
thing from wisdom—it's animal cunning,
devilish conniving. Whenever you're trying
to look better than others or get the better of
others, things fall apart and everyone ends
up at the others' throats.
17-18 Real wisdom, God's wisdom, begins with
a holy life and is characterized by getting
along with others. It is gentle and reason-
able, overflowing with mercy and blessings,
not hot one day and cold the next, not two-
faced. You can develop a healthy, robust
community that lives right with God and en-
joy its results *only* if you do the hard work
of getting along with each other, treating
each other with dignity and honor.

GET SERIOUS

1-2 4 Where do you think all these appalling
wars and quarrels come from? Do you
think they just happen? Think again. They
come about because you want your own
way, and fight for it deep inside yourselves.
You lust for what you don't have and are
willing to kill to get it. You want what isn't
yours and will risk violence to get your
hands on it.
2-3 You wouldn't think of just asking God for
it, would you? And why not? Because you
know you'd be asking for what you have no
right to. You're spoiled children, each want-
ing your own way.
4-6 You're cheating on God. If all you want is
your own way, flirting with the world every
chance you get, you end up enemies of God
and his way. And do you suppose God doesn't
care? The proverb has it that "he's a fiercely
jealous lover." And what he gives in love is

NEW KING JAMES VERSION

6But He gives more grace. Therefore He says:

"God resists the proud,
But gives grace to the humble." [a]

HUMILITY CURES WORLDLINESS

7Therefore submit to God. Resist the devil and he will flee from you. 8Draw near to God and He will draw near to you. Cleanse *your* hands, *you* sinners; and purify *your* hearts, *you* double-minded. 9Lament and mourn and weep! Let your laughter be turned to mourning and *your* joy to gloom. 10Humble yourselves in the sight of the Lord, and He will lift you up.

DO NOT JUDGE A BROTHER

11Do not speak evil of one another, brethren. He who speaks evil of a brother and judges his brother, speaks evil of the law and judges the law. But if you judge the law, you are not a doer of the law but a judge. 12There is one Lawgiver,[a] who is able to save and to destroy. Who[b] are you to judge another?[c]

DO NOT BOAST ABOUT TOMORROW

13Come now, you who say, "Today or tomorrow we will[a] go to such and such a city, spend a year there, buy and sell, and make a profit"; 14whereas you do not know what *will happen* tomorrow. For what *is* your life? It is even a vapor that appears for a little time and then vanishes away. 15Instead you *ought* to say, "If the Lord wills, we shall live and do this or that." 16But now you boast in your arrogance. All such boasting is evil.

17Therefore, to him who knows to do good and does not do *it*, to him it is sin.

RICH OPPRESSORS WILL BE JUDGED

5 Come now, *you* rich, weep and howl for your miseries that are coming upon *you!* 2Your riches are corrupted, and your garments are moth-eaten. 3Your gold and silver are corroded, and their corrosion will be a witness against you and will eat your flesh like fire. You have heaped up treasure in the last days. 4Indeed the wages of the laborers who mowed your fields, which you kept back by fraud, cry out; and the cries of the reapers have reached the ears of the Lord of Sabaoth.[a] 5You have lived on the earth in pleasure and luxury; you have fattened your hearts as[a] in a day of slaughter. 6You have condemned, you have murdered the just; he does not resist you.

BE PATIENT AND PERSEVERING

7Therefore be patient, brethren, until the coming of the Lord. See *how* the farmer waits for the precious fruit of the earth, waiting patiently for it until it receives the early and latter rain. 8You also be patient. Establish your hearts, for the coming of the Lord is at hand.

9Do not grumble against one another, brethren, lest you be condemned.[a] Behold, the Judge is standing at the door!

4:6 [a]Proverbs 3:34 **4:12** [a]NU-Text adds *and Judge.* [b]NU-Text and M-Text read *But who.* [c]NU-Text reads *a neighbor.* **4:13** [a]M-Text reads *let us.* **5:4** [a]Literally, in Hebrew, *Hosts* **5:5** [a]NU-Text omits *as.* **5:9** [a]NU-Text and M-Text read *judged.*

THE MESSAGE

far better than anything else you'll find. It's common knowledge that "God goes against the willful proud; God gives grace to the willing humble."

7-10 So let God work his will in you. Yell a loud
no to the Devil and watch him scamper. Say
a quiet *yes* to God and he'll be there in no
time. Quit dabbling in sin. Purify your inner
life. Quit playing the field. Hit bottom, and
cry your eyes out. The fun and games are
over. Get serious, really serious. Get down
on your knees before the Master; it's the
only way you'll get on your feet.

11-12 Don't bad-mouth each other, friends. It's
God's Word, his Message, his Royal Rule,
that takes a beating in that kind of talk.
You're supposed to be honoring the Mes-
sage, not writing graffiti all over it. God is in
charge of deciding human destiny. Who do
you think you are to meddle in the destiny
of others?

NOTHING BUT A WISP OF FOG

13-15 And now I have a word for you who brashly
announce, "Today—at the latest, tomor-
row—we're off to such and such a city for
the year. We're going to start a business and
make a lot of money." You don't know the
first thing about tomorrow. You're nothing
but a wisp of fog, catching a brief bit of sun
before disappearing. Instead, make it a
habit to say, "If the Master wills it and we're
still alive, we'll do this or that."

16-17 As it is, you are full of your grandiose
selves. All such vaunting self-importance is
evil. In fact, if you know the right thing to do
and don't do it, that, for you, *is* evil.

DESTROYING YOUR LIFE FROM WITHIN

1-3 5 And a final word to you arrogant rich:
Take some lessons in lament. You'll need
buckets for the tears when the crash comes
upon you. Your money is corrupt and your
fine clothes stink. Your greedy luxuries are a
cancer in your gut, destroying your life from
within. You thought you were piling up
wealth. What you've piled up is judgment.

4-6 All the workers you've exploited and
cheated cry out for judgment. The groans of
the workers you used and abused are a roar
in the ears of the Master Avenger. You've
looted the earth and lived it up. But all you'll
have to show for it is a fatter than usual
corpse. In fact, what you've done is con-
demn and murder perfectly good persons,
who stand there and take it.

7-8 Meanwhile, friends, wait patiently for the
Master's Arrival. You see farmers do this all
the time, waiting for their valuable crops to
mature, patiently letting the rain do its slow
but sure work. Be patient like that. Stay
steady and strong. The Master could arrive
at any time.

9 Friends, don't complain about each other.
A far greater complaint could be lodged
against you, you know. The Judge is stand-
ing just around the corner.

New King James Version

10My brethren, take the prophets, who spoke in
the name of the Lord, as an example of suffer-
ing and patience. 11Indeed we count them
blessed who endure. You have heard of the per-
severance of Job and seen the end *intended by*
the Lord—that the Lord is very compassionate
and merciful.
12But above all, my brethren, do not swear,
either by heaven or by earth or with any other
oath. But let your "Yes" be "Yes," and *your* "No,"
"No," lest you fall into judgment.[a]

Meeting Specific Needs

13Is anyone among you suffering? Let him
pray. Is anyone cheerful? Let him sing psalms.
14Is anyone among you sick? Let him call for the
elders of the church, and let them pray over him,
anointing him with oil in the name of the Lord.
15And the prayer of faith will save the sick, and
the Lord will raise him up. And if he has com-
mitted sins, he will be forgiven. 16Confess *your*
trespasses[a] to one another, and pray for one an-
other, that you may be healed. The effective, fer-
vent prayer of a righteous man avails much.
17Elijah was a man with a nature like ours, and
he prayed earnestly that it would not rain; and it
did not rain on the land for three years and six
months. 18And he prayed again, and the heaven
gave rain, and the earth produced its fruit.

Bring Back the Erring One

19Brethren, if anyone among you wanders
from the truth, and someone turns him back,
20let him know that he who turns a sinner from
the error of his way will save a soul[a] from death
and cover a multitude of sins.

5:12 [a]M-Text reads *hypocrisy.* **5:16** [a]NU-Text reads *Therefore confess your sins.* **5:20** [a]NU-Text reads *his soul.*

The Message

10-11 Take the old prophets as your mentors.
They put up with anything, went through
everything, and never once quit, all the time
honoring God. What a gift life is to those
who stay the course! You've heard, of
course, of Job's staying power, and you
know how God brought it all together for
him at the end. That's because God cares,
cares right down to the last detail.

12 And since you know that he cares, let
your language show it. Don't add words like
"I swear to God" to your own words. Don't
show your impatience by concocting oaths
to hurry up God. Just say yes or no. Just say
what is true. That way, your language can't
be used against you.

Prayer to Be Reckoned With

13-15 Are you hurting? Pray. Do you feel great?
Sing. Are you sick? Call the church leaders
together to pray and anoint you with oil in
the name of the Master. Believing-prayer
will heal you, and Jesus will put you on your
feet. And if you've sinned, you'll be for-
given—healed inside and out.

16-18 Make this your common practice: Confess
your sins to each other and pray for each
other so that you can live together whole and
healed. The prayer of a person living right
with God is something powerful to be reck-
oned with. Elijah, for instance, human just
like us, prayed hard that it wouldn't rain, and
it didn't—not a drop for three and a half
years. Then he prayed that it would rain, and
it did. The showers came and everything
started growing again.

19-20 My dear friends, if you know people who
have wandered off from God's truth, don't
write them off. Go after them. Get them
back and you will have rescued precious
lives from destruction and prevented an epi-
demic of wandering away from God.

1 PETER

New King James Version

Greeting to the Elect Pilgrims

1 Peter, an apostle of Jesus Christ,

To the pilgrims of the Dispersion in Pontus, Galatia, Cappadocia, Asia, and Bithynia, 2elect according to the foreknowledge of God the Father, in sanctification of the Spirit, for obedience and sprinkling of the blood of Jesus Christ:

Grace to you and peace be multiplied.

A Heavenly Inheritance

3Blessed *be* the God and Father of our Lord Jesus Christ, who according to His abundant mercy has begotten us again to a living hope through the resurrection of Jesus Christ from the dead, 4to an inheritance incorruptible and undefiled and that does not fade away, reserved in heaven for you, 5who are kept by the power of God through faith for salvation ready to be revealed in the last time.

6In this you greatly rejoice, though now for a little while, if need be, you have been grieved by various trials, 7that the genuineness of your faith, *being* much more precious than gold that perishes, though it is tested by fire, may be found to praise, honor, and glory at the revelation of Jesus Christ, 8whom having not seen[a] you love. Though now you do not see *Him,* yet believing, you rejoice with joy inexpressible and full of glory, 9receiving the end of your faith—the salvation of *your* souls.

10Of this salvation the prophets have inquired and searched carefully, who prophesied of the grace *that would come* to you, 11searching what, or what manner of time, the Spirit of Christ who was in them was indicating when He testified beforehand the sufferings of Christ and the glories that would follow. 12To them it was revealed that, not to themselves, but to us[a] they were ministering the things which now have been reported to you through those who have preached the gospel to you by the Holy Spirit sent from heaven—things which angels desire to look into.

Living Before God Our Father

13Therefore gird up the loins of your mind, be sober, and rest *your* hope fully upon the grace that is to be brought to you at the revelation of Jesus Christ; 14as obedient children, not conforming yourselves to the former lusts, *as* in your ignorance; 15but as He who called you *is* holy, you also be holy in all *your* conduct, 16because it is written, *"Be holy, for I am holy."*[a]

17And if you call on the Father, who without partiality judges according to each one's work, conduct yourselves throughout the time of your stay *here* in fear; 18knowing that you were not redeemed with corruptible things, *like* silver or

1:8 [a]M-Text reads *known.* **1:12** [a]NU-Text and M-Text read *you.*
1:16 [a]Leviticus 11:44, 45; 19:2; 20:7

The Message

1-2 1 I, Peter, am an apostle on assignment by Jesus, the Messiah, writing to exiles scattered to the four winds. Not one is missing, not one forgotten. God the Father has his eye on each of you, and has determined by the work of the Spirit to keep you obedient through the sacrifice of Jesus. May everything good from God be yours!

A New Life

3-5 What a God we have! And how fortunate we are to have him, this Father of our Master Jesus! Because Jesus was raised from the dead, we've been given a brand-new life and have everything to live for, including a future in heaven—and the future starts now! God is keeping careful watch over us and the future. The Day is coming when you'll have it all—life healed and whole.

6-7 I know how great this makes you feel, even though you have to put up with every kind of aggravation in the meantime. Pure gold put in the fire comes out of it *proved* pure; genuine faith put through this suffering comes out *proved* genuine. When Jesus wraps this all up, it's your faith, not your gold, that God will have on display as evidence of his victory.

8-9 You never saw him, yet you love him. You still don't see him, yet you trust him—with laughter and singing. Because you kept on believing, you'll get what you're looking forward to: total salvation.

10-12 The prophets who told us this was coming asked a lot of questions about this gift of life God was preparing. The Messiah's Spirit let them in on some of it—that the Messiah would experience suffering, followed by glory. They clamored to know who and when. All they were told was that they were serving you, you who by orders from heaven have now heard for yourselves—through the Holy Spirit—the Message of those prophecies fulfilled. Do you realize how fortunate you are? Angels would have given anything to be in on this!

A Future in God

13-16 So roll up your sleeves, put your mind in gear, be totally ready to receive the gift that's coming when Jesus arrives. Don't lazily slip back into those old grooves of evil, doing just what you feel like doing. You didn't know any better then; you do now. As obedient children, let yourselves be pulled into a way of life shaped by God's life, a life energetic and blazing with holiness. God said, "I am holy; you be holy."

17 You call out to God for help and he helps—he's a good Father that way. But don't forget, he's also a responsible Father, and won't let you get by with sloppy living.

18-21 Your life is a journey you must travel with a deep consciousness of God. It cost God

NEW KING JAMES VERSION

gold, from your aimless conduct *received* by tra-
dition from your fathers, 19but with the precious
blood of Christ, as of a lamb without blemish
and without spot. 20He indeed was foreordained
before the foundation of the world, but was
manifest in these last times for you 21who
through Him believe in God, who raised Him
from the dead and gave Him glory, so that your
faith and hope are in God.

THE ENDURING WORD

22Since you have purified your souls in obey-
ing the truth through the Spirit[a] in sincere love
of the brethren, love one another fervently with
a pure heart, 23having been born again, not of
corruptible seed but incorruptible, through the
word of God which lives and abides forever,[a]
24because

"All flesh is as grass,
And all the glory of man[a] *as the flower of the grass.*
The grass withers,
And its flower falls away,
25*But the word of the LORD endures forever."*[a]

Now this is the word which by the gospel was
preached to you.

2 Therefore, laying aside all malice, all deceit,
hypocrisy, envy, and all evil speaking, 2as
newborn babes, desire the pure milk of the
word, that you may grow thereby,[a] 3if indeed
you have tasted that the Lord *is* gracious.

THE CHOSEN STONE AND HIS CHOSEN PEOPLE

4Coming to Him *as to* a living stone, rejected
indeed by men, but chosen by God *and* precious,
5you also, as living stones, are being built up a
spiritual house, a holy priesthood, to offer up
spiritual sacrifices acceptable to God through
Jesus Christ. 6Therefore it is also contained in
the Scripture,

"Behold, I lay in Zion
A chief cornerstone, elect, precious,
And he who believes on Him will by no means be put to shame."[a]

7Therefore, to you who believe, *He is* pre-
cious; but to those who are disobedient,[a]

"The stone which the builders rejected
Has become the chief cornerstone,"[b]

8and

"A stone of stumbling
And a rock of offense."[a]

They stumble, being disobedient to the word, to
which they also were appointed.
9But you *are* a chosen generation, a royal
priesthood, a holy nation, His own special peo-

1:22 [a]NU-Text omits *through the Spirit.* **1:23** [a]NU-Text omits *forever.* **1:24** [a]NU-Text reads *all its glory.* **1:25** [a]Isaiah 40:6–8 **2:2** [a]NU-Text adds *up to salvation.* **2:6** [a]Isaiah 28:16 **2:7** [a]NU-Text reads *to those who disbelieve.* [b]Psalm 118:22 **2:8** [a]Isaiah 8:14

THE MESSAGE

plenty to get you out of that dead-end, empty-headed life you grew up in. He paid with Christ's sacred blood, you know. He died like an unblemished, sacrificial lamb. And this was no afterthought. Even though it has only lately—at the end of the ages—become public knowledge, God always knew he was going to do this for you. It's because of this sacrificed Messiah, whom God then raised from the dead and glorified, that you trust God, that you know you have a future in God.

22-25 Now that you've cleaned up your lives by following the truth, love one another as if your lives depended on it. Your new life is not like your old life. Your old birth came from mortal sperm; your new birth comes from God's living Word. Just think: a life conceived by God himself! That's why the prophet said,

The old life is a grass life,
its beauty as short-lived as wildflowers;
Grass dries up, flowers droop,
God's Word goes on and on forever.

This is the Word that conceived the new life in you.

1-3 **2** So clean house! Make a clean sweep of malice and pretense, envy and hurtful talk. You've had a taste of God. Now, like infants at the breast, drink deep of God's pure kindness. Then you'll grow up mature and whole in God.

THE STONE

4-8 Welcome to the living Stone, the source of life. The workmen took one look and threw it out; God set it in the place of honor. Present yourselves as building stones for the construction of a sanctuary vibrant with life, in which you'll serve as holy priests offering Christ-approved lives up to God. The Scriptures provide precedent:

Look! I'm setting a stone in Zion,
a cornerstone in the place of honor.
Whoever trusts in this stone as a foundation
will never have cause to regret it.

To you who trust him, he's a Stone to be proud of, but to those who refuse to trust him,

The stone the workmen threw out
is now the chief foundation stone.

For the untrusting it's
. . . a stone to trip over,
a boulder blocking the way.

They trip and fall because they refuse to obey, just as predicted.

9-10 But you are the ones chosen by God, chosen for the high calling of priestly work, chosen to be a holy people, God's instru-

NEW KING JAMES VERSION

ple, that you may proclaim the praises of Him who called you out of darkness into His marvelous light; 10who once *were* not a people but *are* now the people of God, who had not obtained mercy but now have obtained mercy.

LIVING BEFORE THE WORLD

11Beloved, I beg *you* as sojourners and pilgrims, abstain from fleshly lusts which war against the soul, 12having your conduct honorable among the Gentiles, that when they speak against you as evildoers, they may, by *your* good works which they observe, glorify God in the day of visitation.

SUBMISSION TO GOVERNMENT

13Therefore submit yourselves to every ordinance of man for the Lord's sake, whether to the king as supreme, 14or to governors, as to those who are sent by him for the punishment of evildoers and *for the* praise of those who do good. 15For this is the will of God, that by doing good you may put to silence the ignorance of foolish men— 16as free, yet not using liberty as a cloak for vice, but as bondservants of God. 17Honor all *people.* Love the brotherhood. Fear God. Honor the king.

SUBMISSION TO MASTERS

18Servants, *be* submissive to *your* masters with all fear, not only to the good and gentle, but also to the harsh. 19For this *is* commendable, if because of conscience toward God one endures grief, suffering wrongfully. 20For what credit *is it* if, when you are beaten for your faults, you take it patiently? But when you do good and suffer, if you take it patiently, this *is* commendable before God. 21For to this you were called, because Christ also suffered for us,[a] leaving us[b] an example, that you should follow His steps:

22"*Who committed no sin,*
Nor was deceit found in His mouth";[a]

23who, when He was reviled, did not revile in return; when He suffered, He did not threaten, but committed *Himself* to Him who judges righteously; 24who Himself bore our sins in His own body on the tree, that we, having died to sins, might live for righteousness—by whose stripes you were healed. 25For you were like sheep going astray, but have now returned to the Shepherd and Overseer[a] of your souls.

SUBMISSION TO HUSBANDS

3 Wives, likewise, *be* submissive to your own husbands, that even if some do not obey the word, they, without a word, may be won by the conduct of their wives, 2when they observe your chaste conduct *accompanied* by fear. 3Do not let your adornment be *merely* outward—arranging the hair, wearing gold, or putting on *fine* apparel—

2:21 [a]NU-Text reads *you.* [b]NU-Text and M-Text read *you.*
2:22 [a]Isaiah 53:9 **2:25** [a]Greek *Episkopos*

THE MESSAGE

ments to do his work and speak out for him, to tell others of the night-and-day difference he made for you—from nothing to something, from rejected to accepted.

11-12 Friends, this world is not your home, so don't make yourselves cozy in it. Don't indulge your ego at the expense of your soul. Live an exemplary life among the natives so that your actions will refute their prejudices. Then they'll be won over to God's side and be there to join in the celebration when he arrives.

13-17 Make the Master proud of you by being good citizens. Respect the authorities, whatever their level; they are God's emissaries for keeping order. It is God's will that by doing good, you might cure the ignorance of the fools who think you're a danger to society. Exercise your freedom by serving God, not by breaking the rules. Treat everyone you meet with dignity. Love your spiritual family. Revere God. Respect the government.

THE KIND OF LIFE HE LIVED

18-20 You who are servants, be good servants to your masters—not just to good masters, but also to bad ones. What counts is that you put up with it for God's sake when you're treated badly for no good reason. There's no particular virtue in accepting punishment that you well deserve. But if you're treated badly for good behavior and continue in spite of it to be a good servant, that is what counts with God.

21-25 This is the kind of life you've been invited into, the kind of life Christ lived. He suffered everything that came his way so you would know that it could be done, and also know how to do it, step-by-step.

He never did one thing wrong,
Not once said anything amiss.

They called him every name in the book and he said nothing back. He suffered in silence, content to let God set things right. He used his servant body to carry our sins to the Cross so we could be rid of sin, free to live the right way. His wounds became your healing. You were lost sheep with no idea who you were or where you were going. Now you're named and kept for good by the Shepherd of your souls.

CULTIVATE INNER BEAUTY

1-4 3 The same goes for you wives: Be good wives to your husbands, responsive to their needs. There are husbands who, indifferent as they are to any words about God, will be captivated by your life of holy beauty. What matters is not your outer appearance—the styling of your hair, the jewelry you wear, the cut of your clothes—but your inner disposition.

NEW KING JAMES VERSION

4rather *let it be* the hidden person of the heart,
with the incorruptible *beauty* of a gentle and
quiet spirit, which is very precious in the sight
of God. 5For in this manner, in former times, the
holy women who trusted in God also adorned
themselves, being submissive to their own hus-
bands, 6as Sarah obeyed Abraham, calling him
lord, whose daughters you are if you do good
and are not afraid with any terror.

A WORD TO HUSBANDS

7Husbands, likewise, dwell with *them* with
understanding, giving honor to the wife, as to
the weaker vessel, and as *being* heirs together of
the grace of life, that your prayers may not be
hindered.

CALLED TO BLESSING

8Finally, all *of you be* of one mind, having
compassion for one another; love as brothers,
be tenderhearted, *be* courteous;[a] 9not returning
evil for evil or reviling for reviling, but on the
contrary blessing, knowing that you were called
to this, that you may inherit a blessing. 10For

"He who would love life
And see good days,
Let him refrain his tongue from evil,
And his lips from speaking deceit.
11*Let him turn away from evil and do good;*
Let him seek peace and pursue it.
12*For the eyes of the LORD are on the*
righteous,
And His ears are open to their prayers;
But the face of the LORD is against those
who do evil."[a]

SUFFERING FOR RIGHT AND WRONG

13And who *is* he who will harm you if you be-
come followers of what is good? 14But even if
you should suffer for righteousness' sake, *you*
are blessed. *"And do not be afraid of their*
threats, nor be troubled."[a] 15But sanctify the
Lord God[a] in your hearts, and always *be* ready
to *give* a defense to everyone who asks you a
reason for the hope that is in you, with meek-
ness and fear; 16having a good conscience, that
when they defame you as evildoers, those who
revile your good conduct in Christ may be
ashamed. 17For *it is* better, if it is the will of God,
to suffer for doing good than for doing evil.

CHRIST'S SUFFERING AND OURS

18For Christ also suffered once for sins, the
just for the unjust, that He might bring us[a] to
God, being put to death in the flesh but made
alive by the Spirit, 19by whom also He went and
preached to the spirits in prison, 20who formerly
were disobedient, when once the Divine long-
suffering waited[a] in the days of Noah, while *the*
ark was being prepared, in which a few, that is,
eight souls, were saved through water. 21There is
also an antitype which now saves us—baptism
(not the removal of the filth of the flesh, but the
answer of a good conscience toward God),

3:8 [a]NU-Text reads *humble.* **3:12** [a]Psalm 34:12–16 **3:14** [a]Isaiah 8:12 **3:15** [a]NU-Text reads *Christ as Lord.* **3:18** [a]NU-Text and M-Text read *you.* **3:20** [a]NU-Text and M-Text read *when the longsuffering of God waited patiently.*

THE MESSAGE

4-6 Cultivate inner beauty, the gentle, gracious kind that God delights in. The holy women of old were beautiful before God that way, and were good, loyal wives to their husbands. Sarah, for instance, taking care of Abraham, would address him as "my dear husband." You'll be true daughters of Sarah if you do the same, unanxious and unintimidated.

7 The same goes for you husbands: Be good husbands to your wives. Honor them, delight in them. As women they lack some of your advantages. But in the new life of God's grace, you're equals. Treat your wives, then, as equals so your prayers don't run aground.

SUFFERING FOR DOING GOOD

8-12 Summing up: Be agreeable, be sympathetic, be loving, be compassionate, be humble. That goes for all of you, no exceptions. No retaliation. No sharp-tongued sarcasm. Instead, bless—that's your job, to bless. You'll be a blessing and also get a blessing.

Whoever wants to embrace life
and see the day fill up with good,
Here's what you do:
Say nothing evil or hurtful;
Snub evil and cultivate good;
run after peace for all you're worth.
God looks on all this with approval,
listening and responding well to what he's asked;
But he turns his back
on those who do evil things.

13-18 If with heart and soul you're doing good, do you think you can be stopped? Even if you suffer for it, you're still better off. Don't give the opposition a second thought. Through thick and thin, keep your hearts at attention, in adoration before Christ, your Master. Be ready to speak up and tell anyone who asks why you're living the way you are, and always with the utmost courtesy. Keep a clear conscience before God so that when people throw mud at you, none of it will stick. They'll end up realizing that *they're* the ones who need a bath. It's better to suffer for doing good, if that's what God wants, than to be punished for doing bad. That's what Christ did definitively: suffered because of others' sins, the Righteous One for the unrighteous ones. He went through it all—was put to death and then made alive—to bring us to God.

19-22 He went and proclaimed God's salvation to earlier generations who ended up in the prison of judgment because they wouldn't listen. You know, even though God waited patiently all the days that Noah built his ship, only a few were saved then, eight to be exact—saved *from* the water *by* the water. The waters of baptism do that for you, not by washing away dirt from your skin but by presenting you through Jesus' resurrection

NEW KING JAMES VERSION

through the resurrection of Jesus Christ, [22]who
has gone into heaven and is at the right hand of
God, angels and authorities and powers having
been made subject to Him.

4 Therefore, since Christ suffered for us[a] in the
flesh, arm yourselves also with the same
mind, for he who has suffered in the flesh has
ceased from sin, [2]that he no longer should live
the rest of *his* time in the flesh for the lusts of
men, but for the will of God. [3]For we *have spent*
enough of our past lifetime[a] in doing the will of
the Gentiles—when we walked in lewdness,
lusts, drunkenness, revelries, drinking parties,
and abominable idolatries. [4]In regard to these,
they think it strange that you do not run with
them in the same flood of dissipation, speaking
evil of *you*. [5]They will give an account to Him
who is ready to judge the living and the dead.
[6]For this reason the gospel was preached also to
those who are dead, that they might be judged
according to men in the flesh, but live according
to God in the spirit.

SERVING FOR GOD'S GLORY

[7]But the end of all things is at hand; there-
fore be serious and watchful in your prayers.
[8]And above all things have fervent love for one
another, for *"love will cover a multitude of*
sins."[a] [9]*Be* hospitable to one another without
grumbling. [10]As each one has received a gift,
minister it to one another, as good stewards of
the manifold grace of God. [11]If anyone speaks,
let him speak as the oracles of God. If anyone
ministers, *let him do it* as with the ability
which God supplies, that in all things God may
be glorified through Jesus Christ, to whom be-
long the glory and the dominion forever and
ever. Amen.

SUFFERING FOR GOD'S GLORY

[12]Beloved, do not think it strange concerning
the fiery trial which is to try you, as though
some strange thing happened to you; [13]but re-
joice to the extent that you partake of Christ's
sufferings, that when His glory is revealed, you
may also be glad with exceeding joy. [14]If you are
reproached for the name of Christ, blessed *are*
you, for the Spirit of glory and of God rests upon
you.[a] On their part He is blasphemed, but on
your part He is glorified. [15]But let none of you
suffer as a murderer, a thief, an evildoer, or as a
busybody in other people's matters. [16]Yet if *any-*
one suffers as a Christian, let him not be
ashamed, but let him glorify God in this matter.[a]
[17]For the time *has come* for judgment to be-
gin at the house of God; and if *it begins* with us
first, what will *be* the end of those who do not
obey the gospel of God? [18]Now

"If the righteous one is scarcely saved,
Where will the ungodly and the sinner
appear?"[a]

4:1 [a]NU-Text omits *for us*. **4:3** [a]NU-Text reads *time*.
4:8 [a]Proverbs 10:12 **4:14** [a]NU-Text omits the rest of this verse.
4:16 [a]NU-Text reads *name*. **4:18** [a]Proverbs 11:31

THE MESSAGE

before God with a clear conscience. Jesus has the last word on everything and everyone, from angels to armies. He's standing right alongside God, and what he says goes.

LEARN TO THINK LIKE HIM

1-2 4 Since Jesus went through everything you're going through and more, learn to think like him. Think of your sufferings as a weaning from that old sinful habit of always expecting to get your own way. Then you'll be able to live out your days free to pursue what God wants instead of being tyrannized by what you want.

3-5 You've already put in your time in that God-ignorant way of life, partying night after night, a drunken and profligate life. Now it's time to be done with it for good. Of course, your old friends don't understand why you don't join in with the old gang anymore. But you don't have to give an account to them. They're the ones who will be called on the carpet—and before God himself.

6 Listen to the Message. It was preached to those believers who are now dead, and yet even though they died (just as all people must), they will still get in on the *life* that God has given in Jesus.

7-11 Everything in the world is about to be wrapped up, so take nothing for granted. Stay wide-awake in prayer. Most of all, love each other as if your life depended on it. Love makes up for practically anything. Be quick to give a meal to the hungry, a bed to the homeless—cheerfully. Be generous with the different things God gave you, passing them around so all get in on it: if words, let it be God's words; if help, let it be God's hearty help. That way, God's bright presence will be evident in everything through Jesus, and *he'll* get all the credit as the One mighty in everything—encores to the end of time. Oh, yes!

GLORY JUST AROUND THE CORNER

12-13 Friends, when life gets really difficult, don't jump to the conclusion that God isn't on the job. Instead, be glad that you are in the very thick of what Christ experienced. This is a spiritual refining process, with glory just around the corner.

14-16 If you're abused because of Christ, count yourself fortunate. It's the Spirit of God and his glory in you that brought you to the notice of others. If they're on you because you broke the law or disturbed the peace, that's a different matter. But if it's because you're a Christian, don't give it a second thought. Be proud of the distinguished status reflected in that name!

17-19 It's judgment time for God's own family. We're first in line. If it starts with us, think what it's going to be like for those who refuse God's Message!

If good people barely make it,
What's in store for the bad?

NEW KING JAMES VERSION

19Therefore let those who suffer according to
the will of God commit their souls *to Him* in do-
ing good, as to a faithful Creator.

SHEPHERD THE FLOCK

5 The elders who are among you I exhort, I
who am a fellow elder and a witness of the
sufferings of Christ, and also a partaker of the
glory that will be revealed: 2Shepherd the flock
of God which is among you, serving as over-
seers, not by compulsion but willingly,[a] not for
dishonest gain but eagerly; 3nor as being lords
over those entrusted to you, but being examples
to the flock; 4and when the Chief Shepherd ap-
pears, you will receive the crown of glory that
does not fade away.

SUBMIT TO GOD, RESIST THE DEVIL

5Likewise you younger people, submit your-
selves to *your* elders. Yes, all of *you* be submis-
sive to one another, and be clothed with humil-
ity, for

"God resists the proud,
But gives grace to the humble." [a]

6Therefore humble yourselves under the
mighty hand of God, that He may exalt you in
due time, 7casting all your care upon Him, for
He cares for you.
8Be sober, be vigilant; because[a] your adver-
sary the devil walks about like a roaring lion,
seeking whom he may devour. 9Resist him,
steadfast in the faith, knowing that the same
sufferings are experienced by your brotherhood
in the world. 10But may[a] the God of all grace,
who called us[b] to His eternal glory by Christ Je-
sus, after you have suffered a while, perfect, es-
tablish, strengthen, and settle *you.* 11To Him *be*
the glory and the dominion forever and ever.
Amen.

FAREWELL AND PEACE

12By Silvanus, our faithful brother as I con-
sider him, I have written to you briefly, exhort-
ing and testifying that this is the true grace of
God in which you stand.
13She who is in Babylon, elect together with
you, greets you; and *so does* Mark my son.
14Greet one another with a kiss of love.
Peace to you all who are in Christ Jesus.
Amen.

5:2 [a]NU-Text adds *according to God.* 5:5 [a]Proverbs 3:34
5:8 [a]NU-Text and M-Text omit *because.* 5:10 [a]NU-Text reads
But the God of all grace . . . will perfect, establish, strengthen, and settle you. [b]NU-Text and M-Text read *you.*

THE MESSAGE

So if you find life difficult because you're doing what God said, take it in stride. Trust him. He knows what he's doing, and he'll keep on doing it.

HE'LL PROMOTE YOU AT THE RIGHT TIME

1-3 5 I have a special concern for you church leaders. I know what it's like to be a leader, in on Christ's sufferings as well as the coming glory. Here's my concern: that you care for God's flock with all the diligence of a shepherd. Not because you have to, but because you want to please God. Not calculating what you can get out of it, but acting spontaneously. Not bossily telling others what to do, but tenderly showing them the way.

4-5 When God, who is the best shepherd of all, comes out in the open with his rule, he'll see that you've done it right and commend you lavishly. And you who are younger must follow your leaders. But all of you, leaders and followers alike, are to be down to earth with each other, for—

God has had it with the proud,
But takes delight in just plain people.

6-7 So be content with who you are, and don't put on airs. God's strong hand is on you; he'll promote you at the right time. Live carefree before God; he is most careful with you.

HE GETS THE LAST WORD

8-11 Keep a cool head. Stay alert. The Devil is poised to pounce, and would like nothing better than to catch you napping. Keep your guard up. You're not the only ones plunged into these hard times. It's the same with Christians all over the world. So keep a firm grip on the faith. The suffering won't last forever. It won't be long before this generous God who has great plans for us in Christ—eternal and glorious plans they are!—will have you put together and on your feet for good. He gets the last word; yes, he does.

12 I'm sending this brief letter to you by Silas, a most dependable brother. I have the highest regard for him.

I've written as urgently and accurately as I know how. This is God's generous truth; embrace it with both arms!

13-14 The church in exile here with me—but not for a moment forgotten by God—wants to be remembered to you. Mark, who is like a son to me, says hello. Give holy embraces all around! Peace to you—to all who walk in Christ's ways.

2 PETER

New King James Version

Greeting the Faithful

1 Simon Peter, a bondservant and apostle of
Jesus Christ,

To those who have obtained like precious
faith with us by the righteousness of our God
and Savior Jesus Christ:

2Grace and peace be multiplied to you in the
knowledge of God and of Jesus our Lord, 3as His
divine power has given to us all things that *per-
tain* to life and godliness, through the knowl-
edge of Him who called us by glory and virtue,
4by which have been given to us exceedingly
great and precious promises, that through these
you may be partakers of the divine nature, hav-
ing escaped the corruption *that is* in the world
through lust.

Fruitful Growth in the Faith

5But also for this very reason, giving all dili-
gence, add to your faith virtue, to virtue knowl-
edge, 6to knowledge self-control, to self-control
perseverance, to perseverance godliness, 7to
godliness brotherly kindness, and to brotherly
kindness love. 8For if these things are yours and
abound, *you will be* neither barren nor unfruit-
ful in the knowledge of our Lord Jesus Christ.
9For he who lacks these things is shortsighted,
even to blindness, and has forgotten that he was
cleansed from his old sins.

10Therefore, brethren, be even more diligent
to make your call and election sure, for if you do
these things you will never stumble; 11for so an
entrance will be supplied to you abundantly into
the everlasting kingdom of our Lord and Savior
Jesus Christ.

Peter's Approaching Death

12For this reason I will not be negligent to re-
mind you always of these things, though you
know and are established in the present truth.
13Yes, I think it is right, as long as I am in this
tent, to stir you up by reminding *you*, 14knowing
that shortly I *must* put off my tent, just as our
Lord Jesus Christ showed me. 15Moreover I will
be careful to ensure that you always have a re-
minder of these things after my decease.

The Trustworthy Prophetic Word

16For we did not follow cunningly devised fa-
bles when we made known to you the power
and coming of our Lord Jesus Christ, but were
eyewitnesses of His majesty. 17For He received
from God the Father honor and glory when such
a voice came to Him from the Excellent Glory:
"This is My beloved Son, in whom I am well
pleased." 18And we heard this voice which came
from heaven when we were with Him on the
holy mountain.

The Message

1-2 1 I, Simon Peter, am a servant and apostle
of Jesus Christ. I write this to you whose
experience with God is as life-changing as
ours, all due to our God's straight dealing
and the intervention of our God and Savior,
Jesus Christ. Grace and peace to you many
times over as you deepen in your experience
with God and Jesus, our Master.

Don't Put It Off

3-4 Everything that goes into a life of pleasing
God has been miraculously given to us by
getting to know, personally and intimately,
the One who invited us to God. The best in-
vitation we ever received! We were also
given absolutely terrific promises to pass on
to you—your tickets to participation in the
life of God after you turned your back on a
world corrupted by lust.

5-9 So don't lose a minute in building on what
you've been given, complementing your ba-
sic faith with good character, spiritual un-
derstanding, alert discipline, passionate pa-
tience, reverent wonder, warm friendliness,
and generous love, each dimension fitting
into and developing the others. With these
qualities active and growing in your lives, no
grass will grow under your feet, no day will
pass without its reward as you mature in
your experience of our Master Jesus. With-
out these qualities you can't see what's right
before you, oblivious that your old sinful life
has been wiped off the books.

10-11 So, friends, confirm God's invitation to
you, his choice of you. Don't put it off; do it
now. Do this, and you'll have your life on a
firm footing, the streets paved and the way
wide open into the eternal kingdom of our
Master and Savior, Jesus Christ.

The One Light in a Dark Time

12-15 Because the stakes are so high, even though
you're up-to-date on all this truth and prac-
tice it inside and out, I'm not going to let up
for a minute in calling you to attention be-
fore it. This is the post to which I've been as-
signed—keeping you alert with frequent re-
minders—and I'm sticking to it as long as I
live. I know that I'm to die soon; the Master
has made that quite clear to me. And so I am
especially eager that you have all this down
in black and white so that after I die, you'll
have it for ready reference.

16-18 We weren't, you know, just wishing on a
star when we laid the facts out before you
regarding the powerful return of our Mas-
ter, Jesus Christ. We were there for the pre-
view! We saw it with our own eyes: Jesus re-
splendent with light from God the Father as
the voice of Majestic Glory spoke: "This is
my Son, marked by my love, focus of all my
delight." We were there on the holy moun-
tain with him. We heard the voice out of
heaven with our very own ears.

NEW KING JAMES VERSION

19 And so we have the prophetic word confirmed,[a] which you do well to heed as a light that shines in a dark place, until the day dawns and the morning star rises in your hearts; 20 knowing this first, that no prophecy of Scripture is of any private interpretation,[a] 21 for prophecy never came by the will of man, but holy men of God[a] spoke *as they were* moved by the Holy Spirit.

DESTRUCTIVE DOCTRINES

2 But there were also false prophets among the people, even as there will be false teachers among you, who will secretly bring in destructive heresies, even denying the Lord who bought them, *and* bring on themselves swift destruction. 2 And many will follow their destructive ways, because of whom the way of truth will be blasphemed. 3 By covetousness they will exploit you with deceptive words; for a long time their judgment has not been idle, and their destruction does[a] not slumber.

DOOM OF FALSE TEACHERS

4 For if God did not spare the angels who sinned, but cast *them* down to hell and delivered *them* into chains of darkness, to be reserved for judgment; 5 and did not spare the ancient world, but saved Noah, *one of* eight *people*, a preacher of righteousness, bringing in the flood on the world of the ungodly; 6 and turning the cities of Sodom and Gomorrah into ashes, condemned *them* to destruction, making *them* an example to those who afterward would live ungodly; 7 and delivered righteous Lot, *who was* oppressed by the filthy conduct of the wicked 8 (for that righteous man, dwelling among them, tormented *his* righteous soul from day to day by seeing and hearing *their* lawless deeds)— 9 *then* the Lord knows how to deliver the godly out of temptations and to reserve the unjust under punishment for the day of judgment, 10 and especially those who walk according to the flesh in the lust of uncleanness and despise authority. *They are* presumptuous, self-willed. They are not afraid to speak evil of dignitaries, 11 whereas angels, who are greater in power and might, do not bring a reviling accusation against them before the Lord.

DEPRAVITY OF FALSE TEACHERS

12 But these, like natural brute beasts made to be caught and destroyed, speak evil of the things they do not understand, and will utterly perish in their own corruption, 13 *and* will receive the wages of unrighteousness, *as* those

1:19 [a]Or *We also have the more sure prophetic word.* **1:20** [a]Or *origin* **1:21** [a]NU-Text reads *but men spoke from God.* **2:3** [a]M-Text reads *will not.*

THE MESSAGE

19-21 We couldn't be more sure of what we saw and heard—*God's* glory, *God's* voice. The prophetic Word was confirmed to us. You'll do well to keep focusing on it. It's the one light you have in a dark time as you wait for daybreak and the rising of the Morning Star in your hearts. The main thing to keep in mind here is that no prophecy of Scripture is a matter of private opinion. And why? Because it's not something concocted in the human heart. Prophecy resulted when the Holy Spirit prompted men and women to speak God's Word.

LYING RELIGIOUS LEADERS

1-2 2 But there were also *lying* prophets among the people then, just as there will be lying religious teachers among you. They'll smuggle in destructive divisions, pitting you against each other—biting the hand of the One who gave them a chance to have their lives back! They've put themselves on a fast downhill slide to destruction, but not before they recruit a crowd of mixed-up followers who can't tell right from wrong.

2-3 They give the way of truth a bad name. They're only out for themselves. They'll say anything, *anything*, that sounds good to exploit you. They won't, of course, get by with it. They'll come to a bad end, for God has never just stood by and let that kind of thing go on.

4-5 God didn't let the rebel angels off the hook, but jailed them in hell till Judgment Day. Neither did he let the ancient ungodly world off. He wiped it out with a flood, rescuing only eight people—Noah, the sole voice of righteousness, was one of them.

6-8 God decreed destruction for the cities of Sodom and Gomorrah. A mound of ashes was all that was left—grim warning to anyone bent on an ungodly life. But that good man Lot, driven nearly out of his mind by the sexual filth and perversity, was rescued. Surrounded by moral rot day after day after day, that righteous man was in constant torment.

9 So God knows how to rescue the godly from evil trials. And he knows how to hold the feet of the wicked to the fire until Judgment Day.

PREDATORS ON THE PROWL

10-11 God is especially incensed against these "teachers" who live by lust, addicted to a filthy existence. They despise interference from true authority, preferring to indulge in self-rule. Insolent egotists, they don't hesitate to speak evil against the most splendid of creatures. Even angels, their superiors in every way, wouldn't think of throwing their weight around like that, trying to slander others before God.

12-14 These people are nothing but brute beasts, born in the wild, predators on the prowl. In the very act of bringing down others with their ignorant blasphemies, they themselves will be brought down, losers in the end. Their evil will boomerang on them.

NEW KING JAMES VERSION

who count it pleasure to carouse in the daytime. *They are* spots and blemishes, carousing in their own deceptions while they feast with you, 14having eyes full of adultery and that cannot cease from sin, enticing unstable souls. *They have* a heart trained in covetous practices, *and are* accursed children. 15They have forsaken the right way and gone astray, following the way of Balaam the *son* of Beor, who loved the wages of unrighteousness; 16but he was rebuked for his iniquity: a dumb donkey speaking with a man's voice restrained the madness of the prophet.

17These are wells without water, clouds[a] carried by a tempest, for whom is reserved the blackness of darkness forever.[b]

DECEPTIONS OF FALSE TEACHERS

18For when they speak great swelling *words* of emptiness, they allure through the lusts of the flesh, through lewdness, the ones who have actually escaped[a] from those who live in error. 19While they promise them liberty, they themselves are slaves of corruption; for by whom a person is overcome, by him also he is brought into bondage. 20For if, after they have escaped the pollutions of the world through the knowledge of the Lord and Savior Jesus Christ, they are again entangled in them and overcome, the latter end is worse for them than the beginning. 21For it would have been better for them not to have known the way of righteousness, than having known *it*, to turn from the holy commandment delivered to them. 22But it has happened to them according to the true proverb: *"A dog returns to his own vomit,"*[a] and, "a sow, having washed, to her wallowing in the mire."

GOD'S PROMISE IS NOT SLACK

3 Beloved, I now write to you this second epistle (in *both of* which I stir up your pure minds by way of reminder), 2that you may be mindful of the words which were spoken before by the holy prophets, and of the commandment of us,[a] the apostles of the Lord and Savior, 3knowing this first: that scoffers will come in the last days, walking according to their own lusts, 4and saying, "Where is the promise of His coming? For since the fathers fell asleep, all things continue as *they were* from the beginning of creation." 5For this they willfully forget: that by the word of God the heavens were of old, and the earth standing out of water and in the water, 6by which the world *that* then existed perished, being flooded with water. 7But the heavens and the earth *which* are now preserved by the same word, are reserved for fire until the day of judgment and perdition of ungodly men.

8But, beloved, do not forget this one thing, that with the Lord one day *is* as a thousand years, and a thousand years as one day. 9The Lord is not slack concerning *His* promise, as

2:17 [a]NU-Text reads *and mists.* [b]NU-Text omits *forever.*
2:18 [a]NU-Text reads *are barely escaping.* **2:22** [a]Proverbs 26:11
3:2 [a]NU-Text and M-Text read *commandment of the apostles of your Lord and Savior* or *commandment of your apostles of the Lord and Savior.*

THE MESSAGE

They're so despicable and addicted to pleasure that they indulge in wild parties, carousing in broad daylight. They're obsessed with adultery, compulsive in sin, seducing every vulnerable soul they come upon. Their specialty is greed, and they're experts at it. Dead souls!

15-16 They've left the main road and are directionless, having taken the way of Balaam, son of Beor, the prophet who turned profiteer, a connoisseur of evil. But Balaam was stopped in his wayward tracks: A dumb animal spoke in a human voice and prevented the prophet's craziness.

17-19 There's nothing to these people—they're dried-up fountains, storm-scattered clouds, headed for a black hole in hell. They are loudmouths, full of hot air, but still they're dangerous. Men and women who have recently escaped from a deviant life are most susceptible to their brand of seduction. They promise these newcomers freedom, but they themselves are slaves of corruption, for if they're addicted to corruption—and they are—they're *enslaved.*

20-22 If they've escaped from the slum of sin by experiencing our Master and Savior, Jesus Christ, and then slid back into that same old life again, they're worse than if they had never left. Better not to have started out on the straight road to God than to start out and then turn back, repudiating the experience and the holy command. They prove the point of the proverbs, "A dog goes back to its own vomit" and "A scrubbed-up pig heads for the mud."

IN THE LAST DAYS

1-2 3 My dear friends, this is now the second time I've written to you, both letters reminders to hold your minds in a state of undistracted attention. Keep in mind what the holy prophets said, and the command of our Master and Savior that was passed on by your apostles.

3-4 First off, you need to know that in the last days, mockers are going to have a heyday. Reducing everything to the level of their puny feelings, they'll mock, "So what's happened to the promise of his Coming? Our ancestors are dead and buried, and everything's going on just as it has from the first day of creation. Nothing's changed."

5-7 They conveniently forget that long ago all the galaxies and this very planet were brought into existence out of watery chaos by God's word. Then God's word brought the chaos back in a flood that destroyed the world. The current galaxies and earth are fuel for the final fire. God is poised, ready to speak his word again, ready to give the signal for the judgment and destruction of the desecrating skeptics.

THE DAY THE SKY WILL COLLAPSE

8-9 Don't overlook the obvious here, friends. With God, one day is as good as a thousand years, a thousand years as a day. God isn't late with his promise as some measure late-

NEW KING JAMES VERSION

some count slackness, but is longsuffering toward us,[a] not willing that any should perish but that all should come to repentance.

THE DAY OF THE LORD

10 But the day of the Lord will come as a thief in the night, in which the heavens will pass away with a great noise, and the elements will melt with fervent heat; both the earth and the works that are in it will be burned up.[a] 11 Therefore, since all these things will be dissolved, what manner *of persons* ought you to be in holy conduct and godliness, 12 looking for and hastening the coming of the day of God, because of which the heavens will be dissolved, being on fire, and the elements will melt with fervent heat? 13 Nevertheless we, according to His promise, look for new heavens and a new earth in which righteousness dwells.

BE STEADFAST

14 Therefore, beloved, looking forward to these things, be diligent to be found by Him in peace, without spot and blameless; 15 and consider *that* the longsuffering of our Lord *is* salvation—as also our beloved brother Paul, according to the wisdom given to him, has written to you, 16 as also in all his epistles, speaking in them of these things, in which are some things hard to understand, which untaught and unstable *people* twist to their own destruction, as *they do* also the rest of the Scriptures.

17 You therefore, beloved, since you know *this* beforehand, beware lest you also fall from your own steadfastness, being led away with the error of the wicked; 18 but grow in the grace and knowledge of our Lord and Savior Jesus Christ.

To Him *be* the glory both now and forever. Amen.

3:9 [a]NU-Text reads *you.* **3:10** [a]NU-Text reads *laid bare* (literally *found*).

THE MESSAGE

ness. He is restraining himself on account of you, holding back the End because he doesn't want anyone lost. He's giving everyone space and time to change.

10 But when the Day of God's Judgment does come, it will be unannounced, like a thief. The sky will collapse with a thunderous bang, everything disintegrating in a huge conflagration, earth and all its works exposed to the scrutiny of Judgment.

11-13 Since everything here today might well be gone tomorrow, do you see how essential it is to live a holy life? Daily expect the Day of God, eager for its arrival. The galaxies will burn up and the elements melt down that day—but *we'll* hardly notice. We'll be looking the other way, ready for the promised new heavens and the promised new earth, all landscaped with righteousness.

14-16 So, my dear friends, since this is what you have to look forward to, do your very best to be found living at your best, in purity and peace. Interpret our Master's patient restraint for what it is: salvation. Our good brother Paul, who was given much wisdom in these matters, refers to this in all his letters, and has written you essentially the same thing. Some things Paul writes are difficult to understand. Irresponsible people who don't know what they are talking about twist them every which way. They do it to the rest of the Scriptures, too, destroying themselves as they do it.

17-18 But you, friends, are well-warned. Be on guard lest you lose your footing and get swept off your feet by these lawless and loose-talking teachers. Grow in grace and understanding of our Master and Savior, Jesus Christ.

Glory to the Master, now and forever! Yes!

1 JOHN

New King James Version

What Was Heard, Seen, and Touched

1 That which was from the beginning, which we have heard, which we have seen with our eyes, which we have looked upon, and our hands have handled, concerning the Word of life— 2the life was manifested, and we have seen, and bear witness, and declare to you that eternal life which was with the Father and was manifested to us— 3that which we have seen and heard we declare to you, that you also may have fellowship with us; and truly our fellowship *is* with the Father and with His Son Jesus Christ. 4And these things we write to you that your[a] joy may be full.

Fellowship with Him and One Another

5This is the message which we have heard from Him and declare to you, that God is light and in Him is no darkness at all. 6If we say that we have fellowship with Him, and walk in darkness, we lie and do not practice the truth. 7But if we walk in the light as He is in the light, we have fellowship with one another, and the blood of Jesus Christ His Son cleanses us from all sin.

8If we say that we have no sin, we deceive ourselves, and the truth is not in us. 9If we confess our sins, He is faithful and just to forgive us *our* sins and to cleanse us from all unrighteousness. 10If we say that we have not sinned, we make Him a liar, and His word is not in us.

2 My little children, these things I write to you, so that you may not sin. And if anyone sins, we have an Advocate with the Father, Jesus Christ the righteous. 2And He Himself is the propitiation for our sins, and not for ours only but also for the whole world.

The Test of Knowing Him

3Now by this we know that we know Him, if we keep His commandments. 4He who says, "I know Him," and does not keep His commandments, is a liar, and the truth is not in him. 5But whoever keeps His word, truly the love of God is perfected in him. By this we know that we are in Him. 6He who says he abides in Him ought himself also to walk just as He walked.

7Brethren,[a] I write no new commandment to you, but an old commandment which you have had from the beginning. The old commandment is the word which you heard from the beginning.[b] 8Again, a new commandment I write to

1:4 [a]NU-Text and M-Text read *our.* 2:7 [a]NU-Text reads *Beloved.* [b]NU-Text omits *from the beginning.*

The Message

1-2 1 From the very first day, we were there, tak-
ing it all in—we heard it with our own ears,
saw it with our own eyes, verified it with our
own hands. The Word of Life appeared right
before our eyes; we saw it happen! And now
we're telling you in most sober prose that
what we witnessed was, incredibly, this: The
infinite Life of God himself took shape be-
fore us.
3-4 We saw it, we heard it, and now we're
telling you so you can experience it along
with us, this experience of communion with
the Father and his Son, Jesus Christ. Our mo-
tive for writing is simply this: We want you to
enjoy this, too. Your joy will double our joy!

Walk in the Light

5 This, in essence, is the message we heard
from Christ and are passing on to you: God
is light, pure light; there's not a trace of
darkness in him.
6-7 If we claim that we experience a shared
life with him and continue to stumble around
in the dark, we're obviously lying through
our teeth—we're not *living* what we claim.
But if we walk in the light, God himself being
the light, we also experience a shared life
with one another, as the sacrificed blood of
Jesus, God's Son, purges all our sin.
8-10 If we claim that we're free of sin, we're
only fooling ourselves. A claim like that is
errant nonsense. On the other hand, if we
admit our sins—make a clean breast of
them—he won't let us down; he'll be true to
himself. He'll forgive our sins and purge us
of all wrongdoing. If we claim that we've
never sinned, we out-and-out contradict
God—make a liar out of him. A claim like
that only shows off our ignorance of God.

1-2 2 I write this, dear children, to guide you out
of sin. But if anyone does sin, we have a
Priest-Friend in the presence of the Father:
Jesus Christ, righteous Jesus. When he
served as a sacrifice for our sins, he solved
the sin problem for good—not only ours, but
the whole world's.

The Only Way to Know We're in Him

2-3 Here's how we can be sure that we know God
in the right way: Keep his commandments.
4-6 If someone claims, "I know him well!" but
doesn't keep his commandments, he's obvi-
ously a liar. His life doesn't match his words.
But the one who keeps God's word is the per-
son in whom we see God's mature love. This
is the only way to be sure we're in God. Any-
one who claims to be intimate with God
ought to live the same kind of life Jesus lived.
7-8 My dear friends, I'm not writing anything
new here. This is the oldest commandment
in the book, and you've known it from day
one. It's always been implicit in the Message
you've heard. On the other hand, perhaps it

NEW KING JAMES VERSION

you, which thing is true in Him and in you, be-
cause the darkness is passing away, and the true
light is already shining.
9He who says he is in the light, and hates his
brother, is in darkness until now. 10He who loves
his brother abides in the light, and there is no
cause for stumbling in him. 11But he who hates
his brother is in darkness and walks in dark-
ness, and does not know where he is going, be-
cause the darkness has blinded his eyes.

THEIR SPIRITUAL STATE

12I write to you, little children,
Because your sins are forgiven you for His name's sake.
13I write to you, fathers,
Because you have known Him *who is* from the beginning.
I write to you, young men,
Because you have overcome the wicked one.
I write to you, little children,
Because you have known the Father.
14I have written to you, fathers,
Because you have known Him *who is* from the beginning.
I have written to you, young men,
Because you are strong, and the word of God abides in you,
And you have overcome the wicked one.

DO NOT LOVE THE WORLD

15Do not love the world or the things in the
world. If anyone loves the world, the love of the
Father is not in him. 16For all that *is* in the world—
the lust of the flesh, the lust of the eyes, and the
pride of life—is not of the Father but is of the
world. 17And the world is passing away, and
the lust of it; but he who does the will of God
abides forever.

DECEPTIONS OF THE LAST HOUR

18Little children, it is the last hour; and as
you have heard that the[a] Antichrist is coming,
even now many antichrists have come, by which
we know that it is the last hour. 19They went out
from us, but they were not of us; for if they had
been of us, they would have continued with us;
but *they went out* that they might be made man-
ifest, that none of them were of us.
20But you have an anointing from the Holy
One, and you know all things.[a] 21I have not writ-
ten to you because you do not know the truth,
but because you know it, and that no lie is of the
truth.
22Who is a liar but he who denies that Jesus
is the Christ? He is antichrist who denies the Fa-
ther and the Son. 23Whoever denies the Son
does not have the Father either; he who ac-
knowledges the Son has the Father also.

LET TRUTH ABIDE IN YOU

24Therefore let that abide in you which you
heard from the beginning. If what you heard
from the beginning abides in you, you also will
abide in the Son and in the Father. 25And this is
the promise that He has promised us—eternal
life.

2:18 [a]NU-Text omits *the*. **2:20** [a]NU-Text reads *you all know*.

THE MESSAGE

is new, freshly minted as it is in both Christ and you—the darkness on its way out and the True Light already blazing!

9-11 Anyone who claims to live in God's light and hates a brother or sister is still in the dark. It's the person who loves brother and sister who dwells in God's light and doesn't block the light from others. But whoever hates is still in the dark, stumbles around in the dark, doesn't know which end is up, blinded by the darkness.

LOVING THE WORLD

12-13 I remind you, my dear children: Your sins are forgiven in Jesus' name. You veterans were in on the ground floor, and know the One who started all this; you newcomers have won a big victory over the Evil One.

13-14 And a second reminder, dear children: You know the Father from personal experience. You veterans know the One who started it all; and you newcomers—such vitality and strength! God's word is so steady in you. Your fellowship with God enables you to gain a victory over the Evil One.

15-17 Don't love the world's ways. Don't love the world's goods. Love of the world squeezes out love for the Father. Practically everything that goes on in the world—wanting your own way, wanting everything for yourself, wanting to appear important—has nothing to do with the Father. It just isolates you from him. The world and all its wanting, wanting, wanting is on the way out—but whoever does what God wants is set for eternity.

ANTICHRISTS EVERYWHERE YOU LOOK

18 Children, time is just about up. You heard that Antichrist is coming. Well, they're all over the place, antichrists everywhere you look. That's how we know that we're close to the end.

19 They left us, but they were never really with us. If they had been, they would have stuck it out with us, loyal to the end. In leaving, they showed their true colors, showed they never did belong.

20-21 But you belong. The Holy One anointed you, and you all know it. I haven't been writing this to tell you something you don't know, but to confirm the truth you do know, and to remind you that the truth doesn't breed lies.

22-23 So who is lying here? It's the person who denies that Jesus is the Divine Christ, that's who. This is what makes an antichrist: denying the Father, denying the Son. No one who denies the Son has any part with the Father, but affirming the Son is an embrace of the Father as well.

24-25 Stay with what you heard from the beginning, the original message. Let it sink into your life. If what you heard from the beginning lives deeply in you, you will live deeply in both Son and Father. This is exactly what Christ promised: eternal life, real life!

NEW KING JAMES VERSION

[26]These things I have written to you concern-
ing those who *try to* deceive you. [27]But the
anointing which you have received from Him
abides in you, and you do not need that anyone
teach you; but as the same anointing teaches
you concerning all things, and is true, and is not
a lie, and just as it has taught you, you will[a]
abide in Him.

THE CHILDREN OF GOD

[28]And now, little children, abide in Him, that
when[a] He appears, we may have confidence and
not be ashamed before Him at His coming. [29]If
you know that He is righteous, you know that
everyone who practices righteousness is born of
Him.

3 Behold what manner of love the Father has
bestowed on us, that we should be called chil-
dren of God![a] Therefore the world does not
know us,[b] because it did not know Him.
[2]Beloved, now we are children of God; and it has
not yet been revealed what we shall be, but we
know that when He is revealed, we shall be like
Him, for we shall see Him as He is. [3]And every-
one who has this hope in Him purifies himself,
just as He is pure.

SIN AND THE CHILD OF GOD

[4]Whoever commits sin also commits lawless-
ness, and sin is lawlessness. [5]And you know that
He was manifested to take away our sins, and in
Him there is no sin. [6]Whoever abides in Him
does not sin. Whoever sins has neither seen Him
nor known Him.

[7]Little children, let no one deceive you. He
who practices righteousness is righteous, just as
He is righteous. [8]He who sins is of the devil, for
the devil has sinned from the beginning. For this
purpose the Son of God was manifested, that He
might destroy the works of the devil. [9]Whoever
has been born of God does not sin, for His seed
remains in him; and he cannot sin, because he
has been born of God.

THE IMPERATIVE OF LOVE

[10]In this the children of God and the chil-
dren of the devil are manifest: Whoever does
not practice righteousness is not of God, nor *is*
he who does not love his brother. [11]For this is
the message that you heard from the begin-
ning, that we should love one another, [12]not as
Cain *who* was of the wicked one and murdered
his brother. And why did he murder him? Be-

2:27 [a]NU-Text reads *you abide.* **2:28** [a]NU-Text reads *if.* **3:1** [a]NU-Text adds *And we are.* [b]M-Text reads *you.*

THE MESSAGE

26-27 I've written to warn you about those who are trying to deceive you. But they're no match for what is embedded deeply within you—Christ's anointing, no less! You don't need any of their so-called teaching. Christ's anointing teaches you the truth on everything you need to know about yourself and him, uncontaminated by a single lie. Live deeply in what you were taught.

LIVE DEEPLY IN CHRIST

28 And now, children, stay with Christ. Live deeply in Christ. Then we'll be ready for him when he appears, ready to receive him with open arms, with no cause for red-faced guilt or lame excuses when he arrives.

29 Once you're convinced that he is right and righteous, you'll recognize that all who practice righteousness are God's true children.

1 **3** What marvelous love the Father has extended to us! Just look at it—we're called children of God! That's who we really are. But that's also why the world doesn't recognize us or take us seriously, because it has no idea who he is or what he's up to.

2-3 But friends, that's exactly who we are: children of God. And that's only the beginning. Who knows how we'll end up! What we know is that when Christ is openly revealed, we'll see him—and in seeing him, become like him. All of us who look forward to his Coming stay ready, with the glistening purity of Jesus' life as a model for our own.

4-6 All who indulge in a sinful life are dangerously lawless, for sin is a major disruption of God's order. Surely you know that Christ showed up in order to get rid of sin. There is no sin in him, and sin is not part of his program. No one who lives deeply in Christ makes a practice of sin. None of those who do practice sin have taken a good look at Christ. They've got him all backward.

7-8 So, my dear children, don't let anyone divert you from the truth. It's the person who *acts* right who *is* right, just as we see it lived out in our righteous Messiah. Those who make a practice of sin are straight from the Devil, the pioneer in the practice of sin. The Son of God entered the scene to abolish the Devil's ways.

9-10 People conceived and brought into life by God don't make a practice of sin. How could they? God's seed is deep within them, making them who they are. It's not in the nature of the God-begotten to practice and parade sin. Here's how you tell the difference between God's children and the Devil's children: The one who won't practice righteous ways isn't from God, nor is the one who won't love brother or sister. A simple test.

11 For this is the original message we heard: We should love each other.

12-13 We must not be like Cain, who joined the Evil One and then killed his brother. And why did he kill him? Because he was deep in the practice of evil, while the acts of his

New King James Version

cause his works were evil and his brother's
righteous.
13Do not marvel, my brethren, if the world
hates you. 14We know that we have passed from
death to life, because we love the brethren. He
who does not love *his* brother[a] abides in death.
15Whoever hates his brother is a murderer, and
you know that no murderer has eternal life
abiding in him.

The Outworking of Love

16By this we know love, because He laid
down His life for us. And we also ought to lay
down *our* lives for the brethren. 17But whoever
has this world's goods, and sees his brother in
need, and shuts up his heart from him, how does
the love of God abide in him?
18My little children, let us not love in word or
in tongue, but in deed and in truth. 19And by this
we know[a] that we are of the truth, and shall as-
sure our hearts before Him. 20For if our heart
condemns us, God is greater than our heart, and
knows all things. 21Beloved, if our heart does not
condemn us, we have confidence toward God.
22And whatever we ask we receive from Him,
because we keep His commandments and do
those things that are pleasing in His sight. 23And
this is His commandment: that we should be-
lieve on the name of His Son Jesus Christ and
love one another, as He gave us[a] commandment.

The Spirit of Truth and the Spirit of Error

24Now he who keeps His commandments
abides in Him, and He in him. And by this we
know that He abides in us, by the Spirit whom
He has given us.

4 Beloved, do not believe every spirit, but test
the spirits, whether they are of God; because
many false prophets have gone out into the
world. 2By this you know the Spirit of God:
Every spirit that confesses that Jesus Christ has
come in the flesh is of God, 3and every spirit that
does not confess that[a] Jesus Christ has come in
the flesh is not of God. And this is the *spirit* of
the Antichrist, which you have heard was com-
ing, and is now already in the world.
4You are of God, little children, and have
overcome them, because He who is in you is
greater than he who is in the world. 5They are of
the world. Therefore they speak *as* of the world,
and the world hears them. 6We are of God. He

3:14 [a]NU-Text omits *his brother.* **3:19** [a]NU-Text reads *we shall know.* **3:23** [a]M-Text omits *us.* **4:3** [a]NU-Text omits *that* and *Christ has come in the flesh.*

The Message

brother were righteous. So don't be sur-
prised, friends, when the world hates you.
This has been going on a long time.
14-15 The way we know we've been transferred
from death to life is that we love our broth-
ers and sisters. Anyone who doesn't love is
as good as dead. Anyone who hates a
brother or sister is a murderer, and you
know very well that eternal life and murder
don't go together.
16-17 This is how we've come to understand
and experience love: Christ sacrificed his
life for us. This is why we ought to live sac-
rificially for our fellow believers, and not
just be out for ourselves. If you see some
brother or sister in need and have the means
to do something about it but turn a cold
shoulder and do nothing, what happens to
God's love? It disappears. And you made it
disappear.

When We Practice Real Love

18-20 My dear children, let's not just talk about
love; let's practice real love. This is the only
way we'll know we're living truly, living in
God's reality. It's also the way to shut down
debilitating self-criticism, even when there
is something to it. For God is greater than
our worried hearts and knows more about
us than we do ourselves.
21-24 And friends, once that's taken care of and
we're no longer accusing or condemning
ourselves, we're bold and free before God!
We're able to stretch our hands out and re-
ceive what we asked for because we're do-
ing what he said, doing what pleases him.
Again, this is God's command: to believe in
his personally named Son, Jesus Christ. He
told us to love each other, in line with the
original command. As we keep his com-
mands, we live deeply and surely in him,
and he lives in us. And this is how we expe-
rience his deep and abiding presence in us:
by the Spirit he gave us.

Don't Believe Everything You Hear

1 4 My dear friends, don't believe everything
you hear. Carefully weigh and examine
what people tell you. Not everyone who
talks about God comes from God. There are
a lot of lying preachers loose in the world.
2-3 Here's how you test for the genuine Spirit
of God. Everyone who confesses openly his
faith in Jesus Christ—the Son of God, who
came as an actual flesh-and-blood person—
comes from God and belongs to God. And
everyone who refuses to confess faith in Je-
sus has nothing in common with God. This
is the spirit of antichrist that you heard was
coming. Well, here it is, sooner than we
thought!
4-6 My dear children, you come from God
and belong to God. You have already won a
big victory over those false teachers, for the
Spirit in you is far stronger than anything in
the world. These people belong to the
Christ-denying world. They talk the world's
language and the world eats it up. But we
come from God and belong to God. Anyone

NEW KING JAMES VERSION

who knows God hears us; he who is not of God does not hear us. By this we know the spirit of truth and the spirit of error.

Knowing God Through Love

7Beloved, let us love one another, for love is of God; and everyone who loves is born of God and knows God. 8He who does not love does not know God, for God is love. 9In this the love of God was manifested toward us, that God has sent His only begotten Son into the world, that we might live through Him. 10In this is love, not that we loved God, but that He loved us and sent His Son *to be* the propitiation for our sins. 11Beloved, if God so loved us, we also ought to love one another.

Seeing God Through Love

12No one has seen God at any time. If we love one another, God abides in us, and His love has been perfected in us. 13By this we know that we abide in Him, and He in us, because He has given us of His Spirit. 14And we have seen and testify that the Father has sent the Son *as* Savior of the world. 15Whoever confesses that Jesus is the Son of God, God abides in him, and he in God. 16And we have known and believed the love that God has for us. God is love, and he who abides in love abides in God, and God in him.

The Consummation of Love

17Love has been perfected among us in this: that we may have boldness in the day of judgment; because as He is, so are we in this world. 18There is no fear in love; but perfect love casts out fear, because fear involves torment. But he who fears has not been made perfect in love. 19We love Him[a] because He first loved us.

Obedience by Faith

20If someone says, "I love God," and hates his brother, he is a liar; for he who does not love his brother whom he has seen, how can[a] he love God whom he has not seen? 21And this commandment we have from Him: that he who loves God *must* love his brother also.

5 Whoever believes that Jesus is the Christ is born of God, and everyone who loves Him who begot also loves him who is begotten of Him. 2By this we know that we love the children of God, when we love God and keep His com-

4:19 [a]NU-Text omits *Him*. **4:20** [a]NU-Text reads *he cannot*.

THE MESSAGE

who knows God understands us and listens. The person who has nothing to do with God will, of course, not listen to us. This is another test for telling the Spirit of Truth from the spirit of deception.

God Is Love

7-10 My beloved friends, let us continue to love each other since love comes from God. Everyone who loves is born of God and experiences a relationship with God. The person who refuses to love doesn't know the first thing about God, because God *is* love—so you can't know him if you don't love. This is how God showed his love for us: God sent his only Son into the world so we might live through him. This is the kind of love we are talking about—not that we once upon a time loved God, but that he loved us and sent his Son as a sacrifice to clear away our sins and the damage they've done to our relationship with God.

11-12 My dear, dear friends, if God loved us like this, we certainly ought to love each other. No one has seen God, ever. But if we love one another, God dwells deeply within us, and his love becomes complete in us—perfect love!

13-16 This is how we know we're living steadily and deeply in him, and he in us: He's given us life from his life, from his very own Spirit. Also, we've seen for ourselves and continue to state openly that the Father sent his Son as Savior of the world. Everyone who confesses that Jesus is God's Son participates continuously in an intimate relationship with God. We know it so well, we've embraced it heart and soul, this love that comes from God.

To Love, to Be Loved

17-18 God is love. When we take up permanent residence in a life of love, we live in God and God lives in us. This way, love has the run of the house, becomes at home and mature in us, so that we're free of worry on Judgment Day—our standing in the world is identical with Christ's. There is no room in love for fear. Well-formed love banishes fear. Since fear is crippling, a fearful life—fear of death, fear of judgment—is one not yet fully formed in love.

19 We, though, are going to love—love and be loved. First we were loved, now we love. He loved us first.

20-21 If anyone boasts, "I love God," and goes right on hating his brother or sister, thinking nothing of it, he is a liar. If he won't love the person he can see, how can he love the God he can't see? The command we have from Christ is blunt: Loving God includes loving people. You've got to love both.

1-3 5 Every person who believes that Jesus is, in fact, the Messiah, is God-begotten. If we love the One who conceives the child, we'll surely love the child who was conceived. The reality test on whether or not we love God's children is this: Do we love God? Do

NEW KING JAMES VERSION

mandments. 3For this is the love of God, that we keep His commandments. And His commandments are not burdensome. 4For whatever is born of God overcomes the world. And this is the victory that has overcome the world—our[a] faith. 5Who is he who overcomes the world, but he who believes that Jesus is the Son of God?

THE CERTAINTY OF GOD'S WITNESS

6This is He who came by water and blood—Jesus Christ; not only by water, but by water and blood. And it is the Spirit who bears witness, because the Spirit is truth. 7For there are three that bear witness in heaven: the Father, the Word, and the Holy Spirit; and these three are one. 8And there are three that bear witness on earth:[a] the Spirit, the water, and the blood; and these three agree as one.

9If we receive the witness of men, the witness of God is greater; for this is the witness of God which[a] He has testified of His Son. 10He who believes in the Son of God has the witness in himself; he who does not believe God has made Him a liar, because he has not believed the testimony that God has given of His Son. 11And this is the testimony: that God has given us eternal life, and this life is in His Son. 12He who has the Son has life; he who does not have the Son of God does not have life. 13These things I have written to you who believe in the name of the Son of God, that you may know that you have eternal life,[a] and that you may *continue to* believe in the name of the Son of God.

CONFIDENCE AND COMPASSION IN PRAYER

14Now this is the confidence that we have in Him, that if we ask anything according to His will, He hears us. 15And if we know that He hears us, whatever we ask, we know that we have the petitions that we have asked of Him.

16If anyone sees his brother sinning a sin *which does* not *lead* to death, he will ask, and He will give him life for those who commit sin not *leading* to death. There is sin *leading* to death. I do not say that he should pray about that. 17All unrighteousness is sin, and there is sin not *leading* to death.

KNOWING THE TRUE—REJECTING THE FALSE

18We know that whoever is born of God does not sin; but he who has been born of God keeps himself,[a] and the wicked one does not touch him.

19We know that we are of God, and the whole world lies *under the sway of* the wicked one.

20And we know that the Son of God has come and has given us an understanding, that we may know Him who is true; and we are in Him who is true, in His Son Jesus Christ. This is the true God and eternal life.

21Little children, keep yourselves from idols. Amen.

5:4 [a]M-Text reads *your.* **5:8** [a]NU-Text and M-Text omit the words from *in heaven* (verse 7) through *on earth* (verse 8). Only four or five very late manuscripts contain these words in Greek. **5:9** [a]NU-Text reads *God, that.* **5:13** [a]NU-Text omits the rest of this verse. **5:18** [a]NU-Text reads *him.*

THE MESSAGE

we keep his commands? The proof that we love God comes when we keep his commandments and they are not at all troublesome.

THE POWER THAT BRINGS THE WORLD TO ITS KNEES

4-5 Every God-begotten person conquers the world's ways. The conquering power that brings the world to its knees is our faith. The person who wins out over the world's ways is simply the one who believes Jesus is the Son of God.

6-8 Jesus—the Divine Christ! He experienced a life-giving birth and a death-killing death. Not only birth from the womb, but baptismal birth of his ministry and sacrificial death. And all the while the Spirit is confirming the truth, the reality of God's presence at Jesus' baptism and crucifixion, bringing those occasions alive for us. A triple testimony: the Spirit, the Baptism, the Crucifixion. And the three in perfect agreement.

9-10 If we take human testimony at face value, how much more should we be reassured when God gives testimony as he does here, testifying concerning his Son. Whoever believes in the Son of God inwardly confirms God's testimony. Whoever refuses to believe in effect calls God a liar, refusing to believe God's own testimony regarding his Son.

11-12 This is the testimony in essence: God gave us eternal life; the life is in his Son. So, whoever has the Son, has life; whoever rejects the Son, rejects life.

THE REALITY, NOT THE ILLUSION

13-15 My purpose in writing is simply this: that you who believe in God's Son will know beyond the shadow of a doubt that you have eternal life, the reality and not the illusion. And how bold and free we then become in his presence, freely asking according to his will, sure that he's listening. And if we're confident that he's listening, we know that what we've asked for is as good as ours.

16-17 For instance, if we see a Christian believer sinning (clearly I'm not talking about those who make a practice of sin in a way that is "fatal," leading to eternal death), we ask for God's help and he gladly gives it, gives life to the sinner whose sin is not fatal. There is such a thing as a fatal sin, and I'm not urging you to pray about that. Everything we do wrong is sin, but not all sin is fatal.

18-21 We know that none of the God-begotten makes a practice of sin—fatal sin. The God-begotten are also the God-protected. The Evil One can't lay a hand on them. We know that we are held firm by God; it's only the people of the world who continue in the grip of the Evil One. And we know that the Son of God came so we could recognize and understand the truth of God—what a gift!—and we are living in the Truth itself, in God's Son, Jesus Christ. This Jesus is both True God and Real Life. Dear children, be on guard against all clever facsimiles.

2 JOHN

New King James Version

Greeting the Elect Lady

The Elder,

To the elect lady and her children, whom I love in truth, and not only I, but also all those who have known the truth, 2because of the truth which abides in us and will be with us forever:

3Grace, mercy, *and* peace will be with you[a] from God the Father and from the Lord Jesus Christ, the Son of the Father, in truth and love.

Walk in Christ's Commandments

4I rejoiced greatly that I have found *some* of your children walking in truth, as we received commandment from the Father. 5And now I plead with you, lady, not as though I wrote a new commandment to you, but that which we have had from the beginning: that we love one another. 6This is love, that we walk according to His commandments. This is the commandment, that as you have heard from the beginning, you should walk in it.

Beware of Antichrist Deceivers

7For many deceivers have gone out into the world who do not confess Jesus Christ *as* coming in the flesh. This is a deceiver and an antichrist. 8Look to yourselves, that we[a] do not lose those things we worked for, but *that* we[b] may receive a full reward.

9Whoever transgresses[a] and does not abide in the doctrine of Christ does not have God. He who abides in the doctrine of Christ has both the Father and the Son. 10If anyone comes to you and does not bring this doctrine, do not receive him into your house nor greet him; 11for he who greets him shares in his evil deeds.

John's Farewell Greeting

12Having many things to write to you, I did not wish *to do so* with paper and ink; but I hope to come to you and speak face to face, that our joy may be full.

13The children of your elect sister greet you. Amen.

3 [a]NU-Text and M-Text read *us.* **8** [a]NU-Text reads *you.* [b]NU-Text reads *you.* **9** [a]NU-Text reads *goes ahead.*

The Message

1-2 My dear congregation, I, your pastor, love
you in very truth. And I'm not alone—every-
one who knows the Truth that has taken up
permanent residence in us loves you.
3 Let grace, mercy, and peace be with us in
truth and love from God the Father and from
Jesus Christ, Son of the Father!
4-6 I can't tell you how happy I am to learn
that many members of your congregation
are diligent in living out the Truth, exactly
as commanded by the Father. But permit me
a reminder, friends, and this is not a new
commandment but simply a repetition of
our original and basic charter: that we love
each other. Love means following his com-
mandments, and his unifying command-
ment is that you conduct your lives in love.
This is the first thing you heard, and nothing
has changed.

Don't Walk Out on God

7 There are a lot of smooth-talking charlatans
loose in the world who refuse to believe that
Jesus Christ was truly human, a flesh-and-
blood human being. Give them their true ti-
tle: Deceiver! Antichrist!
8-9 And be very careful around them so you
don't lose out on what we've worked so dili-
gently in together; I want you to get every
reward you have coming to you. Anyone
who gets so progressive in his thinking that
he walks out on the teaching of Christ,
walks out on God. But whoever stays with
the teaching, stays faithful to both the Fa-
ther and the Son.
10-11 If anyone shows up who doesn't hold to
this teaching, don't invite him in and give
him the run of the place. That would just
give him a platform to perpetuate his evil
ways, making you his partner.
12-13 I have a lot more things to tell you, but I'd
rather not use paper and ink. I hope to be
there soon in person and have a heart-to-
heart talk. That will be far more satisfying
to both you and me. Everyone here in your
sister congregation sends greetings.

3 JOHN

New King James Version

Greeting to Gaius

The Elder,

To the beloved Gaius, whom I love in truth:

2 Beloved, I pray that you may prosper in all
things and be in health, just as your soul pros-
pers. 3 For I rejoiced greatly when brethren came
and testified of the truth *that is* in you, just as
you walk in the truth. 4 I have no greater joy than
to hear that my children walk in truth.[a]

Gaius Commended for Generosity

5 Beloved, you do faithfully whatever you do
for the brethren and[a] for strangers, 6 who have
borne witness of your love before the church. *If*
you send them forward on their journey in a
manner worthy of God, you will do well, 7 be-
cause they went forth for His name's sake, tak-
ing nothing from the Gentiles. 8 We therefore
ought to receive[a] such, that we may become fel-
low workers for the truth.

Diotrephes and Demetrius

9 I wrote to the church, but Diotrephes, who
loves to have the preeminence among them,
does not receive us. 10 Therefore, if I come, I will
call to mind his deeds which he does, prating
against us with malicious words. And not con-
tent with that, he himself does not receive the
brethren, and forbids those who wish to, putting
them out of the church.

11 Beloved, do not imitate what is evil, but
what is good. He who does good is of God, but[a]
he who does evil has not seen God.

12 Demetrius has a *good* testimony from all,
and from the truth itself. And we also bear wit-
ness, and you know that our testimony is true.

Farewell Greeting

13 I had many things to write, but I do not
wish to write to you with pen and ink; 14 but I
hope to see you shortly, and we shall speak face
to face.

Peace to you. Our friends greet you. Greet
the friends by name.

4 [a]NU-Text reads *the truth.* **5** [a]NU-Text adds *especially.*
8 [a]NU-Text reads *support.* **11** [a]NU-Text and M-Text omit *but.*

The Message

1-4 The Pastor, to my good friend Gaius: How truly I love you! We're the best of friends, and I pray for good fortune in everything you do, and for your good health—that your everyday affairs prosper, as well as your soul! I was most happy when some friends arrived and brought the news that you persist in following the way of Truth. Nothing could make me happier than getting reports that my children continue diligently in the way of Truth!

Model the Good

5-8 Dear friend, when you extend hospitality to Christian brothers and sisters, even when they are strangers, you make the faith visible. They've made a full report back to the church here, a message about your love. It's good work you're doing, helping these travelers on their way, hospitality worthy of God himself! They set out under the banner of the Name, and get no help from unbelievers. So they deserve any support we can give them. In providing meals and a bed, we become their companions in spreading the Truth.

9-10 Earlier I wrote something along this line to the church, but Diotrephes, who loves being in charge, denigrates my counsel. If I come, you can be sure I'll hold him to account for spreading vicious rumors about us.

As if that weren't bad enough, he not only refuses hospitality to traveling Christians but tries to stop others from welcoming them. Worse yet, instead of inviting them in he throws them out.

11 Friend, don't go along with evil. Model the good. The person who does good does God's work. The person who does evil falsifies God, doesn't know the first thing about God.

12 Everyone has a good word for Demetrius—the Truth itself stands up for Demetrius! We concur, and you know we don't hand out endorsements lightly.

13-14 I have a lot more things to tell you, but I'd rather not use pen and ink. I hope to be there soon in person and have a heart-to-heart talk.

Peace to you. The friends here say hello. Greet our friends there by name.

JUDE

New King James Version

Greeting to the Called

Jude, a bondservant of Jesus Christ, and brother of James,

To those who are called, sanctified[a] by God the Father, and preserved in Jesus Christ:

[2]Mercy, peace, and love be multiplied to you.

Contend for the Faith

[3]Beloved, while I was very diligent to write to you concerning our common salvation, I found it necessary to write to you exhorting you to contend earnestly for the faith which was once for all delivered to the saints. [4]For certain men have crept in unnoticed, who long ago were marked out for this condemnation, ungodly men, who turn the grace of our God into lewdness and deny the only Lord God[a] and our Lord Jesus Christ.

Old and New Apostates

[5]But I want to remind you, though you once knew this, that the Lord, having saved the people out of the land of Egypt, afterward destroyed those who did not believe. [6]And the angels who did not keep their proper domain, but left their own abode, He has reserved in everlasting chains under darkness for the judgment of the great day; [7]as Sodom and Gomorrah, and the cities around them in a similar manner to these, having given themselves over to sexual immorality and gone after strange flesh, are set forth as an example, suffering the vengeance of eternal fire.

[8]Likewise also these dreamers defile the flesh, reject authority, and speak evil of dignitaries. [9]Yet Michael the archangel, in contending with the devil, when he disputed about the body of Moses, dared not bring against him a reviling accusation, but said, "The Lord rebuke you!" [10]But these speak evil of whatever they do not know; and whatever they know naturally, like brute beasts, in these things they corrupt themselves. [11]Woe to them! For they have gone in the way of Cain, have run greedily in the error of Balaam for profit, and perished in the rebellion of Korah.

Apostates Depraved and Doomed

[12]These are spots in your love feasts, while they feast with you without fear, serving *only* themselves. *They are* clouds without water, carried about[a] by the winds; late autumn trees without fruit, twice dead, pulled up by the roots;

1 [a]NU-Text reads *beloved.* **4** [a]NU-Text omits *God.* **12** [a]NU-Text and M-Text read *along.*

The Message

1-2 I, Jude, am a slave to Jesus Christ and brother to James, writing to those loved by God the Father, called and kept safe by Jesus Christ. Relax, everything's going to be all right; rest, everything's coming together; open your hearts, love is on the way!

Fight with All You Have in You

3-4 Dear friends, I've dropped everything to write you about this life of salvation that we have in common. I have to write insisting—begging!—that you fight with everything you have in you for this faith entrusted to us as a gift to guard and cherish. What has happened is that some people have infiltrated our ranks (our Scriptures warned us this would happen), who beneath their pious skin are shameless scoundrels. Their design is to replace the sheer grace of our God with sheer license—which means doing away with Jesus Christ, our one and only Master.

Lost Stars in Outer Space

5-7 I'm laying this out as clearly as I can, even though you once knew all this well enough and shouldn't need reminding. Here it is in brief: The Master saved a people out of the land of Egypt. Later he destroyed those who defected. And you know the story of the angels who didn't stick to their post, abandoning it for other, darker missions. But they are now chained and jailed in a black hole until the great Judgment Day. Sodom and Gomorrah, which went to sexual rack and ruin along with the surrounding cities that acted just like them, are another example. Burning and burning and never burning up, they serve still as a stock warning.

8 This is exactly the same program of these latest infiltrators: dirty sex, rule and rulers thrown out, glory dragged in the mud.

9-11 The Archangel Michael, who went to the mat with the Devil as they fought over the body of Moses, wouldn't have dared level him with a blasphemous curse, but said simply, "No you don't. *God* will take care of you!" But these people sneer at anything they can't understand, and by doing whatever they feel like doing—living by animal instinct only—they participate in their own destruction. I'm fed up with them! They've gone down Cain's road; they've been sucked into Balaam's error by greed; they're canceled out in Korah's rebellion.

12-13 These people are warts on your love feasts as you worship and eat together. They're giving you a black eye—carousing shamelessly, grabbing anything that isn't nailed down. They're—

Puffs of smoke pushed by gusts of wind;
late autumn trees stripped clean of
leaf and fruit,
Doubly dead, pulled up by the roots;

New King James Version

[13]raging waves of the sea, foaming up their own
shame; wandering stars for whom is reserved
the blackness of darkness forever.
[14]Now Enoch, the seventh from Adam,
prophesied about these men also, saying, "Be-
hold, the Lord comes with ten thousands of His
saints, [15]to execute judgment on all, to convict
all who are ungodly among them of all their un-
godly deeds which they have committed in an
ungodly way, and of all the harsh things which
ungodly sinners have spoken against Him."

Apostates Predicted

[16]These are grumblers, complainers, walking
according to their own lusts; and they mouth
great swelling *words*, flattering people to gain
advantage. [17]But you, beloved, remember the
words which were spoken before by the apos-
tles of our Lord Jesus Christ: [18]how they told
you that there would be mockers in the last time
who would walk according to their own ungodly
lusts. [19]These are sensual persons, who cause di-
visions, not having the Spirit.

Maintain Your Life with God

[20]But you, beloved, building yourselves up on
your most holy faith, praying in the Holy Spirit,
[21]keep yourselves in the love of God, looking for
the mercy of our Lord Jesus Christ unto eternal
life.
[22]And on some have compassion, making a
distinction;[a] [23]but others save with fear, pulling
them out of the fire,[a] hating even the garment
defiled by the flesh.

Glory to God

[24]Now to Him who is able to keep you[a] from
stumbling,
And to present *you* faultless
Before the presence of His glory with
exceeding joy,
[25]To God our Savior,[a]
Who alone is wise,[b]
Be glory and majesty,
Dominion and power,[c]
Both now and forever.
Amen.

22 [a]NU-Text reads *who are doubting* (or *making distinctions*). **23** [a]NU-Text adds *and on some have mercy with fear* and omits *with fear* in first clause. **24** [a]M-Text reads *them.* **25** [a]NU-Text reads *To the only God our Savior.* [b]NU-Text omits *Who . . . is wise* and adds *Through Jesus Christ our Lord.* [c]NU-Text adds *Before all time.*

The Message

wild ocean waves leaving nothing on
the beach
but the foam of their shame;
Lost stars in outer space
on their way to the black hole.

14-16 Enoch, the seventh after Adam, prophesied of them: "Look! The Master comes with thousands of holy angels to bring judgment against them all, convicting each person of every defiling act of shameless sacrilege, of every dirty word they have spewed of their pious filth." These are the "grumpers," the bellyachers, grabbing for the biggest piece of the pie, talking big, saying anything they think will get them ahead.

17-19 But remember, dear friends, that the apostles of our Master, Jesus Christ, told us this would happen: "In the last days there will be people who don't take these things seriously anymore. They'll treat them like a joke, and make a religion of their own whims and lusts." These are the ones who split churches, thinking only of themselves. There's nothing to them, no sign of the Spirit!

20-21 But you, dear friends, carefully build yourselves up in this most holy faith by praying in the Holy Spirit, staying right at the center of God's love, keeping your arms open and outstretched, ready for the mercy of our Master, Jesus Christ. This is the unending life, the *real* life!

22-23 Go easy on those who hesitate in the faith. Go after those who take the wrong way. Be tender with sinners, but not soft on sin. The sin itself stinks to high heaven.

24-25 And now to him who can keep you on your feet, standing tall in his bright presence, fresh and celebrating—to our one God, our only Savior, through Jesus Christ, our Master, be glory, majesty, strength, and rule before all time, and now, and to the end of all time. Yes.

REVELATION

New King James Version

Introduction and Benediction

1 The Revelation of Jesus Christ, which God
gave Him to show His servants—things which
must shortly take place. And He sent and signi-
fied *it* by His angel to His servant John, 2who
bore witness to the word of God, and to the tes-
timony of Jesus Christ, to all things that he saw.
3Blessed *is* he who reads and those who hear the
words of this prophecy, and keep those things
which are written in it; for the time *is* near.

Greeting the Seven Churches

4John, to the seven churches which are in
Asia:

Grace to you and peace from Him who is and
who was and who is to come, and from the
seven Spirits who are before His throne, 5and
from Jesus Christ, the faithful witness, the first-
born from the dead, and the ruler over the kings
of the earth.

To Him who loved us and washed[a] us from
our sins in His own blood, 6and has made us
kings[a] and priests to His God and Father, to Him
be glory and dominion forever and ever. Amen.

7Behold, He is coming with clouds, and every
eye will see Him, even they who pierced Him.
And all the tribes of the earth will mourn be-
cause of Him. Even so, Amen.

8"I am the Alpha and the Omega, *the* Begin-
ning and *the* End,"[a] says the Lord,[b] "who is and
who was and who is to come, the Almighty."

Vision of the Son of Man

9I, John, both[a] your brother and companion
in the tribulation and kingdom and patience of
Jesus Christ, was on the island that is called Pat-
mos for the word of God and for the testimony
of Jesus Christ. 10I was in the Spirit on the
Lord's Day, and I heard behind me a loud voice,
as of a trumpet, 11saying, "I am the Alpha and
the Omega, the First and the Last,"[a] and, "What
you see, write in a book and send *it* to the seven
churches which are in Asia:[b] to Ephesus, to
Smyrna, to Pergamos, to Thyatira, to Sardis, to
Philadelphia, and to Laodicea."

12Then I turned to see the voice that spoke
with me. And having turned I saw seven golden
lampstands, 13and in the midst of the seven
lampstands *One* like the Son of Man, clothed
with a garment down to the feet and girded
about the chest with a golden band. 14His head
and hair *were* white like wool, as white as snow,
and His eyes like a flame of fire; 15His feet *were*
like fine brass, as if refined in a furnace, and His
voice as the sound of many waters; 16He had in
His right hand seven stars, out of His mouth
went a sharp two-edged sword, and His counte-
nance *was* like the sun shining in its strength.

1:5 [a]NU-Text reads *loves us and freed;* M-Text reads *loves us and washed.* **1:6** [a]NU-Text and M-Text read *a kingdom.* **1:8** [a]NU-Text and M-Text omit *the Beginning and the End.* [b]NU-Text and M-Text add *God.* **1:9** [a]NU-Text and M-Text omit *both.* **1:11** [a]NU-Text and M-Text omit *I am* through third *and.* [b]NU-Text and M-Text omit *which are in Asia.*

The Message

1-2 1 A revealing of Jesus, the Messiah. God
gave it to make plain to his servants what
is about to happen. He published and deliv-
ered it by Angel to his servant John. And
John told everything he saw: God's Word—
the witness of Jesus Christ!

3 How blessed the reader! How blessed the
hearers and keepers of these oracle words,
all the words written in this book!
Time is just about up.

His Eyes Pouring Fire-Blaze

4-7 I, John, am writing this to the seven
churches in Asia province: All the best to
you from The God Who Is, The God Who
Was, and The God About to Arrive, and
from the Seven Spirits assembled before his
throne, and from Jesus Christ—Loyal Wit-
ness, Firstborn from the dead, Ruler of all
earthly kings.

Glory and strength to Christ, who loves us,
who blood-washed our sins from our lives,
Who made us a Kingdom, Priests for his Father,
forever—and yes, he's on his way!
Riding the clouds, he'll be seen by every eye,
those who mocked and killed him will see him,
People from all nations and all times
will tear their clothes in lament.
Oh, Yes.

8 The Master declares, "I'm A to Z. I'm The
God Who Is, The God Who Was, and The
God About to Arrive. I'm the Sovereign-
Strong."

9-17 I, John, with you all the way in the trial
and the Kingdom and the passion of pa-
tience in Jesus, was on the island called Pat-
mos because of God's Word, the witness of
Jesus. It was Sunday and I was in the Spirit,
praying. I heard a loud voice behind me,
trumpet-clear and piercing: "Write what you
see into a book. Send it to the seven
churches: to Ephesus, Smyrna, Pergamum,
Thyatira, Sardis, Philadelphia, Laodicea." I
turned and saw the voice.

I saw a gold menorah
with seven branches,
And in the center, the Son of Man,
in a robe and gold breastplate,
hair a blizzard of white,
Eyes pouring fire-blaze,
both feet furnace-fired bronze,
His voice a cataract,
right hand holding the Seven Stars,
His mouth a sharp-biting sword,
his face a perigee sun.

NEW KING JAMES VERSION

17And when I saw Him, I fell at His feet as dead. But He laid His right hand on me, saying to me,[a] "Do not be afraid; I am the First and the Last. 18I *am* He who lives, and was dead, and behold, I am alive forevermore. Amen. And I have the keys of Hades and of Death. 19Write[a] the things which you have seen, and the things which are, and the things which will take place after this. 20The mystery of the seven stars which you saw in My right hand, and the seven golden lampstands: The seven stars are the angels of the seven churches, and the seven lampstands which you saw[a] are the seven churches.

THE LOVELESS CHURCH

2 "To the angel of the church of Ephesus write, 'These things says He who holds the seven stars in His right hand, who walks in the midst of the seven golden lampstands: 2"I know your works, your labor, your patience, and that you cannot bear those who are evil. And you have tested those who say they are apostles and are not, and have found them liars; 3and you have persevered and have patience, and have labored for My name's sake and have not become weary. 4Nevertheless I have *this* against you, that you have left your first love. 5Remember therefore from where you have fallen; repent and do the first works, or else I will come to you quickly and remove your lampstand from its place—unless you repent. 6But this you have, that you hate the deeds of the Nicolaitans, which I also hate.

7"He who has an ear, let him hear what the Spirit says to the churches. To him who overcomes I will give to eat from the tree of life, which is in the midst of the Paradise of God." '

THE PERSECUTED CHURCH

8"And to the angel of the church in Smyrna write,

'These things says the First and the Last, who was dead, and came to life: 9"I know your works, tribulation, and poverty (but you are rich); and *I know* the blasphemy of those who say they are Jews and are not, but *are* a synagogue of Satan. 10Do not fear any of those things which you are about to suffer. Indeed, the devil is about to throw *some* of you into prison, that you may be tested, and you will have tribulation ten days. Be faithful until death, and I will give you the crown of life.

11"He who has an ear, let him hear what the Spirit says to the churches. He who overcomes shall not be hurt by the second death." '

THE COMPROMISING CHURCH

12"And to the angel of the church in Pergamos write,

1:17 [a]NU-Text and M-Text omit *to me.* **1:19** [a]NU-Text and M-Text read *Therefore, write.* **1:20** [a]NU-Text and M-Text omit *which you saw.*

THE MESSAGE

I saw this and fainted dead at his feet. His
right hand pulled me upright, his voice reassured me:

17-20 "Don't fear: I am First, I am Last, I'm
Alive. I died, but I came to life, and my life is now forever. See these keys in my hand? They open and lock Death's doors, they open and lock Hell's gates. Now write down everything you see: things that are, things about to be. The Seven Stars you saw in my right hand and the seven-branched gold menorah—do you want to know what's behind them? The Seven Stars are the Angels of the seven churches; the menorah's seven branches are the seven churches."

TO EPHESUS

1 2 Write this to Ephesus, to the Angel of the
church. The One with Seven Stars in his right-fist grip, striding through the golden seven-lights' circle, speaks:

2-3 "I see what you've done, your hard, hard
work, your refusal to quit. I know you can't stomach evil, that you weed out apostolic pretenders. I know your persistence, your courage in my cause, that you never wear out.

4-5 "But you walked away from your first
love—why? What's going on with you, anyway? Do you have any idea how far you've fallen? A Lucifer fall!

"Turn back! Recover your dear early love. No time to waste, for I'm well on my way to removing your light from the golden circle.

6 "You do have this to your credit: You hate
the Nicolaitan business. I hate it, too.

7 "Are your ears awake? Listen. Listen to
the Wind Words, the Spirit blowing through the churches. I'm about to call each conqueror to dinner. I'm spreading a banquet of Tree-of-Life fruit, a supper plucked from God's orchard."

TO SMYRNA

8 Write this to Smyrna, to the Angel of the
church. The Beginning and Ending, the First and Final One, the Once Dead and Then Come Alive, speaks:

9 "I can see your pain and poverty—con-
stant pain, dire poverty—but I also see your wealth. And I hear the lie in the claims of those who pretend to be good Jews, who in fact belong to Satan's crowd.

10 "Fear nothing in the things you're about
to suffer—but stay on guard! Fear nothing! The Devil is about to throw you in jail for a time of testing—ten days. It won't last forever.

"Don't quit, even if it costs you your life. Stay there believing. I have a Life-Crown sized and ready for you.

11 "Are your ears awake? Listen. Listen to
the Wind Words, the Spirit blowing through the churches. Christ-conquerors are safe from Devil-death."

TO PERGAMUM

12 Write this to Pergamum, to the Angel of the
church. The One with the sharp-biting

NEW KING JAMES VERSION

‘These things says He who has the sharp two-edged sword: 13“I know your works, and where you dwell, where Satan’s throne *is*. And you hold fast to My name, and did not deny My faith even in the days in which Antipas *was* My faithful martyr, who was killed among you, where Satan dwells. 14But I have a few things against you, because you have there those who hold the doctrine of Balaam, who taught Balak to put a stumbling block before the children of Israel, to eat things sacrificed to idols, and to commit sexual immorality. 15Thus you also have those who hold the doctrine of the Nicolaitans, which thing I hate.[a] 16Repent, or else I will come to you quickly and will fight against them with the sword of My mouth.

17“He who has an ear, let him hear what the Spirit says to the churches. To him who overcomes I will give some of the hidden manna to eat. And I will give him a white stone, and on the stone a new name written which no one knows except him who receives *it*.” ’

THE CORRUPT CHURCH

18“And to the angel of the church in Thyatira write,

‘These things says the Son of God, who has eyes like a flame of fire, and His feet like fine brass: 19“I know your works, love, service, faith,[a] and your patience; and *as* for your works, the last *are* more than the first. 20Nevertheless I have a few things against you, because you allow[a] that woman[b] Jezebel, who calls herself a prophetess, to teach and seduce[c] My servants to commit sexual immorality and eat things sacrificed to idols. 21And I gave her time to repent of her sexual immorality, and she did not repent.[a] 22Indeed I will cast her into a sickbed, and those who commit adultery with her into great tribulation, unless they repent of their[a] deeds. 23I will kill her children with death, and all the churches shall know that I am He who searches the minds and hearts. And I will give to each one of you according to your works.

24“Now to you I say, and[a] to the rest in Thyatira, as many as do not have this doctrine, who have not known the depths of Satan, as they say, I will[b] put on you no other burden. 25But hold fast what you have till I come. 26And he who overcomes, and keeps My works until the end, to him I will give power over the nations—

27*‘He shall rule them with a rod of iron;*
They shall be dashed to pieces like the
potter’s vessels’[a]—

as I also have received from My Father; 28and I will give him the morning star.

29“He who has an ear, let him hear what the Spirit says to the churches.” ’

2:15 [a]NU-Text and M-Text read *likewise* for *which thing I hate.* **2:19** [a]NU-Text and M-Text read *faith, service.* **2:20** [a]NU-Text and M-Text read *I have against you that you tolerate.* [b]M-Text reads *your wife Jezebel.* [c]NU-Text and M-Text read *and teaches and seduces.* **2:21** [a]NU-Text and M-Text read *time to repent, and she does not want to repent of her sexual immorality.* **2:22** [a]NU-Text and M-Text read *her.* **2:24** [a]NU-Text and M-Text omit *and.* [b]NU-Text and M-Text omit *will.* **2:27** [a]Psalm 2:9

THE MESSAGE

sword draws from the sheath of his mouth—out come the sword words:

13 “I see where you live, right under the shadow of Satan’s throne. But you continue boldly in my Name; you never once denied my Name, even when the pressure was worst, when they martyred Antipas, my witness who stayed faithful to me on Satan’s turf.

14-15 “But why do you indulge that Balaam crowd? Don’t you remember that Balaam was an enemy agent, seducing Balak and sabotaging Israel’s holy pilgrimage by throwing unholy parties? And why do you put up with the Nicolaitans, who do the same thing?

16 “Enough! Don’t give in to them; I’ll be with you soon. I’m fed up and about to cut them to pieces with my sword-sharp words.

17 “Are your ears awake? Listen. Listen to the Wind Words, the Spirit blowing through the churches. I’ll give the sacred manna to every conqueror; I’ll also give a clear, smooth stone inscribed with your new name, your secret new name.”

TO THYATIRA

18 Write this to Thyatira, to the Angel of the church. God’s Son, eyes pouring fire-blaze, standing on feet of furnace-fired bronze, says this:

19 “I see everything you’re doing for me. Impressive! The love and the faith, the service and persistence. Yes, very impressive! You get better at it every day.

20-23 “But why do you let that Jezebel who calls herself a prophet mislead my dear servants into Cross-denying, self-indulging religion? I gave her a chance to change her ways, but she has no intention of giving up a career in the god-business. I’m about to lay her low, along with her partners, as they play their sex-and-religion games. The bastard offspring of their idol-whoring I’ll kill. Then every church will know that appearances don’t impress me. I x-ray every motive and make sure you get what’s coming to you.

24-25 “The rest of you Thyatirans, who have nothing to do with this outrage, who scorn this playing around with the Devil that gets paraded as profundity, be assured I’ll not make life any harder for you than it already is. Hold on to the truth you have until I get there.

26-28 “Here’s the reward I have for every conqueror, everyone who keeps at it, refusing to give up: You’ll rule the nations, your Shepherd-King rule as firm as an iron staff, their resistance fragile as clay pots. This was the gift my Father gave me; I pass it along to you—and with it, the Morning Star!

29 “Are your ears awake? Listen. Listen to the Wind Words, the Spirit blowing through the churches.”

NEW KING JAMES VERSION

THE DEAD CHURCH

3 "And to the angel of the church in Sardis
write,
'These things says He who has the seven
Spirits of God and the seven stars: "I know your
works, that you have a name that you are alive,
but you are dead. 2Be watchful, and strengthen
the things which remain, that are ready to die,
for I have not found your works perfect before
God.[a] 3Remember therefore how you have re-
ceived and heard; hold fast and repent. There-
fore if you will not watch, I will come upon you
as a thief, and you will not know what hour I
will come upon you. 4You[a] have a few names
even in Sardis who have not defiled their gar-
ments; and they shall walk with Me in white, for
they are worthy. 5He who overcomes shall be
clothed in white garments, and I will not blot
out his name from the Book of Life; but I will
confess his name before My Father and before
His angels.
6"He who has an ear, let him hear what the
Spirit says to the churches." '

THE FAITHFUL CHURCH

7"And to the angel of the church in Philadel-
phia write,
'These things says He who is holy, He who is
true, *"He who has the key of David, He who
opens and no one shuts, and shuts and no one
opens"*:[a] 8"I know your works. See, I have set be-
fore you an open door, and no one can shut it;[a]
for you have a little strength, have kept My
word, and have not denied My name. 9Indeed I
will make *those* of the synagogue of Satan, who
say they are Jews and are not, but lie—indeed I
will make them come and worship before your
feet, and to know that I have loved you. 10Be-
cause you have kept My command to persevere,
I also will keep you from the hour of trial which
shall come upon the whole world, to test those
who dwell on the earth. 11Behold,[a] I am coming
quickly! Hold fast what you have, that no one
may take your crown. 12He who overcomes, I
will make him a pillar in the temple of My God,
and he shall go out no more. I will write on him
the name of My God and the name of the city of
My God, the New Jerusalem, which comes down
out of heaven from My God. And *I will write on
him* My new name.
13"He who has an ear, let him hear what the
Spirit says to the churches." '

3:2 [a]NU-Text and M-Text read *My God.* **3:4** [a]NU-Text and M-Text read *Nevertheless you have a few names in Sardis.* **3:7** [a]Isaiah 22:22 **3:8** [a]NU-Text and M-Text read *which no one can shut.* **3:11** [a]NU-Text and M-Text omit *Behold.*

THE MESSAGE

TO SARDIS

1 3 Write this to Sardis, to the Angel of the church. The One holding the Seven Spirits of God in one hand, a firm grip on the Seven Stars with the other, speaks:

"I see right through your work. You have a reputation for vigor and zest, but you're dead, stone-dead.

2-3 "Up on your feet! Take a deep breath! Maybe there's life in you yet. But I wouldn't know it by looking at your busywork; nothing of *God's* work has been completed. Your condition is desperate. Think of the gift you once had in your hands, the Message you heard with your ears—grasp it again and turn back to God.

"If you pull the covers back over your head and sleep on, oblivious to God, I'll return when you least expect it, break into your life like a thief in the night.

4 "You still have a few followers of Jesus in Sardis who haven't ruined themselves wallowing in the muck of the world's ways. They'll walk with me on parade! They've proved their worth!

5 "Conquerors will march in the victory parade, their names indelible in the Book of Life. I'll lead them up and present them by name to my Father and his Angels.

6 "Are your ears awake? Listen. Listen to the Wind Words, the Spirit blowing through the churches."

TO PHILADELPHIA

7 Write this to Philadelphia, to the Angel of the church. The Holy, the True—David's key in his hand, opening doors no one can lock, locking doors no one can open—speaks:

8 "I see what you've done. Now see what *I've* done. I've opened a door before you that no one can slam shut. You don't have much strength, I know that; you used what you had to keep my Word. You didn't deny me when times were rough.

9 "And watch as I take those who call themselves true believers but are nothing of the kind, pretenders whose true membership is in the club of Satan—watch as I strip off their pretensions and they're forced to acknowledge it's you that I've loved.

10 "Because you kept my Word in passionate patience, I'll keep you safe in the time of testing that will be here soon, and all over the earth, every man, woman, and child put to the test.

11 "I'm on my way; I'll be there soon. Keep a tight grip on what you have so no one distracts you and steals your crown.

12 "I'll make each conqueror a pillar in the sanctuary of my God, a permanent position of honor. Then I'll write names on you, the pillars: the Name of my God, the Name of God's City—the new Jerusalem coming down out of Heaven—and my new Name.

13 "Are your ears awake? Listen. Listen to the Wind Words, the Spirit blowing through the churches."

New King James Version

The Lukewarm Church

14“And to the angel of the church of the Laodiceans[a] write,

‘These things says the Amen, the Faithful and True Witness, the Beginning of the creation of God: 15“I know your works, that you are neither cold nor hot. I could wish you were cold or hot. 16So then, because you are lukewarm, and neither cold nor hot,[a] I will vomit you out of My mouth. 17Because you say, ‘I am rich, have become wealthy, and have need of nothing’—and do not know that you are wretched, miserable, poor, blind, and naked— 18I counsel you to buy from Me gold refined in the fire, that you may be rich; and white garments, that you may be clothed, *that* the shame of your nakedness may not be revealed; and anoint your eyes with eye salve, that you may see. 19As many as I love, I rebuke and chasten. Therefore be zealous and repent. 20Behold, I stand at the door and knock. If anyone hears My voice and opens the door, I will come in to him and dine with him, and he with Me. 21To him who overcomes I will grant to sit with Me on My throne, as I also overcame and sat down with My Father on His throne.

22“He who has an ear, let him hear what the Spirit says to the churches.” ’ ”

The Throne Room of Heaven

4 After these things I looked, and behold, a door *standing* open in heaven. And the first voice which I heard *was* like a trumpet speaking with me, saying, “Come up here, and I will show you things which must take place after this.”

2Immediately I was in the Spirit; and behold, a throne set in heaven, and *One* sat on the throne. 3And He who sat there was[a] like a jasper and a sardius stone in appearance; and *there was* a rainbow around the throne, in appearance like an emerald. 4Around the throne *were* twenty-four thrones, and on the thrones I saw twenty-four elders sitting, clothed in white robes; and they had crowns[a] of gold on their heads. 5And from the throne proceeded lightnings, thunderings, and voices.[a] Seven lamps of fire *were* burning before the throne, which are the[b] seven Spirits of God.

6Before the throne *there was*[a] a sea of glass, like crystal. And in the midst of the throne, and around the throne, *were* four living creatures full of eyes in front and in back. 7The first living creature *was* like a lion, the second living creature like a calf, the third living creature had a face like a man, and the fourth living creature *was* like a flying eagle. 8*The* four living creatures, each having six wings, were full of eyes around and within. And they do not rest day or night, saying:

3:14 [a]NU-Text and M-Text read *in Laodicea.* **3:16** [a]NU-Text and M-Text read *hot nor cold.* **4:3** [a]M-Text omits *And He who sat there was* (which makes the description in verse 3 modify the throne rather than God). **4:4** [a]NU-Text and M-Text read *robes, with crowns.* **4:5** [a]NU-Text and M-Text read *voices, and thunderings.* [b]M-Text omits *the.* **4:6** [a]NU-Text and M-Text add *something like.*

The Message

To Laodicea

14 Write to Laodicea, to the Angel of the church. God’s Yes, the Faithful and Accurate Witness, the First of God’s creation, says:

15-17 “I know you inside and out, and find little to my liking. You’re not cold, you’re not hot—far better to be either cold or hot! You’re stale. You’re stagnant. You make me want to vomit. You brag, ‘I’m rich, I’ve got it made, I need nothing from anyone,’ oblivious that in fact you’re a pitiful, blind beggar, threadbare and homeless.

18 “Here’s what I want you to do: Buy your gold from me, gold that’s been through the refiner’s fire. Then you’ll be rich. Buy your clothes from me, clothes designed in Heaven. You’ve gone around half-naked long enough. And buy medicine for your eyes from me so you can see, *really* see.

19 “The people I love, I call to account—prod and correct and guide so that they’ll live at their best. Up on your feet, then! About face! Run after God!

20-21 “Look at me. I stand at the door. I knock. If you hear me call and open the door, I’ll come right in and sit down to supper with you. Conquerors will sit alongside me at the head table, just as I, having conquered, took the place of honor at the side of my Father. That’s my gift to the conquerors!

22 “Are your ears awake? Listen. Listen to the Wind Words, the Spirit blowing through the churches.”

A Door into Heaven

1 4 Then I looked, and, oh!—a door open into Heaven. The trumpet-voice, the first voice in my vision, called out, “Ascend and enter. I’ll show you what happens next.”

2-6 I was caught up at once in deep worship and, oh!—a Throne set in Heaven with One Seated on the Throne, suffused in gem hues of amber and flame with a nimbus of emerald. Twenty-four thrones circled the Throne, with Twenty-four Elders seated, white-robed, gold-crowned. Lightning flash and thunder crash pulsed from the Throne. Seven fire-blazing torches fronted the Throne (these are the Sevenfold Spirit of God). Before the Throne it was like a clear crystal sea.

6-8 Prowling around the Throne were Four Animals, all eyes. Eyes to look ahead, eyes to look behind. The first Animal like a lion, the second like an ox, the third with a human face, the fourth like an eagle in flight. The Four Animals were winged, each with six wings. They were all eyes, seeing around and within. And they chanted night and day, never taking a break:

New King James Version

"Holy, holy, holy,[a]
Lord God Almighty,
Who was and is and is to come!"

9Whenever the living creatures give glory
and honor and thanks to Him who sits on the
throne, who lives forever and ever, 10the twenty-
four elders fall down before Him who sits on the
throne and worship Him who lives forever and
ever, and cast their crowns before the throne,
saying:

11"You are worthy, O Lord,[a]
To receive glory and honor and power;
For You created all things,
And by Your will they exist[b] and were
created."

The Lamb Takes the Scroll

5And I saw in the right *hand* of Him who sat
on the throne a scroll written inside and on
the back, sealed with seven seals. 2Then I saw a
strong angel proclaiming with a loud voice,
"Who is worthy to open the scroll and to loose
its seals?" 3And no one in heaven or on the earth
or under the earth was able to open the scroll, or
to look at it.
4So I wept much, because no one was found
worthy to open and read[a] the scroll, or to look at
it. 5But one of the elders said to me, "Do not
weep. Behold, the Lion of the tribe of Judah, the
Root of David, has prevailed to open the scroll
and to loose[a] its seven seals."
6And I looked, and behold,[a] in the midst of
the throne and of the four living creatures, and
in the midst of the elders, stood a Lamb as
though it had been slain, having seven horns
and seven eyes, which are the seven Spirits of
God sent out into all the earth. 7Then He came
and took the scroll out of the right hand of Him
who sat on the throne.

Worthy Is the Lamb

8Now when He had taken the scroll, the four
living creatures and the twenty-four elders fell
down before the Lamb, each having a harp, and
golden bowls full of incense, which are the
prayers of the saints. 9And they sang a new
song, saying:

"You are worthy to take the scroll,
And to open its seals;
For You were slain,
And have redeemed us to God by Your blood
Out of every tribe and tongue and people
and nation,
10And have made us[a] kings[b] and priests to our
God;
And we[c] shall reign on the earth."

11Then I looked, and I heard the voice of
many angels around the throne, the living crea-
tures, and the elders; and the number of them

4:8 [a]M-Text has *holy* nine times. 4:11 [a]NU-Text and M-Text read *our Lord and God.* [b]NU-Text and M-Text read *existed.* 5:4 [a]NU-Text and M-Text omit *and read.* 5:5 [a]NU-Text and M-Text omit *to loose.* 5:6 [a]NU-Text and M-Text read *I saw in the midst . . . a Lamb standing.* 5:10 [a]NU-Text and M-Text read *them.* [b]NU-Text reads *a kingdom.* [c]NU-Text and M-Text read *they.*

The Message

Holy, holy, holy
Is God our Master, Sovereign-Strong,
The Was, The Is, The Coming.

9-11 Every time the Animals gave glory and honor and thanks to the One Seated on the Throne—the age-after-age Living One—the Twenty-four Elders would fall prostrate before the One Seated on the Throne. They worshiped the age-after-age Living One. They threw their crowns at the foot of the Throne, chanting,

Worthy, O Master! Yes, our God!
Take the glory! the honor! the power!
You created it all;
It was created because you wanted it.

The Lion Is a Lamb

1-2 5I saw a scroll in the right hand of the One Seated on the Throne. It was written on both sides, fastened with seven seals. I also saw a powerful Angel, calling out in a voice like thunder, "Is there anyone who can open the scroll, who can break its seals?"

3 There was no one—no one in Heaven, no one on earth, no one from the underworld—able to break open the scroll and read it.

4-5 I wept and wept and wept that no one was found able to open the scroll, able to read it. One of the Elders said, "Don't weep. Look—the Lion from Tribe Judah, the Root of David's Tree, has conquered. He can open the scroll, can rip through the seven seals."

6-10 So I looked, and there, surrounded by Throne, Animals, and Elders, was a Lamb, slaughtered but standing tall. Seven horns he had, and seven eyes, the Seven Spirits of God sent into all the earth. He came to the One Seated on the Throne and took the scroll from his right hand. The moment he took the scroll, the Four Animals and Twenty-four Elders fell down and worshiped the Lamb. Each had a harp and each had a bowl, a gold bowl filled with incense, the prayers of God's holy people. And they sang a new song:

Worthy! Take the scroll, open its seals.
Slain! Paying in blood, you bought men
and women,
Bought them back from all over the
earth,
Bought them back for God.
Then you made them a Kingdom, Priests
for our God,
Priest-kings to rule over the earth.

11-14 I looked again. I heard a company of Angels around the Throne, the Animals, and the Elders—ten thousand times ten thou-

NEW KING JAMES VERSION

was ten thousand times ten thousand, and thousands of thousands, 12saying with a loud voice:

"Worthy is the Lamb who was slain
To receive power and riches and wisdom,
And strength and honor and glory and blessing!"

13And every creature which is in heaven and on the earth and under the earth and such as are in the sea, and all that are in them, I heard saying:

"Blessing and honor and glory and power
Be to Him who sits on the throne,
And to the Lamb, forever and ever!"[a]

14Then the four living creatures said, "Amen!" And the twenty-four[a] elders fell down and worshiped Him who lives forever and ever.[b]

FIRST SEAL: THE CONQUEROR

6 Now I saw when the Lamb opened one of the seals;[a] and I heard one of the four living creatures saying with a voice like thunder, "Come and see." 2And I looked, and behold, a white horse. He who sat on it had a bow; and a crown was given to him, and he went out conquering and to conquer.

SECOND SEAL: CONFLICT ON EARTH

3When He opened the second seal, I heard the second living creature saying, "Come and see."[a] 4Another horse, fiery red, went out. And it was granted to the one who sat on it to take peace from the earth, and that *people* should kill one another; and there was given to him a great sword.

THIRD SEAL: SCARCITY ON EARTH

5When He opened the third seal, I heard the third living creature say, "Come and see." So I looked, and behold, a black horse, and he who sat on it had a pair of scales in his hand. 6And I heard a voice in the midst of the four living creatures saying, "A quart[a] of wheat for a denarius,[b] and three quarts of barley for a denarius; and do not harm the oil and the wine."

FOURTH SEAL: WIDESPREAD DEATH ON EARTH

7When He opened the fourth seal, I heard the voice of the fourth living creature saying, "Come and see." 8So I looked, and behold, a pale horse. And the name of him who sat on it was Death, and Hades followed with him. And power was given to them over a fourth of the earth, to kill with sword, with hunger, with death, and by the beasts of the earth.

FIFTH SEAL: THE CRY OF THE MARTYRS

9When He opened the fifth seal, I saw under the altar the souls of those who had been slain for the word of God and for the testimony which

5:13 [a]M-Text adds *Amen.* **5:14** [a]NU-Text and M-Text omit *twenty-four.* [b]NU-Text and M-Text omit *Him who lives forever and ever.* **6:1** [a]NU-Text and M-Text read *seven seals.* **6:3** [a]NU-Text and M-Text omit *and see.* **6:6** [a]Greek *choinix;* that is, approximately one quart [b]This was approximately one day's wage for a worker.

THE MESSAGE

sand their number, thousand after thousand after thousand in full song:

The slain Lamb is worthy!
Take the power, the wealth, the wisdom, the strength!
Take the honor, the glory, the blessing!

Then I heard every creature in Heaven and earth, in underworld and sea, join in, all voices in all places, singing:

To the One on the Throne! To the Lamb!
The blessing, the honor, the glory, the strength,
For age after age after age.

The Four Animals called out, "Oh, Yes!" The Elders fell to their knees and worshiped.

UNSEALING THE SCROLL

1-2 6 I watched while the Lamb ripped off the
first of the seven seals. I heard one of the
Animals roar, "Come out!" I looked—I saw a
white horse. Its rider carried a bow and was
given a victory garland. He rode off victori-
ous, conquering right and left.
3-4 When the Lamb ripped off the second
seal, I heard the second Animal cry, "Come
out!" Another horse appeared, this one red.
Its rider was off to take peace from the
earth, setting people at each other's throats,
killing one another. He was given a huge
sword.
5-6 When he ripped off the third seal, I heard
the third Animal cry, "Come out!" I looked.
A black horse this time. Its rider carried a
set of scales in his hand. I heard a message
(it seemed to issue from the Four Animals):
"A quart of wheat for a day's wages, or three
quarts of barley, but all the oil and wine you
want."
7-8 When he ripped off the fourth seal, I
heard the fourth Animal cry, "Come out!" I
looked. A colorless horse, sickly pale. Its
rider was Death, and Hell was close on its
heels. They were given power to destroy a
fourth of the earth by war, famine, disease,
and wild beasts.
9-11 When he ripped off the fifth seal, I saw
the souls of those killed because they had
held firm in their witness to the Word of
God. They were gathered under the Altar,

NEW KING JAMES VERSION

they held. 10And they cried with a loud voice, saying, "How long, O Lord, holy and true, until You judge and avenge our blood on those who dwell on the earth?" 11Then a white robe was given to each of them; and it was said to them that they should rest a little while longer, until both *the number of* their fellow servants and their brethren, who would be killed as they *were*, was completed.

SIXTH SEAL: COSMIC DISTURBANCES

12I looked when He opened the sixth seal, and behold,[a] there was a great earthquake; and the sun became black as sackcloth of hair, and the moon[b] became like blood. 13And the stars of heaven fell to the earth, as a fig tree drops its late figs when it is shaken by a mighty wind. 14Then the sky receded as a scroll when it is rolled up, and every mountain and island was moved out of its place. 15And the kings of the earth, the great men, the rich men, the commanders,[a] the mighty men, every slave and every free man, hid themselves in the caves and in the rocks of the mountains, 16and said to the mountains and rocks, "Fall on us and hide us from the face of Him who sits on the throne and from the wrath of the Lamb! 17For the great day of His wrath has come, and who is able to stand?"

THE SEALED OF ISRAEL

7After these things I saw four angels standing at the four corners of the earth, holding the four winds of the earth, that the wind should not blow on the earth, on the sea, or on any tree. 2Then I saw another angel ascending from the east, having the seal of the living God. And he cried with a loud voice to the four angels to whom it was granted to harm the earth and the sea, 3saying, "Do not harm the earth, the sea, or the trees till we have sealed the servants of our God on their foreheads." 4And I heard the number of those who were sealed. One hundred *and* forty-four thousand of all the tribes of the children of Israel *were* sealed:

5of the tribe of Judah twelve thousand *were* sealed;[a]
of the tribe of Reuben twelve thousand *were* sealed;
of the tribe of Gad twelve thousand *were* sealed;
6of the tribe of Asher twelve thousand *were* sealed;
of the tribe of Naphtali twelve thousand *were* sealed;
of the tribe of Manasseh twelve thousand *were* sealed;
7of the tribe of Simeon twelve thousand *were* sealed;
of the tribe of Levi twelve thousand *were* sealed;
of the tribe of Issachar twelve thousand *were* sealed;

6:12 [a]NU-Text and M-Text omit *behold.* [b]NU-Text and M-Text read *the whole moon.* **6:15** [a]NU-Text and M-Text read *the commanders, the rich men.* **7:5** [a]In NU-Text and M-Text *were sealed* is stated only in verses 5a and 8c; the words are understood in the remainder of the passage.

THE MESSAGE

and cried out in loud prayers, "How long,
Strong God, Holy and True? How long before you step in and avenge our murders?"
Then each martyr was given a white robe
and told to sit back and wait until the full
number of martyrs was filled from among
their servant companions and friends in the
faith.
12-17 I watched while he ripped off the sixth
seal: a bone-jarring earthquake, sun turned
black as ink, moon all bloody, stars falling
out of the sky like figs shaken from a tree in
a high wind, sky snapped shut like a book,
islands and mountains sliding this way and
that. And then pandemonium, everyone and
his dog running for cover—kings, princes,
generals, rich and strong, along with every
commoner, slave or free. They hid in mountain caves and rocky dens, calling out to
mountains and rocks, "Refuge! Hide us from
the One Seated on the Throne and the wrath
of the Lamb! The great Day of their wrath
has come—who can stand it?"

THE SERVANTS OF GOD

1 7Immediately I saw Four Angels standing at
the four corners of earth, standing steady
with a firm grip on the four winds so no wind
would blow on earth or sea, not even rustle
a tree.
2-3 Then I saw another Angel rising from
where the sun rose, carrying the seal of the
Living God. He thundered to the Four Angels assigned the task of hurting earth and
sea, "Don't hurt the earth! Don't hurt the
sea! Don't so much as hurt a tree until I've
sealed the servants of our God on their foreheads!"
4-8 I heard the count of those who were
sealed: 144,000! They were sealed out of
every Tribe of Israel: 12,000 sealed from
Judah, 12,000 from Reuben, 12,000 from
Gad, 12,000 from Asher, 12,000 from Naphtali, 12,000 from Manasseh, 12,000 from
Simeon, 12,000 from Levi, 12,000 from Is-

NEW KING JAMES VERSION

[8]of the tribe of Zebulun twelve thousand
were sealed;
of the tribe of Joseph twelve thousand *were*
sealed;
of the tribe of Benjamin twelve thousand
were sealed.

A MULTITUDE FROM THE GREAT TRIBULATION

[9]After these things I looked, and behold, a
great multitude which no one could number, of
all nations, tribes, peoples, and tongues, stand-
ing before the throne and before the Lamb,
clothed with white robes, with palm branches in
their hands, [10]and crying out with a loud voice,
saying, "Salvation *belongs* to our God who sits
on the throne, and to the Lamb!" [11]All the angels
stood around the throne and the elders and the
four living creatures, and fell on their faces be-
fore the throne and worshiped God, [12]saying:

"Amen! Blessing and glory and wisdom,
Thanksgiving and honor and power and
might,
Be to our God forever and ever.
Amen."

[13]Then one of the elders answered, saying to
me, "Who are these arrayed in white robes, and
where did they come from?"
[14]And I said to him, "Sir,[a] you know."
So he said to me, "These are the ones who
come out of the great tribulation, and washed
their robes and made them white in the blood of
the Lamb. [15]Therefore they are before the
throne of God, and serve Him day and night in
His temple. And He who sits on the throne will
dwell among them. [16]They shall neither hunger
anymore nor thirst anymore; the sun shall not
strike them, nor any heat; [17]for the Lamb who is
in the midst of the throne will shepherd them
and lead them to living fountains of waters.[a]
And God will wipe away every tear from their
eyes."

SEVENTH SEAL: PRELUDE TO THE SEVEN TRUMPETS

8 When He opened the seventh seal, there was
silence in heaven for about half an hour. [2]And
I saw the seven angels who stand before God,
and to them were given seven trumpets. [3]Then
another angel, having a golden censer, came
and stood at the altar. He was given much in-
cense, that he should offer *it* with the prayers of
all the saints upon the golden altar which was
before the throne. [4]And the smoke of the in-
cense, with the prayers of the saints, ascended
before God from the angel's hand. [5]Then the an-
gel took the censer, filled it with fire from the al-
tar, and threw *it* to the earth. And there were
noises, thunderings, lightnings, and an earth-
quake.
[6]So the seven angels who had the seven
trumpets prepared themselves to sound.

FIRST TRUMPET: VEGETATION STRUCK

[7]The first angel sounded: And hail and fire
followed, mingled with blood, and they were

7:14 [a]NU-Text and M-Text read *My lord.* **7:17** [a]NU-Text and M-Text read *to fountains of the waters of life.*

THE MESSAGE

sachar, 12,000 from Zebulun, 12,000 from
Joseph, 12,000 sealed from Benjamin.

9-12 I looked again. I saw a huge crowd, too huge
to count. Everyone was there—all nations
and tribes, all races and languages. And
they were *standing*, dressed in white robes
and waving palm branches, standing before
the Throne and the Lamb and heartily
singing:

Salvation to our God on his Throne!
Salvation to the Lamb!

All who were standing around the Throne—
Angels, Elders, Animals—fell on their faces
before the Throne and worshiped God,
singing:

Oh, Yes!
The blessing and glory and wisdom and
thanksgiving,
The honor and power and strength,
To our God forever and ever and ever!
Oh, Yes!

13-14 Just then one of the Elders addressed me:
"Who are these dressed in white robes, and
where did they come from?" Taken aback, I
said, "O Sir, I have no idea—but you must
know."

14-17 Then he told me, "These are those who
come from the great tribulation, and they've
washed their robes, scrubbed them clean in
the blood of the Lamb. That's why they're
standing before God's Throne. They serve
him day and night in his Temple. The One
on the Throne will pitch his tent there for
them: no more hunger, no more thirst, no
more scorching heat. The Lamb on the
Throne will shepherd them, will lead them
to spring waters of Life. And God will wipe
every last tear from their eyes."

1 8 When the Lamb ripped off the seventh
seal, Heaven fell quiet—complete silence
for about half an hour.

BLOWING THE TRUMPETS

2-4 I saw the Seven Angels who are always in
readiness before God handed seven trum-
pets. Then another Angel, carrying a gold
censer, came and stood at the Altar. He was
given a great quantity of incense so that he
could offer up the prayers of all the holy
people of God on the Golden Altar before
the Throne. Smoke billowed up from the
incense-laced prayers of the holy ones, rose
before God from the hand of the Angel.

5 Then the Angel filled the censer with fire
from the Altar and heaved it to earth. It set
off thunders, voices, lightnings, and an
earthquake.

6-7 The Seven Angels with the trumpets got
ready to blow them. At the first trumpet
blast, hail and fire mixed with blood were

New King James Version

thrown to the earth.[a] And a third of the trees were burned up, and all green grass was burned up.

Second Trumpet: The Seas Struck

8Then the second angel sounded: And *something* like a great mountain burning with fire was thrown into the sea, and a third of the sea became blood. 9And a third of the living creatures in the sea died, and a third of the ships were destroyed.

Third Trumpet: The Waters Struck

10Then the third angel sounded: And a great star fell from heaven, burning like a torch, and it fell on a third of the rivers and on the springs of water. 11The name of the star is Wormwood. A third of the waters became wormwood, and many men died from the water, because it was made bitter.

Fourth Trumpet: The Heavens Struck

12Then the fourth angel sounded: And a third of the sun was struck, a third of the moon, and a third of the stars, so that a third of them were darkened. A third of the day did not shine, and likewise the night.

13And I looked, and I heard an angel[a] flying through the midst of heaven, saying with a loud voice, "Woe, woe, woe to the inhabitants of the earth, because of the remaining blasts of the trumpet of the three angels who are about to sound!"

Fifth Trumpet: The Locusts from the Bottomless Pit

9 Then the fifth angel sounded: And I saw a star fallen from heaven to the earth. To him was given the key to the bottomless pit. 2And he opened the bottomless pit, and smoke arose out of the pit like the smoke of a great furnace. So the sun and the air were darkened because of the smoke of the pit. 3Then out of the smoke locusts came upon the earth. And to them was given power, as the scorpions of the earth have power. 4They were commanded not to harm the grass of the earth, or any green thing, or any tree, but only those men who do not have the seal of God on their foreheads. 5And they were not given *authority* to kill them, but to torment them *for* five months. Their torment *was* like the torment of a scorpion when it strikes a man. 6In those days men will seek death and will not find it; they will desire to die, and death will flee from them.

7The shape of the locusts was like horses prepared for battle. On their heads were crowns of something like gold, and their faces *were* like the faces of men. 8They had hair like women's hair, and their teeth were like lions' *teeth.* 9And they had breastplates like breastplates of iron, and the sound of their wings *was* like the sound of chariots with many horses running into battle. 10They had tails like scorpions, and there were stings in their tails. Their power *was* to hurt men five months. 11And they had as king over them the angel of the bottomless pit, whose

8:7 [a]NU-Text and M-Text add *and a third of the earth was burned up.* **8:13** [a]NU-Text and M-Text read *eagle.*

The Message

dumped on earth. A third of the earth was scorched, a third of the trees, and every blade of green grass—burned to a crisp.

8-9 The second Angel trumpeted. Something like a huge mountain blazing with fire was flung into the sea. A third of the sea turned to blood, a third of the living sea creatures died, and a third of the ships sank.

10-11 The third Angel trumpeted. A huge Star, blazing like a torch, fell from Heaven, wiping out a third of the rivers and a third of the springs. The Star's name was Wormwood. A third of the water turned bitter, and many people died from the poisoned water.

12 The fourth Angel trumpeted. A third of the sun, a third of the moon, and a third of the stars were hit, blacked out by a third, both day and night in one-third blackout.

13 I looked hard; I heard a lone eagle, flying through Middle-Heaven, crying out ominously, "Doom! Doom! Doom to everyone left on earth! There are three more Angels about to blow their trumpets. Doom is on its way!"

1-2 9 The fifth Angel trumpeted. I saw a Star plummet from Heaven to earth. The Star was handed a key to the Well of the Abyss. He unlocked the Well of the Abyss—smoke poured out of the Well, billows and billows of smoke, sun and air in blackout from smoke pouring out of the Well.

3-6 Then out of the smoke crawled locusts with the venom of scorpions. They were given their orders: "Don't hurt the grass, don't hurt anything green, don't hurt a single tree—only men and women, and then only those who lack the seal of God on their foreheads." They were ordered to torture but not kill, torture them for five months, the pain like a scorpion sting. When this happens, people are going to prefer death to torture, look for ways to kill themselves. But they won't find a way—death will have gone into hiding.

7-11 The locusts looked like horses ready for war. They had gold crowns, human faces, women's hair, the teeth of lions, and iron breastplates. The sound of their wings was the sound of horse-drawn chariots charging into battle. Their tails were equipped with stings, like scorpion tails. With those tails they were ordered to torture the human race for five months. They had a king over them, the Angel of the Abyss. His name in Hebrew

NEW KING JAMES VERSION

name in Hebrew *is* Abaddon, but in Greek he has the name Apollyon.

[12]One woe is past. Behold, still two more woes are coming after these things.

SIXTH TRUMPET: THE ANGELS FROM THE EUPHRATES

[13]Then the sixth angel sounded: And I heard a voice from the four horns of the golden altar which is before God, [14]saying to the sixth angel who had the trumpet, "Release the four angels who are bound at the great river Euphrates." [15]So the four angels, who had been prepared for the hour and day and month and year, were released to kill a third of mankind. [16]Now the number of the army of the horsemen *was* two hundred million; I heard the number of them. [17]And thus I saw the horses in the vision: those who sat on them had breastplates of fiery red, hyacinth blue, and sulfur yellow; and the heads of the horses *were* like the heads of lions; and out of their mouths came fire, smoke, and brimstone. [18]By these three *plagues* a third of mankind was killed—by the fire and the smoke and the brimstone which came out of their mouths. [19]For their power[a] is in their mouth and in their tails; for their tails *are* like serpents, having heads; and with them they do harm.

[20]But the rest of mankind, who were not killed by these plagues, did not repent of the works of their hands, that they should not worship demons, and idols of gold, silver, brass, stone, and wood, which can neither see nor hear nor walk. [21]And they did not repent of their murders or their sorceries[a] or their sexual immorality or their thefts.

THE MIGHTY ANGEL WITH THE LITTLE BOOK

10 I saw still another mighty angel coming down from heaven, clothed with a cloud. And a rainbow *was* on his head, his face *was* like the sun, and his feet like pillars of fire. [2]He had a little book open in his hand. And he set his right foot on the sea and *his* left *foot* on the land, [3]and cried with a loud voice, as *when* a lion roars. When he cried out, seven thunders uttered their voices. [4]Now when the seven thunders uttered their voices,[a] I was about to write; but I heard a voice from heaven saying to me,[b] "Seal up the things which the seven thunders uttered, and do not write them."

[5]The angel whom I saw standing on the sea and on the land raised up his hand[a] to heaven [6]and swore by Him who lives forever and ever, who created heaven and the things that are in it, the earth and the things that are in it, and the sea and the things that are in it, that there should be delay no longer, [7]but in the days of the sounding of the seventh angel, when he is about to sound, the mystery of God would be finished, as He declared to His servants the prophets.

JOHN EATS THE LITTLE BOOK

[8]Then the voice which I heard from heaven spoke to me again and said, "Go, take the little

9:19 [a]NU-Text and M-Text read *the power of the horses.* **9:21** [a]NU-Text and M-Text read *drugs.* **10:4** [a]NU-Text and M-Text read *sounded.* [b]NU-Text and M-Text omit *to me.* **10:5** [a]NU-Text and M-Text read *right hand.*

THE MESSAGE

is *Abaddon,* in Greek, *Apollyon*—"Destroyer."

12 The first doom is past. Two dooms yet to come.

13-14 The sixth Angel trumpeted. I heard a
voice speaking to the sixth Angel from the
horns of the Golden Altar before God: "Let
the Four Angels loose, the Angels confined
at the great River Euphrates."

15-19 The Four Angels were untied and let
loose, Four Angels all prepared for the exact
year, month, day, and even hour when they
were to kill a third of the human race. The
number of the army of horsemen was twice
ten thousand times ten thousand. I heard
the count and saw both horses and riders in
my vision: fiery breastplates on the riders,
lion heads on the horses breathing out fire
and smoke and brimstone. With these three
weapons—fire and smoke and brimstone—
they killed a third of the human race. The
horses killed with their mouths and tails;
their serpentlike tails also had heads that
wreaked havoc.

20-21 The remaining men and women who
weren't killed by these weapons went on
their merry way—didn't change their way of
life, didn't quit worshiping demons, didn't
quit centering their lives around lumps of
gold and silver and brass, hunks of stone
and wood that couldn't see or hear or move.
There wasn't a sign of a change of heart.
They plunged right on in their murderous,
occult, promiscuous, and thieving ways.

1-4 **10** I saw another powerful Angel coming
down out of Heaven wrapped in a cloud.
There was a rainbow over his head, his face
was sun-radiant, his legs pillars of fire. He
had a small book open in his hand. He
placed his right foot on the sea and his left
foot on land, then called out thunderously, a
lion roar. When he called out, the Seven
Thunders called back. When the Seven
Thunders spoke, I started to write it all
down, but a voice out of Heaven stopped
me, saying, "Seal with silence the Seven
Thunders; don't write a word."

5-7 Then the Angel I saw astride sea and land
lifted his right hand to Heaven and swore by
the One Living Forever and Ever, who cre-
ated Heaven and everything in it, earth and
everything in it, sea and everything in it,
that time was up—that when the seventh
Angel blew his trumpet, which he was about
to do, the Mystery of God, all the plans he
had revealed to his servants, the prophets,
would be completed.

8-11 The voice out of Heaven spoke to me
again: "Go, take the book held open in the

NEW KING JAMES VERSION

book which is open in the hand of the angel who stands on the sea and on the earth."

9So I went to the angel and said to him, "Give me the little book."

And he said to me, "Take and eat it; and it will make your stomach bitter, but it will be as sweet as honey in your mouth."

10Then I took the little book out of the angel's hand and ate it, and it was as sweet as honey in my mouth. But when I had eaten it, my stomach became bitter. 11And he[a] said to me, "You must prophesy again about many peoples, nations, tongues, and kings."

THE TWO WITNESSES

11 Then I was given a reed like a measuring rod. And the angel stood,[a] saying, "Rise and measure the temple of God, the altar, and those who worship there. 2But leave out the court which is outside the temple, and do not measure it, for it has been given to the Gentiles. And they will tread the holy city underfoot *for* forty-two months. 3And I will give *power* to my two witnesses, and they will prophesy one thousand two hundred and sixty days, clothed in sackcloth."

4These are the two olive trees and the two lampstands standing before the God[a] of the earth. 5And if anyone wants to harm them, fire proceeds from their mouth and devours their enemies. And if anyone wants to harm them, he must be killed in this manner. 6These have power to shut heaven, so that no rain falls in the days of their prophecy; and they have power over waters to turn them to blood, and to strike the earth with all plagues, as often as they desire.

THE WITNESSES KILLED

7When they finish their testimony, the beast that ascends out of the bottomless pit will make war against them, overcome them, and kill them. 8And their dead bodies *will lie* in the street of the great city which spiritually is called Sodom and Egypt, where also our[a] Lord was crucified. 9Then *those* from the peoples, tribes, tongues, and nations will see their dead bodies three-and-a-half days, and not allow[a] their dead bodies to be put into graves. 10And those who dwell on the earth will rejoice over them, make merry, and send gifts to one another, because these two prophets tormented those who dwell on the earth.

THE WITNESSES RESURRECTED

11Now after the three-and-a-half days the breath of life from God entered them, and they stood on their feet, and great fear fell on those who saw them. 12And they[a] heard a loud voice from heaven saying to them, "Come up here." And they ascended to heaven in a cloud, and their enemies saw them. 13In the same hour there was a great earthquake, and a tenth of the city fell. In the earthquake seven thousand peo-

10:11 [a]NU-Text and M-Text read *they.* **11:1** [a]NU-Text and M-Text omit *And the angel stood.* **11:4** [a]NU-Text and M-Text read *Lord.* **11:8** [a]NU-Text and M-Text read *their.* **11:9** [a]NU-Text and M-Text read *nations see . . . and will not allow.* **11:12** [a]M-Text reads *I.*

THE MESSAGE

hand of the Angel astride sea and earth." I went up to the Angel and said, "Give me the little book." He said, "Take it, then eat it. It will taste sweet like honey, but turn sour in your stomach." I took the little book from the Angel's hand and it was sweet honey in my mouth, but when I swallowed, my stomach curdled. Then I was told, "You must go back and prophesy again over many peoples and nations and languages and kings."

THE TWO WITNESSES

1-2 11 I was given a stick for a measuring rod
and told, "Get up and measure God's
Temple and Altar and everyone worshiping
in it. Exclude the outside court; don't mea-
sure it. It's been handed over to non-Jewish
outsiders. They'll desecrate the Holy City
for forty-two months.
3-6 "Meanwhile, I'll provide my two Wit-
nesses. Dressed in sackcloth, they'll proph-
esy for 1,260. These are the two Olive Trees,
the two Lampstands, standing at attention
before God on earth. If anyone tries to hurt
them, a blast of fire from their mouths will
incinerate them—burn them to a crisp just
like that. They'll have power to seal the sky
so that it doesn't rain for the time of their
prophesying, power to turn rivers and
springs to blood, power to hit earth with any
and every disaster as often as they want.
7-10 "When they've completed their witness,
the Beast from the Abyss will emerge and
fight them, conquer and kill them, leaving
their corpses exposed on the street of the
Great City spiritually called Sodom and
Egypt, the same City where their Master
was crucified. For three and a half days
they'll be there—exposed, prevented from
getting a decent burial, stared at by the curi-
ous from all over the world. Those people
will cheer at the spectacle, shouting 'Good
riddance!' and calling for a celebration, for
these two prophets pricked the conscience
of all the people on earth, made it impossi-
ble for them to enjoy their sins.
11 "Then, after three and a half days, the
Living Spirit of God will enter them—
they're on their feet!—and all those gloating
spectators will be scared to death."
12-13 I heard a strong voice out of Heaven call-
ing, "Come up here!" and up they went to
Heaven, wrapped in a cloud, their enemies
watching it all. At that moment there was a
gigantic earthquake—a tenth of the city fell
to ruin, seven thousand perished in the

NEW KING JAMES VERSION

ple were killed, and the rest were afraid and gave glory to the God of heaven.

14The second woe is past. Behold, the third woe is coming quickly.

SEVENTH TRUMPET: THE KINGDOM PROCLAIMED

15Then the seventh angel sounded: And there were loud voices in heaven, saying, "The kingdoms[a] of this world have become *the kingdoms* of our Lord and of His Christ, and He shall reign forever and ever!" 16And the twenty-four elders who sat before God on their thrones fell on their faces and worshiped God, 17saying:

"We give You thanks, O Lord God Almighty,
The One who is and who was and who is to come,[a]
Because You have taken Your great power and reigned.
18The nations were angry, and Your wrath has come,
And the time of the dead, that they should be judged,
And that You should reward Your servants the prophets and the saints,
And those who fear Your name, small and great,
And should destroy those who destroy the earth."

19Then the temple of God was opened in heaven, and the ark of His covenant[a] was seen in His temple. And there were lightnings, noises, thunderings, an earthquake, and great hail.

THE WOMAN, THE CHILD, AND THE DRAGON

12 Now a great sign appeared in heaven: a woman clothed with the sun, with the moon under her feet, and on her head a garland of twelve stars. 2Then being with child, she cried out in labor and in pain to give birth.

3And another sign appeared in heaven: behold, a great, fiery red dragon having seven heads and ten horns, and seven diadems on his heads. 4His tail drew a third of the stars of heaven and threw them to the earth. And the dragon stood before the woman who was ready to give birth, to devour her Child as soon as it was born. 5She bore a male Child who was to rule all nations with a rod of iron. And her Child was caught up to God and His throne. 6Then the woman fled into the wilderness, where she has a place prepared by God, that they should feed her there one thousand two hundred and sixty days.

SATAN THROWN OUT OF HEAVEN

7And war broke out in heaven: Michael and his angels fought with the dragon; and the dragon and his angels fought, 8but they did not prevail, nor was a place found for them[a] in heaven any longer. 9So the great dragon was

11:15 [a]NU-Text and M-Text read *kingdom . . . has become.* **11:17** [a]NU-Text and M-Text omit *and who is to come.* **11:19** [a]M-Text reads *the covenant of the Lord.* **12:8** [a]M-Text reads *him.*

THE MESSAGE

earthquake, the rest frightened to the core
of their being, frightened into giving honor
to the God-of-Heaven.
14 The second doom is past, the third doom
coming right on its heels.

THE LAST TRUMPET SOUNDS

15-18 The seventh Angel trumpeted. A crescendo
of voices in Heaven sang out,

The kingdom of the world is now
the Kingdom of our God and his Messiah!
He will rule forever and ever!

The Twenty-four Elders seated before God
on their thrones fell to their knees, worshiped, and sang,

We thank you, O God, Sovereign-Strong,
WHO IS AND WHO WAS.
You took your great power
and took over—reigned!
The angry nations now
get a taste of *your* anger.
The time has come to judge the dead,
to reward your servants, all prophets and saints,
Reward small and great who fear your Name,
and destroy the destroyers of earth.

19 The doors of God's Temple in Heaven
flew open, and the Ark of his Covenant was
clearly seen surrounded by flashes of lightning, loud shouts, peals of thunder, an earthquake, and a fierce hailstorm.

THE WOMAN, HER SON, AND THE DRAGON

1-2 12 A great Sign appeared in Heaven: a
Woman dressed all in sunlight, standing
on the moon, and crowned with Twelve Stars.
She was giving birth to a Child and cried out
in the pain of childbirth.
3-4 And then another Sign alongside the
first: a huge and fiery Dragon! It had seven
heads and ten horns, a crown on each of the
seven heads. With one flick of its tail it
knocked a third of the Stars from the sky
and dumped them on earth. The Dragon
crouched before the Woman in childbirth,
poised to eat up the Child when it came.
5-6 The Woman gave birth to a Son who will
shepherd all nations with an iron rod. Her
Son was seized and placed safely before
God on his Throne. The Woman herself escaped to the desert to a place of safety prepared by God, all comforts provided her for
1,260 days.
7-12 War broke out in Heaven. Michael and
his Angels fought the Dragon. The Dragon
and his Angels fought back, but were no
match for Michael. They were cleared out of
Heaven, not a sign of them left. The great
Dragon—ancient Serpent, the one called

NEW KING JAMES VERSION

cast out, that serpent of old, called the Devil and
Satan, who deceives the whole world; he was
cast to the earth, and his angels were cast out
with him.
10Then I heard a loud voice saying in heaven,
"Now salvation, and strength, and the kingdom
of our God, and the power of His Christ have
come, for the accuser of our brethren, who ac-
cused them before our God day and night, has
been cast down. 11And they overcame him by
the blood of the Lamb and by the word of their
testimony, and they did not love their lives to the
death. 12Therefore rejoice, O heavens, and you
who dwell in them! Woe to the inhabitants of the
earth and the sea! For the devil has come down
to you, having great wrath, because he knows
that he has a short time."

THE WOMAN PERSECUTED

13Now when the dragon saw that he had
been cast to the earth, he persecuted the woman
who gave birth to the male *Child.* 14But the
woman was given two wings of a great eagle,
that she might fly into the wilderness to her
place, where she is nourished for a time and
times and half a time, from the presence of the
serpent. 15So the serpent spewed water out of
his mouth like a flood after the woman, that he
might cause her to be carried away by the flood.
16But the earth helped the woman, and the earth
opened its mouth and swallowed up the flood
which the dragon had spewed out of his mouth.
17And the dragon was enraged with the woman,
and he went to make war with the rest of her
offspring, who keep the commandments of God
and have the testimony of Jesus Christ.[a]

THE BEAST FROM THE SEA

13 Then I[a] stood on the sand of the sea. And I
saw a beast rising up out of the sea, having
seven heads and ten horns,[b] and on his horns
ten crowns, and on his heads a blasphemous
name. 2Now the beast which I saw was like a
leopard, his feet were like *the feet of* a bear, and
his mouth like the mouth of a lion. The dragon
gave him his power, his throne, and great au-
thority. 3And I saw one of his heads as if it had
been mortally wounded, and his deadly wound
was healed. And all the world marveled and fol-
lowed the beast. 4So they worshiped the dragon
who gave authority to the beast; and they wor-
shiped the beast, saying, "Who *is* like the beast?
Who is able to make war with him?"
5And he was given a mouth speaking great
things and blasphemies, and he was given au-
thority to continue[a] for forty-two months. 6Then
he opened his mouth in blasphemy against God,
to blaspheme His name, His tabernacle, and
those who dwell in heaven. 7It was granted to
him to make war with the saints and to over-

12:17 [a]NU-Text and M-Text omit *Christ.* **13:1** [a]NU-Text reads *he.* [b]NU-Text and M-Text read *ten horns and seven heads.* **13:5** [a]M-Text reads *make war.*

THE MESSAGE

Devil and Satan, the one who led the whole earth astray—thrown out, and all his Angels thrown out with him, thrown down to earth. Then I heard a strong voice out of Heaven saying,

Salvation and power are established!
Kingdom of our God, authority of his Messiah!
The Accuser of our brothers and sisters thrown out,
who accused them day and night before God.
They defeated him through the blood of the Lamb
and the bold word of their witness.
They weren't in love with themselves;
they were willing to die for Christ.
So rejoice, O Heavens, and all who live there,
but doom to earth and sea,
For the Devil's come down on you with both feet;
he's had a great fall;
He's wild and raging with anger;
he hasn't much time and he knows it.

13-17 When the Dragon saw he'd been thrown to earth, he went after the Woman who had given birth to the Man-Child. The Woman was given wings of a great eagle to fly to a place in the desert to be kept in safety and comfort for a time and times and half a time, safe and sound from the Serpent. The Serpent vomited a river of water to swamp and drown her, but earth came to her help, swallowing the water the Dragon spewed from its mouth. Helpless with rage, the Dragon raged at the Woman, then went off to make war with the rest of her children, the children who keep God's commands and hold firm to the witness of Jesus.

THE BEAST FROM THE SEA

1-2 13 And the Dragon stood on the shore of the sea. I saw a Beast rising from the sea. It had ten horns and seven heads—on each horn a crown, and each head inscribed with a blasphemous name. The Beast I saw looked like a leopard with bear paws and a lion's mouth. The Dragon turned over its power to it, its throne and great authority.

3-4 One of the Beast's heads looked as if it had been struck a deathblow, and then healed. The whole earth was agog, gaping at the Beast. They worshiped the Dragon who gave the Beast authority, and they worshiped the Beast, exclaiming, "There's never been anything like the Beast! No one would dare go to war with the Beast!"

5-8 The Beast had a loud mouth, boastful and blasphemous. It could do anything it wanted for forty-two months. It yelled blasphemies against God, blasphemed his Name, blasphemed his Church, especially those already dwelling with God in Heaven. It was permitted to make war on God's holy people and conquer them. It held absolute sway

NEW KING JAMES VERSION

come them. And authority was given him over
every tribe,[a] tongue, and nation. 8All who dwell
on the earth will worship him, whose names
have not been written in the Book of Life of the
Lamb slain from the foundation of the world.
9If anyone has an ear, let him hear. 10He who
leads into captivity shall go into captivity; he
who kills with the sword must be killed with the
sword. Here is the patience and the faith of the
saints.

THE BEAST FROM THE EARTH

11Then I saw another beast coming up out of
the earth, and he had two horns like a lamb and
spoke like a dragon. 12And he exercises all the
authority of the first beast in his presence, and
causes the earth and those who dwell in it to
worship the first beast, whose deadly wound
was healed. 13He performs great signs, so that
he even makes fire come down from heaven on
the earth in the sight of men. 14And he deceives
those[a] who dwell on the earth by those signs
which he was granted to do in the sight of the
beast, telling those who dwell on the earth to
make an image to the beast who was wounded
by the sword and lived. 15He was granted *power*
to give breath to the image of the beast, that the
image of the beast should both speak and cause
as many as would not worship the image of the
beast to be killed. 16He causes all, both small
and great, rich and poor, free and slave, to re-
ceive a mark on their right hand or on their
foreheads, 17and that no one may buy or sell ex-
cept one who has the mark or[a] the name of the
beast, or the number of his name.
18Here is wisdom. Let him who has under-
standing calculate the number of the beast, for it
is the number of a man: His number *is* 666.

THE LAMB AND THE 144,000

14 Then I looked, and behold, a[a] Lamb stand-
ing on Mount Zion, and with Him one hun-
dred *and* forty-four thousand, having[b] His Fa-
ther's name written on their foreheads. 2And I
heard a voice from heaven, like the voice of
many waters, and like the voice of loud thunder.
And I heard the sound of harpists playing their
harps. 3They sang as it were a new song before
the throne, before the four living creatures, and
the elders; and no one could learn that song ex-
cept the hundred *and* forty-four thousand who
were redeemed from the earth. 4These are the
ones who were not defiled with women, for they
are virgins. These are the ones who follow the
Lamb wherever He goes. These were redeemed[a]
from *among* men, *being* firstfruits to God and to
the Lamb. 5And in their mouth was found no de-
ceit,[a] for they are without fault before the throne
of God.[b]

THE PROCLAMATIONS OF THREE ANGELS

6Then I saw another angel flying in the midst
of heaven, having the everlasting gospel to

13:7 [a]NU-Text and M-Text add *and people.* 13:14 [a]M-Text reads *my own people.* 13:17 [a]NU-Text and M-Text omit *or.* 14:1 [a]NU-Text and M-Text read *the.* [b]NU-Text and M-Text add *His name and.* 14:4 [a]M-Text adds *by Jesus.* 14:5 [a]NU-Text and M-Text read *falsehood.* [b]NU-Text and M-Text omit *before the throne of God.*

THE MESSAGE

over all tribes and peoples, tongues and races. Everyone on earth whose name was not written from the world's foundation in the slaughtered Lamb's Book of Life will worship the Beast.

9-10 Are you listening to this? They've made their bed; now they must lie in it. Anyone marked for prison goes straight to prison; anyone pulling a sword goes down by the sword. Meanwhile, God's holy people passionately and faithfully stand their ground.

THE BEAST FROM UNDER THE GROUND

11-12 I saw another Beast rising out of the ground. It had two horns like a lamb but sounded like a dragon when it spoke. It was a puppet of the first Beast, made earth and everyone in it worship the first Beast, which had been healed of its deathblow.

13-17 This second Beast worked magical signs, dazzling people by making fire come down from Heaven. It used the magic it got from the Beast to dupe earth dwellers, getting them to make an image of the Beast that received the deathblow and lived. It was able to animate the image of the Beast so that it talked, and then arrange that anyone not worshiping the Beast would be killed. It forced all people, small and great, rich and poor, free and slave, to have a mark on the right hand or forehead. Without the mark of the name of the Beast or the number of its name, it was impossible to buy or sell anything.

18 Solve a riddle: Put your heads together and figure out the meaning of the number of the Beast. It's a human number: 666.

A PERFECT OFFERING

1-2 14 I saw—it took my breath away!—the Lamb standing on Mount Zion, 144,000 standing there with him, his Name and the Name of his Father inscribed on their foreheads. And I heard a voice out of Heaven, the sound like a cataract, like the crash of thunder.

2-5 And then I heard music, harp music and the harpists singing a new song before the Throne and the Four Animals and the Elders. Only the 144,000 could learn to sing the song. They were bought from earth, lived without compromise, virgin-fresh before God. Wherever the Lamb went, they followed. They were bought from humankind, firstfruits of the harvest for God and the Lamb. Not a false word in their mouths. A perfect offering.

VOICES FROM HEAVEN

6-7 I saw another Angel soaring in Middle-Heaven. He had an Eternal Message to

NEW KING JAMES VERSION

preach to those who dwell on the earth—to
every nation, tribe, tongue, and people— 7saying
with a loud voice, "Fear God and give glory to
Him, for the hour of His judgment has come;
and worship Him who made heaven and earth,
the sea and springs of water."
8And another angel followed, saying, "Bab-
ylon[a] is fallen, is fallen, that great city, because
she has made all nations drink of the wine of the
wrath of her fornication."
9Then a third angel followed them, saying
with a loud voice, "If anyone worships the beast
and his image, and receives *his* mark on his
forehead or on his hand, 10he himself shall also
drink of the wine of the wrath of God, which is
poured out full strength into the cup of His in-
dignation. He shall be tormented with fire and
brimstone in the presence of the holy angels
and in the presence of the Lamb. 11And the
smoke of their torment ascends forever and
ever; and they have no rest day or night, who
worship the beast and his image, and whoever
receives the mark of his name."
12Here is the patience of the saints; here *are*
those[a] who keep the commandments of God and
the faith of Jesus.
13Then I heard a voice from heaven saying to
me,[a] "Write: 'Blessed *are* the dead who die in
the Lord from now on.' "
"Yes," says the Spirit, "that they may rest
from their labors, and their works follow them."

REAPING THE EARTH'S HARVEST

14Then I looked, and behold, a white cloud,
and on the cloud sat *One* like the Son of Man,
having on His head a golden crown, and in His
hand a sharp sickle. 15And another angel came
out of the temple, crying with a loud voice to
Him who sat on the cloud, "Thrust in Your sickle
and reap, for the time has come for You[a] to reap,
for the harvest of the earth is ripe." 16So He who
sat on the cloud thrust in His sickle on the earth,
and the earth was reaped.

REAPING THE GRAPES OF WRATH

17Then another angel came out of the temple
which is in heaven, he also having a sharp sickle.
18And another angel came out from the altar,
who had power over fire, and he cried with a
loud cry to him who had the sharp sickle, say-
ing, "Thrust in your sharp sickle and gather the
clusters of the vine of the earth, for her grapes
are fully ripe." 19So the angel thrust his sickle
into the earth and gathered the vine of the earth,
and threw *it* into the great winepress of the
wrath of God. 20And the winepress was tram-
pled outside the city, and blood came out of the
winepress, up to the horses' bridles, for one
thousand six hundred furlongs.

PRELUDE TO THE BOWL JUDGMENTS

15 Then I saw another sign in heaven, great
and marvelous: seven angels having the
seven last plagues, for in them the wrath of God
is complete.

14:8 [a]NU-Text reads *Babylon the great is fallen,* is fallen, which has made; M-Text reads *Babylon the great is fallen. She has made.* **14:12** [a]NU-Text and M-Text omit *here are those.* **14:13** [a]NU-Text and M-Text omit *to me.* **14:15** [a]NU-Text and M-Text omit *for You.*

THE MESSAGE

preach to all who were still on earth, every
nation and tribe, every tongue and people.
He preached in a loud voice, "Fear God and
give him glory! His hour of judgment has
come! Worship the Maker of Heaven and
earth, salt sea and fresh water!"
8 A second Angel followed, calling out,
"Ruined, ruined, Great Babylon ruined! She
made all the nations drunk on the wine of
her whoring!"
9-11 A third Angel followed, shouting, warn-
ing, "If anyone worships the Beast and its
image and takes the mark on forehead or
hand, that person will drink the wine of
God's wrath, prepared unmixed in his chal-
ice of anger, and suffer torment from fire
and brimstone in the presence of Holy An-
gels, in the presence of the Lamb. Smoke
from their torment will rise age after age.
No respite for those who worship the Beast
and its image, who take the mark of its
name."
12 Meanwhile, the saints stand passionately
patient, keeping God's commands, staying
faithful to Jesus.
13 I heard a voice out of Heaven, "Write this:
Blessed are those who die in the Master
from now on; how blessed to die that way!"
"Yes," says the Spirit, "and blessed rest
from their hard, hard work. None of what
they've done is wasted; God blesses them
for it all in the end."

HARVEST TIME

14-16 I looked up, I caught my breath!—a white
cloud and one like the Son of Man sitting on
it. He wore a gold crown and held a sharp
sickle. Another Angel came out of the Tem-
ple, shouting to the Cloud-Enthroned,
"Swing your sickle and reap. It's harvest
time. Earth's harvest is ripe for reaping."
The Cloud-Enthroned gave a mighty sweep
of his sickle, began harvesting earth in a
stroke.
17-18 Then another Angel came out of the Tem-
ple in Heaven. He also had a sharp sickle.
Yet another Angel, the one in charge of
tending the fire, came from the Altar. He
thundered to the Angel who held the sharp
sickle, "Swing your sharp sickle. Harvest
earth's vineyard. The grapes are bursting
with ripeness."
19-20 The Angel swung his sickle, harvested
earth's vintage, and heaved it into the wine-
press, the giant winepress of God's wrath.
The winepress was outside the City. As the
vintage was trodden, blood poured from the
winepress as high as a horse's bridle, a river
of blood for two hundred miles.

THE SONG OF MOSES, THE SONG OF THE LAMB

1 15 I saw another Sign in Heaven, huge and
breathtaking: seven Angels with seven
disasters. These are the final disasters, the
wrap-up of God's wrath.

NEW KING JAMES VERSION

[2]And I saw *something* like a sea of glass mingled with fire, and those who have the victory over the beast, over his image and over his mark[a] *and* over the number of his name, standing on the sea of glass, having harps of God.
[3]They sing the song of Moses, the servant of God, and the song of the Lamb, saying:

"Great and marvelous *are* Your works,
Lord God Almighty!
Just and true *are* Your ways,
O King of the saints![a]
[4]Who shall not fear You, O Lord, and glorify
Your name?
For *You* alone *are* holy.
For all nations shall come and worship
before You,
For Your judgments have been manifested."

[5]After these things I looked, and behold,[a] the temple of the tabernacle of the testimony in heaven was opened. [6]And out of the temple came the seven angels having the seven plagues, clothed in pure bright linen, and having their chests girded with golden bands. [7]Then one of the four living creatures gave to the seven angels seven golden bowls full of the wrath of God who lives forever and ever. [8]The temple was filled with smoke from the glory of God and from His power, and no one was able to enter the temple till the seven plagues of the seven angels were completed.

16 Then I heard a loud voice from the temple saying to the seven angels, "Go and pour out the bowls[a] of the wrath of God on the earth."

FIRST BOWL: LOATHSOME SORES

[2]So the first went and poured out his bowl upon the earth, and a foul and loathsome sore came upon the men who had the mark of the beast and those who worshiped his image.

SECOND BOWL: THE SEA TURNS TO BLOOD

[3]Then the second angel poured out his bowl on the sea, and it became blood as of a dead *man;* and every living creature in the sea died.

THIRD BOWL: THE WATERS TURN TO BLOOD

[4]Then the third angel poured out his bowl on the rivers and springs of water, and they became blood. [5]And I heard the angel of the waters saying:

"You are righteous, O Lord,[a]
The One who is and who was and who is to
be,[b]
Because You have judged these things.
[6]For they have shed the blood of saints and
prophets,
And You have given them blood to drink.
For[a] it is their just due."

15:2 [a]NU-Text and M-Text omit *over his mark.* **15:3** [a]NU-Text and M-Text read *nations.* **15:5** [a]NU-Text and M-Text omit *behold.* **16:1** [a]NU-Text and M-Text read *seven bowls.* **16:5** [a]NU-Text and M-Text omit *O Lord.* [b]NU-Text and M-Text read *who was, the Holy One.* **16:6** [a]NU-Text and M-Text omit *For.*

THE MESSAGE

2-4 I saw something like a sea made of glass, the glass all shot through with fire. Carrying harps of God, triumphant over the Beast, its image, and the number of its name, the saved ones stood on the sea of glass. They sang the Song of Moses, servant of God; they sang the Song of the Lamb:

Mighty your acts and marvelous,
O God, the Sovereign-Strong!
Righteous your ways and true,
King of the nations!
Who can fail to fear you, God,
give glory to your Name?
Because you and you only are holy,
all nations will come and worship
you,
because they see your judgments are
right.

5-8 Then I saw the doors of the Temple, the Tent of Witness in Heaven, open wide. The Seven Angels carrying the seven disasters came out of the Temple. They were dressed in clean, bright linen and wore gold vests. One of the Four Animals handed the Seven Angels seven gold bowls, brimming with the wrath of God, who lives forever and ever. Smoke from God's glory and power poured out of the Temple. No one was permitted to enter the Temple until the seven disasters of the Seven Angels were finished.

POURING OUT THE SEVEN DISASTERS

1 16 I heard a shout of command from the Temple to the Seven Angels: "Begin! Pour out the seven bowls of God's wrath on earth!"

2 The first Angel stepped up and poured his bowl out on earth: Loathsome, stinking sores erupted on all who had taken the mark of the Beast and worshiped its image.

3 The second Angel poured his bowl on the sea: The sea coagulated into blood, and everything in it died.

4-7 The third Angel poured his bowl on rivers and springs: The waters turned to blood. I heard the Angel of Waters say,

Righteous you are, and your judgments
are righteous,
THE IS, THE WAS, THE HOLY.
They poured out the blood of saints and
prophets
so you've given them blood to drink—
they've gotten what they deserve!

New King James Version

7And I heard another from[a] the altar saying,
"Even so, Lord God Almighty, true and righ-
teous *are* Your judgments."

Fourth Bowl: Men Are Scorched

8Then the fourth angel poured out his bowl
on the sun, and power was given to him to
scorch men with fire. 9And men were scorched
with great heat, and they blasphemed the name
of God who has power over these plagues; and
they did not repent and give Him glory.

Fifth Bowl: Darkness and Pain

10Then the fifth angel poured out his bowl on
the throne of the beast, and his kingdom be-
came full of darkness; and they gnawed their
tongues because of the pain. 11They blasphemed
the God of heaven because of their pains and
their sores, and did not repent of their deeds.

Sixth Bowl: Euphrates Dried Up

12Then the sixth angel poured out his bowl
on the great river Euphrates, and its water was
dried up, so that the way of the kings from the
east might be prepared. 13And I saw three un-
clean spirits like frogs *coming* out of the mouth
of the dragon, out of the mouth of the beast, and
out of the mouth of the false prophet. 14For they
are spirits of demons, performing signs, *which*
go out to the kings of the earth and[a] of the
whole world, to gather them to the battle of that
great day of God Almighty.
15"Behold, I am coming as a thief. Blessed *is*
he who watches, and keeps his garments, lest he
walk naked and they see his shame."
16And they gathered them together to the
place called in Hebrew, Armageddon.[a]

Seventh Bowl: The Earth Utterly Shaken

17Then the seventh angel poured out his
bowl into the air, and a loud voice came out of
the temple of heaven, from the throne, saying,
"It is done!" 18And there were noises and thun-
derings and lightnings; and there was a great
earthquake, such a mighty and great earth-
quake as had not occurred since men were on
the earth. 19Now the great city was divided into
three parts, and the cities of the nations fell. And
great Babylon was remembered before God, to
give her the cup of the wine of the fierceness of
His wrath. 20Then every island fled away, and
the mountains were not found. 21And great hail
from heaven fell upon men, *each hailstone*
about the weight of a talent. Men blasphemed
God because of the plague of the hail, since that
plague was exceedingly great.

The Scarlet Woman and the Scarlet Beast

17 Then one of the seven angels who had the
seven bowls came and talked with me, say-
ing to me,[a] "Come, I will show you the judgment
of the great harlot who sits on many waters,
2with whom the kings of the earth committed
fornication, and the inhabitants of the earth
were made drunk with the wine of her fornica-
tion."

16:7 [a]NU-Text and M-Text omit *another from.* **16:14** [a]NU-Text and M-Text omit *of the earth and.* **16:16** [a]M-Text reads *Megiddo.* **17:1** [a]NU-Text and M-Text omit *to me.*

The Message

Just then I heard the Altar chime in,

Yes, O God, the Sovereign-Strong!
Your judgments are true and just!

8-9 The fourth Angel poured his bowl on the
sun: Fire blazed from the sun and scorched
men and women. Burned and blistered, they
cursed God's Name, the God behind these
disasters. They refused to repent, refused to
honor God.

10-11 The fifth Angel poured his bowl on the
throne of the Beast: Its kingdom fell into
sudden eclipse. Mad with pain, men and
women bit and chewed their tongues,
cursed the God-of-Heaven for their torment
and sores, and refused to repent and change
their ways.

12-14 The sixth Angel poured his bowl on the
great Euphrates River: It dried up to noth-
ing. The dry riverbed became a fine roadbed
for the kings from the East. From the
mouths of the Dragon, the Beast, and the
False Prophet I saw three foul demons crawl
out—they looked like frogs. These are de-
mon spirits performing signs. They're after
the kings of the whole world to get them
gathered for battle on the Great Day of God,
the Sovereign-Strong.

15 "Keep watch! I come unannounced, like a
thief. You're blessed if, awake and dressed,
you're ready for me. Too bad if you're found
running through the streets, naked and
ashamed."

16 The frog-demons gathered the kings to-
gether at the place called in Hebrew *Ar-
mageddon.*

17-21 The seventh Angel poured his bowl into
the air: From the Throne in the Temple came
a shout, "Done!" followed by lightning
flashes and shouts, thunder crashes and a
colossal earthquake—a huge and devastat-
ing earthquake, never an earthquake like it
since time began. The Great City split three
ways, the cities of the nations toppled to
ruin. Great Babylon had to drink the wine of
God's raging anger—God remembered to
give her the cup! Every island fled and not a
mountain was to be found. Hailstones
weighing a ton plummeted, crushing and
smashing men and women as they cursed
God for the hail, the epic disaster of hail.

Great Babylon, Mother of Whores

1-2 17 One of the Seven Angels who carried
the seven bowls came and invited me,
"Come, I'll show you the judgment of the
great Whore who sits enthroned over many
waters, the Whore with whom the kings of
the earth have gone whoring, show you the
judgment on earth dwellers drunk on her
whorish lust."

New King James Version

3So he carried me away in the Spirit into the wilderness. And I saw a woman sitting on a scarlet beast *which was* full of names of blasphemy, having seven heads and ten horns. 4The woman was arrayed in purple and scarlet, and adorned with gold and precious stones and pearls, having in her hand a golden cup full of abominations and the filthiness of her fornication.[a] 5And on her forehead a name *was* written:

MYSTERY, BABYLON THE GREAT,
THE MOTHER OF HARLOTS AND
OF THE ABOMINATIONS
OF THE EARTH.

6I saw the woman, drunk with the blood of the saints and with the blood of the martyrs of Jesus. And when I saw her, I marveled with great amazement.

The Meaning of the Woman and the Beast

7But the angel said to me, "Why did you marvel? I will tell you the mystery of the woman and of the beast that carries her, which has the seven heads and the ten horns. 8The beast that you saw was, and is not, and will ascend out of the bottomless pit and go to perdition. And those who dwell on the earth will marvel, whose names are not written in the Book of Life from the foundation of the world, when they see the beast that was, and is not, and yet is.[a]

9"Here *is* the mind which has wisdom: The seven heads are seven mountains on which the woman sits. 10There are also seven kings. Five have fallen, one is, *and* the other has not yet come. And when he comes, he must continue a short time. 11The beast that was, and is not, is himself also the eighth, and is of the seven, and is going to perdition.

12"The ten horns which you saw are ten kings who have received no kingdom as yet, but they receive authority for one hour as kings with the beast. 13These are of one mind, and they will give their power and authority to the beast. 14These will make war with the Lamb, and the Lamb will overcome them, for He is Lord of lords and King of kings; and those *who are* with Him *are* called, chosen, and faithful."

15Then he said to me, "The waters which you saw, where the harlot sits, are peoples, multitudes, nations, and tongues. 16And the ten horns which you saw on[a] the beast, these will hate the harlot, make her desolate and naked, eat her flesh and burn her with fire. 17For God has put it into their hearts to fulfill His purpose, to be of one mind, and to give their kingdom to the beast, until the words of God are fulfilled. 18And the woman whom you saw is that great city which reigns over the kings of the earth."

The Fall of Babylon the Great

18 After these things I saw another angel coming down from heaven, having great authority, and the earth was illuminated with his glory. 2And he cried mightily[a] with a loud voice, saying, "Babylon the great is fallen, is

17:4 [a]M-Text reads *the filthiness of the fornication of the earth.* **17:8** [a]NU-Text and M-Text read *and shall be present.* **17:16** [a]NU-Text and M-Text read *saw, and the beast.* **18:2** [a]NU-Text and M-Text omit *mightily.*

The Message

3-6 In the Spirit he carried me out in the desert. I saw a woman mounted on a Scarlet Beast. Stuffed with blasphemies, the Beast had seven heads and ten horns. The woman was dressed in purple and scarlet, festooned with gold and gems and pearls. She held a gold chalice in her hand, brimming with defiling obscenities, her foul fornications. A riddle-name was branded on her forehead: GREAT BABYLON, MOTHER OF WHORES AND ABOMINATIONS OF THE EARTH. I could see that the woman was drunk, drunk on the blood of God's holy people, drunk on the blood of the martyrs of Jesus.

6-8 Astonished, I rubbed my eyes. I shook my head in wonder. The Angel said, "Does this surprise you? Let me tell you the riddle of the woman and the Beast she rides, the Beast with seven heads and ten horns. The Beast you saw once was, is no longer, and is about to ascend from the Abyss and head straight for Hell. Earth dwellers whose names weren't written in the Book of Life from the foundation of the world will be dazzled when they see the Beast that once was, is no longer, and is to come.

9-11 "But don't drop your guard. Use your head. The seven heads are seven hills; they are where the woman sits. They are also seven kings: five dead, one living, the other not yet here—and when he does come his time will be brief. The Beast that once was and is no longer is both an eighth and one of the seven—and headed for Hell.

12-14 "The ten horns you saw are ten kings, but they're not yet in power. They will come to power with the Scarlet Beast, but won't last long—a *very* brief reign. These kings will agree to turn over their power and authority to the Beast. They will go to war against the Lamb but the Lamb will defeat them, proof that he is Lord over all lords, King over all kings, and those with him will be the called, chosen, and faithful."

15-18 The Angel continued, "The waters you saw on which the Whore was enthroned are peoples and crowds, nations and languages. And the ten horns you saw, together with the Beast, will turn on the Whore—they'll hate her, violate her, strip her naked, rip her apart with their teeth, then set fire to her. It was God who put the idea in their heads to turn over their rule to the Beast until the words of God are completed. The woman you saw is the great city, tyrannizing the kings of the earth."

Doom to the City of Darkness

1-8 18 Following this I saw another Angel descend from Heaven. His authority was immense, his glory flooded earth with brightness, his voice thunderous:

Ruined, ruined, Great Babylon, ruined!

NEW KING JAMES VERSION

fallen, and has become a dwelling place of demons, a prison for every foul spirit, and a cage for every unclean and hated bird! 3For all the nations have drunk of the wine of the wrath of her fornication, the kings of the earth have committed fornication with her, and the merchants of the earth have become rich through the abundance of her luxury."

4And I heard another voice from heaven saying, "Come out of her, my people, lest you share in her sins, and lest you receive of her plagues. 5For her sins have reached[a] to heaven, and God has remembered her iniquities. 6Render to her just as she rendered to you,[a] and repay her double according to her works; in the cup which she has mixed, mix double for her. 7In the measure that she glorified herself and lived luxuriously, in the same measure give her torment and sorrow; for she says in her heart, 'I sit *as* queen, and am no widow, and will not see sorrow.' 8Therefore her plagues will come in one day—death and mourning and famine. And she will be utterly burned with fire, for strong *is* the Lord God who judges[a] her.

THE WORLD MOURNS BABYLON'S FALL

9"The kings of the earth who committed fornication and lived luxuriously with her will weep and lament for her, when they see the smoke of her burning, 10standing at a distance for fear of her torment, saying, 'Alas, alas, that great city Babylon, that mighty city! For in one hour your judgment has come.'

11"And the merchants of the earth will weep and mourn over her, for no one buys their merchandise anymore: 12merchandise of gold and silver, precious stones and pearls, fine linen and purple, silk and scarlet, every kind of citron wood, every kind of object of ivory, every kind of object of most precious wood, bronze, iron, and marble; 13and cinnamon and incense, fragrant oil and frankincense, wine and oil, fine flour and wheat, cattle and sheep, horses and chariots, and bodies and souls of men. 14The fruit that your soul longed for has gone from you, and all the things which are rich and splendid have gone from you,[a] and you shall find them no more at all. 15The merchants of these

18:5 [a]NU-Text and M-Text read *have been heaped up.* 18:6 [a]NU-Text and M-Text omit *to you.* 18:8 [a]NU-Text and M-Text read *has judged.* 18:14 [a]NU-Text and M-Text read *been lost to you.*

THE MESSAGE

A ghost town for demons is all that's
left!
A garrison of carrion spirits,
garrison of loathsome, carrion birds.
All nations drank the wild wine of her
whoring;
kings of the earth went whoring with
her;
entrepreneurs made millions
exploiting her.

Just then I heard another shout out of Heaven:

Get out, my people, as fast as you can,
so you don't get mixed up in her sins,
so you don't get caught in her doom.
Her sins stink to high Heaven;
God has remembered every evil she's
done.
Give her back what she's given,
double what she's doubled in her
works,
double the recipe in the cup she
mixed;
Bring her flaunting and wild ways
to torment and tears.
Because she gloated, "I'm queen over all,
and no widow, never a tear on my
face,"
In one day, disasters will crush her—
death, heartbreak, and famine—
Then she'll be burned by fire, because
God,
the Strong God who judges her,
has had enough.

9-10 "The kings of the earth will see the smoke of her burning, and they'll cry and carry on, the kings who went night after night to her brothel. They'll keep their distance for fear they'll get burned, and they'll cry their lament:

Doom, doom, the great city doomed!
City of Babylon, strong city!
In one hour it's over, your judgment
come!

11-17 "The traders will cry and carry on because the bottom dropped out of business, no more market for their goods: gold, silver, precious gems, pearls; fabrics of fine linen, purple, silk, scarlet; perfumed wood and vessels of ivory, precious woods, bronze, iron, and marble; cinnamon and spice, incense, myrrh, and frankincense; wine and oil, flour and wheat; cattle, sheep, horses, and chariots. And slaves—their terrible traffic in human lives.

Everything you've lived for, gone!
All delicate and delectable luxury,
lost!
Not a scrap, not a thread to be found!

"The traders who made millions off her kept their distance for fear of getting burned, and cried and carried on all the more:

NEW KING JAMES VERSION

things, who became rich by her, will stand at a
distance for fear of her torment, weeping and
wailing, [16]and saying, 'Alas, alas, that great city
that was clothed in fine linen, purple, and scar-
let, and adorned with gold and precious stones
and pearls! [17]For in one hour such great riches
came to nothing.' Every shipmaster, all who
travel by ship, sailors, and as many as trade on
the sea, stood at a distance [18]and cried out when
they saw the smoke of her burning, saying,
'What *is* like this great city?'

[19]"They threw dust on their heads and cried
out, weeping and wailing, and saying, 'Alas,
alas, that great city, in which all who had ships
on the sea became rich by her wealth! For in one
hour she is made desolate.'

[20]"Rejoice over her, O heaven, and *you* holy
apostles[a] and prophets, for God has avenged
you on her!"

FINALITY OF BABYLON'S FALL

[21]Then a mighty angel took up a stone like a
great millstone and threw *it* into the sea, saying,
"Thus with violence the great city Babylon shall
be thrown down, and shall not be found any-
more. [22]The sound of harpists, musicians,
flutists, and trumpeters shall not be heard in
you anymore. No craftsman of any craft shall be
found in you anymore, and the sound of a mill-
stone shall not be heard in you anymore. [23]The
light of a lamp shall not shine in you anymore,
and the voice of bridegroom and bride shall not
be heard in you anymore. For your merchants
were the great men of the earth, for by your sor-
cery all the nations were deceived. [24]And in her
was found the blood of prophets and saints, and
of all who were slain on the earth."

HEAVEN EXULTS OVER BABYLON

19 After these things I heard[a] a loud voice of
a great multitude in heaven, saying, "Al-
leluia! Salvation and glory and honor and
power *belong* to the Lord[b] our God! [2]For true
and righteous *are* His judgments, because He
has judged the great harlot who corrupted the
earth with her fornication; and He has avenged
on her the blood of His servants *shed* by her."
[3]Again they said, "Alleluia! Her smoke rises up
forever and ever!"

18:20 [a]NU-Text and M-Text read *saints and apostles.*
19:1 [a]NU-Text and M-Text add *something like.* [b]NU-Text and M-Text omit *the Lord.*

THE MESSAGE

Doom, doom, the great city doomed!
Dressed in the latest fashions,
adorned with the finest jewels,
in one hour such wealth wiped out!

17-19 "All the ship captains and travelers by
sea, sailors and toilers of the sea, stood off
at a distance and cried their lament when
they saw the smoke from her burning: 'Oh,
what a city! There was never a city like her!'
They threw dust on their heads and cried as
if the world had come to an end:

Doom, doom, the great city doomed!
All who owned ships or did business
by sea
Got rich on her getting and spending.
And now it's over—wiped out in one
hour!

20 "O Heaven, celebrate! And join in, saints,
apostles, and prophets! God has judged her;
every wrong you suffered from her has been
judged."

21-24 A strong Angel reached for a boulder—
huge, like a millstone—and heaved it into
the sea, saying,

Heaved and sunk, the great city Babylon,
sunk in the sea, not a sign of her ever
again.
Silent the music of harpists and
singers—
you'll never hear flutes and trumpets
again.
Artisans of every kind—gone;
you'll never see their likes again.
The voice of a millstone grinding falls
dumb;
you'll never hear that sound again.
The light from lamps, never again;
never again laughter of bride and
groom.
Her traders robbed the whole earth
blind,
and by black-magic arts deceived the
nations.
The only thing left of Babylon is blood—
the blood of saints and prophets,
the murdered and the martyred.

THE SOUND OF HALLELUJAHS

1-3 19 I heard a sound like massed choirs in
Heaven singing,

Hallelujah!
The salvation and glory and power are
God's—
his judgments true, his judgments just.
He judged the great Whore
who corrupted the earth with her lust.
He avenged on her the blood of his
servants.

Then, more singing:
Hallelujah!
The smoke from her burning billows up
to high Heaven forever and ever and
ever.

NEW KING JAMES VERSION

4And the twenty-four elders and the four living creatures fell down and worshiped God who sat on the throne, saying, “Amen! Alleluia!” 5Then a voice came from the throne, saying, “Praise our God, all you His servants and those who fear Him, both[a] small and great!”

6And I heard, as it were, the voice of a great multitude, as the sound of many waters and as the sound of mighty thunderings, saying, “Alleluia! For the[a] Lord God Omnipotent reigns! 7Let us be glad and rejoice and give Him glory, for the marriage of the Lamb has come, and His wife has made herself ready.” 8And to her it was granted to be arrayed in fine linen, clean and bright, for the fine linen is the righteous acts of the saints.

9Then he said to me, “Write: ‘Blessed *are* those who are called to the marriage supper of the Lamb!’ ” And he said to me, “These are the true sayings of God.” 10And I fell at his feet to worship him. But he said to me, “See *that you do* not *do that!* I am your fellow servant, and of your brethren who have the testimony of Jesus. Worship God! For the testimony of Jesus is the spirit of prophecy.”

CHRIST ON A WHITE HORSE

11Now I saw heaven opened, and behold, a white horse. And He who sat on him *was* called Faithful and True, and in righteousness He judges and makes war. 12His eyes *were* like a flame of fire, and on His head *were* many crowns. He had[a] a name written that no one knew except Himself. 13He *was* clothed with a robe dipped in blood, and His name is called The Word of God. 14And the armies in heaven, clothed in fine linen, white and clean,[a] followed Him on white horses. 15Now out of His mouth goes a sharp[a] sword, that with it He should strike the nations. And He Himself will rule them with a rod of iron. He Himself treads the winepress of the fierceness and wrath of Almighty God. 16And He has on *His* robe and on His thigh a name written:

KING OF KINGS AND
LORD OF LORDS.

THE BEAST AND HIS ARMIES DEFEATED

17Then I saw an angel standing in the sun; and he cried with a loud voice, saying to all the birds that fly in the midst of heaven, “Come and gather together for the supper of the great God,[a] 18that you may eat the flesh of kings, the flesh of captains, the flesh of mighty men, the flesh of horses and of those who sit on them, and the flesh of all *people,* free[a] and slave, both small and great.”

19And I saw the beast, the kings of the earth, and their armies, gathered together to make war against Him who sat on the horse and against His army. 20Then the beast was captured, and with him the false prophet who worked signs in his presence, by which he deceived those who re-

19:5 [a]NU-Text and M-Text omit *both.* **19:6** [a]NU-Text and M-Text read *our.* **19:12** [a]M-Text adds *names written, and.* **19:14** [a]NU-Text and M-Text read *pure white linen.* **19:15** [a]M-Text adds *two-edged.* **19:17** [a]NU-Text and M-Text read *the great supper of God.* **19:18** [a]NU-Text and M-Text read *both free.*

THE MESSAGE

4 The Twenty-four Elders and the Four Animals fell to their knees and worshiped God on his Throne, praising,

Amen! Yes! Hallelujah!

5 From the Throne came a shout, a command:

Praise our God, all you his servants,
All you who fear him, small and great!

6-8 Then I heard the sound of massed choirs, the sound of a mighty cataract, the sound of strong thunder:

Hallelujah!
The Master reigns,
our God, the Sovereign-Strong!
Let us celebrate, let us rejoice,
let us give him the glory!
The Marriage of the Lamb has come;
his Wife has made herself ready.
She was given a bridal gown
of bright and shining linen.
The linen is the righteousness of the
saints.

9 The Angel said to me, “Write this: ‘Blessed are those invited to the Wedding Supper of the Lamb.’ ” He added, “These are the true words of God!”

10 I fell at his feet to worship him, but he wouldn’t let me. “Don’t do that,” he said. “I’m a servant just like you, and like your brothers and sisters who hold to the witness of Jesus. The witness of Jesus is the spirit of prophecy.”

A WHITE HORSE AND ITS RIDER

11-16 Then I saw Heaven open wide—and oh! a white horse and its Rider. The Rider, named Faithful and True, judges and makes war in pure righteousness. His eyes are a blaze of fire, on his head many crowns. He has a Name inscribed that’s known only to himself. He is dressed in a robe soaked with blood, and he is addressed as “Word of God.” The armies of Heaven, mounted on white horses and dressed in dazzling white linen, follow him. A sharp sword comes out of his mouth so he can subdue the nations, then rule them with a rod of iron. He treads the winepress of the raging wrath of God, the Sovereign-Strong. On his robe and thigh is written, KING OF KINGS, LORD OF LORDS.

17-18 I saw an Angel standing in the sun, shouting to all flying birds in Middle-Heaven, “Come to the Great Supper of God! Feast on the flesh of kings and captains and champions, horses and their riders. Eat your fill of them all—free and slave, small and great!”

19-21 I saw the Beast and, assembled with him, earth’s kings and their armies, ready to make war against the One on the horse and his army. The Beast was taken, and with him, his puppet, the False Prophet, who used signs to dazzle and deceive those who had

NEW KING JAMES VERSION

ceived the mark of the beast and those who worshiped his image. These two were cast alive into the lake of fire burning with brimstone. [21]And the rest were killed with the sword which proceeded from the mouth of Him who sat on the horse. And all the birds were filled with their flesh.

SATAN BOUND 1000 YEARS

20 Then I saw an angel coming down from heaven, having the key to the bottomless pit and a great chain in his hand. [2]He laid hold of the dragon, that serpent of old, who is *the* Devil and Satan, and bound him for a thousand years; [3]and he cast him into the bottomless pit, and shut him up, and set a seal on him, so that he should deceive the nations no more till the thousand years were finished. But after these things he must be released for a little while.

THE SAINTS REIGN WITH CHRIST 1000 YEARS

[4]And I saw thrones, and they sat on them, and judgment was committed to them. Then *I saw* the souls of those who had been beheaded for their witness to Jesus and for the word of God, who had not worshiped the beast or his image, and had not received *his* mark on their foreheads or on their hands. And they lived and reigned with Christ for a[a] thousand years. [5]But the rest of the dead did not live again until the thousand years were finished. This *is* the first resurrection. [6]Blessed and holy *is* he who has part in the first resurrection. Over such the second death has no power, but they shall be priests of God and of Christ, and shall reign with Him a thousand years.

SATANIC REBELLION CRUSHED

[7]Now when the thousand years have expired, Satan will be released from his prison [8]and will go out to deceive the nations which are in the four corners of the earth, Gog and Magog, to gather them together to battle, whose number *is* as the sand of the sea. [9]They went up on the breadth of the earth and surrounded the camp of the saints and the beloved city. And fire came down from God out of heaven and devoured them. [10]The devil, who deceived them, was cast into the lake of fire and brimstone where[a] the beast and the false prophet *are.* And they will be tormented day and night forever and ever.

THE GREAT WHITE THRONE JUDGMENT

[11]Then I saw a great white throne and Him who sat on it, from whose face the earth and the heaven fled away. And there was found no place for them. [12]And I saw the dead, small and great, standing before God,[a] and books were opened. And another book was opened, which is *the Book* of Life. And the dead were judged according to their works, by the things which were written in the books. [13]The sea gave up the dead who were in it, and Death and Hades delivered up the dead who were in them. And they were judged, each one according to his works. [14]Then Death and Hades were cast into the lake of fire. This is the second death.[a] [15]And anyone not found written in the Book of Life was cast into the lake of fire.

20:4 [a]M-Text reads *the.* **20:10** [a]NU-Text and M-Text add *also.* **20:12** [a]NU-Text and M-Text read *the throne.* **20:14** [a]NU-Text and M-Text add *the lake of fire.*

THE MESSAGE

taken the mark of the Beast and worshiped his image. They were thrown alive, those two, into Lake Fire and Brimstone. The rest were killed by the sword of the One on the horse, the sword that comes from his mouth. All the birds held a feast on their flesh.

A THOUSAND YEARS

1-3 20 I saw an Angel descending out of
Heaven. He carried the key to the Abyss
and a chain—a huge chain. He grabbed the
Dragon, that old Snake—the very Devil, Satan himself!—chained him up for a thousand years, dumped him into the Abyss, slammed it shut and sealed it tight. No more trouble out of him, deceiving the nations—until the thousand years are up. After that he has to be let loose briefly.

4-6 I saw thrones. Those put in charge of
judgment sat on the thrones. I also saw the souls of those beheaded because of their witness to Jesus and the Word of God, who refused to worship either the Beast or his image, refused to take his mark on forehead or hand—they lived and reigned with Christ for a thousand years! The rest of the dead did not live until the thousand years were up. This is the first resurrection—and those involved most blessed, most holy. No second death for them! They're priests of God and Christ; they'll reign with him a thousand years.

7-10 When the thousand years are up, Satan
will be let loose from his cell, and will launch again his old work of deceiving the nations, searching out victims in every nook and cranny of earth, even Gog and Magog! He'll talk them into going to war and will gather a huge army, millions strong. They'll stream across the earth, surround and lay siege to the camp of God's holy people, the Beloved City. They'll no sooner get there than fire will pour out of Heaven and burn them up. The Devil who deceived them will be hurled into Lake Fire and Brimstone, joining the Beast and False Prophet, the three in torment around the clock for ages without end.

JUDGMENT

11-15 I saw a Great White Throne and the One En-
throned. Nothing could stand before or against the Presence, nothing in Heaven, nothing on earth. And then I saw all the dead, great and small, standing there—before the Throne! And books were opened. Then another book was opened: the Book of Life. The dead were judged by what was written in the books, by the way they had lived. Sea released its dead, Death and Hell turned in their dead. Each man and woman was judged by the way he or she had lived. Then Death and Hell were hurled into Lake Fire. This is the second death—Lake Fire. Anyone whose name was not found inscribed in the Book of Life was hurled into Lake Fire.

NEW KING JAMES VERSION

ALL THINGS MADE NEW

21 Now I saw a new heaven and a new earth, for the first heaven and the first earth had passed away. Also there was no more sea. [2]Then I, John,[a] saw the holy city, New Jerusalem, coming down out of heaven from God, prepared as a bride adorned for her husband. [3]And I heard a loud voice from heaven saying, "Behold, the tabernacle of God *is* with men, and He will dwell with them, and they shall be His people. God Himself will be with them *and be* their God. [4]And God will wipe away every tear from their eyes; there shall be no more death, nor sorrow, nor crying. There shall be no more pain, for the former things have passed away."

[5]Then He who sat on the throne said, "Behold, I make all things new." And He said to me,[a] "Write, for these words are true and faithful."

[6]And He said to me, "It is done![a] I am the Alpha and the Omega, the Beginning and the End. I will give of the fountain of the water of life freely to him who thirsts. [7]He who overcomes shall inherit all things,[a] and I will be his God and he shall be My son. [8]But the cowardly, unbelieving,[a] abominable, murderers, sexually immoral, sorcerers, idolaters, and all liars shall have their part in the lake which burns with fire and brimstone, which is the second death."

THE NEW JERUSALEM

[9]Then one of the seven angels who had the seven bowls filled with the seven last plagues came to me[a] and talked with me, saying, "Come, I will show you the bride, the Lamb's wife."[b] [10]And he carried me away in the Spirit to a great and high mountain, and showed me the great city, the holy[a] Jerusalem, descending out of heaven from God, [11]having the glory of God. Her light *was* like a most precious stone, like a jasper stone, clear as crystal. [12]Also she had a great and high wall with twelve gates, and twelve angels at the gates, and names written on them, which are *the names* of the twelve tribes of the children of Israel: [13]three gates on the east, three gates on the north, three gates on the south, and three gates on the west.

[14]Now the wall of the city had twelve foundations, and on them were the names[a] of the twelve apostles of the Lamb. [15]And he who talked with me had a gold reed to measure the city, its gates, and its wall. [16]The city is laid out as a square; its length is as great as its breadth. And he measured the city with the reed: twelve thousand furlongs. Its length, breadth, and height are equal. [17]Then he measured its wall: one hundred *and* forty-four cubits, *according* to the measure of a man, that is, of an angel. [18]The construction of its wall was *of* jasper; and the city *was* pure gold, like clear glass. [19]The foundations of the wall of the city *were* adorned with all kinds of precious stones: the first foundation *was* jasper, the second sapphire, the third chalcedony, the

21:2 [a]NU-Text and M-Text omit *John.* **21:5** [a]NU-Text and M-Text omit *to me.* **21:6** [a]M-Text omits *It is done.* **21:7** [a]M-Text reads *overcomes, I shall give him these things.* **21:8** [a]M-Text adds *and sinners.* **21:9** [a]NU-Text and M-Text omit *to me.* [b]M-Text reads *I will show you the woman, the Lamb's bride.* **21:10** [a]NU-Text and M-Text omit *the great* and read *the holy city, Jerusalem.* **21:14** [a]NU-Text and M-Text read *twelve names.*

THE MESSAGE

EVERYTHING NEW

1 **21** I saw Heaven and earth new-created.
Gone the first Heaven, gone the first
earth, gone the sea.
2 I saw Holy Jerusalem, new-created, de-
scending resplendent out of Heaven, as ready
for God as a bride for her husband.
3-5 I heard a voice thunder from the Throne:
"Look! Look! God has moved into the neigh-
borhood, making his home with men and
women! They're his people, he's their God.
He'll wipe every tear from their eyes. Death
is gone for good—tears gone, crying gone,
pain gone—all the first order of things
gone." The Enthroned continued, "Look! I'm
making everything new. Write it all down—
each word dependable and accurate."
6-8 Then he said, "It's happened. I'm A to Z.
I'm the Beginning, I'm the Conclusion. From
Water-of-Life Well I give freely to the thirsty.
Conquerors inherit all this. I'll be God to
them, they'll be sons and daughters to me.
But for the rest—the feckless and faithless,
degenerates and murderers, sex peddlers
and sorcerers, idolaters and all liars—for
them it's Lake Fire and Brimstone. Second
death!"

THE CITY OF LIGHT

9-12 One of the Seven Angels who had carried
the bowls filled with the seven final disas-
ters spoke to me: "Come here. I'll show you
the Bride, the Wife of the Lamb." He took me
away in the Spirit to an enormous, high
mountain and showed me Holy Jerusalem
descending out of Heaven from God, re-
splendent in the bright glory of God.
12-14 The City shimmered like a precious gem,
light-filled, pulsing light. She had a wall ma-
jestic and high with twelve gates. At each
gate stood an Angel, and on the gates were
inscribed the names of the Twelve Tribes of
the sons of Israel: three gates on the east,
three gates on the north, three gates on the
south, three gates on the west. The wall was
set on twelve foundations, the names of the
Twelve Apostles of the Lamb inscribed on
them.
15-21 The Angel speaking with me had a gold
measuring stick to measure the City, its
gates, and its wall. The City was laid out in
a perfect square. He measured the City with
the measuring stick: twelve thousand sta-
dia, its length, width, and height all equal.
Using the standard measure, the Angel
measured the thickness of its wall: 144 cu-
bits. The wall was jasper, the color of Glory,
and the City was pure gold, translucent as
glass. The foundations of the City walls
were garnished with every precious gem
imaginable: the first foundation jasper, the
second sapphire, the third agate, the fourth

NEW KING JAMES VERSION

fourth emerald, [20]the fifth sardonyx, the sixth sardius, the seventh chrysolite, the eighth beryl, the ninth topaz, the tenth chrysoprase, the eleventh jacinth, and the twelfth amethyst. [21]The twelve gates *were* twelve pearls: each individual gate was of one pearl. And the street of the city *was* pure gold, like transparent glass.

THE GLORY OF THE NEW JERUSALEM

[22]But I saw no temple in it, for the Lord God Almighty and the Lamb are its temple. [23]The city had no need of the sun or of the moon to shine in it,[a] for the glory[b] of God illuminated it. The Lamb *is* its light. [24]And the nations of those who are saved[a] shall walk in its light, and the kings of the earth bring their glory and honor into it.[b] [25]Its gates shall not be shut at all by day (there shall be no night there). [26]And they shall bring the glory and the honor of the nations into it.[a] [27]But there shall by no means enter it anything that defiles, or causes[a] an abomination or a lie, but only those who are written in the Lamb's Book of Life.

THE RIVER OF LIFE

22 And he showed me a pure[a] river of water of life, clear as crystal, proceeding from the throne of God and of the Lamb. [2]In the middle of its street, and on either side of the river, *was* the tree of life, which bore twelve fruits, each *tree* yielding its fruit every month. The leaves of the tree *were* for the healing of the nations. [3]And there shall be no more curse, but the throne of God and of the Lamb shall be in it, and His servants shall serve Him. [4]They shall see His face, and His name *shall be* on their foreheads. [5]There shall be no night there: They need no lamp nor light of the sun, for the Lord God gives them light. And they shall reign forever and ever.

THE TIME IS NEAR

[6]Then he said to me, "These words *are* faithful and true." And the Lord God of the holy[a] prophets sent His angel to show His servants the things which must shortly take place.

[7]"Behold, I am coming quickly! Blessed *is* he who keeps the words of the prophecy of this book."

[8]Now I, John, saw and heard[a] these things. And when I heard and saw, I fell down to worship before the feet of the angel who showed me these things.

[9]Then he said to me, "See *that you do* not *do that.* For[a] I am your fellow servant, and of your brethren the prophets, and of those who keep the words of this book. Worship God." [10]And he said to me, "Do not seal the words of the prophecy of this book, for the time is at hand. [11]He who is unjust, let him be unjust still; he who is filthy, let him be filthy still; he who is righteous, let him be righteous[a] still; he who is holy, let him be holy still."

21:23 [a]NU-Text and M-Text omit *in it.* [b]M-Text reads *the very glory.* **21:24** [a]NU-Text and M-Text omit *of those who are saved.* [b]M-Text reads *the glory and honor of the nations to Him.* **21:26** [a]M-Text adds *that they may enter in.* **21:27** [a]NU-Text and M-Text read *anything profane, nor one who causes.* **22:1** [a]NU-Text and M-Text omit *pure.* **22:6** [a]NU-Text and M-Text read *spirits of the prophets.* **22:8** [a]NU-Text and M-Text read *am the one who heard and saw.* **22:9** [a]NU-Text and M-Text omit *For.* **22:11** [a]NU-Text and M-Text read *do right.*

THE MESSAGE

emerald, the fifth onyx, the sixth carnelian, the seventh chrysolite, the eighth beryl, the ninth topaz, the tenth chrysoprase, the eleventh jacinth, the twelfth amethyst. The twelve gates were twelve pearls, each gate a single pearl.

21-27 The main street of the City was pure gold, translucent as glass. But there was no sign of a Temple, for the Lord God—the Sovereign-Strong—and the Lamb are the Temple. The City doesn't need sun or moon for light. God's Glory is its light, the Lamb its lamp! The nations will walk in its light and earth's kings bring in their splendor. Its gates will never be shut by day, and there won't be any night. They'll bring the glory and honor of the nations into the City. Nothing dirty or defiled will get into the City, and no one who defiles or deceives. Only those whose names are written in the Lamb's Book of Life will get in.

1-5 22 Then the Angel showed me Water-of-Life River, crystal bright. It flowed from the Throne of God and the Lamb, right down the middle of the street. The Tree of Life was planted on each side of the River, producing twelve kinds of fruit, a ripe fruit each month. The leaves of the Tree are for healing the nations. Never again will anything be cursed. The Throne of God and of the Lamb is at the center. His servants will offer God service—worshiping, they'll look on his face, their foreheads mirroring God. Never again will there be any night. No one will need lamplight or sunlight. The shining of God, the Master, is all the light anyone needs. And they will rule with him age after age after age.

DON'T PUT IT AWAY ON THE SHELF

6-7 The Angel said to me, "These are dependable and accurate words, every one. The God and Master of the spirits of the prophets sent his Angel to show his servants what must take place, and soon. And tell them, 'Yes, I'm on my way!' Blessed be the one who keeps the words of the prophecy of this book."

8-9 I, John, saw all these things with my own eyes, heard them with my ears. Immediately when I heard and saw, I fell on my face to worship at the feet of the Angel who laid it all out before me. He objected, "No you don't! I'm a servant just like you and your companions, the prophets, and all who keep the words of this book. Worship God!"

10-11 The Angel continued, "Don't seal the words of the prophecy of this book; don't put it away on the shelf. Time is just about up. Let evildoers do their worst and the dirty-minded go all out in pollution, but let the righteous maintain a straight course and the holy continue on in holiness."

NEW KING JAMES VERSION

JESUS TESTIFIES TO THE CHURCHES

12“And behold, I am coming quickly, and My
reward *is* with Me, to give to every one accord-
ing to his work. 13I am the Alpha and the
Omega, *the* Beginning and *the* End, the First
and the Last.”[a]
14Blessed *are* those who do His command-
ments,[a] that they may have the right to the tree
of life, and may enter through the gates into the
city. 15But[a] outside *are* dogs and sorcerers and
sexually immoral and murderers and idolaters,
and whoever loves and practices a lie.
16“I, Jesus, have sent My angel to testify to
you these things in the churches. I am the Root
and the Offspring of David, the Bright and
Morning Star.”
17And the Spirit and the bride say, “Come!”
And let him who hears say, “Come!” And let him
who thirsts come. Whoever desires, let him take
the water of life freely.

A WARNING

18For[a] I testify to everyone who hears the
words of the prophecy of this book: If anyone
adds to these things, God will add[b] to him the
plagues that are written in this book; 19and if
anyone takes away from the words of the book
of this prophecy, God shall take away[a] his part
from the Book[b] of Life, from the holy city, and
from the things which are written in this book.

I AM COMING QUICKLY

20He who testifies to these things says,
“Surely I am coming quickly.”
Amen. Even so, come, Lord Jesus!
21The grace of our Lord Jesus Christ *be* with
you all.[a] Amen.

22:13 [a]NU-Text and M-Text read *the First and the Last, the Beginning and the End.* **22:14** [a]NU-Text reads *wash their robes.* **22:15** [a]NU-Text and M-Text omit *But.* **22:18** [a]NU-Text and M-Text omit *For.* [b]M-Text reads *may God add.* **22:19** [a]M-Text reads *may God take away.* [b]NU-Text and M-Text read *tree of life.* **22:21** [a]NU-Text reads *with all;* M-Text reads *with all the saints.*

THE MESSAGE

12-13 “Yes, I'm on my way! I'll be there soon! I'm bringing my payroll with me. I'll pay all people in full for their life's work. I'm A to Z, the First and the Final, Beginning and Conclusion.

14-15 “How blessed are those who wash their robes! The Tree of Life is theirs for good, and they'll walk through the gates to the City. But outside for good are the filthy curs: sorcerers, fornicators, murderers, idolaters—all who love and live lies.

16 “I, Jesus, sent my Angel to testify to these things for the churches. I'm the Root and Branch of David, the Bright Morning Star.”

17 “Come!” say the Spirit and the Bride.
Whoever hears, echo, “Come!”
Is anyone thirsty? Come!
All who will, come and drink,
Drink freely of the Water of Life!

18-19 I give fair warning to all who hear the words of the prophecy of this book: If you add to the words of this prophecy, God will add to your life the disasters written in this book; if you subtract from the words of the book of this prophecy, God will subtract your part from the Tree of Life and the Holy City that are written in this book.

20 He who testifies to all these things says it again: “I'm on my way! I'll be there soon!”
Yes! Come, Master Jesus!

21 The grace of the Master Jesus be with all of you. Oh, Yes!

HARMONY OF THE GOSPELS AND CONCORDANCE

NEW KING JAMES VERSION

Harmony of the Gospels

Date	Event	Location	Matthew	Mark	Luke	John	Related References
	INTRODUCTIONS TO JESUS CHRIST						
	(1) Luke's Introduction				1:1–4		Acts 1:1
	(2) Pre-fleshly state of Christ					1:1–18	Heb. 1:1–14
	(3) Genealogy of Jesus Christ		1:1–17		3:23–38		Ruth 4:18–22 1 Chr. 1:1–4
	BIRTH, INFANCY, AND ADOLESCENCE OF JESUS AND JOHN THE BAPTIST						
7 B.C.	(1) Announcement of Birth of John	Jerusalem (temple)			1:5–25		Num. 6:3
7 or 6 B.C.	(2) Announcement of Birth of Jesus to the Virgin	Nazareth			1:26–38		Is. 7:14
C. 5 B.C.	(3) Song of Elizabeth to Mary	Hill Country of Judea			1:39–45		
	(4) Mary's Song of Praise				1:46–56		Ps. 103:17
5 B.C.	(5) Birth, Infancy, and Purpose for Future of John the Baptist	Judea			1:57–80		Mal. 3:1
	(6) Announcement of Jesus' Birth to Joseph	Nazareth	1:18–25				Is. 9:6, 7
5–4 B.C.	(7) Birth of Jesus Christ	Bethlehem	1:24, 25		2:1–7		Is. 7:14
	(8) Proclamation by the Angels	Near Bethlehem			2:8–14		1 Tim. 3:16
	(9) The Visit of Homage by Shepherds	Bethlehem			2:15–20		
	(10) Jesus' Circumcision	Bethlehem			2:21		Lev. 12:3
4 B.C.	(11) First Temple Visit with Acknowledgments by Simeon and Anna	Jerusalem			2:22–38		Ex. 13:2 Lev. 12
	(12) Visit of the Wise Men	Jerusalem & Bethlehem	2:1–12				Num. 24:17
	(13) Flight into Egypt and Massacre of Innocents	Bethlehem, Jerusalem & Egypt	2:13–18				Jer. 31:15
	(14) From Egypt to Nazareth with Jesus		2:19–23		2:39		
Afterward	(15) Childhood of Jesus	Nazareth			2:40, 51		
A.D. 7–8	(16) Jesus, 12 Years Old, Visits the Temple	Jerusalem			2:41–50		Deut. 16:1–8
Afterward	(17) 18-Year Account of Jesus' Adolescence and Adulthood	Nazareth			2:51, 52		1 Sam. 2:26
	TRUTHS ABOUT JOHN THE BAPTIST						
C. A.D. 28–30	(1) John's Ministry Begins	Judean Wilderness	3:1	1:1–4	3:1, 2	1:19–28	Mal. 3:1
	(2) Man and Message		3:2–12	1:2–8	3:3–14		Is. 40:3
	(3) His Picture of Jesus		3:11, 12	1:7, 8	3:15–18	1:26, 27	Acts 2:38
	(4) His Courage		14:4–12		3:19, 20		
	BEGINNING OF JESUS' MINISTRY						
C. A.D. 30	(1) Jesus Baptized	Jordan River	3:13–17	1:9–11	3:21–23	1:29–34	Ps. 2:7
	(2) Jesus Tempted	Wilderness	4:1–11	1:12, 13	4:1–13		Ps. 91:11
	(3) Calls First Disciples	Beyond Jordan				1:35–51	
	(4) The First Miracle	Cana in Galilee				2:1–11	
	(5) First Stay in Capernaum	(Capernaum is "His" city)				2:12	
	(6) First Cleansing of the Temple	Jerusalem				2:13–22	Ps. 69:9

Date	Event	Location	Matthew	Mark	Luke	John	Related References
A.D. 30	(7) Received at Jerusalem	Judea				2:23–25	
	(8) Teaches Nicodemus about Second Birth	Judea				3:1–21	Num. 21:8, 9
	(9) Co-Ministry with John	Judea				3:22–30	
	(10) Leaves for Galilee	Judea	4:12	1:14	4:14	4:1–4	
	(11) Samaritan Woman at Jacob's Well	Samaria				4:5–42	Josh. 24:32
	(12) Returns to Galilee			1:15	4:15	4:43–45	
	THE GALILEAN MINISTRY OF JESUS						
A.D. 30–32 A.D. 30	(1) Healing of the Nobleman's Son	Cana				4:46–54	
	(2) Rejected at Nazareth	Nazareth			4:16–30		Is. 61:1, 2
	(3) Moved to Capernaum	Capernaum	4:13–17				Is. 9:1, 2
	(4) Four Become Fishers of Men	Sea of Galilee	4:18–22	1:16–20	5:1–11		Ps. 33:9
	(5) Demoniac Healed on the Sabbath Day	Capernaum		1:21–28	4:31–37		
	(6) Peter's Mother-in-Law Cured, Plus Others	Capernaum	8:14–17	1:29–34	4:38–41		Is. 53:4
C. A.D. 30	(7) First Preaching Tour of Galilee	Galilee	4:23–25	1:35–39	4:42–44		
	(8) Leper Healed and Response Recorded	Galilee	8:1–4	1:40–45	5:12–16		Lev. 13:49
	(9) Paralytic Healed	Capernaum	9:1–8	2:1–12	5:17–26		Rom. 3:23
	(10) Matthew's Call and Reception Held	Capernaum	9:9–13	2:13–17	5:27–32		Hos. 6:6
	(11) Disciples Defended via a Parable	Capernaum	9:14–17	2:18–22	5:33–39		
A.D. 31	(12) Goes to Jerusalem for Second Passover; Heals Lame Man	Jerusalem				5:1–47	Ex. 20:10
	(13) Plucked Grain Precipitates Sabbath Controversy	En Route to Galilee	12:1–8	2:23–28	6:1–5		Deut. 5:14
	(14) Withered Hand Healed Causes Another Sabbath Controversy	Galilee	12:9–14	3:1–6	6:6–11		
	(15) Multitudes Healed	Sea of Galilee	12:15–21	3:7–12	6:17–19		
	(16) Twelve Apostles Selected After a Night of Prayer	Near Capernaum		3:13–19	6:12–16		
	(17) Sermon on the Mt.	Near Capernaum	5:1—7:29		6:20–49		
	(18) Centurion's Servant Healed	Capernaum	8:5–13		7:1–10		Is. 49:12, 13
	(19) Raises Widow's Son from Dead	Nain			7:11–17		Job 19:25
	(20) Jesus Allays John's Doubts	Galilee	11:2–19		7:18–35		Mal. 3:1
	(21) Woes Upon the Privileged		11:20–30				Gen. 19:24
	(22) A Sinful Woman Anoints Jesus	Simon's House, Capernaum			7:36–50		
	(23) Another Tour of Galilee	Galilee			8:1–3		
	(24) Jesus Accused of Blasphemy	Capernaum	12:22–37	3:20–30	11:14–23		
	(25) Jesus' Answer to a Demand for a Sign	Capernaum	12:38–45		11:24–26, 29–36		
	(26) Mother, Brothers Seek Audience	Capernaum	12:46–50	3:31–35	8:19–21		
	(27) Famous Parables of Sower, Seed, Tares, Mustard Seed, Leaven, Treasure, Pearl, Dragnet, Lamp Told	By Sea of Galilee	13:1–52	4:1–34	8:4–18		Joel 3:13

Date	Event	Location	Matthew	Mark	Luke	John	Related References
A.D. 31	(28) Sea Made Serene	Sea of Galilee	8:23-27	4:35-41	8:22-25		
	(29) Gadarene Demoniac Healed	E. Shore of Galilee	8:28-34	5:1-20	8:26-39		
	(30) Jairus's Daughter Raised and Woman with Hemorrhage Healed		9:18-26	5:21-43	8:40-56		
	(31) Two Blind Men's Sight Restored		9:27-31				
	(32) Mute Demoniac Healed		9:32-34				
	(33) Nazareth's Second Rejection of Christ	Nazareth	13:53-58	6:1-6			
	(34) Twelve Sent Out		9:35—11:1	6:7-13	9:1-6		1 Cor. 9:14
	(35) Fearful Herod Beheads John	Galilee	14:1-12	6:14-29	9:7-9		
Spring A.D. 32	(36) Return of 12, Jesus Withdraws, 5,000 Fed	Near Bethsaida	14:13-21	6:30-44	9:10-17	6:1-14	
	(37) Walks on the Water	Sea of Galilee	14:22-33	6:45-52		6:15-21	
	(38) Sick of Gennesaret Healed	Gennesaret	14:34-36	6:53-56			
	(39) Peak of Popularity Passes in Galilee	Capernaum				6:22-71 7:1	Is. 54:13
A.D. 32	(40) Traditions Attacked		15:1-20	7:1-23			Ex. 21:17
	(41) Aborted Retirement in Phoenicia: Syro-Phoenician Healed	Phoenicia	15:21-28	7:24-30			
	(42) Afflicted Healed	Decapolis	15:29-31	7:31-37			
	(43) 4,000 Fed	Decapolis	15:32-39	8:1-9			
	(44) Pharisees Increase Attack	Magdala	16:1-4	8:10-13			
	(45) Disciples' Carelessness Condemned; Blind Man Healed		16:5-12	8:14-26			Jer. 5:21
	(46) Peter Confesses Jesus Is the Christ	Near Caesarea Philippi	16:13-20	8:27-30	9:18-21		
	(47) Jesus Foretells His Death	Caesarea Philippi	16:21-26	8:31-38	9:22-25		
	(48) Kingdom Promised		16:27, 28	9:1	9:26, 27		Prov. 24:12
	(49) The Transfiguration	Mountain Unnamed	17:1-13	9:2-13	9:28-36		Is. 42:1
	(50) Epileptic Healed	Mt. of Transfiguration	17:14-21	9:14-29	9:37-42		
	(51) Again Tells of Death, Resurrection	Galilee	17:22, 23	9:30-32	9:43-45		
	(52) Taxes Paid	Capernaum	17:24-27				Ex. 30:11-15
	(53) Disciples Contend About Greatness; Jesus Defines; also Patience, Loyalty, Forgiveness	Capernaum	18:1-35	9:33-50	9:46-62		
	(54) Jesus Rejects Brothers' Advice	Galilee				7:2-9	
c. Sept. A.D. 32	(55) Galilee Departure and Samaritan Rejection		19:1		9:51-56	7:10	
	(56) Cost of Discipleship		8:18-22		9:57-62		

LAST JUDEAN AND PEREAN MINISTRY OF JESUS

Date	Event	Location	Matthew	Mark	Luke	John	Related References
A.D. 32-33 Oct. A.D. 32	(1) Feast of Tabernacles	Jerusalem				7:2, 10-52	
	(2) Forgiveness of Adulteress	Jerusalem				7:53—8:11	Lev. 20:10
A.D. 32	(3) Christ—the Light of the World	Jerusalem				8:12-20	
	(4) Pharisees Can't Meet the Prophecy Thus Try to Destroy the Prophet	Jerusalem—Temple				8:12-59	Is. 6:9
	(5) Man Born Blind Healed; Following Consequences	Jerusalem				9:1-41	

Date	Event	Location	Matthew	Mark	Luke	John	Related References
A.D. 32	(6) Parable of the Good Shepherd	Jerusalem				10:1–21	
	(7) The Service of the Seventy	Probably Judea			10:1–24		
	(8) Lawyer Hears the Story of the Good Samaritan	Judea (?)			10:25–37		
	(9) The Hospitality of Martha and Mary	Bethany			10:38–42		
	(10) Another Lesson on Prayer	Judea (?)			11:1–13		
	(11) Accused of Connection with Beelzebub				11:14–36		
	(12) Judgment Against Lawyers and Pharisees				11:37–54		Mic. 6:8
	(13) Jesus Deals with Hypocrisy, Covetousness, Worry, and Alertness				12:1–59		Mic. 7:6
	(14) Repent or Perish				13:1–5		
	(15) Barren Fig Tree				13:6–9		
	(16) Crippled Woman Healed on Sabbath				13:10–17		Deut. 5:12–15
	(17) Parables of Mustard Seed and Leaven	Probably Perea			13:18–21		
Winter A.D. 32	(18) Feast of Dedication	Jerusalem				10:22–39	Ps. 82:6
	(19) Withdrawal Beyond Jordan					10:40–42	
	(20) Begins Teaching Return to Jerusalem with Special Words About Herod	Perea			13:22–35		Ps. 6:8
	(21) Meal with a Pharisee Ruler Occasions Healing Man with Dropsy; Parables of Ox, Best Places, and Great Supper				14:1–24		
	(22) Demands of Discipleship	Perea			14:25–35		
	(23) Parables of Lost Sheep, Coin, Son				15:1–32		1 Pet. 2:25
	(24) Parables of Unjust Steward, Rich Man and Lazarus				16:1–31		
	(25) Lessons on Service, Faith, Influence				17:1–10		
	(26) Resurrection of Lazarus	Perea to Bethany				11:1–44	
	(27) Reaction to It: Withdrawal of Jesus					11:45–54	
A.D. 33	(28) Begins Last Journey to Jerusalem via Samaria & Galilee	Samaria, Galilee			17:11		
	(29) Heals Ten Lepers				17:12–19		Lev. 13:45, 46
	(30) Lessons on the Coming Kingdom				17:20–37		Gen. 6:1—7:24
	(31) Parables: Persistent Widow, Pharisee and Tax Collector				18:1–14		
	(32) Doctrine on Divorce		19:1–12	10:1–12			Deut. 24:1–4 Gen. 2:23–25
	(33) Jesus Blesses Children: Objections	Perea	19:13–15	10:13–16	18:15–17		Ps. 131:2
	(34) Rich Young Ruler	Perea	19:16–30	10:17–31	18:18–30		Ex. 20:1–17
	(35) Laborers of the 11th Hour		20:1–16				
	(36) Foretells Death and Resurrection	Near Jordan	20:17–19	10:32–34	18:31–34		Ps. 22
	(37) Ambition of James and John		20:20–28	10:35–45			
	(38) Blind Bartimaeus Healed	Jericho		10:46–52	18:35–43		
	(39) Interview with Zacchaeus	Jericho			19:1–10		
	(40) Parable: the Minas	Jericho			19:11–27		

Date	*Event*	*Location*	*Matthew*	*Mark*	*Luke*	*John*	*Related References*
A.D. 33	(41) Returns to Home of Mary and Martha	Bethany				11:55—12:1	
	(42) Plot to Kill Lazarus	Bethany				12:9–11	

JESUS' FINAL WEEK OF WORK AT JERUSALEM

Date	*Event*	*Location*	*Matthew*	*Mark*	*Luke*	*John*	*Related References*
Spring A.D. 33							
Sunday	(1) Triumphal Entry	Bethany, Jerusalem, Bethany	21:1–9	11:1–11	19:28–44	12:12–19	Zech. 9:9
Monday	(2) Fig Tree Cursed and Temple Cleansed	Bethany to Jerusalem	21:10–19	11:12–18	19:45–48		Jer. 7:11
	(3) The Attraction of Sacrifice	Jerusalem				12:20–50	Is. 6:10
Tuesday	(4) Withered Fig Tree Testifies	Bethany to Jerusalem	21:20–22	11:19–26			
	(5) Sanhedrin Challenges Jesus. Answered by Parables: Two Sons, Wicked Vinedressers and Marriage Feast	Jerusalem	21:23—22:14	11:27—12:12	20:1–19		Is. 5:1, 2
	(6) Tribute to Caesar	Jerusalem	22:15–22	12:13–17	20:20–26		
	(7) Sadducees Question the Resurrection	Jerusalem	22:23–33	12:18–27	20:27–40		Ex. 3:6
	(8) Pharisees Question Commandments	Jerusalem	22:34–40	12:28–34			
	(9) Jesus and David	Jerusalem	22:41–46	12:35–37	20:41–44		Ps. 110:1
	(10) Jesus' Last Sermon	Jerusalem	23:1–39	12:38–40	20:45–47		
	(11) Widow's Mite	Jerusalem		12:41–44	21:1–4		Lev. 27:30
	(12) Jesus Tells of the Future	Mt. of Olives	24:1–51	13:1–37	21:5–36		Dan. 12:1
	(13) Parables: Ten Virgins, Talents, The Day of Judgment	Mt. of Olives	25:1–46				Zech. 14:5
	(14) Jesus Tells Date of Crucifixion		26:1–5	14:1, 2	22:1, 2		
	(15) Anointing by Mary at Simon's Feast	Bethany	26:6–13	14:3–9		12:2–8	
	(16) Judas Contracts the Betrayal		26:14–16	14:10, 11	22:3–6		Zech. 11:12
Thursday	(17) Preparation for the Passover	Jerusalem	26:17–19	14:12–16	22:7–13		Ex. 12:14–28
Thursday P. M.	(18) Passover Eaten, Jealousy Rebuked	Jerusalem	26:20	14:17	22:14–16, 24–30		
	(19) Feet Washed	Upper Room				13:1–20	
	(20) Judas Revealed, Defects	Upper Room	26:21–25	14:18–21	22:21–23	13:21–30	Ps. 41:9
	(21) Jesus Warns About Further Desertion; Cries of Loyalty	Upper Room	26:31–35	14:27–31	22:31–38	13:31–38	Zech. 13:7
	(22) Institution of the Lord's Supper	Upper Room	26:26–29	14:22–25	22:17–20		1 Cor. 11:23–34
	(23) Last Speech to the Apostles and Intercessory Prayer	Jerusalem				14:1—17:26	Ps. 35:19
Thursday-Friday	(24) The Grief of Gethsemane	Mt. of Olives	26:30, 36–46	14:26, 32–42	22:39–46	18:1	Ps. 42:6
Friday	(25) Betrayal, Arrest, Desertion	Gethsemane	26:47–56	14:43–52	22:47–53	18:2–12	
	(26) First Examined by Annas	Jerusalem				18:12–14, 19–23	
	(27) Trial by Caiaphas and Council; Following Indignities	Jerusalem	26:57, 59–68	14:53, 55–65	22:54, 63–65	18:24	Lev. 24:16
	(28) Peter's Triple Denial	Jerusalem	26:58, 69–75	14:54, 66–72	22:54–62	18:15–18, 25–27	

Date	Event	Location	Matthew	Mark	Luke	John	Related References
Friday	(29) Condemnation by the Council	Jerusalem	27:1	15:1	22:66–71		Ps. 110:1
	(30) Suicide of Judas	Jerusalem	27:3–10				Acts 1:18, 19
	(31) First Appearance Before Pilate	Jerusalem	27:2, 11–14	15:1–5	23:1–7	18:28–38	
	(32) Jesus Before Herod	Jerusalem			23:6–12		
	(33) Second Appearance Before Pilate	Jerusalem	27:15–26	15:6–15	23:13–25	18:39—19:16	Deut. 21:6–9
	(34) Mockery by Roman Soldiers	Jerusalem	27:27–30	15:16–19			
	(35) Led to Golgotha	Jerusalem	27:31–34	15:20–23	23:26–33	19:16, 17	Ps. 69:21
	(36) 6 Events of First 3 Hours on Cross	Calvary	27:35–44	15:24–32	23:33–43	19:18–27	Ps. 22:18
	(37) Last 3 Hours on Cross	Calvary	27:45–50	15:33–37	23:44–46	19:28–30	Ps. 22:1
	(38) Events Attending Jesus' Death		27:51–56	15:38–41	23:45, 47–49		
	(39) Burial of Jesus	Jerusalem	27:57–60	15:42–46	23:50–54	19:31–42	Ex. 12:46
Friday-Saturday	(40) Tomb Sealed	Jerusalem	27:61–66		23:55, 56		Ex. 20:8–11
	(41) Women Watch	Jerusalem		15:47			

THE RESURRECTION THROUGH THE ASCENSION

Date	Event	Location	Matthew	Mark	Luke	John	Related References
A.D. 33 Dawn of First Day (Sunday, "Lord's Day")	(1) Women Visit the Tomb	Near Jerusalem	28:1–8	16:1–8	24:1–11		
	(2) Peter and John See the Empty Tomb				24:12	20:1–10	
	(3) Jesus' Appearance to Mary Magdalene	Jerusalem		16:9–11		20:11–18	
	(4) Jesus' Appearance to the Other Women	Jerusalem	28:9, 10				
	(5) Guards' Report of the Resurrection		28:11–15				
Sunday Afternoon	(6) Jesus' Appearance to Two Disciples on Way to Emmaus			16:12, 13	24:13–35		1 Cor. 15:5
Late Sunday	(7) Jesus' Appearance to Ten Disciples Without Thomas	Jerusalem			24:36–43	20:19–25	
One Week Later	(8) Appearance to Disciples with Thomas	Jerusalem				20:26–31	
During 40 Days until Ascension	(9) Jesus' Appearance to Seven Disciples by Sea of Galilee	Galilee				21:1–25	
	(10) Appearance to 500	Mt. in Galilee					1 Cor. 15:6
	(11) Great Commission		28:16–20	16:14–18	24:44–49		
	(12) The Ascension	Mt. Olivet		16:19, 20	24:50–53		Acts 1:4–11

CONCORDANCE TO THE NKJV

A

ABASED
I know how to be *a* ... Phil 4:12

ABBA
And He said, "*A* ... Mark 14:36
whom we cry out, "*A* ... Rom 8:15

ABHOR
Therefore I *a* myself ... Job 42:6

ABHORRED
a His own inheritance ... Ps 106:40

ABIDE
the Most High Shall *a* ... Ps 91:1
Him, "If you *a* ... John 8:31
"If you *a* in Me ... John 15:7
a in My love ... John 15:9

ABIDES
He who *a* in Me ... John 15:5
will of God *a* forever ... 1 John 2:17

ABIDING
not have His word *a* ... John 5:38

ABILITY
to his own *a* ... Matt 25:15
a which God supplies ... 1 Pet 4:11

ABLE
shall give as he is *a* ... Deut 16:17
whom we serve is *a* ... Dan 3:17
God is *a* to raise up ... Matt 3:9
fear Him who is *a* ... Matt 10:28
you *a* to drink the ... Matt 20:22
that He is *a* ... 2 Tim 1:12
learning and never *a* ... 2 Tim 3:7
that God was *a* to ... Heb 11:19

ABOLISHED
having *a* in His flesh ... Eph 2:15
Christ, who has *a* ... 2 Tim 1:10

ABOMINABLE
deny Him, being *a* ... Titus 1:16
unbelieving, *a* ... Rev 21:8

ABOMINATION
Yes, seven are an *a* ... Prov 6:16
the scoffer is an *a* ... Prov 24:9
prayer is an *a* ... Prov 28:9
and place there the *a* ... Dan 11:31
the *a* of desolation ... Dan 12:11
the '*a* of desolation,' ... Matt 24:15

ABOMINATIONS
delights in their *a* ... Is 66:3
a golden cup full of *a* ... Rev 17:4

ABOUND
the offense might *a* ... Rom 5:20
sin that grace may *a* ... Rom 6:1
to make all grace *a* ... 2 Cor 9:8
and I know how to *a* ... Phil 4:12

ABOUNDED
But where sin *a* ... Rom 5:20

ABOUNDING
immovable, always *a* ... 1 Cor 15:58

ABOVE
that is in heaven *a* ... Ex 20:4
A it stood seraphim ... Is 6:2
"He who comes from *a* ... John 3:31
I am from *a* ... John 8:23
given you from *a* ... John 19:11
things which are *a* ... Col 3:1
perfect gift is from *a* ... James 1:17

ABSENT
in the body we are *a* ... 2 Cor 5:6

ABSTAIN
we write to them to *a* ... Acts 15:20
A from every form ... 1 Thess 5:22

ABUNDANCE
put in out of their *a* ... Mark 12:44
not consist in the *a* ... Luke 12:15

ABUNDANT
in labors more *a* ... 2 Cor 11:23

ABUNDANTLY
a satisfied with the ... Ps 36:8
may have it more *a* ... John 10:10
to do exceedingly *a* ... Eph 3:20

ACCEPT
offering, I will not *a* ... Jer 14:12
Should I *a* this from ... Mal 1:13

ACCEPTABLE
a time I have heard ... Is 49:8
proclaim the *a* year ... Is 61:2
proclaim the *a* year ... Luke 4:19
is that good and *a* ... Rom 12:2

ACCEPTABLY
we may serve God *a* ... Heb 12:28

ACCEPTED
Behold, now is the *a* ... 2 Cor 6:2
which He made us *a* ... Eph 1:6

ACCESS
whom also we have *a* ... Rom 5:2

ACCOMPLISHED
all things were now *a* ... John 19:28

ACCORD
continued with one *a* ... Acts 1:14

ACCOUNT
they will give *a* ... Matt 12:36
put that on my *a* ... Philem 18

ACCOUNTED
in the LORD, and He *a* ... Gen 15:6
his faith is *a* ... Rom 4:5
God, and it was *a* ... Gal 3:6
God, and it was *a* ... James 2:23

ACCURSED
not know the law is *a* ... John 7:49
of God calls Jesus *a* ... 1 Cor 12:3
to you, let him be *a* ... Gal 1:8

ACCUSATION
over His head the *a* ... Matt 27:37
they might find an *a* ... Luke 6:7

ACCUSE
they began to *a* Him ... Luke 23:2

ACCUSED
while He was being *a* ... Matt 27:12

ACCUSER
a of our brethren ... Rev 12:10

ACCUSING
their thoughts *a* ... Rom 2:15

ACKNOWLEDGE
a my transgressions ... Ps 51:3
In all your ways *a* ... Prov 3:6

ACKNOWLEDGES
a the Son has the ... 1 John 2:23

ACQUAINT
a yourself with Him ... Job 22:21

ACQUAINTED
A Man of sorrows and *a* ... Is 53:3

ACQUIT
at all *a* the wicked ... Nah 1:3

ACT
in the very *a* ... John 8:4

ACTIONS
by Him *a* are weighed ... 1 Sam 2:3

ACTS
of Your awesome *a* ... Ps 145:6

ADD
Do not *a* to His words ... Prov 30:6

ADDED
And the Lord *a* to the ... Acts 2:47
It was *a* because of ... Gal 3:19

ADMONISH
a him as a ... 2 Thess 3:15

ADMONITION
written for our *a* ... 1 Cor 10:11
in the training and *a* ... Eph 6:4

ADOPTION
the Spirit of *a* ... Rom 8:15
waiting for the *a* ... Rom 8:23
to whom pertain the *a* ... Rom 9:4

ADORN
also, that the women *a* ... 1 Tim 2:9

ADORNED
God also *a* themselves ... 1 Pet 3:5
prepared as a bride *a* ... Rev 21:2

ADRIFT
A among the dead ... Ps 88:5

ADULTERER
The eye of the *a* ... Job 24:15

ADULTERERS
nor idolaters, nor *a* ... 1 Cor 6:9
a God will judge ... Heb 13:4

ADULTEROUS
a generation ... Matt 12:39

ADULTERY
You shall not commit *a* ... Ex 20:14
already committed *a* ... Matt 5:28
is divorced commits *a* ... Matt 5:32
another commits *a* ... Mark 10:11
those who commit *a* ... Rev 2:22

ADVANTAGE
a that I go away ... John 16:7
Satan should take *a* ... 2 Cor 2:11

ADVERSARIES
and there are many *a* ... 1 Cor 16:9
terrified by your *a* ... Phil 1:28

ADVERSARY
"Agree with your *a* ... Matt 5:25
opportunity to the *a* ... 1 Tim 5:14
a the devil walks ... 1 Pet 5:8

ADVERSITY
I shall never be in *a* ... Ps 10:6
the day of *a* consider ... Eccl 7:14

ADVICE
in this I give my *a* ... 2 Cor 8:10

ADVOCATE
sins, we have an *A* ... 1 John 2:1

AFAR
and not a God *a* ... Jer 23:23
to you who were *a* ... Eph 2:17
having seen them *a* ... Heb 11:13

AFFAIRS
himself with the *a* ... 2 Tim 2:4

AFFECTION
to his wife the *a* ... 1 Cor 7:3

AFFECTIONATE
Be kindly *a* to one ... Rom 12:10

AFFIRM
you to *a* constantly ... Titus 3:8

AFFLICT
a Your heritage ... Ps 94:5
For He does not *a* ... Lam 3:33

AFFLICTED
To him who is *a* ... Job 6:14
hears the cry of the *a* ... Job 34:28
days of the *a* are evil ... Prov 15:15

Smitten by God, and *a* .... Is 53:4
"O you *a* one .... Is 54:11
being destitute, *a* .... Heb 11:37

AFFLICTING
A the just and taking .... Amos 5:12

AFFLICTION
is, the bread of *a* .... Deut 16:3
a take hold of me .... Job 30:16
and it is an evil *a* .... Eccl 6:2
For our light *a* .... 2 Cor 4:17
supposing to add *a* .... Phil 1:16

AFRAID
garden, and I was *a* .... Gen 3:10
saying, "Do not be *a* .... Gen 15:1
none will make you *a* .... Lev 26:6
ungodliness made me *a* .... Ps 18:4
Whenever I am *a* .... Ps 56:3
one will make them *a* .... Is 17:2
do not be *a* .... Matt 14:27
if you do evil, be *a* .... Rom 13:4
do good and are not *a* .... 1 Pet 3:6

AFTERWARD
a receive me to glory .... Ps 73:24
you shall follow Me *a* .... John 13:36

AGAIN
'You must be born *a* .... John 3:7
having been born *a* .... 1 Pet 1:23

AGAINST
come to 'set a man *a* .... Matt 10:35
or house divided *a* .... Matt 12:25
Me is *a* Me .... Matt 12:30
a the Spirit will not .... Matt 12:31
lifted up his heel *a* .... John 13:18
LORD and *a* His Christ .... Acts 4:26
to kick *a* the goads .... Acts 9:5
a the promises of God .... Gal 3:21
we do not wrestle *a* .... Eph 6:12
I have a few things *a* .... Rev 2:20

AGE
the grave at a full *a* .... Job 5:26
and in the *a* to come .... Mark 10:30

AGED
a one as Paul, the *a* .... Philem 9

AGES
ordained before the *a* .... 1 Cor 2:7

AGONY
And being in *a* .... Luke 22:44

AGREE
that if two of you *a* .... Matt 18:19

AGREED
unless they are *a* .... Amos 3:3

AGREEMENT
what *a* has the temple .... 2 Cor 6:16

AIR
the birds of the *a* .... Gen 1:26
of the *a* have nests .... Luke 9:58
of the power of the *a* .... Eph 2:2
the Lord in the *a* .... 1 Thess 4:17

ALIENATED
darkened, being *a* .... Eph 4:18
you, who once were *a* .... Col 1:21

ALIENS
A have devoured his .... Hos 7:9
Christ, being *a* .... Eph 2:12

ALIKE
esteems every day *a* .... Rom 14:5

ALIVE
I kill and I make *a* .... Deut 32:39
was dead and is *a* .... Luke 15:24
presented Himself *a* .... Acts 1:3
indeed to sin, but *a* .... Rom 6:11
all shall be made *a* .... 1 Cor 15:22
that we who are *a* .... 1 Thess 4:15
and behold, I am *a* .... Rev 1:18
These two were cast *a* .... Rev 19:20

ALLELUIA
Again they said, '*A* .... Rev 19:3

ALLOW
a Your Holy One .... Ps 16:10
a My faithfulness .... Ps 89:33
a Your Holy One .... Acts 2:27

ALLURE
of emptiness, they *a* .... 2 Pet 2:18

ALMOND
a tree blossoms .... Eccl 12:5

ALMOST
a persuade me to .... Acts 26:28

ALOES
of myrrh and *a* .... John 19:39

ALPHA
"I am the *A* and the .... Rev 1:8
"I am the *A* and the .... Rev 22:13

ALTAR
Then Noah built an *a* .... Gen 8:20
'An *a* of earth you .... Ex 20:24
it to you upon the *a* .... Lev 17:11
your gift to the *a* .... Matt 5:23
swears by the *a* .... Matt 23:18
I even found an *a* .... Acts 17:23
We have an *a* from .... Heb 13:10

ALTARS
Even Your *a*, O LORD .... Ps 84:3
and torn down Your *a* .... Rom 11:3

ALTERED
of His face was *a* .... Luke 9:29

ALWAYS
delight, Rejoicing *a* .... Prov 8:30
the poor with you *a* .... Matt 26:11
lo, I am with you *a* .... Matt 28:20
to them, that men *a* .... Luke 18:1
immovable, *a* .... 1 Cor 15:58
Rejoice in the Lord *a* .... Phil 4:4
thus we shall *a* .... 1 Thess 4:17
a be ready to give a .... 1 Pet 3:15

AM
to Moses, "I *A* WHO I .... Ex 3:14
First and I *a* the Last .... Is 44:6
in My name, I *a* .... Matt 18:20
a the bread of life .... John 6:35
a the light of the .... John 8:12
I *a* from above .... John 8:23
Abraham was, I *A* .... John 8:58
"I *a* the door .... John 10:9
a the good shepherd .... John 10:11
a the resurrection .... John 11:25
to him, "I *a* the way .... John 14:6
of God I *a* what I *a* .... 1 Cor 15:10

AMBASSADOR
for which I am an *a* .... Eph 6:20

AMBASSADORS
we are *a* for Christ .... 2 Cor 5:20

AMBITION
Christ from selfish *a* .... Phil 1:16

AMEN
are Yes, and in Him *A* .... 2 Cor 1:20
creatures said, "*A* .... Rev 5:14

ANCHOR
hope we have as an *a* .... Heb 6:19

ANCIENT
Do not remove the *a* .... Prov 23:10
"until the *A* of Days .... Dan 7:22

ANGEL
"Behold, I send an *A* .... Ex 23:20
Manoah said to the *A* .... Judg 13:17
the *A* of His Presence .... Is 63:9
things, behold, an *a* .... Matt 1:20
for an *a* of the Lord .... Matt 28:2
Then an *a* of the Lord .... Luke 1:11
And behold, an *a* .... Luke 2:9
a appeared to Him .... Luke 22:43
For an *a* went down at .... John 5:4
a has spoken to Him .... John 12:29
But at night an *a* .... Acts 5:19
A who appeared to him .... Acts 7:35
immediately an *a* .... Acts 12:23
himself into an *a* .... 2 Cor 11:14
even if we, or an *a* .... Gal 1:8
Then I saw a strong *a* .... Rev 5:2
Jesus, have sent My *a* .... Rev 22:16

ANGELS
If He charges His *a* .... Job 4:18
lower than the *a* .... Ps 8:5
He shall give His *a* .... Ps 91:11
He shall give His *a* .... Matt 4:6
not even the *a* .... Matt 24:36
and all the holy *a* .... Matt 25:31
twelve legions of *a* .... Matt 26:53
And she saw two *a* .... John 20:12
and worship of *a* .... Col 2:18
much better than the *a* .... Heb 1:4
entertained *a* .... Heb 13:2
things which *a* desire .... 1 Pet 1:12
did not spare the *a* .... 2 Pet 2:4
a who did not keep .... Jude 6

ANGER
For His *a* is but for a .... Ps 30:5
gracious, Slow to *a* .... Ps 103:8
Nor will He keep His *a* .... Ps 103:9
around at them with *a* .... Mark 3:5
bitterness, wrath, *a* .... Eph 4:31

ANGRY
Cain. "Why are you *a* .... Gen 4:6
"Let not the Lord be *a* .... Gen 18:30
the Son, lest He be *a* .... Ps 2:12
a man stirs up strife .... Prov 29:22
right for you to be *a* .... Jon 4:4
you that whoever is *a* .... Matt 5:22
"Be *a*, and do not .... Eph 4:26

ANGUISH
remembers the *a* .... John 16:21
tribulation and *a* .... Rom 2:9

ANIMAL
of every clean *a* .... Gen 7:2
set him on his own *a* .... Luke 10:34

ANIMALS
of *a* after their kind .... Gen 6:20
of four-footed *a* .... Acts 10:12

ANNUL
years later, cannot *a* .... Gal 3:17

ANNULS
is confirmed, no one *a* .... Gal 3:15

ANOINT
a my head with oil .... Ps 23:5
when you fast, *a* .... Matt 6:17
a My body for burial .... Mark 14:8
a your eyes with eye .... Rev 3:18

ANOINTED
"Surely the LORD's *a* .... 1 Sam 16:6
destroy the LORD's *a* .... 2 Sam 1:14
"Do not touch My *a* .... 1 Chr 16:22
Because He has *a* .... Luke 4:18
but this woman has *a* .... Luke 7:46
a the eyes of the .... John 9:6
that Mary who *a* .... John 11:2
Jesus, whom You *a* .... Acts 4:27
and has *a* us is God .... 2 Cor 1:21

ANOINTING
But you have an *a* .... 1 John 2:20

ANOTHER
that you love one *a* .... John 13:34

ANSWER
Call, and I will *a* .... Job 13:22
How shall I *a* Him .... Job 31:14
the day that I call, *a* .... Ps 102:2
In Your faithfulness *a* .... Ps 143:1
a turns away wrath .... Prov 15:1
a a fool according .... Prov 26:4
or what you should *a* .... Luke 12:11
you may have an *a* .... 2 Cor 5:12

ANT
Go to the *a* .... Prov 6:6

ANTICHRIST
heard that the *A* .... 1 John 2:18
a who denies the .... 1 John 2:22
is a deceiver and an *a* .... 2 John 7

ANTITYPE
a which now saves us .... 1 Pet 3:21

ANXIETIES
the multitude of my *a* .... Ps 94:19

ANXIETY
A in the heart of man .... Prov 12:25

ANXIOUS
Be *a* for nothing .... Phil 4:6

APART
justified by faith *a* .... Rom 3:28

APOSTLE
called to be an *a* … Rom 1:1
consider the *A* … Heb 3:1

APOSTLES
of the twelve *a* … Matt 10:2
He also named *a* … Luke 6:13
am the least of the *a* … 1 Cor 15:9
none of the other *a* … Gal 1:19
gave some to be *a* … Eph 4:11

APOSTLESHIP
in this ministry and *a* … Acts 1:25
are the seal of my *a* … 1 Cor 9:2

APPAREL
gold rings, in fine *a* … James 2:2
or putting on fine *a* … 1 Pet 3:3

APPEAL
love's sake I rather *a* … Philem 9

APPEAR
and let the dry land *a* … Gen 1:9
also outwardly *a* … Matt 23:28
God would *a* … Luke 19:11
For we must all *a* … 2 Cor 5:10

APPEARANCE
Do not look at his *a* … 1 Sam 16:7
judge according to *a* … John 7:24
those who boast in *a* … 2 Cor 5:12
found in *a* as a man … Phil 2:8

APPEARED
an angel of the Lord *a* … Luke 1:11
who *a* in glory and … Luke 9:31
brings salvation has *a* … Titus 2:11
of the ages, He has *a* … Heb 9:26

APPEARING
Lord Jesus Christ's *a* … 1 Tim 6:14
and the dead at His *a* … 2 Tim 4:1
who have loved His *a* … 2 Tim 4:8

APPEARS
can stand when He *a* … Mal 3:2
who is our life *a* … Col 3:4
the Chief Shepherd *a* … 1 Pet 5:4
that when He *a* … 1 John 2:28

APPETITE
are a man given to *a* … Prov 23:2

APPLE
And my law as the *a* … Prov 7:2

APPLES
fitly spoken is like *a* … Prov 25:11

APPLIED
a my heart to know … Eccl 7:25

APPOINT
For God did not *a* … 1 Thess 5:9

APPOINTED
And as it is *a* for men … Heb 9:27

APPROACH
year, make those who *a* … Heb 10:1

APPROACHING
as you see the Day *a* … Heb 10:25

APPROVE
do the same but also *a* … Rom 1:32

APPROVED
to God and *a* by men … Rom 14:18
to present yourself *a* … 2 Tim 2:15

ARBITRATOR
Me a judge or an *a* … Luke 12:14

ARCHANGEL
the voice of an *a* … 1 Thess 4:16

ARGUMENTS
casting down *a* and … 2 Cor 10:5

ARISE
A, shine … Is 60:1
But the LORD will *a* … Is 60:2
you who sleep, *A* … Eph 5:14

ARK
"Make yourself an *a* … Gen 6:14
him, she took an *a* … Ex 2:3
Bezalel made the *a* … Ex 37:1
in heaven, and the *a* … Rev 11:19

ARM
with an outstretched *a* … Ex 6:6
Have you an *a* like God … Job 40:9
strength with His *a* … Luke 1:51
a yourselves also with … 1 Pet 4:1

ARMED
a strong man, fully *a* … Luke 11:21

ARMIES
And he sent out his *a* … Matt 22:7
surrounded by *a* … Luke 21:20
And the *a* in heaven … Rev 19:14
the earth, and their *a* … Rev 19:19

ARMOR
Put on the whole *a* … Eph 6:11

ARMS
are the everlasting *a* … Deut 33:27
took Him up in his *a* … Luke 2:28

AROMA
the one we are the *a* … 2 Cor 2:16
for a sweet-smelling *a* … Eph 5:2

AROUSED
LORD was greatly *a* … Num 11:10
Then Joseph, being *a* … Matt 1:24

ARRAYED
his glory was not *a* … Matt 6:29
"Who are these *a* … Rev 7:13

ARROGANCE
Pride and *a* and the … Prov 8:13

ARROW
a that flies by day … Ps 91:5

ARROWS
a pierce me deeply … Ps 38:2
Like *a* in the hand of … Ps 127:4

ASCEND
Who may *a* into the … Ps 24:3
If I *a* into heaven … Ps 139:8
'I will *a* into heaven … Is 14:13
see the Son of Man *a* … John 6:62

ASCENDED
You have *a* on high … Ps 68:18
"No one has *a* … John 3:13
"When He *a* on high … Eph 4:8

ASCENDING
the angels of God *a* … John 1:51

ASCRIBE
A strength to God … Ps 68:34

ASHAMED
Let me not be *a* … Ps 25:2
And Israel shall be *a* … Hos 10:6
For whoever is *a* … Mark 8:38
am not *a* of the gospel … Rom 1:16
Therefore God is not *a* … Heb 11:16

ASHES
become like dust and *a* … Job 30:19
in sackcloth and *a* … Luke 10:13

ASIDE
lay something *a* … 1 Cor 16:2
lay *a* all filthiness … James 1:21
Therefore, laying *a* … 1 Pet 2:1

ASK
when your children *a* … Josh 4:6
"*A* a sign for yourself … Is 7:11
whatever things you *a* … Matt 21:22
a, and it will be … Luke 11:9
that whatever You *a* … John 11:22
a anything in My … John 14:14
in that day you will *a* … John 16:23
above all that we *a* … Eph 3:20
wisdom, let him *a* … James 1:5
But let him *a* in faith … James 1:6
because you do not *a* … James 4:2

ASKS
For everyone who *a* … Matt 7:8
you who, if his son *a* … Matt 7:9
Or if he *a* for a fish … Luke 11:11

ASLEEP
But He was *a* … Matt 8:24
some have fallen *a* … 1 Cor 15:6
those who are *a* … 1 Thess 4:15

ASSEMBLING
not forsaking the *a* … Heb 10:25

ASSEMBLY
a I will praise You … Ps 22:22
fast, Call a sacred *a* … Joel 1:14
a I will sing praise … Heb 2:12
to the general *a* … Heb 12:23

ASSURANCE
riches of the full *a* … Col 2:2
Spirit and in much *a* … 1 Thess 1:5
to the full *a* of hope … Heb 6:11

ASSURE
a our heats before … 1 John 3:19

ASSURED
learned and been *a* … 2 Tim 3:14

ASTONISHED
Just as many were *a* … Is 52:14
who heard Him were *a* … Luke 2:47

ASTRAY
one of them goes *a* … Matt 18:12
like sheep going *a* … 1 Pet 2:25

ATONEMENT
the blood that makes *a* … Lev 17:11
for it is the Day of *A* … Lev 23:28
there will be no *a* … Is 22:14

ATTAIN
It is high, I cannot *a* … Ps 139:6
worthy to *a* that age … Luke 20:35
by any means, I may *a* … Phil 3:11

ATTENTION
My son, give *a* to my … Prov 4:20

ATTENTIVE
Let Your ears be *a* … Ps 130:2

ATTESTED
a Man *a* by God to you … Acts 2:22

AUSTERE
because you are an *a* … Luke 19:21

AUTHOR
For God is not the *a* … 1 Cor 14:33
unto Jesus, the *a* … Heb 12:2

AUTHORITIES
a that exist are … Rom 13:1

AUTHORITY
them as one having *a* … Matt 7:29
"All *a* has been given … Matt 28:18
a I will give You … Luke 4:6
and has given Him *a* … John 5:27
You have given Him *a* … John 17:2
the flesh, reject *a* … Jude 8

AUTUMN
a trees without fruit … Jude 12

AVAILS
of a righteous man *a* … James 5:16

AVENGE
Beloved, do not *a* … Rom 12:19
a our blood on those … Rev 6:10

AVENGER
the Lord is the *a* … 1 Thess 4:6

AWAKE
be satisfied when I *a* … Ps 17:15
it is high time to *a* … Rom 13:11
A to righteousness … 1 Cor 15:34

AWAY
the wind drives *a* … Ps 1:4
Do not cast me *a* … Ps 51:11
A time to cast *a* … Eccl 3:5
fait one, And come *a* … Song 2:10
minded to put her *a* … Matt 1:19
and earth will pass *a* … Matt 24:35
"I am going *a* … John 8:21
they cried out, "*A* … John 19:15
unless the falling *a* … 2 Thess 2:3
in Asia have turned *a* … 2 Tim 1:15
heard, lest we drift *a* … Heb 2:1
if they fall *a* … Heb 6:6
can never take *a* … Heb 10:11
world is passing *a* … 1 John 2:17
if anyone takes *a* … Rev 22:19

AWESOME
a is this place … Gen 28:17
God, the great and *a* … Deut 7:21
By *a* deeds in … Ps 65:5
O God, You are more *a* … Ps 68:35
Your great and *a* name … Ps 99:3

AWL
his ear with an *a* … Ex 21:6

AX
If the *a* is dull … Eccl 10:10
And even now the *a* … Matt 3:10

B

BABBLER
"What does this *b* ... Acts 17:18

BABBLINGS
the profane and idle *b* ... 1 Tim 6:20

BABE
the *b* leaped in my ... Luke 1:44
You will find a *B* ... Luke 2:12
for he is a *b* ... Heb 5:13

BABES
Out of the mouth of *b* ... Ps 8:2
revealed them to *b* ... Matt 11:25
of the mouth of *b* ... Matt 21:16
as to carnal, as to *b* ... 1 Cor 3:1
as newborn *b* ... 1 Pet 2:2

BACK
for the fool's *b* ... Prov 26:3
I gave My *b* to those ... Is 50:6
plow, and looking *b* ... Luke 9:62
of those who draw *b* ... Heb 10:39
someone turns him *b* ... James 5:19

BACKBITERS
b, haters of God ... Rom 1:30

BACKBITING
b tongue an angry ... Prov 25:23

BACKSLIDER
The *b* in heart will be ... Prov 14:14

BACKSLIDINGS
And I will heal your *b* ... Jer 3:22

BACKWARD
ten degrees *b* ... 2 Kin 20:11

BAD
b trees bears *b* fruit ... Matt 7:17

BAG
"nor *b* for your ... Matt 10:10

BAKED
b unleavened cakes ... Ex 12:39

BAKER
the butler and the *b* ... Gen 40:1

BALANCES
Falsifying the *b* ... Amos 8:5

BALD
every head shall be *b* ... Jer 48:37

BALDHEAD
Go up, you *b* ... 2 Kin 2:23

BALM
no *b* in Gilead ... Jer 8:22

BANDAGED
and *b* his wounds ... Luke 10:34

BANKERS
my money with the *b* ... Matt 25:27

BANNERS
we will set up our *b* ... Ps 20:5
as an army with *b* ... Song 6:4

BANQUET
b that I have prepared ... Esth 5:4

BANQUETING
He brought me to the *b* ... Song 2:4

BAPTISM
coming to his *b* ... Matt 3:7
b that I am baptized ... Matt 20:22
"But I have a *b* ... Luke 12:50
said, "Into John's *b* ... Acts 19:3
Lord, one faith, one *b* ... Eph 4:5
buried with Him in *b* ... Col 2:12

BAPTISMS
of the doctrine of *b* ... Heb 6:2

BAPTIZE
"I indeed *b* you with ... Matt 3:11
Himself did not *b* ... John 4:2

BAPTIZED
b will be saved ... Mark 16:16
every one of you be *b* ... Acts 2:38
all his family were *b* ... Acts 16:33
Arise and be *b* ... Acts 22:16
were *b* into Christ ... Rom 6:3
I thank God that I *b* ... 1 Cor 1:14
Spirit we were all *b* ... 1 Cor 12:13

BAPTIZING
b them in the name of ... Matt 28:19

BARBARIAN
nor uncircumcised, *b* ... Col 3:11

BARLEY
here who has five *b* ... John 6:9

BARN
the wheat into my *b* ... Matt 13:30

BARNS
reap nor gather into *b* ... Matt 6:26
I will pull down my *b* ... Luke 12:18

BARREN
But Sarai was *b* ... Gen 11:30
"Sing, O *b* ... Is 54:1

BASE
and the *b* things of ... 1 Cor 1:28

BASIN
poured water into a *b* ... John 13:5

BASKET
and put it under a *b* ... Matt 5:15
I was let down in a *b* ... 2 Cor 11:33

BASKETS
they took up twelve *b* ... Matt 14:20

BATHED
to him, "He who is *b* ... John 13:10

BATS
To the moles and *b* ... Is 2:20

BATTLE
b is the LORD's ... 1 Sam 17:47
the *b* to the strong ... Eccl 9:11
became valiant in *b* ... Heb 11:34

BEAR
greater than I can *b* ... Gen 4:13
whom Sarah shall *b* ... Gen 17:21
not *b* false witness ... Ex 20:16
b their Iniquities ... Is 53:11
child, and *b* a Son ... Matt 1:23
A good tree cannot *b* ... Matt 7:18
how long shall I *b* ... Matt 17:17
by, to *b* His cross ... Mark 15:21
whoever does not *b* ... Luke 14:27
are strong ought to *b* ... Rom 15:1
B one another's ... Gal 6:2
b the sins of many ... Heb 9:28

BEARD
the edges of your *b* ... Lev 19:27
Running down on the *b* ... Ps 133:2

BEARING
goes forth weeping, *B* ... Ps 126:6
And He, *b* His cross ... John 19:17
b His reproach ... Heb 13:13

BEARS
Every branch that *b* ... John 15:2

BEAST
You preserve man and *b* ... Ps 36:6
And I saw a *b* rising ... Rev 13:1
the mark of the *b* ... Rev 19:20

BEASTS
like brute *b* ... Jude 10

BEAT
b their swords into ... Is 2:4
spat in His face and *b* ... Matt 26:67

BEATEN
Three times I was *b* ... 2 Cor 11:25

BEAUTIFUL
B in elevation ... Ps 48:2
has made everything *b* ... Eccl 3:11
my love, you are as *b* ... Song 6:4
How *b* upon the ... Is 52:7
indeed appear *b* ... Matt 23:27

BEAUTIFY
b the place of My ... Is 60:13

BEAUTY
"The *b* of Israel is ... 2 Sam 1:19
To behold the *b* ... Ps 27:4
see the King in His *b* ... Is 33:17
no *b* that we should ... Is 53:2

BECAME
b a living being ... Gen 2:7
to the Jews I *b* ... 1 Cor 9:20

BED
I remember You on my *b* ... Ps 63:6
if I make my *b* in hell ... Ps 139:8
"Arise; take up your *b* ... Matt 9:6
be two men in one *b* ... Luke 17:34
and the *b* undefiled ... Heb 13:4

BEDS
sing aloud on their *b* ... Ps 149:5

BEFOREHAND
up, do not worry *b* ... Mark 43:11
told you all things *b* ... Mark 13:23
when He testified *b* ... 1 Pet 1:11

BEG
b you as sojourners ... 1 Pet 2:11

BEGAN
since the world *b* ... Luke 1:70

BEGGAR
there was a certain *b* ... Luke 16:20

BEGGARLY
weak and *b* elements ... Gal 4:9

BEGINNING
b God created the ... Gen 1:1
In the *b* was the Word ... John 1:1
a murderer from the *b* ... John 8:44
True Witness, the *B* ... Rev 3:14
and the Omega, the *B* ... Rev 21:6

BEGOTTEN
I have *b* You ... Ps 2:7
glory as of the only *b* ... John 1:14
loves him who is *b* ... 1 John 5:1

BEGUILING
b unstable souls ... 2 Pet 2:14

BEGUN
Having *b* in the Spirit ... Gal 3:3

BEHALF
you on Christ's *b* ... 2 Cor 5:20

BEHAVE
does not *b* rudely ... 1 Cor 13:5

BEHAVED
blamelessly we *b* ... 1 Thess 2:10

BEHAVIOR
of good *b*, hospitable ... 1 Tim 3:2

BEHEADED
and had John *b* ... Matt 14:10

BEHOLD
B, the virgin shall ... Is 7:14
Judah, "*B* your God ... Is 40:9
"'*B* the Lamb of God ... John 1:36
to them, "*B* the Man ... John 19:5
B what manner of ... 1 John 3:1

BEHOLDING
with unveiled face, *b* ... 2 Cor 3:18

BEING
move and have our *b* ... Acts 17:28
who, *b* in the form of ... Phil 2:6

BELIEVE
tears, "Lord, I *b* ... Mark 9:24
have no root, who *b* ... Luke 8:13
slow of heart to *b* ... Luke 24:25
to those who *b* ... John 1:12
this, that they may *b* ... John 11:42
that you may *b* ... John 20:31
the Lord Jesus and *b* ... Rom 10:9
Christ, not only to *b* ... Phil 1:29
comes to God must *b* ... Heb 11:6
b that there is one ... James 2:19
Even the demons *b* ... James 2:19

BELIEVED
And he *b* in the LORD ... Gen 15:6
Who has *b* our report ... Is 53:1
seen Me, you have *b* ... John 20:29
"Abraham *b* God ... Rom 4:3
whom I have *b* ... 2 Tim 1:12

BELIEVERS
example to the *b* ... 1 Tim 4:12

BELIEVES
The simple *b* every ... Prov 14:15
that whoever *b* in Him ... John 3:16
"He who *b* in the Son ... John 3:36
with the heart brie *b* ... Rom 10:10

BELIEVING
you ask in prayer, *b* ... Matt 21:22

BELLY
On your *b* you shall go ... Gen 3:14

and Jonah was in the *b* .... Jon 1:17
whose god is their *b* .... Phil 3:19

BELOVED
so He gives His *b* .... Ps 127:2
My *b* is mine .... Song 2:16
"This is My *b* .... Matt 3:17
us accepted in the *B* .... Eph 1:6
Luke the *b* physician .... Col 4:14
"This is My *b* .... 2 Pet 1:17

BELT
with a leather *b* .... Matt 3:4

BEND
The wicked *b* their bow .... Ps 11:2

BENEATH
"You are from *b* .... John 8:23

BENEFACTORS
them are called '*b* .... Luke 22:25

BENEFIT
have a second *b* .... 2 Cor 1:15

BESEECH
b you therefore .... Rom 12:1

BESIDE
He leads me *b* the .... Ps 23:2
"Paul, you are *b* .... Acts 26:24

BEST
desire the *b* .... 1 Cor 12:31

BESTOWED
love the Father has *b* .... 1 John 3:1

BETRAY
you, one of you will *b* .... Matt 26:21

BETRAYED
Man is about to be *b* .... Matt 17:22

BETRAYER
See, My *b* is at .... Matt 26:46

BETRAYING
"Judas, are you *b* .... Luke 22:48

BETRAYS
who is the one who *b* .... John 21:20

BETROTH
"I will *b* you to Me .... Hos 2:19

BETROTHED
to a virgin *b* to a man .... Luke 1:27

BETTER
b than sacrifice .... 1 Sam 15:22
It is *b* to trust in .... Ps 118:8
For it is *b* to marry .... 1 Cor 7:9
Christ, which is far *b* .... Phil 1:23
b than the angels .... Heb 1:4
b things concerning .... Heb 6:9

BEWARE
"*B* of false prophets .... Matt 7:15

BEWITCHED
b you that you should .... Gal 3:1

BEYOND
advanced in Judaism *b* .... Gal 1:14

BILLOWS
b have gone over me .... Ps 42:7

BIND
and whatever you *b* .... Matt 16:19
'*B* him hand and foot .... Matt 22:13

BIRD
soul, "Flee as a *b* .... Ps 11:1

BIRDS
b make their nests .... Ps 104:17
"Look at the *b* .... Matt 6:26
have holes and *b* .... Matt 8:20

BIRTH
the day of one's *b* .... Eccl 7:1
Now the *b* of Jesus .... Matt 1:18
will rejoice at his *b* .... Luke 1:14
conceived, it gives *b* .... James 1:15

BIRTHDAY
was Pharaoh's *b* .... Gen 40:20

BIRTHRIGHT
Esau despised his *b* .... Gen 25:34

BISHOP
the position of a *b* .... 1 Tim 3:1
b must be blameless .... Titus 1:7

BIT
and they *b* the people .... Num 21:6

BITE
A serpent may *b* .... Eccl 10:11
But if you *b* and .... Gal 5:15

BITTER
b herbs they .... Ex 12:8
and do not be *b* .... Col 3:19
But if you have *b* .... James 3:14

BITTERLY
And Hezektah wept *b* .... 2 Kin 20:3
went out and wept *b* .... Matt 26:75

BITTERNESS
you are poisoned by *b* .... Acts 8:23
b springing up cause .... Heb 12:15

BLACK
one hair white or *b* .... Matt 5:36
a *b* horse .... Rev 6:5
and the sun became *b* .... Rev 6:12

BLACKNESS
whom is reserved the *b* .... Jude 13

BLACKSMITH
I have created the *b* .... Is 54:16

BLADE
first the *b* .... Mark 4:28

BLAME
be holy and without *b* .... Eph 1:4

BLAMELESS
and that man was *b* .... Job 1:1
body be preserved *b* .... 1 Thess 5:23

BLAMELESSLY
b we behaved .... 1 Thess 2:10

BLASPHEME
b Your name forever .... Ps 74:10
compelled them to *b* .... Acts 26:11
b that noble name .... James 2:7

BLASPHEMED
who passed by *b* Him .... Matt 27:39
great heat, and they *b* .... Rev 16:9

BLASPHEMER
I was formerly a *b* .... 1 Tim 1:13

BLASPHEMES
b the name of the .... Lev 24:16
"This Man *b* .... Matt 9:3

BLASPHEMIES
is this who speaks *b* .... Luke 5:21

BLASPHEMY
but the *b* against .... Matt 12:31
was full of names of *b* .... Rev 17:3

BLEATING
"What then is this *b* .... 1 Sam 15:14

BLEMISH
be holy and without *b* .... Eph 5:27
as of a lamb without *b* .... 1 Pet 1:19

BLEMISHED
to the Lord what is *b* .... Mal 1:14

BLESS
b those who *b* you .... Gen 12:3
You go unless You *b* .... Gen 32:26
"The LORD *b* you and .... Num 6:24
b the LORD at all .... Ps 34:1
b You while I live .... Ps 63:4
b His holy name .... Ps 103:1
b those who curse .... Luke 6:28
B those who .... Rom 12:14
Being reviled, we *b* .... 1 Cor 4:12

BLESSED
B is the man who walks .... Ps 1:1
B is the man to whom .... Ps 32:2
B is the nation whose .... Ps 33:12
B is he who comes .... Ps 118:26
rise up and call her *b* .... Prov 31:28
"*B* are the poor in .... Matt 5:3
B are those who mourn .... Matt 5:4
B are the meek .... Matt 5:5
B are those who hunger .... Matt 5:6
B are the merciful .... Matt 5:7
B are the pure in .... Matt 5:8
B are the peacemakers .... Matt 5:9
B are those who are .... Matt 5:10
B is He who comes .... Matt 21:9
'It is more *b* to give .... Acts 20:35
B be the God and .... Eph 1:3
"*B* are the dead who .... Rev 14:13

BLESSING
And you shall be a *b* .... Gen 12:2
before you today a *b* .... Deut 11:26
shall be showers of *b* .... Ezek 34:26
and you shall be a *b* .... Zech 8:13
that the *b* of Abraham .... Gal 3:14
with every spiritual *b* .... Eph 1:3

BLIND
To open *b* eyes .... Is 42:7
His watchmen are *b* .... Is 56:10
b leads the *b* .... Matt 15:14
to Him, "Are we *b* .... John 9:40
miserable, poor, *b* .... Rev 3:17

BLINDED
and the rest were *b* .... Rom 11:7

BLINDS
a bribe, for a bribe *b* .... Deut 16:19

BLOOD
of your brother's *b* .... Gen 4:10
b shall be shed .... Gen 9:6
b that makes : .... Lev 17:11
hands are full of *b* .... Is 1:15
And the moon into *b* .... Joel 2:31
For this is My *b* .... Matt 26:28
"His *b* be on us and .... Matt 27:25
covenant in My *b* .... Luke 22:20
were born, not of *b* .... John 1:13
b has eternal life .... John 6:54
with His own *b* .... Acts 20:28
propitiation by His *b* .... Rom 3:25
justified by His *b* .... Rom 5:9
through His *b* .... Eph 1:7
brought near by the *b* .... Eph 2:13
against flesh and *b* .... Eph 6:12
peace through the *b* .... Col 1:20
with the precious *b* .... 1 Pet 1:19
b of Jesus Christ His .... 1 John 1:7
our sins in His own *b* .... Rev 1:5
us to God by Your *b* .... Rev 5:9
them white in the *b* .... Rev 7:14
overcame him by the *b* .... Rev 12:11
a robe dipped in *b* .... Rev 19:13

BLOODSHED
me from the guilt of *b* .... Ps 51:14

BLOODTHIRSTY
The LORD abhors the *b* .... Ps 5:6

BLOSSOM
and *b* as the rose .... Is 35:1

BLOT
from my sins, and *b* .... Ps 51:9
and I will not *b* .... Rev 3:5

BLOTTED
your sins may be *b* .... Acts 3:19

BLOW
with a very severe *b* .... Jer 14:17

BLOWS
"The wind *b* where it .... John 3:8

BOAST
puts on his armor *b* .... 1 Kin 20:11
and make your *b* .... Rom 2:17
lest anyone should *b* .... Eph 2:9

BOASTERS
God, violent, proud, *b* .... Rom 1:30

BOASTING
Where is *b* then .... Rom 3:27

BODIES
b a living sacrifice .... Rom 12:1
not know that your *b* .... 1 Cor 6:15
wives as their own *b* .... Eph 5:28

BODILY
b form like a dove .... Luke 3:22
of the Godhead *b* .... Col 2:9

BODY
of the *b* is the eye .... Matt 6:22
those who kill the *b* .... Matt 10:28
this is My *b* .... Matt 26:26
of the temple of His *b* .... John 2:21
deliver me from this *b* .... Rom 7:24
redemption of our *b* .... Rom 8:23
members in one *b* .... Rom 12:4
But I discipline my *b* .... 1 Cor 9:27
b which is broken .... 1 Cor 11:24

baptized into one *b* ... 1 Cor 12:13
are the *b* of Christ ... 1 Cor 12:27
though I give my *b* ... 1 Cor 13:3
It is sown a natural *b* ... 1 Cor 15:44
in the *b* of His flesh ... Col 1:22
our sins in His own *b* ... 1 Pet 2:24

BOILS
Job with painful *b* ... Job 2:7

BOLDLY
therefore come *b* ... Heb 4:16

BOLDNESS
in whom we have *b* ... Eph 3:12
that we may have *b* ... 1 John 4:17

BOND
love, which is the *b* ... Col 3:14

BONDAGE
out of the house of *b* ... Ex 13:14
again with a yoke of *b* ... Gal 5:1

BONDS
"Let us break Their *b* ... Ps 2:3

BONDSERVANTS
B, be obedient to ... Eph 6:5
Masters, give your *b* ... Col 4:1

BONDWOMAN
the one by a *b* ... Gal 4:22

BONE
b clings to my skin ... Job 19:20

BONES
I can count all My *b* ... Ps 22:17
and my *b* waste away ... Ps 31:10
I kept silent, my *b* ... Ps 32:3
the wind, Or how the *b* ... Eccl 11:5
say to them, 'O dry *b* ... Ezek 37:4
of dead men's *b* ... Matt 23:27
b shall be broken ... John 19:36

BOOK
are written in the *b* ... Gal 3:10
in the Lamb's *B* ... Rev 21:27
the prophecy of this *b* ... Rev 22:18

BOOKS
b there is no end ... Eccl 12:12
not contain the *b* ... John 21:25
and *b* were opened ... Rev 20:12

BOOTH
of Zion is left as a *b* ... Is 1:8

BORDERS
and enlarge the *b* ... Matt 23:5

BORE
And to Sarah who *b* ... Is 51:2
b the sin of many ... Is 53:12
b our sicknesses ... Matt 8:17
Himself *b* our sins ... 1 Pet 2:24
b a male Child who was ... Rev 12:5

BORN
A time to be *b* ... Eccl 3:2
unto us a Child is *b* ... Is 9:6
b Jesus who is called ... Matt 1:16
unless one is *b* again ... John 3:3
"That which is *b* ... John 3:6
having been *b* again ... 1 Pet 1:23
who loves Is *b* of God ... 1 John 4:7

BORROWER
b is servant to the ... Prov 22:7

BORROWS
The wicked *b* and does ... Ps 37:21

BOSOM
to Abraham's *b* ... Luke 16:22
Son, who is in the *b* ... John 1:18

BOTTOMLESS
ascend out of the *b* ... Rev 17:8
the key to the *b* ... Rev 20:1

BOUGHT
b the threshing floor ... 2 Sam 24:24
all that he had and *b* ... Matt 13:46
For you were *b* at a ... 1 Cor 6:20
denying the Lord who *b* ... 2 Pet 2:1

BOUND
on earth will be *b* ... Matt 16:19
And see, now I go *b* ... Acts 20:22
who has a husband is *b* ... Rom 7:2
Are you *b* to a wife ... 1 Cor 7:27
Devil and Satan, and *b* ... Rev 20:2

BOUNTIFULLY
and he who sows *b* ... 2 Cor 9:6

BOW
"You shall not *b* ... Ex 23:24
let us worship and *b* ... Ps 95:6
who sat on it had a *b* ... Rev 6:2

BOWED
stood all around and *b* ... Gen 37:7
And they *b* the knee ... Matt 27:29

BOWL
and poured out his *b* ... Rev 16:2

BOWLS
Go and pour out the *b* ... Rev 16:1

BOX
had the money *b* ... John 13:29

BOYS
Shall be full of *b* ... Zech 8:5

BRAIDED
not with *b* hair or ... 1 Tim 2:9

BRANCH
raise to David a *B* ... Jer 23:5
forth My Servant the *B* ... Zech 3:8
b that bears fruit He ... John 15:2

BRANCHES
vine, you are the *b* ... John 15:5

BRASS
become sounding *b* ... 1 Cor 13:1

BRAVE
in the faith, be *b* ... 1 Cor 16:13

BREAD
brought out *b* ... Gen 14:18
shall eat unleavened *b* ... Ex 23:15
not live by *b* alone ... Deut 8:3
b eaten in secret is ... Prov 9:17
B gained by deceit is ... Prov 20:17
Cast your *b* upon the ... Eccl 11:1
for what is not *b* ... Is 55:2
these stones become *b* ... Matt 4:3
not live by *b* alone ... Matt 4:4
this day our daily *b* ... Matt 6:11
eating, Jesus took *b* ... Matt 26:26
"I am the *b* of life ... John 6:48
betrayed took *b* ... 1 Cor 11:23

BREADTH
is as great as its *b* ... Rev 21:16

BREAK
covenant I will not *b* ... Ps 89:34
together to *b* bread ... Acts 20:7

BREAKING
in the *b* of bread ... Acts 2:42
b bread from house to ... Acts 2:46

BREAKS
Until the day *b* ... Song 2:17

BREAST
back on Jesus' *b* ... John 13:25

BREASTPLATE
righteousness as a *b* ... Is 59:17
having put on the *b* ... Eph 6:14

BREASTS
Your two *b* are like ... Song 4:5
b which nursed You ... Luke 11:27

BREATH
nostrils the *b* of life ... Gen 2:7
that there was no *b* ... 1 Kin 17:17
Man is like a *b* ... Ps 144:4
everything that has *b* ... Ps 150:6
"Surely I will cause *b* ... Ezek 37:5
gives to all life, *b* ... Acts 17:25
power to give *b* ... Rev 13:15

BREATHES
indeed he *b* his last ... Job 14:10

BRETHREN
and you are all *b* ... Matt 23:8
least of these My *b* ... Matt 25:40
among many *b* ... Rom 8:29
thus sin against the *b* ... 1 Cor 8:12
over five hundred *b* ... 1 Cor 15:6
perils among false *b* ... 2 Cor 11:26
sincere love of the *b* ... 1 Pet 1:22
we love the *b* ... 1 John 3:14
our lives for the *b* ... 1 John 3:16

BRIBE
you shall take no *b* ... Ex 23:8
b blinds the eyes ... Deut 16:19

BRIBES
hand is full of *b* ... Ps 26:10

BRICK
people straw to make *b* ... Ex 5:7

BRICKS
"Come, let us make *b* ... Gen 11:3

BRIDE
I will show you the *b* ... Rev 21:9
the Spirit and the *b* ... Rev 22:17

BRIDEGROOM
And as the *b* rejoices ... Is 62:5
mourn as long as the *b* ... Matt 9:15
went out to meet the *b* ... Matt 25:1
the friend of the *b* ... John 3:29

BRIDLE
b the whole body ... James 3:2

BRIER
b shall come up the ... Is 55:13

BRIERS
there shall come up *b* ... Is 5:6

BRIGHTER
a light from heaven, *b* ... Acts 26:13

BRIGHTNESS
And kings to the *b* ... Is 60:3
who being the *b* ... Heb 1:3

BRIMSTONE
the lake of fire and *b* ... Rev 20:10

BRING
b back his soul ... Job 33:30
b My righteousness ... Is 46:13
Who shall *b* a charge ... Rom 8:33
b Christ down from ... Rom 10:6
even so God will *b* ... 1 Thess 4:14

BROAD
b is the way that ... Matt 7:13

BROKE
b them at the foot of ... Ex 32:19
He blessed and *b* ... Matt 14:19
b the legs of the ... John 19:32

BROKEN
this stone will be *b* ... Matt 21:44
Scripture cannot be *b* ... John 10:35
body which is *b* ... 1 Cor 11:24

BROKENHEARTED
He heals the *b* And ... Ps 147:3

BRONZE
So Moses made a *b* ... Num 21:9
b walls against the ... Jer 1:18
a third kingdom of *b* ... Dan 2:39

BROOD
"*B* of vipers ... Matt 12:34
hen gathers her *b* ... Luke 13:34

BROOK
disciples over the *B* ... John 18:1

BROOKS
for the water *b* ... Ps 42:1

BROTHER
"Where is Abel your *b* ... Gen 4:9
b offended is harder ... Prov 18:19
b will deliver up ... Matt 10:21
how often shall my *b* ... Matt 18:21
b will rise again ... John 11:23
b goes to law against ... 1 Cor 6:6
Whoever hates his *b* ... 1 John 3:15

BROTHERHOOD
Love the *b* ... 1 Pet 2:17

BROTHERLY
b love continue ... Heb 13:1

BROTHER'S
Am I my *b* keeper ... Gen 4:9
at the speck in your *b* ... Matt 7:3

BROTHERS
is My mother, or My *b* ... Mark 3:33
b are these who hear ... Luke 8:21

BRUISE
He shall *b* your head ... Gen 3:15
the LORD to *b* Him ... Is 53:10

BRUISED
He was *b* for our .... Is 53:5
b reed He will not .... Matt 12:20
BUCKLER
be your shield and *b* .... Ps 91:4
BUFFET
of Satan to *b* me .... 2 Cor 12:7
BUILD
b ourselves a city .... Gen 11:4
"Would you *b* a house .... 2 Sam 7:5
labor in vain who *b* .... Ps 127:1
down, And a time to *b* .... Eccl 3:3
'This man began to *b* .... Luke 14:30
What house will you *b* .... Acts 7:49
"For if I *b* again .... Gal 2:18
BUILDER
foundations, whose *b* .... Heb 11:10
BUILDING
in whom the whole *b* .... Eph 2:21
BUILDS
take heed how he *b* .... 1 Cor 3:10
BUILT
has *b* her house .... Prov 9:1
to a wise man who *b* .... Matt 7:24
having been *b* on the .... Eph 2:20
BULLS
For if the blood of *b* .... Heb 9:13
BULWARKS
Mark well her *b* .... Ps 48:13
BUNDLE
man's *b* of money .... Gen 42:35
BURDEN
Cast your *b* on the .... Ps 55:22
easy and My *b* is light .... Matt 11:30
we might not be a *b* .... 1 Thess 2:9
on you no other *b* .... Rev 2:24
BURDENS
"For they bind heavy *b* .... Matt 23:4
Bear one another's *b* .... Gal 6:2
BURDENSOME
I myself was not *b* .... 2 Cor 12:13
are not *b* .... 1 John 5:3
BURIAL
she did it for My *b* .... Matt 26:12
for the day of My *b* .... John 12:7
BURIED
Therefore we were *b* .... Rom 6:4
and that He was *b* .... 1 Cor 15:4
b with Him in baptism .... Col 2:12
BURN
the bush does not *b* .... Ex 3:3
"Did not our heart *b* .... Luke 24:32
BURNED
If anyone's work is *b* .... 1 Cor 3:15
my body to be *b* .... 1 Cor 13:3
BURNING
b torch that passed .... Gen 15:17
b fire shut up in my .... Jer 20:9
plucked from the *b* .... Amos 4:11
BURNT
lamb for a *b* offering .... Gen 22:7
delight in *b* offering .... Ps 51:16
BURST
the new wine will *b* .... Luke 5:37
BURY
and let the dead *b* .... Matt 8:22
BUSH
from the midst of a *b* .... Ex 3:2
BUSINESS
about My Father's *b* .... Luke 2:49
BUSYBODIES
at all, but are *b* .... 2 Thess 3:11
BUTLER
b did not remember .... Gen 40:23
BUTTER
were smoother than *b* .... Ps 55:21
BUY
Yes, come, *b* wine and .... Is 55:1
"I counsel you to *b* .... Rev 3:18
and that no one may *b* .... Rev 13:17
BUYS
has and *b* that field .... Matt 13:44
BYWORD
has made me a *b* .... Job 17:6

C

CAGE
foul spirit, and a *c* .... Rev 18:2
CAKE
Ephraim is a *c* .... Hos 7:8
CAKES
and love the raisin *c* .... Hos 3:1
CALAMITY
will laugh at your *c* .... Prov 1:26
CALCULATED
c the dust of the .... Is 40:12
CALDRON
this city is the *c* .... Ezek 11:3
CALF
and made a molded *c* .... Ex 32:4
bring the fatted *c* .... Luke 15:23
CALL
C upon Him while He .... Is 55:6
c His name JESUS .... Matt 1:21
c the righteous .... Matt 9:13
Lord our God will *c* .... Acts 2:39
c them My people .... Rom 9:25
c and election sure .... 2 Pet 1:10
CALLED
c the light Day .... Gen 1:5
c his wife's name Eve .... Gen 3:20
I have *c* you by your .... Is 43:1
"Out of Egypt I *c* .... Matt 2:15
city *c* Nazareth .... Matt 2:23
For many are *c* .... Matt 20:16
to those who are the *c* .... Rom 8:28
these He also *c* .... Rom 8:30
c children of God .... 1 John 3:1
CALLING
the gifts and the *c* .... Rom 11:29
For you see your *c* .... 1 Cor 1:26
remain in the same *c* .... 1 Cor 7:20
CALLS
c them all by name .... Ps 147:4
David himself *c* .... Mark 12:37
c his own sheep .... John 10:3
CALM
there was a great *c* .... Matt 8:26
CAMEL
it is easier for a *c* .... Matt 19:24
CAMP
to Him, outside the *c* .... Heb 13:13
CAN
I *c* do all things .... Phil 4:13
CANCER
will spread like *c* .... 2 Tim 2:17
CANOPY
His *c* around Him was .... Ps 18:11
CAPSTONE
bring forth the *c* .... Zech 4:7
CAPTAIN
Which, having no *c* .... Prov 6:7
CAPTIVE
and be led away *c* .... Luke 21:24
He led captivity *c* .... Eph 4:8
CAPTIVES
and make *c* .... 2 Tim 3:6
CAPTIVITY
every thought into *c* .... 2 Cor 10:5
CARCASS
"For wherever the *c* .... Matt 24:28
CARE
"Lord, do You not *c* .... Luke 10:40
how will he take *c* .... 1 Tim 3:5
CARED
he said, not that he *c* .... John 12:6
CAREFULLY
I shall walk *c* all my .... Is 38:15
CARELESS
But, he who is *c* .... Prov 19:16
CARES
No one *c* for my soul .... Ps 142:4
for He *c* for you .... 1 Pet 5:7
CARNAL
c mind is enmity .... Rom 8:7
CARNALLY
c minded is death .... Rom 8:6
CAROUSE
count it pleasure to *c* .... 2 Pet 2:13
CARPENTER
"Is this not the *c* .... Mark 6:3
CARRIED
And *c* our sorrows .... Is 53:4
CARRY
for you to *c* your bed .... John 5:10
it is certain we can *c* .... 1 Tim 6:7
CARRYING
will meet you *c* .... Mark 14:13
CASE
Festus laid Paul's *c* .... Acts 25:14
CASSIA
myrrh and aloes and *c* .... Ps 45:8
CAST
Why are you *c* down .... Ps 42:5
whole body to be *c* .... Matt 5:29
My name they will *c* .... Mark 16:17
by no means *c* out .... John 6:37
c their crowns before .... Rev 4:10
the great dragon was *c* .... Rev 12:9
CASTING
c down arguments .... 2 Cor 10:5
c all your care .... 1 Pet 5:7
CASTS
perfect love *c* out .... 1 John 4:18
CATCH
c Him in His words .... Mark 12:13
now on you will *c* .... Luke 5:10
CATCHES
and the wolf *c* the .... John 10:12
c the wise in their .... 1 Cor 3:19
CAUGHT
him was a ram *c* .... Gen 22:13
her Child was *c* up .... Rev 12:5
CAUSE
hated Me without a *c* .... John 15:25
For this *c* I was born .... John 18:37
CAVES
in dens and *c* of the .... Heb 11:38
CEASE
and night Shall not *c* .... Gen 8:22
He makes wars *c* .... Ps 46:9
tongues, they will *c* .... 1 Cor 13:8
CEASING
pray without *c* .... 1 Thess 5:17
CEDAR
dwell in a house of *c* .... 2 Sam 7:2
CEDARS
the LORD breaks the *c* .... Ps 29:5
CELESTIAL
but the glory of the *c* .... 1 Cor 15:40
CENSER
Aaron, each took his *c* .... Lev 10:1
CERTAINTY
you may know the *c* .... Luke 1:4
CERTIFICATE
a man to write a *c* .... Mark 10:4
CHAFF
be chased like the *c* .... Is 17:13
He will burn up the *c* .... Matt 3:12
CHAIN
pit and a great *c* .... Rev 20:1
CHAINED
of God is not *c* .... 2 Tim 2:9
CHAINS
And his *c* fell off .... Acts 12:7
am, except for these *c* .... Acts 26:29
CHAMBERS
brought me into his *c* .... Song 1:4

CHAMPION
And a *c* went out ... 1 Sam 17:4
CHANGE
now and to *c* my tone ... Gal 4:20
there is also a *c* ... Heb 7:12
CHANGED
c the glory of the ... Rom 1:23
but we shall all be *c* ... 1 Cor 15:51
CHANGERS'
and poured out the *c* ... John 2:15
CHANGES
c the times and the ... Dan 2:21
CHANNELS
c of the sea were seen ... Ps 18:15
CHARIOT
that suddenly a *c* ... 2 Kin 2:11
CHARIOTS
Some trust in *c* ... Ps 20:7
CHARITABLE
you do not do your *c* ... Matt 6:1
c deeds which she ... Acts 9:36
CHARM
C is deceitful and ... Prov 31:30
CHARMS
who sew magic *c* ... Ezek 13:18
CHASE
Five of you shall *c* ... Lev 26:8
CHASTE
present you as a *c* ... 2 Cor 11:2
CHASTEN
a father does not *c* ... Heb 12:7
I love, I rebuke and *c* ... Rev 3:19
CHASTENED
c us as seemed best ... Heb 12:10
CHASTENING
do not despise the *c* ... Job 5:17
Now no *c* seems to be ... Heb 12:11
CHASTENS
the LORD loves He *c* ... Heb 12:6
CHASTISEMENT
The *c* for our peace ... Is 53:5
CHATTER
c leads only to ... Prov 14:23
CHEAT
Beware lest anyone *c* ... Col 2:8
CHEATED
let yourselves be *c* ... 1 Cor 6:7
CHEEK
on your right *c* ... Matt 5:39
CHEEKBONE
my enemies on the *c* ... Ps 3:7
CHEEKS
His *c* are like a bed ... Song 5:13
CHEER
"Son, be of good *c* ... Matt 9:2
CHEERFUL
for God loves a *c* ... 2 Cor 9:7
CHEERFULNESS
shows mercy, with *c* ... Rom 12:8
CHEESE
And curdle me like *c* ... Job 10:10
CHERISHES
but nourishes and *c* ... Eph 5:29
CHERUBIM
above it were the *c* ... Heb 9:5
CHIEF
of whom I am *c* ... 1 Tim 1:15
Zion a *c* cornerstone ... 1 Pet 2:6
CHILD
Train up a *c* in the ... Prov 22:6
For unto us a *C* ... Is 9:6
virgin shall be with *c* ... Matt 1:23
of God as a little *c* ... Mark 10:15
So the *c* grew and ... Luke 1:80
When I was a *c* ... 1 Cor 13:11
She bore a male *C* ... Rev 12:5
CHILDBEARING
she will be saved in *c* ... 1 Tim 2:15

CHILDBIRTH
pain as a woman in *c* ... Is 13:8
CHILDHOOD
c you have known ... 2 Tim 3:15
CHILDLESS
give me, seeing I go *c* ... Gen 15:2
this man down as *c* ... Jer 22:30
CHILDREN
c are a heritage ... Ps 127:3
c rise up and call her ... Prov 31:28
and become as little *c* ... Matt 18:3
"Let the little *c* ... Matt 19:14
the right to become *c* ... John 1:12
now we are *c* of God ... 1 John 3:2
CHOOSE
therefore *c* life ... Deut 30:19
"You did not *c* ... John 15:16
CHOSE
Just as He *c* us in Him ... Eph 1:4
CHOSEN
servant whom I have *c* ... Is 43:10
whom I have *c* ... John 13:18
c the foolish things ... 1 Cor 1:27
Has God not *c* the ... James 2:5
CHRIST
Jesus who is called *C* ... Matt 1:16
"You are the *C* ... Matt 16:16
a Savior, who is *C* ... Luke 2:11
It is *C* who died ... Rom 8:34
to be justified by *C* ... Gal 2:17
been crucified with *C* ... Gal 2:20
C is head of the ... Eph 5:23
to me, to live is *C* ... Phil 1:21
which is *C* in you ... Col 1:27
C who is our ... Col 3:4
Jesus *C* is the same ... Heb 13:8
C His Son cleanses us ... 1 John 1:7
that Jesus is the *C* ... 1 John 5:1
CHRISTIAN
anyone suffers as a *C* ... 1 Pet 4:16
CHRISTIANS
were first called *C* ... Acts 11:26
CHRISTS
"For false *c* and ... Matt 24:24
CHURCH
rock I will build My *c* ... Matt 16:18
c daily those who were ... Acts 2:47
Himself a glorious *c* ... Eph 5:27
as the Lord does the *c* ... Eph 5:29
body, which is the *c* ... Col 1:24
assembly and *c* ... Heb 12:23
CHURCHES
these things in the *c* ... Rev 22:16
CIRCLE
who sits above the *c* ... Is 40:22
CIRCUMCISE
is necessary to *c* them ... Acts 15:5
CIRCUMCISED
among you shall be *c* ... Gen 17:10
who will justify the *c* ... Rom 3:30
if you become *c* ... Gal 5:2
CIRCUMCISION
c is that of the heart ... Rom 2:29
C is nothing and ... 1 Cor 7:19
Christ Jesus neither *c* ... Gal 5:6
CIRCUMSPECTLY
then that you walk *c* ... Eph 5:15
CISTERN
from your own *c* ... Prov 5:15
CITIES
He overthrew those *c* ... Gen 19:25
three parts, and the *c* ... Rev 16:19
CITIZEN
But I was born a *c* ... Acts 22:28
CITIZENS
but fellow *c* with the ... Eph 2:19
CITIZENSHIP
For our *c* is in heaven ... Phil 3:20
CITY
shall make glad the *c* ... Ps 46:4
c has become a harlot ... Is 1:21

How lonely sits the *c* ... Lam 1:1
c that is set on a ... Matt 5:14
He has prepared a *c* ... Heb 11:16
have no continuing *c* ... Heb 13:14
John, saw the holy *c* ... Rev 21:2
CLAP
of the field shall *c* ... Is 55:12
CLAY
pit, out of the miry *c* ... Ps 40:2
We are the *c* ... Is 64:8
blind man with the *c* ... John 9:6
have power over the *c* ... Rom 9:21
CLEAN
He who has *c* hands and ... Ps 24:4
make yourselves *c* ... Is 1:16
c out His threshing ... Matt 3:12
You can make me *c* ... Matt 8:2
"You are not all *c* ... John 13:11
"You are already *c* ... John 15:3
CLEANSE
C me from secret ... Ps 19:12
And *c* me from my sin ... Ps 51:2
How can a young man *c* ... Ps 119:9
might sanctify and *c* ... Eph 5:26
us our sins and to *c* ... 1 John 1:9
CLEANSED
"Were there not ten *c* ... Luke 17:17
CLEANSES
Christ His Son *c* ... 1 John 1:7
CLEAR
of life, *c* as crystal ... Rev 22:1
CLIFF
secret places of the *c* ... Song 2:14
CLIMBS
c up some other way ... John 10:1
CLING
C to what is good ... Rom 12:9
CLINGS
And My tongue *c* ... Ps 22:15
CLOAK
let him have your *c* ... Matt 5:40
using liberty as a *c* ... 1 Pet 2:16
CLODS
The *c* of the valley ... Job 21:33
CLOSE
c friends abhor me ... Job 19:19
CLOSED
The deep *c* around me ... Jon 2:5
CLOTH
a piece of unshrunk *c* ... Matt 9:16
CLOTHE
He not much more *c* ... Matt 6:30
CLOTHED
of skin, and *c* them ... Gen 3:21
A man *c* in soft ... Matt 11:8
naked and you *c* ... Matt 25:36
legion, sitting and *c* ... Mark 5:15
desiring to be *c* ... 2 Cor 5:2
that you may be *c* ... Rev 3:18
CLOTHES
c became shining ... Mark 9:3
many spread their *c* ... Luke 19:36
a poor man in filthy *c* ... James 2:2
CLOTHING
c they cast lots ... Ps 22:18
do you worry about *c* ... Matt 6:28
to you in sheep's *c* ... Matt 7:15
c they cast lots ... John 19:24
CLOTHS
in swaddling *c* ... Luke 2:12
CLOUD
My rainbow in the *c* ... Gen 9:13
day in a pillar of *c* ... Ex 13:21
He led them with the *c* ... Ps 78:14
behold, a bright *c* ... Matt 17:5
of Man coming in a *c* ... Luke 21:27
c received Him out of ... Acts 1:9
by so great a *c* ... Heb 12:1
CLOUDS
Man coming on the *c* ... Matt 24:30
with them in the *c* ... 1 Thess 4:17

- are *c* without water … Jude 12
- He is coming with *c* … Rev 1:7

CLOUDY
- them by day with a *c* … Neh 9:12

CLOVEN
- chew the cud or have *c* … Deut 14:7

CLUSTER
- beloved is to me a *c* … Song 1:14

COAL
- in his hand a live *c* … Is 6:6

COALS
- doing you will heap *c* … Rom 12:20

COBRA
- the lion and the *c* … Ps 91:13

COBRA'S
- shall play by the *c* … Is 11:8

COFFIN
- and he was put in a *c* … Gen 50:26
- touched the open *c* … Luke 7:14

COIN
- if she loses one *c* … Luke 15:8

COLD
- and harvest, *C* and … Gen 8:22
- of many will grow *c* … Matt 24:12
- that you are neither *c* … Rev 3:15

COLLECTION
- concerning the *c* … 1 Cor 16:1

COLT
- on a donkey, A *c* … Zech 9:9
- on a donkey, A *c* … Matt 21:5

COME
- He will *c* and save you … Is 35:4
- who have no money, *C* … Is 55:1
- Your kingdom *c* … Matt 6:10
- "*C* to Me … Matt 11:28
- I have *c* in My … John 5:43
- thirsts, let him *c* … John 7:37
- *c* as a light into the … John 12:46
- O Lord, *c* … 1 Cor 16:22
- the door, I will *c* … Rev 3:20

COMELINESS
- He has no form or *c* … Is 53:2

COMES
- Lord's death till He *c* … 1 Cor 11:26

COMFORT
- and Your staff, they *c* … Ps 23:4
- yes, *c* My people … Is 40:1
- *c* each other … 1 Thess 5:11

COMFORTED
- So Isaac was *c* after … Gen 24:67
- Refusing to be *c* … Jer 31:15

COMFORTER
- She had no *c* … Lam 1:9

COMFORTS
- I, even I, am He who *c* … Is 51:12

COMING
- see the Son of Man *c* … Mark 13:26
- mightier than I is *c* … Luke 3:16
- are Christ's at His *c* … 1 Cor 15:23
- Behold, I am *c* … Rev 3:11
- "Surely I am *c* … Rev 22:20

COMMAND
- *c* I have received … John 10:18
- and I know that His *c* … John 12:50
- If you do whatever I *c* … John 15:14

COMMANDED
- not endure what was *c* … Heb 12:20

COMMANDMENT
- *c* of the LORD is pure … Ps 19:8
- which is the great *c* … Matt 22:36
- "A new *c* I give to … John 13:34
- which is the first *c* … Eph 6:2
- And this is His *c* … 1 John 3:23

COMMANDMENTS
- covenant, the Ten *C* … Ex 34:28
- as doctrines the *c* … Matt 15:9
- *c* hang all the Law … Matt 22:40
- He who has My *c* … John 14:21

COMMANDS
- with authority He *c* … Mark 1:27

COMMEND
- But food does not *c* … 1 Cor 8:8

COMMENDABLE
- patiently, this is *c* … 1 Pet 2:20

COMMENDED
- *c* the unjust steward … Luke 16:8

COMMENDS
- but whom the Lord *c* … 2 Cor 10:18

COMMIT
- "You shall not *c* … Ex 20:14
- into Your hands I *c* … Luke 23:46

COMMITS
- sin also *c* lawlessness … 1 John 3:4

COMMITTED
- *c* Himself to Him who … 1 Pet 2:23

COMMON
- *c* people heard Him … Mark 12:37
- had all things in *c* … Acts 2:44
- concerning our *c* … Jude 3

COMMOTION
- there arose a great *c* … Acts 19:23

COMMUNED
- I *c* with my heart … Eccl 1:16

COMMUNION
- *c* of the Holy Spirit … 2 Cor 13:14

COMPANION
- a man my equal, My *c* … Ps 55:13

COMPANIONS
- while you became *c* … Heb 10:33

COMPANY
- Great was the *c* … Ps 68:11
- to an innumerable *c* … Heb 12:22

COMPARE
- *c* ourselves with … 2 Cor 10:12

COMPARED
- are not worthy to be *c* … Rom 8:18

COMPASSION
- are a God full of *c* … Ps 86:15
- He was moved with *c* … Matt 9:36
- whomever I will have *c* … Rom 9:15
- He can have *c* on those … Heb 5:2

COMPASSIONATE
- the Lord is very *c* … James 5:11

COMPASSIONS
- because His *c* fail not … Lam 3:22

COMPEL
- *c* them to come in … Luke 14:23

COMPELS
- the love of Christ *c* … 2 Cor 5:14

COMPLAINED
- some of them also *c* … 1 Cor 10:10

COMPLAINERS
- These are grumblers, *c* … Jude 16

COMPLAINING
- all things without *c* … Phil 2:14

COMPLAINT
- For the LORD has a *c* … Mic 6:2

COMPLETE
- work in you will *c* … Phil 1:6
- and you are *c* in Him … Col 2:10
- of God may be *c* … 2 Tim 3:17

COMPLETELY
- sanctify you *c* … 1 Thess 5:23

COMPOSED
- But God *c* the body … 1 Cor 12:24

COMPREHEND
- which we cannot *c* … Job 37:5
- the darkness did not *c* … John 1:5

CONCEAL
- of God to *c* a matter … Prov 25:2

CONCEALED
- Than love carefully *c* … Prov 27:5

CONCEIT
- selfish ambition or *c* … Phil 2:3

CONCEITED
- Let us not become *c* … Gal 5:26

CONCEIVE
- the virgin shall *c* … Is 7:14
- And behold, you will *c* … Luke 1:31

CONCEIVED
- in sin my mother *c* … Ps 51:5

CONCERN
- Neither do I *c* myself … Ps 131:1

CONCERNED
- Is it oxen God is *c* … 1 Cor 9:9

CONCESSION
- But I say this as a *c* … 1 Cor 7:6

CONCLUSION
- Let us hear the *c* … Eccl 12:13

CONDEMN
- world to *c* the world … John 3:17

CONDEMNATION
- can you escape the *c* … Matt 23:33
- "And this is the *c* … John 3:19
- Their *c* is just … Rom 3:8
- therefore now no *c* … Rom 8:1

CONDEMNED
- does not believe is *c* … John 3:18
- *c* sin in the flesh … Rom 8:3

CONDEMNS
- Who is he who *c* … Rom 8:34

CONDUCT
- from your aimless *c* … 1 Pet 1:8
- may be won by the *c* … 1 Pet 3:1

CONFESS
- *c* my transgressions … Ps 32:5
- that if you *c* with … Rom 10:9
- every tongue shall *c* … Rom 14:11
- If we *c* our sins … 1 John 1:9

CONFESSED
- *c* that He was Christ … John 9:22

CONFESSES
- *c* that Jesus is the … 1 John 4:15

CONFESSION
- with the mouth *c* … Rom 10:10
- High Priest of our *c* … Heb 3:1
- let us hold fast our *c* … Heb 4:14

CONFIDENCE
- *c* shall be Your … Is 30:15
- Jesus, and have no *c* … Phil 3:3

CONFINED
- the Scripture has *c* … Gal 3:22

CONFIRM
- who will also *c* … 1 Cor 1:8

CONFIRMED
- covenant that was *c* … Gal 3:17
- *c* it by an oath … Heb 6:17

CONFIRMING
- *c* the word through … Mark 16:20

CONFLICT
- to know what a great *c* … Col 2:1

CONFLICTS
- Outside were *c* … 2 Cor 7:5

CONFORMED
- predestined to be *c* … Rom 8:29
- And do not be *c* … Rom 12:2

CONFUSE
- *c* their language … Gen 11:7

CONFUSED
- the assembly was *c* … Acts 19:32

CONGREGATION
- Nor sinners in the *c* … Ps 1:5
- God stands in the *c* … Ps 82:1

CONQUER
- conquering and to *c* … Rev 6:2

CONQUERORS
- we are more than *c* … Rom 8:37

CONSCIENCE
- convicted by their *c* … John 8:9
- strive to have a *c* … Acts 24:16

CONSECRATED
- *c* this house which you … 1 Kin 9:3

CONSENT
- and does not *c* to … 1 Tim 6:3

CONSENTED
- He had not *c* to their … Luke 23:51

CONSENTING
- Now Saul was *c* to his … Acts 8:1

CONSIDER
When I *c* Your heavens .... Ps 8:3
My people do not *c* .... Is 1:3
C the lilies of the .... Matt 6:28
"*C* the ravens .... Luke 12:24
c Him who endured .... Heb 12:3

CONSIST
in Him all things *c* .... Col 1:17

CONSOLATION
if there is any *c* .... Phil 2:1
us everlasting *c* .... 2 Thess 2:16

CONSOLE
c those who mourn .... Is 61:3

CONSTANT
c prayer was .... Acts 12:5

CONSUME
whom the Lord will *c* .... 2 Thess 2:8

CONSUMED
but the bush was not *c* .... Ex 3:2
mercies we are not *c* .... Lam 3:22
beware lest you be *c* .... Gal 5:15

CONSUMING
our God is a *c* fire .... Heb 12:29

CONTAIN
of heavens cannot *c* .... 2 Chr 2:6
c the books that .... John 21:25

CONTEMPT
and be treated with *c* .... Mark 9:12

CONTEMPTIBLE
and his speech *c* .... 2 Cor 10:10

CONTEND
c earnestly for the .... Jude 3

CONTENT
state I am, to be *c* .... Phil 4:11
covetousness: be *c* .... Heb 13:5

CONTENTIONS
sorcery, hatred, *c* .... Gal 5:20

CONTENTIOUS
anyone seems to be *c* .... 1 Cor 11:16

CONTENTMENT
c is great gain .... 1 Tim 6:6

CONTINUAL
a merry heart has a *c* .... Prov 15:15
c coming she weary .... Luke 18:5

CONTINUALLY
heart was only evil *c* .... Gen 6:5
will give ourselves *c* .... Acts 6:4
remains a priest *c* .... Heb 7:3

CONTINUE
Shall we *c* in sin that .... Rom 6:1
C earnestly in prayer .... Col 4:2
Let brotherly love *c* .... Heb 13:1

CONTINUED
c steadfastly in the .... Acts 2:42

CONTRADICTIONS
idle babble and *c* .... 1 Tim 6:20

CONTRARY
to worship God *c* .... Acts 18:13

CONTRIBUTION
to make a certain *c* .... Rom 15:26

CONTRITE
A broken and a *c* .... Ps 51:17
poor and of a *c* spirit .... Is 66:2

CONTROVERSY
For the LORD has a *c* .... Jer 25:31

CONVERSION
describing the *c* .... Acts 15:3

CONVERTED
unless you are *c* .... Matt 18:3

CONVICT
He has come, He will *c* .... John 16:8

CONVICTS
"Which of you *c* .... John 8:46

CONVINCED
Let each be fully *c* .... Rom 14:5

COOKED
c their own children .... Lam 4:10

COOL
and *c* my tongue .... Luke 16:24

COPIES
necessary that the *c* .... Heb 9:23

COPPER
sold for two *c* coins .... Luke 12:6

COPPERSMITH
c did me much harm .... 2 Tim 4:14

COPY
who serve the *c* .... Heb 8:5

CORD
this line of scarlet *c* .... Josh 2:18

CORDS
had made a whip of *c* .... John 2:15

CORNER
was not done in a *c* .... Acts 26:26

CORNERSTONE
become the chief *c* .... Matt 21:42
in Zion A chief *c* .... 1 Pet 2:6

CORRECT
C your son .... Prov 29:17

CORRECTED
human fathers who *c* .... Heb 12:9

CORRECTION
Do not withhold *c* .... Prov 23:13
for reproof, for *c* .... 2 Tim 3:16

CORRECTS
the LORD loves He *c* .... Prov 3:12

CORRODED
and silver are *c* .... James 5:3

CORRUPT
in these things they *c* .... Jude 10

CORRUPTED
for all flesh had *c* .... Gen 6:12
Your riches are *c* .... James 5:2

CORRUPTIBLE
redeemed with *c* .... 1 Pet 1:18

CORRUPTION
Your Holy One to see *c* .... Ps 16:10
c inherit incorruption .... 1 Cor 15:50
having escaped the *c* .... 2 Pet 1:4

COST
and count the *c* .... Luke 14:28

COULD
c remove mountains .... 1 Cor 13:2
which no one *c* number .... Rev 7:9

COUNCILS
deliver you up to *c* .... Mark 13:9

COUNSEL
Who walks not in the *c* .... Ps 1:1
We took sweet *c* .... Ps 55:14
guide me with Your *c* .... Ps 73:24
according to the *c* .... Eph 1:11
immutability of His *c* .... Heb 6:17
"I *c* you to buy from .... Rev 3:18

COUNSELOR
be called Wonderful, *C* .... Is 9:6

COUNSELORS
c there is safety .... Prov 11:14

COUNT
c my life dear to .... Acts 20:24
His promise, as some *c* .... 2 Pet 3:9

COUNTED
Even a fool is *c* .... Prov 17:28
who rule well be *c* .... 1 Tim 5:17

COUNTENANCE
The LORD lift up His *c* .... Num 6:26
with a sad *c* .... Matt 6:16
His *c* was like .... Matt 28:3
of the glory of his *c* .... 2 Cor 3:7

COUNTRY
"Get out of your *c* .... Gen 12:1
that is, a heavenly *c* .... Heb 11:16

COUNTRYMEN
for my brethren, my *c* .... Rom 9:3

COURAGE
strong and of good *c* .... Deut 31:6

COURT
They zealously *c* .... Gal 4:17

COURTEOUS
be tenderhearted, be *c* .... 1 Pet 3:8

COURTS
and into His *c* .... Ps 100:4

COVENANT
I will establish My *c* .... Gen 6:18
the LORD made a *c* .... Gen 15:18
will show them His *c* .... Ps 25:14
sons will keep My *c* .... Ps 132:12
I will make a new *c* .... Jer 31:31
the Messenger of the *c* .... Mal 3:1
cup is the new *c* .... Luke 22:20
He says, "A new *c* .... Heb 8:13
Mediator of the new *c* .... Heb 12:24
of the everlasting *c* .... Heb 13:20

COVENANTS
the glory, the *c* .... Rom 9:4

COVER
He shall *c* you with .... Ps 91:4
c a multitude of sins .... James 5:20

COVERED
Whose sin is *c* .... Ps 32:1
c all their sin .... Ps 85:2
For there is nothing *c* .... Matt 10:26

COVERING
spread a cloud for a *c* .... Ps 105:39

COVERINGS
and made themselves *c* .... Gen 3:7

COVET
"You shall not *c* .... Ex 20:17

COVETED
c no one's silver .... Acts 20:33

COVETOUS
nor thieves, nor *c* .... 1 Cor 6:10

COVETOUSNESS
heed and beware of *c* .... Luke 12:15

COWARDLY
the *c*, unbelieving .... Rev 21:8

CRAFTILY
His people, to deal *c* .... Ps 105:25

CRAFTINESS
deceived Eve by his *c* .... 2 Cor 11:3
in the cunning *c* .... Eph 4:14

CRAFTSMAN
instructor of every *c* .... Gen 4:22

CRAFTY
the devices of the *c* .... Job 5:12
Nevertheless, being *c* .... 2 Cor 12:16

CREAM
were bathed with *c* .... Job 29:6

CREATE
peace and *c* calamity .... Is 45:7

CREATED
So God *c* man in His .... Gen 1:27
Has not one God *c* .... Mal 2:10
c in Christ Jesus .... Eph 2:10
new man which was *c* .... Eph 4:24

CREATION
know that the whole *c* .... Rom 8:22
Christ, he is a new *c* .... 2 Cor 5:17
anything, but a new *c* .... Gal 6:15

CREATOR
Remember now your *C* .... Eccl 12:1
God, the LORD, The *C* .... Is 40:28
rather than the *C* .... Rom 1:25

CREATURE
the gospel to every *c* .... Mark 16:15

CREATURES
firstfruits of His *c* .... James 1:18

CREDIT
For what *c* is it if .... 1 Pet 2:20

CREDITOR
There was a certain *c* .... Luke 7:41

CREEP
sort are those who *c* .... 2 Tim 3:6

CREEPING
c thing and beast of .... Gen 1:24

CREPT
For certain men have *c* .... Jude 4

CRIB
donkey its master's *c* .... Is 1:3

CRIED
the poor who *c* out .... Job 29:12
of the depths I have *c* .... Ps 130:1
CRIES
your brother's blood *c* .... Gen 4:10
CRIMES
land is filled with *c* .... Ezek 7:23
CRIMINALS
also two others, *c* .... Luke 23:32
CROOKED
c places shall be made .... Is 40:4
in the midst of a *c* .... Phil 2:15
CROSS
does not take his *c* .... Matt 10:38
to bear His *c* .... Matt 27:32
down from the *c* .... Matt 27:40
lest the *c* of Christ .... 1 Cor 1:17
boast except in the *c* .... Gal 6:14
the enemies of the *c* .... Phil 3:18
Him endured the *c* .... Heb 12:2
shall not follow a *c* .... Ex 23:2
CROWN
c the year with Your .... Ps 65:11
they had twisted a *c* .... Matt 27:29
obtain a perishable *c* .... 1 Cor 9:25
laid up for me the *c* .... 2 Tim 4:8
on his head a golden *c* .... Rev 14:14
CROWNED
angels, And You have *c* .... Ps 8:5
athletics, he is not *c* .... 2 Tim 2:5
CROWNS
His head were many *c* .... Rev 19:12
CRUCIFIED
"Let Him be *c* .... Matt 27:22
Calvary, there they *c* .... Luke 23:33
lawless hands, have *c* .... Acts 2:23
that our old man was *c* .... Rom 6:6
Jesus Christ and Him *c* .... 1 Cor 2:2
"I have been *c* .... Gal 2:20
CRUCIFY
out again, "*C* Him .... Mark 15:13
CRUEL
hate me with *c* hatred .... Ps 25:19
CRUELTY
the haunts of *c* .... Ps 74:20
CRUSH
of peace will *c* .... Rom 16:20
CRUSHED
every side, yet not *c* .... 2 Cor 4:8
CRUST
man is reduced to a *c* .... Prov 6:26
CRY
and their *c* came up to .... Ex 2:23
Does not wisdom *c* .... Prov 8:1
at midnight a *c* .... Matt 25:6
His own elect who *c* .... Luke 18:7
CRYING
nor sorrow, nor *c* .... Rev 21:4
CRYSTAL
a sea of glass, like *c* .... Rev 4:6
CUBIT
can add one *c* .... Matt 6:27
CUNNING
the serpent was more *c* .... Gen 3:1
c craftiness of deceitful .... Eph 4:14
CUP
My *c* runs over .... Ps 23:5
Then He took the *c* .... Matt 26:27
possible, let this *c* .... Matt 26:39
c is the new covenant .... Luke 22:20
cannot drink the *c* .... 1 Cor 10:21
c is the new .... 1 Cor 11:25
CURE
and to *c* diseases .... Luke 9:1
CURES
and perform *c* .... Luke 13:32
CURSE
c the ground for man's .... Gen 8:21
C God and die .... Job 2:9
"I will send a *c* .... Mal 2:2
law are under the *c* .... Gal 3:10
CURSED
c more than all cattle .... Gen 3:14
from Me, you *c* .... Matt 25:41
CURSES
I will curse him who *c* .... Gen 12:3
CURTAIN
the heavens like a *c* .... Ps 104:2
CUSTOM
according to the *c* .... Acts 15:1
CUT
evildoers shall be *c* .... Ps 37:9
the wicked will be *c* .... Prov 2:22
CYMBAL
or a clanging *c* .... 1 Cor 13:1

D

DAILY
Give us this day our *d* .... Matt 6:11
take up his cross *d* .... Luke 9:23
the Scriptures *d* .... Acts 17:11
DANCE
mourn, And a time to *d* .... Eccl 3:4
And you did not *d* .... Matt 11:17
DANCED
Then David *d* before .... 2 Sam 6:14
DANCING
saw the calf and the *d* .... Ex 32:19
he heard music and *d* .... Luke 15:25
DARE
someone would even *d* .... Rom 5:7
DARK
I tell you in the *d* .... Matt 10:27
shines in a *d* place .... 2 Pet 1:19
DARKENED
their understanding *d* .... Eph 4:18
DARKNESS
d He called Night .... Gen 1:5
Those who sat in *d* .... Ps 107:10
d Have seen a .... Is 9:2
And deep *d* the people .... Is 60:2
body will be full of *d* .... Matt 6:23
cast out into outer *d* .... Matt 8:12
d rather than light .... John 3:19
For you were once *d* .... Eph 5:8
called you out of *d* .... 1 Pet 2:9
d is reserved .... 2 Pet 2:17
and in Him is no *d* .... 1 John 1:5
d is passing away .... 1 John 2:8
DARTS
quench all the fiery *d* .... Eph 6:16
DASH
You shall *d* them to .... Ps 2:9
Lest you *d* your foot .... Matt 4:6
DASHED
infants shall be *d* .... Hos 13:16
DAUGHTER
"Rejoice greatly, O *d* .... Zech 9:9
"Fear not, *d* of Zion .... John 12:15
the son of Pharaoh's *d* .... Heb 11:24
DAUGHTERS
of God saw the *d* .... Gen 6:2
d shall prophesy .... Acts 2:17
DAY
God called the light *D* .... Gen 1:5
And *d* and night .... Gen 8:22
the Sabbath *d* .... Ex 20:8
For a *d* in Your courts .... Ps 84:10
d the LORD has .... Ps 118:24
not strike you by *d* .... Ps 121:6
For the *d* of the LORD .... Joel 2:11
who can endure the *d* .... Mal 3:2
d our daily bread .... Matt 6:11
sent Me while it is *d* .... John 9:4
person esteems one *d* .... Rom 14:5
d will declare it .... 1 Cor 3:13
again the third *d* .... 1 Cor 15:4
with the Lord one *d* .... 2 Pet 3:8
DAYS
d are swifter than a .... Job 7:6
of woman is of few *d* .... Job 14:1
The *d* of our lives are .... Ps 90:10
Before the difficult *d* .... Eccl 12:1
shortened those *d* .... Mark 13:20
raise it up in three *d* .... John 2:20
DAYSPRING
With which the *D* .... Luke 1:78
DEACONS
with the bishops and *d* .... Phil 1:1
d must be reverent .... 1 Tim 3:8
d be the husbands .... 1 Tim 3:12
DEAD
But the *d* know nothing .... Eccl 9:5
d bury their own *d* .... Matt 8:22
not the God of the *d* .... Matt 22:32
this my son was *d* .... Luke 15:24
d will hear the voice .... John 5:25
was raised from the *d* .... Rom 6:4
yourselves to be *d* .... Rom 6:11
be Lord of both the *d* .... Rom 14:9
resurrection of the *d* .... 1 Cor 15:12
And the *d* in Christ .... 1 Thess 4:16
without works is *d* .... James 2:26
And the *d* were judged .... Rev 20:12
DEADLY
drink anything *d* .... Mark 16:18
evil, full of *d* poison .... James 3:8
DEADNESS
the *d* of Sarah's womb .... Rom 4:19
DEAF
d shall be unstopped .... Is 35:5
are cleansed and the *d* .... Matt 11:5
DEAL
My Servant shall *d* .... Is 52:13
DEATH
d parts you and me .... Ruth 1:17
and the shadow of *d* .... Job 10:21
I sleep the sleep of *d* .... Ps 13:3
of the shadow of *d* .... Ps 23:4
house leads down to *d* .... Prov 2:18
who hate me love *d* .... Prov 8:36
swallow up *d* forever .... Is 25:8
no pleasure in the *d* .... Ezek 18:32
who shall not taste *d* .... Matt 16:28
but has passed from *d* .... John 5:24
Nevertheless *d* reigned .... Rom 5:14
D no longer has .... Rom 6:9
the wages of sin is *d* .... Rom 6:23
the Lord's *d* .... 1 Cor 11:26
since by man came *d* .... 1 Cor 15:21
D is swallowed up in .... 1 Cor 15:54
The sting of *d* is sin .... 1 Cor 15:56
is sin leading to *d* .... 1 John 5:16
Be faithful until *d* .... Rev 2:10
shall be no more *d* .... Rev 21:4
which is the second *d* .... Rev 21:8
DEBTOR
I am a *d* both to .... Rom 1:14
that he is a *d* to keep .... Gal 5:3
DEBTORS
as we forgive our *d* .... Matt 6:12
of his master's *d* .... Luke 16:5
brethren, we are *d* .... Rom. 8:12
DECEIT
Nor was any *d* in His .... Is 53:9
philosophy and empty *d* .... Col 2:8
no sin, nor was *d* .... 1 Pet 2:22
mouth was found no *d* .... Rev 14:5
DECEITFUL
deliver me from the *d* .... Ps 43:1
"The heart is *d* .... Jer 17:9
are false apostles, *d* .... 2 Cor 11:13
DECEITFULLY
an idol, Nor sworn *d* .... Ps 24:4
the word of God *d* .... 2 Cor 4:2
DECEITFULNESS
this world and the *d* .... Matt 13:22
DECEIVE
rise up and *d* many .... Matt 24:11
Let no one *d* you with .... Eph 5:6
we have no sin, we *d* .... 1 John 1:8
DECEIVED
"The serpent *d* .... Gen 3:13
the commandment, *d* .... Rom 7:11
deceiving and being *d* .... 2 Tim 3:13

DECEIVER
how that *d* said ... Matt 27:63
This is a *d* and an ... 2 John 7
DECEIVES
heed that no one *d* ... Matt 24:4
DECENTLY
all things be done *d* ... 1 Cor 14:40
DECEPTIVE
you with *d* words ... 2 Pet 2:3
DECISION
in the valley of *d* ... Joel 3:14
DECLARE
The heavens *d* the ... Ps 19:1
d Your name to My ... Ps 22:22
seen and heard we *d* ... 1 John 1:3
DECLARED
and *d* to be the Son of ... Rom 1:4
DECREE
"I will declare the *d* ... Ps 2:7
in those days that a *d* ... Luke 2:1
DEDICATION
it was the Feast of *D* ... John 10:22
DEED
you do in word or *d* ... Col 3:17
DEEDS
because their *d* ... John 3:19
"You do the *d* ... John 8:41
one according to his *d* ... Rom 2:6
you put to death the *d* ... Rom 8:13
DEEP
LORD God caused a *d* ... Gen 2:21
d uttered its voice ... Hab 3:10
"Launch out into the *d* ... Luke 5:4
I have been in the *d* ... 2 Cor 11:25
DEEPER
D than Sheol ... Job 11:8
DEEPLY
But He sighed *d* ... Mark 8:12
DEER
As the *d* pants for the ... Ps 42:1
shall leap like a *d* ... Is 35:6
DEFEATED
and Israel was *d* ... 1 Sam 4:10
DEFEND
D the fatherless ... Is 1:17
DEFENSE
For wisdom is a *d* ... Eccl 7:12
am appointed for the *d* ... Phil 1:17
be ready to give a *d* ... 1 Pet 3:15
DEFILE
also these dreamers *d* ... Jude 8
DEFILED
lest they should be *d* ... John 18:28
and conscience are *d* ... Titus 1:15
DEFILES
mouth, this *d* a man ... Matt 15:11
it anything that *d* ... Rev 21:27
DEFRAUD
d his brother in this ... 1 Thess 4:6
DEGREES
go forward ten *d* ... 2 Kin 20:9
DELICACIES
of the king's *d* ... Dan 1:5
DELICATE
a lovely and *d* woman ... Jer 6:2
DELIGHT
But his *d* is in the ... Ps 1:2
I *d* to do Your will ... Ps 40:8
And I was daily His *d* ... Prov 8:30
And let your soul *d* ... Is 55:2
call the Sabbath a *d* ... Is 58:13
For I *d* in the law of ... Rom 7:22
DELIGHTS
For the LORD *d* in you ... Is 62:4
DELIVER
Let Him *d* Him ... Ps 22:8
I will *d* him and honor ... Ps 91:15
into temptation, But *d* ... Matt 6:13
let Him *d* Him now if ... Matt 27:43
And the Lord will *d* ... 2 Tim 4:18
d the godly out of ... 2 Pet 2:9

DELIVERANCE
not accepting *d* ... Heb 11:35
DELIVERED
who was *d* up because ... Rom 4:25
was once for all *d* ... Jude 3
DELIVERER
D will come out of ... Rom 11:26
DELIVERS
even Jesus who *d* ... 1 Thess 1:10
DELUSION
send them strong *d* ... 2 Thess 2:11
DEMON
Jesus rebuked the *d* ... Matt 17:18
and have a *d* ... John 8:48
DEMONIC
is earthly, sensual, *d* ... James 3:15
DEMONS
authority over all *d* ... Luke 9:1
the *d* are subject ... Luke 10:17
Even the *d* believe ... James 2:19
DEMONSTRATE
faith, to *d* His ... Rom 3:25
DEMONSTRATES
d His own love toward ... Rom 5:8
DEN
cast him Into the *d* ... Dan 6:16
it a '*d* of thieves ... Matt 21:13
DENARIUS
the laborers for a *d* ... Matt 20:2
DENIED
before men will be *d* ... Luke 12:9
Peter then *d* again ... John 18:27
d the Holy One and the ... Acts 3:14
things cannot be *d* ... Acts 19:36
household, he has *d* ... 1 Tim 5:8
DENIES
But whoever *d* ... Matt 10:33
d that Jesus is the ... 1 John 2:22
DENY
let him *d* himself ... Matt 16:24
He cannot *d* Himself ... 2 Tim 2:13
DENYING
but *d* its power ... 2 Tim 3:5
d the Lord who bought ... 2 Pet 2:1
DEPART
scepter shall not *d* ... Gen 49:10
on the left hand, '*D* ... Matt 25:41
will *d* from the faith ... 1 Tim 4:1
DEPARTING
heart of unbelief in *d* ... Heb 3:12
DEPARTURE
d savage wolves will ... Acts 20:29
and the time of my *d* ... 2 Tim 4:6
DEPRESSION
of man causes *d* ... Prov 12:25
DEPTH
nor height nor *d* ... Rom 8:39
Oh, the *d* of the ... Rom 11:33
DEPTHS
our sins Into the *d* ... Mic 7:19
DERISION
shall hold them in *d* ... Ps 2:4
DESCEND
d now from the cross ... Mark 15:32
Lord Himself will *d* ... 1 Thess 4:16
DESCENDANTS
"We are Abraham's *d* ... John 8:33
DESCENDED
He who *d* is also the ... Eph 4:10
DESCENDING
God ascending and *d* ... John 1:51
the holy Jerusalem, *d* ... Rev 21:10
DESERT
d shall rejoice ... Is 35:1
'Look, He is in the *d* ... Matt 24:26
DESERTED
d place by Himself ... Matt 14:13
DESERTS
They wandered in *d* ... Heb 11:38

DESIGN
with an artistic *d* ... Ex 26:31
DESIRABLE
the eyes, and a tree *d* ... Gen 3:6
DESIRE
d shall be for your ... Gen 3:16
Behold, You *d* truth in ... Ps 51:6
"Father, I *d* that ... John 17:24
all manner of evil *d* ... Rom 7:8
Brethren, my heart's *d* ... Rom 10:1
d the best gifts ... 1 Cor 12:31
the two, having a *d* ... Phil 1:23
DESIRED
d are they than gold ... Ps 19:10
One thing I have *d* ... Ps 27:4
DESIRES
shall give you the *d* ... Ps 37:4
the devil, and the *d* ... John 8:44
not come from your *d* ... James 4:1
DESOLATE
any more be termed *D* ... Is 62:4
house is left to you *d* ... Matt 23:38
DESOLATION
the 'abomination of *d* ... Matt 24:15
DESPAIRED
strength, so that we *d* ... 2 Cor 1:8
DESPISE
one and *d* the other ... Matt 6:24
d the riches of His ... Rom 2:4
DESPISED
He is *d* and rejected ... Is 53:3
the things which are *d* ... 1 Cor 1:28
DESPISES
d his neighbor sins ... Prov 14:21
DESPISING
the cross, *d* the shame ... Heb 12:2
DESTITUTE
of corrupt minds and *d* ... 1 Tim 6:5
DESTROY
Why should you *d* ... Eccl 7:16
shall not hurt nor *d* ... Is 11:9
I did not come to *d* ... Matt 5:17
Him who is able to *d* ... Matt 10:28
Barabbas and *d* Jesus ... Matt 27:20
to save life or to *d* ... Luke 6:9
d men's lives but to ... Luke 9:56
d the wisdom of the ... 1 Cor 1:19
able to save and to *d* ... James 4:12
DESTROYED
d all living things ... Gen 7:23
house, this tent, is *d* ... 2 Cor 5:1
DESTRUCTION
You turn man to *d* ... Ps 90:3
d that lays waste ... Ps 91:6
your life from *d* ... Ps 103:4
Pride goes before *d* ... Prov 16:18
whose end is *d* ... Phil 3:19
with everlasting *d* ... 2 Thess 1:9
DESTRUCTIVE
bring in *d* heresies ... 2 Pet 2:1
DETERMINED
d their preappointed ... Acts 17:26
For I *d* not to know ... 1 Cor 2:2
DEVICE
there is no work or *d* ... Eccl 9:10
DEVICES
not ignorant of his *d* ... 2 Cor 2:11
DEVIL
to be tempted by the *d* ... Matt 4:1
prepared for the *d* ... Matt 25:41
of your father the *d* ... John 8:44
give place to the *d* ... Eph 4:27
the snare of the *d* ... 2 Tim 2:26
the works of the *d* ... 1 John 3:8
DEVIOUS
And who are *d* ... Prov 2:15
DEVISES
d wickedness on his ... Ps 36:4
But a generous man *d* ... Is 32:8
DEVOID
who is *d* of wisdom ... Prov 11:12

DEVOTED
Your servant, who is *d* .... Ps 119:38
DEVOUR
For you *d* widows' .... Matt 23:14
bite and *d* one another .... Gal 5:15
whom he may *d* .... 1 Pet 5:8
d her Child as .... Rev 12:4
DEVOURED
wild beast has *d* .... Gen 37:20
birds came and *d* them .... Matt 13:4
of heaven and *d* them .... Rev 20:9
DEVOUT
man was just and *d* .... Luke 2:25
d soldier from among .... Acts 10:7
DEW
God give you Of the *d* .... Gen 27:28
DIADEMS
ten horns, and seven *d* .... Rev 12:3
DIAMOND
d it is engraved .... Jer 17:1
DICTATES
according to the *d* .... Jer 23:17
DIE
it you shall surely *d* .... Gen 2:17
but a person shall *d* .... 2 Chr 25:4
I shall not *d* .... Ps 118:17
born, And a time to *d* .... Eccl 3:2
eat of it and not *d* .... John 6:50
to you that you will *d* .... John 8:24
though he may *d* .... John 11:25
one man should *d* .... John 11:50
the flesh you will *d* .... Rom 8:13
For as in Adam all *d* .... 1 Cor 15:22
and to *d* is gain .... Phil 1:21
for men to *d* once .... Heb 9:27
are the dead who *d* .... Rev 14:13
DIED
And all flesh *d* .... Gen 7:21
in due time Christ *d* .... Rom 5:6
Christ *d* for us .... Rom 5:8
Now if we *d* with .... Rom 6:8
and He *d* for all .... 2 Cor 5:15
for if we *d* with Him .... 2 Tim 2:11
DIES
alive unless it *d* .... 1 Cor 15:36
DIFFERS
for one star *d* from .... 1 Cor 15:41
DILIGENCE
d it produced in you .... 2 Cor 7:11
DILIGENT
d makes rich .... Prov 10:4
DILIGENTLY
d lest anyone fall .... Heb 12:15
DIM
His eyes were not *d* .... Deut 34:7
DIMLY
we see in a mirror, *d* .... 1 Cor 13:12
DINE
come in to him and *d* .... Rev 3:20
DINNER
invites you to *d* .... 1 Cor 10:27
DIP
d your piece of bread .... Ruth 2:14
DIPPED
clothed with a robe *d* .... Rev 19:13
DIRECT
Now may the Lord *d* .... 2 Thess 3:5
DIRT
cast up mire and *d* .... Is 57:20
DISARMED
d principalities .... Col 2:15
DISASTER
will end with *d* .... Acts 27:10
DISCERN
d the face of the sky .... Matt 16:3
senses exercised to *d* .... Heb 5:14
DISCERNED
they are spiritually *d* .... 1 Cor 2:14
DISCERNER
d of the thoughts .... Heb 4:12
DISCERNS
a wise man's heart *d* .... Eccl 8:5
DISCIPLE
he cannot be My *d* .... Luke 14:26
d whom Jesus loved .... John 21:7
DISCIPLES
word, you are My *d* .... John 8:31
but we are Moses' *d* .... John 9:28
DISCIPLINES
he who loves him *d* .... Prov 13:24
DISCORD
And one who sows *d* .... Prov 6:19
DISCOURAGED
lest they became *d* .... Col 3:21
become weary and *d* .... Heb 12:3
DISCRETION
d will preserve you .... Prov 2:11
DISFIGURE
d their faces that .... Matt 6:16
DISGUISES
And he *d* his face .... Job 24:15
DISHONOR
Father, and you *d* Me .... John 8:49
d their bodies among .... Rom 1:24
It is sown in *d* .... 1 Cor 15:43
DISHONORED
But you have *d* the .... James 2:6
DISHONORS
For son *d* father .... Mic 7:6
DISOBEDIENT
out My hands To a *d* .... Rom 10:21
DISORDERLY
for this *d* gathering .... Acts 19:40
DISPENSATION
d of the fullness of .... Eph 1:10
DISPERSION
the pilgrims of the *D* .... 1 Pet 1:1
DISPLEASE
LORD see it, and it *d* .... Prov 24:18
DISPLEASED
they were greatly *d* .... Matt 20:24
it, He was greatly *d* .... Mark 10:14
DISPUTE
there was also a *d* .... Luke 22:24
DISPUTER
Where is the *d* of this .... 1 Cor 1:20
DISPUTES
But avoid foolish *d* .... Titus 3:9
DISQUALIFIED
should become *d* .... 1 Cor 9:27
DISQUIETED
And why are you *d* .... Ps 42:5
DISSENSION
had no small *d* and .... Acts 15:2
DISSIPATION
not accused of *d* .... Titus 1:6
DISSOLVED
the heavens will be *d* .... 2 Pet 3:12
DISTINCTION
compassion, making a *d* .... Jude 22
DISTRESS
d them in His deep .... Ps 2:5
tribulation, or *d* .... Rom 8:35
DISTRESSED
and deeply *d* .... Mark 14:33
DISTRESSES
Bring me out of my *d* .... Ps 25:17
DISTRIBUTED
and they *d* to each as .... Acts 4:35
DISTRIBUTING
d to the needs of the .... Rom 12:13
DITCH
will fall into a *d* .... Matt 15:14
DIVERSITIES
There are *d* .... 1 Cor 12:4
DIVIDE
d the spoil with the .... Prov 16:19
"Take this and *d* .... Luke 22:17
DIVIDED
and the waters were *d* .... Ex 14:21
they were not *d* .... 2 Sam 1:23
"Every kingdom *d* .... Matt 12:25
Is Christ *d* .... 1 Cor 1:13
DIVIDES
at home *d* the spoil .... Ps 68:12
DIVIDING
rightly *d* the word of .... 2 Tim 2:15
DIVINATION
shall you practice *d* .... Lev 19:26
a spirit of *d* met us .... Acts 16:16
DIVINE
d service and the .... Heb 9:1
DIVISION
So there was a *d* .... John 7:43
DIVISIONS
those who cause *d* .... Rom 16:17
persons, who cause *d* .... Jude 19
DIVISIVE
Reject a *d* man after .... Titus 3:10
DIVORCE
her a certificate of *d* .... Deut 24:1
a certificate of *d* .... Mark 10:4
DO
men to *d* to you, *d* .... Matt 7:12
He sees the Father *d* .... John 5:19
without Me you can *d* .... John 15:5
"Sirs, what must I *d* .... Acts 16:30
d evil that good may .... Rom 3:8
or whatever you *d*, *d* .... 1 Cor 10:31
DOCTRINE
What new *d* is this .... Mark 1:27
"My *d* is not Mine .... John 7:16
with every wind of *d* .... Eph 4:14
is contrary to sound *d* .... 1 Tim 1:10
is profitable for *d* .... 2 Tim 3:16
not endure sound *d* .... 2 Tim 4:3
DOCTRINES
commandments and *d* .... Col 2:22
various and strange *d* .... Heb 13:9
DOERS
But be *d* of the word .... James 1:22
DOG
d is better than a .... Eccl 9:4
d returns to his own .... 2 Pet 2:22
DOGS
what is holy to the *d* .... Matt 7:6
d eat the crumbs .... Matt 15:27
But outside are *d* .... Rev 22:15
DOMINION
let them have *d* .... Gen 1:26
d is an everlasting .... Dan 4:34
sin shall not have *d* .... Rom 6:14
glory and majesty, *D* .... Jude 25
DONKEY
d its master's crib .... Is 1:3
and riding on a *d* .... Zech 9:9
colt, the foal of a *d* .... Matt 21:5
d speaking with a .... 2 Pet 2:16
DOOM
for the day of *d* .... Prov 16:4
DOOR
stone against the *d* .... Matt 27:60
to you, I am the *d* .... John 10:7
before you an open *d* .... Rev 3:8
I stand at the *d* .... Rev 3:20
DOORKEEPER
I would rather be a *d* .... Ps 84:10
DOORPOSTS
write them on the *d* .... Deut 6:9
DOORS
up, you everlasting *d* .... Ps 24:7
DOUBLE
from the LORD's hand *D* .... Is 40:2
worthy of *d* honor .... 1 Tim 5:17
DOUBLE-MINDED
he is a *d* man .... James 1:8
DOUBT
faith, why did you *d* .... Matt 14:31

DOUBTING
in faith, with no *d* .... James 1:6
DOUBTS
why do *d* arise in .... Luke 24:38
for I have *d* about you .... Gal 4:20
DOVE
d found no resting .... Gen 8:9
descending like a *d* .... Matt 3:16
DOVES
and harmless as *d* .... Matt 10:16
DOWNCAST
who comforts the *d* .... 2 Cor 7:6
DRAGNET
d that was cast .... Matt 13:47
DRAGON
they worshiped the *d* .... Rev 13:4
He laid hold of the *d* .... Rev 20:2
DRAINED
All faces are *d* .... Joel 2:6
DRANK
them, and they all *d* .... Mark 14:23
DRAW
d honey from the .... Deut 32:13
me to *d* near to God .... Ps 73:28
And the years *d* .... Eccl 12:1
will *d* all peoples .... John 12:32
D near to God and He .... James 4:8
DRAWS
your redemption *d* .... Luke 21:28
DREAM
Now Joseph had a *d* .... Gen 37:5
Your old men shall *d* .... Joel 2:28
to Joseph in a *d* .... Matt 2:13
things today in a *d* .... Matt 27:19
DREAMERS
d defile the flesh .... Jude 8
DREAMS
Nebuchadnezzar had *d* .... Dan 2:1
DRIED
of her blood was *d* .... Mark 5:29
saw the fig tree *d* .... Mark 11:20
DRIFT
have heard, lest we *d* .... Heb 2:1
DRINK
gave me vinegar to *d* .... Ps 69:21
Lest they *d* and forget .... Prov 31:5
follow intoxicating *d* .... Is 5:11
d the milk of the .... Is 60:16
bosom, That you may *d* .... Is 66:11
"Bring wine, let us *d* .... Amos 4:1
that day when I *d* .... Matt 26:29
mingled with gall to *d* .... Matt 27:34
with myrrh to *d* .... Mark 15:23
to her, "Give Me a *d* .... John 4:7
him come to Me and *d* .... John 7:37
do, as often as you *d* .... 1 Cor 11:25
No longer *d* only .... 1 Tim 5:23
DRINKS
to her, "Whoever *d* .... John 4:13
d My blood has .... John 6:54
he who eats and *d* .... 1 Cor 11:29
DRIPPING
His lips are lilies, *D* .... Song 5:13
DROSS
purge away your *d* .... Is 1:25
DROUGHT
in the year of *d* .... Jer 17:8
"For I called for a *d* .... Hag 1:11
DROVE
So He *d* out the man .... Gen 3:24
temple of God and *d* .... Matt 21:12
DROWN
Nor can the floods *d* .... Song 8:7
harmful lusts which *d* .... 1 Tim 6:9
DROWSINESS
d will clothe a .... Prov 23:21
DRUNK
of the wine and was *d* .... Gen 9:21
the guests have well *d* .... John 2:10
"For these are not *d* .... Acts 2:15
and another is *d* .... 1 Cor 11:21
I saw the woman, *d* .... Rev 17:6
DRUNKARD
to and fro like a *d* .... Is 24:20
or a reviler, or a *d* .... 1 Cor 5:11
DRUNKEN
I am like a *d* man .... Jer 23:9
DRUNKENNESS
will be filled with *d* .... Ezek 23:33
not in revelry and *d* .... Rom 13:13
envy, murders, *d* .... Gal 5:21
DRY
place, and let the *d* .... Gen 1:9
made the sea into *d* .... Ex 14:21
It was *d* on the fleece .... Judg 6:40
will be done in the *d* .... Luke 23:31
DUE
pay all that was *d* .... Matt 18:34
d time Christ died .... Rom 5:6
d season we shall .... Gal 6:9
exalt you in *d* time .... 1 Pet 5:6
DULL
heart of this people *d* .... Is 6:10
people have grown *d* .... Matt 13:15
DUMB
the tongue of the *d* .... Is 35:6
DUST
formed man of the *d* .... Gen 2:7
d you shall return .... Gen 3:19
And repent in *d* .... Job 42:6
that we are *d* .... Ps 103:14
counted as the small *d* .... Is 40:15
city, shake off the *d* .... Matt 10:14
of the man of *d* .... 1 Cor 15:49
DUTY
done what was our *d* .... Luke 17:10
DWELL
Who may *d* in Your holy .... Ps 15:1
"I *d* in the high and .... Is 57:15
"I will *d* in them .... 2 Cor 6:16
that Christ may *d* .... Eph 3:17
men, and He will *d* .... Rev 21:3
DWELLING
built together for a *d* .... Eph 2:22
a foreign country, *d* .... Heb 11:9
DWELLS
He who *d* in the secret .... Ps 91:1
but the Father who *d* .... John 14:10
d all the fullness .... Col 2:9
which righteousness *d* .... 2 Pet 3:13
you, where Satan *d* .... Rev 2:13
DWELT
became flesh and *d* .... John 1:14
By faith he *d* in the .... Heb 11:9
DYING
in the body the *d* .... 2 Cor 4:10

E

EAGLE
fly away like an *e* .... Prov 23:5
The way of an *e* .... Prov 30:19
like a flying *e* .... Rev 4:7
EAGLES
up with wings like *e* .... Is 40:31
e will be gathered .... Matt 24:28
EAGLES'
how I bore you on *e* .... Ex 19:4
EAR
shall pierce his *e* .... Ex 21:6
And the *e* of the wise .... Prov 18:15
e is uncircumcised .... Jer 6:10
you hear in the *e* .... Matt 10:27
cut off his right *e* .... John 18:10
not seen, nor *e* heard .... 1 Cor 2:9
"He who has an *e* .... Rev 2:7
EARLY
Very *e* in the morning .... Mark 16:2
arrived at the tomb *e* .... Luke 24:22
EARNESTLY
He prayed more *e* .... Luke 22:44
e that it would not .... James 5:17
you to contend *e* .... Jude 3
EARS
And hear with their *e* .... Is 6:10
"He who has *e* .... Matt 11:15
they have itching *e* .... 2 Tim 4:3
EARTH
to judge the *e* .... 1 Chr 16:33
foundations of the *e* .... Job 38:4
e is the LORD's .... Ps 24:1
You had formed the *e* .... Ps 90:2
there was ever an *e* .... Prov 8:23
e abides forever .... Eccl 1:4
for the meek of the *e* .... Is 11:4
e is My footstool .... Is 66:1
I will darken the *e* .... Amos 8:9
shall inherit the *e* .... Matt 5:5
heaven and *e* pass .... Matt 5:18
e as it is in heaven .... Matt 6:10
treasures on *e* .... Matt 6:19
then shook the *e* .... Heb 12:26
heaven and a new *e* .... Rev 21:1
EARTHLY
"If I have told you *e* .... John 3:12
that if our *e* house .... 2 Cor 5:1
their mind on *e* things .... Phil 3:19
from above, but is *e* .... James 3:15
EARTHQUAKE
after the wind an *e* .... 1 Kin 19:11
there was a great *e* .... Matt 28:2
EARTHQUAKES
And there will be *e* .... Mark 13:8
EASIER
"Which is *e*, to say .... Mark 2:9
"It is *e* for a camel .... Mark 10:25
EAST
goes toward the *e* .... Gen 2:14
wise men from the *E* .... Matt 2:1
many will come from *e* .... Matt 8:11
will come from the *e* .... Luke 13:29
EAT
you may freely *e* .... Gen 2:16
'You shall not *e* .... Gen 3:17
e this scroll .... Ezek 3:1
life, what you will *e* .... Matt 6:25
give us His flesh to *e* .... John 6:52
one believes he may *e* .... Rom 14:2
e meat nor drink wine .... Rom 14:21
I will never again *e* .... 1 Cor 8:13
neither shall he *e* .... 2 Thess 3:10
EATEN
Have you *e* from the .... Gen 3:11
he was *e* by worms .... Acts 12:23
EATS
receives sinners and *e* .... Luke 15:2
"Whoever *e* My flesh .... John 6:54
e this bread will live .... John 6:58
He who *e*, *e* to the .... Rom 14:6
unworthy manner *e* .... 1 Cor 11:29
EDIFICATION
has given me for *e* .... 2 Cor 13:10
rather than godly *e* .... 1 Tim 1:4
EDIFIES
puffs up, but love *e* .... 1 Cor 8:1
EDIFY
but not all things *e* .... 1 Cor 10:23
EDIFYING
of the body for the *e* .... Eph 4:16
ELDER
against an *e* except .... 1 Tim 5:19
ELDERS
the tradition of the *e* .... Matt 15:2
be rejected by the *e* .... Luke 9:22
they had appointed *e* .... Acts 14:23
e who rule well be .... 1 Tim 5:17
lacking, and appoint *e* .... Titus 1:5
e obtained a good .... Heb 11:2
e who are among you I .... 1 Pet 5:1
I saw twenty-four *e* .... Rev 4:4
ELDERSHIP
of the hands of the *e* .... 1 Tim 4:14
ELECT
gather together His *e* .... Matt 24:31
e have obtained it .... Rom 11:7
e according to the .... 1 Pet 1:2
A chief cornerstone, *e* .... 1 Pet 2:6

ELECTION
- call and *e* sure ... 2 Pet 1:10

ELEMENTS
- weak and beggarly *e* ... Gal 4:9
- *e* will melt with ... 2 Pet 3:10

ELEVEN
- numbered with the *e* ... Acts 1:26

ELOQUENT
- an *e* man and mighty ... Acts 18:24

EMBALM
- to *e* his father ... Gen 50:2

ENCOURAGED
- is, that I may be *e* ... Rom 1:12
- and all may be *e* ... 1 Cor 14:31

END
- make me to know my *e* ... Ps 39:4
- shall keep it to the *e* ... Ps 119:33
- *e* is the way of death ... Prov 14:12
- Declaring the *e* ... Is 46:10
- what shall be the *e* ... Dan 12:8
- the harvest is the *e* ... Matt 13:39
- always, even to the *e* ... Matt 28:20
- He loved them to the *e* ... John 13:1
- For Christ is the *e* ... Rom 10:4
- But the *e* of all ... 1 Pet 4:7
- the latter *e* is worse ... 2 Pet 2:20
- My works until the *e* ... Rev 2:26
- Beginning and the *E* ... Rev 22:13

ENDLESS
- and *e* genealogies ... 1 Tim 1:4
- to the power of an *e* ... Heb 7:16

ENDURANCE
- *e* the race that ... Heb 12:1

ENDURE
- as the sun and moon *e* ... Ps 72:5
- His name shall *e* ... Ps 72:17
- persecuted, we *e* ... 1 Cor 4:12

ENDURED
- he had patiently *e* ... Heb 6:15
- *e* as seeing Him who ... Heb 11:27
- consider Him who *e* ... Heb 12:3

ENDURES
- And His truth *e* ... Ps 100:5
- For His mercy *e* ... Ps 136:1
- But he who *e* to the ... Matt 10:22
- *e* only for a while ... Matt 13:21
- for the food which *e* ... John 6:27
- he has built on it *e* ... 1 Cor 3:14
- hopes all things, *e* ... 1 Cor 13:7
- word of the LORD *e* ... 1 Pet 1:25

ENDURING
- the LORD is clean, *e* ... Ps 19:9

ENEMIES
- the presence of my *e* ... Ps 23:5
- *e* will lick the dust ... Ps 72:9
- to you, love your *e* ... Matt 5:44
- *e* will be those ... Matt 10:36
- *e* we were reconciled ... Rom 5:10
- till He has put all *e* ... 1 Cor 15:25
- were alienated and *e* ... Col 1:21
- His *e* are made His ... Heb 10:13

ENEMY
- If your *e* is hungry ... Prov 25:21
- rejoice over me, my *e* ... Mic 7:8
- and hate your *e* ... Matt 5:43
- last *e* that will be ... 1 Cor 15:26
- become your *e* because ... Gal 4:16
- count him as an *e* ... 2 Thess 3:15
- makes himself an *e* ... James 4:4

ENJOY
- richly all things to *e* ... 1 Tim 6:17
- than to *e* the passing ... Heb 11:25

ENJOYMENT
- So I commended *e* ... Eccl 8:15

ENLIGHTEN
- *E* my eyes ... Ps 13:3

ENLIGHTENED
- those who were once *e* ... Heb 6:4

ENMITY
- And I will put *e* ... Gen 3:15
- the carnal mind is *e* ... Rom 8:7
- in His flesh the *e* ... Eph 2:15

ENRAPTURED
- And always be *e* ... Prov 5:19

ENRICHED
- while you are *e* ... 2 Cor 9:11

ENSNARED
- The wicked is *e* ... Prov 12:13

ENSNARES
- sin which so easily *e* ... Heb 12:1

ENTER
- *E* into His gates ... Ps 100:4
- you will by no means *e* ... Matt 5:20
- "*E* by the narrow ... Matt 7:13
- *e* the kingdom of God ... Matt 19:24
- *E* into the joy of your ... Matt 25:21
- and pray, lest you *e* ... Matt 26:41
- "Strive to *e* through ... Luke 13:24
- who have believed do *e* ... Heb 4:3
- *e* the temple till the ... Rev 15:8

ENTERED
- Then Satan *e* Judas ... Luke 22:3
- through one man sin *e* ... Rom 5:12
- ear heard, Nor have *e* ... 1 Cor 2:9
- the forerunner has *e* ... Heb 6:20
- *e* the Most Holy Place ... Heb 9:12

ENTERS
- If anyone *e* by Me ... John 10:9

ENTHRONED
- You are holy, *E* in ... Ps 22:3

ENTIRELY
- give yourself *e* ... 1 Tim 4:15

ENTREAT
- being defamed, we *e* ... 1 Cor 4:13

ENTREATED
- *e* our God for this ... Ezra 8:23

ENVIOUS
- patriarchs, becoming *e* ... Acts 7:9

ENVY
- *e* slays a simple ... Job 5:2
- *e* is rottenness ... Prov 14:30
- not let your heart *e* ... Prov 23:17
- full of *e* ... Rom 1:29
- not in strife and *e* ... Rom 13:13
- love does not *e* ... 1 Cor 13:4
- *e*, murders ... Gal 5:21
- living in malice and *e* ... Titus 3:3

EPISTLE
- You are our *e* written ... 2 Cor 3:2

EPISTLES
- as also in all his *e* ... 2 Pet 3:16

ERR
- My people Israel to *e* ... Jer 23:13

ERROR
- a sinner from the *e* ... James 5:20
- led away with the *e* ... 2 Pet 3:17
- run greedily in the *e* ... Jude 11

ERRORS
- can understand his *e* ... Ps 19:12

ESCAPE
- *e* all these things ... Luke 21:36
- same, that you will *e* ... Rom 2:3
- make the way of *e* ... 1 Cor 10:13
- how shall we *e* if we ... Heb 2:3

ESCAPED
- after they have *e* ... 2 Pet 2:20

ESTABLISH
- seeking to *e* their own ... Rom 10:3
- faithful, who will *e* ... 2 Thess 3:3
- *E* your hearts ... James 5:8
- a while, perfect, *e* ... 1 Pet 5:10

ESTABLISHED
- Your throne is *e* ... Ps 93:2
- built up In Him and *e* ... Col 2:7
- covenant, which was *e* ... Heb 8:6

ESTEEM
- and we did not *e* ... Is 53:3
- *e* others better than ... Phil 2:3

ESTEEMED
- For what is highly *e* ... Luke 16:15

ESTEEMS
- One person *e* one day ... Rom 14:5

ETERNAL
- *e* God is your refuge ... Deut 33:27
- For man goes to his *e* ... Eccl 12:5
- and inherit *e* life ... Matt 19:29
- in the age to come. *e* ... Mark 10:30
- not perish but have *e* ... John 3:15
- you think you have *e* ... John 5:39
- I give them *e* life ... John 10:28
- "And this is *e* life ... John 17:3
- the gift of God is *e* ... Rom 6:23
- are not seen are *e* ... 2 Cor 4:18
- lay hold on *e* life ... 1 Tim 6:12
- *e* life which was ... 1 John 1:2

ETERNITY
- Also He has put *e* ... Eccl 3:11
- One who inhabits *e* ... Is 57:15

EUNUCH
- of Ethiopia, a *e* ... Acts 8:27

EUNUCHS
- made themselves *e* ... Matt 19:12

EVANGELIST
- of Philip the *e* ... Acts 21:8
- do the work of an *e* ... 2 Tim 4:5

EVANGELISTS
- some prophets, some *e* ... Eph 4:11

EVERLASTING
- from *E* is Your name ... Is 63:16
- awake, Some to *e* life ... Dan 12:2
- not perish but have *e* ... John 3:16
- who sent Me has *e* ... John 5:24
- endures to *e* life ... John 6:27
- in Him may have *e* ... John 6:40
- believes in Me has *e* ... John 6:47
- *e* destruction from ... 2 Thess 1:9

EVIDENCE
- *e* of things not seen ... Heb 11:1

EVIDENT
- *e* that our Lord arose ... Heb 7:14

EVIL
- of good and *e* ... Gen 2:9
- knowing good and *e* ... Gen 3:5
- his heart was only *e* ... Gen 6:5
- I will fear no *e* ... Ps 23:4
- *e* more than good ... Ps 52:3
- To do *e* is like sport ... Prov 10:23
- *e* will bow before the ... Prov 14:19
- Keeping watch on the *e* ... Prov 15:3
- *e* All the days of her ... Prov 31:12
- to those who call *e* ... Is 5:20
- of peace and not of *e* ... Jer 29:11
- Seek good and not *e* ... Amos 5:14
- deliver us from the *e* ... Matt 6:13
- "If you then, being *e* ... Matt 7:11
- *e* treasure brings ... Matt 12:35
- everyone practicing *e* ... John 3:20
- done any good or *e* ... Rom 9:11
- Repay no one *e* for ... Rom 12:17
- provoked, thinks no *e* ... 1 Cor 13:5

EVILDOER
- "If He were not an *e* ... John 18:30
- suffer trouble as an *e* ... 2 Tim 2:9

EVILDOERS
- *e* shall be cut off ... Ps 37:9
- from me, you *e* ... Ps 119:115
- iniquity, A brood of *e* ... Is 1:4
- against you as *e* ... 1 Pet 2:12

EXALT
- *e* His name together ... Ps 34:3
- *E* the humble ... Ezek 21:26
- And he shall *e* himself ... Dan 8:25

EXALTATION
- who rejoice in My *e* ... Is 13:3
- brother glory in his *e* ... James 1:9

EXALTED
- Let God be *e* ... 2 Sam 22:47
- I will be *e* among the ... Ps 46:10
- You are *e* far above ... Ps 97:9
- His name alone is *e* ... Ps 148:13
- valley shall be *e* ... Is 40:4
- "Him God has *e* ... Acts 5:31
- And lest I should be *e* ... 2 Cor 12:7
- also has highly *e* ... Phil 2:9

EXALTS
Righteousness *e* ... Prov 14:34
high thing that *e* ... 2 Cor 10:5
e himself above all ... 2 Thess 2:4

EXAMINE
But let a man *e* ... 1 Cor 11:28
But let each one *e* ... Gal 6:4

EXAMPLE
to make her a public *e* ... Matt 1:19
I have given you an *e* ... John 13:15
youth, but be an *e* ... 1 Tim 4:12
us, leaving us an *e* ... 1 Pet 2:21
are set forth as an *e* ... Jude 7

EXAMPLES
to them as *e* ... 1 Cor 10:11
to you, but being *e* ... 1 Pet 5:3

EXCHANGE
give in *e* for his soul ... Matt 16:26

EXCHANGED
Nor can it be *e* ... Job 28:17
e the truth of God for ... Rom 1:25

EXCUSE
now they have no *e* ... John 15:22
they are without *e* ... Rom 1:20

EXCUSES
began to make *e* ... Luke 14:18

EXECUTE
e judgment also ... John 5:27
e wrath on him who ... Rom 13:4

EXECUTES
e justice for me ... Mic 7:9

EXERCISE
e yourself toward ... 1 Tim 4:7

EXHORT
e him as a father ... 1 Tim 5:1
Speak these things, *e* ... Titus 2:15
e one another ... Heb 3:13

EXHORTATION
he who exhorts, in *e* ... Rom 12:8
to reading, to *e* ... 1 Tim 4:13

EXHORTED
know how we *e* ... 1 Thess 2:11

EXIST
by Your will they *e* ... Rev 4:11

EXPECT
an hour you do not *e* ... Luke 12:40

EXPECTATION
the people were in *e* ... Luke 3:15
a certain fearful *e* ... Heb 10:27

EXPLAIN
no one who could *e* ... Gen 41:24
"*E* this parable to us ... Matt 15:15
to say, and hard to *e* ... Heb 5:11

EXPLAINED
He *e* all things to His ... Mark 4:34

EXPOSED
his deeds should be *e* ... John 3:20

EXPOUNDED
He *e* to them in all ... Luke 24:27

EXPRESS
of His glory and the *e* ... Heb 1:3

EXTORTION
they are full of *e* ... Matt 23:25

EXTORTIONERS
e will inherit ... 1 Cor 6:10

EYE
the ear, But now my *e* ... Job 42:5
guide you with My *e* ... Ps 32:8
e is not satisfied ... Eccl 1:8
the apple of His *e* ... Zech 2:8
if your right *e* ... Matt 5:29
it was said, 'An *e* ... Matt 5:38
plank in your own *e* ... Matt 7:3
e causes you to sin ... Matt 18:9
Or is your *e* evil ... Matt 20:15
the *e* of a needle ... Luke 18:25
the twinkling of an *e* ... 1 Cor 15:52
every *e* will see Him ... Rev 1:7
your eyes with *e* salve ... Rev 3:18

EYES
e will be opened ... Gen 3:5
And my *e* shall behold ... Job 19:27
e are ever toward the ... Ps 25:15
The *e* of the LORD are ... Ps 34:15
I will lift up my *e* ... Ps 121:1
but the *e* of a fool ... Prov 17:24
be wise in his own *e* ... Prov 26:5
You have dove's *e* ... Song 1:15
e have seen the King ... Is 6:5
Who have *e* and see ... Jer 5:21
rims were full of *e* ... Ezek 1:18
You are of purer *e* ... Hab 1:13
blessed are your *e* ... Matt 13:16
"He put clay on my *e* ... John 9:15
e they have closed ... Acts 28:27
E that they should not ... Rom 11:8
have seen with our *e* ... 1 John 1:1
the lust of the *e* ... 1 John 2:16
as snow, and His *e* ... Rev 1:14
creatures full of *e* ... Rev 4:6
horns and seven *e* ... Rev 5:6

EYESERVICE
not with *e* ... Eph 6:6

EYEWITNESSES
the beginning were *e* ... Luke 1:2
e of His majesty ... 2 Pet 1:16

F

FABLES
nor give heed to *f* ... 1 Tim 1:4
cunningly devised *f* ... 2 Pet 1:16

FACE
"For I have seen God *f* ... Gen 32:30
f shone while he ... Ex 34:29
sins have hidden His *f* ... Is 59:2
f shone like the sun ... Matt 17:2
dimly, but then *f* ... 1 Cor 13:12
with unveiled *f* ... 2 Cor 3:18
withstood him to his *f* ... Gal 2:11
They shall see His *f* ... Rev 22:4

FADE
We all *f* as a leaf ... Is 64:6
rich man also will *f* ... James 1:11
and that does not *f* ... 1 Pet 1:4

FADES
withers, the flower *f* ... Is 40:7

FAIL
tittle of the law to *f* ... Luke 16:17
faith should not *f* ... Luke 22:32
they will *f* ... 1 Cor 13:8
Your years will not *f* ... Heb 1:12

FAILING
"men's hearts *f* ... Luke 21:26

FAILS
Love never *f* ... 1 Cor 13:8

FAINT
shall walk and not *f* ... Is 40:31

FAINTS
My soul *f* for Your ... Ps 119:81
And the whole heart *f* ... Is 1:5
the earth, Neither *f* ... Is 40:28

FAITH
shall live by his *f* ... Hab 2:4
you, O you of little *f* ... Matt 6:30
not found such great *f* ... Matt 8:10
that you have no *f* ... Mark 4:40
"Increase our *f* ... Luke 17:5
will He really find *f* ... Luke 18:8
are sanctified by *f* ... Acts 26:18
God is revealed from *f* ... Rom 1:17
f apart from the deeds ... Rom 3:28
his *f* is accounted for ... Rom 4:5
those who are of the *f* ... Rom 4:16
f which we preach ... Rom 10:8
f comes by hearing ... Rom 10:17
and you stand by *f* ... Rom 11:20
in proportion to our *f* ... Rom 12:6
Do you have *f* ... Rom 14:22
though I have all *f* ... 1 Cor 13:2
And now abide *f* ... 1 Cor 13:13
For we walk by *f* ... 2 Cor 5:7
the flesh I live by *f* ... Gal 2:20
f are sons of Abraham ... Gal 3:7
But after *f* has come ... Gal 3:25
of the household of *f* ... Gal 6:10
been saved through *f* ... Eph 2:8
one Lord, one *f* ... Eph 4:5
taking the shield of *f* ... Eph 6:16
your work of *f* ... 1 Thess 1:3
for not all have *f* ... 2 Thess 3:2
the mystery of the *f* ... 1 Tim 3:9
I have kept the *f* ... 2 Tim 4:7
in our common *f* ... Titus 1:4
not being mixed with *f* ... Heb 4:2
f is the substance ... Heb 11:1
without *f* it is ... Heb 11:6
says he has *f* ... James 2:14
Show me your *f* ... James 2:18
and not by *f* only ... James 2:24
f will save the sick ... James 5:15
add to your *f* virtue ... 2 Pet 1:5
the patience and the *f* ... Rev 13:10

FAITHFUL
God, He Is God, the *f* ... Deut 7:9
LORD preserves the *f* ... Ps 31:23
eyes shall be on the *f* ... Ps 101:6
But who can find a *f* ... Prov 20:6
the Holy One who is *f* ... Hos 11:12
"Who then is a *f* ... Matt 24:45
good and *f* servant ... Matt 25:23
"He who is *f* in what ... Luke 16:10
Judged me to be *f* ... Acts 16:15
God is *f* ... 1 Cor 1:9
is my beloved and *f* ... 1 Cor 4:17
But as God is *f* ... 2 Cor 1:18
f brethren in Christ ... Col 1:2
who calls you is *f* ... 1 Thess 5:24
This is a *f* saying and ... 1 Tim 1:15
f High Priest in ... Heb 2:17
He who promised is *f* ... Heb 10:23
He is *f* and just to ... 1 John 1:9
Be *f* until death ... Rev 2:10
words are true and *f* ... Rev 21:5

FAITHFULNESS
I have declared Your *f* ... Ps 40:10
Your *f* also surrounds ... Ps 89:8
f endures to all ... Ps 119:90
Great is Your *f* ... Lam 3:23
unbelief make the *f* ... Rom 3:3

FAITHLESS
"O *f* generation ... Mark 9:19
If we are *f* ... 2 Tim 2:13

FALL
a deep sleep to *f* ... Gen 2:21
Let them *f* by their ... Ps 5:10
righteous man may *f* ... Prov 24:16
But the wicked shall *f* ... Prov 24:16
the blind, both will *f* ... Matt 15:14
the stars will *f* ... Matt 24:29
"I saw Satan *f* ... Luke 10:18
take heed lest he *f* ... 1 Cor 10:12
if they *f* away ... Heb 6:6
lest anyone *f* short of ... Heb 12:15
and rocks, "*F* on us ... Rev 6:16

FALLEN
"Babylon is *f* ... Is 21:9
you have *f* from grace ... Gal 5:4
"Babylon is *f* ... Rev 14:8

FALLING
great drops of blood *f* ... Luke 22:44
f away comes first ... 2 Thess 2:3

FALSE
"You shall not bear *f* ... Ex 20:16
I hate every *f* way ... Ps 119:104
f witness shall perish ... Prov 21:28
"Beware of *f* prophets ... Matt 7:15
f christs and *f* ... Matt 24:24
and we are found *f* ... 1 Cor 15:15
of *f* brethren ... Gal 2:4
f prophets have gone ... 1 John 4:1
mouth of the *f* prophet ... Rev 16:13

FALSEHOOD
For their deceit is *f* ... Ps 119:118
Offspring of *f* ... Is 57:4

FALSELY
of evil against you *f* ... Matt 5:11
f called knowledge ... 1 Tim 6:20

FAMILIES
in you all the *f* ... Gen 12:3

the God of all the *f* ... Jer 31:1
in your seed all the *f* ... Acts 3:25

FAMILY
shall mourn, every *f* ... Zech 12:12
f were baptized ... Acts 16:33

FAMINES
And there will be *f* ... Matt 24:7

FAMISH
righteous soul to *f* ... Prov 10:3

FAMISHED
honorable men are *f* ... Is 5:13

FAR
Your judgments are *f* ... Ps 10:5
Be not *f* from Me ... Ps 22:11
The LORD is *f* from ... Prov 15:29
their heart is *f* from ... Matt 15:8
going to a *f* country ... Mark 13:34
though He is not *f* ... Acts 17:27
you who once were *f* ... Eph 2:13

FARMER
The hard-working *f* ... 2 Tim 2:6
See how the *f* waits ... James 5:7

FASHIONED
have made me and *f* ... Job 10:8

FASHIONS
He *f* their hearts ... Ps 33:15

FAST
f as you do this day ... Is 58:4
f that I have chosen ... Is 58:5
"Moreover, when you *f* ... Matt 6:16
disciples do not *f* ... Matt 9:14
I *f* twice a week ... Luke 18:12

FASTED
'When you *f* and ... Zech 7:5
And when He had *f* ... Matt 4:2

FASTING
by prayer and *f* ... Matt 17:21
give yourselves to *f* ... 1 Cor 7:5

FASTINGS
in sleeplessness, in *f* ... 2 Cor 6:5

FAT
and you will eat the *f* ... Gen 45:18
f is the LORD's ... Lev 3:16

FATHER
man shall leave his *f* ... Gen 2:24
and you shall be a *f* ... Gen 17:4
I was a *f* to the poor ... Job 29:16
A *f* of the fatherless ... Ps 68:5
f pities his children ... Ps 103:13
God, Everlasting *F* ... Is 9:6
You, O LORD, are our *F* ... Is 63:16
time cry to Me, 'My *F* ... Jer 3:4
For I am a *F* to Israel ... Jer 31:9
"A son honors his *f* ... Mal 1:6
Have we not all one *F* ... Mal 2:10
Our *F* in heaven ... Matt 6:9
"He who loves *f* ... Matt 10:37
know the *F* ... Matt 11:27
'He who curses *f* ... Matt 15:4
for One is your *F* ... Matt 23:9
"*F* will be divided ... Luke 12:53
F loves the Son ... John 3:35
F raises the dead ... John 5:21
F judges no one ... John 5:22
He has seen the *F* ... John 6:46
F who sent Me bears ... John 8:18
we have one *F* ... John 8:41
of your *f* the devil ... John 8:44
"I and My *F* are one ... John 10:30
'I am going to the *F* ... John 14:28
came forth from the *F* ... John 16:28
that he might be the *f* ... Rom 4:11
one God and *F* of all ... Eph 4:6
"I will be to Him a *F* ... Heb 1:5
down from the *F* ... James 1:17
if you call on the *F* ... 1 Pet 1:17
and testify that the *F* ... 1 John 4:14

FATHERLESS
the helper of the *f* ... Ps 10:14
He relieves the *f* ... Ps 146:9
do not defend the *f* ... Is 1:23
they may rob the *f* ... Is 10:2
You the *f* finds mercy ... Hos 14:3

FATHER'S
you in My *F* kingdom ... Matt 26:29
I must be about My *F* ... Luke 2:49
F house are many ... John 14:2
that a man has his *f* ... 1 Cor 5:1

FATHERS
the LORD God of our *f* ... Ezra 7:27
f trusted in You ... Ps 22:4
our ears, O God, our *f* ... Ps 44:1
f ate the manna ... John 6:31
of whom are the *f* ... Rom 9:5
unaware that all our *f* ... 1 Cor 10:1

FATNESS
of the root and *f* ... Rom 11:17

FAULT
I have found no *f* ... Luke 23:14
does He still find *f* ... Rom 9:19
of God without *f* ... Phil 2:15

FAULTLESS
covenant had been *f* ... Heb 8:7
to present you *f* ... Jude 24

FAULTS
"I remember my *f* ... Gen 41:9
me from secret *f* ... Ps 19:12

FAVOR
granted me life and *f* ... Job 10:12
His *f* is for life ... Ps 30:5
A good man obtains *f* ... Prov 12:2
and stature, and in *f* ... Luke 2:52
God and having *f* ... Acts 2:47

FAVORED
"Rejoice, highly *f* ... Luke 1:28

FAVORITISM
not show personal *f* ... Luke 20:21
God shows personal *f* ... Gal 2:6

FEAR
live, for I *f* God ... Gen 42:18
to put the dread and *f* ... Deut 2:25
said, "Does Job *f* ... Job 1:9
Yes, you cast off *f* ... Job 15:4
The *f* of the LORD is ... Ps 19:9
of death, I will *f* ... Ps 23:4
Whom shall I *f* ... Ps 27:1
Oh, *f* the LORD ... Ps 34:9
There is no *f* of God ... Ps 36:1
The *f* of the LORD is ... Ps 111:10
The *f* of man brings a ... Prov 29:25
F God and keep His ... Eccl 12:13
Let Him be your *f* ... Is 8:13
"Be strong, do not *f* ... Is 35:4
who would not *f* ... Jer 10:7
f Him who is able ... Matt 10:28
"Do not *f* ... Luke 12:32
"Do you not even *f* ... Luke 23:40
And walking in the *f* ... Acts 9:31
given us a spirit of *f* ... 2 Tim 1:7
those who through *f* ... Heb 2:15
because of His godly *f* ... Heb 5:7
F God ... 1 Pet 2:17
love casts out *f* ... 1 John 4:18

FEARED
He is also to be *f* ... 1 Chr 16:25
f God more than ... Neh 7:2
Yourself, are to be *f* ... Ps 76:7
Then those who *f* ... Mal 3:16

FEARFUL
It is a *f* thing to ... Heb 10:31

FEARFULLY
f and wonderfully ... Ps 139:14

FEARING
sincerity of heart, *f* ... Col 3:22
forsook Egypt, not *f* ... Heb 11:27

FEARS
upright man, one who *f* ... Job 1:8
me from all my *f* ... Ps 34:4
nation whoever *f* ... Acts 10:35
f has not been made ... 1 John 4:18

FEAST
and you shall keep a *f* ... Num 29:12
hate, I despise your *f* ... Amos 5:21
every year at the *F* ... Luke 2:41
when you give a *f* ... Luke 14:13
Now the Passover, a *f* ... John 6:4
great day of the *f* ... John 7:37

FEASTING
go to the house of *f* ... Eccl 7:2

FEASTS
the best places at *f* ... Luke 20:46
spots in your love *f* ... Jude 12

FED
and *f* you with manna ... Deut 8:3
f you with milk and ... 1 Cor 3:2

FEEBLE
strengthened the *f* ... Job 4:4
And there was none *f* ... Ps 105:37
And my flesh is *f* ... Ps 109:24
hang down, and the *f* ... Heb 12:12

FEED
ravens to *f* you there ... 1 Kin 17:4
and *f* your flocks ... Is 61:5
to him, "*F* My lambs ... John 21:15
your enemy hungers, *f* ... Rom 12:20
goods to *f* the poor ... 1 Cor 13:3

FEEDS
your heavenly Father *f* ... Matt 6:26

FEET
all things under his *f* ... Ps 8:6
He makes my *f* like the ... Ps 18:33
You have set my *f* ... Ps 31:8
For their *f* run to ... Prov 1:16
Her *f* go down to death ... Prov 5:5
mountains Are the *f* ... Is 52:7
place of My *f* glorious ... Is 60:13
in that day His *f* ... Zech 14:4
two hands or two *f* ... Matt 18:8
began to wash His *f* ... Luke 7:38
wash the disciples' *f* ... John 13:5
f are swift to shed ... Rom 3:15
beautiful are the *f* ... Rom 10:15
things under His *f* ... 1 Cor 15:27
and having shod your *f* ... Eph 6:15
fell at His *f* as dead ... Rev 1:17

FELLOW
begins to beat his *f* ... Matt 24:49
f citizens with the ... Eph 2:19
Gentiles should be *f* ... Eph 3:6
I am your *f* servant ... Rev 19:10

FELLOWSHIP
doctrine and *f* ... Acts 2:42
were called into the *f* ... 1 Cor 1:9
f has righteousness ... 2 Cor 6:14
the right hand of *f* ... Gal 2:9
And have no *f* with the ... Eph 5:11
of love, if any *f* ... Phil 2:1
and the *f* of His ... Phil 3:10
we say that we have *f* ... 1 John 1:6
the light, we have *f* ... 1 John 1:7

FERVENT
f prayer of a ... James 5:16
will melt with *f* ... 2 Pet 3:10

FERVENTLY
love one another *f* ... 1 Pet 1:22

FEW
let your words be *f* ... Eccl 5:2
and there are *f* ... Matt 7:14
but the laborers are *f* ... Matt 9:37
called, but *f* chosen ... Matt 20:16
"Lord, are there *f* ... Luke 13:23

FIDELITY
but showing all good *f* ... Titus 2:10

FIELD
Let the *f* be joyful ... Ps 96:12
"The *f* is the world ... Matt 13:38
and buys that *f* ... Matt 13:44
you are God's *f* ... 1 Cor 3:9

FIERY
LORD sent *f* serpents ... Num 21:6
shall make them as a *f* ... Ps 21:9
burning *f* furnace ... Dan 3:6
concerning the *f* ... 1 Pet 4:12

FIG
f leaves together ... Gen 3:7
"Look at the *f* ... Luke 21:29
'I saw you under the *f* ... John 1:50

FIGHT
"The LORD will *f* ... Ex 14:14

Our God will f for us ... Neh 4:20
My servants would f ... John 18:36
to him, let us not f ... Acts 23:9
F the good f ... 1 Tim 6:12
have fought the good f ... 2 Tim 4:7

FIGHTS
your God is He who f ... Josh 23:10
because my lord f ... 1 Sam 25:28
f come from among ... James 4:1

FIGS
thornbushes or f ... Matt 7:16
or a grapevine bear f ... James 3:12

FILL
f the earth and subdue ... Gen 1:28
"Do I not f heaven ... Jer 23:24
f this temple with ... Hag 2:7
"F the waterpots ... John 2:7
that He might f ... Eph 4:10

FILLED
the whole earth be f ... Ps 72:19
For they shall be f ... Matt 5:6
"Let the children be f ... Mark 7:27
would gladly have f ... Luke 15:16
being f with all ... Rom 1:29
but be f with the ... Eph 5:18
be warmed and f ... James 2:16

FILTHY
with f garments ... Zech 3:3
poor man in f clothes ... James 2:2
oppressed by the f ... 2 Pet 2:7
let him be f ... Rev 22:11

FIND
sure your sin will f ... Num 32:23
waters, For you will f ... Eccl 11:1
seek, and you will f ... Matt 7:7
f a Babe wrapped ... Luke 2:12
f no fault in this Man ... Luke 23:4
f grace to help in ... Heb 4:16

FINDS
f me f life ... Prov 8:35
f a wife f a good ... Prov 18:22
and he who seeks f ... Matt 7:8
f his life will lose ... Matt 10:39
and he who seeks f ... Luke 11:10

FINGER
written with the f ... Ex 31:18
dip the tip of his f ... Luke 16:24
"Reach your f ... John 20:27

FINISH
he has enough to f ... Luke 14:28
has given Me to f ... John 5:36

FINISHED
f the work which You ... John 17:4
He said, "It is f ... John 19:30
I have f the race ... 2 Tim 4:7

FIRE
rained brimstone and f ... Gen 19:24
to him in a flame of f ... Ex 3:2
who answers by f ... 1 Kin 18:24
LORD was not in the f ... 1 Kin 19:12
We went through f ... Ps 66:12
f goes before Him ... Ps 97:3
burns as the f ... Is 9:18
you walk through the f ... Is 43:2
f that burns all the ... Is 65:5
He break out like f ... Amos 5:6
for conflict by f ... Amos 7:4
like a refiner's f ... Mal 3:2
the Holy Spirit and f ... Matt 3:11
f is not quenched ... Mark 9:44
"I came to send f ... Luke 12:49
tongues, as of f ... Acts 2:3
f taking vengeance ... 2 Thess 1:8
and that burned with f ... Heb 12:18
And the tongue is a f ... James 3:6
vengeance of eternal f ... Jude 7
into the lake of f ... Rev 20:14

FIRM
of the hope f to the ... Heb 3:6

FIRMAMENT
Thus God made the f ... Gen 1:7
f shows His handiwork ... Ps 19:1

FIRST
f father sinned ... Is 43:27
desires to be f ... Matt 20:27
f shall be slave ... Mark 10:44
the gospel must f ... Mark 13:10
evil, of the Jew f ... Rom 2:9
f man Adam became ... 1 Cor 15:45
that we who f trusted ... Eph 1:12
Him because He f ... 1 John 4:19
I am the F and the ... Rev 1:17
you have left your f ... Rev 2:4
is the f resurrection ... Rev 20:5

FIRSTBORN
LORD struck all the f ... Ex 12:29
brought forth her f ... Matt 1:25
that He might be the f ... Rom 8:29
invisible God, the f ... Col 1:15
the beginning, the f ... Col 1:18
witness, the f from ... Rev 1:5

FIRSTFRUITS
also who have the f ... Rom 8:23
and has become the f ... 1 Cor 15:20
Christ the f ... 1 Cor 15:23

FISH
had prepared a great f ... Jon 1:17
belly of the great f ... Matt 12:40
five loaves and two f ... Matt 14:17
and likewise the f ... John 21:13

FISHERS
and I will make you f ... Matt 4:19

FIVE
f smooth stones ... 1 Sam 17:40
about f thousand men ... Matt 14:21
and f were foolish ... Matt 25:2

FIXED
is a great gulf f ... Luke 16:26

FLAME
appeared to him in a f ... Ex 3:2
tormented in this f ... Luke 16:24
and His ministers a f ... Heb 1:7
and His eyes like a f ... Rev 1:14

FLAMES
the LORD divides the f ... Ps 29:7

FLAMING
f sword which turned ... Gen 3:24
in f fire taking ... 2 Thess 1:8

FLATTER
They f with their ... Ps 5:9

FLATTERED
Nevertheless they f ... Ps 78:36

FLATTERING
f speech deceive ... Rom 16:18
swelling words, f ... Jude 16

FLATTERS
f his neighbor Spreads ... Prov 29:5

FLATTERY
shall corrupt with f ... Dan 11:32

FLAVOR
the salt loses its f ... Matt 5:13

FLAX
f He will not quench ... Matt 12:20

FLEE
Or where can I f ... Ps 139:7
And the shadows f ... Song 2:17
who are in Judea f ... Matt 24:16
F sexual immorality ... 1 Cor 6:18
f these things and ... 1 Tim 6:11
devil and he will f ... James 4:7

FLESH
bone of my bones And f ... Gen 2:23
shall become one f ... Gen 2:24
f had corrupted their ... Gen 6:12
f I shall see God ... Job 19:26
My f also will rest in ... Ps 16:9
is wearisome to the f ... Eccl 12:12
And all f shall see it ... Is 40:5
"All f is grass ... Is 40:6
out My Spirit on all f ... Joel 2:28
two shall become one f ... Matt 19:5
were shortened, no f ... Matt 24:22
shall become one f ... Mark 10:8
the Word became f ... John 1:14
I shall give is My f ... John 6:51
f profits nothing ... John 6:63
of God, but with the f ... Rom 7:25
on the things of the f ... Rom 8:5
to the f you will die ... Rom 8:13
f should glory in His ... 1 Cor 1:29
"shall become one f ... 1 Cor 6:16
For the f lusts ... Gal 5:17
have crucified the f ... Gal 5:24
may boast in your f ... Gal 6:13
the lust of the f ... 1 John 2:16
has come in the f ... 1 John 4:2

FLESHLY
f wisdom but by the ... 2 Cor 1:12
f lusts which ... 1 Pet 2:11

FLIES
Dead f putrefy the ... Eccl 10:1

FLOAT
and he made the iron f ... 2 Kin 6:6

FLOCK
lead Joseph like a f ... Ps 80:1
He will feed His f ... Is 40:11
you do not feed the f ... Ezek 34:3
my God, "Feed the f ... Zech 11:4
sheep of the f ... Matt 26:31
"Do not fear, little f ... Luke 12:32
there will be one f ... John 10:16
Shepherd the f of God ... 1 Pet 5:2
examples to the f ... 1 Pet 5:3

FLOOD
the waters of the f ... Gen 7:10
them away like a f ... Ps 90:5
the days before the f ... Matt 24:38
bringing in the f ... 2 Pet 2:5
of his mouth like a f ... Rev 12:15

FLOODS
me, And the f of ... Ps 18:4
f on the dry ground ... Is 44:3
rain descended, the f ... Matt 7:25

FLOURISH
the righteous shall f ... Ps 72:7

FLOW
of his heart will f ... John 7:38

FLOWER
As a f of the field ... Ps 103:15
beauty is a fading f ... Is 28:4
grass withers, the f ... Is 40:7
of man as the f ... 1 Pet 1:24

FLOWERS
f appear on the earth ... Song 2:12

FLOWING
'a land f with milk ... Deut 6:3
the Gentiles like a f ... Is 66:12

FLUTE
play the harp and f ... Gen 4:21

FLUTES
instruments and f ... Ps 150:4

FLUTISTS
harpists, musicians, f ... Rev 18:22

FLY
soon cut off, and we f ... Ps 90:10

FOLLOW
f You wherever You go ... Matt 8:19
He said to him, "F ... Matt 9:9
up his cross, and f ... Mark 8:34
will by no means f ... John 10:5
serves Me, let him f ... John 12:26
that you should f ... 1 Pet 2:21
f the Lamb wherever ... Rev 14:4
and their works f ... Rev 14:13

FOLLOWED
f the LORD my God ... Josh 14:8
we have left all and f ... Mark 10:28

FOLLOWS
f Me shall not walk ... John 8:12

FOLLY
taken much notice of f ... Job 35:15
not turn back to f ... Ps 85:8
F is joy to him who is ... Prov 15:21
F is set in great ... Eccl 10:6

FOOD
you it shall be for f ... Gen 1:29

that lives shall be *f* . . . . Gen 9:3
f which you eat shall . . . . Ezek 4:10
the fields yield no *f* . . . . Hab 3:17
That there may be *f* . . . . Mal 3:10
to give them *f* . . . . Matt 24:45
and you gave Me *f* . . . . Matt 25:35
and he who has *f* . . . . Luke 3:11
have you any *f* . . . . John 21:5
they ate their *f* . . . . Acts 2:46
our hearts with *f* . . . . Acts 14:17
destroy with your *f* . . . . Rom 14:15
f makes my brother . . . . 1 Cor 8:13
the same spiritual *f* . . . . 1 Cor 10:3
sower, and bread for *f* . . . . 2 Cor 9:10
And having *f* and . . . . 1 Tim 6:8
and not solid *f* . . . . Heb 5:12
But solid *f* belongs to . . . . Heb 5:14
of *f* sold his . . . . Heb 12:16
destitute of daily *f* . . . . James 2:15

FOODS
f which God . . . . 1 Tim 4:3

FOOL
f has said in his . . . . Ps 14:1
is like sport to a *f* . . . . Prov 10:23
f is right in his own . . . . Prov 12:15
is too lofty for a *f* . . . . Prov 24:7
whoever says, 'You *f* . . . . Matt 5:22
I have become a *f* . . . . 2 Cor 12:11

FOOLISH
I was so *f* and . . . . Ps 73:22
f pulls it down with . . . . Prov 14:1
f man squanders it . . . . Prov 21:20
Has not God made *f* . . . . 1 Cor 1:20
O *f* Galatians . . . . Gal 3:1
were also once *f* . . . . Titus 3:3
But avoid *f* disputes . . . . Titus 3:9

FOOLISHLY
I speak *f* . . . . 2 Cor 11:21

FOOLISHNESS
F is bound up in the . . . . Prov 22:15
devising of *f* is sin . . . . Prov 24:9
of the cross is *f* . . . . 1 Cor 1:18
Because the *f* of God . . . . 1 Cor 1:25

FOOLS
f despise wisdom . . . . Prov 1:7
folly of *f* is deceit . . . . Prov 14:8
F mock at sin . . . . Prov 14:9
We are *f* for Christ's . . . . 1 Cor 4:10

FOOT
will not allow your *f* . . . . Ps 121:3
f will not stumble . . . . Prov 3:23
From the sole of the *f* . . . . Is 1:6
f causes you to sin . . . . Matt 18:8
you dash your *f* . . . . Luke 4:11
If the *f* should say . . . . 1 Cor 12:15

FOOTSTOOL
Your enemies Your *f* . . . . Ps 110:1
Your enemies Your *f* . . . . Matt 22:44

FORBID
said, "Do not *f* . . . . Mark 9:39
"Can anyone *f* . . . . Acts 10:47
f that I should boast . . . . Gal 6:14

FORBIDDING
f to marry . . . . 1 Tim 4:3

FOREFATHERS
conscience, as my *f* . . . . 2 Tim 1:3

FOREHEADS
put a mark on the *f* . . . . Ezek 9:4
seal of God on their *f* . . . . Rev 9:4
his mark on their *f* . . . . Rev 20:4

FOREIGNER
"I am a *f* and a . . . . Gen 23:4
of me, since I am a *f* . . . . Ruth 2:10
to God except this *f* . . . . Luke 17:18

FOREIGNERS
f who were there . . . . Acts 17:21
longer strangers and *f* . . . . Eph 2:19

FOREKNEW
For whom He *f* . . . . Rom 8:29
His people whom He *f* . . . . Rom 11:2

FOREKNOWLEDGE
purpose and *f* of God . . . . Acts 2:23

FOREORDAINED
He indeed was *f* . . . . 1 Pet 1:20

FORESAW
'I *f* the LORD . . . . Acts 2:25

FORESEEING
f that God would . . . . Gal 3:8

FORESEES
A prudent man *f* . . . . Prov 22:3

FORETOLD
have also *f* these days . . . . Acts 3:24
killed those who *f* . . . . Acts 7:52

FOREVER
and eat, and live *f* . . . . Gen 3:22
to our children *f* . . . . Deut 29:29
LORD sits as King *f* . . . . Ps 29:10
Do not cast us off *f* . . . . Ps 44:23
throne, O God, is *f* . . . . Ps 45:6
"You are a priest *f* . . . . Ps 110:4
His mercy endures *f* . . . . Ps 136:1
of our God stands *f* . . . . Is 40:8
My salvation will be *f* . . . . Is 51:6
will not cast off *f* . . . . Lam 3:31
Like the stars *f* . . . . Dan 12:3
and the glory *f* . . . . Matt 6:13
the Christ remains *f* . . . . John 12:34
who is blessed *f* . . . . 2 Cor 11:31
to whom be glory *f* . . . . Gal 1:5
generation, *f* and ever . . . . Eph 3:21
and Father be glory *f* . . . . Phil 4:20
throne, O God, is *f* . . . . Heb 1:8
lives and abides *f* . . . . 1 Pet 1:23
of darkness *f* . . . . Jude 13
power, Both now and *f* . . . . Jude 25
And they shall reign *f* . . . . Rev 22:5

FOREVERMORE
Blessed be the LORD *f* . . . . Ps 89:52
this time forth and *f* . . . . Ps 113:2
behold, I am alive *f* . . . . Rev 1:18

FORGAVE
to repay, he freely *f* . . . . Luke 7:42
God in Christ *f* . . . . Eph 4:32
even as Christ *f* . . . . Col 3:13

FORGET
f the LORD who . . . . Deut 6:12
I will not *f* Your word . . . . Ps 119:16
If I *f* you . . . . Ps 137:5
My son, do not *f* . . . . Prov 3:1
f the LORD your Maker . . . . Is 51:13
f your work and labor . . . . Heb 6:10

FORGETFULNESS
in the land of *f* . . . . Ps 88:12

FORGETS
and immediately *f* . . . . James 1:24

FORGETTING
f those things which . . . . Phil 3:13

FORGIVE
f their sin and heal . . . . 2 Chr 7:14
good, and ready to *f* . . . . Ps 86:5
And *f* us our debts . . . . Matt 6:12
Father will also *f* . . . . Matt 6:14
his heart, does not *f* . . . . Matt 18:35
Who can *f* sins but God . . . . Mark 2:7
f the sins of any . . . . John 20:23
you ought rather to *f* . . . . 2 Cor 2:7
F me this wrong . . . . 2 Cor 12:13
f us our sins and to . . . . 1 John 1:9

FORGIVEN
sins be *f* them . . . . Mark 4:12
to whom little is *f* . . . . Luke 7:47
f you all trespasses . . . . Col 2:13
your sins are *f* . . . . 1 John 2:12

FORGIVENESS
But there is *f* with . . . . Ps 130:4
preached to you the *f* . . . . Acts 13:38
they may receive *f* . . . . Acts 26:18
His blood, the *f* . . . . Eph 1:7

FORGIVES
f all your iniquities . . . . Ps 103:3
is this who even *f* . . . . Luke 7:49

FORGIVING
tenderhearted, *f* . . . . Eph 4:32
and *f* one another . . . . Col 3:13

FORGOT
Joseph, but *f* . . . . Gen 40:23
They soon *f* His works . . . . Ps 106:13

FORGOTTEN
f the God who . . . . Deut 32:18
not one of them is *f* . . . . Luke 12:6
f the exhortation . . . . Heb 12:5
f that he was . . . . 2 Pet 1:9

FORM
earth was without *f* . . . . Gen 1:2
Who would *f* a god or . . . . Is 44:10
f the light and create . . . . Is 45:7
descended in bodily *f* . . . . Luke 3:22
time, nor seen His *f* . . . . John 5:37
For the *f* of this . . . . 1 Cor 7:31
Who, being in the *f* . . . . Phil 2:6
having a *f* of . . . . 2 Tim 3:5

FORMED
And the LORD God *f* . . . . Gen 2:7
f my inward parts . . . . Ps 139:13
say of him who *f* . . . . Is 29:16
"Before I *f* you in . . . . Jer 1:5
Will the thing *f* . . . . Rom 9:20
until Christ is *f* . . . . Gal 4:19

FORMER
f days better than . . . . Eccl 7:10
f rain to the earth . . . . Hos 6:3
f prophets preached . . . . Zech 1:4
your *f* conduct . . . . Eph 4:22
f things have passed . . . . Rev 21:4

FORMS
clay say to him who *f* . . . . Is 45:9
f the spirit of man . . . . Zech 12:1

FORNICATION
"We were not born of *f* . . . . John 8:41
of the wrath of her *f* . . . . Rev 14:8

FORNICATOR
you know, that no *f* . . . . Eph 5:5
lest there be any *f* . . . . Heb 12:16

FORNICATORS
but *f* and adulterers . . . . Heb 13:4

FORSAKE
But I did not *f* . . . . Ps 119:87
father, And do not *f* . . . . Prov 1:8
of you does not *f* . . . . Luke 14:33
never leave you nor *f* . . . . Heb 13:5

FORSAKEN
My God, why have You *f* . . . . Ps 22:1
seen the righteous *f* . . . . Ps 37:25
a mere moment I have *f* . . . . Is 54:7
God, why have You *f* . . . . Matt 27:46
persecuted, but not *f* . . . . 2 Cor 4:9
for Demas has *f* . . . . 2 Tim 4:10

FORSAKING
f the assembling . . . . Heb 10:25

FORSOOK
f God who made him . . . . Deut 32:15
all the disciples *f* . . . . Matt 26:56
with me, but all *f* . . . . 2 Tim 4:16

FORTRESS
is my rock, my *f* . . . . 2 Sam 22:2
my rock of refuge, a *f* . . . . Ps 31:2

FOUND
f a helper comparable . . . . Gen 2:20
a thousand I have *f* . . . . Eccl 7:28
LORD while He may be *f* . . . . Is 55:6
fruit on it and *f* none . . . . Luke 13:6
he was lost and is *f* . . . . Luke 15:24
f the Messiah" (which . . . . John 1:41
and be *f* in Him . . . . Phil 3:9

FOUNDATION
Of old You laid the *f* . . . . Ps 102:25
the earth without a *f* . . . . Luke 6:49
loved Me before the *f* . . . . John 17:24
I have laid the *f* . . . . 1 Cor 3:10
f can anyone lay than . . . . 1 Cor 3:11
us in Him before the *f* . . . . Eph 1:4
not laying again the *f* . . . . Heb 6:1
Lamb slain from the *f* . . . . Rev 13:8

FOUNDATIONS
when I laid the *f* . . . . Job 38:4
And the *f* of the wall . . . . Rev 21:19

FOUNTAIN
will become in him a *f* ... John 4:14

FOUNTAINS
on that day all the *f* ... Gen 7:11
lead them to living *f* ... Rev 7:17

FRAGRANCE
was filled with the *f* ... John 12:3
we are to God the *f* ... 2 Cor 2:15

FREE
'You will be made *f* ... John 8:33
And having been set *f* ... Rom 6:18
Jesus has made me *f* ... Rom 8:2
is neither slave nor *f* ... Gal 3:28
Christ has made us *f* ... Gal 5:1
he is a slave or *f* ... Eph 6:8

FREED
has died has been *f* ... Rom 6:7

FREEDMAN
slave is the Lord's *f* ... 1 Cor 7:22

FREELY
the garden you may *f* ... Gen 2:16
F you have received ... Matt 10:8
f give us all ... Rom 8:32
the water of life *f* ... Rev 22:17

FRIEND
of Abraham Your *f* ... 2 Chr 20:7
f who sticks closer ... Prov 18:24
a *f* of tax collectors ... Matt 11:19
of you shall have a *f* ... Luke 11:5
f Lazarus sleeps ... John 11:11
he was called the *f* ... James 2:23
wants to be a *f* ... James 4:4

FRIENDS
My *f* scorn me ... Job 16:20
the rich has many *f* ... Prov 14:20
one's life for his *f* ... John 15:13
I have called you *f* ... John 15:15
to forbid any of his *f* ... Acts 24:23

FROGS
your territory with *f* ... Ex 8:2
f coming out of the ... Rev 16:13

FRUIT
showed them the *f* ... Num 13:26
brings forth its *f* ... Ps 1:3
f is better than gold ... Prov 8:19
with good by the *f* ... Prov 12:14
like the first *f* ... Is 28:4
does not bear good *f* ... Matt 3:10
good tree bears good *f* ... Matt 7:17
not drink of this *f* ... Matt 26:29
and blessed is the *f* ... Luke 1:42
life, and bring no *f* ... Luke 8:14
and he came seeking *f* ... Luke 13:6
'And if it bears *f* ... Luke 13:9
branch that bears *f* ... John 15:2
that you bear much *f* ... John 15:8
should go and bear *f* ... John 15:16
God, you have your *f* ... Rom 6:22
that we should bear *f* ... Rom 7:4
But the *f* of the ... Gal 5:22
yields the peaceable *f* ... Heb 12:11
Now the *f* of ... James 3:18
autumn trees without *f* ... Jude 12
tree yielding its *f* ... Rev 22:2

FRUITFUL
them, saying, "Be *f* ... Gen 1:22
wife shall be like a *f* ... Ps 128:3
pleasing Him, being *f* ... Col 1:10

FRUITS
Therefore bear *f* ... Matt 3:8
know them by their *f* ... Matt 7:16
of mercy and good *f* ... James 3:17
which bore twelve *f* ... Rev 22:2

FULFILL
for us to *f* all ... Matt 3:15
f the law of Christ ... Gal 6:2
f my joy by being ... Phil 2:2
and *f* all the good ... 2 Thess 1:11
If you really *f* ... James 2:8

FULFILLED
the law till all is *f* ... Matt 5:18
of the Gentiles are *f* ... Luke 21:24
all things must be *f* ... Luke 24:44
of the law might be *f* ... Rom 8:4
loves another has *f* ... Rom 13:8
For all the law is *f* ... Gal 5:14

FULFILLMENT
love is the *f* of the ... Rom 13:10

FULL
and it was *f* of bones ... Ezek 37:1
whole body will be *f* ... Matt 6:22
your joy may be *f* ... John 15:11
You are already *f* ... 1 Cor 4:8
learned both to be *f* ... Phil 4:12

FULLNESS
f we have all received ... John 1:16
But when the *f* of the ... Gal 4:4
filled with all the *f* ... Eph 3:19
Him dwells all the *f* ... Col 2:9

FURNACE
you out of the iron *f* ... Deut 4:20
of a burning fiery *f* ... Dan 3:6
cast them into the *f* ... Matt 13:42
the smoke of a great *f* ... Rev 9:2

FURY
Thus will I spend My *f* ... Ezek 6:12
in anger and *f* On the ... Mic 5:15

G

GAIN
and to die is *g* ... Phil 1:21
rubbish, that I may *g* ... Phil 3:8
is a means of *g* ... 1 Tim 6:5
contentment is great *g* ... 1 Tim 6:6
for dishonest *g* ... 1 Pet 5:2

GAINED
g five more talents ... Matt 25:20

GAINS
g the whole world ... Matt 16:26

GALL
They also gave me *g* ... Ps 69:21
wine mingled with *g* ... Matt 27:34

GAP
and stand in the *g* ... Ezek 22:30

GARDEN
LORD God planted a *g* ... Gen 2:8
g enclosed Is my ... Song 4:12
Eden, the *g* of God ... Ezek 28:13
where there was a *g* ... John 18:1
g a new tomb in ... John 19:41

GARMENT
the hem of His *g* ... Matt 9:20
on a wedding *g* ... Matt 22:11
cloth on an old *g* ... Mark 2:21
all grow old like a *g* ... Heb 1:11
hating even the *g* ... Jude 23

GARMENTS
g did not wear out on ... Deut 8:4
They divide My *g* ... Ps 22:18
from Edom, With dyed *g* ... Is 63:1
"Take away the filthy *g* ... Zech 3:4
man clothed in soft *g* ... Matt 11:8
spread their *g* on the ... Matt 21:8
and divided His *g* ... Matt 27:35
by them in shining *g* ... Luke 24:4
g are moth-eaten ... James 5:2
be clothed in white *g* ... Rev 3:5

GATE
by the narrow *g* ... Matt 7:13
by the Sheep *G* a pool ... John 5:2
laid daily at the *g* ... Acts 3:2
suffered outside the *g* ... Heb 13:12

GATES
up your heads, O you *g* ... Ps 24:7
The LORD loves the *g* ... Ps 87:2
is known in the *g* ... Prov 31:23
Go through the *g* ... Is 62:10
and the *g* of Hades ... Matt 16:18
wall with twelve *g* ... Rev 21:12
g were twelve pearls ... Rev 21:21
g shall not be shut ... Rev 21:25

GATHER
And a time to *g* stones ... Eccl 3:5
g the lambs with His ... Is 40:11
g His wheat into the ... Matt 3:12
sow nor reap nor *g* ... Matt 6:26
Do men *g* grapes from ... Matt 7:16
g where I have not ... Matt 25:26
g together His ... Mark 13:27

GATHERED
g some of every kind ... Matt 13:47
the nations will be *g* ... Matt 25:32

GATHERING
g together of the ... Gen 1:10
g together to Him ... 2 Thess 2:1

GATHERS
The Lord GOD, who *g* ... Is 56:8
together, as a hen *g* ... Matt 23:37

GAVE
to be with me, she *g* ... Gen 3:12
g You this authority ... Matt 21:23
that He *g* His only ... John 3:16
Those whom You *g* ... John 17:12
but God *g* the increase ... 1 Cor 3:6
g Himself for our sins ... Gal 1:4
g Himself for me ... Gal 2:20
g Himself for it ... Eph 5:25

GENERATION
One *g* passes away ... Eccl 1:4
who will declare His *g* ... Is 53:8
and adulterous *g* ... Matt 12:39
this *g* will by no ... Matt 24:34
from this perverse *g* ... Acts 2:40
But you are a chosen *g* ... 1 Pet 2:9

GENERATIONS
be remembered in all *g* ... Ps 45:17
g will call me blessed ... Luke 1:48

GENEROUS
no longer be called *g* ... Is 32:5

GENTILES
g were separated ... Gen 10:5
As a light to the *G* ... Is 42:6
g shall come to your ... Is 60:3
all these things the *G* ... Matt 6:32
into the way of the *G* ... Matt 10:5
revelation to the *G* ... Luke 2:32
g are fulfilled ... Luke 21:24
My name before *G* ... Acts 9:15
poured out on the *G* ... Acts 10:45
a light to the *G* ... Acts 13:47
also the God of the *G* ... Rom 3:29
mystery among the *G* ... Col 1:27
a teacher of the *G* ... 1 Tim 2:7

GENTLE
from Me, for I am *g* ... Matt 11:29
we were *g* among ... 1 Thess 2:7
to be peaceable, *g* ... Titus 3:2
only to the good and *g* ... 1 Pet 2:18
ornament of a *g* ... 1 Pet 3:4

GENTLENESS
love and a spirit of *g* ... 1 Cor 4:21
g, self-control ... Gal 5:23
all lowliness and *g* ... Eph 4:2
Let your *g* be known to ... Phil 4:5
love, patience, *g* ... 1 Tim 6:11

GHOST
supposed it was a *g* ... Mark 6:49

GIFT
it is the *g* of God ... Eccl 3:13
"If you knew the *g* ... John 4:10
but the *g* of God is ... Rom 6:23
each one has his own *g* ... 1 Cor 7:7
though I have the *g* ... 1 Cor 13:2
it is the *g* of God ... Eph 2:8
Do not neglect the *g* ... 1 Tim 4:14
you to stir up the *g* ... 2 Tim 1:6
tasted the heavenly *g* ... Heb 6:4
Every good *g* and ... James 1:17

GIFTS
You have received *g* ... Ps 68:18
and Seba Will offer *g* ... Ps 72:10
how to give good *g* ... Matt 7:11
rich putting their *g* ... Luke 21:1
g differing ... Rom 12:6
are diversities of *g* ... 1 Cor 12:4
and desire spiritual *g* ... 1 Cor 14:1
captive, And gave *g* ... Eph 4:8

GIRD
G Your sword upon Your ... Ps 45:3

- and another will *g* ... John 21:18
- Therefore *g* up the ... 1 Pet 1:13

GIRDED
- a towel and *g* Himself ... John 13:4

GIVE
- *g* you the desires ... Ps 37:4
- Yes, the LORD will *g* ... Ps 85:12
- *G* me understanding ... Ps 119:34
- "*G* to him who asks ... Matt 5:42
- *G* us this day our ... Matt 6:11
- what you have and *g* ... Matt 19:21
- authority I will *g* ... Luke 4:6
- *g* them eternal life ... John 10:28
- commandment I *g* ... John 13:34
- but what I do have I *g* ... Acts 3:6
- *g* us all things ... Rom 8:32
- *G* no offense ... 1 Cor 10:32
- *g* him who has need ... Eph 4:28
- *g* thanks to God ... 2 Thess 2:13
- *g* yourself entirely ... 1 Tim 4:15

GIVEN
- to him more will be *g* ... Matt 13:12
- has, more will be *g* ... Matt 25:29
- to whom much is *g* ... Luke 12:48
- *g* Me I should lose ... John 6:39
- Spirit was not yet *g* ... John 7:39

GIVES
- *g* life to the world ... John 6:33
- "All that the Father *g* ... John 6:37
- The good shepherd *g* ... John 10:11
- not as the world *g* ... John 14:27
- *g* us richly all things ... 1 Tim 6:17
- who *g* to all liberally ... James 1:5
- *g* grace to the humble ... James 4:6

GLAD
- streams shall make *g* ... Ps 46:4
- I was *g* when they said ... Ps 122:1
- make merry and be *g* ... Luke 15:32
- he saw it and was *g* ... John 8:56

GLADNESS
- me hear joy and *g* ... Ps 51:8
- Serve the LORD with *g* ... Ps 100:2

GLORIFIED
- and they *g* the God of ... Matt 15:31
- Jesus was not yet *g* ... John 7:39
- when Jesus was *g* ... John 12:16
- this My Father is *g* ... John 15:8
- "I have *g* You on the ... John 17:4
- *g* His Servant Jesus ... Acts 3:13
- these He also *g* ... Rom 8:30
- things God may be *g* ... 1 Pet 4:11

GLORIFY
- *g* your Father in ... Matt 5:16
- "Father, *g* Your name ... John 12:28
- "He will *g* Me ... John 16:14
- "And now, O Father, *g* ... John 17:5
- death he would *g* ... John 21:19
- therefore *g* God in ... 1 Cor 6:20
- also Christ did not *g* ... Heb 5:5
- ashamed, but let him *g* ... 1 Pet 4:16

GLORIOUS
- *G* things are spoken ... Ps 87:3
- *g* splendor of Your ... Ps 145:5
- habitation, holy and *g* ... Is 63:15
- it to Himself a *g* ... Eph 5:27
- be conformed to His *g* ... Phil 3:21
- *g* appearing of our ... Titus 2:13

GLORY
- show me Your *g* ... Ex 33:18
- *g* has departed from ... 1 Sam 4:21
- Who is this King of *g* ... Ps 24:8
- Your power and Your *g* ... Ps 63:2
- wise shall inherit *g* ... Prov 3:35
- It is the *g* of God to ... Prov 25:2
- *g* I will not give ... Is 42:8
- that they may have *g* ... Matt 6:2
- the power and the *g* ... Matt 6:13
- *g* was not arrayed ... Matt 6:29
- will come in the *g* ... Matt 16:27
- power and great *g* ... Matt 24:30
- "*G* to God in the ... Luke 2:14
- and we beheld His *g* ... John 1:14
- and manifested His *g* ... John 2:11
- not seek My own *g* ... John 8:50
- "Give God the *g* ... John 9:24
- *g* which I had with ... John 17:5
- *g* which You gave Me ... John 17:22
- he did not give *g* ... Acts 12:23
- doing good seek for *g* ... Rom 2:7
- fall short of the *g* ... Rom 3:23
- in faith, giving *g* ... Rom 4:20
- the adoption, the *g* ... Rom 9:4
- the riches of His *g* ... Rom 9:23
- God, alone wise, be *g* ... Rom 16:27
- who glories, let him *g* ... 1 Cor 1:31
- to His riches in g ... Phil 4:19
- appear with Him in *g* ... Col 3:4
- For you are our *g* ... 1 Thess 2:20
- many sons to *g* ... Heb 2:10
- grass, And all the *g* ... 1 Pet 1:24
- to whom belong the *g* ... 1 Pet 4:11
- for the Spirit of *g* ... 1 Pet 4:14
- the presence of His *g* ... Jude 24
- *g* Lord, to receive *g* ... Rev 4:11
- *g* of God illuminated ... Rev 21:23

GLORYING
- Your *g* is not good ... 1 Cor 5:6

GLUTTON
- you say, 'Look, a *g* ... Luke 7:34

GLUTTONS
- *g* shames his ... Prov 28:7
- evil beasts, lazy *g* ... Titus 1:12

GNASHING
- will be weeping and *g* ... Matt 8:12

GO
- 'Let My people *g* ... Ex 5:1
- For wherever you *g* ... Ruth 1:16
- Those who *g* down to ... Ps 107:23
- Where can I *g* from ... Ps 139:7
- to whom shall we *g* ... John 6:68
- *g* you cannot come ... John 8:21
- I *g* to prepare a place ... John 14:2
- shall *g* out no more ... Rev 3:12

GOADS
- to kick against the *g* ... Acts 9:5

GOAL
- I press toward the *g* ... Phil 3:14

GOATS
- his sheep from the *g* ... Matt 25:32
- with the blood of *g* ... Heb 9:12
- *g* could take away ... Heb 10:4

GOD
- *G* created the heavens ... Gen 1:1
- Abram of *G* Most ... Gen 14:19
- and I will be their *G* ... Gen 17:8
- "I am the LORD your *G* ... Ex 20:2
- *G* is a consuming fire ... Deut 4:24
- If the LORD is *G* ... 1 Kin 18:21
- *G* is greater than all ... 2 Chr 2:5
- You have been My *G* ... Ps 22:10
- *G* is our refuge ... Ps 46:1
- *G* is in the midst of ... Ps 46:5
- me a clean heart, O *G* ... Ps 51:10
- Our G is the *G* ... Ps 68:20
- Who is so great a *G* ... Ps 77:13
- Restore us, O *G* ... Ps 80:7
- You alone are *G* ... Ps 86:10
- Exalt the LORD our *G* ... Ps 99:9
- Yes, our *G* is merciful ... Ps 116:5
- For *G* is in heaven ... Eccl 5:2
- Counselor, Mighty *G* ... Is 9:6
- *G* is my salvation ... Is 12:2
- stricken, Smitten by *G* ... Is 53:4
- "*G* with us ... Matt 1:23
- in *G* my Savior ... Luke 1:47
- the Word was with *G* ... John 1:1
- "For *G* so loved the ... John 3:16
- "*G* is Spirit ... John 4:24
- "My Lord and my *G* ... John 20:28
- Christ Is the Son of *G* ... Acts 8:37
- Indeed, let *G* be true ... Rom 3:4
- If *G* is for us ... Rom 8:31
- *G* is faithful ... 1 Cor 1:9
- *G* shall supply all ... Phil 4:19
- and I will be their *G* ... Heb 8:10
- *G* is a consuming fire ... Heb 12:29
- for *G* is love ... 1 John 4:8
- No one has seen *G* ... 1 John 4:12
- *G* Himself will be ... Rev 21:3
- and I will be his *G* ... Rev 21:7

GODDESS
- after Ashtoreth the *g* ... 1 Kin 11:5
- of the great *g* Diana ... Acts 19:35

GODHEAD
- eternal power and *G* ... Rom 1:20
- the fullness of the *G* ... Col 2:9

GODLINESS
- is the mystery of *g* ... 1 Tim 3:16
- *g* with contentment ... 1 Tim 6:6
- having a form of *g* ... 2 Tim 3:5
- to perseverance *g* ... 2 Pet 1:6

GODLY
- who desire to live *g* ... 2 Tim 3:12
- reverence and *g* fear ... Heb 12:28
- to deliver the *g* ... 2 Pet 2:9

GODS
- God is God of *g* ... Deut 10:17
- I said, "You are *g* ... Ps 82:6
- yourselves with *g* ... Is 57:5
- If He called them *g* ... John 10:35
- *g* have come down to ... Acts 14:11

GOLD
- *g* I do not have ... Acts 3:6
- with braided hair or *g* ... 1 Tim 2:9
- a man with *g* rings ... James 2:2
- Your *g* and silver are ... James 5:3
- more precious than *g* ... 1 Pet 1:7
- like silver or *g* ... 1 Pet 1:18
- of the city was pure *g* ... Rev 21:21

GONE
- like sheep have *g* ... Is 53:6

GOOD
- God saw that it was *g* ... Gen 1:10
- but God meant it for *g* ... Gen 50:20
- indeed accept *g* ... Job 2:10
- is none who does *g* ... Ps 14:1
- Truly God is *g* to ... Ps 73:1
- *g* word makes it glad ... Prov 12:25
- on the evil and the *g* ... Prov 15:3
- A merry heart does *g* ... Prov 17:22
- Learn to do *g* ... Is 1:17
- talked to me, with *g* ... Zech 1:13
- they may see your *g* ... Matt 5:16
- "A *g* man out of the ... Matt 12:35
- No one is *g* but One ... Matt 19:17
- For she has done a *g* ... Matt 26:10
- *g* works I have shown ... John 10:32
- went about doing *g* ... Acts 10:38
- *g* man someone would ... Rom 5:7
- in my flesh) nothing *g* ... Rom 7:18
- overcome evil with *g* ... Rom 12:21
- Jesus for *g* works ... Eph 2:10
- fruitful in every *g* ... Col 1:10
- know that the law is *g* ... 1 Tim 1:8
- For this is *g* and ... 1 Tim 2:3
- bishop, he desires a *g* ... 1 Tim 3:1
- for this is *g* and ... 1 Tim 5:4
- prepared for every *g* ... 2 Tim 2:21
- Every *g* gift and ... James 1:17

GOODNESS
- "I will make all My *g* ... Ex 33:19
- and abounding in *g* ... Ex 34:6
- "You are my Lord, My *g* ... Ps 16:2
- Surely *g* and mercy ... Ps 23:6
- That I would see the *g* ... Ps 27:13
- the riches of His *g* ... Rom 2:4
- consider the *g* and ... Rom 11:22
- kindness, *g* ... Gal 5:22

GOSPEL
- The beginning of the *g* ... Mark 1:1
- and believe in the *g* ... Mark 1:15
- *g* must first be ... Mark 13:10
- separated to the *g* ... Rom 1:1
- not ashamed of the *g* ... Rom 1:16
- to a different *g* ... Gal 1:6
- the everlasting *g* ... Rev 14:6

GOVERNMENT
- And the *g* will be upon ... Is 9:6

GRACE
- But Noah found *g* ... Gen 6:8
- *G* is poured upon Your ... Ps 45:2

- The LORD will give *g* ... Ps 84:11
- the Spirit of *g* ... Zech 12:10
- and the *g* of God was ... Luke 2:40
- *g* and truth came ... John 1:17
- And great *g* was upon ... Acts 4:33
- receive abundance of *g* ... Rom 5:17
- is no longer *g* ... Rom 11:6
- For you know the *g* ... 2 Cor 8:9
- *g* is sufficient ... 2 Cor 12:9
- The *g* of the Lord ... 2 Cor 13:14
- you have fallen from *g* ... Gal 5:4
- to the riches of His *g* ... Eph 1:7
- *g* you have been ... Eph 2:8
- *g* was given according ... Eph 4:7
- *G* be with all those ... Eph 6:24
- shaken, let us have *g* ... Heb 12:28
- But He gives more *g* ... James 4:6
- but grow in the *g* ... 2 Pet 3:18

GRACIOUS

- he said, "God be *g* ... Gen 43:29
- I will be *g* to whom I ... Ex 33:19
- at the *g* words which ... Luke 4:22
- that the Lord is *g* ... 1 Pet 2:3

GRAFTED

- In unbelief, will be *g* ... Rom 11:23

GRAIN

- it treads out the *g* ... Deut 25:4
- be revived like *g* ... Hos 14:7
- to pluck heads of *g* ... Matt 12:1
- unless a *g* of wheat ... John 12:24

GRAPES

- brought forth wild *g* ... Is 5:2
- have eaten sour *g* ... Ezek 18:2
- Do men gather *g* ... Matt 7:16
- *g* are fully ripe ... Rev 14:18

GRASS

- The *g* withers ... Is 40:7
- so clothes the *g* ... Matt 6:30
- "All Flesh is as *g* ... 1 Pet 1:24

GRAVE

- my soul up from the *g* ... Ps 30:3
- And they made His *g* ... Is 53:9
- the power of the *g* ... Hos 13:14

GRAVES

- *g* were opened ... Matt 27:52
- *g* which are not ... Luke 11:44
- *g* will hear His voice ... John 5:28

GRAY

- the man of *g* hairs ... Deut 32:25

GREAT

- and make your name *g* ... Gen 12:2
- For the LORD is *g* ... 1 Chr 16:25
- Who does *g* things ... Job 5:9
- *g* is the Holy One ... Is 12:6
- *G* is Your faithfulness ... Lam 3:23
- he shall be called *g* ... Matt 5:19
- one pearl of *g* price ... Matt 13:46
- desires to become *g* ... Matt 20:26
- *g* drops of blood ... Luke 22:44
- appearing of our *g* ... Titus 2:13
- *g* men, the rich men ... Rev 6:15
- Mystery, Babylon the *G* ... Rev 17:5
- the dead, small and *g* ... Rev 20:12

GREATER

- of heaven is *g* ... Matt 11:11
- place there is One *g* ... Matt 12:6
- *g* than Jonah is here ... Matt 12:41
- *g* than Solomon is ... Matt 12:42
- a servant is not *g* ... John 13:16
- "*G* love has no one ... John 15:13
- 'A servant is not *g* ... John 15:20
- who prophesies is *g* ... 1 Cor 14:5
- God is *g* ... 1 John 3:20
- witness of God is *g* ... 1 John 5:9

GREATEST

- little child is the *g* ... Matt 18:4
- but the *g* of these is ... 1 Cor 13:13

GREATNESS

- is the exceeding *g* ... Eph 1:19

GREED

- part is full of *g* ... Luke 11:39

GREEDINESS

- all uncleanness with *g* ... Eph 4:19

GREEDY

- of everyone who is *g* ... Prov 1:19
- not violent, not *g* ... 1 Tim 3:3

GREEK

- written in Hebrew, *G* ... John 19:20
- and also for the *G* ... Rom 1:16
- is neither Jew not *G* ... Gal 3:28

GREEN

- lie down in *g* pastures ... Ps 23:2

GRIEF

- and acquainted with *g* ... Is 53:3
- joy and not with *g* ... Heb 13:17

GRIEVE

- *g* the Holy Spirit ... Eph 4:30

GRIEVED

- earth, and He was *g* ... Gen 6:6
- *g* His Holy Spirit ... Is 63:10
- with anger, being *g* ... Mark 3:5

GROAN

- even we ourselves *g* ... Rom 8:23
- who are in this tent *g* ... 2 Cor 5:4

GROANING

- I am weary with my *g* ... Ps 6:6
- Then Jesus, again *g* ... John 11:38

GROANINGS

- *g* which cannot ... Rom 8:26

GROUND

- "Cursed is the *g* ... Gen 3:17
- you stand is holy *g* ... Ex 3:5
- up your fallow *g* ... Jer 4:3
- others fell on good *g* ... Matt 13:8
- bought a piece of *g* ... Luke 14:18
- God, the pillar and *g* ... 1 Tim 3:15

GROUNDED

- being rooted and *g* ... Eph 3:17

GROW

- truth in love, may *g* ... Eph 4:15
- but *g* in the grace and ... 2 Pet 3:18

GRUDGINGLY

- in his heart, not *g* ... 2 Cor 9:7

GUARANTEE

- in our hearts as a *g* ... 2 Cor 1:22
- us the Spirit as a *g* ... 2 Cor 5:5
- who is the *g* of our ... Eph 1:14

GUIDE

- He will be our *g* ... Ps 48:14
- *g* our feet into the ... Luke 1:79
- has come, He will *g* ... John 16:13

GUIDES

- to you, blind *g* ... Matt 23:16

GUILT

- of your fathers' *g* ... Matt 23:32

GUILTLESS

- *g* who takes His name ... Ex 20:7
- have condemned the *g* ... Matt 12:7

GUILTY

- "We are truly *g* ... Gen 42:21
- world may become *g* ... Rom 3:19
- in one point, he is *g* ... James 2:10

GULF

- you there is a great *g* ... Luke 16:26

H

HABITATION

- Is God in His holy *h* ... Ps 68:5
- but He blesses the *h* ... Prov 3:33
- Jerusalem, a quiet *h* ... Is 33:20
- from His holy *h* ... Zech 2:13
- be clothed with our *h* ... 2 Cor 5:2

HADES

- be brought down to *H* ... Matt 11:23
- *H* shall not ... Matt 16:18
- in torments in *H* ... Luke 16:23
- not leave my soul in *H* ... Acts 2:27
- I have the keys of *H* ... Rev 1:18
- *H* were cast into the ... Rev 20:14

HAIL

- of the plague of the *h* ... Rev 16:21

HAIR

- you cannot make one *h* ... Matt 5:36
- "But not a *h* of your ... Luke 21:18
- not with braided *h* ... 1 Tim 2:9
- *h* like women's *h* ... Rev 9:8

HAIRS

- "But the very *h* ... Matt 10:30

HALLOWED

- the Sabbath day and *h* ... Ex 20:11
- who is holy shall be *h* ... Is 5:16
- heaven, *H* be Your name ... Matt 6:9

HAND

- the *h* of God was ... 1 Sam 5:11
- My times are in Your *h* ... Ps 31:15
- "Sit at My right *h* ... Ps 110:1
- heart is in the *h* ... Prov 21:1
- Whatever your *h* ... Eccl 9:10
- is at his right *h* ... Eccl 10:2
- do not withhold your *h* ... Eccl 11:6
- My *h* has laid the ... Is 48:13
- Behold, the LORD's *h* ... Is 59:1
- are the work of Your *h* ... Is 64:8
- "Am I a God near at *h* ... Jer 23:23
- of heaven is at *h* ... Matt 3:2
- if your right *h* ... Matt 5:30
- do not let your left *h* ... Matt 6:3
- *h* causes you to sin ... Mark 9:43
- sitting at the right *h* ... Mark 14:62
- at the right *h* of God ... Acts 7:55
- The Lord is at *h* ... Phil 4:5
- "Sit at My right *h* ... Heb 1:13
- down at the right *h* ... Heb 10:12

HANDIWORK

- firmament shows His *h* ... Ps 19:1

HANDLE

- *H* Me and see ... Luke 24:39
- do not taste, do not *h* ... Col 2:21

HANDLED

- and our hands have *h* ... 1 John 1:1

HANDS

- took his life in his *h* ... 1 Sam 19:5
- but His *h* make whole ... Job 5:18
- They pierced My *h* ... Ps 22:16
- *h* formed the dry land ... Ps 95:5
- than having two *h* ... Matt 18:8
- "Behold My *h* and ... Luke 24:39
- *h* the print of the ... John 20:25
- his *h* what is good ... Eph 4:28
- the laying on of the *h* ... 1 Tim 4:14
- to fall into the *h* ... Heb 10:31

HANDWRITING

- having wiped out the *h* ... Col 2:14

HANGED

- went and *h* himself ... Matt 27:5

HANGS

- *h* the earth on nothing ... Job 26:7
- Is everyone who *h* ... Gal 3:13

HAPPY

- *H* is the man who has ... Ps 127:5

HARD

- I knew you to be a *h* ... Matt 25:24
- "This is a *h* saying ... John 6:60
- are some things *h* ... 2 Pet 3:16

HARDEN

- But I will *h* his heart ... Ex 4:21
- *h* your hearts as ... Heb 3:8

HARDENED

- But Pharaoh *h* his ... Ex 8:32
- their heart was *h* ... Mark 6:52
- and *h* their hearts ... John 12:40
- lest any of you be *h* ... Heb 3:13

HARDENS

- whom He wills He *h* ... Rom 9:18

HARDSHIP

- *h* as a good soldier ... 2 Tim 2:3

HARLOT

- of a *h* named Rahab ... Josh 2:1
- *h* is one body with ... 1 Cor 6:16
- of the great *h* who ... Rev 17:1

HARLOTRIES

- Let her put away her *h* ... Hos 2:2

HARLOTRY

- are the children of *h* ... Hos 2:4
- For the spirit of *h* ... Hos 5:4

HARLOTS
h enter the .... Matt 21:31
Great, The Mother of *H*. .... Rev 17:5
HARP
Lamb, each having a *h* .... Rev 5:8
HARPS
We hung our *h* Upon the .... Ps 137:2
HARVEST
Seedtime and *h* .... Gen 8:22
"The *h* is past .... Jer 8:20
h truly is plentiful .... Matt 9:37
sickle, because the *h*. .... Mark 4:29
already white for *h*. .... John 4:35
HASTENS
and he sins who *h* .... Prov 19:2
HASTILY
utter anything *h* .... Eccl 5:2
HASTY
Do you see a man *h* .... Prov 29:20
HATE
love the LORD, *h* evil .... Ps 97:10
h every false way .... Ps 119:104
h the double-minded .... Ps 119:113
I *h* and abhor lying .... Ps 119:163
love, And a time to *h* .... Eccl 3:8
You who *h* good and .... Mic 3:2
either he will *h* .... Matt 6:24
HATED
But Esau I have *h* .... Mal 1:3
"And you will be *h* .... Matt 10:22
have seen and also *h* .... John 15:24
but Esau I have *h* .... Rom 9:13
For no one ever *h* .... Eph 5:29
HATEFUL
h woman when she is .... Prov 30:23
in malice and envy, *h* .... Titus 3:3
HATERS
backbiters, *h* of God .... Rom 1:30
HATES
six things the LORD *h* .... Prov 6:16
lose it, and he who *h* .... John 12:25
"If the world *h* .... John 15:18
h his brother is .... 1 John 2:11
HAUGHTY
bring down *h* looks .... Ps 18:27
my heart is not *h* .... Ps 131:1
h spirit before a fall .... Prov 16:18
HEAD
He shall bruise your *h* .... Gen 3:15
and gave Him to be *h*. .... Eph 1:22
For the husband is *h* .... Eph 5:23
HEAL
O LORD, *h* me .... Ps 6:2
h your backslidings .... Jer 3:22
torn, but He will *h* .... Hos 6:1
"*H* the sick .... Matt 10:8
So that I should *h* .... Matt 13:15
sent Me to *h* the .... Luke 4:18
Physician, *h* yourself .... Luke 4:23
HEALED
And return and be *h*. .... Is 6:10
His stripes we are *h* .... Is 53:5
"When I would have *h* .... Hos 7:1
and He *h* them .... Matt 4:24
that you may be *h* .... James 5:16
his deadly wound was *h*. .... Rev 13:3
HEALING
shall arise With *h*. .... Mal 4:2
and *h* all kinds of .... Matt 4:23
tree were for the *h* .... Rev 22:2
HEALINGS
to another gifts of *h*. .... 1 Cor 12:9
HEALS
h all your diseases .... Ps 103:3
Jesus the Christ *h*. .... Acts 9:34
HEALTH
all things and be in *h* .... 3 John 2
HEAR
"*H*, O Israel .... Deut 6:4
Him you shall *h* .... Deut 18:15
H me when I call .... Ps 4:1
O You who *h* prayer .... Ps 65:2
ear, shall He not *h* .... Ps 94:9
h rather than to give .... Eccl 5:1
'Hearing you will *h*. .... Matt 13:14
heed what you *h* .... Mark 4:24
that God does not *h* .... John 9:31
And how shall they *h* .... Rom 10:14
man be swift to *h* .... James 1:19
h what the Spirit says .... Rev 2:7
HEARD
h their cry because of .... Ex 3:7
that they will be *h*. .... Matt 6:7
h the word believed .... Acts 4:4
not seen, nor ear *h* .... 1 Cor 2:9
things that you have *h* .... 2 Tim 2:2
the word which they *h* .... Heb 4:2
which we have *h* .... 1 John 1:1
Lord's Day, and I *h* .... Rev 1:10
HEARER
if anyone is a *h*. .... James 1:23
HEARERS
for not the *h* of the .... Rom 2:13
the word, and not *h* .... James 1:22
HEARING
'Keep on *h* .... Is 6:9
h they do not .... Matt 13:13
h they may hear .... Mark 4:12
or by the *h* of faith .... Gal 3:2
HEARS
out and the LORD *h* .... Ps 34:17
of God *h* God's words .... John 8:47
"And if anyone *h* .... John 12:47
who is of the truth *h*. .... John 18:37
He who knows God *h* .... 1 John 4:6
And let him who *h* .... Rev 22:17
HEART
h was only evil .... Gen 6:5
h rejoices in the LORD .... 1 Sam 2:1
gave him another *h*. .... 1 Sam 10:9
LORD looks at the *h* .... 1 Sam 16:7
his wives turned his *h* .... 1 Kin 11:4
He pierces my *h*. .... Job 16:13
My *h* also instructs me .... Ps 16:7
h is overflowing .... Ps 45:1
h shall depart from me .... Ps 101:4
look and a proud *h*. .... Ps 101:5
with my whole *h* .... Ps 111:1
as he thinks in his *h* .... Prov 23:7
h reveals the man .... Prov 27:19
trusts in his own *h* .... Prov 28:26
The *h* of the wise is .... Eccl 7:4
And a wise man's *h*. .... Eccl 8:5
h yearned for him .... Song 5:4
And the whole *h*. .... Is 1:5
The yearning of Your *h* .... Is 63:15
h is deceitful above .... Jer 17:9
I will give them a *h*. .... Jer 24:7
and take the stony *h* .... Ezek 11:19
yourselves a new *h*. .... Ezek 18:31
are the pure in *h* .... Matt 5:8
is, there your *h* .... Matt 6:21
of the *h* proceed evil .... Matt 15:19
h will flow rivers .... John 7:38
"Let not your *h*. .... John 14:1
Satan filled your *h* .... Acts 5:3
h that God has raised .... Rom 10:9
refresh my *h* in the .... Philem 20
and shuts up his *h* .... 1 John 3:17
HEARTILY
you do, do it *h* .... Col 3:23
HEARTS
God tests the *h* .... Ps 7:9
And he will turn The *h*. .... Mal 4:6
h failing them from .... Luke 21:26
will guard your *h* .... Phil 4:7
of God rule in your *h* .... Col 3:15
HEATHEN
repetitions as the *h* .... Matt 6:7
HEAVEN
called the firmament *H*. .... Gen 1:8
LORD looks down from *h* .... Ps 14:2
word is settled in *h* .... Ps 119:89
For God is in *h* .... Eccl 5:2
"*H* is My throne .... Is 66:1
for the kingdom of *h* .... Matt 3:2
your Father in *h* .... Matt 5:16
On earth as it is in *h*. .... Matt 6:10
"*H* and earth will .... Matt 24:35
Him a sign from *h*. .... Mark 8:11
have sinned against *h* .... Luke 15:18
you shall see *h* .... John 1:51
one has ascended to *h* .... John 3:13
the true bread from *h* .... John 6:32
a voice came from *h* .... John 12:28
sheet, let down from *h* .... Acts 11:5
laid up for you in *h* .... Col 1:5
there was silence in *h*. .... Rev 8:1
Now I saw a new *h*. .... Rev 21:1
HEAVENLY
your *h* Father will .... Matt 6:14
h host praising God .... Luke 2:13
if I tell you *h* things .... John 3:12
blessing in the *h*. .... Eph 1:3
a better, that is, a *h* .... Heb 11:16
the living God, the *h*. .... Heb 12:22
HEAVENS
and the highest *h* .... Deut 10:14
h cannot contain .... 1 Kin 8:27
h declare the glory .... Ps 19:1
For as the *h* are high .... Ps 103:11
behold, I create new *h* .... Is 65:17
and behold, the *h* .... Matt 3:16
h will be shaken .... Matt 24:29
h are the work of Your .... Heb 1:10
h will pass away .... 2 Pet 3:10
HEEDS
h counsel is wise .... Prov 12:15
HEEL
you shall bruise His *h* .... Gen 3:15
has lifted up his *h* .... Ps 41:9
Me has lifted up his *h* .... John 13:18
HEIGHT
nor *h* nor depth .... Rom 8:39
length and depth and *h* .... Eph 3:18
HEIR
He has appointed *h*. .... Heb 1:2
world and became *h* .... Heb 11:7
HEIRS
if children, then *h* .... Rom 8:17
should be fellow *h*. .... Eph 3:6
HELL
shall be turned into *h* .... Ps 9:17
go down alive into *h* .... Ps 55:15
H and Destruction are .... Prov 27:20
be in danger of *h* fire .... Matt 5:22
to be cast into *h* .... Matt 18:9
condemnation of *h* .... Matt 23:33
power to cast into *h* .... Luke 12:5
HELMET
And take the *h* of. .... Eph 6:17
and love, and as a *h* .... 1 Thess 5:8
HELP
May He send you *h*. .... Ps 20:2
A very present *h*. .... Ps 46:1
He is their *h* and .... Ps 115:9
Our *h* is in the name .... Ps 124:8
h my unbelief .... Mark 9:24
and find grace to *h*. .... Heb 4:16
HELPED
fall, but the LORD *h* .... Ps 118:13
of salvation I have *h* .... Is 49:8
h His servant Israel .... Luke 1:54
HELPER
I will make him a *h*. .... Gen 2:18
Behold, God is my *h*. .... Ps 54:4
give you another *H* .... John 14:16
"But when the *H*. .... John 15:26
"The LORD is my *h*. .... Heb 13:6
HELPFUL
all things are not *h* .... 1 Cor 6:12
HELPS
the Spirit also *h* .... Rom 8:26
HEM
and touched the *h*. .... Matt 9:20
HERE
Then I said, "*H* am I .... Is 6:8

HERESIES
dissensions, *h* ... Gal 5:20

HERITAGE
for that is his *h* ... Eccl 3:22
This is the *h* of the ... Is 54:17
of My people, My *h* ... Joel 3:2
The flock of Your *h* ... Mic 7:14

HIDDEN
And my sins are not *h* ... Ps 69:5
Your word I have *h* ... Ps 119:11
h that will not ... Matt 10:26
the *h* wisdom which ... 1 Cor 2:7
bring to light the *h* ... 1 Cor 4:5
have renounced the *h* ... 2 Cor 4:2
rather let it be the *h* ... 1 Pet 3:4
give some of the *h* ... Rev 2:17

HIDE
H me under the shadow ... Ps 17:8
You shall *h* them in ... Ps 31:20
You *h* Your face ... Ps 104:29
darkness shall not *h* ... Ps 139:12
You are God, who *h* ... Is 45:15
"Fall on us and *h* ... Rev 6:16

HIDES
He *h* His face ... Ps 10:11

HIDING
You are my *h* place ... Ps 32:7

HIGH
priest of God Most *H* ... Gen 14:18
For the LORD Most *H* ... Ps 47:2
"I dwell in the *h* ... Is 57:15
know That the Most *H* ... Dan 4:17
up on a *h* mountain by ... Matt 17:1
your mind on *h* things ... Rom 12:16
h thing that exalts ... 2 Cor 10:5
and faithful *H* Priest ... Heb 2:17

HIGHER
you, 'Friend, go up *h* ... Luke 14:10

HIGHWAY
in the desert A *h* ... Is 40:3

HIGHWAYS
h shall be elevated ... Is 49:11
go into the *h* ... Matt 22:9

HILL
My King on My holy *h* ... Ps 2:6
h cannot be hidden ... Matt 5:14
and *h* brought low ... Luke 3:5

HILLS
of the everlasting *h* ... Gen 49:26
of the *h* are His also ... Ps 95:4
up my eyes to the *h* ... Ps 121:1

HINDER
all things lest we *h* ... 1 Cor 9:12

HINDERED
Who *h* you from obeying ... Gal 5:7
prayers may not be *h* ... 1 Pet 3:7

HOLD
right hand shall *h* ... Ps 139:10
h fast that word ... 1 Cor 15:2
h fast and repent ... Rev 3:3

HOLIER
near me, For I am *h* ... Is 65:5

HOLIEST
the way into the *H* ... Heb 9:8

HOLINESS
You, glorious in *h* ... Ex 15:11
I have sworn by My *h* ... Ps 89:35
the Highway of *H* ... Is 35:8
to the Spirit of *h* ... Rom 1:4
spirit, perfecting *h* ... 2 Cor 7:1
uncleanness, but in *h* ... 1 Thess 4:7
be partakers of His *h* ... Heb 12:10

HOLY
where you stand is *h* ... Ex 3:5
day, to keep it *h* ... Ex 20:8
LORD your God am *h* ... Lev 19:2
h seed is mixed ... Ezra 9:2
God sits on His *h* ... Ps 47:8
God, in His *h* mountain ... Ps 48:1
"*H,h,h* ... Is 6:3
child of the *H* Spirit ... Mark 1:18
baptize you with the *H* ... Mark 1:8
who speak, but the *H* ... Mark 13:11
H Spirit will come ... Luke 1:35
H Spirit descended ... Luke 3:22
Father give the *H* ... Luke 11:3
H Spirit will teach ... Luke 12:12
H Spirit was not ... John 7:39
H Spirit has come ... Acts 1:8
all filled with the *H* ... Acts 2:4
receive the *H* Spirit ... Acts 19:2
joy in the *H* ... Rom 14:17
H Spirit teaches ... 1 Cor 2:13
that we should be *h* ... Eph 1:4
were sealed with the *H* ... Eph 1:13
partakers of the *H* ... Heb 6:4
H Spirit sent from ... 1 Pet 1:12
it is written, "Be *h* ... 1 Pet 1:16
moved by the *H* Spirit ... 2 Pet 1:21
anointing from the *H* ... 1 John 2:20
says He who is *h* ... Rev 3:7
For You alone are *h* ... Rev 15:4
is *h*, let him be *h* ... Rev 22:11

HOME
sparrow has found a *h* ... Ps 84:3
to his eternal *h* ... Eccl 12:5
that while we are at *h* ... 2 Cor 5:6
to show piety at *h* ... 1 Tim 5:4

HOMEMAKERS
be discreet, chaste, *h* ... Titus 2:5

HONEY
and with *h* from the ... Ps 81:16
was locusts and wild *h* ... Matt 3:4

HONEYCOMB
than honey and the *h* ... Ps 19:10
fish and some *h* ... Luke 24:42

HONOR
"*H* your father and your ... Ex 20:12
will deliver him and *h* ... Ps 91:15
H and majesty are ... Ps 96:6
H the LORD with your ... Prov 3:9
before *h* is humility ... Prov 15:33
spirit will retain *h* ... Prov 29:23
Father, where is My *h* ... Mal 1:6
is not without *h* ... Matt 13:57
'*H* your father and ... Matt 15:4
h the Son Just as they ... John 5:23
"I do not receive *h* ... John 5:41
but I *h* My Father ... John 8:49
"If I *h* Myself ... John 8:54
him My Father will *h* ... John 12:26
to whom fear, *h* ... Rom 13:7
sanctification and *h* ... 1 Thess 4:4
alone is wise, be *h* ... 1 Tim 1:17
and clay, some for *h* ... 2 Tim 2:20
no man takes this *h* ... Heb 5:4
from God the Father *h* ... 2 Pet 1:17
give glory and *h* ... Rev 4:9

HONORABLE
His work is *h* and ... Ps 111:3
holy day of the LORD *h* ... Is 58:13
providing *h* things ... 2 Cor 8.21
Marriage is *h* among ... Heb 13:4
having your conduct *h* ... 1 Pet 2:12

HONORS
'This people *h* Me ... Mark 7:6
It is My Father who *h* ... John 8:54

HOPE
h He has uprooted ... Job 19:10
also will rest in *h* ... Ps 16:9
My *h* is in You ... Ps 39:7
For You are my *h* ... Ps 71:5
I *h* in Your word ... Ps 119:147
good that one should *h* ... Lam 3:26
to *h*, in *h* believed ... Rom 4:18
h does not disappoint ... Rom 5:5
were saved in this *h* ... Rom 8:24
now abide faith, *h* ... 1 Cor 13:13
life only we have *h* ... 1 Cor 15:19
may know what is the *h* ... Eph 1:18
were called in one *h* ... Eph 4:4
Christ in you, the *h* ... Col 1:27
Jesus Christ, our *h* ... 1 Tim 1:1
for the blessed *h* ... Titus 2:13
to lay hold of the *h* ... Heb 6:18
in of a better *h* ... Heb 7:19
who has this *h* in Him ... 1 John 3:3

HOPED
substance of things *h* ... Heb 11:1

HORSE
and behold, a white *h* ... Rev 6:2
and behold, a white *h* ... Rev 19:11

HOSANNA
H in the highest ... Matt 21:9

HOSPITABLE
Be *h* to one another ... 1 Pet 4:9

HOSTS
The LORD of *h* is with ... Ps 46:7
Praise Him, all His *h* ... Ps 148:2
against spiritual *h* ... Eph 6:12

HOUR
is coming at an *h* ... Matt 24:44
"But the *h* is coming ... John 4:23
save Me from this *h* ... John 12:27
keep you from the *h* ... Rev 3:10

HOUSE
as for me and my *h* ... Josh 24:15
Through wisdom a *h* ... Prov 24:3
better to go to the *h* ... Eccl 7:2
h was filled with ... Is 6:4
h divided against ... Matt 12:25
h shall be called a ... Matt 21:13
make My Father's *h* ... John 2:16
h are many mansions ... John 14:2
publicly and from *h* ... Acts 20:20
who rules his own *h* ... 1 Tim 3:4
the church in your *h* ... Philem 2
For every *h* is built ... Heb 3:4
His own *h*, whose *h* ... Heb 3:6

HOUSEHOLD
the ways of her *h* ... Prov 31:27
be those of his own *h* ... Matt 10:36
h were baptized ... Acts 16:15
saved, you and your *h* ... Acts 16:31
who are of Caesar's *h* ... Phil 4:22

HOUSEHOLDER
h who brings out of ... Matt 13:52

HOUSES
H and riches are an ... Prov 19:14
who has left *h* or ... Matt 19:29
you devour widows' *h* ... Matt 23:14

HOVERING
Spirit of God was *h* ... Gen 1:2

HUMBLE
man Moses was very *h* ... Num 12:3
the cry of the *h* ... Ps 9:12
h shall hear of it and ... Ps 34:2
contrite and *h* spirit ... Is 57:15
A meek and *h* people ... Zeph 3:12
associate with the *h* ... Rom 12:16
gives grace to the *h* ... James 4:6
H yourselves in the ... James 4:10
gives grace to the *h* ... 1 Pet 5:5
h yourselves under the ... 1 Pet 5:6

HUMBLED
as a man, He *h* Himself ... Phil 2:8

HUMBLES
h Himself to behold ... Ps 113:6

HUMILITY
the Lord with all *h* ... Acts 20:19
delight in false *h* ... Col 2:18
mercies, kindness, *h* ... Col 3:12
h correcting those ... 2 Tim 2:25
gentle, showing all *h* ... Titus 3:2
and be clothed with *h* ... 1 Pet 5:5

HUNGER
They shall neither *h* ... Is 49:10
are those who *h* ... Matt 5:6
for you shall *h* ... Luke 6:25
to Me shall never *h* ... John 6:35
hour we both *h* ... 1 Cor 4:11
"They shall neither *h* ... Rev 7:16

HUNGRY
and fills the *h* ... Ps 107:9
gives food to the *h* ... Ps 146:7
'for I was *h* and you ... Matt 25:35
did we see You *h* ... Matt 25:37
to be full and to be *h* ... Phil 4:12

HUNTER
Nimrod the mighty *h* .... Gen 10:9
Esau was a skillful *h* .... Gen 25:27

HURT
h a woman with child .... Ex 21:22
but I was not *h* .... Prov 23:35
another to his own *h* .... Eccl 8:9
They shall not *h* .... Is 11:9
it will by no means *h* .... Mark 16:18
shall not be *h* by the .... Rev 2:11

HUSBAND
She also gave to her *h* .... Gen 3:6
h safely trusts her .... Prov 31:11
your Maker is your *h* .... Is 54:5
now have is not your *h* .... John 4:18
you will save your *h* .... 1 Cor 7:16
the *h* of one wife .... 1 Tim 12

HUSBANDS
H, love your wives .... Eph 5:25
Let deacons be the *h* .... 1 Tim 3:12

HYMN
they had sung a *h* .... Matt 26:30

HYMNS
praying and singing *h* .... Acts 16:25
in psalms and *h* .... Eph 5:19

HYPOCRISY
you are full of *h* .... Matt 23:28
Pharisees, which is *h* .... Luke 12:1
Let love be without *h* .... Rom 12:9
away with their *h* .... Gal 2:13
and without *h* .... James 3:17
malice, all deceit, *h* .... 1 Pet 2:1

HYPOCRITE
and the joy of the *h* .... Job 20:5
For everyone is a *h* .... Is 9:17
also played the *h* .... Gal 2:13

HYPOCRITES
not be like the *h* .... Matt 6:5
do you test Me, you *h* .... Matt 22:18
and Pharisees, *h* .... Matt 23:13

I

IDLE
i Person will suffer .... Prov 19:15
i word men may .... Matt 12:36
saw others standing *i* .... Matt 20:3
they learn to be *i* .... 1 Tim 5:13

IDOL
thing offered to an *i* .... 1 Cor 8:7
That an *i* is anything .... 1 Cor 10:19

IDOLATER
or covetous, or an *i* .... 1 Cor 5:11

IDOLATERS
fornicators, nor *i* .... 1 Cor 6:9
and murderers and *i* .... Rev 22:15

IDOLATRIES
and abominable *i* .... 1 Pet 4:3

IDOLATRY
beloved, flee from *i* .... 1 Cor 10:14
i, sorcery .... Gal 5:20

IDOLS
land is also full of *i* .... Is 2:8
in the room of his *i* .... Ezek 8:12
who regard worthless *i* .... Jon 2:8
You who abhor *i* .... Rom 2:22
yourselves from *i* .... 1 John 5:21
worship demons, and *i* .... Rev 9:20

IGNORANCE
that you did it in *i* .... Acts 3:17
i God overlooked .... Acts 17:30
sins committed in *i* .... Heb 9:7

IGNORANTLY
because I did it *i* .... 1 Tim 1:13

ILLUMINATED
after you were *i* .... Heb 10:32
and the earth was *i* .... Rev 18:1
for the glory of God *i* .... Rev 21:23

IMAGE
Us make man in Our *i* .... Gen 1:26
since he is the *i* .... 1 Cor 11:7
He is the *i* of the .... Col 1:15
and not the very *i* .... Heb 10:1
the beast and his *i* .... Rev 14:9

IMAGINATION
the proud in the *i* .... Luke 1:51

IMITATE
as I also *i* Christ .... 1 Cor 11:1

IMMANUEL
shall call His name *I* .... Is 7:14
shall call His name *I* .... Matt 1:23

IMMORAL
murderers, sexually *i* .... Rev 21:8

IMMORALITY
except sexual *i* .... Matt 5:32
abstain from sexual *i* .... 1 Thess 4:3

IMMORTAL
to the King eternal, *i* .... 1 Tim 1:17

IMMORTALITY
mortal must put on *i* .... 1 Cor 15:53
who alone has *i* .... 1 Tim 6:16

IMMOVABLE
be steadfast, *i* .... 1 Cor 15:58

IMMUTABLE
that by two *i* things .... Heb 6:18

IMPART
that it may *i* grace .... Eph 4:29

IMPENITENT
i heart you are .... Rom 2:5

IMPOSSIBLE
God nothing will be *i* .... Luke 1:37
without faith it is *i* .... Heb 11:6

IMPUTE
the LORD does not *i* .... Ps 32:2

IMPUTED
might be *i* to them .... Rom 4:11
but sin is not *i* .... Rom 5:13

IMPUTES
i righteousness apart .... Rom 4:6

INCORRUPTIBLE
the glory of the *i* .... Rom 1:23
dead will be raised *i* .... 1 Cor 15:52
to an inheritance *i* .... 1 Pet 1:4

INCORRUPTION
corruption inherit *i* .... 1 Cor 15:50

INCREASE
Of the *i* of His .... Is 9:7
Lord "*I* our faith .... Luke 17:5
"He must *i* .... John 3:30
but God gave the *i* .... 1 Cor 3:6

INCREASES
who have no might He *i* .... Is 40:29

INCURABLE
Your sorrow is *i* .... Jer 30:15

INDIGNATION
i which will devour .... Heb 10:27
into the cup of His *i* .... Rev 14:10

INEXCUSABLE
Therefore you are *i* .... Rom 2:1

INEXPRESSIBLE
Paradise and heard *i* .... 2 Cor 12:4
you rejoice with joy *i* .... 1 Pet 1:8

INFALLIBLE
suffering by many *i* .... Acts 1:3

INFIRMITIES
"He Himself took our *i* .... Matt 8:17

INHERIT
love me to *i* wealth .... Prov 8:21
i the kingdom .... Matt 25:34
unrighteous will not *i* .... 1 Cor 6:9
who overcomes shall *i* .... Rev 21:7

INHERITANCE
"You shall have no *i* .... Num 18:20
is the place of His *i* .... Deut 32:9
the portion of my *i* .... Ps 16:5
i shall be forever .... Ps 37:18
He will choose our *i* .... Ps 47:4
will arise to your *i* .... Dan 12:13
God gave him no *i* .... Acts 7:5
and give you an *i* .... Acts 20:32
For if the *i* is of the .... Gal 3:18
we have obtained an *i* .... Eph 1:11
be partakers of the *i* .... Col 1:12
receive as an *i* .... Heb 11:8
i incorruptible .... 1 Pet 1:4

INIQUITIES
i have overtaken me .... Ps 40:12
forgives all your *i* .... Ps 103:3
LORD, should mark *i* .... Ps 130:3
was bruised for our *i* .... Is 53:5
He shall bear their *i* .... Is 53:11
i have separated you .... Is 59:2

INIQUITY
God, visiting the *i* of the .... Ex 20:5
was brought forth in *i* .... Ps 51:5
If I regard *i* in my .... Ps 66:18
i have dominion .... Ps 119:133
i will reap sorrow .... Prov 22:8
A people laden with *i* .... Is 1:4
i is taken away .... Is 6:7
has laid on Him the *i* .... Is 53:6
will remember their *i* .... Hos 9:9
to those who devise *i* .... Mic 2:1
like You, Pardoning *i* .... Mic 7:18
all you workers of *i* .... Luke 13:27
a fire, a world of *i* .... James 3:6

INJUSTICE
i have your fathers .... Jer 2:5

INN
room for them in the *i* .... Luke 2:7
brought him to an *i* .... Luke 10:34

INNOCENCE
washed my hands in *i* .... Ps 73:13

INNOCENT
because I was found *i* .... Dan 6:22
saying, "I am *i* .... Matt 27:24
this day that I am *i* .... Acts 20:26

INQUIRED
Therefore David *i* .... 1 Sam 23:2
the prophets have *i* .... 1 Pet 1:10

INQUIRY
shall make careful *i* .... Deut 19:18

INSANE
images, And they are *i* .... Jer 50:38

INSPIRATION
is given by *i* of God .... 2 Tim 3:16

INSTRUCT
I will *i* you and teach .... Ps 32:8
LORD that he may *i* .... 1 Cor 2:16

INSTRUCTED
This man had been *i* .... Acts 18:25
are excellent, being *i* .... Rom 2:18
Moses was divinely *i* .... Heb 8:5

INSTRUCTION
seeing you hate *i* .... Ps 50:17
Hear *i* and be wise .... Prov 8:33
Give *i* to a wise man .... Prov 9:9
for correction, for *i* .... 2 Tim 3:16

INSTRUCTS
My heart also *i* .... Ps 16:7

INSTRUMENTS
your members as *i* .... Rom 6:13

INSUBORDINATE
for the lawless and *i* .... 1 Tim 1:9

INSUBORDINATION
of dissipation or *i* .... Titus 1:6

INSULTED
will be mocked and *i* .... Luke 18:32
i the Spirit of grace .... Heb 10:29

INSULTS
nor be afraid of their *i* .... Is 51:7

INTEGRITY
in the *i* of my heart .... Gen 20:5
in doctrine showing *i* .... Titus 2:7

INTERCEDE
the LORD, who will *i* .... 1 Sam 2:25

INTERCESSION
of many, And made *i* .... Is 53:12
Spirit Himself makes *i* .... Rom 8:26
always lives to make *i* .... Heb 7:25

INTERCESSOR
that there was no *i* .... Is 59:16

INTEREST
collected it with *i* .... Luke 19:23

INTERPRET
Do all *i*? .... 1 Cor 12:30
pray that he may *i* .... 1 Cor 14:13

INTERPRETATION
to another the *i* … 1 Cor 12:10
of any private *i* … 2 Pet 1:20

INTERPRETATIONS
"Do not *i* belong to … Gen 40:8

INVISIBLE
of the world His *i* … Rom 1:20
is the image of the *i* … Col 1:15
eternal, immortal, *i* … 1 Tim 1:17
as seeing Him who is *i* … Heb 11:27

INWARD
You have formed my *i* … Ps 139:13
God according to the *i* … Rom 7:22
i man is being … 2 Cor 4:16

INWARDLY
i they are … Matt 7:15
is a Jew who is one *i* … Rom 2:29

IRON
i sharpens *i* … Prov 27:17
its feet partly of *i* … Dan 2:33

ISRAEL
"Hear, O *I* … Deut 6:4
For they are not all *I* … Rom 9:6
and upon the *I* of God … Gal 6:16

ITCHING
they have *i* ears … 2 Tim 4:3

J

JEALOUS
God, am a *j* God … Ex 20:5
a consuming fire, a *j* … Deut 4:24
For I am *j* for you … 2 Cor 11:2

JEALOUSY
provoked Him to *j* … Deut 32:16
as strong as death, *j* … Song 8:6
for you with godly *j* … 2 Cor 11:2

JEOPARDY
stand in *j* every hour … 1 Cor 15:30

JESTING
talking, nor coarse *j* … Eph 5:4

JESUS
J Christ was as … Matt 1:18
shall call His name *J* … Matt 1:21
J was led up by the … Matt 4:1
and laid hands on *J* … Matt 26:50
and destroy *J* … Matt 27:20
J withdrew with His … Mark 3:7
J went into … Mark 11:11
they were eating, *J* … Mark 14:22
and he delivered *J* … Mark 15:15
truth came through *J* … John 1:17
J lifted up His eyes … John 6:5
J wept … John 11:35
J was crucified … John 19:20
"This *J* God has raised … Acts 2:32
of Your holy Servant *J* … Acts 4:30
believed on the Lord *J* … Acts 11:17
your mouth the Lord *J* … Rom 10:9
among you except *J* … 1 Cor 2:2
perfect in Christ *J* … Col 1:28
But we see *J* … Heb 2:9
looking unto *J* … Heb 12:2
Revelation of *J* Christ … Rev 1:1
so, come, Lord *J* … Rev 22:20

JOIN
of the rest dared *j* … Acts 5:13

JOINED
and mother and be *j* … Gen 2:24
what God has *j* … Matt 19:6
the whole body, *j* … Eph 4:16

JOINT
j as He wrestled … Gen 32:25
My bones are out of *j* … Ps 22:14
j heirs with Christ … Rom 8:17

JOINTS
and knit together by *j* … Col 2:19
and spirit, and of *j* … Heb 4:12

JOT
one *j* or one tittle … Matt 5:18

JOY
is fullness of *j* … Ps 16:11
j comes in the morning … Ps 30:5
j you will draw … Is 12:3
ashes, The oil of *j* … Is 61:3
shall sing for *j* … Is 65:14
receives it with *j* … Matt 13:20
Enter into the *j* … Matt 25:21
in my womb for *j* … Luke 1:44
there will be more *j* … Luke 15:7
did not believe for *j* … Luke 24:41
My *j* may remain in … John 15:11
they may have My *j* … John 17:13
the Spirit is love, *j* … Gal 5:22
are our glory and *j* … 1 Thess 2:20
j that was set before … Heb 12:2
count it all *j* … James 1:2
with exceeding *j* … 1 Pet 4:13

JOYFUL
Make a *j* shout to the … Ps 100:1
And make them *j* … Is 56:7

JUDGE
The LORD *j* between … Gen 16:5
coming to *j* the earth … 1 Chr 16:33
sword The LORD will *j* … Is 66:16
deliver you to the *j* … Matt 5:25
"*J* not … Matt 7:1
who made Me a *j* … Luke 12:14
j who did not fear God … Luke 18:2
As I hear, I *j* … John 5:30
"Do not *j* according … John 7:24
I *j* no one … John 8:15
j the world but to … John 12:47
this, O man, you who *j* … Rom 2:3
Therefore let us not *j* … Rom 14:13
Christ, who will *j* … 2 Tim 4:1
But if you *j* the law … James 4:11

JUDGES
He makes the *j* of the … Is 40:23
For the Father *j* … John 5:22
he who is spiritual *j* … 1 Cor 2:15
j me is the Lord … 1 Cor 4:4
Him who *j* righteously … 1 Pet 2:23

JUDGMENT
Teach me good *j* … Ps 119:66
from prison and from *j* … Is 53:8
be in danger of the *j* … Matt 5:21
shall not come into *j* … John 5:24
and My *j* is righteous … John 5:30
if I do judge, My *j* … John 8:16
"Now is the *j* … John 12:31
the righteous *j* … Rom 1:32
j which came from one … Rom 5:16
appear before the *j* … 2 Cor 5:10
after this the *j* … Heb 9:27
time has come for *j* … 1 Pet 4:17
a long time their *j* … 2 Pet 2:3
darkness for the *j* … Jude 6

JUDGMENTS
The *j* of the LORD are … Ps 19:9
unsearchable are His *j* … Rom 11:33

JUST
Noah was a *j* man … Gen 6:9
j man who perishes … Eccl 7:15
j shall live by his … Hab 2:4
her husband, being a *j* … Matt 1:19
resurrection of the *j* … Luke 14:14
j persons who need no … Luke 15:7
the Holy One and the *J* … Acts 3:14
dead, both of the *j* … Acts 24:15
j shall live by faith … Rom 1:17
that He might be *j* … Rom 3:26
j men made perfect … Heb 12:23
have murdered the *j* … James 5:6
He is faithful and *j* … 1 John 1:9

JUSTICE
j as the noonday … Ps 37:6
And Your poor with *j* … Ps 72:2
j the measuring line … Is 28:17
the LORD is a God of *j* … Is 30:18
He will bring forth *j* … Is 42:1
J is turned back … Is 59:14
I, the LORD, love *j* … Is 61:8
truth, and His ways *j* … Dan 4:37
'Execute true *j* … Zech 7:9
"Where is the God of *j* … Mal 2:17
And He will declare *j* … Matt 12:18
His humiliation His *j* … Acts 8:33

JUSTIFICATION
because of our *j* … Rom 4:25
offenses resulted in *j* … Rom 5:16

JUSTIFIED
Me that you may be *j* … Job 40:8
words you will be *j* … Matt 12:37
"But wisdom is *j* … Luke 7:35
j rather than the … Luke 18:14
who believes is *j* … Acts 13:39
"That You may be *j* … Rom 3:4
law no flesh will be *j* … Rom 3:20
j freely by His grace … Rom 3:24
having been *j* by … Rom 5:1
these He also *j* … Rom 8:30
that we might be *j* … Gal 2:16
no flesh shall be *j* … Gal 2:16
the harlot also *j* … James 2:25

JUSTIFIES
He who *j* the wicked … Prov 17:15
It is God who *j* … Rom 8:33

JUSTIFY
wanting to *j* himself … Luke 10:29
"You are those who *j* … Luke 16:15
is one God who will *j* … Rom 3:30

K

KEEP
k you wherever you … Gen 28:15
day, to *k* it holy … Ex 20:8
Let all the earth *k* … Hab 2:20
k the commandments … Matt 19:17
"If you love Me, *k* … John 14:15
k through Your name … John 17:11
orderly and *k* the law … Acts 21:24
k the unity of the … Eph 4:3
k His commandments … 1 John 2:3

KEEPER
Am I my brother's *k* … Gen 4:9
The LORD is your *k* … Ps 121:5

KEEPS
k truth forever … Ps 146:6
k the commandment … Prov 19:16
none of you *k* the law … John 7:19
born of God *k* … 1 John 5:18
and *k* his garments … Rev 16:15

KEPT
For I have *k* the … 2 Sam 22:22
these things I have *k* … Matt 19:20
love, just as I have *k* … John 15:10
k back part of the … Acts 5:2
I have *k* the faith … 2 Tim 4:7
who are *k* by the power … 1 Pet 1:5

KEY
taken away the *k* … Luke 11:52
"He who has the *k* … Rev 3:7

KEYS
I will give you the *k* … Matt 16:19
And I have the *k* … Rev 1:18

KILL
k the Passover … Ex 12:21
I *k* and I make alive … Deut 32:39
"Am I God, to *k* … 2 Kin 5:7
A time to *k* … Eccl 3:3
of them they will *k* … Luke 11:49
afraid of those who *k* … Luke 12:4
Why do you seek to *k* … John 7:19
k and eat … Acts 10:13

KILLED
Abel his brother and *k* … Gen 4:8
for Your sake we are *k* … Ps 44:22
and scribes, and be *k* … Matt 16:21
Siloam fell and *k* them … Luke 13:4
k the Prince of life … Acts 3:15
Your sake we are *k* … Rom 8:36
k both the Lord … 1 Thess 2:15

KILLS
the one who *k* the … Matt 23:37
for the letter *k* … 2 Cor 3:6

KIND
animals after their *k* … Gen 6:20
k can come out by … Mark 9:29
suffers long and is *k* … 1 Cor 13:4
And be *k* to one … Eph 4:32

KINDLY
- Julius treated Paul *k* ... Acts 27:3
- *k* affectionate to one ... Rom 12:10

KINDNESS
- For His merciful *k* ... Ps 117:2
- *k* shall not depart ... Is 54:10
- I remember you, The *k* ... Jer 2:2
- by longsuffering, by *k* ... 2 Cor 6:6
- longsuffering, *k* ... Gal 5:22
- and to brotherly *k* ... 2 Pet 1:7

KING
- "Yet I have set My *K* ... Ps 2:6
- The LORD is *K* forever ... Ps 10:16
- And the *K* of glory ... Ps 24:7
- For God is my *K* ... Ps 74:12
- when your *k* is a child ... Eccl 10:16
- and the everlasting *K* ... Jer 10:10
- the LORD shall be *K* ... Zech 14:9
- who has been born *K* ... Matt 2:2
- This Is Jesus The *K* ... Matt 27:37
- "Behold your *K* ... John 19:14
- Now to the *K* eternal ... 1 Tim 1:17
- only Potentate, the *K* ... 1 Tim 6:15
- this Melchizedek, *k* ... Heb 7:1
- *K* of Kings and Lord ... Rev 19:16

KINGDOM
- Yours is the *k* ... 1 Chr 29:11
- *k* is the LORD's ... Ps 22:28
- the scepter of Your *k* ... Ps 45:6
- is an everlasting *k* ... Ps 145:13
- *k* which shall never be ... Dan 2:44
- High rules in the *k* ... Dan 4:17
- "Repent, for the *k* ... Matt 3:2
- for Yours is the *k* ... Matt 6:13
- "But seek first the *k* ... Matt 6:33
- the mysteries of the *k* ... Matt 13:11
- are the sons of the *k* ... Matt 13:38
- of such is the *k* ... Matt 19:14
- back, is fit for the *k* ... Luke 9:62
- against nation, and *k* ... Luke 21:10
- he cannot see the *k* ... John 3:3
- he cannot enter the *k* ... John 3:5
- If My *k* were of this ... John 18:36
- for the *k* of God is ... Rom 14:17
- will not inherit the *k* ... Gal 5:21
- the scepter of Your *k* ... Heb 1:8
- we are receiving a *k* ... Heb 12:28

KINGDOMS
- the *k* were moved ... Ps 46:6
- showed Him all the *k* ... Matt 4:8
- have become the *k* ... Rev 11:15

KINGS
- The *k* of the earth set ... Ps 2:2
- By me *k* reign ... Prov 8:15
- governors and *k* ... Matt 10:18
- *k* have desired to see ... Luke 10:24
- You have reigned as *k* ... 1 Cor 4:8
- and has made us *k* ... Rev 1:6
- that the way of the *k* ... Rev 16:12

KISS
- *K* the Son ... Ps 2:12
- "You gave Me no *k* ... Luke 7:45
- one another with a *k* ... 1 Pet 5:14

KISSED
- they *k* one another ... 1 Sam 20:41
- and *k* Him ... Matt 26:49
- and she *k* His feet and ... Luke 7:38

KNEE
- That to Me every *k* ... Is 45:23
- have not bowed the *k* ... Rom 11:4
- of Jesus every *k* ... Phil 2:10

KNEES
- make firm the feeble *k* ... Is 35:3
- this reason I bow my *k* ... Eph 3:14
- and the feeble *k* ... Heb 12:12

KNEW
- in the womb I *k* ... Jer 1:5
- to them, 'I never *k* ... Matt 7:23
- *k* what was in man ... John 2:25
- He made Him who *k* ... 2 Cor 5:21

KNIT
- be encouraged, being *k* ... Col 2:2

KNOCK
- *k*, and it will be ... Matt 7:7
- at the door and *k* ... Rev 3:20

KNOW
- *k* good and evil ... Gen 3:22
- *k* that I am the LORD ... Ex 6:7
- *k* that my Redeemer ... Job 19:25
- make me to *k* wisdom ... Ps 51:6
- Who can *k* it ... Jer 17:9
- saying, '*K* the LORD ... Jer 31:34
- *k* what hour your ... Matt 24:42
- an oath, "I do not *k* ... Matt 26:72
- the world did not *k* ... John 1:10
- We speak what We *k* ... John 3:11
- *k* that You are ... John 6:69
- My voice, and I *k* ... John 10:27
- If you *k* these things ... John 13:17
- *k* whom I have ... John 13:18
- are sure that You *k* ... John 16:30
- *k* that I love You ... John 21:15
- *k* times or seasons ... Acts 1:7
- and said, "Jesus I *k* ... Acts 19:15
- wisdom did not *k* ... 1 Cor 1:21
- nor can he *k* them ... 1 Cor 2:14
- For we *k* in part and ... 1 Cor 13:9
- *k* the love of Christ ... Eph 3:19
- *k* whom I have ... 2 Tim 1:12
- we *k* that we *k* Him ... 1 John 2:3
- and you *k* all things ... 1 John 2:20
- By this we *k* love ... 1 John 3:16
- *k* that He abides ... 1 John 3:24
- *k* that we are of God ... 1 John 5:19
- "I *k* your works ... Rev 2:2

KNOWLEDGE
- and the tree of the *k* ... Gen 2:9
- unto night reveals *k* ... Ps 19:2
- *k* is too wonderful ... Ps 139:6
- people store up *k* ... Prov 10:14
- *k* spares his words ... Prov 17:27
- and he who increases *k* ... Eccl 1:18
- *k* is that wisdom ... Eccl 7:12
- *k* shall increase ... Dan 12:4
- more accurate *k* ... Acts 24:22
- having the form of *k* ... Rom 2:20
- law is the *k* of sin ... Rom 3:20
- whether there is *k* ... 1 Cor 13:8
- Christ which passes *k* ... Eph 3:19
- is falsely called *k* ... 1 Tim 6:20
- in the grace and *k* ... 2 Pet 3:18

KNOWN
- If you had *k* Me ... John 8:19
- My sheep, and am *k* ... John 10:14
- The world has not *k* ... John 17:25
- peace they have not *k* ... Rom 3:17
- "For who has *k* ... Rom 11:34
- after you have *k* ... Gal 4:9
- requests be made *k* ... Phil 4:6
- *k* the Holy Scriptures ... 2 Tim 3:15

KNOWS
- "For God *k* that in ... Gen 3:5
- *k* what is in the ... Dan 2:22
- *k* the things you have ... Matt 6:8
- and hour no one k ... Matt 24:36
- God *k* your hearts ... Luke 16:15
- searches the hearts k ... Rom 8:27
- *k* the things of God ... 1 Cor 2:11
- *k* those who are His ... 2 Tim 2:19
- to him who *k* to do ... James 4:17
- and *k* all things ... 1 John 3:20

L

LABOR
- Six days you shall *l* ... Ex 20:9
- things are full of *l* ... Eccl 1:8
- has man for all his *l* ... Eccl 2:22
- He shall see the *l* ... Is 53:11
- to Me, all you who *l* ... Matt 11:28
- "Do not *l* for the ... John 6:.27
- knowing that your *l* ... 1 Cor 15:58
- but rather let him *l* ... Eph 4:28
- mean fruit from my *l* ... Phil 1:22
- your work of faith, *l* ... 1 Thess 1:3
- forget your work and *l* ... Heb 6:10
- your works, your *l* ... Rev 2:2

LABORED
- *l* more abundantly ... 1 Cor 15:10
- for you, lest I have *l* ... Gal 4:11

LABORERS
- but the *l* are few ... Matt 9:37

LABORING
- *l* night and day ... 1 Thess 2:9

LABORS
- entered into their *l* ... John 4:38
- creation groans and *l* ... Rom 8:22
- *l* more abundant ... 2 Cor 11:23
- may rest from their *l* ... Rev 14:13

LACK
- What do I still *l* ... Matt 19:20
- "One thing you *l* ... Mark 10:21

LADDER
- and behold, a *l* ... Gen 28:12

LAID
- the place where they *l* ... Mark 16:6
- "Where have you *l* ... John 11:34

LAKE
- cast alive into the *l* ... Rev 19:20

LAMB
- but where is the *l* ... Gen 22:7
- He was led as a *l* ... Is 53:7
- The *L* of God who ... John 1:29
- the elders, stood a *L* ... Rev 5:6
- "Worthy is the *L* ... Rev 5:12
- by the blood of the *L* ... Rev 12:11

LAME
- *l* shall leap like a ... Is 35:6
- blind see and the *l* ... Matt 11:5
- And a certain man *l* ... Acts 3:2

LAMENTATION
- was heard in Ramah, *l* ... Matt 2:18
- and made great *l* ... Acts 8:2

LAMP
- Your word is a *l* ... Ps 119:105
- the *l* of the wicked ... Prov 13:9
- his *l* will be put out ... Prov 20:20
- "Nor do they light a *l* ... Matt 5:15
- "The *l* of the body ... Matt 6:22
- when he has lit a *l* ... Luke 8:16
- *l* gives you light ... Luke 11:36
- does not light a *l* ... Luke 15:8
- burning and shining *l* ... John 5:35

LAMPS
- he made its seven *l* ... Ex 37:23
- and trimmed their *l* ... Matt 25:7

LAMPSTAND
- branches of the *l* ... Ex 25:32
- a basket, but on a *l* ... Matt 5:15
- and remove your *l* ... Rev 2:5

LAND
- *l* that I will show you ... Gen 12:1
- *l* flowing with milk ... Ex 3:8
- They will see the *l* ... Is 33:17
- Bethlehem, in the *l* ... Matt 2:6

LANGUAGE
- whole earth had one *l* ... Gen 11:1
- speak in his own *l* ... Acts 2:6
- blasphemy, filthy *l* ... Col 3:8

LANGUAGES
- according to their *l* ... Gen 10:20

LAST
- He shall stand at *l* ... Job 19:25
- First and I am the *L* ... Is 44:6
- *l* will be first ... Matt 20:16
- the First and the *L* ... Rev 1:11

LATTER
- *l* times some will ... 1 Tim 4:1

LAUGH
- "Why did Sarah *l* ... Gen 18:13
- Woe to you who *l* ... Luke 6:25

LAUGHS
- The Lord *l* at him ... Ps 37:13

LAUGHTER
- your *l* be turned to ... James 4:9

LAW
- stones a copy of the *l* ... Josh 8:32
- The *l* of the LORD is ... Ps 19:7

I delight in Your *l* .... Ps 119:70
Oh, how I love Your *l* .... Ps 119:97
And Your *l* is truth .... Ps 119:142
l will proceed from Me .... Is 51:4
in whose heart is My *l* .... Is 51:7
The *L* is no more .... Lam 2:9
The *l* of truth was in .... Mal 2:6
to destroy the *L* .... Matt 5:17
for this is the *L* .... Matt 7:12
hang all the *L* and the .... Matt 22:40
"The *l* and the .... Luke 16:16
l was given through .... John 1:17
"Does our *l* judge a .... John 7:51
l is the knowledge .... Rom 3:20
because the *l* brings .... Rom 4:15
when there is no *l* .... Rom 5:13
you are not under *l* .... Rom 6:14
For what the *l* could .... Rom 8:3
l that I might live .... Gal 2:19
under guard by the *l* .... Gal 3:23
born under the *l* .... Gal 4:4
l is fulfilled in one .... Gal 5:14
into the perfect *l* .... James 1:25
fulfill the royal *l* .... James 2:8

LAWFUL
Is it *l* to pay taxes .... Matt 22:17
All things are *l* .... 1 Cor 6:12

LAWGIVER
There is one *L* .... James 4:12

LAWLESS
l one will be revealed .... 2 Thess 2:8

LAWLESSNESS
Me, you who practice *l* .... Matt 7:23
l is already at work .... 2 Thess 2:7

LAWYERS
"Woe to you also, *l* .... Luke 11:46

LAY
nowhere to *l* His head .... Matt 8:20
l hands may receive .... Acts 8:19

LAZINESS
l the building decays .... Eccl 10:18

LAZY
l man will be put to .... Prov 12:24
wicked and *l* servant .... Matt 25:26
liars, evil beasts, *l* .... Titus 1:12

LEAD
L me in Your truth and .... Ps 25:5
And do not *l* us into .... Matt 6:13
"Can the blind *l* .... Luke 6:39

LEADS
He *l* me in the paths .... Ps 23:3
And if the blind *l* .... Matt 15:14

LEAF
plucked olive *l* .... Gen 8:11

LEAN
all your heart, And *l* .... Prov 3:5

LEAP
Then the lame shall *l* .... Is 35:6

LEARN
L to do good .... Is 1:17
yoke upon you and *l* .... Matt 11:29

LEARNED
Me The tongue of the *l* .... Is 50:4
have not so *l* Christ .... Eph 4:20
in all things I have *l* .... Phil 4:12

LEARNING
l is driving you mad .... Acts 26:24

LEAST
so, shall be called *l* .... Matt 5:19

LEAVE
a man shall *l* his .... Gen 2:24
For You will not *l* .... Ps 16:10
"I will never *l* .... Heb 13:5

LEAVEN
of heaven is like *l* .... Matt 13:33
l leavens the whole .... Gal 5:9

LEAVES
and they sewed fig *l* .... Gen 3:7
The *l* of the tree .... Rev 22:2

LED
l them forth by the .... Ps 107:7
For as many as are *l* .... Rom 8:14

LEFT
l hand know what your .... Matt 6:3

LEND
"And if you *l* .... Luke 6:34

LENDER
is servant to the *l* .... Prov 22:7

LENDS
ever merciful, and *l* .... Ps 37:26

LENGTH
is your life and the *l* .... Deut 30:20

LEOPARD
or the *l* its spots .... Jer 13:23

LEPERS
"And many *l* were in .... Luke 4:27

LET
"*L* there be light .... Gen 1:3

LETTER
for the *l* kills .... 2 Cor 3:6
or by word or by *l* .... 2 Thess 2:2

LETTERS
does this Man know *l* .... John 7:15

LEVIATHAN
"Can you draw out *L* .... Job 41:1

LEVITE
"Likewise a *L* .... Luke 10:32

LEWDNESS
wickedness, deceit, *l* .... Mark 7:22

LIAR
for he is a *l* and the .... John 8:44
but every man a *l* .... Rom 3:4
we make Him a *l* .... 1 John 1:10
his brother, he is a *l* .... 1 John 4:20

LIARS
"All men am *l* .... Ps 116:11
l shall have their .... Rev 21:8

LIBERALITY
he who gives, with *l* .... Rom 12:8

LIBERALLY
who gives to all *l* .... James 1:5

LIBERTY
year, and proclaim *l* .... Lev 25:10
'To proclaim *l* to the .... Luke 4:18
into the glorious *l* .... Rom 8:21
Lord is, there is *l* .... 2 Cor 3:17
therefore in the *l* .... Gal 5:1

LIE
Do not *l* to one .... Col 3:9
God, who cannot *l* .... Titus 1:2
an abomination or a *l* .... Rev 21:27

LIED
You have not *l* to men .... Acts 5:4

LIES
sin *l* at the door .... Gen 4:7
speaking *l* in .... 1 Tim 4:2

LIFE
the breath of *l* .... Gen 2:7
'For the *l* of the .... Lev 17:11
before you today *l* .... Deut 30:15
He will redeem their *l* .... Ps 72:14
word has given me *l* .... Ps 119:50
She is a tree of *l* .... Prov 3:18
finds me finds *l* .... Prov 8:35
L is more than .... Luke 12:23
l was the light .... John 1:4
so the Son gives *l* .... John 5:21
spirit, and they are *l* .... John 6:63
have the light of *l* .... John 8:12
and I lay down My *l* .... John 10:15
resurrection and the *l* .... John 11:25
you lay down your *l* .... John 13:38
l which I now live .... Gal 2:20
l is hidden with .... Col 3:3
For what is your *l* .... James 4:14
l was manifested .... 1 John 1:2
and the pride of *l* .... 1 John 2:16
has given us eternal *l* .... 1 John 5:11
the Lamb's Book of *L* .... Rev 21:27
right to the tree of *l* .... Rev 22:14
the water of *l* freely Rev22:17
from the Book of *L* .... Rev 22:19

LIFT
I will *l* up my eyes to .... Ps 121:1
Lord, and He will *l* .... James 4:10

LIFTED
your heart is *l* .... Ezek 28:2
in Hades, he *l* up his .... Luke 16:23
the Son of Man be *l* .... John 3:14
"And I, if I am *l* .... John 12:32

LIGHT
"Let there be *l* .... Gen 1:3
The LORD is my *l* .... Ps 27:1
and a *l* to my path .... Ps 119:105
The *l* of the righteous .... Prov 13:9
The LORD gives *l* .... Prov 29:13
Truly the *l* is sweet .... Eccl 11:7
let us walk in the *l* .... Is 2:5
l shall break forth .... Is 58:8
"You are the *l* .... Matt 5:14
"Let your *l* so shine .... Matt 5:16
than the sons of *l* .... Luke 16:8
and the life was the *l* .... John 1:4
darkness rather than *l* .... John 3:19
saying, "I am the *l* .... John 8:12
God who commanded *l* .... 2 Cor 4:6
Walk as children of *l* .... Eph 5:8
You are all sons of *l* .... 1 Thess 5:5
into His marvelous *l* .... 1 Pet 2:9
to you, that God is *l* .... 1 John 1:5
l as He is in the .... 1 John 1:7
says he is in the *l* .... 1 John 2:9
The Lamb is its *l* .... Rev 21:23

LIGHTNING
"For as the *l* .... Matt 24:27
countenance was like *l* .... Matt 28:3

LIGHTNINGS
the throne proceeded *l* .... Rev 4:5

LIGHTS
"Let there be *l* .... Gen 1:14
whom you shine as *l* .... Phil 2:15

LIKENESS
according to Our *l* .... Gen 1:26
carved image—any *l* .... Ex 20:4
when I awake in Your *l* .... Ps 17:15
and coming in the *l* .... Phil 2:7

LILY
the *l* of the valleys .... Song 2:1

LIMIT
to the sea its *l* .... Prov 8:29

LINE
upon precept, *L* upon .... Is 28:10
I am setting a plumb *l* .... Amos 7:8

LINEN
wrapped Him in the *l* .... Mark 15:46

LINGER
salvation shall not *l* .... Is 46:13

LION
l shall eat straw .... Is 11:7

LIONS
the mouths of *l* .... Heb 11:33

LIPS
off all flattering *l* .... Ps 12:3
The *l* of the righteous .... Prov 10:21
But the *l* of .... Prov 20:15
am a man of unclean *l* .... Is 6:5
other *l* I will speak .... 1 Cor 14:21
from evil, And his *l* .... 1 Pet 3:10

LISTEN
you are not able to *l* .... John 8:43
you who fear God, *l* .... Acts 13:16

LISTENS
But whoever *l* to me .... Prov 1:33

LITTLE
Though you are *l* .... Mic 5:2
l ones only a cup .... Matt 10:42
"O you of *l* faith .... Matt 14:31
to whom *l* is forgiven .... Luke 7:47
faithful in a very *l* .... Luke 19:17

LIVE
eat, and *l* forever .... Gen 3:22
a man does, he shall *l* .... Lev 18:5
"Seek Me and *l* .... Amos 5:4
But the just shall *l* .... Hab 2:4

l by bread alone ..... Matt 4:4
"for in Him we *l* ..... Acts 17:28
l peaceably with all ..... Rom 12:18
the life which I now *l* ..... Gal 2:20
If we *l* in the Spirit ..... Gal 5:25
to me, to *l* is Christ ..... Phil 1:21

LIVED
died and rose and *l* ..... Rom 14:9
And they *l* and reigned ..... Rev 20:4

LIVES
but man *l* by every ..... Deut 8:3
but Christ *l* in me ..... Gal 2:20
to lay down our *l* ..... 1 John 3:16
"I am He who *l* ..... Rev 1:18

LIVING
and man became a *l* ..... Gen 2:7
in the light of the *l* ..... Ps 56:13
the dead, but of the *l* ..... Matt 22:32
do you seek the *l* ..... Luke 24:5
the word of God is *l* ..... Heb 4:12
l creature was like a ..... Rev 4:7

LOATHSOME
But a wicked man is *l* ..... Prov 13:5

LOAVES
have here only five *l* ..... Matt 14:17
you ate of the *l* ..... John 6:26

LOCUST
What the chewing *l* ..... Joel 1:4

LOCUSTS
and his food was *l* ..... Matt 3:4

LOFTY
Wisdom is too *l* ..... Prov 24:7

LONG
your days may be *l* ..... Deut 5:16
Who *l* for death ..... Job 3:21
I *l* for Your salvation ..... Ps 119:174
go around in *l* robes ..... Mark 12:38

LONGSUFFERING
is love, joy, peace, *l* ..... Gal 5:22
and gentleness, with *l* ..... Eph 4:2
for all patience and *l* ..... Col 1:11
might show all *l* ..... 1 Tim 1:16
once the Divine *l* ..... 1 Pet 3:20
and consider that the *l* ..... 2 Pet 3:15

LOOK
A proud *l* ..... Prov 6:17
"*L* to Me ..... Is 45:22
l on Me whom they ..... Zech 12:10
say to you, '*L* here ..... Luke 17:23
while we do not *l* ..... 2 Cor 4:18

LOOKED
For He *l* down from ..... Ps 102:19
He *l* for justice ..... Is 5:7
the Lord turned and *l* ..... Luke 22:61
for he *l* to the reward ..... Heb 11:26

LOOKING
the plow, and *l* back ..... Luke 9:62
l for the blessed hope ..... Titus 2:13
l unto Jesus ..... Heb 12:2
l carefully lest ..... Heb 12:15
l for the mercy of ..... Jude 21

LOOKS
The lofty *l* of man ..... Is 2:11
to you that whoever *l* ..... Matt 5:28

LOOSE
and whatever you *l* ..... Matt 16:19
said to them, "*L* him ..... John 11:44

LOOSED
the silver cord is *l* ..... Eccl 12:6

LORD
L is my strength ..... Ex 15:2
L our God, the *L* ..... Deut 6:4
You alone are the *L* ..... Neh 9:6
The *L* of hosts ..... Ps 24:10
Gracious is the *L* ..... Ps 116:5
L surrounds His people ..... Ps 125:2
The *L* is righteous ..... Ps 129:4
L is near to all who ..... Ps 145:18
L is a God of justice ..... Is 30:18
L Our Righteousness ..... Jer 23:6
"The *L* is one ..... Zech 14:9
shall not tempt the *L* ..... Matt 4:7
shall worship the *L* ..... Matt 4:10
Son of Man is also *L* ..... Mark 2:28
who is Christ the *L* ..... Luke 2:11
L is risen indeed ..... Luke 24:34
Me Teacher and *L* ..... John 13:13
He is *L* of all ..... Acts 10:36
with your mouth the *L* ..... Rom 10:9
say that Jesus is *L* ..... 1 Cor 12:3
second Man is the *L* ..... 1 Cor 15:47
the Spirit of the *L* ..... 2 Cor 3:17
that Jesus Christ is *L* ..... Phil 2:11
and deny the only *L* ..... Jude 4
L God Omnipotent ..... Rev 19:6

LORDS
for He is Lord of *l* ..... Rev 17:14

LOSE
save his life will *l* ..... Matt 16:25

LOSES
but if the salt *l* ..... Matt 5:13
and *l* his own soul ..... Matt 16:26

LOSS
count all things *l* ..... Phil 3:8

LOST
save that which was *l* ..... Matt 18:11
and none of them is *l* ..... John 17:12
You gave Me I have *l* ..... John 18:9

LOTS
garments, casting *l* ..... Mark 15:24
And they cast their *l* ..... Acts 1:26

LOUD
cried out with a *l* ..... Matt 27:46
I heard behind me a *l* ..... Rev 1:10

LOVE
l your neighbor as ..... Lev 19:18
l the LORD your God ..... Deut 6:5
Oh, *l* the LORD ..... Ps 31:23
he has set his *l* ..... Ps 91:14
Oh, how I *l* Your law ..... Ps 119:97
l covers all sins ..... Prov 10:12
A time to *l* ..... Eccl 3:8
banner over me was *l* ..... Song 2:4
l is as strong as ..... Song 8:6
do justly, To *l* mercy ..... Mic 6:8
to you, *l* your enemies ..... Matt 5:44
which of them will *l* ..... Luke 7:42
you do not have the *l* ..... John 5:42
If you have *l* for one ..... John 13:35
"If you *l* Me ..... John 14:15
and My Father will *l* ..... John 14:23
l one another as I ..... John 15:12
l has no one than this ..... John 15:13
because the *l* of God ..... Rom 5:5
to *l* one another ..... Rom 13:8
L suffers long and is ..... 1 Cor 13:4
L never fails ..... 1 Cor 13:8
greatest of these is *l* ..... 1 Cor 13:13
For the *l* of Christ ..... 2 Cor 5:14
of the Spirit is *l* ..... Gal 5:22
Husbands, *l* your wives ..... Eph 5:25
the commandment is *l* ..... 1 Tim 1:5
For the *l* of money is ..... 1 Tim 6:10
Let brotherly *l* ..... Heb 13:1
having not seen you *l* ..... 1 Pet 1:8
for "*l* will cover a ..... 1 Pet 4:8
brotherly kindness *l* ..... 2 Pet 1:7
By this we know *l* ..... 1 John 3:16
Beloved, let us *l* ..... 1 John 4:7
for God is *l* ..... 1 John 4:8
There is no fear in l ..... 1 John 4:18
l Him because He ..... 1 John 4:19
loves God must *l* ..... 1 John 4:21
For this is the *l* ..... 1 John 5:3
have left your first *l* ..... Rev 2:4

LOVED
L one and friend You ..... Ps 88:18
Yet Jacob I have *l* ..... Mal 1:2
forgiven, for she *l* ..... Luke 7:47
so *l* the world that ..... John 3:16
whom Jesus *l* ..... John 13:23
"As the Father *l* ..... John 15:9
l them as You have ..... John 17:23
the Son of God, who l ..... Gal 2:20
l the church and gave ..... Eph 5:25
Beloved, if God so *l* ..... 1 John 4:11
To Him who *l* us and ..... Rev 1:5

LOVELY
he is altogether *l* ..... Song 5:16
whatever things are *l* ..... Phil 4:8

LOVES
"He who *l* father or ..... Matt 10:37
l his life will lose ..... John 12:25
l Me will be loved ..... John 14:21
l a cheerful giver ..... 2 Cor 9:7
If anyone *l* the world ..... 1 John 2:15
l God must love his ..... 1 John 4:21

LOVINGKINDNESS
To declare Your l ..... Ps 92:2

LOWER
made him a little *l* ..... Heb 2:7

LOWLINESS
with all *l* and ..... Eph 4:2

LOWLY
for I am gentle and *l* ..... Matt 11:29
in presence am *l* ..... 2 Cor 10:1
l brother glory ..... James 1:9

LUKEWARM
because you are *l* ..... Rev 3:16

LUST
looks at a woman to *l* ..... Matt 5:28
not fulfill the *l* ..... Gal 5:16
You *l* and do not have ..... James 4:2
the *l* of the flesh ..... 1 John 2:16

LUSTS
to fulfill its *l* ..... Rom 13:14
also youthful *l* ..... 2 Tim 2:22
and worldly *l* ..... Titus 2:12
to the former *l* ..... 1 Pet 1:14
abstain from fleshly *l* ..... 1 Pet 2:11
to their own ungodly *l* ..... Jude 18

LUTE
Praise Him with the *l* ..... Ps 150:3

LUXURY
in pleasure and *l* ..... James 5:5
the abundance of her *l* ..... Rev 18:3

LYING
I hate and abhor *l* ..... Ps 119:163
righteous man hates *l* ..... Prov 13:5
not trust in these *l* ..... Jer 7:4
signs, and *l* wonders ..... 2 Thess 2:9

M

MADE
m the stars also ..... Gen 1:16
things My hand has *m* ..... Is 66:2
All things were *m* ..... John 1:3

MADNESS
m is in their hearts ..... Eccl 9:3

MAGIC
m brought their books ..... Acts 19:19

MAGNIFIED
let Your name be *m* ..... 2 Sam 7:26
the Lord Jesus was *m* ..... Acts 19:17
also Christ will be *m* ..... Phil 1:20

MAGNIFIES
"My soul *m* the Lord ..... Luke 1:46

MAGNIFY
m the LORD with me ..... Ps 34:3

MAIDSERVANT
"Behold the *m* ..... Luke 1:38

MAIDSERVANTS
m I will pour out My ..... Acts 2:18

MAJESTY
right hand of the *M* ..... Heb 1:3
eyewitnesses of His *m* ..... 2 Pet 1:16
wise, Be glory and *m* ..... Jude 25

MAKE
"Let Us *m* man in Our ..... Gen 1:26
m you a great nation ..... Gen 12:2
"You shall not *m* ..... Ex 20:4
m Our home with ..... John 14:23

MAKER
M is your husband ..... Is 54:5
has forgotten his *M* ..... Hos 8:14
builder and *m* is God ..... Heb 11:10

MALICE
in *m* be babes ..... 1 Cor 14:20
laying aside all *m* ..... 1 Pet 2:1

MAN
"Let Us make *m*. . . . . . Gen 1:26
m that You are mindful . . . . . . Ps 8:4
of the Son of *M* . . . . . . Matt 24:27
"Behold the *M* . . . . . . John 19:5
by *m* came death . . . . . . 1 Cor 15:21
our outward *m* . . . . . . 2 Cor 4:16
the *m* of God may . . . . . . 2 Tim 3:17
is the number of a *m* . . . . . . Rev 13:18

MANGER
and laid Him in a *m* . . . . . . Luke 2:7

MANIFEST
m Myself to him . . . . . . John 14:21

MANIFESTATION
But the *m* of the . . . . . . 1 Cor 12:7

MANIFESTED
"I have *m* Your name . . . . . . John 17:6
God was *m* in the . . . . . . 1 Tim 3:16
the life was *m* . . . . . . 1 John 1:2

MANIFOLD
the *m* wisdom of God . . . . . . Eph 3:10

MANNA
of Israel ate *m* . . . . . . Ex 16:35
"Our fathers ate the *m* . . . . . . John 6:31

MANNER
Is this the *m* of man . . . . . . 2 Sam 7:19
in an unworthy *m* . . . . . . 1 Cor 11:27
what *m* of love . . . . . . 1 John 3:1

MANSIONS
house are many *m* . . . . . . John 14:2

MANTLE
Then he took the *m* . . . . . . 2 Kin 2:14

MARK
And the LORD set a *m* . . . . . . Gen 4:15
receives the *m* . . . . . . Rev 14:11

MARRED
So His visage was *m* . . . . . . Is 52:14

MARRIAGE
M is honorable among . . . . . . Heb 13:4

MARRIED
But he who is *m* . . . . . . 1 Cor 7:33

MARRY
they neither *m* nor . . . . . . Matt 22:30
forbidding to *m* . . . . . . 1 Tim 4:3

MARRYING
and drinking, *m* . . . . . . Matt 24:38

MARTYRS
the blood of the *m* . . . . . . Rev 17:6

MARVELED
Jesus heard it, He *m* . . . . . . Matt 8:10
so that Pilate *m* . . . . . . Mark 15:5

MARVELOUS
It is *m* in our eyes . . . . . . Ps 118:23
of darkness into His *m* . . . . . . 1 Pet 2:9

MASTER
a servant like his *m* . . . . . . Matt 10:25
greater than his *m* . . . . . . John 15:20
and useful for the *M* . . . . . . 2 Tim 2:21

MASTERS
can serve two *m* . . . . . . Luke 16:13
who have believing *m* . . . . . . 1 Tim 6:2

MATTERS
the weightier *m* . . . . . . Matt 23:23

MATURE
understanding be *m* . . . . . . 1 Cor 14:20
us, as many as are *m* . . . . . . Phil 3:15

MEANT
but God *m* it for good . . . . . . Gen 50:20

MEASURE
a perfect and just *m* . . . . . . Deut 25:15
give the Spirit by *m* . . . . . . John 3:34
to each one a *m* . . . . . . Rom 12:3

MEASURED
m the waters in the . . . . . . Is 40:12
you use, it will be *m* . . . . . . Matt 7:2

MEASURES
house differing *m* . . . . . . Deut 25:14

MEASURING
behold, a man with a *m* . . . . . . Zech 2:1
m themselves by . . . . . . 2 Cor 10:12

MEAT
will never again eat *m* . . . . . . 1 Cor 8:13

MEDIATOR
by the hand of a *m* . . . . . . Gal 3:19
is one God and one *M* . . . . . . 1 Tim 2:5
to Jesus the *M* of the . . . . . . Heb 12:24

MEDICINE
does good, like *m* . . . . . . Prov 17:22

MEDICINES
you will use many *m* . . . . . . Jer 46:11

MEDITATE
but you shall *m* . . . . . . Josh 1:8
M within your heart on . . . . . . Ps 4:4
I will *m* on Your . . . . . . Ps 119:15
m beforehand on . . . . . . Luke 21:14
m on these things . . . . . . Phil 4:8

MEDITATES
in His law he *m* . . . . . . Ps 1:2

MEDITATION
of my mouth and the *m* . . . . . . Ps 19:14
It is my *m* all the day . . . . . . Ps 119:97

MEDIUM
a woman who is a *m* . . . . . . Lev 20:27

MEDIUM'S
shall be like a *m* . . . . . . Is 29:4

MEDIUMS
"Seek those who are *m* . . . . . . Is 8:19

MEEK
with equity for the *m* . . . . . . Is 11:4
Blessed are the *m* . . . . . . Matt 5:5

MEEKNESS
are done in the *m* . . . . . . James 3:13

MEET
prepare to *m* your . . . . . . Amos 4:12
m the Lord in the . . . . . . 1 Thess 4:17

MELODY
singing and making *m* . . . . . . Eph 5:19

MELT
the elements will *m* . . . . . . 2 Pet 3:10

MEMBER
body is not one *m* . . . . . . 1 Cor 12:14

MEMBERS
you that one of your *m* . . . . . . Matt 5:29
do not present your *m* . . . . . . Rom 6:13
neighbor, for we are *m* . . . . . . Eph 4:25

MEMORIAL
and this is My *m* . . . . . . Ex 3:15
also be told as a *m* . . . . . . Matt 26:13

MEMORY
The *m* of the righteous . . . . . . Prov 10:7

MEN
m began to call on the . . . . . . Gen 4:26
make you fishers of *m* . . . . . . Matt 4:19
goodwill toward *m* . . . . . . Luke 2:14
heaven or from *m* . . . . . . Luke 20:4
Likewise also the *m* . . . . . . Rom 1:27
the Lord, and not to *m* . . . . . . Eph 6:7
between God and *m* . . . . . . 1 Tim 2:5

MENSERVANTS
And also on My *m* . . . . . . Joel 2:29
And on My *m* and on . . . . . . Acts 2:18

MERCHANDISE
house a house of *m* . . . . . . John 2:16

MERCIES
give you the sure *m* . . . . . . Acts 13:34

MERCIFUL
LORD, the LORD God, *m* . . . . . . Ex 34:6
He is ever *m* . . . . . . Ps 37:26
Blessed are the *m* . . . . . . Matt 5:7
saying, 'God be *m* . . . . . . Luke 18:13
"For I will be *m* . . . . . . Heb 8:12

MERCY
but showing *m* to . . . . . . Ex 20:6
and abundant in *m* . . . . . . Num 14:18
m endures forever . . . . . . 1 Chr 16:34
M and truth have met . . . . . . Ps 85:10
m is everlasting . . . . . . Ps 100:5
Let not *m* and truth . . . . . . Prov 3:3
For I desire *m* and not . . . . . . Hos 6:6
do justly, To love *m* . . . . . . Mic 6:8
'I desire *m* and not . . . . . . Matt 9:13
And His *m* is on those . . . . . . Luke 1:50
"I will have *m* . . . . . . Rom 9:15
that He might have *m* . . . . . . Rom 11:32
m has made . . . . . . 1 Cor 7:25
as we have received *m* . . . . . . 2 Cor 4:1
God, who is rich in *m* . . . . . . Eph 2:4
but I obtained *m* . . . . . . 1 Tim 1:13
that he may find *m* . . . . . . 2 Tim 1:18
to His *m* He saved us . . . . . . Titus 3:5
that we may obtain *m* . . . . . . Heb 4:16

MERRY
m heart makes a . . . . . . Prov 15:13
we should make *m* . . . . . . Luke 15:32

MESSENGER
"Behold, I send My *m* . . . . . . Mal 3:1
'Behold, I send My *m* . . . . . . Matt 11:10

MESSIAH
Until *M* the Prince . . . . . . Dan 9:25
"We have found the *M* . . . . . . John 1:41

MIDST
God is in the *m* . . . . . . Ps 46:5
I am there in the *m* . . . . . . Matt 18:20

MIGHT
'My power and the *m* . . . . . . Deut 8:17
'Not by *m* nor by . . . . . . Zech 4:6
in the power of His *m* . . . . . . Eph 6:10
honor and power and *m* . . . . . . Rev 7:12

MIGHTIER
coming after me is *m* . . . . . . Matt 3:11

MIGHTY
He was a *m* hunter . . . . . . Gen 10:9
m have fallen . . . . . . 2 Sam 1:19
The LORD *m* in battle . . . . . . Ps 24:8
their Redeemer is *m* . . . . . . Prov 23:11
m has done great . . . . . . Luke 1:49
the flesh, not many *m* . . . . . . 1 Cor 1:26
the working of His *m* . . . . . . Eph 1:19

MILK
come, buy wine and *m* . . . . . . Is 55:1
shall flow with *m* . . . . . . Joel 3:18
have come to need *m* . . . . . . Heb 5:12
desire the pure *m* . . . . . . 1 Pet 2:2

MILLSTONE
m were hung around . . . . . . Matt 18:6
a stone like a great *m* . . . . . . Rev 18:21

MIND
put wisdom in the *m* . . . . . . Job 38:36
perfect peace, Whose *m* . . . . . . Is 26:3
have an anxious *m* . . . . . . Luke 12:29
m I myself serve the . . . . . . Rom 7:25
who has known the *m* . . . . . . Rom 11:34
Be of the same *m* . . . . . . Rom 12:16
in his own *m* . . . . . . Rom 14:5
has known the *m* . . . . . . 1 Cor 2:16
are out of your *m* . . . . . . 1 Cor 14:23
Let this *m* be in you . . . . . . Phil 2:5
love and of a sound *m* . . . . . . 2 Tim 1:7

MINDFUL
is man that You are *m* . . . . . . Ps 8:4
for you are not *m* . . . . . . Matt 16:23
is man that You are *m* . . . . . . Heb 2:6

MINDS
put My law in their *m* . . . . . . Jer 31:33
I stir up your pure *m* . . . . . . 2 Pet 3:1

MINISTER
For he is God's *m* . . . . . . Rom 13:4
you will be a good *m* . . . . . . 1 Tim 4:6

MINISTERS
for they are God's *m* . . . . . . Rom 13:6
If anyone *m* . . . . . . 1 Pet 4:11

MINISTRIES
are differences of *m* . . . . . . 1 Cor 12:5

MINISTRY
But if the *m* of death . . . . . . 2 Cor 3:7
since we have this *m* . . . . . . 2 Cor 4:1
has given us the *m* . . . . . . 2 Cor 5:18
for the work of *m* . . . . . . Eph 4:12
fulfill your *m* . . . . . . 2 Tim 4:5
a more excellent *m* . . . . . . Heb 8:6

MIRACLE
one who works a *m* . . . . . . Mark 9:39

MIRACLES
worked unusual *m* .... Acts 19:11
the working of *m* .... 1 Cor 12:10
MISERY
And remember his *m* .... Prov 31:7
MITES
putting in two *m* .... Luke 21:2
MOCK
Fools *m* at sin .... Prov 14:9
to the Gentiles to *m* .... Matt 20:19
MOCKED
noon, that Elijah *m* .... 1 Kin 18:27
deceived, God is not *m* .... Gal 6:7
MOCKER
Wine is a *m* .... Prov 20:1
MOCKS
He who *m* the poor .... Prov 17:5
MODERATION
with propriety and *m* .... 1 Tim 2:9
MOMENT
in a *m* they die .... Job 34:20
in a *m*, in the .... 1 Cor 15:52
MONEY
be redeemed without *m* .... Is 52:3
And you who have no *m* .... Is 55:1
and hid his lord's *m* .... Matt 25:18
to give him *m* .... Mark 14:11
"Carry neither *m* .... Luke 10:4
I sent you without *m* .... Luke 22:35
be purchased with *m* .... Acts 8:20
not greedy for *m* .... 1 Tim 3:3
m is a root of all .... 1 Tim 6:10
MONEYCHANGERS
the tables of the *m* .... Matt 21:12
MOON
until the *m* is no more .... Ps 72:7
m will not give its .... Mark 13:24
MORNING
Evening and *m* and at .... Ps 55:17
Lucifer, son of the *m* .... Is 14:12
very early in the *m* .... Luke 24:1
the Bright and *M* Star .... Rev 22:16
MORTAL
sin reign in your *m* .... Rom 6:12
and this *m* must put .... 1 Cor 15:53
MORTALITY
m may be swallowed .... 2 Cor 5:4
MOTH
where *m* and rust .... Matt 6:19
MOTHER
because she was the *m* .... Gen 3:20
leave his father and *m* .... Matt 19:5
"Behold your *m* .... John 19:27
The *M* of Harlots .... Rev 17:5
MOUNT
come up to *M* Sinai .... Ex 19:23
They shall *m* up with .... Is 40:31
MOUNTAIN
to Horeb, the *m* .... Ex 3:1
let us go up to the *m* .... Is 2:3
became a great *m* .... Dan 2:35
are you, O great *m* .... Zech 4:7
you will say to this *m* .... Matt 17:20
Him on the holy *m* .... 2 Pet 1:18
MOUNTAINS
m were brought forth .... Ps 90:2
m shall depart And the .... Is 54:10
in Judea flee to the *m* .... Matt 24:16
that I could remove *m* .... 1 Cor 13:2
MOURN
A time to *m* .... Eccl 3:4
are those who *m* .... Matt 5:4
of the earth will *m* .... Rev 1:7
MOURNED
and have not rather *m* .... 1 Cor 5:2
MOURNING
shall be a great *m* .... Zech 12:11
be turned to *m* and .... James 4:9
MOUTH
"Who has made man's *m* .... Ex 4:11
Out of the *m* of babes .... Ps 8:2
knowledge, But the *m* .... Prov 10:14
The *m* of an immoral .... Prov 22:14
And a flattering *m* .... Prov 26:28
m speaking pompous .... Dan 7:8
m defiles a man .... Matt 15:11
m I will judge you .... Luke 19:22
I will give you a *m* .... Luke 21:15
m confession is made .... Rom 10:10
m great swelling words .... Jude 16
vomit you out of My *m* .... Rev 3:16
MOVED
she shall not be *m* .... Ps 46:5
spoke as they were *m* .... 2 Pet 1:21
MUCH
m study is .... Eccl 12:12
to whom *m* is given .... Luke 12:48
MULTIPLIED
of the disciples *m* .... Acts 6:7
of God grew and *m* .... Acts 12:24
MULTIPLY
"Be fruitful and *m* .... Gen 1:22
m the descendants .... Jer 33:22
MULTITUDE
stars of heaven in *m* .... Deut 1:10
In the *m* of words sin .... Prov 10:19
compassion on the *m* .... Matt 15:32
with the angel a *m* .... Luke 2:13
"love will cover a *m* .... 1 Pet 4:8
and behold, a great *m* .... Rev 7:9
MURDER
"You shall not *m* .... Ex 20:13
'You shall not *m* .... Matt 5:21
You *m* and covet and .... James 4:2
MURDERED
up Jesus whom you *m* .... Acts 5:30
MURDERER
He was a *m* from the .... John 8:44
his brother is a *m* .... 1 John 3:15
MURDERERS
and profane, for *m* .... 1 Tim 1:9
abominable, *m* .... Rev 21:8
MURDERS
evil thoughts, *m* .... Matt 15:19
MUSING
while I was *m* .... Ps 39:3
MUTILATION
beware of the *m* .... Phil 3:2
MUZZLE
"You shall not *m* .... 1 Tim 5:18
MYSTERIES
to you to know the *m* .... Matt 13:11
and understand all *m* .... 1 Cor 13:2
MYSTERY
given to know the *m* .... Mark 4:11
wisdom of God in a *m* .... 1 Cor 2:7
I tell you a *m* .... 1 Cor 15:51
made known to us the *m* .... Eph 1:9
the *m* of godliness .... 1 Tim 3:16

N

NAILED
it to the cross .... Col 2:14
NAKED
And they were both *n* .... Gen 2:25
knew that they were *n* .... Gen 3:7
"*N* I came from my .... Job 1:21
'I was *n* and you .... Matt 25:36
but all things are *n* .... Heb 4:13
brother or sister is *n* .... James 2:15
poor, blind, and *n* .... Rev 3:17
NAKEDNESS
or famine, or *n* .... Rom 8:35
n may not be revealed .... Rev 3:18
NAME
Abram called on the *n* .... Gen 13:4
Israel shall be your *n* .... Gen 35:10
This is My *n* forever .... Ex 3:15
shall not take the *n* .... Ex 20:7
and awesome *n* .... Deut 28:58
excellent is Your *n* .... Ps 8:1
n will put their trust .... Ps 9:10
be His glorious *n* .... Ps 72:19
do not call on Your *n* .... Ps 79:6
to Your *n* give glory .... Ps 115:1
above all Your *n* .... Ps 138:2
A good *n* is to be .... Prov 22:1
what is His Son's *n* .... Prov 30:4
be called by a new *n* .... Is 62:2
Everlasting is Your *n* .... Is 63:16
They will call on My *n* .... Zech 13:9
to you who fear My *n* .... Mal 4:2
Hallowed be Your *n* .... Matt 6:9
prophesied in Your *n* .... Matt 7:22
n Gentiles will trust .... Matt 12:21
together in My *n* .... Matt 18:20
will come in My *n* .... Matt 24:5
who believe in His *n* .... John 1:12
comes in his own *n* .... John 5:43
his own sheep by *n* .... John 10:3
through faith in His *n* .... Acts 3:16
there is no other *n* .... Acts 4:12
which is above every *n* .... Phil 2:9
deed, do all in the *n* .... Col 3:17
a more excellent *n* .... Heb 1:4
you hold fast to My *n* .... Rev 2:13
n that you are alive .... Rev 3:1
having His Father's *n* .... Rev 14:1
and glorify Your *n* .... Rev 15:4
n written that no one .... Rev 19:12
NAMED
I have *n* you .... Is 45:4
NAME'S
saved them for His *n* .... Ps 106:8
NARROW
"Enter by the *n* gate .... Matt 7:13
NATION
make you a great *n* .... Gen 12:2
exalts a *n* .... Prov 14:34
n that was not called .... Is 65:1
make them one *n* .... Ezek 37:22
since there was a *n* .... Dan 12:1
n will rise against .... Matt 24:7
"for he loves our *n* .... Luke 7:5
those who are not a *n* .... Rom 10:19
tribe, tongue, and *n* .... Rev 13:7
NATIONS
Why do the *n* rage .... Ps 2:1
I will give You the *n* .... Ps 2:8
n shall serve Him .... Ps 72:11
disciples of all the *n* .... Matt 28:19
who was to rule all *n* .... Rev 12:5
the healing of the *n* .... Rev 22:2
NATURAL
exchanged the *n* .... Rom 1:26
the men, leaving the *n* .... Rom 1:27
did not spare the *n* .... Rom 11:21
n man does not .... 1 Cor 2:14
It is sown a *n* body .... 1 Cor 15:44
NATURE
"We who are Jews by *n* .... Gal 2:15
by *n* children of wrath .... Eph 2:3
of the divine *n* .... 2 Pet 1:4
NEAR
the word is very *n* .... Deut 30:14
upon Him while He is *n* .... Is 55:6
know that it is *n* .... Matt 24:33
kingdom of God is *n* .... Luke 21:31
"The word is *n* .... Rom 10:8
to those who were *n* .... Eph 2:17
for the time is *n* .... Rev 1:3
NEARER
now our salvation is *n* .... Rom 13:11
NEED
the things you have *n* .... Matt 6:8
supply all your *n* .... Phil 4:19
to help in time of *n* .... Heb 4:16
NEGLECT
if we *n* so great a .... Heb 2:3
NEGLECTED
n the weightier .... Matt 23:23
NEIGHBOR
'you shall love your *n* .... Lev 19:18
"You shall love your *n* .... Matt 5:43
"And who is my *n* .... Luke 10:29
"You shall love your *n* .... Rom 13:9

NEVER
in Me shall *n* thirst .... John 6:35
in Me shall *n* die .... John 11:26
Love *n* fails .... 1 Cor 13:8
n take away sins .... Heb 10:11
"I will *n* leave you .... Heb 13:5
prophecy *n* came by .... 2 Pet 1:21

NEW
And there is nothing *n* .... Eccl 1:9
"For behold, I create *n* .... Is 65:17
n every morning .... Lam 3:23
wine into *n* wineskins .... Matt 9:17
of the *n* covenant .... Matt 26:28
n commandment I .... John 13:34
he is a *n* creation .... 2 Cor 5:17
when I will make a *n* .... Heb 8:8
n heavens and a *n* .... 2 Pet 3:13
n name written which .... Rev 2:17
And they sang a *n* .... Rev 5:9
And I saw a *n* heaven .... Rev 21:1
I make all things *n* .... Rev 21:5

NEWNESS
also should walk in *n* .... Rom 6:4

NIGHT
darkness He called *N* .... Gen 1:5
It is a *n* of solemn .... Ex 12:42
pillar of fire by *n* .... Ex 13:22
gives songs in the *n* .... Job 35:10
and continued all *n* .... Luke 6:12
man came to Jesus by *n* .... John 3:2
n is coming when no .... John 9:4
came to Jesus by *n* .... John 19:39
as a thief in the *n* .... 1 Thess 5:2
there shall be no *n* .... Rev 21:25

NINETY-NINE
he not leave the *n* .... Matt 18:12

NOTHING
"I can of Myself do *n* .... John 5:30
Me you can do *n* .... John 15:5
men, it will come to *n* .... Acts 5:3 8
have not love, I am *n* .... 1 Cor 13:2
Be anxious for *n* .... Phil 4:6
For we brought *n* .... 1 Tim 6:7

NOURISHED
"I have *n* and .... Is 1:2

NOURISHES
n and cherishes it .... Eph 5:29

NUMBER
if a man could *n* .... Gen 13:16
teach us to *n* our days .... Ps 90:12
which no one could *n* .... Rev 7:9
His *n* is 666 .... Rev 13:18

O

OATH
for the sake of your *o* .... Eccl 8:2
he denied with an *o* .... Matt 26:72
o which He swore .... Luke 1:73

OATHS
shall perform your *o* .... Matt 5:33

OBEDIENCE
o many will be made .... Rom 5:19
captivity to the *o* .... 2 Cor 10:5
yet He learned *o* .... Heb 5:8

OBEDIENT
you are willing and *o* .... Is 1:19
of the priests were *o* .... Acts 6:7
make the Gentiles *o* .... Rom 15:18
Himself and became *o* .... Phil 2:8
as *o* children .... 1 Pet 1:14

OBEY
God and *o* His voice .... Deut 4:30
His voice we will *o* .... Josh 24:24
o is better than .... 1 Sam 15:22
o God rather than men .... Acts 5:29
and do not *o* the truth .... Rom 2:8
yourselves slaves to *o* .... Rom 6:16
o your parents in all .... Col 3:20
Bondservants, *o* in all .... Col 3:22
those who do not *o* .... 2 Thess 1:8
O those who rule .... Heb 13:17

OBEYED
of sin, yet you *o* .... Rom 6:17

they have not all *o* .... Rom 10:16
By faith Abraham *o* .... Heb 11:8

OBSERVATION
does not come with *o* .... Luke 17:20

OBSERVE
teaching them to *o* all .... Matt 28:20

OBTAIN
also may *o* mercy .... Rom 11:31
o salvation through .... 1 Thess 5:9

OBTAINED
o a part in this .... Acts 1:17
yet have now *o* mercy .... Rom 11:30
endured, he *o* the .... Heb 6:15

OBTAINS
o favor from the LORD .... Prov 8:35

OFFEND
lest we *o* them .... Matt 17:27
than that he should *o* .... Luke 17:2
them, "Does this *o* .... John 6:61

OFFENDED
they were *o* at Him .... Matt 13:57

OFFENSE
and a rock of *o* .... Is 8:14
You are an *o* to Me .... Matt 16:23
by the one man's *o* .... Rom 5:17
the *o* of the cross .... Gal 5:11
sincere and without *o* .... Phil 1:10
And a rock of *o* .... 1 Pet 2:8

OFFENSES
For *o* must come .... Matt 18:7
impossible that no *o* .... Luke 17:1

OFFER
come and *o* your gift .... Matt 5:24
let us continually *o* .... Heb 13:15

OFFERED
to eat those things *o* .... 1 Cor 8:10
so Christ was *o* .... Heb 9:28
o one sacrifice .... Heb 10:12

OFFERING
o You did not require .... Ps 40:6
You make His soul an *o* .... Is 53:10
Himself for us, an *o* .... Eph 5:2
o You did not .... Heb 10:5
o He has perfected .... Heb 10:14

OFFERINGS
and offered burnt *o* .... Gen 8:20
In burnt *o* .... Heb 10:6

OFFICE
sitting at the tax *o* .... Matt 9:9

OFFSPRING
wife and raise up *o* .... Matt 22:24
we are also His *o* .... Acts 17:28
am the Root and the *O* .... Rev 22:16

OFTEN
o I wanted to gather .... Luke 13:34
as *o* as you eat this .... 1 Cor 11:26

OIL
a bin, and a little *o* .... 1 Kin 17:12
very costly fragrant *o* .... Matt 26:7
anointing him with *o* .... James 5:14
and do not harm the *o* .... Rev 6:6

OLD
young, and now am *o* .... Ps 37:25
was said to those of *o* .... Matt 5:21
but when you are *o* .... John 21:18
Your *o* men shall dream .... Acts 2:17
o man was crucified .... Rom 6:6
o things have passed .... 2 Cor 5:17
have put off the *o* man .... Col 3:9
that serpent of *o* .... Rev 20:2

OLDER
o shall serve the .... Gen 25:23
not rebuke an *o* man .... 1 Tim 5:1

OLDEST
beginning with the *o* .... John 8:9

OLIVE
a freshly plucked *o* .... Gen 8:11
o tree which is wild .... Rom 11:24

OMNIPOTENT
For the Lord God *O* .... Rev 19:6

ONCE
died, He died to sin *o* .... Rom 6:10
for men to die *o* .... Heb 9:27
also suffered *o* .... 1 Pet 3:18

ONE
"*O* thing you lack .... Mark 10:21
o thing is needed .... Luke 10:42
I and My Father are *o* .... John 10:30
that they may be *o* .... John 17:11
o accord in the temple .... Acts 2:46
for you are all *o* .... Gal 3:28
to create in Himself *o* .... Eph 2:15
o Lord .... Eph 4:5
o faith .... Eph 4:5
o baptism .... Eph 4:5
o God and Father of .... Eph 4:6
For there is *o* God and .... 1 Tim 2:5
o Mediator between .... 1 Tim 2:5
a thousand years as *o* .... 2 Pet 3:8

OPENED
o not His mouth .... Is 53:7
o the Scriptures .... Luke 24:32
o their understanding .... Luke 24:45
Now I saw heaven *o* .... Rev 19:11

OPENS
him the doorkeeper *o* .... John 10:3
and shuts and no one *o* .... Rev 3:7

OPINION
be wise in your own *o* .... Rom 11:25

OPINIONS
falter between two *o* .... 1 Kin 18:21

OPPORTUNITY
But sin, taking *o* .... Rom 7:8
as we have *o* .... Gal 6:10
but you lacked *o* .... Phil 4:10

OPPRESS
he loves to *o* .... Hos 12:7
o the widow or the .... Zech 7:10
Do not the rich *o* .... James 2:6

OPPRESSED
for all who are *o* .... Ps 103:6
The tears of the *o* .... Eccl 4:1
He was *o* and He was .... Is 53:7
all who were *o* .... Acts 10:38

OPPRESSES
o the poor reproaches .... Prov 14:31

OPPRESSION
have surely seen the *o* .... Ex 3:7
their life from *o* .... Ps 72:14
brought low through *o* .... Ps 107:39
me from the *o* .... Ps 119:134
considered all the *o* .... Eccl 4:1
o destroys a wise .... Eccl 7:7
justice, but behold, *o* .... Is 5:7
surely seen the *o* .... Acts 7:34

ORACLES
received the living *o* .... Acts 7:38
were committed the *o* .... Rom 3:2
principles of the *o* .... Heb 5:12

ORDAINED
o you a prophet .... Jer 1:5
whom He has *o* .... Acts 17:31

ORDER
decently and in *o* .... 1 Cor 14:40

ORDERS
o his conduct aright I .... Ps 50:23

ORDINANCE
resists the *o* of God .... Rom 13:2

ORDINANCES
and fleshly *o* imposed .... Heb 9:10

ORPHANS
will not leave you *o* .... John 14:18
to visit *o* and widows .... James 1:27

OUGHT
These you *o* to have .... Matt 23:23
pray for as we *o* .... Rom 8:26
persons *o* you to be .... 2 Pet 3:11

OUTCAST
they called you an *o* .... Jer 30:17

OUTCASTS
will assemble the *o* .... Is 11:12

OUTRAN
the other disciple *o* ... John 20:4

OUTSIDE
and dish, that the *o* ... Matt 23:26
Pharisees make the *o* ... Luke 11:39
toward those who are *o* ... Col 4:5
to Him, *o* the camp ... Heb 13:13
But *o* are dogs and ... Rev 22:15

OUTSTRETCHED
and with an *o* arm ... Deut 26:8

OUTWARD
at the *o* appearance ... 1 Sam 16:7
adornment be merely *o* ... 1 Pet 3:3

OUTWARDLY
not a Jew who is one *o* ... Rom 2:28

OVERCAME
My throne, as I also *o* ... Rev 3:21
"And they *o* him by ... Rev 12:11

OVERCOME
good cheer, I have *o* ... John 16:33
and the Lamb will *o* ... Rev 17:14

OVERCOMES
of God *o* the world ... 1 John 5:4
o I will give to eat ... Rev 2:7
o shall not be hurt ... Rev 2:11
o shall inherit all ... Rev 21:7

OVERSEER
to the Shepherd and *O* ... 1 Pet 2:25

OVERSEERS
you, serving as *o* ... 1 Pet 5:2

OVERSHADOW
of the Highest will *o* ... Luke 1:35

OVERTHREW
As God *o* Sodom and ... Jer 50:40

OVERTHROW
o the faith of some ... 2 Tim 2:18

OVERTHROWN
and Nineveh shall be *o* ... Jon 3:4

OVERTHROWS
And *o* the mighty ... Job 12:19
o them in the night ... Job 34:25
o the words of the ... Prov 22:12

OVERWHELM
o the fatherless ... Job 6:27

OVERWHELMED
and my spirit was *o* ... Ps 77:3
my spirit is *o* within ... Ps 143:4

OVERWORK
Do not *o* to be rich ... Prov 23:4

OWE
O no one anything ... Rom 13:8

OWED
o him ten thousand ... Matt 18:24

OWN
He came to His *o* ... John 1:11
having loved His *o* ... John 13:1
would love its *o* ... John 15:19
you are not your *o* ... 1 Cor 6:19
But each one has his *o* ... 1 Cor 7:7
For all seek their *o* ... Phil 2:21
from our sins in His *o* ... Rev 1:5

OX
shall not muzzle an *o* ... Deut 25:4
o knows its owner ... Is 1:3
Sabbath loose his *o* ... Luke 13:15
shall not muzzle an *o* ... 1 Cor 9:9

P

PACIFIES
A gift in secret *p* ... Prov 21:14

PAIN
p you shall bring ... Gen 3:16
p as a woman in ... Is 13:8
Why is my *p* perpetual ... Jer 15:18
shall be no more *p* ... Rev 21:4

PAINED
My heart is severely *p* ... Ps 55:4
I am *p* in my very ... Jer 4:19

PAINFUL
for the present, but *p* ... Heb 12:11

PAINS
The *p* of death ... Ps 116:3
having loosed the *p* ... Acts 2:24

PAINT
your eyes with *p* ... Jer 4:30

PALACE
enter the King's *p* ... Ps 45:15
guards his own *p* ... Luke 11:21
evident to the whole *p* ... Phil 1:13

PALACES
Out of the ivory *p* ... Ps 45:8

PALE
behold, a *p* horse ... Rev 6:8

PALM
p branches in their ... Rev 7:9

PALMS
struck Him with the *p* ... Matt 26:67

PAMPERS
p his servant from ... Prov 29:21

PANGS
The *p* of death ... Ps 18:4
labors with birth *p* ... Rom 8:22

PARABLE
do You speak this *p* ... Luke 12:41

PARABLES
rest it is given in *p* ... Luke 8:10

PARADISE
will be with Me in *P* ... Luke 23:43
in the midst of the *P* ... Rev 2:7

PARDON
He will abundantly *p* ... Is 55:7
p all their iniquities ... Jer 33:8

PARDONING
is a God like You, *p* ... Mic 7:18

PARENTS
will rise up against *p* ... Matt 10:21
has left house or *p* ... Luke 18:29
disobedient to *p* ... Rom 1:30

PART
chosen that good *p* ... Luke 10:42
you, you have no *p* ... John 13:8
For we know in *p* ... 1 Cor 13:9
shall take away his *p* ... Rev 22:19

PARTAKE
for we all *p* of that ... 1 Cor 10:17

PARTAKER
in hope should be *p* ... 1 Cor 9:10
Christ, and also a *p* ... 1 Pet 5:1

PARTAKERS
Gentiles have been *p* ... Rom 15:27
know that as you are *p* ... 2 Cor 1:7
qualified us to be *p* ... Col 1:12

PARTIAL
You shall not be *p* ... Lev 19:15

PARTIALITY
that God shows no *p* ... Acts 10:34
doing nothing with *p* ... 1 Tim 5:21
good fruits, without *p* ... James 3:17

PASS
I will *p* over you ... Ex 12:13
When you *p* through the ... Is 43:2
and earth will *p* ... Matt 24:35

PASSED
forbearance God had *p* ... Rom 3:25
High Priest who has *p* ... Heb 4:14
know that we have *p* ... 1 John 3:14

PASSES
of Christ which *p* ... Eph 3:19

PASSION
uncleanness, *p* ... Col 3:5

PASSIONS
gave them up to vile *p* ... Rom 1:26

PASSOVER
It is the LORD's *P* ... Ex 12:11
I will keep the *P* ... Matt 26:18
indeed Christ, our *P* ... 1 Cor 5:7
By faith he kept the *P* ... Heb 11:28

PASTORS
and some *p* and ... Eph 4:11

PASTURE
the sheep of Your *p* ... Ps 74:1
in and out and find *p* ... John 10:9

PASTURES
to lie down in green *p* ... Ps 23:2

PATH
You will show me the *p* ... Ps 16:11

PATHS
He leads me in the *p* ... Ps 23:3
Make His *p* straight ... Matt 3:3
and make straight *p* ... Heb 12:13

PATIENCE
'Master, have *p* ... Matt 18:26
and bear fruit with *p* ... Luke 8:15
labor of love, and *p* ... 1 Thess 1:3
faith, love, *p* ... 1 Tim 6:11
your faith produces *p* ... James 1:3
p have its perfect ... James 1:4
in the kingdom and *p* ... Rev 1:9

PATIENT
rejoicing in hope, *p* ... Rom 12:12
the weak, be *p* ... 1 Thess 5:14

PATIENTLY
if you take it *p* ... 1 Pet 2:20

PATRIARCHS
begot the twelve *p* ... Acts 7:8

PATTERN
p which you were ... Ex 26:30
as you have us for a *p* ... Phil 3:17
p shown you on the ... Heb 8:5

PEACE
you, And give you *p* ... Num 6:26
both lie down in *p* ... Ps 4:8
p have those who ... Ps 119:165
I am for *p* ... Ps 120:7
war, And a time of *p* ... Eccl 3:8
Father, Prince of *P* ... Is 9:6
keep him in perfect *p* ... Is 26:3
p they have not ... Is 59:8
slightly, Saying, '*P* ... Jer 6:14
place I will give *p* ... Hag 2:9
is worthy, let your *p* ... Matt 10:13
that I came to bring *p* ... Matt 10:34
And on earth *p* ... Luke 2:14
if a son of *p* is there ... Luke 10:6
that make for your *p* ... Luke 19:42
leave with you, My *p* ... John 14:27
Me you may have *p* ... John 16:33
Grace to you and *p* ... Rom 1:7
by faith, we have *p* ... Rom 5:1
God has called us to *p* ... 1 Cor 7:15
p will be with you ... 2 Cor 13:11
Spirit is love, joy, *p* ... Gal 5:22
He Himself is our *p* ... Eph 2:14
and the *p* of God ... Phil 4:7
And let the *p* of God ... Col 3:15
faith, love, *p* ... 2 Tim 2:22
meaning "king of *p*," ... Heb 7:2

PEACEABLE
is first pure, then *p* ... James 3:17

PEACEABLY
on you, live *p* ... Rom 12:18

PEACEFUL
in a *p* habitation ... Is 32:18

PEACEMAKERS
Blessed are the *p* ... Matt 5:9

PEARL
had found one *p* ... Matt 13:46

PEARLS
nor cast your *p* ... Matt 7:6
gates were twelve *p* ... Rev 21:21

PENTECOST
P had fully come ... Acts 2:1

PEOPLE
will take you as My *p* ... Ex 6:7
p shall be my *p* ... Ruth 1:16
p who know the joyful ... Ps 89:15
We are His *p* and the ... Ps 100:3
"Blessed is Egypt My *p* ... Is 19:25
to make ready a *p* ... Luke 1:17
take out of them a *p* ... Acts 15:14
who were not My *p* ... Rom 9:25

they shall be My *p* .... 2 Cor 6:16
LORD will judge His *p* .... Heb 10:30
but are now the *p* .... 1 Pet 2:10
tribe and tongue and *p* .... Rev 5:9
they shall be His *p* .... Rev 21:3

PERCEIVE
seeing, but do not *p* .... Is 6:9
may see and not *p* .... Mark 4:12

PERDITION
except the son of *p* .... John 17:12
revealed, the son of *p* .... 2 Thess 2:3
who draw back to *p* .... Heb 10:39

PERFECT
Noah was a just man, *p* .... Gen 6:9
Father in heaven is *p* .... Matt 5:48
they may be made *p* .... John 17:23
and *p* will of God .... Rom 12:2
when that which is *p* .... 1 Cor 13:10
present every man *p* .... Col 1:28
good gift and every *p* .... James 1:17
in word, he is a *p* .... James 3:2
p love casts out fear .... 1 John 4:18

PERFECTED
third day I shall be *p* .... Luke 13:32
or am already *p* .... Phil 3:12
Son who has been *p* .... Heb 7:28

PERFECTION
let us go on to *p* .... Heb 6:1

PERISH
so that we may not *p* .... Jon 1:6
little ones should *p* .... Matt 18:14
in Him should not *p* .... John 3:16
they shall never *p* .... John 10:28
among those who *p* .... 2 Thess 2:10
that any should *p* .... 2 Pet 3:9

PERISHABLE
do it to obtain a *p* .... 1 Cor 9:25

PERISHED
Truth has *p* and has .... Jer 7:28

PERISHING
We are *p* .... Matt 8:25

PERMIT
do not *p* a woman .... 1 Tim 2:12

PERMITS
we will do if God *p* .... Heb 6:3

PERMITTED
p no one to do them .... Ps 105:14
we are *p* .... 2 Cor 4:8

PERSECUTE
when they revile and *p* .... Matt 5:11

PERSECUTED
If they *p* Me .... John 15:20
p, but not forsaken .... 2 Cor 4:9

PERSECUTES
wicked in his pride *p* .... Ps 10:2

PERSECUTION
p arises because of .... Matt 13:21
At that time a great *p* .... Acts 8:1
do I still suffer *p* .... Gal 5:11

PERSECUTOR
a blasphemer, a *p* .... 1 Tim 1:13

PERSEVERANCE
tribulation produces *p* .... Rom 5:3

PERSEVERE
kept My command to *p* .... Rev 3:10

PERSISTENCE
p he will rise and .... Luke 11:8

PERSON
do not regard the *p* .... Matt 22:16
express image of His *p* .... Heb 1:3

PERSUADE
"You almost *p* me .... Acts 26:28

PERSUADED
neither will they be *p* .... Luke 16:31
p that He is able .... 2 Tim 1:12

PERSUASIVE
p words of human .... 1 Cor 2:4

PERVERSE
your way is *p* .... Num 22:32
p man sows strife .... Prov 16:28
from this *p* generation .... Acts 2:40

PERVERT
"You shall not *p* .... Deut 16:19
p the gospel of Christ .... Gal 1:7

PERVERTING
will you not cease *p* .... Acts 13:10

PERVERTS
p his ways will become .... Prov 10:9

PESTILENCE
from the perilous *p* .... Ps 91:3
Before Him went *p* .... Hab 3:5

PESTILENCES
will be famines, *p* .... Matt 24:7

PETITIONS
p that we have asked .... 1 John 5:15

PHARISEE
to pray, one a *P* .... Luke 18:10

PHILOSOPHERS
p encountered him .... Acts 17:18

PHILOSOPHY
cheat you through *p* .... Col 2:8

PHYSICIAN
have no need of a *p* .... Matt 9:12

PHYSICIANS
her livelihood on *p* .... Luke 8:43

PIECES
they took the thirty *p* .... Matt 27:9

PIERCE
a sword will *p* .... Luke 2:35

PIERCED
p My hands and My feet .... Ps 22:16
whom they have *p* .... Zech 12:10
of the soldiers *p* .... John 19:34
p themselves through .... 1 Tim 6:10
and they also who *p* .... Rev 1:7

PIERCING
p even to the division .... Heb 4:12

PILGRIMAGE
heart is set on *p* .... Ps 84:5
In the house of my *p* .... Ps 119:54

PILGRIMS
we are aliens and *p* .... 1 Chr 29:15
were strangers and *p* .... Heb 11:13

PILLAR
and she became a *p* .... Gen 19:26
and by night in a *p* .... Ex 13:21
the living God, the *p* .... 1 Tim 3:15

PILLARS
break their sacred *p* .... Ex 34:13
Blood and fire and *p* .... Joel 2:30
and his feet like *p* .... Rev 10:1

PIT
who go down to the *p* .... Ps 28:1
a harlot is a deep *p* .... Prov 23:27
my life in the *p* .... Lam 3:53
up my life from the *p* .... Jon 2:6
into the bottomless *p* .... Rev 20:3

PITIABLE
of all men the most *p* .... 1 Cor 15:19

PITS
The proud have dug *p* .... Ps 119:85

PITY
for someone to take *p* .... Ps 69:20
p He redeemed them .... Is 63:9
just as I had *p* .... Matt 18:33

PLACE
Come, see the *p* .... Matt 28:6
My word has no *p* .... John 8:37
I go to prepare a *p* .... John 14:2
might go to his own *p* .... Acts 1:25

PLACES
And the rough *p* .... Is 40:4
They love the best *p* .... Matt 23:6
in the heavenly *p* .... Eph 1:3

PLAGUE
bring yet one more *p* .... Ex 11:1

PLAGUES
p that are written .... Rev 22:18

PLANK
First remove the *p* .... Matt 7:5

PLANS
He makes the *p* of the .... Ps 33:10
that devises wicked *p* .... Prov 6:18

PLANT
A time to *p* .... Eccl 3:2
Him as a tender *p* .... Is 53:2
p of an alien vine .... Jer 2:21
p which My heavenly .... Matt 15:13

PLANTED
shall be like a tree *p* .... Ps 1:3
by the roots and be *p* .... Luke 17:6
I *p*, Apollos watered .... 1 Cor 3:6

PLANTS
neither he who *p* .... 1 Cor 3:7

PLATTER
head here on a *p* .... Matt 14:8

PLEASANT
food, that it was *p* .... Gen 3:6
how good and how *p* .... Ps 133:1

PLEASANTNESS
ways are ways of *p* .... Prov 3:17

PLEASE
in the flesh cannot *p* .... Rom 8:8
p his neighbor for his .... Rom 15:2
he may *p* the Lord .... 1 Cor 7:32
is impossible to *p* Him .... Heb 11:6

PLEASED
Then You shall be *p* .... Ps 51:19
in whom I am well *p* .... Matt 3:17
God was not well *p* .... 1 Cor 10:5
testimony, that he *p* .... Heb 11:5

PLEASES
Whatever the LORD *p* .... Ps 135:6

PLEASING
sacrifice, well *p* .... Phil 4:18
for this is well *p* .... Col 3:20
in you what is well *p* .... Heb 13:21

PLEASURE
Do good in Your good *p* .... Ps 51:18
p will be a poor man .... Prov 21:17
shall perform all My *p* .... Is 44:28
your Father's good *p* .... Luke 12:32
to the good *p* of His .... Eph 1:5
for sin You had no *p* .... Heb 10:6
My soul has no *p* .... Heb 10:38
p that war in your .... James 4:1

PLEASURES
Your right hand are *p* .... Ps 16:11
cares, riches, and *p* .... Luke 8:14
to enjoy the passing *p* .... Heb 11:25

PLOW
put his hand to the *p* .... Luke 9:62

PLOWED
You have *p* .... Hos 10:13

PLOWMAN
p shall overtake the .... Amos 9:13

PLUCK
p the heads of grain .... Mark 2:23

PLUCKED
cheeks to those who *p* .... Is 50:6
And His disciples *p* .... Luke 6:1
you would have *p* .... Gal 4:15

PLUNDER
p the Egyptians .... Ex 3:22
The *p* of the poor is .... Is 3:14
house and *p* his goods .... Matt 12:29

PLUNDERED
a people robbed and *p* .... Is 42:22
"And when you are *p* .... Jer 4:30

PLUNDERING
me Because of the *p* .... Is 22:4
accepted the *p* of your .... Heb 10:34

POETS
some of your own *p* .... Acts 171:28

POISON
"The *p* of asps is .... Rom 3:13

POISONED
p by bitterness .... Acts 8:23

POLLUTIONS
have escaped the *p* .... 2 Pet 2:20

POMP
had come with great *p* .... Acts 25:23
POMPOUS
and a mouth speaking *p* .... Dan 7:8
PONDER
P the path of your .... Prov 4:26
PONDERED
p them in her heart .... Luke 2:19
PONDERS
p all his paths .... Prov 5:21
POOR
p will never cease .... Deut 15:11
So the *p* have hope .... Job 5:16
I delivered the *p* .... Job 29:12
p shall eat and be .... Ps 22:26
But I am *p* and needy .... Ps 40:17
Let the *p* and needy .... Ps 74:21
He raises the *p* .... Ps 113:7
slack hand becomes *p* .... Prov 10:4
p man is hated even .... Prov 14:20
has mercy on the *p* .... Prov 14:21
who oppresses the *p* .... Prov 14:31
p reproaches his .... Prov 17:5
Do not rob the *p* .... Prov 22:22
that same *p* man .... Eccl 9:15
The alien or the *p* .... Zech 7:10
"Blessed are the *p* .... Matt 5:3
p have the gospel .... Matt 11:5
"For you have the *p* .... Matt 26:11
sakes He became *p* .... 2 Cor 8:9
should remember the *p* .... Gal 2:10
God not chosen the *p* .... James 2:5
wretched, miserable, *p* .... Rev 3:17
PORTION
O LORD, You, are the *p* .... Ps 16:5
heart and my *p* forever .... Ps 73:26
You are my *p* .... Ps 119:57
I will divide Him a *p* .... Is 53:12
rejoice in their *p* .... Is 61:7
The *P* of Jacob is not .... Jer 10:16
"The LORD is my *p* .... Lam 3:24
and appoint him his *p* .... Matt 24:51
to give them their *p* .... Luke 12:42
give me the *p* .... Luke 15:12
POSSESS
descendants shall *p* .... Gen 22:17
p the land which .... Josh 1:11
"By your patience *p* .... Luke 21:19
p his own vessel .... 1 Thess 4:4
POSSESSED
"The LORD *p* me at .... Prov 8:22
POSSESSING
and yet *p* all things .... 2 Cor 6:10
POSSESSION
as an everlasting *p* .... Gen 17:8
and an enduring *p* .... Heb 10:34
POSSESSIONS
and sold their *p* .... Acts 2:45
POSSIBLE
God all things are *p* .... Matt 19:26
p that the blood .... Heb 10:4
POUR
p My Spirit on your .... Is 44:3
P out Your fury .... Jer 10:25
That I will *p* out My .... Joel 2:28
"And I will *p* .... Zech 12:10
angels, "Go and *p* .... Rev 16:1
POURED
I am *p* out like water .... Ps 22:14
grace is *p* upon Your .... Ps 45:2
strong, Because He *p* .... Is 53:12
and My fury will be *p* .... Jer 7:20
broke the flask and *p* .... Mark 14:3
I am already being *p* .... 2 Tim 4:6
whom He *p* out on us .... Titus 3:6
POVERTY
leads only to *p* .... Prov 14:23
p put in all the .... Luke 21:4
and their deep *p* .... 2 Cor 8:2
p might become rich .... 2 Cor 8:9
tribulation, and *p* .... Rev 2:9
POWER
that I may show My *p* .... Ex 9:16
him who is without *p* .... Job 26:2
p who can understand .... Job 26:14
p belongs to God .... Ps 62:11
p Your enemies shall .... Ps 66:3
gives strength and *p* .... Ps 68:35
a king is, there is *p* .... Eccl 8:4
No one has *p* over the .... Eccl 8:8
'Not by might nor by *p* .... Zech 4:6
the kingdom and the *p* .... Matt 6:13
the Son of Man has *p* .... Matt 9:6
Scriptures nor the *p* .... Matt 22:29
p went out from Him .... Luke 6:19
are endued with *p* .... Luke 24:49
I have *p* to lay it .... John 10:18
"You could have no *p* .... John 19:11
you shall receive *p* .... Acts 1:8
though by our own *p* .... Acts 3:12
man is the great *p* .... Acts 8:10
"Give me this *p* .... Acts 8:19
for it is the *p* .... Rom 1:16
saved it is the *p* .... 1 Cor 1:18
Greeks, Christ the *p* .... 1 Cor 1:24
that the *p* of Christ .... 2 Cor 12:9
greatness of His *p* .... Eph 1:19
the Lord and in the *p* .... Eph 6:10
to His glorious *p* .... Col 1:11
the glory of His *p* .... 2 Thess 1:9
of fear, but of *p* .... 2 Tim 1:7
by the word of His *p* .... Heb 1:3
p of death, that .... Heb 2:14
as His divine *p* .... 2 Pet 1:3
Dominion and *p* .... Jude 25
to him I will give *p* .... Rev 2:26
honor and glory and *p* .... Rev 5:13
POWERFUL
of the LORD is *p* .... Ps 29:4
of God is living and *p* .... Heb 4:12
POWERS
principalities and *p* .... Col 2:15
word of God and the *p* .... Heb 6:5
PRAISE
p shall be of You in .... Ps 22:25
the people shall *p* .... Ps 45:17
P is awaiting You .... Ps 65:1
Let all the peoples *p* .... Ps 67:3
p shall be continually .... Ps 71:6
And the heavens will *p* .... Ps 89:5
Seven times a day I *p* .... Ps 119:164
that has breath *p* .... Ps 150:6
Let another man *p* .... Prov 27:2
let her own works *p* .... Prov 31:31
And your gates *P* .... Is 60:18
He makes Jerusalem a *p* .... Is 62:7
For You are my *p* .... Jer 17:14
Me a name of joy, a *p* .... Jer 33:9
give you fame and *p* .... Zeph 3:20
You have perfected *p* .... Matt 21:16
men more than the *p* .... John 12:43
p is not from men but .... Rom 2:29
Then each one's *p* .... 1 Cor 4:5
should be to the *p* .... Eph 1:12
to the glory and *p* .... Phil 1:11
I will sing *p* to You .... Heb 2:12
the sacrifice of *p* .... Heb 13:15
and for the *p* of those .... 1 Pet 2:14
saying, "*P* our God .... Rev 19:5
PRAISED
daily He shall be *p* .... Ps 72:15
LORD's name is to be *p* .... Ps 113:3
and greatly to be *p* .... Ps 145:3
the Most High and *p* .... Dan 4:34
PRAISES
it is good to sing *p* .... Ps 147:1
and he *p* .... Prov 31:28
PRAISEWORTHY
If there is anything *p* .... Phil 4:8
PRAISING
They will still be *p* .... Ps 84:4
of the heavenly host *p* .... Luke 2:13
in the temple *p* .... Luke 24:53
PRAY
at noon I will *p* .... Ps 55:17
who hate you, and *p* .... Matt 5:44
"And when you *p* .... Matt 6:5
manner, therefore, *p* .... Matt 6:9
"Watch and *p* .... Matt 26:41
"Lord, teach us to *p* .... Luke 11:1
"And I will *p* .... John 14:16
I do not *p* for the .... John 17:9
"I do not *p* for .... John 17:20
p without ceasing .... 1 Thess 5:17
Brethren, *p* for us .... 1 Thess 5:25
Let him *p* .... James 5:13
to one another, and *p* .... James 5:16
say that he should *p* .... 1 John 5:16
PRAYED
p more earnestly .... Luke 22:44
p earnestly that it .... James 5:17
PRAYER
p made in this place .... 2 Chr 7:15
And my *p* is pure .... Job 16:17
A *p* to the God of my .... Ps 42:8
P also will be made .... Ps 72:15
He shall regard the *p* .... Ps 102:17
to the LORD, But the *p* .... Prov 15:8
go out except by *p* .... Matt 17:21
all night in *p* to God .... Luke 6:12
continually to *p* .... Acts 6:4
where *p* was .... Acts 16:13
steadfastly in *p* .... Rom 12:12
to fasting and *p* .... 1 Cor 7:5
always with all *p* .... Eph 6:18
but in everything by *p* .... Phil 4:6
the word of God and *p* .... 1 Tim 4:5
And the *p* of faith .... James 5:15
PRAYERS
though You make many *p* .... Is 1:15
pretense make long *p* .... Matt 23:14
fervently for you in *p* .... Col 4:12
p may not be hindered .... 1 Pet 3:7
which are the *p* .... Rev 5:8
PREACH
time Jesus began to *p* .... Matt 4:17
you hear in the ear, *p* .... Matt 10:27
P the gospel to the .... Luke 4:18
And how shall they *p* .... Rom 10:15
p Christ crucified .... 1 Cor 1:23
I or they, so we *p* .... 1 Cor 15:11
P the word .... 2 Tim 4:2
PREACHED
p that people .... Mark 6:12
out and *p* .... Mark 16:20
of sins should be *p* .... Luke 24:47
p Christ to them .... Acts 8:5
lest, when I have *p* .... 1 Cor 9:27
than what we have *p* .... Gal 1:8
the gospel was *p* .... Heb 4:2
also He went and *p* .... 1 Pet 3:19
PREACHER
they hear without a *p* .... Rom 10:14
I was appointed a *p* .... 1 Tim 2:7
PREACHES
the Jesus whom Paul *p* .... Acts 19:13
p another Jesus .... 2 Cor 11:4
p any other gospel .... Gal 1:9
p the faith which he .... Gal 1:23
PREACHING
p Jesus as the .... Acts 5:42
not risen, then our *p* .... 1 Cor 15:14
PRECEPTS
all His *p* are sure .... Ps 111:7
how I love Your *p* .... Ps 119:159
PRECIOUS
P in the sight of the .... Ps 116:15
She is more *p* than .... Prov 3:15
p things shall not .... Is 44:9
if you take out the *p* .... Jer 15:19
farmer waits for the *p* .... James 5:7
more *p* than gold .... 1 Pet 1:7
who believe, He is *p* .... 1 Pet 2:7
p in the sight of .... 1 Pet 3:4
PREDESTINED
foreknew, He also *p* .... Rom 8:29
having *p* us to .... Eph 1:5
inheritance, being *p* .... Eph 1:11

PREEMINENCE
He may have the *p* .... Col 1:18
loves to have the *p* .... 3 John 9

PREFERENCE
in honor giving *p* .... Rom 12:10

PREJUDICE
these things without *p* .... 1 Tim 5:21

PREMEDITATE
p what you will .... Mark 13:11

PREPARATION
Now it was the *P* .... John 19:14
your feet with the *p* .... Eph 6:15

PREPARE
p a table before me in .... Ps 23:5
P the way of the LORD .... Mark 1:3
p a place for you .... John 14:2

PREPARED
for whom it is *p* .... Matt 20:23
Which You have *p* .... Luke 2:31
mercy, which He had *p* .... Rom 9:23
things which God has *p* .... 1 Cor 2:9
Now He who has *p* .... 2 Cor 5:5
p beforehand that we .... Eph 2:10
God, for He has *p* .... Heb 11:16

PRESENCE
themselves from the *p* .... Gen 3:8
went out from the *p* .... Gen 4:16
P will go with you .... Ex 33:14
afraid in any man's *p* .... Deut 1:17
p is fullness of joy .... Ps 16:11
shall dwell in Your *p* .... Ps 140:13
not tremble at My *p* .... Jer 5:22
shall shake at My *p* .... Ezek 38:20
and drank in Your *p* .... Luke 13:26
full of joy in Your *p* .... Acts 2:28
but his bodily *p* .... 2 Cor 10:10
obeyed, not as in my *p* .... Phil 2:12

PRESENT
we are all *p* before .... Acts 10:33
evil is *p* with me .... Rom 7:21
p your bodies a living .... Rom 12:1
or death, or things *p* .... 1 Cor 3:22
absent in body but *p* .... 1 Cor 5:3
that He might *p* .... Eph 5:27
p you faultless .... Jude 24

PRESERVE
He shall *p* your soul .... Ps 121:7
The LORD shall *p* .... Ps 121:8
loses his life will *p* .... Luke 17:33
every evil work and *p* .... 2 Tim 4:18

PRESERVED
soul, and body be *p* .... 1 Thess 5:23

PRESERVES
For the LORD *p* the .... Ps 31:23
p the souls of His .... Ps 97:10
who keeps his way *p* .... Prov 16:17

PRETENSE
p make long prayers .... Matt 23:14

PRICE
one pearl of great *p* .... Matt 13:46
were bought at a *p* .... 1 Cor 6:20

PRIDE
p serves as .... Ps 73:6
By *p* comes nothing .... Prov 13:10
P goes before .... Prov 16:18
her daughter had *p* .... Ezek 16:49
was hardened in *p* .... Dan 5:20
For the *p* of the .... Zech 11:3
evil eye, blasphemy, *p* .... Mark 7:22
p he fall into the .... 1 Tim 3:6
eyes, and the *p* .... 1 John 2:16

PRIEST
he was the *p* of God .... Gen 14:18
p forever According .... Ps 110:4
So He shall be a *p* .... Zech 6:13
and faithful High *P* .... Heb 2:17
we have a great High *P* .... Heb 4:14
p forever according .... Heb 5:6
Christ came as High *P* .... Heb 9:11

PRIESTHOOD
p being changed .... Heb 7:12
has an unchangeable *p* .... Heb 7:24
generation, a royal *p* .... 1 Pet 2:9

PRIESTS
to Me a kingdom of *p* .... Ex 19:6
Her *p* teach for pay .... Mic 3:11
made us kings and *p* .... Rev 1:6

PRINCE
is the house of the *p* .... Job 21:28
Everlasting Father, *P* .... Is 9:6
Until Messiah the *P* .... Dan 9:25
days without king or *p* .... Hos 3:4
p asks for gifts .... Mic 7:3
"and killed the *P* .... Acts 3:15
His right hand to be *P* .... Acts 5:31
the *p* of the power .... Eph 2:2

PRINCES
to put confidence in *p* .... Ps 118:9
He brings the *p* .... Is 40:23

PRISON
and put him into the *p* .... Gen 39:20
Bring my soul out of *p* .... Ps 142:7
in darkness from the *p* .... Is 42:7
the opening of the *p* .... Is 61:1
John had heard in *p* .... Matt 11:2
I was in *p* and you .... Matt 25:36

PRIZE
the goal for the *p* .... Phil 3:14

PROCEED
of the same mouth *p* .... James 3:10

PROCEEDED
for I *p* forth .... John 8:42

PROCEEDS
by every word that *p* .... Deut 8:3
by every word that *p* .... Matt 4:4
Spirit of truth who *p* .... John 15:26

PROCLAIM
began to *p* it freely .... Mark 1:45
knowing, Him I *p* .... Acts 17:23
drink this cup, you *p* .... 1 Cor 11:26

PROCLAIMED
p the good news .... Ps 40:9
he went his way and *p* .... Luke 8:39

PROCLAIMER
"He seems to be a *p* .... Acts 17:18

PROCLAIMS
good news, Who *p* .... Is 52:7

PRODIGAL
with *p* living .... Luke 15:13

PROFANE
and priest are *p* .... Jer 23:11
tried to *p* the temple .... Acts 24:6
But reject *p* and old .... 1 Tim 4:7

PROFANED
and *p* My Sabbaths .... Ezek 22:8

PROFANENESS
of Jerusalem *p* has .... Jer 23:15

PROFANING
p the covenant of the .... Mal 2:10

PROFESS
They *p* to know God .... Titus 1:16

PROFIT
For what *p* is it to .... Matt 16:26
"For what will it *p* .... Mark 8:36
"For what *p* is it to .... Luke 9:25
her masters much *p* .... Acts 16:16
brought no small *p* .... Acts 19:24
what is the *p* of .... Rom 3:1
seeking my own *p* .... 1 Cor 10:33
Christ will *p* you .... Gal 5:2
about words to no *p* .... 2 Tim 2:14
them, but He for our *p* .... Heb 12:10
What does it *p* .... James 2:14
sell, and make a *p* .... James 4:13

PROFITABLE
It is doubtless not *p* .... 1 Cor 12:1
of God, and is *p* .... 2 Tim 3:16

PROFITS
have not love, it *p* .... 1 Cor 13:3

PROMISE
"Behold, I send the *P* .... Luke 24:49
but to wait for the *P* .... Acts 1:4
"For the *p* is to you .... Acts 2:39
for the hope of the *p* .... Acts 26:6
p might be sure .... Rom 4:16
Therefore, since a *p* .... Heb 4:1
to the heirs of *p* .... Heb 6:17
did not receive the *p* .... Heb 11:39

PROMISED
faithful who had *p* .... Heb 11:11

PROMISES
For all the *p* of God .... 2 Cor 1:20
his Seed were the *p* .... Gal 3:16
having received the *p* .... Heb 11:13
great and precious *p* .... 2 Pet 1:4

PROPER
you, but for what is *p* .... 1 Cor 7:35
but, which is *p* .... 1 Tim 2:10

PROPERLY
Let us walk *p* .... Rom 13:13

PROPHECY
to another *p* .... 1 Cor 12:10
for *p* never came by .... 2 Pet 1:21
is the spirit of *p* .... Rev 19:10
of the book of this *p* .... Rev 22:19

PROPHESIED
Lord, have we not *p* .... Matt 7:22
and the law *p* .... Matt 11:13

PROPHESIES
p edifies the church .... 1 Cor 14:4

PROPHESY
prophets, "Do not *p* .... Is 30:10
The prophets *p* falsely .... Jer 5:31
your daughters shall *p* .... Joel 2:28
Who can but *p* .... Amos 3:8
saying, "*P* to us .... Matt 26:68
your daughters shall *p* .... Acts 2:17
in part and we *p* .... 1 Cor 13:9

PROPHET
raise up for you a *P* .... Deut 18:15
"I alone am left a *p* .... 1 Kin 18:22
I ordained you a *p* .... Jer 1:5
The *p* is a fool .... Hos 9:7
Nor was I a son of a *p* .... Amos 7:14
send you Elijah the *p* .... Mal 4:5
p shall receive a .... Matt 10:41
p is not without honor .... Matt 13:57
by Daniel the *p* .... Mark 13:14
is not a greater *p* .... Luke 7:28
it cannot be that a *p* .... Luke 13:33
who was a *P* .... Luke 24:19
"Are you the *P* .... John 1:21
"This is truly the *P* .... John 6:14
with him the false *p* .... Rev 19:20

PROPHETIC
p word confirmed .... 2 Pet 1:19

PROPHETS
the Law or the *P* .... Matt 5:17
is the Law and the *P* .... Matt 7:12
or one of the *p* .... Matt 16:14
the tombs of the *p* .... Matt 23:29
indeed, I send you *p* .... Matt 23:34
one who kills the *p* .... Matt 23:37
Then many false *p* .... Matt 24:11
Moses and the *p* .... Luke 16:29
are sons of the *p* .... Acts 3:25
p did your fathers not .... Acts 7:52
"To Him all the *p* .... Acts 10:43
do you believe the *p* .... Acts 26:27
by the Law and the *P* .... Rom 3:21
have killed Your *p* .... Rom 11:3
to be apostles, some *p* .... Eph 4:11
this salvation the *p* .... 1 Pet 1:10
because many false *p* .... 1 John 4:1
found the blood of *p* .... Rev 18:24

PROPITIATION
set forth as a *p* .... Rom 3:25
to God, to make *p* .... Heb 2:17
He Himself is the *p* .... 1 John 2:2
His Son to be the *p* .... 1 John 4:10

PROPRIETY
modest apparel, with *p* .... 1 Tim 2:9

PROSPER
they *p* who love you .... Ps 122:6
of the LORD shall *p* .... Is 53:10
against you shall *p* .... Is 54:17
up as he may *p* .... 1 Cor 16:2
I pray that you may *p* .... 3 John 2

PROSPERED
since the LORD has *p* .... Gen 24:56

PROSPERING
His ways are always *p* .... Ps 10:5

PROSPERITY
p all your days .... Deut 23:6
p the destroyer .... Job 15:21
Now in my *p* I said .... Ps 30:6
has pleasure in the *p* .... Ps 35:27
When I saw the *p* .... Ps 73:3
I pray, send now *p* .... Ps 118:25
that we have our *p* .... Acts 19:25

PROSPEROUS
will make your way *p* .... Josh 1:8

PROSPERS
just as your soul *p* .... 3 John 2

PROUD
tongue that speaks *p* .... Ps 12:3
And fully repays the *p* .... Ps 31:23
does not respect the *p* .... Ps 40:4
a haughty look and a *p* .... Ps 101:5
p He knows from afar .... Ps 138:6
Everyone *p* .... Prov 16:5
by wine, He is a *p* .... Hab 2:5
He has scattered the *p* .... Luke 1:51
"God resists the *p* .... 1 Pet 5:5

PROVERB
of a drunkard Is a *p* .... Prov 26:9
one shall take up a *p* .... Mic 2:4
to the true *p* .... 2 Pet 2:22

PROVERBS
three thousand *p* .... 1 Kin 4:32
in order many *p* .... Eccl 12:9

PROVIDE
"My son, God will *p* .... Gen 22:8
"*P* neither gold nor .... Matt 10:9
if anyone does not *p* .... 1 Tim 5:8

PROVIDED
these hands have *p* .... Acts 20:34
p something better .... Heb 11:40

PROVISION
no *p* for the flesh .... Rom 13:14

PROVOKE
"Do they *p* Me to .... Jer 7:19
you, fathers, do not *p* .... Eph 6:4

PROVOKED
p the Most High .... Ps 78:56
his spirit was *p* .... Acts 17:16
seek its own, is not *p* .... 1 Cor 13:5

PRUDENCE
To give *p* to the .... Prov 1:4
wisdom, dwell with *p* .... Prov 8:12
us in all wisdom and *p* .... Eph 1:8

PRUDENT
p man covers shame .... Prov 12:16
A *p* man conceals .... Prov 12:23
The wisdom of the *p* .... Prov 14:8
p considers well .... Prov 14:15
heart will be called *p* .... Prov 16:21
p man foresees evil .... Prov 22:3
Therefore the *p* .... Amos 5:13
from the wise and *p* .... Matt 11:25

PRUDENTLY
Servant shall deal *p* .... Is 52:13

PRUNES
that bears fruit He *p* .... John 15:2

PSALM
each of you has a *p* .... 1 Cor 14:26

PSALMIST
And the sweet *p* .... 2 Sam 23:1

PSALMS
to one another in *p* .... Eph 5:19
Let him sing *p* .... James 5:13

PUNISH
p the righteous is .... Prov 17:26
Shall I not *p* them for .... Jer 5:9

PUNISHED
p them often in every .... Acts 26:11
These shall be *p* .... 2 Thess 1:9

PUNISHES
will you say when He *p* .... Jer 13:21

PUNISHMENT
p is greater than I .... Gen 4:13
you do in the day of *p* .... Is 10:3
p they shall perish .... Jer 10:15
not turn away its *p* .... Amos 1:3
into everlasting *p* .... Matt 25:46
p which was inflicted .... 2 Cor 2:6
Of how much worse *p* .... Heb 10:29
sent by him for the *p* .... 1 Pet 2:14
the unjust under *p* .... 2 Pet 2:9

PURE
a mercy seat of *p* gold .... Ex 25:17
'My doctrine is *p* .... Job 11:4
that he could be *p* .... Job 15:14
of the LORD are *p* .... Ps 12:6
ways of a man are *p* .... Prov 16:2
a generation that is *p* .... Prov 30:12
things indeed are *p* .... Rom 14:20
whatever things are *p* .... Phil 4:8
keep yourself *p* .... 1 Tim 5:22
p all things are *p* .... Titus 1:15
above is first *p* .... James 3:17
babes, desire the *p* .... 1 Pet 2:2
just as He is *p* .... 1 John 3:3

PURER
p eyes than to behold .... Hab 1:13

PURGE
P me with hyssop .... Ps 51:7

PURGED
away, And your sin *p* .... Is 6:7

PURIFICATION
with the water of *p* .... Num 31:23

PURIFIED
all things are *p* .... Heb 9:22
Since you have *p* .... 1 Pet 1:22

PURIFIES
hope in Him *p* himself .... 1 John 3:3

PURIFY
and *p* your hearts .... James 4:8

PURIFYING
p their hearts by .... Acts 15:9
sanctifies for the *p* .... Heb 9:13

PURIM
called these days *P* .... Esth 9:26

PURITY
spirit, in faith, in *p* .... 1 Tim 4:12

PURPOSE
A time for every *p* .... Eccl 3:1
But for this *p* I came .... John 12:27
by the determined *p* .... Acts 2:23
to fulfill His *p* .... Rev 17:17

PURSUE
p righteousness .... Rom 9:30
P love .... 1 Cor 14:1

PURSUES
flee when no one *p* .... Prov 28:1

Q

QUAIL
and it brought *q* .... Num 11:31

QUARREL
He will not *q* nor cry .... Matt 12:19
the Lord must not *q* .... 2 Tim 2:24

QUARRELSOME
but gentle, not *q* .... 1 Tim 3:3

QUEEN
heart, 'I sit as *q* .... Rev 18:7

QUENCH
Many waters cannot *q* .... Song 8:7
flax He will not *q* .... Matt 12:20
q all the fiery .... Eph 6:16
Do not *q* the Spirit .... 1 Thess 5:19

QUENCHED
that shall never be *q* .... Mark 9:43

QUESTIONS
and asking them *q* .... Luke 2:46

QUICKLY
with your adversary *q* .... Matt 5:25
"Surely I am coming *q* .... Rev 22:20

QUIET
aspire to lead a *q* .... 1 Thess 4:11
a gentle and *q* spirit .... 1 Pet 3:4

QUIETNESS
a handful with *q* .... Eccl 4:6
In *q* and confidence .... Is 30:15
of righteousness, *q* .... Is 32:17
that they work in *q* .... 2 Thess 3:12

R

RABBI
be called by men, '*R* .... Matt 23:7

RACA
to his brother, '*R* .... Matt 5:22

RACE
man to run its *r* .... Ps 19:5
r is not to the swift .... Eccl 9:11
I have finished the *r* .... 2 Tim 4:7
with endurance the *r* .... Heb 12:1

RAGE
Why do the nations *r* .... Ps 2:1
'Why did the nations *r* .... Acts 4:25

RAIN
had not caused it to *r* .... Gen 2:5
And the *r* was on the .... Gen 7:12
I will *r* down on him .... Ezek 38:22
given you the former *r* .... Joel 2:23
the good, and sends *r* .... Matt 5:45
"and the *r* descended .... Matt 7:25
that often comes .... Heb 6:7
that it would not *r* .... James 5:17

RAINBOW
"I set My *r* in the .... Gen 9:13
and there was a *r* .... Rev 4:3

RAINED
fire and brimstone .... Luke 17:29

RAINS
righteousness .... Hos 10:12

RAISE
third day He will *r* .... Hos 6:2
in three days I will *r* .... John 2:19
and I will *r* him up at .... John 6:40
and the Lord will *r* .... James 5:15

RAISED
be killed, and be *r* .... Matt 16:21
Just as Christ was *r* .... Rom 6:4
Spirit of Him who *r* .... Rom 8:11
"How are the dead *r* .... 1 Cor 15:35
the dead will be *r* .... 1 Cor 15:52
and *r* us up together .... Eph 2:6

RAISES
"For as the Father *r* .... John 5:21
but in God who *r* .... 2 Cor 1:9

RAN
You *r* well .... Gal 5:7

RANSOM
to give His life a *r* .... Mark 10:45
who gave Himself a *r* .... 1 Tim 2:6

RANSOMED
And the *r* of the LORD .... Is 35:10
redeemed Jacob, And *r* .... Jer 31:11

RASH
Do not be *r* with your .... Eccl 5:2

RASHLY
and do nothing *r* .... Acts 19:36

RAVENOUS
inwardly they are *r* .... Matt 7:15

RAVENS
"Consider the *r* .... Luke 12:24

REACHING
forward to those .... Phil 3:13

READ
day, and stood up to *r* .... Luke 4:16
hearts, known and *r* .... 2 Cor 3:2

READER
the *r* understand .... Mark 13:14

READINESS
the word with all *r* .... Acts 17:11

READING
the prophet Isaiah .... Acts 8:30

READS
Blessed is he who *r* .... Rev 1:3

READY
and those who were *r* .... Matt 25:10

"Lord, I am *r* .... Luke 22:33
Be *r* in season and out .... 2 Tim 4:2
and always be *r*.................... 1 Pet 3:15

REAP
they neither sow nor *r* .... Matt 6:26
you knew that I *r* .... Matt 25:26

REAPED
You have *r* iniquity .... Hos 10:13

REAPERS
are the angels .... Matt 13:39

REAPING
what I did not .... Luke 19:22

REAPS
sows and another *r* .... John 4:37

REASON
"Come now, and let us *r* .... Is 1:18
who asks you a *r* .... 1 Pet 3:15

REASONED
for three Sabbaths *r* .... Acts 17:2

REBEL
if you refuse and *r* .... Is 1:20

REBELLING
more against Him By *r*............. Ps 78:17

REBELLION
hearts as in the *r*.................. Heb 3:8

REBELLIOUS
day long to a *r* people .... Is 65:2

REBUILD
God, to *r* its ruins .... Ezra 9:9
it as in the days of.............. Amos 9:11

REBUKE
Turn at my *r* .... Prov 1:23
R a wise man .... Prov 9:8
is better Than love .... Prov 27:5
R the oppressor .... Is 1:17
sins against you, *r*............... Luke 17:3
Do not *r* an older man .... 1 Tim 5:1
who are sinning *r*.............. 1 Tim 5:20
"The Lord *r* you .... Jude 9
"As many as I love, I *r* .... Rev 3:19

REBUKED
the winds and the .... Matt 8:26
their unbelief .... Mark 16:14
but he was *r* for his .... 2 Pet 2:16

REBUKES
ear that hears the *r*............. Prov 15:31

RECEIVE
believing, you will *r* .... Matt 21:22
and His own did not *r* .... John 1:11
will come again and *r* .... John 14:3
the world cannot *r* .... John 14:17
Ask, and you will *r* .... John 16:24
"*R* the Holy Spirit .... John 20:22
"Lord Jesus, *r* .... Acts 7:59
the Holy Spirit .... Acts 19:2
R one who is weak .... Rom 14:1
the Spirit by the .... Gal 3:2
suppose that he will *r*........... James 1:7

RECEIVED
But as many as *r*................. John 1:12
for God has *r* him .... Rom 14:3
For I *r* from the Lord .... 1 Cor 11:23
Christ .... Col 2:6
R up in glory .... 1 Tim 3:16

RECEIVES
you *r* Me .... Matt 10:40
and whoever *r* Me .... Mark 9:37

RECONCILE
and that He might *r*.............. Eph 2:16

RECONCILED
First be *r* to your .... Matt 5:24
we were *r* .... Rom 5:10
Christ's behalf, be *r* .... 2 Cor 5:20

RECONCILIATION
now received the *r* .... Rom 5:11
to us the word of *r* .... 2 Cor 5:19

RECONCILING
cast away is the *r* .... Rom 11:15
God was in Christ *r* .... 2 Cor 5:19

REDEEM
But God will *r* my soul .... Ps 49:15
their life from .... Ps 72:14
was going to *r* Israel .... Luke 24:21
those who were .... Gal 4:5
us, that He might *r*.............. Titus 2:14

REDEEMED
Let the *r* of the LORD .... Ps 107:2
shall walk there .... Is 35:9
sea a road For the *r* .... Is 51:10
And you shall be *r* .... Is 52:3
and *r* His people .... Luke 1:68
Christ has *r* us from .... Gal 3:13
that you were not *r* .... 1 Pet 1:18
were slain, And have *r* .... Rev 5:9

REDEEMER
For I know that my *R* .... Job 19:25
Our *R* from Everlasting .... Is 63:16

REDEEMING
the time .... Eph 5:16

REDEMPTION
those who looked for *r*........... Luke 2:38
your *r* draws near .... Luke 21:28
grace through the *r* .... Rom 3:24
the adoption, the *r* .... Rom 8:23
sanctification and *r* .... 1 Cor 1:30
In Him we have *r*..................... Eph 1:7
for the day of *r*.................. Eph 4:30
obtained eternal *r*................ Heb 9:12

REED
He will not break .... Is 42:3
shaken by the wind .... Matt 11:7

REFINED
us as silver is *r* .... Ps 66:10

REFINER
He will sit as a *r* .... Mal 3:3

REFORMATION
until the time of *r* .... Heb 9:10

REFRESH
my heart in the Lord .... Philem 20

REFRESHED
his spirit has been *r* .... 2 Cor 7:13
for he often *r* .... 2 Tim 1:16

REFRESHES
the soul of his .... Prov 25:13

REFRESHING
may come from the .... Acts 3:19

REFUGE
eternal God is your *r*........... Deut 33:27
God is our *r* and .... Ps 46:1
who have fled for *r* .... Heb 6:18

REGARD
iniquity in my heart .... Ps 66:18
did not fear God nor *r* .... Luke 18:2

REGARDED
my hand and no one *r* .... Prov 1:24
the lowly state .... Luke 1:48

REGARDS
a rebuke will be .... Prov 13:18

REGENERATION
to you, that in the *r*............ Matt 19:28
the washing of *r*................. Titus 3:5

REGISTERED
So all went to be *r*................ Luke 2:3

REGRETTED
but afterward he *r*............. Matt 21:29

REGULATIONS
yourselves to *r*.......................... Col 2:20

REIGN
"And He will *r* .... Luke 1:33
righteousness will *r* .... Rom 5:17
so grace might *r* .... Rom 5:21
do not let sin *r*..................... Rom 6:12
For He must *r* till He .... 1 Cor 15:25
of Christ, and shall *r* .... Rev 20:6

REIGNED
so that as sin *r* .... Rom 5:21
You have *r* as kings .... 1 Cor 4:8
And they lived and *r* .... Rev 20:4

REIGNS
to Zion, "Your God *r*................. Is 52:7
Lord God Omnipotent *r*........... Rev 19:6

REJECT
"All too well you *r* .... Mark 7:9
R a divisive man .... Titus 3:10

REJECTED
He is despised and *r* .... Is 53:3
r Has become the .... Matt 21:42
many things and be *r*............ Luke 17:25
Moses whom they *r* .... Acts 7:35
to a living stone, *r* .... 1 Pet 2:4

REJECTION
you shall know My *r*............ Num 14:34

REJECTS
he who *r* Me *r* .... Luke 10:16

REJOICE
R in the LORD .... Ps 33:1
of Your wings I will *r*.............. Ps 63:7
Let them *r* before God .... Ps 68:3
Let the heavens *r* .... Ps 96:11
Let the earth *r* .... Ps 97:1
We will *r* and be glad .... Ps 118:24
She shall *r* in time to .... Prov 31:25
R, O young man .... Eccl 11:9
your heart shall *r*................... Is 66:14
Do not *r* over me .... Mic 7:8
do not *r*.......................... Luke 10:20
you would *r* .... John 14:28
but the world will *r*............. John 16:20
and your heart will *r*........... John 16:22
R with those who .... Rom 12:15
and in this I *r* .... Phil 1:18
faith, I am glad and *r* .... Phil 2:17
R in the Lord always .... Phil 4:4
R always .... 1 Thess 5:16
yet believing, you *r* .... 1 Pet 1:8

REJOICED
And my spirit has *r*............... Luke 1:47
In that hour Jesus *r* .... Luke 10:21
Abraham *r* .... John 8:56

REJOICES
glad, and my glory *r*................ Ps 16:9
but *r* in the truth .... 1 Cor 13:6

REJOICING
come again with *r*................ Ps 126:6
he went on his way *r* .... Acts 8:39
confidence and the *r*................ Heb 3:6

RELENT
sworn And will not *r* .... Ps 110:4
sworn And will not *r* .... Heb 7:21

RELENTED
and God *r* from the .... Jon 3:10

RELENTING
I am weary of *r*...................... Jer 15:6

RELIGION
in self-imposed *r* .... Col 2:23
and undefiled *r* .... James 1:27

RELIGIOUS
things you are very *r* .... Acts 17:22

REMAIN
that My joy may *r*................ John 15:11
your fruit should *r* .... John 15:16
"If I will that he *r*.............. John 21:22
the greater part *r*.............. 1 Cor 15:6
are alive and *r*................ 1 Thess 4:15
the things which *r*.................. Rev 3:2

REMAINS
"While the earth *r* .... Gen 8:22
Therefore your sin *r* .... John 9:41
There *r* therefore a .... Heb 4:9

REMEMBER
"*R* the Sabbath day .... Ex 20:8
But we will *r* the name .... Ps 20:7
r Your name in the .... Ps 119:55
R now your Creator .... Eccl 12:1
the former things .... Is 43:18
and their sin I will *r* .... Jer 31:34
In wrath *r* mercy .... Hab 3:2
And to *r* His holy .... Luke 1:72
"*R* Lot's wife .... Luke 17:32
the words of the .... Acts 20:35
R that Jesus Christ .... 2 Tim 2:8
R those who rule .... Heb 13:7

REMEMBERED
Then God *r* Noah................Gen 8:1
His covenant with ....Ex 2:24
His covenant forever ....Ps 105:8
yea, we wept When we *r*............Ps 137:1
And Peter *r* the word ....Matt 26:75
the word of the Lord ....Acts 11:16
REMEMBRANCE
my song in the night ....Ps 77:6
Put Me in *r* ....Is 43:26
do this in *r* of Me ....Luke 22:19
do this in *r* of Me ....1 Cor 11:24
REMISSION
for the *r*...........................Mark 1:4
Jesus Christ for the *r*............Acts 2:38
where there is *r*..................Heb 10:18
REMNANT
The *r* will return ....Is 10:21
time there is a *r*..................Rom 11:5
REMORSEFUL
condemned, was *r*...............Matt 27:3
REMOVE
this cup from Me ....Luke 22:42
your lampstand ....Rev 2:5
REMOVED
Though the earth be *r*..............Ps 46:2
And the hills be *r*....................Is 54:10
this mountain, 'Be *r*............Matt 21:21
REND
So *r* your heart ....Joel 2:13
RENDER
What shall I *r* to the ....Ps 116:12
"*R* therefore to Caesar ....Matt 22:21
RENEW
a steadfast ....Ps 51:10
on the LORD Shall *r*...................Is 40:31
RENEWED
that your youth is *r*.................Ps 103:5
inward man is being *r*..........2 Cor 4:16
and be *r* in the spirit ....Eph 4:23
RENEWING
transformed by the *r* ....Rom 12:2
RENOWN
were of old, men of *r*..............Gen 6:4
REPAID
Shall evil be *r* ....Jer 18:20
REPAY
again, I will *r*...................Luke 10:35
they cannot *r*....................Luke 14:14
R no one evil for evil ....Rom 12:17
is Mine, I will *r*..................Rom 12:19
their parents ....1 Tim 5:4
REPAYS
the LORD, Who fully *r* ....Is 66:6
REPENT
I abhor myself, And *r* ....Job 42:6
"*R*, for the kingdom ....Matt 3:2
you *r* you will all ....Luke 13:3
said to them, "*R* ....Acts 2:38
men everywhere to *r*............Acts 17:30
be zealous and *r* ....Rev 3:19
REPENTANCE
you with water unto *r*...........Matt 3:11
a baptism of *r* for the ....Mark 1:4
persons who need no *r* ....Luke 15:7
renew them again to *r*.............Heb 6:6
found no place for *r* ....Heb 12:17
all should come to *r* ....2 Pet 3:9
REPENTED
it, because they *r* ....Matt 12:41
REPETITIONS
as the heathen do ....Matt 6:7
REPORT
Who has believed our *r* ....Is 53:1
things are of good *r*.................Phil 4:8
REPROACH
R has broken my heart ....Ps 69:20
with dishonor comes *r*............Prov 18:3
not remember the *r* ....Is 54:4
Because I bore the *r* ....Jer 31:19
these things You *r*..............Luke 11:45
lest he fall into *r* ....1 Tim 3:7
esteeming the *r* ....Heb 11:26
and without *r* ....James 1:5
REPROACHED
If you are *r* for the ....1 Pet 4:14
REPROACHES
is not an enemy who *r* ....Ps 55:12
in infirmities, in *r*.............2 Cor 12:10
REPROOF
for doctrine, for *r* ....2 Tim 3:16
REPROOFS
R of instruction are ....Prov 6:23
REPUTATION
seven men of good *r*..............Acts 6:3
made Himself of no *r*...............Phil 2:7
REQUEST
He gave them their *r*............Ps 106:15
For Jews *r* a sign ....1 Cor 1:22
REQUESTS
be made known ....Phil 4:6
REQUIRE
offering You did not *r* ....Ps 40:6
what does the LORD *r*..............Mic 6:8
REQUIRED
your soul will be *r* ....Luke 12:20
him much will be *r*.................Luke 12:48
REQUIREMENTS
keeps the righteous *r* ....Rom 2:26
that was against us ....Col 2:14
RESERVED
"I have *r* for Myself ....Rom 11:4
in heaven for you ....1 Pet 1:4
habitation, He has *r*..................Jude 6
RESIST
an evil person ....Matt 5:39
the Holy Spirit ....Acts 7:51
R the devil and he ....James 4:7
RESISTED
For who has *r* His will ....Rom 9:19
for he has greatly *r* ....2 Tim 4:15
You have not yet *r*...................Heb 12:4
RESISTS
"God *r* the proud ....James 4:6
for "God *r* the proud ....1 Pet 5:5
RESPECT
of the law held in *r* ....Acts 5:34
and we paid them *r* ....Heb 12:9
RESPECTED
And the LORD *r* Abel ....Gen 4:4
REST
is the Sabbath of *r* ....Ex 31:15
to build a house of *r* ....1 Chr 28:2
R in the LORD ....Ps 37:7
fly away and be at *r* ....Ps 55:6
"This is the *r* ....Is 28:12
is the place of My *r* ....Is 66:1
and I will give you *r*.............Matt 11:28
shall not enter My *r* ....Heb 3:11
remains therefore a *r* ....Heb 4:9
that they should *r*.....................Rev 6:11
"that they may *r*.......................Rev 14:13
But the *r* of the dead ....Rev 20:5
RESTED
He had done, and He *r*..............Gen 2:2
"And God *r* on the ....Heb 4:4
RESTORATION
until the times of *r* ....Acts 3:21
RESTORE
R to me the joy ....Ps 51:12
"So I will *r* to you ....Joel 2:25
and will *r* all things ....Matt 17:11
You at this time *r* ....Acts 1:6
who are spiritual *r* ....Gal 6:1
RESTORES
He *r* my soul ....Ps 23:3
RESTRAINS
only He who now *r* ....2 Thess 2:7
RESTRAINT
They break all *r*.........................Hos 4:2
RESTS
quietly in the heart ....Prov 14:33
RESURRECTION
to her, "I am the *r* ....John 11:25
them Jesus and the *r* ....Acts 17:18
the likeness of His *r* ....Rom 6:5
say that there is no *r*............1 Cor 15:12
and the power of His *r* ....Phil 3:10
obtain a better *r*......................Heb 11:35
This is the first *r*.....................Rev 20:5
RETAIN
the sins of any ....John 20:23
RETURN
womb, naked shall he *r* ....Eccl 5:15
Let him *r* to the LORD ....Is 55:7
me, and I will *r*........................Jer 31:18
"*R* to Me ....Zech 1:3
he says, 'I will *r* ....Matt 12:44
RETURNED
astray, but have now *r* ....1 Pet 2:25
RETURNING
evil for evil or ....1 Pet 3:9
RETURNS
As a dog *r* to his own ....Prov 26:11
"A dog *r* to his own ....2 Pet 2:22
REVEAL
the Son wills to *r* Him ....Matt 11:27
His Son in me ....Gal 1:16
REVEALED
things which are *r* ....Deut 29:29
righteousness to be *r* ....Is 56:1
the Son of Man is *r*...............Luke 17:30
the wrath of God is *r* ....Rom 1:18
glory which shall be *r* ....Rom 8:18
the Lord Jesus is *r* ....2 Thess 1:7
lawless one will be *r*.............2 Thess 2:8
ready to be *r* in the ....1 Pet 1:5
when His glory is *r*...................1 Pet 4:13
what we shall be ....1 John 3:2
REVEALER
Lord of kings, and a *r*.............Dan 2:47
REVEALING
waits for the *r* ....Rom 8:19
REVEALS
as a talebearer *r*..................Prov 20:19
His secret to His ....Amos 3:7
REVELATION
Where there is no *r*..............Prov 29:18
it came through the *r* ....Gal 1:12
spirit of wisdom and *r* ....Eph 1:17
He made known to ....Eph 3:3
and glory at the *r*........................1 Pet 1:7
REVERENCE
and *r* My sanctuary ....Lev 19:30
God acceptably with *r*............Heb 12:28
REVERENT
man who is always *r* ....Prov 28:14
their wives must be *r*.............1 Tim 3:11
REVILE
are you when they *r* ....Matt 5:11
God's high priest ....Acts 23:4
REVILED
crucified with Him *r*............Mark 15:32
who, when He was *r* ....1 Pet 2:23
REVIVAL
give us a measure of *r*..............Ezra 9:8
REVIVE
Will You not *r* us ....Ps 85:6
two days He will *r*.....................Hos 6:2
REVIVED
came, sin *r* and I died ....Rom 7:9
REWARD
exceedingly great *r* ....Gen 15:1
look, And see the *r* ....Ps 91:8
Behold, His *r* is with ....Is 40:10
for great is your *r*.....................Matt 5:12
you, they have their *r* ....Matt 6:2
no means lose his *r*.................Matt 10:42
we receive the due *r*..............Luke 23:41
will receive his own *r*.................1 Cor 3:8
cheat you of your *r* ....Col 2:18
for he looked to the *r* ....Heb 11:26
quickly, and My *r* ....Rev 22:12

REWARDS
Whoever *r* evil for . . . Prov 17:13
And follows after *r* . . . Is 1:23

RICH
Abram was very *r* . . . Gen 13:2
The *r* and the poor . . . Prov 22:2
rules over the poor . . . Prov 22:7
man is wise in his . . . Prov 28:11
Do not curse the *r* . . . Eccl 10:20
it is hard for a *r* . . . Matt 19:23
to you who are *r* . . . Luke 6:24
the *r* man's table . . . Luke 16:21
for he was very *r* . . . Luke 18:23
You are already *r* . . . 1 Cor 4:8
though He was *r* . . . 2 Cor 8:9
who desire to be *r* . . . 1 Tim 6:9
of this world to be *r* . . . James 2:5
you say, 'I am *r* . . . Rev 3:17

RICHES
R and honor are . . . Prov 8:18
R do not profit . . . Prov 11:4
in his *r* will fall . . . Prov 11:28
of the wise is their *r* . . . Prov 14:24
and *r* are an . . . Prov 19:14
of the LORD Are *r* . . . Prov 22:4
are not forever . . . Prov 27:24
do you despise the *r* . . . Rom 2:4
make known the *r* . . . Rom 9:23
what are the *r* . . . Eph 1:18
show the exceeding *r* . . . Eph 2:7
the unsearchable *r* . . . Eph 3:8
than the treasures . . . Heb 11:26
To receive power and *r* . . . Rev 5:12

RICHLY
Christ dwell in you *r* . . . Col 3:16
God, who gives us *r* . . . 1 Tim 6:17

RIGHT
the *r* of the firstborn . . . Deut 21:17
"Is your heart *r* . . . 2 Kin 10:15
Lord, "Sit at My *r* . . . Ps 110:1
a way which seems *r* . . . Prov 14:12
clothed and in his *r* . . . Mark 5:15
to them He gave the *r* . . . John 1:12
your heart is not *r* . . . Acts 8:21
seven stars in His *r* . . . Rev 2:1

RIGHTEOUS
also destroy the *r* . . . Gen 18:23
and they justify the *r* . . . Deut 25:1
that he could be *r* . . . Job 15:14
"The *r* see it and . . . Job 22:19
shows mercy and . . . Ps 37:21
I have not seen the *r* . . . Ps 37:25
The LORD loves the *r* . . . Ps 146:8
r is a well of life . . . Prov 10:11
r will be gladness . . . Prov 10:28
r will be delivered . . . Prov 11:21
r will be recompensed . . . Prov 11:31
the prayer of the *r* . . . Prov 15:29
r are bold as a lion . . . Prov 28:1
r considers the cause . . . Prov 29:7
Do not be overly *r* . . . Eccl 7:16
event happens to the *r* . . . Eccl 9:2
with My *r* right hand . . . Is 41:10
By His knowledge My *r* . . . Is 53:11
The *r* perishes . . . Is 57:1
they sell the *r* . . . Amos 2:6
not come to call the *r* . . . Matt 9:13
r men desired to see . . . Matt 13:17
r will shine forth as . . . Matt 13:43
that they were *r* . . . Luke 18:9
this was a *r* . . . Luke 23:47
"There is none *r* . . . Rom 3:10
r man will one die . . . Rom 5:7
Jesus Christ the *r* . . . 1 John 2:1

RIGHTEOUSLY
should live soberly, *r* . . . Titus 2:12
to Him who judges *r* . . . 1 Pet 2:23

RIGHTEOUSNESS
it to him for *r* . . . Gen 15:6
I put on *r* . . . Job 29:14
I call, O God of my *r* . . . Ps 4:1
from the LORD, And *r* . . . Ps 24:5
shall speak of Your *r* . . . Ps 35:28
the good news of *r* . . . Ps 40:9
heavens declare His *r* . . . Ps 50:6
R and peace have . . . Ps 85:10
R will go before Him . . . Ps 85:13
r endures forever . . . Ps 111:3
r delivers from death . . . Prov 10:2
The *r* of the blameless . . . Prov 11:5
the way of *r* is life . . . Prov 12:28
R exalts a nation . . . Prov 14:34
He who follows *r* . . . Prov 21:21
R lodged in it . . . Is 1:21
in the LORD I have *r* . . . Is 45:24
r will be forever . . . Is 51:8
I will declare your *r* . . . Is 57:12
r as a breastplate . . . Is 59:17
r goes forth as . . . Is 62:1
The Lord Our *R* . . . Jer 23:6
to David A Branch of *r* . . . Jer 33:15
The *r* of the righteous . . . Ezek 18:20
who turn many to *r* . . . Dan 12:3
to fulfill all *r* . . . Matt 3:15
exceeds the *r* of the . . . Matt 5:20
to you in the way of *r* . . . Matt 21:32
For in it the *r* . . . Rom 1:17
even the *r* of God . . . Rom 3:22
accounted to him for *r* . . . Rom 4:22
r will reign in life . . . Rom 5:17
might reign through *r* . . . Rom 5:21
ignorant of God's *r* . . . Rom 10:3
might become the *r* . . . 2 Cor 5:21
the breastplate of *r* . . . Eph 6:14
not having my own *r* . . . Phil 3:9
r which we have . . . Titus 3:5
not produce the *r* . . . James 1:20
a preacher of *r* . . . 2 Pet 2:5
a new earth in which *r* . . . 2 Pet 3:13
who practices *r* . . . 1 John 2:29
He who practices *r* . . . 1 John 3:7

RIGHTLY
wise uses knowledge *r* . . . Prov 15:2
r dividing the word . . . 2 Tim 2:15

RISE
for He makes His sun *r* . . . Matt 5:45
third day He will *r* . . . Matt 20:19
third day He will *r* . . . Luke 18:33
be the first to *r* . . . Acts 26:23
in Christ will *r* . . . 1 Thess 4:16

RISEN
there has not *r* . . . Matt 11:11
disciples that He is *r* . . . Matt 28:7
"The Lord is *r* . . . Luke 24:34
then Christ is not *r* . . . 1 Cor 15:13
if Christ is not *r* . . . 1 Cor 15:17
But now Christ is *r* . . . 1 Cor 15:20

RIVER
peace to her like a *r* . . . Is 66:12
he showed me a pure *r* . . . Rev 22:1

RIVERS
By the *r* of Babylon . . . Ps 137:1
All the *r* run into the . . . Eccl 1:7
his heart will flow *r* . . . John 7:38

ROAR
The LORD also will *r* . . . Joel 3:16

ROARING
and the waves *r* . . . Luke 21:25
walks about like a *r* . . . 1 Pet 5:8

ROARS
"The LORD *r* from . . . Amos 1:2
as when a lion *r* . . . Rev 10:3

ROB
"Will a man *r* God . . . Mal 3:8

ROBBED
r other churches . . . 2 Cor 11:8

ROBBER
is a thief and a *r* . . . John 10:1
Barabbas was a *r* . . . John 18:40

ROBBERS
also crucified two *r* . . . Mark 15:27
Me are thieves and *r* . . . John 10:8

ROBBERY
did not consider it *r* . . . Phil 2:6

ROBE
'Bring out the best *r* . . . Luke 15:22
on Him a purple *r* . . . John 19:2
Then a white *r* was . . . Rev 6:11

ROBES
have stained all My *r* . . . Is 63:3
go around in long *r* . . . Luke 20:46
clothed with white *r* . . . Rev 7:9

ROCK
you shall strike the *r* . . . Ex 17:6
and struck the *r* . . . Num 20:11
For their *r* is not . . . Deut 32:31
"The LORD is my *r* . . . 2 Sam 22:2
And who is a *r* . . . 2 Sam 22:32
Blessed be my *R* . . . 2 Sam 22:47
For You are my *r* . . . Ps 31:3
that is higher than . . . Ps 61:2
been mindful of the *R* . . . Is 17:10
shadow of a great *r* . . . Is 32:2
his house on the *r* . . . Matt 7:24
I will build My . . . Matt 16:18
stumbling stone and *r* . . . Rom 9:33
R that followed them . . . 1 Cor 10:4

ROD
Your *r* and Your staff . . . Ps 23:4
shall come forth a *R* . . . Is 11:1
rule them with a *r* . . . Rev 2:27

ROOM
you a large upper *r* . . . Mark 14:15
no *r* for them in the . . . Luke 2:7
into the upper *r* . . . Acts 1:13

ROOT
day there shall be a *R* . . . Is 11:10
because they had no *r* . . . Matt 13:6
of money is a *r* . . . 1 Tim 6:10
lest any *r* of . . . Heb 12:15
I am the *R* and the . . . Rev 22:16

ROOTED
and built up in Him . . . Col 2:7

ROSE
end Christ died and *r* . . . Rom 14:9
buried, and that He *r* . . . 1 Cor 15:4
Jesus died and *r* . . . 1 Thess 4:14

RULE
And he shall *r* . . . Gen 3:16
puts an end to all *r* . . . 1 Cor 15:24
let the peace of God *r* . . . Col 3:15
Let the elders who *r* . . . 1 Tim 5:17
Remember those who *r* . . . Heb 13:7

RULER
to Me The One to be *r* . . . Mic 5:2
by Beelzebub, the *r* . . . Matt 12:24
the *r* of this world . . . John 12:31
'Who made you a *r* . . . Acts 7:27

RULERS
And the *r* take counsel . . . Ps 2:2
"You know that the *r* . . . Matt 20:25
which none of the *r* . . . 1 Cor 2:8
powers, against the *r* . . . Eph 6:12

RULES
That the Most High *r* . . . Dan 4:17
that the Most High *r* . . . Dan 4:32
r his own house well . . . 1 Tim 3:4

RULING
r their children . . . 1 Tim 3:12

RUMORS
hear of wars and *r* . . . Matt 24:6

RUN
r and not be weary . . . Is 40:31
us, and let us *r* . . . Heb 12:1

S

SABAOTH
S had left us a . . . Rom 9:29
ears of the Lord of *S* . . . James 5:4

SABBATH
"Remember the *S* . . . Ex 20:8
S was made for man . . . Mark 2:27

SABBATHS
S you shall keep . . . Ex 31:13

SACRIFICE
to the LORD than *s* . . . Prov 21:3
For the LORD has a *s* . . . Is 34:6
of My offerings they *s* . . . Hos 8:13
LORD has prepared a *s* . . . Zeph 1:7
desire mercy and not *s* . . . Matt 9:13

an offering and a *s* .... Eph 5:2
put away sin by the *s* .... Heb 9:26
no longer remains a *s* .... Heb 10:26
offer the *s* of praise .... Heb 13:15

SACRIFICED
s their sons And their .... Ps 106:37

SACRIFICES
The *s* of God are a .... Ps 51:17
multitude of your *s* .... Is 1:11
priests, to offer up *s* .... Heb 7:27
s God is well pleased .... Heb 13:16

SAFE
he has received him *s* .... Luke 15:27

SAFELY
make them lie down *s* .... Hos 2:18

SAFETY
say, "Peace and *s* .... 1 Thess 5:3

SAINTS
s who are on the earth .... Ps 16:3
does not forsake His *s* .... Ps 37:28
Is the death of His *s* .... Ps 116:15
war against the *s* .... Dan 7:21
Jesus, called to be *s* .... 1 Cor 1:2
the least of all the *s* .... Eph 3:8
be glorified in His *s* .... 2 Thess 1:10
all delivered to the *s* .... Jude 3
shed the blood of *s* .... Rev 16:6

SALT
shall season with *s* .... Lev 2:13
"You are the *s* .... Matt 5:13
s loses its flavor .... Mark 9:50

SALVATION
still, and see the *s* .... Ex 14:13
S belongs to the LORD .... Ps 3:8
is my light and my *s* .... Ps 27:1
God is the God of *s* .... Ps 68:20
joy in the God of my *s* .... Hab 3:18
raised up a horn of *s* .... Luke 1:69
"Nor is there *s* .... Acts 4:12
the power of God to *s* .... Rom 1:16
now is the day of *s* .... 2 Cor 6:2
work out your own *s* .... Phil 2:12
chose you for *s* .... 2 Thess 2:13
neglect so great a *s* .... Heb 2:3

SAMARITAN
a drink from me, a *S* .... John 4:9

SANCTIFICATION
will of God, your *s* .... 1 Thess 4:3

SANCTIFIED
they also may be *s* .... John 17:19
but you were *s* .... 1 Cor 6:11
for it is *s* by the .... 1 Tim 4:5

SANCTIFIES
For both He who *s* .... Heb 2:11

SANCTIFY
s My great name .... Ezek 36:23
"*S* them by Your .... John 17:17
that He might *s* .... Eph 5:26

SANCTUARY
let them make Me a *s* .... Ex 25:8
and the earthly *s* .... Heb 9:1

SAND
descendants as the *s* .... Gen 32:12
innumerable as the *s* .... Heb 11:12

SAT
into heaven, and *S* .... Mark 16:19
And He who *s* there was .... Rev 4:3

SATAN
before the LORD, and *S* .... Job 1:6
"Away with you, *S* .... Matt 4:10
"Get behind Me, *S* .... Matt 16:23
"How can *S* cast out .... Mark 3:23
S has asked for you .... Luke 22:31
to the working of *S* .... 2 Thess 2:9
known the depths of *S* .... Rev 2:24
years have expired, *S* .... Rev 20:7

SATIATED
s the weary soul .... Jer 31:25

SATISFIED
I shall be *s* when I .... Ps 17:15
that are never *s* .... Prov 30:15
of His soul, and be *s* .... Is 53:11

SATISFIES
s the longing soul .... Ps 107:9

SATISFY
s us early with Your .... Ps 90:14
long life I will *s* .... Ps 91:16
for what does not *s* .... Is 55:2

SAVE
Oh, *s* me for Your .... Ps 6:4
s the children of the .... Ps 72:4
s the souls of the .... Ps 72:13
That it cannot *s* .... Is 59:1
s you And deliver you .... Jer 15:20
other, That he may *s* .... Hos 13:10
JESUS, for He will *s* .... Matt 1:21
s his life will .... Matt 16:25
s that which was .... Matt 18:11
let Him *s* Himself if .... Luke 23:35
but to *s* the world .... John 12:47
the world to *s* sinners .... 1 Tim 1:15

SAVED
"He *s* others .... Matt 27:42
That we should be *s* .... Luke 1:71
"Your faith has *s* .... Luke 7:50
might be *s* .... John 3:17
them, saying, "Be *s* .... Acts 2:40
what must I do to be *s* .... Acts 16:30
which also you are *s* .... 1 Cor 15:2
grace you have been *s* .... Eph 2:8
to His mercy He *s* .... Titus 3:5
of those who are *s* .... Rev 21:24

SAVES
antitype which now *s* .... 1 Pet 3:21

SAVIOR
I, the LORD, am your *S* .... Is 60:16
rejoiced in God my *S* .... Luke 1:47
the city of David a *S* .... Luke 2:11
up for Israel a *S* .... Acts 13:23
God, who is the *S* .... 1 Tim 4:10
and *S* Jesus Christ .... Titus 2:13

SAWN
stoned, they were *s* .... Heb 11:37

SAY
"But I *s* to you that .... Matt 5:22
"But who do you *s* .... Matt 16:15

SAYING
This is a faithful *s* .... 1 Tim 1:15

SAYINGS
whoever hears these *s* .... Matt 7:24

SCALES
on it had a pair of *s* .... Rev 6:5

SCARLET
your sins are like *s* .... Is 1:18

SCATTER
I will *s* you among the .... Lev 26:33

SCATTERED
"Israel is like *s* sheep .... Jer 50:17
the sheep will be *s* .... Mark 14:27

SCATTERS
not gather with Me *s* .... Matt 12:30

SCEPTER
s shall not depart .... Gen 49:10

SCHEMER
Will be called a *s* .... Prov 24:8

SCHEMES
sought out many *s* .... Eccl 7:29

SCHISM
there should be no *s* .... 1 Cor 12:25

SCHOOL
daily in the *s* of .... Acts 19:9

SCOFF
They *s* at kings .... Hab 1:10

SCOFFER
"He who corrects a *s* .... Prov 9:7
s is an abomination .... Prov 24:9

SCOFFERS
s will come in the .... 2 Pet 3:3

SCORCHED
And men were *s* with .... Rev 16:9

SCORN
My friends *s* me .... Job 16:20

SCORNS
He *s* the scornful .... Prov 3:34

SCORPIONS
on serpents and *s* .... Luke 10:19
They had tails like *s* .... Rev 9:10

SCOURGE
will mock Him, and *s* .... Mark 10:34

SCOURGES
s every son whom .... Heb 12:6

SCRIBES
"Beware of the *s* .... Mark 12:38

SCRIPTURE
S cannot be broken .... John 10:35
All *S* is given by .... 2 Tim 3:16

SCRIPTURES
S must be fulfilled .... Mark 14:49

SCROLL
eat this *s* .... Ezek 3:1
the sky receded as a *s* .... Rev 6:14

SEA
drowned in the Red *S* .... Ex 15:4
who go down to the *s* .... Ps 107:23
and the *s* obey Him .... Matt 8:27
throne there was a *s* .... Rev 4:6
there was no more *s* .... Rev 21:1

SEAL
stands, having this *s* .... 2 Tim 2:19

SEALED
by whom you were *s* .... Eph 4:30

SEAM
tunic was without *s* .... John 19:23

SE´ANCE
"Please conduct a *s* .... 1 Sam 28:8

SEARCH
glory of kings is to *s* .... Prov 25:2
s the Scriptures .... John 5:39

SEARCHED
s the Scriptures .... Acts 17:11

SEARCHES
For the Spirit *s* .... 1 Cor 2:10

SEASON
Be ready in *s* and out .... 2 Tim 4:2

SEASONED
how shall it be *s* .... Matt 5:13

SEASONS
the times and the *s* .... 1 Thess 5:1

SEAT
shall make a mercy *s* .... Ex 25:17
before the judgment *s* .... 2 Cor 5:10

SEATS
at feasts, the best *s* .... Matt 23:6

SECRET
s things belong .... Deut 29:29
In the *s* place of His .... Ps 27:5
Father who is in the *s* .... Matt 6:6

SECRETLY
He lies in wait *s* .... Ps 10:9

SECRETS
For He knows the *s* .... Ps 44:21
God will judge the *s* .... Rom 2:16

SECT
to the strictest *s* .... Acts 26:5

SECURELY
nation that dwells *s* .... Jer 49:31

SEDUCED
flattering lips she *s* .... Prov 7:21

SEE
in my flesh I shall *s* .... Job 19:26
For they shall *s* God .... Matt 5:8
seeing they do not *s* .... Matt 13:13
rejoiced to *s* My day .... John 8:56
They shall *s* His face .... Rev 22:4

SEED
He shall see His *s* .... Is 53:10
S were the promises .... Gal 3:16
you are Abraham's *s* .... Gal 3:29

SEEDS
the good *s* are the .... Matt 13:38

SEEK
pray and *s* My face 2 Chr 7:14
S the LORD while He Is 55:6
s, and you will find Matt 7:7
of Man has come to *s* Luke 19:10
"You will *s* Me and John 7:34
For all *s* their own Phil 2:21
s those things which Col 3:1

SEEKING
like a roaring lion, *s* 1 Pet 5:8

SEEKS
There is none who *s* Rom 3:11

SEEMS
is a way which *s* Prov 14:12

SEEN
s God face to face Gen 32:30
No one has *s* God at John 1:18
s Me has *s* the John 14:9
things which are not *s* 2 Cor 4:18

SEES
s his brother in need 1 John 3:17

SELF-CONFIDENT
a fool rages and is *s* Prov 14:16

SELF-CONTROL
gentleness, *s* Gal 5:23
to knowledge *s* 2 Pet 1:6

SELF-CONTROLLED
just, holy, *s* Titus 1:8

SELF-SEEKING
envy and *s* exist James 3:16

SELL
s whatever you have Mark 10:21

SEND
"Behold, I *s* you out Matt 10:16
has sent Me, I also *s* John 20:21

SENSES
of use have their *s* Heb 5:14

SENSIBLY
who can answer *s* Prov 26:16

SENSUAL
but is earthly, *s* James 3:15

SENT
unless they are *s* Rom 10:15

SEPARATED
it pleased God, who *s* Gal 1:15

SEPARATES
who repeats a matter *s* Prov 17:9

SEPARATION
the middle wall of *s* Eph 2:14

SERAPHIM
Above it stood *s* Is 6:2

SERIOUS
therefore be *s* and 1 Pet 4:7

SERPENT
s was more cunning Gen 3:1
"Make a fiery *s* Num 21:8
Moses lifted up the *s* John 3:14

SERPENTS
be wise as *s* Matt 10:16

SERVANT
s will rule over a son Prov 17:2
good and faithful *s* Matt 25:21

SERVANTS
are unprofitable *s* Luke 17:10

SERVE
to be served, but to *s* Matt 20:28
but through love *s* Gal 5:13

SERVES
"If anyone *s* Me John 12:26

SERVICE
is your reasonable *s* Rom 12:1
with good will doing *s* Eph 6:7

SERVING
fervent in spirit, *s* Rom 12:11

SET
"See, I have *s* Deut 30:15
s aside the grace Gal 2:21

SETTLE
"Therefore *s* it in Luke 21:14

SETTLED
O LORD, Your word is *s* Ps 119:89

SEVEN
s churches which are Rev 1:4

SEVENTY
"*S* weeks are Dan 9:24

SEVERE
not to be too *s* 2 Cor 2:5

SEVERITY
the goodness and *s* Rom 11:22

SHADE
may nest under its *s* Mark 4:32

SHADOW
In the *s* of His hand Is 49:2
the law, having a *s* Heb 10:1

SHAKE
s the earth Is 2:19
I will *s* all nations Hag 2:7

SHAKEN
not to be soon *s* 2 Thess 2:2

SHAKES
s the Wilderness Ps 29:8

SHAME
never be put to *s* Joel 2:26
to put to *s* the wise 1 Cor 1:27
glory is in their *s* Phil 3:19

SHAMEFUL
For it is *s* even to Eph 5:12

SHARE
to do good and to *s* Heb 13:16

SHARING
for your liberal *s* 2 Cor 9:13

SHARP
S as a two-edged sword Prov 5:4

SHARPEN
s their tongue like a Ps 64:3

SHARPENS
My adversary *s* His Job 16:9

SHARPNESS
I should use *s* 2 Cor 13:10

SHEATH
your sword into the *s* John 18:11

SHEAVES
Bringing his *s* Ps 126:6
gather them like *s* Mic 4:12

SHED
which is *s* for many Matt 26:28

SHEDDING
blood, and without *s* Heb 9:22

SHEEP
s will be scattered Zech 13:7
having a hundred *s* Luke 15:4
and I know My *s* John 10:14
"He was led as a *s* Acts 8:32

SHEEPFOLDS
lie down among the *s* Ps 68:13

SHEET
object like a great *s* Acts 10:11

SHELTER
the LORD will be a *s* Joel 3:16

SHELTERS
s him all the day long Deut 33:12

SHEOL
not leave my soul in *S* Ps 16:10
the belly of *S* I cried Jon 2:2

SHEPHERD
The LORD is my *S* Ps 23:1
His flock like a *s* Is 40:11
'I will strike the *S* Matt 26:31
"I am the good *s* John 10:11
the dead, that great *S* Heb 13:20
S the flock of God 1 Pet 5:2
when the Chief *S* 1 Pet 5:4

SHEPHERDS
"And I will give you *s* Jer 3:15
s have led them astray Jer 50:6

SHIELD
I am your *s* Gen 15:1
truth shall be your *s* Ps 91:4
all, taking the *s* Eph 6:16

SHINE
LORD make His face *s* Num 6:25
among whom you *s* Phil 2:15

SHINED
them a light has *s* Is 9:2

SHINES
heed as a light that *s* 2 Pet 1:19

SHINING
light is already *s* 1 John 2:8

SHIPS
down to the sea in *s* Ps 107:23

SHIPWRECK
faith have suffered *s* 1 Tim 1:19

SHOOT
They *s* out the lip Ps 22:7

SHORT
have sinned and fall *s* Rom 3:23

SHORTENED
those days were *s* Matt 24:22

SHOUT
heaven with a *s* 1 Thess 4:16

SHOW
a land that I will *s* Gen 12:1
s Him greater works John 5:20

SHOWBREAD
s which was not lawful Matt 12:4

SHOWERS
make it soft with *s* Ps 65:10

SHREWDLY
because he had dealt *s* Luke 16:8

SHRINES
who made silver *s* Acts 19:24

SHRIVELED
You have *s* me up Job 16:8

SHUFFLES
with his eyes, He *s* Prov 6:13

SHUNNED
feared God and *s* evil Job 1:1

SHUT
For you *s* up the Matt 23:13

SHUTS
s his eyes from seeing Is 33:15
who opens and no one *s* Rev 3:7

SICK
I was *s* and you Matt 25:36
faith will save the *s* James 5:15

SICKLE
"Thrust in Your *s* Rev 14:15

SICKNESS
will sustain him in *s* Prov 18:14
"This *s* is not unto John 11:4

SICKNESSES
And bore our *s* Matt 8:17

SIDE
The LORD is on my *s* Ps 118:6

SIFT
s the nations with the Is 30:28

SIGH
our years like a *s* Ps 90:9

SIGHING
For my *s* comes before Job 3:24

SIGHT
and see this great *s* Ex 3:3
by faith, not by *s* 2 Cor 5:7

SIGN
will give you a *s* Is 7:14
seeks after a *s* Matt 12:39
For Jews request a *s* 1 Cor 1:22

SIGNS
and let them be for *s* Gen 1:14
cannot discern the *s* Matt 16:3
did many other *s* John 20:30

SILENCE
That You may *s* Ps 8:2
seal, there was *s* Rev 8:1

SILENT
season, and am not *s* Ps 22:2

SILK
covered you with *s* Ezek 16:10

SILLY
They are *s* children .... Jer 4:22
SILVER
may buy the poor for *s* .... Amos 8:6
him thirty pieces of *s* .... Matt 26:15
SIMILITUDE
been made in the *s* .... James 3:9
SIMPLE
making wise the *s* .... Ps 19:7
SIMPLICITY
corrupted from the *s* .... 2 Cor 11:3
SIN
and be sure your *s* .... Num 32:23
Be angry, and do not *s* .... Ps 4:4
s is always before me .... Ps 51:3
soul an offering for *s* .... Is 53:10
And He bore the *s* .... Is 53:12
who takes away the *s* .... John 1:29
"He who is without *s* .... John 8:7
convict the world of *s* .... John 16:8
s entered the world .... Rom 5:12
s is not imputed .... Rom 5:13
s shall not have .... Rom 6:14
Shall we *s* because we .... Rom 6:15
Him who knew no *s* .... 2 Cor 5:21
man of *s* is revealed .... 2 Thess 2:3
we are, yet without *s* .... Heb 4:15
do it, to him it is *s* .... James 4:17
say that we have no *s* .... 1 John 1:8
and he cannot *s* .... 1 John 3:9
SINCERE
and from *s* faith .... 1 Tim 1:5
SINCERITY
simplicity and godly *s* .... 2 Cor 1:12
SINFUL
from me, for I am a *s* .... Luke 5:8
become exceedingly *s* .... Rom 7:13
SING
Let him *s* psalms .... James 5:13
SINGERS
The *s* went before .... Ps 68:25
SINGING
His presence with *s* .... Ps 100:2
and spiritual songs, *s* .... Eph 5:19
SINISTER
Who understands *s* .... Dan 8:23
SINK
I *s* in deep mire .... Ps 69:2
to *s* he cried out .... Matt 14:30
SINNED
You only, have I *s* .... Ps 51:4
"Father, I have *s* .... Luke 15:18
for all have *s* and .... Rom 3:23
that we have not *s* .... 1 John 1:10
SINNER
s who repents than .... Luke 15:7
the ungodly and the *s* .... 1 Pet 4:18
SINNERS
in the path of *s* .... Ps 1:1
the righteous, but *s* .... Matt 9:13
while we were still *s* .... Rom 5:8
many were made *s* .... Rom 5:19
the world to save *s* .... 1 Tim 1:15
such hostility from *s* .... Heb 12:3
SINS
from presumptuous *s* .... Ps 19:13
You, Our secret *s* .... Ps 90:8
The soul who *s* shall .... Ezek 18:4
if your brother *s* .... Matt 18:15
s according to the .... 1 Cor 15:3
the forgiveness of *s* .... Eph 1:7
If we confess our *s* .... 1 John 1:9
propitiation for our *s* .... 1 John 2:2
SISTER
is My brother and *s* .... Matt 12:50
SIT
but to *s* on My right .... Matt 20:23
"*S* at My right hand .... Heb 1:13
I will grant to *s* .... Rev 3:21
SITS
It is He who *s* above .... Is 40:22
so that he *s* as God .... 2 Thess 2:4
SITTING
where Christ is, *s* .... Col 3:1
SKILL
hand forget its *s* .... Ps 137:5
SKILLFULNESS
guided them by the *s* .... Ps 78:72
SKIN
God made tunics of *s* .... Gen 3:21
LORD and said, "*S* .... Job 2:4
Ethiopian change his *s* .... Jer 13:23
SKIP
He makes them also *s* .... Ps 29:6
SKIPPING
upon the mountains, *S* .... Song 2:8
SKULL
to say, Place of a *S* .... Matt 27:33
SKY
s receded as a scroll .... Rev 6:14
SLACK
The Lord is not *s* .... 2 Pet 3:9
SLAIN
is the Lamb who was *s* .... Rev 5:12
SLANDER
whoever spreads *s* .... Prov 10:18
SLANDERERS
be reverent, not *s* .... 1 Tim 3:11
SLANDEROUSLY
as we are *s* reported .... Rom 3:8
SLAUGHTER
led as a lamb to the *s* .... Is 53:7
as sheep for the *s* .... Rom 8:36
SLAVE
commits sin is a *s* .... John 8:34
SLAVES
should no longer be *s* .... Rom 6:6
SLAY
s the righteous .... Gen 18:25
SLEEP
God caused a deep *s* .... Gen 2:21
neither slumber nor *s* .... Ps 121:4
He gives His beloved *s* .... Ps 127:2
and many *s* .... 1 Cor 11:30
We shall not all *s* .... 1 Cor 15:51
SLEEPERS
gently the lips of *s* .... Song 7:9
SLEEPING
"Are you still *s* .... Matt 26:45
SLEEPLESSNESS
in labors, in *s* .... 2 Cor 6:5
SLEEPS
"Our friend Lazarus *s* .... John 11:11
SLEPT
I lay down and *s* .... Ps 3:5
SLIGHTED
is the one who is *s* .... Prov 12:9
SLING
he had, and his *s* .... 1 Sam 17:40
SLIP
Their foot shall *s* .... Deut 32:35
SLIPPERY
set them in *s* places .... Ps 73:18
SLOOPS
all the beautiful *s* .... Is 2:16
SLOW
hear, *s* to speak, *s* .... James 1:19
SLUGGARD
will you slumber, O *s* .... Prov 6:9
SLUMBERING
upon men, While *s* .... Job 33:15
SMALL
And I saw the dead, *s* .... Rev 20:12
SMELL
and he smelled the *s* .... Gen 27:27
SMELLS
s the battle from afar .... Job 39:25
SMITTEN
Him stricken, *S* .... Is 53:4
SMOKE
was filled with *s* .... Rev 15:8
SMOOTH
And the rough places *s* .... Is 40:4
SMOOTH-SKINNED
man, and I am a *s* .... Gen 27:11
SNAIL
s which melts away as .... Ps 58:8
SNARE
is a fowler's *s* .... Hos 9:8
it will come as a *s* .... Luke 21:35
and escape the *s* .... 2 Tim 2:26
SNARED
All of them are *s* .... Is 42:22
SNARES
who seek my life lay *s* .... Ps 38:12
SNATCH
neither shall anyone *s* .... John 10:28
SNATCHES
s away what was .... Matt 13:19
SNEER
And you *s* at it .... Mal 1:13
SNIFFED
They *s* at the wind .... Jer 14:6
SNORTING
s strikes terror .... Job 39:20
SNOW
shall be whiter than *s* .... Ps 51:7
shall be as white as *s* .... Is 1:18
SOAKED
Their land shall be *s* .... Is 34:7
SOAP
lye, and use much *s* .... Jer 2:22
SOBER
the older men be *s* .... Titus 2:2
SOBERLY
think, but to think *s* .... Rom 12:3
SODA
And like vinegar on *s* .... Prov 25:20
SODOMITES
nor homosexuals, nor *s* .... 1 Cor 6:9
SOJOURNER
no *s* had to lodge .... Job 31:32
SOJOURNERS
are strangers and *s* .... Lev 25:23
SOLD
s his birthright .... Gen 25:33
s all that he had .... Matt 13:46
but I am carnal, *s* .... Rom 7:14
SOLDIER
hardship as a good *s* .... 2 Tim 2:3
SOLDIERS
s twisted a crown .... John 19:2
SOLITARILY
heritage, Who dwell *s* .... Mic 7:14
SOLITARY
God sets the *s* in .... Ps 68:6
SOMEBODY
up, claiming to be *s* .... Acts 5:36
SOMETHING
thinks himself to be *s* .... Gal 6:3
SON
Me, 'You are My *S* .... Ps 2:7
is born, Unto us a *S* .... Is 9:6
fourth is like the *S* .... Dan 3:25
will bring forth a *S* .... Matt 1:21
"This is My beloved *S* .... Matt 3:17
Jesus, You *S* of God .... Matt 8:29
are the Christ, the *S* .... Matt 16:16
Whose *S* is He .... Matt 22:42
of the *S* of Man .... Matt 24:37
'I am the *S* of God .... Matt 27:43
of Jesus Christ, the *S* .... Mark 1:1
out, the only *s* .... Luke 7:12
The only begotten *S* .... John 1:18
that this is the *S* .... John 1:34
of the only begotten *S* .... John 3:18
S can do nothing .... John 5:19
s abides forever .... John 8:35
you believe in the *S* .... John 9:35

I said, 'I am the *S* ... John 10:36
behold your *s* ... John 19:26
Jesus Christ is the *S* ... Acts 8:37
by sending His own *S* ... Rom 8:3
not spare His own *S* ... Rom 8:32
live by faith in the *S* ... Gal 2:20
God sent forth His *S* ... Gal 4:4
the knowledge of the *S* ... Eph 4:13
"You are My *S* ... Heb 1:5
though He was a *S* ... Heb 5:8
but made like the *S* ... Heb 7:3
"This is My beloved *S* ... 2 Pet 1:17
denies the *S* ... 1 John 2:23
One like the *S* of Man ... Rev 1:13

SONG
Sing to Him a new *s* ... Ps 33:3
He has put a new *s* ... Ps 40:3
I will sing a new *s* ... Ps 144:9
they sang a new *s* ... Rev 5:9

SONGS
my Maker, Who gives *s* ... Job 35:10
and spiritual *s* ... Eph 5:19

SONS
s shall come from afar ... Is 60:4
He will purity the *s* ... Mal 3:3
you may become *s* ... John 12:36
who are of faith are *s* ... Gal 3:7
the adoption as *s* ... Gal 4:5
in bringing many *s* ... Heb 2:10
speaks to you as to *s* ... Heb 12:5

SOON
For it is *s* cut off ... Ps 90:10

SOOTHED
or bound up, Or *s* ... Is 1:6

SORCERER
But Elymas the *s* ... Acts 13:8

SORCERERS
outside are dogs and *s* ... Rev 22:15

SORCERESS
shall not permit a *s* ... Ex 22:18

SORCERY
idolatry, *s* ... Gal 5:20

SORES
and putrefying *s* ... Is 1:6

SORROW
multiply your *s* ... Gen 3:16
s is continually ... Ps 38:17
And He adds no *s* ... Prov 10:22
Your *s* is incurable ... Jer 30:15
them sleeping from *s* ... Luke 22:45
s will be turned ... John 16:20
s produces repentance ... 2 Cor 7:10
s as others who ... 1 Thess 4:13
no more death, nor *s* ... Rev 21:4

SORROWFUL
But I am poor and *s* ... Ps 69:29
he went away *s* ... Matt 19:22
soul is exceedingly *s* ... Matt 26:38
and I may be less *s* ... Phil 2:28

SORROWS
s shall be multiplied ... Ps 16:4
by men, A Man of *s* ... Is 53:3
are the beginning of *s* ... Matt 24:8

SORRY
s that He had made man ... Gen 6:6
For you were made *s* ... 2 Cor 7:9

SOUGHT
I *s* the LORD ... Ps 34:4
s what was lost ... Ezek 34:4

SOUL
with all your *s* ... Deut 6:5
"My *s* loathes my life ... Job 10:1
s draws near the Pit ... Job 33:22
will not leave my *s* ... Ps 16:10
converting the *s* ... Ps 19:7
He restores my *s* ... Ps 23:3
you cast down, O my *s* ... Ps 42:5
Let my *s* live ... Ps 119:175
No one cares for my *s* ... Ps 142:4
me wrongs his own *s* ... Prov 8:36
When You make His *s* ... Is 53:10
s delight itself ... Is 55:2
The *s* of the father As ... Ezek 18:4
able to destroy both *s* ... Matt 10:28
and loses his own *s* ... Matt 16:26
with all your *s* ... Matt 22:37
your whole spirit, *s* ... 1 Thess 5:23
to the saving of the *s* ... Heb 10:39
his way will save a *s* ... James 5:20
health, just as your *s* ... 3 John 2

SOULS
And will save the *s* ... Ps 72:13
And he who wins *s* ... Prov 11:30
unsettling your *s* ... Acts 15:24
is able to save your *s* ... James 1:21

SOUND
voice was like the *s* ... Ezek 43:2
do not *s* a trumpet ... Matt 6:2
s words which you ... 2 Tim 1:13

SOUNDNESS
him this perfect *s* ... Acts 3:16

SOUNDS
a distinction in the *s* ... 1 Cor 14:7

SOW
s trouble reap ... Job 4:8
Those who *s* in tears ... Ps 126:5
Blessed are you who *s* ... Is 32:20
"They *s* the wind ... Hos 8:7
s is not made alive ... 1 Cor 15:36

SOWER
"Behold. a *s* went ... Matt 13:3

SOWN
s spiritual things ... 1 Cor 9:11
of righteousness is *s* ... James 3:18

SOWS
s the good seed is the ... Matt 13:37
'One *s* and another ... John 4:37
for whatever a man *s* ... Gal 6:7

SPARE
He who did not *s* ... Rom 8:32
if God did not *s* ... 2 Pet 2:4

SPARES
s his rod hates his ... Prov 13:24

SPARK
the work of it as a *s* ... Is 1:31

SPARKLES
it is red, When it *s* ... Prov 23:31

SPARKS
to trouble, As the *s* ... Job 5:7

SPARROW
s has found a home ... Ps 84:3

SPARROWS
than many *s* ... Matt 10:31

SPAT
Then they *s* on Him ... Matt 27:30

SPEAK
only the word that I *s* ... Num 22:35
oh, that God would *s* ... Job 11:5
And a time to *s* ... Eccl 3:7
s anymore in His name ... Jer 20:9
or what you should *s* ... Matt 10:19
to you when all men *s* ... Luke 6:26
s what I have seen ... John 8:38
He hears He will *s* ... John 16:13
Spirit and began to *s* ... Acts 2:4

SPEAKING
envy, and all evil *s* ... 1 Pet 2:1

SPEAKS
to face, as a man *s* ... Ex 33:11
God has sent *s* ... John 3:34
When he *s* a lie ... John 8:44
he being dead still *s* ... Heb 11:4
of sprinkling that *s* ... Heb 12:24

SPEAR
His side with a *s* ... John 19:34

SPEARS
And their *s* into ... Is 2:4

SPECK
do you look at the *s* ... Matt 7:3

SPECTACLE
you were made a *s* ... Heb 10:33

SPEECH
one language and one *s* ... Gen 11:1
his *s* contemptible ... 2 Cor 10:10
s always be with grace ... Col 4:6

SPEECHLESS
your mouth for the *s* ... Prov 31:8

SPEED
they shall come with *s* ... Is 5:26

SPEEDILY
I call, answer me *s* ... Ps 102:2

SPEND
you *s* money for ... Is 55:2
amiss, that you may *s* ... James 4:3

SPENT
"But when he had *s* ... Luke 15:14

SPEW
nor hot, I will *s* ... Rev 3:16

SPIDER
s skillfully grasps ... Prov 30:28

SPIES
men who had been *s* ... Josh 6:23

SPIN
neither toil nor *s* ... Matt 6:28

SPINDLE
her hand holds the *s* ... Prov 31:19

SPIRIT
And the *S* of God was ... Gen 1:2
S shall not strive ... Gen 6:3
S that is upon you ... Num 11:17
portion of your *s* ... 2 Kin 2:9
Then a *s* passed ... Job 4:15
hand I commit my *s* ... Ps 31:5
The *s* of a man is the ... Prov 20:27
s will return to God ... Eccl 12:7
S has gathered them ... Is 34:16
I have put My *S* ... Is 42:1
"The *S* of the Lord ... Is 61:1
S entered me when He ... Ezek 2:2
and a new *s* ... Ezek 18:31
"I will put My *S* ... Ezek 36:27
walk in a false *s* ... Mic 2:11
and He saw the *S* ... Matt 3:16
I will put My *S* ... Matt 12:18
S descending upon ... Mark 1:10
s indeed is willing ... Mark 14:38
go before Him in the *s* ... Luke 1:17
manner of *s* you are of ... Luke 9:55
hands I commit My *s* ... Luke 23:46
they had seen a *s* ... Luke 24:37
"God is *S* ... John 4:24
I speak to you are *s* ... John 6:63
"the *S* of truth ... John 14:17
but if a *s* or an angel ... Acts 23:9
the flesh but in the *S* ... Rom 8:9
does not have the *S* ... Rom 8:9
s that we are children ... Rom 8:16
what the mind of the *S* ... Rom 8:27
to us through His *S* ... 1 Cor 2:10
gifts, but the same *S* ... 1 Cor 12:4
but the *S* gives life ... 2 Cor 3:6
Now the Lord is the *S* ... 2 Cor 3:17
Having begun in the *S* ... Gal 3:3
has sent forth the *S* ... Gal 4:6
with the Holy *S* ... Eph 1:13
the unity of the *S* ... Eph 4:3
stand fast in one *s* ... Phil 1:27
S expressly says that ... 1 Tim 4:1
S who dwells in us ... James 4:5
made alive by the *S* ... 1 Pet 3:18
do not believe every *s* ... 1 John 4:1
you know the *S* ... 1 John 4:2
has given us of His *S* ... 1 John 4:13
S who bears witness ... 1 John 5:6
not having the *S* ... Jude 19
I was in the *S* on the ... Rev 1:10
him hear what the *S* ... Rev 2:7
And the *S* and the ... Rev 22:17

SPIRITS
Who makes His angels *s* ... Ps 104:4
heed to deceiving *s* ... 1 Tim 4:1

SPIRITUAL
s judges all things ... 1 Cor 2:15
However, the *s* is not ... 1 Cor 15:46
s restore such a one ... Gal 6:1

SPIRITUALLY
s minded is life ... Rom 8:6
SPITEFULLY
for those who *s* ... Matt 5:44
SPITTING
face from shame and *s* ... Is 50:6
SPLENDOR
on the glorious *s* ... Ps 145:5
SPOIL
He shall divide the *s* ... Is 53:12
SPOILER
I have created the *s* ... Is 54:16
SPOKE
"No man ever *s* ... John 7:46
I was a child, I *s* ... 1 Cor 13:11
in various ways *s* ... Heb 1:1
s as they were moved ... 2 Pet 1:21
SPOKEN
I have not *s* in secret ... Is 45:19
why am I evil *s* ... 1 Cor 10:30
SPOKESMAN
"So he shall be your *s* ... Ex 4:16
SPONGE
them ran and took a *s* ... Matt 27:48
SPOT
church, not having *s* ... Eph 5:27
Himself without *s* ... Heb 9:14
SPOTS
These are *s* in your ... Jude 12
SPREAD
Then the word of God *s* ... Acts 6:7
SPREADS
s them out like a tent ... Is 40:22
SPRING
Truth shall *s* out of ... Ps 85:11
s send forth fresh ... James 3:11
SPRINGING
a fountain of water *s* ... John 4:14
SPRINGS
And the thirsty land *s* ... Is 35:7
SPRINKLE
"Then I will *s* ... Ezek 36:25
SPRINKLED
having our hearts *s* ... Heb 10:22
SPRINKLING
s that speaks ... Heb 12:24
SPROUT
and the seed should *s* ... Mark 4:27
SQUARES
voice in the open *s* ... Prov 1:20
STAFF
this Jordan with my *s* ... Gen 32:10
Your rod and Your *s* ... Ps 23:4
on the top of his *s* ... Heb 11:21
STAGGER
they will drink and *s* ... Jer 25:16
STAGGERS
As a drunken man *s* ... Is 19:14
STAKES
s will ever be removed ... Is 33:20
STALLS
be no herd in the *s* ... Hab 3:17
STAMMERERS
s will be ready ... Is 32:4
STAMMERING
s tongue that you ... Is 33:19
STAMPING
At the noise of the *s* ... Jer 47:3
STAND
one shall be able to *s* ... Deut 7:24
lives, And He shall *s* ... Job 19:25
ungodly shall not *s* ... Ps 1:5
not lack a man to *s* ... Jer 35:19
And who can *s* when He ... Mal 3:2
that kingdom cannot *s* ... Mark 3:24
he will be made to *s* ... Rom 14:4
Watch, *s* fast in the ... 1 Cor 16:13
for by faith you *s* ... 2 Cor 1:24
having done all, to *s* ... Eph 6:13
S therefore ... Eph 6:14
of God in which you *s* ... 1 Pet 5:12
"Behold, I *s* at the ... Rev 3:20
STANDARD
LORD will lift up a *s* ... Is 59:19
STANDING
they love to pray *s* ... Matt 6:5
and the Son of Man *s* ... Acts 7:56
STANDS
him who thinks he *s* ... 1 Cor 10:12
STAR
For we have seen His *s* ... Matt 2:2
Bright and Morning *S* ... Rev 22:16
STARS
He made the *s* also ... Gen 1:16
born as many as the *s* ... Heb 11:12
STATE
learned in whatever *s* ... Phil 4:11
STATURE
in wisdom and *s* ... Luke 2:52
STATUTE
shall be a perpetual *s* ... Lev 3:17
STATUTES
the *s* of the LORD are ... Ps 19:8
Teach me Your *s* ... Ps 119:12
STAY
S here and watch ... Matt 26:38
STEADFAST
brethren, be *s* ... 1 Cor 15:58
soul, both sure and *s* ... Heb 6:19
Resist him, *s* in the ... 1 Pet 5:9
STEADFASTLY
s set His face to go ... Luke 9:51
And they continued *s* ... Acts 2:42
STEADFASTNESS
good order and the *s* ... Col 2:5
STEADILY
could not look *s* ... 2 Cor 3:13
STEADY
and his hands were *s* ... Ex 17:12
STEAL
"You shall not *s* ... Ex 20:15
thieves break in and *s* ... Matt 6:19
night and *s* Him away ... Matt 27:64
STEM
forth a Rod from the *s* ... Is 11:1
STENCH
there will be a *s* ... Is 3:24
this time there is a *s* ... John 11:39
STEP
s has turned from the ... Job 31:7
STEPS
The *s* of a good man ... Ps 37:23
And established my *s* ... Ps 40:2
the LORD directs his *s* ... Prov 16:9
should follow His *s* ... 1 Pet 2:21
STEWARD
be blameless, as a *s* ... Titus 1:7
STEWARDS
of Christ and *s* ... 1 Cor 4:1
STEWARDSHIP
entrusted with a *s* ... 1 Cor 9:17
STICK
'For Joseph, the *s* ... Ezek 37:16
STICKS
a man gathering *s* ... Num 15:32
STIFF
rebellion and your *s* ... Deut 31:27
STIFF-NECKED
"You *s* and ... Acts 7:51
STILL
When I awake, I am *s* ... Ps 139:18
sea, "Peace, be *s* ... Mark 4:39
STILLBORN
burial, I say that a *s* ... Eccl 6:3
STINGS
like a serpent, And *s* ... Prov 23:32
STIR
I remind you to *s* ... 2 Tim 1:6
STIRRED
So the LORD *s* up the ... Hag 1:14
STIRS
It *s* up the dead for ... Is 14:9
STOCKS
s that were in the ... Jer 20:2
STOIC
and *S* philosophers ... Acts 17:18
STOMACH
Foods for the *s* ... 1 Cor 6:13
STOMACH'S
little wine for your *s* ... 1 Tim 5:23
STONE
him, a pillar of *s* ... Gen 35:14
s shall be a witness ... Josh 24:27
s which the builders ... Ps 118:22
I lay in Zion a *s* ... Is 28:16
take the heart of *s* ... Ezek 36:26
will give him a *s* ... Matt 7:9
s will be broken ... Matt 21:44
s which the builders ... Luke 20:17
those works do you *s* ... John 10:32
Him as to a living *s* ... 1 Pet 2:4
STONED
s Stephen as he was ... Acts 7:59
They were *s* ... Heb 11:37
STONES
Abraham from these *s* ... Matt 3:9
command that these *s* ... Matt 4:3
STONY
fell on *s* ground ... Mark 4:5
STOOPED
And again He *s* down ... John 8:8
STOPPED
her flow of blood *s* ... Luke 8:44
STORE
exist are kept in *s* ... 2 Pet 3:7
STORK
s has her home in the ... Ps 104:17
STORM
He calms the *s* ... Ps 107:29
for a shelter from *s* ... Is 4:6
STRAIGHT
Make *s* in the desert A ... Is 40:3
and make *s* paths for ... Heb 12:13
STRAIGHTFORWARD
that they were not *s* ... Gal 2:14
STRAIN
"Blind guides, who *s* ... Matt 23:24
STRAITS
and desperate *s* ... Deut 28:53
STRANGE
s thing happened ... 1 Pet 4:12
STRANGER
and loves the *s* ... Deut 10:18
I was a *s* and you ... Matt 25:35
STRANGERS
know the voice of *s* ... John 10:5
you are no longer *s* ... Eph 2:19
STRANGLING
that my soul chooses *s* ... Job 7:15
STRAP
than I, whose sandal *s* ... Mark 1:7
STRAW
stones, wood, hay, *s* ... 1 Cor 3:12
STRAY
Who make my people *s* ... Mic 3:5
STRAYED
Yet I have not *s* ... Ps 119:110
some have *s* ... 1 Tim 6:10
STREAM
like a flowing *s* ... Is 66:12
STREAMS
He also brought *s* ... Ps 78:16
STREET
In the middle of its *s* ... Rev 22:2
STREETS
You taught in our *s* ... Luke 13:26

STRENGTH
s no man shall ... 1 Sam 2:9
The LORD is the *s* ... Ps 27:1
is our refuge and *s* ... Ps 46:1
They go from *s* to ... Ps 84:7
S and honor are her ... Prov 31:25
might He increases *s* ... Is 40:29
O LORD, my *s* and my ... Jer 16:19
were still without *s* ... Rom 5:6
s is made perfect ... 2 Cor 12:9

STRENGTHEN
And He shall *s* ... Ps 27:14
S the weak hands ... Is 35:3
s your brethren ... Luke 22:32
s the things ... Rev 3:2

STRENGTHENED
unbelief, but was *s* ... Rom 4:20
stood with me and *s* ... 2 Tim 4:17

STRENGTHENING
s the souls of the ... Acts 14:22

STRENGTHENS
through Christ who *s* ... Phil 4:13

STRETCH
are old, you will *s* ... John 21:18

STRETCHED
I have *s* out my hands ... Ps 88:9
"All day long I have *s* ... Rom 10:21

STRETCHES
For he *s* out his hand ... Job 15:25

STRICKEN
of My people He was *s* ... Is 53:8

STRIFE
man stirs up *s* ... Prov 15:18
even from envy and *s* ... Phil 1:15
which come envy, *s* ... 1 Tim 6:4

STRIKE
The sun shall not *s* ... Ps 121:6
"*S* the Shepherd ... Zech 13:7
'I will *s* the Shepherd ... Matt 26:31

STRINGED
of your *s* instruments ... Amos 5:23

STRIP
S yourselves ... Is 32:11

STRIPES
s we are healed ... Is 53:5
s you were healed ... 1 Pet 2:24

STRIVE
"My Spirit shall not *s* ... Gen 6:3
"*S* to enter through ... Luke 13:24
the Lord not to *s* ... 2 Tim 2:14

STRIVING
for a man to stop *s* ... Prov 20:3

STROKE
with a mighty *s* ... Jer 14:17

STRONG
The LORD *s* and mighty ... Ps 24:8
S is Your hand ... Ps 89:13
"When a *s* man ... Luke 11:21
We then who are *s* ... Rom 15:1
weak, then I am *s* ... 2 Cor 12:10
my brethren, be *s* ... Eph 6:10
were made *s* ... Heb 11:34

STRONGHOLD
of my salvation, my *s* ... Ps 18:2

STRUCK
s the rock twice ... Num 20:11
the hand of God has *s* ... Job 19:21
Behold, He *s* the rock ... Ps 78:20
in My wrath I *s* ... Is 60:10
s the head from the ... Hab 3:13
took the reed and *s* ... Matt 27:30

STUBBLE
do wickedly will be *s* ... Mal 4:1

STUBBORN
"If a man has a *s* ... Deut 21:18

STUBBORN-HEARTED
"Listen to Me, you *s* ... Is 46:12

STUBBORNNESS
do not look on the *s* ... Deut 9:27

STUDIED
having never *s* ... John 7:15

STUMBLE
have caused many to *s* ... Mal 2:8
you will be made to *s* ... Matt 26:31
immediately they *s* ... Mark 4:17
who believe in Me to *s* ... Mark 9:42
For we all *s* in many ... James 3:2

STUMBLED
s that they should ... Rom 11:11

STUMBLES
immediately he *s* ... Matt 13:21

STUMBLING
the deaf, nor put a *s* ... Lev 19:14
But a stone of *s* ... Is 8:14
Behold, I will lay *s* ... Jer 6:21
I lay in Zion a *s* ... Rom 9:33
this, not to put a *s* ... Rom 14:13
of yours become a *s* ... 1 Cor 8:9
and "A stone of *s* ... 1 Pet 2:8
to keep you from *s* ... Jude 24

STUPID
hates correction is *s* ... Prov 12:1

SUBDUE
s all things to ... Phil 3:21

SUBJECT
for it is not *s* ... Rom 8:7
Let every soul be *s* ... Rom 13:1
all their lifetime *s* ... Heb 2:15

SUBJECTED
because of Him who *s* ... Rom 8:20

SUBJECTION
put all things in *s* ... Heb 2:8

SUBMISSION
his children in *s* ... 1 Tim 3:4

SUBMISSIVE
Yes, all of you be *s* ... 1 Pet 5:5

SUBMIT
Therefore *s* to God ... James 4:7
s yourselves to every ... 1 Pet 2:13

SUBSIDED
and the waters *s* ... Gen 8:1

SUBSTANCE
Bless his *s* ... Deut 33:11

SUCCESS
please give me *s* ... Gen 24:12
But wisdom brings *s* ... Eccl 10:10

SUCCESSFUL
Joseph, and he was a *s* ... Gen 39:2

SUDDENLY
s there was with the ... Luke 2:13

SUE
s you and take away ... Matt 5:40

SUFFER
for the Christ to *s* ... Luke 24:46
Christ, if indeed we *s* ... Rom 8:17
in Him, but also to *s* ... Phil 1:29

SUFFERED
s these things and to ... Luke 24:26
for whom I have *s* ... Phil 3:8
after you have *s* ... 1 Pet 5:10

SUFFERING
anyone among you *s* ... James 5:13

SUFFERINGS
I consider that the *s* ... Rom 8:18
perfect through *s* ... Heb 2:10

SUFFERS
Love *s* long and is ... 1 Cor 13:4

SUFFICIENCY
but our *s* is from God ... 2 Cor 3:5

SUFFICIENT
S for the day is Its ... Matt 6:34

SUM
How great is the *s* ... Ps 139:17

SUMMER
and heat, Winter and *s* ... Gen 8:22

SUMPTUOUSLY
fine linen and fared *s* ... Luke 16:19

SUN
So the *s* stood still ... Josh 10:13
s shall not strike you ... Ps 121:6
s returned ten degrees ... Is 38:8
The *s* and moon grow ... Joel 2:10
s shall go down on the ... Mic 3:6
for He makes His *s* ... Matt 5:45
the *s* was darkened ... Luke 23:45
do not let the *s* ... Eph 4:26
s became black as ... Rev 6:12
had no need of the *s* ... Rev 21:23

SUPPER
to eat the Lord's *S* ... 1 Cor 11:20
took the cup after *s* ... 1 Cor 11:25
together for the *s* ... Rev 19:17

SUPPLICATION
by prayer and *s* ... Phil 4:6

SUPPLIES
by what every joint *s* ... Eph 4:16

SUPPLY
And my God shall *s* ... Phil 4:19

SUPPORT
this, that you must *s* ... Acts 20:35

SUPREME
to the king as *s* ... 1 Pet 2:13

SURE
s your sin will find ... Num 32:23
call and elections ... 2 Pet 1:10

SURETY
Be *s* for Your servant ... Ps 119:122
Jesus has become a *s* ... Heb 7:22

SURROUND
LORD, mercy shall *s* ... Ps 32:10

SURROUNDED
also, since we are *s* ... Heb 12:1

SURVIVOR
was no refugee or *s* ... Lam 2:22

SUSPICIONS
reviling, evil *s* ... 1 Tim 6:4

SUSTAIN
S me with cakes of ... Song 2:5

SWADDLING
Him in *s* cloths ... Luke 2:7

SWALLOW
a gnat and *s* a camel ... Matt 23:24

SWEAR
'You shall not *s* ... Matt 5:33
began to curse and *s* ... Matt 26:74

SWEARING
By *s* and lying ... Hos 4:2

SWEARS
but whoever *s* by the ... Matt 23:18

SWEAT
His *s* became like ... Luke 22:44

SWEET
s are Your words ... Ps 119:103
but it will be as *s* ... Rev 10:9

SWEETNESS
mouth like honey in *s* ... Ezek 3:3

SWELLING
they speak great *s* ... 2 Pet 2:18

SWIFT
let every man be *s* ... James 1:19

SWIM
night I make my bed *s* ... Ps 6:6

SWOON
As they *s* like the ... Lam 2:12

SWORD
s which turned every ... Gen 3:24
The *s* of the LORD is ... Is 34:6
'A *s* is sharpened ... Ezek 21:9
Bow and *s* of battle I ... Hos 2:18
to bring peace but a *s* ... Matt 10:34
for all who take the *s* ... Matt 26:52
the *s* of the Spirit ... Eph 6:17
than any two-edged *s* ... Heb 4:12
mouth goes a sharp *s* ... Rev 19:15

SWORDS
shall beat their *s* ... Is 2:4

SWORE
So I *s* in My wrath ... Heb 3:11

SWORN
"By Myself I have *s* ... Gen 22:16
"The LORD has *s* ... Heb 7:21

SYMBOLIC
which things are *s* .... Gal 4:24
SYMPATHIZE
Priest who cannot *s* .... Heb 4:15
SYMPATHY
My *s* is stirred .... Hos 11:8
SYNAGOGUE
but are a *s* of Satan .... Rev 2:9

T

TABERNACLE
t He shall hide me .... Ps 27:5
I will abide in Your *t* .... Ps 61:4
And will rebuild the *t* .... Acts 15:16
and more perfect *t* .... Heb 9:11
TABERNACLES
Feast of *T* was at hand .... John 7:2
TABLE
prepare a *t* before me .... Ps 23:5
dogs under the *t* .... Mark 7:28
of the Lord's *t* .... 1 Cor 10:21
TABLES
and overturned the *t* .... Matt 21:12
TABLET
is engraved On the *t* .... Jer 17:1
TAIL
t drew a third of the .... Rev 12:4
TAKE
t Your Holy Spirit .... Ps 51:11
"*T* My yoke upon .... Matt 11:29
and *t* up his cross .... Mark 8:34
My life that I may *t* .... John 10:17
TAKEN
He was *t* from prison .... Is 53:8
one will be *t* and the .... Matt 24:40
until He is *t* out of .... 2 Thess 2:7
TALEBEARER
t reveals secrets .... Prov 11:13
TALENT
went and hid your *t* .... Matt 25:25
TALK
shall *t* of them when .... Deut 6:7
TALKED
within us while He *t* .... Luke 24:32
TALKERS
both idle *t* and .... Titus 1:10
TAMBOURINE
The mirth of the *t* .... Is 24:8
TARES
the *t* also appeared .... Matt 13:26
TARGET
You set me as Your *t* .... Job 7:20
TARRY
come and will not *t* .... Heb 10:37
TASK
this burdensome *t* .... Eccl 1:13
TASTE
Oh, *t* and see that the .... Ps 34:8
might *t* death for .... Heb 2:9
TASTED
t the heavenly gift .... Heb 6:4
TAUGHT
as His counselor has *t* .... Is 40:13
from man, nor was I *t* .... Gal 1:12
TAUNT
and a byword, a *t* .... Jer 24:9
TAX
t collectors do the .... Matt 5:46
TAXES
t to whom *t* .... Rom 13:7
TEACH
"Can anyone *t* .... Job 21:22
T me Your paths .... Ps 25:4
t you the fear of the .... Ps 34:11
t transgressors Your .... Ps 51:13
So *t* us to number our .... Ps 90:12
t you again the first .... Heb 5:12
TEACHER
for One is your *T* .... Matt 23:8
know that You are a *t* .... John 3:2
named Gamaliel, a *t* .... Acts 5:34
a *t* of the Gentiles in .... 1 Tim 2:7
TEACHERS
than all my *t* .... Ps 119:99
prophets, third *t* .... 1 Cor 12:28
and some pastors and *t* .... Eph 4:11
desiring to be *t* .... 1 Tim 1:7
there will be false *t* .... 2 Pet 2:1
TEACHES
the Holy Spirit *t* .... 1 Cor 2:13
the same anointing *t* .... 1 John 2:27
TEACHING
"*t* them to observe all .... Matt 28:20
t every man in all .... Col 1:28
TEAR
I, even I, will *t* .... Hos 5:14
will wipe away every *t* .... Rev 21:4
TEARS
my couch with my *t* .... Ps 6:6
mindful of your *t* .... 2 Tim 1:4
it diligently with *t* .... Heb 12:17
TEETH
You have broken the *t* .... Ps 3:7
TELL
"Who can *t* if God .... Jon 3:9
t him his fault .... Matt 18:15
whatever they *t* .... Matt 23:3
He comes, He will *t* .... John 4:25
TEMPERATE
prize is *t* in all .... 1 Cor 9:25
husband of one wife, *t* .... 1 Tim 3:2
TEMPEST
And suddenly a great *t* .... Matt 8:24
TEMPLE
So Solomon built the *t* .... 1 Kin 6:14
LORD is in His holy *t* .... Ps 11:4
One greater than the *t* .... Matt 12:6
"Destroy this *t* .... John 2:19
your body is the *t* .... 1 Cor 6:19
grows into a holy *t* .... Eph 2:21
sits as God in the *t* .... 2 Thess 2:4
and the Lamb are its *t* .... Rev 21:22
TEMPLES
t made with hands .... Acts 7:48
TEMPORARY
which are seen are *t* .... 2 Cor 4:18
TEMPT
t the LORD your God .... Matt 4:7
does He Himself *t* .... James 1:13
TEMPTATION
do not lead us into *t* .... Matt 6:13
man who endures *t* .... James 1:12
TEMPTED
forty days, *t* by Satan .... Mark 1:13
lest you also be *t* .... Gal 6:1
in all points *t* .... Heb 4:15
TEMPTER
Now when the *t* came .... Matt 4:3
TENDER
your heart was *t* .... 2 Kin 22:19
TENDERHEARTED
to one another, *t* .... Eph 4:32
TENDS
t a flock and does not .... 1 Cor 9:7
TENT
earthly house, this *t* .... 2 Cor 5:1
TENTMAKERS
occupation they were *t* .... Acts 18:3
TENTS
Than dwell in the *t* .... Ps 84:10
TERRESTRIAL
bodies and *t* bodies .... 1 Cor 15:40
TERRIBLE
is great and very *t* .... Joel 2:11
TERRIFIED
and not in any way *t* .... Phil 1:28
TERRIFY
me with dreams And *t* .... Job 7:14
TERRIFYING
t was the sight .... Heb 12:21
TERROR
are nothing, You see *t* .... Job 6:21
not be afraid of the *t* .... Ps 91:5
TERRORS
consumed with *t* .... Ps 73:19
TEST
said, "Why do you *t* .... Matt 22:18
T all things .... 1 Thess 5:21
but *t* the spirits .... 1 John 4:1
TESTAMENT
where there is a *t* .... Heb 9:16
TESTED
God *t* Abraham .... Gen 22:1
Where your fathers *t* .... Heb 3:9
though it is *t* by fire .... 1 Pet 1:7
TESTIFIED
who has seen has *t* .... John 19:35
which He has *t* .... 1 John 5:9
TESTIFIES
that the Holy Spirit *t* .... Acts 20:23
TESTIFY
t what We have .... John 3:11
t that the Father .... 1 John 4:14
TESTIFYING
was righteous, God *t* .... Heb 11:4
TESTIMONIES
those who keep His *t* .... Ps 119:2
t are my meditation .... Ps 119:99
TESTIMONY
two tablets of the *T* .... Ex 31:18
under your feet as a *t* .... Mark 6:11
no one receives His *t* .... John 3:32
not believed the *t* .... 1 John 5:10
For the *t* of Jesus is .... Rev 19:10
TESTING
came to Him, *t* Him .... Matt 19:3
TESTS
men, but God who *t* .... 1 Thess 2:4
THANK
"I *t* You, Father .... Matt 11:25
t You that I am not .... Luke 18:11
THANKFUL
as God, nor were *t* .... Rom 1:21
THANKFULNESS
Felix, with all *t* .... Acts 24:3
THANKS
the cup, and gave *t* .... Matt 26:27
T be to God for His .... 2 Cor 9:15
THANKSGIVING
His presence with *t* .... Ps 95:2
into His gates with *t* .... Ps 100:4
supplication, with *t* .... Phil 4:6
THEATER
and rushed into the *t* .... Acts 19:29
THIEF
do not despise a *t* .... Prov 6:30
because he was a *t* .... John 12:6
Lord will come as a *t* .... 2 Pet 3:10
THIEVES
And companions of *t* .... Is 1:23
THINGS
in heaven give good *t* .... Matt 7:11
kept all these *t* .... Luke 2:51
share in all good *t* .... Gal 6:6
THINK
t you have eternal .... John 5:39
not to *t* of himself .... Rom 12:3
THINKS
Yet the LORD *t* upon me .... Ps 40:17
For as he *t* in his .... Prov 23:7
t he stands take heed .... 1 Cor 10:12
THIRST
those who hunger and *t* .... Matt 5:6
in Me shall never *t* .... John 6:35
anymore nor *t* anymore .... Rev 7:16
THIRSTS
My soul *t* for God .... Ps 42:2
saying, "If anyone *t* .... John 7:37
freely to him who *t* .... Rev 21:6

THIRSTY
I was *t* and you gave ... Matt 25:35
THISTLES
or figs from *t* ... Matt 7:16
THORN
a *t* in the flesh was ... 2 Cor 12:7
THORNBUSHES
gather grapes from *t* ... Matt 7:16
THORNS
Both *t* and thistles it ... Gen 3:18
some fell among *t* ... Matt 13:7
wearing the crown of *t* ... John 19:5
THOUGHT
You understand my *t* ... Ps 139:2
I *t* as a child ... 1 Cor 13:11
THOUGHTS
The LORD knows the *t* ... Ps 94:11
unrighteous man his *t* ... Is 55:7
"For My *t* are not your ... Is 55:8
Jesus, knowing their *t* ... Matt 9:4
heart proceed evil *t* ... Matt 15:19
The LORD knows the *t* ... 1 Cor 3:20
THREAT
shall flee at the *t* ... Is 30:17
THREATEN
suffered, He did not *t* ... 1 Pet 2:23
THREATENING
to them, giving up *t* ... Eph 6:9
THREATS
still breathing *t* ... Acts 9:1
THREE
hope, love, these *t* ... 1 Cor 13:13
THRESH
It is time to *t* her ... Jer 51:33
THRESHING
t shall last till the ... Lev 26:5
THROAT
t is an open tomb ... Rom 3:13
THRONE
Your *t*, O God, is ... Ps 45:6
Lord sitting on a *t* ... Is 6:1
"Heaven is My *t* ... Is 66:1
for it is God's *t* ... Matt 5:34
will give Him the *t* ... Luke 1:32
"Your *t*, O God, is ... Heb 1:8
come boldly to the *t* ... Heb 4:16
My Father on His *t* ... Rev 3:21
I saw a great white *t* ... Rev 20:11
THRONES
invisible, whether *t* ... Col 1:16
THRONG
house of God in the *t* ... Ps 55:14
THROW
t Yourself down ... Matt 4:6
THROWN
neck, and he were *t* ... Mark 9:42
THRUST
and rose up and *t* ... Luke 4:29
THUNDER
The voice of Your *t* ... Ps 77:18
the voice of loud *t* ... Rev 14:2
THUNDERED
"The LORD *t* from ... 2 Sam 22:14
THUNDERINGS
the sound of mighty *t* ... Rev 19:6
THUNDERS
The God of glory *t* ... Ps 29:3
TIDINGS
I bring you good *t* ... Luke 2:10
TILL
no man to *t* the ground ... Gen 2:5
TILLER
but Cain was a *t* ... Gen 4:2
TILLS
t his land will have ... Prov 28:19
TIME
pray to You In a *t* ... Ps 32:6
for the *t* is near ... Rev 1:3
TIMES
the signs of the *t* ... Matt 16:3
not for you to know *t* ... Acts 1:7
last days perilous *t* ... 2 Tim 3:1
TITHE
And he gave him a *t* ... Gen 14:20
For you pay *t* of mint ... Matt 23:23
TITHES
and to bring the *t* ... Neh 10:37
Bring all the *t* ... Mal 3:10
TITHING
the year of *t* ... Deut 26:12
TITLE
Now Pilate wrote a *t* ... John 19:19
TITTLE
away, one jot or one *t* ... Matt 5:18
TODAY
T I have begotten You ... Ps 2:7
t you will be with Me ... Luke 23:43
"*T*, if you will hear ... Heb 3:7
the same yesterday, *t* ... Heb 13:8
TOIL
t you shall eat of ... Gen 3:17
TOILED
"Master, we have *t* ... Luke 5:5
TOLD
Behold I have *t* ... Matt 28:7
so, I would have *t* ... John 14:2
TOLERABLE
you, it will be more *t* ... Matt 10:15
TOMB
in the garden a new *t* ... John 19:41
TOMBS
like whitewashed *t* ... Matt 23:27
TOMORROW
drink, for *t* we die ... Is 22:13
do not worry about *t* ... Matt 6:34
what will happen *t* ... James 4:14
TONGUE
remember you, Let my *t* ... Ps 137:6
forever, But a lying *t* ... Prov 12:19
t breaks a bone ... Prov 25:15
t should confess that ... Phil 2:11
does not bridle his *t* ... James 1:26
no man can tame the *t* ... James 3:8
every nation, tribe, *t* ... Rev 14:6
TONGUES
From the strife of *t* ... Ps 31:20
speak with new *t* ... Mark 16:17
divided *t*, as of fire ... Acts 2:3
I speak with the *t* ... 1 Cor 13:1
TOOTH
eye for an eye and a *t* ... Matt 5:38
TOPHET
the high places of *T* ... Jer 7:31
TORCH
and like a fiery *t* ... Zech 12:6
TORCHES
When he had set the *t* ... Judg 15:5
come with flaming *t* ... Nah 2:3
TORMENT
You come here to *t* ... Matt 8:29
t ascends forever ... Rev 14:11
TORMENTED
And they will be *t* ... Rev 20:10
TORMENTS
"And being in *t* ... Luke 16:23
TORN
of the temple was *t* ... Matt 27:51
TORTURED
Others were *t* ... Heb 11:35
TOSSED
t to and fro and ... Eph 4:14
TOTTER
drunkard, And shall *t* ... Is 24:20
TOUCH
"If only I may *t* ... Matt 9:21
TOUCHED
t my mouth with it ... Is 6:7
TOUCHES
He *t* the hills ... Ps 104:32
TOWER
t whose top is in the ... Gen 11:4
a watchman in the *t* ... Is 21:5
TRACKED
t our steps So that we ... Lam 4:18
TRADERS
are princes, Whose *t* ... Is 23:8
TRADITION
transgress the *t* ... Matt 15:2
according to the *t* ... Col 2:8
TRAIN
T up a child in the ... Prov 22:6
TRAINED
those who have been *t* ... Heb 12:11
TRAINING
bring them up in the *t* ... Eph 6:4
TRAITOR
also became a *t* ... Luke 6:16
TRAITORS
t, headstrong ... 2 Tim 3:4
TRAMPLE
serpent you shall *t* ... Ps 91:13
swine, lest they *t* ... Matt 7:6
TRAMPLED
t the Son of God ... Heb 10:29
the winepress was *t* ... Rev 14:20
TRANCE
t I saw a vision ... Acts 11:5
TRANSFIGURED
and was *t* before them ... Matt 17:2
TRANSFORMED
this world, but be *t* ... Rom 12:2
TRANSGRESS
do Your disciples *t* ... Matt 15:2
TRANSGRESSED
"Yes, all Israel has *t* ... Dan 9:11
t your commandment ... Luke 15:29
TRANSGRESSES
Whoever *t* and does not ... 2 John 9
TRANSGRESSION
no law there is no *t* ... Rom 4:15
deceived, fell into *t* ... 1 Tim 2:14
TRANSGRESSIONS
mercies, Blot out my *t* ... Ps 51:1
For I acknowledge my *t* ... Ps 51:3
was wounded for our *t* ... Is 53:5
For the *t* of My people ... Is 53:8
TRANSGRESSOR
I make myself a *t* ... Gal 2:18
TRANSGRESSORS
Then I will teach *t* ... Ps 51:13
numbered with the *t* ... Is 53:12
TRAP
of Israel, As a *t* ... Is 8:14
TRAPS
for me, And from the *t* ... Ps 141:9
TRAVEL
You *t* land and sea ... Matt 23:15
TRAVELER
t who turns aside ... Jer 14:8
TRAVELING
lie waste, The *t* ... Is 33:8
TREACHEROUS
are insolent, *t* ... Zeph 3:4
TREACHEROUSLY
"This man dealt *t* ... Acts 7:19
TREAD
You shall *t* upon the ... Ps 91:13
TREADS
an ox while it *t* ... 1 Tim 5:18
t the winepress ... Rev 19:15
TREASURE
and you will have *t* ... Matt 19:21
he who lays up *t* ... Luke 12:21
But we have this *t* ... 2 Cor 4:7
TREASURED
t the words of His ... Job 23:12

TREASURER
Erastus, the *t* of the .... Rom 16:23
TREASURES
it more than hidden *t* .... Job 3:21
I will give you the *t* .... Is 45:3
for yourselves *t* .... Matt 6:19
are hidden all the *t* .... Col 2:3
riches than the *t* .... Heb 11:26
TREATY
Now Solomon made a *t* .... 1 Kin 3:1
TREE
you eaten from the *t* .... Gen 3:11
t Planted by the .... Ps 1:3
like a native green *t* .... Ps 37:35
t bears good fruit .... Matt 7:17
His own body on the *t* .... 1 Pet 2:24
the river, was the *t* .... Rev 22:2
TREES
late autumn *t* without .... Jude 12
the sea, or the *t* .... Rev 7:3
TREMBLE
That the nations may *t* .... Is 64:2
they shall fear and *t* .... Jer 33:9
TREMBLED
Then everyone who *t* .... Ezra 9:4
the earth shook and *t* .... Ps 18:7
and indeed they *t* .... Jer 4:24
TREMBLING
in fear, and in much *t* .... 1 Cor 2:3
t you received .... 2 Cor 7:15
flesh, with fear and *t* .... Eph 6:5
TRENCH
and he made a *t* .... 1 Kin 18:32
TRESPASSES
forgive men their *t* .... Matt 6:14
not imputing their *t* .... 2 Cor 5:19
who were dead in *t* .... Eph 2:1
TRIAL
concerning the fiery *t* .... 1 Pet 4:12
TRIBE
the Lion of the *t* .... Rev 5:5
blood Out of every *t* .... Rev 5:9
TRIBES
t which are scattered .... James 1:1
TRIBULATION
there will be great *t* .... Matt 24:21
world you will have *t* .... John 16:33
with her into great *t* .... Rev 2:22
out of the great *t* .... Rev 7:14
TRIBULATIONS
t enter the kingdom .... Acts 14:22
but we also glory in *t* .... Rom 5:3
t that you endure .... 2 Thess 1:4
TRIED
A *t* stone, a precious .... Is 28:16
TRIMMED
and *t* their lamps .... Matt 25:7
TRIUMPH
always leads us in *t* .... 2 Cor 2:14
TRIUMPHED
the LORD, For He has *t* .... Ex 15:1
TRODDEN
t the winepress alone .... Is 63:3
TROUBLE
few days and full of *t* .... Job 14:1
t He shall hide me .... Ps 27:5
not in *t* as other men .... Ps 73:5
will be with him in *t* .... Ps 91:15
Savior in time of *t* .... Jer 14:8
there are some who *t* .... Gal 1:7
TROUBLED
worried and *t* .... Luke 10:41
shaken in mind or *t* .... 2 Thess 2:2
TROUBLES
Out of all their *t* .... Ps 25:22
will be famines and *t* .... Mark 13:8
him out of all his *t* .... Acts 7:10
TROUBLING
wicked cease from *t* .... Job 3:17
TRUE
He who sent Me is *t* .... John 7:28
Indeed, let God be *t* .... Rom 3:4
whatever things are *t* .... Phil 4:8
Him who is *t* .... 1 John 5:20
for these words are *t* .... Rev 21:5
TRUMPET
deed, do not sound a *t* .... Matt 6:2
t makes an uncertain .... 1 Cor 14:8
For the *t* will sound .... 1 Cor 15:52
TRUST
T in the LORD .... Ps 37:3
T in the LORD with all .... Prov 3:5
Do not *t* in a friend .... Mic 7:5
who *t* in riches .... Mark 10:24
TRUSTED
"He *t* in the LORD .... Ps 22:8
"He *t* in God .... Matt 27:43
TRUSTS
But he who *t* in the .... Ps 32:10
TRUTH
led me in the way of *t* .... Gen 24:48
Behold, You desire *t* .... Ps 51:6
t shall be your shield .... Ps 91:4
And Your law is *t* .... Ps 119:142
t is fallen in the .... Is 59:14
called the City of *T* .... Zech 8:3
you shall know the *t* .... John 8:32
"I am the way, the *t* .... John 14:6
He, the Spirit of *t* .... John 16:13
to Him. "What is *t* .... John 18:38
who suppress the *t* .... Rom 1:18
but, speaking the *t* .... Eph 4:15
your waist with *t* .... Eph 6:14
I am speaking the *t* .... 1 Tim 2:7
they may know the *t* .... 2 Tim 2:25
the knowledge of the *t* .... 2 Tim 3:7
that we are of the *t* .... 1 John 3:19
the Spirit is *t* .... 1 John 5:6
TRY
which is to *t* you .... 1 Pet 4:12
TUMULT
Your enemies make a *t* .... Ps 83:2
TUNIC
Also he made him a *t* .... Gen 37:3
TUNICS
the LORD God made *t* .... Gen 3:21
TURBAN
"Remove the *t* .... Ezek 21:26
TURN
you shall not *t* .... Deut 17:11
"Repent, *t* away from .... Ezek 14:6
on your right cheek, *t* .... Matt 5:39
t them from darkness .... Acts 26:18
TURNED
The wicked shall be *t* .... Ps 9:17
of Israel, They have *t* .... Is 1:4
and how you *t* .... 1 Thess 1:9
TURNING
marvel that you are *t* .... Gal 1:6
or shadow of *t* .... James 1:17
TURNS
A soft answer *t* .... Prov 15:1
that he who *t* .... James 5:20
TURTLEDOVE
t Is heard in our land .... Song 2:12
TUTOR
the law was our *t* .... Gal 3:24
TWIST
unstable people *t* to .... 2 Pet 3:16
TWO
T are better than one .... Eccl 4:9
t shall become one .... Matt 19:5
new man from the *t* .... Eph 2:15
TYPE
of Adam, who is a *t* .... Rom 5:14

U

UNAFRAID
Do you want to be *u* .... Rom 13:3
UNBELIEF
because of their *u* .... Matt 13:58
help my *u* .... Mark 9:24
did it ignorantly in *u* .... 1 Tim 1:13
enter in because of *u* .... Heb 3:19
UNBELIEVERS
yoked together with *u* .... 2 Cor 6:14
UNBELIEVING
Do not be *u* .... John 20:27
u nothing is pure .... Titus 1:15
"But the cowardly, *u* .... Rev 21:8
UNCIRCUMCISED
not the physically *u* .... Rom 2:27
UNCLEAN
I am a man of *u* lips .... Is 6:5
man common or *u* .... Acts 10:28
there is nothing *u* .... Rom 14:14
that no fornicator, *u* .... Eph 5:5
UNCLEANNESS
men's bones and all *u* .... Matt 23:27
flesh in the lust of *u* .... 2 Pet 2:10
UNCLOTHED
we want to be *u* .... 2 Cor 5:4
UNCOVERS
u deep things out of .... Job 12:22
UNDEFILED
incorruptible and *u* .... 1 Pet 1:4
UNDERMINE
And you *u* your friend .... Job 6:27
UNDERSTAND
if there are any who *u* .... Ps 14:2
hearing, but do not *u* .... Is 6:9
"Why do you not *u* .... John 8:43
lest they should *u* .... Acts 28:27
some things hard to *u* .... 2 Pet 3:16
UNDERSTANDING
His *u* is infinite .... Ps 147:5
lean not on your own *u* .... Prov 3:5
u will find good .... Prov 19:8
His *u* is unsearchable .... Is 40:28
also still without *u* .... Matt 15:16
also pray with the *u* .... 1 Cor 14:15
the Lord give you *u* .... 2 Tim 2:7
Who is wise and *u* .... James 3:13
UNDERSTANDS
There is none who *u* .... Rom 3:11
UNDERSTOOD
Then I *u* their end .... Ps 73:17
clearly seen, being *u* .... Rom 1:20
UNDESIRABLE
gather together, O *u* .... Zeph 2:1
UNDIGNIFIED
I will be even more *u* .... 2 Sam 6:22
UNDISCERNING
u, untrustworthy .... Rom 1:31
UNDONE
"Woe is me, for I am *u* .... Is 6:5
UNEDUCATED
that they were *u* .... Acts 4:13
UNFAITHFUL
way of the *u* is hard .... Prov 13:15
UNFAITHFULLY
back and acted *u* .... Ps 78:57
UNFORGIVING
unloving, *u* .... Rom 1:31
UNFORMED
substance, being yet *u* .... Ps 139:16
UNFRUITFUL
and it becomes *u* .... Mark 4:19
UNGODLINESS
heaven against all *u* .... Rom 1:18
UNGODLY
u shall not stand .... Ps 1:5
Christ died for the *u* .... Rom 5:6
UNHOLY
the holy and *u* .... Ezek 22:26
UNINFORMED
the place of the *u* .... 1 Cor 14:16
UNINTENTIONALLY
kills his neighbor *u* .... Deut 4:42
UNITE
U my heart to fear .... Ps 86:11

UNITY
to dwell together in *u* . . . . . Ps 133:1
to keep the *u* of the . . . . . Eph 4:3
UNJUST
commended the *u* . . . . . Luke 16:8
of the just and the *u* . . . . . Acts 24:15
For God is not *u* . . . . . Heb 6:10
UNJUSTLY
long will you judge *u* . . . . . Ps 82:2
UNKNOWN
To The *U* God . . . . . Acts 17:23
UNLEAVENED
the Feast of *U* Bread . . . . . Ex 12:17
UNLOVING
untrustworthy, *u* . . . . . Rom 1:31
UNMERCIFUL
unforgiving, *u* . . . . . Rom 1:31
UNPREPARED
with me and find you *u* . . . . . 2 Cor 9:4
UNPRESENTABLE
u parts have greater . . . . . 1 Cor 12:23
UNPROFITABLE
'We are *u* servants . . . . . Luke 17:10
for that would be *u* . . . . . Heb 13:17
UNPUNISHED
wicked will not go *u* . . . . . Prov 11:21
UNQUENCHABLE
up the chaff with *u* . . . . . Matt 3:12
UNRESTRAINED
that the people were *u* . . . . . Ex 32:25
UNRIGHTEOUS
u man his thoughts . . . . . Is 55:7
u will not inherit the . . . . . 1 Cor 6:9
UNRIGHTEOUSNESS
all ungodliness and *u* . . . . . Rom 1:18
cleanse us from all *u* . . . . . 1 John 1:9
All *u* is sin . . . . . 1 John 5:17
UNRULY
those who are *u* . . . . . 1 Thess 5:14
UNSEARCHABLE
are His judgments . . . . . Rom 11:33
UNSKILLED
only of milk is *u* . . . . . Heb 5:13
UNSPOTTED
to keep oneself *u* . . . . . James 1:27
UNSTABLE
U as water . . . . . Gen 49:4
UNSTOPPED
of the deaf shall be *u* . . . . . Is 35:5
UNTAUGHT
which *u* and unstable . . . . . 2 Pet 3:16
UNTRUSTWORTHY
undiscerning, *u* . . . . . Rom 1:31
UNWASHED
eat bread with *u* hands . . . . . Mark 7:5
UNWISE
Therefore do not be *u* . . . . . Eph 5:17
UNWORTHY
u manner will be . . . . . 1 Cor 11:27
UPHOLD
U me according to . . . . . Ps 119:116
UPHOLDING
u all things by the . . . . . Heb 1:3
UPHOLDS
LORD *u* all who fall . . . . . Ps 145:14
UPPER
show you a large *u* . . . . . Mark 14:15
UPRIGHT
u is His delight . . . . . Prov 15:8
UPRIGHTNESS
princes for their *u* . . . . . Prov 17:26
UPROOT
u the wheat with . . . . . Matt 13:29
URIM
Thummim and Your *U* . . . . . Deut 33:8
US
"God with *u* . . . . . Matt 1:23
If God is for *u* . . . . . Rom 8:31
of them were of *u* . . . . . 1 John 2:19
USE
who spitefully *u* you . . . . . Matt 5:44
u liberty as an . . . . . Gal 5:13
USELESS
one's religion is *u* . . . . . James 1:26
USES
if one *u* it lawfully . . . . . 1 Tim 1:8
USING
u liberty as a . . . . . 1 Pet 2:16
USURY
'Take no *u* or . . . . . Lev 25:36
UTTER
u dark sayings of old . . . . . Ps 78:2
UTTERANCE
the Spirit gave them *u* . . . . . Acts 2:4
UTTERED
which cannot be *u* . . . . . Rom 8:26
UTTERMOST
u those who come . . . . . Heb 7:25
UTTERS
Day unto day *u* speech . . . . . Ps 19:2

V

VAGABOND
you shall be on the . . . . . Gen 4:12
VAIN
the people plot a *v* . . . . . Ps 2:1
you believed in *v* . . . . . 1 Cor 15:2
VALIANT
They are not *v* for the . . . . . Jer 9:3
VALIANTLY
God we will do *v* . . . . . Ps 60:12
VALLEY
shall be exalted . . . . . Is 40:4
VALOR
a mighty man of *v* . . . . . 1 Sam 16:18
VALUE
of more *v* than they . . . . . Matt 6:26
VALUED
It cannot be *v* in the . . . . . Job 28:16
VANISH
knowledge, it will *v* . . . . . 1 Cor 13:8
VANISHED
and He *v* from their . . . . . Luke 24:31
VANITY
of vanities, all is *v* . . . . . Eccl 1:2
VAPOR
best state is but *v* . . . . . Ps 39:5
It is even a *v* that . . . . . James 4:14
VARIATION
whom there is no *v* . . . . . James 1:17
VEGETABLES
and let them give us *v* . . . . . Dan 1:12
is weak eats only *v* . . . . . Rom 14:2
VEHEMENT
of fire, A most *v* . . . . . Song 8:6
VEIL
of the temple was . . . . . Matt 27:51
Presence behind the *v* . . . . . Heb 6:19
VENGEANCE
V is Mine . . . . . Deut 32:35
VENOM
It becomes cobra *v* . . . . . Job 20:14
VESSEL
like a potter's *v* . . . . . Ps 2:9
for he is a chosen *v* . . . . . Acts 9:15
VESSELS
treasure in earthen *v* . . . . . 2 Cor 4:7
VEXED
grieved, and I was *v* . . . . . Ps 73:21
VICE
as a cloak for *v* . . . . . 1 Pet 2:16
VICTIM
And plucked the *v* . . . . . Job 29:17
VICTORY
v that has overcome . . . . . 1 John 5:4
VIEW
"Go, *v* the land . . . . . Josh 2:1
VIGILANT
Be sober, be *v* . . . . . 1 Pet 5:8
VIGOR
nor his natural *v* . . . . . Deut 34:7
VILE
them up to *v* passions . . . . . Rom 1:26
VINDICATED
know that I shall be *v* . . . . . Job 13:18
VINDICATION
Let my *v* come from . . . . . Ps 17:2
VINE
"I am the true *v* . . . . . John 15:1
VINEDRESSER
and My Father is the *v* . . . . . John 15:1
VINEGAR
As *v* to the teeth and . . . . . Prov 10:26
VINES
foxes that spoil the *v* . . . . . Song 2:15
VINEYARD
Who plants a *v* and . . . . . 1 Cor 9:7
VIOLENCE
was filled with *v* . . . . . Gen 6:11
of heaven suffers *v* . . . . . Matt 11:12
VIOLENT
haters of God, *v* . . . . . Rom 1:30
VIPER
And stings like a *v* . . . . . Prov 23:32
VIPERS
to them, "Brood of *v* . . . . . Matt 3:7
VIRGIN
shall conceive . . . . . Is 7:14
"Behold, the *v* shall . . . . . Matt 1:23
VIRGINS
who took their lamps . . . . . Matt 25:1
VIRTUE
to your faith *v* . . . . . 2 Pet 1:5
VISAGE
was marred more than . . . . . Is 52:14
VISIBLE
that are on earth, *v* . . . . . Col 1:16
VISION
in a trance I saw a *v* . . . . . Acts 11:5
to the heavenly *v* . . . . . Acts 26:19
VISIONS
young men shall see *v* . . . . . Joel 2:28
VISIT
orphans and . . . . . James 1:27
VISITATION
God in the day of *v* . . . . . 1 Pet 2:12
VISITED
Israel, for He has *v* . . . . . Luke 1:68
VISITING
the iniquity of the . . . . . Ex 20:5
VISITOR
am a foreigner and a *v* . . . . . Gen 23:4
VITALITY
was turned into the . . . . . Ps 32:4
VOICE
fire a still small *v* . . . . . 1 Kin 19:12
if you will hear His *v* . . . . . Ps 95:7
"The *v* of one crying . . . . . Matt 3:3
And suddenly a *v* . . . . . Matt 3:17
for they know his *v* . . . . . John 10:4
the truth hears My *v* . . . . . John 18:37
If anyone hears My *v* . . . . . Rev 3:20
VOICES
And there were loud *v* . . . . . Rev 11:15
VOID
they are a nation *v* . . . . . Deut 32:28
heirs, faith is made *v* . . . . . Rom 4:14
VOLUME
In the *v* of the book . . . . . Heb 10:7
VOLUNTEERS
Your people shall be *v* . . . . . Ps 110:3
VOMIT
returns to his own *v* . . . . . 2 Pet 2:22
VOW
for he had taken a *v* . . . . . Acts 18:18

VOWS
to reconsider his *v* .... Prov 20:25

W

WAGE
w the good warfare .... 1 Tim 1:18
WAGES
For the *w* of sin is .... Rom 6:23
Indeed the *w* of the .... James 5:4
WAIL
"Son of man, *w* .... Ezek 32:18
WAILING
There will be *w* .... Matt 13:42
WAIT
w patiently for Him .... Ps 37:7
those who *w* on the .... Is 40:31
To those who eagerly *w* .... Heb 9:28
WAITED
w patiently for the .... Ps 40:1
Divine longsuffering *w* .... 1 Pet 3:20
WAITING
ourselves, eagerly *w* .... Rom 8:23
from that time *w* .... Heb 10:13
WAITS
the creation eagerly *w* .... Rom 8:19
WAKE
that whether we *w* .... 1 Thess 5:10
WALK
w before Me and be .... Gen 17:1
Yea, though I *w* .... Ps 23:4
W prudently when you .... Eccl 5:1
"This is the way, *w* .... Is 30:21
be weary, they shall *w* .... Is 40:31
w humbly with your God .... Mic 6:8
W while you have the .... John 12:35
so we also should *w* .... Rom 6:4
For we *w* by faith .... 2 Cor 5:7
W in the Spirit .... Gal 5:16
And *w* in love .... Eph 5:2
that you may *w* worthy .... Col 1:10
and they shall *w* .... Rev 3:4
WALKED
Methuselah, Enoch *w* .... Gen 5:22
The people who *w* .... Is 9:2
in which you once *w* .... Eph 2:2
WALKING
not *w* in craftiness .... 2 Cor 4:2
WALKS
the LORD your God *w* .... Deut 23:14
is the man Who *w* .... Ps 1:1
he who *w* in darkness .... John 12:35
adversary the devil *w* .... 1 Pet 5:8
WALL
then the *w* of the city .... Josh 6:5
you whitewashed *w* .... Acts 23:3
a window in the *w* .... 2 Cor 11:33
Now the *w* of the city .... Rev 21:14
WALLS
By faith the *w* of .... Heb 11:30
WANDER
they have loved to *w* .... Jer 14:10
WANDERED
They *w* in deserts and .... Heb 11:38
WANDERERS
And they shall be *w* .... Hos 9:17
WANDERING
w stars for whom is .... Jude 13
WANDERS
among you *w* .... James 5:19
WANT
I shall not *w* .... Ps 23:1
WANTING
balances, and found *w* .... Dan 5:27
WANTON
have begun to grow *w* .... 1 Tim 5:11
WAR
"There is a noise of *w* .... Ex 32:17
w may rise against .... Ps 27:3
shall they learn *w* .... Is 2:4
going to make *w* .... Luke 14:31
You fight and *w* .... James 4:2

fleshly lusts which *w* .... 1 Pet 2:11
judges and makes *w* .... Rev 19:11
WARFARE
to her, That her *w* .... Is 40:2
w entangles .... 2 Tim 2:4
WARMED
in peace, be *w* .... James 2:16
WARMING
she saw Peter *w* .... Mark 14:67
WARMS
w them in the dust .... Job 39:14
WARN
w those who are .... 1 Thess 5:14
WARNED
Then, being divinely *w* .... Matt 2:12
Who *w* you to flee .... Matt 3:7
WARNING
w every man and .... Col 1:28
WARPED
such a person is *w* .... Titus 3:11
WARRING
w against the law of .... Rom 7:23
WARRIOR
He runs at me like a *w* .... Job 16:14
WARS
you will hear of *w* .... Matt 24:6
Where do *w* and fights .... James 4:1
WASH
w myself with snow .... Job 9:30
W me thoroughly .... Ps 51:2
w His feet with her .... Luke 7:38
said to him, "Go, *w* .... John 9:7
w the disciples' .... John 13:5
w away your sins .... Acts 22:16
WASHED
w his hands before .... Matt 27:24
But you were *w* .... 1 Cor 6:11
Him who loved us and *w* .... Rev 1:5
WASHING
us, through the *w* .... Titus 3:5
WASHINGS
and drinks, various *w* .... Heb 9:10
WASTE
the cities are laid *w* .... Is 6:11
"Why this *w* .... Matt 26:8
WASTED
this fragrant oil *w* .... Mark 14:4
WASTELAND
w shall be glad .... Is 35:1
WASTING
that this man was *w* .... Luke 16:1
WATCH
is past, And like a *w* .... Ps 90:4
"*W* therefore .... Matt 24:42
WATCHED
he would have *w* .... Matt 24:43
WATCHES
Blessed is he who *w* .... Rev 16:15
WATCHFUL
But you be *w* in all .... 2 Tim 4:5
WATCHING
he comes, will find *w* .... Luke 12:37
WATCHMAN
I have made you a *w* .... Ezek 3:17
WATCHMEN
I have set *w* on your .... Is 62:6
WATER
Eden to *w* the garden .... Gen 2:10
I am poured out like *w* .... Ps 22:14
For I will pour *w* .... Is 44:3
given you living *w* .... John 4:10
rivers of living *w* .... John 7:38
can yield both salt *w* .... James 3:12
the Spirit, the *w* .... 1 John 5:8
are clouds without *w* .... Jude 12
let him take the *w* .... Rev 22:17
WATERED
I planted, Apollos *w* .... 1 Cor 3:6
WATERS
me beside the still *w* .... Ps 23:2

Though its *w* roar and .... Ps 46:3
your bread upon the *w* .... Eccl 11:1
thirsts, Come to the *w* .... Is 55:1
fountain of living *w* .... Jer 2:13
living fountains of *w* .... Rev 7:17
WAVE
Its fruit shall *w* .... Ps 72:16
WAVER
He did not *w* at the .... Rom 4:20
WAVERING
of our hope without *w* .... Heb 10:23
WAVES
sea, tossed by the *w* .... Matt 14:24
WAX
My heart is like *w* .... Ps 22:14
WAY
As for God, His *w* .... 2 Sam 22:31
the LORD knows the *w* .... Ps 1:6
Teach me Your *w* .... Ps 27:11
in the *w* everlasting .... Ps 139:24
w that seems right .... Prov 14:12
The *w* of the just is .... Is 26:7
wicked forsake his *w* .... Is 55:7
And pervert the *w* .... Amos 2:7
he will prepare the *w* .... Mal 3:1
and broad is the *w* .... Matt 7:13
will prepare Your *w* .... Matt 11:10
to him, "I am the *w* .... John 14:6
to him the *w* .... Acts 18:26
to have known the *w* .... 2 Pet 2:21
WAYS
For all His *w* are .... Deut 32:4
transgressors Your *w* .... Ps 51:13
w please the LORD .... Prov 16:7
"Stand in the *w* .... Jer 6:16
and owns all your *w* .... Dan 5:23
w are everlasting .... Hab 3:6
unstable in all his *w* .... James 1:8
and true are Your *w* .... Rev 15:3
WEAK
gives power to the *w* .... Is 40:29
knee will be as *w* .... Ezek 7:17
but the flesh is *w* .... Matt 26:41
Receive one who is *w* .... Rom 14:1
God has chosen the *w* .... 1 Cor 1:27
We are *w* .... 1 Cor 4:10
w I became as *w* .... 1 Cor 9:22
For when I am *w* .... 2 Cor 12:10
WEAKENED
w my strength in the .... Ps 102:23
WEAKENS
w the hands of the men .... Jer 38:4
WEAKER
the wife, as to the *w* .... 1 Pet 3:7
WEAKNESS
w were made strong .... Heb 11:34
WEAKNESSES
also helps in our *w* .... Rom 8:26
WEALTH
W gained by .... Prov 13:11
WEALTHY
rich, have become *w* .... Rev 3:17
WEANED
w child shall put his .... Is 11:8
WEAPON
w formed against you .... Is 54:17
WEAPONS
For the *w* of our .... 2 Cor 10:4
WEAR
'What shall we *w* .... Matt 6:31
WEARIED
You have *w* Me with .... Is 43:24
therefore, being *w* .... John 4:6
WEARINESS
say, 'Oh, what a *w* .... Mal 1:13
WEARISOME
and much study is *w* .... Eccl 12:12
WEARY
shall run and not be *w* .... Is 40:31
And let us not grow *w* .... Gal 6:9
do not grow *w* in .... 2 Thess 3:13

WEATHER
'It will be fair *w* .... Matt 16:2
WEDDING
day there was a *w* .... John 2:1
WEEK
the first day of the *w* .... Matt 28:1
WEEKS
w are determined .... Dan 9:24
WEEP
A time to *w* .... Eccl 3:4
You shall *w* no more .... Is 30:19
are you who *w* .... Luke 6:21
do not *w* .... Luke 23:28
w with those who *w* .... Rom 12:15
WEEPING
the noise of the *w* .... Ezra 3:13
They shall come with *w* .... Jer 31:9
There will be *w* .... Matt 8:12
by the tomb *w* .... John 20:11
WEIGH
O Most Upright, You *w* .... Is 26:7
WEIGHED
You have been *w* .... Dan 5:27
WEIGHS
eyes, But the LORD *w* .... Prov 16:2
WEIGHT
us lay aside every *w* .... Heb 12:1
WEIGHTIER
have neglected the *w* .... Matt 23:23
WELFARE
does not seek the *w* .... Jer 38:4
WELL
have done *w* .... Prov 31:29
wheel broken at the *w* .... Eccl 12:6
"Those who are *w* .... Matt 9:12
said to him, '*W* done .... Matt 25:21
WELLS
These are *w* without .... 2 Pet 2:17
WENT
They *w* out from us .... 1 John 2:19
WEPT
out and *w* bitterly .... Matt 26:75
saw the city and *w* .... Luke 19:41
Jesus *w* .... John 11:35
WET
his body was *w* with .... Dan 4:33
WHEAT
w falls into the .... John 12:24
WHEEL
in the middle of a *w* .... Ezek 1:16
WHEELS
noise of rattling *w* .... Nah 3:2
WHERE
not knowing *w* he was .... Heb 11:8
WHIP
A *w* for the horse .... Prov 26:3
WHIRLWIND
Job out of the *w* .... Job 38:1
has His way in the *w* .... Nah 1:3
WHISPER
my ear received a *w* .... Job 4:12
WHISPERER
w separates the best .... Prov 16:28
WHISPERERS
they are *w* .... Rom 1:29
WHISPERINGS
backbitings, *w* .... 2 Cor 12:20
WHITE
clothed in *w* garments .... Rev 3:5
behold, a *w* horse .... Rev 6:2
and made them *w* .... Rev 7:14
WHOLE
w body were an eye .... 1 Cor 12:17
WHOLESOME
not consent to *w* words .... 1 Tim 6:3
WHOLLY
w followed the LORD .... Deut 1:36
WICKED
w shall be silent .... 1 Sam 2:9
w shall be no more .... Ps 37:10
if there is any *w* .... Ps 139:24
w forsake his way .... Is 55:7
And desperately *w* .... Jer 17:9
the sway of the *w* .... 1 John 5:19
WICKEDLY
God will never do *w* .... Job 34:12
WICKEDNESS
LORD saw that the *w* .... Gen 6:5
in the tents of *w* .... Ps 84:10
man repented of his *w* .... Jer 8:6
is full of greed and *w* .... Luke 11:39
sexual immorality, *w* .... Rom 1:29
and overflow of *w* .... James 1:21
WIDE
open your hand *w* .... Deut 15:8
w is the gate and .... Matt 7:13
to you, our heart is *w* .... 2 Cor 6:11
WIDOW
the fatherless and *w* .... Ps 146:9
How like a *w* is she .... Lam 1:1
Then one poor *w* .... Mark 12:42
w has children or .... 1 Tim 5:4
WIDOW'S
And I caused the *w* .... Job 29:13
WIDOWS
w were neglected .... Acts 6:1
visit orphans and *w* .... James 1:27
WIFE
and be joined to his *w* .... Gen 2:24
w finds a good thing .... Prov 18:22
But a prudent *w* .... Prov 19:14
"Go, take yourself a *w* .... Hos 1:2
divorces his *w* .... Mark 10:11
'I have married a *w* .... Luke 14:20
"Remember Lot's *w* .... Luke 17:32
so love his own *w* .... Eph 5:33
the husband of one *w* .... Titus 1:6
bride, the Lamb's *w* .... Rev 21:9
WILD
olive tree which is *w* .... Rom 11:24
WILDERNESS
I will make the *w* .... Is 41:18
of one crying in the *w* .... Matt 3:3
the serpent in the *w* .... John 3:14
WILES
to stand against the *w* .... Eph 6:11
WILL
w be done On earth as .... Matt 6:10
but he who does the *w* .... Matt 7:21
not My *w* .... Luke 22:42
flesh, nor of the *w* .... John 1:13
not to do My own *w* .... John 6:38
w is present with me .... Rom 7:18
and perfect *w* of God .... Rom 12:2
works in you both to *w* .... Phil 2:13
according to His own *w* .... Heb 2:4
work to do His *w* .... Heb 13:21
WILLFULLY
For if we sin *w* .... Heb 10:26
For this they *w* .... 2 Pet 3:5
WILLING
If you are *w* and .... Is 1:19
The spirit indeed is *w* .... Matt 26:41
w that any should .... 2 Pet 3:9
WILLINGLY
by compulsion but *w* .... 1 Pet 5:2
WILLOWS
our harps Upon the *w* .... Ps 137:2
WILLS
to whom the Son *w* .... Matt 11:27
it is not of him who *w* .... Rom 9:16
say, "If the Lord *w* .... James 4:15
WIN
to all, that I might *w* .... 1 Cor 9:19
WIND
the chaff which the *w* .... Ps 1:4
reed shaken by the *w* .... Matt 11:7
"The *w* blows where .... John 3:8
of a rushing mighty *w* .... Acts 2:2
WINDOWS
not open for you the *w* .... Mal 3:10
WINDS
be, that even the *w* .... Matt 8:27
WINDSTORM
And a great *w* arose .... Mark 4:37
WINE
W is a mocker .... Prov 20:1
love is better than *w* .... Song 1:2
Yes, come, buy *w* .... Is 55:1
they gave Him sour *w* .... Matt 27:34
do not be drunk with *w* .... Eph 5:18
not given to much *w* .... Titus 2:3
WINEBIBBERS
Do not mix with *w* .... Prov 23:20
WINEPRESS
"I have trodden the *w* .... Is 63:3
into the great *w* .... Rev 14:19
Himself treads the *w* .... Rev 19:15
WINESKINS
new wine into old *w* .... Matt 9:17
WING
One *w* of the cherub .... 1 Kin 6:24
WINGS
the shadow of Your *w* .... Ps 36:7
With healing in His *w* .... Mal 4:2
WINNOW
You shall *w* them .... Is 41:16
WINS
w souls is wise .... Prov 11:30
WINTER
For lo, the *w* is past .... Song 2:11
flight may not be in *w* .... Matt 24:20
WIPE
w away every tear .... Rev 21:4
WISDOM
for this is your *w* .... Deut 4:6
man who finds *w* .... Prov 3:13
Get *w* .... Prov 4:5
is the beginning of *w* .... Prov 9:10
w is justified by her .... Matt 11:19
Jesus increased in *w* .... Luke 2:52
riches both of the *w* .... Rom 11:33
the gospel, not with *w* .... 1 Cor 1:17
w of this world .... 1 Cor 3:19
not with fleshly *w* .... 2 Cor 1:12
all the treasures of *w* .... Col 2:3
If any of you lacks *w* .... James 1:5
power and riches and *w* .... Rev 5:12
WISE
Do not be *w* in your .... Prov 3:7
who wins souls is *w* .... Prov 11:30
Therefore be *w* as .... Matt 10:16
five of them were *w* .... Matt 25:2
to God, alone *w* .... Rom 16:27
Where is the *w* .... 1 Cor 1:20
not as fools but as *w* .... Eph 5:15
able to make you *w* .... 2 Tim 3:15
WISELY
you do not inquire *w* .... Eccl 7:10
WISER
he was *w* than all men .... 1 Kin 4:31
of God is *w* than men .... 1 Cor 1:25
WISH
w it were already .... Luke 12:49
WISHED
Then he *w* death for .... Jon 4:8
WITCHCRAFT
is as the sin of *w* .... 1 Sam 15:23
WITHDRAW
From such *w* yourself .... 1 Tim 6:5
WITHER
also shall not *w* .... Ps 1:3
WITHERS
The grass *w* .... Is 40:7
The grass *w* .... 1 Pet 1:24
WITHHELD
And your sins have *w* .... Jer 5:25
WITHHOLD
good thing will He *w* .... Ps 84:11
WITHOUT
pray *w* ceasing .... 1 Thess 5:17
w works is dead .... James 2:26

WITHSTAND
you may be able to *w* . . . . . Eph 6:13
WITHSTOOD
I *w* him to his face . . . . . Gal 2:11
WITNESS
all the world as a *w* . . . . . Matt 24:14
This man came for a *w* . . . . . John 1:7
do not receive Our *w* . . . . . John 3:11
Christ, the faithful *w* . . . . . Rev 1:5
beheaded for their *w* . . . . . Rev 20:4
WITNESSED
is revealed, being *w* . . . . . Rom 3:21
WITNESSES
"You are My *w* . . . . . Is 43:10
presence of many *w* . . . . . 1 Tim 6:12
so great a cloud of *w* . . . . . Heb 12:1
WIVES
Husbands, love your *w* . . . . . Eph 5:25
w must be reverent . . . . . 1 Tim 3:11
WOLF
The *w* and the lamb . . . . . Is 65:25
WOLVES
out as lambs among *w* . . . . . Luke 10:3
savage *w* . . . . . Acts 20:29
WOMAN
She shall be called *W* . . . . . Gen 2:23
whoever looks at a *w* . . . . . Matt 5:28
Then the *w* of Samaria . . . . . John 4:9
"*W*, behold your . . . . . John 19:26
natural use of the *w* . . . . . Rom 1:27
His Son, born of a *w* . . . . . Gal 4:4
w being deceived . . . . . 1 Tim 2:14
w clothed with the sun . . . . . Rev 12:1
WOMB
nations are in your *w* . . . . . Gen 25:23
in the *w* I knew you . . . . . Jer 1:5
is the fruit of your *w* . . . . . Luke 1:42
WOMEN
O fairest among *w* . . . . . Song 1:8
w will be grinding . . . . . Matt 24:41
are you among *w* . . . . . Luke 1:28
admonish the young *w* . . . . . Titus 2:4
times, the holy *w* . . . . . 1 Pet 3:5
WONDER
marvelous work and a *w* . . . . . Is 29:14
WONDERFUL
Things too *w* for me . . . . . Job 42:3
name will be called *W* . . . . . Is 9:6
WONDERIFULLY
fearfully and *w* made . . . . . Ps 139:14
WONDERS
"And I will show *w* . . . . . Joel 2:30
signs, and lying *w* . . . . . 2 Thess 2:9
WONDROUS
w works declare that . . . . . Ps 75:1
WONDROUSLY
God, Who has dealt *w* . . . . . Joel 2:26
WOOD
precious stones, *w* . . . . . 1 Cor 3:12
WOODCUTTERS
but let them be *w* . . . . . Josh 9:21
WOOL
They shall be as *w* . . . . . Is 1:18
hair were white like *w* . . . . . Rev 1:14
WORD
w is very near you . . . . . Deut 30:14
w I have hidden . . . . . Ps 119:11
w is a lamp to my feet . . . . . Ps 119:105
Every *w* of God is pure . . . . . Prov 30:5
the *w* of our God . . . . . Is 40:8
for every idle *w* . . . . . Matt 12:36
The seed is the *w* . . . . . Luke 8:11
beginning was the *W* . . . . . John 1:1
W became flesh and . . . . . John 1:14
Your *w* is truth . . . . . John 17:17
Let the *w* of Christ . . . . . Col 3:16
to you in *w* only . . . . . 1 Thess 1:5
by the *w* of His power . . . . . Heb 1:3
For the *w* of God is . . . . . Heb 4:12
does not stumble in *w* . . . . . James 3:2
through the *w* of God . . . . . 1 Pet 1:23
let us not love in *w* . . . . . 1 John 3:18
name is called The *W* . . . . . Rev 19:13
WORDS
Let the *w* of my mouth . . . . . Ps 19:14
The *w* of the wise are . . . . . Eccl 12:11
pass away, but My *w* . . . . . Matt 24:35
You have the *w* of . . . . . John 6:68
not with wisdom of *w* . . . . . 1 Cor 1:17
those who hear the *w* . . . . . Rev 1:3
WORK
day God ended His *w* . . . . . Gen 2:2
people had a mind to *w* . . . . . Neh 4:6
the *w* of Your fingers . . . . . Ps 8:3
Man goes out to his *w* . . . . . Ps 104:23
w is honorable and . . . . . Ps 111:3
will bring every *w* . . . . . Eccl 12:14
For I will *w* a *w* . . . . . Hab 1:5
could do no mighty *w* . . . . . Mark 6:5
"This is the *w* of God . . . . . John 6:29
"I must *w* the works . . . . . John 9:4
w which You have . . . . . John 17:4
know that all things *w* . . . . . Rom 8:28
w is no longer *w* . . . . . Rom 11:6
Do not destroy the *w* . . . . . Rom 14:20
abounding in the *w* . . . . . 1 Cor 15:58
If anyone will not *w* . . . . . 2 Thess 3:10
but a doer of the *w* . . . . . James 1:25
WORKED
which He *w* in Christ . . . . . Eph 1:20
WORKER
w is worthy of his . . . . . Matt 10:10
w who does not need . . . . . 2 Tim 2:15
WORKERS
we are God's fellow *w* . . . . . 1 Cor 3:9
WORKING
Father has been *w* . . . . . John 5:17
through faith in the *w* . . . . . Col 2:12
WORKMANSHIP
For we are His *w* . . . . . Eph 2:10
WORKS
are Your wonderful *w* . . . . . Ps 40:5
And let her own *w* . . . . . Prov 31:31
"For I know their *w* . . . . . Is 66:18
show Him greater *w* . . . . . John 5:20
w that I do he will do . . . . . John 14:12
might stand, not of *w* . . . . . Rom 9:11
same God who *w* . . . . . 1 Cor 12:6
not justified by the *w* . . . . . Gal 2:16
Now the *w* of the flesh . . . . . Gal 5:19
not of *w*, lest anyone . . . . . Eph 2:9
for it is God who *w* . . . . . Phil 2:13
but does not have *w* . . . . . James 2:14
also justified by *w* . . . . . James 2:25
"I know your *w* . . . . . Rev 2:2
their *w* follow them . . . . . Rev 14:13
according to their *w* . . . . . Rev 20:12
WORLD
"The field is the *w* . . . . . Matt 13:38
He was in the *w* . . . . . John 1:10
God so loved the *w* . . . . . John 3:16
His Son into the *w* . . . . . John 3:17
w cannot hate you . . . . . John 7:7
You are of this *w* . . . . . John 8:23
overcome the *w* . . . . . John 16:33
w may become guilty . . . . . Rom 3:19
be conformed to this *w* . . . . . Rom 12:2
loved this present *w* . . . . . 2 Tim 4:10
Do not love the *w* . . . . . 1 John 2:15
w is passing away . . . . . 1 John 2:17
WORLDS
also He made the *w* . . . . . Heb 1:2
WORM
But I am a *w* . . . . . Ps 22:6
w does not die . . . . . Mark 9:44
WORMS
he was eaten by *w* . . . . . Acts 12:23
WORMWOOD
of the star is *W* . . . . . Rev 8:11
WORRY
to you, do not *w* . . . . . Matt 6:25
WORRYING
w can add one . . . . . Matt 6:27
WORSE
w than their fathers . . . . . Jer 7:26
WORSHIP
come to *w* Him . . . . . Matt 2:2
w what you do not . . . . . John 4:22
the angels of God *w* . . . . . Heb 1:6
WORSHIPED
on their faces and *w* . . . . . Rev 11:16
WORSHIPER
if anyone is a *w* . . . . . John 9:31
WORTH
make my speech *w* . . . . . Job 24:25
WORTHLESS
Indeed they are all *w* . . . . . Is 41:29
WORTHLESSNESS
long will you love *w* . . . . . Ps 4:2
WORTHY
present time are not *w* . . . . . Rom 8:18
to walk *w* . . . . . Eph 4:1
the world was not *w* . . . . . Heb 11:38
"*W* is the Lamb who . . . . . Rev 5:12
WOUND
And my *w* incurable . . . . . Jer 15:18
and his deadly *w* . . . . . Rev 13:3
WOUNDED
But He was *w* for our . . . . . Is 53:5
WOUNDING
killed a man for *w* . . . . . Gen 4:23
WOUNDS
Faithful are the *w* . . . . . Prov 27:6
WRANGLINGS
useless *w* of men of . . . . . 1 Tim 6:5
WRATH
speak to them in His *w* . . . . . Ps 2:5
Surely the *w* of man . . . . . Ps 76:10
So I swore in My *w* . . . . . Ps 95:11
W is cruel and anger a . . . . . Prov 27:4
in My *w* I struck you . . . . . Is 60:10
w remember mercy . . . . . Hab 3:2
For the *w* of God is . . . . . Rom 1:18
up for yourself *w* . . . . . Rom 2:5
nature children of *w* . . . . . Eph 2:3
sun go down on your *w* . . . . . Eph 4:26
Let all bitterness, *w* . . . . . Eph 4:31
holy hands, without *w* . . . . . 1 Tim 2:8
So I swore in My *w* . . . . . Heb 3:11
not fearing the *w* . . . . . Heb 11:27
for the *w* of man . . . . . James 1:20
of the wine of the *w* . . . . . Rev 14:8
for in them the *w* . . . . . Rev 15:1
fierceness of His *w* . . . . . Rev 16:19
WRATHFUL
w man stirs up strife . . . . . Prov 15:18
WRESTLE
For we do not *w* . . . . . Eph 6:12
WRETCHED
w man that I am . . . . . Rom 7:24
know that you are *w* . . . . . Rev 3:17
WRETCHEDNESS
let me see my *w* . . . . . Num 11:15
WRINGING
w the nose produces . . . . . Prov 30:33
WRINKLE
not having spot or *w* . . . . . Eph 5:27
WRITE
w them on their hearts . . . . . Heb 8:10
WRITING
the *w* was the *w* . . . . . Ex 32:16
WRITINGS
do not believe his *w* . . . . . John 5:47
WRITTEN
tablets of stone, *w* . . . . . Ex 31:18
your names are *w* . . . . . Luke 10:20
"What I have *w* . . . . . John 19:22
WRONG
done nothing *w* . . . . . Luke 23:41
But he who does *w* . . . . . Col 3:25
WRONGED
We have *w* no one . . . . . 2 Cor 7:2

WRONGS
me *w* his own soul .... Prov 8:36
WROTE
stooped down and *w* .... John 8:6
WROUGHT
And skillfully *w* .... Ps 139:15

Y

YEAR
the acceptable *y*..................... Is 61:2
of sins every *y* .... Heb 10:3
YEARS
and for days and *y* .... Gen 1:14
lives are seventy *y* .... Ps 90:10
when He was twelve *y*........... Luke 2:42
with Him a thousand *y*........... Rev 20:6
YES
let your *Y*' be '*Y*,' .... Matt 5:37
YESTERDAY
For we were born *y*.................. Job 8:9
YOKE
"Take My *y* upon you .... Matt 11:29
YOKED
Do not be unequally *y*........... 2 Cor 6:14
YOUNG
I have been *y* .... Ps 37:25
she may lay her *y* .... Ps 84:3
I write to you, *y* .... 1 John 2:13
YOUNGER
Likewise you *y* people .... 1 Pet 5:5
YOURS
the battle is not *y*.............. 2 Chr 20:15
Y is the kingdom .... Matt 6:13
all Mine are *Y* .... John 17:10
for I do not seek *y*............... 2 Cor 12:14
YOUTH
the sins of my *y* .... Ps 25:7
and *y* are vanity .... Eccl 11:10
I have kept from my *y*.......... Matt 19:20
YOUTHFUL
Flee also *y* lusts .... 2 Tim 2:22
YOUTHS
y shall faint and be .... Is 40:30

Z

ZEAL
The *z* of the LORD of .... 2 Kin 19:31
"*Z* for Your house has .... John 2:17
that they have a *z*.................. Rom 10:2
ZEALOUS
z for good works .... Titus 2:14